W9-ABR-721

KENDAL-ON-HUDSON
LIBRARY
REFERENCE USE ONLY
DO NOT REMOVE

Kendal on Hudson Library
Please Return

# Webster's Biographical Dictionary

*A Merriam-Webster®*

G. & C. Merriam Company, *Publishers*
Springfield, Massachusetts

Copyright © 1980 by G. & C. Merriam Co.

Philippines Copyright 1980 by G. & C. Merriam Co.

Library of Congress Cataloging in Publication Data
Main entry under title:

Webster's biographical dictionary.

1. Biography.
CT103.W4 1980 920'.02 79-23607
ISBN 0-87779-443-X

Webster's Biographical Dictionary principal copyright 1943

All rights reserved. No part of this work covered by the copyrights hereon may be reproduced or copied in any form or by any means—graphic, electronic, or mechanical, including photocopying, recording, taping, or information storage and retrieval systems—without written permission of the publisher.

Made in the United States of America
89RMcN8281

## CONTENTS

# PREFACE

The aim of the editors and publishers of this Merriam-Webster Dictionary is to provide in a single handy volume a work of biographical reference not restricted in its selection of names by considerations of historical period, nationality, race, religion, or occupation, and to supply the reader with full information on the syllabic division and the pronunciation of the names included. Since the Dictionary is intended primarily for English-speaking users, American and British names have been included on a generous scale and often accorded fuller treatment than names of other persons of similar eminence.

There are, of course, many works of biographical reference in English. Most of them, however, are not comparable with this book in either design or scope. Those of unlimited scope are usually many-volumed works; those in one volume are for the most part deliberately limited to a single nationality or race, or to a single occupation or field of endeavor, or to a single historical period. Moreover, a great many biographical dictionaries make no attempt to record pronunciation; and, of those that do, few emphasize this very important matter or offer information approaching in fullness the information provided in this Merriam-Webster book. Fewer still provide syllabic division of names—information of value to printers, writers, and other consultants, and in many instances very difficult to obtain.

Not only does this Dictionary provide pronunciation and syllabic division for the surnames entered but also for titles of rank and in many instances for the place names from which such titles derive. Further, in the section on pages 1628 ff., similar information is given for a very extensive list of prenames in many languages, composed of prenames of persons entered in its Vocabulary—perhaps the most extensive such list obtainable in any single work of reference in English. Most users of this Dictionary are no doubt already familiar with the great difficulties encountered in trying to obtain such information readily from printed sources. The experience of our own editorial staff confirms such an opinion. The pronunciation of the names of many contemporaries was obtained by direct correspondence with those persons or with members of their families or with intimate friends. For many other pronunciations, especially of non-English names, information was contributed by consultants, specialists in various foreign languages, a list of whose names is printed on pages vii, viii, below.

The publishers feel that the convenience of a single volume, the freedom from restriction in the selection of names included, and the fullness of the information on pronunciation and syllabic division more than compensate for its limitations. These limitations are those inherent in any single volume of so broad a scope. They consist in the necessary restriction of the number of names included and in the restriction of the amount of space devoted to each entry. Neither of these restrictions, we believe, is a severe handicap in the present work.

The number of names included (upwards of 40,000) will be found adequate for the usual purposes of most consultants. Only in certain classes of contemporaries may some consultants feel an inadequacy. The names of persons prominent (sometimes only briefly) in sports, in motion pictures, in the contemporary theater, and in radio are so numerous that the editors were compelled, however reluctantly, to curtail their representation to the minimum, relying on the many specialized works of reference and the great volume of current periodical literature in these fields to supply the wants of consultants particularly interested in such names. As for the treatment given each entry, every effort has been made to provide information most likely to be sought by the consultants of this Dictionary. Names of persons included because of a single incident, a single writing, a single discovery, are accorded the briefest treatment, with emphasis duly laid on this single item. In this way, additional space has been obtained to provide longer entries for persons whose lives or works contain many details likely to be sought by the consultant. It will be readily seen, then, that the length of a biography is no measure of the relative importance of the person treated, but rather an indication of editorial judgment of material most likely to prove useful to consultants.

The names and data have been selected as objectively as possible. The selection was made from a large file of names compiled by combining the results of years of reading (especially of newspapers and general and technical periodicals) with check lists of names of persons appearing not only in biographical reference works, such as the *Dictionary of American Biography, Dictionary of National Biography, Chambers's Biographical Dictionary, The Century Cyclopedia of Names, Who's Who in America* (and supplements), *Who's Who* (British), *Who's Who in Latin America, International Who's Who, Current Biography,* and in many specialized works, as various Bible dictionaries, *The Catholic Encyclopedia, The New Catholic Dictionary, The Jewish Encyclopedia, Harper's Encyclopedia of Art,* books of the "Oxford Companion" series, *Grove's Dictionary of Music and Musicians, Hugo Riemanns Musik-Lexikon,* but also in works of general reference, such as the *Encyclopaedia Britannica, Chambers's Encyclopaedia, The New International Encyclopaedia, Larousse du XX^e^ Siècle, Der Grosse Brockhaus, Meyers Lexikon,* Zerolo's *Diccionario Enciclopédico de la Lengua Castellana,* and of historical reference, as *The Cambridge Ancient History, The Cambridge Medieval History, The Cambridge Modern History,* and *Dictionary of American History.* This file contained, of course, many times the number of names that could be included. The editors are neither so naïve nor so opinionated as to think their selections flawless. Infelicities, even errors, of selection are inevitable; but these, the editors believe, are errors of judgment and not the result of bias of any sort. Their correction—indeed, the improvement of the editorial content as a whole, not only of the selection of names but of the data presented—calls for the co-operation of the consultants of this Dictionary. The book is planned to provide the greatest amount of information of value to the largest number of users. The editors will welcome every criticism or suggestion, no matter how minute, designed to further that end.

## THE EDITORIAL STAFF

The planning of this Dictionary has been carried out under the direction of the permanent Editorial Board of G. & C. Merriam Company, consisting of the following members: William Allan Neilson (*chairman*), *Editor in Chief of Merriam-Webster Dictionaries, formerly President of Smith College;* Robert C. Munroe, *President of G. & C. Merriam Company;* John P. Bethel, *General Editor of Merriam-Webster Dictionaries;* Lucius H. Holt, *Managing Editor of Merriam-Webster Dictionaries.* The staff engaged in the editorial work consisted of the following:

EDITOR IN CHIEF

*William Allan Neilson,* M.A., University of Edinburgh; A.M., Ph.D., Harvard University.

GENERAL EDITOR

*John P. Bethel,* B.A., McGill University; A.M., Ph.D., Harvard University.

MANAGING EDITOR

*Lucius H. Holt,* B.A., M.A., Ph.D., Yale University.

ASSISTANT EDITORS

*Everett E. Thompson,* B.A., M.A., Amherst College; Litt.D., Syracuse University.
*Edward F. Oakes,* B.A., Williams College; A.M., Harvard University.
*Edward Artin,* Harvard University.
*Hubert P. Kelsey,* B.A., M.A., University of Michigan.
*Elsie Mag,* A.B., Smith College.
*Joseph A. Palermo,* A.B., Temple University.
*John O. Mayhugh,* B.A., University of Texas.
*Ervina E. Foss,* A.B., Mount Holyoke College.

PROOFREADERS AND EDITORIAL ASSISTANTS

*Hubert H. Roe.*
*Charles Westcott.*
*Anne M. Driscoll*, Smith College.
*Erwin L. Eisold*, B.A., Centre College.
*Lucy C. Rich*, A.B., Vassar College.

CLERICAL ASSISTANTS

*Christine M. Mayher*, Secretary to the General Editor.
*Roberta Teehan.*
*Pearl M. Green.*
*Edith (Moore) Heathcote.*
*Lucille Brouillet*, B.S., Massachusetts State College.
*Eliane (Yelle) Pilon*, B.S.Ed., Worcester (Massachusetts) State Teachers College.
*Grace Kellogg*, B.A., American International College.

Biographies were written by Dr. Bethel, Dr. Holt, Dr. Thompson, Mr. Oakes, Mr. Kelsey, Miss Mag, Mr. Palermo, Miss Foss, Mr. Mayhugh; and verification of this material was done by Mr. Westcott, Miss Foss, Miss Rich, Mr. Roe. All matters concerning pronunciation and syllabic division were under the charge of Mr. Artin, who was assisted by Miss Mag, Mr. Palermo, and others; the Guide to Pronunciation (pages xiv ff.) was prepared by Mr. Artin, the Pronouncing List of Prenames (pages 1628 ff.) by Mr. Artin and Miss Mag. Material for the Tables in the Appendix was compiled by Dr. Thompson and checked and arranged by Mr. Westcott. Cross-referencing was under the charge of Miss Foss, who was assisted by Miss Rich and Miss Brouillet. The proofreading was done by Messrs. Roe, Eisold, and Mayhugh, Miss Driscoll, and Miss Foss. Styling and alphabetizing were done chiefly by Mr. Mayhugh, Mr. Palermo, and Miss Foss.

## CONSULTANTS

Much valuable information and assistance has been supplied by many other persons. To all of these persons the editors and publishers wish to express their grateful appreciation, especially to the following:

Dr. Millar Burrows of Yale University for preparing the biography of Jesus Christ; Dr. Ephraim A. Speiser, Dr. Arthur W. Hummel, and others of the consultants listed below, for correcting the spelling of names or the dates or other details of certain biographies queried to them; Miss Florence E. Birks, of the staff of the City Library, Springfield, Massachusetts, for painstaking and patient co-operation in obtaining or verifying data of all kinds; the very many persons in the United States and in many other countries who have courteously supplied information in response to our letters of inquiry; and the following persons who have supplied information on the pronunciation of names in the fields listed in parentheses after their names (the editors, however, being alone responsible for the interpretation of the information supplied and for the pronunciations as they appear in this Dictionary):

Dr. Rudolph Altrocchi of the University of California (Italian)
Dr. Adriaan Jacob Barnouw of Columbia University (Dutch, Flemish, South African Dutch)
Dr. Robert Pierpont Blake of Harvard University (Georgian)
Dr. William Norman Brown of the University of Pennsylvania (Afghan, Asiatic Indian)
Dr. Joseph Médard Carrière of Northwestern University (Canadian French)
Dr. Pierre Delattre of the University of Oklahoma (French, Old French, Provençal)
Dr. Elliott V. K. Dobbie of Columbia University (Anglo-Saxon)
Dr. Joseph Dunn of the Catholic University of America (Celtic, Brazilian Portuguese)
Dr. William F. Edgerton of the University of Chicago (ancient Egyptian)
Dr. Nabih Amin Faris of Princeton University (Arabic)

Dr. J. D. M. Ford of Harvard University (Portuguese, Spanish)
Dr. Bernhard Geiger of the American Institute for Iranian Art and Archaeology (Persian)
Mr. William Grant, Editor of the Scottish National Dictionary (Scottish)
Dr. Mary R. Haas of the University of Michigan (Siamese)
Dr. Einar Haugen of the University of Wisconsin (Danish, Norwegian)
Dr. Halldór Hermannsson of Cornell University (Icelandic)
Dr. Arthur William Hummel of the Library of Congress (Chinese, Japanese)
Dr. Walter Gilbert Johnson of the University of Illinois (Swedish)
Mr. Anthony J. Klančar of Columbia University (Yugoslav)
Dr. Helge Kökeritz of the University of Minnesota (Swedish)
Miss Maria Lilienthal of Philadelphia, Pennsylvania (Russian)
Dr. Samuel Mendelsohn of Columbia University (Hebrew, Yiddish)
Dr. Karl Heinrich Menges of Columbia University (Mongolian, Tibetan, Turkish)
Dr. George Carpenter Miles of Princeton University (Persian, Turkish)
Dr. Tomás Navarro of Columbia University (Catalan, Spanish)
Professor Ernest D. Nielsen of Grand View College (Danish)
Dr. James A. Notopoulos of Trinity College (modern Greek)
Dr. John B. Olli of the College of the City of New York (Finnish)
Dr. Herbert Penzl of the University of Illinois (German)
Dr. Maxwell Isaac Raphael of Brookline, Massachusetts (Rumanian)
Dr. Joseph John Raymond of The Hotchkiss School (Estonian, Latvian, Lithuanian)
Professor Allen Walker Read of the Illinois Institute of Technology (Middle and early Modern English)
Professor Joseph Remenyi of Western Reserve University (Hungarian)
Dr. Ephraim Avigdor Speiser of the University of Pennsylvania (Akkadian, Assyrian, Babylonian, Sumerian)
Dr. Milivoy Stoyan Stanoyevich of Montclair, New Jersey (Bulgarian, Ukrainian, Yugoslav)
Mr. J. Frank Stimson, Research Assistant in Ethnology and Linguistics, Bishop Museum, Honolulu (Polynesian)
Dr. Morris Swadesh of New York City (Aztec)
Dr. John Reed Swanton of the Bureau of American Ethnology, Smithsonian Institution (American Indian)
Mr. Peter Tyko, Editor of *Dielli*, Boston, Massachusetts (Albanian)
Dr. Charles Frederick Voegelin of Indiana University (American Indian)
Dr. René Wellek of the University of Iowa (Czech)
Dr. Heinz A. Wieschhoff of the University of Pennsylvania (Bantu)
Dr. Edmund Ignace Zawacki of the University of Wisconsin (Polish)
Dr. Anna R. Zollinger of Brooklyn College (Rhaeto-Romanic)

The typesetting and electrotyping of this book were done by the George Banta Publishing Company, of Menasha, Wisconsin, whose staff gave unfailing co-operation and rendered valuable assistance in many ways, notably in the reading of proof. To all members of that staff who were concerned in any way with the making of this Dictionary—and specifically to Mr. C. A. Peerenboom, Mr. George Niedert, and Mr. Adolph Hyson—the editors and publishers express their grateful appreciation.

# EXPLANATORY NOTES

In compiling this Dictionary, the editors have striven for clarity of presentation rather than absolute uniformity in arrangement or rigid consistency in typographical and other mechanical details. Consequently, the basic pattern of arrangement that obtains in general throughout the book has been modified in particular instances, especially in the composite entries (see § 7, below). The typography and punctuation, too, have been adapted to the multifarious nature of the material.

The basic pattern of arrangement and the principal mechanical devices are described and illustrated below.

### BASIC PATTERN OF ARRANGEMENT

The principal details of each entry are given, usually, in the following order: the full name of the person; pronunciation (where not given in a preceding entry or covered in the appendix of prenames, pages 1628 ff.); birth and death dates (where known; with blank space instead of death date for persons still living) or period of existence; nationality, or an equivalent explanatory detail; occupation, or an equivalent descriptive detail.[1] For Americans, the place of birth (as a city or a county) is often included.

Where further information is necessary or desirable, one or more of the following kinds of details are included: family relationships (where significant, especially where there are relationships between two or more persons included in this Dictionary); education[2] (especially in entries of Americans); details of occupational, business, or professional career, or other significant activities; scientific discoveries or inventions; names of literary, musical, artistic, or architectural works.

### MECHANICAL DETAILS OF TYPOGRAPHY AND PUNCTUATION

#### *1. The typography of the entry names.*

The general practice in this Dictionary is to supply rather full information about the names of each person entered. Such information is typically limited, of course, to family name (or surname) and prenames,[3] and, in entries of married women, the maiden surname preceded by the word *nee* (= born). In many entries, however, additional names are also given. These may be of any of the following kinds: assumed names, nicknames (including epithets), titles of dignity or rank. Usually, the main entry is placed at the real surname; sometimes, however, it may be at the pseudonym, or the nickname, or the title. Cross entries are made liberally throughout the book.

(a) The names themselves are printed in heavy-faced type. For the convenience of the consultant, two sizes of heavy-faced type are used: a larger size for surnames and titular names (including prepositions, articles, and other connective elements regarded as parts of such names), a smaller size for prenames. Thus, in the entry

**Cochrane, Thomas.** 10th Earl of **Dundonald.**

the surname (Cochrane) and titular name (Dundonald) are in large heavy-faced type; the prename (Thomas) in smaller heavy-faced type.

(b) Words indicating nature of title are in light roman type, as: Saint, Blessed, Venerable, Abbé, Sir, Chevalier, Cavaliere, Count, Comte, Conde, Conte, Mulai, etc. However, in many Arabic, Persian, Turkish, and other names, words that are actually titles often appear in heavy-faced type as part of the name; for example: Bahadur, Bey, Effendi, Ghazi, Khan, Mirza, Pasha.

(c) Connective words between names, or parts of names, of the same person are in light italic type, as: *or, also, nee, orig. name, nickname.* Connective words between names of different persons are in light roman type. Language labels are in light italic type.

(d) The typical uses of the two sizes of heavy-faced type, and the uses of light roman and light italic type referred to above, are illustrated below.

*Single surname:*

**Scott, Winfield.**
**Scott,** Sir **Walter.**
**Grimm, Jacob** and his brother **Wilhelm.**

*Single names with alternative forms:*

**Barbon** *or* **Barebone** *or* **Barebones, Praisegod** *or* **Praise-God.**
**Scott** *or* **Scot, Reginald** *or* **Reynold.**

*Names containing connective elements:*

**à Beckett, Gilbert Abbott.**
**La Boétie, Étienne de.**
**Le Gallienne, Richard.**
**Leibnitz,** Baron **Gottfried Wilhelm von.**
**Meer, Jan van der.**
**Van Buren, Martin.**

*Compound surname, variously composed:*

**Fournier d'Albe, Edmund Edward.**
**Gatti-Casazza, Giulio.**
**Jiménez de Cisneros, Francisco.**
**Niembsch von Strehlenau, Nikolaus.**
**Ortega y Gasset, José.**
**Ortiz Rubio, Pascual.**
**Zúñiga y Azevedo, Gaspar de.**

*Compound surname with parts separated:*

**Bannerman,** Sir **Henry Campbell-.**
**Bivar, Rodrigo** (*or* **Ruy**) **Díaz de.**
**Carpini, Giovanni de Piano.**

*Surname plus title in same entry:*

**Ginkel, Godert de.** 1st Earl of **Athlone.**
**Craigavon,** 1st Viscount. **James Craig.**
**Lafayette,** Marquis **de. Marie Joseph Paul Yves Roch Gilbert du Motier.**

*Real name plus pseudonym, nickname, or the like:*

**Clemens, Samuel Langhorne.** *Pseudonym* **Mark Twain.**
**Irving,** Sir **Henry.** *Orig. name* **John Henry Brodribb.**

---

[1] In this connection it should be noted that the word *politician* is used in this Dictionary in the general meaning of "a person engaged in politics," and has no derogatory implications.

[2] Names of colleges and universities are usually given in a shortened form in connection with college degrees, appointments, or the like. Thus, "B.A., Chicago" refers to the degree Bachelor of Arts granted by the University of Chicago; "professor, Illinois" means professor in the University of Illinois; "educ. Duke" means educated at Duke University; "grad. Texas A.&M." means graduated from the Agricultural and Mechanical College of Texas. Names of State colleges and universities in the U.S. are often abbreviated to the word *State* preceded by the name or abbreviation of the State. Thus, "Mass. State" means Massachusetts State College; "Mich. State" means Michigan State College of Agriculture and Applied Science; etc.

[3] Variously called also forenames, first names, given names, or Christian names.

**Montez, Lola.** *Stage name of* **Marie Dolores Eliza Rosanna Gilbert.**
**Gatti, Bernardino.** *Known as* **il Soiaro.**
**Tintoretto, Il.** *Real name* **Jacopo Robusti.**
**Greco, El,** *i.e.* the Greek. *Also called* **Domenico.** *Real name: Greek* **Kyriakos Theotokopoulos;** *Spanish* **Domingo Teotocópuli** *or* **Theotocópuli;** *Italian* **Domenico Teotocopulo** *or* **Teoscopoli** *or* **Teoscopuli.**

(e) There are some exceptions to the general practice described and illustrated in § d, above. These exceptions are entries in which the name used for alphabetization is not, in the modern sense, a surname. For practical reasons, all such names have been treated typographically as surnames. Several classes of such names are illustrated by the following:

| | |
|---|---|
| **Homer** | (Greek poet) |
| **John** | (English king) |
| **Pius XI** | (pope) |
| **Gregory of Tours** | (saint) |
| **Henry the Minstrel** | (Scottish bard) |
| **Cino da Pistoia** | (Italian poet) |
| **Chrétien de Troyes** | (French poet) |
| **Genghis Khan** | (Mongol conqueror) |
| **Ali Bey** | (Mameluke ruler) |

### 2. *The spelling and arrangement of foreign-language names.*

It should be noted that many historical persons are entered under the name by which they are best known in English rather than under the form of the name in their native language. Rulers are usually under their equivalent English names; thus, the German kaisers will be found at *Frederick*, *William*, etc., instead of at *Friedrich*, *Wilhelm*, etc.

(a) *Names from languages using the Roman alphabet.*

(i) As a general rule, such names are printed in this Dictionary with the diacritical marks used in the native language, except that in Danish and Norwegian names ø has been printed as ö. In French names, accents have been used with capital as well as lower-case letters (instead of with lower-case letters only, as is the more common practice in books printed in French). Examples:

**Balboa, Vasco Núñez de.**
**Björnson, Björnstjerne.**
**Čapek, Karel.**
**Jebavý, Václav.**
**La Boétie, Étienne de.**

(ii) *German names.* German names containing any of the letters **ä, ö, ü** may admit of variant spellings using **ae, oe, ue** (and vice versa). Not all such variants could be cross-referenced, because of lack of space. Hence if the consultant fails to find such a German name under one spelling, he should look for it under the other.

(iii) *Hungarian names.* In the Hungarian language, the surname or family name comes first, the given or Christian name second. In the name *Kun Béla*, for example, *Kun* is the surname. In this Dictionary, however, in order to avoid confusion, Hungarian names are given in the same order as English names; thus, the name cited above is entered as **Kun, Béla**, and appears as Béla Kun wherever it is mentioned in some other biographical sketch.

In Hungarian names containing a titular element consisting of a name (as a place name) with appended adjectival ending, the adjectival ending is sometimes, in accordance with common practice, rendered by German *von* or French *de*. Thus, in Miklós von Nagybánya Horthy, *von Nagybánya* translates Hungarian *Nagybányai*, the *von* replacing the Hungarian adjectival ending *-i*.

(b) *Names requiring transliteration from a non-Roman alphabet.*

(i) *Arabic names.* As Arabic names have come into English at different periods and through several languages, there is a lack of uniformity in their transliteration. In this Dictionary, most Arabic names are entered under the spelling that accords with the best modern usage in English, but without diacritical marks; usually a transliteration of the full Arabic name with diacritical marks is also given. Example:

**Abd-er-Rahman III.** *Arab.* **'Abd-al-Raḥmān al-Nāṣir.**

Arabic has many compound names. Those containing the elements **Abd** (often combined, as in *Abdul*, *Abd-er-*, etc.), **abu-**, and **ibn-** (see the entries ABD, ABU-, and IBN- in the *Vocabulary*) are alphabetized under those elements. Those beginning with the article **al-** ("the") are alphabetized under the part following the article. Examples:

**abu-Bakr.**
**ibn-al-Farid.**
**ibn-Tufail.**
**Battani, al-.**

(ii) *Chinese names.* Chinese personal names may be quite confusing, since each individual may have several different names—some taken on at different periods of life, others acquired as courtesy names, literary names, or nicknames. For most entries of Chinese names in this Dictionary the customary arrangement of the names is followed: the last or family name is given first with hyphened prename coming second.[4] Examples: **Sun Yat-sen** and **Chiang Kai-shek** (*Sun* and *Chiang* being the family names). Many 20th-century Chinese have adopted the English custom of giving the family name last. In this Dictionary the names of such individuals are treated like English names. Thus, H. H. Kung, whose name in its original Chinese form was K'ung Hsiang-hsi, is entered as **Kung, H. H.**

Chinese dynasties commonly have one name (*T'ang*, *Han*), but the emperors generally had three—dynastic title, reign title, and personal name. For example, one of the emperors of the Manchu dynasty who ruled from 1862 to 1875 had the names *Mu Tsung*, *T'ung Chih*, and *Tsai Shun*. Emperors are entered in this Dictionary under the name generally used in English, the reign title, which was often applied by western writers to the emperor himself. His personal name, which also is sometimes entered in this Dictionary, was by custom forbidden after a ruler ascended the throne. The dynastic title, or temple name, was the posthumous name of the ruler.

For purposes of alphabetizing, a Chinese name is regarded as a single word. Thus, **Li Po** follows **Lipiński** and precedes **Lippe.**

(iii) *Japanese names.* Most Japanese names consist of two elements—family name and a single prename; the prename of one person is seldom used by another. Such names are entered under the surname and treated like English names; for example, **Kagawa, Toyohiko.**

The great shoguns of medieval Japan, who were members of the military clans (*Taira*, *Fujiwara*), as a rule used a single name, as *Yoritomo* and *Iyeyasu*. Although in some reference books such names are expressed in a fuller form (for example, *Minamoto no Yoritomo*, *i.e.* "Yoritomo of the Minamoto clan"), the single name is used in this Dictionary.

[4] Frequently in earlier times only two names were used (for example **Lao-tzu** and **Li Po**) without much consistency in English usage as to the hyphen.

Modern emperors have been known during their lifetime by their personal name (*Mutsuhito, Yoshihito*), but after an emperor's death his reign is always referred to by the era, or reign, name; thus, Mutsuhito's reign (1867–1912) is referred to as the *Meiji Era*.

(iv) *Russian names.* Russians usually have three names, in the following order: a Christian name, a patronymic derived from the father's Christian name, and a surname or family name. All names inflect according to gender. Masculine surnames end commonly in *-in*, *-ov* or *-ev*, or *-ski*. Feminine surnames are almost always inflected forms of masculine surnames. Thus, wives and daughters of men named *Dashkov, Krupski, Tolstoi* would use as surnames *Dashkova, Krupskaya, Tolstaya.* English references, however, often use the masculine form of the surname for both men and women.

Masculine patronymics end in *-ich* or *-vich* ("son of"), feminine patronymics end in *-vna*. Thus, the middle name of each of the sons of a man named Ivan is *Ivanovich* and the middle name of each of his daughters is *Ivanovna*.

Russian names are spelled with little or no consistency in English references, although there has been somewhat more agreement since the revision of the Russian alphabet whereby several letters were dropped. In this Dictionary the editors have avoided spellings introduced into English from French, German, and other languages, except in a few instances (as **Tchaikovsky**) where their use in English has become so widespread as to demand recognition. For the most part, Russian names have been transliterated by essentially the same system used in the etymologies of *Webster's New International Dictionary, Second Edition*, and by several other authorities. Examples (with Russian forms in the revised orthography):

*Christian names*

Андрей = Andrei
Фёдор = Fëdor
Максим = Maksim
Пётр = Pëtr
Семён = Semën
Юрий = Yuri

*Patronymics*

Николаевич = Nikolaevich
Петровна = Petrovna
Сергеевич = Sergeevich
Яковлевич = Yakovlevich

*Surnames*

Андреев = Andreev
Чехов = Chekhov
Дзержинский = Dzerzhinski
Джугашвили = Dzhugashvili
Голицын = Golitsyn
Щедрин = Shchedrin

It will be noted that Russian ы is transliterated as y, not as i. Russian e is transliterated either as e (not as ye) or (where it is pronounced yô) as ë. Compare the remarks on the pronunciation of these letters, pages xx, xxi.

Not all the Russian names in this book, however, have been transliterated by its editors. Many Russians, especially those who have lived abroad or have become citizens of other countries, have shown preference for certain spellings, and the editors have usually felt obliged to follow such personal preferences. Thus, Chaliapin, a naturalized French citizen, is entered at the spelling he himself preferred for English references (*Chaliapin*) rather than at the spelling that accords with the system of transliteration discussed above (*Shalyapin*). Conversely, in cases of Russian citizens having non-Russian names, the editors have sometimes thought it advisable to retain the spelling of the original language (provided, of course, it has a Roman alphabet) rather than transliterate from the Russian form into English; examples: *Witte* and *Wrangel*.

### 3. Syllabic division and pronunciation.

(a) *Syllabic division.* Elsewhere than in the respelling for pronunciation (see section b, below), the syllable division shown for a name indicates, for the guidance of printers, proofreaders, writers, and other interested consultants, those points at which the name may be divided at the end of a line of print or writing. A name may be divided wherever (elsewhere than in the respelling for pronunciation) a centered period, a primary or secondary accent, or a hyphen appears in this Dictionary. The rules for such division, established for each language by long and widespread practice, are in some respects more or less arbitrary; accordingly the division of a name sometimes differs from that of its respelled pronunciation, which attempts to show how the word is syllabified when spoken.

The syllabic division of prenames is, for the most part, given only in the appendix of prenames (pages 1628 ff.).

(b) *Pronunciation.*

(i) Pronunciation is indicated by respelling the names in the familiar Merriam-Webster phonetic alphabet, a full explanation of which is given on page xiv, and a key to which is provided across the foot of every pair of opened pages throughout the Dictionary. The pronunciation respelling is regularly enclosed within parentheses, but if there is an adjacent pair of parentheses serving some other purpose, the pronunciation is enclosed by square brackets.

Every effort has been made to secure accurate information on the pronunciation of all names included. A vast amount of time and effort has been devoted to seeking out the names and addresses of, and corresponding with, relatives, friends, and acquaintances of persons about the pronunciation of whose name there was doubt. The pronunciations of foreign-language names are in large measure based on information supplied by consulting specialists (see pp. vii, viii, above). Occasionally, however, the required information has not been obtained; in such cases, where the editors have felt that a reasonable guess may be made, a pronunciation respelling preceded by a question mark has been given.

Names of identical spelling belonging to different languages are often not divided or pronounced in the same way. Where this is so, the difference has been indicated. In entries in which no division and pronunciation are shown, the division and pronunciation are those of the nearest preceding entry of identical spelling for which these are shown. In a few cases no division and pronunciation are shown because no information on pronunciation could be obtained.

(ii) *Prenames.* Particular attention has been paid to the pronunciation of prenames. Some of these (especially a name susceptible of more than one common pronunciation, for which we have been able to ascertain the pronunciation used by a given bearer) are pronounced in full at the main entry, but—partly to save space, partly to facilitate reference—the pronunciation of such names is usually reserved for an appendix (pages 1628 ff.). Prenames (as those of rulers) that serve as entries in the body of the Dictionary—especially foreign-language variants that serve as alternative entries—have sometimes not been pronounced at the entry. The pronunciation of such prenames should be sought in the prename list.

(iii) *Other names.* Titular names and maiden names have usually been pronounced at the entry under which they occur. Sometimes, however, the maiden name has been left unpronounced if the name is entered, with pronunciation, at its alphabetical place in the body of the Dictionary.

### 4. *Dates.*

Birth and death dates follow the part of the entry devoted to the names and their pronunciation. Typically such dates constitute a separate statement followed by a period. Where internal structure of the entry calls for it, however, as in many composite entries (see § 7, below), such dates may be enclosed in parentheses.

Dates occurring in pairs are printed in full if they are birth and death dates (for example: 1717–1793), but otherwise are usually abbreviated in the conventional way (1717–93).

Dates of both birth and death are given wherever possible. Where one of the dates is omitted because of lack of information, the nature of the single date given is indicated by a prefixed b. (= born) or d. (= died). In entries of living persons a blank space follows the hyphen; for example, the life dates of a person born in 1900 and still alive are recorded thus: 1900– .

Uncertainty about a date (of any sort) is indicated in various ways. When the date assigned to an event is reasonably certain, but not completely so, it is accompanied by a question mark so placed that it can refer to only the date in question; for example: 1717?–1793 (if only the first date is uncertain) or 1717–?1793 (if only the second is uncertain) or 1717?–?1793 (if both dates are uncertain). When the date assigned is merely approximate (within a relatively few years) it is accompanied by the abbreviation c. (= Latin *circa* = English *about*) or, if another abbreviation precedes the date, by the word *about.* Where only the general period of a person's active life is known, the birth and death dates are replaced by a statement qualified by fl. (= Latin *floruit*, flourished), or are omitted altogether if exact dates can be assigned to particular events recorded in the biography.

All dates before the Christian era are accompanied by B.C.; dates after the beginning of the Christian era are accompanied by A.D. only where necessary for complete clarity.

### 5. *Titles of books, periodicals, etc.*

Such titles are printed in italic type.

### 6. *Abbreviations.*

Abbreviations have been used throughout the book wherever it is felt that their use presents little or no difficulty of typography or comprehension. A list of these abbreviations is given on pages xxxiii–xxxvi, below.

### 7. *Composite entries.*

The editors have often found it desirable to treat in a single entry the names of more than one person. The many entries of this sort throughout the Dictionary usually exhibit in composite treatment the members of a single family, dynasty, or the like, or a succession of individuals or families bearing the same title of rank. This plan of treatment is not a mere editorial convenience. Many persons are interested in matters of genealogy and family relationships or are interested in tracing the history of familiar titles of rank. It was felt that such an interest is best served by presenting information of this sort (so far as the physical limitations of this Dictionary permit its inclusion) in composite entries.

In such entries, the surname or title is repeated (for persons other than the first) wherever its repetition seems necessary or desirable for complete clarity.

Composite entries range in complexity from those treating two names (as under **Georges Jules Auguste Cain**) or many names in short space (as the entry at **Károlyi**) to those presenting families of many branches (as the **Douglas** family) often holding several titles of rank (as the **Clifford** family).

Entries of families, dynasties, etc., in general precede other entries of identical spelling (see § 9a, below)—unless the former are treated under the name of one member of the group.

### 8. *Cross references.*

Two general types of cross references are found in this Dictionary: cross entries in the Vocabulary, and cross references in the body of an article. The name to which the consultant is directed is indicated either by the use of special type (light roman capitals and small capitals) or by the placing after the name of the letters *q.v.* (= Latin *quod vide* = *which see*) or, if the reference is to more than one name, *qq.v.* (= Latin *quae vide* = *which* [plural] *see*). Thus:

> **Castlemon, Harry.** Pseudonym of Charles Austin FOSDICK.
> **Colluthus.** Variant of COLUTHUS.
> **Alredus Beverlacensis.** = ALFRED OF BEVERLEY.
> **Cartesius, Renatus.** See René DESCARTES.
> **Smith, Benjamin Eli.** See under Eli SMITH.
> **Badenoch,** Lord of. See *Alexander Stewart* (1343?–?1405), under STEWART family.
> **Temple,** Earls of. See GRENVILLE family.
> **Thomond,** Earls and Marquises of. Titles borne by O'Brien family (*q.v.*).
> **Veturia.** Mother of Coriolanus (*q.v.*).

Cross references with "see" and "cf." are frequently used in the body of a biography. "See" leads to additional information. "Cf." (abbreviation of the Latin word *confer*, meaning "compare") leads to useful, interesting, or related material.

### 9. *Alphabetical arrangement.*

The alphabetical position of any entry is determined first of all by that part of the entry in large heavy-faced type (see § 1, above). For most entries, this is a plain surname, and the ordinary rules of alphabetical sequence govern: surnames follow one another in strict order (**Abbe** preceding **Abbey; Snow** preceding **Snowden**), and entries of persons of the same surname are arranged in the alphabetical order of their prenames (**Jacob** preceding **James**; **James Albert** preceding **James Arthur**; etc.). Numerals, and words printed in light roman type (see § 1b), are disregarded in alphabetizing, except that numerical order governs the arrangement of the members of a series under an entry (as at several of the entries for the name **Henry**).

The following brief statements will clarify the practice of this Dictionary in special cases.

(a) A composite biography of several persons entered under the family (or clan) name precedes the entries of all other persons having this same surname; thus, the **Gordon** family entry precedes all other entries with surname **Gordon.**

(b) For entries such as those at **Henry** or **John** the order of entries is in general as follows: (1) saints; (2) popes; (3) rulers or members of ruling families, where necessary these names being alphabetized by name of country[5]; (4) other persons having the single name; (5) entries in which **Henry** or **John** is a surname; (6) entries in which **Henry** or **John** is followed by a qualifying

[5] For practical purposes, former independent states are treated under the country of which they now form a part. For example, the rulers of León and Castile are alphabetized among the rulers of Spain.

word or phrase (as, **Henry Raspe** and **Henry the Navigator** or **John of Antioch**). All these precede entries in which the letters **Henry** or the letters **John** form the first part of the entry (as **Henryson** or **Johne**).

(c) Names beginning with the prefix **Mc, M'**, or **M'** are all alphabetized as if spelled with the full form of this prefix, **Mac.** In alphabetizing, no distinction is made between these names and other names (such as **Macchiavelli**) in which the initial letters **Mac** are not a prefix. Similarly, names containing the abbreviation **St.** are alphabetized as if this element were spelled in full **Saint.**

(d) In names having a connective element (as a preposition or an article) between the prename and surname (as noted in § 1d above), this element is treated typographically as a part of the surname or titular name.

(i) American and British names containing **De, Van, Von,** or the like, are alphabetized under these connectives unless special circumstances call for special treatment. Thus, **Henry Van Brunt** is entered at **Van Brunt** (following the entry **Vanbrugh**), not at **Brunt.**

(ii) In Swedish, German, Dutch, and other names (except American and British names) such connective elements as **af, ten, ter, till, van, van de, van den, van der, vom, von, von dem, von den, von der, von und zu, zu, zum, zur,** etc., are usually disregarded in alphabetizing when they occur between the prename and surname. Thus, **Gustaf af Geijerstam** is alphabetized at **Geijerstam; Bernhard ten Brink** is alphabetized at **Brink; Jan van der Meer** is alphabetized at **Meer; Friedrich Wilhelm von Bülow** is alphabetized at **Bülow; Christian zu Stolberg** is alphabetized at **Stolberg.**

(iii) In the Romance languages, names of this type are generally alphabetized at that part of the name following such connectives as **d', da, dal, de, de', degli, dei, del, de l', de la, de las, dell', della, delle, de los, des, di, di', do, du,** etc. Thus, **Gustave de Molinari** is alphabetized at **Molinari,** and **Giuliano da Sangallo** is alphabetized at **Sangallo,** the connectives **de** and **da** being disregarded. Names containing **la, le, les,** etc., are alphabetized according to usage or according to the preference of the individual bearing the name, systematic treatment being impossible.

(iv) In some instances, however, where usage in English is so well established that the name is likely to be sought under the connective element, the main entry or a cross entry has been given there. For example, **Hernando de Soto** is entered at **De Soto** and cross-entered at **Soto.**

(e) In names compounded of more than one element: if the surname, or any matter in large heavy-faced type comprising the principal part of an entry (see § 1d, above), is compounded of more than one element, with or without connective elements, it is alphabetized as if these elements formed a single word. Thus the entries

**Apelles.**
**Ap Ellis, Augustine.**
**Apianus, Petrus.**

are alphabetized in the order shown, as if **Ap Ellis** were spelled *Apellis.* Similarly, **Donn-Byrne** follows **Donnay** and precedes **Donndorf.** An exception to this rule is noted under (b), above.

(i) Spanish and Portuguese compound surnames containing **y** or **e** ("and") are alphabetized at the element preceding **y** or **e.** Thus, **José Ortega y Gasset** is entered at **Ortega y Gasset,** not at **Gasset.**

(ii) Sometimes, especially in the Romance languages, usage may require that a compound surname be alphabetized at some element other than the first. For example, **Fernão Lopes de Castanheda** is entered:

**Castanheda, Fernão Lopes de.**

(f) The alphabetization of Arabic, Chinese, Hungarian, and Japanese names has already been discussed, under § 2, above.

# A GUIDE TO PRONUNCIATION

## I. KEY TO THE SYMBOLS USED IN PRONUNCIATION

§ **1.** Accents and Hyphens. The principal accent is indicated by a heavy mark (**′**), and the secondary accent by a lighter mark (′), at the end of the syllable. A syllable having no accent is followed by a centered period, except when it is a final syllable, or occurs immediately before a hyphen in a compound word or name.

Foreign Sounds for which no special symbols are provided are represented by the nearest English equivalents. The division entitled "Elements of Pronunciation of Foreign Names," on pp. xxii ff., presents in compact form a great deal of information on the pronunciation of letters and groups of letters in many foreign languages.

The name of each diacritical symbol is given in parentheses immediately after the symbol.

Symbols Used in Respelling for Pronunciation

**ā** (long a*), as in **āle, fāte, lā′bor** (§ 5).
**ȧ** (half-long a*), as in **chȧ·ot′ic, fȧ·tal′i·ty** (§ 6).
**â** (circumflex a), as in **câre, beâr, âir** (§ 7).
**ă** (short a*), as in **ădd, lămb, făt** (§ 8).
***ă*** (italic short a*), as in ***ă*c·count′, loy′*ă*l** (§ 9).
**ä** (two-dot a), as in **ärm, är·tis′tic, fä′ther** (§ 10).
**ȧ** (one-dot a), as in **ȧsk, stȧff, pȧth** (§ 11).
***ȧ*** (italic one-dot a), as in **so′f*ȧ*, *ȧ*·bound′** (§ 12).
**b**, as in **ba′by, be, bit, bob, but** (§ 13).
**ch**, as in **chair, much, ques′tion** (-ch*ŭ*n) (§ 14).
**d**, as in **day, add′ed** (§ 15).
**d͡ū** (ligatured d-u), as in **ver′d͡ūre** (§ 16).
**ē** (long e*), as in **ēve, mēte, se·rēne′** (§ 17).
**ẹ̄** (hooked long e*), as in **hẹ̄re, fẹ̄ar** (§ 18).
**ė** (half-long e*), as in **ė·vent′, crė·ate′** (§ 19).
**ĕ** (short e*), as in **ĕnd, rĕn·di′tion** (§ 20).
***ĕ*** (italic short e*), as in **si′l*ĕ*nt, nov′*ĕ*l** (§ 21).
**ẽ** (tilde e), as in **mak′ẽr, pẽr·vert′** (§ 22).
**f**, as in **fill, buff, phan′tom** (făn′-), **cough** (kôf) (§ 23).
**g**, as in **go, be·gin′, guy** (gī) (§ 24).
**h**, as in **hat, hen, hide, hot, hurt, a·head′** (§ 25).
**ī** (long i*), as in **īce, spīre, ī·de′a** (§ 26).
**ĭ** (short i*), as in **ĭll, hab′ĭt, bod′y** (bŏd′ĭ) (§ 27).
***ĭ*** (italic short i*), as in **char′*ĭ*·ty, pos′s*ĭ*·ble, d*ĭ*·rect′, A′pr*ĭ*l** (§ 28).
**j**, as in **joke, jol′ly, gem** (jĕm), **edge** (ĕj) (§ 29).
**k**, as in **keep, kick** (kĭk), **cube** (kūb), **cho′rus** (kō′r*ŭ*s), **pique** (pēk) (§ 30).
**ᴋ** (small capital k), as in German **ich** (ĭᴋ), **ach** (äᴋ), Scottish **loch** (lŏᴋ) (§ 31).
**l**, as in **late, leg, lip, lot, full, hol′ly** (§ 32).
**m**, as in **man, men, mine, hum, ham′mer** (§ 33).
**n**, as in **no, on, in′ner, sign** (sīn) (§ 34).
**ɴ** (small capital n): without sound of its own, indicates the nasal tone (as in French or Portuguese) of the preceding vowel or diphthong, as in French **bon** (bôɴ), Portuguese **pão** (pouɴ) (§ 35).
**ng**, as in **sing, sing′er** (sĭng′ẽr), **fin′ger** (fĭng′gẽr), **bank** (băngk), **can′ker** (kăng′kẽr) (§ 36).
**ō** (long o*), as in **ōld, nōte, he′rō** (§ 37).
**ȯ** (half-long o*), as in **ȯ·bey′, tȯ·bac′co, a·nat′ȯ·my** (§ 38).
**ô** (circumflex o), as in **ôrb, lôrd, ôr·dain′, law** (lô), **bought** (bôt), **caught** (kôt), **all** (ôl) (§ 39).
**ŏ** (short o*), as in **ŏdd, nŏt, tŏr′rid, fŏr′est, pŏs·ter′i·ty** (§ 40).
**ŏ̂** (short-circumflex o*), as in **sŏ̂ft, dŏ̂g, clŏ̂th, lŏ̂ss, cŏ̂st** (§ 41).
***ŏ*** (italic short o*), as in **c*ŏ*n·nect′, *ŏ*c·cur′, Bab′y·l*ŏ*n** (§ 42).
**oi**, as in **oil, nois′y, a·void′, goi′ter** (§ 43).
**o͞o** (long double o*), as in **fo͞od, o͞oze, no͞ose, rude** (ro͞od), **true** (tro͞o), **blue** (blo͞o) (§ 44).
**o͝o** (short double o*), as in **fo͝ot, wo͝ol, bo͝or, put** (po͝ot), **pull** (po͝ol), **sure** (sho͝or) (§ 45).
**ou**, as in **out, thou, now** (nou) (§ 46).
**p**, as in **pen, pin, pop, put** (§ 47).
**r**, as in **rap, red, hor′rid, far, fur, curd, rhom′boid** (rŏm′-) (§ 48).
**s**, as in **so, this, haste, cell** (sĕl), **vice** (vīs), **scene** (sēn), **hiss** (hĭs) (§ 49).
**sh**, as in **she, ship, shop, ma·chine′** (-shēn′), **so′cial** (-sh*ă*l) (§ 50).
**t**, as in **time, pat, lat′ter, win′ter, thyme** (tīm) (§ 51).
**t͟h** (barred t-h), as in **t͟hen, t͟hough, smoot͟h, breat͟he** (§ 52).
**th** (plain t-h), as in **thin, through, wealth** (§ 53).
**t͡ū** (ligatured t-u), as in **na′t͡ūre, cul′t͡ūre, pic′t͡ūre** (§ 54).
**ū** (long u*), as in **cūbe, tūne, lūte** (§ 55).
**ů** (half-long u*), as in **ů·nite′, em′ů·late** (§ 56).
**û** (circumflex u), as in **ûrn, fûrl, con·cûr′, fern** (fûrn), **fir** (fûr) (§ 57); for German **ö, oe**, as in **schön** (shûn), **Goe′the** (gû′t*ĕ*); for French **eu**, as in **jeu** (zhû), **seul** (sûl); etc. (§ 57.3).
**ŭ** (short u*), as in **ŭp, tŭb, ŭn′der, ŭn·do′** (§ 58).
***ŭ*** (italic short u*), as in **cir′c*ŭ*s, cir′c*ŭ*m·stance, de′mon** (-m*ŭ*n), **na′tion** (-sh*ŭ*n) (§ 59).
**ü** (umlaut u): for French **u**, as in **me·nu′** (mẽ·nü′); for German **ü**, as in **grün, hübsch**; etc. (§ 60).
**v**, as in **van, vent, vote, re·voke′, re·vive′** (§ 61).
**w**, as in **want, win, weed, wood, a·ward′, per·suade′** (-swād′), **choir** (kwīr) (§ 62).
**y**, as in **yet, yel′low, be·yond′, on′ion** (-y*ŭ*n) (§ 63).
**z**, as in **zone, haze, wise** (wīz), **mu′sic** (-zĭk), **xy′lo·phone** (zī′-) (§ 64).
**zh**, as in **az′ure** (ăzh′ẽr), **gla′zier** (-zhẽr), **pleas′ure** (plĕzh′ẽr), **rouge** (ro͞ozh) (§ 65).
**'** as in **par′don** (pär′d'n), **wres′tle** (rĕs′'l), indicates that a following consonant is syllabic (§ 66); when not followed by a consonant, it indicates that a preceding consonant is voiceless, as in French **nô′tre** (nō′tr'), **meu′ble** (mû′bl'), except after **y**: for its significance in that situation, see § 63.3.

* See § 3.21.

# II. PRELIMINARY EXPLANATIONS

§ **2.** English pronunciation is the basis of the following description of sounds. This Dictionary, in common with other works on pronunciation, uses the same symbols for sounds in different languages that are similar but not identical (e.g., ā for the vowel sound in English *gay* and French *gai*, respectively). Although the differences between English sounds and corresponding sounds in foreign languages are often briefly touched on below, no attempt at detailed differentiation has been made, both because of lack of space and because the assigning of the English value to the symbols transcribing foreign names will usually be found adequate in an English context.

§ **3.** Explanations (chiefly in the form of definitions) of a number of terms which will be used in the description of sounds may advantageously be made here:

§ **3.1.** The **palate** consists of a front, or **hard**, part, and of a back, or **soft**, part. The soft palate is also called the **velum**. The hanging fleshy lobe which constitutes the back part of the soft palate is the **uvula.**

§ **3.2.** Phoneticians distinguish the following parts of the **tongue**: the **point**, or **tip**; the **blade**, including the tip and the part just behind it, lying, when at rest, opposite the ridge just behind the upper front teeth (called the *teethridge*); the **front**,—the middle part of the upper surface, which in rest lies normally opposite the hard palate; the **back**,—the part that rests normally opposite the soft palate.

§ **3.3. front,** *adj.* Uttered with closure or narrowing of the mouth passage at the front of the mouth, or between the front of the tongue (see § 3.2) and the hard palate.

§ **3.4. back,** *adj.* Uttered with closure or narrowing of the mouth passage at the back of the mouth, or between the back of the tongue (see § 3.2) and the soft palate.

§ **3.5. central,** *adj.* Uttered with the tongue intermediate in position between front and back. Also called *mixed.*

§ **3.6. advance,** *v.* To utter with the tongue farther forward.

§ **3.7. retract,** *v.* To utter with the tongue farther back.

§ **3.8. high,** *adj.* Of a vowel, uttered with some part of the tongue high up toward the palate (see § 4). Also called *close.*

§ **3.9. low,** *adj.* Of a vowel, uttered with a wide opening between the tongue and palate (see § 4). Also called *open.*

§ **3.10. mid,** *adj.* Of a vowel, uttered with the tongue intermediate in position between high and low.

§ **3.11.** The terms *high* (or *close*) and *low* (or *open*) are also used relatively. Thus o͝o may be described as a lower or more open vowel than o͞o, though absolutely both o͞o and o͝o are high (or close) vowels.

§ **3.12. tense,** *adj.* Uttered with the tongue and associated muscles in a relatively tense state.

§ **3.13. lax,** *adj.* Uttered with the tongue and associated muscles in a relatively relaxed state.

§ **3.14. round,** *v.* To utter with the lips drawn together laterally so as to form a more or less round opening.

§ **3.15. unround,** *v.* To utter with the lips spread laterally.

§ **3.16. voiced,** *adj.* Uttered with vibration of the vocal cords. Certain consonants are voiced; all vowels are practically always voiced.

§ **3.17. voiceless,** *adj.* Uttered without vibration of the vocal cords. Certain consonants are voiceless.

§ **3.18.** Every language has pairs of consonants that differ chiefly or only in that one member of each pair is voiced while the other is voiceless. English has the following pairs (each sound symbol is accompanied by a key word):

| *Voiced* | | *Voiceless* | |
|---|---|---|---|
| b | **b**an | p | **p**an |
| d | **d**ie | t | **t**ie |
| g | ta**g** | k | ta**ck** |
| t͟h | ei**th**er | th | e**th**er |
| v | **v**an | f | **f**an |
| z | **z**inc | s | **s**ink |
| zh | confu**si**on | sh | Confu**ci**an |
| j | ri**dg**e | ch | ri**ch** |

§ **3.19. quality,** *n.* The identifying character of a vowel sound, determined chiefly by the resonance of the vocal chambers in uttering it.

§ **3.20. quantity** *or* **length,** *n.* The relative duration, or time length, of a speech sound. See § 3.21.

§ **3.21.** The term **long** for the sounds ā, ē, ī, ō, o͞o, ū, and the term **short** for the sounds ă, ĕ, ĭ, ŏ, o͝o, ŭ, have been established in English by long use; and it has been found convenient to retain them in assigning names to these diacritical symbols (and to certain other derivative symbols) in Division I ("Key to the Symbols Used in Pronunciation") of this Guide. Actually, however, these terms are not strictly accurate phonetically, since the difference between each of these pairs of sounds (e.g., between ā and ă) is primarily one of quality rather than of quantity. Hereafter in this Guide the terms are used in their strict phonetic sense, **long** being applied to a sound of relatively great duration, **short** to a sound of relatively small duration.

§ **3.22. fricative,** *adj.* Characterized by frictional rustling of the breath as it is emitted with the mouth passage greatly narrowed, but not closed. Examples: the sounds f, v, s, z.

§ **3.23. trill,** *n.* The rapid vibration of one speech organ against another. See § 48.1.

§ **3.24. retroflex,** *adj.* Of the tongue, having the tip raised and bent back; of sounds, formed thus. See §§ 22, 57.

§ **3.25. obscure,** *adj.* Uttered without stress;—applied to the unstressed vowel symbolized *ȧ, ă, ĕ, ĭ, ŏ,* or *ŭ* in this Dictionary.

§ **3.26. vanish,** *n.* The relatively faint latter part of a diphthong in which the first part has greater stress. Thus, in English, ā often has an ĭ vanish, ō an o͝o vanish.

§ **3.27. open syllable.** A syllable ending in a vowel or diphthong. Example: both syllables of *A′da.*

§ **3.28. closed syllable.** A syllable ending in a consonant. Example: both syllables of *Ed′ward.*

§ **4.** Vowels are often charted or diagramed according to the position that the tongue assumes in uttering them, such position being the chief determinant, or one of the chief determinants, of the quality of each vowel. One common way of charting vowels is shown below. This chart will serve as a rough indication of the relative tongue position of the different vowels.

| | FRONT | CENTRAL | BACK |
|---|---|---|---|
| HIGH | ē<br>ĭ | | o͞o<br>o͝o |
| MID | ā<br>ĕ | û, ẽ, *ȧ*, ŭ | ō |
| LOW | â<br>ă | ȧ | ô<br>ŏ<br>ä |

Note: ī and ū, being diphthongs, are not shown.

# III. DESCRIPTION OF SOUNDS

ā

**§ 5.** As in English **ā**le.
Mid-front tense unrounded. In standard English, usually not a pure, or simple, sound, but diphthongized, beginning at or near the mid-front tense vowel (or, in another variety, at or near the mid-front lax vowel ĕ, as in *met*) and proceeding upward toward ĭ. The second element, or vanish, of the ā sound appears in accented syllables in both England and America when the sound is final or before voiced consonants, as in *day*, *made*. But in America, before voiceless consonants it is usually not prominent and is sometimes lacking, as in *hate*, and in all positions it is less prominent in America and the North of England than in southern England.

**§ 5.1.** In foreign languages, ā is usually a pure sound without vanish, and is often higher and tenser than the corresponding pure English sound, or than the first element of the corresponding diphthongal English sound. In some languages it is so high as to suggest ĭ to many English-speaking persons.

ȧ

**§ 6.** As in English ch**ȧ**otic.
A short sound of ā-like quality, usually without vanish, occurring in unaccented syllables.

â

**§ 7.** As in English c**â**re.
Low-front unrounded, relatively long, having a tongue position between that for ĕ and for ă. In English, it varies from this position to a higher one, near ĕ, and to a lower one, near ă.

ă

**§ 8.** As in English **ă**dd.
Low-front unrounded, the mouth being nearly or quite as wide open as for ä in *art*, but the tongue somewhat farther forward and the front (but not the tip) elevated instead of the back.

There is considerable variation in the sound of ă in standard English. In Southern British speech the sound is noticeably higher than that generally heard in America. To an American of the North or East the word *back* as pronounced by a Southern English speaker often suggests the word *beck*. In the southern United States, however, the ă resembles in quality that of southern England. In the pronunciation of standard English by educated Scotsmen, and by many Northern Englishmen, the ă is replaced by ȧ.

*ă*

**§ 9.** As in English *ă*ccount.
In ordinary English speech, an obscure vowel, like *ȧ* (see § 12). Occasionally in very deliberate speech pronounced ă.

ä

**§ 10.** As in English **ä**rm.
Low-back unrounded. Usually somewhat more advanced in southern England than in America. In New England, however, often more advanced than in southern England, in many cases being actually ȧ (low-central vowel).

ȧ

**§ 11.** As in English **ȧ**sk.
Low-central unrounded, when used in representing the pronunciation of foreign words. In English words in the respelled pronunciation of which ȧ occurs, the low-central pronunciation is rare in standard English outside of New England, the usual pronunciation being ă (low-front vowel) in America and ä (low-back vowel) in southern England. In English words, accordingly, the symbol ȧ is to be regarded as indicating any of three pronunciations.

*ȧ*

**§ 12.** As in English sof*ȧ*.
Mid-central unrounded. Always obscure.

b

**§ 13.** As in English **b**a**b**y.
A voiced sound produced by stopping the breath with the lips. Correlative voiceless stop, p; correlative nasal, m.

ch

**§ 14.** As in English **ch**air.
ch is not a combination of any of the sounds usually borne by *c* and *h* in English, and contains no c or h sound. It is a voiceless sound consisting approximately of t followed by sh (see §§ 51, 50). Voiced correlative, j.

d

**§ 15.** As in English **d**ay.
A voiced sound produced, in English, by stopping the breath by placing the point of the tongue against the teethridge (see § 3.2.). In some languages (e.g., French and Italian) the tongue point is placed against the back of the upper front teeth.

Correlative voiceless stop, t; correlative nasal, n.

d͜ū

**§ 16.** As in English ver**d͜ū**re.
In words in the respelled pronunciation of which this symbol occurs, the pronunciation dū (= dyōō) occurs in most words only in very formal speech. The ligature (‿) indicates that in ordinary speech the dy is usually pronounced j (i.e., d+zh; see § 29). The explanation of this is as follows: The original pronunciation was dy. The sound zh, however, being closer to d than y is, speakers in time began, in accord with a process technically known as assimilation, to take a "path of less resistance" by substituting zh for y.

Also, before consonants the vowel is commonly ẽ or *ŭ*, not ŏŏ.

Correlative sound with voiceless consonant, t͜ū.

ē

**§ 17.** As in English **ē**ve.
High-front tense unrounded. In some languages, higher and tenser than in English.

ē̦

**§ 18.** As in English h**ē̦**re.
Used before r in transcribing English words. The inferior modifier (which is a sign of openness, frequently used by philologists and phoneticians) indicates that, although the full ē pronunciation does sometimes occur in very formal speech, in ordinary speech a more open sound occurs, this open sound being approximately or exactly a lengthened ĭ.

**§ 18.1.** In transcriptions of Danish and South African Dutch, ē̦ represents a long ĭ sound.

ė

**§ 19.** As in English **ė**vent.
A short sound of ē-like quality occurring in unaccented syllables.

ĕ

§ 20. As in English ĕnd.
Mid-front lax unrounded.

ĕ

§ 21. As in English silĕnt.
In ordinary English speech, an obscure vowel, like *ȧ*. Occasionally in very deliberate speech pronounced ĕ.

ẽ

§ 22. As in English makẽr.
Used before r in unaccented syllables. In other languages than English, two sounds—an obscure vowel and an r—are usually pronounced. In types of English in which r is not "dropped," ẽr is pronounced as a single sound—an obscure mid-central vowel uttered with retroflexed tongue (see § 3.24). In types of English in which r final and before a consonant is "dropped," ẽr is pronounced as an obscure mid-central vowel, but without retroflexion.

§ 22.1. ẽ is used for the obscure vowel in French.

f

§ 23. As in English fill.
A voiceless sound produced by the friction of the breath escaping between the closely juxtaposed upper teeth and lower lip. Voiced correlative, v.

g

§ 24. As in English go.
A voiced sound produced by stopping the breath by pressing the back part of the tongue against the soft palate. The tongue is more advanced when the sound occurs with a front vowel (e.g., in *geese* gēs) than when it occurs with a back vowel (e.g., in *goose* gōōs). Correlative voiceless stop, k; correlative nasal, ng.

§ 24.1. In some languages the orthographic spelling *g* sometimes or always stands for a voiced continuant sound articulated, not by making contact between the back of the tongue and the soft palate, but by merely bringing the back of the tongue close to the soft palate—a sound which is the voiced correlative of voiceless ᴋ. This sound is Anglicized as g, and is so represented in this Dictionary. However, in Division IV. ʙ. ("Elements of Pronunciation of Foreign Names") attention is called to some of the better-known languages in which this pronunciation occurs.

h

§ 25. As in English hat.
An impulse of breath occurring, in English, only at the beginning of a syllable before a vowel or before w (e.g., *white* hwīt) or y (e.g., *huge* hūj [= hyōōj]). Usually voiceless in English, but sometimes voiced when between vowels.

ī

§ 26. As in English īce.
A diphthong, not a single sound. Both elements vary somewhat throughout the English-speaking world. In two of the commonest varieties, the diphthong begins with ȧ (low-central vowel) or with ä (low-back vowel) and moves upward toward or to ĭ.

ĭ

§ 27. As in English ĭll.
High-front lax unrounded.

§ 27.1. The symbol ĭ transcribing Polish *y*, Rumanian *ă* and *î*, and the Russian letter transliterated *y* in this Dictionary, stands for a high-central unrounded vowel that has no counterpart in English. ĭ (high-front) is the nearest English equivalent and the usual Anglicization.

ĭ

§ 28. As in English charĭty.
Transcribes a sound that is an obscure mid-central vowel, like *ȧ*, with some speakers, ĭ with others.

j

§ 29. As in English joke.
A voiced sound consisting approximately of d followed by zh (see §§ 15, 65). Voiceless correlative, ch.

k

§ 30. As in English keep.
A voiceless sound produced by stopping the breath by pressing the back part of the tongue against the soft palate. The tongue is more advanced when the sound occurs with a front vowel (e.g., in *keel* kēl) than when it occurs with a back vowel (e.g., in *cool* kōōl). Correlative voiced stop, g; correlative nasal, ng.

ᴋ

§ 31. As in German ich, ach, Scottish loch.
The articulation of this consonant (which occurs in Scottish and in a number of foreign languages—e.g., German and Russian) differs from that of k in that the tongue is merely brought close to the palate, and not actually into contact with it; i.e., the sound is a continuant, and not a stop. As for k and g, in some languages the tongue is more advanced when the sound occurs with a front vowel (e.g., in German *ich* ĭᴋ) than when it occurs with a back vowel (e.g., in German *ach* äᴋ).

l

§ 32. As in English late, full.
In the production of this voiced sound in English, the point of the tongue is in contact with the teethridge, as it is for d. However, whereas for d the breath is completely stopped, for l a passage for the breath is left at both sides, or with some speakers at only one side, of the tongue. Thus l is a continuant, d is a stop.

§ 32.1. As in the case of d, in some languages the tongue point is placed against the back of the upper front teeth rather than against the teethridge.

§ 32.2. While the tongue point is in contact with the teethridge, that part of the tongue behind the point is free to assume a variety of positions. These various positions may roughly be reduced to two: when the front of the tongue is raised toward the hard palate, the l is said to be "clear"; when the back of the tongue is raised toward the soft palate, the l is said to be "dark." In general, in English a clear l is pronounced at the beginning of a syllable; a dark l is pronounced (a) at the end of a syllable, (b) before a consonant, and (c) when the l is syllabic (see § 32.4). The difference between a clear l and a dark l never distinguishes words in English, and the same symbol, l, is accordingly used for both varieties.

§ 32.3. Some languages (e.g., French) have a clear l in all positions. In some languages that have both a clear and a dark l, the incidence of the two is not the same as in English: thus in Polish (which has a separate character, *ł*, for dark l) a dark l may occur at the beginning of a syllable and a clear l at the end of a syllable; and the difference between a clear l and a dark l sometimes distinguishes two words otherwise spelled and pronounced the same (e.g., Polish *lawa*, "lava," *ława*, "bench").

§ 32.4. **Syllabic l** (see § 66). The sound l often forms a syllable by itself, as in *battle* băt′'l, or with other consonants, as in *handled* hăn′d'ld, no vowel whatever being present in the syllable. In pronunciation respellings in this Dictionary a syllabic consonant is preceded by an apostrophe.

### m

§ 33. As in English **m**an.

In the production of this sound, the lips are closed as for b, and prevent the breath from escaping through the mouth; however, the soft palate is lowered and the breath escapes through the nose, producing a nasal resonance. Correlative voiced stop, b; correlative voiceless stop, p.

§ 33.1. **Syllabic m** (see § 66). The sound m sometimes forms a syllable by itself, as in the English suffix *-ism* -ĭz'm and in one pronunciation of *Clapham* klăp′'m (klăp′ăm being another pronunciation), no vowel whatever being present in the syllable. In pronunciation respellings in this Dictionary a syllabic consonant is preceded by an apostrophe.

### n

§ 34. As in English **n**o.

In the production of this sound, the point of the tongue is placed against the teethridge (in some languages, as French and Italian, against the back of the upper front teeth), as for d, and the breath is unable to escape through the mouth; however, the soft palate is lowered and the breath escapes through the nose, producing a nasal resonance. Correlative voiced stop, d; correlative voiceless stop, t.

§ 34.1. **Syllabic n** (see § 66). The sound n often forms a syllable by itself, as in *redden* rĕd′'n, *reddened* rĕd′'nd, no vowel whatever being present in the syllable. In pronunciation respellings in this Dictionary a syllabic consonant is preceded by an apostrophe.

### N

§ 35. As in French bo**N**.

No sound whatever is to be attached to this symbol, which merely indicates that in the utterance of a preceding vowel or diphthong the soft palate is lowered, so that the breath escapes through the nose as well as the mouth, giving the vowel or diphthong a nasal resonance. No trace of any nasal consonant should follow the nasalized vowel unless a nasal consonant is shown in the transcription (see § 35.1). Thus the French word *en* äN consists of only one sound, the vowel ä pronounced with the soft palate lowered.

§ 35.1. In French, a nasal consonant is pronounced after a nasal vowel only in liaison; e.g., *bon accord* bôN′-nȧ′kôr′. In Portuguese and Polish, however, when a nasal vowel is followed by a stop the nasal consonant corresponding in articulation to the stop is usually inserted between the vowel and the stop (m before b, p; n before d, t; ng before g, k). Examples: Polish *bąbel* bôNm′bĕl, Portuguese *campo* käNm′po͞o (contrast French *bambou* bäN′bo͞o′); Polish *pędem* pĕNn′dĕm, Portuguese *conto* kōNn′to͞o (contrast French *contour* kôN′to͞or′); Polish *tęgi* tĕNng′gē, Portuguese *banco* băNng′ko͞o (contrast French *banquette* bäN′kĕt′).

### ng

§ 36. As in English si**ng**.

In the production of this sound, which is not a combination of the sounds n and g, contains no n or g sound, and is a single sound, the back part of the tongue is pressed against the soft palate, as for g, and the breath is unable to escape through the mouth; however, the soft palate is lowered and the breath escapes through the nose, producing a nasal resonance. Correlative voiced stop, g; correlative voiceless stop, k.

### ō

§ 37. As in English **ō**ld.

When accented, ō is usually a diphthong in standard English. In America and in many parts of England, the diphthong begins with the mid-back tense vowel, a pure ō sound, and glides to a vowel resembling o͝o. In the speech of southern England, however, though several varieties of ō exist, the prevailing tendency is to begin the ō sound with the tongue farther forward toward the central position. In the extreme form of this—which is very common in London, Oxford, and Cambridge—the diphthong is approximately ûo͝o, beginning with the û of *hurt* (the unretroflexed mid-central vowel used by those who "drop" their r's; see § 57).

In America the diphthongal character is less marked. Before voiceless consonants, as in *note, oak*, the ō is often nearly or quite pure, without vanish. In any case, the beginning of the American sound is a back vowel, not advanced, though sometimes slightly lowered toward ô. The one symbol ō is here used to indicate all standard varieties.

§ 37.1. In English words in which ō is shown immediately before r in this Dictionary, the vowel is usually ô in southern England, and sometimes in America.

§ 37.2. In foreign languages, ō is usually a pure vowel without vanish, often higher, tenser, and more lip-rounded than the corresponding pure English sound, or than the first element of the corresponding diphthongal English sound.

### ō̇

§ 38. As in English **ō̇**bey.

A short sound of ō-like quality, usually without vanish, occurring in unaccented syllables. Where ō̇ is shown in English words, the sound is frequently the obscure mid-central vowel (like *ȧ*), as in the second syllable of *canopy* kăn′ō̇·pĭ.

§ 38.1. In words belonging to certain foreign languages (as German and Hungarian), ō̇ is also used in accented syllables for a sound resembling a pure ō, but much shorter. Example: German *Gott* gō̇t.

### ô

§ 39. As in English **ô**rb.

Low-back (but higher than ä, which is also low-back), tense, higher and more lip-rounded in southern England than in America; may be long, as in *law* lô, or relatively short, as in *auspicious* ôs·pĭsh′*ŭ*s.

### ŏ

§ 40. As in English **ŏ**dd.

In southern England and to some extent in New England, New York City, and the southern United States, this vowel is low-back (lying between ä and ô, which are also low-back), lax, and slightly rounded. In general in the United States, the sound so transcribed is an entirely unrounded vowel identical in quality with ä and of varying length. Where ŏ is shown before r, however (as in *moral* mŏr′*ă*l), the pronunciation in the United States is often ŏ (with Southern British value) or ô.

§ 40.1. In foreign words, ŏ has a value similar to that which it has in southern England.

### ô̆

§ 41. As in English s**ô̆**ft.

This will be recognized as a combination of the symbols ô and ŏ. It is used in transcribing a class of words which in both America and England are pronounced with either ô or ŏ (or an intermediate sound). When these words are pronounced with ŏ in America, the ŏ usually has, not its usual American value ä, but a value similar to that which it has in southern England.

### *ŏ*

§ 42. As in English c**ŏ**nnect.

In ordinary English speech, an obscure vowel, like *ȧ* (see § 12). Occasionally in deliberate speech pronounced ŏ.

### oi

§ **43**. As in English **oi**l.
A diphthong consisting of ô+ĭ.

### o͞o

§ **44**. As in English f**o͞o**d.
High-back tense rounded. A single vowel, not two.

§ **44.1**. o͞o is also used, in transcribing Swedish and Norwegian *u*, for a high-central rounded long vowel.

### o͝o

§ **45**. As in English f**o͝o**t.
High-back lax rounded. A single vowel, not two.

§ **45.1**. o͝o is also used, in transcribing Norwegian *u*, for a high-central rounded short vowel.

### ou

§ **46**. As in English **ou**t.
A diphthong the first element of which varies throughout the English-speaking world. In what is perhaps the commonest variety, the diphthong begins with ȧ and moves upward to or toward o͝o. In two other common varieties the first element is ă and ä, respectively.

### p

§ **47**. As in English **p**en.
A voiceless sound produced by stopping the breath with the lips. Correlative voiced stop, b; correlative nasal, m.

### r

§ **48**. As in English **r**ap, fa**r**.
In English, this sound is produced by retroflexing the tongue (see § 3.24) and allowing the breath to pass between it and the hard palate. In general, the retroflexion is greater in America and Canada than in southern England. For further information on r in English, see § 57.

§ **48.1**. In foreign languages, in which r is usually more vigorously articulated than in English, two common varieties are the tongue-point trill and the uvular r (see § 3.1). In the tongue-point trill the tongue is in light contact at the sides with the upper molars, and the point and blade are raised toward the front palate and rapidly vibrated up and down against the back part of the teethridge (see § 3.2) by the outgoing voiced breath. In uvular r, the voiced breath passes between the raised back of the tongue and the uvula, causing vibration of the latter (uvular trill) or merely producing a strong fricative sound (uvular scrape). Both the tongue-point trilled r and the uvular r occur in French and in German. Italian and Russian have only the tongue-point trill. Danish r is usually uvular. In Spanish, *rr* is pronounced as a tongue-point trill (transcribed rr in Spanish words in this Dictionary), whereas a single *r* has the same place of articulation but usually consists of only a single flip of the tongue point against the teethridge (transcribed r in Spanish words in this Dictionary).

### s

§ **49**. As in English **s**o.
A voiceless sound produced with the tip and blade of the tongue pressed close to the teethridge, and the point drawn into itself so as to form a very narrow, tubelike channel between the tip and the teethridge. A thread of voiceless breath forced through this channel strikes the points of the teeth (esp. the lower) and produces the characteristic "hissing" sound. Voiced correlative, z.

### sh

§ **50**. As in English **sh**e.
sh is not a combination of the sounds s and h, contains no s or h sound, and is a single voiceless sound, pronounced with the tip and blade of the tongue approaching the hard palate a little farther back than for s. The aperture is wider laterally, so that the current of air passing over the tongue is more spread out like a waterfall than for s, in which it is like a jet. The main body of the tongue is also higher toward the roof of the mouth. The broader stream of air rushes against the teeth much as for s, the mouth requiring to be nearly closed. The position of the tongue is on the whole similar to that for y (cf. § 54). Voiced correlative, zh.

When s and h are in separate syllables, each has its own sound, as in *sheepshead* shēps′hĕd′.

### t

§ **51**. As in English **t**ime.
A voiceless sound produced, in English, by stopping the breath by placing the point of the tongue against the teethridge (see § 3.2). In some languages (e.g., French and Italian) the tongue point is placed against the back of the upper front teeth.
Correlative voiced stop, d; correlative nasal, n.

### t͟h

§ **52**. As in English **t͟h**en.
t͟h is not a combination of the sounds t and h, contains no t or h sound, and is a single voiced sound. The point of the tongue lightly touches the backs or the points of the upper teeth, in some cases protruding a trifle between upper and lower teeth, while breath buzzes through with a fricative sound. Voiceless correlative, th.

### th

§ **53**. As in English **th**in.
Voiceless correlative of t͟h (see § 52).

### tû

§ **54**. As in English na**tû**re.
In words in the respelled pronunciation of which this symbol occurs, the pronunciation tû (=tyo͝o) occurs in most words only in very formal speech. The ligature (‿) indicates that in ordinary speech the ty is usually pronounced ch (i.e., t+sh: see § 14). The explanation of this is as follows: The original pronunciation was ty. The sound sh, however, being closer to t than y is, speakers in time began, in accord with a process technically known as assimilation, to take a "path of less resistance" by substituting sh for y.
Also, before consonants the vowel is commonly ẽ or *ŭ*, not o͝o.
Correlative sound with voiced consonant, dû.

### ū

**55**. As in English c**ū**be.
This symbol represents a combination of two sounds. The first element is y or ĭ, the second element o͞o (in words transcribed ūr in this Dictionary, the second element is usually o͝o; i.e., ūr is yo͝or or ĭo͝or). In words in which ū is shown after certain consonants (notably l, s, z) in this Dictionary, the first element (y or ĭ) is omitted by many or most speakers; e.g., *Lucy*, transcribed lū′sĭ, is often pronounced lo͞o′sĭ.

### ů

§ **56**. As in English **ů**nite.
The sound ū with briefer second element (often lowered to o͝o, even when not preceding r), occurring in unaccented syllables.

### û

§ **57**. As in English **û**rn.
In transcriptions of English words, used only before r in syllables having some degree of accent. In types of

English in which r is not "dropped," ûr is pronounced as a single sound—a mid-central vowel uttered with retroflexed tongue (see § 3.24). In types of English in which r final and before a consonant is "dropped," ûr is pronounced as a mid-central vowel, but without retroflexion.

Whether r is "kept" or "dropped," ûr differs from ĕr in English chiefly in that ûr bears greater stress and is longer than ĕr.

§ **57.1**. In America, consonantal r (as in *red* rĕd) usually has the same tongue position as the mid-central retroflex vowel ûr described above. However, the tongue has this position much more briefly than for ûr, moving immediately toward the position of the following vowel. r (consonant) thus bears the same relation to ûr (retroflex vowel) as w does to o͞o or o͝o, and y does to ē or ĭ (see §§ 62, 63).

§ **57.2**. In some foreign languages (e.g., Czech and Yugoslav) in which r may serve as the vowel in an accented syllable, this r (transcribed ûr in this Dictionary) is not the retroflex vowel described above, but the tongue-point trill (see § 48.1). Examples: Czech *Brno* bûr′nô, Yugoslav *Srbin* sûr′bēn.

§ **57.3**. In names belonging to some foreign languages, û transcribes, not a mid-central vowel, but either of two mid-front rounded vowels, one close (approximately English ā pronounced with rounded lips), the other open (approximately English ĕ pronounced with rounded lips). Examples: French *Richelieu* rē′shē·lyû′ (close), German *Goebbels* gûb′ĕls (open). With speakers of English who "drop" their r's, both of these non-English vowels, the close and the open, are commonly Anglicized as the mid-central unretroflexed vowel (see § 57); hence the use of the symbol û, and the use of one symbol for two different sounds. With speakers of English who do not "drop" their r's, either of these vowels plus a following r is frequently Anglicized as the mid-central retroflexed vowel (see § 57). Thus such speakers would give to *ör* in German *Göring* the sound which they give to *ur* in English *fur*. When no r follows the vowel, however, such speakers are usually unable to use as their Anglicized pronunciation the mid-central unretroflexed vowel, which is usually as foreign to their speech as the mid-front rounded vowels. In such a case, the Anglicizations used are frequently ā for the mid-front close rounded vowel, ĕ for the mid-front open rounded vowel; i.e., the tongue position is approximately the same as for the non-English vowels, but the lip rounding is omitted: see the first sentence in this paragraph. These pronunciations are also often used even when an r follows the vowel. Examples: German *Goethe* gā′tĕ, *Goebbels* gĕb′ĕls, *Göring* gā′rĭng. Cf. § 60.

### ŭ

§ **58**. As in English **ŭ**p.

In America, usually a mid-central unrounded vowel, the highest part of the tongue being a little lower and farther back than for the *ȧ* in *sofa* or ĕr in *better*. In Southern British, it is pronounced with the tongue slightly farther back, being classed by some phoneticians as mid-back tense unrounded.

### *ŭ*

§ **59**. As in English circ***ŭ***s.

Mid-central unrounded. Always obscure.

### ü

§ **60**. As in French men**ü** (mē·n**ü**′), German gr**ü**n.

This symbol transcribes either of two high-front rounded vowels that have no counterpart in English, one close (approximately English ē pronounced with rounded lips), the other open (approximately English ĭ pronounced with rounded lips). These vowels are sometimes Anglicized by omitting the lip rounding; i.e., the close vowel is pronounced as ē, the open as ĭ (cf. § 57.3). Examples: *Tübingen* German tü′bĭng·ĕn, Anglicized tē′bĭng·ĕn; *Müller* German mül′ĕr, Anglicized mĭl′ĕr. Other Anglicizations are yo͞o (= ū) for the close vowel, yo͝o for the open. (Observe that in these pronunciations there occur in succession the two elements that occur simultaneously in the non-English vowels: high-front tongue position, supplied by the y; lip rounding, supplied by the o͞o or o͝o. There is of course in the Anglicized pronunciation the additional element of high-back tongue position, supplied by the o͞o or o͝o.) Examples: *Debussy* French dē·bü′sē′, Anglicized dē·bū′sĭ; *Müller* German mül′ĕr, Anglicized myo͝ol′ĕr (as well as mĭl′ĕr; see above). Still other Anglicizations (as o͞o, o͝o, ŭ, and—where *r* follows the vowel—ûr) occur with less regularity.

### v

§ **61**. As in English **v**an.

A voiced sound produced by the friction of the breath escaping between the closely juxtaposed upper teeth and lower lip. Voiceless correlative, f.

### w

§ **62**. As in English **w**ant.

For this sound, the lips are rounded and the back of the tongue raised as for o͞o or o͝o. However, the tongue has this position much more briefly than for o͞o or o͝o, moving immediately toward the position of the following vowel. w and y are commonly called "semivowels." Cf. §57.1.

### y

§ **63**. As in English **y**et.

For this sound, the lips are unrounded and the front of the tongue (the part behind the blade and tip; see § 3.2) is raised toward the hard palate (whence y is called a palatal sound), as for ē or ĭ. However, the tongue has this position much more briefly than for ē or ĭ, moving immediately toward the position of the following vowel. y and w are commonly called "semivowels." Cf. §57.1.

§ **63.1**. In transcriptions of words from a number of foreign languages, a y following a tongue consonant denotes that that consonant is "palatal" or "palatalized." These two terms are not synonymous. A palatal consonant is one formed with the front of the tongue (the part behind the blade and tip; see § 3.2) near or touching the hard palate, and the tip of the tongue behind the lower front teeth. (The sound y has this articulation [see § 63]; hence the use of y after a consonant to denote that that consonant is palatal.) Common palatal consonants occurring in pronunciations in this Dictionary are ly (the sound of the bold-faced letters in Italian fi**gli**o and Spanish [Castilian pronunciation] o**ll**a), ny (the sound of the bold-faced letters in French a**gn**eau, Italian ba**gn**o, Spanish ca**ñ**ón), dy (the sound of the bold-faced letters in Hungarian **Gy**ula), and ty (the sound of the bold-faced letter in Yugoslav Obrenovi**ć**). Whereas in articulating English l, n, d, t the *tip* of the tongue is in contact with the *teethridge* (see § 3.2), in articulating ly, ny, dy, ty the *front* of the tongue (posterior to the tip; see § 3.2) is in contact with the *hard palate* (posterior to the teethridge), and the *tip* of the tongue is behind the lower front teeth. These palatal sounds can be acquired by placing the tip of the tongue behind the lower front teeth and trying to say l, n, d, t, respectively.

When a consonant (e.g., l, n, d, t) is palatalized, on the other hand, the tip of the tongue is in contact with the teethridge (or, in some languages, with the back of the upper front teeth), as it is for ordinary l, n, d, t. However, the front of the tongue, posterior to the tip, instead of being somewhat low in the mouth as for ordinary l, n, d, t, is brought to or near the hard palate, thus approximating the position which it has in the articulation of a full palatal sound.

§ **63.2**. Palatalization is especially important in Russian. In that language there are a group of five hard, or nonpalatalizing, vowels, and a corresponding group of five soft, or palatalizing, vowels. The palatalizing effect of this group of soft vowels takes, in general, either of two forms: (1) When a soft vowel is immediately preceded by a tongue consonant (except *ch*, *sh*, *shch*, *zh*, which are palatal already), the consonant is palatalized, and a y sound is usually present between the consonant and the vowel. (2) When a soft vowel is initial in a word, or is immediately preceded by another vowel or by a consonant other than a tongue consonant, the palatalization is limited to the presence of a y sound before the vowel. (Certain exceptions to these two statements are noted below.) Whichever of these two forms the palatalization takes, it is indicated in this Dictionary by the symbol y immediately preceding the vowel; e.g., *Esenin* yĭ·syā′nyĭn.

The usual transliteration of the Russian vowels in this Dictionary, and their pronunciation in accented syllables, is as follows (for further information about their pronunciation, see in this Guide Subdivision B of Division IV, entitled "Elements of Pronunciation of Foreign Names"):

| HARD | SOFT |
|---|---|
| a (ȧ) | ya (yȧ) |
| e (â, ā) | e (yâ, yā) |
| y (see § 27.1) | i (yē, ē) |
| o (ô) | ë (yô) |
| u (ōō) | yu (yōō) |

NOTES. It will be observed that the transliteration distinguishes between each pair of hard and soft vowels except hard *e* and soft *e*. However, inasmuch as hard *e* occurs in only two or three genuinely Russian words, one will nearly always be correct in assuming that an *e* in a Russian name is a soft *e*.

Observe that the hard vowel *y* has a value different from that borne by *y* in the soft vowels *ya*, *yu*, where *y* has its usual English value. The letters transliterated *ya*, *yu* are single letters in Russian, the two-letter transliterations being used to distinguish these soft vowels orthographically from the corresponding hard ones. See Russian *y* in "Elements of Pronunciation of Foreign Names" for another value sometimes borne by *y* in Russian names.

*i*, unlike the other soft vowels, does not have a preceding y sound when it is initial, being pronounced simply ē (ĭ in unaccented syllables). *i* is also not palatalized when, as it often does, it forms a diphthong with a preceding vowel.

Observe that, whereas in each of the other four pairs the quality of the hard vowel is the same as that of the second (vocalic) element of the soft vowel, in the pair *y*, *i* this quality is different. After *sh* and *zh* (but not after *ch* and *shch:* see § 14) *i* is pronounced like *y*.

A consonant may also be palatalized in Russian when not followed by a soft vowel (e.g., when final in a word or when medial and followed by another consonant). Such palatalization is indicated orthographically in Russian by a special symbol, not usually transliterated in English and not transliterated in this Dictionary.

§ **63.3**. When the symbol y is final in a word or syllable (e.g., in transcriptions of French and other foreign languages), it is followed by an apostrophe, as a precaution against its being mispronounced by English-speaking persons, who, following the analogy of a common pronunciation of *y* in such positions in English words, might otherwise interpret the symbol as having the value ĭ. Example: *Montaigne* môɴ′tĕn′y′.

### z

§ **64**. As in English **z**one.

A voiced sound produced with the tip and blade of the tongue pressed close to the upper teethridge, and the point drawn into itself so as to form a very narrow, tubelike channel between the tip and the teethridge. A thread of voiced breath forced through this channel strikes the points of the teeth (esp. the lower) and produces the characteristic "buzzing" sound. Voiceless correlative, s.

### zh

§ **65**. As in English a**z**ure (ă**zh**′ẽr; ā′**zh**ẽr).

zh is not a combination of the sounds z and h, contains no z or h sound, and is a single voiced sound, pronounced with the tip and blade of the tongue approaching the hard palate a little farther back than for z. The aperture is wider laterally, so that the current of air passing over the tongue is more spread out like a waterfall than for z, in which it is like a jet. The main body of the tongue is also higher toward the roof of the mouth. The broader stream of air rushes against the teeth much as for z, the mouth requiring to be nearly closed. The position of the tongue is on the whole similar to that for y (cf. § 16). Voiceless correlative, sh.

When z and h are in separate syllables, each has its own sound, as in *hogshead* hŏgz′hĕd.

§ **66**. Certain consonants are capable of constituting the vowel in a syllable, and when they so function are called syllabic consonants. In English the chief such consonants are l, n, and m, which are frequently syllabic in unaccented syllables after certain consonants. No vowel is present in the syllable. The sign of a syllabic consonant in this Dictionary is an apostrophe immediately preceding the consonant, thus: *battle* băt′'l, *harden* här′d'n, *hardened* här′d'nd, *Clapham* klăp′'m.

§ **66.1**. In foreign words (chiefly French), an apostrophe final in a syllable following l or r indicates the unvoicing of these normally voiced sounds, as in French *peuple* pû′pl', *poudre* pōō′dr'.

# IV. ELEMENTS OF PRONUNCIATION OF FOREIGN NAMES

## A. GENERAL OBSERVATIONS

§ 67. **Accent** (**stress**). It is difficult to formulate rules of accentuation for many languages. The following generalizations, however, may prove helpful.

In **Czech**, **Estonian**, **Finnish** (except in names of Swedish origin), **Hungarian**, and **Latvian**, the main accent is always on the first syllable.

In **Danish**, **Dutch**, **German**, **Icelandic**, **Norwegian**, and **Swedish**, the main accent is most often on the first syllable.

In **French**, all syllables (except those containing the vowel ẽ) are stressed, and are followed in this Dictionary by a secondary accent, except the last syllable, which has slightly greater stress than the others, and is followed in this Dictionary by a primary accent.

In **Italian**, the accent is usually on either the penult or the antepenult. When it is on the ultima, the vowel of the ultima bears a grave accent in the Italian orthography.

In **Japanese** all syllables receive fairly even stress. Primary and secondary accent marks are accordingly not used in transcribing Japanese names in this Dictionary.

In **Polish** the accent is almost always on the penult.

In **Portuguese** the accent may be on the penult (which is most often the case), the antepenult, or the ultima.

In **Spanish**, words which bear no written accent are accented on the penult if they end in a vowel or in *n*, *s;* on the ultima if they end in a consonant other than *n*, *s*. Words that are exceptions to this rule bear an acute accent over the vowel of the accented syllable.

In **Turkish**, the main accent is usually on the last syllable, but the other syllables are all distinctly pronounced.

§ 68. **Graphic Accents and Other Modifiers**. A written acute accent over a vowel in Czechslovak, Hungarian, and Icelandic indicates a long vowel. Such a vowel may differ qualitatively as well as quantitatively from the corresponding accentless vowel. A written acute accent over a vowel in Spanish shows where the stress falls when it is irregular (see the preceding section). In French it indicates a particular quality of the vowel, as usually do also the other written accents. In Italian a grave accent over a final vowel indicates that the ultima is the accented syllable. In Portuguese, the acute and circumflex accents are used under certain conditions to indicate a stressed syllable; in addition, they often indicate vowel quality, the acute being used over an open accented vowel, the circumflex over a close accented vowel. Sometimes these accents merely distinguish words otherwise spelled alike. The grave accent (often not used) in Portuguese over a vowel in an unaccented syllable indicates that the vowel is distinctly pronounced and open; sometimes the word bearing it is thereby distinguished from a word otherwise spelled the same, in which the corresponding vowel is slurred.

The mark ¨ has a double function: as a diaeresis, it stands over the second of two vowels and indicates that the two vowels are not to be pronounced as a single sound or as a diphthong, but as two separate sounds, in separate syllables; e.g., in French *Moïse* mô′ēz′ (*oi* in French being ordinarily pronounced wȧ or wä); as an umlaut, it indicates a particular quality of a vowel, different from the quality of the corresponding unmodified vowel; e.g., in German *Grüsse* grü′sĕ (whereas *Gruss* is grōōs).

Other orthographic modifiers, whether attached to vowels or consonants, in these and other languages usually indicate that the modified letter is pronounced differently from the unmodified letter.

§ 69. **Doubled Letters**. A doubled vowel usually has greater length than the corresponding single vowel (e.g., in Estonian and Finnish) or at least greater length than one value of the corresponding single vowel (e.g., in Dutch and German, where, for example, *aa* and *ee*, usually occurring in closed syllables, represent a sound longer than *a* and *e*, respectively, usually have in closed syllables; but are no different in quantity or quality from *a* and *e*, respectively, in open syllables). In such cases, there is often a difference of quality as well as of quantity.

Doubled consonants are pronounced double or prolonged in Arabic, Finnish, Hungarian, Icelandic, Italian, Japanese, Norwegian, Polish, Rumanian, Russian, and Swedish; otherwise they are usually pronounced as a single consonant. The pronunciation of Spanish *ll* and of Icelandic *ll*, *nn* is neither that of the corresponding single letters nor of the single letters doubled or prolonged, being respectively ly (in some dialects, y), d′l, and d′n.

§ 70. **Final Consonants**. In Bulgarian, Czechoslovak, Dutch, German, Polish, and Russian, a final voiced consonant does not have its usual voiced sound, but the corresponding voiceless sound (see § 3.18). The same is usually true in these languages of the same consonants when they precede a voiceless consonant. In French a final consonant or consonant group is often silent.

§ 71. **Vowels**. In general, the values of the vowels in the chief languages other than English are as follows:

**a**: ä or ȧ, long or short. ä is open, ȧ is close.
**e**: when long, ā or â; when short, ĕ or ā. ā is close, ĕ and â are open.
**i**: when long, ē; when short, ĭ or ē. ē is close, ĭ is open.
**o**: ō or ô, long or short. ō is close, ô is open.
**u**: when long, ōō; when short, ŏŏ or ōō. ōō is close, ŏŏ is open.

The vowels **a**, **e**, **o** are often called *strong;* **i**, **u**, *weak*.

The values of the vowels in the chief foreign languages have been rather fully stated in the alphabetized list below. Where, however, a vowel in a specific language is not mentioned, the preceding table will serve as a fair guide.

On the differences between ā, ō in English and in foreign languages, see §§ 5, 37.

In a number of foreign languages, vowel length is of much greater importance than it is in English, two vowels identical in quality but differing in that one is long and the other short often in these languages distinguishing words otherwise pronounced alike (e.g., in German, *Staat* shtät, having long ä, is distinct from *Stadt* shtăt, having short ä). Accordingly, frequent mention of vowel length is made in the list that follows. When foreign words and names are used in an English context, however, such distinctions of length are usually ignored, as they usually are in the pronunciation respellings in the vocabulary of this dictionary.

§ 72. **Scheme of Alphabetization Used**. The letters and letter groups in the list in Subdivision B below have been alphabetized on the following principle: letters without modifier precede letters with modifier, and the latter are alphabetized according to the name of the modifier which they bear. Since some modifiers of letters in foreign languages have no commonly accepted name in English, to facilitate this scheme of alphabetization certain names have had to be invented. Such names are enclosed in quotation marks in the list in the next paragraph. In a few cases, to simplify the alphabetization, an established name is applied to a modifier which happens to be identical in form with, but does not serve the same function as, the modifier properly so called; thus the modifier in Turkish **ğ** is not strictly a breve, but is here so designated.

The names which form the basis of the alphabetization of modified letters are as follows:

| | | | | |
|---|---|---|---|---|
| acute | written | ´ | as in | **é** |
| apostrophe | " | ' | " " | **d'** |
| "bar" | " | ⸝ | " " | **ł** |
| breve | " | ˘ | " " | **ă** |
| cedilla | " | ¸ | " " | **ç** |
| "circle" | " | ° | " " | **å** |
| circumflex | " | ^ | " " | **â** |
| "dot" | " | · | " " | **ż** |
| "double acute" | " | ˝ | " " | **ő** |
| grave | " | ` | " " | **è** |
| "hook" | " | ˛ | " " | **ę** |
| macron | " | ¯ | " " | **ē** |
| "solidus" | " | / | " " | **ø** |
| tilde | " | ~ | " " | **ñ** |
| umlaut | " | ¨ | " " | **ö** |
| "wedge" | " | ˇ | " " | **ž** |

The following examples will illustrate the operation of this principle of alphabetization:

| | | | |
|---|---|---|---|
| **o** | = | **o** | |
| **oa** | = | **o** | + **a** |
| **oi** | = | **o** | + **i** |
| **oí** | = | **o** | + **i acute** |
| **oî** | = | **o** | + **i circumflex** |
| **oj** | = | **o** | + **j** |
| **oy** | = | **o** | + **y** |
| **ó** | = | **o acute** | |
| **ô** | = | **o circumflex** | |
| **ö** | = | **o umlaut** | |
| **ög** | = | **o umlaut** | + **g** |
| **öi** | = | **o umlaut** | + **i** |

Ligatured letters precede the same letters written separately; thus **æ** precedes **ae**, **œ** precedes **oe**.

Language names are in italic type. Under letters or letter groups occurring in more than one language, these language names are arranged alphabetically, thus:

**a** *Czech...*
*Danish...*
*Dutch...*
*Finnish...*
*French...*

Where a number of languages are treated as a single item, the language names within that item are arranged alphabetically, and are alphabetized with respect to other items according to the language name that occurs first. Example:

**d** *Czech...*
*Danish...*
*Dutch, German, Polish, Russian...*
*French...*

## B. VALUES OF SPECIFIC LETTERS AND LETTER GROUPS

NOTE. In the matter that follows, letters are in boldface roman type, sounds are in lightface roman type. Thus when it is stated that, in Rumanian, **e** before **a** is y, the meaning is that the letter **e** before the letter **a** has the sound y; when it is stated that, in closed syllables in Spanish, **e** is ā if the closing consonant is m, n, s, ~~th~~, or th, the meaning is that the letter **e** has the sound ā if the sound at the end of the syllable is m, n, s, ~~th~~, or th.

**a** *Czech:* short ȧ. Cf. Czech **á**.
*Danish:* ȧ, except: ä before or after r.
*Dutch:* ȧ (long when accented) in open syllables, short ä in closed syllables. Cf. South African Dutch **a**.
*Finnish:* short ȧ. Cf. Finnish **aa**.
*French:* usually ȧ, sometimes ä. **am** or **an** final or followed by a consonant is äɴ. Cf. French **â**.
*German:* ä, in general long in accented open syllables and when the spelling is **aa** or **ah**, otherwise short.
*Hungarian:* short ŏ (Southern British value). **aa**, like Hungarian **á**, is long ä.
*Icelandic:* short ä, except: ou before **ng**, **nk**.
*Japanese:* short ä.
*Latvian:* short ä. Cf. Latvian **ā**.
*Polish:* ä.
*Portuguese:* In accented syllables, usually ȧ, except when nasal (see below), or before **l**, **u** in the same syllable (see below), or before prevocalic **m**, **n**, **nh**, when it is ă. In unaccented syllables, usually *ȧ* (but see next sentence). **a** is ä before **l**, **u** in the same syllable, accented or unaccented; ăɴ (see § 35.1) before preconsonantal **m**, **n**, accented or unaccented. **am** at the end of a word is ouɴ.
*Rumanian:* short ä.
*Russian:* ȧ in accented, ŭ or *ȧ* in unaccented, syllables.
*Sanskrit and certain other East Indian languages:* when long, ä; when short, ŭ in accented, *ȧ* in unaccented, syllables.
*South African Dutch:* long ä where European Dutch is long ȧ.
*Swedish:* sometimes long ä, sometimes short ȧ.

**aa** *Danish:* long ô.
*Dutch:* long ȧ.
*Finnish:* long ä. Cf. Finnish **a**.
*German:* long ä.
*Hungarian:* long ä, like Hungarian **á**.
*Norwegian:* long ô.

**aai**
*Dutch, South African Dutch:* when final, long ȧ (in South African Dutch, long ä) + ĭ; before a vowel, long ȧ (in South African Dutch, long ä) + y.

**æ** *Danish:* When long, â. When short: ă before or after r; elsewhere ĕ.
*Icelandic:* ī. Cf. § 26.
*Norwegian:* â when long, ă when short.

**ae** *Flemish:* long ȧ.
*German:* = German **ä** (*q.v.*).

**ai** *Finnish:* ī. Cf. § 26.
*French:* ĕ when short, â when long; sometimes ā. In **aim** or **ain** final or preceding a consonant, ăɴ.
*German:* ī. Cf. § 26.
*Greek (modern):* â.
*Latvian, Lithuanian, Norwegian, Portuguese, Rumanian:* ī. Cf. § 26.

*South African Dutch:* short ä+ĭ, much like English ī: cf. § 26 (whereas South African Dutch **aai** is long ä+ĭ).
*Spanish:* ä′ē̇, much like English ī (see § 26), with the first as the stronger of the two vowels. But when written **aí**, pronounced ä·ē′, with the second as the stronger of the two vowels.

**aim**
*French:* see French **ai.**

**ain**
*French:* see French **ai.**

**aí** *Spanish:* see Spanish **ai.**

**aj** *Czech, Danish:* ī. Cf. § 26.

**am**
*French:* äɴ when final or preceding a consonant; otherwise åm.
*Portuguese:* see Portuguese **a.**

**an** *French:* äɴ when final or preceding a consonant; otherwise ån.
*Portuguese:* see Portuguese **a.**

**ao** *Japanese:* ä+ô.

**aoe**
*Dutch:* ou.

**au** *Dutch:* ou. Cf. § 46; South African Dutch **au.**
*Finnish:* ou. Cf. § 46.
*French:* usually ō; ô before r.
*German:* ou. Cf. § 46.
*Icelandic:* û+ĭ.
*Japanese:* ä+ŏŏ.
*Latvian, Lithuanian, Norwegian, Portuguese, Rumanian:* ou. Cf. § 46.
*South African Dutch:* ō+ŏŏ.
*Spanish:* ä′ŏŏ, much like English ou (cf. § 46), with the first as the stronger of the two vowels. But when written **aú**, pronounced ä·ōō′, with the second as the stronger of the two vowels.
*Swedish:* ou. Cf. § 46.

**auw**
*Dutch:* when final, ou (cf. § 46); before a vowel, ou+v (see Dutch **w**).

**aú** *Spanish:* see Spanish **au.**

**av** *Danish:* ou when not followed by a vowel; when followed by a vowel, åv or, after r, äv.

**ay** *French:* sometimes ā, sometimes ĕ; when followed by a pronounced vowel, å+y, as in *Bayonne* bå′yôn′, or ĕ+y, as in *payer* pĕ′yā′.
*German:* ī, like German **ai.**
*Spanish:* when final, ä+ē̇ (much like English ī: cf. § 26); when followed by a vowel, ä+y.

**aye**
*French:* when final, variously pronounced åy′, ây′, ā, ĕ; when the **e** is pronounced, the **ay** is åy or ĕy, as in *Mayenne* må′yĕn′, *payer* pĕ′yā′.

**á** *Czech:* long ä. Cf. Czech **a.**
*Hungarian:* long ä. Cf. Hungarian **a.**
*Icelandic:* ou. Cf. Icelandic **a.**

**ă** *Rumanian:* short û (mid-central unretroflexed vowel; see § 57) in accented, *ȧ* in unaccented, syllables.

**å** *Norwegian:* long ô, like Norwegian **aa.**
*Swedish:* sometimes long ō, sometimes short ô.

**â** *French:* nearly always ä.
*Rumanian:* high-central tense unrounded vowel having no counterpart in English. Polish *y* and the Russian letter transliterated *y* in this Dictionary are very similarly pronounced. Anglicized as ĭ and so transcribed in this Dictionary.

**à** *French:* å.

**ą** *Lithuanian:* ä, like Lithuanian **a.**
*Polish:* ôɴ. See § 35.1.

**ā** *Latvian:* long ä. Cf. Latvian **a.**

**ã** *Portuguese:* äɴ. **ãe** is äē̇ɴ in Portugal, āē̇ɴ in Brazil. **ão** is ouɴ.

**ä** *Estonian:* ă.
*Finnish:* short ă. Cf. Finnish **ää.**
*German:* long â in open syllables and when followed by **h**, short ĕ in closed syllables.
*Slovak:* short ă.
*Swedish:* before r: ă, long in some cases, short in others; elsewhere, â when long, ĕ when short.

**ää** *Finnish:* long ă. Cf. Finnish **ä.**

**äi** *Finnish:* ă+ĭ.

**äu** *German:* like German **eu** (*q.v.*).

**äy** *Finnish:* ă+ü.

**b** *Czech, Dutch, German, Polish, Russian, South African Dutch:* b, except: unvoiced to p when final or before a voiceless consonant.
*Portuguese:* b, a lip stop, at the beginning of a sentence or of a phrase after a pause, and after consonants except **s**; elsewhere, the lip continuant described under Spanish **b** (*q.v.*).
*Spanish:* Anglicized as b, and so transcribed in all cases in this Dictionary. In Spanish, however, it is a lip stop (see § 13) usually only at the beginning of a sentence and of a phrase after a pause, and after **m** or **n** (**n** in this situation being pronounced m). Elsewhere it is a lip continuant, produced by merely bringing the lips toward each other without their touching each other throughout their whole length. Except: It is p before t; it is p or, more often, silent before s, and is often omitted from the spelling.

**c** *Czech:* ts.
*Danish:* s or ts before **e, i**; elsewhere k.
*Dutch:* s before **e, i, ij, y,** elsewhere k. **cc** is ks before **e, i, ij, y**; elsewhere k.
*French:* s before **e, i, y**; silent after **n** at the end of a word; elsewhere k.
*German:* ts before **e, i, y**; elsewhere, except in **ch, sch** (*qq.v.*), k.
*Hungarian:* ts (but see Hungarian **ch, cs**). Hungarian **cz** is also ts.
*Italian:* k, except as noted below. ch before **e, i,** as in *Ciro* chē′rô. **ci** in turn is ch before another vowel, as in *Ciano* chä′nô. **cc** before **e, i** is t+ch, as in *Ricci* rēt′chē̇ (since the sound ch is really t+sh [see § 14], t+ch is really a prolonged t+sh). **cc** elsewhere is kk. **ch** is k, as in *Chigi* kē′jē̇.
*Latvian, Lithuanian:* ts.
*Norwegian:* s before **e, i, y**; elsewhere k.
*Polish:* ts. **ci** before a vowel is ch.
*Portuguese:* s before **e, i**; usually silent before **ç, t**; elsewhere k.
*Rumanian:* ch before **e, i** (but not before **î**); elsewhere k. **ch** is k.
*Spanish:* th before **e, i** in Castilian Spanish, s before **e, i** in Andalusian, Latin American, and Philippine Spanish; in other situations, k in all types of Spanish, except: often silent before another consonant (e.g., dē′thyô·nä′ryō for *diccionario*).
*Swedish:* s before **ä, e, i, ö, y**; elsewhere k. But see Swedish **ch, sc, sch.**
*Turkish* (*present-day Roman alphabet*): j.
*Yugoslav:* ts.

**cc** *Dutch:* see Dutch **c.**
*French:* ks before **e, i**; elsewhere k.
*Italian:* see Italian **c.**
*Portuguese:* s before **e, i**; elsewhere k.
*Spanish:* occurs before **e, i**; pronounced kth in Castilian Spanish, ks in Andalusian, Latin American, and Philippine Spanish; but the k is often omitted.

**ch** *Catalan:* k when final, elsewhere ch. Cf. Spanish **ch.**
*Czech:* ᴋ (back variety; see § 31).
*Danish:* usually k in proper names, otherwise sh.
*Dutch:* ᴋ (back variety; see § 31) in genuinely Dutch words. But see Dutch **sch.**

*French:* sh; but k in most words derived from Greek.
*German:* ᴋ (see § 31); before **s**, when the **s** belongs to the stem of the word, k; as, *Fuchs* fŏŏks. In words derived from Greek and Latin, k before consonants and back vowels.
*Greek (modern):* ᴋ, front or back according to the accompanying vowel (see § 31).
*Hungarian:* ch, like Hungarian **cs**.
*Italian:* k. Cf. Italian **c**.
*Japanese:* ch.
*Lithuanian:* ᴋ.
*Norwegian:* k, ᴋ, or sh, depending on the pronunciation in the language from which the word comes.
*Polish* ᴋ (back variety; see § 31).
*Portuguese:* sh; but k in words of Greek origin.
*Rumanian:* k.
*Sanskrit and other East Indian languages:* ch.
*Spanish:* ch. Cf. Catalan **ch**.
*Swedish:* k, except: sh in French-derived words.

**ck** *German:* k.

**cs** *Hungarian:* ch.

**cz** *Hungarian:* ts, like Hungarian **c**.
*Polish:* ch.

**ć** *Polish:* a palatalized ts, transcribed tsy. See § 63.1.
*Yugoslav:* a palatal t, transcribed ty (see § 63.1); distinct, in Yugoslav pronunciation, from **č**, which is ch; both characters, however, are usually pronounced ch in English context.

**ç** *French, Portuguese:* s.
*Turkish (present-day Roman alphabet):* ch.

**č** *Czech, Latvian, Lithuanian, Yugoslav:* ch.

**d** *Czech:* dy before **i**, **í**; t at the end of a word or before a voiceless consonant; elsewhere d.
*Danish:* usually t͟h, or th when final, after a vowel: usually silent before **s**, **t**, and after **l**, **n**, **r** (pronounced, however, in the combinations **ldr**, **ndr**, **rdr**); elsewhere d.
*Dutch, German, Polish, Russian:* d, except when final or before a voiceless consonant, where it is t. Cf. South African Dutch **d**.
*French:* generally silent when final.
*Greek (modern):* t͟h.
*Hungarian:* d. **ds** is j̇ (i.e., d+zh: see § 29).
*Norwegian:* usually mute after **l**, **n**, **r** in the same syllable, and in **-stad**; otherwise d.
*Portuguese:* d at the beginning of a sentence and of a phrase after a pause, and after **l**, **n**, **r**; elsewhere t͟h.
*South African Dutch:* d, except: unvoiced to t finally and before **s**; silent after **l**, **n**, **r**; dropped in both pronunciation and spelling when inflection would bring it between a preceding accented vowel and ĕ.
*Spanish:* **d** at the beginning of a sentence and of a phrase after a pause, and after **l** or **n**; elsewhere t͟h. Often silent when final, or between vowels when it follows stressed **a**, **o**, or **u**, or before **s**.
*Swedish:* usually d; t before **s** in some cases; silent in a few situations; silent when initial before **j**.

**dj** *Dutch:* j. Cf. South African Dutch **dj**.
*South African Dutch:* ty. Cf. Dutch **dj**.
*Swedish:* y.
*Yugoslav:* dy, a palatal d (see § 63.1).

**ds** *Hungarian:* j. See Hungarian **d**.

**dt** *German:* t.

**dz** *Czech:* ts when final or before a voiceless consonant; otherwise dz.
*Polish:* usually dz; ts when final or before a voiceless consonant. **dzi** final or before a consonant is jē; **dzi** before a vowel is j; as, *dziwny* jēv′nĭ, *dziarno* jär′nô.

**dź** *Polish:* a palatalized dz, transcribed dzy. See § 63.1.

**dż** *Lithuanian, Polish:* j. See **ż**; § 29.

**dž** *Czech, Lithuanian, Yugoslav:* j (see **ž**; § 29), except: in Czech, ch when final or before a voiceless consonant.

**d'** *Czech:* dy, except: ty when final or before a voiceless consonant. See § 63.1.

**đ** *Yugoslav* (not used in this Dictionary): = Yugoslav **dj** (*q.v.*).

**e** *Czech:* ĕ. Cf. Czech **é**.
*Danish:* variously ḝ (see §§ 18, 18.1), ĭ, ĕ, â, (before or after **r**) ă, or (mostly in unaccented final syllables) ĕ. But see Danish **eg**, **ej**.
*Dutch, German:* in general, long ā in accented open syllables and when doubled or followed by **h**, ȧ in unaccented open syllables, short ĕ in closed syllables, ĕ when final or followed by **l**, **n**, **r** in a final unaccented syllable. Cf. South African Dutch **e**.
*Finnish:* short ĕ. Cf. Finnish **ee**.
*French:* in general: silent when final; in the interior of a word, ẽ or silent, unless followed by a double consonant, when it is ĕ. See French **em**, **en**.
*German:* see Dutch **e**.
*Greek (modern):* When transliterating eta, ē, except: y before another vowel; when transliterating epsilon, â or ĕ. ē being spelled **i** in most European languages, eta is usually transliterated **i** in those languages, and often, by borrowing, in English.
*Hungarian:* short ĕ. **eö**, **ew** are û, like Hungarian **ö** (*q.v.*). Cf. Hungarian **é**.
*Icelandic:* ā (or, strictly, ĕĭ; see § 5) before **ng**, **nk**; elsewhere ĕ.
*Italian:* often short ĕ or long â in syllables bearing primary accent; otherwise ā or ȧ.
*Japanese:* short ĕ.
*Latvian:* ĕ or ă. Cf. Latvian **ē**.
*Lithuanian:* ă.
*Norwegian:* sometimes long ā, sometimes short ĕ; before **r**, long â and short ă; obscure in **-en**, **-er**, **-et**.
*Polish:* ĕ.
*Portuguese:* in accented syllables, ā or â; in unaccented syllables, ĕ, ė, or (before another vowel) y. See Portuguese **em**, **en**.
*Rumanian:* ĕ, except: at the beginning of a word, usually yĕ; before **a**, y.
*Russian:* practically always a soft vowel (see § 63.2), and pronounced: in accented syllables, yā if the vowel in the following syllable is soft, yâ if the vowel in the following syllable is hard; in unaccented syllables, yĕ or yĭ.
*South African Dutch:* differs from European Dutch in that **e** in accented open syllables, and **ee**, are long ĭ, transcribed ḝ in this Dictionary (see §§ 18, 18.1). **ê** is long â.
*Spanish:* ā in open syllables (but ĕ if preceded or followed by rr, or followed by h); ĕ in closed syllables (but ā if the closing consonant is m, n, s, t͟h, or th).
*Swedish:* variously long ā, short ĕ, long â and short ă (before **r**), ĕ (esp. in the endings **-e**, **-el**, **-er**).
*Yugoslav:* ĕ.

**ea** *Rumanian:* yä.

**eau**
*French:* ō.

**ee** *Dutch:* long ā.
*Finnish:* long â. Cf. Finnish **e**.
*German:* long ā.

**eeu**
*South African Dutch:* ḝ (see South African Dutch **e**)+ŏŏ. Cf. Dutch **eeuw**.

**eeuw**
*Dutch:* When final, long ā+ŏŏ; before a vowel, ā+v (see Dutch **w**). Cf. South African Dutch **eeu**.

**eg** *Danish:* usually ī.
*Norwegian:* ī before **l**, **n**; elsewhere āg.

**ei** *Czech:* ĕ+ĭ, much like English ā (see § 5).
*Dutch, South African Dutch:* Anglicized as ī (i.e., ȧ+ĭ; see § 26), and so represented in this Dictionary. In Dutch, however, it is ĕ+ĭ. Cf. Dutch **ij**, Flemish **ey**.
*Finnish:* ā or, strictly, ĕĭ. See § 5.
*French:* â or ĕ; **eil, eill** are ây or ĕy. But see French **eim, ein.**
*German:* ī.
*Greek (modern):* ē, ê, or, before another vowel, y.
*Icelandic:* ā or, strictly, ĕĭ. See § 5.
*Japanese:* ĕ+ê, much as English ā. See § 5.
*Latvian, Lithuanian:* ā or, strictly, ĕĭ. See § 5.
*Norwegian:* ā or, strictly, ĕĭ. See § 5.
*Portuguese:* ā+ê or â+ê, much like English ā (see § 5); in some parts of Portugal, ă+ê.
*Rumanian:* ĕ+ĭ, much like English ā. See § 5.
*Spanish:* ĕʹê, much like English ā (see § 5), with the first as the stronger of the two vowels. But when written **eí**, pronounced â·ēʹ, with the second as the stronger of the two vowels.

**eim**
*French:* when final or followed by a consonant, ăN; otherwise â or ĕ+m.

**ein**
*French:* when final or followed by a consonant, ăN; otherwise â+n or ĕ+n.

**eí** *Spanish:* see Spanish **ei.**

**ej** *Danish:* ī.

**em**
*French:* preceding a consonant, äN; when final or preceding a vowel, the **e** is ē, ĕ, or, by syncope, silent, and the **m** is m.
*Portuguese:* āNm in an accented syllable before **b, p** (see § 35.1); ēNm or āNm in an initial unaccented syllable before **b, p**; when final in a word, ăêN in Portugal, āêN in Brazil. Cf. Portuguese **e.**

**en** *French:* usually äN when final or preceding a consonant; but **ien** in this position is yăN. See French **e.**
*Portuguese:* when final, or in an accented syllable before a consonant, āN (but see **ens** below); in an initial unaccented syllable before a consonant, ēN or āN; final **ens** is ăêNsh in Portugal, āêNs in Brazil. See § 35.1.

**ens**
*Portuguese:* see Portuguese **en.**

**eö** *Hungarian:* û, like Hungarian **ö** (*q.v.*).

**eu** *Dutch, South African Dutch:* û (long mid-front close rounded vowel: see § 57.3).
*Finnish:* ĕ+ŏŏ.
*French:* generally û, a mid-front rounded vowel, sometimes close, sometimes open. See § 57.3.
*German:* Anglicized as oi, and so represented in this Dictionary. See § 43. The second vowel, however, is ü in German. Cf. German **äu.**
*Portuguese:* sometimes ā+ŏŏ, sometimes â+ŏŏ.
*Swedish:* â+ōō.

**ew**
*Hungarian:* û, like Hungarian **ö** (*q.v.*).

**ey** *Flemish:* like Dutch **ei** (*q.v.*).
*French:* sometimes ā, sometimes ĕ.
*German:* ī, like German **ei.**
*Icelandic:* ā or, strictly, ĕĭ. See § 5.
*Spanish:* when final, ĕ+ê (much like English ā; see § 5); followed by a vowel, ā+y or ĕ+y (see Spanish **e**).

**é** *Czech:* long â. Cf. Czech **e.**
*French:* ā.
*Hungarian:* long ā. Cf. Hungarian **e.**
*Icelandic:* yĕ.

**ê** *French:* usually long â, sometimes short ĕ.
*South African Dutch:* long â.

**ė** *Lithuanian:* = Lithuanian **ē** = ā.

**è** *French:* long â or short ĕ.

**ę** *Lithuanian:* ă, like Lithuanian **e.**
*Polish:* ĕN (see § 35.1).

**ē** *Latvian, Lithuanian:* ā.

**ë** *Russian:* yô. Occurs in accented syllables only. See § 63.2.

**ě** *Czech:* yĕ.

**f** *Icelandic:* f at the beginning of a syllable; sometimes v when medial or final; b before **n.**
*Japanese:* the voiceless correlative of the voiced lip continuant described under Spanish **b** (*q.v.*); transcribed f in this Dictionary.
*Russian:* f. See Russian **v.**
*Swedish:* usually f; in a few words which preserve the old orthography, v; silent before **v.**

**ff** *Russian:* see Russian **v.**

**g** in all languages: in general, g, except as noted below.
*Catalan:* j before **e, i** (not h or K as in Spanish); elsewhere g.
*Danish:* medially and finally, usually the continuant sound described in § 24.1, represented by g in this Dictionary; when final, sometimes the stop k or g; sometimes silent, esp. after **i, u**; elsewhere usually the stop g. But **eg** is usually ī, **ög** is often oi.
*Dutch:* In general: initial in a syllable, and before **d**+a vowel, **g** is the voiced continuant described in § 24.1, represented by g in this Dictionary; elsewhere it is K. **gg** is the voiced continuant. Cf. Dutch **gh**; South African Dutch **g, gh.**
*Finnish:* occurs only in **ng**, pronounced ng.
*Flemish:* initially, a stop g, not, as in Dutch, the continuant sound described in § 24.1; otherwise as in Dutch.
*French:* zh immediately preceding **e, i, y**; silent when final after **n, r,** and before **t**; elsewhere g. Cf. French **gh, gu.**
*German:* Not uniform in all parts of Germany. It is treated as follows in one form of German and in this Dictionary: stop g before a vowel or a voiced consonant; K when final or before a voiceless consonant.
*Greek (modern):* y before the front vowels ē, ê, ĕ, â; elsewhere it is the sound described in § 24.1, represented by g in this Dictionary. Except: it is a stop g in the combination **ng**, pronounced ngg; this g is palatalized before ē, ê, ĕ, â, the pronunciation then being nggy (see § 63.1).
*Hungarian:* g (but see Hungarian **gy**). **gh** is also g.
*Icelandic:* gy before **i** (see § 63.1); otherwise g.
*Italian:* g, except as noted below. j before **e, i,** as in *Giso* jēʹzô. *gi* in turn is j before another vowel, as in *Giusto* jōōsʹtô. **gg** before **e, i** is d+j, as in **Baggio** bädʹjô (since the sound j is really d+zh [see § 29], d+j is really a prolonged d+zh). **gg** elsewhere is gg. **gh** is g, as in *Ghisi* gēʹzē. **gl** is usually ly before **i** (see § 63.1), but gl in a few words. **gli** before a vowel is ly. **gn** is ny (see § 63.1).
*Japanese:* g in all situations in some dialects; medially, ng in other dialects.
*Norwegian:* y before front vowels; k before **s, t** in the same syllable; ng before **n**; silent before **j**; elsewhere usually g.
*Polish:* k when final or before a voiceless consonant; otherwise g.
*Portuguese:* zh before **e, i**; following a vowel or **s** and preceding **a, o, u, l, r,** it is the continuant sound described in § 24.1, represented by g in this Dictionary; elsewhere stop g.
*Rumanian:* j before **e, i**; otherwise g. **gh** is g.
*Russian:* in general, k when final, elsewhere g.
*South African Dutch:* K, except: g, a stop, when preceded by **r** (sometimes **l**) and followed by *ĕ*; sh

before **e**, **i** in Greek and Latin loan words; dropped in both pronunciation and spelling when inflection would bring it between a preceding accented vowel and a following *ĕ*. Cf. Dutch **g**; South African Dutch **gh**.

*Spanish:* before **e**, **i**, like Spanish **j** (*q.v.*); at the beginning of a sentence and of a phrase after a pause, and after **n**, stop g; elsewhere it is the sound described in § 24.1, represented by g in this Dictionary; except: often silent before another consonant (e.g., dē′nō for *digno*).

*Swedish:* before **ä**, **e**, **i**, **ö**, **y**, and after **l**, **r** in the same syllable, y; before **s**, **t**, often k; before **n**, ng; silent before **j**; elsewhere g (but see **ng**). **gg** is gg.

**gg** *Dutch:* see Dutch **g**.

*Italian:* see Italian **g**.

**gh** *Dutch, Flemish:* the continuant sound described in § 24.1, represented by g in this Dictionary. Cf. South African Dutch **gh**.

*French, Hungarian, Italian, Rumanian:* g.

*South African Dutch:* g, a stop, as in English *go*. Cf. Dutch **gh**.

**gj** *Norwegian, Swedish:* y.

*Yugoslav:* = Yugoslav **dj** = dy.

**gl** *Italian:* see Italian **g**.

**gn** *French, Italian:* ny. See § 63.1.

*Norwegian, Swedish:* ngn.

**gu** *French:* variously g, gw, or gü.

*Italian:* gw.

*Portuguese:* g before **e**, **i**; gw before **a**. See Portuguese **g**.

*Spanish:* gw before **a**, **o**; g before **e**, **i** unless written **gü**, when it is gw. See Spanish **g**.

**gy** *Hungarian:* dy. See § 63.1.

**ǵ** *Yugoslav* (not used in this Dictionary): = Yugoslav **dž** = j.

**g'** *Latvian:* a palatalized d, transcribed dy. See § 63.1.

**ğ** *Turkish* (*present-day Roman alphabet*): with **e**, **i**, **ö**, **ü**: y; with **a**, **ı**, **o**, **u** it is the continuant sound described in § 24.1, represented by g in this Dictionary.

**h** *Arabic, Persian, Turkish:* pronounced after a vowel in the same syllable, but omitted in the Anglicized pronunciation.

*Czech:* Anglicized as h, and so represented in this Dictionary, except when final. In Czech, however, the sound here transcribed h is actually the voiced continuant described in § 24.1. Final **h** is unvoiced, becoming ᴋ (see § 31).

*Danish:* silent before **j**, **v**; elsewhere h. But see Danish **ch**.

*Dutch, South African Dutch:* in European Dutch, like English h; in South African Dutch, the same sound voiced. Both are transcribed h in this Dictionary.

*French:* with most speakers, completely silent in all situations. However, elision and liaison take place before initial **h** ("mute **h**") in some words, but not before initial **h** ("aspirated **h**") in others. Thus: *l'herbe* lĕrb, *les herbes* lā-zĕrb′, but *la hase* lȧ äz′, *les hases* lā äz′.

*German:* after a vowel in an accented syllable, usually silent, indicating merely that the vowel is long; elsewhere (but cf. German **ch**, **sch**, **th**), usually h.

*Hungarian:* h, except: silent in **gh**, **th**, and when final; **ch** is ch.

*Italian:* always silent.

*Norwegian:* silent before **j**, **v**; elsewhere h.

*Polish:* h with some speakers, ᴋ (back variety; see § 31) with others.

*Portuguese:* always silent. But cf. Portuguese **ch**, **lh**, **nh**.

*Rumanian:* usually h before a vowel; ᴋ before a consonant and at the end of a syllable, and before a vowel in Greek loan words.

*Sanskrit and other East Indian languages:* pronounced after a consonant in the same syllable, but omitted in the Anglicized pronunciation.

*Spanish:* silent. But cf. Spanish **ch**.

*Swedish:* h, except: silent before **j**, **v**. But cf. Swedish **ch**, **sch**.

*Yugoslav:* before a vowel, h; elsewhere, ᴋ.

**hj** *Danish, Norwegian, Swedish:* y, the **h** being silent.

**hv** *Danish, Norwegian, Swedish:* v, the **h** being silent.

*Icelandic:* sometimes hw, sometimes kw.

**ı** *Turkish* (*present-day Roman alphabet*): û (unretroflexed mid-central vowel; see § 57). [Turkish **ı** (no dot; corresponding capital, **I**) is a different letter from Turkish **i** (corresponding capital, **İ**).]

**i** *Czech:* short ĭ. Cf. Czech **í**.

*Danish:* sometimes ē (long or short), sometimes ĭ.

*Dutch:* in general, long ē in accented, ē̇ in unaccented, open syllables; short ĭ in closed syllables. See §§ 3.27, 3.28. Cf. Dutch **ij**, South African Dutch **i**.

*Finnish:* short ĭ. Cf. Finnish **ii**.

*French:* usually ē; when nasalized by a following **m** or **n**, ăɴ; before a vowel, usually y.

*German:* in general, long ē in accented, ē̇ in unaccented, open syllables, short ĭ in closed syllables. See §§ 3.27, 3.28.

*Greek* (*modern*): transliterates iota and, sometimes (owing to the influence of the Roman-alphabet languages of continental Europe, in which **i** is often or usually ē), eta; in either case, pronounced ē in accented, ē̇ in unaccented, syllables, **y** when preceding another vowel.

*Hungarian:* short ĭ. Cf. Hungarian **í**.

*Icelandic:* long ē before **ng**, **nk**; elsewhere short ĭ.

*Italian:* ē, except: usually y when unaccented before another vowel.

*Japanese:* ē̇. **ii** is ē̇+ē̇.

*Latvian:* short ĭ. Cf. Latvian **ī**.

*Lithuanian:* ĭ.

*Polish:* ē; before another vowel, **y**. But see Polish **ci**, **dzi**, **si**, **zi**.

*Portuguese:* When accented: ē, except: ĭ before **l** final or followed by a consonant (but not before **lh**) and before **u**. When unaccented: ē̇, *ĕ*, or (before another vowel) y. See Portuguese **im**, **in**.

*Rumanian:* usually short ē when not accompanying another vowel; before another vowel, y; after another vowel, forms the second half of a diphthong; at the end of a word following a consonant, silent or very lightly pronounced. **ii** is long ē.

*Russian:* On its pronunciation in accented syllables, see § 63.2. In unaccented syllables, it is yĭ or ĭ. Except: After a vowel, **i** frequently forms the second half of a diphthong; in that case it is not preceded by a y sound, but is pronounced much like the second element of the English diphthongs oi, ī (see §§ 43, 26). **i** is also used to transcribe a diphthong variously pronounced (according to its position in the word or to the dialect of Russian being spoken) ûĭ, long ē, ĭē, or ĭ. Thus the common ending **-ski** in Russian names has a double vowel in the Russian spelling, a single vowel in the English transliteration. The regular transliteration would be **ii**, but this has been rejected by most English transcribers as clumsy; and furthermore a single **i** adequately represents one pronunciation (the fourth above) of the combination. Some transcribers use **y** for this double vowel, but this transcription is used in this Dictionary only where well-established usage compels it. The consonant sounds g, k, ᴋ preceding this combination are not palatalized.

*South African Dutch:* long û (mid-central vowel, without retroflexion: see § 57) in accented open syllables, where it is written **î**; short û in accented closed syllables; ĕ in unaccented syllables.
*Spanish:* ē in accented, ė in unaccented, syllables, except: unaccented before another vowel, y.
*Swedish:* sometimes long ē, sometimes short ĭ.
*Turkish (present-day Roman alphabet):* ĭ or ē. [Turkish **i** (corresponding capital, **İ**) is a different letter from Turkish **ı** (no dot; corresponding capital, **I**).]

**ie** *Dutch:* ē, longer before **r** than in other positions. **ië** is ė+ĕ, **ieë** is ē+ĕ.
*Finnish:* yĕ.
*German:* sometimes a single vowel ē; sometimes two vowels, ė·ĕ, ē′ĕ, ė·ē′, or ė·ā′.
*Latvian:* yĕ or yă (see Latvian **e**).

**ieë**
*Dutch:* see Dutch **ie**.

**ieuw**
*Dutch:* when final, long ē+o͝o; before a vowel, long ē+v (see Dutch **w**).

**ië** *Dutch:* see Dutch **ie**.

**ii** *Finnish:* long ē. Cf. Finnish **i**.
*Japanese:* ė+ė.
*Rumanian:* long ē. Cf. Rumanian **i**.

**ij** *Dutch:* like Dutch **ei** (*q.v.*), except: in the suffix **-lijk**, ĕ.

**im**
*French:* in general: ăɴ when final or followed by a consonant; elsewhere ēm.
*Portuguese:* when final or before a consonant, ēɴ (see § 35.1); elsewhere ēm when accented, ėm when unaccented.

**in** *French:* in general: when final or before a consonant, ăɴ; elsewhere ēn.
*Portuguese:* before a consonant, ēɴ (see § 35.1); elsewhere ēn when accented, ėn when unaccented.

**iu** *Finnish:* yo͞o.

**í** *Czech, Hungarian, Icelandic:* long ē. Cf. Czech, Hungarian, Icelandic **i**.

**î** *French:* ē.
*Rumanian:* like Rumanian **â** (*q.v.*).
*South African Dutch:* see South African Dutch **i**.

**į** *Lithuanian:* ĭ, like Lithuanian **i**.

**ī** *Latvian:* long ē. Cf. Latvian **i**.

**j** *Czech:* y, except: after a vowel it is pronounced ĭ and forms the second half of a diphthong. Thus **aj** is ȧĭ, i.e., ī (see § 26).
*Danish:* y, except: after a vowel it is pronounced ĭ and forms the second half of a diphthong (see Danish **aj**, **ej**, **öj**). **sj** is sh.
*Dutch, South African Dutch:* y, except: zh in French loan words.
*Finnish:* y.
*French:* zh.
*German:* y.
*Hungarian:* y, except: after a vowel it is pronounced ĭ or ė, and forms the second half of a diphthong.
*Icelandic:* y.
*Italian:* y.
*Japanese;* j.
*Latvian:* y.
*Lithuanian:* y.
*Norwegian:* y, except: **kj** is ᴋ (front variety; see § 31); **sj**, **skj** are sh.
*Polish:* y.
*Portuguese:* zh.
*Rumanian:* zh.
*Sanskrit and other East Indian languages:* j.
*Spanish:* Anglicized as h, and so represented in this Dictionary; actually, however, ᴋ (back variety; see § 31) in Spanish.
*Swedish:* y, except: **kj** is ch (i.e., t+sh; see § 14) or, strictly, t+the front variety of ᴋ (see § 31); **sj** is sh; **skj**, **stj** are sh; **tj** is like **kj**. In **dj**, **gj**, **hj**, **lj** the first letter is silent, all being pronounced y.
*Turkish (present-day Roman alphabet):* zh.
*Yugoslav:* y, except: following a vowel and not followed by another vowel it is pronounced ė or ĭ and forms the second half of a diphthong; in the combinations **dj** (or **gj**), **lj**, **nj**, it denotes a palatal consonant (see § 63.1), **dj** or **gj** being dy, **lj** ly, and **nj** ny.

**k** *Czech:* k, except: voiced to g before **d**, **z**.
*Dutch:* k, except: g (a stop consonant as in English *go*, not the continuant usual for Dutch **g**; see § 24.1; see Dutch **g**) before **b**, **d**.
*Greek (modern):* ky before ē, ė, ĕ, â; elsewhere k. Except: ky, k are voiced to gy, g respectively in the combination **nk**, pronounced nggy before ē, ė, ĕ, â, elsewhere ngg.
*Icelandic:* ky before **e**, **i**; otherwise k.
*Norwegian:* k, except: **ki** before a vowel is ᴋ (front variety; see § 31); **sk** before **e**, **i**, **y** is sh, elsewhere sk; **skj** is sh.
*Swedish:* before **ä**, **e**, **i**, **ö**, **y** at the beginning of an accented syllable, or of a syllable preceding the accented syllable, usually ch (i.e., t+sh; see § 14) or, strictly, t+the front variety of ᴋ (see § 31); elsewhere k. But see Swedish **kj**, **sk**, **skj**.

**kh** *Arabic, Persian:* ᴋ.
*Greek (modern)* (transliterating Greek chi): ᴋ, front or back (see § 31) according as it occurs with front or back vowels.
*Russian:* ᴋ (back variety; see § 31) or, by some, h.
*Sanskrit and other East Indian languages:* k+h. The h is omitted in the Anglicized pronunciation.

**kj** *Swedish:* see Swedish **j**.

**k'** *Latvian:* ty. See § 63.1.

**l** *Czech:* l; a prolonged l may function as the vowel in an accented syllable in Czech, as in *Vltava*. In the utterance of this syllabic l, the back of the tongue has approximately the position of English ŭ (see § 32.2), and ŭl, as the nearest English equivalent, is the transcription used in this Dictionary.
*French:* a clear l (see § 32.2), except: sometimes silent before **s**, **n**, **d**, **t**, **x**, and finally; **il** and **ille** final following a vowel sound are y' (see § 63.3), as in *Corneille* kôr′nâ′y'; **lh** is ly; **ll** is l, except that medial **ill**, and **ille** final following a consonant sound, are sometimes ē+y, sometimes ē+l.
*Greek (modern):* palatalized (i.e., ly; see § 63.1) before ē, ė; elsewhere l.
*Lithuanian:* clear before **e**, **i**, **y**; dark elsewhere. See § 32.2.
*Polish:* clear l (see §§ 32.2, 32.3). Cf. Polish **ł**.
*Portuguese:* final and preceding a consonant, dark; elsewhere, clear. See § 32.2.
*Russian:* before certain vowels, a palatalized l, represented by ly in this Dictionary (see §§ 63.1, 63.2); when it is not palatalized, it is always dark (see §§ 32.2, 32.3).

**lh** *French:* ly, y, or (when **h** is the first letter of a word) l.
*Portuguese:* ly (a palatal l; see § 63.1).

**lj** *Swedish:* y, the **l** being silent.
*Yugoslav:* ly (a palatal l; see § 63.1).

**ll** *Catalan:* l, not ly as in Castilian Spanish.
*French:* see French **l**.
*Icelandic:* d'l.
*Spanish:* in general, ly (see § 63.1) in Castilian Spanish, y in Andalusian, Latin American, and Philippine Spanish. Other pronunciations occur, but are not recorded in this Dictionary. See Catalan **ll**.

*Welsh:* a voiceless l. It can be approximated by pronouncing an h before l.

**ly** *Hungarian:* ly (a palatal l; see § 63.1).

**l'** *Latvian, Slovak:* ly.

**ł** *Polish:* dark l (see §§ 32.2, 32.3); in transcriptions in this Dictionary, not differentiated from clear l. Cf. Polish **l**.

**m** *Czech:* m, except: sometimes syllabic ('m: see § 66) in unaccented syllables.

*French, Portuguese:* when final following a vowel, or following a vowel and preceding a consonant, usually indicates nasalization of the vowel (see **am**, **em**, etc.; see § 35); elsewhere m.

**mp**

*Greek (modern):* when not the last letter and the first letter, respectively, of the elements of a compound, pronounced, and sometimes transliterated, mb.

**n** before **g**, **k**, and any letter or letter combination pronounced as a back ᴋ (see § 31) is ng in most languages.

*Czech:* ny before **i**, **í** (see § 63.1); elsewhere n.

*French:* when final following a vowel, or following a vowel and preceding a consonant, usually indicates nasalization of the vowel (see **an**, **en**, etc.; see § 35); elsewhere n.

*Greek (modern):* ny before ē, ê (see § 63.1); elsewhere n. Except: ng in the combinations **nch**, **ng**, **nk**, where **n** often transliterates gamma; **np** is mb.

*Italian:* n, except: ng before k, g; m before f, v.

*Portuguese:* following a vowel and preceding a consonant, usually indicates nasalization of the vowel (see **an**, **en**, etc.; see § 35); elsewhere n. (**n** occurs at the end of a word only in a few learned words, is pronounced, and does not nasalize the preceding vowel.)

*Spanish:* n, except: ng before g, k, h; m before **b**, **p**, **v**; usually silent when it immediately precedes **m**, and in the prefix **trans-**.

**ng** *Danish, Dutch, Finnish, German, Norwegian, South African Dutch, Swedish:* usually ng as in English *singer*, not ngg as in English *finger*. Where, however, **n** and **g** are the last and first letters, respectively, of the elements of a compound, each letter retains its own sound.

**nh**

*Portuguese:* ny. See § 63.1.

**nj** *Yugoslav:* ny. See § 63.1.

**nn**

*Icelandic:* d'n after a diphthong or a vowel bearing an acute accent; otherwise nn.

**nt** *Greek (modern):* when not the last letter and the first letter, respectively, of the elements of a compound, pronounced, and sometimes transliterated, nd.

**ny** *Hungarian:* ny. See § 63.1.

**ń** *Polish:* ny. See § 63.1.

**n'** *Latvian:* ny. See § 63.1.

**ñ** *Spanish:* ny. See § 63.1.

**ň** *Czech:* ny. See § 63.1.

**o** *Czech:* short ô. Cf. Czech **ó**.

*Danish:* variously ō, ŏ, or ŏ (Southern British value; see § 40).

*Dutch:* long ō in accented, ŏ in unaccented, open syllables; sometimes short ŏ (Southern British value; see § 40), sometimes short ô, in closed syllables. **oo** is long ō. Cf. South African Dutch **o**.

*Finnish:* short ŏ (Southern British value; see § 40). Cf. Finnish **oo**.

*French:* ô, except: ō when followed by an unpronounced **s**; usually when followed by the sound **z**; when in a final syllable and not followed by a pronounced consonant. Cf. French **ô**.

*German:* in general, long ō in accented open syllables and when doubled or followed by **h**, otherwise ŏ (see § 38.1).

*Greek (modern):* ô, whether transliterating omicron or omega.

*Hungarian:* ŏ (like ō, but shorter). **oo**, like Hungarian **ó**, is long ō.

*Icelandic:* short ŏ (Southern British value; see § 40), except: long ō before **ng**, **nk**. Cf. Icelandic **ó**.

*Italian:* often ô in syllables bearing primary accent; otherwise ō or ŏ.

*Japanese:* usually ŏ (short), sometimes ō (long).

*Latvian:* wô. Cf. Latvian **ō**.

*Lithuanian:* ô.

*Polish:* ô. Cf. Polish **ó**.

*Portuguese:* in accented syllables, ô or ō; in unaccented syllables, o͞o, ô, or ŏ; preceding an accented vowel, w. See Portuguese **om**, **on**.

*Rumanian:* short ŏ (Southern British value; see § 40). See Rumanian **oa**.

*Russian:* ô in accented, ŭ, ŭ, or ô in unaccented, syllables.

*South African Dutch:* long o͞o in open syllables, short ŏ (Southern British value; see § 40) in closed syllables. **oo** is long o͞o. **ô** is long ô. Cf. Dutch **o**.

*Spanish:* ō in open syllables (but ô if preceded or followed by rr, or followed by h); ô in closed syllables (but ō if followed by s).

*Swedish:* When long: sometimes a sound lying between o͞o and ō, and transcribed o͞o in this Dictionary; sometimes ō. When short: sometimes ô, sometimes o͝o.

*Yugoslav:* ō in accented, ŏ in unaccented, syllables.

**oa** *Rumanian:* wä.

**œ** *French:* ā in Greek loan words. **œi** is ûy'. **œu** is û.

**oe** *Dutch:* short o͞o, except: long o͞o before **r**.

*German:* = German **ö** (*q.v.*), except: usually two vowels in Greek and Latin loan words; long ō in Low German geographical names.

**oei**

*Dutch, South African Dutch:* when final, long o͞o+ĭ; before a vowel, long o͞o+y.

**oi** *Finnish:* oi.

*French:* sometimes wȧ, sometimes wä.

*German:* oi, except: long ō in Low German names.

*Greek (modern):* ē, ê, or, before another vowel, y.

*Lithuanian:* oi.

*Portuguese:* sometimes ō+ê or ô+ê, sometimes w+ē.

*Rumanian:* oi.

*South African Dutch:* oi. Cf. South African Dutch **ôi**.

*Spanish:* oi, with the first as the stronger of the two vowels. But when written **oí**, pronounced ô·ē', with the second as the stronger of the two vowels.

**oí** *Spanish:* see Spanish **oi**.

**oî** *French:* sometimes wȧ, sometimes wä.

**oj** *Czech:* oi.

**om**

*French:* when final or followed by a consonant, ôɴ; elsewhere, ô or ō+m.

*Portuguese:* when final or followed by **b**, **p**, ōɴ (see § 35.1); elsewhere, a nonnasal vowel (see Portuguese **o**)+m.

**on** *French:* when final or followed by a consonant, ôɴ; elsewhere, ô or ō+n.

*Portuguese:* when followed by a consonant, ōɴ (see § 35.1); elsewhere, a nonnasal vowel (see Portuguese **o**)+n.

**oo** *Dutch:* long ō. Cf. South African Dutch **oo**.

*Finnish:* long ô. Cf. Finnish **o**.

*German:* long ō.

*South African Dutch:* long o͞o. Cf. Dutch **oo**.

**ooi**

*Dutch, South African Dutch:* when final, long ō (in

South African Dutch, long o͞o)+ĭ; before a vowel, long ō (in South African Dutch, long o͞o)+y.

**ou** *Czech:* long ô+o͝o.
*Dutch:* short ŏ (Southern British value; see § 40)+o͝o; transcribed ou in this Dictionary, though different from the English sound so transcribed (see § 46). Cf. South African Dutch **ou**.
*Finnish:* ŏ+o͝o; transcribed ou.
*French:* o͞o; w before a pronounced vowel.
*Greek (modern):* o͞o.
*Japanese:* ô+o͝o.
*Portuguese:* in unaccented syllables, ō; in accented syllables, ō in some sections of Portugal and in Brazil, ō+o͝o in other sections of Portugal.
*South African Dutch:* ō+o͝o. Cf. Dutch **ou**.

**ouw**
*Dutch:* when final, ou (see Dutch **ou**); before a vowel, ou+v (see Dutch **w**).

**ov** *Danish:* often a diphthong, ou.

**ow** *German:* in Low German names, long ō.

**oy** *Flemish:* long ō+ĭ.
*French:* wȧ.
*German:* oi.
*Spanish:* when final, oi; when followed by a vowel, ō+y or ô+y.

**ó** *Czech:* long ō. Cf. Czech **o**.
*Hungarian:* long ō.
*Icelandic:* long ō. Cf. Icelandic **o**.
*Polish:* o͞o, like Polish **u**.

**ô** *French:* ō.
*Slovak:* wô.
*South African Dutch:* long ô.

**ôi** *South African Dutch:* differs from South African Dutch **oi** in that ô, the first element of the diphthong (see § 43), is longer.

**ő** *Hungarian:* û (long mid-front close rounded vowel; see § 57.3). Distinct from Hungarian **ö** (*q.v.*).

**ō** *Latvian:* ō. Cf. Latvian **o**.

**ø** *Danish, Norwegian* (not used in this Dictionary): another way of writing **ö**.

**õe** *Portuguese:* ōēɴ.

**ö** in various languages: usually a mid-front rounded close or open vowel, represented by û in this Dictionary. See § 57.3.
*Danish:* û, mid-front rounded close or open vowel. But **ög**, **öj** are oi.
*Hungarian:* û (short mid-front open rounded vowel; see § 57.3). Distinct from Hungarian **ő** (*q.v.*). **eö** has the same sound as **ö**.
*Icelandic:* ûĭ before **ng**, **nk**; elsewhere û.

**ög** *Danish:* oi.

**öi** *Finnish, Norwegian:* ûĭ

**öj** *Danish:* oi.

**öv** *Danish:* often a diphthong, û+o͝o.

**öy** *Finnish:* û+ü.
*Norwegian:* ûĭ.

**p** *French:* sometimes silent when final.
*Greek (modern):* p, except in **mp** (*q.v.*), **np** (see Greek **n**).
*Portuguese:* p, except: generally silent before **t**, **ç**, **s**.
*Spanish:* p, except: usually silent before **s**, **t**, and often omitted from the spelling.

**ph** in all languages: usually f in words of Greek origin.

**q** *Arabic:* Anglicized as k, and so transcribed in this Dictionary. In Arabic, however, the point of contact between tongue and soft palate is farther back than for k.

**qu** *Czech:* kv.
*Danish:* kv.
*Dutch:* kv.
*French:* usually k; in a few words, kw or kü.
*German:* kv.
*Italian:* kw.
*Norwegian:* kv.
*Portuguese:* in general, kw before **a**, k before **e**, **i**.
*Spanish:* k.

**qv** *Swedish:* kv.

**r** in various foreign languages: see § 48.1.
*Czech:* sometimes syllabic (see § 57.2); otherwise r. Cf. Czech **ř**.
*French:* often silent in final **-er**, and sometimes in final **-ers**, both of which are then pronounced ā.
*Yugoslav:* sometimes syllabic (see § 57.2); otherwise r.

**rn** *Icelandic:* d'n.

**rr** *Spanish:* see § 48.1.

**rz** *Polish:* zh, except: unvoiced to sh at the end of a word, before a voiceless consonant, and after a voiceless consonant in the same syllable.

**r'** *Latvian:* ry. See § 63.1.

**ř** *Czech:* approximately r+zh, except: r+sh when final or before a voiceless consonant.

**s** *Danish:* always s.
*French:* s, except: z between vowels; frequently silent when final.
*German:* s, except: z between vowels and initial before a vowel, in some parts of Germany; usually sh when followed by **p** or **t** in the same syllable, except in parts of northern Germany, where it is s. **ss** is s.
*Hungarian:* sh (but see Hungarian **cs**, **ds**, **sz**, **zs**). **ss** is also pronounced sh, sometimes lengthened.
*Italian:* when initial before a voiced consonant, z; between vowels, frequently z; otherwise s. But see Italian **sc**.
*Polish:* s. **si** before a vowel is sh.
*Portuguese:* When initial, or when following a consonant and preceding a vowel, s; between vowels, z; before a voiceless consonant, sh in Portugal, s in Brazil. At the end of a word: sh in Portugal, s in Brazil, before a pause or a voiceless consonant; zh in Portugal, z in Brazil, before a voiced consonant; z before a vowel. **sc** before **e**, **i**, **y** is s. **ss** is s.
*Swedish:* after **r**, s with some speakers, sh with others; otherwise s, except in **sc**, **sch**, **sj**, **sk**, **skj**, **stj** (*qq.v.*).

**sc** *French:* s before **e**, **i**, **y**; otherwise sk.
*Italian:* sh before **e**, **i**; otherwise sk. **sch** is sk.
*Portuguese:* see Portuguese **s**.
*Swedish:* sometimes sh, sometimes s.

**sch**
*Danish:* sh.
*Dutch:* sᴋ initially; s medially, finally, and before inflectional endings. Cf. South African Dutch **sch**.
*German:* sh.
*Italian:* sk.
*South African Dutch:* sk where European Dutch is sᴋ.
*Swedish:* sh.

**si** *Polish:* when final or followed by a consonant, sē; when followed by a vowel, sh.

**sj** *Danish, Norwegian, South African Dutch, Swedish:* sh.

**sk** *Norwegian:* sh before **e**, **i**, **y**; otherwise sk. **skj** is sh.
*Swedish:* in general, sh before accented **ä**, **e**, **i**, **ö**, **y**, elsewhere sk. **skj** is sh.

**skj**
*Norwegian, Swedish:* sh.

**ss** *Hungarian:* sh, sometimes lengthened.

**ssch**
*Dutch:* s.

**stj**
*Swedish:* sh.

**sz** *German* (usually written **ss** in roman type): s.
*Hungarian:* s.
*Polish:* sh. **szcz** is sh+ch.

**ś** *Polish:* sy. See § 63.1.

**ść** *Polish:* palatalized s+palatalized ts (see § 63.1), transcribed stsy in this Dictionary.

**ş** *Rumanian, Turkish (present-day Roman alphabet):* sh.
**š** *Czech, Latvian, Lithuanian, Yugoslav:* sh.
**t** *Czech:* ty (see § 63.1) before **i, í**; elsewhere t.
*Dutch:* t, except: ts or s in **ti**+vowel in Latin loan words (e.g., *Fabritius* fȧ·brē′(t)sē̇·ûs).
*French:* t, except: often silent when final; final **ts** is often silent; **ti**+a vowel is frequently sy.
*German:* t, except: ts in **ti**+a vowel in Latin loan words (e.g., *Curtius* kŏŏr′tsē̇·ŏŏs).
*Greek (modern):* t, except in **nt** (*q.v.*).
*Swedish:* t, except: ts in **t**+unaccented **i** in Latin loan words; **ti** in **-tion** preceded by a consonant, in Latin loan words, is sh; **tj** is ch (i.e., t+sh; see § 14) or, strictly, t+the front variety of K (see § 31); **stj** is sh.
**th** *Danish, German, Norwegian:* t, except: t+h when the last letter and the first letter respectively of the elements of a compound.
*French:* t.
*Greek (modern):* th.
*Hungarian:* t.
*Icelandic:* transliterates either of two letters, one of which (occurring only at the beginning of a syllable) is th, the other of which is t̶h̶.
*Portuguese:* t.
**tj** *Norwegian:* ky.
*Swedish:* see Swedish **t**.
**ts** *Hungarian:* ch (i.e., t+sh; see Hungarian **s**; see § 14).
**tsch**
*German:* ch. See § 14.
**ty** *Hungarian:* ty. See § 63.1.
**tz** *German:* ts.
**t'** *Czech:* ty. See § 63.1.
**ţ** *Rumanian:* ts.
**u** *Czech:* short ŏŏ. Cf. Czech **ú, ů, qu**.
*Danish:* ōō and ŏŏ.
*Dutch, South African Dutch:* long ü in open accented syllables, short ü in open unaccented syllables (see § 3.27); short û (mid-front rounded open vowel; see § 57.3) in closed syllables (see § 3.28). **uu** is ü, long except in French loan words. **-um** in geographical names is *-ŭm*.
*Finnish:* short ŏŏ. Cf. Finnish **uu**.
*French:* usually ü; before another vowel, often forms a diphthong with it. But see French **gu, qu, um, un**.
*German:* in general, ōō (long when accented) in open syllables and preceding **h**, otherwise short ŏŏ.
*Greek (modern):* Except as strongly established usage requires otherwise, modern-Greek upsilon is transliterated **u** in this Dictionary only when the upsilon occurs in combination with a preceding omicron (transliterated **ou** and pronounced ōō) or a following iota (transliterated **ui** and pronounced ē or ē̇). A upsilon standing alone is pronounced ē or ē̇, and is regularly transliterated **y**. A upsilon preceding another vowel (except iota: see above) is pronounced y and transliterated **y**. Except after omicron (see above), a upsilon following a vowel is pronounced f before a voiceless consonant, v elsewhere, and transliterated **v**. In a few cases, however, this postvocalic modern-Greek upsilon has been transliterated **u**, as in transliterations of ancient Greek.
*Hungarian:* short ŏŏ. Cf. Hungarian **ú**.
*Icelandic:* long ōō before **ng, nk**; elsewhere, a short mid-front rounded open vowel (see § 57.3), transcribed ẽ before **r** in unaccented syllables, elsewhere û.
*Italian:* ōō, except: when unaccented before a vowel, w.
*Japanese:* usually short, sometimes long; ŏŏ and ōō respectively.
*Latvian:* short ŏŏ. Cf. Latvian **ū**.
*Lithuanian:* short ŏŏ.
*Norwegian:* a high-central rounded vowel, close and long or open and short, Anglicized respectively ōō and ŏŏ and so represented in this Dictionary.
*Polish:* ōō.
*Portuguese:* ōō, except: usually w when unaccented before another vowel (but **gu, qu** before **e, i** are g, k, respectively, unless the **u** bears a diaeresis, when they are gw, kw, respectively). See Portuguese **um, un**.
*Rumanian:* short ōō; after a vowel, forms the second half of a diphthong; silent after an **i** preceded by a vowel (e.g., **oiu** is oi).
*Russian:* ōō in accented, ŏŏ in unaccented, syllables.
*Spanish:* ōō, except: when unaccented before a vowel, w.
*Swedish:* sometimes a long high-central close rounded vowel, Anglicized as ōō and so represented in this Dictionary; sometimes a short vowel resembling English ŭ, and so represented in this Dictionary.
**ui** *Dutch, South African Dutch:* Anglicized as oi, and so represented in this Dictionary. The Dutch sound, however, is û (mid-front open rounded vowel; see § 57.3)+ü.
*Greek (modern):* ē, ē̇, or, before another vowel, y. See Greek **u**.
*Portuguese:* sometimes ōō+ē̇, sometimes w+ē.
*Rumanian:* ōō+ĭ.
**uj** *Czech:* ŏŏ+ĭ.
**um**
*French:* when final, ôm when **um** is the Latin ending **um**, otherwise ûɴ; before a consonant, ûɴ; before a vowel, üm.
*Portuguese:* when final or before **b, p**, ōōɴ (see § 35.1); otherwise ōōm.
**un**
*French:* when final or followed by a consonant, ûɴ; otherwise ün.
*Portuguese:* before a consonant, ōōɴ (see § 35.1); otherwise ōōn.
**uo** *Finnish:* wŏ.
*Lithuanian:* wô.
**uu**
*Dutch:* see Dutch **u**.
*Finnish:* long ōō. Cf. Finnish **u**.
**uy** *Dutch:* like Dutch **ui** (*q.v.*).
**ú** *Czech:* long ōō. Cf. Czech **u, ů**.
*Hungarian:* long ōō. Cf. Hungarian **u**.
*Icelandic:* long ōō. Cf. Icelandic **u**.
**ů** *Czech:* long ōō. Cf. Czech **u, ú**.
**û** *French:* ü.
**ű** *Hungarian:* ü (long high-front close rounded vowel; see § 60). Distinct from Hungarian **ü** (*q.v.*).
**ų** *Lithuanian:* short ŏŏ, like Lithuanian **u**.
**ū** *Latvian:* long ōō. Cf. Latvian **u**.
*Lithuanian:* long ōō. Cf. Lithuanian **u**.
**ü** *Estonian, German, Turkish (present-day Roman alphabet):* ü (see § 60).
*Hungarian:* ü (short high-front open rounded vowel; see § 60). Distinct from Hungarian **ű** (*q.v.*).
**v** *Czech:* when final or before certain (chiefly voiceless) consonants, f; elsewhere, v.
*Danish:* v, except: often silent after **l**; after a short vowel, pronounced ŏŏ and forms the second half of a diphthong.
*German:* in general, f in all positions in genuinely German words, v in words still regarded as more or less foreign.
*Greek (modern):* (1) transliterating beta: v; (2) transliterating upsilon after certain vowels: see Greek **u**.
*Russian:* v, except: f finally and before voiceless con-

sonants. (The transliterations **ff** and **f**, common in English for the Russian letter when final, are in general not used in this Dictionary.)
*South African Dutch:* f in all positions.
*Spanish:* Anglicized as v, and so transcribed in this Dictionary. In Spanish, however, it does not have the sound of English v, being pronounced exactly like Spanish **b** (*q.v.*).

**w** *Czech:* v.
*Danish:* v.
*Dutch, South African Dutch:* in European Dutch, similar to the lip continuant described under Spanish **b**; in South African Dutch, like English v. Both are transcribed v in this Dictionary.
*French:* sometimes w, sometimes v.
*German:* v. But see German **ow**.
*Hungarian:* occurs only in **ew** (*q.v.*).
*Norwegian:* v.
*Polish:* v, except: unvoiced to f finally and before a voiceless consonant.
*Swedish:* v.

**x** *French:* usually silent when final; s in a few words; otherwise ks or gz.
*Portuguese:* most commonly sh; in learned words, ks or s; in the prefix **ex-** preceding an accented syllable, the **x** is z when a vowel immediately follows.
*Spanish:* usually ks; before a consonant, often s; between two vowels the second of which is accented, sometimes gz.

**y** *Czech:* short ĭ, like Czech **i**. Cf. Czech **ý**.
*Danish:* ü (high-front close rounded vowel, long or short; see § 60).
*Dutch:* long ē in accented, ė in unaccented, open syllables; short ĭ in closed syllables. Cf. Flemish **y**, South African Dutch **y**.
*Finnish:* ü (short high-front open vowel; see § 60). Cf. Finnish **yy**.
*Flemish:* like Dutch **ij** (*q.v.*).
*French:* as consonant, y; as vowel, ē.
*German:* ē, ė, and ĭ, like German **i** (*q.v.*), except in learned words from the Greek, in which it is frequently ü (close in open syllables and long when accented; open and short in closed syllables; see §§ 60, 3.27, 3.28).
*Greek (modern):* usually transliterates a upsilon not accompanied by another vowel (see Greek **u**) and is pronounced ē in accented, ė in unaccented, syllables; sometimes used instead of **g** for gamma, and instead of **i** for iota, when these letters are pronounced y (see Greek **g** and **i**).
*Hungarian:* a vowel, short ĭ, except in **gy**, **ly**, **ny**, **ty**, where it indicates that the preceding consonant is palatal (see § 63.1), even when these combinations are final; thus *király* is kĭ′räl·y′, not kĭ′rä·lĭ. **gy** is pronounced dy. Cf. Hungarian **ý**.
*Icelandic:* short ĭ. Cf. Icelandic **ý**.
*Japanese:* always a consonant, y.
*Lithuanian:* ē.
*Norwegian:* ü (high-front close rounded vowel, long or short; see § 60).
*Polish:* a high-central unrounded vowel that has no counterpart in English; Anglicized as ĭ, and so transcribed in this Dictionary.
*Russian:* (1) Transliterating one of the Russian hard vowels (see § 63.2), **y** has the sound described in § 27.1, transcribed ĭ in this Dictionary. (2) In **ya**, **yu** (*qq.v.*), which transliterate two of the Russian soft vowels (see § 63.2), it indicates the y sound that forms the first element of these sounds. (3) Sometimes, esp. at the end of a word, **y** transliterates a Russian diphthong pronounced û+ĭ. The regular transcription would be **yi**, but this has been rejected by most transcribers as misleading and clumsy. (4) In a system of transcription not regularly used in this Dictionary, but a few examples of which well-established usage has compelled it to adopt, **y** is also used to transcribe another diphthong one pronunciation of which is identical with that of the diphthong described in (3) above. On this point see Russian **i**.
*Slovak:* like Polish **y** (*q.v.*).
*South African Dutch:* ĕ+ĭ, much like English ā (see § 5).
*Spanish:* as a consonant, y; as a vowel, ē; after another vowel and not bearing an acute accent, it serves as the second half of a diphthong.
*Swedish:* ü, close or open; see § 60.
*Turkish (present-day Roman alphabet):* y.

**ya** *Russian:* yȧ in accented, yŭ or yȧ in unaccented, syllables. See § 63.2.

**yi** *Finnish:* ü+ĭ.

**ym**
*French:* when final or followed by a consonant, ăɴ; otherwise ēm.

**yö** *Finnish:* ü+û.

**yu** *Russian:* yōō in accented, yŏŏ in unaccented, syllables. See § 63.2.

**yy** *Finnish:* ü (long high-front close vowel; see § 60). Cf. Finnish **y**.

**ý** *Czech:* long ē, like Czech **í**. Cf. Czech **y**.
*Icelandic:* long ē. Cf. Icelandic **y**.

**z** *Czech:* z, except: unvoiced to s finally and before a voiceless consonant.
*Danish:* s.
*French:* often mute when final; otherwise usually z.
*German:* ts. But cf. German **sz**.
*Hungarian:* z. But see Hungarian **cz**, **sz**, **zs**.
*Icelandic:* s.
*Italian:* generally ts, but not infrequently dz. **zz** is tts or ddz, i.e., a prolonged t followed by an s, or a prolonged d followed by a z.
*Polish:* z, except: unvoiced to s when final or before a voiceless consonant. (But see Polish **cz**, **dz**, **rz**, **sz**.) **zi** before a vowel is zh.
*Portuguese:* initially and between vowels, z; when final before a pause or a voiceless consonant, sh; when final before a voiced consonant, zh.
*Russian:* z, except: unvoiced to s when final or before a voiceless consonant.
*South African Dutch:* s.
*Spanish:* th in Castilian Spanish, s in Andalusian, Latin American, and Philippine Spanish.
*Swedish:* s.

**zh** *Russian:* zh, except: unvoiced to sh finally and before a voiceless consonant.

**zi** *Polish:* see Polish **z**.

**zs** *Hungarian:* zh.

**zz** *Italian:* see Italian **z**.

**ź** *Polish:* zy. See § 63.1.

**ż** *Lithuanian:* zh.
*Polish:* zh, except: unvoiced to sh finally and before a voiceless consonant.

**ž** *Czech:* zh, except: unvoiced to sh when final.
*Latvian, Lithuanian, Yugoslav:* zh.

# ABBREVIATIONS USED IN THIS BOOK

*ab.*...........about
*A.B.*..........Artium Baccalaureus (Bachelor of Arts)
*Acad.*.........Academy
*A.D.*..........Anno Domini (in the year of our Lord)
*ad int.*.......ad interim
*Adj.*..........Adjutant
*adm.*..........admitted
*A.E.&M.P.*....Ambassador Extraordinary and Minister Plenipotentiary
*A.E.&P.*......Ambassador Extraordinary and Plenipotentiary
*A.E.F.*........American Expeditionary Force, or Forces
*Afr.*..........Africa; African
*Agric.*........Agricultural; Agriculture
*A.I.F.*........Australian Imperial Forces
*Ala.*..........Alabama
*Alban.*........Albanian
*Alta.*.........Alberta (province of Canada)
*Am.*...........America(n)
*A.M.*..........Artium Magister (*Lat.*, Master of Arts)
*A.&M.*.........Agricultural and Mechanical (College)
*amb.*..........ambassador
*Amer.*.........America(n)
*anc.*..........ancient
*Angl.*.........Anglicized
*anon.*.........anonymous, anonymously
*Apoc.*.........Apocrypha(l)
*Apr.*..........April
*A.R.A.*........Associate of the Royal Academy
*Arab.*.........Arabic
*Ariz.*.........Arizona
*Ark.*..........Arkansas
*art(s)*........article(s)
*A.-S.*.........Anglo-Saxon
*As. Ind.*......Asiatic Indian
*Assn.*.........Association
*assoc.*........associate; associated; association
*asst.*.........assistant
*A.T.S.*........Auxiliary Territorial Service
*Atty.*.........Attorney
*Atty. Gen.*....Attorney General
*Aug.*..........August
*A.V.*..........Authorized Version (of the Bible)
*b.*............born
*B.A.*..........Baccalaureus Artium (Bachelor of Arts)
*Bab.*..........Babylonian
*B.Arch.*.......Bachelor of Architecture
*B.C.*..........before Christ; British Columbia
*B.C.E.*........Bachelor of Chemical Engineering; Bachelor of Civil Engineering
*B.C.L.*........Bachelor of Civil Law
*B.D.*..........Bachelor of Divinity
*B.E.*..........Bachelor of Education; Bachelor of Engineering
*B.E.F.*........British Expeditionary Force, or Forces
*Belg.*.........Belgian; Belgium
*bet.*..........between
*B.F.A.*........Bachelor of Fine Arts
*biog(s).*......biography; biographies
*bk(s).*........book(s)
*B.L.*..........Bachelor of Laws; Bachelor of Letters
*B.Lit(t).*.....Bachelor of Literature, or of Letters (*Lat.*, Baccalaureus Lit[t]erarum)
*B.M.E.*........Bachelor of Mining Engineering; Bachelor of Mechanical Engineering
*B.Mech.E.*....Bachelor of Mechanical Engineering
*B.Mus.*........Bachelor of Music
*B.Ph.*.........Bachelor of Philosophy
*Braz.*.........Brazilian
*Brig. Gen.*....Brigadier General
*Brit.*.........Britain; British
*bro(s).*.......brother(s)
*B.S.* or *B.Sc.*..Bachelor of Science
*B.S.Ed.*.......Bachelor of Science in Education
*Bulg.*.........Bulgarian
*Bull.*.........Bulletin
*B.W.I.*........British West Indies
*c.*............circa (*Lat.*, about)
*Cal.* or *Calif.*..California
*Calif. Inst. Tech.*.......California Institute of Technology
*Can.*..........Canada; Canadian
*Can. Fr.*......Canadian French
*Cantab.*.......Cantabrigiensis (*Lat.*, of Cambridge)
*Capt.*.........Captain
*Cath.*.........Catholic
*C.B.*..........Chirurgiae Baccalaureus (*Lat.*, Bachelor of Surgery); Companion of the Bath
*C.B.E.*........Companion (of the Order) of the British Empire
*cc.*...........cubic centimeter(s)
*C.C.N.Y.*......College of the City of New York
*C.E.*..........Civil Engineer
*Celt.*.........Celtic
*cent(s).*......century, centuries
*cf.*...........compare (Lat. *confer*)
*ch.*...........chargé d'affaires
*Ch.*...........Church
*chap(s).*......chapter(s)
*Ch.B.*.........Chirurgiae Baccalaureus (*Lat.*, Bachelor of Surgery)
*Chin.*.........Chinese
*Ch.M.*.........Chirurgiae Magister (*Lat.*, Master of Surgery)
*Chron.*........Chronicles (book of Bible)
*Cie* [no period].Compagnie (*French*, Company)
*C.I.E.*........Companion (of the Order) of the Indian Empire
*CIO*...........Congress of Industrial Organizations; formerly, Committee for Industrial Organization
*cm.*...........centimeter(s)
*C.M.*..........Chirurgiae Magister (*Lat.*, Master of Surgery)
*Co.*...........Company; County
*Col.*..........Colossians (book of Bible); Colonel
*Coll.*.........College
*collab.*.......collaborated; collaboration; collaborator
*colloq.*.......colloquial; colloquially
*Coll. (of) Phys. & Surg.*......College of Physicians and Surgeons
*Colo.*.........Colorado
*Com.*..........Commander; Commodore
*Comm.*.........Commission; Committee
*Conn.*.........Connecticut
*cont.*.........continued
*Cor.*..........Corinthians (book of Bible)
*Corp.*.........Corporation
*cr.*...........created
*cu.*...........cubic

# Abbreviations Used in This Book

*d.* . . . . . . . . . . . . died; penny, pence (*Lat.*, denarius, denarii)
*Dan* . . . . . . . . . . . Daniel (book of Bible); Danish
*D.A.R.* . . . . . . . . Daughters of the American Revolution
*dau* . . . . . . . . . . . daughter
*D.B.E.* . . . . . . . . Dame (Commander, Order) of the British Empire
*D.C.* . . . . . . . . . . District of Columbia
*D.D.* . . . . . . . . . . Doctor of Divinity
*D.D.S.* . . . . . . . . Doctor of Dental Surgery
*Dec* . . . . . . . . . . . December
*Del* . . . . . . . . . . . Delaware
*Dem* . . . . . . . . . . Democrat; Democratic
*Dem.-Rep* . . . . . Democratic-Republican
*Den* . . . . . . . . . . . Denmark
*dept(s)* . . . . . . . . department(s)
*Deut* . . . . . . . . . . Deuteronomy (book of Bible)
*D.F.C.* . . . . . . . . Distinguished Flying Cross
*dict* . . . . . . . . . . dictionary
*dim* . . . . . . . . . . . diminutive
*div* . . . . . . . . . . . division; divorced
*D.Lit.* or *D.Litt.* Doctor of Literature, or of Letters (*Lat.*, Doctor Lit[t]erarum)
*D.M.S.* . . . . . . . . Doctor of Medical Sciences
*D.Mus* . . . . . . . . Doctor of Music
*D.* (or *Dr.*) *P.H.* Doctor of Public Health, or Hygiene
*D.Phil* . . . . . . . . Doctor of Philosophy
*Dr* . . . . . . . . . . . . Doctor
*D.-R.* . . . . . . . . . Democratic-Republican
*D.S.* or *D.Sc.* . . Doctor of Science
*D.S.C.* . . . . . . . . Distinguished Service Cross
*D.S.M.* . . . . . . . . Distinguished Service Medal
*D.S.O.* . . . . . . . . (Companion of the) Distinguished Service Order
*D.S.T.* . . . . . . . . Doctor of Sacred Theology
*D.T.* . . . . . . . . . . Doctor of Theology
*Du* . . . . . . . . . . . . Dutch
*D.V.* . . . . . . . . . . Douay Version (of the Bible)
*E.* . . . . . . . . . . . . East
*E.Afr.* . . . . . . . . . East Africa(n)
*Eccles* . . . . . . . . . Ecclesiastes (book of Bible)
*ed(s)* . . . . . . . . . . edition(s); editor; edited
*educ* . . . . . . . . . . educated
*E.E.* . . . . . . . . . . Electrical Engineer; Envoy Extraordinary
*E.E.&M.P.* . . . . Envoy Extraordinary and Minister Plenipotentiary
*e.g.* . . . . . . . . . . . exempli gratia (*Lat.*, for example)
*E.M.* . . . . . . . . . . Engineer of Mines
*Encyc. Brit.* . . . . Encyclopaedia Britannica
*Eng* . . . . . . . . . . . England; English
*Eph* . . . . . . . . . . . Ephesians (book of Bible)
*erron* . . . . . . . . . erroneous; erroneously
*esp* . . . . . . . . . . . especially
*Esq* . . . . . . . . . . . Esquire
*est.* or *estab.* . . . established
*Esth* . . . . . . . . . . Esther (book of Bible)
*Eston* . . . . . . . . . Estonian
*et al* . . . . . . . . . . et alii or et aliae (*Lat.*, and others)
*etc.* . . . . . . . . . . . et cetera (*Lat.*, and others; and the rest; and so forth)
*Eur* . . . . . . . . . . . Europe; European
*exc* . . . . . . . . . . . except; exception
*Exod* . . . . . . . . . . Exodus (book of Bible)
*Ezek* . . . . . . . . . . Ezekiel (book of Bible)
*f.* . . . . . . . . . . . . . following
*Feb* . . . . . . . . . . . February
*Fed* . . . . . . . . . . . Federalist
*fem* . . . . . . . . . . . feminine
*ff.* . . . . . . . . . . . . following
*Finn* . . . . . . . . . . Finnish
*fl.* . . . . . . . . . . . . flourished (*Lat.* floruit)
*Fla* . . . . . . . . . . . Florida
*Flem* . . . . . . . . . . Flemish
*F.&M.* . . . . . . . . . Franklin and Marshall College
*Fr.* . . . . . . . . . . . . French
*Fredk* . . . . . . . . . Frederick
*freq* . . . . . . . . . . . frequently
*F.R.S.* . . . . . . . . . Fellow of the Royal Society
*ft.* . . . . . . . . . . . . foot; feet
*Ft.* . . . . . . . . . . . . Fort
*Ga* . . . . . . . . . . . . Georgia
*Gael* . . . . . . . . . . Gaelic
*Gal* . . . . . . . . . . . Galatians (book of Bible)
*gen* . . . . . . . . . . . generally
*Gen* . . . . . . . . . . . Genesis (book of Bible); General
*Gent* . . . . . . . . . . Gentleman
*Geol* . . . . . . . . . . geological; geology
*Geom* . . . . . . . . . geometrical; geometry
*Ger* . . . . . . . . . . . German; Germany
*G.H.Q.* . . . . . . . . General Headquarters
*Gov* . . . . . . . . . . . Governor
*govt* . . . . . . . . . . . government
*Gr.* . . . . . . . . . . . . Greek
*grad* . . . . . . . . . . . graduate; graduated
*Gr. Brit.* . . . . . . . Great Britain
*Grk* . . . . . . . . . . . Greek
*Hab* . . . . . . . . . . . Habakkuk (book of Bible)
*Hag* . . . . . . . . . . . Haggai (book of Bible)
*Heb* . . . . . . . . . . . Hebrew; Hebrews (book of Bible)
*hist.*, *Hist.* . . . . . historical; history
*H.M.* . . . . . . . . . . His (*or* Her) Majesty, or Majesty's
*H.M.S.* . . . . . . . . His (*or* Her) Majesty's Ship
*hon* . . . . . . . . . . . honorary
*Hon* . . . . . . . . . . . Honorable
*Hos* . . . . . . . . . . . Hosea (book of Bible)
*h.p.* . . . . . . . . . . . horsepower
*hr(s)* . . . . . . . . . . hour(s)
*Hung* . . . . . . . . . . Hungarian; Hungary
*Icel* . . . . . . . . . . . Icelandic
*i.e.* . . . . . . . . . . . . id est (*Lat.*, that is)
*Ill.* . . . . . . . . . . . . Illinois
*illust* . . . . . . . . . . illustrated; illustration
*in.* . . . . . . . . . . . . inch(es)
*Inc.*, *inc.* . . . . . . Incorporated
*incl* . . . . . . . . . . . including
*Ind* . . . . . . . . . . . Indiana
*Inst* . . . . . . . . . . . Institute; Institution
*Introd* . . . . . . . . . introduction
*Ir.* . . . . . . . . . . . . Irish
*Ire* . . . . . . . . . . . . Ireland
*Isa* . . . . . . . . . . . . Isaiah (book of Bible)
*Ital* . . . . . . . . . . . Italian
*I.W.W.* . . . . . . . . Industrial Workers of the World
*Jan* . . . . . . . . . . . January
*Jap* . . . . . . . . . . . Japanese
*J.D.* . . . . . . . . . . Juris, or Jurum, Doctor (*Lat.*, Doctor of Law, or Laws)
*Jer* . . . . . . . . . . . Jeremiah (book of Bible)
*Josh* . . . . . . . . . . Joshua (book of Bible)
*Jr.*, *jr.* . . . . . . . . Junior
*Kans* . . . . . . . . . . Kansas
*K.B.* . . . . . . . . . . Knight (of the Order) of the Bath
*K.C.* . . . . . . . . . . King's Counsel
*K.C.B.* . . . . . . . . Knight Commander (of the Order) of the Bath
*K.C.S.I.* . . . . . . . Knight Commander (of the Order) of the Star of India
*Ky* . . . . . . . . . . . . Kentucky
*l.* . . . . . . . . . . . . . line
*La* . . . . . . . . . . . . Louisiana
*Lam* . . . . . . . . . . Lamentations (book of Bible)
*lat* . . . . . . . . . . . . latitude
*Lat* . . . . . . . . . . . Latin; Latinized
*lb(s)* . . . . . . . . . . pound(s) (*Lat.*, libra)

*Levit*.......... Leviticus (book of Bible)
*Lieut*.......... Lieutenant
*lit*............ literature; literary; literal
*Lith*.......... Lithuania; Lithuanian
*Litt.D*......... Litterarum Doctor (Doctor of Letters)
*ll*............. lines
*LL.B*.......... Legum Baccalaureus (Bachelor of Laws)
*LL.D*......... Legum Doctor (*Lat.*, Doctor of Laws)
*log*........... logarithm
*Ltd*........... Limited
*m*............. married; mile(s)
*M*............ Monsieur
*M.A*.......... Master of Arts
*Macc*......... Maccabees
*Maj*.......... Major
*Mal*.......... Malachi (book of Bible)
*Man*.......... Manitoba
*manuf*......... manufacturer; manufacturing
*Mar*.......... March
*M.Arch*....... Master of Architecture
*masc*.......... masculine
*Mass*.......... Massachusetts
*math.*, *Math*.... mathematical; mathematics
*Matt*.......... Matthew (book of Bible)
*M.B*.......... Medicinae Baccalaureus (*Lat.*, Bachelor of Medicine); Musicae Baccalaureus (*Lat.*, Bachelor of Music)
*M.B.A*........ Master in, or of, Business Administration
*Md*........... Maryland
*M.D*.......... Medicinae Doctor (Doctor of Medicine)
*Me*........... Maine
*M.E*.......... Mining, or Mechanical, Engineer
*Med*.......... Medical
*M.E.E*........ Master of Electrical Engineering
*Messrs*........ Messieurs
*Met.E*......... Metallurgical Engineer
*Mex*.......... Mexico; Mexican
*mfg.*, *Mfg*...... manufacturing
*mfr(s)*......... manufacturer(s)
*Mich*.......... Michigan
*Mil*........... Military
*min(s)*........ minute(s)
*Minn*......... Minnesota
*min.p*......... minister plenipotentiary
*Miss*.......... Mississippi
*M.I.T*......... Massachusetts Institute of Technology
*M.L*.......... Master of Laws
*Mlle*.......... Mademoiselle
*Mme*.......... Madame
*Mo*........... Missouri
*mod*.......... modern
*Mont*......... Montana
*M.P*.......... Member of Parliament
*Mr*........... Mister
*Mrs*.......... Mistress
*MS.*, *ms*....... manuscript
*M.S.* or *M.Sc.*. Master of Science
*M.S.Agr*....... Master of Scientific Agriculture
*MSS.*, *mss*..... manuscripts
*Mt(s)*......... Mount; Mountain(s)
*Mus*.......... Museum; music
*Mus.B*........ Musicae Baccalaureus (*Lat.*, Bachelor of Music)
*Mus.D*........ Musicae Doctor (*Lat.*, Doctor of Music)
*N*............ North
*N.A*.......... National Army
*N.Am(er)*...... North America(n)
*Nat*.......... National; Natural
*N.B*.......... New Brunswick
*N.C*.......... North Carolina
*N.Dak*........ North Dakota
*N.E*.......... Northeast
*Nebr*.......... Nebraska
*Neh*........... Nehemiah (book of Bible)
*Neth*.......... Netherlands
*Nev*........... Nevada
*Newf*.......... Newfoundland
*N.H*.......... New Hampshire
*N.J*........... New Jersey
*N.Mex*........ New Mexico
*no(s)*......... number(s) (*Lat.*, numero)
*Nor*........... Norway
*Norw*.......... Norwegian
*Nov*........... November
*N.S*........... Nova Scotia
*N.S.D.A.P*..... Nationalsozialistische Deutsche Arbeiterpartei (National Socialist German Workers Party—official title of German Nazi party)
*N.S.W*........ New South Wales
*N.T*........... New Testament
*Num*.......... Numbers (book of Bible)
*N.W*.......... Northwest
*N.Y*.......... New York
*N.Y.U*........ New York University
*N.Z*........... New Zealand
*Obad*.......... Obadiah (book of Bible)
*obs*............ obsolete
*obsoles*......... obsolescent
*occas*.......... occasional; occasionally
*Oct*........... October
*Okla*.......... Oklahoma
*O.M*.......... Order of Merit
*Ont*........... Ontario
*opp*........... opposed; opposite
*Ore*........... Oregon
*orig*........... original; originally
*O.T*........... Old Testament
*Oxon*.......... Oxoniensis (*Lat.*, of Oxford)
*oz(s)*.......... ounce(s)
*p*............. page
*Pa*............ Pennsylvania
*pat*............ patented
*P.E.I*......... Prince Edward Island
*P.E.N*......... (International Association of) Poets, Playwrights, Editors, Essayists, and Novelists
*Penn. State*.... Pennsylvania State College
*perh*........... perhaps
*Pers*........... Persian
*Ph.B*.......... Philosophiae Baccalaureus (*Lat.*, Bachelor of Philosophy)
*Ph.D*.......... Philosophiae Doctor (*Lat.*, Doctor of Philosophy)
*Phil*........... Philippians (book of Bible)
*Phila*.......... Philadelphia
*Ph.M*......... Philosophiae Magister (*Lat.*, Master of Philosophy)
*Phys*.......... Physician(s)
*P.I*........... Philippine Islands
*pl*............. plural
*P.O*........... Post Office
*Pol*........... Poland; Polish
*Poly*.......... Polytechnic (Institute or School)
*Port*.......... Portugal; Portuguese
*pp*............ pages
*P.R*........... Puerto Rico
*Pres*.......... President
*prob*.......... probably
*prod*.......... produced
*Prof*.......... Professor
*pron*.......... pronounce; pronounced; pronunciation
*prond*......... pronounced
*Prot*.......... Protestant

*Prot. Episc.*.....Protestant Episcopal
*Prov.*..........Proverbs (book of Bible); province
*pseud.*.........pseudonym
*pub(l)*.........published
*Q.C.*...........Queen's Counsel
*qq.v.*..........quae vide (*Lat.*, which see)
*Que.*...........Quebec
*q.v.*...........quod vide (*Lat.*, which see)
*R.A.*...........Royal Academician
*R.A.F.*.........Royal Air Force
*R.A.M.C.*......Royal Army Medical Corps
*R.C.*...........Roman Catholic
*Rep.*...........Republican
*res.*...........residence
*rev.*...........revised
*Rev.*...........Revelation (book of Bible); Reverend; Review
*R.F.A.*.........Royal Field Artillery
*R.F.C.*.........Royal Flying Corps
*R.I.*...........Rhode Island
*R.N.*...........Royal Navy
*R.N.R.*.........Royal Naval Reserves
*Rom.*...........Romans (book of Bible)
*R.P.I.*.........Rensselaer Polytechnic Institute
*R.R.*...........Railroad
*RSFSR*.......Russian Socialist Federated Soviet Republic
*Rum.*...........Rumanian
*Russ.*..........Russian
*R.V.*...........Revised Version (of the Bible)
*Ry.*............railway
*s.*.............shilling; shillings
*S.*.............South; Saint (*Ital.*, Santo)
*S.Afr.*.........South Africa(n)
*Sam.*...........Samuel (book of Bible)
*S.Am(er).*......South America(n)
*Sask.*..........Saskatchewan
*S.B.*...........Scientiae Baccalaureus (*Lat.*, Bachelor of Science)
*S.C.*...........South Carolina
*Sc.D.*..........Scientiae Doctor (*Lat.*, Doctor of Science)
*Scot.*..........Scottish
*S.D.*...........Scientiae Doctor (*Lat.*, Doctor of Science)
*S.Dak.*.........South Dakota
*S.E.*...........Southeast
*sec(s)*.........second(s)
*Secy.*..........secretary
*Sem.*...........Seminary
*Sept.*..........September
*Serb.*..........Serbian
*sing.*..........singular
*S.J.D.*.........Scientiae Juridicae Doctor (*Lat.*, Doctor of Juridical Science)
*Skr.*...........Sanskrit
*S.M.*...........Scientiae Magister (Master of Science)
*S.M.U.*.........Southern Methodist University
*Sou.Afr.Du.*....South African Dutch
*Span.*..........Spanish
*S.P.C.C.*.......Society for Prevention of Cruelty to Children
*specif.*........specific; specifically
*sq.*............square
*Sr., sr.*.......Senior
*SS.*............Saints (*Ital.*, Santi; *Lat.*, Sancti)
*St.*............Saint; Street
*S.T.B.*.........Sacrae Theologicae Baccalaureus (*Lat.*, Bachelor of Sacred Theology); Scientiae Theologicae Baccalaureus (*Lat.*, Bachelor of Theological Science)
*S.T.D.*.........Sacrae Theologicae Doctor (*Lat.*, Doctor of Sacred Theology); Scientiae Theologicae Doctor (*Lat.*, Doctor of Theological Science)
*Ste.*...........Sainte (*French*, feminine of Saint)
*S.T.L.*.........Sacrae Theologicae Licentiatus (*Lat.*, Licentiate of Sacred Theology)
*Sts.*...........Saints
*suppl.*.........supplement; supplementary
*Surg.*..........Surgeon(s)
*S.W.*...........Southwest
*Swed.*..........Swedish
*Switz.*.........Switzerland
*T.C.U.*.........Texas Christian University
*Tech.*..........Technical; (Institute or School of) Technology; (Poly)technic Institute
*Tenn.*..........Tennessee
*Tex.*...........Texas
*T.H.*...........Territory of Hawaii
*Theol.*.........Theological; Theology
*Thess.*.........Thessalonians (book of Bible)
*Tim.*...........Timothy (book of Bible)
*tr.* or *trans(l)*...translated; translation
*Turk.*..........Turkish
*U.*.............University
*U.C.L.A.*.......University of California at Los Angeles
*U.K.*...........United Kingdom
*Ukrain.*........Ukrainian
*UN*.............United Nations (Organization)
*Univ(s)*........University; Universities
*UNRRA*......United Nations Relief and Rehabilitation Administration
*U.S.*...........United States (of America)
*U.S.A.*.........United States of America; United States Army
*U.S.C.G.*.......United States Coast Guard
*U.S.M.A.*.......United States Military Academy
*U.S.M.C.*.......United States Marine Corps
*U.S.N.*.........United States Navy
*U.S.N.A.*.......United States Naval Academy
*U.S.N.R.*.......United States Naval Reserve
*U.S.S.*.........United States Ship
*U.S.S.R.*.......Union of Soviet Socialist Republics
*usu.*...........usual(ly)
*v.*.............versus
*Va.*............Virginia
*var(s).*........variant(s)
*V.C.*...........Victoria Cross
*V.I.*...........Virgin Islands
*viz.*...........videlicet (*Lat.*, namely)
*V.M.I.*.........Virginia Military Institute
*vol(s).*........volume(s)
*V.P.I.*.........Virginia Polytechnic Institute
*vs.*............versus
*Vt.*............Vermont
*W.*.............West
*Wash.*..........Washington
*W.C.T.U.*.......Woman's Christian Temperance Union
*W.I.*...........West Indies
*Wis.*...........Wisconsin
*W.&J.*..........Washington and Jefferson College
*W.&L.*..........Washington and Lee University
*wr.*............written
*W.Va.*..........West Virginia
*Wyo.*...........Wyoming
*Yid.*...........Yiddish
*Y.M.C.A.*.......Young Men's Christian Association
*yr(s).*.........year(s)
*Yugo.*..........Yugoslavian
*Y.W.C.A.*.......Young Women's Christian Association
*Zech.*..........Zechariah (book of Bible)
*Zeph.*..........Zephaniah (book of Bible)

# A
# DICTIONARY OF NAMES OF NOTEWORTHY PERSONS

## WITH PRONUNCIATIONS AND CONCISE BIOGRAPHIES

**Aa'ge·sen** (ô'gĕ·s'n) *or* **Aa'ge·son** (ô'gĕ·s'n), **Svend.** fl. 1185. Earliest Danish historian; author of *Compendiosa Historia Regum Daniae,* recording Danish history from 300 to 1185.

**Aahmes.** See AHMOSE.

**Aa'li'** *or* **A'li'** (ä'lē'), **Mehemet.** 1815–1871. Turkish pasha and diplomat; five times grand vizier (1852 ff.); took part in London conference (1871) on Black Sea question.

**Aal'to** (äl'tō), **Alvar.** 1898–1976. Finnish architect and furniture designer. Architect of business buildings, as Sunila Pulp Mill at Kotka, hospitals, as sanatorium at Paimio, libraries, as library at Viipuri, theaters, stores, and private dwellings. To U.S. (1940); accepted position on M.I.T. faculty. His wife, **Aino** (d. 1949), collaborator with him in architectural work and furniture designing.

**Aan'rud** (ôn'rōōd), **Hans.** 1863–1953. Norwegian poet, playwright, and author of stories of peasant life.

**Aa're·strup** (ô'rĕ·strōōp), **Carl Ludvig Emil.** 1800–1856. Danish lyric poet.

**Aar'on** (âr'ŭn). Traditional founder of Hebrew priesthood; first Jewish high priest. Brother of Moses (*q.v.*), with whom, according to Biblical book of *Exodus,* he led the Israelites out of Egypt (c. 1200 B.C. according to some authorities). Succeeded by his son Eleazar; another son, Ithamar, was ancestor of Eli.

**Aa'sen** (ô'sĕn), **Ivar Andreas.** 1813–1896. Norwegian philologist; instrumental in establishing from popular dialects an accepted literary language (Landsmaal) by means of his *Grammar* (1848) and his *Dictionary of Norse Popular Speech* (1850).

**Abad.** See ABBAD.

**Abaelard** *or* **Abailard.** See Peter ABELARD.

**Abafi, Michael.** See APAFFY.

**A'ban'court'** (ȧ'bäɴ'kōōr'), **Charles Xavier Joseph de Fran'que·ville'** (fräɴk'vēl') **d'.** 1758–1792. French minister of war (1792); slain in massacre at Versailles (Sept. 9, 1792).

**A'ba·no** (ä'bä·nō), **Pietro d'. Peter of Abano.** 1250?–?1316. Italian philosopher and physician; denounced by Inquisition for heresy and magic.

**Abarbanel.** Variant of ABRABANEL.

**A'bas·cal'** (ä'bäs·käl'), **José Fernando.** Marqués **de la Con·cor'dia** (kông·kôr'thyä). 1743–1821. Spanish statesman and general. Governor of Cuba (1796); viceroy of Peru (1804–16).

**Abassides** *or* **Abassids.** Variants of ABBASSIDES.

**Abate** *or* **Abati, Niccolo dell'.** See ABBATE.

**A'bau'zit'** (ȧ'bō'zēt'), **Firmin.** 1679–1767. French Protestant theologian, philosopher, and scientist. Sir Isaac Newton acknowledged indebtedness to him for corrections in mathematical work.

**Ab'ba A·ri'ka** (ȧb'bä ȧ·rĭ'kä). *Usually called* **Rab** (răb; *Heb.* räv). d. 247 A.D. Babylonian rabbi; founded Jewish Academy of Sura (on Euphrates); probably greatest of haggadists of Babylonian schools.

**Ab·bad' I** (ăb·bäd') *or* **A·bad'** (ȧ·bäd'). *In full* **'Abbād ibn-Muḥammad abu-'Amr.** d. 1042. Founder of Abbadide dynasty of Seville. King (1023–42); as cadi of Seville, seized occasion of anarchy in Córdoba to secure control of Seville and establish new throne. His son **Abbad II,** *Arab.* **al-Mu'taḍid** (reigned 1042–68); poet and patron of letters; his policy harmful to Spanish Moslems; forced to pay tribute to Ferdinand I of Castile. His son **Abbad III,** *Arab.* **al-Mu'tamid** (reigned 1068–91); seized Córdoba; held a gay court, giving rise to many legends; aroused enmity of Christians, esp. of Alfonso VI of Castile; called to his aid Moslems (Almoravides) of Africa, who defeated Alfonso (1086); later (1091) deposed by them and sent into exile; died (1095) in Morocco.

**Ab'bad·ides** (ăb'ȧ·dīdz) *or* **Ab'bad·ids** (ăb'ȧ·dĭdz). Short-lived Mohammedan dynasty founded by Abbad I and ruling (1023–91) at Seville in southern Spain, following the Western Caliphate; overthrown by the Almoravides.

**Ab'ba'die'** (ȧ'bȧ'dē'), **Antoine Thom'son** (tŏm's'n) **d'** (1810–1897) and his brother **Arnaud Michel d'** (1815–1893). Explorers, b. Dublin; moved to France (1818); conducted scientific explorations in Abyssinia (1838–48).

**Ab·bas'** (ăb·bäs'). *In full* **al-'Abbās ibn-'Abd-al-Muṭṭalib.** 566?–652. Paternal uncle of Mohammed. Rich merchant of Mecca; one of chief apostles of Islam; ancestor of dynasty of Abbassides (*q.v.*).

**Ab·bas′, abu-al-** (*à*·bo͝ol′ăb·bäs′). *Also* **Abu'l-Abbas.** *Known as* **al-Saffāḥ,** *i.e.* the bloodshedder. 721?–754. Descendant of Abbas, uncle of Mohammed. Founder and first caliph (750–754) of Abbasside dynasty; removed capital of Islam from Al Kufa.

**Abbas I.** 1813–1854. Pasha of Egypt (1848–54). Grandson of Mehemet Ali (*q.v.*). After Ibrahim Pasha's death (1848), made regent, later (1849) pasha of Egypt; murdered by slaves.

**Abbas II.** *In full* **Ab·bas′ Hil′mi Pa′sha** (ăb·bäs′ hĭl′mĭ pä′shä). 1874–1944. Khedive of Egypt (1892–1914). Son of Tewfik Pasha. Co-operated with British officials in matters of justice, taxation, irrigation, reconquest of Sudan, etc. (1900–14); deposed when British protectorate over Egypt established (1914). See HUSSEIN KAMIL.

**Abbas.** Name of three shahs of Persia: **Abbas I the Great.** 1557–?1628. Shah (1586–1628). Son of Shah Mohammed. Defeated the Uzbeks near Herat (1597) and drove them from Persia; fought long wars with Turks and Tatars; defeated Turks at Basra (1605) and at Sultanieh (1618); added greatly to Persian territory; besieged and took Baghdad (1623); made many reforms in the country. **Abbas II.** 1632–1667. Shah (1642–67); son of Safi I; regained Kandahar (1648). **Abbas III.** Shah (1732–36); child ruler, last of the Safawid dynasty; deposed. See NADIR SHAH.

**Abbas Effendi.** See ABDUL BAHA.

**Ab·bas′ Mir′za′** (ăb·bäs′ mēr′zä′). 1783–1833. Persian prince. Son of Fath Ali. Unsuccessful in preventing Russia from taking Persian provinces in Caucasus; won against Turks at Erzurum (1821); lost Armenia in second Russian war (1826–28); was guaranteed succession to throne but died before his father.

**Ab′bas·sides** (ăb′*à*·sīdz) *or* **Ab′bas·ids** (ăb′*à*·sĭdz). Mohammedan dynasty ruling in Eastern Caliphate (37 caliphs; 750–1258). Founded by Abbas, descendant of, and named for, Abbas, uncle of Mohammed. Shiite and Persian in origin, succeeding purely Arab Ommiad dynasty; established its capital at Baghdad (762); overthrown and its capital destroyed by Mongols under Hulagu.

**Ab·ba′te** (äb·bä′tā), *also* **A·ba′te** (ä·bä′tā) *or* **A·ba′ti** (ä·bä′tē), **Niccolo dell'.** 1512?–1571. Italian painter, esp. of frescoes.

**Ab′be** (ăb′ē), **Cleveland.** 1838–1916. American meteorologist, b. New York City. Director, Cincinnati Observatory (1868); began issuing weather reports (Sept. 1, 1869). Joined weather service of U.S. at its organization (Jan. 3, 1871); retired (1916).

**Ab′be** (äb′ĕ), **Ernst.** 1840–1905. German physicist and industrialist. Directed research for optical firm of Carl Zeiss (from 1866); partner (1875); took over management of firm after death of Zeiss (1888) and reorganized it (1896) into a co-operative industry with advanced labor regulations. Also established (1889) with his own fortune the Carl-Zeiss-Stiftung for scientific research and social betterment. Noted for work in optics and improvements in optical glass and instruments, esp. the microscope.

**Ab′bey** (ăb′ĭ), **Edwin Austin.** 1852–1911. American painter, b. Philadelphia. *Harper's Weekly* staff illustrator. To London (1878). Illustrations for *Selections from the Poetry of Robert Herrick* (1882) favorably received; those for *Old Songs* (1889) caused Pennell to call him "the greatest living illustrator." Executed panels, illustrating the *Quest of the Holy Grail,* for Boston Public Library (1890–1902). Exhibited at Royal Academy (1890 ff.). Requested by King Edward (1902) to paint coronation picture. Engaged (1911) on group of murals at Pennsylvania State Capitol in Harrisburg.

**Abbey, Henry Eugene.** 1846–1896. American impresario, b. Akron, Ohio. In partnership with John B. Schoeffel (from 1876) and Maurice Grau (from 1882). Managed appearances of William H. Crane and Stuart Robson, the elder Sothern, Henry Irving, and Edwin Booth. Introduced to America Sarah Bernhardt (1880), Jean and Édouard de Reszke, Emma Eames, and Calvé; managed Adelina Patti's American tour (1889–90). Manager of Metropolitan Opera House, New York (1883–84, 1891–96), with Grau as business manager.

**Ab′bon′ of Fleu′ry′** (à′bôɴ′ ŭv flû′rē′). *Lat.* **Ab′bo Flo′ri·a·cen′sis** (ăb′ō flō′rĭ·*à*·sĕn′sĭs). 945?–1004. French theologian and chronicler.

**Ab′bot** (ăb′ŭt), **Anthony.** Pseudonym of Charles Fulton OURSLER.

**Abbot, Charles Greeley.** 1872–1973. American astrophysicist, b. Wilton, N.H. Grad. M.I.T. (1894). Assistant (1895), director (1907), Smithsonian Astrophysical Observatory; secretary, Smithsonian Institution (1928). Carried on research on solar radiation. Author of *The Sun* (1911), *The Earth and the Stars* (1925), *The Sun and the Welfare of Man* (1929).

**Abbot, Ezra.** 1819–1884. American Biblical scholar, b. Jackson, Me.; member of New Testament committee for revision of English Bible (1871 ff.).

**Abbot, George.** 1562–1633. English prelate, b. Guildford, Surrey. Archbishop of Canterbury (from 1611). One of translators of New Testament in King James Bible.

**Abbot, Henry Larcom.** 1831–1927. Engineer officer, U.S. Army, b. Beverly, Mass. Served through Civil War. Appointed (1857) to assist Capt. Andrew A. Humphreys (*q.v.*) in investigating flood-protection questions of the lower Mississippi. Appointed to command Engineer Battalion at Willett's Point, N.Y. (1865); developed Engineer School of Application. Member (1904) of board of consulting engineers to determine plan of a Panama canal.

**Ab′bott** (ăb′ŭt), **Austin.** 1831–1896. American lawyer and author, b. Boston. Son of Jacob Abbott. Collaborated with his brother Benjamin in production of legal compendiums (1855–70) and brought out similar works thereafter independently (1873–95).

**Abbott, Benjamin Vaughan.** 1830–1890. American lawyer and author, b. Boston. Son of Jacob Abbott. Grad. N.Y.U. (1850). Adm. New York bar (1852). In collaboration with his brother Austin, published (between 1855 and 1870) numerous law treatises, reports, and digests. Appointed (1864) secretary of New York Code Commission; drafted penal code which became basis of present law. Appointed (1870) one of commissioners to revise Statutes of the United States.

**Abbott, Charles.** 1st Baron **Ten′ter·den** (tĕn′tēr·d'n; -dĕn). 1762–1832. English jurist, b. Canterbury. Chief justice (from 1818).

**Abbott, Charles Conrad.** 1843–1919. American naturalist and author, b. Trenton, N.J. Author of *Days out of Doors, Upland and Meadow, Travels in a Treetop,* and many other works of a semipopular character.

**Abbott, Claude Colleer.** 1889–1971. English educator and poet; professor of English, Durham (1932 ff.); author of *Poems* (1921), *Ploughed Earth* (1930), etc.

**Abbott, Edwin Abbott.** 1838–1926. English clergyman and writer. Headmaster, City of London School (1865–89). Author of *A Shakespearian Grammar* (1870), *Francis Bacon* (1885), and theological works. His brother **Evelyn** (1843–1901) was a classical scholar; author of *History of Greece* (3 vols., 1888–1900).

**Abbott, George.** 1887– . American playwright and producer, b. Forestville, N.Y. B.A., Rochester (1911).

Actor on legitimate stage (1913); began writing and directing plays and motion pictures (1919); director for Paramount Pictures (1927–30); theatrical producer in New York. Coauthor of *Three Men on a Horse* (with J. C. Holm), *Love 'em and Leave 'em* (with J. V. A. Weaver), *Coquette* (with Ann Preston Bridgers); author of *The Boys from Syracuse* (musical comedy adapted from Shakespeare's *Comedy of Errors*).

**Abbott, Grace.** 1878–1939. American social worker, b. Grand Island, Nebr.; chief of Child Labor Division of Children's Bureau, Washington, D.C. (1921–34). Her older sister, **Edith** (1876–1957), dean (from 1924) of School of Social Service Administration, U. of Chicago; author of *Women in Industry* (1910), books on the immigration problem, *The Tenements of Chicago* (1936), *Public Assistance* (1939).

**Abbott, Jacob.** 1803–1879. American Congregational clergyman and author, b. Hallowell, Me. Father of Benjamin Vaughan, Austin, and Lyman Abbott. Grad. Bowdoin (1820). Founded in Boston (1829) Mount Vernon School for girls. Won immediate success with *The Young Christian* (1832); withdrew (1835) from pulpit to devote himself to writing of juveniles, including the *Rollo* books (28 vols.: *Rollo at Play, Rollo's Travels*, etc.), *Harper's Story Books* (36 vols.).

**Abbott, Lemuel.** 1760–1803. English portrait painter.

**Abbott, Lyman.** 1835–1922. American Congregational clergyman, author, and editor, b. Roxbury, Mass. Son of Jacob Abbott. Grad. N.Y.U. (1853). Editor, *Illustrated Christian Weekly* (1870). Joined Henry Ward Beecher (1876) in editorship of *Christian Union*, succeeding him (1881) as editor in chief and continuing when paper changed to *The Outlook* (1893). After death of Beecher, succeeded (1890) to pulpit of Plymouth Congregational Church in Brooklyn; retired (1899) to devote himself to editorship of *The Outlook*. Author of *Theology of an Evolutionist* (1897), *Henry Ward Beecher* (1903), *The Great Companion* (1904), *The Spirit of Democracy* (1910).

**Abbott, Wilbur Cor'tez** (kôr'tĕz). 1869–1947. American historian, b. Kokomo, Ind. Professor, Yale (1908–20), Harvard (1920–37).

**Abd** (ăbd). Arabic word (meaning "servant") used as an initial element in Semitic proper names.

**Abd-al-.** See also names beginning ABDUL.

**Abd-al-A·ziz'** (ȧb·dŏŏl'ă·zēz'). *Often* **Abd-el-Aziz.** *Arab.* **'Abd-al-'Azīz ibn-Mūsa ibn-Nuṣayr.** d. 716. Son of Musa. First emir (713–716) of conquered region of southern Spain; made Seville his capital.

**Abd-al-Aziz IV,** Mulai. *Also* **Abd-el-Aziz** *or* **Abdul-Aziz.** 1878–1943. Sultan of Morocco (1894–1908) of Filali dynasty. His modern ideas, friendliness to foreigners, and high taxes led to unrest; forced to yield to French influence; last years of reign (1904–08) marked by exploits of bandit Raisuli (*q.v.*); deposed by revolt led by his brother Abd-al-Hafiz, who succeeded him.

**Abd-al-Aziz ibn-Saud.** See IBN-SAUD.

**Abd-al-Ha·fiz'** (ȧb·dŏŏl'hȧ·fēz'). *Also* Mulai **Hafiz** *or* **Abdul-Hafiz.** 1875?– . Sultan of Morocco (1908–12) of Filali dynasty. Placed on throne by revolt that deposed his brother Abd-al-Aziz IV; forced to abdicate by French, who established protectorate (1912).

**Abd-al-Kadir.** See ABD-EL-KADER.

**Abdallah.** See also ABDULLAH.

**Abd·al·lah'** *or* **Abd·ul·lah'** (ȧb·dŏŏl·lä'), *i.e., literally,* Servant of God. *Arab.* **'Abd-Allāh ibn-'Abd-al-Muṭṭalib.** 545?–570. Father of Mohammed, b. Mecca. Cf. ABD-AL-MUTTALIB.

**Abdallah.** *In full* **'Abd·al·lāh' ibn-Yā·sīn'** (ȧb·dŏŏl-lä' ĭb''n yä·sēn'). d. 1058? Learned and pious Moslem; founder of Almoravides, sect in northwestern Africa and Spain; taught and organized Berber and Negro tribes of western Sahara region; killed in battle, but his successors founded Marrakech (1062) in Morocco and carried conquest to Spain. See Yusuf IBN-TASHFIN.

**Abd·al'la·tif'** (ȧb·dŏŏl'lȧ·tēf'). *Arab.* **'Abd al-Latif al-Baghdadi.** 1162?–1231. Arab physician, traveler, and historian, b. Baghdad; wrote an account of Egypt.

**Abd-al-Ma·lik'** (ȧb·dŏŏl'mȧ·lĭk'). *Arab.* **'Abd-al-Malik ibn-Marwān.** 646?–705. Fifth Ommiad caliph (685–705) of Baghdad. Son of Marwan I. Spent first years of reign in putting down revolts of rival caliphs; with aid of his general al-Hajjaj, united Islam; at war with Byzantine emperors, esp. Justinian II, but results indecisive; first caliph to coin purely Arabic money; made improvements in administration and established Arabic as official language.

**Abd-al-Mu'min** (ȧb·dŏŏl·mōō'mĭn) *or* **Abdul-Mu-min.** *Arab.* **'Abd-al-Mu'min ibn-'Ali.** 1094?–1163. Arab leader of North Africa and founder of Almohade dynasty. Member of a Berber tribe of Atlas region; favored by ibn-Tumart, founder of sect of Almohades; after ibn-Tumart's death (c. 1130), assumed title of caliph and conquered (1140–47) cities of North Africa and Morocco; put end to Almoravide dynasty (1147); passed over into Spain, taking Córdoba (1148), Almería (1151), and Granada (1154), and extended his rule over Mohammedan Spain; gained control of Tunis and Tripoli (1158–60).

**Abd-al-Mut'ta·lib** (ȧb·dŏŏl·mŏŏt'tȧ·lĭb). *Arab.* **'Abd-al-Muṭṭalib.** d. 578. Grandfather of Mohammed, and his guardian for about two years. Cf. ABDALLAH (545?–570).

**Abd-al-Rahman** *or* **Abd-ar-Rahman.** Variants of ABD-ER-RAHMAN.

**Abd-al-Rahman.** = IBN-KHALDUN.

**Abd-al-Wahab.** Founder of sect of Wahabis. See MOHAMMED IBN-ABD-AL-WAHAB.

**Abd-el-Aziz.** Variant of ABD-AL-AZIZ.

**Abd-el-Ka'der** *or* **Abd-al-Ka'dir** (ȧb·dŏŏl·kä'dĭr). 1807?–1883. Arab leader in Algeria and emir of Mascara. Joined Arab tribes of Oran in opposition to French; emir (or dey) of Mascara (1832 ff.); united many tribes (1832–34); secured favorable treaty from France; twice again fought France (1835–37, 1840–41); driven into Morocco; secured help of Moroccan sultan, Abd-er-Rahman, but both defeated (1844) at Isly by French under Bugeaud; surrendered (1847) and became prisoner of France; freed by Napoleon III (1852). Lived at Bursa (1852–55), later at Damascus.

**Abd-el-Ka'dir** (ȧb·dŏŏl·kä'dĭr). *Arab.* **'Abd-al-Qā-dir.** 14th-century Arabian historian of music.

**Abd'-el-Krim'** (*Angl.* ăb'dĕl·krĭm'). *Also* **Abdel Krim.** *Arab.* **'Abd-al-Ka·rīm'** (ȧb·dŏŏl'kȧ·rēm'). 1885–1963. Leader of Moors in Rif region, Morocco. Made emir (1922); successful in war with Spanish (1921–24). Attacked French zone (1925); defeated by combined French and Spanish (1926); exiled to Réunion (1926).

**Abdenago.** See SHADRACH.

**Ab'der·hal'den** (äp'dĕr·häl'dĕn), **Emil.** 1877–1950. Swiss chemist and physiologist; taught in German universities.

**Abd-er-Rah·man'** (ȧb·dŏŏr'ră·män'). *Also* **Abd-ar-Rah·man'** *or* **Abd·ur'rah·man'.** Name of five Ommiad emirs of Western Emirate (later Caliphate) of Córdoba, esp.:

**Abd-er-Rahman I.** *Arab.* **'Abd-al-Raḥmān ibn-Mu'āwiyah.** 731–788. Grandson of Hisham, 10th Ommiad caliph of Damascus. Emir (756–788). Escaped Abbasside massacre (750) of members of house of Ommiad; gained mastery of southern Spain by victory on

Guadalquivir River (756); made Córdoba his capital and built its famous mosque; opposed invasion (778) in Ebro Valley by Charlemagne (*q.v.*), who, however, was called back before any battle was fought, except the legendary rearguard action against Roland (source of *Chanson de Roland*).

**Abd-er-Rahman II.** 788–852. Emir (822–852). Patron of music and letters; built many fine structures in Córdoba.

**Abd-er-Rahman III.** *Arab.* **'Abd-al-Raḥmān al-Nāṣir.** 891–961. Emir (912–929); caliph (929–961). Brought Moslem Spain under strong central government; seized part of Morocco in opposition to Fatimid caliphs; at war with kings of León and Navarre during much of his reign, defeating them in several battles; assumed title of caliph (929); during his reign, Ommiad caliphate of Spain reached zenith of its power; built strong fleet; made Córdoba most important center of learning in Europe.

**Abd-er-Rahman.** *Also* **Abd-ar-Rahman** *or* **Abdurrahman.** *Arab.* **'Abd-al-Raḥmān.** d. 732. Arab emir of Spain (731–732). Governor of southern Gaul (721); led Saracen army through western Pyrenees into France (732); met Franks under Charles Martel at Tours, near Poitiers (732); defeated and killed in great battle.

**Abd-er-Rahman.** *Also* **Abd-ur-Rahman.** 1778–1859. Sultan of Fez and Morocco (1822–59). Involved in disputes with Austria, Spain, and England because of piracy practiced by his subjects; sided with Abd-el-Kader (1844) in war against France; both badly defeated by Bugeaud in battle of Isly (1844); made peace with France.

**Abd'-er-Rah·man' Khan** (äb'dĕr·rŭ·män' kän). *Also* **Abdurrahman Khan.** 1830?–1901. Amir of Afghanistan (1880–1901); grandson of Dost Mohammed (*q.v.*).

**Abdias.** See OBADIAH.

**Abdool.** Former variant of ABDUL.

**Abdul.** See also names beginning ABD-AL- and ABD-EL-.

**Abd'ul-A·ziz'** (äb'dŭl·ä·zēz'). 1830–1876. Sultan of Turkey (1861–76). Son of Mahmud II; brother and successor of Abdul-Medjid I. First sultan to visit Western Europe (1867); established Bulgarian exarchate; came under Russian influence (1870); failing to quell revolt in Herzegovina and Bosnia (1875), deposed on demand of foreign powers; committed suicide or murdered.

**Abdul-Aziz ibn-Saud.** See IBN-SAUD.

**Abd'ul Ba·ha'** (äbd'o͝ol bă·hä'), *i.e., literally,* Servant of Baha. *Real name* **Ab·bas' Ef·fen'di** (äb·bäs' ĕ·fĕn'dĭ). 1844–1921. Persian Bahai leader. Imprisoned (1868–1908) at Akka (Acre), Turkish penal colony on the Mediterranean south of Beyrouth; succeeded his father, Bahaullah (*q.v.*), as Bahai leader (1892–1921); freed from prison during regime of Young Turks. Journeyed through Europe and U.S. (1911–13); preached and expanded the Bahai religion; during World War (1914–19) lived in Palestine; knighted (1920; Sir Abdul Baha Bahai) by England for his services. See SHOGHI EFFENDI.

**Abd'ul-Ha·mid'** (äb'dŭl·hä·mēd'). *Also written* **Abdu-l-Hamid** *and* **Abd-ul-Hamid.** Name of two sultans of Turkey:

**Abdul-Hamid I.** 1725–1789. Sultan (1774–89). Son of Ahmed III. Succeeded his brother Mustafa III. Reign notable for two disastrous wars (1768–74, 1787–92) with Russia: (1) inherited from Mustafa, at end of which, by Treaty of Küchük Kainarja (1774), Crimea was lost; (2) against Russia and Austria, not settled till reign of his successor, Selim III, by Treaty of Jassy (1792).

**Abdul-Hamid II.** 1842–1918. Sultan (1876–1909). Son of Abdul-Medjid I; succeeded his brother Murad V. Long reign marked by many events of great importance to Turkey; insurrection in Balkans led to war with Russia (1877–78); lost most of his possessions in Europe by Treaty of San Stefano (1878). Promised reforms which were not carried out; responsible for Armenian outrages (1895–96); avoided demands for redress or reform by inciting powers against each other. Driven to war with Greece by revolts in Crete (1896–97). His misgovernment finally led to prolonged period (1896–1908) of discontent and increasing strength of Young Turk movement; faced with their revolutionary activity, restored (1908) constitution of 1876; deposed by unanimous vote of parliament; exiled to Salonika (1909), but returned to Constantinople (1912); confined (1915–18) at Magnesia (Manisa).

**Abd'ul Ke·rim' Pa·sha'** (äb'dŭl kĕ·rēm' pä·shä'). 1811–1883. Turkish general; took part in Crimean War (1853–56), and campaigns against Serbia (1876); in command in Russo-Turkish War (1877–78), but banished for failure.

**Abdullah.** See also ABDALLAH.

**Abd·ul'lah** (äb·do͞ol'ä), **Ach'med** (äk'mĕd). *Pen name* **A. A. Na'dir** (nä'dĕr). *Full name* **Achmed Abdullah Nadir Khan el-Durani el-Iddrissyeh.** 1881–1945. Fiction writer; b. Kabul, Afghanistan. Educ. in India, England, France, Germany. Served in British Indian and Ottoman armies. In recent years resident in U.S. Author of short stories, novels, and plays.

**Abdullah et Taaisha.** See KHALIFA.

**Abd·ul·lah'** (*or* **Abd·al·lah'**) **ibn-Hu·sein'** (*ȧ*b·do͞ol·lä' ĭb''n·ho͞o·sīn'). 1882–1951. King of Jordan (Trans-Jordan); second son of Husein ibn-Ali (*q.v.*); made amir of British mandate of Trans-Jordan (1921); became king (1946) when country got its independence.

**Abd'ul-Me·djid' I** *or* **Abd'ul Me·jid'** (äb'dŭl mĕ·jēd'). 1823–1861. Sultan of Turkey (1839–61). Son of Mahmud II. At his accession Turkish Empire threatened by attacks of Mehemet Ali, rebellious viceroy of Egypt; defeated at Nisib (1839); his rights protected by powers in Treaty of London (1840) and Straits Convention (1841). Began to carry out reforms of predecessors, aided by chief adviser, Reshid Pasha; issued decrees granting various rights to citizens; reforms not very successful because of strong opposition of reactionary Moslems. Founded (1851) Order of Medjidie. Engaged in war with Russia (Crimean War, 1853–56), securing alliance (1854) with England and France. Succeeded by his brother Abdul-Aziz.

**Abd'ul-Me·djid' (II) Ef·fen'di** (ĕ·fĕn'dē). *Also* **Abd'ul Me·jid'.** 1868–1944. Caliph at Constantinople (1922–24). Only surviving son of Sultan Abdul-Aziz. Scholar and patron of arts and music. At end of war with Greece (1924), office of sultan abolished by Mustafa Kemal Pasha; proclaimed caliph of Constantinople in succession to his cousin Mohammed VI. Treaty of Lausanne signed (1923) during caliphate; with establishment of republic (1923), his position nominal; to Switzerland on abolition (Mar. 3, 1924) of caliphate by President Atatürk of Turkey.

**Abd·ul-Wah·hab'** (*ȧ*b·do͞ol'wă·häb'). *Arab.* **'Abd-al-Wahhāb.** 1691–1787. Mohammedan reformer, b. in Arabia. Educ. Basra; founder of puritanical movement in Islam, started in Nejd; sought to restore primitive form as taught by Mohammed; his teachings spread rapidly in central Arabia and his followers (Wahabis) attained power, esp. in 20th century under ibn-Saud.

**Abdurrahman** *or* **Abd-ur-Rahman.** Variants of ABD-ER-RAHMAN.

**A·be** (ä·bĕ), **Iso** *or* **Isoh.** 1865–1949. Japanese politician, b. in Fukuoka prefecture. Educ. Doshisha (Kyoto), Hartford Theological Sem., U.S. (1891–94), and Berlin

U.; professor at Waseda U., Tokyo (1899–1928); member, House of Representatives (from 1928); organizer (1927) and leader of opposition Social Mass party, merged (1939) with Fascist party.

**Abe, Nobuyuki.** 1875–1953. Japanese general, b. in Ishikawa prefecture. Lieutenant general (1932); commander in chief of Formosan army; supreme war councilor (1934–36); prime minister (1939–40); sought more peaceful relations with Russia and U.S.

**à Becket, Thomas.** See BECKET.

**à Beck'ett** (*à* běk'ět; -ĭt), **Gilbert Abbott.** 1811–1856. English journalist, humorist, and playwright; member of original staff of *Punch;* author of *Comic History of England* (1848), *Comic History of Rome* (1852), etc. Two sons, **Gilbert Arthur** (1837–1891) and **Arthur William** (1844–1909), were also journalists and writers, contributors to *Punch.*

**Abednego.** See SHADRACH.

**Abeilard.** See Peter ABELARD.

**A'bel** (ä'bĕl), **Carl.** 1837–1906. German philologist; author of *Linguistic Essays* (1880), *Slavic and Latin* (1883).

**A'bel** (ā'bĕl), Sir **Frederick Augustus.** 1827–1902. English chemist, b. London; chemist to War Department (1854–88); inventor of cordite (with James Dewar), also of the Abel tester (adopted as official government standard, 1879) for determining flash point of petroleum; author of works on explosives.

**Abel, John Jacob.** 1857–1938. American pharmacologist and physiological chemist, b. Cleveland. Grad. U. of Michigan (1883); did research on chemical composition of animal tissues and fluids; isolated compound known as *epinephrine.*

**A'bel** (ä'bĕl), **Karl Friedrich.** 1725–1787. German virtuoso on the viola da gamba, and composer. With Johann Christian Bach, conducted Bach-Abel Concerts in London (1765–82).

**A'bel** (ä'bĕl), **Niels Henrik.** 1802–1829. Norwegian mathematician; known for research in theory of elliptic functions. Cf. Karl G. J. JACOBI.

**Ab'e·lard** (ăb'ĕ·lärd), **Peter.** *Fr.* Pierre **A'bé'lard'** *or* **A'bai'lard'** (à'bā'lȧr'). *Surname also* **Abaelard** *or* **Abeilard.** 1079–1142. French philosopher and theologian, b. near Nantes. Master of a school of philosophy (1091–1113); student of theology under Anselm of Laon (1113–17). Teacher of philosophy (1117–21). Secretly married Héloïse, incurring anger of her uncle Fulbert, whose hirelings mutilated him. Withdrew to monastery; persecuted; his nominalistic doctrines declared heretical (1121). Wandered from monastery to monastery; condemned for heresy (1140); died (1142) on way to Rome to present defense. Body given to Héloïse, then prioress of the Paraclete (founded by him); she was buried beside him (1164); both entombed at Paris (1817).

**A'be·lin** (ä'bĕ·lĭn), **Johann Philipp.** *Pseudonyms* **Go'tho·fre'dus** (gō'tō·frā'dŏŏs) *or* **Johann Ludwig Gott'fried** (gŏt'frēt) *or* **Philipp Ar'la·ni·bä'us** (är'lä·nē·bȧ'ŏŏs). d. bet. 1634–37. German historian, b. Strasbourg. Founded *Theatrum Europaeum* (21 vols., 1633–1738), illustrated serial work on world history.

**A'bell** (ā'bĕl), **Thomas.** d. 1540. English priest. Chaplain to Catherine of Aragon. Published *Invicta Veritas* (1533), opposing ecclesiastical claims of Henry VIII. Executed at Smithfield (1540).

**A'ben** (ä'bân). Spanish form for Arabic *ibn* ("son of") used in transliteration of names.

**A·ben'cer·ra'ges** (*à*·bĕn'sĕ·rā'jĕz). *Span.* **A'ben·cer·ra'jes** (ä'bân·thĕr·rä'hās). A 15th-century family of Moors in Granada, famed in romance for their feud with the family of the Zegris.

**A'ben·ez'ra** *or* **A'ben-Es'ra** (ȧ'bĕn·ĕz'rä). = IBN EZRA.

**Ab'er·corn** (ăb'ĕr·kôrn), Earls, marquises, and dukes of. Titles in Scottish peerage borne by members of Hamilton family, including: **James Hamilton** (1575?–1618), eldest son of Claud Hamilton (see under HAMILTON family); created (1606) 1st earl of Abercorn for services as commissioner of union with England. His son **James** (fl. 1617–1634), 2d earl; created Baron **Stra·bane'** (str*à*·băn') in Irish peerage; succeeded as duke of **Châ'tel'he·rault'** (shä'tĕl'rō'); on death (1651) of 2d duke of Hamilton, became male representative of house of Hamilton.

**James Hamilton** (1656–1734), 6th earl; great-grandson of 1st earl; aided in defense of Derry (1689); created Viscount Strabane (Irish peerage, 1701); privy councilor of England, as was his son **James** (d. 1744), 7th earl. **James** (1712–1789), 8th earl, Viscount Hamilton (English peerage), son of 7th earl, summoned to Irish House of Peers (1736); representative Scottish peer (1761–86); his nephew, 9th earl, was created (1790) marquis of Abercorn.

**James Hamilton** (1811–1885), 10th Earl, 2d Marquis, and 1st Duke of Abercorn; grandson of 1st marquis; lord lieutenant of Ireland (1866–68, 1874–76). **James** (1838–1913), 2d duke; son of 1st duke; eldest brother of Lord George Francis Hamilton (*q.v.*); official figurehead of Irish landlords in land war; opposed home rule. **James Albert Edward** (1869–1953), 3d duke; son of 2d duke; a leader of Unionist party in Ulster; governor general of Northern Ireland (1922–45).

**Ab'er·crom'bie,** *or* **Ab'er·crom'by** (ăb'ĕr·krŏm'bĭ; -krŭm'bĭ), **James.** 1706–1781. British general, b. in Banffshire, Scotland. Commander of British forces in America at attack on French at Ticonderoga (1758); defeated; recalled to England (1758).

**Abercrombie, John.** 1780–1844. Scottish physician and pathologist.

**Abercrombie, Lascelles.** 1881–1938. English poet and critic, b. in Cheshire. Professor of English literature, Leeds (1922–29), U. of London (1929–35). Author of *Interludes and Poems* (1908), *Emblems of Love* (1912), *Deborah* (a play; 1913), *Theory of Art* (1922), *Principles of English Prosody* (1923), *Twelve Idylls* (1928).

**Abercrombie, Leslie Patrick.** 1879–1957. English architect; specialist in town planning.

**Ab'er·crom'by** (ăb'ĕr·krŏm'bĭ; -krŭm'bĭ), Sir **Ralph.** 1734–1801. British general, b. Menstry, Scotland. Led expeditionary force that conquered St. Lucia and Trinidad (1795–96). Commanded troops in Mediterranean (1800); defeated French at Alexandria (1801) and died of wounds received there. Credited with restoring discipline and efficiency to British army. His brother Sir **Robert** (1740–1827), also a British general, served in America in French and Indian War and American Revolution; aided Cornwallis in conquering Tipu Sahib (1792); commanded in second Rohilla War. Sir Ralph's 3d son, **James** (1776–1858), 1st Baron **Dun·ferm'line** (dŭn-fûrm'lĭn; dŭm-), was called to bar at Lincoln's Inn (1801); M.P. (1807–30); judge advocate general (1827); chief baron of exchequer of Scotland (1830); master of the mint in Earl Grey's cabinet (1834); speaker of House of Commons (1835–39).

**Aberdare,** Baron. See Henry Austin BRUCE.

**Ab'er·deen'** (ăb'ĕr·dēn'; ăb'ĕr·dēn). See GORDON family.

**Aberdeen and Te·mair'** (tĕ·mâr'). See GORDON family.

**Ab'er·hart** (ā'bĕr·härt), **William.** 1878–1943. Canadian political leader, b. near Seaforth, Ontario. Educ. Queen's U. Premier of Alberta (1935–43).

**Ab'er·nath'y** (ăb'ĕr·năth'ĭ), **Ralph David.** 1926– American clergyman; president of Southern Christian Leadership Conference (from 1968).

**Ab′er·ne′thy** (ăb′ẽr·nē′thĭ; -nĕth′ĭ), **John.** 1764–1831. English surgeon, b. London. Known for his lectures on anatomy and for his operation for ligation of the external iliac artery (1797).

**A′bert** (ä′bẽrt), **Johann Joseph.** 1832–1915. Composer, b. Kochowitz, Bohemia. Court Kapellmeister, Stuttgart (1867–88). Wrote operas, symphonies, etc. His son **Hermann** (1871–1927), music historian and editor.

**A′betz** (ä′bĕts), **Heinrich Otto.** 1903–1958. German propagandist and Nazi official. Studied art; taught drawing; worked for Franco-German rapprochement; propagandist for Nazis (from 1932); expelled from France (1935) but soon returned as member of embassy staff; appointed (Aug., 1940) ambassador to Vichy government and high commissioner of occupied France.

**Ab′gar** (ăb′gär). *Lat.* **Ab′ga·rus** (ăb′gȧ·rŭs). A title (not a personal name) of the 29 rulers (99 B.C.–217 A.D.) of Osrhoëne, northwestern Mesopotamia, with capital at Edessa. According to tradition, related by Eusebius, **Abgar V (Uk·kā′mā** [ōōk·kä′mä]), a leper, wrote a letter to Jesus and received an answer (*Abgarus Letters;* undoubtedly apocryphal); later (29 A.D.) he was visited and cured by Judas (or Thaddaeus), one of the disciples.

**A′bich** (ä′bĭκ), **Wilhelm Hermann.** 1806–1886. German geologist and traveler, b. Berlin; author of *Geologische Forschungen in den Kaukasischen Ländern* (3 vols., 1878–87).

**A·bi′jah** (ȧ·bī′jȧ). *Also* **A·bi′jam** (ȧ·bī′jăm). *In Douay Bible* **A·bi′a** (ȧ·bī′ȧ). Second king of Judah (c. 917–915 B.C.); son and successor of Rehoboam (*2 Chron.* xii. 16; *1 Kings* xiv. 31).

**A′bild·gaard** (ä′bĭl·gôr), **Nikolaj Abraham.** 1743?–1809. Danish historical painter; director of Copenhagen Academy (from 1789).

**A·bim′e·lech** (ȧ·bĭm′ĕ·lĕk). In Bible (*Judges* ix. 1–57), a son of Gideon who killed all his 70 brothers except one (Jotham) and made himself king of Shechem.

**A·bin′a·dab** (ȧ·bĭn′ȧ·dăb). In Bible: (1) second son of Jesse and elder brother of David (*1 Sam.* xvii. 13); (2) a son of Saul, killed with father at battle of Gilboa (*1 Sam.* xxxi. 2).

**Abinger,** Baron. See James SCARLETT.

**Ab′ing·ton** (ăb′ĭng·tŭn), **Frances** *or* **Fanny,** *nee* **Bar′ton** (bär′t′n). 1737–1815. English actress. Flower girl; street singer; domestic servant. Played at Drury Lane (1764–82) under Garrick until his death; at Covent Garden (1782–90); last appearances 1797–99. Created thirty characters, including Lady Teazle (1777).

**A·bish′a·i** (ȧ·bĭsh′â·ī; ăb′ĭ·shī). *In Douay Version* **A·bis′a·i** (ȧ·bĭs′â·ī; ăb′ĭ·sī). In Bible (*2 Sam.* ii. 18), a nephew and loyal follower of David and valiant soldier.

**A′bleiges′** (ȧ′blâzh′), **Jacques d′.** 14th-century French legal compiler; compiled (c. 1389) collection of old, chiefly customary, laws known as *Grand Coutumier de France* or *Coutumier de Charles VI.*

**A·ble·si′mov** (ŭ·blyĭ·syē′môf), **Aleksandr Anisimovich.** 1742–1784. Russian playwright; wrote *The Miller,* first successful Russian opera; first to represent Russian folk life on stage.

**Ab′ner** (ăb′nẽr). In Bible (*1 Sam.* xiv. 50–51), a cousin of Saul and commander in chief of army during Saul's reign. After Saul's death, opposed David; killed by Joab, David's commander (*2 Sam.* ii–iii).

**Ab′ney** (ăb′nĭ), Sir **William de Wive′les·lie** (wĭv′′lz·lĭ). 1843–1920. English chemist and physicist. Specialist in fields of photographic chemistry, stellar photometry, color photography, spectroscopy.

**aboo–** *or* **abou–.** See names beginning ABU-.

**Abool–** *or* **Aboul–.** See names beginning ABU-AL-, ABUL-, ABU′L. Cf. ABU-.

**Ab–o′–th′–Yate.** Pseudonym of Benjamin BRIERLEY.

**A′bout′** (ȧ′bōō′), **Edmond François Valentin.** 1828–1885. French journalist, novelist, and playwright. Author of *Le Roi des Montagnes* (1856), *L'Homme à l'Oreille Cassée* (1861), *Le Nez d'un Notaire* (1862), *Madelon* (1863).

**A·boyne′** (ȧ·boin′), Viscounts and 5th earl of. See earls and marquises of *Huntly* under GORDON family.

**A′bra·ba·nel′** (*Span.* ä′brä·bä·nĕl′; *Port.* ă′brȧ·bȧ·nĕl′) *or* **A′bar·ba·nel′** (*Span.* ä′bär·bä·nĕl′; *Port.* ă′bẽr·bȧ·nĕl′) *or* **A′bra·va·nel′** (*Span.* ä′brä·vä·nĕl′; *Port.* ă′brȧ·vȧ·nĕl′). Name of old Jewish family of southern Europe, esp. of Spain, Portugal, and Italy, distinguished as physicians, scholars, poets, and benefactors of Jewish people. Oldest branch lived in Seville; members include: **Isaac Abrabanel** (1437–1508), theologian, Bible commentator, and statesman, b. Lisbon; treasurer of Alfonso V of Portugal (to 1481); served later in financial capacity to Ferdinand and Isabella of Castile and also to governments of Naples and Venice; his commentaries on Bible exerted wide influence; wrote philosophical works and apologetics in defense of Jewish doctrine of the Messiah. His son **Judah León Abrabanel** (d. 1535), physician and poet, known in Spanish literary history as **Le·ón′ He·bre′o** (lā·ôn′ â·brā′ō) *or* **Le′o He·brae′us** (lē′ō hē·brē′ŭs), *i.e.* Leo the Hebrew; his *Dialoghi di Amore* (in Italian) was used by Castiglione in his *Courtier.*

**A′bra·ham** (ā′brȧ·hăm) *or* **A′bram** (ā′brăm). Traditional patriarch of Jews (*Gen.* xi. 26–xxv. 10), father of Isaac and of Ishmael and grandfather of Jacob. Cf. LOT.

**A′bra·ham a Sanc′ta** (*or* **San′ta**) **Cla′ra** (ä′brä·häm ä zängk′tä [zän′tä] klä′rä). *Real name* **Hans Ulrich Me′ger·le** (mā′gẽr·lĕ). 1644–1709. Roman Catholic preacher and satirist, b. in Baden. Augustinian monk (1662); court preacher at Vienna (1677); attacked vices of contemporary life.

**Abraham ben Meïr.** See IBN EZRA.

**A′bra·ham ibn Da·ud′** *or* **A′bra·ham ben Da′vid** (ā′brȧ·hăm bĕn dā′vĭd). *Arab.* **I·brā′hīm′ ibn–Da·ud′** (ĭ·brä′hēm′ ĭb′′n dä·wōōd′). *Often spoken of as* **ibn–Daud.** 1110?–1180. Jewish philosopher and historian, b. Toledo, Spain. First prominent Jewish advocate of Aristotelian system of knowledge. Wrote *Sepher Haqabala* (*Book of Tradition*), a chronological history down to 1161; in Arabic, *'Emunah Ramah* (*Sublime Faith*), his chief philosophical work.

**A′bra·ham of An′ti·och** (ā′brȧ·hăm ŭv ăn′tĭ·ŏk). Ninth-century Syrian founder of a sect (Abrahamites) who denied divinity of Christ.

**Abrantès,** Duc **d′.** See Andoche JUNOT.

**A·breu′** (ȧ·brâ′ōō), **Antônio Lim′po de** (lēɴm′pōō thē). 1797–1883. Brazilian statesman; aided in securing reforms under Dom Pedro II.

**Abreu, João Ca·pis·tra′no de** (kȧ·pēs·tră′nōō thē). 1853–1927. Brazilian historian; professor, Rio de Janeiro (1883–99); author of works dealing with early history of Brazil.

**A·bruz′zi** (ä·brōōt′tsē), Duke of the. **Luigi Amedec Giuseppe Maria Ferdinando Francesco,** Prince of **Sa·voy′–A·o′sta** (sȧ·voi′ä·ôs′tä). 1873–1933. Italian naval officer and explorer; son of Amadeus, Duke of Aosta, King of Spain (1870–73). First to ascend Mt. St. Elias in Alaska (1897); commander of Italian fleet in World War (until 1917).

**Ab′sa·lom** (ăb′sȧ·lŏm). In Bible (*2 Sam.* xiii–xix), third son of David; murdered his brother Ammon and fled; on return, advised by Ahithophel (*q.v.*), stirred up rebellion against father; killed by Joab in flight from battle. Dryden's satirical poem *Absalom and Achitophel* (1681) is based on story of Absalom.

**Ab'sa·lon** (ăp'sȧ·lŏn) *or* **Ax'el** (ăk'sĕl). 1128–1201. Danish soldier, statesman, and archbishop of Lund (1178–1201). Counselor and general under Waldemar I and Canute VI; delivered Denmark from Wendish pirates; conquered Mecklenburg and Estonia.

**Abt** (äpt), **Franz.** 1819–1885. German composer, esp. of songs, including *When the Swallows Homeward Fly.*

**abu–.** Arabic name prefix meaning "father." In names, the first compound element beginning with *abu-* is less commonly used to designate a person than the second (or final) compound element; thus, for **abu–Abdallah Mohammed ibn–Batuta,** see IBN-BATUTA.

**abu–'Abdullāh.** See BOABDIL.

**abu–al–.** See also names beginning ABUL-.

**abu–al–Abbas** *or* **Abu'l–Abbas.** See ABBAS.

**a·bu–al–A·la' al–Ma·ar'ri** (ȧ·bo͝ol'ȧ·lä' ăl'mȧ·ăr'rī). *Arab.* **abu–al–'Alā' al–Ma'arri.** 973–1057. Arabic poet and philosopher, b. near Aleppo; totally blind at early age. His writings, marked by rationalism and pessimistic skepticism, exerted influence on many generations.

**a·bu–al–A·ta'hi·yah** (ȧ·bo͝ol'ă·tä'hĭ·yă). *Also* **Abu'l–Atahiya.** *Arab.* **abu–al–'Atāhiyah.** 748–828? Arabic religious poet, b. Anbar on Euphrates. Lived at Al Kufa and Baghdad in time of caliphs Harun al-Rashid and al-Mamun. Known as father of Arabic sacred poetry; his poems were characterized by simplicity and moral earnestness.

**a·bu–al–Fa·raj' al–Is'fa·ha'ni** (ȧ·bo͝ol'fă·răj' ăl·ĭs'-fă·hä'nĭ). *Also* **Abu'l Faraj.** *Arab.* **abu–al–Faraj al–Iṣfahāni.** 897?–967. Arabian scholar and historian, b. Isfahan, Persia; lived chiefly at Baghdad and Aleppo; noted esp. for *Kitāb al-Aghāni* (*Book of Songs*), treasury and source of Arabian poetry and literature, esp. of pre-Islamic and early Moslem periods.

**Abubacer.** See IBN-TUFAIL.

**a·bu'–Bakr'** (ȧ·bo͞o'băk'ĕr). *Also* **Abu Bekr** (bĕk'ĕr). 573–634. Mohammedan leader; first caliph (632–634). Father of Aisha, wife of Mohammed; one of first of Mohammed's followers; chosen successor on Mohammed's death (632); fought successfully against Persia and Byzantine emperor, Heraclius.

**a·bu'–Ha·ni'fah** (ȧ·bo͞o'hă·nē'fă). *Properly* **al–Nu–'man ibn–Thabit.** 699–767. Mohammedan jurist, b. Al Kufa, prob. of Persian origin. Founder of one of schools of Moslem law (Hanafites); merchant by profession; overseer of craftsmen under al-Mansur in building of Baghdad.

**abu–Jafar Abdallah.** = al-MANSUR (712?–775).

**Abul–** *or* **Abu'l–.** See also names beginning ABU-AL-. Cf. ABU-.

**Abu'l Faraj.** See ABU-AL-FARAJ AL-ISFAHANI.

**Abulfaraj** *or* **Abulfaragius.** See BAR-HEBRAEUS.

**A·bu–l Fazl'** *or* **A·bul'fazl'** (ȧ·bo͝ol'făz''l). 1551–1602. Moslem vizier and historiographer of the Mogul emperor Akbar. Led in literary movement of period; author of *Akbar Namah* (in Persian; a history of Akbar's reign) and *Ain-i-Akbari* (*Institutes of Akbar*).

**A·bul'fe·da'** *or* **A·bul'fi·da'** (ȧ·bo͝ol'fĭ·dä'). *Arab.* **abu–al–Fidā'.** 1273–1331. Arabian geographer and historian, b. Damascus. Descendant of Ayyub, father of Saladin. Took part in several campaigns against the crusaders (1285–98); entered service of Mameluke sultan al-Nasir (1298); governor of principality of Hama (1310–31); given title of sultan (1320); wrote several historical works, esp. an epitome of the history of mankind, valuable as a source for Saracenic history between 700 and 1200.

**A·bul' Gha'zi Ba'ha·dur' Khan** (ä·bo͝ol' gä'zē bä'-hä·do͝or' kän). 1603–1664. Turkish historian and ruler (1643–64) of Khwarazm (Khiva). As khan, fought Kalmucks and Turkomans; author of history of Mongols and Tatars (Fr. transl., 2 vols., 1871–74).

**Abu'l Ḥasan.** See JUDAH HA-LEVI.

**Abu'l Hasan al–Ashari.** = al-ASHARI.

**Abul Kalam Azad.** See AZAD.

**A·bul' Ka'sim** (ȧ·bo͝ol' kä'sĭm). *Arab.* **abu–al–Qāsim Khalaf ibn–'Abbās al–Zahrāwi.** *Lat.* **Al'bu·ca'sis** (ăl'bû·kā'sĭs). d. ?1013. Arab surgeon, b. near Córdoba. Court physician of Emir Hakam II; wrote *al-Taṣrīf,* a résumé of Arabian medical knowledge of the time; partly translated into Latin and other languages and for several centuries used as manual of surgery.

**Abul Qasim** (*or* **Kasim**) **Mansur.** See FIRDAUSI.

**A·bul' We·fa'** (ȧ·bo͝ol' wĕ·fä') *or* **A·bul' Wa·fa'** (wȧ-fä'). 940–998. Persian astronomer and mathematician; worked with trigonometric functions and constructed tables of tangents and cotangents.

**abu–Mashar.** See ALBUMAZAR.

**Abumeron.** See AVENZOAR.

**a·bu'–Nu·was'** (ȧ·bo͞o'no͝o·wäs'). *Arab.* **abu–Nuwās.** *Orig.* **al–Ḥasan ibn–Hāni'.** 756?–?810. Arabic lyric poet, b. in Susiana (Khuzistan), of humble origin. Lived at Basra and Baghdad; friend of caliphs Harun al-Rashid and al-Amin; known esp. for poems of love and wine.

**a·bu'–Tam·mam'** (ȧ·bo͞o'tăm·mäm'). *Arab.* **abu–Tammām Ḥabīb ibn–Aws.** 807–?845. Arabian poet, b. near lake of Tiberias, Syria. Court poet in Baghdad; noted esp. for anthology (*Dīwān al-Ḥamāsah*) of Arabian poets, known in English as the *Hamasa,* most valuable of all such collections of Arabic literature.

**a·bu'–U·bay'da** (ȧ·bo͞o'o͝o·bī'dă). *Also* **Abu Ubaida.** *Arab.* **abu–'Ubaydah Ma'mar ibn–al–Muthannā.** 728–?825. Arabian scholar, b. Basra, of Jewish parents. Kharijite in religion and politics; defender of non-Arab Moslems; wrote some 200 treatises on grammar and philology, also *al-Mathalīb* (*Book of the Arabs' Faults*); summoned to Baghdad (803) by Harun al-Rashid.

**A·ca'cius** (ȧ·kā'shŭs; -shĭ·ŭs). fl. 4th century. Bishop of Caesarea; founder of a religious sect (Acacians) that maintained that the Father and the Son were like in will alone.

**Ac'cia·juo'li** (ät'chī·wô'lē) *or* **Ac'cia·jo'li** (ät'chä-yô'lē), **Donato.** 1428–1478. Florentine scholar and statesman; gonfalonier of Florence (1473); biographer of Hannibal, Scipio, and Charlemagne.

**Ac'ci·us** (ăk'shĭ·ŭs) *or* **At'ti·us** (ăt'ĭ·ŭs), **Lucius.** 170?–?90 B.C. Roman tragic poet and prose writer, known esp. for his adaptations of Greek dramas.

**Ac·col'ti** (äk·kôl'tē), **Benedetto.** 1415–1466. Italian jurist and historian. Chancellor of Florentine Republic (1459); author (with his brother **Leonardo**) of a Latin history of the First Crusade, credited with being basis for Tasso's *Jerusalem Delivered.* His son **Bernardo** (1465–1536) was an Italian poet, known for his recitations of impromptu verse.

**Ac'co·ram·bo'ni** (äk'kô·räm·bô'nē), **Vittoria.** 1557?–1585. An Italian lady whose first husband was murdered (1581) in order that she might marry Orsini, Duca di Bracciano. After the duke's death (1585), she was murdered at the instigation of a relative of his. Her story is used in John Webster's play *The White Devil or Vittoria Corombona.*

**Ac·cor'so** (äk·kôr'sō), **Francesco.** *Lat.* **Franciscus Ac·cur'si·us** (ă·kûr'shĭ·ŭs; -shŭs). Name of two Italian jurists, father (1185?–?1260) and son (1225–1293).

**Acernus, Sebastian.** See KLONOWIC.

**Acevedo de Toledo, Pedro Enríquez.** See Conde de FUENTES.

**Achab.** See AHAB.

**A·chad' Ha·am'** (ȧ·ĸäd' hä·äm'). *Pseudonym of* **Ash'er Ginz'berg** (ăsh'ẽr gĭnz'bûrg). 1856–1927. Jewish writer, b. in Ukraine; advocate of cultural and spiritual Zionism.

**Ach'ae·men'i·dae** (ăk'ē·mĕn'ĭ·dē). *Also* **Ach'ae·men'i·des** (ăk'ē·mĕn'ĭ·dēz). Name of ruling house of ancient Persia, derived from its founder, **A·chaem'e·nes** (ȧ·kĕm'ē·nēz; ȧ·kē'mē·nēz) of 7th century B.C. Early rulers were Teispes (son of Achaemenes), Cyrus, and Cambyses, kings of Anshan (or Anzan); Cyrus the Great, founder of the Persian Empire, and his son Cambyses (II); by a collateral line (according to Herodotus) from Teispes, Darius I and his successors down to Darius III, overthrown by Alexander the Great (331 B.C.).

**A'chan** (ā'kăn). In Bible (*Joshua* vii), an Israelite whose act of stealing caused defeat of his people, who thereupon stoned him to death.

**A·chard'** (ä·shär'), **Franz Karl.** 1753–1821. German chemist, b. Berlin, pioneer in beet-sugar industry.

**A'chard'** (á'shär'), **Louis Amédée Eugène.** 1814–1875. French novelist.

**A·cha'ri·us** (äk·kä'rĭ·ŭs), **Erik.** 1757–1819. Swedish physician and botanist; pupil of Linnaeus; authority on lichens.

**Achaz.** See AHAZ.

**A'chen·bach** (ä'ĸĕn·bäĸ), **Andreas.** 1815–1910. German landscape and marine painter. His brother and pupil **Oswald** (1827–1905) was also a landscape painter. Andreas's son **Max** (1858?–1898) was a Wagnerian tenor, under stage name **Max Al·va'ry** (äl·vä'rē); at Metropolitan Opera House, N.Y., for several seasons (1884 ff.).

**A'chen·wall** (ä'ĸĕn·väl), **Gottfried.** 1719–1772. German statistician, b. Elbing; regarded by some as founder of science of statistics.

**A'che·ry'** (àsh'rē'), **Jean Luc D'.** 1609–1685. French Benedictine monk; noted for his collection of medieval manuscripts.

**Ach'e·son** (ăch'ĕ·s'n), **Dean Gooderham.** 1893–1971. Am. lawyer and statesman; U.S. secy. of state (1949–1953), author of *Present at the Creation* (1969), etc.

**Ach'e·son** (ăch'ĕ·s'n), **Edward Goodrich.** 1856–1931. American inventor, b. Washington, Pa. Assistant to Thomas Edison (1880–81); discovered silicon carbide.

**A·chil'les Ta'ti·us** (ȧ·kĭl'ēz tā'shĭ·ŭs; tā'shŭs). fl. 4th century A.D. Greek rhetorician; author of a romance, *Leucippe and Cleitophon.*

**Achitophel.** See AHITHOPHEL.

**Achmed** *or* **Achmet.** Variants of AHMED.

**A'ci·da'li·us** (ä'tsē·dä'lē·o͝os; *Angl.* ăs'ĭ·dā'lĭ·ŭs, -dāl'-yŭs), **Va'lens** (vä'lĕns; *Angl.* vā'lĕnz). 1567–1595. German classical philologist, critic, and poet in Latin.

**Ack'er·mann** (äk'ẽr·män), **Alexander.** See AGRICOLA.

**Ackermann, Konrad Ernst.** 1712–1771. German actor. Opened (1765) in Hamburg a theater, later regarded as setting standard for German acting.

**Ack'er'mann'** (á'kĕr'män'), **Louise Victorine,** *nee* **Cho'quet'** (shô'kĕ'). 1813–1890. French poet.

**Ack'er·mann** (äk'ẽr·män; *Angl.* ăk'ẽr·măn), **Rudolph.** 1764–1834. Inventor and art publisher, b. in Saxony. Established print shop and art school, London (1795); patented (1801) method for waterproofing paper and cloth; credited with establishing art lithography in Eng.

**Ack'land** (ăk'lănd), **Rodney.** 1908– . English playwright; author of *Improper People* (1929), *The Old Ladies* (1935), *Remembrance of Things Past* (1938), and *Sixth Floor* (1939).

**Ack·té'–Ja·lan'der** (àk·tā'yà·làn'dĕr), **Aino,** *nee* **Stoe'mer–Ack·té'** (stû'mĕr-). 1876–1944. Finnish opera singer; m. General Bruno Jalander; with Metropolitan Opera Company, New York (1903–04, 1904–05).

**Ac'land** (ăk'lănd), Sir **Henry Wentworth.** 1815–1900. English physician; regius professor of medicine, Oxford (1858–94).

**Acland, John Dyke.** d. 1778. English soldier and politician. Major of infantry in Burgoyne's expedition; wounded and taken prisoner in battle of Saratoga (1777). His wife, Lady **Christian Henrietta Caroline Acland** (1750–1815), accompanied him on Burgoyne's campaign (1776–77).

**Açoka.** See ASOKA.

**A·con'zio** (ä·kōn'tsyô) *or* **A·con'cio** (ä·kōn'chô), **Jacopo.** *Lat.* **Jacobus A·con'ti·us** (ȧ·kŏn'shĭ·ŭs). 1492?–?1565. Writer, b. Trent, Italy; lived much of his life in England; published (1565) *The Stratagems of Satan*, notable attempt to find a basis of dogma common to all Christians.

**A·cos'ta** (ȧ·kôsh'tȧ), **Gabriel,** *later* **Uriel.** *Also called* **Uriel da Cos'ta** (dȧ kôsh'tȧ). c. 1591–?1647. Portuguese philosopher, b. Oporto; converted from Roman Catholicism to Judaism; fled to Amsterdam; excommunicated by Amsterdam synagogue as atheist (c. 1624–c. 31).

**A·cos'ta** (ä·kōs'tä), **Joaquín.** 1795?–1852. Colombian soldier and historian, b. Guaduas. Soldier in Bolívar's army (1819); spent several years in Paris writing his *Compendio Histórico del Descubrimiento y Colonización de la Nueva Granada* (pub. 1848).

**Acosta, José de.** 1539?–1600. Spanish missionary; author of *Historia Natural y Moral de las Indias* (1590).

**Acosta, Julio.** 1872–1954. Costa Rican political leader; president of Costa Rica (1920–24).

**Acquaviva, Claudio.** See AQUAVIVA.

**A·cre'li·us** (ȧ·krē'lĭ·ŭs; *Swed.* ä·krā'lĭ·ŭs), **Israel.** 1714–1800. Swedish Lutheran clergyman. Missionary to Christina, now Wilmington, Delaware (1749–56). Author of *History of New Sweden* (1759).

**Acropolita, Georgius.** See AKROPOLITES.

**Ac'ton** (ăk'tŭn), 1st Baron. **John Emerich Edward Dal'berg–Ac'ton** (dôl'bûrg-). 1834–1902. English historian; son of Sir Richard E. Acton and the daughter of the duc de Dalberg (see DALBERG family). Regius professor of modern history, Cambridge (1895–1902). Leader of English liberal Roman Catholics hostile to dogma of papal infallibility. Planned, as editor, *Cambridge Modern History;* lectures on modern history and French Revolution (published posthumously).

**Acton,** Sir **John Francis Edward.** 1736–1811. English officer in service of Tuscany and Naples, b. in France. Commander in chief of Neapolitan navy, minister of finance, and prime minister under Ferdinand I, King of the Two Sicilies; on entry of French into Naples fled to Sicily (1806).

**A·cu'ña** (ä·ko͞o'nyä), **Cristóbal de.** 1597–?1676. Spanish Jesuit missionary, b. Burgos; to South America; accompanied Pedro Teixeira on exploratory trip down Amazon (1637–39); author of *Nuevo Descubrimiento del Gran Río de las Amazonas* (1641).

**Acuña, Hernando de.** 1500?–1580. Spanish poet, soldier, and diplomat; known esp. for translation of Olivier de La Marche's popular allegorical poem *Le Chevalier Délibéré* into Spanish quintillas (five-line stanzas) under title *El Caballero Determinado* (1553).

**Acuña de Figueroa, Francisco.** See FIGUEROA.

**A·da·chi** (ä·dä·chē), **Kenzo.** 1864–1948. Japanese politician, b. Kumamoto. In Okuma cabinet (1914–15); minister of communications (1925–27), of home affairs (1929–31); responsible for overthrow of Minseito cabinet and abandonment of gold standard (1931); organized (1932) and led (1932–39) National League (Kokumin Domei), a semi-Fascist party.

**Adachi, Mineichiro.** 1869–1934. Japanese jurist, b.

Yamagata. President, International Court of Justice at The Hague (1931–33).

**A'dad·ni·ra'ri** (ä'däd·nē·rä'rē) *or* **Ha'dad-ni·ra'ri** (hä'däd-). Name of several kings of Assyria: **Adadnirari I** (reigned 1305–1277 B.C.); defeated Kassites in the south; extended boundaries of empire; succeeded by his son Shalmaneser I. **Adadnirari II** (reigned 911–889 B.C.); resumed southeastern campaigns, annexing new regions along the Tigris; defeated Babylonian king (909); reconquered Aramaeans in northwest (907–903); made treaty with Babylonians; succeeded by his son Tukulti-Ninurta II. **Adadnirari III** *or* **IV** (reigned 811–782 B.C.); extended conquests to west, esp. in the Orontes Valley; see SEMIRAMIS.

**A·dair'** (ȧ·dâr'), **James.** 1709?–?1783. Pioneer in America (1735–70), b. in Ireland. His *History of the American Indians* (1775) advanced theory that Indians are descendants of ancient Jews.

**Ad'al·bert** *or* **Ad'el·bert** (ăd''l·bērt; *Ger.* ä'däl·bĕrt, ä'dĕl·bĕrt), Saint. *Czech* **Voj'těch** (voi'tyĕк). 955?–997. Bohemian prince and prelate; bishop of Prague (983); failing to convert his people, abandoned his diocese and retired (988) to monastery near Rome; sent back to Prague (992) by Pope John XV; again left and preached gospel among Hungarians, Poles, and Prussians; murdered by a heathen priest. Known as "Apostle of the Prussians."

**Ad'al·bert** (ăd''l·bērt; *Ger.* ä'däl·bĕrt). 1000?–1072. German ecclesiastic. Archbishop of Hamburg and Bremen (c. 1043). As papal legate (1053) spread Christianity among the Wends. Endeavored unsuccessfully to form Germany, England, and Scandinavia into an independent northern patriarchate.

**A'dal·bert** (ä'däl·bĕrt). *In full* **Heinrich Wilhelm Adalbert.** 1811–1873. Prince of Prussia. Nephew of Frederick William III. Engaged in organizing first German fleet; chief of Prussian navy (1849); admiral (1854).

**A'dam** (ä'däm). Family of Bavarian painters, including: **Albrecht** (1786–1862), painter of battle scenes and horses; and his sons **Ben'no** [bĕn'ō] (1812–1892), painter of animals, **Franz** (1815–1886), painter of animals and battle scenes, and **Eugen** (1817–1880), genre painter and painter of battle scenes.

**A'dam'** (à'däɴ'). Family of French sculptors, including: **Jacob Sigisbert** (1670–1747) and his sons **Lambert Sigisbert** (1700–1759), **Nicolas Sébastien** (1705–1778), and **François Balthasar Gaspard** (1710–1761).

**A'dam** (ä'däm), **Franz.** 1815–1886. German painter, b. Milan, Italy. Works, chiefly battle scenes, include *Attack of the Chasseurs d'Afrique at Sedan.*

**Ad'am** (ăd'ăm), **Jean.** 1710–1765. Scottish poetess, b. near Greenock.

**A'dam'** (à'däɴ'), **Jean Louis.** 1758–1848. French pianist and composer. His son **Adolphe Charles** (1803–1856) composed comic operas, ballet music, and military and piano pieces.

**Adam, Juliette,** *nee* **Lamber.** *Pen names* **La Mes'sine'** (mĕ'sēn') *and* **Juliette Lam'ber'** (läɴ'bâr') *and* Comte **Paul Va'si'li'** (và'zē'lē'). 1836–1936. French writer, b. Verberie; founded (1879) and edited *La Nouvelle Revue;* author of novels and miscellaneous works. Her second husband, **Antoine Edmond Adam** (1816–1877), was prefect of police in Paris during Franco-Prussian War.

**A'dam** (ä'däm), **Karl.** 1876–1966. German theologian; professor at Tübingen (from 1919).

**A'dam'** (à'däɴ'), **Paul.** 1862–1920. French symbolist novelist; author of *La Ville Inconnue,* etc.

**Adam, Quirin François Lucien.** 1833–1918. French jurist and philologist, b. Nancy; author of studies of native American Indian languages (Cree, Ojibway, Tupi).

**Ad'am** (ăd'ăm), **Robert.** 1728–1792. Scottish architect, b. Kirkcaldy; son of **William Adam** (1689–1748), an architect. Most important of four brothers, the others being **John, James, William.** Architect (1762–68) to King George III. With James and William, built the Adelphi section of London (1769–71). With James, built many public buildings and private mansions. The brothers introduced a light decorative style of furniture characterized by wreaths, paterae, the honeysuckle, and the fan ornament.

**Adam,** Sir **Ronald Forbes.** 1885– . British lieutenant general; deputy chief of imperial general staff (1938–39); commanding officer of 3d army corps (1939–40), of northern command (1940–41); adjutant general to the forces (1941); general (1942–46).

**A'dam' de la Halle'** (à'däɴ' dē là àl'). *Called* **Adam le Bos'su'** (lē bô'sü'). 1235?–1285. French trouvère, musician, and playwright, b. Arras. Composed lyrics, love songs, motets, rondeaus, and dramatic pieces. Author of *Le Jeu de la Feuillée* (performed about 1260), known as the earliest French comedy, and *Le Jeu de Robin et Marion,* earliest comic opera.

**Adam le Roi.** See ADENET LE ROI.

**Ad'am of Bre'men** (ăd'ăm ŭv brā'mĕn; brĕm'ĕn). *Ger.* **A'dam von Bre'men** (ä'däm fōn brā'mĕn). d. 1076? German ecclesiastical historian, author of *Gesta Hammaburgensis Ecclesiae Pontificum.*

**Ad'am Sco'tus** (ăd'ăm skō'tŭs) *or* **Adam An'gli·cus** (ăng'glĭ·kŭs). fl. 1180. Scottish theologian, known for his sermons and treatises (pub. 1518).

**A'dam von Ful'da** (ä'däm fōn fŏŏl'dä). b. 1450? German music theorist and composer; author of *De Musica* (1490).

**A'dam·ber'ger** (ä'däm·bĕr'gēr), **Valentin.** *Stage name in Italy* **A'da·mon'ti** (ä'dä·mōn'tē). 1743–1804. Austrian operatic tenor and teacher of singing, b. Munich. His daughter **Antonie** (1790–1867), b. Vienna, was an actress.

**A·dam'i** (ȧ·dăm'ĭ), **John George.** 1862–1926. British pathologist, b. Manchester, England; educ. Cambridge, Breslau, Paris; professor, McGill U., Montreal, Canada (1892 ff.). Author of *Principles of Pathology* (1908), *Medical Contributions to the Study of Evolution* (1918), etc.

**Ad'a·mic** (ăd'ȧ·mĭk; ȧ·dăm'ĭk), **Louis.** *Orig. surname* **A·da'mič** (ä·dä'mēch). 1899–1951. Author, b. Blato, Dalmatia (now in Yugoslavia); to U.S. (1913); naturalized (1918). Author of *Dynamite* (1931), *The Native's Return* (1934), *Cradle of Life* (1936), *My America* (1938), *From Many Lands* (1940), *Two-Way Passage* (1942), etc.

**Ad'am·nan** (ăd'ăm·năn; ȧ·dăm'năn) *or* **Ad'om·nan** (ăd'ŏm·năn; ȧ·dŏm'năn) *or* **Eu'nan** (ô'năn), Saint. 625?–704. Irish ecclesiastic, b. Donegal, Ulster; abbot of Iona (679–704); author of a biography of Saint Columba.

**Adamonti.** Stage name of Valentin ADAMBERGER.

**A'da·mow'ski** (ä'dä·môf'skē), **Ti'mo'thée'** (tē'mô'tā'), *Pol.* **Ty'mo·te'usz** (tĭ'mô·tĕ'ōōsh). 1858–1943. Polish violinist in U.S., b. Warsaw; to U.S. (1879) as solo violinist to Clara Louise Kellogg; organized (1888) Adamowski String Quartet; played with Boston Symphony Orchestra; taught at New England Conservatory. His brother **Joseph** (1862–1930), violoncellist, b. Warsaw, taught in Germany and Russia (1883–87); to America (1889); member of Boston Symphony Orchestra (1889–1907) and of Adamowski Quartet and Trio; professor of cello at New England Conservatory (from 1903). **Antoinette A'da·mow'ska** (ä'dä·môf'skä), *nee* **Szu·mow'ska** [shōō·môf'skä] (1868–1938), wife of Joseph (m. 1896), was a pianist and teacher; b. Lublin, Poland; to America (1894); played on tours in Europe and America; played with Boston, Cincinnati, and New York symphony orchestras; member of Adamowski Trio; taught at New England Conservatory and privately.

**Ad'ams** (ăd'ămz), **Abigail**, *nee* **Smith.** 1744–1818. b. Weymouth, Mass. Wife of John Adams, second President of the United States. Her grandson Charles Francis Adams published two volumes of her letters.

**Adams, Alvin.** 1804–1877. American pioneer in the express business (Adams Express Co.); b. Andover, Vt.

**Adams, Arthur Henry.** *Pseudonym* **James James.** 1872–1936. Writer, b. Lawrence, N.Z. Author of novels, as *Honeymoon Dialogues, The Brute, Galahad Jones, Grocer Greatheart;* poetry, as *Maoriland, The Nazarene, London Streets;* plays, as *Tapu, Mrs. Pretty and the Premier.*

**Adams, Bertram Martin,** *called* **Bill.** 1879– . Writer of stories and verse, b. in England of American parentage.

**Adams, Brooks.** 1848–1927. American historian, b. Quincy, Mass. Son of Charles Francis Adams (1807–1886). Grad. Harvard (1870). Author of *Law of Civilization and Decay* (1895), *The New Empire* (1902), *The Theory of Social Revolutions* (1913), etc.

**Adams, Charles Christopher.** 1873–1955. American zoologist, b. Clinton, Ill. Author of *Guide to the Study of Animal Ecology,* etc.

**Adams, Charles Follen.** 1842–1918. American merchant and poet, b. Dorchester, Mass. Author of German dialect poems, as in *Leedle Yawcob Strauss, and Other Poems* (1877) and *Dialect Ballads* (1888).

**Adams, Charles Francis:** 1807–1886. American lawyer, diplomat, and author, b. Boston. Son of John Quincy Adams. Member, U.S. House of Representatives (1858–61). Minister to Great Britain (1861–68) through Civil War; one of U.S. arbitrators on commission to settle *Alabama* claims (1871–72). Edited two volumes of letters of Abigail Adams, *Works of John Adams* (10 vols., 1850–56; with a biography), and *Memoirs of John Quincy Adams* (12 vols., 1874–77).

**Adams, Charles Francis.** 1835–1915. American lawyer, railroad expert, and historian, b. Boston; son of Charles Francis Adams (1807–1886). Served through Civil War. Chairman, Massachusetts Board of Railroad Commissioners (1872–79); appointed chairman of government directors (1878) and president (1884), Union Pacific Railroad; forced out (1890) by Jay Gould. Author of *A College Fetich* (1883), *Some Modern College Tendencies* (1906), *Railroads: Their Origin and Problems* (1878), *Biography of Richard Henry Dana* (1890), *Life of Charles Francis Adams* (1900), *Trans-Atlantic Historical Solidarity* (1913).

**Adams, Charles Francis.** 1866–1954. American lawyer and financier, b. Quincy, Mass. Grandson of Charles Francis Adams (1807–1886). U.S. secretary of the navy (1929–33).

**Adams, Charles Kendall.** 1835–1902. American educator, b. Derby, Vt. Professor of history, U. of Michigan (1867–85); president of Cornell (1885–92), of U. of Wisconsin (1892–1901).

**Adams, Comfort Avery.** 1868–1958. American electrical engineer, b. Cleveland. Grad. Case School (1890). Professor of engineering (1906–36), Harvard. Author of *Dynamo Design Schedules.*

**Adams, Ephraim Douglas.** 1865–1930. American historian and educator, b. Decorah, Iowa; author of books on British and American history.

**Adams, Frank Dawson.** 1859–1942. Canadian geologist; professor, McGill U., Montreal (1894–1931); author of *The Birth and Development of the Geological Sciences.*

**Adams, Frank Ramsay.** 1883–1963. American novelist and writer of musical comedies, b. Morrison, Ill.

**Adams, Franklin Pierce.** *Known as* **F. P. A.** 1881–1960. American journalist and humorist, b. Chicago. Conducted column "The Conning Tower," in New York *World* (1922–31), New York *Herald-Tribune* (1931–37), New York *Post* (1938–41). Author of *Tobogganing on Parnassus* (1910), *In Other Words* (1912), *By and Large* (1914), *So there!* (1922), *Christopher Columbus* (1931), *The Diary of Our Own Samuel Pepys* (1935), etc.; one of regular members of "Information Please" radio program.

**Adams, Frederick Upham.** 1859–1921. American inventor and author, b. Boston, Mass. Inventor in field of street-lighting and railroad equipment (1884–93). Founded (1893) and edited reform magazine *The New Time.* Wrote works on engineering and social problems, and several novels.

**Adams, George Burton.** 1851–1925. American educator and historian, b. Fairfield, Vt. Professor of history, Yale (1888–1925). Author of *Civilization during the Middle Ages* (1894).

**Adams, Hannah.** 1755–1831. American author, b. Medfield, Mass.; compiler of *Dictionary of Religions.*

**Adams, Harry William.** 1868–1947. English landscape painter.

**Adams, Henry Brooks.** 1838–1918. American historian, b. Boston. Son of Charles Francis Adams (1807–1886). Secretary to his father in Washington (1860–61) and London (1861–68). Assistant professor of history at Harvard, and editor of *North American Review* (1869–76). Author of *The Life of Albert Gallatin, The Writings of Albert Gallatin* (3 vols., 1879), *History of the United States* (9 vols., 1889–91), covering Jefferson and Madison administrations, *Mont-Saint-Michel and Chartres* (1904), *The Education of Henry Adams* (1906), *A Letter to American Teachers of History* (1910).

**Adams, Henry Carter.** 1851–1921. American economist and author, b. Davenport, Iowa. Professor, U. of Michigan (1886–1921). Author of *Public Debts* (1887), *The Science of Finance* (1898), *American Railway Accounting* (1918).

**Adams, Herbert.** 1858–1945. American sculptor, b. Concord, Vt. Executed busts of John Marshall, William Ellery Channing, William Cullen Bryant, and Joseph Story, for American Hall of Fame; also the bronze doors of St. Bartholomew's Church, New York City, and those of the Congressional Library, Washington, D.C.

**Adams, Herbert Baxter.** 1850–1901. Historian and political scientist, b. Shutesbury, Mass. Grad. Amherst (1872); Ph.D., Heidelberg (1876). Professor, Johns Hopkins (1876–1901). An organizer, and first secretary, American Historical Association (1884). Author of *Life and Writings of Jared Sparks* (2 vols., 1893), etc.

**Adams, James Trus'low** (trŭs'lō). 1878–1949. American essayist and historian, b. Brooklyn, N.Y. Grad. Yale (1900); New York stockbroker (1900–12). Served in military intelligence division through World War. Author of *Founding of New England* (1921), *The Epic of America* (1931), *The March of Democracy* (2 vols., 1932–33), *America's Tragedy* (1935), *The Living Jefferson* (1936), *Empire on the Seven Seas* (1940), *Dictionary of American History* (1940; with R. V. Coleman), etc.

**Adams, John.** 1735–1826. Second president of the United States, b. Braintree (now Quincy), Mass. Elected delegate (1774) to First Continental Congress; in congress until appointment (1777–78) as commissioner to France. Made minister to United Provinces (1780); negotiated a loan from Dutch bankers (1782). Joined Jay and Franklin in Paris (1782) to negotiate treaty of peace with Great Britain. Envoy to Great Britain (1785–88).

Elected vice-president (1788, 1792) and president (1796) of United States; defeated by Jefferson for presidency (1800) and retired to private life. Author of *Thoughts on Government* (1776), *A Defence of the Constitutions of Government of the United States of America* (3 vols., 1787–88). Signer of Declaration of Independence. Elected to American Hall of Fame (1900).

**Adams, John.** 1760?–1829. British seaman; mutineer (*alias* **Alexander Smith**) on H.M.S. *Bounty* (1789); founded colony on Pitcairn Island.

**Adams, John Couch** (ko͞och). 1819–1892. English astronomer; educ. Cambridge. Discoverer, independently of Leverrier (*q.v.*), of the planet Neptune (1843–46). Professor of astronomy, Cambridge (1858); prosecuted researches in the theory of secular acceleration of the moon's mean motion, and the November meteors.

**Adams, John Quin′cy** (kwĭn′zĭ). 1767–1848. Sixth president of the United States, b. Braintree (now Quincy), Mass. Son of John Adams, second President of the United States. Elected to U.S. Senate (1803); resigned (1808). Minister to St. Petersburg (1809–11). Appointed justice of Supreme Court (1811), but declined. One of negotiators (1814) of peace after War of 1812. Minister to Great Britain (1815). Secretary of state under Monroe (1817–25). President of the United States (1825–29); defeated by Andrew Jackson for second term. Representative in Congress (1831–48). Author of *Memoirs* (12 vols.; ed. by Charles Francis Adams; pub. 1874–77), *Writings* (7 vols.; ed. by W. C. Ford; pub. 1913). Elected to American Hall of Fame (1905).

**Adams, Joseph Quin′cy** (kwĭn′sĭ). 1881–1946. American Shakespearean scholar, b. Greenville, S.C. Professor, Cornell (1919–31). Director, Folger Shakespeare Library, Washington, D.C. (from 1931). General editor, *The New Variorum Shakespeare*. Author of *Shakespearean Playhouses* (1917); editor of *Chief Pre-Shakespearean Dramas* (1924), *The Adams Shakespeare* (1929), etc.

**Adams, Lé·o′nie** (lā·ō′nĭ) **Fuller.** 1899– . American poet, b. Brooklyn, N.Y.; m. William Troy (1933); writer of lyrical verse, as in *Those Not Elect* (1925), *High Falcon* (1929), *This Measure* (1933).

**Adams, Maude.** *Real name* **Maude Kis·kad′den** (kĭs·kăd′'n). *Adopted her mother's maiden name* (Adams) *as stage name.* 1872–1953. American actress, b. Salt Lake City. Joined E. H. Sothern company, New York (1888); with Charles Frohman Stock Company; later, in supporting roles with John Drew. Starred in *Little Minister* (1897–98), *L'Aiglon* (1900–01), *Peter Pan* (1906–07), *What Every Woman Knows* (1908–09), *Chantecler* (1910–11), etc. Teacher of dramatics, Stephens Coll. (Mo.)

**Adams, Moses.** Pseudonym of George William BAGBY.

**Adams, Oscar Fay.** 1855–1919. American author, b. Worcester, Mass. Author of *The Story of Jane Austen's Life* (1891), *The Archbishop's Unguarded Moment* (1899). Compiler of a *Dictionary of American Authors* (1897).

**Adams, Samuel.** 1722–1803. American revolutionary patriot and statesman, b. Boston. Unsuccessful in business. Tax collector of Boston (1756–64). Member of Massachusetts legislature (1765–74); leader of radicals therein. Instrumental in maintaining activities of Committees of Correspondence among American colonies. A leader in agitation that led up to Boston Tea Party. Delegate (1774–75) to First and Second Continental Congresses; signed Declaration of Independence. Member of Congress (to 1781). Lieutenant governor of Massachusetts (1789–93), governor (1794–97).

**Adams, Samuel Hopkins.** 1871–1958. American journalist, b. Dunkirk, N.Y. On staff New York *Sun* (1891–1900), *McClure's Magazine* (1903–05). Author of *The Great American Fraud* (1906), *Average Jones* (1911), *Success* (1921), *Revelry* (1926), *The Flagrant Years* (1929), *The Gorgeous Hussy* (1934), *It Happened One Night* (motion picture; 1934), *Maiden Effort* (1937), *Incredible Era* (1939), *The Harvey Girls* (1942), etc.

**Adams, Sarah,** *nee* **Flow′er** (flou′ẽr). 1805–1848. English poet and hymn writer; m. William Bridges Adams (1834). Author of *Vivia Perpetua* (a dramatic poem; 1841), *Nearer, My God, to Thee* (1840).

**Adams, Thomas.** 1871–1940. British architect; specialist in town planning.

**Adams, Walter Sydney.** 1876–1956. American astronomer, b. Antioch, Syria. Grad. Dartmouth (1898). Astronomer (from 1909), director (from 1923), Mount Wilson Observatory of Carnegie Institution, Pasadena, Calif.

**Adams, Will.** *Jap. title* **An·jin Sa·ma** (än·jēn sä·mä), *i.e.* "Mr. Pilot." 1575?–1620. English navigator, b. Gillingham, near Chatham. First Englishman to visit Japan. Early apprenticed to mercantile marine; entered British navy; engaged (1598) as pilot major for Dutch fleet of five vessels bound for the Indies, of which, after a voyage of hardships, one ship reached Kyushu (1600); summoned to shogun at Osaka; his life spared by Iyeyasu; because of his knowledge of ships, shipbuilding, navigation, etc., held by shogun as adviser (1600–20), rendering valuable services to the Japanese; given an estate near Yokosuka; married a Japanese woman; attempted to establish trade with England through Captain John Saris of Bantam (1613); undertook voyages to Siam and Cochin China (1616–18).

**Adams, William Henry Davenport.** 1828–1891. English writer and editor; founded and edited *Scottish Guardian* (1870–78); compiler of *Concordance to Shakespeare's Plays* (1886).

**Adams, William Taylor.** *Pseudonym* **Oliver Op′tic** (ŏp′tĭk). 1822–1897. American author, b. Bellingham, Mass. Teacher in Boston public schools (1845–65). Chief works are various series of books for boys.

**Ad′ams–Ac′ton** (ăd′ămz·ăk′tŭn), **John.** 1830–1910. English sculptor, b. Acton Hill. His *Gladstone* is in Liverpool, *General Napier* in London, and the mausoleum of John and Charles Wesley in Westminster Abbey.

**Ad′am·son** (ăd′ăm·s'n), **William.** 1863–1936. English trade-unionist and politician; secretary for Scotland in Macdonald's first British Labor cabinet (1924).

**Adamson, William Charles.** 1854–1929. American legislator, b. Bowdon, Ga. Member, U.S. House of Representatives (1897–1917); introduced Adamson Act, making eight hours a normal day for railroad labor.

**Adans le Roi.** See ADENET LE ROI.

**A′dan′son′** (à′däɴ′sôɴ′), **Michel.** 1727–1806. French naturalist, b. Aix; author of *Les Familles Naturelles des Plantes* (1763).

**Ad′dams** (ăd′ămz), **Jane.** 1860–1935. American social settlement worker and peace advocate, b. Cedarville, Ill. Grad. Rockford Coll. (1881). With Ellen Gates Starr, opened social settlement of Hull-House, Chicago (1889); its resident head (1889–1935). Became acknowledged leader of social settlement work in U.S. President, International Congress of Women (1919); presided at conventions at The Hague (1915, 1922), Zurich (1919), Vienna (1921), Washington (1924). Shared Nobel peace prize with Nicholas Murray Butler (1931). Author of *Democracy and Social Ethics* (1902), *Twenty Years at Hull House* (1910), *A New Conscience and an Ancient Evil* (1911), *The Second Twenty Years at Hull House* (1930), etc. Elected to American Hall of Fame (1965).

**Ad′der·ley** (ăd′ẽr·lĭ), **Charles Bowyer.** 1st Baron **Nor′ton** (nôr′t'n). 1814–1905. English statesman. Grad. Oxford (1835). Helped found Church of England Canterbury colony, New Zealand (1849). Undersecretary for the colonies (1866); carried through act (1867) creating Dominion of Canada. President, Board of Trade (1874–78).

**Ad'dicks** (ăd'ĭks), **John Edward O'Sul'li·van** (ō·sŭl'ĭ·văn). 1841–1919. American promoter and politician, b. Philadelphia. Pioneer in production of illuminating gas; president, Bay State Gas Co. (1884), Brooklyn Gas Co. (1892). Promoter, with Thomas W. Lawson, of Amalgamated Copper Co. Campaigned (1889–1906) to obtain U.S. senatorship from Delaware by bribery and corruption; defeated (1906) by H. A. Du Pont. Fall in price of copper, and receivership of Bay State Gas Co., brought financial collapse and charges of fraud.

**Ad'ding·ton** (ăd'ĭng·tŭn), **Henry.** 1st Viscount **Sid'mouth** (sĭd'mŭth). 1757–1844. English Tory statesman. Speaker, House of Commons (1789–1801); first lord of treasury and chancellor of exchequer (1801–04); home secretary (1812–21), his repressive measures helping to provoke Peterloo Massacre (1819).

**Ad'di·son** (ăd'ĭ·s'n), **Christopher.** 1st Viscount **Addison.** 1869-1951. English physician and politician, b. Hogsthorpe, Lincolnshire. Minister of munitions (1916–17); minister in charge of reconstruction (1917); first minister of health (1919–21); minister without portfolio (1921); minister of agriculture and fisheries (1930–31); secretary of state for dominion affairs (1945–47).

**Addison, John.** 1766?–1844. English player on the contrabass and composer of popular operettas.

**Addison, Joseph.** 1672–1719. English essayist, poet, and statesman, b. Milston, Wilts. Son of **Lancelot Addison** (1632–1703), clergyman and writer. Grad. Oxford. Latin verse commended by Dryden. Traveled in Europe on pension in preparation for diplomatic service (1699–1703). Wrote, at request of Lord Halifax, *The Campaign* (1704), celebrating Marlborough's victory at Blenheim. Undersecretary of state; secretary to lord lieutenant of Ireland (till 1710); M.P. (from 1708). Started *Whig Examiner*, a periodical (1710). Contributed essays to Steele's *Tatler* (1709–11); with Steele produced the nonpolitical *Spectator*, writing half the 555 papers of social satire and literary criticism (1711–12). His tragedy *Cato*, produced at Drury Lane (1713), was successful, partly because of popular interpretation as a defense of the Whigs. Contributed a few papers to Steele's *Guardian* and to a revived *Spectator* (1714). Secretary for Ireland (1715). m. Charlotte, Countess Dowager of Warwick (1716). One of lords commissioners of trade (1716); secretary of state under Sunderland (1717–18); retired on a pension of £1500 a year (1718). See Sir Richard STEELE and Thomas TICKELL.

**Addison, Julia de Wolf'** (dĕ wŏŏlf'), *nee* **Gibbs** (gĭbz). 1866– . American artist and writer of books on art, b. Boston; m. Daniel Dulany Addison (1889). Painter of murals; designer of ecclesiastical ornament, mosaic, etc.; illuminator on vellum. Writer of music for Easter and Christmas carols and for songs, including *The Night Hath a Thousand Eyes* (1888).

**Addison,** Sir **Percy,** *in full* **Albert Percy.** 1875-1952. British naval officer; served in World War (1914–18); rear admiral (1923), vice-admiral (1929), admiral (retired 1933).

**Addison, Thomas.** 1793–1860. English physician. M.D., Edinburgh (1815). Discovered "Addison's disease" (1855) when physician at Guy's Hospital, London.

**Addums, Mozis.** Pseudonym of George William BAGBY.

**Ade** (ād), **George.** 1866–1944. American humorist and playwright, b. Kentland, Ind. Grad. Purdue (1887). In newspaper work (1887–1900). Author of *Fables in Slang* (contributed to Chicago *Record*, 1890–1900), *The Girl Proposition* (1902), *Breaking into Society* (1903), *Knocking the Neighbors* (1912), *Single Blessedness* (1922), *The Old-Time Saloon* (1931), and the plays *The Sultan of Sulu* (1902), *The County Chairman* (1903), *The College Widow* (1904), *Father and the Boys* (1907), and several photoplays.

**A'dee** (ā'dē), **Alvey Augustus.** 1842–1924. American diplomat, b. Astoria, N.Y. Served forty-seven years in U.S. State Department, as chief of the Diplomatic Bureau (1878–82), 3d assistant secretary of state (1882–86), 2d assistant secretary of state (1886–1924).

**Ad'e·la** (ăd'ĕ·lȧ). 1062?–1137. Daughter of William the Conqueror; m. Stephen Henry, Count of Blois and Chartres. Mother of Stephen, King of England, whose title to the throne derived through her.

**A'de·laer** (ȧ'dĕ·lẽr) *or* **A'de·ler** (-lẽr), **Cort Si'vert·sen** (sē'vẽrt·s'n). *Orig. name* **Cort Sivertsen.** 1622–1675. Danish naval commander, b. in Norway. Captain in service of Venice (1642–61); admiral, Danish service (1663).

**Ad'e·laide** (ăd'ĕ·lād), Saint. *Ger.* **A'del·heid** (ä'dĕl·hīt). 931?–999. Daughter of King Rudolf II of Burgundy; m. Lothair (d. 950), son of King Hugh of Italy. Imprisoned by Berengar II (950); appealed to Otto I, King of Germany, who came to her rescue and married her (951). As queen mother during reign of Otto II (973–983), had much influence in administering state affairs. Joint regent with Empress Theophano for Otto III (983–991), sole regent (991–996). Died at cloister in Selz, Alsace (Dec. 16, 999).

**Ad'e·laide** (ăd'ĕ·lād). 1792–1849. Daughter of George, Duke of Saxe-Meiningen; m. (1818) William, Duke of Clarence, who became William IV of England.

**A'dé'la'ïde'** (ȧ'dā'lȧ'ēd'). *In full* **Adélaïde Eugénie Louise.** 1777–1847. Princess of **Or'lé'ans'** (ôr'lā'äɴ'), b. Paris; sister of Louis Philippe; influential in persuading him to accept the crown (1830).

**Ad'e·lard** (ăd'ĕ·lärd) *or* **Æth'el·hard** (ăth'ĕl·härd) of Bath. 12th-century English traveler and writer on mathematics and natural science.

**Ad'el·bert** (ăd''l·bẽrt; *Ger.* ä'dĕl·bĕrt). Variant of ADALBERT.

**Adeler.** See ADELAER.

**A'de·lung** (ä'dĕ·lŏŏng), **Johann Christoph.** 1732–1806. German philologist and grammarian, b. in Pomerania; author of *Grammatisch-Kritisches Wörterbuch der Hochdeutschen Mundart* (5 vols., 1774–86), *Über den Deutschen Stil* (3 vols., 1785–86), etc. His nephew **Friedrich von Adelung** (1768–1843) was also a philologist.

**Adelwlf, Adelwold.** Variants of ETHELWULF, ETHELWOLD.

**A'de·nau'er** (ä'd'n·ou'ẽr; ăd''n-), **Konrad.** 1876–1967. German lawyer; chancellor of West Germany (1949–63).

**A'de·net' le Roi'** (ȧd'nĕ' lē rwä'). *Also* **A'dam'** (ȧ'däɴ'), **A'dans'** (ȧ'däɴts'), **A'de·nès'** (ȧ'dē·nĕs'), *or* **A'de·nez'** (ȧ'dē·nāts'), **le Roi.** 13th-century French trouvère; adapted chansons de geste to fashionable forms.

**A'de·od'a·tus** (ā'dē·ŏd'ȧ·tŭs). Name of two popes: **Adeodatus I;** see DEUSDEDIT. Saint **Adeodatus II;** pope (672–676). See *Table of Popes*, Nos. 68, 77.

**Adhemar** (*or* **Adhémar**) **de Bourbon.** See AIMAR DE BOURBON.

**Ad·her'bal** (ăd·hûr'băl). Joint king of Numidia (118–113 B.C.) with his brother Hiempsal (to c. 117) and cousin Jugurtha; ousted and slain by Jugurtha (*q.v.*).

**Ad'ler** (äd'lẽr), **Alfred.** 1870–1937. Viennese psychologist and psychiatrist. At first a Freudian, later opposed Freud's emphasis on sex and advanced own theory of the inferiority complex to explain psychopathic cases. Author of *The Theory and Practice of Individual Psy-*

*chology* (1918), *The Science of Living* (1929), *The Pattern of Life* (1930), etc.

**Ad'ler** (ăd'lẽr), **Cyrus**. 1863–1940. American Jewish scholar, educator, and author, b. Van Buren, Ark. Grad. U. of Pennsylvania and Johns Hopkins. With Smithsonian Institution and U.S. National Museum (1892–1908). President, Dropsie College, Philadelphia (from 1908); president, Jewish Theological Seminary of America, New York (1924–40). Editor on *Jewish Encyclopedia;* editor of *American Jewish Year Book* (from 1899).

**Ad'ler** (ăd'lẽr), **Fe'lix** (fē'lĭks). 1851–1933. Educator and ethical reformer, b. Alzey, Ger.; to U.S. (1857); grad. Columbia (1870). Founder (1876) and lecturer, N.Y. Society for Ethical Culture. Professor of political and social ethics, Columbia (from 1902). Author of *Creed and Deed* (1877), *Life and Destiny* (1905), *Religion of Duty* (1905), *An Ethical Philosophy of Life* (1918).

**Ad'ler** (äd'lẽr), **Friedrich**. 1827–1908. German architect and archaeologist, b. Berlin. Designed churches in Berlin. Active in excavations at Olympia (1875–81). Author esp. of books on medieval architecture in Germany.

**Ad'ler** (ăd'lẽr, äd'lẽr), **George J.** 1821–1868. Philologist, b. Leipzig, Germany; to U.S. (1833).

**Ad'ler** (äd'lẽr), **Kaspar**. See Kaspar AQUILA.

**Ad'ler** (ăd'lẽr), **Mortimer Jerome**. 1902– . American philosopher and educator.

**Ad'ler** (ăd'lẽr; äd'lẽr), **Nathan Marcus**. 1803–1890. Jewish rabbi, b. in Hanover. Chief rabbi of London (1844); suggested United Synagogues Act (passed 1870). His son **Hermann** (1839–1911), b. in Hanover, was also British chief rabbi (from 1891). Another son, **El'kan** (ĕl'kăn) **Nathan** (1861–1946), lawyer, is author of works on Jewish history, literature, and religion.

**Ad'ler** (äd'lẽr), **Viktor**. 1852–1918. Austrian Social Democrat leader, b. Prague. Moved to Vienna (1855). Leader of Social Democratic party, and member of the Reichsrat (from 1907). Advocated Austrian union with German Reich. His son **Friedrich** (1879–1960), an Austrian Socialist politician, assassinated (1916) Count Karl von Stürgkh; death sentence commuted.

**Ad'ler·beth** (äd'lẽr·bĕt), **Gudmund Göran**. 1751–1818. Swedish poet and playwright; translator of Vergil, Horace, Ovid, and Old Norse poetry.

**Ad'ler·creutz** (äd'lẽr·krûüts), Count **Karl Johan**. 1757–1815. Swedish general, b. in Finland. Defeated in Finland by Russians (1808); led party which deposed Gustavus IV (1809); served in Germany against Napoleon I (1813), in Norway (1814).

**Ad'ler·spar're** (äd'lẽr·spär'rĕ), Count **Georg**. 1760–1835. Swedish general, statesman, editor, and writer. Active in revolt leading to overthrow of Gustavus IV (1809).

**Ad'lum** (ăd'lŭm), **John**. 1759–1836. American pioneer in grape growing and wine making, b. York, Pa. Produced the Catawba grape; author of *Adlum on Making Wine* (1826).

**Ad'olf** (ăd'ŏlf; *Ger.* ä'dôlf). Variant of ADOLPHUS.

**Ad'olf** (ăd'ŏlf; *Ger.* ä'dôlf) **of Nas'sau** (năs'ô; *Ger.* näs'ou). *Lat.* **A·dol'phus** (ȧ·dŏl'fŭs). 1250?–1298. King of Germany (1292–98); son of Walram II; elected to succeed Rudolf I of Hapsburg; claimed title to Holy Roman Empire but never crowned; at war in Meissen and Thuringia (1294–96); deposed (1298) and killed soon after in battle of Göllheim. See NASSAU, 1.

**Adolf of Nassau.** *Full name* **William August Charles Frederick Adolf.** 1817–1905. Duke of Nassau (1839–66; see NASSAU). Forced to relinquish duchy to Prussia as result of Prussian victory over Austria; renounced all claims to duchy (1867); grand duke of Luxemburg (1890–1902).

**A·dol'phus** (ȧ·dŏl'fŭs). Variant of ADOLF.

**Adolphus, John.** 1768–1845. English lawyer and historian, b. London. Author of a history of the reign of George III (1802). His son **John Leycester** (1795–1862), lawyer and writer, wrote *Letters to Richard Heber* (1821), proving Scott's authorship of the Waverley Novels.

**A·dol'phus Fred'er·ick** (frĕd'ẽr·ĭk; frĕd'rĭk). *Swed.* **Adolf Fredrik.** 1710–1771. King of Sweden (1751–71). Son of Christian Augustus (1673–1726), Duke of Schleswig-Holstein-Gottorp. Bishop of Lübeck (1727–50); favored by Empress Elizabeth of Russia; through her influence made heir to throne of Sweden (1743); m. (1744) Louisa Ulrica, sister of Frederick the Great. Deprived of all power as ruler by council of state and by party factions.

**Adolphus Frederick.** See CAMBRIDGE.

**A'dor'** (ȧ'dôr'), **Gustave.** 1845–1928. Swiss statesman; member (from 1889) and president (1902), National Council; president, Swiss Confederation (1919).

**A'drets'** (ȧ'drĕ'), Baron **des. François de Beau'mont'** (bō'môɴ'). 1513–1587. French Huguenot commander noted for ferocity and cruelty; abandoned Protestantism and fought the Protestants (1567).

**A'dri·an** (ā'drĭ·ăn) *or* **Ha'dri·an** (hā'-). Name of six popes (see *Table of Popes*, Nos. 95, 106, 109, 169, 186, 220), especially:

**Adrian I.** d. 795. Pope (772–795). Summoned Charlemagne to drive back Lombards who were threatening Rome (773–774); founder of temporal power of the popes; presided over Second Nicene Council (787).

**Adrian IV.** *Real name* **Nicholas Break'spear** (brāk'spēr). 1100?–1159. Pope (1154–59), b. near St. Albans, England. Cardinal bishop of Albano (1146); raised to papal see (1154), the only Englishman ever to become pope; in conflict with Emperor Frederick I because of his vigorous insistence upon papal supremacy as defined by Gregory VII; gave Ireland to Henry II of England (1154).

**Adrian VI.** 1459–1523. Pope (1522–23), b. Utrecht, Holland. Vice-chancellor of U. of Louvain; chosen tutor (1506) to Archduke Charles (later Charles V); grand inquisitor (1516) and regent (1520) of Spain; created cardinal (1517) by Leo X; as pope, failed in efforts to reform church and to oppose advances of Turks.

**Adrian.** Roman emperors. See HADRIAN.

**A'dri·an** (ā'drĭ·ăn), **Edgar Douglas.** 1889–1977. English physiologist. Grad. Trinity Coll., Cambridge. Author of *The Basis of Sensation* (1928). Corecipient with Sir Charles Sherrington of the Nobel prize (1932) in medicine and physiology for joint discoveries relating to the function of the neurons.

**A'dri·a'ni** (ä'drē·ä'nē), **Giovanni Battista.** 1513–1579. Florentine statesman; author of a history covering the period 1536–74 (pub. 1583).

**A'dri·a'no di Bo·lo'gna** (ä'drē·ä'nō dē bō·lō'nyä). = Adriano BANCHIERI.

**A'dy** (ŏ'dĭ), **Endre.** 1877–1919. Hungarian lyrical poet.

**A'dye** (ā'dĭ), Sir **John Miller.** 1819–1900. British general and writer on military subjects.

**Æ** *or* **A.E.** Pseudonym of George William RUSSELL.

**Ædde.** See EDDI.

**Ædilberct.** See ETHELBERT (552?–616).

**Ægelbriht.** Variant of ETHELBERT (d. 794).

**Ae·gi'di** (â·gē'dē), **Ludwig Karl.** 1825–1901. German jurist, politician, and publicist; b. Tilsit.

**Ae·gid'i·us of As·si'si** (ē·jĭd'ĭ·ŭs ŭv äs·sē'zē). *Also known as* Blessed **Giles** (jīlz). d. 1262. One of original companions of Saint Francis of Assisi. His sayings, advice, and answers to questions collected and published under title *Dicta* (Eng. transl., *The Golden Words of the Blessed Brother Giles*, 1906).

**Aeh′ren·thal** (â′rĕn·täl), Count **von. Alois Le′xa** (lĕk′sä). 1854–1912. Austro-Hungarian statesman, b. in Bohemia. Ambassador to Bucharest (1895), to St. Petersburg (1899); foreign minister (1906–12). Instrumental in Austrian annexation of Bosnia and Herzegovina (1908); created count (1909).

**Aeken, Hieronymus van.** See Hieronymus BOSCH.

**Ælf′heah′** (ălf′hâ′äK). *Known as* Saint **Al′phege** (ăl′fĕj). 954–1012. English prelate; bishop of Winchester (984); archbishop of Canterbury (1006). Obtained from Olaf Tryggvesson promise not to invade England (994); captured and killed by Danes.

**Ælfled.** See ETHELFLEDA.

**Ælfred.** See ALFRED (849–901).

**Æl′fric** (ăl′frĭk). *Called* **Gram·mat′i·cus** (gră·măt′ĭ·kŭs). c. 955–c. 1020. English abbot and writer. Abbot of Cernel (now Cerne Abbas), later of Eynsham. Author of a Latin and English grammar and glossary, two books of homilies (first pub. 1844–46), and *Lives of the Saints.*

**Ae′li·an** (ē′lĭ·ăn). *Lat.* **Claudius Ae′li·a′nus** (ē′lĭ·ā′nŭs). Roman rhetorician of 3d century A.D. (or earlier); author, in Greek, of works commonly known by Latin titles, as *De Natura Animalium* and *Variae Historiae.*

**Aelred,** Saint. See ETHELRED.

**Aelst** (älst), **Evert van** (1607–1657) and his nephew **Willem van** (1625?–after 1683). Dutch still-life painters.

**Ae·mil′i·a′nus** (ē·mĭl′ĭ·ā′nŭs). 206?–253. Roman emperor, b. in Mauritania. Governor of Pannonia and Moesia in reign of Gallus; after successful campaign against barbarians on Danube, elected emperor by his soldiers (253); died few months later.

**Aemilius, Paulus.** See Paolo EMILIO.

**Aemilius Paulus, Lucius.** See PAULUS.

**Aeneas Silvius** (*or* **Sylvius**). See Pope PIUS II.

**Ae·ne′as Tac′ti·cus** (ē·nē′ăs tăk′tĭ·kŭs). Greek writer on military subjects, of 4th century B.C.

**Ae·nes′i·de′mus** (ē·nĕs′ĭ·dē′mŭs). Greek Skeptic philosopher; taught in Alexandria, prob. in 1st century B.C.

**A·ë′no·bar′bus** (ā·ē′nō·bär′bŭs; ā·ĕn′ō-). Variant of AHENOBARBUS.

**Ae·pi′nus** (â·pē′nŏŏs), **Franz Maria Ulrich Theodor Hoch.** 1724–1802. German physicist; lived in St. Petersburg (1757–98); conducted researches in electricity and magnetism, including the original double-touch method of magnetizing.

**Aert′sen** *or* **Aerts′zen** (ärt′sĕn), **Pieter.** 1508?–?1575. Dutch realistic painter of still life, homely scenes, and religious and historical subjects.

**Aes′chi·nes** (ĕs′kĭ·nēz; *esp. Brit.,* ēs′-). 389–314 B.C. Athenian orator; political opponent of Demosthenes in Athenian assembly, advocating appeasement policy in dealing with Philip of Macedon. Forced into exile (330).

**Aes′chy·lus** (ĕs′kĭ·lŭs; *esp. Brit.,* ēs′-). 525–456 B.C. Greek tragic dramatist, b. Eleusis, Attica. According to tradition, served in Athenian armies in Persian wars and was engaged at Marathon, Artemisium, Salamis, and Plataea. In annual competitions at Athens won first prize in tragedy thirteen times (between 484 and 468). Of his many plays (perhaps 90 in all) only seven have survived: *The Suppliants, The Persians* (*Persae*), *Seven against Thebes, Prometheus Bound,* and the Orestean trilogy (*Oresteia*), *Agamemnon, Choephoroi,* and *Eumenides.* See SOPHOCLES.

**Ae′sop** (ē′sŏp). Reputed Greek author of *Aesop's Fables;* said to have lived about 620–560 B.C., to have been ugly and deformed, and to have been born a slave. The sources of a number of the fables have been traced to earlier literature.

**Ae·so′pus** (ē·sō′pŭs), **Clodius.** *Also called* **Ae′sop.** Roman tragedian of 1st century B.C.; friend of Cicero.

**Æthelbald.** See EADBALD.

**Æthelbald, Æthelberht, Æthelbert, Æthelflaed, Æthelred, Æthelwold, Æthelwulf.** Variants of ETHELBALD, ETHELBERT, ETHELFLEDA, etc.

**Æthelhard.** See ADELARD.

**Æthelstan.** See ATHELSTAN.

**A·ë′ti·on** (ā·ē′shĭ·ŏn; -tĭ·ŏn). Greek painter of 4th century B.C., known esp. for his painting of marriage of Alexander and Roxana.

**A·ë′ti·os** (ā·ē′shĭ·ŏs; -tĭ·ŏs). *Lat.* **A·ë′ti·us** (ā·ē′shĭ·ŭs). fl. about 500 A.D. Greek physician and compiler of a medical work.

**A·ë′ti·us** (ā·ē′shĭ·ŭs), **Flavius.** 396?–454. Roman general; successful in holding Roman boundaries in Gaul against barbarian attacks (434 ff.); won his most famous victory, over Attila and the Huns, at Châlons (June, 451); put to death in Rome by Emperor Valentinian III.

**A·ë′ti·us** (ā·ē′shĭ·ŭs) **of Antioch.** *Called* "the Atheist" *or* "the Ungodly." d. 367. Syrian theologian, b. Antioch. Founder (c. 350) of an extreme sect of Arians, known as Aetians, Anomoeans, or Eunomians (after Eunomius, his disciple), whose doctrine was that the Son of God was a created being and hence essentially unlike (Greek *anomoios*) God; banished by Constantius (359) but brought back by Julian (c. 361).

**A·fa·na′siev** (ŭ·fŭ·nä′syĕf), **Aleksandr Nikolaevich.** 1826–1871. Russian scholar; writer on folklore and national Slav poetry. Educ. Moscow U. Employee (1849–56), chief (1856–62), Department of Foreign Archives, Moscow.

**Af·fon′so.** *Modern* **A·fon′so** (ȧ·fōN′sōō). Portuguese forms of ALFONSO.

**Af′fre** (ä′fr′), **Denis Auguste.** 1793–1848. French Roman Catholic prelate; archbishop of Paris (1840); during Revolution of 1848 mortally wounded at barricades in Paris while attempting to persuade insurgents to submit to authority.

**af Geijerstam.** See GEIJERSTAM.

**A′fing·er** (ä′fĭng·ẽr), **Bernhard.** 1813–1882. German sculptor, b. Nuremberg, Bavaria.

**af Leopold, Carl Gustaf.** See LEOPOLD.

**A·fon′so.** *Older* **Af·fon′so** (ȧ·fōN′sōō). Portuguese forms of ALFONSO.

**A·fra′ni·us** (ȧ·frā′nĭ·ŭs), **Lucius.** Roman comic poet of 1st century B.C., an imitator of Menander. Fragments of his works are extant.

**Afranius, Lucius.** d. 46 B.C. Roman general; follower of Pompey, with whose aid he was elected consul (60 B.C.); defeated by Caesar in Spain (49); joined Pompey and was present at disastrous battles of Pharsalus (48) and Thapsus (46); captured and executed.

**Af′ri·ca′nus** (ăf′rĭ·kā′nŭs), **Scipio.** See SCIPIO AFRICANUS.

**Africanus, Sextus Julius.** 3d-century Christian traveler and historian; author of a history of the world from creation to 221 A.D., in which he reckoned period between creation and Christ's birth at 5499 years, and antedated Christ's birth by three years. His chronology adopted by most Eastern churches.

**af Wirsén, Carl David.** See WIRSÉN.

**Af·ze′li·us** (ăf·zē′lĭ·ŭs; *Swed.* äv·sā′lĭ·ŭs), **Adam.** 1750–1837. Swedish botanist; founded Linnaean Institute at Uppsala (1802); published Linnaeus's *Autobiography* (1823).

**Afzelius, Arvid August.** 1785–1871. Swedish pastor, writer, and collector of Swedish folk songs.

**A′gag** (ā′găg). In Bible (*1 Sam.* xv), king of Amalekites; killed by Samuel after Saul had spared life.

**A′ga Khan′** (ä′gȧ kän′). Title of three heads of Ismailian sect of British Indian Mohammedans:

**Aga Khan I.** *Orig. name* **Hasan Ali Shah.** 1800–1881. Traced descent from rulers of Egypt and Persia and from Fatima, daughter of Mohammed; governor of province of Kerman; after quarrel with shah, emigrated to India; as spiritual head of important sect of Mohammedans of India, greatly aided British government; checked frontier tribes; granted title of "His Highness the Aga Khan"; acknowledged as leader by other Moslem communities in Africa and Asia. His work continued by his son **Aga Khan II** (d. 1885).

**Aga Khan III.** *Real name* **Aga Sultan Sir Mahomed Shah.** 1877–1957. Son of Aga Khan II. Head of Ismaili Mohammedans (1885–1957). Eur. educ.; on viceroy's council (1902–04); founded Aligarh U. for Mohammedans (1910); aided Gr. Brit. greatly in World War I; worked for strong and free Turkey; auth. of *India in Transition* (1918).

**Aga Khan IV.** *In full* **H. H. Shah Karim Aga Khan IV.** 1936– . Grandson of Aga Khan III. Head, Ismaili Mohammedans (1957– ).

**Aga Mohammed Khan.** Variant of AGHA MOHAMMED KHAN.

**Aganoor Pompili, Vittoria.** See POMPILI.

**Ag'a·pe'tus** (ăg'ȧ·pē'tŭs). Name of two popes. See *Table of Popes*, Nos. 57, 130.

**Agapida,** Friar **Antonio.** A pseudonym of Washington IRVING.

**Agar.** See HAGAR.

**A'gar** (ā'gär), **Herbert Sebastian.** 1897– . American poet and miscellaneous writer, b. New Rochelle, N.Y. Editor (from 1940), Louisville (Ky.) *Courier-Journal.* Author of volumes of verse (with his wife; see Eleanor Carroll CHILTON), and of *Bread and Circuses* (1930), *The People's Choice* (1933; awarded Pulitzer prize for history), *Land of the Free* (1935), *Pursuit of Happiness* (1938), *A Time for Greatness* (1942), etc.

**A'gardh** (ä'gärd), **Karl Adolf.** 1785–1859. Swedish bishop of Karlstad (1834 ff.) and algologist.

**A·ga'si·as of Eph'e·sus** (ȧ·gā'shĭ·ăs, ĕf'ē·sŭs). fl. 100 B.C. Greek sculptor; son of Dositheus. His name is inscribed on base of statue known as *Borghese Gladiator.*

**Ag'as·siz** (ăg'ȧ·sē), **Alexander.** 1835–1910. American zoologist, b. Neuchâtel, Switzerland. Son of Jean Louis Agassiz. To U.S. (1849). Mine superintendent at Calumet, Mich. (1867 ff.); president, Calumet Mining Co. On zoological exploration trips to west coast of S. America (1875), the Gulf Stream in American waters (1877), West Indies (1878), Hawaii coral reefs (1885), S. American and U.S. coastal waters (1891), Bahamas (1892), Bermuda and Florida reefs (1894), Australian Great Barrier Reef (1896), Pacific waters between San Francisco and the Marquesas (1899–1900), waters between Peru and Easter Island (1904). Author of *North American Acalephae* (1865), *Embryology of the Starfish* (1865), *North American Starfishes* (1877), etc.

**Ag'as·siz** (ăg'ȧ·sē; *Fr.* à'gà'sē'), **Louis,** *in full* **Jean Louis Rodolphe.** 1807–1873. Naturalist, b. Môtier-en-Vully, Switzerland. Published *The Fishes of Brazil* (1829) from study of collection turned over to him by von Martius. At Paris (1831–32); associated with Cuvier and von Humboldt; published *Recherches sur les Poissons Fossiles* (5 vols., 1833–34) from notes and material furnished by Cuvier. Professor of natural history, Neuchâtel (1832–45). Published *History of the Fresh Water Fishes of Central Europe* (1839–42), *Études Critiques sur les Mollusques Fossiles* (1840–45), *Nomenclator Zoologicus* (1842–46). Interested in glacial action over Europe; published *Études sur les Glaciers* (2 vols., 1840), *Système Glaciaire* (1846), *Nouvelles Études et Expériences sur les Glaciers Actuels* (1847). To U.S. (1846) for lectures at Cambridge; professor of natural history, Lawrence Scientific School, Harvard (1848–73). Began collections now in Harvard Museum of Comparative Zoology (1859). Naturalized citizen of U.S. (1861). Varied active teaching life with zoological exploration, as in Brazil (1865), Cuban waters (1869), around Cape Horn to California (1871). Established (1873) Anderson School of Natural History, a summer school on Penikese Island in Buzzards Bay. Of a planned ten-volume work, *Contributions to the Natural History of the United States,* four volumes were completed (1857 ff.). Elected to American Hall of Fame (1915). His second wife, **Elizabeth Cabot,** *nee* **Car'y** [kâr'ĭ] (1822–1907), was a founder of Radcliffe College (1879) and its president (1894–1902).

**A'gate** (ā'gȧt), **Frederick Styles.** 1803–1844. American painter, b. Sparta, N.Y. One of group which initiated National Academy of Design (1826). Exhibited at National Academy (1826–44). His brother **Alfred T.** (1812–1846) was artist on Wilkes Exploring Expedition (1838–42).

**Agate, James Evershed.** 1877–1947. English dramatic critic, b. Manchester.

**Ag'a·tha** (ăg'ȧ·thȧ), Saint. Sicilian Christian martyr of 3d century who, according to legend, was tortured by the Roman governor whose advances she had resisted. Patron saint of Malta.

**Ag'a·thar'chi·des** (ăg'ȧ·thär'kĭ·dēz). *Also* **Ag'a·thar'chus** (-thär'kŭs). Greek historian and geographer of 2d century B.C.

**Ag'a·thar'cus** (ăg'ȧ·thär'kŭs). Athenian painter of 5th century B.C., said to have originated scene painting.

**A·ga'thi·as** (ȧ·gā'thĭ·ăs; ȧ·găth'ĭ·ăs). Byzantine Greek writer of 6th century A.D.; author of love poems, epigrams, and a history of contemporary times.

**Ag'a·tho** (ăg'ȧ·thō), Saint. Pope (678–681).

**A·gath'o·cles** (ȧ·găth'ō·klēz). 361–289 B.C. Tyrant of Syracuse (316–304 B.C.), king (304–289 B.C.); b. Thermae, Sicily, of humble origin. Gained power through patronage; declared ruler of Syracuse (316); controlled most of Sicily; after defeat by Hamilcar, carried war into Africa (310) where campaign was successful; returned to Sicily (307) where his despotic rule was made complete (305); invaded Italy and Corcyra (300–295).

**Ag'a·thon** (ăg'ȧ·thŏn). Athenian tragic poet of late 5th century B.C.; friend of Euripides and Plato. Scene of Plato's *Symposium* is laid in his house.

**Agee, Fanny Heaslip.** See Fanny Heaslip LEA.

**A'gee** (ā'jē, -jē), **James.** 1909–1955. American author, playwright, and critic; b. Knoxville, Tennessee.

**Ag'e·la'das** (ăj'ĕ·lā'dăs) *or* **Hag'e·la'das** (hăj'-). Greek sculptor of late 6th and early 5th centuries B.C., from Argos; reputed teacher of Myron, Phidias, and Polycletus.

**Ag'e·san'der** (ăj'ĕ·săn'dẽr). Greek sculptor of late 1st century B.C., from Rhodes; collaborated with Polydorus and Athenodorus in carving Laocoön group.

**A·ges'i·la'us II** (ȧ·jĕs'ĭ·lā'ŭs). d. about 360 B.C. King of Sparta (c. 400–360 B.C.) and noted general; commanded against Persians in Asia Minor (396) and against Corinthian league of Greek states (battle of Coronea, 394); defended Sparta brilliantly (370–369, 362); died in Egypt commanding Spartan mercenaries.

**Aggeus.** See HAGGAI.

**A·gha'** (*or* **A·ga'**) **Mo·ham'med Khan'** (ä·gä' mō·häm'măd kän'). 1720–1797. Shah of Persia (1794–97); founder of the Kajar dynasty. Contended in civil war (1779–94) against reigning Zand dynasty and overthrew its chief ruler, Karim Khan, and successors 1779–94; jealous of Russian interference; murdered. Succeeded by his nephew Fath Ali.

**Agh'lab·ite** (ăg'lȧ·bīt; ăg·lăb'īt) *or* **Agh'lab·id** (ăg'lȧ·bĭd; ăg·lăb'ĭd). Arab Sunnite dynasty, ruling (800–909) in North Africa with capital at Kairouan. Founded by **Ibrahim ibn-al-Agh·lab'** (-ăg·lăb'), *or* **Ibrahim I,** sent out as governor by Harun al-Rashid; some of Aghlabite emirs harried coasts of Italy, France, Corsica, and Sardinia, and conquered Sicily (by 902); dynasty destroyed by Fatimids.

**A'gi·as** (ā'jĭ·ăs). Greek cyclic poet of 8th century B.C.; author of epic narrating story of homeward voyage of Achaean warriors from siege of Troy.

**A'gis** (ā'jĭs). Name of four kings of Sparta: **Agis I,** legendary founder (c. 11th century B.C.) of royal line. **Agis II,** king (c. 426–399 B.C.); victor in battle of Mantinea (418). **Agis III,** king (338–331 B.C.); revolted against Macedonian rule; killed in battle. **Agis IV,** king (244–?241 B.C.); instituted measures of reform involving redistribution of land and admission of Perioeci to Spartan political life; opposed by his colleague Leonidas II; sentenced to death by ephors.

**Ag'nes** (ăg'nĕs; -nĭs), Saint. Roman Catholic virgin martyr; according to legend, suffered martyrdom at Rome (304 A.D.). Patron saint of young girls, who formerly observed St. Agnes's Eve (Jan. 20–21) with quaint rites intended to reveal their future husbands. The superstition forms background of Keats's *Eve of St. Agnes.*

**Ag'nes** (ăg'nĕs; -nĭs; *Ger.* äg'nĕs). d. after 1114. German princess; daughter of Holy Roman Emperor Henry IV; m. 1st (1079) Frederick, Duke of Swabia, by whom she was mother of Frederick (d. 1147; m. Judith, daughter of Henry the Black of the Guelph family; father of Emperor Frederick I Barbarossa) and Conrad III, first emperor of the Hohenstaufen (*q.v.*) line; m. (1106) 2d Leopold III, Margrave of Austria of the Babenberg (*q.v.*) line, by whom she was mother of Leopold IV, Margrave of Austria, Henry Jasomirgott, 1st Duke of Austria, and the historian Otto, Bishop of Freising.

**Agnes de Castro.** See Ines de CASTRO.

**A·gne'si** (ä·nyâ'zē), **Maria Gaetana.** 1718–1799. Italian woman mathematician; professor, U. of Bologna (from 1752); author of *Istituzioni Analitiche* (1748). Her sister **Maria Teresa** (1724–?1780) was a pianist and composer of cantatas, piano concertos, and five operas.

**Ag'new** (ăg'nū), **David Hayes.** 1818–1892. American surgeon and educator, b. Lancaster Co., Pa. Professor, U. of Pennsylvania (1871–89).

**Agnew, Spi'ro** (Spēr'ō) **Theodore.** 1918– . American politician; U.S. vice-president (from 1969).

**A'gno·lo** (ä'nyō·lō). See AGOSTINO.

**Agnolo, Baccio d'.** 1460?–1543. Florentine wood carver and architect; carved many of the decorations in church of Santa Maria Novella and the Palazzo Vecchio; in Florence designed Villa Borghese, Bartolini Palace, etc.

**Ag'non** (äg'nŏn), **Shmuel Yosef.** 1888–1970. Israeli author, b. Galicia. Shared Nobel prize in literature (1966) with Nelly SACHS.

**Ag'o·rac'ri·tus** (ăg'ō·răk'rĭ·tŭs). Greek sculptor of 5th century B.C.; studied under Phidias; reputed sculptor of a statue of Nemesis (at Rhamnus).

**A'go·sti'ni** (ä'gō·stē'nē) *or* **A'go·sti'no** (-nō), **Paolo.** d. 1629. Italian musician; conductor of pope's orchestra in St. Peter's Rome; composer, esp. of sacred music.

**A'go·sti'no** (ä'gō·stē'nō) and **A'gno·lo** (ä'nyō·lō). Italian architects of early 14th century, who designed the Porta Romagna, the church and convent of St. Francis, and other buildings in Siena.

**A'go·sti'no di Duc'cio** (dē dōōt'chō). 1418–1498. Italian sculptor and architectural decorator, best known for work on façade of San Bernardino in Perugia.

**Agostino Veneziano.** See Agostino VENEZIANO.

**A'goult'** (ȧ'gōō'), Comtesse **d'. Marie Catherine Sophie de Fla'vi'gny'** (dē flȧ'vē'nyē'). *Pseudonym* **Da'niel' Stern'** (*Fr.* dȧ'nyĕl' stĕrn'; *Ger.* dä'nyĕl shtĕrn'; *Eng.* dăn'yĕl stûrn'). 1805–1876. French writer, b. Frankfort on the Main; m. comte d'Agoult (1827). Noted for liaison with Franz Liszt, Hungarian composer, by whom she had three daughters, one of whom, Cosima, became wife of Richard Wagner. Author of *Histoire de la Révolution de 1848* (1851).

**A'gra·mon'te** (ä'grä·mōn'tā), **Aristides.** 1869–1931. Cuban bacteriologist, b. Camagüey. Grad. Coll. Phys. and Surg., Columbia (1892). With Walter Reed, Jesse Lazear, and James Carroll, member U.S. army board that discovered transmission of yellow fever by mosquitoes. Cuban secretary of public health (1922).

**Agramonte, Ignacio.** 1841–1873. Cuban revolutionist, b. Puerto Príncipe; commissioned under Céspedes, became a leader of revolts (1868–69) against Spain.

**A·gre'da** (ä·grā'thä), **María de.** *Real name* **María Fer·nán'dez Co'ro·nel'** (fĕr·nän'dāth kō'rō·nĕl'). *Religious name* Sor **Ma·rí'a de Je·sús'** (sôr mä·rē'ä thā hā·sōōs'). 1602–1665. Spanish nun, b. Agreda; superior of Immaculate Conception Convent at Agreda; adviser to Philip IV; on basis of alleged divine revelation, wrote life of Virgin Mary (later destroyed) and *Mística Ciudad de Diós* (1670; banned by Pope Innocent XI).

**A·gri'co·la** (*Ger.* ä·grē'kō·lä; *Angl.* ȧ·grĭk'ō·lȧ), **Alexander.** *Real surname* **Ackermann.** 1446?–1506. German composer of chansons, motets, masses, and magnificats.

**Agricola, Christoph Ludwig.** 1667–1719. German landscape and portrait painter.

**Agricola, Georgius.** *Real name* **Georg Bau'er** (bou'ĕr). 1494–1555. German mineralogist and scholar, b. in Saxony. Author of *De Re Metallica* (1530).

**A·gric'o·la** (ȧ·grĭk'ō·lȧ), **Gnaeus Julius.** 37–93 A.D. Roman soldier; father-in-law of Tacitus. Governor of Aquitania (74–78); consul (78) and governor of Britain; pacified Britain to northern boundary of Perth and Argyll (78–84). Subject of Tacitus's *Agricola.*

**A·gri'co·la** (*Ger.* ä·grē'kō·lä; *Angl.* ȧ·grĭk'ō·lȧ), **Johann Friedrich.** 1720–1774. German composer, organist, and writer on music.

**Agricola, Johannes.** *Real name* **Johannes Snei'der** (snī'dĕr), *later* **Schnit'ter** (shnĭt'ĕr). *Also called* **Ma·gis'ter Is·le'bi·us** (mä·gĭs'tĕr ĭs·lā'bē·ōōs). 1494?–1566. German Protestant reformer, b. Eisleben, Saxony. Disciple of Luther. Proponent of Antinomianism, opposing Melanchthon and Luther.

**Agricola, Martin.** *Real name* **Martin Sohr** (zōr) *or* **So're** (zō'rĕ). 1486–1556. German Protestant church musician and composer; attempted to improve musical notation.

**Ag·ri'co·la** (*Finn.* åg·rĭ'kō·lå; *Angl.* ȧ·grĭk'ō·lȧ), **Michael.** 1506?–1557. Bishop of Åbo; one of first to write in Finnish vernacular; published version of New Testament in Finnish (1548).

**A·gri'co·la** (*Du.* ȧ·grē'kō·lȧ; *Angl.* ȧ·grĭk'ō·lȧ), **Rodolphus.** *Real name* **Roelof Huys'man** *or* **Huys'mann** (hīs'män). 1443–1485. Dutch scholar, painter, musician, and promoter of classical studies, esp. in Germany.

**A·grip'pa I** *and* **II** (ȧ·grĭp'ȧ). Name frequently used, esp. by Josephus, for HEROD AGRIPPA I and II.

**A·grip'pa** (ä·grĭp'ä; *Angl.* ȧ·grĭp'ȧ), **Cornelius Heinrich.** *Called* **A·grip'pa von Net'tes·heim** (ä·grĭp'ä fōn nĕt'ĕs·hīm). 1486?–1535. German physician, theologian, and student of the occult.

**A·grip'pa** (ȧ·grĭp'ȧ), **Marcus Vipsanius.** 63–12 B.C. Roman general and statesman, of humble origin; son-in-law and adviser of Emperor Augustus. Suppressed disorders in Gaul and Germany (38 B.C.); consul (37). Appointed naval commander; defeated Sextus Pompeius at Mylae and Naulochus (36); aedile (33); largely responsible for naval victory over Antony at Actium (31); consul (27). Succeeded Marcellus as chief minister (c. 23); tribune (18–12); governor in the East, *i.e.* Syria (from c. 23).

**Agrippa, Menenius.** See MENENIUS AGRIPPA.

**Ag'rip·pi'na** (ăg'rĭ·pī'nȧ). Name of two Roman women: **Agrippina** the elder, *known also as* **Vip·sa'ni·a Agrippina** [vĭp·sā'nĭ·ȧ] (13 B.C.?–33 A.D.), daughter of M. Vipsanius Agrippa and of Julia, daughter of Augustus; wife of Germanicus Caesar and mother of Caligula; regarded as one of noblest and most heroic women of antiquity; accompanied her husband on all his campaigns; on his death (19 A.D.) returned to Italy; incurred hatred of Tiberius; banished to island of Pandataria, near Naples; died of starvation, perhaps voluntarily but under suspicious circumstances. Her daughter **Agrippina** the younger (15?–59 A.D.), b. at Oppidum Ubiorum, later named Colonia Agrippina after her (modern Cologne); m. 1st Domitius Ahenobarbus by whom she was mother of Nero, 2d Crispus Passienus, 3d (49 A.D.) her uncle Emperor Claudius, whom she poisoned (54); destroyed many of the Roman nobility and (50) excluded Britannicus, son of Claudius, from the throne; caused many scandals; sought to rule through her son Nero, but was put to death by him.

**A·gua'do** (ä·gwä'thō), **Alejandro María.** Marqués **de las Ma·ris'mas** (thā läs mä·rēs'mäs). 1784–1842. Financier, b. Seville, Spain. Financial agent of Ferdinand VII; later, became naturalized French citizen; amassed huge fortune; bequeathed valuable paintings to the Louvre.

**A·güe'ro y Be'tan·court'** (ä·gwā'rō ē bā'täng·kōōrt'), **Aristides de.** 1865–1933. Cuban diplomat; Cuba's representative to first Assembly of League of Nations; member of Council of League of Nations (1927–30); presided over council (1928).

**A'gues'seau'** (á'gĕ'sō'), **Henri François d'.** *Real surname* **Da'gues'seau'.** 1668–1751. French jurist, b. Limoges. Chancellor of France (1717–18, '20–22, '37–50).

**A'gui·lar'** (ä'gē·lär'; *Angl.* ă·gwĭl'ēr), **Grace.** 1816–1847. English writer, b. of Spanish Jewish parents. Author of *The Spirit of Judaism* (1842) and the novels *Home Influence* (1847), *Vale of Cedars* (1850), etc.

**A'gui·le'ra** (ä'gē·lā'rä), **Ventura Ruiz** (rōō·ēth'). 1820–1881. Spanish poet, b. Salamanca. To Madrid (1843); political journalist. His works include collections of poems, as *Elegías* (1862), *La Arcadia Moderna* (1875), and prose works, including short novels.

**A'gui·nal'do** (ä'gē·näl'dō), **Emilio.** 1869–1964. Filipino leader, b. near Cavite, Luzon. Commander of Filipino forces in rebellion against Spain (1896–98); led insurrection against American authority (Feb., 1899–1901); captured by Funston (Mar., 1901). Took oath of allegiance to U.S.; retired from public life.

**A·guir're** (ä·gēr'rā), **José Sá'enz de** (sä'ānth thā). 1630–1699. Spanish cardinal and author, b. Logroño.

**A·guir're** (ä·gēr'rā), **Lope de.** 1508?–1561. Spanish adventurer, b. Oñate, Biscay; to America and participated in insurrections in Peru; joined Pedro de Urzúa's expedition in search of El Dorado (1559); gained control of expeditionary party through murder of Urzúa and of his successor, Guzmán (1561); led expedition down Amazon as pirate band; plundered Indian villages and island of Margarita.

**Aguirre Cer'da** (sĕr'thä), **Pedro.** 1879–1941. Chilean statesman; president of Chile (1938–41).

**A'gu·ja'ri** (ä'gōō·yä'rē), **Lucrezia.** 1743–1783. Italian operatic soprano, noted for the extremely high range of her voice; known as **La Ba'star·del'la** (lä bäs'tär·dĕl'lä) because of her illegitimate birth.

**A'gus·tín'** (ä'gōōs·tēn'), **Antonio.** *Lat.* **Antonius Au'gus·ti'nus** (ô'gŭs·tī'nŭs). 1517–1586. Spanish jurist, b. Saragossa; archbishop of Tarragona.

**A'hab** (ā'hăb). *In Douay Version* **A'chab** (ā'kăb). d. ?853 B.C. 7th king of Israel (c. 875–853 B.C.). Son and successor of Omri. During most of reign (*1 Kings* xvi. 29–xxii. 40), kingdom at peace; established friendly relations with foreign states, esp. by marriage with Jezebel, Phoenician princess, daughter of king of Sidon; their daughter Athaliah married Jehoram, King of Judah, thus strengthening alliance with southern kingdom; brought large force to join allies that withstood (854) Shalmaneser of Assyria at Karkar; killed in battle against Benhadad of Damascus. Jezebel's foreign religion (worship of Baal) aroused strong opposition in Israel, esp. from Elijah (*q.v.*). Succeeded by sons Ahaziah and Jehoram.

**A·has'u·e'rus** (ȧ·hăz'ū·ē'rŭs). Name, as used in the Bible, of two unidentified kings of Persia: (1) the great king whose capital was at Shushan, modern Susa (see *Ezra* iv. 6 and *Esther* i–x), sometimes identified with Xerxes the Great, but chronological and other data conflict; (2) the father of Darius the Mede (*Daniel* vi. 1 and ix. 1).

**A'haz** (ā'hăz). *Also Assyrian* **Je·ho'a·haz** (jē·hō'ȧ·hăz). *In Douay Version* **A'chaz** (ā'kăz). d. ?720 B.C. King of Judah (c. 735–c. 720 B.C.). Son of Jotham. Made coruler by father (c. 741); threatened by siege of Jerusalem by kings of Syria and Israel; called upon Tiglath-pileser III of Assyria for aid, contrary to advice of prophet Isaiah; forced to pay tribute to Assyria; in Bible (*2 Kings* xvi; *2 Chron.* xxviii), his idolatry and sacrilege denounced by Isaiah, Hosea, and Micah; succeeded by son Hezekiah.

**A'ha·zi'ah** (ā'hȧ·zī'ȧ). *In Douay Bible* **Och'o·zi'as** (ŏk'ō·zī'ăs). Name of two kings in Biblical history: (1) **Ahaziah.** d. ?851 B.C. King of Israel (c. 853–c. 851 B.C.). Son of Ahab and Jezebel. Helpless before revolt of Moab; succeeded by brother Jehoram (*1 Kings* xxii. 40, 51–53; *2 Kings* i). (2) **Ahaziah.** d. ?844 B.C. King of Judah (?844 B.C.); ruled about one year (*2 Kings* viii. 25–29). Son of Jehoram and Athaliah; slain by Jehu; succeeded by Athaliah (*q.v.*).

**A·he'no·bar'bus** (ȧ·hē'nō·bär'bŭs; ȧ·hĕn'ō-). Name of plebeian Roman family, including notably: **Gnaeus Domitius Ahenobarbus,** tribune (104 B.C.), pontifex maximus (103), consul (96), and censor (92); his son **Lucius Domitius,** consul (54 B.C.), successor to Caesar as governor of Gaul (49), follower of Pompey in civil wars, slain in flight after battle of Pharsala (48); Lucius's son **Gnaeus Domitius,** governor of Bithynia (40 B.C.), consul (32), deserted from Antony to Octavius at Actium (31) and died shortly thereafter—the **E'no·bar'bus** (ē'nō·bär'bŭs; ĕn'ō-) of Shakespeare's *Antony and Cleopatra.* **Gnaeus Domitius,** grandson of Gnaeus Domitius (consul 32); m. Agrippina, dau. of Germanicus Caesar; father of Emperor Nero.

**A·hi'jah** (ȧ·hī'jȧ). *In Douay Version* **A·hi'as** (ȧ·hī'ăs). In Bible, prophet who foretold accession of Jeroboam as king and, later, death of Jeroboam's son (*1 Kings* xi. 29 ff.; xiv. 1 ff.).

**A·hith'o·phel** (ȧ·hĭth'ō·fĕl). *In Vulgate and Douay Version* **A·chit'o·phel** (ȧ·kĭt'ō·fĕl). In Bible (*2 Sam.* xv. 12; xvi. 23; xvii. 1–23), counselor of King David; on failure of his advice to Absalom, killed himself. See ABSALOM.

**Ahl** (äl), **Henry Hammond.** 1869–1953. American muralist and portrait painter, b. Hartford, Conn.

**Ah'le** (ä'lĕ), **Johann Rudolph.** (1625–1673) and his son **Johann Georg** (1651–1706). German organists and composers.

**Ahl′gren** (äl′grān), **Ernst.** *Pseudonym of* **Victoria Maria Be′ne·dicts′son** (bĕ′nĕ·dĭkts′sôn), *nee* **Bru·ze′li·us** (brōō·zā′lĭ·ŭs). 1850–1888. Swedish novelist and short-story writer.

**Ahl′quist** (äl′kvĭst), **August Engelbert.** 1826–1889. Finnish philologist, poet, and traveler in Russia and Siberia.

**Ahl′wardt** (äl′värt), **Theodor Wilhelm.** 1828–1909. German Orientalist and librarian.

**Ahmad.** *Arab.* **Aḥmad.** See also AHMED.

**Ahmad Shah** *or* **Ah′mad Shah Dur·ra′ni** (ä′mȧd shä dŏŏr·rä′nē). 1724–1773. Amir of Afghanistan (1747–73). Hereditary chief of Abdali tribe of Afghans; held command under Nadir Shah. Founded (1747) Afghan kingdom of Kandahar, changing name of his tribe to Durrani; warlike ruler, acquiring great wealth, including Koh-i-noor diamond. Six times invaded Punjab (1748–52); defeated Mogul emperor (1756) and seized Delhi, his action causing great disorder in northern India; lost Punjab to Marathas, but in great battle at Panipat (1761) defeated combined Marathas and Sikhs. Never ruled permanently in India; kept state in two Afghan capitals, Kabul and Kandahar.

**Ah·med′** (ä·mĕt′). *Also* **Ach·med′** *or* **Ach·met′** (äκ·mĕt′). Name of three Ottoman sultans of Turkey:

**Ahmed I.** 1589–1617. Sultan (1603–17). Son of Mohammed III. First part of reign humane and efficient; in peace treaty with Austria (1606), abolished annual tribute paid by her; fought unsuccessful war with Persia (1602–12); in last years gave himself up to pleasure.

**Ahmed II.** 1642–1695. Sultan (1691–95). Son of Ibrahim and brother of Sultan Suleiman II. Confirmed Mustafa Kuprili as grand vizier; soon after accession, his army defeated with great loss at Slankamen (1691) by Louis William I of Baden; Hungary lost to Turks; succeeding disasters hastened death.

**Ahmed III.** 1673–1736. Sultan (1703–30). Son of Mohammed IV and brother and successor of Mustafa II. Afforded refuge to Charles XII of Sweden after his defeat at Poltava (1709); forced by this into war with Russia, terminated by Peace of the Pruth (1711). Took Morea and Ionian Islands from Venetians (1715); invaded Hungary, but army badly defeated (1716) at Peterwardein by Prince Eugene of Savoy; Belgrade occupied (1717); lost considerable territory by Treaty of Passarowitz (1718). In war with Persia (1730), defeated by Nadir Shah. Deposed by revolt of Janizaries and died in prison.

**Ah′med** (ă′măd). *In full* **Si′di Ah′med–esh–She·rif′ es–Se·nu′si** (sē′dĭ ă′măd·ăsh·shă·rēf′ ăs·să·nōō′sĭ). 1872–1933. Chief sheik of the Senusi (1902–18); grandson of al-Senusi, founder of Senusi sect. In World War fought on side of Turkey and Germany; later (after 1921) worked for Pan-Islamism at Ankara; died at Medina.

**Ahmed Arabi.** See ARABI PASHA.

**Ahmed Bey Zogu.** See ZOG I.

**Ah′med el–Be·da·wi′** (ă′măd ȧl·bă·dă·wē′). *Arab.* **Aḥmad al–Badawi.** 1200?–1276. Saint and miracle worker of Egyptian Mohammedans, supposed to have been born in Fez, Morocco. Center of worship of his followers was at Tanta in Nile delta.

**Ahmed Fuad Pasha.** See FUAD I.

**Ahmed ibn–Hanbal.** = IBN-HANBAL.

**Ah′med ibn–Tu·lun′** (ă′măd ĭb″n·tōō·lōōn′). *Arab.* **Aḥmad ibn–Tūlūn.** 835–884 A.D. Founder of Mohammedan dynasty (868–905) of Tulunids in Egypt. Son of Turkish slave from Fergana; made lieutenant to governor; made Egypt independent of Baghdad by building strong army; improved irrigation and erected many public buildings.

**Ahmed Pasha.** See (1) Claude Alexandre de BONNEVAL; (2) DJEZZAR.

**Ah·med′ Ri·za′ Bey** (ä·mĕt′ rē·zä′ bā). 1870?–1930. Turkish statesman; member, Young Turk party; president, Turkish parliament (1908); member, Turkish peace commission (1920).

**Ah·med′ Shah** (ä·măd′ shä) *or* **Ah·med′ Mir·za′** (mēr·zä′). 1898–1930. Shah of Persia (1909–25), last of Kajar line. Son of Mohammed Ali. Succeeded to throne on deposition of his father (1909); ruled under regency (1909–14); crowned shah (1914). Moved to Paris (1923); on refusal to return, was deposed by National Assembly which chose Riza Shah Pahlavi as his successor.

**Ahmed Tewfik Pasha.** See TEWFIK PASHA.

**Ah·med′ Ve·fik′ Pa·sha′** (ä·mĕt′ vĕ·fĭk′ pä·shä′). 1819–1891. Turkish statesman and educationist, b. Constantinople. Educ. at Paris. Spent early years compiling educational books. Entered diplomatic service (1849); ambassador to France (1860–61). Vali at Bursa (1879–82) where he did remarkable work for local improvement.

**Ah′mose** (ä′mōs) *or* **A·ma′sis** (ȧ·mā′sĭs) *or* **A·mo′sis** (ȧ·mō′sĭs). Name of two kings of ancient Egypt:

**Ahmose I** *or* **Amasis I;** *also* **Aaḥ′mes** (ä′mĕs) *or* **Ah′mes** (ä′mĕs). First king of XVIIIth (Diospolite) dynasty; reigned (c. 1580–57 B.C.). Re-established government at Thebes; expelled the Hyksos (see APOPHIS III); recovered Nubia. Father of Amenhotep I.

**Ahmose II** *or, usually,* **Amasis II.** A king of the XXVIth (Saite) dynasty; reigned (c. 569–525 B.C.). Defeated and succeeded Apries (*q.v.*); founded Naucratis as market for the Greeks. Kingdom threatened by supremacy of Cyrus in Babylon.

**Ahn** (än), **Johann Franz.** 1796–1865. German educator; known for his methods of teaching modern languages.

**A′ho** (ȧ′hŏ), **Juhani.** *Real name* **Juhani Bro′feldt** (brōō′fĕlt). 1861–1921. Finnish prose writer; author esp. of satirical, realistic, and historical novels.

**Ah′rens** (ä′rĕns), **Heinrich.** 1808–1874. German jurist and philosophical writer.

**A·hui′zotl** (ä·wē′sō·t'l). d. 1502. King or chief of the Aztecs (1486–1502). Completed great temple at Tenochtitlan; subdued neighboring tribes; built aqueduct from Chapultepec to Lake of Texcoco. Succeeded by Montezuma II.

**Ai′bling·er** (ī′blĭng·ẽr), **Johann Kaspar.** 1779–1867. German composer of church music; cofounder in Venice of Odeon Conservatory of Music.

**Ai′card′** (ā′kȧr′), **François Victor Jean.** 1848–1921. French poet, novelist, and playwright, b. Toulon. Author of *Poèmes de Provence* (1874), *Le Père Lebonnard* (1889), *Maurin des Maures* (1908), etc.

**Ai′dan** (ā′d'n), Saint. d. 651. Irish monk of Iona; set out to evangelize Northumbria (635). First bishop of Lindisfarne; supported by King Oswald; later won favor of King Oswin, last king of Deira.

**Aidan.** d. 606. A West Scottish king (of Dalriada).

**A′ï′dé′** (ȧ′ē′dā′; ī·dā′), **Charles Hamilton.** 1826–1906. Poet and novelist, b. Paris, of Armenian father and English mother. Educ. Bonn. Served seven years in British army. Author of verse, as *Eleanore* (1856), *Songs without Music* (1882), and novels, as *Rita* (1859), *The Marstons* (1868), *Passages in the Life of a Lady* (1887).

**Ai′guil′lon′** (ā′gwē′yôN′), Duc **d′. Emmanuel Armand Vi′gne·rot′ du Ples′sis′ de Ri′che·lieu′** (vēn′yē·rō′ dü plĕ′sē′ dē rē′shē·lyû′). 1720–?1788. French military commander and politician; great-grandnephew of Cardinal Richelieu. Fought in Seven Years' War; minister of foreign affairs under Louis XV (1770–74). See René MAUPEOU. His son **Armand de Vignerot du Plessis de Richelieu,** Duc **d'Aiguillon** (b. 1750), was a deputy of the nobility in the States-General (1789), and (from 1792) an émigré serving in royalist army.

**A·i·ka·wa** (ä·ē·kä·wä), **Yoshisuke.** 1880– . Japanese financier. Studied steel business in U.S., part of the time as laborer in a Pittsburgh mill; organizer and president of Manchuria Industrial Development Corp.

**Ai′ken** (ā′kĕn), **Charles Avery.** 1872–1965. American painter and graphic artist, b. Georgia, Vt. Known for his watercolors of flowers and landscapes.

**Aiken, Conrad Potter.** 1889–1973. American poet, critic, and writer of fiction, b. Savannah, Ga. Grad. Harvard (1911). Author of volumes of verse, as *Earth Triumphant* (1914), *Turns and Movies* (1916), *Priapus and the Pool* (1922), *Selected Poems* (1929; awarded Pulitzer prize), *John Deth* (1930), *Time in the Rock* (1936), *Brownstone Eclogues* (1942), *Collected Poems* (1953, 1970); novels, as *Blue Voyage* (1927), *Great Circle* (1933), *King Coffin* (1935), *Conversation* (1940); *Collected Short Stories* (1950); *Ushant* (autobiography; 1952); *Collected Criticism* (1968).

**Aiken, George L.** 1830–1876. American actor and playwright, b. Boston. Dramatized *Uncle Tom's Cabin* (1852).

**Ai′kens** (ā′kĕnz), **Andrew Jackson.** 1830–1909. American newspaper editor and publisher, b. Barnard, Vt. Organized (1864) a plan for distributing to newspapers a ready-to-print page, including advertising matter, since developed into the Western Newspaper Union.

**Aik′man** (āk′măn), **William.** 1682–1731. Scottish portrait painter.

**Ail′ly′** (à′yē′), **Pierre d′.** 1350–1420. French cardinal, theologian, and advocate of church reform; prominent at Council of Constance (1414–18) which condemned Huss to death. Called "Hammer of Heretics."

**Ailred,** Saint. See Ethelred.

**Ai′mard′** (ĕ′màr′), **Gustave.** *Pseudonym of* **Olivier Gloux** (glōō). 1818–1883. French traveler and writer, b. Paris. Author of novels of adventure, including *The Trappers of Arkansas* (1858), *Arizona Bandits* (1882), etc.

**Ai′mar′** [ĕ′màr′] (*or* **Ad′he′mar′** *or* **Ad′hé′mar′** [à′dā′màr′]) **de Bour′bon′** (dĕ bōōr′bôN′). 9th-century French baron; ancestor of house of Bourbon.

**Aime** (ām; *Fr. also* âm), **Val′cour** (văl′kōōr; *Fr.* vàl′-kōōr′). 1798–1867. American pioneer sugar planter, b. St. Charles Parish, La.; built first sugar refinery in U.S.

**Ai′me·ric′ de Pe′gui′lhan′** (ĕ′mĕ·rēk′ dĕ pā′gē′län′). Provençal troubadour of 13th century, from Toulouse.

**Ai′moin′** (ĕ′mwăN′). 960?–1010. French abbé and chronicler; author of *Histoire des Francs*, etc.

**Ain′ger** (ān′jĕr), **Alfred.** 1837–1904. English clergyman; biographer of Charles Lamb and George Crabbe.

**Ain′mil′ler** (īn′mĭl′ĕr), **Max Emanuel.** 1807–1870. German artist and painter on glass.

**Ains′lie** (ānz′lĭ), **Douglas.** 1865–1948. English poet, literary critic, and philosopher; translator of works of Benedetto Croce.

**Ainslie, Hew.** 1792–1878. Poet, b. in Ayrshire, Scotland; in America (from 1822). Writer of light verse.

**Ainslie,** Sir **Robert.** 1730?–1812. English diplomat and numismatist. Ambassador to Constantinople (1776–92). Collector of ancient eastern and North African coins.

**Ains′worth** (ānz′wûrth; -wĕrth), **Fred Crayton.** 1852–1934. American army officer; adjutant general, U.S. army (1907–12); introduced card-index filing system for keeping records of army personnel.

**Ainsworth, Henry.** 1571–?1623. English separatist clergyman and rabbinical and Oriental scholar. Educ. Cambridge. To Amsterdam (1593) where he joined a group of Brownists. Author of a Brownist confession of faith and coauthor of a defense of Brownism. Noted esp. for his exegetic works on the Old Testament. Cf. Robert Browne (d. 1633).

**Ainsworth, Robert.** 1660–1743. English lexicographer; compiler of a Latin-English dictionary (1736).

**Ainsworth, William Harrison.** 1805–1882. English novelist, b. Manchester. Publisher in London; edited *Bentley's Miscellany*, *Ainsworth's Magazine*, and *New Monthly* (from 1840). Most of his 39 novels are historical, including *Rookwood* (1834), *Jack Sheppard* (1839), *Old St. Paul's* (1841), *Guy Fawkes* (1841), *Windsor Castle* (1843), *The Flitch of Bacon* (1854), and *Boscobel* (1872), several illustrated by Cruikshank.

**Ainsworth, William Newman.** 1872–1942. American Methodist Episcopal bishop, b. Camilla, Ga. Elected bishop (1918); president, Anti-Saloon League of America (from 1935).

**Aird** (ârd), Sir **John.** 1833–1911. British construction engineer, b. London, of Scottish father and English mother. Constructed Aswan and Asyut dams (1898–1902).

**Aird, Thomas.** 1802–1876. Scottish poet; author of *Martzoufle* (1826), *Old Bachelor in the Scottish Village* (1845).

**Air′y** (âr′ĭ), Sir **George Biddell.** 1801–1892. English astronomer. Astronomer royal (1835–81); equipped Royal Observatory at Greenwich with newly designed instruments; adopted more rapid methods of calculation; reduced all lunar and planetary observations made at Greenwich from 1750–1830; conducted expeditions to observe transit of Venus (1874), and reduced data.

**A′i·sha** *or* **A′ye·sha** (ä′ĭ·shă). *Arab.* **′Ā′i·shah** (ä′ĭ·shă). See under Mohammed (the Prophet).

**A′ïs′sé′** (à′ē′sā′). 1694?–1733. A Circassian slave girl, bought in infancy by French ambassador at Constantinople and educated at Paris. Her *Letters* (pub. 1787 with notes by Voltaire) depict social life in Paris at beginning of 18th century.

**Ais′tulf** (īs′tōōlf) *or* **As′tolf** (ăs′tŏlf). d. 756. King of the Lombards (749–756). Besieged and captured Ravenna (750–751); hostile to Rome and the pope; at war with the Franks under Pepin (754); forced to promise return of papal domains, later breaking promise; besieged Rome (756) but defeated by Pepin (*q.v.*).

**Ait′ken** (āt′kĕn), **John.** 1839–1919. British physicist; investigator of atmospheric dust, dew, cyclones, etc.

**Aitken, Robert.** 1734–1802. Printer, b. Dalkeith, Scotland. Opened bookstore in Philadelphia (1771); published first complete English Bible printed in America (1782).

**Aitken, Robert.** 1800–1873. Scottish clergyman, b. Crailing. Withdrew temporarily (1824–40) from Church of England; leader of Aitkenites.

**Aitken, Robert Grant.** 1864–1951. American astronomer, b. Jackson, Calif. Director, Lick Observatory (1930–35); discovered over 3000 double stars.

**Aitken, Robert Ingersoll.** 1878–1949. American sculptor, b. San Francisco. Executed McKinley monument (in Golden Gate Park, San Francisco), George Rogers Clark monument (at U. of Virginia), busts of Thomas Jefferson, Daniel Webster, Benjamin Franklin, Henry Clay (in Hall of Fame), equestrian statue of Gen. O. O. Howard (in Gettysburg National Park), etc.

**Aitken, William Maxwell.** See Beaverbrook.

**Ai′ton** (ā′t′n), **William.** 1731–1793. Scottish botanist. Director of Kew Gardens (1759–93); published catalogue *Hortus Kewensis* (1789), an enlarged edition of which was brought out (1810–13) by his son and successor, **William Townsend** (1766–1849).

**Ai'va·zov'ski** (ī'vŭ·zôf'skĭ; *Russ.* -skû·ĭ), **Ivan Konstantinovich.** 1817–1900. Russian marine painter, b. in Crimea, of Armenian descent.

**A'jal'bert'** (á'zhál'bâr'), **Jean.** 1863–1947. French lawyer, poet, novelist, and writer of books of travel.

**A·ka·hi·to** (ä·kä·hē·tō). fl. 8th century A.D. One of chief poets of golden age of Japanese poetry.

**Ak'bar** (ăk'bär; *in Eng., also* -bär). [Arab. *akbar* very great.] *Properly* **Ja·lal'–ud–Din' Mu·ham'mad** (jȧ·lä'lo͝od·dēn' mo͝o·hăm'măd). *Known as* **Akbar the Great.** 1542–1605. Emperor of Hindustan (1556–1605), third of Mogul dynasty, b. Umarkot, Sind, while his father, Humayun, was in exile. With Bairam Khan, won back empire from Hindus at Panipat (1556); ruled (1556–60) under regency of Bairam Khan; dismissed him (1560). Spent early years of reign in continual warfare; successfully invaded Punjab (1566); subjugated Rajput kingdoms (1561–69); conquered Gujarat (1572–73) and later (1593) annexed it; conquered Bengal (1576) and Kashmir (1586–92); annexed Sind (1592); finally ruled empire comprising all of northern India. Excelled as organizer and administrator of conquered provinces; introduced many reforms, abolished extortion, developed trade, and was most tolerant toward the many religious faiths of India; ably supported by his vizier, Abu-l Fazl. Built Fatehpur Sikri as his capital (1570–85). Led expedition (1598) which finally subdued Deccan (1601). Last years troubled by rebellious conduct of his son Prince Selim (later Jahangir).

**Ak'bar Khan** (ŭk'băr kän). d. 1849. Afghan leader; son of Dost Mohammed. After capture (1839) of his father by British in first Afghan War, gathered Afghan army, attacked British in retreat from Kabul, murdering (1841) British envoy Sir William H. Macnaghten, and (1842) massacred almost entire force of 3000; defeated a few months later by Sir George Pollock.

**A'ked** (ā'kĕd; -kĭd), **Charles Frederic.** 1864–1941. Clergyman, b. Nottingham, England; ordained to Baptist ministry (1886); pastor, Pembroke Chapel, Liverpool (1890–1907). To U.S. (1907); pastor, Fifth Ave. Baptist Church, N.Y. (1907–11), First Congregational Church, San Francisco (1911–15), First Congregational Church of Kansas City (1919–24), All Souls' Church, Los Angeles (from 1925). Author of *The Courage of the Coward* (1905), *The Divine Drama of Job* (1913), etc.

**Ake'ley** (āk'lĭ), **Carl Ethan.** 1864–1926. American taxidermist, sculptor, naturalist, and explorer, b. Clarendon, N.Y. Made exploring trips (1896, 1905) to Africa for specimens for Field Museum and (1909, 1921–22, 1926) American Museum of Natural History; died in Africa. His sculptures include *The Wounded Comrade, The Charging Herd, The Nandi Spearmen;* inventor of the Akeley cement gun and of a naturalist's motion-picture camera. Married (1924) **Mary L. Jobe** (jōb), explorer (notably in northern Canadian Rockies, 1914–18) and author, who accompanied him on his last expedition, assuming charge of it at his death.

**a Kempis, Thomas.** See THOMAS A KEMPIS.

**Aken, Hieronymus van.** See Hieronymus BOSCH.

**A'ken·side** (ā'kĕn·sīd), **Mark.** 1721–1770. English poet and physician. Grad. Leiden U. (1744). Practiced in London; physician to queen (1761). Author of *Pleasures of the Imagination* (1744), *Hymn to the Naiads* (1746), and other verse.

**A'ker·man** (ā'kẽr·măn), **Amos Tappan.** 1821–1880. American lawyer, b. Portsmouth, N.H. Practiced in Georgia; served in Confederate army through Civil War. Attorney general of U.S. (1870–71).

**A'kers** (ā'kẽrz), **Benjamin Paul.** 1825–1861. American sculptor, b. Saccarappa (now part of Westbrook), Me. His works include *Una and the Lion* and *The Dead Pearl Diver.* For his wife **Elizabeth Chase Akers** see Elizabeth Chase ALLEN.

**Akhenaten, Akhenaton, Akhnaton.** Variants of IKHNATON.

**Akh'tal, al–** (ȧl·ăk'tăl). *Arab.* **al–Akhṭal;** *orig.* **Ghiyāth ibn–Ḥārith.** 640?–?710. Christian Arabic poet, b. in Iraq. One of three (see JARIR and al-FARAZDAQ) great contemporary poets of Ommiad period noted for their style and technique; wrote satires and panegyrics; champion esp. of Ommiad cause against theocratic party.

**A·khund' of Swat'** (ä·ko͞ond' ŭv swät'). *Real name* **Abd·ul' Gha·fur'** (ȧb·do͝ol' gȧ·fo͞or'). 1794–1874. Mohammedan saint of Swat valley in mountains of northwestern frontier of India; exerted great influence for many years over Mohammedans of Central Asia; friendly to British.

**A·ki'ba ben Jo'seph** (ȧ·kĭ'vä bĕn jō'zĕf; -zĭf). c. 50–132 A.D. Jewish teacher (rabbi) and martyr in Palestine. Chief teacher of great rabbinical school at Jaffa; introduced new method of interpreting Jewish oral law (Halakah) which developed as foundation of the Mishnah; exerted very great influence on later rabbis. Supported Bar Cocheba in revolt against Hadrian (132); taken prisoner by Romans and suffered martyrdom by being flayed alive. One of the ten martyrs mentioned in Jewish penitential prayer.

**A'kins** (ā'kĭnz), **Zoë.** 1886–1958. American poet and playwright, b. Humansville, Mo.; m. Capt. Hugo Cecil Levinge Rumbold (1932). Author of poetry, as *Interpretations* (1911), *The Hills Grow Smaller* (1937), and plays, as *Déclassée* (1919), *Daddy's Gone a-Hunting* (1921), *A Royal Fandango* (1924), *The Greeks Had a Word For It* (1929), *The Old Maid* (1935), *The Little Miracle* (1936), and a novel, *Forever Young* (1941). Recipient of Pulitzer drama prize (1934–35).

**Ak'ro·po·li'tes** (ăk'rō·pō·lī'tēz), **Ge·or'gi·os** (jē·ôr'jĭ·ōs). *Lat.* **Geor'gi·us Ac'ro·po·li'ta** (jôr'jĭ·ŭs [jē·ôr'-] ăk'rō·pō·lī'tȧ). 1217?–1282. Byzantine historian and diplomat; negotiated pact reuniting Greek and Latin churches (1274); author of a history of Byzantine empire from 1204 to 1261.

**A·ksa'kov** (ŭ·ksȧ'kôf), **Sergei Timofeevich.** 1791–1859. Russian novelist, b. in Ufa government; author of realistic and humorous novels and valuable descriptions of contemporary life. His elder son, **Konstantin Sergeevich** (1817–1860), poet and dramatist, ardent Slavophile, wrote *The Prince Lupuvitski* and *Moscow Delivered in 1812.* Another son, **Ivan Sergeevich** (1823–1886), was a writer and leading Slavophile; in government service (1842–52); editor of Moscow *Sbornik* (1852; later suppressed); in Crimean War (1855–56); established several papers (1861–67) devoted to union of Slavic nations, but all were suppressed; in Russo-Turkish War (1877–78), influential supporter of liberation of Balkan Slavs; edited the *Rus* (1880–85), a Moscow weekly serving interests of Slavophile party.

**Akunian, Ilse.** See FRAPAN-AKUNIAN.

**al–.** For Arabic names beginning *al-*, see the second element.

**A·la'–ad–Din'** (ä·lä'ĕd·dēn') *or* **A·la' ed–Din'.** *Anglicized* **A·lad'din** (ȧ·lăd'ĭn). Name of several early Seljuk princes (13th and 14th centuries), esp.: **Ala–ad–Din** (fl. 1340); son of Othman, founder of Ottoman Empire; aided his brother Sultan Orkhan I in organizing new Ottoman Empire, esp. in formation of Janizaries and standing army.

**Al'a·bas'ter** (ăl'ȧ·băs'tẽr) *or* **Ar·blas'tier** (är·blăs'tyẽr), **William.** 1567–1640. English clergyman and poet in Latin; author of *Roxana*, a tragedy (pub. 1632).

**A'la'coque'** (à'là'kôk'), Saint **Marguerite Marie.** 1647–1690. French nun; founder of devotion to Sacred Heart of Jesus. Canonized (1920) by Benedict XV.

**Aladdin** *or* **Ala ed-Din.** See ALA-AD-DIN.

**Alain.** Pseudonym of Émile Auguste CHARTIER.

**A'lain' de Lille'** (à'lăN' dẽ lēl'). *Lat.* **A·la'nus ab** (*or* **de**) **In'su·lis** (*à*·lā'*nŭs*) ăb [dē] ĭn'sū·lĭs). 1114?–?1203. French philosopher, theologian, and alchemist; called "the Universal Doctor." Author of *De Planctu Naturae*, satire on human vices; the encyclopedic poem *Anticlaudianus*, treatise on morals.

**A'lain'-Four'nier'** (à'lăN'fōōr'nyā'). *Pen name of* **Henri Alain Fournier.** 1886–1914. French novelist; missing after World War I battle of Sept. 22, 1914; author of *Le Grand Meaulnes* (1913).

**Alam,** Shah. See (1) BAHADUR SHAH I; (2) SHAH ALAM.

**A'la·mán'** (ä'lä·män'), **Lucas.** 1792–1853. Mexican historian and statesman, b. Guanajuato. Held offices in administrations of Santa Anna and his followers, esp. as minister of foreign relations; organized government archives and founded National Museum. Opposed democratic form of government; responsible for much of hostile attitude between Mexico and U.S. (1823–53). Author of two valuable works on Mexican history.

**A'la·man'ni** (ä'lä·män'nē) *or* **A'le·man'ni** (ä'lā-), **Luigi.** 1495–1556. Italian poet. Conspired against Giulio de' Medici; fled to Venice, thence to France where he spent most of life, chiefly at court. His works include lyrics, epigrams, blank-verse satires, etc.

**Alamgir.** See AURANGZEB.

**A'la·mi'nos** (ä'lä·mē'nōs), **Antonio** *or* **Antón.** fl. 1499–1520. Spanish navigator; with Columbus (1499, 1502); pilot on Córdoba and Cortes expeditions to Mexico (1517–20); discoverer of Bahama channel (1520).

**Al'an** (ăl'*ăn*), **William.** = William ALLEN (1532–1594).

**Alanbrooke,** Viscount. See Sir Alan Francis BROOKE.

**Alane, Alexander.** See ALESIUS.

**Alanus ab** (*or* **de**) **Insulis.** See ALAIN DE LILLE.

**A'lar·cón'** (ä'lär·kôn'), **Hernando de.** 16th-century Spanish explorer in America, with Coronado; explored Gulf of California and lower Colorado River (1540–41).

**Alarcón, Pedro Antonio de.** 1833–1891. Spanish writer and statesman, b. Guadix; educ. under Jesuits. As radical journalist, published *El Eco de Occidente*, founded *La Redención*, and edited *El Látigo*. Participated as volunteer in Moroccan campaign (1859). Elected deputy; member, council of state (1875–81); minister to Norway and Sweden; member, Royal Spanish Acad. (1875 ff.). Known esp. for short stories and sketches of Spanish rustic life, as *El Sombrero de Tres Picos* (1874) and *El Niño de la Bola* (1880). Other works include *Juicios Literarios y Artísticos* (1873), *Amores y Amoriós* (1875), *Cosas Que Fueron* (1882); the chronicle *Diario de un Testigo de la Guerra de Africa* (1860); novels, as *El Escándalo* (1875), *El Capitán Veneno* (1881), and *La Pródiga* (1882); and *Historia de Mis Libros* (1889).

**A'lar·cón' y Men·do'za** (ē män·dō'sä; -thä), **Juan Ruiz** (rōō·ēs'; -ēth') **de.** 1580?–1639. Spanish dramatist, b. Mexico. A leading representative of the golden age. To Spain (1600–08, 1611 ff.); lawyer at Seville (1606); in service of marqués de Salinas, Madrid (1611 ff.); member, Council of the Indies (1626 ff.). Associated with Tirso de Molina. His plays include *El Semejante de Sí Mismo*, *La Verdad Sospechosa* (imitated by Corneille in *Le Menteur*), *Las Paredes Oyen*, *El Examen de Maridos*, *El Tejedor de Segovia*, and *Ganar Amigos.*

**A'lard'** (à'làr'), **Jean Delphin.** 1815–1888. French violinist and composer; professor at the Conservatoire, Paris (1843–75).

**Al'a·ric** (ăl'*à*·rĭk). 370?–410. Gothic king and conqueror, b. on island at mouth of Danube. Under Emperor Theodosius, commanded Gothic auxiliaries (394); failing to receive high command in Roman army after Theodosius's death (395), left Roman service, was elected king of Visigoths, and invaded Greece (395–396) until checked by Stilicho. Appointed governor in Illyricum by Emperor Arcadius as bribe; built up strong military forces; invaded (400) and ravaged Italy until checked by Stilicho (402 or 403). Bribed by Emperor Honorius with appointment as prefect of western Illyricum; again invaded Italy (408); besieged, captured (Aug. 24, 410), and plundered Rome.

**Alaric II.** d. 507 A.D. King of Visigoths (484–507). Set up commission to make abstract of Roman laws and imperial decrees (generally known as *Breviarum Alaricianum* or *Breviary of Alaric*) to form code for his Roman subjects. Defeated and killed by Clovis in battle near Poitiers; succeeded by his son Amalaric (*q.v.*), who was under protection of Theodoric, King of the Ostrogoths, as regent (507–526).

**A'las** (ä'läs), **Leopoldo.** *Pseudonym* **Cla·rín'** (klä·rēn'). (1852–1901). Spanish novelist, b. Zamora. Professor of law, U. of Oviedo. Known esp. for his analytical novel *La Regenta* (1884–85).

**a Lasco, Johannes.** See Jan ŁASKI.

**A·la'-ud-din'** (*à*·lä'ōōd·dēn'). d. 1315. Second king of Khilji dynasty in India (1295–1315). Led plundering expedition into Malwa; on return murdered his uncle Jalal-ud-din and usurped throne; reign marked by plots and revolts, invasions of Mongols, raids in the Deccan, and wars with Rajputs. Name also borne by two sultans of Bahmani dynasty of the Deccan: **Ala-ud-din I** *or* **Za·far' Khan** [*zà*·făr' kän] (reigned 1347–58) and **Ala-ud-din II** (reigned 1435–57).

**Alaungpaya.** See ALOMPRA.

**Á'la·va** (ä'lä·vä), **Miguel Ricardo de.** 1771–1843. Spanish soldier and statesman, b. Vitoria; participated in Peninsular War under Wellington (1811 ff.); promoted brigadier general; in service of Ferdinand VII (1815); liberal leader (1820) and president (1822) of the Cortes; aided in deposition of Ferdinand (1822); fled to England after restoration of Ferdinand by French (1823); in service of Maria Christina against Don Carlos; ambassador to London (1834), Paris (1835); retired to France after La Granja insurrection.

**Alba,** Duke of. See ALVA.

**Al'ban** (ôl'b*ă*n), Saint. First British martyr. According to Bede, put to death (c. 304) for sheltering Christian cleric who converted him.

**Al·ban'** (*Ger.* äl·bän') *or* **Al·ba'nus** (*Ger.* äl·bä'nōōs; *Eng.* ăl·bā'n*ŭ*s), **Mat·thi'as** [*Ger.* mä·tē'äs; *Eng.* m*ă*·thī'*ă*s] (1621–1712) and his sons **Mi'cha·el** [*Ger.* mĭ'kä·ĕl; *Eng.* mī'k'l] (1677–?1722) and **Jo'seph** [*Ger.* yō'zĕf; *Eng.* jō'zĕf, -zĭf] (1680–1722). Tirolese violinmakers.

**Al·ba'ni** (äl·bä'nē). Name of illustrious family of Rome that left Albania (16th century) to take refuge in Italy from Turkish invasions. Several of its members became distinguished as Roman prelates: (1) **Alessandro** (1692–1779), nephew of Pope Clement XI; cardinal (1721) and collector of art works; built (c. 1760) Villa Albani near Rome, in which was assembled a notable collection of classical sculpture. (2) **Giovanni Francesco** = Pope CLEMENT XI. (3) **Giovanni Girolamo** (1504–1591), legal scholar and cardinal.

**Al·ba'ni** (äl·bä'nē), Madame. *Stage name of* **Em'ma' La'jeu'nesse'** (ĕm'mà' là'zhû'nĕs'). 1852–1930. Canadian operatic and oratorio singer, b. Chambly, Quebec; made London debut in *La Sonnambula* at Covent Garden (1872); m. Ernest Gye, operatic impresario (1878).

**Al·ba′ni** (äl·bä′nē) *or* **Al·ba′no** (äl·bä′nō), **Francesco.** 1578–1660. Italian painter of Eclectic school. Known esp. for his representations of the Holy Family and for his frescoes on mythological subjects.

**Al′ba·ny** (ôl′bȧ·nĭ), Duke of. English title held by members of Stewart family (*q.v.*), including royal Stuarts James I and Charles I and II of England.

**Al′ba·ny** (ôl′bȧ·nĭ), Countess of. **Louise Maximiliana Caroline Stuart.** 1753–1824. Daughter of Gustavus Adolphus, Prince of Stolberg-Gedern; b. Mons, Belgium; m. (1772) the Young Pretender (see Charles Edward STUART, d. 1788); mistress of Alfieri, Italian poet, later of Fabre, a French artist.

**Albategnius** *or* **Albatenius.** See al-BATTANI.

**Al′bee** (ôl′bē; -bē), **Edward F.** 1857–1930. American theater manager, b. Machias, Me. Associated with B. F. Keith in organizing and directing Keith-Albee Vaudeville Circuit (from 1883); president (1914). His grandson, **Edward Franklin** (1928– ), an American playwright, b. Washington, D. C. Author of *Who's Afraid of Virginia Woolf?* (1962), etc.

**Albee, Ernest.** 1865–1927. American philosopher, b. Langdon, N.H.; author of *History of English Utilitarianism* (1902).

**Albee, Fred Houd′lett** (hōōd′lĕt; -lĭt). 1876–1945. American orthopedic surgeon, b. Alna, Me.

**Al′be·marle** (ăl′bē·märl), Duke of. See George MONCK.

**Albemarle,** Earls of. See Arnold Joost van KEPPEL.

**Al·bé′niz** (äl·bā′nēth), **Isaac.** 1860–1909. Spanish pianist and composer of operas, zarzuelas, and many piano pieces, including suites *Iberia* and *Catalonia.*

**Albéniz, Pedro.** 1795–1855. Spanish organist and composer of pianoforte music; teacher at Madrid.

**Al·ber′di** (äl·bĕr′thē), **Juan Bautista.** 1814–?1886. Argentine statesman, jurist, and philosopher, b. Tucumán. Champion of Argentine democracy; author of *Objeto de un Congreso Americano, Bases para la Organización Política de la Confederación Argentina,* etc.

**Al′ber·dingk Thijm′** (äl′bĕr·dĭngk tīm′), **Josephus Albertus.** 1820–1889. Dutch author and art critic; sought to arouse interest in art and literature of Middle Ages; also wrote fiction, poetry, and drama.

**Al′ber·ic I** (ăl′bĕr·ĭk). d. 925. Lombard adventurer; helped expel Saracens from Italy. Said to have ruled Rome despotically and to have been murdered by Romans; m. Marozia, daughter of Theodora. His son **Alberic II** (d. 954) was elected Roman senator.

**Al′be·ro′ni** (äl′bā·rō′nē), **Giulio.** 1664–1752. Cardinal and statesman, b. Parma, Italy. Negotiated marriage of Philip V and Elizabeth Farnese. Prime minister of Spain (1715–19); foreign policy led to war disastrous to Spain; banished from Spain (1719).

**Al′bert** (ăl′bĕrt), Saint. See ETHELBERT (d. 794).

**Albert I** and **V.** Dukes of Austria. See ALBERT I and II, Kings of Germany.

**Albert** the Pious. *Ger.* **Albrecht.** 1559–1621. Archduke of Austria. Son of Emperor Maximilian II. Brought up at Spanish court; educated for the church. Governor of Spanish Netherlands (1595); m. (1599) the Infanta **Isabella,** *Span.* **Isabel Clara Eugenia** (1566–1633), daughter of Philip II of Spain, who had received (1598) the Low Countries from her father. Defeated in attempt to conquer Dutch (Nieuport, 1600); took Ostend after siege (1601–04); made twelve-year truce with Netherlands (1609). At his death Isabella remained nominal ruler of Netherlands (1621–33).

**Albert.** *Full Ger. name* **Albrecht Friedrich Rudolf.** Duke of **Te′schen** (tĕsh′ĕn). 1817–1895. Archduke of Austria; son of Archduke Charles Louis. Austrian army leader and military writer. Served in Italy and Sardinia (1848–49); commanded Austrians in Venetia (1860–63); field marshal (1863); led Austrian army at Custoza (1866); commander in chief, Austrian army (1866); inspector general of the army (1866–95).

**Al′bert I** (ăl′bĕrt; *Fr.* àl′bâr′; *Flem.* äl′bĕrt). *In full* **Albert Lé′o′pold′** (*Fr.* lā′ô′pôl′; *Flem.* lā′ō·pōlt) **Clé′ment′** (klā′mäN′) **Ma′rie′** (mà′rē′) **Mein′rad** (mīn′rät). 1875–1934. King of the Belgians (1909–34). Second son of Philip, Count of Flanders; nephew of Leopold II. Attended military school; member of Belgian Senate (1893–98); interested in developing Belgian commerce, industry, and transport; m. (1900) Elizabeth, a duchess of Bavaria; became heir apparent (1905); visited Belgian Congo (1909); became king (1909). Strengthened army to maintain Belgium's neutrality (1909–13); forced (Aug. 2, 1914) to answer Germany's ultimatum; led Belgian army in historic and disastrous retreat (Aug.–Oct., 1914); preserved Belgian defenses around Ypres throughout World War I (1914–18); led Belgian and French forces in final general Allied offensive through Belgium (Sept.–Nov., 1918). Conducted works of reconstruction (1919–34); brought about stabilization of currency and new monetary system (1926).

**Albert,** Prince. *In full* **Albert Francis Charles Augustus Emmanuel of Saxe-Coburg-Gotha.** 1819–1861. Prince consort of England. Younger son of Ernest I, Duke of Saxe-Coburg-Gotha. Studied at Brussels and Bonn (1836–38); traveled in Italy with his mentor, Baron von Stockmar; cultivated music and painting; m. Queen Victoria of England, his first cousin (1840); at first met public mistrust and prejudice. Active in promotion of science, art, and philanthropy; suggested International Exhibition (1851). Bought Balmoral. Counseled conciliatory attitude in Trent affair (1861).

**Albert,** *Ger.* **Al′brecht** (äl′brĕKt). Name of two kings of Germany:

**Albert I** of Austria. 1250?–1308. King of Germany (1298–1308). Son of Rudolf I. Duke of Austria (1282–1308). Opposed Adolf of Nassau; elected king in his place (1298); recognized by pope (1303); unsuccessful against Thuringia but strengthened Hapsburg rule; befriended peasant class and encouraged towns; murdered by his nephew John the Parricide; his daughter Agnes married (1296) King Andrew III of Hungary.

**Albert II.** 1397–1439. King of Germany (1438–39); first Holy Roman emperor of house of Hapsburg (*q.v.*). Duke of Austria (1404–39) as Albert V; m. daughter of Emperor Sigismund. Short reign marked by wars with Turks and disturbances in Hungary and Bohemia.

**Albert I.** *Ger.* **Albrecht.** *Called* **Albert the Bear.** 1100?–1170. First important margrave of Brandenburg (1150–70), and first of Ascanian dynasty; founder of ruling house of Anhalt. See BRANDENBURG.

**Albert.** *Called* **Al′ci·bi′a·des** (ăl′sĭ·bī′ȧ·dēz; *Ger.* äl′tsē·bē′ä·dĕs). 1522–1557. Margrave of Brandenburg, b. Ansbach. Son of Casimir, Margrave of Brandenburg. Prince of **Kulm′bach-Bay·reuth′** [kōōlm′-bäK·bī·roit′] (1541). Though a Protestant, embraced cause of Charles V at Schmalkalden; later conspired against emperor (1551); instrumental in negotiating Treaty of Chambord (1552) with France; returned to cause of Charles V (1552); defeated twice (1553) in attempt to ratify territorial claims; fled to France (1554).

**Albert III.** *Called* **A·chil′les** (ȧ·kĭl′ēz; *Ger.* ä·KĭI′ĕs) *and* **U·lys′ses** (ū·lĭs′ēz; *Ger.* ōō·lüs′ĕs). 1414–1486. Elector of Brandenburg. Son of Frederick I, Elector of Brandenburg. Succeeded to principality of Ansbach (1440); inherited Bayreuth from his brother John (1464). Elector of Brandenburg (1470–86). Author of *Dispositio Achillea*

(1473), legally establishing the custom of primogeniture.

**Albert II.** *Ger.* **Albrecht.** 1318–1379. Son of Prince Henry II, the Lion. Prince of Mecklenburg (1329–48); first duke (from 1348) of reigning house of Mecklenburg.

**Albert.** *Ger.* **Albrecht.** 1490–1568. 1st Duke of Prussia. Son of Frederick of Ansbach. Grand master (last) of Teutonic Knights (1511–25). Attempted unsuccessfully to regain independence of Prussia from Poland (1519). Succeeded (Treaty of Cracow, 1525) in gaining Prussia as hereditary secular duchy; became disciple of Luther and introduced Reformation in Prussia. Founded (1544) U. of Königsberg, a Protestant university.

**Albert III.** *Ger.* **Albrecht.** *Called* **Albert the Bold.** 1443–1500. Duke of Saxony. Founder of Albertine line (*q.v.*). Son of Frederick the Gentle. Joint ruler of Saxony (1464–85) with his older brother Ernest (*q.v.*); received eastern and western portions, including Meissen, in division of dominions (1485). See also ERNESTINE LINE.

**Albert.** 1828–1902. King of Saxony (1873–1902). Son of King John of Saxony. As crown prince, commanded Saxon army corps, and later, army of the Meuse in Franco-Prussian War; inspector general and field marshal (1871).

**Albert.** *Ger.* **Albrecht.** 1865–1939. Duke of Württemberg, b. Vienna. Son of Philip, Duke of Württemberg. Entered Württemberg military service (1885); inspector general (1913); served through World War; commanded German fourth army on Western Front; field marshal (1916). Heir presumptive to Württemberg throne until 1918.

**Albert I.** Prince of **Monaco.** See MONACO.

**Albert.** *Ger.* **Albrecht Ka'si·mir** (kä'zē·mēr). Duke of **Saxe'–Te'schen** (săks'tĕsh'ĕn). 1738–1822. Second son of Augustus III, King of Poland. Lost battle of Jemappes (1792) and retired to Vienna.

**Albert.** *Ger.* **Albrecht.** 1340?–1412. Duke of Mecklenburg (1384–1412) as Albert III; king of Sweden (1365–89). Nephew of Magnus II of Sweden. Waged civil war with Magnus and Magnus's son Haakon of Norway (1364–71); took Magnus prisoner (1365); became figurehead, deprived of power by Council of Nobles (1371); defeated and taken prisoner (1389) at Falköping by Margaret of Denmark; released, and renounced throne (1395); retired to Mecklenburg.

**Albert** the Blessed. d. 1215. Patriarch of Jerusalem, b. Parma. At request of hermits of Mt. Carmel drew up first definite rule of Order of Carmelites, a rule so rigorous that it was mitigated later by Pope Innocent IV.

**Albert.** *Commonly called* **Albert of Brandenburg.** 1490–1545. Archbishop of Magdeburg (1513); archbishop and elector of Mainz (1514); cardinal (1518). Entrusted with publication of indulgence for the building of the new St. Peter's, Rome, in part of Germany; appointed Tetzel subcommissioner.

**Albert.** Count **von Bollstädt.** See ALBERTUS MAGNUS.

**Al'bert'** (àl'bâr'). *Real name* **Alexandre Mar'tin'** (màr'tăN'). *Known as* **Albert the Workingman.** 1815–1895. French mechanic and politician; involved in revolutions of 1830 and 1848; follower of Louis Blanc. Member of provisional government (1848); first workingman to enter a government in France. Condemned to life imprisonment for his part in revolution of 1848; pardoned by Louis Napoleon (1859).

**Albert, Charles d'** and **Honoré d'.** See duc de LUYNES.

**Albert, Eugen D'.** See D'ALBERT.

**Al'bert** (äl'bĕrt), **Heinrich.** 1604–1651. German composer, poet, and organist; considered creator of present form of German lied.

**Albert, Joseph.** 1825–1886. German photographer. Discovered and introduced an improved photogelatin engraving process (albertype) permitting more than a thousand copies to be made from one plate.

**Al'bert Edward** (ăl'bērt). 1841–1910. Prince of Wales. See EDWARD VII.

**Albert the Great.** See ALBERTUS MAGNUS.

**Al·ber'ti** (äl·bĕr'tē), **Domenico.** 1717?–?1739. Italian musician; composed sonatas in which melody is supported by broken-chord bass accompaniment known now as Alberti bass.

**Al·ber'ti** (äl·bĕr'tē), **Friedrich August von.** 1795–1878. German geologist and mining engineer; gave (1834) name of Trias or Triassic system to lowest major division of Mesozoic era.

**Alberti, Leon Battista.** 1404–1472. Italian architect, painter, organist, and writer. Designed church of Sant'Andrea at Mantua and church of San Francesco at Rimini, façade of Santa Maria Novella at Florence, and Palazzo Strozzi. Credited with being first to investigate scientifically the laws of perspective.

**Al'ber·tine line** (ăl'bēr·tĭn; -tēn). *Also known as* **Wit'ten·berg line** (vĭt'ĕn·bĕrk). Younger line of Wettin family (*q.v.*), established (1485) by division of electoral duchy of Saxony between Ernest and Albert III (*qq.v.*; see also ERNESTINE LINE), sons of Frederick the Gentle. At division received eastern and western portions; gained electoral dignity and much territory (1547) from Ernestine line when it was defeated in war of the League of Schmalkalden; acquired various lands and titles in Germany (1569–1815); retained Saxony, which later (1806) became a kingdom; electors of Saxony also kings of Poland (1697–1763). See especially electors of Saxony: MAURICE, AUGUSTUS, JOHN GEORGE I–IV, AUGUSTUS II and III of Poland, and kings of Saxony: ANTHONY, FREDERICK AUGUSTUS I–III, JOHN, ALBERT, GEORGE.

**Al'ber·ti·nel'li** (äl'bār·tē·nĕl'lē), **Mariotto.** 1474–1515. Italian painter. Collaborated with Fra Bartolommeo on *Last Judgment* and other paintings.

**Al'ber·ti'ni** (äl'bār·tē'nē), **Luigi.** 1871–1941. Italian journalist and politician. Joined staff of *Corriere della Sera* (1896), managing editor (1900–25); advocated Italian entry in World War; senator (from 1914). A delegate to Washington Conference; opponent of Fascism.

**Al·ber'tis** (äl·bĕr'tēs), **Luigi Maria d'.** 1841–1901. Italian explorer in Malay Archipelago and New Guinea (1871–78).

**Al·ber'tus Mag'nus** (ăl·bûr'tŭs măg'nŭs), Saint. *Real name* **Al'bert** (*Ger.* äl'bĕrt), Count **von Boll'städt** (bôl'shtĕt). *Called* **Albert the Great** *and* **Universal Doctor** *or* **Doc'tor U'ni·ver·sa'lis** (dŏk'tēr ū'nĭ·vēr-sā'lĭs; dŏk'tôr). 1193? (or 1206?)–1280. German scholastic philosopher, theologian, scientist, and writer, b. in Swabia. Entered Dominican order (1223); taught in various German schools, at Paris (1245), and at Cologne (1248–54), where Thomas Aquinas was his pupil. Provincial of Dominicans in Germany (1254–59); bishop of Ratisbon (1260–62). Retired and spent rest of life (mostly at Cologne) in scholarly and scientific pursuits, notably in preparing commentaries on Aristotle and an attempt to unite theology and Aristotelianism. His extensive knowledge, esp. of chemistry and physical sciences, gave him reputation of being a magician. Author of *Summa de Creaturis, Summa Theologiae* (incomplete), and many other writings. Beatified (1622); named doctor of the church, and canonized, by Pius XI (1932).

**Al'ber·y** (ăl'bēr·ĭ), **James.** 1838–1889. English playwright, b. London; author of *Two Roses* (1870), *Pink Dominos, Apple Blossoms,* etc.

**Al'bi·no'ni** (äl'bē·nō'nē), **Tommaso.** 1674–1745. Italian violinist and composer of cantatas, sonatas, concertos, and over fifty operas. J. S. Bach used several of his themes for compositions.

**Al·bin'o·va'nus Pe'do** (ăl·bĭn'ō·vā'nŭs pē'dō). Roman poet, of 1st century A.D.; friend of Ovid; author of an epic on exploits of Germanicus Caesar in Germany.

**Al·bi'nus** (ăl·bī'nŭs), **Decimus Clodius Septimius.** d. 197 A.D. Roman general; proclaimed emperor in Gaul on death of Pertinax (193); defeated and beheaded by Severus (197).

**Albinus, Spurius Postumius.** fl. latter half of 4th century B.C. Roman consul (334, 321 B.C.); commander at battle of Caudine Forks.

**Al'boin** (ăl'boin; -bō·ĭn). d. 573. King of the Lombards (c. 565–573). In alliance with the Avars destroyed the Gepidae (c. 566); killed Cunimund, King of the Gepidae, and married his daughter Rosamund. Led Lombards, Saxons, and others into northern Italy, establishing kingdom of Lombardy with capital at Pavia, captured after three-year siege (569–572). Aided Belisarius in his conquest of Italy. According to legend, murdered by his wife.

**Al·bo'ni** (äl·bō'nē), **Marietta.** Contessa **Pe'po·li** (pâ'pō·lē). 1823–1894. Italian operatic contralto.

**Al'bor·noz'** (äl'bôr·nôth'), **Gil Álvarez Carillo de.** 1310–1367. Spanish prelate and soldier, b. Cuenca; archbishop of Toledo (1337 ff.); participated in campaigns against Moors; to court of Pope Clement VI at Avignon; created cardinal. Legate to Rome in service of Innocent VI, secured restoration of papal authority in Papal States (1353–62); legate to Bologna in service of Urban V (1367).

**Al'brecht** (äl'brĕKt). German form of ALBERT.

**Al'brechts·ber'ger** (äl'brĕKts·bĕr'gẽr), **Johann Georg.** 1736–1809. Austrian contrapuntist, theorist, composer, and teacher of music; author of *Gründliche Anweisung zur Komposition* (1790).

**Albrecht von Eyb.** See EYB.

**Al'bret'** (ál'brĕ'). Name of a Gascon family holding a lordship in the Landes from the 11th century and including: **Charles d'Albret,** constable of France in command at Agincourt (1415); killed in the battle. **Jean d'Albret** (d. 1516), king of Navarre by his marriage (1484) with Catherine de Foix. Their son **Henri d'Albret,** King of Navarre (see HENRY II of Navarre); made a duke of France (1550); m. Margaret, sister of Francis I of France. **Charlotte d'Albret,** sister of Jean; m. (1499) Cesare Borgia. **Jeanne d'Albret** (1528–1572), Queen of Navarre (1562–72), daughter of Henri, m. (1548) Anthony of Bourbon; their son was Henry IV, King of France. See (1) BOURBON; (2) LA TOUR D'AUVERGNE.

**Al'bright** (ôl'brīt), **Jacob.** 1759–1808. American preacher, b. near Pottstown, Pa. Converted to Methodism (1790). Organized classes (1800) among his converts. Annual conference (1807) adopted name "The Newly Formed Methodist Conference," and elected Albright a bishop. Methodists refused to recognize the movement, later known as the *Evangelical Association* and more recently as the *Evangelical Church.*

**Albright, Malvin Marr.** 1897– . American sculptor, b. Chicago.

**Al·briz'zi** (äl·brēt'tsē), Contessa **d'. Isabella Te'o·to'chi** (tā'ō·tô'kē). 1770?–1836. Italian writer whose home in Venice was a rendezvous for Byron, Alfieri, and other celebrities. Author of essays on distinguished contemporaries, a biography of Vittoria Colonna (1836), etc.

**Albucasis.** See ABUL KASIM.

**Al'bu·maz'ar** (ăl'bŭ·măz'ẽr) *or* **Al'bu·mas'ar** (-măs'ẽr). *Also* **a·bu'–Ma'shar** (ȧ·bōō'mă'shăr). *Arab.* **abu-Ma'shar Ja'far ibn-Muḥammad.** 805–886. Arab astrologer and astronomer, b. in Balkh. Lived at Baghdad; author of about 50 works, the most important translated into Latin: *Flores Astrologici* (1488), *De Magnis Conjunctionibus* (1489), *Introductorium in Astronomiam* (1506); in spite of certain fantastic ideas on astral influences, contributed considerably to astronomical knowledge, esp. on laws of tides. Used as title character (a charlatan) of a play (1614) by Thomas Tomkis, later revived by Dryden and Garrick.

**Albuquerque,** Duques **de.** See Francisco FERNÁNDEZ DE LA CUEVA.

**Al'bu·quer'que** (äl'bōō·kĕr'kĕ; *Angl.* ăl'bŭ·kûr'kē), **Affonso de.** *Old Port.* **Affonso d'Al'bo·quer'que** (däl'bōō-). *Called* **Affonso o Gran'de** (ōō grăNn'dĕ), *i.e.* the Great. 1453–1515. Viceroy of Portuguese Indies and founder of Portuguese empire in the East, sometimes called "the Portuguese Mars," b. Alhandra, near Lisbon. Spent youth at court of Alfonso V; took part in expedition against Turks and in battle of Otranto (1481); chief equerry to King John II (1489). Made first journey in Indian fleet to the East (1503–04); viceroy of Portuguese lands in Asia (1506); made prisoner at Cannanore by Almeida (1508–09) but released; captured Goa (1510) and made it chief Portuguese city in the East; gradually (1510–15) secured control of Malabar coast, Ceylon, Sunda Isles, Malacca, and Ormuz; replaced and ordered home by King Emanuel (1515). Died at sea near Goa; life written (pub. 1557) by his natural son **Braz** *or* **Bla'si·us** (blā'zĭ·ŭs; -zhĭ·ŭs), *later* **Affonso, Albuquerque** (1500–1580).

**Albuquerque, Joaquim Mou·si'nho de** (mō·zē'nyōō thē). 1855–1902. Portuguese colonial officer. Secretary general of Portuguese India; governor of Lourenço Marques; commanded in war in Mozambique (1895–96), subduing rebellion.

**Albuquerque, Mathias d'.** d. 1646? Portuguese general, b. prob. in Brazil. Governor of Pernambuco (1624, 1629). Served Portugal against Spain (1640–44); won battle of Montijo, or Campo Mayor (May, 1644); created count of Allegrete and grandee of Portugal.

**Al·cae'us** (ăl·sē'ŭs). fl. about 600 B.C. Greek lyric poet, b. Mytilene. Exiled because of political enemies. Wrote in the Aeolic dialect hymns, drinking and love songs, and political odes against tyrants; invented the Alcaic meter.

**Alcalá Zamora y Torres, Niceto.** See ZAMORA Y TORRES.

**Al·cam'e·nes** (ăl·kăm'ē·nēz). fl. ?440 B.C. Greek sculptor of Lemnos and Athens.

**Alcántara, Saint Peter of.** See PETER OF ALCÁNTARA.

**Al·cá'zar** (äl·kä'thär), **Baltasar de.** 1530–1606. Spanish poet and epigrammatist.

**Alcester,** Baron. See *Frederick Beauchamp Paget Seymour,* under SEYMOUR family, ¶3.

**Al·cia'ti** (äl·chä'tē), **Andrea.** 1492–1550. Italian jurist; among first to make historical study of Roman law; author of legal works and a book of emblems, or moral lessons, in Latin verse (1522).

**Al'ci·bi'a·des** (ăl'sĭ·bī'ȧ·dēz). c. 450–404 B.C. Athenian general and politician; friend of Socrates. Educ. in house of Pericles, his uncle. In Peloponnesian War (431–404) persuaded Athenians to join alliance against Spartans; a leader in unsuccessful expedition against Syracuse (415). Accused of mutilating statues of Hermes; escaped to Sparta and there induced revolt of Ionians against Athens; lost confidence of Spartans. Regained confidence of Athenians (411–409) by helping defeat Spartan fleet and recover Cyzicus, Chalcedon, and Byzantium; returned to Athens (407); appointed general but dismissed after defeat at Notium (407); fled to Phrygia, where he was murdered.

**Al·cid'a·mas** (ăl·sĭd'ȧ·măs). fl. 4th century B.C. Greek rhetorician and sophist, b. Elaea, Asia Minor; pupil of Gorgias; instructor at Athens.

**Al'ci·phron** (ăl'sĭ·frŏn). fl. 2d or 3d century A.D. Greek rhetorician; author of fictitious letters in pure Attic dialect professedly written by common people in Athens, constituting character sketches and giving details of domestic life, manners, etc.

**Alc·mae'on** (ălk·mē'ŏn). fl. 6th century B.C. Greek physician and Pythagorean philosopher; said to be first to make anatomical dissections.

**Alc'mae·on'i·dae** (ălk'mē·ŏn'ĭ·dē). A powerful Athenian family, to which Alcibiades (*q.v.*) and Pericles (*q.v.*) belonged, leaders in politics of 6th and 5th centuries B.C.

**Alc'man** (ălk'măn). fl. 7th century B.C. Founder of Doric lyric poetry, b. a slave in Lydia but freed at Sparta. Composed choral songs, hymns, paeans, etc.

**Al'cock** (ôl'kŏk), **John.** 1430–1500. English prelate. Bishop of Rochester, Worcester, and Ely; twice lord chancellor; founded Jesus College, Cambridge (1496).

**Alcock,** Sir **John William.** 1892–1919. English aviator, b. in Manchester. Served as captain in World War I; bombed Constantinople; captured by Turks (1917). Pilot of plane, with Arthur Whitten Brown as navigator, which made first nonstop transatlantic flight, Newfoundland to Ireland, 1960 miles in 16 hrs., 12 mins. (June 14, 1919). Knighted (1919).

**Alcock,** Sir **Rutherford.** 1809–1897. English diplomat. Practiced medicine (to 1844). Consul at Fuchow, China (1844); first consul general in Japan (1858–65); minister at Peking (1865–71). Author of *The Capital of the Tycoon* (2 vols., 1863), *Art and Art Industries in Japan* (1878).

**Al'co·fo·ra'do** (äl'kōō·fōō·rä'thōō), **Marianna.** 1640–1723. Portuguese Franciscan nun; author of five letters (pub. anonymously at Paris, 1669) to her deserting lover, Noël Bouton, afterwards Comte de Chamilly.

**Alcofribas Nasier.** Anagrammatic pseudonym of François RABELAIS.

**Al'cott** (ôl'kŭt), **Amos Bronson.** 1799–1888. American transcendentalist, teacher, and writer, b. near Wolcott, Conn. Itinerant peddler in Virginia and Carolinas (1818–23). Teacher in small towns of Connecticut (1823–27), Boston (1828–30), Germantown, Pa. (1831–33). Opened school in Boston (1834) which failed (1837–39). Established co-operative community, Fruitlands, near Harvard, Mass. (1844); abandoned (1845). Absorbed in transcendental philosophy, lectured at intervals (1853–59). Appointed superintendent of schools, Concord, Mass. (1859). Family poverty relieved by success of his daughter Louisa's *Little Women* (1868). Started Concord Summer School of Philosophy and Literature (1879) which continued until his death (1888). Author of *Observations on the Principles and Methods of Infant Instruction* (1830), *The Doctrine and Discipline of Human Culture* (1836), *Ralph Waldo Emerson* (1865).

**Alcott, Louisa May.** 1832–1888. Daughter of Amos Bronson Alcott. American author, b. Germantown, Pa. Nurse in Union hospital at Georgetown during Civil War. Her letters of this period, revised, were published (1863) under title *Hospital Sketches.* Editor, *Merry's Museum,* a magazine for children (1867). Achieved great success with first volume of *Little Women* (1868), followed by second volume (1869). Other works include *An Old Fashioned Girl* (1870), *Little Men* (1871), *Aunt Jo's Scrap-Bag* (6 vols., 1872–82), *Jo's Boys* (1886).

**Al'cuin** (ăl'kwĭn) *or* **Al·bi'nus** (ăl·bī'nŭs). *Anglo-Saxon name* **Ealh'wi'ne** (ă'ălκ·wĭ'nĕ). *Adopted surname* **Flac'cus** (flăk'ŭs). 735–804. English scholar. Aided Charlemagne in revival of learning at court of Franks (781). Upheld orthodoxy against adoptionist heresy at council held at Frankfort (794). Abbot of Tours (796). Author of manuals of instruction in grammar, rhetoric, and dialectics; theological, Biblical, and hagiological works; metrical annals.

**Al'da** (äl'dä), **Frances.** *Original name* **Frances Davis.** 1883–1952. Operatic soprano, b. Christchurch, New Zealand. Studied under Marchesi in Paris; made debut at Opéra Comique (1904), at N.Y. as Gilda (1908); m. (1910; divorced 1928) Giulio Gatti-Casazza, director of Metropolitan Opera House. Author of *Men, Women, and Tenors* (1937).

**Al·da'ma** (äl·dä'mä), **Juan.** d. 1811. Mexican army officer and patriot. Took part in uprising of 1810–11; supported Hidalgo y Costilla; betrayed and shot. Cf. Ignacio José ALLENDE.

**Al·da'nov** (ŭl·dá'nôf), **M. A.** *Pseudonym of* **Mark Aleksandrovich Lan·dau'** (lŭn·dou'). *Also known as* **Landau-Aldanov.** 1886–1957. Russian publicist and novelist, b. Kiev. Author of *The Thinker,* trilogy on French Revolution, *The Fifth Seal* (trans. 1943), etc.

**Al'de·gre'ver** (äl'dĕ·grā'vẽr), **Heinrich.** *Real surname* **Trip'pen·me'ker** (trĭp'ĕn·mā'kẽr). 1502–?1560. German painter, engraver, and goldsmith, of Soest in Westphalia; one of the Little Masters. Works include two series of *The Wedding Dancers,* also historical, allegorical, and Biblical subjects, ornaments, portraits, etc.

**Al'den** (ôl'dĕn), **John.** 1599?–1687. One of pilgrims on *Mayflower,* landing at Plymouth, Mass. (1620). A signer of Mayflower Compact; moved to Duxbury. Deputy from Duxbury (1641–49); treasurer of Duxbury (1656–58). Governor's assistant (1633–41, 1650–86). Deputy governor (1664–65, 1677). See Myles STANDISH.

**Al'den·ham** (ôl'dĕn·ăm; ôld'năm), 1st Baron. **Henry Hucks Gibbs.** 1819–1907. English banker and scholar. Director, Bank of England (1853–1901); governor (1875–77). Aided in preparation of *Oxford English Dictionary;* edited texts for Early English Text Society.

**Al'der** (äl'dẽr), **Kurt.** 1902–1958. German chemist, shared Nobel prize in chemistry (1950) with Otto DIELS.

**Al'der·man** (ôl'dẽr·măn), **Edwin Anderson.** 1861–1931. American educator, b. Wilmington, N.C. Grad. North Carolina (1882). Professor of education (1893–96), president (1896–1900), North Carolina; president, Tulane (1900–04); president, U. of Virginia (from 1904).

**Al'der·son** (ôl'dẽr·s'n), Sir **Edwin Alfred Hervey.** 1859–1927. English soldier. Lieutenant general (1914); first commander of Canadian corps in France (1915–16); inspector general of Canadian forces (1916–18).

**Ald'helm** (ăld'hĕlm). 640?–709. English scholar. Abbot of Malmesbury (c. 673); bishop of Sherborne (705); built churches and monasteries. Wrote Latin verse, a treatise on Latin prosody, including his famous 101 riddles, as well as songs in English.

**Aldighero da Zevio.** See ALTICHIERO DA ZEVIO.

**Al'din** (ôl'dĭn), **Cecil Charles Windsor.** 1870–1935. English artist. Illustrated Kipling's *Jungle Book* (1894–95), Dickens's *Pickwick Papers* (1910). Author of *The Romance of the Road* (1928), *Ratcatcher to Scarlet* (1926), *Dogs of Character* (1927), etc.

**Al'ding·ton** (ôl'dĭng·tŭn), **Richard.** 1892–1962. English poet and novelist. Educ. Dover College and London U.; m. (1913) "H.D.," American imagist poet (see Hilda DOOLITTLE), 2d Netta McCulloch (1937). Served in World War I (1916–18); traveled Europe, North Africa, B.W.I. (1928–39); resident of U.S. (from 1939). Author of translations from Greek, French, and medieval Latin; a life of Voltaire (1926); verse (collected editions 1929, 1931, 1934, 1940) including *Images* (1915), *Images of*

*War* (1919), *Images of Desire* (1919), *A Fool i' the Forest* (first long poem; 1925), *A Dream in the Luxembourg* (1930), *Life Quest* (1935), *The Crystal World* (1938); novels, as *Death of a Hero* (1929), *All Men Are Enemies* (1933), *Very Heaven* (1937), *Rejected Guest* (1939); short stories, and the autobiographical *Life for Life's Sake* (1941).

**Al·di'ni** (äl·dē'nē), **Giovanni.** 1762–1834. Italian physicist; nephew of Luigi Galvani. Professor, U. of Bologna; founder, National Institute of Italy.

**Al'dis** (ôl'dĭs), **Mary,** *nee* **Reynolds.** 1872–1949. American water-color artist and writer; **m.** Arthur Taylor Aldis (1892). Author of *Plays for Small Stages* (1915), *The Princess Jack* (1915), *Drift* (1918), *No Curtain* (1935), etc.

**Al'do·bran·di'ni** (äl'dô·brän·dē'nē). Noble family of Florence (from 12th century) including: **Silvestro Aldobrandini** (1499–1558); teacher of law at Pisa; led revolt against Medici; banished (1530) because of resistance to imperial army of Charles V; became advocate of Pope Paul III. His son **Ippolito** (1536–1605) became Pope Clement VIII. Ippolito's nephew **Pietro** (1571–1621); cardinal; archbishop of Ravenna under Pope Paul V.

**Al'dred** (ăl'drĕd; -drĭd) *or* **Eal'dred** (ă'ăl·drĕd) *or* **Al'red** (ăl'rĕd; -rĭd). d. 1069. English ecclesiastic; bishop of Worcester (1044); archbishop of York (1060). Crowned William I (1066), Matilda (1068).

**Al'drich** (ôl'drĭch), **Bess,** *nee* **Stree'ter** (strē'tēr). 1881–1954. American writer, b. Cedar Falls, Iowa; m. (1907) Charles S. Aldrich (d. 1925). Author of short stories and novels, including *A White Bird Flying* (1931), *Spring Came on Forever* (1935), *Song of Years* (1939), etc.

**Al'drich** (ôl'drĭch; *Brit. usu.* -drĭj), **Henry.** 1647–1710. English scholar; dean, Christ Church, Oxford (1689 till death). Designed Peckwater quadrangle of Christ Church. Adapted anthems and church music; wrote humorous verse; author of *Artis Logicae Compendium* (1691), long used as a textbook.

**Aldrich, Nelson Wilmarth.** 1841–1915. American financier and statesman, b. Foster, R.I. Member, U.S. House of Representatives (1878–81), U.S. Senate (1881–1911). Leading Republican; identified esp. with tariff and currency legislation. Name attached to Aldrich-Vreeland Currency Act (1908) and Payne-Aldrich Tariff Act (1909).

**Aldrich, Richard.** 1863–1937. American music critic, b. Providence, R.I. Educ. Harvard and in Germany. Music critic, New York *Times* (1902–24); editor of a series of biographies of musicians; author of *A Guide to Parsifal* (1904), *A Guide to the Nibelungen Ring* (1905), etc.

**Aldrich, Thomas Bailey.** 1836–1907. American author and editor, b. Portsmouth, N.H. Editor, *Every Saturday*, Boston (1865–74), *Atlantic Monthly* (1881–90). Author of stories, as *The Story of a Bad Boy* (1870), *Marjorie Daw* (1873), and of several volumes of poems.

**Aldrich, Thomas Bell.** 1861–1938. American chemist, b. Port Jefferson, N.Y. Studied at Albany Normal School (1879–82); Ph.D., Jena (1892). Known for work on adrenaline, esp. determination of the structural formula and molecular weight of the hormone, after its isolation by Jokichi Takamine (*q.v.*).

**Al'drich–Blake'** (-blāk'), Dame **Louisa Brandreth,** *nee* **Aldrich.** 1865–1925. English surgeon, b. in Essex. Grad. London U. (1892; M.D., 1894); master in surgery, first woman to be so qualified (1895). Dean, London School of Medicine for Women (1914).

**Al'dridge** (ôl'drĭj), **Ira Frederick.** *Called* **the African Ros'ci·us** (rŏsh'ĭ·ŭs). 1805?–1867. American Negro actor. Personal attendant to Edmund Kean and encouraged by him to study for stage. Successful in England and Germany. Leading roles include Othello, Lear, Macbeth.

**Al'dring·en** (äl'drĭng·ĕn) *or* **Al'dring·er** (-ēr) *or* **Al'tring·er** (äl'trĭng·ēr), Count **Johann.** 1588–1634. General in imperial German army during Thirty Years' War. Supported Wallenstein (1625); succeeded Tilly as commander of Catholic League army (1632); as field marshal conducted successful campaign in Bavaria and Swabia against Swedes.

**Al'dro·van'di** (äl'drô·vän'dē), **Ulisse.** *Lat.* **Ulysses Al'dro·van'dus** (ăl'drô·văn'dŭs). 1522–1605. Italian naturalist; director of botanical garden established (1586) at his instigation by senate of Bologna; author of *Natural History*, noteworthy for its illustrations.

**Aldus Manutius.** See MANUTIUS.

**A'le·an'dro** (ä'lā·än'drô), **Girolamo.** *Lat.* **Hieronymus Al'e·an'der** (ăl'ē·ăn'dēr). 1480–1542. Italian scholar and cardinal. Rector of U. of Paris. Papal representative on missions to Germany, Netherlands, and France; opposed Luther at Diet of Worms. Compiler of Greek-Latin lexicon (1512); author of letters and reports concerning his various missions against Luther.

**A'le·ar'di** (ä'lā·är'dē), **Aleardo.** *Orig. surname* **Gaetano.** 1812–1878. Italian poet and patriot. Took part in insurrection (1848) against Austrian control of Lombardy; imprisoned (1852, 1859). To Verona after expulsion of Austrians from Lombardy; became senator. Author of ode on maritime cities of Italy (1856) and other poems, as *Canti* (1864).

**A'lec·san'dri** *or* **A'lex·an'dri** (ä'lĕk·sän'drē), **Vasile.** 1821–1890. Rumanian lyric poet. Active in revolutionary movement (1848); fled to Paris. Rumanian minister for foreign affairs (1859–60); minister to France (1885). Published Rumanian popular songs (1844, 1852, 1853); author of lyrics and dramas, as *Despot Voda* (1880), *Ovidiu* (1885).

**A'le·grí'a** (ä'lā·grē'ä), **Ciro.** 1909–1967. Peruvian novelist; exiled for political activity, settled (1934) in Chile; author of *The Golden Serpent* (1935), *The Starving Dogs*, and *Broad and Alien Is the World* (1941).

**Aleichem, Shalom** *or* **Sholem.** See Solomon RABINOWITZ.

**A'leix·an'dre** (ȧ'lĕk·sȧn'drĕ), **Vincente.** 1898– Spanish poet. Wrote *Espadas como labios* (1932), *Historia del corazón* (1954), etc.; awarded Nobel prize for literature (1977).

**A·le'khine** *or* **A·lje'chin** (ŭ·lyā'kyĭn), **Alexander.** *Russ. name* **Aleksandr Aleksandrovich A·le'khin.** 1892–1946. Chess master, b. Moscow, Russia. Won world championship from Capablanca (1927); defended it successfully (1928, 1934); lost it (1935), regaining it (1937). Author of books on chess.

**A·le·kse'ev** *or* **A·le·xe'iev** (ŭ·lyĭ·ksyā'yĕf), **Evgeni Ivanovich.** 1845–?1917. Russian admiral. Commanded Russian squadron in Far East during Chinese-Japanese War (1894–95); chief of Russian fleet in Far East at opening of Russo-Japanese War (1904); dismissed from service (1905) because of defeats.

**Alekseev** *or* **Alexeiev, Mikhail Vasilievich.** 1857–1918. Russian general. Served in army (1876–90); took part in Russo-Japanese War (1904–05); general (1904). Chief of staff at outbreak of World War (1914); won victory in Galicia campaign; commander on Northwestern Front (1915); chief of imperial general staff (1915–16). Fought with Denikin against Bolshevik rule (1917–18).

**A·le·ksei'** *or* **A·le·xei'** (ŭ·lyĭ·ksyā'ĭ). = ALEXIS.

**A·lem'** (ä·lān'), **Leandro.** 1842?–1896. Argentine politician, b. Buenos Aires. Organizer (1887) and leader of radical party Unión Cívica, later (1891 ff.) called Unión Cívica Radical; banished (1893).

**A'le·mán'** (ä'lā·män'), **Mateo.** 1547?–?1610. Spanish novelist. Grad. Seville U. (1564). His picaresque novel *Guzmán de Alfarache* (1599; part II, 1604) ran through about sixteen editions in five years and was translated into French (1600), English (1623), and Latin (1623). Said to have become printer in Mexico City (c. 1609).

**Alemanni, Luigi.** See ALAMANNI.

**Alemán Val·dés'** (väl·dās'), **Miguel.** 1902– . Mexican lawyer, b. Sayula, Veracruz. LL.B., U. of Mexico (1928); justice of superior court of appeals (1930); senator; governor of Veracruz (1936–40); minister of government (1940–45); president of Mexico (1946–52).

**A'lem'bert'** (á'läN'bâr'), **Jean Le Rond'** (lẽ rôN') **d'.** 1717?–1783. French mathematician and philosopher, b. Paris. Son of Mme. de Tencin (*q.v.*); associate of Diderot in editing the *Encyclopédie.*

**A'len'çon'** (á'läN'sôN'). A French ducal house several times established. The third house (from c. 1285) included: **Charles de Valois, Duc d'Alençon,** brother of Philip VI of France, killed at Crécy (1346); and **Charles IV, Duc d'Alençon** (1489–1525), husband (1509) of Margaret of Navarre; constable of France, whose cowardice caused loss of battle of Pavia (1525) and capture of Francis I. House re-established (1566–74) for **François, Duc d'Alençon** (1554–1584), later Duc **d'An'jou'** [däN'zho͞o'] (1574–84), son of Henry II and Catherine de Médicis, a suitor of Queen Elizabeth of England.

**A'ler** (ä'lẽr), **Paul.** 1656–1727. German Jesuit and educator, b. in Luxemburg; author of *Gradus ad Parnassum* (1702), dictionary of prosody once used in English schools as aid in Latin versification.

**A·le'si·us** (*à*·lē'zhĭ·*ŭ*s; -shĭ·*ŭ*s; *Ger.* ä·lā'zē·o͞os), *properly* **A'less** (ä'lĕs), **Alexander.** *Also called* **Alexander Al'ane** (ăl'*ă*n). 1500–1565. Scottish Lutheran theologian; educ. Edinburgh; imprisoned; fled to Germany (1532). Professor of theology, Frankfort on the Oder; dean (1543), twice rector, U. of Leipzig.

**A'les·san'dri Pal'ma** (ä'lā·sän'drē päl'mä), **Arturo.** 1868–1950. Chilean lawyer and statesman, b. near Linares, of Italian lineage. A leader of the Liberal group; minister of finance (1913–18), and of the interior (1918–20); president of Chile (1920–25); attempted many social and political reforms, but forced out by the depression and an army revolt (1924); recalled from Europe (1925) but soon again expelled; again president (1932–38). His son **Jorge Alessandri Ro·drí'guez** (rō-thrē'gās) (1895–1970), lawyer and university professor. President of Chile (1958–64).

**A·les'si** (ä·lĕs'sē), **Galeazzo.** 1512–1572. Italian architect; friend and imitator of Michelangelo.

**Al'ex·an'der** (ăl'ĕg·zăn'dẽr; ăl'ĭg-; *Brit. also* -zän'-). Name of eight popes (see *Table of Popes,* Nos. 6, 156, 170, 181, 206, 216, 239, 243), especially:

**Alexander III.** *Real name* **Orlando Ban'di·nel'li** (bän'dē·nĕl'lē). d. 1181. Pope (1159–81); b. Siena, Italy. Had long contest (1159–76) with Emperor Frederick I Barbarossa; excommunicated Frederick; opposed by three antipopes (elected 1159, 1164, 1168); forced to seek refuge in France (1162–65); victorious over Frederick at battle of Legnano (1176); also successful in contest with Henry II of England, finally winning recognition of papal supremacy and canonization of Thomas à Becket.

**Alexander IV.** *Real name* **Rinaldo Con'ti** (kōn'tē), of house of **Se'gni** (sā'nyē). d. 1261. Pope (1254–61); b. Anagni, Italy. Nephew of Gregory IX. Almost continuously in conflict with Hohenstaufens, esp. with Manfred of Sicily; driven from Rome, spent last years at Viterbo; established Inquisition in France; founded order of Augustinian hermits (1256).

**Alexander V.** *Real name in Gr.* **Petros Phi'lar·gos** (fē'lär·gôs). *Ital.* **Pietro di Can'di·a** (dē kän'dyä). 1340?–1410. Pope (1409–10). Created cardinal (1405); elected pope by Council of Pisa in attempt to heal Western Schism; never reached Rome to occupy papal throne.

**Alexander VI.** *Real name* **Ro·dri'go** (rō·thrē'gō) **Lan·zol' y Bor'ja** (län·thôl' ē bôr'hä). See BORGIA. 1431?–1503. Pope (1492–1503); b. near Valencia, Spain. Nephew of Pope Calixtus III. Made cardinal bishop (1476); had many mistresses, esp. Vannozza (Giovanna) dei Cattanei (1470–92), who bore him several children (see Cesare BORGIA and Lucrezia BORGIA), and Giulia Farnese; elected to papacy through bribery; formed league against Naples (1493); issued bull (May 4, 1493) dividing New World between Spain and Portugal; unsuccessfully opposed Charles VIII of France in his invasion of Naples (1494); joined (1495) Holy League with the emperor, Milan, Venice, and Spain to expel Charles; ordered execution of Savonarola (1498); aided in downfall of the Sforza (1500); destroyed power of houses of Orsini and Colonna; instituted censorship of books (1501). Directed all his efforts to increase temporal power of pope and to family aggrandizement; patronized great artists, esp. Bramante, Raphael, Michelangelo.

**Alexander VII.** *Real name* **Fabio Chi'gi** (kē'jē). 1599–1667. Pope (1655–67); b. Siena. Created cardinal (1652); lost Avignon (1662) in conflict with Louis XIV; issued bull against Jansenists; a patron of literature and architecture; built colonnade in piazza of St. Peter's.

**Alexander I.** Prince **Alexander Joseph of Bat'ten·berg** (băt''n·bûrg; *Ger.* bät'ĕn·bĕrk). 1857–1893. First prince of Bulgaria (1879–86). Second son of Prince Alexander of Hesse-Darmstadt and his morganatic wife, Countess von Haucke (see BATTENBERG); nephew of Czar Alexander II of Russia. Served in Hessian army and (1877–78) in Russian army in Russo-Turkish War. Elected (1879) prince of new autonomous principality, Bulgaria; under influence of Russia (1879–83) but restored (1883) constitution of 1879 and encouraged development of political parties. After successful revolution (1885) in Eastern Rumelia, became governor of district; led army in war with Serbia (1885), winning several battles. Overthrown (1886) by conspiracy fomented by Russians; kidnaped, but restored; abdicated; granted title of Count **von Har'te·nau** (här'tĕ·nou); retired to Austria.

**Alexander.** 886?–913. Son of Basil I. Nominally, joint ruler of Eastern Roman Empire with his brother Leo VI (886–912), but took no part in affairs. Regent for Constantine VII (912–913).

**Alexander I and II.** Surnames of PTOLEMY IX and X.

**Alexander.** Name of two kings of Epirus:

**Alexander I.** d. 326 B.C. Brother of Olympias, mother of Alexander the Great; made king of Epirus by Philip of Macedon; during festivities at his marriage with Philip's daughter Cleopatra, Philip was slain by Pausanias (336); killed at battle of Pandosia.

**Alexander II.** Succeeded to throne (272 B.C.); invaded Macedonia (264), but defeated by Demetrius II and later temporarily driven from Epirus.

**Alexander.** 1893–1920. King of Greece; second son of King Constantine. Succeeded to throne on father's deposition by Allies (June 14, 1917); entrusted administration of government to Premier Venizelos; approved Greece's entry into World War on side of Allies. Died (Oct. 25, 1920) as result of bite from pet monkey.

**Alexander.** Name of five kings of Macedonia:

**Alexander I** (reigned 498–454 B.C.).
**Alexander II** (reigned 369–368 B.C.).
**Alexander III.** *Known as* **Alexander the Great.** 356–323 B.C. Succeeded his father, Philip II of Macedon (336); conquered Thrace and Illyria, destroyed Thebes, and gained ascendancy over all Greece (335); started expedition to East to attack Persia (334); won battles of Granicus (334) and Issus (333); conquered Tyre and Gaza, occupied Egypt, and founded Alexandria (332); destroyed Persian power in battle of Arbela (331); invaded eastern Persia (330–327) and northern India (326); defeated Porus on the Hydaspes (326); withdrew from India to Persia (325–324); died of fever in Babylon.
**Alexander IV.** 323–310 B.C. Posthumous son of Alexander the Great and Roxana; put to death with his mother by order of Cassander.
**Alexander V.** Third son of Cassander; shared throne (297–294 B.C.) with his brother Antipater; murdered by order of Demetrius.

**Alexander.** Name of three emperors (czars) of Russia of Romanov (*q.v.*) dynasty:
**Alexander I.** *Russ.* **Aleksandr Pavlovich.** 1777–1825. Emperor (1801–25), b. St. Petersburg. Eldest son of Paul I; m. (1793) Princess (Louise Marie) Elisabeth of Baden. Placed on throne by conspiracy forcing abdication of Paul. Gained some liberal ideas (1796–1800) from Frédéric C. de La Harpe, Swiss republican; began reign with sweeping reforms; made senate the supreme high court (1801); established ministries (1802); encouraged education and science. Joined coalition against Napoleon (1805); present at Austerlitz (1805); joined with Prussia but, after defeats (1807) of Eylau and Friedland, signed Treaty of Tilsit. Fought successful war against Turkey (1806–12); became rival of Napoleon, resulting in French invasion of Russia (1812); helped destroy Napoleon's army in retreat. Held strong position in Europe (1813–15); present at battles of Dresden and Leipzig (1813); entered Paris with allies (1814); took part in Congress of Vienna (1815); formed Holy Alliance (1815) and took part in conferences that followed it. Last years of reign (1820–25) marked by reactionary policies, embittered feelings, increasing popular discontent. Succeeded by his brother Nicholas I.
**Alexander II.** *Russ.* **Aleksandr Nikolaevich.** 1818–1881. Son of Nicholas I. Emperor (1855–81). Carefully educated and given military training; traveled in Germany; m. (1841) Maria, afterwards known as Maria Alexandrovna, daughter of Grand Duke Louis II of Hesse-Darmstadt. Signed Treaty of Paris (1856) terminating Crimean War. Had strong convictions for reforms; emancipated serfs (1861), his greatest achievement; reorganized army and government administration; established regular system of courts and founded schools. Put down Polish insurrection (1863–64); friendly to Germany in Franco-Prussian War (1870–71); waged war with Turkey (1877–78); extended boundaries of Russia in Caucasus and Central Asia (1868–81). Shortly after death of wife (1880), m. Ekaterina Dolgorukova. In spite of good done by his reforms, many added burdens placed upon peasants; certain repressive measures caused unrest; activity of Nihilists increased (1879–81); killed by bomb in St. Petersburg.
**Alexander III.** *Russ.* **Aleksandr Aleksandrovich.** 1845–1894. Son and successor of Alexander II. Emperor (1881–94). Became heir apparent on death (1865) of his elder brother Nicholas; m. (1866) daughter of Christian IX of Denmark (see MARIA FËDOROVNA). During years before accession (1865–81) showed open disapproval of some of father's policies; succeeded to throne on father's assassination; crowned (1883). Continued reactionary policies; countenanced persecutions, esp. of Jews; did not favor foreign influences, but himself interfered in affairs of Balkan states, esp. Bulgaria; continued Russian advance in Central Asia, even to frontier of Afghanistan (1884–85), bringing about crisis with England. Opposed any close union with Germany, but became virtual ally of France (1891–94); succeeded by his son Nicholas II.

**Alexander.** *Russ.* **Aleksandr Mikhailovich.** 1866–1933. Russian grand duke; brother-in-law of Emperor Nicholas II; m. (1894) Xenia (b. 1875), daughter of Alexander III. Their eldest daughter, Irina Aleksandrovna, married (1914) Prince Feliks Yusupov, an assassin of Rasputin.

**Alexander.** Name of three kings of Scotland:
**Alexander I.** 1078?–1124. Fourth son of Malcolm Canmore and Margaret, grandniece of Edward the Confessor. Succeeded his brother Edgar as king (1107); quelled insurrection of northern clans; contested claims of York and Canterbury to supremacy over see of St. Andrews.
**Alexander II.** 1198–1249. Great-grandnephew of Alexander I. Succeeded his father, William the Lion (1214); entered into league with English barons to resist King John; invaded England (1215); m. (1221) Joan, eldest sister of Henry III; repelled Norse invasion (1230); repelled Henry's demand for homage; settled dispute at Newcastle (1244); died of fever on expedition to wrest Hebrides from Norway.
**Alexander III.** 1241–1286. Son of Alexander II. Succeeded to kingdom (1249); m. (1251) Margaret, daughter of Henry III; defeated Norwegian invasion (1263); united Hebrides and Isle of Man to kingdom; assisted Henry III against barons (1264); induced recognition of granddaughter Margaret, daughter of Eric of Norway, called "Maid of Norway," as heir presumptive; subject of *Lament for Alisaundre,* one of earliest Scottish poems.

**Alexander.** Name of three rulers of the Serbs:
**Alexander Kar′a·geor′ge·vich** (kăr′*ȧ*·jôr′jĕ·vĭch). *Serbian* **A·lek′san′dar Ka·ra′djor′dje·vić** (ä·lĕk′sän′-där kä·rä′dyôr′dyĕ·vēt′y′). 1806–1885. Prince of Serbia 1842–58). Son of Karageorge (*q.v.*). Officer in Russian army; chosen prince to succeed Miloš Obrenović; weak and vacillating in his policy, at times pro-Russian and at others pro-Austrian; deposed by National Assembly (1848); accused of complicity in murder of Prince Michael (1868) but pardoned.
**Alexander I O·bre′no·vich** (ō·brĕ′nō·vĭch). *Serbian* **Aleksandar O·bre′no·vić** (ô·brĕ′nô·vēt′y′). 1876–1903. King of Serbia (1889–1903). Son of Milan and Queen Natalie. On father's abdication proclaimed king under regency; assumed full authority (1893); abolished (1894) Constitution of 1888; made unpopular marriage (1900) with Madame Draga Mashin; after several arbitrary acts, murdered with Queen Draga by group of officers; last of Obrenovich family. Succeeded by King Peter I.
**Alexander I.** 1888–1934. Son of Peter I and grandson of Alexander Karageorgevich; b. Cetinje, Montenegro. Prince regent of Serbia (1914–21) and king of Yugoslavia (1921–34). As youth lived at Geneva; to Serbia (1909), taking oath as heir apparent; took part in Balkan Wars (1912–13). Because of King Peter's ill health, appointed regent (1914); commander in chief of Serbian armies during World War (1914–19); became (1921) king of new Serb-Croat-Slovene State (now Yugoslavia); m. (1922) Princess Maria of Rumania. Because of disturbed condition of kingdom, especially after assassination of Stefan Radić (1928), abolished Constitution of 1921 and dismissed parliament (1929); did much to secure friendly

relations with neighboring countries. Assassinated at Marseille (Oct. 9, 1934) by Macedonian terrorist; succeeded by his son Peter II under regency council.

**Alexander,** Mrs. Pseudonym of Annie French HECTOR.

**Alexander, Albert Victor.** 1st Earl **Alexander of Hills'bor·ough** (hĭlz'bŭ·rŭ; -brŭ). 1885–1965. British Labor politician; first lord of the admiralty (1929–31, 1940–46); minister of defense (1947–50).

**Alexander,** Sir **George.** *Orig. name* **George Sam'son** (săm's'n). 1858–1918. English actor and manager; manager, St. James's Theatre, London (1891–1918).

**Alexander, Grover Cleveland.** 1887–1950. American baseball player, b. St. Paul, Nebr.; pitcher in National League for 20 years (Philadelphia, Chicago, St. Louis).

**Alexander, Harold Rupert Leofric George.** 1st Earl **Alexander of Tu'nis** (tū'nĭs). 1891–1969. British general; educ. Sandhurst; served in France (1914–18) and northwest frontier, India (1935); commander of the 1st division (1938–40); in charge of evacuation of British army from Dunkirk; commander on Burma front (Mar., 1942); commander in chief in Middle East (Aug., 1942); deputy allied commander in chief in North Africa (Feb., 1943), then in Mediterranean theater, commanding invasions of Sicily (July, 1943) and Italy (Sept., 1943); field marshal (Nov., 1944) and allied commander in chief in Italy (1944–45); governor general of Canada (1946–52).

**Alexander, Hartley Burr.** 1873–1939. American philosopher, educator, and writer, b. Lincoln, Nebr. Grad. U. of Nebraska (1897); Ph.D., Columbia (1901). Associate editor (1903–08), *Webster's New International Dictionary;* professor of philosophy, Nebraska (1908–27), Scripps Coll. (from 1927). Author of poems (especially on American Indian themes), works on North American and Latin American folklore, philosophy, etc. Special editor for Southwestern United States loan words, *Webster's New International Dictionary, Second Edition.*

**Alexander,** Sir **James Edward.** 1803–1885. British general and explorer, b. in Scotland. Explored central Africa (1836–37). Responsible for preservation of Cleopatra's Needle. Author of travel books.

**Alexander, Jerome.** 1876–1959. American chemist, b. New York City; specialist in chemistry of colloids; pioneer in ultramicroscopy.

**Alexander, John Henry.** 1812–1867. American scientist, b. Annapolis, Md. Urged standardization of weights and measures. Author of *History of the Metallurgy of Iron* (1840), *A Universal Dictionary of Weights and Measures, Ancient and Modern* (1850).

**Alexander, John White.** 1856–1915. American painter, b. Allegheny, Pa. Illustrator on staff of *Harper's* (1874 ff.). Studied abroad (1877 ff.). Kept studio at Paris (1890–1901), New York (1901–15). His works include portraits, as of Rodin, Grover Cleveland, Andrew Carnegie, W. D. Howells, Mark Twain, Alphonse Daudet, Robert L. Stevenson, Thomas Hardy, Walt Whitman, Joe Jefferson as Bob Acres, Maude Adams as L'Aiglon; murals, as six lunettes (*Evolution of the Book*) in Library of Congress, Washington; and paintings, as *The Pot of Basil* (Boston Museum), *The Green Bow* (Luxembourg), *Study in Black and Green* and *The Engagement Ring* (both in Metropolitan Museum, New York).

**Alexander, Joshua Willis.** 1852–1936. American lawyer, b. Cincinnati. U.S. secretary of commerce (1919–21).

**Alexander, Peter.** British Shakespearean scholar; professor, Glasgow (from 1935); author of *Shakespeare's Life and Art* (1939).

**Alexander, Samuel.** 1859–1938. Philosopher, b. Sydney, Australia. Educ. U. of Melbourne and Balliol Coll., Oxford. Professor of philosophy, Victoria U. of Manchester (1893–1924); Herbert Spencer Lecturer, Oxford (1927). Member, Order of Merit (1931). Author of *Space, Time, and Deity* (Gifford lectures; pub. 1920), *Spinoza and Time* (1921), *Art and the Material* (1925), *Beauty and Other Forms of Value* (1933).

**Alexander, Stephen.** 1806–1883. American astronomer, b. Schenectady, N.Y. Grad. Union Coll. (1824). Professor, Princeton (1840–77). Directed party to Labrador to observe solar eclipse (1860). One of original fifty members of National Academy of Sciences (1862).

**Alexander,** Sir **William.** Earl of **Stir'ling** (stûr'lĭng). 1567?–1640. Scottish poet. Tutor to earl of Argyle, Prince Henry Frederick, and Prince Charles (later Charles I of England). Received grant of Nova Scotia and New Brunswick (1621); secretary of state for Scotland (1626 till death). Author of *Monarchicke Tragedies; Paraenesis to the Prince* (a poem, 1604); *Doomesday* (a sacred epic; part I, 1614).

**Alexander, William.** *Known as* Lord **Stirling.** 1726–1783. American Revolutionary officer, b. New York City. Unsuccessfully claimed earldom of Stirling (1756–62). Member, Council of New Jersey; suspended because of opposition to Stamp Act. Captured British transport at Sandy Hook (1776). Brigadier general in Continental army; had part in exposing the Conway Cabal (1778); served on court of inquiry to decide fate of John André (1780).

**Alexander, William.** 1824–1911. Irish Anglican prelate; educ. Brasenose, Oxford; bishop of Derry (1867–93); archbishop of Armagh and primate of all Ireland (1893 till death); author of *St. Augustine's Holiday* (poems, 1886) and theological works. His wife, **Cecil Frances,** *nee* **Hum'phreys** [hŭm'frĭz] (1818?–1895; m. 1850), wrote tracts in connection with Oxford Movement and hymns, including *There Is a Green Hill Far Away* and *Jesus Calls Us o'er the Tumult.*

**Alexander, William Lindsay.** 1808–1884. Scottish clergyman. Educ. Edinburgh and St. Andrews. Congregational pastor, Edinburgh (1835–77); reviser of Old Testament (1870); professor (1854) and principal (1877), Theological Hall, Edinburgh.

**Alexander Ba'las** (bā'lăs). d. 145 B.C. King of Syria (150–145). Of obscure origin; claimed to be son of Antiochus IV Epiphanes. Usurped throne with help of Romans, killing Demetrius I; m. Cleopatra Thea. Defeated and killed in battle near Antioch by Demetrius II and Ptolemy VI Philometor. Succeeded by his son Antiochus VI.

**Alexander John I.** Prince of Rumania. = Alexandru Ioan CUZA.

**Alexander** (*Russ.* **Aleksandr**) **Nev'ski** (nĕv'skĭ; nĕf'-; *Russ.* ŭ·lyĭ·ksân'dẽr nyăf'skû·ĭ). 1220?–1263. Russian saint and hero, b. Vladimir; son of Prince Yaroslav of Novgorod. Became prince of Novgorod (1238); defeated Swedes (1240) in great battle near site of present Leningrad, on Neva river (whence his name *Nevski*); defeated Livonian knights (1242) on ice of Lake Peipus. On father's death (1246), became grand duke of Kiev and Novgorod and (1252) of Vladimir; vassal of Mongols throughout his rule, but on friendly terms with them. Order of Alexander Nevski was founded (1725) by Peter the Great in his honor.

**Alexander of Aph'ro·dis'i·as** (ăf'rō·dĭz'ĭ·ăs). fl. about 200 A.D. Greek philosopher of Aphrodisias in Caria. Lecturer on peripatetic philosophy at Athens.

**Alexander of Hales** (hālz). *Known as* **Doc'tor Ir·ref'ra·ga'bi·lis** (dŏk'tẽr ĭr·rĕf'rȧ·găb'ĭ·lĭs; dŏk'tôr). d. 1245. English scholastic theologian and philosopher. Franciscan (1222 ff.); author of *Summa Theologiae,* attempted correlation of Augustinianism and newly introduced writings of Aristotle and Arabs.

**Alexander of Tral'les** (trăl'ēz). *Lat.* **Alexander Tral'li·a'nus** (trăl'ĭ·ā'nŭs). fl. 6th century A.D. Greek physician; practiced at Rome; notable for his *Twelve Books on Medicine.*

**Alexander Se·ve'rus** (sē·vēr'ŭs), **Marcus Aurelius.** *Original name* **A·lex'i·a'nus Bas'si·a'nus** (ȧ·lĕk'sĭ·ā'nŭs băs'ĭ·ā'nŭs). 208?–235. Roman emperor (222–235), b. in Phoenicia. Son of Gessius Marcianus and first cousin of Heliogabalus. To Rome (218); adopted by Heliogabalus (221) and created caesar; became emperor (222). Reigned in peace for some years; waged war with Ardashir of Persia (231–233), defeating him; after return to Rome, set out (234) to subdue revolt of Germans; waylaid and killed by mutinous soldiers. Just and wise ruler; pagan, but reverenced Christian doctrines.

**Alexander the Paph'la·go'ni·an** (păf'lȧ·gō'nĭ·ăn; -gōn'yăn) fl. 2d cent. A.D. Roman impostor of Paphlagonia; established fraudulent oracle, exposed by Lucian.

**Al'ex·an'der·son** (ăl'ĕg·zăn'dēr·s'n; ăl'ĭg-), **Ernst** (ûrnst) **Fred'er·ik** (frĕd'ēr·ĭk; frĕd'rĭk) **Wer'ner** (vûr'nēr). 1878–1975. Electrical and radio engineer and inventor, b. Uppsala, Sweden; to U.S. (1901). Associated with General Electric Co. (from 1902). Inventions include a high-frequency alternator, multiple-tuned antenna, vacuum-tube telephone transmitter, and tuned radio-frequency receiver. Pioneer in television, electric ship propulsion, and railroad electrification.

**Al'ex·an'dra** (ăl'ĕg·zăn'drȧ; ăl'ĭg-; *Brit. also* -zän'-). 1844–1925. Eldest daughter of Christian IX of Denmark and Louise, daughter of Landgrave William of Hesse. Queen consort of Edward VII of England whom she married (1863) when he was prince of Wales.

**A·le·xan'dra** (*Russ.* **A·lek·san'dra**) **Fe·o'do·rov'na** (*Russ.* ŭ·lyĭ·ksån'drŭ fyĭ·ô'dŭ·rôv'nŭ). *Orig.* **A'lix Vic·to'ri·a He·le'ne Lu·i'se Be·a'trix** (ä'lĭks vĭk·tō'rē·ä hā·lā'nĕ lōō·ē'zĕ bā·ä'trĭks). 1872–1918. Empress of Russia (1894–1917). Daughter of Grand Duke Louis IV of Hesse-Darmstadt; granddaughter of Queen Victoria; m. (1894) Nicholas II, Emperor of Russia. Superstitious and pious, caused scandals by her relations with the religious fanatic Rasputin; taken prisoner (1917) by Bolsheviks and killed. See ROMANOV family.

**Alexandri, Vasile.** See ALECSANDRI.

**A·le·xei'** *or* **A·le·ksei'** (ŭ·lyĭ·ksyā'ĭ). = ALEXIS.

**Alexeiev.** See ALEKSEEV.

**A·lex'is** (ȧ·lĕk'sĭs). fl. 4th and 3d centuries B.C. Greek dramatist of Middle Comedy; credited with over two hundred plays.

**Alexis.** *Russ.* **Aleksei.** Name of several members of Russian imperial family, including:

**Alexis I Mikhailovich.** 1629–1676. Second czar of Romanovs (1645–76); son of Michael. First ten years of reign (1645–55) stormy period of internal troubles and insurrections. Gained control over eastern Ukraine (1654) by treaty with Chmielnicki; fought war against Poland in two campaigns (1654–56, 1660–67); secured Smolensk; waged unsuccessful war with Sweden (1656–61); suppressed with difficulty great peasant revolt (1670–71). Extended Russian lands, esp. eastward in Asia; introduced reforms by revision of laws, but these new laws were often a hardship for peasants; prepared Russia for work of his son Peter the Great (1689–1725); m. (1) Maria Miloslavski, mother of Fëdor III and Ivan V, and (2) Natalya Narishkina, mother of Peter the Great.

**Alexis Petrovich.** 1690–1718. Czarevitch; eldest son of Peter the Great by Eudoxia (Lopukhina). Opposed father's reforms; fled to Vienna and Naples (1717); made head of conspiracy; seized, condemned to death, and tortured; executed, probably on Peter's orders; m. (1711) Charlotte Christine Sophie (1694–1715), daughter of Duke Louis of Brunswick-Wolfenbüttel; their son ruled (1727–30) as Peter II.

**Alexis Aleksandrovich.** 1850–1908. Grand duke, b. St. Petersburg. Brother of Alexander III; uncle of Nicholas II. Commander in chief of Russian fleet during Russo-Japanese War; disasters forced his resignation (1905).

**Alexis Nikolaevich.** 1904–1918. Czarevitch; youngest child and only son of Emperor Nicholas II. Seized with parents and sisters by Bolsheviks during revolution (1917); executed (July, 1918).

**A'lex'is'** (ȧ'lĕk'sē'), **Pierre Nord.** See NORD ALEXIS.

**A·lex'is** (ä·lĕk'sĭs), **Willibald.** Pseudonym of Wilhelm HÄRING.

**A·lex'i·us** (ȧ·lĕk'sĭ·ŭs), Saint. Roman Christian of 5th century; founder of order whose members were known as Alexians or Cellites.

**Alexius** *or* **Alexis.** Name of five rulers of Eastern Roman Empire:

**Alexius I Com·ne'nus** (kŏm·nē'nŭs). 1048–1118. Emperor (1081–1118); nephew of Emperor Isaac Comnenus; talented soldier; raised by his followers to supplant Nicephorus III; defended empire against Scythians, Turks, and Normans; his domains invaded by First Crusade (1096–99); his life (*Alexiad*) written by his daughter Anna Comnena (*q.v.*).

**Alexius II Comnenus.** 1168?–1183. Emperor (1180–83); son of Manuel I; deposed and murdered by his uncle Andronicus I.

**Alexius III An'ge·lus** (ăn'jĕ·lŭs). d. 1210. Emperor (1195–1203); brother of Isaac Angelus, whom he drove from throne; in turn deposed by army of crusaders (1203) who besieged Constantinople and reinstated Isaac; died in exile.

**Alexius IV Angelus.** d. 1204. Emperor (1203–04), reigning six months; son of Isaac II Angelus; put to death by Alexius V.

**Alexius V.** *Known as* **Du'cas Mour'tzu·phlos** (*Mod. Gr.* thōō'käs mōōr'tsōō·flôs). d. 1204. Emperor (1204); attempted defense of Constantinople against crusaders (Fourth Crusade); driven out, arrested in Morea, and executed. Latin Empire established (1204); see BALDWIN I.

**Alexius I.** *Called* **Grand Comnenus.** 1180?–1222. Of younger Comnenus line (see COMNENUS); grandson of Emperor Andronicus I. First emperor of Trebizond (1204–22). With his brother David Comnenus, seized Trebizond and coastland of northeastern Asia Minor when Constantinople was taken by crusaders (1204). Attacked Nicaean emperor, Theodore I Lascaris, in Bithynia, but defeated. Founded dynasty that lasted more than 250 years (1204–1461).

**Al'eyn** (ăl'ĭn), **Charles.** d. 1640. English historical poet.

**Al·fa'no** (äl·fä'nō), **Franco.** 1877–1954. Italian composer of instrumental and chamber music and, esp., operas; completed Puccini's unfinished *Turandot.*

**Alfarabius.** See al-FARABI.

**Al·fa'ro** (äl·fä'rō), **Eloy.** 1864–1912. Ecuadorian general and political leader, b. Monte Cristi. Led uprising against President Cordero (1893–95); declared himself anticlerical dictator (1895); president of Ecuador (1897–1901 and 1907–11). Led the revolt (1906) that deposed President Lisardo García; became constitutional president (1907). Reduced power of Roman Catholic Church; completed railroad from Quito to Guayaquil (1908). Murdered in uprising of 1912. His son **Colón Eloy (1891–1957)**, diplomat; Ecuadorian minister to various Central American countries (to 1933), to U.S. (from 1933); ambassador to U.S. (1936–44).

**Alfaro, Ricardo J.** 1882–1971. Panamanian lawyer and diplomat, b. Panama; secretary of government and justice (1918–22); minister to U.S. (1922–30, 1933–36); member of the Hague Tribunal (1929–41); president of Panama (1931–32); foreign minister (from 1945).

**Al·fie′ri** (äl·fyâ′rē), **Cesare.** Marchese **di So·ste′gno** (sō·stā′nyō). 1796–1869. Italian statesman, b. Turin. Active in furthering Italian unification; formed and headed third constitutional ministry (Aug.–Oct., 1848); president, Piedmont senate (1856–60).

**Alfieri,** Conte **Vittorio.** 1749–1803. Italian tragic dramatist. Inherited fortune; from seventeenth year traveled for nearly seven years through England and Europe. Fell in love at 26 with Marchesa Turinetti di Prie, who inspired his first tragedy, *Cleopatra* (produced 1775), the success of which decided him on a literary career. Settled in Turin (1773); moved to Florence (c. 1776) to study Tuscan for his playwriting; there met countess of Albany (*q.v.*), who became his mistress. Author of 19 tragedies, all classical in form, including *Saul, Sofonisba, Antigone,* and *Maria Stuart;* an autobiography; sonnets; odes; six comedies; and a satire against France, *Misogallo.* His plays and poems, which show his love of freedom and hatred of tyranny, served to revive the national spirit in Italy.

**Al·fon′so** (ăl·fŏn′sō; -zō; *Ital.* äl·fôn′sō). Name of two kings of Naples:

**Alfonso I.** King of Sicily (1416–58) and of Naples (1443–58). See ALFONSO V, King of Aragon (1416–58).

**Alfonso II.** 1448–1495. King of Naples (1494–95). Son of Ferdinand I, King of Naples. Fought against Florentines (1479) and Turks (1481); unpopular as king, resigned (1495) in favor of his son Ferdinand as Charles VIII of France threatened Naples. Father of Ferdinand II.

**Al·fon′so** (ăl·fŏn′sō; -zō). *Anglicized form of Port.* **A·fon′so,** *older* **Af·fon′so** (ȧ·fōɴ′sōō). Name of six kings of Portugal, the first four being of the House of Burgundy (*q.v.*):

**Alfonso I.** *Port.* **Affonso Henriques.** 1112–1185. First king of Portugal (1139–85). Son of Henry of Burgundy; succeeded father as count of Portugal (1112–39); seized throne (1128) from his mother, who had acted as regent. Freed country from León (1130–39); won great victory over Moors at Ourique (1139); crowned first king of an independent Portugal (1139); captured Lisbon with aid of English crusaders (1147); defeated Moors and took Santarem (1171); won a second time at Santarem (1184). Established (c. 1162) Order of Aviz (see AVIZ). Generally regarded as saint by Portuguese.

**Alfonso II.** *Called* **Affonso o Gor′do** (ōō gōr′dōō), *i.e.* the Fat. 1185–1223. Son of Sancho I. King (1211–23). Won victory over Moors at Alcácer do Sal (1217); excommunicated by Pope Honorius III.

**Alfonso III.** 1210–1279. Son of Alfonso II. King (1248–79). Added Algarve to Portugal (1250).

**Alfonso IV.** *Called* **Affonso o Bra′vo** (ōō brȧ′vōō), *i.e.* the Brave. 1290–1357. Son of Diniz. King (1325–57). Reign marked by disastrous civil war with his son Pedro.

**Alfonso V** of house of Aviz (*q.v.*). *Called* **Affonso o A·fri·ca′no** (ōō ă·frē·kă′nōō), *i.e.* the African. 1432–1481. Son of Edward; b. at Cintra. King (1438–81). After father's death (1438) engaged with his uncle Pedro in fierce struggle for regency; assumed government (1448); defeated Pedro (1449); conducted successful campaign in Morocco (1458–71); married his niece Juana la Beltraneja (see JUANA OF PORTUGAL); failed in attempt to seize Castile and León (1476); abdicated (1476) in favor of his son John but forced to return; signed treaty with Castile (1479). During his reign Portuguese voyages made along west coast of Africa almost to equator (see Prince HENRY).

**Alfonso VI** of house of Braganza (*q.v.*). 1643–1683. Son of John IV. King (1656–83). Paralyzed at age of three; led dissolute life, drove queen regent, Luisa de Guzmán, from court (1662); overcome by Dom Pedro (see PEDRO II) and exiled to Terceira (1667). Throne occupied during rest of his life (1667–83) by Pedro as regent.

**Al·fon′so** (ăl·fŏn′sō; -zō; *Span.* äl·fôn′sō) *or* **Al·phon′so.** *Also* **A·lon′so** (ȧ·lŏn′zō; *Span.* ä·lôn′sō). Name of five kings of Aragon:

**Alfonso I.** *Called* **Alfonso el Ba′tal·la·dor′** (ĕl bä′tä·lyä·thôr′), *i.e.* the Battler. d. 1134. King (1104–34). Also sometimes, as husband of Queen Urraca, known as Alfonso VII of León (1109–34). Granted divorce from Urraca by Pope; continually at war with Castile and León; won Saragossa from Moors (1118).

**Alfonso II.** 1152–1196. King (1162–96). Patron of Provençal poetry.

**Alfonso III.** 1265–1291. Son of Pedro III. King (1285–91). Granted wide powers to nobles (1287).

**Alfonso IV.** 1299–1336. King (1327–36).

**Alfonso V.** *Called* **Alfonso el Mag·ná′ni·mo** (ĕl mäg·nä′nē·mō), *i.e.* the Magnanimous. 1385–1458. Son of Ferdinand I. King (1416–58) and, as Alfonso I, king of Sicily (1416–58) and of Naples (1443–58). Made heir to throne of Naples by Joanna II (1420); disinherited (1423). Captured Naples (1442) and enforced claims. Patron of learning.

**Alfonso** *or* **Alphonso.** *Also* **Alonso.** Name of five kings of Castile: **Alfonso I, II, III** = ALFONSO VI, VII, VIII of León and Castile. **Alfonso X** and **XI** (after union of León and Castile, 1230) = ALFONSO X and XI of León and Castile. See also ALFONSO XII and XIII of Spain.

**Alfonso** *or* **Alphonso.** *Also* **Alonso.** Name of eleven kings of León and Castile:

**Alfonso I.** d. 757. King of León and Asturias (739–757); drove Moors out of Galicia and León.

**Alfonso II.** d. 842. King of León and Asturias (791–842); held court at Oviedo.

**Alfonso III.** 848–912. King of León and Asturias (866–910); faced with revolts of nobles and of his sons; abdicated.

**Alfonso IV.** d. 933. King of León and Asturias (925–930); abdicated.

**Alfonso V.** d. 1027. King of León and Asturias (999–1027); warred with Moors in Portugal.

**Alfonso VI.** *Called* **Alfonso el Bra′vo** (ĕl brä′vō), *i.e.* the Valiant. d. 1109. King of León (1065–1109) and, as Alfonso I, king of Castile (1072–1109); father of Teresa, wife of Henry of Burgundy (*q.v.*); two kingdoms temporarily united (1072); recovered Toledo from Moors; defeated by Abbad III (1086). Reign notable for exploits of the Cid.

**Alfonso VII.** *Called* **El Em′pe·ra·dor′** (ĕl ām′pā·rä·thôr′), *i.e.* the Emperor. *Also known as* **Alfonso II** of Castile. d. 1157. King of León and Castile united (1126–57); m. (1128) Berengaria, daughter of Ramón Berenguer IV; founded Order of Alcántara (1156).

**Alfonso VIII.** *Also known as* **Alfonso III** of Castile. d. 1214. King of Castile (1158–1214); won great victory over Moors at Navas de Tolosa (1212).

**Alfonso IX.** *Also known as* **Alfonso VIII** of León. d. 1230. King of León (1188–1230); m. (1197) Berengaria of Castile; founded U. of Salamanca (c. 1220).

**Alfonso X.** *Called* **Alfonso el Sa′bi·o** (ĕl sä′byō), *i.e.* the Learned. 1226?–1284. King of Castile and León (1252–84); candidate for office of Holy Roman emperor (1257) but not elected; engaged in civil wars and war with Moors (1261–66); Pamplona seized by French;

promulgated code of laws, *Las Siete Partidas*, basis of Spanish jurisprudence; notable as poet and leader of intellectual life.

**Alfonso XI.** d. 1350. King of Castile (1312–50); as ally of Alfonso IV of Portugal, defeated Moors near Tarifa (1340). See also ALFONSO XII and XIII, of Spain.

**Alfonso** *or* **Alphonso.** *Also* **Alonso.** Name of two Bourbon kings of Spain (see also ALFONSO of León and Castile):

**Alfonso XII.** *Full name* **Francisco de A·sís′** (ä·sēs′) **Fernando Pío Juan María Gregorio Pelayo.** 1857–1885. King (1874–85). Proclaimed by army at end of civil war; suppressed Carlist opposition (1876); summoned Cortes which made new constitution (1876); under influence of prime minister, Cánovas del Castillo.

**Alfonso XIII.** *Full name* **León Fernando María Isidro Pascual Antonio.** 1886–1941. Posthumous son of Alfonso XII and Maria Christina. King (1886–1931). Under regency of his mother (1886–1902), during which period Spain lost Philippines and last possessions in America in Spanish-American War (1898); m. Princess Victoria of Battenberg (1906). His reign marked by rioting in Madrid and Barcelona (1909–11) over trouble in Morocco, Spanish neutrality in World War (1914–19), cabinet crisis (1922), and defeat of Spanish in Morocco (1923) by Moors under Abd-el-Krim. Appointed Primo de Rivera dictator (1923–25). National Assembly opened (1927); period marked by strikes, riots, and declaration of martial law (1930). Forced to abdicate (1931); lived in exile (1931–41).

**Al′ford** (ôl′fẽrd), **Henry.** 1810–1871. English clergyman and scholar. Grad. Cambridge (1832). Edited New Testament in Greek with collation of readings (1841–61); published sermons, hymns, and poems. Dean of Canterbury (1857–71). First editor of *Contemporary Review* (1866–70).

**Alfraganus.** See al-FARGHANI.

**Al′fred** *or* **Æl′fred** (ăl′frĕd; -frĭd). *Called* **Alfred the Great.** 849–899. King of the West Saxons. Fifth son of Ethelwulf. Assisted his brother Ethelred I against Danes; succeeded Ethelred as king (871); fought Danes at Wilton (871). Met second invasion of Danes under Guthrum with victory at Edington in Wiltshire (878). Captured London (885 or 886), received submission of Angles and Saxons, and recognized as sovereign of all England. Waged war (893–97) against Danes; finally, with improved navy, forced invading Danes to withdraw (897), and consolidated England round his kingdom as center. Compiled best laws of earlier kings; divided parts of Mercia according to shire system for first time; promoted learning, bringing to Wessex many famous scholars. Author of free translations from Latin (amounting to recastings) of *Pastoral Care* by Gregory the Great, histories by Bede and Orosius (*q.v.*), and Boethius's *Consolation of Philosophy.*

**Al′fred** (ăl′frĕd; -frĭd), Prince. *In full* **Alfred Ernest Albert.** 1844–1900. Duke of **Ed′in·burgh** [ĕd′′n·bûr′ō; -bŭ·rŭ; ĕd′ĭn-] (1865–93) and of **Saxe–Coburg–Gotha** (1893–1900). Second son and fourth child of Queen Victoria. Captain in British navy (1866); admiral (1893). Married (1874) Grand Duchess Marie Alexandrovna, dau. of Alexander II of Russia; had four daughters: (1) Marie, Queen of Rumania, (2) Victoria Melita, who married Grand Duke Cyril of Russia, (3) Alexandra, Princess of Hohenlohe-Langenburg, and (4) Beatrice, who married Alfonso, infante of Spain.

**Al′fred,** *or* **Al′u·red** (ăl′ū·rĕd), **of Bev′er·ley** (bĕv′-ẽr·lĭ). *Lat.* **Al′u·re′dus,** *or* **Al·re′dus, Bev′er·la·cen′sis** (ăl′ū·rē′dŭs [ăl·rē′dŭs] bĕv′ẽr·lȧ·sĕn′sĭs). fl. 1143. English chronicler.

**Alf·vén′** (ȧl·vān′), **Hannes.** 1908– . Swedish physicist; shared 1970 Nobel prize in physics with Louis NÉEL, for work in plasma physics.

**Alfvén, Hugo.** 1872–1960. Swedish composer of symphonies, choral music, songs, and piano pieces.

**Al·gar′di** (äl·gär′dē), **Alessandro.** 1602–1654. Italian baroque sculptor and architect; known esp. for his portraiture. Studied with Lodovico Carracci; succeeded Bernini as court sculptor. Executed *Retreat of Attila from Rome,* one of largest alto-relievos in the world, and a monument of Pope Leo XI (both in St. Peter's); designed façade of Church of Sant'Ignazio at Rome, etc.

**Al′ga·rot′ti** (äl′gä·rôt′tē), Conte **Francesco.** 1712–1764. Italian philosopher and critic. Friend of Frederick the Great and Voltaire. Author of *Newtonian Philosophy for Ladies* (1733), *Essays on the Fine Arts,* etc.

**Algazel.** See al-GHAZZALI.

**Al′ger** (ăl′jẽr), **Horatio.** 1832–1899. American Unitarian clergyman and author, b. Revere, Mass. Grad. Harvard (1852). Writer of more than 100 enormously popular books for boys, including the *Ragged Dick* (1867), *Luck and Pluck* (1869), and *Tattered Tom* (1871) series.

**Alger, Russell Alexander.** 1836–1907. American politician, b. Lafayette, Ohio. Served in Civil War; rose from ranks to colonelcy. Elected governor of Michigan (1884). U.S. secretary of War (1897); resigned (1899) at McKinley's request because of criticism directed against War Dept. for inefficiency. U.S. senator (1902–07).

**Algirdas.** Lithuanian form for OLGIERD.

**Al′ha·zen′** (ăl′hă·zĕn′). *Arab.* **abu–'Ali al–Ḥasan ibn–al–Haytham.** 965?–?1039. Arab astronomer and optician, b. Basra. Failed in attempt to regulate annual overflow of Nile; wrote more than 100 works on mathematics, astronomy, philosophy, and medicine; chief work, *Kitāb al-Manāẓir,* a treatise on optics (pub. in Latin with title *Opticae Thesaurus,* 1572) influential in development of that science in Middle Ages.

**Al′hu·ce′mas** (ä′lōō·thā′mäs), Marqués **de. Manuel Gar·cí′a Pri·e′to** (gär·thē′ä prē·ā′tō). 1860–1938. Spanish politician, b. Astorga, León. Prime minister of Spain (1917–18; 1922–23); overthrown by Gen. Primo de Rivera.

**A·li′** (ă·lī′). *Arab.* **'Ali ibn–abi–Ṭālib.** 600?–661. Fourth caliph (656–661). Cousin and, as husband of Fatima, son-in-law of Mohammed, and one of his first converts; accompanied him to Medina (622); disappointed at succession (632) of abu-Bakr as caliph; opposed by Aisha; as fourth caliph, succeeded Othman; his rule stormy and full of civil conflicts; defeated Aisha at battle of Basra (656); assassinated at Al Kufa by three members of Kharijite sect. See ALIDS.

**A′li′.** *Commonly known as* **A′li′ Pa·sha′** (ä′lē′ pä·shä′). *Called* **The Lion of Ja′ni·na** [yä′nē·nä] (*mod.* **Io·an′-ni·na** [yô·ä′nyē·nä]). 1741–1822. Turkish pasha, b. Tepeleni, Albania; son of an Albanian bey. Gained power through unscrupulous means; as pasha of Janina (1788), powerful in Albania; several times changed allegiance to Napoleon or England; plotted against the Porte. Established barbarous culture at court in Janina described by Byron in *Childe Harold's Pilgrimage.*

**Ali, Mehemet.** See MEHEMET ALI.

**A·li′** (ä·lē′), **Muhammad.** *Original name* **Cassius Marcellus Clay, Jr.** 1942– American heavyweight boxer, b. Louisville, Kentucky.

**A·li′** (ă·lī′), Mulai. 1610?–?1655. Sultan of Morocco (1650–55); founder of dynasty still ruling Morocco.

**A′li′ Bey** (ä′lē′ bā). 1728–1773. Mameluke ruler (bey) of Egypt (1766–73), b. in Abkhasia in the Caucasus. In boyhood sold as slave into Egypt; became a Mameluke bey; seized government (1766) and declared Egypt independent of Turkey; made wide conquests; defeated and taken prisoner in battle.

**Ali Bey.** See Domingo BADÍA Y LEBLICH.

**A·li' ibn-Hu·sein'** (ä·lē' ĭb''n·hōō·sīn'). 1878–1935. Last king of independent kingdom of Hejaz (1924–25). Eldest son of King Husein ibn-Ali. Emir of Medina during father's reign; led Arab forces against Turkey in World War; made king (1924) on father's abdication; forced to resign by ibn-Saud; lived (1925–35) with his brother King Faisal at Baghdad in Iraq, at times acting as regent of Iraq.

**Ali Mohammed of Shiraz.** See the BAB.

**A·li' Var'di Khan** (ä·lē' vär'dē kän). *Also* **Allahvardi Khan.** *Real name* **Mir'za Mu·ham'mad A·li'** (mēr'zä mōō·häm'măd ä·lē'). 1676–1756. Nawab of Bengal (1740–56). Of obscure birth; became governor of Bihar; made prime minister by Nawab Shuja-ud-din. Revolted against nawab's son and successor; usurped throne (1740); continuously at war with marauding Marathas (1741–51); gave English permission to fortify Calcutta (1742). In old age, favored his grandson Siraj-ud-daula (*q.v.*).

**Al'ice Maud' Mar'y** (ăl'ĭs môd' mâr'ĭ). 1843–1878. Princess of Great Britain and Ireland. Duchess of Saxony. Grand Duchess of **Hesse'–Darm'stadt** (hĕs'-därm'stät; -shtät). Second daughter of Queen Victoria; m. (1862) Louis of Hesse who became grand duke (as Louis IV) of Hesse-Darmstadt (1877–92). Their fourth daughter, Alix, married Czar Nicholas II of Russia. Founder of Women's Union for Nursing Sick and Wounded in War. See also BATTENBERG.

**Al'ids** (ăl'ĭdz). (1) Descendants of Caliph Ali, son-in-law of Mohammed; established Shiite sect in Persia; their leaders who revolted (762–763) put down by Abbassides. (2) Dynasty of Idrisids in Morocco (788–974); founded by Idris ibn-Abdullah, great-grandson of Caliph Ali's son Hasan; overthrown by Berbers.

**Alighieri, Dante.** See DANTE.

**Alimentus, Lucius Cincius.** See CINCIUS ALIMENTUS.

**A·lin'** (à·lēn'), **Oscar Josef.** 1846–1900. Swedish historian and politician.

**Al'i·son** (ăl'ĭ·s'n), **Archibald.** 1757–1839. Scottish Episcopal clergyman; author of *Taste* (1790), a book of essays admired by Jeffrey. His elder son, **William Pulte'ney** [pŭlt'nĭ; pōlt'nĭ] (1790–1859), was professor of medicine, Edinburgh U. (1822–56) and author of medical works. His younger son, Sir **Archibald** (1792–1867), was a historian; called to Scottish bar (1814); as sheriff of Lanarkshire suppressed riots (1837); author of *History of Europe during the French Revolution* (10 vols., 1833–42, and in continuation, 9 vols., 1852–59), and biographies and an autobiography. The latter's son, Sir **Archibald** (1826–1907), was an army officer in Crimean War and in Sepoy Mutiny; second in command of Ashanti expedition; led Highland brigade at Tell el-Kebir in Egyptian campaign; general (1887); author of *On Army Organisation* (1869).

**Al'kan'** (àl'käN'), **Charles Valentin Mor'hange'-** (mô'räNzh'-). 1813–1888. French pianist and composer.

**Alk'mar** (älk'mär) *or* **Alk'maar** (älk'mär), **Hin'rek** (hĭn'rĕk), **Hen'drik** (hĕn'drĭk), *or* **Hein'rik** (hīn'rĭk), **van** (vän). Author of *Reinke de Vos* (written 1487; pub. 1498), Low German version of *Reynard the Fox*, translated or adapted from the Dutch.

**Al·lac'ci** (äl·lät'chē), **Le·o'ne** (lā·ō'nā). *Lat.* **Leo Al·la'ti·us** (ă·lā'shĭ·ŭs). 1586–1669. Greek theologian, scholar, and author. Vatican librarian (from 1661); compiler of *Drammaturgia*, catalogue of Italian musical dramas to 1666.

**Allahvardi Khan.** See ALI VARDI KHAN.

**Al'la'mand'** (à'là'mäN'), **Jean Nicolas Sébastien.** 1713–1787. Naturalist and physicist; b. Lausanne, Switzerland. Professor, U. of Leiden; first to explain phenomena of Leyden jar.

**Al'lan** (ăl'ăn), **David.** 1744–1796. Scottish painter. Awarded gold medal of St. Luke's for historical composition, *Origin of Painting; or the Corinthian Maid Drawing the Shadow of her Lover.* Painted portraits, London. Illustrated Allan Ramsay's *Gentle Shepherd.* Known as "Scottish Hogarth" for humorous descriptive paintings such as *Scotch Wedding, Highland Dame,* etc.

**Allan, George.** Pseudonym of Mite KREMNITZ.

**Allan,** Sir **Hugh.** 1810–1882. Financier and shipowner, b. in Scotland. Identified with Canada (from 1826). Founded Allan Line of steamships (1856); one of projectors of Canadian Pacific Railway. His brother **Andrew** (b. 1822), associated with him in founding Allan Line, succeeded him (1882) in its presidency.

**Allan,** Sir **William.** 1782–1850. Scottish historical painter. Traveled in Russia (1805–14); known esp. for scenes of Russian life, and scenes from Scottish history.

**Allatius, Leo.** See Leone ALLACCI.

**All'butt** (ôl'bŭt), Sir **Thomas Clifford.** 1836–1925. English physician; grad. Cambridge (1860). Regius professor of physics, Cambridge (1892 till death). Invented short clinical thermometer (1866); described hyperpiesia apart from kidney disease (1895); demonstrated aortic origin of angina pectoris (1894). Author of *System of Medicine* (8 vols., 1896–99). Thought to have been original of Lydgate in George Eliot's *Middlemarch.*

**Allegri, Antonio** and **Pomponio.** See CORREGGIO.

**Al·le'gri** (äl·lā'grē), **Gregorio.** 1582?–1652. Italian composer. Member, Sistine choir (from 1629). His *Miserere* is sung annually in the Sistine Chapel on Good Friday.

**Al'leine** (ăl'ĭn), **Joseph.** 1634–1668. English Puritan clergyman. Educ. Oxford. Ejected from Anglican living (1662) for nonconformity; frequently fined and imprisoned for evangelical preaching. Wrote *An Alarm to the Unconverted* (1672).

**Alleine, Richard** (1611–1681) and his brother **William** (1614–1677). English Puritan clergymen. Both ejected from Anglican livings under Act of Uniformity (1662); ministered semiprivately thereafter. Richard wrote *Vindiciae Pietatis* (1663) and other religious works.

**Al'len** (ăl'ĕn; -ĭn), **Alexander Viets Griswold.** 1841–1908. American Episcopal clergyman, educator, and author; b. Otis, Mass.

**Allen, Arthur Augustus.** 1885–1964. American ornithologist, b. Buffalo, N.Y. Asst. professor (1915–25), professor (from 1925), Cornell. Author of *The Book of Bird Life* (1930), etc.

**Allen, Bennet Mills.** 1877–1963. American zoologist and embryologist, b. Greencastle, Ind. Author of studies on germ cells, influence of glands of internal secretion upon growth, etc.

**Allen, Charles Herbert.** 1848–1934. American banker and politician, b. Lowell, Mass. Grad. Amherst (1869). Assistant secretary of navy (1898–1900); first U.S. governor of Puerto Rico (1900–02).

**Allen, Edgar.** 1892–1943. American anatomist and endocrinologist, b. Canon City, Colo.; Ph.B. (1915), Ph.D. (1921), Brown U.; professor of anatomy, U. of Mo. (1923–33; dean of medical school, 1929–33), Yale (from 1933); known for research on sex hormones.

**Allen, Elisha Hunt.** 1804–1883. American lawyer and politician. Practiced law, Bangor, Me. (1828 ff.). Member, U.S. House of Representatives (1841–43). Consul at Honolulu (1850–56); minister of finance under king of Hawaii (1856–57); chancellor and chief justice (1857–76); Hawaiian minister to U.S. (1876–83).

**Allen,** **Elizabeth,** *nee* **Chase.** *Pseudonym* **Florence Per′cy** (pûr′sĭ). 1832–1911. American poet, b. Strong, Me.; m. Marshall S. M. Taylor (1851; divorced), B. P. Akers (1860; d. 1861), E. M. Allen (1865). Author of poem *Rock Me to Sleep* (1860).

**Allen, Ethan.** 1738–1789. American Revolutionary soldier, b. Litchfield, Conn. Served (1757) during French and Indian War. Associated with early Vermont (then known as New Hampshire grants) history (from 1769). Colonel commanding Green Mountain Boys (1770–75). On orders from Connecticut, seized, with Benedict Arnold, Fort Ticonderoga (May 10, 1775). Captured at Montreal and held prisoner (1775–78). Exchanged; returned to Vermont; major general of militia. Presented to Congress Vermont's claims to independence and recognition (1778). Involved (1780–83) with brothers (including Ira Allen, *q.v.*) in negotiations with British, perhaps undertaken to force American Congress to recognize Vermont's claims. Settled in Burlington (1787).

**Allen, Florence Ellinwood.** 1884–1966. American judge, b. Salt Lake City, Utah. Grad. Western Reserve (1904); LL.B., N.Y.U. (1913). Judge, Ohio court of common pleas (1921–26), supreme court of Ohio (2 terms, 1922–34), U. S. circuit court of appeals (from 1934). First woman in America to be state supreme-court judge.

**Allen, Francis Richmond.** 1843–1931. American architect, b. Boston. Studied at École des Beaux-Arts, Paris (1877–78). Member, Allen & Collens, designers especially of collegiate and church buildings in modern Gothic style, as at Williams and Vassar colleges, Union Theological Seminary, etc.

**Allen, Fred Hovey.** 1845–1926. American Congregational clergyman and writer, b. Lyme, N.H. Introduced in U.S. process of making photogravure reproductions of paintings. Author of *Masterpieces of Modern German Art,* first book to be illustrated by photogravure plates made in U.S. (1884), *Popular History of the Reformation* (1887), *Grand Modern Paintings* (1888).

**Allen, Frederic Sturges.** 1861–1920. American lexicographer, b. Norwalk, Conn. Grad. Yale (1884), LL.B. (1892). Lawyer in Conn. and New York City (1892–1903). General editor, *Webster's New International Dictionary* (pub. 1909); compiler of *Allen's Synonyms and Antonyms* (1920).

**Allen, Frederick Lewis.** 1890-1954. American editor and author, b. Boston. Assistant editor (1921), associate editor (1931), editor (1941), *Harper's Magazine.* Author of *Only Yesterday* (1931), *The Lords of Creation* (1935), *Since Yesterday* (1940), etc.

**Allen, Frederick Madison.** 1879–1964. American physician, b. Des Moines, Iowa; authority on diabetes.

**Allen, Glover Morrill.** 1879–1942. American zoologist, b. Walpole, N.H. A.B. (1901), Ph.D. (1904), Harvard. Curator of mammals (from 1907) and associate professor of zoology (from 1928), Harvard. Author of *Birds and their Attributes* (1925), *Bats* (1939), etc. Special editor for terms in ornithology and mammalogy, *Webster's New International Dictionary, Second Edition.*

**Allen, Grant,** *in full* **Charles Grant Blair·fin′die** (blâr-fĭn′dĭ). *Pseudonyms* **Cecil Pow′er** (pou′ẽr) *and* **J. Arbuthnot Wilson.** 1848–1899. British author, b. near Kingston, Ontario. B.A., Oxon. (1871). Professor of mental and moral philosophy in college for Negroes, Jamaica (1873); returned to England (1876). Author of *Physiological Aesthetics* (1877), *The Evolutionist at Large* (1881), and thirty works of fiction, beginning with *Philistia* (1884) and including *The Devil's Die* (1888), *The Woman Who Did* (1895), *The British Barbarians* (1896).

**Allen, Henry Tureman.** 1859–1930. American general, b. Sharpsburg, Kentucky. Served in Spanish-American War. With Mexican expedition (1916). In command of ninetieth division in France in World War, and of American forces of occupation in Germany (1919).

**Allen, Hervey,** *in full* **William Hervey.** 1889–1949. American author, b. Pittsburgh, Pa. Grad. U. of Pittsburgh (1915). Author of *Israfel* (a biography of E. A. Poe; 1926) and the novels *Anthony Adverse* (1933), *Action at Aquila* (1937), *It Was Like This* (1940), etc.

**Allen, Horace Newton.** 1858–1932. American Presbyterian clergyman, b. Delaware, Ohio. Grandnephew of Ethan Allen. Medical missionary (1884) and U.S. minister (1897–1905) to Korea.

**Allen, Horatio.** 1802–1890. American civil engineer, b. Schenectady, N. Y. Engineer with Delaware and Hudson Co. (1825–29). Ran first locomotive over new railroad (Honesdale, Pa.; Aug. 9, 1829). President, Erie Railroad (1843). Consulting engineer for Brooklyn Bridge, Panama Railroad.

**Allen,** Sir **Hugh Percy.** 1869–1946. English organist. Organist of New College, Oxford (1901–18); conductor, London Bach choir; director, Royal College of Music (1918). Professor of music, Oxford (from 1918).

**Allen, Ira.** 1751–1814. Brother of Ethan Allen (*q.v.*). American Revolutionary politician, b. Cornwall, Conn. A leader in agitation to obtain statehood for Vermont. Involved (1780–91) in negotiations with British. Assisted in founding U. of Vermont (1789).

**Allen,** Sir **James.** 1855–1942. New Zealand statesman, b. S. Australia. M.P., New Zealand (1887–1920); high commissioner in London for N.Z. (1920–26); member, Legislative Council, N.Z. (from 1927).

**Allen, James Lane.** 1849–1925. American novelist, b. near Lexington, Ky. Engaged in school and college teaching (1872–85). Author of *Flute and Violin, and Other Kentucky Tales and Romances* (1891), *A Kentucky Cardinal* (1894), *Aftermath* (1895), *The Choir Invisible* (1897), *The Reign of Law* (1900), *The Mettle of the Pasture* (1903).

**Allen, Joel Asaph.** 1838–1921. American zoologist and author, b. Springfield, Mass. Accompanied Agassiz to Brazil (1865). Curator of birds, Harvard Museum of Comparative Zoology (1867–85); of birds and mammals, American Museum of Natural History, New York (1885–1921). Author of *The American Bisons, Living and Extinct* (1876), *History of North American Pinnipeds* (1880).

**Allen, Joel Nott.** 1866–1940. American portrait painter, b. Ballston Spa, N.Y.

**Allen, John.** 1810–1892. American dentist, b. in Broome Co., N.Y. Devised modern denture, with porcelain teeth attached to platinum plate (patent granted, 1851).

**Allen, John F.** 1829–1900. American engineer, b. in England. Invented valve motion that made high-speed steam engines possible, an inclined-tube vertical water-tube boiler, and a system of pneumatic riveting.

**Allen, Joseph Henry.** 1820–1898. American Unitarian clergyman and author, b. Northboro, Mass. Joint editor with his brother **William Francis** (1830–1889) and with J. B. Greenough of a widely used school series of Latin manuals.

**Allen. Josiah Allen's Wife.** Pseudonym of Marietta HOLLEY.

**Al′len** (äl′ĕn), **Karl Ferdinand.** 1811–1871. Danish historian; author of *History of the Three Northern Kingdoms* (5 vols., 1864–72).

**Al′len** (ăl′ĕn; -ĭn), **Percy Stafford.** 1869–1933. English classical scholar and educator; president, Corpus Christi Coll., Oxford; student of the Renaissance.

**Allen, Ralph.** *Called* **the Man of Bath** (bàth). 1694–

1764. English philanthropist. Deputy postmaster, Bath. Amassed fortune by devising and forming new system of direct postal routes for England and Wales. Original of Allworthy in Fielding's *Tom Jones*.

**Allen, Richard.** 1760–1831. American Negro bishop, b. Philadelphia; slave. One of founders of African Methodist Episcopal Church, and its bishop (1816–31).

**Allen, Thomas.** 1542–1632. English mathematician, antiquary, and collector of astronomical, astrological, and historical manuscripts.

**Allen, Thomas.** 1849–1924. American painter, b. St. Louis.

**Allen, Viola.** 1869–1948. American actress, b. Huntsville, Ala.; m. Peter Duryea (1906). Played in *The Masqueraders, Under the Red Robe, The Christian, The Eternal City*, etc., and in Shakespearean plays and modern comedies.

**Allen, William.** 1532–1594. English cardinal. Opened English Roman Catholic seminary at Douai (1568), later moved to Reims (1578). Created cardinal (1587). At time of Armada supported claims of Philip II; urged Roman Catholics of England to rise against Elizabeth. Made librarian at Vatican. Douay Bible begun under his direction. Served on commission for revision of Vulgate.

**Allen, William.** 1784–1868. American Congregational clergyman, educator, and author, b. Pittsfield, Mass. Grad. Harvard (1802). President, Dartmouth (1817–19), Bowdoin (1819–31, 1833–38). Compiler of *American Biographical and Historical Dictionary* (1809).

**Allen, William Francis.** 1830–1889. See under Joseph Henry ALLEN.

**Allen, William Henry.** 1784–1813. American naval officer, b. Providence, R.I. In command of *Argus;* killed in engagement with British brig *Pelican* (1813).

**Allen, Zachariah.** 1795–1882. American inventor, b. Providence, R.I. Invented first hot-air house-heating system (1821) and an automatic steam-engine cutoff (1834).

**Al'len·by** (ăl'ĕn·bĭ), **Edmund Henry Hynman.** 1st Viscount **Allenby.** 1861–1936. English field marshal. Served in Bechuanaland (1884–85), Zululand (1888), and in cavalry operations in Boer War. Commanded cavalry in France in World War; as commander in chief of Egyptian Expeditionary Force, took Beersheba and Gaza (1917), entered Jerusalem (Dec. 9, 1917), and won sweeping victory over Turks at Megiddo (1918). Raised to peerage as Viscount Allenby of Megiddo and Felixstowe (1919). High commissioner for Egypt (1919–25). His life written by Sir Archibald Wavell (1940).

**Al·len'de** (ä·yān'dā), **Ignacio José.** 1779–1811. Mexican army officer and patriot. Companion of Juan Aldama in uprising of 1810–11; supported Hidalgo y Costilla; betrayed and shot.

**Al'ler·ton** (ăl'ĕr·t'n; -tŭn), **Isaac.** 1586?–1659. One of *Mayflower* Pilgrims (1620). Assistant governor of colony, under Bradford (1621–25). Agent of colony to deal with financial backers in England; exceeded authority (1630) by borrowing in colony's name to purchase goods for trading purposes; repudiated by colony (1631). Lived in New Haven colony (1644–59).

**Al'les·tree** (ăl'ĕs·trē), **Richard.** 1619–1681. English clergyman and scholar. Served on side of king in Civil War. Canon, Christ Church College, Oxford (1660); regius professor of divinity (1663–79); provost of Eton (1665). Author of *The Whole Duty of Man.*

**Al'ley** (ăl'ĭ), **Rewi.** 1897– . New Zealand industrial organizer, of Anglo-Irish descent, in China. Named by his father after Rewi Te Manipoto, a Maori chieftain. Served in World War I; sheep farmer in New Zealand; to China and became factory inspector for municipal council of Shanghai; after Japanese invasion (1937), began, with approval of Chiang Kai-shek, establishing small industrial co-operatives throughout China to make up for productive areas lost to Japan.

**Al'leyn** (ăl'ĭn; ăl'ān; ă·lēn'). Variant of ALLEN.

**Alleyn, Edward.** 1566–1626. English actor. One of earl of Worcester's players (1586); then with other companies, esp. the Lord Admiral's company. With Henslowe, built Fortune Theatre at Cripplegate (1600). Made last appearances in *Tamburlaine, Jew of Malta*, and *Faustus* (1604). Founded and endowed Dulwich College (1613–16); directed its affairs (1617–22).

**Al'li·bone** (ăl'ĭ·bōn), **Samuel Austin.** 1816–1889. American editor and librarian, b. Philadelphia. Compiler of *A Critical Dictionary of English Literature and British and American Authors* (1st vol., 1858; 2d & 3d vols., 1871).

**Al'lin** (ăl'ĭn), **Norman.** 1884– . English concert and operatic basso; principal basso at Covent Garden, London (from 1918).

**Allin,** Sir **Thomas.** 1612–1685. English admiral; defeated Dutch off Isle of Wight and French off Dungeness (1666); served against Barbary pirates (1668–70).

**Al'ling·ham** (ăl'ĭng·ăm), **William.** 1824–1889. Irish poet. Author of *Day and Night Songs* (1854), *Laurence Bloomfield in Ireland* (narrative in couplets on Irish life, 1864), *Irish Songs and Poems* (1887). Editor, *Fraser's Magazine* (1874–79).

**Al'li·son** (ăl'ĭ·s'n), **Fred.** 1882–1974. American physicist, b. Glade Spring, Va.; professor, Ala. Poly. Inst. (from 1922); credited with developing magneto-optic method of analysis leading to discovery of chemical elements 85 and 87.

**Allison, William Boyd.** 1829–1908. American lawyer and political leader, b. in Perry Township, Ohio; moved to Dubuque, Iowa (1855). Member, U.S. House of Representatives (1862–70), U.S. Senate (1872–1908); coauthor of Bland-Allison Act of 1878. Chairman of committee on appropriations, U.S. Senate (1881–1908).

**All'man** (ôl'măn), **George James.** 1812–1898. Irish biologist. Professor of botany, Dublin (1844); regius professor of natural history, Edinburgh (1855–70). Made studies in morphology of coelenterates and polyzoans.

**All'mers** (äl'mērs), **Hermann.** 1821–1902. German writer and poet; author of *Marschenbuch* (1858), *Römische Schlendertage* (1868), *Elektra* (drama, 1872), etc.

**Al'lon** (ăl'ŭn), **Henry.** 1818–1892. English Congregational minister. Held London pastorate (1844–92); published *Congregational Psalmist* (1852 ff.); edited *British Quarterly Review* (1877–86). His son **Henry Erskine** (1864–1897), composer of sonatas and choral works.

**Al·lo'ri** (äl·lō'rē), **Alessandro.** 1535–1607. Italian painter of Florentine school; imitator of Michelangelo. His son **Cristofano** (1577–1621), also portrait painter of Florentine school, is known esp. for *Judith with the Head of Holofernes, St. Julian, Sacrifice of Isaac* (in Pitti Palace), and *Isabella of Aragon at the Feet of Charles VIII* (in Louvre).

**Al'lott** *or* **Al'lot** (ăl'ŭt), **Robert.** fl. 1600. English editor of miscellany of Elizabethan poetry entitled *England's Parnassus* (1600).

**Al'lou·ez'** (à'lwā'), **Claude Jean.** 1622–1689. Jesuit missionary in America, b. Saint-Didier, Haute Loire, France. Penetrated new regions about Lake Superior (1665–75) establishing missions; continued Marquette's work among the Illinois (1676–89).

**All'port** (ôl'pōrt), **Gordon Willard.** 1897–1967. American psychologist, b. Montezuma, Ind. A.B. (1919), Ph.D. (1922), Harvard; asst. professor (1930–36), associate professor (1937–42), professor (from 1942), Harvard. Author of *Personality—a Psychological Interpretation* (1937), etc.

**All'ston** (ôl'stŭn), **Washington.** 1779–1843. American artist and author, b. Waccamaw, S.C. Studied in Europe. Paintings include *Belshazzar's Feast* (Boston Athenaeum), *The Flood*, and *A Spanish Girl* (Metropolitan Museum of Art, New York). Author of *The Sylphs of the Seasons with other Poems* (1813), *Monaldi* (1841), and a novel.

**Al'mack** (ôl'măk), **William.** d. 1781. Scottish founder of famous Almack's Assembly Rooms, King St., St. James's, London (1765). His surname is said to be a syllabic transposition of an original patronymic McCaul or McCall.

**Al·ma'gro** (äl·mä'grō), **Diego de.** 1475?–1538. Spanish soldier, b. near Ciudad Real. To Panama (1514); joined Pizarro in plan for exploration (1522); took part in first voyage to south (1524–25). Took part in Pizarro's conquest of Peru, joining expedition at Cajamarca (1533); quarreled violently with Pizarro but soon reconciled; joined march on Cuzco. Led expedition of conquest to Chile (1535–36); returned (1537), claimed Cuzco, and captured it by surprise; defeated (1538) in ensuing war with Alonso de Alvarado and Hernando Pizarro; captured and executed. His son **Diego** (1520–1542), b. in Panama, of an Indian mother, accompanied him to Chile; made governor of Peru at Pizarro's death (1541); later defeated by royalists and executed.

**Almansor** *or* **Almanzor.** See al-MANSUR.

**Al'ma-Tad'e·ma** (ăl'mȧ·tăd'ē·mȧ), Sir **Lawrence.** 1836–1912. Painter, b. Dronrijp, Netherlands. Studied at Academy of Antwerp and under Baron Hendrik Leys. Settled in England (1869); naturalized (1873). Member, Order of Merit. His first paintings dealt with Frankish subjects; then followed an ancient Egyptian series and (after 1865) studies of Greek and Roman life. Important works include *Tarquinius Superbus* (1867), *Wine Shop* (1869), *Un Jongleur* (1870), *Roses of Heliogabalus* (1888), *Conversion of Paula* (1898). Exhibited at St. Louis World's Fair (1904) *Coliseum*, *Shrine of Venus*, and *Caracalla*. His daughter **Laurence** (d. 1940) was a writer of novels, poems, plays, and essays.

**Al'ma·zán'** (äl'mä·sän'), **Juan Andreu.** 1891–1965. Mexican army commander, b. in Guerrero. Served with Madero (1910); commanded army zone of Monterrey (from 1924). Unsuccessful candidate for presidency of Mexico (1940).

**Al·mei'da** (äl·mā'ē·thȧ), **Antônio José de.** 1866–1929. Portuguese physician and statesman. Prime minister (1916–17); president of Portugal (1919–23). Author of *Affronta* (1896), etc.

**Almeida, Brites de.** fl. 1386. Portuguese heroine who led townspeople of Aljubarrota in resistance to Spanish invasion of Portugal and alone killed seven Spaniards. Known as "Portuguese Joan of Arc."

**Almeida, Francisco de.** 1450?–1510. Portuguese soldier; first viceroy of Portuguese India (1505–09); established forts and trading posts in Cochin, Ceylon, and Sumatra.

**Almeida, Guilherme de.** 1890-1969. Brazilian lawyer (1912–23) and writer, b. in São Paulo. Author of verse, as *Messidor* (5 eds., 1919–35), *Era uma Vez...* (1922, 1927), *Nós* (1922, 1927, 1930), *Você* (1931), *Poetas de França* (translations, 1936), and prose, including *Do Sentimento Nacionalista na Poesia Brasileira* (1925) and *Rilmo, Elemento de Expressão* (1926).

**Almeida, Nicoláo To·len·ti'no de** (tōō·lăNn·tē'nōō thē). 1745?–1811. Portuguese satirist of contemporary manners.

**Al·mei'da–Gar·rett'** (äl·mā'ē·thȧ·gȧr·rĕt'), **Visconde de. João Baptista da Sil'va Lei·tão'** (thȧ sĭl'vȧ lā·ē·touN'). 1799–1854. Portuguese poet, dramatist, and statesman, b. Oporto. Spent boyhood in Azores; attended U. of Coimbra. Took part in revolt of 1820; expatriated; returned (1826). Helped Dom Pedro gain throne; appointed minister of interior; member of national Cortes, supporting democratic principles. Led romantic movement in Portuguese literature; collected for his *Romanceiro* (1851–53) 32 early Portuguese ballads and romances; composed the epic *Camões* (1825), the long poem *Dona Branca* (1826), etc. Worked to found national theater; wrote historical prose dramas, including *Auto de Gil Vicente* (1838) and *Frei Luiz de Sousa* (1844).

**Al'mo·hades** (ăl'mō·hādz; -hădz) *or* **Al'mo·hads** (-hădz). *Arab.* **Mu·waḥ·ḥi·dūn'** (mōō·wă·hĭ·dōōn'), *i.e.* Unitarians. Arab dynasty established in North Africa and Spain (1147–1269) by Islamitic sect of Almohades, founded (c. 1130) by ibn-Tumart (*q.v.*). Actual founder of dynasty was Abd-al-Mumin (*q.v.*), who conquered Morocco and southern Spain, overthrowing Almoravides. Its greatest ruler among his successors was Yaqub al-Mansur (see at MANSUR). Power of dynasty declined after disastrous defeat by Christians at Navas de Tolosa (1212); terminated in Spain (1232) and in Africa (1269).

**Al'mond** (ôl'mŭnd), **Linda,** *nee* **Stevens.** American writer; m. Huston Berley Almond (1909); author of children's books, esp. a series of Peter Rabbit stories.

**Al·mon'de** (äl·mŏn'dĕ), **Philips van.** 1644–1711. Dutch admiral. Commander of Dutch fleet at victory at La Hogue (1692), and, with Sir George Rooke, of allied fleet that destroyed Spanish fleet in Bay of Vigo (1702).

**Al·mon'te** (äl·mŏn'tā), **Juan Nepomuceno.** 1804?–1869. Mexican general and statesman; reputed son of Morelos. Educ. in U.S. Served under Santa Anna in Texas; captured at battle of San Jacinto (1836); minister to U.S. (1841–46, 1853), to France (1857, 1866); twice unsuccessful candidate for presidency.

**Al·mo'ra·vides** (ăl·mō'rȧ·vīdz; ăl'mō·rä'vīdz) *or* **Al·mo'ra·vids** (ăl·mō'rȧ·vĭdz; ăl'mō·rä'vĭdz). *Arab.* **al–Mu·rā'bi·ṭūn'** (ăl'mōō·rä'bĭ·tōōn'), *i.e.* the hermits. A Moslem (Berber) dynasty established (1062) by Almoravides sect in North Africa; later ruled (1090–1147) in Spain. Its founder, Yusuf ibn-Tashfin (see IBN-TASHFIN), made Marrakech its African capital; in Spain its power centered in Seville, but in spiritual matters the emirs acknowledged supremacy of Abbasside caliphs of Baghdad; overcome by Almohades (1147).

**Alm'qvist** (älm'kvĭst), **Karl Jonas Ludvig.** 1793–1866. Swedish writer, b. Stockholm. Grad. U. of Uppsala (1815). Author of romances, esp. the series *The Book of the Thorn-Rose* (1832–35), lyrics, songs, dramas, socialistic novels, etc.

**Aln'wick** (ăn'ĭk), **William of.** d. 1449. English ecclesiastic; bishop of Norwich and Lincoln. Confessor to young King Henry VI; codified statutes and customs of Lincoln cathedral.

**A. L. O. E.,** *i.e.* A Lady of England. Pseudonym of Charlotte Maria TUCKER.

**A'lo·i'si** (ä'lō·ē'zē), Baron **Pompeo.** 1875–1949. Italian diplomat; minister to Denmark (1920–22), Rumania (1923–25), Albania (1926–27); ambassador to Japan (1928–29), Turkey (1930–32). Chief of cabinet in ministry of foreign affairs (1932–36); Italian representative on League of Nations council (1932–36). Author of *Ars Nipponica.*

**A·lom'pra** (ȧ·lŏm'prȧ). *Also* **Aloung P'Houra** *and* **Alaungpaya.** 1711–1760. Founder of last Burmese dynasty. With small force seized Ava (1753); rebuilt Rangoon (1753); overcame Peguans (1757) who ruled Burma at the time.

**A·lon'so** (ȧ·lŏn'zō; *Span.* ä·lôn'sō). Variant of ALFONSO.

**A·lon'zo** (ä·lôn'sō), **Mateo.** 1878– . Argentine sculptor; studied at Barcelona, Spain. His most notable work, *Christ of the Andes*, a statue (unveiled 1904), 26 feet high, molded in bronze from old Argentine cannon, stands on granite pedestal at Uspallata Pass on Chile-Argentine border as symbol of perpetual peace between the two countries.

**Aloung P'Houra.** See ALOMPRA.

**Aloysius Gonzaga,** Saint. See GONZAGA.

**Alp Ars·lan'** (älp ärs·län'), *i.e.* Courageous Lion. *Orig. name* **Mo·ham'med** (mōō·häm'mäd). 1029–1072. Second sultan of Seljuk Turks (1063–72). Great-grandson of Seljuk. Succeeded his father, Daud, as ruler of Khurasan (1059). Conquered Georgia and Armenia (1064); defeated Byzantine Emperor Romanus Diogenes at Manzikert (1071) and took him prisoner; released him for ransom; by this victory, established Seljuk Empire of Rum in Asia Minor. Began conquest of Turkestan. Succeeded by his son Malik Shah.

**Al'phand'** (al'fäN'), **Jean Charles Adolphe.** 1817–1891. French civil engineer. In charge, under Haussmann, of improvements in public parks of Paris (from 1854).

**Alphege,** Saint. See ÆLFHEAH.

**Al·phon'sa** (ăl·fŏn'sȧ; -zȧ), Mother. *Real name* **Rose Hawthorne.** 1851–1926. Youngest daughter of Nathaniel Hawthorne; m. (1871) George Parsons Lathrop (d. 1898). Converted to Roman Catholic faith (1891); founded sisterhood, Servants of Relief for Incurable Cancer; established home, Hawthorne, N.Y. (1901), and served there (1901–26).

**Al·phon'so** (ăl·fŏn'sō; -zō; *Span.* äl·fôn'sō). Variant of ALFONSO.

**Alphonsus Liguori.** See LIGUORI.

**Al·pi'ni** (äl·pē'nē), **Prospero.** *Lat.* **Prosper Al·pi'nus** (ăl·pī'nŭs). 1553–1617. Italian botanist and physician; credited with first account of coffee plant published in Europe.

**Alred.** See ALDRED.

**Alredus Beverlacensis.** = ALFRED OF BEVERLEY.

**Als'berg** (ăls'bûrg), **Carl Lucas.** 1877–1940. American biochemist, b. New York City. Grad. Columbia; studied in Germany. Authority on food chemistry.

**Al'sop** (ôl'sŭp), **Richard.** 1761–1815. American author, b. Middletown, Conn.; one of Hartford wits. Collaborated in writing *The Echo*, verse satire which appeared in *American Mercury* (between 1791 and 1805; publ. in book form, 1807). Among other works is *A Poem, Sacred to the Memory of George Washington* (1800).

**Al'sted** *or* **Al'stedt** (äl'shtĕt), **Johann Heinrich.** 1588–1638. German Protestant theologian and philosopher; wrote also on music and history.

**Al'strö'mer** *or* **Al'stroe'mer** (äl'strû'mẽr), **Jonas.** 1685–1761. Pioneer of Swedish industrialism. Engaged in ship brokerage in England (1710–24); returned to Sweden; established a woolen factory, and then a sugar refinery. Introduced better breeds of sheep; improved methods in tanning, shipbuilding, etc., and in cultivation of potatoes and dye plants.

**Alt** (ält), **Rudolf von** (1812–1905) and his brother **Franz** (1821–1914). Viennese painters, esp. in water colors.

**Al'ta·mi'ra y Cre·ve'a** (äl'tä·mē'rä ē krā·vā'ä), **Rafael.** 1866–1951. Spanish jurist and historian. Educ. Valencia U. Professor, history of Spanish law, Oviedo U. (1897–1910); professor, Madrid (1914–36), U. of Mexico. Judge, Permanent Court of International Justice (1922–45). Author of works on history of law, on Spanish law, and on Spanish history.

**Al·tamsh'** (ȧl·tŭmsh'). *More correctly* **Il·tut'mish** (ĭl·tōōt'mĭsh). d. 1236. Third and greatest sultan of Delhi of Slave Dynasty (1211–36). Born a slave; m. daughter of Kutb-ud-din. Strengthened and enlarged Mohammedan empire of northern India; conquered governors of Lower Bengal and of Sind; escaped destruction by Genghis Khan (1221–22), whose hordes stopped at the Indus; destroyed Ujjain (1234), capital of ancient Hindu kingdom of Vikramaditya (*q.v.*); built Kutb Minar, supposedly most perfect tower in the world, at Delhi (1231–32). Succeeded by Raziya (*q.v.*).

**Alt'dor'fer** (ält'dôr'fẽr), **Albrecht.** 1480?–1538. German painter, esp. of landscapes, architect, and engraver on copper and wood; one of the Little Masters. Works include *Holy Family* (at Vienna), *Alexander's Victory at Arbela* (at Munich), etc.

**Al'ten** (äl'tĕn), Count **Karl August von.** *Eng.* Sir **Charles Alten.** 1764–1840. Hanoverian general; in Hanoverian army (1776–1803), British army (1803–15), serving under Wellington in Peninsular War and at Waterloo; again in Hanoverian army (from 1818); Hanoverian minister of war (1837).

**Al'ten·berg** (äl'tĕn·bĕrk), **Peter.** *Real name* **Richard Eng'län'der** (ĕng'lĕn'dẽr). 1862?–1919. Austrian writer of brief prose poems.

**Al'ten·stein** (äl'tĕn·shtīn), **Karl.** Baron **vom Stein** (shtīn) **zum Altenstein.** 1770–1840. Prussian statesman. Minister of finance (1808–10), of public worship and education (1817–38).

**Al'ter** (ôl'tẽr), **David.** 1807–1881. American physicist and physician, b. in Westmoreland Co., Pa. Investigated spectral analysis; discovered that certain elemental gases have spectra peculiar to themselves, thus making possible spectroscopic determination of chemical nature of gases.

**Alt'geld** (ôlt'gĕld), **John Peter.** 1847–1902. American political leader, b. in Germany. Governor of Illinois (1892–96), first Democratic governor of state since Civil War.

**Al'then'** (al'tĕn'), **Jean.** 1711–1774. Son of Persian governor; enslaved by Turks; escaped to France; introduced madder plant into France.

**Althorp,** Viscounts. See *Earls Spencer* under SPENCER family.

**Alt'house** (ôlt'hous), **Paul Shearer.** 1889–1954. American operatic and concert tenor, b. Reading, Pa.; made debut with Metropolitan Opera Co., N.Y. (1913).

**Al·thu'si·us** (ăl·thū'zhĭ·ŭs; *Ger.* äl·tōō'zē·ŏŏs) *or* **Alt'hu'sen** (ält'hōō'zĕn) *or* **Alt'hus'** (ält'hōōs'; äl'tōōs'), **Johannes.** 1557–1638. German jurist; defender of democratic principles.

**Al'ti·chie'ro da Ze'vio** (äl'tē·kyâ'rō dä dzâ'vyō). *Also* **Al'di·ghe'ro da Ze'vio** (äl'dē·gâ'rō). 14th-century Italian painter, esp. of frescoes.

**Alt'man** (ôlt'măn), **Benjamin.** 1840–1913. American merchant and art collector, b. New York City. His small dry-goods store (opened 1865) developed into B. Altman & Co. department store (incorporated 1913).

**Alt'mey'er** (ôlt'mī'ẽr), **Arthur Joseph.** 1891–1972. American government administrator; in federal government service (from 1933); member (1935–1946), chairman (from 1937), U.S. Social Security Board.

**Al'ton'** (al'tôN'), **Eduard Josef d'.** 1772–1840. Anatomist, archaeologist, and engraver, b. Aquileja, Austria. Studied in Italy and Austria; professor of archaeology and history of art, Bonn (from 1826). Made the first chalk drawings on stone (1802); author of *Die Naturgeschichte des Pferdes* (1810–17), illustrated with his own engravings; coauthor of *Vergleichende Osteologie* (1821–28). His son **Eduard** (1803–1854), anatomist, b. Sankt Goar, Prussia, was professor at Halle (1834); author of handbook of comparative human anatomy (1850).

**Altringer,** Count **Johann.** See ALDRINGEN.

**Alt'schu'ler** (ält'shōō'lẽr), **Modest.** 1873– . Violoncellist, b. in Russia. In U.S. (from 1896); organized and conducted (1903–20) Russian Symphony Orchestra in New York and on tour; introduced in U.S. works of leading contemporary Russian composers; conductor, Los Angeles Symphony Society (1929).

**Alt'shel'er** (ôlt'shĕl'ẽr), **Joseph Alexander.** 1862–1919. American editor and author, b. Three Springs, Ky. Wrote several series of adventure books for boys.

**Alured of Beverley.** *Lat.* **Aluredus Beverlacensis.** = ALFRED OF BEVERLEY.

**Al'va** (ăl'vȧ; *Span.* äl'vä) *or* **Al'ba** (ăl'bȧ; *Span.* äl'bä), Duke of. **Fernando Ál'va·rez de To·le'do** (äl'vä·rāth thā tō·lā'thō). 1508–1582. Spanish general. Commander under Charles V (1535–56); important factor in victory of Mühlberg (1547) over Elector John Frederick of Saxony; commanded imperial forces in Italy (1553–59); sent by Philip II to suppress Dutch revolt in Netherlands (1567); set up Council of Troubles (Blood Council) to punish enemies of Spain; campaign (1567–73) marked by extreme cruelty, suppressing all opposition and executing Counts Egmont, Horn, and many others; defeated William of Orange; led expedition (1580–81) that conquered Portugal, defeating Dom Antônio, last of the house of Aviz.

**Al'va·ra'do** (äl'vä·rä'thō), **Alonso de.** 1490?–1554. Spanish soldier, b. Burgos. Served under Cortes in conquest of Mexico (1519–21); in Peru (1534); defeated by Almagro's forces in battle of Abancay (1537); active in civil wars in Peru (1538–42); marshal and governor of Cuzco (c. 1552); killed in revolt in Charcas.

**Alvarado, Juan Bautista.** 1809–1882. Mexican political leader in California, b. Monterey, Calif. Governor of virtually independent Dept. of California (1836–41).

**Alvarado, Pedro de.** 1495?–1541. Spanish soldier, b. Badajoz. Companion of Grijalva (1518) and of Cortes in conquest of Mexico (1519–21); in command of Mexico City (1520) when Cortes went against Narváez on coast; in "la noche triste" (see CORTES) saved his own life by famous leap ("Alvarado's leap"); led expedition to Guatemala (1523–27); returned from Spain to Guatemala as governor (1530–34); led expedition (1534) against Quito, but persuaded by Pizarro to retire; in Mexico (1540–41).

**Álvares de Azevedo, Manuel Antônio.** See AZEVEDO.

**Al'va·rez** (äl'vȧ·rĕsh), **Francisco.** 16th-century Portuguese traveler; lived six years in Abyssinia; wrote account of the country (c. 1527).

**Ál'va·rez** (äl'vä·rās), **Juan.** 1790?–1867. Mexican general, of Indian descent, b. Atoyac, Guerrero. Took part in revolution for Mexican independence (1821); joined Santa Anna to overthrow Iturbide (1823); fought in war with U.S. (1846–47); first governor of Guerrero (1849); leader in revolt against Santa Anna (1855); acting president of Mexico (Oct.–Dec., 1855); led reform movements; determined opponent of Maximilian and French invasion (1861–67).

**Ál'va·rez** (äl'vä·rāth), **Luis.** 1836–1901. Spanish historical, genre, and portrait painter; b. Madrid.

**Al'va·rez** (ăl'vȧ·rĕz), **Walter Clement.** 1884–1978. American physician, b. San Francisco. Head of division of medicine, Mayo Clinic, Rochester, Minn. (1926–50). His son, **Luis Walter** (1911– ), a physicist, received the Nobel prize in physics (1968).

**Ál'va·rez de Cienfuegos** (äl'vä·rāth), **Nicasio.** See CIENFUEGOS.

**Ál'va·rez de Pe·rei'ra y Cu·be'ro** (äl'vä·rāth thā pā·rĕ'ē·rä ē kōō·bā'rō), **José.** 1768–1827. Spanish sculptor; executed statue of Ganymede and busts of Charles IV and Queen María Luisa. His son **José Álvarez y Bou·gel'** [ē bō·ōō·hĕl'] (1805–1830) was also a sculptor.

**Al'va·rez do O'ri·en'te** (äl'vȧ·rēzh thōō ō'rē·änn'tĕ), **Fernão.** 1540?–?1595. Portuguese poet, b. Goa; author of the pastoral *Lusitânia Transformada.*

**Ál'va·rez Ga'to** (äl'vä·rāth gä'tō), **Juan.** 1433?–1496. Spanish poet, b. Madrid.

**Ál'va·rez Quintero** (äl'vä·rāth), **Serafín** and **Joaquín.** See QUINTERO.

**Alvary, Max.** Stage name of Max ACHENBACH.

**Al've·ar'** (äl'vā·är'), **Carlos María de.** 1789–1853. Leader in war for Argentine independence, b. in Misiones territory, Uruguay. Educ. in England. A rival of San Martín; compelled surrender of Montevideo (1814); defeated by Artigas; succeeded Gervasio Antonio Posadas as dictator (1815). Governor of Buenos Aires; forced to flee to Brazil (1820); minister to U. S. (1823). Commanded Argentine army against Brazil in Uruguay (1826); won battle of Ituzaingó (1827). Banished by Rosas (after 1829); lived many years in U. S.

**Alvear, Marcelo Torcuato de.** 1868–1942. Argentine diplomat and Radical political leader, b. Buenos Aires. Took part in revolutions (1890, 1893, 1905); national deputy (1912–17); minister to France (1917–22); president of Argentina (1922–28); exiled (1931–32).

**Al'vens·le'ben** (äl'vĕns·lā'bĕn), **Gustav von.** 1803–1881. Prussian general; led fourth army corps (1866–71), which played important part at Beaumont (1870), etc. His brother **Konstantin von Alvensleben** (1809–1892) commanded third army corps in Franco-Prussian War; retired as general of infantry (1873).

**Alverstone,** Viscount. See Richard Everard WEBSTER.

**Alves, Francisco de Paula Rodrigues.** See RODRIGUES ALVES.

**Alviella, Goblet d'.** See GOBLET D'ALVIELLA.

**Al'vin'czy** (ŏl'vĭn'tsē; äl'-), **Josef.** Baron **von Bor'be·rek** (bôr'bĕ·rĕk). 1735–1810. Austrian general, b. in Transylvania. Served in Seven Years' War and war with Turks (1788–92); led Austrian division in Netherlands (1792–93); commander in Italy (1796); defeated by Napoleon at Arcole (1796) and Rivoli (1797); field marshal (1808).

**Al'y·at'tes** (ăl'ĭ·ăt'ēz). King of Lydia; father of Croesus (*q.v.*). During reign (c. 617–560 B.C.) made conquests in Asia Minor which established Lydian empire.

**A·lyp'i·us** (ȧ·lĭp'ĭ·ŭs). fl. about 360 A.D. Greek theorist and writer on music; author of *Introduction to Music,* key to musical system of notation of ancient Greeks.

**Al'zog** (äl'tsōk), **Johannes Baptist.** 1808–1878. German Roman Catholic church historian; author of *Lehrbuch der Universalkirchengeschichte* (1840).

**Al'zon'** (ål'zôn'), **Emmanuel Marie Joseph Maurice Dau'dé'** (dō'dā') **d'.** 1810–1880. French ecclesiastic; founder (1844) of establishment at Nîmes for religious instruction, which developed (1850) into religious congregation called Augustinians of the Assumption (Assumptionists).

**Am'a·das** (ăm'ȧ·dăs) *or* **Am'i·das** (ăm'ĭ·dăs), **Philip.** 1550–1618. English navigator; with Raleigh (1584–85) and Grenville (1585) expeditions to West Indies and America.

**A'made'** (å'måd'), **Albert d'.** 1856–1941. French army officer; head of French force co-operating with British in attack on Dardanelles during World War.

**A'ma·dé** (ŏ'mŏ·dā), Baron **László.** 1703–1764. Hungarian poet; composer of popular patriotic songs. His songs published (1836) by Hungarian pianist Count **Tádé Amadé** (1782?–1845), who also discovered and aided Franz Liszt.

**A'ma·de'o** (ä'mä·dā'ō) *or* **O'mo·de'o** (ō'mō·dā'ō),

Giovanni Antonio. *Lat.* **Am'a·de'us** (ăm'ȧ·dē'ŭs). 1447?–1522. Italian Renaissance sculptor and architect, b. Pavia. His works include sculptures in Colleoni Chapel at Bergamo and sarcophagus of St. Lanfrancus in church of St. Lanfrancus near Pavia. Aided in designing Milan cathedral.

**Am'a·de'us** (ăm'ȧ·dē'ŭs). *Fr.* **A'mé'dée'** (ȧ'mā'dā'). Name of eight counts of Savoy. Count **Amadeus VIII** was created (1416) first duke of Savoy (see SAVOY).

**Amadeus IX.** 1435–1472. Duke of Savoy (1465–72); m. Yolande, daughter of Charles VII of France and sister of Louis XI; their son was Philibert I, Duke of Savoy.

**Am'a·de'us** (ăm'ȧ·dē'ŭs). *Ital.* **A'me·de'o** (ä'mā·dâ'ō). *Span.* **A'ma·de'o** (ä'mä·thā'ō). *In full* **Amedeo Ferdinando Maria di Sa·vo'ia** (dē sä·vô'yä). 1845–1890. Son of King Victor Emmanuel II of Italy; b. Turin. Duke of Aosta and king of Spain (1870–73), elected by Spanish Cortes after unsuccessful attempt to persuade prince of Hohenzollern (see LEOPOLD) to accept crown following revolution (1868) that deposed Isabella; attempted to exercise authority, but disliked by populace and opposed by all factions; abdicated (1873) following outbreak of Carlist civil war. See duke of the ABRUZZI.

**A'ma·dor' de los Rí'os** (ä'mä·thôr' thā lōs rē'ōs), **José.** 1818–1878. Spanish critic and historian.

**A'ma·dor' Guer·re'ro** (ä'mä·thôr' gĕr·rĕ'rō), **Manuel.** 1833–1909. Panamanian physician; a leader in Panama's struggle for independence; first president of republic (1904–08).

**A·mal'a·ric** (ȧ·măl'ȧ·rĭk). 502?–531 A.D. King of Visigoths (526–531); ruled Spain and part of Languedoc. Son of Alaric II (*q.v.*).

**Am'a·la·sun'tha** (ăm'ȧ·lȧ·sŭn'thȧ) *or* **Am'a·la·su·en'tha** (-sū·ĕn'thȧ) *or* **Am'a·la·swin'tha** (-swĭn'thȧ). 498–?535 A.D. Dau. of Theodoric (*q.v.*), King of Ostrogoths; left with two children at death of her husband Eutharic; succeeded her father as regent (526–?535) for her son; murdered.

**Am'a·lek** (ăm'ȧ·lĕk). *In Douay Version* **Am'a·lech** (-lĕk). In Bible, a grandson of Esau (*Gen.* xxxvi. 12) and ancestor of Amalekites.

**A·ma'li·a** (ä·mä'lē·ä). *In full* **Anna Amalia.** Duchess of **Saxe'–Wei'mar** (săks'vī'mär). 1739–1807. Wife (m. 1756) of Ernest Augustus Constantine, Duke of Saxe-Weimar (d. 1758). Regent (1758–75) for son Duke Charles Augustus. Patroness of literature and art.

**A·ma'li·e** (ä·mä'lē·ĕ). *In full* **Marie Friederike Amalie.** Princess of **Ol'den·burg** (ôl'dĕn·bŏŏrk). 1818–1875. Queen of Greece (1836–62) as wife of King Otto (m. 1836).

**A·ma'li·e Au·gu'ste** (ou·gŏŏs'tĕ). 1788–1851. Daughter of Maximilian I, King of Bavaria; m. (1806) Eugène de Beauharnais; had two sons and four daughters. See LEUCHTENBERG.

**A·ma'li·e Ma·ri'e Frie'de·ri'ke Au·gu'ste** (mä·rē'ĕ [mä·rē'] frē'dĕ·rē'kĕ ou·gŏŏs'tĕ). *Pseudonym* **Amalie Hei'ter** (hī'tĕr). 1794–1870. Duchess of Saxony; sister of King Frederick Augustus II and King John of Saxony. Dramatist and composer; author of *Die Fürstenbraut*, *Der Majoratserbe*, and *Der Oheim*.

**A·mal'ric** (ȧ·măl'rĭk; ăm'ăl·rĭk). *Also* **A·mau'ry** (ȧ·mô'rĭ; *Fr.* ȧ'mō'rē'). Name of two kings of Jerusalem: **Amalric I** (1135–1174); brother of Baldwin III; king (1162–74); struggled (1164–74) with Nureddin for control of Egypt, three times invading it; attacked by Saladin (1170); scholar and jurist. **Amalric II** (1144–1205); brother of Guy of Lusignan; m. (1197) Isabella, daughter of Amalric I and half sister of Sibylla, Guy of Lusignan's wife; king of Cyprus (1194–1205); titular king of Jerusalem (1197–1205); secured truce with Mohammedans (1198–1203).

**A·mal'ric of Be'na** (bē'nȧ). *Fr.* **A'mal'ric' de Bène'** (ȧ'mȧl'rēk' dē bân') *or* **A'mau'ri' de Char'tres** (ȧ'mō'rē' dē shȧr'tr'). d. 1204? French theologian and mystical philosopher, b. Bène, near Chartres. Founded Amalricians, pantheistic sect; doctrines condemned by Pope Innocent III (1204), by synod at Paris (1209), and by Lateran Council (1215).

**Aman.** See HAMAN.

**A'man'–Jean'** (ȧ'mäN'zhäN'), **Edmond.** 1860?–1936. French painter, esp. of portraits.

**A'man·ul'lah Khan** (ŭ'mȧn·ōōl'lä kän). 1892–1960. Amir of Afghanistan (1919–29); son of Habibullah Khan. Assumed crown on murder of his father; made treaties with Great Britain and Russia (1921); introduced reforms which led to revolt (1928); forced to abdicate; lived in Rome (1929 ff.); sought German aid (1941) in attempt to regain throne.

**A'ma·ra Sin'ha** (ŭ'mȧ·rȧ sĭN'hȧ). Sanskrit grammarian and poet of 4th century A.D.; author of *Amara-Kosha* (*Treasury of Amara*), collection of Sanskrit roots (in 3 books).

**A·ma'ri** (ä·mä'rē), **Michele.** 1806–1889. Italian historian and statesman. Member of Carbonari. Twice exile in France to avoid punishment for opposition to Bourbon rule of Naples; returned to Italy (1859). Taught Arabic at Pisa (1859), later at Florence. Senator (1861 ff.); minister of instruction (1862–64). Author of *La Guerra del Vespro Siciliano*, *Storia dei Musulmani in Sicilia*, and a bibliography of Arabic sources for history of Sicily.

**Am'a·sa** (ăm'ȧ·sȧ; ȧ·mā'sȧ). In Bible (*2 Sam.* xvii. 25; xx. 4–12), son of David's half sister Abigail and cousin of Joab; captain of Absalom's army; slain by Joab.

**Amasias.** See AMAZIAH.

**Amasis.** Kings of ancient Egypt. See AHMOSE.

**A·ma'ti** (ä·mä'tē). Name of Italian family of violinmakers of Cremona in 16th and 17th centuries. **Andrea Amati** (1530?–?1611) is credited with being designer of modern violin. His brother **Nicola** (fl. 1568–1586) made principally bass viols. Andrea's sons **Antonio** (1550?–1638) and **Girolamo** *or* **Geronimo** (1556?–?1630) made violins, violas, and violoncellos. Most famous member of family, Girolamo's son **Nicolò** *or* **Nicola** (1596–1684), teacher of Antonio Stradivari and of Andrea Guarnieri, improved on violin and developed grand Amati. His son **Girolamo** *or* **Geronimo** (1649–1740) was last of family to achieve distinction.

**A·ma'to** (ä·mä'tō), **Giovanni Antonio d'.** *Called* **Il Vec'chio** (vĕk'kyō), *i.e.* the old [man]. 1475–1555. Neapolitan painter of religious subjects.

**Amato, Pasquale.** 1879–1942. Operatic baritone, b. Naples, Italy. A leading baritone in Buenos Aires, and at La Scala in Milan. In U. S. at Metropolitan Opera House (1908 ff.).

**Amauri de Chartres.** See AMALRIC OF BENA.

**Amaury.** See AMALRIC.

**A'mau'ry'–Du'val'** (ȧ'mō'rē'dü'vȧl'), **Eugène Emmanuel.** *Real surname* **Pi'neux'–Du'val'** (pē'nû'-). 1808–1885. French painter, esp. of church murals and frescoes. See DUVAL family.

**Am'a·zi'ah** (ăm'ȧ·zī'ȧ). *In Douay Bible* **Am'a·si'as** (-sī'ăs). d. ?780 B.C. King of Judah (798–?780). Son of Joash. Conquered Edomites (798); challenged Joash, King of Israel; defeated and taken prisoner; assassinated at Lachish; succeeded by Uzziah (*2 Kings* xiv; *2 Chron.* xxv–xxvii).

**Am·bed'kar** (ȧm·bād'kĕr), **Bhimrao Ramji.** 1893–1956.

Hindu lawyer and social worker; educ. Columbia (1917), Bonn, and London School of Economics; ardent worker for abolition of caste, finally forcing Gandhi to take up untouchables as political issue; appointed (July, 1942) minister of labor in Indian cabinet.

**Am′ber′ger** (ăm′bĕr′gẽr), **Christoph.** 1500?–?1562. German portrait painter, b. Nuremberg; executed portraits of emperor Charles V, Sebastian Münster, etc.

**Am·bi′o·rix** (ăm·bī′ō·rĭks). Chief of Gallic tribe, the Eburones; their leader in campaigns against Romans (54–53 B.C).

**Am′boise′** (äN′bwȧz′), **Georges d′.** 1460–1510. Archbishop of Rouen (1493–98). On accession of Louis XII (1498) became cardinal and prime minister; active in French campaigns in northern Italy (1499–1503). Ambitious to become pope, but twice passed over; legate for life in France (1503).

**Am′broise′** (äN′brwȧz′) *or* **Am′brose** (ăm′brōz). Late 12th-century French chronicler of the Third Crusade.

**Am′bronn** (äm′brôn), **Leopold Friedrich August.** 1854–1930. German astronomer, b. Meiningen.

**Am′bros** (äm′brôs), **August Wilhelm.** 1816–1876. Music historian, composer, pianist, and critic, b. in Bohemia; author of *Geschichte der Musik* (1862–78).

**Am′brose** (ăm′brōz), *Lat.* **Am·bro′si·us** (ăm·brō′zhĭ·ŭs; -zĭ-), Saint. 340?–397. Bishop of Milan and father of the church, b. Trier. Consecrated bishop of Milan (374). Opposed Arianism; presided at church synod in Aquileia (381) which deposed Arian leaders Palladius and Secundianus. Remained in Milan during its occupation by Gauls, working for relief of poor; forced to flee Milan after assassination of Valentinian (392). Works include homiletic commentaries, as *De Spiritu Sancto, De Mysteriis,* and hymns, as *Deus Creator Omnium* and *Veni Redemptor Gentium.*

**Am·bro′si·us** (äm·brō′zē·ōōs), **Hermann Gustav Oskar.** 1897– . German composer, b. Hamburg; composed four symphonies, choral works, chamber music, etc.

**Am′drup** (ȧm′drōōp), **Georg Karl.** 1866–1947. Danish naval officer, b. Copenhagen. Charted east coast of Greenland (1898–99; 1900).

**Amédée, Amedeo.** French and Spanish forms, respectively, of AMADEUS.

**A·meer′ A·li′** (ă·mēr′ ă·lē′), **Syed.** Also **Seyyid Amir Ali.** 1849–1928. Indian jurist and Islamic leader. Grad. in arts and law, U. of Calcutta; held Tagore law professorship, U. of Calcutta (1884–85); judge of high court of Calcutta (1890–1904). Retired to live in England. Appointed Indian judge to Privy Council (1909) by Lord Morley.

**A′me·ghi′no** (ä′mā·gē′nō), **Fio·ri′no** (fyō·rē′nō). 1854?–1911. Argentine anthropologist and paleontologist, of Italian birth.

**A′me·lot′ de La Hous′saye′** (ȧm′lō′ dẽ lȧ ōō′sā′), **Abraham Nicolas.** 1634–1706. French publicist and historian; author of *Histoire du Gouvernement de Venise* (1676).

**Amen, Jacob.** See Jacob AMMANN.

**A·men′do·la** (ä·mĕn′dō·lä), **Giovanni.** 1882–1926. Italian politician, b. Naples. Professor of theoretical philosophy, U. of Pisa; opposed Fascist policies; died as result of beatings inflicted by political opponents.

**A′men·em·het′** (ä′mĕn·ĕm·hĕt′) *or* **A′men·em·hat′** (-hät′). Name of four kings of ancient Egypt of XIIth (Theban) dynasty: **Amenemhet I;** founder of dynasty (see MENTUHOTEP V); reigned (c. 2000–1970 B.C.), the last ten years with his son Sesostris as coregent; centralized authority of king; strengthened worship of Amen (Amon); erected pyramid at El Lisht. **Amenemhet II;** son of Sesostris I; reigned (c. 1938–1903 B.C.); coregent with his father (1938–1935 B.C.) and with his son Sesostris II (1906–1903); enjoyed reign of prosperity; increased trade with Punt. **Amenemhet III;** son of Sesostris III; reigned (c. 1849–1801 B.C.); one of great monarchs of Middle Kingdom; kept Egypt at high level of prosperity; developed mines in Sinai region; established vast irrigation system, esp. in Faiyum (Lake Moeris). His son **Amenemhet IV;** reigned (c. 1801–1792 B.C.).

**A′men·ho′tep** (ä′mĕn·hō′tĕp) *or* **Am′e·no′phis** (ăm′ē·nō′fĭs). Name of four kings of ancient Egypt of XVIIIth (Diospolite) dynasty: **Amenhotep I;** second king of dynasty; son of Ahmose I; reigned (c. 1557–1540 B.C.); invaded Nubia; fought wars with Libyans and Syrians (cf. THUTMOSE I). **Amenhotep II;** son of Thutmose III and Queen Hatshepsut; reigned (c. 1447–1420 B.C.); coregent with his father for one year; faced by revolts in Asia; fought successful campaigns in northern Palestine and on Euphrates (1447 B.C.); by firm rule kept Nubia under control; succeeded by his son Thutmose IV. **Amenhotep III;** last of great rulers of Middle Kingdom; son of Thutmose IV; reigned (c. 1411–1375 B.C.); m. Tiy; led successful expedition into Upper Nubia above second cataract; held supremacy in Asia, acknowledged by Babylonia; reign an era of magnificence and prosperity; his capital, Thebes, developed into great monumental city; erected temples, pylons, hypostyle halls (as at Karnak), colossi (Colossi of Memnon, near Thebes), obelisks, etc. His son **Amenhotep IV** = IKHNATON.

**A′mer·bach** (ä′mẽr·bäĸ), **Hans.** 1444–?1513. German printer in Basel. Published (1480–1512) over 70 works including those of St. Augustine (1506) and St. Ambrose. His son **Bonifacius** (1496?–1562), Swiss jurist and scholar, was a friend of Erasmus. Bonifacius's son **Basilius** (1533–1591) was a jurist and art collector.

**A′me·ri′ghi** (ä′mā·rē′gē) *or* **A′me·ri′gi** (-jē). Variant of *Merisi* (see Michelangelo da CARAVAGGIO).

**Amerigo Vespucci.** *Lat.* **Americus Vespucius.** See VESPUCCI.

**A′mer·ling** (ä′mẽr·lĭng), **Friedrich von.** 1803–1887. Austrian portrait painter.

**A′mer·y** (ā′mẽr·ĭ), **Leopold Charles Maurice Stennett.** 1873–1955. English publicist and statesman, b. in India. Educ. Oxford. On editorial staff, London *Times* (1899–1909); completed *Times History of the South African War* (7 vols., 1909). M.P. as Unionist (1911); served in army in Flanders and Near East (1914–16). First lord of admiralty (1922–24); secretary of state for colonies (1924–29) and for dominion affairs (1925–29), for India (1940–45). Author of *The Empire in the New Era* (1928), *The Forward View* (1935), etc.

**Ames** (āmz), **Adelbert.** 1835–1933. American general, b. Rockland, Me. Served through Civil War; brevetted major general (1866). U. S. senator from Mississippi (1870–74); governor of Mississippi (1874–76); appointed brigadier general in Spanish-American War (1898).

**Ames, Fisher.** 1758–1808. American statesman, b. Dedham, Mass. Member, U. S. House of Representatives (1789–97). Supported Hamilton's policies; opposed commercial retaliation against Great Britain (1794); distrusted democratic tendencies and policies advocated by Jefferson. His writings and speeches collected in *Works of Fisher Ames* and *Speeches of Fisher Ames in Congress.*

**Ames, James Barr.** 1846–1910. American educator, b. Boston. Grad. Harvard (1868), Harvard Law School (1872). Professor of law (1877–95), dean (1895–1910), Harvard Law School. Adapted successfully Langdell system of teaching law by study of cases; prepared case books. Author of *Lectures on Legal History* (pub. 1913).

**Ames, Joseph.** 1689–1759. English bibliographer and antiquarian, b. Yarmouth. Compiler of *Typographical Antiquities* (1749), regarded as foundation of English bibliography.

**Ames, Joseph Alexander.** 1816–1872. American portrait painter, b. Roxbury, Mass.

**Ames, Joseph Sweetman.** 1864–1943. American physicist, b. Manchester, Vt. Researcher in electrodynamics and spectroscopy. Member (1917 ff.), chairman (1927–39), National Advisory Committee for Aeronautics. President of the Johns Hopkins U. (1929–35). Special editor for physics, aeronautics and aviation, *Webster's New International Dictionary, Second Edition.*

**Ames, Mary,** *nee* **Clem′mer** (klĕm′ẽr). 1839–1884. American writer, b. Utica, N.Y.; m. Rev. Daniel Ames (divorced 1874), Edmund Hudson (1883). Author of *Memorial of Alice and Phoebe Cary* (1873), *Ten Years in Washington* (1874), *Poems of Life and Nature* (1882), and novels.

**Ames, Oakes.** 1804–1873. American financier and politician, b. Easton, Mass. Made fortune in Oliver Ames & Sons, shovel manufacturers. Member, U.S. House of Representatives (1863–73). Involved in affairs of Union Pacific Railroad construction and Crédit Mobilier; sold shares of Crédit Mobilier to members of Congress to forestall investigation (1867–68); exposed by investigating committee (1872–73) and publicly censured by vote of House of Representatives (1873). His son **Oliver** (1831–1895) was governor of Massachusetts (1886, 1887, 1888).

**Ames, Oakes.** 1874–1950. Grandson of Oakes AMES (1804–1873). American botanist, b. North Easton, Mass. (A.B., Harvard (1898). On staff (1899–1922), director (1910–22), Harvard botanical garden; professor of botany, Harvard (1926–41); presented to Harvard (1940) his orchid herbarium of 57,000 specimens. Author of many works on orchids, esp. a serial work, *Orchidaceae*, of which seven volumes have been published (1942).

**Ames, Oliver.** 1807–1877. American manufacturer, b. Plymouth, Mass. Associated with brother, Oakes Ames, in shovel manufacture. Acting president, Union Pacific Railroad (1866–68), president (1868–71); director of other railroads. His son **Frederick Lothrop** (1835–1893) was a capitalist interested in railroads, banks, real estate, etc.

**Ames, Winthrop.** 1871–1937. Grandson of Oakes AMES (1804–1873). American theatrical producer, b. North Easton, Mass. Managed theaters in Boston and New York (1905–32); built Little Theater (1912) and Booth Theater, New York (1913); produced *Snow White*, first play in New York City especially for children; revived Gilbert and Sullivan operas.

**Am·fi·te·a′trov** (ŭm·fyĭ·tyĭ·ȧ′trôf), **Aleksandr Valentinovich.** 1862–1923. Russian novelist, publicist, and playwright.

**Am′herst** (ăm′ẽrst; -ûrst), **Jeffrey.** Baron **Amherst.** 1717–1797. British officer in America, b. in Kent, England. Ordered (1758) to America to command army against French fortress of Louisburg; Louisburg capitulated (July 27, 1758). Commander in chief in North America (1759); captured Ticonderoga (July 27) and Crown Point (Aug. 4). Attacked Montreal and captured it (Sept. 8, 1760). Appointed governor general of British North America (1760–63). Created baron (1776), field marshal (1796).

**Amherst, William Pitt.** Earl **Amherst of A′ra·kan′** (ä′rä·kän′; ăr′ȧ·kăn′). 1773–1857. Nephew of Jeffrey Amherst. Envoy to Peking (1816–17); governor general of India (1823); conducted successful war on king of Burma (1824–26); retired to England (1828).

**A·mi′ci** (ä·mē′chē), **Giovanni Battista.** 1786?–?1863. Italian astronomer and opticist; developed reflecting telescope, achromatic microscope, polarization apparatus.

**Amicis, Edmondo De.** See DE AMICIS.

**Amidas, Philip.** See AMADAS.

**A′miel′** (ȧ′myĕl′), **Henri Frédéric.** 1821–1881. Swiss poet and philosopher. Professor of aesthetics and moral philosophy at Geneva academy; author of *Journal Intime* (pub. in part, 1883–84), an introspective diary.

**A′mi·go′ni** (ä′mē·gō′nē), **Jacopo.** 1675–1752. Venetian painter, esp. of portraits and mythological subjects.

**A·min′, al-** (ăl·ă·mēn′). *Arab.* **al-Amīn.** 785?–813. Abbasside caliph of Baghdad (809–813); son and successor of Harun al-Rashid; opposed by his brother al-Mamum, who besieged Baghdad (813); murdered for surrendering.

**A′miot′** *or* **A′myot′** (ȧ′myō′), **Jean Joseph Marie.** 1718–1793. French Jesuit; missionary to China (from 1740); author of books on China and a Manchu grammar.

**Amir Ali, Seyyid.** See Syed AMEER ALI.

**Am′man** (äm′än), **Johann Konrad.** 1669–?1724. Swiss physician; wrote on instruction of deaf and dumb.

**Amman, Jost.** 1539–1591. Swiss engraver in Nuremberg. Executed many woodcuts for editions of Bible (1564–71), 115 woodcuts for a book on arts and trades (1568), copperplate engravings of a series of kings of France, etc.

**Am′ma·na′ti** (äm′mä·nä′tē), **Bartolommeo.** 1511–1592. Florentine architect and sculptor.

**Am′man** (äm′än) *or* **A′men** (ä′mĕn), **Jacob.** Swiss Mennonite bishop; led (1693–97) schism from Mennonite church in Switzerland and Alsace; followers known as Amish or Amish Mennonites.

**Am′men** (ăm′ĕn), **Daniel.** 1819–1898. American naval officer and author, b. in Ohio. Participated in attack on Port Royal (1861), Fort McAllister (1863), Fort Fisher (1864–65).

**Am′mers-Kül′ler** (äm′ẽrs·kül′ẽr), **Johanna** (*called* **Jo**) **van.** 1884–1966. Dutch novelist, playwright, and short-story writer, b. Delft; married (1904) and lived in London; published 3 plays and her first success, the novel *The House of Joy;* moved to Amsterdam; published *The Rebel Generation* (1925). Other works include *Jenny Heysten's Career* (1930), *Tantalus* (1930), *No Surrender* (1931), *The House of Tavelinck* (1939).

**Am′mi·a′nus Mar′cel·li′nus** (ăm′ĭ·ā′nŭs mär′sĕ·lī′nŭs). fl. second half of 4th century A.D. Roman soldier and historian, b. Antioch of Greek family. Author of a Latin history of Roman Empire from Nerva to death of Valens (96–378), constituting a continuation of Tacitus' history; of 31 original books, 18 are extant, covering period from 353 to 378.

**Am′mi·ra′to** (äm′mē·rä′tō), **Scipione.** 1531–1601. Italian historian; author of *Istorie Fiorentine*, covering history of Tuscany to 1574.

**Ammon.** See BEN-AMMI.

**Am′mon** (äm′ōn), **Christoph Friedrich von.** 1766–1850. German Protestant theologian.

**Am·mo′ni·us** (ă·mō′nĭ·ŭs). *Called* **Ammonius Li·thot′o·mus** (lĭ·thŏt′ō·mŭs). fl. 3d century B.C. Greek surgeon; introduced practice of lithotrity.

**Ammonius.** *Surnamed* **Sac′cas** (săk′ăs), *i.e.* sack bearer, from his early occupation as a porter. Alexandrian philosopher of 1st half of 3d century A.D. Founder of Neoplatonism; teacher of Plotinus, Longinus, Origen, etc. Said to have attempted to harmonize doctrines of Plato and Aristotle.

**Ammonius of Alexandria.** Alexandrian Christian philosopher of 3d century; reputed author of a harmony of the Gospels and a work on the agreement of the teachings of Moses and Jesus.

**A'mon'tons'** (á'môN'tôN'), **Guillaume.** 1663–1705. French physicist; investigated phenomena of friction; invented system of long-distance signaling through a series of stations.

**A'mo·ret'ti** (ä'mô·rāt'tē), **Carlo.** 1741–1816. Italian naturalist and geographer.

**A'mo·ry** (ā'mô·rĭ), **Thomas.** 1691?–1788. English author of Irish descent. Author of *Memoirs, Containing Lives of Several Ladies of Great Britain* (1755) and *Life of John Buncle, Esq.* (1756–66).

**A'mos** (ā'mŏs). Minor Hebrew prophet of 8th century B.C.; herdsman of Tekoa, near Bethlehem, whose reproofs, exhortations, and visions, addressed to Israel, are recorded in Old Testament book of *Amos.*

**A'mos** (ā'mŏs), Sir **Maurice Sheldon.** 1872–1940. British jurist; educ. Cambridge; admitted to bar (1897); judicial adviser to government of Egypt (1919–25); professor of comparative law, London U. (1932–37). Author of *The English Constitution* (1930), *The American Constitution* (1938), etc.

**Amosis.** Kings of ancient Egypt. See AHMOSE.

**Am'père'** (äN'pâr'), **André Marie.** 1775–1836. French scientist, b. near Lyons. Professor of physics, Collège de France, Paris (1824). Discovered important principles in field of magnetism and electricity; formulated law (Ampère's law) which forms basis of study of electrodynamics. Invented astatic needle, which made invention of astatic galvanometer possible. The ampere, or unit of intensity of an electric current, is named after him. His son **Jean Jacques Antoine** (1800–1864), essayist and literary historian, wrote *Histoire Romaine à Rome* (1858), etc.

**Am'phis** (ăm'fĭs). fl. 4th century B.C. Greek writer of comedies.

**Ampt'hill** (ăm(p)t'(h)ĭl), Barons. See RUSSELL family.

**Am·pu'dia** (äm·pōō'thyä), **Pedro de.** fl. 1840. Mexican general; commanded Mexican army on Rio Grande at beginning of Mexican War (1846); surrendered to General Taylor at Monterrey (1846).

**Am'ra·phel** (ăm'rȧ·fĕl; ăm·rā'-). In Bible (*Gen.* xiv), king of Shinar; possibly, but improbably, to be identified with the Babylonian king Hammurabi (*q.v.*).

**Amr ibn-al-As** (ăm·rōōb'nĭl·äs'). *In Eng. sometimes* **Am·ru'** (ăm·rōō'). *Arab.* **'Amr ibn-al-'Āṣ.** 594?–664. Arab general and statesman, of tribe of Koreish. Strong opponent of Mohammed in his earlier years, but converted to Islam (629); one of abu-Bakr's great generals; took part in conquest of Syria (633); sent (639) by Caliph Omar I to subdue Egypt; seized Pelusium and defeated Egyptians at Heliopolis (640); first Mohammedan governor of Egypt (642–644); recalled to subdue Alexandria (645–646); later falsely accused of ordering destruction of Alexandrine Library; after death of Caliph Othman (656), sided with Muawiyah against Ali in civil strife; vicegerent of Egypt (658–664); administration efficient; projected canal to unite Mediterranean and Red seas.

**'Amr' ibn-Bahr'** (ăm'ĕr ĭb''n·bär'). *Surnamed* **al-Jā'ḥiẓ** (äl·jä'hĭz), *i.e.* the goggle-eyed. 773?–869. Arab writer; known as founder of Arabic prose style; author of books on rhetoric, morals, etiquette, etc.

**Amr ibn-Kul·thum'** (ăm·rōōb'nĭ·kōōl·thōōm'). *Arab.* **'Amr ibn-Kulthūm.** d. 600 A.D.? Pre-Islamic Arabian poet, notable especially for odes.

**Amru.** See AMR IBN-AL-AS.

**Amru-'l-Kais.** See IMRU'-AL-QAYS.

**Ams'dorf** (äms'dôrf), **Nikolaus von.** 1483–1565. German Protestant theologian. Supported Luther; aided in translation of Bible. Bishop of Naumburg (1542–46).

**Am'she·witz** (?ăm'shĕ·wĭts), **J. H.** 1882–1942. English mural and portrait painter.

**Ams'ler** (äms'lẽr) *or* **Ams'ler-Laf'fon** (-läf'ōn), **Jakob.** 1823–1912. Swiss mathematician; invented (1854) a form of planimeter adapted for measuring irregular plane areas.

**Amsler, Samuel.** 1791–1849. Swiss engraver; employed at Rome (from 1816), Munich (from 1829); known esp. for engravings of works of Raphael.

**Am'stutz** (ăm'stŭts), **Noah Steiner.** 1864– . American engineer and patent attorney, b. in Wayne County, Ohio. Originated first phototelegraphy system and first automatic half-tone engraving machine; wrote *Handbook of Photo Engraving* (1907).

**A'mul·ree** (ā'mŭl·rē), 1st Baron. **William Warrender Mackenzie.** 1860–1942. British jurist; authority on local government.

**A'mund·sen** (ä'mōōn·sĕn), **Roald.** 1872–1928. Norwegian polar explorer, b. Borge. Navigated Northwest Passage and fixed position of North Magnetic Pole (1903–06). Discovered South Pole (Dec., 1911). Completed Northeast Passage (1920); flew across North Pole with Lincoln Ellsworth (1926). Disappeared (June, 1928) on flight to rescue Nobile who was lost returning from North Pole. Author of *North West Passage* (1908), *The South Pole* (1912), *The North East Passage* (1918–20), *Our Polar Flight* (with Lincoln Ellsworth; 1925), *First Crossing of the Polar Sea* (with Lincoln Ellsworth; 1927), *My Life as an Explorer* (1927). See Lincoln ELLSWORTH.

**Amurath.** See MURAD.

**A'my** (ā'mĭ), **Ernest Valentine.** 1892– . American engineer, b. New York City. E.E., Columbia (1917). With N.Y. Edison Co. (1910–20), Radio Corp. of America (1922–28); consulting engineer (from 1928). Inventor and coinventor of sound-absorbing blocks, devices for noise reduction in radio, and aerial systems for radio.

**A·myn'tas** (ȧ·mĭn'tȧs). Name of three kings of Macedonia: **Amyntas I** (d. 498 B.C.), fifth in descent from Perdiccas; acknowledged himself tributary vassal to Persian sovereign, Darius Hystaspis. **Amyntas II** (reigned 394–370 B.C.), father of Philip of Macedon and nephew of Perdiccas II. **Amyntas III** (reigned 360–359 B.C.; d. 336), grandson of Amyntas II; excluded from throne (359) by his uncle Philip of Macedon; executed (336) by Alexander the Great for plotting against him.

**Amyntor, Gerhard von.** Pseudonym of Dagobert von GERHARDT.

**A'myot'** (á'myō'), **Jacques.** 1513–1593. French scholar, b. Melun. Bishop of Auxerre (1570). Translator of ancient classics, esp. of Plutarch's *Lives* (1559), his translation of which forms the basis for the English translation by Thomas North (1579).

**Amyot, Jean Joseph Marie.** See AMIOT.

**A'my'raut'** (á'mē'rō'), **Moïse.** *Lat.* **Moses Am'y·ral'dus** (ăm'ĭ·răl'dŭs). 1596–1664. French Protestant theologian. His liberal form of Calvinism (Amyraldism) had many adherents in colonial New England.

**An'a·char'sis** (ăn'ȧ·kär'sĭs). fl. 600 B.C. Scythian philosopher; visited Athens and became acquainted with Solon; reputed author of many epigrams and letters.

**Anacharsis Cloots.** See CLOOTS.

**An'a·cle'tus** (ăn'ȧ·klē'tŭs) *or* **Cle'tus** (klē'tŭs), Saint. Third pope (bishop of Rome; 79?–?90).

**Anacletus II.** *Orig.* **Pietro Pier'le·o'ni** (pyâr'lā·ō'nē). Antipope (1130–38) elected in opposition to Innocent II; excommunicated (1134) by Council of Pisa.

**A·nac're·on** (ȧ·năk'rē·ŏn). 572?–?488 B.C. Greek lyric poet, b. in coastal city of Teos, Asia Minor. Said to have served in Greek forces resisting invasion of Cyrus the

Great (545); reputed tutor of Polycrates of Samos and, later, a favored courtier in king's retinue. After death of Polycrates, invited by Hipparchus to Athens; met Simonides and other literary men of the time. Famed for satires, and esp. for lyrics and hymns. His short lyrics celebrating love and wine have fixed term "Anacreontics" for a class of poetry of this kind. Only fragments of his verse are extant, including notably two short hymns to Artemis and Dionysus. A collection of some 60 lyrics published under Anacreon's name in 1554 is now regarded as spurious.

**A·nag'nos** (ȧ·năg'nŏs), **Mi'chael** (mī'kĕl; -k'l). 1837–1906. Educator, b. in Epirus, Greece. Educ. U. of Athens. To U.S. (c. 1867); head of Perkins Institution (for the blind), Watertown, Mass. (1876–1906).

**A·nan' ben Da'vid** (ȧ·nän' bĕn dā'vĭd). fl. 8th century A.D. Jewish religious leader in Persia. Founder (c. 765) of sect of Karaites, within Judaism, but opposed to rabbinism and Talmudism; unsuccessful candidate for exilarch; particular doctrine (Ananism) developed in his work *The Book of the Precepts* (pub. c. 770).

**A'nand** (ä'nȧnd), **Mulk** (mo͝olk) **Raj** (räj). 1905– . Indian novelist and critic; works include a trilogy of novels of contemporary India with a sepoy hero, *Lal Singh*, *The Village* (1939), *Across the Black Waters* (1940), and *The Sword and the Sickle* (1942).

**A'nan·da** (ä'nȧn·dȧ). fl. 5th century B.C. Favorite disciple of Buddha.

**A·nan·da Ma·hi·dol** (ä·nän·tä mä·hēd·dōn). 1925–1946. King of Thailand (1935–46), under regency of three (1935–40). Son of Mahidol, brother of King Prajadhipok. Educ. Switzerland (until 1938); made first state visit to Thailand in 1938. Assassinated.

**An'a·ni'as** (ăn'ȧ·nī'ăs) and his wife **Sap·phi'ra** (să·fī'rȧ) *or, in Douay Version,* **Sa·phi'ra.** In Bible early Christians who were struck dead for lying to the Apostle Peter (*Acts* v. 1–11).

**An'as·ta'si·a** (ăn'ăs·tā'shĭ·ȧ; -shȧ; -zhĭ·ȧ; -zhȧ). Name of two Christian martyrs, the first slain during reign of Nero (54–68), the second (Saint Anastasia), during persecution under Diocletian (c. 303 or 304).

**Anastasia Romanovna.** See ROMANOV.

**An'as·ta'si·us** (ăn'ăs·tā'shĭ·ŭs; -shŭs; -zhĭ·ŭs; -zhŭs). (1) Name of four popes (see *Table of Popes*, Nos. 39, 50, 121, 168), especially: **Anastasius IV.** d. 1154. Pope (1153–54); b. Rome. Settled controversy in regard to candidature of Frederick I for emperor; issued interdict against Arnold of Brescia. (2) Name of an antipope (855) in time of Benedict III.

**Anastasius.** Name of two rulers of Eastern Roman Empire:

**Anastasius I.** 430?–518. Emperor (491–518), a palace official, b. Dyrrhachium (Durazzo), raised to throne for his ability and integrity; m. widow of Zeno (491); put down revolt in Asia Minor (492–496); fought indecisive war with Persia (502–505); empire invaded by Huns, Slavs, and Bulgarians (507–512); built Anastasian Wall (512) from Propontis (Sea of Marmara) to Euxine (Black Sea) to keep out barbarians; made (506) Anastasian law and rescript; suspected of being Monophysite.

**Anastasius II.** d. 721. Emperor (713–716); organized strong army and navy; overthrown by mutiny; retired to Thessalonica and became monk; slain by Leo III.

**Anastasius.** *Called* **Anastasius Bib'li·o·the·car'i·us** (bĭb'lĭ·ō·thē·kâr'ĭ·ŭs). fl. 9th century. Librarian of the Vatican; translated *Acts* of Council of Constantinople (869) from Greek into Latin.

**An'ax·ag'o·ras** (ăn'ăk·săg'ō·răs). 500?–428 B.C. Greek philosopher, b. Clazomenae. Taught in Athens for 30 years (c. 462–c. 432), his pupils including Pericles, Euripides, and possibly Socrates; charged with impiety and banished from Athens for life. First to introduce dualistic explanation of universe: held that all natural objects are composed of infinitesimally small particles, or atoms, containing mixtures of all qualities, and that mind or intelligence acts upon masses of these particles to produce objects we see. Among his other tenets were beliefs that heavenly bodies are masses of stone cast from the earth, and that animals and man sprang from warm moist clay.

**An'ax·ar'chus** (ăn'ăk·sär'kŭs). fl. about 350 B.C. Greek philosopher. Disciple of Democritus; adherent of atomism and eudaemonism.

**A·nax'i·man'der** (ȧ·năk'sĭ·măn'dēr). 611–547 B.C. Greek astronomer and philosopher of Miletus; disciple of Thales. Credited with discovery of obliquity of the ecliptic, introduction of sundial, and invention of geographical maps. Taught that the first principle, or primary substance, is eternal and indestructible matter (the boundless or the infinite) containing within itself all contraries, such as heat and cold, moist and dry, and that the phenomenal universe has been evolved through the separation of these contraries and the creative union of those elements which have an affinity for each other, such as heat and moisture.

**An'ax·im'e·nes of Lamp'sa·cus** (ăn'ăk·sĭm'ē·nēz ŭv lămp'sȧ·kŭs). fl. 4th century B.C. Greek rhetorician and historian. Wrote histories of Philip of Macedon and of Greece, and an epic on Alexander; probable author of *Rhetorica ad Alexandrum*, usually attributed to Aristotle.

**Anaximenes of Mi·le'tus** (mī·lē'tŭs; mĭ-). Greek philosopher of 6th century B.C.; held that air is the primary substance and that all things are derived from it by varying degrees of compression or rarefaction.

**An'ce·lot'** (äɴs'lō'), **Jacques Arsène François Polycarpe.** 1794–1854. French dramatist, poet, and novelist. His wife, **Marguerite Virginie,** *nee* **Char'don'** [shȧr'dôɴ'] (1792–1875), also wrote for the theater.

**An'chi·e'ta** (äɴ'shē·ā'tȧ), **José de.** 1533–1597. Portuguese Jesuit missionary, b. Canary Islands. To Brazil (1553); founded college for conversion of Indians. Author of an Indian grammar and works on Brazil. Called "Apostle of Brazil."

**An'cil'lon'** (äɴ'sē'yôɴ'), **Charles.** 1659–1715. Jurist and writer, b. Metz; fled to Berlin after revocation of Edict of Nantes (1685); councilor of king of Prussia; author of works on revocation of Edict of Nantes. His great-grandson **Jean Pierre Frédéric,** *or* **Johann Peter Friedrich** (1767–1837), b. Berlin, was pastor of French Reformed Church in Berlin; royal historiographer (1803); Prussian secretary of state for foreign affairs (1832).

**Anc'kar·ström** *or* **An'kar·ström** (àng'kȧr·strûm), **Johan Jakob.** 1762–1792. Swedish army officer; assassin of King Gustavus III of Sweden (1792).

**An·co'na** (äng·kō'nä) **Alessandro d'.** 1835–1914. Italian critic, journalist, and scholar; author of *Origini del Teatro in Italia* (1877).

**An'cre** (äɴ'kr'), Marquis **d'. Concino Con·ci'ni** (kōn·chē'nē). d. 1617. Italian adventurer, b. Florence. To France in suite of Marie de Médicis when she married Henry IV (1600). With his wife, Leonora Galigai, stirred up queen's enmity against Henry. After Henry's death (1610) bought marquisate of Ancre in Picardy; made marshal and prime minister (1613). Assassinated.

**An'cus Mar'ci·us** (ăng'kŭs mär'shĭ·ŭs; mär'shŭs). Fourth legendary king (641–616 B.C.) of early Rome; a Latin, grandson of Numa Pompilius. Supposed to have founded plebeian class.

**An'czyc** (än'chĭts), **Władysław Ludwik.** 1824–1883.

Polish writer, b. Vilna; author of comedies and poems; translator of German and French classics.

**An′der·le′dy** (ăn′dẽr·lā′dĕ), **Anton Maria.** 1819–1892. General of Jesuit order; b. Valais, Switzerland.

**An′dersch** (ăn′dẽrsh), **Carl Samuel.** 1732–1777. German anatomist.

**Andersen.** See also ANDERSON and ANDERSSON.

**An′der·sen** (ȧn′ẽr·s'n), **Hans Christian.** 1805–1875. Danish author, b. Odense, Denmark, son of a poor shoemaker. Educated at expense of generous patrons. His early novels were *The Improvvisatore* (1835), *O. T.* (1836), *Only a Fiddler* (1837). His chief claim to fame, however, rests on his *Fairy Tales* (first series, 1835; second series, 1838–42; third series, 1845; others at irregular intervals; last series, 1871–72). Among the best-known of the Fairy Tales are *The Fir Tree, The Ugly Duckling, The Tinder-Box, The Red Shoes, Little Claus and Big Claus, The Swineherd, The Snow Queen.*

**Andersen Nexö, Martin.** See NEXÖ.

**Anderson.** See also ANDERSEN and ANDERSSON.

**An′der·son** (ăn′dẽr·s'n), **Alexander.** 1775–1870. American engraver, b. New York City. Made first wood engravings in America (1794).

**Anderson, Alexander.** *Pseudonym* **Sur′face·man** (sûr′fĭs·măn). 1845–1909. Scottish poet; railway track layer (surfaceman). Author of *A Song of Labour and other Poems* (1873), *Songs of the Rail* (1878). Librarian, Edinburgh University (1880).

**Anderson, Benjamin M.** 1886–1949. American economist, b. Columbia, Mo. Taught economics, Columbia U. (1911–13), Harvard (1913–18); economist, Chase National Bank, N.Y. (1920–39); professor of economics, U.C.L.A. (1939–46).

**Anderson, Carl David.** 1905– . American physicist, b. New York City; for discovery of positron (1932), awarded (with Victor Franz Hess) 1936 Nobel prize for physics.

**Anderson, Carl Thomas.** 1865–1948. American cartoonist, b. Madison, Wis. Author of *How to Draw Cartoons Successfully* (1935); creator of comic strip *Henry.*

**Anderson, Chandler Parsons.** 1866–1936. American lawyer, b. Lakeville, Conn.; B.A., Yale (1887); at Harvard Law School (1888–89); adm. to bar (1891); practiced, New York City. Engaged esp. in international arbitration; counselor, U.S. Department of State (1910–13); U.S. arbitrator on British-American pecuniary claims arbitration (1913–23); U.S. commissioner, mixed claims commission between U.S. and Germany (from 1923). An editor of *American Journal of International Law.*

**Anderson, David.** 1880-1953. English bridge and tunnel engineer; responsible for design and construction of Southwark Bridge, Tyne Bridge, Wearmouth Bridge, Tees Bridge, Londonderry Bridge, Mersey Tunnel, etc.

**Anderson,** Sir **David Murray.** 1874–1936. British admiral. First governor and commander in chief (1933–36) of Newfoundland as crown colony.

**Anderson,** Sir **Edmund.** 1530–1605. English lawyer. Educ. Lincoln College, Oxford. Lord chief justice of common pleas (1582); took part in trials of Mary, Queen of Scots (1586), and Sir Walter Raleigh (1603).

**Anderson, Edwin Hatfield.** 1861–1947. American librarian, b. Zionsville, Ind. Organizer (1895), librarian (1895–1904), Carnegie Library, Pittsburgh, Pa.; director, N.Y. Public Library (1913–34).

**Anderson, Elizabeth,** *nee* **Gar′rett** (găr′ĕt). **1836–1917.** English physician and pioneer in movement for admission of women to professions. Opened (1866) in London a dispensary for women, now the Elizabeth Garrett Anderson Hospital. M.D., U. of Paris (1870); m. J. G. S. Anderson (1871); first English woman mayor (Aldeburgh, 1908).

**Anderson, Elizabeth,** *nee* **Mil′bank** (mĭl′băngk). 1850–1921. American philanthropist, b. New York City; m. (1887) Abram A. Anderson, portrait painter. Created Milbank Memorial Fund (1905), income to be used to "improve the physical, mental, and moral condition of humanity." See also Joseph MILBANK.

**Anderson, Isabel.** See under Larz ANDERSON.

**Anderson, James.** 1739–1808. Scottish economist, b. near Edinburgh. Author of *An Inquiry into the Nature of the Corn Laws* (1777), anticipating theory of rent called after Ricardo. Inventor of a two-horse plow without wheels, often called Scotch plow.

**Anderson, John.** 1726–1796. Scottish professor of physics, U. of Glasgow. Author of *Institutes of Physics* (1786). Bequeathed property for founding Anderson College, Glasgow.

**Anderson,** Sir **John.** Viscount **Wa′ver·ley** (wā′vẽr·lĭ). 1882–1958. British civil servant. Entered colonial office (1905), permanent undersecretary (1922–32); governor of Bengal (1932–37); M.P. (1938); lord privy seal (1938–39); home secretary and minister of home security (1939–40) in charge of interning of enemy aliens and building of air-raid shelters (one type of shelter being named for him); lord president of the council (1940–43); chancellor of the exchequer (1943–45).

**Anderson, Joseph.** 1757–1837. American jurist and political leader, b. White Marsh, Pa. Served through Revolutionary War; senator from Tennessee (1797–1815); first comptroller, U.S. Treasury (1815–36).

**Anderson,** Dame **Judith.** *Original name* **Frances Margaret Anderson.** 1898– . Actress, b. Adelaide, Australia. On U.S. stage from 1918, playing leading parts in *Cobra* (1924), *Strange Interlude* (1930), *As You Desire Me* (1930–31), *Mourning Becomes Electra* (1931), *The Old Maid* (1935), etc.

**Anderson, Karl.** 1874–1956. Brother of Sherwood Anderson. American portrait painter and illustrator.

**Anderson,** Sir **Kenneth Arthur Noel.** 1891–1959. British general; served in World War I, in India (1930–31), at Dunkirk (1940); commander, 1st army (1942), in East Africa (1945); lieut. general (1943); governor of Gibraltar (1947–52); general (1949).

**An′der·son** *or* **An′ders·son** (ȧn′dẽr(s)·sôn), **Lars.** *Lat.* **Laurentius An·dre′ae** (ăn·drē′ē). 1480?–1552. Swedish reformer, b. Strengnäs; with Olaus Petri, published translation of New Testament (1526).

**An′der·son** (ăn′dẽr·s'n), **Larz.** 1866–1937. American diplomat, b. Paris, France; grad. Harvard (1888). U.S. minister to Belgium (1911–12); ambassador to Japan (1912–13). His wife, **Isabel,** *nee* **Perkins** (1876–1948), b. Boston, author of books and plays for young people.

**Anderson, Marian.** 1902– . American concert contralto, b. Philadelphia. Began singing career (1924); appeared on concert stage in Europe; recital in New York (Dec. 30, 1935), subsequently appearing successfully throughout U.S. Awarded Spingarn medal (1939).

**An′der·son** (ăn′dẽr·s'n), **Mary.** 1872–1964. Labor union leader, b. Lidköping, Sweden; to U.S. (1888). Employee in clothing factory, Chicago, and for 18 years in shoe factory. Director, Women's Bureau, U.S. Department of Labor (1919–44).

**Anderson, Mary Antoinette.** 1859–1940. American actress, b. Sacramento, Calif. Chief roles include Juliet (debut role, Louisville, Ky., 1875), Rosalind in *As You Like It,* Bianca in *Fazio,* Clarice in *Comedy and Tragedy,* and Perdita in *A Winter's Tale.* Married Antonio de Navarro (1889), retired, and settled in England.

**Anderson, Mary Reid,** *nee* **Mac·ar′thur** (măk·är′thẽr).

1880–1921. English labor organizer; m. W. C. Anderson (1911). Organized National Federation of Women Workers.

**Anderson, Maxwell.** 1888–1959. American playwright, b. Atlantic, Pa. Grad., U. of North Dakota (1911); M.A., Stanford (1914). Taught school, then worked as a journalist to 1924. Dramatic works include *What Price Glory* (with Laurence Stallings, 1924), *Saturday's Children* (1927), *Elizabeth the Queen* (1930), *Mary of Scotland* (1933), *Valley Forge* (1934), *Winterset* (1935), *High Tor* (1936), *Key Largo* (1939), *The Eve of St. Mark* (1942), *Anne of the Thousand Days* (1948), *Lost in the Stars* (1949), *The Bad Seed* (1955).

**Anderson, Philip Warren.** 1923– . American physicist. With Bell Laboratories (1949– ), visiting professor, Cambridge U. (1967– ); awarded (with Sir Nevill F. Mott and John H. Van Vleck) Nobel prize for physics (1977).

**An'der·son** (ăn'dēr·s'n), **Ras'mus** (răs'mŭs) **Björn** (byûrn). 1846–1936. American author, editor, and diplomat, b. Albion, Wis. U.S. minister to Denmark (1885–89). Author of *The Scandinavian Languages* (1873), *America not Discovered by Columbus* (1874), *Viking Tales of the North* (1877), etc.; translator of many Scandinavian works.

**Anderson, Richard H.** 1821–1879. American army officer, b. Statesburg, S.C. Grad. U.S.M.A., West Point (1842). Confederate brigadier general (1861), major general (1862), lieutenant general, temporary (1864).

**Anderson, Robert.** 1750–1830. Scottish editor and critic, b. in Lanarkshire. Edited *A Complete Edition of the Poets of Great Britain* (14 vols., 1792–1807).

**Anderson, Robert.** 1805–1871. American army officer, b. in Kentucky. Grad. U.S.M.A., West Point (1825). In command of Fort Sumter at time of Confederate attack.

**Anderson, Rudolph Martin.** 1876–1961. Canadian zoologist, b. in Iowa, U.S.A. Zoologist, Geological Survey of Canada (1913–20); chief of division of biology and consulting zoologist, department of mines and resources, Ottawa (1920–46). Author of books on Canadian mammals and wild animal life. Special editor (furs and fur-bearing animals), *Webster's New International Dictionary, Second Edition.*

**Anderson, Sherwood.** 1876–1941. American poet, novelist, and story writer, b. Camden, Ohio. Newspaper editor in Marion, Va. Author of *Windy McPherson's Son* (1916), *Mid-American Chants* (poems, 1918), *Winesburg, Ohio* (1919), *Poor White* (1920), *The Triumph of the Egg* (1921), *Many Marriages* (1922), *A Story Teller's Story* (1924), *Dark Laughter* (1925), *Beyond Desire* (1933), *Puzzled America* (1935), *Kit Brandon* (1936), *Home Town* (1940), etc. *Sherwood Anderson's Memoirs* (1942) and his *Letters* (1953) published posthumously.

**Anderson, Thomas David.** 1853–1933. Amateur astronomer of Edinburgh, Scotland; discovered two new stars (1892, 1901) in constellations of Auriga and Perseus.

**Anderson, Thomas Victor.** 1881–1972. Canadian soldier, b. Ottawa. Grad. Royal Military Coll., Kingston (1900); B.Sc., McGill (1901). Taught engineering, Royal Mil. Coll. (1902–06); served in World War I (1915–17; wounded; D.S.O.); quartermaster general of Canada (1935–38); chief of general staff (1938–40); inspector general, central Canada (1940–1942).

**Andersson.** See also ANDERSEN and ANDERSON.

**An'ders·son** (än'dērs·sôn), **Karl Johan.** 1827–1867. Swedish explorer in southwestern Africa; with Galton in Damaraland (1850); continued alone to Lake Ngami (1854); penetrated to Okavango River (1858–59).

**Andersson, Nils Johan.** 1821–1880. Swedish botanist; author of works on botany of Scandinavia and Lapland, and also on Swedish expedition around world (1851–53).

**Andino, Tiburcio Carías.** See CARÍAS ANDINO.

**An'dler'** (äN'dlâr'), **Charles.** 1866–1933. French educator and author of books on German state socialism and Pan-Germanism; b. Strasbourg.

**An·doc'i·des** (ăn·dŏs'ĭ·dēz). b. 440 B.C.? Athenian politician and orator.

**An·dra'da** (äNn·drä'thȧ), **Antonio de.** 1580?–1634. Portuguese Jesuit missionary in East Indies and Tibet.

**An·dra'da e Sil'va** (ē sĭl'vȧ), **José Bonifácio de.** *Called also* **José Bonifácio.** 1763?–1838. Brazilian statesman and geologist. Advocate of Brazilian independence under Pedro I; one of Pedro's ministers (1821); after independence declared, minister of interior and of foreign affairs (1822). Banished to France (1823), for democratic principles, with his brothers **Antônio** (1773–1845) and **Martim** (1776–1844), also radical statesmen.

**An'drade** (ăn'drād), **Edward Neville da Costa.** 1887–1971. English physicist. Educ. University Coll., London; U. of Heidelberg; Cambridge; U. of Manchester. Professor, Artillery Coll., Woolwich (1920–28), U. of London (1928–1949). Author of *The Structure of the Atom, The Mechanism of Nature, Simple Science* (with Julian Huxley), *The New Chemistry*, etc.

**An·dra'de** (äNn·drä'thĕ), **Gomes Freire de.** See FREIRE DE ANDRADE.

**An'drae** (än'drā), **Walter.** 1875–1956. German archaeologist, b. near Leipzig. Engaged in excavations in Babylonia and Assyria (1899–1913); author of books on Assyrian culture.

**An'dral'** (äN'dràl'), **Gabriel.** 1797–1876. French physician, b. Paris; professor, U. of Paris (1828–66); author of *Clinique Médicale* (1823–56).

**An'drás·sy** (ŏn'drä·shĭ), Count **Gyula.** 1823–1890. Hungarian statesman. Exiled for participation in revolt of 1848; obtained amnesty (1857) and returned to Austria. Elected to diet (1861); vice-president of diet (1865); first constitutional prime minister (1867); foreign minister (1871). Plenipotentiary at Congress of Berlin (1878). His son Count **Gyula** (1860–1929) entered Austrian Abgeordnetenhaus (1884); minister of interior (1906–09); foreign minister (1918); deputy in Hungarian National Assembly (1922); imprisoned (1921) for implication in attempt to restore Charles I to throne.

**An'dré** (än'drā; ăn'drĭ), **John.** 1751–1780. British soldier; son of Genevese parents. Joined Royal Fusiliers in Canada (1774); aide-de-camp to General Grey and Sir Henry Clinton; made adjutant general by Clinton, with rank of major. Appointed to negotiate with Benedict Arnold for betrayal of West Point to British; captured by Americans while returning toward New York in civilian clothes with negotiation papers in his boots; hanged as spy.

**An'dré'** (äN'drā'), **Louis Joseph Nicolas.** 1838–1913. French general, b. Nuits-Saint-Georges. Minister of war (1901–05); effected reforms in French army.

**Andreä.** See also ANDREAE.

**An·dre'ä** (än·drā'ä), **Jakob.** 1528–1590. German Lutheran theologian and writer. Active in organizing Lutheran Church throughout Germany and in producing *Formula of Concord*, second part of *Book of Concord*, published (1580) to end controversies among Lutheran groups. His grandson **Johann Valentin Andreä** (1586–1654) was a Protestant theologian and satirical writer. See Christian ROSENKREUTZ.

**Andrea del Sarto.** See SARTO.

**An'dre·a'des** (än'thrâ·ä'thĕs), **Andreas.** 1876–1935. Greek economist; representative of Greece at League of Nations assembly (1923–24, 1929).

**Andreae.** See also ANDREÄ.

**An·dre′ae** (ăn·drē′ē), **Laurentius.** See Lars ANDERSON.

**An·dre′ae** (än·drā′â), **Wilhelm Friedrich.** 1888–1962. German political economist and sociologist, b. Magdeburg. Professor, Giessen (from 1933).

**An′dre·a′ni** (än′drâ·ä′nē), **Andrea.** 1540?–1623. Italian engraver on wood in chiaroscuro, b. Mantua. His chief works include *The Deluge* and *The Destruction of Pharaoh's Host* (both after Titian) and *The Triumph of Julius Caesar* (10 prints after Mantegna).

**An·dre′as** (än·drā′äs), **Willy.** 1884– . German historian, b. Karlsruhe. Author of *Deutschland vor der Reformation* (1932), etc.

**An′dree** (än′drā), **Karl Theodor.** 1808–1875. German geographer and journalist; founded and edited (1861–75) *Globus.* His son **Richard** (1835–1912) was a geographer, ethnologist, writer, and editor of *Globus* (1891–1903). Richard's wife (m. 1903), **Marie An′dree–Eysn′** [-ī′z′n] (1847–1929), was a folklorist.

**An·drée′** (àn·drā′), **Salomon August.** 1854–1897. Swedish aeronaut; lost while attempting flight in balloon to north polar region.

**An·dre′ev** (ŭn·dryā′yĕf), **Andrei Andreevich.** 1895–1971. Russian Soviet politician; member of Communist party (1914); secretary of central committee of Communist party in U.S.S.R. (1935–1946).

**An·dre′ev,** *more commonly in English reference* **An·dre′yev, Leonid Nikolaevich.** 1871–1919. Russian novelist and writer of short stories, plays, etc., b. Orel. Lawyer and police-court reporter; his early stories noticed by Gorki, who helped him at beginning of career; published first collection of stories (1901); at time of revolution (1917), bitterly opposed Bolsheviki; forced to leave Russia after loss of possessions; died in poverty in Finland. Author of *The Red Laugh* (1904), *To the Stars* (1905), *The Life of Man* (1906; mystery play), *Savva* (1906; poetic drama), *Love of One's Neighbor* (1908), *Anathema* (1909), *The Seven Who Were Hanged* (1909), *Silence and Other Stories* (1910), *He Who Gets Slapped* (1916), and *S. O. S.* (1919).

**An′dre·i′ni** (än′drâ·ē′nē), **Francesco.** fl. 16th and early 17th centuries. Italian comedian; leader of troupe touring Italy and France. His wife, **Isabella** (1562–1604), b. Padua, was an actress in the troupe; author of a pastoral fable (1588). Their son **Giovanni Battista** (1578?–?1650), actor, playwright, and poet, wrote *L'Adamo,* a sacred drama from which Milton reputedly borrowed some scenes of *Paradise Lost.*

**An′dre·o′li** (än′drâ·ô′lê), **Giorgio.** 1465?–?1555. Italian potter and majolica painter at Gubbio from about 1485 to 1552; inventor (c. 1518) of a noted luster for his pottery.

**An′dré′os′sy′** *or* **An′dré′os′si′** (äN′drā′ô′sē′), Comte **Antoine François.** 1761–1828. French general and diplomat. Served in revolutionary army and under Napoleon. Napoleon's ambassador at London, Vienna, and Constantinople.

**An·drés′** (än·drās′), **Juan.** 1740–1817. Spanish Jesuit writer in Italy; author of *Dell'Origine, dei Progressi, e dello Stato Attuale d'Ogni Letteratura* (7 vols., 1782–99), etc.

**An′drew** (ăn′drōō). In Bible, one of the twelve apostles (*Matt.* iv. 18 and x. 2; *Mark* i. 16 and iii. 18; *Luke* vi. 14; *John* i. 40; *Acts* i. 13); brother of (Simon) Peter; according to tradition, suffered martyrdom by crucifixion, in Achaia.

**Andrew.** *Hung.* **An′drás** (ŏn′dräsh). Name of three kings of Hungary of Árpád dynasty:

**Andrew I.** d. 1060. King (1046–60). Banished by King Stephen, lived in Poland and Russia; overthrew Peter Orseolo (1046); engaged in three campaigns (1049–52) against Emperor Henry III; independence acknowledged (1052); dethroned by his brother Béla.

**Andrew II.** 1175–1235. King (1205–35). Son of Béla III. His extravagance and generosity brought financial troubles; forced to grant estates to nobles who reduced Hungary almost to anarchy. m. Gertrude of Meran, murdered (Sept., 1213) by nobles. On advice of pope set out with large army on crusade to Holy Land (1217); sailed from Venice to Acre, but expedition failed. On return found Hungary in frightful condition; nobles extorted from him (1222) the Golden Bull (Hungarian Magna Charta) which limited the monarchy, granted people annual assembly, and preserved rights of feudal nobles. Married three times; father, by his first wife, of St. Elizabeth of Hungary. See LADISLAS III.

**Andrew III.** *Called* **Andrew the Venetian.** d. 1301. Last king of Árpád dynasty (1290–1301). Grandson of Andrew II. At beginning of reign forced to contest claims of Charles Martel, son of king of Naples, and of Albert of Hapsburg, son of Emperor Rudolf; defeated Charles (1291); made peace with Hapsburgs by marrying (1296) Agnes of Austria, daughter of Albert I, Emperor of Germany.

**Andrew, James Osgood.** 1794–1871. American Methodist Episcopal bishop, b. in Wilkes County, Ga. Chosen bishop (1832). His holding of slaves was issue which, at general conference of the church (1844), resulted in division of Methodist Episcopal Church into northern and southern branches (1845); chosen one of first bishops of Methodist Episcopal Church, South (1846).

**Andrew, John Albion.** 1818–1867. Governor of Massachusetts (1861–66); b. Windham, Me.

**Andrew, Samuel.** 1656–1738. American Congregational clergyman and educator, b. Cambridge, Mass. Active in founding of Yale College (1701); its rector (1707–19).

**Andrew of Wyntoun.** See WYNTOUN.

**An′drewes** (ăn′drōōz), **Sir Christopher Howard.** 1896– . English physician; asst. resident physician, hospital of Rockefeller Inst., New York City (1923–25); on scientific staff, National Inst. for Medical Research, London (from 1927). Known esp. for work on viruses.

**Andrewes, Lancelot.** 1555–1626. English prelate and scholar, of vast patristic learning. Educ. Cambridge. Bishop of Chichester (1605), Ely (1609), Winchester (1619); privy councilor for England and Scotland. A favorite preacher at courts of Elizabeth, James I, and Charles I. One of Westminster ten translators of Pentateuch and historical books for Authorized Version of Bible (1607).

**An′drews** (ăn′drōōz), **Avery de La′no** (dĕ lā′nō). 1864–1959. American lawyer and army officer, b. Massena, N.Y. Grad. U.S.M.A., West Point (1886). Practiced law, New York City (from 1891). Police commissioner, New York City (1895–98). Served in Spanish-American War; brigadier general, asst. chief of staff to Gen. Pershing, World War.

**Andrews, Charles Freer.** 1871–1940. British publicist; active career chiefly in India; friend and interpreter of Gandhi, as in *Mahatma Gandhi's Ideas.*

**Andrews, Charles McLean.** 1863–1943. American historian and educator, b. Wethersfield, Conn. Grad., Trinity (1884), Ph.D., Johns Hopkins (1889). Professor, Bryn Mawr (1889–1907), Johns Hopkins (1907–10), Yale (1910–31). Authority on colonial American history and institutions. Author of *The Historical Development of Modern Europe* (2 vols., 1896, 1898), *A Short History of England* (1912), *The Colonial Background of the American Revolution* (1924, 1931), *Colonial Period of American History* (4 vols., 1934–38), etc.

**Andrews, Charlton.** 1878–1939. American educator, critic, playwright, and novelist, b. Connersville, Ind. Author of the plays *His Majesty the Fool* (1913), *Ladies' Night* (with Avery Hopwood, 1920), and *Don't Believe It* (1930); other works include *The Technique of Play Writing* (1915), *The Affair of the Syrian Dagger* (1937).

**Andrews, Elisha Benjamin.** 1844–1917. American educator, b. Hinsdale, N.H. Served in Civil War. President, Denison U. (1875–79), Brown U. (1889–98); chancellor, U. of Nebraska (1900–08). Author of *The United States in Our Own Time* (1903), *The History of the United States* (6 vols., 1913).

**Andrews, Ethan Allen.** 1787–1858. American educator, b. New Britain, Conn. Editor of a Latin-English lexicon (1850; translated from Freund's Latin-German lexicon), original of *Harpers' Latin Dictionary.*

**Andrews, Frank Maxwell.** 1884–1943. American army officer, b. Nashville, Tenn.; grad. U.S.M.A. (1906); served in Philippine Islands and Hawaii; with aviation section of Signal Corps in U.S. (1917–20); with U.S. army of occupation in Germany (1920–23); executive officer, Kelly Field (1923–25); colonel (1935); organizer and first commander (temporary major general) of G. H. Q. Air Force (1936–39); head of U.S. Caribbean defense command (Jan., 1942); lieut. general, head of Middle East command (Nov., 1942), of U.S. forces in Europe (Feb., 1943); killed in airplane crash, Iceland (May, 1943).

**Andrews, John Miller.** 1871–1956. Northern Ireland statesman; minister of labor (1921–37), finance (1937–40); prime minister of Northern Ireland (1940–43).

**Andrews, John Oliver.** 1896– . English military aviator; served in World War (1914–18); transferred to R.A.F. (1919); director of armament development in air ministry (from 1939).

**Andrews, Lancelot.** 1555–1626. = Lancelot ANDREWES.

**Andrews, Launce′lot** (lôns′lŏt) **Winchester.** 1856–1938. Chemist, b. London, Canada. Professor, State U. of Iowa (1885–1904); research chemist in Chicago (1915–21). Author of *An Introduction to the Study of Qualitative Analysis* (1891).

**Andrews, Lorrin.** 1795–1868. American missionary, b. East Windsor (now Vernon) Conn. Missionary in Hawaii (1828–41). Member, royal privy council of Hawaii (1846–59); first associate justice of supreme court of Hawaii (1852–55).

**Andrews, Mary Raymond,** *nee* **Ship′man** (shĭp′măn). d. 1936. American novelist, b. Mobile, Ala. m. (1884) William Shankland Andrews. Author of *A Good Samaritan* (1906), *Enchanted Forest* (1909), *Eternal Masculine* (1913), *Eternal Feminine* (1916), *Yellow Butterflies* (1922), *Lost Commander* (1929), etc.

**Andrews, Roy Chapman.** 1884–1960. American naturalist, explorer, and author, b. Beloit, Wis. On expeditions to Alaska (1908), Borneo, etc. (1909–10), northern Korea (1911–12), Alaska (1913); headed expeditions (1916–30) of American Museum of Natural History to Tibet, China, Burma, Mongolia, and Central Asia, esp. The Gobi. Known esp. for discoveries of geological strata, dinosaur eggs, remains of largest known land mammals, and evidences of ancient human life. With American Museum of Natural History (from 1906); its director (1935–41). Author of *Across Mongolian Plains* (1921), *On the Trail of Ancient Man* (1926), *The New Conquest of Central Asia* (1932), *This Business of Exploring* (1935), etc.

**Andrews, Thomas.** 1813–1885. Irish physicist and chemist. Educ. Glasgow U.; M.D., Edinburgh (1835). Professor, Belfast (1849–79). By experiments in liquefaction of gases, established conceptions of critical temperature and critical pressure.

**Andrews, Thomas.** 1847–1907. English metallurgical chemist and ironmaster, b. Sheffield. Pioneer in microscopic study of metals; investigated resistance of metals to concussion at different temperatures, and strength of steel rails and railway axles.

**Andrews, William Draper.** 1818–1896. American inventor of a centrifugal pump.

**Andreyev.** Variant of ANDREEV.

**An′drić** (än′drĭch), **Ivo.** 1892–1975. Yugoslav writer, b. in Bosnia. Awarded Nobel prize in literature (1961); wrote *The Bridge on the Drina* (1945), etc.

**An′dri′eux′** (äN′drē′û′), **François Guillaume Jean Stanislas.** 1759–1833. French poet and playwright; author of several comedies, as *Les Étourdis* (1788), *Helvétius* (1802), *La Comédienne* (1816), and of verse narratives, as *Le Meunier Sans-Souci* (1797).

**Andrieux, Louis.** 1840–1931. French politician, b. Trévoux. Member, chamber of deputies (1876–77, 1882 ff.). Prefect of police, Paris (1879–81). Organized Boulangist group of socialist republicans (1890). Author of *Souvenirs d'un Ancien Préfet de Police* (2 vols., 1885).

**An·dris′cus** (ăn·drĭs′kŭs). Greek adventurer of 2d century B.C. Passed himself off as son of Perseus, King of Macedon; seized throne (149 B.C.); defeated by Metellus (148 B.C.); sent as captive to Rome and executed.

**An′dro·clus** (ăn′drō·klŭs) *or* **An′dro·cles** (ăn′drō·klēz). Roman slave of 1st cent. A.D.; according to story of Apion and Aulus Gellius, spared in arena by lion from whose foot he had extracted a thorn years before in Africa. Story used by George Bernard Shaw in *Androcles and the Lion.*

**An′dro·ni′cus** (ăn′drō·nī′kŭs; ăn·drŏn′ĭ·kŭs). Name of three emperors of Eastern Roman Empire:

**Andronicus I Com·ne′nus** (kŏm·nē′nŭs). 1110?–1185. Grandson of Alexius I Comnenus; emperor (1183–85); taken captive by Seljuks (1141); at court of Emperor Manuel (1152–80); regent for Emperor Alexius II, whom he killed (1183); ruled vigorously; tried to destroy power of nobles; overthrown by Isaac Angelus.

**Andronicus II Pa′lae·ol′o·gus** (pā′lē·ŏl′ō·gŭs; păl′ē-). 1260–1332. Son of Michael VIII; emperor (1282–1328). When Osmanli Turks seized Bithynia, called Roger di Flor and his Catalan Grand Company to fight them; after defeating Turks, Roger's company turned against the empire, devastating Thrace and Macedonia (1303–11); at war with grandson Andronicus (1320–28); abdicated.

**Andronicus III Palaeologus.** 1296?–1341. Emperor (1328–41); rebellious in youth; forced Andronicus II to abdicate; defeated by Stephen Dushan of Serbia.

**Andronicus IV** is name sometimes given to son of John V Palaeologus who usurped throne (1376–79).

**Andronicus, Lucius Livius.** See LIVIUS ANDRONICUS.

**Andronicus of Rhodes** (rōdz). fl. 1st century B.C. Greek Peripatetic philosopher in Rome; arranged, catalogued, and published works of Aristotle (c. 70 B.C.); expounded Aristotelian philosophy.

**An′dros** (ăn′drŏs), Sir **Edmund.** 1637–1714. British colonial governor in America, b. on island of Guernsey. Governor of province of New York (1674). Appointed (1686) governor of "Dominion of New England," formed by uniting the several New England colonies; interfered with colonists' rights and customs; colonies revolted (1689), imprisoned him, and resumed separate existences. Sent to England for hearing, but charges not pressed. Governor of province of Virginia (1692–97). Lieutenant governor of Guernsey (1704–06).

**An·dro′ti·on** (ăn·drō′shĭ·ŏn). fl. 4th century B.C. Athenian orator; pupil of Isocrates; attacked by Demosthenes.

**An'drou'et'** (äN'drōō'ĕ'). *Known as* **Androuet Du Cer'ceau'** (sĕr'sō'). Name of family of French architects, including: **Jacques** (1515?–?1584), known esp. as author of several illustrated books on architecture; two of his sons, **Baptiste** (1560?–?1602), successor of Pierre Lescot as architect of the Louvre (1578), and **Jacques** (d. 1614), architect in chief of royal buildings; and Baptiste's son **Jean** (d. after 1649), known as "architect of Louis XIII," designer of the Hôtel de Sully, Paris (1624).

**A'nel'** (ȧ'nĕl'), **Dominique.** 1679?–?1730. French surgeon; invented new method of operating for aneurysm.

**A·ne'rio** (ä·nâ'ryô), **Felice.** 1560?–?1614. Italian composer of church music. Succeeded Palestrina as composer for the papal chapel. His brother **Giovanni Francesco** (1567?–?1621) was also a composer, esp. of church music.

**Anet, Claude.** Pseudonym of Jean SCHOPFER.

**A'ne·than'** (ȧn'täN'), Baron **Jules Joseph d'.** 1803–1888. Belgian statesman, b. Brussels. Conservative leader; premier (1870–71); senate president (1884–86).

**A'neu·rin** (ä'nĕ·ōō·rĕn) *or* **A'nei·rin** (ä'nī·rĕn). fl. 603. Welsh bard. Son of a chief of the Gododin, tribe living on sea coast south of Firth of Forth. Wrote epic *Gododin* on defeat of Britons by Saxons at Cattraeth (c. 603); probably present at battle as bard and priest.

**An·fin·sen** (an'fin·s'n), **Christian Boehmer.** 1916– . Biochemist, b. Monessen, Pa. Ph.D., Harvard, 1943. Shared 1972 Nobel prize in chemistry with Stanford Moore and William Stein for work on chemistry of enzymes.

**An·fos'si** (än·fôs'sē), **Pasquale.** 1727–1797. Italian composer; pupil of Piccinni; Kapellmeister, St. John Lateran (1791–97). Composed many operas and oratorios.

**Angarita, Isaías Medina.** See MEDINA ANGARITA.

**An'gas** (ăng'gȧs), **George Fife.** 1789–1879. English merchant and shipowner, b. Newcastle upon Tyne. Commissioner for formation of colony of South Australia (1834); emigrated to Adelaide, South Australia (1851); regarded as a founder of South Australia.

**An'gel** (ān'jĕl), **John.** 1881–1960. English sculptor; to U.S. (1925); carved statuary on Cathedral of St. John the Divine in New York, a crucifixion group for St. Louis, Mo., etc.

**An'ge·la Me·ri'ci** (än'jâ·lä mȧ·rē'chē), Saint. 1474?–1540. Italian Roman Catholic religious, b. Desenzano del Garda; tertiary of St. Francis; founded order of Ursulines at Brescia (1535). Canonized (1807).

**An'ge·li** (ăn'jĕ·lī). See ANGELUS.

**An'ge·li** (än'jâ·lē), **Heinrich von.** 1840–1925. Genre and portrait painter in Vienna (from 1862), b. in Hungary.

**Angelico,** Fra. See Giovanni da FIESOLE.

**An'gell** (ān'jĕl), **George Thorndike.** 1823–1909. American reformer, b. Southbridge, Mass. An organizer of Massachusetts Society for Prevention of Cruelty to Animals. Founded magazine *Our Dumb Animals* (1868).

**Angell, James Burrill.** 1829–1916. American educator and diplomat, b. near Scituate, R.I. Grad. Brown (1849). President, U. of Vermont (1866–71), Michigan (1871–1909). U.S. minister to China (1880–81), Turkey (1897–98).

**Angell, James Rowland.** 1869–1949. Son of James Burrill Angell. American educator and psychologist, b. Burlington, Vt. Grad. U. of Michigan (1890), A.M., Michigan (1891) and Harvard (1892); studied abroad, chiefly at U. of Berlin and Halle. Professor (1894–1919), acting president (1918–19), U. of Chicago. President of Yale U. (1921–37). Author of *Psychology* (1904), *American Education* (1937), etc.

**Angell, Joseph Kinnicutt.** 1794–1857. American lawyer and writer of legal treatises, b. Providence, R.I.

**Angell,** Sir **Norman.** *Orig. name* **Ralph Norman Angell Lane.** 1872–1967. English author and lecturer. Educ. at Lycée de St. Omer, France, and in Geneva. Spent youth as rancher, prospector, and newspaperman in western U.S. (to 1898). Editor, *Galignani's Messenger* (1899–1903), *Foreign Affairs* (1928–31). Invented The Money Game, series of card games designed to teach elements of economics. Author of *The Great Illusion* (1910), *The Great Illusion, 1933* (1933), *America's Dilemma* (1940), and other works on international affairs, finance, and peace. Awarded 1933 Nobel peace prize.

**Angelo, Michael.** See MICHELANGELO.

**An'ge·lus** (ăn'jĕ·lŭs). *Pl.* **An'ge·li** (-lī). Byzantine family that furnished rulers of Eastern Roman Empire: Isaac II Angelus, Alexius III Angelus, and Alexius IV Angelus. Michael VIII Palaeologus was direct descendant of family; another ruling house was established by Michael Angelus Comnenus as despots of Epirus (1204–1318).

**An'ge·lus Si·le'si·us** (ăn'jĕ·lŭs sĭ·lē'shĭ·ŭs; -zhĭ·ŭs; sī-). *Real name* **Johannes Scheff'ler** (shĕf'lẽr). 1624–1677. German religious poet and mystic; author of *Cherubinischer Wandersmann* (1657).

**An'ge·ly'** (äN'zhẽ·lē'), **Lou'is** (lōō'ē). 1787?–1835. German dramatist. Adapted many French comedies.

**Angers, David d'.** See DAVID D'ANGERS.

**An'ger·stein** (ăng'gẽr·stīn), **John Julius.** 1735–1823. British merchant, philanthropist, and patron of fine arts, b. in Russia. Underwriter at Lloyd's (1756). Collected paintings, purchased at his death by British government as nucleus of National Gallery.

**An'ger·ville** (ăn'jẽr·vĭl), **Richard.** = Richard de BURY.

**An'ge·vins** (ăn'jĕ·vĭnz; *Fr.* äNzh'văN'). See ANJOU and PLANTAGENET.

**Anghiera** *or* **Anghera, Pietro Martire d'.** See PETER MARTYR.

**An'gil·bert** (ăng'gĭl·bûrt), Saint. c. 740–814. Frankish Latin poet, and privy councilor to Charlemagne; abbot of Centula, now Saint-Riquier, Picardy (790 ff.); friend of Alcuin; honored at court by name "Homer." Father, by Charlemagne's daughter Bertha, of the historian Nithard.

**An'gio·lie'ri** (än'jô·lyâ'rē), **Cecco.** 1250?–?1312. Italian humorous poet; author chiefly of autobiographical poems. Appears in one of *Decameron* tales.

**Anglerius, Petrus Martyr.** See PETER MARTYR.

**Anglesey.** (1) Earl of. See Arthur ANNESLEY. (2) Marquis of. See Henry William PAGET.

**An'glin** (ăng'glĭn), **Margaret Mary.** 1876–1958. Actress, b. Ottawa, Canada; m. Howard Hull (1911). Played leading parts on American stage in *Camille* (1903–04), etc. Known especially for roles in Shakespearean plays and Greek tragedies, as Sophocles's *Electra* and *Antigone*, and Euripides's *Medea*. Her father, **Timothy Warren Anglin** (1822–1896), Canadian journalist and legislator, was twice (1874–77, 1878) speaker of Dominion House of Commons. Her brother **Francis Alexander Anglin** (1865–1933) was a Canadian supreme court judge (1909–33).

**An'gou'lême'** (äN'gōō'lâm'). French title of nobility derived from countship in southwest France dating from 9th century and held by several families, becoming crown appanage (1373) under Charles V and possession of House of Orléans. Among counts of Angoulême were John, a son of Louis I, Duc d'Orléans (see ORLÉANS), and John's son Charles. Countship was made a duchy (1515) by Charles's son Francis I, with whom Angoulême branch of House of Valois (see VALOIS) began to rule as kings of France (1515–89). See also MARGARET OF NAVARRE and individual ANGOULÊME entries below.

**Angoulême,** Duc **d'. Charles de Va'lois'** (dē vȧ'lwȧ'). 1573–1650. French general and politician; natural son of Charles IX of France and Marie Touchet. Commander under Henry IV. Implicated in Verneuil conspiracy; sentenced to life imprisonment; freed by Louis XIII (1616). Army commander and diplomat for Louis XIII. One of his sons, **Louis Emmanuel de Valois,** Duc **d'Angoulême** (1596–1653), was also an army commander.

**Angoulême,** Duc **d'. Louis Antoine de Bour'bon'** (dē bo͝or'bôɴ'). 1775–1844. Last dauphin of France; eldest son of Charles X; renounced throne (1830); proclaimed (1836) by Legitimists as Louis XIX; lived in exile. His wife, **Marie Thérèse Charlotte** (1778–1851), was as a child imprisoned in the Temple with her parents Louis XVI and Marie Antoinette; after their execution, known as "Orphan of the Temple" until her release (1795); remained ardent ultraroyalist throughout life.

**Ång'ström** (ông'strûm; *Angl.* ăng'strŭm), **Anders Jonas.** 1814–1874. Swedish astronomer and physicist. Educ. U. of Uppsala, and member of faculty from 1839. Studied light; angstrom unit, used in expressing length of light waves, named in his honor. Made spectral analyses, esp. of sun and aurora borealis; identified hydrogen in solar atmosphere (1862). His son **Knut Johan** (1857–1910), also a physicist at U. of Uppsala, investigated solar radiation and photographed infrared spectrum.

**An'guier'** (äɴ'gyā'), **François** (1604–1669) and his brother **Michel** (1614–1686). French sculptors.

**An·gui'scio·la** (äng·gwē'shô·lä) *or* **An·gus'so·la** (äng·go͞os'sô·lä), **Sofonisba.** 1535?–?1626. Italian portrait painter, known esp. for her self-portraits.

**An'gus** (ăng'gŭs), Earls of. See (1) UMFRAVILLE; (2) under DOUGLAS family.

**An'halt** (än'hält). German duchy and its ruling house, which originated with Albert the Bear (*q.v.*), Margrave of Brandenburg. On death (1252) of Albert's grandson Henry I, district (then a county) divided into three parts; succession of unions and redivisions (1570–1863); final unification effected (1863) under Leopold IV Frederick (1817–1871). Recent rulers: Leopold IV (1863–71), Frederick I (1871–1904), Frederick II (1904–abdicated 1918). Most important division (during 17th–19th centuries) was **An'halt-Des'sau** (-dĕs'ou) branch. Among princes of the line were Leopold I (1676–1747), Leopold II (1700–1751), and Moritz (1712–1760), all distinguished generals. See individual biographies.

**A'ni'cet'-Bour'geois'** (ȧ'nē'sĕ'bo͞or'zhwȧ'), **Auguste.** 1806–1871. French writer of vaudeville pieces and melodramas, chiefly in collaboration.

**An'i·ce'tus** (ăn'ĭ·sē'tŭs), Saint. Pope (bishop of Rome; 154?–?165).

**Aniello, Tommaso.** See MASANIELLO.

**A'ni·muc'cia** (ä'nē·mo͞ot'chä), **Giovanni.** 1500?–1571. Italian composer of sacred music. Maestro di cappella at St. Peter's (1555–71). Called "Father of the Oratorio," because oratorio said to have developed from his *Laudi Spirituali*, performed in oratory of Saint Philip Neri. His brother **Paolo** (d. 1563), composer of motets and madrigals, was maestro di cappella at the Lateran (1550–52).

**A'nis·feld'** (ä'nĭs·fĕlt'; *Russ.* ŭ·nyĭs·fyāl'y't), **Boris Israelevich.** 1879– . Painter and stage decorator, b. in Russia; to U.S. (1917). Employed by Diaghilev for work with Russian ballet.

**An'jou'** (äɴ'zho͞o'; *Angl.* ăn'jo͞o). French noble family, established in 9th century. (Name derived from county in western France.) There have been several houses of Anjou:

FIRST HOUSE: **Fulk I** (fo͝olk) **the Red,** *Fr.* **Foulques le Roux** (fo͞olk' lē ro͞o'), first count (888?–938); **Fulk II** (ruled 942–958); **Geoffrey I,** *Fr.* **Geoffroi** (ruled 958–987); **Fulk III Ner'ra'** [nĕ'rȧ'] (c. 970–1040; ruled 987–1040); **Geoffrey II Mar·tel'** [mär·tĕl'; *Fr.* mȧr'tĕl'] (1006–1060; ruled 1040–60); **Geoffrey III** (ruled 1060–67); **Fulk IV le Ré'chin'** [rā'shăɴ'] (ruled 1068–1109); **Fulk V the Young,** *Fr.* **Foulques le Jeune** [lē zhûn'] (1092–1143; ruled 1109–29), later king of Jerusalem (1131–43), at war (1112–19) with Henry I, King of England; Fulk's son **Geoffrey IV the Handsome,** sometimes known as **Geoffrey Plantagenet** (1113–1151; ruled 1129–49), m. (1129) Henry I's daughter Matilda; their son **Henry,** count (1149), m. (1152) Eleanor of Aquitaine, adding Aquitaine to Anjou, and, on death (1154) of Stephen, King of England, recognized as his successor, first of English house of Anjou (Plantagenets).

SECOND HOUSE: Plantagenet kings of England, esp. first three: **Henry II** (ruled 1154–89), **Richard I** (ruled 1189–99), and **John** (ruled 1199–1216). Much English land in France lost by John to Philip II of France (1202–04); countship of Anjou attached to France. Other Plantagenets (*q.v.*) to Richard II (d. 1399) also called Angevins, but none after John were counts of Anjou.

THIRD HOUSE: Kings of Naples and Sicily. Anjou given (1246) by King Louis IX as appanage to his brother **Charles,** Count of Provence, later (1266–85) king of Naples and Sicily; succeeded as king by his son **Charles II** (1285–1309). Charles II had five children, from whom descended five different but interrelated lines of European rulers: (1) HUNGARY—from oldest son, **Charles Martel** (1272?–1295), king in opposition (1290–95) to Andrew III. Other members of line include **Charles Robert,** founder of Anjou line of Hungary (1308–42); **Louis the Great,** King of Hungary (1342–82), Poland (1370–82); and **Mary** (ruled 1382–95), who married Sigismund, later Holy Roman Emperor. (2) NAPLES—from second son, **Robert;** succeeded his father, Charles II, as king of Naples (1309–43); succeeded in turn by granddaughter, **Joanna I,** Queen of Naples (1343–82), who adopted Louis of Anjou (see 4, below). (3) NAPLES—from third son, **John,** Duke of **Du·raz'zo** (do͞o·rät'tsô). His grandson was **Charles III,** King of Naples (1381–86), succeeded by his son **Ladislas** (1386–1414) and daughter **Joanna II** (1414–35), with whom direct line became extinct. (4) FRANCE, ANJOU, AND NAPLES—from fourth child, **Margaret;** m. Charles de Valois (see CHARLES DE VALOIS). Their son **Philip** chosen (1328), as Philip VI, first king of France of House of Valois; countship united to crown. Philip succeeded by son **John II** (1350–64); countship raised to duchy (1360) and bestowed by John on his second son, **Louis I,** Count of Provence (1339–84) and Duke of Anjou (1360–84). Louis adopted by Joanna I as her successor to throne of Naples (1382–84); titular king only. Next two dukes also titular kings only: **Louis II** (reigned 1389–99) and **Louis III** (reigned 1417–34). Louis II's second son, **René,** married Isabella of Lorraine (see LORRAINE); king of Naples (1435–42) after death of Joanna II (see 3, above), but driven out by Alfonso I (see 5, below). René's daughter Margaret of Anjou (*q.v.*) married King Henry VI of England. (5) ARAGON AND NAPLES—from fifth child, **Blanche;** m. James II, King of Aragon. From them descended **Alfonso V** (1416–58), who as Alfonso I was king of Naples (1443–58). His natural son **Ferdinand I** succeeded as king of Naples (1458–94), followed by **Alfonso II** (ruled 1494–95) and **Ferdinand II** (ruled 1495–96), last of house of Anjou in Naples. Meanwhile, duchy of Anjou had reverted to French throne (1480); bestowed several times later, especially (1574–84) on François, son of Henry II (see under ALENÇON), but on his death (1584) became definitively part of royal domain. Title duke of Anjou also borne by other French kings and members of royal family (as Philip, later Philip V of Spain) but without implying territorial sovereignty.

**Ankarström.** See ANCKARSTRÖM.

**An'ker Lar'sen** (äng'kẽr lär's'n), **Johannes.** 1874–1957. Danish novelist; author of *The Philosopher's Stone* (Eng. trans., 1924), *Martha and Mary* (1925; Eng. trans., 1926), etc.

**Anlaf Sitricson.** See OLAF SITRICSON.

**An'na** (ăn'ȧ). See also HANNAH.

**An'na Com·ne'na** (ăn'ȧ kŏm·nē'nȧ). 1083–?1148. Learned Byzantine author; daughter of Emperor Alexius I Comnenus; m. Nicephorus Bryennius. Conspired (1118) against Emperor John II, her brother; retired with her mother, Irene, to convent, where she wrote *Alexiad,* a history, partly (2 books) on reigns from Isaac Comnenus to Alexius, partly (13 books) on reign of Alexius.

**An'na I·va'nov·na** (än'nŭ ĭ·vȧ'nôv·nŭ), *better* **I·o·an'nov·na** (ĭ·ô·än'nôv·nŭ). *Eng.* **Anne.** 1693–1740. Romanov empress of Russia (1730–40). Younger daughter of Ivan V and niece of Peter the Great. m. (1710) Frederick William, Duke of Courland (d. 1711). Elected to throne by supreme council under conditions practically vitiating her authority; foiled council by dismissing it, exiling or executing its members; surrounded herself with German favorites whose leader was Biron (*q.v.*). Intervened successfully in War of Polish Succession (1733–35); in alliance with Austria, fought war against Turks (1736–39); secured Azov by treaty of Belgrade (1739); secured succession to her great-nephew Ivan VI.

**An'na Le·o·pol'dov·na** (än'nŭ lyĭ·ŭ·pōl'y'·dŭv·nŭ) *or* **Anna Kar'lov·na** (kär'lŭv·nŭ). *Real name* **Elisabeth Katharina Christine.** 1718–1746. b. Rostock, Germany. Daughter of Charles Leopold, Duke of Mecklenburg-Schwerin; niece of Anna Ivanovna (*q.v.*); m. (1739) Anthony Ulrich (1714–1776), Prince of Brunswick. Grand duchess; regent (1740–41) of Russia during reign of her infant son, Ivan VI; imprisoned (1741–46) with husband after Ivan's deposition.

**An'na** (ăn'ȧ) **of Denmark.** 1532–1585. See AUGUSTUS, Elector of Saxony.

**Anne** (ăn), Saint. Mother of Virgin MARY.

**Anne** (ăn). 1665–1714. Queen of Great Britain and Ireland (1702–14), of house of Stuart. Second daughter of James II and Anne Hyde. Educ. in Protestant faith; m. (1683) George, Prince of Denmark (d. 1708). After accession to throne suffered domination of duke and duchess of Marlborough (see *Sarah Jennings Churchill* under John CHURCHILL) till alienated from them because of their Whig sympathies; this estrangement (1710) followed by Tory ministry of Harley and St. John. Indulged in patronage of the church; granted crown revenues to form "Queen Anne's Bounty" (1704). Dismissed Marlborough in supporting terms of Treaty of Utrecht (signed 1713). Most important public event of her reign was Act of Union with Scotland (1707).

**Anne' de Bre·tagne'** (än' dẽ brẽ·tän'y'). *Eng.* **Anne of Brittany.** 1477–1514. Daughter of Duke Francis II of Brittany and Marguerite de Foix. m. (1491) Charles VIII of France (d. 1498) and (1499) Louis XII. Through her, Brittany united to crown of France.

**Anne' de France'** (än' dẽ fräNs'). *Also* **Anne' de Beau'jeu'** (bō'zhû'). 1460–1522. Eldest daughter of Louis XI of France and Charlotte de Savoie. Regent of France (1483–91) during minority of her brother Charles VIII.

**Anne of Austria** (ăn). *Fr.* **Anne' d'Au'triche'** (än' dō'trēsh'). 1601–1666. Daughter of Philip III of Spain; b. Madrid; m. (1615) Louis XIII of France; virtually separated (1620–43) through influence of Cardinal Richelieu. Took some part in conspiracies against husband. Queen regent for her son Louis XIV (1643–61); chose Cardinal Mazarin as prime minister.

**Anne of Bohemia.** 1366–1394. Queen of England; consort of Richard II. Daughter of Emperor Charles IV by Elizabeth of Pomerania. Delayed in arrival in England by Wat Tyler's uprising; m. (1382) Richard II; interceded with Richard in behalf of City of London, which had been shorn of its privileges for refusing him a loan, and gained pardon (1392); died of pestilence.

**Anne of Cleves** (klēvz). 1515–1557. Fourth wife of Henry VIII; daughter of John, Duke of Cleves, leader of Protestants of western Germany. Selected by Thomas Cromwell on death of Jane Seymour as wife for Henry, to ally him with German Protestants against emperor. m. at Greenwich (1540); marriage declared null by Parliament at Henry's request a few months later. Buried in Westminster Abbey.

**Anne of Denmark.** 1574–1619. Queen of James I of England. Daughter of Frederick II of Denmark and Norway. m. (1589) James after death (1587) of his mother, Mary, Queen of Scots; crowned at Windsor (1603); appeared in masques by Jonson and Dekker.

**Annes'ley** (ănz'lĭ), **Arthur.** 1st Earl of **An'gle·sey** (ăng'g'l·sĭ). 1614–1686. English statesman, b. Dublin. Member, Richard Cromwell's parliament (1658). President, council of state, aiding in restoration of Charles II (1660). Lord privy seal (1672–82).

**An'nett** (ăn'ĕt; -ĭt), **Henry Edward.** 1871–1945. English pathologist; educ. University Coll., Liverpool. Member of Liverpool School of Tropical Medicine expedition to West Africa (1891), and director of second expedition (1900); directed expeditions to Uruguay (1905), West Indies (1906–07). Professor of comparative pathology, U. of Liverpool (1906–11); superintendent of research laboratories, Higher Runcorn (1911–22); lecturer in animal pathology, U. of Liverpool (1922–28); cancer researcher (1931–38).

**An'ning** (ăn'ĭng), **Mary.** 1799–1847. English collector of natural curiosities. Discovered skeleton of ichthyosaurus (1811), later first specimens of plesiosaurus and pterodactyl.

**An'no** (ăn'ō) *or* **Han'no** (hăn'ō), Saint. d. 1075. Archbishop of Cologne (1056); headed uprising of princes against regency of Agnes of Poitou (1062), kidnaped her son King Henry IV, taking him to Cologne, and usurped regency; killed (1075). Canonized (1183).

**Annunzio, Gabriele D'.** See D'ANNUNZIO.

**A·nouilh'** (ȧ'nōō'ē), **Jean.** 1910– . French dramatist, b. Bordeaux, France.

**An'que·til'-Du'per'ron'** (äNk'tēl'dü'pĕ'rôN'), **Abraham Hyacinthe.** 1731–1805. French Orientalist; editor and translator of the *Avesta* (1771); author of *Législation Orientale* (1778), *Oupanichads* (1804), etc. His brother **Louis Pierre Anquetil** (1723–1806) was an abbé and historian.

**An·rep'** (ŭn·ryâp'), **Boris.** fl. 1920–1930. Russian mosaicist in England. Works include a pavement in National Gallery, London (*Labours of Life, Pleasures of Life,* and *Awakening of the Muses*), one in Tait Gallery, London, representing Blake's *Marriage of Heaven and Hell,* and one in the Greek Cathedral, London, representing prophet Ezekiel.

**Ansano di Pietro.** See SANO DI PIETRO.

**Ans′char** (ăns′kär), Saint. *Also called* Saint **Ans·char′i·us** (ăns·kâr′ĭ·ŭs), **Ans′gar** (ăns′gär), **Ans·gar′i·us** (ăns·gâr′ĭ·ŭs), *or* **Ans′kar** (ăns′kär). 801–865. Frankish missionary to Denmark, Sweden, and Germany. First archbishop of Hamburg-Bremen (857).

**An′schütz** (än′shüts), **Ottomar.** 1846–1907. German photographer, b. Lissa, Posen. Conducted experiments in high-speed photography; invented a tachyscope built on principle of stroboscope to reproduce men and animals in motion, a forerunner of motion-picture machine.

**An′schütz-Kämp′fe** (än′shüts·kĕmp′fĕ), **Hermann.** 1872–1931. German engineer, b. Zweibrücken. Inventor of gyrocompass (1908).

**Ans′dell** (ănz′dĕl), **Richard.** 1815–1885. English animal painter. A.R.A. (1861); R.A. (1870). Best-known works include *Stag at Bay, The Combat.*

**An′se·gis** (ăn′sē·jĭs) *or* **An′se·gi′sus** (ăn′sē·jī′sŭs), Saint. 770?–?833. Abbot of Fontanelle (from 823). Collected laws and decrees of Charlemagne and Louis le Débonnaire in *Quatuor Libri Capitularium Regum Francorum,* known commonly as *Capitularies* (completed 827).

**An′selm** (ăn′sĕlm), Saint. 1033–1109. Scholastic philosopher, b. Aosta, Piedmont. Settled in abbey of Bec; elected prior (1063), abbot (1078); wrote treatises *Monologion* and *Proslogion.* Appointed archbishop of Canterbury by William Rufus (1093); embroiled with William Rufus over his refusal to accept episcopal pall from king and with Henry I over his refusal to consecrate prelates invested by king; suffered exile by each in turn; reconciled with Henry through compromise (1107). During exile wrote treatise on the atonement, *Cur Deus Homo.* Canonized (1494) by Alexander VI.

**Anselm of Laon** (läɴ). *Fr.* **An′selme′ de Laon′** (äɴ′sĕlm′ dē läɴ′). d. 1117. French theologian; author of *Glossa Interlinearis,* interlinear gloss of Latin scriptures.

**An′selm of Luc′ca** (ăn′sĕlm, lo͝ok′kä), Saint. 1036?–1086. Italian Benedictine ecclesiastic, b. Mantua; nephew of Pope Alexander II (also known as Saint Anselm of Lucca). Bishop of Lucca; partisan of Gregory VII; known esp. for ecclesiastical reforms.

**An′ser′met′** (äɴ′sĕr′mĕ′), **Ernest.** 1883–1969. Swiss orchestral conductor; known esp. for his interpretations of modern music, esp. of Stravinsky; principal conductor of Diaghilev's Ballet Russe (1915 ff.).

**Ansgar** *or* **Ansgarius** *or* **Anskar,** Saint. See ANSCHAR.

**An′son** (ăn′s'n), **Adrian Constantine.** 1851–1922. American professional baseball player, b. Marshalltown, Iowa; manager, National League team, Chicago (1879–97); known as batter.

**Anson, George.** Baron **Anson.** 1697–1762. English admiral. Commanded squadron in Pacific, inflicted damage on Spanish commerce, circumnavigated world (1740–44); defeated French off Finisterre (1747); first lord of admiralty (1751–56, 1757–62); admiral of fleet (1761). Effected reforms in naval administration, raising navy to high efficiency.

**Anson,** Sir **William Reynell.** 1843–1914. English jurist; author of standard texts, as *The Principles of the English Law of Contract* (1879), *The Law and Custom of the Constitution* (I, 1886; II, 1892).

**Ans′pach** (ănz′păk). *English form of German* **Ans′bach** (äns′bäκ). See CAROLINE OF ANSPACH.

**Ans′pa′cher** (äns′pä′kẽr), **Louis Kauf′man** (kouf′măn). 1878–1947. American playwright, b. Cincinnati, Ohio. m. (1905) Kathryn Kidder (d. 1939). Author of *Tristan and Isolde* (poetical drama, 1904), *Embarrassment of Riches* (1906), *The Glass House* (1912), *All the King's Horses* (1920), *A Way of Life* (1937), etc.

**An′sted** (ăn′stĕd; -stĭd), **David Thomas.** 1814–1880. English geologist.

**An′ster** (ăn′stẽr), **John.** 1793–1867. Irish poet. Called to Irish bar (1824); regius professor of Civil law, Dublin (1850–67). Translated Goethe's *Faust* (pub. 1835, 1864).

**An′stett** (än′shtĕt), **Jo·hann′** (yō·hän′) **Pro·ta′si·us** (prō·tä′zē·o͝os) **von** (fōn). 1766–1835. Russian diplomat.

**An′stey** (ăn′stĭ), **Christopher.** 1724–1805. English poet. Scholar and fellow of King's Coll., Cambridge. Published *New Bath Guide,* an immediate success, praised for original humor (1766).

**Anstey, F.** Pseudonym of Thomas Anstey GUTHRIE.

**An·tal′ci·das** (ăn·tăl′sĭ·dăs). Spartan naval commander and diplomat of 4th century B.C. Negotiated successfully for Persian aid against Athens (388) and commanded Sparta's fleet in operations near the Hellespont (the Dardanelles); forced peace (Peace of Antalcidas, 386) on Athens by terms of which Asia Minor was acknowledged as subject to Persia, and other Greek cities (except islands of Lemnos, Imbros [Imroz Adaya], and Skyros, which remained Athenian) were recognized as independent. Continued on friendly relations with Artaxerxes until Sparta's defeat at Leuctra (371).

**An·ta·ra′** (ăn·tă·ră′) *or* **An′tar** (ăn′tăr). *Arab.* **'Antarah ibn-Shaddād al-'Absi.** 525?–?615. Arab warrior hero and poet, b. a Christian slave. Took part in fierce war between two Arab tribes and became famous for his deeds of valor; wrote battle songs and poems (of which only one is completely extant) about contests of pagan Bedouins; hero of extremely popular Arabic romantic literature, esp. of a portentous compilation known as *Antar.*

**An′te·la′mi** (än′tā·lä′mē), **Benedetto.** fl. 1177–1233. Italian sculptor.

**An·te′nor** (ăn·tē′nôr; -nẽr). Athenian sculptor of 6th century B.C.; executed bronze statues of Harmodius and Aristogiton placed by Athenians in the Ceramicus, carried off by Xerxes to Susa, and returned to Athens by Alexander the Great.

**An′ter·us** (ăn′tẽr·ŭs) *or* **An′ter·os** (-ŏs), Saint. Pope (bishop of Rome; 235–236).

**An·tevs′** (än·tĕfs′), **Ernst Valdemar.** 1888– . Geologist, b. in Sweden; Ph.D., U. of Stockholm (1917). Research associate, Carnegie Institution in U. S. (1922–23, 1928–29, 1934 ff.). On various geological expeditions; known esp. for work relating to glacial geology, tree growth as indicator of climate, and Quaternary geology and climate of southwest U.S.

**An′theil** (ăn′tīl), **George.** 1900–1959. American concert pianist and composer, exponent of futurism; b. Trenton, N. J.; pupil of Constantin von Sternberg and (1914 ff.) Ernest Bloch; lived in Germany and France; associated with motion pictures, as composer and assoc. producer. Compositions include *Zingareska* (1921), *Ballet Mécanique* (1925), operas *Transatlantic* (1929) and *Helen Retires* (1932), orchestral works, as *Archipelago* (1933), the ballet *Dreams* (1935), sonatas, quartets, etc.

**An·the′mi·us** (ăn·thē′mĭ·ŭs). d. 472. Roman emperor (467–472). Son-in-law of Marcian, Emperor of the East. Appointed emperor by Emperor Leo I on advice of Ricimer, his counselor; defeated Huns in Dacia (466, 468); his daughter married Ricimer (467); later, quarreled with Ricimer, who brought Olybrius and army and besieged Rome; killed in the assault.

**Anthemius of Tral′les** (trăl′ēz). Sixth-century Greek mathematician and architect; planned (with Isidorus of Miletus) and built (532–537) church of Saint Sophia at Constantinople for Emperor Justinian.

**An·theu′nis** (än·tû′nĭs), **Gen′til′** (zhäɴ′tēl′) **Theodoor.**

1840–1907. Belgian poet; author of lyrics in Flemish.

**An'thoine'** (äN'twȧn'), **François Paul.** 1860–1944. French general in World War.

**An'thon** (ăn'thŭn), **Charles.** 1797–1867. American classical scholar, b. New York City. Professor, Columbia (1820–67). Edited texts and classical dictionaries.

**An'tho·ny** (ăn'tô·nĭ; -thô·nĭ), Saint. c. 250–350. First Christian monk, b. in middle Egypt. Ascetic from age of twenty; withdrew to solitude of a height near the Nile; emerged only to organize communities of anchorites and, late in life, to attack Arianism. Subject of legends recording temptations that beset him and his struggles against forces of evil. Regarded as founder of Christian monachism.

**Anthony.** *In full* **Anthony Clemens Theodore.** *Ger.* **Anton Klemens Theodor.** 1755–1836. King of Saxony; succeeded (1827) his brother Frederick Augustus I; coregent (1830) with nephew Frederick Augustus II; sanctioned constitutional government (1831).

**Anthony, C. L.** See Dodie SMITH.

**Anthony, Joseph.** 1897– . American journalist and editor, b. New York City. Editor, *Golden Book Magazine.* Author of *The Gang* (1921), *Casanova Jones* (verse novel; 1930), and screen plays (from 1935).

**Anthony, Katharine Susan.** 1877–1965. American writer, b. Roseville, Ark. Grad. U. of Chicago (1905). Author of *Feminism in Germany and Scandinavia* (1915), *Labor Laws of New York* (1917), and biographies, as *Margaret Fuller* (1920), *Catherine the Great* (1925), *Queen Elizabeth* (1929), *Marie Antoinette* (1932), *Louisa May Alcott* (1938).

**Anthony, Mark.** See Marcus ANTONIUS (83?–30 B.C.).

**Anthony, Susan Brownell.** 1820–1906. American woman-suffrage advocate, b. Adams, Mass. Organizer, The National Woman Suffrage Association (1869); lecturer and campaigner for woman suffrage; president, National Am. Woman Suffrage Association (1892–1900). Elected to Am. Hall of Fame (1950). See Elizabeth STANTON.

**Anthony of Bour'bon** (bo͝or'bŭn). *Fr.* **An'toine' de Bour'bon'** (äN'twȧn' dẽ bo͝or'bôN'). 1518–1562. Duke of Vendôme and king of Navarre (1555–62). Son of Charles de Bourbon, Duc de Vendôme; b. in Picardy; m. (1548) Jeanne d'Albret (see ALBRET), heiress to throne of Navarre. Weak and irresolute on religious question; at first joined his brother Louis, Prince de Condé; involved in conspiracy against Francis II (1560); after this joined Catholic forces; killed in assault on Rouen. Father of Henry of Navarre (Henry IV of France). See BOURBON.

**Anthony of Pad'u·a** (păd'ū·ȧ), Saint. 1195–1231. Franciscan monk, b. Lisbon, Portugal. Taught theology in Italy and France; known as great preacher; provincial of his order in northern Italy (1227). Canonized (1232) by Gregory IX.

**Antias, Valerius.** See VALERIUS ANTIAS.

**An·tig'o·nus** (ăn·tĭg'ô·nŭs). Name of two kings of Judea:

**Antigonus I.** 135?–104 B.C. Coregent (105–104) with his brother Aristobulus. Killed as result of court intrigue.

**Antigonus II.** *Called* **Mat'ta·thi'as** (măt'ȧ·thī'ăs). 80?–37 B.C. King (40–37), last of the Hasmonaean dynasty. Son of Aristobulus II. Taken by Pompey as prisoner to Rome (63); escaped, but again prisoner (56); failed to secure Caesar's aid to throne of Judea; defeated by Herod (42); with help of Parthians, became king (40); drove Herod from Jerusalem; overcome by Romans (37) and put to death at Antioch.

**Antigonus.** Name of three kings of Macedonia, the **An·tig'o·nids** (ăn·tĭg'ô·nĭdz):

**Antigonus I.** *Called* **Antigonus Cy'clops** (sī'klŏps) *or* **Mon'oph·thal'mos** (mŏn'ŏf·thăl'mŏs), *i.e.* the one-eyed. 382–301 B.C. King (306–301). One of generals of Alexander the Great; after death of Alexander (323), received provinces of Greater Phrygia, Lycia, and Pamphylia; made war against Perdiccas and Eumenes (322–316) and, later, against others of the Diadochi, with varying success (cf. PTOLEMY I); attempted to gain sole control of Asia. Assumed title of king (306); invaded Egypt; with his son Demetrius Poliorcetes, overwhelmed at Ipsus (301) by Lysimachus and Seleucus; killed in the battle.

**Antigonus II Gon'a·tas** (gŏn'ȧ·tăs). 319?–239 B.C. Grandson of Antigonus I. King (283–239), assuming title on death of his father, Demetrius Poliorcetes, and attaining full control (276); twice expelled (before 277 and 273) from his kingdom by Pyrrhus of Epirus.

**Antigonus III Do'son** (dō'sŏn). d. 221 B.C. King (229–221). Nephew of Antigonus Gonatas and cousin of Demetrius II, whom he succeeded, marrying his widow; supported Achaean League; defeated Spartans at Sellasia (221).

**Antigonus of Ca·rys'tus** (kȧ·rĭs'tŭs). fl. 250 B.C. Greek sculptor and author, b. Carystus, Euboea; lived at Athens and Pergamum; wrote biographies and works on art.

**An·tim'a·chus of Col'o·phon** (ăn·tĭm'ȧ·kŭs, kŏl'ô·fŏn) *or* **of Clar'os** (klâr'ŏs; klā'rŏs). fl. about 400 B.C. Greek poet; author of epic *Thebais* and elegy *Lydē*, both praised by Plato.

**An'tin** (ăn'tĭn), **Mary.** 1881–1949. Writer, b. Polotsk, Russia; to U.S. (1894). Educ. Teachers Coll., Columbia, and Barnard Coll.; m. (1901) Amadeus William Grabau (*q.v.*). Author of *From Polotzk to Boston* (1899), *The Promised Land* (1912), and *They Who Knock at Our Gates* (1914).

**An'ti·no'ri** (än'tē·nô'rē), Marchese **Orazio.** 1811–1882. Italian explorer, b. Perugia. Explored White Nile region (1859–61), northern Abyssinia (1869), and Shoa (1876). One of founders of Italian Geographical Society.

**An·tin'o·üs** (ăn·tĭn'ô·ŭs). 117–138 A.D. Page and favorite of Emperor Hadrian at Rome; noted for his beauty; drowned himself in Nile; subject of many works of art.

**An·ti'o·chus** (ăn·tī'ô·kŭs). Name of four kings of Commagene, reigning during period 62 B.C.–72 A.D.; at war with or under control of Rome; Commagene finally made Roman province.

**Antiochus.** Name of thirteen kings of the Seleucidae of Syria, forming dynasty reigning 280–64 B.C.:

**Antiochus I.** *Called* **Antiochus So'ter** (sō'tẽr), *i.e.* the preserver. 324–261 B.C. King (280–261 B.C.). Son of Seleucus I Nicator. Fought at Ipsus (301); associated with father as ruler (292); m. his stepmother, Stratonice (*q.v.*); won great victory over Gauls in Asia Minor (275); waged indecisive war (276–273) against Ptolemy II Philadelphus of Egypt; made alliance with Antigonus Gonatas of Macedonia; had difficulty in keeping great Seleucid empire intact; waged war against Eumenes I of Pergamum (263–261); killed in battle.

**Antiochus II.** *Called* **Antiochus The'os** (thē'ŏs), *i.e.* the divine. 286–247 B.C. King (261–247 B.C.). Son of Antiochus I. Waged long and ineffectual war with Ptolemy II (c. 260–252); expelled tyrant Timarchus from Miletus (258) and was given surname Theos for this deliverance; lost (c. 250) Bactria (Balkh) to Diodotus and Parthia to the Arsacids (*q.v.*); m. 1st Laodice, by whom he was father of Seleucus II (who succeeded him) and Antiochus Hierax, 2d (c. 252) Berenice, daughter of Ptolemy II, as token of peace with Egypt; abandoned her (247); supposedly poisoned by Laodice.

**Antiochus III.** *Called* **Antiochus the Great.** 242–187 B.C. King (223–187 B.C.). Younger son of Seleucus II and great-grandson of Antiochus I. Suppressed revolts in Media and Persia (220); faced with attempt to make Asia Minor independent (223–220), finally overcame usurper Achaeus after two-year siege of Sardis (215–213); at war with Ptolemy IV Philopator (219–217), who defeated him at Raphia (217); recovered Armenia (212); made successful invasion of Parthia, Media, and Bactria (210–205); formed coalition (202) with Philip V of Macedon against Egypt (see PTOLEMY V); reduced all of southern Syria (202), defeated Egyptians at Paneas (198), and invaded Thrace (195–194); gave refuge to Hannibal (195); quarreled with Rome (193); defeated by Romans at Thermopylae (191) and his fleets beaten twice (191, 190) off western and southern coasts of Asia Minor; completely defeated (190) by Romans under P. Scipio Africanus at Magnesia (Manisa), near Ephesus; made peace (188), giving up all Asia Minor (cf. EUMENES II); killed while plundering temple in Elymaïs. Succeeded by his sons Seleucus IV and Antiochus IV.

**Antiochus IV.** *Called* **Antiochus E·piph'a·nes** (ē·pĭf'ȧ·nēz), *i.e.* the illustrious. d. 163 B.C. King (175–163). Son of Antiochus III. Sent as hostage to Rome (189); educated there; seized throne when his brother Seleucus IV was murdered; waged war with Egypt (171–168); captured Pelusium (169); defeated both Ptolemy VI and VII; declared Judaism illegal (168); undertook second campaign against Egypt (168) but forced by Rome to give it up; destroyed Jewish temples in Syria; his intolerance and stringent methods against Jewish religion brought on Wars of the Maccabees (167–160); lost Jerusalem, but made successful expedition to Armenia and Persia (cf. ALEXANDER BALAS).

**Antiochus V.** *Called* **Antiochus Eu'pa·tor** (ū'pȧ·tôr), *i.e.* of a good father. 173–162 B.C. Son of Antiochus IV. King (163–162) under regency of Lysias; made peace with Jews; overthrown and killed by his cousin Demetrius I Soter.

**Antiochus VI.** *Called* **Antiochus Theos** *and* **Antiochus Epiphanes Di'o·ny'sus** (dī'ō·nī'sŭs). d. 142 B.C. Boy king (145–142), under regent at Antioch, in opposition to Demetrius II. Son of Alexander Balas and Cleopatra Thea (*qq.v.*).

**Antiochus VII.** *Called* **Antiochus Eu·er'ge·tes** (ū·ûr'jē·tēz) *and* **Antiochus Si·de'tes** (sī·dē'tēz). 158?–?129 B.C. King (138?–?129). Son of Demetrius I and brother of Demetrius II; m. Cleopatra Thea (her 3d husband); at war with Jews (138–134); destroyed Jerusalem (133); killed in Parthian War.

**Antiochus VIII.** *Called* **Antiochus Phil'o·me'tor** (fĭl'ō·mē'tôr) *and* **Antiochus Gry'pus** (grī'pŭs), *i.e.* the hook-nosed. d. 96 B.C. Son of Demetrius II Nicator and Cleopatra Thea. Joint ruler with his mother (125–121); sole king (121–115); forced to divide realm with Antiochus IX (115–96). Father of Seleucus VI and Demetrius III.

**Antiochus IX.** *Called* **Antiochus Phi·lop'a·tor** (fĭ·lŏp'ȧ·tôr) *and* **Antiochus Cyz'i·ce'nus** (sĭz'ĭ·sē'nŭs). d. 95 B.C. King (115–95). Seleucid pretender; son of Antiochus VII. As rival ruler, at war with Antiochus VIII; drove him from Antioch, but lost it (112).

**Antiochus X.** *Called* **Antiochus Eu'se·bes** (ū'sē·bēz), *i.e.* the pious. d. 92 B.C. Son of Antiochus IX. King (95–93) in opposition to his cousin Demetrius III.

**Antiochus XI.** *Called* **Antiochus Epiphanes Phil'a·del'phus** (fĭl'ȧ·dĕl'fŭs). d. 92 B.C. Son of Antiochus VIII. King (92). Defeated by Antiochus X.

**Antiochus XII.** *Called* **Antiochus Dionysus.** d. 85 B.C. Son of Antiochus VIII.

**Antiochus XIII.** *Called* **Antiochus A'si·at'i·cus** (ā'zhĭ·ăt'ĭ·kŭs; ā'shĭ-). King (69–64 B.C.). Son of Antiochus X. Received large part of Syria from Lucullus (69), losing it when it was made a Roman province (B.C. 64) by Pompey.

**Antiochus Hi'er·ax** (hī'ẽr·ăks), *i.e.* the hawk. d. 226 B.C. Son of Antiochus II of Syria and Laodice; younger brother of Seleucus II. Aided by Ptolemy III Euergetes of Egypt, waged war against his brother (241?–236); given Asia Minor to rule; defeated in war with Attalus I of Pergamum (229–228); fled to Thrace (227).

**Antiochus of As'ca·lon** (ăs'kȧ·lŏn). Greek philosopher of 1st century B.C.; works no longer extant; only knowledge of him based on mention by Cicero and Sextus Empiricus.

**Antiochus of Syracuse.** fl. 5th century B.C. Greek historian. His writings, on history of Sicily and colonizing of Italy, used as source material by later historians, esp. by Thucydides.

**Antipas.** See HEROD ANTIPAS.

**An·tip'a·ter** (ăn·tĭp'ȧ·tẽr). 398?–319 B.C. Macedonian general and statesman. Father of Cassander (*q.v.*). Ambassador of Philip of Macedon to Athens (346); negotiated peace after battle of Chaeronea (338); suppressed Spartan revolt under Agis III by victory at Megalopolis (331); regent of Macedonia during Alexander's expedition in East (334–323); at division of empire after Alexander's death, left in command in Macedonia; associated with his son-in-law Craterus (323–321) in rule; died while fighting to make his position secure.

**Antipater.** *Called* **Antipater the Id'u·mae'an** (ĭd'ū·mē'ăn). d. 43 B.C. Procurator of Judea (47–43). Father of Herod the Great. Supported Hyrcanus II against Aristobulus II; gained influence in Judea after Pompey seized Jerusalem (63); later, on decline of Pompey's power, made friends with Caesar; aided him at Alexandria (47); rewarded with Roman citizenship and appointment as procurator; assassinated.

**An·tiph'a·nes** (ăn·tĭf'ȧ·nēz). 408?–?334 B.C. Greek playwright; settled in Athens and began (c. 387) writing comedies, only fragments of which are extant.

**An'ti·phon** (ăn'tĭ·fŏn). 480?–411 B.C. Attic orator and writer of speeches for litigants, especially in murder cases; condemned to death (411) for his part in conspiracy of the Four Hundred (wealthy citizens) to maintain control of Athens.

**Antiphon.** fl. 5th century B.C. Greek mathematician and philosopher.

**An·tis'the·nes** (ăn·tĭs'thē·nēz). 444?–after 371 B.C. Athenian philosopher; studied under Socrates; founder of the Cynic school.

**An'toine'** (äɴ'twȧn'), Père. See ANTONIO DE SEDILLA.

**Antoine, André.** 1857?–1943. French actor and theater manager, b. Limoges. Founded (1887) Théâtre Libre, where new methods of dramatic presentation were tried. Opened (1897) Théâtre Antoine where, with his own company, he produced many contemporary plays; managed the Odéon (1906–13).

**Antoine, Jacques Denis.** 1733–1801. French architect; designer of the mint in Paris.

**Antoinette, Marie.** See MARIE ANTOINETTE.

**An·to·kol'ski** (ŭn·tŭ·kôl'y'·skû·ĭ; *Angl.* ăn'tō·kôl'skĭ), **Mark Matveevich.** 1843–1902. Russian sculptor, b. Wilno, of Jewish parentage; resided permanently in Paris (1880 ff.). Most of works in Alexander III Museum, Leningrad. Specialized in portrait statues, as of Ivan the Terrible (his most famous; bought by Emperor Alexander II and cast in bronze) and of Turgenev.

**An'tom·mar'chi** (än'tôm·mär'kē), **Francesco.** 1780?–1838. Corsican physician to Napoleon at St. Helena (from 1818); exhibited (1822) alleged Napoleonic death mask; wrote *Les Derniers Moments de Napoléon* (1823).

**An′to·nel′li** (än′tō·nĕl′lē), **Giacomo.** 1806–1876. Italian prelate and statesman; minister of finance, Papal States (1845); created cardinal (1847); prime minister (1848); accompanied Pius IX to Gaeta (1848) and, on return to Rome (1850), re-established absolute power of papal administration; secretary of foreign affairs (from 1850); stanch opponent of Italian unification.

**An′to·nel′lo da Mes·si′na** (än′tō·nĕl′lō dä mās·sē′nä). 1430?–1479. Sicilian painter; reputed to have introduced oil painting into Italy; among his works are *St. Jerome* and *Salvator Mundi* (National Gallery, London), *Madonna del Rosario* (Messina), *Crucifixion* (Antwerp), *St. Sebastian* (Dresden).

**An′to·ne′scu** (än′tō·nĕ′skōō), **Ion.** 1882–1946. Rumanian general, b. in Transylvania; educ. in French military schools; served in Rumanian army in World War; military attaché in Rome and London; general; chief of staff (1937); suspended from army (Nov., 1938) and imprisoned as one of leaders of abortive revolt; released and made minister of war; forced to resign and again arrested (July, 1940) for opposing territorial concessions to Russia; released and appointed premier (Sept. 5, 1940); as dictator forced Carol's abdication; removed from office (1944); executed as war criminal.

**An·to′ni·a** (ăn·tō′nĭ·ȧ; -tōn′yȧ). Name of three Roman women: (1) **Antonia Major.** fl. 1st century A.D. Daughter of Marcus Antonius and Octavia and grandmother of Emperor Nero. (2) Her younger sister, **Antonia Minor.** 36 B.C.–37 A.D. Wife of Nero Claudius Drusus; mother of Emperor Claudius and of Germanicus Caesar and Livilla. Died soon after accession of her grandson Caligula. (3) **Claudia Antonia.** d. 66 A.D. Daughter of Emperor Claudius; put to death by Nero.

**Antonides. Joannes.** See Jan Antonisz van der GOES.

**An′to·ni′nus** (ăn′tō·nī′nŭs), Saint. *Real name* **Antonio Pie·roz′zi** (pyā·rôt′tsē). *Also called* **Antonio De′ For′ci·glio′ni** (dā fōr′chē·lyō′nē). 1389–1459. Italian Dominican friar; papal theologian, Council of Florence (1439); archbishop of Florence (1446); canonized (1523) by Adrian VI. Among his works are *Summa Theologica* (pub. 1477), *Summa Confessionalis*, and the chronicle *Summa Historialis*.

**Antoninus, Marcus Aurelius.** See (1) CARACALLA, (2) MARCUS AURELIUS, (3) HELIOGABALUS.

**Antoninus Pi′us** (pī′ŭs). *Full name* **Ti′tus Au·re′li·us Ful′vus Boi·o′ni·us Ar′ri·us** (tī′tŭs ô·rē′lĭ·ŭs [ô·rēl′yŭs] fŭl′vŭs boi·ō′nĭ·ŭs ăr′ĭ·ŭs). 86–161 A.D. Roman emperor (138–161). b. Lanuvium, of family originally from southern Gaul. Proconsul in Asia; adopted (138) by Emperor Hadrian and succeeded him (138); m. (138) Annia Galeria Faustina; enjoyed remarkably peaceful and prosperous reign—no wars, revolts, conspiracies of any kind recorded, except in northern Britain where earth wall (Wall of Antonine) built by Roman governor from Forth to Clyde to keep out Pict and Scot invasions; literature encouraged, trade and communications advanced; his daughter Faustina married his nephew Marcus Aurelius (*q.v.*), whom he adopted as successor; also adopted Lucius Verus (see VERUS).

**An·tô′nio,** Dom (dōɴ ăɴn·tō′nyōō). 1531–1594. Grand prior of Crato and claimant to Portuguese throne (1580) as natural son of Louis, Duke of Beja (1506–1545), second son of King Emanuel. Defeated by duke of Alva; fled to Paris. Last of house of Aviz (see AVIZ).

**An·to′nio** (än·tō′nyō), **Nicolás.** 1617–1684. Spanish bibliographer; author of *Bibliotheca Hispana* (1672–96), index of Spanish authors from reign of Augustus (27 B.C.–14 A.D.) to 1670.

**An·to′nio de Se·dil′la** (än·tō′nyō thā sā·thē′lyä). *Known as* Père **An′toine′** (pâr äɴ′twȧn′). 1748–1829. Spanish Capuchin priest in New Orleans, b. in Granada, Spain. To Louisiana (1780); curé of parish of St. Louis of New Orleans (1785). Accused (1790) of trying to introduce Inquisition; bound in irons and shipped back to Spain. Reinstated in his parish (1795) by king of Spain. Dispute (1805) with vicar-general of Louisiana decided in Antoine's favor by king. Secret agent for Spanish government (1813–16).

**An·to′ni·us** (ăn·tō′nĭ·ŭs; -tōn′yŭs), **Gaius.** *Nickname* **Antonius Hy′bri·da** (hī′brĭ·dȧ). fl. 63–42 B.C. Roman politician and administrator; consul with Cicero (63); governor in Macedonia; censor (42).

**Antonius, Marcus.** 143–87 B.C. Roman orator; consul (99); censor (97); as follower of Sulla, executed by order of Marius and Cinna (87).

**Antonius, Marcus.** *Known in English as* **Mark,** *or* **Marc, An′to·ny** (ăn′tō·nĭ) *or* **An′tho·ny** (ăn′tō·nĭ; -thō·nĭ). 83?–30 B.C. Roman orator, triumvir, and soldier; grandson of Marcus Antonius (143–87); member of old patrician family related through his mother to Julius Caesar. To Greece (58); took part in campaigns (58–56) against Aristobulus II and in Palestine and Egypt; aided Caesar in Gaul (54); through Caesar's influence became successively quaestor, augur, and tribune of the plebs; commanded left wing of Caesar's army at Pharsalus (48); consul with Caesar (44). After Caesar's death (44), influenced Romans by his oratory to drive out the assassins; found Octavius (see AUGUSTUS) a rival; defeated by forces of senate (43); triumvir (43), receiving Asia as his command; with Octavius defeated republican forces at Philippi (42). Visited Athens, then Asia to punish Cleopatra; succumbed to her charms and followed her to Egypt (41); in division of Roman world by triumvirate, took East (40–36); m. (40) Octavia as second wife, but returned to Cleopatra, living voluptuously; suffered serious defeat by Parthians (36); settled in Alexandria, alienating his Roman support (34). Rivalry with Octavius increased; deprived of his power (32) by senate; with Cleopatra, completely defeated by Octavius at Actium (31); fled to Egypt; deserted by army, committed suicide. Appears as character in literature, esp. in Shakespeare's *Antony and Cleopatra* and *Julius Caesar* and Dryden's *All for Love.* See also Marcus Aemilius LEPIDUS.

**An′to·ny** (ăn′tō·nĭ). Variant of ANTHONY.

**Antony, Mark** *or* **Marc.** See Marcus ANTONIUS (83?–30 B.C.).

**An·tyl′lus** (ăn·tĭl′ŭs). fl. 2d or 3d century A.D. Greek physician and surgeon.

**Anushirvan.** See KHOSRAU I.

**An·va·ri′** *or* **An·wa·ri′** (än·vȧ·rē′). *In full* **Auad–ud-din Ali Anvari.** fl. 12th century. Persian lyric poet, b. in Khurasan. Long enjoyed favor of Persian rulers, but finally banished to Balkh. His principal poems, including lyrics and elegies, collected in the *Divan;* his longest poem, *The Tears of Khorassan,* translated into English by William Kirkpatrick (1754–1812), British army officer and Persian scholar.

**An′ville′** (äɴ′vēl′), **Jean Baptiste Bour′gui′gnon′** (bōōr′gē′nyôɴ′) **d′.** 1697–1782. French geographer and cartographer. Royal geographer (1719); wrote on ancient geography and meteorology, with maps scientifically prepared; author of *Atlas Général* (pub. between 1737 and 1780).

**An′za** (än′sä), **Juan Bautista de.** 1735–1788. Spanish explorer on Pacific coast of America, b. Fronteras, Mexico. Founded San Francisco (1776). Governor of New Mexico (1777–88).

**An'zen·gru'ber** (än'tsĕn·grōō'bẽr), **Ludwig.** 1839–1889. Viennese playwright and novelist.

**An'zi·lot'ti** (än'tsē·lôt'tē), **Dionisio.** 1869–1950. Italian jurist; president, Permanent Court of International Justice (1928–30).

**A·o·ki** (ä·ō·kē), Viscount **Shuzo.** 1844–1914. Japanese diplomat. Educ. at Tokyo and in Germany; minister to Germany (1874–85); vice-minister and minister of foreign affairs (1885–91); minister to Germany and England (1894–99); m. German baroness Elisabeth von Rahden; negotiated (1894) Aoki-Kimberley Treaty with Great Britain, abolishing extraterritoriality; privy councilor (1899–1905); became first Japanese ambassador to U.S. (1905–09).

**A·o'sta** (ä·ôs'tä), Duke of. (1) = AMADEUS, King of Spain. (2) His grandson **Emanuele Filiberto** (1869–1931), Duke of Aosta and Prince of Savoy; cousin of King Victor Emmanuel III; Italian general; in World War, commanded Third Army, stationed on the Isonzo; successful until Caporetto (1917), when he conducted retreat to the Piave; made marshal (1926). (3) His son Prince **Amedeo Umberto** (1898–1942), Duke of Aosta, married (1927) Princess Anna of France. Viceroy of Italian East Africa (1937–41); commander in chief of Italian forces in East African campaigns (1939–41); surrendered to British (1941).

**A'paf·fy** (ŏ'pŏf·fĭ) *or* **A'pa·fi** (ŏ'pŏ·fĭ) *or* **A'ba·fi** (ŏ'bŏ·fĭ), **Mi'chael** (mī'kĕl; -k'l). 1632–1690. A Szekler, prince of Transylvania (1661–90) as Michael I; ruled as vassal of the Porte (1661–86); recognized suzerainty of Emperor Leopold I. His son **Michael (II) Apafi** (1677–1713) succeeded him as prince (1690–97); acknowledged vassalage to Hapsburgs, Transylvania becoming part of Hungary; abdicated (1697).

**A'pel** (ä'pĕl), **Johann August.** 1771–1816. German author. His ghost story *Die Jägerbraut,* in collection *Gespensterbuch* (1810–14), furnished text for Weber's opera *Der Freischütz.*

**A·pel'les** (ȧ·pĕl'ēz). Greek painter of 4th century B.C., b. in Ionia; regarded as greatest painter of antiquity. Court painter of Philip of Macedon and Alexander the Great. His paintings (no copies of which are extant) included one of Alexander grasping a thunderbolt, Artemis with a chorus of maidens, Aphrodite rising from the sea, and portraits of Clitus, Archelaus, and Antigonus.

**Ap El'lis** (ăp ĕl'ĭs), **Augustine.** 1886–1969. British military aviator; served in World War (1914–18); in command of flying training schools (from 1931).

**Ap'i·a'nus** (ăp'ĭ·ā'nŭs; ā'pĭ-; *Ger.* ä'pē·ä'nōōs), **Pe'trus** (pē'trŭs; *Ger.* pā'trōōs). *Latin name of* **Peter Bie'ne·witz** (bē'nĕ·vĭts) *or* **Ben'ne·witz** (bĕn'ĕ·vĭts). 1501?–1552. German astronomer, mathematician, and geographer. Author of *Cosmographia* (1524); printed some of earliest maps of America. His son **Philippus,** *Ger.* **Philipp** (1531–1589), was also a mathematician and geographer.

**A·pi'ci·us** (ȧ·pĭsh'ĭ·ŭs), **Marcus Gavius.** fl. 14–37 A.D. Roman epicure; said to have spent vast fortune in satisfying desire for rare foods.

**A'pi·on** (ā'pĭ·ŏn; ăp'ĭ·ŏn). Greek grammarian and anti-Semite of 1st century A.D.; head of deputation sent by citizens of Alexandria to Emperor Caligula to complain against Jews (38); his strictures against the Jews were refuted by Josephus in *Against Apion.* Settled in Rome and taught rhetoric. Tale of Androcles and the lion is from one of his books.

**A'pol'li'naire'** (á'pô'lē'nâr'), **Guillaume.** *In full* **Guillaume Apollinaire de Kos'tro·wit'sky** (kôs'trô·vēt'skĭ). 1880–1918. Man of letters in France, b. Rome, of Polish parentage. Associated with advanced literary and artistic movements, and with a poetical group whose work was marked by exoticism, irony, and occasional buffoonery; wrote novels, essays, plays, and many bizarre fantasies.

**A·pol'li·nar'is of La·od'i·ce'a** (ȧ·pŏl'ĭ·nâr'ĭs ŭv lā·ŏd'ĭ·sē'ȧ). d. ?390 A.D. Teacher of rhetoric, and controversial theologian; bishop of Laodicea, Syria (from c. 362). When Emperor Julian prohibited Christians from teaching the classics, collaborated with his father (**Apollinaris** the elder, fl. 335–362, an Alexandrian who taught grammar at Berytus and Laodicea) in converting Old Testament into poems and dramas and New Testament into dialogues in imitation of Plato; opposed Arianism; set forth his own beliefs (Apollinarianism), establishing sect condemned as heretical by several church councils; his teachings widely accepted in Syria and neighboring lands; author of poems and religious works, most of which have been lost.

**Apollinaris Si·do'ni·us** (sī·dō'nĭ·ŭs; sĭ·dō'-), **Gaius Sollius.** 430?–?487. Early Christian prelate, politician, and writer, b. Lyon. As a favorite of Emperor Anthemius, appointed governor of Rome (467); later raised to rank of patrician and senator. Entered church; consecrated bishop of Clermont (472). Author of nine books of letters and poems valued as source material for 5th-century political and literary history.

**A·pol'lo·do'rus** (ȧ·pŏl'ō·dō'rŭs). *Known as* **Ski·ag'ra·phos** (skī·ăg'rȧ·fŏs), *i.e.* the Shadow Painter. fl. 5th century B.C. Athenian painter; said to have introduced improvements in chiaroscuro and perspective.

**Apollodorus.** Athenian grammarian of 2d century B.C.; author of book on gods and Greek heroic age valued as source book on ancient mythology.

**Apollodorus of Ca·rys'tus** (kȧ·rĭs'tŭs). Greek playwright at Athens (300–260 B.C.); author of 47 comedies, and five times winner of prize for comedy.

**Apollodorus of Damascus.** fl. 2d century A.D. Greek architect; a favorite of Emperor Trajan; designed Forum Trajanum at Rome and triumphal arches at Benevento and Ancona. Banished and put to death by Emperor Hadrian.

**Ap'ol·lo'ni·us** (ăp'ŏ·lō'nĭ·ŭs). *Known as* **Apollonius Mo'lon** (mō'lŏn). Greek rhetorician of 1st century B.C.; teacher at Rhodes, particularly of Cicero and Caesar.

**Apollonius Dys'co·lus** (dĭs'kō·lŭs), *i.e.* the Crabbed. fl. 1st half of 2d century A.D. Alexandrian scholar; one of greatest of Greek grammarians; made first critical study of Greek syntax; only four of his many works extant. Father of the grammarian Aelius Herodianus (*q.v.*).

**Apollonius of Per'ga** (pûr'gȧ). Greek mathematician of 3d century B.C.; known esp. for treatise on conic sections.

**Apollonius of Rhodes** (rōdz) *or* **Apollonius Rho'di·us** (rō'dĭ·ŭs). Greek epic poet of late 3d and early 2d century B.C. Author of an epic, *Argonautica,* based on legend of the Argonauts.

**Apollonius of Tral'les** (trăl'ēz). fl. 2d century B.C. Greek sculptor; collaborated with his brother Tauriscus in executing marble group known as *Farnese Bull.*

**Apollonius of Ty'a·na** (tī'ȧ·nȧ). Greek Neo-Pythagorean philosopher of 1st century A.D.; traveled in India, visiting Babylon and Nineveh en route; regarded by many contemporaries as magician and miracle worker.

**A·pol'los** (ȧ·pŏl'ŏs). *In Douay Version* **A·pol'lo** (-ō). In Bible, a 1st-century Christian; Alexandrian Jew instructed in Christian doctrine by Aquila and Priscilla at Ephesus (*Acts* xviii. 24 ff.); an eloquent preacher, esp. at Corinth (*1 Cor.* i. 12); thought by some to be author of *Epistle to the Hebrews.*

**Ap′o·phis** (ăp′ō·fĭs). *Also* **A·po′pi** (ä·pô′pē) *or* **A·pe′pi** (ä·pĕ′pē). Name of three Hyksos kings of ancient Egypt. **Apophis III** (c. 1600 B.C.), king over wide territory with capital at Avaris (Pelusium?) in the delta; defeated and driven out of Egypt by Ahmose I.

**Ap′per·ley** (ăp′ẽr·lĭ), **Charles James.** *Pseudonym* **Nim′rod** (nĭm′rŏd). 1777?–1843. Welsh sporting writer. Author of *The Chase, the Turf, and the Road* (1837) and a series of sporting memoirs.

**Ap′pert′** (ȧ′pâr′), **François.** d. 1840? Parisian chef; invented (1804) process for preserving food in hermetically sealed containers. His brother **Benjamin Nicolas Marie** (1797–?1847) was an educator and philanthropist; active in urging prison reform.

**Ap′pia** (äp′pyä), **A′dolphe′** (ȧ′dôlf′). 1862–1928. Stage producer, b. Geneva, Switzerland; pioneer in developing technique of stage lighting. Among his notable stage productions were Byron's *Manfred,* with music by Schumann, in Paris (1903); Gluck's *Orfeo ed Euridice* (1913); Wagner's *Tristan und Isolde* (1923), *Rheingold* (1924), *Die Walküre* (1924).

**Ap·pia′ni** (äp·pyä′nē), **Andrea.** 1754–1817. Italian painter known esp. for his frescoes at Monza and in Church of Santa Maria, Milan; called "Painter of the Graces." First court painter to Napoleon.

**Ap′pi·a′nus** (ăp′ĭ·ā′nŭs) *or* **Ap′pi·an** (ăp′ĭ·ăn). Roman historian of 2d century A.D., orig. from Alexandria. Of the original 24 books of his history of Rome, *Romaïka,* written in Greek, eleven complete books and fragments of others are extant.

**Appius Claudius.** See CLAUDIUS (Roman gens).

**Ap′ple·by** (ăp′'l·bĭ), **John Francis.** 1840–1917. b. Westmoreland, N.Y. American inventor of a cartridge magazine and automatic feed device for rifles (pat. 1864) and of a grain binder (pat. 1878, 1879).

**Ap′ple·gath** (ăp′'l·găth), **Augustus.** 1788–1871. English inventor of vertical printing press.

**Appleseed, Johnny.** See John CHAPMAN (1774–1845).

**Ap′ple·ton** (ăp′'l·tŭn; -t'n), **Daniel.** 1785–1849. American publisher, b. Haverhill, Mass. With his son **William Henry** (1814–1899) founded D. Appleton & Co., book publishers (1838).

**Appleton,** Sir **Edward Victor.** 1892–1965. English physicist, b. Bradford, Eng. Awarded Nobel prize in physics (1947) for discovery of an electrically charged layer in the ionosphere (Appleton layer).

**Appleton, Nathan** (1779–1861) and his brother **Samuel** (1766–1853). b. New Ipswich, N.H. Pioneers in cotton-cloth manufacture, at Waltham, Lowell, Lawrence (Mass.), and Manchester (N.H.); among founders of Lowell, Mass.

**Ap′po·nyi** (ŏp′pô·nyĭ). Name of Hungarian noble family including: Count **Antal György Apponyi** (1751–1817), founder of Apponyi Library, Pressburg. His grandson Count **György** (1808–1899), court chancellor (1846), Conservative party leader (to 1848) and, later, Nationalist party leader supporting Deák in efforts to negotiate Austro-Hungarian Ausgleich. Count György's son Count **Al′bert** (ŏl′bĕrt) **György** (1846–1933), member of Esterházy and Wekerle cabinets (1917), head of Hungarian peace delegation in Paris (1920), and speaker of Képviselöház (1920 ff.).

**Appuleius, Lucius.** See APULEIUS.

**A·pra′ksin** *or* **A·prax′in** (ŭ·prá′ksyĭn), **Fëdor Matveevich.** 1671–1728. Russian admiral. Entered service of Czar Fëdor (1681) and of Peter the Great (1683); became favorite of Peter; governor of Archangel (1692); one of most influential members of imperial court (after 1700). Admiral of Russian navy; built ships, wharves, fortresses; defeated Swedes (1708), saving St. Petersburg from destruction. Created count (1709). Captured Viborg (1710); defeated Swedish fleet (1713), with result that Baltic provinces by Treaty of Nystad (1721) became Russian; won several other naval victories in Turkey and Persia. His nephew Count **Stepan Fëdorovich Apraksin** (1702–1760), general, served in war against Turks (1737); made general in chief (1746) and marshal (1756); strongly opposed to German influence; in Seven Years' War, defeated Prussians at Gross-Jägersdorf (1757); involved in court intrigue; died in prison.

**Ap′ri·es** (ăp′rĭ·ēz). *Known in Bible as* Pharaoh **Hoph′ra** (hŏf′rȧ). King (c. 588–569 or 566 B.C.) of ancient Egypt of XXVIth (Saite) dynasty. Son of Psamtik II. Aided Jews under Zedekiah in their revolt against Babylon but could not prevent Nebuchadnezzar from taking Jerusalem (586); had strong navy which seized Cyprus and Phoenician coast; defeated in expedition against Cyrene. See AHMOSE II.

**Ap′u·le′ius,** *sometimes* **Ap′pu·le′ius** (ăp′ū·lē′yŭs), **Lucius.** Philosopher and rhetorician of 2d century A.D.; best known for *Metamorphoses,* or *The Golden Ass,* story in which the hero is transformed into an ass, in which form he meets with many amusing adventures, and is finally restored to his own person with aid of Isis.

**A′qua·vi′va** (ä′kwä·vē′vä) *or* **Ac′qua·vi′va** (äk′kwä-vē′vä), **Claudio.** 1543?–1615. Italian ecclesiastic; fifth general of Society of Jesus (1581–1615).

**Aq′ui·la** (ăk′wĭ·lȧ). In Bible, 1st-century Christian, a Jew of Pontus; with wife **Pris·cil′la** (prĭ·sĭl′ȧ), lived for time at Rome till driven out by edict of Claudius (49); tentmakers at Corinth, where St. Paul lodged with them (*Acts* xviii. 1–3); accompanied Paul to Ephesus, where they instructed Apollos in Christian doctrine.

**Aquila.** *Called* **Aquila of Pon′tus** (pŏn′tŭs) *or* **Aquila Pon′ti·cus** (pŏn′tĭ·kŭs). fl. 130 A.D. Translator of Old Testament; b. Sinope, Pontus; became Christian; later, proselyte to Judaism and reputedly disciple of Rabbi Akiba ben Joseph. Best known for his literal translation of Old Testament from Hebrew into Greek, extant only in fragments.

**Aquila.** See ARNO.

**Aq′ui·la** (ăk′wĭ·lȧ; *Ger.* ä′kvē·lä), **Kaspar.** *Orig. surname* **Adler.** 1488–1560. Bavarian Protestant theologian; friend of Luther and his assistant in translation of Bible.

**Aquin, Louis Claude d′.** See DAQUIN.

**A·qui′nas** (ȧ·kwī′năs), Saint **Thomas.** *Also* **Thomas of A·qui′no** (ä·kwē′nô). 1225?–1274. Italian scholastic philosopher, often called the Angelic Doctor (Lat. *Doctor Angelicus*) and Prince of Scholastics (Lat. *Princeps Scholasticorum*); b. in family castle at Roccasecca, near Aquino. Educ. under Benedictines at Monte Cassino, and at U. of Naples. Entered Dominican order (1243); to Paris (1245) and Cologne; studied under Albertus Magnus (1248–52); established theological school at Cologne; teacher at Cologne (to c. 1252), Dominican monastery of St. Jacques, Paris (1252–61), Italy (1261 ff.). Canonized by Pope John XXII (1323); proclaimed doctor of the church (1567) by Pius V; declared patron of Catholic schools (1880). Known particularly as systematizer of Catholic theology and for philosophical system known now as Thomism. Author of *Summa Theologica, Summa de Veritate Catholicae Fidei contra Gentiles, Quaestiones Disputatae, Quodlibeta, Catena Aurea, Opuscula Theologica,* and a commentary on Peter Lombard's *Sententiae.*

**A·ra′bi Pa′sha** (ȧ·rä′bĭ pä′shä). *More correctly* **Ah′med A·ra′bi** (ä′măd). 1841?–1911. Egyptian revolutionist, b. in Lower Egypt. Served twelve years as conscript soldier in Egyptian army; after dismissal on unproved charges became leader of discontented Nationalists;

acquired great influence (1881) over Khedive Tewfik Pasha (*q.v.*); undersecretary for war (1882); dismissed from ministry (1882) on intervention of British; defeated at Tell el-Kebir (Sept. 13, 1882) by General Wolseley; captured, tried, and sentenced to death, later to life imprisonment; sent to Ceylon; pardoned and returned to Egypt (1901).

**A'ra'go'** (à'rà'gō'; *Angl.* ăr'ȧ·gō), **François,** *in full* **Dominique François Jean.** 1786–1853. French scientist, b. Estagel. Investigated chromatic polarization of light; showed importance of undulatory theory of light; in field of electromagnetism, discovered principle of the development of magnetism by rotation. Appointed director of Paris observatory (1830); determined planetary diameters with greatest exactness. Took part in July revolution (1830); minister of war and marine in provisional government (1848); responsible for abolition of slavery in French colonies; opposed election of Louis Napoleon as president of France; refused to take oath of allegiance after coup d'état of 1851. His brother **Jacques** (1790–1855) was a traveler, novelist, and playwright. Another brother, **Étienne Vincent** (1802–1892), was a poet, playwright, and politician. François's son **Emmanuel** (1812–1896), vigorous opponent of Louis Napoleon, was minister of justice (1870), later of the interior; member, National Assembly (1871–76); senator (1876–80); ambassador to Switzerland (1880–94).

**A'ra'gon'** (à'rà'gôɴ'), **Louis.** 1897– . French novelist, poet, and essayist; a leader of Dadaists and later of surrealists. Among his works are *Feu de Joie* (1920), *Le Libertinage* (1924), *Le Paysan de Paris* (1926), *Les Cloches de Bâle* (1935), *Les Voyages de l'Impériale* (1940).

**A·ra'ia** (ä·rä'yä), **Francesco.** c. 1700–c. 1770. Italian composer; Kapellmeister, St. Petersburg (c. 1734–59); composed first opera produced in Russian, *La Clemenza di Tito* (1751; Russian libretto by F. G. Volkov).

**A·ra·i Ha·ku·se·ki** (ä·rä·ē hä·kŏŏ·sĕ·kē). 1657–1725. Japanese scholar, historian, and philosopher. Author of *Hankampu* (1701), history of daimios from 1600 to 1680; *Tokushi Yoron,* history of Japan; autobiography (1716).

**A·rak·che'ev** or **A·rak·che'yev** (ŭ·rŭk·chă'yĕf), **Aleksei Andreevich.** 1769–1834. Russian soldier and statesman. Favorite of Emperor Paul and commander of his bodyguard; made count (1799); political adviser to Alexander I (1801–25); minister of war (1806).

**A·ra·ki** (ä·rä·kē), **Sadao.** 1877–1966. Japanese general, b. Tokyo, of a Samurai family. Fought in Russo-Japanese War; in World War, in Japanese military mission to Moscow; minister of war (1932–34); member of cabinet advisory council (1937–38); minister of education (1938–40); sentenced as war criminal to life imprisonment in 1948; released in 1955 because of failing health.

**Ar'am** (âr'ăm), **Eugene.** 1704–1759. English schoolmaster and murderer. Self-taught philologist; recognized in advance of scholars the Indo-European affinities of Celtic, and disputed the derivation of Latin from Greek. Convicted of murder on evidence by an accomplice; executed and hung in chains. Subject of a romance by Bulwer-Lytton and a ballad by Thomas Hood.

**A·ran'da** (ä·rän'dä), Conde **de. Pedro Pablo A·bar'ca y Bo·le'a** (ä·bär'kä ē bō·lā'ä). 1718–1799. Spanish statesman, b. Saragossa; general in Spanish army; ambassador to Poland (1760–66); president, council of Castile, and prime minister (1766–73); suppressed uprisings in Madrid; effected expulsion of Jesuits (1767); ambassador to France (1773–87); president, council of state (1792); banished to Aragon.

**A·ra'nha** (ȧ·rä'nyȧ), **José Pereira da Graça.** See Graça Aranha.

**Aranha, Oswaldo.** 1894–1960. Brazilian lawyer and diplomat, b. Alegrete, Rio Grande do Sul; a leader in Vargas revolution (1930); minister of justice (1930) and finance (1931); ambassador to U.S. (1934–38); minister of foreign affairs (1938–44).

**A'rany** (ŏ'rŏn·y'), **János.** 1817–1882. Hungarian poet; professor of Hungarian language and literature at Nagykörös Gymnasium (1851–60). Member (from 1858), secretary (1865–79), Hungarian Acad. Among his works are an epic trilogy comprising *Toldi, The Love of Toldi,* and *Toldi's Evening; King Buda's Death* (epic, 12 cantos); *The Siege of Murány;* and many ballads and lyrics. His son **László** (1844–1898) was also a poet.

**A·ras'** (ä·räs'), **Tevfik Rustu** *or* **Tewfik Rushdi.** 1883–1972. Turkish diplomat; active in Turkish revolution (1908–09) and war for independence (1919–23); minister of foreign affairs (1925–38); ambassador to Great Britain (from 1939).

**A·ra'tor** (ȧ·rā'tẽr; -tôr). fl. 6th century A.D. Ligurian Christian poet; author of *De Actibus Apostolorum,* an apostolic history in verse.

**A·ra'tus of Sic'y·on** (ȧ·rā'tŭs ŭv sĭsh'ĭ·ŏn; sĭs'ĭ-). Greek general and statesman of 3d century B.C.; strategos of Achaean League (245 ff.). Fought Spartans under Cleomenes, finally, with aid from Antigonus of Macedonia, defeating Cleomenes at Sellasia (221), but with result that Macedonia became dominating power in Achaean League. Waged defensive war with Aetolians (221–219).

**Aratus of So'li** (sō'lī). c. 315–c. 245 B.C. Greek physician and poet; author of didactic poems *Phainomena* and *Diosēmeia,* later popular in Rome. Verse from his opening invocation to Zeus quoted by St. Paul (*Acts* xvii. 28) in his speech on Mars' Hill (or Areopagus), Athens.

**A·ra·u'jo de A·ze·ve'do** (ȧ·rȧ·ōō'zhōō thē ȧ·zĕ·vā'thōō), **Antônio de.** Conde **da Bar'ca** (thȧ bär'kȧ). 1754–1817. Portuguese statesman and diplomat, b. Sa, near Ponte de Lima; ambassador to The Hague (1789), Berlin (1797), St. Petersburg (1802); minister of foreign affairs (1804 ff.); prime minister (1807–08); to Rio de Janeiro with Portuguese court (March, 1808); founded schools of fine arts, medicine, and chemistry at Rio de Janeiro; minister of marine for colonies of Brazil; prime minister (1817).

**A·ra·u'jo Por'to–A·le'gre** (pôr'tōō·ȧ·lâ'grĕ), **Manuel de.** 1806–1879. Brazilian poet, painter, and architect, b. in Rio Pardo. Studied at Rio de Janeiro, Paris, and in Italy; professor (1837 ff.), Academy of Art, Rio de Janeiro; appointed (1859) consul general at Stettin, Germany; created (1870) baron **de San'to Ân'ge·lo** (dĕ săɴn'tōō ăɴ'zhĕ·lōō). Designed church at Sant'Ana, and Bank of Brazil in Rio; wrote several plays, including *Colombo* (1866), and a volume of poems, *Brasilianas.*

**Ar'ber** (är'bẽr), **Edward.** 1836–1912. English man of letters; editor of *English Reprints,* a series of accurate texts of works previously accessible only in rare editions, of *An English Garner* of old tracts and poems (1877–96), *British Anthologies* (1899–1901), and *A Christian Library* (1907).

**Arber, Werner.** 1929– . Swiss microbiologist. At U. of Geneva (1960–70), U. of Basel (1970– ); awarded (with Daniel Nathans and Hamilton O. Smith) Nobel prize for physiology or medicine (1978).

**Arblastier, William.** See William Alabaster.

**Arblay,** Madame **d'.** See Fanny Burney.

**Ar'bo·gast** (är'bō·găst). Frankish general in Roman army; sent by Emperor Theodosius against usurper Maximus (388 A.D.); defeated Maximus. Appointed chief minister to Western emperor, Valentinian II, young brother-in-law of Theodosius; killed Valentinian and proclaimed his own candidate, Eugenius, emperor. Defeated by Theodosius (394); committed suicide.

**Ar'bois' de Ju'bain'ville'** (ár'bwȧ' dẽ zhü'băɴ'vēl'), **Marie Henri d'.** 1827–1910. French archaeologist and philologist; professor of Celtic language and literature, Collège de France (from 1882); founder of *Revue Celtique.*

**Ar'bo·le'da** (är'bō·lā'thä), **Julio.** 1817–?1862. Colombian poet and patriot. Leader of successful revolt of Conservatives (1856); assumed presidency (1860); assassinated. His short poems notable for their excellence.

**Ar·bós'** (är·bōs'), **Enrique Fernández.** 1863–1939. Spanish violinist, orchestra conductor, and composer.

**Ar'buck'le** (är'bŭk''l), **John.** 1839–1912. American coffee merchant and sugar refiner, b. Pittsburgh. Said to be largest individual owner of his day of shipping under American registry. See H. O. HAVEMEYER.

**Ar·buth'not** (är·bŭth'nŭt; är'bŭth·nŏt). **John.** 1667–1735. Scottish physician and writer. M.D., St. Andrews (1696); physician in ordinary to Queen Anne (1709). Close friend of Swift. Author of witty political pamphlets, including one (*The History of John Bull,* a satire against the duke of Marlborough) which popularized and fixed modern conception of John Bull as the typical Englishman; a founder and contributor to *Memoirs of Martinus Scriblerus;* author of medical and scientific papers.

**Arbuthnot,** Sir **Robert Keith.** 1864–1916. English rear admiral; in command of first cruiser squadron at battle of Jutland (May 31, 1916); sank with his cruiser, *Defence,* destroyed by German fire.

**Arc, Joan of.** *Fr.* **Jeanne d'Arc.** See JOAN OF ARC.

**Ar'ca·delt** (är'kȧ·dĕlt) *or* **Ar'cha·delt** (är'kȧ·dĕlt) *or* **Ar'cha·det** (är'kȧ·dĕt), **Jakob.** 1514?–after 1557. Dutch composer of madrigals, masses, and motets; resident in Rome (1539–55) and Paris (1555 ff.).

**Ar·ca'di·us** (är·kā'dĭ·ŭs). 377?–408. First emperor of Eastern Roman Empire (395–408); b. in Spain. Son of Roman Emperor Theodosius I, at whose death Roman Empire was divided (see HONORIUS). Lived in luxury and complete indifference to affairs of empire, while government administered by: (1) Rufinus, praetorian prefect, murdered (395); (2) Eutropius, eunuch, deposed and beheaded (399); (3) his wife, Eudoxia (d. 404), who had great influence over him (see EUDOXIA); (4) Anthemius, praetorian prefect (404–408). During his reign Alaric the Goth ruled Balkan region (396–401); Gainas, Gothic general, seized and held Constantinople (400), but driven out the same year; Patriarch Chrysostom (*q.v.*) persecuted by Eudoxia and exiled (404).

**Ar'ce** (är'thā), **Gaspar Núñez de.** See NUÑEZ DE ARCE.

**Ar'ce** (är'sā), **Manuel José.** 1783?–1847. First president of Central America (1825–29), b. San Salvador.

**Ar·ces'i·la'us** (är·sĕs'ĭ·lā'ŭs) *or* **Ar·ces'i·las** (är·sĕs'ĭ·lăs). 316–241 B.C. Athenian philosopher; in his teachings reacted against Stoic dogmatism and attempted to return to thought and method of Socrates and Plato.

**Arch** (ärch), **Joseph.** 1826–1919. English social reformer. Agricultural laborer; founded National Agricultural Laborers' Union (1872); M.P. (1885–86, 1892–1902).

**Archadelt** *or* **Archadet, Jakob.** See ARCADELT.

**Ar·cham'bault** (är·shăm'bō), **Anna Margaretta.** d. 1956. American portrait painter and miniaturist.

**Arch'bold** (ärch'bōld), **John Dustin.** 1848–1916. American oil magnate, b. Leesburg, Ohio. Identified with Standard Oil Co. (1882–1911), a dominant figure in its organization; after dissolution forced by U. S. Supreme Court decision (1911), became president of Standard Oil Co. of New Jersey (1911–16).

**Arch'dale** (ärch'dāl), **John.** 1642?–?1717. Colonial governor of Carolina (1694–98).

**Ar'che·la'us** (är'kē·lā'ŭs). d. 399 B.C. King of Macedonia (413–399 B.C.); natural son of Perdiccas II; patron of Greek art and literature.

**Archelaus.** See HEROD ARCHELAUS.

**Archelaus.** fl. 5th century B.C. Greek philosopher; reputedly a teacher of Socrates.

**Archelaus.** Name of three Cappadocians:

**Archelaus.** fl. 1st century B.C. A general of Mithridates VI Eupator. Sent by Mithridates (88–87 B.C.) with large fleet and army to hold Greece against Romans; won Athens and other Greek peoples to his aid, but fought indecisive battle near Thespiae; lost Piraeus to Sulla (86); also badly defeated by Sulla at Chaeronea and Orchomenus (86); discredited by Mithridates, became friend and ally of Rome.

**Archelaus.** d. 55 B.C. Son of the preceding. High priest at Comana (63); m. Berenice (IV), daughter of Ptolemy Auletes of Egypt; king of Egypt for a few months (56); killed in battle against Aulus Gabinius, proconsul of Syria.

**Archelaus.** *Called* **Archelaus Si·si'nes** (sĭ·sī'nēz). d. 17 A.D. Grandson of Archelaus of Comana. King of Cappadocia (40 B.C.–17? A.D.); made king by Mark Antony, whom he deserted after Actium (31 B.C.); his kingdom extended by Octavian (20 B.C.); deposed by Tiberius and died in prison in Rome, Cappadocia being made Roman province.

**Ar'chen·holz** (är'kĕn·hōlts), **Johann Wilhelm von.** 1743–1812. German historian and editor. Author of *England und Italien* (5 vols., 1785), *Annalen der Britischen Geschichte* (20 vols., 1789–98), *Geschichte des Siebenjährigen Krieges* (1793).

**Ar'cher** (är'chẽr), **Branch Tanner.** 1790–1856. Texas patriot, b. in Virginia; to Texas (1831). Active in measures for Texan independence; Texas secretary of war under President Lamar.

**Archer, Frederic.** 1838–1901. Organist, b. Oxford, England; to U.S. (1881). Conducted Boston Oratorio Society (1887–88), Pittsburgh Orchestra (1896–98); popularized organ recitals in U.S.

**Archer, Frederick.** 1857–1886. English jockey.

**Archer, Frederick Scott.** 1813–1857. English photographer and sculptor; invented collodion process in photography (1850).

**Archer, James.** 1823–1904. Scottish portrait painter; best known for costume paintings and paintings of children.

**Archer, Thomas.** 1789–1848. English actor and playwright, b. Bath. Author of *Asmodeus, Blood Royal, The Black Doctor, The King's Ransom,* etc.

**Archer, William.** 1856–1924. Scottish dramatic critic and playwright. Educ. Edinburgh U.; trained as lawyer. Dramatic critic on London *Figaro* (1879–81). Introduced Ibsen to English stage by translation of *The Pillars of Society* (produced 1880) and other Ibsen plays. Author of *Masks or Faces?* (1888) and *Play-making* (1912); wrote several plays, one (*The Green Goddess,* 1923) a successful melodrama.

**Ar·cher'mus of Chi'os** (är·kûr'mŭs, kī'ŏs). fl. 6th century B.C. Greek sculptor.

**Ar·ches'tra·tus** (är·kĕs'trȧ·tŭs). fl. 4th century B.C. Greek poet, from Gela in Sicily.

**Ar'chiac'** (ȧr'shyȧk'), Vicomte **d'. Étienne Jules Adolphe Des'mier' de Saint'-Si'mon'** (dā'myā' dẽ săɴ' sē'môɴ'). 1802–1868. French geologist.

**Ar'chi·as** (är'kĭ·ăs). fl. 8th century B.C. Greek colonizer, from Corinth; founded (734) Syracuse, Sicily.

**Archias, Aulus Licinius.** 120–after 61 B.C. Greek poet,

b. Antioch, Syria; to Rome (102 B.C.); received Roman citizenship through citizenship granted him (93) in Heraclea, one of towns allied with Rome; defended by Cicero (*Pro Archia*, 61) against charge that he had obtained citizenship illegally.

**Ar'chi·da'mus** (är'kĭ·dā'mŭs). Name of five kings of Sparta, including: **Archidamus II** (reigned 476–427 B.C.), who commanded Spartan forces at beginning of Peloponnesian War (431–427). **Archidamus III** (reigned 360–338 B.C.), who defended Sparta against Epaminondas (362), supported Phocians in Sacred War (355–346), and commanded mercenary army in Italy protecting the Tarentines (338).

**Ar·chig'e·nes** (är·kĭj'ē·nēz). Greek eclectic physician at Rome in time of Trajan (98–117 A.D.).

**Ar·chil'o·chus** (är·kĭl'ō·kŭs). Greek lyric poet and writer of lampoons, of 7th century B.C. Among works are hymns, elegies, and satirical verse in iambic measure, which he is credited with introducing.

**Ar'chi·me'des** (är'kĭ·mē'dēz). 287?–212 B.C. Greek mathematician and inventor, b. Syracuse. Studied at U. of Alexandria. Known especially for work in mechanics and hydrostatics; credited with devising a screw (Archimedean screw) for raising water. Discovered principle (Archimedean principle) that a body immersed in fluid loses in weight by an amount equal to the weight of the fluid displaced; according to legend, he was seeking method for determining purity of gold in King Hiero's crown, and shouted *Eureka* (I have found it) on discovering method determined by above principle.

**Ar·chi·pen'ko** (*Ukrain.* ŭr·kyĭ·pyăn'kô; *Russ.* ŭr·kyē'-pyĕn·kô), **Aleksandr Porfirievich.** 1887–1964. American (Russ.-born) sculptor. Resident of Paris (1908–21), Berlin (1921–23), and U.S. (from 1923); U.S. citizen (1928). Work represented in many museums; leader of radical modernists; rejected cubism, attempting to attain pure, abstract sculpture, introducing many innovations.

**Ar·chy'tas of Ta·ren'tum** (är·kī'tăs, tȧ·rĕn'tŭm). fl. 400–365 B.C. Greek Pythagorean philosopher, scientist, and general; contemporary of Plato; solved problem of doubling the cube; advanced the study of acoustics and music by his investigations; first to distinguish harmonic progression from arithmetical and geometric progression; credited with inventing pulley. Author of moral aphorisms, esp. on happiness.

**Ar'co** (är'kō), **Alonso del.** *Called* **El Sor·dil'lo de Pe·re'da** (ĕl sôr·thē'lyō thā pā·rā'thä). 1625–1700. Spanish painter, b. Madrid; pupil of Antonio de Pereda; notable for religious canvases and portraits.

**Ar'çon'** (ȧr'sôN'), **Jean Claude Éléonore Le Mi'chaud'** (mē'shō') **d'.** 1733–1800. French engineer, officer, and military writer; inventor of unsinkable floating batteries used at siege of Gibraltar (1782); technical adviser to Committee of Public Safety and to Directory.

**Ar'cos'** (ȧr'kōs'), **René.** 1881– . French writer; one of group (unanimists) with Jules Romains and Duhamel who founded school known as "l'Abbaye"; author of *L'Âme Essentielle* (1901), *L'Île Perdue* (1913), *Le Mal* (1916), *Caserne* (1921), *Autrui* (1926), etc.

**Arc·ti'nus of Mi·le'tus** (ärk·tī'nŭs, mī·lē'tŭs, mĭ-). Greek cyclic poet of 8th century B.C.; author of *Aethiopis*.

**Arc·tow'ski** (ärts·tôf'skē), **Henryk.** 1871–1958. Polish scientist, b. Warsaw. Professor of geophysics and meteorology, U. of Lwów (from 1920); at Smithsonian Institution (from 1939).

**Ar'da·shir** (är'dȧ·shĭr). *Later Persian form of* **Artaxerxes.** Name of three kings of Persia of dynasty of the Sassanidae (*q.v.*): **Ardashir I.** Reigned (c. 226–241). Gained control of region around Persepolis (212); put brothers to death; began war against Persis (Fars) and Carmania (Kerman); defeated and killed Artabanus V, the Parthian king (226 or 227); founded Sassanian empire with Ctesiphon as its capital; established orthodox Zoroastrianism as official religion; extended kingdom but not successful against Armenia; at war with Rome (231–233); defeated by Alexander Severus (233); associated his son Shapur I on throne with him (241). **Ardashir II.** Reigned (379–383). Son of Ormizd II. Governor (or king) of Adiabene; made king of Persia at age of 70; quarreled with court nobles; deposed. **Ardashir III.** 621–630. Considered by some as king (628–630); raised to throne at age of seven during period of chaos following murder of Khosrau II; murdered.

**Ar'di·gò'** (är'dē·gô'), **Roberto.** 1828–1920. Italian positivist philosopher; professor, Padua (1881–1909); author of *Opere Filosofiche* (11 vols., 1882–1912).

**Ardilaun,** Baron. See under GUINNESS family.

**Ar·di'ti** (är·dē'tē), **Luigi.** 1822–1903. Italian composer and operatic conductor; conducted in Havana, New York (1847 ff., 1878 ff.), London, St. Petersburg, and Vienna; his works include the operas *I Briganti* (1841), *Il Corsaro* (1846), and *La Spia* (1856).

**Ar'doin** (är'doin; -dō·ĭn). *Also* **Ar'du·in** (är'dŭ·ĭn). Marquis of **I·vre'a** (ē·vrâ'ä). d. 1015? Raised revolt in northern Italy against Otto III (997–1000); became king of the Lombards (1002); waged wars against Emperor Henry II (1004, 1013–14); deposed (1014).

**A'ren'berg'** (ȧ'răN'bâr'), Prince **Auguste Marie Raymond d'.** *Known as* Comte **de La Marck'** (dē lȧ mȧrk'). 1753–1834. Politician; delegate of French nobility in States-General (1789); friend of Mirabeau. After Mirabeau's death (1791), emigrated to Austria; commissioned (1793) major general in Austrian army; served as agent of Austria in negotiations with French.

**A'rène'** (ȧ'rân'), **Paul Auguste.** 1843–1896. French writer and Provençal poet; best known for his tales of Provence.

**A·ren'ski** (ŭ·ryān'skû·ĭ; *Angl.* ȧ·rĕn'skĭ), **Anton Stepanovich.** 1861–1906. Russian composer, b. Novgorod. Studied under Rimski-Korsakov (1879–82). Composer of operas, as *A Dream on the Volga* (1892), *Raphael* (1894), and *Nal and Damayanti* (1899), two symphonies, and songs, choruses, and piano pieces.

**Ar'e·tae'us of Cap'pa·do'ci·a** (ăr'ē·tē'ŭs; kăp'ȧ·dō'-shĭ·ȧ, -shȧ). fl. 1st to 2d century A.D. Greek physician and writer; lived at Rome.

**Ar'e·tas** (ăr'ĕ·tăs). Name of several kings of Nabataeans of Arabia Petraea, esp. **Aretas IV,** father-in-law of Herod Antipas (*q.v.*), whom he attacked and defeated (36 A.D.) after Herod had divorced his daughter to marry Herodias.

**A're·tin'** (ä'rā·tēn'), Baron **Johann Christoph von.** 1773?–1824. Bavarian jurist and writer on politics and law. His son Baron **Karl Maria von Aretin** (1796–1868) was a historian.

**A're·ti'no** (ä'rā·tē'nō), **Guido.** See GUIDO D'AREZZO.

**Aretino, Leonardo.** See Leonardo BRUNI.

**Aretino, Pietro.** 1492–1556. Italian satirist, b. Arezzo. Studied literature and painting, Perugia; protégé of Leo X, Clement VII (to 1525), and Giovanni de' Medici (1525–27); settled in Venice (1527). Known esp. for satirical attacks on powerful contemporaries, winning him nickname of Scourge of Princes. Among his works are *Ragionamenti* (1532–34), *Orazia* (tragedy in verse; 1546), the comedies *La Cortigiana* (1534) and *La Talanta* (1550), and six volumes of letters (1537–57).

**Aretius Felinus.** See Martin BUCER.

**Arezzo, d'.** See (1) GUIDO D'AREZZO; (2) GUITTONE D'AREZZO; (3) NICCOLÒ D'AREZZO.

**Ar′fe** (är′fā). Name of family of Spanish silversmiths and goldsmiths of German or Flemish origin, including **Enrique de Arfe** (fl. 1500–1543), his son **Antonio de Arfe** (fl. 1566), and Antonio's son **Juan de Arfe y Vil′la·fa′ñe** [ē vē′lyä·fä′nyā] (1535–?1603), known as "the Spanish Cellini."

**Ar′gall** (är′gôl; -g'l), Sir **Samuel**. 17th-century English mariner and adventurer. First to sail northern route direct to Virginia (1609). Captured Pocahontas (1612), took her to Jamestown, where she was converted, married John Rolfe, and (1616) sailed to England with her husband in Argall's vessel. Broke up French settlements on Maine and Nova Scotia coast (1613). Deputy governor, Virginia (1617–19). Admiral, British naval force (1625) that captured £100,000 in prize cargoes.

**Ar′gand′** (ȧr′gäN′; *Angl.* är′gănd), **Aimé**. 1755–1803. Swiss physicist, inventor of a lamp (Argand lamp) with a burner that produced brighter illumination by means of current of air introduced into middle of flame through a circular wick.

**Ar′ge·lan′der** (är′gĕ·län′dẽr), **Friedrich Wilhelm August**. 1799–1875. Prussian astronomer. Astronomer, Åbo Observatory (1823); professor, Bonn (1837). Introduced scientific observations of variable stars; studied progressive motion of solar system in space; published a celestial atlas; determined position of thousands of stars. See Eduard SCHÖNFELD.

**Ar′gens′** (ȧr′zhäNs′), Marquis **d'. Jean Baptiste de Boy′er′** (bwȧ′yā′). 1704–1771. French writer, esp. of political pamphlets (*Lettres Juives, Lettres Chinoises,* etc.) and memoirs. Lived twenty-five years in Prussia; a favorite of Frederick II; director of fine arts at Berlin Academy.

**Ar′gen·so′la** (är′hän·sō′lä), **Bartolomé Le′o·nar′do** (lā′ō·när′thō) **de** (1562–1631) and his brother **Lupercio Leonardo de** (1559–1613). Sometimes called "the Spanish Horaces." Spanish poets, b. Barbastro, Aragon; educ. U. of Huesca; protégés of Maria of Austria; historiographers of Aragon (Lupercio, 1599–1613; Bartolomé, 1613 ff.); in retinue of count of Lemos, viceroy of Naples (1610); wrote in imitation of the classics; among Bartolomé's works is *Conquista de las Islas Molucas* (1609); Lupercio's works include dramas, as *Isabela* and *Alejandra,* and a continuation of Zurita y Castro's *Anales de la Corona de Aragón* (completed in part by Bartolomé); their collected poems were published under title *Rimas* (1634).

**Ar′gen′son′** (ȧr′zhäN′sôN′), **de Voy′er′** (vwȧ′yā′) **d'.** Notable French family, including: **Marc René de Voyer d'Argenson** (1652–1721), president of council of finance and keeper of the seals under Louis XIV (1718). His son **René Louis de Voyer** (1694–1757), Marquis **d'Argenson,** called **d'Argenson la Bête** (bât), foreign minister of France (1744–47), author of political essays and memoirs. Another son, **Marc Pierre de Voyer** (1696–1764), Comte **d'Argenson,** councilor of state (1724), secretary of war (1743–57), founder of École Militaire in Paris, friend of Voltaire and patron of Diderot and d'Alembert (who dedicated the *Encyclopédie* to him). René Louis's son **Marc Antoine René de Voyer** (1722–1787), Marquis **de Paul′my′** (pō′mē′) **d'Argenson,** secretary of war (1757–58), ambassador to Switzerland, Poland, Venice. Marc Pierre's grandson **Marc René de Voyer d'Argenson** (1771–1842), army officer and government official during French Revolution and under Napoleon, friend of Lafayette and opponent of Bourbons.

**Ar′gen·ti′na, La** (lä är′jĕn·tē′nȧ; *Span.* är′hän·tē′nä). *Real name* **Antonia Mer·cé′** (mĕr·sā′). 1890?–1936. Argentine dancer, b. Buenos Aires. Studied at Madrid; toured Europe and U. S. (from 1927) as head of own company of Spanish dancers.

**Ar′gi·ro′pu·lo** (är′jē·rō′pōō·lō), **Giovanni**. Italian form of Johannes ARGYROPOULOS.

**Argote y Góngora, Luis de.** See GÓNGORA Y ARGOTE.

**Ar′gout′** (ȧr′gōō′), Comte **Antoine Maurice Apollinaire d'.** 1782–1858. French financier; governor of Bank of France (from 1834); minister of finance (1836).

**Ar·güel′les** (är·gwā′lyās), **Agustín**. 1776–1844. Spanish liberal statesman, b. Ribadesella, Asturias; member of the Cortes (1812 ff.); imprisoned (1814–20); minister of interior (1820–21); fled to England (1823–32); president, chamber of deputies; guardian to Queen Isabella. Often called "the Spanish Cicero."

**Ar·guel′lo** (är·gā′yō), **Luis Antonio**. 1784–1830. b. San Francisco. Governor of California under Mexican rule (1822–25), first native-born Californian to hold this post; led expedition to Columbia River region (1821).

**Ar·gyll′** (är·gīl′), Earls, marquises, and dukes of. Titles in Scottish peerage of branch of Campbell family, including: **Colin Campbell,** 1st earl (created 1457). His son **Archibald,** 2d earl, killed at Flodden (1513), was succeeded by his son **Colin** (d. 1530), 3d earl, father of **Archibald** (d. 1558), 4th earl, who embraced Reformation principles. His son **Archibald** (1530–1573), 5th earl, deserted party of John Knox for espousal of cause of Mary, Queen of Scots; coconspirator in murder of Darnley; commanded Mary's forces at Langside (1568); submitted to James VI's party (1571); lord high chancellor of Scotland (1572). His grandnephew **Archibald** (1598–1661), 1st marquis and 8th earl, took side of Covenanters (1638); ravaged lands of earl of Atholl and Ogilvies, royalists (1640); forced Charles I to accept terms of Scottish parliament (1641); defeated by Montrose at Inverlochy and at Kilsyth (1645); supported Charles II after his sympathies for Cromwell estranged by execution of Charles I (1649); submitted to Cromwell's troops (1652); at Restoration (1660) tried before Scottish parliament on charges of collaboration with Roundheads; beheaded at Edinburgh. His son **Archibald** (1629–1685), 9th earl, fought at Dunbar as Highland Royalist; submitted, at Charles's direction, to Cromwell (1655); imprisoned for suspected Royalist plot (1657–60); commissioned to disarm Highlands (1667); opposed arbitrary measures of James, Duke of York, against Covenanters; opposed Scottish test act (1681); imprisoned on charge of treason and sentenced to death; escaped to Holland; planned invasion in league with Rye House conspirators (1683); led unsuccessful invasion of Scotland to co-operate with Monmouth's rebellion (1685); taken prisoner and beheaded. His son **Archibald** (1651?–1703), 1st duke (created 1701), joined William of Orange at The Hague; commissioner to offer Scottish crown to William and Mary; restored to title and estates (1689); shared with earl of Breadalbane (see John CAMPBELL) and Sir John Dalrymple (*q.v.*) infamy of massacre of Macdonalds of Glencoe for nonsubmission (1692). His son **John** (1678–1743), 2d duke, and duke of **Green′wich** (*Brit.* grĭn′ĭj, grĕn′-) in English peerage (created 1719); promoted, as royal commissioner, union of Scotland and England; fought under Marlborough at Oudenarde and Malplaquet; engaged in political intrigue, first against Marlborough; dissatisfied with Tory reward, turned Whig again; recovered influence at accession of George I (1714); played into hands of Tories (1721) to secure patronage of Scotland; field marshal (1736); defended Edinburgh against punishment for Porteous riot (1736); portrayed in Scott's *Heart of Midlothian.* Died without issue, causing succession to pass to his brother Archibald (see below) and thence to

Campbells of Mamore, descendants of younger son of 9th earl. **Archibald** (1682–1761), 3d duke, brother of 2d duke, was lord high treasurer of Scotland (1705); promoted union; Scottish representative peer (1707); justice general (1710); Walpole's chief adviser in Scotland; keeper of the Great Seal (1734–61). **George John Douglas** (1823–1900), 8th duke, published pamphlets against disruption of Church of Scotland; lord privy seal (1852–55); postmaster general (1855–58); secretary of state for India (1868–74); opposed Tory policy in Eastern question (1877–80); lord privy seal under Gladstone (1880–81); disapproved Irish land bill and opposed Irish home rule (1886); adherent of cataclysmal school in geology; author of *The Reign of Law* (1866), *Primeval Man* (1869), *The Unity of Nature* (1884), *The Unseen Foundations of Society* (1893). His son **John Douglas Sutherland** (1845–1914), 9th duke, m. Princess Louise, 4th daughter of Queen Victoria (1871); governor general of Canada (1878–83); unionist M. P. (1895–1900); author of poems, tales, and reminiscences.

**Ar′gy·ro·pou′los** (är′jĭ·rō·po͞o′lŏs; *mod. Greek* är′yē·rô′po͞o·lôs) *or* **Ar′gy·ro·pu′lus** (är′jĭ·rō·pū′lŭs), **Johannes.** 1416?–?1486. Greek scholar, b. Constantinople. Professor at Florence (1456) and Rome (1471), his students including Lorenzo de' Medici, Angelus Politian, Johann Reuchlin. Translated parts of Aristotle's works into Latin.

**Ar′i·a·ra′thes** (ăr′ĭ·ȧ·rā′thēz). Name of nine Persian rulers of northern Cappadocia, the last seven forming an independent dynasty ruling from c. 255 to 36 B.C.

**A′rias** (ä′ryäs), **Arnulfo.** 1897–     . Panamanian politician; educ. in Panama and U.S. (U. of Chicago; M.D., Harvard); gave up practice of medicine for diplomatic service; minister to Italy, France, Great Britain; delegate to League of Nations; president of Panama (1940–41, 1949–51, 1968); exiled for Fascist sympathies.

**Arias, Harmodio.** 1886–1962. Panamanian political leader, b. Penonomé. Provisional president of Panama (1931) after revolution that deposed President Arosemena; elected president (1932–36).

**Arias de Ávila, Pedro.** See PEDRARIAS.

**A′rias Mon·ta′no** (ä′ryäs môn·tä′nō), **Benito.** *Lat.* **Benedictus Ar′i·as Mon·ta′nus** (âr′ĭ·ăs mŏn·tā′nŭs). 1527–1598. Spanish theologian and Orientalist; known esp. as editor of Antwerp Polyglot Bible (8 vols., 1569–73).

**Ar′i·o·bar·za′nes** (ăr′ĭ·ō·bär·zā′nēz). Name of three kings of Pontus and three kings of Cappadocia:

**Ariobarzanes I,** Satrap of Pontus (5th century B.C.), father of Mithridates I. **Ariobarzanes II** (reigned 363–337 B.C.) revolted from Artaxerxes and established independence of Pontus. **Ariobarzanes III** (reigned 266–?240 B.C.).

**Ariobarzanes I,** King of Cappadocia (93–63 B.C.), retained throne with Roman aid against attacks by Mithridates. His son **Ariobarzanes II** (reigned c. 63–51 B.C.). The latter's son **Ariobarzanes III** (reigned c. 51–42 B.C.) took side of Pompey against Caesar; pardoned by Caesar; put to death (42) by Cassius.

**A·ri′on** (ȧ·rī′ŏn). Semilegendary Greek poet of 7th century B.C.; resident at court of Periander, Tyrant of Corinth; reputedly first poet to use dithyramb; only a fragment of his work extant.

**A′ri·o′sti** (ä′rē·ôs′tē), **Attilio.** 1660?–?1740. Italian operatic composer, b. Bologna; court Kapellmeister, Berlin (1698); on first board of directors (with Handel and Bononcini) of London Academy of Music (1720); among his operas are *Dafne* (1686), *La Festa d'Imeneo* (1700), *Amor tra Nemici* (1708), and *Coriolano* (1723).

**A′ri·o′sto** (ä′rē·ôs′tō), **Lodovico.** 1474–1533. Italian poet, b. Reggio Emilia. Entered diplomatic and military service of Ippolito, Cardinal d'Este (1503); to glorify house of Este, began (1506) best-known work, the chivalric epic poem *Orlando Furioso* (pub. in 40 cantos, 1516; in 46 cantos, 1532; sequel to Boiardo's *Orlando Innamorato*); broke with Cardinal d'Este (1517) and entered service of cardinal's brother Alfonso d'Este, Duke of Ferrara; appointed governor of Garfagnana (1522–25); retired to Ferrara (1525–33). Author also of comedies, as *La Cassaria* (1508), *Gli Suppositi* (1509), *Il Negromante* (1520), and *La Lena* (1529), satires, sonnets, odes, Latin poems, etc.

**Ar′i·o·vis′tus** (ăr′ĭ·ō·vĭs′tŭs). fl. 71?–58 B.C. Germanic tribal chief, leader of the Suevi; crossed Rhine into Gaul (c. 61); aided Sequani against Aedui; defeated (58) by Caesar at Vesontio (Besançon).

**A·ris′ta** (ä·rēs′tä), **Mariano.** 1802–1855. Mexican general, b. in San Luis Potosí. Took part in Mexican attempt to overcome Texan Revolution (1836); commander of Mexican army; defeated by Z. Taylor at Palo Alto and Resaca de la Palma (1846); minister of war under Herrera (1848–51); president of Mexico (1851–53).

**Ar′is·tag′o·ras** (ăr′ĭs·tăg′ō·răs). d. 497 B.C. Tyrant of Miletus. Regent while his brother-in-law Histiaeus was at court of Darius; unsuccessfully attacked Naxos (500 B.C.); incited Ionian cities to revolt against Persia; secured Athenian aid and burned Sardis (499); driven out by Persians and fled to Thrace.

**Ar′is·tar′chus** (ăr′ĭs·tär′kŭs). 220?–?150 B.C. Greek grammarian and critic; originally from Samothrace, but, as librarian, resident chiefly in Alexandria; edited Homer, Hesiod, Pindar, Aeschylus, Sophocles, and other Greek authors; first to arrange *Iliad* and *Odyssey* in 24 books. Known as the Coryphaeus of Grammarians.

**Aristarchus of Sa′mos** (sā′mŏs). Greek astronomer of 3d century B.C.; credited with maintaining that earth rotates on its own axis and revolves about sun; showed method of estimating relative distances of sun and moon from earth from angle formed by them at observer's eye when moon is at first or third quarter.

**Ar′is·ti′des** *or* **Ar′is·tei′des** (ăr′ĭs·tī′dēz). *Called* **Aristides the Just.** 530?–?468 B.C. Athenian statesman. Commanded contingent at Marathon (490 B.C.); elected chief archon (489–488). Urged maintenance of Athens as military instead of naval power, opposing Themistocles; ostracized (c. 485). Returned to Athenian service (480); as strategos (480–479), loyally supported Themistocles in Salamis campaign; commanded Athenian contingent at Plataea (479). Commanded Athenian squadron off Byzantium (478 or 477); entrusted by members of Delian Confederacy with fixing assessments of states in confederacy. Remained influential in Athenian policy until his death.

**Aristides** *or* **Aristeides.** Greek Christian apologist of 2d century; author of apology for Christian faith known as *Apology of Aristides*, of which a complete manuscript in a Syriac version was found by Dr. J. Rendel Harris on Mt. Sinai (1889).

**Aristides** *or* **Aristeides, Publius Aelius.** *Surnamed* **The′o·do′rus** (thē′ō·dō′rŭs). Greek rhetorician of 2d century A.D.; resident in Smyrna. After destruction of Smyrna by earthquake (178), wrote to Emperor Marcus Aurelius Antoninus and persuaded him to rebuild city.

**Aristides** *or* **Aristeides, Quin·til′i·a′nus** (kwĭn·tĭl′ĭ·ā′nŭs). Greek writer of 1st century A.D. or later; author of treatise on music regarded as most important ancient book on this subject.

**Aristides** (*or* **Aristeides**) **of Thebes** (thēbz). Greek painter of 4th century B.C.

**Ar′is·tip′pus** (ăr′ĭs·tĭp′ŭs). 435?–?356 B.C. Greek philosopher, orig. from Cyrene; studied under Socrates. Founded Cyrenaic school, teaching that pleasure is chief end of life and immediate pleasures are preferable.

**A·ris'to·bu'lus** (*ȧ*·rĭs'tō·bū'l*ŭ*s; är'ĭs·tō-). Greek historian, of 4th century B.C., originally from Cassandreia; accompanied Alexander the Great and wrote account of his campaigns.

**Aristobulus.** fl. c. 160 B.C. Alexandrian Jew; Peripatetic philosopher; wrote on the Pentateuch; by quotations from Greek poets and philosophers attempted to prove Greek indebtedness to Jewish religious ideology; genuineness of his work, most of it now lost, subject of much controversy among scholars.

**Aristobulus.** Name of several members of Hasmonaean family of Palestine. For **Aristobulus I (Judah)** and **II**, see MACCABEES.

**Aristobulus III.** 52–35 B.C. Grandson of Aristobulus II and brother of Mariamne, second wife of Herod the Great; made high priest (36–35 B.C.) on intercession of Cleopatra and Antony; killed by Herod, who was suspicious of his plans. Cf. ARISTOBULUS, son of Herod the Great.

**Aristobulus.** d. 6 B.C. Son of Herod the Great by his second wife, Mariamne the Hasmonaean; half brother of Herod Philip, Herod Archelaus, and Herod Antipas; father of Herod Agrippa I and Herodias. With his brother Alexander, educ. at Rome (23–17); designated as a probable heir; involved in family intrigues; accused of treason and condemned to death; with Alexander put to death by Herod.

**Aristogiton** *or* **Aristogeiton.** See HARMODIUS.

**Ar'is·tom'e·nes** (ăr'ĭs·tŏm'ē·nēz). Semilegendary national hero of Messenia in 7th century B.C.; leader of revolt against Sparta; credited with marvelous deeds of valor in the war.

**Ar'is·toph'a·nes** (ăr'ĭs·tŏf'*ȧ*·nēz). 448?–?380 B.C. Athenian playwright; regarded as one of greatest writers of comedies of all time. Of his more than 40 comedies, which gave satiric expression to his strong, conservative prejudices against certain trends and personalities in the Athens of his day, only 11 are extant: *The Acharnians* (425), *The Knights* (424), *The Clouds* (423), *The Wasps* (422), *The Peace* (421), *The Birds* (414), *Lysistrata* (411), *The Thesmophoriazusae* (411), *The Frogs* (405), *The Ecclesiazusae* (393), *Plutus* (388).

**Aristophanes of By·zan'ti·um** (bĭ·zăn'shĭ·*ŭ*m; bĭ-; -tĭ·*ŭ*m). 257?–?180 B.C. Greek scholar; orig. from Byzantium; settled in Alexandria; became chief librarian of the museum there (c. 197). Edited works of Hesiod, Homer, Anacreon, Pindar, Aristophanes (the playwright), etc.; compiled lists of foreign and rare words and expressions.

**Ar'is·tot'le** (ăr'ĭs·tŏt''l). 384–322 B.C. Greek philosopher, b. Stagira, Greek colony on northwestern shore of Aegean Sea; hence sometimes called "the Stagirite." Son of court physician of Amyntas II. Studied (367–347) under Plato at academy in Athens; tutored Alexander the Great (c. 342–335); taught in Athens as head of Peripatetic school (335–322). His treatises, in large part consisting of lectures delivered to his disciples in his school at Athens, may be classified as works in logic, metaphysics, natural science, ethics and politics, rhetoric and poetics. Among his writings on logic (called later the *Organon*) are *Prior Analytics* (2 books), *Posterior Analytics* (2 books), and *Sophisms.* His great philosophical work is *Metaphysics* (13 books). In field of natural science are *Physics* (8 books), *On the Heavens* (4 books), *On Beginning and Perishing* (2 books), *Parts of Animals* (4 books), *Generation* (5 books), *On the Soul* (*De Anima*), and *On Plants* (2 books). In field of ethics and politics are *Nicomachean Ethics* (10 books) and *Politics* (8 books). In field of rhetoric and poetics are *Rhetoric* (3 books) and *Poetics*, of which only his treatment of tragedy and epic poetry has been preserved.

**Ar'is·tox'e·nus** (ăr'ĭs·tŏk'sē·n*ŭ*s). Greek Peripatetic philosopher of 4th century B.C.; orig. from Tarentum (Taranto), disciple of Aristotle; only extant work a musical treatise, *Elements of Harmony* (3 books).

**A·ri·su·ga·wa** (ä·rē·so͝o·gä·wä). Name of royal Japanese family originating in 17th century with a son of Emperor Go-Yozei (d. 1638). Two modern members of family have been prominent: **Arisugawa Ta·ru·hi·to** [tä·ro͝o·hē·tō] (1835–1895), adoptive uncle of emperor; heir presumptive; led imperial troop against rebels at time of restoration (1868–69); suppressed Satsuma rebellion (1877); made field marshal; took part in Chinese-Japanese War. His brother **Arisugawa Ta·ke·hi·to** [tä·kĕ·hē·tō] (1862–1913); entered navy; served (1879–82) in British navy; took part in war with China; admiral superintendent of naval base at Yokosuka; representative of emperor abroad.

**A·ri·ta** (ä·rē·tä), **Hachiro.** 1884–1965. Japanese diplomat. Vice-minister for foreign affairs (1932–33); ambassador to Belgium (1934–36), China (1936); foreign minister (1936–37, 1938–40); member of House of Peers.

**A·ri'us** (*ȧ*·rī'*ŭ*s; âr'ĭ·*ŭ*s). d. 336 A.D. Greek ecclesiastic at Alexandria; taught doctrine (Arianism) that God is alone, unknowable, and separate from every created being, that Christ is a created being and not God in the fullest sense, and is to be worshiped as a secondary deity, and that in the incarnation the Logos assumed a body but not a human soul. Arianism condemned as heretical in general councils of Nicaea (325) and Constantinople (381). See ATHANASIUS.

**Arjumand Banu.** See under SHAH JAHAN.

**Ar'kell** (är'k'l; är·kĕl'), **Reginald.** 1882–1959. English journalist, playwright, and librettist; librettist or lyricist for many revues and musical comedies; author of *Colombine and Other Verses* (1912), *Meet These People* (1928), *Green Fingers* (1934), and *War Rumours* (1939).

**Ark'wright** (ärk'rīt), Sir **Richard.** 1732–1792. English inventor and manufacturer. Inventor of spinning frame (pat. 1769), first machine capable of producing cotton thread of the firmness and hardness required in the warp; patented additional improvements (1775). See Jedediah STRUTT.

**Ar'land'** (år'läN'), **Marcel.** 1899– . French writer, b. Varennes; author of novels, as *Terres Étranges* (1923), *L'Ordre* (1929; awarded Goncourt prize), *Antarès* (1932), and *La Vigie* (1935), and essays, including *La Route Obscure* (1924), *Essais Critiques* (1931).

**Ar'len** (är'lĕn), **Michael.** *Orig.* **Di·kran'** (dĭ·krän') **Kou·youm'djian** (ko͞o·yo͞om'jyän). 1895–1956. British novelist and playwright, b. in Bulgaria of Armenian parents. Educ. Malvern Coll.; naturalized British subject (1922). Author of *The London Venture* (1920), *These Charming People* (1923), *The Green Hat* (1924), *Man's Mortality* (1933), *The Crooked Coronet* (1937), *The Flying Dutchman* (1939), etc.

**Ar'lin'court'** (år'lăN'ko͞or'), Vicomte **d'. Charles Victor Pré'vot'** (prā'vō'). 1789–1856. French poet and novelist; author of *Le Solitaire* (novel), *La Caroléide* (poem), and *Le Brasseur Roi* (historical romance).

**Ar'ling·ton** (är'lĭng·t*ŭ*n), 1st Earl of. **Henry Ben'net** (bĕn'ĕt; -ĭt). 1618–1685. English statesman. Fought with royal forces in Civil War; after Restoration, keeper of privy purse; secretary of state (1662–74); in charge of foreign affairs in the Cabal; terminated triple alliance with Holland and Sweden; largely responsible for Dutch war (1672–74); arranged for Charles II terms of secret treaty of Dover (1670) with Louis XIV; unsuccessfully impeached on charges of corruption and betrayal of trust (1674).

**Ar'liss** (är'lĭs), **George.** 1868–1946. Actor, b. and educ. London. Made debut at London (1887); appeared on N.Y. stage (1901) with Mrs. Patrick Campbell. Began career in motion pictures in U.S. (1920); played leading roles in *Darling of the Gods, Green Goddess, Old English, Disraeli, House of Rothschild, Cardinal Richelieu, Iron Duke, East Meets West,* etc. Author of autobiography *Up the Years from Bloomsbury* (1927).

**Ar·lot'to Mai·nar'di** (är·lôt'tô mī·när'dē). *Called* **Il Pio·va'no** (ēl pyô·vä'nô). 1395–1483. Italian burlesque poet; works known only in a French translation, *Patron de l'Honnête Raillerie, Contenant les Brocards, Bons Mots, Agréables Tours et Plaisantes Rencontres de Pievano Arlotto* (1650).

**Ar'ma'gnac'** (ȧr'mȧ'nyȧk'). Noble French house (c. 10th century–1503), supporters of house of Orléans (see ORLÉANS), including: **Bernard VII** (d. 1418), Comte **d'Armagnac,** leader of Orleanist party (hence known as Armagnacs) in struggle with Burgundians during reign of Charles VI; constable of France (1415); killed by mob in Paris when Burgundians gained control of city (1418). **Jean V** (1420?–1473), Comte **d'Armagnac,** grandson of Bernard VII; formed incestuous union with his sister; deprived of his possessions (1460) by Charles VII; executed by royal troops (1473). See also NEMOURS family.

**Ar'mand'** (ȧr'mäɴ'), **Charles.** *Assumed name of* **Armand Tu'fin'** (tü'făɴ') *or* **Tef'fin'** (tĕ'făɴ'). Marquis **de La Rouë'rie'** (rwȧ'rē'; *also* rōō'rē') *or* **Roua'rie'** (rwȧ'rē'). 1756–1793. French army officer; served in American Continental army during Revolutionary War (1777–82); royalist adherent and agitator in France (from 1783).

**Ar'mans·perg** (är'mäns·pĕrк), Count **Joseph Ludwig von.** 1787–1853. German statesman, b. in Lower Bavaria. Accompanied King Otto to Greece; served as member of regency (1832–35) and chancellor of state (1835–37), in Greece.

**Arm'brus'ter** (ärm'brōōs'tēr), **Charles Hubert.** 1874–1957. English civil servant in Africa; specialist in Amharic; prepared *Amharic Grammar* (1908), *Amharic-English Vocabulary* (1920), etc.

**Ar'men·da·riz'** (är'mān·dä·rēth'), **José de.** Marqués **de Cas'tel·fuer'te** (käs'tĕl·fwĕr'tā). 1670?–?1740. Spanish commander in War of Spanish Succession (1701–14). Viceroy of Peru (1724–36).

**Arm'felt** (ȧrm'fĕlt), Baron **Karl Gustaf von.** 1666–1736. Swedish general; commander in chief of Swedish army in Finland. His great-grandson Count **Gustaf Mauritz Armfelt** (1757–1814), Swedish statesman and general, b. in Finland, distinguished himself in war against Russia (1788–90); member of regency council after death of Gustavus III (1792); charged with treason; fled to Russia; later restored to important offices and commands; entered Russian service in Finland (1811).

**Armin, Friedrich Sixt von.** See SIXT VON ARMIN.

**Ar'min** (är'mĭn), **Robert.** fl. 1600–1610. English actor; prominent in roles of Shakespeare's clowns and fools; member of cast of Ben Jonson's *Alchemist* (1610); author of *Nest of Ninnies* (1608).

**Ar·min'i·us** (är·mĭn'ĭ·ŭs; *Ger.* är·mē'nē·ōōs) *or* **Ar·min'** (är·mēn'). *Sometimes called* **Her'mann** (hĕr'män). 17 B.C.?–21 A.D. German national hero; chief of the Cherusci. Served in Roman armies (1–6 A.D.) and became Roman citizen. Returned home and organized rebellion of Cherusci against Roman governor Varus; cut off outlying forces and annihilated three Roman legions in surprise attack, probably in Teutoburger Wald (9 A.D.), forcing back Roman frontier from Elbe to Rhine; attacked by Germanicus Caesar (15 A.D.) and defeated (16 A.D.). Fought successfully against Marbo, king of the Marcomanni.

**Ar·min'i·us** (är·mĭn'ĭ·ŭs; *Du.* är·mē'nē·ûs), **Jacobus.** *Real name* **Jacob Har'men·sen** (här'mĕn·sĕn) *or* **Her'mansz** (hĕr'mäns). 1560–1609. Dutch Reformed theologian; promulgator of doctrines known as Arminianism, now held notably by Methodists in America and Wesleyans in Great Britain. Studied at Leiden, at Geneva under Bèze, and at Basel. Preacher, Amsterdam (1588–1603); professor of theology, Leiden (from 1603). At first defended Calvinistic doctrine of predestination, but soon adopted views of opponents. Engaged in bitter theological controversies, esp. (from 1604) with his colleague Gomarus, rejecting doctrine of absolute predestination and favoring chiefly doctrines of universal redemption and conditional predestination or election. His teachings influenced anti-Calvinistic Remonstrance or "Five Articles" (1610) of his disciples (later called Remonstrants).

**Ar'mi·stead** (är'mĭ·stĕd; -stĭd), **George.** 1780–1818. American army officer, b. New Market, Va. Defended Fort McHenry against British (1814), and saved Baltimore. Cf. Francis Scott KEY.

**Armistead, Lewis Addison.** 1817–1863. American army officer, b. New Bern, N.C. In U.S. army (1839–61), Confederate army (1861–63); brigadier general (1862). Killed in Pickett's charge at Gettysburg.

**Ar'mi·tage** (är'mĭ·tĭj), **Edward.** 1817–1896. English historical painter; executed frescoes in Houses of Parliament.

**Armitage, Merle.** 1893–1975. American impresario, b. Mason City, Iowa. Managed bookings for Alice Nielsen, John McCormack, Schumann-Heink, Mary Garden, and others; directed publicity for Diaghilev ballet and for Pavlova. A founder (1924) and general manager (1924–30), Los Angeles Grand Opera Assoc.; manager, Philharmonic Auditorium (from 1933). Among his many books are *Biography of Rockwell Kent* (1932), *Igor Stravinsky* (1936), *George Gershwin* (1938), and *So-called Abstract Art* (1939).

**Ar'mi·tage–Smith'** (-smĭth'), Sir **Sydney Armitage.** 1876–1932. English financial expert; British treasury representative, Paris Peace Conference (1919); secretary general, Reparation Commission (1924–30).

**Ar'mour** (är'mēr), **Jean.** Wife of Robert BURNS.

**Armour, John Douglas.** 1830–1903. Canadian judge. Grad. Toronto U. (1850); chief justice of court of Queen's Bench (1887); chief justice, Ontario (1900); judge of supreme court of Canada (1902).

**Armour, Norman.** 1887– . American diplomat; A.B., Princeton (1909); LL.B., Harvard (1913); U.S. minister to Haiti (1932–35), Canada (1935–38); ambassador to Chile (1938–39), Argentina (1939–44), Spain (1945); asst. secretary of state (1947–49).

**Armour, Philip Danforth.** 1832–1901. American industrialist, b. Stockbridge, N.Y. Developed Armour & Co. (1870), meat packers, from pork-packing plant established by his brother **Herman Ossian** (1837–1901). Philip became head of Armour & Co. (1875); responsible for methods of utilizing waste products, introduction of refrigeration, preparation of canned meats, vast expansion of dealings; founded Armour Institute of Technology (1893). See Frank W. GUNSAULUS. His son **Jonathan Ogden** (1863–1927) carried on the business.

**Arm'stead** (ärm'stĕd; -stĭd), **Henry Hugh.** 1828–1905. English sculptor. Silversmith (to 1863); sculptor (1863 ff.); employed on Albert Memorial and public buildings.

**Arm'strong** (ärm'strŏng), **Archibald.** d. 1672. Court

jester to King James I (of England); introduced as character in Scott's *Fortunes of Nigel.*

**Armstrong, David Maitland.** 1836–1918. American artist, b. near Newburgh, N.Y. m. (1866) Helen Neilson, niece of Hamilton Fish. U.S. consul to Papal States (1869–72). During his last years specialized in stained glass. Father of Hamilton Fish ARMSTRONG, Helen Maitland ARMSTRONG. and Margaret Neilson ARMSTRONG.

**Armstrong, Edward.** 1846–1928. English historian. Lecturer on history, Queen's Coll., Oxford. Author of *Elisabeth Farnese, Lorenzo de' Medici, Emperor Charles V, French Wars of Religion.*

**Armstrong, Edwin Howard.** 1890–1954. American electrical engineer, b. New York City. E.E., Columbia (1913). Did research at Columbia U. (1914–35); professor, Columbia (from 1936). Captain and major, Signal Corps, U.S. army (1917–19). His inventions in field of radio include regenerative circuit (1912), superheterodyne circuit (1918), superregenerative circuit (1920); developed frequency-modulation system of radio.

**Armstrong, Hamilton Fish.** 1893–1973. Son of David Maitland Armstrong (*q.v.*). Am. writer and editor, b. New York City. Managing editor (1922–28) and editor (1928–72), *Foreign Affairs.* Author of *The New Balkans* (1926), *Hitler's Reich—The First Phase* (1933), etc., and a memoir, *Those Days* (1963).

**Armstrong, Harry,** *orig.* **Henry W.** 1879–1951. b. Somerville, Mass. American composer of the music of *Sweet Adeline* (1903; words by Richard H. Gerard).

**Armstrong, Helen Maitland.** 1869–1948. American artist, b. in Florence, Italy; dau. of David Maitland Armstrong (*q.v.*). Designer and painter of stained-glass windows, mural decorations, etc.

**Armstrong, Henry Edward.** 1848–1937. English chemist; recipient of Davy Medal (1911).

**Armstrong, John** *or* **Johnnie.** d. about 1528. Leader of gang of highwaymen along Scottish border; appeared before James V (of Scotland) and offered to aid in suppressing border marauders; seized and hanged; became subject of a number of ballads.

**Armstrong, John.** 1709–1779. Scottish physician and poet.

**Armstrong, John.** 1758–1843. American army officer and diplomat, b. Carlisle, Pa. Served through American Revolution; wrote a series of anonymous letters (1783) in effort to force Congress to pay arrears to army officers. U.S. senator (1800–02, 1803–04); U.S. minister to France (1804–10); as secretary of war (1813–14), held in large part responsible for military failures in War of 1812.

**Armstrong, Louis,** *in full* **Daniel Louis.** *Known as* **Satchmo.** 1900–1971. American jazz musician, b. New Orleans, La. Recordings number about 1500; appeared in many movies; composed *Sister Kate,* etc.

**Armstrong, Margaret Neilson.** 1867–1944. American writer, b. New York City; daughter of David Maitland Armstrong (*q.v.*). Author of *Fanny Kemble: a Passionate Victorian* (1938), *Murder in Stained Glass* (1939), and *Trelawny: a Man's Life* (1940).

**Armstrong, Martin Donisthorpe.** 1882– . English poet and fiction writer, b. Newcastle upon Tyne. Author of *Exodus, and Other Poems* (1912), *The Puppet Show* (1922), *Sir Pompey and Madame Juno* (1927), *Lover's Leap* (1932), *General Buntop's Miracle* (1934), etc.

**Armstrong, Neil Alden.** 1930– . American astronaut, b. Ohio. Performed first manual docking maneuver in space (1966); commanded Apollo XI to moon with Edwin Aldrin and Michael Collins, first man to stand on the moon (1969).

**Armstrong, Nellie.** See MELBA.

**Armstrong, Paul.** 1869–1915. American playwright, b. Kidder, Mo. Wrote popular melodramas, including *Salomy Jane* (1907), *Via Wireless* (1908; with Winchell Smith), *Alias Jimmy Valentine* (1909).

**Armstrong, Samuel Chapman.** 1839–1893. American educator, b. in Hawaii. Founded (1868) and headed Hampton Normal and Industrial Institute.

**Armstrong,** Sir **Thomas Henry Wait.** 1898– English organist and composer; organist, Exeter Cathedral (1928–33) and Christ Church Cathedral, Oxford (1933–55); composer esp. of choral works.

**Armstrong,** Sir **Walter.** 1850–1918. English critic and writer; director, National Art Gallery, Dublin (1892).

**Armstrong, William George.** Baron **Armstrong of Crag′side** (krăg′sīd). 1810–1900. English inventor. Invented hydroelectric machine which produced frictional electricity (1840–45), a hydraulic crane (1846), breech-loading gun made of successive rings of metal shrunk upon an inner steel barrel with rifle bore (c. 1855), prototype of all modern artillery, a breech-loading gun with wire-wound cylinder (1880). Founder (1847) of Elswick Engineering Works; merged (1927) its armament and shipbuilding with Vickers' Sons and Co. to form Vickers Armstrongs, Ltd.

**Arm′strong-Jones′** (-jōnz′), **Antony Charles Robert. Earl of Snow′don** (snō′d'n). 1930– . Married Princess Margaret Rose of Great Britain (1960).

**Arn.** See ARNO.

**Ar′na·bol′di** (är′nä·bôl′dē), **Alessandro.** 1827–1898. Italian lyric poet.

**Arnaldo da Brescia.** See ARNOLD OF BRESCIA.

**Arnaldus Villanovanus.** See ARNAUD DE VILLENEUVE.

**Ar′na·son** (är′nä·sŏn), **Jón.** 1819–1888. Icelandic writer; author of *Popular Legends of Iceland* (1862–64).

**Ar′naud′** (år′nō′), **François Thomas Marie de Ba′cu′-lard′** (bå′kü′lår′) **d′.** 1718–1805. French man of letters; literary correspondent of Frederick the Great in Paris (1748–50); accompanied Frederick to Berlin (1750); returned to France (1755); wrote series of romances under general title *Épreuves de Sentiment* (12 vols., 1772–81).

**Arnaud, Henri.** 1641–1721. Waldensian pastor and soldier; led group of Waldenses against allied French and Savoyard armies to regain native Vaudois valleys (1689–90); secured repatriation of Waldenses (1690–98); lived in Württemberg (1698–1721); wrote *Histoire de la Glorieuse Rentrée des Vaudois dans leurs Vallées* (1710).

**Arnaud Daniel.** See DANIEL.

**Ar′naud′ de Ville′neuve′** (år′nō′ dĕ vēl′nûv′). *French form of Lat.* **Ar·nal′dus Vil′la·no·va′nus** (är·năl′dŭs vĭl′ȧ·nō·vā′nŭs) *and Eng.* **Arnold of Vil′la·no′va** (vĭl′ȧ·nō′vȧ). 1235?–?1312. Physician, astrologer, and alchemist, probably of Spanish (Catalan) origin. Taught philosophy and medicine at Barcelona and Paris. Discovered poisonous property of carbon monoxide gas and of decayed meat.

**Ar′nauld′** (år′nō′), **Antoine.** 1560–1619. French lawyer; famous for his speech (1594) against Jesuits and in favor of U. of Paris. His 20 children included: **Robert Arnauld d'An′dil′ly′** [däɴ′dē′yē′] (1589–1674), lawyer, theological writer. **Jacqueline Marie Arnauld** (1591–1661), known as **Mère′ An′gé′lique′** (mâr′ äɴ′zhā′lēk′), abbess of Port-Royal, Paris. **Jeanne Catherine Agnès Arnauld** (1593–1671), Jansenist nun, author of religious books. **Henri Arnauld** (1597–1692), Jansenist prelate; bishop of Angers (1649); one of four bishops refusing to sign acceptance of pope's bull condemning Jansen's *Augustinus.* **Antoine Arnauld** (1612–1694), known as "the Great Arnauld," philosopher and Jansenist theologian; famed for his controversial writings; religious director of nuns at Port-Royal; author of *La Perpétuité de la Foi* (in collaboration with Nicole; 1669–79), etc. A daughter of Robert Arnauld d'Andilly, **Angélique Arnauld** *or* **Angélique de Saint'-Jean'** [săN'zhäN'] (1624–1684), abbess of Port-Royal (1678 ff.); author of *Mémoires pour Servir à l'Histoire de Port-Royal.*

**Ar'nault'** *or* **Ar'naut'** (ȧr'nō'). Variant of ARNAUD.

**Arnault, Antoine Vincent.** 1766–1834. French author of dramas, fables, and memoirs.

**Arnd** *or* **Arndt** (ärnt), **Johann.** 1555–1621. German Lutheran theologian and religious writer; author of *Vom Wahren Christentum* (1609; Eng. transl. *True Christianity*).

**Arndt** (ärnt), **Ernst Moritz.** 1769–1860. German patriot and author, b. on island of Rügen, son of former Swedish serf. Educ. U. of Greifswald and Jena (1791–94). His *Versuch einer Geschichte der Leibeigenschaft in Pommern und Rügen* (1803) led to abolition of serfdom by Swedish king. Professor of history, Greifswald (1806; 1810–11); attacked Napoleon in *Geist der Zeit* (1806 ff.); fled to Stockholm (1806–09); associated in Russia with Baron vom Stein against Napoleon (1812). Returned to Germany and fired German spirit against oppressors with his song, *Was Ist des Deutschen Vaterland?* and other songs, pamphlets, and patriotic poems.

**Arne** (ärn), **Thomas Augustine.** 1710–1778. English musical composer; m. (1736) **Cecilia Young** (1711–1789), oratorio and concert singer. Wrote music for Joseph Addison's *Rosamund* (1733), Fielding's *Tom Thumb, or the Opera of Operas* (1733), Milton's *Comus* (1738), Thomson and Mallet's *Masque of Alfred* (which includes the song *Rule Britannia*; 1740). Composed oratorios *Abel* (1755) and *Judith* (1764), many songs, as those for *Tempest* (1746), light operas, and incidental music. Cf. Theophilus CIBBER. His son **Michael** (1741?–1786) was a harpsichordist and composer.

**Ar·nei'ro** (ĕr·nā'ē·rōō), Visconde **de. José Augusto Fer·rei'ra** (fĕr·rā'ē·rȧ) **Vei'ga** (vā'ē·gȧ). 1838–1903. Portuguese composer; known for his *Te Deum* and the operas *L'Elisir di Giovinezza* and *La Derelitta.*

**Ar'neth** (är'nĕt), **Alfred von.** 1819–1897. Austrian historian; author of *Prinz Eugen von Savoyen* (3 vols., 1858), *Geschichte Maria Theresias* (10 vols., 1863–79), etc.

**Arneth, Joseph Ca'la·san'za** (kä'lä·zän'tsä) **von.** 1791–1863. Austrian archaeologist and numismatist. His son **Alfred** (1819–1897) was a diplomat and author of several works on history of Austria.

**Ar'nim** (är'nĭm), Countess **Elizabeth Mary von.** See Elizabeth Mary RUSSELL.

**Arnim** *or* **Arn'heim** (ärn'hīm), **Hans Georg von.** 1581–1641. German diplomat and general in Thirty Years' War; b. Boitzenburg, Prussia. Successively in the service of Sweden (1613), Poland (1621), the emperor (1626), and Saxony (1631).

**Arnim,** Count **Harry Karl Kurt Eduard von.** 1824–1881. German diplomat. Ambassador at Rome (1864–70); supported German bishops at Vatican Council in protest against dogma of papal infallibility. Participated (1871) in peace negotiations between Germany and France. Ambassador at Paris (1872–74); recalled (1874) because of differences with Bismarck.

**Arnim, Jürgen von.** 1889?–1962. German army officer; tank expert; colonel general, in command in northern Tunisia (Jan., 1943); captured by British 1st army on Cap Bon peninsula (May 12, 1943).

**Arnim, Ludwig Joachim,** *or* **Achim, von.** 1781–1831. German romantic poet and novelist. Published, with Clemens Brentano, *Des Knaben Wunderhorn* (3 vols., 1805–08), a collection of legends and folk songs. Author of *Der Wintergarten* (1809), *Halle und Jerusalem* (1811), *Schaubühne* (1813), *Die Kronenwächter* (1817), etc. His wife, **Elisabeth** *or* **Bettina** (1785–1859), sister of Clemens Brentano, and correspondent of Goethe, was author of *Goethes Briefwechsel mit einem Kinde* (1835; in part supposedly fictitious), *Die Günderode* (1840), etc.

**Arniston,** Lord. See DUNDAS of Arniston.

**Ar'no** (är'nō) *or* **Arn** (ärn) *or* **Aq'ui·la** (ăk'wĭ·lȧ). 750?–821. German clergyman; archbishop of Salzburg (from 798); highly esteemed by Charlemagne and Pope Leo III.

**Ar'no** (är'nō), **Peter.** *Real name* **Curtis Ar'noux** (är'nōō) **Peters.** 1904–1968. American cartoonist; grad. Yale (1922); contributor to *New Yorker;* exhibitor in New York, London, and Paris; cartoons collected in *Peter Arno's Parade* (1929), *Peter Arno's Circus* (1931), *The Low-Down,* etc.

**Ar·no'bi·us** (är·nō'bĭ·ŭs). *Sometimes called* **Arnobius A'fer** (ā'fẽr). fl. 300 A.D. Early Christian apologist in northern Africa; author of *Adversus Gentes* (7 books), apparently written to rebut charges that contemporary troubles were due to impiety of Christian belief and were existent particularly since the Christian religion had become established in the Roman Empire.

**Ar'nold** (är'n'ld), **Benedict.** 1741–1801. American army officer, traitor, b. Norwich, Conn.; m. (1779) Margaret Shippen (*q.v.*). With Ethan Allen, captured Fort Ticonderoga (1775). A leader of unsuccessful campaign to capture Quebec (1775). Brigadier general (1776). Stopped British thrust from Canada down Lake Champlain (1776). Major general (1777). Repulsed British force in Mohawk Valley (1777); aided in forcing Burgoyne's surrender. In command at Philadelphia (1778–79); court-martialed for irregularities and reprimanded. Began treasonable correspondence with British (1779). In command at West Point (1780); arranged to surrender West Point to British; plot discovered (Sept. 23, 1780). Fled to British; led raids in Virginia (1780) and Connecticut (1781). To England (Dec., 1781), where he spent rest of life in disgrace and poverty.

**Arnold, Bion Joseph.** 1861–1942. American electrical engineer, b. Casnovia, Mich.; expert on electric traction and subways.

**Ar'nold** (är'nôlt), **Christoph.** 1650–1695. German peasant astronomer; early observer of comets (1682, 1686) and of transit of Mercury across sun (1690).

**Ar'nold** (är'n'ld), Sir **Edwin.** 1832–1904. English poet and journalist. M.A., Oxon. (1856); won Newdigate prize (1852). Principal, Deccan Coll., Bombay, India (1856–61). Editor of *Daily Telegraph* (1873). Author of *The Light of Asia* (poem on life and teachings of Buddha, 1879), and other poems and translations on life and thought of the East.

**Arnold, George.** 1834–1865. American poet and miscellaneous writer, b. New York City.

**Arnold, Henry Harley.** 1886–1950. American general, b. Gladwyne, Pa.; grad. U.S.M.A., West Point (1907); in army aviation (1911); awarded trophy for 30-mile flight (1912) and as commander of U.S. army Alaskan flight (1934); chief of U.S. Army Air Corps (1938); chief of U.S. air forces (June, 1941); lieutenant general (Dec., 1941); general (Mar., 1943); general of the army (Dec., 1944); general of the air force (May, 1949). Author of *Air Men and Aircraft* (1929), etc.

**Arnold, Matthew.** 1822–1888. English poet and critic. Son of Dr. Thomas Arnold of Rugby; uncle of Mary Augusta Ward (*q.v.*). Grad. Balliol, Oxford (1844); Newdigate prizeman (1843). Inspector of schools (1851–86). Professor of poetry, Oxford (1857–67). Lectured in

America (1883–84, 1886). His poetical works include *The Strayed Reveller and other Poems* (1849), *Empedocles on Etna and other Poems* (1852), *Poems* (containing *Sohrab and Rustum*, *Scholar-Gipsy*, and *Requiescat;* 1853), *New Poems* (containing *Thyrsis* and *A Southern Night;* 1867), and *Poems* (two-volume collection containing *Rugby Chapel;* 1869). Critical essays include *On Translating Homer* (1861; vol. 2, 1862), *On the Study of Celtic Literature* (1867), two series of *Essays in Criticism* (1865, 1888), *Culture and Anarchy* (1869), *Literature and Dogma* (1873).

**Arnold, Ralph.** 1875– . American geologist and petroleum engineer, b. Marshalltown, Iowa. With U.S. Geological Survey (1900); geologist (1908–09). Investigated oil fields of Texas, Wyoming, Mexico, Trinidad, Venezuela, etc. Author of *Two Decades of Petroleum Geology* and *Petroleum in the United States and Possessions*, etc.

**Arnold, Samuel.** 1740–1802. English organist and composer. Wrote operas, including *Maid of the Mill* (1765), afterpieces, pantomimes, and oratorios, including *The Cure of Saul* (1767).

**Arnold, Samuel Greene.** 1821–1880. American historical writer, b. Providence, R.I. Lieutenant governor, Rhode Island (1852, 1861, 1862); U.S. senator (1862–63). Author of *History of Rhode Island and Providence Plantation* (1859).

**Arnold, Thomas.** 1795–1842. English educator. Grad. Oxford (1814). Ordained in Church of England (1818). Headmaster of Rugby (1828–42); introduced mathematics, modern history, and modern languages to curriculum; strongly influenced development of modern public schools in England. Regius professor of history at Oxford (1841). Author of five volumes of sermons, edition of Thucydides, and three-volume history of Rome. His son **Thomas** (1823–1900), colonial school inspector, embraced Roman Catholicism (1856); professor of English literature in new Roman Catholic university at Dublin; published manual of English literature. See also Matthew ARNOLD.

**Arnold, Thomas Kerchever.** 1800–1853. English clergyman; editor of school classics.

**Arnold, Thurman Wesley.** 1891–1969. American lawyer, b. Laramie, Wyo. A.B., Princeton (1911); LL.B., Harvard (1914). Professor, Yale (1931–37). Asst. attorney general of U.S. (1938–43); judge, U.S. court of appeals for D.C. (1943–45). Author of *The Folklore of Capitalism* (1937), *Democracy and Free Enterprise* (1942), etc.

**Ar·nold′** (ŭr·nôl′y′t), **Yuri von.** 1811–1898. Russian composer and musicologist, b. St. Petersburg.

**Ar′nold of Bre′scia** (är′n′ld ŭv brā′shä). *Ital.* **Ar·nal′do da Bre′scia** (är·näl′dō dä brā′shä). 1100?–1155. Italian political reformer; student of Abelard; combated corruption of clergy; led popular revolt against bishop of Brescia; silenced by 2d Lateran Council (1139); condemned (with Abelard) by Council of Sens (1140); fled to Switzerland (until 1143); called to Rome (1145); forced Pope Eugene III into exile; patterned reformed government after Roman republic; forced to flee by interdict of Adrian IV (1155); betrayed by Frederick I; executed at Rome (1155).

**Arnold of Villanova.** See ARNAUD DE VILLENEUVE.

**Ar′nold von Winkelried** (är′nōlt). See WINKELRIED.

**Ar′nold–For′ster** (är′n′ld·fôr′stẽr), **Hugh Oakeley.** 1855–1909. English writer and political leader; grandson of Dr. Thomas Arnold of Rugby. Grad. Oxford (1877). Unionist M.P. (1892–1909). Secretary of state for war under Balfour (1903–05). Author of *English Socialism of Today* (1908) and works on army matters.

**Ar′nold·son** (ȧr′no͝old·sôn), **Klas Pontus.** 1844–1916. Swedish writer, politician, and pacifist. Member of Riksdag (1882–87); advocated permanent neutrality. Edited liberal and pacifist periodicals. Co-winner (with Fredrik Bajer) of 1908 Nobel peace prize. Author of *Hope of the Centuries, a Book on World Peace* (1900).

**Arnoldson, Sigrid.** 1860–1943. Swedish operatic soprano; m. (1889) Maurice Fischof. Sang chiefly in Moscow and St. Petersburg.

**Ar·nol′fo di Cam′bio** (är·nôl′fō dē käm′byō). 1232?–?1300. Florentine architect; pupil of Nicola Pisano; built Church of Santa Croce, Florence (1295 ff.); began reconstruction of Cathedral of Florence (1296). Thought by some to be identical with **Arnolfo da Fi·ren′ze** (dä fē·rĕn′tsā), Florentine sculptor of tabernacles in churches of San Pietro fuori le mura (Rome) and St. Cecilia in Trastevere (Rome), and tomb of Boniface VIII in Vatican grottoes.

**Ar′nott** (är′nŏt), **Neil.** 1788–1874. Scottish physician. M.A., Aberdeen (1805); M.D. (1814). East India Company ship's surgeon in China service (1807–09); practiced at London (1811–55). Made many inventions, esp. in ventilation and smokeless grates. Published *Elements of Physics* (1827–29), etc.

**Ar′nould′** (ȧr′no͞o′), **Sophie.** 1744–1802. French opera singer (1757–78), b. Paris; known as a wit; her salon frequented by d'Alembert, Diderot, and Rousseau.

**Arn′stein** (ärn′stīn; -shtīn), **Karl.** 1887–1974. American airship designer and builder, b. Prague, Bohemia. Educ. U. of Prague. With Zeppelin Co., Friedrichshafen, Germany (1919–24). To U.S. (1924); naturalized (1930). Technical director of aircraft construction, Goodyear Tire and Rubber Co., Akron, Ohio (1924); vice-president and chief engineer, Goodyear-Zeppelin Corp. (from 1925). Designer of numerous commercial and military airships.

**Ar′nulf** (är′no͝olf). 850?–899. Natural son of Carloman of Bavaria. Margrave, later duke, of Carinthia. Deposed Charles III; elected king of Germany, or the East Franks (887). Holy Roman emperor (887–899; crowned 896). Won great victory over Northmen at Louvain (891); led successful expedition against Moravians (892); invaded Italy and stormed Rome (894–895).

**A′ron·hold** (ä′rôn·hôlt), **Siegfried Heinrich.** 1819–1884. German mathematician; professor at Berlin (1863–83); a founder of mathematical theory of invariants and investigator of plane curves of third and fourth orders.

**A′ro·se·me′na** (ä′rō·sā·mā′nä), **Florencio Harmodio.** 1873–1945. President of Panama (1928–31). His brother **Juan Demóstenes** (1879–1939) was also president of Panama (1936–39; died in office).

**Arouet, François Marie.** See VOLTAIRE.

**Arouj.** See BARBAROSSA I.

**Arp, Bill.** Pseudonym of Charles Henry SMITH.

**Arp** (ärp), **Jean** *or* **Hans** (häns). **1887–1966.** French artist, b. Strasbourg. Studied at Weimar (1906–09), Paris, Lucerne, Zurich (1911–12), and Munich (1912). A founder of Dadaism, Zurich (1916); member of surrealist group of painters, Paris (from 1925).

**Arp** (ärp), **Ju′li·us** (yo͞o′lē·o͝os). 1858– . Lepidopterist, b. Holstein, Ger.; to Brazil (1881), naturalized (1920). Presented his collection of 25,000 specimens of butterflies to Museu Nacional at Rio de Janeiro.

**Ár′pád** (är′päd). d. 907. National hero of Hungary; semilegendary Magyar chief; founder of Hungarian monarchy; supposed to have led Magyars into Hungary (c. 875), conquered much territory, and invaded Italy; founder of dynasty of Árpád, whose first crowned king was St. Stephen (997–1038) and last, Andrew III (d. 1301).

**Arpino,** Cavaliere **d'.** See Giuseppe CESARI.

**Ar'ran** (ăr'ăn), Earls of. See (1) HAMILTON family; (2) *James Stewart* (d. 1596), under STEWART family.

**Ar·ra'u** (är·rä'o͞o), **Claudio.** 1903– . Chilean pianist; studied and made debut in Germany; visited U.S. (1924); on tour in South America and in Europe; on tour in U.S. (1940, 1941).

**Ar're·bo** (ä'rĕ·bō), **Anders Christensen.** 1587–1637. Danish poet; author of *Hexaëmeron* (1641).

**Ar'rest'** (à'rĕ'), **Heinrich Ludwig d'.** 1822–1875. German astronomer; professor, U. of Leipzig (1852) and Copenhagen (1857); known for his discoveries of comets and his studies of nebulae.

**Ar·rhe'ni·us** (är·rā'nĭ·ŭs), **Svante August.** 1859–1927. Swedish physicist and chemist, b. near Uppsala. Studied at U. of Uppsala; professor, U. of Stockholm (1895); director, Nobel Institute for Physical Chemistry (from 1905). Established electrolytic dissociation theory, for which he received 1903 Nobel prize for chemistry. Author of works on biological chemistry, electrochemistry, physical chemistry, and astronomy.

**Ar'rhi·dae'us** (ăr'ĭ·dē'ŭs). Natural son of Philip II of Macedon; elected king of Macedonia by soldiers of Alexander the Great in Babylon after Alexander's death (323 B.C.); put to death (317) by order of Olympias, former wife of Philip II, and mother of Alexander.

**Ar'ri·a** (ăr'ĭ·ȧ). d. 42 A.D. Roman matron; wife of **Cae·ci'na Pae'tus** (sē·sī'nȧ pē'tŭs), who was involved in a conspiracy against the emperor, Claudius, and was condemned to death; determined not to survive her husband, stabbed herself and handed dagger to him with remark, "Paetus, it doesn't hurt."

**Ar·ria'ga** (ȧr·ryȧ'gȧ), **Manuel José de.** 1842–1917. Portuguese statesman and first constitutional president of Republic of Portugal (1911–15), b. Horta, Azores. Studied law but entered politics early as Republican deputy during reign of Louis I; actively engaged in revolutionary movement (1910) that overthrew King Manuel and established republic; poet, writer on jurisprudence, and orator; resigned presidency (1915).

**Ar'ri·an** (ăr'ĭ·ăn). *Lat.* **Flavius Ar'ri·a'nus** (ăr'ĭ·ā'nŭs). fl. 2d century A.D. Greek historian, originally from Nicomedia (Izmet), Bithynia. Governor of Cappadocia (131–137); archon of Athens (147–148). Author of *Anabasis of Alexander* (life of Alexander the Great), *Indica* (description of India), *Periplus of the Euxine*, and of two books on philosophy of Epictetus.

**Ar·ria'za y Su'per·vie'la** (är·ryä'thä ē so͞o'pĕr·vyā'lä), **Juan Bautista de.** 1770–1837. Spanish poet, b. Madrid; author of *Las Primicias* (1797), the didactic poem *Emilia* (1803), *Poesías Patrióticas* (1810; including the ode *Profecía del Pirineo*), and *Poesías Líricas* (6th edition, 1829–32).

**Ar'ri·va·be'ne** (är'rē·vä·bâ'nā), Conte **Giovanni.** 1787–1881. Italian economist. Political exile in England and Belgium (1820–59); returned to Italy (1860); senator. Influential in improving Italian economic conditions.

**Ar'rol** (ăr'ŭl), Sir **William.** 1839–1913. Scottish bridge builder; constructed new Tay bridge (1882–87), Forth bridge (1883–90), Tower bridge, London (1886–94), Nile bridge at Cairo.

**Ar·rom'** (är·rôn') *or* **Ar·rón'** (är·rôn'). **Cecilia Francisca Josefa de.** = Fernán CABALLERO.

**Ar'row** (ăr'ō), **Kenneth Joseph.** 1921– . Economist, b. New York City. Ph.D., Columbia, 1951. Shared 1972 Nobel prize for economics with John Richard Hicks for work on theory of general economic equilibrium.

**Ar'row·smith** (ăr'ō·smĭth), **Aaron** (1750–1823) and his nephew **John** (1790–1873). English geographers and map makers.

**Ars,** Curé of. See Saint Jean Baptiste Marie VIANNEY.

**Ar'sa·ces** (är'sȧ·sēz). Name of several (by some considered a title of all) kings of the Arsacidae of Parthia including: **Arsaces I.** King (c. 250–248 B.C.). Scythian chief; led revolt against Seleucid king, Antiochus II (250); established new kingdom. Some authorities say he ruled 37 years, thus identifying him with Tiridates (*q.v.*). **Arsaces VI** *or* **Mithridates I.** King (171–138 B.C.). See MITHRIDATES I. See also FIRUZ I and PHRAATES I.

**Ar·sac'i·dae** (är·săs'ĭ·dē) *or* **Ar·sac'ids** (är·săs'ĭdz; är'sȧ·sĭdz). Dynasty of Parthian rulers (about 30 kings, of whom very little is known), founded by Arsaces I (*q.v.*) on dissolution of Seleucid Empire (c. 250 B.C.). Last ruler (see ARTABANUS) overthrown (c. 226 A.D.) by Ardashir, founder of Sassanid Empire (see SASSANIDAE).

**Ar·se'ni·us Au·to'ri·a'nus** (är·sē'nĭ·ŭs ô·tō'rĭ·ā'nŭs). 13th-century patriarch of Constantinople; deposed and banished (1261) by Emperor Michael VIII, whom he had excommunicated for blinding his ward John IV.

**Ar'ses** (är'sēz). *In some sources called* **Xerxes III.** King of Persia (338–336 B.C.); son of Artaxerxes III (*q.v.*); murdered by eunuch Bagoas.

**Ar·sin'o·ë** (är·sĭn'ō·ē). Name of several women prominent in Egyptian history:

**Arsinoë.** fl. 4th century B.C. Concubine of Philip of Macedon; m. Lagus, founder of dynasty of Ptolemies; mother of Ptolemy I of Egypt.

**Arsinoë I.** d. 247 B.C. Daughter of Lysimachus of Thrace; m. (c. 285) as 1st wife, Ptolemy II Philadelphus, by whom she was mother of Ptolemy III; banished to Coptos.

**Arsinoë II.** 316–271 B.C. Daughter of Ptolemy I and Berenice I; m. 1st (c. 300) Lysimachus, King of Thrace; on his death, m. 2d Ptolemy Keraunos, but immediately exiled by him and her children slain; fled to Egypt and m. 3d (276) her brother Ptolemy II Philadelphus as second wife; a nome of Egypt and several cities named after her.

**Arsinoë III.** d. ?205 B.C. Daughter of Ptolemy III Euergetes and Berenice II; m. her brother Ptolemy IV Philopator; put to death by him; mother of Ptolemy V Epiphanes.

**Arsinoë IV.** d. 41 B.C. Daughter of Ptolemy XI Auletes and sister of Cleopatra; captured by Romans and led in triumph through Rome; killed by order of Antony.

**Ar'son'val'** (ȧr'sôN'vȧl'), **Jacques Arsène d'.** 1851–1940. French physicist, b. Borie. Director, laboratory of biological physics, Collège de France (1882); professor (1894). Devised first reflecting galvanometer containing a moving coil (d'Arsonval galvanometer), and a magnetotelephone. Conducted experiments in the mechanical equivalent of heat, and in high-frequency oscillating electric current of low voltage and high amperage (d'Arsonval current), esp. as valuable in treatment of certain diseases. Invented an instrument (d'Arsonval instrument) for measuring a direct current of electricity.

**Ar'ta·ba'nus** (är'tȧ·bā'nŭs). Name of four kings of Parthia, of Arsacidae, esp.: **Artabanus I** (d. ?124 B.C.), king (127–?124 B.C.), killed fighting the Tocharians (Scythians). **Artabanus II** (d. 40 A.D.), king (10?–40 A.D.), made peace with Rome. **Artabanus V** *or* **IV** (d. 226 or 227), king (209–?227), last of Arsacids, defeated and killed in battle of Hormuz by Ardashir of Persia, founder of Sassanidae dynasty.

**Ar'ta·ba'zus** (är'tȧ·bā'zŭs). Name of several distinguished Persians, esp.: (1) A general under Xerxes; commanded Parthians and Chorasmians in expedition against Greece (480 B.C.); warned Mardonius not to fight at Plataea (479); after Persian defeat, led his part of army (40,000 men) in retreat through Thessaly, Macedonia, and Thrace to Byzantium. (2) A general in reigns of Artaxerxes III and Darius III. Led revolt (356 B.C.) but later (c. 349) pardoned; attended Darius in battle of Arbela (331); rewarded by Alexander.

**Ar'ta·pher'nes** (är'tȧ·fûr'nēz). *More correctly* **Ar·taph're·nes** (är·tăf'rē·nēz). fl. late 6th century B.C. Persian general, brother of King Darius Hystaspis. Satrap of Sardis; took active part in suppressing Ionian revolt (499–498). His son **Artaphernes** (fl. 5th century B.C.) was a Persian general; with Datis, commanded Persian army that invaded Greece and was defeated at Marathon (490); led Lydians in expedition of Xerxes I against Greece (481).

**Ar'ta·xer'xes** (är'tăg·zûrk'sēz; -tăk·sûrk'-; -tȧ·zûrk'-). *Pers.* **Ar'takh·shat'ra'** (är'täκ·shät'rä'), *later* **Ar·dashir** (see ARDASHIR). Name of three Persian kings:

**Artaxerxes I.** *Called* **Lon·gim'a·nus** (lŏn·jĭm'ȧ·nŭs). d. 424 B.C. King (464–424). Son of Xerxes I; father of Xerxes II, Sogdianus, and Darius II. Killed his father's murderer, the vizier Artabanus (464). In general, enjoyed peaceful reign; put down rebellion in Bactria (Balkh) and more serious one in Egypt (460–454); kept Persia neutral during Samian and Peloponnesian wars; sanctioned practice of Jewish religion in Jerusalem (458); appointed Nehemiah governor of Judea (445).

**Artaxerxes II.** *Called* **Mne'mon** (nē'mŏn). d. 359 B.C. King (404–359). Son of Darius II. Near beginning of his reign (401), faced by revolt of his brother Cyrus (see CYRUS, the younger), whom he defeated and killed at Cunaxa (401). Reign marked by many rebellions; concluded with Sparta peace of Antalcidas (386); his expeditions against Egypt (385–383, 374–372) failed completely. Rebuilt royal palace at Susa; effected changes in Persian religion, restoring worship of early gods.

**Artaxerxes III.** *Orig.* **O'chus** (ō'kŭs). d. 338 B.C. King (359–338). Son of Artaxerxes II. At accession, murdered most of his relatives; attempted to subjugate Egypt; failed at first; defeated by princes of Sidon, Cyprus, etc., and (346) by Greek generals in Egypt; later, with great cruelty, succeeded in subduing Egypt (343); slain by eunuch Bagoas, an Egyptian who had been put in authority; succeeded by his son Arses (*q.v.*).

**Ar·te'di** (är·tē'dĭ), **Peter.** 1705–1735. Swedish naturalist; left materials for scientific study of fishes, edited by his friend Linnaeus (1738).

**Ar'te·mi·do'rus Dal'di·a'nus** (är'tē·mĭ·dō'rŭs dăl'dĭ·ā'nŭs). fl. 2d cent. A.D. Greek soothsayer and interpreter of dreams; author of *The Interpretation of Dreams*, which throws light on religious rites, myths, and opinions of the ancients.

**Artemidorus of Eph'e·sus** (ĕf'ē·sŭs). fl. about 100 B.C. Greek geographer; his work (in 11 books now lost) much used by Strabo and others.

**Ar'te·mis'i·a** (är'tē·mĭz'ĭ·ȧ; -mĭsh'ĭ·ȧ). Name of two queens of Asia Minor: (1) Queen of Halicarnassus and Cos; subject to Persian king; joined fleet of Xerxes in expedition against Greece (480 B.C.); showed much bravery and skill in battle of Salamis. (2) Queen of Caria (d. about 350 B.C.); m. her brother Mausolus; succeeded as ruler (352–350) at his death; in his memory, erected Mausoleum at Halicarnassus (completed c. 350), one of the Seven Wonders of the (ancient) World.

**Ar'te·vel'de** (är'tĕ·vĕl'dĕ), **Jacob van.** 1290?–1345. Flemish statesman; reputedly a brewer, hence called the "Brewer of Ghent"; supported England in Anglo-French war (1335); all-powerful governor of Flanders (1336–45). His son **Philip** (1340?–1382) headed revolt of Ghent against count of Flanders (1381); defeated and killed at Roosebeke (1382). Story of Philip's career theme of drama (*Philip van Artevelde*, 1834), by Sir Henry Taylor.

**Ar'thois'** (år'twå') *or* **Ar'tois', Jacques d'.** 1613–?1684. Flemish landscape painter, esp. of scenes near Brussels, his birthplace.

**Ar'thur** (är'thẽr). Real or legendary 6th-century king of the Britons; perhaps son of Uther Pendragon. Led British army (c. 516) against invading Saxons; probably won victory at Mount Badon (c. 520); said to have died at battle of Camlan (537). As central figure of great cycle of romance, said to have held court, with his wife Guinevere, at Caerleon on the Usk, and to have instituted order of Knights of the Round Table, and is traditionally supposed to have been taken to mythical island of Avalon to be healed of his wounds after battle of Camlan.

**Arthur.** Duke *or* Count **of Brit'ta·ny** (brĭt'ȧ·nĭ). 1187–1203. Posthumous son of Geoffrey, 4th son of Henry II, by Constance of Brittany. Claimant to throne of England on death of King Richard (1199); captured by his uncle King John (1202); murdered at Rouen, probably by John's order. Appears as character in Shakespeare's *King John*.

**Arthur, Chester Alan.** 1829–1886. President of the United States, b. Fairfield, Vt. Collector of port of New York (1871–78). Vice-president, United States (Mar. 4–Sept. 19, 1881); president (1881–85) on death of Garfield.

**Arthur, Julia.** *Real name* **Ida Lewis.** 1869–1950. Actress, b. Hamilton, Ont.; m. Benjamin B. Cheney, Jr.; on stage (from 1880); played in A. M. Palmer's company in New York and in Henry Irving's company in London.

**Arthur, Timothy Shay.** 1809–1885. American writer, b. near Newburgh, N.Y.; advocate of temperance; achieved immense popularity with *Ten Nights in a Barroom and What I Saw There* (1854).

**Ar·ti'gas** (är·tē'gäs), **José Gervasio.** 1764–1850. Uruguayan general, b. Montevideo; captain in Spanish army in Uruguay; led Gauchos in revolt for independence (1811); defended Uruguayan independence against Argentines and Brazilians; captured Montevideo from Argentines (1815) and lost it to Portuguese (1817); defeated by Portuguese at Tacuarembó (1820); fled to Paraguay (1820 ff.).

**Ar'tois'** (år'twå'), Comte **d'.** Title granted (1757) by Louis XV of France to his grandson Charles Philippe (later Charles X).

**Artois, Jacques d'.** See ARTHOIS.

**Ar'tôt'** (år'tō'). Professional name of Belgian musical family, originally surnamed **Mon'ta'gney'** (môɴ'tå'nyā'), including: **Maurice Montagney Artôt** (1772–1829), horn player and conductor; his sons **Jean Désiré** (1803–1887), horn player, and **Alexandre Joseph** (1815–1845), violinist and composer; Jean Désiré's daughter **Marguerite Joséphine Désirée** (1835–1907), operatic singer.

**Ar·tsy·ba'shev** *or* **Ar·tzy·ba'sheff** (ŭr·tsĭ·bå'shĕf), **Mikhail Petrovich.** 1878–1927. Russian realistic novelist, b. in south Russia; great-grandson of Kosciusko. Author of novels *Sanin* (pub. 1907) and *The Breaking Point* (1915) and plays *The Law of the Savage*, *Jealousy*, *Enemies*, and *War* (Russian *Voina*, 1918). Father of Boris Artzybasheff (*q.v.*).

**Ar·tu'si** (är·tōō'sē), **Giovanni Maria.** 1550?–1613. Italian composer and musical theorist; combated innovations in music; composed *Canzonette* (for 4 voices, 1598) and *Cantate Domino;* wrote *L'Arte del Contrappunto Ridotta in Tavole* (1586), *Delle Imperfezioni della Musica Moderna* (1600), *Considerazioni Musicali* (1607), etc.

**Ar·tzy·ba'sheff** (ŭr·tsĭ·bå'shĕf), **Boris.** 1899–1965. American illustrator and writer, b. Kharkov, Russia; son of Mikhail Artsybashev (*q.v.*); to U.S. (1919); naturalized (1926). Illustrator of books by Edmund Wilson,

Padraic Colum, Rabindranath Tagore, Balzac, and Nansen. Author of *Poor Shaydullah* (1931) and *Seven Simeons* (1937).

**Ar'un·del** (ăr'ŭn·d'l), Earl of. Title in English peerage of branch of Fitzalan family having common ancestry with Stewart family (*q.v.*), which passed (1580), to Howard family, including: **Richard Fitz·al'an** [fĭts-ăl'ăn] (1267–1302), 1st earl; fought for Edward I against Welsh and Scots and in Gascony. His son **Edmund** (1285–1326), 2d earl; faithful to Edward II; captured and executed by Queen Isabella and Mortimer. His son **Richard** (1307–1376), 3d earl, and Earl **Wa·renne'** [wä·rĕn'] (or Earl of **Surrey**); fought at Crécy, siege of Calais, and naval battle off Winchelsea; regent of England (1355). His son **Richard** (1346–1397), 4th earl, and Earl of Surrey; won naval victory against French and Spanish off Margate (1387); active in Gloucester faction opposing Richard II; imprisoned and beheaded. See Thomas I MOWBRAY. His son **Thomas** (1381–1415), 5th earl; restored to title and estates by Henry IV; one of leaders of expedition to help Burgundy (1411); lord treasurer under Henry V. His kinsman **John Fitzalan,** Lord **Mal·trav'ers** [măl·trăv'ẽrz] (1385–1421), 6th earl; succeeded by his son **John** (1408–1435), 7th earl, who served Henry VI with distinction in the field. John's son **Humphrey** (d. 1438), 8th earl; succeeded by John's brother **William** (1417–1488), 9th earl. **Henry Fitzalan** (1511?–1580), 12th earl; opposed passing over of Mary and Elizabeth in royal succession in favor of Lady Jane Grey; under Mary held high appointments; leader of Catholic nobility, twice imprisoned under suspicions of implication in Catholic plots, under Elizabeth. For later earls see *Earls of Arundel* under HOWARD family.

**Arundel, Thomas.** 1353–1414. English prelate. Bishop of Ely (1374); archbishop of York (1388); archbishop of Canterbury (1396). Banished for assisting in movement for regency in derogation of Richard II's authority; returned with Henry IV, whom he crowned. Chancellor (1399, 1407, 1412); bitter opponent of Lollards.

**Ar'un·dell** (ăr'ŭn·dĕl), Lady **Blanche.** 1583–1649. Daughter of earl of Worcester; m. Thomas Arundell of Wardour in Wiltshire; defended Wardour Castle for nine days against Parliamentary army attacks (1643). Her son **Henry Arundell** (1606?–1694), 3d Baron **Arundell of War'dour** (wôr'dẽr), fought for Charles I; dislodged Parliamentary forces from Wardour Castle (1644); privy councilor (1686); lord privy seal (1687).

**Ar'vède' Ba'rine'** (ȧr'vĕd' bȧ'rēn'). *Pseudonym of* Mme. **Charles Vin'cens'** (văN'säN'). 1840–1908. French writer and critic; author of *L'Œuvre de Jésus Ouvrier* (1879), *Portraits de Femmes* (1887), *Bernardin de Saint-Pierre* (1891), *Alfred de Musset* (1893), *Louis XIV et la Grande Mademoiselle, 1652–1693* (1905).

**Ar'wids·son** (ȧr'vĭts·sôn), **Adolf Ivar.** 1791–1858. Poet, b. in Finland; banished (1822) by Russian authorities; settled in Sweden; director, Royal Library, Stockholm (1843–58).

**Ar'ya·bha'ta** *or* **Ar'ya·bhat'ta** (är'yȧ·bŭt'ȧ). b. 476 A.D. Indian mathematician and astronomer, b. Pataliputra (Patna) during Gupta era. Maintained theory of rotation of earth round its axis and explained cause of eclipses of sun and moon; his only work, *Aryabhatiya,* treated of astronomy and mathematics (quadratic equations, table of sines, and other rules of algebra and trigonometry).

**Arz von Straus'sen·burg** (ärts fôn shtrou'sĕn·bo͝orK), Baron **Artur.** 1857–1935. Austro-Hungarian general, b. in Transylvania. Distinguished himself in World War as commander of 6th army corps on Russian front. Succeeded Conrad von Hötzendorf as chief of general staff (1917); proposed common offensive with German forces on the Isonzo which drove Italians beyond the Piave (1917); led new unsuccessful attack on Italians (1918). Author of *Zur Geschichte des Grossen Krieges 1914–1918* (1924).

**A'sa** (ā'sȧ). d. about 875 B.C. 3d king of Judah (c. 915–875). Successor and son of Abijah (or Abijam). Most of long reign peaceful (*1 Kings* xv. 8–25); zealous in destruction of idols and strange altars (*2 Chron.* xiv. 1–5); fought and defeated large Ethiopian army (*2 Chron.* xiv. 9–15); sought help from Benhadad of Damascus against Baasha; succeeded by Jehoshaphat (*1 Kings* xv. 18 ff.).

**A·sa·ka·wa** (ä·sä·kä·wä), **Kwan-Ichi.** 1873–1948. Educator, b. in Japan. Educ. Waseda U. (Tokyo), Dartmouth, and Yale (Ph.D., 1902). Teacher of history, Yale (from 1907); professor (1937–42); writer on Japanese history and institutions. Special editor for Japanese terms, *Webster's New International Dictionary, Second Edition.*

**A'sam** (ä'zäm). Family of Bavarian artists, including: **Hans Georg** (1649?–1711) and his sons **Cosmas Damian** (1686–?1742) and **Egid Quirin** (1692–?1750), best known for their frescoes in Bavarian churches.

**As'björn'sen** (äs'byûrn'sĕn), **Peter Christen.** 1812–1885. Norwegian writer, naturalist, realistic poet, and collector of Norwegian folklore.

**As'bur'y** (ăz'bẽr'ĭ; -bẽr·ĭ; -brĭ), **Francis.** 1745–1816. Methodist Episcopal bishop, b. near Birmingham, Eng. Missionary of Methodism to U.S. (1771); recalled (1775) but refused to return; became citizen of Delaware (1778). Prominent in formation of Methodist Episcopal Church in U.S. (1779–84); consecrated as superintendent at conference in Baltimore (1784); assumed title of bishop (1785); ruled new church in U.S. until his death. Cf. John and Charles WESLEY.

**Asbury, Herbert.** 1891–1963. American journalist and author, b. Farmington, Mo. On staff of New York *Sun* (1916–20), *Herald* (1920–24), *Herald Tribune* (from 1924). Served in France in World War (1918–19). Author of *A Methodist Saint* (a life of Bishop Francis Asbury; 1927), *The Gangs of New York* (1928), *Life of Carry Nation* (1929), *The Barbary Coast* (1933), *The French Quarter* (1936), *Sucker's Progress* (1938), *Gem of the Prairie* (1940), *The Golden Flood* (1942), etc.

**Ascanian dynasty.** See BRANDENBURG.

**As·cá'su·bi** (äs·kä'so͞o·bē), **Hilario.** 1807–1875. Argentine poet, b. Buenos Aires. Minister to France (1864). Author of *Santos Vega, Paulino Lucero,* depicting Gaucho life.

**Asch** (ȧsh; *Angl.* ăsh), **Sholem** *or* **Shalom** *or* **Sholom.** 1880–1957. Yiddish novelist and playwright, b. Kutno, near Warsaw, Poland. Educ. in Hebrew schools and rabbinical coll., Poland; began writing (1901), at first in Hebrew, later in Yiddish or German; to U.S. on visit (1910), to reside (1914); naturalized (1920); lived in Paris (1925), in Russia (1928). Author of plays including *Mottke the Thief* (1917) and *The God of Vengeance* (pub. in U.S., 1918), and fiction including *Uncle Moses* (1920), *Kiddush Ha-Shem* (1926), *The Mother* (1930), *The Three Cities* (1933), *The War Goes On* (1937), *Song of the Valley* (1939), *The Nazarene* (1939), *Children of Abraham* (1942). His son **Nathan** (1902–1964), b. Warsaw; to U.S. (1915); naturalized; author of *The Office* (1925), *Love in Chartres* (1927), *Pay Day* (1930), *The Valley* (1935), *The Road* (1937).

**As'cham** (ăs'kăm), **Roger.** 1515–1568. English writer and scholar. B.A. and fellow, St. John's, Cambridge (1534). Secretary to Sir Richard Morison, English ambassador to Charles V, Holy Roman Emperor (1550–53). Latin secretary to Queen Mary; tutor, and later secretary, to Queen Elizabeth. Prebendary of York (1559). Author of *Toxophilus*, treatise on archery (1545), and esp. of *The Scholemaster*, treatise on practical education (begun 1563; pub. 1570).

**Asch′bach** (äsh′bäĸ), **Joseph von.** 1801–1882. Austrian historian; author of *Geschichte Kaiser Sigismunds* (4 vols., 1838–45), of histories of Visigoths and Moors in Spain, etc.

**Asche** (ăsh), **John Stanger Heiss Oscar.** 1872–1936. Australian actor, playwright, and theatrical manager, b. Geelong, Australia. Managed Adelphi Theatre, London (1904) and His Majesty's Theatre (1907). Toured Australia (1909, 1912–13). Author of *The Spanish Main* (play; 1915), *Chu Chin Chow* (musical play; 1916), etc.

**As′cle·pi′a·des of Bi·thyn′i·a** (ăs′klē·pī′ȧ·dēz, bĭ·thĭn′ĭ·ȧ). fl. 100 B.C. Greek physician. Opposed Hippocrates's theory of disease; taught that disease results from unharmonious motion of corpuscles of which body is composed; recommended simple treatments, as diet, bathing, and exercise; credited with being first to distinguish between acute and chronic diseases.

**Asclepiades of Sa′mos** (sā′mŏs). fl. 3d century B.C. Greek poet and epigrammatist; reputedly friend of Theocritus. A variety of logaoedic verse is called Asclepiadean after him.

**A′sco·li** (äs′kō·lē), **Cecco d′.** See CECCO D'ASCOLI.

**Ascoli, Graziadio Isaia.** 1829–1907. Italian comparative philologist; professor, Milan (from 1860); founder and editor of *Archivio Glottologico Italiano* (1873–1912).

**As·co′ni·us Pe′di·a′nus** (ăs·kō′nĭ·ŭs pē′dĭ·ā′nŭs; pĕd′ĭ-). Roman scholar, of 1st century A.D., prob. from Padua, but long resident in Rome; prepared commentaries on Cicero's speeches.

**Ascue, Anne.** See ASKEW.

**A·sel′li** (ä·sĕl′lē) *or* **A·sel′lio** (ä·sĕl′lyō), **Gasparo.** *Lat.* **Gaspar A·sel′li·us** (ȧ·sĕl′ĭ·ŭs). 1581–1626. Italian physician and anatomist; discovered the lacteal vessels while dissecting a dog (1623?).

**A·sen′** *or* **As·sen′** (ȧ·sān′). Medieval Bulgarian dynasty (1186–1258), probably of Vlach origin. **John,** *or* **Ivan, Asen I** (d. 1196) and his brother **Peter Asen** (d. 1197); boyars in control of fortresses near Trnovo; founded second Bulgarian empire; declared independence from Byzantium; defeated Byzantine Emperor Isaac Angelus near Stara Zagora (1190). Rule taken over (1197) by younger brother, Kaloyan (*q.v.*) or Yoannitsa.

**John Asen II** (ruled 1218–41); son of John Asen I; greatest of family; soldier and able monarch; added Epirus, Macedonia, and part of Albania to his realm; conquered Serbia, and assumed title of czar of the Greeks and Bulgars. Succeeding rulers of dynasty were **Ka·li′man** (kȧ·lē′mȧn) **I** (ruled 1241–46), **Michael Asen** (ruled 1246–57), and **Kaliman II** (ruled 1257–58), with whom male line became extinct. See CONSTANTINE ASEN.

**Aser.** See ASHER.

**Ash** (ăsh), **Edwin Lancelot Hope′well–** (hōp′wĕl-; -wĕl-). 1881–1964. English neurologist; author of *Mind and Health* (1910), *Nerves and the Nervous* (1911), *The Problem of Nervous Breakdown* (1919), *Melancholia in Everyday Practice* (1934), etc.

**Ash, John.** 1724?–1779. English Baptist minister. Published a *New and Complete Dictionary of the English Language* (2 vols., 1775), including most of Bailey's vocabulary, and provincial terms.

**Ash·a·ri′, al–** (ăl′ăsh·ȧ·rē′). *Arab.* **abu–al–Ḥasan ′Ali al–Ash′ari.** 873–?935. Arab theologian, b. Basra. Convert from orthodoxy to Mutazilite beliefs; publicly repudiated (912) Mutazilism and returned to orthodox beliefs; at Baghdad, by his argumentation and writings (about 100 bks.), laid foundations of Sunnite theology.

**Ash′bee** (ăsh′bē), **Charles Robert.** 1863–1942. English architect and art connoisseur, b. Isleworth. Founder and director, Guild of Handicraft. Author of *Craftsmanship in Competitive Industry, Modern Silverwork, The Treatises of Benvenuto Cellini, Book of Cottages and Little Houses,* etc., also of verse.

**Ash′bourne** (ăsh′bōrn; -bûrn), 1st Baron. **Edward Gibson.** 1837–1913. Irish jurist and politician; M.P. (1875–85); attorney general for Ireland (1877–80); lord chancellor of Ireland (1885, 1886–92, 1895–1906).

**Ash′bur′ton** (ăsh′bûr′t'n), 1st Baron. **John Dun′ning** (dŭn′ĭng). 1731–1783. English lawyer. M.P. (1768–82). Known for defense of East India Company (1762), and of Wilkes (1763); author of a resolution in Parliament that "the influence of the crown has increased, is increasing, and ought to be diminished" (1780).

**Ashburton,** 1st Baron of 2d creation. See BARING family.

**Ash′by** (ăsh′bĭ), **Henry.** 1846–1908. English physician, b. in Surrey. M.D., U. of London (1878). Lecturer on diseases of children (1880–1908), Owens Coll. and Victoria U. (both at Manchester). Widely known as authority in pediatrics.

**Ash′croft** (ăsh′krŏft), Dame **Peggy,** *in full* **Edith Margaret Emily.** 1907– . English actress; roles in *Dear Brutus, The Land of Heart's Desire, Othello* (as Desdemona to Paul Robeson's Othello), *Merchant of Venice, School for Scandal, The Importance of Being Earnest.*

**Ashe** (ăsh), **John.** 1720?–1781. American revolutionary commander, b. Grovely, N.C. His defeat at Briar Creek, Ga. (1778) enabled British to gain Georgia and access to the Carolinas.

**Ashe, Thomas.** 1836–1889. English schoolmaster and poet.

**Ash′er** (ăsh′ẽr). *In Douay Version* **A′ser** (ā′sẽr). In Bible, Jacob's eighth son (*Gen.* xxx. 12–13); ancestor of one of twelve tribes of Israel.

**Ash′ford** (ăsh′fẽrd), **Bailey Kelly.** 1873–1934. American surgeon, b. Washington, D.C. Grad. Georgetown U. (M.D., 1896), Army Medical School (1898); surgeon in Puerto Rico in Spanish-American War. Known for his work on, and campaign against, hookworm disease in Puerto Rico.

**Ashford, Margaret Mary,** *known as* **Daisy.** 1881–1972. English author; m. (1920) James Devlin. Known particularly for *The Young Visiters; or Mr. Salteena's Plan* (written at age of 9; pub. 1919).

**A·shi′** (ȧ·shē′), Rabbi. 352–427 A.D. Hebrew scholar of Babylon; chief editor of Talmud. At early age head of famous rabbinical school at Sura, Babylonia; spent 50 years in compiling the Gemara.

**A·shi·ka·ga** (ä·shē·kä·gä). Japanese shogunate (1338–1568), with capital at Kyoto. Its period of rule characterized by political instability, gradual breakdown of feudal system, increase in foreign trade, and activity in literature and art. Among its more prominent members were the shoguns Takauji, Yoshimitsu, and Yoshimasa (*qq.v.*); during its rule, the Portuguese (1542) and St. Xavier (1549) entered Japan.

**Ashkenazi, Elijah.** See Elijah LEVITA.

**Ash′ley** (ăsh′lĭ), **William Henry.** 1778?–1838. American fur trader and explorer, b. Powhatan Co., Va. In upper Missouri River region (1822–23), Green River, Wyoming (1824–25), and westward nearly to Great Salt Lake (1826).

**Ashley,** Sir **William James.** 1860–1927. English economist. Grad. Balliol, Oxford (1881); professor, U. of Toronto (1888–92), Harvard (1892–1901), U. of Birmingham (1901–25). Author of *Introduction to English*

*Economic History and Theory* (1888, 1893; a standard work), *Tariff Problem* (1903), *Gold and Prices* (1912).

**Ashley Cooper,** *recently* **Ashley-Cooper,** *conventionally* **Ashley** *only.* Family name of earls of SHAFTESBURY.

**Ash′mead** (ăsh′mēd), **Isaac.** 1790–1870. American printer, b. Germantown, Pa. Founded (1819) Sunday and Adult School Union, which became American Sunday School Union.

**Ash′mead-Bart′lett** (-bärt′lĕt; -lĭt), Sir **Ellis.** 1849–1902. English political leader, b. Brooklyn, of American parents; to England in boyhood. Grad. Oxford (1872). Conservative M.P. (1880–84, 1885 to death); civil lord of admiralty (1885, 1886–92); field observer in Boer War (1899); ardent imperialist. Author of *The Battlefields of Thessaly* (1897). His son **Ellis** (1881–1931) was a journalist and war correspondent; M.P. (1924–26). For Sir Ellis's younger brother, **William Lehman,** see under Baroness BURDETT-COUTTS.

**Ash′mole** (ăsh′mōl), **Elias.** 1617–1692. English antiquarian. Royalist in Civil War. Published (1672) exhaustive history of Order of the Garter. Presented collection of rarities to Oxford (1677), nucleus of Ashmolean Museum.

**A·sho′ka** (*ȧ*·shō′k*ȧ*). Variant of ASOKA.

**Ash′ton** (ăsh′t*ŭ*n), **Algernon Bennet Langton.** 1859–1937. English musical composer. Educ. Leipzig (1863–79), Frankfort (1880–81). Professor of piano at Royal College of Music (1885–1910). Composed chamber music, sonatas, instrumental quartets and quintets, piano pieces, and songs.

**Ashton, Ernest Charles.** 1873–1957. Canadian physician and army officer; staff surgeon, Brantford General Hospital (1901–15); chief of Canadian general staff (1935–38); inspector general of military forces in Canada (from 1939).

**Ashton, Helen.** 1891–1958. English novelist, b. London; m. (1927) Arthur Edward North Jordan. Author of *A Lot of Talk* (1927), *Doctor Serocold* (1930), *Bricks and Mortar* (1932), *Family Cruise* (1934), *People in Cages* (1937), *William and Dorothy* (1938), etc.

**Ashton,** Sir **William.** 1881–1963. English-born landscape painter in Australia.

**Ashton, Winifred.** Real name of Clemence DANE.

**A′shur·ba′ni·pal** (ä′sho͝or·bä′nē·päl). *Also* **As′sur·ba′ni·pal** *and* **A′sur·ba′ni·pal** (ä′so͝or-). King of Assyria (669–626 B.C.). Son of Esarhaddon. By some identified, but probably erroneously, with Sardanapalus (*q.v.*). Seized control of delta region and Memphis in Egypt (667) defeating Taharka; recognized Necho I as chief of lords of delta region in Egypt (664) and Necho's son Psamtik as regent (663); lost Egypt to Psamtik (c. 660–654); defeated (c. 652) Cimmerians, who had overrun Asia Minor; overcame revolt of his older brother, Shamash-shum-ukin, ruler over Babylon (668–648); subdued Elam (642–639). Records of his reign remain very full for 30 years (669–639), but none exist for latter part. Last years marked by attacks of Scythians on north and northeast and by rapid rise of Media and Chaldea. Able administrator; devoted to art and literature; raised Assyria to height of power; brought in many captives of conquered races, who erected buildings. Remains of his palace at Nineveh, inner walls of which were lined with remarkable sculptures in relief, were unearthed at Kuyunjik, near Mosul.

**A′shur-dan′** (ä′sho͝or·dän′). Name of three kings of Assyria, esp. **Ashur-dan III** (reigned 772–754 B.C.), whose disastrous reign marked decline of Assyrian power.

**A′shur·na′sir·pal** (ä′sho͝or·nä′zĭr·päl). *Also* **As′sur·na′sir·pal** *or* **A′sur·na′zir·pal** (ä′so͝or·nä′zĭr·päl). Name of two kings of Assyria: **Ashurnasirpal I** (reigned 1038–1020 B.C.). **Ashurnasirpal II** *or* **III** (reigned 884–859 B.C.); one of great conquerors of Assyria; extended boundaries east, west, and north, and moved capital city from Nineveh to Calah (Kalakh); succeeded by his son Shalmaneser III.

**Asiaticus.** See ANTIOCHUS XIII of Syria.

**Asinius Pollio, Gaius.** See POLLIO.

**Askanian dynasty.** = ASCANIAN DYNASTY (see BRANDENBURG).

**As′ke·na′zy** (äs′kĕ·nä′zĭ), **Szymon.** 1867–1935. Polish historian; professor, U. of Lemberg (1897–1914); author of *Napoleon and Poland* (3 vols., 1918); Polish representative at League of Nations.

**As′kew** *or* **As′cue** (ăs′kū), **Anne.** 1521–1546. English Protestant martyr. Burned at stake at Smithfield for refusing to recant her opinions on transubstantiation.

**Asklepiades.** Variant of ASCLEPIADES.

**As′kwith** (ăs′kwĭth), **George Ranken.** 1st Baron **Askwith.** 1861–1942. English industrial conciliator; grad. Oxford. Chief industrial commissioner (1911–19); umpire, Scottish Coal Conciliation Board (1913–15); chairman, government arbitration committee under Munitions of War Acts (1915–17). Author of *Industrial Problems and Disputes* (1920), etc.

**As′ma′ī, al-** (ăl·ăs′mă·ē). *Arab.* **al-Aṣma′ī ′Abd-al-Malik ibn-Quraib.** c. 739–831. Arab scholar; tutor to son of Harun al-Rashid; strove to keep Arab language and literature free from foreign influences; author of *Book of Distinction, Book of the Wild Animals,* etc. Believed by some to have written the romance *Antar.*

**Asmonaean.** Variant of HASMONAEAN.

**Asmus.** See Matthias CLAUDIUS.

**As′nyk** (äs′nĭk), **Adam.** *Pseudonym* **El-y** (ĕl′ĭ). 1838–1897. Polish poet and dramatist, b. Kalisz. His lyrics, among the best in Polish literature, are intellectual and philosophical.

**A·so′ka** (*Pali; pron.* *ȧ*·sō′k*ȧ*) *or* **A·ço′ka** (*Skr.; pron.* *ȧ*·shō′k*ȧ*). *Called* **Asoka the Great.** d. 232 B.C. King of Magadha (273–232) of Maurya dynasty. Son of Bindusara and grandson of Chandragupta. Brought kingdoms of Bengal and Orissa into his great domain (corresponding to nearly all of modern India, Afghanistan, and Baluchistan); brought Kalinga war to successful close (261); converted from Brahmanism to Buddhism (about 261); became zealous supporter of Buddhism, making it the state religion; convoked great Buddhist councils, esp. at Pataliputra (Patna), his capital; left edicts on Buddhism engraved on rocks and pillars in various parts of India that are today records of great value.

**As·pa′si·a** (ăs·pā′shĭ·*ȧ*; -zhĭ·*ȧ*). 470?–410 B.C. Greek adventuress and consort of Pericles, b. probably at Miletus. Noted for her beauty, wit, and learning; at Athens won affection and esteem of Pericles, who married her after divorcing his first wife; exerted great influence over him in many of his public acts; her position in Athenian society still a question of dispute; bore one son named Pericles.

**Aspasia** the Younger. *Real name, according to Plutarch,* **Mil′to** (mĭl′tō). fl. 5th–4th century B.C. Greek beauty, b. in Phocaea (Foça), Asia Minor; presented to Cyrus the Younger, who placed her in his harem and named her Aspasia after the wife of Pericles; on death of Cyrus, became property of Artaxerxes; later claimed by Darius when he was named heir to Persian throne; created priestess by Artaxerxes to prevent her transfer to Darius.

**As′per** (äs′pĕr), **Hans.** 1499–1571. Swiss painter, miniaturist, and woodcut designer; best known for portraits.

**A′sper·ti′ni** (äs′pâr·tē′nē), **Amico.** 1475–1532. Italian painter; pupil and imitator of Francia.

**As'pi·nall** (ăs'pĭ·n'l), Sir **Algernon Edward.** 1871–1952. English vice-president and secretary of West India Committee (1898–1938); author of *The Pocket Guide to the West Indies, West Indian Tales of Old,* and *A Wayfarer in the West Indies.*

**As'pin·wall** (ăs'pĭn·wôl), **William Henry.** 1807–1875. American merchant, b. New York City; promoter of Pacific Mail Steamship Co. (1848) and Panama Railroad (1850–55).

**Asp'land** (ăsp'lănd), **Robert.** 1782–1845. English Unitarian minister.

**As'quith** (ăs'kwĭth), **Herbert Henry.** 1st Earl of **Ox'ford** (ŏks'fẽrd) **and Asquith.** 1852–1928. English statesman. Grad. Balliol, Oxford (1874). Liberal M.P. (1886–1918, 1920–24). Home secretary (1892–95); chancellor of the exchequer (1905–08); prime minister (1908–16). Obtained passage of Parliament Act (1911), abolishing veto power of House of Lords, Home Rule Bill for Ireland, and Welsh Disestablishment Act. Formed (1915) coalition cabinet with Unionists; forced out by Lloyd George (1916). His second wife, **Mar'got** (mär'gō), *orig.* **Emma Alice Margaret** (1864–1945; m. 1894), daughter of Sir Charles Tennant, Glasgow merchant and patron of art, wrote *Autobiography* (1922) and other similar books including *Octavia* (1928) and *More Memories* (1933).

Children of 1st earl: **Raymond**, eldest son; killed in action (1916). **Herbert** (1881–1947), lawyer and author; called to bar (1907); captain in R.F.A. on western front (1915–18); author of verse, as *The Volunteer, A Village Sermon, Pillicock Hill, Poems 1912–1933, Youth in the Skies* (1940), and of the novels *Wind's End, Young Orland, Roon,* and *Mary Dallon.* **Elizabeth** (1897–1945), Princess **Bibesco** by marriage (1919) with Prince Antoine Bibesco (see BIBESCO family); author of *I Have only Myself to Blame* (1921), *Balloons* (1923), *There is No Return* (1927), *Portrait of Caroline* (1931).

**As'se·lyn** *or* **As'se·lin** (äs'ĕ·lĭn), **Jan.** 1610–1652. Dutch landscape painter, b. near Amsterdam.

**As'se·ma'ni** (äs'sā·mä'nē), **Giu·sep'pe** (jōō·zĕp'pā) **Si·mo'ne** (sē·mō'nā). *Arab.* **al'-Sam·a'ni** (ăs'săm·ä'nē). 1687–1768. Syrian Orientalist, b. Tripoli, Syria. Custodian in Vatican Library; made two extensive journeys (1717, 1735) in East collecting Oriental manuscripts for Vatican; created titular archbishop of Tyre; author of several works on Oriental manuscripts, esp. *Bibliotheca Orientalis Clementino-Vaticana* (4 vols., 1719–28). His nephew **Stefano E·vo'dio** (ā·vô'dyō) **Assemani** (1709?–1782), Orientalist and author, b. Tripoli, was custodian in Vatican Library. Another nephew, **Giuseppe A'lo·y'sio** (ä'lō·ē'zyō) **Assemani** (1710–1782), was professor of Oriental languages at Rome. A grandnephew, **Simone Assemani** (1752–1821), b. Tripoli, educ. at Rome, missionary in Syria, was appointed (1785) professor of Oriental languages at Padua; wrote valuable treatise on numismatics (1787) and a work (1787) on Arabic culture, literature, and customs before Mohammed.

**Assen.** Variant of ASEN.

**As'ser** (ăs'ẽr). d. 909? Welsh monk. Studied in household of Alfred the Great six months of each year; wrote life of Alfred. Bishop of Sherborne.

**As'ser** (äs'ẽr), **Tobias Michael Carel.** 1838–1913. Dutch jurist and statesman, b. Amsterdam. Professor of law, Amsterdam (1862–93); member, Dutch council of state (1893); minister of state (1904). Author of several works on international law. Corecipient, with A. H. Fried, of 1911 Nobel peace prize.

**Assisi,** Saint **Francis of.** See FRANCIS OF ASSISI.

**As'sol'lant'** (ȧ'sô'läɴ'), **Jean Baptiste Alfred.** 1827–1886. French writer, esp. of juveniles. Spent some years in U. S. and wrote *Scènes de la Vie aux États-Unis* (1858); his charge that Sardou's play *Uncle Sam* plagiarized this book was dismissed by jury of French authors.

**Assurbanipal.** Variant of ASHURBANIPAL.

**Assurnasirpal.** Variant of ASHURNASIRPAL.

**Ast** (äst), **Georg Anton Friedrich.** 1778–1841. German philologist and writer on philosophy.

**A·staire'** (ȧ·stâr'), **Fred.** *Orig. surname* **Aus'ter·litz** (ôs'tẽr·lĭts). 1899– . American actor and dancer, b. Omaha, Nebr. Starred in musical comedies (with his sister **Adele** from 1916 until her marriage, 1932) and motion pictures (often with Ginger Rogers), including *Gay Divorcee, Roberta, Follow the Fleet,* and *Carefree.*

**As'tell** (ăs't'l), **Mary.** 1668–1731. English author. Wrote (1694) *A Serious Proposal to Ladies,* proposing an establishment for religious retirement of women to be conducted by Church of England; attacked in *Tatler* (No. 52) under name of **Mad'o·nel'la** (măd'ō·nĕl'ȧ).

**As'tle** (ăs''l), **Thomas.** 1735–1803. English antiquary and paleographer; keeper of records, Tower of London (1783); author of *The Origin and Progress of Writing* (1784).

**Ast'ley** (ăst'lĭ), Sir **Jacob.** Baron **Astley.** 1579–1652. English Royalist general. Served in Thirty Years' War. In Civil War commanded infantry at Edge Hill, Gloucester, Naseby; taken prisoner at Stow (1646), and paroled.

**Astley, Philip.** 1742–1814. English equestrian; joined British regiment of light horse (1759); proprietor of circus and hippodrome (known as "Astley's"), London (1770); opened Astley's Royal Amphitheatre, London (1798).

**Astolf.** See AISTULF.

**As'ton** (ăs'tŭn), **Francis William.** 1877–1945. English physicist. Educ. Birmingham and Cambridge universities. Fellow of Trinity College, Cambridge (from 1920). Discovered number of isotopes in several nonradioactive elements by means of mass spectra; awarded 1922 Nobel prize in chemistry. Author of *Isotopes* (1922), *Mass Spectra and Isotopes* (1933), and papers on electric discharge in gases.

**Aston, William George.** 1841–1911. British diplomat and philologist, b. Ireland. M.A. (1863), Queen's U., Ireland. In legation and consular service in Japan and Korea (1864–89). Author of grammars of Japanese spoken and written languages, of *Annals of Ancient Japan* (a translation, 1896), *History of Japanese Literature* (1899), and *Shinto* (1905).

**As'tor** (ăs'tẽr), **John Jacob.** 1763–1848. German-American fur trader and financier, b. Duchy of Baden, Germany. To U.S. (1784); entered fur trade; incorporated American Fur Co. (1808), Pacific Fur Co. (1810). Founded (1811) Astoria, at mouth of Columbia River, as trading post, but lost it to British (1813). Made large and profitable loans to U.S. government (1814); invested heavily in New York real estate; monopolized Mississippi Valley (by 1817) and upper Missouri (1822–34) fur trade. Sold fur interests (1834); devoted himself to administering his fortune. His son **William Backhouse** (1792–1875) administered Astor estate (1848–75); his grandson **John Jacob** (1822–1890) served on McClellan's staff in Civil War, and administered Astor estate (1875–90); his great-grandson **John Jacob** (1864–1912) managed Astor estate (from 1890), served in Spanish-American War, lost his life in *Titanic* disaster.

**Astor, William Waldorf.** 1st Viscount **Astor of He'ver** (hē'vẽr) **Castle.** 1848–1919. Great-grandson of John Jacob Astor. British financier and journalist, b. New York City. Defeated in campaign (1881) for governor of New York State; U.S. minister at Rome (1882–85); published novels *Valentino* (1886) and *Sforza* (1889). To

England (1890); naturalized British subject (1899); proprietor, *Pall Mall Gazette* and *Pall Mall Magazine*. His eldest son, **Waldorf** (1879–1952), 2d viscount, educ. Oxford, served in World War as inspector of quartermaster-general services (1914–17); parliamentary secretary to prime minister (1918), to ministry of food (1918), and to ministry of health (1919–21); owner of *Observer*. His wife **Nancy,** *nee* **Lang′horne** [lăng′ẽrn] (1879–1964), b. Greenwood, Va., m. 1st (1897; divorced 1903) Robert Gould Shaw (d. 1930), 2d (1906) Waldorf Astor; M.P. (1919–45), succeeding her husband in House of Commons when he entered House of Lords as 2d Viscount Astor, thus first woman to sit in British Parliament. Their son, **William Waldorf** (1907–1966), 3d viscount, educ. Oxford, was parliamentary private secretary to Sir Samuel Hoare (1936–37) and to secretary of state for home affairs (1937 ff.). The 2d viscount's brother, **John Jacob** (1886–1971), 1st Baron **Astor of Hever,** army officer, aide-de-camp to viceroy of India (1911–14), served through World War I ; engaged in newspaper business as chairman of Times Publishing Co.

**A·stor′ga** (äs·tôr′gä), Baron **d'. Emanuele Gioacchino Cesare Rin·cón′** (rĕng·kōn′). 1680–?1755. Sicilian composer; known esp. for his *Stabat Mater* (c. 1707); also wrote operas, including *Dafni* (1709).

**As′trid** (ăs′trĭd; *Swed.* ås′-). *In full* **Astrid So·fi′a Lo′vi·sa′ Thy′ra** (sō·fē′ȧ lōō′vĭ·sä′ tü′rä). 1905–1935. Queen of the Belgians. Daughter of Prince Charles, brother of king of Sweden; m. (1926) Prince Leopold (later Leopold III) of Belgium.

**As′truc′** (às′trük′), **Jean.** 1684–1766. French physician. Besides medical works, wrote *Conjectures sur les Mémoires Originaux dont il Paraît que Moïse s'est Servi pour Composer le Livre de la Genèse* (1753), beginning of modern scholarly textual investigation of sources of Pentateuch.

**As′trup** (äs′trōōp), **Eivind.** 1871–1895. Norwegian arctic explorer, b. Oslo. With Peary in Greenland (1891–92, 1893–95).

**As·tu′rias** (äs·tōō′ryäs), Príncipe **de.** *Eng.* Prince of the **As·tu′ri·as** (ăs·tū′rĭ·ȧz). Title (1388–1931) of heir to Spanish throne.

**Asturias, Miguel Angel.** 1899–1974. Guatemalan writer; awarded Nobel prize in literature (1967). Wrote *The President* (1946), *Men of Corn* (1949).

**As·ty′a·ges** (ăs·tī′ȧ·jēz). Last king of Media (reigned c. 584–550 B.C.). Son of Cyaxares. According to Herodotus, Astyages's daughter Mandane married Cambyses and was mother of Cyrus the Great. Attacked Cyrus; seized by his own troops in mutiny; held captive by Cyrus, who seized kingdom. See HARPAGUS.

**Asurbanipal.** Variant of ASHURBANIPAL.

**Atahiyah.** See ABU-AL-ATAHIYAH.

**At′a·hual′pa** (ăt′ȧ·wäl′pȧ; *Span.* ä′tä·wäl′pä) *or* **A′ta·ba′li·pa** (ä′tä·bä′lē·pä). 1500?–1533. Last Inca king of Peru. On death (1525) of his father, Huayna Capac, disputed kingdom with his half brother Huáscar, whom he defeated and captured; at Cajamarca was treacherously arrested (1532) and condemned to death by Pizarro on his refusal to become a Christian; killed by strangulation.

**Atatürk, Kemal.** See KEMAL ATATÜRK.

**At′a·ul′phus** (ăt′ȧ·ŭl′fŭs). *Latinized form of* **At′a·wulf** (ăt′ȧ·wŏŏlf) *or* **At′a·ulf** (ăt′ȧ·ŭlf). d. 415 A.D. King of the Visigoths; brother-in-law and successor (410) of Alaric. Withdrew Goths from Italy into Gaul; made alliance with Emperor Honorius, whose half sister Galla Placidia he married; led army across Pyrenees into Spain; assassinated at Barcelona.

**Atch′i·son** (ăch′ĭ·s'n), **Joseph Anthony.** 1895– . American sculptor and painter, b. Washington, D.C.

**A·thal′a·ric** (ȧ·thăl′ȧ·rĭk). 516–534. Grandson and successor (526) of Theodoric, king of Ostrogoths in Italy.

**Ath′a·li′ah** (ăth′ȧ·lī′ȧ). *In Douay Bible* **Ath′a·li′a** (-ȧ). d. 836 B.C. Queen of Judah (c. 842–836). Daughter of Ahab and wife of Jehoram, King of Judah. On death of her son King Ahaziah (*q.v.*), usurped throne (*2 Kings* xi) and exterminated all sons of Ahaziah except Joash, who six years later was made king as result of priestly insurrection; slain in revolt. Subject of Racine's tragedy *Athalie.*

**A·than′a·gild** (ȧ·thăn′ȧ·gĭld). d. 547. King of Visigoths in Spain (534); father of Brunhilde (*q.v.*).

**A·than′a·ric** (ȧ·thăn′ȧ·rĭk). d. 381. Chief of Visigoths in Dacia (c. 366–380). Defeated (369) by Roman Emperor Valens, and (376) by Huns; died in Byzantium while seeking aid from Emperor Theodosius.

**Ath′a·na′si·us** (ăth′ȧ·nā′shĭ·ŭs; -sĭ·ŭs; -shŭs), Saint. *Called* **Athanasius the Great.** 293?–373. Greek father of the church; lifelong opponent of Arianism; controversialist, for many years referred to as "Athanasius contra mundum"; also known as "Father of Orthodoxy." Early a student of theology; attended Council of Nicaea (325) as deacon. Patriarch of Alexandria (328–373). Refused to obey command of emperor to reinstate Arius; tried by partisan Council of Tyre (325) and exiled to Trier, Germany; advocated Homoousian doctrine; allowed to return to Alexandria (337) by Constantius; again exiled (339 or 340) by powerful Arians; found asylum with Pope Julius I; vindicated (343) by Western Council at Sardica; allowed to return to his see (346); worked in peace ten years; wrote *Defense against the Arians;* exiled third time (356–362); lived mostly with Egyptian hermits; during this exile wrote, among other books, his greatest doctrinal work, *Discourses against the Arians;* in Alexandria (362) but soon exiled for fourth time (362) by Julian; brought back (363) by Jovian and driven out a fifth time (365) by Valens; soon restored and during last years (366–373) continued his labors at Alexandria. Author of *History of the Arians, On the Decrees of the Nicene Synod,* and a series of festal epistles. Not author of Athanasian Creed, which originated later (5th or 6th century).

**Ath′el·stan** *or* **Æth′el·stan** (ăth′ĕl·stăn). 895–940. King of England. Son of King Edward the Elder; grandson of King Alfred. Crowned king of West Saxons and Mercians (c. 924); made Northumbria tributary; invaded Scotland (933 or 934); defeated league of Welsh, Scots, and Danes at Brunanburh (937) and established himself king of greater part of what is now England.

**Ath′e·nae′us** (ăth′ē·nē′ŭs). Greek scholar of late 2d and early 3d century A.D., of Naucratis, Egypt. His only extant work, *The Deipnosophists* (15 books), contains much miscellaneous information, not only about foods but also about contemporary music, songs, dances, games, and other social diversions.

**Ath′e·nag′o·ras** (ăth′ē·năg′ō·răs). Athenian Christian apologist of 2d century; his *Apology,* or *Legatio Pro Christianis,* addressed to Emperor Marcus Aurelius Antoninus, defends Christians against charges of atheism, incest, and cannibalism.

**Athenas, Georges.** See Marius and Ary LEBLOND.

**A·the′no·do′rus** (ȧ·thē′nō·dō′rŭs). Greek sculptor of 1st century B.C., from Rhodes; collaborated with Agesander and Polydorus in carving Laocoön group.

**Athenodorus.** Two Stoic philosophers of 1st century B.C.: **Athenodorus Ca′na·ni′tes** [kā′nȧ·nī′tēz] (c. 74 B.C.–7 A.D.), a tutor of Octavius; **Athenodorus Cor·dyl′i·on** [kôr·dĭl′ĭ·ŏn] (d. after 47 B.C.), librarian at Pergamum.

**Ath′er·ton** (ăth′ẽr·tŭn; -t'n), **Gertrude Franklin,** *nee*

**Horn** (hôrn). 1857–1948. American novelist, b. San Francisco, m. George H. Bowen Atherton (d. 1887). Author of *The Californians* (1898), *The Conqueror* (1902), *Tower of Ivory* (1910), *Mrs. Balfame* (1916), *Black Oxen* (1923), *The Sophisticates* (1931), *Golden Peacock* (1936), *The House of Lee* (1940), *The Horn of Life* (1942), etc.

**Ath·lone′** (ăth·lōn′), 1st Earl of. See Godert de GINKEL.

**Athlone,** 1st Earl of (2d creation). **Alexander Augustus Frederick William Alfred George Cam′bridge** (kām′-brĭj). 1874–1957. British army officer. Bro. of Queen Mary and uncle of George VI; m. Princess Alice, granddaughter of Queen Victoria. Served in Matabele campaign (1896), Boer War (1899–1900), World War (1914–19); governor general of Union of South Africa (1923–31); governor general of Canada (1940–45).

**Ath′oll** *or* **Ath′ole** (ăth′ŭl), Earls, marquises, and dukes of. Original form **Atholl** restored 1893. Scottish titles held by members of **Murray** line after reversion (1595) of earldom to crown on death of 5th earl of Stewart line (see *earls of Atholl,* under STEWART family), including: **John Murray** (d. 1642), 1st earl of Murray line; led men on king's side in Civil War; imprisoned (1640) by marquis of Argyll. His son **John** (1631–1703), 2d earl and 1st marquis; Royalist leader; supported rising in favor of Charles II, under command of 9th earl of Glencairn (1653); held high offices after Restoration, including justice-generalship of Scotland (1670–78); deprived on joining in remonstrance to king against Lauderdale's severities inflicted on Covenanters (1678); lord lieutenant of Argyll (1684); captured earl of Argyll (1685); wavered at revolution; implicated in Jacobite plots and intrigues; pardoned; acted as negotiator in pacification of Highlands. John's (1631–1703) son **John** (1660–1724), 2d marquis and 1st duke (created 1703); supported William and Glorious Revolution (1688) in spite of urging of his bro., Lord Charles Murray, earl of Dunmore (*q.v.*) to support King James; kept clear of Jacobite plot against Queen Anne despite intrigues of Simon Lord Lovat and his tool, duke of Queensberry; secured Queensberry's downfall (1703); privy councilor, lord privy seal (1703); opposed union (1705–07); took no part in invasion of 1708; deprived on accession of George I; remained faithful to government despite sons' participation in Jacobite rebellion (1715); captured (1717) Rob Roy Macgregor. John's (1660–1724) son **James** (1690?–1764), 2d duke; lord privy seal (1733–63); keeper of the great seal and lord justice general (1763). James's brother George was a Jacobite general (see Lord George MURRAY) and father of **John** (1729–1774), 3d duke, who sold the sovereignty of Isle of Man to the treasury (1765). His son **John** (1755–1830), 4th duke, was created Earl Strange in peerage of Great Britain (1786). Sir **John James Hugh Henry Stewart-Murray** (1840–1917), 7th duke (succeeded 1864); inherited the Percy barony (1865); lord lieutenant of Perth (from 1878); hon. colonel in Black Watch (1903). His son **John George Stewart-Murray** (1871–1942), 8th duke, British cavalry officer, educ. Eton, served on Nile expedition (1896–98) in battles of Atbara and Khartoum (1898), and in South Africa (1899–1902); commanded Scottish cavalry in Gallipoli and Egypt in World War. M.P. (1910–17). His wife (m. 1899), **Katharine Marjory** (1874–1960), daughter of Sir James Henry Ramsay; educ. Royal College of Music; organizer and member of many charitable services and of educational, agricultural, hospital, and other committees; M.P. (1923–38).

**Ath′ol·stan** (ăth′ŭl·stăn), 1st Baron. **Hugh Graham.** 1848–1938. Canadian journalist, b. Huntingdon, Que.; founder (1869) and proprietor of Montreal *Star.*

**Athulf.** Variant of ETHELWULF.

**At′kins** (ăt′kĭnz), Sir **Ivor** (ī′vẽr) **Algernon.** 1869–1953. English organist and choirmaster of Worcester Cathedral (from 1897); president, Royal Coll. of Organists (1935, 1936). Composer of *Hymn of Faith* (with libretto arranged by Sir Edward Elgar).

**At′kin·son** (ăt′kĭn·s'n), **Brooks,** *in full* **Justin Brooks.** 1894– . American dramatic critic, b. Melrose, Mass. Grad. Harvard (1917). Dramatic critic, New York *Times* (1925–42). Author of *Skyline Promenades* (1925), *Henry Thoreau, the Cosmic Yankee* (1927), *East of the Hudson* (1931), etc.

**Atkinson, Edward.** 1827–1905. American textile manufacturer and writer on economic subjects; b. Brookline, Mass.

**Atkinson, Eleanor,** *nee* **Stack′house** (stăk′hous). 1863–1942. American writer; m. (1891) Francis Blake Atkinson. Author of *Mamzelle Fifine* (1903), *Greyfriars Bobby* (1912), *Johnny Appleseed* (1915), *Poilu, a Dog of Roubaix* (1918), etc.

**Atkinson,** Sir **Harry Albert.** 1831–1892. New Zealand statesman, b. and educ. in England; to N.Z. (1855). Prime minister (1876–77, 1883–84, 1887–91); successful in abolition of provinces and in introduction of economies in public expenditure.

**Atkinson, John.** 1835–1897. American Methodist Episcopal clergyman, b. Deerfield, N.Y. Author of *The Centennial History of American Methodism, 1784–1816* (1884) and the hymn *Shall We Meet Beyond the River.*

**Atkinson, John Augustus.** 1775–1831. English painter. Lived in Russia (1784–1801); exhibited at Royal Academy (1802–29); made book plates representing Russian manners and customs (1803–04) and panorama of St. Petersburg (1805); exhibited (1812) *Seven Ages,* pictorial representation of famous passage in Shakespeare's *As You Like It,* and (1819) his masterpiece, *Battle of Waterloo.*

**Atkinson, Louisa.** See Caroline L. W. CALVERT.

**Atkinson, Thomas.** 1807–1881. American Protestant Episcopal bishop, b. in Dinwiddie County, Va. Consecrated bishop of North Carolina (1853). Instrumental in reuniting northern and southern branches of church after Civil War.

**Atkinson, Thomas Dinham.** 1864–1948. English architect and writer; architect to dean and chapter of Winchester Cathedral and to warden and fellows of Winchester Coll. Author of *English Architecture* (1904), *Key to English Architecture* (1936), etc.

**Atkinson, Thomas Witlam.** 1799–1861. English architect. Wrote and illustrated journals (1858, 1860) of his travels in western Siberia.

**At′kyns** (ăt′kĭnz), Sir **Edward.** 1587–1669. English jurist; defended Prynne before Star Chamber on libel charge resulting from publication of *Histriomastix.*

**Atli.** See ATTILA.

**A·tos′sa** (ȧ·tŏs′ȧ). fl. 6th century B.C. Persian queen; wife of (1) her brother Cambyses, (2) of the Magian Smerdis, and (3) of Darius I Hystaspis (*q.v.*); mother of Xerxes I. Exerted great influence over Darius.

**Atossa.** Nickname of duchess of Marlborough (see under John CHURCHILL).

**At′ta·lus** (ăt′ȧ·lŭs). Name of three kings of Pergamum, the Attalids:

**Attalus I.** *Surnamed* **So′ter** (sō′tẽr). 269–197 B.C. King (241–197). Refused tribute to Gauls of Galatia; defeated them decisively (before 230); became master of all Asia Minor west of Mt. Taurus, defeating Antiochus Hierax in three battles (229–228); ally of Rome against Philip V of Macedon (211–204); patron of arts. Father of Eumenes II and Attalus II.

**Attalus II.** *Surnamed* **Phil'a·del'phus** (fĭl'ȧ·dĕl'fŭs). 220–138 B.C. King (160?–138). Able soldier; frequently sent as ambassador to Rome; succeeded his brother Eumenes II as king; as patron of arts, kept Pergamum as center of Hellenistic culture.

**Attalus III.** *Surnamed* **Phil'o·me'tor** (fĭl'ō·mē'tôr). 171–133 B.C. King (138–133). Nephew of Attalus II. Eccentric sovereign, represented as dilletante in literature and art; bequeathed his kingdom to Rome.

**Attalus, Flavius Priscus.** d. after 416. Emperor of Rome (409–410). Probably Ionian Greek; prefect of Rome when it was besieged by Alaric (409); proclaimed emperor by Alaric in place of Honorius; deposed by Alaric (410); banished by Honorius (416).

**At'tar** (ăt'ẽr). *Pers.* **'Aṭ·ṭār'** (ät·tär'), *i.e., literally,* perfume, attar of roses, *hence* druggist. *In full* **Farid ud-din Attar.** *Also* **Ferid Eddin Attar.** *Pers.* **Farīd ud-dīn 'Aṭṭār,** *literally* pearl of the faith, druggist. *Real name* **Mohammed ibn-Ibrahim.** 1119–?1229. Persian mystic poet, b. Nishapur. Druggist by trade (hence the name *Attar*); student of Sufism; traveled extensively in Egypt, India, and Turkestan; spent most of life at Nishapur. Wrote many poems, his most famous being *Mantiq ut-Tair* (Language of Birds), a very popular allegorical poem of 4600 couplets containing a complete survey of the life and doctrine of the Sufis; author also of *Pandnāmah* (Book of Counsel), *Bulbul Nāmah* (Book of the Nightingale), and a book of memoirs of the Mohammedan saints.

**Attendolo, Giacomuzzo.** See SFORZA.

**At'ter·berg** (ȧt'tẽr·băr'y'), **Kurt.** 1887– . Swedish composer and orchestra conductor; best known for his symphonies.

**At'ter·bom** (ȧt'tẽr·bo͝om), **Per Daniel Amadeus.** 1790–1855. Swedish poet, philosopher, and literary historian. Author of *The Flowers* (1812), *The Island of Blessedness* (1823), *Swedish Seers and Poets* (6 vols., 1841–55), etc.

**At'ter·bur'y** (ăt'ẽr·bĕr'ĭ; -bẽr·ĭ), **Francis.** 1662–1732. English ecclesiastic and controversialist. Educ. Oxford. Dean of Carlisle (1704); bishop of Rochester and dean of Westminster (1713). Deprived and banished for complicity in Jacobite plots (1723).

**Atterbury, William Wallace.** 1866–1935. American railway executive, b. New Albany, Ind. Grad. Yale (1886). Apprentice in Altoona (Pa.) shops of Pennsylvania Railroad (1886); rose to presidency of railroad (1925–35). During World War, director of construction and operation of U.S. military railways in France (1917–19).

**At'ter·idge** (ăt'ẽr·ĭj), **Harold Richard.** 1886–1938. American librettist, b. Lake Forest, Ill.; wrote esp. for revues, including the series *The Passing Show* (10 annual editions, 1912 ff.) and *Artists and Models.*

**At'ti·cus** (ăt'ĭ·kŭs), **Titus Pomponius.** 109–32 B.C. Original name Titus Pomponius; surname Atticus added because of his long residence in Athens. Roman literary patron; intimate friend and correspondent of Cicero; edited Cicero's letters written to him.

**Atticus Herodes.** See HERODES ATTICUS.

**At'ti·la** (ăt'ĭ·lȧ). 406?–453. King of the Huns (433?–453); known as "the Scourge of God." At first (433–441) occupied with wars with other barbarian tribes; extended his power over central Europe; exacted large tribute and concessions from Theodosius II, Emperor of the East; overran Balkan countries (447–450), causing great destruction. On refusal (450) of tribute by Emperor Marcian, turned his armies to West; invaded Gaul (451) but forced to give up siege of Orléans; retired to Catalaunian Plains on Marne; defeated there, in battle of Châlons-sur-Marne (June, 451), one of decisive battles of history, by combined armies of Romans under Aëtius and Visigoths under Theodoric and Thorismond; pursued across Rhine. Invaded northern Italy (452), devastating region and destroying Aquileia; yielded to intercession of Pope Leo I and recrossed Alps; died suddenly on eve of new invasion of Italy. Appears under name **Et'zel** (ĕt'sĕl) as legendary king in *Nibelungenlied* and as **At'li** (ät'lē) in *Volsunga Saga.* See also HONORIA.

**Attius, Lucius.** See ACCIUS.

**Att'lee** (ăt'lē; -lē), 1st Earl **Clement Richard.** Viscount **Prestwood.** 1883–1967. English labor leader and politician, b. London. Grad. Oxford; studied law; lecturer (1913–22), London School of Economics; undersecretary for war (1924); postmaster general (1931); leader of Labor opposition in Commons (1935); member of war cabinet, as lord privy seal (1940), minister of dominion affairs and deputy prime minister (1942); prime minister (1945–51).

**At'tucks** (ăt'ŭks), **Crispus.** 1723?–1770. American mulatto or, perhaps, of mixed Negro and Indian blood; leader of mob in "Boston Massacre" and one of three men killed by fire of British troops.

**Att'wood** (ăt'wo͝od), **Thomas.** 1765–1838. English musician and composer. Pupil under Mozart (1785); organist (1796 till death), St. Paul's Cathedral, London. Composed two coronation anthems, glees, and *The Soldier's Dream* and other songs.

**Attwood, Thomas.** 1783–1856. English political reformer; son of Birmingham banker; organized Political Union (1830) for reform of franchise; M.P. (1832–39); supported Chartists.

**At'wa'ter** (ăt'wô'tẽr; -wŏt'ẽr), **Wilbur Olin.** 1844–1907. American agricultural chemist, b. Johnsburg, N.Y. Professor, Wesleyan U. (1873–1907). Director (1875–77), first state agricultural station in U.S., Middletown, Conn. Founder and chief, Office of Experiment Stations, U.S. Dept. of Agriculture (1888 ff.). Conducted experiments in calorimetry.

**At'wood** (ăt'wo͝od), **George.** 1746–1807. English mathematician. Grad. Trinity, Cambridge (1769). Author of mathematical works and inventor of Atwood's machine for verifying laws of acceleration of motion.

**Atwood, Wallace Walter.** 1872–1949. American geologist and geographer, b. Chicago. Grad. U. of Chicago (1897). Professor, Harvard (1913–20). President of Clark U. (1920–46). Founder and editor of *Economic Geography* (1925). Author of *The World At Work* (1931), *The Growth of Nations* (1936), etc. Special editor for physical geography, *Webster's New International Dictionary, Second Edition.*

**Au'ba'nel'** (ō'bȧ'nĕl'), **Théodore.** 1829–1886. French Provençal poet, b. Avignon. A leader of group (Félibrige) of Provençal writers striving for maintenance and purification of Provençal as a literary language.

**Au'ber'** (ō'bâr'), **Daniel François Esprit.** 1782–1871. French composer; pupil of Cherubini. Writer of grand operas and comic operas, his works including *La Muette de Portici, Fra Diavolo, Le Philtre, Le Domino Noir,* etc. Regarded as founder of French grand opera. Duet "Amour Sacré de la Patrie," in *La Muette de Portici,* said to have been used as signal, in Brussels, for revolution of 1830.

**Au'bert'** (ō'bâr'), **Jacques.** d. 1753. French violinist and composer; author of opera *La Reine des Péris,* and violin sonatas, ballets, etc.

**Aubert, Louis François Marie.** 1877–1968. French pianist and composer; author of the opera *La Forêt Bleue,* the symphonic poem *Habanera,* a fantasia for piano and orchestra, many songs, piano pieces, etc.

**Au'bi'gnac'** (ō'bē'nyȧk'), Abbé **d'. François Hé'de·lin'** (ā'dlăN'). 1604–1676. French dramatic critic; author of

*Pratique du Théâtre* (1657), and *Conjectures Académiques sur l'Iliade* (pub. 1715) in which he was one of first to question authorship of Homeric poems.

**Au'bi'gné'** (ō'bē'nyā'), **Jean Henri Merle d'.** See MERLE D'AUBIGNÉ.

**Aubigné, Théodore Agrippa d'.** 1552–1630. French Huguenot commander and author; served under Condé and Henry of Navarre; in exile at Geneva (from 1620). Wrote poetical works, satire, and histories.

**Au'bi'gny'** (ō'bē'nyē'), Seigneurs of. See *earls and dukes of Lennox*, under STEWART family.

**Au'brey** (ô'brĭ), **John.** 1626–1697. English antiquary. Educ. Oxford. Author of *Miscellanies* (1696), consisting of ghost stories and folklore, and of *Minutes of Lives* (first pub. 1813), including vivid portrayals of Bacon, Milton, Raleigh, Hobbes, and others.

**Au'bry' de La Bou'char'de·rie'** (ō'brē' dē là bōō'-shȧr'dē·rē'), Comte **Claude Charles.** 1773–1813. French artillery general under Napoleon; killed at Leipzig.

**Au'bry' de Mont'di'dier'** (môɴ'dē'dyā'). French knight of Charles V's court; murdered (1371) by a companion, and revenged, according to legend, by his dog.

**Au'bus'son'** (ō'bü'sôɴ'), **Pierre d'.** 1423–1503. French grand master of Knights of St. John of Jerusalem (from 1476); defended Rhodes against Turks (1480); created cardinal (1489). See JEM.

**Au'chin·closs** (ô'kĭn·klŏs), **Louis Stanton.** 1917– . Am. lawyer and author, b. New York.

**Au'chin·leck'** (ô'kĭn·lĕk'; ô'kĭn-), Sir **Claude John Eyre.** 1884– . British general; educ. Wellington Coll. and Sandhurst; served with distinction in Egypt, Aden, and Mesopotamia during World War I (D.S.O., 1917); active in operations against Mohmands on northwest frontier of India (1933, 1935); instrumental in mechanizing Indian army; transferred to England (1939), he led the ineffectual expedition occupying Narvik in Norway (1940); head of Southern Command, England; commander in chief in India (1940–41 and 1943); general (1941) and commander in chief in the Middle East (1942); field marshal (1946); supreme commander in India and Pakistan (1947).

**Auch·mu'ty** (ôk·mū'tĭ), Sir **Samuel.** 1756–1822. British general, b. New York. Served in British army during American Revolution, in India, at Cape, in Egypt, in campaign against Buenos Aires (1806–08), and in Java; commander in chief in Ireland (1821). His father, **Samuel** (1722–1777), was rector (1764–77) of Trinity Church, New York.

**Auckland,** Baron, and Earl of. See William and George EDEN.

**Au'de·bert'** (ōd'bâr'), **Jean Baptiste.** 1759–1800. French naturalist and engraver; produced plates illustrating animals and birds.

**Aude'lay** (ôd'lĭ), **John.** = John AWDELAY.

**Au'den** (ô'd'n), **Wystan Hugh.** 1907–1973. Am. (English-born) poet; educ. Oxford; m. (1935) Erika Mann (*q.v.*); to U.S. (1939); returned to England (1972). Author of *Poems* (1930), *The Orators* (1932). *The Dance of Death* (1933), *Look, Stranger!* (1936), *Another Time* (1940), *The Double Man* (1941), *Collected Poetry* (1945), *The Dyer's Hand* (essays; 1962), *About the House* (1965), *Collected Shorter Poems* (1966), *Collected Longer Poems* (1968), *City Without Walls* (1969). Editor of *Oxford Book of Light Verse* (1938). Frequent collaborator with Christopher Isherwood (*q.v.*), as in *The Dog Beneath the Skin* (play; 1935), *The Ascent of F6* (play; 1936), *On the Frontier* (play; 1938), *Journey to a War* (1939); collaborator also with Louis MacNeice in *Letters from Iceland* (1937); with Chester Kallman, wrote opera librettos, as for Stravinsky's *Rake's Progress* (1951).

**Au'dif'fret'–Pas'quier'** (ō'dē'frĕ'pä'kyā'), Duc **Edme Armand Gaston d'.** 1823–1905. French statesman; president of National Assembly (1875); appointed senator for life (1875); president of senate (1876–79).

**Aud'ley** *or* **Aude'ley** (ôd'lĭ), Sir **James.** 1316?–1386. English knight. One of original knights companions of Order of the Garter, instituted (c. 1348) by Edward III. Fought under Black Prince in France; governor of Aquitaine (1362); grand seneschal of Poitou (1369).

**Aud'ley** (ôd'lĭ), **Thomas.** Baron **Audley of Wal'den** (wôl'dĕn). 1488–1544. English lord chancellor. Presided as speaker of "black parliament" (1529); lord chancellor (1533) after supporting Henry VIII in divorcing Catherine of Aragon; presided at trial of Sir Thomas More (1535); tried Anne Boleyn (1536); carried through parliament attainder of Thomas Cromwell and dissolution of Henry's marriage with Anne of Cleves (1540); founded Magdalene College, Cambridge.

**Au'dou·in'** (ō'dwăɴ'), **Jean Victor.** 1797–1841. Pioneer French entomologist.

**Au'dran'** (ō'dräɴ'), **Edmond.** 1842–1901. French composer of oratorios, operettas, and vaudeville pieces. His father, **Marius** (1816–1887) was a singer.

**Au'du·bon** (ô'dōō·bŏn; -dū-; -bŭn), **John James.** 1785–1851. American ornithologist and artist, b. in Haiti; natural son of Jean Audubon, a French mercantile agent, and a Creole woman; legally adopted (1794) in Nantes, France, as son of Jean Audubon and his wife. To America (1803); settled near Philadelphia. To Kentucky (1808); opened general store in Louisville, transferring later to various other cities; began painting birds from life; bankrupt in business (1819); to Cincinnati; voyaged down Mississippi observing and painting birds; tutor and drawing teacher in New Orleans and St. Francisville, La.; took his work to England, seeking a publisher (1826). *Birds of America* (1827–38), *Ornithological Biography* (1839), and (with MacGillivray) *Synopsis of the Birds of North America* (1839) established his reputation. Settled (1841–51) on his estate, now Audubon Park, New York City, working at but not completing *The Viviparous Quadrupeds of North America* (with Bachman). Elected to American Hall of Fame (1900).

**Aue, Hartmann von.** See HARTMANN VON AUE.

**Au'en·brug'ger von Au'en·brugg** (ou'ĕn·brŏŏg'ĕr fôn ou'ĕn·brŏŏk), **Leopold.** 1722–1809. Physician in Vienna; discoverer of percussion method of detecting diseases of thorax and lungs.

**Au'er** (ou'ĕr), **Le'o·pold** (lā'ô·pôlt). 1845–1930. Hungarian violinist and teacher. Professor (1868), Conservatory of Music, St. Petersburg; director (1888–92), Russian Imperial Music Society symphony concerts. To N.Y. (1918); became famed as teacher; among pupils were Heifetz, Mischa Elman, and Zimbalist.

**Au'er·bach** (ou'ĕr·bäκ), **Berthold.** 1812–1882. German novelist and story writer; known esp. for his pictures of life in Black Forest. His fiction includes *Spinoza* (1837), *Schwarzwälder Dorfgeschichten* (1st series, 1843), *Barfüssele* (1856), *Edelweiss* (1861), *Auf der Höhe* (1865).

**Au'ers·perg** (ou'ĕrs·pĕrκ), Count **Anton Alexander von.** *Pseudonym* **Anastasius Grün** (grün). 1806–1876. Poet and statesman of liberal sympathies, b. in Austria.

**Auersperg,** Prince **Carlos.** 1814–1890. Austrian statesman. Member, Bohemian diet; president, Austrian upper chamber (1861); defended constitutional system against clerical and feudal reaction, and championed unity of the empire; president, Austrian ministry (1867–68); supported Liberal cabinet of his brother Prince **Adolf Wilhelm** (1821–1885), who was premier (1871–79) of Cisleithan reform ministry. Adolf's son Prince **Karl** (1859–1927) was a member (1894–1902) of Lower Austrian diet, and for several years leader of Constitution party in upper chamber.

**Auerstædt,** Duc **d'.** See Louis Nicolas DAVOUT.

**Auer von Welsbach, Aloys** and **Carl.** See WELSBACH.

**Auf'fen·berg** (ouf'ĕn·bĕrK), Baron **Josef von.** 1798–1857. German dramatist; author of *Pizarro* (1823), *Die Spartaner, Alhambra, Das Nordlicht von Kasan,* etc.

**Auf'fen·berg von Ko·ma'rów** (ouf'ĕn·bĕrK fôn kō-mä'rōōf), Baron **Moritz.** 1852–1928. Austro-Hungarian general, b. Troppau. Commanding general, Sarajevo (1909); minister of war (1911; dismissed, 1912); commanded 4th Austrian army at beginning of World War; victorious at Komarów (1914); imprisoned (1915) on charges of irregularities as war minister; acquitted.

**Auf'recht** (ouf'rĕKt), **Theodor.** 1822–1907. German Sanskrit scholar and philologist, b. in Upper Silesia. Professor of Sanskrit, Edinburgh (1862), Bonn (1875–89). Cofounder, with Adalbert Kuhn, of *Zeitschrift für Vergleichende Sprachforschung.*

**Au'ge·reau'** (ōzh'rō'), **Pierre François Charles.** Duc **de Ca'sti·glio'ne** (käs'tē·lyō'nā). 1757–1816. French soldier, b. Paris; distinguished himself at Lodi and Castiglione (1796); carried through coup d'état of 18 Fructidor (Sept. 4, 1797); created marshal of France by Napoleon; served in Napoleonic armies throughout empire period.

**Au'gier'** (ō'zhyā'), **Émile,** *in full* **Guillaume Victor Émile.** 1820–1889. French poet and dramatist, b. Valence. Grandson of C. A. G. Pigault-Lebrun. His plays, chiefly comedies of manners and social satires, include *Gabrielle* (1849), *Le Gendre de Monsieur Poirier* (with Jules Sandeau; 1854), *Le Mariage d'Olympe* (1855), *Les Lionnes Pauvres* (1858), *Les Effrontés* (1861), *Maître Guérin* (1864), *Lions et Renards* (1869), *Madame Caverlet* (1876), *Les Fourchambault* (1878).

**Au'gust** (ou'gōōst). German form of AUGUSTUS.

**August.** *In full* **Friedrich Wilhelm Heinrich August.** 1779–1843. Prince of Prussia; nephew of Frederick the Great. Served in Prussian army against Napoleon, esp. as brigade and corps commander in campaigns of 1813–15.

**Au·gus'ta** (ô·gŭs'tȧ; *Ger.* ou·gōōs'tä). d. 1772. Princess of Saxe-Coburg-Gotha; m. (1736) Frederick Louis, Prince of Wales. Mother of George III of England.

**Au·gu'sta** (ou·gōōs'tä). *In full* **Marie Luise Katharina Augusta.** 1811–1890. Empress of Germany as wife of William I (*q.v.*).

**Au·gus'ta Vic·to'ri·a** (ô·gŭs'tȧ vĭk·tō'rĭ·ȧ). *Ger.* **Au·gu'ste Vik·to'ri·a** (ou·gōōs'tĕ vĭk·tō'rē·ä). 1858–1921. Empress of Germany as wife of William II (*q.v.*).

**Au'gus·tine** (ô'gŭs·tēn; ô·gŭs'tĭn), Saint. *Lat.* **Aurelius Au'gus·ti'nus** (ô'gŭs·tī'nŭs). 354–430. Early Christian church father and philosopher, b. Tagaste (Souk-Ahras) in eastern Numidia. Originally a Manichaean; came under influence of Bishop Ambrose of Milan; after passing through spiritual crisis, converted to Christianity and baptized (Easter, 387). Returned to Tagaste and ordained priest (391); consecrated bishop, with right of succession to Hippo in proconsular Africa (395); bishop of Hippo (396–430). By sermons, pastoral letters, and books, came to exercise enormous influence throughout Christian world; stood forth esp. as champion of orthodoxy against Manichaeans, Donatists, and Pelagians. His most famous works are *De Civitate Dei* (*The City of God*) and his autobiography, *Confessiones.*

**Augustine,** Saint. *Also* **Aus'tin** (ôs'tĭn). d. 604. First archbishop of Canterbury; known as the "Apostle of the English." Sent (596), with forty monks, as missionary to the English by Pope Gregory I; baptized Ethelbert, King of Kent (597); consecrated bishop of the English (597) at Arles; archbishop (601); founded monastery of Christ Church, Canterbury.

**Augustinus, Antonius.** See Antonio AGUSTÍN.

**Augustsohn, W.** Pseudonym of Wilhelm von KOTZEBUE.

**Augustulus, Romulus.** See ROMULUS AUGUSTULUS.

**Au·gus'tus** (ô·gŭs'tŭs). *Original name* **Ga'ius Oc·ta'vi·us** (gā'yŭs ŏk·tā'vĭ·ŭs). *After his adoption* **Gaius Julius Caesar Oc·ta'vi·a'nus** (ŏk·tā'vĭ·ā'nŭs). *Sometimes known in early life as* **Octavianus,** *Eng.* **Oc·ta'vi·an** (ŏk·tā'vĭ·ăn). 63 B.C.–14 A.D. First Roman emperor (27 B.C.–14 A.D.). Son of Octavius and Atia (daughter of Julia, youngest sister of Julius Caesar); b. Rome. Carefully educated; talents brought him into favor of his great-uncle Julius Caesar, who adopted him as son and heir (45 B.C.). After death of Caesar (44 B.C.), gained control in Italy, aided by Cicero; joined Mark Antony and Lepidus in establishing Second Triumvirate (43 B.C.), receiving at first Africa, Sardinia, and Sicily as his domains; with Antony, defeated Brutus and Cassius at Philippi (42 B.C.); after Philippi, received Italy as his portion. His sister Octavia married Antony (40 B.C.). Fought Sicilian War against Pompey (38–36 B.C.); rivalry with Antony finally settled by defeat of Antony and Cleopatra at battle of Actium (31 B.C.). Became sole ruler of Roman world; closed temple of Janus (27 B.C.); received title of "Augustus" (exalted, sacred), conferred by senate (27 B.C.), and, later, other titles; retained consular office, but sometimes granted it to others for certain periods; inaugurated reforms and beneficial laws. Made his stepson Tiberius his heir and successor (4 A.D.); added to empire by victories in Spain, Pannonia, Dalmatia, and Gaul, but his legions suffered terrible defeat (9 A.D.; see ARMINIUS), when army of Publius Quintilius Varus (*q.v.*) was totally destroyed by Germans; died on journey to Campania. A ruler of administrative ability and initiative; promoted agriculture and the arts, his reign (Augustan age) marking golden age of Latin literature. Married (1) Claudia, who had no children; (2) Scribonia, whose daughter Julia married three times and had five children by her second husband (see AGRIPPINA); (3) Livia Drusilla (divorced wife of Tiberius Claudius Nero), who had two sons (stepsons of Augustus), Tiberius, later emperor, and Drusus (d. 9 B.C. at age of 30). Met with domestic sorrows throughout his life, esp. because of conduct of his daughter Julia, who was banished for her excesses, and because he had no son, and his nephew, grandsons, and favorite stepson, Drusus, all died young.

**Au·gus'tus** (ô·gŭs'tŭs). *Ger.* **Au'gust** (ou'gōōst). 1526–1586. Elector of Saxony (1553–86). Son of Henry the Pious; brother of Maurice, whom he succeeded. Embraced Lutheranism (1574) through influence of his wife (m. 1584) **Anna,** daughter of Christian III of Denmark; instrumental in securing adoption (1580) of *Formula Concordiae,* a creed of Lutheran orthodoxy; as ruler, introduced many reforms and improvements.

**Augustus.** Name of three kings of Poland:

**Augustus I.** See SIGISMUND II AUGUSTUS (1548–1572).

**Augustus II.** *Called* **Augustus the Strong.** 1670–1733. King (1697–1704, 1709–33); b. Dresden. Elector of Saxony (1694–1733) under name of **Frederick Augustus I.** Made alliance (1701) with Peter the Great, but forced by Charles XII of Sweden to give up crown (1704–09) to Stanislas I Leszczyński; restored after battle of Poltava (1709).

**Augustus III.** 1696–1763. Son of Augustus II; b. Dresden. Elector of Saxony (1733–63) under name of **Frederick Augustus II.** King (1734–63). Supported Prussia in first Silesian War (1740–42) but sided with

Austria in second Silesian War (1744–45); defeated and forced to pay indemnity; electorate occupied by Prussians during Seven Years' (third Silesian) War (1756–63).

**Augustus William.** *Ger.* **August Wilhelm.** 1722–1758. Prince of Prussia, of Hohenzollern line. Brother of Frederick the Great. Not successful as military leader; deprived of command (1757) by Frederick. Father of Frederick William II, who succeeded Frederick the Great as king of Prussia. See HOHENZOLLERN.

**Au'lard'** (ō'lȧr'), **François Alphonse.** 1849–1928. French historian, esp. of French Revolution.

**Auletes.** See PTOLEMY XI.

**Aul'noy'** (ō'nwȧ') *or* **Au'noy',** Comtesse **d'.** **Marie Catherine Ju'mel' de Ber'ne·ville'** (zhü'mĕl' dē bĕr'nē·vēl'). 1650?–1705. French author; best known for her fairy tales *L'Oiseau Bleu, La Belle aux Cheveux d'Or, Fortunée,* etc.

**Aulus Gellius.** See GELLIUS.

**Au'male'** (ō'mȧl'). Name of French family of nobility derived from a town in Normandy near Dieppe, which became a county (11th century), later a duchy (1547). Dukedom of Aumale was first granted by King Henry II to Claude I and François de Lorraine, ducs de Guise (see GUISE and LORRAINE). Duchy passed (1618) to ducal house of Nemours (Savoy), thence to Louis XIV by purchase (1675), and finally to House of Orléans (*q.v.*). Holders of the dukedom of Aumale include: **Claude II de Lor'raine'** [lô'rân'] (1526–1573), soldier; opposed to Coligny and Huguenots; favored massacre of St. Bartholomew; killed at siege of La Rochelle. His son **Charles** (1555?–1631), a leader of Holy (or Catholic) League after death (1588) of duc de Guise; refused submission to Henry IV; spent last years in exile. **Henri Eugène Philippe Louis d'Or'lé'ans'** [dôr'lā'äN'] (1822–1897); son of Louis Philippe, King of France; army officer and administrator; governor general of Algeria (1847–48); general of division (1873); author of *Histoire des Princes de Condé* and other political and historical works.

**Au·mon'ier** (ô·mŏn'yā; -mō'nyā; -mŏn'ĭ·ā; -mō'nĭ·ā), **James.** 1832–1911. English landscape painter. Worked as designer of calicoes (till after 1873). Devoted himself to painting English countryside, as in *When the Tide is Out, Sunday Evening, Sheep Washing.* His nephew **Stacy Aumonier** (1887–1928) began as a landscape painter and decorative designer; became an entertainer, reciting his own character sketches; began (1913) writing short stories and novels, including *Olga Bardel* and *Heartbeat* (1922).

**Aungerville** *or* **Aungervyle, Richard.** See Richard de BURY.

**Aunoy.** See AULNOY.

**Au'rang·zeb** *or* **Au'rung·zeb** (ô'rŭng·zĕb; ou'-; *Hindustani* ä'ŏŏ·rŭng·zāb) *or* **Au'rung·zebe** (ô'rŭng·zēb; ou'-; *Hindustani* ä'ŏŏ·rŭng·zēb). 1618–1707. Sixth emperor of Hindustan (1658–1707) of Mogul dynasty. Son of Shah Jahan. Rebelled against father and usurped throne (1658); kept father in prison at Agra fort (1658–66); caused death of his three brothers (1659–61). Assumed title of **A'lam·gir** (ä'lȧm·gēr), *i.e.* Conqueror of the World. At war with Sivaji, leader of the Marathas (1662–80), who remained independent. After long contest (1666–88), his generals conquered Mohammedan kingdoms of Bijapur and Golconda, these conquests bringing him in touch with English at Madras and at Surat and Calcutta (founded 1690). Renewed wars with Marathas (1689–1705), these rebellions and wars weakening Mogul power, then at its widest extent; forced to find shelter in Ahmadnagar (1706). By his religious bigotry, alienated both Mohammedans and Hindus.

**Aurel.** Pseudonym of Marie Antoinette MORTIER.

**Au·re'li·an** (ô·rē'lĭ·ăn; -rēl'yăn). *Full Latin name* **Lucius Domitius Au·re'li·a'nus** (ô·rē'lĭ·ā'nŭs). *Called* **Res'ti·tu'tor Or'bis** (rĕs'tĭ·tū'tôr ôr'bĭs; -tū'tēr), *i.e.* Restorer of the Roman Empire. 212?–275. Roman emperor (270–275); of humble origin. From common soldier rose to high military positions under emperors Valerian and Claudius II; elected emperor by army (270). Drove Goths across Danube, but gave up Dacia; in war with Palmyra (271–273), defeated its queen, Zenobia (*q.v.*), destroyed city, and carried Zenobia as prisoner to Rome; reconquered Egypt (273); recovered Gaul and Britain from Tetricus (274); began fortification walls of Rome. Killed by conspirators among his officers.

**Aurelianus, Caelius.** See CAELIUS AURELIANUS.

**Au·re'li·us** (ô·rē'lĭ·ŭs; -rēl'yŭs). See (1) COMMODUS; (2) CONSTANTINE I (Roman emperor); (3) NUMERIANUS; (4) PROBUS.

**Aurelius, Marcus.** *In full* **Marcus Aurelius Antoninus.** See (1) MARCUS AURELIUS; (2) CARACALLA.

**Aurelius Vic'tor** (vĭk'tēr), **Sextus.** fl. 4th century A.D. Roman historian; author of a short history of the Roman emperors.

**Au'relle' de Pa'la'dines'** (ô'rĕl' dē pȧ'lȧ'dēn'), **Louis Jean Baptiste d'.** 1804–1877. French general; served in Crimean and Franco-Prussian wars; elected senator for life (1875).

**Aurevilly, Jules Barbey d'.** See BARBEY D'AUREVILLY.

**Au'ric'** (ô'rēk'), **Georges.** 1899– . French composer; his works include a comic opera (*La Reine de Cœur*) and several ballets. See Arthur HONEGGER.

**Au·ri'fa·ber** (ou·rē'fä·bēr; ou'rē·fä'bēr), *Latinized from* **Gold'schmied** (gôlt'shmēt), **Johann.** 1517–1568. German Lutheran theologian; appointed professor at Rostock (1550) on recommendation of Melanchthon. Not to be confused with **Johann Aurifaber** (1519–1575), also a Lutheran theologian, friend and assistant of Luther, an editor of Luther's works, and vigorous opponent of Melanchthon.

**Au'riol'** (ô'ryôl'), **Vincent.** 1884–1966. French lawyer, b. Revel, Haute-Garonne. Elected to Chamber of Deputies (1914); Socialist leader; minister of finance (1936), of justice (1938). Interned (1940–43). Member Constituent Assembly (1945); minister of state; first president of Fourth Republic (1947–54).

**Au·ri'spa** (ou·rēs'pä), **Giovanni.** 1369?–1459. Sicilian scholar and humanist. Traveled in Near East (1414 ff.); returned with 238 manuscripts of classical Greek authors, as Arrian, Pindar, Xenophon, Plato, Sophocles, Strabo, Aeschylus. His translations include Hierocles's *Liber in Pythagorae Aurea Carmina Latinitate Donatus* (1474) and *Philisci Consolatoria*...(1510).

**Aurungzeb** *or* **Aurungzebe.** See AURANGZEB.

**Aus'lan'der** (ôs'lăn'dēr), **Joseph.** 1897–1965. American poet, b. Philadelphia. Grad. Harvard (1917). Instructor, Harvard (1919–23); lecturer in poetry, Columbia U. (from 1929). Author of *Sunrise Trumpets* (1924), *Cyclops' Eye* (1926), *Hell in Harness* (1930), *No Traveler Returns* (1933), *More Than Bread* (1936); coeditor, *The Winged Horse* (a poetry anthology; 1927); translator, *Fables of La Fontaine* (1930), *Sonnets of Petrarch* (1931).

**Au·so'ni·us** (ô·sō'nĭ·ŭs), **Decimus Magnus.** fl. 4th century A.D. Roman scholar, of Bordeaux; entrusted by Valentinian with education of Gratian, heir apparent; honored by Gratian when he became emperor; consul (379 A.D.). Author of prose summaries of *Iliad* and *Odyssey,* memorial verses on Roman emperors, and a number of idylls.

**Aus'ten** (ôs'tĕn; -tĭn). See GODWIN-AUSTEN; ROBERTS-AUSTEN.

**Austen, Jane.** 1775–1817. English novelist, b. at parsonage of Steventon, Hampshire; unmarried; lived at home, after father's death, with mother and sisters, successively at Bath, Southampton, and Chawton, Hampshire; moved (1817) to Winchester for medical advice and died there. During the period 1796 to 1798 wrote *Pride and Prejudice* (pub. 1813), *Sense and Sensibility* (1811), and *Northanger Abbey* (posthumously, 1818); desisted from writing because of discouragement over inability to find a publisher; during period 1811 to 1816 wrote *Mansfield Park* (1814), *Emma* (1816), and *Persuasion* (posthumously, 1818).

**Aus'tin** (ôs'tĭn), Saint. See AUGUSTINE (d. 604).

**Austin, Alfred.** 1835–1913. English poet laureate. Grad. London U. (1853); called to bar (1857); journalist (1866–96); joint editor (with W. J. Courthope), later editor, of *National Review* (1883–95); poet laureate (1896). Author of 20 volumes of verse (1871–1908), including *Savonarola* (1881), *Conversion of Winckelmann* (1897), *Sacred and Profane Love* (1908).

**Austin, Frederic.** 1872–1952. English baritone and composer. Member Royal Opera, Covent Garden; principal baritone, Beecham Opera Co. Composer of Hammersmith version of *Beggar's Opera* and *Polly*, of music to plays, and festival music. His brother **Ernest** (1874–1947), composer of orchestral works, chamber music, and tone poems.

**Austin, Frederick Britten.** 1885–1941. English author and playwright. Author of *The Shaping of Lavinia* (1911), *A Saga of the Sword* (1928), *The Road to Glory* (1935), *Forty Centuries Look Down* (1936), and many other novels, also short stories, and *The Thing that Matters* (a play, 1921).

**Austin, Herbert.** 1st Baron **Austin.** 1866–1941. English motorcar manufacturer; in engineering works in Australia (to 1890); to England to take charge of manufacture of Wolseley sheep-shearing machine (1890); started manufacture of Austin motorcars (1905).

**Austin, John.** 1790–1859. English jurist; professor of jurisprudence, University College, London (1828–32); author of *Province of Jurisprudence Determined* (1832), *Lectures on Jurisprudence* (1861–63). His wife **Sarah,** *nee* **Taylor** (1793–1867), translated and edited German and French historical texts, including Ranke's *History of the Popes* (1840; the occasion for Macaulay's essay on the subject) and *History of the Reformation in Germany* (1845), and Guizot's *English Revolution* (1850). See also Lucie DUFF-GORDON.

**Austin, Mary,** *nee* **Hunter.** 1868–1934. American novelist and playwright, b. Carlinville, Ill.; grad. Blackburn U. (1888); m. Stafford W. Austin (1891). Author of the novels *The Land of Little Rain* (1903), *Lost Borders* (1909), *The Lovely Lady* (1913), *The Man Jesus* (1915), *The Land of Journeys' Ending* (1924), *Starry Adventure* (1931), the plays *The Arrow Maker* (1911), *The Man Who Didn't Believe in Christmas* (1916), an autobiography, *Earth Horizon* (1932), etc.

**Austin, Stephen Fuller.** 1793–1836. American colonizer in Texas, b. in southwestern Va. Carried out (1822) colonization plans of his father, **Moses** (1761–1821); directed (1822–32) government in the colony, encouraging immigration from U.S., maintaining peace and order. Imprisoned in Mexico City (1833–34) for urging Texas statehood and separation from Coahuila. Secretary of state, Republic of Texas (1836).

**Austin, William.** 1778–1841. American lawyer and writer b. Lunenburg, Mass.; author of *Peter Rugg, the Missing Man* (1824).

**Austin, William Lane.** 1871–1949. American statistician, b. in Scott County, Miss. Ph.B. (1897), LL.B. (1898), U. of Mississippi. On staff of census bureau (from 1900); director of U.S. census (1933 ff.).

**Aus'tral** (ôs'trăl), **Florence.** *Stage name of* **Florence Wilson.** 1894–1968. Australian concert and opera singer, b. Melbourne. Made debut (1922) in grand opera at Covent Garden as Brünnehilde; toured England as soloist; m. (1925) John Amadio, flutist; made American debut (1925); toured America (1926); appeared in Berlin (1930) as Brünnehilde; toured U.S., Canada, and Australia.

**Auteroche, Jean Chappe d'.** See under Claude CHAPPE.

**Au·tol'y·cus** (ô·tŏl'ĭ·kŭs). fl. c. 310 B.C. Greek astronomer and mathematician of Pitane in Aeolia. Author of earliest entirely preserved Greek mathematical work; wrote on motion of points on a revolving sphere, and on apparent rising and setting of fixed stars.

**Au'tran'** (ō'träN'), **Joseph.** 1813–1877. French poet, b. Marseilles; author of *La Fille d'Eschyle, Le Cyclope* (verse drama), etc.

**Auvergne.** See LA TOUR D'AUVERGNE.

**Au'wers** (ou'vẽrs), **Arthur von.** 1838–1915. German astronomer. Astronomer, Imperial Academy of Sciences, Berlin (from 1866); made observations on transits of Venus (1874, 1882), proper motion of fixed stars, positions of stars, etc.

**Aux·en'ti·us** (ôk·sĕn'shĭ·ŭs). d. 374? Bishop of Milan; Arian; prominent in opposing Nicene Creed.

**Au'zoux'** (ō'zōō'), **Louis.** 1797–1880. French physician; inventor of a paste enabling him to make accurate anatomical models; popularized study of anatomy.

**A'va·ku'mo·vić** (ä'vä·kōō'mô·vēt'y'; *Angl.* -vĭch), **Jovan.** 1841–1928. Serbian statesman, b. Belgrade. Minister of justice (1887); premier (1892–93). President of provisional government (1903).

**Á'va·los** (ä'vä·lōs), **Fernando Francisco de.** Marqués **de Pe·sca'ra** (pȧ·skä'rä). 1489–1525. Spanish soldier, b. in Kingdom of Naples; m. (1509) Vittoria Colonna (see COLONNA); commander in chief in service of Charles V; engaged at Ravenna (1512), Milan (1521), La Bicocca (1522), Pavia (1525); approached by Giovanni Morone, chancellor of Duke Francesco Maria Sforza of Milan, in conspiracy against Charles V; joined conspirators and, later, disclosed plans to Charles.

**A'van·dale** (ā'văn·dāl; ăv'ăn-), Baron. See *Andrew Stewart* (d. 1488), under STEWART family.

**A·van'zo** (ä·vän'tsō), **Jacopo.** fl. latter half of 14th century. Italian painter.

**Avebury,** Baron. See Sir John LUBBOCK.

**A'vé'-Lal'le·mant'** *or* **A'vé'-Lal'le·ment'** (ȧ'vā'lȧl'-mäN'), **Robert Christian Berthold.** 1812–1884. German scholar and traveler in Brazil; author of books recounting his journeys.

**Ave'ling** (āv'lĭng), **Edward Bibbins.** 1851–1898. Son-in-law of Karl Marx. English scientist and socialist reformer.

**Aveling, Francis Arthur Powell.** 1875–1941. English psychologist; professor, U. of London; author of *The Immortality of the Soul, Science and Faith, Modernism,* and *Psychology.*

**A'vel·la·ne'da** (ä'vȧ·lyä·nā'thä), **Alonso Fernández de.** See FERNÁNDEZ DE AVELLANEDA.

**A'vel·la·ne'da** (ä'vȧ·yä·nā'thä), **Nicolás.** 1836–1885. Argentine journalist, educator, and author, b. in Tucumán; president of Argentina (1874–80).

**A'vel·la·ne'da y Ar'te·a'ga** (ä'vȧ·(l)yä·nā'thä ē är'-tȧ·ä'gä), **Gertrudis Gó'mez de** (gō'mās [-māth] thȧ). *Pseudonym* **La Pe're·gri'na** (pā'rȧ·grē'nä). 1814–1873. Spanish writer, b. Puerto Príncipe (Camagüey), Cuba; to Spain (1836); m. (1846) Pedro Sabater (d. 1846), governor of Madrid, and (1854) Verduzo Masieu (d. 1863); known particularly as a poet and dramatist. Her works include novels, as *El Mulato Sab* (1839), *Dos Mujeres* (1842), *Espatolino* (1844); dramas, as *Leoncia* (1840), *Saúl* (1849), *Baltasar* (1858); lyrics, as *Poesías Líricas* (1841).

**A'vem·pa'ce** *or* **A'ven·pa'ce** (ä'vȧm·pä'thā). *Arab.* **abu-Bakr Muḥammad ibn-Yaḥya ibn-Bājjah.** *Often known as* **ibn-Baj'jah** (ĭb''n·bäj'jă) *or* **ibn-al-Ṣā'igh.** d. 1138. Spanish-Arabian philosopher, scientist, and poet, b. Saragossa; lived at Seville and Granada; wrote several treatises on astronomy and medicine which have not survived; most important work, a philosophical treatise on the conduct of the individual; influenced Averroës; held by Moslem writers to be an atheist.

**A've·na'ri·us** (ä'vȧ·nä'rē·o͞os; *Angl.* ăv'ē·nâr'ĭ·ŭs), **Richard.** 1843–1896. Nephew of Richard Wagner. German positivist philosopher, b. Paris. Professor of philosophy, Zurich (1877–96); set forth principle of economy of thinking, also theory (Empiriokritizismus) of pure experience in relation to environment and knowledge. Author of *Kritik der Reinen Erfahrung* (1888–90), *Der Menschliche Weltbegriff* (1891), etc. His brother **Ferdinand** (1856–1923), poet and writer on art, founded art journal *Kunstwart* (1887); wrote *Wandern und Werden* (1881), *Lebe!* (1883), *Stimmen und Bilder* (1897), etc.; compiled anthologies of poems.

**A've·nel'** (ȧv'nĕl'), Vicomte **Georges d'.** 1855–1939. French writer, esp. of treatises on economic history and issues, including *Richelieu et la Monarchie Absolue* (4 vols., 1884–90), *Histoire Économique de la Propriété, 1200–1800* (5 vols., 1894–1909), *L'Évolution des Moyens de Transport* (1920), etc.

**A've·nol'** (ȧv'nôl'), **Joseph Louis Anne.** 1879–1952. French statesman; financial delegate of France in London (1916–23); deputy secretary-general (1923–32) and secretary-general (1933–40), League of Nations.

**A'ven·ti'nus** (ä'vĕn·tē'no͞os; *Angl.* ăv'ĕn·tī'nŭs), **Johannes.** *Real name* **Johannes Tur'mair** *or* **Thur'mayr** (to͞or'mīr). 1477–1534. Bavarian historian; author of *Annales Boiorum* (pub. 1554), a history of Bavaria.

**Av'en·zo'ar** (ăv'ĕn·zō'ĕr; -zō·är') *or* **A·bu'me·ron'** (ȧ·bo͞o'mĕ·rŏn'). *Arab.* **a·bu'-Mar·wān'** (ȧ·bo͞o'măr·wän') **'Abd-al-Malik ibn-abi-al-'Alā'.** *Surnamed* **ibn-Zuhr'** (ĭb''n·zo͞or') *or* **ibn-Zohr'** (ĭb''n·zōr'). 1091?–1162. Arab physician in Spain, b. Seville. Physician and vizier to Abd-al-Mumin, founder of Almohade dynasty; protested against quackery and superstition in medicine; author of six important medical works, three of which survive; great admirer of Galen; taught Averroës.

**A·ver'chen·ko** (ŭ·vyär'chĕn·kô; *Ukrainian* ŭ·vyĕr·chăn'kô), **Arkadi Timofeevich.** 1881–1925. Russian writer of parodies, one-act plays, and short stories.

**A've·re'scu** (ä'vĕ·rĕ'sko͞o), **Alexandru.** 1859–1938. Rumanian general and statesman; as minister of war (1907), undertook reorganization of Rumanian army. Chief of general staff (1912); commanded attack on Bulgaria (1913); held army command in World War. As prime minister (1918), conducted peace negotiations with Central Powers; again prime minister of Rumania (1920–21, 1926–27).

**Averlino** *or* **Averulino, Antonio di Pietro.** See FILARETE.

**A·ver'ro·ës** *or* **A·ver'rho·ës** (ȧ·vĕr'ō·ēz; ăv'ēr·ō'ēz). *Frequently known as* **ibn-Rushd'** (ĭb''n·ro͝osht'). *Arab.* **abu-al-Walīd Muḥammad ibn-Aḥmad ibn-Rushd.** 1126–1198. Spanish-Arabian philosopher and physician, b. Córdoba. Lived in Morocco for several years (from 1153); cadi of Seville (1169) and, later, of Córdoba; sent by caliphs on important missions; suspected by al-Mansur and interned (1195); died in Morocco. Wrote many treatises on jurisprudence, astronomy, grammar, and medicine; his greatest works, commentaries on Aristotle. Had more influence on succeeding Jewish and Christian thought than on Arabian; his philosophy, developed as Averroism, does not greatly differ from later Christian Scholasticism.

**A'ver·y** (ā'vẽr·ĭ), **Elroy McKendree.** 1844–1935. American educator and author, b. Erie, Mich. Author of textbooks in physics and chemistry, and a twelve-volume *History of the United States and its People.*

**A'vi·a'nus** (ā'vĭ·ā'nŭs) *or* **A'vi·a'ni·us** (-ā'nĭ·ŭs; -ān'yŭs), **Flavius.** fl. 4th century A.D. (or later). Latin writer of fables.

**Avicebrón.** See IBN-GABIROL.

**Av'i·cen'na** (ăv'ĭ·sĕn'ȧ). *Also known as* **ibn-Si'na** (ĭb''n·sē'nä). *Arab.* **abu-'Ali al-Ḥusayn ibn-Sīna.** 980–1037. Arab physician and philosopher, b. in village near Bokhara. Studied at Bokhara; received court position (997); traveled in Khwarazm (Khiva) and Persia; made vizier at Buyid court at Hamadan; compelled by soldiers to resign; imprisoned, but escaped to Isfahan; court physician (1024); traveled widely. Wrote about 100 works; his greatest, *The Canon,* a system of medicine, long regarded in Orient as medical textbook of great authority (often translated, first by Gerard of Cremona, 12th century); also works on theology, metaphysics, logic, mathematics, etc. His philosophy (Avicennism) is based on Aristotle but includes Neoplatonic ideas.

**A'vi·e'nus** (ā'vĭ·ē'nŭs), **Rufus Festus.** fl. 4th century A.D. Roman poet; translated Aratus's *Phainomena* and paraphrased Dionysius's *Periegesis* under title *Descriptio Orbis Terrae;* wrote also descriptions of coasts of Mediterranean, Black, and Caspian seas.

**Á'vi·la** (ä'vē·lä), **Gil Gon·zá'lez de** (gôn·thä'lāth). c. 1578–1658. Spanish historian, b. Ávila; historiographer of Castile (1612 ff.); author of *Historia de la Vida y Hechos del Rey Don Enrique III de Castilla* (1638).

**Ávila, Juan de.** 1494?–1569. Spanish preacher, b. Almodóvar del Campo; called "the Apostle of Andalusia"; author of *Epistolario Espiritual* (1578).

**Ávila, Pedro Arias de** *or* **Pedrarius de.** See PEDRARIAS.

**Ávila Camacho, Manuel.** See CAMACHO.

**Ávila y Zú'ñi·ga** (ē tho͞o'nyē·gä), **Luis de.** c. 1500–1564. Spanish historian, b. Placencia; author of *Comentario de la Guerra de Alemania Hecha por Carlos V en 1546 y 1547* (1547).

**Avilés, Pedro Menendez de.** See MENENDEZ DE AVILÉS.

**A'vi·son** (ā'vĭ·s'n), **Charles.** 1710?–1770. English organist and composer of concertos and sonatas. Author of *Essay on Musical Expression* (1752).

**A·vi'tus** (ȧ·vī'tŭs), **Marcus Maecilius.** d. 456 A.D. Emperor of the West (455–456), b. Auvergne. Master of armies of Gaul (c. 450); chosen emperor with help of Visigoths; deposed by Ricimer.

**Avitus,** Saint **Sextus Alcimus Ecdicius.** d. about 525. Bishop of Vienne, France (from 490); opponent of Arianism. Author of homilies and poems.

**A'viz** (ȧ'vēsh) *or* **A'vis** (ȧ'vēsh). Name of Portuguese dynasty (1385–1580) derived from order of knighthood (Aviz) founded by King Alfonso I and named from town in eastern Portugal. House founded by John the Great (John I), Grand Master of Order of Aviz, natural son of Peter I of house of Burgundy; succeeding rulers were: Edward, Alfonso V, John II, Emanuel, John III, Sebastian, and Henry (d. 1580). Portugal was a dependency of Spain (1580–1640). See Dom ANTÔNIO.

**A'vo·ga'dro** (ä'vō·gä'drō), Count **Amedeo.** 1776–1856. Italian chemist and physicist, b. Turin; author of hypothesis (Avogadro's hypothesis or law, 1811) that equal volumes of all gases at same temperature and pressure contain equal numbers of molecules.

**Avon,** Earl of. See Anthony EDEN.

**Awde'lay** *or* **Awde'ley** (ôd'lā), **John.** fl. 1559–1577. English printer; reputed author of *Fraternitye of Vacabondes* (1565).

**à Wood, Anthony.** See Anthony WOOD.

**A'xa·ya'catl** (ä'shä·yä'kä·t'l) *or* **A'xa·ya·ca'tzin** (ä'shä·yä·kä'tsēn). 15th-century Aztec emperor (1464–77) and conqueror; said to be father of Montezuma II.

**Axel.** See ABSALON.

**Ax'el·rod** (ăk'sĕl·rŏd), **Julius.** 1912– . American biochemist, b. New York City. Shared Nobel prize in physiology and medicine (1970) with Bernard Katz and Ulf von Euler.

**A·ya'la** (ä·yä'lä), **Eusebio.** 1875–1942. Paraguayan politician. Held various official positions (1910–21); provisional president of Paraguay (1921–23); forced to resign; minister to U.S. (1925); again president (1932–36); deposed by Col. Rafael Franco.

**Ayala, Juan Manuel de.** Spanish commander (Mar.–Nov., 1775) of ship that made first exploration of Bay of San Francisco.

**Ayala, Pedro López de.** See LOPEZ DE AYALA.

**Ayala, Ramón Pérez de.** See PÉREZ DE AYALA.

**Ayala y Her·re'ra** (ē ĕr·rĕ'rä), **Adelardo Ló'pez** (lō'pāth) **de.** 1828–1879. Spanish dramatist and politician, b. Guadalcanal, Badajoz; elected deputy (1857); minister of colonies under Alfonso XII (1875); president, chamber of deputies (1878). His dramatic works include *Un Hombre de Estado* (1851), *Castigo y Perdón* (1851), *Los Dos Guzmanes* (1851), *Rioja* (1854), *El Tejado de Vidrio* (1854), *El Tanto por Ciento* (1861), *El Nuevo Don Juan* (1863), and *Consuelo* (1878).

**Ay'de·lotte** (ā'dĕ·lŏt), **Frank.** 1880–1956. American educator, b. Sullivan, Ind. Grad. Indiana U. (1900). Rhodes scholar at Oxford (1905–07). Professor of English, M.I.T. (1915–21). President, Swarthmore Coll. (1921–40); president, Institute of Advanced Study, Princeton (from 1939). American secretary, Rhodes trustees (1918–53). Author of *Elizabethan Rogues and Vagabonds* (1913), *The Oxford Stamp* (1917), etc.

**Ayer** (âr), **Edward Everett.** 1841–1927. American industrialist, b. Kenosha, Wis. A founder, and first president, of Field Museum of Natural History, Chicago.

**Ayesha** *or* **Ayeshah.** Variant of *Aisha* (see MOHAMMED, the Prophet).

**Aylesford,** Earl of. See FINCH family.

**Ayles'worth** (ālz'wûrth; -wĕrth), Sir **Allen Bristol.** 1854–1952. Canadian constitutional lawyer. Educ. Toronto U. Minister of justice (1906–11); agent before Hague Tribunal regarding Atlantic fisheries (1910).

**Ayl·lón'** (ī·lyōn'), **Lucas Váz'quez** [väth'kāth] (*or* **Vás'quez** [väs'kāth]) **de.** 1475?–1526. Spanish explorer. In Santo Domingo (1502–20); attempted settlement on American mainland, probably on what is now South Carolina coast (1526); died there.

**Ayl'mer** (āl'mĕr), Sir **Fenton John.** 1862–1935. British general; served in attempt to relieve Kut-el-Amara (1916).

**Aylmer, John.** 1521–1594. English ecclesiastic. Grad. Cambridge (1541). Tutor to Lady Jane Grey; because of opposition to doctrine of transubstantiation had to flee to Continent until accession of Elizabeth (1558); bishop of London (1576); notorious for arbitrary and unconciliatory attitude to Puritans and Roman Catholics; assailed in Martin Marprelate tracts.

**Aylmer, Matthew.** Baron **Aylmer.** d. 1720. British naval officer, b. in Ireland. Commander at Beachy Head (1690); vice-admiral (1694); commander in chief of fleet (1709–11, 1714–20). As governor of Greenwich Hospital (1714–20), established school for sons of seamen.

**Aymer de Valence.** See de VALENCE.

**Ay'rer** (ī'rĕr), **Jakob.** 1543?–1605. German dramatic poet; many of his plays published under title *Opus Theatricum* (1618).

**Ayres** (ârz), **Anne.** 1816–1896. Protestant religious, b. London, Eng.; to U.S. (1836); consecrated (1845) Sister of The Holy Communion, at New York City, the first woman in America to become a Protestant sister.

**Ayres, Leonard Porter.** 1879–1946. American educator and statistician, b. Niantic, Conn. Grad. Boston U. (1902). Director, departments of education and statistics, Russell Sage Foundation (1908–20). Vice-president, Cleveland Trust Co. (from 1920). Economic adviser on Dawes Plan commission (1924). Chief statistician, War Department (1940 ff.). Author of books on education, and of *Price Changes and Business Prospects* (1921), *Business Recovery Following Depression* (1922), *Economics of Recovery* (1933), *Inflation* (1936).

**Ayres, Ruby Mildred.** 1883–1955. English novelist; m. (1909) Reginald William Pocock. Wrote *Richard Chatterton, V.C.*, *The Remembered Kiss*, *The Bachelor Husband*, *Compromise*, *Silver Wedding* (play; produced 1932), *Big Ben* (1939), *The Constant Heart* (1941).

**Ayr'ton** (âr't'n), **William Edward.** 1847–1908. English electrical engineer and inventor. Educ. University College, London. In Indian telegraph service (1868) after study under Lord Kelvin; taught physics in Tokyo and London; professor of electrical engineering, South Kensington (1884–1908). Author of *Practical Electricity* (1887). His first wife, **Matilda,** *nee* **Chap'lin** [chăp'lĭn] (1846–1883; m. 1872), pioneer woman doctor, took high honors in examinations, Surgeons' Hall, Edinburgh (1870, 1871); opened school for midwives in Japan (1873); M.D., Paris (1879); practiced at Royal Free Hospital, London, and in Algiers and Montpellier. His second wife, **Hertha,** *nee* **Marks** [märks] (1854–1923; m. 1885), was a scientist; studied at Girton College (1876 ff.); awarded medal for researches on electric arc and on sand ripples (1906); collaborated with husband on admiralty reports on electric searchlights; invented an antigas fan (1915).

**Ays'cough** (ăs'kū), **Anne.** = Anne ASKEW.

**Ays'cough** (ās'kō), **Florence,** *nee* **Whee'lock** (hwē'lŏk). 1878–1942. American writer, b. in Shanghai; daughter of a Canadian father. m. Francis Ayscough (d. 1933) and (1935) Prof. Harley Farnsworth MacNair. Lecturer on Chinese subjects. Author of *Fir-Flower Tablets* (with Amy Lowell; poems translated from Chinese) and of various interpretations of Chinese culture.

**Ays'cough** (ăs'kū), **John.** Pseudonym of Monsignor Count BICKERSTAFFE-DREW.

**Ays'cue** (ăs'kū; ās'kū), Sir **George.** d. 1671. British admiral. Sent by parliament to reduce Barbados and visit Virginia (1651–52); lost his command after indecisive battle with Dutch off Plymouth (1652); naval adviser to Sweden till Restoration; served in second Dutch war (1664–66), becoming admiral of the white; prisoner in Holland (1666–67).

**Ay'ton** *or* **Ay'toun** (ā't'n), Sir **Robert.** 1570–1638. Scottish poet; author of lyrics and many Latin and English panegyrics.

**Ay'toun** (ā't'n), **William Ed'mond·stoune** (ĕd'mŭn·stŭn). 1813–1865. Scottish poet and parodist. Educ. U. of Edinburgh and at Aschaffenburg, Germany; began contributions to *Blackwood's* (1836); professor of rhetoric and belles lettres, U. of Edinburgh (1845). Author of *Poland, Homer, and other Poems* (1832), *Lays of the Scottish Cavaliers* (1848), *Firmilian, a Spasmodic Tragedy* (1854); collaborated with Sir Theodore Martin in *The Bon Gaultier Ballads* (1845) and *Poems and Ballads of Goethe* (1858); annotated collection of *Ballads of Scotland* (1858).

**A·yub′ Khan** (ā·ē·ōōb′ [ī·ōōb′] kän). 1855–1914. Amir of Afghanistan (1880–81). Youngest son of Shere Ali. After father's death, took possession of Herat (1879); after preliminary victory over the British, was defeated by Gen. Roberts (1880); defeated by Abd-er-Rahman Khan (1881) and driven from Herat; lived in exile in Persia and (1887–1914) as state prisoner at Rawalpindi.

**Ay·yub′id** (ī·yōōb′ĭd) *or* **A·yub′ite** (ī·yōōb′īt). Moslem dynasty (1169–1250) established in Egypt (1173) by Saladin and named from his father, Ayyub ibn-Shadhi (d. 1173), a Kurd who served as a general in Syria and Mesopotamia; extended its power over Nubia, Hejaz, and Yemen; fought Europeans in Third, Fourth, and Fifth crusades; overthrown by Mamelukes.

**A·zad′** (ä·zäd′), **A·bul′ Ka·lam′** (ȧ·bŏŏl′ kȧ·läm′). 1888–1958. Indian Moslem politician, b. Mecca, Arabia; supporter of Gandhi; president, All-India Congress (several times 1923 ff., including 1941).

**A·za′ña** (ä·thä′nyä), **Manuel.** 1880–1940. President of Spanish Republic (1936–39). Lawyer; leader of liberal politicians. Editor and author; wrote biography of Juan Valera. Active in overthrow of Alfonso XIII (1931); minister of war in first republican ministry; premier (1931–33); attempted many reforms; arrested and imprisoned (Oct., 1934); led Republican left; again premier (1936); elected president (May, 1936); after civil war (1936–39) had driven government into northeast Spain, left for Paris (Feb., 1939); resigned (Mar., 1939).

**A·zan·chev′ski** (ŭ·zŭn·chăf′skû·ĭ; *Angl.* -skĭ), **Mikhail Pavlovich.** 1838 (or 1839)–1881. Russian composer, b. Moscow; director, St. Petersburg Conservatory (1870–76), to which he gave his large music library. Composer esp. of chamber music.

**A·za′ra** (ä·thä′rä), **Félix de.** 1746–1811. Spanish soldier, naturalist, and traveler; to Paraguay (1781) as one of commission to fix boundaries of Spanish and Portuguese possessions; returned to Spain (1801). Author of *Voyage dans l'Amérique Méridionale* (1809), etc. His brother **José Nicolás** (1731–1804), diplomat; envoy to papal court (1765); ambassador to France (1798).

**Az′a·ri′ah** (ăz′ȧ·rī′ȧ). *In Douay Bible* **Az′a·ri′as** (-ăs). = Uzziah, King of Judah.

**A·ze′glio** (ä·dzâ′lyō), Marchese **d'. Massimo Ta′-pa·rel′li** (tä′pä·rĕl′lē). 1798–1866. Italian statesman and author, b. Turin. Son-in-law of Manzoni. Leader in risorgimento; helped foment revolution (1848) and secure reforms of Pius IX through polemic writings; wounded at Vicenza (1848). Premier of Sardinia (1849–52); favored house of Savoy as rulers of united Italy. His works include two historical novels, *Ettore Fieramosca* (1833) and *Niccolò de' Lapi* (1841); polemic writings, as *Degli Ultimi Casi di Romagna* (1846) and *Il Lutto di Lombardia* (c. 1847); and an autobiography, *I Miei Ricordi* (pub. 1873).

**A·ze·ve′do** (ȧ·zĕ·vā′thōō). **Antônio de Araujo de.** See Araujo de Azevedo.

**Azevedo, Manuel Antônio Ál′va·res de** (äl′vȧ·rĕz thē). 1831–1852. Brazilian lyric poet, b. São Paulo; author of *Lira dos Vinte Anos* (a volume chiefly of elegies).

**A′ze·ve′do y Zúñiga** (ä′thâ·vā′thō; ä′sā-). = Gaspar de Zúñiga y Azevedo.

**A′zo** (ä′dzō) *or* **Az′zo** (äd′dzō). *Lat.* **Az′o·li′nus Por′ci·us** (ăz′ō·lī′nŭs pôr′shĭ·ŭs). 1150?–?1230. Italian jurist; professor of law at Bologna; author of *Summa Codicis* and *Apparatus ad Codicem.*

**Azorín.** See José Martínez Ruiz.

**A′zu·ma** (ä′zōō·mä), **Tokuho.** 1909– . Japanese dancer, b. Tokyo. Head of Azuma school of dancing.

**A·zu′ni** (ä·dzōō′nē), **Domenico Alberto.** 1749–1827. Sardinian jurist; author of *Dizionario Universale Ragionato della Giurisprudenza Mercantile* (1786–88), *Sistema Universale dei Principii del Diritto Marittimo* (1795), etc.

# B

**Baa′de** (bä′dĕ), **Walter.** 1893–1960. German-born astronomer in America; Ph.D., Göttingen (1919). Member of staff, Hamburg observatory (1919–31); astronomer at Mount Wilson observatory, Pasadena, Cal. (1931–1958).

**Baa′der** (bä′dẽr), **Franz Xaver von.** 1765–1841. German Roman Catholic mystical philosopher, theologian, and writer.

**Ba′al Shem′-Tob′** *or* **-Tov′** (bȧ′äl shäm′tōv′), *i.e.* "kind, or good, master of the Holy Name." *Known also, from his initials, as* **BEShT** (bĕsht). *Real name* **Is′ra·el** (ĭz′rā·ĕl; -rĭ·ĕl) **ben El′i·e′zer** (ĕl′ĭ·ē′zẽr). 1700?–1760. Jewish teacher, healer, and popular idol; founder of modern Hasidism in Poland. Served in Galicia and Poland as teacher, mediator in civil suits, slaughterer, and tavern keeper. Learned healing powers of plants; wrote amulets; prescribed cures; said to have worked miracles with name of God; won large following and settled in Miedzyboz, Podolia (c. 1740). Taught disciples by means of oral sayings and parables; upheld a pantheistic doctrine and communion with God through joyous worship; opposed asceticism.

**Baarle, Caspar van.** See Casparus Barlaeus.

**Ba′a·sha** (bā′ȧ·shȧ). *In Douay Version* **Ba′a·sa** (-sȧ). d. 888? B.C. King of Israel (911–888?). Killed Nadab, son of Jeroboam I, and seized throne (*1 Kings* xv. 27–34); waged war with Asa of Judah.

**Bab** (băb), **the,** *i.e.* "the Gate." *Title of* Mirza (*or* Sayid) **Ali Mohammed of Shiraz.** 1819–1850. Founder of Babism (1844–45), modern religious sect of Persia. First taught at Shiraz; influenced large number of Persian Moslems; persecuted and imprisoned; condemned to death as heretic of Islam; executed (July 9, 1850) in public square of Tabriz; his mission taken over by Bahaullah (*q.v.*).

**Bab** (bäp), **Julius.** 1880–1955. German playwright and dramatic critic, b. Berlin.

**Babar.** See Baber.

**Bab′bage** (băb′ĭj), **Charles.** 1792–1871. English mathematician and mechanical genius. M.A., Cantab. (1817). Devoted 37 years, large part of fortune, and government grants, to perfecting a calculating machine refused (1842) by the government. Invented an ophthalmoscope

(1847) but failed to make it known. Instrumental in founding the Astronomical and Statistical societies. Author of *On Economy of Machines and Manufactures* (1832) and *Ninth Bridgewater Treatise* (1837).

**Bab'bitt** (băb'ĭt), **Benjamin Tal'bot** (tăl'bŭt). 1809–1889. American inventor, b. Westmoreland, N.Y.; obtained over 100 patents, including soap processes, an ordnance projector, steam boilers, etc.

**Babbitt, Irving.** 1865–1933. American scholar and educator, b. Dayton, Ohio. A.B., Harvard (1889). On teaching staff (1894–1933), professor of French literature (from 1912), Harvard. Founder (with Paul Elmer More) of modern humanistic movement. Author of *Literature and the American College* (1908), *The New Laokoön* (1910), *The Masters of Modern French Criticism* (1912), *Rousseau and Romanticism* (1919), *Democracy and Leadership* (1924).

**Babbitt, Isaac.** 1799–1862. American inventor, b. Taunton, Mass. Invented a journal box (pat. 1839); suggested that it be lined with an alloy now known as Babbitt metal.

**Bab'cock** (băb'kŏk), **Edwina Stanton.** 1877– . American short-story writer and poet, b. Nyack, N.Y. Author of *Greek Wayfarers and Other Poems* (1916), *Nantucket Windows* (1925), etc.

**Babcock, George Herman.** 1832–1893. American inventor, b. near Otsego, N.Y. Invented a polychromatic printing press, a job printing press, and (with Stephen Wilcox) improvements in boiler design. President (1881–93), Babcock, Wilcox & Company, boiler manufacturers.

**Babcock, Harold De·los'** (dḗ·lŏs'). 1882-1968. American physicist, b. Edgerton, Wis.; B.S., U. of California (1907). Member of staff, Mount Wilson observatory, Pasadena, Cal. (from 1909); specialist in spectroscopy.

**Babcock, James Francis.** 1844–1897. American chemist, b. Boston. State assayer of liquors, Massachusetts (1875–85); established "three per cent limit" in definition of an intoxicating liquor. City inspector of milk, Boston (1885 ff.); enforced laws against adulteration. Inventor of Babcock fire extinguisher.

**Babcock, Orville E.** 1835–1884. American army officer, b. Franklin, Vt. Served through Civil War; aide-de-camp (1864–65) to General Grant. Private secretary (1869–77) to President Grant. Accused of implication in Whisky Ring; acquitted (1876) as result of Grant's deposition regarding his excellent character.

**Babcock, Stephen Moulton.** 1843–1931. American agricultural chemist, b. Bridgewater, N.Y. Professor of agricultural chemistry, Wisconsin (1887–1913). Specialist in chemistry of milk; deviser of a test (Babcock test, 1890) for determining amount of fat in milk.

**Babcock, Winnifred,** *nee* **Eaton.** *Pseudonym* **Onoto Watanna.** 1879– . American writer, b. Nagasaki, Japan; m. (1901) B. W. Babcock. Author of *The Old Jinriksha* (1895), *A Japanese Nightingale* (1901; later dramatized), *Daughters of Nijo* (1904), *Honorable Miss Moonlight* (1912), and *His Royal Nibs* (1925).

**Ba'be·lon'** (bȧ'blôɴ'), **Ernest Charles François.** 1854–1924. French numismatist and archaeologist; author of *Traité des Monnaies Grecques et Romaines* (7 vols., 1901–26), *Le Rhin dans l'Histoire* (2 vols., 1916–17), etc.

**Ba'ben·berg** (bä'bĕn·bĕrĸ). Name of Franconian family that held margraviate (976–1156) and duchy (1156–1246) of Austria, including: first margrave, **Leopold** *or* **Lu'it·pold I** [lōō'ĭt·pōlt] (976–994); best known, **Leopold III,** the Pious (1096–1136; canonized 1485); and **Frederick II,** Duke of Austria and Styria (1230–46), last of Babenbergs. Possessions passed (1278) to Rudolf I, founder of house of Hapsburg (*q.v.*). See *Table* (*in Appendix*) for AUSTRIA.

**Ba'ber** *or* **Ba'bur** *or* **Ba'bar** (bä'bẽr), *i.e.* Tiger. *Mongol nickname of* **Zahir ud-Din Muhammad.** 1483–1530. Founder of Mogul dynasty of India; emperor (1526–30). Descendant of Tamerlane and Genghis Khan. Succeeded his father as king of Fergana (1495); conquered Samarkand (1497); lost both kingdoms (1501); crossed Hindu Kush and besieged and captured Kabul (1504); attempted to reconquer Samarkand but was completely defeated by Uzbeks (1514); made raids into India (1519–24); led small army across Indus (1525) and defeated (1526) much larger army of Ibrahim Lodi, Afghan sultan, at Panipat; occupied Delhi and Agra and established Mogul empire; defeated Hindus in a second great battle (1527) near Agra; extended power to east; began organizing new realm; wrote *Memoirs.*

**Ba'beş** (bä'bĕsh), **Victor.** 1854–1926. Rumanian physician and bacteriologist, b. Vienna. Discovered genus (*Babesia*) of protozoans in blood of animals, one species of which causes Texas fever in cattle; discovered granules that take stain in bacteria, and hemorrhagic bacteria in man; demonstrated penetration of certain bacteria through unbroken skin or mucosa; prepared an antitubercular serum; worked on immunizing properties of blood of immunized animals.

**Babet la Bouquetière.** See François Joachim de Pierre de BERNIS.

**Ba'beuf'** *or* **Ba'bœuf'** (bȧ'bûf'), **François Émile.** *Pseudonym* **Grac'chus'** (grȧk'küs') **Babeuf.** 1760–1797. French agitator; journalist during French Revolution, advocating communistic theories (Babouvism); involved in conspiracy to overthrow Directory and re-establish constitution of 1793; stabbed himself before being summoned to guillotine.

**Ba'bi'net'** (bȧ'bē'nĕ'), **Jacques.** 1794–1872. French physicist, b. Lusignan; invented various apparatus for use in physics.

**Bab'ing·ton** (băb'ĭng·tŭn), **Anthony.** 1561–1586. English Roman Catholic conspirator. Served as page to Mary, Queen of Scots. Induced (1586) by John Ballard, a priest, to organize a conspiracy (Babington's plot or conspiracy) to murder Elizabeth, lead a general Catholic uprising, and release Mary; detected by Walsingham's spies; executed with Ballard and a dozen others.

**Babington, Charles Cardale.** 1808–1895. English botanist and archaeologist. B.A., Cantab. (1830); professor of botany, Cambridge (1861); a founder of Entomological Society (1833) and Cambridge Antiquarian Society (1840). Author of *Manual of British Botany* (1843), *Flora of Cambridgeshire* (1860), etc.

**Ba'bo** (bä'bō), **Joseph Marius von.** 1756–1822. German dramatist; author of *Otto von Wittelsbach.*

**Ba'bri·us** (bā'brĭ·ŭs). Writer of fables (in Greek), possibly living in Syria in 1st century A.D. (or later).

**Bab'son** (băb's'n), **Roger Ward.** 1875–1967. American financial statistician, b. Gloucester, Mass. Grad. M.I.T. (1898). Founder of Babson's Statistical Organization and also of Babson Institute; lecturer on statistics and economics.

**Babur.** See BABER.

**Ba·car'di** (bȧ·kär'dĭ). *Span.* **Ba·car·dí'** (bä'kär·thē'). Name of family of distillers, in Spain for about 300 years, whose business was removed (1862) to Cuba, where members of family, esp. **Facundo** (1892–1932) and **Luis J.,** have conducted it successfully, their rum (trademarked Bacardi) being well known.

**Bac·cel'li** (bät·chĕl'lē), **Alfredo.** 1863–1955. Italian poet and novelist; wrote philosophical poems and novels, as *The Way of Light* and *In the Shadow of the Conquered.*

**Baccelli, Guido.** 1832–1916. Italian physician and politician. Taught medicine, U. of Rome. Member, chamber of deputies (from 1874); minister of public instruction in various cabinets (from 1880–1900); senator (1890); minister of agriculture (1901–03).

**Bac·chyl'i·des** (bă·kĭl'ĭ·dēz). Greek lyric poet, of 5th century B.C., rival of Pindar. Only fragments of works are extant, containing *Odes of Victory* (*Epinikia*) and *Dithyrambs*.

**Bac'ci** (bät'chē), **Baccio Maria.** 1888– . Florentine painter; works include *La Miracolata*, *Barca all'Elba*, *La Convalescente*, *Ragazza Napoletana*, *Temporale d'Agosto*, etc.

**Bac'cio** (bät'chō). See Baccio BANDINELLI.

**Bac·cioc'chi** (bät·chôk'kē), **Felice Pasquale.** 1762–1841. French army officer, b. in Corsica. m. (1797) Maria Anna Elisa Buonaparte (see under BONAPARTE), sister of Napoleon. General in army; senator of France (1804). Crowned with his wife when she became grand duchess of Tuscany (1809).

**Baccio d'Agnolo.** See AGNOLO.

**Baccio della Porta.** See Fra BARTOLOMMEO.

**Bach** (bäκ). Family of German musicians and composers, including: **Hans** (d. 1626), called "the Player," a professional musician; and his sons **Johann(es)** (1604–1673), organist at Erfurt; **Christoph** (1613–1661), organist and town musician at Weimar; **Heinrich** (1615–1692), organist at Arnstadt. Christoph's son **Ambrosius** (1645–1695), town musician at Eisenach; and his sons **Johann Christoph** (1671–1721), organist at Ohrdruf; and **Johann Sebastian** (for J. S. Bach and his sons and grandson see entry Johann Sebastian BACH). Another **Johann Christoph** (1642–1703), son of Heinrich, organist at Eisenach (from 1665) and composer, esp. of vocal music; his work includes motets, 44 preludes for chorals, a saraband with 12 variations for clavier, the cantata *Es Erhob Sich ein Streit*, etc. His son **Nikolaus** (1669–1753), organist and director of university music at Jena; composer of orchestral suites, a mass in E minor, a comic operetta, etc. **Johann Michael** (1648–1694), another son of Heinrich, organist at Gehren (from 1673); composer of vocal and instrumental music; father-in-law of Johann Sebastian Bach.

**Bach** (bȧκ), **Aleksei Nikolaevich.** 1857–1946. Russian chemist. Educ. U. of Kiev. Joined revolutionary party (1881); lived abroad (1885–1917); returned to Russia after Revolution of 1917; organized biochemical inst. of public health office in Moscow (1920); known for work on oxidation processes in living organisms.

**Bach** (bäκ), Baron **Alexander von.** 1813–1893. Austrian statesman. Minister of justice (1848); minister of interior (1849; deposed 1859); succeeded Schwarzenberg (1852) as leader of Austrian ministry. Advocated absolutism and centralization of Hapsburg monarchy; negotiated concordat with pope (1855); ambassador to Holy See (1859–67).

**Bach, Johann Sebastian.** 1685–1750. German organist, composer, and master contrapuntist. Son of Ambrosius Bach and brother of Johann Christoph Bach (1671–1721), his first music teachers. Student and chorister, Michaelisschule, Lüneburg (1700–03); violinist, royal chapel orchestra, Weimar (1703); organist, Arnstadt (1703); studied organ under Buxtehude, Lübeck (1705); organist, Mühlhausen (1707); court organist, Weimar (1708); court concertmeister, Weimar (1714–17); court Kapellmeister, Köthen (1717–23); cantor, Thomasschule, and director of university music, Leipzig (from 1723); honorary court composer, Dresden (1736). Visited Frederick the Great at Potsdam (1747); improvised there on the various newly invented pianos and tried the chief church organs; died totally blind (1750). Composed very large library of church, vocal, and instrumental music, including: *Vocal:* about 200 church cantatas (also secular cantatas); a mass in B minor; Christmas, Easter, and Ascension oratorios; passions according to St. Matthew and St. John; magnificats, motets, hymns, etc. *Instrumental:* (for organ) preludes, fugues, toccatas, fantasias, sonatas, and preludes for chorals; (for clavier) concertos, partitas, suites, inventions, fantasias, sonatas, toccatas, capriccios, variations, including 48 preludes and fugues (*The Well-Tempered Clavier*), *Musical Offering*, on a theme suggested by Frederick the Great; also, *Art of Fugue*, chamber and orchestral music, and other sonatas, concertos, etc., for keyed and stringed instruments. Four of his sons and a grandson were musicians of importance: **Wilhelm Friedemann** (1710–1784); called "the Halle Bach"; organist at Dresden (1733–47), at Halle (1747–64); composer of concertos, sonatas, fantasias for organ and clavier, etc. **Karl Philipp Emanuel** (1714–1788); called "the Berlin, or Hamburg, Bach"; composer and pioneer in establishing the sonata form; chamber musician to Frederick the Great, Berlin (1740); director of church music, Hamburg (from 1767); works include numerous concertos and sonatas for the clavier and piano, songs, church and chamber music, and a treatise called *The True Art of Clavier Playing* (1753). **Johann Christoph Friedrich** (1732–1795); called "the Bückeburg Bach"; chamber musician (1750) and Kapellmeister (1756) at Bückeburg; composer of motets, church and secular cantatas, 3 oratorios, 6 quartets for flute and stringed instruments, and clavier sonatas. **Johann Christian** (1735–1782); called "the Milan, or London, Bach"; cathedral organist, Milan (1760); music master to Queen Charlotte Sophia, London (1762); cofounder of Bach-Abel concerts (1765); composer of operas, oratorios, many arias and cantatas, clavier concertos, chamber music, symphonies, overtures, etc. **Wilhelm Friedrich Ernst** (1759–1845); son of J. C. F. Bach; organist, pianist, and composer; Kapellmeister at Berlin (1789), and later music teacher of royal family; works include cantatas, songs, and piano pieces.

**Bach, Julius Karl von.** 1847–1931. German engineer, b. Stollberg. Aided in development of Zeppelin dirigible.

**Bach, Paul.** See Rudolf BAUMBACH.

**Bache** (bāch), **Alexander Dallas.** 1806–1867. American physicist, b. Philadelphia. Professor, Pennsylvania (1828–36, 1842–43). President, Girard College (1836–42). Superintendent, U.S. Coast Survey (1843–67). First president, National Academy of Sciences; one of incorporators of Smithsonian Institution.

**Bache, Benjamin Franklin.** 1769–1798. American journalist, b. Philadelphia. Founded the Philadelphia *General Advertiser* (later known as the *Aurora*); attacked Washington and Adams; arrested (June 26, 1798) for libeling president; released on parole. His son **Franklin** (1792–1864) was a chemist and educator, b. Philadelphia. With George Bacon Wood, published a *Pharmacopoeia* (1830), which became basis of the *United States Pharmacopoeia*, and compiled a *Dispensatory of the United States of America*.

**Bache, Francis Edward.** 1833–1858. English violinist, organist, and composer of a trio, two operas, a concerto, etc. His brother **Walter** (1842–1888), pupil and exponent of Liszt, whose works he popularized in England, was a concert pianist and professor of pianoforte at Royal Academy.

**Bache, Richard.** 1737–1811. Merchant, b. in Yorkshire, Eng.; to New York (1765); m. (1767) Sarah, daughter of Benjamin Franklin; succeeded Franklin as postmaster general.

**Bachelin, Olivier.** See Olivier BASSELIN.

**Bach'el·ler** (băch'ĕ·lẽr), **Irving Addison.** 1859–1950.

American novelist, b. Pierpont, N.Y. B.S., St. Lawrence U. (1882). Journalist in New York (to c. 1900). Author of *The Master of Silence* (1890), *Eben Holden* (1900), *D'ri and I* (1901), *Keeping Up With Lizzie* (1911), *A Man for the Ages* (1919), *A Candle in the Wilderness* (1930), *The Oxen of the Sun* (1935), *A Boy for the Ages* (1937), etc.

**Ba'cher** (bä'ĸĕr), **Karl.** 1884– . Austrian poet, fiction writer, and playwright.

**Ba'cher** (bä'ĸĕr), **Otto Henry.** 1856–1909. American etcher and illustrator, b. Cleveland, Ohio.

**Bachiacca** *or* **Bacchiacca, Il.** See Francesco UBERTINI.

**Bach'man** (băk'măn), **John.** 1790–1874. American Lutheran clergyman and naturalist, b. Rhinebeck, N.Y. Associated with J. J. Audubon (from 1831); collaborator in *The Viviparous Quadrupeds of North America* (3 vols., 1845–49).

**Bacho, John.** See BACONTHORPE.

**Bach'rach** (băk'răk), **David, Jr.** 1845–1921. American inventor, b. Germany; to U.S. (1850). With Louis Edward Levy (*q.v.*) invented a photoengraving process (1875); founded Bachrach, Inc., photographers.

**Bachur, Elijah.** See Elijah LEVITA.

**Ba·cic'cio** (bä·chēt'chō), **Il.** *Real name* **Giovanni Battista Gaul'li** (goul'lē). 1639–1709. Italian painter; student of Bernini; among his paintings are *Madonna and Child* and *St. Francis Xavier Dying* (both at Rome).

**Back** (băk), Sir **George.** 1796–1878. English explorer. Sailed with Franklin on arctic expeditions of discovery (1818, 1819, 1825); led two expeditions to explore remaining North American coastline (1833, 1836). Admiral (1857). Wrote narratives of voyages.

**Back'er** (bäk'ĕr), **Jakob Adriaensz.** 1608–1651. Dutch painter. Works include *Lady Regents of the Amsterdam Orphan Asylum* and *Guild of Archers* (both in Amsterdam).

**Backers, Americus.** See under John BROADWOOD.

**Back'house** (băk'ŭs), Sir **Roger Roland Charles.** 1878–1939. British admiral; served in World War (1914–18); admiral (1934); commanded home fleet (1935); first sea lord and chief of naval staff (1938); admiral of the fleet (1939).

**Back'huy'sen** *or* **Bak'hui'sen** *or* **Bak'huy'sen** (bäk'hoi'sĕn), **Ludolf.** 1631–1708. Dutch marine painter and etcher. His many paintings include *Rough Sea at the Mouth of the Maas* (now in the Louvre), a coast scene (in Amsterdam), and others in London, The Hague, etc.

**Back'lund** (bȧk'lŭnd), **Johan Oskar.** 1846–1916. Swedish astronomer; investigator of celestial mechanics. Director (from 1895) of observatory at Pulkova, Russia.

**Bäck'ström** (bĕk'strûm), **Per Johan Edvard.** 1841–1886. Swedish writer; author of several volumes of verse and a number of dramas, including the successful tragedy *Dagvard Frey* (1876).

**Back'us** (băk'ŭs), **Isaac.** 1724–1806. American clergyman, b. Norwich, Conn. Separatist from Congregational Church (1746). New Light minister (1748–56). Organizer (1756) and pastor (1756–1806), Baptist Church, Middleborough, Mass. Champion of religious liberty. Author of *A History of New England, with Particular Reference to the Denomination of Christians Called Baptists* (1777–96).

**Back'well** (băk'wĕl; -wĕl), **Edward.** d. 1683. English goldsmith and Lombard Street banker; originator of bank-note system; intermediary in financial transactions between Charles II and Louis XIV.

**Ba'cler' d'Albe'** (bȧ'klâr' dȧlb'), Baron. **Louis Albert Guis'lain'** (gē'läN'). 1762–1824. French painter, esp. of landscapes and battle pictures; officer in Napoleonic armies; made *Carte du Théâtre des Campagnes de Bonaparte en Italie.*

**Ba'con** (bā'kŭn), **Delia Salter.** 1811–1859. American writer, b. Tallmadge, Ohio. Sister of Leonard Bacon (*q.v.*). Worked in England (1853–57) to prove theory that Shakespearean plays were written by group headed by Lord Bacon. Author of *Philosophy of the Plays of Shakspere Unfolded* (1857), origin of so-called Baconian theory. Violently insane (1857–59).

**Bacon, Francis.** 1st Baron **Ver'u·lam** (vĕr'ōō·lăm; vĕr'ū-) [*from Lat.* Verulamium, *present St. Albans*] *and* Viscount **St. Al'bans** (sȧnt ôl'bănz). 1561–1626. English philosopher and author. Son of Nicholas Bacon. Educ. Trinity Coll., Cambridge (1573–75). M.P. (1584 ff.). Attached himself to earl of Essex, Elizabeth's favorite (1591); instrumental in conviction of Essex on charge of treason (1601). Paid court to James I; commissioner for arranging union with Scotland (1604). m. (1606) Alice Barnham, daughter of London alderman. Solicitor general (1607); attorney general (1613); lord chancellor and raised to peerage (1618); promoted increase of monopoly patents which enabled Buckingham's brothers to acquire wealth; confessed himself guilty of bribery and corrupt dealing in chancery suits (1621); fined £40,000 (later remitted by king), banished from parliament and court, and pardoned (1621). Chief literary works include *Essays* (1597 ff.; complete collection of 58 pub. 1625), concise expressions of practical wisdom and full of shrewd observations; *De Sapientia Veterum* (1609); *History of Henry VII* (1622); *Apophthegms New and Old* (1624), a collection of anecdotes and witticisms. Chief philosophical works include *Advancement of Learning* (1605), a survey in English of state of knowledge, as an introduction to a projected (but never completed) *Instauratio Magna*, or encyclopedia of all knowledge; *Novum Organum* (1620), in Latin, key to his system for the new systematic analysis of knowledge, intended to replace the deductive logic of Aristotle with inductive method in interpreting nature; *De Augmentis Scientiarum* (1623), a completion in Latin of the *Advancement.* Legal writings include *Maxims of the Law* (1630), *Reading on the Statute of Uses* (1642).

**Bacon, Frank.** 1864–1922. American actor and playwright, b. Marysville, Cal. To New York (1906); played in *The Fortune Hunter, The Miracle Man, The Cinderella Man.* With Winchell Smith, wrote *Lightnin'*, which had long uninterrupted run in New York (Aug. 26, 1918 to Aug. 27, 1921).

**Bacon, Henry.** 1866–1924. American architect, b. Watseka, Ill. Designed Lincoln Memorial, Washington, D.C.; Public Library, Paterson, N.J.; Court of the Four Seasons, Panama-Pacific Exposition, San Francisco. Collaborated with Daniel Chester French in various memorials to famous Americans.

**Bacon, John.** See BACONTHORPE.

**Bacon, John.** 1740–1799. English sculptor. Won first gold medal awarded for sculpture by Royal Academy (1769); A.R.A. (1770). His monuments to Pitt in Westminster Abbey and to Dr. Johnson in St. Paul's Cathedral are among his chief works.

**Bacon, Josephine Dodge,** *nee* **Das'kam** (dăs'kăm). 1876–1961. American writer, b. Stamford, Conn. A.B., Smith (1898); m. (1903) Selden Bacon. Among her many works are *The Imp and the Angel* (1901), *Poems* (1903), *Memoirs of a Baby* (1904), *Biography of a Boy* (1910), *The Strange Cases of Dr. Stanchon* (1913), *To-Day's Daughter* (1914), *Square Peggy* (1919), *Counterpoint* (1927), *Kathy* (1933), *The House by the Road* (1937), *The Root and the Flower* (1939).

**Bacon, Leonard.** 1802–1881. American Congregational clergyman, b. Detroit, Mich. Brother of Delia Bacon (*q.v.*). Pastor, First Church, New Haven, Conn. (from 1825). One of founders and editor of *The Independent.* Leader in antislavery movement. Author of *Slavery Discussed in Occasional Essays* (1846), *The Genesis of the New England Churches* (1874). His son **Leonard Woolsey** (1830–1907) was also a Congregational clergyman and writer.

**Bacon, Leonard.** 1887–1954. American poet, b. Solvay, N.Y. Author of *Ulug Beg* (1923), *Animula Vagula* (1926), *Guinea Fowl and Other Poultry* (1927), *Lost Buffalo* (1930), *Sunderland Capture and Other Poems* (1940; awarded Pulitzer prize).

**Bacon, Nathaniel.** 1647–1676. American colonial leader of Bacon's Rebellion, b. in England. Emigrated to America (1673); settled in Virginia; tried to force Governor Berkeley to institute reforms; declared by Berkeley to be a rebel. At head of colonial force, captured Jamestown (1676); burned it; required citizens to take oath of fidelity to himself. Initiated conciliatory policy, but died before it could show results.

**Bacon,** Sir **Nicholas.** 1509–1579. Father of Francis Bacon. English lawyer; lord keeper of great seal (1558 to death) under Queen Elizabeth; received full jurisdiction of lord chancellor (1559); managed church matters with Cecil; advocated strict measures against Mary, Queen of Scots.

**Bacon, Peggy.** 1895– . American painter, etcher, illustrator, caricaturist, and writer, b. Ridgefield, Conn.; m. (1920; divorced 1940) Alexander Brook. Author of *Funerealities* (1925), *Ballad of Tangle Street* (1929), *The Terrible Nuisance* (1931), *Off With Their Heads* (1934), *Catcalls* (1935), etc.

**Bacon, Robert.** 1860–1919. American banker and diplomat, b. Jamaica Plain, Mass. Partner in J. P. Morgan & Co. (1894–1903). Asst. secretary of state (1905–09); secretary of state (1909). U.S. ambassador to France (1909–12). On Pershing's staff in World War (1917); chief of American military mission at British general headquarters (1918).

**Bacon, Roger.** 1214?–1294. English philosopher and man of science; called "the Admirable Doctor"—in Latin, "Doc'tor Mi·ra'bi·lis" (dŏk'tẽr mĭ·răb'ĭ·lĭs; dŏk'tôr). Studied at Oxford and Paris; settled at Oxford as Franciscan monk. Experimented in alchemy and optics; knew how to make gunpowder; accused of dealing in black magic. Confined (1257) in Paris for ten years under suspicion by Franciscan order for heretical writings. Prepared a rectified calendar (1263). Prepared on request of Pope Clement IV encyclopedic *Opus Majus* (1268), embracing treatises on grammar, logic, mathematics, physics, philology, and philosophy. Confined again (1278–92). Wrote *Compendium Studii Theologiae* (1292); other works include *Opus Secundum, Opus Tertium.*

**Bacon, Thomas.** 1700?–1768. Anglican clergyman in Maryland, b. on Isle of Man. To Maryland (1745); compiler of *Laws of Maryland* (1765).

**Ba'con·thorpe** (bā'kŭn·thôrp) *or* **Bacon** *or* **Ba'cho** (bā'kō), **John.** d. 1346. English Carmelite scholar; called "the Resolute Doctor." Grandnephew of Roger Bacon. Author of over 120 commentaries. Anticipated Wycliffe in teaching subordination of priestly to kingly power. Expositor of doctrines of Arab Averroës.

**Ba'csá·nyi** (bŏ'chä·nyĭ), **János.** 1763–1845. Hungarian poet; author of patriotic poem *The Valor of the Magyars* (1785); published volume of verse (1827); author of number of fine elegies.

**Baculard d'Arnaud.** See ARNAUD.

**Bad'by** (băd'bĭ), **John.** d. 1410. Lollard martyr; vehemently denied transubstantiation; burned at stake for heresy.

**Ba·deau'** (bă·dō'), **Adam.** 1831–1895. American officer, b. New York City. Military secretary to General Grant (1864–69); author of *Military History of Ulysses S. Grant* (3 vols., 1868, 1881) and *Grant in Peace* (1887).

**Ba'den** (bä'dĕn). German dynasty of 800 years' duration, originating with Hermann, Duke of Carinthia, who assumed title of margrave of Baden (1112); not influential in political history until 1771; lands of family, frequently divided and reunited, became electorate (1803) and grand duchy (1806). Recent rulers (with dates of reigns): Charles Frederick (1738–1811), Charles (1811–18), Louis (1818–30), Leopold (1830–52), Frederick I (1852–1907), Frederick II (1907–abdicated 1918). See also MAXIMILIAN, Prince of Baden.

**Ba·de'ni** (bä·dā'nē), Count **Kasimir Felix.** 1846–1909. Austrian statesman, b. in Galicia. Governor of Galicia (1888); prime minister of Austria-Hungary (1895–97); attempted by ordinance to place Czech language on par with German in Bohemia and Moravia; violently opposed by German-speaking deputies and forced to resign (1897).

**Bad'e·noch** (băd''n·ŏκ), Lord of. See *Alexander Stewart* (1343?–?1405), under STEWART family.

**Ba'den-Pow'ell** (bā'd'n·pō'ĕl). Surname of children of **Baden Powell** (1796–1860), Savilian professor of geometry, Oxford (1827–60), known for investigations in optics and radiation. Among his children were: (1) Sir **George Smyth** [smĭth] **Baden-Powell** (1847–1898), publicist. M.A., Oxon. (1878). Conservative M.P. (1885–98); commissioner on administration of West Indian colonies (1882), details of Malta constitution (1887), and Behring sea fisheries (1891). Author: *Protection and Bad Times* (1879). (2) **Robert Stephenson Smyth** (1857–1941), 1st Baron **Baden-Powell** of **Gil'well** (gĭl'wĕl), soldier. Educ. Charterhouse. Commanded Ashanti levies; chief staff officer, Matabele campaign (1896–97); held Mafeking through 215-day siege by Boers until relieved (1900); made major general; lieutenant general (1908). Inaugurated Boy Scouts (1908) and, with his sister **Agnes** (1858–1945), the Girl Guides (1910). Author of works on army tactics and on scouting and the autobiographical *Lessons of a Lifetime* (1933). (3) **Baden Fletcher Smyth** (1860–1937), soldier. Educ. Charterhouse. Served in New Guinea; on staff through Boer War; bombing and camouflage officer in World War. Invented man-lifting kites (1894); refounded Aeronautical Society (1897). Author of books on travel, ballooning, aeronautics.

**Badī' al-Zamān.** See al-HAMADHANI.

**Ba·dí'a y Le·blich'** (bä·thē'ä ē lā·blēk'), **Domingo.** *Also called* **A·li' Bey el'-Ab·bas'si** (ä·lē' bā' ĕl'äb·bä'sē). 1766–1818. Spanish traveler, b. Barcelona; studied Arabic at Valencia; disguised as Mussulman, visited Morocco (1803–05), Tripoli, Cyprus, Egypt, Mecca (1807; first Christian known to be there since institution of Islam), Jerusalem (1807), and Constantinople (1807); prefect of Córdoba (1812); to Paris after fall of Napoleon. Author of *Voyages d'Ali-Bei en Afrique et en Asie pendant les Années 1803–07* (1814).

**Ba'di·us** (bā'dĭ·ŭs), **Jodocus.** *Lat. name of* **Josse Bade** (bȧd). 1462–?1535. Flemish printer, b. near Brussels. Studied in Italy; professor of Greek and Latin at Lyon. Settled in Paris (c. 1495) and began his independent printing work (c. 1500). Published over 400 volumes, notable for excellent typography and textual accuracy.

**Ba·do'glio** (bä·dô'lyō), **Pietro.** 1871–1956. Italian soldier, b. Grazzano Monferrato, Alessandria. Officer in World War; promoted general (1919); succeeded Diaz as chief of general staff (1919–21); signed armistice for Italy. Ambassador to Brazil (1924). Chief of general staff (1925–28, 1933–40); marshal (1926); governor general of Libya (1928–33); commanded Italian forces in Ethiopian campaign (1935–36), in European war (1940). Succeeded Mussolini as premier (1943–44).

**Baduila.** See TOTILA.

**Baeda.** See Saint BEDE.

**Bae'de·ker** (bā'dĭ·kẽr; *Ger.* bâ'-), **Karl.** 1801–1859. German publisher. Established in Coblenz (1827); issued (1829) a guidebook to Coblenz, followed by a series of world-famous travel handbooks in German, French, and English for most European countries, parts of North America and the Orient, etc.

**Baeke'land** (bāk'lănd; *Flem.* bä'kĕ·länt), **Leo Hendrik.** 1863–1944. Chemist and inventor, b. Ghent, Belgium; educ. U. of Ghent. To U.S. (1889); manufacturer of photographic papers of his own invention; known esp. for discovery of the synthetic resin Bakelite.

**Baer** (bâr), **George Frederick.** 1842–1914. American lawyer and industrialist, b. near Lavansville, Pa. President (1901 ff.), Reading Company; headed resistance to United Mine Workers of America in great strike (1902).

**Baer** (bâr), **Karl Ernst von.** 1792–1876. Estonian naturalist and pioneer embryologist. Studied medicine at Dorpat. To Germany; did research on embryology of chick and on other animals; discovered human ovum and the notochord; showed that the various organs of vertebrates are derived from germ layers by differentiation. Appointed librarian of Academy of Sciences of St. Petersburg (1834). Author of *Über Entwicklungsgeschichte der Thiere* (2 vols., 1828–37), *Untersuchungen über die Entwicklung der Fische* (1835), etc.

**Baer** (bâr), **William Jacob.** 1860–1941. American painter, b. Cincinnati, Ohio; studied in Munich (1880–84); painted portraits and genre pictures (1885–92), and miniatures thereafter, including *Aurora, Summer, Nymph,* and *Primavera.*

**Baerle, Caspar van.** See Casparus BARLAEUS.

**Baer'lein** (bâr'līn), **Henry.** 1875–1960. English journalist and novelist.

**Baert** (bärt), **Jean.** Variant of Jean BART.

**Baert'son** (bärt'sôn), **Albert.** 1866–1922. Belgian painter, as of *Petite Cour au Bord de l'Eau* (in the Luxembourg), *Chalands sous la Neige* (Brussels), *Petite Place Flamande, le Soir* (Antwerp).

**Bae'yer** (bâ'yẽr), **Adolf,** *in full* **Johann Friedrich Wilhelm Adolf, von.** 1835–1917. German organic chemist. Professor at Munich (1875–1915). Known esp. for synthesis of indigo, and of arsenicals, phthaleins, etc. Awarded 1905 Nobel prize for chemistry. His father, **Johann Jacob Baeyer** (1794–1885), German soldier and geologist, was president of Central Bureau of European Surveys at Berlin (1864) and of Berlin Geodetic Institute (1869).

**Bá'ez** (bä'ās), **Cecilio.** 1862–1941. Paraguayan jurist and statesman, b. Asunción; educ. U. of Asunción. President of Paraguay (1906); professor of Civil law, rector (1934 ff), U. of Asunción; minister of foreign affairs (1937 ff.). Author of *Resumen de la Historia del Paraguay* (1910), *Lecciones de Derecho Civil* (1916), *Historia Colonial del Paraguay y Río de la Plata* (1926), *Cantos Épicos al Paraguay,* etc.

**Ba'ez** (bä'ĕz; bīz), **Joan.** 1941– . Am. folk singer, b. Staten Island, N.Y. m. (1968) David Victor Harris.

**Baf'fin** (băf'ĭn), **William.** 1584–1622. English navigator. Pilot on several expeditions in search of Northwest Passage (1612–16); discoverer of Baffin Bay; sailed to latitude 77°45', a record not surpassed for 236 years. First on record to determine longitude by lunar observation.

**Bag'by** (băg'bĭ), **George William.** *Pseudonym* **Moses Adams** *or* **Mo'zis Ad'dums** (mō'zĭs ăd'ŭmz). 1828–1883. American humorist and lecturer, b. in Buckingham County, Va. His lectures include *Bacon and Greens, Women Folks, The Disease Called Love.*

**Bage'hot** (băj'ŭt), **Walter.** 1826–1877. English economist and journalist. M.A., University Coll., London (1848); entered father's shipowning and banking business (1852); editor of *Economist* (1860 till death). Author of *The English Constitution* (1867) and *Lombard Street* (1873), books of description and analysis by a scientific observer; *Physics and Politics* (1869), applying evolutionary theory to politics; *Literary Studies* (1879) and *Economic Studies* (1880).

**Bag'ge·sen** (bäg'ĕ·sĕn; bäg'ĕ·zĕn), **Jens Immanuel.** 1764–1826. Danish poet and satirical humorist. Traveled extensively in Germany, Switzerland, and France; adopted German as second mother tongue. Engaged in literary feuds against romanticism, esp. against Oehlenschläger. Author of *Comical Tales* (1785), *Labyrinthen* (1791), *Parthenais* (in German; 1804), *There Was a Time When I was Very Little* (a Danish song), etc.

**Bag'ley** (băg'lĭ), **William Chandler.** 1874–1946. American educator and writer, b. Detroit. Grad. Mich. State (1895); Ph.D., Cornell (1900). Professor of education, Teachers Coll., Columbia (1917–40); president, National Council of Education (1931–37).

**Ba·glio'ni** (bä·lyō'nē), Cavaliere **Giovanni.** 1571–1644. Italian art historian and painter; called "Il Sor'do del Ba·roz'zo" (ēl sōr'dō dāl bä·rôt'tsō); paintings in St. John Lateran, St. Peter's; wrote *Le Vite de' Pittori, Scultori, Architetti, ed Intagliatori dal Pontificato di Gregorio XIII del 1572 fino a' Tempi di Urbano VIII nel 1642* (1642).

**Ba·gli'vi** (bä·lyē'vē), **Giorgio.** 1669–?1707. Italian physician; propounded theory (solidism) that the solid parts of the body are the seat of disease.

**Ba'gna·ca·val'lo, Il** (ēl bä'nyä·kä·väl'lō). *Real name* **Bartolommeo Ra·men'ghi** (rä·mĕng'gē). 1484–1542. Italian painter; studied under Francia and Raphael; work influenced by Dosso Dossi; aided Raphael in decoration of Vatican; painted *Crucifixion* (St. Peter's, Bologna), *Madonna with Saints* (Bologna), *Circumcision* (Louvre), etc.

**Bag'nold** (băg'nŭld), **Enid.** 1889– . English writer; m. (1920) Sir Roderick Jones. Auth., *A Diary Without Dates* (1917), *Sailing Ships* (verse; 1918), *National Velvet* (novel; 1935), *The Squire* (novel; 1938), etc.

**Bag'ot** (băg'ŭt), Sir **Charles.** 1781–1843. English diplomat and administrator. M.A., Oxon. (1804). Minister to France (1814), U.S. (1815–20); ambassador to St. Petersburg (1820), The Hague (1824). Governor general of Canada (1841–43).

**Ba·gra·ti·on'** (bŭ·grŭ·tyĭ·ôn'), Prince **Pëtr Ivanovich.** 1765–1812. Russian general, of noble Georgian family. Entered Russian army (1782); served under Suvorov; at siege of Ochakov (1788) and in Polish campaign (1792, 1794); in campaigns in Italy and Switzerland (1799) and Austro-Russian War (1805) against French; noted for successful resistance to greatly superior force at Hollabrunn near Vienna (1805); fought at Austerlitz (1805), Eylau and Friedland (1807), and in campaign against Turks (1809–10); in war with French (1812), defeated at Mogilëv and mortally wounded at Borodino.

**Ba·ha' al-Din'** (bă·hä' ŏŏd·dēn'). *Also* **Be·ha' ud-Din'** (bă·hä' ŏŏd·dēn') *and* **Bo'had·din'** (bō'ă·dēn'). *Arab.* **Bahā'-al-Dīn ibn-Shaddād.** 1145–1234. Arab writer and statesman, b. Mosul. Secretary and biographer of Saladin; cadi of Jerusalem (1188–93); after Saladin's death (1193), cadi of Aleppo (1193–1231).

**Baha al-Din Zu·hayr′** (zōō·hīr′). *Arab.* **Bahā' al-Din Zuhayr.** 1186–1258. Arab poet. Secretary in Egyptian government and court poet of the Ayyubids; noted for polished and delicate productions.

**Ba·ha′dur Shah** (bȧ·hä′dōōr shä′). Name of two rulers of Hindustan of Mogul dynasty. **Bahadur Shah I.** *Also called* Shah **Alam.** d. 1712. Son and successor of Aurangzeb; known before accession as Prince **Muazzim;** defeated his brother and assumed crown; ruled 1707–12. **Bahadur Shah II.** *Orig.* **Mohammed Bahadur Shah.** 1768?–1862. Last ruler (nominal only) of Mogul dynasty of Hindustan (1837–57); affairs of his realm controlled by East India Company; at time of Sepoy Mutiny (1857) fled to tomb of Humayun, south of Delhi; captured by Major Hodson; tried for rebellion, found guilty, and sentenced to imprisonment for life (1858); died at Rangoon.

**Ba·ha′ul·lah′** (bä·hä′ōōl·lä′), *i.e.* Splendor of God. *Real name* Mirza (*i.e.* Prince) **Husayn Ali.** 1817–1892. Persian religious leader, b. Teheran. Founder of Bahaism. Became follower of the Bab (1850); persecuted and imprisoned (1852); exiled to Baghdad; preached Babism successfully in Baghdad; exiled to Constantinople, then Adrianople, and finally to Akka (Acre), near Mt. Carmel; claimed (1863) to be leader promised by the Bab; took title Bahaullah as head of new Bahai faith; preached and wrote much during years of exile. Succeeded by his son Abdul Baha (*q.v.*).

**Bah′ma·ni** (bä′mȧ·nē; *Arab.* bä·mä·nē′). Mohammedan dynasty of the Deccan, founded by Ala-ud-din (*q.v.*). Its fourteen members ruled (1347–1526) all provinces south of the Vindhya Hills.

**Bahr** (bär), **Hermann.** 1863–1934. Austrian journalist, playwright, and theater manager. Champion successively of naturalism, romanticism, and symbolism. Author of *Zur Kritik der Moderne* (1890), *Das Konzert* (1900), *Der Meister* (1903), *Himmelfahrt* (1916), *Der Unmensch* (1920), *Der Inwendige Garten* (1927), etc.

**Bah·ram′** (bä·räm′). *Also* **Vah·ram′** (vä·räm′) *or* **Va′rah·ran′** (vä′rä·rän′) *or* **Va·ra′nes** (vȧ·rā′nēz). Name of five kings of the Sassanidae of Persia, esp.: **Bahram V.** *Called* **Gor** (gôr), *i.e.* wild ass. Son of Yazdegerd I and father of Yazdegerd II. King (420–440). Began persecution of Christians, which led to war with Rome; defeated (422); granted same toleration to Christianity that Zoroastrianism received in Roman Empire. Great hunter; a favorite in Persian tradition; mentioned in Omar Khayyám's *Rubáiyát* xviii.

**Bahrdt** (bärt), **Karl Friedrich.** 1741–1792. German Protestant rationalistic theologian. Dismissed from professorship (1766–75) at Leipzig and Erfurt because of profligacy and at Giessen because of his heretical translation of New Testament (1773–75). Lectured and engaged in controversial writing, Halle, Prussia (1779–89); imprisoned (1789) because of his satire *Das Religionsedikt;* spent last ten years of life as innkeeper. Other works include *Briefe über die Bibel im Volkston* (1782) and an autobiography (4 vols., 1790).

**Bah·ri′** (bȧ·rē′) *or* **Bah′rites** (bȧ′rīts; bä′-). One of the two (see also BURJI) Mameluke dynasties of Egypt, having 24 sultans (ruled 1250–1390). Originated in purchased bodyguard of an Ayyubid sultan who settled his slaves on an island in the Nile—hence the name (from Arab. *baḥr,* large river, the Nile). Bahri were chiefly Turks and Mongols; many of the sultans were slaves that rose to be army commanders and seized power.

**Baḥur, Elijah.** See Elijah LEVITA.

**Baḥ′ya ibn-Pa·qu′da.** *In full* **Baḥ′ya ben Jo′seph ibn Pa·ku′da** (bȧ′yä bĕn jō′zĕf [-zĭf] ĭb′′n pȧ·kōō′dä). 11th-century Jewish writer on religion; resident in Saragossa, Spain; author of a treatise in Arabic translated as *Duties of the Heart.*

**Bai** *or* **Baj** (bä′ē), **Tommaso.** 1660?–1714. Italian tenor and composer; Kapellmeister, Vatican (1713–14); wrote a celebrated *Miserere.*

**Baibars.** See BAYBARS.

**Bai·da′wi, al-** (ăl′bī·dä′wĭ). *Arab.* **'Abdallāh ibn-'Umar al-Baidāwi.** d. 1286? Mohammedan critic, b. in Fars, Persia. Cadi of Shiraz; wrote a commentary on the Koran accepted by the Sunnites; author of other treatises, including a history of Persia.

**Ba′ïf′** (bȧ′ēf′), **Jean Antoine de.** 1532–1589. French poet; one of The Pléiade; author of *Passe-Temps* and *Mimes, Enseignements et Proverbes.* Unsuccessfully tried to introduce unrhymed verse of the ancients into French poetry.

**Bai′kie** (bā′kĭ), **James.** 1866–1931. Scottish clergyman and Egyptologist, b. in Midlothian. Author of *The Story of the Pharaohs* (1st ed., 1908), *The Sea-Kings of Crete* (1st ed., 1910), *Lands and People of the Bible* (1914), *A Century of Excavations* (1923), *A History of Egypt* (2 vols., 1929), *The Ancient East and its Story* (1929), etc.

**Baikie, William Balfour.** 1825–1864. Scottish naturalist and philologist. M.D., Edinburgh. Naval surgeon (1848). Surgeon and naturalist on Niger expedition (1854); wrecked on second expedition (1859); settled at Lokoja, setting up native commonwealth with himself as head. Compiled vocabularies of 50 native dialects; translated portions of Bible into Hausa.

**Bailén,** Duque **de.** See Francisco Javier de CASTAÑOS.

**Bai′ley** (bā′lĭ), Sir **Abe.** 1864–1940. South African financier and politician, b. Cradock, Cape Colony (Cape of Good Hope). To Transvaal in gold rush of 1880; amassed fortune from mining; friend of Cecil Rhodes; aided in organizing Union of South Africa; served in Boer War (1899–1902). Member, Transvaal Legislative Assembly (1910–24).

**Bailey, Florence Augusta,** *nee* **Mer′ri·am** (mĕr′ĭ·ăm). 1863–1948. American ornithologist, b. Locust Grove, N.Y.; sister of Clinton Hart Merriam (*q.v.*) and wife (1899) of Vernon Bailey (*q.v.*). Grad. Smith (1886). Author of *Birds Through an Opera Glass* (1889), *Handbook of Birds of the Western United States* (1902), *Cave Life in Kentucky* (1933), etc.

**Bailey, Gamaliel.** 1807–1859. American antislavery advocate, b. Mount Holly, N.J. Edited (1836–46) *Cincinnati Philanthropist,* first antislavery paper in West, and (1847–59) *National Era,* a Washington (D.C.) weekly journal under auspices of American and Foreign Anti-Slavery Society.

**Bailey, Guy Winfred.** 1876–1940. American educator, b. Hardwick, Vt.; A.B., U. of Vermont (1900); Vermont secretary of state (1908–17); president of U. of Vermont (from 1920).

**Bailey, Henry Christopher.** 1878–1961. English writer, esp. of detective stories; creator of fictional amateur detective Reggie Fortune, as in *Mr. Fortune Speaking, Clue for Mr. Fortune, The Bishop's Crime,* and of the criminal lawyer Joshua Clunk, as in *Orphan Ann* (1941).

**Bailey, James Anthony.** 1847–1906. American circus owner, b. Detroit. Combined (1881) his circus with that of P. T. Barnum (*q.v.*). See also RINGLING.

**Bailey, James Montgomery.** 1841–1894. American journalist, known as the "Danbury News Man," b. Albany, N.Y. Served in Civil War; captured at Gettysburg. Bought (1865) *Danbury Times,* Danbury, Conn., and merged it (1870) with the *Jeffersonian* to form the *Danbury News,* a weekly paper that became famous for the wit and humor with which real and fictitious news items were presented.

**Bailey, Liberty Hyde.** 1858–1954. American horticulturist and botanist, b. South Haven, Mich. Grad. Mich. State (1882). Professor of horticulture (1888–1903) and director of agricultural experiment station (1903–13), Cornell. Known for research on North American sedges, blackberries, raspberries, and New World palms, as well as work on rural problems and education. Editor of *Cyclopedia of American Agriculture, Cyclopedia of American Horticulture, Standard Cyclopedia of Horticulture;* author of *Hortus* (dictionary of gardening), *How Plants Get their Names,* etc.

**Bailey, Nathan** *or* **Nathaniel.** d. 1742. English lexicographer. Author of *An Universal Etymological English Dictionary* (1721), an interleaved copy of which formed basis of Dr. Johnson's dictionary.

**Bailey, Philip James.** 1816–1902. English poet of the "spasmodic school." Studied at Glasgow. Author of *Festus* (1839), based on story of Faust, greatly altered in later editions.

**Bailey, Solomon Irving.** 1854–1931. American astronomer, b. Lisbon, N.H. Grad. Boston U. (1881); sent (1889) to Peru to determine best location for southern station for Harvard College observatory; selected Arequipa; in charge of work there (from 1892); established (1893) highest scientific station in the world, on top of El Misti (19,000 feet). Asst. professor of astronomy (1893), associate professor (1898), professor (1913–25), Harvard. Author of articles on meteors, stellar photometry, variable stars, star clusters, etc.

**Bailey, Temple,** *in full* **Irene Temple.** d. 1953. American novelist, b. Petersburg, Va.; author of *Glory of Youth* (1913), *The Trumpeter Swan* (1920), *The Gay Cockade* (1921), *Peacock Feathers* (1924), *Silver Slippers* (1928), *Enchanted Ground* (1933), *Fair as the Moon* (1935), etc.

**Bailey, Vernon.** 1864–1942. American biologist, b. Manchester, Mich. Chief field naturalist, U.S. Biological Survey (retired 1933). Author of *Spermophiles of the Mississippi Valley* (1893), *Life Zones and Crop Zones of New Mexico* (1913), *Beaver Habits and Beaver Farming* (1923), *Mammals of Oregon* (1936), etc. See Florence Augusta BAILEY.

**Bail'lar'ger'** (bȧ'yȧr'zhā'), **Jules Gabriel François.** 1806–1891. French physician; known for his skill in treating mental disorders.

**Bail'let'** (bȧ'yĕ'), **Adrien.** 1649–1706. French priest and scholar; author of *Les Vies des Saints,* etc.

**Bail'lie** (bā'lĭ), Lady **Grizel.** 1665–1746. Scottish poet. As a child, carried food to her father, Sir Patrick Hume, who had been forced into hiding, and messages to the imprisoned patriot Robert Baillie of Jerviswood (whose son George she married, 1692); shared parents' exile in Utrecht (1684–88). Some of her ballads are included in Allan Ramsay's *Tea-Table Miscellany.*

**Baillie, Joanna.** 1762–1851. Scottish dramatist and poet. From youth, lived in London and with her sister in Hampstead. Author of *Fugitive Verses* (anon.; 1790), a series of *Plays on the Passions* (1798, 1802, 1812), three volumes of dramas (1836). Her play *De Montfort* was produced by Kemble and Mrs. Siddons; *The Family Legend* (1810) was most successful. Her brother **Matthew** (1761–1823) was a physician; author of *Morbid Anatomy of Some of the Most Important Parts of the Human Body,* an early treatise on pathology.

**Baillie, Robert.** 1599–1662. Scottish clergyman. Professor of divinity, Glasgow U. (1642); sent to Westminster Assembly (1643); principal, Glasgow U. (1661). His *Letters and Journals* are of historical importance.

**Baillie-Hamilton.** Family name of the earls of HADDINGTON.

**Baillie of Jer'vis·wood** (jär'vĭs·wŏŏd; jûr'vĭs-), **Robert.** d. 1684. Scottish politician and conspirator; hanged for treason at Edinburgh (Dec. 4, 1684).

**Bail'lon'** (bȧ'yôɴ'), **Ernest Henri.** 1827–1895. French physician and naturalist, b. Calais; author of *Dictionnaire de Botanique* and *Histoire des Plantes.*

**Bail'lot'** (bȧ'yō'), **Pierre Marie François de Sales** (sȧl). 1771–1842. French violinist; composer for violin and author of books on violin playing, notably *Méthode de Violon* (with Rode and Kreutzer).

**Bail'ly'** (bȧ'yē'), **Jean Sylvain.** 1736–1793. French scholar and politician, b. Paris. Author of histories of ancient, modern, and East Indian astronomy. President of States-General (1789); mayor of Paris (1789); imposed martial law and called out National Guard to keep order (1791); lost popularity; guillotined (Nov. 10).

**Bai'ly** (bā'lĭ), **Edward Hodges.** 1788–1867. English sculptor. Studied under Flaxman (1807); R.A. (1821). Established reputation with *Eve at the Fountain* (1818); executed figures on Marble Arch, and statue of Nelson in Trafalgar Square, London.

**Baily, Francis.** 1774–1844. English astronomer. Made fortune on stock exchange and retired from business (1825). A founder of Royal Astronomical Society (1820); revised several star catalogues and improved *Nautical Almanac;* first to describe fully (1836) the phenomenon of bright spots (Baily's beads) observed along moon's disk during total eclipse of sun. Author of *Account of the Rev. John Flamsteed* (1835) and works on life annuities.

**Bain** (bān), **Alexander.** 1810–1877. Scottish electrician, b. Thurso; inventor of chemical telegraph.

**Bain, Alexander.** 1818–1903. Scottish psychologist. Educ. U. of Aberdeen; taught philosophy (1841–45). Secretary, London board of health (1848–50); examiner in logic and moral philosophy, U. of London (1857–62); member of the circle including Grote and J. S. Mill; professor of logic and English literature, U. of Aberdeen (1860–80). Known for his application to psychology of the findings of physiology and for elevating standard of education in Scotland. Author of *The Senses and the Intellect* (1855), *Emotions and the Will* (1859), *Mental and Moral Science,* a condensation of his philosophical writings (1868), *Logic* (1870), *Mind and Body* (1872), *Education as a Science* (1879), biographies of James and J. S. Mill (1882), and works on grammar and rhetoric; edited Grote's minor works (1873); founded the periodical *Mind* (1876).

**Bain, Francis William.** 1863–1940. British writer, b. Bothwell, Lanark; author of *Christina of Sweden, The Principle of Wealth Creation, The English Monarchy and its Revolutions, A Heifer of the Dawn, An Incarnation of the Snow, An Echo of the Spheres,* etc.

**Bain'bridge** (bān'brĭj), **William.** 1774–1833. American naval officer, b. Princeton, N.J. Served in war with Tripoli (1801–05) and in War of 1812.

**Baines** (bānz), **Edward** (1774–1848) and his son Sir **Edward** (1800–1890). English journalists. Proprietors of the Leeds *Mercury.* Members of parliament. Champions of reform; advocated separation of church and state; opposed governmental interference in education. Wrote historical books.

**Baines, Frederick Ebenezer.** 1832–1911. Promoter of British post office telegraph system. Advocated successfully acquisition by government of telegraph systems (1856–70); organized parcel post service (1883).

**Ba·i'ni** (bä·ē'nē), **Giuseppe.** 1775–1844. Italian clergyman, composer, musical critic; Kapellmeister, Vatican (1818 ff.); composed a *Miserere;* wrote *Memorie Storico-Critiche della Vita e delle Opere di Giovanni Pierluigi da Palestrina* (2 vols., 1828).

**Bain′ville′** (băɴ′vēl′), **Jacques.** 1879–1936. French journalist, b. Vincennes. A founder of modern royalist movement and of royalist journal *L'Action Française.* Author of historical and political works.

**Bai·rak·dar′** (bī·räk·där′), **Mustafa.** 1775–1808. Grand vizier of Ottoman Empire; marched on Constantinople (1808) to reinstate Selim III, who had been deposed by Janizaries; deposed Mustafa IV; made Mahmud II sultan, Selim having been killed; committed suicide to avoid capture by Janizaries.

**Baird** (bârd), Sir **David.** 1757–1829. Scottish soldier. Served as captain in India; prisoner there (1780–84); returned to last war against Tippoo (1791–99); served in campaigns in Egypt (1801–02), Cape of Good Hope (1805–06), Copenhagen (1807); second in command in Spain (1808); lost left arm at Coruña; K.B. (1809); baronet (1810); general (1814). On several occasions passed over in choice of commander. Commander in chief in Ireland (1820–22).

**Baird, Henry Martyn.** 1832–1906. American Presbyterian clergyman, b. Philadelphia. Author of books on history of the Huguenots.

**Baird, James.** 1802–1876. Scottish ironmaster; liberal benefactor of Church of Scotland; deputy lieutenant for counties of Ayr and Inverness; founder (1871) of Baird Lectures for defense of orthodox religious education.

**Baird, John L.** 1888–1946. Scottish inventor. Educ. Royal Technical College and Glasgow U. Inventor of Televisor, early practical television apparatus, and of Noctovisor, a device for seeing in the dark by invisible rays.

**Baird, John Lawrence.** 1st Baron **Stone′ha′ven** (stōn′hā′vĕn). 1874–1941. British diplomat and politician; governor general of Australia (1925–30).

**Baird, Spencer Fullerton.** 1823–1887. American zoologist, b. Reading, Pa. Asst. secretary (1850–78), secretary (1878 ff.), Smithsonian Institution, Washington, D.C. First U.S. fish commissioner (1871 ff.). Works include *Catalogue of North American Mammals* (1857), *Catalogue of North American Birds* (1858), *A History of North American Birds* (with T. M. Brewer and R. Ridgway).

**Bairns′fa′ther** (bârnz′fä′thẽr), **Bruce.** 1888–1959. English soldier, artist, and journalist, b. in India; son of army major. Served in France (from 1914); captain (1915); transferred to war office (1916) for work abroad. Creator of famous "Old Bill" cartoons. Wrote and illustrated *Fragments from France* (6 vols.); *The Better 'Ole; Bullets and Billets; From Mud to Mufti; Old Bill, M.P.1.*

**Ba′ius** (bā′yŭs) *or* **Ba′jus** (bā′jŭs), **Mi′chael** (mī′kĕl; -k'l). *Latinized name of* **Mi′chel′ de Bay′** (mē′shĕl′ dē bā′). 1513–1589. Belgian Catholic theologian; professor at Louvain (1575). His doctrines on free will, predestination, and grace, containing germ of Jansenism, condemned by Pope Pius V.

**Baj, Tommaso.** See BAI.

**Baj′a·zet′** (băj′ȧ·zĕt′). *Also* **Ba·ya·zid′** (bī·yä·zēd′) *and* **Ba·ye·zid′** (bī·yĕ·zēd′). Name of two sultans of Ottoman Empire:

**Bajazet I.** *Called* **Yil·de·rim′** (yĭl·dĭ·rĭm′), *i.e.* lightning. 1347–1403. Sultan (1389–1403). Son of Murad I. Strangled younger brother, Yakub; first to take title "sultan"; overran countries of southeastern Europe and Asia Minor; at Nicopolis (Nikopol, Bulgaria), defeated (1396) allied Christian army of Poles, Hungarians, and French; led army against Mongol invader Tamerlane; defeated near Angora (1402) and taken prisoner.

**Bajazet II.** 1447–1513. Sultan (1481–1512). Son of Mohammed II. Strengthened Turkish power in Europe by wars with Poland, Hungary, and (1499–1502) Venice; threatened by Mamelukes of Egypt (1488–91); engaged in long struggle with Persia; last years of reign troubled by rivalry and revolts of three sons; built several fine mosques, esp. in Adrianople and Constantinople (1505); forced to abdicate (1512) in favor of son Selim.

**Baj′er** (bī′ẽr), **Fredrik.** 1837–1922. Danish statesman and writer. Member of Folketing (1872–95); founder of Danish Peace Society (1882); founder (1891) and president, International Peace Bureau, Bern. Author of *The Scandinavian Neutrality System* (1906) and other works on neutrality. Co-winner (with Klas Arnoldson) of 1908 Nobel peace prize.

**Ba′ji Ra′o** (bä′jē rä′ōō). Name of two Maratha peshwas:

**Baji Rao I.** d. 1740. Second peshwa (1720–40); son of Balaji Vishvanath. Organized his nation against Moslem powers in north; came to terms with his southern rival, the Nizam of Hyderabad (1731); conquered Gujarat, Malwa, and Bundelkhand, and (1737) threatened Delhi; made league with Rajputs against Moguls (1739).

**Baji Rao II.** d. 1852. Seventh and last peshwa (1795–1818); son of Raghunath Rao. Opposed by Holkar (*q.v.*) Maratha dynasty; forced to seek aid from British; signed Treaty of Bassein (1802) with Indian government; after Second Maratha War (1802–04) in which other Maratha houses were defeated, retained rule at Poona as British subsidiary; later, in Third Maratha War (1817–18), defeated by British; retired as pensioner at Bithur, near Cawnpore.

**Baj′pai** (bäj′pī), Sir **Girja Shankar.** 1891–1954. Indian statesman and diplomat; educ. Oxford. Envoy of India to U.S. (1941–47).

**Bajus, Michael.** See Michael BAIUS.

**Baj′za** (boi′zŏ), **József.** 1804–1858. Hungarian journalist, theater manager, and poet; editor of *Kritikai Lapok* (*Critical Leaves;* 1831–36), *Athenaeum* (1837–43), and *Figyelmezö* (*Observer*); director of National Theater at Pest (1837). Published volume of verse (1835).

**Bake′less** (bāk′lĕs; -lĭs), **John Edwin.** 1894– American writer and editor, b. Carlisle, Pa.; A.B., Williams (1918); Ph.D., Harvard (1936). On editorial staff of *Living Age* (1921–25, 1928–29) and *The Forum* (1926–28); literary editor, *Literary Digest* (1937–38). Teacher of journalism, N.Y.U. (from 1927). Author of *The Economic Causes of Modern War* (1921), *Christopher Marlowe*...(1937), etc.

**Ba′ker** (bā′kẽr), Sir **Benjamin.** 1840–1907. English civil engineer. In association with Sir John Fowler, planned Forth bridge (Scotland), underground railways, the Tower bridge, and Blackwall tunnel (all in London), and assisted in Upper Egypt with Aswan and Asyut dams (completed 1902).

**Baker, Benjamin A.** 1818–1890. American actor, playwright, and manager, b. New York City. Introduced the topical play, with *A Glance at New York in 1848* (1848), *New York As It Is* (1848).

**Baker, Benjamin Franklin.** 1811–1889. American musician, b. Wenham, Mass. Established Boston Music School (1857). Composed *Stars of the Summer Night* (vocal quartet; 1865), *The Storm King* (cantata; 1856).

**Baker, Burtis,** *in full* **Samuel Burtis.** 1882– . American portrait, figure, landscape, and still-life painter; b. Boston.

**Baker, Ernest A.** 1869–1941. English librarian and man of letters; B.A., London (1892). First director, U. of London School of Librarianship (1919–34). Compiler of several anthologies; author notably of *History of the English Novel* (10 vols., 1924–39).

**Baker, Frank Collins.** 1867–1942. American zoologist, b. Warren, R.I. Curator, natural history museum, U. of Illinois (from 1918). Author of *A Naturalist in*

*Mexico* (1895), *The Lymnaeidae of North and Middle America* (1911), *Fresh Water Mollusca of Wisconsin* (1928), etc.

**Baker, George Augustus.** 1821–1880. American portrait painter, b. New York City. His son **George Augustus** (1849–1910) was a lawyer and writer; author of a volume of society verse *Point Lace and Diamonds* (1875), *Bad Habits of Good Society* (1876), and some comedies.

**Baker, George Fisher.** 1840–1931. American financier, b. Troy, N.Y. A founder (1863), president (from 1877), board chairman (from 1909), First National Bank, New York City. Benefactor of Harvard School of Business Administration. His son **George** (1878–1937) succeeded him (1931) as head of the bank.

**Baker, George Pierce.** 1866–1935. American educator, b. Providence, R.I. A.B., Harvard (1887). Taught English at Harvard (1888–1924; professor from 1905); made reputation as teacher of dramatic composition in his course in play writing (English 47 in the college catalogue, hence the phrase "The 47 Workshop"). Professor of the history and technique of the drama and director of the university theater, Yale (1925–35). Author of *The Development of Shakespeare as a Dramatist* (1907), *Dramatic Technique* (1919). Edited various Elizabethan plays and *Plays of the 47 Workshop*, *Yale One-Act Plays*, *Yale Long Plays* (4 vols.). Special editor for drama terms, *Webster's New International Dictionary, Second Edition.*

**Baker, Henry.** 1698–1774. English naturalist. Invented a system of instruction for deaf-mutes. Conducted, with his father-in-law, Daniel Defoe, *Universal Spectator and Weekly Journal* (1728–31). Received Copley gold medal (1744) for microscopical experiments on saline particles. Author of philosophical poem on the universe, as well as works on microscopy.

**Baker,** Sir **Henry Williams.** 1821–1877. English clergyman and hymn writer; editor of *Hymns Ancient and Modern* (1861), the most representative collection of hymns in use in Church of England.

**Baker,** Sir **Herbert.** 1862–1946. English architect; commenced practice in South Africa, at first for Cecil Rhodes; designed Groote Schuur for Rhodes, Government House and Union buildings for South African government at Pretoria, cathedrals at Capetown, Pretoria, and Salisbury in Rhodesia. Established offices in London; designed Rhodes House at Oxford, Bank of England buildings, India House at Aldwych, and Winchester College war memorial. Also designed secretariat and legislative buildings for new capital at Delhi, India.

**Baker, Lorenzo Dow.** 1840–1908. American sea captain and merchant, b. Wellfleet, Mass. First importer of bananas from Jamaica (1870); one of organizers of Boston Fruit Co. (1885); managing director of Jamaica division, United Fruit Co. (1897 ff.).

**Baker, Marcus.** 1849–1903. American geographer, b. Kalamazoo, Mich. Member, U.S. Geological Survey (1886 ff.). Prepared report for U.S. government on Venezuelan boundary question; retained by Venezuela as an expert in this case. A founder and manager, National Geographic Society.

**Baker, Newton Diehl.** 1871–1937. American lawyer and statesman, b. Martinsburg, W.Va. B.A., Johns Hopkins (1892); LL.B., Washington and Lee (1894). Practiced at Martinsburg, then at Cleveland, Ohio; city solicitor (1902–12) and mayor (1912–16), Cleveland. U.S. secretary of war (1916–21). Member, Permanent Court of Arbitration at The Hague (1928). Awarded medal by National Institute of Social Sciences (1933) "for services to humanity."

**Baker, Ray Stannard.** 1870–1946. American journalist and author, b. Lansing, Mich. B.S., Michigan State (1889). On staff of Chicago *Record* (1892–97), *McClure's Magazine* (1899–1905), *American Magazine* (1906–15); director of press bureau for American Commission to Negotiate Peace, Paris (1919). Authorized biographer of Woodrow Wilson. Author of *Seen in Germany* (1901), *The Spiritual Unrest* (1910), *Woodrow Wilson and World Settlement, a History of the Peace Conference* (3 vols., 1922), *Woodrow Wilson—Life and Letters* (8 vols., 1927–39), the autobiographical *Native American* (1941), and, under pseudonym **David Gray′son** (grā′s'n), *Adventures in Contentment* (1907), *Adventures in Friendship* (1910), *Adventures in Understanding* (1925), *Adventures in Solitude* (1931).

**Baker,** Sir **Richard.** 1568–1645. English writer of a widely used *Chronicle of the Kings of England* (from Roman period to 1625).

**Baker,** Sir **Samuel White.** 1821–1893. English traveler and explorer. Founded agricultural colony in Ceylon (1848 ff.); supervised construction of railway from Danube to Black Sea (1859–60); explored Nile tributaries in Abyssinia (1861–62); discovered Lake Albert (1864); as governor general of equatorial regions of Nile, took steps to suppress slave trade and establish administration (1869–74). Author of accounts of explorations, as *Ismaïlia* (1874), of *Wild Beasts and Their Ways* (1890) on big-game hunting, etc. His younger brother **Valentine** (1827–1887), known as **Baker Pa·sha′** (pä·shä′), served in Kaffir War (1852–53) and Crimean War (1854–56); in sultan's service in Russo-Turkish War (1877–78); in Egyptian service and commander of police (1882–87); defeated (1884) by Osman Digna near Suakin; author of *Clouds in the East* (1876), *War in Bulgaria* (1879).

**Baker, Sara Josephine.** 1873–1945. American pediatrician, b. Poughkeepsie, N.Y. M.D., Woman's Medical Coll., New York Infirmary (1898). Director, Bureau of Child Hygiene, New York City (1908–23); organized first bureau of child hygiene under government control and thus aided in establishing in New York City lowest baby death rate of any large city. Author of *Healthy Mothers* (1923), *Healthy Babies* (1923), *Child Hygiene* (1925), *Fighting for Life* (1939), etc.

**Baker, Thomas Stockham.** 1871–1939. American educator, b. Aberdeen, Md. A.B. (1891) and Ph.D. (1895), Johns Hopkins. President, Carnegie Tech. (1922–35). Active in cause of international peace.

**Baker, Valentine.** See under Sir Samuel White BAKER.

**Bake′well** (bāk′wĕl; -wĕl), **Robert.** 1725–1795. English agriculturist. A pioneer in practice of systematic inbreeding; produced Leicestershire breed of sheep and Dishley, or New Leicestershire Longhorn, breed of cattle; first to establish on a large scale the letting of rams for breeding.

**Bakhuisen** *or* **Bakhuysen, Ludolf.** See BACKHUYSEN.

**Bak′hui′zen van den Brink** (bäk′hoi′zĕn vän dĕn brĭngk′), **Reinier Cornelius.** 1810–1865. Dutch historian, critic, and fiction writer. Coeditor of *De Gids* (1837–43); government archivist (from 1850).

**Bakin** *or* **Kyo·ku·tei Ba·kin** (kyō·kōō·tā bä·kēn). 1767–1848. Japanese novelist, b. Tokyo. Wrote 142 novels, of which best known is *Hakkenden* (*Tale of Eight Dogs*), in 106 volumes (1814–41).

**Bak·ri′, al-** (ăl′băk·rē′) *or* **al-Bek·ri′** (ăl′bĕk·rē′). *Arab.* **abu-'Ubayd al-Bakri.** 1040?–1094. Arab geographer, b. Córdoba, Spain. Student of poetry and philology; author of important medieval work on geography, *The Book of Roads and Kingdoms*, extant only in part.

**Bakst** (bȧkst), **Lé′on′** (lā′ôN′) **Nikolaevich.** *Orig. sur-*

*name* **Rosenberg.** 1866?–1924. Russian painter and decorative artist, b. St. Petersburg, of Jewish parents. Studied at Imperial Acad. of Arts and at Paris. At St. Petersburg and Moscow (1900–06), painted genre scenes and portraits; to Paris (1906); began painting stage settings. Won universal recognition as chief artist of scenery for Russian ballets produced by Diaghilev, including *Cleopatra, Scheherazade, Salome, Daphnis and Chloe;* designed stage settings for Wolf-Ferrari's opera *Secret of Suzanne*, Musorgski's *Boris Godunov*, D'Annunzio's *La Pisanelle* and *Saint Sébastien*, and Pavlova's *Orientale* (N.Y., 1914) and *Istar* (Paris, 1924). Founded liberal school of painting in Russia; first visited U.S. 1922.

**Ba·ku′nin** (bŭ·kōō′nyĭn), **Mikhail Aleksandrovich.** 1814–1876. Russian anarchist and writer, b. in Tver government, of aristocratic family. Educ. St. Petersburg military school; served in Imperial Guard; traveled in Germany, France, and Switzerland (1841–47). Refused to return to Russia at government's demand and lost his property; expelled from Paris (1847) because of violent speech urging Poles and Russians to overthrow absolute monarchy; active in European revolutionary movements (1848–49); sentenced to death in Austria but handed over (1851) to Czarist government; sent to eastern Siberia (1855); escaped, returning to Europe via Japan and U.S. (1861). Leading anarchist in Europe (1861–76); worked with Marx and Engels; expelled (1872) from First International for his militant views; developed Bakuninism, esp. in *God and the State* (pub. 1882). His ideas gained considerable power in Spain (1870–73) and, at times, in other European countries; his doctrines (principal tenets: atheism, destruction of the state, and ultraindividualistic rights) established Nihilism in Russia.

**Bala.** See BILHAH.

**Ba′laam** (bā′lăm). In Bible, a diviner summoned by Moabite king **Ba′lak** (bā′lăk), *in Douay Version* **Ba′lac** (-lăk), to curse the Israelites; story of his journey, of his being rebuked by his ass, and of his blessing instead of cursing the Israelites, told in *Num.* xxii–xxiv.

**Ba·la·ba′nov** (bȧ·lŭ·bȧ′nôf), **Angelica.** *Russ.* **Anzhelika Ba·la·ba′no·va** (bȧ·lŭ·bȧ′nŭ·vŭ). 1878–1965. Russian revolutionist, b. near Kiev. Studied in Zurich, Brussels, Berlin, Leipzig, London. Assoc. editor with Mussolini of *Avanti.* Worked with Lenin and Trotsky in Russian Revolution; first secretary of Third International. Disillusioned by events, left Russia and became teacher of languages in Vienna. Author of *My Life as a Rebel* (1938).

**Balafré, le.** Nickname of **François** and **Henri I de Lorraine,** Ducs **de Guise.** See GUISE family.

**Ba′la·guer′ y Ci·re′ra** (bä′lä·gĕr′ ē thē·rä′rä), **Víctor.** 1824–1901. Spanish poet, scholar, and statesman, b. Barcelona. Professor of history, U. of Barcelona; leader of liberal party at Barcelona (1843–68); minister of public works (1872), colonies, and finance; senator; known esp. for studies in Catalonian history and legends; leader in establishment of Catalan Juegos Florales (a literary fiesta) at Barcelona. Author of lyric poem *El Trovador de Montserrat* (1850), *Historia de Cataluña y de la Corona de Aragón* (1860–63), *Historia Política y Literaria de los Trovadores* (6 vols., 1877–80), *Tragedias* (1879), *Poesías Completas* (1884), and epic trilogy *Los Pirineos* (1892).

**Ba′la·ji** (bä′lä·jē). Name of two Maratha peshwas:

**Balaji Vish′va·nath** (vĭsh′vȧ·nät). d. 1720. Peshwa (Brahman chief minister) of Maratha raja (1714–20); became actual head of Maratha confederacy, as successors of Sivaji lost power; first ruling peshwa; marched to Delhi to support usurpers (1718); secured imperial grant of revenues of the Deccan (1720); succeeded by his son.

**Balaji Ba′ji Ra′o** (bä′jē rä′ōō). d. 1761. Third peshwa (1740–61); grandson of Balaji Vishvanath. Strengthened the confederacy, making Poona the capital (1750); ruled during zenith of Maratha power; renewed invasion of upper India (1760); made alliance with other Hindu powers; totally defeated in great battle at Panipat (1761) by Afghans under Ahmad Shah Durrani.

**Balak.** *In Douay Version* **Balac.** See under BALAAM.

**Ba·la′ki·rev** (bŭ·lä′kyĭ·ryĕf), **Mili Alekseevich.** 1837–1910. Russian composer, b. Nizhni Novgorod (Gorki). To St. Petersburg (1855); friend of Glinka; attracted attention as brilliant pianist; had especially close relations with Tchaikovsky. Cofounder (1862) of the Free School of Music at St. Petersburg; director (1883–94) of Imperial Capella. Composer of two symphonic poems (*Russia* and *Tamara*), music to *King Lear*, pianoforte fantasy *Islamy*, and many Russian folk songs.

**Bal′an·chine′** (băl′ăn·chĭn′), **George.** *Orig. name* **Georgi Ba·lan·chi·vad′ze** (bŭ·lŭn·chĭ·väd′zyĕ). 1904– . Am. (Russ.-born) choreographer; ballet master with Diaghilev Company in Paris (1924–29); to U.S. (1933); with Metropolitan Opera House, N.Y. (1934–37). Director of New York City Ballet.

**Ba′lard′** (bȧ′lȧr′), **Antoine Jérôme.** 1802–1876. French chemist, b. Montpellier. Discoverer of bromine; devised process for extracting sodium sulphate from sea water.

**Ba′las·sa** (bŏ′lŏsh·shŏ), Baron **Bálint.** 1551–1594. Hungarian Renaissance lyric poet; author of patriotic and martial poems, love lyrics, religious hymns, and adaptations from Latin and German literature.

**Ba′lázs** (bŏ′läzh), **Béla.** *Pen name of* **Her′bert Bau′er** (hĕr′bĕrt bou′ẽr). 1884–1949. Hungarian journalist and poet; editor of *Tag*, Vienna; author of *Der Mantel der Träume* (1923), *Der Phantasieführer* (1925), *Das Richtige Himmelsblau* (1925), etc.

**Bal′ban** (bŭl′bȧn). d. 1287. Next-to-last king of Slave Dynasty of Delhi (1266–87). Able general and minister (1246–66) of sultan Nasir-ad-din; became sultan (1266). His reign disturbed by conflicts with Mongols, wild tribes of India, and Rajputs; crushed revolt in Bengal.

**Bal′bi** (bäl′bē), **Adriano.** 1782–1848. Italian geographer; author of *Atlas Ethnographique du Globe* (1826), *Abrégé de Géographie* (1832).

**Balbi, Gasparo.** 16th-century Venetian merchant and traveler; author of *Viaggio all'Indie Orientali* (1590), first European account of India beyond the Ganges.

**Bal·bi′nus** (băl·bī′nŭs), **Decimus Caelius.** d. 238 A.D. Roman emperor (238); poet and orator. After death of Gordian, when Rome threatened by Maximin, proclaimed by senate joint emperor with Pupienus Maximus. See GORDIANUS III.

**Bal′bo** (bäl′bō), **Cesare.** Conte **di Vi·na′dio** (vē·nä′dyō). 1789–1853. Italian statesman and historical writer. Served in administrative capacities under Napoleon (1807–14). In Piedmontese army (until 1821); accused of complicity in revolution of 1821; fled to France (to 1826). Associated with Cavour in founding of risorgimento. Appointed first premier of Piedmont (1848). His works include *Storia d'Italia sotto ai Barbari* (1830), *Vita di Dante* (1839), *Meditazioni Storiche* (1842), *Delle Speranze d'Italia* (1843).

**Balbo, Italo.** 1896–1940. Italian aviator and statesman. Embraced Fascist movement in Ferrara (1919); member of "quadrumvirate" in march on Rome (1922). General of national militia (1923); first minister of aviation (1929–33). Commanded mass transatlantic flights to Brazil (1929) and U.S. (summer, 1933). Promoted air marshal (1933); governor of Libya (Nov., 1933). Killed in air crash over Tobruk (June, 1940). Wrote three books of memoirs.

**Bal·bo'a** (băl·bō'ă; *Span.* bäl·bō'ä), **Vasco Nú'ñez de** (nōō'nyāth thā). 1475–1519. Spanish explorer, b. Jerez de los Caballeros. Sailed to America with Rodrigo de Bastidas (1500); settled in Hispaniola. To Darien (1510); governor of settlement (1512). Discovered Pacific Ocean (Sept. 25, 1513) and, as "El Mar del Sur," *i.e.* South Sea, took formal possession of it for Spain (Sept. 29); made other journeys of exploration (1513–14). Served (1514–17) under Pedrarias, new governor of Panama, with whom he had unfriendly relations and disputes; accused (probably falsely) of sedition; condemned and executed.

**Bal·bue'na** (bäl·bwā'nä), **Bernardo de.** 1568–1627. Spanish poet, b. Valdepeñas; ordained priest; lived in Mexico, Spain, and West Indies; bishop of Puerto Rico. Author of epic on national hero Bernardo del Carpio, *El Bernardo o La Victoria de Roncesvalles* (1624); also of *La Grandeza Mejicana* (poem; 1609) and *Siglo de Oro en las Selvas de Erífile* (pastoral tales; 1608).

**Bal'bus** (băl'bŭs), **Lucius Cornelius.** fl. 1st century B.C. Roman politician, b. Gades (Cádiz); admitted to Roman citizenship by Pompey. Aided in forming 1st triumvirate; accompanied Caesar to Spain (61) and Gaul (58). Acquitted (56) of charge of illegally exercising citizenship rights. Opposed Pompey. Consul (40).

**Balcarres,** Earls of. See LINDSAY family.

**Balch** (bôlch), **Emily Greene.** 1867–1961. American economist and sociologist, b. Jamaica Plain, Mass.; professor, Wellesley Coll. (1913–18); international secretary, Women's International League for Peace (1919–22), honorary president (from 1936); shared with John R. Mott (*q.v.*) 1946 Nobel prize for peace.

**Bal'der·ston** (bôl'dẽr·stŭn), **John Lloyd.** 1889–1954. American playwright, b. Philadelphia. War correspondent in Europe (1915–31). Author of *Berkeley Square* (1929), etc. Collaborator in writing *Dracula* (1927), and scenarios for motion pictures *Lives of a Bengal Lancer, Berkeley Square, Prisoner of Zenda,* etc.

**Bal'di** (bäl'dē), **Bernardino.** 1553–1617. Italian mathematician and miscellaneous writer. Author of *Cronica dei Matematici* (pub. 1707).

**Bal·di'ni** (bäl·dē'nē), **Baccio.** 1436?–?1487. Florentine engraver; engraved, from sketches by Botticelli, *The Prophets, The Sibyls,* and Dante's *Inferno.*

**Bal'di·nuc'ci** (bäl'dē·nōōt'chē), **Filippo.** 1624–1696. Florentine art historian; author of first history of copper engraving, first lexicon of technical terms, and (pub. 1681–1728) *Notizie de' Professori del Disegno da Cimabue in qua (dal 1260 sino al 1670).*

**Bal'di·vie'so** (bäl'dē·vyā'sō), **Enrique.** 1901– . Bolivian statesman and writer, b. Tupiza, Potosí; professor of constitutional law, U. of La Paz (1932; 1939 ff.); minister of public instruction (1935), war (1935–36), foreign relations (1936), foreign affairs (1937); founder and leader of Bolivian Socialist party (1936 ff.); vice-president of Bolivia (1938). Works include poems, plays, and miscellaneous prose writings.

**Bal'do·mir'** (bäl'dō·mēr'), **Alfredo.** 1884–1948. Uruguayan soldier and politician, b. Montevideo. Minister of national defense, with rank of general (1935); president of Uruguay (1938–43).

**Bal'do·vi·net'ti** (bäl'dō·vē·nāt'tē) *or* **Bal'dui·net'ti** (bäl'dwē·nāt'tē), **Alessio.** 1425?–1499. Florentine decorative artist and painter; known esp. for his frescoes in Church of Santa Trinità, Florence.

**Bal'dung** (bäl'dōōng), **Hans.** *Called* **Hans Grien** (grēn) *or* **Grün** (grün). 1476?–1545. German painter, engraver, and designer for woodcuts and glass painting; contemporary of Dürer. Works include an altarpiece with scenes from life of Christ and Mary (Freiburg Cathedral) and allegories, crucifixions, portraits, etc.

**Bald'win** (bôld'wĭn). *Fr.* **Bau'douin'** (bō'dwăN'). Name of two emperors of Constantinople (Empire of Romania):

**Baldwin I.** 1171–?1205. Son of Baldwin V, Count of Hainaut. Count of Flanders as Baldwin IX and of Hainaut as Baldwin VI (1195–?1205). A leader of the Fourth Crusade (1202–04). On capture of Constantinople (1204) by crusaders, elected first Latin emperor. Beaten by Greeks and Bulgarians at Adrianople (1205); captured and slain.

**Baldwin II.** 1217–1273. Nephew of Baldwin I and son of Peter of Courtenay. Last Latin emperor of Constantinople (1228–61). Under regency of John of Brienne during minority (1228–37). Kingdom greatly reduced; financial situation desperate. Sold holy relics of Byzantium to Saint Louis of France. Driven out of Constantinople by Michael VIII Palaeologus (1261). Yielded rights to Charles of Anjou (1267).

**Baldwin.** Name of five kings of Jerusalem, belonging to family of counts of Flanders:

**Baldwin I.** 1058–1118. Brother of Godfrey of Bouillon; king (1100–18); increased Latin kingdom by taking Acre (1104), Berytus (Beyrouth), and Sidon (1110).

**Baldwin II.** *Known as* **Baldwin de Burgh** (dĕ bûrg'). d. 1131. Nephew of Baldwin I; count of Edessa (1100–18); king (1118–31); captured by Arabs on way to aid Edessa (1124); released (1125); left his kingdom greatly enlarged to his son-in-law Fulk V of Anjou (see ANJOU).

**Baldwin III.** 1130?–1162. Grandson of Baldwin II and son of Fulk V of Anjou; king (1143–62); Second Crusade in his reign (1147–49).

**Baldwin IV.** 1160–1185. Son of Amalric I; leper; reign (1174–83) much disturbed by Mussulman attacks.

**Baldwin V.** d. 1186. Nephew of Baldwin IV; king in name only (1183–86).

**Baldwin.** *Fr.* **Baudouin.** Name of nine counts of Flanders (9th century–1205), including:

**Baldwin I.** *Called* **Bras' de fer'** (brȧ' dẽ fâr'), *i.e.* Iron Arm. d. 879. Founder of countship.

**Baldwin V.** *Called* **le Dé'bon'naire'** (lẽ dā'bō'nâr'). d. 1067. Count (1036–67); in conflicts with Emperor Henry III; regent of France (1060–66) during minority of Philip I; accompanied his daughter Matilda's husband, William of Normandy, in invasion of England (1066).

**Baldwin VII.** d. 1119. Ally of Louis VI against England.

**Baldwin VIII.** = BALDWIN V, Count of Hainaut.

**Baldwin IX.** = BALDWIN I, Emperor of Constantinople.

**Baldwin.** *Fr.* **Baudouin.** Name of six counts (c. 1070–1205) of **Hai'naut'** (ĕ'nō') including:

**Baldwin IV.** 1099–1171. Count (1120–71).

**Baldwin V.** 1150–1195. Count (1171–95).

**Baldwin VI.** = BALDWIN I, Emperor of Constantinople.

**Baldwin, Abraham.** 1754–1807. American political leader, b. North Guilford, Conn. Moved to Georgia (1783–84). A founder of U. of Georgia, orig. Franklin Coll. Member, Congress of the Confederation (1785), U.S. House of Representatives (1790–99), U.S. Senate (1799–1807).

**Baldwin, Evelyn Briggs.** 1862–1933. American meteorologist and arctic explorer, b. Springfield, Mo. On Peary expedition to North Greenland (1893–95); on expedition to Franz Josef Land (1898–99); discovered and explored Graham Bell Island (1899); organized and led Baldwin-Ziegler polar expedition (1901–02).

**Baldwin, Frank Stephen.** 1838–1925. b. New Hartford,

Conn. American inventor of a calculating machine (1902), later redesigned (with J. R. Monroe) as Monroe calculating machine.

**Baldwin, Henry.** 1780–1844. American jurist, b. New Haven, Conn. Member (from Pennsylvania), U.S. House of Representatives (1817–22). Associate justice, U.S. Supreme Court (1830–44).

**Baldwin, James.** 1924– . Am. writer, b. New York. Author of *Go Tell It on the Mountain* (1953), *Nobody Knows My Name* (1961), *The Fire Next Time* (1963), etc.

**Baldwin, James Mark.** 1861–1934. American psychologist, b. Columbia, S.C. Grad. Princeton (1884). Studied at Leipzig, Berlin, and Tübingen (1884–85). Professor, U. of Toronto (1889–93), Princeton (1893–1903), Johns Hopkins (1903–09) and National U. of Mexico (1909–13). Specialist in child psychology and social psychology. Founder, with James McKeen Cattell (*q.v.*), and editor (1894–1909), *Psychological Review*. Editor of *Dictionary of Philosophy and Psychology* (1901–06).

**Baldwin, Loammi.** 1740–1807. American engineer and army officer, b. North Woburn, Mass. Served in American Revolution (1775–77, invalided home). First grower of Baldwin apples. His son **Loammi** (1780–1838) was also a civil engineer; constructor of dry docks at the Charlestown (Mass.) and Norfolk (Va.) navy yards.

**Baldwin, Matthias William.** 1795–1866. American industrialist, b. Elizabethtown, N.J. Manufactured stationary engines (from 1827) and locomotives (from 1831). Formed M. W. Baldwin Co., now the Baldwin Locomotive Works.

**Baldwin, Robert.** 1804–1858. Canadian statesman. Solicitor general of Upper Canada (1840); after Act of Union, formed first Canadian administration to accept responsible government, acting as attorney general of Upper Canada (1842, 1848–51); revised judicial system; introduced municipal system in Ontario.

**Baldwin, Simeon Eben.** 1840–1927. American jurist, b. New Haven, Conn. Professor, Yale Law School (1869–1919). President, American Bar Association (1890). Chief justice, Connecticut supreme court (1907–10). Governor of Connecticut (1910–14). Works include *A Digest of All the Reported Cases...of Connecticut* (2 vols., 1871–82), *Modern Political Institutions* (1898), *American Railroad Law* (1904), *The American Judiciary* (1905), *The Relations of Education to Citizenship* (1912). His father, **Roger Sherman Baldwin** (1793–1863), also a lawyer, was governor of Connecticut (1844–46).

**Baldwin, Stanley.** 1st Earl **Baldwin of Bewd′ley** (būd′lĭ). 1867–1947. English statesman. Educ. Trinity College, Cambridge (B.A., 1888); active head of iron and steel manufactories (c. 1892–c. 1916). Financial secretary to treasury (1917–21); president, board of trade (1921–22); as chancellor of exchequer (1922–23), arranged with aid of Montagu Norman funding of British debt to U.S. (1922); Conservative prime minister and first lord of the treasury (1923–24, 1924–29, 1935–37); lord president of the council (1931–35). Author of *Classics and the Plain Man* (1926), *This Torch of Freedom* (1935), *Service of Our Lives* (1937).

**Baldwin, William.** fl. 1547. English writer of verse and plays; superintended publication of, and contributed plays to, *Mirror for Magistrates* (1559).

**Baldwin of Redvers.** See REDVERS.

**Bale** (bāl), **John.** 1495–1563. English author and bishop of Ossory. Author of controversial works in Protestant cause, of a Latin history of English literature, and of *King John*, first English historical play.

**Ba′len** (bä′lĕn), **Hendrick van.** 1575–1632. Flemish historical painter, b. Anvers. Pupil of Adam van Noort; studied in Italy; first master of van Dyck. His works, represented in museums at Amsterdam, Dresden, Munich, Vienna, etc., include *Repose of the Holy Family* (Lille, France).

**Bal′es·tier′** (băl′ĕs·tēr′), **Charles Wolcott.** 1861–1891. American publisher and writer, b. Rochester, N.Y. Sent to London (1888) to obtain original English manuscripts for publication. Formed partnership with William Heinemann for publishing an English library to compete with Tauchnitz. Secured right to publish Kipling's work in U.S.; collaborated with Kipling in *The Naulahka* (1892). His sister **Caroline** married Kipling (1892).

**Balfe** (bălf), **Michael William.** 1808–1870. Irish operatic composer and singer. Appeared as Figaro in Rossini's *Barbiere di Siviglia* in Paris (1827); produced his first opera, *I Rivali di Se Stessi*, at Palermo (1830), his first in England being *Siege of Rochelle* (1835). Other operas include *Maid of Artois* (1836); *Falstaff* (1838); *The Bohemian Girl*, including the well-known song "I dreamt I dwelt in marble halls" (1843); *The Sicilian Bride* (1852); and *Rose of Castile* (1857).

**Bal′four** (băl′fo͝or), **Alexander.** 1767–1829. Scottish novelist; author of *Campbell* (1819) and *The Foundling of Glenthorn* (1823), etc.

**Balfour, Andrew.** 1873–1931. Scottish surgeon, tropical health authority, and novelist. Grad. Edinburgh U. (1898). Served in Boer War. Served on health commissions in Mesopotamia, Egypt, etc. during World War; health commissioner for Mauritius (1921) and Bermuda (1923). Director in chief of Wellcome Bureau of Scientific Research, London; director of London School of Hygiene and Tropical Medicine (from 1923). Author of *By Stroke of Sword*, *The Golden Kingdom*, and other novels, and of *Public Health and Preventive Medicine* (with C. J. Lewis, 1902), *Health Problems of the Empire* (1924), etc.

**Balfour, Arthur James.** 1st Earl of **Balfour.** 1848–1930. English philosopher and statesman. Educ. Trinity Coll., Cambridge. Conservative M.P. (1874–85, 1886–1905, 1906–11); one of so-called "Fourth party" (1880). To Berlin Congress (1878) as secretary to uncle Lord Salisbury; chief secretary for Ireland (1887–91); first lord of the treasury (1892, 1895, 1900) and government leader in Commons (1895); prime minister (1902–05); unionist leader of opposition (1906); first lord of admiralty, succeeding Winston Churchill (1915), held other offices in coalition ministry; foreign secretary (1916–19); headed mission to U.S. for establishing Anglo-Saxon solidarity (Apr., 1917); made declaration (Balfour Declaration, Nov., 1917) that British government favored establishment in Palestine of national home for Jewish people, without prejudice to civil and religious rights of existing non-Jewish communities; attended Paris Peace Conference as foreign secretary; representative to League of Nations; leading British delegate to Washington Disarmament Conference (1921–22). Author of *A Defence of Philosophic Doubt* (1879), *Essays and Addresses* (1893), *The Foundations of Belief* (1895), *Theism and Humanism* (1915), *Theism and Thought* (1923). His younger brother **Francis Maitland** (1851–1882), b. in Edinburgh, was a morphologist; author of a monograph on elasmobranch fishes and a textbook of comparative embryology (1880–81). See also Eleanor M. SIDGWICK.

**Balfour,** Sir **Graham,** *in full* **Thomas Graham.** 1858–1929. British educator and author, b. Chelsea. Lived with his cousin R. L. Stevenson at Vailima (1891–94); wrote authoritative *Life of Robert Louis Stevenson* (1901). In educational administrative work (from 1902).

**Balfour** of Pit′ten·dreich′ (pĭt′′n·drēk′), Sir **James.** d. 1583. Scottish judge and political intriguer.

**Balfour** of Kin′loch (kĭn′lŏκ) **John.** Scottish Covenanter, whom Scott in *Old Mortality* confused with **John Balfour** (d. 1688), 3d Baron **Balfour of Bur′leigh** *or* **Bur′ley** [bûr′lĭ].

**Balfour, John Hutton.** 1808–1884. Scottish physician and professor of botany at Edinburgh U. (from 1845). His son Sir **Isaac Bayley** (1853–1922), b. Edinburgh, was also a botanist; professor, Edinburgh U. (from 1888); curator, Royal Botanic Garden, Edinburgh.

**Balfour, Robert.** 1550?–?1625. Scottish professor of Greek and philosopher; author of a volume of commentaries on Aristotle (1618–20).

**Balfour of Bur′leigh** (bûr′lĭ), 6th Baron. Alexander **Hugh Bruce.** 1849–1921. Scottish administrator. In British cabinet as secretary for Scotland (1895–1903). Lord rector, Edinburgh U. (1896); chancellor, St. Andrews U. (1900). Author of *An Historical Account of the Rise and Development of Presbyterianism in Scotland* (1911).

**Ba′liev** (bȧ′lyĕf), **Nikita.** 1877–1936. Russian theatrical manager; served in Russo-Japanese War (1904–05). On staff of Moscow Art Theater. Assembled semiprivate amateur cabaret which he developed into professional company known as Chauve-Souris, appearing in Russia (1917–19), Constantinople (1919–20), Paris (1920–22), New York (1922–23), and on tour of U.S., and, later (until 1934), in Paris, London, and New York by turns.

**Bal′iol** *or* **Bal′liol** (bāl′yŭl). Anglo-Norman family founded by **Guido** *or* **Guy**, holder of Ballieul and other fiefs in Normandy, and including: **John de Baliol** (d. 1269); great-great-grandson of Guido; founder of Balliol College, Oxford, by gift of lands (c. 1263) and by gifts in his will and from his widow Devorguila. His son **John de Baliol** (1249–1315); claimed Scottish throne on death (1290) of Margaret, Maid of Norway, by right of his maternal grandmother, daughter of David, grandson of David I; supported by William of Douglas at Berwick; claim allowed by Edward I of England, whose overlordship Baliol acknowledged; crowned at Scone (1292); made alliance with Philip IV of France; brought to submission by Edward I of England (1296); died in exile in Normandy. **Edward de Baliol** (d. 1363); eldest son of the preceding; invaded Scotland (1332) with aid of Edward III of England and barons disinherited by Robert Bruce; defeated Sir Archibald Douglas and supporters of David II at Halidon Hill (1333); crowned at Scone; unseated by Scottish patriots (1334); restored to throne by Edward III; surrendered kingdom to Edward III (1356).

**Ball** (bôl), **Albert.** 1896–1917. English pilot in Royal Flying Corps; destroyed 43 enemy planes during World War; V.C. (posthumous).

**Ball,** Sir **Alexander John.** 1759–1809. British naval officer; served in Mediterranean under Nelson; engaged at Abukir Bay (1798) and in reduction of Malta (1798–1800); governor of Malta; rear admiral (1805).

**Ball, Ernest R.** 1878–1927. American vaudeville actor; composer of popular songs, as *Love Me and the World is Mine* and *Mother Machree.*

**Ball, Frances.** *Known as* Mother **Frances Mary Theresa.** 1794–1861. English religious; founder (1822) of the Loretto, or Loreto, nuns, also called Ladies of Loretto, established near Dublin, Ireland, and now represented in Ireland, England, India, Canada, and the United States.

**Ball, Francis Elrington.** 1863–1928. Irish scholar, b. in County Dublin. Authority on Swift; editor of *The Correspondence of Jonathan Swift* (1910–14).

**Ball** (bäl), **Hugo.** 1886–1927. German writer; one of founders of Dadaism. Author of *Byzantinisches Christentum* (1923), *Die Folgen der Reformation* (1924), etc.

**Ball** (bôl), **John.** d. 1381. English priest; expounder of doctrines of Wycliffe; influential in stirring up Wat Tyler's rebellion; executed.

**Ball, John.** 1818–1889. Irish Alpinist and politician, b. Dublin. First president, Alpine Club (founded 1857); author of *Alpine Guide* (1863–68). Undersecretary for colonies (1855–57).

**Ball, John.** 1861–1940. British golf champion; amateur champion eight times between 1888 and 1912; first amateur to win open championship (1890) and to win both amateur and open championships in one year (1890).

**Ball, John Thomas.** 1815–1898. Irish jurist, b. Dublin; lord chancellor of Ireland (1875–80).

**Ball,** Sir **Robert Staw′ell** (stō′ĕl). 1840–1913. Irish astronomer and mathematician, b. Dublin. Educ. Trinity College, Dublin. Royal astronomer of Ireland (1874–92). Professor, Cambridge (1893–1913). Author of *Elements of Astronomy* (1880, 1900), *The Story of the Heavens* (1885, 1905), and other popular texts.

**Ball, Thomas.** 1819–1911. American sculptor, b. Charlestown, Mass. Among his chief works are a life-size bust of Daniel Webster completed a few days before Webster's death; busts of Rufus Choate, William H. Prescott, and Henry Ward Beecher; equestrian statue of George Washington (now in Public Garden, Boston); statue of St. John the Evangelist (1875; now in Forest Hills Cemetery); *Emancipation,* a group with Lincoln and a kneeling slave (1875; now in Washington, D.C.); and statues of Daniel Webster (1876; now in Central Park, New York), Sumner (1878; now in Public Garden, Boston), Josiah Quincy (1879; now in front of City Hall, Boston).

**Bal′la·gi** (bŏl′lŏ·gĭ), **Mór.** *Orig.* **Mo′ritz Bloch** (mō′rĭts blôκ). 1818–1891. Hungarian theologian and grammarian, of Jewish descent; accepted Protestant faith (1843); professor of theology at Budapest (1855–78). Compiled Hungarian-German dictionary (2 vols., 1854–57).

**Bal′lance** (băl′ăns), **John.** 1839–1893. New Zealand journalist and statesman, b. in Ulster. Served in Maori war (1867). Member of three ministries; as prime minister (1891–93) imposed progressive land tax and progressive income tax and carried out other reform measures.

**Bal′lanche′** (bȧ′läɴsh′), **Pierre Simon.** 1776–1847. French philosopher and writer; member of salon of Mme. Récamier.

**Bal′lan·tine** (băl′ăn·tīn), **James.** 1808–1877. Scottish poet; reviver of art of glass painting, and maker of stained-glass windows.

**Ballantine, William.** 1812–1887. English lawyer. Prosecuted murderer Franz Müller (1864); led case for Tichborne Claimant (1871); defended gaekwar of Baroda (1875).

**Bal′lan·tyne** (băl′ăn·tīn), **James.** 1772–1833. Scottish printer. Proprietor and editor of *Kelso Mail;* published Walter Scott's works (1802 ff.); with brother **John** (1774–1821), associated with Walter Scott in printing and publishing (from 1808) until ruined by bankruptcy of Constable and Co. (1826); thereafter editor of *Weekly Journal.*

**Ballantyne, Robert Michael.** 1825–1894. Nephew of James Ballantyne. Scottish writer of "story books for young folks" beginning with *Hudson's Bay* (1848), based upon his six years' service with Hudson's Bay Co., and including *The Young Fur Traders* (1856), *Ungava* (1857), *The Gorilla Hunters* (1862), etc.

**Ballantyne, Thomas.** 1806–1871. British journalist, b. Paisley. One of four original proprietors of *Manchester Examiner.* Later, editor of *Liverpool Journal,*

*Mercury, Statesman,* and *Old St. James's Chronicle.* Associated with Cobden and Bright in agitation against corn laws; published (1841) *Corn Law Repealer's Handbook.*

**Ballard, John.** d. 1586. English Jesuit priest; instigated Babington's plot; executed.

**Ballard, Philip Boswood.** 1865–1950. British educator, b. Maesteg, Wales. Educational inspector, London (1906–30). Author of *Obliviscence and Reminiscence, Mental Tests,* texts on teaching methods, etc.

**Ballenden** *or* **Ballentyne, John.** See BELLENDEN.

**Bal'lin** (bäl'ĕn), **Albert.** 1857–1918. German shipowner. Associated with Hamburg-American Steamship Line as director of passenger traffic (1886) and director general (from 1899). Author of German-American shipping agreement (1902).

**Bal'lin·ger** (băl'ĭn·jẽr), **Richard Achilles.** 1858–1922. American lawyer, b. Boonesboro, Iowa. U.S. secretary of interior under Taft (1909–11). Became center of attack by forest conservation group headed by Gifford Pinchot (*q.v.*). Accused by a subordinate, Louis R. Glavis, of impeding investigation of certain coal land claims in Alaska; discharged Glavis for insubordination. Controversy investigated by Congress; investigation became practically a trial of Taft's conservation policy. Cleared of wrongdoing by the investigating committee; resigned office (March, 1911).

**Balliol.** See BALIOL.

**Bal'li·vián'** (bä'yē·vyän'), **Enrique Bustamante y.** See BUSTAMANTE Y BALLIVIÁN.

**Ballivián, José.** 1804–1852. Bolivian general, b. La Paz. Fought under presidents Sucre and Santa Cruz; won battle of Ingaví (1841). President of Bolivia (1841–48). His son **Adolfo** (1831–1874) was a soldier, statesman, and diplomat; president of Bolivia (1873–74).

**Ballot, C. H. D. Buys.** See BUYS BALLOT.

**Bal·lou'** (bă·lōō'), **Adin.** 1803–1890. American clergyman, b. Cumberland, R.I. Founder (1841) and president (1841–51) of a Utopian community, Hopedale Community, Milford, Mass.; after its dissolution (1856), remained (till 1880) as pastor of Hopedale (Unitarian) Parish. Author of *Practical Christian Socialism* (1854), *Primitive Christianity and Its Corruptions* (1870).

**Ballou, Hosea.** 1771–1852. American clergyman, b. Richmond, N.H. One of early leaders of Universalism in U.S. Editor of *Universalist Magazine* (1819–28), *Universalist Expositor* (1830 ff.). His grandnephew **Hosea** (1796–1861), also a Universalist clergyman, was first president of Tufts College. **Ma·tu'rin** (mă·tū'rĭn) **Murray** (1820–1895), son of the latter, founded one of the first American illustrated periodicals; a founder and first editor of Boston *Daily Globe.*

**Bal'ma·ce'da** (bäl'mä·sā'thä), **José Manuel.** 1842–1891. Chilean statesman and Liberal leader, b. Santiago. Deputy in congress (from 1870); minister to Argentina (1878–81); minister of foreign affairs (1881–86). President of Chile (1886–91); defeated after severe fighting in civil war (1891); committed suicide (Sept. 19).

**Bal'mer** (bäl'mẽr), **Johann Jakob.** 1825–1898. German mathematician and physicist; discoverer of a formula (Balmer's formula) expressing the connection between the frequencies of the radiations in the main series of the spectrum of hydrogen.

**Balmerino,** Barons. See ELPHINSTONE family.

**Bal'mes** (bäl'mās), **Jaime Luciano.** 1810–1848. Spanish philosopher, b. Vich, Catalonia; educ. U. of Cervera; ordained priest (1833); professor of mathematics at Vich; author of *La Religión Demostrada al Alcance de los Niños* (1841), *El Protestantismo Comparado con el Catolicismo en Sus Relaciones con la Civilización Europea* (4 vols., 1842–44), *Filosofía Fundamental* (4 vols., 1846), etc.

**Bal'mont** (bál'y'·mŭnt), **Konstantin Dmitrievich.** 1867–1943. Russian symbolist poet, b. in Vladimir government. Resident in Paris (after 1918). Translator of many English and other classic writers into Russian. Volumes of his original verse include *Under the Northern Sky* (1894), *Silence* (1898), *In Boundless Space* (1895), *The Liturgy of Beauty* (1905), *The Bird of Flame* (1907).

**Bal·nav'es** (băl·năv'ĕs; -ĭs), **Henry.** 1512?–1579. Scottish lord of session under James V; imprisoned on account of his Protestantism. Author of *The Confession of Faith* (1584). One of Bothwell's judges (1567).

**Balsamo, Giuseppe.** Real name of Count Alessandro di CAGLIOSTRO.

**Bal'ta** (bäl'tä), **José.** 1816–1872. Peruvian soldier and politician, b. Lima. Supported Prado and served in his cabinet (1865–67); one of leaders in revolution that deposed Prado (1868). President of Peru (1868–72); murdered in army mutiny.

**Bal'tard'** (bál'tár'), **Louis Pierre.** 1764–1846. French architect and engraver; professor at École Polytechnique and École des Beaux-Arts. His son **Victor** (1805–1874) was also an architect; studied at École des Beaux-Arts; best known as architect of huge iron and glass structure housing general market (Halles Centrales) of Paris; appointed architect (1853) of Paris Hôtel de Ville.

**Bal'ta·za·ri'ni** (bäl'tä·tsä·rē'nē). *Known in France as* **Bal'tha'zar' de Beau'joy'eulx'** (bál'tá'zár' dē bō'-zhwá'yû'). 16th-century Italian violinist; intendant of music to Catherine de Médicis; contributed to the early development of classical ballet.

**Bal'ti·more** (bôl'tĭ·mōr), Lord. Appellation of barons Baltimore of Baltimore in Ireland, members of English family that obtained patent for and colonized Maryland. See George CALVERT.

**Bal'ti·more** (bôl'tĭ·mōr; -mẽr), **David.** 1938– . American microbiologist. At Salk Institute for Biological Studies (1965–68), Massachusetts Institute of Technology (1968– ); awarded (with Renato Dulbecco and Howard Temin) Nobel prize for physiology or medicine (1975).

**Ba·łuc'ki** (bä·lōōts'kē), **Michał.** 1837–1901. Polish novelist and playwright, b. Cracow. Educ. U. of Cracow. Author of novels, including *The Awakening* (his first; under pseudonym **El·pi'don** [ĕl·pē'dōn]; 1863), *A Romance without Love* (1870), *Sabina* (1871), and *The Parson's Niece* (1872), many comedies, as *Hunting a Husband* (1869), *The Emancipated* (1873), and *The Open House* (1883), and historical and literary essays.

**Ba'luze'** (bá'lüz'), **Étienne.** 1630–1718. French historian; author of *Vitae Paparum Avenionensium;* editor of historical documents.

**Bal'zac'** (bál'zák'; *Angl.* bôl'zăk, băl'zăk), **Honoré de.** *Orig. family name* **Bals'sa'** (bál'sá'). 1799–1850. French novelist, b. Tours. Received early education under Oratorians at Vendôme; to Paris (1818); studied law for three years; earned livelihood as editor, printer, typefounder, etc., while writing under various pseudonyms and in collaboration with others; achieved first success (1829) with historical novel in imitation of Scott, *Le Dernier Chouan,* a tale of Brittany in 1799; thereafter sustained output of both masterpieces and less successful works. Associate of Hugo, Vigny, Lamartine, and George Sand; m. (1850) Madame Evelina Hanska, Polish lady and owner of estates in Russia. Considered greatest novelist of France and founder of the realistic novel; through his novels (with their more than 2000 characters from all phases of contemporary life) sought to demonstrate molding effect of social environment on raw material of human personality; conceived plan of presenting comprehensive picture of contemporary French society under general title *La Comédie Humaine* (first series pub. 1842; pub. posthumously in 47 vols.), including such subdivisions as "Scènes de la Vie Privée," "Scènes de la Vie Parisienne," "Scènes de la Vie Militaire," "Études Philosophiques." Among his works are *La Physiologie du Mariage* (1829), short stories, as *El Verdugo, La Maison du Chat qui Pelote, Le Bal de Sceaux, La Peau de Chagrin,* the novels *La Vendetta, Gobseck* (1830), *Un Épisode sous la Terreur* (1831), *Le Colonel Chabert, Louis Lambert* (1832), *Eugénie Grandet* (1833), *Le Père Goriot* (1834), *La Fille aux Yeux d'Or* (1835), *Le Lis dans la Vallée* (1835), *L'Enfant Maudit* (1836), *Le Curé de Village* (1837), *Mémoires de Deux Jeunes Mariées* (1841), *Une Ténébreuse Affaire* (1841), *La Fausse Maîtresse* (1842), *Splendeurs et Misères des Courtisanes* (1843), *Modeste Mignon* (1844), *Les Paysans* (1845), *L'Envers de l'Histoire Contemporaine* (1845), *La Cousine Bette* (1847), *Le Cousin Pons* (1847), plays, as *Mercadet* (1838) and *Vautrin* (1839), and *Contes Drolatiques* (1832–37; Eng. tr. *Droll Stories*).

**Balzac,** Seigneur **de. Jean Louis Guez** (gâz). 1597?–1654. French prose writer; regarded as a master of prose style in his period; author of *Lettres* (1624), *Le Prince* (1631), *Discours* (1644), *Le Barbon* (1648), *L'Aristippe* (1658).

**Bam'ber'ger** (bäm'bĕr'gẽr), **Ludwig.** 1823–1899. German politician and economist. Implicated in Revolution of 1848 as editor of radical *Mainzer Zeitung;* participated in republican uprising in Palatinate; forced to live in exile; banker, Paris (1853–66). Returned to Germany after amnesty (1866); National Liberal member of Reichstag (1871–80); helped found Reichsbank; defended gold standard; opposed doctrinaire socialism and Bismarck's protectionist policy. Leader of so-called secessionists (1880); cofounder of German Liberal party (1884–93); opposed colonial policy of Germany. Author of *Erlebnisse aus der Pfälzischen Erhebung* (1849), *Monsieur de Bismarck* (1868), *Die Fünf Milliarden* (1873), *Erinnerungen* (1899), etc.

**Bamboccio, Il.** Nickname of Pieter van LAAR.

**Bam'ford** (băm'fẽrd), **Samuel.** 1788–1872. English weaver and poet; deeply interested in welfare of laboring classes; author of *Passages in the Life of a Radical, Early Days,* etc.

**Bamp'ton** (bămp'tŭn), **John.** 1690?–1751. English clergyman. Endowed Bampton lectures, 8 divinity sermons to be delivered annually at Oxford.

**Bampton, Rose.** 1909– . American operatic contralto, b. Cleveland, Ohio. Member Metropolitan Opera Company, New York; made debut in 1932.

**Ba'na** (bä'nȧ). fl. 7th century A.D. Sanskrit author at court of King Harsha (*q.v.*). Wrote lyric poems, dramas, and romances, esp. *Kādambarī,* a poetical novel relating the fortunes of a princess of that name, and *Harshacharita* (*i.e.* Deeds of Harsha), an account of the events of Harsha's reign.

**Banbury,** Earl of. See KNOLLYS family.

**Ban'ces Can·da'mo** (bän'thās kän·dä'mō), **Francisco Antonio de.** 1662–1704. Spanish dramatic poet, b. Sahugo, Asturias; successor to Calderón de la Barca as official poet.

**Ban·chie'ri** (bäng·kyâ'rē), **Adriano.** 1567?–1634. Italian musician and writer on music; composer of church music, symphonies, dramatic pieces in madrigal style, etc.; author of works on organ playing and on counterpoint; founded Accademia de' Floridi, Bologna.

**Ban'co** (bäng'kō), **Nanni d'An·to'nio di** (dän·tô'nyō dē). 1374–?1420. Florentine sculptor and architect; studied under Donatello; among his works are the Porta della Mandola of the Duomo and *Saint Philip* (Or-San-Michele, Florence).

**Ban'croft** (băn'krŏft; băng'-), **Aaron.** 1755–1839. American Unitarian clergyman, b. Reading, Mass. An organizer (1825) and president (1825–36) of American Unitarian Association.

**Bancroft, Cecil Franklin Patch.** 1839–1901. American educator, b. New Ipswich, N.H. Principal, Phillips Academy, Andover, Mass. (1873–1901).

**Bancroft, Edward.** 1744–1821. American scientist and secret agent, b. Westfield, Mass. Settled in Dutch Guiana; author of *Natural History of Guiana* (1769). Settled in London, England; discovered important dyes for use in textile manufacture. During American Revolution, served as secret agent for American commissioners in Paris; alleged also to have sold information on American affairs to British government (1776–78).

**Bancroft, Frederic.** 1860–1945. American historian, b. Galesburg, Ill. A.B., Amherst (1882); Ph.D., Columbia (1885). Author of *The Negro in Politics* (1885), *The Public Life of Carl Schurz* (1908), *Calhoun and the Nullification Movement in South Carolina* (1928), *Slave-Trading in the Old South* (1931), etc. Editor of *Speeches, Correspondence and Public Papers of Carl Schurz* (6 vols., 1913).

**Bancroft, George.** 1800–1891. American historian, b. Worcester, Mass. Teacher (1822–31); publication of first and second volumes (1834, 1837) of his *History of the United States* brought public recognition. Appointed (1837) collector of the port, Boston. U.S. secretary of the navy (1845–46); established United States Naval Academy, Annapolis. U.S. minister to Great Britain (1846–49). Worked on his history (vol. III, 1840; IV, 1852; V, 1852; VI, 1854; VII, 1858; VIII, 1860; IX, 1866; X [final volume], 1874). Supported Lincoln through Civil War. Wrote for Andrew Johnson his first annual message as president (1865). U.S. minister to Germany (1867–74). Additional works include *Literary and Historical Miscellanies* (1855), *History of the Formation of the Constitution of the United States* (2 vols., 1882), *Martin Van Buren to the End of his Public Career* (1889). Elected to American Hall of Fame (1910).

**Bancroft, Hubert Howe.** 1832–1918. American publisher and writer, b. Granville, Ohio. Works include *West American Historical Series* (39 vols., 1875–90), prepared under his direction from his large library of works on the western American region, *Resources of Mexico* (1893), *The New Pacific* (1900).

**Bancroft, Richard.** 1544–1610. English prelate. B.A., Cantab. (1567). Leader of Anglicans; combated Martin Marprelate tracts; sponsored canons against Puritanism among clergy. Bishop of London (1597); archbishop of Canterbury (1604). Overseer of translations of Bible for Authorized Version.

**Bancroft,** Sir **Squire.** 1841–1926. English actor and theatrical manager; son of Secundus Bancroft White Butterfield; took name Bancroft at marriage (1867) to Marie Effie Wilton (1839–1921), actress and manager. Managed jointly with wife Prince of Wales's Theatre in London (1867–79), producing and acting in plays of T. W. Robertson as a specialty; rebuilt and managed Haymarket Theatre (1880–85).

**Bancroft, Wilder Dwight.** 1867–1953 American chemist, b. Middletown, R.I. Grad. Harvard (1888). Taught physical chemistry at Cornell (1903–37). Founder and editor (1896–1932), *Journal of Physical Chemistry.* Author of *The Phase Rule* (1897), *Applied Colloid Chemistry* (1932), etc.

**Bandeira, Bernardo de Sá da.** See SÁ DA BANDEIRA.

**Ban'del** (băn'dĕl), **Ernst von.** 1800–1876. German sculptor of colossal statue (unveiled 1875) of the national hero Arminius (near Detmold).

**Ban'de·lier'** (băn'dĕ·lēr'), **Adolph Francis Alphonse.** 1840–1914. Swiss-American explorer and archaeologist, b. Bern, Switzerland; to Highland, Ill. (1848). Researches in New Mexico and Arizona (1880–89) and in Peru and Bolivia (1892–1903). On staff of Museum of Natural History, N.Y. (1903 ff.). Wrote on archaeology of southwestern U.S., Mexico, and Central and South America.

**Ban·del'lo** (bän·dĕl'lō), **Matteo.** 1480?–1562. Piedmontese Dominican and writer of novelle. Tutor of Lucrezia Gonzaga (Mantua, 1515–21). Lived at Milan (1521–26); adviser to Cesare Fregoso, an Italian general (c. 1528–41); fled to France; bishop of Agen (1550–54). Author of *Rime* (1537) and *Lodi* (1545), both in honor of Lucrezia; known esp. for his *Novelle* (vols. 1–3, 1554; vol. 4, 1573). The novelle were translated into French (1565) by Belleforest (*q.v.*), and the tales in Painter's *Palace of Pleasure* are largely drawn from them; they provided source material for several Shakespearean and other Elizabethan plays (through Belleforest or Painter) and for Lope de Vega, Byron, and others.

**Ban·die'ra** (bän·dyâ'rä), **Attilio** (1811?–1844) and his brother **Emilio** (1819–1844). Italian patriots; headed abortive revolt against Austrian rule.

**Ban'di·nel'li** (bän'dē·nĕl'lē), **Baccio** *or* **Bartolommeo.** 1493–1560. Florentine sculptor; among his works are *Hercules and Cacus* (Florence), *Adam and Eve* (Florence), and bas-reliefs in choir of cathedral of Florence.

**Ba·nér'** (bȧ·nār') *or* **Ban·ner'** (bȧn·nār'), **Johan.** 1596–1641. Swedish general in Thirty Years' War. Served under Gustavus Adolphus against Russia and Poland; commander of right wing, Breitenfeld (1631); commander, Swedish forces in south Germany (1632); field marshal (1634) gained victories at Wittstock (1636) and Chemnitz (1639).

**Ba'ner·jea** (bȧ'nôr·jē), Sir **Surendranath.** 1848–1925. Indian political leader, b. Calcutta. Founded (1876) Indian Association in Bengal; twice president, Indian National Congress. Founded Ripon College, Calcutta (1882). Considered father of Indian nationalism.

**Bánf'fy** (bänf'fĭ), Baron **Dezső** *or* **De'si·de'ri·us** (dā'zē·dā'rē·ŏŏs). 1843–1911. Hungarian statesman; prime minister of Hungary (1895–99).

**Ban'field** (băn'fēld), **Edmund James.** 1852–1923. Australian naturalist; long a dweller on a remote southern Pacific island. Author of *The Confessions of a Beachcomber*, *My Tropic Isle*, and *Tropic Days.*

**Bang** (bȧng), **Bernhard Laurits Frederik.** 1848–1932. Danish veterinarian; originated (1892) method of eradicating tuberculosis from dairy herds, discovered bacterium of infectious abortion, or Bang's disease (1896).

**Bang, Hermann Joachim.** 1857?–1912. Danish writer. Author of novels *Families Without Hope* (1880), *Fädra* (1883), *Eccentric Tales* (1885), *Tine* (1889), *The Gray House* (1901), and essays, poems, and critical works.

**Bange** (bänzh), **Charles Valérand Ra'gon'** (rȧ'gôN') **de.** 1833–1914. French artillery colonel, b. Balignicourt. Creator of artillery system adopted by French army (1877–81) and fundamentally that existing at outbreak of World War; first to use effectively the screw principle in cannon breechblock mechanism.

**Bangs** (băngz), **John Kendrick.** 1862–1922. American humorist, b. Yonkers, N.Y. Works include *Tiddledywink Tales* (1891), *Coffee and Repartee* (1893), *The Idiot* (1895), *A House-boat on the Styx* (1896), and lectures, as *The Evolution of a Humorist, From Adam to Ade, Salubrities I Have Met.*

**Ba'nim** (bā'nĭm), **John.** 1798–1842. Irish poet, playwright, and novelist; called the "Scott of Ireland." His *Damon and Pythias* produced (1821) at Covent Garden, with Macready and Kemble as principals. Author, in conjunction with his brother **Michael** (1796–1874), of series of *Tales of the O'Hara Family* (6 vols., 1825–26), depicting somber side of Irish peasant life. John also wrote longer novels, including *The Denounced* (1829). Michael also wrote *Father Connell* (1842), *Clough Fion* (1852), *Town of the Cascades* (1864).

**Bank'head** (băngk'hĕd), **John Hollis.** 1872–1946. American lawyer; U.S. senator from Ala. (from 1931). His brother **William Brockman** (1874–1940), lawyer, member U.S. House of Representatives (1917–40; speaker 1936–40). W. B. Bankhead's daughter **Tallulah Brockman** (1903–1968), stage and screen actress.

**Banks** (băngks), Sir **Edward.** 1769?–1835. English building contractor, orig. a day laborer; builder (after plans of John Rennie) of London bridge, Waterloo bridge, and Southwark bridge.

**Banks, George Linnaeus.** 1821–1881. English journalist, poet, and dramatist. His wife (m. 1846), **Isabella,** *nee* **Var'ley** [vär'lĭ] (1821–1897), best known as **Mrs. Linnaeus Banks,** was a novelist and poet; assisted him in his editorship of various journals; her most popular novel was *The Manchester Man* (1872).

**Banks,** Sir **Joseph.** 1743–1820. English naturalist. Educ. Christ Church, Oxford. Accompanied Cook's expedition round the world, in the *Endeavour,* equipped by himself (1768–71); visited Hebrides and Iceland (1772). President of Royal Society (1778–1820). Aided settlement in New South Wales. His library and collections now in British Museum.

**Banks, Nathan.** 1868–1953. American entomologist, b. Roslyn, N.Y.; grad. Cornell (1889). Curator of insects, museum of comparative zoology, Harvard (from 1916); compiler of catalogues of the Acarina and of Nearctic Neuroptera and Heteroptera.

**Banks, Nathaniel Prentiss.** 1816–1894. American army officer, b. Waltham, Mass. Governor of Massachusetts (1858–61). Served through Civil War as major general; received thanks of Congress (1864) for capture of Port Hudson (1863). Member, U.S. House of Representatives (1853–57, 1865–73, 1875–79, 1889–91; speaker 1856–57).

**Banks, Thomas.** 1735–1805. English sculptor. Gold medalist, Royal Academy (1770); studied in Italy (1772–79); in Russia (1781) executed *Armed Neutrality* for Empress Catherine and sold to her *Cupid Catching a Butterfly.* His *Shakespeare Attended by Painting and Poetry* now in Stratford on Avon.

**Banks,** Sir **William Mitchell.** 1842–1904. Scottish surgeon and anatomist; grad. Edinburgh (1864); an originator of method of operating for cancer of the breast.

**Ban'na·tyne** (băn'ȧ·tīn), **George.** 1545–?1608. Scottish collector of Scottish poems of the 15th and 16th century (compiled in ms., 1568; pub. 1873–1902). Patron of the Bannatyne Club, a literary club founded (1823) under presidency of Sir Walter Scott.

**Ban'ne·ker** (băn'ĭ-kẽr), **Benjamin.** 1731–1806. Mathematician and astronomer, b. Ellicott, Md. Helped survey site of District of Columbia. Published almanac (1791ff.); defended intellectual equality of Negro in correspondence with Thomas Jefferson.

**Banner, Johan.** See Johan BANÉR.

**Bannerman,** Sir **Henry Campbell-.** See CAMPBELL-BANNERMAN.

**Ban'ning'** (bȧ'năNzh'), **Émile.** 1836–1898. Belgian official and writer; superintendent of archives in ministry of foreign affairs. Active participant in creation of Congo Free State. Author of historical and political treatises, notably several on African colonization and administration.

**Ban'ning** (băn'ĭng), **Margaret,** *nee* **Cul'kin** (kŭl'kĭn). 1891– . American novelist, b. Buffalo, Minn.; grad. Vassar (1912); m. (1914) Archibald Tanner Banning. Author of *This Marrying* (1920), *Prelude to Love* (1929), *The First Woman* (1935), *Too Young to Marry* (1938), *Out in Society* (1940), *Women For Defense* (1942), etc.

**Ban'nis·ter** (băn'ĭs·tẽr), **Charles.** 1738?–1804. English actor and bass singer. Made debut (1762) at Haymarket. His son **John** (1760–1836), comedian, created Don Whiskerandos in Sheridan's *Critic* (1779); played Charles Surface, Parolles, George Barnwell, Sir Anthony Absolute, Bob Acres, Tony Lumpkin; acting manager of Drury Lane (1802–03).

**Bannister, Roger Gilbert.** 1929– . English athlete and physician. First man to run the mile in under four minutes (3 minutes 59.4 seconds) at Oxford, Eng. (May 6, 1954).

**Ban'se** (bän'zĕ), **Ewald Hermann August.** 1883–1953. German geographer and political and military philosopher; author of many books on geography, geology, and travels in Near East and books on psychological warfare (as *Raum und Volk im Weltkrieg*, 1933, and *Wehrwissenschaft*) credited with influencing Hitler and his associates in their conduct of diplomacy and military operations.

**Ban'ting** (băn'tĭng), Sir **Frederick Grant.** 1891–1941. Canadian research physician. Grad. U. of Toronto; served in World War I (1915–19); practiced medicine, London, Ont. (until 1921); professor, U. of Toronto (from 1923); began research on internal secretion of the pancreas, U. of Toronto (1921); working under the direction of J. J. R. Macleod, discovered (with Charles H. Best) the hormone insulin (1922) now used as a specific remedy for diabetes. Awarded jointly with J. J. R. Macleod the 1923 Nobel prize for physiology and medicine, which was shared with C. H. Best and J. B. Collip for their part in discovery of insulin.

**Banting, William.** 1797–1878. English undertaker and writer (1863) on a dietetic method (Bantingism) of reducing corpulence.

**Ban'tock** (băn'tŭk), Sir **Granville.** 1868–1946. English composer. Operatic conductor (1896); director, School of Music, Birmingham and Midland Institute (1900); professor of music, Birmingham U. (1908–34). Prolific composer of operas, symphonic poems, overtures, as well as a drama *Rameses II* (1891), a choral symphony *Atlanta in Calydon* (1912), choral songs and dances, etc.

**Ban'vard** (băn'värd), **John.** 1815–1891. American painter and writer, b. New York City. Drifted down Mississippi in a flatboat (1840) painting scenes along the way for his *Panorama*, exhibited throughout U.S. and in England. Painted *The Orison* (1861), from which first American chromolithograph was made.

**Ban'ville'** (bäɴ'vēl'), **Théodore de.** 1823–1891. French writer, b. Moulins. Author of pieces for the theater, including *Le Cousin du Roi* (verse comedy; 1857), *Les Fourberies de Nérine* (verse comedy; 1864), *Diane au Bois* (verse comedy; 1864), *Gringoire* (prose comedy; 1866), *Riquet à la Houppe* (fairy comedy; 1884). His volumes of verse include *Odes Funambulesques*, *Trente-six Ballades Joyeuses*, *Sonnailles et Clochettes*. Among his critical works are *Petit Traité de Poésie Française* and *Critiques*. He also wrote tales, as *Contes Héroïques* (1884) and *Contes Bourgeois* (1885), a novel *Marcelle Rabbe* (1891), and sketches, as *Esquisses Parisiennes* (1859) and *Les Camées Parisiens* (1866–73).

**Ban'zes Candamo** (bän'thās). = BANCES CANDAMO.

**Ba'our'-Lor'mian'** (bȧ'ōōr'lôr'myäɴ'), **Pierre Marie François Louis.** 1770–1854. French poet and playwright; author of the tragedies *Omasis* (1806) and *Mahomet II* (1810).

**Ba'que·ri'zo Mo·re'no** (bä'kā·rē'sō mō·rā'nō), **Alfredo.** 1859–1951. Ecuadorian political leader; president of Ecuador (1916–20); provisional president (1931–32).

**Bär** (bâr), **Karl Ernst von.** See BAER.

**Bar** (bär), **Karl Ludwig von.** 1836–1913. German jurist; author of treatises on German and international law.

**Bar·ab'bas** (bȧ·răb'ăs; bär·ăb'ăs). In Bible, prisoner released by Pilate instead of Jesus (*Matt.* xxvii. 15–26; *Mark* xv. 6–15; *Luke* xxiii. 16–25; *John* xviii. 39–40).

**Bar'a·dai'** (băr'ȧ·dī'), **Jacob.** *Lat.* **Jacobus Bar'a·dae'us** (băr'ȧ·dē'ŭs). *Arab.* **al-Bar'da'i'** (ăl·băr'dă·ē'), *i.e.* the man in rags. d. 578. Syrian monk, b. near Edessa; founded Jacobite Church (so named after him), a branch of Syrian Monophysites. Consecrated bishop of Edessa (c. 543); as prelate of Syrian Arabs, journeyed over countries and islands of Near East (c. 543–578), preaching, ordaining, and consecrating bishops.

**Ba'ra'guay' d'Hil'liers'** (bȧ'rȧ'gā' dēl'yā'). Name of two French army commanders: **Louis** (1764–1812), one of Napoleon's generals in Italy, Egypt, and Spain; and his son **Achille** (1795–1878), marshal of France (from 1854).

**Bar'ak** (bâr'ăk; bā'răk). *In Douay Version* **Bar'ac** (bâr'ăk; bā'răk). In Bible, Israelite who led army that defeated Canaanites under Sisera (*Judges* iv). See DEBORAH.

**Ba·ra'ka** (bȧ·rä'kȧ), **Imamu Amiri** *Orig. name* **(Everett) LeRoi Jones.** 1934– . Poet and playwright, b. Newark, N.J. Grad. Howard Univ. (1954). Works include *Preface to a Twenty-Volume Suicide Note* (1961), poems; *The Dutchman* (1964), *The Toilet* (1964), *The Slave* (1966), plays; *The System of Dante's Hell* (1965), a novel; *Black Music* (1968), essays.

**Ba·ra'nov** (bŭ·rȧ'nôf), **Aleksandr Andreevich.** 1746–1819. Russian Alaskan fur trader. In Alaska 28 years (1790–1818); first governor of Russian America.

**Ba'rante'** (bȧ'räɴt'), Baron **de. Amable Guillaume Prosper Bru'gière'** (brü'zhyâr'). 1782–1866. French historian and diplomat. Ambassador to Turin (1830), St. Petersburg (1835). Author of *Histoire des Ducs de Bourgoyne* (1824), *Histoire de la Convention Nationale* (1851–53), etc.

**Bá'rány** (bä'rän·y'), **Robert.** 1876–1936. Austrian physician; specialist in otology. Taught at U. of Uppsala (from 1917). Investigated physiology and pathology of balancing apparatus in inner ear. Awarded 1914 Nobel prize in medicine.

**Ba'rat'** (bȧ'rȧ'), Saint **Madeleine Sophie.** 1779–1865. b. Joigny, Burgundy. French founder (1800) of Society of the Sacred Heart of Jesus.

**Ba'ra'tier'** (bȧ'rȧ'tyā'), **Albert Ernest Augustin.** 1864–1917. French army officer; member of Marchand mission (1896) which reached Fashoda (1898); general of division in World War I; died in front-line trench before Reims.

**Ba'ra·tie'ri** (bä'rä·tyâ'rē), **Oreste.** 1841–1901. Italian general, b. Condino, Italian Tirol; served under Garibaldi in Sicily (1860); governor of Eritrea (1891); undertook campaign of conquest against Abyssinians; defeated decisively at battle of Aduwa (March, 1896); retired from army (1896); author of *Memorie d'Africa* (1897).

**Ba·ra·tyn'ski** (bŭ·rŭ·tĭn'skû·ĭ; *Angl.* -skĭ), **Evgeni Abramovich.** 1800–1844. Russian lyric poet. In early life a soldier; while on garrison duty in Finland, wrote (c. 1825) *Eda*, with a Finnish heroine; his philosophy pessimistic, his poems gloomy and melancholy. His best lyrics include *On the Death of Goethe*, *Finland*, *The Last Death*, *The Gypsy Girl*, *The Ball*, and *The Steamboat*.

**Bar·ba·ce'na** (băr·bȧ·sā'nȧ), Marquês **de.** Feliberto

**Cal·dei′ra Brant Pon′tes** (käl·dā′rȧ bräNnt′ pōNn′-tēs). 1772–1841. Brazilian soldier and statesman, b. near Mariana, Minas Gerais. Commanded Brazilian army against Uruguay, but was defeated at Ituzaingó (1827) and relieved of command; accompanied (1828) Queen Maria II of Portugal to Europe and there defended her rights; prime minister of Brazil (1829–30).

**Bar′ba·ra** (bär′bȧ·rȧ), Saint. 3d-century virgin martyr. Depicted on left of Virgin Mary in Raphael's *Sistine Madonna.*

**Barbarelli, Giorgio.** See Il GIORGIONE.

**Bar′ba·ri** (bär′bä·rē), **Jacopo de′.** *Known in Germany as* **Jakob Walch** (välk). 1440?–?1516. Italian painter and engraver; painter to Elector Frederick the Wise (1503–05); court painter at Brussels (from 1510) to Archduchess Margaret. His paintings represented in museums in Venice, Munich, Dresden, Berlin, and Augsburg; among his plates are *Judith, Adoration of the Magi, The Dying Cleopatra,* and *Mars and Venus.*

**Bar′ba·ros′sa** (bär′bȧ·rŏs′ȧ). Nickname of FREDERICK I, Holy Roman Emperor.

**Barbarossa.** Name of two Algerian corsairs, orig. Greeks, who became Moslem pirates.

**Barbarossa I. Horush** *or* **Arouj** *or* **Koruk.** 1473?–1518. Became sea rover; for some time served Mamelukes; together with brother Khizr, raided Spanish coast and towns of Tunis and Algeria; killed by Spaniards.

**Barbarossa II.** *Orig.* **Khizr.** *Better known by adopted name* **Khair ed-Din,** *also spelled* **Khaireddin** *and* **Chaireddin.** 1466?–1546. Took command of pirates on death of his brother Barbarossa I; secured aid of Selim I, Turkish sultan, who made him his deputy in northern Africa (1516); defeated Spanish at Algiers (1519); acted as pasha for Sultan Suleiman (1529); evacuated (1533) thousands of Moors driven out of Spain by Inquisition; seized Tunis (1534); defeated by expedition of Charles V, commanded by Andrea Doria (1535); gained victory near Actium (1538); controlled much of Mediterranean (1541–44); died at Constantinople.

**Bar′ba′roux′** (bȧr′bȧ′ro͞o′), **Charles Jean Marie.** 1767–1794. French revolutionist. Member of Girondist group in Convention; voted for execution of Louis XVI. Opposed Robespierre; proscribed as enemy of republic (May, 1793) and guillotined (July 25, 1794).

**Barbatelli, Bernardino.** See Bernardino POCCETTI.

**Barbatus.** See Ulrich HAN.

**Bar′bauld** (bär′bōld; -bō), **Anna Letitia,** *nee* **Ai′kin** (ā′kĭn). 1743–1825. English author; m. Rev. Rochemont Barbauld (1774); with him conducted boys' boarding school in Suffolk (1774–85). Author of volumes of verse, anthologies, etc., and of *Hymns in Prose for Children.*

**Bar′ba′zan′** (bȧr′bȧ′zäN′), Sire **Arnaud Guillaume de.** *Called* **Che·va′lier′ sans re·proche′** (shē·vȧ′lyā′ säN rē·prôsh′). 1360–?1431. French general of Charles VII; defeated English and Burgundian army at La Croisette (1430).

**Barbellion, W. N. P.** Pseudonym of Bruce Frederick CUMMINGS.

**Bar′bé′-Mar′bois′** (bȧr′bā′mȧr′bwä′), Marquis **François de.** 1745–1837. French politician, b. Metz. Minister of finance under Napoleon (1801); negotiated sale of Louisiana to U.S. Created peer of France by Louis XVIII; became minister of justice.

**Bar′ber** (bär′bẽr), **Donn.** 1871–1925. American architect, b. Washington, D.C. Works include National Park Bank, New York; Travelers Insurance Building, Aetna Life Insurance Building, and Supreme Court Building, Hartford, Conn.; Department of Justice Building, Washington, D.C.

**Barber, Edwin Atlee.** 1851–1916. American archaeologist, b. Baltimore, Md. Studied prehistoric relics in western U.S.; specialist in ceramics; author of *The Pottery and Porcelain of the United States* (1893), *Maiolica of Mexico* (1908), *Hispano-Moresque Pottery* (1915).

**Barber, Francis.** 1751–1783. American Revolutionary officer, b. Princeton, N.J. Served throughout American Revolution; led battalion in final assault at Yorktown.

**Barber, John Warner.** 1798–1885. American engraver and historian, b. East Windsor, Conn.

**Barber, Samuel.** 1910– . Am. composer, b. West Chester, Pa. Composed *Vanessa, Piano Concerto,* etc.

**Bar′be·ri′ni** (bär′bā·rē′nē). Powerful Tuscan family, prominent in history of papacy in 17th century; rose to power in 16th century through commerce; excited jealousy of other noble families by its wealth and power; forced to flee to France after defeat by duke of Parma (1641–44); re-established in Rome (1652). Prominent members include **Maffeo** (1568–1644), who became Pope Urban VIII (*q.v.*), and his nephews the three brothers **Francesco** (1597–1679), cardinal, vice-chancellor, founder of Barberini Library, **Taddeo** (b. 1647), commander of papal forces, prefect of Rome, prince of Palestrina, and **Antonio** (1608–1671), cardinal, archbishop of Reims; high chamberlain to Urban VIII.

**Bar′be·ri′ni** (bär′bā·rē′nē) *or* **da Bar′be·ri′no** (dä bär′bā·rē′nō), **Francesco.** 1264–1348. Italian poet; contemporary and associate of Dante; among his works are *Documenti d'Amore* and *Del Reggimento e Costumi di Donna,* valuable source book for 13th-century manners.

**Bar·be′ro** (bär·bā′rō), **Andrés José Camilo.** 1877– . Paraguayan physician, educator, and statesman, b. Asunción; professor (1901–14) and dean (1906), Asunción; minister of agriculture (1937) and national economy (1938–1939). Author of *Higiene Municipal y Rural* (1917), *Plantas Medicinales del Paraguay* (1917), etc.

**Bar′bey′ d'Au′re·vil′ly′** (bȧr′bā′ dôr′vē′yē′), **Jules.** 1808–1889. French man of letters; author of biographical essays, literary criticisms, and novels, as *Une Vieille Maîtresse* (1851), *L'Ensorcelée* (1854), *Un Prêtre Marié* (1865), *Une Histoire Sans Nom* (1884).

**Bar′bié′ du Bo′cage′** (bȧr′byā′ dü bô′kȧzh′), **Jean Denis.** 1760–1825. French geographer; professor at the Sorbonne (1809).

**Bar′bier′** (bȧr′byā′), **Antoine Alexandre.** 1765–1825. French bibliographer; compiler of *Dictionnaire des Ouvrages Anonymes et Pseudonymes* (1806–08); author of *Nouvelle Bibliothèque d'un Homme de Goût* (1808–10).

**Barbier, Henri Auguste.** 1805–1882. French poet, best remembered for *Les Iambes* (1831), a series of political and social satires of the monarchy of Louis Philippe.

**Barbier, Paul Jules.** 1825–1901. French playwright and librettist, b. Paris. Frequent collaborator with Michel Carré (as in *Cora ou l'Esclavage*); author of libretto for Offenbach's *Contes d'Hoffmann.*

**Bar·bie′re** (bär·byâ′râ), **Domenico del.** *Called* **Domenico Fio′ren·ti′no** (fyō′rân·tē′nō). 1501–1565. Italian painter, sculptor, and engraver; collaborator with Il Rosso and Primaticcio at Fontainebleau and Troyes.

**Bar·bie′ri** (bär·byā′rē), **Francisco A·sen′jo** (ä·sān′hō). 1823–1894. Spanish composer, known esp. for his zarzuelas.

**Bar·bie′ri** (bär·byâ′rē), **Giovanni Francesco.** See GUERCINO.

**Bar′bi·rol′li** (bär′bĭ·rŏl′ĭ; -rōl′ĭ), Sir **John.** 1899–1970. Orchestra conductor, b. London, of Italian father and French mother. Served in World War I (1914–18). Violoncellist with International String Quartet (1920–24); succeeded Toscanini (1936) as conductor of New York Philharmonic Orchestra.

**Bar′bon** (bâr′bŏn), **Nicholas.** d. 1698. English economist. First to institute fire insurance in England; author of treatises on money.

**Bar′bon** (bâr′bŏn) *or* **Bare′bone′** (bâr′bōn′) *or* **Bare′bones′** (bâr′bōnz′), **Praise′god′** *or* **Praise′-God′** (prāz′gŏd′). 1596?–1679. English leather seller, Anabaptist, and member of Fifth Monarchy Men, after whom "Barebone's Parliament" (1653) was nicknamed; published defense of pedobaptism (1642); opposed restoration of Charles II (1660); imprisoned in Tower (till 1662). It has been said, but without proof, that he had two brothers named (1) Christ-came-into-the-world-to-save Barebone and (2) If-Christ-had-not-died-thou-hadst-been-damned Barebone, the latter shortened to Damned Barebone (*Dict. of National Biography*).

**Bar·bo′sa** (bĕr·bô′zȧ), **Ruy.** 1849–1923. Brazilian jurist, b. São Salvador. Aided in drafting (1890) constitution of Brazil; member, Permanent Court of International Justice (1921).

**Barbosa du Bocage, Manuel María.** See BOCAGE.

**Bar′bou′** (bär′bōō′). Name of family of French printers, including: **Jean** (fl. 1539), of Lyon, who printed (1539) a fine edition of works of Clément Marot; his son **Hugues** (fl. 1580), of Limoges, who printed (1580) an edition of Cicero's *Letters to Atticus;* **Joseph** (d. 1737), of Paris; **Jean Joseph** (d. 1752), of Paris; and **Joseph Gérard** (1715–1813), of Paris, who printed (about 1750) a series of Latin classics.

**Bar′bour** (bär′bĕr), **Clarence Augustus.** 1867–1937. American Baptist clergyman and educator, b. Hartford, Conn. A.B., Brown (1888); grad. Rochester Theol. Sem. (1891); ordained (1891); president and professor, Rochester Theol. Sem. (1915–29); president of Brown U. (1929–37). Author of several religious books.

**Barbour, James.** 1775–1842. American statesman, b. Barboursville, Va. Governor of Virginia (1812–15); U.S. senator (1815–25); U.S. secretary of war (1825–28); U.S. minister to Great Britain (1828–29). His brother **Philip Pendleton** (1783–1841), American jurist, b. Barboursville, Va. was associate justice of U.S. Supreme Court (1836–41).

**Barbour, John.** 1316?–1395. Scottish poet. Archdeacon of Aberdeen (from 1357). Author of the *Brus* (1375), a national epic about Robert Bruce, the war of independence, and the battle of Bannockburn. Probable author of *Legend of Troy* and *Legends of the Saints*, translations.

**Barbour, Oliver Lorenzo.** 1811–1889. American lawyer, b. Cambridge, N.Y.; compiler of *Reports of Cases in Law and Equity in the Supreme Court of the State of New York* (67 vols., covering years 1847–77), known as *Barbour's Supreme Court Reports.*

**Bar′busse′** (bär′büs′), **Henri.** 1873–1935. French editor and author, b. Asnières. Served in World War; after the war, became a zealous internationalist. Writer of poetry, novels, and essays. His *Le Feu*, story of a squad in the trenches during the World War, awarded Goncourt prize (1916). Among his other works are *Pleureuses* (poetry; 1895), the novels *Les Suppliants* (1903), *L'Enfer* (1908), and *Les Enchaînements* (1925), the essay collections *Paroles d'un Combattant* and *La Lueur dans L'Abîme* (1921), and the critical study *Zola* (1932).

**Bar′ca** (bär′kȧ) *or* **Bar′cas** (bär′kȧs). Surname of Hannibal's father, Hamilcar, and some other Carthaginian generals. See HAMILCAR BARCA.

**Bar′ca** (bär′kȧ), Conde **da.** See Antônio de ARAUJO DE AZEVEDO.

**Bar′clay** (bär′klĭ; -klā). English family of bankers, including: **James** (fl. 1736), admitted into banking partnership by brother-in-law Joseph Freame; **Robert J. P.** (1843–1913), during whose administration Barclays Bank Limited was organized by merger of a number of banking houses; **Robert Leatham** (1869–1939).

**Barclay, Alexander.** 1475?–1552. Priest and poet, probably of Scottish birth. Author of *The Ship of Fools* (*The Shyp of Folys*, 1508), part translation, part imitation, of Sebastian Brant's *Narrenschiff* (1494), *The Castell of Laboure, Egloges* (the first eclogues in English).

**Barclay, Edwin.** 1882–1955. President of Liberia (1930–1944).

**Barclay, Florence Louisa,** *nee* **Charles′worth** (chärlz′-wûrth). 1862–1921. English novelist. Author of sentimental romances, including *The Rosary* (1909), *Mistress of Shenstone* (1910), *The Broken Halo* (1913), *White Ladies of Worcester* (1917).

**Barclay,** Sir **George.** fl. 1696. British conspirator; involved in assassination plot against King William III (1696); executed.

**Barclay, John.** 1582–1621. Scottish satirical poet. Author of *Satyricon* (1603–07), politico-satirical romance directed against Jesuits; a supplement *Icon Animorum* (1614); *Argenis*, an allegory alluding to political faction and conspiracy, in Latin (1621).

**Barclay, John.** 1734–1798. Scottish clergyman. Author of *Without Faith, Without God* (1769). Founded (1773) a sect called Barclayites or Bereans (cf. *Acts* xvii. 10 ff.). His nephew **John Barclay** (1758–1826), M.D., Edinburgh (1796), was author of a number of treatises on anatomy.

**Barclay, Robert.** 1648–1690. Scottish Quaker. Imprisoned several times; received, with William Penn and other Quakers, patent of East New Jersey, and made nominal governor (1682–88). Author of *The Apology* (1676), standard exposition of Quaker tenets.

**Barclay, Robert H.** d. 1837. British naval officer, b. in Scotland. Commanded British flotilla on Lake Erie (1813); defeated by Commodore O. H. Perry.

**Barclay,** Sir **Thomas.** 1853–1941. Lawyer and publicist, b. in Scotland. Educ. University Coll., London, and Universities of Paris, Bonn, and Jena. Identified with agitation for better international understanding (since 1900).

**Barc·lay′ de Tol′ly** (bŭrk·lī′ dĕ tô′lyĭ), Prince **Mikhail.** 1761–1818. Russian field marshal, of Scottish descent. Entered army, serving in Turkish War (1788–89), in campaign against Sweden (1790), and in Poland (1792, 1794); major general under Bennigsen at Pultusk (1806); as a foreigner, disliked by Russian national party, but appointed (1810) minister of war by Emperor Alexander; commander in chief of Army of the West (1812); his defeat at Smolensk forced him to yield command to Kutusov, but his Fabian tactics, unpopular with Russians, finally brought about defeat of Napoleon's invasion; commanded right wing at Borodino (1812); after brilliant service at Bautzen (1813) again made commander in chief; served also at Dresden, Leipzig, and capture of Paris; made prince and field marshal.

**Bar Co′che·ba** *or* **Bar Kokh′ba** (bär′ kōĸ′vä), **Si′mon** (sī′mŭn). *Also* **Bar Co·zi′ba** (kŏ·zē′vȧ). d. 135 A.D. Hebrew leader of insurrection against Romans (132–135) in later years of Hadrian's rule; at first successful, but finally slain at village of Bethar, near Caesarea.

**Bar′croft** (bär′krŏft), Sir **Joseph.** 1872–1947. English physiologist. Educ. Cambridge. Professor, Royal Institution (1923–26), Cambridge (1926–37). Author of *The Respiratory Function of the Blood, Features in the Architecture of Physiological Function*, and *The Brain and Its Environment.*

**Barcynska,** Countess. See Oliver SANDYS.

**Bard** (bärd), **John.** 1716–1799. American physician, b. Burlington, N.J. Introduced (with Peter Middleton) systematic dissection of corpses for purposes of instruction. First to report a case of extrauterine fetus (1760). His son **Samuel** (1742–1821) was physician to George Washington in New York after American Revolution and was instrumental in establishing first New York medical school and the New York hospital. Samuel's son **William** (1778–1853) organized and headed New York Life Insurance and Trust Co. (1830–47).

**Bar′das** (bär′dȧs). d. 866. Brother of Byzantine Empress Theodora; coregent with her for Michael III (842–856); exercised control of affairs (856–866).

**Bar·deen′** (bär·dēn′), **John.** 1908– . Am. physicist, b. Madison, Wis. Shared 1956 Nobel prize in phsyics with William Shockley and Walter Brattain; shared a second Nobel prize in physics in 1972 with Leon N. Cooper and John R. Schrieffer.

**Bar′de·sa′nes** (bär′dē·sā′nēz) *or* **Bar·dai·san′** (băr·dī·sän′). 154–223? Syrian Christian poet and theologian, b. Edessa. Active in introducing Christianity into Edessa; founded a Gnostic sect (Bardesanists); wrote many hymns long used in Christian churches.

**Bar′di** (bär′dē), **Giovanni.** Conte **del Ver′nio** (dāl vĕr′nyō). 1534?–?1612. Italian scholar and music patron, b. Florence. Member of Pope Clement VIII's court. Said to have originated idea of the opera, and to have had first operas performed in his home.

**Bardiya.** See SMERDIS.

**Bar′dolf** *or* **Bar′dolph** (bär′dŏlf; bär·dŏlf′), **Thomas.** 5th Baron **Bardolf.** 1368–1408. English soldier; involved in Hotspur's rebellion (1403); joined Northumberland (1405) and invaded northern England. A character in Shakespeare's *Henry IV*.

**Bar′doux′** (bȧr′dōō′), **Agénor.** 1829–1897. French politician. Member, National Assembly (1871); minister of public instruction (1877–79); senator for life (1882). His son **Achille Octave Marie Jacques** (1874–1959), journalist and literary critic.

**Barebone** *or* **Barebones, Praisegod.** See BARBON.

**Ba′rents** (bä′rĕnts), **Willem.** d. 1597. Dutch navigator; commanded several expeditions that reached Novaya Zemlya in searching for a northeast passage to eastern Asia; discovered Spitsbergen (1596). Barents Island and Barents Sea named in his honor.

**Ba′rère′ de Vieu′zac′** (bȧ′râr′ dē vyû′zȧk′), **Bertrand.** 1755–1841. French lawyer and revolutionist, b. Tarbes. Member of States General (1789) and of National Convention (1792); defended the Terror, becoming known, because of his eloquence, as "The Anacreon of the Guillotine." Secret agent under Napoleon. Proscribed at Restoration as regicide; in exile until amnesty of 1830.

**Ba·ret′ti** (bä·rāt′tē), **Giuseppe Marc′Antonio.** *Pseudonym* **Aristarco Scan′na·bu′e** (skän′nä·bōō′ā). 1719–1789. Italian critic, b. Turin. Lived in England (1751–60, 1765 ff.); friend of Johnson, Burke, Garrick, Reynolds. Among his works are *Dissertation on Italian Poetry* (1753), *Dictionary and Grammar of the Italian Language* (1760), *Lettere Familiari* (1762–63; published in English as *A Journey from London to Genoa*, 1770), *Discours sur Shakespeare et M. de Voltaire* (1777).

**Bar′fod** (bär′fōōth), **Paul Frederik.** 1811–1896. Danish historian and politician; advocated union of Norway, Sweden, and Denmark. Author of *History of Denmark, 1319–1670* (6 vols., 1885–93).

**Bargeny,** Barons. See *Sir John Hamilton of Lettrick*, under HAMILTON family.

**Bar′giel** (bär′gēl), **Woldemar.** 1828–1897. German composer.

**Bargone, Frédéric Charles.** See Claude FARRÈRE.

**Bar′ham** (băr′ăm), Baron. See *Sir Charles Middleton*, under John MIDDLETON.

**Barham, Richard Harris.** *Pseudonym* **Thomas In′golds·by** (ĭng′gŭl(d)z·bĭ). 1788–1845. English humorous writer. Educ. Brasenose College, Oxford; priest in ordinary of Chapel Royal (1824). Author of *The Ingoldsby Legends* (metrical tales first published in *Bentley's Miscellany*, 1837 ff.).

**Bar′–He·brae′us** *or* **Bar′he·brae′us** (bär′hē·brē′ŭs), **Gregorius.** *Arab.* **abu–al–Faraj ibn–al–'Ibri.** *Anglicized* **A·bul′fa·raj′** (ȧ·bōōl′fă·răj′). *Latinized* **Ab′ul·fa·ra′gi·us** (ăb′ŭl·fȧ·rā′jĭ·ŭs). 1226–1286. Syrian scholar and catholicos of Jacobite Church; son of Jewish physician who became Christian. Became monk at Antioch (c. 1243); awarded bishopric of Aleppo (1252); archbishop of Eastern Jacobites (1264); last classical author in Syriac literature; author (in Arabic) of epitomized history of the world and of commentaries (in Syriac and Arabic) on Aristotle; also wrote other treatises on theology, philosophy, and science.

**Ba·ria′tin·ski.** Variant of BARYATINSKI.

**Barine, Arvède.** See ARVÈDE BARINE.

**Bar′ing** (bâr′ĭng). Name of English family and financial and commercial house. Sir **Francis** (1740–1810), grandson of German Lutheran immigrant and cloth manufacturer, established, with his brother John, banking house in London; director of East India Company. His son **Alexander** (1774–1848), 1st Baron **Ash′bur′ton** (ăsh′bûr′t′n), extended firm's banking operations in U.S.; M.P. (1806–35), opposed to reform; negotiated settlement of boundary between Maine and Canada (in Webster-Ashburton Treaty, 1842). One grandson of Sir Francis, **Charles Thomas** (1807–1879) was bishop of Durham; another, Sir **Francis Thornhill** (1796–1866), Baron **North′brook** (nôrth′brŏŏk), was chancellor of the exchequer (1839–41); first lord of the admiralty (1849–52). **Thomas George** (1826–1904), 1st Earl of **Northbrook,** son of the preceding, was a statesman; viceroy of India (1872–76). **Edward Charles** (1828–1897), 1st Baron **Rev′el·stoke** (rĕv′'l·stōk), a third grandson of Sir Francis, followed Thomas as head of firm; his 4th son, **Maurice** (1874–1945), journalist and author, wing commander in reserve of Royal Air Force (1925), is author of poems, plays, novels, and books on Russia and Russian literature. Another grandson of Sir Francis, **Evelyn** (1841–1917), 1st Earl of **Cro′mer** (krō′mẽr), was appointed (1883) British agent and consul general with plenipotentiary diplomatic rank to advise Egyptian government; obtained loan to spend on irrigation (1885), which increased revenue and forestalled bankruptcy; completed land survey and lowered land tax; conducted deliberate campaign for reform of railways, justice, and education; successfully installed Abbas as Tewfik Pasha's successor as khedive (1892) and checked nationalist movement; resigned (1907); author of *Modern Egypt* (1908) and *Ancient and Modern Imperialism* (1910).

**Bar′ing–Gould′** (bâr′ĭng·gōōld′), **Sab′ine** (săb′ĭn). 1834–1924. English author. Rector of Lewtrenchard, North Devon (1881). Author of *Lives of the Saints* (15 vols., 1872–77), theological works, and hymns, including "Onward Christian Soldiers"; *Book of Were-Wolves* (1865) and other studies in legend and folklore; one opera, *The Red Spider* (1898); and numerous novels including *Mehalah* (1880), *John Herring* (1883), *Cheap Jack Zita* (1893), *The Broom Squire* (1896).

**Bar–Jesus.** See ELYMAS.

**Bar′ker** (bär′kẽr), **Benjamin Fordyce.** 1818–1891. American gynecologist, b. Wilton, Me.

**Barker,** Sir **Ernest.** 1874–1960. Eng. historian; fellow and lecturer, Oxford (1898–1920); principal, King's College, London (1920–27); professor of political science,

Cambridge (1928–39); author of *Political Thought in England from Herbert Spencer to To-day* (1915), *Greek Political Theory* (1918), *The Crusades* (1923), *Church, State, and Study* (essays; 1930), *Oliver Cromwell and the English People* (1937), *Ideas and Ideals of the British Empire* (1941).

**Barker, Harley Granville–.** See GRANVILLE-BARKER.

**Barker,** Sir **Herbert Atkinson.** 1869–1950. English surgeon; known for his skill in manipulative surgery, curing without operation or orthopedic appliances.

**Barker, James Nelson.** 1784–1858. American dramatist and politician, b. Philadelphia. Produced *The Indian Princess, or La Belle Sauvage* (1808). Mayor of Philadelphia (1819–20). Collector of the port of Philadelphia (1829–38).

**Barker, J. Ellis.** 1870–1948. English journalist, lecturer, and historian, b. Cologne, Germany. Author of *British Socialism, Modern Germany, The Great Problems of British Statesmanship*, and of treatises on health and ways to maintain it.

**Barker, Lewellys Franklin.** 1867–1943. American physician, b. Norwich, Ont., Canada. Grad. U. of Toronto (1890); studied in Germany. Professor, Johns Hopkins U. (1905–13); chief physician, Johns Hopkins Hospital (1905–13). Author of *The Nervous System and Its Constituent Neurones* (1899), *The Clinical Diagnosis of Internal Diseases* (1916), *The Young Man and Medicine* (1927), *Psychotherapy* (1940), *Time and the Physician* (autobiography; 1942).

**Barker, Robert.** 1739–1806. Scottish portrait painter and drawing teacher; reputed inventor of panoramas.

**Barker, Thomas.** 1769–1847. English painter of landscapes and rustic scenes, including *The Woodman* and *Old Tom.* His son **Thomas Jones** (1815–1882) was a painter of portraits and military subjects; known for scenes of Franco-Prussian and Crimean wars.

**Bark'hau'sen** (bärk'hou'zĕn), **Heinrich.** 1881–1956. German physicist and electrical engineer. Author of *Probleme der Schwingungserzeugung* (1907), *Elektronenröhren*, etc.

**Bark'la** (bärk'lȧ), **Charles Glover.** 1877–1944. English physicist. Professor, U. of London (1909–13), Edinburgh (1913–44). Nobel prize in physics (1917). Author of papers on electric waves, X rays, and secondary rays.

**Bar'kley** (bär'klĭ), **Alben William.** 1877–1956. American politician, b. in Graves Co., Ky. Admitted to bar (1901). Member, U.S. House of Representatives (1913–27); U.S. senator from Kentucky (1927–49), majority leader (1937–47); U.S. vice-president (1949–53).

**Bar'kly** (bär'klĭ), Sir **Henry.** 1815–1898. English colonial governor; governor of British Guiana (1848–53), Jamaica (1853–56), Victoria (1856–63), Mauritius (1863–70), Cape of Good Hope (1870–77).

**Bar Kokhba.** See BAR COCHEBA.

**Bar'lach** (bär'läκ), **Ernst.** 1870–1938. German artist, sculptor, playwright, and poet, b. Wedel, Holstein. After early success in sculpture, won fame by plays *Der Tote Tag* (1912), *Der Arme Vetter* (1918), *Die Echten Sedemunds* (1920), *Die Sündflut* (1924).

**Bar·lae'us** (bär·lē'ŭs), **Casparus.** *Latinized form of* **Caspar van Baar'le** *or* **Baer'le** (bär'lĕ). 1584–1648. Dutch poet and historian. Author of *Poemata* (Latin poems; 1628), *Rerum per Octennium in Brasilia* (1647).

**Bar'low** *or* **Bar'lowe** (bär'lō), **Arthur.** 1550?–?1620. English navigator; with Philip Amadas explored (1584) coast of what is now North Carolina. His letter to Sir Walter Raleigh (printed in vol. 3 of Hakluyt's *Voyages*) caused Raleigh to select Roanoke Island for colony.

**Bar'low** (bär'lō), **George.** 1847?–1914. English poet, b. London; author of *Poems and Sonnets* (1871) and *The Pageant of Life* (1888); wrote English version of libretto of Gounod's *Ave Maria* at Gounod's request.

**Barlow, Jane.** 1860–1917. Irish novelist and author of stories, sometimes in verse, of Irish village life, as *Irish Idylls* (1892), *Ghostbereft* (1902).

**Barlow, Joel.** 1754–1812. American poet and diplomat, b. Redding, Conn. Served in American Revolution. Appointed (1795) U.S. consul to Algiers; arranged treaties with Tunis, Algiers, and Tripoli. U.S. minister to France (1811). Works include two epic poems, *The Vision of Columbus* (1787) and *The Columbiad* (1807).

**Barlow, Peter.** 1776–1862. English mathematician and optician. Master in Royal Military Academy, Woolwich (1806–47). Devised means of rectifying errors in ships' compasses. Known for *Mathematical and Philosophical Dictionary* (1814).

**Bar'me·cides** (bär'mē·sīdz). *Better* **Bar'ma·kids** (bär'mȧ·kĭdz) [from Arab. *barmak*, chief priest]. Wealthy and influential Persian family at Baghdad (c. 752–803) under Abbassides of eastern caliphate; furnished several viziers; under Caliph Harun al-Rashid, family destroyed because of fear of their power. Members include **Kha'led ibn-Bar'mak** (κä'lĭd ĭb''n băr'măk), *Arab.* **Khālid,** general and finance minister under abu-al-Abbas and two succeeding caliphates (c. 752–785); his son **Yah'ya** (yă'yä), *Arab.* **Yaḥya** (died c. 803), tutor of Harun in his youth and later vizier under Harun; Yahya's two sons, **Fazl** (făz''l), *Arab.* **al-Faḍl,** and **Ja'far** [jă'făr] (the Giafar of *Arabian Nights*), powerful in the state and intimate companions of the caliph until destroyed by him.

**Bar'na·bas** (bär'nȧ·băs), **Jo'ses** (jō'sēz; -zĕz) *or* **Joseph.** In Bible, Cyprian Levite early converted to Christianity (*Acts* iv. 36–37); assisted in work of church at Antioch (*Acts* xi. 22 ff.); accompanied Paul on his first missionary journey, but later, after a disagreement, separated from him and went to Cyprus (*Acts* xiii–xv).

**Bar'nard** (bär'nẽrd), Lady **Anne,** *nee* **Lindsay.** 1750–1825. English author of ballad *Auld Robin Gray* (1771); m. (1793) Andrew Barnard, colonial secretary at Cape of Good Hope.

**Barnard, Christiaan Neethling.** 1922– . South African surgeon. Performed first successful human heart transplant operation (1967).

**Barnard, Edward Emerson.** 1857–1923. American astronomer, b. Nashville, Tenn. Appointed junior astronomer, Lick Observatory (1887–95); astronomer, Yerkes Observatory (1895–1923). Discovered 5th satellite of Jupiter and the nebulous ring around Nova Aurigae. Photographed comets and sections of the Milky Way.

**Barnard, Frederick.** 1846–1896. English engraver and black-and-white artist, b. London. Illustrated Household Edition (1871–79) of Dickens's works.

**Barnard, Frederick Augustus Porter.** 1809–1889. American educator, b. Sheffield, Mass. Grad. Yale (1828). Teaching (1828–56). President, U. of Mississippi (1856–58); chancellor (1858–61). President, Columbia U. (1864–89). Favored opening of Columbia's educational opportunities to women; Barnard College, Columbia, named in his honor.

**Barnard, George Grey.** 1863–1938. American sculptor, b. Bellefonte, Pa. Studied at Art Institute of Chicago and École des Beaux-Arts, Paris (1884–87). Taught sculpture in Art Students' League of New York (1900–04). Among his works are *The Urn of Life*, including nineteen figures (Carnegie Museum), two groups containing 31 statues (at Harrisburg, Pa., capitol), *God Pan* (Columbia U.), *Rising Woman* and *Adam and Eve* (on Rockefeller estate at Pocantico Hills, N.Y.), portrait bust of Lincoln (Metropolitan Museum of Art, N.Y.), *Mother Earth and Her Child, Refugee, Prodigal Son* (a group), and *Builder.*

**Barnard, Henry.** 1811–1900. American educator, b. Hartford, Conn. Grad. Yale (1830). Active in improving public-school system, esp. in Connecticut and Rhode Island (1837–55). Chancellor, U. of Wisconsin (1858–60); president, St. John's College, Annapolis, Md. (1866–67). First U.S. commissioner of education (1867–70). Editor, *American Journal of Education* (1855–82). Compiler of *Library of Education* (52 vols.).

**Bar·nar′do** (bär·när′dō; bẽr-), **Thomas John.** 1845–1905. British physician and philanthropist, b. in Ireland. Known for his establishment (from 1867) in England and British possessions of Dr. Barnardo's Homes for orphaned and destitute children.

**Bar·na′to** (bär·nä′tō), **Bar′nett** (bär′nĕt; -nĭt), *called* **Bar′ney** (bär′nĭ). *Orig. name* **Barnett I′saacs** (ī′zȧks; -zĭks). 1852–1897. English speculator. Made fortune in Kimberley diamond mines; joined interests with Cecil Rhodes (1888); engineered Kaffir boom in mining stocks (1895); suicide at sea.

**Bar′nave′** (bȧr′nȧv′), **Antoine Pierre Joseph Marie.** 1761–1793. French politician; prominent Jacobin in States General (1789). Later, advocated constitutional monarchy; impeached for treasonable correspondence with king (1792); guillotined (Nov. 29, 1793).

**Barn′by** (bärn′bĭ), Sir **Joseph.** 1838–1896. English composer and conductor. Director of music at Eton (1875–92); second principal of Guildhall School of Music (1892–96). Composed hymn tunes, part songs including *Sweet and Low,* the cantata *Rebekah,* anthems, and other sacred music.

**Barnes** (bärnz), **Albert.** 1798–1870. American Presbyterian clergyman in Philadelphia (1830–70); b. Rome, N.Y.

**Barnes, Barnabe.** 1569?–1609. English lyric poet. Author of *Parthenophil and Parthenophe* (1593), a separate volume of sonnets (1595), a tragedy *The Divil's Charter* (1607).

**Barnes, Ernest William.** 1874–1953. English clergyman and mathematician. Bishop of Birmingham. Author of monographs and articles on gamma functions, integral functions, linear difference equations, etc.

**Barnes, George Nicoll.** 1859–1940. British labor leader, b. in Scotland. General secretary, Amalgamated Society of Engineers (1896–1908); Labor M.P. (1906–22); member of war cabinet (1917); British delegate to Paris peace conference (1919) and first assembly of League of Nations (1921). Author of *From Workshop to War Cabinet* (1923), *Industrial Conflict: The Way Out* (1924), *The History of the International Labour Organization* (1926).

**Barnes, Harry Elmer.** 1889–1968. American educator and sociologist, b. Auburn, N.Y. Grad. Syracuse (1913). Professor, Clark U. (1920–23), Smith (1923–30); in newspaper editorial work (from 1929). Author of *Sociology before Comte* (1917), *Social History of the Western World* (1921), *Progress of American Penology* (1922), *The Genesis of the World War* (1926), *The Twilight of Christianity* (1929), *History of Western Civilization* (2 vols., 1935), *An Economic History of the Western World* (1937), *An Intellectual and Cultural History of the Western World* (1937), etc.

**Barnes, John Gorell.** 1st Baron **Gor′ell** (gŏr′ĕl) **of Bramp′ton** (brăm(p)′tŭn). 1848–1913. English jurist; B.A., Cantab.; called to bar (1876); judge of probate, divorce, and admiralty division (1892), and president (1905–09). His son **Ronald Gorell** (1884– ), 3d Baron, journalist, soldier, and poet; educ. Oxford. On staff of London *Times* (1910–15). Served in World War (1914–18; captain, 1916; major, 1918). After the war, chairman of Boulton Paul Aircraft, Ltd.; member of many government boards and commissions. Editor, *Cornhill Magazine.* Author of *Babes in the African Wood* (1911), *Love Triumphant, and Other Poems* (1913), *Days of Destiny* (1917), *Pilgrimage* (1920), *The Spirit of Happiness* (1925), *Many Mansions* (1926), *Gauntlet* (1931), *Unheard Melodies* (1934), *In the Potter's Field, and Other New Poems* (1936), *Last of the English, and Other New Poems* (1939), etc.

**Barnes, Juliana.** See Juliana BERNERS.

**Barnes, Margaret,** *nee* **Ayer** (âr). 1886–1967. American author, b. Chicago. A.B., Bryn Mawr (1907). m. (1910) Cecil Barnes. Began writing in 1926. Author of a dramatization of Edith Wharton's *Age of Innocence* (produced 1928); with Edward Sheldon, the plays *Jenny* (1929) and *Dishonored Lady* (1930); *Prevailing Winds* (short stories; 1928); and the novels *Years of Grace* (awarded Pulitzer prize, 1930), *Westward Passage* (1931), *Within This Present* (1933), *Edna, His Wife* (1935), *Wisdom's Gate* (1938).

**Barnes, Mary Downing,** *nee* **Shel′don** (shĕl′dŭn). 1850–1898. Daughter of the educator Edward Austin Sheldon (1823–1897). American educator, b. Oswego, N.Y. Educ. U. of Michigan; Cambridge, Eng.; and Zurich. Professor of history, Wellesley (1876–80), Oswego Normal School (1882–84), Stanford (1891–96). Reputed first teacher in U.S. to use Pestalozzian method in teaching history. Her husband (m. 1884), **Earl Barnes** (1861–1935), was professor of education at Stanford (1891–97), and a lecturer; author of *Studies in Education* (2 vols., 1897), *Where Knowledge Fails* (1907), *Women in Modern Society* (1912), etc.

**Barnes, Robert.** 1495–1540. English martyr. Prior, Austin friars, Cambridge; examined by Wolsey for Puritanical preaching (1526); abjured under pressure; imprisoned; escaped to Continent (1528) and met Luther; returned to England (1531); conducted diplomatic negotiations for Henry VIII; reverted to Lutheranism; burnt for heresy under the Six Articles.

**Barnes, Ronald Gorell.** See under John Gorell BARNES.

**Barnes, Thomas.** 1785–1841. Editor of London *Times* (1817–41).

**Barnes, William.** 1801–1886. English poet, philologist, and clergyman. Master of a Dorchester boys' school; executed wood cuts; B.D., St. John's Cambridge (1850). Author of *Hwomely Rhymes* (1859) and *Poems of Rural Life* (1879), both in Dorset dialect; *Philological Grammar* (1854); *Outline of English Speechcraft* (1878).

**Barnes, William Emery.** 1859–1939. English ecclesiastic and educator. Educ. Cambridge; Hulsean professor of divinity, Cambridge (1901–34); specialist in study of Old Testament and Aramaic subjects.

**Bar·nett′** (bär·nĕt′), **Eugene Epperson.** 1888–1970. Y.M.C.A. executive, b. Leesburg, Fla. A.B., Emory U. (1907). General secretary of Y.M.C.A.'s national council and international committee (1941 ff.).

**Bar′nett** (bär′nĕt; -nĭt), **John.** 1802–1890. English singer and composer; son of a Prussian immigrant (named Beer). Composed operas *Mountain Sylph* (prod. 1834) and *Fair Rosamond* (prod. 1837). His nephew **John Francis Barnett** (1837–1916) was a pianist, professor of music, and composer; known for his oratorio *The Raising of Lazarus* (prod. 1876), cantatas, quartets, quintets, etc.

**Barnett, Morris.** 1800–1856. English actor and playwright; author of several comedies, as *Monsieur Jacques* and *The Serious Family,* adapted from French plays.

**Barnett, Samuel Augustus.** 1844–1913. English clergyman. B.A., Wadham College, Oxford. Aided in founding

(1884) Toynbee Hall, a university settlement in Whitechapel district, London, the first social settlement house; its first warden (1884–96); instrumental in educational and housing reform; canon of Bristol (1894–1906), Westminster (1906–13). Author of *Practicable Socialism* (1888).

**Bar'ne·veldt** *or* **Bar'ne·veld** (bär'nĕ·vĕlt), **Jan van Ol'den** (vän ŏl'dĕn). 1547–1619. Dutch statesman; champion of Dutch independence. Grand pensionary, Province of Holland (1586); as leader of Republican party, opposed designs and warlike policies of Maurice of Nassau; negotiated treaty with Spain (1609); sided with Remonstrants (Arminians) in religious strife (1617) against Maurice and the Gomarists (Calvinists); illegally arrested (1618); condemned as traitor and executed (1619).

**Bar'ney** (bär'nĭ), **Joshua.** 1759–1818. American naval officer, b. in Maryland. Served through American Revolution; captured three times by British; captured British frigate *General Monk* (1782). In French service (1796–1802). Privateer during War of 1812. Joined force at Bladensburg defending Washington; defeated after heroic resistance, wounded, and captured (1814).

**Barn'field** (bärn'fēld), **Richard.** 1574–1627. English poet. Author of *The Affectionate Shepherd* (1594), and of sonnets in the style of Shakespeare.

**Bar'num** (bär'nŭm), **Phineas Taylor.** 1810–1891. American showman, b. Bethel, Conn. Opened "American Museum" of curios (1842). Exhibited the dwarf Tom Thumb (see Charles Sherwood STRATTON) with great success in U.S. and England. Brought Jenny Lind to U.S. for concert tour (1850). Opened "The Greatest Show on Earth" in Brooklyn (1871); combined with Bailey (1881) to form Barnum and Bailey Circus; imported Jumbo, a huge African elephant bought from Royal Zoological Society in London. Connected with circus business until his death. See also RINGLING.

**Barnum, Zenus.** 1810–1865. American hotelkeeper and capitalist, b. near Wilkes-Barre, Pa. Organized North American Telegraph Co. (1848–49) to run telegraph line between Washington and New York; merged company with American Telegraph Co. (1859), with himself as president.

**Barocchio, Giacomo.** See Giacomo da VIGNOLA.

**Ba·roc'ci** (bä·rôt'chē) *or* **Ba·roc'cio** (bä·rôt'chō), **Federigo.** 1528–1612. Italian painter; studied under Battista Franco; influenced by Raphael and Correggio; among his works are *La Madonna del Popolo* (Uffizi Gallery), *Christ Crucified* (Cathedral of Genoa), *Burning of Troy* (Borghese Palace).

**Ba'roche'** (bȧ'rôsh'), **Pierre Jules.** 1802–1870. French minister of interior during presidency of Louis Napoleon (1850–51); president of council of state, with rank of minister (1851); resigned (1869).

**Ba·ro'da** (bȧ·rō'dȧ), Maharaja Gaekwar of. Sir **Sa'ya·ji Ra'o III** (sŭ'yä·jē rä'ōō). 1863–1939. Succeeded as gaekwar (1875) as a descendant of Maratha founder of family. Invested with full ruling powers (1881); carefully educated; extremely wealthy, gave large sums to British government during World War for airplanes, trucks, relief funds, etc.; representative of India at Imperial Conference (1937); author of several books.

**Ba·ro'ja** (bä·rô'hä), **Pío.** 1872–1956. Spanish author, b. San Sebastián. Physician in Basque country; baker and journalist; wrote many novels (earliest 1900) based on Basque life and Carlist wars, *Memorias de un Hombre de Acción* (20 vols., 1913–31), and many volumes of essays (1900–32).

**Ba'ron'** (bȧ'rôN'), **Michel.** *Real name* **Michel Boy'ron'** (bwȧ'rôN'). 1653–1729. French actor in tragedy and comedy, and playwright. Author of *L'Homme à Bonnes Fortunes* (1686).

**Bar'on·dess'** (băr'ŭn·dĕs'), **Joseph.** 1867–1928. Jewish leader, b. Kamenets Podolsk, Russia; to U.S. (1888). Active in Zionist movement and various social reforms.

**Ba·ro'ni·us** (bȧ·rō'nĭ·ŭs), **Caesar.** *Ital.* **Cesare Ba·ro'nio** (bä·rô'nyō). 1538–1607. Italian ecclesiastical historian. Joined Oratory of St. Philip Neri (1557); superior (1593); confessor to Clement VIII; apostolic prothonotary (1595); cardinal (1596); Vatican librarian (1597). Commissioned by St. Philip Neri to write Roman Catholic reply to Protestant *Magdeburg Centuries*, the *Annales Ecclesiastici a Christo Nato ad Annum 1198* (12 vols., 1588–1607).

**Ba'ross** (bŏ'rôsh), **Gábor** *or* **Ga'bri·el** (*Ger.* gä'brē·ĕl). *Ennobled as* **von Bel'lus** (fôn bĕl'ōōsh). 1848–1892. Hungarian statesman. As minister of communications (1886) and of merged departments of commerce and communications (1890), he was in charge of unifying railroad system of Austria-Hungary, uniting post and telegraph systems, and fixing tariff zones on railroads, canals, etc., in Hungary.

**Barozzi, Giacomo.** See Giacomo da VIGNOLA.

**Barr** (bär), **Amelia Edith,** *nee* **Hud'dle·ston** (hŭd''l·stŭn). 1831–1919. Novelist, b. in Lancashire, England; m. Rev. Robert Barr (1850); to U.S., living in Texas (1854–68) and New York City. Wrote voluminously, chiefly fiction, including *Jan Vedder's Wife* (1885), *The Maid of Maiden Lane* (1900), *The House on Cherry Street* (1909).

**Barr, Archibald.** 1855–1931. Scottish engineer and inventor; educ. Glasgow U.; professor of civil engineering and mechanics, Glasgow U. (1889–1913); with William Stroud (*q.v.*) invented naval and military range finders, height finders, naval gunfire-control instruments, pressure pumps, etc.; chairman of company (Barr & Stroud, Ltd., Glasgow) for manufacturing these instruments.

**Barr, Robert.** 1850–1912. Editor and novelist, b. Glasgow, Scotland. Educ. in Toronto, Canada. Editor in Detroit, Mich., and London, Eng., and coeditor with Jerome K. Jerome in London. Author of *The O'Ruddy* (1904; with Stephen Crane).

**Barra, Francisco León de la.** See DE LA BARRA.

**Bar'rande'** (bȧ'räNd'), **Joachim** (zhō'ȧ'kēm'). 1799?–1883. French geologist and paleontologist; authority on Silurian formations.

**Bar'ras** (băr'ăs), **Charles M.** 1826–1873. American playwright; author of *The Black Crook* (first produced at Niblo's Garden, New York, 1866, and often revived), not to be confused with a later *Black Crook* (prod. 1872) by T. & H. Paulton.

**Bar'ras'** (bȧ'rȧs'), Vicomte **Paul François Jean Nicolas de.** 1755–1829. French revolutionist. Member of National Convention; voted for execution of Louis XVI. Took prominent part in overthrow of Robespierre (July 27, 1794). As commander in chief, appointed by Convention, called Napoleon Bonaparte to keep order in Paris. Member of Directory (1795); secured appointment of Bonaparte to command army in Italy. Arranged marriage of Bonaparte with Joséphine de Beauharnais. At height of his power from 1797 to 1799; suspected by Napoleon of intrigues to aid restoration of monarchy (from 1799); not again in Paris until after Restoration (1815).

**Bar'ratt** (băr'ăt), Sir **Arthur Sheridan.** 1891– . British air marshal, b. in India; educ. for army; served with Royal Flying Corps in France (1914–18); with Royal Air Force from 1919; senior instructor at staff college, Andover; senior air staff officer, headquarters,

India (1932–34); commandant of staff college (1936–39); chief, R.A.F. in France and air marshal (1940); commander, Army Co-operation (1940–43), Technical Training (1943–45); inspector general, R.A.F. (1945–47).

**Bar·ré′** (bă·rā′; băr′ē), **Isaac.** 1726–1802. British soldier, b. Dublin, of French parentage. Wounded at Quebec, under Wolfe. M.P. (1761–90); opposed Lord North's ministry and taxation of American colonies; treasurer of navy (1782). Eponym of Barre, Vt., and of Wilkes-Barre, Pa.

**Bar·re′da La′os** (bär·rĕ′thä lä′ōs), **Felipe.** 1884– . Peruvian lawyer. Editor of *La República*, Lima (1926–30); ambassador to Argentina and Uruguay (1930–38); delegate to Permanent Court of International Justice at The Hague.

**Bar·rei′ro** (bär·rĕ′ē·rō), **Cândido.** d. 1880. President of Paraguay (1878–80).

**Bar′rell** (băr′ĕl), **Joseph.** 1869–1919. American geologist and engineer, b. New Providence, N.J. B.S. (1892), E.M. (1893), M.S. (1897), Lehigh; Ph.D., Yale (1900). Professor of geology (from 1908), Yale. Known for work relating to igneous intrusions, regional geology, geological time, isostasy, and origin of the earth.

**Bar′rère′** (bȧ′râr′), **Camille Eugène Pierre.** 1851–1940. French diplomat; ambassador to Italy (1897 ff.); played important part in influencing Italy to join Allies in World War.

**Bar′rès′** (bȧ′rĕs′), **Auguste Maurice.** 1862–1923. French writer and politician. Boulangist member, Chamber of Deputies (1889–93). Author of novels preaching restoration of national energy to France (*Les Déracinés*, 1897; *L'Appel au Soldat*, 1900; *Leurs Figures*, 1902), and of a series called *Les Bastions de l'Est* (*Au Service de l'Allemagne*, 1905; *Colette Baudoche*, 1909). His *l'Âme Française et la Guerre* is a collection of articles written day by day during the World War.

**Bar′rett** (băr′ĕt; -ĭt), **Charles Simon.** 1866–1935. American organizer of farmers, b. Pike County, Georgia. President, National Farmers' Union (1906–28). Representative of National Board of Farm Organizations and National Farmers' Union at peace conference, Paris (1918–19).

**Barrett, Eaton Stannard.** 1786–1820. Irish poet. Author of *Woman and other Poems* (1810) and political satires.

**Barrett, Elizabeth.** See BROWNING.

**Barrett, John.** 1866–1938. American journalist and diplomat, b. Grafton, Vt. A.B., Dartmouth (1889). U.S. minister to Siam (1894–98), Argentina (1903–04), Panama (1904–05), Colombia (1905–06). Director-general, Pan American Union, Washington, D.C. (1907–20). Author of *Admiral George Dewey* (1899), *Pan American Union...* (1911), *Panama Canal...* (1913), *Pan American Commerce...* (1919), *The Call of South America* (1924), etc.

**Barrett, Lawrence.** 1838–1891. American actor, b. Paterson, N.J. Joined Boston Museum Company (1858, 1859). Served in Civil War (1861–62). In partnership with Booth (1886–91); excelled in Shakespearean roles.

**Barrett,** Sir **William Fletcher.** 1844–1925. British physicist, b. Jamaica, West Indies. Professor, Royal College of Science, Dublin (1873–1910). One of founders of Society for Psychical Research (1882). Did research on magnetism, radiant heat, sound, and vision. Joint author, *Introduction to Practical Physics* (1892), *On Swedenborg* (1912), etc.

**Barrett, Wilson.** 1846–1904. English actor, playwright, and theater manager, b. in Essex. Manager of Court Theatre, London (1879), Princess Theatre, London (1881), Lyceum Theatre, London (1899). Toured in U.S. five times (between 1886 and 1897). Author of *Nowadays* (1889), *The Sign of the Cross* (1895), etc.

**Bar·ret′to** (bă·rĕt′ō), **Larry.** *In full* **Laurence Brevoort Barretto.** 1890–1971. American novelist, b. Larchmont, N.Y. Author of *A Conqueror Passes* (1924), *To Babylon* (1925), *Old Enchantment* (1928), *Horses in the Sky* (1929), *The Indiscreet Years* (1931), *Tomorrow Will Be Different* (1936), *Journey Through Time* (1940), etc.

**Barrey, Lodowick.** See Lodowick BARRY.

**Barri, Giraldus de.** See GIRALDUS DE BARRI.

**Bar′rias′** (bȧ′ryȧs′), **Félix Joseph.** 1822–1907. French historical painter. His brother **Louis Ernest** (1841–1905) was a sculptor.

**Bar′rie** (băr′ĭ), Sir **James Matthew.** 1860–1937. Scottish novelist and dramatist. Grad. Edinburgh U. (1882). Editorial writer, *Nottingham Journal* (1883). Began career as man of letters with *Auld Licht Idylls* (1888), *A Window in Thrums* (1889), *Little Minister* (1891); after *Sentimental Tommy* (1895) turned from fiction to writing for the theater; first play *Walker, London* (1893) a success, followed by *Professor's Love Story* (1895); came to full development as dramatist of manners and fantasy, producing (1903) *Quality Street, The Admirable Crichton*, and *Little Mary; Peter Pan* (1904), elaborated from an episode in *Little White Bird* (1902); *Alice-Sit-by-the-Fire* (1905); and *What Every Woman Knows* (1908); developed a favorite theme, the folly of worldly success, in *The Will* (1913) and in *The Twelve Pound Look;* produced among his World War plays *A Kiss for Cinderella* (1916); continued to mingle the everyday world and dreamland, whimsical humor and human tragedy, with further reaches into dreamland in his closing period, with *Dear Brutus* (1917), *Mary Rose* (1920), and the enigmatical *Shall We Join the Ladies?* (1922). Presents autobiographical account of early life in *Margaret Ogilvy* (1894).

**Bar′rière′** (bȧ′ryâr′), **Théodore.** 1823–1877. French playwright, b. Paris. Author of *Les Filles de Marbre* (1853), *Les Faux Bonshommes* (1856), etc.

**Bar·ri′li** (bär·rē′lē), **Antonio Giulio.** 1836–1908. Italian novelist. Fought under Garibaldi (1866, 1867). Founded and edited *Caffaro* (1872–87). Member, Chamber of Deputies (1876–79). Professor, Genoa (1889). Wrote two plays, literary criticism, as *Il Rinnovamento Letterario Italiano* (1890), and many novels, as *Il Capitan Dodero* (1865), *Come un Sogno* (1875), *L'Olmo e l'Edera* (1877).

**Bar′ring·ton** (băr′ĭng·tŭn), **E.** See L. Adams BECK.

**Barrington, George.** *Real name* **George Wal′dron** (wôl′drŭn). 1755–c. 1840. Irish writer; transported to New South Wales as an incorrigible pickpocket (1790) but granted emancipation for disclosing a projected mutiny on shipboard; made superintendent of convicts, later high sheriff of Parramatta, N.S.W. Author of histories of New South Wales and New Holland (now Australia).

**Barrington, John Shute.** 1st Viscount **Barrington.** 1678–1734. English lawyer and champion of civil rights of Protestant dissenters; emissary to Scotland to win Presbyterian support for union with England. His 4th son, **Daines** (1727–1800), lawyer, antiquarian, and naturalist, was Welsh judge (1757) and second justice of Chester (1778–85); author of *Observations on the Statutes* (1766) with learned notes.

**Barrington, Rutland.** *Real name* **George Barrington Rutland Fleet** (flēt). 1853–1922. English actor and singer, esp. in Gilbert and Sullivan operas.

**Bar′rios** (bär′ryōs), **Justo Rufino.** 1835?–1885. Guatemalan general and political leader, b. San Lorenzo.

Commander in chief of army (1871–73); president of Guatemala (1873–85); killed in action in war with El Salvador. His nephew **José María Reina Barrios** (1853–1898) was president of Guatemala (1892–98); assassinated.

**Bar'ron** (băr'ŭn), **Clarence Walker.** 1855–1928. American editor and publicist, b. Boston. On staff of Boston *Transcript* (1875–84). Founder (1887) and president, Boston News Bureau; founder, Philadelphia News Bureau (1897). Editor of *Barron's Financial Weekly;* manager of Dow, Jones & Co., New York, publishers of *Wall Street Journal* (1901). Author of *The Federal Reserve Act* (1914), *The Audacious War* (1915), *The Mexican Problem* (1917), *War Finance* (1919), *A World Remaking* (1920).

**Bar'ros** (bär'rōōsh), **João de.** 1496–1570. Portuguese historian, b. Viseu. Governor of Portuguese Guinea; treasurer of Portuguese India (1528). Known esp. for *Ásia* (vols. 1–3, 1552–63; vol. 4, 1615), history of the Portuguese in East Indies to 1539, known in English as *Decades.*

**Bar'ros A·ra'na** (bär'rōs ä·rä'nä), **Diego.** 1830–1907. Chilean historian, b. Santiago. Studied law; professor, history of literature, Santiago; known esp. as authority on history of Chile. Author of *Historia de la Guerra del Pacífico* (2 vols., 1880–81), *Historia General de Chile* (16 vols., 1884–1902), etc.

**Bar'ros Bor·go'ño** (bär'rōs bôr·gō'nyō), **Luis.** 1858–1943. Chilean writer, diplomat, and statesman, b. Santiago. Professor of history, U. of Santiago. Minister of war and marine (1889, 1902), war (1892), foreign affairs (1894, 1918–19); vice-president of Chile; acting president (Oct. to Dec., 1925); ambassador to Argentina (to 1938). His works include *La Misión del Vicario Apostólico Don Juan Muzi...* (1883), *El Vice-Almirante Patricio Lynch, 1824–1886* (1886), *La Cuestión del Pacífico y las Nuevas Orientaciones de Bolivia* (1922; Eng. transl., 1924).

**Bar'ros Jar'pa** (bär'rōs här'pä), **Ernesto.** 1894– . Chilean lawyer and statesman, b. Chillán; educ. U. of Chile. Minister of foreign affairs (1921; again 1941 ff.) and finance and interior (1932); professor of international public law, U. of Chile. Author of *Solución de los Conflictos Internacionales* (1915), *Hacia la Solución* (1927), and *La Conferencia de la Paz y el Convenio sobre Arreglo Pacífico de los Conflictos Internacionales.*

**Bar'ros Lu'co** (bär'rōs lōō'kō), **Ramón.** b. 1835. President of Chile (1910–15).

**Bar·ro'so** (băr·rō'zōō), **Gustavo.** 1888–1959. Brazilian jurist, writer, and journalist, b. Fortaleza, Ceará; educ. for bar at Fortaleza (1907–09) and Rio de Janeiro (1910–11). Editor, *Jornal do Ceará* (1908–09) and *Jornal do Comércio* (1911–13). Secretary, Brazilian delegation to Versailles peace conference (1919); director, National Historical Museum (1922 ff.). Works include *Terra de Sol* (1912), *Heróis e Bandidos* (1917), *Ao Som da Viola* (1921), *Coração da Europa* (1922), *O Brasil em Face do Prata* (1930), *Luz e Pó* (1932), *A Viagem Submarina* (1934), *História Secreta do Brasil* (2 vols., 1936, 1937), *Reflexões dum Bóde* (1937), and *Coração de Menino* (1939).

**Bar'rot'** (bá'rō'), **Camille Hyacinthe Odilon.** 1791–1873. French statesman, b. Villefort. Leader of "dynastic opposition" in chamber of deputies (after 1830); one of leaders of reform movement of 1847; appointed president of Council of State (1848) by Thiers. In ministry during presidency of Louis Napoleon; resigned (1849). Councilor f state (1872).

**Bar'row** *or* **Bar'rowe** (băr'ō), **Henry.** d. 1593. English church reformer. B.A., Cantab. (1570). Influenced by Brownists. Imprisoned, with John Greenwood, for denying authority of ecclesiastical dignitaries, and hanged at Tyburn for recusancy. By some considered a founder of Congregationalism.

**Bar'row** (băr'ō), **Isaac.** 1630–1677. English mathematician and theologian. First Lucasian professor of mathematics at Cambridge (1663), resigned (1669) in favor of his pupil Isaac Newton. Author of *Methods of Tangents,* controversial pieces including *Pope's Supremacy* (1680), and *Sermons.*

**Barrow,** Sir **John.** 1764–1848. English traveler; secretary to ambassador to China (1792), and to governor of Cape of Good Hope (1797). Secretary of the admiralty (1804–06, 1807–45). Founder of Royal Geographical Society (1830). Promoted Arctic exploration. Author of accounts of his voyages and travels.

**Bar'rows** (băr'ōz), **David Prescott.** 1873–1954. American educator and ethnologist, b. Chicago. Grad. Pomona (1894). Director of education, Philippine Islands (1903–09). Professor of education (1910) and of political science (1911), dean of faculties (1913), president (1919–23), U. of California. Author of *A History of the Philippines* (1903), etc.

**Barrows, Samuel June.** 1845–1909. American Unitarian clergyman and prison reformer, b. New York City. Influential in passage of New York's first probation law and of a federal parole law.

**Bar'ry** (băr'ĭ; *Fr.* bá'rē'), Comtesse **du.** See Du Barry.

**Bar'ry** (băr'ĭ), **Alfred.** 1826–1910. English clergyman, b. London. Educ. Cambridge. Canon of Worcester (1871) and Westminster (1881). Primate of Australia (1884–89), metropolitan of New South Wales, and bishop of Sydney. Rector of St. James's, in Piccadilly (1895–1900).

**Barry, Ann Street.** See under Spranger Barry.

**Barry,** Sir **Charles.** 1795–1860. English architect. Built Travellers' Club (1831), and Reform Club (1837), and Bridgewater House (1847), London; won competition for best designs for Houses of Parliament (1836); occupied in building them (1840–60). His son **Edward Middleton** (1830–1880), also an architect, built new Covent Garden Theatre, extensions to National Gallery, Charing Cross Hotel. Another son, Sir **John Wolfe Wolfe-Barry** [wŏŏlf'băr'ĭ] (1836–1918), was a civil engineer; studied under Sir John Hawkshaw; planned and directed extensions of London's electric railway systems; built Barry docks, at Barry, near Cardiff, the Tower bridge and new Kew bridge over the Thames; British representative on International Suez Commission (1892–1906).

**Barry, Elizabeth.** 1658–1713. English actress. Coached by her lover the earl of Rochester, appeared successfully as Queen Isabella in *Mustapha* (1673); created over one hundred different roles in comedy, including Lady Brute in *Provoked Wife.*

**Barry, James.** 1741–1806. Irish historical painter. Brought to London by Edmund Burke (1763); executed six pictures on "Human Culture" on walls of Society of Arts (1777–83); professor of painting at Royal Academy (1782–99). Known for *Adam and Eve, Venus Rising from the Sea, Death of General Wolfe.*

**Barry, John.** 1745–1803. American naval officer, b. in County Wexford, Ireland. Settled in Philadelphia (1760). Entered naval service in American Revolution; performed brilliant exploits in command of American war vessels.

**Bar'ry** *or* **Bar'rey** (băr'ĭ), **Lodowick.** 17th-century English dramatist; known as author of *Ram Alley or Merry Tricks* (1611), included in second and later editions of Dodsley's *Old Plays.*

**Bar'ry** (băr'ĭ), **Martin.** 1802–1855. English physician and embryologist. M.D., Edinburgh (1833). Demonstrated penetration of ova by spermatozoa (1843).

**Barry, Philip.** 1896–1949. American playwright, b. Rochester, N.Y. A.B., Yale (1919); grad. student, Harvard (1919–22). Author of *You and I* (1922), *In a Garden* (1925), *White Wings* (1926), *Paris Bound* (1927), *Holiday* (1929), *Hotel Universe* (one-act play; 1930), *Tomorrow and Tomorrow* (1931), *The Animal Kingdom* (1932), *The Joyous Season* (1933), *Bright Star* (1935), *Here Come the Clowns* (1938), *The Philadelphia Story* (1939), etc.

**Barry,** Sir **Redmond.** 1813–1880. Irish colonial judge. Called to Irish bar (1838); to Australia (1839); first solicitor general of Victoria (1851); acting chief justice, supreme court; founder and first chancellor of U. of Melbourne (1853).

**Barry, Spran'ger** (?sprăn'jẽr). 1719–1777. Irish actor. Made London debut (1746) at Drury Lane as Othello; alternated with Garrick as Hamlet and Macbeth; with Mrs. Cibber as Juliet, rivaled Garrick's Romeo; built theater in Dublin (1758) and Cork (1761); returned to Drury Lane under Garrick (1767); to Covent Garden (1774) with wife. Among his roles were Mahomet in Johnson's *Irene* (1749) and Young Norval in Home's *Douglas* (1757). His wife (m. 1768), **Ann,** *nee* **Street** (1734–1801), Mrs. Dancer by an early marriage, played Cordelia to Barry's Lear in Dublin (1758); made last appearance in most successful part, as Lady Randolph in *Douglas* (1798).

**Barry, William Farquhar.** 1818–1879. American army officer, b. New York City. Chief of artillery on W. T. Sherman's staff (1864–65); organized and headed Artillery School, Fort Monroe, Va. (1867–77).

**Barry, William Francis.** 1849–1929. English Roman Catholic priest and author of essays, romantic novels, *The New Antigone* (1887) on modern views of marriage, and books on Newman and Renan.

**Barry, William Taylor.** 1785–1835. American lawyer, b. Lunenburg, Va. U.S. postmaster general (1829–35).

**Bar'ry·more** (băr'ĭ·mōr), **Maurice.** *Real name* **Herbert Blythe** (blīth). 1847–1905. Actor, b. in India. On English stage (1872–75) and American stage (1875 ff.). Leading man for Madame Modjeska (1881–84, 1886); played in support of Lily Langtry, Olga Nethersole, Mrs. Fiske; m. (1876) **Georgiana Emma Drew** (1856–1893), daughter of John Drew, herself an actress excelling in comedy. Their three children, **Lionel** (1878–1954), **Ethel** (1879–1959; m. Russell Griswold Colt; divorced, 1923), and **John** (1882–1942), all succeeded on legitimate stage. Lionel has starred in numerous motion pictures, as *Rasputin and the Empress* (with Ethel and John; 1933). Ethel starred in *A Doll's House* (1905), *Alice-Sit-by-the-Fire* (1906), *The Constant Wife* (1926), etc. John played Hamlet (1924–25) and starred in motion pictures, as *Beau Brummel, Don Juan,* etc.

**Barse** (bärs), **George Randolph,** Jr. 1861–1938. American figure and portrait painter; painted eight panels for Library of Congress.

**Bar·sot'ti** (bär·sôt'tē), **Charles.** 1850–1927. Editor, b. near Pisa, Italy; settled in New York City (1872). Established *Il Progresso* (1880), first Italian daily newspaper in U.S.

**Bar'stow** (bär'stō), Mrs. **Montagu.** = Baroness Orczy.

**Bar·su'mas** (bär·sōō'măs) *or* **Bar·su'ma** (-mȧ). *Also* **Bar–So'ma** (băr·sō'mä). 435?–489. Syrian monk. As bishop or metropolitan of Nisibis (Nusaybin), established a theological school; chief founder of Nestorianism in Persia.

**Bart** (bȧr) *or* **Barth** (bȧrt), **Jean.** 1651?–1702. French soldier of fortune. His courage and success as commander of privateer in war against Dutch led Louis XIV to appoint him captain of a frigate (1686) and squadron commander (1697).

**Bar'tas'** (bȧr'tȧs'), Seigneur **du. Guillaume de Sal'luste'** (dē sȧ'lüst'). 1544–1590. French poet; author of *La Semaine* (epic of the Creation, 1578), and the incomplete universal history *La Seconde Semaine.* His works translated into English by Josuah Sylvester (*q.v.*).

**Bar'tel** (bär'tĕl), **Kazimierz.** 1882– 1941. Polish mathematician and statesman; prime minister for a few months after Piłsudski's coup d'état (May, 1926) and again after Piłsudski's retirement (June, 1928–Apr., 1929; Dec., 1929–Mar., 1930). Professor of mathematics in Lemberg (from 1930).

**Bar'tels** (bär'tĕls), **Adolf.** 1862–1945. German journalist, poet, and writer. Author of *Deutsche Dichtung der Gegenwart* (1897), *Geschichte der Deutschen Literatur* (1901–02), *Martin Luther* (1903), *Lessing und die Juden* (1918), *Meine Lebensarbeit* (1932), etc.

**Bartels, Hans von.** 1856–1913. German painter of seascapes, fishing scenes, etc.

**Bar'ten·stein** (bär'tĕn·shtīn), Baron **Johann Christoph von.** 1689–1767. Austrian statesman, b. Strasbourg. Secretary of state and adviser of Charles VI and Maria Theresa (1727–53); director, Austrian foreign affairs during struggle for recognition of Pragmatic Sanction; vice-chancellor, political and financial affairs (1753).

**Bar'tet'** (bȧr'tĕ'), **Jeanne Julia.** *Real surname* **Regnault'** (rē·nyō'). 1854–1941. French actress.

**Barth** (bärt), **Heinrich.** 1821–1865. German explorer, b. Hamburg. Traveled through North Africa and Nile Valley, Palestine, Syria, Asia Minor, and Greece (1845–47), through the Sahara and Sudan (1850–55), and again in Greece, Asia Minor, and Turkey. His accounts of his travels notable for accuracy and breadth of information.

**Barth** (bȧrt), **Jean.** See Jean Bart.

**Barth** (bärt), **Karl.** 1886–1968. Swiss Protestant Reformed theologian and educator; champion of dialectic theology. Author of *Der Römerbrief* (1919), *Das Wort Gottes und die Theologie* (1924), *Christliche Dogmatik* (1927), *Credo* (1935), etc. Associate editor, *Zwischen den Zeiten* (1922–33). His brother **Peter** (1888–1940), clergyman; editor of *Calvini Opera Selecta* (1926 ff.).

**Barth, Paul.** 1858–1922. German writer on philosophical and sociological subjects, b. in Silesia. Professor, U. of Leipzig.

**Barth, Theodor.** 1849–1909. German editor and political leader. Liberal member of Reichstag (1881–84, 1885–98, 1901–03). Founded (1883) and edited (1883–1907) *Die Nation.*

**Bar·thé'** (bär·tā'), **Richmond.** 1901– . American Negro sculptor, b. in Mississippi; studied at Chicago Art Inst.; awarded Julius Rosenwald fellowship; first exhibited in New York (1931). Among his works are *Blackberry Woman, African Boy Dancing, Lindy Hop, Negro Mother, Harmonica Player,* and a number of portrait busts.

**Bar'thel** (bär'tĕl), **Max.** 1893– . German poet and novelist; author of *Verse aus den Argonnen* (1916), *Arbeiterseele,* and the novels *Das Spiel mit der Puppe* (1925), *Der Putsch* (1927), and *Der Mensch am Kreuz* (1927).

**Bar'thé'le·my'** (bȧr'tāl'mē'), **Auguste Mar'seille'** (mȧr'sâ'y'). 1796–1867. French poet and satirist, b. Marseille; collaborated (1824–34) with Joseph Méry (*q.v.*) in political satires, including *La Villéliade* (against the minister Villèle, 1827), *La Peyronnéide* (against the minister Peyronet), *Napoléon en Égypte* (1828), *Waterloo* (1829); also collaborated in founding and editing weekly journal, *Némésis*, attacking (1831–32) government of Louis Philippe.

**Barthélemy,** Marquis **François de.** 1750?–1830. French statesman and diplomat; negotiated treaties of Basel (1795); member of Directory (1797); transported to Guiana for royalist sympathies (1797–99). Created senator by Napoleon; deserted Napoleon and favored (1814) Louis XVIII; created peer of France by Louis XVIII.

**Barthélemy, Jean Jacques.** 1716–1795. French abbé and scholar; author of *Voyage du Jeune Anacharsis en Grèce* (1788), an account of the government, customs, and buildings of ancient Greece as they might have appeared to a traveler in ancient times.

**Barthélemy Saint′-Hi′laire′** (săɴ′tē′lâr′), **Jules.** 1805–1895. French journalist, savant, and politician, b. Paris. Minister of foreign affairs (1880–81). Translated Aristotle.

**Barthema, Lodovico di.** See Lodovico di VARTHEMA.

**Bar′thez′** (bȧr′tâz′) *or* **Bar′thès′** (bȧr′tâs′), **Paul Joseph.** 1734–1806. French medical writer and philosopher; collaborator with Diderot and d'Alembert on the *Encyclopédie.*

**Bar′thol′di′** (bȧr′tôl′dē′; *Angl.* bär·thŏl′dĭ), **Frédéric Auguste.** 1834–1904. French sculptor, b. Colmar; known esp. for his colossal figures, as the Statue of Liberty (*Liberté Éclairant le Monde* or *Liberty Enlightening the World*), presented (1885, unveiled 1886) by the French people to the U.S. and located on Bedloe's Island in New York harbor, and *Le Lion de Belfort*, commemorating defense of Belfort in Franco-Prussian War.

**Bar′tholdt** (bär′tōlt), **Richard.** 1855–1932. American editor and legislator, b. in Germany; to U.S. as a boy. Editor, St. Louis *Tribune* (1885–92). Member, U.S. House of Representatives (1893–1915). Author of *From Steerage to Congress* (1930).

**Bar·tho′lin** (bär·to͝o′lĭn), **Kaspar.** 1585–1629. Danish physician. Professor of medicine (1613), then of divinity, U. of Copenhagen. Author of *Institutiones Anatomicae* (1611). His son **Thomas** (1616–1680), known for his observations on the lymphatics, was professor of anatomy at Copenhagen (from 1648); enlarged his father's *Institutiones Anatomicae*, and defended Harvey's doctrine of the circulation of the blood.

**Bar′tho·lo·mae′** (bär′tō·lō·mâ′), **Christian.** 1855–1925. German philologist, b. near Bayreuth. Professor of Sanskrit, Heidelberg (from 1909). Author of *Altiranisches Wörterbuch* (1904), etc.

**Bar·thol′o·mae′us An′gli·cus** (bär·thŏl′ō·mē′ŭs [-tŏl′-] ăng′glĭ·kŭs) *or* **Bar·thol′o·mew** (bär·thŏl′ō·mū) **the Englishman.** fl. 1230–1250. English Franciscan friar; professor of theology, Paris; author of *De Proprietatibus Rerum* (first printed c. 1470; Eng. transl. by Trevisa, 1398), an encyclopedia of the Middle Ages. Frequently confused with a 14th-century English Franciscan, **Bartholomew de Glan′ville** [dĕ glăn′vĭl] (d. 1360?).

**Bar′tho′lo′mé′** (bȧr′tô′lô′mā′), **Paul Albert.** 1848–1928. French painter and sculptor, b. Thiverval. Among his works are *Le Secret*, *Jeune Fille Pleurant*, and *Jeune Fille Priant;* his *Monument aux Morts* is in Père Lachaise cemetery, and his *La Victoire* in the Place du Carrousel, both in Paris.

**Bar·thol′o·mew** (bär·thŏl′ō·mū), Saint. In Bible, one of twelve apostles (*Matt.* x. 3; *Mark* iii. 18; *Luke* vi. 14; *Acts* i. 13). His day in Roman and Anglican churches is Aug. 24 (at Rome, Aug. 25) and in Eastern Church, June 11. Cf. NATHANAEL.

**Bartholomew, John.** 1831–1893. Scottish cartographer. His son **John George** (1860–1920), educ. Edinburgh U., also a cartographer, was a founder of Royal Scottish Geographical Society (1884); cartographer to the king (from 1913); introduced layer system of contour coloring in topographic maps; his best-known work, the [London] *Times Survey Atlas of the World*, completed (1921) after his death.

**Bar′thou′** (bȧr′to͞o′), **Jean Louis.** 1862–1934. French lawyer and statesman, b. Oloron-Sainte-Marie. Practiced law (from 1884). Held appointments in various cabinets, as minister of public works (1895, 1906, 1909–10), interior (1896–98), justice (1913). As premier of France (Mar.–Dec., 1913), secured passage of act to extend term of compulsory army service from two years to three, thus adding 170,000 effectives to army. Again held cabinet posts (1917–21); became minister of justice (1922) under Poincaré; headed French delegation to Genoa conference; elected senator; appointed president of reparation commission. Again minister of justice under Poincaré (1926) and Briand (1929). As minister of foreign affairs (1934), directed efforts to secure French security by means of accords with Little Entente, Soviet Russia, Great Britain; arranged visit to France by King Alexander of Yugoslavia in connection with his proposed eastern European agreement similar to Locarno agreements; killed in vain attempt to prevent assassination of Alexander in Marseille (Oct. 9).

**Bar′ti·mae′us** (bär′tĭ·mē′ŭs). *In Douay Version* **Bar′ti·me′us** (-mē′ŭs). In Bible, a blind man healed by Jesus at Jericho (*Mark* x. 46 ff.).

**Bartimeus.** Pseudonym of Lewis RITCHIE.

**Bart′let** (bärt′lĕt; -lĭt), **James Vernon.** 1863–1940. English professor of church history, Mansfield Coll., Oxford (1900). Author of *Studies in the Synoptic Problem* (1911), *Christian Worship* (1936), etc.

**Bart′lett** (bärt′lĕt; -lĭt), **Ellis Ashmead-.** See ASHMEAD-BARTLETT.

**Bartlett, Enoch.** 1779–1860. American merchant of Dorchester, Mass., for whom Bartlett pear is named. This pear, known in France and England as the "bon chrétien," was introduced to America by Captain Thomas Brewer and grown on his farm at Roxbury, Mass.; later distributed by Bartlett under his own name after he had bought Brewer's farm.

**Bartlett,** Sir **Frederic Charles.** 1886–1969. British psychologist; educ. Cambridge and London (B.A., 1909). Professor, Cambridge (1931–52). Author of *Psychology and Primitive Culture* (1923), *The Problem of Noise* (1934), etc.

**Bartlett, Frederic Clay.** 1873–1953. American painter, esp. of murals; b. Chicago.

**Bartlett, Homer Newton.** 1845–1920. American musician and composer, b. Olive, N.Y.

**Bartlett, John.** 1820–1905. American publisher, b. Plymouth, Mass.; with Little, Brown & Co. (from 1863); compiled *Familiar Quotations* (1855), *Complete Concordance to Shakespeare's Dramatic Works and Poems* (1894).

**Bartlett, John Russell.** 1805–1886. American bibliographer and librarian, b. Providence, R.I. Bookdealer, New York (1836–50). Secretary of state, Rhode Island (1855–72). Aided in collection and care of library of John Carter Brown, Providence. Works include *Dictionary of Americanisms* (1848), *Records of the Colony of Rhode Island, 1636–1792* (10 vols.), etc.

**Bartlett, Josiah.** 1729–1795. American physician and Revolutionary leader, b. Amesbury, Mass. Practiced medicine, Kingston, N.H. (1750–95). Delegate to Continental Congress (1775–76, 1778–79); signer of Declaration of Independence. Associate justice (1782–88), chief justice (1788–90), superior court of New Hampshire. "President" of New Hampshire (1790, 1791, 1792) and its first governor (1793–94).

**Bartlett, Paul Wayland.** 1865–1925. American sculptor, b. New Haven, Conn. Studied in Paris. Among his notable works are *Bear Tamer* (in Metropolitan Museum, N.Y.), *Columbus* and *Michelangelo* (Library of Congress, Washington), *Lafayette* (in court of Louvre, Paris; 1908), *Puritans* (on Hartford, Conn., capitol building), *Robert Morris* (Philadelphia; 1924), *Franklin* (Waterbury; 1921), *Alexander Agassiz* and *Gen. Joseph Warren* (Boston).

**Bartlett, Robert Abram.** 1875–1946. Known as "Captain Bob Bartlett." Arctic explorer, b. Brigus, Newfoundland. On Peary expedition (1897–98); commanded the *Roosevelt* on arctic voyage (1905–09). On Canadian government arctic expedition (1913–14) commanded the *Karluk*, which was crushed by ice near Wrangel Island (Jan., 1914); crossed ice to Siberia, with one Eskimo, and returned with rescuers for his companions. Commanded expedition to north Greenland (1917); on expeditions to N.W. Alaska and Arctic Ocean (1925), north Greenland and Ellesmere Land (1926), Siberia (1928), Labrador (1929), Greenland (1930 ff.); Arctic (1942–45). Author of *Last Voyage of the Karluk* (1916), *Sails over Ice* (1934), etc.

**Bartlett, Samuel Colcord.** 1817–1898. American Congregational clergyman and educator, b. Salisbury, N.H. Grad. Dartmouth (1836). President, Dartmouth College (1877–92).

**Bartlett, Vernon.** 1894– . English journalist and novelist; founder and editor of *World Review*. Radio broadcaster on foreign affairs (1928–34). Author of *Mud and Khaki* (1916); *Topsy Turvy* (1927), *This is My Life* (1938), etc.

**Bar′tók** (bŏr′tōk), **Béla.** 1881–1945. Hungarian composer; professor at institute of music, Budapest (1907 ff.); to U.S. (1940). Regarded as a leader of contemporary national Hungarian music. Published collections of over 6,000 Hungarian, Rumanian, and Arabian folk tunes; composer of operas, pantomimes, orchestral suites, symphonic poems, concertos for piano and orchestra, violin sonatas, and piano pieces.

**Bar′to·li** (bär′tō·lē), **Adolfo.** 1833–1894. Italian literary scholar. Author of *I Primi Secoli della Letteratura Italiana* (1870–79), *Storia della Letteratura Italiana* (7 vols., 1878–89), etc.

**Bartoli, Daniello.** 1608–1685. Italian Jesuit priest; wrote *Storia della Compagnia di Gesù* (1653–73).

**Bartoli, Pietro San′ti** (sän′tē). *Sometimes called* **Il Pe′ru·gi′no** (ēl pā′rōō·jē′nō). c. 1635–1700. Italian painter and engraver; studied under Poussin; engraved after ancient monuments and Renaissance works; published *Admiranda Romanorum Antiquitatum Vestigia* and *Pitture Antiche delle Grotte di Roma* (1706).

**Bar′to·li′ni** (bär′tō·lē′nē), **Lorenzo.** 1777–1850. Italian sculptor, b. in Tuscany. Studied under Lemot, Paris (1797 ff.). Sent by Napoleon to found school of sculpture at Carrara (1808). Among his works are the group *Charity* (Florence) and portrait busts, as of Napoleon, Mme. de Staël, Lord Byron, Liszt.

**Bar′to·lom·me′o** (bär′tō·lōm·mâ′ō), **Fra.** *Orig.* **Bar′to·lom·me′o di Pa′go·lo del Fat′to·ri′no** (dē pä′gō·lō dāl fät′tō·rē′nō). *Called familiarly* **Bac′cio del′la Por′ta** (bät′chō dāl′lä pôr′tä). 1475–1517. Florentine painter. Studied under Piero di Cosimo. Follower of Savonarola; retired to Dominican convent of San Marco (1500–04)—hence often called **Il Fra′te** (ēl frä′tā); visited Venice (1508). Teacher and student of Raphael; associated with Albertinelli (1509–12); influenced by Leonardo, Bellini, Giorgione. His work includes *Apparition of the Virgin to St. Bernard* (Florentine Academy), *Marriage of Saint Catherine* (Louvre), the nude *St. Sebastian* (Pézenas), *Christ at Emmaus* (San Marco), *Madonna della Misericordia* (Cathedral of Lucca), *St. Mark* and, with Albertinelli, *Madonna and Saints* (both in the Pitti Palace), *Assumption* (Berlin), *Last Judgment* (Uffizi Gallery).

**Bar′to·loz′zi** (bär′tō·lōt′tsē), **Francesco.** 1727–1815. Italian engraver, b. Florence. Grandfather of Madame Vestris (see under Charles MATHEWS). Associate of Cipriani; engraved after works of Guercino, Annibale Carracci, Giordano, Reynolds, Gainsborough, Cosway, Angelica Kauffmann. To England (1764); engraver to king; one of original members of British Royal Academy (1768). Head of Royal Academy at Lisbon (1802–15).

**Bar′to·lus** (bär′tō·lŭs). *Ital.* **Bar′to·lo** (bär′tō·lō). 1314–1357. Italian jurist; professor at Pisa and Perugia; among his works are treatises *On Procedure* and *On Evidence*, and *Commentary on the Code of Justinian* (1588–89).

**Bar′ton** (bär′t'n), **Andrew.** d. 1511. Scottish naval officer; cleared Scottish coast of Flemish pirates (1506), signalizing his success by sending James IV three barrels filled with pirates' heads. Accused of piracy. Hero of the old ballad *Sir Andrew Barton.*

**Barton, Benjamin Smith.** 1766–1815. American physician and naturalist, b. Lancaster, Pa. Author of *Elements of Botany* (1803), first elementary botany written by an American.

**Barton, Bernard.** 1784–1849. English poet; called "Quaker poet." Bank clerk, Woodbridge (1809–49).

**Barton, Bruce.** 1886-1967. American businessman, author, and politician, b. Robbins, Tenn. A.B., Amherst (1907). In magazine editorial work (1907–18); head of advertising agency in New York City (1918–67); member, U.S. House of Representatives (1937–41). Author of *More Power to You* (1917), *Better Days* (1924), *The Man Nobody Knows* (1925), *The Book Nobody Knows* (1926), *What Can a Man Believe?* (1927), *On the Up and Up* (1929). His father, **William Eleazar** (1861–1930), b. Sublette, Ill., was a Congregational clergyman and author; pastor, Oak Park, Ill. (1899–1924); author of many religious books and books about Abraham Lincoln.

**Barton, Clara,** *in full* **Clarissa Harlowe.** 1821–1912. Founder of American Red Cross, b. Oxford, Mass. Schoolteacher (1836–54); clerk in patent office, Washington, D.C. (1854–61). During Civil War, solicited and distributed supplies for the wounded. In Europe (1869–73), gave aid during Franco-Prussian War, in association with International Red Cross, an organization created by international agreement at Geneva (1864). Campaigned (1877–82) to have U.S. sign Geneva agreement; succeeded (1882), and became first president (1882–1904) of American Red Cross. Her works include *History of the Red Cross* (1882), *A Story of the Red Cross* (1904), *Story of My Childhood* (1907).

**Barton, Derek Harold Richard.** 1918– . English chemist. Shared Nobel prize in chemistry (1969) with Odd Hassel.

**Barton,** Sir **Edmund.** 1849–1920. Australian statesman. Speaker of legislative assembly, New South Wales (1883–87); attorney general (1889, 1891–93); led delegation presenting Australian Commonwealth Constitution bill to British Parliament (1900); first prime minister of Australian Commonwealth (1901–03); judge of Australian high court (1903–1920).

**Barton, Elizabeth.** 1506?–1534. Tavern servant at Aldington. After nervous illness, uttered prophecies and rebukes of those in power, which were believed by many to be divinely inspired; examined by ecclesiastical commission which pronounced her professions sincere. Became Benedictine nun (1527); often referred to as "the nun of Kent" or "the holy maid of Kent." Inveighed against Henry VIII's divorce from Catherine of Aragon; her denunciations adjudged treasonable; condemned with several ecclesiastics; executed at Tyburn (April 20).

**Barton, Frances** *or* **Fanny**. See Frances ABINGTON.

**Barton, George Aaron**. 1859–1942. Educator, b. in East Farnham, Quebec, Canada. Grad. Haverford Coll. (1882). Professor of Semitic languages, Bryn Mawr (1891–1922), Pennsylvania (1922–32).

**Barton, William**. 1748–1831. American Revolutionary officer, b. Warren, R.I. Noted for daring capture (1777) of the British brigadier general, Prescott, in the latter's house at Newport. Imprisoned (honorably) at Danville, Vt. (1810–24) for refusing to pay judgment on his land in Vermont; judgment paid by Lafayette on his visit to U.S. (1824–25).

**Bar′tram** (bär′trăm), **John**. 1699–1777. American botanist, b. near Darby, Pa. Cousin of Humphry Marshall (*q.v.*). Self-taught botanist. Started garden (1728) near Philadelphia; made experiments in hybridizing. Corresponded and exchanged plants with English horticulturist Peter Collinson (from 1733) and with Linnaeus. His garden, a favorite resort of Franklin and Washington, now a part of Philadelphia's park system, contains many giant trees planted by Bartram himself. Designated by Linnaeus the greatest contemporary "natural botanist." His son **William** (1739–1823) was also a naturalist; published (1791) an account of his travels through southeastern U.S. in search of plant and animal specimens.

**Bartsch** (bärch), **Johann Adam Bernhard von**. 1757–1821. Viennese engraver and writer on art. Custodian of collection of engravings, Imperial Library (1816–21). Author of *Le Peintre-Graveur* (21 vols., 1803–21).

**Bartsch, Karl**. 1832–1888. German philologist and critic. Professor of Germanic and Romance philology, Rostock (1858–71), Heidelberg (1871–88). Editor, *Germania* (1868–88); compiler of selections (chrestomathies) of Old French and Provencal literature; translator and editor of the *Nibelungenlied;* editor of *Parzival* (1870–71) and other medieval works; translator of Burns and Dante, etc.

**Bartsch, Paul**. 1871–1960. Zoologist, b. in Silesia, Germany; to U.S. while young. Grad. State U. of Iowa (1896). Curator, division of marine invertebrates, U.S. National Museum, Washington, D.C. (1914).

**Bartsch, Rudolf Hans**. 1873–1952. Austrian novelist, b. Graz. Author of *Zwölf aus Steiermark* (1906), *Schwammerl* (1912), etc.

**Bar′uch** (bâr′ŭk; bā′rŭk). In Bible, secretary of prophet Jeremiah (*Jer.* xxxvi) and reputed author of book of *Baruch* (in Protestant Apocrypha; a canonical book of Roman Catholic Old Testament).

**Ba′ruch** (bär′o͞ok), **Bernard Man′nes** (măn′ĕs). 1870–1965. American businessman and statesman. A.B., C.C.N.Y. (1889). In brokerage business, New York City. Appointed by President Wilson member of Advisory Commission of Council for National Defense (1916); chosen chairman of Committee on Raw Materials, Minerals and Metals; also, chairman of War Industries Board (1918–19). Associated with American Commission to Negotiate Peace, in Paris (1919), as member of drafting committee on economic section; member of Supreme Economic Council and chairman of raw materials division. Also, member of president's conference for capital and labor (1919) and president's agricultural conference (1922); appointed (1934) by President Roosevelt chairman of a committee to recommend legislation to take profits out of war; presented to Senate military affairs committee (1937) his recommendations for wartime industrial mobilization; chairman of special commission on rubber (1942); appointed to atomic energy committee of United Nations (1946). Author of *Making of Economic and Reparation Sections of Peace Treaty* (1920). His father, **Simon** (1840–1921) was a physician; b. Germany; to U.S.; in Confederate army in Civil War (1862–65); practiced medicine, Camden, S.C. (1865–81), New York City (1881); performed operation for appendicitis (1888), said to be first in America. Influential in introducing hydrotherapy.

**Ba′ruch** (bä′ro͝oκ), **Löb**. Original name of Ludwig BÖRNE.

**Bar′us** (bâr′ŭs), **Carl**. 1856–1935. American physicist, b. Cincinnati, Ohio. Ph.D., U. of Würzburg, Germany (1879). Professor (1895–1926), dean of graduate department (1903–26), Brown U. Author of *The Measurement of High Temperatures* (1889), *Condensation of Atmospheric Moisture* (1895), *Condensation Induced by Nuclei and by Ions* (4 parts, 1907–10), *Interferometer Experiments in Acoustics* (3 vols., 1921–25), etc.

**Bar′well** (bär′wĕl; -wĕl), Sir **Henry Newman**. 1877–1959. Australian lawyer; educ. Whinham Coll., St. Peter's Coll., Adelaide U.; LL.B. (1899). Premier and attorney general of South Australia (1920–24); commonwealth senator (1925–28); agent general for South Australia (1928–33).

**Bar′wick** (băr′ĭk), **John**. 1612–1664. English clergyman; B.A., Cantab. (1635); Royalist in sympathy (1642); settled in London and with brothers supplied Charles I, and Charles II, with news of rebel plans. Imprisoned in Tower of London (1650–52). Royal chaplain (1660); dean of Durham (1660), St. Paul's (1661).

**Bary, Heinrich Anton de**. See DE BARY.

**Ba·rya′tin·ski** (bŭ·ryȧ′tyĭn·skû·ĭ; *Angl.* -skĭ), Prince **Aleksandr Ivanovich**. 1814–1879. Russian field marshal. Given command of army in Caucasus by Emperor Alexander II, conducting three successful campaigns against Caucasian tribes (1856–59); stormed Gunib, captured leader Shamyl (1859); appointed field marshal.

**Ba′rye′** (bȧ′rē′), **Antoine Louis**. 1795–1875. French sculptor, esp. of animal figures; b. Paris.

**Bar′zun** (bär′zŭn; bär·zŭn′), **Jacques**. 1907– . American historian, b. France. To U.S. (1920); at Columbia U. (1927). Author of *Berlioz and the Romantic Century* (1950) and books on music, art, education, etc.

**Ba·sa·na′vi·čius** (bä·sä·nä′vĭ·cho͞os), **Jonas**. 1851–1927. Lithuanian scholar and statesman. Published (from 1875) works on Lithuanian mythology and folklore. Founded and edited (1883–86) *Ausra*. At time of Russian troubles (1905), settled at Vilna, convoked a national assembly, and served as its president. Member, Lithuanian national council (1917–18).

**Basarab**. See BESSARABA.

**Bascio, Matteo da**. See MATTEO DA BASCIO.

**Bas′com** (băs′kŭm), **John**. 1827–1911. American educator, b. Genoa, N.Y. President, U. of Wisconsin (1874–87). Professor of political science, Williams (1891–1903).

**Ba′se·dow** (bä′zĕ·dō), **Johann Bernhard**. 1724?–1790. German teacher, educational reformer, and author. Established the Philanthropinum, a model school for children, at Dessau (1774). Author of *Elementarwerk* (4 vols., 1774), and other works on pedagogy.

**Basedow, Karl von**. 1799–1854. German physician; one of first to recognize and describe (1840) exophthalmic goiter (Basedow's disease).

**Bash′ford** (băsh′fẽrd), **Henry Howarth**. 1880–1961. English physician and fiction writer; author of *The*

*Corner of Harley Street*, *The Happy Ghost*, *The Harley Street Calendar*, etc.

**Bashford, James Whitford.** 1849–1919. American Methodist bishop and educator, b. Fayette, Wis. President, Ohio Wesleyan (1889–1904). Elected bishop (1904); labored in China (1904–15). Obtained copy of Japan's Twenty-one Demands on China (1915) and revealed their nature to President Wilson. Opposed Japanese militaristic policy in China. Works include *China and Methodism* (1906), *Christian Missions* (1906), *China: an Interpretation* (1916).

**Bash·kir′tsev** (bŭsh·kyĕr′tsĕf), **Marie.** *Russ.* **Marya Konstantinovna Bash·kir′tse·va** (-tsĕ·vŭ). 1860–1884. Russian painter and diarist, b. near Poltava, of wealthy and noble family. Enjoyed excellent education and acquaintance with best society in European cities; studied painting at Paris under Robert-Fleury and Bastien-Lepage; exhibited in the Salon (1880; *Meeting*, a pastel, 1884). Author of *Journal*, covering most of her life, remarkable human document that caused much discussion (pub. Paris, 1887; Eng. transl., 1890), and of *Letters*, correspondence with Guy de Maupassant (pub. 1891).

**Ba·sho** (bä·shō). *Also known as* **Ma·tsu·o** (mä·tso͞o·ō) **Basho.** *Real name* **Matsuo Mu·ne·fu·sa** (mo͞o·nĕ·fo͞o·sä). 1644–1694. One of the greatest of Japanese poets; a mystic; esp. skillful in composing hokku.

**Bas′il** (băz′ĭl; -'l) *or* **Ba·sil′i·us** (bȧ·sĭl′ĭ·ŭs; -zĭl′-), Saint. *Known as* **Basil the Great.** 330?–?379 A.D. Early church father, b. Caesarea, Cappadocia. Brother of Gregory of Nyssa (*q.v.*). Studied at Byzantium and Athens; visited Syria and Egypt to learn from hermits there and led monastic life for a time (c. 360); ordained (c. 365). Became bishop of Caesarea (370); devoted himself to stamping out heresies, esp. Arianism; improved liturgy and organized monastic institutions on basis of hard work, charitable services, and communal life to replace asceticism of hermits; known as founder of monastic institutions. Works include *De Spiritu Sancto*, *Moralia*, and *Regulae*.

**Basil.** Name of two rulers of Eastern Roman Empire:

**Basil I.** *Called* **Basil the Macedonian.** 812?–886. Son of an officer of court of Emperor Michael III. Emperor (867–886); founded Macedonian dynasty. Companion of Michael; joint ruler with him (866–867). Caused Michael's death. One of the great Byzantine rulers; reformed finances; began recodification of laws; generally successful with armies and fleets; *Prochiron* issued (c. 878). Tried to end schism between Eastern and Western churches; unsuccessful.

**Basil II.** 958?–1025. Son of Romanus II. Emperor (976–1025). Crowned at age of two (960). Empire ruled by his mother, Theophano (963), by Nicephorus Phocas (963–969) and by John I Zimisces (969–976) as his guardians. Nominally joint emperor (976–1025) with his brother Constantine VIII, but latter took no part in government. Waged incessant warfare for 50 years; suppressed revolt in Asia Minor (979). Fought long war (986–1018) against Bulgarians, finally subduing them; hence called **Bul′ga·roc′to·nus** (bŭl′gȧ·rŏk′tō·nŭs), *i.e.* slayer of Bulgarians.

**Basil.** *Russ.* **Va·si′li** (vŭ·syē′lyû·ĭ). Name of four rulers of Russia:

**Basil I Dmi′tri·e·vich** (d'myē′tryĭ·yĕ·vyĭch). 1371–1425. Grand duke of Moscow (1389–1425). Son of Demetrius Donskoi. Annexed Nizhni Novgorod; at war with Tatars and Lithuanians.

**Basil II.** *Called* **Tëm′ny** (tyôm′nû·ĭ), *i.e.* the blind. 1415–1462. Son of Basil I. Grand duke of Moscow (1425–62). Reign marked by anarchy and long civil war; realm suffered from serious attacks of Tatars (1443, 1451) and Lithuanians; Russian Church became virtually independent (1448).

**Basil III I·va′no·vich** (ĭ·vá′nŭ·vyĭch). 1479–1533. Grand duke (1505–33). Son of Ivan the Great. Incorporated ancient principalities into Muscovy: Pskov (1510), Smolensk (1514), Ryazan (1517); established Russian influence on the Volga.

**Basil (IV) Shui′ski** (sho͞o′ĭ·skû′ĭ). d. 1612. Russian boyar; seized Muscovite throne (1606) in time of troubles after Boris Godunov; caused death of Pseudo-Demetrius; deposed (1610) and carried off to Warsaw.

**Bas′i·li′des** (băs′ĭ·lī′dēz; băz′-). d. about 140 A.D. Gnostic of Alexandria, b. probably in Syria; founder of heretical sect of Basilidians. Wrote commentaries on Gospel (*Exegetica;* 24 books; extant only in extracts). His system of philosophy (Basilidian Gnosticism) has an elaborate cosmology.

**Bas′i·lis′cus** (băs′ĭ·lĭs′kŭs; băz′-). d. 478. Emperor of the East (476–477). Brother-in-law of Emperor Leo I. Sent by Leo (468) in command of expedition to Carthage against Genseric, the Vandal chieftain; defeated and banished; deposed Zeno; later (477) deposed by Zeno.

**Bas′ker·ville** (băs′kẽr·vĭl), **John.** 1706–1775. English typographer. Worked as stone carver, writing master, and manufacturer of japanned goods; began to study typefounding (1750); pioneer manufacturer of fine printing paper and inks; produced quarto of Vergil (1757) and editions of Milton (1758), the Bible (1763), and Latin authors (1772–73); printer to Cambridge U. (1758–68).

**Bas′nage′** (bä′nȧzh′) *or* **Basnage de Beau′val′** (dẽ bō′vȧl′), **Jacques.** 1653–1725. French Protestant theologian and historian; exile in Holland after revocation of Edict of Nantes: aided diplomatically in arranging Triple Alliance at The Hague (1717); author of *Histoire des Juifs* (5 vols., 1706), etc.

**Ba′sov** (bä′sŏf), **Nikolai Gennadievich.** 1922– . Soviet physicist. Shared Nobel prize in physics (1964) with C. Townes and A. Prochorov.

**Bass** (băs), **Edward.** 1726–1803. American Protestant Episcopal bishop, b. Dorchester, Mass. Pastor, Newbury, Mass. (1752–1803). Consecrated first bishop of Massachusetts (1797), his bishopric including Rhode Island and New Hampshire.

**Bass, George.** d. 1812? English explorer of coast of New South Wales and discoverer of Bass Strait (1798).

**Bass, Michael Thomas.** 1799–1884. English brewer. Took control of firm founded (1777) by grandfather William Bass (b. 1720) for brewing Burton beer; Liberal M.P. (1848–83). His son **Michael Arthur** (1837–1909) was M.P. (1865–86); friend of Gladstone; raised to peerage as Baron **Bur′ton** [bûr′t'n] (1886).

**Bas·sa′ni** (bäs·sä′nē), **Giovanni Battista.** 1657–1716. Italian composer, chiefly of religious pieces, as oratorios, masses, psalms, etc.

**Bas·sa′no** (bäs·sä′nō), Duc **de.** See Hughes Bernard MARET.

**Bassano,** *orig.* **Pon′te** (pōn′tā), **Jacopo** *or* **Giacomo da.** 1510–1592. Venetian painter; known esp. as one of earliest Italian genre painters; works include genre paintings, portraits, as of Tasso and Ariosto, and Biblical scenes, as *Christ Driving the Money Changers out of the Temple* and *Good Samaritan* (both in National Gallery, London). His sons **Francesco Bassano** (1549–1592), **Leandro Bassano** (1557–1623), **Giambattista da Ponte** (1553–?), and **Girolamo da Ponte** (1560–1662) were also painters.

**Basse** (băs), **William.** d. 1653? English poet. Author of *Sword and Buckler* (1602); best known by *Epitaph on Shakespeare* and *Angler's Song*, quoted by Walton.

**Bas′se·lin′** (bȧs′lăN′) *or* **Ba′che·lin′** (bȧsh′lăN′),

**Olivier.** 15th-century French song writer, esp. of drinking songs.

**Bas'set'** (bȧ'sĕ'), **René.** 1855–1924. French orientalist, b. Lunéville. Director, École Supérieure des Lettres in Algiers (from 1894). Author of *La Poésie Arabe Antéislamique* (1880), *Nouveaux Contes Berbères* (1897), *Grammaire, Dialogues et Dictionnaire Touaregs* (1908), etc.

**Bas'sett** (băs'ĕt; -ĭt), **John Spencer.** 1867–1928. American historian, b. Tarboro, N.C.; author of *Life of Andrew Jackson* (2 vols., 1911), *A Short History of the United States* (1913), *The Lost Fruits of Waterloo* (1918), *Our War with Germany* (1919), *Expansion and Reform* (1926).

**Bas'si** (bäs'sē), **Matteo da.** See MATTEO DA BASCIO.

**Bassi, Ugo.** 1800–1849. Italian priest and patriot; known as stirring preacher; joined Garibaldi at Rieti as chaplain (c. 1848); captured by Austrians near Comacchio: tortured and executed (Aug. 8, 1849).

**Bassianus.** See (1) ALEXANDER SEVERUS, (2) CARACALLA, (3) HELIOGABALUS.

**Bas'so** (băs'ō), **Hamilton,** *in full* **Joseph Hamilton.** 1904–1964. American novelist, b. New Orleans. Educ. Tulane U. Journalist in New Orleans (1927); assoc. editor, *New Republic* (1935–37). Author of *Cinnamon Seed* (1934), *Courthouse Square* (1936), *Days Before Lent* (1939), *The View from Pompey's Head* (1954).

**Bas'som'pierre'** (bȧ'sôN'pyâr'), Baron **François de.** 1579–1646. French soldier and statesman. Favorite of Henry IV; member of party adhering to cause of Marie de Médicis (from 1610); created marshal of France (1622). Ambassador to Spain and to Switzerland; on diplomatic mission in England. Confined by Richelieu in Bastille (1631–43); wrote there *Mémoires*, interesting as sources of contemporary history.

**Bas'ta·ble** (băs'tȧ·b'l), **Charles Francis.** 1855–1945. Irish political economist, b. in County Cork. Grad. Trinity Coll., Dublin. Professor, Dublin U. (1882–1932). Author of books on international commerce and public finance.

**Bastardella, La.** See Lucrezia AGUJARI.

**Bastard of Orléans, the.** = Jean DUNOIS.

**Ba'sti·an** (bäs'tē·än), **Adolf.** 1826–1905. German ethnologist and traveler, b. Bremen. Traveled in every continent (1851–66). Professor, Berlin (after 1866) and director of its ethnological museum (1886). Author of *Die Völker des Östlichen Asien* (Jena, 1866–71), etc.

**Bas'ti·at'** (bȧs'tyȧ'), **Claude Frédéric.** 1801–1850. French economist, advocate of free trade, and opponent of socialism; author of *Sophismes Économiques*, *Propriété et Loi*, *Protectionnisme et Communisme*, *Capital et Rente*, and *Les Harmonies Économiques* (unfinished).

**Bas·ti'das** (bäs·tē'thäs), **Rodrigo de.** b. 1460? Spanish explorer of northern coast of South America (1500–02); founded Santa Marta, Colombia (1525).

**Bas'tide'** (bȧs'tēd'), **Jules.** 1800–1879. French politician, b. Paris. Participated in revolt in Paris (1832); condemned to death, but escaped; pardoned (1834). Journalist (from 1834). Took active part in 1848 revolution; minister of foreign affairs, succeeding Lamartine (1848).

**Bas'ti·en'-Le·page'** (bȧs'tyăN'lē·pȧzh'), **Jules.** 1848–1884. French painter, b. Damvillers; pupil of Cabanel; esp. successful in painting peasant scenes; his works include *Jeanne d'Arc* (Metropolitan Museum of Art, New York).

**Ba't'a** (bȧ'tyȧ), **Tomáš.** 1876–1932. Czechoslovak industrialist, b. Zlín, Moravia; founder of large shoe manufactory; killed in airplane accident.

**Ba'taille'** (bȧ'tä'y'), **Félix Henry.** 1872–1922. French poet and playwright, b. Nîmes. His plays include *Maman Colibri* (1904), *La Marche Nuptiale* (1905), *Poliche* (1905), *La Femme Nue* (1908), *La Vierge Folle* (1910); author also of several volumes of verse, as *La Divine Tragédie*, containing war poems (1917).

**Batch'el·ler** (băch'ĕ·lēr), **George Sherman.** 1837–1908. American lawyer, b. Batchellerville, N.Y. Served through Civil War. U.S. judge in international tribunal for legal administration of Egypt (1876–85, 1898–1908). Asst. secretary of treasury (1889–91); U.S. minister to Portugal (1891–97).

**Bate'man** (bāt'măn), **Henry Mayo.** 1887–1970. British caricaturist, b. in Australia. Contributor of humorous drawings to *Punch* and other publications; known esp. for depiction of embarrassing situations, as "The Guardsman who Dropped his Rifle."

**Bate'man** (bāt'măn), **Kate Josephine.** 1843–1917. American actress; m. (1866) Dr. George Crowe. With her sister Ellen, appeared as child prodigy at age of three. Under P. T. Barnum's management (1851–54). Acted with Henry Irving (between 1875–77).

**Bates** (bāts), **Arlo.** 1850–1918. American educator and writer, b. East Machias, Me. Editor, *Boston Sunday Courant* (1880–93). Professor of English, M.I.T. (1893–1918). Besides novels (as *Mr. Jacobs*, 1883) and poetry (*Sonnets in Shadow*, 1887), wrote *Talks on Writing English* (1896–1901), *Talks on Teaching Literature* (1906).

**Bates, Blanche.** 1873–1941. American actress and singer, b. Portland, Ore.; starred in *Madame Butterfly* (1900), *Under Two Flags*, *The Girl of the Golden West*, etc.; retired (1926); again on stage for brief period (1933).

**Bates, Daisy.** 1860?–1951. English welfare worker among Australian aborigines. To Australia (1899) as *Times* correspondent to investigate treatment of aborigines; became absorbed in welfare work and lived among aborigines for thirty-five years. Visited Canberra (1933) at invitation of commonwealth government to discuss welfare of native tribes. Created C.B.E. (1933). Author of *The Passing of the Aborigines* (1938).

**Bates, Edward.** 1793–1869. American lawyer, b. in Goochland Co., Va. Attorney general in Lincoln's cabinet (1861–64). His brother **Frederick** (1777–1825) was governor of Missouri (1824–25).

**Bates, Ernest Sutherland.** 1879–1939. American educator and author, b. Gambier, Ohio. A.B., Michigan (1902); Ph.D., Columbia (1908). Professor, U. of Arizona (1908–15), Oregon (1915–25); in editorial work, N.Y. (1926–39). Author of *The Friend of Jesus* (1928), *The Story of Congress* (1936), *The Story of the Supreme Court* (1936), *Biography of the Bible* (1937); editor of *The Bible Designed to be Read as Living Literature* (1936).

**Bates, Harry.** 1850?–1899. English sculptor, b. Stevenage. Studied in Paris under Rodin. Works include *Queen Victoria* (Dundee), equestrian statue of Lord Roberts (Calcutta).

**Bates, Henry Walter.** 1825–1892. English naturalist. Journeyed to upper Amazon (1848); returned to England (1859) with 8000 species of insects new to science. Author of *The Naturalist on the Amazon* (1863).

**Bates, Herbert Ernest.** 1905–1974. English novelist and short-story writer. Author of *The Two Sisters* (1926), *A House of Women* (1936), *Spella Ho* (1938), *The Purple Plain* (1947), *Love for Lydia* (1952), *The Darling Buds of May* (1958).

**Bates, John Coalter.** 1842–1919. American army officer, b. in St. Charles County, Mo. Served through Civil War; in Cuba during Spanish-American War; in Philippines (1899) during the Philippine insurrection. Retired (1906) as lieutenant general.

**Bates, Joshua.** 1788–1864. American financier, b. Weymouth, Mass. Partner in Baring Bros. & Co., international bankers (1828–64). Chief founder of Boston Public Library.

**Bates, Katharine Lee.** 1859–1929. American educator and author, b. Falmouth, Mass. A.B., Wellesley (1880). Professor of English at Wellesley (1891–1925). Author of *College Beautiful and Other Poems* (1887), *Rose and Thorn* (1889), *Sunshine and Other Verses for Children* (1890), *Hermit Island* (1891), *America the Beautiful and Other Poems* (1911), *Fairy Gold* (1916), etc.

**Bates, Ralph.** 1899– . British novelist; served in World War (1914–18) and on Loyalist side in Spanish civil war. Author of *Lean Men*, *The Olive Field*, *Sirocco*, *The Miraculous Horde* (short stories; 1939), *The Fields of Paradise* (1940), *The Undiscoverables* (1942), etc.

**Bate′son** (bāt′s'n), **William.** 1861–1926. English biologist and pioneer in study of genetics. Educ. St. John's, Cambridge; from early research on *Balanoglossus* formulated his then revolutionary theories on the evolution of vertebrates, since generally accepted; explored fauna of salt lakes of western Central Asia and northern Egypt (1886–87); championed Mendel in *Mendel's Principles of Heredity—a Defence* (1902); delivered Silliman lectures at Yale (1907), subsequently published as *Problems of Genetics* (1913); special editor, *Webster's New International Dict.* (1909); director, John Innes Horticultural Institution, Surrey, England (1910–26). His sister **Mary** (1865–1906), English historian, lectured at Newnham College, Cambridge (1888–1906); special student of early English monastic and municipal institutions; edited many works for antiquarian societies; author of *Laws of Breteuil* (1900–01), *Mediaeval England* (1903), *Borough Customs* (2 vols., 1904–06), etc.

**Bath** (båth), Earls of. See William PULTENEY.

**Bath,** 1st Marquis of. See Thomas THYNNE.

**Bá′tho·ry** *or* **Bá′tho·ri** (bä′tō·rĭ). Noble family of Hungary originating in 13th century, including: **Stephen** (see STEPHEN BÁTHORY), King of Poland; succeeded as prince of Transylvania (1576–81) by his brother **Chri′stoph** (krĭs′tōf), who invited Jesuits into his lands. Christoph's son **Si′gis·mund** (zē′gĭs·mo͝ont), *Hung.* **Zsigmond** (1572–1613), Prince of Transylvania (1581–98); instructed by Jesuits; joined league of Christian princes against Turks (1588); under influence of Jesuits, abdicated in favor of Emperor Rudolf (1598) in order to enter priesthood; regretted action and unsuccessfully sought to regain lands; forced to flee to Bohemia (1602). Stephen's son **Gabriel,** *Hung.* **Gábor** (1589–1613), Prince of Transylvania (1608–13); because of his cruelty, driven from country and murdered; last of the family. Stephen's niece **Elizabeth Báthory** (d. 1614); known in legend and history for extreme cruelty; said to have killed more than 600 maidens and bathed in their blood; died in prison.

**Bath–she′ba** (băth·shē′bȧ; băth′shē·bȧ). *In Douay Version* **Beth·sa′be·e** (bĕth·sā′bē·ē). In Bible, wife of Uriah the Hittite; committed adultery with David and later, after David had caused death of Uriah, became his 2d wife (*2 Sam.* xi); mother of Solomon (*2 Sam.* xii. 24).

**Bath′urst** (băth′ûrst; -ẽrst), **Allen.** 1st Earl **Bathurst.** 1684–1775. English political leader and patron of literature; friend of Pope. Tory M.P. (1705–12); in upper house impeached directors of South Sea scheme; privy councilor (1742). His uncle **Ralph Bathurst** (1620–1704) was a clergyman and physician; ordained (1644); compelled to abandon active public ministry by Civil War; studied medicine (M.D., Oxon., 1654); practiced medicine during Commonwealth; for some time physician to navy; one of originators of Royal Society; chaplain to Charles II (1663); as president (from 1664) rebuilt Trinity College; vice-chancellor of Oxford (1673–76). **Henry,** 2d earl (1714–1794), son of the 1st earl, M.P. (1735–54), was lord chancellor (1771–78) as Baron **Aps′ley** (ăps′lĭ); lord president of the council (1779–82). **Henry,** 3d earl (1762–1834), grandson of 1st earl, held several offices under Pitt and successors.

**Bathurst, Charles.** See BLEDISLOE.

**Bath′y·cles** (băth′ĭ·klēz). Greek sculptor, of Magnesia (Manisa), of 6th century B.C.; commissioned by Spartans to carve marble throne for statue of Apollo (c. 550 B.C.).

**Ba·tis′ta y Zal·dí′var** (bä·tēs′tä ē säl·dē′vär), **Fulgencio.** 1901–1973. Cuban soldier and political leader, b. in Oriente province. Worked at various trades (before 1921); soldier in national army (1921–23); clerk at staff headquarters. Took part in revolt against President Gerardo Machado (1931–33); led coup that deposed Céspedes (1933); made colonel and commander of Cuban constitutional army (1933). As dictator, controlled administration (1933–40) of provisional and de facto governments; caused impeachment of President Miguel M. Gómez (1936); approved selection of President Laredo Bru (1936–40); president (1940–44; 1952–58); regime overthrown by Fidel Castro (1958); went into exile Jan. 1, 1959.

**Bat′lle** (bät′yā), **Lorenzo.** 1812–?1872. Uruguayan general and political leader, b. Montevideo. President of Uruguay (1868–72). His son **José Batlle y Or·dó′ñez** [ē ôr·thō′nyās] (1856–1929), journalist and statesman, b. Montevideo, was leader of Liberals (Colorados); president of Uruguay (1903–07, 1911–15).

**Bat′man** (băt′măn), **John.** 1800–1840. Australian colonizer, b. Parramatta, N.S.W. Reputed founder of Victoria colony, Australia; colonized Port Phillip (1835 ff.).

**Ba·to′ni** (bä·tō′nē) *or* **Bat·to′ni** (bät·tō′nē), **Pompeo Girolamo.** 1708–1787. Italian painter; known esp. for his portraits, as of Emperor Joseph II, Leopold II, Clement XII; also painted *Marriage of Saint Catherine* (Quirinal, Rome), *Madonna* (Louvre), *Hercules* (Pitti Palace).

**Bat·ta′ni, al–** (ăl′băt·tä′nē). *Arab.* **abu–'Abdullāh Muḥammad ibn–Jābir al–Battāni.** *Lat.* **Al′ba·teg′ni·us** (ăl′bȧ·tĕg′nĭ·ŭs) *or* **Al′ba·te′ni·us** (ăl′bȧ·tē′nĭ·ŭs). c. 850–929. Arab astronomer; greatest of his time; conducted original research work at Rakka for more than forty years (877–918); corrected some of Ptolemy's results; determined with greater accuracy obliquity of the ecliptic and length of tropical year and of seasons; introduced use of sines in mathematical calculations. Author of *De Motu Stellarum* (first pub. at Nuremberg, 1537).

**Bat′ten·berg** (băt′'n·bûrg; *Ger.* bät′ĕn·bĕrk). Title of family of German counts; title died out (c. 1314) and was revived (1851) for a royal branch, including the following three sons and two grandsons of Prince **Alexander** (1823–1888; son of Louis II, Grand Duke of Hesse-Darmstadt; *q.v.*) and Julia Teresa, Countess von Haucke (1825–1895), a Pole; title renounced (1917) by members living in England in favor of the surname Mountbatten. Prince **Louis Alexander of Battenberg** (1854–1921); naturalized British subject; m. (1884) Princess Victoria, daughter of Alice Maud Mary, Duchess of Saxony; rear admiral in navy (1904); commander in chief of Atlantic fleet (1908–10); admiral (1919); created marquis of **Mil′ford Ha′ven** [mĭl′fẽrd hā′vĕn] (1917). His elder son, **George Louis Victor Henry Sergius Mount·bat′ten** [mount·băt′'n] (1892–1938), 2d Marquis of Milford Haven; lieutenant in British navy (1914); present at battles of Helgoland (1914), Dogger Bank (1915), and Jutland (1916); became commander (1926). For Prince Louis Alexander of

Battenberg's younger son, Prince **Louis Francis of Battenberg** (1900– ), see Viscount Louis MOUNTBATTEN. Prince Louis Alexander's brother Prince **Alexander Joseph of Battenberg** (1857–1893) became Alexander I of Bulgaria (*q.v.*). Another brother, Prince **Henry Maurice of Battenberg** (1858–1896); m. Princess Beatrice (1857–1944), daughter of Queen Victoria (1885); naturalized British subject; governor of Isle of Wight; died of fever with Ashanti expeditionary force.

**Bat'ter·son** (băt'ẽr·s'n), **James Goodwin.** 1823–1901. American businessman and insurance pioneer, b. Wintonbury, now Bloomfield, Conn. In stonecutting business (to 1863). Founder (1863) and president (1863–1901) of Travelers Insurance Co., Hartford, the first accident-insurance company in America.

**Bat'teux'** (bȧ'tû'), **Charles.** 1713–1780. French abbé, critic, and man of letters; author of *Cours de Belles-Lettres* (1750).

**Bat'tey** (băt'ĭ), **Robert.** 1828–1895. American physician, b. Augusta, Ga. Pioneer in abdominal surgery, esp. in ovariotomy.

**Bat'thyány** (bŏt'tyän·y'). An old noble family of Hungary, including: **Károly József** (1698?–1772), Prince of Batthyány; field marshal in Austrian service; distinguished himself in War of Austrian Succession, esp. at Pfaffenhofen (1745); ban of Croatia (1764). **Lajos** (1806?–1849), Count of Batthyány; premier of first Hungarian ministry (1848); sought vainly to avoid breach with Austria; arrested and executed by Austrians (1849). **Kázmér** (1807–1854), Count of Batthyány; minister of foreign affairs (1849); fled with Kossuth to Turkey after insurrection; in France (1851–54). **Tivadar** (1859–1931), Count of Batthyány; organizer of Independence party (1921).

**Bat·ti'sti** (bät·tēs'tē), **Cesare.** 1875–1916. Italian journalist and patriot; founded journal *Il Popolo* in Trentino, attacking Austrian dictatorship. To Italy on outbreak of World War (1914); joined Alpine chasseurs; wounded, captured, condemned as a traitor, and hanged by the Austrians.

**Bat'ti·sti'ni** (bät'tēs·tē'nē), **Mattia.** 1857–1928. Italian operatic and concert baritone; known for his bel canto.

**Battoni, Pompeo Girolamo.** See BATONI.

**Ba'tu Khan'** (bä'tōō kän'). d. 1255. Mongol ruler. Grandson of Genghis Khan and son of Juji. Under Ogadai led army that conquered Russia, Poland, and Hungary (1237–41); aided by the great general Subotai; defeated Henry, Duke of Silesia, near Liegnitz (1241) and captured Pest; recalled to Karakorum by death of Ogadai; lived in great splendor at Sarai as khan of the Golden Horde, or Western Kipchaks (1241–55), his realm extending from Lake Balkhash to Hungary. Succeeded by his brother Birkai.

**Ba'tyush·kov** (bȧ'tyŏŏsh·kôf), **Konstantin Nikolaevich.** 1787–1855. Russian poet and essayist.

**Batz** (bȧts), Baron **Jean de.** 1761?–1822. French royalist; attempted to rescue Louis XVI and royal family.

**Bau'de·laire'** (bōd'lâr'), **Charles Pierre.** 1821–1867. French poet, b. Paris. Translator of tales of Edgar Allan Poe; author of *Petits Poèmes en Prose*, *Curiosités Esthétiques*, and esp. of a single celebrated and influential volume of verse, *Les Fleurs du Mal* (1857). Regarded, with Verlaine and Mallarmé, as a leader of the decadents, a 19th-century French group concerning themselves with the aesthetic motives characteristic of decadent or hypercivilized society, and cultivating the abnormal and neurotic in subject and treatment. Died half insane from long addiction to drugs.

**Bau'de·locque'** (bōd'lôk'), **Jean Louis.** 1746–1810. French surgeon and obstetrician.

**Bau'dis·sin** (bou'dĭ·sĭn), Count **Wolf Heinrich von.** 1789–1878. German literary critic and translator. In Danish diplomatic service (1810–14); resident in Dresden (from 1827).

**Bau'ditz** (bou'dĭts), **Sophus.** 1850–1915. Danish novelist; author of *Stories of a Hunting Lodge* (1889).

**Bau'douin'** (bō'dwăN'). 1930– . King of Belgium (1951– ). Son of Leopold III.

**Baudouin.** See BALDWIN (of Flanders, Hainaut, etc.).

**Bau'dril'lart'** (bō'drē'yȧr'), **Jacques Joseph.** 1774–1832. French agronomist and author. His son **Henri Joseph Léon** (1821–1892) was an economist; professor in Collège de France (1866). His grandson **Henri Marie Alfred** (1859–1942), prelate and historian, is author of *Philippe V et la Cour de France* and *L'Église Catholique, la Renaissance et le Protestantisme.*

**Bau'dry'** (bō'drē'), **Paul Jacques Aimé.** 1828–1886. French portrait painter and muralist. Murals by him are in Palais de Justice and in foyer of Grand Opéra at Paris.

**Bau'er** (bou'ẽr), **Andreas Friedrich.** 1783–1860. German mechanic; associate of Friedrich König (*q.v.*).

**Bauer, Bruno.** 1809–1882. German rationalistic philosopher, theologian, and historical writer. Lecturer on theology (1834–42); deprived of license (1842) as result of destructive effect of his criticism of Bible. Author of *Kritik der Evangelischen Geschichte des Johannes* (1840), *Kritik der Evangelischen Synoptiker* (1840), etc.

**Bauer, Georg.** See Georgius AGRICOLA.

**Bauer, Gustav.** 1870–1944. German politician; entered Reichstag (1912) and became (1919–20) premier of peace-treaty (Treaty of Versailles) ministry; vice-chancellor and minister of treasury (1921–22).

**Bauer, Harold.** 1873–1951. Piano virtuoso, b. London, Eng. Made debut as pianist in Paris (1893); first appeared in U.S. with Boston Symphony Orchestra (1900). On many tours through Europe and U.S.; appeared frequently with Ossip Gabrilówitsch in two-piano recitals, often in support of symphony orchestras. Especially known as an interpreter of Brahms, Schumann, and Franck.

**Bauer, Herbert.** See Béla BALÁZS.

**Bauer, Karoline.** 1807–1877. German actress; m. 1st (1829) Prince Leopold of Coburg (later king of the Belgians), 2d (1844) Count Ladislas de Broel-Plater of Poland. Wrote *Posthumous Memoirs*, bitterly attacking King Leopold and Baron Stockmar.

**Bauer, Louis Agricola.** 1865–1932. American astronomer and physicist.

**Bauer, Marius A'lex'an'dre** (ȧ'lĕk'säN'dr') **Jacques** (zhäk). 1864–1932. Dutch painter and etcher, esp. of scenes from Oriental life.

**Bauer, Otto.** 1881–1938. Austrian political leader; foreign minister (1919); leader of Social Democratic party and of 1934 Socialist revolt.

**Bauer, Walter.** 1904– . German fiction writer.

**Bau'ern·feind** (bou'ẽrn·fīnt), **Karl Maximilian von.** 1818–1894. German engineer. Director, Technical College of Munich (1868–74, 1880–83). Inventor of prismatic cross used in surveying. Author of *Zur Brückenbaukunde* (1854), etc.

**Bau'ern·feld** (bou'ẽrn·fĕlt), **Eduard von.** 1802–1890. Viennese playwright. Author of *Die Bekenntnisse* (1834), *Bürgerlich und Romantisch* (1835), *Grossjährig* (1846), and many other comedies, drawing-room pieces, poems, etc.

**Bau'hin'** (bō'ăN'), **Gaspard.** 1560–1624. Swiss botanist and anatomist; professor, Basel (from 1588); author of *Theatrum Anatomicum* (1621), *Pinax Theatri Botanici* (1623). His brother **Jean** (1541–1613), physician and botanist at Basel, wrote *Historia Universalis Plantarum Nova et Absolutissima* (completed by others, 1650).

**Baum** (boum), **Johann Peter**. 1869–1916. German poet and novelist.

**Baum** (bäm), **Lyman Frank**. 1856–1919. American journalist and playwright, b. Chittenango, N.Y. On editorial staff of newspapers in South Dakota and Chicago (from 1880). Author of *Mother Goose in Prose* (1897), *Wonderful Wizard of Oz* (1900), and other humorous and extravagant tales, esp. the series of books dealing with mythical country of "Oz." *Wonderful Wizard of Oz* was turned into a highly successful musical comedy under title *Wizard of Oz* (prod. 1901) and later provided the scenario for a motion picture of the same name.

**Baum** (boum), **Vicki**. 1888-1960. Novelist, b. in Vienna, Austria; m. Richard Lert (1916). To Berlin (1926); engaged in editorial work. To U.S. (1931); settled in Los Angeles, Cal. Author of *Grand Hotel* (a novel later successfully dramatized and scenarized), *And Life Goes On* (1932), *Men Never Know* (1935), *A Tale From Bali* (1937), *Shanghai* (1939), *Grand Opera* (1942), etc.

**Bau'mann'** (bō'män'), **Émile**. 1867-1941. French novelist, b. Lyon. Author of *L'Immolé* (1908), *La Fosse aux Lions* (1911), *Saint Paul* (1925), etc.

**Bau'mann** (bou'män), **Oskar**. 1864–1899. Austrian traveler and explorer in Africa. Geographer, Congo expedition (1885); explored Fernando Po (1886), Usambara (1888), German East Africa, etc. (1890–95); ascertained source of Kagera river.

**Baum'bach** (boum'bäĸ), **Rudolf**. 1840–1905. German lyric and narrative poet; resident in Austria (1865–85); author of *Zlatorog* (1875), *Lieder eines Fahrenden Gesellen* (1878), *Trug-Gold* (a story of the 17th century, 1878; under pseudonym **Paul Bach** [bäĸ]), *Horand und Hilde* (1879), *Spielmannslieder* (1882), *Die Lindenwirtin* and other drinking songs, etc.

**Bau'mé'** (bō'mā'), **Antoine**. 1728–1804. French chemist, b. Senlis. Discovered improvements in processes for purifying saltpeter, bleaching, making sal ammoniac, etc. Invented a hydrometer (Baumé hydrometer) and devised two scales (Baumé scales) for graduating this instrument, one for use in measuring liquids heavier than water and one for liquids lighter than water.

**Bäu'mer** (boi'mẽr), **Gertrud**. 1873–1954. A leader of feminist movement in Germany; author of *Handbuch der Frauenbewegung* (5 vols., from 1901), *Die Frau in der Krisis Unserer Kultur* (1926), etc.

**Bau'mes** (bô'mĕs), **Caleb Howard**. 1863–1937. American lawyer and politician, b. Bethlehem, N.Y. Admitted to bar (1898); began practice in Newburgh, N.Y. Member, New York State assembly (1909–13) and New York State senate (1919–37). As chairman of N.Y. State joint legislative committee (1926) to draft changes in code of criminal procedure and penal law, his name is associated with the several statutes passed (1926) as amendments, including esp. the statute (Baumes Law) providing life imprisonment for persons under a fourth conviction for a felony or for certain misdemeanors.

**Baum'gar'ten** (boum'gär'tĕn), **Alexander Gottlieb**. 1714–1762. German philosopher; considered by some the founder of modern aesthetics. Professor, Frankfurt an der Oder (from 1740). Author of *Metaphysica* (1739), *Aesthetica Acromatica* (1750–58; unfinished), etc.

**Baumgarten, Hermann**. 1825–1893. German historian. Professor, Karlsruhe (1861–72), Strasbourg (1872–89). Author of *Karl V und die Deutsche Reformation* (1889), etc.

**Baumgarten, Michael**. 1812–1889. German Protestant theologian, b. in Holstein. Professor, Rostock (1850). Opposed Lutheran hierarchy; removed from professorship (1858).

**Baum'gart'ner** (boum'gärt'nẽr), **Gallus Jakob**. 1797–1869. Swiss politician and writer; leader of Liberal party (to 1841) and then joined Ultramontane party; member of Ständerat (1857–60). Author of *Die Schweiz... 1830–50* (4 vols., 1853–66), etc.

**Baum'stark** (boum'shtärk), **Anton**. 1800–1876. German classical philologist, b. Sinzheim, Baden. Professor, Freiburg (1836–71); author of *Urdeutsche Staatsaltertümer* (1873), etc.

**Baur** (bour), **Ferdinand Christian**. 1792–1860. German Protestant theologian, scholar, and Biblical critic. Professor, Tübingen (1826–60); founder of Tübingen school of theology. Author of *Das Manichäische Religionssystem* (1831), *Die Christliche Gnosis...* (1835), *Lehrbuch der Christlichen Dogmengeschichte* (1847), etc.

**Bausch** (boush). Name of family of manufacturers of optical instruments, including the following members: **John Jacob** (1830–1926), b. Süssen, Württemberg, Germany; to U.S. (1849); founder (1853; with Henry Lomb) and president, Bausch & Lomb Optical Co., Rochester, N.Y. His sons **Edward** (1854–1944), b. Rochester, N.Y., chairman of Bausch & Lomb, inventor of scientific devices, and author of *Manipulation of the Microscope*, and **William** (1861–1944), b. Rochester, N.Y., secretary (1909–35) and vice-president (from 1935) of Bausch & Lomb. **Carl Louis Bausch** (1887– ); grandnephew of John Jacob Bausch; b. Syracuse, N.Y.; M.E., Syracuse (1909); entered Bausch & Lomb as machinist (1909), becoming mechanical engineer (1921) and vice-president in charge of research and engineering (1935).

**Bau'tain'** (bō'tăN'), **Louis Eugène Marie**. 1796–1867. French abbé, theologian, and philosopher.

**Baux** (bō), Princes of. See ORANGE.

**Ba·var'i·a** (bȧ·vâr'ĭ·ȧ), House of. A ruling German family, originating with counts of Wittelsbach (12th century). See WITTELSBACH.

**Ba'vi·us** (bā'vĭ·ŭs). Roman poet of 1st century B.C.; of inferior talent and malicious nature; enemy of Vergil and Horace.

**Bax** (băks), Sir **Arnold Edward Trevor**. 1883–1953. English composer. Studied at Royal Academy of Music (1900–05). Compositions include symphonic poems, as *The Garden of Fand* (1916), *Tintagel* (1917), and *November Woods* (1917), and symphonies, including *Romantic Overture* and *London Pageantry* (1937). His brother **Clifford** (1886–1962), dramatist and poet, produced *The Poetasters of Ispahan* (1912), *The Rose without a Thorn* (1932), *The House of Borgia* (1935); author also of *Midsummer Madness* (1924), *Pretty Witty Nell* (1932), *Ideas and People* (1936).

**Bax, Ernest Belfort**. 1854–1926. English philosophical writer. Helped William Morris to found Socialist League and edited with Morris its organ, *The Commonweal;* with Morris, wrote *Socialism, its Growth and Outcome* (1894); author of *The Problem of Reality* (1893); *The Real, the Rational and the Alogical* (1920), and a history of philosophy.

**Bax'ter** (băks'tẽr), **James Phinney.** 1893–1975. American educator, b. Portland, Me. A.B. (1914), Williams; A.M. (1923), Ph.D. (1926), Harvard. Teacher of history, Harvard (1925–37), professor (1936–37); president, Williams Coll. (1937–61). His grandfather **James Phinney** (1831–1921), b. Gorham, Me., merchant and historian; editor of *Documentary History of Maine* (10 vols.); author of *Sir Ferdinando Gorges and his Province of Maine* (1890), *The Pioneers of New France in New England* (1894), etc.

**Baxter, John.** 1781–1858. English bookseller and printer; first to use ink roller; publisher of the illustrated "Baxter's Bible." His son **George** (1804–1867), invented oil-color printing (Baxter print).

**Baxter, Richard.** 1615–1691. English Puritan scholar and writer. Ordained (1638); became moderate nonconformist; elected minister at Kidderminster (1641); chaplain in Cromwell's army (1645–47); forced out of Church of England by Act of Uniformity (1662). Prepared *Reformed Liturgy* for Savoy conference; unsuccessful at conference in attempt to gain terms that would allow moderate dissenters to remain in Church of England; declined bishopric of Hereford. Suffered course of persecution climaxed by imprisonment by chief justice Jeffreys (1685) on charge of libeling the church in his *Paraphrase on the New Testament;* released after 18 months. Author of *Saints' Everlasting Rest* (1650), *Call to the Unconverted* (1657), a number of theological works, and the autobiographical *Reliquiae Baxterianae* (1696).

**Baxter, Robert Dudley.** 1827–1875. English economist; wrote treatises on taxation, revenues, national debts, etc.

**Bay, Michel de.** See Michael BAIUS.

**Ba'yard'** (bȧ'yȧr'; *Angl.* bā'ẽrd), Seigneur **de. Pierre Ter'rail'** (tĕ'rȧ'y'). 1473?–1524. French hero, renowned for knightly character; known as "Chevalier sans peur et sans reproche." Distinguished himself in Italian campaigns of Charles VIII, Louis XII, and Francis I, esp. in victory of Marignano (1515) and in defense of Mézières (1521); killed in battle at Sesia River in Italy.

**Bay'ard** (bī'ärd; -ẽrd), **James Asheton.** 1767–1815. American lawyer, b. Philadelphia. Member, U.S. House of Representatives (1797–1803); in Jefferson-Burr disputed election thrown into House of Representatives for decision (1800), intermediary who secured understanding with Jefferson resulting in Jefferson's election. U.S. senator from Delaware (1805–13). One of three Americans chosen by President Madison to negotiate terms of treaty of peace with Great Britain (1813–14), resulting in Treaty of Ghent (1814). One son, **Richard Henry** (1796–1868), was U.S. senator from Delaware (1836–39, 1840–45); another son, **James Asheton** (1799–1880), was U.S. senator from Delaware (1851–64, 1867–69). A son of the latter, **Thomas Francis** (1828–1898), was U.S. senator from Delaware (1869–85), U.S. secretary of state (1885–89), and first U.S. ambassador to Great Britain (1893–97).

**Ba'yard'** (bȧ'yȧr'), **Jean François Alfred.** 1796–1853. French playwright, esp. in collaboration with Scribe and others.

**Bayazid** *or* **Bayezid.** See BAJAZET.

**Bay·bars'** *or* **Bai·bars'** (bī·bärs'). *Also* **Bi·bars'.** Name of two Mameluke sultans of Bahri dynasty:

**Baybars I.** *Arab.* **al-Malik al-Ẓāhir Rukn-al-Dīn Baybars.** 1233–1277. Sultan (1260–77). Turkish slave, sold into Damascus; made commander in bodyguard by Ayyubid sultan al-Salih; real founder of Mameluke power; made Egypt center of Moslem world; broke strength of crusaders in Syria; successful in wars against Armenians and Seljuks; destroyed Syrian branch of Ismailian order of Assassins (1272).

**Baybars II.** d. 1309. Sultan (1308–09). Circassian slave of Sultan Qalawun; seized throne, interrupting long rule of al-Nasir.

**Bay'er** (bī'ẽr; *Angl.* bā'-), **Friedrich.** 1825–1880. German industrialist after whom Friedrich Bayer and Co. (founded at Elberfeld, 1850; became [1881] Farbenfabriken vorm. Friedrich Bayer und Co.) was named. A chemist of this company developed and patented aspirin (c. 1899).

**Bay'er** (bī'ẽr), **Johann.** 1572–1625. German astronomer. Published *Uranometria* (1603), 51 astronomical maps based on observations of his predecessors; introduced use of Greek and Latin characters to distinguish stars of a constellation in the order of their brightness.

**Bayer, Karl Robert Emmerich von.** *Pseudonym* **Robert Byr** (bür). 1835–1902. Austrian novelist and writer on military subjects; in military service (1852–62); author of *Gita* (4 vols., 1877), *Lydia* (1885), *Der Weg zum Glück* (1890), *Sternschnuppen* (1897), etc.

**Bayes** (bāz), **Nora.** *Professional name of* **Dora Gold'berg** (gōld'bûrg). 1880–1928. American actress; widely known in vaudeville and musical comedy.

**Bayeux, Thomas of.** See THOMAS OF BAYEUX.

**Bayle** (bâl), **Pierre.** 1647–1706. French philosopher and critic. Born in Protestant faith; converted to Roman Catholicism; returned (1670) to Protestantism. Professor, Rotterdam (1681); defender of liberty of thought and religious toleration; removed because of skeptical beliefs (1693). Compiled (1697) *Dictionnaire Historique et Critique*, in which he analyzed and criticized accepted historical and philosophical tenets. Regarded as founder of 18th-century rationalism.

**Bay'ley** (bā'lĭ), **Victor.** 1880– . British official in India and novelist; on staff of Indian State Railways; author of *Carfax of the Khyber* (1935), *Liquid Fury* (1936), *Frontier Fires* (1937), *City of Fear* (1938), *North-West Mail* (1939), *Dynamite* (1940), etc.

**Bayley, William Shirley.** 1861–1943. American geologist, b. Baltimore. Member of faculty, U. of Illinois (from 1907); professor (1913–31). Author of *Minerals and Rocks* (1915), *Descriptive Mineralogy* (1916), etc.

**Bay'lis** (bā'lĭs), **Lilian Mary.** 1874–1937. English theater manager; lessee of Old Vic Theatre, London (from 1898), and Sadler's Wells Theatre, London (from 1931).

**Bay'liss** (bā'lĭs), Sir **William Maddock.** 1860–1924. English physiologist. Taught physiology, University Coll., London (1888–1924; professor from 1912). In collaboration with Professor Ernest Henry Starling, presented papers on significant researches, including venous and capillary pressures (1894), innervation of the intestine (1898–99), discovery of the hormone secretin manufactured by glands on the wall of the small intestine (1902). His use of saline injections for amelioration of surgical shock was widely adopted among troops in 1918. Author of *Nature of Enzyme Action* (1908), *Principles of General Physiology* (1915), *The Vaso-motor System* (1923).

**Bayliss,** Sir **Wyke.** 1835–1906. English painter and writer on art; best known for his paintings of church interiors; author of *The Higher Life in Art* (1879), etc.

**Bay'lor** (bā'lẽr), **Robert Emmet Bledsoe.** 1793?–1873. American jurist and Baptist clergyman, b. in Kentucky. In Texas (from 1839). Associate justice, Texas supreme court (1841–45); U.S. district judge (1845–61). Instrumental in obtaining charter for first Baptist college in Texas, named Baylor University (now at Waco, Tex.) in his honor.

**Bay'ly** (bā'lĭ), **Ada Ellen.** *Pseudonym* **Edna Ly'all** (lī'ăl). 1857–1903. English novelist and supporter of women's rights and political liberal movements. Author of *Won by Waiting* (1879), *Donovan* (1882), *Doreen* (1894), *The Hinderers* (1902).

**Bayly,** Sir **Lewis.** 1857–1938. British admiral; commander in chief of western approaches (1915–19); did much to promote close ties between Great Britain and U.S. Author of *Pull Together!* (memoirs; 1939).

**Bayly, Thomas Haynes.** 1797–1839. English author and song writer; educ. Oxford; author of songs and ballads, as "I'd be a butterfly" and "She wore a wreath of roses," 36 dramatic pieces, including the farce *Perfection*, and five novels, including *The Aylmers*.

**Baynes** (bānz), **Thomas Spencer**. 1823–1887. English philosopher. Professor, St. Andrews (1864). Editor of ninth edition of *Encyclopaedia Britannica* (1873–87). See William Robertson SMITH.

**Ba'zaine'** (bȧ'zân'), **François Achille**. 1811–1888. A Marshal of France. Served in Crimean War (1854–56); in Italy (1859); as head of French army in Mexico (1863). Appointed marshal (1864). Commanded main French armies in Franco-Prussian War; defeated at Vionville, Mars-la-Tour, and Gravelotte; besieged in Metz; surrendered (Oct. 27, 1870). Court-martialed (1873); sentence of death commuted to twenty years' imprisonment. Escaped from prison (1874); fled to Spain and lived there in exile.

**Baz'al·gette** (băz''l·jĕt; -jĭt), Sir **Joseph William**. 1819–1891. English civil engineer. Carried out construction of London's main drainage system (1858–75) and Thames embankment (1862–74).

**Bazán, Emilia Pardo**. See PARDO BAZÁN.

**Ba'zan'court'** (bȧ'zäN'kōōr'), Baron **César de**. 1810–1865. French author of novels, histories, and military works, including *Noblesse Oblige* (novel, 1851), *L'Expédition de Crimée*...(1857), *La Campagne d'Italie de 1859*...(1859–60).

**Ba'zard'** (bȧ'zȧr'), **Saint'-A'mand'** (săN'tȧ'mäN'). 1791–1832. French socialist, b. Paris. Organizer of French Carbonari; follower of Saint-Simon.

**Ba'zin'** (bȧ'zăN'), **François Emmanuel Joseph**. 1816–1878. French composer, esp. of light operas; b. Marseille.

**Bazin, René François Nicolas Marie**. 1853–1932. French novelist, b. Angers; writer also of travel books and biography. His novels include *Stéphanette* (1884), *Une Tache d'Encre* (1888), *La Terre qui Meurt* (1898), *Les Oberlé* (1901), *Donatienne* (1903), *L'Isolée* (1905), *Le Blé qui Lève* (1907); among his volumes of short stories are *Contes de Bonne Perrette* (1897) and *Récits de la Plaine et de la Montagne* (1904).

**Bazzi, Giovanni Antonio de'**. See Il SODOMA.

**Baz·zi'ni** (bäd·dzē'nē), **Antonio**. 1818–1897. Italian violinist and composer; director, conservatory of Milan (1882); composed violin pieces, overtures (as to *King Lear* and *Saul*), six quartets and a quintet for string instruments, the symphonic poem *Francesca da Rimini*, the opera *Turandot* (1867), etc.

**Beach** (bēch), **Amy Marcy**, *nee* **Che'ney** (chē'nĭ). 1867–1944. American pianist and composer, b. Henniker, N.H.; m. (1885) Henry Harris Aubrey Beach (d. 1910). Appeared with Boston Symphony Orchestra and other orchestras. Among her compositions are *The Minstrel and the King*, *Rose of Avontown*, *The Chambered Nautilus*, *Panama Hymn*, *Gaelic Symphony* (for piano and violins), and piano pieces and songs.

**Beach, Chester**. 1881–1956. American sculptor, b. San Francisco. Studied in Paris (1904–07). Among his works are *Fountain of the Waters* and *Twelve Signs of the Zodiac* (Fine Arts Garden, Cleveland, Ohio) and portrait busts, as *Peter Cooper*, *Asa Gray*, *Eli Whitney*, *Samuel F. B. Morse*, and *Walt Whitman*.

**Beach,** Sir **Michael Edward Hicks**. See HICKS BEACH.

**Beach, Moses Yale**. 1800–1868. American journalist and inventor, b. Wallingford, Conn. Bought New York *Sun* (1838); its editor (1838–48); turned it over (1848) to his sons **Moses Sperry** (1822–1892) and **Alfred Ely** (1826–1896). *Sun* sold (1868) to Charles A. Dana.

**Beach, Rex Ellingwood**. 1877–1949. American writer, b. Atwood, Mich. Educ. Rollins Coll., Winter Park, Fla. (1891–96); studied law, but turned to writing stories of adventure. Among his best-known tales are *Pardners* (1905), *The Spoilers* (1906), *The Barrier* (1907), *Going Some* (1910), *The Ne'er-do-Well* (1911), *The Net* (1912), *The Auction Block* (1914), *Oh, Shoot* (1921), *The Goose Woman* (1925), *Don Careless* (1928), *Son of the Gods* (1929), *Alaskan Adventures* (1933), *Jungle Gold* (1935), etc. Collaborator in dramatizing some of his books, as *The Spoilers*, *Going Some*.

**Beach, Thomas Miller**. 1841–1894. British secret-service agent. Served in Federal army in American Civil War under name of **Henry le Car'on** (lĕ kăr'ŭn); became major (1865). Became secret agent (1867); returned to U.S. and joined Fenians; informed British and Canadian governments of Fenian plans on several occasions (1866, 1868, 1871, 1879); left America (1888); gave evidence against Irish agitators (1889). Wrote *Twenty-five Years in Secret Service* (1892).

**Beaconsfield,** Earl of. See DISRAELI.

**Bea'dle** (bē'd'l), **George Wells**. 1903– . Am. biologist, b. Wahoo, Neb. Awarded Nobel prize in physiology and medicine (1958) with Edward L. Tatum and Joshua Lederberg.

**Bea'han** (bē'ăn), **Charles**. 1904– . American playwright, b. Clearfield, Pa. Collaborator in writing and producing plays for stage and motion pictures, including *Jarnegan*, *One Night of Love*, *Murder by the Clock*, *Dangerous Nan McGrew*, etc. Author of the novels *The Island God Forgot* and *Night for a Lady*.

**Beal** (bēl), **Gifford Reynolds**. 1879–1956. American painter, b. New York City. A.B., Princeton (1900). Studied under William M. Chase. Among his better-known paintings are *Across the Valley* (water color; Metropolitan Museum of Art, N.Y.), *Freight Yards, Hudson River* (Syracuse Museum of Art), *The Puff of Smoke* (Chicago Art Institute).

**Beal, William James**. 1833–1924. American botanist and educator, b. Adrian, Mich. Student under Agassiz and Asa Gray. Professor, Michigan State College (1871–1910); experimented with hybridization of grains. Author of *The New Botany* (1881), *The Grasses of North America* (2 vols., 1887), *Seed Dispersal* (1898).

**Beale** (bēl), **Dorothea**. 1831–1906. English educator. Head teacher (1857) of Clergy Daughters' School, Casterton, Westmorland (the "Lowood" of *Jane Eyre*); principal of Cheltenham Ladies' College (1858–1906); helped found St. Hilda's College at Cheltenham (1885), for women secondary-school teachers, and St. Hilda's Hall at Oxford (1893), for women teachers.

**Beale, Edward Fitzgerald**. 1822–1893. American naval officer, courier, and pioneer, b. in District of Columbia. With Kit Carson, crept through Mexican lines (1846) to carry news to Commodore Stockton of Kearny's desperate position after his defeat at San Pascual. Courier across the country six times (1847–49); brought first authentic news (1848) of gold discoveries in California. Superintendent of Indian affairs for California and Nevada (1852–65).

**Beale, Lionel Smith**. 1828–1906. English physiologist and microscopist. M.B., London (1851); professor of physiology and anatomy (1853–69), pathological anatomy (1869–76), medicine (1876–96), King's College, London. Discoverer of "Beale's cells." Author of *The Structure and Growth of the Tissues* (1865), *Disease Germs* (1872), *Bioplasm* (1872).

**Beale, Truxtun**. 1856–1936. American diplomat, in Persia (1891–92), Greece, Rumania, and Serbia (1892–94).

**Beall** (bēl), **John Yates**. 1835–1865. American Confederate soldier, b. in Jefferson County, Va. In Canada (1864); attempted to seize Federal warship on Lake Erie and free Confederate prisoners; hanged as spy.

**Beals** (bēlz), **Carleton.** 1893– . American journalist and publicist, b. Medicine Lodge, Kans. B.A., California (1916). Special correspondent in Italy (1920–22), Mexico (1923, 1925–28), Central America (1928), Europe (1929), Cuba (1932–33), South America (1934). Lecturer on Mexican-American relations. Author of *Rome or Death* (1923), *Mexico* (1923), *Brimstone and Chili* (1927), *Mexican Maze* (1931), *Banana Gold* (1932), *Fire on the Andes* (1934), *America South* (1937), *American Earth* (1939), *Pan America* (1940), the autobiographical works *Glass Houses* (1938) and *The Great Circle* (1940).

**Bean** (bēn), **Tarleton Hoffman.** 1846–1916. American ichthyologist, b. Bainbridge, Pa. Curator, department of fisheries, U.S. National Museum (1880–95); director, New York Aquarium (1895–98). Head of fish culture activities in New York State (1906–16). Author of *Oceanic Ichthyology* (with G. B. Goode; 1895) and of descriptive lists of fishes of Pennsylvania, Long Island, New York, Bermuda.

**Beard** (bẽrd), **Charles Austin.** 1874–1948. American historian and educator, b. Knightstown, Ind. Ph.B., DePauw (1898); Ph.D., Columbia (1904). Professor of politics, Columbia (1907–17). Director of Training School for Public Service, New York City (1917–22). Author of *Development of Modern Europe* (with J. H. Robinson; 2 vols., 1907), *American Government and Politics* (1910), *American City Government* (1912), *Economic Interpretation of the Constitution* (1913), *History of the American People* (with W. C. Bagley; 1918); *Economic Basis of Politics* (1922), *American Party Battle* (1928), etc. m. (1900) **Mary Rit′ter** [rĭt′ẽr] (1876–1958), Ph.B., DePauw (1897), his collaborator in writing *American Citizenship* (1913), *History of the United States* (1921), *The Rise of American Civilization* (4 vols., 1927–42), *The Making of American Civilization* (1937), etc.

**Beard, Daniel Carter,** *known as* **Dan.** 1850–1941. American painter, illustrator, and organizer of Boy Scout movement in U.S., b. Cincinnati, Ohio; son of James Henry Beard. Studied at Art Students' League, New York (1880–84). Teacher of animal drawing, Woman's School of Applied Design (1893–1900). Originator and founder (1910) of first Boy Scout society in America. (See Sir Robert S. S. Baden-Powell.) Mt. Beard, a peak adjoining Mt. McKinley, was named in his honor. Author of *American Boys' Handy Book* (1882), *Outdoor Handy Book* (1900), *Boy Pioneers and Sons of Daniel Boone* (1909), *Shelters, Shacks, and Shanties* (1914), *Signs, Signals, and Symbols* (1918), *American Boys' Book of Camplore and Woodcraft* (1920), *Wisdom of the Woods* (1927), etc.

**Beard, George Miller.** 1839–1883. American neurologist, b. Montville, Conn. Noted for his researches in electrotherapeutics, neurasthenia, and mental disease. Author of *Eating and Drinking* (1871), *The Medical and Surgical Uses of Electricity* (1871; with Alphonso D. Rockwell), *Nervous Exhaustion* (1880), *American Nervousness* (1881).

**Beard, James Henry.** 1812–1893. American artist, b. Buffalo, N.Y. Studio in Cincinnati. Among his portraits are those of Henry Clay, John Quincy Adams, General William Henry Harrison, General Taylor, and General Sherman. His brother **William Holbrook** (1824–1900) was noted for his humorous animal pictures. James's son **James Carter** (1837–1913) wrote illustrated articles on plant and animal life for the magazines, and illustrated Theodore Roosevelt's *Hunting Trip of a Ranchman* (1886). Another son, **Thomas Francis** (1842–1905), was editor and cartoonist on *Judge* during the Blaine campaign (1884) and illustrator (1885–1905) for the *Ram's Horn*, a Chicago religious weekly. See also Daniel Carter Beard.

**Beard, Mary,** *nee* **Ritter.** See Charles Austin Beard.

**Beards′ley** (bẽrdz′lĭ), **Aubrey Vincent.** 1872–1898. English artist in black and white. Worked in architect's office; became ornamental illustrator of books, including *Morte d'Arthur*, *Rape of the Lock*, *Mademoiselle de Maupin*, Oscar Wilde's *Salome.* Art editor of *Yellow Book* (1894).

**Bear′sted** (bâr′stĕd; -stĭd), 1st Viscount. **Marcus Sam′u·el** (săm′ū·ĕl). 1853–1927. English financier. Founded Shell Transport and Trading Company (1897), amalgamated with Royal Dutch Petroleum Company (1907), an oil-producing, refining, and distributing organization. Lord Mayor of London (1902–03).

**Bea′ton** *or* **Be′thune** (bē′t'n), **David.** 1494–1546. Scottish Roman Catholic prelate and statesman. Educ. St. Andrews, Glasgow, and Paris. Sent by James V on missions to France; keeper of privy seal (1528); appointed cardinal under the title of St. Stephen in the Coelian Hill (1538); succeeded his uncle as archbishop of St. Andrews (1539); led party committed to French alliance and opposed to English alliance; upon failure in attempt to assume regency, put in custody by regent Arran (1543); chancellor of Scotland (1543); had George Wishart, preacher of Reformation, arrested, tried for heresy, and burned at stake (1546); murdered in revenge by John and Norman Leslie and William Kirkcaldy. His uncle **James Beaton** (1470?–1539) was lord treasurer (1505–06), chancellor (1513–26); archbishop of Glasgow (1509); archbishop of St. Andrews and primate of Scotland (1522); influenced king to ally himself with France rather than England. David's nephew **James Beaton** (1517–1603) was a trusted adviser of the queen regent, widow of James V; was consecrated last Roman Catholic archbishop of Glasgow of the old hierarchy (1552); lived in Paris as Scottish ambassador (1560–1603).

**Be′a·tri′ce Por′ti·na′ri** (bā′ä·trē′chā pōr′tē·nä′rē). 1266–1290. Wife of Simone de' Bardi. Florentine noblewoman immortalized by Dante (*q.v.*) in his *Vita Nuova* and *Divina Commedia.*

**Beat′tie** (bē′tĭ), **James.** 1735–1803. Scottish poet. M.A., Marischal College, Aberdeen (1753); studied divinity; became professor of moral philosophy there (1760). Author of descriptive poem on progress of genius, the *Minstrel* (1st part, 1771; 2d, 1774) in Spenserian stanzas, of minor poems *The Hermit* and *Retirement*, and of *Essay on... Truth*, attacking Hume (1770).

**Beat′ty** (bē′tĭ), **David.** 1st Earl of the **North Sea** and of **Brooks′by** (bro͝oks′bĭ). 1871–1936. British admiral. Entered navy (1884); rear admiral (1910); vice-admiral (1915); admiral (1919); in command of battle cruiser squadron; at Heligoland Bight (1914); at Dogger Bank (1915), at which *Blücher* was sunk; led squadron against German fleet in battle of Jutland (1916); admiral of the fleet (1919); 1st sea lord of admiralty (1919–27); attended Washington conference on limitation of armaments (1921).

**Beatty,** Sir **Edward Wentworth.** 1877–1943. Canadian lawyer and executive. Educ. Toronto U. Chairman and president of Canadian Pacific Railway (1918–42); chancellor of McGill U. (since 1921).

**Beatus Rhenanus.** (1) Pseudonym of Theodor Birt; (2) see Beatus Rhenanus.

**Beau′champ** (bē′chăm), Barons. See *Edward Seymour* (1539?–1621, 1561–1612), under Seymour family.

**Beau′champ′** (bō′shäN′), **Alphonse de.** 1767–1832. French publicist and author of *Histoire de la Vendée et des Chouans* (1806).

**Beau′champ** (bē′chăm), **Richard de.** Earl of **War′wick** (wŏr′ĭk). 1382–1439. English soldier. Defeated Owen Glendower (1403); fought Percys at Shrewsbury (1403); visited Holy Land (1408); suppressed Lollard uprising (1414); took part in Henry V's French campaigns (1415 ff.); had charge of education of Henry VI; lieutenant of France and Normandy (1437). His father **Thomas** (d. 1401), whom he succeeded as earl, joined magnates under Gloucester in overthrowing Richard II (Dec., 1387); imprisoned for treason in Beauchamp Tower (1397); released by Henry IV.

**Beau′clerc** (bō′klâr). See HENRY I of England.

**Beau′clerk** (bō′klâr), **Topham.** 1739–1780. Descendant of Charles II and Nell Gwyn; intimate friend (after 1757) of Dr. Johnson; m. (1768) Lady **Diana Spencer** (1734–1808), an amateur painter and illustrator of Dryden's *Fables*, immediately after her divorce from Lord Bolingbroke.

**Beau′court′** (bō′kōōr′), Marquis **de. Gaston du Fresne** (dü frân). 1833–1902. French historian, b. Paris; author of *Histoire de Charles VII* (1881–92).

**Beau′fort** (bō′fērt). Name of an English noble family which sprang illegitimately from the union of John of Gaunt, duke of Lancaster, of Beaufort castle in Anjou, and Catherine, the widow of Sir Hugh Swynford, and which was legitimized by parliament (1397), but excluded from royal succession. Its members include: **John Beaufort** (1373?–1410), Earl of **Som′er·set** (sŭm′ēr·sĕt; -sĭt); eldest of 3 sons of this union (see Henry BEAUFORT; Thomas BEAUFORT); assisted Richard II against the lords appellants (1397); made marquis of **Dor′set** (dôr′sĕt; -sĭt) by Richard II; became admiral of the fleet. His daughter **Jane** *or* **Joan** (d. 1445) married James I of Scotland, whose murderers she punished fiercely. His older son **John** (1403–1444), 1st Duke of Somerset, commanded Henry V's forces in France (1439 ff.); with his younger brother **Edmund** (cr. earl of Dorset, 1442; killed at St. Albans, 1455), 2d Duke of Somerset, recaptured Harfleur (1440). For Margaret, daughter of the 1st duke, see Margaret BEAUFORT. **Henry** (1436–1464), 3d Duke of Somerset, son of Edmund, shared in the struggle against Richard, Duke of York; defeated by Yorkists at Newnham Bridge (April, 1460) but successful at Wakefield (Dec., 1460); shared attainder of Henry VI (1461); captured and beheaded (1464).

**Beaufort,** Dukes of. See SOMERSET family.

**Beau′fort′** (bō′fôr′), Duc **de. François de Ven′dôme′** (dē väɴ′dōm′). 1616–1669. French officer and politician; son of César de Bourbon, Duc de Vendôme; conspired with Cinq-Mars against Richelieu (1642); in exile until Richelieu's death. Further conspiracy led to imprisonment (1643–48); a leader of the Fronde (1648–49). Loyal to Louis XIV (from 1653); appointed to high naval command; killed in action (June 25, 1669). Called "Roi des Halles" (rwä dā ȧl), *i.e.* "King of the Markets," because of the boldness and coarseness of his language.

**Beau′fort** (bō′fērt), Sir **Francis.** 1774–1857. English rear admiral. Devised "Beaufort's scale" (1805), for indicating wind velocities. Surveyed entrance to Río de la Plata (1807) and southern coast of Asia Minor (1811–12). Hydrographer to navy (1829–55).

**Beaufort, Henry.** 1377?–1447. English cardinal and statesman; second son of John of Gaunt by Catherine Swynford. Bishop of Lincoln (1398), Winchester (1404). Chancellor (1403–04, 1413–17, 1424–26). Papal legate in crusade against Hussites (1427–31). Crowned Henry VI king of France and England (1431). Repelled attempt of Gloucester to deprive him of his see (1432). Failed in missions of peace to France (1439, 1440).

**Beaufort, Margaret.** Countess of **Rich′mond and Der′by** (rĭch′mŭnd, där′bĭ). 1443–1509. Heiress of John of Gaunt; daughter of John Beaufort, 1st Duke of Somerset; m. (1455) Edmund Tudor, Earl of Richmond (see TUDOR family). After triumph of Yorkists (1461), confined at Pembroke; m. Henry Stafford, son of duke of Buckingham; m. (c. 1482) Thomas Stanley, 1st Earl of Derby; after accession of Richard III, emerged from retirement to promote alliance of her party to Yorkist house of Woodville by marriage (1486) of her son Henry Tudor (later Henry VII) to Princess Elizabeth, daughter of Elizabeth Woodville. Remembered as "Lady Margaret," generous patron of education; under influence of her Romanist confessor, John Fisher, endowed divinity professorships at Oxford and Cambridge; enriched foundation that opened as Christ's Coll., Cambridge (1505), and corporation that refounded monastic house as St. John's Coll., Cambridge (1508); early patron of Caxton and Wynkyn de Worde.

**Beaufort,** Sir **Thomas.** d. 1427. 3d son of John of Gaunt by Catherine Swynford. English commander; admiral of fleet in the north (1403); commanded royal forces in Scrope's rebellion (1405); captain of Calais (1407); chancellor (1410–12); engaged in wars with French (1412–27); created duke of **Ex′e·ter** [ĕk′sē·tēr] (1416); member of council under Gloucester's protectorate (1422 ff.).

**Beau′har′nais′** (bō′ȧr′nĕ′). Name of a noble French family of Orléanais. Prominent members include: **Alexandre,** Vicomte **de Beauharnais** (1760–1794), French army officer, b. in Martinique; fought under Rochambeau in American Revolution; deputy of nobility to States-General (1789); general in chief, army of the Rhine (1793); charged with responsibility for surrender of Mainz; guillotined (July 23, 1794). His wife, **Joséphine de Beauharnais,** *nee* **Marie Joséphine Rose Ta′scher′ de la Pa′ge·rie′** [tȧ′shâr′ dē lȧ pȧzh′rē′] (1763–1814); b. in Martinique; m. Napoleon Bonaparte (Mar. 9, 1796); crowned empress of the French at Napoleon's coronation (Dec. 2, 1804); divorced by Napoleon (1809). A son of Alexandre and Joséphine, **Eugène de Beauharnais** (1781–1824); b. Paris; served with Napoleon in Egypt (1798–99); made by Napoleon viceroy of Italy (1805); m. Princess Amalie Auguste of Bavaria (1806); formally adopted by Napoleon and made heir apparent to crown of Italy (1806); commanded army corps in Russian campaign (1812); retired to Bavaria (after 1814) and became (1817) duke of **Leuch′ten·berg** (loiк′tĕn·bĕrк) and prince of **Eich′stätt** (īк′shtĕt). For sons and daughters of Eugène, see LEUCHTENBERG. Eugène's sister **Hortense de Beauharnais** (1783–1837); m. (1802) Louis Bonaparte, King of Holland; mother of Napoleon III. **Stéphanie de Beauharnais** (1789–1860), niece of Joséphine and adopted dau. of Napoleon; m. (1806) Charles, grand duke of Baden.

**Beau′jan′** (bō′zhäɴ′), **Émile Ambroise Amédée.** 1821–1888. French lexicographer; collaborator in Littré's *Dictionnaire de la Langue Française* (1863–72).

**Beau′lieu′** (bō′lyû′), Baron **Jean Pierre de.** 1725–1819. Austrian general; defeated by Napoleon Bonaparte at Lodi (1796).

**Beau′ma′noir′** (bō′mȧ′nwȧr′), Sire **de. Philippe de Ré′mi′** (dē rā′mē′). 1250–1296. French jurist; author of *Coutumes de Beauvoisis*, a source book for study of old French law.

**Beau′mar′chais′** (bō′mȧr′shĕ′; *Angl.* bō′mär·shā′), **Pierre Augustin Ca′ron′** (kȧ′rôɴ′) **de.** 1732–1799. French playwright and man of affairs, b. Paris. At first, like his father, a clockmaker; then engaged in commercial and financial affairs; attracted public attention when, in connection with litigation over inheritance at the death of his business partner, he published in his own vindication four *Mémoires*, wittily attacking judicial injustice. Financed purchase of supplies for American colonies during American Revolution. Chiefly known as author of *Le Barbier de Séville* (first performed 1775) and *Le Mariage de Figaro* (first performed 1784), comedies which later inspired operas by Rossini and Mozart.

**Beau'mont'** (bō'môɴ'), **André.** See Jean CONNEAU.

**Beaumont, Élie de,** *in full* **Jean Baptiste Armand Louis Léonce Élie de.** 1798–1874. French geologist; professor, Collège de France (1832); published *Carte Géologique de France* (1841), *Notices sur les Systèmes de Montagnes* (1852), etc.

**Beaumont, Éon de.** See ÉON DE BEAUMONT.

**Beau'mont** (bō'mŏnt; -mŭnt), **Francis.** 1584–1616. English dramatist. Educ. Oxford; entered Inner Temple (1600); wrote commendatory verses for plays of Ben Jonson (1607–11); began (c. 1606) intimate collaboration with fellow bachelor John Fletcher in composition of about fifty comedies and tragedies; m. (1613) Ursula, daughter of Henry Isley of Sundridge, Kent. Probably sole author of *The Woman Hater* (c. 1607); collaborations with Fletcher include *The Knight of the Burning Pestle, The Scornful Lady, Philaster, The Maid's Tragedy, A King and No King, Cupid's Revenge, The Coxcomb.*

**Beaumont,** Sir **George Howland.** 1753–1827. English patron of art and landscape painter. Knew Dr. Johnson, Sir Joshua Reynolds; entertained Scott, Rogers, Byron, Wordsworth; befriended Coleridge, Wilkie, Landseer.

**Beaumont,** Sir **John.** 1583–1627. English poet; elder brother of Francis, the dramatist. Known chiefly for *Metamorphosis of Tobacco* (1602), written in smooth couplets, and *Bosworth Field* (a volume of poems, 1629).

**Beaumont, Joseph.** 1616–1699. English divine and poet, b. in Suffolk; author of *Psyche* (epic poem; 1648).

**Beaumont, Robert de.** Earl of **Leices'ter** (lĕs'tẽr). 1104–1168. Chief justiciar of England. Son of Robert de Beaumont, Count of Meulan, warrior at Hastings and counselor of William II and Henry I. With his twin brother, **Waleran** (1104–1166), aided and advised Stephen (1137). Made his peace with Henry II; in charge of kingdom in king's absences in France. Chief justiciar jointly with Richard de Lucy (1153–66).

**Beaumont, William.** 1785–1853. American surgeon, b. in Connecticut. Studied process of digestion by exhaustive experiments with patient whose stomach was exposed by gunshot wound (1822). His work *Experiments and Observations on the Gastric Juice and the Physiology of Digestion* (1833) is greatest single contribution ever made to the knowledge of gastric digestion.

**Beau'mont' de La Bon'ni'ère'** (bō'môɴ' dē lȧ bô'nē'nyâr'), **Gustave Auguste de.** 1802–1866. French publicist; author, with Tocqueville, of *Traité du Système Pénitentiaire aux États-Unis* (1833) and *Marie, ou l'Esclavage aux États-Unis* (1835), etc.

**Beaune** (bōn), **Florimond de.** 1601–1652. French mathematician; his work paved way for study of integral calculus.

**Beau'ne·veû'** (bōn'vû'), **André.** fl. 1360–1403. Flemish-born French sculptor and miniaturist; sculptor of the tombs of Philip VI and Charles V of France.

**Beau'nis'** (bō'nēs'), **Henri Étienne.** 1830–1921. French physiologist and psychologist. Founder (1889) at Sorbonne of first laboratory of physiological psychology.

**Beau're·gard** (bō'rē·gärd; *Fr.* bōr'gȧr'), **Pierre** (pyâr) **Gus'tave'** (güs'tȧv') **Tou'tant'** (tōō'täɴ') **de.** 1818–1893. American army officer, b. near New Orleans, La. Grad. U.S.M.A., West Point (1838). Served through Mexican War. Superintendent, U.S.M.A., West Point, at outbreak of Civil War; resigned to enter Confederate army. As brigadier general, in command at bombardment of Fort Sumter; served through Civil War; at Bull Run, Shiloh (as general), Corinth. Manager, the Louisiana lottery (1870–88). Commissioner of public works, New Orleans (1888 ff.). Author of *Principles and Maxims of the Art of War* (1863), *A Commentary on the Campaign and Battle of Manassas* (1891).

**Beaurepaire.** See QUESNAY DE BEAUREPAIRE.

**Beau'temps'–Beau'pré'** (bō'täɴ'bō'prā'), **Charles François.** 1766–1854. French hydrographic engineer.

**Beauvais, Vincent of.** See VINCENT OF BEAUVAIS.

**Beauval, Jacques Basnage de.** See Jacques BASNAGE.

**Beau'voir'** (bō'vwȧr'), **Roger de.** *Real name* **Édouard Roger de Bul'ly'** (bü'yē'). 1809–1866. French poet, playwright, and novelist of the romantic period; b. Paris. His wife, **Éléonore Léocadie,** *nee* **Doze** [dōz] (1822–1859), was an actress and author of several comedies.

**Beauvoir, Simone de.** *In Full* **Simone Lucie Ernestine Marie Bertrand de Beauvoir.** 1908– . Fr. author. Wrote *The Second Sex* (1953), *The Mandarins* (1956), etc.

**Beaux** (bō), **Cecilia.** 1863–1942. American painter, b. Philadelphia. Studied under William Sartain and at Académie Julian and Lazar School in Paris. Excelled in portraiture, especially in painting women and children. Work represented in all important public collections in U.S., and in Luxembourg Gallery in Paris and the Uffizi Gallery in Florence. Among her best-known paintings are *Last Days of Infancy, Mother and Daughter, The Dreamer, A New England Woman, Dorothea and Francesca, The Cynthia.*

**Bea'ver·brook** (bē'vẽr·brŏŏk), 1st Baron. **William Maxwell Ait'ken** (āt'kĕn). 1879–1964. British newspaper publisher, b. Newcastle, New Brunswick, Canada. Made fortune through amalgamation of Canadian cement mills. Canadian government representative at western front in World War I; took charge of Canadian war records; British minister of information (1918). Member of British war cabinet (1940–Feb., 1942), as minister for aircraft production (1940–41), minister of state (1941), minister of supply (1941); sent to U.S. (Feb., 1942) to supervise British supply agencies. Publisher of *The Daily Express* and other newspapers; author of *Canada in Flanders* (1916), *Politicians and the Press* (1925), *Politicians and the War* (2 vols.; 1928, 1932), *Resources of the British Empire* (1934).

**Beaz'ley** (bēz'lĭ), Sir **Charles Raymond.** 1868–1955. English historian and geographer. M.A., Oxon. (1893). Professor of history, U. of Birmingham (1909–33). Author of *Dawn of Modern Geography* (3 vols., 1897, 1901, 1906), *Voyages and Travels: 16th–17th centuries* (1902), *History of Russia* (1918), *The Road to Ruin* (1932), etc.

**Beazley,** Sir **John Davidson.** 1885–1970. British archaeologist, b. Glasgow, Scotland; professor atOxford (1925–56); author of works on early Greek art.

**Be'bel** (bā'bĕl), **August.** 1840–1913. German Social Democratic leader and writer. Joined German labor movement (1861); converted to socialism by Liebknecht; chairman, committee of German workingmen's unions (1867); cofounder of Social Democratic party, Eisenach (1869). Deputy to North German diet (1867–71); member of newly formed Reichstag (1871–81, 1883–1913). Sentenced with Liebknecht (1872) to imprisonment of two years and nine months on charges of high treason and lese majesty against German emperor, and subsequently (1886) on further charges. Resident of Berlin (from 1890) as recognized leader of Social Democratic party and editor of *Vorwärts.* Author of *Unsere Ziele*

(1870), *Der Deutsche Bauernkrieg* (1876), *Die Frau und der Sozialismus* (1883), *Christentum und Sozialismus* (1892), *Aus Meinem Leben* (1910–14), etc.

**Bec′ca·fu′mi** (bāk′kä·fōō′mē), **Domenico**. *Orig. name* **Domenico di Pa′ce** (dē pä′chā). *Called* **Il Mec′che·ri′no** (ēl māk′kā·rē′nō). 1486–1551. Italian painter and sculptor; rival of Sodoma; known esp. for his designs of scenes from the Old Testament for pavement in cathedral of Siena (1517–25, 1544, 1546); among his other works are frescoes in Siena city hall, and pieces of sculpture, as marble figures of the apostles for cathedral of Siena.

**Bec·ca′ri** (bāk·kä′rē), **Odoardo**. 1843–1920. Italian botanist and traveler in New Guinea, East Indies, and East Africa; founder of *Nuovo Giornale Botanico Italiano* (1869).

**Bec′ca·ri′a** (bāk′kä·rē′ä), Marchese **di. Cesare Bo′ne·sa′na** (bō′nā·sä′nä). 1738–1794. Italian economist and jurist, b. Milan. Professor of law and economy, Milan (1768); anticipated in his lectures economic theories of Adam Smith, and theories of Malthus on population and subsistence. Councilor of state and magistrate (1771). On commission for reform of civil and criminal jurisprudence in Lombardy (1790). Author of *Tratto dei Delitti e delle Pene* (1764), which condemns confiscation, capital punishment, and torture, and advocates prevention of crime by education; his ideas had widespread effects, influencing Catherine II of Russia and the French revolutionary code.

**Beccaria, Giovanni Battista**. 1716–1781. Italian physicist; experimented with atmospheric electricity and spread knowledge of Franklin's electrical researches; chief work, *Dell'Elettricismo Naturale ed Artifiziale* (1753).

**Bé′champ′** (bā′shäN′), **Pierre Jacques Antoine**. 1816–1908. French physician, surgeon, and chemist, b. near Dieuze. Author of *Les Microzymas dans leurs Rapports avec l'Hétérogénie, l'Histogénie, la Physiologie et la Pathologie* (1883).

**Beche**, Sir **Henry Thomas de la**. See DE LA BECHE.

**Becher**, Lady **Eliza**. See Eliza O'NEILL.

**Bech′er** (bĕK′ẽr), **Johann Joachim**. 1635–1682. German chemist, political economist, and physician. Suggested establishment of German colonies in South America. Carried on experiments for transmuting the Danube sand into gold. Advanced (with Stahl) the phlogiston theory of combustion. Author of *Physica Subterranea* (1669), on the nature of minerals and other substances.

**Bech′stein** (bĕK′shtīn), **Johann Matthäus**. 1757–1822. German zoologist and forester; founder of a school of forestry; director (from 1800) of Academy of Forestry at Dreissigacker. Author of *Die Forst- und Jagdwissenschaft nach allen ihren Teilen* (14 vols., 1818–27).

**Bechstein, Ludwig**. 1801–1860. German epic poet, novelist, and folklorist. Librarian, ducal library, Meiningen (1831); archivist (1848). Author of poems *Die Haimonskinder* (1830) and *Faustus* (1833), the novel *Das Tolle Jahr* (1833), the tale *Fahrten eines Musikanten* (1836–37), and collections of folk tales and fairy stories.

**Bechterev** *or* **Bechterew**. Variants of BEKHTEREV.

**Beck** (bĕk), Sir **Adam**. 1857–1925. Canadian public utility operator and financier, b. Baden, Ontario. Chairman, Ontario Hydro-Electric Power Commission (1906). Member, Ontario legislature (1905–19), Ontario ministry (1905).

**Beck** (bĕk) *or* **Beek** (bāk), **David**. 1621–1656. Dutch portrait painter; pupil and assistant of Van Dyck. Worked mostly at courts of England, France, and Denmark, and in service of Queen Christina of Sweden.

**Beck** (bĕk), **James Montgomery**. 1861–1936. American lawyer, b. Philadelphia. Solicitor general of U.S. (1921–25); member, U.S. House of Representatives (1927–34). Author of *War and Humanity* (1916), *The Constitution of the United States* (1922), etc.

**Beck** (bĕk), **Jean Baptiste**. 1881–1943. Educator and musician, b. in Alsace. Educ. in Paris and Strassburg. To U.S.; professor of Romanic languages, U. of Illinois (1911–14), Bryn Mawr (1914–20), Pennsylvania (from 1920); also, professor of the history of music at Curtis Inst. of Music (1924–32). Discoverer of the key to translation of medieval music. Author of *Die Melodien der Troubadours* (1909), *Corpus Cantilenarum Medii Aevi* (1927).

**Beck** (bĕk), **Józef**. 1894–1944. Polish statesman, b. Warsaw. Served in Piłsudski's Polish legion in World War. Military attaché at Paris (1922–23). Polish minister of foreign affairs (1932–39).

**Beck** (bĕk), **Karl**. 1817–1879. Poet, b. in Hungary; resident in Vienna (from 1848) as an editor of the *Lloyd*. Author of *Nächte: Gepanzerte Lieder* (1838), *Der Fahrende Poet* (1838), *Stille Lieder* (1839), the tragedy *Saul* (1841), the novel in verse *Janko, der Ungarische Rosshirt* (1842), *Lieder vom Armen Manne* (1846), *Jadwiga* (1863), and other poetic works reflecting the spirit and life of his native Hungary.

**Beck, Lily Adams**. *Pseudonyms* **E. Bar′ring·ton** (băr′ĭng·tŭn) *and* **Louis Mores′by** (mōrz′bĭ). d. 1931. English writer. Granddaughter of Sir Fairfax Moresby (*q.v.*). Lived many years in Orient; traveled in Little Tibet; lived in Canada (1919–30); d. in Japan. Author of many short stories, her first volume under title *The Ninth Vibration* (1922); a fictionalized life of Buddha, *The Splendour of Asia; The Story of Oriental Philosophy* (1928); a number of historical romances.

**Beck, Theodric Romeyn** (1791–1855) and his brother **John Brodhead** (1794–1851). American physicians, b. Schenectady, N.Y.; collaborated in *Elements of Medical Jurisprudence* (1823). Another brother, **Lewis Caleb** (1798–1853), was author of books on botany, chemistry, and mineralogy.

**Beck′e** (bĕk′ĕ), **Friedrich**. 1855–1931. Austrian mineralogist and geologist; inventor of a method for determining minerals by means of their light-refractive properties.

**Becke** (bĕk), **George Lewis** (*or* **Louis**). 1855?–1913. Australian fiction writer, b. Port Macquarie, New South Wales; author of adventure stories, *By Reef and Palm, The Ebbing of the Tide, The Mutineer*, etc.

**Beck′er** (bĕk′ẽr), **Albert Ernst Anton**. 1834–1899. German composer of church music, a symphony in G minor, an opera (*Loreley*), an oratorio, chamber music, and vocal compositions.

**Becker, Carl Heinrich**. 1876–1933. German oriental scholar and politician, b. Amsterdam. Professor, colonial institute, Hamburg (1908) and Bonn (1913). Secretary of state in Prussia (1919, 1925); member of Prussian cabinet (1921). Author of *Islamstudien* (1924), etc.

**Becker, Carl Lotus**. 1873–1945. American historian, b. in Blackhawk County, Iowa. Professor of European history, Cornell (from 1917). Author of *Beginnings of the American People* (1915), *Our Great Experiment in Democracy* (1924), *Modern History* (1931), *Progress and Power* (1936), *The Declaration of Independence* (1942).

**Becker, George Ferdinand**. 1847–1919. American scientist, b. New York City. Educ. Harvard, Heidelberg, Berlin. On U.S. geological survey work (1879 ff.). Studied South African gold fields (1896), mineral resources of the Philippines (1898). Pioneer in investigation of chemicophysical problems.

**Becker, Jean** (zhäN). 1833–1884. Musician, b. Mannheim, Germany. Violinist in Florence, Italy (from 1866); member of Florentine Quartet. Three children, **Jean'ne** [zhä'nĕ] (1859–1893), pianist, **Hans** (1860–1917), violist and violinist, and **Hugo** (1864–1941), violoncellist, were accomplished musicians. Hugo made concert tour of U.S. (1901–02).

**Becker, Julius Maria.** 1887– . German writer of plays, fiction, and verse.

**Becker, Karl Ferdinand.** 1775–1849. German philologist. Physician (from 1815) at Offenbach. Made researches in philology; author of *Organismus der Sprache* (1827) and the textbooks *Ausführliche Deutsche Grammatik* (1836–39) and *Der Deutsche Stil* (1848).

**Becker, Karl Ferdinand.** 1804–1877. German organist and writer on music. Organist, Leipzig (from 1825); revised Forkel's *Systematisch-Chronologische Darstellung der Musikliteratur* (1836–39); author of *Die Hausmusik in Deutschland im 16., 17., und 18. Jahrhundert* (1840).

**Becker, Karl Ludwig Friedrich.** 1820–1900. German genre and historical painter. His paintings include *Belisarius Begging* (1850), frescoes of the Niobidensaal (Berlin Museum), *The Doge in Council* (1864), *Charles V Visiting Fugger* (1870; now in National Gallery, Berlin), *Dürer in Venice* (1873), etc.

**Becker, May,** *nee* **Lam'ber·ton** (lăm'bẽr·t'n; -tŭn). 1873–1958. American critic and author, b. New York City; m. Gustave L. Becker (1894; divorced, 1911). On staff of *Literary Review*, New York *Evening Post* (1915–24), *Saturday Review of Literature* (1924–33), book section of New York *Herald Tribune*. Author of *A Reader's Guide Book* (1923), *First Adventures in Reading* (1936), *Choosing Books for Children* (1937), etc., and a series of *Golden Tales* (*of Our America*, 1929; *of the Old South*, 1930; *of New England*, 1931; *of the Prairie States*, 1932; *of the Far West*, 1935; *of Canada*, 1938; *of the Southwest*, 1939), *Introducing Charles Dickens* (1940), *Growing up with America* (1941).

**Becker, Nikolaus.** 1809–1845. German poet, best known for his song of the Rhine (1840) beginning "Sie sollen ihn nicht haben, den freien deutschen Rhein," which inspired notably Alfred de Musset's answer "Nous l'avons eu, votre Rhin allemand" (1841).

**Becker, Rudolf Zacharias.** 1752–1822. German popular writer and journalist. Edited *Allgemeiner Reichsanzeiger* (from 1791), *Nationalzeitung der Deutschen* (1796), etc.; arrested and imprisoned at Magdeburg (1811–13) by French because of article in latter publication. Author of *Noth- und Hülfsbüchlein* (1788), *Mildheimisches Liederbuch* (1799), and a description of his experiences in prison (1814).

**Becker, Wilhelm Adolf.** 1796–1846. German classical archaeologist; professor at Leipzig (from 1842). Author of *Gallus* (1838) and *Charikles* (1840), romances of ancient everyday Greek and Roman life, *Handbuch der Römischen Alterthümer* (begun 1843; completely revised later by Marquardt and Mommsen); etc.

**Becker-Modersohn, Paula.** See under Otto MODERSOHN.

**Beck'et** (bĕk'ĕt; -ĭt), **Thomas à** (*ȧ*; ä). *Also* Saint **Thomas Becket.** 1118?–1170. English prelate, of Norman parentage. Sent by Theobald, archbishop of Canterbury, to study canon law at Bologna and Auxerre. Vigorous chancellor under Henry II (1155–62); organized campaign and fought in war with Toulouse (1159). Made archbishop of Canterbury (1162) by Henry and became uncompromising defender of rights of Church against lay power; refused to seal Constitutions of Clarendon, and fled to France (1164); persuaded Pope Alexander III to suspend bishops who crowned Prince Henry in his absence, and forced king to reconciliation (1170); refused absolution of bishops; murdered by four overzealous knights of Henry's court. Canonized (1172). Shrine plundered by Henry VIII (1538) and name of saint expunged from English church calendar.

**Beck'ett** (bĕk'ĕt; -ĭt), Sir **Edmund.** 1st Baron **Grim'thorpe** (grĭm'thôrp). 1816–1905. English lawyer, architect, horologist, and controversialist. After accumulating fortune at the bar, interested himself in church architecture, clockmaking (superintended construction of Big Ben), and religious controversies. Author of *A Rudimentary Treatise on Clock and Watch Making* (1850), *A Book on Building, Civil and Ecclesiastical* (1876), etc.

**Beckett, Gilbert Abbott à, Gilbert Arthur à, Arthur William à.** See À BECKETT.

**Beckett, Samuel.** 1906– . Irish author and playwright, b. Dublin. To Paris (1937). Awarded the Nobel prize in literature (1969).

**Beck'ford** (bĕk'fẽrd), **William.** 1760–1844. English man of letters and art collector. His Gothic novel *Vathek*, written in French (1782), is best known in the anonymous and unauthorized English translation which was published (1786) the year before the French original. Secluded himself in magnificent residence, "Fonthill," with a 260-foot tower. Author of travel sketches including *Dreams, Waking Thoughts and Incidents* (1783) and satires on the minor novel.

**Beck'mann** (bĕk'män), **Johann.** 1739–1811. German technologist and educator; professor of economics, Göttingen (from 1770); author of a history of inventions, *Beiträge zur Geschichte der Erfindungen* (1780–1805).

**Beck'nell** (bĕk'n'l), **William.** 1790?–?1832. American pioneer, b. in Kentucky. Traced Santa Fe trail (1822), which became main commercial route to southwest.

**Beck'with** (bĕk'wĭth), Sir **George.** 1753–1823. English army officer and colonial governor; lieutenant general (1805); governor of Bermuda (1797), St. Vincent (1804), Barbados (1808); conquered Martinique (1809) and Guadaloupe (1810); commanded English troops in Ireland (1816–20). His brother Sir **Thomas Sydney** (1772–1831) served in Denmark (1807) and Peninsular campaign (1808–11); commander in chief at Bombay, India (1829); lieutenant general (1830). Their nephew **John Charles Beckwith** (1789–1862), an army officer; at Waterloo (1815); settled in Piedmont among Waldenses and endeavored to reawaken evangelical faith.

**Beckwith, James Carroll.** 1852–1917. American painter, b. Hannibal, Mo. Studied New York and Paris; kept studio with John Singer Sargent in Paris (1874–78). Among his best-known portraits are those of Theodore Roosevelt, Mark Twain, Paul du Chaillu.

**Beckx** (bĕks), **Pierre Jean.** 1795–1887. Belgian ecclesiast, b. Sichem. Entered Society of Jesus (1819); confessor to duke Ferdinand of Anhalt-Köthen; Jesuit procurator in Austria (1847); to Belgium (1848) on expulsion of Jesuits from Austria; rector of Jesuit college at Louvain; aided in re-establishing Jesuits in Austria; supported Cardinal Szcitowsky, Primate of Hungary, in successful effort to reinstate Jesuits and found novitiate at Tyrnau (Trnava). General of Society of Jesus (1853–84; resigned); influential adviser to Pope Pius IX. Author of *Der Monat Maria.*

**Becque** (bĕk), **Henry François.** 1837–1899. French dramatist, b. Paris. Author of *Les Corbeaux* (1882) and *La Parisienne* (1885) which marked rise of realistic or naturalistic school in the French drama.

**Béc'quer** (bĕ'kẽr), **Gustavo Adolfo.** 1836–1870. Spanish poet, b. Seville, of German descent; earned living at Madrid as hack writer and translator of foreign novels (c. 1854–70); author of the prose tales *Leyendas Españolas* and verse, including *Volverán las Oscuras*

*Golondrinas, Olas Gigantes que Os Rompéis Bramando,* and *Cuando Me Lo Contaron Sentí el Frío.*

**Bec'que·rel'** (bĕ'krĕl'). Family of French physicists, including: **Antoine César** (1788–1878); one of creators of science of electrochemistry; invented thermoelectric needle for determining internal bodily temperatures; investigated atmospheric electricity, galvanometers, and electric conductivity of metals. His son **Alexandre Edmond** (1820–1891); b. Paris; investigator especially of the solar spectrum and in fields of magnetism, electricity, and optics. Alexandre Edmond's son **Antoine Henri** (1852–1908); b. Paris; awarded (together with Pierre Curie and Madame Curie) the Nobel prize in physics (1903) for his investigations of uranium and radioactive substances; the rays emitted by a radioactive substance are known as "Becquerel rays."

**Be·daux'** (bĕ·dō'), **Charles Eugène.** 1887–1944. Efficiency engineer, b. France; to U.S. (c. 1908). Originator of the Bedaux, or point, system of wage payment.

**Bed'dard** (bĕd'ärd), **Frank Evers.** 1858–1925. English zoologist, b. Dudley. Naturalist to the *Challenger* expedition commission (1882–84); prosector of the Zoological Society of London (1884–1915). Investigated an order (Oligochaeta) of worms which includes the earthworms. Author of *Animal Coloration* (1892), *The Structure and Classification of Birds* (1898), *Mammalia* (in the *Cambridge Natural History,* 1902), etc.

**Bed'doe** (bĕd'ō), **John.** 1826–1911. English surgeon and anthropologist; B.A., London (1851); M.D., Edinburgh (1853); surgeon with army during Crimean War; author of *Stature and Bulk of Man in the British Isles* (1870), *The Races of Britain* (1886), etc.

**Bed'does** (bĕd'ōz), **Thomas.** 1760–1808. English physician and scientific writer. M.D., Oxon. (1786). m. (1794) Anna, sister of Maria Edgeworth. Established at Clifton a "pneumatic institution" for treatment of diseases by inhalation of gases (1798), with Humphry Davy as superintendent. His son **Thomas Lovell** (1803–1849), dramatist and poet, led a wandering life in Europe as a physician; wrote *The Bride's Tragedy* (pub. 1822) and continued revising *Death's Jest Book,* an incoherent macabre drama, from 1825 throughout his life.

**Bede** (bēd) *or* **Bae'da** (bē'dȧ) *or* **Be'da** (bē'dȧ), Saint. 673–735. English scholar, historian, and theologian; known since 9th century as "the Venerable Bede." Ordained (703); associated with monastery at Jarrow throughout life; taught Greek, Latin, Hebrew, and theology. Concluded (731) his ecclesiastical history of England, *Historia Ecclesiastica Gentis Anglorum.* Author of *Historia Abbatum,* a history of the abbots of Wearmouth and Jarrow, and of *De Natura Rerum,* on physical science. Made a Doctor of the Church by Pope Leo XIII.

**Bede, Cuthbert.** Pseudonym of Edward BRADLEY.

**Be·del'** (bĕ·dĕl'), **Maurice.** 1883–1954. French novelist; winner of Prix Goncourt (1927) with *Jérôme, 60° Latitude Nord;* author also of *Fascisme An VII, Zulfu, La Nouvelle Arcadie,* etc.

**Be·dell'** (bĕ·dĕl'), **Frederick.** 1868–1958. American physicist, b. Brooklyn, N.Y.; grad. Yale (1890). Professor of applied electricity, Cornell (1904–37); consulting physicist, Pasadena, Calif. Investigator of alternating electric currents and of aerodynamics.

**Bed'ford** (bĕd'fẽrd), Earls and dukes of. See JOHN OF LANCASTER, Jasper TUDOR, and RUSSELL family.

**Bedford, Francis.** 1799–1883. English bookbinder; assistant to the bookbinder Charles Lewis (1786–1836) and successor in his business; partner (1841–50) of John Clarke, who was skilled in binding books in tree-marbled calf; protégé of duke of Portland.

**Bedford,** Sir **Frederick George Denham.** 1838–1913. British naval officer; served in Crimean War; lord of the admiralty (1889–92, 1895); commander in chief, North American station (1895–1903); governor of Western Australia (1903–09).

**Bé'dier'** (bā'dyā'), **Charles Marie Joseph.** 1864–1938. French author and scholar in medieval French literature, b. Paris. Published prose adaptation of *Roman de Tristan et Yseult* (1900), a critical edition of *Chanson de Roland* (1921), and a study entitled *La Formation des Légendes Épiques* (1908–13), advancing the theory that the medieval epic cycles developed along the routes followed by pilgrims.

**Bed·mar'** (bāth·mär'), Marqués **de. Alfonso de la Cue'va** (thā lä kwā'vä). 1572–1655. Spanish politician; ambassador to Venice (1607); formed unsuccessful conspiracy against Venetian Republic (1618; theme of Otway's *Venice Preserved*); president, Council of Flanders (1622); created cardinal (1622); returned to Spain and was made bishop of Oviedo.

**Be'dos' de Celles'** (bā'dôs' dē sĕl'), **François.** 1706–1779. French Benedictine monk; author of *L'Art du Facteur d'Orgues* (3 vols., 1766–78), a work on organ construction.

**Bed'well** (bĕd'wĕl; -wĕl), **William.** 1561?–1632. Father of Arabic studies in England; educ. Cambridge; translator of mathematical works, including one on use of carpenter's square; compiler of an Arabic lexicon; one of translators of King James Bible (1604–11).

**Bee'be** (bē'bē), **Charles William.** 1877–1962. American naturalist and explorer, b. Brooklyn, N.Y. Grad. Columbia (1898). Curator of ornithology (from 1899) and director of department of scientific research, N.Y. Zoological Society; originator of the collection of living birds in the N.Y. Zoological Park. Headed scientific expeditions to Nova Scotia, Mexico, S. America, the Himalayas, Borneo, etc. Investigator of land and water vertebrates in neotropical countries and of marine life in Bermuda waters. Author of *Two Bird Lovers in Mexico* (1905), *Jungle Peace* (1918), *Galápagos, World's End* (1923), *Jungle Days* (1925), *The Arcturus Adventure* (1925), *Pheasants—Their Lives and Homes* (1926), *Beneath Tropic Seas* (1928), *Half Mile Down* (1934), *Book of Bays* (1942), etc. See Elswyth THANE.

**Beebe, Lucius Morris.** 1902–1966. American journalist, b. Wakefield, Mass. Joined staff of New York *Herald-Tribune* (1929); author of *Fallen Stars* (1921), *Corydon and Other Poems* (1924), *François Villon* (1925), *Boston and the Boston Legend* (1935), etc.

**Bee'cham** (bē'chăm), **Thomas.** 1820–1907. English manufacturer of pills (formula patented 1847); retired (1895), and was succeeded by his son Sir **Joseph** (1848–1916), who was father of the musician Sir Thomas Beecham (*q.v.*).

**Beecham,** Sir **Thomas.** 1879–1961. English conductor and impresario; son of Sir Joseph Beecham, manufacturer of Beecham's pills. Initiated (1906) and conducted (1907–09) New Symphony and Beecham Symphony concert orchestras in London, introducing works of Frederick Delius; produced and conducted operas, many for the first time in London, as Strauss's *Salome;* associated with first appearance of Russian ballet (1911–12); produced Russian operas (1913), in which Chaliapin made his first English appearances; added (1914) to repertoire of opera and ballet *Prince Igor, Coq d'Or, Daphnis and Chloë,* among others. Suspended operatic production because of financial loss (1920); returned (1920) to orchestral conducting of symphonies; many tours in U.S. and elsewhere.

**Bé'e·che Ar·güel'lo** (bā'ā·chā är·gwā'yō), **Octavio.**

1866– . Costa Rican jurist and diplomat; minister to U.S. (1920–22); minister of foreign relations (1930–31); president, Supreme Court of Justice (1935).

**Bee'cher** (bē'chẽr), **Charles Emerson.** 1856–1904. American paleontologist, b. Dunkirk, N.Y. Curator and professor, Yale (from 1888); known chiefly for contributions on development and structure of trilobites and brachiopods.

**Beecher, Henry Ward.** 1813–1887. American clergyman, b. Litchfield, Conn. Son of Lyman Beecher. Pastor, Plymouth Congregational Church, Brooklyn, N.Y. (1847–87); powerful and convincing speaker of wide influence throughout country. Against slavery; favored woman suffrage. Charged (1874) by Theodore Tilton with adultery with Mrs. Tilton; a trial (1875) lasting six months resulted in a jury disagreement, but the scandal overshadowed his last years. Plymouth Church remained loyal to him; lectured widely throughout country. Died suddenly, March 8, 1887. Elected to American Hall of Fame (1900).

**Beecher, Lyman.** 1775–1863. American Presbyterian clergyman, b. New Haven, Conn. Held pastorates in Boston (1826–32) and Cincinnati (1832–42). President, Lane Theological Seminary, Cincinnati (1832–52); accused by conservative groups of heresy; acquitted by synod. Among his thirteen children were: **Catharine Esther** (1800–1878); conducted girls' schools in Hartford, Conn. (1824–32) and Cincinnati (1832–37); propagandist for female higher education and antisuffragist. **Edward** (1803–1895); Congregational clergyman and educator; founded *The Congregationalist* (1849). **Harriet Elizabeth** (see Harriet Beecher STOWE). **Henry Ward** (see Henry Ward BEECHER). **Thomas Kinnicut** (1824–1900); Congregational clergyman at Elmira, N.Y. (1854–1900); pioneer in "institutional church" movement.

**Bee'chey** (bē'chĭ), Sir **William.** 1753–1839. English painter. Made portrait painter to Queen Charlotte (1793); his works include *Brother and Sister* (Louvre) and, his best, *Cavalry Review in Hyde Park* (Kensington Palace, London). His son **Frederick William** (1796–1856), rear admiral and geographer, accompanied Franklin's scientific polar expedition (1818) and Parry's (1819); surveyed coasts of North Africa (1821–23), South America (1835), and Ireland (1837); author of geographical works.

**Beeding, Francis.** Pseudonym; see John Leslie PALMER.

**Beek, David.** See David BECK.

**Beer** (bēr), **George Louis.** 1872–1920. American historian, b. on Staten Island, N.Y. Successful tobacco merchant (1893–1903); retired to devote himself to historical study. Author of *British Colonial Policy, 1754–1765* (1907), *The Origins of the British Colonial System, 1578–1600* (1908), *The English-Speaking Peoples* (1917), etc.

**Beer** (bār), **Jakob Liebmann.** Real name of Giacomo MEYERBEER.

**Beer** (bār), **Michael.** 1800–1833. German playwright; brother of Giacomo Meyerbeer (*q.v.*). His most successful play was the tragedy *Strensee* (1829), for which Meyerbeer wrote an overture and incidental music.

**Beer** (bēr), **Thomas.** 1889–1940. American author, b. Council Bluffs, Iowa. B.A., Yale (1911); studied law, Columbia (1911–13). In World War I, served in France as lieutenant. Author of *Fair Rewards* (1922), *Stephen Crane* (1923), *Sandoval* (1924), *The Mauve Decade* (1926), *The Road to Heaven* (1928), *Hanna* (1929), *Mrs. Egg and Other Barbarians* (1933).

**Beer** (bār), **Wilhelm.** 1797–1850. Brother of Giacomo Meyerbeer (*q.v.*). German banker and astronomer. Established an observatory in the Tiergarten of Berlin, and (with J. H. von Mädler) made studies of Mars and the moon (1828–40); made a detailed map of the moon (1834–36).

**Beer'bohm** (bēr'bōm), **Max.** 1872–1956. English critic, essayist, and caricaturist; half brother of Sir Herbert Beerbohm Tree (*q.v.*). Educ. Oxford. Succeeded G. B. Shaw as dramatic critic of *Saturday Review* (1898). m. (1910) Florence Kahn of Memphis, Tenn.; resident in Rapallo, Italy (from 1910). Author of essays, *The Happy Hypocrite* (1897), *More* (1899), *And Even Now* (1920), *Variety of Things* (1928); *Zuleika Dobson*, his one novel, a satirical story of an adventuress at Oxford (1911); *A Christmas Garland*, a collection of parodies of contemporary authors (1912); and among the volumes of pictorial caricatures, *Twenty-five Gentlemen* (1896), *The Poet's Corner* (1904), *Rossetti and His Circle* (1922), *Observations* (1925).

**Beerbohm Tree,** Sir **Herbert.** See TREE.

**Bee'ren·brouck** (bā'rĕn·brouk), **Charles Joseph Marie Ruys** (rois) **de.** 1874?–1936. Dutch statesman; leader of Catholic party; three times premier of the Netherlands.

**Beer'-Hof'mann** (bār'hōf'män; -hôf'-), **Richard.** 1866–1945. Austrian poet, playwright, and novelist; author of *Jakobs Traum* (1918), *Der Junge David* (1934), *Vorspiel zum König David* (1936), etc.

**Beer'naert** (bār'närt), **Auguste Marie François.** 1829–1912. Belgian statesman, b. Ostend. Minister of public works (1873–78), agriculture and industry (1884); president of the council and minister of finance (1884–94); president of Chamber of Deputies (1895). Member of International Peace Conference (1899, 1907); recipient, with Baron d'Estournelles de Constant, of Nobel peace prize (1909).

**Beers** (bērz), **Clifford Whittingham.** 1876–1943. American mental hygienist, b. New Haven, Conn. Ph.B., Yale (1897). In business, New York City (1898–1900, 1904–06). Suffered mental breakdown; entered sanitarium; made careful study of his own case and of his mental recovery; published famous book, *A Mind That Found Itself* (1908; 24th ed., 1939). Devoted himself thereafter to promotion of mental hygiene movement; founded (1908) Connecticut Society for Mental Hygiene, first society of its kind; founded National Commission for Mental Hygiene (1909), American Foundation for Mental Hygiene (1928), International Commission for Mental Hygiene (1930), and International Foundation for Mental Hygiene (1931). Awarded gold medal (1933) of National Institute of Social Sciences for "distinguished services for the benefit of mankind."

**Beers, Ethel Lynn.** *Nee* **Ethelinda Eliot.** 1827–1879. American poet, b. Goshen, N.Y.; m. (1846) William H. Beers. Author of *All Quiet along the Potomac* (1879).

**Beers, Henry Augustin.** 1847–1926. American educator, b. Buffalo, N.Y. Taught English literature at Yale, (1871–1916); professor emeritus (1916–26). Authority on English romanticism of 18th and 19th centuries.

**Beers** (bārs), **Jan van.** 1821–1888. Flemish poet; author of verse written in Flemish, including *Dreams of Youth* (1853), *The Illusions of Life* (1859), *Sentiment and Life* (1869), etc.

**Bees'ly** (bēz'lĭ), **Edward Spencer.** 1831–1915. English historian. Educ. Wadham College, Oxford; led, with Frederic Harrison and John Henry Bridges, English Positivist movement; professor of history, U. of London (1859–1889); editor, *Positivist Review* (1893). Author of translations and biography of Comte.

**Bees'ton** (bēs'tŭn), Sir **William.** fl. 1702. British colonial administrator; to Jamaica (1660); lieutenant governor of the colony (1693–1702).

**Bee'tho'ven** (bā'tō'vĕn; *Ger.* bāt'hō'-), **Ludwig van** (vän; fän). 1770–1827. German composer, of Flemish descent, b. in Bonn. Received early musical education from his father and from Neefe. Held various positions (1783–92) as second court organist, opera band conductor, etc.; formed intimate and lasting friendships in exclusive circles of Bonn, notably with Count Ferdinand von Waldstein and von Breuning family. In Vienna briefly (1787) to study with Mozart; sent again to Vienna by elector of Cologne (1792); studied with Haydn, Albrechtsberger, and Salieri. Resident in Vienna (from 1792) as pianist and composer; gained many influential friends and patrons, including Prince Lichnowsky, Prince Lobkowitz, Ferdinand Ries, etc. Made public debut as pianist in his concerto in C major (1795) and published three trios for piano, violin, and violoncello (opus 1); appeared for first time in his own concert 1800. Suffered from defective hearing (from c. 1798); became totally deaf (c. 1819); last years clouded by illness and worry. In his sonatas and symphonies, developed musical forms of his predecessors, as in his use of a greater variety of key relationship in change from one movement to another, lengthening of the introduction, insertion of chorus in the finale (as in ninth symphony), and development of third movement from a minuet to a scherzo. His instrumental compositions include 9 symphonies (1800–23), esp. the 3d, or *Eroica* (1804), the 5th (1808), the 6th, or *Pastoral* (1808), and the 9th, or *Choral* (1823); numerous sonatas for piano solo (*The Moonlight Sonata, Pathétique*) and for piano and other instruments (*The Kreutzer Sonata*, dedicated to Rodolphe Kreutzer); 5 concertos for piano and orchestra (1795–1809); a violin concerto in D (1806); 21 sets of variations for piano solo; string trios and quartets, quintets, etc.; overtures; minuets, including the *Minuet in G;* music to *Prometheus* (1801) and to *Egmont* (1810); the orchestral fantasia *The Battle of Vittoria* (1813; called the Battle Symphony). His vocal compositions include the oratorio *Mount of Olives* (1803), the opera *Fidelio* (1805; revised 1806 and 1814), 2 masses (C major, 1807, and *Missa Solemnis* in D, 1824), cantatas, canons, songs, etc.

**Beets** (bāts), **Nikolaas.** 1814–1903. Dutch poet and writer. Professor of theology, Utrecht (1874–84). Author of the poems *Korenbloemen* (1853), *Najaarsbladen* (1881), etc.; prose writings *José* (1834), *De Masquerade* (1836), and *Camera Obscura* (1839), a collection of tales and sketches of life and manners in Holland written under pseudonym **Hil'de·brand** (hĭl'dĕ·bränt); literary criticism and works on theology, etc.

**Bef'froy' de Rei'gny'** (bā'frwȧ' dĕ rā'nyē'), **Louis Abel.** *Pseudonym* **Cou'sin' Jacques'** (kōō'zăN' zhäk'). 1757–1811. French writer of farces.

**Be'ga** (bā'gȧ), **Cornelis.** 1620–1664. Dutch painter and etcher; pupil of Adriaen van Ostade. Portrayed humorous scenes from low peasant life including *Peasants' Concert* (now in Amsterdam Museum) and *Rustic Interior* (Louvre).

**Be'ga·rel'li** (bā'gä·rĕl'lē), **Antonio.** 1498?–1565. Italian terra-cotta sculptor, b. Modena; chief master of Emilian school in high Renaissance period. His works include a Pietà in Sant'Agostino, *Madonna with the Christ Child* in Galleria Estense, *Madonna di Piazza* in Museo Civico, *Descent from the Cross* in San Francisco (all in Modena), and statues in San Benedetto Pò.

**Be'gas** (bā'gäs), **Karl.** 1794–1854. German religious, historical, and portrait painter; adherent successively of Nazarene (German Pre-Raphaelite), romanticist, and realist schools. Studied at Paris with Gros (1813–22) and in Italy (1822–24) as court painter to king of Prussia; professor, Royal Academy, Berlin (from 1824). His works include frescoes in various Berlin churches; *Christ on the Mount of Olives, Baptism of Christ, Tobias and the Archangel, Henry IV at Canossa, Lorelei, Die Mohrenwäsche;* and portraits of Jacob Grimm, Meyerbeer, von Humboldt, and other contemporaries. His son **Oskar** (1828–1883) was a portrait, genre, and historical painter; painted *Descent from the Cross* for Michaeliskirche, Berlin; later works include landscapes, portraits of Peter von Cornelius, Crown Prince Frederick, General von Moltke, and William I, and mural decorations in Berlin Rathaus. Another son, **Reinhold** (1831–1911), was a sculptor of the realistic school; studied under Rauch, Berlin; conducted master studio at academy (1876–1903); his sculptures include *Pan Consoling a Deserted Nymph,* colossal group *Borussia* surmounting Berlin Bourse, Schiller monument in Berlin, *Mercury and Psyche* (National Gallery, Berlin), monument of Alexander von Humboldt, portrait busts of William I, Frederick III, William II, Bismarck, and Moltke, marble sarcophagi of Frederick III and his empress (in Potsdam), and a bronze group *Germania* surmounting Reichstag building. Another son, **Adalbert** (1836–1888), was a painter and etcher, known esp. for his copies of old masters and portraits of women. Another son, **Karl** (1845–1916), was a sculptor; created esp. genre groups, portrait busts, and decorative monuments, including monument commemorating Franco-Prussian war (1898; in Kassel), and *Boar Hunt* (Berlin Tiergarten).

**Beg'bie** (bĕg'bĭ), **Harold.** 1871–1929. English journalist and author of novels, largely didactic, and biographies, including one of General William Booth.

**Begg** (bĕg), **Alexander.** 1839–1897. Canadian pioneer and historian, b. Quebec. Early settler and merchant in Manitoba; author of *The Creation of Manitoba* (1871), *Ten Years in Winnipeg* (1879), *History of the North-West* (3 vols., 1894–95), etc.

**Bé'gin'** (bā'zhăN'), **Louis Nazaire.** 1840–1925. Canadian cardinal. B.A., Laval U., Quebec; professor of theology, Laval U. (1868–84); bishop of Chicoutimi (1888); coadjutor to Cardinal Taschereau (1891); archbishop of Quebec (1898); led a campaign of social action (1907 ff.); created cardinal (1914).

**Be·gin** (bĕ·gēn', bā'gĭn), **Menahem.** 1913– . Israeli politician. Prime minister (1977– ); awarded (with Anwar el-Sadat) Nobel prize for peace (1978).

**Bé'gon'** (bā'gôN'), **Michel.** 1638–1710. French administrator in French West Indies, Canada, Rochefort, and La Rochelle; patron of science. The plant genus *Begonia* named in his honor.

**Bé'guine'** (bā'gēn'), **Léonard Michel.** 1855–1929. French sculptor. Awarded medal of honor (1926) for his statue *Victoire 1918.* Other works include *David Vainqueur* (in bronze), *Charmeuse* (in marble), *De Longperrier* (a portrait bust).

**Be·ha'ghel** (bȧ·hä'gĕl), **Otto.** 1854–1936. German philologist; professor at Giessen (from 1888); editor in chief (1888–92) of *Germania,* a philological magazine; author of books on German language, including *Deutsche Syntax* (4 vols., 1923–32).

**Be'haim** (bā'hīm) *or* **Bö'heim** (bû'hīm), **Martin.** 1459?–?1507. German navigator and geographer, b. Nuremberg. Traveled through Europe as merchant (1476–84); to Portugal (1484), said to have introduced various improvements in nautical instruments there; constructed (1492) a terrestrial globe, still preserved at Nuremberg, showing erroneous geographical conceptions previous to the discovery of America.

**Be'haim** (bā'hīm) *or* **Be'ham** (bā'häm) *or* **Be'heim** (bā'hīm), **Michel.** 1416–1474. German Meistersinger,

b. Sulzbach. Soldier and court singer in Hungary, Norway, the Palatinate, and elsewhere. Author of *Buch von den Wienern* (pub. 1843) dealing with siege (1462) of imperial palace at Vienna, and of short historical poems, esp. of Turkey and Hungary, spiritual and secular songs.

**Bé'haine'** (bā'än'), **René.** 1880–1966. French novelist, b. at Vervins. Author of *Histoire d'une Société*, in successive volumes (from 1899), including *La Conquête de la Vie, Les Survivants, Si Jeunesse Savait, L'Enchantement du Feu, Avec les Yeux de l'Esprit.*

**Bé'hal'** (bā'äl'), **Auguste.** 1859–1941. French chemist; professor, U. of Paris and École de Pharmacie. Author of treatises on organic chemistry.

**Be'ham** (bā'häm), **Hans Sebald.** 1500–1550. German painter, engraver, and woodcutter; one of "Little Masters"; settled in Frankfurt (1531); works include miniatures for two prayer books of Cardinal Albert of Mainz, four paintings (on a table top) from the life of David, hundreds of woodcuts designed esp. as illustrations for history books and Bibles, 252 copper engravings, and 18 etchings. His brother and pupil, **Bar'thel** (bär'tĕl) (1502–1540), likewise a painter and engraver and one of the "Little Masters," was court painter to Duke William IV of Bavaria in Munich; works include 17 portraits of Bavarian dukes and more than 90 engravings.

**Be'han** (bē'ăn), **Brendan Francis.** 1923–1964. Irish author and playwright; wrote *The Quare Fellow* (1954), *The Hostage* (1958), *Borstal Boy* (1958), etc.

**Beha ud-Din.** See BAHA AL-DIN.

**Behm** (bām), **Ernst.** 1830–1884. German geographer and statistician, b. Gotha. Founder (1866) and editor (1866–78) of *Das Geographische Jahrbuch;* editor in chief (from 1878) of *Petermanns Mitteilungen;* statistician (from 1876) of *Der Gothaische Hofkalender*, the Almanach de Gotha.

**Behmen, Jakob.** See Jakob BÖHME.

**Behn** (bān; bĕn), **Aph'ra** *or* **Af'ra** (ăf'rȧ) *or* **Aph'a·ra** (ăf'ȧ·rȧ) *or* **Ay'fa·ra** (ā'fȧ·rȧ), *nee* **Johnson.** 1640–1689. English dramatist and novelist. Lived from childhood (to 1658) in Surinam, West Indies; met Oroonoko, "the royal slave"; m. merchant named Behn (d. 1666); served as spy in Antwerp; unrewarded; imprisoned for debt. First English woman professional writer; author of vivacious, rather coarse comedies including *Forc'd Marriage* (1671), *The Rover* (1677), *False Count* (1682), a satirical play, *The Roundheads*, attacking Puritans, of poems and translations, of novels and tales, including *Oroonoko* (c. 1678).

**Behnc'ke** (bāng'kĕ), **Paul.** 1866–1937. German admiral; took part in the battle of Jutland (1916); as chief of naval staff (1920–24), rebuilt German navy.

**Behr'end** (bâr'ĕnd), **Bernard Arthur.** 1875–1932. American electrical engineer, b. in Switzerland. Designer of electric machinery and inventor of electric devices. Author of *The Induction Motor* (1900), etc.

**Behr'ends** (bâr'ĕn(d)z), **Adolphus Julius Frederick.** 1839–1900. American clergyman, b. Nijmegen, Holland; to Ohio at age of five. In Baptist ministry (to 1876) and Congregationalist ministry (from 1876).

**Beh'rens** (bā'rĕns), **Peter.** 1868–1940. German architect and artist, b. in Hamburg. Developed modern industrial architectural style, as in General Electric Co. structures in Berlin. Designed workers' apartment buildings in Vienna and abbey of St. Peter at Salzburg.

**Beh'ring** (*Dan.* bā'rĕng; *Angl.* bēr'ĭng, bĕr'-, bâr'-). Variant of BERING.

**Beh'ring** (bā'rĭng), **Emil von.** 1854–1917. German bacteriologist. Professor, Marburg (from 1895); pioneer in immunology. Worked with Shibasaburo Kitazato in Robert Koch's laboratory in Berlin. Discovered diphtheria antitoxin and bovovaccine, protective against tuberculosis in cattle. Awarded 1901 Nobel prize in medicine. See Pierre ROUX.

**Behr'man** (bâr'măn), **Samuel Nathaniel.** 1893–1973. American playwright, b. Worcester, Mass. A.B., Harvard (1916). Author of plays including *The Second Man* (1927), *Serena Blandish* (1928), *Brief Moment* (1932), *Biography* (1933), *Love Story* (1934), *End of Summer* (1936), *Wine of Choice* (1938), *No Time for Comedy* (1939), *The Talley Method* (1940), *Fanny* (1954).

**Beil'by** (bēl'bĭ), Sir **George Thomas.** 1850–1924. Scottish industrial chemist. Improved process of distillation of shale oil and invented a synthetic process of manufacturing alkaline cyanides. Advanced original hypothesis on crystalline and vitreous states of solids, in *Aggregation and Flow of Solids* (1921). As director (1917–24) of Fuel Research Board, studied production of oil from coal by carbonization.

**Beil'stein** (bīl'shtīn), **Friedrich Konrad.** 1838–1906. German chemist, b. in Russia. Professor, Institute of Technology, St. Petersburg (from 1866). Author of *Handbuch der Organischen Chemie* (Hamburg, 1880–83), which describes thousands of organic compounds.

**Bein** (bīn), **Albert.** 1903– . Playwright, b. Kishinev, Rumania; to U.S. as a child; settled in Chicago; author of *Little Ol' Boy* (1933), *Let Freedom Ring* (1935; based on Grace Lumpkin's novel, *To Make My Bread*), *Heavenly Express* (1940).

**Beis'sel** (bī'sĕl), **Johann Conrad.** 1690–1768. Clergyman, b. Eberbach, Germany; to Pennsylvania (1720). Founded (c. 1730) at Ephrata, Pa., "Economy," a community of Solitary Brethren of the Community of Seventh-Day Baptists (Dunkers). His hymns and melodies have influenced American hymnology.

**Beit** (bīt), **Alfred** (1853–1906) and his brother Sir **Otto** (1865–1930). British financiers and philanthropists; sons of a Hamburg merchant. Alfred, in association with Cecil Rhodes in South African diamond fields, amassed enormous fortune; both brothers trustees under Rhodes's will to carry out South African projects, including a university.

**Beith** (bēth), **John Hay.** *Pseudonym* **Ian Hay.** 1876–1952. Scottish novelist and playwright. Grad. Cambridge (1898). Officer in Argyll and Sutherland Highlanders, B.E.F. Early novels include *Pip* (1907), *A Man's Man* (1909), *A Safety Match* (1911), *The First Hundred Thousand* (1915), *Carrying On* (1917), *The Last Million* (1918), *Paid, With Thanks* (1925).

**Bé'jart'** (bā'zhȧr'). Family of French actors in comedy, including **Madeleine** (1618–1672), **Joseph** (1622–1659), **Louis** (1630–1678), and **Armande Grésinde Claire Élisabeth** (1642–1700), wife of Molière (1662 until his death in 1673) and of the actor Guérin d'Estriché. All acted in the plays of Molière.

**Beke** (bēk), **Charles Tilstone.** 1800–1874. English geographer. Explorer of Abyssinia; first to determine course of Blue Nile; explored alleged position of Mt. Sinai. Wrote *Discoveries of Sinai in Arabia and of Midian* (1878).

**Be'ke'sy** (bā'kā'shĭ; -kĕ-), **Georg von.** 1899–1972. Hungarian-born American physiologist. To the U.S. (1949). Awarded Nobel prize in physiology and medicine (1961).

**Bekh'te·rev** (byāK'tyĭ·ryĕf), **Vladimir Mikhailovich.** 1857–1927. Russian neuropathologist; founded psychoneurological institute in St. Petersburg (1907); author of *The Nerve Currents in Brain and Spinal Cord* (1882), *The Functions of the Nervous Centers* (1909), *Nervous System Diseases* (1911), etc.

**Bek'ker** (bĕk'ĕr), **August Immanuel.** 1785–1871. German classical scholar and philologist. Professor, Berlin (from 1810); prepared critical editions of Plato, Aristotle, Photius, and other Greek authors; edited Byzantine, Provençal, and Old French authors; wrote *Anecdota Graeca* (1814–21), etc.

**Bekker, Balthasar.** 1634–1698. Dutch Protestant theologian. Pastor, Amsterdam (1679–92); suspected of Cartesianism and deposed (1692) following publication of his *De Betoverde Wereld* (1691) condemning belief in witchcraft, the devil, and magical powers.

**Bekker, Elizabeth,** *called* **Betje.** 1738–1804. Dutch novelist; m. Adriaan Wolff (d. 1777). Coauthor (with Aagje Deken) of *De Historie van Mejuffrouw Sara Burgerhart* (1782), *De Historie van den Heer Willem Levend* (1784–85), *Brieven van Abraham Blankaart* (1787–89), *Historie van Mejuffrouw Cornelia Wildschut* (1793–96); collection of poems (3 vols., 1785–86).

**Bekri, al-.** See al-BAKRI.

**Bél** (bāl), **Mátyás.** *Lat.* **Matthias Be'li·us** (bē'lĭ·ŭs). 1684–1749. Hungarian scholar; appointed historiographer to Emperor Charles VI; author of *Notitia Hungariae Novae Historico-Geographica*, dedicated to the emperor.

**Bé'la** (bā'lŏ). Name of four kings of Hungary of the Árpád dynasty, especially:

**Béla III.** d. 1196. King (1173–96). Educ. Constantinople; favored and introduced Byzantine customs and culture; m., as 2d wife, Margaret, sister of Philip Augustus of France; fought two wars (1181–88, 1190–91), only partly successful, against Venice to recover Dalmatia; aided Isaac II Angelus against Bulgarians.

**Béla IV.** 1206–1270. King (1235–70). Son of Andrew II (*q.v.*). Inherited much-disturbed kingdom from his father; spent most of reign in attempt to restore peace and order; m. Maria, daughter of Nicaean emperor, Theodore Lascaris. First and greatest event of reign was his overwhelming defeat in great Mongol invasion (1237–41; see BATU KHAN), all Hungary being overrun and devastated; forced to flee to Adriatic; after Mongol withdrawal, defeated (1246) Frederick of Austria, last of Babenbergs, who had seized western provinces of Hungary; fought off other foreign enemies (Serbs, Tatars); engaged in war (1265–70) with Ottokar of Bohemia over possession of Styria. Succeeded by his son Stephen V.

**Bel'a·fon'te** (bĕl'ȧ·fŏn'tē), **Harry.** 1927– . Am. singer and actor, b. New York City.

**Belaiev.** Incorrect variant of BELYAEV.

**Be·lain'** (bē·lăN'), **Pierre.** Sieur **d'Es'nam'buc'** (dā'năN'bük') *or* **d'É'nam'buc'.** 1570?–1636. French privateer; founded first French colonies in West Indies, in Saint Christopher (c. 1625), later, at Martinique and Guadeloupe.

**Béla Kun.** See Béla KUN.

**Be'lal·cá'zar** (bā'läl·kä'thär; -sär) *or* **Be'nal·cá'zar** (bā'näl-), **Sebastián de.** *Real name* **Sebastián Mo·ya'no** (mō·yä'nō). 1495?–?1550. Spanish conquistador, b. in Estremadura; to America (1519); conquered Nicaragua (1524); participated in Pizarro's conquest of Peru (1532); defeated Inca chief Rumiñahui at Quito (1533); established cities of Quito and Guayaquil; invaded Popayán (now southwestern Colombia) in search for El Dorado; governor of Popayán (1538).

**Be·las'co** (bĕ·lăs'kō), **David.** 1854–1931. American playwright and producer, b. San Francisco. Stage manager, Madison Square Theater, New York City (1880–87) and later of the Lyceum; then, owner and manager of Belasco Theater, New York City. Widely known because of his success in developing talents of actors and in his methods of stage setting and lighting. Author of or collaborator in: *May Blossom* (1884), *Lord Chumley* (1887), *The Heart of Maryland* (1895), *The Girl of the Golden West* (1905), *The Return of Peter Grimm* (1911), *Laugh, Clown, Laugh* (1923), etc. Among notable actors appearing in plays produced by him were E. H. Sothern, Mrs. Leslie Carter, Blanche Bates, David Warfield, Ina Claire.

**Be'la·ún'de y Diez Can·se'co** (bā'lä·ōōn'dā ē thyās kän·sā'kō), **Víctor Andrés.** 1883–1966. Peruvian diplomat, scholar, and writer, b. Arequipa; known in U.S. as one of foremost exponents of Pan-Americanism.

**Bel'cher** (bĕl'chẽr), Sir **Edward.** 1799–1877. English naval officer. Employed on coastal surveys of Africa, western America, East Indies (1830–47); commanded Arctic expedition in search of Sir John Franklin (1852); admiral (1872). Author of narratives of voyages.

**Belcher, James,** *called* **Jem.** 1781–1811. English prize fighter. Successful until he lost an eye (1803); became publican. A kind of handkerchief is called *belcher* after him.

**Belcher, Jonathan.** 1682–1757. American colonial governor, b. Cambridge, Mass. Governor of Massachusetts and New Hampshire (1730–41). Governor of New Jersey (1747–57).

**Bel'ci·kow'ski** (bĕl'tsē·kôf'skē), **Adam.** 1839–1909. Polish essayist and playwright, b. in Cracow. Author of literary studies and esp. historical dramas, including *King Don Juan* (1869), *Hunyadi* (1870), *The Oath* (1878), *King Boleslav the Bold* (1882).

**Bel·cre'di** (bĕl·krā'dē), Count **Richard.** 1823–1902. Austrian statesman. Governor of Bohemia (1864); succeeded Schmerling as minister of state and prime minister (1865–67), favoring strongly conservative policy; president of administrative court of justice (1881–95).

**Be'lesme'** *or* **Bel'lême'** (bĕ'lâm'), **Robert of.** Earl of **Shrews'bur·y** (shrōōz'bẽr·ĭ; shrōz'-). fl. 1098. Supported Robert's rebellion against William I (1077); revolted against Henry I (1102) and was banished from England; returned as ambassador of king of France (1112); was thereupon seized, tried for old crimes, and imprisoned for life.

**Bel'gio·io'so** (bāl'jō·yō'sō), Principessa **di. Cristina Tri·vul'zio** (trē·vōōl'tsyō). 1808–1871. Italian patriot and author. Lived in Paris (1830–48); founded and edited *La Gazzetta Italiana* in behalf of Italian nationalism. Raised at own expense volunteer corps for Charles Albert (c. 1848). Exiled (1849–61). Founded (after 1861) *Italia* and *Perseveranza.* Among her works are *Souvenirs d'Exil* (1850), *Histoire de la Maison de Savoie* (1860), *Réflexions sur l'État Actuel de l'Italie et sur son Avenir* (1869).

**Bel'grand'** (bĕl'grăN'), **Marie François Eugène.** 1810–1878. French hydrographic engineer; installed sewerage system in Paris and built reservoirs of Montsouris. Author of *Les Travaux Souterrains de Paris, les Eaux, les Aqueducs* (1875).

**Bel·gra'no** (bĕl·grä'nō), **Manuel.** 1770–1820. Argentine general and patriot; in command of northern forces, defeated royalists in battles of Tucumán (1812) and Salta (1813); was defeated (1813) in campaigns in north (Bolivia) and replaced (1814) by San Martín.

**Belhaven,** Barons. See under HAMILTON family.

**Be'li'dor'** (bā'lē'dôr'), **Bernard Fo'rest' de** (fō'rĕ' dē). 1693?–1761. French engineer; author of *Cours de Mathématiques, Traité des Fortifications,* etc.

**Be·lin'ski** (byĭ·lyēn'skû·ĭ; *Angl.* -skĭ), **Vissarion Grigorievich.** 1811–1848. Russian literary critic, son of army surgeon. Educ. Moscow U.; member of intimate group of "idealist" young authors; wrote first literary criticism in magazine articles (1834); edited Moscow *Observer* (1838–39). To St. Petersburg (1839); contributed to literary journals; passed through several phases

(1840–48) of criticism—realism, didacticism, enthusiasm for art, etc.; wrote series of long essays on great writers of Russian literature. His writings (complete works, 12 vols., 1859–62) form foundation of Russian literary criticism.

**Bel'i·sar'i·us** (bĕl'ĭ·sâr'ĭ·ŭs). 505?–565. General of Eastern Roman Empire, b. in Illyria. Served under Emperor Justinian I. Soldier in early youth in eastern armies (529–532). m. (531) Antonina, favorite of Empress Theodora. Saved Justinian by suppressing Nika riot (532). Led expedition that overthrew Vandal kingdom in Africa (533–534). Sent by emperor to subdue Goths in Italy; conquered Sicily (535) and southern Italy (536–537); occupied Rome (536) and defended it for a year (537–538); seized Ravenna (540). Led forces against Persians (541–542). Sent again to Italy (544–548) but with inadequate forces and without Justinian's full support; replaced by Narses (548). In Constantinople in retirement (548–559). Repelled barbarian invaders (559). In later years in disfavor.

**Belisha, Leslie Hore-.** See HORE-BELISHA.

**Bel'jame'** (bĕl'zhám'), **Alexandre.** 1842–1906. French educator; author of *Le Public et les Hommes de Lettres en Angleterre au XVIIIe Siècle;* editor of critical texts of certain of Shakespeare's plays and of poems by Shelley and Tennyson.

**Bel'knap** (bĕl'năp), **Jeremy,** *orig.* **Jeremiah.** 1744–1798. American Congregational clergyman, b. Boston. Author of *History of New Hampshire* (3 vols., 1784, 1791, 1792); *American Biography* (2 vols., 1794, 1798).

**Belknap, William Worth.** 1829–1890. American army officer and politician, b. Newburgh, N.Y. Served through Civil War; brigadier general (from 1864). U.S. secretary of war in Grant's cabinet (1869); impeached for malfeasance in office (1876); resigned.

**Bell** (bĕl), **Acton, Currer,** *and* **Ellis.** Pseudonyms respectively of Anne, Charlotte, and Emily BRONTË.

**Bell, Alexander Melville.** 1819–1905. Educator, b. Edinburgh, Scotland. A teacher of science of correct speech (1843 ff.); developed idea of a physiological alphabet which would present visually the articulating position of the vocal organs for each sound. Moved to Washington, D.C. (1881); naturalized (1897). Author of *Visible Speech: the Science of Universal Alphabetics* (1867), *The Principles of Elocution, The Standard Elocutionist.* His son **Alexander Graham** (1847–1922), b. Edinburgh, came to U.S. (1871) as teacher of speech for the deaf; naturalized (1882). Developed telephone (1873–76; patented 1876, 1877); cf. Elisha GRAY and Johann P. REIS. Invented photophone, which transmitted first wireless telephone message (June 3, 1880), induction balance and telephone probe for detection of bullets in human body (1881), and recorder for Edison's phonograph; solved (with Langley *et al.*) problem of stability of balance in a flying machine; founded Volta Bureau for increase of knowledge relating to deaf. Elected to American Hall of Fame (1950).

**Bell, Andrew.** 1753–1832. Scottish clergyman and educator. While superintendent of an orphanage in Madras, India, originated monitorial system (Bell, or Madras, system) of school education, in which older pupils (monitors) instruct the younger.

**Bell, Aubrey FitzGerald.** 1881–1950. British writer, esp. of books on Spanish and Portuguese literature; compiled anthology *Oxford Book of Portuguese Verse* (1925).

**Bell,** Sir **Charles.** 1774–1842. Scottish anatomist. Surgeon to Middlesex hospital (1812–36); professor of surgery, Edinburgh (1836). Discovered distinct functions of sensory and motor nerves; announced discovery in his *Anatomy of the Brain* (1811) and established it by his *Nervous System* (1830). His eldest brother, **John** (1763–1820), surgeon, was author of *Anatomy* (3 vols., 1793–1802) and *Principles of Surgery* (3 vols., 1801–07). Another brother, **George Joseph** (1770–1843), jurist, professor at Edinburgh (1822), was member of commissions resulting in Scottish judicature act (1825) and in Scottish bankruptcy act (1839).

**Bell, Charles Frederic Moberly.** 1847–1911. English journalist, b. Alexandria, Egypt. Founded *Egyptian Gazette* (1880). Correspondent of London *Times* on Egyptian questions; manager, London *Times* (1890); published *Encyclopaedia Britannica,* 9th ed. (1898); started literary organ (1897–1901), later *The Times Literary Supplement;* established The Times Book Club (1905).

**Bell, Clark.** 1832–1918. American authority on medical jurisprudence; b. Whitesville, N.Y. Established and edited *Medico-Legal Journal* (1884).

**Bell, Clive,** *in full* **Arthur Clive Howard.** 1881–1964. English critic in art and literature. Educ. Cambridge. Author of *Art* (1914), *Since Cézanne* (1922), *Proust* (1929), *Account of French Painting* (1931). m. **Vanessa** (1879–1961), dau. of Sir Leslie Stephen (*q.v.*; see also Leonard WOOLF) and fellow member of Bloomsbury group. Their son **Julian** (1908–1937), poet, author of *We did not Fight* (1935), *Work for the Winter* (poems; 1936), was fatally wounded while driving ambulance for loyalists in Spanish civil war.

**Bell, Digby Valentine.** 1849–1917. American comedian and operatic baritone, b. Milwaukee; starred in Gilbert and Sullivan operas; later, in vaudeville and motion pictures.

**Bell, George.** 1814–1890. English publisher; founder of G. Bell & Sons, London. His son and successor **Edward** (1844–1926) was a student of ancient architecture; author of *Architecture of Ancient Egypt,* etc.

**Bell, George Joseph.** See under Sir Charles BELL.

**Bell, Gertrude Margaret Lowthian.** 1868–1926. English traveler, archaeologist, and government official; granddaughter of Sir Isaac Lowthian Bell. Grad. Oxford. Traveled into interior of Arabia to Haïl (1913); appointed to military intelligence staff, then as political secretary at Baghdad (1917); helped mold post-war administration of Mesopotamia, siding with forces bringing Faisal to throne of Iraq (1921). Author of *The Desert and the Sown* (1907), *Amurath to Amurath* (1911), and the archaeological work *The Palace and Mosque of Ukhaidir* (1914).

**Bell, Henry.** 1767–1830. Scottish engineer, b. in West Lothian; originator of steam navigation in Europe; designed, and ran successfully on the Clyde (1812–20), the three-horsepower steamboat *Comet.*

**Bell, Henry Glassford.** 1803–1874. Scottish mercantile lawyer and man of letters. Founded *Edinburgh Literary Journal* (1828). Author of a vindication of Mary, Queen of Scots (1830), *Summer and Winter Hours* (1831). Figures as "Tallboys" in John Wilson's *Noctes Ambrosianae.*

**Bell, Henry Thomas Mackenzie.** 1856–1930. English poet; author of *Spring's Immortality and other poems* (1893), *Poetical Pictures of Great War* (1915, 1916, 1917, 1919).

**Bell,** Sir **Isaac Lowthian.** 1816–1904. Scottish metallurgical chemist and industrialist. Founded, with his brothers, the Clarence iron-smelting works on the Tees. Author of metallurgical and chemical papers.

**Bell, Jacob.** 1810–1859. English pharmaceutical chemist. Founded (1841) Pharmaceutical Society of Great Britain; established *Pharmaceutical Journal* and superintended it for 18 years; submitted (1851), as M.P., legislative proposals for regulating practice of pharmacy.

**Bell, James Franklin.** 1856–1919. American army officer, b. Shelbyville, Ky. Grad. U.S.M.A., West Point (1878). Served in Philippine Islands (1898–99); awarded Congressional Medal of Honor for gallantry in action on island of Luzon. Chief of staff, U.S. army (1906–10). Major general (1907). Commander of 77th division, National army, at Camp Upton (1917).

**Bell, John.** 1691–1780. Scottish traveler; sent with Russian embassies to Persia, China, and Constantinople; author of *Travels* (1763).

**Bell, John.** 1763–1820. See under Sir Charles BELL.

**Bell, John.** 1797–1869. American lawyer, b. near Nashville, Tenn. Member, U.S. House of Representatives (1827–41). U.S. secretary of war (1841). Member, U.S. Senate (1847–59). Nominee (1860) of the Constitutional Union party for president of the United States; gained only electoral votes of Tennessee, Kentucky, and Virginia.

**Bell, John.** 1811–1895. English sculptor. Chief works, all in London, include Wellington Monument at the Guildhall (1855–56), Guards' Memorial in Waterloo Place (1858–60), and American group in Albert Memorial (1873).

**Bell, John Joy.** 1871–1934. Scottish journalist and author. Established reputation as humorist with his *Wee MacGreegor* (1902; dramatized, 1912). Other works include *Mistress M'Leerie* (1903), *Courtin' Christina* (1913), *Mr. Craw* (1924).

**Bell, John Keble.** *Pseudonym* **Keble Howard.** 1875–1928. English playwright and journalist; editor of *The Sketch* (1902–04); dramatic critic, *Daily Mail* (1904–08); founder of Croydon Repertory Theatre (1913). Among his plays are *Compromising Martha* (1906), *The Embarrassed Butler* (1912), and *Lord Babs* (1925). Author of many light prose sketches, as *The Bachelor Girls* (1907), *Puck and Mr. Purley* (1920), *Paradise Island* (1926).

**Bell, Julian.** See under Clive BELL.

**Bell, Lilian.** Mrs. **Arthur Hoyt Bogue** (bōg). 1867–1929. American fiction writer, b. Chicago. Among her books are *Love Affairs of an Old Maid* (1893), *Why Men Remain Bachelors, and Other Luxuries* (1906), *Angela's Quest* (1910), *The Land of Don't-Want-To* (1916).

**Bell, Neil.** Pseudonym of Stephen SOUTHWOLD.

**Bell,** Sir **Robert.** 1800–1867. Irish journalist and man of letters. Contributed, to *Lardner's Cabinet Cyclopaedia*, articles on history of Russia and lives of English poets; wrote continuation of Mackintosh's *History of England.* Author of three comedies and of tales. Known esp. for annotated ed. of the English poets (24 vols., 1854–57).

**Bell, Robert.** 1841–1917. Canadian geologist. Naturalist and geologist of expeditions (1884, 1885, 1897) to Baffin Bay and south coast of Baffin Land. Director of Geological Survey of Canada.

**Bell, Thomas.** 1792–1880. English dental surgeon and naturalist. Lectured on dental surgery and comparative anatomy at Guy's Hospital, London (1817–61). Professor of zoology, King's College, London (1836). Author of books on British animals; edited Gilbert White's *Natural History of Selborne* (1877).

**Bell, Vanessa.** See Clive BELL.

**Bell, William Melvin.** 1860–1933. American clergyman of United Brethren in Christ, b. in Whitley County, Ind. Ordained (1882); elected bishop (1905); senior bishop (1921); in charge of eastern district, including Atlantic and Gulf states (1917–29).

**Bel'la** (bĕl'lä), **Stefano della.** 1610–1664. Italian designer and engraver; known esp. for his engravings of military episodes, executed for Richelieu, as *Siege of Arras, Siege of Saint-Omer,* etc.

**Bel'laigue'** (bĕ'lĕg'), **Camille.** 1858–1930. French music critic, historian, and biographer. On staff of *Revue des Deux Mondes* and *Temps* (from 1885). Author of *La Musique Française au XIXe Siècle* (2 vols., 1890), and biographies of Mozart (1906), Mendelssohn (1907), and Gounod (1910).

**Bellamont** *or* **Bellomont,** Earl of. See Richard COOTE.

**Bel'la·my** (bĕl'ȧ·mĭ), **Edward.** 1850–1898. American author, b. Chicopee Falls, Mass. His Utopian romance *Looking Backward* (1888) presented a method of economic organization, socialistic in nature, guaranteeing material equality corresponding to political equality of citizens. Its enormous success inspired an unsuccessful sequel, *Equality* (1897).

**Bellamy, George Anne** [*by mistake for* **Georgiana**]. 1731?–1788. English actress. Illegitimate daughter of James O'Hara, 2d Baron Tyrawley, diplomat; educ. at convent in Boulogne. Appeared first in *Love for Love* at Covent Garden (1742); played Juliet to Garrick's Romeo in rivalry with Barry and Mrs. Cibber (1750); author of an *Apology* (6 vols., 1785).

**Bel'la·my** (bĕl'ȧ·mē), **Jacobus.** 1757–1786. Dutch poet; champion of blank verse; author of sentimental, patriotic, and Anacreontic poems.

**Bel'la·my** (bĕl'ȧ·mĭ), **Joseph.** 1719–1790. American Congregational clergyman, b. Cheshire, Conn. Author of *True Religion Delineated* (1750).

**Bel'lan'gé'** (bĕ'läN'zhā'), **Joseph Louis Hippolyte** (1800–1866) and his son **Eugène** (1837–1895). French painters, esp. of war scenes.

**Bel'lar·mine** (bĕl'är·mĭn; -mēn), **Robert.** *Ital.* **Roberto Francesco Romolo Bel'lar·mi'no** (bāl'lär·mē'nō). 1542–1621. Italian prelate and controversialist. Entered Society of Jesus (1560); aided in revision of Vulgate (1591); rector, Roman Coll. (1592); created cardinal (1599); archbishop of Capua (1602–05). Declared doctor of the church by Pius XI; beatified (1924). Known esp. for his theological disputations, as with James I of England and William Barclay of Aberdeen, who denied temporal power of pope.

**Bel'la·vi'tis** (bāl'lä·vē'tēs), Conte **Giusto.** 1803–1880. Italian mathematician; known for his work in projective, descriptive, and analytical geometry.

**Bel'lay'** (bĕ'lā'), **Guillaume du.** Seigneur **de Lan'gey'** (dē läN'zhā'). 1491–1543. French general and diplomat. Employed by Francis I on missions to England (1529–30 and later), in negotiations for purpose of uniting German princes against Charles V (1532–36), and in Italy as governor of Turin (1537–39) and then of Piedmont (1539–42). His work on contemporary history, *Ogdoades,* lost except for fragment inserted in *Mémoires* of his brother **Martin** (d. 1559). Another brother, **Jean** (1492?–1560), was bishop of Paris (1532), cardinal, and bishop of Ostia (1555).

**Bellay, Joachim du.** 1522–1560. French poet, b. Liré near Angers; called "the French Ovid" and "Prince of the Sonnet." Nephew of Guillaume and Jean du Bellay. Became friend of Ronsard and member of the group of poets known as The Pléiade, whose ideas he embodied in his *Défense et Illustration de la Langue Française* (1549). His volumes of sonnets are *Olive* (1550) and especially *Les Antiquités de Rome* and *Les Regrets.* Other works include *Vers Lyriques, Divers Poèmes* (1552), *Les Jeux Rustiques.*

**Bel'leau'** (bĕ'lō'), **Remi.** 1528–1577. French man of letters, b. Paris. Member of group known as The Pléiade. Author of descriptive and pastoral poetry, including *Petites Inventions* (1557) and *Bergerie* (1565, 1572).

**Belle'fo'rest'** (bĕl'fô'rĕ'), **François de.** 1530–1583.

French writer; compiler of tragedies from Bandello's novels, including stories used by Shakespeare.

**Belle′gambe′** (bĕl′gäɴb′), **Jean.** 1470–1534. Flemish painter; called by his contemporaries "the Master of Color." Many of his paintings are in the museum at Douai.

**Belle′garde′** (bĕl′gärd′), Count **Heinrich von.** 1756–1845. Austrian general and statesman, b. Dresden. Transferred from Saxon army to Austrian service (1771). Won distinction as general chief of staff in French Revolution; concluded with Napoleon armistice of Leoben (1797). General chief of staff of Austrian army in Italy (1800); president of war council (1805); field marshal (from 1806); commander of forces in Napoleonic campaigns; governor general of Galicia (1809–13). Commander in chief of Austrian forces in Italy (1813–15); governor general of Lombardy and Venetia (1814). President of war council and minister of state (1820–25).

**Belle′-Isle′** (bĕ′lēl′), Duc **de. Charles Louis Auguste Fou′quet′** (fōō′kĕ′). 1684–1761. Grandson of Nicolas Fouquet. Marshal of France. Served in War of the Spanish Succession (1701–14), Spanish War (1718), War of the Polish Succession (1733), and War of the Austrian Succession (1740–48). As minister of war (1758) introduced useful reforms in army administration during Seven Years' War.

**Bellême, Robert of.** See BELESME.

**Bel′len·den** (bĕl′ĕn·dĕn) *or* **Bal′len·den** (băl′ĕn·dĕn) *or* **Bal′len·tyne** (băl′ĕn·tīn), **John.** fl. 1533–1587. Scottish ecclesiastic and poet; translator of Livy and of Boece's *Historia Scotorum* into Scottish vernacular (1536).

**Bellenden,** Sir **John.** d. 1577. Scottish lawyer; privy councilor of Mary, Queen of Scots (1561); involved in murder of Rizzio; joined nobles against Mary and Bothwell; privy councilor of Regent Murray; aided in framing pacification of Perth (1573).

**Bellenden, William.** d. ?1633. Scottish classical scholar; diplomatic agent in France of James VI and Mary, Queen of Scots; author of treatises illustrating Roman history by extracts from Latin authors.

**Bel′ler·by** (bĕl′ĕr·bĭ), **John Roth′er·ford** (rŭth′ĕr·fērd). 1896– . English economist. Educ. Leeds and Harvard. Member of staff, International Labor Office, League of Nations (1921–27); technical adviser, International Economic Conference, Geneva (1927); prof. of economic science, Liverpool (1930–32). Author of texts on monetary stability and other economic subjects.

**Bel′ler·mann** (bĕl′ĕr·män), **Johann Gottfried Heinrich.** 1832–1903. German composer and writer on music. Professor, U. of Berlin (from 1866). Composer chiefly of vocal music, including psalms, motets, and choruses for Greek plays. Author of a historical exposition of mensural music (1858), a treatise on counterpoint (1862), and other theoretical works.

**Bel′lew** (bĕl′ū; bĕ·lōō′; bĕ·lū′), **John Chippendall Montesquieu.** *Orig. surname* **Hig′gin** (hĭg′ĭn). 1823–1874. English clergyman; assumed mother's maiden surname, Bellew (1844); chaplain of St. John's Cathedral, Calcutta (1851–55); one of foremost preachers of his day; entered Roman Catholic Church (1868) as a layman and devoted himself to literature and public readings. His son **Harold Kyrle Bellew** (1855–1911) was an actor on the English and American stage.

**Bel′li** (bĕl′lē), **Giuseppe Gioacchino.** 1791–1863. Italian popular poet; wrote satirical sonnets on Roman life, as *I Sonetti Romaneschi* (pub. 1886–89).

**Bel′lin·cio′ni** (bāl′lēn·chō′nē), **Gemma.** 1864–1950. Italian opera singer, b. at Como; m. Roberto Stagno. Created role of Santuzza in première of *Cavalleria Rusticana;* also created principal soprano roles in *Fedora, A Santa Lucia, Lorenza, La Cabrera, Sapho,* and others.

**Bel′ling** (bĕl′ĭng), **Rudolf.** 1886–1972. German sculptor, b. in Berlin. Studied at Berlin Academy. Associated with development of abstract sculpture in Germany; in Turkey (from 1933).

**Bel′ling·ham** (bĕl′ĭng·ăm; -hăm), **Richard.** 1592?–1672. American colonial governor, b. Boston, Lincolnshire, England. Settled (1634) at Boston, Mass. Governor of Massachusetts colony (1641, 1654, 1665–72).

**Bel′lings·hau′sen** (bĕl′ĭngs·hou′zĕn), **Fabian Gottlieb von.** *Russ.* **Faddei Faddeevich Bel·lings·gau′sen** (bĕ·lyĭngs·gou′zyĕn). 1778–1852. Russian admiral and explorer, b. on Oesel Island, Livonia. Joined Russian navy (1797); officer on first Russian circumnavigation of globe (1803); given command (1819) by Emperor Alexander I of expedition of exploration to Antarctic which discovered (1819–21) and named Peter I Island and Alexander I Island; participated in operations against Varna (1828); commander of Baltic fleet.

**Bel·li′ni** (bāl·lē′nē). Venetian family of painters including:

**Iacopo** (c. 1400–c. 1470), its founder; pupil of Gentile da Fabriano; initiator of Venetian school of painting; father-in-law of Andrea Mantegna. His works include *The Crucified One, Annunciation, Crucifixion, Adoration of the Kings,* and two sketchbooks (in British Museum and Louvre).

His son **Gentile** (1429?–1507); official painter to the Venetian state (1474); to Constantinople (1479–80) to paint for sultan; introduced oil painting in Venetian mural decoration. His works include restorations of decorations by Gentile da Fabriano in ducal palace, three pageant pictures representing miracles performed by a relic of the Cross, *Preaching of St. Mark,* portraits, etc.

Another son, **Giovanni** (1430?–1516); leading painter of Venetian school; master of Giorgione, Titian, Palma Vecchio, etc.; known chiefly for his altarpieces and Madonnas.

**Bellini, Lorenzo.** 1643–1704. Italian physician and anatomist; discoverer of the action of nerves on muscles, and of the excretory ducts (Bellini's ducts) of the kidneys.

**Bellini, Vincenzo.** 1801–1835. Italian opera composer, b. Catania, Sicily. Studied under Zingarelli and others in Naples (1819–27); settled in Paris (1833). Composed melodic operas including *Adelson e Salvina* (1825), *Bianca e Fernando* (1826), *Il Pirata* (1827), *I Capuleti ed i Montecchi* (1830), *La Sonnambula* (1831), *Norma* (1831), and *I Puritani* (1835), also sacred music, various instrumental and choral works, etc.

**Bell′mann** (bĕl′măn), **Karl Mikael.** 1740–1795. Swedish lyrical and humorous poet, b. Stockholm. Author of *Fredmans Epistlar* (1790), *Fredmans Sånger* (1791), and other religious poems, improvisations, satires, parodies, and esp. drinking and love songs.

**Bel′lo** (bā′yō), **Andrés.** 1780?–1865. Spanish-American scholar and author, b. Caracas, Venezuela. London agent of Venezuelan revolutionary government (1810–29). On staff of Chilean government; edited civil code of Chile; Chilean representative in several cases of international arbitration. Rector, U. of Chile (from 1843).

**Bel′loc** (bĕl′ŏk; -ŭk), **Hilary,** *in full* **Joseph Hilary Pierre** (pyâr). *Pen name* **Hi·laire′** (hĭ·lâr′) **Belloc.** 1870–1953. English author. Son of French barrister and English mother; naturalized British subject (1902); grad. Oxford (1895); newspaper and magazine writer; M.P. (1906–10). Author of essays, verse, novels, history, biography, criticism, including *The Path to Rome* (1902;

a travel journal), *Bad Child's Book of Beasts* (1896; nonsense verse), *Cautionary Tales* (1907; light verse), the novels *Mr. Clutterbuck's Election* (1908), *The Girondin* (1911), *The Green Overcoat* (1912), and *The Man Who Made Gold* (1930); *History of England* (1925–31), *Marie Antoinette* (1910), *Richelieu* (1929), *Wolsey* (1930), *Cromwell* (1934), *Characters of the Reformation* (1936), *The Crisis of our Civilization* (1937), *The Great Heresies* (1938), *The Last Rally* (1940); *Elizabeth: Creature of Circumstance* (1942).

**Belloc, Marie Adelaide.** *Pen name* Mrs. **Belloc Lowndes** (loundz). 1868–1947. English novelist; sister of Hilary Belloc; m. Frederic Sawrey Lowndes. Author of historical works, novels (beginning with *The Philosophy of a Marquise*, 1899), and esp. murder and mystery stories, as *The Chink in the Armour* (1912), *Who Rides on a Tiger* (1936), and the autobiographical *I, too, have lived in Arcadia* (1941).

**Bel'lo Co'de·si'do** (bā'yō kō'thā·sē'thō), **Emilio.** 1868–1963. Chilean statesman, b. Santiago; minister of industry and public works (1898), justice (1900), foreign affairs (1901, 1904, 1919), interior (1905), state (1924), national defense (1932–38); minister to Mexico (1901) and Bolivia (1919); councilor of state (1909–12); president, council of government (1925); arbitrator in Honduras-Guatemala frontier dispute (1930).

**Bel·lo'ni Ga'ray·co'e·che'a** (bā·yō'nē gä'rī·kō'ā·chā'ä), **José Le·on'cio** (lā·ôn'syō). 1882– . Uruguayan sculptor, b. Montevideo; professor, Industrial School of Morcolti, Switzerland (1900–07), and at Montevideo (from 1913). Works include bust of Artigas, *William Tell*, *La Carreta*, *El Aguatero*, etc.

**Bel'lonte'** (bĕ'lôNt'), **Maurice.** 1893?– . French aviator. See Dieudonné COSTE.

**Bel·lo'ri** (bāl·lô'rē), **Giovanni Pietro.** 1636?–1700. Italian antiquary and writer on art.

**Bel'lot'** (bĕ'lō'), **Joseph René.** 1826–1853. French naval officer; joined English polar expeditions.

**Bellotto, Bernardo.** See under Antonio CANALETTO.

**Bel'low** (bĕl'ō), **Saul.** 1915– . Am. writer, b. Canada. To U.S. (1924); wrote *The Adventures of Augie March* (1953), *Herzog* (1964), *Mr. Sammler's Planet* (1970), *Humboldt's Gift* (1975); awarded Nobel prize for literature (1976).

**Bel'lows** (bĕl'ōz), **Albert Fitch.** 1829–1883. American painter, b. Milford, Mass. Excelled in water-color paintings, chiefly of rural scenes. Did notable work in large etchings during his later years. Author of *Water Color Painting* (1868).

**Bellows, George Wesley.** 1882–1925. American artist and lithographer, b. Columbus, Ohio. Educ. Ohio State U. Known as a leader among the realists. Paintings include *Emma and Her Children* (Boston Museum of Fine Arts), *Portrait of My Mother* (Chicago Art Institute), *Polo Game at Lakewood, New Jersey* (in Columbus [Ohio] Gallery of Fine Arts), *Stag at Sharkey's* (Cleveland [Ohio] Museum), *Up the Hudson* (Metropolitan Museum, New York City), *North River* (Pennsylvania Academy of Fine Arts, Philadelphia).

**Bellows, Henry Whitney.** 1814–1882. American Unitarian clergyman, b. Boston. Pastor in New York City (1839–82). Founder and president, United States Sanitary Commission, which cared for sick and wounded during Civil War. Active in cause of civil-service reform.

**Bel'loy'** (bĕ'lwȧ'), **Dormont de.** *Real name* **Pierre Laurent Buy'rette'** (bü·ē'rĕt'). 1727–1775. French actor and playwright; first to introduce native, instead of classic, heroes on French stage. Author of *Le Siège de Calais* (1765), *Gaston et Bayard* (1771), etc.

**Bellune,** Duc **de.** See Claude VICTOR.

**Bel'mont** (bĕl'mŏnt), **Au'gust** (ô'gŭst). 1816–1890. Banker, b. Alzei, in Rhenish Palatinate; to U.S. (1837). Established banking house, August Belmont & Co.; naturalized. Consul general for Austria in U.S. (1844–50). U.S. minister to the Netherlands (1853–57). Supported Union during Civil War. Noted art connoisseur and sportsman. Father of **Perry** (1850–1947), lawyer, member of U.S. House of Representatives (1881–89); and **August** (1853–1924), banker, head of August Belmont & Co., m. Eleanor Robson (*q.v.*).

**Bel'mon'tet'** (bĕl'môN'tĕ'), **Louis.** 1799–1879. French poet and playwright, b. Montauban.

**Be'loch** (bā'lôK), **Karl Julius.** 1854–1929. German historian in Italy, b. in Lower Silesia. Professor of ancient history, U. of Rome (1879–1912, 1913–18, 1924–29), Leipzig (1912–13). Author of *Griechische Geschichte* (4 vols., 1893–1904), *Römische Geschichte bis zum Beginn der Punischen Kriege* (1926), etc.

**Be·lon'** (bē·lôN'), **Pierre.** 1517–1564. French naturalist; author of *Histoire Naturelle des Étranges Poissons Marines*, and *Histoire de la Nature des Oyseaux*.

**Be·lot'** (bē·lō'), **Adolphe.** 1829–1890. French dramatist and novelist, b. in Guadeloupe. Collaborator with Alphonse Daudet in *Sapho* (1885), a comedy.

**Belotto, Bernardo.** See under Antonio CANALETTO.

**Be'low** (bā'lō), **Fritz von.** 1853–1918. Prussian general, b. Danzig. In World War I, commanded army corps, notably in battle of Masurian Lakes (1914); commanded 2d army at St. Quentin (1915–16), 1st army at Cambrai and Rethel (1916–18), and 9th army on the Somme (1918). His brother **Otto** (1857–1944) was also a general; commanded 8th army at Tannenberg and Masurian Lakes (1915–16), 6th, and later the 14th, army, against Italy (1917), and the new 1st army (1918).

**Bel'sham** (bĕl'shăm), **Thomas.** 1750–1829. English Unitarian clergyman; author of religious treatises. His brother **William** (1752–1827), historian and political writer, wrote historical studies designed to support Whig principles.

**Bel·shaz'zar** (bĕl·shăz'ēr). *Corruption of Babylonian* **Bel-shar-usur.** Crown prince of Babylonia; son of Nabonidus (*q.v.*). In command of armies of northern Babylonia, apparently conjointly with his father, king of Babylon, when it was taken by Cyrus (539 B.C.); nothing known of his fate except statement in Biblical book of Daniel (v. 30).

**Belt** (bĕlt), **Thomas.** 1832–1878. English geologist and naturalist. Geologist in Australian gold fields (1852–62); in charge of gold mines in Nova Scotia (1862 ff.), Nicaragua (1868–72). Author of scientific papers on glacial period and of *The Naturalist in Nicaragua* (1874).

**Bel·traf'fio** (bāl·träf'fyō) *or* **Bol·traf'fio** (bōl-), **Giovanni Antonio.** 1467–1516. Italian painter; pupil of Leonardo da Vinci.

**Bel·tra'mi** (bāl·trä'mē), **Eugenio.** 1835–1900. Italian mathematician and physicist; known esp. for research in non-Euclidean geometry.

**Beltraneja, la.** See under JUANA OF PORTUGAL.

**Bel·trán' y Mas'ses** (bĕl·trän' ē mä'sās), **Federico.** 1885–1949. Spanish painter; known esp. for portraits, fete and ballet scenes, and decorative ensembles.

**Bely, Andrei.** See Boris BUGAEV.

**Be·lya'ev** (byĭ·lyȧ'yĕf), **Mitrofan Petrovich.** 1836–1904. Russian music publisher; founded (1885) press to publish modern Russian compositions; instituted orchestral and chamber concerts for performance of such compositions. Rimski-Korsakov, Borodin, Liadov, and Glazunov joined in writing a string quartet in his honor.

**Bel·zo'ni** (bāl·tsō'nē), **Giovanni Battista.** 1778–1823. Italian explorer and archaeologist. Explored Egyptian antiquities (1815–19); opened temple of Abu-Simbel (1817); discovered tomb of Seti I, Thebes (1817); opened second pyramid of Giza; transferred bust *Young Memnon* (now in British Museum) from Thebes to Alexandria.

**Bel·zú'** (bĕl·sōō'), **Manuel Isidoro.** 1808–1866. Bolivian general, b. La Paz; president of Bolivia (1848–55); assassinated.

**Bem** (bĕm), **Józef.** 1795–1850. Polish general, b. Tarnów, Galicia. Distinguished himself in Polish revolution (1830–31); fled to Paris. Took part in insurrection in Vienna (1848), joining Hungarian army; commanded army of Transylvania (1848); made brilliant campaign with small force, defeating Austrians at Piski (1849); drove Austrians and Russians into Walachia but was badly defeated (1849) by superior forces at Schässburg (Sighişoara); escaped to Turkey; embraced Islam and became a pasha; revered by Szeklers.

**Bem'bo** (bĕm'bō), **Pietro.** 1470–1547. Italian writer and ecclesiastic, b. Venice. Secretary to Leo X (1513); historiographer of Venetian republic (1529); created cardinal (1539). Restored classic tradition in Italian language and literature. Author of *Gli Asolani* (1505), *Prose della Volgar Lingua* (1525), etc.

**Be'mel·mans** (bē'mĕl·mănz), **Ludwig.** 1898–1962. American painter, illustrator, and writer, b. in Tirol, of Belgian father and Bavarian mother; to U.S. (1914); naturalized (1918). Author and illustrator of *Hansi* (1934), *My War with the U.S.* (1937), *Life Class* (1938), *Madeline* (1939), *Small Beer* (1939), *Donkey Inside* (1941), *I Love You, I Love You, I Love You* (1942), etc.

**Be'mis** (bē'mĭs), **Samuel Flagg.** 1891–1973. American historian and educator, b. Worcester, Mass. A.B., Clark (1912); Ph.D., Harvard (1916). Professor, George Washington U. (1924–34), Yale (1935–1960). Author of *Jay's Treaty. . .*(1923), *Pinckney's Treaty. . .*(1926; awarded Pulitzer prize), *A Diplomatic History of the United States* (1936), *John Quincy Adams and the Foundation of American Foreign Policy* (1949; awarded Pulitzer prize), etc.

**Bé'mont'** (bā'môɴ'), **Charles.** 1848–1939. French historian, b. Paris; author of works on English and European history.

**Bem'rose** (bĕm'rōz), **William.** 1831–1908. English publisher; best known for his works on wood carving and pottery.

**ben** (bĕn). Hebrew word for "son"; used often as part of a name, as **Akiba ben Joseph,** *i.e.* Akiba, son of Joseph. Corresponding term in Arabic names is IBN-.

**Benadad.** See BENHADAD.

**Benalcázar, Sebastián de.** See BELALCÁZAR.

**Ben'–am'mi** (bĕn'ăm'ī). *In Douay Version* **Am'mon** (ăm'ŏn). In Bible, son of Lot, ancestor of Ammonites (*Genesis* xix. 38).

**Bé'nard'** (bā'nȧr'), **Henri Jean Émile.** 1844–? . French architect; designed a number of churches, the Salle des Fêtes and Tribunal de Commerce at Le Havre; won first prize (1899) for his design in international competition for plans for U. of California buildings.

**Be'na·ven'te y Mar·tí'nez** (bā'nä·vān'tā ē mär·tē'-nāth), **Jacinto.** 1866–1954. Spanish dramatist, b. Madrid. Educ. U. of Madrid; traveled in France, England, Russia (1885–92), and, later, in U.S. and South America; member, Spanish Acad. (c. 1913 ff.); awarded Nobel prize in literature (1922). His plays, notable for satirical quality and realism, include *El Nido Ajeno, El Marido de la Téllez, Más Fuerte que el Amor, La Losa de los Sueños, Señora Ama, La Malquerida, La Vertud Sospechosa, La Otra Honra,* and *La Ciudad Alegre y Confiada.*

**Be'na·vi'des** (bā'nä·vē'thās), **Óscar Raimundo.** 1876–1945. Peruvian soldier and statesman, b. Lima. Served with French army (five years), Peruvian army (from 1894); chief of general staff, Peru (1913); chief of governing junta during revolution (1914); provisional president of Peru (1915). Minister to Italy (1917–20), Spain (1931), England (1932–33). Chief of national defense (1933); president of Peru (1933–39); ambassador to Spain (1940) and to Argentina (1941).

**Be'na·vi'des y Diez Can·se'co** (ē thyās kän·sā'kō), **Alfredo.** 1881– . Peruvian diplomat, b. Lima. Consul at Le Havre (1909), Bordeaux (1909), Bremen (1911); in foreign office as chief of consular bureau (1913), of diplomatic bureau (1914–20). Minister of marine and aviation (1931); minister to Great Britain (from 1933). Author of *Escalafón Diplomático del Perú* (1914) and *Colección de Actos Internacionales en Vigor para la República del Perú* (2 vols.).

**Ben'bow** (bĕn'bō), **John.** 1653–1702. English naval officer; commander in chief of squadron in blockade of Dunkirk (1696) and in West Indies (1698–1700); vice-admiral (1701); failed in pursuit of French naval commander Ducasse (1702) because of mutiny of officers; died of wounds.

**Bence'–Jones'** (bĕns'jōnz'), **Henry.** 1814?–1873. English physician and chemist.

**Bench'ley** (bĕnch'lĭ), **Robert Charles.** 1889–1945. American humorist, b. Worcester, Mass. A.B., Harvard (1912). On staff, successively, of Curtis Publishing Co. of Philadelphia, New York *Tribune, Vanity Fair,* New York *World, Life, New Yorker.* Actor in motion-picture "shorts" (1929 and from 1937); in radio work (from 1937). Author of *Of All Things* (1921), *Love Conquers All* (1922), *The Early Worm* (1927), *The Treasurer's Report* (1930), *No Poems* (1932), *From Bed to Worse* (1934), *My Ten Years in a Quandary* (1936), *After 1903, What?* (1938), etc.

**Benck'en·dorff** (*Ger.* bĕng'kĕn·dôrf) *or* **Ben'ken·dorf** (*Russ.* byăng'kyĭn·dôrf). Russian family of German origin, settled in Livonia in 16th century, including: **Aleksandr Khristoforovich** (1783–1844); general and statesman; engaged in campaigns against Napoleon (1813–15); later, director of police in Russia. **Aleksandr Konstantinovich** (1849–1917); entered diplomatic service (1868); at Rome (1869–77); in retirement (1877–86); first secretary at Vienna (1886–97); minister at Copenhagen (1897–1903); ambassador in London (1903–16); influential in furthering Anglo-Russian friendship and forming Triple Entente (1907); died in London.

**Ben'da** (bĕn'dä). Family of Bohemian musicians in Germany, whose chief members include: **Franz** *or* **František** (1709–1786); violinist and composer for violin; concertmeister of Frederick II of Prussia (from 1771), in which position his brother **Joseph** (1724–1804) succeeded him. Another brother, **Georg** *or* **Jiří** (1722–1795); clavierist, violinist, and oboist; introduced music drama with spoken text; Kapellmeister to duke of Gotha (1748–78); composed operettas, cantatas, masses, etc., and melodramas including *Ariadne auf Naxos* (1774), *Medea* (1778), *Pygmalion* (1780). Two sons of Franz, b. in Potsdam: **Friedrich Wilhelm Heinrich** (1745–1814), violinist and clavierist, royal chamber musician (1765–1810), composer of 3 operas, 2 oratorios, cantatas, and instrumental music; and **Karl Hermann Heinrich** (1748–1836), violinist and composer of chamber music, concertmeister of royal opera. Georg's son **Friedrich Ludwig** (1746–1792); b. Gotha; director of concerts at Königsberg (1789) and composer of comic operas, violin concertos, an oratorio, etc.

**Ben'da'** (băɴ'dȧ'), **Julien.** 1867–1956. French philosophical and critical writer, b. Paris. His works include *Mon Premier Testament* (1910), the analytical novel *L'Ordination* (1912), *Le Bergsonisme ou une Philosophie sur la Mobilité* (1912), *La Fin de l'Éternel* (1929), etc.

**Benda, Pauline.** See SIMONE.

**Ben'da** (bĕn'dȧ), **Władysław The'o·dor** (thē'ō·dôr). 1873–1948. Painter and illustrator, b. Poznań, Poland; to U.S. (1899); naturalized (1911). Illustrator for magazines and books; creator of a type of masks, known as Benda masks, used on the stage.

**Ben Da'vid** *or* **Ben·da'vid** (bĕn·dā'vĭd; *Ger.* dä'vēt, -vĭt, -fēt, -fĭt), **Lazarus.** 1762–1832. German philosopher and mathematician. Lecturer on Kantian philosophy, Vienna; expelled from Vienna (1797); director of a Jewish school, Berlin. Author of *Über den Ursprung unserer Erkenntnis* (1802), etc.

**Ben'de·mann** (bĕn'dĕ·män), **Eduard.** 1811–1889. German painter of Düsseldorf school; pupil of Schadow. Professor, Dresden Academy (1838–59); director, Düsseldorf Academy (1859–67). Works include *Die Trauernden Juden in Babylon*, *Die Wegführung der Juden in die Babylonische Gefangenschaft*, *Penelope*, many large frescoes and historical pictures in royal castle at Dresden, illustrations for *Nibelungenlied* (1841), portraits, etc.

**Ben'der** (bĕn'dẽr), **Harold Herman.** 1882–1951. American philologist, b. Martinsburg, W.Va. A.B., Lafayette (1903); Ph.D., Johns Hopkins (1907); further study in Germany. Faculty member (from 1909), professor of Indo-Germanic philology (from 1918), chairman of department of Oriental languages and literatures (from 1927), Princeton. Special editor for etymology and philology, *Webster's New International Dictionary, Second Edition.* Author of *On the Lithuanian Word-Stock as Indo-European Material* (1920), *A Lithuanian Etymological Index* (1921), *The Home of the Indo-Europeans* (1922), etc.

**Ben'dix** (bĕn'dĭks), **Max.** 1866–1945. American orchestra conductor, b. Detroit. Concertmeister, Theodore Thomas Orchestra (1886–96). Organized and conducted Max Bendix String Quartet. Founded Bendix Music Bureau, New York (c. 1915). Music director, N.Y. Metropolitan Opera House, Royal English Opera, St. Louis Municipal Opera. Conductor at expositions at Chicago (1893), St. Louis (1904), San Francisco (1915), Chicago (1933).

**Bendix, Vincent.** 1882–1945. American inventor and industrialist, b. Moline, Ill. Interested himself in improving equipment of automobiles; developed Bendix electric self-starter. President and manager, Bendix Products Corporation, and Bendix Brake Co., manufacturers of self-starters, brakes, carburetors, etc., for automobiles; president, Bendix Aviation Corp.

**Bendl** (bĕn'd'l), **Karel.** 1838–1897. Czech composer, b. Prague. Wrote several Czech national operas, esp. *Lejla* (1868), *Břetislav and Jitka* (1870), and *Černahorci* (1881), and a ballet, masses, cantatas, and many Czech songs and choruses.

**Be'ne·dek** (bā'nĕ·dĕk), **Ludwig August von.** 1804–1881. Austrian general, b. in Hungary. Served with distinction in Galician, Italian, and Hungarian campaigns (1846–49) and as commander, 8th army corps, at Solferino (1859); successively chief of general staff, military governor of Hungary, and commander in chief of Austrian army in Venetia and Alpine provinces (1860); commander, army of the north (1866); disastrously defeated (1866) by Prussians at Königgrätz (Sadowa); suspended from command (1866).

**Be·ne'den** (bĕ·nā'dĕn), **Pierre** (pyâr) **Jo'seph'** (zhō'zĕf') **van.** 1809–1894. Belgian zoologist; professor at Catholic U. of Louvain (from 1836); writer on the Cetacea, parasites, etc. His son **Eduard van Beneden** (1846–1910), professor at Leiden, was an embryologist.

**Be'ne·det'ti** (bā'nā·dāt'tē), Comte **Vincente.** 1817–1900. French diplomat, b. in Corsica. Ambassador at Berlin (1864). Forced himself upon king of Prussia at Ems (July 13, 1870) to demand in name of French government a solemn renunciation of candidacy of Prince Leopold of Hohenzollern-Sigmaringen to throne of Spain, this blunder giving Bismarck the casus belli necessary to precipitate Franco-Prussian War.

**Be'ne·dicks'** (bĕ'nĕ·dĭks'), **Carl Axel Fredrik.** 1875–1958. Swedish physicist; professor, Stockholm (1911); director of Metallographical Institute, Stockholm (1920–35); received Edlund award (1904), and Carnegie gold medal for metallurgical research (1908).

**Ben'e·dict** (bĕn'ē·dĭkt). Name of fifteen popes (see *Table of Popes*, Nos. 62, 81, 104, 117, 133, 135, 136, 145, 147, 154, 194, 197, 247, 249, 260) and three antipopes, especially:

**Benedict III.** d. 858. Pope (855–858). Election opposed by Emperor Lothair; did much in rebuilding of Rome after Saracen raids.

**Benedict VIII.** d. 1024. Pope (1012–24). b. Rome. Son of Count Gregory of Tusculum and brother of Pope John XIX. Crowned Henry II as emperor (1014); defeated Saracens and took Sardinia from them; reformed clergy; held synod at Pavia (1022).

**Benedict IX.** 1012?–1056. Pope (1032–44, 1045, 1047–48); called "the Boy Pope." Nephew of Benedict VIII. Obtained election through simony; his profligacy aroused much opposition; twice deposed; regained papal see a third time (1047), but in this last period held to be antipope to Clement II.

**Benedict X.** *Real name* **John Min'ci·us** (mĭn'shĭ·ŭs; -sĭ·ŭs). Pope (1058–59). By some held to be antipope.

**Benedict XIII.** *Real name* **Pietro Francesco Or·si'ni** (ôr·sē'nē). 1649–1730. Pope (1724–30). Created cardinal (1672); scholarly and upright, but yielded to guidance of unscrupulous Cardinal Coscia; exerted influence for peace. For Benedict XIII, antipope at Avignon (1394–1423), see Pedro de LUNA.

**Benedict XIV.** *Real name* **Prospero Lam'ber·ti'ni** (läm'bâr·tē'nē). 1675–1758. Pope (1740–58); b. Bologna. Cardinal (1728); archbishop of Bologna (1731); in two bulls (1742, 1744), settled controversies concerning Indian and Chinese rites; greatly encouraged education, literature, and science; liberal in policy toward foreign powers; his collected works, first published in 12 volumes (1747–51), include *On the Beatification and Canonization of Saints.*

**Benedict XV.** *Real name* **Giacomo del'la Chie'sa** (dāl'lä kyâ'zä). 1854–1922. Pope (1914–22); b. Pegli, near Genoa. Papal nuncio at Madrid (1883–87) with Cardinal Rampolla; archbishop of Bologna (1907); cardinal (1914); elected pope soon after World War began (1914); made many attempts to bring end to war (1914–18); determined opponent of Modernism; published (1918) completed *Codex Juris Canonici.*

*Antipopes:* **Benedict XIII.** *Real name* **Pedro de Luna** (*q.v.*). 1328?–?1423. Antipope at Avignon (1394–1423). **Benedict XIV.** Antipope (1424?).

**Benedict, Erastus Cornelius.** 1800–1880. American lawyer, b. Branford, Conn. Author of *American Admiralty* (1850), long accepted as standard.

**Benedict, Francis Ga'no** (gā'nō). 1870–1957. American chemist, b. Milwaukee; grad. Harvard (1893). Director, nutrition laboratory, Carnegie Institution, Washington, D.C. (1907–37).

**Ben'e·dict** (bĕn'ē·dĭkt; *Ger.* bā'nā·dĭkt), Sir **Julius.** 1804–1885. Pianist, composer, and conductor, b. Stuttgart, Germany. Orchestra conductor, Vienna (1823), Naples (1825). Resident in London (from 1835) as pianist, opera conductor, and concert director (Drury Lane, Covent Garden, etc.); accompanied Jenny Lind on her American tours (1850–51); became British subject; knighted (1871). His compositions include operas, cantatas, oratorios, and 2 symphonies.

**Benedict, Leopold.** See Morris WINCHEVSKY.

**Benedict, Ruth Fulton.** 1887–1948. American anthropologist, b. New York City. Her major work was *Patterns of Culture* (1934).

**Ben′e·dict Bi′scop** (bĕn′ê·dĭkt bĭsh′ŏp), Saint. Also **Biscop Ba′du·cing′** (bä′do͝o·chĭng[g]′). 628?–690. English ecclesiastic. Conducted Theodore of Tarsus from Rome to Canterbury (669); built monasteries of St. Peter at Wearmouth (674), and St. Paul at Jarrow (682); teacher of Bede; introduced stone-built church and art of glassmaking into England.

**Benedict of Nur′si·a** (nûr′shĭ·*ā*; -sh*ā*), Saint. 480?–?543. Founder of monasticism in western Europe; established (c. 529) monastery on Monte Cassino, which became head of Benedictine order; formulated strict rules, *Regula Monachorum,* to govern monks.

**Benedictsson, Victoria Maria.** Real name of Ernst AHLGREN.

**Be′ne·dix** (bā′nȧ·dĭks), **Roderich Julius.** 1811–1873. German playwright, and author of miscellaneous historical and critical writings on the theater.

**Ben′e·field** (bĕn′ĕ·fēld), **John Barry.** 1877– . American journalist and writer, b. Jefferson, Tex. B.Litt., Texas (1902). On staff of New York *Times,* Brooklyn *Standard Union,* Dallas *News.* Author of *The Chicken-Wagon Family* (1925), *Short Turns* (1926), *Bugles in the Night* (1927), *Valiant Is the Word for Carrie* (1935), etc.

**Be′ne·ke** (bā′nĕ·kĕ), **Friedrich Eduard.** 1798–1854. German empirical psychologist, philosopher, and educator. Professor, Berlin (from 1832). Charged with Epicureanism for his *Grundlegung zur Physik der Sitten* (1822) opposing Hegel's philosophy; author also of *Lehrbuch der Psychologie als Naturwissenschaft* (1833), *Pragmatische Psychologie* (1850), etc.

**Be·nel′li** (bȧ·nĕl′lē), **Sem** (sĕm). 1877–1949. Italian dramatist; known esp. for his *La Cena delle Beffe* (1909), produced in Paris under title *La Beffa* (1910) and in New York as *The Jest* (1919); his *L'Amore dei Tre Re* (1909) has been set to music.

**Be′neš** (bĕ′nĕsh), **Eduard.** 1884–1948. Czechoslovak statesman, b. Kožlany. Educ. universities of Prague, Paris, and Dijon; professor in Prague (1909–15). Disciple of Masaryk; worked in Paris (1915–19) with Masaryk in Czech nationalist movement; Czech delegate at peace conference (1919–20). Foreign minister of new state of Czechoslovakia (1918–35); prime minister (1921–22); member of Council of League of Nations (1923–27); a cofounder of Little Entente; lecturer in sociology in Prague U. (1922–38). Elected president of Czechoslovakia (1935); resigned (Oct., 1938) on German occupation of Sudetenland. Appointed professor of sociology, U. of Chicago (1939). President of the Czechoslovak government in England (1939–45); returned to Czechoslovakia (1945); re-elected (1946).

**Be·nét′** (bĕ·nā′), **William Rose.** 1886–1950. American poet, novelist, and editor, b. Fort Hamilton, N.Y. Ph.B., Yale (1907). On staff of *Century Magazine* (1911–18), New York *Evening Post Literary Review* (1920–24), *Saturday Review of Literature* (from 1924). Among his volumes of verse are *Merchants from Cathay* (1913), *The Falconer of God* (1914), *Moons of Grandeur* (1920), *Man Possessed* (1927), *Starry Harness* (1933), *Golden Fleece* (1935), *The Dust Which Is God* (1941; awarded Pulitzer prize). His novels include *The First Person Singular* (1922), *Flying King of Kurio* (juvenile; 1926). m. as 2d wife Elinor Wylie (*q.v.*). His brother **Stephen Vincent** (1898–1943), b. Bethlehem, Pa.; B.A., Yale (1919); author of *Five Men and Pompey* (1915), *Young Adventure* (1918), *Heavens and Earth* (1920), *The Beginning of Wisdom* (1921), *Tiger Joy* (1925), *John Brown's Body* (1928), *Ballads and Poems* (1931), *The Devil and Daniel Webster* (1937), *Thirteen O'Clock* (1937), *Tales before Midnight* (1939), *Western Star* (1943), *America* (pub. 1944), etc.

**Ben′e·zet′** (bĕn′ĕ·zĕt′), **Anthony.** *Fr.* **Antoine Bé′né′zet′** (bā′nā′zĕ′). 1713–1784. Am. educator, b. Fr. Became Quaker in London (1727); to Philadelphia (1731). Interested in antislavery cause, education of Negroes, temperance, and the condition of the Indians.

**Ben′fey** (bĕn′fī), **Theodor.** 1809–1881. German Sanskrit scholar and comparative philologist. Professor, Göttingen (1848–81). Author of *A Dictionary of Greek Roots* (1839–42), *Complete Grammar of the Sanskrit Language* (1852), *Sanskrit-English Dictionary* (1866).

**ben-Gabirol.** See IBN-GABIROL.

**Beng′el** (bĕng′ĕl), **Johann Albrecht.** 1687–1752. German Protestant theologian and scholar. Master of a theological seminary, Denkendorf (1713–41). Author of a critical study of New Testament (1734); first to classify New Testament manuscripts into Asiatic and African families; author also of *Ordo Temporum* (1741), and *Gnomon Novi Testamenti* (1742), an exegetical commentary.

**Ben′gough** (bĕn′gō), **John Wilson.** 1851–1923. Canadian cartoonist, b. Toronto; on staff of Montreal *Star* and Toronto *Globe;* published two volumes of poetry (*Verses Grave and Gay,* 1895; *In Many Keys,* 1902) and several political brochures, as *The Gin Mill Primer* (1898) and *The Whole Hog Book* (1911).

**Ben-Gu·rion** (bĕn′go͝or·yôn′), **David.** *Orig. name* **David Gruen.** 1886–1973. Israeli statesman, b. Poland; to Palestine (1906); proclaimed independence of Israel (1948); head of provisional govt. (1948–49); prime minister (1949–53; 1955–63).

**Ben′ha′dad** *or* **Ben′-Ha′dad** (bĕn′hā′dăd). *In Douay Version* **Ben′a′dad** (bĕn′ā′dăd). Name of three kings of Damascus:

**Benhadad I.** fl. 900 B.C. Ally of Asa, King of Judah; fought Baasha of Israel (*2 Chron.* xvi).

**Benhadad II** *or* **Ha′dad·e′zer** (hā′dăd·ē′zẽr). fl. 854 B.C. Defeated by Ahab, King of Israel (*1 Kings* xx. 1–34); joined in coalition with Ahab, defeating Shalmaneser III of Assyria at Karkar (854).

**Benhadad III.** fl. 805 B.C. Son of Hazael. Defeated by Joash, King of Israel (*2 Kings* xiii. 24–25).

**Ben′ham** (bĕn′ăm), Sir **William Gurney.** 1859–1944. English journalist, and compiler of *Benham's Book of Quotations* (1907).

**Be′nin·ca′sa** (bā′nĕng·kä′sä), **Ursula.** 1547–1618. Italian religious; founded (1583) Oblate Sisters of the Immaculate Conception of the Blessed Virgin Mary, an order whose members were known as Theatines, or Theatine nuns.

**Be·ní′tez** (bȧ·nē′tās), **Justo Pastor.** 1896– . Paraguayan diplomat and journalist, b. Asunción. Minister of justice and public instruction, interior, finance, war, foreign affairs (1930–34); minister to Brazil (1935–38) and Bolivia (1938–1939). Author of *Ideario Político* (1919), *Jornadas Democráticas* (1921–22), *El Liberalismo en el Paraguay* (1930), *La Revolución de los Comuneros* (1938), etc.

**Ben′ja·min** (bĕn′j*ā*·mĭn). In Bible, youngest of Jacob's twelve sons (*Gen.* xxxv. 16–18; xlii–xlv), son of Rachel, ancestor of one of twelve tribes of Israel.

**Benjamin, Arthur.** 1893–1960. British pianist and composer, b. Sydney, Australia. Professor, Royal College of Music, London (from 1921). Received Carnegie award (1924) for the string quartet *Pastoral Fantasia.* Composer also of operas, piano and violin pieces, orchestral music, choral works, and songs.

**Benjamin, Asher.** 1773–1845. American architect and writer, b. Greenfield, Mass. His writings spread late colonial designs throughout New England.

**Benjamin, Judah Philip.** 1811–1884. Lawyer, b. in St. Thomas, British West Indies; to Charleston, S.C., while a child. U.S. senator from Louisiana (1853–61); attorney general in Jefferson Davis's cabinet (1861); transferred to war department (1861–62); secretary of state (1862–65); extremely unpopular because of advocacy of plan to arm slaves for Confederate service, but retained confidence of Davis. Escaped to England (1865); built up large and profitable legal practice there; queen's counsel (1872–83).

**Benjamin, Park.** 1809–1864. American editor and minor poet, b. in British Guiana; to Norwich Conn., at age of four. His son **Park** (1849–1922) was a patent lawyer, editor in chief of *Appleton's Cyclopaedia of Applied Mechanics* (1881–92), and author of books on electricity.

**Ben'ja'min'** (bäN'zhȧ'măN'), **René.** 1885–1948. French novelist, playwright, and essayist, b. in Paris. On staff of *Gil Blas* and *Écho de Paris.* Wounded at Verdun (1914). His novel *Gaspard* was awarded Goncourt prize (1915); other works include *Grandgoujon* (1918), *La Farce de la Sorbonne* (1921), *Vie Prodigieuse d'Honoré de Balzac* (1925), *Sacha Guitry* (1933), *Chronique d'un Temps Troublé* (1938), etc.

**Ben'ja'min'-Cons'tant'** (bäN'zhȧ'măN'kôNs'täN'). 1845–1902. = Benjamin CONSTANT.

**Ben'ja·min of Tu·de'la** (bĕn'jȧ·mĭn ŭv to͞o·thä'lä). d. 1173. Spanish Jewish traveler, b. in Navarre, Spain; visited France, Italy, Greece, Palestine, Persia, borders of China, Egypt, and Sicily (1159–1173); known esp. for *Massa 'ot* (*Travels*).

**Benkendorf.** See BENCKENDORFF.

**Ben·lliu're y Gil'** (bān·lyo͞o'rā ē hēl'), **José.** 1855–1936. Spanish painter, b. Valencia; best known for paintings of Spanish and Italian folk life. His brother **Mariano** (1862–1947), sculptor.

**Benn** (bĕn), **William Wedgwood.** 1877–1960. English political leader. B.A., London (1898). Liberal M.P. (1906–27), Labour M.P. (1927–31, 1937–42). Served in yeomanry and air force in World War I (1914–15). Secretary of state for India (1929–31).

**Benn'dorf** (bĕn'dôrf), **Otto.** 1838–1907. German archaeologist; professor in Zurich (1869), Munich (1871), Prague (1872), Vienna (1877); director of Austrian Archaeological Institute (1898).

**Ben'net** (bĕn'ĕt; -ĭt), **Henry.** See Earl of ARLINGTON.

**Bennet, Sanford Fillmore.** 1836–1898. American physician and hymn writer, b. Eden, N.Y.; author of *In the Sweet By and By.*

**Ben'nett** (bĕn'ĕt; -ĭt), **Alfred William.** 1833–1902. English botanist; collaborated with G. Murray in *Handbook of Cryptogamic Botany* (1889); wrote *Flora of Alps* (2 vols., 1896–97).

**Bennett, Arnold,** *in full* **Enoch Arnold.** 1867–1931. English novelist and dramatist. Abandoned law to become assistant editor of *Woman* (1893); abandoned editorship (1900) to devote himself to literature. Made reputation as a master in fiction with *Old Wives' Tale* (1908). Treated in infinite detail ugly, sordid life in the "Five Towns," centers of the pottery industry, in the trilogy of novels *Clayhanger* (1910), *Hilda Lessways* (1911), *These Twain* (1916). Dramatized his novel *Buried Alive* (1908) as *Great Adventure* (1913) and wrote, with Edward Knoblock, the play *Milestones* (1912). Other works include *Riceyman Steps* (1923), *Lord Raingo* (1926), *Accident* (1929).

**Bennett, Charles Edwin.** 1858–1921. American Latin scholar, b. Providence, R.I. Professor, Cornell (1892–1921); author of *A Latin Grammar* (1895, with many later editions), *Appendix to Bennett's Latin Grammar* (1895; revised, 1907, as *The Latin Language*), numerous other textbooks, and translations.

**Bennett, Floyd.** 1890–1928. American aviator, b. near Warrensburg, N.Y. With Byrd in MacMillan expedition to northwestern Greenland (1925); pilot with Byrd in flight over North Pole (May 9, 1926); received Congressional Medal of Honor. Floyd Bennett Airport, Brooklyn, named in his honor.

**Bennett, Henry Gordon.** 1887–1962. Australian soldier; served in World War I (1915–18); major general, commanding 8th division of Australian Imperial Force (1940), all Australian forces in Malaya (1941); escaped from Singapore when it surrendered to Japanese (Feb., 1942); lieutenant general (Mar., 1942).

**Bennett, James Gordon.** 1795–1872. Editor, b. Keith, Banffshire, Scotland; to Halifax, Nova Scotia (1819). On staff of *New York Enquirer* (1826–28), and its successor, *Morning Courier and New York Enquirer* (1829–32). Started New York *Herald* (May 6, 1835), a one-cent daily newspaper; remained its editor until his retirement (1867). His son **James Gordon** (1841–1918) succeeded him; sent Stanley to Africa to find Livingstone (1869–71); financed expedition (1875) to search for a northwest passage and expedition (1879–81) of George W. DeLong to the Arctic; established (1887) Paris edition of New York *Herald;* joined John W. Mackay in Commercial Cable Co. which laid transatlantic cables and broke Gould monopoly. Suddenly broke off marriage engagement (1877); horsewhipped by fiancée's brother; fought duel; resident in Paris (from 1877). Established Gordon Bennett international trophies in yachting and automobile and aeronautical racing.

**Bennett, James William.** 1891– . American writer, b. Mitchell, Ind. A.B., Stanford (1916). American vice-consul at Shanghai, China (1918–19) and Sydney, Australia (1919). Author of *Plum Blossoms and Blue Incense* (1926), *The Manchu Cloud* (1927), *Chinese Blake* (1930), *Spinach Jade* (1939), etc.

**Bennett, John Hughes.** 1812–1875. English physician. M.D., Edinburgh (1837). Introduced systematic lectures on histology, Edinburgh (1841); professor of institutes of medicine, Edinburgh (1843–74). Pioneer in use of microscope in clinical pathology.

**Bennett, Richard.** 1872–1944. American actor and producer, b. in Cass County, Ind.; associated as producer with Charles Frohman (1896–1908); appeared in *Charley's Aunt, Royal Family, What Every Woman Knows, Jarnegan, The Barker;* father of **Constance** (1905–1965), b. New York City, motion-picture actress (debut in *Cytherea,* 1924; later starred in many productions) and of **Joan** (1910– ), b. Palisades, N.J., actress, on stage (debut with father in *Jarnegan,* 1928) and in many motion pictures.

**Bennett, Richard Bedford.** Viscount **Bennett.** 1870–1947. Canadian statesman; minister of justice and attorney general (1921); prime minister (1930–35).

**Bennett, William Cox.** 1820–1895. English song writer.

**Bennett,** Sir **William Sterndale.** 1816–1875. English pianist and composer. Intimate friend (from 1832) of Mendelssohn; professor of music at Cambridge (1856); principal, Royal Academy of Music (1868). Composed

*Naiads* (overture; 1837), *The May Queen* (cantata; 1858), *Paradise and Peri* (overture; 1862), *Symphony in G Minor* (1864), *Woman of Samaria* (oratorio; 1867), *Ajax* (1872).

**Bennewitz, Peter.** Real name of Petrus APIANUS.

**Ben–Nez.** See Morris WINCHEVSKY.

**Ben′nig·sen** (bĕn′ĭκ·sĕn), Count **Le′vin** (lā′vēn) **Au′gust** (ou′go͝ost) **The′o·phil** (tā′ô·fēl). 1745–1826. Russian general, b. in Brunswick, of Hanoverian family. Entered Russian service (1773); fought against Turks (1774, 1778), in Poland (1793–94), and at Derbent in Persian War (1796); active in conspiracy that led to assassination of Emperor Paul (1801); in Napoleonic Wars, fought at Pułtusk (1806) and commanded at Eylau (1807); in French attack (1812), won victory over Murat but retired because of difference with Kutuzov; later, commanded Russian army on right wing at Leipzig (1813); made count by the emperor. His son Count **Alexander Levin** (1809–93) was a distinguished Hanoverian statesman.

**Ben′nig·sen** (bĕn′ĭκ·sĕn), **Rudolf von.** 1824–1902. German statesman and political leader, b. in Hanover. Leader of liberal opposition in lower chamber; cofounder and leader of German National Verein (1859–67), which joined National Liberal party. Member (1867–83) and president (1873–79), Prussian Assembly; member (1871–83, 1887–98) of German Reichstag and leader of National Liberal party; warmly supported Bismarck; later (1878 ff.), opposed Bismarck's economic policy and laws against Socialists; chief administrator, Province of Hanover (1888–97). His son **Rudolf** (1859–1911) was first governor of German New Guinea (1899–1902).

**Ben′no** (bĕn′ō), Saint. 1010–1106. Bishop of Meissen (1066) and missionary among the Wends. His canonization (1523) by Pope Adrian VI violently attacked by Luther in *Wider den Neuen Abgott.* Patron saint of Bavaria and of Munich; his remains deposited (1576) in latter place.

**Be·nois′** (byĭ·noi′), **Aleksandr Nikolaevich.** 1870–1960. Russian painter; known esp. for his painting of scenery for Stravinsky's ballet *Petruchka* and for ballets of Diaghilev.

**Be·noît′** (bẽ·nwȧ′), **Pierre.** 1886–1962. French novelist, b. Albi; author of *Koenigsmark, L'Atlantide, Pour Don Carlos, Le Lac Salé, L'Oublié,* etc.

**Benoît, Pierre Léonard Léopold,** *also known as* **Peter.** 1834–1901. Belgian composer; director of Antwerp Conservatory of Music; leader in Flemish musical school; composer of oratorios, operas, cantatas, religious dramas, hymns, and songs.

**Benoît de Sainte′-Maure′** *or* **Sainte′-More′** (dẽ săNt′môr′). 12th-century French trouvère; author of a verse *Chronique des Ducs de Normandie* for his patron, Henry II of England. His *Roman de Troie,* founded on works of Dares Phrygius and Dictys Cretensis, was used in Latin version by Guido delle Colonne and became a source for retellings (as by Boccaccio, Chaucer, and Shakespeare) of the Troilus and Cressida story.

**Benozzo Gozzoli.** See GOZZOLI.

**Ben′se·rade′** (băNs′rȧd′), **Isaac de.** 1613–1691. French poet and dramatist; under patronage of Richelieu and Mazarin. Best known for a sonnet, *Job,* taken as rivaling a sonnet by Voiture entitled *Uranie* and initiating a literary civil war between adherents (Jobelins and Uranins) of the two poets at court.

**Ben′son** (bĕn′s'n), **Edward White.** 1829–1896. English prelate. B.A., Cantab. (1852); first head master of Wellington College (1859–72); bishop of Truro (1877); archbishop of Canterbury (1882); sponsored legislation reforming church patronage and discipline; opposed Welsh disestablishment (1893); delivered historically important judgment at trial of Dr. Edward King, Bishop of Lincoln, charged with ritual offenses (1889–90). Author of *Cyprian* (1897) and *The Apocalypse* (1900). His eldest son, **Arthur Christopher** (1862–1925), master at Eton (1885–1903), master of Magdalene College, Cambridge (1915–25); editor with Viscount Esher of *Correspondence of Queen Victoria* (1907); author of a biography of his father, monographs (in *English Men of Letters Series,* 1904–06) on Rossetti, FitzGerald, and Pater, and *From a College Window* (1906), *Beside Still Waters* (1907), *Memories and Friends* (1924). His third son, **Edward Frederic** (1867–1940), novelist; engaged in archaeological work at Athens (1892–95) and in work of Hellenic Society in Egypt; author of society novel *Dodo* (1893), novels of modern Greece, as *The Capsina* (1899), and clever fiction including *The Challoners* (1904), *David of Kings* (1924), *Mezzanine* (1926). His fourth son, **Robert Hugh** (1871–1914), clergyman; took Anglican orders (1894); received into Roman Catholic Church (1903), ordained (1904); popular as preacher and as writer of semimystical fiction, as *The Light Invisible* (1903), historical fiction, as *By What Authority* (1904), and modern novels.

**Benson,** Sir **Frank Robert.** 1858–1939. English actor-manager. As student at Oxford produced Greek play *Agamemnon;* founded touring repertory company, and school of acting; produced many of Shakespeare's plays; organized 26 of annual Stratford-on-Avon Shakespeare festivals. For his brother **Godfrey Rathbone,** see Baron CHARNWOOD.

**Benson, Frank Weston.** 1862–1951. American painter, b. Salem, Mass. Studied at Museum of Fine Arts in Boston (1880–83) and Académie Julian in Paris (1883–85). Teacher at Museum of Fine Arts in Boston (from 1889). Excels in painting women and children, often in outdoor scenes of brilliant light and color. Among well-known paintings are *My Little Girl, In the Spruce Woods, Pomona, Moonlight at Sea, Eleanor.* Painted the murals *The Seasons* and *The Three Graces* (in Congressional Library at Washington, D.C.).

**Benson, Louis FitzGerald.** 1855–1930. American hymnologist, b. Philadelphia. Grad. U. of Pennsylvania (1874); Princeton Theological Seminary (1887); in Presbyterian ministry (from 1887); devoted himself to hymnology (from 1894). Editor of various church hymnals; author of *Hymns and Verses* (1897), etc.

**Benson, Richard Meux** (mūks). 1824–1915. English ecclesiastic. Founded at Oxford (1865) an Anglican Society of Mission Priests of St. John the Evangelist, often called "Cowley Fathers"; established branch in Boston, Mass. (1870–71).

**Benson, Stella.** 1892–1933. English novelist, poet, and short-story writer; m. (1921) J. C. O'Gorman Anderson of Chinese customs service. Author of *I Pose* (1915), *Living Alone* (1919), *Good-Bye, Stranger* (1926), *Tobit Transplanted* (in U.S., *The Far-away Bride*) (1931).

**Benson, William Shepherd.** 1855–1932. American naval officer, b. Macon, Ga. Grad., U.S.N.A., Annapolis (1877). Promoted through the grades to captain (1909) and rear admiral (1915); chief of naval operations (1915–19); served on special commissions abroad during World War I and in Paris (1919) as naval adviser to American Commission to Negotiate Peace; retired (1919). Chairman, U.S. Shipping Board (1920).

**Bent** (bĕnt), **Charles.** 1799–1847. American pioneer, b. Charleston, Va. (now W.Va.). Fur trapper in Colorado and New Mexico (1823–47). With his brother **William** (1809–1869), built trading post, Bent's Fort, near present La Junta (1828–52). William became first permanent white settler in Colorado and that state's most prominent citizen. Another brother, **Silas** (1820–1887), was an American naval officer (from 1836); accompanied Perry on his trip to Japan; made extensive hydrographic surveys in Pacific.

**Bent, James Theodore.** 1852–1897. English explorer and archaeologist. B.A., Oxon. (1875). Made archaeological journeys to Greece, Asia Minor, Abyssinia, Arabia, the Bahrein Islands, South Africa. Made excavations of ruins of the Great Zimbabwe in Mashonaland (1891).

**Ben'tham** (bĕn'thăm), **Jeremy.** 1748–1832. English jurist and philosopher; one of chief expounders of utilitarianism. M.A., Oxon. (1766). Called to bar (1772); wrote criticism of Blackstone's *Commentaries* as showing antipathy to reform (1776). Made recommendations in *View of the Hard Labour Bill* (1778) for improvement in mode of criminal punishment, published later in *Rationale of Punishment and Rewards* (1825). Made trip to Russia (1785–88) to visit his brother (see below); there wrote *Defence of Usury* (printed 1787), his first essay in economics, following the principles of Adam Smith. Published (1789) work on administration of justice, *Introduction to the Principles of Morals and Legislation*, expounding his basic ethical doctrine that morality of actions is determined by utility, that is, the capacity for rendering pleasure or preventing pain, according to which the object of all conduct and legislation is "the greatest happiness of the greatest number"—the key phrase of Benthamism (suggested by Priestley's *Essay on the First Principles of Government*, 1768, and earlier used in Hutcheson's *Ideas of Beauty and Virtue*, 1725). Studied poor law question (1797–98). Wrote several treatises developed in *Rationale of Judicial Evidence* (edited by J. S. Mill, 1825). Aided in establishing *Westminster Review* (1823) to spread philosophical radicalism; working on codification of laws and *Constitutional Code* (1st vol., 1827) at his death. His nephew and secretary (1826–32), **George** (1800–1884), was an English botanist; studied law; wrote *Outlines of a New System of Logic* (1827), setting forth for first time principle of the qualification of the predicate; author of *Handbook of British Flora* (1858); produced for government works on flora of Hong Kong and Australia; collaborated with Joseph Hooker in *Genera Plantarum* (7 vols., 1862–83). Jeremy's brother Sir **Samuel** (1757–1831) was a naval architect and engineer; colonel in Russian service; superintendent of shipbuilding yard at Kritchev.

**Ben'tinck** (bĕn'tĭngk), **William.** 1st Earl of **Port'land** [pōrt'lănd; pôrt'-] (2d creation). 1649?–1709. English soldier and diplomat, b. in Holland; descendant of a noble family from the Palatinate. Trusted agent of William III; made privy councilor (1689); helped arrange treaty of Ryswick (1697); negotiated and signed treaties of partition (1698, 1700). His eldest son **Henry** (1680–1724) was created 1st duke of Portland (1716). His great grandson **William Henry Cav'en·dish** (kăv'ĕn·dĭsh) **Bentinck** (1738–1809), 3d Duke of Portland; son of William (1709–1762), 2d duke; assumed by license additional name Cavendish; lord chamberlain under Rockingham (1765) and lord lieutenant of Ireland (1782); prime minister (1783); home secretary (1794–1801); lord president of the council (1801–05) under Pitt; again prime minister (1807–09). Lord **William Cavendish Bentinck** (1774–1839), 2d son of 3d duke, a lieutenant colonel at Marengo, was governor of Madras (1803); recalled (1807) on account of a Sepoy mutiny at Vellore (1806); governor general of Bengal (1828–33), effecting financial and judicial reform, suppression of Thugs, and abolition of suttee (1829); first governor general of India (1833). Lord **William George Frederic Cavendish Bentinck** (1802–1848), son of 4th duke, was a devotee of horse racing; M.P. (1828–48); leader of anti-Peel protectionists (1846–47).

**Bent'ley** (bĕnt'lĭ), **Edmund Clerihew.** 1875–1956. English writer of detective fiction, as *Trent's Last Case* (1912), *Trent Intervenes* (1938), etc.; originator of a type of humorous pseudo-biographical verse known as clerihews. His son **Nicolas Clerihew** (1907–    ), writer and illustrator of humorous works, including *Die? I Thought I'd Laugh* (1936), *Ballet Hoo* (1937), *Le Sport* (1939), *Animal, Vegetable, and South Kensington* (1940).

**Bent'ley** (bĕnt'lĭ), **John Francis.** 1839–1902. English ecclesiastical architect. Developed an English form of Gothic in building and decorating churches and convents; designed and built in Byzantine style the Roman Catholic cathedral in Westminster (1894 ff.).

**Bentley, Phyllis Eleanor.** 1894–    . English novelist; in early years, teacher, secretary, lecturer, and reviewer by turns; author of novels with Yorkshire background, including *The Spinner of the Years* (1928), *The Partnership* (1928), *Carr* (1929), *Trio* (1930), *Inheritance* (1932), *A Modern Tragedy* (1934), *Freedom, Farewell!* (1936), *Take Courage* (1940), *Manhold* (1941).

**Bentley, Richard.** 1662–1742. English clergyman, scholar, and critic. B.A., Cantab. (1680). Won reputation as classical scholar by critical letter to Mill (1691). Delivered first Boyle lectures, *A Confutation of Atheism* (1692). Proved in controversy (1697–99) with Charles Boyle (*q.v.*) spuriousness of *Epistles of Phalaris*, evoking Jonathan Swift's *Battle of the Books*. Master of Trinity College, Cambridge (1700–42); tried and nearly ejected for despotic rule. Known for critical texts of classical authors.

**Bentley, Richard.** 1794–1871. English publisher; founder of *Bentley's Miscellany* (1837–68), of which Dickens was first editor, succeeded by Ainsworth. His son **George** (1828–1895) was also a publisher in London.

**Ben'ton** (bĕn't'n; -tŭn), **Frank.** 1852–1919. American apiculturist, b. Coldwater, Mich.; investigated bee culture in Asia, Africa, and Europe (1880–91); author of *The Honey Bee* (1896), *Bee Keeping* (1897), etc.

**Benton, Thomas Hart.** 1782–1858. American political leader, b. Hillsboro, N.C.; father of Jessie Frémont (*q.v.*). To St. Louis, Mo. (1815). Member, U.S. Senate (1821–51); defender of sound money; supported Jackson in his campaign against the national bank; often called "Old Bullion." In slavery issue, opposed secession; defeated (1850) for Senate because of stand on slavery issue. Member, U.S. House of Representatives (1853–55). Author of *Thirty Years' View* (1854–56), his political autobiography.

His grandnephew **Thomas Hart Benton** (1889–1975); American painter, b. Neosho, Mo.; studied at Chicago Art Institute (1906–07) and in Académie Julian, Paris, France (1908–11); served as private in World War; has devoted himself to vigorous and realistic portraiture of people representing ordinary life and occupations of American Middle West, among well-known paintings being *Cotton Pickers, Lonesone Road, Meal, Homestead,* and *Susanna and the Elders;* his paintings of farm life, especially, have won prizes in many exhibitions; director, department of painting, Kansas City (Mo.) Art Institute (from 1935); his murals include *The Arts of Life in America* (Whitney Museum of American Art, in New York City), *History of Indiana* painted for Indiana Building at Century of Progress Exhibition in Chicago (1933), and *History of Missouri* for State House at Jefferson City, Mo.

**Bent'zel-Stern'au** (bĕn'tsĕl·shtĕr'nou), Count **Christian Ernst zu.** 1767–1849. German statesman and writer. Minister of finance, grand duchy of Frankfurt (1812). Author esp. of satirical tales and novels.

**Ben'-Ya·hu'da** (bĕn'yȧ·hōō'dȧ) *or* **Ben'-Ye·hu'da** (bĕn'yĕ-), **E'li·e'ser** (ĕ'lĭ·ĕ'zẽr). 1858–1922. Hebrew scholar and Zionist; b. in Lithuania, son of Jehudah Perlman; studied medicine in Paris; to Palestine (1881); in U.S. (1914–18); instrumental in introducing Hebrew as language of daily speech in Palestine, modernizing the language by addition of new words. Compiler of great Hebrew lexicon (unfinished at time of his death).

**Benz** (bĕnts), **Karl.** 1844–1929. German engineer; pioneer in construction of motor-driven vehicles (first car driven through streets of Munich, 1886). Founded firm of Benz & Co., Mannheim, to manufacture motor cars. Cf. Gottlieb DAIMLER.

**Beolco, Angelo.** See Il RUZZANTE.

**Beö'thy** (bû'tĭ), **Zsolt.** 1848–1922. Hungarian educator; professor, Budapest (from 1882); author of history of Hungarian literature (1896).

**Bé'rain'** (bā'răɴ'), **Jean.** 1639?–1711. French architect and designer; director of fetes in court of Louis XIV. His designs, costumes, decorations, etc., mark transition from style of Louis XIV to that of Louis XV.

**Bé'ran'ger'** (bā'räɴ'zhā'), **Pierre Jean de.** 1780–1857. French lyric poet, b. Paris. Liberal in political sympathies; his chansons, including *Le Roi d'Yvetot* and *Le Vieux Drapeau*, gained immense popularity with the masses of the French people.

**Bé'rard'** (bā'rär'), **Christian.** 1902–1949. French painter, b. Paris; identified with neoromantic school; his paintings include *Après le Nain* and *Sur la Plage.*

**Bérard, Joseph Frédéric.** 1789–1828. French physician and philosopher.

**Bérard, Léon.** 1876–1960. French lawyer and politician; member, chamber of deputies (1910–27) and senate (from 1927); minister of public instruction (1917, 1919–20, 1926–28); minister of justice and vice-president of council (1931–32); minister of justice (1935).

**Bérard, Victor.** 1864–1931. French scholar and publicist; student of Greek classics; translator of *Odyssey;* author of treatises on current affairs.

**Bé'raud'** (bā'rō'), **Henri.** 1885–1958. French novelist and political essayist; author of *Le Vitriol de la Lune* (1921; Goncourt prize), *Le Martyre de l'Obèse* (1922), *Les Lurons de Sabolas* (1932), *Ciel de Suie* (1934), *Trois Ans de Colère* (essays; 1937), etc.

**Béraud, Jean.** 1849?–?1935. Portrait and genre painter, b. St. Petersburg, Russia, of French parentage; studied under Bonnat in Paris; known esp. for his paintings of religious subjects and Paris scenes.

**Berceo, Gonzalo de.** See GONZALO DE BERCEO.

**Ber'chem** *or* **Ber'ghem** (bĕr'ᴋĕm), **Nicolaes Pietersz.** 1620–1683. Dutch landscape painter and etcher.

**Ber'chère'** (bĕr'shâr'), **Narcisse.** 1819–1891. French painter, esp. of Oriental scenes.

**Ber·chet'** (bâr·shā'), **Giovanni.** 1783–1851. Italian poet, b. Milan; political exile in England, France, Germany (1821–47); his works include *Lettera Semiseria* (manifesto of the Romantic movement in Italy, 1816), political and patriotic poems, and a collection of ballads.

**Berch'told** (bĕrᴋ'tōlt), Count **Leopold von.** 1863–1942. Austro-Hungarian statesman, b. Vienna. Ambassador at St. Petersburg (1907–11); foreign minister (1912–15); signed Austrian ultimatum to Serbia (1914) preceding World War.

**Berck·hey'de** (bĕrk·hī'dĕ), **Gerrit** (1638–1698) and his brother **Job** (1630–1693). Dutch painters, b. Haarlem. Gerrit's paintings include chiefly street scenes and views of public places; Job's paintings, chiefly landscapes and architectural and genre subjects.

**Ber'co·vici** (*Rum.* bĕr'kō·vēch; *Angl.* bûr'kō·vē'sē), **Kon'rad** (*Rum.* kŏn'räd). 1882–1961. American novelist and short-story writer, of Rumanian birth; to U.S. (1916); author of *Around the World in New York* (1918), *Ghitza* (1919), *Ileana—The Marriage Guest* (1925), *The Story of the Gypsies* (1928), *That Royal Lover* (1931), *Against the Sky* (1932), *The Incredible Balkans* (1933), and many articles and tales about gypsies.

**Ber'da·nier'** (bûr'd'n·ẽr'), **Paul Frederick.** 1879–1961. American painter and etcher, b. Frackville, Pa. Best known for landscapes and prints.

**Ber·dya'ev** (byĕr·dyȧ'yĕf), **Nikolai Aleksandrovich.** 1874–1948. Russian philosopher; author of *Freedom and the Spirit* (Eng. tr., 1935), and *The Destiny of Man* (Eng. tr., 1937), *Solitude and Society* (Eng. tr., 1938), *Spirit and Reality* (Eng. tr., 1939).

**Be'rend** (bā'rĕnt), **Alice.** *Pen name of* **Alice Berend Brein'ling·er** (brīn'lĭng·ẽr). 1878– . German novelist and playwright.

**Be'rendt** (bā'rĕnt), **Karl Hermann.** 1817–1878. German physician and ethnologist; fled Germany after political upheavals (1848–49); to Nicaragua (1851–55), Mexico (1855–62), Yucatán (1864?), Guatemala (1874 ff.). Author of *Analytical Alphabet of the Mexican and Central American Languages* (1869), *Los Indigenas de la América Central y sus Idiomas* (1878), etc.

**Ber'en·gar** (bĕr'ĕn·gär). *Ital.* **Be'ren·ga'rio** (bā'răng·gä'ryō). *Lat.* **Ber'en·gar'i·us** (bĕr'ĕn·gâr'ĭ·ŭs). Name of two kings of Italy: **Berengar I** (d. 924); grandson of Louis the Pious; marquis of Fri'u·li (frē'ōō·lē; frē·ōō'lē) and king of the Lombards (888–889, 898–924); Holy Roman emperor (915–924); defeated by Duke Guy of Spoleto; crowned emperor, last of the Italian line, by Pope John X (915); had troubled reign; called in Hungarians as allies. His grandson **Berengar II** (d. 966); overcame Hugh of Provence (945); king (950–961); overthrown by Emperor Otto I (961); became feudatory of Germany; died a prisoner at Bamberg.

**Ber'en·gar'i·a** (bĕr'ĕn·gâr'ĭ·ȧ). *Span.* **Be'ren·gue'la** (bā'rĕng·gā'lä). 1108–1149. Daughter of Ramón Berenguer IV, Conde de Barcelona. Queen of Castile; m. (1128), as 2d husband, Alfonso VII of León and Castile; defended Toledo against Moors (1139); famous for her beauty.

**Berengaria.** d. 1230? Daughter of Sancho VI of Navarre. Queen of England; wife of Richard I. Joined Richard at Reggio, Italy (1191), when on (Third) Crusade to Holy Land; m. Richard (1191) at Limassol, Cyprus; accompanied him to Acre; resided there (1191–92) during campaign against Saracens; lived at Poitou during Richard's imprisonment (1192–94) in Germany; possibly estranged after his release; after Richard's death (1199) lived mostly at Le Mans in Maine.

**Berengaria.** *Sp.* **Berenguela.** 1171–1246. Daughter of Alfonso VIII (III) of Castile and Eleanor Plantagenet (daughter of Henry II of England); 2d wife of Alfonso IX (VIII) of León; marriage (1197) stopped wars, but annulled (1214) by Pope Innocent III on ground of kinship; after death of her father Alfonso (1214) and her brother Henry I (1217), queen for a few months (1217); proclaimed her son Ferdinand (III) king (1217).

**Bé'ren'ger'** (bā'räɴ'zhā'). *Called* **Bérenger de Tours** (dē tōōr'). *Lat.* **Ber'en·gar'i·us** (bĕr'ĕn·gâr'ĭ·ŭs). 998–1088. French ecclesiastic, b. Tours, France; attacked (c. 1045) dogmas of transubstantiation and the real presence; condemned for heresy; recanted; spent last years as an ascetic.

**Bérenger, René.** 1830–1915. French jurist and legislator, b. Valence. Minister of public works in cabinet of Casimir-Périer; elected senator for life (1875). Interested in judicial and prison reforms; author of "Bérenger laws" favoring or granting immunity to first offenders; prominent in move to suppress exhibition of indecent pictures and inscriptions (hence his nickname "Père la Pudeur").

**Bérenger, Victor Henry.** 1867–1952. French author, politician, and diplomat, b. Rugles. Ambassador to U.S. (1926).

**Berenguela.** Spanish form of BERENGARIA.

**Be'ren·guer'** (bā'rĕng·gĕr'), **Ramón.** Name of four counts of Barcelona (1017–1162), esp. Ramón Berenguer IV (count, 1131–62), who married **Pe'tro·nil'la** (pā'trô·nē'lyä), queen (1137–62) of Aragon, daughter of Ramiro II, and by her was father of Alfonso II of Aragon (1162–96) and of Berengaria, queen of Castile.

**Ber'e·ni'ce** (bĕr'ĕ·nī'sē). Name of several Egyptian princesses, esp.: (1) **Berenice I** (d. before 283 B.C.); wife and half sister of Ptolemy I Soter and granddaughter of Cassander; mother of Ptolemy II Philadelphus. (2) **Berenice** (d. 246 B.C.); daughter of Ptolemy II Philadelphus; m. Antiochus II Theos (*q.v.*). (3) **Berenice II** of Cyrene (d. 216? B.C.); m. Ptolemy III Euergetes; subject of legend giving rise to name of the constellation *Coma Berenices;* mother of Ptolemy IV Philopator. See CONON of Samos.

**Berenice** *or* **Ber·ni'ce** (bẽr·nī'sē; bûr-). Name of two Jewish princesses: (1) Daughter of Salome (sister of Herod the Great) and mother by Aristobulus of Herod Agrippa I. (2) Eldest daughter of Herod Agrippa I. 28? A.D.–after 75 A.D. Married three times; m. as 2d husband her uncle Herod of Chalcis (*q.v.*), and as 3d, Polemon, King of Cilicia; left latter to live at court of her brother Herod Agrippa II; Paul appeared before her, Herod Agrippa, and Festus (c. 60) at Caesarea (*Acts* xxv. 13–xxvi. 32); retired with Herod to live at Rome (75); noted for her beauty; mistress of Titus.

**Ber'en·son** (bĕr'ĕn·s'n), **Bernhard.** 1865–1959. Art critic and author, b. in Lithuania. A.B., Harvard (1887). m. (1900) Mary Logan Smith, daughter of Hannah Whitall Smith (*q.v.*). Author of *Venetian Painters of the Renaissance* (1894), *The Study and Criticism of Italian Art* (1901, 1902, 1915), *Essays in Mediaeval Art* (1930), etc.

**Be'rent** (bĕ'rĕnt), **Wacław.** 1873–1940. Polish fiction writer, b. Warsaw.

**Be·re'ra** (bā·râ'rä), **Orlando.** 1915?– . Italian violinist, b. Ferrara. Soloist with New York Philharmonic Orchestra (1938).

**Ber'es·ford** (bĕr'ĭz·fẽrd; bĕr'ĭs-), Lord **Charles William de la Poer.** 1st Baron **Beresford.** 1846–1919. British naval officer, b. in Ireland. Took part in bombardment of Alexandria (1882) and Nile expedition (1884–85); advocate of big navy program in parliament; full admiral (1906). Author of *The Betrayal,* a protest against Lord Fisher's shipbuilding policy (1912), *Life of Nelson and his Times* (1898–1905), etc.

**Beresford, John Davys.** 1873–1947. English novelist. Architect by profession. Earned reputation as writer with biographical trilogy about an architect, *Jacob Stahl* (1911), *A Candidate for Truth* (1912), *The Invisible Event* (1915). Other works include *God's Counterpoint* (1918), *The Monkey Puzzle* (1925), *Love's Illusion* (1930), *Cleo* (1937), *Snell's Folly* (1939), *Strange Rival* (1940).

**Beresford, William Carr.** Viscount **Beresford.** 1768–1854. British general. Natural son of 1st marquis of Waterford. Served in Nova Scotia (1786) and in Europe; made reputation in Egypt (1801–03) and at taking of Cape of Good Hope (1805); served through Peninsular War; reorganized Portuguese army; won victory of La Albuera (1811); commanded center of army in battles of Nivelle, the Nive, and Orthez (1814); general (1825); made master general of ordnance by Wellington (1828).

**Berg** (bĕrk), **Alban.** 1885–1935. Austrian composer of songs, piano sonata, orchestral works, chamber concerto, lyric suite, etc.

**Berg, Friedrich W. R.** See Fëdor Fëdorovich BERK.

**Ber'gaigne'** (bĕr'gĕn'y'), **Abel Henri Joseph.** 1838–1888. French Sanskrit scholar; professor at Sorbonne.

**Bergamasco, Il.** See Giovanni Battista CASTELLO.

**Ber'gen** (bûr'gĕn), **Edgar John.** 1903– . American ventriloquist and comedian, b. Chicago; achieved success on radio and in motion pictures with famous dummy "Charlie McCarthy" (first radio appearance Dec. 17, 1936) and, later, with "Mortimer Snerd."

**Ber'ger** (bĕr'gẽr), **Ludwig.** 1777–1839. German pianist and composer; teacher of pianoforte in Berlin (from 1815); among his pupils were Mendelssohn, Taubert, Henselt, Fanny Hensel, etc.

**Ber'ger** (bûr'gẽr), **Vic'tor** (vĭk'tẽr) **L.** 1860–1929. Socialist editor and leader, b. in Austria; to U.S. (1878); settled in Milwaukee. Editor, Milwaukee *Daily Vorwaerts* (1892–98), *Social Democratic Herald* (1900), Milwaukee *Leader* (Socialist daily newspaper; from 1911). Pioneer in U.S. in organizing Socialists. Member, U.S. House of Representatives (1911–13), first Socialist elected to Congress; elected again (1918 and again 1919) but excluded by Congress on ground of disloyalty to U.S. (1919); finally elected and seated (1923–29). Sentenced to prison for 20 years on charge of giving aid and comfort to the enemy in time of war (1918–19); sentence reversed by U.S. Supreme Court (1921).

**Bergerac, Cyrano de.** See CYRANO DE BERGERAC.

**Ber'ge·rat'** (bĕr'zhẽ·rȧ'), **Auguste Émile.** 1845–1923. French poet, playwright, and literary critic; b. Paris.

**Ber'gey** (bûr'gĭ), **David Hendricks.** 1860–1937. American bacteriologist, b. Montgomery County, Pa. Grad. Pennsylvania (1884). On faculty (1903–32), professor (1926–32), director of laboratory of hygiene (1928–31), Pennsylvania. Authority on classification of bacteria. Author of *The Principles of Hygiene* (1901), etc.

**Bergh** (bûrg), **Christian.** 1763–1843. American shipbuilder, b. near Rhinebeck, N.Y. Opened shipyard on East River, New York City (?1785); retired from business (1837). His son **Henry** (1811–1888) founded American Society for the Prevention of Cruelty to Animals (1866), and served as its first president; instrumental in founding Society for the Prevention of Cruelty to Children (1875).

**Bergh** (băr'y'), **Johan Edvard.** 1828–1880. Swedish landscape painter, b. Stockholm; professor, Stockholm (from 1861).

**Bergh** (bĕrk), **Pieter Theodor Helvetius van den.** 1799–1873. Dutch poet and playwright; author of the comedy *The Nephew* (1837).

**Berg'haus** (bĕrk'hous), **Heinrich.** 1797–1884. German geographer and cartographer. His nephew **Hermann** (1828–1890) was also a cartographer; prepared new edition of Heinrich's *Physikalischer Atlas* (1886).

**Berghem.** See BERCHEM.

**Ber'gi·us** (bĕr'gē·ŏŏs), **Friedrich.** 1884–1949. German chemist; founder of a technical research laboratory in Hanover. Investigated effect of high pressure on chemical actions; developed processes for production of motor fuels by hydrogenation of coal under pressure and for production of sugar from wood. Awarded (with Karl Bosch) 1931 Nobel prize for chemistry.

**Bergk** (bĕrk), **Theodor.** 1812–1881. German classical scholar and philologist. Author of *Poetae Lyrici Graeci*

(3 vols., 1843), editions of Sophocles (2d ed., 1868) and Aristophanes (1872), etc.

**Berg'man** (bär'y'·män), **Torbern Olof.** 1735–1784. Swedish analytical chemist and physicist. Professor, U. of Uppsala. First to obtain nickel in a pure state (1775). Author of *Elective Attractions* (1775) and *Opuscula Physica et Chemica* (1779–90).

**Berg'mann** (běrк'män), **Ernst von.** 1836–1907. Latvian-born German surgeon. Specialist in brain surgery. Pioneered in aseptic methods. His son **Gustav von Bergmann** (1878–1955), b. Würzburg, also a physician.

**Berg'ner** (běrg'nẽr), **Elisabeth.** 1900– . British (Austrian-born) actress; m. Paul Czinner. Appeared in stage and motion-picture plays; in America (from 1935) in *Escape Me Never, As You Like It, Dreaming Lips,* etc.

**Ber·gon'zi** (bär·gôn'tsē), **Carlo.** c. 1686–1747. Violin maker of Cremona, Italy; pupil of Stradivarius. His son **Michelangelo** and grandsons **Niccolò, Zosimo,** and **Carlo** were also violinmakers.

**Berg'söe** (běrк'sû), **Jörgen Wilhelm.** 1835–1911. Danish naturalist and novelist. Among his novels are *Piazza del Popolo* (1866) and *Who Was He?* (1878).

**Berg'son'** (běrg'sôɴ'; *Angl.* běrg's'n), **Henri.** 1859–1941. French philosopher, b. Paris. Professor, Collège de France (1900–21). Elements of his philosophical theory (known as Bergsonism) found in his *Essai sur les Données Immédiates de la Conscience* (1889), *Matière et Mémoire* (1897), *Le Rire* (1900), *L'Évolution Créatrice* (1906), *L'Énergie Spirituelle* (1920), *Durée et Simultanéité* (1922). Awarded Nobel prize in literature (1927).

**Berg'ström** (běrк'strûm), **Hjalmar.** 1868–1914. Danish playwright. Author of *When King David Grew Old* (1902), *Lynggaard & Co.* (1905), *Karen Borneman* (1907), *In the Swim* (1910), *The Way to God* (1912), etc.

**Be'ring** (bā'rēng; *Angl.* bẹr'ĭng, běr'-, bâr'-), **Vitus.** 1680–1741. Danish navigator. Employed by Russians on expeditions (from 1725) to discover whether Asia and North America were connected; sailed from Kamchatka to Alaska (1741). Bering Sea and Bering Strait, discovered by him, are named in his honor.

**Bé'riot'** (bā'ryō'), **Charles Auguste de.** 1802–1870. Belgian violinist and composer; father of **Charles Wilfrid de Bériot** (1833–1914), piano virtuoso and composer; b. Paris; taught at Paris Conservatory.

**Be·ris'so** (bȧ·rē'sō), **Cesáreo Leonardo.** 1887– . Uruguayan military aviator; founder (1913) and instructor (from 1916), Military School of Aviation, Los Cerrillos, Canelones; director, Escuela Militar de Aplicación (1922–31). First pilot to make nonstop flight from Santiago de Chile to Buenos Aires (1929).

**Be'ri·ya** (byā'ryĭ·yŭ) *or* **Beria, Lavrenti Pavlovich.** 1899–1953. Soviet leader, b. in Georgia; chief of public security organization in Caucasus (1921–31); commissar for internal affairs (1938–46) and public security (1941–46); a vice-chairman of Council of People's Commissars (from 1941).

**Berk** (byärk), Count **Fëdor Fëdorovich.** *Ger. name* **Friedrich Wilhelm Rembert Berg** (běrк). 1793?–1874. Russian field marshal, b. in Livonia. Served in Russo-Turkish campaign (1828–29) and against Poles (1831); made general; minister to Austria (1849); governor of Finland (1854–61); put down insurrection in Poland (1863); made field marshal (1865).

**Ber'ke·feld** (běr'kĕ·fĕlt), **Wilhelm.** 1836–1897. German owner of kieselguhr mines; inventor of Berkefeld filter (impassable to microscopic organisms) and proprietor of factory at Celle for its manufacture.

**Berke'ley** (bûrk'lĭ; *Brit. usu.* bärk'-), **George.** 1685–1753. Irish philosopher. M.A. and fellow, Dublin U. (1707); presented by Swift at English court (1713); lecturer in divinity, Greek, and Hebrew, Dublin U. (1721–24); dean of Derry (1724); obtained (1725) charter for college in Bermudas, but government grant never paid; lived in America (1728–31); made bishop of Cloyne (1734); retired to Oxford (1752). In *Essay towards a New Theory of Vision* (1709), *A Treatise concerning the Principles of Human Knowledge* (1710), and *Three Dialogues between Hylas and Philonous* (1713), his system of subjective idealism (Berkeleianism), which taught that the essence of all save spiritual being is perceptibility and hence that so-called material things exist only in being perceived. Author also of *Alciphron, or the Minute Philosopher* (1733), on freethinking in antithesis to his theory that all nature is the language of God.

**Berkeley, John.** 1st Baron **Berkeley of Strat'ton** (străt''n). d. 1678. English Royalist officer. Surrendered Exeter to Fairfax (1646); on admiralty staff (1660); lord lieutenant of Ireland (1670); ambassador at Congress of Nijmegen (1676–77). One of first proprietors, with Carteret, of New Jersey (1664), providing government under the "Concessions."

**Berkeley, Miles Joseph.** 1803–1889. English clergyman; author of *Introduction to Cryptogamic Botany* (1857) and *Outlines of British Fungology* (1860).

**Berkeley,** Sir **William.** 1606–1677. Colonial governor, b. Bruton, Somersetshire, Eng. Governor of Virginia (1642–76); his policies led to Bacon's Rebellion (1676).

**Ber'ken** (běr'kĕn), **Ludwig van.** *Also* **Louis de Ber'quen'** (lwē dē běr'kĕn'). Fifteenth-century lapidary at Bruges, credited with establishing (c. 1470) guild of lapidaries, with inventing regular plan of arrangement of facets in gems to increase color effects, and with discovering (c. 1476) the method of cutting diamond with diamond and devising a wheel for use in this method.

**Berk'ley** (bûrk'lĭ; *Brit.* bärk'lĭ), **James John.** 1819–1862. English engineer; constructed first railway line in India, from Bombay to Thana, 20 miles (1853); completed Bombay-Calcutta-Madras-Nagpur line (1856).

**Berk'man** (bûrk'măn; běrk'män), **Alexander.** 1870–1936. Polish-born anarchist; emigrated to U.S. During Homestead (Pa.) strike disorders, stabbed Henry Clay Frick, then head of Carnegie Steel Co.; confined in penitentiary (1892–1906). Associate of Emma Goldman in publishing anarchist magazine *Mother Earth;* convicted with Emma Goldman of obstructing conscription (1917), imprisoned (1917–19), and deported to Russia (1919). Later, resided in France; suicide (1936).

**Berk'shire** (bûrk'shĭr; -shẽr; *Brit. usu.* bärk'-), Earls of. See under HOWARD family.

**Ber'la'ge** (běr'lá'gĕ), **Hendrik Petrus.** 1856–1934. Dutch architect; codesigned Panopticon, Amsterdam (1882); designed Amsterdam Bourse (1903), in modern style which he introduced in Holland.

**Ber'le** (bûr'lē), **Adolf Augustus.** 1895–1971. American diplomat, b. Boston, Mass. LL.B., Harvard (1916); practiced law in Boston and New York; asst. secretary of state (1938–44); U.S. ambassador to Brazil (1945–46).

**Ber'lich·ing·en** (běr'lĭк·ĭng·ĕn), **Götz,** *or* **Gottfried, von.** 1480–1562. German feudal knight, b. Jagsthausen, now in Württemberg. Fought in service of various princes (from 1497); at siege of Landshut (1504), lost his right hand, for which an iron one was substituted—hence the nickname "Götz with the Iron Hand"; led numerous feuds, notably against Nuremberg and Electorate of Mainz; twice (1512, 1518) put under ban for private warfare and robbery. Served Duke Ulrich of Württemberg against Swabian League and in defense of Möckmühl (1519); captured and imprisoned at Heilbronn (1519–22). Forced by rebels to lead them in Peasants' Revolt (1525); seized and imprisoned at Augsburg by

Swabian League (1528–30). Fought under Charles V against Turks (1542) and France (1544). His autobiography (pub. 1731) used by Goethe as a source for the drama *Götz von Berlichingen* (1773; tr. by Sir Walter Scott, 1799).

**Ber'lier'** (bĕr'lyā'), **Jean Baptiste.** 1843–1911. French engineer; known esp. for his proposed underground railway system (since realized), including passage under Seine.

**Ber·lin'** (bûr·lĭn'), **Irving.** *Real name* **Israel Ba·line'** (bȧ·lēn'). 1888– . Song writer, b. in Russia; to U.S. as a child (1893); educ. in New York public schools. Among his song successes are *Alexander's Ragtime Band, Oh, How I Hate to Get Up in the Morning, All Alone, Remember, Always, Because I Love You, Russian Lullaby.* Composer of lyrics for *Music Box Revues, Ziegfeld Follies,* and other musical comedies and revues.

**Ber'li·ner** (bûr'lĭ·nẽr), **E'mile** (ā'mĭl). 1851–1929. Inventor, b. in Hanover; to U.S. (1870). Invented the Berliner loose-contact telephone transmitter or microphone (1877); perfected various features of telephone; introduced (pat. 1878) use of induction coil in transmitter. Invented a talking machine (1887) and a method of duplicating disk records; invented and first used (1908) lightweight rotating-cylinder internal-combustion motor later used for airplanes; invented (1925) acoustic tile and acoustic cells for insuring good acoustics in halls, etc.

**Ber'lioz'** (bĕr'lyôz'), **Louis Hector.** 1803–1869. French composer, b. La Côte-Saint-André. Noted as pioneer of modern orchestration and as creator of program music. His compositions include *Symphonie Fantastique, Roméo et Juliette, La Damnation de Faust, Les Troyens* (in two parts, *La Prise de Troie* and *Les Troyens à Carthage*). His wife was the Irish actress Harriet Constance Smithson (*q.v.*).

**Ber'man'** (bĕr'mäN'; *Angl.* bûr'măn, bâr'măn). Name of two Russian-born painters of the Neo-Romanticist group: **Lé'o'nide'** (lā'ô'nēd') *or* **Le'o·nid** (lē'ō·nĭd) **Berman** (1896– ), known usually by his prename only, having dropped the surname to avoid confusion with his brother; marine painter, b. Peterhof; resident and citizen of France. His brother **Eu'gène'** (û'zhân'; ü'-) **Berman** (1899–1972), painter and theatrical designer, b. St. Petersburg; resident in France (1919 ff.) and in the U.S. (from 1937).

**Bermúdez, Remigio Morales.** See MORALES BERMÚDEZ.

**Ber·mu'do** (bĕr·mōō'thō). Name of three kings of Asturias and León: **Bermudo I.** *Called* **El Diá'co·no** (ĕl dyä'kō·nō), *i.e.* the Deacon. d. 791. King (788–791). **Bermudo II.** d. 999. King (982–999); defeated by Moors (992). **Bermudo III.** 1016–1037. King (1027–37); killed in battle; under his successor, León and Castile temporarily united.

**Bern, Dietrich von.** See THEODORIC the Great.

**Ber'na·be'i** (bār'nä·bâ'ē), **Giuseppe Ercole.** 1620?–1687. Italian composer of operas and church music. His son **Giuseppe Antonio** (1649?–1732), also an operatic composer and writer of church music, succeeded him (1688) as court Kapellmeister at Munich.

**Ber·nac'chi** (bâr·näk'kē), **Antonio.** 1685–1756. Italian castrato; engaged by Handel for his London theater; founded voice school in Bologna (1736); teacher of Raff; composed vocal pieces and religious music.

**Ber·nac'chi** (bẽr·năk'ĭ; bûr-), **Louis Charles.** 1876–1942. Scientist and explorer, b. in Tasmania. Educ. Melbourne U. Physicist to Southern Cross Antarctic expedition (1898) and to Scott's Antarctic expedition (1901–04). Explored British Namaqualand (1905) and upper Amazon (1906). Author of scientific articles on terrestrial magnetism, meteorology, seismology, etc.

**Ber'na'dette' of Lourdes** (bĕr'nȧ'dĕt', lōōrd; *Angl.* bûr'nȧ·dĕt'). *Real name* **Bernadette Sou'bi'rous'** (sōō'bē'rōō'). 1844–1879. French peasant girl, b. Lourdes; joined Sisters of Charity at Nevers (1866); took perpetual vows (1878). Her visions of Our Lady at Lourdes, instructing her to make known miraculous healing powers She would impart to its waters, led to establishment of Lourdes as a shrine. Canonized (1933).

**Ber'na·dotte** (bûr'nȧ·dŏt; *Fr.* bĕr'nȧ'dôt'). Name of family of old lineage of Béarn, France, whose earliest known member (17th century) owned estate in Pau known as "Bernadotte." **Jean Baptiste Jules Bernadotte** (1763?–1844); general under Napoleon; elected (1810) heir to throne of Sweden; king (1818–44) as Charles XIV John (*q.v.*); founder of present Swedish royal line. Succeeding rulers have been Oscar I (ruled 1844–59), Charles XV (1859–72), Oscar II (1872–1907), Gustavus V (1907–1950), Gustavus VI (from 1950). See *Table (in Appendix)* for SWEDEN.

**Ber'na'nos'** (bĕr'nȧ'nôs'), **Georges.** 1888–1948. French novelist, b. Paris.

**Ber'nard** (*Eng.* bûr'närd, -nẽrd, bẽr·närd', bûr·närd'). See also BERNHARD.

**Ber'nard'** (bĕr'nȧr'), **Charles de.** *In full* **Pierre Marie Charles de Bernard du Grail de la Vil'lette'** (dẽ bĕr'nȧr' dü grȧ'y' dẽ lȧ vē'lĕt'). 1804–1850. French novelist; author of *La Femme de Quarante Ans,* etc.

**Bernard, Claude.** 1813–1878. French physiologist, b. Saint-Julien. Investigated chemical phenomena of digestion, glycogenic function of the liver, and the sympathetic nervous system. Awarded grand prize in physiology three times by Académie des Sciences.

**Ber'nard** (bûr'nẽrd), Sir **Francis.** 1712–1779. Colonial governor in America, b. in England. Appointed governor of New Jersey (1758–60); transferred to governorship of Massachusetts (1760–69). Aroused bitter opposition by his policies; removed from office (1769) and returned to England. His son Sir **Thomas** (1750–1818) was a lawyer and philanthropist in England.

**Ber'nard'** (bĕr'nȧr'), **Jean Jacques.** 1888– . French playwright and novelist; works include the plays *Le Voyage à Deux* (1911), *Martine* (1922), *L'Arne en Peine* (1926), *Le Roy de Malousie* (1928), and the novels *Le Roman de Martine* (1929), *Madeleine Landier* (1933).

**Ber'nard** (bûr'nẽrd), **John Henry.** 1860–1927. Irish churchman and philosopher; archbishop of Dublin (1915–19); provost of Trinity Coll. (1919–27). Author of Kantian and Biblical commentaries.

**Ber·nard'** (bẽr·närd'; bûr-), **Moun'ta·gue** (mŏn'tȧ·gū). 1820–1882. English lawyer. First professor of international law, Oxford (1859–74).

**Ber'nard'** (bĕr'nȧr'), **Simon.** 1779–1839. French military engineer, b. Dôle, France. In French army (1797–1814); aide-de-camp to Napoleon (1813–14); with Napoleon at Waterloo (1815). To U.S. (1815); planned coast defenses (1815–30). Returned to France (1830); French minister of war (1834, 1836–39).

**Bernard, Tristan.** *Real name* **Paul Bernard.** 1866–1947. French playwright, esp. of farce comedy, and novelist, b. Besançon. His works include *L'Anglais tel qu'on le Parle* (1899), *Triplepatte* (1906), and the novel *Mémoires d'un Jeune Homme Rangé* (1899).

**Ber'nard' de Chartres** (bĕr'nȧr' dẽ shȧr'tr'). *Surnamed* **Syl'ves'tris'** (sēl'vĕs'trēs'; *Angl.* sĭl·vĕs'trĭs). 12th-century French Platonist philosopher.

**Ber'nard' de Ven'ta'dour'** (väN'tȧ'dōōr'). 12th-century troubadour and song writer.

**Ber·nard' of Clair'vaux'** (bẽr·närd' ŭv klĕr'vō'; bĕr'-

nȧr′-dŭv), Saint. 1091–1153. French ecclesiastic; known as "Thaumaturgus of the West"; founder and first abbé of Cistercian monastery of Clairvaux. Became influential in papal court of Innocent II. Bitter opponent of rationalistic philosophy of Abélard and of all heresies. Called (1146) Christians in France to second crusade (started 1147). His writings consist of epistles, sermons, and theological treatises, including *De Contemptu Dei*, *De Consideratione*, *De Diligendo Deo*, *Adversus Abaelardum*, etc. Canonized (1173) by Pope Alexander III; named Doctor of the Church by Pope Pius VIII.

**Bernard of Clu′ny′** (klü′nē′) *or* **of Mor′laix′** (môr′lĕ′). 12th-century Benedictine monk in Abbey of Cluny in northern France; author of Latin poem *De Contemptu Mundi*, the beginning of which was translated by John Mason Neale into three hymns: *Jerusalem the Golden*, *The World is Very Evil*, and *For Thee, O Dear, Dear Country.*

**Bernard of Men′thon′** (mäɴ′tôɴ′), Saint. 923–1008. Roman Catholic priest; archdeacon of Aosta; founded (c. 962) hospices on Great and Little Saint Bernard; patron of Alpinists.

**Ber·nar′des** (bĕr·nȧr′dēs), **Arthur,** *or* **Artur, da Sil′va** (dȧ sĭl′vȧ). 1875–1955. Brazilian statesman, b. Viçosa, Minas Gerais; educ. for bar at São Paulo; federal deputy (1909); senator; secretary of finance, Minas Gerais state government; president of Minas Gerais (1918–22); president of Brazil (1922–26); suppressed revolution in São Paulo; senator (1927 ff.); political exile (1932–34); professor of Brazilian studies, U. of Lisbon (1934).

**Ber·nar′des Pi·men′ta** (bĕr·nȧr′dēsh pē·mäɴn′tȧ), **Diogo.** 1540?–?1605. Portuguese poet, b. Ponte de Lima; known esp. for pastoral lyrics, elegies, and idyls; author of *Varias Rimas ao Bom Jesús* (1594), *O Lima* (1596), and *Rimas Varias: Flores do Lima* (1596).

**Ber′nar′din′ de Saint′-Pierre′** (bĕr′nȧr′dăɴ′ dē săɴ′pyâr′), **Jacques Henri.** 1737–1814. French writer, b. Le Havre; resident in Île de France (now Mauritius) for three years (1768–71). Precursor of French romantic movement; wrote *Voyage à l'Île de France* and *Études de la Nature* (1784–88); best remembered for romance *Paul et Virginie* (1788).

**Ber′nar·di′no of Sie′na** (bār′när·dē′nō, syâ′nä), Saint. 1380–1444. Italian Franciscan monk; known esp. as a preacher; vicar-general of Franciscan order (1438); introduced strict Observantine rule into the order.

**Ber·nar′do del Car′pio** (bĕr·när′thō thĕl kär′pyō). Spanish semilegendary hero of 9th century; reputed son of Ximena, sister of Alfonso II of León, and Don Sancho, Conde de Saldaña. Distinguished himself in wars against Moors. Became central figure in Spanish romances, ballads, and plays; portrayed by Lope de Vega as national hero and conqueror of Roland at Roncesvalles.

**Ber′nau′er** (bĕr′nou′ẽr), **Agnes.** d. 1435. Daughter of an Augsburg baker; m. Albert, son of Ernest, Duke of Bavaria-Munich; when Albert acknowledged the marriage, Ernest had her seized, convicted of witchcraft, and drowned in Danube. The tale is material for several German dramas.

**Ber′nays** (bĕr′nīs), **Jakob.** 1824–1881. German classical philologist and writer on philosophy. His brother **Michael** (1834–1897), literary historian and critic, was professor at Munich (1873–90).

**Ber′ne·ker** (bĕr′nĕ·kẽr), **Erich.** 1874–1937. German Slavic scholar.

**Ber′ners** (bûr′nẽrz), 2d Baron. **John Bour′chier** (bou′chẽr). 1467–1533. English translator and author. Chancellor of exchequer (1516); negotiator of alliance between Henry VIII of England and Charles I of Spain (1518). Translator of Froissart's *Chronicles* (1523–25), and *The Golden Boke of Marcus Aurelius* (1534) from a French version of Guevara's *El Reloj de Príncipes.*

**Berners,** 14th Baron. See Gerald Hugh TYRWHITT.

**Ber′ners** (bĕr′nẽrz) *or* **Bernes** (bĕrnz) *or* **Barnes** (bärnz), **Juliana.** b. 1388? English woman, said to have been prioress of Sopwell nunnery; reputed author of a treatise on hunting in the *Book of St. Albans* (printed c. 1486).

**Bern′hard** (bĕrn′härt). Duke of **Saxe′-Wei′mar** (săks′vī′mär). 1604–1639. German general, b. Weimar. Son of John, Duke of Weimar; brother of Ernest I the Pious (*q.v.*). Served in Protestant cause in Thirty Years' War; in Swedish army, commanded at Lützen (1632) after death of Gustavus Adolphus; defeated at Nördlingen (1634); abandoned by Sweden, made alliance with Richelieu; won victory at Rheinfelden (1638) and captured Breisach (1638).

**Bernhard.** 1649–1706. Founder (1680) of Saxe-Meiningen (*q.v.*) branch of Ernestine line of Saxony. A descendant, **Bernhard Erich Freund** (froint) [II] (1800–1882), was duke of Saxe-Meiningen (1803–66; under regent, 1803–21); after supporting Austria against Prussia (1866), forced to resign in favor of son George. His grandson **Bernhard** (1851–1926), officer in Prussian army (1870–1903), inspector general (1903–09), field marshal (after 1909), was duke of Saxe-Meiningen (1914–18; abdicated).

**Bernhard, Georg.** 1875–1944. German journalist; editor, *Vossische Zeitung;* fled from Germany (1933); edited émigré paper (*Tageszeitung*) in Paris (from 1933).

**Bernhard, Karl.** Pseudonym of Andreas Nicolai de SAINT-AUBAIN.

**Bern·har′di** (bĕrn·här′dē), **Friedrich von.** 1849–1930. Prussian general and military writer, b. St. Petersburg. Head of military history department of general staff, Berlin (1898); commander, 31st cavalry brigade (1900) and 7th division (1904); commanding general, 7th army corps, at Münster (1908–09). Fought in World War I on eastern front (1915) and on western front as corps leader (1918); took part in battle of Armentières. Author of *Germany and the Next War* (1st Eng. tr., 1911), *Deutschlands Heldenkampf 1914–18* (1921).

**Bern′hard of Lip′pe-Bie′ster·feld** (bĕrn′härt ŭv lĭp′ĕ·bē′stẽr·fĕlt). 1911– . German prince; m. (1937) Princess Juliana of Orange, heiress to throne of Netherlands; Queen (1947). See LIPPE.

**Bern′hardt** (bûrn′härt; *Fr.* bĕr′nȧr′), **Sar′ah** (sâr′ȧ; sā′rȧ; *Fr.* sȧ′rȧ′). *Orig. name* **Rosine Ber′nard′** (bĕr′nȧr′). 1844–1923. French actress, b. Paris. *Known as* "the Divine Sarah." m. Jacques Damala, a Greek actor (1882); separated (1883). With Comédie Française (1872–80); played successful roles in *Le Sphinx*, *Phèdre*, *Hernani*, *Ruy Blas.* On tour in England, U.S., and European countries, acting chiefly in *Adrienne Lecouvreur*, *Froufrou*, and *La Dame aux Camélias* (1880–82). Starred in a series of Sardou's plays, including *Fédora*, *Théodora*, *La Tosca* (1883–93). Became proprietress of Théâtre de la Renaissance (1893); appeared there in Sardou's *Gismonda* and Rostand's *La Princesse Lointaine.* Leased (1899) Théâtre des Nations (renamed Théâtre Sarah-Bernhardt); acted in Rostand's *L'Aiglon* and a French rendition of *Hamlet.* Leg amputated (1914), but continued her career; scored triumph in Tristan Bernard's *Jeanne Doré.* Made member of Legion of Honor (1914).

**Bern·har′dy** (bĕrn·här′dē), **Gottfried.** 1800–1875. German classical scholar and philologist.

**Ber′ni** (bĕr′nē), **Francesco.** 1497–1536. Italian satirist and burlesque poet.

**Bernice.** See BERENICE.

**Ber'ning·haus** (bûr'nĭng·hous), **Oscar Edmund.** 1874–1952. American painter; best known for his murals.

**Ber·ni'ni** (bår·nē'nē), **Giovanni Lorenzo.** 1598–1680. Italian sculptor, architect, and painter, b. Naples. Protégé of Urban VIII and succeeding popes. Dominant influence on European sculpture for more than century; creator of Berninesque style. Succeeded Maderna as architect of St. Peter's (1629). Designed Scala Regia in Vatican; completed Barberini Palace; constructed fountains of Piazza Navona, Trevi, Barberini, etc.; redecorated Lateran and bridge of Sant'Angelo. Submitted designs for restoration of Louvre. His sculpture includes *David* and *Apollo and Daphne* (both in Villa Borghese), *Rape of Proserpine* (Villa Lodovisi), *Louis XIV* (Versailles).

**Ber'nis'** (bĕr'nēs'), **François Joachim de Pierre** (pyâr) **de.** 1715–1794. French cardinal and statesman. Ambassador to Venice (1752); councilor of state (1755); represented France in diplomatic negotiations with Austria before Seven Years' War. Created cardinal (1758). Ambassador to Rome (1769); obtained (1773) from Pope Clement XIV suppression of Jesuits. Called, from his little poems and "bouquets poétiques," **Ba'bet' la Bou'que·tière'** (bȧ'bĕ' lȧ bo͝ok'tyâr').

**Ber·noul'li** (*Ger.* bĕr·no͝ol'ē; *Fr.* bĕr'no͞o'yē'). Name of a family of mathematicians and scientists of Basel, Switzerland, including: **Jakob** *or* **Jacques** (1654–1705); professor of mathematics at U. of Basel (from 1687); author of *Conamen Novi Systematis Cometarum* (1682), *Dissertatio de Gravitate Aetheris* (1683), *Ars Conjectandi* (pub. posthumously), etc. His brother **Johann** *or* **Jean** (1667–1748); professor of mathematics at U. of Basel (from 1705); pioneer in exponential calculus. Their nephew **Nikolaus** *or* **Nicolas** (1687–1759); professor of mathematics at Padua, then of law and logic at U. of Basel. Johann's three sons: **Nikolaus** *or* **Nicolas** (1695–1726), professor of jurisprudence at Bern, then of mathematics at St. Petersburg; **Da'ni·el** (*Ger.* dä'nē·ĕl; *Fr.* dȧ'nyĕl') (1700–1782), professor of mathematics at St. Petersburg, of anatomy, botany, and physics, and then of philosophy, at U. of Basel, author of *Hydrodynamica* (1738) and works on acoustics, astronomy, etc.; and **Johann** *or* **Jean** (1710–1790), professor of eloquence and of mathematics, known for his contribution to theories of heat and light. Two sons of the last named: **Johann** *or* **Jean** (1744–1807), astronomer to the Academy of Berlin, author of *Recueil pour les Astronomes* (Berlin, 1772–76); and **Jakob** *or* **Jacques** (1758?–1789), professor of physics at U. of Basel, then of mathematics at St. Petersburg. **Christoph** *or* **Christophe** (1782–1863); naturalist and professor at U. of Basel; author of scientific works on mechanics, etc. **Johann Jakob** (1831–1913); archaeologist and professor at U. of Basel; writer on Greek and Roman iconography. **Karl Albrecht** (1868–1937); author of novels and plays.

**Bern'stein** (bĕrn'shtīn), **Aaron.** 1812–1884. German political and scientific writer, b. Danzig.

**Bernstein, Eduard.** 1850–1932. German Social Democratic writer and politician. Joined Social Democrats (1872); coeditor of *Sozialdemokrat* (1881–90) in Zurich (until 1888) then as exile in London; associate of Engels; proponent of revisionism (1889) which aimed at a modified Marxian socialism, evolutionary rather than revolutionary. Returned to Germany (1901); member of Reichstag (1902–06, 1912–18, 1920–28); joined Independents following split in Social Democratic party (1916); rejoined Majority Socialists (1919). Author of *Die Voraussetzungen des Sozialismus und die Aufgaben der Sozialdemokratie* (1899), etc.

**Bernstein, Elsa,** *nee* **Por'ges** (pôr'gĕs). *Pseudonym* **Ernst Ros'mer** (rŏs'mẽr). 1866– . Austrian dramatist, b. Vienna; m. (1890) writer Max Bernstein, in Munich. Wrote modern dramas and historical tragedies.

**Bern'stein'** (bĕrn'stĕn'), **Henry Léon Gustave Charles.** 1876–1953. French dramatist, b. Paris. Author of *Le Détour* (1902), *Le Voleur* (1906), *Samson* (1907), *L'Assaut* (1912), *Judith* (1922), *Le Venin* (1927), etc.

**Bern'stein** (bûrn'stīn), **Herman.** 1876–1935. Journalist, playwright, and author, b. in Russia; to U.S. (1893). European correspondent, New York *Times* (1908, 1909, 1911, 1912). Founder (1914) and editor (1914–16) of Jewish daily paper *The Day;* editor, *The American Hebrew* (1916–19). Russian correspondent, New York *Herald* (1917, 1918); published "Willy-Nicky" telegrams (messages between German kaiser and Russian emperor in 1914). Editor of weekly *Jewish Tribune* (1923–28). U.S. minister to Albania (1930–33). Author of *The Flight of Time* (poems; 1899), *In the Gates of Israel* (1902), *Celebrities of our Time* (interviews; 1925). Adapter of plays from Russian and German.

**Bern'stein** (bûrn'stīn), **Leonard.** 1918– . Amer. conductor, composer, pianist, and author, b. Lawrence, Mass. Conductor of New York Philharmonic (1958–69). Composed symphonies, operas, and ballets; wrote musical score for *West Side Story* (1957), etc.

**Bern'stein** (bûrn'stēn), **Theresa Ferber.** 1903– . Am. painter, b. Philadelphia; m. William Meyerowitz.

**Bern'storff** (bĕrn'shtôrf), Count **von.** Title of several members of a German family of statesmen and diplomats in Danish, Prussian, and German service, including: **Johann Hartwig Ernst** (1712–1772); b. Hanover; entered Danish service (1733); ambassador at Paris (1744–50); foreign minister (1751–70); preserved neutrality of Denmark in Seven Years' War; advocated friendly alliance with Sweden; concluded treaties with France (1758) and Russia (1767) esp. relative to Holstein (Gottorp) exchange; furthered trade and commerce, a public health program, emancipation of peasants, and other reforms; patron of arts and learning; dismissed (1770) as a result of Struensee's intrigues; recalled (1772). His nephew **Andreas Peter** (1735–1797); b. Hanover; entered Danish service (1758); dismissed (1770) and recalled (1772) with his uncle; foreign minister (1773); concluded defensive anti-Swedish alliance with Russia (1773); joined unwillingly armed neutrality compact (1780) with Russia, Prussia, and Sweden and a separate agreement with Great Britain; dismissed (1780); recalled (1784); took part in reform movements, including emancipation of Danish peasants (1788). Andreas's son **Christian Günther** (1769–1835); b. Copenhagen; in Danish service (1787–1818); ambassador at Berlin (1789–94) and Stockholm (1794–97); succeeded his father as secretary of state (1797); head of ministry and foreign minister (1800–10); Danish ambassador at Vienna (1811) and Berlin (1816); entered Prussian diplomatic service as foreign minister (1818–32). Christian's nephew **Albrecht** (1809–1873); Prussian ambassador successively at Munich, Vienna, and Naples (1845–54); at London (1854–61, 1862–73); foreign minister (1861–62). Albrecht's son **Johann-Heinrich** (1862–1939); b. London; entered German diplomatic service (1889); councilor of embassy at London (1902–06); consul general, Cairo (1906); ambassador at Washington (1908–17); endeavored, without support from his government, to further President Wilson's attempts at mediation preceding America's entry into World War I and to promote better understanding between U.S. and Germany; ambassador at Constantinople (1917–18); member, Democratic party in Reichstag (1921–28); chairman, German

League of Nations Union and vice-chairman, League of Nations; German delegate to disarmament conferences (1929–31).

**Berodach-baladan.** Erroneous variant of MERODACH-BALADAN (*2 Kings* xx. 12).

**Be·ros'sus** (bĕ·rŏs'ŭs) *or* **Be·ro'sus** (-rō'sŭs). Babylonian priest of 3d century B.C.; author of a history of Babylonia (in Greek), parts of which have been preserved as extracts in works of Josephus and Eusebius.

**Ber'quin'** (bĕr'kăN'), **Arnaud.** 1749?–1791. French writer, esp. of books for children; known as "the Children's Friend."

**Berrettini, Pietro.** See Pietro da CORTONA.

**Ber'ru·gue'te** (bĕr'rōō·gā'tā), **Alonso.** c. 1486–1561. Spanish sculptor and painter; pupil of Michelangelo; court sculptor, painter, and chamberlain to Charles V.

**Ber'ry'** (bĕ'rē'). Duchy of central France which became (1360) an appanage of French reigning house. Title of duc de Berry held by many princes, esp. (1) **Jean de France** (dē fräNs). 1340–1416. 1st duke; 3d son of John II of France. Extortionate governor of Languedoc (1380–88); coregent of France (1392) with his brother Philip the Bold, Duke of Burgundy (see PHILIP). Involved in feud between houses of Orléans and Burgundy (from c. 1396); patron of arts and literature. (2) **Charles.** 1685–1714. Grandson of Louis XIV; 3d son of Louis, the grand dauphin. (3) King Louis XVI (*q.v.*). (4) **Charles Ferdinand de Bour'bon'** (dē bōōr'bôN'). 1778–1820. Last duke; 2d son of comte d'Artois (afterward King Charles X of France). In exile (1789–1814); served in Condé's army and in Russia; m. Anna Brown in England; left her on his family's refusal to acknowledge the marriage. Returned to France (1814); m. (1816) **Marie Caroline Ferdinande Louise** of Naples (1798–1870), by whom he had two children, **Louise Marie Thérèse d'Ar'tois'** [dȧr'twȧ'] (1819–1864), who became duchess of Par'ma (pär'mȧ; *Ital.* -mä), and Henri, Duc de Bordeaux and later Comte de Chambord (see CHAMBORD). Assassinated at Paris.

**Ber'ry** (bĕr'ĭ), **Edward Wilber.** 1875–1945. American paleontologist; authority on classification and evolution of plants, esp. of southeastern North America, equatorial America, and South America.

**Berry, Martha McChesney.** 1866–1942. American educator, b. near Rome, Ga. Founder of Berry schools for underprivileged children of back-country districts in Georgia and vicinity. Awarded Roosevelt memorial medal for services to nation (1925); in nationwide poll (1931), voted one of twelve greatest American women.

**Berry, Mary.** 1763–1852. English author; literary executor of Horace Walpole, who bequeathed to her and her sister **Agnes** (1764–1852) his house, "Little Strawberry Hill." Author of *Life of Rachel Wriothesley* (1819) and *Social Life of England and France from 1660–1830* (1828–31).

**Ber'ry'er'** (bĕ'rē'yā'), **Pierre Nicolas.** 1757–1841. French lawyer; counsel for defense in trial of Marshal Ney. His son **Pierre Antoine** (1790–1868), also a lawyer, aided in defense of Marshal Ney.

**Ber·se'zio** (bâr·sâ'tsyō), **Vittorio.** 1830–1900. Italian playwright and novelist.

**Bert** (bâr), **Paul.** 1833–1886. French physiologist and politician. Governor general of Annam and Tonkin (1886). Author of scientific works, including *Leçons d'Anatomie et de Physiologie Animales* (1885).

**Ber'taut'** (bĕr'tō'), **Jean.** 1552–1611. French Roman Catholic prelate and poet.

**Ber'tha** (bûr'thȧ). d. 783. Daughter of Caribert, Count of Laon; m. Pepin the Short; mother of Charlemagne.

**Bertha of Burgundy.** See ROBERT II of France.

**Ber'the·lot'** (bĕr'tē·lō'), **Henri Mathias.** 1861–1931. French general; reorganized Rumanian army; commander in Vesle sector, western front (1918).

**Berthelot, Pierre Eugène Marcelin.** 1827–1907. French chemist and statesman, b. Paris. Elected senator for life (1881); minister of public instruction (1886–87); minister of foreign affairs (1895–96). Best known for his researches in explosives, dyestuffs, the synthesis of organic compounds, and especially in field of thermochemistry, a science based largely on his observations.

**Ber'thier'** (bĕr'tyā'), **Louis Alexandre.** Prince **de Neu'châ'tel'** (nû'shä'tĕl'). Duc **de Va'lan'gin'** (vȧ'läN'zhăN'). Prince **de Wa'gram'** (vȧ'grȧm'; *Ger.* vä'gräm). 1753–1815. Marshal of France. Served under Lafayette in American Revolution; with Napoleon in Italy and Egypt; minister of war (1799–1808); created marshal (1804); Napoleon's chief of staff (1808–14). After 1814, supported cause of Louis XVIII. Author of *Mémoires* (pub. 1827).

**Berthold,** Meister. See Berthold SCHWARZ.

**Ber'thol'let'** (bĕr'tô'lĕ'), Comte **Claude Louis.** 1748–1822. French chemist. Superintendent of dyeing processes in France (1784); discovered new method of bleaching (1789). One of founders of l'École Polytechnique; professor of chemistry there. One of savants with Napoleon in Egypt. Named senator by Napoleon (1804); created count. With Lavoisier (*q.v.*) and others, devised system of chemical nomenclature that serves as basis of system still in use. Voted for deposition of Napoleon (1814). Created peer by Louis XVIII. His works include *Éléments de l'Art de la Teinture* (1791) and *Essai de Statique Chimique* (1803).

**Ber'thoud'** (bĕr'tōō'), **Ferdinand.** 1727–1807. Swiss inventor of marine clocks.

**Ber'ti** (bĕr'tē), **Domenico.** 1820–1897. Italian scholar and statesman; active in risorgimento; professor of philosophy, Turin (1849–60), Rome (1870–77); member of parliament (1849 ff.); minister of education (1866–67), commerce (1881–84).

**Ber'tie** (bär'tĭ), **Francis Leveson.** 1st Viscount **Bertie.** 1844–1919. English diplomat; ambassador at Rome (1903–04), Paris (1905–18).

**Ber'til'lon'** (bĕr'tē'yôN'; *Angl.* bûr'tĭ·lŏn), **Alphonse.** 1853–1914. French anthropologist and criminologist, b. Paris. As chief of department of identification in prefecture of police of the Seine, Paris, devised system (Bertillon system) of identifying criminals by anthropometric measurements. Author of *Identification Anthropométrique*, etc. His brother **Jacques** (1851–1922), statistician and criminologist, wrote *La Statistique Humaine en France* (1880). His father, **Louis Adolphe** (1821–1883), was a physician and statistician.

**Ber'tin'** (bĕr'tăN'). Family of French journalists, including: **Louis François Bertin** (1766–1841) and his brother **Louis François Bertin de Veaux** [vō] (1771–1842), cofounders of *Journal des Débats* (changed by Napoleon I to *Journal de l'Empire*, 1805–14); and two sons of the older Louis François, **François Édouard** (1797–1871) and **Louis Marie Armand** (1801–1854), who continued editorship of *Journal des Débats* (Armand, 1841–54; Édouard, 1854–71).

**Bertin,** Chevalier **Antoine de.** 1752–1790. French poet; author of *Voyage de Bourgogne* (1777) and collections of elegies and love lyrics.

**Bertin, Louis Émile.** 1840–1924. French naval engineer; naval construction adviser to Japanese government (c. 1885–90) and influential in determining type of Japanese warships.

**Bertin, Louise Angélique.** 1805–1877. French poet and

composer of the operas *Guy Mannering*, *Le Loup-garou*, *Fausto*, and *La Esméralda*.

**Ber'ti'ni'** (bĕr'tē'nē'), **Jérôme Henri.** 1798–1876. French pianist and composer, esp. for piano.

**Ber'to·li'ni** (bär'tô·lē'nē), **Francesco.** 1836–1909. Italian historian; pioneer among Italian scholars in application of German critical methods.

**Ber'ton'** (bĕr'tôN'), **Pierre Mon'tan'** (môN'täN'). 1727–1780. French musician; orchestra leader (from 1755), and later director, of the Opéra, Paris. His son **Henri Montan Berton** (1764–1844), was a composer, esp. of light opera. Henri's natural son **François Montan Berton** (1784–1832) composed several operas presented at the Opéra Comique.

**Ber·to'ni** (bâr·tō'nē), **Ferdinando Giuseppe.** 1725–1813. Italian organist and composer of over forty operas (including *Orfeo* and *Quinto Fabio*), fifteen oratorios, and much church music.

**Ber'trand'** (bĕr'träN'), **Alexandre.** 1820–1902. French archaeologist.

**Bertrand, Gabriel Émile.** 1867–1962. French biochemist, at Pasteur Institute (from 1900).

**Bertrand,** Comte **Henri Gratien.** 1773–1844. French general under Napoleon in all campaigns of the empire; accompanied Napoleon to Elba and St. Helena.

**Bertrand, Joseph Louis François.** 1822–1900. French mathematician.

**Bertrand, Louis Marie Émile.** 1866–1941. French novelist, biographer, and writer of books of travel; b. Spincourt.

**Bertrand, Marcel Alexandre.** 1847–1907. French geologist; pioneer in study of tectonics.

**Bertrand de Bar'-sur'-Aube'** (dē bär'sür'ōb'). 13th-century French poet; author of several chansons de geste.

**Bertrand de Born.** See Bertrand de BORN.

**Ber'tuch** (bĕr'tōōk), **Friedrich Justin.** 1747–1822. German writer, publisher, and bookdealer. Translator of *Don Quixote* (1775–76).

**Bé'rulle'** (bā'rül'), **Pierre de.** 1575–1629. French cardinal (1627); founder (1611) of Congregation of the Oratory, in France; a pioneer in Catholic renaissance.

**Beruni, al-.** See al-BIRUNI.

**Ber'vic'** (bĕr'vēk'), **Charles Clément.** *Orig. surname* **Bal'vay'** (bål'vā'). 1756–1822. French engraver. His plates include a Laocoön and a portrait of Louis XVI.

**Ber'wick** (bĕr'ĭk), Duke of. **James Fitz·james'** (fĭts·jāmz'; fĭts'jāmz). 1670–1734. Natural son of James II, King of England. Soldier in Hungary, England, Flanders; suppressed Camisards in Languedoc (1705); created marshal of France (1706). Served as French commander in War of the Spanish Succession and War of the Polish Succession. Killed at siege of Philippsburg (1734).

**Berwick, Mary.** Pseudonym of *Adelaide Anne Procter* (see under Bryan Waller PROCTER).

**Ber·ze'li·us** (bẽr·zē'lĭ·ŭs; bûr-; *Swed.* bĕr·sā'lĭ·ŭs), Baron **Jöns Jakob.** 1779–1848. Swedish chemist; grad. U. of Uppsala (1802). Taught medicine and pharmacy at Stockholm (from 1807) and chemistry (from 1815). Created baron because of scientific achievements (1835). Determined atomic and molecular weights of many substances, using oxygen as a standard; experimented in electrolysis and developed the dualistic theory originated by Lavoisier; discovered the elements selenium, cerium, and thorium, and first isolated columbium, silicon, etc.; introduced present system of writing chemical symbols and formulas; improved analytical methods, esp. the blowpipe method; advocated classification of minerals according to chemical composition.

**Ber'ze·vi'czy** (bĕr'zĕ·vĭ'tsĭ), **Albert von** (fôn). 1853–1936. Hungarian politician and writer; author of *Italy* (1898), *Queen Beatrice* (1908), and *History of Absolutism* (2 vols., 1921–26).

**Bes'ant** (bĕz''nt), **Annie,** *nee* **Wood.** 1847–1933. English theosophist and Indian political leader; m. Rev. Frank Besant (1867). Associated, under pseudonym **Ajax,** with Charles Bradlaugh in propaganda for free thought and limitation of population. Joined Theosophical Society (1889); devoted pupil of Madame Blavatsky; president of society (1907–33). Founded Central Hindu College at Benares (1898); organized India Home Rule League; president, Indian National Congress (1917). Author of many publications on theosophy, including *Reincarnation* (1892), *Karma* (1895), *Theosophy and the New Psychology* (1904); on India, as *The Religious Problem in India* (1902); and an *Autobiography* (1893).

**Be·sant'** (bē·zănt'; bĕ-; *orig.* bĕz''nt), Sir **Walter.** 1836–1901. English novelist. Coauthor, with James Rice, of a series of novels, including *Ready-Money Mortiboy* (1872) and *The Seamy Side* (1881). Sole author of novels upon social conditions, including *All Sorts and Conditions of Men* (1882) and *Children of Gibeon* (1886), and of critical and biographical works.

**Be'se·ler** (bā'zĕ·lẽr), **Wilhelm Hartwig.** 1806–1884. Prussian political leader in Schleswig-Holstein, b. in Oldenburg. President, provisional government of Schleswig-Holstein (1848); defended independence of the duchies; governor, with Count Friedrich von Reventlow, of the duchies (1849–51). Translated Macaulay's *History of England* (1852–60). His nephew **Hans Hartwig von Beseler** (1850–1921), general; retired as infantry general (1907); recalled (1914) as head of 3d reserve corps in World War; led siege of Antwerp (1914) and Novogeorgievsk (1915); as governor general of Poland (1915–18) and colonel general, attempted to organize a Polish government and army under German control.

**BEShT.** See BAAL SHEM-TOB.

**Bes'kow** (bĕs'kôv), Baron **Bernhard von.** 1796–1868. Swedish dramatist, poet, and historian.

**Bes'nard'** (bā'når'), **Paul Albert.** 1849–1934. French painter and etcher of impressionistic school, b. Paris. Brilliant colorist; painter of portraits, landscapes, and murals, and in water colors, pastels, and oils.

**Bes·sa·ra'ba** (*Russ.* byĕs·sŭ·rá'bŭ) *or* **Ba'sa·rab'** (*Rum.* bä'sä·räb'). Family of Walachian voivodes, prominent in southeastern Europe from 13th to 18th century, after whom province of Bessarabia is named.

**Bes·sar'i·on** (bĕ·sâr'ĭ·ŏn), **Johannes** *or* **Basilius.** 15th-century Roman Catholic prelate and Greek scholar, b. Trebizond. Archbishop of Nicaea (1437). Exerted himself to effect union of Greek and Latin churches; supported Roman Church in councils of Ferrara and Florence. Cardinal (1439); invested with title of Latin patriarch of Constantinople (1463). Translated Aristotle's *Metaphysics* and Xenophon's *Memorabilia;* collected library of Greek manuscripts presented to Venetian Senate and made nucleus of library of St. Mark.

**Bessborough,** Earls of. See PONSONBY family.

**Bes'sel** (bĕs'ĕl), **Friedrich Wilhelm.** 1784–1846. Prussian astronomer, b. Minden. Director of observatory at Königsberg (from 1813); calculated orbit of Halley's comet (1804); made (1838) first authenticated determination of distance of a star (61 Cygni) from the earth; introduced consideration of the personal equation of observers and worked out theory of instrumental errors; invented mathematical functions (Bessel functions) used in mathematical physics and astronomy.

**Bes'se·mer** (bĕs'ĕ·mẽr), Sir **Henry.** 1813–1898. English engineer and inventor. Obtained patents (1855 ff.) for manufacture of steel by decarbonization of melted pig iron by means of a blast of air (Bessemer process); established steel works at Sheffield (1859) making a specialty of gunmaking and, later, steel rails. Cf. William KELLY.

**Bes'se·nye'i** (bĕ'shĕ·nyĕ'ĭ), **György.** 1747–1811. Hungarian playwright and poet. Author of the tragedy *Agis*, *The Philosopher* (first true comedy in Hungarian language; 1777), the epic *King Matthias*, and biographical, historical, and philosophical works.

**Bes'sey** (bĕs'ĭ), **Charles Edwin.** 1845–1915. American botanist; pioneer in present laboratory methods of teaching biology.

**Bes'sie** (bĕs'ĭ), **Alvah Cecil.** 1904– . American writer, b. New York City. Author of *Dwell in the Wilderness* (novel; 1935), *Men in Battle* (on the Spanish civil war; 1939), *Bread and a Stone* (novel; 1941), etc.

**Bes'sières'** (bĕ'syâr'), **Jean Baptiste.** Duc **d'Is'trie'** (dēs'trē'). 1766–1813. Marshal of France. Served under Napoleon. Marshal (1804) and duke of Istria (1809).

**Bess of Hardwick.** See Elizabeth TALBOT.

**Best** (bĕst), **Charles Herbert.** 1899–1978. Canadian physiologist; head of department of physiology (1929–65), U. of Toronto. Associated with F. G. Banting (*q.v.*) and others in discovery of insulin.

**Best, William Thomas.** 1826–1897. English organist; editor of works of Handel and Bach; composer of anthems and fugues.

**Bestia.** See CALPURNIUS BESTIA.

**Bes·tu'zhev** (byĭs·too'zhĕf), **Aleksandr Aleksandrovich.** 1797?–1837. Russian novelist and poet; with Ryleev, wrote *The Polar Star* (1823); under pseudonym **Cos'sack Mar·lin'ski** (kŏs'ăk [-ăk] mŭr·lyēn'skû·ĭ; *Angl.* -skĭ), wrote (after 1830) many novels based on experiences in Caucasus, as *Ammalat Bek* and *Mullah Nur.*

**Bestuzhev-Ryu'min** (-ryoo'myĭn), Count **Aleksei Petrovich.** 1693–1766. Russian statesman; influential during reigns of Anna Ivanovna (1730–40) and Elizabeth (1741–62); imperial chancellor (1744); favored alliance of Russia, Austria, England, and Saxony to offset that of France and Prussia; briefly successful (1747) until Treaty of Aix-la-Chapelle changed situation (1748); his influence reduced by Anglo-Prussian alliance (1756); dismissed (1759); recalled on Catherine II's accession (1762) and created field marshal.
His brother **Mikhail Petrovich** (1688–1760) was a diplomat; represented Russia at several European capitals, esp. Copenhagen (1705), London (1720–21), Stockholm (1721–26, 1732–39), Warsaw (1726–30), and Berlin (1730–32); instrumental in bringing about Swedish-Russian War (1741–43); successful in mission to Versailles (1756–60).

**Bestuzhev-Ryumin, Konstantin Nikolaevich.** 1829–1897. Russian historian.

**Be'tan·court'** (bā'tän-koor'), **Romulo.** 1908– . Venezuelan statesman. Provisional president (1945–47); president (1959–63).

**Betham-Edwards, Matilda Barbara.** See under Amelia Ann Blanford EDWARDS.

**Be'the** (bā'tĕ), **Hans Albrecht.** 1906– . Am. physicist, b. Germany. Ph.D., Munich (1928); taught at universities in Germany (to 1933), in England (1933–35). To U.S. (1935); at Cornell U. Research in astrophysics and nuclear physics. Fermi Award (1961); Nobel prize in physics (1967).

**Beth'ell** (bĕth''l), **John.** American inventor of the pressure process (pat. 1838) for impregnating wood with preservatives, a process in general use at present esp. for timber on railroads.

**Bethell, Richard.** 1st Baron **West'bur·y** (wĕst'bĕr·ĭ; -brĭ). 1800–1873. English judge. Attorney general (1856–58); lord chancellor (1861–65); advocate of law reform and codification.

**Bé'then'court'** (bā'tän'koor'), **Jean de.** d. 1425? French navigator; conqueror of Canary Islands (1402–06).

**Beth'len** (bĕt'lĕn), **Gabriel,** *Hung.* **Gábor.** *Full surname* **Bethlen von Ik'tár** (fôn ĭk'tär). 1580–1629. Prince of Transylvania (1613–29) and king of Hungary (1620–29). Member of prominent Protestant family. Overthrew Gabriel Báthory (1613) and was chosen his successor; at beginning of Thirty Years' War (1619), took up arms against Austrian Hapsburgs; took Pressburg and threatened Vienna; after defeat of Czechs at White Mountain (1620), made peace (1621) with Emperor Ferdinand and renounced title of king of Hungary; m. (1625), as 2d wife, Catherine, sister of Elector George William of Brandenburg and sister-in-law of Gustavus Adolphus. Known as one of "three great Magyars" of his time.

**Bethlen,** Count **Stephen,** *Hung.* **István.** 1874–1947. Hungarian statesman, b. in Transylvania, of same family as Gábor Bethlen. Elected to parliament as Liberal (1901); active in counterrevolutionary movement against Béla Kun (1918–19); his estates confiscated by Rumania (1920). Prime minister (1921–31) by appointment of Regent Horthy; settled dispute with Austria over Burgenland (1921); secured aid of League of Nations in financial reconstruction (1923); made treaty of friendship with Italy (1927). Active in party politics (1931–35); retired (1939).

**Beth'mann-Holl'weg** (bāt'män·hôl'vāκ), **Moritz August von.** 1795–1877. German jurist and statesman. Counselor of state (1845); member of upper chamber (1849–52) and lower chamber (1852–55) of Prussian parliament and leader of Moderate Constitutional (*Wochenblatt*) party; minister of public worship and education (1858–62). His grandson **Theobald von Bethmann-Hollweg** (1856–1921), statesman, chancellor of German empire (1909–17); advocated extension of Prussian franchise, autonomy for Alsace-Lorraine, and other reforms; referred to Belgian neutrality treaty as "scrap of paper" (1914); failed, during World War I, to restrict submarine warfare; forced out of office by Hindenburg and Ludendorff (1917).

**Bethsabee.** See BATH-SHEBA.

**Be'thune** (bē't'n), **David** and **James.** See BEATON.

**Be·thune'** (bȧ·thūn'), **Mary,** *nee* **Mc·Leod'** (mȧk-loud'). 1875–1955. American Negro educator, b. Mayesville, S.C.; taught in various mission schools in Georgia and Florida (1895–1904); opened (1904) at Daytona Beach, Fla., small school, Daytona Normal and Industrial Institute, which merged (1923) with Cookman Institute into Bethune-Cookman College, a coeducational college; president of college (from 1923); appointed (1936) director of Division of Negro Affairs of the National Youth Administration.

**Bé'thune'** (bā'tün'), **Maximilien de.** See SULLY.

**Bet'je·man** (bĕch'ĕ·măn), Sir **John.** 1906– . English poet. Collections of poems include *Collected Poems* (1958), *Summoned by Bells* (1960), *High and Low* (1966). Knighted (1969). Named poet laureate in 1972.

**Bet'ter·ton** (bĕt'ẽr·tŭn; -t'n), **Thomas.** 1635?–1710. English actor. Joined Sir William Davenant's company (1661); m. (1662) Mary Saunderson (d. 1712), actress; managed Dorset Garden Theatre (1671). Played Timon, Lear, Troilus in Shakespearean adaptations by Dryden, Shadwell, Tate; ruined by speculation (1692); resigned management of Haymarket Theatre (1709) and retired;

last appearance as Melantius in *The Maid's Tragedy* (1710).

**Betti di Biagio, Bernardino.** See PINTURICCHIO.

**Bet'ti·nel'li** (bāt'tē·nĕl'lē), **Saverio.** 1718–1808. Italian writer and critic; entered Society of Jesus (1736); attacked Dante's literary reputation in *Lettere Dieci di Virgilio agli Arcadi* (1756); also wrote critical essays.

**Betto di Biagio, Bernardino di.** See PINTURICCHIO.

**Betts** (bĕts), **Louis.** 1873–1961. American portrait painter.

**Betts, Samuel Rossiter.** 1786–1868. American jurist; known for his decisions on admiralty law.

**Betz** (bĕts), **Franz.** 1835–1900. German baritone.

**Beuckelszoon** *or* **Beukelszoon** *or* **Beuckels, Jan.** See JOHN OF LEIDEN.

**Beu'dant'** (bû'dän'), **François Sulpice.** 1787–1852. French mineralogist and physicist, b. Paris.

**Beu'mel·burg** (boi'mĕl·bōōrk), **Werner.** 1899–1963. German journalist and author of historical novels.

**Beur'non'ville'** (bûr'nôn'vēl'), Comte **de,** *later* Marquis **de. Pierre de Riel** (ryĕl). 1752–1821. Marshal of France. Minister of war (1793); ambassador to Berlin (1800) and to Madrid (1802). Supported Louis XVIII (1814); named marshal (1816) and marquis (1817). His nephew Baron **Étienne Martin de Beurnonville** (1779–1876) was also a French general.

**Beust** (boist), Count **Friedrich Ferdinand von.** 1809–1886. German statesman. Prime minister of Saxony (1853–66). Chief opponent of Bismarck (esp. 1863–71). Austrian foreign minister (1866); prime minister (1867); chancellor of Austrian empire (1867–71). Reorganized empire as a dualistic Austro-Hungarian union (1867); dismissed (1871); ambassador to London (1871–78) and Paris (1878–82).

**Bev'an** (bĕv'ăn), **A·neu'rin** (ȧ·nī'rĭn). 1897–1960. British statesman. Minister of health (1945–51); introduced National Health Service (1948); minister of labor (1951).

**Bev'er·idge** (bĕv'ẽr·ĭj), **Albert Jeremiah.** 1862–1927. American political leader and historian, b. in Highland County, Ohio. Member, U.S. Senate (1899–1911). Author of *The Life of John Marshall* (2 vols., 1916, 1919).

**Beveridge, William Henry.** 1st Baron **Tug'gal** (tŭg'ăl). 1879–1963. English economist, b. in India; M.A., B.C.L. (1902), Oxon.; director of labor exchanges (1909–16); 2d secretary (1916–18), permanent secretary (1919), Ministry of Food; director, London School of Economics (1919–37); chairman, Unemployment Insurance Statutory Committee (1934–44); as chairman of Inter-Departmental Committee on Social Insurance and Allied Services (1941–42) brought out (1942) comprehensive report embodying proposals for postwar social security in Great Britain.

**Bev'in** (bĕv'ĭn), **Ernest.** 1881–1951. British labor leader, b. in Somersetshire. Devoted to labor-union organization (from c. 1909); gained prominence by speech before Transport Workers' Court of Inquiry (1920); negotiated merger of 32 unions into national organization, Transport and General Workers' Union (1922), and became general secretary; chairman, general council of Trades Union Congress (1936–37); minister of labor and national service (1940–45); secretary of state for foreign affairs (from 1945).

**Bew'ick** (bū'ĭk), **Thomas.** 1753–1828. English wood engraver and restorer of wood engraving to popularity. Illustrated Gay's *Fables* (1779), *General History of Quadrupeds* (1790), *History of British Birds* (1797), *The Chillingham Bull* (1789). Assisted in illustrating Gay's *Fables* by brother **John** (1760–1795) and in *Fables of Esop* by son **Robert Elliot** (1788–1849).

**Bexley,** Baron. See Nicholas VANSITTART.

**Bey'e·ren** (bī'yĕ·rĕn), **Abraham van.** 1620?–?1675. Dutch painter, esp. of genre pictures and still life.

**Bey'er·lein** (bī'ẽr·līn), **Franz Adam.** 1871–1949. German novelist and playwright.

**Beyle, Marie Henri.** Real name of STENDHAL.

**Bey'rich** (bī'rĭk), **Heinrich Ernst.** 1815–1896. German paleontologist and geologist.

**Bey'schlag** (bī'shläk), **Willibald.** 1823–1900. German Protestant theologian; leader of the Evangelical Union to protect German Protestant interests (from 1886). His son **Franz** (1856–1935), geologist, directed Prussian Geological Institution (1903–23).

**Bèze** (bâz), **Théodore de.** *Lat.* **Theodorus Be'za** (bē'zȧ). 1519–1605. French Protestant theologian; adopted Protestantism at Geneva (1548); with Calvin, became leader of Reformation in France; succeeded Calvin on latter's death (1564).

**Be·zout'** (bē·zōō'), **Étienne.** 1730–1783. French mathematician.

**Bha'ra·vi** (bä'rȧ·vĭ). Hindu poet (7th cent.); reputed author of the epic *Kirātārjunīya*, based on an episode in the Indian national epic of the *Mahābhārata.*

**Bhar'tri·ha'ri** (bŭr'trĭ·hŭ'rĭ). fl. 1st half of 7th century A.D. Hindu poet, philosopher, and grammarian; greatest Sanskrit writer of verse; author of three widely translated *Satakas*, the first 100 stanzas under title *Good Conduct*, the second, *Passion of Love*, and the third, *Renunciation*. Author also of *Vakyapadiya.*

**Bhas'ka·ra A·char'ya** (bäs'kȧ·rȧ ä·chär'yȧ), *i.e.* Bhaskara the Learned [Sanskrit *ācārya*, teacher]. b. 1114. Hindu astronomer and mathematician.

**Bha'va·bhu'ti** (bŭ'vȧ·bōō'tĭ). fl. 700 A.D. Sanskrit dramatist, b. probably in Berar, Central India. Author of *Mālatī-Mādhava*, sometimes called the Hindu *Romeo and Juliet; Mahāvīra-charita*, a story of Rama; and *Uttararāma-charita*, a romantic tale of Rama.

**Bia'lik** (byä'lĭk) *or* **Bya'lik, Chaim Nachman.** 1873–1934. Hebrew poet, b. in Volhynia, southern Russia. Aroused great emotion among Jews with early poem *In the City of Slaughter* (1903), written after Jewish pogrom of Kishinev; influential in revival of Hebrew; strong supporter of Zionist movement. To Berlin (1921); partner in publishing firm, later transferred to Tel Aviv, Palestine; visited England and America (1926).

**Bian'chi** (byäng'kē), **Francesco.** 1752–1810. Italian conductor and composer of about seventy operas (including *Merope* and *Alzira*), oratorios, etc.

**Bianchi, Nicomede.** 1818–1886. Italian historian.

**Bian'chi-Fer·ra'ri** (-fâr·rä'rē), **Francesco.** *Sometimes called* **Il Fra're** (ēl frä'rā). 1460?–1510. Italian painter; reputed teacher of Correggio at Ferrara.

**Bian·chi'ni** (byäng·kē'nē), **Francesco.** 1662–1729. Italian astronomer. Observed spots on planet Venus; asserted that it rotates in 24⅓ days. Appointed by Clement XI secretary of commission to reform calendar.

**Bian'co** (byäng'kō), **Margery,** *nee* **Williams.** 1881–1944. Author, b. London, Eng.; educ. in U.S.; m. (1904) Francesco Bianco (1878–1946) of Turin, Italy. Writer of fiction, esp. for children, as *The Velveteen Rabbit* (1922).

**Biandrata, Giorgio.** See BLANDRATA.

**Biard** (byȧr), **Auguste.** 1798–1882. French genre painter, b. Lyon.

**Bi'as of Pri·e'ne** (bī'ăs, prī·ē'nē). Greek sage of 6th century B.C. One of so-called Seven Wise Men of Greece, or Seven Sages; known esp. for maxims.

**Bibaculus, Marcus Furius.** See FURIUS.

**Bibars.** See BAYBARS.

**Bibb** (bĭb), **George Mortimer.** 1776–1859. American lawyer, b. in Prince Edward Co., Va.; U.S. senator from

Kentucky (1811–14, 1829–35); U.S. secretary of treasury (1844–45).

**Bib·bie′na** (bĕb·byâ′nä). See BIBIENA.

**Bibbiena, Bernardo Do·vi′zio da** (dô·vē′tsyô dä). 1470–1520. Italian poet; cardinal (1513); legate to France (1518). Translated comedies of Plautus; wrote *La Calandria* (1521), an early Italian comedy.

**Bi′ber** (bē′bĕr), **Heinrich Johann Franz von.** 1644–1704. German violinist and composer; a founder of German school of violin playing. His compositions include musical dramas, church music, and violin music.

**Bi·be′sco** (bē·bĕ′skō). *Rum.* **Bi·be′scu** (-skōō). Name of a Rumanian boyar house, including: **George Demetrius** (1804–1873), hospodar of Walachia, who, returning from exile (1834–41), led opposition to government of Prince Alexandru Ghika and brought about his deposition (1842); became hospodar (1843); elected prince (1845); overthrown by insurrection excited by opposition to his dependence upon Russia; approved new constitution and resigned (1849). His brother **Bar′bo** (bär′bō) **Demetrius,** *Rum.* **Barbu Dimitrie** (1799–1869), Prince **Stir·bey′,** *Rum.* **Ştir·beiu′** (shtēr·bā′), Walachian statesman; took name of his uncle Barbo Stirbey, who adopted him; took part in uprising of Alexandru Ypsilanti; minister of finance under Alexandru Ghika; secretary of state, minister of public instruction, minister of justice (1831–37), minister of interior under his brother George (1844), on whose fall he fled to Paris (1847); as hospodar of Walachia (1849–56), took reins of government; strove for Rumanian unity; on election of Cuza, retired to France. Prince **George** (zhôrzh) (1834–1902); son of George Demetrius Bibesco; served in French army, taking part in Mexican campaign and campaign of 1870. His son Prince **George** [zhôrzh] **Va′len′tin′** [vá′läN′tăN′] (1880–1941); Rumanian industrialist and aviator; ambassador to Paris (1906); president, International Aeronautical Federation (1930–41). Prince George Valentin's wife, Princess **Marthe** (mårt) **Lu′cie′** (lü′sē′) (1890– ); novelist and playwright; conducted Red Cross hospital during World War; her many works, written chiefly in French, include *The Eight Paradises,* a record of travel in Asia (crowned by French Academy when she was 18), *Isvor, the Land of Willows, A Daughter of Napoleon, Egyptian Day, Leaves of the Calendar* (1939); and (under pseudonym **Lu′cile′ De·caux′** [lü′sēl′ dē·kō′]) *Katia, Louison,* and *Loulou, Prince Imperial.* Prince **An′toine′** (äN′twån′) (1878–1951); diplomat and author; cousin of Prince George Valentin Bibesco; counselor, London and Petrograd legations; minister in Washington (1920–26), Madrid (1927–31); delegate, International Commission on Danube; author of the plays *Jealousy, Married Life, Which?* and *The Heir.* For his wife, Princess **Elizabeth,** see under Herbert Henry ASQUITH.

**Bi·bie′na** (bē·byâ′nä) *or* **Bib·bie′na** (bĕb·byâ′nä), **Gal′li** (gäl′lē) **da** (dä). Italian family of architects and artists: **Ferdinando** (1657–1743) and his three sons, **Alessandro** (1687–1769), **Giuseppe** (1696–1756), **Antonio** (1700–1744).

**Bibl** (bē′bĕl), **Viktor.** 1870–1947. Austrian historian.

**Bibliander.** See Theodor BUCHMANN.

**Bibliophile Jacob.** Pseudonym of Paul LACROIX.

**Bib′u·lus** (bĭb′ū·lŭs), **Marcus** (*erroneously* **Lucius**) **Calpurnius.** d. 48 B.C. Roman politician; opponent of Julius Caesar; consul with Caesar (59 B.C.); endeavored to block all measures sponsored by Caesar.

**Bic′ci** (bēt′chē), **Ersilio.** 1845– . Italian poet.

**Bi′chat′** (bē′shà′), **Marie François Xavier.** 1771–1802. French pioneer in scientific histology and pathological anatomy.

**Bick′er·staff** (bĭk′ẽr·stáf), **Isaac.** A pseudonym adopted by (1) Jonathan SWIFT in pamphlet (1708) chronicling death of John Partridge; (2) Richard STEELE in the *Tatler* (1709–11); (3) Benjamin WEST, American mathematician, in almanacs pub. (from 1768) in Boston.

**Bick′er·staffe** (bĭk′ẽr·stáf), **Isaac.** c. 1735–c. 1812. Irish playwright. Author esp. of comedies and comic operas.

**Bickerstaffe-Drew** (-drōō′), Monsignor Count **Francis Browning Drew.** 1858–1928. English Roman Catholic clergyman and author. Chaplain to British fighting services (1886–1919); private chamberlain of Pope Leo XIII (1891) and Pope Pius X (1903); prothonotary apostolic (1912); decorated and mentioned in dispatches in World War; retired (1919). Author, under pseudonym **John Ays′cough** (ăs′kū), of 20 novels, including *Rosemary, Dromina,* and *A Prince in Petto.*

**Bick′er·steth** (bĭk′ẽr·stĕth; -stĭth), **Edward.** 1786–1850. English evangelical clergyman. Collector of over 700 hymns in *Christian Psalmody* (1833). His son **Edward Henry** (1825–1906), bishop of Exeter (1885–1900), wrote *Yesterday, To-day, and For Ever* (1866), and hymns including *Peace, Perfect Peace.*

**Bick′nell** (bĭk′n′l), **Frank Alfred.** 1866–1943. American landscape painter.

**Bi′da′** (bē′dá′), **Alexandre.** 1823–1895. French painter, esp. of Bible scenes.

**Bi′dault′** (bē′dō′), **Georges.** 1899– . French educator and politician. Helped found Catholic daily *L'Aube* (1932) and wrote for it on foreign affairs (1932–39); joined underground movement (1941); president of National Council of Resistance (1943–44); foreign minister of France (from 1944); provisional president (1946).

**Bid′dle** (bĭd′'l), **Francis.** 1886–1968. American lawyer, b. Paris, France; B.A. (1909), LL.B. (1911), Harvard; member of Philadelphia law firms (1915–39); special assistant U.S. attorney (1922–26); judge, U.S. Circuit Court of Appeals (1939–40); solicitor general of U.S. (1940); attorney general of U.S. (1941–45). His brother **George** (1885–1973), b. Philadelphia, painter and sculptor; works in U.S. and foreign museums.

**Biddle, James.** 1783–1848. American naval officer, b. Philadelphia. First lieutenant in command of *Wasp* (1812), which captured *Frolic;* given command of *Hornet* (1813–15); commanded *Ontario,* which entered Columbia River (1817); negotiated (1846) first treaty between U.S. and China.

**Biddle, John.** 1615–1662. Founder of English Unitarianism. M.A., Oxon. (1641); schoolmaster, Gloucester; imprisoned for publishing refutations of deity of Holy Spirit; released by decree of oblivion (1652); imprisoned for *A Twofold Catechism* (1654); banished by Cromwell to Scilly Isles (1655), to save his life.

**Biddle, Nicholas.** 1786–1844. American financier, b. Philadelphia. Appointed by Monroe a director of Bank of the United States (1819); elected its president (1822). Center of attack by Jackson against bank; new charter refused; secured state charter, and bank became (Mar. 1, 1836) "The Bank of the United States of Pennsylvania." Biddle resigned (1839) and retired.

**Bid′lack** (bĭd′lăk), **Benjamin Alden.** 1804–1849. American diplomat, b. Paris, N.Y. U.S. chargé d'affaires in New Granada (Colombia); negotiated (1846) with New Granada a treaty including right of way across Isthmus of Panama.

**Bi′dou′** (bē′dōō′), **Henry.** 1873–1943. French dramatic and literary critic.

**Bid′pai** (bĭd′pī) *or* **Pil′pay** (pĭl′pī) *or* **Pil′pai** (pĭl′pī). Reputed author of Indian fables. His original Sanskrit tales no longer extant; chief early editions, *Panchatantra* and its abridgment *Hitopadesa*, translated into Pahlavi (6th century A.D.) for a Persian king; further translations made into old Syriac (6th century) and Arabic (8th century) from this work. In introduction to the Arabic translation, author of original fables called Bidpai, chief of Indian philosophers; actually *Bidpai* is Sanskrit *vidyāpati*, "chief pundit" (at a court), and not a proper name.

**Bid′well** (bĭd′wĕl; -wĕl), **Shelford.** 1848–1909. English pioneer in telephotography.

**Bie′ber·bach** (bē′bēr·bäκ), **Ludwig.** 1886– . German mathematician.

**Bieberstein.** See MARSCHALL VON BIEBERSTEIN.

**Bie′der·mann** (bē′dēr·män), **Felix.** See Felix DÖRMANN.

**Biedermann, Friedrich Karl.** 1812–1901. German politician, publicist, and historian. Member (1848) of preliminary parliament, Frankfurt, and of German National Assembly; as member of Saxon diet favored (1849–50) union under Prussian leadership. Leader of Saxon National Liberal party in Saxon diet (1869–76); member of German Reichstag (1871–74).

**Bièfve** (byâv), **Édouard de.** 1809–1882. Belgian historical and portrait painter.

**Biel** (bēl), **Gabriel.** 1425?–1495. German scholastic philosopher. Author of *Epitome et Collectorium ex Occamo*, an exposition on the nominalistic teachings of William of Ockham; etc.

**Bie′la** (bē′lä), **Wilhelm von.** 1782–1856. German astronomer; observed (1826) periodic comet (Biela's comet; first seen in 1772) which separated (1846) into two comets.

**Bielinski.** Variant of BELINSKI.

**Biel′ski** (byĕl′skē), **Marcin.** 1495?–1575. Polish historian and poet, b. Biała. Wrote first history in Polish language; his history of Poland (pub. 1597) completed by his son **Joachim** (1540–1599).

**Bienewitz, Peter.** Real name of Petrus APIANUS.

**Bien′ville′** (byăN′vēl′; *Angl.* bĭ·ĕn′vĭl, byĕn′-), Sieur **de. Jean Baptiste Le Moyné** (lē·mwȧn′). 1680–1768. Son of Charles Lemoyne (*q.v.*). Provincial governor in America, b. Canada. Explorer of lower Mississippi and Red River (1699). Lieutenant of the king in Louisiana (1700); governor of the colony (1701–12, 1718–26, 1733–43); founder of New Orleans (1718).

**Bier** (bēr), **August.** 1861–1949. German surgeon.

**Bier′baum** (bēr′boum), **Otto Julius.** 1865–1910. German poet, novelist, and miscellaneous writer.

**Bierce** (bērs), **Ambrose Gwinnett.** 1842–?1914. American journalist and short-story writer, b. in Meigs County, Ohio. Served through Civil War. Reputation as witty and caustic writer established by *The Fiend's Delight* (1872), *Nuggets and Dust Panned Out in California* (1872), *Cobwebs from an Empty Skull* (1874). Contributed column of "Prattle" in San Francisco *Examiner* (1887–96). Later work became cynical, often bitter and gruesome. Disappeared into Mexico (1913) and fate unknown. Other works include *Tales of Soldiers and Civilians* (1891), *Can Such Things Be?* (1893), *Devil's Dictionary* (1906).

**Bier′stadt** (bēr′stăt; *Ger.* bēr′shtät), **Albert.** 1830–1902. American landscape painter of Hudson River school, b. Solingen, Germany; to U.S. (1831). His paintings include *Sunshine and Shadow*, *Rocky Mountains*, *Valley of the Yosemite*, studies of the Sierra Nevada, and the historical paintings *Discovery of the Hudson River*, *Settlement of California*, and *Entrance into Monterey*.

**Bies·ter′** (byĕsh·tär′; bēs′tēr), **João Ernesto.** 1829–1880. Portuguese dramatist.

**Biè′vre** (byâ′vr′), Marquis **de. Georges François Ma′re′schal′** (mȧ′rā′shȧl′). 1747–1789. French writer; best known for his puns and bons mots.

**Big′e·low** (bĭg′ē·lō), **Erastus Brigham.** 1814–1879. American inventor, b. West Boylston, Mass. Invented power looms for use in carpet weaving and in manufacturing gingham, silk brocatel, and pile fabrics.

**Bigelow, Jacob.** 1786–1879. American physician and botanist, b. Sudbury, Mass. Author of *Florula Bostoniensis* (1814; standard manual of New England botany until Gray's *Manual* of 1848), *American Medical Botany* (3 vols., 1817, 1818, 1820), etc. His son **Henry Jacob** (1818–1890) was a prominent New England surgeon.

**Bigelow, John.** 1817–1911. American writer and diplomat, b. Bristol (now Malden), N.Y. Coeditor and co-owner, with William Cullen Bryant, of New York *Evening Post* (1848–61). U.S. consul general at Paris (1861–65); U.S. minister to France (1865–66). Author of *France and the Confederate Navy, 1862–68* (1888), *Life of Benjamin Franklin* (1874), etc.

**Bigelow, Poultney.** 1855–1954. American traveler, journalist, and author, b. New York City. Founded *Outing* (1885), first American magazine devoted esp. to amateur sport. Expelled from Russia because of political writings (1892); correspondent for London *Times* in Spanish-American War (1898). Personal friend of long standing of German Kaiser Wilhelm II. Author of *History of the German Struggle for Liberty, 1806–1848* (4 vols., 1903), *Prussianism and Pacifism* (1919), *Japan and Her Colonies* (1923), etc.

**Bigg** (bĭg), **John Stanyan.** 1828–1865. English poet and journalist; member of spasmodic school (see under Sydney DOBELL), as shown in *Night and the Soul* (1854).

**Big′gers** (bĭg′ērz), **Earl Derr** (?dĕr). 1884–1933. American writer, b. Warren, Ohio. Best known for his character "Charlie Chan," a Chinese detective, central figure in several novels, later used in stage and motion-picture versions. Author also of popular success *Seven Keys to Baldpate* (1913; later dramatized and filmed), *The Agony Column* (1916), etc.

**Biggers, John David.** 1888–1973. American glass manufacturer. Director of production, Office of Production Management (1941); minister to Great Britain in charge of production, co-ordination, and lend-lease (Aug., 1941); returned to private life (Oct., 1941).

**Biggs** (bĭgz), **Hermann Michael.** 1859–1923. American physician; pioneer in preventive medicine. Introduced diphtheria antitoxin in U.S. (1894). Headed work in New York City for prevention of tuberculosis; as State commissioner of health, developed division of infant and maternity welfare.

**Bigham, John Charles.** See 1st Viscount MERSEY.

**Big′low** (bĭg′lō), **Hosea.** Pseudonym of James Russell LOWELL.

**Bi′gnon′** (bē′nyôN′), **Louis Pierre Édouard.** 1771–1841. French statesman and historian. Designated by Napoleon in his will to write history of France from time of Consulate; wrote *Histoire de France depuis le 18–Brumaire jusqu'en 1812* (1829–38).

**Bi′god** (bī′gŏd). English noble family, prominent in 12th and 13th centuries and including: **Hugh** (d. ?1176), 1st Earl of **Norfolk**; active in rebellions against Henry I, Stephen, and Henry II. **Roger** (d. 1221), 2d earl, and son of Hugh; joined barons against John (1215) and had part in securing Magna Charta. **Roger** (d. 1270), 4th earl and grandson of 2d earl; at first supported Henry III against Simon de Montfort but later joined de Montfort's party. **Roger** (1245–1306), 5th and last earl and nephew of 4th earl, took arms in protest against taxation without national consent.

**Bigordi, Domenico di Tommaso.** See GHIRLANDAJO.

**Bi'gour'dan'** (bē'gōōr'däN'), **Guillaume.** 1851–1932. French astronomer.

**Bi·ha'ri Lal** (bĭ·hä'rĭ läl'). fl. 17th century A.D. Hindi poet, b. in Gwalior. Resided at court of Jaipur; wrote *Satsāi* (completed 1662), collection of amorous verses (c. 700 distichs) in Hindi idiom of Mathura, the poet's home.

**Bijns** *or* **Byns** (bīns), **Anna.** 1494?–1575. Flemish poet; known as "Sappho of Brabant."

**Bik'a·ner'** (bĭk'ȧ·nẽr'; *native pron.* bē·kŭ·năr), Maharaja of. Sir **Gan'ga Singh'ji Ba·ha'dur** (gŭng'gä sĭN'hȧ·jē bȧ·hä'dŏŏr). 1880–1943. Indian soldier and statesman. Maharaja (1880–1943); assumed full ruling powers (1898); officer in British army (from 1900); general (1937); served in China campaign (1901) in command of Bikaner Camel Corps; in World War I (1914–15); awarded Kaisar-i-Hind medal; representative of India at several imperial conferences (1917, 1919, 1930); at League of Nations (1924, 1930); at Indian Round Table Conference in London (1930–31).

**Bi·ke'las** (vē·kâ'läs), **Demetrios.** 1835–1908. Greek poet and historian; translated several of Shakespeare's plays into modern Greek; author of patriotic hymns, and of *The Greeks of the Middle Ages* (1878) and *Greek, Byzantine and Modern* (1893).

**Bil'der·dijk** (bĭl'dẽr·dīk), **Willem.** 1756–1831. Dutch poet, scholar, and critic.

**Bildsöe, J. A. D. J.** See Jens JENSEN.

**Bil'fing·er** (bĭl'fĭng·ẽr) *or* **Bülf'fing·er** (bül'fĭng·ẽr), **Georg Bernhard.** 1693–1750. German philosopher of Leibnitz-Wolffian school and mathematician. Author of *Dilucidationes Philosophicae* (1725), an exposition of Wolffian metaphysics.

**Bil'hah** (bĭl'hȧ). *In Douay Version* **Ba'la** (bā'lȧ). In Bible, handmaid of Jacob's wife Rachel (*Gen.* xxix. 29). See JACOB.

**Bil'ha·na** (bĭl'hȧ·nȧ). fl. 11th century A.D. Indian poet b. in Kashmir. Lived at court of Vikramaditya VI. Author of a famous love song in 50 strophes, *Chauraspanchāsika*, and an epic.

**Bil'laud'-Va'renne'** (bē'yō'vȧ'rĕn'), **Jean Nicolas.** 1756–1819. French revolutionary politician; member of Commune and influential in instigating September Massacres (1792); supported Robespierre against Hébert and Danton but later aided in his overthrow. Prosecuted as Terrorist; transported to Guiana (1795); refused pardon offered by Napoleon; released (1816); to Haiti, where he died.

**Bil'le** (bĕl'ĕ), **Steen Andersen.** 1797–1883. Danish admiral and minister of marine. Commanded expedition to South America and a scientific expedition around the world in the *Galatea* (1845–47); commanded second squadron in war against Germany (1848). Minister of marine (1852–53, 1860–68); commander of a mission to China (1869).

**Bil'ling·hurst** (bĭl'ĭng·hûrst; *Span.* bē'lĕng·gōōrst'), **Guillermo Enrique.** 1851–1915. Peruvian businessman and radical political leader, b. Arica, of English father and native Peruvian mother. President of Peru (1912–14); forced to resign by military coup d'état; sent into exile in Panama.

**Bil'lings** (bĭl'ĭngz), **Henry.** 1901– . American painter and author.

**Billings, John Shaw.** 1838–1913. American physician and librarian; in medical service, U.S. army (1861–95). Fostered growth of surgeon general's library in Washington. With Dr. Robert Fletcher, prepared *Index-Catalogue* (16 vols., 1880–95). Also with Dr. Fletcher, published *Index Medicus* (1879–95), a monthly guide to current medical literature. Chief librarian, New York Public Library (1896–1913).

**Billings, Josh.** Pseudonym of Henry Wheeler SHAW.

**Billings, Warren K.** See under T. J. MOONEY.

**Bil'ling·ton** (bĭl'ĭng·tŭn), **Elizabeth,** *nee* **Weich'sel** (vīk'sĕl). 1768–1818. English opera singer; daughter of a German oboist; m. (1783) James Billington, double-bass player; sensation at Covent Garden (1786); toured Italy (1794 ff.); appeared at Covent Garden and Drury Lane on alternate nights (1801), and at King's Theatre in Italian opera (1802–11).

**Bill'roth** (bĭl'rōt), **Albert Christian Theodor.** 1829–1894. German surgeon. Professor at Vienna (from 1867); made important contributions to histology and pathology; advanced military surgery. Also a pianist; at his house his friend Brahms played much of his chamber music before its public performance.

**Bil'ly the Kid** (bĭl'ĭ thē kĭd'). *Real name* **William H. Bon'ney** (bŏn'ĭ). 1859–1881. American desperado, b. New York City. As youth lived in Kansas, Colorado, New Mexico. Most notorious outlaw of American southwest, a legendary glamour surrounding his career.

**Bil'ney** *or* **Byl'ney** (bĭl'nĭ), **Thomas.** 1495?–1531. English martyr; denounced prayers to saints and image worship; burned as heretic.

**Bim'bi·sa'ra** (bĭm'bĭ·sä'rȧ). d. 554? B.C. An early king of Magadha (582–554); regarded as founder of the greatness of the kingdom; friend and protector of Gautama Buddha.

**Bin'chois'** (băN'shwȧ'), **Gilles** *or* **Égide.** 15th-century Flemish composer.

**Binck** (bĭngk), **Jakob.** 1500?–1569. German portrait painter and engraver.

**Binder, Mathilde.** See under Alexander KAUFMANN.

**Bindusara.** *In full* **Bin'du·sa'ra A·mi'tra·gha'ta** (bĭn'dōō·sä'rȧ ȧ·mĭ'trȧ·gä'tȧ). d. 273 B.C. Second king of Magadha (298–273) of Maurya dynasty. Son of Chandragupta and father of Asoka.

**Bi'net'** (bē'nĕ'; *Angl.* bē·nā'), **Alfred.** 1857–1911. French psychologist, b. Nice. Director, laboratory of physiological psychology, Sorbonne, Paris. Collaborated with Théodore Simon in establishing standard by which degrees of intelligence may be measured; devised tests (Binet, or Binet-Simon, tests) for measuring intelligence by this standard. Author of *Introduction à la Psychologie Expérimentale* (1894), *Les Idées Modernes sur les Enfants* (1910), etc.

**Binet, Satané.** Pseudonym of Francisque SARCEY.

**Bi'net'-Val'mer'** (bē'nĕ'vȧl'mâr'), **Jean.** *Known as* **Jean Binet de Valmer.** 1875–1940. Swiss-born novelist; naturalized in France (1914).

**Bin'ger'** (băN'zhā'), **Louis Gustave.** 1856–1936. French explorer and administrator, b. Strasbourg. Explored west African region north of Ivory Coast and established French protectorate; governor of Ivory Coast (1893).

**Bing'ham** (bĭng'ăm), **George Caleb.** 1811–1879. American painter; studios successively at Jefferson City, St. Louis, Kansas City; excelled in portrait and genre painting.

**Bingham, George Charles.** 3d Earl of **Lu'can** (lū'kăn). 1800–1888. English soldier; directed charge of heavy brigade of cavalry at Balaklava (1854); covered with two regiments retirement of light brigade; censured by Lord Raglan (1855); general (1865); field marshal (1887).

**Bingham, Hiram.** 1789–1869. American missionary, b. Bennington, Vt. Missionary at Honolulu (1820–40). Reduced Hawaiian language to writing; with associates, translated Bible into Hawaiian. His son **Hiram** (1831–1908) was missionary to Gilbert Islands (1857–64, 1873–75) and did for Gilbert language what his father had done for Hawaiian. The latter's son **Hiram** (1875–1956) explored Bolívar's route across Venezuela and Colombia (1906–07), Spanish trade route from Buenos Aires to Lima (1908–09), Inca ruins in Peru (1911–15); U.S. senator from Conn. (1925–33).

**Bingham, Joseph.** 1668–1723. English clergyman; author of *Origines Ecclesiasticae* (10 vols., 1708–22).

**Bingham, Robert Worth.** 1871–1937. American newspaper publisher and diplomat; publisher of Louisville *Courier-Journal* and Louisville *Times.* U.S. ambassador to Great Britain (1933–37).

**Bingham, Theodore Alfred.** 1858–1934. American army officer; retired (1904) with rank of brigadier general; police commissioner, New York City (1906–09).

**Bingham, William.** 1752–1804. American political leader, b. Philadelphia. Founder and director, Bank of North America (chartered Dec. 31, 1781), first bank in the country. Served in Continental Congress (1786–89), Pennsylvania Assembly (1790–95), U.S. Senate (1795–1801). Founder of Binghamton, N.Y.

**Bin′ney** (bĭn′ĭ), **Amos.** 1803–1847. American zoologist.

**Binney, Horace.** 1780–1875. American lawyer and legal writer.

**Binney, Thomas.** 1798–1874. English nonconformist clergyman; noted pulpit orator.

**Binns** (bĭnz), **Archie.** 1899– . American writer; served in U.S. army (1918); sailor; newspaper reporter; editor, Leonard Scott Publication Co.; author of *Maiden Voyage* (1931), *Lightship* (1934), *Backwater Voyage* (1936), *The Laurels are Cut Down* (1937), *The Land is Bright* (1939), *The Roaring Land* (1942).

**Binns, Charles Fergus.** 1857–1934. Authority on ceramics, b. Worcester, Eng. Associated with Royal Porcelain Works, Worcester, Eng. (1872–96); to U.S.; director of New York State Coll. of Ceramics (1900–31). Consulting editor on ceramic terms for *Webster's New International Dictionary, Second Edition.*

**Binns, John Alexander.** 1761?–1813. American farmer, b. in Loudoun County, Va. Introduced use of gypsum as fertilizer; experimented with crop rotation and deep plowing. Originator of so-called "Loudoun system" of soil treatment. Author of *A Treatise on Practical Farming* (1803).

**Bin′yon** (bĭn′yŭn), **Laurence.** 1869–1943. English poet and art historian; educ. Oxford; in charge of Oriental prints and drawings, British Museum (1913–32). Author of works on Chinese, Japanese, and Indian art, and of volumes of verse (*Collected Poems,* 1931; *The North Star,* 1941), blank verse dramas (including *Paris and Oenone,* 1906; *Boadicea,* 1925), and a verse translation of Dante's *Commedia* (*Inferno,* 1933; *Purgatorio,* 1938).

**Binz** (bĭnts), **Karl.** 1832–1913. German physician and pharmacologist.

**Bin′zer** (bĭn′tsẽr), Baron **August Daniel von.** 1793–1868. German author and song writer.

**Bi′on** (bī′ŏn). fl. 3d century B.C. Greek philosopher, of Borysthenes, Sarmatia. Author of *Diatribae,* popular satires directed against gods, scientists, and men of wealth.

**Bion.** fl. 3d or 2d century B.C. Greek pastoral poet, b. near Smyrna; lived probably in Sicily. Best known of extant poems, *Epitaphios Adonidos* (*Lament for Adonis*).

**Biondo, Flavio.** See FLAVIO BIONDO.

**Biot** (byō), **Jean Baptiste.** 1774–1862. French mathematician, physicist, and astronomer, b. Paris. From his investigations of the polarization of light, formulated Biot's law; founder of saccharimetry by use of polariscope. His son **Édouard Constant** (1803–1850) was a Chinese scholar, translator of *Tcheou li,* and compiler of a gazetteer of China.

**Bi·ra′go** (bē·rä′gō), Baron **Karl von.** 1792–1845. Austrian military engineer.

**Bi′rague′** (bē′rȧg′), **René de.** 1506?–1583. Cardinal and statesman, b. Milan, Italy. Conducted diplomatic missions for Francis I and Henry II of France; influential in court of Catherine de Médicis; chancellor (1573).

**Biran, Maine de.** See MAINE DE BIRAN.

**Birch** (bĭrk), **Christian Andreas.** See under BIRCH-PFEIFFER.

**Birch** (bûrch), **Samuel.** 1813–1885. English Egyptologist.

**Birch, Thomas.** 1705–1766. English historian, clergyman, and editor of state papers.

**Birch, Thomas.** 1779–1851. Painter, b. in England; to Philadelphia as a child. Painter of landscapes, marines, and some naval battle scenes, as *Engagement of the Constitution and the Guerrière* (now at U.S. Naval Academy, Annapolis).

**Birch′-Pfeif′fer** (bĭrk′pfī′fẽr), **Charlotte Karoline,** *nee* **Pfeiffer.** 1800–1868. German actress and dramatist; m. (1825) **Christian Andreas Birch** (1793–1868) of Copenhagen, author. See Wilhelmine von HILLERN.

**Bird** *or* **Birde** (bûrd). See also BYRD.

**Bird** (bûrd), **Arthur.** 1856–1923. American musician, b. Cambridge, Mass.; composer of a symphony and of orchestral and instrumental music.

**Bird, Edward.** 1772–1819. English painter; best-known work, *The Field of Chevy Chace.*

**Bird, Isabella Lucy.** See BISHOP.

**Birds′eye′** (bûrdz′ī′), **Clarence.** 1886–1956. American executive and inventor, b. Brooklyn, N.Y. President, Birds Eye Frosted Foods (1930–34), Birdseye Electric Co. (1935–38); food technologist (from 1939). Trademark "Birds Eye," applied to frozen foods, is name of process developed by him.

**Bird′wood** (bûrd′wo͝od), Sir **George Christopher Molesworth.** 1832–1917. Anglo-Indian official and writer on Indian botany, art, and folklore, b. in India. Medical practitioner in Bombay (1858–68). Served 30 years in India office. His brother **Herbert Mills** (1837–1907), Anglo-Indian judge, gained reputation for independence of action; active in educational and scientific movements. The latter's son Field Marshal Sir **William Riddell** (1865–1951) was military secretary to Kitchener in South Africa (1902); commanded Australasian forces at Gallipoli and at western front (1914–18); commander in chief in India (1925).

**Biren, Ernst Johann.** See BIRON.

**Birge** (bûrj), **Edward A′sa·hel** (ā′s'l; ā′sȧ·ĕl). 1851–1950. American zoologist and limnologist, b. Troy, N.Y. Grad. Williams Coll. (1873). Professor (from 1879), president (1918–25), U. of Wisconsin. His nephew **Raymond Thayer Birge** (1887– ), physicist.

**Bir′ger** (bĭr′yẽr). Name of several rulers of Sweden:

Earl **Birger Bro′sa′** (bro͞o′sȧ′). *Sometimes known as* **Birger I.** d. 1202. Controlled affairs (1195–1202) during reign of his son-in-law Sverker; kept country at peace.

**Birger of Bjäl′bo′** (byĕl′bo͞o′). d. 1266. Created earl (1248); regent (1250–66) during minority of son Waldemar; founder of Folkung dynasty (*q.v.*); led crusade to Finland (1249–50); conquered part of it and founded Tavastehus (Häme); made commercial treaties with Lübeck and England; said to have founded Stockholm; made wise laws.

**Birger II.** 1280–1321. Son of Magnus I; nominally king (1290–1302) under regency; crowned (1302), king (1302–18); engaged in civil war with brothers (1306–10); caused their imprisonment and death (1317–18); exiled to Denmark (1318).

**Birgitta,** Saint. See BRIDGET.

**Bir'kai** (bĭr'kī). d. 1267. Mongol ruler. Grandson of Genghis Khan and brother of Batu Khan. Converted to Islam; succeeded Batu as khan of Golden Horde (1255–67); built a new capital on banks of lower Volga; ruled independent of Mongols in north; allied with Islamic forces (1262) against Il-khan Hulagu, his cousin.

**Birk'beck** (bûr(k)'bĕk), **George.** 1776–1841. English physician and founder of mechanics' institutions, first in Glasgow, originating present system of popular scientific education. Founder and councilor of University College, London (1827).

**Bir'ken·head** (bûr'kĕn·hĕd), 1st Earl of. **Frederick Edwin Smith.** 1872–1930. English lawyer and statesman. Conservative M.P. (1906–18); opposed Parliament Bill (1911); attorney general (1915); lord chancellor (1919–22); secretary of state for India (1924–28). Known for his Law of Property Act (1922) and other legal reform measures. Father of novelist Lady Eleanor Furneaux Smith (*q.v.*) and of **Frederick Winston Furneaux Smith** (1907–1975), 2d earl, who biographized him in *The First Phase* (1933) and *The Last Phase* (1935).

**Bir'ket-Smith'** (bēr'kĕt·smĭt'), **Kaj.** 1893– . Danish ethnologist and polar explorer; accompanied ethnographic exploration to northern Greenland (1918); with Rasmussen (1921–23); on Danish-American Alaskan expedition (1933). Made special study of Eskimos.

**Bir'kett** (bûr'kĕt; -kĭt), **Herbert Stanley.** 1864–1942. Canadian surgeon, b. Hamilton, Ont.; M.D., McGill; professor of otolaryngology (1895–1931), McGill; asst. director-general, Canadian Army Medical Corps (1918).

**Birk'hoff** (bûr'kôf), **George David.** 1884–1944. American mathematician, b. Overisel, Mich.; A.B., Harvard (1905), Ph.D., Chicago (1907); assistant professor of mathematics, Harvard (1912–19), professor (1919–44); known for researches in dynamics and on systems of differential equations; author of *Relativity and Modern Physics* (1923), *The Origin, Nature, and Influence of Relativity* (1925), *Dynamical Systems* (1928), *Aesthetic Measure* (1933), *Basic Geometry* (coauthor; 1941).

**Birmingham, George A.** Pseudonym of James Owen HANNAY.

**Bir'ney** (bûr'nĭ), **James Gillespie.** 1792–1857. American antislavery leader; executive secretary, American Anti-Slavery Society (1837 ff.). "Liberty Party" candidate for president (1840, 1844). Policy was to accomplish abolition of slavery by political means and moral suasion. Father of **James** (1817–1888), lawyer and diplomat; **William** (1819–1907), lawyer and Civil War general; and **David Bell** (1825–1864), Civil War general.

**Bi'ró** (bĭ'rō), **Ludwig.** 1880–1950. Hungarian novelist, playwright, and scenarist, b. Vienna.

**Bi'ron'** (bē'rôɴ'), Baron **de. Armand de Gon'taut'** (dẽ gôɴ'tō'). *Called* **Le Boi'teux'** (lẽ bwȧ'tû'). 1524?–1592. Marshal of France (from 1577); killed at siege of Épernay. His son **Charles de Gontaut** (1562–1602), Duc **de Biron;** surnamed "The Thunderbolt of France"; commanded armies of Henry IV; created duke and peer (1598). Charles's great-grandnephew **Armand Louis de Gontaut** (1747–1793), Duc **de Biron**; known under title of Duc **de Lau'zun'** (lō'zûɴ'), fought in American Revolution; represented nobility in States-General (1789); favored Revolutionary policies; held military commands (1792–93); guillotined.

**Bi'ron** (*Russ.* byē'rôn), **Ernst** (ĕrnst) **Jo·hann'** (yō·hän'). *Orig. surname* **Büh'ren** (*Ger.* bü'rĕn). Duke of **Kur'land** (ko͝or'lănd). 1690–1772. Russian statesman. Became favorite of Anna Ivanovna on her accession (1730); chamberlain and virtual ruler of Russia during her reign (1730–40). On death of Empress Anna, assumed regency for infant Ivan VI (1740); as result of palace revolution, was imprisoned (1740) and banished to Siberia (1741), but permitted (1742) by new empress, Elizabeth, to reside at Yaroslavl.

**Bir'rell** (bĭr'ĕl), **Augustine.** 1850–1933. English political leader and man of letters. Chief secretary for Ireland (1907–16). Author of volumes of essays *Obiter Dicta* (1884) and *More Obiter Dicta* (1924), and of biographies of Charlotte Brontë (1885), William Hazlitt (1902), and Frederick Locker-Lampson (1920).

**Birt** (bĭrt), **Theodor.** 1852–1933. German classical philologist and writer. Author of *Das Antike Buchwesen* (1882), *Zur Kulturgeschichte Roms* (1909), *Aus dem Leben der Antike* (1918), and poems (under pseudonym **Be·a'tus Rhe·na'nus** [*Ger.* bā·ä'to͞os rā·nä'no͞os; *Eng.* bē·ā'tŭs rē·nā'nŭs]), etc.

**Bi·ru'ni, al-** (ăl'bē·ro͞o'nē). *Arab.* **abu-al-Rayḥān Muḥammad ibn-Aḥmad al-Bīrūni.** 973–1048. Arabian scholar and author, of Persian descent. A Shiite with agnostic leanings; taught and studied in India (c. 1000); lived (1017–48) at Ghazni, capital of Mahmud; corresponded with Avicenna; wrote excellent description and history of India and treatises on mathematics, astrology, and astronomy.

**Bis'bee** (bĭz'bē), **William Henry.** 1840–1942. American army officer; engaged at Murfreesboro, in Atlanta campaign, and in battle of Jonesboro, Ga., in Civil War, and in Cuba in Spanish-American War (1898) and in Philippines (1899–1902). Brigadier general (Oct., 1901).

**Bi'schof** (bĭ'shōf; -shôf), **Karl Gustav Christoph.** 1792–1870. German chemist and geologist.

**Bi'schoff** (bĭ'shôf), **Theodor Ludwig Wilhelm.** 1807–1882. German anatomist and physiologist.

**Biscop** *or* **Bischop** *or* **Bisschop, Simon.** See Simon EPISCOPIUS.

**Bish'op** (bĭsh'ŭp), Sir **Henry Row'ley** (rō'lĭ). 1786–1855. English composer of operas, burlettas, and incidental music to Shakespeare's plays; remembered esp. for his glees and songs; introduced air of "Home, Sweet Home" into *Clari* (1823); first musician to be knighted (1842). His second wife, **Ann,** *nee* **Riv'i·ère'** [rĭv'ĭ·âr'] (1810–1884), operatic singer, toured continent (1839–46), North America (1847), Australia (1855).

**Bishop, Isabella Lucy,** *nee* **Bird.** 1832–1904. English traveler, lecturer, and writer; author of *Englishwoman in America* (1856), *The Hawaiian Archipelago* (1875), *Unbeaten Tracks in Japan* (1880), and *The Yangtse Valley and Beyond* (1899). First woman fellow of Royal Geographical Society (1892).

**Bishop, John Peale.** 1892–1944. American writer, b. Charles Town, W.Va. Resided chiefly in France (from c. 1930). Author of *Green Fruit, Many Thousands Gone, Now With His Love,* etc.

**Bishop, Joseph Bucklin.** 1847–1929. American journalist and author, b. Seekonk, Mass. On staff of New York *Tribune* (1870–83), *Evening Post* (1883–1900), *Globe* (1900–05). Secretary, Isthmian Canal Commission (1905–14). Author of *Issues of a New Epoch* (1904), *The Panama Gateway* (1913), *Theodore Roosevelt and His Time, Shown in his Letters* (2 vols., 1920), etc.; editor of *Theodore Roosevelt's Letters to His Children* (1919).

**Bishop, William Avery.** 1894–1956. Canadian military aviator, b. Owen Sound, Ont. Educ. Royal Military Coll., Kingston. Member of Canadian Expeditionary Force in France (1914); transferred to Royal Flying Corps (1915); awarded Victoria Cross and officially credited with bringing down 72 enemy aircraft. Group captain, Royal Canadian Air Force (1931); air vice-marshal of Canada (1936); air marshal (1938), and director of air-force recruiting (1940).

**Bis'marck** (bĭz'märk; *Ger.* bĭs'-), *in full* **Bis'marck-Schön'hau'sen** (-shûn'hou'zĕn), Prince **Otto Eduard Leopold von.** 1815–1898. Prussian statesman and first chancellor of German Empire, b. Schönhausen; called "the Iron Chancellor." Studied law at Göttingen and Berlin (1832–35). In Prussian civil (1836–39) and military service. Member, United Diet of Prussia (1847), second chamber of Prussian Diet (1849), and Erfurt Parliament (1850). Prussian ambassador to Germanic Diet at Frankfurt (1851–58); strongly opposed Austrian predominance and advocated consolidation of German people under Prussian leadership. Ambassador to Russia (1859) and France (1862). President of Prussian cabinet, and foreign minister (1862); engaged in struggle with diet over army reorganization, the budget, and prerogatives of the crown; declared (1862) that German problems must be solved by "blood and iron." Defeated Denmark (with co-operation of Austria) in Schleswig-Holstein war (1864); created count (1865); broke again with Austria over Schleswig-Holstein question in Seven Weeks' War, and with Italy's help gained decisive victory (1866) at Königgrätz (Sadowa). Reorganized German Bund, excluding Austria, as North German Confederation under leadership of Prussia (1866); gained triumphs in Franco-Prussian war (1870–71); took part in neutralization of Luxemburg; succeeded in winning over south German states to join confederation, and gained prestige among German people. Became first chancellor of new German Empire at Versailles, and created prince (1871). Engaged in unsuccessful struggle (*Kulturkampf*, 1872 ff.) with Roman Catholics; put through many economic and social reforms, including workmen's compulsory insurance and government ownership of industrial enterprises; advocated strong colonial and international policy, and protective tariff. Presided over international Congress of Berlin (1878); concluded Triple Alliance (Dreibund) of Germany, Italy, and Austria-Hungary (1882) to make Germany secure against France and Russia. Disagreed with William II and resigned (1890) with titles of Duke of **Lau'en·burg** (lou'ĕn·bŏŏrk) and colonel general of cavalry; reconciled with emperor (1894). Author of *Gedanken und Erinnerungen* (1898).

His son Prince **Herbert Nikolaus von Bismarck-Schönhausen** (1849–1904) served in Franco-Prussian War (1870); entered diplomatic service (1873); private secretary to his father (1877–81); counselor of German legation, London (1882) and St. Petersburg (1884); secretary of state (1886); Prussian minister of state (1888); presided at Samoan conference, Berlin, between Germany, England, and U.S. (1889); retired from diplomatic service after resignation of his father (1890). Member of Reichstag (1881–89, 1893, 1898). Another son, Count **Wilhelm Albrecht Otto von Bismarck-Schönhausen** (1852–1901), served in Franco-Prussian war (1870–71); member of Reichstag (1878–81) and Prussian chamber (1882–85); served in imperial chancellery (1878–79, 1881–84); president, province of Hanover (1889); governor of East Prussia (1895). Herbert's son Prince **Otto von Bismarck-Schönhausen** (1897– ) served in World War (from 1917); member, German National People's party, Reichstag (1924); entered diplomatic service (1927); counselor of embassy, London (1928).

**Bis'pham** (bĭs'făm), **David Scull.** 1857–1921. American baritone, b. Philadelphia. Sang at Covent Garden, London, and Metropolitan Opera House, New York (1896–1909).

**Bis'sell** (bĭs''l), **George Edwin.** 1839–1920. American sculptor.

**Bissell, George Henry.** 1821–1884. American petroleum pioneer, b. Hanover, N.H. Organized (1854) first oil company in U.S., to develop oil lands in Pennsylvania.

**Bis'sen** (bēs''n), **Hermann Wilhelm.** 1798–1868. Danish sculptor. Studied under Thorvaldsen.

**Bis'sing** (bĭs'ĭng), Baron **Moritz Ferdinand von.** 1844–1917. German general; cavalry general of 7th army corps (1901–07); governor general of Belgium (1914–17); colonel general (1915–17). Aimed to separate Flemish and Walloons in Belgium under a German protectorate. His son Baron **Friedrich Wilhelm** (1873–1956), Egyptologist, was assistant in Egyptian museum at Cairo (1897–1903); professor, Munich (1906–22) and Utrecht (1922–26).

**Bis'so·la'ti–Ber'ga·ma'schi** (bēs'sô·lä'tē·bār'gä·mäs'kē), **Leonida.** 1857–1920. Italian politician. Editor of Italian socialist organ *L'Avanti* (1896); member of parliament (1897) and leader of revisionist group of Italian Social Democratic party; seceded and founded Reformist Socialist party (1912); favored freedom of Libya and Italy's participation in World War on side of entente; minister without portfolio (1916–18).

**Bis'son'** (bē'sôɴ'), **Alexandre Charles Auguste.** 1848–1912. French author of comedies.

**Bittenfeld, Karl Eberhard Herwarth von.** See HERWARTH VON BITTENFELD.

**Bit'ter** (bĭt'ẽr), **Karl Hermann.** 1813–1885. Prussian statesman and writer on music. Prussian minister of finance (1879–82); active in re-establishing stability of Prussian finances and in bringing German railroads under government control. Author of *Johann Sebastian Bach* (1865), etc.

**Bitter, Karl Theodore Francis.** 1867–1915. Sculptor, b. Vienna, Austria; to U.S. (1888); naturalized. His four figures *Architecture, Sculpture, Painting, Music,* adorn front of Metropolitan Museum, N.Y.

**Bit'tin·ger** (bĭt''n·jẽr), **Charles.** 1879–1970. American painter and physicist; director Duxbury Color Laboratory (from 1919).

**Bitt'ner** (bĭt'nẽr), **Julius.** 1874–1939. Austrian composer of choruses, songs, and esp. operas.

**Bit'zi·us** (bĭ'tsē·ŏŏs), **Albert.** *Pseudonym* **Jeremias Gott'helf** (gôt'hĕlf). 1797–1854. Swiss novelist; author esp. of works depicting village life in Switzerland.

**Bivar, Rodrigo** (*or* **Ruy**) **Díaz de.** See the CID.

**Bix'by** (bĭks'bĭ), **Horace Ezra.** 1826–1912. Mississippi River pilot, b. Geneseo, N.Y. Friend, and for a time partner, of Samuel Clemens (Mark Twain).

**Bix'io** (bēk'syô), **Nino,** *in full* **Girolamo Nino.** 1821–1873. Italian soldier. Commanded Roman troops against French (1849); commanded vessel in Sicilian campaign (1860); captured Reggio (1860); promoted lieutenant general; forced surrender of Civitavecchia (1870). Elected to chamber of deputies (1866); senator (1870). His brother **Jacques Alexandre Bix'io'** [bēk'syō'] (1808–1865) was a French publicist and politician.

**Bi'zet'** (bē'zĕ'), **Alexandre César Léopold,** *called* **Georges.** 1838–1875. b. Paris. French composer of the operas *Les Pêcheurs de Perles* (1863), *La Jolie Fille de Perth* (1867), *L'Arlésienne* (1872), and *Carmen* (1875), an overture, *Patrie,* and many songs and piano compositions.

**Bjerk'nes** (byărk'nās), **Vilhelm.** 1862–1951. Norwegian physicist. Proposed theory of electric resonance that aided in development of wireless telegraphy (1895). His son **Jakob Aall Bonnevie** (1897– ), meteorologist, Bergen observatory (from 1918).

**Björk'man** (byûrk'măn), **Edwin Au'gust** (ô'gŭst). 1866–1951. Journalist, writer, and translator of Scandinavian authors; b. Stockholm, Sweden; to U.S. (1891).

**Björn'son** (byûrn'sŏn), **Björnstjerne.** 1832–1910. Norwegian poet, dramatist, novelist, and political and social leader; winner of 1903 Nobel prize in literature. Educ. Royal Frederick U., Christiania (1852); fought, as dramatic critic, for release of Norwegian theater from Danish influence. Theater manager, Bergen (1857–59); editor of *Aftenbladet*, Christiania (1859); director, Christiania theater (1865–67); editor of *Norsk Folkeblad* (1866). Author of *Poems and Songs*, a collection (1870), including the national anthem *Ja, Vi Elsker Dette Landet;* an epic cycle, *Arnljot Gelline* (1870); the peasant novels and tales *Synnöve Solbakken* (1857), *Arne* (1858), *A Happy Boy* (1860), *The Fisher Maiden* (1868); the novels *Magnhild* (1877), *Flags are Flying in Town and Port* (1884), *In God's Way* (1889); the plays *Between the Battles* (1857), *Lame Hulda* (1858), *King Sverre* (1861), *Sigurd the Bastard* (trilogy; 1862), *Mary Stuart in Scotland* (1864), *The Newly Married* (1865), *A Bankruptcy* (1875), *The King* (1877), *Beyond Human Power* (1883), *Paul Lange and Tora Parsberg* (1898); etc. His son **Björn** (1859–1942), actor and playwright, was director of National Theater, Christiania (1899–1907) and of Hebbel Theater, Berlin (1908–09).

**Black** (blăk), **Adam.** 1784–1874. Scottish publisher. Acquired copyrights of *Encyclopaedia Britannica* (1827), Scott's Waverley Novels (1851), and De Quincey's works (1861).

**Black, Hugh.** 1868-1953. Scottish-American clergyman; professor of practical theology, Union Theol. Seminary, New York (since 1906); known as fine preacher.

**Black, Hugo La Fayette.** 1886–1971. American politician and jurist, b. Harlan, Ala. LL.B., Alabama (1906); practiced law in Birmingham, Ala.; U.S. senator from Alabama (1927–37). Associate justice, U.S. Supreme Court (1937–71).

**Black, Jeremiah Sullivan.** 1810–1883. American lawyer, b. near Stony Creek, Pa. U.S. attorney general in Buchanan's cabinet (1857–60); exposed California land title frauds; attacked squatter sovereignty. U.S. secretary of state (1860–61) during difficult months just preceding Civil War.

**Black, Joseph.** 1728–1799. Scottish chemist. M.D., Edinburgh (1754); wrote doctoral thesis on causticization, which laid foundations of quantitative analysis. Evolved theory of latent heat; measured latent heat of steam; founded doctrine of specific heats (1760).

**Black, William.** 1841–1898. Scottish journalist and novelist. War correspondent for London *Morning Star* during Seven Weeks' War (1866). Author of *A Daughter of Heth* (1871). *A Princess of Thule* (1874), etc.

**Blackbeard.** See Edward TEACH.

**Black'burne** (blăk'bûrn; -bẽrn), **Francis.** 1782–1867. Irish lawyer. Attorney general for Ireland (1830–34, 1841); lord chancellor of Ireland (1852, 1866); prosecuted O'Connell and presided at trial of Smith O'Brien.

**Blackburne, Joseph Henry.** 1841–1924. English chess player.

**Black'ett** (blăk'ĕt; -ĭt), **Patrick Maynard Stuart.** 1897–1974. Baron **Blackett.** British physicist. Professor, Birkbeck Coll., London (1933–37), Manchester U. (1937–53), and Imperial College of Science and Technology, London (1953–67); created life peer (1969). Known for work on cosmic rays, and esp. on the meson; a discoverer of the positron. Nobel prize in physics (1948).

**Black' Hawk'** (blăk' hôk'). *Indian name* **Ma-ka-tae-mish-kia-kiak.** 1767–1838. American Indian (Sac) chieftain, b. near present Rock Island, Ill. Black Hawk War (summer, 1832) ended by victory of U.S. Army troop. Black Hawk carried to Washington, given audience with President Jackson (1833), and returned to own country. His *Autobiography of Black Hawk* (1833) is an American classic.

**Black'ie** (blăk'ĭ), **John Stuart.** 1809–1895. Scottish scholar and man of letters. Made translations in verse of *Faust* (1834), Aeschylus (1850), and the *Iliad* (1886); professor of Greek, Edinburgh (1852–82); founded and endowed Celtic chair, Edinburgh (1882).

**Black'lock** (blăk'lŏk), **Thomas.** 1721–1791. Scottish poet; blind from infancy; one of first to attribute genius to Burns.

**Black'more** (blăk'mōr), Sir **Richard.** 1650?–1729. English physician and poetaster; praised by Dr. Johnson.

**Blackmore, Richard Doddridge.** 1825–1900. English novelist. Author of *Lorna Doone* (1869), *Springhaven* (1887), etc.

**Black'mun** (blăk'mŭn), **Harry Andrew.** 1908– . Am. jurist, b. Nashville, Ill. LL.B., Harvard (1932); associate justice, U.S. Supreme Court (1970– ).

**Black Prince, the.** = EDWARD, Prince of Wales (1330–1376), son of Edward III; probably so called from the color of his armor.

**Black'stone** (blăk'stōn; *Brit.* -stŭn), Sir **William.** 1723–1780. English jurist; author of *Commentaries on the Laws of England* (4 vols., 1765–69), best-known history of the doctrines of English law, influential in U.S.

**Black'well** (blăk'wĕl; -wẽl), **Elizabeth.** 1821–1910. American physician, b. Bristol, Eng.; to U.S. (1832). M.D., Geneva Medical School of Western N.Y. (1849). First woman doctor of medicine in modern times. Opened private dispensary in New York (1850), which became incorporated (1857) into New York Infirmary and College for Women. Settled in England (1869); professor of gynecology in London School of Medicine for Women (1875–1907).

**Blackwell, Henry Brown.** 1825–1909. American editor, b. Bristol, Eng. Brother of Elizabeth Blackwell. Pioneer woman-suffrage advocate; m. (May 1, 1855) Lucy Stone (*q.v.*). Editor of *Woman's Journal* (1870?–1909). His daughter **Alice Stone Blackwell** (1857–1950), b. East Orange, N.J.; also an advocate of woman's suffrage; assisted in editing *Woman's Journal;* edited the paper *The Woman's Column* (1885–1905); author of *Armenian Poems* (1896), *Songs of Russia* (1906), etc.

**Blackwell, Lucy Stone.** See Lucy STONE.

**Black'wood** (blăk'wŏŏd), **Algernon.** 1869–1951. English novelist and traveler. Farmed in Canada; ran hotel in Toronto; joined staff of New York *Sun* and New York *Times;* entered dried-milk business.

**Blackwood, Frederick Temple Hamilton-Temple-.** 1st Marquis of **Duf'fer·in and A'va** (dŭf'ẽr·ĭn, ä'vȧ). 1826–1902. British diplomat and administrator, b. Florence; son of 4th Baron Dufferin, of the Irish Blackwoods, who were of ancient Scottish stock. Educ. Oxford; active in relieving famine distress in Ireland (1846–48); entered House of Lords (1850) as Baron **Clan'de·boye'** (klăn'dĕ·boi'); lord in waiting to Queen Victoria (1849–52, 1854–58); commissioner to inquire into massacres in Levant (1860); undersecretary for India (1864–66); as governor general of Canada (1872–78), quieted agitators and strengthened imperial connection; ambassador at St. Petersburg (1879–81), Constantinople (1881–82); commissioner in Egypt (1882–83) to establish reorganization after Arabi Pasha's defeat at Tell el-Kebir; as governor general of India (1884–88), settled land question tactfully, pacified amir of Afghanistan, settled crisis with Russia by delimiting northwest frontier, and annexed Upper Burma (1886); ambassador at Rome (1889–91), Paris (1891–96). His mother, Lady **Helen Se·li'na** (sĕ·lē'nȧ) **Sheridan**

(1807–1867), Countess of **Dufferin** and Countess of **Gifford,** was a poet; granddaughter of Richard Brinsley Sheridan; m. 1st (1825) 4th Baron Dufferin and 2d (1862) George Hay, Earl of Gifford; author (under pseudonym **Im·pul'si·a Gush'ing·ton** [ĭm·pŭl'sĭ·*ȧ* gŭsh'ĭng·tŭn]) of sentimental and humorous ballads.

**Blackwood, William.** 1776–1834. Scottish publisher. Founder of *Edinburgh Encyclopaedia* (1810); founder and editor of *Edinburgh Monthly Magazine* (1817), which soon became *Blackwood's Magazine.* Founded publishing house of William Blackwood & Sons (c. 1816). His son **John** (1818–1879) succeeded an elder brother as editor (1845) of *Blackwood's* and as head of publishing business (1852); published George Eliot's *Scenes of Clerical Life* in *Blackwood's,* and most of her novels in book form.

**Blaeu** *or* **Blaeuw** *or* **Blauw** (blou), **Willem Janszoon.** 1571–1638. Dutch mathematician, geographer, and astronomer; founder of a publishing firm at Amsterdam, known esp. for its terrestrial and celestial globes; author of *Novus Atlas* (1634–62). His sons **Cornelius** (d. 1650) and **Jan** (d. 1673) continued the firm; Jan published *Atlas Magnus* (11 vols., 1650–62).

**Bla'ga** (blä'gä), **Lucian.** 1895–1961. Rumanian poet and playwright, known esp. for his dramatization of Rumanian folk myths.

**Blá'ha-Mi'keš** (blä'hȧ·mĭ'kĕsh), **Záboj.** 1887– . Czech pianist and composer.

**Blaich** (blīk), **Hans Erich.** *Pseudonyms* **Dr. Owl'glass'** (oul'glȧs') *and* **Ra'ta·tös'kr** (rä'tä·tûs'kẽr). 1873–1945. German writer and translator. Author of folk tales, often humorous; editor of *Simplicissimus* (1912–24, 1933–35); translator of Rabelais, Aristophanes, Montaigne, Cervantes, etc.

**Blaine** (blān), **James Gillespie.** 1830–1893. American statesman, b. West Brownsville, Pa. Newspaper editor, Augusta, Me. (1854–60). Member, U.S. House of Representatives (1863–76); speaker (1869–75). U.S. senator (1876–81). Unsuccessful candidate for Republican presidential nomination (1876, 1880). U.S. secretary of state (1881). Republican nominee for president (1884); in campaign, Rev. S. D. Burchard called Democratic party "the party whose antecedents are rum, Romanism, and rebellion," losing many votes for Blaine; lost election to Grover Cleveland. U.S. secretary of state (1889–92).

**Blain'ville'** (blăN'vēl'), **Henri Marie Du'cro'tay' de** (dü'krô'tā' dẽ). 1777–1850. French zoologist and physician; succeeded Cuvier (1832) as professor in Museum of Natural History, Paris.

**Blair** (blâr), **Hugh.** 1718–1800. Scottish Presbyterian clergyman. Professor of rhetoric, Edinburgh U. (1762–83); defended authenticity of Macpherson's Ossianic poems; author of *Lectures on Rhetoric* (1783).

**Blair, James.** 1655–1743. Educator, b. in Scotland; to America (1685). Founder and first president of College of William and Mary (1693–1743).

**Blair, John.** 1732–1800. American jurist, b. Williamsburg, Va. Associate justice, U.S. Supreme Court (1789–96).

**Blair, Montgomery.** 1813–1883. American lawyer, b. in Franklin County, Ky. Postmaster general in Lincoln's cabinet (1861–64).

**Blair, Robert.** 1699–1746. Scottish clergyman; author of *The Grave* (1743), a poem in blank verse, later illustrated by William Blake.

**Blaise** *or* **Blaize,** Saint. See BLASIUS.

**Blake** (blāk), **George.** 1893–1961. English journalist and novelist; author of *Vagabond Papers* (1922), *David and Joanna* (1936), *Late Harvest* (1938), etc.

**Blake,** Dame **Louisa Brandreth Aldrich-.** See ALDRICH-BLAKE.

**Blake, Lyman Reed.** 1835–1883. American inventor, b. South Abington, Mass. Shoe manufacturer; invented a form of shoe that could be sewed and a machine (pat. 1858; known as the McKay machine for the promoter, Gordon McKay) for sewing soles to uppers.

**Blake, Nicholas.** See Cecil Day LEWIS.

**Blake, Robert.** 1599–1657. English admiral. As Parliamentarian in Civil War, took part in defense of Bristol against Royalists (1643) and Lyme (1643–44). As admiral and general of the sea, pursued Prince Rupert's fleet to the Mediterranean and destroyed bulk of it (1650). Fought engagements, breaking naval supremacy of Holland (1652–53). Destroyed Turkish pirate fleet (1655); destroyed Spanish West Indian fleet at Santa Cruz (1657).

**Blake, William.** 1757–1827. English artist, poet, and mystic. Apprenticed to an engraver (1771–78); employed new process of printing from etched copper plates in series of his own lyrical poems, hand-illustrated and colored, beginning with *Songs of Innocence* (1789), and *Songs of Experience* (1794), the last named including the poem *Tiger! Tiger! burning bright.* Illustrated Mary Wollstonecraft's works (1791) and Young's *Night Thoughts* (1793–1800). Executed and engraved many religious designs, his best *Inventions to the Book of Job* (1820–26); occupied at time of death in engraving designs for Dante's *Divina Commedia.* Author of mystical and metaphysical works including *Prophetic Books* (1793–1804), and of symbolic poems terminating with *Milton* (1804) and *Jerusalem* (1804–18).

**Blake'lock** (blāk'lŏk), **Ralph Albert.** 1847–1919. American painter, b. New York City. Among his works are *Pipe Dance* (Metropolitan Museum, New York), *From St. Ives to Lelant* (St. Louis Museum), *Colorado Plains* (Corcoran Gallery, Washington, D.C.), and *Canoe Builders, Sunset,* and *Moonrise* (National Gallery of Art, Washington, D.C.).

**Blake'ney** (blāk'nĭ), Baron **William.** 1672–1761. British army commander; lieutenant governor of Minorca on its capture by the French (1756).

**Blakes'lee** (blāks'lē), **Albert Francis.** 1874–1954. American botanist, b. Geneseo, N.Y.; A.B., Wesleyan (1896), Ph.D., Harvard (1904); taught at Harvard, Radcliffe, and (1907–15) Conn. Agricultural Coll.; resident investigator in plant genetics (from 1915; director of department 1936–41), Carnegie Station for Experimental Evolution, Cold Spring Harbor, L.I.

**Bla'mey** (blā'mĭ), Sir **Thomas Albert.** 1884–1951. Australian soldier. Served in World War I (1914–18), on Turkish front; chief of staff, Australian Corps (1918) and Australian Imperial Force (1919). Lieutenant general, commanding A.I.F. in Middle East (1940); engaged in defense of Greece (1941); deputy commander in chief of British forces in Middle East (1941); returned to Australia with part of Middle East A.I.F. and appointed (Mar., 1942) commander of all ground forces in Australia.

**Bla·mire'** (blȧ·mīr'), **Susanna.** 1747–1794. English poet; called "Muse of Cumberland"; author of North Country lyrics and poems in Scots dialect.

**Blanc** (bläN), **Louis,** *in full* **Jean Joseph Charles Louis.** 1811–1882. French socialist leader, regarded as founder of state socialism, b. Madrid, Spain. Journalist; founded (1839) *Revue du Progrès,* organ for his socialist doctrines. Gained prominence through his *Organisation du Travail* (1840) and *Histoire de Dix Ans, 1830–1840* (1841), the latter an attack upon policies and methods of Louis Philippe's government. Member of provisional government in revolution of 1848; forced government to adopt principle of guarantee of employment to workingmen; discredited by failure of policies as put into effect by politicians unfriendly to him; took refuge in England (1848–70). Returned to France; elected to Chamber of Deputies (1871). Author of *Histoire de la Révolution Française* (12 vols., 1847–62) and many political pamphlets. His brother **Auguste Alexandre Philippe Charles** (1813–1882) was an art critic; author of *Les Artistes de mon Temps* (1876), etc.

**Blanc** (blän), **Ludwig Gottfried.** 1781–1866. German clergyman, philologist, and Dante scholar.

**Blanca.** Spanish form of BLANCHE.

**Blanchan, Neltje.** Pseudonym of Neltje DOUBLEDAY.

**Blan'chard'** (blän'shàr'), **François.** 1753–1809. French aeronaut; inventor of a parachute. Crossed English Channel (1785) by balloon, with John Jeffries (*q.v.*).

**Blan'chard** (blăn'chẽrd; -shẽrd), **Samuel Laman.** 1804–1845. English journalist, poet, and essayist.

**Blanchard, Thomas.** 1788–1864. American inventor, b. Sutton, Mass. Invented automatic tack-manufacturing machine, a lathe for turning gun barrels, a method of turning irregular forms from a pattern, etc.

**Blanche** (blànsh), **August Theodor.** 1811–1868. Swedish dramatist and novelist.

**Blanche** (blänsh), **Jacques Émile.** 1861–1942. French portrait painter, b. Paris.

**Blanche of Cas·tile'** (blànch, kăs·tēl'). 1187?–1252. Daughter of Alfonso IX, King of Castile. m. (1200) Louis, son of Philip Augustus, King of France. Queen of France during Louis VIII's reign (1223–26); queen regent during minority (1226–36) of her son Louis IX and again (1248–52) during his absence on a crusade.

**Blanche of Na·varre'** (nȧ·vär'). *Span.* **Blan'ca de Na·var'ra** (bläng'kä thā nä·vär'rä). Name of three queens: (1) Queen of France. 1331–1398. Daughter of Philip III, King of Navarre; m. (1349) Philip VI of Valois, King of France; left valuable collection of manuscripts. (2) Queen of Aragon. 1385?–1441. Daughter of Charles III of Navarre; m. 1st, Martin, King of Sicily, and 2d (1420), John of Aragon; mother of Prince Charles of Viana. (3) Queen of Castile. 1424–1462. Daughter of John of Aragon (see under 2, above); m. (1440) Henry IV of Castile; divorced (1453).

**Blan'co** (bläng'kō), **Antonio Guzmán.** See GUZMÁN BLANCO.

**Blan'co–Fom·bo'na** (-fôm·bō'nä), **Rufino.** 1874–1944. Venezuelan diplomat, writer, and publisher, b. Caracas. Exiled from Venezuela (1910) for opposition to Juan Vicente Gómez; resident in Madrid (1914); founded publishing house there (1915). Author of *Cuentos de Poeta* (1900), *El Hombre de Hierro* (1907), *Tragedias Grotescas* (1928), *El Secreto de la Felicidad* (1932), etc.

**Blan'co White** (bläng'kō hwīt'), **Joseph.** See WHITE.

**Blan'co y E·re'nas** (bläng'kō ē ā·rā'näs), **Ramón.** Marqués **de Pe'ña Pla'ta** (thā pā'nyä plä'tä). 1831–1906. Spanish soldier and statesman, b. San Sebastián; served in Cuba during war for independence (1868–77); participated in Spanish annexation of Santo Domingo; governor of Mindanao; colonel general in Spanish civil war (1871); captain general of Catalonia (1877–79, 1882, 1887–93). Governor general of Cuba (1879–81, 1897–98); resisted invasion of U.S. troops.

**Bland** (blănd), **Edith** and **Hubert.** See Edith NESBIT.

**Bland, James A.** 1854–1911. American Negro song writer, b. Flushing, Long Island, N.Y.; author of *Oh Dem Golden Slippers, In the Evening by the Moonlight, Carry me back to Old Virginny*, etc.

**Bland, Richard.** 1710–1776. American statesman, b. in Virginia. Delegate to Continental Congresses (1774, 1775). Author of *Inquiry into the Rights of the British Colonies* (1766), earliest published defense of colonies' stand on taxation.

**Bland, Richard Parks.** 1835–1899. American lawyer. Member, U.S. House of Representatives from Missouri (1873–95, 1897–99). Leader of congressional free silver bloc; coauthor of Bland-Allison Act (1878) remonetizing silver. Defeated by W. J. Bryan (1896) for presidential nomination.

**Blan·dra'ta** (blän·drä'tä) *or* **Bian·dra'ta** (byän-), **Giorgio.** 1515?–?1588. Italian physician and polemic. Defended anti-Trinitarian views against Calvin and Reformed theologians (1566); introduced Unitarian doctrines in Poland and Transylvania.

**Bland'-Sut'ton** (blănd'sŭt''n), Sir **John.** 1855–1936. English surgeon and writer; author of *Evolution and Disease* (1890), *The Story of a Surgeon* (1930), etc.

**Blane** (blān), Sir **Gilbert.** 1749–1834. Scottish physician. Accompanied Admiral Rodney to West Indies (1779, 1782); introduced use of lime juice in navy as a scurvy preventive, subsequently (1795) made obligatory; improved sanitary conditions in navy; made baronet for transport of sick and wounded of Walcheren expedition (1812); instrumental in framing rules that became basis of modern quarantine regulations.

**Blan'qui'** (blän'kē'), **Jérôme Adolphe.** 1798–1854. French economist, b. Nice. His brother **Louis Auguste** (1805–1881) was an extreme Socialist agitator; took prominent part in revolutions of 1839, 1848, 1871; first public advocate of dictatorship of the proletariat.

**Blasch'ka** (blăsh'kä; *Angl.* blăsh'kȧ), **Leopold** (d. 1895) and his son **Rudolph** (1857–1939). German artists in glass; makers (from 1886) esp. of glass flowers for Harvard U. botanical museum.

**Blasch'ke** (bläsh'kĕ), **Wilhelm.** 1885–1962. German mathematician.

**Blas'co–I·bá'ñez** (bläs'kō·ē·bä'nyāth; -nyās), **Vicente.** 1867–1928. Spanish novelist, b. Valencia. As ardent republican, forced to flee to Paris (1889) and Italy (1895); imprisoned (1896–97); deputy (1898–1907); to Argentina (1910–13) on colonizing expedition; to Europe (1914) as supporter of Triple Entente; after World War, retired to villa on Riviera. Works include *Arroz y Tartana* (1894), *Flor de Mayo* (1895), *La Barraca* (1898; his first great success), *Entre Naranjos* (1900), *Cañas y Barro* (1902; considered by many his masterpiece), *La Catedral* (1903; Eng. tr. *The Shadow of the Cathedral*), *El Intruso* (1904), *La Bodega* (Eng. *The Fruit of the Vine*), *La Maya Desnuda* (1906), *Sangre y Arena* (1908; Eng. tr. *Blood and Sand*), *Los Muertos Mandan* (1909), *Los Argonautas* (1914), *Los Cuatro Jinetes del Apocalipsis*, by which he is best known abroad (1916; Eng. tr. *The Four Horsemen of the Apocalypse*, 1918), *Mare Nostrum* (1918), *Los Enemigos de la Mujer* (1919), *El Paraíso de las Mujeres* (1922), *El Papa del Mar* (1926), and *A los Pies de Venus* (1926), and historical works, as *La Argentina y Sus Grandezas* (1910) and *Historia de la Guerra Europea* (9 vols.).

**Blä'ser** (blâ'zẽr), **Gustav.** 1813–1874. German sculptor. Carved many portrait busts, as of Abraham Lincoln (Washington, D.C.), etc.

**Bla·ser'na** (blä·zĕr'nä), **Pietro.** 1836–?1918. Italian physicist and acoustician.

**Blash'field** (blăsh'fēld), **Edwin Howland.** 1848–1936. American painter, esp. of genre pictures, portraits, and murals. Decorated central dome of Library of Congress at Washington, D.C., and parts of the capitol buildings in Minnesota, Iowa, South Dakota, and Wisconsin.

**Bla'si·us** (blā'zhĭ·ŭs; -zĭ·ŭs) *or* **Blaise** (blāz) *or* **Blaize** (blāz), Saint. d. 316. Christian bishop of Sebaste (Sivas), Armenia; patron saint of wool combers, because reputedly martyred by having his flesh torn with wool-combers' irons before he was beheaded.

**Blasnavac.** = BLAZNAVAC.

**Blass** (bläs), **Friedrich Wilhelm.** 1843–1907. German classical scholar and philologist.

**Blatch** (blăch), **Harriot,** *nee* **Stan′ton** (stăn′t′n; -tŭn). 1856–1940. Daughter of Elizabeth Cady Stanton. American woman-suffrage leader and lecturer. m. (1882) William Henry Blatch. Author of *Mobilizing Woman Power* (1918), *A Woman's Point of View* (1919), *Elizabeth Cady Stanton...*(1921).

**Blatch′ford** (blăch′fẽrd), **Samuel.** 1820–1893. American jurist, b. New York City. Associate justice, U.S. Supreme Court (1882–93).

**Blau·velt′** (blô·vĕlt′), **Lillian Evans.** 1874–1947. American concert soprano; sang before Queen Victoria (1899); soloist at Handel festival, London (1900); sang Coronation Ode during coronation festivities of Edward VII (1902).

**Blauw.** See BLAEU.

**Bla·vat′sky** (*Angl.* blȧ·văt′skĭ), **Elena Petrovna.** *Russ. surname* **Bla·vat′ska·ya** (blŭ·vȧt′skȧ·yŭ). *Nee* **He′le·na Hahn** (hā′lā·nä hän′). 1831–1891. Russian traveler and theosophist, b. Ekaterinoslav (Dnepropetrovsk). Daughter of German nobleman; granddaughter of Princess Helena Dolgoruki; m. (1848) Gen. Nikifor Vasilievich Blavatsky; soon left him; visited Tibet and India; became interested in spiritism and occult sciences; to U.S. (1873); with Henry Steel Olcott, organized (1875) Theosophical Society; organized branch in Bombay, India (1879); established official journal, *The Theosophist;* many of her so-called miracles demonstrated (1884) as fraudulent by Society for Psychical Research; to Italy (1885). At time of her death, had 100,000 followers in various parts of world. Author of *Isis Unveiled* (2 vols., 1877), *The Secret Doctrine* (2 vols., 1888), *The Key to Theosophy* (1889), and *The Voice of Silence* (1889).

**Blaze** (bläz), **François Henri Joseph.** *Called* **Cas′til′-Blaze′** (kȧs′tēl′-). 1784–1857. French musician and music critic. His son **Ange Henri** (1813–1888), called **Blaze de Bu′ry′** (dẽ bü′rē′), was a poet, music critic, and translator; author of *Musiciens Contemporains* (1856), a translation of Goethe's *Faust*, etc.

**Blaz·na′vac** (bläz·nä′väts), **Milivoje Petrović.** 1826–1873. Serbian soldier and statesman; member of regency during minority of Prince Milan (1868–72).

**Blease** (blēz), **Coleman Livingston.** 1868–1942. American politician; governor of South Carolina (1911–15); U.S. senator (1925–31).

**Blech** (blĕĸ), **Leo.** 1871–1958. German conductor and composer. Studied with Humperdinck (1895–98).

**Ble′chen** (blĕ′ĸĕn), **Karl.** 1798–1840. German painter, esp. of landscapes.

**Bled′is·loe** (blĕd′ĭs·lō), 1st Viscount. Sir **Charles Bath′urst** (băth′ûrst; -ẽrst). 1867–1958. English statesman. Governor general and commander in chief of New Zealand (1930–35).

**Bleek** (blāk), **Friedrich.** 1793–1859. German Biblical scholar. His son **Wilhelm Heinrich Immanuel** (1827–1875), philologist, lived in Cape Town (from 1856); author of *Comparative Grammar of South African Languages* (1862–69), *The Origin of Language* (Eng. tr., 1869), *Specimens of Bushman Folklore* (Eng. tr., 1911), etc.

**Blei** (blī), **Franz.** 1871–1942. Austrian writer in Germany; essayist, satirist, novelist, and playwright.

**Bleib′treu** (blīp′troi), **Georg.** 1828–1892. German painter of battle scenes, esp. of War of Liberation, German-Danish war of 1849, and wars of 1866 and 1870–71. His son **Carl** (1859–1928), poet, critic, and novelist, wrote *Dies Irae* (1882; depicting battle scenes), *Schlechte Gesellschaft* (1885), *Geschichte der Englischen Literatur* (1887), etc.

**Blen′kin·sop** (blĕng′kĭn·sŏp), **John.** 1783–1831. English pioneer in locomotive engineering; patented (1811) a double-cylinder locomotive working by means of a racked rail and a toothed wheel, successfully tested (1812) and used thereafter. Cf. Richard TREVITHICK.

**Blen′ner·has′set** (blĕn′ẽr·hăs′ĕt; -ĭt), Lady **Charlotte.** *Nee* Countess **von Ley′den** (fôn lī′dĕn). 1843–1917. German biographer of Mme. de Staël, Cardinal Newman, and others.

**Blen′ner·has′sett** (blĕn′ẽr·hăs′ĕt; -ĭt), **Harman.** 1765–1831. American conspirator, b. in Hampshire, Eng.; to U.S. (1796). Associate of Aaron Burr (from 1805) in conspiracy to invade Mexico; arrested (1806–07), but not tried.

**Blé′riot′** (blā′ryō′; *Angl.* blā′rĭ·ō, blĕr′ĭ·ō), **Louis.** 1872–1936. French engineer and pioneer aviator, b. Cambrai. Manufactured a monoplane and in it was first to fly the English Channel in a heavier-than-air machine, taking off from Calais and landing near Dover (July 25, 1909).

**Bles′** (blĕs′), **Hen′ri met de** (häɴ′rĭ mĕt dĕ). *Known also as* **Hen·ri′cus Bles′si·us** (hĕn·rī′kŭs blĕs′ĭ·ŭs). 1480?–?1550. Flemish painter; his *L'Adoration des Mages* hangs in Munich and his landscapes *Paysages Historiques* in Venice.

**Bles′sing·ton** (blĕs′ĭng·tŭn), Countess of. *Nee* **Marguerite Pow′er** (pou′ẽr). 1789–1849. Irish woman of letters; m. (1818) Charles John Gardiner, 1st Earl of Blessington. Attracted to her soirées distinguished men of art, letters, and fashion. Author of personal reminiscences, including *Conversations with Lord Byron* (1834), *Idler in Italy* (1839–40), *Idler in France* (1841), and many novels.

**Bleu′ler** (bloi′lẽr), **Eugen.** 1857–1939. Swiss psychiatrist.

**Bley′le** (blī′lĕ), **Karl.** 1880– . Austrian composer.

**Bli′cher** (blē′kẽr), **Steen Steensen.** 1782–1848. Danish lyric poet and novelist. Author of a translation of Ossian (1807–09); the collected tales *Jydske Romanzer, Nationalnoveller*, etc. (1833–36); *Poems* (1835–36); etc.

**Blick′ens·der′fer** (blĭk′ĕnz·dûr′fẽr), **George.** 1850?–1917. American inventor, notably of typewriter bearing his name.

**Bligh** (blī), **William.** 1754–1817. English naval officer. Accompanied Captain Cook as sailing master on third voyage round world (1772–75); commanded *Bounty* on voyage to Tahiti (1787) to obtain breadfruit plants for introduction in West Indies; cast adrift in open boat with 18 men by mutinous crew led by Fletcher Christian (1789); reached Timor, in East Indies, after voyage of 4000 miles. Sailed again (1791) for breadfruit and succeeded in establishing the plant in the West Indies. Governor, New South Wales (1805–08); imprisoned by mutinous soldiers (1808–10). Vice-admiral (1814).

**Blind** (blĭnt), **Karl.** 1826–1907. German political agitator and author of numerous political essays, biographies, articles on Germanic folklore, etc.

**Blind Harry** *or* **Blind Hary** (blīnd). See HENRY THE MINSTREL.

**Blinn** (blĭn), **Hol′brook** (hōl′bro͝ok). 1872–1928. American actor.

**Bliss** (blĭs), Sir **Arthur Edward Drummond.** 1891–1975. English composer.

**Bliss, Cornelius Newton.** 1833–1911. American merchant; in dry goods house, Boston (1848–66); in textile manufacturing business, New York (from 1866). U.S. secretary of interior (1897–98).

**Bliss, Daniel.** 1823–1916. American missionary to Syria (1855–1902). Founder of Syrian Protestant College (chartered 1864, opened 1866), now called American University, Beyrouth, and its president for 36 years. A son, **Harvard Sweetser** (1860–1920), succeeded him in presidency. Another son, **Frederick Jones** (1859–1937), b. in Syria, conducted archaeological research in Palestine (1891–1900).

**Bliss, Philip Paul.** 1838–1876. American evangelist; with Ira Sankey, published *Gospel Songs* (1874), including "Hold the Fort" and "Pull for the Shore."

**Bliss, Tasker Howard.** 1853–1930. American army officer; grad. U.S.M.A., West Point (1875). Engaged in Cuba and Puerto Rico in Spanish-American War (1898); chief of staff with rank of general (1917). Member of supreme war council in France (1917–18) and of American Commission to Negotiate Peace (1918–19).

**Bliv'en** (blĭv'ĕn), **Bruce.** 1889– . American journalist, b. Emmetsburg, Iowa. Managing editor (1923–30), president and editor (from 1930), *The New Republic.*

**Blixen,** Baroness. See Isak DINESEN.

**Bloch** (blôk), **Carl Heinrich.** 1834–1890. Danish historical and religious painter.

**Bloch** (*Fr.* blôk; *Angl.* blŏk), **Er'nest'** (*Fr.* ĕr'nĕst'; *Angl.* ûr'nĕst, -nĭst). 1880–1959. Composer, b. Switz.; to U.S. (1916); naturalized (1924). Founder and dir. (1920–25), Cleveland Inst. of Mus.; dir. (1925–30), San Francisco Cons. of Mus.; in Eur. (1930–39); returned to U.S. (1939). Composed lyric drama *Macbeth,* symphonies, as *America,* symphonic poems, suites for piano and strings, concertos, sonatas, chamber music, etc.

**Bloch** (blŏk), **Felix.** 1905– . American physicist, b. Zurich, Switz. To U.S. (1934). Awarded Nobel prize in physics (1952) with E. Purcell.

**Bloch** (*Fr.* blôk; *Pol.* blôĸ), **Jean de** (zhäɴ dē). 1836–1902. Polish financier, peace advocate, and writer, b. Radom, of Jewish parents. Author of important work on war (7 vols.; pub. St. Petersburg, 1898) which appeared in English abridged form as *The Future of War in its Technical, Economic, and Political Relations* (1899) and in England as *Is War Now Impossible?* (1899); upheld thesis that modern war would be so terrible and so expensive that no country would enter upon it; many of his individual predictions very accurate.

**Bloch** (blôk), **Jean Richard.** 1884–1947. French novelist and playwright.

**Bloch** (blŏk), **Konrad.** 1912– . American biochemist, b. Germany. To U.S. (1936). Awarded Nobel prize in physiology and medicine (1964).

**Bloch** (blŏĸ), **Markus Elieser.** 1723–1799. German physician and ichthyologist; known for his *Allgemeine Naturgeschichte der Fische* (12 vols., 1782–95).

**Bloch** (blŏĸ), **Moritz.** See Mór BALLAGI.

**Block** (blŏk), **Herbert Lawrence.** *Pseud.* **Her'block** (hûr'blŏk). 1909– . Am. editorial cartoonist, b. Chicago. His works have appeared in collections published in 1952, 1955, 1958, 1964, etc.

**Block** (blôk), **Mau'rice'** (mō'rēs'), *orig.* **Mo'ritz** (mō'rĭts). 1816–1901. Economist, b. Berlin; moved to France and became naturalized French citizen; served in ministry of agriculture (1844–52) and in bureau of statistics (1852–62). Author of *L'Europe Politique et Sociale* (1869), *Petit Manuel d'Économie Pratique* (1890), etc.

**Blockx** (blŏks), **Jan.** 1851–1912. Belgian composer of symphonies, cantatas, an oratorio, songs, the operas *Maître Martin* and *Herberg Prinses,* etc.

**Blodg'ett** (blŏj'ĕt; -ĭt), **Katharine Burr.** 1898– . American physicist. Discovered (1939) coating process to eliminate reflections in glass.

**Bloem** (blûm), **Walter.** 1868–1951. German playwright and novelist. His son **Walter Julius** (1898– ), novelist.

**Bloe'maert** (blōō'märt), **Abraham.** 1564–1651. Dutch painter and engraver, esp. of landscapes and religious and mythological pieces.

**Bloe'men** (blōō'mĕn), **Pieter van.** *Called* **Stan'daert** (stän'därt). 1651–1720. Flemish battle and animal painter. His brother **Jan Frans van Bloemen** (1656?–?1748), landscape painter, was called in Italian **O'riz·zon'te** (ō'rēd·dzōn'tā), from the beautiful horizons in his landscapes.

**Blois** (blwä). See HENRY OF BLOIS; PETER OF BLOIS; STEPHEN (king of England).

**Blois.** A countship of north central France, originating c. 9th century; countships of **Tou'raine'** (tōō'rân') and **Char'tres** (shär'tr') added (11th to 13th century). First count, as vassal of dukes of France, **The'o·bald I** [thē'ō·bôld] (d. about 975). Early counts took part in crusades, especially **Louis de Blois** (1167?–1205), count (1191); grandson of King Louis VII; became subject of Richard I of England; joined Fourth Crusade (1202); made duke of **Ni·cae'a** (nī·sē'ȧ); killed at Adrianople. Countship passed (1218) to Margaret, sister of Louis, and later (1230–1397) to **Châ'til'lon'** (shä'tē'yôɴ') branch: Mary of **A'vesnes'** (ȧ'vân') and her husband, Hugh of Châtillon, an ancestor of Charles de Blois (*q.v.*). Countship sold (1397) to Louis I, Duc d'Orléans (see ORLÉANS); united (1498) with crown by accession of Louis XII, grandson and second successor of Louis I of Orléans.

**Blois** *or* **Châ'til'lon'** (shä'tē'yôɴ'), **Charles de.** 1319–1364. Nephew of Philip VI of France. Claimant to duchy of Brittany; proclaimed duke (1341); captive in England (1347–56); killed at battle of Auray. See BLOIS.

**Blois, François Louis de.** *Lat.* **Franciscus Ludovicus Blo'si·us** (blō'zhĭ·ŭs; -zĭ·ŭs). 1506–1566. Flemish mystical writer, b. near Liége; became a Benedictine (1520) and abbot of monastery in Hainaut (1530). Wrote in Latin; works translated into nearly all European languages. Among his best-known works are *Institutio Spiritualis, Consolatio Pusillanimium* (*Comfort for the Faint-Hearted*), *Sacellum Animae Fidelis* (*The Sanctuary of the Faithful Soul*), *Speculum Monachorum* (*Mirror for Monks*).

**Blok** (blôk), **Aleksandr Aleksandrovich.** 1880–1921. Russian symbolist poet; m. daughter of scientist Mendeleev; much influenced by Vladimir Soloviëv and by events of attempted revolution (1905) and by Bolshevik Revolution (1917). His greatest work, an apologia for Revolution of 1917, *The Twelve* (Eng. transl. 1920).

**Blok** (blŏk), **Petrus Johannes.** 1855–1929. Dutch historian.

**Blom'berg** (blôm'bĕrĸ), **Werner von.** 1878–1946. German army officer; minister of war in Hitler's cabinet (1933–38).

**Blom'field** (blōōm'fēld), **Charles James.** 1786–1857. English prelate of Church of England. Bishop of London (1828–56); mediator in Tractarian movement. Edited plays of Aeschylus and Greek lyric poets. His son Sir **Arthur William** (1829–1899) was architect to Bank of England (1883); associated with Arthur Edmund Street, son of George Edmund Street (*q.v.*) in erection of Law Courts in London (1881); known as a restorer of churches and for his revived Gothic. Sir Arthur William's nephew Sir **Reginald** (1856–1942), architect and author; worked chiefly in domestic and civil architecture and garden designs; author of *The Formal Garden in England* (with F. Inigo Thomas; 1892), *A History of Renaissance Architecture in England* (1897).

**Blom'maert** (blôm'ärt), **Philippe Marie.** 1808?–1871. Flemish scholar; devoted himself to resurrection of Flemish language.

**Blom′strand** (blo͞om′strȧnd), **Christian Wilhelm.** 1826–1897. Swedish mineralogist and chemist.

**Blön′dal** (blûn′däl), **Sigfús.** 1874– . Icelandic scholar, critic, and lexicographer.

**Blon′del′** (blôɴ′dĕl′). *Also* **Blondel de Nesle** (nĕl′). 12th-century French trouvère; according to tradition, located imprisoned Richard, Cœur de Lion, in a castle by means of a song they had jointly composed, Blondel singing one verse under the castle walls and Richard answering from his prison window.

**Blondel, André Eugène.** 1863–1938. French physicist; author of treatises on high-frequency alternating currents and radioelectric waves.

**Blondel, François.** Sieur **des Croi′settes′** (dā krwä′zĕt′). 1617–1686. French architect; builder of Porte St. Denis, Paris; author of *Cours d'Architecture*, etc.

**Blondel, Hippolyte Marie Georges.** 1856–1948. French historian and economist. Author of *La Politique Protectionniste en Angleterre* (1904), *L'Éducation Économique du Peuple Allemand* (1908), etc. His brother **Maurice** (1861–1949), philosopher, was professor at U. of Aix-Marseille.

**Blondel, Jacques François.** 1705–1744. French architect; designed city reconstruction in Metz and Strasbourg. Author of treatises on architecture.

**Blon′din′** (blôɴ′dăɴ′; *Angl.* blŏn′dĭn), **Charles.** *Real name* **Jean François Gra′ve·let′** (grȧ′vlĕ′). 1824–1897. French tightrope walker, b. Saint-Omer; crossed Niagara Falls on tightrope (1855, 1859, 1860). See G. A. Farini.

**Blood** (blŭd), **Thomas.** 1618?–1680. Irish adventurer. Attempted to assassinate duke of Ormonde (1670). Succeeded in stealing English crown (1671) but arrested with it while in flight. Contrived personal interview with Charles II; pardoned and restored to his Irish estates.

**Bloom** (blo͞om), **Sol.** 1870–1949. American politician, b. Pekin, Ill. Settled in New York City (1903); engaged in real estate and construction business. Member, U.S. House of Representatives (from 1923); chairman, foreign affairs committee of the house (1940 ff.).

**Bloom, Ursula.** English writer, b. Chelmsford; m. 1st (1916) Arthur Brownlow Denham-Cookes (d. 1918) and 2nd (1925) Charles Gower Robinson. Author of *The Great Beginning* (1924), *Tarnish* (1929), *Pastoral* (1934), *These Roots Go Deep* (1939), etc.

**Bloom′er** (blo͞om′ẽr), **Amelia,** *nee* **Jenks** (jĕngks). 1818–1894. American pioneer in social reform, b. Homer, N.Y.; m. (1840) Dexter C. Bloomer. Wrote articles on education, unjust marriage laws, woman's suffrage. Became notorious as advocate of dress reform for women; in lecture work, wore proposed new woman's costume, the full trousers of which came to be called "bloomers."

**Bloom′field** (blo͞om′fēld), **Leonard.** 1887–1949. American philologist and educator, b. Chicago. A.B., Harvard (1906), Ph.D., Chicago (1909). Asst. professor, Illinois (1913–21); professor, Ohio State U. (1921–27); professor of Germanic philology, Chicago (1927–40); professor of linguistics, Yale (from 1940). Author of *Introduction to the Study of Language* (1914), *Menomini Texts* (1928), *Language* (1933), *Plains Cree Texts* (1934), etc.

**Bloomfield, Maurice.** 1855–1928. Philologist, b. Bielitz, Austria; to U.S. (1859). Professor of Sanskrit and comparative philology, Johns Hopkins (1881–1926). Author of *Vedic Concordance* (1906), etc.

**Bloomfield, Robert.** 1766–1823. English shoemaker and poet; author of *The Farmer's Boy* (1800), and of *Rural Tales* (1802), *Wild Flowers* (1806), *The Banks of the Wye* (1811).

**Bloor** (blo͝or), **Ella Reeve.** *Nee* **Ella Reeve** (rēv). *Called* **Mother Bloor.** 1862–1951. American Communist leader and writer; joined Socialist party (1900) as organizer; active in many strikes for betterment of conditions of labor; after Russian Revolution (1917) became identified with international socialist workers.

**Blore** (blōr), **Edward.** 1787–1879. English artist and architect; built Sir Walter Scott's Abbotsford (c. 1816).

**Blos** (blōs), **Wilhelm.** 1849–1927. German statesman and Social Democratic journalist (1872); member of Reichstag (1881–1918); Württemberg state president (1918–20).

**Blosius, Franciscus Ludovicus.** See François Louis de Blois.

**Blos′som** (blŏs′ŭm), **Henry Martyn.** 1866–1919. American playwright, b. St. Louis; author of *Checkers* (dramatized from his story *Checkers*, 1897), *Mlle. Modiste*, *The Yankee Consul*, *The Man from Cook's*, *The Red Mill.*

**Blou′et′** (blo͞o′ĕ′), **Paul.** *Pseudonym* **Max O'Rell′** (măks ō·rĕl′). 1848–1903. French writer; resident in England (from 1872). Author of *John Bull et son Île* (1883), *Les Chers Voisins* (1885), *Jonathan et son Continent* (1889), *Un Français en Amérique* (1891), etc.

**Blount** (blŭnt), **Charles.** Earl of **Dev′on·shire** (dĕv′ŭn·shĭr; -shẽr). 8th Baron **Mount′joy′** (mount′joi′). 1563–1606. English soldier. Great-grandson of William Blount (*q.v.*), 4th baron. Supporter of Essex; lord deputy of Ireland (1601); put down earl of Tyrone's rebellion and subdued most of Ireland (1603). See Penelope Devereux.

**Blount, Charles.** 1654–1693. English deist and writer of freethinking books: the first, *Anima Mundi* (1679); the best known, *The Two First Books of Apollonius Tyaneus* (1680), the latter said to derive in part from the manuscript writings of Lord Herbert of Cherbury.

**Blount** *or* **Blunt** (blŭnt), **Edward.** fl. 1588–1632. English printer. Freeman of Stationers' Company (1588); publisher of Florio's *Italian and English Dictionary* (1598), of Florio's translation of Montaigne's *Essays* (1603), and, with Isaac Jaggard, of first folio edition of Shakespeare's works (1623).

**Blount,** Sir **Edward Charles.** 1809–1905. English banker in France.

**Blount, James Henderson.** 1837–1903. American lawyer and diplomat, b. in Jones County, Ga. U.S. special commissioner to Hawaii (1893); investigation convinced him that American interests had been responsible for revolution that overthrew Queen Liliuokalani and established U.S. protectorate; ordered U.S. flag lowered and protectorate ended; action supported by President Cleveland.

**Blount, Thomas.** 1618–1679. English antiquarian and lexicographer. Author of *Glossographia* (1656), a dictionary of difficult words; *Nomolexicon*...(1670), a dictionary of obscure legal terms.

**Blount,** Sir **Walter.** d. 1403. English soldier; accompanied Black Prince to Spain (1367) and, probably, John of Gaunt to Castile (1386); killed at battle of Shrewsbury when mistaken for Henry IV (1403). Character (called "Blunt") in Shakespeare's *Henry IV.*

**Blount, William.** 4th Baron **Mount′joy′** (mount′joi′). d. 1534. English statesman and patron of learning; brought Erasmus to England. Great-grandfather of Charles Blount (*q.v.*), 8th baron.

**Blount, William.** 1749–1800. American political leader, b. in Edgecombe County, N.C. Served in American Revolution. Member, U.S. congress (1782, 1783, 1786, 1787); delegate to Constitutional Convention (1787). Governor of territory south of Ohio River (1790). First U.S. senator from Tennessee (1796–97); expelled from senate on charge of plotting to aid British to get control of Spanish Florida and Louisiana.

**Blow** (blō), **John.** 1648–1708. English composer of ecclesiastical services, anthems, and occasional odes. Organist in Westminster Abbey (1669–80; 1695–1708); succeeded by William Croft (*q.v.*).

**Blow, Susan Elizabeth.** 1843–1916. American educator, b. St. Louis, Mo.; opened in St. Louis first public kindergarten in U.S. (1873).

**Blü'cher** (blü'kĕr; *Angl.* blōō'chĕr, -kĕr), **Gebhard Leberecht von.** Prince of **Wahl'statt** (väl'shtät). *Nicknamed* **Mar'schall Vor'wärts** (mär'shäl fôr'-vĕrts; fōr'-), *i.e.* Marshal Forward. 1742–1819. Prussian field marshal, b. Rostock. Entered Swedish service (1756); captured by Prussians in Seven Years' War and entered Prussian service as lieutenant; discharged from army by Frederick the Great (1770); engaged in farming in Pomerania. Rejoined army as major (1787); took part in Dutch campaign; distinguished himself in campaigns against France (1793–94); lieutenant general (1801); governor of Münster (1803). Served in campaign of 1805–06, notably at Auerstedt; surrendered to French (1806) at Ratkow, near Lübeck; exchanged for French general Victor; general and commander in Pomerania (1809–11). After outbreak of War of Liberation, led Prussian troops under Russian command at Lützen, Bautzen, Haynau, etc. (1813); commander in chief of Silesian army (Prussians and Russians). Served (1813) in war against Napoleon; defeated Macdonald at Katzbach and Marmont at Möckern; crossed the Elbe at Wartenburg; first to enter Leipzig; field marshal general. Crossed Rhine (1814) and besieged Napoleon at La Rothière; suffered defeats and forced to retreat (1814); defeated Napoleon at Laon and entered Paris (1814); created Prince of Wahlstatt (in Silesia); commander of Prussian forces in Belgium (1815); defeated at Ligny; aided Wellington in victory at Waterloo (La Belle Alliance); occupied Paris. Awarded special Iron Cross by Frederick William III.

**Blü'cher** *or* **Blue'cher** (*Russ.* blyōō'kyĕr), **Vasili Konstantinovich.** *Assumed name; real name unknown.* 1889–1938. Russian general. Common soldier in World War I; took part in Russian Revolution (1917) and fought against Kolchak and Wrangel (1919–20); commander of forces in Russian Far East (1921–22); drove Japanese out of Vladivostok (1922); military adviser to Kuomintang, Canton (1924–27); called General **Ga-lin** (jē·ä'lōōn') by Chinese; aided Chiang Kai-shek in northern campaign (1926–28) but left him, returning to Moscow, when Chiang repudiated Communists; given command in eastern Siberia (1929); developed Khabarovsk; mysteriously dismissed (1938) and disappeared.

**Blu'dov** (blōō'dôf), Count **Dmitri Nikolaevich.** 1785–1864. Russian statesman, b. in Vladimir government. Entered diplomatic service (1800); by Nicholas I, made secretary of state (1826), minister of interior (1837), minister of justice and member of imperial council (1839); created count (1842). Worked for betterment of serfs; officially signed ukase abolishing serfdom (1861).

**Blue** (blōō), **Rupert.** 1868–1948. American sanitary authority. Staff member (1892–1920), surgeon general (1912–20), U.S. Public Health Service.

**Bluh'me** (blōō'mĕ), **Christian Albrecht.** 1794–1866. Danish statesman. Minister president (1852–53); minister president and foreign minister (1864–65).

**Blum** (blōōm), **Ernest.** 1836–1907. French journalist and playwright; collaborator with Labiche, and others.

**Blum** (blōōm), **Karl Ludwig.** 1786–1844. Prussian musician, composer, and stage manager; introduced French vaudeville into Germany.

**Blum** (blōōm), **Léon.** 1872–1950. French political leader, b. Paris. Leader of Socialist party, then of Popular Front, a group of leftist, labor, and middle-of-the-road parties; premier of France (June 4, 1936–June 21, 1937); carried through radical reforms affecting banking, labor, and agriculture; prisoner of Germans (1941–45); provisional president (1946).

**Blum** (blōōm), **Robert.** 1807–1848. German political agitator, writer, and orator, b. Cologne. Liberal leader in Leipzig; founder and leader of German Catholic movement (1845). Organized Liberal party of Saxony in Revolution of 1848; vice-president, preliminary parliament at Frankfurt; leader of leftists, National Assembly; delivered congratulatory address to democrat insurgents, Vienna (1848) and joined students' corps; sentenced to death and shot (1848). His son **Hans** (1841–1910) was a jurist and writer.

**Blum'berg** (blŭm'bĕrg'; blōōm'-), **Baruch Samuel.** 1925– . American virologist. With National Institutes of Health (1957–64), Institute for Cancer Research (1964– ), U. of Pennsylvania (1970– ); awarded (with D. Carleton Gajdusek) Nobel prize for physiology or medicine (1976).

**Blu'me** (blōō'mĕ), **Karl Ludwig.** 1796–1862. German botanist; author of works on flora of East Indies.

**Blu'men·bach** (blōō'mĕn·bäk), **Johann Friedrich.** 1752–1840. German zoologist and anthropologist. Professor of medicine, Göttingen (1776–1835). First to make zoology dependent upon comparative anatomy; called founder of modern anthropology; pioneer in craniology; first to classify human species as Caucasian, Mongolian, Ethiopian, American, and Malayan.

**Blu'men·feld** (blōō'mĕn·fĕlt; *Russ.* blyōō'myĕn·fyĕly't), **Feliks Mikhailovich.** 1863–1931. Russian pianist.

**Blu'men·schein** (blōō'mĕn·shīn), **Ernest L.** 1874–1960. American painter. His wife (m. 1905), **Mary Shepard,** *nee* **Greene** (1869–1958) also a painter.

**Blu'men·thal** (blōō'mĕn·täl), **Jakob.** 1829–1908. German pianist and composer; to London (1848); pianist to Queen Victoria (1848–1901).

**Blumenthal,** Count **Leonhard von.** 1810–1900. Prussian general; chief of staff, Austro-Prussian forces against Denmark (1864), army of crown prince against Austria (1866), and in Franco-Prussian war (1870–71).

**Blumenthal, Oskar.** 1852–1917. German playwright and critic. Dramatic critic and editor, *Berliner Tageblatt* (1875–87); founder and director (1888–97), Lessing Theater, Berlin.

**Blu'mer** (blōō'mĕr), **Johann Jakob.** 1819–1875. Swiss jurist, statesman, and historian.

**Blunck** (blōōngk), **Hans Friedrich.** 1888–1961. German author of verse, fiction, and plays.

**Blun'den** (blŭn'dĕn), **Edmund Charles.** 1896–1974. English poet. Fellow and tutor in English literature, Merton Coll., Oxford (1931–43). Author of verse collected in *Poems, 1914–30* and *Poems, 1930–40* and of prose works *Undertones of War* (1928), *Life of Leigh Hunt* (1930), *The Face of England* (1932), *Charles Lamb and His Contemporaries* (1934), *Keats's Publisher* (1936), *Thomas Hardy* (1941).

**Blundevill, Ranulf** *or* **Randulf de.** See Earl of CHESTER.

**Blunt** (blŭnt). See also BLOUNT.

**Blunt, John Henry.** 1823–1884. English High-Church theologian and ecclesiastical historian.

**Blunt, Wilfrid Scaw'en** (skō'ĕn). 1840–1922. English poet and traveler. After travels in Near East and India, became ardent anti-imperialist and critic of white exploitation of native races, and active supporter of Mohammedan aspirations and of nationalism in Egypt, Ireland, and India. Author of the poems *Love Sonnets of Proteus* (1880) and *Esther* (1892); a novel in verse, *Griselda* (1893); and *My Diaries* (1919, 1920).

**Bluntsch'li** (blo͝onch'lē), **Johann Kaspar.** 1808–1881. Swiss legal scholar and statesman; professor, Zurich (1833), Munich (1848), Heidelberg (1861). One of founders (1873) of Inst. of International Law, Ghent. Chief works, *Allgemeines Staatsrecht* (2 vols., 1852) and *Das Moderne Völkerrecht* (1868).

**Bly, Nellie.** Pseudonym of Elizabeth Cochrane SEAMAN.

**Bly'den** (blī'd'n), **Edward Wilmot.** 1832–1912. Negro scholar, diplomat, and author, b. St. Thomas, West Indies; to U.S. (1845). President, Liberia College (from 1880); Liberian minister to court of St. James's (1892).

**Blythe, Herbert.** See Maurice BARRYMORE.

**Bo'ab·dil'** (bō'äb·thēl'). *Span. corruption of Arab.* **a·bu'-'Ab·dul'lāh** (ȧ·bo͞o'ȧb·do͝ol'lä). *Called* **El Chi'co** (ĕl chē'kō), *i.e.* the little. *Ruled as* **Mo·ham'-med XI** (*Arab.* mo͝o·hăm'măd). d. 1533 or 1534. Last Moorish king of Granada (1482–83, 1486–92). Dethroned (1482) his father, abu-al-Hasan; attacked Lucena (1483), but defeated there by Castilians and taken prisoner; reinstated (1486) by Spaniards on condition of paying tribute; latter part of reign troubled by civil war; driven from Granada (1492) by Ferdinand and Isabella; crossed to Africa and retired to Fez.

**Boa'den** (bō'd'n), **James.** 1762–1839. English journalist, playwright, and Shakespearean scholar; exposed (1796) the Ireland Shakespearean forgeries; published (1837) a treatise on Shakespeare's sonnets, identifying "Mr. W. H." with William Herbert, afterwards earl of Pembroke.

**Bo'a·di·ce'a** (bō'ăd·ĭ·sē'ȧ) *or, more correctly,* **Bou·dic'ca** (bo͞o·dĭk'ȧ). d. 62 A.D. Queen of the Iceni, Britons of Norfolk and Suffolk. Led revolt of Iceni and Trinovantes (Britons of Essex and Suffolk) against Romans; defeated by Roman governor Suetonius Paulinus, took poison.

**Bo'a·ner'ges** (bō'ȧ·nûr'jēz). In Bible (*Mark* iii. 17), appellation, explained as "sons of thunder," given by Jesus to apostles James and John (*qq.v.*), sons of Zebedee.

**Bo'as** (bō'ăs), **Franz** (frănts). 1858–1942. American anthropologist and ethnologist, b. Westphalia, Germany. To America; carried on investigations in North America, Mexico, and Puerto Rico (1886–1931); taught anthropology at Columbia (from 1896; professor from 1899); curator of anthropology, American Museum of Natural History (1901–05). Authority on anthropometry and on linguistics of North American tribes. Author of *The Mind of Primitive Man* (1911), *Kultur und Rasse* (1913), *Anthropology and Modern Life* (1928), etc.

**Bo'as** (bō'ăz), **Frederick S.** 1862-1957. English literary historian. Author of *Shakespeare and his Predecessors* (1896), *University Drama in the Tudor Age* (1914), *Marlowe and his Circle* (1929), etc.

**Bo'az** (bō'ăz). *In Douay Version* **Bo'oz** (bō'ŏz). In Bible, second husband of Ruth (*q.v.*).

**Bo'ba·dil'la** (bō'bä·thē'(l)yä), **Francisco de.** d. 1502. Spanish officer; succeeded Columbus as viceroy of Indies (1499); on arrival at Santo Domingo (1500), imprisoned Columbus, sending him back to Spain in chains; recalled, under arrest, to Spain (1502).

**Bobbs** (bŏbz), **William Conrad.** 1861–1926. American publisher; entered employ of Merrill, Meigs & Co., booksellers, Indianapolis (1879). President, Bobbs-Merrill Co., from its organization (1895).

**Bobillier, Marie.** See Michel BRENET.

**Bo·bo·ry'kin** (bŭ·bŭ·rĭ'kyĭn), **Pëtr Dmitrievich.** 1836–1921. Russian dramatist, novelist, and critic.

**Bob'ri·kov** (bôb'ryĭ·kôf), **Nikolai Ivanovich.** 1839–1904. Russian general; as governor general (1898–1903), ruthless in Russification of Finland; granted dictatorial powers (1903); assassinated.

**Bo·brzyń'ski** (bô·bzhĭn'y'·skē), **Michał.** 1849–1935. Polish historian.

**Bo'cage'** (bô'kȧzh'), **Jean Denis Barbié du.** See BARBIÉ DU BOCAGE.

**Bo·ca'ge** *or* **Boc·ca'ge** (bo͞o·kȧ'zhĕ), **Manuel Maria Bar·bo'sa du** (bĕr·bô'zȧ tho͞o). *Academic name* **El·ma'no Sa·di'no** (ĕl·mă'no͞o sȧ·thē'no͞o). 1765–1805. Portuguese poet; leader of Nova Arcádia group of poets; works include the revolutionary and antireligious poems *Verdades Duras*, sonnets, and cantatas, as *Hero and Leander*.

**Boc'cac·ci'no** (bŏk'kät·chē'nō), **Boccaccio.** 1467?–?1524. Italian painter; known esp. for his frescoes in cathedral of Cremona.

**Boc·cac'cio** (bôk·kät'chō; *Angl.* bō·kä'chē·ō, -chō), **Giovanni.** 1313–1375. Italian writer, b. Paris; to Naples (1323) to study accounting; frequented court of Robert d'Anjou; met his chief source of inspiration, Maria dei Conti d'Aquino (called "Fiammetta" in his writings), illegitimate daughter of Robert d'Anjou, King of Naples. To Florence (c. 1340); lived subsequently at Ravenna (1346), Forlì (1348); formed close friendship with Petrarch, at Florence (1350); engaged in diplomatic missions for Florence (1351, 1354, 1365, 1367); appointed lecturer on Dante, in Florence (1373). Known as father of classic Italian prose, because of his celebrated collection of 100 novelle, the *Decameron* (first pub. 1353). His other works include the romance *Il Filocopo* (1331–38), the verse narratives *Il Filostrato* (c. 1338), *La Teseide* (c. 1341), and *Il Ninfale Fiesolano*, the pastoral romances *Ameto*, *L'Amorosa Visione*, and *L'Amorosa Fiammetta* (c. 1341), the prose romance *Il Corbaccio* (c. 1354), sonnets, a *Life of Dante* with commentary, the Latin prose works *De Genealogiis Deorum Gentilium* (1351–60), *De Casibus Virorum Illustrium* and *De Claris Mulieribus* (1356–64), and *De Montibus, Sylvis*, etc., and a vol. of Latin eclogues. His writings have been used as source books by many subsequent writers, as Chaucer, Shakespeare, D'Annunzio, et al.

**Boc'cage'** (bô'kȧzh'), **Marie Anne Fi'quet' du** (fē'kĕ' dü). *Nee* **Marie Anne Le Page'** (lē pȧzh'). 1710–1802. French poet; author of the long poems *Le Paradis Terrestre* (imitation of Milton; 1748), *La Colombiade*, etc. Visited Voltaire at Ferney.

**Boc'ca·li'ni** (bŏk'kä·lē'nē), **Traiano.** 1556–1613. Italian satirist.

**Boc'ca·ne'ra** (bŏk'kä·nā'rä) *or* **Bo'ca·ne'gra** (bō'kä·nā'grä) *or* **Boc'ca·ni'gra** (bŏk'kä·nē'grä). Genoese family of statesmen, soldiers, and financiers, including: **Simone** (1300?–1363), first doge of Genoa (1339–44, 1356–63), and his brother **Egidio**, Admiral of Castile.

**Boc'che·ri'ni** (bŏk'kā·rē'nē), **Luigi.** 1743–1805. Italian composer and violoncellist. His *Minuet in A* is well known.

**Boc'chus** (bŏk'ŭs). Name of two kings of Mauretania: **Bocchus I** at first fought with son-in-law Jugurtha against Romans, but later (106 B.C.) delivered him to Sulla. His son **Bocchus II** (d. 33 B.C.); aided Caesar and later sided with Octavian against Antony; confirmed by Octavian in his kingdom; ruled jointly with his younger brother **Bo'gud** (bō'gŭd).

**Boc·cio'ni** (bôt·chō'nē), **Umberto.** 1882–1916. Italian futurist painter and sculptor.

**Boc·co'ne** (bôk·kō'nā), **Paolo.** 1633–1704. Sicilian botanist.

**Bo'chart'** (bô'shȧr'), **Samuel.** 1599–1667. French Huguenot theologian and philologist.

**Bock** (bôk), **Fedor von.** 1880–1945. German army commander, b. in Cüstrin. Served in World War (1914–18); remained with Reichswehr, commanding its 2d division (as lieutenant general; 1931) and as one of its three group commanders (1935); his forces occupied Austria and aided in taking over Sudetenland (1938–39); colonel general and chief of northern armies in invasion of Poland (1939), and of armies on central (Moscow) front in Russian campaign (1941); relieved of command when he failed to take Moscow; commander southern Russia (1942); again relieved after failure at Stalingrad.

**Bock, Hieronymus.** *Lat.* **Tra′gus** (trā′gŭs; *Ger.* trä′gōōs). 1489?–1554. German botanist and physician; regarded by some as one of founders of science of botany.

**Bock** (bôk), **Karl.** 1849– . Danish explorer and ethnographer; carried on researches in Sumatra, Borneo, Siam, and Laos.

**Bock′el·mann** (bôk′ĕl·män), **Rudolf.** 1892– . German Wagnerian baritone.

**Bockelson** *or* **Bockold, Jan.** See JOHN OF LEIDEN.

**Böckh** (bûk), **August.** 1785–1867. German classical philologist and antiquary. Professor, Berlin (from 1811). Author of *Corpus Inscriptionum Graecarum* (books 1–2, 1825) by which he established science of Greek epigraphy, *Zur Geschichte der Mondzyklen bei den Hellenen,* on ancient chronology (1855), etc.

**Böck′ing** (bûk′ĭng), **Eduard.** 1802–1870. German jurist and scholar; editor of critical texts of legal classics.

**Böck′lin** (bûk′lēn), **Arnold.** 1827–1901. Swiss painter; best known for landscapes, often graced with mythological figures.

**Bocs′kay** (bôch′koi), **István.** 1557–1606. Hungarian national leader and prince of Transylvania (1604–06), b. in Cluj. Led Hungarian revolutionists against Emperor Rudolf (1604–06); secured Treaty of Vienna (1606) with religious freedom to Protestants of Hungary; said to have been poisoned.

**Bo·danz′ky** (bō·dänts′kē), **Ar′tur** (är′tōōr). 1877–1939. Conductor and composer, b. Vienna. Conducted at Covent Garden (1914), Metropolitan Opera Company, New York City (1915–39).

**Bo′de** (bō′dĕ), **Johann Elert.** 1747–1826. German astronomer. Director of Berlin observatory (1786–1825); author of *Uranographia* (1801), a collection of star maps and a catalogue of 17,240 stars and nebulae, 12,000 more than had appeared in earlier charts. Bode's law, which expresses the relative distances of the planets from the sun, though named after him, had been previously discovered by the German mathematician J. D. Titius (1729–1796).

**Bode, Johann Joachim Christoph.** 1730–1793. German musician, bookdealer, and translator. Translated Sterne, Fielding, Goldsmith, Burney, Montaigne, etc.

**Bode, Wilhelm von.** 1845–1929. German art critic and museum director; general director of all royal museums in Prussia (1906–20). Published historical studies, notably of Dutch and Flemish paintings, Italian and German sculpture, and crafts.

**Bo′del′** (bô′dĕl′), **Jean.** d. 1210. French trouvère. Author of a chanson de geste, *Chanson des Saxons,* on the conquest of Saxony by Charlemagne; a miracle play; and the poem *Congé,* a farewell to his friends and patrons as he was about to be confined in a lepers' colony.

**Bo′den·heim** (bō′d'n·hīm), **Maxwell.** 1893-1954. American writer, b. Hermanville, Miss. Author of poetry, as *Minna and Myself* (1918), *Against This Age* (1925), *Bringing Jazz* (1930); fiction, as *Blackguard* (1923), *Crazy Man* (1924), *Replenishing Jessica* (1925), *Virtuous Girl* (1930), *Duke Herring* (1931); and volumes of essays.

**Bo′den·stedt** (bō′dĕn·shtĕt), **Friedrich Martin von.** 1819–1892. German poet and writer. Author of *Lieder des Mirza-Schaffy* (1851), translations from Russian (Lermontov, Pushkin, Turgenev), Persian (Hafiz, Omar Khayyám) and English (Shakespeare), etc.

**Bo′den·stein** (bō′dĕn·shtīn), **Andreas Rudolf.** Real name of KARLSTADT.

**Bodenstein, Max.** 1871–1942. German chemist; known for work in physical chemistry and electrochemistry, esp. that relating to equilibrium and velocity of gaseous reactions and to photochemical reactions; credited with discovery of chain reaction.

**Bo′dhi·dhar′ma** (bō′dĭ·dŭr′mȧ). *Also called* **Ta′mo′** (dä′mô′). d. about 530 A.D. Buddhist monk from southern India; to China (520) as Buddhist missionary; known as first Buddhist patriarch of China; founded contemplative school of Buddhism in China.

**Bo′di′chon′** (bô′dē′shôN′), **Barbara Leigh Smith.** 1827–1891. English advocate of women's rights; a founder of Girton College; water-color painter.

**Bo′din′** (bô′dăN′), **Jean.** 1530–1596. French political economist. Author of *Methodus ad Facilem Historiarum Cognitionem* (1566) and *Relation de ce qui s'est Passé en l'Assemblée du Tiers État de France en 1576; la République* (1576).

**Bo′dio** (bô′dyō), **Luigi.** 1840–1920. Italian political economist and statistical authority.

**Bod′ley** (bŏd′lĭ), **George Frederick.** 1827–1907. English architect. Designer of many churches, including Episcopal cathedrals at Hobart Town, Tasmania, and Washington, D.C.; exponent of 14th-century English Gothic; friend of pre-Raphaelites.

**Bodley,** Sir **Thomas.** 1545–1613. English diplomat and founder of Bodleian library at Oxford; minister to The Hague (1589–96).

**Bod′mer** (bōd′mĕr), **Johann Jakob.** 1698–1783. Swiss scholar and critic. Edited, with Breitinger, *Die Discourse der Mahlern* (1721–23), a weekly critical journal modeled after Addison's *Spectator.* Awakened interest in Germany in Middle High German and English literature, notably by his editions of *Paradise Lost* (1732) and part of *Nibelungenlied* (1757) and his studies on the Minnesingers (1758–59); engaged (from c. 1741) in successful literary war with Gottsched, championing emancipation of German literature from French classic tradition and importance of feeling rather than reason in poetry.

**Bo·do′ni** (bō·dō′nē), **Giambattista.** 1740–1813. Italian printer and type designer; designed first roman type of style now called "modern," a typical current form being known as "Bodoni book"; published editions of Homer's *Iliad,* Vergil, and multilingual edition of Lord's Prayer.

**Bödt′cher** (bût′kĕr), **Ludwig Adolph.** 1793–1874. Danish lyric poet.

**Boë, Franz de le.** See Franciscus SYLVIUS.

**Bo·ece′** (bō·ēs′). Obsolete English form of (Anicius Manlius Severinus) BOETHIUS.

**Bo·ece′** (bō·ēs′) *or* **Bo·e′thi·us** (bō·ē′thĭ·ŭs), **Hector.** *Also sometimes* **Boyce** (bois). *Family name* **Boyis** (bois). 1465?–1536. Scottish historian; friend of Erasmus; first principal, U. of Aberdeen (1505). Known for his fabulous and legendary *Historia Scotorum* (1527).

**Boe′he** (bû′ĕ), **Ernst.** 1880–1938. German conductor and composer.

**Boeh′ler** (bû′lĕr), **Peter.** 1712–1775. Moravian bishop (from 1748), b. Frankfurt-am-Main, Prussia; to America (1738) as missionary. Headed Moravians of Georgia in migration to site at Bethlehem, Pa.

**Boehm** (bām; bûm), Sir **Joseph Edgar.** 1834–1890. British sculptor, of Hungarian parentage; removed to London (1862) as portrait sculptor; produced busts, figures, and equestrian statues, including sarcophagus of Dean Stanley in Westminster Abbey and Wellington statue at Hyde Park Corner.

**Boehm** (bām; bûm), **Martin**. 1725–1812. American United Brethren bishop, b. in Lancaster County, Pa. Consecrated bishop of Mennonite Church (1759). Excluded, because of liberal views and association with persons of other sects, from Mennonite communion; joined with Philip William Otterbein (*q.v.*) and others to found new church, United Brethren in Christ (1789; first annual conference, 1800), and chosen, with Otterbein, its bishop.

**Boehm** (bûm), **Max Hildebert**. 1891– . German ethnologist; formulator of German attitudes regarding Germans outside Reich boundaries; author of *Europa Irredenta* (1923) and *Das Eigenständige Volk* (1932).

**Boehm, Theobald**. See Böhm.

**Boehme** *or* **Boehm, Jakob**. See Jakob Böhme.

**Boehn** (bûn), **Max von**. 1850–1921. German general in World War I (1914–18).

**Boe'kel·mann** (bo͝ok'ĕl·măn), **Ber·nar'dus** (bĕr·när'-dŭs). 1838–1930. Pianist, b. Utrecht, Netherlands; settled in U.S. (1866) and taught in New York City; promoted public appreciation of chamber music.

**Boelck'e** (bûl'kĕ), **Oswald**. 1891–1916. German flier in World War. See Max Immelmann.

**Bo'ëll'mann'** (bô'ĕl'màn'), **Léon**. 1862–1897. French organist and composer.

**Boer'haa've** (bo͞or'hä'vĕ), **Hermann**. 1668–1738. Dutch physician. Professor of medicine and botany (1709) and of chemistry (1718), Leiden. Author of *Institutiones Medicae in Usus Annuae Exercitationis Domesticos Digestae* (1708) and *Aphorismi de Cognoscendis et Curandis Morbis* (1709), encyclopedic medical books widely translated; *Elementa Chemiae* (1724); etc.

**Boes'set'** (bwä'sĕ'), **Antoine** (1585–1643) and his son **Jean Baptiste** (1612?–1685) and Jean Baptiste's son **Claude Jean Baptiste** (1636?–?1700). French court musicians and composers of ballets, airs, etc.

**Bo·e'thi·us** (bô·ē'thĭ·ŭs), **Anicius Manlius Severinus**. 480?–?524. Roman philosopher. Friend of Theodoric, Ostrogoth ruler of Rome (493–526), who made him consul (510); later, accused of conspiring against Theodoric, arrested, imprisoned at Pavia, and finally executed without trial (524). His greatest work, *De Consolatione Philosophiae* (Eng. title, *The Consolation of Philosophy*), written while he awaited his fate in prison at Pavia. Translated and wrote commentaries on certain of Aristotle's works and wrote independent treatises on logic, arithmetic, music, and theology.

**Boethius, Hector**. See Boece.

**Bo·ë'thus** (bô·ē'thŭs). Greek sculptor of 2d century B.C., perhaps from Chalcedon; known for his carvings of children, esp. for a group representing a boy struggling with a goose.

**Boétie, Étienne de la**. See Étienne de La Boétie.

**Bo·e'ti·us** (bô·ē'shĭ·ŭs). Variant of Boethius.

**Boëx, J. H. H.** and **S. J. F.** See J. H. Rosny.

**Bo'gan** (bō'găn), **Louise**. 1897–1970. American poet, b. Livermore Falls, Me.; author of *Body of This Death* (1923), *Dark Summer* (1929), *The Sleeping Fury* (1937).

**Bo·gar'dus** (bô·gär'dŭs), **Emory Stephen**. 1882– . American sociologist and educator.

**Bogardus, James**. 1800–1874. American inventor, b. Catskill, N.Y.; inventor of a dry gas meter, a method for manufacturing postage stamps, etc.

**Bo'gart** (bō'gärt; -gĕrt), **John**. 1836–1920. Am. engineer. Consulting engineer for hydroelectric power development from Niagara Falls. Advisory engineer, Rapid Transit Commission, New York City; prepared plans for subway system and tunnels under Hudson River.

**Bo·gatz'ky** (bô·gäts'kē), **Karl Heinrich von**. 1690–1774. German hymn writer; author of *Das Güldene Schatzkästlein der Kinder Gottes* (tr. into English as Bogatzky's *Golden Treasury*).

**Bog·da·no'vich** (bŭg·dŭ·nô'vyĭch), **Ippolit Fëdorovich**. 1743–1803. Russian poet.

**Bo'ger·man** (bō'gĕr·män), **Jan**. 1576–1637. Dutch theologian. Translator of Dutch version of Bible.

**Bo'gert** (bō'gĕrt), **George H**. 1864–1944. American painter, esp. of landscapes and marines.

**Boggs** (bŏgz), **Frank Myers**. 1855–1926. American landscape and marine painter.

**Boggs, Lillburn W**. 1792–1860. American politician, b. Lexington, Ky. Governor of Missouri (1836–40); expelled Mormons from state by use of militia.

**Bo·go·lju'bow** (bŭ·gŭ·lyo͞o'bôf), **E. D.** *Russ.* **Efim Dmitrievich Bogolyubov**. 1889–1952. Russian chess master.

**Bo·go·lyu'bov** (bŭ·gŭ·lyo͞o'bôf), **Aleksei Petrovich**. 1824–1896. Russian historical and genre painter.

**Bo·go·raz'** (bŭ·gŭ·räs'), **Vladimir Germanovich**. 1865–1936. Russian ethnographer; member of Jesup Expedition studying tribes of northern Pacific Coast; best known to American anthropologists by his account of Chukchi tribes of Siberia; author also of novels under pseudonym **Tan** (tàn).

**Bogud**. See under Bocchus.

**Bogue** (bōg), Mrs. **Arthur Hoyt**. See Lilian Bell.

**Bogue, David**. 1750–1825. Scottish preacher, orig. a Presbyterian, later an independent congregationalist. A founder of London Missionary Society, etc.

**Bo'gu·sław'ski** (bô'go͞o·släf'skē), **Wojciech**. 1759?–1829. Polish actor and playwright; regarded as creator of the Polish theater; wrote esp. comedies.

**Bohaddin**. See Baha al-Din.

**Böheim, Martin**. See Behaim.

**Bo'he·mund** (bō'ĕ·mŭnd). *Fr.* **Bo'hé'mond'** (bô'ā'-môɴ'). Name of several Norman princes of Antioch or (for later rulers) counts of Tripoli. **Bohemund I** (1056?–1111); prince (1099–1111); eldest son of Robert Guiscard; fought with his father against Emperor Alexius Comnenus (1080–85); in civil strife with his brother Roger (1086–89); became (1089) prince of Otranto (or Tarentum); a leader of First Crusade (1096–99), esp. at siege and capture of Antioch (1097–98); entered Jerusalem (1099); captured and imprisoned by Moslems (1100–03); defeated at Haran (1104); returned to Europe; m. Constance, daughter of Philip I of France; unsuccessful in war with Alexius; prince of Antioch (1108–11) only as vassal of Alexius. His son **Bohemund II** (1108–1131); prince (1126–30). **Bohemund III** (d. 1201); grandson of Bohemund II; prince (1163–99). **Bohemund VII** (d. 1287); last of the name; count of Tripoli (1275–87).

**Böh'lau** (bû'lou), **Helene**. 1859–1940. German novelist; m. (1886) Friedrich Arndt, called Omar al-Rashid Bey (d. 1910).

**Boh'le** (bō'lĕ), **Ernst Wilhelm**. 1903–1960. German National Socialist (Nazi) leader, b. Bradford, Eng.; brought up in South Africa. Appointed, by Hitler, Gauleiter (divisional leader) for German nationals living abroad and for German merchant seamen; made chief (1937) of foreign organization in German Foreign Office and honorary state secretary.

**Boh'len** (bō'lĕn), **Charles Eustis**. 1904–1974. Am. diplomat, b. Clayton, N.Y. Entered U.S. foreign service (1929); ambassador to U.S.S.R. (1953–57), to the Philippines (1957–59), and to France (1962–68). Author of memoir, *Witness to History 1929–1969* (1973).

**Boh·lin'** (bo͞o·lēn'), **Karl Petrus Theodor**. Swedish astronomer; dir. of Stockholm Observatory (1897–1927).

**Böhl von Faber, Cecilia** and **Johann Nikolaus.** See Fernán CABALLERO.

**Böhm** (bûm), **Georg.** 1661–1733. German organist and clavichordist.

**Böhm** *or* **Boehm** (bûm), **Theobald.** 1794–1881. German flutist and composer.

**Böhm'-Ba'werk** (bûm'bä'vĕrk) *or* **Böhm von Bawerk, Eugen.** 1851–1914. Austrian economist and statesman; minister of finance (1895, 1897–98, 1900–04). Cofounder and representative of so-called Austrian school, which advanced an economic theory of a system of value based upon the final utility concept; carried on researches on capital and interest.

**Böh'me** (bû'mĕ), **Herbert.** 1907– . German poet.

**Böh'me** (bû'mĕ) *or* **Böhm** (bûm), **Jakob.** *Surname also* **Boeh'me** (bû'mĕ) *or* **Boehm** (bûm) *or, esp. in English,* **Beh'men** (bā'mĕn). 1575–1624. German theosophist and mystic, b. near Görlitz, Prussia. Settled in Görlitz as shoemaker (1599). Author of *Aurora, oder die Morgenröte im Aufgang* (1612; pub. 1634), manuscript of which condemned as heretical by ecclesiastical authorities, and of *Von den Drei Prinzipien des Göttlichen Wesens* (1619), *Mysterium Magnum* (1623), *Der Weg zu Christo* (1624), etc. His philosophy, concerned especially with problem of evil, rests on thesis of dualism of God and explains evil as necessary because of existence in divine nature of a principle complementary and antithetical to goodness. His writings translated into other languages, notably in England, where Mrs. Jane Lead became a leader of the Philadelphians, a Boehmenist sect.

**Böh'mer** (bû'mẽr), **Johann Friedrich.** 1795–1863. German historian, esp. of German medieval history.

**Böhm'-Er'mol·li** (bûm'ĕr'mô·lĭ), Baron **Eduard von.** 1856–1941. Austrian general; led second army in Serbia and Galicia during World War; distinguished himself at Lemberg (1915); led summer offensive against Russians (1917); field marshal general (1918); led advance on Podolia and commanded forces in Ukraine (1918).

**Bohn** (bōn), **Henry George.** 1796–1884. English publisher and translator, of German parentage. Issued "guinea catalog" of old books (1841); republished at cheap rate editions of standard works and translations in history, science, philosophy, theology, etc. (1846 ff.); revised Lowndes's *Bibliographer's Manual of English Literature* (6 vols., 1864).

**Böh'ner** (bû'nẽr), **Johann Ludwig.** 1787–1860. German pianist and composer.

**Bohr** (bōr), **Niels.** 1885–1962. Danish physicist; professor, Copenhagen (1916); head of Institute for Theoretical Physics (1920). Proposed a theory of atomic structure (Bohr theory) resulting from consideration of spectroscopic data, according to which the atom represents a dynamic system of electrons rotating in orbits around a nucleus, from which radiation is emitted only during the passage of an electron from an orbit of higher energy to one of lower energy; adapted the quantum theory to atomic structure. Awarded 1922 Nobel prize in physics. His son **Aage Niels** (1922– ), a physicist, was director of the Nordic Institute for Theoretical Physics (1962– ); awarded (with Ben Roy Mottelson and L. James Rainwater) Nobel prize for physics (1975).

**Böht'lingk** (bût'lĭngk), **Otto von.** 1815–1904. German Sanskrit scholar and Orientalist. See Rudolf von ROTH.

**Bohun, de** (dĕ bōōn). Name of an English family, long resident on the Welsh Marches, founded by the Norman **Humphrey de Bohun** (d. 1187), supporter of Henry II in the rebellion of Prince Henry, "the Young King" (1173). His grandson **Henry** (1176–1220), made (1199) 1st earl of **Her'e·ford** (hĕr'ĕ·fẽrd), died on pilgrimage to Holy Land (1220); his successors fluctuated between loyalty to the king and defiance of the king in baronial cause, the 2d earl, **Humphrey V** (d. 1274), created earl of **Es'sex** (ĕs'ĕks; -ĭks), joining federation of barons (1258) and joining king against de Montfort (1263); the 3d earl, **Humphrey VII** (d. 1298), joining earl of Norfolk in refusing to serve in Gascony (1297); the 4th earl, **Humphrey VIII,** being taken prisoner as a follower of king at Bannockburn (1314) and slain as a baronial supporter at Boroughbridge (1322); and the male line becoming extinguished (1373) on death of **Humphrey X,** who had inherited earldom of Northampton from his father. The coheiresses of the three earldoms were married to members of royal family, **Eleanor** (1374) to Thomas of Woodstock, and **Mary** (1397) to Henry of Bolingbroke, afterwards Henry IV.

**Bo·iar'do** (bô·yär'dô), **Matteo Maria.** Conte **di Scan·dia'no** (skän·dyä'nô). 1434–1494. Italian poet. Known esp. for his uncompleted historical epic *Orlando Innamorato* (69 cantos, 1482; pub. 1487) in which he treated Carolingian epic material in the style of the Arthurian cycle of romances and which served as point of departure for Ariosto's *Orlando Furioso.*

**Boi'chut'** (bwȧ'shü'), **Edmond Just Victor.** 1864–1941. French general in World War; later, crushed Abd-el-Krim revolt in Morocco (1926).

**Boi'e** (boi'ĕ), **Heinrich Christian.** 1744–1806. German writer; in Göttingen (1769) and center of group of poets there (Göttingen Dichterbunde).

**Bo'iel'dieu'** (bô'yĕl'dyû'), **François Adrien.** 1775–1834. French composer, esp. of musical scores of comic operas, as *Les Deux Lettres* (1796), *La Famille Suisse* (1797), *Le Calife de Bagdad* (1800), *Jean de Paris* (1812), *La Dame Blanche* (1825), etc. Frequent collaborator with Cherubini, Isouard, Kreutzer, and others. Father of **Adrien Louis Victor** (1816–1883), also a musician, and composer of several comic opera scores.

**Boi'leau'-Des'pré'aux'** (bwȧ'lō'dā'prā'ō'), **Nicolas.** 1636–1711. French critic and poet, b. Paris. Studied law; admitted to bar (1656). Author of *Satires* (1666), several volumes of *Épîtres* (beginning 1669), *L'Art Poétique* (1674). Boileau's works, esp. his *L'Art Poétique,* are regarded as establishing the principles on which the classical literature of France is based.

**Boil'ly'** (bô'yē'), **Louis Léopold.** 1761–1845. French genre and portrait painter and lithographer.

**Boisbaudran, Lecoq de.** See LECOQ DE BOISBAUDRAN.

**Bois'go'bey'** (bwä'gô'bā'), **Fortuné Cas'tille' du** (kȧs'tē'y' dü). 1824–1891. French writer of detective fiction.

**Bois'guil'le·bert'** (bwä'gē'y'·bâr'), Sieur **de. Pierre Le Pe·sant'** (lẽ pẽ·zäN'). 1646–1714. French economist; anticipated principal teachings of 18th-century physiocrats.

**Bois-Reymond, Du.** See DU BOIS-REYMOND.

**Bois'ro'bert'** (bwä'rô'bâr'), **François Le Mé'tel'** (lẽ mā'tĕl') **de.** 1592–1662. French poet; friend of Richelieu; assisted in establishment of French Academy and (1634) one of its first members.

**Bois'so'nade'** (bwȧ'sô'nȧd'), **Jean François.** 1774–1857. French classical scholar.

**Bois'sou'dy'** (bwȧ'sōō'dē'), **Antoine Philippe Thomas Joseph Bau'che·ron' de** (bōsh'rôN' dẽ). 1864–1926. French general in World War.

**Bois'sy' d'An'glas'** (bwȧ'sē' däN'glȧs'), Comte **François Antoine de.** 1756–1826. French statesman; member of States-General (1789); aided in overthrow of Robespierre; member of Committee of Public Safety (1794); president of Council of Five Hundred; senator under Napoleon and peer of France under Louis XVIII.

**Bo'i·to** (bô'ē·tō), **Arrigo**. 1842–1918. Italian composer and librettist; known chiefly for his opera *Mefistofele*, which marks transition in Italian opera from mere tunefulness to dramatic emphasis. Author also of several novels, under the anagram **To·bi'o Gor'ria** (?tô·bē'ô gôr'ryä).

**Bo·jar'do** (bô·yär'dô). = BOIARDO.

**Boj'e** (boi'ĕ), **Heinrich Christian**. = BOIE.

**Boj'er** (boi'ẽr), **Johan**. 1872–1959. Norwegian novelist and playwright.

**Bok** (bŏk), **Edward William**. 1863–1930. Editor, b. in Den Helder, Netherlands; to U.S. as child (1869). In employ of Henry Holt & Co. and Charles Scribner's Sons. Organized (1886) Bok Syndicate to handle publication of Beecher's sermons. Editor in chief, *The Ladies' Home Journal* (1889–1919). Donated fund of $100,000 for American peace award for best plan to establish universal peace (1923). Author of *Why I Believe in Poverty* (1915), *The Americanization of Edward Bok* (1920), *A Man From Maine* (1923), *Twice Thirty* (1924), *Dollars Only* (1926), *Perhaps I Am* (1928). See Cyrus H. K. CURTIS.

**Bokelson, Jan**. See JOHN OF LEIDEN.

**Bol** (bŏl), **Ferdinand**. 1616–1680. Dutch portrait and religious painter and etcher. Studied under Rembrandt.

**Bol·di'ni** (bôl·dē'nē), **Giovanni**. 1845–1931. Italian genre and portrait painter; worked in France (from 1872).

**Boldrewood, Rolf**. Pseudonym of Thomas Alexander BROWNE.

**Bo'le·slav** (bô'lĕ·släf). Name of two dukes of Bohemia:

**Boleslav I** (d. 967); duke (929–967); constantly at war with Germans; forced to accept their sovereignty (950); made conquests to the east. His son **Boleslav II** (d. 999); duke (967–999); continued policies of father; saw final success of Christian faith; founded bishopric of Prague (973).

**Bo'le·slav** (bō'lĕ·slăv; bŏl'ĕ-). *Also* **Bo'le·slas** (bō'lĕ·slås; -släs; bŏl'ĕ-) *and* **Bo'le·slaus** (-slôs). *Pol.* **Bo·le'sław** (bô·lĕ'släf). Name of five kings of Piast dynasty of Poland:

**Boleslav I.** *Called* **Chro'bry** (krô'brĭ), *i.e.* the Mighty. (d. 1025). Son of **Miesz'ko** (myĕsh'kô), converted Christian Polish prince. First king of Poland (992–1025); seized Lusatian marches and held them against Emperor Otto III; continued wars against Emperor Henry II; made peace of Bautzen (1018), much to Poland's advantage.

**Boleslav II.** *Called* **the Bold.** 1039?–1083. Son of Casimir I. King (1058–79); seized Kiev (1069); crowned king (1076), throwing off German rule; excommunicated and deposed.

**Boleslav III.** *Called* **Wry-mouthed.** 1086–1138. King (1102–38); enlarged kingdom; overcame Pomerania; defeated emperors Henry V and Lothair II.

**Boleslav IV.** 1127–1173. King (1146–73); overcome by Emperor Frederick I.

**Boleslav V.** *Called* **the Chaste.** 1221–1279. King (1227–79); reign marked by internal dissensions and by Mongol invasion (1237–41).

**Bol'eyn** (bo͝ol'ĭn; bo͝o·lĭn'; bo͝o·lēn'), **Anne**. 1507–1536. Second queen of Henry VIII. Attached to service of Queen Claude of France (c. 1519–22); became mistress of Henry (1527); secretly married to him (January, 1533), whereupon Henry's marriage to Catherine of Aragon declared null by Archbishop Cranmer; gave birth to future Queen Elizabeth I (September, 1533). Charged with criminal intercourse with several paramours and condemned to death by unanimous vote of an assembly of 26 peers; beheaded. Her father, Sir **Thomas Boleyn** (1477–1539), Earl of **Wilt'shire** (wĭlt'shĭr; -shẽr), was an English statesman.

**Bo·lin'** (bo͝o·lēn'), **Andreas Wilhelm**. 1835–1924. Swedish-Finnish philosopher, wrote on Leibnitz (1864), Ludwig Feuerbach (1891), Spinoza (1894).

**Bol'ing·broke** (bŏl'ĭng·bro͝ok). Surname given Henry (later Henry IV of England) from his birthplace.

**Bolingbroke**, 1st Viscount. **Henry St. John** (sĭn'jŭn). 1678–1751. English statesman and orator. Tory M.P. (1701). Secretary for war (1704–08); foreign secretary (1710), sharing leadership of party with Harley, negotiated Treaty of Utrecht (1713); created viscount (1712); contrived dismissal of Harley (1714). Fled to Paris on accession of George I and the consequent change of ministry (1714); started negotiations with James Stuart, the "Old Pretender" (1715), whose accession to the throne was desired by many Tories; served James as private secretary (1715–16) but eventually alienated from Stuart cause by its insistence on Roman Catholicism. Attainted (1715); pardoned (1723), but excluded by Walpole from House of Lords. Became associate of Pope and Swift and wrote (c. 1730) the philosophy for Pope's *Essay on Man;* failed in intrigues to unseat Walpole and retired to France (1735). Author of *Letters on the Study of History* (1752), laying down precepts endorsed by Voltaire, *Idea of a Patriot King* (1749), advocating benevolent despotism, etc.

**Bo'lin·ti·nea'nu** (bô'lēn·tē·nyä'no͞o), **Dimitrie**. 1819–1872. Rumanian journalist, politician, and writer of plays, legends, ballads, elegies, etc.

**Bo·li'tho** (bô·lī'thō), **Henry Hector**. 1898– . British writer, b. in New Zealand; to England (1922). Author of *The Islands of Wonder* (1920), *The New Zealanders* (1928), the novel *Judith Silver* (1929), *Albert the Good* (1932), *Victoria, the Widow and her Son* (1934), *The House in Half Moon Street* (1936), *Edward VIII* (1937), *George VI* (1937), etc.

**Bolitho, William**. *Full name* **William Bolitho Ry'all** (rī'ăl). 1891–1930. British journalist and author, b. S. Africa. Variously newsboy, laborer, and student; served in World War I; London correspondent for Manchester *Guardian* and New York *World*. Author of *Italy Under Mussolini, Twelve Against the Gods*, etc.

**Bo·lí'var** (bô·lē'vär), **Si·món'** (sē·môn'). *Anglicized* **Si'mon Bol'i·var** (sī'mŭn bŏl'ĭ·vẽr). *Known as* **El Li'ber·ta·dor'** (ĕl lē'bẽr·tä·thôr'), *i.e.* the Liberator. 1783–1830. South American soldier, statesman, and revolutionary leader, b. Caracas, Venezuela. Fought under Miranda in revolt against Spanish in Venezuela (1810); compelled to flee. Planned and led Venezuelan revolution and seized Caracas (1812–13); finally defeated in Venezuela and left for Cartagena, Colombia (1814); captured Bogotá (1814) but defeated and went into exile in Jamaica; fled to Haiti and planned another revolution in Venezuela, which was successful (1815–18); entered New Granada (Colombia), raised small army, and defeated Spanish at Boyacá (1819); made president of new republic of Colombia and given almost supreme power (1819); won battle of Carabobo (June, 1821), final victory for independence of Venezuela. Marched south to Quito (1821) and Peru; arrived in Callao (Sept. 1, 1823) after Gen. San Martín, "Protector of Peru," had resigned and left the country; defeated Spanish in battle of Junín (Aug. 6, 1824), which victory, with that of Sucre at Ayacucho (Dec. 9, 1824), freed Peru from Spain. President (actually dictator) of Peru (1824–27); visited Upper Peru (1825), organizing new republic (named *Bolivia* after him); returned to Bogotá (1828); resigned as supreme chief of Colombia (1830); died (Dec. 17, 1830) on estate near Santa Marta, Colombia.

**Böll** (bûl), **Heinrich.** 1917– . German writer, b. Cologne. Novels include *Der Zug war pünktlich* ("The train was on time," 1949), *Ansichten eines Clowns* ("The Clown," 1963), *Gruppenbild mit Dame* ("Group portrait with lady," 1971). Awarded Nobel prize for literature 1972.

**Bol'land** (bŏl'änt), **Gerardus Johannes Petrus Josephus.** 1854–1922. Dutch philosopher; opposed Catholicism, socialism, theosophy, and Freemasonry; edited Hegel's works.

**Bol'land'** (*Fr.* bô'läɴ'; *Flem.* bŏl'änt; *Angl.* bŏl'ănd), **Jean de.** 1596–1665. Flemish Jesuit hagiologist; editor (from c. 1643) of *Acta Sanctorum*, or *Lives of the Saints*, which was continued after his death by his collaborators and successors, known as Bollandists. See Heribert ROSWEYDE.

**Bol'ley** (bŏl'ĭ), **Henry Luke.** 1865–1956. American plant pathologist, b. Manchester, Ind. Known for work on control of plant diseases, esp. of grains.

**Boll'man** (bôl'män; *Angl.* bōl'măn), **Ju'stus** (yōōs'tōōs; *Angl.* jŭs'tŭs) **E'rich** (ā'rĭκ; *Angl.* ĕr'ĭk). 1769–1821. b. Hoya, Hanover; to U.S. (1796). Confidential agent of Aaron Burr (1806–07); imprisoned; released on decision of Supreme Court; told Burr's plans to Jefferson (1807) and denied these were directed against U.S.; testified at Burr's trial.

**Bologna, Pellegrino da.** See Pellegrino TIBALDI.

**Bo'logne'** (bô'lôn'y'), **Jean** (zhäɴ). *Known in Italy as* **Giovanni da Bo·lo'gna** (dä bô·lō'nyä). 1529?–1608. Flemish sculptor attached (1558) to court of the Médicis in Florence.

**Bolognese, Il.** See Giovanni Francesco GRIMALDI.

**Bo'lo Pa'scha** (*Ger.* bō'lō pä'shä). *Fr.* **Bo'lo' Pa'cha'** (bô'lō' pȧ'shȧ'). d. 1918. Assumed name of a German World War I agent in France who spread pacifist and defeatist propaganda (hence the term *Boloism*); executed in France (1918).

**Bols** ( bōlz), Sir **Louis Jean.** 1867–1930. British army officer. In World War I, served under General Allenby, in France with third army as brigadier general (1915), and in Palestine as chief of staff; major general (1917); effected capture of Jerusalem and final defeat of Turks in Syria. Governor of Bermuda (1927–30).

**Bol'swert** (bŏl'svĕrt), **Boetius Adam van** (1580–1633), **Schelte van** (1581?–1659). Dutch engravers, brothers.

**Bolté, Charles L.** 1895– . American army officer; grad. Armour Tech. (1917); served in World War I; in World War II, chief of staff, U.S. forces in British Isles (from May, 1941).

**Bol'ton** (bōl't'n), **Dukes and Duchess of.** See PAULET; Lavinia FENTON.

**Bolton, Charles Knowles.** 1867–1950. American antiquary; especially interested in early Americana.

**Bolton, Guy.** 1884– . Playwright, b. at Broxbourne, Herts, Eng. Practicing architect in New York City; turned (1913) to writing for stage (esp. musical comedy) and motion pictures. His stage successes include *Sally, Lady Be Good;* as collaborator, *Rio Rita, Anything Goes, Girl Crazy;* his scenarios include *The Love Parade, The Camels are Coming, The Murder Man.*

**Boltraffio, Giovanni Antonio.** See BELTRAFFIO.

**Bolt'wood** (bōlt'wŏŏd), **Bertram Borden.** 1870–1927. American scientist, b. Amherst, Mass. Professor of radiochemistry, Yale (1910–27). Specialist in field of radioactivity; discoverer of the element ionium.

**Boltz'mann** (bôlts'män), **Ludwig.** 1844–1906. Austrian physicist; studied kinetic theory of gases; won recognition in Germany of Maxwell's electromagnetic theory of light; demonstrated Stefan's, or Stefan-Boltzmann, law relating to radiation from a black body.

**Bo'lyai** (bô'lyoi), **Farkas.** 1775–1856. Hungarian mathematician; professor, Maros-Vásárhely (from 1802). Author of *Tentamen Juventutem Studiosam in Elementa Matheseos Purae Introducendi* (1832–33) in which fundamentals of geometry treated in new way. His son **János** (1802–1860), also a mathematician, wrote supplement to above work entitled *Appendix Scientiam Spatii Absolute Veram Exhibens*, essay on non-Euclidean geometry.

**Bol·za'no** (bôl·tsä'nō), **Bernhard.** 1781–1848. Roman Catholic theologian, philosopher, and mathematician, b. Prague; a formulator of modern mathematical theory of functions.

**Bomba.** See FERDINAND II, King of the Two Sicilies.

**Bom'berg** (bŏm'bĕrκ), **Daniel.** d. 1549. Dutch printer (in Venice, 1516–49), notably of editions of Hebrew Bible and Talmud.

**Bom'pard'** (bôɴ'pȧr'), **Louis Maurice.** 1854–1935. French diplomat; ambassador to St. Petersburg (1902–07), Constantinople (1909–14); senator (1919).

**Bom·tem'po** (bōɴn·tāɴm'pōō), **João Domingos.** 1775–1842. Portuguese pianist and composer.

**Bon.** See BUON.

**Bo·nac'ci-Bru'na·mon'ti** (bô·nät'chê brōō'nä·mōn'tê), **Maria Alinda.** 1841–1903. Italian lyric poet.

**Bo'nald'** (bô'nȧl'), Vicomte **Louis Gabriel Ambroise de.** 1754–1840. French publicist and philosopher; an émigré during French Revolution; returned to France (1806) and became minister of instruction under Napoleon (1808); extreme conservative in his policies.

**Bo'na·parte** (bō'nȧ·pärt; *Fr.* bô'nȧ'pȧrt'). *It.* **Buo'na·par'te** (bwô'nä·pär'tā). A Corsican family of Italian origin to which belonged Napoleon I, Emperor of the French. Napoleon's parents were **Carlo Buonaparte** (1746–1785), a Corsican lawyer, and **Maria Letizia Ra'mo·li'no** [rä'mô·lē'nô] (1750–1836). Their children (in chronological order) were:

(1) **Joseph** (1768–1844); member of Council of Five Hundred (1798); councilor of state (1799); made by Napoleon king of Naples (1806–08), king of Spain (1808–13); resident in U.S. (1815–32) under name of Comte de Sur'vil'liers' (sür'vē'lyā').

(2) **Napoleon** (1769–1821); see NAPOLEON I.

(3) **Maria Anna Elisa** (1777–1820); m. (1797) Felice Pasquale Bacciocchi (*q.v.*); made by Napoleon princess of **Luc'ca** (lōōk'kä) and **Piom·bi'no** [pyôm·bē'nô] (1805), grand duchess of **Tus'ca·ny** [tŭs'kȧ·nĭ] (1809).

(4) **Lucien** (1775–1840); as president of Council of Five Hundred (1799) aided Napoleon in securing dictatorship of France; ambassador to Madrid (1800); negotiated peace treaty between Spain and Portugal (1801); exiled for opposing Napoleon's policies (1810); on way to U.S., captured by English; held as prisoner of state in England; prince of **Ca·ni'no** [kä·nē'nô] (1814). Among his eleven children were:

(a) **Charles Lucien Jules Laurent** (1803–1857), Prince of Canino and of **Mu'si·gna'no** (mōō'zē·nyä'nô); naturalist; resident of Philadelphia (1822–28); author of *American Ornithology, or History of Birds Inhabiting the United States not given by Wilson* (1825–33). See Alexander WILSON.

(b) **Lae·ti'ti·a** [lē·tĭsh'ĭ·ȧ; -tĭsh'yȧ; -tĭsh'ȧ] (1804–1872); m. (1821) Thomas Wyse, English diplomatist.

(c) **Louis Lucien** (1813–1891); phonetician and philologist; investigator of Basque language; created prince (1863) by Napoleon III.

(d) **Pierre Napoléon** (1815–1881); created prince (1852) by Napoleon III; shot journalist Victor Noir (1870) but acquitted of murder. Pierre's son Prince **Roland** (1858–1924) was a geographer.

(5) **Louis** (1778–1846); m. (1802) Hortense de Beauharnais; made by Napoleon king of Holland (1806); abdicated (1810) and assumed title of comte **de St.-Leu** (săN'lû'). His third son, Charles Louis Napoleon, was Emperor Napoleon III (*q.v.*).
(6) **Maria Paulina,** *orig.* **Carlotta** (1780–1825); m. 1st (1797) Charles Victor Emmanuel Leclerc; 2d (1803) Prince Camillo Borghese (*q.v.*) and became duchess of **Gua·stal'la** (gwäs·täl'lä).
(7) **Maria Annunciata,** *later* **Carolina** (1782–1839); m. (1800) Marshal Joachim Murat and became queen of Naples (1808); known (after 1815) as Comtesse **Li·po'na** (lē·pō'nä).
(8) **Jérôme** (1784–1860); lieutenant on expedition to Haiti (1803); took refuge from British in U.S.; m. (1803) Elizabeth Patterson (1785–1879) of Baltimore; marriage annulled (1805) by French council of state; m. Princess Catherine of Württemberg; made by Napoleon king of Westphalia (1807); after Napoleon's abdication, settled in Florence; returned to France (1848); created marshal of France (1850). His daughter **Matilde** (1820–1904), m. Prince Anatolic Demidov.
**Napoléon Joseph Charles Paul** (1822–1891); called Prince Napoleon; also known as **Plon'-Plon'** (plôN'-plôN'); son of Jérôme and Princess Catherine; general in Crimean war; m. (1859) Princess Clotilde, daughter of Victor Emmanuel II of Sardinia; corps commander in war of 1859; his liberal political views caused conflict with Napoleon III; death of prince imperial made him head of family (1879); as pretender to throne, exiled from France (1886) with his son Prince **Victor** (1862–1926).

**Bo'na·parte** (bō'nȧ·pärt), **Charles Joseph.** 1851–1921. American lawyer, b. Baltimore, Md. Son of Jérôme Bonaparte; grandson of Jérôme, King of Westphalia. U.S. secretary of navy (1905–06); U.S. attorney general (1906–09).

**Bonaparte, Elizabeth,** *nee* **Patterson.** 1785–1879. Wife of Jérôme Bonaparte, daughter of William Patterson, b. in Baltimore; m. (1803) but marriage not recognized by Napoleon and annulled by French council of state (1805); lived most of the time in Europe (1815–40); grandmother of **Jerome Napoleon Bonaparte** (1830–1893), American soldier and French army officer.

**Bon'ar** (bŏn'ẽr), **Horatius.** 1808–1889. Scottish clergyman and writer of three series of *Hymns of Faith and Hope* (1857–66), including "I heard the voice of Jesus say."

**Bonar Law, Andrew.** See Bonar LAW.

**Bon'a·ven·tu'ra** (bŏn'ȧ·vĕn·tū'rȧ; *Ital.* bō'nä·vān-tōō'rä) *or* **Bon'a·ven'ture** (bŏn'ȧ·vĕn'tūr), Saint. *Real name* **Giovanni di Fi·dan'za** (dē fē·dän'tsä). 1221–1274. Italian scholastic philosopher, b. in Tuscany. Called "the Seraphic Doctor." Entered Franciscan order (c. 1242); professor of theology, Paris (1253); general of Franciscans (1257); bishop of Albano (1273); created cardinal by Gregory X (1273). Venerated during his lifetime; appears as saint in Dante's *Paradiso;* canonized by Sixtus IV (1482); declared doctor of the church by Sixtus V (1587). A leading medieval writer and mystic; his works include *Itinerarium Mentis in Deum, Reductio Artium in Theologiam, Biblia Pauperum, Speculum Mariae Virginis, Breviloquium.*

**Bon'a·ven·tu'ra** (bŏn'ȧ·vĕn·tū'rȧ), Father. Pseudonym of Charles Edward Stuart (*q.v.*), used in visit to England (1753); also so called in Scott's *Redgauntlet.*

**Bonavino, Cristoforo.** Real name of Ausonio FRANCHI.

**Bon'champ'** (bôN'shäN'), Marquis **Charles Melchior Artus de.** 1760–1793. French general; Vendean leader; mortally wounded at battle of Cholet (Oct. 19, 1793).

**Bon'ci** (bōn'chē), **Alessandro.** 1870–1940. Italian tenor; sometime rival of Caruso.

**Bon'com·pa'gni di Mom·bel'lo** (bōng'kôm·pä'nyē dē môm·bĕl'lō), **Carlo.** Conte **di Sam·po'ro** (dē säm·pô'rō). 1804–1880. Italian jurist and statesman; active in cause of Italian unification.

**Boncour, Joseph Paul-.** See PAUL-BONCOUR.

**Bond** (bŏnd), **Carrie,** *nee* **Jacobs.** 1862–1946. American song writer, b. Janesville, Wis.; m. (1887) Dr. Frank L. Bond (d. 1895). Among her widely successful songs are *A Perfect Day, Just A-wearyin' for You, I Love You Truly, God Remembers When the World Forgets, Do You Remember?* Also wrote books for children and an autobiography.

**Bond,** Sir **Edward Augustus.** 1815–1898. English librarian; principal librarian, British Museum (1878–88).

**Bond, Hugh Lennox.** 1828–1893. American jurist; ended Ku Klux Klan terror by decisions in South Carolina cases. Released on habeas corpus writs South Carolina canvassers imprisoned by State supreme court in attempt to carry the State for Tilden, thus making Hayes's election possible.

**Bond, Oliver.** 1760?–1798. Irish revolutionist; intellectual leader of organization for establishing an Irish republic independent of England; charged with treason (1798) and died in prison.

**Bond, Shadrach.** 1773?–1832. American political leader, b. in Baltimore County, Md. Emigrated to Illinois region (c. 1791). First governor of State of Illinois (1818–22).

**Bond, William Bennett.** 1815–1906. Canadian Anglican leader and vigorous reformer and temperance advocate; bishop of Montreal (1878); archbishop and metropolitan (1901); primate of all Canada (1904).

**Bond, William Cranch.** 1789–1859. American astronomer; director of Harvard Observatory (1839–59). His son **George Phillips** (1825–1865) was also director of Harvard College Observatory (1859–65); specialist in use of photography in mapping the sky, measuring brightness of stars and double stars; discoverer of Hyperion, satellite of Saturn, and the crape ring.

**Bond'field** (bŏn(d)'fēld), **Margaret Grace.** 1873–1953. English trade unionist and labor leader; M.P. (1923–31); parliamentary secretary to ministry of labor (1924); minister of labor (1929–31); first woman minister in British government.

**Bon'di** (bôn'dē), **Clemente.** 1742–1821. Italian Jesuit and poet; translated Vergil, Ovid's *Metamorphoses;* wrote love poems and humorous satire.

**Bone** (bōn), **Henry.** 1755–1834. English enamel painter to George III, George IV, and William IV. His son **Henry Pierce** (1779–1855) was also an enamel painter.

**Bone,** Sir **Muirhead.** 1876–1953. Scottish etcher and painter. Official artist during World War, on western front and with the fleet (1916–18); known for *The Great Gantry* (1906), *Ayr Prison, The Shot Tower, Liberty's Clock,* etchings in dry point. His brother Sir **David William** (1874–1959); master mariner; author of novels of seafaring life.

**Bonehill,** Captain **Ralph.** See Edward STRATEMEYER.

**Bo·nel'li** (bō·nĕl'lē), **Francesco Andrea.** 1784–1830. Italian naturalist; best known for his entomological studies.

**Bo·nel'li** (bō·nĕl'ĭ), **Richard.** *Real surname* **Bunn** (bŭn). 1894– . American baritone. With Chicago Civic Opera Company (1925) and Metropolitan Opera Company of New York (from 1932).

**Bo'ner** (bō'nẽr), **Ulrich.** *Latinized surname* **Bo·ne'ri·us** (bō·nēr'ĭ·ŭs; *Ger.* bō·nā'rē·ōōs). 14th-century Swiss writer of fables. Collected fables under title *Der*

*Edelstein* (c. 1350; printed 1461), one of first German books to be printed; collection published by Breitinger (*q.v.*) in *Fabeln aus den Zeiten der Minnesinger* (1757).

**Bone′steel** (bōn′stēl), **Charles Hartwell.** 1885–1964. American army officer; grad. U.S.M.A., West Point (1908); advanced through the grades to colonel (1937), brigadier general (1940), major general (1941); commander of U.S. forces in Iceland (Sept., 1941); supreme commander of Allied forces in Iceland (April, 1942).

**Bon·fi′gli** (bôn·fē′lyē), **Benedetto.** 15th-century Italian painter, b. Perugia; reputed master of Perugino.

**Bon′ghi** (bông′gē), **Ruggiero** *or* **Ruggero.** 1828–1895. Italian scholar, writer, and statesman, b. Naples. Active in national movement (1848); Conservative member, chamber of deputies (1860 ff.); minister of education (1874–76). Founded *La Stampa*, Turin (1863). His works include *Opere di Platone* (1858), *Pio IX e il Papa Futuro* (1877), *La Storia di Roma* (3 vols., 1884–88).

**Bon′heur′** (bô′nûr′), **Rosa,** *in full* **Marie Rosalie.** 1822–1899. French painter; known esp. for her paintings of animals. Among her notable paintings are *Tillage in Nivernais* (Luxembourg) *Studies of Animals* (Bordeaux Musée), and *Horse Fair* (Metropolitan Museum of Art in New York). Her brother **Auguste** (1824–1884) was also a landscape and animal painter.

**Bon′homme′** (bô′nôm′), **Jacques.** Pseudonym of Guillaume CALE.

**Bo′ni** (bō′nī), **Albert.** 1892– . American publisher. Secretary-treasurer, Boni & Liveright, Inc. (1918–19); president, Albert & Charles Boni, Inc. (from 1923); an organizer of Washington Square Players, which became Theatre Guild.

**Bo′ni** (bô′nē), **Giacomo.** 1859–1925. Italian architect and archaeologist; known for restorations of Doges' Palace and campanile in Venice and for excavations of Roman Forum and Palatine.

**Bon′i·face** (bŏn′ĭ·fās), Saint. *Orig. name* **Win′frid** (wĭn′frĭd) *or* **Wyn′frith** (wĭn′frĭth). 680?–755. English Benedictine missionary, b. in Devonshire. Called "Apostle of Germany." Authorized by Pope Gregory II, preached and organized church in Bavaria, Thuringia, Friesland, and Hesse (719 ff.); bishop (723); archbishop (732); entrusted with reformation of Frankish church (741); archbishop of Mainz (748); resigned his see to continue evangelization of Friesland (754); set upon, with his followers, by a mob and killed at Dokkum, West Friesland.

**Boniface.** Name of nine popes (see *Table of Popes*, Nos. 42, 55, 66, 67, 69, 112, 138, 193, 203), especially:

**Boniface I,** Saint. d. 422. Pope (bishop of Rome; 418–422); b. Rome. Recognized by Emperor Honorius; supported St. Augustine; famous as an organizer.

**Boniface VII.** By some regarded as an antipope (974), but in the lists as pope (984–985).

**Boniface VIII.** *Real name* **Benedetto Ca′e·ta′ni** (kä′ā·tä′nē). 1235?–1303. Pope (1294–1303); b. Anagni. As pope, concerned himself with many European affairs; endeavored esp. to end wars; issued (1296) the bull *Clericis laicos* directed against Philip IV of France, forbidding collection of taxes on church property without consent of Holy See; issued (1301) the bull *Ausculta Fili*, reproach against Philip, and (1302) *Unam Sanctam* asserting temporal as well as spiritual supremacy of pope; as a result of quarrel with Philip, made prisoner at Anagni (1303) by Philip's Italian aides; died within a month.

**Boniface IX.** *Real name* **Pietro To′ma·cel′li** (tō′mä·chĕl′lē). d. 1404. Pope (1389–1404); b. Naples. Acquired almost absolute power in Rome; spent great sums in fortifications; quarreled with Richard of England and opposed Louis of Anjou in his claim to Naples.

**Boniface.** Count of **Montferrat.** See MONTFERRAT.

**Bo′ni′face′** (bô′nē′fȧs′), **Joseph Xavier.** See Xavier SAINTINE.

**Bon′i·face of Sa·voy′** (bŏn′ĭ·fās, sȧ·voi′). d. 1270. Archbishop of Canterbury; elected through influence of his niece Eleanor, queen of Henry III of England; consecrated (1245). Initiated visitation of Canterbury (1250); supported bishops against exactions by king and pope (1256), but shifted to side of king and (1263) confirmed papal excommunication of rebel barons.

**Bon′i·fa′ci·us** (bŏn′ĭ·fā′shĭ·ŭs). d. 432 A.D. Roman governor of Africa. Reputed to have invited Vandals into that province (c. 429); later, warred upon Vandals and defended city of Hippo from them. Died from wounds received in duel with Aëtius (*q.v.*).

**Bonifacius.** See Saint BRUNO of Querfurt.

**Bo′ni·fa′zio Ve′ro·ne′se** (bō′nē·fä′tsyō vā′rō·nā′sā). *Sometimes* **Bonifazio Ve′ne·zia′no** (vā′nā·tsyä′nō). *Properly* **Bonifazio di Pi·ta′ti** (dē pē·tä′tē). 1487–1553. Italian painter of the Venetian school; pupil of Palma Vecchio.

**Bo·nil′la** (bō·nē′yä), **Manuel.** 1849–1913. Honduran political leader, b. Juticalpa. Led revolt against President Policarpo Bonilla (1900); president of Honduras (1903–07); with El Salvador as an ally and with aid of Lee Christmas, American soldier of fortune, engaged in war (1907) with Zelaya of Nicaragua; was defeated and fled to U.S.; led revolution against President Dávila (1910–11); elected president (1911) and inaugurated (Feb., 1912), serving until death.

**Bonilla, Policarpo.** 1858–1926. Honduran Liberal leader; aided by President Zelaya of Nicaragua; president of Honduras (1894–1900); overthrown by Manuel Bonilla (1900) and held in prison (1900–06); Honduran representative at Peace Conference at Paris (1919).

**Bo·nil′la y San Mar·tín′** (bō·nē′lyä ē sän mär·tēn′), **Adolfo.** 1875–1926. Spanish jurist and scholar.

**Bo′nin′** (bô′năN′), **Charles Eudes.** 1865–1929. French explorer in western China, Mongolia, etc. (1893–1900).

**Bo·nin′** (bō·nēn′), **Eduard von.** 1793–1865. Prussian general; war minister (1852–54, 1858–59); commanding general of 8th army corps at Coblenz.

**Bon′ing·ton** (bŏn′ĭng·tŭn), **Richard Parkes.** 1801?–1828. English landscape and genre painter; associated with Delacroix in new conception of historical painting; instrumental in introducing methods of Constable and other English water-colorists to painters of Barbizon school. Known for purity and brilliance of his coloring.

**Bonivard, François de.** See BONNIVARD.

**Bonn** (bôn), **Moritz Julius.** 1873–1965. German economist. Author of works chiefly on world economy and world politics, including *Nationale Kolonialpolitik* (1910), *Amerika und sein Problem* (1925), *Geld und Geist* (1927), etc.

**Bon′nard′** (bô′nár′), **Abel.** 1883-1968. French writer. Author of books of verse, a novel, and two volumes of travel sketches, *En Chine* (1923), which won for him Grand Prix de Littérature from French Academy (1924).

**Bonnard,** Chevalier **Bernard de.** 1744–1784. French poet.

**Bonnard, Pierre.** 1867–1947. French painter; identified with modernist group.

**Bon′nas′sieux′** (bô′nȧ′syû′), **Jean Marie.** 1810–1892. French sculptor; carved colossal statue *Notre-Dame de France* at Le Puy.

**Bon′nat′** (bô′nȧ′), **Léon Joseph Florentin.** 1833–1922. French painter. Attained great success in early career for his religious paintings; later, succeeded as portrait painter.

**Bonne'chose'** (bôn'shōz'), **François Paul Émile Bois'nor'mand' de** (bwä'nôr'mäN' dẽ). 1801–1875. French librarian and author esp. of histories, as of France (1834) and England (1858–59), and of *Bertrand Du Guesclin* (1866), *Lazare Hoche* (1867), etc.

**Bonne'mère'** (bôn'mâr'), **Joseph Eugène.** 1813–1893. French historian.

**Bon'ner** *or* **Bon'er** (bŏn'ẽr), **Edmund.** 1500?–1569. English prelate; sent to Rome (1533) to appeal in behalf of Henry VIII, who had been excommunicated after marriage with Anne Boleyn (1533). Bishop of London (1539); imprisoned (1549–53) for insistence that royal supremacy was in abeyance during Edward VI's minority. Restored to bishopric at accession of Mary (1553) and became principal agent in Marian persecution of Reformers; refused oath of supremacy at accession of Elizabeth and was deposed (1559); died in prison.

**Bon'net'** (bô'nĕ'), **Charles.** 1720–1793. Swiss naturalist and philosopher. Credited with discovery of parthenogenesis while studying aphids; defended incasement theory.

**Bonnet, Georges.** 1889–1973. French politician and diplomat; held various cabinet posts (1926 ff.); ambassador to U.S. (1937); minister of foreign affairs (1938–39) at time of Munich conference. Member of parliament (1956–1968).

**Bonnet, Henri.** 1888–1978. French diplomat and historian, b. Châteauponsac; member, League of Nations secretariat (1920–31); ambassador to U.S. (from 1945).

**Bon'ne·val'** (bôn'vál'), Comte **Claude Alexandre de.** 1675–1747. *Known as* **Ah·med'** (ä·mĕt'), *or* **Ach·met'** (äκ·mĕt'), **Pa·sha'** (pä·shä'). French soldier in Italy and Netherlands (1701). Quarreled, fled to Austria, and served under Prince Eugene against France and Turkey. Quarreled with Eugene; embraced Islamism; general in Turkish army; banished from Turkey.

**Bon'ne·ville** (bŏn'ẽ·vĭl), **Benjamin Louis Eu'la·lie** (ū'lȧ·lē) **de.** 1796–1878. American army officer, b. Paris, France. Explored northwestern country (1832–35); served in Mexican War and Civil War. Subject of Washington Irving's *Adventures of Captain Bonneville* (1837).

**Bonne'ville'** (bôn'vēl'), **Nicolas de.** 1760–1828. French writer; appointed president of one of Paris districts at outbreak of French Revolution (1789); reputed to be first to suggest formation of garde nationale; imprisoned during Terror and persecuted under Empire. Among his many books are *Histoire de l'Europe Moderne* (1789–92), *Poésies* (1793).

**Bon'ney** (bŏn'ĭ), **Thomas George.** 1833–1923. English geologist; professor, University College, London (1877–1901); specialist in petrology and glaciology.

**Bonney, William H.** See BILLY THE KID.

**Bon'nier'** (bô'nyā'), **Gaston.** 1853–1922. French botanist; specialist in plant physiology and anatomy.

**Bon'ni'vard'** *or* **Bo'ni'vard'** (bô'nē'vȧr'), **François de.** 1496–1570. Swiss ecclesiastic and politician; prior of St. Victor near Geneva (1514) and opponent of Duke Charles of Savoy, who was plotting to obtain control of Geneva; arrested by duke at Lausanne (1530) and confined in Castle of Chillon (in subterranean dungeon from 1532); freed when the Bernese captured Chillon (Mar. 29, 1536). Hero of Lord Byron's poem *The Prisoner of Chillon.*

**Bono.** See BUON.

**Bo·no'mi** (bô·nô'mē), **Giuseppe.** 1739–1808. Italian architect; practiced in England (from 1767); influential in revival of Greek renaissance style. His son **Joseph** (1796–1878) was a sculptor and draftsman; known as an illustrator of Egyptological publications.

**Bo'non·ci'ni** (bō'nôn·chē'nē) *or* **Buo'non·ci'ni** (bwô'-). Italian family of musicians of 17th and 18th centuries, including: **Giovanni Maria** (1640–1678); musical theorist and composer. His son **Giovanni Battista** (c. 1672–c. 1752); operatic composer; known for his rivalry with Handel (London, 1716); composer of oratorios (as *Il Giosuè*), symphonies, chamber music, and operas. Another son, **Marcantonio** (c. 1675–1726); composer of operas, cantatas, and oratorios.

**Bon'pland'** (bôN'pläN'), **Aimé Jacques Alexandre.** *Real surname* **Gou'jaud'** (gōō'zhō'). 1773–1858. French naturalist. Traveled with Alexander von Humboldt (1799–1804) in Mexico, the Andes, etc., and collected many new species of plants; professor of natural sciences in Buenos Aires (1818–21). Imprisoned (1821–30) by dictator of Paraguay. Author of *Plantes Équinoxiales* (1805), etc.

**Bon'sal** (bŏn's'l), **Stephen.** 1865–1951. American journalist; New York correspondent in Balkans (1885), Morocco (1889), Macedonia (1890), China (1895), Cuba (1897–98), Philippines (1901), Venezuela (1903), Russia (1907), Mexico (1910–11). Secretary to governor general of Philippine Islands (1913). With A.E.F. in France (1918). Among his books are *Morocco as It Is* (1892), *Heyday in a Vanished World* (1937).

**Bon'sels** (bôn'zĕls), **Waldemar.** 1881–1952. German writer of verse, fiction, and travel books.

**Bon'stet'ten'** (*Fr.* bôn'stā'tĕn'; *Ger.* bôn'shtĕt'ĕn), **Charles Victor de** *or* **Karl Viktor von.** 1745–1832. Swiss man of letters. Among his works are *Recherches sur la Nature et les Lois de l'Imagination* (1807), *Études de l'Homme* (1821).

**Bon'temps'** (bôN'täN'), **Roger.** Pseudonym of Roger de COLLERYE.

**Bon'va'lot'** (bôN'vá'lō'), **Pierre Gabriel Édouard.** 1853–1933. French explorer and author. Traveled through central Asia and Turkestan (1882), through Persia and the Pamirs (1885–87) and with Prince Henri d'Orléans from Siberia to Tonkin (1889–90).

**Bonvicino, Alessandro.** See Il MORETTO.

**Bon'vin'** (bôN'văN'), **François.** 1817–1887. French genre and still-life painter.

**Bon'vin** (bŏn'vĭn), **Lud'wig** (lŏŏd'vĭg). 1850–1939. Jesuit priest, musician, and composer, b. in Switzerland; music director at Canisius College, Buffalo, N.Y. (1887–1907); authority on Gregorian music; composer of orchestral, choral, and church music.

**Bon'wick** (bŏn'(w)ĭk), **James.** 1817–1906. Australian archivist, b. London; writer on early Australian history; compiled *Historical Records of New South Wales* (7 vols., 1893–1901).

**Boole** (bōōl), **George.** 1815–1864. English mathematician and logician. Professor, Queen's College, Cork (from 1849). Author of *Treatise on Differential Equations* (1859), *Treatise on the Calculus of Finite Differences* (1860), other mathematical works, and *An Investigation of the Laws of Thought on Which Are Founded the Mathematical Theories of Logic and Probabilities* (1854), in which he elaborates his method of applying mathematics to logic.

**Boone** (bōōn), **Daniel.** 1734–1820. American pioneer, b. near Reading, Pa. Moved to North Carolina (1750); made trips to Kentucky region (1767, 1769–71). Guided settlers into Kentucky (1775); erected fort (1775) on site of what is now Boonesboro; his land titles there invalidated (after 1780). After some years in western Virginia (1788–98), moved into region of what is now Missouri and secured a grant of land (c. 1799), his grant being confirmed to him by Congress (1814). Elected to American Hall of Fame (1915).

**Booth** (bōōth; *Brit. usu.* bōōth). Family of actors on American stage, including: **Junius Brutus** (1796–1852), b. London; acted at Covent Garden (1817–20), and, in support of Edmund Kean, at Drury Lane (1820); on U.S. stage (from 1821) with occasional tours to England; chief roles, Othello, Iago, Richard III, Shylock. His son **Junius Brutus** (1821–1883), actor and manager. Another son, **Edwin Thomas** (1833–1893); on New York stage (1862–73); toured England and Continent (1880–82); appeared with Lawrence Barrett (1887–89, 1890–91) and Mme. Modjeska (1889–90); chief roles: Hamlet, King Lear, Romeo, Othello, Iago, Benedict, Brutus, Richelieu, Sir Giles Overreach. Elected to American Hall of Fame (1925). Another son, **John Wilkes** (1838–1865); achieved success in Shakespearean roles (1860–63); intrigued to kidnap Lincoln (1864) and then to assassinate him; shot and killed Lincoln at Ford's Theater, Washington (Apr. 14, 1865); escaped, but was shot, or killed himself (Apr. 26, 1865).

**Agnes Booth.** *Nee* **Marian Agnes Land Rookes** (rōōks). 1846–1910. Actress; wife of younger Junius Brutus; b. Sydney, Australia; to U.S. in childhood; m. 1st (1861) Harry Perry (d. 1863), 2d (1867) Junius Brutus Booth (d. 1883), and 3d (1885) John B. Schoeffel; appeared in support of Edwin Forrest, Edwin Booth, E. A. Sothern, Lawrence Barrett; leading woman in Palmer's company, at Madison Square Theater, New York (1890).

**Booth, Ballington.** See under William Booth.

**Booth, Barton.** 1681–1733. English tragic actor. Engaged by Betterton (1700); his best roles include Ghost to Wilks's Hamlet, Cato in Addison's tragedy, Brutus, Lear, Othello, Henry VIII, Hotspur.

**Booth, Charles.** 1840–1916. English shipowner and sociological writer. Author of *Life and Labour of the People in London* (1891–1903); instrumental in obtaining passage of Old Age Pensions Act (1908).

**Booth, Evangeline Cory.** See under William Booth.

**Booth,** Sir **Felix.** 1775–1850. English distiller and chief contributor to Capt. James Clark Ross's North American expedition of discovery (1829–33); after him Boothia Felix peninsula is named.

**Booth, George.** 1st Baron **Del'a·mere** (dĕl'ȧ·mēr) *or* **de la Mer** (dĕl'ȧ·mär). 1622–1684. English political and military leader; member of Long Parliament; treasurer at war (1655); leader of so-called New Royalists, who joined with Cavaliers in attempt to effect the Restoration (1659); one of twelve members of Parliament sent to The Hague to summon Charles II. His second son, **Henry** (1652–1694), 2d Baron Delamere and 1st Earl of **War'ring·ton** (wŏr'ĭng·tŭn), was imprisoned for implication in Rye House Plot (1683); acquitted of charge of complicity in Monmouth's rebellion (1685); took up arms for William of Orange (1688); chancellor of exchequer (1689–90).

**Booth, William.** *Known as* **General Booth.** 1829–1912. English religious leader and founder of Salvation Army. Experienced conversion (1844); after 9 years as regular preacher of Methodist New Connexion, became independent itinerant revivalist (1861); m. (1855) **Catherine Mum'ford** (mŭm'fērd) (1829–1890), a preacher in public (1860) and later known as "Mother of the Salvation Army"; founded mission in Whitechapel, London (1865), which became (1878) the Salvation Army, with a program of social reforms and charities in city slums and among paupers and criminals; introduced the army in America, Australia, Europe, India, Japan. Author of *In Darkest England and the Way Out* (1890).

His eldest son, **William Bramwell** (1856–1929), chief organizer and chief of staff of Salvation Army (1880–1912) and on father's death general of the army (1912–29); m. (1882) **Florence Eleanor So'per** [sō'pēr] (1861–1957), a worker in the army (from 1880), and organizer of rescue work among women (1912), who bore him **Catherine Bramwell** (1883– ), in command of women's social work in Great Britain and Ireland (1926), and **Mary Booth** (1885–1969) in command of Salvation Army operations in Germany (1924–29).

**Ballington** (1859–1940), second son of William, was in charge of Salvation Army in Australia (1885–87) and in U.S. (1887–1896); withdrew from army after disagreement with father on method of operation in America; organized similar body, the Volunteers of America (1896); m. (1886) **Maud Charles'worth** [chärlz'wûrth] (1865–1948), who had helped his sister **Catherine Booth'-Clib'born** [-klĭb'ôrn] (1859–1955), to organize branches of the army in Paris and in Switzerland, and who aided her husband in founding of the volunteers and directed its prison work, was one of founders of Parent-Teachers Association, and author of *Branded* (1897) and *After Prison, What?* (1903).

**Emma Moss Booth'-Tuck'er** [-tŭk'ēr] (1860–1903), another daughter of William Booth; in charge of training homes of the army (1880–88); m. (1888) **Frederick St. George de La·tour'** [dĕl'ȧ·tōōr'] **Booth-Tucker** (1853–1929; assumed name Booth in 1888), Anglo-Indian, who resigned from Indian civil service to inaugurate Indian branch of Salvation Army (1882), served as secretary of international work in London (1891–96) and as commander in U.S. (1896–1905); author of *Life of General William Booth* (1898) and *Farm Colonies of the Salvation Army* (1903).

**Evangeline Cory Booth** (1865–1950), seventh child of William Booth, was commander of the army in London five years, in Canada nine years, national commander in U.S. (1904–34); elected general of international organization (1934); also orator, musician, poet, and author of *Love is All* (1925), *Songs of the Evangel* (1927), *Towards a Better World* (sermons, 1928), *Woman* (1930).

**Boothe** (bōōth), **Clare.** 1903– . American playwright; m. George Tuttle Brokaw (divorced, 1929) and (1935) Henry R. Luce (*q.v.*). On editorial staff of *Vogue* (1930), *Vanity Fair* (1931–34). Member, U.S. House of Representatives (1943–47); ambassador to Italy (1953–57). Author of *The Women* (1937), *Kiss the Boys Goodbye* (1938), *Margin for Error* (1939).

**Boott** (bōōt), **Kirk.** 1790–1837. American manufacturer, b. Boston. Pioneer in cotton textile manufacturing; associate of Nathan and Samuel Appleton at Lowell, Mass.

**Booz.** See Boaz.

**Bopp** (bŏp), **Franz.** 1791–1867. German philologist, founder of science of comparative philology. Carried on researches, esp. in Sanskrit mss., at Paris and London (1812 ff.); professor, Berlin (1821–64). Author of a Sanskrit grammar (1829–32) and glossary (1830), a comparative grammar of Indo-European languages (1833–52), and of studies on the Celtic, Caucasian, Malayo-Polynesian, Albanian, and other languages.

**Bor** (bôr), **Pieter Christiaanszoon.** 1559–1635. Dutch historian; author of . . . *Wars of the Netherlands* (1595 ff.), now used as a source book.

**Bo'ra** (bō'rä), **Katharina von.** 1499–1552. Wife of Martin Luther, b. Saxony. Cistercian nun in Nimbschen, Saxony (1515–23); adopted Lutheran doctrines and fled to Wittenberg (1523); married Luther (1525).

**Bo'rah** (bō'rȧ), **William Edgar.** 1865–1940. American lawyer and statesman; adm. to bar (1889); practiced in Boise, Idaho (1891–1940). U.S. senator from Idaho (1907–40): chairman, Senate foreign relations committee (from 1924). Strongly opposed World Court and entrance of United States into League of Nations; advocated disarmament conference (1920–21).

**Borandon,** Saint. See BRENDAN.

**Bor·bón'** (bôr·bôn'). Spanish form of BOURBON.

**Bor'chard** (bôr'chẽrd), **Edwin.** 1884–1951. American authority on international law, b. New York City. Law librarian of Congress (1911–13; 1914–16); professor of law, Yale Law School (from 1917). U.S. technical adviser at Conference on Codification of International Law (1930) and U.S. representative on the Committee of Experts for Inter-American Codification of International Law.

**Bor'chardt** (bôr'kärt), **Ludwig.** 1863–1938. German Egyptologist.

**Borch'gre·vink** (bŏrk'grā·vĕngk), **Carsten Egeberg.** 1864–1934. Norwegian naturalist and explorer. Member of first party to land on Antarctic Continent (1895); in command of Sir George Newnes's *Southern Cross* expedition (1898), first expedition to winter on the Antarctic Continent (at Cape Adare, 1899); explored Ross Sea and by sledge as far south as 78° 50'.

**Bor'da'** (bôr'dȧ'), **Jean Charles de.** 1733–1799. French mathematician and nautical astronomer.

**Bor'deaux'** (bôr'dō'), Duc de. See Comte de CHAMBORD.

**Bordeaux, Henry.** 1870–1963. French novelist; known esp. for tales of French family life; author also of critical works.

**Bor'den** (bôr'd'n), **Gail.** 1801–1874. American inventor, b. Norwich, N.Y. To Kentucky (1815), Indiana Territory (1816), Mississippi (1822), Texas (about 1829). Invented a meat biscuit (1851); condensed milk (1853, patent granted 1856).

**Borden, Lizzie Andrew.** 1860–1927. Central figure in unsolved murder mystery. After discovery (Aug. 4, 1892) of dead bodies of her wealthy father and stepmother in their Fall River (Mass.) home, accused of their murder, tried, but acquitted.

**Borden,** Sir **Robert Laird.** 1854–1937. Canadian lawyer and statesman, b. Nova Scotia. M.P. (from 1896); leader of Conservative opposition in House of Commons (1901); prime minister (1911–20); delegate of Canada at Paris Peace Conference (1919); representative of Canada on Council of League of Nations.

**Bor'det'** (bôr'dĕ'), **Jules.** 1870–1961. Belgian bacteriologist. Director, Pasteur Institute, Brussels (from 1901). Known for work in immunology and serology; codiscoverer of complement fixation on which Wassermann test for diagnosis of syphilis is based; received 1919 Nobel prize in medicine.

**Bor·do'ne** (bôr·dō'nā), **Pa·ris'** (pä·rēs'). 1500–1571. Venetian painter; pupil of Titian; worked in Venice, Treviso, Crema, Augsburg, and in France.

**Bordoni, Faustina.** See under Johann Adolf HASSE.

**Bo'ré'** (bô'rā'), **Jean Étienne.** 1741–1820. b. in Louisiana Territory. Pioneer in production of sugar in region near New Orleans (1795); mayor of New Orleans (1803).

**Bo'rel'** (bô'rĕl'), **Félix Édouard Émile.** 1871–1956. French mathematician; known for work in infinitesimal calculus and the calculus of probabilities.

**Borel d'Haute'rive'** (dō'trēv'), **Joseph Pétrus.** 1809–1859. French writer of the extreme romantic school; author of a collection of verse, *Rhapsodies* (1831), and two works of fiction.

**Bo·rel'li** (bô·rĕl'lē), **Giovanni Alfonso.** 1608–1679. Italian physicist and astronomer; founder of iatrophysical school. Credited with discovery of parabolic path of comets; sought to explain motion of Jupiter's satellites by laws of attraction; attempted to apply laws of mechanics to motions of the animal body in *De Motu Animalium* (1680–81).

**Bor·ge'se** (bôr·jā'sā), **Giuseppe Antonio.** 1882–1952. Writer and scholar, b. Sicily. To U.S. (1931); naturalized (1938); professor of Italian literature, Chicago (1936).

**Bor·ghe'se** (bôr·gā'sā). Family of Italian noblemen, orig. from Siena, including: **Camillo** (1552–1621), elected to papacy as Paul V (*q.v.*). His nephew Cardinal **Scipione Borghese,** *real name* **Caf'fa·rel'li** [käf'fä·rĕl'lē] (d. 1633); built Villa Borghese and founded its celebrated art collection. Prince **Camillo Filippo Lodovico Borghese** (1775–1832); aided French in invasion of Italy and governed Piedmont (1807–14) under French rule; sold Borghese art collection (returned in part, 1815) to Napoleon for Piedmontese national domains; m. (1803) Maria Paulina Buonaparte (1780–1825), Napoleon's sister (see BONAPARTE).

**Bor·ghe'si** (bôr·gā'sē), Conte **Bartolommeo.** 1781–1860. Italian numismatist and epigraphist.

**Bor'gia** (bôr'jä). *Orig. Span. form* **Bor'ja** (bôr'hä). Italian family of Spanish origin, influential in the papacy and in Italy in 15th and 16th centuries, from time of election (1455) of **Alfonso** as Pope Calixtus III (*q.v.*). His nephew **Rodrigo,** who became (1492) Pope Alexander VI (*q.v.*), was, before election as pope, father by Roman woman, Vannozza dei Cattanei, of five children, including **Giovanni** (d. 1497; received duchy of Gandía from king of Spain; murdered, probably at instigation of Cesare), Cesare, and Lucrezia.

**Cesare.** *Eng.* **Caesar.** 1475 or 1476–1507. Created archbishop of Valencia (1492) and cardinal (1493); sent as papal legate (1497) to Naples to crown Frederick of Aragon king; relinquished cardinal's office (1498); to France as legate (1498) to carry to Louis XII pope's bull annulling Louis's marriage; granted duchy of Valentinois; m. (1499) Charlotte d'Albret, sister of king of Navarre; despite failure to conquer all of Romagna, made its duke (1501) by his father; seized cities and districts in central Italy (Piombino, Urbino, Pesaro, etc.), acting with extreme cruelty and treachery, spreading terror in all Italy; opposed by enemies, esp. Pope Julius II (elected 1503); forced to surrender castles to pope; arrested in Naples by Gonzalo de Córdoba and sent to Spain (1504); imprisoned for two years (1504–06); escaped, fled to Navarre, and killed in siege of castle at Viana. His character favorably portrayed by Machiavelli in his *Principe.*

**Lucrezia.** *Eng.* **Lucretia.** 1480–1519. Duchess of **Fer·ra'ra** (fār·rä'rä); b. Rome. Married three times by her father, Pope Alexander VI, for political reasons: (1) to Giovanni Sforza (1493), lord of Pesaro; marriage annulled (1497) when pope's friendliness to Naples made alliance with Sforzas undesirable; (2) to nephew of king of Naples, Alfonso of Aragon (1498), Duke of Bisceglie, murdered (1500) by order of her brother Cesare; (3) with great splendor in Rome to Alfonso of Este, son and heir to duke of Ferrara (1501), who became duke (1505). Set up at Ferrara brilliant court where gathered learned men, poets, and artists, among them Ariosto, Cardinal Bembo, Titian, Dosso Dossi, and Aldus Manutius; devoted rest of her life to education and charity. Cleared by recent research of many accusations of crime and vice.

**Bor'gia** (bôr'jä), **Stefano.** 1731–1804. Italian cardinal and antiquary; known esp. for his archaeological collection.

**Bor'glum** (bôr'glŭm), **Gut'zon** (gŭt's'n), ***in full*** **John Gutzon de la Mothe** (dĕl'ȧ·mŏt'). 1867–1941. American sculptor, b. Idaho. Studios in London and Paris (c. 1894–1901) and in New York (from 1901). Among works are equestrian statue of Sheridan (Washington,

D.C.), large head of Lincoln (Capitol, Washington, D.C.), bronze group *Mares of Diomedes* (Metropolitan Museum of Art, New York), and statues of Beecher, Altgeld, Huntington, William Jennings Bryan, and figures of apostles for Cathedral of St. John the Divine, New York. Designed and began carving Confederate memorial on face of Stone Mountain, Ga., but after controversy with members of association destroyed designs, models, and work. Designed and carved figures of Presidents Washington, Jefferson, Lincoln, and T. Roosevelt, first national memorial federally authorized, financed by State of South Dakota on Mt. Rushmore in the Black Hills. Also painter. His brother **Solon Hannibal** (1868–1922), b. Ogden, Utah, was also a sculptor.

**Borgo, Luca di.** See Luca PACIOLI.

**Bor'go·gno'ne** (bōr'gô·nyō'nâ), **Il.** See Jacques COURTOIS.

**Borgognone, Ambrogio.** *Real name* **Ambrogio Ste'fa·ni** (stā'fä·nē; stâ'fä·nē), *or* **di Ste'fa·no** (-nō), **da Fos·sa'no** (fôs·sä'nô). fl. 1473–1524. Italian painter; known esp. for his decorations in the Certosa (Pavia), as *The Crucifixion* and altars of St. Ambrose and St. Siro.

**Bo'ri** (bô'rē), **Lu·cre'zia** (lōō·krā'tsyä). *Nee* **Lu·cre'cia Bor'ja Gon·zá'lez de Rian'cho** (lōō·krā'thyä bôr'hä gôn·thä'lāth thā ryän'chō). 1887–1960. Spanish lyric soprano; with Metropolitan Opera Co., N.Y. (1913 ff.).

**Bo'ring** (bō'rĭng), **Edwin Gar'ri·gues** (găr'ĭ·gūz). 1886–1968. American psychologist; known for work on theoretical psychology, psychophysics, and sensation.

**Bo'ris** (bō'rĭs; bŏr'ĭs; *Bulg.* bô·rĭs', bô'rĭs). Name of three rulers of Bulgaria:

**Boris I.** d. 907. Czar (852–889). Defeated in campaigns against Germans (853) and Serbs (860); converted to Christianity (865) after persuasion by Michael III, Byzantine emperor; accepted (866–870) primacy of Rome; strong sovereign who did much to spread Christianity in Bulgaria; abdicated (889) and retired to monastery; returned briefly (893) to depose his son Vladimir.

**Boris II.** Czar (969–972). Forced to abdicate.

**Boris III.** 1894–1943. King (czar) of Bulgaria (1918–43). Eldest son of Ferdinand I; b. Sofia. Succeeded on his father's abdication; christened (1896) an Orthodox Catholic; m. (1930) Princess Giovanna, daughter of Victor Emmanuel III of Italy. During events that led up to World War II, he tried to steer a neutral course; but sided with Germany (1941).

**Boris Godunov.** See GODUNOV.

**Bor'ja** (bôr'hä), Saint **Francisco de.** Duque **de Gan·dí'a** (gän·dē'ä). *Ital.* **Francesco Bor'gia** (bôr'jä). 1510–1572. Spanish Jesuit, b. Gandía. Attendant at court of Charles V (1528); accompanied Charles to Africa (1535) and in Provence (1536); viceroy of Catalonia. Succeeded father as duke (1543); resigned viceroyalty and interested himself in forwarding work of Society of Jesus. Joined Jesuit order; ordained priest; commissary general of order in Spain, Portugal, and the Indies (1554); succeeded Laynez as general of Society of Jesus (1565). Beatified by Urban VIII (1624) and canonized by Clement X (1671).

**Bör'je·son'** (bûr'yĕ·sôn'), **Johan Laurentius Helenus.** 1835–1910. Swedish sculptor. Works include equestrian statue of Charles X Gustavus (Malmö) and *Youth with a Tortoise* (Stockholm).

**Bör'jes·son'** (bûr'yĕs·sôn'), **Johan.** 1790–1866. Swedish lyric poet; author of the historical drama *Erik XIV* (1846).

**Bor'ke·nau** (bôr'kĕ·nou), **Franz.** 1900–1957. German writer; left-wing member of German Labor party; author of *The Spanish Cockpit* (1938), *New German Empire* (1939), etc.

**Bor'lase** (bôr'lăs), **William.** 1695–1772. English clergyman, antiquary, and naturalist. Author of *Antiquities of Cornwall* (1754), *Natural History of Cornwall* (1758), etc.

**Bor'laug** (bôr'lôg), **Norman Ernest.** 1914– . Am. agronomist, b. Cresco, Iowa. Awarded Nobel peace prize (1970) for development of new crop strains of wheat and rice to ease world hunger.

**Bor'mann** (bôr'män), **Martin Ludwig.** 1900–?1945. German Nazi leader; joined Nazi party (1925); member of highest governing body of the Nazi party (from 1933). Rudolf Hess's chief of staff (1933–41) and successor as Hitler's 3d deputy; reported dead (1945) but sentenced to death in absentia as war criminal (1946).

**Born** (bôrn), **Bertrand de.** Vicomte **de Haute'fort'** (dē ōt'fôr'). 12th-century French soldier and troubadour; played important part in encouraging sons of Henry II of England to rebellion; composed satires and lyrics of love and war; mentioned by Dante in the *Divina Commedia* (*Inferno* XXVIII, 134).

**Born** (bôrn), **Ignaz von.** 1742–1791. Austrian mineralogist and metallurgist. Introduced process of extracting silver from ores by amalgamation; introduced improvements in mining, salt working, and bleaching.

**Born, Max.** 1882–1970. German physicist; known for work on the theory of relativity, the quantum theory, the space-lattice theory of crystals, and atomic structure. Awarded Nobel prize in physics (1954) with W. Bothe.

**Bör'ne** (bûr'nĕ), **Ludwig.** *Orig.* **Löb Ba'ruch** (bä'rōōĸ). 1786–1837. German political writer and satirist, of Jewish decent. Embraced Christianity and changed name (1818); to Paris (1830). Published journals, in which he criticized the German stage and politics, and worked for political freedom and social reforms; became a leader of new literary party "Young Germany," and engaged in bitter controversy with Heine.

**Bor'neil'** (bôr'nâ'y'), **Giraud de.** 1150?–?1220. French troubadour, mentioned by Dante in the *Divina Commedia* (*Purgatorio* xxvi).

**Bor'net'** (bôr'nĕ'), **Jean Baptiste Édouard.** 1828–1911. French botanist, authority on red algae and lichens. See Gustave Adolphe THURET.

**Bor'nier'** (bôr'nyā'), Vicomte **Henri de.** 1825–1901. French poet and playwright.

**Bor'no'** (bôr'nō'), **Louis Eustache Antoine François Joseph.** 1865–1942. Haitian lawyer and public official, b. Port-au-Prince. Member of Permanent Court of International Justice at The Hague (1919–22); president of Haiti for two terms (1922–30).

**Bo·ro·din'** (bŭ·rŭ·dyēn'), **Aleksandr Porfirevich.** 1834–1887. Russian composer and chemist; promoter of new Russian musical school. Studied medicine and chemistry; became military physician. Author of articles and monographs on chemistry. Devoted much leisure time to study of music and was stimulated by friendship with Balakirev and Liszt; composer of opera *Prince Igor* (begun 1869; completed by Rimski-Korsakov and Glazunov, 1889), containing the Polovtsi dances popularized by the Diaghilev troupe, and of the symphonic poem *In the Steppes of Central Asia* (1880), symphonies, string music, songs.

**Borodin, Mikhail Markovich.** *Orig. surname* **Gru·sen·berg'** (grōō·zyĕn·byārk'). 1884–1953. Russian diplomat and political adviser. Joined Russian Social Democratic party (1903); after Russian Revolution (1917), became active Communist worker; called to Canton (1923) by Sun Yat-sen as political adviser to Kuomintang; head of Communist government (1924–27) established at Hankow; broke with Chiang Kai-shek (1927) and forced to return to Russia.

**Bo'ro·je·vić von Boj'na** (bō'rô·yĕ·vēt·y' fôn boi'nä),

Baron **Svetozar.** 1856–1920. Commander in Austrian army; b. in Croatia. In World War, leader of 3d army at Przemyśl (1914), commander of 5th army in 11 battles on Isonzo front, and field marshal general and commander in chief of Austrian army on the Italian front (1918).

**Bo'ro'tra'** (bô'rô'trà'), **Jean.** 1898– . French lawn tennis player. Member of Davis Cup team (1925–33) that won cup (1927) and successfully defended it (1928–32). Secretary general of physical education under Vichy government (1940).

**Bor'ough** (bûr'ô), *or* **Bur'rough** (bûr'ô). Name of an English family including the following members whose accounts appear in Hakluyt: **Stephen** (1525–1584), navigator; master of first English ship to sail around North Cape (named by him) to Russia (1553); in charge of three ships sent to open trade relations with Muscovy (1560). His brother **William** (1536–1599), comptroller of queen's navy; vice-admiral under Drake in Cádiz expedition (1587); in command of ship against Armada (1588). **Christopher** (fl. 1579–1587), son of Stephen, interpreter of Russian for the Muscovy Company's expedition to Media and Persia (1579).

**Borovský, Havel.** Pseudonym of Karel HAVLÍČEK.

**Bo·row'ski** (bô·rŏf'skĭ), **Fe'lix** (fē'lĭks). 1872–1956. Composer and educator, b. Burton, Eng.; to U.S. (1897). President, Chicago Musical Coll. (1916–25); superintendent, Chicago Civic Music Association (1926–32); professor of musicology, Northwestern U. (from 1937). Composer of many orchestral works, chamber music, etc.

**Bor'rel'ly'** (bô'rĕ'lē'), **Alphonse Louis Nicolas.** 1842–1926. French astronomer; discoverer of a number of variable stars, nebulae, comets, and small planets.

**Bor'ro·me'o** (bōr'rô·mâ'ô), Saint **Carlo.** 1538–1584. Italian nobleman and ecclesiastic. Created cardinal and archbishop of Milan (1560); known esp. for his ecclesiastical reforms. Founded order of Oblates of St. Ambrose (1578). His nephew Conte **Federigo** (1564–1631), also a cardinal and archbishop of Milan, founded Ambrosian Library at Milan (1609).

**Bor'ro·mi'ni** (bōr'rô·mē'nē), **Francesco.** 1599–1667. Italian architect and sculptor. Associated with Maderna and Bernini; master of baroque style. Known esp. for façade of Sant'Agnese in Piazza Navona, Rome.

**Bor'row** (bŏr'ō), **George.** 1803–1881. English author and linguist. Educ. chiefly in Edinburgh; familiar with seven languages (by 1819); neglected study of law to acquire languages, including Romany. To London as compiler (1824); produced *Celebrated Trials* (1825). Tramped through England, met gypsies and road girl celebrated as Isopel Berners. As agent of Bible Society, toured Russia, Spain, Portugal, Morocco (1833–40), studying language of each country; published translation of Danish ballads (1826) and, in Russia, *Targum*, translations from thirty languages and dialects (1835). m. widow of naval officer (1840) and settled at Oulton Broad, Norfolk, making several excursions through Celtic Britain; welcomed gypsies to camp on his estate and cultivated their friendship; compiled lexicon of Romany (1874). Author of *The Zincali, or the Gypsies in Spain* (1841), *The Bible in Spain*, which made him famous (1843), *Lavengro* (1851) and its sequel *Romany Rye* (1857), both dealing with gypsy life, and *Wild Wales* (1862).

**Bort, Léon Philippe Teisserenc de.** See TEISSERENC DE BORT.

**Bort·nyan'ski** (bŭrt·nyån'skû·ĭ; *Angl.* -skĭ), **Dmitri Stephanovich.** 1752–1825. Russian composer; pupil of Galuppi. Director (1779–1825) of Court Church Choir, Petrograd, later (from 1796) named Imperial Chapel Choir, which he reformed and brought to high state of efficiency.

**Bor'ton** (bôr't'n), **Stockton.** 1852–1907. American inventor, b. Moorestown, N.J. Associated with Willcox & Gibbs Sewing Machine Co. (1880–1907); developed and perfected high-speed sewing machine, receiving more than fifty patents for his inventions.

**Boru, Brian.** See BRIAN.

**Bo'ry' de Saint' Vin'cent'** (bô'rē' dē săN' văN'säN'), **Jean Baptiste Georges.** 1778?–1846. French geographer and naturalist. Explored Mauritius, Réunion, St. Helena, Morea, the Cyclades.

**Bos, Hieronymus.** See BOSCH.

**Bo'san·quet** (bō'z'n·kĕt; -kĭt), **Bernard.** 1848–1923. English Hegelian philosopher; disciple of T. H. Green. Author of *The Essentials of Logic* (1895), *Philosophical Theory of the State* (1899).

**Bos'boom-Tous'saint'** (bŏz'bōm·tōō'săN'), **Anna Louisa Geertruida,** *nee* **Toussaint.** 1812–1886. Dutch historical and romantic novelist; author of *Het Huis Lauernesse* (1840), a cycle (1846–55) dealing with Robert Dudley's adventures in Low Countries. Married (1851) **Johannes Bosboom** (1817–1891), Dutch church and architectural painter.

**Bos·cán' Al'mo·ga·ver'** (bŏs·kän' äl'mô·gä·vĕr'), **Juan.** 1493?–1542. Spanish poet; at court of Charles V, Granada (1519 ff.); adapted Italian meters and verse forms to Spanish poetry; credited with founding Italian school of poetry in Spain.

**Bos·caw'en** (bŏs·kô'ĕn; -kô'ĕn), **Edward.** 1711–1761. English naval officer. Known as "Old Dreadnought." Won distinction at taking of Porto Bello (1739) and siege of Cartagena (1741); won victory off Finisterre (1747); intercepted French squadron off Newfoundland, capturing 2 ships and 1500 men (1755); admiral (1758); assisted at taking of Louisburg and island of Cape Breton (1758); defeated French Toulon fleet in Lagos Bay (1759).

**Bosc' d'An'tic'** (bôsk' däN'tēk'), **Louis Augustin Guillaume.** 1759–1828. French naturalist. His father, **Paul** (1726–1784), was physician to Louis XV.

**Bosch** (bŏs) *or* **Bos, Hieronymus.** *Real name* **Hieronymus van Ae'ken** (ä'kĕn) *or* **van A'ken.** 1450?–1516. Dutch painter, b. Hertogenbosch, Netherlands. Painter of religious pictures, genre pieces, caricatures, and fantastic representations of devils, monstrosities, and other gruesome subjects.

**Bosch, Jan van den.** See Jan VAN DEN BOSCH.

**Bosch** (bŏsh), **Karl.** 1874–1940. German industrial chemist. Adapted the Haber process (for the synthesis of ammonia) to the commercial production of ammonia; awarded, jointly with Friedrich Bergius, the 1931 Nobel prize in chemistry. See Fritz HABER.

**Bosch, Robert August.** 1861–1942. German engineer and industrialist; founder of Robert Bosch Co., Stuttgart, manufacturers of magnetos, igniters, automatic lubricators, and other equipment for power-driven engines and vehicles.

**Bo'sco** (bôs'kô), Don **Giovanni.** 1815–1888. Italian priest; founded order of Salesian Fathers (1864).

**Bos'co·vich** (bôs'kô·vēch), **Ruggiero Giuseppe.** 1711–1787. Italian mathematician, astronomer, and physicist, b. Ragusa, Dalmatia. Joined Jesuits (1725); taught in Rome (1740), Pavia, Milan; first in Italy to write in advocacy of Newton's theories. Advanced a molecular theory of matter (1758).

**Bose** (bōs; bŏs; bŏsh), Sir **Ja·ga·dis'** (jȧ·gȧ·dēs') **Chan'dra** (chŭn'drȧ) *or* **Chun'der** (chŭn'dĕr). 1858–1937. Indian physicist and plant physiologist. Professor, Presidency College, Calcutta (1885–1915); founder and director of Bose Research Institute, Calcutta. Invented device similar to the wireless coherer and an instrument for indicating the refraction of electric waves, and an instrument (the crescograph) for rendering perceptible the growth of plants. Author of *Response in the Living and Non-Living, The Physiology of Photosynthesis, The Nervous Mechanism of Plants*, etc.

**Bose, Sub·has'** (sho͝ob·häsh'; so͝ob·häsh') **Chan'dra** (chŭn'drȧ). 1897–1945. Hindu politician and nationalist; supported Gandhi and joined Swaraj party (c. 1920); advocated complete independence for India; many times imprisoned; president of All-India Trades Union Congress (1929–31); wrote *The Indian Struggle* (1935); president of the Indian National Congress (1939).

**Bo'sio'** (bô'zyō'; bô'zyō), **François Joseph.** 1769?–1845. French sculptor; carved bas-reliefs of Column Vendôme in Paris, statue of Louis XIV in Paris, and portrait busts of Napoleon, Joséphine, Louis XVIII, etc.

**Bos'quet'** (bôs'kĕ'), **Pierre Jean François.** 1810–1861. French army officer; division commander in French army in Crimea; won victory at Alma; saved British army at Inkerman; wounded in assault on the Malakoff (Sept. 8, 1855); created senator and marshal of France (1856).

**Boss** (bŏs), **Lewis.** 1846–1912. American astronomer; director, Dudley Observatory, Albany, N.Y. (from 1876). Compiler of two catalogues of stars.

**Bos'si** (bôs'sē), Baron **Giuseppe Carlo Aurelio de'.** 1758–1823. Italian politician and poet.

**Bossi, Marco Enrico.** 1861–1925. Italian composer.

**Bos'su'** (bô'sü'), **Adam le.** See ADAM DE LA HALLE.

**Bossu, René Le.** See LE BOSSU.

**Bos'su' d'Ar'ras', le** (lẽ bô'sü' dȧ'räs'). = ADAM DE LA HALLE.

**Bos'suet'** (bô'sü·ĕ'), **Jacques Bénigne.** 1627–1704. French Roman Catholic prelate, b. Dijon. Tutor to the dauphin (1670–81); bishop of Meaux (1681); renowned as pulpit orator. Author of *Oraisons Funèbres*, etc.

**Bos'sut'** (bô'sü'), **Charles.** 1730–1814. French mathematician; edited works of Pascal.

**Bos'ton** (bŏs'tŭn), **Thomas.** 1677–1732. Scottish Presbyterian clergyman. One of the twelve "Marrow Men," defenders of *The Marrow of Modern Divinity* by "E.F." (perhaps the English theologian Edward Fisher, fl. 1627–55) advocating Calvinism, against charge of Scottish General Assembly that it was too free in offers of salvation (1720). Author of *The Fourfold State* (1720), and *Crook in the Lot*, once a favorite in rural Scotland.

**Bo'ström** (bo͞o'strûm), **Christoffer Jakob.** 1797–1866. Swedish philosopher. Championed "rational idealism," in which true reality is represented as spiritual only; held theory that society as well as the individual is a thought of God, and the ultimate ideal of political development is a rational system of states in harmonious obedience to a constitutional monarch.

**Bost'wick** (bŏst'wĭk), **Arthur Elmore.** 1860–1942. American librarian; on staff of New York Public Library (1895–99; 1901–09); librarian of St. Louis Public Library (1909–38).

**Bos'well** (bŏz'wĕl; -wĕl), **James.** *Called* **Boz'zy** (bŏz'ĭ). 1740–1795. Scottish lawyer and biographer of Samuel Johnson. Son of **Alexander Boswell,** Lord **Au'chin-leck'** (ô'kĭn·lĕk'; ô'kĭn-), lord justiciary. Acquainted with Voltaire, Rousseau, Wilkes (in Italy), General Paoli. Met Dr. Johnson in London (1763), visited him frequently (1772–84), toured Hebrides with him (1773), was elected member of Literary Club (1773); took notes unceasingly of Dr. Johnson's conversations. Succeeded to father's estate (1782); called to English bar (1786); to London (1789). Author of *Account of Corsica* (1768), *Journal of Tour to Hebrides* (1786), *Life of Samuel Johnson*, masterpiece of biography (1791), letters (ed. by C. B. Tinker, 1924), and miscellaneous writings, as in the Malahide collection (pub. 1928 ff., after acquisition from a descendant, Lord Talbot de Malahide). His eldest son, Sir **Alexander** (1775–1822), antiquary and poet, issued reprints of old poems from his private press; Conservative M.P. (1818–21). A younger son, **James** (1778–1822), lawyer, assisted E. Malone with second edition of Shakespeare, and edited third variorum Shakespeare (1821).

**Bos'worth** (bŏz'wûrth; -wẽrth), **Joseph.** 1789–1876. English clergyman and philologist. Author of *An Anglo-Saxon Dictionary* (1838), which was edited and enlarged after his death by Professor **Thomas Northcote Tol'ler** [tŏl'ẽr] (part I, 1882; part II, 1898; supplement, 1908).

**Bosworth, William Welles.** 1869–1966. American architect; practiced in Boston and New York. Among structures designed by him are Rockefeller home at Pocantico Hills, N.Y., American Telephone and Telegraph Co. office building in New York City, buildings for M.I.T. at Cambridge, Mass.

**Bote'ler** (bŭt'lẽr). Former variant spelling of BUTLER.

**Bo·te'lho de Ma·ga·lhães'** (bo͞o·tā'lyo͞o thĕ mă·gȧ-lyāēNs'), **Benjamin Constant.** *Also known as* **Benjamin Cons·tant'** (kōNs·tăNnt'). 1833–91. Brazilian diplomat.

**Bo·te'ro** (bō·tā'rō), **Giovanni.** 1540–1617. Italian writer and political economist; known for his theories on growth of population.

**Bot'e·tourt** (bŏt'ĕ·tŏt), Baron **de. Norborne Berke'-ley** (bûrk'lĭ; *Brit. usu.* bärk'-). 1718?–1770. Colonial governor of Virginia (1768–70), of same family as William Berkeley (1608?–1677).

**Boteville, Francis** and **William.** See William THYNNE.

**Bo'tha** (bō'tȧ), **Louis.** 1862–1919. South African soldier and statesman, b. Natal. Commanded Boer army before Ladysmith; defeated British at Colenso; commander in chief (1900). Carried on peace negotiations; became first prime minister of Transvaal (1907); headed Transvaal delegation at union convention (1908–09); first prime minister of Union of South Africa (1910–19). Put down Afrikaner revolt against intervention in World War I, and won surrender of German forces in South West Africa (1915); with Jan Smuts attended Paris peace conference as representative of South Africa (1919).

**Bo'the** (bō'tĕ), **Walther.** 1891–1957. German physicist. Awarded Nobel prize in physics (1954) with Max Born. Developed and worked with coincidence method.

**Both'mer** (bōt'mẽr), Count **Felix von.** 1852–1937. Bavarian general; led 2d Bavarian reserve corps at Lorraine (1914) and German forces in Galicia (1915–16); colonel general of 19th army, Lorraine (1918).

**Both'well** (bŏth'wĕl; -wĕl; bŏth'-), 4th Earl of. **James Hep'burn** (hĕb'ẽrn; -ûrn). 1536?–1578. Scottish Protestant nobleman. Husband of Mary, Queen of Scots. Educ. by his granduncle, Patrick Hepburn, Bishop of Moray. Adherent of French party, supported government of Mary of Guise, queen regent, whom his father, **Patrick** (1512?–1556), 3d earl, brought to Stirling (1543). Imprisoned for conspiracy to seize person of young Queen Mary (1562); escaped to France until recalled by Mary, who took refuge with him after murder of Rizzio (1566). Superintended murder of Darnley (1567); acquitted of murder; kidnaped Mary (April 24, 1567); married Mary (May 15, 1567); made Duke of **Ork'ney** (ôrk'nĭ) and **Shet'land** (shĕt'lănd). Driven by wrath of nobles into separating from queen and fleeing to Orkney and Shetland, thence to Norway; died insane, prisoner of Danish king. His nephew **Francis Stewart Hepburn,** 5th earl (d. 1624), son of a natural son of James V, called by his mother's name, joined Catholic rebellion against James VI, attempted to capture king (1591), was denounced by James as a pretender to throne (1592), fled to Normandy (1594); d. Naples.

**Bot'olph** (bŏt'ŏlf; bō'tŏlf; bô·tôlf') *or* **Bot'ulph** (bŏt'ŭlf; bō'tŭlf; bô·tŭlf'), Saint. d. 680. English Benedictine monk and founder of a monastery probably on site of present Boston (Botolphstown).

**Botsares, Markos.** See BOZZARIS.

**Bots'ford** (bŏts'fẽrd), **George Willis.** 1862–1917. American historian; professor, Columbia Univ. (1910–17). Author of textbooks on ancient history.

**Bott** (bôt), **Jean** (zhäɴ) **Joseph.** 1826–1895. German violinist and composer.

**Bot'ta** (*It.* bôt'tä; *Fr.* bô'tȧ'), **Carlo Giuseppe Guglielmo.** 1766–1837. Italian physician and historian; exiled to France (c. 1792). His son **Paul Émile** (1802–1870), French archaeologist, directed search for Assyrian antiquities in ruins near Khorsabad.

**Bot'te·si'ni** (bōt'tā·zē'nē), **Giovanni.** 1821?–1889. Italian musician and composer; reputed world's greatest contrabassist. Director, Conservatory of Parma (after 1871). Among his compositions are the opera *Cristoforo Colombo* (1847), oratorio *Garden of Olivet* (1887), symphonies, a quartet, and overtures.

**Bött'ger** (bût'gẽr), **Adolf.** 1815–1870. German poet; translator of works of Byron (1840), poems by Pope, Goldsmith, Milton, and Ossian, and Longfellow's *Hiawatha.*

**Bött'ger** (bût'gẽr) *or* **Bött'cher** (bût'κẽr) *or* **Böt'ti·ger** (bût'ĭ·gẽr), **Johann Friedrich.** 1682–1719. German maker of porcelains. With E. von Tschirnhaus, produced white china and a reddish-brown stoneware called Böttger ware; established factory at Dresden, later (1710) removed to Meissen, for production of Dresden china, which he is credited with originating.

**Bot'ti·cel'li** (bōt'tē·chĕl'lē; *Angl.* bŏt'ĭ·chĕl'ĭ), **Sandro.** *Orig.* **Alessandro di Mariano de'i Fi'li·pe'pi** (dā'ē fē'lē·pā'pē). 1444?–1510. Italian painter, b. Florence. Pupil of Fra Filippo Lippi; protégé of many great Florentine families, and esp. of Lorenzo di Pierfrancesco de' Medici, a cousin of Lorenzo the Magnificent. Assisted in decoration of Sistine Chapel (c. 1482). Follower of Savonarola (after 1497). Among his works are *The Life of Moses, The Temptation of Christ,* and *Punishment of Korah, Dathan, and Abiram* (frescoes, all in Sistine Chapel), *Fortitude, Adoration of the Magi, The Magnificat, Spring, Birth of Venus* (*Venus Anadyomene*), *Calumny, Coronation of the Virgin, Annunciation* (all in Uffizi Gallery), *Nativity, Mars and Venus* (both in National Gallery, Florence), several Madonnas, and illustrations for Dante's *Divina Commedia* (Berlin Museum and Vatican Library).

**Bötticher, Paul Anton.** See Paul Anton de LAGARDE.

**Böt'ti·ger** (bût'ĭ·gẽr), **Johann Friedrich.** See BÖTTGER.

**Böttiger, Karl August.** 1760–1835. German philologist and archaeologist.

**Böt'ti·ger** (bût'tĭ·gẽr), **Karl Vilhelm.** 1807–1878. Swedish poet and literary historian.

**Bot'tin'** (bô'tăɴ'), **Sébastien.** 1764–1853. French government administrator and statistician; edited *Almanach du Commerce de Paris* (1819–53), later acquired by another company and published under name *Annuaire du Commerce Didot-Bottin* and referred to commonly as "Bottin."

**Bot·tome'** (bŏ·tōm'), **Phyllis.** 1884–1963. English writer of novels and short stories, b. England, dau. of American clergyman; m. (1917) A. Ernan Forbes Dennis. First novel, *Raw Material* (1905). Engaged in relief work in Vienna (1919 ff.), her experiences in Vienna serving as basis for *Old Wine.* Other books: *Private Worlds* (1934), *Level Crossing* (1936), *Danger Signal* (1939), *Mortal Storm* (1940), *London Pride* (1941).

**Bot'tom·ley** (bŏt'ŭm·lĭ), **Gordon.** 1874–1948. English poet and dramatist; student of Elizabethans. His works on Shakespearean themes include plays *King Lear's Wife* (1915) and *Gruach* (1921), on Icelandic saga material the one-act tragedy *The Riding to Lithend* (1909), on Renaissance Italy three dramatic eclogues *A Vision of Giorgione* (1910), and on Scottish themes the one-act plays *The White Widow* (1936). Author also of lyric verse, as in *Chambers of Imagery* (2 vols., 1907, 1912).

**Bottomley, Horatio William.** 1860–1933. English newspaper editor and proprietor. Established weekly *John Bull,* vehicle of rabid patriotism during World War. M.P. (1906–12, 1918–22). Convicted of misappropriation of funds held in trust (1922), and imprisoned for 5 years.

**Botulph,** Saint. See Saint BOTOLPH.

**Bo'tyov** (bō'tyôf), **Khristo.** *Properly* **Khristo Botyov Pet'kov** (pĕt'kôf). 1847–1876. Bulgarian patriot and poet; attacked Turks and Bulgarian landed proprietors; forced to flee to Rumania. Attempted to raise Bulgarians in revolt against Turks but was killed (May 20, 1876). Excelled as lyric poet (*Poems,* 1875).

**Botzaris, Markos.** See BOZZARIS.

**Bou'bou·li'na** (bōō'bōō·lyē'nä), **Laskarina.** 1783–1825. Patriotic Greek woman, who, during Greek war for independence, armed three ships (1823) and commanded them against Turks; killed in action.

**Bou'chard'** (bōō'shȧr'), **Charles Jacques.** 1837–1915. French physician and biologist. One of first to advocate union of laboratory with clinic and to point out importance of microbiology in medical studies.

**Bou'ché'** (bōō'shā'), **Lou'is** (lōō'ĭ). 1896–1969. American painter, b. New York City; painted murals in International Music Hall at Rockefeller Center, New York, and in Department of Justice building in Washington, D.C.

**Bou'ché'-Le·clercq'** (bōō'shā'lē·klâr'), **Louis Théodore Auguste.** 1842–1923. French historian.

**Bou'cher'** (bōō'shā'), **Alfred.** 1850–1934. French sculptor; studied under Dubois.

**Boucher, François.** 1703–1770. French painter; court painter (1765) and favorite of Mme. de Pompadour; known esp. for historical and pastoral paintings and genre pieces.

**Bou'cher** (bou'chẽr), **Jonathan.** 1738–1804. Anglican clergyman, b. Cumberland, Eng.; in Virginia (1759–75). Author of *A View of the Causes and Consequences of the American Revolution* (1797). His glossary of obsolete and provincial words was published (1807) as *A Supplement to Dr. Johnson's Dictionary of the English Language.*

**Bou'cher'** (bōō'shā'), **Pierre.** Sieur **de Bou'cher'ville'** (bōō'shā'vēl'). 1622–1717. French pioneer in Canada (from 1635). Governor of Three Rivers; author of *Histoire Véritable et Naturelle des Mœurs et des Productions de la Nouvelle France* (1663).

**Boucher de Crève'cœur' de Perthes'** (dē krĕv'kûr' dē pĕrt'), **Jacques.** 1788–1868. French archaeologist and writer of tragedies, fiction, etc. Employed by Napoleon in diplomatic missions; collected Roman and Celtic antiquities; first to prove that man had existed in Pleistocene period. Author of *Antiquités Celtiques et Antédiluviennes* (1847–65).

**Boucher-Desnoyers.** See Auguste G. L. B. DESNOYERS.

**Bou'chor'** (bōō'shôr'), **Joseph Félix.** 1853–1937. French painter; known for paintings of historic episodes of World War (1914–18).

**Bouchor, Maurice.** 1855–1929. French poet and playwright; also designed and worked marionettes.

**Bou'ci·cault** (bōō'sĭ·kō) *or* **Bour'ci·cault** (bōōr'sĭ·kō),

Dion. *Orig.* **Dionysius Lardner Bour′si·quot** (bo͝or′-si·kō). 1820?–1890. Actor and playwright, b. Dublin, Ireland; educ. in England; to New York (1853), with reputation already established. A leading figure on N.Y. stage (1853–62; again 1872–90). Among his plays are *The Octoroon* (1859); *The Colleen Bawn* (1860); *Arrah-na-Pogue* (1864); *The O'Dowd* (1873); *The Shaughraun* (1874); last appearance (1886) in his play *The Jilt.* His son **Dion,** *in full* **Dionysius George** (1859–1929), was also an actor and theater manager, in U.S., England, and Australia.

**Bou′ci′quaut′** (bo͞o′sē′kō′). *Properly* **Jean Le Mein′gre** (lē măN′gr'). d. 1368. French soldier; served under King John, who named him marshal of France. His son **Jean,** *known as* **Boucicquaut II** (1366?–1421), named marshal of France by King Charles VI (1391), accompanied John the Fearless on crusade against Turks (1396); governed Genoa for Charles VI (1401–09); taken prisoner at Agincourt (1415).

**Bou′det′** (bo͞o′dĕ′), Comte **Jean.** 1769–1809. French general; recovered Guadeloupe (1794); distinguished himself under Napoleon at Essling and Aspern (1809).

**Boudicca.** See BOADICEA.

**Bou′din′** (bo͞o′dăN′), **Eugène Louis.** 1825–1898. French painter.

**Bou′di·not** (bo͞o′d'n·ō), **Elias.** 1740–1821. American Revolutionary patriot and philanthropist, b. Philadelphia. Member from N.J., Continental Congress (1777, 1778, 1781–84), U.S. House of Representatives (1789–95). Director, U.S. mint (1795–1805).

**Boué** (bwā), **Ami.** 1794–1881. Geologist, b. Hamburg; cofounder of geological society of France; author of *Mémoires Géologiques et Paléontologiques* (1832), etc.

**Bouet′-Wil′lau′mez′** (bwĕ′vē′yō′mâz′), Count **Louis Édouard.** 1808–1871. French admiral and explorer in Africa.

**Bouf′flers′** (bo͞o′flâr′), Chevalier (*later* Marquis) **Catherine Stanislas Jean de.** 1738–1815. French poet and courtier; brigadier of infantry (1780) and field marshal (1784). Governor of Senegal (1785–88). Émigré in Prussia (1789–1800); lived in retirement on his estates (from 1800).

**Boufflers,** Duc **Louis François de.** 1644–1711. Known as "Chevalier de Boufflers." French lieutenant general (1681) and marshal of France (1694); defended Lille against Prince Eugene (1708) and successfully managed retreat after Malplaquet (1709).

**Bou′gain′ville′** (bo͞o′găN′vēl′), **Louis Antoine de.** 1729–1811. French navigator. Aide-de-camp to Montcalm in Canada (1756); served in Germany in Seven Years' War (1761–63); made unsuccessful attempt to colonize Falkland Islands; commanded first French expedition around the world (1766–69) and visited Tuamotu, Tahiti, the Samoan group, part of the New Hebrides, the Louisiade and New Britain archipelagoes; took part in American Revolution; made a senator and count by Napoleon I. An island of Solomon group and two straits in Solomon and New Hebrides groups bear his name; tropical flowering vine Bougainvillaea named for him.

**Bough′ton** (bou′t'n), **George Henry.** 1833–1905. Painter, b. England; brought up at Albany, N.Y.; resided (after 1861) in London. Chose as chief subjects early American colonial life; illustrator of *Rip Van Winkle* (1893) and *Knickerbocker History* (1886.)

**Boughton, Rutland.** 1878–1960. English composer, esp. of ballets, music dramas, and choral dramas.

**Bou′guer′** (bo͞o′gâr′), **Pierre.** 1698–1758. French hydrographer and mathematician; professor of hydrography, Havre (1730); measured intensity of light of sun as compared with that of moon and thus became one of founders of photometry; sent to Peru (with Godin, La Condamine, and Jussieu, 1735) to measure a degree of the meridian near the equator; invented a heliometer.

**Bou′gue·reau′** (bo͞o′grō′), **Adolphe William.** 1825–1905. French painter; studied under Picot; among his decorative paintings are those for Hôtel Bartholony, including *L'Amour, L'Amitié, La Fortune, Le Printemps, L'Été, La Danse.* Among his religious paintings are *Les Saintes Femmes au Tombeau du Christ, La Vierge, Jésus et Saint Jean.*

**Bou′hé′lier′** (bo͞o′ā′lyā′), **Saint-Georges de.** *Real name* **Georges de Bouhélier-Le·pel′le·tier′** (-lē·pĕl′-tyā′). 1876–1947. French writer; author of verse, fiction, and plays.

**Bou′il·het′** (bo͞o′yĕ′), **Louis.** 1822–1869. French lyric poet and playwright; close friend of Flaubert.

**Bouil′laud′** (bo͞o′yō′), **Jean.** 1796–1881. French physician; one of first to attempt to identify a definite area of the brain as connected with a particular function; studied relationship between lesions of brain and the loss of power of speech.

**Bouil′lé′** (bo͞o′yā′), Marquis **François Claude Amour de.** 1739–1800. French general; commander at Metz (1789); plotted with Louis XVI to get him out of France (1791), but failed and fled to England; joined Condé's army.

**Bouil′lon′** (bo͞o′yôN′). French family of nobility, deriving its name from medieval duchy and town of Bouillon, now part of Luxembourg province, Belgium. The duchy once belonged to the crusader Godefroy (see GODFREY OF BOUILLON); later it came under the houses of **La Marck** (là märk′) and **La Tour′ d'Au′vergne′** (là to͞or′ dō′vĕr′ny'). Members of the latter house in the 16th and 17th centuries were: **Henri de La Tour d'Auvergne,** Duc **de Bouillon** (1555–1623), marshal of France and Calvinist supporter of Henry IV; his elder son **Frédéric Maurice** (1605–1652), duke, soldier, and enemy of Richelieu; and his second son, Marshal Turenne (see TURENNE).

**Robert III de La Marck.** Comte **de Bouillon.** *Also known as* **Seigneur de Fleu′ranges′** (flû′räNzh′) *and* **Le Jeune A′ven′tu′reux′** (lē zhûn à′väN′tü′rû′). 1491?–?1537. French soldier; boyhood companion of Francis I; created marshal of France, and defended Pérouse (1537). His *Mémoires* important source material for history of Louis XII. See LA MARCK.

**Bouil′ly′** (bo͞o′yē′), **Jean Nicolas.** 1763–1842. French playwright and novelist.

**Bou′lain′vil′liers′** (bo͞o′lăN′vē′lyā′), **Henri de.** Comte **de Saint′-Saire′** (săN′sâr′). 1658–1722. French historian.

**Bou′lan′ger′** (bo͞o′läN′zhā′), **Georges Ernest Jean Marie.** 1837–1891. French general, b. Rennes. Served at siege of Metz (1870) but escaped to Paris; commanded army of occupation in Tunis (1884–85) but recalled; minister of war (1886–87); arrested (1887) and deprived of command (1888) for disobedience of orders; aroused popular enthusiasm among elements antagonistic to government; called "Man on Horseback" because he often appeared mounted before Paris crowds; elected deputy from several departments (1889) on platform demanding reform of constitution; movement (Boulangism), to which Bonapartists and party of revenge upon Germany attached themselves, became dangerous (1889); accused of conspiracy by Tirard ministry; fled to Brussels without awaiting trial, later to island of Jersey (1889); committed suicide.

**Boulanger, Gustave Rodolphe Clarence.** 1824–1888. French painter, best known for his Oriental scenes.

**Boulanger, Louis.** 1806–1867. French painter. Painted portraits of Hugo, Balzac, Dumas père, and other notables; religious pictures *Saint Marc, Mater Dolorosa*, etc.

**Bou'lay' de la Meurthe'** (bōō'lā' dē lȧ mûrt'), **Antoine Jacques Claude Joseph.** 1761–1840. French political leader; member of Council of Five Hundred; opposed Jacobinism and despotic policies of Directory. During the Empire, aided in drafting the Code Civil des Français. Banished by Louis XVIII (1815); returned to France (1819) and lived in retirement.

**Boule** (bōōl), **Charles André.** See BOULLE.

**Boule, Pierre Marcellin.** 1861–1942. French paleontologist. Known for work on geology of mountains of central France and on human and other mammalian fossils.

**Boul'ger** (bōl'jẽr), **Demetrius Charles.** 1853–1928. English historian; writer esp. on Asiatic subjects.

**Boul'lay'** (bōō'lā'), **Pierre François Guillaume.** 1777–1869. French pharmacist; with Jean Baptiste André Dumas, formulated and published etherin theory (1828). His son **Félix Polydore** (1806–1835), was also a pharmaceutical chemist; a pupil and collaborator of Dumas.

**Boulle** *or* **Boule** (bōōl), **André Charles.** *Corruptly in English* **Buhl.** 1642–1732. French cabinetmaker; established in Louvre palace as cabinetmaker to king (from 1672). Introduced furniture decorated by inlaying metals, tortoise shell, mother of pearl, and other colored materials on ebony or ebonized wood, a style called buhlwork. Upon his death title of cabinetmaker to king passed to his four sons, **Jean Philippe, Pierre Benoît, Charles André,** and **Charles Joseph.**

**Boul'longne'** (bōō'lôɴn'y') *or* **Bou'logne'** (bōō'lôn'y'), **Bon** (1649–1717) and his brother **Louis de** (1654–1733). French painters.

**Boul'ton** (bōl't'n; -tŭn), **Matthew.** 1728–1809. English manufacturer and engineer. Invented process of steel inlay; became partner of James Watt (1775) and with him established plant for manufacturing steam engines; established new copper coinage for Great Britain (1797).

**Bou·quet'** (bōō·kā'), **Henry.** 1719–1765. British officer in America, b. Switzerland. To America (1756). Served (1758) in expedition against Fort Duquesne. Naturalized by Maryland and Pennsylvania. Instrumental in crushing the Indian rebellion under Pontiac (1763).

**Bou'quet'** (bōō'kĕ'), Dom **Martin.** 1685–1754. French Benedictine monk who began editing of *Rerum Gallicarum et Francicarum Scriptores* (8 vols., 1738–52), a collection of historical documents.

**Bou'quet' de la Grye'** (bōō'kĕ' dē lȧ grē'y'), **Jean Jacques Anatole.** 1827–1909. French hydrographic engineer.

**Bou'ras'sa'** (bōō'rȧ'sȧ'), **Henri.** 1868–1952. Grandson of Louis Joseph Papineau. French-Canadian journalist and politician, b. Montreal. Contributor to *Le Nationaliste* in Montreal (from 1897); editor of independent newspaper *Le Devoir* (from 1910). Member of Dominion House of Commons (1896–99; 1900–07; 1925; 1926); Nationalist party leader (from 1900). Opposed French-Canadian support of British policy in Boer War and Canadian participation in the World War.

**Bour'ba'ki'** (bōōr'bȧ'kē'), **Charles Denis Sauter.** 1816–1897. French general; served in Crimean War (1854–55) and Italian campaign (battle of Solferino, 1859); commanded Imperial Guard at Metz (1870) and failed to break through Prussian lines; retired (1881).

**Bour'bon** (bōōr'bŭn; *Fr.* bōōr'bôɴ'). French royal family, named from a castle and seigniory in central France, whose descendants formed ruling dynasties in France, Spain, and Naples. Its remote ancestor (9th century) was Baron **Ai'mar** (ī'mär; ĕ'mȧr'), one of whose descendants, an heiress of Bourbon, married (1272) **Robert de France** (1256–1318), Count of **Cler'mont'** (klĕr'môɴ'), 6th son of Louis IX. Barony raised to a duchy and peerage (1327). The eldest branch: Robert's son **Louis I** (1279–1341), 1st Duc **de Bourbon** and **Peter I, Louis II, John I, Charles I,** and **John II,** with whom the eldest line as rulers became extinct; others of the eldest line were **Charles** (1435–1488), Cardinal de Bourbon, collector of tapestries and books, son of Charles I and brother of John II, and last of the male line, Charles (1490–1527), Duc de Bourbon (*q.v.*). There were many collateral branches, especially those of Vendôme, Condé, Montpensier, Conti, Soissons, and Parma. See also CHARLES, dukes of Parma. The most important royal lines:
*France:* Henry IV, first Bourbon king of France (1589–1610), was Henry (III) of Navarre, son of **Anthony of Bourbon** (d. 1562), Duke of **Ven'dôme'** (väɴ'dōm'), who married (1548) Jeanne d'Albret, a descendant in the fifth generation of Charles V, Valois king of France; successors of Henry IV were (1610–1793) Louis XIII, XIV, XV, XVI, and during the Restoration (1814–30), Louis XVIII and Charles X, and Louis Philippe (1830–48) of the Bourbon-Orléans line.
*Spain:* Philip V, first Bourbon king of Spain (1700–24, 1724–46), was great-grandson of Philip IV (1621–65), who had married Elizabeth, daughter of Henry IV of France; successors of Philip V were Louis (1724) and (1746–1931) Ferdinand VI, Charles III and IV, Ferdinand VII, Isabella II, Alfonso XII and XIII.
*Naples:* Charles IV, founder of Neapolitan Bourbon branch, was third son of Philip V of Spain and was made king of Naples and Sicily (1735); acceded to throne of Spain (1759) as Charles III and resigned Naples to his son Ferdinand, who as Ferdinand IV of Naples was expelled by Napoleon (1805) and restored as Ferdinand I (1815–25), King of the Two Sicilies; successors of Ferdinand were Francis I, Ferdinand II, and Francis II, whose kingdom became a part of the new Italy (1860); this branch is extinct.
*Orléans,* a younger house, sometimes known as **Bourbon-Orléans:** originated from Philippe, Duke of Orléans, brother of Louis XIV, whose great-great-great-grandson was Louis Philippe, King of France (1830–48); members of this branch have in recent years been the chief claimants to the throne of France. See entries at ORLÉANS. See *Tables* (*in Appendix*) for FRANCE and SPAIN, and individual biographies of all rulers mentioned above.

**Bourbon,** Duc **Charles de.** *Commonly called* **Con'né'ta'ble de Bour'bon'** (kô'nā'tȧ'bl' dē bōōr'bôɴ'), *i.e.* Constable Bourbon. 1490–1527. Of younger branch of House of Bourbon; son of Gilbert, Count of Montpensier. Became duke (1505); created constable of France (1515) for bravery at battle of Marignano. Quarreled with King Francis I and (1523) concluded private alliance with Emperor Charles V and Henry VIII of England; aided Imperial army in driving French from Italy (1524); unsuccessfully besieged Marseille (1524); took part in defeat of Francis at Pavia (1525); made duke of Milan by Charles V (1526). Led army of Spanish and German mercenaries in attack on Rome (1527) and mortally wounded, it is said, by Benvenuto Cellini.

**Bourbon,** Cardinal **Charles de.** 1523–1590. Uncle of Henry IV. Archbishop of Rouen and cardinal; Catholic leader; proclaimed king as Charles X by the Guises (1589); died soon after their defeat by Henry IV.

**Bourbon,** Duc **Louis Henri de.** Prince **de Con'dé'** (dē kôɴ'dā'). *Generally known by his title* **Mon·sieur' le Duc'** (mē·syû' lē dük'). 1692–1740. Member of council for education of Louis XV in his minority; profited by Law's Mississippi scheme; prime minister (1723–26); exiled by his successor, Cardinal de Fleury.

**Bourbon–Orléans.** Name of French noble family. See ORLÉANS, 4.

**Bour′chier** (bou′chẽr), **Arthur.** 1864–1927. English actor and manager. m. Violet Vanbrugh, actress (1894). Actor-manager, Garrick Theatre (1900–06); joined Sir Herbert Beerbohm Tree (1910). Chief parts: Macbeth, Shylock, Iago, King Henry VIII, Bottom, John Silver (in *Treasure Island*), Old Bill (in *The Better 'Ole*).

**Bourchier, John.** See BERNERS.

**Bourchier, Thomas.** 1404?–1486. English prelate, descendant of King Edward III. Archbishop of Canterbury (1454); lord chancellor (1455). Became Yorkist (1459). Crowned Edward IV (1461) and his queen, Elizabeth Woodville (1465). Installed as cardinal (1473). Crowned Richard III (1483), and Henry VII (1485), and married Henry VII to Elizabeth of York (1486).

**Bourcicault.** See BOUCICAULT.

**Bour′da′loue′** (bo͞or′dȧ′lo͞o′), **Louis.** 1632–1704. French Jesuit theologian; professor at Bourges; court preacher (from 1670), known for saintly character and fervid eloquence.

**Bour′deau′** (bo͞or′dō′), **Louis.** 1824–1900. French philosopher; author of *Le Problème de la Mort* (1892) and *Le Problème de la Vie* (1901). His nephew **Jean** (1848–1928), was a student of philosophy and of socialism.

**Bour′delle′** (bo͞or′dĕl′), **Émile.** 1861–1929. French sculptor; collaborator with Rodin (to c. 1902).

**Bour·dil′lon** (bẽr·dĭl′yŭn), **Francis William.** 1852–1921. English poet. Author of poem *The Night Has a Thousand Eyes*, etc.

**Bourdin, Maurice.** See Antipope GREGORY VIII.

**Bour′don′** (bo͞or′dôN′), **Sébastien.** 1616–1671. French painter, chiefly of historical themes.

**Bourdon de l'Oise′** (dẽ lwȧz′), **François Louis.** c. 1758–1798. Leader among French Revolutionists; aided in convicting and executing Louis XVI; aided in overthrow of Robespierre (1794); turned Royalist in sympathies; proscribed by Directory; transported to French Guiana.

**Bour′gault′–Du′cou′dray′** (bo͞or′gō′dü′ko͞o′drā′), **Louis Albert.** 1840–1910. French composer, esp. of choral works; compiled collections of folk tunes.

**Bour′ge·lat′** (bo͞or′zhẽ·lȧ′), **Claude.** 1712–1779. French veterinarian; founded and directed at Lyon (1761) first veterinary school in Europe.

**Bour′geois′** (bo͞or′zhwȧ′), **Auguste.** See ANICET-BOURGEOIS.

**Bourgeois, Émile.** 1857–1934. French historian; professor at U. of Paris.

**Bourgeois, Léon Victor Auguste.** 1851–1925. French statesman, b. Paris. Premier of France (1895–96); headed French delegation to Hague Peace Conferences (1899; 1907); member, Permanent Court of Arbitration at The Hague. One of drafters of the Covenant of the League of Nations (1919); chairman of first meeting of league. Awarded Nobel peace prize for year 1920.

**Bour′geois** (bo͞or′zhwä), Sir **Peter Francis.** 1756–1811. English landscape painter to George III (1794).

**Bour′get′** (bo͞or′zhĕ′), **Charles Joseph Paul.** 1852–1935. French critic, poet, and novelist, b. Amiens. Earliest work was verse, as *La Vie Inquiète* (1874), *Les Aveux* (1882). First novel *L'Irréparable* (1884). Wrote on causes of French pessimism. Among other works are *Un Cœur de Femme* (1890), *Cosmopolis* (1893), *Un Saint* (1894), *Un Divorce* (1904), *Le Sens de la Mort* (1915), *Le Danseur Mondain* (1925), *Nos Actes nous Suivent* (1927).

**Bour′gogne′** (bo͞or′gôn′y'). French spelling of BURGUNDY.

**Bourguignon, Le.** See Jacques COURTOIS.

**Bou′ri′gnon′** (bo͞o′rē′nyôN′), **Antoinette.** 1616–1680. Flemish religious visionary who believed herself in direct communion with God and divinely appointed to restore the spirit of the gospel; taught that Christianity consisted not in faith and practice but in internal emotion and supernatural impulse. Bourignianism spread through Holland and into Scotland, where a solemn renunciation of it is still, in the Established Church of Scotland, required from every entrant to ministry at time of his ordination.

**Bour′i·not** (bo͞or′ĭ·nō), Sir **John George.** 1837–1902. Canadian historian. Founder (1860) and first editor, Halifax *Herald.* Author of *Manual of the Constitutional History of Canada* (1888), a standard textbook, and other historical texts.

**Bourke, de.** Family name of earls and marquises of CLANRICARDE.

**Bourke-White, Margaret.** See under Erskine CALDWELL.

**Bour′mont′** (bo͞or′môN′), **Louis Auguste Victor de.** Comte **de Ghaisnes** (dẽ gân). 1773–1846. French soldier and politician; an émigré (1789), but returned to France to serve under Napoleon; wounded at Lützen (1813); commissioned general of division (1814). Commanded division in French army during the Hundred Days; went over to Louis XVIII's side four days before Waterloo (1815). Minister of war (1829); commander in chief of Algerian expedition (1830); created marshal of France.

**Bourne** (bōrn), **Edward Gaylord.** 1860–1908. American historian. Author of *Essays in Historical Criticism* (1901), *Spain in America* (1904), etc.

**Bourne** (bōrn), **Francis.** 1861–1934. English Roman Catholic prelate; archbishop of Westminster (1903); cardinal (1911).

**Bourne** (?bōrn; bo͝orn), **Hugh.** 1772–1852. English carpenter and preacher. Cut off from Wesleyan connection (1808). Founder of the first society of Primitive Methodists (1810).

**Bourne** (bōrn), **Jonathan, Jr.** 1855–1940. American lawyer and politician; U.S. senator from Oregon (1907–13); author of the Parcel Post Law.

**Bourne** (?bōrn; bo͝orn), **Richard.** d. 1682. English missionary among American Indians; took charge religious services, Sandwich, Mass.; to Indian settlement at Mashpee, Mass. (1658); ordained, by John Eliot, pastor of Indian Church at Mashpee (1670).

**Bour′rienne′** (bo͞o′ryĕn′), **Louis Antoine Fau′ve·let′** (fōv′lĕ′) **de.** 1769–1834. French diplomat; private secretary of Napoleon (1797). Offered services to Louis XVIII; named minister of state. Author of *Mémoires sur Napoléon*...(1829).

**Bour′sault′** (bo͞or′sō′), **Edme.** 1638–1701. French playwright and miscellaneous writer; commissioned by Louis XIV to write *Véritable Étude des Souverains* (1671) for the education of the dauphin.

**Bousbecq** *or* **Bousebecque, Augier Ghislain de.** See Augier Ghislain de BUSBECQ.

**Bous·set′** (bo͞o·sĕ′), **Wilhelm.** 1865–1920. German theologian, New Testament critic, and historian of religion.

**Bous′sin′gault′** (bo͞o′săN′gō′), **Jean Baptiste Joseph Dieudonné.** 1802–1887. French agricultural chemist.

**Bou′ter·wek** (bo͞o′tẽr·vĕk), **Friedrich.** 1766?–1828. German writer on philosophy and history of literature.

**Bou′tet′ de Mon′vel′** (bo͞o′tĕ′ dẽ môN′vĕl′), **Louis Maurice.** 1851–1913. French painter and illustrator; best known for his illustrations of books for children, as *Chansons de France, Jeanne d'Arc.*

**Bout′my′** (bo͞o′mē′), **Émile.** 1835–1906. French educator and writer; founded (1872) and directed École Libre des Sciences Politiques, Paris.

**Bou'ton'** (bōō'tôN'), **Charles Marie.** 1781–1853. Fr. scene painter in Paris; later an associate of Daguerre in inventing and exhibiting the diorama (1822).

**Bouton, Noël.** See comte de CHAMILLY.

**Bou'troux'** (bōō'trōō'), **Étienne Émile Marie.** 1845–1921. French philosopher and educator.

**Bouts** (bouts), **Dierik** *or* **Dirk** *or* **Thierry.** *Erroneously* **Stu'er·bout** (stü'ẽr·bout). 1410?–1475. Dutch painter of landscapes, portraits, and religious scenes.

**Bout'well** (bout'wĕl; -wĕl), **George Sewall.** 1818–1905. American political leader; governor of Massachusetts (1851, 1852). Member of Congress (1863–69). A leader in impeachment of Andrew Johnson. U.S. secretary of the treasury (1869–73). U.S. senator (1873–77).

**Bou'vard'** (bōō'vár') *or* **Bou'vart'** (-vár'), **Alexis.** 1767–1843. French astronomer; discovered eight comets; observed irregularities of planet Uranus.

**Bou'vier'** (bōō'vyā'), **Alexis.** 1836–1892. French novelist, playwright, and song writer; made success with his radical song *La Canaille.*

**Bou'vi·er** (bōō'vĭ·ă; bōō'vyā'; bōō·vēr'), **John.** 1787–1851. Jurist, b. Codogno, Italy; to U.S. (1802) and studied law. Practiced in Philadelphia (from 1822). Best known for his *Law Dictionary*...(1839) and *The Institutes of American Law* (4 vols., 1851).

**Bovadilla.** Variant of BOBADILLA.

**Bo·vard'** (bô·värd'), **Marion McKinley.** 1847–1891. American educator; associated in founding of U. of Southern California (1880), and its first president (1880–91). Another member of this family, **George Finley Bovard** (1856–1932), was president of U. of Southern California (1903–21).

**Bo·ve'ri** (bô·vā'rē), **Theodor.** 1862–1915. German zoologist; known for researches in cytology, esp. on fertilization in ascarids and sea-urchin eggs; believed in the individuality of chromosomes.

**Bo·vet'** (bô'vĕ'), **Daniel.** 1907– Italian physiologist, b. Switzerland. Awarded Nobel prize in physiology and medicine (1957).

**Bo'vet'** (bô'vĕ'), **Marie Anne de.** *Pen name of* Marquise **Guy de Bois'-Hé'bert'** (dẽ bwä'ā'bâr'). 1860– . French author of novels, works of travel, and translations from English books.

**Bo'vey** (bō'vĭ), **Wilfrid.** 1882–1956. Canadian lawyer, soldier, and writer, b. Montreal. Called to Quebec bar (1907); practiced law. Served in World War. Author of *Canadien,* study of the French Canadian, *Life Insurance Law,* and *The French-Canadians Today* (1939).

**Bow'dich** (bou'dĭch), **Thomas Edward.** 1791–1824. English traveler in Africa; influenced British government to take over direct control of Gold Coast.

**Bow'ditch** (bou'dĭch), **Nathaniel.** 1773–1838. American mathematician and astronomer, b. Salem, Mass., descendant of family from Dorsetshire, Eng. Self-educated; mathematical prodigy. Made five sea voyages (between 1795 and 1803). Prepared (1799) 1st American edition of J. H. Moore's standard work, *The Practical Navigator,* which he expanded and published as *The New American Practical Navigator* (1802), simultaneously with a new edition of Moore's work by the same English publishers. Over sixty editions of this work have appeared since that time. Translated, with commentaries, first four volumes of Laplace's *Celestial Mechanics* (1829–39). President, Essex Fire and Marine Insurance Co. (1804–23); actuary, Massachusetts Hospital Life Insurance Co. (1823–38). His 3d son, **Henry Ingersoll** (1808–1892), physician, b. Salem, Mass.; practiced, Boston (from 1834); forwarded public-health movements; author of *Public Hygiene in America* (1877). Nathaniel's grandson **Charles Pickering Bowditch** (1842–1921), archaeologist; professor, Harvard; financed and led expeditions to Yucatán and Central America studying Maya remains. Author of *The Numeration, Calendar Systems, and Astronomical Knowledge of the Mayas* (1910). His brother **Henry Pickering** (1840–1911), physiologist, b. Boston; professor, Harvard (1871–1906); established first physiological laboratory in U.S.; dean, Harvard medical faculty (1883–93); with Sir Michael Foster, editor of *Journal of Physiology* (1877–98).

**Bowd'ler** (boud'lẽr), **Thomas.** 1754–1825. English editor of Shakespeare; published *Family Shakespeare* (10 vols., 1818), an expurgated version omitting or modifying parts "which cannot with propriety be read aloud in a family"—which gave rise to the opprobrious word *bowdlerize;* edited Gibbon's *History* similarly.

**Bow'doin** (bō'd'n), **James.** 1726–1790. American merchant and Revolutionary leader, b. Boston. Member, Constitutional Convention (1779). Governor of Mass. (1785–87). Bowdoin College (chartered 1794) is named in his honor. His son **James** (1752–1811) was U.S. minister to Spain (1804–08), and conducted in Paris negotiations with Napoleon's ministers regarding the Florida purchase.

**Bow'ell** (bō'ĕl), Sir **Mackenzie.** 1823–1917. Canadian statesman, b. England; to Canada (1833). Editor, Belleville (Ont.) *Intelligencer.* Member of Canadian Parliament (1867–92); prime minister of Canada (1894–96). Member of Canadian Senate, and leader of Conservative opposition (1896–1906).

**Bow'en** (bō'ĕn), **Charles Synge Christopher.** Baron **Bowen.** 1835–1894. English jurist; junior counsel against claimant in famous Tichborne Case; judge of queen's bench and knighted (1879); lord of appeal in ordinary (1893).

**Bowen, Elizabeth Dorothea Cole.** 1899–1973. Irish novelist and short-story writer; m. Alan Cameron (1923). Author of *The Hotel* (1927), *To the North* (1932), *The Cat Jumps* (short stories; 1934), *The Death of the Heart* (1939), *Bowen's Court* (family history; 1942) *The Heat of the Day* (1949).

**Bowen, Francis.** 1811–1890. American philosopher; professor, Harvard (from 1853). Author of *Treatise on Logic* (1864), *Modern Philosophy, from Descartes to Schopenhauer and Hartmann* (1877).

**Bowen, George.** 1816–1888. American missionary in India (1848–88). Known as "the white saint of India."

**Bowen,** Sir **George Ferguson.** 1821–1899. English colonial administrator. First governor of Queensland (1859); conciliated Maoris and settlers as governor of New Zealand (1868–72); governor of Victoria, Australia (1872), Mauritius (1879), Hongkong (1882); privy councilor (1886).

**Bowen, Ira Sprague.** 1898–1973. American astronomer, b. Seneca Falls, N. Y. Known for work on atomic structure, cosmic rays, and nebular spectra.

**Bowen, Marjorie.** Pseudonym of Gabrielle Margaret LONG.

**Bow'er** (bou'ẽr), **Archibald.** 1686–1766. Scottish Jesuit and ecclesiastical historian.

**Bower, Frederick Orpen.** 1855–1948. English botanist.

**Bower,** Sir **Hamilton.** 1858–1940. British army officer. While in Chinese Turkestan (1890) made collection (known as "Bower manuscript") of ancient Sanskrit records inscribed on birch bark.

**Bow'er** (bō'ẽr) *or* **Bow'mak'er** (bō'māk'ẽr), **Walter.** 1385?–1449. Scottish chronicler. One of authors of *Scotichronicon,* completed 1447, which he abridged as *The Book of Cupar.*

**Bow'er·bank'** (bou'ẽr·băngk'), **James Scott.** 1797–1877. English naturalist and paleontologist. One of founders of London Clay Club (1836), an organization for study of fossils of Tertiary period.

**Bow'ers** (bou'ẽrz), **Claude Ger·nade'** (zhẽr·näd'). 1878–1958. American journalist, historian, and diplomat; on staff of New York *World* (1923–31), New York *Journal* (1931–33). U.S. ambassador to Spain (1933–39), to Chile (1939–53). Author of *The Party Battles of the Jackson Period* (1922), *Jefferson and Hamilton* (1925), *The Tragic Era—The Revolution After Lincoln* (1929), *Jefferson in Power* (1936), *Spanish Adventures of Washington Irving* (1940).

**Bowers, H. R.** 1883–1912. British naval officer (lieutenant), who accompanied Captain Robert Falcon Scott (*q.v.*) on his last and ill-fated Antarctic expedition (1912).

**Bowes-Lyon.** Family name of Queen ELIZABETH of England (b. 1900).

**Bow'ie** (bōō'ĭ; bō'ĭ), **James.** 1799–1836. Reputed inventor of bowie knife. American soldier, b. Burke Co., Ga. Settled in Texas (1828); naturalized Mexican citizen (1830). Leader in opposition to central Mexican government (1832). Colonel in Texan army (1835–36). Killed at the Alamo (Mar. 6, 1836).

**Bow'ker** (bou'kẽr), **Richard Rogers.** 1848–1933. American editor and author; editor of *The Library Journal* (from 1876), *Publishers' Weekly* (from 1884), *The Readers' Guide in Economic, Social and Political Science* (with George Iles; 1891). Author of *Work and Wealth* (1883), *Electoral Reform* (1889), *Of Business* (1901), *Of Politics* (1901), *Of Religion* (1903), *Economic Peace* (1923), etc.

**Bowles** (bōlz), **Caroline Anne.** See under Robert SOUTHEY.

**Bowles, Chester Bliss.** 1901– . Am. statesman and author, b. Springfield, Mass. Governor of Conn. (1949–51); ambassador to India and Nepal (1951–53) and India (1963–69). Author of influential books on foreign affairs.

**Bowles, Francis Tiffany.** 1858–1927. Grandson of Samuel Bowles (1797–1851). American naval constructor; grad. U.S.N.A., Annapolis (1879); in U.S. navy (to 1903); rear admiral (from 1901); chiefly a constructor in U.S. naval yards; president, Fore River Shipbuilding Corp., Quincy, Mass.

**Bowles, Samuel.** 1797–1851. American editor, b. Hartford, Conn. Published Hartford *Times* (1819–22), a weekly paper; founded Springfield *Republican*, Springfield, Mass. (weekly, 1824–44; daily, from 1844). His son **Samuel** (1826–1878) succeeded to control of paper at father's death; by vigor and independence of his policies and excellence of news reports made the *Republican* eminent among newspapers of the time. His son **Samuel** (1851–1915) took over control of paper (1878).

**Bowles, William Lisle.** 1762–1850. English clergyman and poet. Broke away from commonplaces of 18th-century poetry in *Fourteen Sonnets* (1789), hailed as revival of natural poetry by Wordsworth, Coleridge, Southey. Aroused controversy with Campbell and Byron over Pope's poetical merits.

**Bow'ley** (bō'lĭ), **Albert Jesse.** 1875–1945. American army officer; grad. U.S.M.A., West Point (1897); served in Spanish War (1898), Philippines, and World War I as artillery officer; lieutenant general (1939).

**Bowmaker, Walter.** See BOWER.

**Bow'man** (bō'măn), **Isaiah.** 1878–1950. American geographer and educator, b. Waterloo, Ont., Canada. Taught Yale (1905–15); director, American Geographical Society, N.Y. (1915–35); president, Johns Hopkins (1935–48). Advisor to Pres. Wilson at Paris Peace Conference (1918–19). Authority on physiography and political geography.

**Bowman, John Gabbert.** 1877–1962. American educator; chancellor (1921–45), U. of Pittsburgh.

**Bowman,** Sir **William.** 1816–1892. English ophthalmic surgeon. One of first to become expert in use of ophthalmoscope; known esp. for investigations upon minute structure of eye, kidney, and striped muscles. Bowman's capsule, glands, and membrane are named after him.

**Bowne** (boun), **Borden Parker.** 1847–1910. American philosopher. Author of *Personalism*, expounding doctrine that ultimate reality consists of a plurality of spiritual beings or independent persons (1908). See George H. HOWISON.

**Bow'ring** (bou'rĭng), Sir **John.** 1792–1872. English consular agent and linguist. Literary executor of Jeremy Bentham, edited works (11 vols., 1843). Superintendent of trade in China (1849); governor of Hongkong (1854); negotiated treaty of commerce with Siam (1855). Translator, and compiler of anthologies of eastern European poetry; author of poems and hymns, including *In the cross of Christ I glory*.

**Bow'yer** (bō'yẽr), **William.** 1699–1777. English printer. Called "the learned printer." Educ. Cambridge. Printer to Society of Antiquaries (1736), to Royal Society (1761), to House of Commons and House of Lords (1767). His father **William** (1663–1737) was one of twenty printers allowed by Star Chamber (1700).

**Box'all** (bŏk'sôl; -s'l), Sir **William.** 1800–1879. English portrait painter.

**Boy.** Pseudonym of Tadeusz ŻELEŃSKI.

**Bo·ya'dzhi·ev** (bô·yä'jĕ·yĕf), **Kliment.** 1865– Bulgarian general; commanded 1st Bulgar army in Serbia during World War.

**Boyce** (bois), **Hector.** See Hector BOECE.

**Boyce, Neith.** See under Hutchins HAPGOOD.

**Boyce,** Sir **Rubert William.** 1863–1911. English pathologist, hygienist, and specialist in tropical diseases and sanitation.

**Boyce, William.** 1710–1779. English ecclesiastical composer. Composer (1736) and organist (1758) to Chapel Royal.

**Boy·cott** (boi'kŏt; -kŭt), **Charles Cunningham.** 1832–1897. Retired British army captain, agent for estates in County Mayo (1873), and conspicuous victim (1880) of the economic and social ostracizing practice of Irish Land League agitators which came to be called "boycotting" or a "boycott."

**Boyd** (boid), **Alan Stephenson.** 1922– . American lawyer; U.S. secretary of transportation (1967–69).

**Boyd** (boid), **Ernest.** 1887–1946. Irish critic and essayist; member of editorial staff, N.Y. *Evening Post* (1920–22); editor *American Spectator* (1932). Author of *Ireland's Literary Renaissance* (1916, 1922), *Studies in Ten Literatures* (1925).

**Boyd** (boid), **Federico.** 1851–1924. Panamanian political leader, prominent in events leading to independence of Panama (1903). His son **Augusto Samuel** (1879–1957), surgeon and statesman; head surgeon of Santo Tomás Hospital, Panama (1905–36); vice-president (1936–39), and president (1939–40), of Panama. Another son, **Jorge Eduardo** (1886– ), lawyer and diplomat; represented Panama as counsel or delegate at international meetings (1911–36); attorney general of Panama (1924–26); ambassador to U.S. (from 1939).

**Boyd** (boid), **Henry.** d. 1832. Irish vicar; first translator of Dante's *Inferno* into English verse (1785); translator of whole *Divina Commedia* into English verse (1802).

**Boyd, James.** 1888–1944. American novelist; 1st lieut. in A.E.F., in action at St.-Mihiel and in Meuse-Argonne offensive (1918). Author of *Drums* (1925), *Marching On* (1927), *Long Hunt* (1930), *Roll River* (1935).

**Boyd, Thomas Alexander.** 1898–1935. American writer; author of *Through the Wheat* (1923), *Shadow of the Long Knives* (1928), *Mad Anthony Wayne* (1929), *Lighthorse Harry Lee* (1931).

**Boyd, Zachary.** 1585?–1653. Scottish minister; author of *The Last Battel of the Soul in Death* (1629); *Zion's Flowers*, quaint poems, once commonly called "Boyd's Bible."

**Boy'dell** (boi'dĕl), **John.** 1719–1804. English engraver and publisher of prints. Sheriff of London (1785); lord mayor (1790). Commissioned artists to paint illustrations of Shakespeare's works (engravings from which published in edition of Shakespeare, 1802); built Shakespeare gallery in Pall Mall, London (1786).

**Boy'den** (boi'd'n), **Seth.** 1788–1870. American inventor; invented process for making patent leather (1819); malleable cast iron (1826; patent issued, 1831); sheet iron; a hat-shaping machine. Manufactured locomotives, stationary steam engines. His brother **Uriah Atherton** (1804–1879) devised an improved turbine water wheel (1844).

**Boyd Orr** (boid'ôr), Lord **John.** 1880–1971. British nutritionist, b. Scotland. First director of UN Food and Agriculture Organization (1945–49); awarded Nobel peace prize (1949).

**Bo'ye** (bô'yĕ), **Caspar Johannes.** 1791–1853. Danish pastor, romantic poet, and dramatist, b. Norway.

**Bo·yé'** (bô·yĭ'), **Martin Hans.** 1812–1909. Scientist, b. Copenhagen, Denmark. To U.S. (1836). Disclosed nickel deposits in Pennsylvania ores; refined the oily product from cottonseed, getting cottonseed oil.

**Boy'-Ed'** (boi'āt'), **Ida.** *Nee* **Ida Ed.** 1852–1928. German novelist; m. Carl J. Boy (1870). Her son **Carl von Boy-Ed,** naval attaché in Washington at outbreak of World War I; acted as German agent in U.S.

**Boy'en** (boi'ĕn), **Hermann von.** 1771–1848. Prussian general; director of War Department (1810–12); general chief of staff in War of Liberation. Minister of war (1814–19); retired (1819). Recalled (1840) as councilor of state and general of infantry; war minister (1841–47).

**Boy'er'** (bwà'yā'), **A'bel'** (à'bĕl'). 1667–1729. French Huguenot settler in England (1689); compiler of a French-English and English-French lexicon, and histories of William III (1702) and Queen Anne (1722).

**Boyer,** Baron **Alexis de.** 1757?–1833. French surgeon. Imperial family surgeon to Napoleon (1804); consulting surgeon to Louis XVIII (1823), Charles X, and Louis Philippe. Author of *Traité Complet d'Anatomie* (4 vols., 1797–99), etc.

**Boyer, Jean Pierre.** 1776–1850. President of Haiti (1818–43), b. Port-au-Prince. A free mulatto; joined Pétion and Christophe in move to establish republic; succeeded Pétion (1818) as president of southern portion; after death of Christophe (1820), brought whole island under his control; driven out by revolution (1843).

**Boyer d'A'gen'** (dà'zhäN'), **Augustin.** *Orig. name* **Jean Auguste Boyer.** 1857–bet. 1943–46. French writer; author esp. of historical, artistic, and religious studies.

**Boy'e·sen** (boi'ĕ·sĕn), **Hjalmar Hjorth.** 1848–1895. Author and educator, b. Norway; to U.S. (1869); professor of German, Cornell (1874–80) and Columbia (1880–95). Author of fiction, verse, critical essays, etc.

**Boyle** (boil). Family name of earls of **Cork** (kôrk) and of **Or'rer·y** (ŏr'ĕr·ĭ), including: **Richard** (1566–1643), 1st Earl of Cork, founder of house of Cork and Orrery. Called the "Great Earl of Cork"; b. Canterbury; educ. Cambridge; tried his fortunes in Ireland (1588); acquitted on two charges of embezzling records; purchased Sir Walter Raleigh's Irish possessions; introduced manufactures, built bridges and harbors; amassed fortune; a lord justice (1629) and lord high treasurer (1631), of Ireland; helped to bring about impeachment of Strafford, his rival in Ireland; suppressed Irish rebellion of 1641. His 7th son was the famous physicist and chemist (see Robert BOYLE). His 3d son, **Roger** (1621–1679), Baron **Brog'hill** (brŏg'hĭl) and 1st Earl of Orrery, soldier and dramatist, held general's command in Ireland under Cromwell (1650) and membership in Cromwell's privy council; became convinced of hopelessness of Richard Cromwell's cause and secured Ireland for Charles II; author of *Parthenissa*, a romance (1665–67), *A Treatise on the Art of War* (1677), and rhymed tragedies. **Charles** (1676–1731), 4th Earl of Orrery, after whom as patron George Graham named his astronomical invention the orrery, a kind of planetarium; grandson of Roger Boyle, 1st Earl of Cork; edited *Epistles of Phalaris*, which were shown spurious by Richard Bentley, satirized by Swift in his *Battle of the Books* (1704); fought at Malplaquet; a negotiator of Treaty of Utrecht; imprisoned in Tower of London as a Jacobite (1721). **Richard** (1695–1753), 3d Earl of **Bur'ling·ton** (bûr'lĭng·tŭn) and 4th Earl of Cork; great grandson of 1st earl of Cork; privy councilor (1714); lord high treasurer of Ireland (1715); patron of literature and art. **John** (1707–1762), 5th Earl of Cork and 5th Earl of Orrery, son of 4th Earl of Orrery, was a friend of Swift, Pope, and Dr. Johnson; known chiefly for his rancorous and grudgingly commendatory *Remarks on the Life and Writings of Jonathan Swift* (1751) and a translation of the letters of Pliny the Younger (1751).

**Boyle, Edward Courtney.** 1883–1967. English naval officer. Commander of submarine, which raided Sea of Marmara (1915); retired as rear admiral (1932).

**Boyle, Kay.** 1903– . American short-story writer.

**Boyle, Richard Vicars.** 1822–1908. English civil engineer; engineer in chief for imperial Japanese railways (1872–77).

**Boyle, Robert.** 1627–1691. British physicist and chemist, b. at Lismore Castle, Munster, Ireland. See BOYLE family. Settled at Oxford (1654) and devoted himself to chemistry and natural philosophy; one of first members of group that became the Royal Society. Improved air pump and invented a compressed-air pump; experimented in pneumatics; investigated specific gravities, refractive powers, crystals, electricity, etc.; discovered importance of air in propagation of sound; held that atoms of one kind of matter constitute all substances, the atoms having different arrangements and movements in different substances. Author of *New Experiments Physico-Mechanical touching the Spring of the Air and its Effects* (1660); answered criticism of this work with his *Defense Against Linus* (1662), in which he enunciated the law (Boyle's law) that the volume of a gas varies inversely as the pressure; author also of *The Sceptical Chemist* (1661), *Origin of Forms and Qualities According to the Corpuscular Philosophy* (1666), *Memoirs for the Natural History of the Human Blood* (1684), and of moral and religious essays. By his will founded *Boyle Lectures*, for defense of Christianity against unbelievers.

**Boy'lesve'** (bwà'lâv'), **René.** *Pseudonym of* **René Tar'di'vaux'** (târ'dē'vō'). 1867–1926. French novelist.

**Boyl'ston** (boil'stŭn), **Zabdiel.** 1679–1766. American physician; inoculated patients against smallpox (1721), first such practice in America.

**Boyn'ton** (boin't'n; -tŭn), **Henry Walcott.** 1869–1947. American writer, author of *Life of Washington Irving* (1901), *Bret Harte* (1903), *James Fenimore Cooper* (1931). His brother **Percy Holmes** (1875–1946), author of *The Challenge of Modern Criticism* (1931), *Literature and American Life* (1936), etc.

**Boyron, Michel.** See Michel BARON.

**Boz** (bŏz). Pseudonym of Charles DICKENS.

**Boze′man** (bōz′măn), **John M.** 1835–1867. American pioneer; opened Rocky Mountain trail now known as Bozeman Pass.

**Boz′za·ris** (bôt′sä·rēs; *often Angl.* bō·zăr′ĭs, -zär′ĭs), **Mar′co** (mär′kō). *Also* **Mar′kos** (mär′kôs) **Bot′za·ris** *or* **Bot′sa·res** (bôt′sä·rēs). 1788?–1823. Greek patriot; hero of Greek war of independence; famed for defense of Missolonghi against Turks (1822–23); killed in action near Carpenisi (Aug. 20, 1823). His last battle subject of poem by Fitz-Greene Halleck (*q.v.*).

**Brab′a·zon** (brăb′ȧ·z'n), **Reginald.** 12th Earl of **Meath** (mēth). 1841–1929. British philanthropist; initiated recognition of Empire Day (May 24).

**Brabourne,** Baron. See KNATCHBULL-HUGESSEN.

**Brac′cio da Mon·to′ne** (brät′chō dä mōn·tō′nā), **Andrea.** 1368–1424. Italian condottiere. Secured sovereignty of Perugia (1416); captured Rome (1417); created count of Foggia (1421); crowned prince of Aquila and Capua (1423); commanded Neapolitan forces against Sforza (1424).

**Brac′cio·li′ni** (brät′chō·lē′nē), **Francesco.** 1566–1645. Italian ecclesiastic and poet; known esp. for his satire *Lo Scherno degli Dei* (1618–26) and for *La Croce Riacquistata* (1605–11), an imitation of Tasso's *Gerusalemme Liberata.*

**Bracciolini, Poggio.** See POGGIO BRACCIOLINI.

**Brac′co** (bräk′kō), **Roberto.** 1862–1943. Italian playwright, novelist, and essayist.

**Brace** (brās), **Charles Loring.** 1826–1890. American social-service worker, b. Litchfield, Conn. Instrumental in establishing Children's Aid Society (1853).

**Brace′gir′dle** (brās′gûr′d'l), **Anne.** 1663?–1748. English actress. Appeared (1688) as Lucia in Shadwell's *Squire of Alsatia;* closely associated with plays of Congreve; created Almeria in *Mourning Bride* (1697), and Belinda in Vanbrugh's *Provoked Wife;* played tragic roles in Shakespearean adaptations; retired (1707).

**Bra′chet′** (brȧ′shĕ′), **Auguste.** 1844–1898. French philologist; author of *Grammaire Historique de la Langue Française* (1867), *Dictionnaire Étymologique de la Langue Française* (1870), etc.

**Bracht** (bräKt), **Eugen Felix Prosper.** 1842–1921. German landscape painter.

**Brack′en** (brăk′ĕn), Sir **Brendan.** 1901–1958. Brit. newspaper publisher and politician. Parliamentary private secretary to Churchill (1940–41); minister of information (1941–45); 1st lord of admiralty (May–Aug., 1945).

**Brack′en·bur′y** (brăk′ĕn·bĕr′ĭ; -bĕr·ĭ), Sir **Henry.** 1837–1914. English soldier. Chief of staff in Zulu War (1879–80); accompanied Nile expeditionary force (1884–85); director general of ordnance in Boer War (1899–1902); general (1901).

**Brack′en·bur′y** *or* **Brak′en·bur′y** (brăk′ĕn·bĕr′ĭ; -bĕr·ĭ), Sir **Robert.** d. 1485. Constable of Tower of London; refused to obey Richard III's order to murder two young sons of Edward IV; gave keys of Tower to Sir James Tyrrell, who carried out the order.

**Brack′ley** (brăk′lĭ), Viscounts of. See EGERTON family.

**Brack′man** (brăk′măn), **Robert.** 1898– . American painter, b. Odessa, Russia; to U.S. as a child; best known for still lifes, figure studies, and portraits.

**Bracq** (bråk), **Jean Charlemagne.** 1853–1934. Educator and publicist, b. Cambrai, France; to U.S. (1871); professor of Romance languages, Vassar (1892–1918). Writer on French Protestantism, Anglo-French relations, and contemporary French literature.

**Brac′que·mond′** (bråk′môN′), **Félix Joseph Auguste.** 1833–1914. French painter and etcher.

**Brac′ton** (brăk′tŭn) *or* **Brat′ton** (brăt′'n) *or* **Bret′ton** (brĕt′'n), **Henry de.** d. 1268. English ecclesiastic and judge. Author of first systematic treatise on laws of England in Middle Ages.

**Brad′bur·y** (brăd′bĕr·ĭ), Sir **John Swanwick.** 1st Baron **Bradbury.** 1872–1950. English treasury official. Joint permanent secretary to the treasury (1913–19); principal British representative on reparations commission, Paris (1919–25). Treasury notes issued during World War bearing his signature sometimes called "Bradburies." Cf. Sir Norman F. W. FISHER.

**Brad′dock** (brăd′ŭk), **Edward.** 1695–1755. Commander in chief of British forces in America (1754). Led expedition against Fort Duquesne (1755); surprised by attack of force of French and Indians (July 9, 1755) and defeated with loss of over half his force; died of wounds (July 13).

**Brad′don** (brăd′'n), Sir **Edward Nicholas Coventry.** 1829–1904. English official in India (till 1878). Premier of Tasmania (1894–99); senior member for Tasmania in first Australian Commonwealth parliament (1901). His sister **Mary Elizabeth** (1837–1915) was a writer; m. (1874) publisher John Maxwell; won success as novelist with *Lady Audley's Secret* (1862); author of 80 novels and many plays.

**Brade, James.** See BRAID.

**Brad′ford** (brăd′fērd), **Francis Scott.** 1898–1961. American mural painter.

**Bradford, Gamaliel.** 1863–1932. American biographer, b. Boston. Author of *Lee, the American* (1912), *Confederate Portraits* (1914), *Union Portraits* (1916), *Damaged Souls* (1923), *Darwin* (1926), *D. L. Moody—A Worker in Souls* (1927), *Daughters of Eve* (1930), *The Quick and the Dead* (1931), etc. His father, **Gamaliel** (1831–1911), a Boston banker, wrote *The Lesson of Popular Government* (1899).

**Bradford, John.** 1510?–1555. English Protestant martyr. Chaplain to Bishop Ridley (1550) and to Edward VI (1553). Accused of sedition on accession of Queen Mary; tried before Bishop Gardiner; condemned as heretic and burned at Smithfield.

**Bradford, Roark.** 1896–1948. American fiction writer. Among his books are *Ol' Man Adam an' His Chillun* (1928; see Marc CONNELLY), *John Henry* (1931; dramatized, 1940, with music by Jacques Wolfe), *Let the Band Play Dixie* (short stories, 1934), *The Three-Headed Angel* (1937).

**Bradford, William.** 1590–1657. Pilgrim Father. b. Austerfield, Yorkshire, Eng. Joined a separatist group, the Brownists (1606); went with this group to Amsterdam (1609), seeking freedom of worship; moved to Leiden (1609), and became citizen of that city. Sailed with Pilgrims for New World (1620); a signer of the Mayflower Compact (1620). Governor of Plymouth Colony (April 1621–32; 1635; 1637; 1639–43; 1645–56). Author of *History of Plymouth Plantation* (pub. in full, 1856).

**Bradford, William.** 1663–1752. Printer, b. Barnwell, Leicestershire, Eng. To Pennsylvania (1685); associated in founding of first paper mill in America (1690); established printing press in Philadelphia; moved to New York (1693); crown printer (1693–1742); official printer to New Jersey (almost continuously 1703–33). His press turned out first legislative proceedings published in America, first New York paper money (1709), first American Book of Common Prayer (1710), first drama written in American colonies (1714), first history of New York (1727), first newspaper to appear in New York, *New York Gazette* (1725). His son **Andrew** (1686–1742), appointed (about 1715) official printer to the province, founded and published *American Weekly Mercury,* first newspaper in Philadelphia (1719). Andrew's nephew **William** (1722–1791), known as "patriot printer of 1776," founded and edited *Weekly Advertiser, or Pennsylvania Journal* (1742). His son **Thomas** (1745–1838) founded *Merchants' Daily Advertiser*, Philadelphia (1797). Another son, **William** (1755–1795), was attorney general of U.S. (1794–95).

**Bradford, William.** 1823?–1892. American marine painter, esp. of arctic whaling scenes.

**Brad'laugh** (brăd'lô), **Charles.** 1833–1891. English secularist and social and political reformer. Free-thought lecturer under name of "Iconoclast." Publisher of *National Reformer* (1860); prosecuted (1876) with Mrs. Annie Besant for republishing Malthusian *Fruits of Philosophy*, his winning of this case effective in nullifying restrictions on the freedom of the press then remaining. Associated with Mrs. Besant's work (1874–85). M.P. (1880), asserted his right to affirm instead of swearing on Bible; re-elected, but excluded by the house, each year until 1886; championed bill permitting members to affirm, which became law (1888).

**Brad'ley** (brăd'lĭ), **Andrew Cecil.** 1851–1935. English literary critic. Author of *Shakespearean Tragedy* (1904), a series of objectively reasoned studies in dramatic construction and character interpretation organic in the leading tragedies of Shakespeare; *Oxford Lectures on Poetry* (1909). His brother **Francis Herbert** (1846–1924), philosopher, attacked utilitarianism in *Ethical Studies* (1876); pointed out limitations in J. S. Mill's system, in *Principles of Logic* (1883); expounded in *Appearance and Reality* (1893) and *Essays on Truth and Reality* (1914) metaphysical basis of his absolute idealism.

A half brother, **George Granville Bradley** (1821–1903), clergyman and scholar, succeeded Stanley as dean of Westminster (1881); biographer of Dean Stanley (1892). His son **Arthur Granville** (1850–1943), historian and author of *Life of Wolfe* (1895), *Canada in the Twentieth Century* (1903), *A Book of the Severn* (1919), *Romance of Wales* (1929), and topographical works.

**Bradley, Charles Henry.** 1860–1922. American educator, first to introduce sloyd classes in U.S.

**Bradley, Charles Schenck.** 1853–1929. American inventor; invented a rotary converter, a process for producing aluminum, a process for fixation of atmospheric hydrogen.

**Bradley, Edward.** *Pseudonym* **Cuthbert Bede** (bēd). 1827–1889. English clergyman, author and illustrator of *Adventures of Mr. Verdant Green, an Oxford Freshman* (1853–56); illustrated his own verse and prose.

**Bradley, Henry.** 1845–1923. English self-taught philologist and lexicographer. His review of first part of *New English Dictionary* (commonly called *Oxford English Dictionary*) attracted attention to his extraordinary philological knowledge; engaged as an editor (1889); senior editor (1915–23) on death of Sir James Murray. Cofounder of Society for Pure English (1913). Revised F. H. Stratmann's *Middle English Dictionary* (1891). Author of "The Goths" (1888) for the *Story of the Nations* series, *Making of English* (1904), *English Place-names* (1910).

**Bradley, James.** 1693–1762. English astronomer. Discovered aberration of light (announced 1729) and nutation of earth's axis (announced 1748).

**Bradley, Joseph P.** 1813–1892. American jurist. Associate justice, U.S. Supreme Court (1870–92).

**Brad'ley, O'mar** (ō'mär) **Nelson.** 1893– . Am. gen., b. Clark, Mo.; grad. U.S.M.A. (1915); World War II commander; Tunisia (1943), Europe (1943–45); adm. veterans' affairs (1945–47); chief of staff, U.S. Army (1948–49); chm., U.S. joint chiefs of staff (1949–53).

**Brad'shaw** (brăd'shô), **George.** 1801–1853. English printer; originator of railway timetables (1839), developed into well-known series of Bradshaw's railway guides.

**Bradshaw, Henry.** 1831–1886. English antiquary and bibliographer.

**Bradshaw, John.** 1602–1659. English judge. Presided at trial of Charles I and pronounced sentence (1649).

**Brad'street** (brăd'strēt), **John M.** American lawyer and businessman; established in Cincinnati (1849) Bradstreet's Improved Mercantile Agency, later (1876) called The Bradstreet Co., merged (1933) with R. G. Dun & Co. to form Dun & Bradstreet, Inc., a concern furnishing financial data and credit ratings of American businesses and businessmen, now located in New York City.

**Bradstreet, Simon.** 1603–1697. English provincial governor in America. To America (1630); secretary, Massachusetts Bay Colony (1630–36); instrumental in forming New England Confederation (1643 ff.), of which he was commissioner (1646–79); governor of the colony (1679–86; 1689–92). His wife, **Anne,** *nee* **Dudley** (1612?–1672), to America (1630), was first woman poet writing in English in American colonies; author of *The Tenth Muse* (1650).

**Brad'war·dine** (brăd'wẽr·dēn), **Thomas.** 1290?–1349. English prelate and mathematician. Called "the Profound Doctor." Chaplain and confessor to Edward III (1338); archbishop of Canterbury (1349); died of plague. Author of *De Causa Dei*, directed against Pelagianism, and of treatises on geometrical problems.

**Bra'dy** (brā'dĭ), **Alice.** See under William A. Brady.

**Brady, Henry Bowman.** 1835–1891. English naturalist and pharmacist; authority on fossil and recent foraminifera.

**Brady, James Buchanan.** 1856–1917. American financier, b. New York City. Bellboy; employee of New York Central R.R.; salesman for railroad supply house (1879); successful as financier; known as "Diamond Jim" because of collections of diamonds and other jewels; endowed James Buchanan Brady Urological Institute, Johns Hopkins (1912).

**Brady, Mathew B.** 1823?–1896. American photographer. Accompanied Union armies, taking photographs (1861–65) which became basis for pictorial history of Civil War.

**Brady, Nicholas.** 1659–1726. Irish Anglican clergyman; collaborator with Nahum Tate in metrical version of Psalms (licensed 1696).

**Brady, William A.** 1863–1950. American theatrical producer and manager, b. San Francisco. Leased Manhattan Theater, New York (1896); proprietor of the Playhouse, New York; president, National Association of the Motion Picture Industry (1915–20). Also managed the pugilists James J. Corbett and James J. Jeffries; m. (1899, as 2d wife) **Grace George** (1880–1961), actress, b. in New York, who made her New York debut in *The New Boy* (1894), subsequently starring in many plays. His dau. **Alice Brady** (1892–1939), also an actress, appeared successfully in Gilbert and Sullivan opera; starred on the stage in *Forever After* and later in motion pictures.

**Brae'ke·leer** (brä'kĕ·lār), **Ferdinand de.** 1792–1883. Belgian painter, esp. of small genre pictures. His son **Henri** (1840–1888), also a painter, is represented in museums at Amsterdam, Antwerp, Brussels.

**Braeme, Charlotte Monica.** See Bertha M. Clay.

**Bra'ga** (brä'gä), **Gaetano.** 1829–1907. Italian violoncellist and composer of a celebrated *Serenade*.

**Bra'ga** (brá'gȧ), **Teófilo.** 1843–1924. Portuguese scholar and writer, b. Ponta Delgada, Azores. One of founders of Portuguese modern school of poetry; author of more than 100 volumes, many of them notable in history, history of literature, and philosophy. Active in movement for republic; head of provisional government (1910–11) after dethronement of King Manuel; interim president of Portugal (May to Oct., 1915).

**Bra·gan′za** (brȧ·găn′zȧ) *or* **Bra·gan′ça** (brȧ·găN′sȧ). Name of a dynasty of Portugal (1640–1910) and of the collateral house of Brazil (1822–1889), derived from name of district in northern Portugal (now Bragança).

The Portuguese dynasty was founded by John IV (1640–56), who was followed by Alfonso VI, Pedro II (whose sister Catherine married Charles II of England), John V, Joseph Emanuel, Maria I and Pedro III, Maria I (alone), John VI (regent 1792–1816; king 1816–26), Pedro IV, Maria II (Dom Miguel), Pedro V, Louis I, Carlos I, and Manuel (deposed 1910, when Portugal became a republic).

The Brazilian house (1822–1889) was established (1815) when John VI (then regent) of Portugal declared the colony of Brazil a kingdom under the Portuguese monarchy. John's son Dom Pedro I (same as Pedro IV of Portugal) was chosen (1822) "Constitutional Emperor and Perpetual Defender" of the new independent state in South America; Dom Pedro I abdicated (1831) and was succeeded by his son Pedro II (1831–89), who was forced to abdicate (1889, when Brazil became a republic).

**Brag′don** (brăg′dŭn), **Claude.** 1866–1946. American theosophist and architect; author of books on theosophy and architecture.

**Bragg** (brăg), **Braxton.** 1817–1876. American army officer; grad. U.S.M.A., West Point (1837). Entered Confederate army (1861); general (Apr. 12, 1862). Won battle of Chickamauga; unsuccessfully besieged Chattanooga; relieved of field command (Dec., 1863); military adviser to President Davis (1864–65). His brother **Thomas** (1810–1872) was attorney general of the Confederate States of America (1861–62).

**Bragg,** Sir **William Henry.** 1862–1942. English physicist. Educ. King William's College, Isle of Man, and Cambridge U. Professor, Adelaide U., South Australia (1886–1908), Leeds U. (1909–15), U. of London (1915–23); professor of chemistry at Royal Institution and director of Davy-Faraday research laboratory (from 1923); director of Royal Institution. Pioneered, with his son William as associate, in the study of crystalline structure by means of X rays; co-winner, with son William, of 1915 Nobel prize in physics. Author of *Studies in Radioactivity* (1912), *X-rays and Crystal Structure* (with his son; 1915), *The World of Sound* (1920), *Concerning the Nature of Things* (1925), *The Universe of Light* (1933). His son Sir **William Lawrence** (1890–1971), b. South Australia; educ. St. Peter's College, Adelaide, and Cambridge; professor of physics, Victoria U., Manchester (1919–37); Cavendish professor of experimental physics, Cambridge (from 1938); author of *The Crystalline State* (1934), *Atomic Structure of Minerals* (1937).

**Bra′ham** (brā′ăm), **John.** *Real surname* **Abraham.** 1774?–1856. English tenor singer; in London sustained leading position in opera, oratorio, and concert for forty years.

**Bra′he** (brä′ĕ), Count **Per.** 1602–1680. Swedish soldier and statesman. Served under Gustavus Adolphus (1626–32); directed peace negotiations with Poland (1635). Governor general of Finland (1637–40; 1648–54). Founder (1640) and chancellor (1646–80) of U. of Åbo. High bailiff, Sweden (1641), and member of regency during minorities of Christina (1632–44) and Charles XI (1660–72).

**Bra′he** (brä′ĕ), **Tycho.** 1546–1601. Danish astronomer. Established with royal aid observatory on island of Hven in The Sound (1576); in Bohemia under patronage of Rudolph II (1599), where he had Kepler as assistant (1600). Rejected Copernican system and held that the five planets revolved about the sun, which in turn revolved about the immobile earth; discovered new star (Tycho's star) in Cassiopeia (1572) and variations of the moon; corrected values of many astronomical quantities and recorded positions of stars and planets, his observations published by Kepler in the *Rudolphine Tables.* Author of *Astronomiae Instauratae Mechanica* (1598), describing his life, discoveries, instruments, etc., and of *Astronomiae Instauratae Progymnasmata* (1602–03, edited by Kepler).

**Brah′ma·gup′ta** (brŭ′mȧ·go͝op′tȧ). 588–?660. Hindu astronomer; wrote (628) a work on astronomy containing important chapters on mathematics.

**Brahms** (bräms; *freq. Angl.* brämz), **Johannes.** 1833–1897. German composer and pianist, b. Hamburg. Director of court concerts and of a choral society in Detmold (1854–58); lived in Vienna (from 1862); conductor of the Singakademie (1863–64) and concerts of the Gesellschaft der Musikfreunde (1872–75). His compositions include: (1) instrumental works for orchestra: two serenades (1860), four symphonies (1876–86), the *Academic Festival* and *Tragic* overtures (1881), a violin concerto (1879), and a double concerto for violin and violoncello (1888); (2) chamber music: sonatas for piano and violin, violoncello, or clarinet; 5 trios, 3 quartets, and a quintet, for piano and other instruments; 3 string quartets; 2 string quintets; 2 string sextets; a quintet for clarinet and other instruments; (3) piano works: sonatas, a scherzo in E-flat minor, variations, two rhapsodies, Hungarian dances, waltzes, and smaller pieces; (4) organ works: preludes for chorals, a fugue in A-flat minor; (5) vocal works: *German Requiem* (1868), *Rinaldo,* a cantata (1869), *Rhapsody* (1870), *Schicksalslied* (1871), *Triumphlied* (1872), *Nänie* (1881), *Gesang der Parzen* (1883), choruses, and songs.

**Braid** *or* **Brade** (brād), **James.** 1795?–1860. British surgeon and writer on hypnotism, b. in Scotland. Practiced in Manchester; investigated mesmerism, proving its subjective nature and demonstrating that no magnetic influence passed from operator into subject; originated term *neurohypnotism,* later shortened to *hypnotism.*

**Braid′wood** (brād′wo͝od), **Thomas.** 1715–1806. Scottish teacher of deaf mutes; opened in Edinburgh first school for deaf mutes in the British Empire.

**Braille** (brä′y′; *Angl.* brāl), **Louis.** 1809–1852. French teacher of the blind; himself blind from age of three, devoted himself to study of music; organist in Paris. Teacher of the blind (from 1828); devised system of raised-point writing for literature and music (known as *Braille*), which has been widely adopted for instruction of the blind throughout the world.

**Brai·low′sky** (brŭ·ĭ·lôf′skû·ĭ; *Angl.* brī·lôf′skĭ), **Alexander.** 1896– . Russian concert pianist; appeared in New York (1924, 1938, and later seasons).

**Brails′ford** (brāls′fẽrd), **Henry Noel.** 1873–1958. English journalist. Editor, *New Leader* (1922–26). Author of *Shelley, Godwin, and their Circle, How the Soviet Works* (1927), *Rebel India* (1932), *Voltaire* (1935).

**Brai′nard** (brā′nẽrd), **David Legge.** 1856–1946. American army officer and arctic explorer. On Lady Franklin Bay Arctic Expedition (1881–84), explored Grinnell Land and the northwest coast of Greenland; with two companions reached the most northerly point attained up to that time (May 13, 1882).

**Brainard, John Gardiner Calkins.** 1796–1828. American poet; assoc. editor, *Connecticut Mirror* (1822–27).

**Brai′nerd** (brā′nẽrd), **David** (1718–1747) and his brother **John** (1720–1781). American missionaries among the Indians.

**Braith** (brīt), **Anton.** 1836–1905. German painter of animals, esp. cattle.

**Brai′thwaite** (brā′thwāt), **John.** 1797–1870. English engineer; built first practical steam fire engine (c. 1829) and, with Ericsson, a caloric engine (1833).

**Braithwaite, William Stanley Beaumont.** 1878–1962. American Negro poet, critic, and anthologist; author of *Lyrics of Life and Love* (1904), *Our Essayists and Critics of Today* (1920), *Sandy Star* (verse; 1926), *Frost on the Green Leaf* (short stories; 1928).

**Brakelond.** See JOCELIN DE BRAKELOND.

**Bra′ley** (brā′lĭ), **Berton.** 1882–1966. American poet and novelist.

**Bra′mah** (brä′mȧ), **Ernest.** *Pen name of* **Ernest Bramah Smith.** 1869?–1942. English writer of detective fiction, as *The Wallet of Kai Lung* (1900). Created the fictional detective Max Carrados.

**Bram′ah** (brăm′ȧ; brä′mȧ), **Joseph.** 1748–1814. English engineer; inventor of a safety lock (1784) and of a hydraulic press (1795), both known by his name, and of a printing machine for bank notes, etc.

**Bra·man′te** (brä·män′tā). *Incorrectly called* **Bramante Laz′za·ri** (läd′dzä·rē). *Real name* **Donato d'A′gno·lo** (dä′nyō·lō) *or* **d'An′ge·lo** (dän′jā·lō). 1444–1514. Italian architect; worked chiefly in Milan (1472–99) and in Rome (1499–1514); employed by Popes Alexander VI and Julius II. Inaugurator of a Renaissance style in architecture, often called "Bramantesque." Drew up plans (carried out only in part) for reconstruction of St. Peter's.

**Bramantino, Il.** See Bartolommeo SUARDI.

**Bram′bach** (brăm′bäĸ), **Kaspar Joseph.** 1833–1902. German composer of chamber music, piano pieces, the opera *Ariadne*, and secular cantatas and other choral works. His brother **Wilhelm** (1841–1932), classical philologist and music historian, was librarian at Karlsruhe (1872–1904).

**Bram·bil′la** (bräm·bēl′lä), **Paolo.** 1786–1838. Italian composer of operatic, religious, and concert music. His daughters **Marietta** (1807–1875), **Teresa** (1813–1895), **Annetta,** and **Giuseppina** (d. 1903) were celebrated singers.

**Bram′hall** (brăm′hôl), **John.** 1594–1663. English prelate in Ulster. Anglican bishop of Derry (1634); archbishop of Armagh (1661); speaker, Irish House of Lords (1661). Argued against Hobbes on freedom of the will.

**Brampton,** Baron. See Sir Henry HAWKINS.

**Bram′well** (brăm′wĕl; -wĕl), **George William Wilshere.** Baron **Bramwell.** 1808–1892. English judge. Drafted, with Mr. Justice Willes, Common Law Procedure Act (1852); raised to the bench (1856) and to court of appeal, as lord justice (1876). His brother Sir **Frederick Joseph** (1818–1903) designed one of earliest successful railroad locomotives, and was an expert authority on municipal and waterworks engineering; one of first to specialize as a technical consultant, expert legal witness, and arbitrator, in technological matters.

**Branch** (brȧnch), **Anna Hempstead.** 1875?–1937. American poet; grad. Smith (1897); awarded first of Century prizes for best poem by a college graduate, with *The Road 'Twixt Heaven and Hell* (1898).

**Branch, John.** 1782–1863. American political leader; governor of North Carolina (1817–20); U.S. senator (1823–29); secretary of the navy (1829–31); governor of Florida Territory (1834–45).

**Branck′er** (brăngk′ẽr), Sir **William Sefton.** 1877–1930. English military officer. Organizer of national air service; officer in Royal Flying Corps (1914–18), major general (1917); first recipient of Air Force Cross (1918); air vice-marshal (1924); killed in disaster of airship *R. 101.*

**Bran′cuşi** (brän′kōōsh), **Constantin.** 1876–1957. Rumanian sculptor; associated with ultramodern school of art, esp. with symbolism. Among works are *The Kiss, New-Born, Leda,* and *Mlle. Pogany.*

**Brand** (bränt), **Hennig.** *Also* **Brandt.** d. about 1692. German alchemist of Hamburg; discovered the element phosphorus (1669).

**Brand** (bränt), Sir **Johannes Henricus** *or* **Jan Hendrik.** 1823–1888. South African statesman. President, Orange Free State (1864–88); defeated Basutos (1865–69); declined to desert policy of friendship towards British to become president of Transvaal (1871).

**Brand** (brănd), **John.** 1744–1806. English clergyman and antiquary.

**Brandan,** Saint. See BRENDAN.

**Brande** (brănd), **Dorothea,** *nee* **Thompson.** 1893–1948. American writer; m. 2d, Seward Collins (1936); on editorial staff, *American Review* (from 1933); author of *Wake Up and Live* (1936), *Letters to Philippa* (1937), *My Invincible Aunt* (1938), etc.

**Brande, William Thomas.** 1788–1866. English chemist. Successor of Sir Humphry Davy at Royal Institution; author of *Manual of Chemistry* and *Dictionary of Pharmacy and Materia Medica.*

**Bran′deis** (brăn′dīs), **Louis Dem′bitz** (dĕm′bĭts). 1856–1941. American jurist, b. Louisville, Ky. LL.B., Harvard (1877); practiced in Boston (1879–1916). Appeared (1907–14) as special counsel for the people in legal proceedings involving constitutionality of Oregon and Illinois women's ten-hour laws, Ohio nine-hour law, California eight-hour law, and Oregon minimum-wage law; also, as counsel for interests opposing monopoly of transportation in New England by N.Y., N.H.&H. Railroad (1907–13). Associate justice, U.S. Supreme Court (1916–39; retired). Author of *Other People's Money* (1914), *Business, a Profession* (1914), *The Curse of Bigness,* etc.

**Bran′den·burg** (brăn′dĕn·bûrg; *Ger.* brän′dĕn·bŏŏrĸ), House of. German royal family (Ascanian dynasty) founded (c. 1142) by Margrave Albert the Bear (*q.v.*), whose descendants added territory (12th–13th centuries); especially prosperous during joint reign (1220–67) of John I and Otto III and reign of Waldemar (1303–19); became extinct (1320). Possession of the mark disputed by several claimants; acquired (1323) by Louis of Bavaria, only to be lost by his successors; declined greatly in influence; by treaty, all rights transferred (1373) to Emperor Charles IV; reverted (1411) to Emperor Sigismund, by whom it was conferred (1417) on Burgrave Frederick of Nuremberg. See House of PRUSSIA.

**Bran′den·burg** (brän′dĕn·bŏŏrĸ), **Erich.** 1868–1946. German historian.

**Bran′den·bur′ger** (brän′dĕn·bŏŏr′gẽr), **Clemens.** 1879– German historian in Brazil.

**Bran′des** (brän′dĕs), **Georg Morris.** *Orig. surname* **Co′hen** (kō′ĕn). 1842–1927. Danish literary critic and historian, b. Copenhagen. Disciple of Comte, Taine, Mill, and Spencer; champion of materialism, esp. in literature. Taught at U. of Copenhagen (1872–77); accused of radicalism; journalist, writer, and lecturer, Berlin (1877–82); public lecturer, Copenhagen (from 1882); professor of aesthetics, U. of Copenhagen (from 1902). Author of *Aesthetic Studies* (1868), *Main Currents in Nineteenth-Century Literature* (6 vols., 1872–90), lives of Esaias Tegnér, Lassalle (1877), and Beaconsfield (1879), *Sören Kierkegaard* (1877), *Danish Poets* (1884), *Impressions of Russia* (1888), monographs on Shakespeare (1895–96), Goethe (1915), Voltaire (1916–17), and others, *The Jesus Myth* (1925). His brother **Carl Edvard Brandes** (1847–1931), critic, playwright, and politician, was coeditor of radical paper *Politiken*, Copenhagen (from 1884); minister of finance (1913–20).

**Bran′des** (brän′dĕs), **Johannes Christian.** 1735–1799. German actor and dramatist.

**Bran′dis** (brän′dĭs), **Christian August.** 1790–1867. German classical philologist and historian of philosophy.

**Brandis,** Sir **Dietrich.** 1824–1907. Forestry expert, b. Bonn, Germany. Inspector general of Indian forests (1864–83); adviser of British and American forestry students (1888–96).

**Brandl** (brän′d′l), **Alois.** 1855–1940. Austrian Anglicist and literary historian. President, German Shakespeare Society (1903–21) and coeditor of its yearbook (1899–1918). Re-edited Tieck translation of Shakespeare (1897); author of *Samuel Taylor Coleridge und die Englische Romantik* (1886), *Mittelenglische Literatur* (1893), *William Shakespeare* (1894), *Lebendige Sprache* (1928–32), etc.

**Bran′don** (brăn′dŭn), Dukes of. Title of dukes of Hamilton, first bestowed on 4th duke. See marquises and dukes of HAMILTON.

**Brandon,** Viscount. See Charles GERARD.

**Brandon, Charles.** 1st Duke of **Suf′folk** (sŭf′ŭk). d. 1545. English soldier. Served Henry VIII as squire and on various diplomatic missions; m. Henry's sister Mary of France (*q.v.*); commanded unsuccessful invasion of France (1523) and at capture of Boulogne (1544).

**Brandon, Richard.** d. 1649. English executioner of Charles I; son of **Gregory Brandon,** London hangman.

**Brandt.** See also BRAND and BRANT.

**Brandt** (brănt, *Ger.* bränt), **Willy.** *Real name* **Herbert Frahm** (′främ). 1913– . West German statesman. Mayor of West Berlin (1957–66); chancellor of West Germany (1969–74). Nobel peace prize (1971).

**Brandts′-Buys′** (bränts′bois′). Family of Dutch musicians including: **Henry** (1851–1905), choral conductor (from 1878) in Amsterdam; his nephew **Jan** (1868–1933), composer (in Ragusa, Italy, from 1920); and Jan's cousin **Johann Sebastian** (1879– ), music critic and writer on modern and Javanese music.

**Bran′ford** (brăn′fẽrd), **Frederick Victor.** 1892– . English poet; author of *Titans and Gods* (1922), *The White Stallion* (1924).

**Brang′wyn** (brăng′wĭn), Sir **Frank.** 1867–1956. British painter and mural decorator, b. at Bruges, of Welsh extraction. Known for richness of color in his decorative panels, skillful technique in etchings (*London Bridge, Notre Dame, The Paper Mill*), and designs for stained glass, tapestry, book decoration, and metalwork. Also known for broad treatment and correct drawing in his pictures.

**Bran′ko·vić** (brän′kō·vēt′y′; *Angl.* -vĭch). Name of a reigning Serbian family of 14th and 15th centuries, including: **Vuk** (d. 1398), reputed traitor at Kosovo (1389); his son **George** [jôrj] (1367–1456); sided first with Hungarians, then with Turks; built new capital at Semendria (Smederevo); his sons driven out of Serbia by Turks (by 1459).

**Bran′ly′** (bräN′lē′), **Édouard.** 1844–1940. French physicist; inventor (1890) of coherer (so called by Sir Oliver Lodge in 1894) that made wireless telegraphy possible.

**Brann** (brăn), **William Cowper.** 1855–1898. American journalist; founded *The Iconoclast* (1891; Waco, Tex.), a journal designed "to break foolish idols and shatter false ideals"; by violent attacks on what he considered sham, fraud, and humbug stirred up hostility; killed in pistol fight on streets of Waco (1898). Author of *Brann the Iconoclast* (2 vols.), etc.

**Bran′nan** (brăn′ăn), **Samuel.** 1819–1889. American pioneer; adopted Mormon faith (1842); led colony of Mormons to California (1846). Published *California Star* (1847), first newspaper in San Francisco.

**Bran′ner** (brăn′ẽr), **John Casper.** 1850–1922. American geologist; investigated mineral deposits and suitability of soil for growth of cotton in Brazil (1874–84).

**Brans′combe** (brăns′kŭm), **Gena.** 1881– . Canadian composer; m. John Ferguson Tenney (1910). Composer of choral drama *Pilgrims of Destiny, Festival Prelude,* symphonic suite *Quebec,* chamber music, and choral works.

**Brant** (brănt), **Joseph.** *Indian name* **Tha·yen′da·ne′-ge·a** (thȧ·yĕn′dȧ·nā′gē·ȧ). 1742–1807. Mohawk Indian chief. Educ. in charity school in Lebanon, Conn.; became member of Anglican Church. In American Revolution given captain's commission by British, honored on trip to England, painted in Mohawk regalia by Romney. Commanded Indian forces co-operating with St. Leger's expedition, fought fiercely at battle of Oriskany (Aug. 6, 1777); responsible for the Cherry Valley massacre (1778); with Tories ravaged Mohawk Valley. Assigned land in Canada after Revolution; persuaded British (1785) to indemnify Iroquois for their losses in the war.

**Brant** *or* **Brandt** (bränt), **Sebastian.** 1457?–1521. German humanist and satiric poet. Author of satirical didactic poem *Narrenschiff* (1494), the source of *The Shyp of Folys* by Alexander Barclay (*q.v.*).

**Bran′ting′** (brȧn′tĭng′), **Karl Hjalmar.** 1860–1925. Swedish Socialist leader and statesman; co-winner (with Christian Lange) of Nobel peace prize for 1921. Editor of the *Socialdemokraten,* Stockholm (1886–1917). Cofounder (1889) and leader, Swedish Social Democratic Labor party; member, 2d chamber of the Riksdag (from 1897); minister of finance, Liberal Socialist cabinet (1917–18); presided at Stockholm Conference (1917) and other conferences on international social democracy; advocated neutrality for Sweden but sympathized with Allies in World War I. Prime minister (1920, 1921–23, 1924–25); first representative of Sweden, Assembly of League of Nations, and member of Council (1922–25).

**Bran′tôme′** (bräN′tōm′), Seigneur **de. Pierre de Bour′deilles′** (dē bo͝or′dâ′y′). 1535?–1614. French chronicler; served in army against Huguenots; author of *Mémoires* (pub. 1665–66), treasured for account of important people and events of period.

**Braque** (brȧk), **Georges.** 1882–1963. French painter; identified with ultramodern group of painters; an early exponent of Fauvism, and one of founders of cubism. Painted still-life studies and a few landscapes.

**Bras′cas′sat′** (brȧs′kȧ′sȧ′), **Jacques Raymond.** 1804–1867. French landscape and animal painter.

**Bras de Fer.** See François de LA NOUE.

**Bra·shear′** (bră·shẹr′), **John Alfred.** 1840–1920. American scientist; maker of lenses for telescopes.

**Brash′er** (brăsh′ẽr), **Rex.** 1869–1960. American ornithologist; painter of birds in natural colors; author of *Birds and Trees of North America* (12 vols., 1934).

**Bras′i·das** (brăs′ĭ·dȧs). d. 422 B.C. Spartan general in early phases of Peloponnesian War; relieved Methone (431 B.C.), repulsed Athenian attack on Megara (428), captured Athenian colony of Amphipolis (424), and defeated Cleon before Amphipolis (422).

**Bras′lau** (brăs′lou), **Sophie.** 1892–1935. American operatic contralto, with Metropolitan Opera Company.

**Bras'seur' de Bour'bourg'** (brȧ'sûr' dẽ bo͝or'bo͝or'), **Charles Étienne.** 1814–1874. French clergyman and ethnographer; missionary in Mexico and Central America (1848–64); archaeologist to French scientific expedition to Mexico (1864); translated into French *Popol Vuh*, sacred book of Quiché Indians.

**Bras'sey** (brăs'ĭ), **Thomas.** 1805–1870. English railway contractor. His eldest son, **Thomas** (1836–1918), Earl **Brassey,** became secretary to the admiralty (1883–85), governor of Victoria, Australia (1895–1900); author of an encyclopedic work, *The British Navy* (1882–83); founder of the *Naval Annual* (1886); his wife (m. 1860), **Anna (Annie),** *nee* **All'nutt** [ôl'nŭt] (1839–1887), was author of *The Voyage in the Sunbeam* (1878) and *Last Voyage* (1889).

**Bras'sin'** (brȧ'săɴ'), **Lou'is** (lo͞o'ē). 1840–1884. Belgian pianist and composer, in Berlin (1866), Brussels (1869–79), and St. Petersburg. His brother and pupil **Leopold** (1843–1890) was court pianist at Coburg; another brother, **Gerhard** (1844–?1885), violinist and composer of solos, concertmeister, Gothenburg, Sweden; teacher, Berlin (1874–75); conductor, Breslau (1875–80).

**Brath'waite** *or* **Brath'wait** *or* **Brath'wayte** (brăth'-wāt), **Richard.** 1588–1673. English poet. Author of *A Strappado for the Devil* (1615), a collection of satires, and *Barnabae Itinerarium*, doggerel verse in English and Latin (1638).

**Bră·ti·a'nu** (brȧ·tĭ·ä'no͞o). Name of politically prominent Rumanian family, including among its members: **Ioan** (1822–1891), active in Rumanian rebellion against Russia and Turkey (1848); forced to take refuge in France; returned to Rumania (1857) and rose to leadership in Liberal party; aided in fall of Cuza and election of Prince Charles of Hohenzollern as king; prime minister (1867–68, 1876–88); succeeded as prime minister by his brother **Dimitrie** (1818–1892), who had been politically opposed to him (from c. 1856). Ioan's son **Ion** (1864–1927) was prime minister (1909–11; 1913–18; Dec., 1918–Sept., 1919; 1922–26; June–Sept., 1927) and virtual dictator of country (from 1922); succeeded as prime minister by his brother **Vintilă** (1867–1930), who was forced out of office (1928) by Iuliu Maniu (*q.v.*), leader of Peasant party.

**Brat'tain** (brăt''n), **Walter Houser.** 1902– . American physicist, b. Amoy, China. Researcher at Bell Telephone Lab.; awarded Nobel prize in physics (1956) with J. Bardeen and W. Shockley.

**Brat'tle** (brăt''l), **Thomas.** 1658–1713. American merchant; treasurer, Harvard (1693–1713). Chief organizer of Brattle Street Church, Cambridge, Mass.; waged controversy with the Mathers; condemned Salem witchcraft proceedings (1692).

**Bratton, Henry de.** See BRACTON.

**Brau'chitsch** (brou'kĭch), **Heinrich Alfred Hermann Walther von.** 1881–1948. German army officer, b. Berlin. Major general (1931); Reichswehr chief of artillery (1932); commander of East Prussian military area (1933); colonel general and commander in chief of German army (1938). Planned and carried out German occupation of Austria and Czechoslovakia, conquest of Poland, and movements in war against France and Great Britain (1939), and Russia (1941); relieved of command by Hitler (1941); interned by British (1945).

**Brau'er** (brou'ẽr), **Friedrich.** 1832–1904. German entomologist; proposed (1885) the system of classification of Insecta which is in general use today.

**Braun** (broun), **August Emil.** 1809–1856. German archaeologist.

**Braun, Heinrich.** 1854–1927. German Social Democratic writer and politician. Cofounder (1883) of Social Democrat paper *Die Neue Zeit;* member of Reichstag (1903); Prussian minister of agriculture (1919). His wife **Lily,** *nee* **von Kretsch'mann** [krāch'män; krĕch'-] (1865–1916), a Socialist, daughter of Gen. Hans von Kretschmann, was author of *Aus Goethes Freundeskreisen* (1892), *Im Schatten der Titanen* (1908), the novel *Lebenssucher* (1917), and works on social questions.

**Braun, Karl.** 1822–1893. German political leader and writer; advocate of German unity and industrial freedom; member of Reichstag (1867–87) and of Supreme Court, Leipzig (1879–87).

**Braun, Karl Ferdinand.** 1850–1918. German physicist. Professor of physics and director of Physical Institute at Strassburg (from 1895). Discovered method in wireless telegraphy of increasing energy of sending station, and of gaining control of direction of effective radiation by arrangement of antennas; invented a cathode-ray tube (Braun tube). Awarded (jointly with Marconi) the 1909 Nobel prize for physics.

**Braun, Kaspar.** 1807–1877. German wood engraver.

**Braun, Otto.** 1872–1955. Prussian political leader. Social Democratic member of Prussian Chamber of Deputies (1913), of German National Assembly, Weimar (1919–20), and of Reichstag (1920 ff.); minister of agriculture (1918–21); prime minister of Prussia (1920–21, 1921–25. 1925–33); in Switzerland (from 1933).

**Braun, Wernher von.** 1912-1977. Am. rocket expert, b. Germany. Helped develop German World War II rockets. To U.S. (1945); worked on U.S. space program.

**Brau'ne** (brou'nĕ), **Christian Wilhelm.** 1831–1892. German anatomist.

**Brau'ner** (brou'nẽr), **Bohuslav.** 1855–1935. Czech chemist; known for work in inorganic chemistry, esp. on grouping of elements in Mendeleev's periodic system, atomic weights, and rare elements.

**Braun'fels** (broun'fĕls), **Walter.** 1882–1954. German pianist and composer.

**Braunschweig.** See BRUNSWICK.

**Brauwer, Adriaen.** See BROUWER.

**Bra'vo** (brä'vō), **Luis González.** See GONZÁLES BRAVO.

**Bravo, Nicolás.** 1787?–1854. Mexican general and political leader, b. Chilpancingo. One of leaders who overthrew Iturbide (1823); vice-president of Mexico (1824–27). Led rebellion against President Guadalupe Victoria (1827); defeated and banished (1828). Acting president (1839, 1842–43), also president for a few days (1846).

**Bra'vo-Mu·ril'lo** (-mo͞o·rē'lyō), **Juan González.** 1803–1873. Spanish statesman; a founder and editor of first law journal in Spain, *Boletín de Jurisprudencia* (1835 ff.); member of Cortes (1837, 1839); proscribed as enemy of Espartero and fled to France (1840–43). Minister of justice (1847), public instruction and finance (1849); prime minister (1851–52); exiled (1854–56); engaged in diplomatic missions (1856–68). Accompanied Queen Isabella II on flight to Bayonne after revolution (1868).

**Braw'ley** (brô'lĭ), **Benjamin Griffith.** 1882–1939. American Baptist clergyman and educator. Professor of English, Atlanta Baptist Coll. (1906–10), Howard U. (1910–12), Morehouse Coll. (1912–20), Shaw U. (1923–31), Howard U. (1931–39). Author of *A Short History of the American Negro* (1913), *The Negro in Literature and Art* (1918), *The Negro Genius* (1937), etc.

**Brawne** (brôn), **Fanny.** See John KEATS.

**Brax'ton** (brăks'tŭn), **Carter.** 1736–1797. American Revolutionary political leader, b. Newington, Va. Member, Continental Congress (1775–76; 1777–83; 1785); signer of the Declaration of Independence.

**Bray** (brā), **Anna Eliza,** *nee* **Kempe** (kĕmp). 1790–1883. English novelist; m. (1818) Charles Alfred Stothard (see under Thomas STOTHARD); m. (1823?) Rev. Edward Atkyns Bray, writer. Wrote (1826–74) historical romances, the most popular based on histories of Devon and Cornwall families.

**Bray, Thomas.** 1656–1730. English clergyman. Sent by bishop of London to organize Anglican church in Maryland (1699); founder of Society for the Propagation of the Gospel.

**Bray′ley** (brā′lĭ), **Edward Wedlake.** 1773–1854. English topographer and archaeologist; collaborator with John Britton in topographical books.

**Braz Pe·rei′ra Go′mes** (brȧs′ pĕ·rā′rȧ gō′mēs), **Wenceslau.** 1868–1966. Brazilian political leader and industrialist. President of Minas Gerais (1909–10); vice-president of Brazil (1910–14), president (1914–18).

**Braz′za′** (brȧ′zȧ′), **Pierre Paul François Camille Sa′vor′gnan′ de** (sȧ′vôr′nyäN′ dē). *Real name* **Braz′za Sa′vor·gna′ni** (brät′tsä sä′vôr·nyä′nē). 1852–1905. French explorer in Africa. Explored region of Ogowe River (1875–78); later, traversed Gabon, reached Stanley Pool, founded Brazzaville (now capital of French Equatorial Africa), and placed region under French protection (1879–82); returned to Congo (1883); commissioner-general (1886–98).

**Breadalbane,** Earl of. See John CAMPBELL.

**Breakspear, Nicholas.** = Pope ADRIAN IV.

**Bré′al′** (brā′ȧl′), **Michel Jules Alfred.** 1832–1915. French philologist. Author of *Dictionnaire Étymologique Latin* (1885), *Essai de Sémantique* (1897), etc. Translator of Bopp's comparative grammar (1867–72).

**Breas′ted** (brĕs′tĕd; -tĭd), **James Henry.** 1865–1935. American Orientalist, archaeologist, and historian, b. Rockford, Ill. On staff of U. of Chicago (1894–1935), professor of Egyptology and Oriental history (1905–33). Director of various archaeological expeditions to Egypt and Mesopotamia (1919–20, and after 1925). Among his many books are *A History of Egypt* (1905), *Development of Religion and Thought in Ancient Egypt* (1912), *Ancient Times* (1916), re-edited as *Conquest of Civilization* (1926), *The Dawn of Conscience* (1933).

**Bré′beuf′** (brā′bûf′), **Jean de.** 1593–1649. French Jesuit missionary among Huron Indians in Canada; put to death by Iroquois; canonized (June 29, 1930).

**Brecht** (brĕKt), **Bertolt** *or* **Bert.** 1898–1956. German playwright and poet. In exile (from 1935).

**Breck′en·ridge** (brĕk′ĕn·rĭj), **Hugh Henry.** 1870–1937. American painter.

**Breckenridge, Lester Paige.** 1858–1940. American mechanical engineer; designed dynamometer cars for determining train resistance on railroads (1897–99); invented automatic recording machine (1901); known also for work on smokeless combustion and on power production.

**Breck′in·ridge** (brĕk′ĭn·rĭj), **John Cabell.** 1821–1875. American lawyer and statesman, b. near Lexington, Ky. Member, U.S. House of Representatives (1851–55); vice-president of U.S. (1857–61); presidential candidate, southern faction Democratic party (1860); U.S. senator (1861). Joined Confederate army (1861); secretary of war, Confederate States of America (1865). His grandfather **John** (1760–1806), b. near Staunton, Va., U.S. senator (1801–05); attorney general of U.S. (1805–06).

**Bre′de·ro** (brā′dĕ·rō), **Gerbrand Adriaanszoon.** 1585–1618. Dutch playwright and poet; author of lyrics (pub. 1622) and of farces and comedies.

**Bre′de·ro′de** (brā′dĕ·rō′dĕ), Count **Hendrik van.** 1531–1568. b. Brussels, descendent of ancient counts of Holland. Leader of nobles ("les Gueux," or "The Beggars") in struggle against Spanish rule in the Netherlands; took part (1566) in drawing up the "Compromise" of nobles, at Breda, and the petition of grievances presented to Margaret of Parma; made unsuccessful attempt to raise army at Antwerp; fled to Germany (1567).

**Bre·di′chin** (bryĭ·dyē′chyĭn), **Fëdor Aleksandrovich.** 1831–1904. Russian astronomer; director of observatory, Moscow (1873–90), Pulkovo (1890–95); known for work on the forms of comets and the structure of meteors.

**Bre′dig** (brā′dĭK), **Georg.** 1868–1944. German chemist; deviser of a method (Bredig method) of preparing colloids by electrical disintegration.

**Bre′dow** (brā′dō), **Adalbert von.** 1814–1890. Prussian general; cavalry officer in war of 1866; led charge at Vionville-Mars-la-Tour, Franco-Prussian War (1870); lieutenant general (1871).

**Breen** (brēn), **Patrick.** d. 1868. Pioneer in America, b. in Ireland, to U.S. (1828). One of 36 survivors of 81 in party, led by George Donner, isolated on way to California by blizzard (Nov., 1846); his diary contains vivid account of the tragedy.

**Breese** (brēz), **Kidder Randolph.** 1831–1881. American naval officer, b. Philadelphia. Accompanied Commodore Matthew C. Perry's expedition to Japan (1852). Served through Civil War; fleet captain under Porter (1864–66); led assault on Fort Fisher (Jan. 15, 1865).

**Bre′feld** (brā′fĕlt), **Ludwig.** 1837–1907. Prussian jurist; minister of commerce and trade (1896–1901). His brother **Oskar** (1839–1925), botanist, carried on researches in mycology and is credited with introducing gelatin cultures in bacteriology.

**Bre′gen·dahl** (brĭ′gĕn·dȧl), **Marie.** 1867–1940. Danish writer of fiction and poetry.

**Bré′guet′** (brā′gĕ′), **Abraham Louis.** 1747–1823. French mechanician and watchmaker; built instruments of great accuracy, including astronomical clocks and marine chronometers; made improvements in watches, as the use of the ruby as a bearing. His grandson **Louis François Clément** (1804–1883), physicist and watchmaker, was in charge of building first electric telegraph line along Rouen railway; invented device to protect telegraphic apparatus from atmospheric electricity, and system of electric clocks for transmitting time to a distance. **Antoine** (1851–1882), son of Louis François Clément, was an electrical engineer and industrialist; inventor of an electrical recording anemometer. **Louis Charles** (1881–1955), manufacturer of airplanes, descendant of Abraham Louis, equipped first helicopter to rise perpendicularly with a passenger.

**Brehm** (brām), **Alfred Edmund.** 1829–1884. German zoologist; founder (1867) and director (1867–75), Berlin Aquarium. Author of *Tierleben* (6 vols., 1864–69), *Das Leben der Vögel* (2d ed., 1867–68), etc. His father, **Christian Ludwig** (1787–1864), pastor and ornithologist, made a collection of over 9000 birds, almost entirely European.

**Brehm, Bruno von.** 1892– . Viennese novelist and art historian, b. in Yugoslavia.

**Breinlinger, Alice Berend.** See Alice BEREND.

**Brei′ting·er** (brī′tĭng·ẽr), **Johann Jakob.** 1701–1776. Swiss scholar. As collaborator with Bodmer (*q.v.*) on *Die Discourse der Mahlern*, engaged in famous Swiss opposition to literary influence of Gottsched and the rationalists. His own more constructive *Kritische Dichtkunst* (2 vols., 1740) influenced literary ideals of Klopstock, Goethe, and Schiller through championship of irrational elements of poetry, esp. English. His *Fabeln aus den Zeiten der Minnesinger* (1757) helped pave way for later interest of romanticists in literature of Middle Ages.

**Breit′kopf** (brīt′kôpf). Family of German printers and publishers, including: **Bernhard Christoph** (1695–1777), founder of Leipzig printing (1719) and publishing (from 1725) firm, known (from 1795) as Breitkopf and Härtel. His son and successor (from 1745), **Johann Gottlob Im-**

manuel (1719–1794), typographical expert, developed (from 1750) movable music type; improved musical notation and German characters; devised method of printing maps and Chinese characters from movable pieces; wrote several treatises on printing. Johann's son **Christoph Gottlob** (1750–1800) gave up the business (1795) to G. C. Härtel.

**Breit'mann** (brīt'măn; -män), **Hans** (häns). Pseudonym of Charles Godfrey LELAND.

**Bre'ke·len·kam** (brā'kĕ·lĕn·käm), **Quirijn van.** 1620?–1668. Dutch painter, esp. of scenes from folk life, market scenes, and domestic and workshop interiors.

**Bre'ma** (brā'mȧ), **Ma'rie** (mä'rĭ). *Real name* **Min'ny Fehr'mann** (mĭn'ē fār'män). 1856–1925. English opera singer.

**Bre'mer** (brā'mẽr), **Fredrika.** 1801–1865. Novelist, b. in Finland; moved to Sweden (1805). Author of *Sketches of Everyday Life*, a series of romances (1828 ff.), of *Hertha* (1856) and *Father and Daughter* (1858), in which she advocates equal rights for women, etc.

**Bre'mond'** (brā'môɴ'), **Henri.** 1855–1933. French literary critic and historian.

**Brenainn,** Saint. See BRENDAN.

**Bren'dan** (brĕn'dăn) *or* **Bren'ainn** (brĕn'ĭn) *or* **Bran'dan** (brăn'dăn) *or* **Bo·ran'don** (bô·răn'dŭn), Saint. 484–577. Hero of a legendary voyage (565–573) to the promised land of saints on western islands, basis of popular medieval legend *Navigation of St. Brendan;* founder of a monastery at Clonfert (?553). Also called **Brendan of Clon'fert** (klŏn'fẽrt), *or* **Brendan, son of Finn'lo·ga** (fĭn'lô·ĸȧ), to distinguish him from another Irish saint, **Brendan of Birr** [bĭr] (490?–573).

**Bren'del** (brĕn'dĕl), **Karl Franz.** 1811–1868. German writer on music; supported "New German" movement of Wagner and Liszt.

**Brendel, Martin.** 1862–1939. German astronomer.

**Bre·net'** (brē·nĕ'), **Michel.** *Pseudonym of* **Marie Bo'bil'lier'** (bô'bē'lyā'). 1858–1918. French writer on music.

**Bren'nan** (brĕn'ăn), **Francis.** 1894–1968. Am. Roman Catholic leader and cardinal, b. Pa. First Amer. member of Sacred Roman Rota (1940), dean (1959).

**Brennan, Frederick Hazlitt.** 1901–1962. American journalist, b. St. Louis; fiction writer, and playwright.

**Brennan, Louis.** 1852–1932. Irish inventor of a dirigible torpedo and a gyroscopic monorail railway system.

**Brennan, William Joseph,** Jr. 1906– American lawyer, b. Newark, N.J.; justice Supreme Court, N.J. (1952–56); associate justice, U.S. Supreme Court (from1956).

**Bren'ner** (brĕn'ẽr), **Elias.** 1647–1717. Swedish archaeologist and numismatist, b. Finland. His wife, **Sophia Elisabeth,** *nee* **We'ber** [vā'bẽr] (1659–1730), was a lyric poet.

**Bren'ner** (brĕn'ẽr), **Vic'tor** (vĭk'tẽr) **Da'vid** (dā'vĭd). 1871–1924. Sculptor, b. Shavli, Russia. To U.S. (about 1890). Designed Lincoln cent (issued 1909).

**Brennglas, Adolf.** Pseudonym of Adolf GLASSBRENNER.

**Bren'nus** (brĕn'ŭs). Semilegendary Gallic chieftain of 4th century B.C. Led an invasion of Italy, defeated Roman army, and plundered and burned city of Rome, besieging the capitol until bought off by offer of 1000 pounds of gold. According to legend, during weighing of gold, a Roman tribune protested against use of false weights by the Gauls, whereupon Brennus cast his sword on the scale with the exclamation, "Vae Victis!" *i.e.* "Woe to the vanquished!"

**Brennus.** Gallic leader in invasion of Greece (279 B.C.); defeated before Delphi; said to have killed himself.

**Brent** (brĕnt), **Charles Henry.** 1862–1929. Protestant Episcopal bishop, b. Newcastle, Ontario, Canada. Pastorate in Boston (1891–1901). Bishop of the Philippine Islands (1901–18); bishop of western New York (1918–26); bishop in charge of churches in Europe (1926–28).

**Bren·ta'no** (brĕn·tä'nō), **Clemens.** 1778–1842. Brother of Bettina von Arnim (*q.v.*). German dramatist, novelist, and romantic poet. Became fervid Roman Catholic (1818) and withdrew to monastery of Dülmen, near Münster (1818–24) to be near the nun Anna Katharina Emmerich (*q.v.*), whose revelations he recorded. Compiled (1805–08), with his brother-in-law Ludwig von Arnim, *Des Knaben Wunderhorn,* a collection of German folk songs. Author of plays, stories, and patriotic, spiritual, and commemorative poems. His nephew **Franz** (1838–1917) was a philosopher; Roman Catholic priest (1864–73); professor in Würzburg (1872), in Vienna (1874–80); resident largely in Florence (from 1895); author of books on Aristotle, and of works on psychology, logic, ethics. Franz's brother **Lujo** *or* **Ludwig** (1844–1931), political economist, investigated trade unionism in England (1868), championed the working class, advocated free trade, and opposed the wage-fund theory; professor successively (1872–91) in Breslau, Strassburg, Vienna, Leipzig, and (1891–1914) Munich.

**Brentford,** Earl of. See Patrick RUTHVEN.

**Brentford,** Viscount. See Sir William JOYNSON-HICKS.

**Bren'ton** (brĕn't'n; -tŭn), **William.** d. 1674. English colonist in America. To Massachusetts Colony (1634); to Portsmouth, R.I. (1639); a founder of Newport, R.I. (1639); deputy governor of Portsmouth and Newport (1640–47; 1662–65); president of Providence Plantations (1660–62); governor of Rhode Island and Providence Plantations under charter of 1663 (1666–69).

**Brenz** (brĕnts), **Johann.** 1499–1570. Lutheran reformer; took active part in Reformation as disciple of Luther; coauthor of *Syngramma Suevicum* (1525) and proponent of Ubiquitarian theory; forced to flee (1548); provost, Stuttgart (from 1553).

**Brere'ley** *or* **Brier'ley** (brẹ̄r'lĭ), **Roger.** 1586–1637. English clergyman and poet; founder of the Familist sect of Grindletonians.

**Brere'ton** (brâr't'n), **Lewis Hyde.** 1890–1967. American army officer, b. Pittsburgh; grad. U.S.N.A. (Annapolis) but transferred to army (1911); in military aviation; served in World War I; head of air force in Philippines (1941) and Middle East (1942) and of all U.S. forces in Middle East (1943); head of 9th Air Force and later of allied airborne forces in W. Europe.

**Brere'ton** (brẹ̄r't'n), Sir **William.** 1604–1661. English military commander in Cromwell's Roundhead army.

**Brescia, Arnold of** (*Ital.* **Arnaldo da**). See ARNOLD OF BRESCIA.

**Brescia, Moretto da.** = Il MORETTO.

**Brescianino, Girolamo.** See MUZIANO.

**Bresh·kov'sky** (*Angl.* brĕsh·kôf'skĭ), **Catherine.** *Russ. name* **Ekaterina Konstantinovna Bresh'ko–Bresh·kov'ska·ya** (bryäsh'kô·bryĭsh·kôf'skŭ·yŭ). *Called* **Ba'bush·ka** (bȧ'bo͝osh·kŭ) *and* "Grandmother of the Russian Revolution." 1844–1934. Russian revolutionist, b. near Vitebsk, Little Russia, of wealthy and noble family. Devoted life to welfare of Russian peasant. Left home (1870) to spread revolutionary doctrine; at Kiev, joined followers of Bakunin; imprisoned, St. Petersburg (1874–78), exiled to Siberia (1878); kept much of the time in close confinement; on release (1896) joined agitation for agrarian revolution; fled to Switzerland (1900); visited U.S. (1904–05), but returned to Russia (1905) to take part in abortive revolution; imprisoned (1907–10), and again banished to Siberia; released by Kerensky (1917); forced to flee after Bolsheviks came to power; lectured in U.S. (1919); spent last years in Czechoslovakia.

**Bressano, Girolamo.** See MUZIANO.

**Bress'lau** (brĕs'lou), **Harry.** 1848–1926. German historian and paleographer.

**Bre·teuil'** (brē·tû'y'), Baron **de. Louis Auguste le Ton'ne·lier'** (tô'nē·lyā'). 1730–1807. French politician and diplomat; secretary of state to king's household (1783–88); central figure in group opposed to Calonne and upholding king's autocratic powers; his return to ministry (July 12, 1789) signal for outbreak of the Revolution. Émigré (1789–1802).

**Bre·ton'** (brē·tôɴ'), **André.** 1896–**1966.** French poet, essayist, and critic; member of the Dadaists, and a founder of the surrealist movement; editor (from 1924) of *La Révolution Surréaliste.*

**Breton, Jules Adolphe.** 1827–1906. French painter and writer; excelled in painting scenes of rustic life. His painting *The First Communion* was sold for $45,000 (1886) and greatly increased his reputation; other paintings: *Bénédiction des Blés* (Luxembourg), *Plantation d'un Calvaire* (Lille). Author of *Les Champs et la Mer* (1875) and *Jeanne* (1880), verse; *La Vie d'un Artiste* (1890), *Un Peintre Paysan* (1896). His brother **Émile Adélard** (1831–1902) was a landscape painter.

**Bret'on** (brĕt''n) *or* **Brit'ton** *or* **Brit'taine** (brĭt''n), **Nicholas.** 1551?–c.1623. English poet. Author of satirical, religious, romantic, and pastoral works in prose and verse, including the pastoral *Passionate Shepheard* (1604), and an idyll in prose, *Wits Trenchmour* (1597).

**Bre·tón' de los Her·re'ros** (brā·tôn' dā lōs ĕr·rĕ'rōs), **Manuel.** 1796–1873. Spanish dramatist. Member, Spanish Acad. (1837 ff.); director, Biblioteca Nacional (1847–73). Author of some 360 plays, including *A la Vejez Viruelas* (1824), *Me Voy de Madrid* (1828), *Marcela* (1831), *A Madrid Me Vuelvo* (1836), *Muérete ¡y Verás...!* (1837), *Escuela del Matrimonio* (1852), and lyric and satiric poems.

**Bre·tón' y Her·nán'dez** (brā·tôn' ē ĕr·năn'dāth), **Tomás.** 1850–1923. Spanish composer; director, Madrid conservatory. Composer of zarzuelas, operas, an orchestral suite, oratorio, and chamber music.

**Bre·ton'neau'** (brē·tô'nō'), **Pierre.** 1778–1862. French physician; known for descriptions of typhoid fever and diphtheria; credited with performing first successful tracheotomy for diphtheria; first used the term *diphthérie,* which was adapted in English as *diphtheria;* enunciated a theory of specific causes of infectious diseases.

**Bret'schnei'der** (brĕt'shnī'dēr), **Karl Gottlieb.** 1776–1848. German Protestant theologian; edited Melanchthon's works (1834–48) in *Corpus Reformatorum.*

**Brett** (brĕt). Family name of Viscount ESHER.

**Brett, George Howard.** 1886–1963. American army officer; grad. Virginia Military Institute. Served in Philippine scouts (1910); 2d lieutenant, cavalry, U.S. army (1911); transferred to signal corps for air training (1915). Major general, acting chief of air corps, U.S. army (1940); lieutenant general, U.S. army, and deputy supreme commander under General Wavell in the Far East (Jan., 1942), under General MacArthur (Mar., 1942); head of U.S. Caribbean defense command (1942–45)

**Brett, John Watkins** (1805–1863) and his younger brother **Jacob.** English pioneers in submarine **telegraphy.** Established submarine telegraphic communication between England and France (1850). Associated in syndicate with Cyrus Field in laying first transatlantic cable (1858), which failed after transmitting a few messages.

**Bretton, Henry de.** See BRACTON.

**Breu'er** (broi'ĕr), **Josef.** 1842–1925. Austrian physician; known esp. for work on the ear and on psychoanalysis; author (with Freud) of *Studien über Hysterie* (1895).

**Breu'er** (broi'ĕr), **Mar·cel'** (?mär·sĕl') **Lajos.** 1902– Architect, b. in Hungary; M.A., Bauhaus, Weimar (1924); director, Bauhaus, Dessau (1925–28); practiced as architect in Berlin (1928–31), while traveling in European countries (1931–35), in London (1935–37); associate professor, Harvard U. (1937–46) and partner of Walter Gropius (*q.v.*) in architectural firm, Cambridge Mass. His interests range from large hospital and factory projects through private housing (including interior designs and prefabricated houses), to pioneer work in furniture design (tubular steel 1925, aluminum 1933, plywood 1935).

**Breuer, Peter.** 1856–1930. German sculptor.

**Breughel.** See BRUEGHEL.

**Breuil** (brû'y'), Abbé **Henri Édouard Prosper.** 1877–**1961.** French archaeologist; authority on paleolithic art

**Breul** (broil), **Karl Hermann.** 1860–1932. Germanic scholar and writer in England; author of revisions of *New German Dictionary* (from 1906), editions of German classics, *The Romantic Movement in German Literature* (1927), etc.

**Bre·voort'** (brē·vōrt'; -vôrt'), **James Ren'wick** (rĕn'-wĭk). 1832–1918. American landscape painter.

**Brew'er** (brōō'ĕr), **David Josiah.** 1837–1910. American jurist, b. Smyrna, Asia Minor, son of a missionary; associate justice, U.S. Supreme Court (1889–1910); member Venezuela boundary and arbitration commissions.

**Brewer, Ebenezer Cobham.** 1810–1897. English clergyman and schoolmaster; compiler of *Dictionary of Phrase and Fable* (1870).

**Brewer, Thomas Mayo.** 1814–1880. American ornithologist.

**Brewer, William Henry.** 1828–1910. American scientist; assistant to J. D. Whitney in geological survey of California (1860–64); collected about 2000 species of plants of California; professor of agriculture, Yale (1864–1903). Instrumental in establishing, in Connecticut, the first agricultural experiment station in U.S., and in organizing Yale Forestry School (1900).

**Brew'ster** (brōō'stēr), **Benjamin Harris.** 1816–1888. American lawyer; U.S. attorney general (1881–85); prosecuted the accused in star-route fraud **cases.**

**Brewster, Chauncey Bunce.** 1848–1941. American Protestant Episcopal clergyman; bishop of Connecticut (1899–1928; resigned). His brother **Benjamin** (1860–1941) was bishop of Maine (1916–41).

**Brewster,** Sir **David.** 1781–1868. Scottish physicist, b. Jedburgh. Discovered biaxial crystals. Invented a kaleidoscope (1816); improved on the stereoscope. Advocated adoption of refractive system in lighthouses.

**Brewster, George Thomas.** 1862–1943. American sculptor; carved Robert E. Lee bust in Hall of Fame.

**Brewster, King'man** (kĭng'măn). 1919– . American educator; president of Yale (from 1963).

**Brewster, William.** 1567–1644. American pioneer, b. in England. Bailiff and postmaster, Scrooby, Eng. (1590–1608). Emigrated to Holland (1608), settled at Leiden (1609); in printing business (1609–19). Sailed to America on the *Mayflower* (1620). Leader of church and influential in management of affairs of Plymouth Colony.

**Brezh'nev** (brĕzh'nyĕf), **Leonid I.** 1906– . Russian politician; president of U.S.S.R. (1960–64; 1977– ); first secretary of the Communist party (from 1964).

**Březina, Otakar.** Pseudonym of Václav JEBAVÝ.

**Brian** (brēn; *Angl.* brī'ăn). *Known in Eng. as* **Brian Bo·ru'** (bô·rōō'; -rōō') *or in Irish writings as* **Brian Bo·ram'ha** *or* **Bo·raim'he** *or, less correctly,* **Bo·roim'he, Bo·rum'ha** (*all pronounced* bô·rōō'; -rōō'), etc. 926–1014. King of Ireland (1002–14); slain while defeating Danes at battle of Clontarf, near Dublin.

**Bri'an'chon'** (brē'äN'shôN'), **Charles Julien.** 1785–1864. French mathematician. Discovered theorem named for him, concerning a hexagon circumscribed to a conic, set forth in his *Sur les Surfaces Courbes du Second Degré* (1808).

**Bri'and'** (brē'äN'), **Aristide.** 1862–1932. French statesman, b. Nantes. Journalist; contributor to Radical and Socialist journals; deputy (1902–19), at first as Socialist-Radical; founded *L'Humanité* (1904) with Jean Jaurès; chiefly responsible for draft of law separating church and state (1905–06). Prime minister (1909–11); confronted by general strike on French railroads (1910) called by Confédération Générale du Travail (C.G.T.); broke it by "calling to the colors" all railroad workers; again prime minister (1913); minister of justice in Viviani's cabinet (1914–15); head of coalition government (1915–17); retired (1917–21). Again prime minister (1921–22); French representative at Washington Conference (1921–22); delegate to League of Nations (1924); minister of foreign affairs (1925–32); prime minister (1925–26) during period of depreciation of the franc. Awarded Nobel peace prize for 1926 with Gustav Stresemann; influential as foreign minister in policy of rapprochement with Germany as marked by Locarno treaties and in entry of Germany into the League of Nations; with Secretary Kellogg of U.S. developed Kellogg-Briand Pact, multilateral treaty for renunciation of war (1927–28); again prime minister (1929); issued memorandum for plan for "United States of Europe" (1930).

**Bri'ard'** (brē'är'), **Étienne.** 16th-century French type founder of Avignon; in designing type for musical notation, he introduced round notes instead of angular notes, and separate notes instead of ligatures.

**Bride** of Kildare, Saint. See Brigid.

**Bridge** (brĭj), **Ann.** 1889– . *Pseud.* **Lady O'Malley.** English writer of novels and short stories, including *Peking Picnic* (1932), *Enchanter's Nightshade* (1937) and *Four-Part Setting* (1939).

**Bridge, Frank.** 1879–1941. English orchestra conductor; composer of chamber and orchestral music.

**Bridge,** Sir **John Frederick.** 1844–1924. English organist, composer, and antiquary. Organist of Westminster Abbey (1882–1918); composer of oratorios and cantatas, choral ballads, church music. His brother **Joseph Cox** (1853–1929) was organist of Chester Cathedral (1877–1925) and professor of music, U. of Durham (1908–29).

**Bridg'er** (brĭj'ẽr), **James.** 1804–1881. American pioneer and scout, b. Richmond, Va. First white man known to have visited Great Salt Lake.

**Bridg'es** (brĭj'ĕz; -ĭz), **Calvin Blackman.** 1889–1938. American geneticist.

**Bridges, John.** d. 1618. English clergyman; author of work (1587) which provoked Martin Marprelate tracts; bishop of Oxford (1604); reputed among contemporary Puritan writers to be author of *Gammer Gurton's Needle.* He was possibly a collaborator (see also William Stevenson and Bishop John Still).

**Bridges, John Henry.** 1832–1906. English medical inspector, student of Comtist philosophy, and a leader in English positivist movement. Author of *Five Discourses on Positive Religion* (1882) and works on social reform; edited Roger Bacon's *Opus Majus* (1897).

**Bridges, Robert Seymour.** 1844–1930. English poet; poet laureate (1913–30). Practiced medicine in hospitals (1875–82). Lived in Berkshire, pursuing poetry and music (till 1904); here wrote his one long narrative poem, *Eros and Psyche* (1885), and eight dramas. Engaged in metrical experimentation and inaugurated, in pamphlet *On Prosody of Paradise Regained and Samson Agonistes* (1889), new development in English verse, giving freedom to natural accentuation and allowing fresh flexibility of rhythm. Published *The Spirit of Man* (1916), a prose and verse anthology "designed to bring fortitude," and war poems collected in *October* (1920). Founded (1913) with Henry Bradley, and others, Society for Pure English, which became active in 1919; advocated, in *English Pronunciation* (1913), closer correspondence between the written and spoken forms of words. His magnum opus, *The Testament of Beauty* (begun 1926, pub. 1929), sums up his aesthetic and spiritual experience. His prose works include *Milton's Prosody* (1893) and *John Keats, a Critical Essay* (1895).

**Bridges,** Sir **Tom,** *in full* **George Tom Molesworth.** 1871–1939. English cavalry officer. Commanded 19th division in World War; headed war mission in U.S. (1918); governor of South Australia (1922–27).

**Bridges,** Sir **William Throsby.** 1861–1915. British major general; commander of first Australian contingent in World War; mortally wounded at Gallipoli.

**Bridg'et** (brĭj'ĕt; -ĭt) *or* **Brig'it** (brĭj'ĭt) *or* **Bir·git'ta'** (bĭr·gĭt'tȧ') *or* **Bri·git'ta'** (brĭ-), Saint. 1303?–1373. Swedish Roman Catholic nun and mystic; patroness of Sweden. m. (1316) Ulf Gudmarsson; mother of St. Catherine of Sweden. After husband's death (1344) devoted herself to religion and asceticism; founded at Vadstena (c. 1344; estab. 1370) the Brigittine order, or Order of the Saviour, for men and women, on basis of Augustinian rule. Author of *Revelationes,* accounts of visions she had had from early childhood. Canonized by Boniface I (1391).

**Bridget** of Kildare, Saint. See Brigid.

**Bridge'wa'ter** (brĭj'wô'tẽr; -wŏt'ẽr), Earls and dukes of. See Egerton family.

**Bridg'man** (brĭj'măn), **Frederic Arthur.** 1847–1927. American painter; painted much in Brittany, Algiers, and Egypt; known for paintings reconstructing scenes from antiquity, esp. in Egypt; author of *Winters in Algeria,* with his own illustrations (1889).

**Bridgman, Herbert Lawrence.** 1844–1924. American journalist and explorer, b. Amherst, Mass. Business manager, *Brooklyn Standard Union* (1887–1924). Friend and patron of Peary, who named cape in northeastern Greenland in his honor and who notified him first of discovery of North Pole (Sept. 6, 1909). Instrumental in exposing falsity of Cook's claims.

**Bridgman, Laura Dewey.** 1829–1889. American blind deaf-mute, educated by use of a raised alphabet devised by Dr. S. G. Howe, head of the Perkins Institution in Boston; first blind deaf-mute successfully educated by systematic means.

**Bridgman, Percy Williams.** 1882–1961. American physicist, b. Cambridge, Mass. A.B. (1904), Ph.D. (1908), Harvard. Taught physics, Harvard (from 1910); professor (1919). Awarded 1946 Nobel prize for physics for research and publications on high pressure.

**Bri'die** (brī'dĭ), **James.** *Pseudonym of* **O. H. Ma'vor** (mā'vẽr). 1888–1951. Scottish physician and playwright; nephew of James Mavor; served in World War; practiced in Glasgow. Author of plays, including *The Anatomist* (1931), *Jonah and the Whale* (1932), *Marriage is no Joke* (1934), *Colonel Wotherspoon* (1934), *Moral Plays* (1936), *The King of Nowhere* (1938).

**Bridport,** Viscount. See Hood family.

**Briefs** (brēfs), **Götz.** 1889– . German economist.

**Brie'ger** (brē'gẽr), **Johann Friedrich Theodor.** 1842–1915. German Protestant theologian and historian, esp. of the Reformation.

**Brienne, John of.** See John of Brienne.

**Brienne, Loménie de.** See Loménie de Brienne.

**Bri'er·ley** (brī'ẽr·lĭ), **Benjamin.** *Pseudonym* **Ab'-**

**o'-th'-Yate'** (ăb'ŭ·thē·yāt'; ȧb'-). 1825–1896. English weaver and writer of stories and verses in Lancashire dialect.

**Brier'ley** (brēr'lĭ), **Roger**. See BRERELEY.

**Bri'eux'** (brē'û'), **Eugène**. 1858–1932. French dramatist. Newspaper reporter and editor. Scored first success with *Blanchette*, demonstrating ill effects of education of girls of working classes (1892). Most of his plays deal with present-day social problems. Among his plays are *Les Bienfaiteurs* (1896), *L'Évasion* (1896), *Les Trois Filles de M. Dupont* (1897), *La Robe Rouge*, dealing with injustices of the law (1900), *Maternité* (1903), *Les Hannetons*, a comedy (1906), *La Femme Seule* (1912), *L'Avocat* (1922), *La Famille Lavolette* (1926).

**Brif'fault** (brē'fō), **Robert Stephen**. 1876–1948. English surgeon and novelist, b. London. Practiced in New Zealand; served in World War; retired from medical practice (1919). Author of *The Making of Humanity* (1919), *The Mothers* (1927), *Sin and Sex* (1931), *Europa* (1935), *Europa in Limbo* (1937).

**Briggs** (brĭgz), **Charles Augustus**. 1841–1913. American clergyman and Biblical scholar; Professor, Union Theological Seminary (1874–1913). Tried for heresy by Presbytery of N.Y. (1892); suspended by General Assembly from Presbyterian ministry; became Episcopal clergyman (1900). His condemnation and suspension caused Union Theological Seminary to sever Presbyterian connections and become independent and undenominational.

**Briggs, Clare A.** 1875–1930. American cartoonist, b. Reedsburg, Wis. Staff member, New York *Tribune* (from 1914); among his creations, *Skin-nay*, *The Days of Real Sport*, *When a Feller Needs a Friend*, *Ain't It a Grand and Glorious Feeling*, *Mr. and Mrs.*

**Briggs, Henry**. 1556?–1631. English mathematician. Grad. Cambridge (1581). Professor of geometry, Gresham College, London (1596–1620). Proposed decimal system of common (or Briggsian) logarithms now universally used; calculated and published logarithmic tables. His works include *Arithmetica Logarithmica* (1624) and *Trigonometria Britannica* (completed by Henry Gellibrand).

**Briggs, Le Baron Russell**. 1855–1934. American educator; professor of English, Harvard (from 1890), dean of the college (1891–1902), and dean of the faculty (1902–25). Also, president of Radcliffe (1903–23). Trained in his select composition course many well-known poets and authors.

**Briggs, Lyman James**. 1874–1963. American physicist; with U.S. Department of Agriculture (1896–1920); chief, division of mechanics and sound, National Bureau of Standards (1920–33); asst. director of research and testing (1926–33), director (1933–45).

**Brig'ham** (brĭg'ăm), **Amariah**. 1798–1849. American alienist; founded (1844) *American Journal of Insanity*, now *American Journal of Psychiatry*.

**Brigham, Emma Frances**. 1855–1881. American sculptor; m. Eugene Winslow Durkee (1878). Carved bust of Maria Mitchell, the original of which is at Vassar College and a replica in the American Hall of Fame.

**Brigham, William Tufts**. 1841–1926. American scientist; director of Bishop Museum of Ethnology, Honolulu (1888–1918); author of books on Hawaiian history and culture.

**Brig'house'** (brĭg'hous'), **Harold**. 1882–1958. English dramatist; author of *Hobson's Choice* (1916), *The Game* (1920), and other plays, and of several novels.

**Bright** (brīt), Sir **Charles Tilston**. 1832–1888. English telegraph engineer. Engineer-in-chief of Atlantic Telegraph Company (1856), which laid first transatlantic cable, between Ireland and Newfoundland (1858); consulting engineer in laying of Atlantic cables of 1865 and 1866; with Josiah Latimer Clark, improved method of applying asphalt covering to submarine cables.

**Bright, James Wilson**. 1852–1926. American philologist; pioneer in scientific study of English philology in United States. Author of *Outlines of Anglo-Saxon Grammar* (1891); editor of an *Anglo-Saxon Reader*.

**Bright, John**. 1811–1889. English orator and statesman, son of Rochdale cotton-mill owner, of Quaker stock. Took part in opposition to principle of church rates (1834–41); M.P. (almost continuously, 1843–89); with Richard Cobden contributed to defeat of corn laws (1838–46), and engaged in free-trade agitation and in movements for financial reform, electoral reform, and religious freedom. Denounced policy that led to Crimean War (1854); supported the North in American Civil War (1861); admirer of Lincoln; advocated Irish disestablishment (1868). President of Board of Trade under Gladstone (1868–70); chancellor of duchy of Lancaster (1873, 1880), resigned (1882) on British intervention in Egyptian affairs. Last spoke in House of Commons (1887) in opposition to Gladstone's Irish home-rule policy. His sister **Margaret** (1818–1890), advocate (from 1870) of temperance reform and woman suffrage, m. (1839) Samuel Lucas.

**Bright, Mary Chavelita**. See George EGERTON.

**Bright, Mynors**. 1818–1883. English scholar; decipherer and editor of Pepys's *Diary* (1875–79).

**Bright, Richard**. 1789–1858. English physician; at Guy's Hospital, London (1820–43). Published *Reports of Medical Cases* (vol. 1, 1827), containing first description and diagnosis of Bright's disease. His son **James Franck** (1832–1920), educator; master, University Coll., Oxford (1881–1906); author of *History of England* (5 vols., 1875–1904).

**Bright, Timothy**. 1551?–1615. English inventor of modern shorthand. Abandoned medical profession to take holy orders. Granted by Queen Elizabeth (1588) exclusive privilege for fifteen years of teaching and of printing shorthand according to his system, which had an alphabetical basis as regards initial letters.

**Bright' Eyes'** (brīt' īz'). **Su·sette' La Flesche'** (sōō·zĕt' lȧ flĕsh'). 1854–1903. American Indian writer and lecturer, b. in Nebraska reservation; daughter of Omaha chief who was son of French trader and Omaha woman. Educ. in mission school; aroused public sympathy (1878) by account of sufferings of Indians forcibly removed by U.S. government from South Dakota to Indian Territory; speaking tour in eastern U.S. (1879) effective in causing abandonment of policy of arbitrary removals of Indians; m. Thomas H. Tibbles (1881).

**Brig'id** (brĭj'ĭd; brē'ĭd) of Kil·dare' (kĭl·dâr'), Saint. *Also* **Bridg'et** (brĭj'ĕt; -ĭt), **Brig'it** (brĭj'ĭt; brē'ĭt), **Brighid** (brēd), **Bride** (brīd). 453–523. A patron saint of Ireland, daughter of a prince of Ulster and his bondmaid. Freed from parental control by king of Ulster because of extraordinary piety; founded four monasteries, the chief of these at Kildare. Commemorated Feb. 1.

☞ Do not confuse with St. BRIDGET of Sweden (*q.v.*).

**Brigit** *or* **Brigitta** of Sweden, Saint. See BRIDGET.

**Bril** *or* **Brill** (brĭl), **Paul** (1554–1626) and his brother **Mathys** (1550–1584). Flemish landscape painters.

**Brill** (brĭl), **Abraham Arden**. 1874–1948. American psychiatrist, b. in Austria. Lecturer on abnormal psychology and psychoanalysis, N.Y.U. (1914–25), on psychoanalysis and psychosexual sciences, Columbia (from 1929). Chiefly known as translator of works of Jung and Freud and as expositor of their doctrines.

**Brill, Nathan Edwin**. 1860–1925. American physician;

investigator of a form of typhus that from his accounts became known as Brill's disease.

**Bril'lat'-Sa'va'rin'** (brē'yȧ'sȧ'vȧ'răN'), **Anthelme.** 1755–1826. French politician and writer; member of the National Assembly; fled to Switzerland during the Terror (1792), and to U.S. (1793). Returned to Paris (1796); judge of the Court of Cassation during the Consulate. Best known for his *Physiologie du Goût*, a literary work on gastronomy (1825).

**Bril'louin'** (brē'ywăN'), **Louis Marcel.** 1854–1948. French physicist; known for work on structure of crystals, viscosity of liquids and gases, radiotelegraphy, and relativity.

**Brin** (brēn), **Benedetto.** 1833–1898. Italian naval engineer and cabinet minister. Minister of marine (1876–78, 1884–91, 1896–98), for foreign affairs (1892–93). Leader in development of modern Italian navy; designed several cruisers.

**Brind'ley** (brĭn(d)'lĭ), **James.** 1716–1772. English canal engineer. Constructed, without written calculations or drawings, canal from Manchester to the Mersey at Runcorn that became the Manchester Ship Canal; built 365 miles of canals.

**Bri·nell'** (brĭ·nĕl'), **Johann August.** 1849–1925. Swedish engineer. Introduced at Paris International Exposition (1900) the Brinell machine, an apparatus for measuring the hardness of metals and alloys.

**Brin'ig** (brĭn'ĭg), **Myron.** 1900– . American novelist, b. Minneapolis.

**Brink, Bernhard ten** (tĕn brĭngk'). 1841–1892. Dutch philologist, b. Amsterdam. Professor, Marburg (1870–73), Strassburg (from 1873). Author of *Chaucer Studien ...*(1870), *Geschichte der Englischen Literatur* (1877 ff.), and lectures on Shakespeare (1893).

**Brink, Jan ten.** 1834–1901. Dutch critic, novelist, and literary historian.

**Brink'man** *or* **Brinck'man** (brĭngk'măn), Baron **Carl Gustav von.** 1764–1847. Swedish diplomat and poet; friend and correspondent of Tegnér, Schleiermacher, the Humboldts. Ambassador to Prussian court at Memel (1807) and to London (1808–10). Author of *Gedichte von Selmar* (1789) in German, and of *Tankebilder* (1828), etc., in Swedish.

**Brin'ley** (brĭn'lĭ), **Daniel Putnam.** 1879–1963. American mural painter.

**Brin'ton** (brĭn't'n; -tŭn), **Daniel Garrison.** 1837–1899. American anthropologist; pioneer in study of anthropology in U.S. Author of *The American Race* (1891), etc.

**Brin'vil'liers'** (brăN'vē'lyā'), Marquise **de. Marie Madeleine,** *nee* **d'Au'bray'** (dō'brā'). 1630?–1676. Notorious French poisoner; discovered and beheaded (1676).

**Bri'on** (brē'ôn), **Friederike Elisabeth.** 1752–1813. Alsatian woman; resident (from 1760) in Sesenheim, near Strasbourg, where she became friend of Goethe; served as inspiration for his early lyrics, appears in *Dichtung und Wahrheit*, and is said to be original of Maria in *Götz von Berlichingen* and of Gretchen in *Faust*.

**Bri·ón'** (brē·ōn'), **Luis.** 1782–1821. South American naval commander, b. in Curaçao, of Dutch parentage. Joined Bolívar (1812 ff.), commanding rebel fleet in Venezuelan and Colombian revolutions; supplied, outfitted, and commanded fleet for Bolívar's later campaigns (1815, 1816); defeated Spaniards on Margarita Island; member, Congress of Angostura, which proclaimed Colombian independence (1819).

**Bri·o'schi** (brē·ôs'kē), **Francesco.** 1824–1897. Italian mathematician; known esp. for work on theory of invariants, fifth-degree and sixth-degree equations, and elliptic functions.

**Briosmo.** See Andrea Riccio.

**Bris'bane** (brĭz'bān; -bān), **Albert.** 1809–1890. American advocate of Fourierism, b. Batavia, N.Y. Author of *Social Destiny of Man* (1840), *Association* (1843), and other expositions of Fourierism. His son **Arthur** (1864–1936), b. Buffalo, N.Y., was a journalist; began on staff of New York *Sun* (1883); editor of New York *Evening Journal* (1897–1921) and Chicago *Herald and Examiner* (from 1918); influential as an editorial writer and columnist in these and other Hearst journals.

**Brisbane,** Sir **Thomas Makdougall.** 1773–1860. Scottish soldier and astronomer. Major general (1813); governor of New South Wales (1821–25). Established observatory at Paramatta, near Sydney (1822), and a magnetic observatory at Makerstoun, Scotland (1841); in Australia catalogued 7385 stars. Brisbane, Australia, is named after him.

**Brissac,** Comte de. See Charles de Cossé.

**Bris'son'** (brē'sôN'), **Eugène Henri.** 1835–1912. French political leader; president of Chamber of Deputies (1881–85; 1894–98; 1904–05; 1906–12); premier of France (1885–86; 1898). Strongly anticlerical.

**Bris'sot'** (brē'sō'), **Jacques Pierre.** *Surnamed* **de War'ville'** (dē vȧr'vēl'). 1754–1793. French journalist and ardent Revolutionary leader; author of two works on philosophy of law (1781, 1782); imprisoned in Bastille; one of the mob that stormed the Bastille (July 14, 1789); member of diplomatic committee of the Legislative Assembly; a moderate in the Convention; leader of the Girondists, or Brissotins; guillotined in Paris (Oct. 31, 1793).

**Bris'tol** (brĭs't'l), Countess of. See under Pierrepont family.

**Bristol,** Earls of. See Digby; Hervey.

**Bristol, Mark Lambert.** 1868–1939. American naval officer; grad. U.S.N.A., Annapolis (1887); served in Spanish-American War (1898) and in World War; U.S. high commissioner to Turkey (1919 ff.); commander of Asiatic fleet with rank of admiral (1927); chairman of navy general board (1930–32).

**Bris'tow** (brĭs'tō), **Benjamin Helm.** 1832–1896. American lawyer, b. Elkton, Ky. U.S. solicitor general (1870–72); secretary of treasury (1874–76); obtained evidence and convictions against the Whisky Ring.

**Bristow, George Frederick.** 1825–1898. American musician and composer; with N.Y. Philharmonic Society (1842–82), conductor (1851–62). Composer of church and concert music, oratorios, cantatas, etc.

**Bri·tan'ni·cus** (brĭ·tăn'ĭ·kŭs). *Orig.* **Claudius Tiberius Ger·man'i·cus** (jûr·măn'ĭ·kŭs; jēr-). 41–55 A.D. Son of Emperor Claudius and Messalina. Surnamed Britannicus in honor of his father's triumph in Britain (43 A.D.). Considered heir to throne until execution of his mother (48); through influence of Agrippina, set aside in succession in favor of her son Nero; poisoned by Nero. Subject of Racine's tragedy *Britannicus*.

**Brit'tain** (brĭt''n), **Marion Luther.** 1866–1953. American educator; A.B., Emory U. (1886); president of Georgia Tech. (1922–44).

**Brittain, Vera.** 1893?–1970. English free-lance journalist and lecturer; m. (1925) George E. G. Catlin. Served as nurse in London, Malta, and France (1915–19). Author of *Testament of Youth* (1933), and *Poems of the War and After* (1934), *A Testament of Friendship* (1940).

**Brit'ta·ny** (brĭt''n·ĭ), Duke or count of. English title held by Geoffrey (1158–1186), son of Henry II, by Geoffrey's son Arthur (1187–1203), and by Geoffrey's widow's second husband, Ranulf de Blundevill, earl of Chester; by Charles de Blois (1319–1364), who married the daughter of, and succeeded, Guy of Brittany

(d. 1331); lastly by Francis II of Brittany (1459–1488).

**Brit'ten** (brĭt''n), **Benjamin.** *In full* **Edward Benjamin Britten.** 1913–1976. British composer. His works include *A Midsummer Night's Dream* (1960), etc.

**Brit'ton** (brĭt''n), **John.** 1771–1857. English antiquary; created popular taste for books on topography. Author, with F. W. Brayley, of first nine volumes of *The Beauties of England and Wales* (1801–14); author of *Cathedral Antiquities of England* (14 vols., 1814–35), etc.

**Britton, Nathaniel Lord.** 1859–1934. American botanist; author of *Illustrated Flora of the Northern United States, Canada, and the British Possessions*...(1896–98; with Addison Brown), *Flora of Bermuda* (1918). m. (1885) **Elizabeth Gertrude Knight** (1858–1934), botanist; specialist in anatomy and classification of North American mosses.

**Britton, Thomas.** 1654?–1714. English coal dealer, known as the "musical small-coal man." Had a famous musical club over his shop, where Handel and other performers took part in concerts (1678).

**Briusov.** Variant of Bryusov.

**Bri'zeux'** (brē'zû'), **Julien Auguste Pélage.** 1806–1858. French poet, known esp. for his Breton eclogues and idylls; translated Dante's *Divina Commedia.*

**Broad** (brôd), **Charlie Dun·bar'** (dŭn·bär'). 1887–1971. English philosopher; professor, Cambridge (1933–53); president, Society for Psychical Research (1935). Author of *Perception, Physics, and Reality* (1914), etc.

**Broad'bent** (brôd'bĕnt), Sir **William Henry.** 1835–1907. English physician. Carried on researches on cancer, aphasia, and paralysis, advancing a hypothesis to explain some of the manifestations in hemiplegia; active in movements for prevention and cure of tuberculosis.

**Broadbottom, Geffery.** Pseudonym of earl of Chesterfield.

**Broad'hurst** (brôd'hûrst), **George H.** 1866–1952. English playwright and fiction writer; to U.S. (1882); theatrical manager and producer in New York; to England (1926) and devoted himself esp. to short-story writing. Author of plays *Bought and Paid For* (with Arthur Hornblow), *Why Smith Left Home, A Fool and His Money, The Mills of the Gods, The Law of the Land.*

**Broad'wood** (brôd'wŏŏd), **John.** 1732–1812. British piano manufacturer, b. in Scotland; m. (1769) daughter of **Burkhard Tschu'di** (chōō'dē), better known as **Bur'kat Shu'di** (bŏŏr'kät shōō'dē), a Swiss, founder of a piano factory in London (c. 1728). Partner (1770) with Shudi, and (1773) with Shudi's son **Burkat**; sole proprietor (1782–95); admitted to partnership his sons **James** (1795) and **Thomas** (1807), the firm becoming John Broadwood & Sons. Co-operated with **A·me'ri·cus Back'ers** (ȧ·mā'rē·kûs băk'ẽrs), Dutch piano maker, in manufacturing first grand piano in England; introduced improvements in piano mechanism, as did his grandson **Henry Fowler Broadwood** (1811–1893). A descendant of John's, **Henry John Tschudi Broadwood** (d. 1911), was patented the barless grand piano.

**Bro'ca'** (brô'kȧ'), **Paul.** 1824–1880. French surgeon and anthropologist. Discovered seat of articulate speech in the brain (1861); authority on aphasia.

**Bro'card'** (brô'kȧr'), **Henri.** 1845–1922. French mathematician after whom Brocard's circle is named.

**Broc'chi** (brôk'kē), **Giovanni Battista.** 1772–1826. Italian naturalist and geologist.

**Brock** (brŏk), **Arthur Clutton-.** See Clutton-Brock.

**Brock, Charles Edmund.** 1870–1938. English illustrator and portrait painter.

**Brock,** Sir **Isaac.** 1769–1812. British soldier. Commanded garrison at Quebec (1806–10); major general (1811); forced surrender of General William Hull's forces at Detroit (1812); hence popularly the "hero of Upper Canada"; killed at battle of Queenston Heights.

**Brock, Lynn.** Pseudonym of Alister McAllister.

**Brock,** Sir **Thomas.** 1847–1922. English sculptor.

**Brock'dorff–Rant'zau** (brŏk'dôrf·rän'tsou), Count **Ulrich von.** 1869–1928. German statesman; minister in Copenhagen (1912–18); foreign minister (1919) and leader of German peace delegation at Versailles; resigned (1919) because of his opposition to Germany's signing of Treaty of Versailles. Ambassador to Moscow (1922); opposed membership in League of Nations and the Locarno Pact.

**Brock'es** (brôk'ĕs), **Barthold Heinrich.** 1680–1747. German poet; author of a collection of religious and nature poems, and of translations of Pope's *Essay on Man* (1740) and Thomson's *Seasons* (1745).

**Brock'haus** (brôk'hous), **Friedrich Arnold.** 1772–1823. German publisher, b. Westphalia. Founded (1805) book business in Amsterdam, organized as firm of F. A. Brockhaus, printers and publishers; transferred to Leipzig (1817). Publications of firm include encyclopedia *Brockhaus' Konversations-Lexikon* (begun 1796, copyright bought 1808; 15th ed., *Der Grosse Brockhaus,* 20 vols. and suppl., 1928–35); Ersch and Gruber's *Allgemeine Enzyklopädie der Wissenschaften und Kunste* (from 1831); as well as yearbooks, pocket editions, and books on popular science and travel. Friedrich Arnold's sons **Friedrich** (1800–1865) and **Heinrich** (1804–1874) and later Heinrich's sons and grandsons carried on the business. Another son of Friedrich Arnold, **Hermann** (1806–1877), b. Amsterdam, was an Orientalist; professor of Indology, Leipzig (from 1848); edited various Sanskrit and Persian works; also edited journal of German Oriental Society (1852–65) and Ersch and Gruber's *Allgemeine Enzyklopädie* (from 1856, vols. 62–99). His son **Friedrich Arnold** (1838–1895), b. Dresden, was a jurist. Heinrich's grandson **Heinrich** (1858–1941) was an art historian; professor, Leipzig (1892–1913); director of the Historical Art Institute, Florence (1897–1912).

**Brock'hurst** (brŏk'hûrst), **Gerald L.** 1890– . English portrait painter and etcher.

**Brock'way** (brŏk'wā), **Howard.** 1870–1951. American composer, b. Brooklyn. Boston Symphony Orchestra produced his *Sylvan Suite* (1901) and his *Symphony* (1907). Composer also of choral music, songs, and piano pieces.

**Brod** (brōt), **Max.** 1884–1968. German writer, b. Prague, of Jewish parents. Author of fiction, lyric poems, a play, and works on pacifism and Zionism.

**Brod'e·rip** (brŏd'rĭp), **William John.** 1789–1859. English lawyer and naturalist; a founder of Zoological Society of London. Author of *Leaves from the Note-Book of a Naturalist* (1852), etc.

**Bro'deur'** (brô'dûr'), **Louis Philippe.** 1862–1924. Canadian statesman, b. Belœil, Que. Member of Canadian House of Commons (from 1891), speaker (1901). First head of Canadian naval service (1910). Judge of Supreme Court of Canada (1911).

**Brod'head** (brŏd'hĕd), **John Romeyn.** 1814–1873. American historian, b. Philadelphia, of Dutch and English descent. Author of *History of the State of New York* (vol. 1, period 1609–64, pub. 1853; vol. 2, period 1664–91, pub. 1871).

**Brod'hun** (brōd'hōōn), **Eugen.** 1860– . German physicist. With Otto Lummer, invented a photometer (Lummer-Brodhun photometer) based on principle of total reflection and using a combination of two right-angled prisms.

**Bro'die** (brō'dĭ), Sir **Benjamin Collins.** 1783–1862.

English surgeon. Opposed homeopathy; promoted conservative treatment of diseases of the joints, which effected reduction in number of amputations. His son Sir **Benjamin Collins** (1817–1880), a chemist, investigated allotropic forms of carbon.

**Brodribb, John Henry** and **Sydney.** See Sir Henry IRVING.

**Brod'rick** (brŏd'rĭk), **William St. John Fremantle.** 1st Earl of **Mid'le·ton** (mĭd''l·tŭn). 1856–1942. English political leader. Conservative M.P. (1880–1906); financial secretary to war office (1886–92); secretary for war (1900–03), for India (1903–05). His uncle **George Charles Brodrick** (1831–1903), journalist and educator; 2d son of 7th Viscount Midleton; on staff of London *Times* (1860–72); warden of Merton Coll., Oxford (1881–1903); author of *English Land and English Landlords* (1881), and a popular history of Oxford U.

**Brod'sky** (brôt'skû·ĭ; *Angl.* -skĭ), **Adolf.** 1851–1929. Russian violinist, b. Taganrog. Settled at Manchester, England (1895), as director of Royal Coll. of Music (1895–1929).

**Bro·dziń'ski** (brô·jĕn'y'·skē), **Kazimierz.** 1791–1835. Polish poet and scholar; professor of Polish literature, Warsaw (from 1826); best-known poetical work, *Wiesław* (1820).

**Broek'hui'zen** (brōōk'hoi'zĕn), **Jan van.** *Latinized* **Janus Brouk·hu'si·us** (brōōk·hū'zĭ·ŭs). 1649–1707. Dutch classical scholar and poet. Author of Latin poems *Carmina* (1684), editions of Propertius (1702) and Tibullus (1707), and Dutch poems (1677) modeled after those of Pieter Hooft.

**Brofeldt, Juhani.** Real name of Juhani AHO.

**Brof·fe'rio** (brôf·fâ'ryô), **Angelo.** 1802–1866. Italian poet, lawyer, and politician; liberal member of Piedmontese parliament (1848–66); opponent of Cavour. Author of plays, historical and political works, dialect poems (*Canzoni Piedmontesi*), and an autobiography.

**Bro'gan** (brō'găn), Sir **Denis William.** 1900–1974. British political scientist; author of *The American Political System* (1933), *France under the Republic* (1940), etc.

**Brö'ger** (brû'gĕr), **Karl.** 1886–1944. German poet, b. Nuremberg; author of popular war song, *Kamerad, als wir Marschiert* (1916).

**Brög'ger** (brûg'gĕr), **Waldemar Christofer.** 1851–1940. Norwegian geologist and mineralogist.

**Broghill,** Baron. See BOYLE family.

**Bro'glie'** (*Fr.* brô'glē'; *Ital.* brô'lyâ), **de.** Name of a noble French family of Piedmontese origin, including comtes, ducs, and princes **de Broglie: Victor Maurice** (1647?–1727), comte, army commander under Louis XIV; suppressed Protestant activities in the Cévennes; marshal of France (1724). His son **François Marie** (1671–1745), comte, and (1742) duc, also a soldier; led campaigns in Flanders, Germany, and Italy, under Louis XIV; marshal of France (1734); commanded army of Bohemia (1741). François Marie's son **Victor François** (1718–1804), duc, also a soldier; in Seven Years' War in command at battle of Bergen (1759), won battle of Corbach (1760); commanded troops assembled near Versailles at outbreak of French Revolution (1789); withdrew to Germany (1790); commanded force of émigrés operating in Champagne (1792); in British service (1794) and Russian service (1797). Victor François's son **Victor Claude** (1757–1794), prince, also a soldier; favored Revolutionary cause (1789) and was president of Constituent Assembly (1791); adjutant general, army of the Rhine (1792); guillotined, Paris (1794). Victor Claude's son **Achille Charles Léonce Victor** (1785–1870), duc, statesman; member of Chamber of Peers (1814); minister of the interior and of public worship and instruction (1830), of foreign affairs (1832–34); president of the council (1835); retired from political life (after 1851); author of four volumes of *Souvenirs.* Achille's son **Jacques Victor Albert** (1821–1901), prince, then duc, statesman and historian; member of National Assembly (1871); ambassador to Great Britain (1871); premier and minister of foreign affairs (1873–74); president of the council and minister of justice (1877); retired (1885); author of *L'Église et l'Empire Romain au IVe Siècle* (1856), *Frédéric II et Marie Thérèse* (1883), *Frédéric II et Louis XV* (1885), *Marie Thérèse Impératrice* (1888). Jacques Victor Albert was grandfather of **Maurice** (1875–1960), duc, and **Louis Victor de Broglie** (1892– ), both physicists; Maurice best known for his researches in nuclear physics, X rays, and radioactivity; Louis Victor, recipient of 1929 Nobel prize for physics and professor at U. of Paris (from 1932), best known for his research on the quantum theory and his discovery of the wave character of electrons.

**Bro'glio** (brô'lyô), **Emilio.** 1814–1892. Italian statesman and writer, b. Milan. Active in revolutionary movement in Lombardy (1848); member, parliament (1861–76). Known esp. for his epistolary treatise on income tax, *Dell'Imposta sulla Rendita* (25 letters to Cavour; pub. 1856).

**Bro'gny'** *or* **Bro'gni'** (brô'nyē'), Cardinal **de.** *Ecclesiastical title of* **Jean Al'lar'met'** (à'làr'mĕ') *or* **d'A'lou'zier'** (dà'lōō'zyā'). *Also known as* Cardinal **de Vi'viers'** (dē vē'vyā') *or* Cardinal **d'Os'tie'** (dôs'tē'). 1342–1426. French ecclesiastic; president of the Council of Constance (1415–17), which condemned John Huss.

**Broke** (brŏŏk) *or* **Brooke, Arthur.** d. 1563. English translator who wrote first English version of story of Romeo and Juliet (1562), Shakespeare's main source.

**Broke** (brŏŏk), Sir **Philip Bowes Vere.** 1776–1841. English naval officer. Commander of the *Shannon* (1807–13), in which he captured American frigate *Chesapeake* off Boston (June 1, 1813), receiving severe wound in the action; rear admiral (1830).

**Brome** (brōōm), **Richard.** d. 1652. English dramatist. Servant, later friend, of Ben Jonson; collaborator with Ben Jonson's son and with Thomas Heywood. Made reputation with *The Northern Lass* (1632). Author of comedies of actual life and romantic comedies. His *Jovial Crew* (1641) last play to be acted before closing of theaters by the Puritans under Cromwell (1642).

**Bro·me'li·us** (brōō·mā'lĭ·ŭs), **Olaf.** 1639–1705. Swedish botanist.

**Brom'field** (brŏm'fēld), **Louis.** 1896–1956. American writer; author of *The Green Bay Tree* (1924), *Early Autumn* (awarded Pulitzer prize; 1926), *The Strange Case of Miss Annie Spragg* (1928), *The Rains Came* (1937), *Night in Bombay* (1939), *Wild is the River* (1941), *Mrs. Parkington* (1943), etc.

**Brom'ley** (brŭm'lĭ; brŏm'-), Sir **Thomas.** 1530–1587. English judge; lord chancellor who presided over trial of Mary, Queen of Scots (1586).

**Bronck** (brŏngk), **Jonas** (jō'năs). *Also* **Bronk** (brŏngk) *or* **Brunk** (brŭngk). d. 1643? Danish pioneer in America; first settler in upper New York City, in district now the borough of Bronx, named after him; Bronxville, Bronx Park, and Bronx River, also named after him.

**Brönd'sted** (brûn'stĕth), **Peter Oluf.** 1780–1842. Danish archaeologist. Made excavations and carried on research in Greece (1810–13).

**Bron'gniart'** (brôɴ'nyàr'), **Alexandre.** 1770–1847. French mineralogist and geologist. Director of Sèvres porcelain factory (from 1800), where he revived art of painting on glass and developed ceramic chemistry. Author of *Classification Naturelle des Reptiles,* making the division into saurians, batrachians, chelonians, ophidians (1805), *Essai sur la Géographie Minéralogique des Environs de Paris* (with Cuvier, 1811), *Traité des Arts Céramiques* (1844). His son **Adolphe Théodore** (1801–1876), botanist, was professor at the Museum of Natural History; authority on pollen and on classification and distribution of fossil plants and seeds; pioneer in plant physiology; author of a catalogue of plants in the museum, the basis for the system of classification used in Germany.

**Bronikowski, Friedrich von Oppeln–.** See OPPELN-BRONIKOWSKI.

**Bronn** (brôn), **Heinrich Georg.** 1800–1862. German zoologist and paleontologist; author of work on rock formations, and translator of Darwin's *Origin of Species*.

**Bron′nen** (brôn′ĕn), **Arnolt.** 1895–1959. German playwright and novelist.

**Bron′sart von Schel′len·dorf** (brôn′zärt fôn shĕl′ĕn·dôrf), **Hans.** *Professional name* **Hans von Bronsart.** 1830–1913. German pianist and composer; studied with Liszt; intendant, court theater at Hanover (1867–87) and Weimar (1887–95). His wife **Ingeborg**, *nee* **Starck** [shtärk] (1840–1913), was also a pianist and composer. Hans's brother **Paul** (1832–1891), entered Prussian army (1849); chief of division in Franco-Prussian War (1870–71); made preliminary negotiations with Napoleon III for French surrender at Sedan; Prussian minister of war (1883–89); increased standing army and introduced magazine rifle; general, 1st army corps, Königsberg (1889). Another brother, **Walter** (1833–1914), served in Prussian army in campaigns of 1864 and 1866, and as chief of general staff, 9th army corps, in war of 1870–71; commanding general of 3d (1888) and 10th (1890) army corps; war minister (1893–96). Paul's son **Friedrich** (1864– ) joined Prussian guards (1882); with German military mission in Turkey (1913); chief of staff, Turkish headquarters, during World War (1914–17); leader, Prussian infantry division in France (1918).

**Brön′sted** (brûn′stĕth), **Johannes Nicolaus.** 1879–1947. Danish chemist.

**Bronstein, Leib** (*or* **Lev**) **Davydovich.** See Leon TROTSKY.

**Bron′të** (brŏn′tē). Name of a family of English novelists, daughters of **Patrick** (1777–1861), Irish Anglican clergyman; named, before coming to England, Brunty or Prunty; perpetual curate of Haworth, Yorkshire (from 1820); eccentric in habits; m. (1812) Maria Branwell of Penzance, Cornwall. Their three daughters, **Charlotte** (1816–1855), **Emily Jane** (1818–1848), and **Anne** (1820–1849), after attending an oppressive boarding school for clergymen's daughters and teaching for a time, took to literature, publishing a volume of poems (1846) under the respective pseudonyms of **Cur′rer** (kûr′ẽr), **Ellis**, and **Acton Bell;** produced novels reflecting the domestic unhappiness and the penury of their lives. Charlotte returned to Roehead as teacher (1835–38), governess (1839, 1841); studied languages, with Emily, in Brussels (1842); taught in Brussels (1843); had her first novel *The Professor* rejected by Smith & Elder; achieved success with *Jane Eyre* (1847), a strong, emotional narrative of the struggles of an orphan governess against wretched conditions and thwarted love for her sardonic employer, which brought to the Victorian novel new vitality and truthfulness to character; produced *Shirley* (1849) and *Villette* (1853); m. Arthur Bell Nicholls, her father's curate (1854). Her sister Emily Jane produced only one novel, *Wuthering Heights* (1848), a highly imaginative story of intense passion set against somber background of Yorkshire moors, in which a wild gypsy is prompted by disappointed love to ghoulish measures of vindictiveness. The youngest sister, Anne, produced *Agnes Grey* (1848), and *The Tenant of Wildfell Hall* (1848). Patrick's only son, **Patrick Branwell** (1817–1848) was a drunkard and opium addict.

**Bron·zi′no, Il** (ēl brôn·dzē′nō). *Also* **Agnolo** *or* **Angiolo di Co′si·mo** (dē kô′zē·mō). 1502–1572. Florentine painter. Pupil of Raffaelino del Garbo and Pontormo; court painter to Cosimo I of Florence.

**Brook** (bro͝ok), **Alexander.** 1898– . American painter, b. Brooklyn, N.Y.; m. Peggy Bacon (1920; divorced 1940); best known as an easel painter.

**Brooke** (bro͝ok), Baron. See Sir Fulke GREVILLE.

**Brooke,** Lord. See Leopold G. F. M. GREVILLE.

**Brooke,** Sir **Alan Francis.** 1st Viscount **Al′an·brooke′** (ăl′ăn·bro͝ok′). 1883–1963. British soldier, b. France; served in World War I; expert in gunnery and anti-aircraft warfare; major general (1935), lieutenant general (1938); in command of newly formed Mobile Division (1938–39), Anti-Aircraft Corps (1938–39), Anti-Aircraft Command (1939), Southern Command (1939, 1940), 2d Army Corps, British Expeditionary Force (1939–40); commander in chief of home forces (1940–41); chief of Imperial General Staff (1941); accompanied Churchill on international conferences (1942–43); field marshal (1944).

**Brooke, Arthur.** See BROKE.

**Brooke, Basil Stan′lake** (stăn′lāk). 1st Viscount **Brooke′bor′ough** (bro͝ok′bûr′ō; -bŭ·rŭ). 1888–1973. Politician of Northern Ireland; educ. in England; served in World War I (1914–18); M.P. (1929 ff.), prime minister of Northern Ireland (1943–63).

**Brooke, Edward William.** 1919– . American statesman, b. Washington, D.C. First Negro popularly elected to U.S. Senate (1967; from Mass.)

**Brooke, Henry.** 1703?–1783. Irish poet and novelist. Author (1735) of philosophical poem *Universal Beauty*, said to have suggested Darwin's *Botanic Garden;* tragedy *Gustavus Vasa* (1739); and two novels, *Juliet Grenville* (1774) and *The Fool of Quality* (1765–70).

**Brooke, Henry James.** 1771–1857. English mineralogist; described thirteen new mineral species; first introduced (in articles for the *Encyclopaedia Metropolitana*) the six groups, or systems, according to which forms of crystals are commonly classified.

**Brooke,** Sir **James.** 1803–1868. English soldier, raja of Sarawak, b. Benares, son of Bengal civil servant. Set out (1838) in private schooner to bring civilization to Malay Archipelago; aided Raja Muda Hassim in suppressing rebellion; made governor of Sarawak with title of raja (1841); reformed government; governor of British colony Labuan; left Sarawak (1863). His nephew Sir **Charles Anthony Johnson Brooke** (1829–1917), name orig. Johnson, joined him (1852), assumed name Brooke and succeeded him as second raja (1868); was succeeded in turn by his son Sir **Charles Vyner** (1874–1963), third raja, who continued expeditions in suppression of head-hunting and the program of benevolent government.

**Brooke, John Rutter.** 1838–1926. American officer in Union Army, b. Montgomery Co., Pa. Commanded brigade at Antietam, regiment at Fredericksburg, brigade at Chancellorsville and Gettysburg; severely wounded at Cold Harbor. Major general in command of 1st Corps at Chickamauga Park, Ga. (1897); led troops in skirmishes in Puerto Rico; military governor of Puerto Rico, and of Cuba (Jan. to Dec., 1899).

**Brooke, Rupert.** 1887–1915. English poet, son of a master at Rugby. Grad. Cambridge; traveled in America and New Zealand (1913–14). Commissioned in Royal Naval Division (1914). Author of *Poems* (1911), *1914 and other Poems* (1915), *Letters from America* (1916).

**Brooke, Stopford Augustus.** 1832–1916. Irish preacher

and man of letters. Church of England clergyman (1857–80); seceded from Church of England (1880); preached as Unitarian minister at Bedford Chapel, Bloomsbury (1876–95). Author of life of F. W. Robertson (1865) and works on English literature.

**Brooke-Popham,** Sir **Henry Robert Moore.** See POPHAM.

**Brookes** (bro͝oks), Sir **Norman Everard.** 1877–1968. Australian tennis champion and businessman, b. Melbourne. Member of Australasian Davis Cup tennis team (1914, 1919, 1920); with Gerald L. Patterson, won American national doubles championship (1919); pioneer in introduction of scientific game. Chairman of a paper and an insurance company; partner in William Brookes & Co., graziers. Knighted (1939).

**Brook′ings** (bro͝ok′ĭngz), **Robert Somers.** 1850–1932. American merchant and philanthropist, b. Cecil Co., Md. Successful in woodenware business, St. Louis (1867–96); president of corporation, Washington U. (1897–1928). A founder of Institute for Government Research, Washington, D.C. (1918), Institute of Economics (1922), and Robert Brookings Graduate School of Economics and Government (1924), all three of which were merged (1927) into the Brookings Institution, devoted to public service through research and training in the social sciences, located in Washington, D.C.

**Brooks** (bro͝oks), **Alfred Hulse.** 1871–1924. American scientist; with U.S. Geological Survey, field work in Alaska (1898–1916, 1919–24). Author of *Geography and Geology of Alaska* (1906).

**Brooks, Allan.** 1869–1946. English painter and illustrator, b. Etawah, India. D.S.O. (1919). Interested esp. in ornithology; painted twenty-four plates of birds to complete Louis Agassiz Fuertes's volume, *Birds of Massachusetts.*

**Brooks, Charles Stephen.** 1878–1934. American essayist and playwright; author of *Journeys to Bagdad* (1915), *There's Pippins and Cheese to Come* (1917), *Chimney-Pot Papers* (1919), *Wappin' Wharf* (a play; 1921), *Roundabout to Canterbury* (1926), *A Window at the Inn* (a play; 1934), etc.

**Brooks, Charles William Shirley.** 1816–1874. English journalist and novelist. Editorial writer, *Illustrated London News;* joined staff of *Punch* (1851), editor (1870). Author of several novels including *Aspen Court* (1855) and *Sooner or Later* (1868).

**Brooks, Gwendolyn.** 1917– . U.S. poet, b. Topeka, Kansas; grew up in Chicago. Collections include *A Street in Bronzeville* (1945); *Annie Allen* (1949), Pulitzer prize 1950; *Selected Poems* (1963).

**Brooks, Henry Harlow.** 1871–1936. American physician; served in U.S. medical corps in World War I; known as pathologist and diagnostician.

**Brooks, Maria,** *nee* **Gow′en** (gou′ĕn). *Pen name* **Ma·rí′a del Oc′ci·den′te** (mä·rē′ä thĕl ôk′sē·thān′tā). 1794?–1845. American poet, b. Medford, Mass. m. John Brooks (1810). Author of *Judith, Esther, and Other Poems* (1820), *Zóphiël* (1833), *Idomen* (1843).

**Brooks, Phillips.** 1835–1893. American Episcopal bishop, b. Boston. Grad. Harvard (1855). Pastorates: Philadelphia (1859–69); Trinity Church, Boston (1869–91). Consecrated bishop (1891). Author of the hymn *O Little Town of Bethlehem* (1868). Elected to American Hall of Fame (1910).

**Brooks, Preston Smith.** 1819–1857. b. Edgefield, S.C. Member, U.S. House of Representatives (1852–57); physically assaulted Senator Charles Sumner in U.S. Senate chamber after Sumner's verbal attack on his uncle, **Andrew Pickens Butler** (1796–1857), U.S. senator (1846–57).

**Brooks, Richard Edwin.** 1865–1919. American sculptor.

**Brooks, Van Wyck.** 1886–1963. American essayist, critic, and translator. Editor, *The Freeman* (1920–24). Author of *The Wine of the Puritans* (1909), *America's Coming-of-Age* (1915), *The Ordeal of Mark Twain* (1920), *The Pilgrimage of Henry James* (1925), *The Life of Emerson* (1932), *The Flowering of New England, 1815–1865* (1936), *New England Indian Summer, 1865–1915* (1940). See Alfred KREYMBORG.

**Brooks, William Keith.** 1848–1908. American zoologist; professor, Johns Hopkins (1876–1908), head of biological department (from 1894).

**Broom** (bro͞om), **Robert.** 1866–1951. South African morphologist and paleontologist, b. Paisley, Scotland. M.D., Glasgow (1895). Professor of zoology and geology, Victoria College, Stellenbosch, South Africa (1903–10). Author of works on comparative anatomy and vertebrate paleontology.

**Broome** (bro͞om), **William.** 1689–1745. English scholar; translated about a third of text and provided most of the notes for Pope's *Odyssey* (1722–26). Satirized in the *Dunciad.*

**Bro′phy** (brō′fĭ), **John.** 1899–1965. English novelist. Edited, with Eric Partridge, *Songs and Slang of the British Soldier: 1914–1918* (1930). First novel, *The Bitter End* (1928); others, *Flesh and Blood* (1931), *Ramparts of Virtue* (1936), *Gentleman of Stratford* (1939), *Ridiculous Hat* (1939), *Green Glory* (1940).

**Bro′que·ville′** (brôk′vēl′), Comte **Charles de.** 1860–1940. Belgian statesman; premier (1911–17; 1932–34).

**Broschi, Carlo.** See Carlo FARINELLI.

**Bro′sio** (brô′zyô), **Manlio.** 1897– . Italian diplomat. Secy. general of the North Atlantic Treaty Organization (from 1964).

**Brosse** (brôs), **Salomon de.** 1565?–1627. French architect. Architect of Marie de Médicis (1614); designed Luxembourg Palace (1615–20), portal of Church of Saint Gervais (1616), the main hall of the Palais de Justice (1618).

**Brosses** (brôs), **Charles de.** 1709–1777. French scholar. First to employ geographical divisions Australasia and Polynesia. Author of *Histoire des Navigations aux Terres Australes* (1756), *Du Culte des Dieux Fétiches* (1760), *Formation Mécanique des Langues* (1765).

**Broth′ers** (brŭth′ẽrz), **Richard.** 1757–1824. British naval officer, b. in Newfoundland; discharged on half pay (1783). Self-announced apostle of new religion, claiming crown of England as descendant of David; committed to Newgate (1795), later to a lunatic asylum (till 1806).

**Brotherton, Thomas of.** See THOMAS OF BROTHERTON.

**Brou′ckère′** (bro͞o′kâr′), **Charles Marie Joseph Ghislain de.** 1796–1860. Belgian economist and politician. Brother of **Henri Marie Joseph Ghislain** (1801–1891), Belgian premier (1852–55).

**Brough** (brŭf), **Robert.** 1872–1905. Scottish portrait painter, influenced by modern French training.

**Brougham** (bro͞om; bro͞o′ăm), **Henry Peter.** Baron **Brougham and Vaux.** 1778–1868. Scottish jurist and political leader. Founder, with Sydney Smith and Jeffrey, of *Edinburgh Review* (1802). Practiced at English bar (1808); M.P. (1810); carried measure making slave trade felony; defended Queen Caroline as her attorney general in trial (1820); a founder of London University (1828); persuaded by Whigs to accept chancellorship under Grey (1830–34); by famous speech (1831) helped pass Reform Bill; remodeled judicial committee of privy council (1833), a lasting reform; estranged from Whigs. Continued for 30 years to hear appeals in judicial cases before privy council and House of Lords; advocated immediate abolition of slavery (1838). He is the original of the "learned friend" in Peacock's *Crotchet Castle.* The brougham (carriage) is named after him.

**Brough'ton** (brô't'n), **Rhoda.** 1840–1920. English novelist. Made reputation for audacity with *Cometh Up as a Flower* (1867) and *Not Wisely but Too Well* (1867).

**Broughton de Gyfford,** Baron. See John Cam HOBHOUSE.

**Broukhusius, Janus.** See Jan van BROEKHUIZEN.

**Broun** (brōōn), **Matthew Heywood Campbell.** 1888–1939. American journalist, b. Brooklyn, N.Y. On staff, New York *Morning Telegraph* (1908–09; 1910–12), *Tribune* (1912–21), *World* (1921–28), the Scripps-Howard newspapers (from 1928); writer of column *It Seems to Me.* Among his books are *Pieces of Hate* (1922), *Gandle Follows His Nose* (1926).

**Brounck'er** *or* **Broun'ker** (brŭng'kẽr), **William.** 2d Viscount **Brouncker** of Cas'tle Ly'ons (kȧs''l lī'ŭnz). 1620?–1684. Irish mathematician. First president of Royal Society (1662–77); an early user of continued fractions; intimate of Pepys.

**Brou·noff'** (brōō·nôf'), **Pla·ton'** (plŭ·tôn'). 1863–1924. Pianist and composer, b. Elisavetgrad, Russia; to U.S. (1891); settled in New York City as pianist, lecturer, and teacher. Composer of a cantata, overture, anthems, etc.; also, the symphony *Palestine* and the opera *Ramona.*

**Brous'sais'** (brōō'sĕ'), **François Joseph Victor.** 1772–1838. French physician; author of *Examen de la Doctrine Médicale Généralement Adoptée* (1816), which sets forth theory that disease is result of spread of irritation in one part by physiological sympathy to other parts.

**Brous'son'net'** (brōō'sô'nĕ'), **Pierre Marie Auguste.** 1761–1807. French physician and naturalist. Credited with introducing Angora goat and Merino sheep into France.

**Brou'wer** *or* **Brau'wer** (brou'wẽr), **Adriaen.** 1606?–1638. Flemish genre and landscape painter; among his famous works are *Peasants Feasting, The Smoker* (Louvre), *The Drinker, Tavern Interior.*

**Brow'der** (brou'dẽr), **Earl Russell.** 1891–1973. American Communist politician, b. Wichita, Kans. Joined Communist party (1919); its general secretary (1930–45); its nominee for president of the United States (1936, 1940).

**Brown** (broun). See also BROUN and BROWNE.

**Brown, Aaron Venable.** 1795–1859. American lawyer; member, U.S. House of Representatives (1839–45); governor of Tennessee (1845–47); U.S. postmaster general (1857–59).

**Brown, Addison.** 1830–1913. American jurist and botanist, b. West Newbury, Mass. District judge, southern district of New York (1881–1901); with N. L. Britton, wrote *Illustrated Flora of the Northern United States, Canada, and the British Possessions* (3 vols., 1896–98).

**Brown, Alexander.** 1764–1834. Financier, b. County Antrim, Ireland; to U.S. (1800). Settled in Baltimore, Md.; built up mercantile and banking house, Alexander Brown & Sons, with world-wide connections. One son, Sir **William** (1784–1864), started in Liverpool firm of Brown, Shipley, & Co., was benefactor of city of Liverpool. A second son, **John A.** (1788–1872), organized Brown Bros. & Co., Philadelphia (1818). A third, **James** (1791–1877), established Brown Bros. & Co., New York (1825). Another son, **George** (1787–1859), was an organizer of Baltimore and Ohio Railroad and its treasurer (1827–34); head of Alexander Brown & Sons (1834–59).

**Brown, Alice.** 1857–1948. American writer, b. Hampton Falls, N.H.; author of *Fools of Nature, The Road to Castaly* (verse), *Tiverton Tales, The Mannerings* (1906), *Children of Earth* (play; 1915), *The Black Drop* (1919), *The Willoughbys* (1935), etc.

**Brown, Arthur Judson.** 1856–1963. American Presbyterian clergyman; secretary, Presbyterian Board of Foreign Missions (1895–1929).

**Brown, Arthur Whitten.** 1886–1948. British aviator, b. in Glasgow. Served in World War I; navigator of airplane piloted by John & William Alcock (*q.v.*) on first nonstop airplane flight across Atlantic Ocean (June 14, 1919).

**Brown, Bartholomew.** American musicologist; teacher, Boston (fr. 1800); an editor of *Bridgewater Collection* (see Nahum MITCHELL).

**Brown, Benjamin Gratz** (grăts). 1826–1885. American lawyer, b. Lexington, Ky. Identified with free-soil movement in Missouri, and later in formation of Republican party. U.S. senator (1863–67). Governor of Missouri (1871–73). Vice-presidential nominee (1872).

**Brown, Carleton.** 1869–1941. American philologist and educator; author, editor, and compiler of works on English literature of the Middle Ages.

**Brown, Charles Armitage.** 1786–1842. English man of letters; intimate companion of Keats (1817–20).

**Brown, Charles Brockden.** 1771–1810. American novelist, b. Philadelphia. Author of *Wieland* (1798); *Ormond* (1799); *Edgar Huntly* (1799); *Arthur Mervyn* (1799–1800). First American novelist to gain international reputation.

**Brown, Charles Reynolds.** 1862–1950. American Congregational clergyman and educator; dean of Divinity School, Yale (1911–28).

**Brown, Crum,** *in full* **Alexander Crum.** 1838–1922. Scottish chemist. With John Gibson formulated the Crum Brown-Gibson rule.

**Brown, Elmer Ellsworth.** 1861–1934. American educator; professor, science and art of teaching, U. of California (1893–1906). U.S. commissioner of education (1906–11), chancellor, New York U. (1911–33).

**Brown** (broun), **Ernest.** 1881–1962. British politician, b. Torquay; M.P. (1923 ff.); minister of labor (1935–40), of national service (1939–40); secretary for Scotland (1940–41); minister of health (1941–43); chancellor of Duchy of Lancaster (1943–45).

**Brown, Ernest William.** 1866–1938. Mathematician, b. Hull, England; to U.S.; professor, Haverford (1891–1907), Yale (1907–32). Investigated celestial mechanics.

**Brown, Ford Madox.** 1821–1893. English historical painter, b. at Calais, France. Grandson of John Brown (1735–1788), Scottish Brunonian physician (*q.v.*). Studied art on Continent; accepted Dante Gabriel Rossetti as pupil (1848); closely allied with Pre-Raphaelite group. Executed twelve wall paintings for Manchester town hall, illustrating town's history (1878). Biography written by his grandson Ford Madox Ford (*q.v.*). His son **Oliver Madox** (1855–1874), novelist and water-colorist, exhibited *Exercise* in Royal Academy (1870); author of *The Black Swan* (previously pub. as *Gabriel Denver,* 1873).

**Brown, Francis.** 1784–1820. American clergyman and educator, b. Chester, N.H. President, Dartmouth College (1815–20), during litigation accompanying Dartmouth College Case. His son, **Samuel Gilman** (1813–1885), clergyman, was president of Hamilton College (1867–81). Samuel's son **Francis** (1849–1916), Semitic scholar, was president of Union Theological Seminary (1908–16) and editor in chief of the *Hebrew and English Lexicon of the Old Testament* (1886–1906).

**Brown, George.** 1787–1859. See Alexander BROWN.

**Brown, George.** 1818–1880. Canadian journalist and political leader, b. Edinburgh; founder of Toronto *Globe* (1844). Advocated in Canadian parliament laicization of Ontario schools, representation by population, federation of British colonies in North America, and purchase of northwest territories. His father, **Peter** (1784–1863), founded *The Banner* in Toronto (1843), a politico-religious paper.

**Brown, George Douglas.** *Pen name* **George Douglas.** 1869–1902. Scottish novelist; author of *The House with the Green Shutters* (1901), depicting harsher aspects of Scottish life in dissent from sentimentality of kailyard school.

**Brown, George Loring.** 1814–1889. American landscape painter.

**Brown, Gerard Baldwin.** 1849–1932. English art historian; professor of fine arts, Edinburgh (1880–1930). Author of *The Fine Arts* (1891), *The Arts in Early England* (2 vols., 1903), etc.

**Brown, Goold.** 1791–1857. American grammarian, b. Providence, R.I. Author of *Institutes of English Grammar* (1823), *Grammar of English Grammars* (1851).

**Brown, Henry Billings.** 1836–1913. American jurist; associate justice, U.S. Supreme Court (1890–1906).

**Brown, Henry Kirke.** 1814–1886. American sculptor, b. Leyden, Mass. Works: Washington (equestrian) and Lincoln (both, Union Square, New York); Gen. Winfield Scott and Gen. Nathanael Greene (both equestrian, Washington, D.C.); *Angel of the Resurrection* (Greenwood Cemetery).

**Brown, Horatio Robert Forbes.** 1854–1926. British historian; succeeded Rawdon Lubbock Brown in work of calendaring state papers in Venetian archives concerning English history. Author of works on history and life of Venice, biography of J. A. Symonds (1895), and *Dalmatia* (1925).

**Brown, Jacob Jennings.** 1775–1828. American army officer, b. Bucks County, Pa. In War of 1812, defended American base at Sacket's Harbor, on Lake Ontario (May, 1813); in command in western New York, at Battle of Niagara (July 25, 1814), and the defense of Fort Erie.

**Brown, James.** 1791–1877. See Alexander BROWN.

**Brown, James.** 1800–1855. American publisher. Organized partnership with Charles Coffin Little (1837) which developed (1847) into Little, Brown & Co., of Boston.

**Brown** of Priest′field (prēst′fēld), **John.** 1627?–1685. Scottish Covenanter martyr, shot in wife's presence by direction of John Graham of Claverhouse.

**Brown, John.** 1715–1766. English clergyman; educ. Cambridge; author of an *Essay on the Characteristics of Lord Shaftesbury,* defending utilitarian philosophy (1751), *An Estimate of the Manners and Principles of the Times,* a bitter satire (1757), as well as tragedies, odes, and writings on music.

**Brown, John.** 1735–1788. Scottish physician; founder of the Brunonian system of medicine, based on the doctrine that disease consists in excess or deficiency of excitation of the body by external agents; declared practice of bloodletting erroneous; author of *Elementa Medicinae* (1780), expounding his theory of medicine.

**Brown, John.** 1736–1803. See Nicholas BROWN.

**Brown, John.** *Called* **Old Brown of O′sa·wat′o·mie** (ō′sȧ·wŏt′ō·mĭ; ŏs′ȧ-). 1800–1859. American abolitionist fanatic, b. Torrington, Conn. Obsessed with idea of abolishing slavery by force (from 1856); in revenge for a proslavery massacre at Lawrence, Kans., massacred five slavery adherents at Pottawatomie (May 24, 1856); made heroic stand at Osawatomie (August, 1856) against raid by proslavery adherents from Missouri. Conceived plan of establishing new state as refuge for negroes and base of operations for freeing slaves; received financial aid from Massachusetts abolitionists; seized Harpers Ferry, Va., and government arsenal there (Oct. 16–17, 1859), intending this action as signal for general insurrection of slaves. Overpowered, convicted of treason; hanged (Dec. 2, 1859). Regarded by northern sympathizers as a martyr, and commemorated in marching song "John Brown's body."

**Brown, John.** 1810–1882. Scottish physician and essayist; friend of Thackeray and Ruskin. Author of *Horae Subsecivae, i.e.* Leisure Hours, treating (vol. 1, 1858) of the practice of medicine, and (vols. 2 & 3, 1861, 1882) of poetry, art, and human character; *Rab and His Friends,* classic story of an old scarred mastiff attending upon mistress and master through their sickness and death (1859); *Marjorie Fleming,* an essay upon the ten-year-old prodigy of Sir Walter Scott (1863); *John Leech and other Papers* (1882). His great-grandfather **John** (1722–1787) of Had′ding·ton (hăd′ĭng·tŭn), Scottish preacher and scholar; author of explanation of Westminster Confession (1758), and of *Self-interpreting Bible* (1778).

**Brown,** Sir **John.** 1816–1896. English steel manufacturer; originated at Sheffield use of rolled-steel armor plating for war vessels (1860).

**Brown, John A.** 1788–1872. See Alexander BROWN.

**Brown, John Carter.** 1797–1874. See Nicholas BROWN.

**Brown, John George.** 1831–1913. American genre painter; b. Durham, Eng., to U.S. (about 1853); noted esp. for paintings of street urchins.

**Brown, John Macmillan.** 1846–1935. Educator, b. Irvine, Scotland; professor, Canterbury University College, New Zealand; chancellor, U. of New Zealand (from 1923); author of *Maori and Polynesian, The Riddle of the Pacific, Peoples and Problems of the Pacific,* etc.

**Brown, John Mason.** 1900–1969. American literary critic, b. Louisville, Ky. Author of *To All Hands* (1943), *Daniel Boone* (1952), etc.

**Brown, Joseph Rogers.** 1810–1876. American inventor, b. Warren, R.I. Devised precision instruments, calipers, and protractors. With Lucian Sharpe, founded J. R. Brown & Sharpe (1853), incorporated (1868) as Brown and Sharpe Manuf. Co.

**Brown, Lancelot.** 1715–1783. Known as "Capability Brown." English landscape gardener; laid out gardens at Kew and Blenheim.

**Brown, Martha,** *nee* **Mc·Clel′lan** (mȧ·klĕl′ăn). 1838–1916. American temperance lecturer and organizer, b. Baltimore; m. (1858) W. Kennedy Brown. An organizer of the Prohibition party (1869), and a founder of National Woman's Christian Temperance Union.

**Brown, Nicholas.** 1729–1791. American businessman, b. Providence, R.I. With his brothers in foreign trading and domestic manufacture, as Nicholas Brown & Co. (from 1762). Revolutionary cannon made from iron ore taken from their deposits of bog ore at Scituate and cast in their furnace. Supplied clothing and munitions to American army. Instrumental in locating, in Providence, Rhode Island College, later (1804) named Brown University. His brothers were: **Joseph** (1733–1785), **John** (1736–1803), and **Moses** (1738–1836). Moses introduced cotton manufacturing into Rhode Island (1789 ff.) and aided a Quaker school in Providence, ultimately (1904) named Moses Brown School. Nicholas's grandson **John Carter Brown** (1797–1874), assembled library of Americana, now at Brown University.

**Brown, Oliver Madox.** See Ford Madox BROWN.

**Brown, Olympia.** 1835–1926. American minister and suffragist, b. Prairie Ronde, Mich. Ordained (1863) minister of Universalist Church, first woman in America in ministry of a regular church; m. (1873) John Henry Willis. President, Wisconsin Woman's Suffrage Assn. (1887–1917).

**Brown, Peter.** See under George BROWN (1818–1880).

**Brown, Peter Hume.** 1849–1918. Scottish historian. Biographer of George Buchanan, John Knox, and

Goethe; author of *History of Scotland* (1899–1909).

**Brown, Rawdon Lubbock.** 1803–1883. English historical research student, in Venice (1833–83); editor of *Calendar of State Papers...Relating to English Affairs ...in the Archives of Venice* (pub. 1864–84).

**Brown, Robert.** 1773–1858. Scottish botanist. Naturalist on Flinders's expedition to Australia (1801–05); collected new plant species. Discovered gymnospermism. Demonstrated vibratory movement (Brownian movement) of microscopic particles. Curator of botanical dept. in British Museum (1827). His adoption of Jussiaean system of classification furthered its general adoption in place of Linnaean.

**Brown, Robert.** 1842–1895. Scottish naturalist and geographer. Author of *Manual of Botany* (1874), *Science for All* (5 vols., 1877–82), *Peoples of the World* (5 vols., 1882–85), etc.

**Brown, Roy.** 1879–1956. American landscape painter.

**Brown, Samuel Gilman.** See Francis BROWN.

**Brown, Sidney George.** 1873–1948. English electrical engineer and inventor, b. Chicago, Ill. Educ. University College, London. Invented the relay and magnetic shunt which first relayed messages over long submarine cables (1899), the single-point iridium microphonic relay (1908), the granular carbon microphone relay much used in radiotelegraphy, a gyroscopic compass for marine use (1914) and one for air-service use, a gun directional compass, an airplane speed indicator (1930).

**Brown, Solyman.** 1790–1876. American clergyman and dentist, b. Litchfield, Conn. Congregational clergyman (1813–17); classics teacher (1820–32); Swedenborgian minister (from 1822). Practiced dentistry (1834–50); known as a founder of dentistry as an organized profession.

**Brown, Sterling Allen.** 1901– . American Negro poet; b. Washington, D.C.; teacher in the South (from 1922); professor of English, Howard U.; author of *Southern Road* (1932), *A Negro Looks at the South* (1943).

**Brown, Thomas,** the younger. Pseudonym of Thomas MOORE.

**Brown, Thomas.** 1663–1704. English writer of satirical verses, including *I do not love thee, Dr. Fell*, written while at Oxford; London hack writer.

**Brown, Thomas.** 1778–1820. Scottish metaphysician; coadjutor (from 1810) of Dugald Stewart as professor of moral philosophy, Edinburgh; defended Hume's doctrine of causality as not inconsonant with religion; made advances toward associational psychology; wrote commonplace poems after model of Pope and Akenside.

**Brown, Thomas Edward.** 1830–1897. British poet, b. Isle of Man. Schoolmaster (1858–93). Author of *Betsy Lee, a Foc's'le Yarn* (1873) and other books of verse, mostly in Anglo-Manx dialect.

**Brown, Walter Folger.** 1869–1961. American lawyer and politician; U.S. postmaster general (1929–33).

**Brown,** Sir **William.** 1784–1864. See Alexander BROWN.

**Brown, William Adams.** 1865–1943. American theologian; ordained in Presbyterian ministry (1893); professor of theology, Union Sem. (1898–1936). Author of *The Essence of Christianity* (1902), *Modern Theology...* (1914), *The Church, Catholic and Protestant* (1935), etc.

**Brown, William Henry.** 1884–1939. American botanist; plant physiologist (1911–23), director (1924–33), Bureau of Science, Manila; professor, U. of Philippines (1919–24); lecturer in botany, Johns Hopkins (1933–39).

**Brown, Zenith,** *nee* **Jones.** *Pseudonyms* **Leslie Ford** and **David Frome** (frōm). 1898– . American novelist, b. Smith River, Calif.; m. Ford K. Brown. Best known for her detective fiction and for creation of character Mr. Pinkerton, as in *Mr. Pinkerton Goes to Scotland Yard* (1934) and *Mr. Pinkerton Grows a Beard* (1935).

**Browne** (broun). See also BROUN and BROWN.

**Browne, Charles Albert.** 1870–1947. American agricultural chemist; chief, Bureau of Chemistry, U.S. Department of Agriculture (1923–27); chief, chemical and technical research (1927–35); supervisor of chemical research (from 1935). Specialist in chemistry of sugar.

**Browne, Charles Farrar.** *Originally* **Brown.** *Pseudonym* **Artemus Ward.** 1834–1867. American humorist, b. near Waterford, Me. Learned printer's trade. First of his humorous articles in Cleveland (Ohio) *Plain Dealer* (1858). On staff of *Vanity Fair*, New York (1859); lectured through country (1861–66); on English tour (1866–67); died in England. Author of *Artemus Ward, His Book* (1862), *Artemus Ward, His Travels* (1865).

**Browne, Edward Granville.** 1862–1926. English Orientalist. Lecturer in Persian (1888–92), professor of Arabic (1902–26), Cambridge.

**Browne, Edward Harold.** 1811–1891. English theological teacher and writer. His *Exposition of the Thirty-nine Articles* (2 vols., 1850, 1854) long a standard authority.

**Browne, George Elmer.** 1871–1946. American painter

**Browne, Hab'lot** (hăb'lō) **Knight.** *Known as* **Phiz** (fĭz). 1815–1882. English painter. Abandoned line engraving for etching and water-color painting. Preferred to his rival applicant, W. M. Thackeray, as illustrator, in succession to Robert Seymour (d. 1836), of *Pickwick Papers;* illustrated other Dickens novels and those of Lever and Ainsworth.

**Browne, Isaac Hawkins.** 1705–1760. English poet and wit. Author of parodies on contemporary poets, and of Latin poem *De Animi Immortalitate* (1754). Called by Dr. Johnson one of first wits of the country.

**Browne, Lewis.** 1897–1949. Rabbi and author, b. London, Eng.; to U.S. (1912). Rabbi (1920–26). Writer and lecturer (from 1926). Author of *This Believing World* (1926), *Why Are Jews Like That?* (1929), *Blessed Spinoza* (1932), *Oh, Say, Can You See?* (1937), etc.

**Browne** (broun), Count **Maximilian Ulysses von.** Baron **de Camus** and **Mountany.** 1705–1757. Austrian field marshal, b. in Switzerland, son of Irish Jacobite exile in service of Emperor Charles VI. Commanded Maria Theresa's army in Silesia during War of Austrian Succession, and in Seven Years' War; field marshal (1753); defeated by Frederick the Great at Lobositz (1756) and Prague (1757).

**Browne, Porter Emerson.** 1879–1934. American novelist and playwright, b. Beverly, Mass. Author of plays *A Fool There Was* (1906), *The Spendthrift* (1908), *A Girl of Today* (1915), *The Bad Man* (1920); novels *A Fool There Was* (1908), *Scars and Stripes* (1917).

**Browne, Ralph Cowan.** 1880–1960. American roentgenologist and inventor; inventor of electrical system and mechanism adopted by U.S. government in North Sea mine barrage during World War, and of portable X-ray apparatus, an air-lift mine pump, a form of high-resistance transmitter used in telephony.

**Browne, Robert.** 1550?–?1633. English separatist clergyman; founder of Brownists, predecessors of the Independents, or Congregationalists. Emigrated with followers to Middelburg, Zeeland (1581); issued books enunciating Independency, circulation of which was punishable in England by death. Returned to England (1584); excommunicated; after qualified submission to bishop, appointed master of Stamford grammar school (1586); accepted episcopal ordination (1591); rector of Achurch, Northamptonshire (1591–1631).

**Browne,** Sir **Samuel James.** 1824–1901. British army officer, b. and served in India; general (1888); inventor of the sword belt called the "Sam Browne belt."

**Browne,** Sir **Thomas.** 1605–1682. English physician and author. Practiced medicine, Norwich (from 1637); aided, by his professional evidence, in condemnation of two women as witches (1664). Author of *Religio Medici,* confessions of a skeptic (1643, following surreptitious edition published without his knowledge in 1642), which was inserted in Index Expurgatorius; *Pseudodoxia Epidemica,* storehouse of out-of-the-way learning (1646); *Hydriotaphia: Urne-Buriall* (1658); and a mystical treatise, *The Garden of Cyrus* (1658), showing how the quincunx pervades the universe.

**Browne, Thomas.** 1870–1910. English painter and black-and-white artist; created the American comic-strip characters Weary Willie and Tired Tim.

**Browne, Thomas Alexander.** *Pseudonym* **Rolf Bol′dre-wood** (rŏlf bōl′dẽr·wo͝od). 1826–1915. Australian novelist, b. London; son of one of founders of Melbourne. Engaged in agriculture and cattle breeding; police magistrate; commissioner of gold fields (till 1895). Author of *Robbery under Arms* (tale of the bushranger Captain Starlight; 1888), *The Squatter's Dream* (tale of sheep raisers; 1890), *Old Melbourne Memories* (1895), *The Babes in the Bush* (1900), *In Bad Company* (1901), and other novels of Australian life.

**Browne, William.** 1591–?1643. English pastoral poet; author of *Britannia's Pastorals* (book I, 1613; II, 1616; III, 1852) and *The Shepheards Pipe,* including eclogues by other poets (1614).

**Brow·nell′** (brou·nĕl′; brou′nĕl), **Thomas Church.** 1779–1865. American Episcopal bishop and educator, b. Westport, Mass. Consecrated bishop (1819). First president (1823–31), Washington College, now Trinity College, Hartford, Conn.

**Brownell, William Crary.** 1851–1928. American journalist and literary critic; on staff New York *World* (1871–79), *The Nation* (1879–81). Author of *French Traits* (1889), *French Art* (1892), *Victorian Prose Masters* (1901), *American Prose Masters* (1909), *Criticism* (1914), *Standards* (1917), *The Genius of Style* (1924), *Democratic Distinction in America* (1927).

**Brown′ing** (broun′ĭng), **Elizabeth Barrett.** *Maiden name* **Elizabeth Moul′ton** (mōl′t'n; -tŭn), *later* **Barrett** (name assumed by father, Edward Moulton, on succeeding to estate in Jamaica). 1806–1861. English poet. Read Homer in Greek at eight; translated *Prometheus Bound* (1833); wrote many original poems. As result of injury to spine in saddling a horse at fifteen, semi-invalid for years; regained strength some time previous to her marriage (1846) to Robert Browning but always delicate; expressed hesitation to burden him with invalid wife in *Sonnets from the Portuguese,* written in secret, first seen by Robert Browning, and published in 1850. Sympathized with struggle of Florentines for freedom in *Casa Guidi Windows* (1851). Completed *Aurora Leigh* (1856), expressing her "highest convictions in work and art." Bitterly disappointed by peace of Villafranca. Last work *Poems before Congress* (1860).

**Browning, John Moses.** 1855–1926. American designer of firearms, b. Ogden, Utah, son of gunsmith. Designed sporting firearms manufactured by Winchester, Remington, Stevens, and Colt companies; organized with brother **Matthew** a gunmaking firm. Inventor of Browning automatic pistol, model of 1911, Browning machine gun, model of 1917, Browning automatic rifle, model of 1918, used in World War. His brother **Jonathan Edmund** (1859–1939), skillful mechanic and inventor, co-operated with him in inventing and building of machine guns, repeating rifles, and automatic pistol; patented (1940) automatic rifle operated by expansion of gases from the explosion.

**Browning, Orville Hickman.** 1806–1881. American lawyer, b. Harrison County, Ky. U.S. senator (1861–63). U.S. secretary of the interior (1866–69).

**Browning, Oscar.** 1837–1923. English historical writer and educationalist.

**Browning, Robert.** 1812–1889. English poet; son of clerk in Bank of England, having literary and artistic tastes, and a mother having passion for music. Showed Shelleyan influence in first published work, *Pauline* (anon., 1833); wrote earliest of his dramatic lyrics, *Porphyria's Lover* (1834), in Russia; published long dramatic narrative poems *Paracelsus* (1835) and *Sordello* (1840). Urged by Macready, wrote tragedy *Strafford,* produced at Covent Garden (1837), followed by other plays, including *Pippa Passes, Return of the Druses, Blot in the 'Scutcheon, Colombe's Birthday;* published these plays along with *Dramatic Romances and Lyrics* (under the title *Bells and Pomegranates,* 1841–46); contributed to *Hood's Magazine* (1844–45) six poems including *The Bishop Orders his Tomb at Saint Praxed's* and *The Flight of the Duchess.* m. (1846) Elizabeth Barrett (see Elizabeth Barrett BROWNING) and lived for next fifteen years more or less in seclusion, mainly in Italy; published only *Christmas Eve* and *Easter Day* (1850) and *Men and Women* (1855; including *Fra Lippo Lippi*); returned to London upon wife's death (1861), and in psychological monologues of *Dramatis Personae* (1864; including *Prospice, Rabbi Ben Ezra, A Death in the Desert, Caliban upon Setebos*) found his best form; wrote *The Ring and the Book* (1864–69), story of a Roman murder case in 12 books, in which each of the participants in the trial independently narrates episode of the crime from his own point of view—often regarded as Browning's masterpiece. Turned increasingly to speculation and analytical disquisition in later writings on variety of subjects, including *Fifine at the Fair* (1872), *Red Cotton Nightcap Country* (1873), *The Inn Album* (1875); returned to direct narrative in *Dramatic Idylls* (1879, 1880; including *Pheidippides*). Showed failing powers of objectivity in last works; for example, *Jocoseria* (1883), *Ferishtah's Fancies* (1884), *Asolando* (1889, appearing the day of his death). Buried in Westminster Abbey.

His son **Robert Wie′de·mann** (?wē′dĕ·măn) **Barrett** (1849–1912), b. at Florence, studied art at Antwerp and practiced painting and sculpture; edited *Love Letters of Robert and Elizabeth Barrett Browning* (1899).

**Brown′low** (broun′lō), Barons. See CUST.

**Brownlow, William Gannaway.** 1805–1877. Called "the Fighting Parson." American political leader, b. Wythe Co., Va. Methodist itinerant preacher (1826–36). Editor, Jonesboro (Tenn.) *Whig and Independent* (1839–49); Knoxville (Tenn.) *Whig* (1849–61), when it was suppressed because of Union sympathies. Active in leadership of Union sympathizers (from 1863). Governor of Tennessee (1865–69). U.S. senator (1869–75).

**Brown′rigg** (broun′rĭg), Sir **Robert.** 1759–1833. British soldier; lieut. general (1808); served in Walcheren expedition (1809); governor of Ceylon (1811–20); conquered Kandyan kingdom (1814–15); general (1819).

**Brown′-Sé′quard′** (broun′sā′kȧr′; -sā′kwȧr′), **Charles Édouard.** 1817?–1894. Physician and physiologist, b. Port Louis, Mauritius, of American and French parentage. Known esp. for investigations of physiology and pathology of spinal cord, and of blood, animal heat, and internal secretions of organs; advocated hypodermic injection of a fluid prepared from testicles of sheep as means of invigorating human beings and prolonging life.

**Brown′son** (broun′s'n), **Orestes Augustus.** 1803–1876. American clergyman and writer, b. Stockbridge, Vt.

Universalist minister (1826–29); Unitarian minister (1832–44); converted to Roman Catholicism (1844).

**Broz** (brōz) *or* **Bro'zo·vich** (brō'zô·vĭch; *Yugo.* -vēt'y'), **Josip.** Called **Ti'to** (tē'tô). 1892– . Yugoslav premier, b. Zagorye, Croatia. Metal worker, labor leader; partisan leader during World War II; marshal of the People's Army and president of National Liberation Council (1943); prime min. (1945-53); pres. (from 1953).

**Bro'žik** (brô'zhĭk), **Václav.** 1851–1901. Czech painter.

**Bruce** (brōōs) *or in early use* **de Bruce** (dĕ; dê). Surname of old Scottish family of Norman descent founded by **Robert de Bruce I,** *also* **Braose** *or* **Breaux** *or* **Brus** (d. 1094?), from Bruis, a castle near Cherbourg, follower of William the Conqueror. It includes:

**Robert VI** (1210–1295); son of **Robert V** (d. 1245) and Isabel, niece of the Scottish king William the Lion; called the "Competitor" (with John de Baliol); recognized as heir presumptive (1238–41); one of fifteen regents during minority of Alexander III; fought on side of Henry III against barons; at arbitration of Edward I lost his claim to crown to Baliol (1292).

**Robert VIII** (1274–1329), king and liberator of Scotland; called "the Bruce"; grandson of Robert VI; at first paid homage, as had his father, **Robert VII** (1253–1304), to Edward I of England as king of Scotland (1296); in arms against Edward (1298); publicly adhered to Edward during invasion (1302–04); murdered John Comyn, nephew of Baliol (1306); crowned as Robert I, King of Scotland, at Scone (1306); defeated by English army at Methven (1306), took refuge on coast of Ireland; excommunicated and outlawed; returned (1307) and in two years wrested most of Scotland from English; routed Edward II's army at Bannockburn (1314) and took Stirling Castle; subdued Hebrides (1316); repulsed English again and again until final treaty (1328) at Northampton by which Edward III recognized independence of Scotland and Bruce's right to throne; died of leprosy.

**Edward** (d. 1318), King Robert's younger brother, subdued Galloway (1308); aided Ulster chieftains to expel English; crowned king of Ireland (1315).

**David** (1324–1371), son of King Robert; succeeded his father as David II (1329); crowned king of Scotland, with his queen, Joan, daughter of Edward II of England, at Scone (1331); retired to France upon dispersal of adherents by Edward III at Halidon Hill (1333); invaded England, taken prisoner at Neville's Cross (1346); ransomed (1357) for 100,000 marks to be paid in ten years; proposed bequeathing crown to son of Edward III of England in return for remission of fine; died childless.

**Bruce.** Name of English family holding earldom of **El'gin** (ĕl'gĭn). Prominent members of family are **Robert** (d. 1685), 2d earl; lord chamberlain of England (1685). His son **Thomas** (1655?–1741), 3d earl; imprisoned as Jacobite (1696); resided in Brussels (1696–1741). **Thomas** (1766–1841), 7th earl of Elgin and 11th earl of **Kin·car'dine** (kĭng·kär'dĭn; kĭn-); British diplomat; arranged while envoy to the Porte for conveyance of collection called the "Elgin marbles," including the Parthenon frieze, from the Acropolis of Athens to British Museum (1803–12). His son **James** (1811–1863), 8th earl of Elgin and 12th earl of Kincardine; diplomat; governor of Jamaica (1842); governor general of Canada (1847–54); envoy to China and Japan to negotiate treaties; first viceroy of India directly appointed by the crown (1862). Sir **Frederick William Adolphus** (1814–1867), youngest son of 7th earl; diplomat; served in Hongkong (1844), Bolivia (1848), Uruguay (1851), Egypt (1853), and as envoy to China (1858) and to Washington (1865). **Victor Alexander** (1849–1917), 9th earl of Elgin and 13th earl of Kincardine; b. in Canada, son of 8th earl; viceroy of India during period of frontier uprisings (1894–99); chairman of royal commission to examine conduct of Boer War; colonial secretary in Campbell-Bannerman's ministry (1905–08).

**Bruce, Alexander Hugh.** See BALFOUR OF BURLEIGH.

**Bruce, Arthur Loring.** Pseudonym of Francis Welch CROWNINSHIELD.

**Bruce,** Sir **David.** 1855–1931. British physician and bacteriologist, specialist in tropical diseases, b. Melbourne, Australia. M.B. and C.M., Edinburgh. Entered Royal Army Medical Corps (1883); first described (1887) the small bacterium that causes undulant fever (also called Malta, or Mediterranean, fever), and traced the bacterium to milk of Maltese goats. Served in South Africa (1894–1901); discovered organism that causes nagana (1895?); member of Army Medical Advisory Board (1902–11). To Uganda to investigate sleeping sickness (1903, with Nabarro and Castellani; again 1908–10); to Malta to investigate Mediterranean fever (1904–06); to Nyasaland to investigate connection between human and animal diseases (1911–14). Major general (1912).

**Bruce, David Kirkpatrick Este.** 1898-1977. Amer. diplomat, b. Baltimore, Md. U.S. ambassador to France (1949–52), West Germany (1957–59), and Great Britain (1961–69).

**Bruce, Henry Austin.** 1st Baron **Ab'er·dare'** (ăb'ēr-dâr'; *Welsh* ȧ'bĕr·dȧr'). 1815–1895. English political leader. Home secretary (1869–73); lord president of council (1873–74); administrative director (from 1882) of company formed by Sir George Dashwood Taubman Goldie for exploration and commercial exploitation in West Africa, which became Royal Niger Co. First chancellor, U. of Wales (1894).

**Bruce, James.** 1730–1794. Scottish explorer in Africa. British consul, Algiers (1763–65); rediscovered source of Blue Nile (1770). Author of *Travels to Discover the Source of the Nile* (5 vols., 1790).

**Bruce, Michael.** 1746–1767. Scottish poet and schoolmaster. His poems published by Rev. John Logan, who himself claimed authorship of *Ode to the Cuckoo.*

**Bruce, Stanley Melbourne.** Viscount. 1883–1967. Australian statesman. Prime minister of Australia (1923–29). Representative on council of League of Nations (1933–35), and president of council (1935). Represented Australia at imperial and world economic conferences (1923–33); high commissioner for Australia in London (1933–45); Australian representative in British war cabinet (1942–45).

**Bruce, William Cabell.** 1860–1946. American lawyer, politician, and biographer, b. Va.; practiced law in Baltimore; U.S. senator, Maryland (1923–29). Author of *Benjamin Franklin, Self-Revealed* (2 vols.), *John Randolph of Roanoke* (2 vols.; 1923), etc.

**Bruce, William Speirs.** 1867–1921. British polar explorer and naturalist. Studied medicine, Edinburgh; on polar expeditions (1892–99); leader of Scottish national antarctic expedition to explore Weddell Sea (1902–04); visited Spitsbergen seven times (1906–20).

**Bruch** (brŏŏκ), **Max.** 1838–1920. German composer and conductor. Composer of epic cantatas, oratorios, orchestral works, and chamber music.

**Bru'che·si'** (brü'shā'zē'), **Louis Joseph Paul Napoléon.** 1855–1939. Canadian prelate, b. Montreal. Roman Catholic archbishop of Montreal (from 1897). Established Anti-Alcoholic League (1907) and order of nurses, Sisters of Hope.

**Bruck** (brŏŏk), Baron **Karl Ludwig von.** 1798–1860. Austrian statesman; delegate to National Assembly, Frankfurt (1848); minister of commerce (1848–51);

helped carry out many commercial and customs reforms; minister of finance (1855–60); failed in contemplated reforms and in meeting obligations resulting from Italian war of 1859; committed suicide.

**Brück′e** (brük′ĕ), **Ernst Wilhelm von.** 1819–1892. German physician and physiologist; known for researches in histology and the physiology of the circulation of the blood, studies of digestion, nervous system, sense organs, and speech.

**Bruck′er** (brŏŏk′ẽr), **Johann Jakob.** 1696–1770. German philosopher; author of *Historia Critica Philosophiae* (5 vols., 1742–44), first history of philosophy in Germany.

**Brück′ner** (*Ger.* brük′nẽr), **Alexander.** 1834–1896. Russian historian, b. St. Petersburg; to Germany (1891); author of works on Russian history, mostly in German.

**Brückner, Alexander.** 1856–1939. Austrian Slavic scholar; authority on medieval Polish literature.

**Bruck′ner** (brŏŏk′nẽr), **Anton.** 1824–1896. Austrian composer and organist; professor, Vienna Conservatory (1871). His compositions include 9 symphonies, 3 grand masses, a string quintet (1879), a Te Deum (1885), a requiem, and choral works.

**Brück′ner** (brük′nẽr), **Eduard.** 1862–1927. German geographer and meteorologist; specialist in climatology and glaciology.

**Brückner, Wilhelm.** 1884– . German National Socialist leader; joined Reichswehr (1919) and National Socialist German Workers' party (1923); led "Munich Regiment" in uprising of 1923; imprisoned 5½ months; general secretary of society for German propaganda in foreign lands, Bavaria (1924–28); leader in Sturmabteilung and member of Hitler's permanent escort (1930).

**Brudenell, James Thomas.** See earl of CARDIGAN.

**Brue′ghel** *or* **Brue′gel** *or* **Breu′ghel** (brû′gĕl). Family of Flemish painters, including: **Pieter** the Elder (1520?–1569), called "Peasant Brueghel" and "the Droll," whose paintings were chiefly of peasant life, landscapes, and Biblical and fantastic scenes. His sons **Pieter** the Younger (1564?–?1638), called "Hell Brueghel," painter of rural and genre subjects in his father's style and esp. of paintings of infernal regions, devils, and flames; and **Jan** the Elder (1568–1625), called "Velvet Brueghel" and "Flower Brueghel," painter esp. of flowers and of landscapes with Biblical and mythological figures and animals, and of landscapes and background for many figure painters, notably Rubens. Jan's sons **Jan** the Younger (1601–1678), pupil of his father and painter of landscapes and flowers, and **Ambrose** (1617–1675), painter of flowers and fruits. **Abraham** (1631–?1690), son of Jan the Younger, painter of still life in the Italian-Flemish style. **Jan Baptist** (1670–1719), great-grandson of Jan the Elder, painter of flowers and fruits.

**Brue′ning** (brü′nĭng). = BRÜNING.

**Bru′ere′** (brü′yâr′), **Robert Walter.** 1876– . American authority on industrial relations; director, Bureau of Industrial Research, New York (1917–23); assoc. editor, *The Survey* (1923–28); research secretary, J. C. Penney Foundation (1928–30). Author of *Increasing Home Efficiency* (with his wife, **Martha,** *nee* **Bens′ley** [bĕnz′lĭ]; 1912), *The Coming of Coal* (1922), *The Man With a Thousand Partners* (1931).

**Brues** (brōōz), **Charles Thomas.** 1879–1955. American entomologist, b. Wheeling, W.Va. On staff, entomology department, Harvard (from 1909, professor from 1935). Special editor for entomology, *Webster's New International Dictionary, Second Edition.* Author of *A Key to the Families of North American Insects* (1915), and *Classification of Insects* (1932), both with A. L. Melander, and of *Insects and Human Welfare* (1920).

**Bru′eys′** (brü′ĕs′), **David Augustin de.** 1640–1723. French writer; author of religious treatises; collaborator with Palaprat (*q.v.*) in several successful comedies, as *Le Concert Ridicule* (1689), *Le Grondeur* (1691), *Le Muet* (1691), *L'Avocat Patelin* (1706).

**Brug′mann** (brŏŏg′män), **Karl.** 1849–1919. German philologist of the neogrammarian (Junggrammatiker) school. Professor of Sanskrit and comparative philology, Freiburg (1884) and Leipzig (1887). Author of *Nasalis Sonans in der Indogermanischen Grundsprache* (1876), *Morphologische Untersuchungen* (with Osthoff; 5 vols., 1878–90; vol. 6, 1910), *Grundriss der Vergleichenden Grammatik der Indogermanischen Sprachen* (1886–93).

**Bru′gna·tel′li** (brōō′nyä·tĕl′lē), **Luigi Gasparo.** 1761–1818. Italian mineralogist and chemist; reputed to have invented a process of electroplating (1805).

**Bru′gnon′** (brü′nyôɴ′), **Jacques.** 1895– . French lawn-tennis player; member of Davis Cup team (1925–33) that won cup (1927) and successfully defended it (1928–32).

**Brugsch** (brŏŏksh), **Heinrich Karl.** 1827–1894. German Egyptologist. Worked on deciphering of demotic Egyptian and published first book, *Scriptura Aegyptiorum Demotica* (1848), while still a student at the gymnasium; professor, Göttingen (1868); director of school of Egyptology, Cairo (1870). Author of hieroglyphic-demotic dictionary (1867–82), Egyptian grammar, and writings on geography, history, religion, etc., of ancient Egypt.

**Brühl** (brül), Count **Heinrich von.** 1700–1763. Saxon statesman; won favor of Augustus III; prime minister in virtual control of Saxony and Poland (1746–63); induced Augustus to side against Prussia in Seven Years' War, and fled with him to Warsaw after loss of Saxon army (1756); returned to Dresden (1763). His library (62,000 volumes) forms part of the Royal Library, Dresden.

**Bruhns** (brōōns), **Karl Christian.** 1830–1881. German astronomer. Professor and director of observatory, U. of Leipzig (1860); discovered six comets.

**Bruis, Pierre de.** See Pierre de BRUYS.

**Bru′lat′** (brü′lȧ′), **Paul.** 1866–1925. French novelist.

**Bru′lé′** (brü′lā′), **Étienne.** 1592?–1633. French adventurer in America. To Quebec (1608) with Champlain. Went into western wilderness (1610); lived with Huron Indians, assembling furs for the French (1618–29). First European to traverse four of the five Great Lakes. Killed and eaten by Indians.

**Brüll** (brül), **Ignaz.** 1846–1907. Austrian pianist and composer; wrote 10 operas, orchestral and chamber music, songs, piano compositions.

**Brülow** *or* **Brüllow.** See BRYULOV.

**Brum** (brōōm), **Baltasar.** 1883–1933. Uruguayan jurist, journalist, and political leader; president of Uruguay (1919–23); set forth in a speech (1920) the "Brum doctrine" (American league of nations).

**Bru′mi·di** (?brōō′mē·dē), **Constantino.** 1805–1880. Painter, b. Rome, Italy; to U.S. (1852); became naturalized citizen. Chief work, frescoes in Capitol, Washington, D.C.

**Brum′mell** (brŭm′ĕl), **George Bryan.** *Called* **Beau** (bō) **Brummell.** 1778–1840. English dandy; friend of prince of Wales, afterward George IV; a gambler, fled from creditors to Calais (1816); British consul at Caen (1830–32); died in French asylum for insane.

**Bru′moy′** (brü′mwȧ′), **Pierre.** 1688–1742. French Jesuit and scholar; best known for his *Le Théâtre des Grecs* (1730).

**Brun** (brōōn), Saint. See BRUNO.

**Brun** (brûɴ), **Charles Le.** See Charles LE BRUN.

**Brun** (brōōn), **Friederike Sophie Christiane,** *nee* **Mün′ter**

(mün′tẽr). 1765–1835. German writer; m. (1783) Konstantin Brun, in Copenhagen. Author of poems (1795), prose writings (1799–1801), *Briefe aus Rom* (1816), accounts of her travels in Russia, Switzerland, and southern Europe. Friend of Madame de Staël and Sismondi.

**Brunck** (brûNk), **Philippe.** 1729–1803. French classical scholar; author of an anthology of Greek poets, *Analecta,* and editions of Greek and Latin classics.

**Brune** (brün), **Guillaume Marie Anne.** 1763–1815. French army officer; marshal of France (1804); murdered by royalist mob during the White Terror at Avignon (Aug. 2, 1815).

**Bru′neau′** (brü′nō′), **Alfred.** 1857–1934. French composer and music critic; identified with ultramodern movements in music; critic on staff of *Revue Indépendante, Gil Blas, Figaro, Le Matin;* composer of operas and of several volumes of critical writings.

**Brunechildis** *or* **Brunehilde** *or* **Brunehaut.** See BRUNHILDE.

**Bru·nel′** (brōō·nĕl′), Sir **Marc Is′am·bard** (ĭz′ăm·bärd). 1769–1849. Inventor and engineer, b. in France. To New York (1793) as refugee of French Revolution; practiced as architect and engineer; to England (1799); invented method of making ships' blocks; constructed Thames Tunnel (1825–43). His son **Isambard Kingdom** (1806–1859) was a designer and builder of railroads, bridges, tunnels, steamships, docks, etc.; as chief engineer, built most of Great Western Railway (from 1833) and introduced broad gauge; built the *Great Western,* first steamship for regular transatlantic trips (1838), *Great Britain,* first ocean screw steamship (1845), and *Great Eastern,* largest steamship of its time (1858).

**Bru′nel·le′schi** (brōō′nāl·lās′kē) *or* **Bru′nel·le′sco** (-kō), **Filippo.** 1377?–1446. Italian architect, b. Florence. Reputed founder of Renaissance architecture and first to establish soundly scientific theory of perspective. Designed and constructed dome of Santa Maria del Fiore Cathedral in Florence, which in some measurements exceeds St. Peter's, Rome (1420 ff.). Among his other works are the Pitti Palace, Church of San Lorenzo, Capella dei Pazzi, and Ospedale degl'Innocenti (all in Florence).

**Bru′net′** (brü′nĕ′), **Jean.** 1823–1894. French poet, b. Avignon; one of the seven poets who founded Félibrige.

**Brunet, Jacques Charles.** 1780–1867. French bibliographer; published *Manuel du Libraire et de l'Amateur de Livres* (1810).

**Bru′net′-De·baines′** (-dẽ·bĕn′), **Charles Fortuné Louis.** 1801–1862. French architect; architect of the Invalides (1860); laid remains of Napoleon in tomb prepared for him there.

**Bru′ne·tière′** (brü′nẽ·tyâr′), **Vincent de Paul Marie Ferdinand.** 1849–1906. French critic; professor of literature, École Normale, Paris (1886); lecturer at the Sorbonne (1893); editor, *Revue des Deux Mondes* (1893). Author of *Études Critiques* (8 vols., 1880–1907), *L'Évolution de la Poésie Lyrique* (1894), etc.

**Brunetto Latini.** See Brunetto LATINI.

**Brun′fels** (brōōn′fĕls), **Otto.** 1488?–1534. German physician and botanist; called "father of botany"; author of *Contrafayt Kreuterbuch,* first of 16th-century herbals, describing for first time the native plants of Germany.

**Brun·hil′de** (brōōn·hĭl′dĕ) *or* **Bru′ne·hil′de** (brōō′-nĕ·hĭl′dĕ) *or* **Bru′ne·chil′dis** (brōō′nĕ·kĭl′dĭs) *or* **Bru′ne·haut′** (brü′nẽ·ō′). d. 613. Daughter of Athanagild, King of Visigoths; queen of Austrasia by virtue of marriage (561) to Sigebert, King of Austrasia. Induced Sigebert to war against Chilperic, King of Neustria, who had murdered his wife Galeswintha (Brunhilde's sister) in order to marry his mistress Fredegund, who later (575) murdered Sigebert. Sought to rule Austrasia as regent for her son Childebert; opposed by nobles and forced to flee to Burgundy; continued to be troublemaker until, at age of 80, she was captured by Clotaire II and executed by being dragged to death by a wild horse.

**Brun′hoff′** (brü′nôf′), **Jean de.** 1899–1937. French author and illustrator of children's stories, notably a series on Babar, the little elephant.

**Bru′ni** (brōō′nē) *or* **Bru′no** (brōō′nō), **Leonardo.** *Sometimes called* **Leonardo A′re·ti′no** (ä′râ·tē′nō). 1369–1444. Italian humanist, b. Arezzo. Apostolic secretary; chancellor of Florentine Republic (1427). Known esp. as promoter of Greek learning by literal translations into Latin of Plutarch, Demosthenes, Aristotle, and Plato. Author, in Italian, of biographies of Dante and Petrarch.

**Brü′ning** (brü′nĭng), **Heinrich.** 1885–1970. German statesman. Member (1924–33) and leader (1929), Center party in Reichstag; proponent of the "Lex Brüning," dealing with tax reforms (1925). Chancellor (1930–32) and director of German foreign policy (1931); leader of Center party (1933); lecturer and tutor, Harvard (1937–39); Littauer professor of government, Harvard (1939).

**Brun′lees** (brŭn′lēz), Sir **James.** 1816–1892. Scottish civil engineer. Planned the São Paulo railway in Brazil; assisted in the Mersey railway; constructed Avonmouth dock, Bristol (1868–77).

**Brunn** (brōōn), **Heinrich von.** 1822–1894. German archaeologist. Carried on researches in Italy (1843–53); professor, Munich (1865–94). Author of works on ancient Greek and Roman art.

**Brunne, Robert de.** See Robert MANNYNG.

**Brun′ner** (?brŭn′ẽr), **Arnold William.** 1857–1925. American architect, b. New York City.

**Brun′ner** (brōōn′ẽr), **Constantin.** *Pseudonym of* **Leo Wert′hei′mer** (vĕrt′hī′mẽr). 1862–1937. German philosopher.

**Brunner, Heinrich.** 1840–1915. Jurist and law historian, b. Upper Austria. Professor (1866–72) successively at Lemberg, Prague, and Strasbourg, and (from 1873) at Berlin. Author of *Deutsche Rechtsgeschichte* (1887–92), etc.

**Brunner, Johann Conrad.** 1653–1727. Swiss anatomist; made researches on the pancreas and on glands (Brunner's glands) in the duodenum.

**Brunner, Sebastian.** 1814–1893. Austrian Roman Catholic theologian and writer; author of poems including *Der Nebeljungen Lied,* a satirical attack on Hegelians (1845), the novel *Die Prinzenschule zu Möpselglück* (1847), humorous tales, attacks on Schopenhauer, Goethe, Heine, and others.

**Brün′now** (brün′ō), **Franz Friedrich Ernst.** 1821–1891. German astronomer.

**Brun′now** (*Ger.* brōōn′ō), Count **Philipp.** 1797–1875. Russian diplomat, b. Dresden, Germany; ambassador at London (1840–54), Frankfort and Berlin (1855–58), again London (1858–74); represented Russia at congresses of the Holy Alliance, at Congress of Paris (1856), and at London conferences (1864, 1871); created count (1871).

**Bru′no I** (brōō′nō) *or* **Brun** (brōōn), Saint. 925–965. Called "the Great." Son of Henry I, the Fowler, and brother of Otto the Great. Archbishop of Cologne and duke of Lorraine; scholar and patron of learning. Imperial chancellor (940); distinguished himself in victory (953) over Conrad of Lorraine in the latter's rebellion against his father-in-law, Otto.

**Bru′no** (brōō′nō), **Giordano.** 1548?–1600. Italian philosopher, b. Nola. Forced to leave Dominican order because of unorthodoxy (c. 1576); traveled widely, lecturing, teaching, and writing (to 1592). Champion of Copernican cosmology; opponent of Aristotelian logic; ardent Lullianist; expounded monadism. Arrested by Inquisition (1592) and burned at stake (Feb. 17, 1600). Influenced philosophical thought of Böhme, Leibnitz, Spinoza, Schelling, and Hegel.

**Bruno, Leonardo.** See BRUNI.

**Bru′no of Co·logne′** (brōō′nō, kō·lōn′), Saint. 1030?–1101. Founder of Carthusian order of monks, b. Cologne. Director of schools in Rheims diocese (1057); withdrew to wild mountain (Chartreuse) near Grenoble, France, and founded (1086) order of Carthusians; adviser to Pope Urban II at Rome (1090); established (?1094) second Carthusian monastery (Della Torre) in Calabria.

**Bru′no** (brōō′nō) *or* **Brun** (brōōn) *or* **Bruns** (brōōns) **of Quer′furt** (kvär′fōōrt), Saint. *Religious name* **Bon′i·fa′ci·us** (bŏn′ĭ·fā′shĭ·ŭs; *Ger.* bō′nē·fä′tsē·ōōs). 970?–1009. German missionary prelate and martyr. Archbishop (1004) and apostle to heathen Prussians; massacred with eighteen companions (1009).

**Bru′not′** (brü′nō′), **Ferdinand.** 1860–1938. French philologist; professor at the Sorbonne (1900).

**Bruns′wick** (brŭnz′wĭk). *Ger.* **Braun′schweig** (broun′-shvīk). A princely German house, descended from the Welf family (see WELF). The German duchy of Brunswick, with Lüneburg, which was created (1235) in the Welf family, was divided at the death of Duke Ernst (1546) into: (1) Elder branch, **Bruns′wick–Wol′fen·büt′tel** (vôl′fĕn·büt′ĕl), later **Brunswick;** and (2) younger branch, **Bruns′wick–Lü′ne·burg** (lü′nĕ·bōōrk), or Hanover (*q.v.*). Seat of duchy transferred from Wolfenbüttel to Brunswick (1754). A branch line, **Bruns′wick–Be′vern** (-bā′vĕrn), founded (1666) by Ferdinand Albert I, succeeded the direct line (1735). Most important rulers of the house were:

**Karl I.** 1713–1780. Duke (1735–80).

**Karl Wilhelm Ferdinand.** 1735–1806. Son of Karl I and nephew of Frederick the Great. German general, b. at Wolfenbüttel. Duke (1780–1806). Won renown in Seven Years' War; as ruler, representative of the "benevolent despots" of 18th century; as Prussian field marshal, commanded army that invaded Holland (1787) and army of allies against French (1792); defeated at Valmy (1792); resigned command (1794) because of interference of Prussian king; sent on diplomatic mission to Russia (1803); again in command of Prussian army, defeated and mortally wounded at Auerstedt.

**Friedrich Wilhelm.** 1771–1815. Duke (1813–15); son of Karl Wilhelm Ferdinand. General in Napoleonic wars (1809); lived in England after battle of Wagram (1809–13); commanded new army (1813–15); killed at Quatre Bras.

**Karl II.** 1804–1873. Duke (1815–30); son of Friedrich Wilhelm. Began administration of duchy (1823); unpopular and driven out (1830); retired to Geneva.

**Wilhelm.** 1806–1884. Duke (1830–84); brother of Karl II. Granted new constitution (1832); long and prosperous reign; with his death, direct (elder) Brunswick line became extinct; duchy passed to Ernest Augustus (*q.v.*), Duke of Cumberland, and his son Ernest Augustus, last duke (1913–18; abdicated).

**Brun′ton** (brŭn′t'n; -tŭn), Sir **Thomas Lauder.** 1844–1916. Scottish physician. Did research on circulation, physiological action of drugs, etc.; discovered value of amyl nitrate in treatment of angina pectoris (1867).

**Brunton, William.** 1777–1851. Scottish engineer and builder of early marine steam engines.

**Brusasorci, Il.** See Domenico RICCIO.

**Brush** (brŭsh), **Charles Francis.** 1849–1929. American scientist, b. Euclid, Ohio. Pioneer investigator of methods of electric lighting; inventor of Brush electric arc light, a storage battery, and other devices used in modern electrical engineering. Awarded Rumford medal (1899) and Edison medal (1913).

**Brush, Edward Nathaniel.** 1852–1933. American physician and psychiatrist; editor, *American Journal of Psychiatry* (1904–33).

**Brush, George de Forest.** 1855–1941. American figure and portrait painter.

**Brush, George Jarvis.** 1831–1912. American mineralogist; professor, Sheffield Scientific School, Yale (from 1855); director (1872–98).

**Brush, Katharine,** *nee* **Ing′ham** (ĭng′ăm). 1902–1952. American writer; m. Thomas Stewart Brush (1920; divorced), Hubert Charles Winans (1929). Author of *Young Man of Manhattan* (1930), *Red-Headed Woman* (1931), *The Boy from Maine* (1942), and short stories.

**Bru·si′lov** (brōō·syē′lôf), **Aleksei Alekseevich.** 1853–1926. Russian soldier; in World War, led army invading Galicia (1914) and counterattacking in Volhynia (1915); succeeded (1916) Gen. Ivanov in command of all Russian armies south of Pripyat marshes; made successful offensive (June–Nov., 1916) against Austrians; appointed to supreme command by coalition cabinet (1917); accepted Bolshevik regime but not active in its service; retired (1924).

**Brusius.** See Pierre de BRUYS.

**Bru′tus** (brōō′tŭs), **Decimus Junius.** *Surnamed* **Al·bi′nus** (ăl·bī′nŭs). d. 43 B.C. Roman general; served under Caesar in Gaul; governor of Gaul. Joined conspiracy against Caesar and one of his assassins (not to be confused with Marcus Junius BRUTUS). Executed by order of Antony.

**Brutus, Decimus Junius.** Roman consul (138 A.D.); patron of literature.

**Brutus, Lucius Junius.** Roman consul (509 B.C.), one of first two in Roman history. According to legend, took leading part in expulsion of Tarquins, sentenced own two sons to death when they conspired to restore Tarquins; killed in single combat with Aruns, a son of Tarquinius Superbus. See Publius VALERIUS PUBLICOLA.

**Brutus, Marcus Junius.** 85?–42 B.C. Roman politician and conspirator; sided with Pompey against Caesar, but pardoned by Caesar after Pompey's defeat at Pharsala (48 B.C.). Governor of Cisalpine Gaul (46); praetor in Rome (44). Headed conspiracy against Caesar and was one of his assassins. After Caesar's death (44), raised army in Macedonia; defeated at Philippi (42) by combined forces of Antony and Octavius. Committed suicide.

**Bruyère, Jean de La.** See Jean de LA BRUYÈRE.

**Bruyn** (broin), **Bar′thel** (bär′tĕl) *or* **Bar′tho·lo·mä′us** (bär′tō·lō·mâ′ōōs). 1493?–?1555. German religious and portrait painter.

**Bruyn** (broin), **Kornelis Philander de.** 1652–?1726. Dutch traveler and painter; author of *Voyage to the Levant* (1698), containing more than 200 engravings, and *Travels in Muscovy, Persia* (1711), with 300 plates.

**Bru·ys′** (brü·ē′) *or* **Bru·is′** (brü·ē′), **Pierre de.** *Lat.* **Petrus Bru′si·us** (brōō′zhĭ·ŭs; -zĭ·ŭs). d. about 1126. French religious reformer; studied under Abelard; advocated abolition of infant baptism, prayers for the dead, veneration of the cross, and church buildings; his followers were known as Petrobrusians; burned as a heretic (c. 1126).

**Bry** (brē; brī), **Théodore de** (1528–1598) and his son **Jean Théodore de** (1561–1623). Flemish engravers; established printing and engraving firm in Frankfort, Germany.

**Bry'an** (brī'ăn), Sir **Francis**. d. 1550. English soldier and poet; favorite of Henry VIII; sent on several missions to France and Rome; called "vicar of hell" for his desertion of Anne Boleyn; contributed verses to *Tottel's Miscellany*.

**Bryan, William Jennings**. 1860–1925. Known as "The Commoner." American lawyer and political leader, b. Salem, Ill. Grad. Illinois College (1881). Member, U.S. House of Representatives (1891–95). Allied himself with free-silver advocates (1894–96). Famous cross-of-gold speech in Democratic convention, Chicago, won him nomination for presidency (1896); defeated by McKinley. Nominated again (1900); campaigned as antiexpansionist and anti-imperialist; defeated by McKinley-Roosevelt ticket. Edited (from 1901) the *Commoner*, weekly paper. Nominated third time for the presidency (1908); defeated by Taft. In Democratic convention of 1912, instrumental in swinging nomination to Woodrow Wilson. U.S. secretary of state (1913–15); resigned because of lack of sympathy with Wilson's policy after sinking of *Lusitania*. Supported Wilson's renomination in convention (1916). Lecturer on Chautauqua circuit and at religious assemblies. Hostile to ideas of evolution; one of prosecuting attorneys in case against Dayton, Tenn., teacher, John T. Scopes (*q.v.*), indicted for teaching evolution in his classes (1925). Cross-examined by Clarence Darrow, of counsel for the defense, his ignorance of discoveries of modern science exposed. Died suddenly (July 26, 1925), a few days after the trial had ended. His brother **Charles Wayland** (1867–1945) was governor of Nebraska (1923–25, 1931–35) and Democratic candidate for vice-president of the United States (1924). See also Ruth Bryan ROHDE.

**Bryan, William Lowe**. 1860–1955. American educator; professor of philosophy, Indiana (1885–1902), and president (1902–37).

**Bry'ant** (brī'ănt), Sir **Arthur Wynne Morgan**. 1899– English lecturer, editor, historical writer, and producer of pageants. Author of books on the England of Charles II and of a biography of Samuel Pepys.

**Bryant, Henry Grier**. 1859–1932. American geographer and explorer; second in command, Peary Relief Expedition (1892); commanded Peary Auxiliary Expedition (1894); commanded expedition exploring Mt. St. Elias, Alaska (1897).

**Bryant, Jacob**. 1715–1804. English classical scholar and collector of books. Author of treatises on ancient mythology, Homeric questions, and theology.

**Bryant, William Cullen**. 1794–1878. American poet and editor, b. Cummington, Mass. Attended Williams College (1810–11); practiced law, Great Barrington, Mass. (1815–25); retired to devote himself to writing. Early works, *Thanatopsis* and *To a Waterfowl*, pub. in *North American Review* (1817), and *Rizpah*, *Monument Mountain*, *Autumn Woods*, and *Forest Hymn*, pub. in *United States Literary Gazette* (1824–25). Co-owner and co-editor, New York *Evening Post* (1829–78). Published *The Fountain, and Other Poems* (1842), *The White-Footed Doe, and Other Poems* (1844), *The Flood of Years* (1876), *A Lifetime* (1877). Some of his lines have become household quotations, as: "Truth, crushed to earth, shall rise again," from *The Battlefield;* "The melancholy days are come, the saddest of the year," from *The Death of the Flowers*. Elected to American Hall of Fame (1910).

**Bry·ax'is** (brī·ăk'sĭs). Greek sculptor of 4th century B.C.; one of four sculptors (see TIMOTHEUS) who collaborated in executing mausoleum at Halicarnassus.

**Bryce** (brīs), **George**. 1844–1931. Canadian historian. A founder of University of Manitoba (1877), and head of faculty of science (1891–1904). Author of histories of Manitoba (1882) and Hudson's Bay Company (1900) and of Canadian biographies.

**Bryce, James**. Viscount **Bryce**. 1838–1922. British jurist, historian, and diplomat, b. Belfast, Ireland, of a Scottish family. Grad. Oxford (1862); author of monograph *Holy Roman Empire* (1864); regius professor of Civil law, Oxford (1870–93). Undersecretary for foreign affairs under Gladstone (1886) and chief secretary for Ireland in Campbell-Bannerman cabinet (1905–06). Ambassador to the U.S. (1907–13); signer of Anglo-American arbitration treaty (1911); member, Hague Tribunal (1913). Author of *The American Commonwealth* (1888), classic work on American government, and *Modern Democracies* (1922), and of studies of South Africa and South America.

**Brydg'es** (brĭj'ĕz; -ĭz). Family name of barons and dukes of CHANDOS.

**Brydges**, Sir **Samuel Egerton**. 1762–1837. English author of bibliographical and genealogical works.

**Bry·en'ni·us** (brī·ĕn'ĭ·ŭs), **Nicephorus**. 1062?–1137. Byzantine soldier and historian; defended Constantinople against Godfrey of Bouillon (1097); aided in defeat of Malik Shah, Seljuk sultan of Iconium (1116); m. Anna Comnena, daughter of Alexius; wrote history of period 1057–1079, completed by his wife.

**Bry'gos** (brī'gŏs). Greek potter of early 5th century B.C.; famed for paintings on vases.

**Bryu'lov** (*Russ.* bryōō'lôf), **Aleksandr Pavlovich**. *Orig. family name* **Brül'low** *or* **Brü'low** (*Ger.* brü'lō). 1798–1877. Russian architect, of German descent. His brother **Karl Pavlovich** (1799–1852) painted portraits, genre scenes, a few historical subjects, and many religious pictures.

**Bryu'sov** (bryōō'sôf), **Valeri Yakovlevich**. 1873–1924. Russian symbolist poet, playwright, and novelist.

**Buachalla, Dómhnall ua.** See Donal BUCKLEY.

**Bu·at'** (bü·à'), **Edmond Alphonse Léon**. 1868–1923. French general in the World War.

**Bu·bas'tite** (bū·băs'tīt). Name of a dynasty (the XXIId) of Egyptian kings of Libyan origin, reigning about 945 to 745 B.C., derived from name of its capital, Bubastis, in the Nile delta. See *Table* (*in Appendix*) for EGYPT.

**Bu'ber** (bōō'bĕr), **Martin**. 1878–1965. Jewish religious scholar, philosopher, and writer, b. Vienna; worked for development of Hasidism and recognition of cultural significance of Judaism.

**Bub'na von Li'tic** (bŏŏb'nä fôn lĭ'tyĭts), Count **Ferdinand von**. 1768?–1825. Austrian field marshal (1809); fought in battle of Leipzig (1813); governor general of Lombardy (1818).

**Bu'ca·re'li y Ur·sú'a** (bōō'kä·rä'lē ē ōōr·sōō'ä), **Antonio María**. 1717–1779. Spanish general and administrator; governor of Cuba (1760–71); viceroy of New Spain (1771–79).

**Buc·cleuch'** (bŭ·klōō'). An old Scottish ducal family tracing descent from Sir Richard le Scott (1249–85) but taking origin in grants of land by James II of Scotland to Sir Walter Scott of Kirkurd and Buccleuch (c. 1452). The family includes Sir Walter Scott of Branxholm and Buccleuch (1490?–1552), whose life furnished material for *The Lay of the Last Minstrel* and whose great-grandson Sir Walter Scott (1565–1611) was raised to the peerage (1606), his successor being created earl (1619). From a branch of the family, through "Auld Wat" Scott (1550?–?1629) and his son William Scott of Harden, was descended Sir Walter Scott, author of the Waverley novels, etc. The dukedom came into being (1663) on marriage of Countess Anne Scott, daughter of 2d earl, to duke of Monmouth (the rebel, 1649–1685), who at that time assumed surname Scott and was created 1st duke of Buccleuch. His grandson, 2d duke, was succeeded by 2d duke's grandson, **Henry Scott** (1746–1812), 3d Duke of Buccleuch and 5th Duke of **Queensberry;** traveled abroad with Adam Smith as tutor; first president of Royal Society of Edinburgh (1783); succeeded (1810) William Douglas (see *dukes of Queensberry*, under DOUGLAS family). His grandson **Walter Francis Scott** (1806–1884), 5th Duke of Buccleuch and 7th Duke of Queensberry; M.A., Cantab. (1827); lord privy seal (1842–46); lord president of council (1846); built pier and breakwater at Granton (1835–42); chancellor of Glasgow U. (1877).

**Bu'cer** (bo͞o'tsẽr) *or* **But'zer** (bo͞o'tsẽr), **Martin.** *Real surname* **Kuh'horn** (ko͞o'hôrn). 1491–1551. German Protestant reformer. In Dominican order (1506–21); convert to Luther's doctrines (from 1518); engaged in spreading doctrines of Reformation in Strasbourg (1523), Ulm, and Cologne; mediated in differences between Luther and Zwinglians; helped draw up Tetrapolitan Confession for Diet of Augsburg (1530); brought about Wittenberg Concordat between Luther and south Germans (1536); tried to unite Protestants and Roman Catholics in Diet of Ratisbon (1541); refused to sign Augsburg Interim (1548). Professor of theology, Cambridge U. (1549–51), at Cranmer's invitation; worked for Reformation in England. Author, under pseudonym **A·re'ti·us Fe·li'nus** (*ȧ*·rē'shĭ·*ŭ*s fē·lī'n*ŭ*s; *Ger.* ä·rā'tsē·o͝os fā·lē'no͝os), of a work on the Psalms (1529).

**Buch** (bo͞oK), Baron **Christian Leopold von.** 1774–1853. German geologist and paleontologist; became a plutonist; demonstrated importance of volcanic processes.

**Buch, Walter.** 1883–1949. German National Socialist. Sturmabteilung leader, Munich (1923); member of Reichstag (1928); leader of party (1933); group leader of Schutzstaffel (1934).

**Buch'an** (bŭk'ăn; *Scot.* bŭK'ăn). One of the seven original Scottish earldoms, held first by the Comyn family (*q.v.*); for a century and a half by the Stewart family, including Sir Alexander (1343?–?1405), the "Wolf of Badenoch"; and after 1617 by the Erskine family (see David Steuart ERSKINE, 11th earl).

**Buchan, Alexander.** 1829–1907. Scottish meteorologist. Secretary (1860) of Scottish Meteorological Society, which inaugurated observatory on summit of Ben Nevis (1883). Author of *The Handy Book of Meteorology* (1867), *Report on Atmospheric Circulation* (1889), etc.

**Buchan, Elspeth,** *nee* **Simpson.** 1738–1791. Founder (1783) of a Scottish fanatical sect, the Buchanites. Persuaded followers that she was the woman of Revelation xii.

**Buchan,** Sir **John.** 1st Baron **Tweeds'muir** (twēdz'mūr). 1875–1940. Scottish author and governor general of Canada, b. Perth. Served on headquarters staff, British army in France (1916–17); director of information under Lloyd George (1917–18); M.P. (1927–35); governor general of Canada (1935–40). Author of many novels of adventure, including *John Burnet of Barns* (1898), *Greenmantle* (1916), *John Macnab* (1925), historical and biographical studies, as of Cromwell (1934), Augustus (1937), and autobiography, *Pilgrim's Way* (1940).

**Buchan, William.** 1729–1805. Scottish physician; author of *Domestic Medicine; or The Family Physician* (1769), a popular work on medicine.

**Bu·chan'an** (bů·kăn'ăn; b*ŭ*-), **Edgar Simmons.** 1872–1932. British paleographer; specialized in translation of ancient palimpsests and theological documents. Resident in U.S. (1914–30) and in Australia (from 1930). Center of sensational controversy (1923) over a palimpsest in possession of Hispanic Society of America, which he declared to date from 1st or 2d century and to challenge entire King James Version of the Bible; his statement was disputed and the manuscript withdrawn before it could be fully deciphered.

**Buchanan, Franklin.** 1800–1874. American naval officer, b. Baltimore. By order of Secretary of Navy Bancroft, submitted plan for naval school at Annapolis; became first superintendent, U.S. Naval Academy (1845–47). In command of Perry's flagship (1853) on expedition to Japan. Joined navy of the Confederacy (1861); admiral in command at battle of Mobile Bay; captured (Aug. 5, 1864).

**Buchanan, George.** 1506–1582. Scottish humanist and author. Satirized Franciscan friars on urging of James V; imprisoned by Cardinal Beaton; fled to Bordeaux, where he taught in different colleges; had Montaigne as student. Openly took side of Calvinists on return to Scotland; moderator of General Assembly (1567). Vouched that Casket Letters were in handwriting of Mary, Queen of Scots; charged Mary, in *Detectio Mariae Reginae*, with murder of Darnley; tutor to James VI (1570–78); occupied last years with *De Juri Regni apud Scotos* (1579), confuting absolutism with doctrine that kings exist by will of people, and *Rerum Scoticarum Historia* (1582). Author of tragedies and much Latin verse.

**Buchanan,** Sir **George.** 1831–1895. English physician and exponent of sanitary science. Chief agent in eradicating typhus fever, reducing mortality from tuberculosis, and controlling cholera. His eldest son, Sir **George Seaton** (1869–1936), hygienist, was senior medical officer, Ministry of Health (1919–34).

**Buchanan,** Sir **George Cunningham.** 1865–1940. British civil engineer, specialist in harbor, dock, and river works.

**Buchanan,** Sir **George William.** 1854–1924. British diplomatist of Scottish family; ambassador at St. Petersburg (1910–18).

**Buchanan, James.** 1791–1868. Fifteenth president of the United States, b. near Mercersburg, Pa. Grad. Dickinson College (1809). Adm. to bar, Lancaster, Pa. (1812); volunteer in the War of 1812; member, U.S. House of Representatives (1821–31). U.S. minister to Russia (1832–34). U.S. senator (1834–45). Secretary of state (1845–49). U.S. minister to Great Britain (1853–56). President of the United States (1857–61) during years just preceding Civil War; failed to meet challenge of South Carolina's secession (Dec. 20, 1860), and endeavored to avoid the issue of civil conflict.

**Buchanan, Robert Williams.** 1841–1901. British poet and novelist, b. Staffordshire. Attacked Swinburne in *Session of the Poets* (in *Spectator*, 1866) and Pre-Raphaelites in *The Fleshly School of Poetry* (in *Contemporary Review*, 1871). Author of *Ballads of Life, Love, and Humour* (1882), and a series of novels and plays.

**Bu·cha'rin.** Variant of BUKHARIN.

**Bu'cher** (bū'kẽr), **John Emery.** 1872–1943. American chemist; inventor of a process for nitrogen fixation, and processes for making magnesium, beryllium, and aluminum.

**Bü'cher** (bü'Kẽr), **Karl.** 1847–1930. German economist; student esp. of historical development of European economics.

**Bu'cher** (bo͞o'Kẽr), **Lothar.** 1817–1892. German publicist and diplomat; member Bismarck's foreign ministry (1864–86); negotiated agreement between Lassalle and

Bismarck; in writings attacked economic tenets of Liberals.

**Buch'holtz** (bo͝ok'hôlts), **Johannes.** 1882–1940. Danish playwright, novelist, and short-story writer.

**Buch'man** (bo͝ok'măn), **Frank Nathan Daniel.** 1878–1961. American evangelist, founder of Oxford Group movement (at Oxford University, 1921). Grad. Muhlenberg College (1899); as director Christian work, Penn. State College (1909–15), evolved art of "changing" lives of students and a religion called A First Century Christian Fellowship; missionary under Y.M.C.A. auspices in Japan, Korea, India; extension lecturer, Hartford Theological Foundation (1916–21). Organizer of groups in South Africa, South America, Canada, U.S., Scandinavian countries; carried on extensive campaign for "Moral Rearmament" in Great Britain (1939).

**Buch'mann** (bo͝ok'män), **Theodor.** *Known by Grecized form of surname* **Bi·bli·an'der** (bē·blē·än'dẽr). 1500?–1564. Swiss theologian and Oriental scholar; succeeded Zwingli as professor of Protestant theology at Zurich.

**Buch'ner** (bo͞oκ'nẽr), **Eduard.** 1860–1917. German chemist; demonstrated that alcoholic fermentation of sugars is due to action of enzymes contained in yeast and not to physiological processes in yeast cells; awarded 1907 Nobel prize in chemistry. His brother **Hans** (1850–1902), hygienist and bacteriologist, demonstrated that there are present in blood serum substances that protect the organism against infection.

**Büch'ner** (bü κ'nẽr), **Georg.** 1813–1837. German poet; author of dramatic poem *Dantons Tod* (1835), a comedy *Leonce und Lena* (in manuscript), a tragedy *Woyzeck.* His sister **Luise** (1821–1877), poet and novelist, wrote *Die Frauen und ihr Beruf* (1855), in which she championed women's rights. Their brother **Friedrich Karl Christian Ludwig** (1824–1899) was a physician and materialistic philosopher. Another brother, **Alexander** (1827–1904), literary historian and novelist, was professor of literature, Valenciennes (1857–62) and Caen (1862–97).

**Buch'ner** (bo͞oκ'nẽr), **Johann Andreas.** 1783–1852. German pharmacist; credited with discovering salicin and berberine; instrumental through his writings in establishing pharmacy on scientific basis.

**Buch'ser** (bo͝ok'sẽr), **Frank.** 1828–1890. Swiss painter and etcher; painted portraits of Union and Confederate leaders, including Lincoln, Andrew Johnson, Lee, Grant, and Sherman.

**Buck** (bŭk), **Carl Darling.** 1866–1955. American philologist; professor of Sanskrit and Indo-European comparative philology, Chicago (1900–33).

**Buck, Dudley.** 1839–1909. American organist and composer, b. Hartford, Conn. His compositions include choral and organ pieces, esp. church music (anthems, hymns, Te Deums, etc.), as well as concert cantatas.

**Buck, Eugene Edward,** *called* **Gene.** 1885–1957. American librettist, song writer, and producer (of Ziegfeld *Follies* 1912–26 and *Midnight Frolic* 1914–26); president (from 1914), American Society of Composers, Authors, and Publishers.

**Buck, Pearl,** *nee* **Sy'den·strick'er** (sī'd'n·strĭk'ẽr). 1892–1973. American novelist, b. Hillsboro, W.Va.; m. John Lossing Buck (1917; divorced, 1935), Richard J. Walsh (1935). Author of *The Good Earth* (1931; awarded Pulitzer prize, 1932), *Sons* (1932), *The Mother* (1934), *A House Divided* (1935), *House of Earth* (1935), *The Exile* (1936), *Fighting Angel* (1936), *The Patriot* (1939), *Other Gods* (1940), *Dragon Seed* (1942). Awarded Nobel prize in literature (1938).

**Bucke** (bŭk), **Richard Maurice.** 1837–1902. English-born psychologist and psychiatrist in Canada.

**Buckholdt, Johann.** See JOHN OF LEIDEN.

**Buckhurst,** Baron. See Thomas SACKVILLE.

**Buck'ing·ham** (bŭk'ĭng·ăm; -hăm), Earls, marquises, and dukes of [county of]. Title of earl in English peerage was conferred upon Walter Giffard of Normandy by William the Conqueror (or perhaps by William Rufus) and returned to crown (1176); conferred (1377) on Thomas of Woodstock, son of Edward III, borne by his son Humphrey; at Humphrey's death it passed, through his sister Anne, to her son Humphrey Stafford, who was created duke of Buckingham (1444); remained in Stafford family until attainder and execution of Edward, 3d duke (1521). (See THOMAS OF WOODSTOCK; Humphrey, Henry, and Edward STAFFORD.) Title of earl (second creation) conferred (1617) by James I on George Villiers, followed by titles of marquis (1618), and duke (1623), latter two titles becoming extinct with death of 2d duke, that of earl claimed by line of doubtful legitimacy (till 1774). (See George VILLIERS, 1st and 2d dukes.) Title of duke of Buckingham and Normanby, conferred (1703) on John Sheffield and became extinct on death of his son in 1735. (See John SHEFFIELD.)

☞ Do not confuse with earls of BUCKINGHAMSHIRE.

**Buckingham,** Marquises and dukes of [town of]. Marquisate in English peerage conferred (1784), belonged (till 1889); to members of Grenville family (*q.v.*) elevated to dukedom of Buckingham and Chandos (1822).

**Buckingham, James Silk.** 1786–1855. English traveler, lecturer, and author of travel books; established *Athenaeum* in London (1828).

**Buckinghamshire,** Earls of. See John HOBART.

**Buck'land** (bŭk'lănd), **William.** 1784–1856. English geologist; dean of Westminster (from 1845); author of *Reliquiae Diluvianae* (1823) and the Bridgewater Treatise *Geology and Mineralogy considered with Reference to Natural Theology* (1836). His son **Francis Trevelyan** (1826–1880), surgeon and naturalist, was inspector of salmon fisheries (1867–80); known esp. for researches in fish culture.

**Buck'le** (bŭk''l), **George Earle.** 1854–1935. English journalist. Editor, *The Times* London (1884–1912). Author of vols. 3–6 (1914–20) of *Life of Disraeli,* completing vols. 1–2 (1910–12) written by W. F. Monypenny (*q.v.*). Editor of letters of Queen Victoria.

**Buckle, Henry Thomas.** 1821–1862. English historian; author of *History of Civilization in England* (1st vol., 1857; 2d, 1861); adopted scientific method of writing history, with attention to each country's physical conditions, climate, soil, etc.

**Buck'ley** (bŭk'lĭ), **Donal.** *Gaelic* **Dómh'nall ua Bu'a·chal·la** (t͟hū'năl ō bū'ȧ·κă·lȧ). 1866– . Irish political administrator. Member, Dail Eireann (1919–23); governor general (seanascal), Irish Free State (1932–37).

**Buckley, James Monroe.** 1836–1920. American Methodist Episcopal clergyman; editor, *Christian Advocate* (1880–1912). Author of *Oats or Wild Oats?* (1885), etc.

**Buckley, Samuel Botsford.** 1809–1883. American naturalist. Texas state geologist (1866–67; 1874–77). His name is perpetuated in Buckley's Peak, in the Great Smoky range, and in the genus of plants *Buckleya.*

**Buck'ner** (bŭk'nẽr), **Simon Bol'i·var** (bŏl'ĭ·vẽr). 1823–1914. American army officer, b. Hart Co., Ky. Grad. U.S.M.A., West Point (1844). Served through Mexican War. Joined the Confederate army; brigadier general (1861); surrendered to Grant at Fort Donelson (1862); exchanged (1862); lieut. general (from 1864). Editor, Louisville *Courier* (1868). Governor of Kentucky (1887–91). Candidate for vice-president on the sound-money Democratic ticket (1896). His son **Simon Bolivar**

(1886–1945), army officer, b. Munfordville, Ky.; grad. (1908) U.S.M.A. (West Point); commandant, U.S.M.A. (1933–36); commanding gen. in Alaska (July 1940–June 1944); lieut. gen. (1943); commanding gen. in invasion of Okinawa (1945); killed in action.

**Buck′stone** (bŭk′stōn; *Brit.* -stŭn), **John Baldwin.** 1802–1879. English comedian and writer of plays and farces, including *Luke the Labourer* and *Ellen Wareham.* First London appearance in 1823; lessee and actor-manager, Haymarket Theatre (1853–78). His daughter **Lucy Isabella** (1858–1893) and son **Rowland** (1860–1922) were also actors.

**Budaeus.** See Guillaume BUDÉ.

**Budd** (bŭd), **William.** 1811–1880. English physician; advocated disinfection to prevent spread of contagious diseases; recommended measures that stamped out Asiatic cholera in Bristol and the rinderpest in England (1866); proved contagious nature of typhoid fever in his *Typhoid Fever; Its Nature, Mode of Spreading, and Prevention* (1873).

**Bud′de** (bo͝od′ĕ), **Emil Arnold.** 1842–1921. German physicist; constructed one of first practical metal-filament electric lamps.

**Budde, Karl Ferdinand Reinhard.** 1850–1935. German evangelical theologian.

**Bud·de′us** (bo͞o·dā′o͞os), **Johann Franz.** *Real surname* **Bud′de** (bo͝od′ĕ). 1667–1729. German Lutheran theologian and scholar.

**Buddha.** See GAUTAMA BUDDHA.

**Bud′dha·gho′sa** (*Pali* bo͝od′dȧ·gō′sȧ; *Skr.* -shȧ). fl. early 5th century A.D. Indian Buddhist scholar and author, b. a Brahman near Buddh Gaya, northern India. Went to Anuradhapura, Ceylon, to study Buddhist texts; translated many of these Singhalese commentaries into Pali; returned to Buddh Gaya and continued his writing; author of many works, esp. *Visuddhi Magga* ("The Path of Purity"), a long summary of Buddhist doctrine.

**Bud′dle** (bŭd′'l), **Adam.** d. 1715. English botanist; possessed large collection of mosses and grasses; genus *Buddleia* named for him.

**Bu′dé′** (bü′dā′), **Guillaume.** *Lat.* **Bu·dae′us** (bū·dē′ŭs). 1468–1540. French scholar; friend of Erasmus. Appointed royal librarian by Francis I; responsible for Francis's foundation of library at Fontainebleau, later moved to Paris as Bibliothèque National; responsible also for Francis's foundation of Collège de France (1530). By his writings, influenced revival of interest in Greek language and literature.

**Bu·dën′ny** (bo͞o·dyôn′nû·ĭ; *Angl.* bo͞o·dĕn′ĭ), **Semën Mikhailovich.** 1883–1973. Russian soldier, b. southern Russia. Entered Russian army (1903); active in Revolution of 1917; joined Red army (1918); cavalry leader; active in campaign against Denikin and Wrangel (1919–20) and in Polish War (1920); member of Union Central Executive Committee (1922); inspector of cavalry (1924); member of Union Commissariat of Agriculture (1931); marshal of Soviet Union (from 1935); commander of Moscow Military District (1937–40); member of Central Committee of Communist party (from 1939); first vice-commissar of defense (1940); in command of southern front (July–Nov., 1941) in war with Germany.

**Budge** (bŭj), Sir **Ernest Alfred Wallis.** 1857–1934. English archaeologist. Assyrian and Hebrew scholar at Cambridge; keeper of Egyptian and Assyrian antiquities, British Museum (1893–1924); conducted excavations in Egypt, the Sudan, and Mesopotamia.

**Bud′ge** (bo͞ot′gĕ), **Julius.** 1811–1888. German physiologist.

**Budg′ell** (bŭj′ĕl), **Eustace.** 1686–1737. English essayist and miscellaneous writer, cousin of Joseph Addison.

**Bu′ell** (bū′ĕl), **Don Carlos.** 1818–1898. American army officer; brigadier general of volunteers at outbreak of Civil War; major general (March 21, 1862). Relieved of command after battle of Perryville (October 8, 1862), for failure to pursue Confederate force; resigned (1864).

**Buell, Raymond Leslie.** 1896–1946. American publicist; president, Foreign Policy Assoc. (1933–39). Author of *Contemporary French Politics* (1920), *International Relations* (1925), *The Native Problem in Africa* (2 vols., 1928), and *Poland, Key to Europe* (1939).

**Buer′ger** (bür′gẽr), **Le′o** (lē′ō). 1879–1943. Physician and surgeon, b. Vienna, Austria; to U.S. while young; m. (1913) Germaine Schnitzer. Practiced in New York City; Buerger's disease is named for him.

**Bu·fa′no** (bo͞o·fä′nō), **Beniamino.** 1898–1970. Sculptor, b. near Rome, Italy; to U.S. as a child. Studied in New York under Paul Manship. To China, where he studied Chinese glazing and carved bust of Sun Yat-sen. Selected by San Francisco Municipal Art Commission (1937) to carve colossal statue of Saint Francis at Christmas Tree Point, dominating the city.

**Buff** (bo͝of), **Charlotte.** 1753–1828. Friend and companion of Goethe, in Wetzlar (1772); the original of Lotte in *Die Leiden des Jungen Werthers;* m. (1773) Georg Christian Kestner. Subject of Thomas Mann's novel *Lotte in Weimar.*

**Buffalo Bill.** Sobriquet of William Frederick CODY.

**Buf′fing·ton** (bŭf′ĭng·tŭn), **Adelbert Rinaldo.** 1837–1922. American army officer; coinventor with William Crozier (*q.v.*) of the Buffington-Crozier disappearing gun carriage.

**Buf′fon′** (bü′fôN′), Comte **Georges Louis Leclerc de.** 1707–1788. French naturalist; director of Jardin du Roi (now Jardin des Plantes) and of royal museum (1739). Admitted to French Academy (1753), his inaugural address being the celebrated *Discours sur le Style.* Author (with others) of *Histoire Naturelle* (44 vols., 1749–1804), completed by B. G. E. de Lacépède.

**Bu′ford** (bū′fẽrd), **John.** 1826–1863. American army officer; grad. U.S.M.A., West Point (1848); brigadier general, Union army (1862); brilliant cavalry commander; major general (1863).

**Bu·ga′ev** *or* **Bu·ga′yev** (bo͞o·gȧ′yĕf), **Boris Nikolaevich.** *Pseudonym* **Andrei Be′ly** (byā′lû·ĭ). 1880–1934. Russian symbolist poet and novelist.

**Bu′geaud′ de la Pi′con′ne·rie′** (bü′zhō′ dẽ lȧ pē′-kôn′rē′), **Thomas Robert.** 1784–1849. French soldier; created marshal of France (1843) and duc d'Isly (1844). Served in Africa (1836–47); governor of Algeria (1840); won battle of Isly, in Morocco (1844).

**Bu′gen·ha′gen** (bo͞o′gĕn·hä′gĕn), **Johann.** *Called* **Pom′er·a′nus** (pŏm′ẽr·ā′nŭs) *or* **Dr. Pom′mer** (pôm′-ẽr). 1485–1558. German Protestant reformer, b. Pomerania. Won over to Luther (1520); professor (1525), Wittenberg; organized Protestant church in Brunswick (1528), Hamburg (1539), Lübeck (1530), Pomerania (1534), Denmark (1537), and Schleswig-Holstein (1542); general superintendent, electorate of Saxony (1539). Assisted Luther in translating Bible; translated Bible into Low German (1533); drew up Leipzig Interim with Melanchthon (1548).

**Bug′ge** (bo͝og′gĕ), **Elseus Sophus.** 1833–1907. Norwegian philologist; professor, Christiania (from 1866). Author of critical works, notably on the Edda songs and the northern, Celtic, Romance, and Etruscan languages.

**Bu′giar·di′ni** (bo͞o′jär·dē′nē), **Giuliano.** 1475–1554. Florentine painter; pupil of Ghirlandaio and Albertinelli; friend and associate of Michelangelo.

**Buhl** (bo͞ol), **Charles André.** See Charles André BOULLE.

**Büh'ler** (bü'lẽr), **Hans Adolf.** 1877–1951. German painter, designer, and etcher.

**Bühler, Johann Georg.** 1837–1898. German Sanskrit scholar and Indologist; engaged in researches in Indian philology, archaeology, religion, and epigraphy; professor of Sanskrit and Indology, Vienna (1881).

**Buh'tu·ri, al-** (ăl·bo͝o'to͞o·rē). *Arab.* **Walīd ibn-'Ubayd al-Buḥturi.** 820–897. Arab court poet of the Abbasids at Baghdad.

**Bu'ick** (bū'ĭk), **David D.** 1855–1929. American pioneer automobile manufacturer; originally a plumber, sold his business and went into debt developing the Buick automobile; lost control of manufacturing company; at time of death was clerk in a Detroit trade school.

**Bu·il'** (bo͞o·ēl'), **Bernardo.** c. 1450–1520. Spanish Benedictine monk, b. Catalonia; accompanied Columbus on 2d trip to America as apostolic vicar of New World (1493); joined opponents of Columbus, returning to Spain (1494) to prefer charges against him; abbot of Cuxa Convent (c. 1495–1520).

**Bu·is'son'** (bü·ē'sôɴ'), **Ferdinand.** 1841–1932. French educator; successively inspector, inspector general, and director (1879) of elementary teaching; professor of science of education, the Sorbonne, Paris (from 1896). Edited *Dictionnaire de Pédagogie.* Awarded (with Ludwig Quidde) Nobel peace prize (1927).

**Bu·kha'ri, al-** (ăl'bo͞o·ĸä'rē). *Arab.* **Muḥammad ibn-Ismā'īl al-Bukhāri.** 810–870. Arab author, b. Bokhara, of an Iranian family. Traveled throughout Moslem world collecting traditions ("hadiths"); out of 600,000, selected 7275 which he classified and issued as *Ṣaḥīḥ* ("sincere book"), a collection affording basis of Mohammedan law and next to Koran in canonical importance and in influence on Moslem mind.

**Bu·kha'rin** (bo͞o·ĸä'ryĕn), **Nikolai Ivanovich.** 1888–1938. Russian Communist leader and editor. Educ. Moscow; joined Social Democratic party; his activities brought many arrests, imprisonments, and banishments (1902–17); with Lenin, published *Pravda* in Austria; edited (1916) *Novy Mir* (*The New World*) in New York City; after Russian Revolution (1917), member of Central Committee of Communist party in Russia; leader of Left Wing Bolshevists; member of Politburo (1918–29); head of Third International (1926–29); expelled from Communist party (1929); again admitted to favor (1934) but suspected of support of Trotsky and subversive activities; expelled (1937), arrested, and tried; executed with other Bolshevik leaders (1938); wrote several works on Communism.

**Bü'lau** (bü'lou), **Friedrich.** 1805–1859. German professor of applied philosophy (1836) and political science (1840), Leipzig.

**Bulck'e** (bo͝ol'kĕ), **Karl.** 1875– . German author.

**Bülffinger, Georg Bernhard.** See Georg Bernhard BILFINGER.

**Bul'fin** (?bo͝ol'fĭn), Sir **Edward Stanislas.** 1862–1939. British army officer in World War; general (1925).

**Bul'finch** (bo͝ol'fĭnch), **Charles.** 1763–1844. American architect (Massachusetts State House; Conn. State House; India Wharf, Boston; New South Church, Boston; Maine State Capitol). Succeeded Latrobe as architect of National Capitol (1817–30). His son **Thomas** (1796–1867), b. Newton, Mass., was author of *The Age of Fable* (1855).

**Bul·ga'kov** (bo͞ol·gȧ'kôf), **Mikhail Afanasievich.** 1891–1940. Russian novelist and playwright.

**Bul·ga'nin** (bo͝ol·gȧ'nyĭn), **Nikolai Aleksandrovich.** 1895–1975. Russian political leader; premier of the Soviet Union (1955–58).

**Bul·ga'rin** (bo͝ol·gȧ'ryĭn), **Faddei** [*Eng.* **Thaddeus**] **Venediktovich.** 1789–1859. Russian writer, b. Lithuania, of Polish origin; to St. Petersburg (1820) to engage in journalism; founded (1825) *Northern Bee,* political daily; an extreme absolutist, using influence against such men as Pushkin and Gogol; wrote several novels, the best, *Ivan Vyzhigin* (1829).

**Bul'ga·ris** *or, better,* **Voul'ga·res** (vo͞ol'gä·rĕs), **Demetrios.** 1803–1878. Greek statesman; premier of Greece (1855–57). Took part in revolution that forced King Otto from throne (1862) and was premier under King George I (1863–64, 1865, 1866, 1868, 1871, 1874).

**Bul'ga·rus** (bŭl'gȧ·rŭs). d. 1166. Italian jurist; one of so-called Four Doctors of Bologna, renowned for knowledge of Roman law, the other three being **Mar·ti'nus** [mär·tī'nŭs] (d. before 1166), **Hu'go** [hū'gō] (d. c. 1168), and **Ja·co'bus** [jȧ·kō'bŭs] (d. 1178). Bulgarus and Martinus were friends and advisers of Emperor Frederick Barbarossa; by advice of the Four Doctors, attempt was made to reimpose neglected regalian rights upon Lombard towns at Diet of Roncaglia (1158).

**Bulke'ley** (bŭlk'lĭ), **Morgan Gardner.** 1837–1922. American insurance executive and politician, b. East Haddam, Conn. First president, Aetna Life Insurance Co. (1879–1922). In baseball, first president of the National League (1876). Governor of Connecticut (1889–93); U.S. senator (1905–11).

**Bulke'ley** *or* **Bulk'ley** (bŭlk'lĭ), **Peter.** 1583–1659. Founder and first minister of Concord, Mass. (1635); b. Bedfordshire, Eng.

**Bull** (bo͝ol), **Ephraim Wales.** 1806–1895. American horticulturist, b. Boston, Mass. Developed the Concord grape, first exhibited in 1853.

**Bull, George.** 1634–1710. English theologian. Anglican bishop of St. David's (1705). Chief theological work, *Defensio Fidei Nicenae* (1685), shows that the doctrine of the Trinity was held by ante-Nicene fathers.

**Bull** (bo͝ol), **Jacob Breda.** 1853–1930. Norwegian author of plays, satires, historical and modern novels, fairy tales, poems, biographies, and, esp., stories and sketches of his homeland.

**Bull** (bo͝ol), **John.** 1563?–1628. English organist to James I and composer of instrumental music. A Roman Catholic, fled England (1613); organist of Antwerp Cathedral (1617–28). Credited with composition of an early form (1619) of the air of *God Save the King.*

**Bull** (bo͝ol), **Ole Bornemann.** 1810–1880. Norwegian violinist. Studied under Spohr (briefly) and Paganini. Toured as virtuoso throughout Europe and five times (1843–79) through North America; founded a national theater, Bergen; lost fortune in attempt to found Norwegian colony in Pennsylvania (1852); resident in Cambridge, Massachusetts, during last years of life. His violin compositions include solos, concertos, and, esp., fantasias on national themes.

**Bull** (bo͝ol), **William Tillinghast.** 1849–1909. American surgeon, b. Newport, R.I. Grad. Harvard (1869). Practiced, New York City. Especially known for skill in abdominal operations, and treatment of hernia and cancer. One of first American surgeons to adopt antisepsis.

**Bul'lant'** (bü'läɴ'), **Jean.** 1515?–1578. French architect; architect for Henry II and Catherine de Médicis.

**Bul'lard** (bo͝ol'ẽrd), **Arthur.** *Pseudonym* **Albert Edwards.** 1879–1929. American journalist and writer; foreign correspondent for various magazines (1905–17; 1921 ff.); served in U.S. state department's Russian division (1919–21). Author of *Panama* (1911), *The Barbary Coast* (1913), *Mobilizing America* (1917), *The Stranger* (1920), etc.

**Bullard, Robert Lee.** 1861–1947. American army officer, b. Youngsboro, Ala.; grad. U.S.M.A., West Point

(1885). Served in Philippine Islands during insurrection, and on Mexican border (1915–16); brigadier general (June, 1917); major general (Aug., 1917); commanded 1st division, A.E.F. (Dec. 14, 1917–July 14, 1918), 3d corps (July 14, 1918–Oct. 11, 1918); lieutenant general (Oct. 16, 1918); commanded 2d army, A.E.F. Retired (1925).

**Bul'len** (bo͝ol'ĕn), **Arthur Henry**. 1857–1920. English man of letters. Rediscovered Thomas Campion's lyrics (1889). Edited Marlowe, Middleton, and other Elizabethan dramatists.

**Bullen, Frank Thomas**. 1857–1915. English seaman, lecturer, and author. Author of *The Cruise of the Cachelot* (1898), *Told in the Dog Watches* (1910), and other books on sea life.

**Bul'ler** (bo͝ol'ẽr), Sir **Redvers Henry**. 1839–1908. British general; commander in chief in Boer War until coming of Roberts; relieved Ladysmith; retired (1901) because of indiscreet reply to criticism of South African failures.

**Buller,** Sir **Walter Lawry**. 1838–1906. New Zealand jurist and ornithologist, author of *Manual of the Birds of New Zealand* (1882).

**Bul'lett** (bo͝ol'ĕt; -ĭt), **Gerald**. 1893–1958. English novelist, short-story writer, and essayist.

**Bul'ling·er** (bo͝ol'ĭng·ẽr), **Heinrich**. 1504–1575. Swiss reformer; disciple of Zwingli; at Zwingli's death (1531), head of Reformation in German Switzerland; shared in drawing up first Helvetic Confession (1536); concluded (1549) with Calvin the *Consensus Tigurinus*, on the Lord's Supper; prepared second Helvetic Confession (1566).

**Bul'litt** (bo͝ol'ĭt), **William Christian**. 1891–1967. American diplomat, b. Philadelphia. On staff, Philadelphia *Public Ledger* (1915–17). Assistant in U.S. Department of State (1917–18); U.S. ambassador to Russia (1933–36), to France (1936–41), at large (1941–42); special assistant to secretary of the navy (1942). Enlisted in French army (1944).

**Bul'loch** (bo͝ol'ŭk), **James Dunwody**. 1823–1901. American naval officer. Agent of Confederacy in England and France during the Civil War.

**Bul'lock** (bo͝ol'ŭk), **Charles Jesse**. 1869–1941. American economist. Professor, Harvard (1908–35).

**Bul'lo·kar** (bo͝ol'ō·kär), **John**. 1580?–?1641. English physician and lexicographer. Published *An English Expositor* (1616, 3d ed. 1641), one of the earliest English dictionaries, long a rival of Cockeram's *Dictionarie*. Probably a son of **William Bullokar** (fl. 1586), educator; advocate of spelling reform; translator of Aesop's *Fables* (1585); compiler of an English grammar (1586).

**Bully, Édouard Roger de**. Real name of Roger de BEAUVOIR.

**Bul'mer** (bo͝ol'mẽr), **William**. 1757–1830. English printer; best known for his printing of a fine edition of Shakespeare.

**Bul'nes** (bo͝ol'nās), **Manuel**. 1799–1866. Chilean soldier and Conservative leader; in command of Chilean army at Yungay (1839) and at capture of Lima; president of Chile for two terms (1841–51).

**Bü'low** (bü'lō), Baroness **Frieda von** (1857–1909) and her sister **Margarete von** (1860–1884). German novelists.

**Bülow,** Baron **Friedrich Wilhelm von.** Count **Bülow von Den'ne·witz** (dĕn'ĕ·vĭts). 1755–1816. Prussian general; governor of East and West Prussia (1812); lieut. general (1813); defeated (1813) Oudinot at Luckau and Grossbeeren, and Ney at Dennewitz; served with distinction at Leipzig (1813), Laon and Montmartre (1814); with Blücher at Waterloo (1815); infantry general and count of Dennewitz (1814); commanding general, Königsberg (1814–15). His brother Baron **Dietrich Adam Heinrich von Bülow** (1757–1807), soldier and military writer, served in Prussian army (1773–89); satirized Prussian army system in *Der Feldzug von 1805* (1806).

**Bülow,** Baron **Heinrich von.** 1791–1846. Prussian statesman. Served in War of Liberation (1813–14); secretary to embassy in London (1817) and Berlin (1819) under von Humboldt; ambassador to England (1827); signed (1831) London treaty regarding Belgian neutrality and championed a customs union; delegate to the diet (1841–42); foreign minister (1842–45).

His nephew **Bernhard Ernst von Bülow** (1815–1879), statesman, b. in Holstein, was in Danish civil service (1839–48); represented Holstein and Lauenburg at Frankfurt Diet (1852–62); state minister of Mecklenburg-Strelitz (1862–67); ambassador for the two Mecklenburg duchies in Berlin (1868); secretary of state for foreign affairs (from 1873) with rank of Prussian state minister.

The latter's son Prince **Bernhard von Bülow** (1849–1929), statesman and diplomat, b. in Holstein; served in war of 1870–71; served (1876–88) with embassies at Rome, Vienna, Athens, Paris, and St. Petersburg; secretary of Berlin Congress (1878); minister at Bucharest (1888–93) and ambassador at Rome (1893–97); through Holstein's influence became secretary of state for foreign affairs, Berlin (1897–1900); negotiated purchase of Caroline and other islands from Spain; created count (1899). Succeeded Hohenlohe as imperial chancellor (1900–09) and Prussian minister president (from 1900); effected fall of French foreign minister Delcassé (1905) and brought about the Algeciras conference (1906) following the Moroccan crisis; created prince (1905); attempted a foreign policy of friendly relations, esp. with England, but failed (1908); resigned as chancellor (1909) following split on budget question; as ambassador extraordinary to Rome (1914) attempted unsuccessfully to keep Italy out of war. Author of *Deutsche Politik* (1916).

Prince von Bülow's nephew **Bernhard Wilhelm von Bülow** (1885–1936) served in department of foreign affairs (1917–19) and again (from 1923) as head of League of Nations department; took part in peace negotiations at Brest-Litovsk and Versailles; director of European division of foreign affairs (1927–30); secretary of state of foreign office (1930–34); author of works chiefly on diplomacy and the World War.

**Bülow, Karl von.** 1846–1921. German general commanding 3d army corps (1903–12); colonel general and army inspector (1913); commanded 2d army in World War; field marshal general (1915).

**Bülow, Karl Eduard von.** 1803–1853. German writer; translated Manzoni's *I Promessi Sposi* (2d ed., 1837); compiled *Novellenbuch* (4 vols., 1834–36), a collection of 100 tales from the old Italian, Spanish, French, English, Latin, and German; wrote *Novellen* (3 vols., 1846–48), *Heinrich von Kleists Leben und Briefe* (1848).

His son Baron **Hans Guido von Bülow** (1830–1894), pianist and conductor, studied under Hauptmann, Richard Wagner in Zurich (1850–51), and Liszt in Weimar; made first concert tour (1853); teacher, Stern Conservatory, Berlin (1855–64); m. (1857) Liszt's daughter Cosima, who later married Richard Wagner (*q.v.*); as conductor of royal opera, Munich (1864), directed first performances of *Tristan* (1865) and *Die Meistersinger* (1868); director of Royal Conservatory, Munich (1867); on various concert tours in London and U.S. (1875–76, 1889–90); director of Abonnementskonzerte, Hamburg (from 1886), and philharmonic concerts, Berlin. Edited works of Beethoven, Cramer,

Chopin, and others; composed music for Shakespeare's *Julius Caesar*, etc.

**Bu'loz'** (bü'lō'), **François.** 1803–1877. French journalist; editor of *Revue des Deux Mondes* (1831). His son **Charles** (1843–1905) succeeded him as editor of *Revue des Deux Mondes* (1877–93).

**Bult'haupt** (bŏŏlt'houpt), **Heinrich.** 1849–1905. German poet, critic, and dramatist.

**Bult'mann** (bŏŏlt'män), **Rudolf.** 1884–1976. German theologian. His writings deny the existence of Jesus as a historical personage. Author of *Geschichte der Synoptischen Tradition* (1921), *Jesus* (1926), etc.

**Bul'wer** (bŏŏl'wẽr), **William Henry Lytton Earle.** Baron **Dal'ling** (dôl'ĭng) **and Bulwer.** *Known as* Sir **Henry Bulwer.** 1801–1872. English diplomat, brother of Baron Lytton (*q.v.*). As secretary of legation, concluded important commercial treaty at Constantinople (1837); ambassador at Madrid (1843–48); concluded Clayton-Bulwer Treaty (1850) between United States and Great Britain guaranteeing mutual control and protection of Isthmian canal; ambassador at Constantinople (1858–65).

**Bulwer–Lytton.** See LYTTON.

**Bum'pus** (bŭm'pŭs), **Hermon Carey.** 1862–1943. American educator and biologist; authority on museums, marine biology, and outdoor education.

**Bu'nau'-Va'ril'la'** (bü'nō'vȧ'rē'yȧ'), **Philippe Jean.** 1860–1940. French engineer. Engaged in early French endeavors to construct a Panama canal (1884–89, 1894); minister from new republic of Panama to U.S. (1903); negotiated treaty by which U.S. acquired control of Panama Canal Zone (Hay-Bunau-Varilla Treaty, 1903).

**Bun'bur·y** (bŭn'bẽr·ĭ; -bẽr'ĭ), **Henry William.** 1750–1811. English caricaturist and author.

**Bunce** (bŭns), **William Gedney.** 1840–1916. American landscape painter, esp. of scenes in Venice, Italy.

**Bunche** (bŭnch), **Ralph Johnson.** 1904–1971. Amer. diplomat, b. Detroit, Mich. Awarded Nobel peace prize (1950) for his work as U.N. mediator in Palestine conflict (1948–49).

**Bun'ge** (*Russ.* bŏŏng'gĕ; *Ger.* bŏŏng'ĕ), **Alexander von.** 1803–1890. Russian botanist and traveler in Siberia, north China, the Altai, the Volga steppes, central Russia, and Central Asia. His brother **Friedrich Georg** (1802–1897), legal historian, was authority on laws of Livonia, Esthonia, and Kurland. Sons of Alexander are **Gustav** (1844–1920), physiologist, and **Alexander** (1851– ), physician, zoologist, and traveler in Siberia.

**Bun'ge** (bŏŏng'hā), **Augusto.** 1877–1943. Argentine physician and politican; interested in educational and social problems. His brother **Alejandro** (1880–1943), engineer and economist; director general of census (1916–20, 1922–24); founder, *Revista de Economía Argentina.* Their sister **Delfina Bunge de Gál'vez** (thā gäl'vās), writer, m. Manuel Gálvez. Among her works are *Simplement* (poems in French; 1911), *Nuestra Señora de Lourdes* (1916; 3 editions), *La Nouvelle Moisson* (poems in French; 1919), *El Tesoro del Mundo* (1923), *Tierras del Mar Azul* (1928), *El Reino de Dios* (1934), *Viaje Abrededor de Mi Infancia* (1938), and school textbooks.

**Bun'ge** (bŏŏng'gĕ), **Nikolai Khristianovich.** 1823–1895. Russian political economist; prime minister (1887).

**Bu'nin** (bōō'nyĭn), **Ivan Alekseevich.** 1870–1953. Russian poet and novelist, b. Voronezh. Author of verse (first poems pub. 1888), realistic novels, dealing mostly with decay of Russian nobility, short stories, and translations into Russian of Longfellow's *Hiawatha*, Byron's *Manfred* and *Cain*, and Tennyson's *Lady Godiva.* Awarded Nobel prize for literature (1933).

**Bun'ker** (bŭng'kẽr), **Ellsworth.** 1894– . American diplomat; ambassador to South Vietnam (from 1967).

**Bunn** (bŭn), **Alfred.** 1796?–1860. English theatrical manager. Called "Poet Bunn." Manager of Drury Lane and Covent Garden (1833–48). Produced Balfe's operas: wrote and translated libretti.

**Bun'ner** (bŭn'ẽr), **Henry Cuyler.** 1855–1896. American writer, b. Oswego, N.Y. On staff of *Puck,* humorous weekly. Contributor of light familiar verse and short stories to magazines. Author of *Short Sixes* (1890), *Zadoc Pine* (1891), *Made in France* (1893).

**Bunny.** See Carl Emil SCHULTZE.

**Bun'sen** (bŏŏn'zĕn; *Angl.* bŭn's'n), Baron **Christian Karl Josias von.** 1791–1860. Prussian diplomat, lay theologian, and scholar, b. in Waldeck. Through Niebuhr's influence became (1818–38) successively Prussian secretary of embassy, chargé d'affaires, and resident minister at Rome; favorite of Frederick William III and friend of Frederick William IV; obtained (1830) from Pope Pius VIII brief making concessions on mixed marriages in Prussian dominions; recalled from Rome when brief proved ambiguous (1838). Negotiated in London (1841) for Anglo-Prussian Protestant bishopric in Jerusalem; ambassador to England (1842–54); defended German rights in Schleswig-Holstein against Denmark, reluctantly signed London protocol (1852). Member, Herrenhaus (from 1857); created baron (1857).

**Bunsen, Robert Wilhelm.** 1811–1899. German chemist. Professor, Heidelberg (1852–89). With Kirchhoff, pioneered in spectrum analysis. Invented Bunsen burner, the ice calorimeter, and a zinc-carbon electric cell (Bunsen cell); designed Bunsen disk photometer; demonstrated brilliance of flame of magnesium burned in air; formulated (with Roscoe) reciprocity law; discovered (with Kirchhoff, 1860) the elements cesium and rubidium.

**Bun'ting** (bŭn'tĭng), **Jabez.** 1779–1858. English Wesleyan Methodist minister; president of Wesleyan Theological Institute (1835) and secretary of Wesleyan Missionary Society for 18 years.

**Buntline, Ned.** Pseudonym of Edward Z. C. JUDSON.

**Bun'yan** (bŭn'yăn), **John.** 1628–1688. English preacher and writer, son of tinsmith, b. Elstow, near Bedford. Enlisted in Parliamentary army (1644–46); moved by two devotional books of his wife's, gave up amusements and swearing and joined nonconformist church in Bedford (1653); left by death of wife (c. 1656) with four young children; remarried (c. 1659); began to preach (1657) and published first writings against Quakers (1656, 1657); imprisoned for preaching without license (1660–72) until released by Charles II's Declaration of Indulgence; in prison, preached to prisoners, wrote nine of his books, including *Grace Abounding to the Chief of Sinners* (1666), *The Holy City* (1666); imprisoned again for short time (1675) during which his *Pilgrim's Progress* (pub. 1678) is supposed to have been written; continued to preach and write. Principal later works: *The Life and Death of Mr. Badman* (1680), *The Holy War* (1682).

**Buol'-Schau'en·stein** (bŏŏl'shou'ĕn·shtīn), Count **Karl Ferdinand von.** 1797–1865. Austrian statesman; prime minister and minister of foreign affairs (1852–59); signed Treaty of Paris (1856).

**Buon** (bwôn) *or* **Buo'no** (bwô'nō). *Also* **Bon** (bôn) *or* **Bo'no** (bô'nō). Family of Venetian architects and sculptors, including: **Giovanni** (d. 1442?), his son **Bartolomeo** (d. 1464?), whose main works were Ca'd'Oro (c. 1430) and the Porta della Carta of Doge's palace, Venice; and **Bartolomeo** the younger (1450?–1529), architect of Republic of Venice (1505), designer of the Procuratie Vecchie, and restorer of the tower of St. Mark.

**Buonaccorsi, Pietro.** See Perino del VAGA.

**Buonaparte.** Italian spelling of BONAPARTE.

**Buonarroti, Michelangelo.** See MICHELANGELO.

**Buo′nar·rot′ti** (bwô′när·rôt′tē), **Filippo Michele.** 1761–1837. Revolutionist, b. Pisa; descendant of Michelangelo. Naturalized French citizen; active in French Revolution; imprisoned and deported for part in Babeuf conspiracy (1796–1812).

**Buon′del·mon′te** (bwôn′dâl·mōn′tâ) *or* **Buon′del·mon′ti** (-tē). 13th-century Florentine nobleman and Guelph leader whose assassination (Easter Sunday, 1215) served as pretext for beginning of civil war between Guelphs and Ghibellines.

**Buoninsegna, Duccio di.** See DUCCIO DI BUONINSEGNA.

**Buononcini.** See BONONCINI.

**Buonvicino.** See Il MORETTO.

**Bur′bage** (bûr′bĭj), **James.** d. 1597. English actor. One of earl of Leicester's players (1574); erected first English playhouse, The Theatre, in Shoreditch (1576); converted a house into Blackfriars Theatre (1596). His son **Richard** (1567?–1619) had reputation as actor (by 1588); played chief parts in plays of Shakespeare, Ben Jonson, and Beaumont and Fletcher (1595–1618), excelling in tragedy; with his brother, removed fabric of The Theatre from Shoreditch to the Bankside (1598) and, taking Shakespeare, Heming, and Condell as partners, established Globe Theatre as a summer playhouse.

**Bur′bank** (bûr′băngk), **Luther.** 1849–1926. American horticulturist, b. Lancaster, Mass. Took up market gardening (1868); developed the Burbank potato, first practical result of his experiments with plants. Moved to Santa Rosa, California (1875); began experiments to develop more and better varieties of cultivated plants. He developed new and improved varieties of plums, berries, lilies, roses, poppies, tomatoes, corn, squash.

**Bur′chard** (bûr′chẽrd), **Samuel Dickinson.** 1812–1891. American Presbyterian clergyman; pastor, New York City (1839–79). In speech in support of Blaine (1884) he used the words: "We are Republicans and don't propose to leave our party and identify ourselves with the party whose antecedents are rum, Romanism, and rebellion." These words probably responsible for Blaine's loss of New York State's vote and the election.

**Bur′chell** (bûr′chĕl), **William John.** 1782 –1863. English naturalist. Explored for specimens in South Africa (1810–15) and South America (1826–29); many plant and animal species named after him.

**Burch′field** (bûrch′fēld), **Charles Ephraim.** 1893–1967. American painter; devoted himself to landscape painting (from 1929).

**Bur·chiel′lo** (bo͝or·kyĕl′lō), **Domenico.** *Orig. surname* **di Gio·van′ni** (dē jō·vän′nē). 1404–1449. Florentine barber poet; known esp. for his burlesque sonnets and obscure humor.

**Bürck′el** (bür′kĕl), **Josef.** 1895–1944. German National Socialist administrator; member of Reichstag (1930–34); governor of Saarland (from 1935); directed Nazi annexation of Austria after military occupation; Gauleiter of Lorraine (Aug., 1940).

**Burck′hard** (bo͝ork′härt), **Max Eugen.** 1854–1912. Austrian writer and theater director; director of the Vienna court theater (1890–98) and champion of modern drama. Author of essays and critical works chiefly on jurisprudence and the theater, of novels and tales, and of comedies and verse.

**Burck′hardt** (bo͝ork′härt). See Georg SPALATIN.

**Burckhardt, Jakob.** 1818–1897. Swiss historian of art and culture.

**Burckhardt, Johann Karl.** 1773–1825. Mathematician and astronomer, b. Leipzig; naturalized French citizen (1799); published lunar tables (1812).

**Burckhardt, Johann Ludwig.** 1784–1817. Swiss traveler in Egypt, Arabia, and the Levant; author of *Travels in Nubia, Notes on the Bedouins and Wahabys,* etc.

**Bur′dach** (bo͝or′däκ), **Karl Friedrich.** 1776–1847. German physiologist; specialist in anatomy of nervous system.

**Burdach, Konrad.** 1859–1936. German philologist.

**Bur·dett′** (bûr·dĕt′; bẽr-), Sir **Francis.** 1770–1844. English political leader; m. Sophia Coutts, daughter of rich banker (1793). In parliament (from 1796); opposed war with France, urged parliamentary reform, prison reform, removal of Catholic disabilities, abolition of flogging in the army; championed free speech. His daughter was the philanthropist Angela Georgina Burdett-Coutts (*q.v.*).

**Bur·dett′–Coutts′** (-ko͞ots′), Baroness **Angela Georgina.** 1814–1906. English philanthropist; daughter of Sir Francis Burdett (*q.v.*) and granddaughter of Thomas Coutts (*q.v.*). Inherited grandfather's fortune (1837) and assumed surname Coutts. Built and endowed churches and schools; endowed three colonial bishoprics; established industries to relieve distress; established shelter for fallen women; presented market to London for supplying fish in poor district; built model dwellings; aided emigration schemes; raised Turkish relief fund (1877–78); effected many other benefactions. Created peeress (1871); first woman presented with freedom of city of London (1872).

Her husband (m. 1881), American-born **William Lehman Ash′mead–Bart′lett** (ăsh′mēd·bärt′lĕt; -lĭt) **Burdett-Coutts** (1851–1921), younger brother of Sir Ellis Ashmead-Bartlett (*q.v.*), was special commissioner to Russo-Turkish War for Turkish relief fund; obtained royal license to assume wife's surname (1882); assisted in development of his wife's philanthropic schemes; in parliament, pressed through reform of army medical service and advocated railway reform.

**Bur·dette′** (bûr·dĕt′; bẽr-), **Robert Jones.** 1844–1914. American Baptist clergyman, humorist, and author; best known for his lecture *The Rise and Fall of the Moustache* (1876).

**Bur′don–San′der·son** (bûr′d'n·sän′dẽr·s'n), Sir **John Scott.** 1828–1905. English physiologist; first Waynflete professor of physiology, Oxford (1882–95) and regius professor of medicine (1895–1903). Despite much antivivisectionist opposition, made researches in physiology and pathology.

**Buren, Anna van.** See EGMONT.

**Bu′resch** (bo͞o′rĕsh), **Karl.** 1878–1936. Austrian statesman; chancellor (1931–32) and minister of foreign affairs (1932) in coalition cabinets; minister of finance (1933–35) successively in Dollfuss and Schuschnigg cabinets; minister without portfolio in reorganized Schuschnigg cabinet (1935); governor of Austrian Postal Savings Bank (1936).

**Burg** (bo͝orκ), **Paul.** *Pseudonym of* **Paul Schaum′burg** (shoum′bo͝orκ). 1884– . German historical novelist.

**Bür′ger** (bür′gẽr), **Gottfried August.** 1747–1794. German romantic poet and writer of ballads; associated at Göttingen with young literary circle including Voss and two Stolbergs and became leading contributor and editor (from 1778) of their publication *Musenalmanach* (founded 1770). Translator of Homer (in part; 1776) and Shakespeare. Author of ballads *Lenore* (1773; considered his masterpiece), *Die Kuh* (1784), *Der Wilde Jäger* (1785), *Der Kaiser und der Abt* (1785), and *Lenardo und Blandine.* Editor of first German version of *Baron Munchausen,* with additions of his own (see R. E. RASPE).

**Bürger, Hugo.** Pseudonym of Hugo LUBLINER.

**Bur′ger** (bo͝or′gẽr), **Konrad.** 1856–1912. German librarian and bibliographer.

**Bür'ger** (bür'gẽr), **Lucian.** Pseudonym of Charlotte NIESE.

**Bur'ger** (bo͝or'gẽr), **Ludwig.** 1825–1884. German painter and illustrator.

**Bur'ger** (bûr'gẽr), **Warren Earl.** 1907– . American jurist; chief justice, U.S. Supreme Court (from 1969).

**Bur'gess** (bûr'jĕs; -jĭs), **Albert Franklin.** 1873–1953. American economic entomologist.

**Burgess, Charles Frederick.** 1873–1945. American chemical engineer and inventor; inventor of electrolytic process for purifying iron, of various alloys, of improvements in dry cells.

**Burgess, Edward.** 1848–1891. American yacht designer, b. West Sandwich, Mass. Designed the international yacht race winners *Puritan* (1885), *Mayflower* (1886), *Volunteer* (1887).

**Burgess, Frank Gelett.** 1866–1951. American humorist and illustrator, b. Boston. Editor, *Lark*, San Francisco (1895–97), where first appeared his well-known *Purple Cow* jingle. Author and illustrator of many whimsical books, including *Goops and How to Be Them* (1900), *Are You a Bromide?* (1907), *Why Men Hate Women* (1927), *Look Eleven Years Younger* (1937).

**Burgess, George Kimball.** 1874–1932. American physicist, b. Newton, Mass. With National Bureau of Standards, Washington, D.C. (from 1903); director of the bureau (from 1923). Engaged in metallurgical and pyrometric researches.

**Burgess, Hugh.** English inventor; with his partner Charles Watt invented soda process for wood pulp for paper (1851–54); to U.S. (1854) and built plant at Roger's Ford, Pa., for making paper pulp from wood by this process. Cf. Benjamin C. TILGHMAN.

**Burgess, James.** 1832–1916. Scottish mathematician and archaeologist; author of *The Ancient Temples and Sculptures of India* (1897–1910).

**Burgess, John William.** 1844–1931. American educator, b. Giles Co., Tenn.; professor of political science, Amherst (1873–76), Columbia (1876–1912). Author of *Political Science and Comparative Constitutional Law* (2 vols., 1890), *Reconstruction and the Constitution* (1902), *Russian Revolution and the Soviet Constitution* (1919), *The Sanctity of Law...*(1927), etc.

**Burgess, Thornton Waldo.** 1874-1965. American writer, b. Sandwich, Mass. Successful in writing nature stories and animal tales for children, including *Burgess Bedtime Stories* in daily press. Author of *Burgess Bird Book for Children* (1919), *Burgess Animal Book...*(1920), *Burgess Flower Book...*(1923), *Tales from the Story Teller's House* (1937), etc.

**Burgh** (bûrg), **de.** Family name of earls and marquises of CLANRICARDE.

**Burgh, Hubert de.** d. 1243. Chief justiciar of England (1215–32), of Norman-Irish birth. Chamberlain to King John (1201); jailer, according to the chronicler Ralph of Coggeshall, of Arthur, Duke of Brittany, whom he refused to blind and mutilate at order of King John (cf. Shakespeare's *King John* iv. 1.); a leader in expulsion of French from England (1216–17); regent and chief minister for Henry III; created earl of Kent (1227); called to render account of administration by Henry III, charged with treason (1231) and outlawed; pardoned and restored to his estates and title (1234); last of justiciars to hold major political powers.

**Burgh'ley** (bûr'lĭ), Barons. See CECIL family.

**Bürgi, Joost** *or* **Jobst.** See Justus BYRGIUS.

**Bur'gin** (bûr'jĭn), **George Brown.** 1856–1944. English novelist.

**Burgk'mair** (bo͝ork'mīr), **Hans.** 1473–1531. German painter and wood engraver, b. Augsburg; friend of Dürer; helped introduce Italian Renaissance style into Germany. His paintings include religious works, portraits, frescoes, landscapes, etc.

**Burgmein.** See RICORDI family.

**Burg'mül'ler** (bo͝ork'mül'ẽr), **Johann Friedrich Franz.** 1806–1874. Composer, b. Ratisbon, Bavaria; naturalized French citizen; wrote chiefly ballet and light piano music. His brother **Norbert** (1810–1836) wrote songs and orchestral and chamber music.

**Bur·goyne'** (bûr·goin'; bûr'goin), **John.** 1722–1792. British army officer and dramatist. Commanded expedition from Canada against American colonies (1776); forced to surrender at Saratoga (1777); participated in impeachment of Warren Hastings. Author of plays including *The Maid of the Oaks*, brought out by Garrick (1775), and *The Heiress* (1786). His natural son Sir **John Fox Burgoyne** (1782–1871), military engineer; inspector general of fortifications (1845–68); general (1855); field marshal (1868).

**Bur'gun·dy** (bûr'gŭn·dĭ). *Fr.* **Bour'gogne'** (bo͞or'-gôn'y'). Name of two ruling houses:

(1) Ducal house of Burgundy, a region in western central Europe which from 5th century to 15th had varying boundaries, was at different times a county, duchy, kingdom, etc., and was often divided, most of it becoming finally (end of 15th century) a part of France. Two lines of ducal house: (a) Capetian line (1032–1361), from **Robert I** (d. 1075), Duke of **Burgundy,** son of King Robert of France (996–1031), through eleven rulers to Duke **Philippe de Rou'vre** [dẽ ro͞o'vr'] (1345–1361; reigned 1350–61), with whose death the line became extinct. (b) Cadet line (1363–1477) re-established by John the Good, King of France (1350–64), whose mother, Jeanne de Bourgogne (1293–1348), was a daughter of Duke Robert II (reigned 1272–1305) of Burgundy (Capetian line). This second line comprised dukes of Burgundy at height of their power: Philip the Bold, founder, John the Fearless, Philip the Good, and Charles the Bold (see individual biographies; see also MARY OF BURGUNDY). On the death of Charles (1477), the duchy proper passed to France. Dukedom revived for Louis (1682–1712), dauphin of France, grandson of Louis XIV, and father of Louis XV.

(2) A dynasty of Portugal originating with Henry of Burgundy (1057–?1112); grandson of Robert I, 1st Duke of Burgundy; appointed (1094) count of Portugal by his father-in-law, Alfonso VI of León and Castile; succeeded (1112) by his son Alfonso I, who made Portugal an independent kingdom (1139). There were nine kings of this dynasty (1139–1383): Alfonso I, Sancho I, Alfonso II, Sancho II, Alfonso III, Diniz, Alfonso IV, Pedro I, and Ferdinand I. Line became extinct with Ferdinand I (d. 1383) and was succeeded by the House of Aviz. See *Table* (*in Appendix*) for PORTUGAL.

**Bu'ri·án von Ra'jecz** (bo͞o'rĭ·än fôn rŏ'yĕts), Count **Stephan von.** 1851–1922. Austro-Hungarian statesman; succeeded Count von Berchtold (*q.v.*) as foreign minister (1915–16); again foreign minister (Apr. 15–Oct. 25, 1918).

**Bu'ri'dan'** (bü'rē'däɴ'; *Angl.* bū'rĭ·dăn, -d'n), **Jean.** d. after 1358. French scholastic philosopher, reputed (prob. erroneously) to have posed famous problem that has become known as "Buridan's ass," used to prove the inability of the will to act between two equally powerful motives.

**Bur·ji'** (bo͝or·jē'). One of the two (see also BAHRI) Mameluke dynasties of Egypt, having 23 sultans (1382–1517). Originated in a bodyguard, chiefly Circassian slaves, founded by a Bahri sultan; quartered in towers of the citadel (hence name, from Arab. *burj*, tower).

Nearly all rulers of dynasty corrupt and incompetent; brought Egypt to low state politically and economically.

**Burke** (bûrk), **Billie.** 1886–1970. American actress; m. (1914) Florenz Ziegfeld. Leading woman in John Drew's company presenting *My Wife* (1907); also starred in *Love Watches* (1908), *Suzanne* (1911), *Caesar's Wife* (1919), *Happy Husbands* (1929), *Vinegar Tree* (1931), and in motion pictures.

**Burke, Edmund.** 1729–1797. British statesman and orator, b. Dublin, of Protestant father and Roman Catholic mother. Brought up a Protestant; entered Middle Temple (1750) but abandoned legal studies for literary work; published *Vindication of Natural Society,* satire upon Bolingbroke (1756), and *On the Sublime and Beautiful* (1756). M.P. through influence of his patron, Ralph, 2d Earl Verney (1765); gained high position among Whigs through eloquence on American question and vigorous opposition to George III's policy of court domination and arbitrary rule; issued political pamphlets *On the Present State of the Nation* replying to Grenville on commerce and finance (1769), and *Thoughts on the Present Discontents,* accusing Tory government of suppressing public opinion, as in Wilkes case (1770); advocated liberal treatment of colonies in speeches *American Taxation* (1774) and *Conciliation with America* (1775); championed free trade with Ireland and Catholic emancipation; denounced use of Indians in American war (1778); forced North to resign. Paymaster of the forces under Rockingham (1782) and in succeeding coalition government; saw, in rout of Whigs and Pitt's ascendancy, an end of his cherished hope for political office; took active part in investigation of East India Company and urged impeachment of Warren Hastings, opening the case (1788), and delivering nine-day speech in reply to defense (1794); supported Wilberforce in advocating abolition of slave trade (1788–89); appeared as champion of the old order in opposition to atheistical Jacobinism in *Reflections on the French Revolution* (1790) and a series of writings mounting in passionate denunciation and reaching climax in *Letters on a Regicide Peace* (1795–97); quarreled with Fox and Whigs (1791); retired from parliament on pension (1794), defending its acceptance in the *Letter to a Noble Lord* (1796), eloquently rhetorical exposition of constitutional principle.

**Burke, Edward Raymond.** 1881–1968. American lawyer and politician; practiced law, Omaha, Nebr. Member, U.S. House of Representatives (1933–35); U.S. senator from Nebraska (1935 ff.). Cosponsor with James Wolcott Wadsworth of the Selective Training and Service Act (1940).

**Burke, Fielding.** Pseudonym of Olive Tilford DARGAN.

**Burke, John.** 1787–1848. Irish genealogist. Compiler (1826) of the first dictionary of baronets and peers in alphabetical order, known as *Burke's Peerage,* and of a dictionary of commoners, later known as *Burke's Landed Gentry* (1833–38). His son Sir **John Bernard** (1814–1892), genealogist and expert in heraldry; Ulster king-of-arms (1853); keeper of state papers in Ireland (1855); re-edited his father's *Peerage* annually (1847–92), also his *Landed Gentry;* published *Vicissitudes of Families* (1859–63).

**Burke, Kenneth Du·va'** (dōō·vä'). 1897– . American writer of philosophic and literary criticism; b. Pittsburgh, Pa. Educ. Ohio State and Columbia. Author of *Towards a Better Life...*(1932), *Permanence and Change: an Anatomy of Purpose* (1935), *Attitudes Toward History* (2 vols., 1937), etc.

**Burke, Robert O'Hara.** 1820–1861. Irish explorer, b. County Galway. To Australia (1853). Led exploratory expedition for Philosophical Institute of Victoria (1860); with companion, W. J. Wills (*q.v.*), crossed Australian continent (from south to north), the first white men to do so; died of starvation on return trip.

**Burke, Thomas.** 1886–1945. English novelist and short-story writer; first popular success *Limehouse Nights,* featuring Quong Lee, Chinatown philosopher (1917). Author of further Limehouse stories, autobiographical novel *The Wind and the Rain* (1924), *Flower of Life* (1929), *Night Pieces* (1935), *Travel in England* (1943), etc.

**Burke, Thomas Henry.** 1829–1882. Irish undersecretary; murdered in Dublin by the Invincibles, a branch of the Fenian secret society, led by James Carey.

**Burke, Victor.** 1882–1958. American bacteriologist; professor of bacteriology (from 1921), head of department (from 1925), Washington State College. Author of *The Cyclogasteridae* (1930); special editor for bacteriology, *Webster's New International Dictionary, Second Edition.*

**Burke, William.** 1792–1829. Irish criminal. Accomplice of William Hare; hanged at Edinburgh for smothering victims in order to sell the bodies for dissection (hence the verb *burke,* meaning to murder by suffocation).

**Bür'kel** (bür'kĕl), **Heinrich.** 1802–1869. Bavarian painter of landscapes, chiefly of the Alps.

**Bur'kitt** (bûr'kĭt), **Francis Crawford.** 1864–1935. English Biblical scholar; author of writings on early church history, New Testament texts, and sources for life of Jesus.

**Bur'leigh** (bûr'lĭ). See BALFOUR OF BURLEIGH.

**Burleigh,** 3d Baron **Balfour of.** See John BALFOUR.

**Burleigh,** Barons. See CECIL family.

**Burleigh, Harry Thacker.** 1866–1949. American singer and composer, b. Erie, Pa. Arranged over 100 Negro spirituals, including *Little Mother of Mine, Deep River,* etc. Spingarn medal (1917).

**Bur'le·son** (bûr'lĕ·s'n), **Albert Sidney.** 1863–1937. American lawyer and politician; member, U.S. House of Representatives (1899–1913); U.S. postmaster general (1913–21).

**Burleson, Edward.** 1798–1851. Pioneer in Texas (1831); b. Buncombe County, N.C.; in command of Texan troops at capture of San Antonio (Dec. 10, 1835); vice-president of Texas (1841).

**Bur'ley** (bûr'lĭ), Sir **Simon.** 1336–1388. English soldier and courtier. Guardian and tutor to Richard II; negotiated Richard's marriage with Anne of Bohemia; adviser of Richard in struggle for absolute power.

**Bur'lin·game** (bûr'lĭn·gām; -lĭng·gām), **Anson.** 1820–1870. American lawyer and diplomat; member, U.S. House of Representatives (1855–61). U.S. minister to China (1861–67). Appointed (1868) by Chinese government head of delegation to visit U.S. and Europe, and make treaties. Burlingame concluded convention with U.S. (Burlingame Treaty, July 28, 1868), establishing reciprocal rights of citizens of the two countries. His son **Edward Livermore** (1848–1922), b. Boston, was editor of *Scribner's Magazine* (1887–1914). Anson's grandson **William Roger** (1889–1967), author, b. New York City; engaged in Meuse-Argonne offensive (1918); author of *Susan Shane* (1926), *High Thursday* (1928), *The Heir* (1930), *March of the Iron Men* (1938), *Engines of Democracy* (1940).

**Burlington,** Earl of. See BOYLE family.

**Bur·liuk'** (bŏŏr·lyōōk'), **David.** 1882–1967. Russian painter, b. Kharkov. Identified with ultramodern movement; leader in painting during Russian revolutionary period. To U.S. (1922); represented in many important exhibitions.

**Bur'man** *or* **Bur'mann** (bûr'män). Dutch family of scholars, including **Pieter** the elder (1668–1741), classical scholar; editor of Latin writers including Quintilian

(1720) and Ovid (1727); author of *Sylloge Epistolarum* (5 vols., 1727), a contribution to the history of scholarship, and works on Roman antiquities. His nephew **Johannes** (1706–1779), botanist; author of works on flora of India and Africa. Johannes's brother **Pieter** the younger (1714–1778), classical scholar; edited Vergil (1746), a Latin anthology (1759), Aristophanes (1760), Claudian (1760; begun by his uncle).

**Bur'man** (bûr'măn), **Ben Lucien.** 1895– . American journalist and author, b. Covington, Ky.; served in 2d division. A.E.F.; wounded at Soissons; author of *Mississippi* (1929; filmed and called *Heaven on Earth*, 1931) and *Steamboat Round the Bend* (1933; filmed 1935).

**Bur'mei'ster** (bōōr'mī'stẽr), **Hermann.** 1807–1892. German naturalist and traveler in South America.

**Bur'me'ster** (bōōr'mā'stẽr), **Willy.** 1869–1933. German concert violinist. Studied under Joachim (1882–85).

**Bur'na·by** (bûr'nȧ·bĭ), **Frederick Gustavus.** 1842–1885. English cavalry officer and traveler. As correspondent for *The Times* of London, traveled with Gordon in the Sudan (1875); made journey on horseback across Russian steppes in midwinter (1875), and across Armenia and Asia Minor (1876), described in *Ride to Khiva* (1876), and *On Horseback through Asia Minor* (1876).

**Bur·nand'** (bûr·nănd'; bẽr-), Sir **Francis Cowley.** 1836–1917. English playwright, and editor of *Punch* (1880–1906). Author of many burlesques, including *Black-eyed Susan* (1866), *Cox and Box* (with music by Sir Arthur Sullivan, produced 1867), *The Colonel* (1881); of farces adapted from the French; and *Happy Thoughts* (1866), orig. a series in *Punch*.

**Burne'-Jones'** (bûrn'jōnz'), Sir **Edward Co'ley** (kō'lĭ). *Orig. surname* **Jones.** 1833–1898. English painter and designer. Educ. Exeter College, Oxford, where acquainted with William Morris; began painting under guidance of Rossetti (1856); little known until he exhibited large oil paintings (1877–78), *Le Chant d'Amour, Days of Creation, The Beguiling of Merlin, The Mirror of Venus;* among best-known paintings are *The Golden Stairs* (1880), *King Cophetua and the Beggar Maid* (1884), *The Depths of the Sea* (1886); engaged upon various decorative series, for example *The Briar Rose*, four large paintings depicting the fairy tale of the Sleeping Beauty (1890); furnished many stained-glass designs, as for Christ Church Cathedral, Oxford (1859).

**Bur·nell'** (bûr·nĕl'; bẽr-), **Arthur Coke** (kōk). 1840–1882. English Sanskrit scholar.

**Burnell, Robert.** d. 1292. English bishop. Lord chancellor and chief adviser of Edward I (1274–92).

**Burnes** (bûrnz), Sir **Alexander.** 1805–1841. British traveler and official in India; assassinated at Kabul.

**Bur'net** (bûr'nĕt; -nĭt), **Dana.** 1888–1962. American author; published *Poems* (1915), *The Shining Adventure* (1916), *Angel Food* (comedy, 1927), *The Boundary Line* (drama, 1931).

**Burnet,** Sir **Frank Macfarlane.** 1899– . Australian medical scientist. Awarded Nobel prize in physiology and medicine (1960) with P. Medawar.

**Burnet, Gilbert.** 1643–1715. English bishop and historian, b. Edinburgh, of Scottish family. Professor of divinity, Glasgow (1669–74); strongly anti-Catholic; reproved Charles II for his dissolute living; fled to Holland on accession of James II; outlawed (1687). Counseled William and Mary, accompanied them to England (1688), and preached their coronation sermon. Bishop of Salisbury (1689), influential at court during life of Queen Mary; his pamphlet defending Broad Church position, the *Exposition of the Thirty-nine Articles* (1699), condemned as heterodox by lower house of convocation; as member of an ecclesiastical commission appointed, after Mary's death, to distribute vacant church livings, devised the scheme known (after 1704) as Queen Anne's Bounty. Author of *History of the Reformation* (3 vols., 1679–1714), *History of my Own Time* (2 vols., 1723–34). His son **William** (1688–1729) was appointed (1720) governor of provinces of New York and New Jersey; transferred to governorship of Massachusetts (1728).

**Burnet, John.** 1863–1928. Scottish classical scholar; in his *Greek Philosophy: Thales to Plato* (1914), he ascribed to Socrates much doctrine believed by scholars Plato's own, put into mouth of Socrates.

**Burnet, Thomas.** 1635?–1715. English clergyman. Educ. Cambridge; master of Charterhouse (1685–1715). Author of *Telluris Theoria Sacra* (1681), a fanciful cosmogony praised by Addison. His *Archaeologiae Philosophicae* (1692), treating Mosaic account of fall of man as allegory, gave great offense and precluded his clerical advancement.

**Bur·nett'** (bûr·nĕt'; bẽr-), **Frances Eliza,** *nee* **Hodg'son** (hŏj's'n). 1849–1924. Writer, b. Manchester, England; to U.S. (1865); settled near Knoxville, Tenn.; m. Dr. Swan Moses Burnett (1873), divorced (1898); m. Stephen Townesend (1900). Chief works, *Little Lord Fauntleroy* (1886), *Editha's Burglar* (1888), *Sara Crewe* (1888), *The Pretty Sister of José* (1889), *Little Saint Elizabeth* (1890), *T. Tembarom* (1913); plays, with William Gillette, *Esmeralda* (presented, 1881); *A Lady of Quality* (1896), *The First Gentleman of Europe* (produced by Frohman, 1897).

**Bur'nett** (bûr'nĕt; -nĭt), **James.** See Lord MONBODDO.

**Bur·nett'** (bûr·nĕt'; bẽr-; bûr'nĕt, -nĭt), **Peter Hardeman.** *Orig.* **Burnet.** 1807–1895. b. Nashville, Tenn. Pioneer in California; first governor of the state (1849–51).

**Burnett, Whit.** 1899–1973. American editor, b. Salt Lake City; journalist and foreign correspondent in Europe; m. (1930, div. 1941) **Martha Fo'ley** [fō'lĭ] (journalist, b. Boston), with whom he founded (in Vienna, 1931; transferred to New York, 1933) and edited magazine *Story*, until she succeeded (1941) Edward J. O'Brien (*q.v.*) as editor of annual anthologies *Best Short Stories.* Burnett married novelist **Hallie South'gate** (South'gāt), with whom he continued to edit *Story* until 1971.

**Burnett,** Sir **William.** 1779–1861. Scottish physician general of British navy; physician in ordinary to king (1835); patentee of a disinfecting fluid (Burnett's fluid, a strong solution of zinc chloride) with which wood, fabrics, etc., may be impregnated (or burnettized), to prevent decay.

**Burnett, William Riley.** 1899– . American novelist; author of *Little Caesar* (1929), *Iron Man* (1930), *The Giant Swing* (1932), *Dark Hazard* (1933), *High Sierra* (1940), *The Quick Brown Fox* (1942). *Nobody Lives Forever* (1944), *The Asphalt Jungle* (1949).

**Bur'ney** (bûr'nĭ), Sir **Cecil.** 1858–1929. British naval officer; conducted Scutari affair successfully (1913); commanded first battle squadron at Jutland (1916); admiral of the fleet (1920).

**Burney,** Dr. **Charles.** 1726–1814. English organist and musical historian; father of Fanny Burney (*q.v.*). Composed *Alfred, Robin Hood,* and *Queen Mab* for Drury Lane Theatre (1745–50); organist at Chelsea Hospital (1783–1814). Author of *History of Music* (4 vols., 1776–89). His eldest son, **James** (1750–1821), naval officer, twice sailed with Captain Cook; wrote histories of discoveries in the Pacific and *History of the Buccaneers of America* (1816); his second son, **Charles** (1757–1817), classical scholar, collected rare books and manuscripts ultimately bought for British Museum.

**Burney, Fanny,** *orig.* **Frances.** 1752–1840. English

novelist; daughter of Dr. Charles Burney, musician. Author of *Evelina* (anonymously; 1778), *Cecilia* (1782), *Camilla* (1796), *The Wanderer* (1814); m. (1793) General **d'Ar'blay** (där'blā; *Fr.* dȧr'blā'), a French refugee; with husband in Paris (1802–12); after Waterloo, passed rest of life in England. Edited her father's *Memoirs* (1832); published *Diary and Letters* (1842–46).

**Burn'ham** (bûr'năm), 1st Baron. **Edward Le'vy-Law'son** (lē'vĭ·lô's'n). 1833–1916. English newspaper proprietor, son of Joseph Moses Levy, founder of the *Daily Telegraph*. Assumed surname Lawson under uncle Lionel Lawson's will (1875). Editor, London *Daily Telegraph* (from c. 1855) and managing proprietor (1885–1903); transformed newspaper from plain chronicle to lively and entertaining vehicle of news and opinions; organized appeals for funds in support of charitable, patriotic, and cultural projects; sponsored Assyrian archaeological expedition of George Smith (1873); raised to peerage (1903).

His eldest son, **Harry Lawson Webster Lawson** (1862–1933), 1st Viscount **Burnham**; educ. Oxford; succeeded father (1903) as director of conduct and policy of *Daily Telegraph*, which he sold (1927); Liberal (1885–95), later Unionist (1910–16), M.P.; helped draft Representation of the People Act, known as Reform Act of 1918; president of International Labor Conference of League of Nations (1921–22); presided over joint committees making award of "Burnham scales" of teachers' salaries.

**Burnham, Daniel Hudson.** 1846–1912. American architect, b. Henderson, N.Y. With John W. Root, organized Burnham & Root, architects (1873); after death of Root (1891), formed firm of G. H. Burnham & Co. Chief of construction for Chicago World's Fair (1893); chairman, commission of experts appointed for planning development of Washington, D.C. (1901); consultant on city planning for Cleveland, San Francisco, Manila. Submitted (1909) a plan of Chicago, later carried out. Among his buildings: Montauk Building, Chicago; Flatiron Building, New York; Union Railroad Station, Washington, D.C.

**Burnham, Frederick Russell.** 1861–1947. American explorer, b. Tivoli, Minn.; discovered buried treasure in ruins of ancient civilization in Rhodesia. Served as chief of scouts of British army in Boer War (1900–01); on surveys on Volta River, West Africa (1902); explored Congo basin region (1903–04). Discovered remains of Maya civilization, Mexico (1908); collaborated with John Hays Hammond in diverting the Yaqui River through canals into a 700-square-mile delta.

**Burnham, Sherburne Wesley.** 1838–1921. American astronomer, b. Thetford, Vt. Shorthand reporter (1858–88). On staff of Lick Observatory (1888–92); senior astronomer at Yerkes Observatory (1897–1914). Known for catalogues of 1274 new double stars that he discovered and of all known double stars (over 12,000) visible in Northern Hemisphere.

**Bur'nouf'** (bür'nōōf'), **Jean Louis.** 1775–1844. French philologist; author of *Méthode pour Étudier la Langue Grecque* (1814), *Méthode pour Étudier la Langue Latine* (1840). His son **Eugène** (1801–1852) was an Orientalist, noted for researches in Zend language. A relative, **Émile Louis Burnouf** (1821–1907), was also an Orientalist; author of *Méthode pour Étudier la Langue Sanscrite* (1859), *Essai sur le Véda* (1863), a collaborator on *Dictionnaire Classique Sanscrit-Français* (1863–64).

**Burns** (bûrnz), **Anthony.** 1834–1862. American Negro slave, b. Stafford Co., Va. Fled and arrested in Boston (May 24, 1854) on charge of theft; recognized as fugitive slave. Protests against his return to Virginia culminated in riots and calling out of armed troops. Returned to Virginia; bought out of slavery; studied at Oberlin College (1857–62); pastor of a Negro Baptist church, St. Catherine's, Canada.

**Burns,** Sir **George** (1795–1890) and his brother **James** (1789–1871). Scottish shipowners; operated line of small sailing vessels between Liverpool-Belfast-Glasgow (from 1824); gradually began use of steam navigation; founded, with capitalists including Samuel Cunard (*q.v.*), the Cunard Company (1839).

**Burns, James Henry.** 1885– . American army officer; grad. U.S.M.A., West Point (1908); promoted through the grades to colonel (1919), major general (1940); chief of army ordnance (April, 1942).

**Burns, John.** 1858–1943. English labor leader. Left school at age of ten; worked as engineer in England, on shipboard, and on West African coast. Socialist labor organizer; radical M.P. (1892–1918); cabinet member as president of local government board (1905–14) and as president of Board of Trade (1914); resigned on declaration of war.

**Burns, Robert.** 1759–1796. Scottish national poet, b. Alloway, near Ayr; son of a cotter. Educ. by his father; worked as farm laborer (1772); wrote early poems including *Death of Poor Mailie*. Farmed, with brother Gilbert, 118 acres at Mossgiel (1784–88), and wrote some of best poems including *The Jolly Beggars*, *Halloween*, *The Cotter's Saturday Night*, *Holy Willie's Prayer*, *To a Mouse* (1785), and *The Twa Dogs* and other more satirical works (1786). Gave (1786) written declaration of marriage to **Jean Ar'mour** [är'mẽr] (1767–1834) of Mauchline; arranged with John Wilson, Kilmarnock printer, for edition of poems to obtain passage money to Jamaica to become plantation overseer; success of this edition (1786) caused him to abandon West Indian venture and to move to Edinburgh; lionized in Edinburgh literary circles. On proceeds of second edition (1787) traveled through border towns; took farm at Ellisland (1788–91) and married Jean Armour; wrote *Tam o' Shanter* and *Auld Lang Syne* (c. 1789). Gave up Ellisland and became exciseman at Dumfries; contributed 200 songs to James Johnson's *Scots Musical Museum* (1787–1803). Supplied about 100 songs (on invitation of George Thomson, collector of Celtic airs) for *Scottish Airs with Poetry*, including lyrics, as *John Anderson, my Jo*, *Comin' thro' the Rye*, and such humorous poems as *Address to the Deil* and *To a Louse*, receiving in remuneration only a shawl, a picture, and £5. Joined Dumfriesshire Volunteers (1794); developed rheumatic fever from exposure; buried with military honors.

**Burns, William John.** 1861–1932. American detective, b. Baltimore. Director, bureau of investigation, U.S. Department of Justice (1921–24). Founder, and for many years president, of William J. Burns International Detective Agency.

**Burn'side** (bûrn'sīd), **Ambrose Everett.** 1824–1881. American army commander, b. Liberty, Ind. Grad. U.S.M.A., West Point (1847). Brigadier general (1861); major general (1862); in command of Army of Potomac (Oct., 1862); unsuccessful in Fredericksburg campaign; relieved of command (1863); assigned to Department of the Ohio (until Nov. 16, 1863). With Army of the Potomac, under Grant, before Petersburg (1864), failed to follow up advantage after explosion of a mine; blamed by court of inquiry; resigned commission (1865). Governor of Rhode Island (1866–69). U.S. senator (1875–81). Lent his name to type of side whiskers such as he wore—"burnsides."

**Bur'pee** (bûr'pē; -pē), **Washington Atlee.** 1858–1915. American seedsman; b. Sheffield, New Brunswick, Canada; to U.S. as a child. Started in seed business (1876) and developed W. Atlee Burpee & Co., mail-order seed house, with head offices at Philadelphia, which has been continued by his sons **David** (president) and **W. Atlee, Jr.** (secretary-treasurer).

**Burr** (bûr), **Aaron.** 1716–1757. American Presbyterian clergyman and educator, b. Fairfield, Conn. President, College of New Jersey, now Princeton (1748–57).

**Burr, Aaron.** 1756–1836. Son of Aaron Burr (1716–1757). American Revolutionary officer and political leader, b. Newark, N.J. Grad. Princeton (1772). Served in army from outbreak of Revolution (until 1779); practiced law, New York City (from 1783). U.S. senator (1791–97). In election of 1800, tied with Jefferson for the presidency, each receiving 73 votes; when election was thus thrown into Congress, Burr disclaimed competition for the office, and Jefferson was elected on the 36th ballot; Burr became vice-president of the United States (1801–05). Mortally wounded Alexander Hamilton in duel (July 11, 1804), at Weehawken, N.J. Conspired to seize territory from Spanish America and create a new republic in Southwest; arrested (1807); tried for treason; acquitted (1807). Went abroad (1808), and tried to interest authorities in France and England in his schemes; failed; returned to U.S. (1812); resumed practice of law in New York. His daughter **Theodosia** (1783–1813), wife of Joseph Alston, was lost at sea.

**Burr, Amelia Josephine.** 1878–1966. American poet; m. Rev. Carl Hopkins Elmore (1921); author of *In Deep Places* (1914), *Life and Living* (1916), *The Silver Trumpet* (1918), *Hearts Awake* (1919).

**Burr, William Hubert.** 1851–1934. American civil engineer; consulting engineer to municipal depts. of New York City (1893–1904); member, Isthmian Canal Commission (1899, 1904).

**Burr, Willie Olcott.** 1843–1921. American newspaper proprietor and editor, b. Hartford, Conn.; joined (1861) staff of Hartford *Times*, of which his father, **Alfred Edmund** (1815–1900), had been proprietor and editor from its establishment as a daily paper (1841); became proprietor and editor (1890).

**Bur'rhus** (bûr'ŭs). Variant of BURRUS.

**Bur'ritt** (bûr'ĭt), **Elihu.** 1810–1879. American linguist and advocate of international peace, b. New Britain, Conn. Apprenticed to a blacksmith. Called "the Learned Blacksmith." Founded *Christian Citizen* (1844), advocating international peace; edited it (1844–51). Organized Brussels Peace Congress (1848). Lectured on international peace (1851–61).

**Burrough.** See BOROUGH.

**Bur'roughs** (bûr'ōz), **Edgar Rice.** 1875–1950. American writer of adventure stories; known chiefly as creator of Tarzan (*Tarzan of the Apes*, 1914; *The Return of Tarzan*, 1915; etc.).

**Burroughs, George.** 1650?–1692. American clergyman; accused of witchcraft (1692), tried, convicted, and executed at Salem; only clerical victim of witchcraft.

**Burroughs, John.** 1837–1921. American naturalist, b. near Roxbury, N.Y. Teacher (1854–63); clerk in Treasury Dept., Washington, D.C. (1863–73); lived (from 1873) on a farm near Esopus, N.Y.; built a secluded cabin, called "Slabsides," back in the hills (1895), and spent much time there. Friend (from 1863) of Walt Whitman, whom he honored in his first published book, *Notes on Walt Whitman as Poet and Person* (1867). His nature essays began to appear in the *Atlantic* (1865). His first nature book, *Wake-Robin*, a book on birds (pub. 1871). Other works: *Winter Sunshine* (1875), *Birds and Poets* (1877), *Locusts and Wild Honey* (1879), *Pepacton* (1881), *Fresh Fields* (1885), *Signs and Seasons* (1886), *Indoor Studies* (1889), *Literary Values* (1902), *Ways of Nature* (1905), *Bird and Bough* (1906), *Camping and Tramping with Roosevelt* (1907), *The Summit of the Years* (1913), *The Breath of Life* (1915), *Field and Study* (1919).

**Burroughs, William Seward.** 1857–1898. b. Rochester, N.Y. American inventor of a key-set recording and adding machine (patented 1888), earliest adding machine to be successfully marketed.

**Bur'rows** (bûr'ōz), **Ronald Montagu.** 1867–1920. English archaeologist; conducted archaeological excavations at Pylos and Sphacteria (1895–96) and in Boeotia (1905, 1907).

**Bur'rus** (bûr'ŭs), **Sextus Afranius.** d. 63 A.D. Roman general; commander of Praetorian Guard (52 A.D.). Associated with Seneca in education of Nero and, after death of Claudius (54), used influence with Praetorian Guard to assure Nero's undisputed succession to throne. As adviser to Nero, refused to approve certain assassinations ordered by emperor.

**Bur'si·an** (bŏŏr'zē·än), **Konrad.** 1830–1883. German classical philologist and archaeologist.

**Bürstenbinder, Elisabeth.** Real name of E. WERNER.

**Burt** (bûrt), **Maxwell Struthers.** 1882–1954. American writer, b. Baltimore. Cattle ranchman in Wyoming (from 1908); president, Bar B.C. Ranch Co. (until 1937). Author of *In the High Hills* (1914), *Songs and Portraits* (book of verse; 1921), *Chance Encounters* (1921), *The Interpreter's House* (1924), *The Diary of a Dude Wrangler* (1924), *The Delectable Mountains* (1926), *Festival* (1931), *Escape from America* (1936). His wife (m. 1913), **Katherine,** *nee* **New'lin** [nū'lĭn] (1882– ), fiction writer; author of *The Branding Iron* (1919), *"Q"* (1922), *Beggars All* (1933).

**Bur'ton** (bûr't'n), **Harold Hitz** (hĭts). 1888–1964. American jurist, b. Jamaica Plain, Mass.; A.B., Bowdoin (1909), LL.B., Harvard (1912); practiced law (in Cleveland from 1919); mayor of Cleveland (1935–40); U.S. senator (1941–45); associate justice, U.S. Supreme Court (1945–58).

**Bur'ton,** Baron. **Michael Arthur Bass.** See under Michael Thomas BASS.

**Burton, Ernest DeWitt.** 1856–1925. Am. theologian and educator; president, U. of Chicago (1923–25).

**Burton, Frederick Russell.** 1861–1909. American musician. Studied native Indian music at first hand; author of *Songs of the Ojibway Indians* (1903, amplified into *American Primitive Music*, 1909), *Strongheart* (1908), *Redcloud of the Lakes* (1909). Composer of *Hiawatha*, and *The Legend of Sleepy Hollow*, cantatas.

**Burton,** Sir **Frederick William.** 1816–1900. Irish water-color painter. Portrait painter in Dublin; director of National Gallery, London (1874–94).

**Burton, John Hill.** 1809–1881. Scottish historian. Achieved reputation with *Life of David Hume* (1846); editor, with Sir John Bowring, of Bentham's works.

**Burton, Marion LeRoy.** 1874–1925. American Congregational clergyman and educator; president, Smith College (1910–17), U. of Minnesota (1917–20), U. of Michigan (1920–25).

**Burton, Richard Eugene.** 1861–1940. American poet, b. Hartford, Conn. Professor of literature, Rollins (from 1933). Author of *Dumb in June* (1895), *Memorial Day* (1897), *Lyrics of Brotherhood* (1899), *Song of the Unsuccessful* (1900), *From the Book of Life* (1909), *Poems of Earth's Meaning* (1917), etc.

**Burton,** Sir **Richard Francis.** 1821–1890. British explorer and Orientalist, of English family settled in Ireland. Joined Indian army (1842); recorded experiences in *Scinde, or the Unhappy Valley* (1851); made pilgrimage to Mecca (1853) disguised as Pathan, which he described in *Personal Narrative* (1855); with Speke, explored

Somaliland (1854), Lake Tanganyika region (1858), described in *First Footsteps in East Africa* (1856); British consul at Fernando Po (1861–65), Damascus (1869–71), Trieste (1872); accompanied Captain Cameron to Gold Coast (1881–82); published translations of Camoëns (1880) and of *Arabian Nights* (16 vols., 1885–88). His wife, **Isabel**, *nee* **Ar'un·dell** [ăr'ŭn·dĕl] (1831–1896), shared his wanderings after marriage (1861); wrote travel narratives and his biography.

**Burton, Robert.** *Pseudonym* **De·moc'ri·tus Junior** (dē·mŏk'rĭ·tŭs). 1577–1640. English clergyman and author. Vicar, St. Thomas's, Oxford (1616–40). Author of Latin comedy *Philosophaster* (1606; acted 1618) and of *The Anatomy of Melancholy*, a medical treatise upon the causes and symptoms and the cure of melancholy and upon love melancholy and religious melancholy, including a storehouse of miscellaneous learning, a picture of contemporary life and thought, and a sketch of a Utopia (1621).

**Burton, Theodore Elijah.** 1851–1929. American lawyer and politician; member, U.S. House of Representatives (1889–91, 1895–1909, 1921–29) and U.S. Senate (1909–15). Author of *Life of John Sherman* (1906), *Corporations and the State* (1911), *The Constitution...*(1923), etc.

**Burton, William Meriam.** 1865–1954. American chemist and industrialist; introduced process of cracking petroleum (1912). Awarded Willard Gibbs medal (1918) and Perkins medal (1921) in recognition of his work in the chemistry of petroleum.

**Bur'ton–O'pitz** (-ō'pĭts), **Russell.** 1875–1954. American physiologist; author of *Text Book of Physiology* (1920).

**Bu'ry'** (bü'rē'), **Ange Henri Blaze de.** See under François Blaze.

**Bu'ry** (?bū'rĭ; bĕr'ĭ), **John Bagnell.** 1861–1927. Irish historian; regius professor of modern history, Cambridge (1902–27). Author of a history of Greece, and several histories of the later Roman Empire.

**Bur'y** (bĕr'ĭ), **Richard de.** *Orig. name* **Richard Aun'ger·ville** *or* **Aun'ger·vyle** (oun'jĕr·vĭl). 1287–1345. English ecclesiastic, scholar, and collector of books and manuscripts, b. Bury St. Edmunds. Tutor to Edward of Windsor, afterwards Edward III; bishop of Durham (1333); ambassador at Paris, in Hainaut, Germany, and Scotland. Author of *Philobiblon* (1473), autobiographical sketch designed as handbook on collecting and preserving books.

**Bus'becq'** (büz'bĕk') *or* **Bus'beck'** (büz'bĕk') *or* **Bous'becq'** (bōōz'bĕk') *or* **Bou'se·becque'** (bōōz'-bĕk'), **Augier Ghislain de.** 1522–1592. Flemish diplomat; ambassador of Emperor Ferdinand I to sultan at Constantinople (1554–62); ambassador of Emperor Rudolph II at Paris. Author of volume of letters written from Turkey, *Legationis Turcicae Epistolae Quatuor* (1589).

**Bus'by** (bŭz'bĭ), **Richard.** 1606–1695. English clergyman and schoolmaster; headmaster of Westminster (1638–95), numbering among his pupils South, Dryden, Locke, Prior, Atterbury; traditionally a severe disciplinarian; edited Greek and Latin grammars.

**Busch** (bŏŏsh), **Moritz.** 1821–1899. German writer and journalist; press agent, companion, and confidant of Bismarck (from 1870). Author of *Graf Bismarck und seine Leute* (1878), *Unser Reichskanzler* (1884), etc.

**Busch, Wilhelm.** 1832–1908. German humorous illustrator and poet; illustrator for *Fliegende Blätter* (1859–71); author of humorous and satirical illustrated verse.

**Busch, Wilhelm.** 1861–1929. German historian.

**Bu'sche** (bŏŏsh'ĕ), **Hermann von dem** (fŏn dĕm). *Called* **Pa·si'phi·lus** (pä·zē'fē·lōōs; *Angl.* pȧ·sĭf'ĭ·lŭs). 1468–1534. German scholar and humanist; author of *Vallum Humanitatis*, 3 books of epigrams in defense of humanism (1518).

**Bü'sching** (büsh'ĭng), **Anton Friedrich.** 1724–1793. German geographer; author of the unfinished *Neue Erdbeschreibung* (11 parts, 1754–92) that laid foundation of modern statistical geography.

**Busch'mann** (bŏŏsh'män), **Johann Karl Eduard.** 1805–1880. German philologist; collaborated with the brothers von Humboldt and helped edit Alexander von Humboldt's *Kosmos*. Author of comparative grammar of dialects of Malaysia and Polynesia (1840).

**Bu'sem·baum** (bōō'zĕm·boum) *or* **Bu'sen·baum** (bōō'zĕn·boum), **Hermann.** 1600–1668. German Jesuit theologian; author of *Medulla Theologiae Moralis* (1650), which was later condemned for its sections on regicide and publicly burned (1757) by the Parliament of Toulouse.

**Bush** (bŏŏsh), **Vannevar.** 1890–1974. American electrical engineer, b. Everett, Mass. Dean of engineering and vice-president, M.I.T. (1932–38); president, Carnegie Institution of Washington (1939–55). Devised machine for solving differential equations. Director, Office of Scientific Research and Development (1941–46).

**Bush'–Brown'** (bŏŏsh'broun'), **Henry Kirke.** 1857–1935. American sculptor; among his notable works are equestrian statues *Gen. G. G. Meade* and *Gen. John F. Reynolds* at Gettysburg, *Indian Buffalo Hunt* at Chicago Exposition of 1893, equestrian statue *General Anthony Wayne* for Valley Forge, *Lincoln Memorial* at Gettysburg, and portrait bust of his uncle Henry Kirke Brown for American Hall of Fame.

**Bush'nell** (bŏŏsh'nĕl), **David.** 1742?–1824. American inventor; invented submarine boat ("Bushnell's turtle"); predecessor of modern submarine.

**Bushnell, Horace.** 1802–1876. American Congregational clergyman, b. Bantam, Conn. Pastorate: Hartford, Conn. (1833–61); inspired liberal preacher and writer.

**Bu·si'ri, al–** (ăl'bōō·sē'rē). *Arab.* **Sharaf-al-Dīn Muḥammad al-Būṣīri.** 1213–?1296. Arab poet of Berber extraction; lived in Egypt; author of famous ode *al-Burdah* ("The Prophet's Mantle") in praise of Mohammed, which has acquired almost sacred character and has been subject of many commentaries and translations.

**Busk** (bŭsk), **George.** 1807–1886. English surgeon, zoologist, and paleontologist; authority on Bryozoa.

**Bus'ken Hu·et'** (bûs'kĕn hü·wĕt'), **Conrad.** 1826–1886. Dutch theologian, literary critic, and writer.

**Bu·son** (bōō·sŏn), **Yosa.** 1716–1783. Japanese painter.

**Bu·so'ni** (bōō·zō'nē), **Ferruccio Benvenuto.** 1866–1924. Italian pianist and composer; taught at Helsingfors (1888–90), Moscow (1890–91), Boston (1891–93), Berlin (1894 ff.). Director, Conservatory of Bologna (1913–15). Considered greatest piano technician after Liszt and Rubinstein. Among his works are operas, a symphonic poem, concertos, suites, compositions for piano and for orchestra, chamber music.

**Bus'se** (bŏŏs'ĕ), **Hermann Eris.** 1891–1947. German novelist.

**Busse, Karl.** 1872–1918. German author of verse, essays, literary history, and novels, chiefly with German-Polish borderland background.

**Bus'sy'** (bü'sē'), Comte **de.** **Roger de Ra'bu'tin'** (dē rȧ'bü'tăN'). *Known also as* **Bussy-Rabutin.** 1618–1693. French soldier and writer; best known as author of *Histoire Amoureuse des Gaules* (1665).

**Bus'sy'–d'Am'boise'** (-däN'bwȧz'), Seigneur **Louis de.** 1549–1579. French nobleman; took advantage of St.

Bartholomew's Massacre (1572) to murder one of his relatives to whom he owed money; pillaged Anjou, of which he was governor (1576); was assassinated by husband of a woman he had seduced. Appears in Dumas père's *La Dame de Monsoreau* and, as central figure, in George Chapman's drama *Bussy d'Ambois*.

**Bus'ta·man'te** (bōōs'tä·män'tā), **Anastasio.** 1780–1853. Mexican general and political leader, b. Jiquilpán, Michoacán. Fought in Spanish army against revolutionists (as early as 1808), but (1821) supported Iturbide and Plan of Iguala (form of government); vice-president of the republic under Guerrero (1829) but, with Santa Anna, led revolt against him. President of Mexico (1829–32); driven out by Santa Anna but, after latter's downfall (1836), again president (1837–39; nominally until Sept., 1841).

**Bustamante, Carlos María de.** 1774–1848. Mexican historian, soldier, and statesman, b. Oaxaca. Editor, *Diario de Méjico* (1805 ff.); army officer in first Mexican war for independence (1812); interned at Vera Cruz; aided in Iguala declaration of independence; as secretary to Santa Anna, accompanied him on march to capital (1821); founded weekly newspaper *La Avispa de Chilpancingo*. Author of works on modern Mexican history.

**Bustamante y Bal'li·vián'** (ē bä'yē·vyän'), **Enrique.** 1883–1937. Peruvian writer and diplomat, b. Lima; edited *La Prensa, La Nación, La Opinión Nacional, El Perú* (Lima), and *El Triunfo* (Havana); prefect of departments of Junín and Arequipa. Author of *Elogios, Poemas Paganos y Místicos* (1910), *Arias de Silencio* (1916), *Epopeia do Trópico* (in Portuguese), *Odas Vulgares* (1927), and *Junín, Poemas* (1930).

**Bustamante y Sirvén, Antonio Sánchez de.** See SÁNCHEZ DE BUSTAMANTE Y SIRVÉN.

**Butch'er** (bōōch'ẽr), **Samuel Henry.** 1850–1910. British classical scholar; collaborated with Andrew Lang in prose translation of *Odyssey* (1879), one of the best translations extant. Author of *Aristotle's Theory of Poetry and Fine Art* (1895) and other works on Greek subjects.

**Bute** (būt), Earls and marquises of. See under STEWART family.

**Bu'te·nandt** (bōō'tē·nänt), **Adolph.** 1903– . German chemist; known for work on sex hormones, esp. isolation of androsterone and investigation of chemical structure of progestin. Declined share of 1939 Nobel prize for chemistry because of Nazi decree prohibiting acceptance.

**But'ler** (bŭt'lẽr). Family name: (1) of earls, marquises, and dukes of ORMONDE; (2) of earls of OSSORY.

**Butler, Alban.** 1711–1773. English Roman Catholic hagiographer. Author of *Lives of the Principal Saints* (4 vols., 1756–59). His nephew **Charles** (1750–1832), conveyancer, availed himself (1791) of provisions of Roman Catholic Relief Act (1791) and became first Roman Catholic to be called to bar since 1688; writer on legal and theological subjects.

**Butler, Alfred J.** 1850–1936. English scholar; author of *Ancient Coptic Churches of Egypt* (1884), *Court Life in Egypt* (1887), *The Arab Conquest of Egypt* (1902), *Islamic Pottery* (1926), *Sport in Classic Times* (1930). His son **Harold Beresford** (1883–1951), served as secretary to foreign trade dept. of foreign office (1916), to ministry of labor (1917), to labor commission of Peace Conference (1919); deputy director (1920–32), director (1932–38) of International Labor Office; appointed British minister to U.S. (1942).

**Butler, Amos William.** 1860–1937. American anthropologist, zoologist, and ornithologist; a founder of the American Anthropological Society and American Association of Mammalogists; founder, International Committee on Mental Hygiene. Author of *Birds of Indiana*, and of sociological papers.

**Butler, Andrew Pickens.** See Preston Smith BROOKS.

**Butler, Benjamin Franklin.** 1795–1858. American lawyer, b. Columbia County, N.Y. U.S. attorney general (1833–38); secretary of war (1836–37). His son **William Allen** (1825–1902), lawyer and writer, b. Albany, N.Y., was author of *Nothing to Wear* (1857).

**Butler, Benjamin Franklin.** 1818–1893. American lawyer, army officer, and politician, b. Deerfield, N.H. Entered Union service at outbreak of Civil War; commanded land forces in capture of New Orleans (May 1, 1862); military governor, New Orleans (May 1–Dec. 16, 1862); by his arbitrary government, caused protest and charges of corruption. In command, districts of eastern Virginia and North Carolina (1863); in New York, to preserve order during elections of 1864. Member, U.S. House of Representatives (1867–75; 1877–79). Governor of Massachusetts (1882–84). Candidate of Anti-Monopoly and National (Greenback) parties for president (1884).

**Butler, Charles.** 1750–1832. See Alban BUTLER.

**Butler, Edward Cuthbert.** 1858–1934. Irish scholar and authority on mysticism, b. Dublin. Abbot of Downside Abbey, Bath, England (1906–22); president of English Benedictine Congregation (1914–21). Author of *Benedictine Monachism* (1919, 1924) and of *Western Mysticism* (1922, 1927), treating of contemplation and views of SS. Augustine, Gregory, Bernard.

**Butler, Ellis Parker.** 1869–1937. American humorist, b. Muscatine, Iowa. Worked as bill clerk, salesman, store clerk (to 1897); moved to New York (1897) and devoted himself to writing. Made first great success with *Pigs is Pigs* (1906). Among other books were *Confessions of a Daddy* (1907), *That Pup* (1908), *Red Head* (1916), *Jibby Jones* (1923), *Pigs, Pets, and Pies* (1927), and *Hunting the Wow* (1934).

**Butler, George.** 1774–1853. English clergyman and educator. Headmaster of Harrow (1805–29); chancellor of Peterborough (1836), dean (1842). His four sons won distinguished honors at the universities. The eldest son, **George** (1819–1890), was public examiner at Oxford and principal of various schools, whose wife, **Josephine Elizabeth,** *nee* **Grey** (1828–1906), was an advocate of women's higher education, a social reformer influential in securing repeal of Contagious Diseases Act and reform of law affecting white slave traffic, and author of memoirs and reminiscences. The third son, **Arthur Gray** (1831–1909), was master at Rugby (1858–62), first headmaster of reconstituted Haileybury College (1862–67), and dean and tutor at Oriel College, Oxford (1875–97). The youngest son, **Henry Montague** (1833–1918), was headmaster of Harrow (1859–85), dean of Gloucester (1885–86), and master of Trinity College, Cambridge (1886–1918). A grandson, Sir **George Geoffrey Gilbert Butler** (1887–1929), educ. Cambridge, was lecturer in history (1910) and librarian (1912) of Corpus Christi College, Cambridge; member of Balfour mission to U.S. (1917); member of royal commission on government of Ceylon (1927).

**Butler, Harold Beresford.** See under Alfred J. BUTLER.

**Butler, Howard Crosby.** 1872–1922. American archaeologist; by invitation of Turkish government, explored ruins at Sardis (between 1910 and 1922).

**Butler, John.** 1728–1794. American Loyalist, b. New London, Conn. At outbreak of American Revolution, recruited (1777–78) force of Indians and rangers, "Butler's Rangers," who invaded Wyoming Valley, Pa. (1778); defeated Continentals there, with atrocities committed by the Indians (Wyoming Massacre, July 3, 1778). Was defeated (1779) near Elmira, N.Y. Joined in British raid through Mohawk Valley (1780). British commissioner of Indian affairs at Niagara, Canada, following Revolutionary War. His son, **Walter N.** (d. 1781), commanded Butler's Rangers in attack on Cherry Valley, N.Y. (Cherry Valley Massacre, Nov. 11, 1778).

**Butler, Joseph.** 1692–1752. English theologian. Of Presbyterian family, joined Church of England as a youth; rector of Stanhope (1725–40); clerk of the closet to queen (1736), to king (1746); bishop of Bristol (1738); dean of St. Paul's (1740); bishop of Durham (1750). Author of *Fifteen Sermons* (1726) and of *The Analogy of Religion* (1736).

**Butler, Marion.** 1863–1938. American lawyer and politician. U.S. senator from North Carolina (1896–1901); author of law establishing R.F.D.; secured first favorable report on bill to establish postal savings banks; advocated parcel post; led fight to appropriate funds for building first submarine. Aided in organizing cotton and tobacco co-operative marketing associations.

**Butler, Nicholas Murray.** 1862–1947. American educator, b. Elizabeth, N.J. A.B. (1882) and Ph.D. (1884), Columbia. Professor of philosophy and education, Columbia (1890–1902); president of Columbia (1902–45), Barnard (1904–45), Bard (1928–45), New York Post-Graduate Med. School (1931–45). An organizer and first president (1886–91) of New York Coll. for the Training of Teachers, now Teachers Coll., affiliated with Columbia. Chairman, Lake Mohonk Conference on International Arbitration (1907, 1909, 1910, 1911, 1912); president, Carnegie Endowment for International Peace (1925–45). Awarded, jointly with Jane Addams, Nobel peace prize (1931). Received Republican electoral vote for vice-president of U.S. (1912), the regular candidate having died prior to election. Author of books on educational and public problems.

**Butler, Pierce.** 1866–1939. American jurist; b. in Dakota Co., Minn.; practiced law in St. Paul (from 1897); assoc. justice, U.S. Supreme Court (1923–39).

**But'ler** (bŭt'lẽr), **Richard Austen.** 1902– . British politician, b. in India; educ. Cambridge; undersecretary for India (1932–37), for foreign affairs (1938–41); minister of education (1941–45), of labor (1945).

**Butler,** Sir **Richard Harte Keatinge.** 1870–1935. English army officer; major general (1915), corps commander (1918); head of Western Command (1924–28).

**Butler, Samuel.** 1612–1680. English satirical poet. Page to countess of Kent (c. 1628), wife of Henry, 7th Earl of Kent; clerk to puritan justices of the peace; secretary (1661) to 2d earl of Carbery, lord president of the marches, who appointed him steward of Ludlow Castle. Author of *Hudibras*, a much-quoted mock-heroic poem in octosyllabic couplets satirizing the hypocrisy, churlishness, greed, pride, and casuistry of the Presbyterians and Independents (parts I, 1663; II, 1664; III, 1678).

**Butler, Samuel.** 1835–1902. English satirist. Son of Rev. **Thomas** and grandson of **Samuel** (1774–1839), headmaster of Shrewsbury school and bishop of Lichfield. Sheep rancher in New Zealand (1859–64); his first book, *A First Year in Canterbury Settlement*, edited and published (1863) by his father. Began to study painting and exhibited at Royal Academy regularly (1868–76). First important literary work anonymous *Erewhon* (1872), a utopian novel of a land divested of machinery; the next an ironic defense of Christian evidences, *The Fair Haven* (1873). Attacked Darwin's law of natural selection in series of works, proposing that variations are due to striving of individuals and handed on through "unconscious memory." Recorded topographical study of Italian Switzerland with wit and humor and scenic appreciation in *Alps and Sanctuaries of Piedmont and the Canton Ticino* (1881) and *Ex Voto* (1888). Studied music and, with H. Festing Jones, composed gavottes, minuets, a cantata, and an oratorio. In pamphlets and in *The Authoress of the Odyssey* (1897), developed theory that the author of the *Odyssey* was a woman of Trapani in Sicily. Published life and letters of his grandfather (1896). Advanced view that Shakespearean sonnets were addressed to a man of humble birth (1899). Chief work, *The Way of All Flesh* (written 1873–85, pub. 1903), an iconoclastic philosophical novel largely autobiographical, satirizing family life in mid-Victorian England.

**Butler, Smedley Darlington.** 1881–1940. American officer, U.S. Marine Corps; brigadier general (1921), major general (1929). Engaged at capture of Veracruz (1914) and awarded Congressional Medal of Honor; also engaged at capture of Ft. Rivière, Haiti (1917).

**Butler, Walter N.** See John BUTLER.

**Butler, William Allen.** See under Benjamin Franklin BUTLER.

**Butler, William Archer.** 1814?–1848. Irish Anglican clergyman; professor of moral philosophy, Trinity College, Dublin (1837–48).

**Butler,** Sir **William Francis.** 1838–1910. British army officer, b. Ireland. Served in India (1860), Canada (1867–73), Ashanti War (1873–74), Zulu War (1879), the Sudan (1884–85). Commanded British troops at Alexandria (1890–93); ordered home from command in Boer War because of expression of views not approved by government (1899); lieutenant general (1900). His wife (m. 1877), **Elizabeth Southerden,** *nee* **Thompson** (1844–1933), was a Swiss-born English painter of military and battle scenes.

**Butler, William Orlando.** 1791–1880. American lawyer and army officer, b. Jessamine Co., Ky. Candidate for vice-president on Cass ticket (1848).

**Butler, Zebulon.** 1731–1795. American army officer, b. Ipswich, Mass. Served in French and Indian War. Led settlers (1769) into Wyoming Valley, Pa. Raised small force in Wyoming Valley which was defeated by Butler's Rangers (see John BUTLER).

**But'le·rov** (bo͞ot'lyĕ·rôf), **Aleksandr Mikhailovich.** 1828–1886. Russian chemist; credited with discovery of the tertiary alcohols.

**Bütsch'li** (büch'lē), **Otto.** 1848–1920. German zoologist. Investigated developmental history of invertebrates, anatomical structure of nematodes, and constitution of protoplasm; pioneered in study of nuclear and cell division.

**Butt** (bŭt), **Archibald.** 1865–1912. American army officer; served in Philippines and in Cuba during the American occupation; military aide to Presidents T. Roosevelt and Taft; lost on *Titanic* (Apr. 15, 1912). Selections from his letters published as *Letters of Archie Butt* (1924) and *Taft and Roosevelt* (1930).

**Butt,** Dame **Clara.** 1873–1936. English contralto ballad and oratorio singer; m. (1900) R. Kennerley Rumford, baritone; cycle *Sea Pictures* composed specially for her by Sir Edward Elgar (1899).

**Butt, Isaac.** 1813–1879. Irish lawyer and nationalist leader; as leader of coalition between Irish Protestants and other nationalists, inaugurated home-rule movement (1870).

**But'ter** (bŭt'ẽr), **Nathaniel.** d. 1664. English printer and journalist.

**But'ter·field** (bŭt'ẽr·fēld), **Daniel.** 1831–1901. American army officer; chief of staff, Army of the Potomac (1863) and at battle of Gettysburg, under Meade. Hooker's chief of staff at battle of Lookout Mountain. With Sherman in famous march to the sea.

**Butterfield, William.** 1814–1900. English architect.

Erected new buildings at Oxford U. and Rugby school; excelled in Gothic.

**But'ter·ick** (bŭt'ẽr·ĭk), **Ebenezer.** 1826–1903. American inventor; tailor and shirtmaker by trade; invented paper patterns (Butterick patterns) for shirts, suits, dresses, etc.

**Butt'mann** (bo͝ot'män), **Philipp Karl.** 1764–1829. German classical scholar.

**But'ton** (bŭt''n), Sir **Thomas.** d. 1634. English navigator. Sent on expedition to search for Northwest Passage; explored coasts of Hudson Bay (1612–13).

**But'trick** (bŭt'rĭk), **George Arthur.** 1892– . Clergyman, b. Northumberland, Eng.; to U.S. as a young man. Ordained in Congregational ministry (1915). Pastor, Madison Avenue Presbyterian Church, New York City (from 1927).

**Buttrick, Wallace.** 1853–1926. American Baptist clergyman, b. Potsdam, N.Y. Secretary, general education board established by John D. Rockefeller to promote education (1902–17); president of board (1917–23); chairman (1923–26).

**Butzer, Martin.** See BUCER.

**Bux·höw'den** (bo͝oks·hûv'dĕn), Count **Friedrich Wilhelm von.** 1750–1811. Russian general, b. Livonia; commanded Russian left wing at Austerlitz (1805).

**Bux'te·hu'de** (bo͝oks'tĕ·ho͞o'dĕ), **Dietrich.** 1637–1707. Swedish-born organist and composer in Germany.

**Bux'ton** (bŭks'tŭn), Sir **Thomas Fowell.** 1786–1845. English philanthropist. Accumulated fortune in brewing business. M.P. (1818–37); advocated amelioration of criminal law and prison discipline (1816–20); advocated abolition of slavery in British dominions (1822–33) and repression of African slave trade (1839–40). His third son and biographer, **Charles** (1823–1871), was advocate in parliament of church reform, disestablishment, and security of tenure in Ireland; urged clemency for mutineers after Sepoy mutiny, and opposed retributive measures against Governor Eyre of Jamaica for his conduct in the uprising of 1865. Charles's son **Sydney Charles** (1853–1934), 1st Earl **Buxton,** was undersecretary for colonies (1892–95); postmaster general (1905–10); president of Board of Trade (1910–14); largely responsible for writing and enactment of acts on copyright, unemployment insurance, pilotage, bankruptcy; governor general of South Africa (1914–20); created earl in 1920. Sir **Thomas Fowell Buxton** (1837–1915), grandson of Sir Thomas (1786–1845), was active in church missions, antislavery movement, and forest conservation; governor of South Australia (1895–98). His sons **Edward No'el-Bux'ton** [nō'ĕl-] (1869–1948), 1st Baron **Noel-Buxton** (cr. 1930), and **Charles Roden Buxton** (1875–1942) were attacked by a Turkish assassin while on mission to secure neutrality of Bulgaria (Oct., 1914); coauthors of books upon postwar problems in the Balkans and Near East. Edward was minister of agriculture and fisheries (1924, 1929–30); changed surname to Noel-Buxton (1930). Charles was principal of Morley College (1902–10), Liberal M.P. (1910), treasurer of Independent Labor party (1924–27) and author of works upon home rule, essays, and reviews.

**Bux'torf** (bo͝oks'tôrf), **Johannes,** the Elder. 1564–1629. German Protestant Hebraist; authority on rabbinical literature; author of *Lexicon Hebraicum et Chaldaicum* (1607), *Biblia Hebraica Rabbinica* (4 vols., 1618–19). His son **Johannes,** the Younger (1599–1664), also a Hebraist, completed and published his *Concordantiae Bibliorum Hebraicorum* (1639) and *Lexicon Chaldaicum, Talmudicum, et Rabbinicum* (1639).

**Bu'yids** (bo͞o'yĭdz) *or* **Bu'yides** (-yĭdz) *or* **Bu·way'hids** (bo͞o·wī'hĭdz). A Persian Shiite dynasty (932–1055) founded by the Dailamites. It seized Baghdad and controlled caliphs until overthrown by Seljuk sultans.

**Buys' Bal·lot'** (bois'bä·lŏt'), **Christoph Hendrik Didericus.** 1817–1890. Dutch meteorologist. Director, Royal Dutch Meteorological Institute, Utrecht (from 1854); advocated uniform system of meteorological observations; formulated a law (Buys Ballot's law) for determining from the direction of the wind the location of the area of lower barometric pressure; used successfully a system of storm signals.

**Buys'se** (boi'sĕ), **Cyriel.** 1859–1932. Flemish novelist, known as a realist.

**Byalik, Chaim Nachman.** See BIALIK.

**Byelinsky.** Variant of BELINSKI.

**Byeluy.** Variant of *Bely.* See Boris BUGAEV.

**By'ers** (bī'ẽrz), **William Newton.** 1831–1903. American surveyor and pioneer; b. Madison Co., Ohio; to Colorado (c. 1858); founded at Denver (1859) first newspaper in state, *Rocky Mountain News,* of which he was publisher and editor (until 1878). The mineral *byerite* is named for him.

**Byles** (bīlz), **Mather.** 1707–1788. American Congregational clergyman and writer of essays and light verse.

**Byng** of Vi'my (bĭng' ŭv vē'mĭ; *Fr.* vē'mē'), 1st Viscount. **Julian Hedworth George Byng.** 1862–1935. British military commander, 7th son of 2d earl of Strafford. Served in Boer War; made skillful withdrawal from Dardanelles (1915); commanded Canadian division at capture of Vimy Ridge (Apr., 1917); commanding third army, executed on Cambrai front surprise attack with tanks that broke Hindenburg line (Nov., 1917); governor general of Canada (1921–26); commissioner of (London) Metropolitan Police (1928–31); field marshal (1932).

**Byng** (bĭng), **Andrew.** 1574–1651. English scholar. One of the translators of the Authorized Version of the Bible.

**Byng, George.** Viscount **Tor'ring·ton** (tŏr'ĭng·tŭn). 1663–1733. British admiral, b. in Kent. Captain (1688); present at Beachy Head (1690), and, as rear admiral, at taking of Gibraltar (1704); admiral of the fleet (1718); destroyed Spanish fleet off Cape Passero (1718); first lord of Admiralty (1727–33). His fourth son, **John** (1704–1757), was in navy (from 1718); rear admiral (1745); his squadron was defeated in defending Minorca and threatened by French fleet (1756); sentenced by court martial for neglect of duty (1757) and shot.

**Byn'kers·hoek** (bĭng'kẽrs·ho͝ok), **Cornelis van.** 1673–1743. Dutch jurist; member (from 1703) and president (from 1724), Supreme Council of Holland, Zeeland, and West Friesland. Author of works on international and Roman and Dutch Civil Law.

**Byn'ner** (bĭn'ẽr), **Witter.** 1881–1968. American writer; literary editor for publishing companies (1902–15). President, Poetry Society of America (1920–22). Author of poetry, as *Grenstone Poems* (1917), *The Beloved Stranger* (1919), *Caravan* (1925), *Eden Tree* (1931), etc.; plays, *Tiger* (1913), *Iphigenia in Tauris* (1915), *Cake* (1926); translations, *A Book of Love* (1923; from French of Charles Vildrac) and *The Jade Mountain* (verse from Chinese poets of the T'ang dynasty; with Kiang Kang-hu).

**Byns, Anna.** See Anna BIJNS.

**Byr, Robert.** Pseudonym of Karl Robert Emmerich von BAYER.

**Byrd** (bûrd), **Richard E've·lyn** (ē'vĕ·lĭn). 1888–1957. American polar explorer, b. Winchester, Va., son of **Richard Evelyn** (1860–1925). Grad. U.S.N.A., Annapolis (1912); ensign, U.S. navy (1912); commander, U.S. air forces in Canada (July–Nov., 1918). In charge of aviation unit, Navy-MacMillan Polar Expedition (1925); with Floyd Bennett flew by airplane over North Pole and back to Kings Bay, Spitzbergen (1926); with three companions, made 42-hour transatlantic flight from New York to France (1927); flew over South Pole (1929); on expeditions to antarctic (1928–30; 1933–35), discovering Edsel Ford Mountains, Marie Byrd Land; rear admiral (1930) in recognition of his work of exploration. Equipped expedition to Antarctica with novel device, a monster snow cruiser (1939), recalled expedition after refusal of additional appropriation by Congress (1940); received new special award of gold star for attachment to Distinguished Service Medal (Oct., 1940). Author of *Skyward* (1928), *Little America* (1930), *Discovery* (1935), *Alone* (1938). His brother **Harry Flood** (1887–1966) was governor of Virginia (1926–30); U.S. senator (from 1933).

**Byrd** *or* **Bird** (bûrd), **William.** 1540?–1623. English organist and composer; granted, with Tallis, 21-year monopoly of issuing printed music and music paper (1575); Catholic recusant; founder of school of English madrigalists (c. 1588); composed church music.

**Byrd, William.** 1652–1704. b. London, Eng. Tobacco planter, fur trader, and merchant in Virginia; member, council of state (from 1683) and its president (1703). His son **William** (1674–1744) was also a member of council of state (from 1709) and its president (1743–44).

**Byr'gi·us** (bûr'jĭ·ŭs), **Justus.** *Lat. form of* **Joost** *or* **Jobst Bür'gi** (bür'gē). 1552–1632. Swiss mathematician; invented astronomical instruments; constructed a celestial globe; compiled a table of logarithms.

**Byrne** (bûrn), **Donn.** See Brian Oswald DONN-BYRNE.

**Byrne, James.** 1857–1942. American lawyer and educator; practiced law in New York (from 1883). Regent, U. of the State of New York (1916–37), and chancellor (1933–37).

**Byrnes** (bûrnz), **James Francis.** 1879–1972. American jurist, b. Charleston, S.C.; admitted to bar (1903); member U.S. House of Representatives (1911–25); U.S. senator from S.C. (1931–41); associate justice, U.S. Supreme Court (1941–42); director of economic stabilization (1942–43), of war mobilization (1943–45); secretary of state (1945–47). Governor of S.C. (1951–55).

**Byrns** (bûrnz), **Joseph W.** 1869–1936. American lawyer and politician, b. Cedar Hill, Tenn. Practiced law at Nashville (from 1891). Member, U.S. House of Representatives (1909–36), majority leader (1933–35), speaker (1935–36).

**By'rom** (bī'rŭm), **John.** 1692–1763. English poet, hymnologist, and inventor of a shorthand system (copyrighted 1742). His collected poems published (1773) and diary (1854–57); author of phrase "tweedledum and tweedledee," and of hymn *Christians, awake, salute the happy morn.*

**By'ron** (bī'rŭn), **George Gordon.** 6th Baron **Byron.** 1788–1824. English poet, b. London, son of **John,** a libertine, and Catherine Gordon, a Scottish heiress; and grandson of John (1723–1786; *q.v.*); lived with mother at Aberdeen until on the death of his great uncle (1798) he succeeded to barony created for an ancestor John (d. 1652; *q.v.*); educ. Harrow and Trinity College, Cambridge, where he published (1807) volume of poems, *Hours of Idleness,* which was fiercely assailed by *Edinburgh Review;* replied in witty satirical poem *English Bards and Scotch Reviewers* (1809). Traveled in Portugal, Spain, Greece, Turkey, swimming the Hellespont (May 3, 1810); addressed *Maid of Athens* to Theresa Macri, his hostess's daughter; spoke twice in House of Lords (1812); sprang into fame with publication of first two cantos of *Childe Harold's Pilgrimage,* a narrative poem of travels through southern Europe by an imaginary pilgrim (1812); published (1813–14) Turkish tales in verse *The Giaour, The Bride of Abydos, The Corsair, Lara,* which were as popular as *Childe Harold.* m. (Jan., 1815) **Anne Isabella Mil'banke** [mĭl'băngk] (1792–1860), a mathematician and heiress who gave birth (1815) to Augusta Ada, returned to her father's protection (Jan., 1816), and became Baroness Wentworth (1856). Signed deed of separation from wife and left England (1816), never to return; traveled in Switzerland with Shelley; wrote *Childe Harold,* canto iii (1816) and *The Prisoner of Chillon* (1816); lived at or near Venice (1816–19); had a child, Allegra, by Jane Clairmont (1817); finished canto iv of *Childe Harold* (related in the first person) and began (1818) *Don Juan,* a satirical epic poem narrating adventures of a handsome libertine. Took Teresa, Countess Guiccioli, from her husband (1819); composed historical dramas *Marino Faliero, Sardanapalus, The Two Foscari,* and *Cain, a Mystery* (1821). Joined Leigh Hunt in *The Liberal* magazine (1822), in which he took revenge upon Southey with *The Vision of Judgment;* was present at the cremation of Shelley (1822); in the *Prophecy of Dante* (1821) denounced tyranny and spoke out as champion of liberty for oppressed in Italy. Adapted a German tale as *Werner* (1822), a successful play with Macready in leading part; after death of daughter Allegra composed his last play *The Deformed Transformed* (1824); after completing *The Island* (1823), based on Bligh's account of mutiny on the *Bounty,* continued *Don Juan;* accepted invitation of Prince Mavrokordatos to join Greek insurgents in struggle for independence, enlisted a regiment, advanced large sums; died at Missolonghi of malaria. Took additional name Noel (1815), adopted it (1822) as prerequisite to reception of inheritance from wife's relative Lady Noel.

**Byron, Henry James.** 1834–1884. English playwright; author of *Our Boys* (played Jan., 1875 to Apr., 1879) and *The Upper Crust,* and of one novel, many farces, burlesques, pantomimes, etc.

**Byron, John.** 1st Baron **Byron.** 1600?–1652. English Cavalier commander in many battles of Civil War.

**Byron, John.** 1723–1786. English navigator. Called "Foul-weather Jack." Grandfather of the poet Byron. As midshipman with Anson, shipwrecked on Chile coast (1741); his account of this shipwreck used by Lord Byron in *Don Juan;* commanded exploratory voyage round the world (1764–66); governor of Newfoundland (1769–72); rear admiral (1775); worsted off Grenada (1779).

**Byron, Robert.** 1905–1941. English scholar; author of *Europe in the Looking Glass* (1927), *The Byzantine Achievement* (1929), *The Birth of Western Painting* (1930), *First Russia, then Tibet* (1933), *The Road to Oxiana* (1937).

**By'ström** (bü'strûm), **Johan Niklas.** 1783–1848. Swedish sculptor.

**By'wa'ter** (bī'wô'tẽr; -wŏt'ẽr), **Hector Charles.** 1884–1940. British journalist and naval authority; engaged in intelligence work in World War I (1914–18). Naval correspondent, London *Daily News* and *Observer* (1923–28), and European naval correspondent, Baltimore *Sun* (1921–30). Author of *Sea Power in the Pacific* (1921), *Navies and Nations* (1927), and *Cruisers in Battle* (1939).

**Bywater, Ingram.** 1840–1914. English classical scholar; regius professor of Greek, Oxford (1893–1908).

**Byzantinus, Josephus.** = Josephus GENESIUS.

# C

**Ca'a·ma'ño** (kä'ä·mä'nyō), **José María Plácido.** 1838–1901. Ecuadorian political leader, b. Guayaquil. Banished (1882) for conspiring against dictator Veintemilla; led expedition against Guayaquil (1883) and drove out Veintemilla. Provisional president of Ecuador (1883–84), president (1884–88); minister to Washington (1889–90); lived in Spain (1895–1901).

**Ca'bal·le'ro** (kä'bä·yā'rō), **Bernardino.** 1831–1885. Paraguayan general and political leader, b. in Brazil. Active in war against Argentina, Brazil, and Uruguay (1865–70); taken prisoner (1870); minister of war; acting president of Paraguay after death of Barreiro (1880–82); president (1882–85; died in office).

**Ca'bal·le'ro** (kä'bä·lyā'rō), **Fernán.** *Pseudonym of* **Ce·ci'li·a Fran·cis'ca Jo·se'fa de Ar·rom'** (thā·thē'lyä frän·thēs'kä hō·sā'fä thā är·rōn'), *nee* **Böhl von Fa'ber** (bûl' fōn fä'bẽr). 1797?–1877. Spanish novelist, b. Morges, Switzerland, of German and Spanish parentage; educ. Germany (1805–13); to Cádiz (1813); m. (1) Antonio Planells y Bardaxi (d. 1817), (2) Francisco Ruiz del Arco (d. 1833), (3) Antonio de Arrom, or Arrón, de Ayala (d. about 1859). Considered founder of modern novel in Spain and, more specifically, of local-color novel; made first collection of Spanish popular tales and poems, *Cuentos y Poesías Populares Andaluces* (1859, 1877). Author of novels, some written originally in French or German, *La Gaviota* (1849), *La Familia Albareda* (1880), *Clemencia* (1887), and *Elia;* collections of short stories, as *Cuadros de Costumbres* and *Relaciones; Epistolario,* letters (pub. 1922). Her father, **Johann Nikolaus Böhl von Faber** (1770–1836), scholar and businessman, b. Hamburg, published *Floresta de Rimas Antiguas Castellanas* (3 vols., 1821–25) and *Teatro Español anterior a Lope de Vega* (1832).

**Caballero, Francisco Largo.** See LARGO CABALLERO.

**Ca'bal·le'ro y Fer·nán'dez de Ro'das** (ē fĕr·nän'-däth thā rō'thäs), **Antonio.** 1816–1876. Spanish soldier; fought in Carlist wars, in national revolution (1868), and battle of Alcolea; governor of Cuba (1869–70).

**Ca'bal·le'ro y Las'tres** (kä'bä·yā'rō ē läs'trās), **Ernesto.** 1872– . Peruvian naval officer, b. Lima; supervised construction in France of first South American submarines (1909); rear admiral (1930); naval attaché in U.S., Italy, Greece, Spain.

**Ca'ba'nel'** (kȧ'bȧ'nĕl'), **Alexandre.** 1823–1889. French painter; studied under Picot; professor at École des Beaux-Arts (Paris); known as historical, genre, and portrait painter. His works include *La Naissance de Vénus, Le Repos de Ruth, Françoise de Rimini* (in Amiens museum), *Christ au Jardin des Oliviers* (in Valenciennes museum).

**Ca'ba'nis'** (kȧ'bȧ'nēs'), **Pierre Jean Georges.** 1757–1808. French physician and philosopher. Administrator of hospitals in Paris; professor of hygiene (1795), later of legal medicine and history of medicine (1799), Medical School of Paris; sympathizer with Revolutionists; physician to Mirabeau; member of Council of Five Hundred; senator. Disciple of philosopher Condillac, the scope of whose work he extended; regarded the soul as a faculty, not an entity; often called founder of modern physiological psychology; changed from a materialistic to a vitalistic point of view. Author of *Traité du Physique et du Moral de l'Homme* (1802).

**Ca'bar·rús'** (kä'bär·rōōs'), Conde **Francisco de.** 1752–1810. Spanish financier, of French ancestry; represented Spain at Congress of Rastatt (1797); developed trade with Philippines; served as minister of finance under Ferdinand VII and Joseph Bonaparte. See Jeanne M. I. T. TALLIEN.

**Cab'ell** (kăb'ĕl), **James Branch.** 1879–1958. American novelist and essayist, b. Richmond, Va. A.B., William and Mary (1898). Journalist with New York *Herald* (1899–1901) and Richmond *News* (1901); editor, *The American Spectator* (1932–35). Contributor to magazines (from 1902); first came to notice with the novel *Jurgen* (1919), attacked for immorality and temporarily suppressed. Many of his novels have their scenes laid in the imaginary country of Poictesme, esp. a series referred to as the "Biography of Manuel," purporting to trace lineage of its nobility from Dom Manuel, Count of Poictesme, to his Virginia descendants. Among his works are *The Eagle's Shadow* (1904), *The Line of Love* (1905), *Gallantry* (1907), *Chivalry* (1909), *The Cords of Vanity* (1909), *The Soul of Melicent* (1913; reissued 1920 as *Domnei*), *The Rivet in Grandfather's Neck* (1915), *The Certain Hour* (1916), *Jurgen* (1919), *Figures of Earth* (1921), *The High Place* (1923), *The Music from behind the Moon* (1926), *The Silver Stallion* (1926), *Townsend of Lichfield* (1930), *These Restless Heads* (1932), *Smirt* (1934), *Ladies and Gentlemen* (1934), *Smith* (1935), *Preface to the Past* (1936), *Smire* (1937), *The King Was in His Counting House* (1938), *The First Gentleman of America* (1942), etc.

**Ca·be'ro Dí'az** (kä·bā'rō thē'äs), **Alberto.** 1874– . Chilean lawyer and diplomat, b. Santiago. Senator (from 1925); president of senate (1932); minister of national defense (1938); ambassador to U.S. (from 1939).

**Ca'bes'taing'** (kȧ'bĕs'tä'ny') *or* **Ca'bes'tan'** (-täɴ') *or* **Ca'bes'tant'** (-täɴ'), **Guillaume de.** Late 12th-century Provençal troubadour, author of a number of love lyrics. According to legend, he loved Marguerite, wife of Raymond of Château Roussillon, and was therefore slain by Raymond, his heart torn from his body, cooked, and served to Marguerite, who, having learned what she had eaten, committed suicide by starvation, declaring that since she had eaten such noble food her lips should touch no other.

**Ca'bet'** (kȧ'bĕ'), **Étienne.** 1788–1856. Political radical, b. Dijon, France. Involved in revolution of 1830; exiled for radical articles (1834–39). Influenced by Robert Owen, led a group to Nauvoo, Ill. (1849), to found a utopian community, called Icaria; its president (1849–56); became American citizen (1854); withdrew from community after dissension (1856).

**Ca·be'za de Va'ca** (kä·bā'thä thā vä'kä), **Álvar Núñez.** 1490?–?1557. Spanish colonial official and explorer, b. Jerez de la Frontera. Soldier in campaigns in Italy, Spain, and Navarre (1511–26). Treasurer of expedition of Narváez (1527–28); wrecked on island on Texas coast and imprisoned by Indians (1528); escaped and finally reached Mexico City via northern Mexico (1530–36); returned to Spain (1537). Led expedition to Río de la Plata region, across southern Brazil 1000 miles to Asunción (1541–42). Colonial governor in Paraguay (1542–44); deposed and sent to Spain (1544–45); imprisoned (1551–56). His reports of Narváez expedition led directly to expeditions of Niza (1539) and Coronado (1540–42).

**Ca'ble** (kā'b'l), **George Washington.** 1844–1925. American author, b. New Orleans, La. Served in Confederate army; self-educated; clerk in New Orleans business house (1869–79). After success of first book, *Old Creole Days* (1879), made writing his profession; other works include *The Grandissimes* (1884), *The Creoles of Louisi-*

*ana* (1884), *Dr. Sevier* (1885), *Bonaventure* (1888), *Strange True Stories of Louisiana* (1889), *The Cavalier* (1901), *The Flower of the Chapdelaines* (1918).

**Cab′ot** (kăb′ŭt), **George.** 1752–1823. American businessman and politician, b. Salem, Mass. Educ. Harvard (1766–68); in shipping business (1768–95); U.S. senator (1791–96); leading member of federalist group called the Essex Junto.

**Cabot, John.** *Ital.* **Giovanni Ca·bo′to** (kä·bō′tō). 1450–1498. Italian navigator and explorer, b. Genoa. Naturalized citizen of Venice (1476); visited Mecca; moved to England (c. 1484); sailed from Bristol (1497) in the *Mathew*, under patent from Henry VII, in search of route to Asia; landed after 52 days on Cape Breton Island; made second voyage (1498), explored east and west coasts of Greenland, reached Baffin Land and Newfoundland, explored coast south to 38th parallel.

His son **Sebastian** (1476?–1557), b. Venice, made map of Gascony and Guienne for Henry VIII of England (1512); map maker to Ferdinand the Catholic (1512–16); prepared to sail on voyage of discovery, which was canceled (1517); pilot major to Emperor Charles V (1519–26, 1533–44); commander of Venetian expedition from Seville in search of Tarshish and Ophir, which explored the La Plata (1526–30); published engraved map of world (1544); granted pension by Edward VI (1549); restricted privileges of German Hanseatic merchants of the Steelyard (1551); founded, and made governor of, company of Merchant Adventurers of London (1551), which sent expeditions (1553, 1555–56) to search for northeast passage to the east, effecting trade with Russia as result.

**Cabot, Richard Clarke.** 1868–1939. American physician, b. Brookline, Mass. A.B. (1889), M.D. (1892), Harvard. With Mass. General Hospital (from 1898), chief of medical staff (1912–21); teacher (from 1903), professor of clinical medicine (1919–33), Harvard Medical School; professor of social ethics, Harvard (1920–34). Author of *Clinical Examination of the Blood* (1896), *Physical Diagnosis* (1901), *Social Service and the Art of Healing* (1909), *Differential Diagnosis* (2 vols., 1911–15), *What Men Live By* (1914), *Social Work* (1919), *Facts on the Heart* (1926), *The Meaning of Right and Wrong* (1933), *Christianity and Sex* (1937), etc.

**Ca·bral′** (kȧ·bräl′), **Pedro Álvares.** 1460?–?1526. Portuguese navigator. After da Gama's return, sent by King Emanuel I of Portugal in command of fleet of 13 vessels to establish trade with East Indies (1500–01). For some unknown reason, took westward course; carried by wind and current to coast of Brazil (Apr. 22, 1500) and took possession of it in name of Portugal. Continued voyage to East; lost four ships in storm off Cape of Good Hope; reached Calicut, India; established trading post there. Nothing known of him after his return.

**Ca·bre′ra** (kä·brā′rä), **Luis.** 1876–1954. Mexican lawyer, b. Zacatlán. Professor of Civil law (1907–08) and director (1912), National School of Jurisprudence, Mexico City; deputy (1912, 1917); secretary of finance (1914–17, 1919–20); member, Mexican-American Mixed Claims Commission (1916–17); in law practice, Mexico City (from 1920). Author of *El Cantar de los Cantares* (1919), *Obras Políticas* (1920), *La Herencia de Carranza* (1920), *Musa Peregrina* (1929), *El Balance de la Revolución* (1931), *Veinte Años Después* (1937), etc.

**Cabrera, Manuel Estrada.** See ESTRADA CABRERA.

**Cabrera, Ramón.** Conde **de Mo·rel′la** (mō·rā′lyä). 1806–1877. Spanish Carlist general, noted for his cruelty; commander of Carlist troops (1833–40, 1848–49); defeated; retired to France.

**Cabrera Bobadilla Cerda y Mendoza.** See Conde de CHINCHÓN.

**Ca·bril′lo** (kä·brē′(l)yō), **Juan** (hwän) **Ro·drí′guez** (rō·thrē′gāth; -gās). d. 1543. Explorer in America, b. in Portugal. To Mexico with Narváez (1520); with Cortes at capture of Mexico City (1521). Made explorations on west coast of Mexico, northward to San Diego Bay, Santa Catalina Island, Santa Barbara Channel.

**Ca·bri′ni** (kȧ·brē′nē), Saint **Frances Xavier.** *Known as* **Mother Cabrini.** 1850–1917. Roman Catholic Saint, b. Italy. Founded Missionary Sisters of the Sacred Heart (1880). To U.S. (1889); naturalized (1909). Canonized (1946), becoming first American saint.

**Cac·ci′ni** (kät·chē′nē), **Giulio.** *Called also* **Giulio Ro·ma′no** (rō·mä′nō). 1550?–1618. Italian singer and composer, b. Rome; pioneer in monody, dramatic recitative, and operatic style. Settled in Florence (1564) and entered service of grand duke of Tuscany. His works include the musical dramas *The Rape of Cephalus* (1597), and *Euridice* (1600, later than the *Euridice* of Jacopo Peri, *q.v.*), the collection of canzonets and madrigals for one voice with basso continuo *Nuove Musiche* (1602; new series, 1614), etc.

**Cá′ce·res** (kä′sȧ·rās), **Andrés Avelino.** 1836–?1923. Peruvian general, political leader, and diplomat, b. Ayacucho. Military attaché at Peruvian legation in Paris (1857–60); fought in War of the Pacific (1879–83); general; after capture of Lima by Chileans, head of provisional government (1883); led Peruvians who refused to accept Treaty of Ancón (1884) and overcame President Iglesias, whom Chileans supported in civil war (1885–86); president of Peru (1886–90); minister to France and Great Britain (1890–94); again president (1894–95), but defeated by party of Piérola; left Peru (1895), returned (1903); minister to Italy (1905–11).

**Cáceres, Zoila Aurora.** 1877– . Peruvian writer, b. Lima; daughter of Andrés Avelino Cáceres, former president of Peru; educ. Sorbonne, Paris; lectured at Sorbonne (1908), U. of San Marcos, Lima (1911), Athenaeum, Madrid (1921), and National Inst. of Panama (1925). Author of *Mujeres de Ayer y de Hoy* (1910), *España en la Poesía del Perú* (1913), *Ignacio Merino Pintor Peruano* (1919), *La Ciudad del Sol* (1927), *La Princesa Sumática* (1929), *Mi Vida con Gomes Carrillo*, and *El Arte Pictórico en el Perú.*

**Ca′chin′** (kȧ′shăN′), **Marcel.** 1869–1958. French Socialist political leader.

**Ca·dal′so y Váz′quez** (kä·thäl′sō ē väth′kāth), **José de.** 1741–1782. Spanish writer, b. Cádiz; educ. Paris; traveled in England, Germany, and Italy; entered Spanish army; promoted colonel; founded school of poets at Salamanca. Author of *Sancho García, Conde de Castilla* (tragedy; 1771), *Eruditos a la Violeta* (satire; 1772), and verse, including *Noches Lúgubres* (1773) and *Cartas Marruecas* (1793).

**Ca′ Da Mo′sto** *or* **Ca′da Mo′sto** *or* **Ca′da·mo′sto** (kä′dä·mōs′tō), **Alvise** (*or* **Luigi**) **da.** 1432?–?1511. Venetian navigator and explorer; explored west coast of Africa under commission from Prince Henry of Portugal (1455–56); discovered Cape Verde Islands (1456). Author of *Il Libro della Prima Navigazione per Oceano alle Terre de' Negri della Bassa Etiopia* (1507).

**Cad′bur·y** (kăd′bĕr·ĭ; -brĭ; -bĕr′ĭ), **George.** 1839–1922. English industrialist and social reformer, b. Birmingham. Son of **John** (1801–1889; founder of Cadbury Brothers, cocoa and chocolate manufacturers); entered father's business (1856); with his brother **Richard** (d. 1899) took over management (1861); promoted welfare, educational work, and improved housing for employees. His wife (m. 1888), **Elizabeth Mary,** *nee* **Taylor** (1858–1935), was a social worker and philanthropist.

**Cade** (kād), **John,** *known as* **Jack.** d. 1450. English rebel leader. Landed proprietor claiming name Mortimer, possibly a relation of duke of York; asserted by government after his death to have been Irishman banished for murder (1449) and to have served in French wars under name of Aylmer. Leader of Kentish rebellion (May–July, 1450) in protest against court corruption, maladministration, oppressive taxation; defeated Henry VI's forces at Sevenoaks (June 18); entered London (July 3); forced lord mayor and judges to condemn to death Lord Saye-and-Sele and William Crowmer, sheriff of Kent, hated instrument of oppressive taxation; refused readmission to city on exaction of forced contributions; repulsed at London Bridge; hunted down after dispersion of army under amnesty and killed at Heathfield (July 12).

**Cad′ell** (kăd′'l), **Francis**. 1822–1879. Scottish explorer in Australia. Served East India Company and in Opium War (1840–41); explored Murray River and tributaries in Australia (1848–59); murdered by his crew.

**Cadell, Robert**. 1788–1849. Scottish publisher; partner (1811–26) in Edinburgh house of Constable & Co.; after its failure, dissolved partnership and began business again alone; realized fortune by several editions of Scott's works.

**Ca·de′ras** (kä·dā′räs), **Gian** (jän) **Fa·dri′** (fä·drē′). 1830–1891. Rhaeto-Romanic lyric poet; published *Rimas* (1865), *Nuovas Rimas* (1879), *Fluors Alpinas* (1883), *Sorrirs e Larmas* (1887); also wrote comedies, *Il Farmacist* (1864) and *Patüfla* (1866).

**Cad′il·lac** (kăd′'l·ăk; *Fr.* kȧ′dē′yȧk′), Sieur **Antoine de la Mothe** (dē lȧ mȯt′). 1658–1730. French administrator in America, b. in Gascony, France. Officer in French army. To America (1683); in command of post at Mackinac (1694); obtained grant of land at what is now Detroit; settled large French colony on site (1701); recalled (1711). Governor of Louisiana (1713–16). Lived in Gascony (after 1717).

**Cad′man** (kăd′măn), **Charles Wakefield**. 1881–1946. American composer, b. Johnstown, Pa. Music critic, Pittsburgh *Dispatch;* organist in Pittsburgh churches, and for Pittsburgh Male Chorus. Made special study of North American Indian songs and flute pieces; on basis of this study, wrote a number of popular Indian songs and several Indian operas (*The Land of the Misty Water, The Garden of Death, Shanewis*). Also composed a cantata (*The Vision of Sir Launfal*), song cycles (*White Enchantment, The Morning of the Year*), suites for orchestra, piano, stringed instruments, operettas, and grand operas (*Garden of Mystery, A Witch of Salem*).

**Cadman, Samuel Parkes**. 1864–1936. Congregational clergyman, b. Wellington, Eng. Educ. Wesleyan Coll., in Richmond, Surrey. To U.S. (1890); pastor of Metropolitan Temple, New York City (1895–1901) and Central Congregational Church, Brooklyn (1901–36). President (1924–28), and radio minister (1928–36), Federal Council of Churches of Christ in America; first radio preacher. Author of *The Victory of Christmas* (1909), *Charles Darwin and Other English Thinkers* (1911), *William Owen...*(1912), *Ambassadors of God* (1920), *Christianity and the State* (1924), *Imagination and Religion* (1926), *Every Day Questions and Answers* (1930), *The Pursuit of Happiness* (1935), etc.

**Cad′mus** (kăd′mŭs), **Paul**. 1904– . American painter, b. New York City. Studied at National Academy of Design and Art Students' League, New York; worked three years as commercial artist; spent two years in Europe (1931–33). His paintings include *The Fleet's In, Greenwich Village Cafeteria, Coney Island.*

**Ca·dog′an** (kȧ·dŭg′ăn), **William**. 1st Earl **Cadogan**. 1675–1726. Irish soldier and diplomat. As quartermaster general to Marlborough (1701–11), organized march of allies to Danube, acted as chief of staff at Blenheim, commanded advance guard in victory of Oudenarde, was dangerously wounded at Mons. Under Jacobite party, lost rank and emoluments (1712); restored to lieutenant generalship (1714); lieutenant of ordnance (1714–18); as plenipotentiary signed third Barrier Treaty between Great Britain, Holland, and the emperor (1715); waged last campaign against Jacobite insurrection (1715–16), restored order in Scotland; general (1717); negotiated Quadruple Alliance (1720); commander in chief (1722). His brother **Charles** (1691–1776), 2d Baron Cadogan, served in Marlborough's later campaigns and in Scotland (1715); general (1761). A descendant, **George Henry Cadogan** (1840–1915), 5th earl, grandnephew of 1st duke of Wellington, was undersecretary of state for war (1875), for colonies (1878), lord privy seal (1886–92), lord lieutenant of Ireland (1895–1902).

**Cadore**, Duc **de**. See Jean Baptiste Nompère de CHAMPAGNY.

**Ca·dor′na** (kä·dōr′nä), Conte **Carlo**. 1809–1891. Italian statesman and lawyer. Supporter of Gioberti; deputy (1848 ff.); president, chamber of deputies (1850–55); senator (1858 ff.); minister of education (1848–49, 1858–59); prefect of Turin (1864); minister of interior (1868); ambassador to London (1869); president, council of state (1875). Author of *La Politica di Cavour nelle Relazioni fra la Chiesa e lo Stato* (1882), *Dell'Espansione Coloniale dell'Italia* (1885).

His brother **Raffaele** (1815–1897), general, took part in national movements (1848, 1859, 1866) and in Crimean War (1854–56); deputy in Sardinian parliament (1848 ff.); minister of war, Tuscany (1859); crushed insurrection in Sicily as military commandant (1866); captured and occupied Rome (Sept. 20, 1870); senator (1871 ff.); commanding general in Turin (1873–77). Author of *La Liberazione di Roma nel 1870* (1889).

Raffaele's son Conte **Luigi** (1850–1928), soldier; on general staff (1896); commander, 7th army corps, Genoa (1910); chief of general staff (1914 ff.); commander in chief of Italian armies (1915–17); conducted operations on the Isonzo; captured Gorizia; succeeded in chief command by Diaz after Italian retreat (Nov., 1917); member, supreme war council of Allies; created marshal of Italy by Mussolini (1923). Author of *Il Generale Raffaele Cadorna nel Risorgimento Italiano* (1903), *La Guerra alla Fronte Italiana* (2 vols., 1921).

**Ca′dou′dal′** (kȧ′do͞o′dȧl′), **Georges**. 1771–1804. French royalist conspirator; leader of Chouan uprising (1799); implicated in plot formed by Pichegru and Moreau (1803); guillotined (June 25, 1804).

**Cad·wal′a·der** (kăd·wŏl′ȧ·dēr). d. 634. See CAEDWALLA.

**Cadwalader, John**. 1742–1786. American Revolutionary officer, b. Philadelphia. Brigadier general of Pennsylvania militia (Apr., 1777); engaged at Princeton, Brandywine, and Germantown. Supported Washington in winter of 1777–78; challenged General Conway to duel on charge that Conway was undermining Washington's authority; severely wounded Conway, who later confessed to his intrigue (Conway Cabal) and left the army. His father, **Thomas** (1708?–1799), was a Philadelphia physician and surgeon.

**Cad·wal′a·dr** (kăd·wŏl′ȧ·dēr). d. 1172. Welsh prince; son of Gruffydd, King of Gwynedd (North Wales). Expelled by Owain Gwynedd, his elder brother; fled to Ireland; returned with army of Irish Danes, who blinded him in pique when he became reconciled to Owain Gwynedd without fighting; after further strife, fled to

England; restored to his lands (1159) by Henry II.

**Cadwallon.** See CAEDWALLA.

**Ca'dy** (kā'dĭ), **Hamilton Perkins.** 1874–1943. American chemist, b. Morris Co., Kans. A.B. (1897), Ph.D. (1903), Kansas; professor, Kansas (from 1911). Authority on helium and other rare gases in natural gas.

**Cae·cil'i·us** (sē·sĭl'ĭ·ŭs; -sĭl'yŭs). Greek scholar of early 1st century A.D., from Calacte, in Sicily. Only fragments of his works are extant, including *On the Style of the Ten Orators*, *History of the Servile Wars*, *On Rhetoric*.

**Cae·cil'i·us Sta'ti·us** (stā'shĭ·ŭs; -shŭs) *or* **Statius Caecilius.** 219?–?166 B.C. Roman comedist; b. in Gaul, taken to Rome as a slave. His plays, extant only in fragments, were adapted from Greek playwrights, esp. Menander.

**Cae·ci'na** (sē·sī'nȧ). *In full* **Aulus Caecina A'li·e'nus** (ā'lĭ·ē'nŭs; ăl'ĭ-). Roman general in Spain. After death of Nero (68 A.D.), supported Galba, and later Vitellius; commanded part of army of Vitellius in campaign in Italy; when confronted with Vespasian's army, turned traitor and attempted unsuccessfully to induce his contingents to desert to Vespasian. Involved in plot against Vespasian (79 A.D.); executed by Titus.

**Caed'mon** (kăd'mŭn). fl. 670. Earliest English Christian poet. A herdsman who, according to Bede, received divine call in a dream to sing of "the beginning of created things," which he obeyed in the dream and afterwards from memory wrote in verses previously unknown; composed additional verses and put into verse Scriptural passages translated for him; accepted by Abbess Hilda as inmate of monastery at Whitby, where he continued to write poetry on sacred themes; generally recognized as a saint. Probably author of only part of so-called Caedmon poems, paraphrases of parts of *Genesis*, *Exodus*, *Daniel*, and poems on lamentations of fallen angels, descent into hell, the temptation; accepted author of nine-line *Hymn*, supposed to be his first song, preserved in Northumbrian version of Bede's Latin paraphrase.

**Caed·wal'la** (kăd·wŏl'ȧ) *or* **Cad·wal'a·der** (kăd·wŏl'ȧ·dẽr) *or* **Cad·wal'lon** (kăd·wŏl'ŭn). d. 634. King of Gwynedd (North Wales). Allied with Penda of Mercia, defeated Northumbrians near Doncaster and killed Edwin (633); defeated and killed by Oswald, Edwin's nephew.

**Cae'li·us Au·re'li·a'nus** (sē'lĭ·ŭs ô·rē'lĭ·ā'nŭs). Physician of 5th century A.D. (or earlier) in Numidia, orig. from Rome; author of treatises on chronic and acute diseases, largely translated from works by Soranus of Ephesus.

**Caelius Ru'fus** (rōō'fŭs), **Marcus.** d. 48 B.C. Roman politician; tribune (52 B.C.); aedile (50); friend and correspondent of Cicero, a number of his letters being preserved. Supported Caesar against Pompey; made praetor (48). Embittered by failure to receive higher honors, attempted to organize revolt; killed by some of soldiers he tried to bribe. Defended by Cicero (in oration *Pro Caelio*) against charge of attempted poisoning brought by Catullus's mistress.

**Cae'pi·o** (sē'pĭ·ō), **Quintus Servilius.** Roman general. Consul (106 B.C.); governor in Gaul (105); defeated by the Cimbri; deprived of office and property; expelled from Roman Senate; convicted of misconduct and imprisoned.

**Cae'ru·lar'i·us** *or* **Ce'ru·lar'i·us** (sẹ̄r'ōō·lâr'ĭ·ŭs; sẽr'-; -ū·lâr'-), **Michael.** Patriarch of Constantinople (1043–59) through imperial favor; revived and brought to completion (1054) schism between Greek and Roman church prepared by Photius; excommunicated by Leo IX (1054); banished by Isaac I (1059); died in exile.

**Caesalpinus, Andreas.** See Andrea CESALPINO.

**Cae'sar** (sē'zẽr), **Gaius Julius.** 100 B.C.–44 B.C. Roman general and statesman. m. (83 B.C.) Cornelia (d. 67?), daughter of Lucius Cinna, head of popular party in Rome; identified himself with popular party and became chief rival of Sulla, head of oligarchic party. Quaestor (68 B.C.); curule aedile (65); pontifex maximus (63); praetor (62); propraetor in Spain (61); m. Pompeia, a relative of Pompey. Succeeded in reconciling the two influential statesmen in Rome, Pompey and Crassus, and with them formed an alliance (First Triumvirate, 60); elected consul (59) and proconsul in Gaul and Illyricum (58); m. (59) Calpurnia. Made military reputation in Gaul, defeating the Helvetii and Ariovistus (58) and the Belgi (57), invading Britain (55, 54), crossing Rhine (55, 53), and subduing revolt under Vercingetorix (52). When senate, induced by Pompey, voted that he should disband his army by a given date or be regarded as an enemy to the state, led army across the Rubicon (49), small river that separated his province from Italy, and moved against Pompey in Rome, beginning actual fighting of civil war; quickly mastered all Italy; pursued Pompey to Thessaly and decisively defeated him at Pharsalus (48). Roman dictator (from 49); aided Cleopatra (49) and brought her to Rome; defeated Pharnaces at Zela (47) and remnants of Pompey's forces at Thapsus (46) and Munda (45). Offered the crown (Feb. 15, 44), but refused it. Murdered by group of nobles, including Brutus and Cassius, in senate building on ides of March (Mar. 15, 44). Renowned also as orator and writer; his works on the Gallic wars, *Commentaries* (*De bello Gallico*) and civil war (*De bello civili*) regarded as models of clear, concise, and vigorous historical composition. While head of Roman state, effected many reforms, including reform of the calendar (Julian calendar; introduced 46 B.C.); prevented by death from completing other reforms he planned, including codifying the law, draining Pontine marshes, enlarging harbor at Ostia, building canal through Isthmus of Corinth.

**Caesar, Irving.** 1895– . American lyricist and librettist, b. New York City. Author of popular songs and of lyrics for George White's *Scandals* (1929, 1931), and for musical comedies *No, No, Nanette*, *Sweetheart Time*, *No Foolin'*, *Transatlantic Rhythm*, etc.

**Caesar,** Sir **Julius.** 1558–1636. English judge and philanthropist; son of Adelmare Caesar (orig. Cesare Adelmare), a medical adviser to Queens Mary Tudor and Elizabeth, descended from Italian dukes de' Cesarini; M.A., Oxon. (1578); judge of admiralty (1584); chancellor of exchequer (1606); master of rolls (1614–36).

**Cae·sar'i·us of Arles** (sē·zâr'ĭ·ŭs, ärl), Saint. 470?–543. Bishop of Arles (502–542), b. near Cabillonum (Chalon-sur-Saône) of a noble Roman family. Took habit at Lérins (489); bishop of Arles (502); obtained pallium from Pope Symmachus and became apostolic vicar of Gaul and Spain; presided over councils of Agde (506), Arles (524), Carpentras (527), Vaison and Orange (529), the last of which defended Augustinian doctrines against Semi-Pelagianism; introduced many ecclesiastical reforms and founded several monasteries, including one for his sister Caesaria.

**Caesarius of Hei'ster·bach** (hī'stẽr·bäĸ). 1180?–?1240). Cistercian monk of Cologne; author (in Latin) of works on history of Cologne, as *Catalogus Archiepiscoporum Coloniensium* (pub. 1879) and a biography of Archbishop Engelbert of Cologne (pub. 1843), collections of miscellaneous stories, as *Dialogus Miraculorum* (pub. 1851) and *VIII Libri Miraculorum* (3 books, pub. 1901). etc.

**Ca'e·ta'ni** (kä'ȧ·tä'nē) *or* **Ga'e·ta'ni** (gä'-). Italian noble family, prominent since election (1294) of **Benedetto Caetani** to papacy (see BONIFACE VIII). One branch, holding title of duke of **Ser'mo·ne'ta** (sār'-mō·nā'tä), includes: **Guglielmo**, who received the duchy from Pope Pius III (1503); **Francesco**, 7th duke, who acquired by marriage the county of Caserta (1642); **Michelangelo** (1804–1882), duke, Italian patriot, and student of Dante; his son **Onorato** (1842–1917), Italian senator and for a short period minister of foreign affairs; Onorato's sons **Leone** (1869–1935), duke, a student of Islam, and **Gelasio** (1877–1934), an Italian ambassador to U.S. Another branch acquired title duke of **Lau'ren·za'na** (lou'rān·tsä'nä), by marriage (1606).

**Caf'fa·rel'li** (käf'fä·rĕl'lē). *Stage name of* **Gaetano Ma'jo·ra'no** (mä'yō·rä'nō). 1703–1783. Italian singer.

**Caf'fa'rel'li'** (kȧ'fȧ'rĕ'lē'). French family of Italian origin, including the four brothers: **Louis Marie Joseph Maximilien** (1756–1799), general under Napoleon; **Charles Ambroise** (1758–1826), a prefect under Napoleonic regime; **Louis Marie Joseph** (1760–1845), Comte de Caffarelli, councilor of state under Napoleon; **François Marie Auguste** (1766–1849), general under Napoleon.

**Caf'fery** (kăf'rĭ; -ēr·ĭ), **Jefferson.** 1886–1974. American diplomat, b. Lafayette, La.; entered diplomatic service 1911; U.S. ambassador to Cuba (1934–37), Brazil (1937–44), France (1944–49), Egypt (1949–55).

**Caf'fi** (käf'fē), **Ippolito.** 1809–1866. Italian painter. Studied at Venice Academy; taught drawing in Rome.

**Caf'fié'ri'** (kȧ'fyā'rē'). Family of French sculptors of Italian origin, including: **Philippe** (1634–1716); his sons **François Charles** (1667–1729) and **Jacques** (1678–1755); a son of François, **Charles Philippe** (1695–1766); and a son of Jacques, **Jean Jacques** (1725–1792), most renowned of the family, sculptor of statues and busts.

**Cage** (kaj), **John Milton, Jr.** 1912– . Amer. composer, b. Los Angeles. Interested in aleatoric music; devised the "prepared piano." Composed *Imaginary Landscape No. 4* (1951), *Water Music* (1952), *Music for Amplified Toy Pianos* (1960), etc.; essays and lectures on music collected in *Silence* (1961), *A Year from Monday* (1967), etc.

**Ca'glia·ri** *or* **Ca'lia·ri** (kä'lyä·rē). Family of Venetian painters including: **Paolo** = Paolo VERONESE; his brother and pupil **Benedetto** (1538–1598), whose works include *Saint Agatha* (in Church of Sts. Peter and Paul, Murano) and *Rape of Proserpine* (Venice Acad.); Veronese's sons **Gabriele** (1568–1661), who assisted in completion of Veronese's unfinished works, and **Carlo**, *called* **Carletto** (1570–1596), whose works include *Saint Catherine* (Florence) and *Virgin and Saints* (Venice).

**Ca·glio'stro** (kä·lyôs'trō), Count **Alessandro di.** *Real name* **Giuseppe Bal'sa·mo** (bäl'sä·mō). 1743–1795. Italian impostor, b. at Palermo of poor parentage. As assistant to apothecary in a monastery, picked up some knowledge of chemistry and medicine; traveled in Greece, Egypt, Arabia, Persia, Rhodes, and Malta; assumed title of count; in Italy, married Lorenza Feliciani, who accompanied and assisted him. Traveled widely in Europe, posing as a physician, alchemist, necromancer, and freemason; practiced many frauds to obtain money, selling love philters, elixirs of youth, etc.; in London, posed as founder of a kind of freemasonry; in Paris, involved, with Cardinal de Rohan (*q.v.*) and others, in affair of the diamond necklace and confined in Bastille; in Rome, condemned to death for being a heretic, but sentence commuted to life imprisonment.

**Ca'gnat'** (kȧ'nyȧ'), **René Louis Victor.** 1852–1937. French classical archaeologist. Professor of epigraphy and Roman antiquities, Collège de France (1887). Author of *Étude Historique sur les Impôts Indirects Chez les Romains* (1882), *Explorations Épigraphiques et Archéologiques en Tunisie* (1883–86), *L'Armée Romaine d'Afrique* (1892), *À Travers le Monde Romain* (1912).

**Ca'gni** (kä'nyē), **Umberto.** 1863?–1932. Italian explorer. Joint leader with duke of the Abruzzi of polar expedition (1900); led sledge party that attained a point 239.15 miles from North Pole. Accompanied duke of the Abruzzi on ascent of Mt. St. Elias, Alaska, also of Ruwenzori, Africa (1906). Leader of government expedition to investigate fate of Nobile flight to North Pole (1928).

**Ca'gniard' de la Tour'** (kȧ'nyȧr' dē lȧ to͞or'), **Charles.** 1777–1859. French engineer and physicist; inventor of a blowing machine and of a siren used for determining number of vibrations corresponding to sounds of various pitches.

**Ca·gno'la** (kä·nyô'lä), Marchese **Luigi.** 1762–1833. Italian architect, b. Milan; known especially for his two triumphal arches in Milan, Porta Di Marengo and Arco della Pace, the latter surpassed in size only by Arc de Triomphe, Paris; other works include the campanile at Urgnano and chapel of Santa Marcellina in Milan.

**Ca'han** (kȧ'hȧn), **Abraham.** 1860–1951. Author, b. Vilna; to U.S. (1882); editor of *Jewish Daily Forward*, New York. Author of *Yekl, A Tale of the New York Ghetto*, *White Terror and the Red*, *The Rise of David Levinsky*, and an autobiography (5 vols.; in Yiddish).

**Ca'hill** (kā'hĭl), **Marie.** 1874–1933. American actress, b. Brooklyn, N.Y.; m. (1903) Daniel V. Arthur. Starred in *The Wild Rose* (1902), *Sally in Our Alley* (1902), *Nancy Brown* (1903), *Molly Moonshine* (1905), *Marrying Mary* (1906–07), etc.

**Cahill, Thaddeus.** 1867–1934. American inventor, b. Mt. Zion, Iowa. Studied at Oberlin (1884–85), also in various laboratories; LL.B. (1892), LL.M. (1893), D.C.L. (1900), George Washington U. Removed laboratory from Washington to Holyoke, Mass. (1902), then to New York (1911). Invented electric typewriter and the telharmonium, a device for producing music at distant points by means of alternating currents of electricity controlled by an operator who plays on a keyboard; also invented devices for heat engines, composing machines, and wireless telephony.

**Ca'ia·phas** (kā'yȧ·fȧs; kī'ȧ-), **Joseph.** *In Douay Version* **Ca'i·phas** (kā'ĭ·fȧs). Jewish high priest (from c. 18 A.D. to 36 A.D.). Sought death of Jesus; presided at council that condemned him to death (*Matthew* xxvi. 57–68); took part in trial of Peter and John (*Acts* iv ).

**Cail'lard** (kāl'ērd), Sir **Vincent Henry Penalver.** 1856–1930. English financial expert. Grad. Royal Military Acad., Woolwich; commissioned in Royal Engineers (1876). President, council of administration of Ottoman public debt (1883–98; resigned); instrumental in securing British participation in building the Baghdad Ry. Financial director, Vickers Co. (1906–27); negotiated for share in reconstruction of Turkish fleet, arsenals, and dockyards.

**Cail'laux'** (kȧ'yō'), **Eugène Alexandre.** 1822–1896. French civil engineer and politician; minister of public works (1874) and of finance (1877).

**Joseph Caillaux** (1863–1944), his son. Member of chamber of deputies (1898); minister of finance (1899–1902, 1906–09, 1911); premier of France (1911–12); again minister of finance (1913–14); accused of financial irregularities in office by editor of *Le Figaro*, Gaston Calmette, who was afterwards shot and killed in his office by Caillaux's wife (Mar. 16, 1914); advocated policy of making peace with Germany during World War; arrested (Dec., 1917) and convicted of having had correspondence with the enemy; in prison (1920–23); again finance minister (1925).

**Cail'la'vet'** (kȧ'yȧ'vĕ'), **Gaston Arman de.** 1870–1915. French journalist and playwright; collaborator with R. de Flers in a number of comic operas and comedies.

**Caillet, Guillaume.** See CALE.

**Cail'le·tet'** (kȧ'y'·tĕ'), **Louis Paul.** 1832–1913. French physicist and industrialist; devoted himself to study of metallurgy and liquefaction of gases; credited with liquefying oxygen, nitrogen, and other gases considered theretofore as unliquefiable (1877–78).

**Cail'liaud'** (kȧ'yō'), **Frédéric.** 1787–1869. French explorer in Egypt and Nubia.

**Cail'lié'** *or* **Cail'lé'** (kȧ'yā'), **René Auguste.** 1799–1838. French explorer in Africa. In order to reach Timbuktu from Senegal, learned Arabic, studied as convert to Islam, posed as Arab from Egypt, and joined caravan going inland; reached Timbuktu a year later after many hardships (1827–28); crossed Sahara to Morocco with another caravan; received prize of Geographical Society of Paris for being first white man to journey to Timbuktu and return safely.

**Cain** (kăN), **Georges Jules Auguste.** 1853–1919. French painter and author; his paintings include *Une Barricade en 1830*, *Rixe au Café de la Rotonde*, *Mort des Derniers Montagnards;* his writings include *Coins de Paris* (1905), *Anciens Théâtres de Paris* (1906), *Les Environs de Paris* (1912–13), etc. His brother **Henri** (1859–1937), painter, especially of genre scenes and portraits; author of librettos for light operas; collaborator in several plays, as *Sapho* (after Alphonse Daudet: with Arthur Bernède, 1897), *Les Mirages* (also with Bernède).

**Cain** (kān), **James Mallahan.** 1892– . American journalist, b. Annapolis, Md.; author of *The Postman Always Rings Twice* (detective story, 1934; play, 1936).

**Cain, Richard Harvey.** 1825–1887. American Negro clergyman and political leader, b. of free parents in Greenbrier Co., Va. Joined African Methodist Episcopal Church (about 1844); ordained (1862). Member, U.S. House of Representatives (1873–75, 1877–79). Bishop (1880) of Louisiana and Texas diocese.

**Caine** (kān), Sir **Hall,** *in full* **Thomas Henry Hall.** 1853–1931. English novelist. Educ. Isle of Man and Liverpool. On staff of Liverpool *Mercury.* To London at invitation of Dante Gabriel Rossetti and was his guest until Rossetti's death (1882); published *Recollections of Rossetti* (1882). In later years, lived on Isle of Man; member of Manx legislature (from 1901). Author of *Shadow of a Crime* (1885), *Son of Hagar* (1886), *The Deemster* (1887), *The Bondman* (1890), *The Manxman* (1894), *The Christian* (1897), *The Woman Thou Gavest Me* (1913), *The Master of Man* (1921), and *Life of Christ* (posthumous, 1938). Several of his novels have been dramatized.
His brother **William Ralph Hall** (1865–1939), journalist and writer; on staff of Liverpool *Mercury;* editor of *Court Circular*, *Family Churchman*, and *Household Words;* director and manager, Isaac Pitman & Sons, Ltd. Author of a number of books on the Isle of Man, including *The Isle of Man* (1909), *The Kingdom of Man and the Isles* (1919), *The Story of Sodor and Man* (1925); compiler of anthologies *Humorous Poems of the Century* (1890) and *Love Songs of England* (1893).

**Caiphas.** See CAIAPHAS.

**Caird** (kârd), **Edward.** 1835–1908. Scottish philosopher and theologian. Educ. Glasgow and St. Andrews; B.A., Oxon. (1863). Professor of moral philosophy, Glasgow (1866–93); succeeded Jowett as master of Balliol Coll., Oxford (1893–1906); with T. H. Green, founded English neo-Hegelian school of philosophy; advocate of higher education for women. Author of *Philosophy of Kant* (1878), *Hegel* (1883), *Evolution of Religion* (1891–92), *Evolution of Theology in the Greek Philosophers* (1904). His brother **John** (1820–1898), clergyman and philosopher; M.A., Glasgow (1845); professor of theology, Glasgow (1862); principal (1873); author of *An Introduction to the Philosophy of Religion* (1880), expounding Hegel.

**Cairnes** (kârnz), **John Elliott.** 1823–1875. Irish economist. M.A., Dublin (1854); professor of political economy at Dublin (1856–61), Galway (1861–66), University Coll., London (1866–72); regarded by contemporaries as second only to J. S. Mill. Author of *The Slave Power* (1862) and treatises on political economy, treating it as almost a pure science and defending the wage-fund theory.

**Cairns** (kârnz), **Hugh McCalmont.** 1st Earl **Cairns.** 1819–1885. Irish lawyer, parliamentary orator, and statesman. B.A., Dublin (1838). British solicitor general (1858); in parliament won reputation by brilliant speeches (1858); attorney general and lord justice of appeal (1866); leader of Conservative party in House of Lords (1869–74); opposed disestablishment of Irish church and Irish land bill (1870); lord chancellor of England (1868, 1874–80); made memorable speech in criticism of Gladstone's policy in Transvaal (1881).

**Cairns, John.** 1818–92. Scottish Presbyterian clergyman. M.A., Edinburgh (1841); joint professor of systematic theology and apologetics (1876), and principal (1879), United Presbyterian Theological Coll.; author of religious works.

**Cai·ro'li** (kī·rô'lē), **Benedetto.** 1825–1889. Italian statesman, b. Pavia. Prime minister of Italy (1878, 1879–81); lost office following French seizure of Tunis.

**Caitanya.** See CHAITANYA.

**Caithness.** Title of Scottish earldom held by SINCLAIR family.

**Ca'ius** (kā'yŭs; kī'ŭs). Variant of GAIUS.

**Caius** (kēz; *orig.* kāz), **John.** *Real surname* **Kees** (kāz), **Keys** (kāz), **Kay** (kā), *or* **Key** (kā). 1510–1573. English physician. Educ. Gonville Hall, Cambridge; studied medicine under Vesalius at Padua; M.D. (1541); lecturer on anatomy, London (1544–64); one of physicians to Edward VI, Mary Tudor, Elizabeth. Enlarged and refounded his old college as Gonville and Caius College (1557); master (1559–73). Author of critical, antiquarian, and scientific works.

**Ca·jan'der** (kȧ·yȧn'dĕr), **Aino Kaarlo.** 1879–1943. Finnish forestry expert and statesman, b. Uusikaupunki. Educ. Helsingfors U.; professor of forestry there (1911–34); chief of forestry in Finland (1918 ff.). Prime minister (1922, 1924, 1937–40); minister of defense (1928–29); deputy (1929–33).

**Caj'e·tan** (kăj'ē·tăn), Cardinal. *Lat.* **Caj'e·ta'nus** (-tā'nŭs). *Ital.* **Ga'e·ta'no** (gä'ā·tä'nō). *Real name* **Tommaso de Vi'o** (dā vē'ō). 1469–1534. Italian cardinal, b. Gaeta; papal legate at Augsburg (1518); summoned Luther before his tribunal.

**Cajetan of Thie'ne** (tyâ'nâ), Saint. *Ital.* **Gaetano Tie'ne** (tyâ'nâ). *Lat.* **Cajetanus.** 1480–1547. Italian lawyer and religious reformer; founded (with G. P. Caraffa, later Pope Paul IV, *q.v.*) the Oratory of Divine Love, which developed into an order of the clerks regular known as the Theatines.

**Ca'ji·gal' de la Ve'ga** (kä'hē·gäl' dā lä vā'gä), **Francisco Antonio.** 1695–1777. Spanish colonial governor, b. Hoz, Santander. Governor of Santiago, Cuba (1738–47); successfully repelled attack of English fleet under Admiral Vernon (1741); governor general of Cuba (1747–60); viceroy pro tem of Mexico (1760–61).

**Cajori, Florian.** 1859–1930. American mathematician,

b. Switzerland; to U.S. (1875). B.S., Wisconsin (1883), Ph.D., Tulane (1894). Professor of physics (1889–98), mathematics (1898–1918), dean of engineering (1903–18), Colorado Coll.; professor of history of mathematics, California (from 1918).

**Čak′ste** *or* **Chak′ste** (chäk′stâ), **Jānis.** *Also* **Tschak′-ste.** 1859–1927. Latvian politician. Chairman of people's council (1918) after proclamation of Latvian republic; president, Latvian constituent assembly (1920). Unanimously elected first president of Latvia (1922); re-elected (1925); died in office.

**Calabrese, Il (Cavaliere).** See Mattia PRETI.

**Ca′la·mat′ta** (kä′lä·mät′tä), **Luigi.** 1802–1869. Italian engraver, b. Civitavecchia. To Paris (1822); studied with Ingres; professor, École des Beaux-Arts, Brussels (1837 ff.), Brera Acad., Milan (1861 ff.). His engravings include a death mask of Napoleon, portraits of Ingres, Paganini, Guizot, George Sand, and *Francesca da Rimini, La Gioconda, Madonna di Foligno.*

**Ca′lame′** (kȧ′lȧm′), **Alexandre.** 1810–1864. Swiss landscape painter, illustrator, lithographer, and etcher. Studied under Diday in Geneva (1829) and traveled in Europe and England. His works include *Ruins of Paestum* (now in Leipzig), Alpine scenes, as *Mount Rosa at Sunrise* and *Bernese Oberland* (Leipzig), *The Four Seasons* (Geneva), *Lake of the Four Cantons* (London), and *Wetterhorn* (Basel), and lithographs, sketches, and etchings esp. of Swiss Alps.

**Cal′a·mis** (kăl′ȧ·mĭs). Greek sculptor, of early 5th century B.C.; carved statues of various deities, as Apollo, Aphrodite, Hermes.

**Ca·lam′i·ty Jane** (kȧ·lăm′ĭ·tĭ jān′). *Sobriquet of* **Martha Jane Burke.** 1852?–1903. American horsewoman and frontier character, esp. in Deadwood, South Dakota; known as marksman.

**Cal′a·my** (kăl′ȧ·mĭ), **Edmund.** 1600–1666. English Puritan clergyman, b. London, of Huguenot parents; B.A., Cantab. (1619); attached himself to Calvinist party; resigned church office on enforcement of ceremonial observances (1636); active defender of Presbyterian cause; one of principal authors of *Smectymnuus*, assailing Bishop Joseph Hall's claim of divine right of episcopacy; member of Westminster Assembly (1643); opposed execution of Charles I; declined bishopric at Restoration; imprisoned for preaching without license. Father of **Edmund** (1635?–1685), M.A., Cantab. (1658), Presbyterian minister, and **Benjamin** (1642–1686), M.A., Cantab. (1668), High-Church clergyman. **Edmund** (1671–1732), Presbyterian minister, son of the younger Edmund, was a prolific writer; known for his biography of the 2000 ministers ejected from Church of England by Act of Conformity.

**Ca′lan·drel′li** (kä′län·drĕl′ē), **A′le·xan′der** (ä′lĕ·ksän′-dẽr). 1834–1903. Sculptor, b. Berlin, of Italian parents; studied at Berlin Acad.; later worked under Drake; known esp. for his monuments, as equestrian statue of Frederick William IV (before National Gallery, Berlin), statue of Peter von Cornelius (Berlin), etc.

**Ca′las′** (kȧ′läs′), **Jean.** 1698–1762. French Calvinist merchant of Toulouse; judicially convicted on a baseless charge of murdering his son **Marc Antoine** (a suicide) to prevent the son from becoming a Roman Catholic; executed by being broken on the wheel.

**Ca′la·san′zio** (kä′lä·sän′thyō), San **José.** *English* Saint **Joseph of Ca′la·san′za** (kä′lä·sän′thä; *Angl.* kăl′ȧ·săn′zȧ). 1556–1648. Spanish priest, b. Calasanza, Aragon; founder of Piarist order; canonized (1767) by Clement XIII.

**Cal′car** *or* **Kal′kar** (käl′kär) *or* **Kalck′er** (käl′kẽr), **Jan Stevenszoon van.** 1499?–?1550. Landscape and portrait painter and designer of woodcuts, b. Calcar, Duchy of Cleves. Active in Dordrecht, Venice (c. 1536; as disciple of Titian), and Naples. His works include illustrations for anatomical work of Vesalius *De Humani Corporis Fabrica* (1543), and imitations of works of Titian and Raphael. Portrait of Councilor Melchior von Brauwiller of Cologne (1540; now in Louvre) is also ascribed to him.

**Cal·da′ni** (käl·dä′nē), **Leopoldo Marco Antonio.** 1725–1813. Italian anatomist and physiologist; professor, Bologna (1755), Padua (1771–1805); advocate of irritability theory of Albrecht von Haller; published with his nephew anatomical plates entitled *Icones Anatomicae* (4 vols., 1801–14) and *Explicatio Iconum Anatomicarum* (5 vols., 1802–14).

**Cal·da′ra** (käl·dä′rä), **Antonio.** 1670–1736. Italian composer; studied in Venice under Legrenzi; assistant Kapellmeister, Vienna (from 1716); composed much church music including masses, motets, and cantatas, over 70 operas, 36 oratorios, chamber music, etc.

**Caldara, Polidoro.** See CARAVAGGIO.

**Cal′de·cote** (kôl′dĕ·kŭt), 1st Viscount (cr. 1939). Sir **Thomas Walker Hobart In′skip** (ĭn′skĭp). 1876–1947. English jurist and government official, b. Bristol. Educ. Cambridge; called to bar (1899). Served in Admiralty naval intelligence division (1915–18) and head of naval law branch (1918). M.P. (1918–29, 1931–39); solicitor general (1922–24, 1924–28, 1931–32); attorney general (1928–29, 1932–36); minister for co-ordination of defense (1936–39); secretary of state for dominion affairs (1939; 1940); lord chancellor (1939–40); leader of the House of Lords (1940).

**Cal′de·cott** (kôl′dĕ·kŭt), **Randolph.** 1846–1886. English artist and illustrator. Did illustrations for Washington Irving's *Old Christmas* (1876) and *Bracebridge Hall* (1877) and for children's favorites, such as *The House that Jack Built;* worked for *The Graphic;* contributed to *Punch.*

**Caldeira Brant Pontes, Feliberto.** See Marquês de BARBACENA.

**Cal′der** (kôl′dẽr), **Alexander Stirling.** 1870–1945. American sculptor, b. Philadelphia. Studied at Pennsylvania Academy of Fine Arts and in Paris under Chapu and Falguière. Sculptor of John James Audubon and William Penn in American Hall of Fame. Represented by works in Metropolitan Museum of Art of New York, St. Louis Art Museum, Pennsylvania Academy of Fine Arts, etc. His father, **Alexander Milne Calder** (1846–1923), sculptor, b. Aberdeen, Scotland; studied art in Edinburgh, London, and Philadelphia; designed and carved many art pieces for Philadelphia, including an equestrian statue of General Meade for Fairmount Park and work on the municipal building. A. S. Calder's son **Alexander** (1898–1976), b. Philadelphia; grad. Stevens Inst. (1919); best known for his original constructions of bent wire, metal, etc., of two types termed by him *stabiles* ("static abstract sculptures") and *mobiles* ("plastic forms in motion").

**Calder,** Sir **Robert.** 1745–1818. British naval officer, b. in Scotland. Took part in battle of Cape St. Vincent (1797); rear admiral (1799); outmaneuvered by French squadron (1801); failed to win complete victory over Villeneuve; censured for error of judgment; admiral (1810).

**Cal′de·rón′** (käl′dā·rōn′), **Francisco García.** 1832–1905. Peruvian statesman, b. Arequipa. Member of congress (1867); after occupation of Lima by Chilean army (1881) and flight of President Piérola, elected president of Peru (1881); sought aid of U.S., but made prisoner by Chileans, who sent him to Valparaiso; returned to Lima (1886); president of senate; rector of U. of San Marcos. Father of Francisco and Ventura GARCÍA CALDERÓN.

**Cal′der·on** (kôl′dẽr·ŏn), **Philip Hermogenes.** 1833–1898. British painter. Son of a Spanish Protestant clergyman and professor in London; studied in Paris under Picot; exhibited *Broken Vows* (1857); R.A. (1867); keeper of Royal Academy (1887); exhibited *The Renunciation of St. Elizabeth of Hungary* (1891); leader of so-called St. John's Wood school of genre painters. His son **George** (1868–1915), dramatist; educ. Oxford; student of Russian literature, dialects, and folklore; author of *The Fountain* (1909), *Revolt* (1912), *Cromwell: Mall of Monks*, and a book of travel impressions, *Tahiti* (pub. 1921); served in British army at Dardanelles in World War I; reported missing (1915).

**Cal′de·rón′** (käl′dȧ·rôn′), **Serafín Estébanez.** See ESTÉBANEZ CALDERÓN.

**Cal′de·rón′ de la Bar′ca** (käl′dȧ·rôn′ dȧ lä bär′kä; *Angl.* kôl′dẽr·ŏn), **Pedro.** 1600–1681. Spanish dramatist and poet, b. Madrid. Educ. under Jesuits at Madrid; grad. (1619), U. of Salamanca. Entered Spanish army (to c. 1630); created knight, Order of Santiago (1637), by Philip IV; served in campaign against Catalan rebels (1640); retired (1643); pensioned (1645). Entered Order of St. Francis (1650), priest (1651); honorary chaplain to Philip IV (1663); superior, Brotherhood of San Pedro, Madrid. Author of 120 *comedias*, 80 *autos*, and 20 smaller pieces (*entremeses*, etc.), including *La Hija del Aire*, *El Tetrarca de Jerusalén*, *El Médico de Su Honra*, *El Alcalde de Zalamea*, *La Dama Duende*, *El Secreto a Voces*, *La Cena de Baltasar*, *El Príncipe Constante*, *El Mágico Prodigioso*, *La Devoción de la Cruz*, *La Vida Es Sueño*, *El Purgatorio de San Patricio*, *Peor Está Que Estaba*, and *Astrólogo Fingido*.

**Cal′de·rón′ Guar′dia** (käl′dȧ·rôn′ gwär′thyä), **Rafael Ángel.** 1900–1970. President of Costa Rica (1940–44).

**Cal′der·wood** (kôl′dẽr·wo͝od), **David.** 1575–1650. Scottish Presbyterian apologist. M.A., Edinburgh (1593). Banished for refusing to surrender roll of signatures to a remonstrance; defended Presbyterianism in *The Altar of Damascus* (1621); author of a *History of the Kirk of Scotland* (abridged edition pub. 1678).

**Calderwood, Henry.** 1830–1897. Scottish philosopher. Educ. Edinburgh; professor of moral philosophy, Edinburgh (1868); first chairman of Edinburgh school board. Author of *The Philosophy of the Infinite* (1854) criticizing Sir William Hamilton's agnostic tendencies, and of *Evolution and Man's Place in Nature* (1893).

**Cal′di·cott** (kôl′dĭ·kŭt), **Alfred James.** 1842–1897. English conductor, and composer of two cantatas, *The Widow of Nain* (1881) and *A Rhine Legend* (1883), and part songs, operettas, and glees; director of London College of Music (1892–97).

**Cald′well** (kôld′wĕl; -wĕl; kŏld′-), **Anne.** 1876–1936. American librettist and song writer, b. Boston; m. James O'Dea; author of librettos for musical comedies including *The Top of the World*, *The Nest Egg*, *Pom-Pom*, *The Sweetheart Shop*, *The Magnolia Lady*, and of lyrics for *Peg o' My Dreams* (1924) and *The City Chap* (1925); collaborated on songs for *Babes in Toyland* and *Flying Down to Rio;* composed the popular songs *Kalua* and *Wait Till the Cows Come Home.*

**Caldwell, Erskine Preston.** 1903– . Am. author, b. White Oak, Ga. Educ. universities of Virginia and Pennsylvania. Worked as journalist, cotton picker, stagehand, professional football player, book reviewer, and editor; wrote scenarios for Metro-Goldwyn-Mayer (1933–34). Author of *The Bastard* (1929), *Poor Fool* (1930), *American Earth* (1931), *Tobacco Road* (1932; subsequently dramatized, breaking [1939] record for number of New York performances formerly held by *Abie's Irish Rose*), *God's Little Acre* (1933), *We Are the Living* (1933), *Journeyman* (1935), *Kneel to the Rising Sun* (1935), *Some American People* (1935), *All-Out on the Road to Smolensk* (1942). Collaborator with his second wife, **Margaret**, *nee* **Bourke-White** (bûrk′hwīt′) (1906–1971), photographer, in pictorial books *You Have Seen Their Faces* (1937), *North of the Danube* (1938), *Shooting the Russian War* (1942).

**Caldwell, Otis William.** 1869–1947. American botanist and educator, b. Lebanon, Ind. B.S., Franklin Coll., Ind. (1894), Ph.D., Chicago (1898). Associate professor of botany (1907–13), professor and dean of University Coll. (1913–17), U. of Chicago; professor of education, Teachers College, Columbia (1917–35). Author of *Laboratory and Field Manual of Botany* (1901), *Introduction to Botany* (1914), *Then and Now in Education* (1923), *Introduction to Science* (with F. D. Curtis, 1929), etc.

**Caldwell, Taylor,** *in full* **Janet Taylor.** 1900– . Novelist, b. near Manchester, Eng.; to U.S. (1907); m. as 2d husband Marcus Reback (1931). Author of *Dynasty of Death* (1938), *The Eagles Gather* (1940), *The Earth is the Lord's* (1941), *The Strong City* (1942).

**Cale** (kȧl) *or* **Cail′let′** (kȧ′yĕ′), **Guillaume.** d. 1358. French peasant insurgent leader of the Jacquerie (1358); captured, tortured, and beheaded.

**Ca′leb** (kā′lĕb). In Bible, one of twelve Israelites sent to spy out land of Canaan; took part in its conquest; one of those appointed by Moses to parcel it out (*Numbers* xiii. 6, 30; xiv. 6, 24, 38; xxxiv. 19; *Joshua* xiv. 6–15; xv. 13–19).

**Ca·le′nus** (kȧ·lē′nŭs), **Quintus Fufius.** d. 41 B.C. Roman general; tribune of people (61 B.C.); praetor (59); served under Julius Caesar in Gaul (51) and Spain (49); consul (47). Joined Mark Antony after Caesar's death and commanded Antony's forces in north Italy; died while preparing to attack Octavian.

**Ca′le·pi′no** (kä′lȧ·pē′nō) *or* **Ca·le′pio** (kä·lâ′pyō), **Ambrogio.** 1435–1511. Italian lexicographer and Augustinian monk. His Latin-Italian dictionary (1502) developed in successive editions and enlargements into a polyglot of eleven languages (1590), re-edited by Facciolati (*q.v.*) as a seven-language polyglot (1718) and by Forcellini (*q.v.*) as *Totius Latinitatis Lexicon* (1771). Hence the term *calepin* for a dictionary.

**Calgacus.** = GALGACUS.

**Cal·houn′** (kăl·ho͞on′), **John.** 1806–1859. American lawyer. President, constitutional convention at Lecompton, Kansas (1857); blamed, perhaps unjustly, for the Lecompton proslavery constitution.

**Calhoun, John Caldwell.** 1782–1850. American lawyer, b. near Calhoun Mills, S.C. Grad. Yale (1804). Member, U.S. House of Representatives (1811–17). U.S. secretary of war (1817–25). Vice-president of U.S. (1825–32). Champion of states' rights; instrumental in guiding South Carolina policy during nullification crisis (1832–33). U.S. senator (1832–43). U.S. secretary of state (1844–45). U.S. senator (1845–50). Champion of slavery and southern cause in Senate debates.

**Calhoun, William James.** 1848–1916. American lawyer and diplomat, b. Pittsburgh, Pa. On investigating mission to Cuba (1897). Member, Interstate Commerce Commission (1898–1900). U.S. confidential agent to Venezuela (1905–08). U.S. minister to China (1909–13).

**Caliari.** See CAGLIARI.

**Caliban.** Pseudonym of Richard NORDHAUSEN.

**Ca·lig′u·la** (kȧ·lĭg′ū·lȧ). *Real name* **Gaius Caesar.** 12 A.D.–41 A.D. Roman emperor (37–41). Youngest son of Germanicus Caesar (nephew of Tiberius) and Agrippina, b. probably at Antium (Porto d'Anzio). Brought up in camps among soldiers; nicknamed Caligula because in youth he wore *caligae*, or military shoes. Declared heir to throne by Tiberius; for a short time ruled with moderation; suffered severe illness (c. 38) after which his reign marked by extreme cruelty and tyranny; undoubtedly insane; delighted in torture and bloodshed; made his horse a consul. Murdered by members of praetorian cohorts led by Chaerea.

**Că·li·ne'scu** (kȧ·lē·nĕ'skōō), **Armand.** 1893–1939. Rumanian lawyer and statesman; leader in National Peasant party; minister of interior (1937–39); under orders from King Carol, endeavored to suppress Iron Guards, pro-Nazi organization; premier of Rumania (March 7, 1939); slain by Iron Guardists (Sept. 21, 1939).

**Calippus.** Variant of CALLIPPUS.

**Ca·lix'tus** (kȧ·lĭks'tŭs). *More properly* **Cal·lis'tus** (kă·lĭs'tŭs). Name of three popes (see *Table of Popes*, Nos. 16, 162, 211), especially:

**Calixtus II.** *Real name* **Gui'do of Vienne** (gwē'dō, vyĕn) *or* **of Burgundy.** d. 1124. Pope (1119–24); expelled Antipope Gregory (VIII) from Rome (1121); concluded (1122) Concordat of Worms with Henry V of Germany on question of investiture.

**Calixtus III.** *Real name* **Alfonso Bor'gia** (bôr'jä). 1378–1458. Pope (1455–58); b. in Spain; uncle of Pope Alexander VI; attempted unsuccessful crusade against Turks. An antipope (in office 1168–78) also is known as **Calixtus III.**

**Ca·lix'tus** (kä·lĭks'tōōs; *Angl.* kȧ·lĭks'tŭs) *or* **Ca·lixt'** (kä·lĭkst'), **Georg.** *Orig surname* **Cal'li·sen** (käl'ē·zĕn). 1586–1656. German Lutheran theologian, b. Medelby, Schleswig. Traveled extensively in Europe and England and became acquainted with leading reformers; professor of theology, Helmstedt (after 1614). Upheld reunion of Lutheran and Reformed Protestant sects with each other and with Roman Catholic Church, and became involved in syncretistic controversy with orthodox opponents. Author of *Disputationes de Praecipuis Religionis Christianae Capitibus*, *Epitome Theologiae Moralis* (1634), etc.

**Cal'kins** (kô'kĭnz), **Clinch,** *in full* **Marion Clinch.** d.1968. American writer; m. Mark Merrell. Author of a book of verse, and of *Some Folks Won't Work* (1930), *Spy Overhead* (1937), etc.

**Calkins, Mary Whiton.** 1863–1930. American philosopher and psychologist, b. Hartford, Conn.; taught at Wellesley (1891–1930); her works include *Der Doppelte Standpunkt in der Psychologie* (1905), *The Persistent Problems of Philosophy* (1907).

**Calkins, Norman Allison.** 1822–1895. American educator, b. Gainesville, N.Y. In *Primary Object Lessons for a Graduated Course of Development* (1861), introduced to U.S. principles of object teaching set forth by Pestalozzi.

**Calkins, Phineas Wolcott.** 1831–1924. American clergyman, b. Corning, N.Y. Grad. Yale (1856); studied at Union Theol. Sem., and U. of Halle, Ger. Ordained in Congregational ministry (1862); pastor in Philadelphia (1864–66), Buffalo (1866–80), Newton, Mass. (1880–95), Kansas City, Mo. (1896–98), Woburn, Mass. (1898–1907). Author of *Keystones of Faith* (1888), *Parables for Our Times* (1901).

His son **Raymond** (1869– ), Congregational clergyman, b. Buffalo. Educ. Harvard (A.B., 1890) and Harvard Divinity School (1893–95); ordained (1896); pastor in Pittsfield, Mass. (1896–1903), Portland, Me. (1903–12), Cambridge, Mass. (1912–40). Author of *The Christian Idea in the Modern World* (1918), *The Eloquence of Christian Experience* (1927), *The Holy Spirit* (1930), *Religion and Life* (1935), etc.

**Cal'la·ghan** (kăl'ȧ·hăn; -găn), Sir **George Astley.** 1852–1920. English naval officer. Commanded naval brigade that relieved legations in Peking during Boxer uprising (1900); commander in chief of home fleets (1911–14); admiral of the fleet (1917–18).

**Cal'la·ghan** (kăl'ȧ·hăn), **Morley Edward.** 1903– Canadian novelist and story writer, b. Toronto. B.A., Toronto (1925). Author of *Strange Fugitive* (1928), *Native Argosy* (1929), *Broken Journey* (1932), *They Shall Inherit the Earth* (1935), *More Joy in Heaven* (1936).

**Cal'la·han** (kăl'ȧ·hăn), **James Morton.** 1864–1956. American educator, b. Bedford, Ind. A.B., Indiana (1894); Ph.D., Johns Hopkins (1897). Professor and head of department of history and political science, West Virginia U. (1902–29) and research professor there (from 1929). Author of *Confederate Diplomacy* (1901), *The American Expansion Policy* (1903), *The Monroe Doctrine and International Relations*, etc.

**Cal'las** (kăl'ăs), **Maria Meneghini** (mĕn'ĕ·gē'nē). 1923–1977. Amer. soprano, b. New York City. Sang leading operatic roles throughout the world.

**Call'cott** (kôl'kŭt), Sir **Augustus Wall.** 1779–1844. English landscape painter; R.A. (1810); surveyor of royal pictures (1834). Exhibited landscapes, as *The Mouth of the Tyne* (1818), and figure paintings, as *Milton Dictating to his Daughter* (1840). His wife, Lady **Callcott** (1786–1844), *nee* **Maria Dundas,** widow of Capt. Thomas Graham, R.N.; author of books about India, Rome, and South America, and of *Little Arthur's History of England* (1836). His older brother **John Wall** (1766–1821), musician and composer; author of *Musical Grammar* (1806); known for his glees and catches, as *O beauteous fair* and *Dull repining sons of care.* J. W. Callcott's son **William Hutchins** (1807–1882), composer of songs and glees, including *The last man*, and the anthem *Give peace in our time, O Lord.*

**Cal·le'ja del Rey'** (kä·(l)yĕ'hä thĕl rĕ'ē), **Félix María.** Conde **de Cal'de·rón'** (thā käl'dā·rôn'). 1750–1820. Spanish general, called "the Butcher"; b. Medina del Campo. To Mexico (1789); defeated Hidalgo (*q.v.*) at Puente de Calderón, near Guadalajara (1811), and Hidalgo's successor Morelos; known for his cruel treatment of prisoners; viceroy of Mexico (1813–16).

**Cal'len·dar** (kăl'ĕn·dẽr), **Hugh Longbourne.** 1863–1930. English physicist. Educ. Cambridge. Professor, McGill U., Montreal (1893–98), University Coll., London (1898–1902), Imperial Coll. of Science, London (1902–30). Known for investigations relating to steam and to thermometry; invented a compensated air thermometer (1891) and a radio balance (1910). Author of *Callendar Steam Tables* (1915) and *Properties of Steam and Thermodynamic Theory of Turbines* (1920).

**Cal'les** (kä'yās), **Plutarco Elías.** 1877–1945. Mexican political leader, b. in Sonora. Schoolteacher, farmer, and tradesman in Sonora; soldier under Obregón and Carranza (1913–15); governor of Sonora (1917); held cabinet positions under Carranza (1919–20) and Obregón (1920–24); in bitter struggle with Huerta for supremacy (1923–24). President of Mexico (1924–28); carried out reforms; administration marked by struggle between church and state. Contended for control with President Cárdenas (1935–36); driven into exile in U.S. (1936).

**Cal'li·as** (kăl'ĭ·ăs). Athenian soldier and diplomat; fought at Marathon (490 B.C.); sent on mission (c. 445) to Artaxerxes, King of Persia, but apparently failed in his object. His grandson **Callias** commanded Athenian infantry in victory at Corinth (392 B.C.) and headed mission which negotiated peace of Callias (371); ridiculed by Aristophanes for his extravagance.

**Cal·lic'ra·tes** (kă·lĭk'rȧ·tēz). Greek architect, of 5th

century B.C.; collaborated with Ictinus in designing the Parthenon. Cf. PHIDIAS.

**Cal'li·crat'i·das** (kăl'ĭ·krăt'ĭ·dăs). d. 406 B.C. Spartan admiral; succeeded Lysander (406 B.C.). Killed at battle of Arginusae.

**Cal'lières' Bon'ne·vue'** (kȧ'lyâr' bôn'vü'), Chevalier **Louis Hector de.** 1646–1703. French army officer; governor of Montreal (1684); succeeded Frontenac as governor general of Canada (1699).

**Cal·lim'a·chus** (kă·lĭm'ȧ·kŭs). Greek sculptor, of late 5th century B.C.; reputed inventor of the Corinthian column, and first to use the running drill in carving folds in drapery, etc.

**Callimachus.** Greek scholar, of 3d century B.C., b. in Cyrene; head of a school in Alexandria, and chief librarian of Alexandrian library. Of about 800 works ascribed to him, only 6 hymns, 64 epigrams, and a few fragments are extant.

**Cal'li·ni'cus** (kăl'ĭ·nī'kŭs). See SELEUCUS II.

**Callinicus.** Egyptian architect; credited with invention of Greek fire, used in burning Saracen fleet in battle off Byzantium (c. 670 A.D.).

**Cal·li'nus** (kă·lī'nŭs). Greek poet of Ephesus, of 8th or perhaps 7th century B.C.; said to be earliest writer of elegiacs, and creator of political and martial elegies. Only a few fragments extant.

**Cal·lip'pus** *or* **Ca·lip'pus** (kȧ·lĭp'ŭs). Greek astronomer, of 4th century B.C., b. in Cyzicus, Asia Minor; instituted Callippic cycle or period, a period of 76 years, equal to 4 Metonic cycles minus a day (=27,759 days).

**Callisen, Georg.** See Georg CALIXTUS.

**Cal·lis'the·nes** (kă·lĭs'thē·nēz). 360?–?328 B.C. Greek philosopher and historian; relative and disciple of Aristotle. Accompanied Alexander the Great on eastern expedition; criticized Alexander for adopting Oriental ways; accused of plotting against king; imprisoned; died in prison. Author of a history of Greece from 387 to 357, and other historical works, none extant.

**Cal·lis'tra·tus** (kă·lĭs'trȧ·tŭs). Athenian orator and general whose brilliant defense of his policy in allowing the Thebans to occupy Oropus on their promise (later violated) to surrender it on demand influenced Demosthenes to study oratory; executed (355 B.C.).

**Callistus.** See Popes CALIXTUS.

**Cal'lot'** (kȧ'lō'), **Jacques.** 1592–1635. French painter and engraver, b. Nancy. Studied in Rome and Florence; returned to Nancy, in service of duke of Lorraine. Portrayed war scenes; etched genre sketches; first artist to raise etching to an independent art. His famous etchings include *Pont-Neuf, Madonna of the Impruneta,* the two series *Capricci* and *Le Gueux.*

**Call'well** (kôl'wĕl; -wĕl), Sir **Charles Edward.** 1859–1928. English soldier, b. London. Educ. Royal Military Acad.; served in India, Natal, and South Africa; retired (1909). Recalled (1914); on duty at War Office (1914–16); planned organization of Dardanelles campaign; on mission to Russia (1916); on duty in ministry of munitions (1916–17); major general (1917). Author of *Small Wars, their Principles and Practice* (1896), *Tactics of Today* (1900), *The Dardanelles* (1919), *The Experiences of a Dug-Out 1914–1918* (1920), etc.

**Cal'mette'** (kȧl'mĕt'), **Gaston.** 1858–1914. French journalist; editor of *Le Figaro:* killed in his office by Mme. Caillaux (Mar. 16, 1914; see under Joseph CAILLAUX). His brother **Albert Léon Charles** (1863–1933), bacteriologist; founder (1891) and director (1891–93) of bacteriological institute at Saïgon; founder (1896) and director (1896–1919) of Pasteur Institute at Lille; developed an antitoxin for vaccination of newborn infants against tuberculosis.

**Ca'lo·mar'de** (kä'lō·mär'thā), **Francisco Tadeo de.** 1775–1842. Spanish ultraroyalist statesman, b. Villel, Aragon. Educ. for law at Saragossa. Stanch supporter of Ferdinand VII; occupied posts in council for Indies and in ministry of justice (1814–15); secretary of Cámara del Real Patronato (1823) and minister of justice (1823–33); fled to France (1833) after unsuccessful attempt to insure succession of Don Carlos to Spanish throne.

**Ca'lonne'** (kȧ'lôn'), **Charles Alexandre de.** 1734–1802. French minister of finance under Louis XVI; b. Douai. Held government positions at Douai, Metz (1768), and Lille (1774); controller general of finance (1783); found state treasury in hopeless disorder, with no money and no credit; began policy of display and new loans which after three years (1784–86) reached absolute limits; opened Assembly of Notables (1787); proposed taxation of nobles and clergy; opposed; removed from office. Lived in England (1787–1802); allowed by Napoleon to return to France; died a month later.

**Ca'lov** (kä'lôf), **Abraham.** *Orig. surname* **Ka'lau** (kä'lou). *Latinized surname* **Ca·lo'vi·us** (kȧ·lō'vĭ·ŭs). 1612–1686. German theologian; professor of theology, Wittenberg (from 1650); championed Lutheran orthodoxy; attacked esp. the syncretism of Calixtus; opposed Calvinists, Arminians, Socinians, and Pietists; author of *Systema Locorum Theologicorum* (12 vols., 1665–77).

**Calprenède.** See LA CALPRENÈDE.

**Cal·pur'ni·a** (kăl·pûr'nĭ·ȧ). Wife of Julius Caesar (from 59 B.C.); endeavored to dissuade him from going to senate on day of his assassination.

**Cal·pur'ni·us Bes'ti·a** (kăl·pûr'nĭ·ŭs bĕs'chĭ·ȧ; bĕs'tĭ·ȧ), **Lucius.** Roman general and politician of 2d century B.C.; tribune (121 B.C.) and consul (111). Commanded army against Jugurtha; bribed to conclude disgraceful peace; tried and condemned by Roman Senate. Another **Lucius Calpurnius Bestia,** perhaps his grandson, tribune (63 B.C.), was associated with conspiracy of Catiline; selected to give signal for revolt by speech against Cicero.

**Calpurnius Piso.** See PISO.

**Calpurnius Sic'u·lus** (sĭk'ū·lŭs), **Titus.** Roman pastoral poet of 1st century A.D.; of his works, 7 eclogues, a panegyric, and a few fragments are extant.

**Cal'vaert** *or* **Cal'vart** (käl'värt), **Denis.** Called **De·nis' le Fla'mand'** (dē·nē' lē flȧ'mäɴ'). 1540?–1619. Flemish painter; studio in Bologna, Italy, where many of his best works are preserved.

**Cal'vé'** (kȧl'vā'), **Emma.** *Stage name of* **Emma de Ro'quer'** (dē rô'kā'). 1858–1942. French operatic soprano; made professional debut at Brussels (1882) as Marguerite in *Faust;* sang thereafter in Paris, Italy, England, Spain, Russia, and U.S.; especially successful in roles in *Cavalleria Rusticana, Sapho, Carmen.*

**Cal'ver·ley** (kăl'vẽr·lĭ), **Charles Stuart.** 1831–1884. English poet and parodist. Educ. Harrow (where known as an athlete and writer of Latin verse), Oxford (1850–52), Cambridge (1852–59; M.A., 1859); barrister (1865); invalided by skating accident (1866). Best known for his humorous verse, as in *Verses and Translations* (1862) and *Fly Leaves* (1872); rendered Theocritus into scholarly English verse.

**Cal'vert** (kăl'vẽrt), **Caroline Louisa Waring.** 1834–1872. Australian author of tales of Australia, under maiden name **Louisa At'kin·son** (ăt'kĭn·s'n). Collected botanical specimens for government. Genus *Atkinsonia* and species *Epaeris calvertiana* named after her.

**Calvert, George.** 1st Baron **Bal'ti·more** (bôl'tĭ·mōr). 1580?–1632. English proprietor in America, b. Yorkshire, Eng. Grad. Trinity Coll., Oxford (1597). M.P. (from 1609); knighted (1617). Secretary of state and member of privy council (1619); announced conversion to Roman Catholic faith (1625); resigned secretaryship of state; created baron (1625). Granted Newfoundland (1622); objected to it because of climate; granted territory comprising what is now Maryland (1632), but died before charter was issued. Charter issued (1632) to his son **Cecilius** (1605–1675), 2d baron. George's second son, **Leonard** (1606–1647), was governor of Maryland province (1634–47). Cecilius's son **Charles** (1637–1715), 3d baron, was governor of Maryland (1661–75) and proprietor (1675–1715).

**Calvert, Louis.** 1859–1923. Actor, b. Manchester, Eng.; naturalized American citizen. Achieved prominence in Shakespearean roles, acting with Sir Henry Irving, Ellen Terry, Sir Herbert Tree; also appeared in modern plays, as by Ibsen, Shaw, and Barrie.

**Cal'ver·ton** (kăl'vẽr·t'n; -tŭn), **Victor Francis.** 1900–1940. American writer and lecturer, b. Baltimore. A.B., Johns Hopkins (1921). Founder (1923) and editor of *The Modern Monthly;* wrote *The Newer Spirit* (1925), *The Bankruptcy of Marriage* (1928), *American Literature at the Crossroads* (1931), *The Passing of the Gods* (1934), etc.

**Cal'vin** (kăl'vĭn; *Fr.* kȧl'văN'), **John.** *Orig.* **Jean Chau'vin'** (shō'văN') *or* **Caul'vin'** (kōl'văN'). 1509–1564. French theologian and reformer, b. Noyon, Picardy. Studied in Paris, Orléans, and Bourges. Gradual convert to doctrines of Reformation; openly declared his acceptance of them (c. 1528). Banished from Paris (1533); took refuge in Basel, Switzerland, where he published his famous *Institution Chrétienne* (1536; translated as *Institutes of the Christian Religion*). To Geneva; joined Farel in trying to establish theocratic government over city; driven out by popular revolt (1538); retired to Strassburg as professor and pastor of its French church. Recalled to Geneva (1541), succeeded in establishing theocratic government; had controversies with various heretics, one of whom, Servetus, was burned at the stake (1553). Founded at Geneva (1559) an academy where he taught theology. His Genevan government served as focal point for defense of Protestantism throughout Europe, and his zeal and his writings brought into one body of doctrine (known as *Calvinism*) the scattered and unsystematic reformed opinions of the period.

**Calvin, Melvin.** 1911– . Amer. chemist, b. St. Paul, Minn. With Univ. of Calif. at Berkeley (1937). Known for research on photosynthesis. Awarded Nobel prize in chemistry (1961).

**Cal·vi'si·us** (kăl·vĭsh'ĭ·ŭs; -vĭsh'ŭs), **Se'thus** (sē'thŭs). *Real name* **Seth Kall'witz** (zāt kăl'vĭts). 1556–1615. German musician and theorist. Musical director, St. Paul's Church, Leipzig (1581); cantor, Schulpforte, (1582); cantor of St. Thomas's School and musical director of churches, Leipzig (from 1594); took active part in establishing harmony as a separate branch from counterpoint. Composer esp. of church music; author of *Exercitationes Musicae* (1600–11), etc.

**Cal'vo** (käl'vō), **Carlos.** 1824–1906. Argentine diplomat and jurist, b. Buenos Aires. In consular service (1852–58); deputy (1859); Paraguayan chargé d'affaires, Paris and London (1860–64); Argentine minister plenipotentiary to Berlin (1883), Russia (1889), Austria (1890), Paris (1899). Formulated Calvo doctrine (more widely known as *Drago doctrine;* cf. Luis María DRAGO). Authority on international law; author of *Le Droit International Théorique et Pratique* (6 vols., 1863), *Recueil Complet des Traités, Conventions, etc., de l'Amérique Latine* (15 vols., 1862–69), *Annales Historiques de la Révolution de l'Amérique Latine* (5 vols., 1864–75), all pub. also in Spanish.

**Cal'vus** (kăl'vŭs), **Gaius Licinius Macer.** Roman orator and poet, of 1st century B.C. Little of his work has survived.

**Cal'za·bi'gi** (käl'tsä·bē'jē), **Raniero da.** 1714–1795. Italian poet; collaborator of Gluck to attain proper balance between music and action of drama; wrote libretti for Gluck's *Orfeo, Alceste*, and *Paride ed Elena.*

**Cam** (kouN) *or* **Cão** (kouN), **Diogo.** *Span.* **Diego Ca'no** (kä'nō). fl. 1480–1486. Portuguese navigator. In service of Alfonso V and John II; discovered mouth of Congo (1484); explored West African coast south to 22d parallel.

**Ca·ma'cho** (kä·mä'chō), **Manuel Ávila.** 1897–1955. Mexican politician and soldier, b. Teziutlán, Puebla state. Joined revolutionary forces under Huerta (1914); continued in active military service (1914–29); became known as successful arbitrator; president of Mexico (1940–46).

**Cam'ba'cé'rès'** (käN'bȧ'sā'rĕs'), Duc **de. Jean Jacques Ré'gis'** (rā'zhēs'). 1753–1824. French jurist and statesman, b. Montpellier. Member of the Convention (1792); president, Committee of Public Safety (1794) and Committee of Five Hundred (1796); minister of justice (1799); second consul (1799). Friend and chief counselor of Napoleon; archchancellor of the Empire (1804); created duke of Parma (1808).

**Cam'bert'** (käN'bâr'), **Robert.** 1628?–1677. French composer, b. Paris; a founder of opera in France. Musical superintendent to Anne of Austria (1666); composed *La Pastorale* (1659; text by Abbé Pierre Perrin), regarded as first French comedy in music; associated with Perrin as director of Académie Royale de Musique of the Paris opera house (patent obtained by Perrin, 1669); with him produced his *Pomone* (1671; text by Perrin), regarded as first real French opera; took refuge in London (1672) following dispossession of Perrin's right by court composer and intendant, Lully; said to have become master of music to Charles II of England.

**Cam·bia'so** (käm·byä'zō) *or* **Cam·bia'si** (-zē), **Luca.** 1527–1585. Genoese painter; studied under his father, **Giovanni Cambiaso;** friend and collaborator of Giovanni Battista Castello; called to Spain by Philip II to assist in frescoing the Escorial (1583); among his works are *Martyrdom of St. George, Rape of the Sabines*, and a *Pietà* (all at Genoa), and fresco *Paradise* in Escorial.

**Cam·bi'ni** (käm·bē'nē), **Giovanni Giuseppe.** 1746–1825. Italian violinist and composer in France; b. Leghorn; settled in Paris (1770); composed over 60 symphonies, 144 string quartets, 19 operas, ballets, etc.

**Cambio, Arnolfo di.** See ARNOLFO DI CAMBIO.

**Cam'bon'** (käN'bôN'), **Joseph.** 1754?–1820. French financier and politician. Member of the Convention (1792); voted for execution of Louis XVI. Authority on matters of finance; published detailed statement of the public debt. Exiled after Restoration (1815).

**Cambon, Pierre Paul.** 1843–1924. French diplomat, b. Paris; in home government service (1870–82) and diplomatic service (1882–1920); ambassador at Madrid (1886), Constantinople (1890), London (1898–1920). His brother **Jules Martin** (1845–1935), diplomat; ambassador at Washington (1897–1902), Madrid (1902–07), Berlin (1907–14).

**Cambon, Victor.** 1852–1927. French economist and publicist; author of *L'Allemagne au Travail* (1909), *Derniers Progrès de l'Allemagne* (1916), *Notre Avenir* (1918), *L'Industrie Organisée d'après les Méthodes Américaines* (1920), etc.

**Cambrensis, Giraldus.** See GIRALDUS DE BARRI.

**Cam'bridge** (kām'brĭj), Duke of. A title of English nobility held by: (1) Three infant sons of James II (title cr. 1661), none of whom lived to maturity. (2) George II, prior to accession as king (title held 1706–27). (3) **Adolphus Frederick** (1774–1850), seventh son of George III; served in Hanoverian and British armies; cr. duke of Cambridge (1801); privy councilor (1802); field marshal (1813); viceroy of kingdom of Hanover (1816–37); m. (1818) **Augusta** (1797–1889), daughter of Frederick, Landgrave of Hesse-Cassel. (4) His son and successor, **George William Frederick Charles** (1819–1904), 2d duke; served in Hanoverian army (1837) and British army; commanded division in Crimean War (1854); succeeded Lord Hardinge as commander in chief (1856); field marshal (1862); criticized many of changes inaugurated (1870, 1880) in army, opposing short service, formation of army reserve, and linking of battalions; chief personal aide-de-camp to Queen Victoria (1882–95).

**Cambridge,** Marquis of. See Adolphus Charles, Duke of TECK.

**Cambridge,** Earl of. A title of English nobility, originally united with earldom of Huntingdon and held by Plantagenet kings, which was bestowed: (1) on other Plantagenets, including Edmund of Langley and several dukes of York; (2) in 1619 on James Hamilton, 2d Marquis of Hamilton, and held by his sons James and William, 1st and 2d dukes of Hamilton (see HAMILTON family); (3) in 1659 on Henry, Duke of Gloucester, brother of Charles II.

**Cambridge, Ada.** *Maiden name of* Mrs. **George Frederick Cross.** 1844–1926. Australian novelist, b. in England; resident of Victoria (after 1870). Author of *A Marked Man* (1891), *The Three Miss Kings* (1891), *The Hand in the Dark* (1913).

**Cambridge, Richard Owen.** 1717–1802. English satirical poet. Educ. Oxford; lived in Twickenham (from 1751). Author of mock epic poem, the *Scribleriad* (1751), with Martin Scriblerus hero.

**Cam'bronne'** (käN'brôn'), Comte **Pierre Jacques Étienne.** 1770–1842. French general; served with distinction in campaigns of 1812, 1813, 1814; accompanied Napoleon to Elba; commanded division of Imperial Guard at Waterloo (1815).

**Cam·by'ses** (kăm·bī'sēz). fl. first half of 6th century B.C. King of Anshan; m. Mandane, daughter of Astyages, King of Media; father of Cyrus the Great. Sometimes called **Cambyses I,** King of Persia.

**Cambyses (II).** d. 522 B.C. King of Persia (529–522 B.C.). Son of Cyrus the Great. Secretly murdered younger brother Smerdis before setting out to conquer Egypt; defeated Psamtik III at Pelusium (525); added Nile Valley as far as Nubia to Persian Empire; failed in expeditions against Ammon and Ethiopia; died while returning to Persia (522) after learning of usurpation of his throne by "false Smerdis." See SMERDIS.

**Cam'den** (kăm'dĕn), Earls and marquis of. See Sir Charles PRATT.

**Camden, William.** 1551–1623. English antiquary and historian. Educ. Oxford; traveled in various parts of England collecting archaeological material; second master of Westminster School (1575); headmaster (1593–97), traveling during vacations; Clarenceux king-of-arms (1597–1623). Compiled *Britannia,* an account in Latin of British Isles from earliest times (first pub. 1586); printed list of epitaphs found in Westminster Abbey (1600); wrote a history of reign of Queen Elizabeth (1615, 1625).

**Camel** *or* **Camellus, George Joseph.** See KAMEL.

**Cam'e·rar'i·us** (kăm'ẽr·âr'ĭ·ŭs; *Ger.* kä'mȧ·rä'rē·ŏŏs), **Joachim.** *Surname Latinized from Ger.* **Kam'mer·mei'ster** (käm'ẽr·mī'stẽr), *i.e.* "chamberlain," *added to orig. family name* **Lieb'hard** (lēp'härt) *because of hereditary family office of chamberlain to prince bishop of Bamberg.* 1500–1574. German classical scholar. Professor of Greek, Erfurt (1518) and Nuremberg (1526); embraced Reformation and became friend of Melanchthon at Wittenberg (1521); attended Diet of Augsburg as delegate from Nuremberg and helped Melanchthon formulate Augsburg Confession (1530); took part in university reform and helped develop Latin and Greek studies at Tübingen (1535) and Leipzig (from 1541). Author of handbooks of grammar, translations and editions of classical texts (notably of Plautus, 1552), an edition of Melanchthon's letters (1569), biographies of Helius Eobanus Hessus (1553) and of Melanchthon (1566), *Epistolae Familiares,* a contribution to the history of his time, etc. His son **Joachim** (1534–1598), physician and botanist, specialized in cultivation of rare plants.

**Camerarius, Rudolf Jakob.** 1665–1721. German physician and botanist of Tübingen; known for work on the reproductive organs of plants.

**Cam'er·on** (kăm'ẽr·ŭn), **Basil.** 1885– . Orchestra conductor, b. Reading, Eng. Studied in Berlin (1901–03). Served in World War; wounded in action (1918). Conducted Hastings Municipal Orchestra (1923–30), Harrogate Municipal Orchestra (1924–30), Royal Philharmonic Society concerts at London (1928–31), British Broadcasting Company symphony concerts at London (1928–33), San Francisco Symphony Orchestra (1930–32), Seattle Symphony Orchestra (1932–38).

**Cameron,** Sir **David Young.** 1865–1945. British painter and etcher; educ. Glasgow and Edinburgh; represented in leading English, Australian, and Canadian galleries. Collections of his etchings appeared in *Paris Etchings* (1904) and *Etchings in Belgium* (1907); also made etchings to illustrate *The Compleat Angler,* etc.

**Cameron, Donald** (1695?–1748). See CAMERON OF LOCHIEL.

**Cameron, Edgar Spier** (spīr). 1862–1944. American figure, landscape, and mural painter, b. Ottawa, Ill. Studied in Chicago Academy of Design, Art Students' League in New York, Académie Julian and École des Beaux-Arts (Paris). Art critic on Chicago *Tribune* (1891–1900). Executed murals for supreme court library of Springfield, Ill.

**Cameron,** Sir **Ewen** *or* **Evan.** See CAMERON OF LOCHIEL.

**Cameron, John.** 1579?–1625. Scottish theologian. Protestant minister, Bordeaux (1608–17); professor of divinity, Saumur (1618–20, 1623–24), Montaubon (1624); disliked in Scotland and France for his doctrine of passive obedience; stabbed in street in Montaubon. Called founder of moderate Calvinistic school of Saumur, often called *Cameronites.*

**Cameron, Margaret.** See Margaret Cameron KILVERT.

**Cameron, Richard.** d. 1680. Scottish Covenanter, founder of religious sect of Reformed Presbyterians, popularly called Cameronians. Schoolmaster; tutor; on return from Holland (1680) resisted reinstatement of Episcopal Church in Scotland; preached in fields; renounced allegiance to Charles II (1680); killed in skirmish in hills of Ayrshire, the survivors of which were amnestied and formed nucleus of the famous Cameronian regiment of British army.

**Cameron, Simon.** 1799–1889. American financier and politician, b. in Lancaster County, Pa. U.S. senator (1845–49, 1857–61, 1867–77); controlled Republican political machine in Pennsylvania (1857–77). U.S. secretary of war (1861–62); criticized for manner of awarding army contracts. U.S. minister to Russia (1862). His son **James Donald** (1833–1918) succeeded him in control of Republican machine in Pennsylvania; U.S. secretary of war (1876–77); senator (1877–97).

**Cameron, Verney Lovett.** 1844–1894. English explorer

in Africa. Served in British navy (1857–83); in Abyssinian campaign (1868); leader of Royal Geographic Society's expedition to aid Livingstone (1873); sent Livingstone's papers to England; explored southern half of Lake Tanganyika; first European to cross equatorial Africa east to west (1875). Author of *Across Africa* (1877) and, with Sir R. F. Burton, *To the Gold Coast for Gold* (1883).

**Cameron of Loch·iel′** (lŏk·ēl′). Appellation of: (1) Sir **Ewen** *or* **Evan Cameron** (1629–1719), Scottish highland chieftain; led clan against forces of Commonwealth (1652); submitted to Monck and was received at Charles II's court (1660); raised his clan to join John Graham of Claverhouse in battle of Killiecrankie (1689); sent clan to join in earl of Mar's uprising (1715); said to have killed last wolf in Scotland. (2) His grandson **Donald Cameron** (1695?–1748), called "the Gentle Lochiel," chieftain of Clan Cameron; reluctantly supported Prince Charles Edward (1745); took Edinburgh (1745); fought at Prestonpans; captured Falkirk; wounded at Culloden (1746); escaped with Prince Charles Edward to France (1746).

**Ca·mil′lus** (kȧ·mĭl′ŭs), **Marcus Furius.** d. about 365 B.C. Roman soldier and statesman. Captured Veii after ten-year siege; saved Rome from complete destruction in Gallic invasion under Brennus (*q.v.*); five times elected dictator; aided in securing passage of Licinian laws (367 B.C.); died of plague.

**Cam′maerts** (käm′ärts), **Émile.** 1878–1953. Belgian poet, writer, and patriot, b. Brussels; settled in England (1908) but remained Belgian subject. Translator of Ruskin and Chesterton into French. Author of *Les Bellini* (essay on art criticism), of plays, of verse written during World War and translated into English by his wife, Tita Brand, including *Belgian Poems* (1915), *New Belgian Poems* (1916), and *Messines and Other Poems* (1918), of *Through the Iron Bars* (account of Belgium's suffering in World War; Eng. trans., 1918), of *Poèmes Intimes* (1922), and of *Discoveries in England* (1930), *The Laughing Prophet* (1937), *The Child of Divorce* (1938), *The Keystone of Europe* (1939), etc.

**Cam′mann** (kăm′ăn), **George Philip.** 1804–1863. American physician in New York; inventor of the binaural stethoscope.

**Cam′ma·ra′no** (käm′mä·rä′nō), **Salvatore.** d. 1852. Italian librettist; wrote libretti of *Lucia di Lammermoor*, *Il Trovatore*, etc.

**Ca·mões′** (kȧ·mōĕɴsh′), *Eng. spelling* **Cam′o·ëns** (kăm′ō·ĕnz; kȧ·mō′ĕnz), **Luiz Vaz de** (vȧzh thĕ). 1524–1580. Portuguese poet, b. Lisbon. Educ. U. of Coimbra (1539–42). To Lisbon (1542); banished from court (c. 1547) as result of conflicts arising from his passion for a lady in the queen's retinue, Caterina de Ataide (the "Natercia" of his verse). Participated in campaign of John III against Morocco, losing right eye (1550); to India (1553–69) as common soldier; led adventurous life; clashed with Portuguese authorities at Goa over alleged abuses; imprisoned. Returned to Lisbon (1570); gained patronage of King Sebastian; reinstated at court. Author of *Os Lusíadas* (Eng. *The Lusiad*, better *Lusiads;* composed, 1556 ff.; pub., 1572), his masterpiece, treating in ottava rima the chief episodes in Portuguese history; wrote also sonnets, odes, elegies, satires, epigrams, and comedies, including *Os Amphitryões* and *Filodemo.* Notable for his development of Portuguese lyric to its highest point and for his influence on national drama.

**Camp** (kămp), **Walter Chauncey.** 1859–1925. American football coach, b. New Britain, Conn. Grad. Yale (1880). In employ of New Haven Clock Co. (from 1883). Football coach, Yale (1888); influential in shaping American football rules; originator of practice of choosing an all-America football team (from 1889). Deviser of the "Daily Dozen," a series of simple calisthenic exercises.

**Cam·pa′gna** (käm·pä′nyä), **Gerolamo.** c. 1549–after 1626. Venetian sculptor, b. Verona; pupil of Cattaneo at Verona and Venice. His works include statue of Doge Leonardo Loredano on tomb in church of Santi Giovanni e Paolo at Venice, statue of St. Justina over portal of Arsenal, altar of San Giorgio Maggiore, statue of St. Anthony in church of San Giacomo di Rialto (all in Venice), statue of Duke Federico Montefeltro (at Urbino), and bronze statues on façade of Palazzo del Consiglio (at Verona).

**Cam′pa·gno′la** (käm′pä·nyô′lä), **Domenico.** c. 1484–c. 1563. Italian painter; worked chiefly in Padua; thought to have assisted Titian in decoration of Scuola del Santo, Padua. His paintings include frescoes in Scuola del Santo and Scuola del Carmine (Padua), *Birth of Christ* (in Vienna Academy), *Holy Family* (Pitti Palace), *Four Prophets* (Venetian Academy), *Madonna* (Museo Civico, Padua); other works include engravings, woodcuts, and many pen-and-ink drawings.

**Campagnola, Giulio.** 1482–?1515. Italian engraver and painter; engraved chiefly after Giorgione, as *The Astrologer*, *The Samaritan*, *Two Nude Women.* His technique of engraving anticipated stippling.

**Cam′pa·gno′li** (käm′pä·nyô′lē), **Bartolomeo.** 1751–1827. Italian violinist and composer. Studied in Bologna and Modena, and under Nardini in Florence; in service of duke of Courland, Dresden (1780–83); conductor of Gewandhaus concerts, Leipzig (1797–1816); court Kapellmeister, Neustrelitz (from 1826). Composed 41 caprices for viola, a violin school (1797), concertos and sonatas for violin and flute, etc.

**Cam′pan′** (käɴ′päɴ′), **Jeanne Louise Henriette,** *nee* **Ge·net′** (zhĕ·nĕ′). 1752–1822. French educator; first lady of the bedchamber to Marie Antoinette (c. 1769–89). Opened girls' boarding school at Saint-Germain (1794); appointed by Napoleon (1807) head of a school for daughters, sisters, and nieces of officers of the Legion of Honor. Author of *Mémoires sur la Vie Privée de Marie Antoinette* (1822).

**Campaña, Pedro.** See Peter de KEMPENER.

**Cam′pa·na′ri** (käm′pä·nä′rē), **Giuseppe.** 1858–1927. Italian cellist and dramatic baritone. Made debut as opera singer in New York City (1893), and sang in first American performance of *Pagliacci;* member, Metropolitan Opera Company (1895–98).

**Cam′pa·nel′la** (käm′pä·nĕl′lä), **Tommaso,** *orig.* **Giovanni Domenico.** 1568–1639. Italian philosopher, b. Stilo, Calabria; opponent of scholasticism and Aristotelian logic. Dominican monk (from c. 1583); studied at Naples and Cosenza; taught at Rome and Naples; imprisoned (1599–1626) on charges of heresy and conspiracy against Spanish rule; forced to flee to France (1634); protégé of Louis XIII and Richelieu. Known especially for his *Civitas Solis* ("City of the Sun"), written during imprisonment, a description of a utopian state similar to that of Plato's *Republic.* His works, over 80 in all, also include *Philosophia Sensibus Demonstrata* (1591), *De Sensu Rerum et Magia* (1620), *Philosophia Epilogistica Realis* (printed with *Civitas Solis*, 1623), and *Atheismus Triumphatus*...(1636).

**Cam′pa·ni′ni** (käm′pä·nē′nē), **Italo.** 1846–1896. Italian operatic tenor. Studied in Parma and under Lamperti in Milan; sang at La Scala in Milan (1869), in Bologna (1871), London (1872), and New York (1873); later toured in U.S. and Russia; lived chiefly in New York (after 1883). His brother **Cleofonte** (1860–1919), conductor, studied at Parma conservatory (1870–78) and

Milan; conductor, Parma Opera (1883); as assistant conductor, Metropolitan Opera, N.Y. (1883), conducted first American production of Verdi's *Otello* (1887); conductor, Covent Garden, London (1897–1902), La Scala, Milan (1903–06); toured in Europe and South America; conductor and general artistic director, Manhattan Opera House, New York City (1906–09); conductor and director (1910–19) and general manager (from 1913), Chicago Opera Company.

**Cam·pa'nus** (kăm·pā'nŭs), **Johannes.** 13th-century Italian mathematician, b. Novara; chaplain to Pope Urban IV; wrote commentaries on Euclid.

**Camp'bell** (kăm'bĕl; *in U.S., also* kăm'ĕl). Family name of earls, marquises, and dukes of ARGYLL.

**Campbell, Alexander.** 1788–1866. Founder of the Disciples of Christ, b. in County Antrim, Ireland. To U.S. (1809); settled first in Washington, Pa.; pastor, Brush Run, Pa., church (1813), affiliated with a Baptist association; was refused license as preacher. Itinerant undenominational preacher (1813–27). Founded (1823) and edited (1823–30) *Christian Baptist*, edited *Millennial Harbinger* (1830–63), using these magazines to promulgate his reforms and his criticism of current Baptist organization and practice. His followers, known as Disciples of Christ (nicknamed Campbellites), were dropped from Baptist affiliation and from about 1827 began to form a new and separate denomination. Founded Bethany College, Bethany, W.Va. (1840); president (1840–66). Coalescence of churches of the Christian Connection with churches of the Disciples of Christ formed a vigorous organization, spreading through Kentucky, Tennessee, Ohio, and westward. Chief work: *The Christian System* (1839). Cf. John McLEOD CAMPBELL.

**Campbell,** Sir **Alexander.** 1822–1892. Canadian politician. Postmaster general (1867–73, 1879, 1880, 1885–87); senator (1867); minister of militia (1879), of justice (1881); lieutenant governor of Ontario (1887–92).

**Campbell,** Sir **Archibald.** 1769–1843. British army officer. Served in India (1788–99), in Portugal (1808–20); Portuguese commander at Lisbon (1816–20); conducted Burmese War (1824–26); governor of British Burma (1826–29); lieutenant governor of New Brunswick, Canada (1831–37); lieutenant general (1838).

**Campbell,** Sir **Colin.** Baron **Clyde** (klīd). 1792–1863. British military commander, b. Glasgow. Original surname **Mac·li'ver** (măk·lē'vẽr) changed to *Campbell* through error of duke of York (1807). Served in Peninsular War (1810–13), in West Indies (1819–26), in China (1842–46), in India (1846–53); commanded first division in Crimean War (1854–55). Commander in chief in India (1857–60); relieved Lucknow (1857); suppressed Sepoy Mutiny (1857–58); cr. baron Clyde (1858); field marshal (1862).

**Campbell, Douglas Houghton.** 1859–1953. American botanist, b. Detroit. Ph.M. (1882) and Ph.D. (1886), Michigan; studied in Germany (1886–88). Professor, Stanford (from 1891). Author of *Elements of Structural and Systematic Botany* (1890), *Structure and Development of Mosses and Ferns* (1895), *Plant Life and Evolution* (1911), *Outline of Plant Geography* (1926), etc.

**Campbell, George.** 1719–1796. Scottish theologian. Principal of Marischal Coll., Aberdeen (1759–92) and professor of divinity (1771–92). Author of *Dissertation on Miracles* (1762) and of *Philosophy of Rhetoric* (1776), resembling and rivaling the lectures of Blair.

**Campbell,** Sir **George.** 1824–1892. British administrator in India, b. and educ. in Scotland. Entered Indian civil service (1842); employed by governor general to write official account of Sepoy Mutiny (1857); judge of high court of Bengal (1862); chief commissioner of Central Provinces (1867); lieutenant governor of Bengal (1871–74). Author of *Ethnology of India* (1865).

**Campbell, George Washington.** 1769–1848. Lawyer, b. in Sutherland, Scotland; to America as a child. Grad. Princeton (1794); U.S. secretary of the treasury (1814); U.S. senator from Tenn. (1815–18); U.S. minister to Russia (1818–21).

**Campbell, James.** 1812–1893. American lawyer, b. Philadelphia; U.S. postmaster general (1853–57).

**Campbell, James Dykes.** 1838–1895. Scottish merchant (in Mauritius 1873–81) and author of a biography, long the standard biography, of Coleridge (1894).

**Campbell, John.** 1st Earl of **Lou'doun** (lou'd'n). 1598–1663. Scottish organizer of the subscribers to the National Covenant. Lord chancellor of Scotland (1641–60); frequent envoy from parliament to Charles I (1642–47); fought at Dunbar (1650) and in Scottish uprising (1653); heavily fined by Charles II (1662). His great grandson **John Campbell** (1705–1782), 4th Earl of Loudoun, British general, b. in Ayrshire, Scotland; entered army (1727); commander in chief in America (1756); lost Forts Oswego and William Henry; failed in planned invasion of Canada; recalled (Dec., 1757); acting commander, British troops in Portugal (1762–63); general (1770).

**Campbell, John.** 1st Earl of **Bread·al'bane** (brĕd-ôl'băn). 1635–1716. Scottish politician. Attempted to dispossess male heir to earldom of Caithness; his claim rejected by privy council; submitted to William III (1689) and employed to bribe Highland chiefs to submit; with Argyll, organized massacre of Macdonalds of Glencoe (1692); joined, but soon withdrew from, Jacobite rising (1715).

**Campbell, John.** 1653–1728. Journalist, b. in Scotland; emigrated to Massachusetts (c. 1695); postmaster at Boston (from 1702). Publisher of Boston *News-Letter* (1704–22), first regular newspaper in America.

**Campbell, John.** 1708–1775. Scottish man of letters in London; agent for Georgia (1765–75); author of *Military History of Prince Eugene and Duke of Marlborough* (1736), *Lives of British Admirals* (4 vols., 1742, 1744).

**Campbell, John.** 1st Baron **Campbell.** 1779–1861. British jurist, b. in Fife, Scotland. Called to bar in England (1806); M.P. (1830); took active part in law reform, largely by abolition of obstructive technicalities; solicitor general (1832); attorney general (1834–41); chief justice of queen's bench (1850); lord chancellor (1859). Author of *Lives of the Lord Chancellors* (1845–47), *Lives of the Chief Justices* (1849, 1857).

**Campbell, John Archibald.** 1811–1889. American jurist, b. Washington, Ga. Educ. U.S.M.A., West Point (3 years). Associate justice, U.S. Supreme Court (1853); resigned (1861). Assistant secretary of war in Confederate cabinet (1862–65).

**Campbell** of **Is'lay** (ī'lȧ; ī'lā), **John Francis.** 1822–1885. Scottish writer of Highland folklore; government official; Gaelic scholar. Author of *Popular Tales of the West Highlands* (4 vols., 1860–62).

**Campbell, John McLeod.** 1800–1872. Scottish theologian. Educ. Glasgow and Edinburgh; ejected from ministry in Church of Scotland because of his views on personal assurance of salvation and on universality of the atonement (1831); preached without remuneration, Glasgow (1833–59). His followers known as Campbellites; cf. Alexander CAMPBELL, 1788–1866.

**Campbell, Joseph.** 1879–1944. Irish poet, b. Belfast; under his Gaelic name (**Seo'samh Mac Cathm'haoil** [shō'săf măk kă'wĭl]) published *The Rushlight* (1906), *The Mountainy Singer* (1909), etc.

**Campbell, Levin H.** 1886– . American army officer; grad. U.S.N.A., Annapolis, but transferred to the army; advanced through the grades to colonel (1940); lieut. general (April, 1945) and chief of ordnance, U.S. army.

**Campbell, Lewis.** 1830–1908. Scottish classical scholar. Educ. Glasgow and Oxford; professor of Greek and Gifford lecturer, St. Andrews (1863–94). Edited Sophocles, translated Sophocles and Aeschylus into English verse, completed Jowett's translation of Plato's *Republic* (1894).

**Campbell,** Sir **Malcolm.** 1885–1948. English businessman and automobile racer; on staff of Lloyds, London (1906). Served through World War (1914–18; air pilot 1916–18). Began motor racing as hobby (1910); subsequently established (chiefly at Daytona Beach, Fla., and Salt Lake City, Utah) many world records for speed. Author of *Speed* (1931), *The Romance of Motor-Racing* (1936), *The Roads and the Problem of their Safety* (1937), etc.

**Campbell,** Mrs. **Patrick.** *Nee* **Beatrice Stella Tan'ner** (tăn'ẽr). 1867–1940. English actress; m. 1st, Patrick Campbell (1884; killed in South Africa, 1900), 2d, George Frederick Myddleton Cornwallis-West (1914). On professional stage (from 1888); appeared in *The Second Mrs. Tanqueray, The Masqueraders, The Notorious Mrs. Ebbsmith, Little Eyolf, Magda, Hedda Gabler, Pygmalion;* well known also in roles of Ophelia, Lady Teazle, Lady Macbeth, and Juliet.

**Campbell, Reginald John.** 1867–1956. English clergyman, b. London. Educ. Oxford; ordained in Congregational ministry (1895); minister of City Temple, London (1903–15), where his sermons were credited with teaching a new theology; ordained in Church of England ministry (1916); chancellor of Chichester Cathedral (from 1930). Author of many religious books, including *A Faith for To-day* (1900), *Christianity and the Social Order* (1908), *The War and the Soul* (1916), *Problems of Life* (1919), *The Call of Christ* (1933), *The Peace of God* (1936).

**Campbell, Robert.** See Robert MACGREGOR, 1671–1734.

**Campbell, Roy,** *in full* **Ignatius Roy Dunnachie.** 1901–1957. British poet, b. Durban, South Africa. War correspondent of the *Tablet;* served in Spain during Spanish Civil War. Author of *The Flaming Terrapin, Adamastor, Flowering Reeds, Broken Record, Flowering Rifle.*

**Campbell, Thomas.** 1763–1854. Associated with his son Alexander Campbell (*q.v.*) in founding and organizing the Church of the Disciples of Christ.

**Campbell, Thomas.** 1777–1844. British poet, b. and educ. Glasgow. Studied law in Edinburgh (1797) and worked as tutor; published his didactic poem *The Pleasures of Hope* (1799), treating of contemporary subjects, including French Revolution, partition of Poland, Negro slavery, which scored a success; man of letters in or near London (1803–44); pensioned by crown (1805); published *Specimens of the British Poets* (1819), selections with short lives; edited *New Monthly Magazine* (1820–30); lord rector of Glasgow (1826–29); buried in Westminster Abbey. Remembered chiefly for his stirring patriotic and war lyrics, including *Hohenlinden, Ye Mariners of England, The Soldier's Dream, The Battle of the Baltic* (mostly written 1800–01).

**Campbell,** Lord **William.** d. 1778. English administrator in America. Appointed governor of Nova Scotia (1766), of South Carolina (1773); arrived at Charleston June 17, 1775; attempted unsuccessfully to keep colony loyal.

**Campbell, William.** 1876–1936. American metallurgist, b. Gateshead, England. Grad. King's Coll., London (1892); studied at Oxford (1892–94), Durham U. (B.S., 1897), Royal School of Mines, London (1899–1901); Ph.D., Columbia (1903). Taught at Columbia U. School of Mines (1904–36). Metallographist connected with U.S. Geological Survey (1907–21).

**Campbell, William Edward March.** See William MARCH.

**Campbell, William Wallace.** 1862–1938. American astronomer, b. Hancock County, Ohio. B.S., Michigan (1886). Astronomer (1891–1930), director (1901–30), Lick Observatory, Calif.; president, U. of Calif. (1923–30). In charge of eclipse expeditions to India (1898), Georgia (1900), Spain (1905), Flint Island (1908), Russia (1914), Washington (1918), Western Australia (1922). Author of *The Elements of Practical Astronomy* (1899), *Stellar Motions* (1913), and *Stellar Radial Velocities* (with J. H. Moore; 1928).

**Campbell, William Wilfred.** 1861–1918. Canadian poet, b. in Ontario. Anglican clergyman (1885–91; resigned); entered Canadian civil service (1891). Author of *Lake Lyrics* (1889), *Beyond the Hills of Dream* (1899), *Collected Poems* (1905), *Poetic Tragedies* (1908); editor, *Oxford Book of Canadian Verse* (1906).

**Camp'bell–Ban'ner·man** (-băn'ẽr·măn), Sir **Henry.** 1836–1908. British statesman, b. Glasgow; son of Sir James Campbell (Lord Provost of Glasgow, 1840–43); assumed name Bannerman under maternal uncle's will (1872). M.A., Cantab. (1861). Liberal M.P. (1868–1908); financial secretary to war office (1871–74, 1880–82); chief secretary for Ireland (1884–85); secretary for war (1886, 1892–95); supported Gladstone's home-rule policy for Ireland; leader of Liberals in House of Commons (1899); advocated conciliatory measures toward conquered Boers, and denounced British "methods of barbarism" in South Africa (1901). Prime minister (1905–08), on Balfour's resignation; ended importation of indentured Chinese labor into South Africa; granted Boer ex-republics responsible government; led campaign against House of Lords; advocated arbitration of international disputes and limitation of armaments, alliances with great naval powers.

**Cam'pe** (käm'pĕ), **Joachim Heinrich.** 1746–1818. German writer and educator. Studied theology; tutor to Humboldt family, Berlin (1769 and 1774–75); helped reorganize school system as educational adviser in Brunswick (1786–1805); took over Brunswick educational book house (1787–1808), which he developed largely through publication of his own works. Author of juveniles, including *Robinson der Jüngere* (1779–80; based on Defoe; translated into many languages), works on education, and works on German language, including *Wörterbuch der Deutschen Sprache* (5 vols., 1807–11).

**Cam·peg'gio** (käm·pād'jō), **Lorenzo.** 1474?–1539. Italian papal legate. Studied law at Pavia and Bologna; bishop of Feltri (1512); cardinal (1517); sent to England (1518), ostensibly to urge crusade against Turks; made bishop of Salisbury by Henry VIII (1524–34); archbishop of Bologna (1524); as colegate with Wolsey to hear Henry VIII's suit to divorce Catherine of Aragon (1528–29), was under papal instructions not to offend Catherine's nephew Charles V of France; failed to satisfy Henry; assisted at coronation of Charles V (1530).

**Cam'pen·hout** (käm'pĕn·hout), **François van.** 1779–1848. Belgian violinist, composer, and tenor singer. His works include several operas, cantatas, choruses, religious music, and songs, notably the music of the Belgian national air, *La Brabançonne* (written during revolution of 1830).

**Cam'per** (käm'pẽr), **Pieter.** 1722–1789. Dutch anatomist and naturalist. Educ. at Leiden. Professor at Franeker (1750), Amsterdam (1755), Groningen (1763–73). Known for work in human and comparative anatomy, also in surgery and obstetrics; attempted to determine the degree of human intelligence by measuring the facial angle; discovered the large air content of the bones of birds.

**Camperdown,** Earl of. See under Adam DUNCAN.

**Cam·pe′ro** (käm·pā′rō), **Narciso.** 1813–1896. Bolivian soldier. Minister of war (1872); president of Bolivia (1880–84); in war with Chile, commanded Peruvian and Bolivian armies at Tacna; defeated (1880).

**Camp′hau′sen** (kämp′hou′zĕn), **Ludolf.** 1803–1890. Prussian statesman. Banker in Cologne (1826); member, Rhenish Provincial Diet (1843) and General Diet of States, Berlin (1847); president of Prussian ministry (March–June, 1848); Prussian plenipotentiary at Frankfurt (1849); proposed closer confederation of states under Prussian leadership; sat in Prussian upper chamber (1849–51) and in Erfurt Parliament (1850). His brother **Otto von Camphausen** (1812–1896), statesman and financial expert; member of lower chamber (1849, 1850–52) and of Erfurt Parliament (1850); president of shipping trade (1854); member, Prussian Herrenhaus (1860); minister of finance (1869) and vice-president of state ministry (1873); resigned offices (1878) following conflict with Bismarck on latter's protective tariff.

**Camphausen, Wilhelm.** 1818–1885. German painter; studied under Alfred Rethel and at Düsseldorf Acad., where he taught (from 1859). His works include historical and battle scenes, equestrian portraits of German princes, statesmen, and soldiers, also sketches for woodcuts and lithographs. Author and illustrator of a diary of the Schleswig-Holstein campaign, *Ein Maler auf dem Kriegsfeld* (1865).

**Camp′huy′sen** (kämp′hoi′sĕn), **Dirk Rafelsz.** 1586–1627. Dutch painter, religious poet, and theologian; deserted art for theology; preacher in Vleuten, near Utrecht (1616); deprived of post because of Arminian views (1619); lived subsequently in poverty, and resided in Dokkum as dealer in flax; author of a translation of the Psalms, the volume *Comforting Rhymes* (1624), etc. His nephew **Raphael** (1597?–1657), painter esp. of moonlight scenes, including a *Winter Landscape* (now in Leipzig). Another nephew, **Govaert** (1624?–1672), painter and engraver; court painter at Stockholm (c. 1653–63); painted esp. landscapes with animals in Paul Potter's style, stable interiors, and farmyard scenes.

**Cam′pi** (käm′pē). 16th-century Italian family of painters in Cremona, including: **Galeazzo Campi** (1477–1536), pupil and imitator of Boccaccino, painter chiefly of religious pictures. His son **Giulio** (c. 1502–1572), pupil of Giulio Romano in Mantua; chief works include high altar in San Abbondio at Cremona (1527) and frescoes in Santa Margherita at Cremona (1547). Another son, **Antonio** (d. 1591?), known also as an architect and writer; imitator of Correggio; employed in several Italian cities and by Philip II in Madrid; works include the painting *Birth of Christ* in church of San Paolo in Milan and a chronicle of Cremona decorated with original engravings. A third son, **Vincenzo** (1536–1591), pupil of his brother Giulio, painter chiefly of portraits, as in Bergamo Gallery, and of still-life and genre scenes, as in the Brera at Milan. **Bernardino Campi** (1522–c. 1590), pupil of Giulio Campi, influenced chiefly by Giulio Romano and Correggio; chief work frescoes in cupola of San Sigismondo at Cremona; author of *Parere sopra la Pittura* (1584).

**Campin, Robert.** See under Le Maître de FLÉMALLE.

**Cam′pin′chi′** (käɴ′păɴ′kē′), **César.** 1882–1941. French criminal lawyer and politician; minister of marine; opposed policy of appeasement adopted at Munich (1938); fled to North Africa when French army was defeated (June, 1940).

**Cam′pi·on** (kăm′pĭ·ŭn; -pyŭn), **Edmund.** 1540–1581. English Jesuit martyr. Son of London bookseller; M.A., Oxon. (1564); Anglican deacon (1568?); suspected of papist leanings, escaped to Douai; joined Jesuits (1573); professor of rhetoric, Prague. Sent to England (1580) with Robert Parsons (*q.v.*) on mission to coerce temporizing Catholics; distributed at Oxford commencement (1581) audacious attack on Anglican Church; indicted for conspiracy to dethrone queen; racked three times; executed as traitor. Beatified (1886).

**Campion, Thomas.** 1567–1620. English poet and musician. Gentleman pensioner, Cambridge (1581); doctor of physic (1606); practiced medicine in London. Wrote masques and composed music for them, for court occasions (1607–17); wrote *Poemata*, a collection of epigrams, elegies, etc., in Latin (1595), *Observations on the Arte of English Poesie* advocating rhymeless verse on model of classical quantitative verse (1602), and a textbook on counterpoint (1617?). Remembered chiefly for graceful and musical lyrics, including *Cherry Ripe; Come, Cheerful Day;* and *Whether Men Do Laugh or Weep.*

**Cam·pís′te·guy** (käm·pēs′tā·gē), **Juan.** 1859–1937. Uruguayan political leader, of Basque descent, b. Montevideo. Teacher and journalist; took part in overthrow of Santos government (1886); engaged in various social projects (1891–96); secretary of treasury (1897, 1899). President of Uruguay (1927–31).

**Cam′pis′tron′** (käɴ′pēs′trôɴ′), **Jean Galbert de.** 1656–1723. French playwright. Author of *Virginie* (1683), the opera *Acis et Galatée* (1686), the tragedies *Phocion, Alcibiade, Phraate,* and *Juba,* the comedy *Le Jaloux Désabusé.*

**Cam′po·a·mor′ y Cam′po·o·so′rio** (käm′pō·ä·môr′ ē käm′pō·ō·sō′ryō), **Ramón de.** 1817–1901. Spanish poet, philosopher, and statesman, b. Navia, Asturias. Educ. at Santiago and Madrid; studied medicine; deputy to Cortes; governor of Alicante and Valencia (1854); councilor of state (after 1874); senator. Author of political tracts, as *Polémicas con la Democracia* (1862), philosophical treatises, as *La Filosofía de las Leyes* (1846) and *La Metafísica y la Poética* (1891), poems, as *Ternezas y Flores* (1840), *Fábulas Morales y Políticas* (1842), *Colón* (16 cantos, 1853, 1857), *El Drama Universal* (1869), *Los Buenos y los Sabios* (1881), and *Los Amores de Juana* (1882), and verse plays, as *Dies Irae* (1873) and *El Palacio de la Verdad* (1871).

**Cam′po·ma′nes** (käm′pō·mä′nās), Conde **de. Pedro Ro·drí′guez** (rō·thrē′gāth). 1723–1802. Spanish statesman and economist, b. in Asturias. President of council (1788–93); director, Royal Acad. of History; studied economic causes of Spain's impoverishment and pursued policy of economic reform. Author of *Tratado de la Regalía de la Amortización* (1765), *Discurso sobre el Fomento de la Industria Popular* (1771), and *Discurso sobre la Educación Popular de los Artesanos y Su Fomento* (1774–76).

**Cam′pos** (käm′pōs), **Rubén.** 1876– . Mexican educator, b. Guanajuato. Official in secretariat of public education (1898–1919, 1922 ff.). Author of *El Folklore y la Música Mexicana, El Folklore Literario de México, La Producción Literaria de los Aztecas, Tradiciones y Legendas Mexicanas.*

**Cam′pos Sal′les** (kăɴm′pōōs säl′ēs), **Manuel Fer·raz′**

**de** (fĕr·ràz′ ~~thĕ~~). 1841-1913. Brazilian lawyer and politician, b. Campinas, São Paulo state. Deputy (1884–89); minister of justice (1889 ff.); governor of São Paulo (1896–1898). President of Brazil (1898–1902).

**Cam′pra′** (kän′prȧ′), **André.** 1660–1744. French opera composer. Kapellmeister, Toulon cathedral (1679), Arles (1681), Toulouse (1683–94); to Paris (1694); royal Kapellmeister (from 1722). Composed ballet operas *L'Europe Galante* (1697) and *Le Carnaval de Venise* (1699), other operas including *Tancrède* (1702) and *Les Fêtes Vénitiennes* (1710), five books of motets (1695–1720), three books of cantatas (1708–28), a mass (1700), psalms, etc.

**Ca′muc·ci′ni** (kä′mōōt·chē′nē), **Vincenzo.** c. 1773–1844. Italian historical painter; chief representative of academic classical period in Italy.

**Ca′mus′** (kȧ′mü′), **Albert.** 1913–1960. French novelist, essayist, and playwright, b. Algeria. To Paris (1940); active in Fr. resistance during World War II. Awarded Nobel prize in literature (1957). Author of *The Stranger* (1942), *The Plague* (1947), *The Rebel* (1951), *The Fall* (1956), etc.

**Camus, Armand Gaston.** 1740–1804. French politician; member of States-General (1789), of the Convention (1792); president of Council of Five Hundred (1796–97). Author of *Lettres sur la Profession d'Avocat,* etc.

**Can′a·chus** (kăn′ȧ·kŭs). fl. late 6th century B.C. Greek sculptor, of Sicyon; known esp. for two statues of Apollo, one for Miletus and one for Thebes.

**Ca·na′le** (kä·nä′lā), **Michele Giuseppe.** 1808–1890. Italian historian; professor, Genoa; author of histories, plays, and historicoromantic novels.

**Ca′na·le′jas y Mén′dez** (kä′nä·lĕ′häs ē män′dāth), **José.** 1854–1912. Spanish statesman, b. El Ferrol. Educ. Madrid; became member of Cortes (1881); held several cabinet offices (between 1888 and 1902); president of Cortes (1906); premier (1910–11); accomplished separation of church and state, securing passage of anticlerical measures. Author of *El Partido Liberal* (1912) and volumes of speeches.

**Ca′na·let′to** (kä′nä·lāt′tō), **Antonio.** *Orig. surname* **Ca·na′le** (kä·nä′lā) *or* **Ca·nal′** (kä·näl′). 1697–1768. Venetian painter; studied under his father, Bernardo Canale; worked chiefly in Venice, also in Rome (1719–46), London (1746–56); known particularly for his urban scenes, esp. of Venice; his works found chiefly in Windsor Castle, in National Gallery in London (as *View on the Grand Canal, Regatta on the Grand Canal*), in the Louvre (as *Palace of the Doges, Piazza San Marco*), and in galleries of Turin and Dresden.
His nephew and pupil **Bernardo Be·lot′to** (bā·lôt′tō) *or* **Bel·lot′to** (bāl·lôt′tō) (1720–1780), also called **Canaletto** *or* **Canale,** was also a painter and etcher of Venetian scenes; worked in Rome, Milan, Dresden (1746–58, 1761–66), Vienna (1758–60), and Warsaw; his works found at Dresden and Vienna.

**Ca′na·li′zo** (kä′nä·lē′sō), **Valentín.** 1797?–?1847. Mexican general, b. Monterrey. Acting president of Mexico during Santa Anna's absences (1843, 1844); impeached for arbitrary acts (1844); banished (1845); allowed to return and served in war against U.S. (1846–47); in command of Mexican retreat after Cerro Gordo.

**Canares** *or* **Canaris.** Variants of KANARES, KANARIS.

**Can′by** (kăn′bĭ), **Edward Richard Sprigg.** 1817–1873. American army officer, b. in Kentucky; grad. U.S.M.A., West Point (1839); served through Mexican War and Civil War; murdered by Indian envoys in conference.

**Canby, Henry Sei′del** (sī′d'l). 1878–1961. American author and editor, b. Wilmington, Del. Ph.B. (1899), Ph.D. (1905), Yale. Teacher of English, Yale (from 1900; with rank of professor from 1922). Assistant editor, *Yale Review* (1911–20); editor, "Literary Review" of New York *Evening Post* (1920–24); editor, *Saturday Review of Literature* (1924–36). Author of *The Short Story in English* (1909), *College Sons and College Fathers* (1915), *Education by Violence* (1919), *Everyday Americans* (1920), *Definitions* (1st series, 1922, 2d series, 1924), *American Estimates* (1929), *Classic Americans* (1931), *The Age of Confidence* (1934), *Alma Mater* (1936), *Thoreau* (1939), *Handbook of English Usage* (1942), etc.

**Can·crin′** (kän·krēn′), Count **Georg.** *Russ. name* **Egor Frantsevich Kan·krin′** (kŭn·kryēn′). 1774–1845. Russian statesman, b. Hanau, Germany. To Russia (1796); entered Russian army; commissary general (1812); accompanied Czar Alexander I to Paris (1814). Russian minister of finance (1823–44). Author of *International Wealth, National Wealth, and Political Economy* (1820), etc.

**Can′da·ce** (kăn′dȧ·sē; kăn·dā′sē). According to inscriptions, a title (*Katake*) meaning "queen." Name of several queens of Ethiopia (Meroë), esp.: (1) Queen (or queen regent) who waged war with Roman governor of Egypt, was defeated (c. 22 B.C.) and her capital, Napata, destroyed. (2) Queen ruling at Meroë; her eunuch converted (c. 60 A.D.) by Philip (*Acts* viii. 27).

**Can·da′mo** (kän·dä′mō), **Francisco Antonio de Bances.** See BANCES CANDAMO.

**Candamo, Manuel.** 1842–1904. Peruvian journalist and politician, b. Lima. Provisional president (1895), president (1903–04; died in office).

**Can′di·do** (kän′dē·dō), **Pietro.** *Italian name of* **Pe′ter Can′did** (pē′tẽr kăn′dĭd). *Orig.* **Pieter de Wit′** (dĕ vĭt′) *or* **de Wit′te** (vĭt′ĕ). 1548?–1628. Flemish painter, b. Bruges; studied under Vasari in Italy; court painter at Munich (from 1586). Best known for his murals (as in the Residenz, Munich) and altarpieces.

**Can·dio′ti** (kän·dyō′tē), **Alberto María.** 1889– . Argentine diplomat and writer. In consular service (1913–29); minister to Yugoslavia and Greece (1930–34), Colombia and Ecuador (1935–39); ambassador to Colombia (1939–42), Mexico (1942– ). Author of *En la Penumbra de la Tarde* (1917), *Die Friedensbewegung in Süd- und Mittelamerika* (1922), *Historia de la Institución Consular en la Antigüedad y en la Edad Media* (1923), *El Jardín del Amor* (1936), *Incertidumbre* (1944), etc.

**Candish, Thomas.** See CAVENDISH.

**Can′dler** (kăn′dlẽr), **Asa Griggs.** 1851–1929. American manufacturer, b. in Carroll County, Ga. Developed manufacture and marketing of Coca-Cola. His brother **Warren Akin** (1857–1941), Methodist Episcopal clergyman; A.B., Emory Coll. (1875); president, Emory Coll. (1888–98); bishop, Methodist Episcopal Church, South (from 1898); author of *History of Sunday Schools* (1880), *High Living and High Lives* (1901), *The Christ and the Creed* (1927), etc.

**Can′dlish** (kăn′dlĭsh), **Robert Smith.** 1806–1873. Scottish Free Church leader. Minister of St. George's, Edinburgh (1834–73); took a leading part (from 1843) in formation of independent Free Church, and succeeded Thomas Chalmers as its controlling spirit (1847); principal of New College, Edinburgh (1862).

**Can′dolle′** (käN′dôl′), **Augustin Pyrame de.** 1778–1841. Swiss botanist. Educ. Geneva; moved to Paris (1796). His *Historia Plantarum Succulentarum* (4 vols., 1799–1803) and *Astragalogia* (1802) attracted notice of Cuvier and J. B. Lamarck, who entrusted him with publication of third edition of *Flore Française* (1803–15), the introduction to which contained first exposition of his natural system of plant classification; made botanical and agricultural survey of France in six summers for French government (1806–12); botanist and director of botanical garden (1807), professor of botany (1810), U. of Montpellier; professor of natural science and co-director (with son) of botanical garden at Geneva (1816–34). Attempted in his *Prodromus Systematis Regni Vegetabilis* (pub. 1824–74; based on his earlier *Regni Vegetabilis Systema Naturale*, of which only 2 vols. were published, 1819 and 1821), to set forth a complete natural system of plant classification but finished only 7 vols. His son **Alphonse Louis Pierre Pyrame de Candolle** (1806–1893), b. Paris, succeeded him as professor at Geneva and, in collaboration with his son **Anne Casimir Pyrame** (1836–1925), continued his *Prodromus Systematis...*; author also of *Géographie Botanique Raisonnée* (1855), *Lois de la Nomenclature Botanique* (1867), etc.

**Cane Grande della Scala.** See SCALA.

**Ca·ñe'te** (kä·nyā'tā), **Manuel.** 1822–1891. Spanish poet, dramatist, and critic, b. Seville; secretary to Infanta Doña Isabella (later queen of Spain); dramatic critic on *Ilustración Española y Americana* (1883–91). Author of verse and of plays, as *Un Rebato en Granada* (1845), *El Duque de Alba* (1845), and (with Tamayo y Baus) *La Esperanza de la Patria.*

**Ca·ne'va** (kä·nâ'vä), **Carlo.** 1845–1922. Italian soldier; in Austrian army (1863–66); in Italian army (1867 ff.); served in Abyssinian campaign (1896); lieutenant general (1902); commander in chief, Tripoli expeditionary force (1911); recalled (1912); member of senate (1912 ff.); presided over commission investigating Caporetto disaster (1917).

**Canfield, Dorothy.** See Dorothy Canfield FISHER.

**Can'ga Ar·güel'les** (käng'gä är·gwā'lyās), **José.** 1770–1843. Spanish statesman, b. in Asturias. Deputy to constituent Cortes (1812); exiled by Ferdinand VII (1814); minister of finance (1820–21); exile in England (1823–29). Author of *Elementos de la Ciencia de Hacienda* (1825), *Diccionario de Hacienda, con Aplicación a España* (1827), *Observaciones sobre la Guerra de la Península* (5 vols., 1833–36), and verse translation of odes of Sappho.

**Cange, du.** See DU CANGE.

**Can Grande.** See under SCALA.

**Ca·ni'na** (kä·nē'nä), **Luigi.** 1795–1856. Italian archaeologist and architect; architect at Rome (1818 ff.); directed excavation of Tusculum (1839) and the Appian Way (1848). Author of *L'Architettura Antica* (9 vols., 1834–44), *Foro Romano* (1845), *Gli Edifizii di Roma Antica* (6 vols., 1846–56), *Descrizione dell'Antico Tuscolo* (1841).

**Canino,** Prince of. See under BONAPARTE.

**Ca·ni'sius** (kȧ·nĭsh'ŭs; -ĭ·ŭs), Saint **Peter,** *Lat.* **Petrus.** *Orig. name* **Pieter De Hondt** (dĕ hônt'). 1521–1597. Jesuit theologian in Germany, b. Nijmegen. Entered Jesuit order (1543), and founded at Cologne first house of that order in Germany; influential in re-establishing Roman Catholicism in parts of Germany and in Poland; first provincial of Jesuit order in Germany (1556); prepared a catechism in Latin, *Summa Doctrinae Christianae* (1555). Beatified (1869); canonized (1925).

**Ca'nitz** (kä'nĭts), **Friedrich Rudolf Ludwig von.** 1654–1699. Prussian diplomat and poet; minister plenipotentiary in peace negotiations at Ryswick. Author of odes, satires, and elegies, chiefly imitations of Latin and French models.

**Canmore.** See MALCOLM III (of Scotland).

**Can'na·bich** (kän'ä·bĭκ), **Christian.** 1731–1798. German violinist, conductor, and composer; concertmeister and music director at court of Duke Karl Theodor at Mannheim (1757) and later (1778) at Munich. Composer of symphonies, violin concertos, chamber music, operas, and ballets.

**Can'nan** (kăn'ăn), **Gilbert.** 1884–1955. English novelist and playwright; educ. Cambridge; called to bar (1908); dramatic critic on *Star* (1909–10). Author of *Peter Homunculus* (1909), *Little Brother* (1912), *Old Mole* (1914), *Windmills* (verse; 1915), *Mummery* (1918), *Pugs and Peacocks* (1921), and the plays *Miles Dixon* (1910), *James and John* (1911), *Mary's Wedding* (1912), *The Arbour of Refuge* (1913), *The Release of the Soul* (1920), etc.

**Can'ning** (kăn'ĭng), **George.** 1770–1827. British statesman, b. London, of an English family that had settled in Ireland (1618). Through aid of an uncle, educ. at Oxford, where he was noted as a Jacobin. M.P. (1793); supported Pitt, partly because of fear of French Revolution; brilliant orator; undersecretary for foreign affairs in Pitt's administration (1796–99); supported ministry by his periodical the *Anti-Jacobin* (1797–98); barred from advancement because of poverty and direction of merciless wit against Whigs, yet influential as chief confidant of Pitt; left office of treasurer of navy on Pitt's death (1806). Foreign secretary (1807–10); planned seizure of Danish fleet; fought duel with Castlereagh (1809), occasioned by latter's failure to co-operate in vigorous war policy. After twelve years in minor offices, succeeded Castlereagh as foreign secretary and leader of House of Commons (1822), and real director of cabinet. Succeeded Liverpool as prime minister and chancellor of the exchequer (1827); promoted policy of non-intervention and fostered liberal and nationalist movements in Europe; acknowledged independence of revolted Spanish colonies in America (1823); shielded Greece against Turkish aggression (1825–27); established British independence of Holy Alliance; contended for Catholic emancipation and laid groundwork for repeal of corn laws.

His third son, **Charles John** (1812–1862), Earl Canning, governor general of India (1856–62); brought war with Persia to successful conclusion (1857); on own responsibility, intercepted troops en route to China for service against Taiping rebels, and diverted them to India to help quell Sepoy Mutiny (1857); nicknamed "Clemency Canning" because of refusal to make reprisals; re-established order in North India according to a liberal policy (1859–62); first viceroy of India (1858).

**Canning, Hubert George de Burgh.** See CLANRICARDE.

**Canning,** Sir **Samuel.** 1823–1908. English pioneer in manufacture and submersion of submarine telegraphic cable. Engineer in chief of Atlantic cable-laying expeditions (1865–66, 1869) in steamship *Great Eastern;* laid cables from England to Malta and Alexandria.

**Canning,** Sir **Stratford.** 1st Viscount **Stratford de Red'cliffe** (rĕd'klĭf). 1786–1880. British diplomat; called "the Great Elchi." 1st cousin of George Canning. Educ. Cambridge. Minister plenipotentiary at Constantinople (1810–12); negotiated treaty of Bucharest between Russia and Turkey (1812). As plenipotentiary to Switzerland (1814–18), aided in establishing federal government there. Minister to U.S.A. (1820–24). Sent on missions, among others, to obtain general recognition of Greek independence from Turkey (1825), to negotiate settlement of Greek affairs with French and Russian envoys (1828). M.P. (1828–41). Ambassador at Constantinople (1842–58). Author of verses and pamphlets.

**Can'niz·za'ro** (kän'nēd·dzä'rō), **Stanislao.** 1826–1910. Italian chemist, b. Palermo. Assistant in chemistry at Pisa, later at Turin; took part in Sicilian Revolution (1848); fled to Paris (1849); professor of physical chemistry, National Coll. of Alexandria (1851); professor of chemistry, Geneva (1855), Palermo (1861), Rome (1871); senator (1871). Discovered Cannizzaro reaction; clearly defined distinction between molecular and atomic weights; amplified Avogadro's hypothesis and applied it to the atomic theory; showed method of deducing atomic weights of elements in volatile compounds from molecular weights of the compounds.

**Cannizzaro, Tommaso.** 1838–1916. Italian poet, b. Messina, Sicily; author of *La Voir* (1862, in French), *In Solitudine* (2 vols., 1877–80), *Antivespro* (1882), *Cianfrusaglie* (1884), and prose works, as *L'India* (1899), *Garibaldi e Mazzini* (1900).

**Can'non** (kăn'ŭn), **Annie Jump.** 1863–1941. American astronomer, b. Dover, Del. B.S., Wellesley (1884); studied at Radcliffe. Assistant (1896–1911), curator of astronomical photographs (1911–38), Harvard Observatory. Observed visually many variable stars of long period; in photographic work, discovered 300 variable stars, five new stars, and one spectroscopic binary; catalogued 286,000 stellar spectra, filling ten quarto volumes; compiled bibliography of variable stars comprising about 200,000 references.

**Cannon, George Quayle.** 1827–1901. Mormon leader, b. Liverpool, Eng. Convert to Mormonism (1840). To U.S. (1842); settled at Nauvoo, Ill.; emigrated to Salt Lake City, Utah (1847). Delegate, U.S. House of Representatives (1873–81). Fined and imprisoned (1888) for polygamy. An executor of will of Brigham Young; member, Council of Apostles, Mormon Church (from 1859); first councilor (from 1880).

**Cannon, Harriet Starr.** 1823–1896. b. Charleston, S.C. Founder and mother superior, Sisterhood of St. Mary, incorporated 1865, an Episcopal sisterhood.

**Cannon, Henry White.** 1850–1934. American banker, b. Delhi, N.Y. U.S. comptroller of currency (1884–86); president, Chase National Bank (1886–1904). His brother **James Graham** (1858–1916), president, Fourth National Bank, New York (1910–14); author of books on clearinghouse methods and administration.

**Cannon, James.** 1864–1944. American Methodist Episcopal clergyman, b. Salisbury, Md. A.B., Randolph-Macon (1884), A.M., Princeton (1889), B.D., Princeton Theol. Sem. (1888). Admitted to Virginia Conference of the Methodist Episcopal Church, South (1888). President, Blackstone Coll. for Girls (1894–1918). Elected bishop (1918); supervisor of missions in Mexico, Cuba, Africa, and Brazil (from 1918). Member of executive committee, Anti-Saloon League of America (from 1902), and of its administrative committee (from 1927), and chairman of its national legislative committee (from 1914); also chairman of executive committee of World League Against Alcoholism (from 1919). Leader of Southern Democrats opposed to Alfred E. Smith in presidential campaign of 1928 because of his antiprohibition stand.

**Cannon, Joseph Gurney.** 1836–1926. Called "Uncle Joe." American politician, b. New Garden, N.C. Adm. to bar (1858). Practiced, Danville, Ill. Member, U.S. House of Representatives (1873–91; 1893–1913; 1915–23); speaker (1903–11). Leader of the reactionary Republicans. As speaker, accused of autocratic methods in controlling house procedure; power of speaker overthrown (March, 1910) by combination of Democrats and insurgent Republicans.

**Cannon, Walter Bradford.** 1871–1945. American physiologist, b. Prairie du Chien, Wis. A.B. (1896), M.D. (1900), Harvard. Teacher (from 1899), professor (from 1906), Harvard Medical School. Known for work on movements of stomach and intestines, effects of emotions on bodily processes, the autonomic nervous system, etc.; discovered a substance (called by him *sympathin*) which is produced by stimulation of sympathetic nerves and which causes stimulation of certain organs. Author of *A Laboratory Course in Physiology* (1910), *Traumatic Shock* (1923), *The Wisdom of the Body* (1932), etc. His wife, **Cornelia,** *nee* **James** (1876–1969), novelist, b. St. Paul, Minn.; A.B., Radcliffe (1899); author of *The Pueblo Boy* (1926), *Red Rust* (1928), *Heirs* (1930), *The Fight for the Pueblo* (1934), etc.

**Cannon, William Austin.** 1870–1958. American botanist, b. Washington, Mich. A.B., Stanford (1899), Ph.D., Columbia (1902). On staff, department of botanical research, Carnegie Institution of Washington (from 1906), research associate (from 1925). Authority on desert plants and roots.

**Ca'no** (kä'nō), **Alonso.** *Called* **El Gra'na·di'no** (ĕl grä'nä·thē'nō). 1601–1667. Spanish painter, sculptor, and architect; b. Granada; appointed court painter (1638); canon of Granada (1651 ff.); chief architect, Granada Cathedral (1667 ff.). Works include design for Granada Cathedral façade, statuettes of the Virgin, busts of Adam and Eve, and a cycle of paintings, *Seven Joys of the Virgin.*

**Cano, Diego.** See Diogo CAM.

**Cano, Juan Sebastián del.** *Also* **Juan Sebastián de El Ca'no** *or* **El·ca'no** (ĕl·kä'nō). d. 1526. Spanish navigator, b. Guetaria. Commanded *Concepción,* one of Magellan's five ships (1519 ff.); after death of Magellan and deposition of Carabello, became commander of expedition; arrived in Spain (Sept. 6, 1522), with one ship, *Victoria,* via Moluccas and Cape of Good Hope, first to circumnavigate earth by sailing westward.

**Cano, Melchor.** 1509–1560. Spanish theologian. Entered Dominican order (1523), priest (1531); theologian to Council of Trent (1551); rector at college of Valladolid (1553); prior at Salamanca (1557) and provincial of Castile (1560); bitter opponent of Jesuits. Author of *De Locis Theologicis,* inquiry into sources of theological knowledge.

**Ca·non'i·cus** (kȧ·nŏn'ĭ·kŭs). 1565?–1647. Sachem of Narragansett Indians; friendly with English; ceded land comprising present state of Rhode Island to Roger Williams.

**Ca·no'va** (kä·nô'vä), **Antonio.** 1757–1822. Italian sculptor, b. Possagno, Treviso; founder of modern classic school of sculpture; marks transition from baroque style to classicism of Thorvaldsen. To Rome (1779) on pension from Venetian government; called to Paris to execute commissions for Napoleon (1802, 1805, 1810); sent to Paris (1815) by Pius VII to recover art treasures taken from Rome; created marquis of Ischia; perpetual president, Academy of St. Luke. His works include *Orpheus, Eurydice, Daedalus and Icarus, Theseus Vanquishing the Minotaur, Cupid and Psyche* (Louvre), monument to Pope Clement XIV (church of Santi Apostoli, Rome), *Venus and Adonis* (Naples Museum), *Hebe Pouring Nectar* (Berlin), *Perseus* (Vatican), *Venus* and *Napoleon* (Pitti Palace), *Three Graces* (Leningrad), *Venus Borghese* (Villa Borghese, Rome), *Paris* (Munich), *Theseus and the Centaur* (Vienna), *Mars and Venus* (London).

**Cá'no·vas del Cas·til'lo** (kä'nō·väs thĕl käs·tē'lyō), **Antonio.** 1828–1897. Spanish statesman and writer, b. Málaga. Educ. Madrid. Deputy to Cortes (1852); chargé d'affaires, Rome (1854); minister of interior (1864), of colonies (1865); banished (1868–69). A leader in securing restoration of Bourbons (Alfonso XII, 1874); premier (1875–79, 1879–81, 1884–85, 1890–92, 1895–97); prepared law for abolition of Negro slavery; set up plan granting autonomy to Cuba. Author of verse, several volumes of literary studies, a life of Estébanez Calderón, and of *Problemas Contemporáneos* (3 vols., 1884–90), *Estudios del Reinado de Felipe IV* (3 vols., 1888–90), and *Historia General de España* (10 vols., 1890–97).

**Can'ro'bert'** (kän'rô'bâr'), **François Certain.** 1809–1895. French army commander. General and aide-de-camp to Louis Napoleon (1850); active in coup d'état (Dec. 2, 1851). French commander in Crimean War (1854–55); marshal of France (1855). Commanded Army of Rhine (1870); taken prisoner at Metz (Oct. 27, 1870). Elected senator (1876).

**Can'ta·cu·zene'** (kăn'tȧ·kū·zēn'). *Lat.* **Can'ta·cu·ze'nus** (kăn'tȧ·kū·zē'nŭs). *Rum.* **Can'ta·cu·zi'no** (kän'tä·kōō·zē'nō). Name of a Byzantine and a later Rumanian family including **John VI Cantacuzene** (*q.v.*), Emperor of Eastern Roman Empire (1347–55), and descendants of his who became distinguished in Rumania (17th–19th centuries): **Şerban Cantacuzino** (1640–1688), Hospodar of Walachia (1679–88); compelled to serve under Turks at siege of Vienna (1683); national benefactor; introduced Indian corn; influential in substituting Rumanian for Slavonic language in liturgy. **Gheorge** (1837–1913), Rumanian public official; head of Conservative party (1899–1905); premier of Rumania (1905–07).

**Can'ta·cu·zene'** (kăn'tä·kōō·zān'; *Russ.* kŭn·tŭ·kōō'-zyān), Princess. *Nee* **Julia Dent Grant.** 1876– . American author, b. Washington, D.C.; granddaughter of President Grant; m. Major General Prince Cantacuzene, Count Speransky, of Russia (1899). Author of *Revolutionary Days* (1919), *Russian People* (1920), *My Life Here and There* (1921).

**Can'ta·ri'ni** (kän'tä·rē'nē), *also* **da Pe'sa·ro** (dä pā'zä·rō), **Simone.** *Called* **Il Pe'sa·re'se** (ēl pā'zä·rā'sā). 1612–1648. Italian painter and etcher; b. near Pesaro; imitator of Guido Reni. His paintings include *Holy Family* (in Louvre), *Magdalen* (church of San Filippo, Pesaro), *Transfiguration* (Brera, Milan), *Portrait of Guido* (Bologna gallery); his etchings include *Jupiter, Neptune, and Pluto Honoring the Arms of Cardinal Borghese.*

**Can'te·lupe** *or* **Can'ti·lupe** (kăn'tĭ·lōōp), **Walter de.** d. 1266. English prelate. 2d son of **William de Cantelupe** (d. 1239), 1st Baron Cantelupe, a constant adherent of King John and of Henry III. Justice itinerant (1231); bishop of Worcester (1236–66); defended pluralities against papal legate Otho (1237); opposed archbishop Boniface's claim of right of visitation (1251) and papal demands for money (1252, 1255); took part in excommunicating infringers of Magna Carta (1253); one of 24 representatives who set up Provisions of Oxford (1258); supported Simon de Montfort's cause and won over Oxford University to popular side. His nephew **Thomas de Cantelupe** (1218?–1282), prelate and saint; educ. Paris and Orléans; taught canon law at Oxford; favored Montfort party; chancellor of England (Feb.–Aug., 1265); bishop of Hereford (1275–82); chief adviser of Edward I; led opposition to Archbishop Peckham (1279); appealed against Peckham to Rome in dispute over jurisdiction; excommunicated by Peckham; went to Rome; died at Orvieto. Canonized by Pope John XXII (1320).

**Can'te·mir'** (kän'tĕ·mēr'). *Russ.* **Kan·te·mir'** (kŭn·tyĕ·myēr'). Moldavian family of Tatar origin, including: **Con'stan·tin'** (kŏn'stän·tēn'), Prince of Moldavia (1685–93). His brother **Di·mi'tri·e** [dē·mē'-trē·yĕ] (1673–1723), Prince of Moldavia (1710–11), joined Peter the Great in war against Turks, placing Moldavia under Russian sovereignty; also known as linguist and writer, author of *History of the Growth and Decay of the Ottoman Empire.* Demetrius's son **An·ti·och'** [ŭn·tyĭ·ôκ'] (1709?–1744), poet and diplomat; Russian minister to Great Britain (1732–38) and France (1738); known as writer of satires and as translator.

**Can'te·rac'** (kän'tȧ·räk'), **José.** c. 1775–1835. Spanish general; of French descent and birth. To America (1815) as brigadier general; to Peru (1818) to assist in quelling revolt; fought several campaigns with La Serna in upper Peru; member of military cabal which deposed viceroy Joaquín de la Pezuela in favor of La Serna (1821); lieutenant general and commander in chief of royalist forces in Peru; defeated by Bolívar at Junín (1824); commanded reserves at Ayacucho (1824); to Spain; appointed captain general of New Castile (Jan., 1835).

**Canterbury,** Viscounts. See MANNERS-SUTTON.

**Canth** (känt), **Ulrika Vilhelmina,** *called* **Minna.** *Nee* **Jo'hans·son** (yŏ'häns·sŏn). 1844–1897. Finnish writer and feminist; author of novels including *Hanna* (1886) and *Poor Folk* (1886), and plays including *The Invasion* (1882), *The Preacher's Family* (1890), and *Anna Liisa* (1895).

**Can'til'lon'** (kän'tē'yôn'), **Richard.** 1680?–1734. Irish economist; merchant in London and Paris; author of *Essai sur la nature du commerce en général* (1755), with which economics as a science was said by Jevons to have originated.

**Can·ti'lo** (kän·tē'lō), **José María.** 1877–1953. Argentine diplomat. Minister to Paraguay (1916–19), Portugal (1919–27), Switzerland (1927–32); ambassador to Uruguay (1930–33), Italy (1933–38); member, Council of League of Nations; minister of foreign affairs (1938–41). Author of *Les Jardins de France* (poetry; 1906), *Los Desorbitados* (a novel), *La Ganga* (short stories), etc.

**Cantilupe.** See CANTELUPE.

**Cant'lie** (kănt'lĭ), Sir **James.** 1851–1926. Scottish physician. Educ. Aberdeen U. and Charing Cross Hospital, London, where he became a demonstrator of anatomy (1872), assistant surgeon (1877), and surgeon (1887). With cholera expedition in Egypt (1883); dean of College of Medicine for Chinese in China (1889–96); returned to London and became plague officer for London County Council; consulting surgeon, North Eastern Railway Co.; consulting surgeon, Seamen's Hospital Society. Founder (1921) and president (1921–23) of Royal Society of Tropical Medicine and Hygiene; founder and coeditor, *Journal of Tropical Medicine.* Author of *Naked Eye Anatomy, Beri-beri, Tropical Surgery, Degeneration Amongst Londoners* (1885), *Physical Efficiency* (1906), etc.

**Can'ton** (kăn't'n; -tŭn), **John.** 1718–1772. English physicist. Elected to Royal Society for paper on making artificial magnets (1749); first in England to verify Franklin's hypothesis of identity of lightning and electricity; invented an electroscope and an electrometer; demonstrated compressibility of water in refutation of Florentine academicians (1762); discovered phosphorescent substance known as Canton's phosphorus (1768).

**Canton, William.** 1845–1926. English poet and journalist, b. on Chinese island of Chusan, son of an English colonial official. Teacher and journalist in London (1867–76), Glasgow (1876–91); manager of Isbister & Co., publishers, London (1891). Author of verse, including *Through the Ages: the Legend of a Stone Axe* (1873) and *A Lost Epic and Other Poems* (1887), of a series of books for his daughter Winifred Vida Canton including *The Invisible Playmate* (1894), *W. V. Her Book* (1896), *A Child's Book of Saints* (1898), and *In Memory of W. V.* (1901), and of a *History of the British and Foreign Bible Society* (1901–10).

**Can·to′ni** (kän·tō′nē), **Carlo**. 1840–1906. Italian philosopher; professor, Pavia (1878 ff.); disciple of Kant.

**Can′tor** (kăn′tẽr), **Eddie**. 1892–1964. American comedian, b. New York City. In vaudeville and burlesque; later in musical comedies (as *Kid Boots*, 1923–26, and *Whoopee*, 1929–30), in motion pictures (from 1926; starred in *The Thief of Bagdad*, *Roman Scandals*, etc.), and on radio.

**Can′tor** (kän′tôr), **Georg**. 1845–1918. German mathematician, b. St. Petersburg; professor, Halle (from 1872). Developed a theory of irrational numbers, an arithmetic of the infinite, and the theory of sets of points; introduced transfinite numbers.

**Cantor, Moritz Benedikt**. 1829–1920. German mathematician; professor at Heidelberg (1863–1913); author of *Vorlesungen über Geschichte der Mathematik* (3 vols., 1880–98; a 4th vol. later prepared under his supervision), a history of mathematics to 1799.

**Can·tù′** (kän·tōō′), **Cesare**. 1804?–1895. Italian historian. Professor of belles-lettres, Sondrio. Known especially for his historical works, as *Storia Universale* (35 vols., 1838–47), *Storia degli Italiani* (6 vols., 1854); author also of the historical romance *Margherita Pusterla*, describing prison life (1837), and a volume of poems (1870).

**Can·tú′** (kän·tōō′), **Federico**. 1908– . Mexican painter; traveled and studied in U.S. and Europe; assisted Rivera on frescoes for secretariat of public education, Mexico City.

**Cant′well** (kănt′wĕl; -wĕl), **Robert Emmett**. 1908– . American novelist, b. Little Falls, Wash.; associate editor of *Time* (from 1938); author of *Laugh and Lie Down* (1931) and *The Land of Plenty* (1934), proletarian novels about the lumber-mill industry in the Northwest.

**Can′u·le′ius** (kăn′ū·lē′yŭs), **Cneius** *or* **Gnaeus**. Roman politician; tribune (c. 445 B.C.); sponsored the lex Canuleia, making marriages between patricians and plebeians legal.

**Ca·nute′** (kȧ·nūt′) *or* **Cnut** (k′nōōt) *or* **Knut** (k′nōōt). *Anglo-Saxon* **Cnūt** (k′nōōt). *Danish* **Knud** (k′nōōth). Name of six kings of Denmark, two of whom were also kings of England.

**Canute II** of Denmark (994?–1035), *known as* "the Great." Son of Sweyn Forkbeard, King of the Danes. King of England (1016–35) and of Denmark (1018–35). Fled to Denmark (1014); returned and waged war with Edmund Ironside (1015–16); defeated Edmund at Assandun in Essex but allowed him to rule in the south (1016); thoroughly conquered all England after Edmund's death (1016–18); chosen by witan as king of all England (1017); m. (1017) Emma of Normandy, widow of King Ethelred; in Denmark for a few months (1019) to strengthen his hold there; at first cruel, but during most of reign (1020–35) an able, just, and popular ruler; strongly supported the church; defeated attempt (1026) of kings of Norway and Sweden to conquer Denmark; overcame Swedish fleet and damaged their combined fleet; made pilgrimage to Rome (1026–27); became king of Norway (1028–35); subject of many legends.

**Canute III**, his son by his second wife; better known as Hardecanute (*q.v.*), king of Denmark and England.

**Canute IV** (d. 1086), *called* "the Saint." Grandnephew of Canute II. King of Denmark (1080–86); strong supporter of the church; tried to invade England (1085); murdered by rebels. Canonized (1100); patron saint of Denmark.

**Canute V** (d. 1157). Son of Magnus. King of Denmark (1147–57); ruled in Jutland; waged civil war with Sweyn III; assassinated.

**Canute VI** (1163–1202). Son of Waldemar the Great. King of Denmark (1182–1202); crowned as coregent (1170); extended Danish dominion over Pomerania and Holstein; came into conflict with Emperor Frederick I Barbarossa; styled himself "king of the Danes and Wends."

**Ca·nute′ La′vard** (kȧ·nūt′ lä′vär). 1094?–1131. Prince of Denmark. Son of Eric I. Became duke of Sles′vig (*Dan.* slĭs′vē) (1115); brought German culture to Denmark; ruler of Wendish tribes on frontier; assassinated.

**Cão, Diogo**. See Diogo CAM.

**Caoil′te** (kēl′tĕ). Famous Fenian poet of third century A.D.

**Ca′pa·blan′ca y Grau·per′ra** (kä′pä·bläng′kä ē grau·pĕr′rä), **José Raoul**. 1888–1942. Cuban chess master. Grad. Columbia (1910); official in Cuban foreign office (from 1913). Defeated Marshall, of U.S. (1909); won first place in masters' tournament at San Sebastian, Spain (1911); defeated Lasker in match for world's championship at Havana (1921); defeated by Alekhine (1927); author of books on chess.

**Capac, Manco**. See MANCO CAPAC.

**Cap′de·vi′la** (käp′thā·vē′lä), **Arturo**. 1889– . Argentinian professor and writer, b. Córdoba; author of *Babel y el Castellano* (awarded national literary grand prize), *La Dulce Patria*, *La Fiesta del Mundo*, *Los Románticos*, *Branca D'Oria*, *Los Incas*, etc.

**Ča′pek** (chä′pĕk), **Karel**. 1890–1938. Czech journalist, playwright, and miscellaneous writer. Educ. U. of Prague, and in Paris and Berlin. On staff of *Národní Listy*, Prague (1919–23) and *Lidové Noviny* (from 1923). Author of plays, including *R. U. R.* (*Rossum's Universal Robots*; 1920), *The Life of the Insects*, also known as *The World We Live In* (1921; with his brother **Josef**, 1887–1945), *The Makropoulos Secret* (1922), *Adam the Creator* (1927; with his brother), *The White Scourge* (1936; produced in England under title *Power and Glory*), and *The Mother* (1937), of novels, including *The Manufacture of the Absolute* (1922), *Krakatit* (1924), *War with the Newts*, and the *Cheat* (unfinished; Eng. trans. 1941), and of miscellaneous writings, including volumes of short stories and *Letters from England* (1924), *The Gardener's Year*, *Conversations with T. G. Masaryk*, *Criticism of Words* (1920).

**Ca′pel** (kā′pĕl), **Arthur**. Baron **Capel of Had′ham** (hăd′ăm). 1610?–1649. English Royalist leader. Lieutenant general of Shropshire, Cheshire, and North Wales; escorted queen to Paris (1646); aided Charles I's escape to Isle of Wight (1647); one of leaders of Second Civil War (1648); beheaded. His son **Arthur** (1631–1683), Earl of Essex; lord lieutenant of Hertfordshire (1660), of Wiltshire (1668), of Ireland (1672–77); opposed grants to Charles II's favorites and opposed his Catholic leanings; first lord of treasury (1679); on discovery of Rye House Plot (1683) sent to Tower; found with throat cut, probably a suicide.

**Capel, Thomas John**. 1836–1911. English Roman Catholic priest. Established Roman Catholic University at Kensington (1874–78); London pulpit orator and successful proselytizer; figured as Monsignor Catesby in Disraeli's *Lothair* (1870); to California (1883); prelate in charge of district of northern California.

**Ca′pell** (kā′pĕl), **Edward**. 1713–1781. English Shakespearean commentator. Deputy inspector of plays (1737); published edition of Shakespeare's plays (10 vols., 1768) and a complete commentary, *Notes and Various Readings to Shakespeare* (1779–83).

**Capella, Martianus**. See MARTIANUS CAPELLA.

**Ca·pel′le** (kä·pĕl′ĕ), **Eduard von**. 1855–1931. German naval officer; vice-admiral (1909); admiral (1913); succeeded von Tirpitz as secretary of the navy (1916–18);

put in effect (1917) unrestricted submarine warfare against Allies, esp. Great Britain.

**Ca·pel'lo** (kä·pĕl'lō; -päl'lō) *or* **Cap·pel'lo** (käp·pĕl'lō; -päl'lō), **Bianca.** 1542?–1587. Italian adventuress, b. Venice. Mistress of Francesco de' Medici, Duke of Tuscany; simulated pregnancy and palmed off on him as his own son a child of the people; caused assassination of all her accomplices in this deceit; m. Francesco (1579) and was proclaimed grand duchess of Tuscany four months later.

**Capello, Luigi.** 1859–1941. Italian soldier. Commanded army which captured Gorizia (Aug., 1916); commanded 2d army in Italian offensive on Bainsizza plateau (1917); retired (July, 1918). Opponent of Fascism; arrested (Nov., 1925) and accused of being involved in plot to kill Mussolini; sentenced to 30 years' penal servitude.

**Ca'pen** (kā'pĕn), **Elmer Hewitt.** 1838–1905. American educator, b. Stoughton, Mass.; president, Tufts College (1875–1905). His son **Samuel Paul** (1878–1956), b. Somerville, Mass., chancellor, U. of Buffalo (from 1922).

**Ca'pern** (kā'pẽrn), **Edward.** 1819–1894. English poet, known as "the rural postman of Bideford"; employed in lace factory at Tiverton, Devonshire. Author of *Poems* (1856), *The Devonshire Melodist* (1862), *Wayside Warbles* (1865).

**Ca'per·ton** (kā'pẽr·t'n; -tŭn), **William Banks.** 1855–1941. American naval officer, b. Spring Hill, Tenn. Grad. U.S.N.A., Annapolis (1875); rear admiral (Feb., 1913); commanded naval forces at Vera Cruz (1915), intervening in Haiti (1915–16), suppressing Santo Domingo revolution (1916); commander in chief of U.S. Pacific fleet, with rank of admiral (1916–19).

**Capet, Hugh.** See HUGH CAPET; CAPETIAN.

**Ca·pe'tian** (kȧ·pē'shăn) dynasty. *Fr.* **Ca'pé'tien'** (kȧ'pā'syăN'). The third dynasty of French kings, derived from its first ruler, Hugh Capet; ruled (987–1328), through 14 kings in the direct line; followed by Valois dynasty (1328). For collateral branches see BURGUNDY, ANJOU, VALOIS, ORLÉANS, BOURBON. Members of family earlier than Hugh Capet include **Robert the Strong** (d. 866), Count of **An'jou'** (äN'zhōō'; *Angl.* ăn'jōō), founder of the family; his sons, the counts of Paris, **Eudes** (ûd) *or* **O'do** [ō'dō] (reigned 888–898) and **Robert I** (reigned 922–923); and **Hugh the Great** (*q.v.*), Duke of France and Count of Paris, son of Robert I and father of Hugh Capet. These counts often considered as kings of France because they held the power much of the time (888–987), although the last of the Carolingians were the nominal kings. See *Table* (*in Appendix*) for FRANCE.

**Cap'grave** (kăp'grāv), **John.** 1393–1464. English chronicler and hagiologist. Joined order of Augustinian hermits and resided most of life in friary at King's Lynn, Norfolk; provincial of order in England. Author of *Nova Legenda Angliae*, a catalogue of English saints, in Latin, printed by Wynkyn de Worde (1516, 1527), *The Chronicle of England* (from Creation to 1417) in English, and *Liber de illustribus Henricis*.

**Capistrano.** See JOHN OF CAPISTRANO.

**Ca'pi·to** (kä'pē·tō; *as Lat.*, kăp'ĭ·tō), *orig.* **Köp'fel** (kûp'fĕl), **Wolfgang Fa·bri'ci·us** (fä·brē'tsē·ōōs; *as Lat.*, fȧ·brĭsh'ĭ·ŭs; -brĭsh'ŭs). 1478–1541. German clergyman, supporter of Martin Luther in the Reformation. Roman Catholic priest at Basel (1515) and in service of Archbishop Albert, at Mainz (1520). To Strasbourg (1523); became leader of Reformation movement in that vicinity; endeavored to reconcile Lutherans and Swiss reformers. One of chief authors (1530) of Tetrapolitan Confession submitted to Diet of Augsburg, and of First Helvetic Confession (1536).

**Cap·ma'ny y Mon'pa·la'u** (käp·män'y' ē môm'pä·lä'ōō), **Antonio de.** 1742–1813. Spanish philologist and historian, b. Barcelona; officer in Spanish army; member of Cortes at Cádiz (1812–13); fought against Napoleonic domination. Author esp. of works on Castilian philology and on history of Barcelona; compiled French-Spanish dictionary (1805).

**Capnio.** See Johann REUCHLIN.

**Capodistrias, Capo d'Istria.** See KAPODISTRIAS.

**Ca·po'te** (kȧ·pō'tē), **Truman.** 1924– . Amer. author, b. New Orleans. Wrote *Other Voices, Other Rooms* (1948), *Breakfast at Tiffany's* (1958), *In Cold Blood* (1965), *Thanksgiving Visitor* (1968), etc.

**Cap'pel'** (kȧ'pĕl'), **Louis.** *Lat.* **Ludovicus Cap·pel'lus** *or* **Ca·pel'lus** (kȧ·pĕl'ŭs). 1585–1658. French Protestant clergyman; professor of Hebrew, later of theology, at theological seminary at Saumur; known for his critical studies of Old Testament texts, especially their orthography and pointing.

**Cappello, Bianca.** See CAPELLO.

**Cap'per** (kăp'ẽr), **Arthur.** 1865–1951. American editor and politician, b. Garnett, Kans. On staff (from 1884), proprietor and publisher (from 1892), Topeka, Kans., *Daily Capital;* proprietor and publisher of other Kansas papers and of several rural magazines, including *Capper's Weekly*, *Capper's Farmer*, *Kansas City Kansan.* Governor of Kansas (1915–19), U.S. senator (1919–49).

**Cap'pon** (kăp'ŭn), **James.** 1855–1939. Canadian educator, b. in Scotland; educ. Glasgow; to Canada (1888); professor of English and dean of arts faculty, Queens U., Kingston, Can. Author of *Studies in Canadian Poetry*, *Bliss Carman...*, *Canada and the Empire*, and *A School of Idealism.*

**Cap·po'ni** (käp·pō'nē), Marchese **Gino.** 1792–1876. Florentine statesman and scholar; prime minister of Tuscany (1848); head of council of state (1859) which prepared union of Tuscany and Piedmont; created senator by King Victor Emmanuel of Italy (1860). Author of *Storia della Republica di Firenze* (1875).

**Capponi, Piero.** 1447?–1496. Florentine statesman and soldier; diplomat in service of Lorenzo de' Medici (to 1492); opposed party of the Medicis after Lorenzo's death (1492); as head of Florence, negotiated favorable terms with invading Charles VIII of France (1494); killed while leading Florentine army against Pisa.

**Capps** (kăps), **Edward.** 1866–1950. American educator, b. Jacksonville, Ill. A.B., Illinois Coll. (1887), Ph.D., Yale (1891). Professor of Greek, U. of Chicago (1892–1907), of classics, Princeton (1907–36); American editor of Loeb Classical Library; managing editor of *Classical Philology* (1906–07). Author of *From Homer to Theocritus*, *The Greek Stage According to the Extant Dramas*, *Greek Comedy*, etc.

**Capps, Washington Lee.** 1864–1935. American naval officer, b. Portsmouth, Va. Grad. U.S.N.A., Annapolis (1884); B.S., Glasgow (1888). On Dewey's staff (1898–99); chief constructor, U.S. navy, and chief of bureau of construction and repair, with rank of rear admiral (1903–10); general manager, Emergency Fleet Corporation (1917); retired (1928).

**Cap'ra** (kăp'rȧ), **Frank.** 1897– . Motion-picture director, b. Palermo, Sicily; to U.S. (1903). Director for Columbia Studios, Hollywood, Calif. Pictures produced under his direction include *Power of the Press*, *Ladies of Leisure*, *It Happened One Night* (1934), *Mr. Deeds Goes to Town* (1936), *Lost Horizon*, *Mr. Smith Goes to Washington*, *You Can't Take It With You* (1938). Received Motion Picture Academy award (1934, 1936, 1938).

**Ca·pra'ra** (kä·prä'rä), **Giovanni Battista.** 1733–1810. Italian ecclesiastical diplomat. Nuncio to Cologne,

Lucerne, Vienna; cardinal (1792); bishop of Iesi (1793); at Napoleon's request, legate to France to complete negotiations for Concordat of 1801; archbishop of Milan (1802); officiated at coronation of Napoleon as king of Italy (1805). Author of *Concordat et Recueil des Bulles et Brefs de N. S. Pie VII sur les Affaires de l'Église en France* (1802).

**Ca·pri′vi** (kä·prē′vē), Count **Leo von.** 1831–1899. German soldier and statesman. Entered Prussian army (1849); chief of staff of 10th army corps in Franco-Prussian War (1870–71). Appointed chief of the admiralty (1883); reorganized German navy. Commanding general, 10th army corps, in Hanover (1888). Succeeded Bismarck (1890) as imperial chancellor (resigned 1894) and president of Prussian ministry (resigned 1892).

**Ca′pron** (kā′prŭn), **Horace.** 1804–1885. American farm expert, b. Attleboro, Mass.; U.S. commissioner of agriculture (1867–71); agricultural adviser to Japanese government (1871–75).

**Ca·pro′ni** (kä·prō′nē), **Gianni.** 1886–1957. Italian airplane builder; constructed biplane bomber during World War, later developed as a triplane, and bombers used in Spanish Civil War and in world war (1939 ff.).

**Ca·pua′na** (kä·pwä′nä), **Luigi.** 1839–1915. Italian writer and literary critic, b. in Sicily; professor, history of literature, U. of Catania (1895 ff.); leader with Verga of Sicilian realists. Author of novels and short stories including *Profili di Donne* (1878), *Giacinta* (1879), *Il Profumo* (1890), *Il Marchese di Roccaverdina* (1901), *La Sfinge, Homo*, and *Le Paesane*, of plays, as *Giacinta* and *Malia*, and of critical works, as *Teatro Italiano Contemporaneo* (1865), *Studi sulla Letteratura Contemporanea* (5 vols., 1882–87), *Cronache Letterarie* (1899).

**Ca′pus′** (kȧ′pü′), **Alfred.** 1858–1922. French journalist and playwright, b. Aix; political editor of *Figaro* (1914–22). His plays include *Brignol et sa Fille* (1894), *La Veine* (1901), *La Châtelaine* (1902), *Monsieur Piégeois* (1905), *Les Deux Hommes* (1908), *Hélène Ardouin* (1913), *La Traversée* (1920).

**Car′a·cal′la** (kăr′ȧ·kăl′ȧ). *Real name* **Marcus Aurelius An′to·ni′nus** (ăn′tō·nī′nŭs). *Orig. name* **Bas′si·a′nus** (băs′ĭ·ā′nŭs). 188–217 A.D. Nicknamed Caracalla from name of long hooded tunic or coat, worn by Gauls, which he introduced. Roman emperor (211–217); son of Lucius Septimius Severus; b. at Lugdunum (Lyon). Became (211) joint emperor with his brother Geta (*q.v.*); caused murder of Geta (212) and persuaded praetorian guards to proclaim him sole ruler; had many (20,000 according to Dio Cassius) of Geta's relatives, friends, etc., killed, including the jurist Papinian. His reign spent in various provinces where excesses and extravagance were indulged in; with a motive of avarice, granted Roman citizenship to all free inhabitants of the empire; in campaigns against Gauls, Germans, and Parthians practiced extreme cruelty and treachery. Assassinated by Macrinus, Roman prefect at Edessa. The Baths (Thermae) of Caracalla and Arch of Septimius Severus erected in Rome by senate (205–207) in honor of the emperor and his two sons.

**Caracci.** Variant of CARRACCI.

**Ca·rac′cio·li** (kä·rät′chō·lē) *or* **Ca·rac′cio·lo** (-lō). Neapolitan noble family, including: **Marino Caraccioli** (1459?–1538), diplomat, cardinal (1535), imperial governor of Milan. Ser **Giovanni** (1480–1550), prince of Melfi, marshal of France, governor of Piedmont (1545 ff.). Saint **Francesco** (1563–1608), founder of Clerici Regulares Minores (1588). **Domenico,** Marchese **di Caraccioli** (1715–1789), governor of Sicily (1781, 1786), minister of foreign affairs under Ferdinand IV of Naples. **Luigi Antonio** (1721–1803), Parisian writer, as of *Lettres Interessantes du Pape Clément XIV.* Principe **Francesco** (1752–1799), revolutionist; admiral; in service of Ferdinand IV of Naples (to 1798); in service of Parthenopean Republic (1799); successfully prevented landing of British and Sicilian fleet; arrested at capture of Naples by Cardinal Ruffo.

**Ca·rac′ta·cus** (kȧ·răk′tȧ·kŭs) *or* **Ca·rat′a·cus** (kȧ·răt′ȧ·kŭs). *English* **Ca·rad′oc** (kȧ·răd′ŭk). *Welsh* **Ca·ra′dawg** (kă·ră′doug). British chieftain of the Catuvellauni. Leader in resisting Roman invasion under Aulus Plautius (43–47); after defeat withdrew into south Wales; defeated by Ostorius Scapula, governor of Britain, in Shropshire (50 A.D.); sent captive to Rome.

**Ca·ra′fa** (kä·rä′fä), **Michele Enrico.** 1787–1872. Composer of operas, b. Naples, of noble family. Cavalry officer under Murat, King of Naples; took part in Russian campaign (1812); decorated by Napoleon; retired from army after Napoleon's fall; lived in Naples (1814–27), Paris (1827–72); naturalized French citizen; professor of composition, Paris Conservatory (1840). His operas include *Il Fantasma, Il Vascello di Occidente, Gabriele, Ifigenia, Berenice, Le Solitaire, La Violette, La Fiancée de Lammermoor, Masaniello*, and *La Prison d'Édimbourg.*

**Ca′ra·gia′le** (kä′rä·jä′lĕ), **Ioan Luca.** 1853–1912. Rumanian writer; author of satirical comedies, as *The Stormy Night* (1879) and *The Lost Letter* (1884), and of short stories, as *The Easter Torch* (1889), *The Sin* (1892).

**Ca′ra·thé′o·do·ry′** (kä′rä·tā′ô·thô·rē′), **Constantin.** 1873–1950. Mathematician, b. Berlin; prof., Munich; his publications deal with calculus of variations.

**Ca·rau′si·us** (kȧ·rô′zhĭ·ŭs), **Marcus Aurelius.** 245?–293. Roman usurper in Britain. Originally a Menapian pilot on Scheldt; served Roman Emperor Maximian against revolted Gauls (286); put in command of Roman fleet at Boulogne to ward off Frankish and Saxon pirates, enriched himself by plunder; set himself up as emperor in Britain (287); defeated Maximian's fleet.

**Ca′ra·vag′gio** (kä′rä·väd′jō), **Michelangelo da.** *Real name* **Michelangelo Me·ri′si** (mā·rē′zē) *or* **Me·ri′sio** (mā·rē′zyō). c. 1565–1609. Italian painter, b. at Caravaggio; founder of naturalistic school. Painted chiefly plebeian types in their natural surroundings; influenced Ribera; in Rome (c. 1585–87); protégé of Cardinal del Monte; forced to leave Rome after killing companion in quarrel; to Palestrina, Naples, Malta, Catania, Syracuse (Sicily), etc. His works include *The Entombment of Christ* (Vatican), *Card Players* (Rome and Dresden), *Gipsy Fortune Teller* (in Palazzo dei Conservatori, Rome), *Love as a Ruler, Love Conquered*, and *St. Matthew Writing the Gospel* (all in Berlin Museum), *Death of Mary* (Louvre), *Christ and the Apostles at Emmaus* (London), and portraits, as *Grand Master of the Knights of Malta* (Louvre) and a self-portrait (Uffizi Gallery).

**Caravaggio, Polidoro da.** *Real name* **Polidoro Cal·da′ra** (käl·dä′rä). c. 1495–1543. Italian painter, b. at Caravaggio; pupil of Raphael; known especially as frieze decorator in Vatican, his works being known chiefly through etchings of Bartoli, Alberti, etc.; among his canvases are *Christ Bearing the Cross* (in Naples Gallery), *Cephalus and Procris* (in Vienna Museum).

**Car′a·way** (kăr′ȧ·wā), **Hattie Wyatt.** 1878–1950. Am. politician, b. Bakerville, Tenn. First woman to be elected to the U.S. Senate (1933); served as senator from Arkansas (1931–45).

**Carbajal, Francisco de.** See CARVAJAL.

**Car′bia** (kär′byä), **Romulo.** 1885– . Argentinian historian, b. Buenos Aires. Author of *La Nueva Historia del Descubrimiento de América* (1936), etc.

**Car′bo·nell′ y Ri·ve′ro** (kär′bō·nĕl′y′ ē rē·vā′rō), **José Manuel.** 1880– . Cuban statesman. Officer in

Cuban war; general in civil war (1906). Founded *El Ateneo de la Habana* (1902); coeditor, with brother Néstor, of *Letras* (1905–17); founded *Anales* of Academia Nacional de Artes y Letras; editor, *Evolucion de la Cultura Cubana.* Delegate to fourth (1910) and sixth (1928) Pan-American conferences; minister to Brazil (1934–37); ambassador to Mexico (from 1937). Author of several volumes of verse and many critical works on Cuban literature. His brother **Néstor** (1883– ), diplomat; in educational, police, and editorial work in Havana (1909–28); minister, Cuban Pan-American office (1924–28); secretary-general, Pan-American Conference (1928); minister to Argentina (1928–33), Colombia (1934); ambassador to Peru (from 1943). Author of *El Ayuntamiento de La Habana* (1918; with E. S. Santovenia), *Próceres* (1919), biographical studies of Martí (1923, 1933), and *Prosas Oratorias* (1927).

**Car'butt** (kär'bŭt), **John.** 1832–1905. Photographer, b. Sheffield, Eng.; to U.S. in 1853; devised new gelatin-covered dry plate for use in photography; introduced the orthochromatic plate, giving correct color values in photography.

**Car'ca·no** (kär'kä·nō), **Giulio.** 1812–1884. Italian writer. Secretary to provisional government, Milan (1848); professor, Academy of Fine Arts, Milan (1859); secretary and director of studies, Istituto Lombardo (1868); senator (1876 ff.). Author of romances, as *Angiola Maria* (1839) and *Damiano* (1850), tragedies, translations from Shakespeare, and several volumes of poetry.

**Cár'ca·no** (kär'kä·nō), **Miguel Ángel.** 1889– . Argentine statesman; negotiated Anglo-Argentine commercial treaty (signed 1933); minister of agriculture (1935–38); ambassador to France (1938–41), to Great Britain (1941–45). Writer on economics and political theory.

**Cárcano, Ramón José.** 1860–1946. Argentine lawyer and writer; member of the legislature (1883–86; 1913 ff.); director of post and telegraph (1887–90); governor of Córdoba (1913–16; 1925–28); ambassador to Brazil (1933–39). Author of *El General Quiroga y la Expedición al Desierto* (1882), *Perfiles Contemporáneos* (1885), *Estudios Coloniales* (1895), *Juan Facundo Quiroga*, etc.

**Car'cel'** (kȧr'sĕl'), **Bertrand Guillaume.** 1750–1812. French clockmaker; inventor (c. 1800) of the Carcel lamp, in which the oil is pumped by clockwork into the wick tube.

**Car'co'** (kȧr'kō'), **Fran'cis'** (fräN'sēs'). *Orig. surname* **Car'co'pi'no'** (kȧr'kô'pē'nō'). 1886–1958. French novelist and poet; author of *La Bohème et Mon Cœur* (1912), *Chansons Aigres-Douces* (1912), *Au Vent Crispé du Matin* (1913), *Les Innocents* (novel; 1917), *L'Homme Traqué* (1922), *Perversité* (1925), *Nostalgie de Paris* (1941), etc.

**Car·da'no** (kär·dä'nō), **Geronimo** *or* **Girolamo.** *Eng.* **Jerome Car'dan** (kär'dăn; -d'n). *Lat.* **Hieronymus Car·da'nus** (kär·dā'nŭs). 1501–1576. Italian mathematician, physician, and astrologer. Grad. in medicine, Padua. Public lecturer in geometry at Milan (1534); professor of medicine, Pavia (1559), Bologna (1562); arrested for heresy or debt or both (1570); on release, moved to Rome (1571); pensioned by Pope Gregory XIII. Successful as a physician, being summoned to Scotland, where he cured the archbishop (1552). In *Ars Magna* (1545), gave as his own the cubic solution which he had obtained from Tartaglia, its discoverer, thus giving rise to a controversy; published *De Subtilitate Rerum* (1551) and *De Rerum Varietate* (1557) containing scientific speculation and information on contemporary physical knowledge; also wrote works on astronomy, astrology, rhetoric, medicine, etc., and an autobiography, *De Propria Vita* (1576). See N. TARTAGLIA.

**Car'den** (kär'd'n), Sir **Sackville Hamilton.** 1857–1930. British naval officer; vice-admiral, commander of Mediterranean squadron (1914–15) in its attempt to silence Turkish forts at Dardanelles; retired with rank of admiral (1917).

**Car'de·nal'** (kȧr'dē·nȧl'), **Pierre.** 13th-century Provençal poet, sometimes termed "Juvenal of the Provençals" because of vigor of his satire.

**Cár'de·nas** (kär'thā·näs), **García López de.** Spanish explorer in America; with Coronado's expedition (1540–42) to New Mexico; penetrated to Grand Canyon of Colorado River.

**Cárdenas, Lázaro.** 1895–1970. Mexican soldier and radical leader, b. in Michoacan state. Joined revolutionary forces (1913); brigadier general (1924); follower of Gen. Calles; provisional governor of Michoacán (1920), governor (1928–32); minister of interior (1931); minister of war and marine (1933). President of Mexico (1934–40); launched Six-Year Plan; administration marked by plans for redistribution of land, industrial and transportation development, renewal of struggle with Roman Catholic Church, and expropriation (1938) of foreign-owned oil properties. Commander, forces on Pacific coast (1941), Mexican army (1945); minister of defense (1943–45).

**Cárdenas y E·char'te** (ē ā·chär'tā), **Raúl de.** 1884– . Cuban statesman; deputy from Havana province (1911 ff.); secretary to Cuban president (1933); attorney general of Supreme Court (1934); secretary of justice (1934). Author of *El Recurso de Inconstitucionalidad* (1912) and *La Política de los Estados Unidos en el Continente Americano* (1921).

**Cardi da Cigoli, Lodovico.** See CIGOLI.

**Car'di·gan** (kär'dĭ·găn), 7th Earl of. **James Thomas Brude'nell** (brōōd'nĕl). 1797–1868. English soldier. M.P. (1818–29); entered army (1824); lieut. colonel by purchase (1830); unpopular because of his unconciliatory temper; fought duel with one of his own officers (1840). Commander of cavalry, led the "Six Hundred" in the famous charge of the Light Brigade, in battle of Balaklava in Crimean War (1854); first man to reach the Russian lines; lieut. general (1861).

**Car'di'nal'** (kȧr'dē'nȧl'), **Pierre.** = Pierre CARDENAL.

**Car·do'zo** (kär·dō'zō), **Benjamin Nathan.** 1870–1938. American jurist, b. New York City. A.B., Columbia (1889). Adm. to bar (1891); practiced in New York; justice, supreme court of New York (1914–28). Associate justice, U.S. Supreme Court (1932–38). Author of *The Nature of the Judicial Process* (1921), *The Growth of the Law* (1924), *The Paradoxes of Legal Science* (1928), etc.

**Car·duc'ci** (kär·dōōt'chē), **Bartolommeo.** *Span.* **Bartolomé Car·du'cho** (kär·thōō'chō). 1560–1608. Italian painter, b. Florence. Accompanied his master Federigo Zuccaro to Spanish court (1585); protégé of Philip II and III; painted frescoes in Escorial library and several altarpieces in church of San Felipe el Real. His works include *Holy Eucharist, Descent from the Cross, St. Francis Receiving the Stigmata, Adoration of the Kings.* His brother **Vincenzo,** *Span.* **Vicente** (1568?–1638), accompanied him to Spain (1585); painter to Spanish court (1609 ff.); protégé of Philip III and IV. His works include *Martyrdom of St. Andrew* (in cathedral at Toledo), and 54 paintings for the El Paular monastery (now in the Prado); author of the dialogue *De las Excelencias de la Pintura* (1633).

**Carducci, Giosuè.** *Early pseudonym* **E·no'tri·o Ro·ma'no** (ā·nô'trē·ō rō·mä'nō). 1835–1907. Italian poet, b. Valdicastello, Tuscany. Professor of literary history, Bologna (1861–1904). Awarded Nobel prize for literature (1906). Stanch classicist; attempted to introduce classical metrical schemes into Italian poetry; considered national poet of modern Italy. Author of historical studies in literary criticism, including *Storia del Giorno di Parini* (1892), *La Poesia Barbara nei Secoli XV e XVI* (1881), and of many volumes of verse, including *Satana e Polemiche Sataniche* (1879), *Odi Barbare* (1887), *Nuovi Odi Barbare* and *Terze Odi Barbare* (1888–89). Representative poems are *Inno a Satana, Il Bove, Pianto Antico, Funere Mersit Acerbo, Ça Ira* (12 sonnets on French Revolution), *Alle Fonti del Clitumno, In Una Chiesa Gotica, La Chiesa di Polenta,* and *Alla Stazione.*

**Card′well** (kärd′wĕl; -wĕl), **Edward.** 1787–1861. English theologian. M.A., Oxon. (1812); Camden professor of ancient history (1826–31); principal of St. Alban Hall, Oxford (1831–61); published editions of Aristotle's *Ethics*, Greek New Testament, and Josephus's *History of the Jewish War*, and projected a history of Church of England.

His nephew **Edward** (1813–1886), Viscount Cardwell, statesman and military reformer; B.A., Oxon. (1835); M.P. (1842); supported Peel and free-trade policy; president of Board of Trade in Aberdeen's coalition ministry (1852–55); carried Merchant Shipping Act (1854), consolidating all existing shipping laws; secretary for Ireland (1859–61); secretary for colonies (1864–66); refused to keep British troops in colonies during peacetime unless colonies paid for them; abolished penal transportation (1868); laid foundations for federation in Canada; secretary for war under Gladstone (1868–74); abolished commissions by purchase and instituted short-service system and the reserve in army.

**Careless, William.** See William CARLOS.

**Ca·rew′** (kȧ·rōō′), **Bamfylde Moore.** 1693–?1770. English vagabond; son of a Devonshire rector; ran away from school to join Gypsies, of whom he was eventually chosen king; clever sharper; transported to Maryland; escaped despite heavy iron collar; returned to wandering life in England and Scotland.

**Carew, George.** Baron **Carew of Clop′ton** (klŏp′tŭn) *and* Earl of **Tot′nes** (tŏt′nĕs). 1555–1629. English soldier. Educ. Oxford; held a command in Irish wars against earl of Desmond (1575–83); master of ordnance in Ireland (1588–92); on Essex's expedition to Cadiz (1596) and Azores (1597); ambassador to France (1598). President of Munster, Ireland (1600–03); after failure of Essex, repressed rebellion of earl of Tyrone with ruthlessness. Master general of ordnance (1608–17); governor of Guernsey (1610–21).

**Carew, Richard.** 1555–1620. English poet and antiquary. Educ. Oxford; M.P. (1584); high sheriff of Cornwall (1586). Translator of five cantos of Tasso's *Jerusalem Delivered* (1594); published *Survey of Cornwall* (1602).

**Carew, Thomas.** 1595?–?1645. English poet, one of Cavalier Poets. B.A., Oxon. (1611); secretary to Lord Herbert of Cherbury (1619); served in court of Charles I; friend of Sir John Suckling, Ben Jonson, Davenant; admirer of Donne; his masque *Coelum Britannicum* acted at Whitehall (1633). Author chiefly of short brilliant lyrics of sensuous order, as *He that loves a rosy cheek*, his longest poem being *A Rapture.*

**Car′ey** (kâr′ĭ), **Henry.** 1st Baron **Huns′don** (hŭnz′dŭn). 1524?–1596. English soldier and diplomat; son of Anne Boleyn's sister; envoy to France (1564, 1591), to Scotland (1587); governor of Berwick (1568–87); commissioner on treason trials (1585–95) and to try Mary, Queen of Scots (1586). His youngest son, **Robert** (1560?–1639), 1st Earl of **Mon′mouth** (mŏn′mŭth; mŭn′-), soldier; fought in Netherlands (1587), against Armada (1588), in Normandy (1591); warden of Scottish border (1593–1603); by sixty hours of riding carried news of Queen Elizabeth's death to James VI of Scotland (1603); followed Charles, Prince of Wales, to Spain (1623).

**Carey, Henry.** d. 1743. English poet and composer. Reputed illegitimate son of George Savile, Marquis of Halifax. Published first poems (1713); wrote farces, burlesques, and songs, and often the accompanying music, for London stage (1715–39), including *Chrononhotonthologos*, a burlesque of contemporary theatrical bombast (1734), and *A Wonder; or the Honest Yorkshireman*, a ballad opera (1735). Author and composer of *Sally in our Alley* (now usually sung to tune borrowed from *The Country Lasse*, not Carey's); rumored to be author of words and music of *God Save the King.* His posthumous son **George Saville** (1743–1807) failed as actor; successful as vocalist and mimic (1770–1807); author of masques, farces, burlettas, operas, songs.

**Carey, Henry Charles.** 1793–1879. American economist, b. Philadelphia; son of Mathew Carey. In publishing business (1817–35); retired to devote himself to study and writing. Author of *Principles of Political Economy* (3 vols., 1837, 1838, 1840); *The Principles of Social Science* (3 vols., 1858–59); etc.

**Carey, James.** 1845–1883. Dublin builder and town councilor, originally a bricklayer; a founder of the Invincibles (1881); directed assassination (1882) of Lord Frederick Cavendish and T. H. Burke in Phoenix Park, Dublin; betrayed Fenians and by his evidence caused execution of five associates; shot at sea on way to Natal by Patrick O'Donnell, a bricklayer sent by the Invincibles to avenge the deaths.

**Carey, Mathew.** 1760–1839. Publisher, b. Dublin, Ireland. Editor, *Freeman's Journal*, Dublin (1780–83); *Volunteer's Journal* (1783–84). Fled to America (1784) to escape prosecution for attacks on British government; founded *Pennsylvania Herald* (1785), *Columbian Magazine* (1786); publisher and bookseller in Philadelphia (from 1790). See Henry Charles CAREY.

**Carey, Rosa Nou·chette′** (nōō·shĕt′). 1840–1909. English writer of stories for girls, including *Nellie's Memories* (1868), *Wee Wifie* (1869), *Only the Governess* (1888), *The Mistress of Brae Farm* (1908).

**Carey, William.** 1761–1834. English Orientalist and missionary; shoemaker by trade. Helped found Baptist Missionary Society; one of first missionaries to go to India (1793); established church, school, and printing press at Serampore (1799–1801); professor of Sanskrit in college at Fort William near Calcutta (1801–30); issued translations (known as *Serampore versions*) of the Scriptures in nearly 40 languages and dialects; compiled grammars and dictionaries of Mahratta, Sanskrit, Punjabi, and other native languages; edited the *Ramayana* (1806–10).

**Car′gill** (kär′gĭl), **Donald.** 1619?–1681. Scottish Covenanter. Ejected from his parish for rebuking Charles II's conduct (1662); wounded at Bothwell Bridge (1679) during insurrection by Scottish Covenanters; with Richard Cameron (*q.v.*) declared Charles II deposed and excommunicated (1680); beheaded for treason.

**Car′hart** (kär′härt), **Henry Smith.** 1844–1920. American physicist, b. Coeymans, N.Y. Grad. Wesleyan (1869). Teacher at Michigan (1886–1909). Known for work in electricity, especially on standard cells (devising the Carhart-Clark cell) and primary batteries; author of textbooks and treatises.

**Carhart, Paul Worthington.** 1871–1933. American

orthoëpist and lexicographer, b. Jackson, Mich. Ph.B., Yale (1894); studied phonetics abroad under Sweet and Viëtor (1900–02). Phonetician on staff of G. & C. Merriam Co., publishers of Webster's Dictionaries (1898–1900, 1902–33); managing editor (1928–33).

**Ca·rí'as An·di'no** (kä·rē'äs än·dē'nō), **Tiburcio.** 1876–1969. Honduran general; president of Honduras (1933–49).

**Cariès.** See CARRIÈS.

**Ca'ri·gna'no** (kä'rē·nyä'nō). The cadet, or Savoy-Carignan, branch of house of Savoy (*q.v.*).

**Carilef.** See WILLIAM OF SAINT CARILEF.

**Ca·ri'nus** (kȧ·rī'nŭs). d. 285. Roman emperor (283–285). Elder son of emperor Carus (*q.v.*). Appointed (282) governor of western provinces, as his father and brother (Numerianus) left on expedition against Persians; on death of Carus (283) left joint emperor with Numerianus; indulged in violent excesses, but displayed some bravery and military skill against barbarians; fought with Diocletian; won decisive battle near Margum in Moesia; killed by one of his officers.

**Ca·ris'si·mi** (kä·rēs'sē·mē), **Giacomo.** c. 1604–1674. Italian composer, b. Marino. Kapellmeister, Assisi (1624–28), St. Apollinaris, Rome (1628–84); among his pupils were Bononcini, Scarlatti, and Charpentier. Marks transition from polyphonic style of Palestrina school to monodic style of founders of opera; originator of chamber cantata; developed instrumental accompaniment to motet; one of originators of oratorio. His compositions include masses, motets, and the oratorios *Jephthah*, *Judicium Salomonis*, *Baltazar*, and *Jonas*. Author of *Ars Cantandi* (1696).

**Carl.** Variant of KARL.

**Carl** (kärl), **William Crane.** 1865–1936. American organist, b. Bloomfield, N.J. Studied in Paris under Guilmant. Organist in Newark, N.J. (1882–92) and at First Presbyterian Church, New York City (1892–1936). Founded and directed Guilmant Organ School, New York City (1899).

**Car·lén'** (kȧr·lān'), **Emilie,** *nee* **Smith** (smĭt). 1807–1892. Swedish novelist and feminist; leader of a literary coterie in Stockholm. Author of *Waldemar Klein* (1838), *The Rose of Tistelö* (1842), *The Hermit* (1846), *The Merchant's House on the Cliff* (1860). Married 1st (1827) Dr. Axel Flygare (d. 1833), 2d (1841) **Johan Gabriel Carlén** (1814–1875), writer, author of *Romances of Swedish Life* (1846).

**Carle'ton** (kärl'tŭn; -t'n), Sir **Guy.** 1st Baron **Dor'ches'ter** (dôr'chĕs'tẽr; -chĭs·tẽr). 1724–1808. British soldier and administrator, b. in County Tyrone, Ireland. Served in America (1758–62); acting governor of Quebec (1766–70); governor of Quebec and commander of British forces in Canada (1775–77); repelled attack of Montgomery and Benedict Arnold on Quebec (1775–76); defeated Arnold on Lake Champlain and took Crown Point (1776); superseded as commander by Burgoyne (1777); succeeded Sir Henry Clinton as commander in chief in America (1782–83); governor of Quebec (1786–91, 1793–96); general (1793).

**Carleton, Henry Guy.** 1856–1910. American playwright, b. Fort Union, N.Mex. Chief plays, *The Gilded Fool* (1892), *Butterflies* (1894).

**Carleton, Mark Alfred.** 1866–1925. American plant pathologist, b. Jerusalem, Ohio. B.S. (1887), M.S. (1893), Kansas State Coll. Cerealist with U.S. Department of Agriculture (from 1894); introduced grain crops from foreign countries, notably Kubanka wheat from western Asia; founded durum wheat industry.

**Carleton, Will,** *in full* **William McKendree.** 1845–1912. American poet, b. near Hudson, Mich.; author of *Farm Ballads* (1873), *City Ballads* (1875); best-known poem, *Over the Hill to the Poor House.*

**Carleton, William.** 1794–1869. Irish novelist. Son of a cottier; attended hedge schools; tutor in Dublin. Author of stories delineating Irish peasant life, reflecting its pathos and humor, including two series of *Traits and Stories of the Irish Peasantry* (1830, 1833) and a long powerful novel *Fardorougha the Miser* (1837); alienated many Irishmen by unsparing criticism in later stories, including *The Tithe Proctor* (1849), *The Squanders of Castle Squander* (1852).

**Car'li** *or* **Car'li-Rub'bi** (kär'lē·rōōb'bē), Conte **Giovanni Rinaldo.** 1720–1795. Italian economist and antiquary. Professor of astronomy and navigation, Padua (1744); president, council of commerce, Milan (1753); president, school of finance, Milan (1771). His works include *Delle Origini e del Commercio della Moneta e dell' Istituzione delle Zecche d'Italia* (1754–60), *Sul Libero Commercio dei Grani* (1771), *Antichità Italiche* (1771), *Lettere Americane* (2 vols., 1780–81).

**Car·lile'** (kär·līl'; kär'līl), **John Snyder.** 1817–1878. American lawyer, b. Winchester, Va. Member, U.S. House of Representatives (1855–57; 1861); influential in creation of State of West Virginia; U.S. senator from West Virginia (1861–65).

**Carlile, Richard.** 1790–1843. English freethinker and reformer. Journeyman tinsmith in London; disciple of Thomas Paine; vendor of *Black Dwarf*, a prohibited radical weekly (1817); printed Southey's *Wat Tyler* and other free-thought papers; imprisoned for publishing his *Political Litany* and again (1819–25) for publishing Paine's works; published journal *The Republican* (1819–26), despite imprisonment of his wife, sister, and shopmen as his accomplices; edited a weekly *The Gorgon* and (1830) opened hall for free discussion; imprisoned for refusing to pay church rates (1830–33, 1834–35).

**Carlingford,** Baron. See Chichester Samuel FORTESCUE.

**Car·lisle'** (kär·līl'; kär'līl), Earls of. Title in English peerage held by James Hay (*q.v.*) and (from 1661) by the Howard family (*q.v.*).

**Carlisle, John Griffin.** 1835–1910. American lawyer, b. in Campbell County (now Kenton County), Ky. Member, U.S. House of Representatives (1877–90); speaker (1883–89); identified with movement for tariff reform; U.S. senator (1890–93); U.S. secretary of the treasury (1893–97); noted for sound-money policy.

**Carlo Alberto, Carlo Emanuele, Carlo Felice.** See CHARLES ALBERT, CHARLES EMMANUEL, CHARLES FELIX.

**Car'lo·man** (kär'lō·măn; *Fr.* kȧr'lô'mäɴ'). *Ger.* **Karl'mann** (kärl'män). (1) d. 754. Son of Charles Martel. Mayor of the palace (741–747) jointly with his brother Pepin the Short; administered eastern Frankish kingdom; fought wars with Germans and strengthened power of church; retired to a monastery (747) and later to Monte Cassino (750).

(2) 751–771. Son of Pepin the Short. King of Eastern Franks (768–771); joint king of the Franks with his brother Charlemagne (*q.v.*).

(3) 828–880. Son of Louis the German and father of the Emperor Arnulf. Duke of Bavaria (865–876); king of Bavaria and Carinthia (876–880). Crowned king of the Lombards at Pavia (877).

**Carloman.** d. 884. Son of Louis II. King of France, joint ruler with his brother Louis III (879–882); sole ruler (882–884); reigned in south (Aquitaine and Burgundy); at war with Northmen.

**Car'los** (kär'lōs). Spanish form of CHARLES.

**Car'los I** (kȧr'lōōsh). *Eng.* **Charles I.** 1863–1908. King of Portugal (1889–1908). Son of King Louis I and

Maria Pia; b. Lisbon. Strained relations with Great Britain (1889–90) over acts of Portuguese colonists in South Africa; suspended constitution (1907); appointed João Franco dictator; discontent aroused because of Franco's measures; assassinated with eldest son, Louis, in streets of Lisbon.

**Car′los** (kär′lŏs; *Span.* -lōs), Don (dŏn; *Span.* dôn). Name of several princes of Spain:

(1) See CHARLES, Prince of Viana.

(2) Don **Carlos de Aus′tri·a** [thā ous′trē·ä] (1545–1568), eldest son of Philip II and Maria of Portugal, b. Valladolid. Prince of Asturias and heir to Spanish throne; his betrothal to Elizabeth of Valois, daughter of Henry II of France, suddenly annulled and Elizabeth married to his father; accused (1567) of plotting against father's life; died in prison, possibly murdered. Subject of Schiller's tragedy *Don Carlos* (1801) and of dramas by Alfieri, Chénier, Otway, Núñez de Arce, etc.

(3) Don **Carlos de Bor·bón′** (bôr·bôn′). See CHARLES III of Spain.

(4) Don **Carlos** 1st, *full name* **Carlos María Isidro de Borbón** (1788–1855), second son of Charles IV and brother of Ferdinand VII (*q.v.*); became pretender to Spanish throne when Ferdinand, persuaded by his wife Maria Christina, abrogated statute in favor of male heirs and secured throne to his daughter Isabella II (1833); supported by Basques and Catalonians, proclaimed king as Charles V; revolted, but in Carlist wars (1833–39) overcome by government forces; fled to France (1839); resigned pretensions (1845) to his son Don Carlos 2d.

(5) Don **Carlos** 2d, *full name* **Carlos Luis Fernando de Borbón,** Conde **de Mon′te·mo·lín′** [môn′tā-mō·lēn′] (1818–1861); recognized by Carlists as Charles VI (1845); made prisoner during insurrection (1860); released on signing renunciation of claims; died without issue, claims passing to youngest brother, Don Juan (*q.v.*), who abdicated (1868) in favor of his son Don Carlos 3d.

(6) Don **Carlos** 3d, *full name* **Carlos María de los Do·lo′res** (lōs thō·lō′rās) **de Borbón** (1848–1909); published proclamation claiming Spanish throne as Charles VII (1872); entered Spain (1873); waged civil war (1873–76); fled to France; gave up struggle, but did not relinquish claims; expelled from France (1881) for Orleanist sympathies; abdicated (1909) in favor of his son Don Jaime of Madrid (b. 1870).

**Car′los** (kâr′lŏs) *or* **Care′less** (kâr′lĕs; -lĭs), **William.** d. 1689. English Royalist officer who, after battle of Worcester, shared with Prince Charles (later Charles II) his hiding place in a hollow oak (the "Royal Oak") at Boscobel, Shropshire (Sept. 6 and 7, 1651); escaped to France; later in service of Charles II.

**Car·lo′ta** (kär·lō′tä). *Incorrectly* **Car·lot′ta** (kär·lŏt′ȧ). *Eng.* **Charlotte.** *Full name* **Marie Charlotte Amélie Augustine Victoire Clémentine Léopoldine.** 1840–1927. Empress of Mexico (1864–67). Only dau. of Leopold I of Belgium; b. Laeken, near Brussels; m. (1857) Maximilian, Archduke of Austria; accompanied him to Mexico (1864) when he was given imperial crown; sent by Maximilian (1866) to Europe to secure aid from Napoleon III and the pope against Mexican republicans; realizing failure of her husband's cause became hopelessly insane; confined in château near Brussels (1879–1927).

**Car·lo′ta** (kär·lō′tä). *Eng.* **Charlotte.** *In full* **Joaquina Carlota de Bor·bón′** (thā bôr·bôn′). 1775–1830. Queen of Portugal. Dau. of Charles IV of Spain; m. (1790) John VI of Portugal; marriage unhappy; publicly disavowed by John, then regent (1806); fled with royal family to Brazil (1808); encouraged son Dom Miguel in revolt against Dom Pedro and Maria (1828–30).

**Carlovingian** dynasty. See CAROLINGIAN dynasty.

**Carl′sen** (kärl′s′n), **E·mil′** (ē·mēl′). 1853–1932. Painter, b. Copenhagen, Denmark; to U.S. (1872). Best known for his still-life and marine paintings. His son **Dines** (1901–1966), also an artist.

**Carl′son** (kärl′s′n), **An′ton** (ăn′tōn) **Julius.** 1875–1956. American physiologist, b. in Sweden; to U.S. (1891). B.S., Augustana Coll., Ill. (1898), Ph.D., Stanford (1902). Taught at U. of Chicago (1904–40). Did research on the heart and circulation, lymph, saliva, the thyroids, the parathyroids, the pancreas, immune bodies, also on metabolism, gastric secretion, and hunger.

**Carl′son, Evans Fordyce.** 1896–1947. American soldier, b. Sydney, N.Y.; served in China (1927–29), Nicaragua (1930–33), in China and Japan (1933–36); as U.S. observer traveled with Chinese 8th Route Army (1937–39); recorded experiences and observations in *Twin Stars of China* and *The Chinese Army* (1940); led guerrilla unit ("Carlson's Raiders") which attacked Japanese on Little Makin Island (1942) and Guadalcanal.

**Carl′son** (kärl′sôn), **Fredrik Ferdinand.** 1811–1887. Swedish historian and politician. Professor, Uppsala (1849–77); member of Riksdag (1850–66, 1878–87); minister of public worship (1863–70, 1875–78). Author of a *History of Sweden* (seven volumes, 1855–85). His son **Ernst** (1854–1909), historian; professor at Göteborg; member of Riksdag (1897–1905); wrote *Charles XII in Saxony, Sweden and Prussia 1701–1709,* etc.

**Carl′son** (kärl′s′n), **John Fa′bi·an** (fā′bĭ·ăn; fāb′yăn). 1875–1945. Landscape painter, b. in Sweden; to U.S. (1886). Studied at Art Students' League in Buffalo and New York; head instructor of landscape painting, Art Students' League, New York. Author of *Elementary Principles of Landscape Painting* (1928).

**Carlstadt.** See KARLSTADT.

**Carl′ton** (kärl′t′n; -tŭn), **Effie,** *nee* **Crock′ett** (krŏk′ĕt; -ĭt). 1857–1940. American actress; author, under pen name **Effie Can′ning** (kăn′ĭng), of the lullaby *Rock-a-Bye Baby* (orig. copyright, 1887).

**Car·lyle′** (kär·līl′; kär′līl), **Thomas.** 1795–1881. Scottish essayist and historian, b. Ecclefechan, Dumfriesshire, son of a stonemason. Educ. Annan Academy and Edinburgh U., where he studied arts course and divinity. Taught mathematics, Annan (1814); schoolmaster at Kirkcaldy (1816); tutor to Charles Buller (1822–24). Wrote articles for Brewster's *Edinburgh Encyclopaedia;* translated Legendre's *Geometry* and Goethe's *Wilhelm Meister;* wrote *Life of Schiller* (1824). Met Coleridge, Hazlitt, and other literary men in London (1824); m. (1826) Jane Baillie Welsh; settled in Edinburgh; wrote essays for *Edinburgh Review;* formed friendship with Jeffrey. Moved to Craigenputtock (1828); wrote the autobiographical *Sartor Resartus* (pub. in *Fraser's Magazine,* 1833–34), a speculative discussion of creeds and systems of philosophy under guise of a philosophy of clothes; corresponded with Goethe. Settled in London in Cheyne Row, Chelsea (1834–81), whence often called the "Sage of Chelsea." His *French Revolution* (1837), published despite burning of manuscript for most of first volume by John Stuart Mill's servant, established his reputation as one of foremost men of letters; began lectures (1837), one course of which was *Heroes and Hero Worship* (pub. 1840). Attacked shams and corruption of modern society in *Chartism* (1839), *Past and Present* (1843), *Latter Day Pamphlets* (1850); in *Oliver Cromwell* (1845) revolutionized contemporary estimate of Cromwell; biographized his friend John Sterling (1851); devoted himself (1851–

65) to his *History of Frederick the Great*, making two trips to Germany (1852, 1858) for research. After death of his wife (1866) discovered from her diary extent of her privations and suffering from his want of consideration for her because of absorption in his work. Made plea for Germany during Franco-Prussian War (1870–71); suffered failing health and paralysis of right hand (1872); buried in Ecclefechan. His *Reminiscences* (written, 1866; published without editing by Froude, 1881), containing harsh comments upon individuals and misanthropic passages written in periods of nervous depression, prejudiced the popular estimate of his genius.

His wife, **Jane Baillie**, *nee* **Welsh** (1801–1866), daughter of a Scottish physician, descendant of John Knox; wrote a tragedy at age of 14; wished to marry her teacher, Edward Irving, who was bound by previous engagement; corresponded with Carlyle; declined to become engaged to him (until 1825); married (1826); more tractable with visitors than Carlyle; suffered from Carlyle's temper and his absorption in work; victim (1845–57) of jealousy over Lady Ashburton's friendship with Carlyle; became an invalid (1858).

His younger brother, **John Aitken** (1801–1879), M.D., Edinburgh (1825), traveling physician to countess of Clare in Italy (1831–37), and to duke of Buccleuch (1838–43); translated Dante's *Inferno* into prose (1849); student of Icelandic.

**Car′ma·gno′la** (kär′mä·nyô′lä). *Orig. name* **Francesco Bus·so′ne** (bōōs·sō′nā). Conte **di Ca′stel·nuo′vo** (käs′tâl·nwô′vō). c. 1390–1432. Italian condottiere, b. at Carmagnola; in service of Filippo Maria Visconti, Duke of Milan (1416–23); subdued Bergamo, Brescia, Parma, Piacenza, Genoa, and other cities; after break with Visconti, led Venetians against Milan (1436); convicted of treason by Venetian Council of Ten after unsuccessful campaign; beheaded (Apr. 5, 1432) despite intercession of doge.

**Car′man** (kär′măn), **William Bliss**. 1861–1929. Canadian poet, b. Fredericton, N.B. Educ. U. of New Brunswick, U. of Edinburgh (1882–83), Harvard (1886–88). On staff successively of New York *Independent*, *Current Literature*, *Atlantic Monthly*. His many volumes of verse include *Low Tide on Grand Pré* (1893), *A Sea-Mark* (1895), *Ballads of Lost Haven* (1897), *By the Aurelian Wall* (1898), *Sappho* (1902), *Pipes of Pan* (1903–05), *Daughters of Dawn* (1912), *April Airs* (1916), *Later Poems* (1921). Collaborated with Richard Hovey in *Songs from Vagabondia* (1894), *More Songs from Vagabondia* (1896), and *Last Songs from Vagabondia* (1900). Prose essays collected in *Kinship of Nature* (1904), *The Poetry of Life* (1905), etc.

**Carmarthen,** Marquises of. See Thomas and Francis OSBORNE.

**Carmen Sylva.** Pseudonym of ELIZABETH, Queen of Rumania.

**Car′mer** (kär′mẽr), **Carl Lamson**. 1893– . American poet and novelist, b. Cortland, N.Y. Ph.B., Hamilton (1914), M.A., Harvard (1915); served in World War; teacher of English; professor, U. of Alabama (1924–27); asst. editor, *Vanity Fair* (1928–29), *Theatre Arts Monthly* (1929–33). Author of *Frenchtown* and *Deep South* (verse), *Stars Fell on Alabama* (1934), *Listen for a Lonesome Drum* (1936), *Genesee Fever* (1941), *America Sings* (1942).

**Car′mi′chael** (kär′mī′kĕl; -k'l; kär·mī′-), Sir **Thomas David Gibson**. Baron **Carmichael of Skir′ling** (skûr′lĭng). 1859–1926. British colonial administrator and art connoisseur, b. Edinburgh. B.A., Cantab. (1881). Governor of Victoria, Australia (1908–11), Madras (1911–12), Bengal (1912–17).

**Car′mo·dy** (kär′mô·dĭ), **John Michael**. 1882?–1963. American federal administrator, b. Towanda, Pa. In business (1900–26); editor of *Coal Age* and *Factory and Industrial Management*, New York City (1927 ff.). Chairman, Bituminous Coal Labor Board (1933); chief engineer in Civil Works Administration and Federal Emergency Relief Administration (1933–35); served also on National Labor Relations Board. Rural electrification (1936–39) and Federal works (1939–41) administrator; member Maritime Commission (1941–47).

**Car·mo′na** (kẽr·mō′nȧ), **Antonio Oscar de Fra·go′so** (dĕ frȧ·gō′zōō). 1869–1951. Portuguese general and statesman, b. Lisbon. Made prime minister and minister of war by military decree (1926); virtually dictator; faced with revolts in Oporto and Lisbon (1927); suppressed outbreaks with aid of monarchists; reconstructed cabinet (1927); elected president by plebiscite (1928); re-elected (1935 and 1942).

**Car′mon′telle′** (kȧr′môɴ′tĕl′), **Louis.** *Professional name of* **Louis Car′ro′gis′** (kȧ′rô′zhē′). 1717–1806. French painter, engraver, and writer; published collections of proverbs and plays, *Proverbes Dramatiques* (8 vols., 1768–81) and *Théâtre de Campagne* (1775). Among his paintings were portraits of Philidor, Boufflers, Grimm.

**Car′nall** (kär′näl), **Rudolf von.** 1804–1874. German mining engineer after whom the mineral carnallite is named; active in founding German Geological Society.

**Car·nar′von** (kär·när′vŭn; kẽr-), Earls of. See HERBERT family, 3.

**Car·ne′a·des** (kär·nē′ȧ·dēz). 214?–129 B.C. Greek skeptic philosopher; founder in Athens of what is known as the New, or Third, Academy. Cf. CLITOMACHUS.

**Car·ne′gie** (kär·nā′gĭ; -nĕg′ĭ; kär′nĕ·gĭ; *the first was his own pron.*), **Andrew.** 1835–1919. Industrialist and humanitarian, b. Dunfermline, Scotland. To U.S. (1848); settled in Allegheny, Pa. Held minor positions in cotton textile factory and telegraph company; secretary to superintendent, Pittsburgh division, Pennsylvania Railroad; served in military transportation section, U.S. War Dept., through Civil War. Entered iron and steel business (1865); concentrated on steel industry (from 1873); chief owner, Homestead Steel Works, by 1888; controlled seven other manufactories; consolidated his interests into Carnegie Steel Co. (1899); merged this company with United States Steel Corp. (1901), and retired. Devoted rest of life to distribution of huge fortune for benefit of society, in accordance with views expressed in his article "Wealth" in *North American Review* (June, 1889). Benefactions include large contributions for public libraries, public education, and international peace; endowed Carnegie Corporation of New York with $125,000,000 to support his benefactions after his death.

**Car·nei′ro Le·ão′** (kẽr·nā′rōō lē·ouɴ′), **Honorio Hermeto.** Marquês **de Pa·ra·ná′** (thĕ pȧ·rȧ·nä′). 1801–1856. Brazilian statesman; minister of justice (1832–33); prime minister (Jan., 1843–Feb., 1844; 1854–56); president of Rio de Janeiro (1841 ff.), Pernambuco (1849 ff.).

**Car′ney** (kär′nĭ), **Julia**, *nee* **Fletcher.** 1823–1908. American verse writer, b. Boston. Author of *Little Things* (1845), containing the verses beginning *Little drops of water, little grains of sand.*

**Car′ni·cer′ y Bat′lle** (kär′nē·sâr′ ē bät′lyā), **Ramón.** 1789–1855. Spanish composer, b. Tárrega, Catalonia. Professor of composition, Madrid conservatory (1830–54). Contributed to formation of national opera in Spain. Composer of Italian operas, symphonies, religious works, and songs including Chilean national anthem *Dulce Patria.*

**Carnock,** Baron. See Sir Arthur NICOLSON.

**Car'not'** (kȧr'nō'). Name of a Burgundian family prominent during French Revolution and after.

**Joseph François Claude** (1752–1835), jurist, b. Nolay; advocate at Dijon assembly and active in revolutionary movement; procureur général at Dijon; author of law commentaries (1812–1823).

**Lazare Nicolas Marguerite** (1753–1823), his brother; *called* "le grand Carnot" (lẽ gräN); statesman and general, b. Nolay; deputy to Legislative Assembly (1791) and National Convention (1792); member, Committee of Public Safety (1793); called "Organizer of Victory" for his work while in charge of organization and direction of the armies (1793–95); president of the Convention (1795); member of the Directory (1795–97), and twice its president; fled to Switzerland and Germany at coup d'état of Fructidor (1797) to escape proscription on account of supposed Royalist sympathies; minister of war (1800–01); member of Tribunate (1802–07); governor of Antwerp (1814); Napoleon's minister of interior during Hundred Days (1815); exiled by Louis XVIII (1815); lived in Warsaw and Magdeburg (1815–23). Author of works on mathematics and military strategy including a work on fortification *De la défense de places fortes* (1810), soon accepted as standard for most European armies.

**Nicolas Léonard Sadi** (1796–1832), elder son of Lazare; physicist, pioneer in thermodynamics, b. Paris; entered Polytechnic School (1812); served in engineer corps (1814–28); engaged in research; published (1824) his famous essay on heat, *Réflexions sur la Puissance Motrice du Feu;* his theory, later developed by other scientists, notably Lord Kelvin, was in substance the second law of thermodynamics (*Carnot's principle*); devised a reversible engine to investigate theories on energy produced and heat applied under ideal conditions; also added to knowledge of principle now known as conservation of energy; died of cholera.

**Lazare Hippolyte** (1801–1888), younger son of Lazare; politician and journalist, b. Saint-Omer; lived in exile with his father (1815–23); elected deputy from Paris (1839–48), voting with extreme Radical Left; in Legislative Assembly (1850–51), opposed to Louis Napoleon; although elected to National Assembly several times, did not take his seat until 1864; again deputy (1871–75); made life senator (1875); author of several works on history and biography.

**Sadi,** *in full* **Marie François Sadi** (1837–1894), son of Lazare Hippolyte. Fourth president of the French Republic, b. Limoges. Entered engineering profession; made prefect of Department of Seine-Inférieure (1871); Republican member of National Assembly (1871–76); in Chamber of Deputies (1876–80); twice cabinet officer (1880–81, 1885–86). Elected president to succeed Grévy (1887–94); administration marked by his tact and ability, especially in meeting crises of Boulangist agitation (1889) and Panama scandals (1892); assassinated by an Italian anarchist.

**Ca'ro** (kä'rō), **Heinrich.** 1834–1910. German industrial chemist; one of the founders of the coal-tar dye industry.

**Ca'ro** *or* **Ka'ro** (kä'rō), **Joseph ben Ephraim.** 1488–1575. Jewish Talmudist and codifier of Jewish religious laws, b. in Spain or Portugal. Exiled from Spain with parents (1492); migrated to Nicopolis (Bulgaria), Adrianople, Salonika, and Constantinople; settled in Palestine (c. 1535). Author of *Beth Joseph* (or *House of Joseph,* a commentary on the religious lawbook *Arba Turin* of Jacob ben Asher; 4 parts, 1550–59) and of *Shulhan Aruck* (or *Arranged Table,* an authoritative code of Jewish religious and civil law based chiefly on Talmud; 4 parts, 1565). *Maggid Mesharim* (pub. 1646), a kind of diary containing discussions with a personified Mishnah as his heavenly mentor, is also ascribed to him.

**Ca'ro** (kä'rō), **Miguel Antonio.** 1843–1909. Colombian politician and author, b. Bogotá. Relative of Rafael Núñez. Editor of conservative journal and partly responsible for 1886 constitution. Vice-president of Colombia (1892–94), and president (1894–98) at death of Núñez. Writer on philosophy, politics, and history; known esp. for poetry, as in collection *Horas de Amor.*

**Ca'ro** (kä'rō), **Nikodem.** 1871–1935. German chemist; with Adolf Frank (*q.v.*), developed cyanamide process for nitrogen fixation.

**Carobert.** = CHARLES I of Hungary.

**Ca'rol** (kä'rŏl; *Angl.* kăr'ŭl). *Eng.* **Charles.** Name of two kings of Rumania:

**Carol I.** *Orig.* **Karl Eitel Friedrich.** 1839–1914. Prince of Rumania (1866–81); first king of Rumania (1881–1914). Second son of Prince Charles Anthony of Hohenzollern-Sigmaringen (see CHARLES ANTHONY and HOHENZOLLERN) and brother of Leopold; entered military service; m. (1869) Elizabeth (*q.v.*), Princess of Wied; elected prince (1866) after deposition of Alexandru Ioan Cuza; aided Russia in war against Turkey (1877), independence of Rumania being recognized by Treaty of Berlin (1878); proclaimed king (1881); made secret alliance with Austria (1883); promoted economic development of country; declared war on Bulgaria (1913) in Second Balkan War; proclaimed neutrality at beginning of World War (1914), though sympathizing with Germany. Succeeded by his nephew Ferdinand I.

**Carol II.** 1893–1953. King (1930–40). Eldest son of Ferdinand I; b. Sinaia. Contracted morganatic marriage (1917) with Mme. Zizi Lambrino; divorced her to marry (1921) Princess Helen of Greece, by whom he was father of King Michael (*q.v.*). Renounced (1925) right of succession to throne, deserted wife, and went to Paris (where he was known as M. Carol Ca'rai·man' [kä'rī-män']) to live in exile with Mme. Magda Lupescu; formally divorced Princess Helen (1928). Returned to Rumania by airplane (1930); supplanted his son Michael as king; reign marked by continued attempts to please both Russia and Germany; broke with National Peasant party which had at first supported him; tried unsuccessfully to become dictator; driven from throne (1940) by German influence; fled with Mme. Lupescu to Spain; to Cuba (1941), Mexico (1942).

**Carolan, Torlogh.** See O'CAROLAN.

**Car'o·line Ma·til'da** (kăr'ō·lĭn mȧ·tĭl'dȧ). 1751–1775. Queen of Denmark; wife of Christian VII, King of Denmark. Posthumous daughter of Frederick Louis, eldest son of George II of England. Married (1766); gave birth to son, later King Frederick VI; treated with coldness and neglect by profligate husband; involved in amour with court physician, Struensee (*q.v.*), who became all-powerful in palace (1770) and chief minister (1771); arrested with Struensee (1772); confessed guilt; divorced; spent last years in Hanover.

**Car'o·line of Ans'pach** (kăr'ō·lĭn ŭv ănz'păk). *In full* **Wilhelmina Carolina.** 1683–1737. Queen of Great Britain and Ireland, wife of George II. Daughter of John Frederick, Margrave of Brandenburg-Ansbach. Married (1705) George Augustus, Electoral Prince of Hanover; went to England on accession of George I (1714); gathered distinguished circle including Pope, Gay, Chesterfield, and Lord Hervey; connived at husband's amour with Henrietta Howard; crowned queen (1727); kept Sir Robert Walpole in power; appointed bishops rather for learning than orthodoxy; regent during absence of king on four occasions; hated her eldest son Frederick.

**Caroline of Bruns′wick** (brŭnz′wĭk). *In full* **Amelia Elizabeth Caroline.** 1768–1821. Queen of Great Britain and Ireland, wife of George IV. Daughter of Charles William Ferdinand, Duke of Brunswick-Wolfenbüttel. Forced as bride (1795) upon prince of Wales by George III; persecuted by prince's mistresses; deserted by profligate husband after birth of Princess Charlotte Augusta (1796); censured for improprieties and unguarded speech (1806); traveled on Continent; on death of George III (1820) refused offer of settlement on condition of renouncing title of queen; held popular support and secured abandonment of bill in House of Lords divorcing her on ground of adultery with Bergami (1820); forcibly excluded from Westminster Hall on coronation day (1821).

**Car′o·lin′gi·an** (kăr′ō·lĭn′jĭ·ăn) *or* **Car′lo·vin′gi·an** (kär′lō·vĭn′jĭ·ăn) dynasty. Second Frankish dynasty of kings and emperors, succeeding Merovingian dynasty; ruled in France from Pepin the Short (751) to death of Louis V (987) and in Germany to death of Louis III, the Child (911). See *Tables* (*in Appendix*) for FRANCE and HOLY ROMAN EMPIRE.

**Carolsfeld.** See SCHNORR VON CAROLSFELD.

**Carolus-Duran.** See DURAN.

**Carolus Magnus.** See CHARLEMAGNE.

**Ca′ron′** (kä′rôɴ′), **Pierre Augustin.** Original name of BEAUMARCHAIS.

**Caron, René Édouard.** 1800–1876. Canadian jurist and politician; judge, Court of Queen's Bench (1853); lieutenant governor, Province of Quebec (1873–76).

**Ca′ron·de·let′** (kä′rôn·dā·lĕt′; *Angl.* kȧ·rŏn′dĕ·lĕt′), Barón **Francisco Luis Héctor de.** 1748?–1807. Spanish administrator in America, b. Noyelles, Flanders. Governor of Louisiana and West Florida (1791–95); after sale of West Florida to France, continued as governor of Louisiana (1795–97); governor general of Quito, Ecuador (1799–1807).

**Ca·roth′ers** (kȧ·rŭth′ẽrz), **Wallace Hume.** 1896–1937. American chemist, b. Burlington, Iowa. B.S., Tarkio Coll. (1920), Ph.D., Illinois (1924); teacher (1921–28); research chemist, E. I. Du Pont de Nemours and Co., Wilmington, Del. (from 1928). Patented (1937) synthetic material nylon, patent being issued posthumously and assigned to du Pont company.

**Ca·ro′to** (kä·rô′tô), **Giovanni Francesco.** c. 1480–1555. Veronese painter; pupil of Liberale and Mantegna. His works include frescoes in church of Sant'Eufemia, *Annunciation* in San Girolamo, altar of San Fermo Maggiore, and several panels in Pinacoteca Communale (all in Verona).

**Ca′ro·vé′** (kä′rô·vā′), **Friedrich Wilhelm.** 1789–1852. German philosopher; advocate of a universal religion of humanity, founded on Christianity but having neither hierarchy nor dogma.

**Carp** (kärp), **Petrache.** 1837–1919. Rumanian statesman; prime minister of Rumania (1900–01, 1911–12).

**Car·pac′cio** (kär·pät′chō), **Vittore.** b. before 1460–d. before 1526. Venetian painter; influenced by Gentile Bellini. His works include *History of St. Ursula* (series of nine pictures including particularly *Dismissal of the Ambassadors*, *Departure of the Betrothed Pair*, and *St. Ursula's Dream*), *Life of St. George* (another nine-picture series), six scenes from the life of Mary, a series *Life of St. Stephen*, also *Presentation in the Temple* (Venetian Acad.), *Death of the Virgin* (Ferrara), and *Madonna Enthroned* (London).

**Car·pa′ni** (kär·pä′nē), **Giuseppe.** 1752–1825. Italian librettist and musicographer; author of Milanese dialect poems, librettos, as *Camilla* (music by Paer), *La Passione di Gesù Cristo* (music by Weigl), translations of French and German operas, a translation of Haydn's oratorio *Creation*, and critical works, as *Le Haydine ovvero Lettere sulla Vita e le Opere del Celebre Maestro Giuseppe Haydn* (1812), *Le Rossiniane ossia Lettere Musico-Teatrali* (1824).

**Car′peaux′** (kȧr′pō′), **Jean Baptiste.** 1827–1875. French sculptor; studied at Beaux-Arts, Paris (to 1844) and in Rome (1845–50). Notable works include *La Danse* (on façade of Opéra, Paris), *Les Quatre Parties du Mond* (in gardens of Luxembourg), and portrait busts of Napoleon III, Alexandre Dumas fils, Princess Mathilde, the painter Gérome, etc.

**Car′pen·ter** (kär′pĕn·tẽr), **Edward.** 1844–1929. English writer, b. Brighton. Educ. Cambridge; in Anglican ministry (1869–74); visited U.S. (1877) and met Emerson, Holmes, Lowell, Bryant, and Whitman; settled in Derbyshire (1883), devoting himself to study and writing; became interested in socialist movements inspired by Hyndman and William Morris; lectured on socialism. Author of *Chants of Labour* (1888), *Civilization, its Cause and Cure* (1889), *Angels' Wings* (1898), *Love's Coming of Age* (1896), *Iolaus* (1902), *The Art of Creation* (1904), *My Days and Dreams* (1916).

**Carpenter, Edward Childs.** 1872–1950. American author, b. Philadelphia. Financial editor, Philadelphia *Inquirer* (1905–16). Author of novels, as *The Chasm* (1903), *Captain Courtesy* (1906), *The Code of Victor Jallot* (1907), *The Easy Mark* (1912), and a number of plays, including *The Cinderella Man* (1916), *The Bachelor Father* (1928), *Whistling in the Dark* (1932).

**Carpenter, Ford Ashman.** 1868–1947. American meteorologist and aeronaut, b. Chicago. With U.S. weather service (1888–1919); manager, department of meteorology and aeronautics, Los Angeles Chamber of Commerce (from 1919); radio broadcaster (1923–35); international balloon pilot; inventor of meteorological devices.

**Carpenter, George Lyndon.** 1872–1948. Salvation Army general, b. Newcastle, New South Wales; entered Salvation Army (1892), general (1939–46).

**Carpenter, John Alden.** 1876–1951. American composer, b. Park Ridge, Ill. A.B., Harvard (1897); studied music at Harvard under John K. Paine, in England under Sir Edward Elgar, and in Chicago under Bernhard Ziehn; in business (1897–1936). Composer of an orchestral suite (*Adventures in a Perambulator*), a concertino for piano and orchestra, a symphony, a ballet pantomime (*The Birthday of the Infanta*), a ballet (*Skyscrapers*), a symphonic poem (*Sea Drift*), and many songs.

**Carpenter, Lant.** 1780–1840. English Unitarian minister. Educ. Glasgow; minister and master of boarding school in Exeter (1805–17), at Bristol (from 1817); had Harriet and James Martineau as pupils; for infant baptism substituted infant dedication; drowned off Leghorn. His daughter **Mary** (1807–1877), educational and social reformer; opened girls' school at Bristol (1829); organized a "working and visiting society" (1835); founded a ragged school, Bristol (1846), reformatories, an industrial school (1859); visited India in interests of female education and prison management (1866, 1868, 1869, 1875); author of treatises on reformatories, juvenile delinquents, young convicts. His son **William Benjamin** (1813–1885), physiologist; grad. in medicine, Edinburgh (1839); professor of physiology at Royal Institution, London (1844); professor of forensic medicine, University Coll., London; took part in expedition for deep-sea exploration (1868–71); advocated doctrine of vertical circulation of ocean currents distinct from horizontal currents; author of a handbook on microscopy and treatises on principles of general, comparative, human, and mental physiology (1839–74).

William's son **Joseph Estlin** (1844–1927), Unitarian clergyman; M.A., University Coll., London (1863); grad. from divinity course in Manchester New Coll., London; professor (from 1875), principal (1906–15), Manchester New Coll.; also, lecturer in comparative religion, Oxford (1914–24); author of *The Composition of the Hexateuch*... (1902), *The Bible in the Nineteenth Century* (1903), and *The Johannine Writings*...(1927).

**Carpenter, Louis George.** 1861–1935. American consulting engineer, b. Orion, Mich. B.S. (1879), M.S. (1883), Michigan State. Professor, Colorado State (1888–1911). Expert in irrigation litigation in Colorado, Kansas, Wyoming, etc.

**Carpenter, Rhys.** 1889– . American archaeologist, b. Cotuit, Mass. A.B. (1908) and Ph.D. (1916), Columbia; B.A. (1911) and M.A. (1914), Oxon. Teacher of classical archaeology; professor at Bryn Mawr (1918–55); director, American School of Classical Studies, Athens, Greece (1927–32, 1946–48). Author of *Tragedy of Etarre* (1912), *The Sun-thief, and Other Poems* (1914), *The Plainsman, and Other Poems* (1920), *The Land Beyond Mexico* (1921), *The Esthetic Basis of Greek Art* (1921), *The Greeks in Spain* (1925), *The Sculpture of the Nike Parapet* (1929), *The Humanistic Value of Archaeology* (1933), *The Defenses of Acrocorinth* (1935).

**Carpenter, William Benjamin.** See under Lant CARPENTER.

**Carpenter, William Henry.** 1853–1936. American educator, b. Utica, N.Y. Educ. Cornell, Leipzig, Freiburg (Ph.D., 1881); also, A.B., Hamilton (1881). Taught Germanic languages and literature at Columbia (1883–1926; professor from 1895); also provost of Columbia (1912–26). Author of *Grundriss der Neuisländischen Grammatik* (1881), and numerous technical articles.

**Car'pen'tier'** (kȧr'päɴ'tyā'; *Angl.* kär'pĕn·tēr'), **Georges.** 1894– French pugilist; won light-heavyweight championship of the world by knocking out Battling Levinsky in four rounds (1920); defeated by Dempsey in fourth round of fight for heavyweight championship (1921); lost light-heavyweight crown to Battling Siki (1922).

**Car'pen'tier'** (kȧr'päɴ'tyā'), **Jules Adrien Marie Louis.** 1851–1921. French railroad engineer; inventor of many precision instruments, esp. for measuring electric, optical, and photographic powers; a pioneer of the periscope and of cinematograph apparatus.

**Car'pi** (kär'pē), **Girolamo da.** *Orig.* **Girolamo de' Sel·la'ri** (sȧl·lä'rē). 1501–1556. Italian painter; pupil of Garofalo; directed architectural work on pontifical palaces under Paul III. His paintings include a *Pietà* (in Pitti Palace), *Adoration of the Magi* (at Bologna), *Holy Family* (in Capitol, Rome), *Descent of the Holy Ghost* (in church of St. Francis, Rovigo).

**Carpi, Ugo da.** c. 1455–c. 1523. Italian wood engraver. Formerly held to be inventor of printing in chiaroscuro; actually, he improved original German technique and originated the term *chiaroscuro.* His prints, chiefly after Raphael and Parmigianino, include *Sybil, Descent from the Cross, Massacre of the Innocents, Diogenes.*

**Car·pi'ni** (kär·pē'nē), **Giovanni de Pia'no** (dȧ pyä'nō). 1182? or 1200?–?1252. Franciscan monk, b. near Perugia; one of first Europeans to explore the Mongol empire. Companion and disciple of St. Francis of Assisi; head of Catholic mission sent by Pope Innocent IV to the khan of Tatary to protest against Mongols' invasion of Christian lands and to gain information about them; started from Lyon on April 16, 1245, reached destination on July 22, 1246, after suffering many hardships; dismissed by khan with letter to pope bearing information of no significance; returned to Kiev on June 9, 1247, and finally to pope at Lyon. His *Liber Tartarorum*, containing information concerning the regions and peoples visited, was not published in its entirety until 1839.

**Carpio, Bernardo del.** See BERNARDO DEL CARPIO.

**Car·poc'ra·tes** (kär·pŏk'rȧ·tēz). Gnostic of Alexandria in 2d century A.D.; founded Gnostic sect of Carpocratians; taught doctrine that men can attain to a higher degree of illumination than that of Jesus.

**Carp'zov** (kärp'tsôf). Distinguished Saxon family, including notably: **Benedikt** (1565–1624), jurist, professor at Wittenberg and chancellor of Saxony. His son **Benedikt** (1595–1666), jurist, and professor at Leipzig; author of *Practica Nova Imperialis Saxonica Rerum Criminalium* (1635), *Jurisprudentia Romano-Saxonica*, and *Jurisprudentia Ecclesiastica seu Consistorialis* (1649).

**Carr** (kär), **Benjamin.** 1769–1831. Musician, b. in England; to U.S. (1793), settling at Philadelphia. Composer of *The Archers* (an opera, 1796), *Masses, Vespers, and Litanies* (1805), etc.

**Carr, Eugene Asa.** 1830–1910. American brigadier general, b. Concord, N.Y. Served through Civil War; awarded Congressional Medal of Honor for gallantry at battle of Pea Ridge.

**Carr, Gene.** 1881–1959. American comic-strip artist, b. New York City. On staff of New York *Herald*, Philadelphia *Times*, New York *Journal*, New York *World*. Creator of comic-strip series including *Lady Bountiful, All the Comforts of Home, The Prodigal Son, Father, Willie Wise, The Jones Boys, Flirting Flora, Little Nell.*

**Carr, Howard.** 1880–1960. English composer and operatic conductor, b. Manchester. Music editor for Australian broadcasting commission. Composer of symphonic and orchestral works, songs, and theatrical pieces.

**Carr, Joseph Bradford.** 1828–1895. American brigadier general, b. Albany, N.Y.; held center of Union line at Gettysburg.

**Carr, Robert.** Viscount **Roch'es'ter** (rŏch'ĕs'tēr; -ĭs-tēr). Earl of **Som'er·set** (sŭm'ēr·sĕt; -sĭt). d. 1645. Scottish favorite of James I of England; a cadet of Ker of Ferniehirst (see KERR family). Commended to James I by good looks and high animal spirits; substituted by James for his constitutional adviser; loaded with honors; given Sir Walter Raleigh's manor of Sherborne (1609); created viscount Rochester (1611), earl of Somerset (1613). Enamored of Lady Frances Howard, wife of earl of Essex; opposed in his marriage to countess of Essex upon her obtaining of a decree of nullity, by his confidant in the intrigue, Sir Thomas Overbury, who was found poisoned in the Tower (1613); married countess of Essex (1613); attached himself to wife's great-uncle the earl of Northampton, and Spanish party; lord chamberlain (1614); dislodged as favorite by George Villiers (1614). With his wife (who pleaded guilty and was pardoned, 1616) accused of murdering Overbury (1615); prosecuted by Francis Bacon; imprisoned in Tower (until 1622); later pardoned.

**Carr,** Sir **Robert.** d. 1667. English colonial administrator; appointed (1664), with Nicolls, Maverick, and Cartwright, a commissioner to New England; with Nicolls, captured New Amsterdam from the Dutch (1664) and renamed it New York; encountered opposition to his authority in Massachusetts and New Hampshire, but governed Maine (1666–67).

**Car·rac'ci** *or* **Ca·rac'ci** (kä(r)·rät'chē). Bolognese family of painters; founders of the Eclectic school and Accademia degli Incamminati. Their joint works include frescoes in Palazzo Farnese at Rome and Palazzo Fava at Bologna (latter depicting scenes from *The Aeneid* and voyage of the Argonauts) and a frieze (story of Romulus) in Palazzo Magnani at Bologna.

**Lodovico Carracci** (1555–1619), pupil of Prospero Fontana at Bologna; studied works of Italian masters at Parma, Mantua, and Venice; worked chiefly at Bologna; noted teacher.

**Annibale** (1560–1609), Lodovico's cousin; studied at Parma and Venice; influenced by Correggio, Titian, and Veronese.

**Agostino** (1557–1602), Annibale's brother; known also as an engraver; studied painting under Fontana, and engraving under Tibaldi at Bologna and Cornelis Cort at Venice; friend of Tintoretto.

**Antonio Marziale** (1583–1618), natural son of Agostino; works include frescoes in Church of San Bartolommeo del Isola (Rome) and *The Flood* (Louvre).

**Car·ran′za** (kär·rän′thä), **Bartolomé de.** 1503–1576. Spanish theologian, b. Miranda, Navarre; professor of theology at Valladolid; confidant of Charles V and Philip II; confessor to Mary Tudor; theologian at Council of Trent; archbishop of Toledo; imprisoned (1559–67) by Inquisition on charges of heresy evinced in his *Comentario sobre el Catequismo Cristiano;* reimprisoned at Rome (1567–76).

**Car·ran′za** (kär·rän′sä; *Angl.* kă·răn′zȧ), **Venustiano.** 1859–1920. Mexican revolutionist and political leader, b. Cuatro Ciénegas, Coahuila. Took part in local revolt in Coahuila (1893); held various state offices; governor at time of Madero revolution (1911), in which he supported Madero; after Madero's assassination (1913), became leader of Constitutionalists; successful in opposition to Victoriano Huerta; proclaimed "First Chief" of Mexico (Aug.–Nov., 1914); adopted program of social and economic reform; unfriendly to U.S.; attacked by forces of Villa and Emiliano Zapata; provisional president (Oct., 1915–Mar., 1917); recognized by U.S. (1915) but Villa raids into U.S. territory resulted in American punitive expedition (1916); accepted Constitution of 1917; elected president (1917–20); kept Mexico neutral in World War; forced to leave capital by Obregón; defeated in battle and murdered in Puebla state (May 21).

**Car·ra′ra** (kär·rä′rä), **Francesco.** 1805–1888. Italian jurist, b. Lucca; instructor in criminal law, U. of Pisa; deputy (1865–70); senator (1876 ff.). Opposed capital punishment. Known especially for his *Programma del Corso di Diritto Criminale* (13 vols., 1879–86); author also of *Opuscoli di Diritto Criminale* (7 vols., 1878–80) and *Lineamenti di Pratica Legislativa Penale* (2d ed., 1882).

**Car′ras·quil′la** (kär′räs·kē′yä), **Tomás.** 1858–1941. Colombian novelist; author of *Frutos de mi Tierra* (1896), *Salve Regina* (1903), *Grandeza* (1910), *El Padre Casafus* (1914), *Ligia Cruz* (1926), *Dimitas Arias*, *En la Diestra de Dios Padre*, etc.

**Car′ré′** (kȧ′rā′), **Albert.** 1852–1938. French theatrical producer, b. Strasbourg; succeeded Carvalho as director of Opéra-Comique (1898–1912, 1918–25); director of Comédie Française (1914–1918). Author of the comedy *Le Docteur Jojo* and the libretto for *La Basoche.*

**Carré, Michel.** 1819–1872. French playwright and librettist; author or coauthor (often with Paul Jules Barbier) of *Galatée* (1852), *La Statue* (1861), *Mignon* (1867), *Paul et Virginie* (1877), *Polyeuchte* (1878), etc.

**Car′rel** (kăr′ĕl; kă·rĕl′; *Fr.* kȧ′rĕl′), **A·lex′is** (ȧ·lĕk′sĭs; *Fr.* ȧ′lĕk′sē′). 1873–1944. French surgeon and biologist, b. Sainte-Foy-lès-Lyon, France. L.B. (1890), M.D. (1900), U. of Lyon. Prosector, U. of Lyon (1900–02); in U.S.A. (1905–39); on staff (1906–12), member (1912–39; emeritus), Rockefeller Institute for Medical Research; in military medical service, France (1914–19); in France on special mission for French Ministry of Public Health (from 1939). Developed methods for suturing blood vessels and transplantation of organs; awarded 1912 Nobel prize for physiology and medicine; successful in cultivating chicken heart tissue outside of the body for period of many years; developed the Carrel-Dakin treatment of wounds by regular intermittent irrigation with Dakin's solution (see H. D. DAKIN); assisted by Charles A. Lindbergh on construction of the perfusion pump, used in keeping organs alive outside of the body. Author of *Man, the Unknown* (1935), *The Culture of Organs* (with Lindbergh; 1938).

**Car′rel′** (kȧ′rĕl′), **Nicolas Armand.** 1800–1836. French journalist and political leader; founder, with Thiers and Mignet, and editor (1830–36) of *Le National*, in Paris; mortally wounded in duel.

**Car·re′ño** (kär·rē′nyō), **Teresa.** 1853–1917. Venezuelan piano virtuoso, composer, and singer; composer of a string quartet, many piano works, and a Venezuelan festival hymn (not the national anthem, which was written by J. Landaeta).

**Carreño de Mi·ran′da** (thā mē·rän′dä), **Juan.** 1614–1685. Spanish painter, b. Avilés, Asturias; succeeded Velázquez as court painter and portraitist. Works include portraits, as of Charles II, and religious paintings.

**Car·rer′** (kär·rĕr′), **Luigi.** 1801–1850. Venetian poet and scholar; professor of belles-lettres, U. of Padua; director, Museo Correr, Venice. His works include *Poesie* (1831), *L'Anello di Sette Gemme* (1838), *Ballate* (1838).

**Car·re′ra** (kär·rē′rä), **José Miguel de.** 1785–1821. Chilean revolutionist, b. Santiago. Served in Europe in Spanish army; joined revolutionary movement in Chile (1810) with his brothers **Juan José** and **Luis** (both shot as rebels at Mendoza, 1818); overthrew conservative junta (1811); dissolved congress and established new government, ruling as military dictator (1811–13); replaced by Bernardo O'Higgins (1813); made pretense of aiding O'Higgins at Rancagua (1814); fled to Buenos Aires and U.S.A.; after return to Buenos Aires (1816), attempted to stir up rebellion against Chile; captured and executed at Mendoza.

**Carrera, Rafael.** 1814–1865. Guatemalan revolutionist and political leader, b. Guatemala City, of mixed white and Indian parentage. Active against anticlerical Liberal revolt (1837); led Guatemalan insurgents and finally destroyed Central American Federation (1839); proclaimed Guatemala independent (1839); dominated Guatemala as dictator (1840–65) and, for much of the time, Central American states also; president of Guatemala (1844–48, 1854–65); made president for life (1854); led war against El Salvador (1850–53, 1863); illiterate and conservative, strongly favored the church.

**Car·re′ra** (kär·râ′rä), **Valentino.** 1834–1895. Italian dramatist; employed in Italian customs department (to 1878); attempted to found popular movement in modern drama. Author of *La Quaderna di Nanni* (1870), *Galateo Nuovissimo* (1875), *Bastoni fra le Ruote* (1884) *La Filosofia di Giannina* (1885).

**Car·re′ra An·dra′de** (kär·rē′rä än·drä′thā), **Jorge.** 1903– . Ecuadorian poet; author of *Estanque Inefable* (1922), *La Guirnalda del Silencio* (1926), *Boletines de Mar y Tierra* (1930), *La Hora de las Ventanas Iluminadas* (1937), etc.

**Car′rère′** (kȧ′râr′), **Jean.** 1865–1932. French journalist and poet; war correspondent in Transvaal during Boer War (1899–1902); author of *L'Aube* (1891), *Premières Poésies* (1893), *Les Buccins d'Or* (1918), *Les Chants Orphiques* (1923), etc.

**Car·rère'** (kȧ·râr'), **John Merven.** 1858–1911. American architect, b. of American parentage in Rio de Janeiro, Brazil. Received diploma, École des Beaux-Arts, Paris (1882). In office of McKim, Mead and White, New York (1883–84). With Thomas Hastings, formed firm of Carrère and Hastings, New York (1886). Examples of their work: hotels Ponce de Leon (1887) and Alcazar (1888), St. Augustine, Fla.; Central Congregational Church, Providence, R.I. (1891); Royal Bank of Canada, Montreal (1906); Carnegie Institution, Washington, D.C. (1906); Memorial Hall, Yale Univ. (1906); U.S. Senate and U.S. House of Representatives office buildings, Washington, D.C.; New York Public Library (completed 1911).

**Car'rey'** (kȧ'rā'), **Jacques.** 1646–1726. French painter whose drawings of the Parthenon (1673–74) before its bombardment by the Venetians have been of great value to students of Greek art.

**Car'rier'** (kȧ'ryā'), **Jean Baptiste.** 1756–1794. French revolutionist; member of the Convention; sent on mission to Normandy and Brittany; notorious for his cruelty in executing sentences of revolutionary tribunal in Nantes (1793–94); guillotined in Paris (Dec. 16, 1794).

**Car'rier'-Bel'leuse'** (-bĕ'lûz'), *properly* **Carrier de Belleuse, Albert Ernest.** 1824–1887. French sculptor; studied under David d'Angers; among his works are *L'Amour et l'Amitié, Jupiter et Hébé, Bacchante.*

**Car·rie'ra** (kär·ryâ'rä), **Rosalba.** 1675–1757. Italian painter, b. Venice; known to her contemporaries chiefly for her portraits, miniatures, and pastels.

**Car'rière'** (kȧ'ryâr'), **Eugène.** 1849–1906. French painter and lithographer; studied at École des Beaux-Arts (Paris), and under Cabanel; identified with impressionist group of painters in France.

**Car·ri·ere'** (kä·rē·âr'), **Moriz.** 1817–1895. German philosopher; professor, Munich (from 1853). Author esp. of books on aesthetics.

**Car'riès',** *orig.* **Ca'riès'** (kȧ'ryĕs'), **Jean Joseph Marie.** 1855–1894. French sculptor and ceramist.

**Car·ril'lo** (kär·rē'yō), **Braulio.** 1800–1845. Costa Rican jurist and politician. Chief justice of supreme court; president of Costa Rica (1834–37, 1838–41); deposed (1841). To Salvador and practiced law; assassinated (1845).

**Carrillo, Julián.** 1875–1965. Mexican violinist and composer. Studied in San Luis Potosí and in Leipzig; director, National Conservatory of Music, Mexico City (1913); director, American Symphony Orchestra, New York (1915), and National Orchestra of Mexico, Mexico City (1919). Introduced new musical theory which he called *Sonido 13* (1925 ff.); author of many musical treatises.

**Car'ring·ton** (kăr'ĭng·tŭn), Lord. See Sir *Archibald Primrose* (1616–1679), under PRIMROSE family.

**Carrington, FitzRoy.** 1869–1954. Connoisseur of engravings and etchings, b. Surbiton, Surrey, Eng.; bro. of Hereward Carrington (*q.v.*). To U.S. (1886); with Frederick Keppel & Co., art dealers in New York (1892–1913; member of firm from 1899); curator of department of prints, Boston Museum of Fine Arts (from 1913). Author of *Engravers and Etchers* (1917); compiler and editor of *Prints and Their Makers* (1916); editor (from 1911) of *The Print Collectors' Quarterly.*

**Carrington, Henry Beebee.** 1824–1912. American lawyer, soldier, and writer, b. Wallingford, Conn.; served through Civil War; brigadier general (from 1862). Author of *Battles of the American Revolution* (1876), *The Six Nations* (1892), *Washington, the Soldier* (1898).

**Carrington, Hereward Hubert Lavington.** 1880– . American psychologist and psychical researcher, b. in Jersey, Channel Islands; bro. of FitzRoy Carrington; educ. in England; to U.S. (1899). Author of *The Physical Phenomena of Spiritualism* (1907), *Death Deferred* (1912), *The Natural Food of Man* (1912), *Side Show and Animal Tricks* (1913), *Modern Psychical Phenomena* (1919), *Magic for Everyone* (1927), *Houdini and Conan Doyle* (with B. M. L. Ernst; 1932), *Introduction to the Maniac* (1937), etc.

**Carrington, Richard Christopher.** 1826–1875. English astronomer. Educ. Cambridge (1844–48); observer to Durham U. (1849–52); built private observatory, near Reigate, Surrey (1853); mapped stars and sunspots; discovered systematic drift of photosphere.

**Car·rión'** (kär·ryōn'), **Gerónimo.** 1812–1873. Ecuadorian politician, b. Loja. President of Ecuador (1865–67); united Ecuador with Peru and Chile in alliance against Spain; resigned (Nov., 1867).

**Car'ro·dus** (kăr'ō·dŭs), **John Tiplady.** 1836–1895. English violinist; debut as soloist, London (1863); leader at Covent Garden (1869); leader of (British) Philharmonic.

**Carrogis, Louis.** See CARMONTELLE.

**Car'roll** (kăr'ŭl), **Charles.** *Known as* **Charles Carroll of Car'roll·ton** (kăr'ŭl·tŭn; -t'n). 1737–1832. American Revolutionary leader, b. Annapolis, Md. Educ. Paris and London. Member, committee of correspondence and committee of safety (1775), Maryland convention (1776), Continental Congress (1776–78); signer of Declaration of Independence. U.S. senator (1789–92).

**Carroll, Daniel.** 1730–1796. American patriot. Delegate, Continental Congress (1780–84), Constitutional Convention (1787); representative from Maryland, U.S. House of Representatives (1789–91).

**Carroll, Earl.** 1893–1948. American theatrical producer, b. Pittsburgh, Pa. After aviation experience in World War and later, turned to the stage. Wrote lyrics and music for *So Long Letty* and *Canary Cottage;* author of *The Love Mill, The Lady of the Lamp,* etc. Producer of revues, the Earl Carroll *Vanities* (from 1923), largely his own work.

**Carroll, Gladys Hasty.** 1904– . American novelist, b. Rochester, N.H.; author of *As the Earth Turns* (1933; dealing with Maine farm life), *A Few Foolish Ones* (1935), *Neighbor to the Sky* (1937).

**Carroll, Howard.** 1854–1916. American journalist, author, and playwright, b. Albany, N.Y. His comedy *The American Countess* (1884) had a run of 200 performances in New York.

**Carroll, James.** 1854–1907. Physician, b. Woolwich, Eng.; to Canada (1869) and shortly afterwards to U.S. Private, U.S. army (1874–83); hospital steward (1883–98). M.D., Univ. of Maryland (1891). Acting assistant surgeon, U.S. army (1898–1902); lieutenant, Medical Corps (1902–07); major (1907). Assisted Walter Reed (*q.v.*) in Cuba in investigations of yellow fever; for scientific purposes, had himself infected with the disease by a mosquito. Professor of bacteriology and pathology, Columbian Univ. and Army Medical School (1902–07).

**Carroll, John.** 1735–1815. American Roman Catholic prelate, b. Upper Marlboro, Md. Educ. in France; became Jesuit priest; after suppression of Jesuit order (1773), returned to America (1774). Consecrated bishop (Aug. 15, 1790); founded Georgetown College (1791); his see being created an archdiocese (1808), became first archbishop of Baltimore.

**Carroll, John.** 1892–1959. American painter, b. Wichita, Kans. Educ. U. of California (1913–15); studied painting under Frank Duveneck, Cincinnati. Ensign, U.S. navy (1917–19). Professor of painting, Art Students' League, New York (1926), Society of Arts and Crafts, Detroit (from 1930). His *White Lace* in Toledo, Ohio, museum;

his work represented also in Pennsylvania Academy of Fine Arts in Philadelphia, Los Angeles Museum of Fine Arts, Indianapolis Institute of Art, Newark Museum of Art, etc.

**Carroll, Lewis.** Pseudonym of Charles Lutwidge DODGSON.

**Carroll, Paul Vincent.** 1900–1968. Playwright, b. Dundalk, Ireland. Author of *Things that are Caesar's* (1934), *Shadow and Substance* (1937), *White Steed* (1939), *Plays for my Children* (1939).

**Carrucci, Jacopo.** See Jacopo da PONTORMO.

**Car·ruth'ers** (kă·rŭth'ẽrz), **Alexander Douglas Mitchell.** 1881–1962. English naturalist; educ. Cambridge. On collecting and exploring expeditions in Congo region (1905–06), Russian Turkestan and Bokhara (1907–08), northwest Arabia (1909), Mongolia and Central Asia (1910–11), Syria and Asia Minor (1913). Author of *Unknown Mongolia* (1913), *The Desert Route to India* (1930), *Arabian Adventure* (1935), and *Northern Najd* (1938).

**Carruthers, Robert.** 1799–1878. Scottish journalist. Editor of *Inverness Courier* (1828–78); edited Pope's works with a memoir (4 vols., 1853); compiler, with Robert Chambers, of *Chambers's Cyclopaedia of English Literature* (1844).

**Car'son** (kär's'n), **Christopher,** *known as* **Kit** (kĭt). 1809–1868. American trapper, scout, and Indian agent, b. in Madison Co., Ky. Ran away from home (1826); joined expedition to California (1829–31); trapper (1831–42); guide, Frémont's expeditions (1842, 1843, 1845); after battle of San Pascual (Dec. 6, 1846), when Kearny's force was surrounded, crawled at night through investing troops and summoned aid from San Diego. Appointed Indian agent (1853–61); served in southwest against Indians during Civil War.

**Carson, Edward Henry.** Baron **Carson of Dun·cairn'** (dŭn·kârn'; dŭn-). 1854–1935. British jurist and politician, b. Dublin. Educ. Trinity Coll., Dublin. Called to bar; queen's counsel at Irish bar (1889) and English bar (1894); M.P. (1892–1921). Solicitor general for Ireland (1892); solicitor general (1900–06); attorney general (1915); first lord of admiralty (1917); member of war cabinet, without portfolio (1917–18); lord of appeal in ordinary (1921–29).

**Carson, Rachel Louise.** 1907–1964. Am. scientist and author, b. Springdale, Pa. Her books concerned environmental problems; author of *Under the Sea Wind* (1941), *The Sea Around Us* (1951), *Silent Spring* (1966), etc.

**Car'stares** *or* **Car'stairs** (kär'stârz), **William.** 1649–1715. Scottish clergyman and adviser to William of Orange; popularly nicknamed "Cardinal Carstares." Studied at Edinburgh (1663–67); transferred to Utrecht (1669–72) on father's outlawry as Covenanter; agent of William of Orange among disaffected in Scotland in preparation for 9th earl of Argyll's proposed invasion according to Rye House Plot (1683); put to torture of boot and thumbscrew; on release became chaplain to William of Orange, whom he accompanied to England (1688); king's chief adviser in Scottish affairs (1693–1702). Principal of Edinburgh U. (1703–15).

**Car'stens** (kär'stĕns), **Asmus Jakob.** 1754–1798. German painter and designer; b. near Schleswig; studied in Copenhagen and Italy; professor, Academy of Art, Berlin (1790); lived in Rome (from 1792). Among his works are drawings representing scenes from Greek mythology (as a series of twenty-four Argonaut plates), Dante's *Divina Commedia*, Ossian's poems, and Shakespeare's plays. His drawings are credited with influencing German art.

**Cars'well** (kärz'wĕl; -wĕl), **Donald.** 1882–1940. British journalist and writer, b. Glasgow; M.A., Glasgow (1904); on staff of Glasgow *Herald* (1904–12), London *Times* (1912–17). Author of *Trial of Ronald Tree* (1925), *Brother Scots* (1927), *Sir Walter...*(1930), *Trial of Guy Fawkes...*(1934). His wife (m. 1915), **Catherine Roxburgh,** *nee* **Mac·far'lane** [măk·fär'lăn] (1879–1946), also a writer; m. (1st) Herbert P. M. Jackson (1903; marriage annulled, 1908); dramatic critic for Glasgow *Herald* (1907–11); author of the novels *Open the Door* (1920), *The Camomile* (1922), and a biography of Robert Burns (1930); collaborator with husband in *The Scots Week-end* (1936).

**Carte** (kärt), **Richard D'Oy'ly** (doi'lĭ). 1844–1901. English operatic impresario. Joined his father, a flutist, in musical-instrument business (1861); composed operettas. Became successful concert and lecture agent; produced Gilbert and Sullivan's *Trial by Jury* (1875), *Sorcerer* (1877), *H.M.S. Pinafore* (1878); formed partnership with Gilbert and Sullivan; sent Oscar Wilde, who was caricatured in Gilbert and Sullivan's *Patience*, to lecture in U.S. on aesthetic philosophy (1882); often had five companies performing Gilbert and Sullivan operas in U.S.; built Savoy Theatre, first public building in England lighted by electricity (1881), where rest of Gilbert and Sullivan operas (the last *The Grand Duke*, 1896) and other operas were performed; organized touring companies that continued to operate after his death; built an unsuccessful Royal English Opera House (1891).

**Carte, Thomas.** 1686–1754. English historian. B.A., Oxon. (1702), M.A., Cantab. (1706); strong Jacobite; resigned as reader at Bath Abbey rather than take oaths to George I (1715); secretary to Bishop Atterbury, fled to France (1722–28); published his *Life of Ormonde* (1736) and *General History of England* (4 vols., 1747–55).

**Car'ter** (kär'tẽr), **Elizabeth.** 1717–1806. English poet and translator. Contributed verse to *Gentleman's Magazine*; published poems (1738, 1762); expert linguist; translator from French and Italian; translator of Epictetus (1758); friend of Dr. Johnson, who praised her Greek scholarship.

**Carter, Franklin.** 1837–1919. American educator, b. Waterbury, Conn.; grad. Williams (1862); president, Williams College (1881–1901).

**Carter, Frederick.** d. 1967. English painter and etcher; studied in Paris and Antwerp. Published series of drawings and etchings on the *Comedy of Masks;* drew decorations for books by Cyril Tourneur and others. Author of *The Dragon of Revelation* (1932), *D. H. Lawrence and the Body Mystical* (1932), *Gold like Glass* (1932).

**Carter, Henry.** Original name of Frank LESLIE.

**Carter, Henry Alpheus Peirce** (pẽrs). 1837–1891. Hawaiian statesman, b. Honolulu, of American parentage. In mercentile business (from 1854); developed great sugar plantations and markets, negotiated (1876) treaty with U.S. putting Hawaiian sugar on free list for importation. Hawaiian minister of interior (1880–82); Hawaiian minister to U.S. (1883–91).

**Carter, Henry Rose.** 1852–1925. American physician, b. in Caroline Co., Va.; in marine hospital service (from 1879); specialist in study of yellow fever and malaria.

**Carter, Howard.** 1873–1939. English archaeologist, b. in Norfolk. On archaeological survey work in Egypt (from 1890); assisted Flinders Petrie at Tell el-Amarna (1892); served Egyptian government as inspector-general of antiquities department. Associated with 5th earl of Carnarvon (*q.v.*, under HERBERT family, 3) in important Egyptian excavations (1907–12; 1919–23) culminating (1922) in discovery of tomb of Tutankhamen of XVIIIth Egyptian dynasty (c. 1350 B.C.).

**Carter, James Gordon.** 1795–1849. American educational reformer, b. Leominster, Mass.; pioneer advocate of establishment of normal schools.

**Carter, Jimmy,** *in full* **James Earl, Jr.** 1924– . Thirty-ninth president of the U.S. (1977– ), b. Plains, Ga. In navy (1946-53); Georgia legislator (1962–66) governor of Georgia (1971–75).

**Carter,** Mrs. **Leslie.** 1862–1937. American actress, b. Lexington, Ky.; m. 1st Leslie Carter (1880), 2d W. L. Payne (1906); made New York debut (1890); starred in (among other plays) *The Heart of Maryland, Zaza, La Tosca,* and *The Second Mrs. Tanqueray.*

**Carter, Nick.** Pseudonym of the author or authors (from c. 1870) of a series of dime novels, chiefly detective stories and tales of adventure. The character Nick Carter was reputedly invented by **John R. Coryell** (1848–1924), American professional writer of popular fiction, and turned over by him to two other professional writers **Thomas Chal′mers** [chăl′mẽrz] **Har′baugh** [här′bô] (1849–1924) and **Frederick Van Rensselaer Dey** [dā] (1861?–1922). These authors are also reputed to have written some of the romantic novels that have appeared under the pseudonym Bertha M. Clay (*q.v.*).

**Carter, William Samuel.** 1859–1923. American labor leader, b. Austin, Tex.; president, Brotherhood of Locomotive Firemen and Enginemen (1909–22); official of U.S. Railway Administration during World War emergency (1918–20).

**Car′ter·et** (kär′tẽr·ĕt; -ĭt), Sir **George.** 1610?–1680. British naval officer and colonial proprietor, b. on island of Jersey. Second in command against Sallee pirates (1637); comptroller of English navy (1639); succeeded his uncle (Sir **Philip de Carteret,** 1584–1643) as lieutenant governor of Jersey; subdued Parliamentary party on island and sent out privateers in Royalist cause; surrendered Jersey to Parliamentary force (1651); vice-admiral in French navy. At Restoration, M.P. (1661–69) and privy councilor; treasurer of navy (1661–67), censured by House of Commons for mismanagement of navy funds (1669); one of eight to receive grant of Carolina (1663); proprietor (from 1664), with Lord John Berkeley, of territory between Hudson and Delaware rivers, named New Jersey because of his former governorship of island of Jersey; deputy treasurer of Ireland (1667–73).

**Car′ter·et** (kär′tẽr·ĕt; -ĭt), **John.** Earl **Gran′ville** (grăn′vĭl). 1690–1763. English orator, diplomat, and statesman. Grandson of Sir George Carteret; succeeded father as 2d Baron Carteret of Hawnes [hônz] (1695). Educ. Oxford; entered House of Lords (1711); lord lieutenant of Devonshire (1716–21). Envoy to Sweden (1719), gained access to Baltic for British commerce, arranged peace treaties among Baltic powers (1719–20). Secretary of state under Walpole (1721–24). As lord lieutenant of Ireland (1724–30), ordered prosecution of publisher of *Drapier's Letters;* despite this became friend of Jonathan Swift. Opposed Walpole (1730–42); real head of administration (1742–44), though only secretary of state, with policy of supporting Maria Theresa; hated for his partiality to house of Hanover; advised George II to exclude William Pitt from office (1746); failed to form ministry (1746); lord president of council (1751–63).

**Carteret, Philip.** 1639–1682. Colonial governor in America, b. in Jersey, Channel Islands; distant cousin of Sir George Carteret. Governor of New Jersey (1664–76), and, after division of province, of East New Jersey (1676–82); had early difficulties collecting rents for the proprietors; in conflict with Andros, governor of New York, over collections of customs duties (1680–81).

**Carteret, Philip.** d. 1796. English navigator. Commanded second vessel in Wallis's expedition for exploration of Southern Hemisphere (1766); separated from first vessel in Straits of Magellan; discovered Pitcairn Island and Queen Charlotte Islands, explored St. George's Channel; retired as rear admiral (1794).

**Carteromaco.** Pseudonym of Niccolò FORTEGUERRI.

**Cartesius, Renatus.** See René DESCARTES.

**Car′tha·lo** (kär′thȧ·lō). Carthaginian general in Third Punic War (149–146 B.C.).

**Car′tier′** (kȧr′tyā′), Sir **George Étienne.** 1814–1873. Canadian statesman, b. in St. Antoine, Que. Practiced law (from 1835); took part in Papineau's rebellion (1837); Conservative member of legislature (1848); attorney general (1856). Joint prime minister with Sir John Macdonald (1858–62); supported building of Grand Trunk Railway and Canadian Pacific; carried his native province into federation (1867). Minister of militia and defense under Sir John Macdonald (1867–73); defeated by Roman Catholic clerical influence (1872); died in England.

**Cartier, Jacques.** 1491–1557. French sailor and explorer. Made three voyages to Canada, exploring (1534) Gulf of St. Lawrence, sailing (1535) up St. Lawrence River to site of Montreal, and attempting to colonize (1541–42) in Canada. Known as the discoverer of the St. Lawrence River.

**Car′ton** (kär′t'n; -tŭn), **Richard Claude.** *Real surname* **Critch′ett** (krĭch′ĕt; -ĭt). 1856–1928. English actor and playwright, b. London. On stage (1875–85); with Cecil Raleigh wrote melodrama *The Great Pink Pearl* (1885); thereafter devoted himself to writing plays, esp. comedies.

**Car′ton′ de Wiart** (kȧr′tôɴ′ dẽ vyȧr′), **Henry.** 1869–1951. Belgian statesman; member of Chamber of Representatives (from 1896); instrumental in securing passage of law providing for proportional representation (1899); premier of Belgium (1919–21).

**Car′touche′** (kȧr′to͞osh′). *Nickname of* **Louis Dominique Bour′gui′gnon′** (bo͞or′gē′nyôɴ′). 1693–1721. Head of a band of thieves in Paris (c. 1709–21); caught by police and broken on the wheel (Nov. 28, 1721). His supposed exploits have been the subject of various plays. The name *cartouche* has become, in French, the ordinary term applied to similar criminals.

**Cart′wright** (kärt′rĭt), **Edmund.** 1743–1823. English inventor. M.A., Oxon. (1766); country clergyman. After visit to cotton-spinning mill (1784), conceived idea of applying machinery to weaving; patented a power loom (1785–87) which was improved and developed into the modern power loom; built a weaving mill (1787); patented a wool-combing machine (1789–92); bankrupt (1793); patented an alcohol engine (1797); rewarded with £10,000 by Parliament (1809).

His brother **John** (1740–1824), parliamentary reformer, called "father of reform"; served in navy (1758?–70); chief magistrate in Newfoundland (1765–70); warm supporter of American colonists in resistance to taxation (1774–75); major of militia (1775–90); devoted himself to writing in favor of strengthening the navy, manhood suffrage, annual parliaments, abolition of slavery, emancipation of Greece; indicted for sedition and fined (1820).

**Cart′wright** (kärt′rĭt), **Peter.** 1785–1872. American Methodist clergyman, b. in Amherst Co., Va. Itinerant preacher (from 1803) in Kentucky and (1824) Illinois.

**Cartwright,** Sir **Richard John.** 1835–1912. Canadian statesman. M.P. (1863); minister of finance (1873), of trade and commerce (1896); Canada's representative on Anglo-American joint high commission at Quebec (1898–99); senator (1904); acting prime minister in absence of Laurier at imperial conference in London (1907).

**Cartwright, Thomas.** 1535?–1603. English Puritan clergyman. Left Cambridge on Queen Mary's accession (1553); M.A., Cantab. (1560); attacked use of surplice (1565); professor of divinity, Cambridge (1569–70); deprived of post by John Whitgift, vice-chancellor; lectured against constitution of Church of England; imprisoned for nonconformity; clergyman to English residents at Antwerp and Middelburg; author of exegetical treatises.

**Cartwright, William.** 1611–1643. English dramatist. M.A., Oxon. (1635); a florid preacher in university; junior proctor of university (1643). Author of *The Ordinary* (1635?), a play ridiculing Puritans, and of fantastic plays, including *The Royal Slave* (1636).

**Car′ty** (kär′tĭ), **John Joseph.** 1861–1932. American electrical engineer, b. Cambridge, Mass. Educ. Cambridge Latin School. Chief engineer, New York Telephone Co. (1889–1907); chief engineer (1907–19), vice-president (1919–30), American Telephone and Telegraph Co. Pioneer in switchboard construction and the development of the telephone, for which he made many inventions.

**Ca′rus** (kä′ro͝os), **Carl Gustav.** 1789–1869. German physician and philosopher. Adherent of Schelling in philosophy; sought to explain consciousness and the development of the soul. Author of works on gynecology, comparative anatomy, physiology, psychology, and the psyche.

**Carus, Julius Victor.** 1823–1903. German zoologist; professor, Leipzig (from 1853); author of a history of zoology; translator of most of Darwin's works.

**Car′us** (kâr′ŭs), **Marcus Aurelius.** 223?–283. Roman emperor (282–283), b. in Dalmatia. Prefect of Praetorian Guard; chosen emperor by soldiers (282) on murder of Probus; successful in campaign against Sarmatians in Illyricum; proceeded against Persians; killed on the Tigris. Succeeded by his two sons, Carinus and Numerianus (*qq.v.*).

**Ca′rus** (kä′ro͝os), **Paul.** 1852–1919. Editor and philosopher, b. Ilsenburg, Germany; educ. Strassburg, Tübingen; to U.S. (c. 1884); settled in Chicago. Editor (from 1887), *Open Court*, a forum for discussion of religion and ethics, also (from 1890) the *Monist;* established Open Court Publishing Co., to publish philosophical and scientific treatises. Author of *Monism, its Scope and Import* (1891), *Religion and Science* (1893), *The Surd of Metaphysics* (1903), *God* (1908), *The Principle of Relativity in the Light of the Philosophy of Modern Science* (1913), etc.

**Ca·ru′so** (kä·ro͞o′zô; *Angl.* kȧ·ro͞o′sō, -zō), **Enrico,** *orig.* **Er·ri′co** (âr·rē′kō). 1873–1921. Tenor singer, b. Naples, Italy. Studied singing while working as mechanic and factory accountant (1883–93). Appeared on Italian stage (1894–98); at St. Petersburg and Buenos Aires (1898–99); at La Scala, Milan (1899–1900); made world-wide reputation; sang in Italy and abroad (1900–03). First appeared at Metropolitan Opera House, New York (Nov. 21, 1903) in *Rigoletto,* with great success; established as leading tenor of Metropolitan company. Had large repertoire, comprising more than forty operas.

**Ca′rus Ster′ne** (kä′ro͝os shtĕr′nĕ). *Pseudonym of* **Ernst Ludwig Krau′se** (krou′zĕ). 1839–1903. German popular writer on natural science; contributed to spread of Charles Darwin's theories.

**Carvaille, Léon.** See Léon CARVALHO.

**Car′va·jal′** (kär′vä·häl′) *or* **Car′ba·jal′** (-bä-), **Francisco de.** 1464–1548. Spanish soldier, b. Arévalo. Fought under Gonzalo de Córdoba and was at Ravenna and Pavia (1525) and sack of Rome (1527); to Mexico (1528); sent by Hernando Cortes to Peru (1536) to aid Francisco Pizarro; as field marshal under Vaca de Castro, overcame Diego de Almagro at Chupas (1542); joined Gonzalo Pizarro against Pedro de la Gasca; taken prisoner and executed.

**Carvajal, Tomás José González-.** See GONZÁLEZ-CARVAJAL.

**Car·va′lho** (kĕr·vȧ′lyo͞o), **José da Sil′va** (thȧ sĭl′vȧ). 1782–1845. Portuguese statesman; judge (1810); active in revolution of 1820 and in provisional government; minister of justice under John VI (1821–23); seconded Dom Pedro in conflict with Dom Miguel, the Usurper; minister of finance (1832–36); aided in establishing constitution of Dom Pedro (1842); appointed councilor of state.

**Car′va′lho′** (kȧr′vȧ′yō′), **Léon.** *Orig.* **Léon Car′vaille′** (kȧr′vä′y′). 1825–1897. French basso and theater director, b. Mauritius; sang at Opéra Comique, Paris (1847); director of Théâtre Lyrique (1855) and Opéra Comique (1876–87; 1891–97). His wife, **Marie Caroline Félix,** *nee* **Mio′lan′** [myô′läɴ′] (1827–1895), renowned singer at Théâtre Lyrique and Opéra Comique.

**Car·va′lho** (kĕr·vȧ′lyo͞o), **Ronald de.** 1893–1935. Brazilian lawyer, diplomat, and writer; counselor of embassy, Paris (1931–33); secretary to president of Brazil (1933 ff.). Author of *Luz Gloriosa* (1913), *História da Literatura Brasileira* (1919), *Toda a América* (1926), and *Rabelais e o Riso do Renascimento* (1931).

**Carvalho e Mello, Sebastião José de.** See Marquês de POMBAL.

**Car′ver** (kär′vẽr), **George Washington.** 1864–1943. American Negro botanist, b. of slave parents in Missouri. Stolen with his mother and carried into Arkansas; bought back by his master, who raised him. B.S. (1894), M.S. Agr. (1896), Iowa State. In charge of greenhouse, Iowa State; teacher, Tuskegee Institute (from 1896), director of its department of agricultural research; collaborator, division of mycology and disease survey, Bureau of Plant Industry, U.S. Department of Agriculture (from 1935). Known esp. for his researches on industrial uses of the peanut.

**Carver, John.** 1576?–1621. First governor of Plymouth Colony, b. in Nottinghamshire or Derbyshire, England. Emigrated to Holland (1609); joined Pilgrims at Leiden; contributed liberally to finance the group. Agent of Pilgrims (1617–20), in getting charter and financial aid in England for expedition to New World. Chartered the *Mayflower*, gathered the London Pilgrims together, and sailed from London (July 15, 1620). Elected governor under Mayflower Compact (Nov. 11, 1620).

**Carver, Jonathan.** 1710–1780. American explorer of Lake Superior and much of Minnesota. Began his travels (1766) at suggestion of Major Robert Rogers; went to England (1769) and published his *Travels in Interior Parts of America* (1778) and a treatise on tobacco (1779).

**Carver, Thomas Nixon.** 1865-1961. American economist, b. Kirkville, Iowa. A.B., Southern Calif. (1891), Ph.D., Cornell (1894). Professor, Oberlin (1894–1900) and Harvard (from 1902). Author of *The Distribution of Wealth* (1904), *Principles of Political Economy* (1919), *The Essential Factors of Social Evolution* (1935), etc.

**Carver, Willard.** 1866–1943. American chiropractor, b. Maysville, near Davenport, Iowa. LL.B., Drake (1891), grad. Parker School of Chiropractic, Ottumwa, Iowa (1906). Founder, Carver Chiropractic Institute, New York City (1919), Carver Chiropractic U., Denver, Colo. (1923). Author of *Carver's Chiropractic Analysis* (1909), *Applied Psychology* (1914), *Psycho-Bio-Physiology* (1919), etc.

**Car′y** (kâr′ĭ), **Alice** (1820–1871) and her sister **Phoebe** (1824–1871). American poets, b. near Cincinnati. Authors of *Poems of Alice and Phoebe Cary* (1849). Phoebe is best known for her poem *One Sweetly Solemn Thought* (1852).

**Cary, Edward.** 1840–1917. American newspaper editor, b. Albany, N.Y. Educ. Union College. Editor, New York *Times* (1871–1917).

**Cary, Elisabeth Luther.** 1867–1936. American literary and art critic, b. Brooklyn, N.Y.; on staff of New York *Times* (1908–36); author of *Alfred Tennyson*...(1898), *Robert Browning*...(1899), *Ralph Waldo Emerson*... (1904), *The Art of William Blake* (1907), etc.

**Cary, Henry Francis.** 1772–1844. English clergyman and translator, b. Gibraltar, of Irish extraction. M.A., Oxon. (1796); published translation in blank verse of Dante's *Inferno* (1805) and of *Purgatorio* and *Paradiso* (1812); translated Aristophanes' *Birds* (1824), and Pindar (1832).

**Cary, Lucius.** See Viscount FALKLAND.

**Cary, Phoebe.** See Alice CARY.

**Ca'sa** (kä'sä), **Giovanni della.** 1503–1556. Italian prelate and writer. Protégé of Alessandro Farnese (Paul III); archbishop of Benevento (1544); fought against Italian Reformation; prepared index of prohibited books (1549); papal secretary of state under Paul IV. Author of manual of polite conduct *Il Galateo ovvero De' Costumi*, his best-known work (1558), translations of Thucydides, and many poems notable for their style.

**Ca'sa'bian'ca'** (kȧ'zȧ'byäN'kȧ'), **Louis de.** 1755?–1798. French naval officer who, with his son **Gia'co'mo'** (zhyȧ'kô'mō'), aged 10, went down with his ship, the *Orient*, in battle of the Nile. The incident is subject of a poem, *Casabianca* (1829), by Felicia Hemans.

**Ca·sals'** (käs·äls'), **Pablo**, *in full* **Pablo** (*or* **Pau** [pou]) **Carlos Salvador De·fil'ló** (dā·fē'lō) **de Casals.** 1876–1973. Spanish violoncellist, conductor, and composer b. Catalonia; professor, conservatory of music, Barcelona (1897); toured France, England, South America, and U.S. (1901, 1903–04, 1914–16); settled in Prades, France (1939); to Puerto Rico (1956); composer of works for violoncello and piano, violin and piano, and orchestral and choral works.

**Ca'sa·no'va** (kä'sä·nô'vä; *Angl.* kăs'ȧ·nō'vȧ, kăz'ȧ-), **Francesco.** 1727–1805. Italian painter and etcher; brother of Giovanni Jacopo Casanova (*q.v.*). Painter to the king at Paris and member of the Academy; known for his battle paintings, including *Hannibal Crossing the Alps* and a series painted for Catharine of Russia. Another brother, **Giovanni Battista** (1730–1795), also a painter, was director of the Dresden Academy (from 1764).

**Casanova** *or* **Casanova de Sein'galt'** (dē săN'gȧl'), **Giovanni Jacopo.** 1725–1798. Italian adventurer, b. Venice, of family of actors. Educ. for priesthood; showed brilliance of mind and wit; expelled for scandalous conduct from Seminary of St. Cyprian (1741). Secretary in household of Cardinal Aquaviva; entered Venetian army at Corfu; by turns preacher, abbé, alchemist, cabalist, gambler, violin player, for nearly 20 years visiting capitals of Europe, as far as Constantinople, alternately in fortune and in distress; skeptic and sensualist; involved in one intrigue after another. Imprisoned as spy on return to Venice (1755) but made a marvelous escape (1756), narration of which became his stock in trade; director of state lotteries in Paris, accumulated fortune; agent of Louis XV; declined post offered by Frederick II in Berlin (1764); made acquaintance of the great, including the pope (who bestowed upon him the papal order of the Golden Spur), Empress Catherine, Voltaire, von Haller, Mme. de Pompadour, Cagliostro. Traveled to Russia, whence forced to flee because of a scandal and a duel; finding lettre de cachet on return to Paris, fled to Spain; expelled from Madrid (1769); police spy for Venetian inquisitors (from 1774); exiled for satirical libel upon one of patrons (1782); librarian for Count von Waldstein at Dux Castle in Bohemia. Author of *Mémoires Écrits par Lui-Même* (12 vols., 1826–38), a clever and cynical record of his rogueries and amours.

**Casas, Bartolomé de las.** See LAS CASAS.

**Ca·sa'ti** (kä·sä'tē), **Gaetano.** 1838–1902. Italian explorer in southern Anglo-Egyptian Sudan and neighboring central African region (1879–83); joined Emin Pasha (1883) and was sent on a mission to a native king, who held him prisoner; escaped and returned to Emin Pasha (1888).

**Ca·sau'bon** (kȧ·sô'bŭn; *Fr.* kȧ'zō'bôN'), **Isaac.** 1559–1614. Theologian and classical scholar, b. Geneva, of French-Huguenot refugee parents. Professor of Greek at Geneva (1582–96), Montpellier (1596–99); corresponded with Joseph Scaliger; summoned to Paris by Henry IV but prevented from receiving professorship by Catholic opposition. Feeling insecure after murder of king, crossed to England (1610); favorably received by James I and made prebendary of Canterbury and Westminster; welcomed by Anglican bishops as having reached theological position midway between Puritanism and Romanism; forced to share increasing unpopularity of James and bishops; persecuted by Jesuit pamphleteers after failure of attempt to buy his recantation and adoption of Romanism; spent last years on assignment by king and bishops to refute the *Annales* of Baronius; buried in Westminster Abbey. With Scaliger and Lipsius, member of famous triumvirate of 16th-century classical scholars. Author of commentaries on Theophrastus (1592), Suetonius (1595), Persius (1605), Polybius (1609, unfinished till 1617), of a revision, with commentary, of Athenaeus (his most ambitious work; 1600), of a diary, *Ephemerides* (began 1597, pub. 1850). His son **Florence Étienne Méric** (1599–1671), classical scholar; M.A., Oxon. (1622); edited works of Marcus Aurelius (1643), Terence, Epictetus (1659).

**Cas'ca** (kăs'kȧ), **Publius Servilius.** d. after 42 B.C. First among the assassins of Julius Caesar to strike Caesar.

**Case** (kās), **Anna.** 1889– . American operatic soprano, b. Clinton, N.J. Debut with Metropolitan Opera Company (1909); member of company (1909–17); also on concert stage in U.S., Europe, and Canada; m. (1931) Clarence H. Mackay.

**Case, Everett Needham.** 1901– . American educator, b. North Plainfield, N.J. A.B., Princeton (1922); B.A., Cambridge, Eng. (1924); president, Colgate U. (1942– ).

**Case, Leonard.** 1820–1880. American lawyer and philanthropist, b. Cleveland, Ohio; grad. Yale (1842); founder and benefactor of Case School of Applied Science, Cleveland, Ohio.

**Case, Thomas.** 1844–1925. English philosopher and educator, b. Liverpool. Educ. Oxford. On faculty at Oxford (from 1870), professor (1889–1910), president of Corpus Christi Coll. (1904–24). Author of *Realism in Morals* (1877), *Physical Realism* (1888).

**Ca·sel'la** (kä·sĕl'lä), **Alfredo.** 1883–1947. Italian pianist and composer. Studied at Paris Conservatory; first known in Paris as concert pianist, director of Trocadéro popular concerts, and music critic; instructor, Conservatorio di Santa Cecilia, Rome (from 1915); founded *Società Italiana di Musica Moderna* (1917); leader of Italian modernist movement in music. Composer of operas, symphonies, rhapsodies (as *Italia*), suites (as *Le Couvent sur l'Eau*), *Elegia Eroica*, *Pagine di Guerra*, *Concerto Romano*, ballets (as *La Giara*, *Ballets Suédois*), chamber music, songs, and piano pieces. Author of *L'Evoluzione della Musica* (1919), *Igor Stravinski* (1923), the autobiography *21+26* (1932), *Il Pianoforte* (1937).

**Caselli, Jean.** Pseudonym of Henry CAZALIS.

**Case'ment** (kās'mĕnt), Sir **Roger David.** 1864–1916. British consular agent and Irish rebel. Distinguished himself in investigation for British government of conduct of rubber trade of Upper Congo (1903) and in investigation of atrocities by Anglo-Peruvian Amazon Company (1910); knighted. Joined Irish Nationalists in opposition to Redmond and to participation of Irishmen in World War; to Berlin (1914) to seek assistance in gaining Irish independence; landed from German submarine near Tralee (1916); hanged by British as traitor.

**Cases, Las.** See LAS CASES.

**Ca'sey** (kā'sĭ), **Edward Pearce.** 1864–1940. American architect, b. Portland, Me. C.E. (1886), Ph.B. (1888), Columbia; studied at École des Beaux-Arts, Paris (1888–91). Practiced in New York City. Architect for completion of Congressional Library, Washington, D.C.; winner of first prize in competition for Grant monument in Washington, D.C. (1902); architect of New York State monuments on fields of Antietam and Gettysburg.

**Casey, Joseph.** 1814–1879. American jurist, b. in Washington Co., Md. Reporter of decisions, supreme court of Pennsylvania (1855–61); published *Pennsylvania State Reports*, known as *Casey's Reports*. Judge, U.S. Court of Claims (1861–63); chief justice of the reorganized court (1863–70).

**Casey, Richard Gardiner.** Baron **Casey.** 1890– . Australian soldier and diplomat, b. Brisbane; served in World War I; Australian minister to United States (1940–42); British minister of state in the Middle East (1942–43); governor of Bengal (1944–46); governor-general of Australia (from 1965).

**Cas'grain'** (käz'grăN'; käs'-), **Henri Raymond.** 1831–1904. Canadian historian, b. Rivière Ouelle, Quebec. Ordained Roman Catholic priest (1856); rector, Quebec basilica (1860–73). Author of *Biographies Canadiennes* (1885), *Montcalm et Lévis* (2 vols., 1891), etc. His nephew **Thom'as** (tŏm'ăs) **Chase** (chās) **Casgrain** (1852–1916), lawyer and politician; postmaster general of Canada (1914–16).

**Casgrain, Philippe Ba'by'** (bȧ'bē'). 1826–1917. Canadian lawyer and historian, b. Quebec. Author of *Les Plaines d'Abraham* (1900), *La Maison de Montcalm* (1902), *Notre Système Judiciaire* (1911).

**Cas'i·mir** (kăz'ĭ·mĭr). *Pol.* **Ka·zi'mierz** (kä·zē'-myĕsh). *Ger.* **Ka'si·mir** (kä'zē·mēr). Name of kings of Poland: **Casimir I** (1015–1058), called "the Peaceful" and "the Restorer"; king (1040–58); proclaimed king (1034) but revolt of nobles led to anarchy; fled to Hungary; lost Kraków and Gniezno to duke of Bohemia; with help of Holy Roman Emperor Henry III (1041), reconquered much lost territory and restored Christianity; succeeded by Boleslav II. **Casimir II** (1138–1194), called "the Just"; son of Boleslav III; king (1177–94); organized Polish senate and introduced laws protecting peasants. **Casimir III** (1309–1370), called "the Great"; son of Ladislas Lokietek; king (1333–70); stopped war with Teutonic Knights; worked with Hungary to establish order (1335–53); seized principality of Galicia (1340); defeated Lithuanians (1353); codified laws of Great and Little Poland (1347) and befriended peasants (hence also known as "Peasants' king"); laid foundations for U. of Cracow (1364); last of Piast dynasty. **Casimir IV** (1427–1492), son of Ladislas II Jagello; king (1447–92); in youth, grand duke of Lithuania; subjugated Teutonic Knights after thirteen-year war (1454–66), terminated by (2d) Peace of Thorn (1466), by which the order surrendered Pomerania, West Prussia, and other lands; unpopular, because of much trouble with subjects; founded (1467) Polish Diet (Sejm); his reign a golden age of culture for Poland. **Casimir V** = JOHN II CASIMIR.

**Ca'si'mir'-Pé'rier'** (kȧ'zē'mēr'pā'ryā'), **Jean Paul Pierre.** 1847–1907. French statesman, 5th president of the Republic; b. Paris, son of Auguste Casimir Périer (see PÉRIER). Decorated for conduct in Franco-Prussian War (1870–71); entered public service (1871); elected to Chamber of Deputies (1874); undersecretary in departments of public instruction and war (1877–79); vice-president (1890–93), president (1893), Chamber of Deputies; prime minister (1893–94). Elected president after assassination of Carnot (1894–95); unexpectedly resigned and retired to private business, presumably because of belief that office of executive had become too restricted. Witness at Zola trial, but implication of connection with Dreyfus case never proved.

**Caskoden,** Sir **Edwin.** Pseudonym of Charles MAJOR.

**Cas'lon** (kăz'lŏn), **William.** 1692–1766. English type founder; produced type excelling in legibility, which was used in England and America and on Continent till about 1800, revived about 1845 by Chiswick Press. His son **William** (1720–1778) became partner (1742) and carried on his father's business.

**Cas·pa'ri** (käs·pä'rē), **Karl Paul.** 1814–1892. German Protestant theologian; professor, Oslo, Norway (1857).

**Cass** (kăs), **Lewis.** 1782–1866. American lawyer, b. Exeter, N.H. Served through War of 1812. Governor of Michigan Territory (1813–31); responsible for constructive administration in opening up this territory, visiting Indian tribes in Lake Superior region on 5000-mile canoe trip. U.S. secretary of war (1831–36); U.S. minister to France (1836–42); U.S. senator (1845–48). Democratic candidate for president (1848); defeated by Taylor. U.S. senator (1849–57); U.S. secretary of state (1857–60).

**Cassagnac.** See GRANIER DE CASSAGNAC.

**Cas·san'der** (kă·săn'dẽr). 350?–297 B.C. King of Macedonia (316–297 B.C.). Son of Antipater; failed to be named successor on Antipater's death (319); supported by many Greek states, waged successful war (319–317) against Macedonian regent Polysperchon; seized Olympias, mother of Alexander, and put her to death (316); m. (316) Alexander's half sister Thessalonica, for whom he built and named a city in Macedonia. Engaged in war with Antigonus (315–311); caused murder of Roxana and her son (310); waged Four Years' War against Demetrius I (307–304); joined forces with Lysimachus, Ptolemy, and Seleucus against Antigonus, who was defeated and slain at Ipsus (301); in complete control of Macedonia and Greece. Cf. BERENICE I.

**Cas·satt'** (kă·săt'), **Alexander Johnston.** 1839–1906. American railroad executive, b. Pittsburgh, Pa. Grad. Rensselaer Polytechnic Inst. (1859). In service of Pennsylvania Railroad (1861–82), first vice-president (1880–82), retired; recalled as president (1899–1906). His sister **Mary** (1845–1926), artist, b. Allegheny City, Pa.; studied in Europe (1868–74); studio in Paris (from 1874); associated with leaders of the impressionistic school; excelled in painting mothers and children.

**Casse'grain'** (käs'grăN'), **Guillaume.** fl. 17th century. French sculptor in service of Louis XIV.

**Cassegrain, N.** fl. 17th century. French physician; professor, Collège de Chartres; inventor of the Cassegrainian telescope, a form of reflecting telescope (1672); author of a treatise on proportions of the megaphone.

**Cas'sel** (kăs''l), Sir **Ernest Joseph.** 1852–1921. Financier and philanthropist, b. Cologne, Germany. Clerk in banking firm of Elspacher. Member (1870–84) of house of Bischoffscheim and Goldschmidt in London, England; naturalized (1878). Set up own business (1884); reorganized finances of Uruguay and of railroads in Sweden, Mexico, and U.S.; issued Mexican and Chinese government loans; financed Nile dams and irrigation work and founded National Bank of Egypt; created State Bank of Morocco and National Bank of Turkey; privy councilor (1902).

**Cas′sel** (kȧs′sĕl), **Gustav,** *in full* **Karl Gustav.** 1866–1945. Swedish economist; professor in Stockholm (from 1904); lecturer, Oxford U. (1932); financial expert with Swedish delegation at Genoa conference (1922); Swedish delegate at international economic conference, Geneva (1927); called in by League of Nations (1920–21) for opinion on currency problems, and by U.S. committee on currency and finance (1928); delegate, world economic conference, London (1933). Author of *The Theory of Social Economics* (1918; translated 1923), *Fundamental Thoughts in Economics* (1925), *Recent Monopolistic Tendencies in Industry and Trade* (1927), *Quantitative Thinking in Economics* (1935), *The Downfall of the Gold Standard* (1936).

**Cas′sell** (kăs′'l), **John.** 1817–1865. English publisher; son of a publican; apprenticed to carpenter; self-educated; started publishing business to supply reading for instruction of working classes (1850), issued educational magazines and *Cassell's Magazine* (from 1852).

**Casseres, Benjamin de.** See De Casseres.

**Cas′si·a′nus** (kăs′ĭ·ā′nŭs), **Johannes.** *Also known as* **Johannes Mas·sil′i·en′sis** (mă·sĭl′ĭ·ĕn′sĭs) *and* **Johannes Er′e·mi′ta** (ĕr′ē·mī′tȧ). 360?–?435. Monk and theologian; lived in Egypt as anchorite (385–400); founded monastery and convent at Marseilles (c. 415); credited by some with being founder of Semi-Pelagianism; promoted monasticism in western Europe.

**Cas′sin** (kăs′ĭn), **John.** 1813–1869. American ornithologist, b. in Delaware Co., Pa.; ornithologist on Perry's expedition to Japan (1853).

**Cassin, René.** 1887– . French statesman. Awarded Nobel peace prize (1968) for work on human rights. Pres., UN Human Rights Commission (1946–68).

**Cas′si′ni′** (kȧ′sē′nē′). Family of French astronomers including: **Jean Dominique** (1625–1712), b. near Nice; professor at Bologna (1650); later became French citizen; first director of the Paris observatory; discovered four of Saturn's satellites (1671–84); observed a dark division in Saturn's ring; made earliest systematic observation of zodiacal light; determined parallax of sun, obliquity of ecliptic, and eccentricity of earth's orbit; in mathematics, discovered Cassinian oval. His son **Jacques** (1677–1756), b. Paris; succeeded him as director of Paris observatory (1712); known for work to determine figure of the earth. **César François Cassini de Thu′ry′** [dē tü′rē′] (1714–1784), son of Jacques, and his successor as director of the Paris observatory (1756); began topographical map of France (1744); specialized in geodesy. Comte **Jacques Dominique de Cassini** (1748–1845), son of César and his successor as director of Paris observatory (1784–93); completed César's map of France (pub. 1793). Vicomte **Alexandre Henri Gabriel de Cassini** (1784–1832), son of Jacques Dominique; published *Opuscules Phytologiques* (1826).

**Cas′si·o·do′rus** (kăs′ĭ·ō·dō′rŭs), **Flavius Magnus Aurelius.** Roman statesman and writer. Government official under Theodoric and Athalaric; retired (c. 540 A.D.) to devote himself to study and writing. Founded monasteries, in which he required the monks to copy and translate Greek works. Among his works are panegyrics on the Gothic kings and queens, a philosophical treatise *De Anima,* an encyclopedia of literature and art, and *Variae,* a collection of the decrees of Theodoric and his successors, the regulations of government offices, etc., forming a valuable source for information about the Ostrogothic kingdom in Italy. His *History of the Goths* has been lost.

**Cas·si′rer** (kä·sē′rēr), **Ernst.** 1874–1945. German philosopher; taught at Berlin U. (1905–19), Hamburg U. (1919–33), Oxford (1933–35), Göteborg (1936–41), Yale (1941–44), Columbia (1944–45). His works, chiefly on the philosophical foundations of natural science and psychology, include *Das Erkenntnisproblem in der Philosophie und Wissenschaft der Neueren Zeit* (3 vols., 1906–19), *Determinismus und Indeterminismus in der Modernen Physik* (1937).

**Cas′si·us** (käs′ē·ŏŏs), **Andreas.** 1640?–?1673. German physician and chemist, b. Schleswig; discoverer of purple pigment known as purple of Cassius.

**Cas′si·us** (kăsh′ĭ·ŭs; kăsh′ŭs; kăs′ĭ·ŭs), **Avidius.** d. 175 A.D. Roman general, b. in Syria. First distinguished himself in Parthian War (162–165 A.D.). On rumor of death of Emperor Aurelius was encouraged to proclaim himself emperor; killed by his own officers.

**Cassius Dio.** = Dio Cassius.

**Cassius Lon·gi′nus** (lŏn·jī′nŭs), **Gaius.** Roman general and conspirator. Distinguished himself in Parthian War (53 B.C.); sided with Pompey against Caesar and fought at Pharsalus (48); pardoned by Caesar. Headed conspiracy against Caesar (44) and was one of the actual assassins. Defeated at Philippi, he ordered his freedman to kill him (42 B.C.).

**Cassius Longinus, Gaius.** Roman jurist; consul (30 A.D.); governor of Syria (45–50); banished by Nero (65), recalled by Vespasian. Author of *Libri Juris Civilis* (10 books).

**Cassius Longinus, Quintus.** A relative of Cassius Longinus the conspirator. Roman politician of 1st century B.C.; as governor of Further Spain (54 B.C.), notorious for severity of his administration.

**Cassius Par·men′sis** (pär·mĕn′sĭs), **Gaius.** Roman politician. One of the assassins of Julius Caesar (44 B.C.). After battle of Philippi (42), joined Sextus Pompeius in Sicily; after Pompeius's defeat at Naulochus, joined Antony and fought at Actium (31); fled to Athens; captured and executed by Octavius. Author of satires, epigrams, elegies, and plays.

**Cassius Vec′el·li′nus** (vĕs′ĕ·lī′nŭs) *or* **Vic′el·li′nus** (vĭs′-), **Spurius.** Roman semilegendary political and military leader of late 6th and early 5th centuries B.C.

**Cas′si·ve·lau′nus** (kăs′ĭ·vē·lô′nŭs) *or* **Cas′si·vel·lau′nus** (-vĕ·lô′nŭs). *Welsh* **Cas·wal′lawn** (kăs·wȧl′oun) *or* **Cas·wal′lon** (-oun). fl. 54 B.C. British prince. Chief of Catuvellauni (in Hertfordshire, Buckinghamshire, Berkshire); opposed Julius Caesar's second expedition into Britain (54 B.C.).

**Ca·sta′gno** (käs·tä′nyō), **Andrea del.** 1423–1457. Florentine painter; succeeded Masaccio as outstanding realist. His works include frescoes in church of Sant' Apollonia, portraits of Dante, Petrarch, Boccaccio, and others, an equestrian portrait of Niccolò da Tolentino (Florence cathedral), *Crucifixion* (church of Santa Maria Novella), and a mural in Palazzo del Podestà representing the enemies of Cosimo de' Medici hanging by their feet, whence his sobriquet "An′dre·i′no de·gl'Im′pic-ca′ti" (än′drā·ē′nō dā·lyēm′pēk·kä′tē).

**Ca·stal′di** (käs·täl′dē), **Pamfilo.** 1398–?1490. Italian physician and printer, b. Feltre. Thought by some to have invented printing from movable types, the invention later supposedly revealed to Gutenberg by Castaldi's pupil Johann Fust (*q.v.*); used types of Murano glass.

**Castalio.** See Castellio.

**Castañeda, Jorge Ubico.** See UBICO CASTAÑEDA.

**Cas·ta·nhe'da** (kȧsh·tȧ·nyā'thȧ), **Fernão Lo'pes de** (lō'pĕzh thĕ). d. 1559. Portuguese historian, b. Santarém; lived in India (1528–1548); author of *História do Descobrimento e Conquista da Índia pelos Portugueses* (8 vols., 1551–61).

**Cas·ta'ños** (käs·tä'nyōs), **Francisco Javier de.** Duque **de Bai·lén'** (bī·lān'). 1758–1852. Spanish soldier, b. in Biscay; defeated French under General Dupont de l'Étang at Bailén (1808); commanded Spanish army, under Wellington, at Vitoria (1813); president, council of Castile (1833); opponent of Carlists; became the guardian of Queen Isabella (1843).

**Cas'te·lar' y Ri·poll'** (käs'tȧ·lär' ē rē·pôl'y'), **Emilio.** 1832–1899. Spanish statesman, orator, and writer, b. Cádiz. Professor of history, Madrid (1856–65, 1868–75); exiled to France (1866–68); deputy to the Cortes (1869); advocate of republic and separation of church and state; minister of foreign affairs after proclamation of republic (1873); prime minister (Sept., 1873–Jan., 1874); deputy (1876–93). Author of *La Civilización en los Cinco Primeros Siglos del Cristianismo* (1859), *Historia del Movimiento Republicano en Europa* (2 vols., 1873–74), *Historia del Descubrimiento de América* (1892), and biographies of Byron and Fra Filippo Lippi.

**Cas'te·lein'** (käs'tĕ·līn'), **Matthijs de.** 1488?–1550. Flemish poet and critic; an outstanding leader of the Rederijkerskamers, or Chambers of Rhetoric; author of many plays, including *Historie van Pyramus ende Thisbe,* and of *Const van Rhetoriken* (finished 1548; pub. 1555), first treatise on Flemish versification, containing also ballads, songs, etc.

**Castelfranco, Giorgione da.** See Il GIORGIONE.

**Ca'stel·la'ni** (käs'tāl·lä'nē), **Aldo.** 1877–1971. Physician, b. Florence, Italy. M.D., Florence (1899); studied at Bonn and London School of Tropical Medicine. Investigated sleeping sickness in Uganda (1902–03); professor, Ceylon Medical Coll. (1903–15), Royal U. of Naples (1915–19), and in U.S. at Tulane (1926) and Louisiana State U. medical school (1932); surgeon general to Italian forces in Ethiopian campaign (1935–36). Known for work on tropical diseases, esp. for investigations of the organisms causing sleeping sickness and yaws, also for work in dermatology and bacteriology. See also Sir David BRUCE and D. N. NABARRO.

**Cas'tel·la'nos** (käs'tȧ·(l)yä'nōs), **Juan de.** 1522–1606. Spanish soldier, priest, and poet, b. Seville; to South America as a youth; cura of Tunja, Colombia; known particularly for his *Elegías de Varones Ilustres de Indias* (pub. 1588, 1619), a versified chronicle of the exploits of Columbus, Bobadilla, Aguirre, and other early conquistadors.

**Cas'tel·la'nos** (käs'tȧ·yä'nōs), **Julio.** 1905–1947. Mexican painter and etcher, b. Mexico City; painted fresco for Melchor Ocampo School in Coyoacán; successful in stage designs.

**Ca·stel'li** (käs·tĕl'ē), **Ignaz Franz.** 1781–1862. Austrian journalist, poet, and dramatist; author of over 200 plays (mostly adapted from French originals), chiefly satirizing weaknesses of the Viennese.

**Cas·tel'li·o** (kăs·tĕl'ĭ·ō) *or* **Cas·ta'li·o** (-tā'lĭ·ō), **Sebastianus.** *Latinized name of* **Sébastien Châ'til'lon'** (shä'tē'yôN') *or* **Châ'teil'lon'** (shä'tā'yôN'). 1515–1563. French Protestant theologian and humanist; forced to relinquish rectorship at Geneva (1545) because of deviations from Calvinist doctrine; translated the Bible into French and Latin.

**Ca·stel'lo** (käs·tĕl'lō), **Giovanni Battista.** *Called* **Il Ber'ga·ma'sco** (ēl bār'gä·mäs'kō). 1509?–1569. Italian painter and architect, b. at or near Bergamo; associated with Genoese school; called to Madrid by Philip II (1567); aided in restoration of the Alcázar (Madrid) and in construction of Escorial.

**Cas·tel'lo–Bran'co** (kȧsh·tĕ'lōō·brăNng'kōō), **Camillo.** Visconde **de Cor·re'ia–Bo·te'lho** (kōōr·rā'yȧ·bōō·tā'lyōō). 1826–1890. Portuguese writer, b. Lisbon; known particularly for novels of manners, as *Amor de Perdição* (1862) and *Amor de Salvação* (1864).

**Cas'tel'nau'** (kȧs'tĕl'nō'), Comte **de. Francis de la Porte** (dē lȧ pôrt'). 1812–1880. French naturalist and traveler; visited Canadian lakes, U.S., and Mexico (1837–41); led government scientific expedition to equatorial South America (1843–47); French consul at Melbourne (from 1862).

**Castelnau, Michel de.** Sieur **de la Mau'vis'sière'** (dē lȧ mō'vē'syâr'). 1520?–1592. French diplomat; ambassador to England (1575–85); attempted to negotiate marriage between Queen Elizabeth and duc d'Alençon.

**Castelnau, Noël Marie Joseph Édouard de Cu'rières' de** (dē kü'ryâr' dē). 1851–1944. French general; commanded 2d army in Lorraine (1914) and group of armies constituting French center (1915); chief of staff to General Joffre (Dec., 1915); had share in early defense of Verdun (1916); commanded group of armies in eastern France at time of armistice. Member, Chamber of Deputies (1919–24).

**Castelnuovo,** Conte **di.** See CARMAGNOLA.

**Ca'stel·nuo'vo** (käs'tāl·nwô'vō), **Enrico.** 1839–1915. Italian novelist, b. Florence. Author of *Racconti e Bozzetti* (1872), *Il Professore Romualdo* (1878), *Prima di Partire* (1890), *Il Ritorno dell'Aretusa* (1901).

**Ca'stel·ve'tro** (käs'tāl·vā'trō), **Lodovico.** 1505–1571. Italian critic and philologist, b. Modena. Forced to flee to Chiavenna on charges of heresy (1561). His works include a translation and exposition of Aristotle's *Poetics* (1570), commentaries on Cicero's *Rhetorica* (1553), Dante, and Petrarch.

**Ca'sti** (käs'tē), **Giambattista.** 1724–1803. Italian poet and adventurer; imperial court poet under Francis I (Vienna); settled at Paris (1798). His works include *Novelle Galanti in Ottave Rime* (1793), the political satire *Gli Animali Parlanti* (1802), a satire on court of Catherine II of Russia (1803), and librettos for operas of Paisiello, as *Il Re Teodoro* (1784).

**Ca'sti·glio'ne** (käs'tē·lyō'nā), Duc **de.** See Pierre François Charles AUGEREAU.

**Castiglione,** Conte **Baldassare.** 1478–1529. Italian diplomat and writer, b. near Mantua. Attached to courts of Milan (1496–1500) and Urbino (1504 ff.); commander of papal troops; sent by Clement VII on diplomatic mission to Spain (c. 1526); after sack of Rome by Bourbons (1527), accused of treachery; settled in Spain; bishop of Ávila. Known particularly for his celebrated dialogue on ideal courtly life *Il Cortegiano,* sometimes called *Il Libro d'Oro* (1528; Eng. title *The Courtier;* 1st Eng. trans. by Sir Thomas Hoby, 1561).

**Castiglione,** Conte **Carlo Ottavio.** 1784–1849. Italian numismatist and philologist, b. Milan; coeditor (with Cardinal Mai) of Ulfilas' Gothic Biblical fragments; known also for contributions in Oriental numismatics and literature.

**Castiglione, Giovanni Benedetto.** *Called* **Il Grechet'to** (ēl grȧ·kāt'tō). 1616–1670. Italian painter and etcher, b. Genoa; court painter to duke of Mantua (1664 ff.); known especially for his animal paintings; among his works are several studies of Noah and the animals of the Ark and of Jacob with his herds.

**Ca'sti·glio'ni** (käs'tē·lyō'nē), **Arturo.** 1874–1953. American physician and historian of medicine, b. Trieste, Italy; professor, U. of Padua (1922–38); lecturer, Yale

(1939), professor (from 1943); naturalized (1946); author of *Storia della Medicina* (1927; American ed. 1940), etc.

**Castil-Blaze.** See BLAZE.

**Cas·ti'lho** (kȧsh·tē'lyōō), Visconde **Antônio Feliciano de.** 1800–1875. Portuguese poet, b. Lisbon; educ. U. of Coimbra; head of Romantic school in Portugal. Author of verse, as in *Amor e Melancolia* (1822), *A Primavera* (1822), *A Noite do Castelo* (1836), and *Escavações Poéticas* (1844), translations, as of Ovid's *Metamorphoses* (1841), and free adaptations of Shakespeare's *Midsummer Night's Dream*, Goethe's *Faust*, etc.

**Cas·til'la** (käs·tē'yä), **Miguel Hi·dal'go y** (ē·thäl'gō ē). 1753–1811. Mexican priest and patriot; led revolution for independence; executed (1811).

**Castilla, Ramón.** 1797?–1867. Peruvian general and political leader; fought under Sucre in war for independence (1820–26) and in civil wars of Peru (1841–45); minister of war (1837); president of Peru (1845–51); led revolution which overthrew President José Echenique, becoming president for second term (1855–62); abolished slavery (1856); proclaimed new constitution (1860).

**Cas'til·le'jo** (käs'tē·lyĕ'hō), **Cristóbal de.** 1490?–?1550. Spanish poet; ordained priest; secretary to Ferdinand I at Vienna (1525–?50). His works (collected edition, expurgated by Inquisition, 1573) include ballads, *Diálogo entre el Autor y Su Pluma*, and satirical poems, as *Diálogo Que Habla de las Condiciones de las Mujeres.*

**Castillejos,** Marqués **de los.** See Juan PRIM Y PRATS.

**Cas'til·le'ro Re'yes** (käs'tē·yā'rō rā'yās), **Ernesto de Jesús.** 1889– Panamanian educator. Professor of history, Colegio de Artes y Oficios, Escuela Normal de Institutoras, and National Inst. (1929–35); superintendent of schools, Panama (1936–40).

**Cas·til'lo** (käs·tē'lyō), **Bernal Díaz del.** See DÍAZ DEL CASTILLO.

**Castillo, Ignacio María del.** Conde **de Bil·ba'o** (bēl·bä'ō). 1817–1893. Spanish general; governor of Cuba (1883–84).

**Cas·til'lo** (käs·tē'yō), **Ramón S.** 1873–1944. Argentine jurist and politician; minister of public instruction (1936); minister of the interior (1936–37); vice-president of Argentina (1938–40); acting president (1940–42); president (1942–43), on resignation of Roberto M. Ortiz.

**Cas·til'lo Ná'je·ra** (käs·tē'yō nä'hā·rä), **Francisco.** 1886–1954. Mexican physician and diplomat. M.D. (1903), U. of Mexico; professor of urology (1919) and director (1920), army medical school; member, international commission for campaign against yellow fever (1921–25). Minister to China (1922–24), Belgium (1927–30), Holland (1930–32), France (1933–35); delegate to League of Nations; ambassador to U.S. (1935–45); foreign minister (1945–46). Author of *The Campaign against Yellow Fever in Mexico* (1923), *Un Siglo de Poesía Belga, 1830–1930* (1931), *El Gavilán* (1934).

**Cas·til'lo Sa·lór'za·no** (käs·tē'lyō sä·lôr'thä·nō), **Alonso de.** 1584?–?1647. Spanish writer, b. Tordesillas; author of humorous poems, plays, and, esp., picaresque novels, as *La Niña de los Embustes* (1634) and *La Garduña de Sevilla* (1642).

**Cas'tle** (kȧs''l), **Egerton.** 1858–1920. English journalist, novelist, and playwright. Educ. Paris, Glasgow, and Cambridge; newspaper publisher in Liverpool; on staff of *Saturday Review* (1885–94). Among his numerous works are *Consequences* (novel; 1891), *Saviolo* (play; with W. H. Pollock; 1893), *Young April* (romance; 1899), *The Star-Dreamer* (1903), *Panther's Cub* (1910), *The Hope of the House* (1915), *Wolf Lure* (1917), *New Wine* (1919). His wife, **Agnes,** *nee* **Sweet'man** [swēt'măn] (d. 1922), collaborated with him in many novels, including *The Pride of Jennico* (1898; later dramatized) and *The Bath Comedy* (1899; dramatized as *Sweet Kitty Bellairs*).

**Castle, Vernon Blythe.** *Orig.* **Vernon Blythe** (blīth). 1887–1918. Dancer and aviator, b. Norwich, Eng.; to U.S. (1906); on stage (from 1907); assumed name Castle. His dancing popular in Paris (1912), and later in New York; originated the one-step, turkey trot, Castle walk. Aviator in Royal Flying Corps (from 1916); killed in aviation accident, Fort Worth, Tex. (Feb. 15, 1918). His wife, **Irene,** *nee* **Foote** [fŏŏt] (1893?–1969), dancer; m. Vernon Castle (1911), 2d Robert E. Treman, 3d Frederick McLaughlin, 4th George Enzinger (1946); author of *Modern Dancing* (with Vernon Castle; 1914), *My Memories of Vernon Castle* (1918).

**Castle, William Ernest.** 1867–1962. American zoologist, b. Alexandria, Ohio. A.B., Harvard (1893); Ph.D., Harvard (1895); teacher at Harvard (from 1897; professor 1908–37). Author of *Heredity in Relation to Evolution and Animal Breeding* (1911), *Genetics and Eugenics* (1916), etc.

**Castlemaine.** (1) Earl of. See Roger PALMER. (2) Countess of. See Barbara VILLIERS.

**Castlemon, Harry.** Pseudonym of Charles Austin FOSDICK.

**Castlereagh,** Viscount. See Robert STEWART (1769–1822).

**Cast'ner** (kăst'nẽr), **Hamilton Young.** 1859–1899. American chemist, b. Brooklyn, N.Y. Educ. Brooklyn Polytech. Inst. and Columbia Coll. School of Mines. Invented an electrolytic method of manufacturing caustic soda and chlorine from sodium chloride.

**Cas'trén'** (kȧs'trān'), **Matthias Alexander.** 1813–1852. Finnish ethnologist and philologist. Collected ballads and legends illustrative of Finnish mythology; professor of Finnish language and literature (1851), chancellor (1852), U. of Helsingfors. Regarded as founder of Ural-Altaic philology.

**Castriota, George.** See SCANDERBEG.

**Cas'tro** (käs'trō), **Américo.** 1885–1972. Spanish scholar, b. Rio de Janeiro. Educ. in Spain and Paris; professor, Madrid U. (1913–36) and Princeton U. (1940–53); ambassador to Berlin (1931–32). Author of *Vida de Lope de Vega* (1919), *Les Grands Romantiques Espagnols* (1922), *El Pensamiento de Cervantes* (1925), etc.

**Castro, Cipriano.** 1858?–1924. Venezuelan general and dictator, b. near San Antonio, Táchira state. Led insurrection against President Ignacio Andrade (1899); became "supreme military leader" (1899–1901); provisional president (1901–02); elected president (1902–08); his administration marked by many revolts, and by despotic acts. Chiefly notorious for involving Venezuela in serious difficulties with foreign powers, notably with Germany, England, Italy, and Belgium as creditor nations (1902–07; their blockade of Venezuelan ports bringing about U.S. intervention, 1902), with U.S. (1904–08) because of confiscation of American properties in Venezuela, and with Colombia and France (1905). Deposed by revolution led by vice-president Gómez (1908) and never allowed to return despite many attempts, as one through U.S. (1916).

**Castro, Cristóbal Va'ca de** (vä'kä thā). d. 1558. Spanish administrator; member, audiencia of Valladolid; sent to Peru by Charles V. On assassination of Pizarro assumed government of Peru; suppressed rebellion of younger Almagro (Sept., 1542) and executed him.

**Cas'tro** (kȧsh'trōō), **Eugênio de.** 1869–1944. Portuguese symbolist poet, b. Coimbra; professor of French, U. of Coimbra; author of *Cristalizações da Morte* (1884), *Oaristos* (1890), *Sagramor* (1895), *Salomé* (1896), *Poesias*

*Escolhidas* (1902), and dramas, as *O Anel de Policrates* (1907).

**Castro, Fidel.** 1927– Cuban political leader, b. Mayarí. Led revolution against President Fulgencio Batista (1959); premier (from 1959).

**Cas'tro** (käs'trō), **Inés** (*or* **Inez** *or sometimes, Anglicized,* **Agnes**) **de.** 1320?–1355. Spanish noblewoman, descendant of royal family of Castile; m. (1354) Dom Pedro secretly; murdered at Coimbra by order of Alfonso who feared serious political consequences from the unequal union. Episode was celebrated by novelists and poets, esp. by Camoëns in *The Lusiad* and by Antônio Ferreira in *Inês de Castro.*

**Cas'tro** (kȧsh'trōō), **João de.** 1500–1548. Portuguese naval commander, b. Lisbon; placed in command of fleet to rid European seas of pirates (1543). To Portuguese India (1545) as viceroy ad interim; defeated Mahmud Shah III, King of Gujarat; relieved city of Diu; subdued Malacca; appointed viceroy (1547) by John III.

**Cas'tro** (käs'trō), **José María.** 1818–1893. Costa Rican statesman, b. San José. President of Costa Rica (1847–49, 1866–68); called "Founder of the Republic."

**Castro, Juan José.** 1895–1968. Argentine orchestra conductor and composer.

**Castro, Manuel Fernández de.** See FERNÁNDEZ DE CASTRO.

**Castro y Bell·vís'** (ē bĕl·y'·vēs'), **Guillén de.** 1569–1631. Spanish dramatist, b. Valencia; best known for *Las Mocedades del Cid,* source for Corneille's *Le Cid.*

**Castro y Velasco, Antonio Acisclo Palomino de.** See PALOMINO.

**Cas'tro·vie'jo** (käs'trō·vyĕ'hō), **Ramón.** 1904– Spanish-born American ophthalmologist.

**Ca·struc'cio Ca'stra·ca'ni de'gli An'tel·mi·nel'li** (käs·trōōt'chō käs'trä·kä'nē dā'lyē än'tāl·mē·nĕl'lē). 1281–1328. Italian soldier and Ghibelline leader; conquered Lucca and Pistoia; assumed control of Pisa; created imperial vicar and duke of Lucca (1327).

**Caswallawn** *or* **Caswallon.** See CASSIVELAUNUS.

**Cas'well** (kăz'wĕl; -wĕl), **Richard.** 1729–1789. American Revolutionary officer, b. in Cecil Co., Md.; delegate to Continental Congress (1774–76); colonel in Revolutionary army; governor of North Carolina (1776–80; 1785–87).

**Cat** (kăt), **Christopher.** fl. 1703–1733. English tavernkeeper, of "The Cat and Fiddle" in London, meeting place of the Kit-cat Club, a social club for Whigs.

**Ca'ta·la'ni** (kä'tä·lä'nē), **Angelica.** 1780–1849. Italian operatic soprano.

**Ca'tar·giu'** (kä'tär·jōō'), **Lascăr.** 1823–1899. Rumanian statesman; prime minister of Rumania (1866, 1871–76, 1889, 1891–95); leader in Senate of Conservative opposition to Brătianu (1876–88).

**Ca·te'na** (kä·tā'nä), **Vincenzo di Bia'gio** (dē byä'jō). c. 1470–1531. Venetian painter; pupil of Bellini. His works include *Holy Trinity* (church of San Simeone Grande, Venice), *Knight Adoring the Christ Child* (National Gallery, London), *Christ Giving the Keys to St. Peter* (Boston).

**Caterina.** Italian form of CATHERINE.

**Cates'by** (kāts'bĭ), **Mark.** 1679?–1749. English naturalist and traveler. In America (1712–19, 1722–25), studying flora and fauna. Author of *The Natural History of Carolina, Florida, and the Bahama Islands.*

**Catesby, Robert.** 1573–1605. English conspirator, son of Roman Catholic squire; took part in rebellion of earl of Essex (1601); named accomplice in Rye Plot (1603) to seize James I and force concessions of religious tolerance; chief instigator of Gunpowder Plot (1604–05); betrayed by Francis Tresham; killed resisting arrest.

**Cath'a·rine** (kăth'ȧ·rĭn). See CATHERINE.

**Catharine Jagello.** See JAGELLON.

**Cath'cart** (kăth'kĕrt; -kärt), Sir **William Schaw.** 1st Earl **Cathcart.** 1755–1843. English soldier and diplomat. Son of **Charles Cathcart** (1721–1776; 9th Baron Cathcart, ambassador to Russia 1768–71). Commanded an irregular corps, the "British legion," in America (1777–80); served in Low Countries (1793–95); commander in chief in Ireland (1803–05); bombarded Copenhagen (1807); general (1812); ambassador at St. Petersburg (1814–21).

His son **Charles Murray** (1783–1859), 2d earl, styled Lord **Green'ock** [grĭn'ŭk] (1807–43); soldier; served in Italy and Sicily (1805–06), at Walcheren (1809), in Iberian Peninsula (1810–12), as quartermaster general (1814–23), at Waterloo; commander in chief in Canada (1846–49); general (1854); discovered new mineral, greenockite (1841).

Sir **George** (1794–1854), soldier; 3d son of 1st earl; aide-de-camp to Wellington at Waterloo and in France (1815–18); commander in chief in South Africa (1852–54); conquered Kaffirs and Basutos; killed at battle of Inkerman.

**Ca'the·li'neau'** (kȧt'lē'nō'), **Jacques.** 1759–1793. French Royalist; leader of Vendeans in uprising of 1793; died (July 4, 1793) of wounds received leading assault on Nantes.

**Cath'er** (kăth'ēr), **Willa Sibert.** 1873–1947. American novelist, b. Winchester, Va. B.A., Nebraska (1895); on staff of Pittsburgh *Daily Leader* (1898–1901); associate editor of *McClure's Magazine* (1906–12). Author of *April Twilights* (verse; 1903), and the novels *Alexander's Bridge* (1912), *O Pioneers* (1913), *The Song of the Lark* (1915), *My Ántonia* (1918), *Youth and the Bright Medusa* (1920), *One of Ours* (1922; awarded Pulitzer prize), *A Lost Lady* (1923), *The Professor's House* (1925), *My Mortal Enemy* (1926), *Death Comes for the Archbishop* (1927), *Shadows on the Rock* (1931), *Obscure Destinies* (1932), *Lucy Gayheart* (1935), *Not Under Forty* (1936), *Sapphira and the Slave Girl* (1940).

**Cath'er·ine** (kăth'ēr·ĭn). Name of three wives of king Henry VIII of England. See (1) CATHERINE OF ARAGON; (2) Catherine HOWARD; (3) Catherine PARR.

**Catherine** *or* **Catharine.** Name of two empresses of Russia:

**Catherine I.** *Russ.* **Ekaterina Alekseevna.** *Orig. name* **Marfa Ska·vron'ska·ya** (skŭ·vrôn'skŭ·yŭ). 1684?–1727. Empress (1725–27). Of Livonian peasant origin; m. a Swedish dragoon; taken prisoner at Marienburg (1702); became serf of Prince Menshikov. Attracted attention of Peter I the Great and became his mistress (1703); exerted influence over Peter and became his adviser; saved his life in campaign against Turks on the Prut (1711); m. Peter as his second wife (1712); crowned empress (1724). Succeeded Peter as Catherine I (1725); during short peaceful reign, relied upon Prince Menshikov; established supreme privy council; founded Russian Academy of Sciences. Succeeded by grandson Peter II.

**Catherine II.** *Called* **Catherine the Great.** *Russ. name* **Ekaterina Alekseevna.** *Orig. name (Anglicized)* **Sophia Augusta Frederica of An'halt-Zerbst'** (än'-hält·tsĕrpst'). *Called* "the Semiramis of the North." 1729–1796. Empress (1762–96). Married (1745) Peter (later Peter III), nephew of Empress Elizabeth; soon became estranged from Peter, both being subjects of much court scandal; soon after Peter's accession (1762), deposed him with help of her paramour Grigori Orlov, Potëmkin, Princess Dashkova, and others; usurped throne (1762). During her reign, serfdom and misery among peasants increased but frontiers of empire extended by large conquests; participated in partitions of Poland (1772, 1793, 1795); won victories over Turks in war (1768–72) and by Treaty of Küchük Kainarja (1774); annexed Crimea (1783); engaged in second war with Turks (1787–92), concluding favorable Treaty of Jassy (1792); although German, identified herself completely with Russian people; corresponded with Voltaire; disciple of the Encyclopedists. Followed by son Paul I.

**Ca'the·rine' de Foix** (kȧ'trēn'). See Foix.

**Ca'the·rine' de Mé'di'cis'** (kȧ'trēn' dē mā'dē'sēs'). *Ital.* **Ca'te·ri'na de' Me'di·ci** (kä'tā·rē'nä dā mâ'dē·chē; *Angl.* mĕd'ĕ-, mā'dē-). 1519–1589. Daughter of Lorenzo de' Medici, b. Florence (see Medici). Married (1533) Henry, second son of Francis I of France. Became queen of France (1547). Had four sons, three of whom became kings of France; began to assert herself in government when eldest, Francis II, became king (1559); regent during minority of Charles IX (1560–63) and had practically complete control during his entire reign (1560–74); exerted some influence over Henry III (1574–89). Stirred up wars between Catholics and Huguenots; sided with either as selfishness dictated, but generally with Catholics; planned Massacre of St. Bartholomew (1572).

**Cath'er·ine Howard** (kăth'ēr·ĭn). See Catherine Howard.

**Catherine of Alexandria,** Saint. d. about 307. Christian virgin and martyr, b. Alexandria; according to legend, beheaded after failure of attempt to torture her on a spiked wheel.

**Catherine of Ar'a·gon** (ăr'ȧ·gŏn). 1485–1536. 1st Queen of Henry VIII of England; mother of Mary I. Daughter of Ferdinand and Isabella of Spain; m. (1501) Arthur, Prince of Wales (d. 1502), marriage not consummated; betrothed (1503) to Prince Henry, with papal dispensation, but unmarried while Henry VII extorted new demands from her father. Married Henry VIII (1509); gave birth to, but lost, four children (1510–14); regent during Henry's invasion of France (1513). Informed by Henry (1526) that cohabitation must cease pending decision of validity of marriage with brother's widow; appeared before legatine court of Cardinals Campeggio and Wolsey (1529), after which case was revoked to Rome; abandoned by Henry (1531) and separated from her daughter Princess Mary. Refused to yield title of queen for princess-dowager after Archbishop Cranmer's declaration of nullity of her marriage (1533); passed rest of life in religious devotion, a prisoner, fearing poison; refused to swear to new act of succession (1534); dictated last letter of forgiveness to Henry.

**Catherine of Bo·lo'gna** (bō·lō'nyä), Saint. 1413–1463. Roman Catholic religious, b. Bologna; abbess of order of Poor Clares and founder of their convent of the Holy Sacrament at Bologna.

**Catherine of Bra·gan'za** (brȧ·găn'zȧ). 1638–1705. Queen of Charles II of England. Daughter of John IV, Duke of Braganza and (after 1640) King of Portugal; m. (1662) to Charles II; forced by Charles to receive his mistress Lady Castlemaine and to live in retirement; subjected to schemes for dissolution of marriage because of childlessness (1667–70); accused by Titus Oates of design to poison king and by Whigs of complicity in Popish Plot (1678–80); shielded from these attacks by king; abandoned for duchess of Portsmouth; reconciled Charles on his deathbed with Catholic Church. Retired to Lisbon (1693); regent of Portugal for her brother Peter II (1704–05), gaining successes over Spain.

**Catherine of Gen'o·a** (jĕn'ō·ȧ), Saint. 1447–1510. Roman Catholic mystic.

**Catherine of Ric'ci** (rēt'chē), Saint. c. 1552–c. 1589. Dominican nun, prioress of convent at Prato in Toscana; noted for wisdom.

**Catherine of Sie'na** (syâ'nä), Saint. 1347–1380. Roman Catholic religious, b. Siena; renowned for ecstatic visions and revelations; responsible for decision of Pope Gregory XI to leave Avignon and return to Rome (1377), and for the recognition of Pope Urban VI (1380). Author of letters and of devotional works.

**Catherine of Sweden,** Saint. c. 1330–1381. Swedish religious; daughter of Saint Bridget, whom she succeeded as abbess of the convent of the Brigittines at Vadstena.

**Catherine of Va'lois'** (vȧ'lwȧ'). 1401–1437. Queen of Henry V of England; mother of Henry VI. Daughter of Charles VI of France. Married Henry (1420); crowned in Westminster Abbey (1421). After Henry's death in France (1423), may have been legally married to Owen Tudor (*q.v.*) by whom she was mother of three sons and a daughter, the eldest son (Edmund, cr. earl of Richmond 1453) being father of Henry VII.

**Catherine of Würt'tem·berg** (vür'tĕm·bĕrк). 1783–1835. Daughter of King Frederick I of Württemberg. m. (1807) Jérôme Bonaparte on demand of Napoleon; queen of Westphalia (1807–13); accompanied husband in exile (1813–15).

**Cat'i·line** (kăt'ĭ·līn; -'l·īn). *Full Lat. name* **Lucius Sergius Cat'i·li'na** (kăt'ĭ·lī'nȧ). 108?–62 B.C. Roman politician; quaestor (77 B.C.); praetor (68); governor of Africa (67–66). Entered into conspiracy to assassinate the consuls and plunder Rome (63); foiled by Cicero, then a consul. Attacked by Cicero in speeches in senate and forum; fled to army of Manlius, his ally in Etruria; defeated (62) and slain.

**Ca'ti'nat'** (kȧ'tē'nȧ'), **Nicolas de.** 1637–1712. French soldier; commanded Italian army (1690–96) and forced duke of Savoy to sue for peace; created marshal of France.

**Cat'lin** (kăt'lĭn), **George.** 1796–1872. American artist, traveler, and author, b. Wilkes-Barre, Pa. Devoted himself (from 1829) to study of American Indians; executed series of Indian portraits (painted 1829–38) now in National Museum, Washington, D.C., and of Indian sketches, in American Museum of Natural History, New York. Author of *Life Among the Indians* (1867), etc.

**Ca'to** (kā'tō), **Dionysius.** Supposed author, in 3d century (or later) A.D., of *Dionysii Catonis Disticha de Moribus ad Filium,* collection of moral apothegms much admired in Middle Ages.

**Cato, Marcus Porcius.** *Known as* **Cato the Censor** *and* **Cato the Elder.** 234–149 B.C. Roman statesman, b. in Tusculum. Quaestor (204 B.C.); aedile (199); praetor (198); consul (195); censor (184). Endeavored to restore by legislation what he believed to be the high morals and simplicity of life characteristic of early days of the republic; champion of anti-Carthaginian policy and chiefly responsible for bringing on Third Punic War, ending every speech in the Roman senate with the words *Ceterum censeo Carthaginem esse delendam* ("For the rest, I vote that Carthage should be destroyed"). His only extant work is *De Agricultura,* or *De Re Rustica.*

His great-grandson **Marcus Porcius Cato,** *surnamed* **U'ti·cen'sis** (ŭ'tĭ·sĕn'sĭs) [from Utica, city of his death]. *Known as* **Cato the Younger.** 95–46 B.C. Roman Stoic philosopher. Served against Spartacus (72 B.C.); military tribune in Macedonia (67); quaestor (65); tribune of the people (62); praetor (54). Supported Cicero against Catiline, and Pompey against Caesar. Committed suicide on learning of Caesar's decisive victory at Thapsus (46).

**Cato, Publius Valerius.** Roman scholar and poet of 1st century B.C.; a native of Cisalpine Gaul.

**Ca'tron** (?kā'trŭn), **John.** 1786?–1865. American jurist, b. probably in Pennsylvania; moved to Tennessee (1812); first chief justice of Tennessee (1831–34); associate justice, U.S. Supreme Court (1837–65).

**Ca'troux'** (kȧ'trōō'), **Georges.** 1879–1969. French general; educ. St. Cyr; served in World War I; gov. gen. of Indo-China (1939–40); Free French high commissioner and General de Gaulle's representative in Near East (1940); commander in chief in Levant (1941–43); negotiated between de Gaulle and Giraud (1943); gov. gen. of Algeria (1943–44); amb. to Russia (1945–46).

**Cats** (käts), **Jakob.** 1577–1660. Dutch poet and statesman; grand pensionary of Holland (1636) and keeper of the great seal (1648–51).

**Catt** (kăt), **Carrie Chapman,** *nee* **Lane.** 1859–1947. American woman-suffrage leader and lecturer, b. Ripon, Wis. Educ. State College of Iowa; high school principal, and superintendent of schools, Mason City, Iowa; m. Leo Chapman (1884; d. 1886), 2d George William Catt (1890; d. 1905). State lecturer and organizer, Iowa Woman Suffrage Association (1890–92); on staff of National American Woman Suffrage Association (from 1892), president (1900–04; 1915–47); also, president International Woman Suffrage Alliance (1904–23). A leader in campaign resulting in adoption of 19th amendment to U.S. Constitution (1920).

**Cat·tell'** (kă·tĕl'), **William Cassaday.** 1827–1898. American Presbyterian clergyman, b. Salem, N.J. President, Lafayette College (1863–83). His son **James McKeen Cattell** (1860–1944), psychologist; A.M., Lafayette (1883), Ph.D., Leipzig (1886); professor and head of department of psychology, U. of Penn. (1888–91), Columbia (1891–1917); author of papers on psychological measurements, individual differences, applied psychology, education, etc.; editor of *Psychological Review* (1894–1904), *Science* (from 1894), *Scientific Monthly* (from 1900), *American Naturalist* (from 1907), *School and Society* (1915–39), also of *American Men of Science* (from 1906), *Leaders in Education* (from 1932).

**Cat'ter·mole** (kăt'ẽr·mōl), **George.** 1800–1868. English water-colorist, architectural and topographical draftsman, and illustrator; illustrated *Waverley Novels.*

**Cat'ton** (kăt'n), **Charles Bruce.** 1899–1978. Amer. writer and editor, b. Petoskey, Mich. Editor of the *American Heritage* magazine (1954–59). Author of *Mr. Lincoln's Army* (1951), *Glory Road* (1952), *Stillness at Appomatox* (1953), *The Coming Fury* (1961), etc.

**Ca·tul'lus** (kȧ·tŭl'ŭs), **Gaius Valerius.** 84?–54 B.C. Roman lyric poet, b. Verona. Among his poems, chiefly lyrics, over 100 in number, are many addressed to "Lesbia," who has been identified as Clodia, notorious sister of Clodius, and wife (63–59 B.C.) of Quintus Metellus Celer. Regarded as one of the greatest lyric poets in Rome's literary history.

**Cat'u·lus** (kăt'ū·lŭs). Name of a family of ancient Rome, of the Lutatian gens, including notably: **Gaius Lutatius,** consul (242 B.C.), commander of fleet (241 B.C.) that defeated Carthaginian fleet of the Aegates (Aegadian Isles). **Quintus Lutatius** (152?–87 B.C.), consul with Marius (102 B.C.), and his colleague in defeating (101) the Cimbri at Vercellae (Vercelli); committed suicide (87). His son **Quintus Lutatius** (d. 60 B.C.), consul (78), joined Pompey in defeating Lepidus (77), censor (65), supporter of Cicero in his attack against Catiline (63).

**Cau'chon'** (kō'shôN'), **Pierre.** d. 1442. French Roman Catholic prelate; bishop of Beauvais (1420–29); judge at trial of Joan of Arc (1431).

**Cau'chy'** (kō'shē'), **Augustin Louis.** 1789–1857. French mathematician, b. Paris. Held three professorships in Paris; refused to take oath required by Louis Philippe and went into exile (1830); taught at Turin; returned to Paris (1837); professor of mathematical astronomy at Sorbonne (1848). Known for important researches in pure and applied mathematics, esp. in calculus; invented calculus of residues; developed wave theory in optics; worked on theory of elasticity.

**Cau'er** (kou'ẽr). Family of German sculptors, including: **Emil** (1800–1867), whose chief works are statues of persons prominent in Reformation, as Sickingen, Hutten, Melanchthon; his sons **Karl** (1828–1885), designer of Garfield memorial at Cleveland, Ohio, and **Robert** (1831–1893); Karl's three sons, **Hugo** (1864–1918), **Ludwig** (1866–1947), and **Emil** (1867–1946); Robert's son **Stanislaus** (1867–1943).

**Cau'lain'court'** (kō'lăN'kōōr'), Marquis **Armand Augustin Louis de.** 1772–1827. French soldier and diplomat; served in Revolutionary and Napoleonic armies; general and aide-de-camp to Napoleon (1802). Ambassador to Russia (1807–11). Created duc de Vicence (1808) and a senator (1813); minister of foreign affairs (1813–14, and during the Hundred Days). His brother **Auguste Jean Gabriel** (1777–1812), general; aide-de-camp to Berthier (1804); general of brigade (1806); served in Spain, Portugal, and Russia; killed in battle of Moscow.

**Cau'mont'** (kō'môN'), **Arcisse de.** 1802–1873. French scholar; founder of science of archaeology in France.

**Caus** (kō) *or* **Cauls** (kō) *or* **Caulx** (kō) *or* **Caux** (kō), **Salomon de.** 1576–?1626. Norman engineer and architect in England and Germany. In book on motive power of water, anticipated steam engine (1615).

**Causse, Charles.** See Pierre MAËL.

**Caus'sin' de Per'ce·val'** (kō'săN' dẽ pĕr'sẽ·vȧl'), **Jean Jacques Antoine.** 1759–1835. French Orientalist. His son **Armand Pierre** (1795–1871) was professor of Arabic, Collège de France (from 1822); author of *Essai sur l'Histoire des Arabes avant l'Islamisme* (1847).

**Caut'ley** (kôt'lĭ), Sir **Proby Thomas.** 1802–1871. English engineer and paleontologist. Member of council of India (1858–68); presented Indian fossils to British Museum.

**Ca'vai'gnac'** (kȧ'vĕ'nyȧk'). French family, including: **Jean Baptiste** (1762–1829), lawyer and revolutionist; as member of National Convention (1792), voted for death of Louis XVI; member of Council of Five Hundred; exiled as regicide after Restoration. His two sons **Éléonore Louis Godefroy** (1801–1845), journalist and politician, active in revolutionary events and intrigues (1830–34), and **Louis Eugène** (1802–1857), army commander; served in Algeria (1832–48); as minister of war (1848), suppressed uprising in Paris; chief of the executive body (June–Dec., 1848); unsuccessful candidate for president of France (Dec., 1848). **Jacques Marie Eugène Godefroy** (1853–1905), son of Louis Eugène; member of various ministries (from 1892); declared (1898) before Chamber of Deputies his belief in Dreyfus's guilt. **Eugène** (1876– ), son of Jacques; historian; author of *Histoire Financière d'Athènes* (1909), *Histoire de l'Antiquité* (1912 ff.), etc.

**Ca'val·can'ti** (kä'väl·kän'tē), **Guido.** c. 1250–1300. Florentine poet and philosopher; leading Florentine poet before Dante, who called him his "first friend"; wrote in *dolce stil nuovo.*

**Ca'val·ca·sel'le** (kä'väl·kä·sĕl'lā), **Giovanni Battista.** 1820–1897. Italian art historian and critic, b. Legnano; inspector of Museo Nazionale, Florence (1867), and general director of fine arts in Rome. His works, written in collaboration with Joseph Archer Crowe (*q.v.*), include *Early Flemish Painters* (1857), *New History of Italian*

*Painting* (1864), *Titian* (1876), and *Raphael* (1883).

**Ca'va'lier'** (kȧ'vȧ'lyā'), **Jean.** 1681–1740. French military leader of the Camisards. Son of a peasant; baker at Geneva; led Huguenot insurgents in the Cévennes (1702); defeated superior forces but made submission (1704), failing to obtain liberty of conscience; explained the revolt to Louis XIV. Served under duke of Savoy and with English in Spain (1706).

**Ca'va·lie'ri** (kä'vä·lyâ'rē), **Emilio de'.** *Also* **Emilio del Ca'va·lie're** (-rā). 1550?–1602. Italian composer, b. Rome; inspector general of arts at Medici court (1589 ff.); one of originators of figured-bass (basso continuo) accompaniment. Known esp. for dramatic compositions, as *Disperazione di Filene, Il Satiro, Giuoco della Cieca,* and *La Rappresentazione di Anima e di Corpo* (regarded as the first oratorio).

**Cavalieri, Francesco Bonaventura.** 1598–1647. Italian mathematician. At early age, became a Jesuit; professor at Bologna (1629). Originated the method of indivisibles which he published in 1635 and by means of which was able to solve problems proposed by Kepler.

**Cavalieri, Lina.** See under Lucien MURATORE.

**Ca'val·le'ro** (kä'väl·lâ'rō), Conte **Ugo.** 1880?–1943. Italian general; in Ethiopia, under duke of Aosta (1938–39); marshal and successor to Marshal Badoglio as commander in chief in campaign against Greece (1940–41); chief of staff, Italian high command (1941–43).

**Ca·val'li** (kä·väl'lē), **Francesco.** *Orig.* **Pietro Francesco Ca·let'ti-Bru'ni** (kä·lāt'tē·bro͞o'nē). 1602?–1676. Italian composer, b. Crema. Protégé of Federigo Cavalli, a Venetian nobleman; pupil of Monteverdi; organist (1665), Kapellmeister (1668–76) in church of San Marco, Venice; aided in development of modern opera by innovations, as introduction of solos and set numbers. His works include operas and religious music.

**Ca·val·li'ni** (kä'väl·lē'nē), **Pietro.** c. 1250–c. 1330. Italian painter and mosaicist, Rome; thought to have influenced Cimabue and Giotto. Among works ascribed to him are frescoes in upper church of St. Francis Assisi, and frescoes and mosaics in church of San Paolo fuori le Mura.

**Ca·val'lo** (kä·väl'lō), **Tiberio,** *Angl.* **Tiberius.** 1749–1809. Italian physicist in England. Invented delicate instruments for measuring the quantity and force of electricity.

**Ca'val·lot'ti** (kä'väl·lôt'tē), **Felice Carlo Emmanuele.** 1842–1898. Italian politician and writer. Fought under Garibaldi (1860, 1866); member of parliament (1873–98); leader of extreme Left (1886 ff.); ardent supporter of Irredentists; bitter opponent of Crispi; killed in his thirty-third duel. His works include lyric poetry and plays.

**Cav'an** (kăv'ăn), 10th Earl of. **Frederic Rudolph Lam'bart** (lăm'bärt). 1865–1946. British soldier; served in South Africa (1901) and in World War (1914–18); in charge of operations of 10th Italian army on Piave front (1918). General (1921); chief of imperial general staff (1922–26); field marshal (1932).

**Ca'va·nil'les** (kä'vä·nē'lyās), **Antonio José.** 1745–1804. Spanish botanist; director of botanical gardens at Madrid (1801); author of *Icones et Descriptiones Plantarum Hispaniae* (6 vols., 1791–1801).

**Ca'vaz·zo'la** (kä'vät·tsô'lä) *or* **Ca'vaz·zuo'la** (-tswô'lä), **Il** (ēl). *Real name* **Paolo Mo·ran'do** (mō·rän'dō). 1486–1522. Veronese painter. His works include *Baptism of Christ, Madonna in Glory* (an altarpiece), *St. Rocco* and *Madonna and St. John the Baptist* (both in National Gallery, London), and portraits.

**Cave** (kāv), **Edward.** 1691–1754. English printer. Printer and journalist at Norwich; employed in post office, London; supplied country newspapers with London newsletters; founded and edited *Gentleman's Magazine* (1731–54) under pseudonym of "Sylvanus Urban, Gent."; issued reports of debates in House of Commons upon which Samuel Johnson had his first employment.

**Cave, George.** 1st Viscount **Cave.** 1856–1928. English jurist, b. London; educ. Oxford. Called to bar (1880); king's counsel (1904); M.P. (1906–18); privy councilor (1915); member of British cabinet (1915–19); lord chancellor of England (1922–28). His wife (m. 1885), **Anne,** *nee* **Math'ews** (măth'ūz), author of memoirs, including *Memories of Old Richmond* (1922), *Odds and Ends of My Life* (1929).

**Cave, William.** 1637–1713. English ecclesiastical historian and patristic scholar; M.A., Cantab. (1660); chaplain to Charles II; canon of Windsor (1684). Author of *Apostolici* (1677), a history of apostles and fathers of first three centuries.

**Ca've·do'ni** (kä'vâ·dō'nē), Don **Celestino.** 1795–1865. Italian numismatist and antiquary.

**Ca've·lier'** (kȧ'vē·lyā'), **Pierre Jules.** 1814–1894. French sculptor; notable works include *Pénélope Endormie, Abélard, La Poésie, L'Histoire,* and portrait busts.

**Cav'ell** (kăv''l), **Edith Louisa.** 1865–1915. English nurse. First matron of medical institute in Brussels, which became Red Cross hospital (1914); assisted about 200 English, French, and Belgian soldiers to escape to Dutch border (Nov., 1914–July, 1915); arrested by Germans, admitted her successful efforts; condemned to death by court-martial; shot (Oct. 12, 1915) along with a Belgian, Philippe Baucq, who had furnished guides.

**Cav'en·dish** (kăv'ĕn·dĭsh). Pseudonym of Henry JONES (1831–1899).

**Cavendish.** English family, members of which bear titles of marquis of **Har'ting·ton** (här'tĭng·tŭn) and duke of **Dev'on·shire** (dĕv'ŭn·shĭr; -shēr); descended from Sir **John Cavendish** (d. 1381), chief justice of King's Bench (1372–81), who was beheaded by Jack Straw's followers, and from Sir **William Cavendish** of Cavendish, Suffolk (1505?–1557), founder of the house, who was treasurer of royal chamber under Henry VIII, Edward VI, and Mary, and whose third wife, Bess of Hardwick (see Elizabeth TALBOT), brought Chatsworth to the family. Members of the family include the following.

**George** (1500–?1562), brother of Sir William; gentleman usher (from 1526); biographer of Cardinal Wolsey (1557).

**William** (d. 1626), Sir William's second son; cr. first earl of Devonshire (1618); uncle of (1st) duke of Newcastle (*q.v.*).

**William** (1640–1707), 1st Duke of Devonshire; Sir William's great-grandson; a leader of anticourt and anti-Romanist party in House of Commons (1666–78); aided in raising the north country in favor of William of Orange; argued for James II's deposition (1689); cr. (1694) duke of Devonshire and marquis of Hartington.

**William** (1720–1764), 4th Duke of Devonshire; great-grandson of 1st duke; lord lieutenant of Ireland (1755–56); prime minister (1756–57); lord chamberlain (1757–62).

**Henry** (1731–1810), another great-grandson of 1st duke; chemist and physicist; studied at Cambridge (1749–53); lived a wealthy bachelor in seclusion, carrying on scientific experimentation; determined specific gravity of hydrogen, the true nature of which he was the first to recognize, and carbon dioxide; discovered (before 1783) that water results from union of hydrogen and oxygen; discovered composition of nitric acid; apparently isolated argon without knowing it; anticipating certain researches of Coulomb and Faraday in electricity, devised ways of measuring capacity of apparatus, using "inch of electricity" as unit; discovered specific inductive capacity, introduced idea of potential under name of "degree of electricification"; devised Cavendish experiment, for estimating density of earth (1798). The Cavendish Laboratory at Cambridge U. is named for him.

**Georgiana** (1757–1806), daughter of 1st Earl Spencer, wife of 5th duke of Devonshire; a reigning queen of society; friend of Fox, Sheridan, Selwyn, Dr. Johnson; a beauty whose portrait was painted by Sir Joshua Reynolds and Gainsborough, both as child and as duchess.

**Spencer Comp'ton** [kŭmp'tŭn] (1833–1908), 8th duke; M.A., Cantab. (1854); Liberal M.P. (1857); visited President Lincoln in U.S. (1862); war secretary in Lord Russell's government (1866); postmaster general under Gladstone; chief secretary for Ireland (1870–74); led Liberal party in House of Commons (1875–80); declined offer of premiership (1880); secretary of state for India under Gladstone (1880–82), war secretary (1882–85); partly responsible for sending Gordon back to Sudan and failing to support him; consistently opposed Gladstone's Irish home-rule policy, favoring coercion; with Joseph Chamberlain, founded new party of Liberal Unionists; declined premiership (1886, 1887); joined Salisbury's coalition government as president of council (1895–1902), continued under Balfour (1902–03); opposed to fiscal policy and, as a free trader, opposed to tariff reform; resigned (1903).

Lord **Frederick Charles** (1836–1882), bro. of 8th duke; B.A., Cantab. (1858); chief secretary for Ireland (1882); murdered, with Undersecretary Burke, by Irish Invincibles in Phoenix Park, Dublin.

**Victor Christian William** (1868–1938), *known as* Lord **Hartington;** 9th duke; nephew of 8th duke; educ. Cambridge; M.P. (1891–1908); financial secretary to treasury (1903–05); governor general of Canada (1916–21); secretary of state for colonies (1922–24); high steward of Cambridge (from 1923).

**Cavendish** *or* **Can'dish** (kăn'dĭsh), **Thomas.** 1555?–1592. English navigator, third circumnavigator of the globe. Imitating Drake, sailed with three ships (1586) to Brazil; discovered Port Desire (Puerto Deseado, Patagonia); passed Strait of Magellan; captured Spanish treasure galleon; returned home via Philippines, Moluccas, Java, Cape of Good Hope, with only one ship, the *Desire*, after 2 years and 50 days. Attempted second voyage with five ships (1591); unable to pass Strait of Magellan; died at sea.

**Cavendish, William.** Duke of **Newcastle.** See NEWCASTLE.

**Cavendish Bentinck.** See BENTINCK.

**Ca'ven'tou'** (kȧ'väN'to͞o'), **Joseph Bienaimé.** 1795–1877. French chemist; codiscoverer (with Pelletier) of quinine.

**Ca·vi'glia** (kä·vē'lyä), **Enrico. 1862–1945. Italian army** officer; lieutenant general commanding corps which broke Austrian lines on Bainsizza plateau (1917); commanded army which shared in victory of Vittorio Veneto (1918); general (1919); expelled D'Annunzio from Fiume (Dec., 1920).

**Ca·vour'** (kä·vo͞or'), Conte **Camillo Ben'so di** (bĕn'sō dē). 1810–1861. Italian statesman, b. Turin. Educ. Turin military academy; lieutenant of engineers (1826–31); retired to family estate at Leri, Piedmont, and devoted himself to agriculture and travel (to 1847). Founded, with Count Cesare Balbo, *Il Risorgimento*, organ for Italian national movement (1847); took part in war against Austria (1848); after Piedmont was granted new constitution, became member of chamber of deputies, Sardinia (1848). Premier (1852–59); joined alliance of France, England, and Turkey against Russia (1854); dispatched Sardinian troops under La Marmora to Crimea (1855); gained admission of Sardinia to Congress of Paris (1856); formed alliance with Napoleon III against Austria (Plombières, 1858); assumed ministry of war (1859) during Italian War; resigned premiership after Napoleon's private peace with Austria at Villafranca (1859). Again premier (1860–61); ceded Nice and Savoy to France in return for unification of northern Italy; secretly aided Garibaldi in Sicilian expedition (1860); secured union of central and southern Italy (except Rome and Venetia) to Piedmont through plebiscites. His works have been published as *Opere Politico-Economiche del Conte Camillo di Cavour* (1855), *Discorsi Parlementari del Conte Camillo di Cavour* (1863–80).

**Caw'drey** (kô'drĭ), **Robert.** fl. 1604. English lexicographer; published *The Table Alphabetical of Hard Words* (1604).

**Ca·wein'** (kȧ·wīn'), **Madison Julius.** 1865–1914. American poet, b. Louisville, Ky. Author of *Blooms of the Berry* (1887), *Lyrics and Idyls* (1890), *Poems of Nature and Love* (1893), *Shapes and Shadows* (1898), *Kentucky Poems* (1902), etc.

**Ca·xi'as** (kȧ·shē'ȧs), Duque **de. Luiz Alves de Li'ma e Sil'va** (thĕ lē'mȧ ē sĭl'vȧ). 1803–1880. Brazilian general and statesman, b. Rio de Janeiro. Commander in chief of Brazilian army in war against Argentina (1851–52); as marshal (1862), commanded forces in successful war against Paraguay (1866–69); made duke by Emperor Dom Pedro I. Prime minister (1850, 1856–57, 1861–62, 1875–78). See Francisco de LIMA E SILVA.

**Cax'ton** (kăks'tŭn), **William.** 1422?–1491. First English printer. Apprenticed (1438) to London silk merchant; merchant on his own account at Bruges (1446–70); as governor of English merchants in Low Countries (1465–69), negotiated commercial treaties with dukes of Burgundy. Translated popular medieval romance *The Recuyell of the Historyes of Troye* (1469–71), finished at request of Duchess Margaret of Burgundy, sister of Edward IV. Learned printing in Cologne (1471–72); set up press, in partnership with Colard Mansion; printed his *Recuyell*...(1474 or 1475) and another translation, *The Game and Playe of the Chesse;* returned to England (1476); established press at Westminster; issued an indulgence by Abbot Sant (1476), first known piece of printing from Caxton press in England; issued (1477) first dated book printed in England, Earl Rivers's *The Dictes and Sayings of the Philosophers* (a translation from the French); contributed an eighth book to Higden's *Polychronicon* (revising John de Trevisa's work and bringing narrative to 1460).

**Cay'ley** (kā'lĭ), **Arthur.** 1821–1895. English mathematician; educ. Cambridge (1842); called to bar (1849); Sadlerian professor of pure mathematics, Cambridge (1863–95). Contributed in 966 mathematical papers new theories, as his theory of matrices, a new subject, abstract geometry, and additions to existing theories; also contributed to theoretical dynamics and spherical and physical astronomy. His brother **Charles Bagot** (1823–1883), b. near St. Petersburg; educ. London and Cambridge; known for his translations in verse of Dante (1851), Aeschylus (1867), Homer (1877), Petrarch (1879).

**Cay'lus'** (kā'lüs'), Comtesse **de. Marie Marguerite Le Va'lois' de Vil'lette' de Mur'çay'** (lē vȧ'lwȧ' dē vē'lĕt' dē mür'sā'). 1673–1729. Niece of Mme. de Maintenon; m. comte de Caylus (1686; d. 1704). Her son **Anne Claude Philippe de Tu'bières'** (tü'byâr'), Comte **de Caylus** (1692–1765), was an archaeologist; published *Recueil d'Antiquités Egyptiennes, Étrusques,*

*Grecques, Romaines, et Gauloises* (7 vols., 1752–67); interested also in art and engraving.

**Ca'za'lès'** (kȧ'zȧ'lĕs'), **Jacques Antoine Marie de.** 1758–1805. French politician; deputy of the nobility in States-General (1789); defended royal authority; member of National Assembly; joined Mirabeau in effort to organize conservative liberal party; émigré (1792–1803).

**Ca'za'lis'** (kȧ'zȧ'lēs'), **Henry.** *Pseudonyms* **Jean Ca·sel'li** (kä·sĕl'lē; kȧ'zĕ'lē') and **Jean La'hor'** (lȧ'ôr'). 1840–1909. French physician and poet; author of *Chants Populaires de l'Italie* (1865), *L'Illusion* (1875–93), etc. Wrote also *Histoire de la Littérature Hindoue*, and treatises on medical subjects.

**Ca'za'mian'** (kȧ'zȧ'myäN'), **Louis.** 1877–1965. French scholar and authority on English literature; professor at Sorbonne, Paris (from 1909). Author of *Modern England* (1911), *Histoire de la Littérature Anglaise* (with Émile Legouis; 1924), *Essais en Deux Langues* (1939), etc.

**Ca'zin'** (kȧ'zăN'), **Jean Charles.** 1841–1901. French painter and ceramic artist. Director, École des Beaux-Arts, Paris (1868); to England (1871), designed ceramics for Fulham pottery. Best known for his landscapes, as *Souvenir de Fête, The Journey's End, The Marne, The Bathers*, and for religious works, including *Judith, Tobit*, and *Hagar and Ishmael.*

**Ca'zotte'** (kȧ'zôt'), **Jacques.** 1719–1792. French writer; author of *Le Diable Amoureux* (1772), and of a continuation of *The Arabian Nights* centering about an imaginary submarine meeting place (Domdaniel) near Tunis. Guillotined in Paris as a Royalist (1792).

**Cead'da** (chă'ȧd·dȧ) *or* **Chad** (chăd), Saint. d. 672. English prelate. An Angle of Northumbria; succeeded Cedd (*q.v.*) as bishop of East Saxons (664); bishop of Lindisfarne (see later removed to York; 665?–669); bishop of Mercians (c. 670); died of plague.

**Ce·án'–Ber·mú'dez** (thȧ·äm'bĕr·mōō'thāth), **Juan Agustín.** 1749–1829. Spanish art historian and painter, b. Gijón; author of *Diccionario Histórico de los Más Ilustres Profesores de las Bellas Artes en España* (6 vols., 1800), etc.

**Cé'ard'** (sā'ȧr'), **Henri.** 1851–1924. French novelist and playwright.

**Ce'bes** (sē'bēz). fl. 5th century B.C. Greek philosopher, of Thebes; disciple and friend of Socrates. An interlocutor in Plato's *Phaedo.*

**Cebes of Cyz'i·cus** (sĭz'ĭ·kŭs). Greek Stoic philosopher of 2d century A.D.

**Cec'chi** (chāk'kē), **Giovanni Maria.** 1518–1587. Italian dramatist; wrote religious plays and comedies.

**Cec'co d'A'sco·li** (chāk'kō däs'kō·lē). *Popular name of* **Francesco de'gli Sta'bi·li** (dā'lyē stä'bē·lē). c. 1257–1327. Italian poet and philosopher, b. Ascoli; professor of astrology, U. of Bologna (1322); burned at stake for heresy. Author of a commentary on Sacrobosco's *Sphaera Mundi* and of *L'Acerba*, an encyclopedic poem attacking Dante's *Divina Commedia.*

**Čech** (chĕK), **Svatopluk.** 1846–1908. Czech poet. Educ. Prague; influenced by Byron; representative of distinctly national poetry. His verse includes epics (as *The Adamites, The Angels*, and *The Dreams*), satires, and lyrics.

**Cec'il** (sĕs''l; sĕs'ĭl; sĭs''l). An English family descended from David Cyssell or Sisseld or Cecill, sheriff of Northamptonshire (1532–33) and three times M.P., through his grandson William Cecil, Lord Burghley (see below), whose two sons were founders of two branches of the family, the elder line comprising the earls and marquises of **Ex'e·ter** (ĕk'sē·tēr), the younger line the earls and marquises of **Salis'bur·y** (sôlz'bĕr·ĭ; -brĭ).

**William Cecil** (1520–1598), 1st Baron **Burgh'ley,** *sometimes* **Bur'leigh** (bûr'lĭ). Statesman; educ. Cambridge (1535–41); secretary to lord protector, Somerset; as secretary of state (1550–53), abolished some commercial monopolies; during reign of Queen Mary, conformed to Roman Catholicism and escorted Cardinal Pole from Brussels (1554). As chief secretary of state (1558–72) became the shrewd originator and cautious director of Elizabeth I's policy; organized a network of spies to detect plots against the queen (1570); cr. (1571) Baron Burghley of Burghley (or Burleigh); lord high treasurer (1572–98); assumed responsibility for execution of Mary, Queen of Scots (1587). Succeeded as queen's adviser by his son Robert Cecil (see below).

ELDER LINE:

**Thomas Cecil** (1542–1623), 1st Earl of Exeter and 2d Baron Burghley; son of 1st baron by his first wife, sister of the Greek scholar Sir John Cheke. Soldier; served in Scotland (1573), in Low Countries (1585), against Armada (1588); helped crush rising under earl of Essex (1601).

Sir **Edward** (1572–1638), Viscount **Wim'ble·don** (wĭm'b'l·dŭn); 3d son of 2d baron; held various commands in Low Countries (1596–1610); bungled Spanish expedition (1625), letting treasure ships reach Cadiz; avoided censure as favorite of Buckingham. The 10th earl of Exeter was created marquis of Exeter (1801).

**David George Brown'low Cecil** [broun'lō] (1905– ), Lord Burghley; son and heir of 5th marquis of Exeter; educ. Cambridge; track athlete; M.P. (1931–43); parliamentary secretary; with ministry of aircraft production (1942–43); governor of Bermuda (1943–45).

YOUNGER LINE:

**Robert Cecil** (1563?–1612), 1st Earl of Salisbury and 1st Viscount **Cran'borne** (krăn'bôrn); son of 1st Baron Burghley by his second wife, dau. of Sir Anthony Cooke, ecclesiastical commissioner. Statesman; conducted foreign affairs as secretary of state (1596–1608); secured accession of James VI of Scotland to English throne (1603) as James I; continued as secretary and chief minister under James I, in charge of administration of national affairs; lord treasurer (1608); often called "crooked-backed earl."

**Robert Arthur Talbot Gas'coyne–Cec'il** [găs'koin-] (1830–1903), 3d Marquis of Salisbury. Statesman; B.A., Oxon. (1849); wrote pungent articles for *Quarterly Review* (from 1860); secretary for India (1866–67, 1874–78), for foreign affairs (1878); leader of opposition in House of Lords on death of Beaconsfield (1881); helped defeat Gladstone's home-rule bill (1893); opponent of democracy and radical ideas of progress. Prime minister and foreign secretary (1885–86, 1886–92, 1895–1902); followed imperialist but cautiously conciliatory policy; annexed Burma; strengthened hold on Upper Nile and Zanzibar; secured open door in China; reconquered Sudan (1896); refused to avenge Armenian massacres (1897); retired, after conducting Boer War (1902), in favor of his nephew A. J. Balfour.

**James Edward Hubert Gascoyne–Cecil** (1861–1947), 4th marquis; eldest son of 3d marquis. Tory leader; educ. Oxford; M.P. (1885); served in Boer War; lord privy seal (1903–05); president of Board of Trade (1905); joined diehards in struggle over Parliament bill; critical of coalition government in World War; lord president of council (1922–23); lord privy seal (1924–29); leader of House of Lords (1925–29).

**Robert,** *in full* **Edgar Algernon Robert, Cecil** (1864–1958), 1st Viscount **Cecil of Chel'wood** (chĕl'wŏŏd); 3d son of 3d marquis. Educ. Oxford; M.P. (1906–23), opposed to Joseph Chamberlain's tariff policy; minister of blockade (1916–18); asst. secretary of state for foreign affairs (1918); participated in drafting League of Nations Covenant. Member of Stanley Baldwin's first and second cabinets; representative on disarmament committee at Geneva, resigned from cabinet because of failure of cabinet to support compromise of cruiser question with U.S. (1927); president of League of Nations Union. Awarded Nobel peace prize (1937). Author of *Our National Church* and *The Way of Peace* (1928).

Lord **Hugh Richard Heathcote Cecil** (1869–1956), 5th son of 3d marquis. B.A., Oxon. (1891); M.P. (1895–1906, 1910–37); with Winston Churchill, headed group of independents in House of Commons; resisted tariff reform, limitation of powers of House of Lords, and the Parliament bill; member of Royal Flying Corps (1915); spoke with authority on ecclesiastical questions and Church of England prayer-book proposals; provost of Eton (1936)

**Robert Arthur James Gascoyne-Cecil** (1893–1972), 5th marquis, eldest son of 4th marquis; secretary of state for dominion affairs (1940–42, 1943–45); leader of House of Lords (1942–45, 1951–57); lord president of the Council (1952–57). His brother Lord **Edward Christian David Cecil** (1902– ), writer; author of *Sir Walter Scott* (1933), *Early Victorian Novelists* (1934), *Jane Austen* (1935), *The Young Melbourne* (1939).

**Ce·cil'i·a** (sē·sĭl'ĭ·ȧ; -sĭl'yȧ; sē·sēl'-), Saint. d. 230 (or, according to some, 176). Christian martyr, b. Rome. In spite of vow of celibacy, was compelled to marry young nobleman; converted husband to Christianity and with him suffered martyrdom. According to legend, she both sang and played musical instruments; hence, she is patron saint of music.

**Cedd** (chĕd) *or* **Ced'da** (chĕd'dȧ), Saint. d. 664. English prelate; brother of St. Ceadda (*q.v.*). Christianized East Saxons; bishop of East Saxons (654); founded and ruled monastery at Lastingham, Yorkshire; attended council of Whitby (664); died of plague.

**Ceiriog.** See John Ceiriog HUGHES.

**Ce'ja·dor' y Frau'ca** (thĕ'hä·thôr' ē frou'kä), **Julio.** 1864–1927. Spanish Hispanic philologist, b. Saragossa; author of *La Lengua de Cervantes* (1905), *Fraseología o Estilística Castellana* (4 vols., 1921–25), etc.

**Če'la·kov'ský** (chĕ'lȧ·kôf'skē), **František Ladislav.** 1799–1852. Bohemian poet; published collection of Slavic folk songs (1822–27), *Centifolia* (1840), etc. His son **Ladislav** (1834–1902), botanist, professor at Prague (1882), wrote *Prodromus der Flora von Böhmen* (1867–81), *Die Gymnospermen* (1890), etc.

**Celano, Thomas of.** See THOMAS OF CELANO.

**Cé'leste'** (sā'lĕst'), Mme. 1815–1882. French dancer and actress in England and America.

**Cel'es·tine** (sĕl'ĕs·tīn; sē·lĕs'tĭn, -tīn). Name of five popes (see *Table of Popes*, Nos. 43, 165, 175, 179, 192), especially:

**Celestine I,** Saint. d. 432. Pope (bishop of Rome; 422–432); convoked Council of Ephesus (431) which condemned the Nestorian heresy; reputed to have sent Palladius (431) and Saint Patrick (432) as missionaries to Ireland.

**Celestine III.** *Real name* **Giacinto Bo·bo'ne** (bō-bō'nā). 1106?–1198. Crowned Henry VI of Germany emperor (1191); confirmed statutes of the Teutonic Order of Knights (1192).

**Celestine V,** Saint. *Real name* **Pietro di Mur·ro'ne** (mo͝or·rō'nā) *or* **Mo·ro'ne** (mō·rō'nā). 1215–1296. Benedictine monk; lived many years as a hermit; founded order of Celestines (c. 1254); elected pope (1294) at age of eighty; resigned after five months; kept in confinement by Boniface VIII to prevent a schism.

An antipope (1124) also was known as **Celestine II.**

**Céline, Louis-Ferdinand.** See Louis Fuch DESTOUCHES.

**Cel'lier** (?sĕl'yā), **Alfred.** 1844–1891. English composer, esp. of light operas.

**Cel·li'ni** (chĕ·lē'nē; *Ital.* chāl·lē'nē), **Benvenuto.** 1500–1571. Italian goldsmith and sculptor, b. Florence. Pupil of Michelangelo, Bandinelli, and Marconi; banished from Florence as result of duel (1523); employed at Rome; protégé of Clement VII; worked under Michelangelo; to France in service of Francis I (1540); returned to Florence as protégé of Cosimo de' Medici (1545). Works include bronze relief *Nymph of Fontainebleau* (Louvre), bronze busts of Cosimo de' Medici (National Museum, Florence) and Bindo Aldoviti (Gardner collection, Boston), life-size *Crucifixion* (Escorial), gold saltcellar of Francis I (Vienna museum), many decorative works in gold, designs for medals, coins, etc. His *Autobiography*, invaluable as record of Renaissance life in Italy, is a classic of Italian literature.

**Cé'lo'ron' de Blain'ville'** (sā'lô'rôN' dē blăN'vēl'), **Pierre Joseph de.** 1693–1759. French officer and explorer in America, b. Montreal. Commandant of post at Michilimackinac (1734–42); headed expedition (1749) which went down Ohio River, nailing signs to trees and burying lead plates along riverbanks with inscriptions asserting French sovereignty over region; in command at Detroit (1750–53); died of wounds.

**Cel'si·us** (sĕl'sĭ·ŭs; -shĭ·ŭs; *Swed.* sĕl'sĭ·ŭs), **Anders.** 1701–1744. Swedish astronomer, b. Uppsala. Professor, Uppsala (1730–44); builder and director of observatory at Uppsala (1740); published collections of observations by himself and others on the aurora borealis (1733); on French expedition to measure degree of meridian in polar regions (1736); advocated introduction of Gregorian calendar; first to describe (1742) centigrade thermometer, hence also called *Celsius thermometer.*

His uncle **Olaf Celsius** (1670–1756), professor of theology and Oriental languages at Uppsala; also a botanist, teacher of Linnaeus, and authority on plants mentioned in Bible. His son **Olaf** (1716–1794), professor of history, U. of Uppsala (1747), and bishop of Lund (1777).

**Cel'so de As·sis' Fi·guei·re'do** (sĕl'so͞o thē ȧ·sēs' fē-gā·ē·rā'tho͞o), Conde **Affonso.** 1860–1938. Brazilian writer and historian. Dean, faculty of law, Rio de Janeiro. Author of several volumes of verse and of *O Imperador no Exilio* (1893), *Guerrilhas* (1895), *Giovannina* (play, 1896), *Imitação de Cristo* (1898), *Oito Anos de Parlamento...*, and *Páginas Avulsas* (1928).

**Cel'sus** (sĕl'sŭs). Platonist philosopher of 2d century A.D.; author of first notable attack on Christianity, in his *True Word* or *True Account*, answered by Origen (*q.v.*) in his *Contra Celsum.*

**Celsus, Aulus Cornelius.** Roman writer of early 1st century A.D.; compiler of an encyclopedia on agriculture, medicine, military science, law, and philosophy, of which only the 8 books on medicine are extant.

**Celsus, Publius Juventius.** 67?–?130 A.D. Roman jurist, whose works (now lost) were often quoted by other legal authorities.

**Cel'tis** (tsĕl'tĭs; *as Lat.*, sĕl'-) *or* **Cel'tes** (tsĕl'tĕs; sĕl'-tēz), **Con·ra'dus** (kôn·rä'do͝os; *Lat.* kŏn·rā'dŭs). *Original name* **Konrad Pick'el** (pĭk'ĕl). 1459–1508. German humanist and poet (in Latin). Studied under Agricola in Heidelberg; professor at Ingolstadt (1492–97) and Vienna (from 1497); promoted and systematized study of classics, esp. Greek; discovered Peutingerian table (cf. Konrad PEUTINGER) and the Latin plays of Roswitha (*q.v.*). His works include *Ars Versificandi et Carminum* (1486), verse, as in *Amores* (1502) and *Oden* (1513), histories, notably of Nuremberg, and editions of classical authors.

**Cen′ci** (chĕn′chē), **Beatrice.** 1577–1599. Young Roman woman, daughter of **Francesco Cenci** (1549–1598), a man of great wealth but cruel and vicious nature; suffered much from her father's brutality; conspired with her brother and stepmother to secure father's death. Francesco was killed in his bed (Sept. 9, 1598) by Beatrice's friend Olimpio Calvetti and a hired assassin; Cenci family arrested and finally confessed the crime; were refused pardon by pope, despite efforts to obtain mercy for them; all executed (Sept. 11, 1599). Beatrice and her story have been the subject of a number of literary works, including a tragedy by Shelley and a novel by Guerrazzi.

**Cen′drars′** (säɴ′drȧr′), **Blaise.** 1887–1961. French poet and fiction writer; author of *Séquences* (1912), *L'Or...* (1925), *Rhum* (1930), *Hors la Loi* (1936), *La Vie Dangereuse* (1938), etc.

**Cen·ni′ni** (chān·nē′nē), **Cennino.** c. 1370–c. 1440. Italian painter; known chiefly for his treatise on 14th-century painting *Trattato della Pittura* (1437, pub. 1821).

**Cen′so·ri′nus** (sĕn′sō·rī′nŭs). Roman scholar of 3d century A.D., whose only extant work is *De Die Natali* (238 A.D.).

**Cen·te′no Val′le·nil′la** (sān·tā′nō vä′yȧ·nē′yä), **Pedro.** 1904– . Venezuelan painter and diplomat.

**Cent·liv′re** (sĕnt·lĭv′ẽr; -lē′vẽr), **Susanna.** 1667?–1723. English dramatist and actress. Left a widow at 17, wrote plays, her first a tragedy, *The Perjured Husband* (1700); appeared first in her own comedy *Love at a Venture* (1706); m. (1706) Joseph Centlivre, chief cook to Queen Anne; wrote among her comedies *The Gamester* (1705), *The Busy Body* (1709), *A Bold Stroke for a Wife*, one of the characters in which is Simon Pure (1718), *The Wonder! a Woman Keeps a Secret* (1714).

**Cen′tu·rión′** (sān′tōō·ryôn′), **Emilio.** 1894– . Argentine painter. Professor of drawing (1920–38) and director (from 1938), National Preparatory School of Fine Arts; professor, National Acad. of Fine Arts (1922–31).

**Ceph′i·sod′o·tus** (sĕf′ĭ·sŏd′ō·tŭs). Name of two Greek sculptors of 4th century B.C.: Cephisodotus the Elder, a close relative of Praxiteles; Cephisodotus the Younger, a son of Praxiteles.

**Ce′po·la** (chā′pō·lä; *sometimes Anglicized* sĕp′ō·lȧ), **Bartolommeo.** 15th-century Italian lawyer; author of a treatise on legal technicalities which gave rise to phrase *devices of Cepola*, to designate "technical devices, evasions, and quibbles for dragging out law suits and circumventing laws" (*Webster's New International Dictionary, 2d Ed.*).

**Ce·rac′chi** (chā·räk′kē), **Giuseppe.** c. 1751–1802. Italian sculptor, in Rome, London (1775 ff.), U.S. (1790 ff.), Austria, Paris (1796 ff.); involved in conspiracy against life of Napoleon (Paris, 1800); executed with fellow conspirators (1802). His works include portrait busts of Sir Joshua Reynolds, George Washington (in Boston Athenaeum), Benjamin Franklin (in Penn. Academy), and Alexander Hamilton (in Penn. Academy; replica in American Hall of Fame).

**Cerano, Il.** See Giovanni Battista CRESPI.

**Ceraunus.** See PTOLEMY KERAUNOS.

**Cer′dic** (chĕr′dĭch). d. 534. Founder of West Saxon kingdom. Landed near Southampton (495); defeated Britons (508) and at Charford, Hampshire (519); conquered Isle of Wight (530).

**Cer′do** (sûr′dō). 2d-century Syrian Gnostic, founder of sect known as Cerdonians. Cf. MARCION.

**Ce′re·a′lis** (sẹ̄r′ē·ā′lĭs), **Petillius.** Roman general; related to emperor Vespasian; as consul, suppressed revolt of Civilis (70 A.D.); governor of Britain (71), where he defeated the Brigantes.

**Ce·re′zo** (thȧ·rā′thō), **Mateo.** 1635–1685. Spanish painter; b. Burgos; leading representative of Madrid school; works include *Ascension of the Virgin* and *Betrothal of St. Catharine* (the Prado), *Saint Jerome* (Leipzig), and *Christ in Agony* (Burgos Cathedral).

**Ce·rin′thus** (sē·rĭn′thŭs). Heresiarch of 1st century A.D., probably of Syria; founder of sect whose members were known as Cerinthians.

**Cer′mak** (sûr′măk), **An′ton** (ăn′tŏn) **Jo′seph** (jō′zĕf; -zĭf). 1873–1933. American politician, b. Prague, Bohemia; to U.S. as infant. In real estate business, Chicago (1908–33); mayor of Chicago (1931–33). Fatally wounded (Feb. 15, 1933; died Mar. 6) in Miami, Fla., by bullet intended for President-elect F. D. Roosevelt.

**Cer·nu′schi** (chȧr·nōōs′kē), **Enrico.** 1821–1896. Italian economist; to France (1850) after participating in nationalist insurrections (Milan, 1848; Rome, 1849); a director of Bank of Paris; known esp. as champion of bimetallism.

**Cer·nu′schi** (chȧr·nōōs′kē; *sometimes Hispanicized* sȧr-nōōs′chē), **Félix.** 1907– . Argentine physicist, b. Montevideo, Uruguay; Ph.D., Cantab. (1938). Professor, U. of Tucumán, Argentina. Among his articles published in scientific journals are *Sur les Neutrons* (1937), *An Elementary Theory of Condensation* (1939), *Super-Novae in the Neutron-Core Stars* (1939), *A Tentative Theory of the Origin of Cosmic Rays* (1939), *On the Behavior of Matter at Extremely High Temperatures and Pressures* (1939).

**Cerny, Frederick.** Pseudonym of Frederick GUTHRIE.

**Cerrito, Francesca.** See under Charles SAINT-LÉON.

**Cerro, Luis M. Sánchez.** See SÁNCHEZ CERRO.

**Cerularius, Michael.** See CAERULARIUS.

**Cer·van′tes Sa′a·ve′dra** (thĕr·vän′tās sä′ä·vā′thrä; *Angl.* sẽr·văn′tēz), **Miguel de.** 1547–1616. Spanish novelist, b. Alcalá de Henares. Said to have studied under Jesuits at Seville (1564–65) and at U. of Salamanca (c. 1582–84). At Rome (1569); in service of Cardinal Giulio Acquaviva (c. 1570–74); left hand maimed in battle of Lepanto (1571)—hence nicknamed **El Man′co** [*i.e.*, "the handless one"] **de Le·pan′to** (ĕl mäng′kō thȧ lȧ·pän′tō); served also in engagements at Navarino, Corfu, and Tunis; garrisoned at Palermo (1574); captured by Algerian pirates while returning to Spain (1575); held for ransom, Algeria (1575–80). To Madrid (1580); m. Catalina de Salazar y Palacios (1584); essayed play writing (to 1587); commissary of Seville (1588–93); tax collector, Granada (1594–97); imprisoned for three months (1597); at Valladolid (1604–05); protégé of count of Lemos (1613 ff.); tertiary of Saint Francis, Alcalá de Henares (1613 ff.). His masterpiece is *Don Quixote* (*Don Quijote de la Mancha;* part I, 1605; part II, 1615), novel burlesquing chivalric romances of the day. His minor works include the pastoral novel *Galatea* (1585), many early plays (two extant: *El Trato de Argel* and *La Numancia*), *Novelas Ejemplares* (12 tales; 1613), *Viaje al Parnaso* (rhymed criticism of contemporary poets; 1614), *Ocho Comedias y Ocho Entremeses Nuevos, Nunca Representados* (1615), *Pérsiles y Sigismunda* (1616), and many poems, esp. sonnets.

**Cer·ve′ra y To·pe′te** (thĕr·vā′rä ē tō·pā′tā), **Pascual.** Conde **de Je·rez′** (hȧ·rāth′). Marqués **de San′ta A′na** (sän′tä ä′nä). 1839–1909. Spanish naval commander, b. Medina-Sidonia. Educ. naval academy at San Fernando (1848–51); naval officer in Morocco (1859), Philippines, Cuba (1868–78), etc.; minister of marine; admiral; adjutant to queen regent; head of Spanish commission to London naval conference (1891). Commander of Spanish squadron in Spanish-American War (1898); defeated and taken prisoner in attempt to break American blockade in harbor of Santiago de Cuba (July 3, 1898); returned to Spain (Sept., 1898). Vice-admiral (1901); chief of staff, Spanish navy (1902); senator (1903 ff.).

**Ce'sal·pi'no** (chā'zäl·pē'nō), **Andrea.** *Lat.* **Andreas Caes'al·pi'nus** (sĕz'ăl·pī'nŭs; sĕs'-). 1519–1603. Italian philosopher, botanist, and physician. Professor of materia medica and director of botanical garden, Pisa (1555). Anticipated Linnaean system of classification in his *De Plantis* (1583), to which Linnaeus acknowledged indebtedness.

**Cesare, Carlo de.** See DE CESARE.

**Ce'sa·ri** (chā'zä·rē), **Antonio.** 1760–1828. Italian lexicographer; Oratorian; champion of Renaissance purity in language; works include an augmented re-edition of the *Vocabolario della Crusca* (1806–09), *Le Bellezze di Dante* (1824–26), and translations from the classics.

**Cesari, Giuseppe.** Cavaliere **d'Ar·pi'no** (där·pē'nō). *Called* **Il Giu'sep·pi'no** (ēl jōō'zāp·pē'nō). 1568?–1640. Italian painter; representative of a manneristic school distinct from the Carraccis' Eclectic school and Caravaggio's naturalistic school. His works include *Ascension* in church of St. John Lateran, frescoes in the Capitol and in Borghese chapel of Santa Maria Maggiore (Rome), cartoons for mosaics in dome of St. Peter's.

**Ce'sa·ri'ni** (chā'zä·rē'nē), Cardinal **Giuliano.** *Known as* Cardinal **Jul'ian** (jōōl'yăn). 1398–1444. Italian ecclesiastical diplomat. Counselor to Pope Martin V; cardinal (1426); preached and led unsuccessful crusade against Hussites (1431). President, Council of Basel (1431 ff.); prominent in negotiations at Council of Ferrara-Florence (1438 ff.); legate to Poland from Pope Eugene IV to incite crusade against Turks; killed in ensuing battle of Varna (1444).

**Cesarion.** See PTOLEMY XIV.

**Ce'sa·rot'ti** (chā'zä·rôt'tē), **Melchiorre.** 1730–1808. Italian poet; professor of Hebrew and Greek, Padua (1768 ff.); influenced Italian literature by his translation of Macpherson's *Ossian* (1763); among his other works are *Pronea*, *Saggio sulla Filosofia delle Lingue* (1785), and translations, as of Homer's *Iliad*.

**Ces·no'la** (chāz·nô'lä), **Luigi Palma di.** 1832–1904. Army officer and archaeologist, b. near Turin, Italy. Officer in Italian army (1849–59); to U.S. (c. 1860); served in Union army through Civil War; awarded Congressional Medal of Honor; naturalized (1865). U.S. consul, Cyprus (1865–76); explored ruins on Cyprus; his collection of archaeological objects purchased by Metropolitan Museum of Art, New York City. Director, Metropolitan Museum (1879–1904).

**Cés'pe·des** (sās'pā·thās), **Carlos Manuel de.** 1819–1874. Cuban revolutionist, b. Bayamo. Finished education in Spain; took part in Prim y Prats' revolution (1843); after return to Cuba led armed revolt (1868), which began Ten Years' War; elected president of revolutionists (1869); deposed (1873), after growing discontent; killed (1874), probably by Spanish soldiers. His son **Carlos Manuel de Céspedes y Que·sa'da** [ē kā-sä'thä] (1871–1939), lawyer and diplomat (at Washington, 1913–22); provisional president of Cuba (Aug. 12–Sept. 5, 1933).

**Cés'pe·des** (thās'pā·thās), **Pablo de.** 1538–1608. Spanish painter and writer, b. Córdoba; author of *Arte de la Pintura* (poem; 1649); his paintings include *Last Supper* (in Córdoba cathedral and in Seville museum), *Ascension of Christ* (in Madrid Academy), and frescoes in Seville Cathedral.

**Ce'sti** (chās'tē), **Marc'Antonio.** 1623–1669. Italian composer; Kapellmeister, Florence (1646 ff.); assistant Kapellmeister to Leopold I, Vienna (1666–69). His works include operas, as *Il Pomo d'Oro* (1667), and cantatas known particularly as first to be performed on stage.

**Ces'ti·us** (sĕs'tĭ·ŭs), **Gaius.** Roman praetor and tribune of the people; his tomb, known as the Pyramid of Cestius, stands near the gate of St. Paul, Rome. Keats and Shelley were buried nearby.

**Cet'e·way'o** (sĕt'ē·wā'ō; kĕt-; *Zulu* kĕ·chwä'yō). *Also* **Cet'y·way'o** *or* **Cet'ti·way'o** *or* **Ke·tchwa'yo** (kĕ-chwä'yō) *or* **Ke·tshwa'yo** (-chwä'-). d. 1884. Zulu chief recognized as king by British (1872) but who rebelled (1878) against British rule, the Zulus destroying a British regiment at Isandhlwana (or Isandula) (1879); captured (1879), held prisoner in Cape of Good Hope (1879–82), and taken to England (1882); attempt by British government to reinstate him as king of the Zulus failed.

**Ce·the'gus** (sē·thē'gŭs), **Gaius Cornelius.** Roman politician of 1st century B.C.; involved in Catiline's conspiracy; executed (Dec. 5, 63 B.C.).

**Cethegus, Marcus Cornelius.** d. 196 B.C. Roman general and politician; consul (204). As proconsul in Cisalpine Gaul (203), helped in defeating Hannibal's brother Mago and driving his Carthaginian army from Italy.

**Ce·ti'na** (thā·tē'nä), **Gutierre de.** c. 1520–c. 1570. Spanish lyric poet, b. Seville; a leading Spanish Petrarchist; known esp. for his madrigal *Ojos Claros Serenos*.

**Ceu'len** (kû'lĕn), **Cornelius Janssen van.** See JANSSEN VAN CEULEN.

**Ceu'len** *or* **Keu'len** (kû'lĕn), **Ludolph van.** 1540–1610. Dutch mathematician; professor of fortification at Leiden; known for computations of the value of $\pi$ (*Ludolphian*, or *Ludolph's*, *number*), which he finally carried to 35 decimal places.

**Ce'va** (châ'vä), **Giovanni** (1647?–?1734) and his brother **Tommaso** (1648–1736). Italian mathematicians; Giovanni originated *Ceva's theorem* (which concerns lines through the vertices of a triangle); Tommaso wrote *Opuscula Mathematica* (1699) and a Latin poem, *Puer Jesus*.

**Cé'zanne'** (sā'zàn'), **Paul.** 1839–1906. French painter, a leader of postimpressionism, b. Aix-en-Provence. Studio at Aix (from 1879). Excelled in still-life painting and in landscapes. Among his notable works are *Joueurs de Cartes*, *La Maison du Pendu*, *Les Baigneurs*, *Bouquet de Fleurs*, *Scène Champêtre*, *Léda au Cygne*, *La Cour de Village*.

**Cha'ba'neau'** (shà'bà'nō'), **Camille Jean Eugène.** 1831–1908. French philologist; author of... *La Conjugaison Française* (1868), *La Langue et la Littérature du Limousin* (1892), etc.

**Cha'ba'nel'** (shà'bà'nĕl'), **Noël.** 1613–1649. French Jesuit missionary in America; to Canada (1643); assigned to mission among Huron Indians; murdered by a renegade Huron (Dec. 8, 1649). One of group known as Jesuit Martyrs of North America canonized by Pope Pius XI (June 29, 1930).

**Cha'bannes'** (shà'bàn'). Name of an old French family of Limousin, prominent in 15th century; esp.: **Jacques de Chabannes** (1400?–1453), general in Hundred Years' War; served with Joan of Arc under Charles VII; took part in Praguerie revolt (1440); captain of écorcheurs; pardoned and aided in expulsion of English from Normandy and Guienne. His brother **Antoine** (1411?–1488), Comte **de Dam'mar'tin'** (dà'màr'tăN'); general in Hundred Years' War; took part in Praguerie revolt; captain of écorcheurs; presided over commission that procured conviction of Jacques Cœur; loyal officer under Louis XI.

**Cha'bas'** (shà'bàs'), **François Joseph.** 1817–1882. French Egyptologist; known esp. for translations of hieroglyphic and hieratic writings.

**Chabas, Paul Émile.** 1869–1937. French painter; pupil of Bouguereau and Robert-Fleury; among his works are *Crépuscule*, *Nageuse*, and the famous *Matinée de Septembre* (*September Morn*).

**Cha'bot'** (shá'bō'), **François.** 1759–1794. French revolutionist politician. Capuchin monk; withdrew from order at outbreak of French Revolution (1789). Member of Legislative Assembly (1791) and National Convention (1792); a violent extremist; introduced motion to make Notre Dame the "Temple of Reason," and originated term "the Mountain" for extremist group occupying the top seats in the Convention; accused of bribery; condemned with Danton group; guillotined at Paris (Apr. 5, 1794).

**Chabot, Philippe de.** Seigneur **de Bri'on'** (brē'ôN'). Comte **de Char'ny'** (shár'nē'). Marquis **de Bu'san'çois'** (bü'zäN'swá'). 1480–1543. French soldier; defended Marseilles (1524); envoy in Italy (1529) to negotiate ratification of Treaty of Cambrai by Charles V; commander in chief of troops fighting duke of Savoy (1535); reputed to be first to suggest colonization of Canada.

**Cha'bri·as** (kā'brĭ·ăs). d. 357 B.C.? Athenian general; defeated Spartans at Aegina (388 B.C.), and again near Thebes (378); defeated Spartan fleet off Naxos (376); held Athenian naval command at outbreak of Social War (357); killed at siege of Chios.

**Cha'bri'er** (shá'brē'ā'), **Alexis Emmanuel.** 1841–1894. French composer. Compositions include two operettas, *L'Étoile* (1877) and *L'Éducation Manquée* (1879), symphonic work *España* (1883), choral works, operas, piano works, songs, etc.

**Cha·cón'** (chä·kōn'), **Lázaro.** 1873–1931. Guatemalan soldier and politician, b. Teculután. President of Guatemala (1926–30); settled boundary dispute with Honduras.

**Chacón y Cal'vo** (ē käl'vō), **José María.** 1893– . Cuban lawyer, diplomat, and writer; in Madrid as secretary of Cuban legation (1918–26) and embassy (1926–34); head of Dirección de Cultura, in Cuba (from 1937). Author of *Orígenes de la Poésia en Cuba* (1913), *Ensayo de Literatura Cubana* (1922), *Cedulario Cubano, las Orígines de la Colonización* (1929), etc.

**Chacón y Cas'tel·lón'** (käs'tā·yōn'), **Luis.** 1670–?1717. Cuban soldier, b. Havana; captain general of Cuba (1702–06, 1707–08, 1711–13); led expedition (1707) against English in Carolina.

**Cha'cor'nac'** (shá'kôr'nák'), **Jean.** 1828–1873. French astronomer; published (1856) ecliptic atlas of the sky continued by Paul Henry (*q.v.*).

**Chad,** Saint. See CEADDA.

**Chad'bourne** (chăd'bẽrn), **Paul Ansel.** 1823–1883. American educator, b. North Berwick, Me. First president, Mass. Agricultural Coll. (1866–67), again president (1882–83); president, U. of Wisconsin (1867–70); Williams Coll. (1872–81).

**Chad'dock** (chăd'ŭk), **Charles Gilbert.** 1861–1936. American neurologist, b. Jonesville, Mich. M.D., Michigan (1885); studied at Munich and Paris. Professor, St. Louis U. (from 1892). Author of *Outline of Psychiatry.*

**Chad'er·ton** (chăd'ẽr·t'n; -tŭn), **Laurence.** 1536?–1640. English Puritan theologian; son of Roman Catholic gentleman; became Protestant at Cambridge; B.A., Cantab. (1567); chosen by founder to be first master of Emmanuel Coll. (1584–1622); one of translators of Authorized Version of Bible (1607–11).

**Chad'wick** (chăd'wĭk), Sir **Edwin.** 1800–1890. English sanitary reformer. Poor-law commissioner (1833); laid foundation of systems of government inspection by experts; commissioner of board of health (1848–54).

**Chadwick, French Ensor.** 1844–1919. American naval officer, b. Morgantown, Va. (now W.Va.). Chief of staff, under Admiral Sampson, at battle of Santiago de Cuba (July 3, 1898).

**Chadwick, George Alexander.** 1840–1923. Church of England clergyman and poet; ordained (1863); dean of Armagh (1886–96); bishop of Derry and Raphoe (1896–1915). Author of *Poems, Chiefly Sacred* (1900).

**Chadwick, George Whitefield.** 1854–1931. American conductor and composer, b. Lowell, Mass. Studied in Boston and (1877–80) Europe. Organist in Boston; also, director of New England Conservatory of Music (from 1897). Composer of three symphonies, overtures, choral pieces, string quartets, songs, and organ and piano works.

**Chadwick, Hector Munro.** 1870–1947. English philologist; educ. Cambridge; professor of Anglo-Saxon, Cambridge (from 1912). Author of *Studies in Old English* (1899), *Studies in Anglo-Saxon Institutions* (1905), *The Heroic Age* (1912), *An Early Irish Reader* (1927), *Russian Heroic Poetry* (1932).

**Chadwick, Henry.** 1824–1908. Sports writer, b. Exeter, Eng.; to U.S. (1837); on staff of New York *Times*, Brooklyn *Eagle*, New York *Clipper*. Fostered professional baseball; compiled annual baseball handbook (beginning 1869), which later became *Spalding's Official Base Ball Guide.*

**Chadwick,** Sir **James.** 1891–1974. English physicist, b. Manchester. Lecturer and asst. director of radioactive research, Cavendish Laboratory, Cambridge; professor of physics, Univ. of Liverpool (1935–43). Discovered the neutron (1932); awarded 1935 Nobel prize for physics; chief British adviser at Los Alamos (N.M.) laboratory (1943–45).

**Chae're·a** (kēr'ē·ȧ), **Gaius Cassius.** Roman soldier and conspirator; assassin of Emperor Caligula (Jan. 24, 41 A.D.); executed by order of new emperor, Claudius (Jan. 25, 41 A.D.).

**Chae·re'mon** (kē·rē'mŏn). Stoic philosopher and scholar in Alexandria; called to Rome (49 A.D.) to assist in education of Nero; author of a *History of Egypt*, and treatises on astrology, comets, hieroglyphics, etc.

**Chaf'fee** (chăf'ē), **Adna Romanza.** 1842–1914. American army officer, b. Orwell, Ohio. Served through Spanish-American War; commanded American troops in capture of Pekin, China, at time of Boxer rebellion (1900); lieutenant general and chief of staff, U.S. army (1904–06; retired). His son **Adna Romanza** (1884–1941), army officer; grad. U.S.M.A., West Point (1906); staff officer in France in World War I; advocate of mechanized army; organized U.S. army's first mechanized brigade; brigadier general (1938); appointed to organize and command the armored force of U.S. army.

**Cha·gall'** (shŭ·gál'), **Marc.** 1887– . Russian painter, b. Vitebsk; studied under Bakst in St. Petersburg and (1910–14) Paris; to U.S. (1941); returned to France (1948). Identified with impressionist and cubist schools; known esp. for scenes of Russian folk life.

**Cha'gas** (shá'gȧs), **Carlos.** 1879–1934. Brazilian physician and bacteriologist.

**Chagatai.** Variant of JAGATAI.

**Chai·kov'ski** (chī·kôf'skû·ĭ; *Angl.* -skĭ), **Nikolai Vasilievich.** 1850–1926. Russian revolutionist, b. Vyatka; educ. St. Petersburg. At early age became involved in liberal political agitation; took refuge in Kansas, where he founded a community of people "seeking God within themselves"; returned to Europe after its failure; forced to live in exile. After Russian revolution (1917), opposed Bolsheviks; president of northern government on Archangel front; again driven into exile.

**Chaikovski, Pëtr Ilich.** See TCHAIKOVSKY.

**Chail'lé'-Long'** (shȧ'yā'lông'), **Charles.** 1842–1917. American army officer and explorer, b. in Somerset Co., Md. Served in Union army through Civil War. Appointed officer in Egyptian army (1869); chief of staff under General Gordon (1874); sent by khedive on mission to Uganda (1875). Returned to New York; studied law; practiced in Egypt (1882); in Paris (1882–87). U.S. consul general, Korea (1887–89). Author of *Naked Truths of Naked People* (1876), *The Three Prophets: Chinese Gordon, Mohammed-Ahmed (El Maahdi), Arabi Pasha* (1884), *My Life in Four Continents* (1912).

**Chaillu.** See Du Chaillu.

**Chain** (chān), **Ernst Boris.** 1906–1979. English biochemist, b. Germany. Awarded Nobel prize in medicine and physiology (1945) with A. Fleming and H. Florey for their discovery and development of penicillin.

**Chaireddin.** See Barbarossa II.

**Chai·tan'ya** *or* **Cai·tan'ya** (chī·tŭn'yȧ). 1485–1527. Indian mystic, b. Nadia, Bengal. Renounced the world (c. 1510); settled in Orissa, teaching a religious system later adopted by his followers, the Caitanyas, a Vaishnava sect; taught that caste was subordinate to faith in Krishna. Believed by followers to be an incarnation of Krishna.

**Cha'it Singh** (chä'ĭt sĭɴ'hȧ). Raja of Benares (1773–80), a zamindar under British East India Company, which assessed him for large sums annually (1778–80) as war contribution; because of refusal to pay, suspected by Warren Hastings (*q.v.*) of planning revolt; arrested and deposed (1781). This treatment of him figured prominently in trial of Hastings (1788–95).

**Cha·jug'** (kȧ·yōōj'), **Jehuda.** 11th-century Hebrew grammarian, known as the "Prince of Hebrew Grammarians"; his works aided early translators of Bible.

**Cha'ka** (chä'kă). 1773–1828. Zulu chief (1800–28); conqueror of most of southeastern Africa; assassinated.

**Cha'kri'** (chäk'rē'). Dynasty of kings of Siam (Thailand), founded by Chao P'ya Chakri, a pure Siamese, who established order in country after Burmese invasion and ruled as King Rama I (1782–1809). Succeeding rulers: Rama II–VI, Prajadhipok, and Ananda Mahidol.

**Chakste, Jānis.** See Čakste.

**Chal·con'dy·les** (kăl·kŏn'dĭ·lēz) *or* **Chal'co·con'dy·las** (kăl'kô·kŏn'dĭ·lȧs), **Demetrius.** 1424–1511. Greek scholar, b. Athens. To Italy under patronage of Cardinal Bessarion (1447); professor, Padua (1463); called to Florence by Lorenzo de' Medici (1479); taught in Milan (1492). Published editions of Homer, Isocrates, and Suidas; credited with contributing to revival of letters in Italy. His brother **Laonicus** wrote a history of the Byzantine empire from 1298 to 1463.

**Chal'grin'** (shȧl'grăɴ'), **Jean François Thérèse.** 1739–1811. French architect; architect to Monsieur (later Louis XVIII); architect of Luxembourg palace, church of Sainte Philippe du Roule, Collège de France, etc.

**Cha·lia'pin** (shŭ·lyȧ'pyĭn), **Feodor Ivanovitch.** *Russ.* **Feodor Ivanovich Sha·lya'pin** (shŭ·lyȧ'pyĭn). 1873–1938. Russian operatic basso. Sang in St. Petersburg (1894) and in chief cities of Europe and U.S. thereafter; long a member of Metropolitan Opera Co., N.Y. Left Russia (1927); settled in Paris; naturalized. His most successful performances included roles in *Faust*, Glinka's *A Life for the Czar*, Rimski-Korsakov's *Maid of Pskov*, *Sadko*, and *Mozart and Salieri*, Boito's *Mefistofele*, Massenet's *Don Quichotte*, Musorgski's *Boris Godunov*. Well known also as concert singer; credited with popularizing *The Song of the Volga Boatmen* and *The Song of the Flea*.

**Chalk'hill** (chôk'hĭl), **John.** fl. 1600. English poet. Author of a pastoral, *Thealma and Clearchus* (1683), published by Izaak Walton.

**Chal'le·mel'-La'cour'** (shȧl'mĕl'lȧ'kōōr'), **Paul Armand.** 1827–1896. French statesman. Professor of philosophy at Pau (1849), of French literature at Zurich (1856–59). Member, Chamber of Deputies (1873); senator (1876); ambassador to Russia (1879), England (1880); minister of foreign affairs (1883); again senator (1885); president of Senate (1893).

**Chal'lis** (chăl'ĭs), **James.** 1803–1882. English astronomer; educ. Cambridge; Plumian professor of astronomy, Cambridge (1836–82). Using Leverrier's computations, sought unknown planet indicated by behavior of Uranus and actually observed it (Aug. 4, 1846), without knowing it, before its announced discovery as Neptune. Invented a transit reducer (1849) and a meteoroscope (1848); introduced collimating eyepiece (1850).

**Chal'lo·ner** (chăl'ô·nẽr), **Richard.** 1691–1781. English Roman Catholic prelate. Studied at Douai (1704), professor of philosophy (1713–20), of divinity (1720–30); carried on controversy with Conyers Middleton on popery and paganism (1737); coadjutor in London (1741); vicar apostolic in London (1758). Re-edited Douay Bible (1749–50). Author of historical works and *Garden of the Soul* (a popular manual of devotion).

**Chal'mers** (chä'mẽrz), **Alexander.** 1759–1834. Scottish journalist and biographer. M.A., Aberdeen; editor of works of Shakespeare, Fielding, Johnson, Warton, Pope, Gibbon, Bolingbroke; published *General Biographical Dictionary* (32 vols., 1812–17), *Glossary to Shakespeare* (1797).

**Chalmers, George.** 1742–1825. Scottish antiquary. Educ. Aberdeen and Edinburgh; emigrated to Maryland (1763); lawyer in Baltimore (till American Revolution); chief clerk to privy council, London (1786–1825). Author of pamphlets on American colonies (1777–82), and biographies.

**Chalmers, George Paul.** 1836–1878. Scottish portrait and landscape painter.

**Chalmers, James.** 1782–1853. Scottish bookseller; suggested an adhesive postage stamp (1834), claimed invention, but yielded to Sir Rowland Hill priority in making known plans for its use.

**Chalmers, James.** 1841–1901. Scottish missionary to New Guinea; killed and eaten by cannibals at Goaribari Island.

**Chalmers,** Sir **Mackenzie Dalzell.** 1847–1927. English jurist, b. Nonington. Educ. Oxford, called to bar (1869); in Indian civil service (1869–72); practiced in London (from 1872). Best known for his skill in drafting legal codifications for adoption by British Parliament.

**Chalmers, Thomas.** 1780–1847. Scottish theologian and preacher. Gained wide reputation as preacher at Glasgow and as administrator of poor relief; professor of moral philosophy, St. Andrews (1823–28), of theology, Edinburgh (1828–43). Leader of evangelical section of Church of Scotland; led withdrawal of 470 ministers from general assembly to constitute Free Church of Scotland (1843); principal of Free Church Coll., Edinburgh (1843–47). Author of *Institutes of Theology* and philosophical and devotional treatises.

**Chal'mers** (chăl'mẽrz), **Thomas Hardie.** 1884–1966. American operatic baritone, b. New York City; studied in Florence, Italy; member, Metropolitan Opera Company, New York (1917–25). Also actor, as in Ibsen's *Wild Duck* and O'Neill's *Beyond the Horizon* and *Mourning Becomes Electra*, and (from 1927) director and editor of motion pictures and news reels.

**Cha'lon'** (shȧ'lôɴ'). A Burgundian princely house, princes of Orange (*q.v.*). **Philibert de Chalon** (1502–1530), last of the house, entered service of Emperor Charles V to avenge himself on Francis I, who had seized

Orange; won fame at siege of Fuenterrabia (1523); viceroy of Naples (1528); killed at siege of Florence.

**Cha'lon'** (shà'lôN'), **John James** (1778–1854) and his brother **Alfred Edward** (1780–1860). English painters, b. Geneva; John James, landscape and genre painter, is known for his *Napoleon on Board the Bellerophon;* Alfred Edward, miniature painter, for his *John Knox Reproving Queen Mary's Ladies.*

**Chal'o·ner** (chăl'ō·nĕr), Sir **Thomas.** 1521–1565. English diplomat and poet; educ. Oxford and Cambridge; envoy to Scotland (1551, 1552, 1555–56); ambassador to France (1553), to Emperor Ferdinand (1559), to Spain (1561–64); author of Latin verses.

**Chalotais.** See LA CHALOTAIS.

**Cha'luk·ya** (chä'lŏŏk·yȧ). A medieval Hindu dynasty ruling in the Deccan (c. 500–753). Its most famous king, **Pu'la·ke'sin II** [pōō'lȧ·kā'shĭn] (608–642), a contemporary of Harsha, was defeated (642) by the Pallava king (see PALLAVA) Narasimha-varman; later, Chalukyas joined with the Cholas (*q.v.*) and under Vikramaditya II overthrew the Pallavas (740); this early dynasty terminated (753) but eastern Chalukyas ruled (c. 610–c. 1074) at Vengi, near east coast, north of modern Masulipatam; continually at war with Cholas until absorbed by them (c. 1074). Another branch of dynasty was restored to power (973–c. 1190) at Kalyani (western Hyderabad); its most distinguished sovereign was Vikramaditya VI (1075–1125).

**Cham.** Pseudonym of Count Amédée de NOÉ.

**Cham'ber·lain** (chām'bĕr·lĭn), Sir **Austen,** *in full* **Joseph Austen.** 1863–1937. British statesman; eldest son of Joseph Chamberlain (*q.v.*) and half brother of Neville Chamberlain (*q.v.*). Educ. Rugby and Cambridge. His father's secretary during home-rule controversy; Unionist M.P. (1892); civil lord of admiralty (1895–1900); financial secretary to treasury (1900–02); postmaster general (1902); chancellor of exchequer (1903–06); supported father's tariff policy of imperial preference. Secretary of state for India (1915–17); resigned after assuming responsibility for Mesopotamia affair; member of war cabinet (1918). As chancellor of exchequer (1919–21), called for heavy income tax, super tax, excess profits tax; Conservative leader of House of Commons and lord privy seal (1921–23); co-operated with Lloyd George's administration, made settlement with Sinn Fein, urged creation of Irish Free State (1921). Foreign secretary (1924–29); handled with firmness situation upon Sir Lee Stack's murder in Cairo (1924); conducted diplomacy leading to signing of Locarno Pact (1925); awarded Nobel peace prize (jointly with Charles G. Dawes, 1925); attended all meetings of Council and Assembly of League of Nations and facilitated Germany's entry into league (1926); supported Kellogg Peace Pact (1927–28). First lord of admiralty (1931); opposed Four-Power Pact (1933) and revision of Treaty of Versailles. Author of *Peace in Our Time* (1928).

**Chamberlain, Basil Hall.** 1850–1935. English Japanese scholar; professor of Japanese and philology, Imperial U. of Tokio. Author of *The Classical Poetry of the Japanese* (1880), *Handbook of Colloquial Japanese* (4th ed., 1907), *Japanese Poetry* (1910), *Japanese Grammar* (1924), *Things Japanese* (6th ed., 1927), etc.

**Chamberlain, Charles Joseph.** 1863–1943. American botanist, b. Sullivan, Ohio. A.B., Oberlin (1888), Ph.D., Chicago (1897). On teaching staff, U. of Chicago (from 1897); professor (1915–29). Author of *Methods in Plant Histology* (1901), *The Living Cycads* (1919), *Gymnosperms, Structure and Evolution* (1935), etc.

**Chamberlain, George Agnew.** 1879–1966. American novelist, b. São Paulo, Brazil, of American parentage. Educ. Princeton. U.S. consul general, Mexico City, Mexico (1917–19). Author of *Through Stained Glass* (1915), *John Bogardus* (1916), *White Man* (1919), *Cobweb* (1921), *Lost* (a play; 1926), *No Ugly Ducklings* (1927), *When Beggars Ride* (1930), *The Auction* (1932), *Two on Safari* (1934), *In Defense of Mrs. Maxon* (1938), etc.

**Chamberlain, George Earle.** 1854–1928. American politician, b. near Natchez, Miss. Governor of Oregon (1902–09). U.S. senator (1909–21); as chairman, Military Affairs Committee (from 1913), instrumental in putting through measures for selective draft, food control, and war financing.

**Chamberlain, Houston Stewart.** 1855–1927. Publicist, b. Southsea, England; resident at Dresden (1885–89). Vienna (1889–1908), Bayreuth (1908–27); naturalized German citizen (1916); m., 2d (1908), Eva Wagner, daughter of Richard Wagner. Author of *Die Grundlagen des Neunzehnten Jahrhunderts* (1899), translated as *The Foundations of the Nineteenth Century* (2 vols., 1911).

**Chamberlain, John.** 1553–1627. English letter writer, b. London; educ. Cambridge. Collection of his letters (written between 1597 and 1626) edited by Norman Egbert McClure, *The Letters of John Chamberlain* (2 vols., 1939).

**Chamberlain, John Rensselaer.** 1903– . American writer and editor, b. New Haven, Conn. Ph.B., Yale (1925). On staff of New York *Times* (1926–36; book columnist 1933 ff.); book editor, *Scribner's Magazine* (1936–38), *Harper's Magazine* (from 1939). Author of *Farewell to Reform* (1932), *The American Stakes* (1940).

**Chamberlain, Joseph.** 1836–1914. British statesman, b. London. Expanded his father's screw-manufacturing business in Birmingham (1854–74), retired with fortune; championed nonconformist opposition to denominationalism; as mayor of Birmingham (1873–76), campaigned to improve municipal housing and sanitation. M.P. (1876), as John Bright's colleague; prompted reorganization of Liberal party. Member of second Gladstone cabinet; gained passage of act for reforming laws of bankruptcy (1883), Patent Act (1883), Merchant Shipping Bill (1884); opposed coercion in Ireland; negotiated Kilmainham Treaty with Parnell (1882); proposed scheme of semi-home-rule (1885); opposed Irish land purchase bill; resigned. Entered third Gladstone cabinet as president of local government board (1886); resigned on introduction of home-rule bill (1886). Led Liberal Unionists in attempt to force Gladstone to modify home-rule bill; sent to U.S. to negotiate settlement of fisheries dispute between Canada and U.S. (1887–88). Leader of Liberal Unionists in Parliament and colonial secretary in third Salisbury cabinet (1895); instrumental in passing of Workmen's Compensation Act (1897); an imperial federationist, aimed to tighten bond between Great Britain and self-governing colonies; accused of privity in Jameson Raid (New Year's, 1896), acquitted by House of Commons committee; effected passage of Commonwealth of Australia Bill (1900) settling differences between colonial and imperial delegates; his attempt at conciliation of grievances of Transvaal uitlanders against the burghers (1897), especially the franchise, met by demand from President Kruger of British withdrawal from South Africa which precipitated Boer War; visited South Africa (1902), first secretary of state to visit an overseas colony on political matters; sought conciliation of rival races and dealt successfully with Transvaal financiers. Resigned on refusal of government to grant tariff preference to colonial grain and food, important to his ambition for closer political union of empire through mutually preferential commerce; launched unofficial speaking campaign (1903–06); brought about crushing defeat of Unionist party under Balfour (1906) on issue of imperial fiscal union; withdrew from public life and suffered paralytic stroke (1906). His program of imperial preference adopted in part in 1919, wholly in 1932. Largely instrumental in founding Birmingham U. (1900); its first chancellor (1901). Father of Austen and Neville Chamberlain (see separate entries).

**Chamberlain, Joshua Lawrence.** 1828–1914. American army officer and educator, b. Brewer, Me. Served through Civil War; designated to receive surrender of Confederate army. Awarded Congressional Medal of Honor for defense of Little Round Top in battle of Gettysburg. Governor of Maine (1866–70). President of Bowdoin Coll. (1871–83).

**Chamberlain, Neville,** *in full* **Arthur Neville.** 1869–1940. British statesman; son of Joseph Chamberlain (*q.v.*) and half brother of Sir Austen Chamberlain (*q.v.*). Educ. Mason Coll., Birmingham. Managed an estate on Andros Island, Bahamas (1890–97). Made success in hardware manufacture in Birmingham; as lord mayor (1915–16), established municipal bank, the first in England. M.P. (1918); postmaster general (1922–23); minister of health (1923, 1924–29); chancellor of exchequer (1923–24, 1931–37); chairman of Unionist party (1930–31). Succeeded Baldwin as prime minister (May 28, 1937); as leader of Conservative party, emphasized urgency of British rearmament (1937). Set forth foreign policy calling for avoidance of war by appeasement; sought to keep war in Spain from spreading; sought to draw Mussolini away from Hitler by concessions; recognized union of Austria with Germany; conflicted with foreign secretary Anthony Eden (who resigned Feb., 1938) over policy toward totalitarian powers. Conferred with Hitler at Berchtesgaden about Sudeten Germans; received increased demands from Hitler at Bad Godesberg; met with Daladier, Mussolini, and Hitler at Munich (Sept. 29–30, 1938), agreed to partition of Czechoslovakia; received vote of confidence on return home with Anglo-German amity declaration. Made Anglo-Italian pact by which Italy agreed to retain status quo in Mediterranean, recognize British water rights in Lake Tana, and withdraw from Spanish territory after civil war in return for British recognition of Italian title to Ethiopia (Nov., 1938); maintained nonintervention committee in supervision of war in Spain (1938); signed reciprocity trade treaty with U.S. (Jan., 1939); recognized Franco government in Spain (Feb., 1939). Forced to abandon appeasement and make switch in policy; pledged armed assistance to Poland (Mar., 1939) and to Rumania and Greece (Apr., 1939); forced to violate pledge by Baldwin (reaffirmed by himself) of no conscription in peace time (Apr., 1939). Declared war on Germany (Sept. 3, 1939) after German invasion of Poland, took Winston Churchill into government as first lord of admiralty and Anthony Eden as secretary for dominions; signed 15-year mutual assistance pact with Turkey (Oct., 1939); attacked in House of Commons for failure to send effective help to Finland (March, 1940), as well as for lack of aggressiveness in prosecution of war; following military disaster in Norway, failed to get vote of confidence and resigned as prime minister (May 10, 1940); became lord president of the council in Churchill cabinet; died (Nov., 1940) after illness of several weeks.

**Chamberlain,** Sir **Neville Bowles.** 1820–1902. British army officer in India; b. Rio de Janeiro, son of British consul general. Served through Afghan War (1839–42), Gwalio campaign (1843); commanded Punjab frontier force (1854–57); distinguished himself during Sepoy Mutiny (1857–58); commander in chief of Madras army (1876–81); general (1877); field marshal (1900).

**Chamberlain, Owen.** 1920– . Amer. nuclear physicist, b. San Francisco. Taught at Univ. of Calif. at Berkeley (1948– ). Awarded Nobel prize in physics (1959) with Emilio Segrè for discovery of antiprotons.

**Cham'ber'land'** (shäN'bĕr'läN'), **Charles Édouard.** 1851–1908. French bacteriologist; collaborated with Pasteur; invented an unglazed porcelain filter.

**Cham'ber·layne** (chām'bẽr·lān; -lĭn), **William.** 1619–1679. English poet; practiced as physician; author of *Pharonnida* (a romance in verse, 1659), etc.

**Cham'ber·lin** (chām'bẽr·lĭn), **Clarence Duncan.** 1893– . American aviator, b. Denison, Iowa. Pilot of monoplane *Columbia* (with C. A. Levine as passenger) in record nonstop flight from Roosevelt Field, N.Y., to Germany, landing at Eisleben, Saxony, a distance of 3911 miles in 42 hours and 31 mins. (June 4–6, 1927). Author of *Record Flights* (1928).

**Chamberlin, Thomas Chrowder.** 1843–1928. American geologist, b. Mattoon, Ill. Grad. Beloit (1866); professor, Beloit (1873–82). Specialized in study of glacial deposits and their evidence as to climatic conditions in past ages. President, U. of Wisconsin (1887–92). Professor of geology, and director of Walker Museum, U. of Chicago (1892–1928). Founded *Journal of Geology* (1893), editor in chief (1893–1922). Formulated, with F. R. Moulton, the planetesimal, or spiral-nebula, hypothesis to account for origin of the earth. Author of *The Geology of Wisconsin* (4 vols., 1873–82), *General Treatise on Geology* (with R. D. Salisbury; 1906), *The Origin of the Earth* (1916), *The Two Solar Families* (1928), etc.

His son **Rollin Thomas** (1881–1948), geologist, b. Beloit, Wis.; S.B., Chicago (1903), Ph.D. (1907); teacher (1912–48), Chicago; editor, *Journal of Geology* (from 1928).

**Chamberlin, William Henry.** 1897–1969. American journalist and writer, b. Brooklyn. Correspondent for *Christian Science Monitor* in Moscow (1922–34), Far East (1935–39), and France (1939). Author of *Soviet Russia* (1930), *The Soviet Planned Economic Order* (1931), *Russia's Iron Age* (1934), *The Russian Revolution 1917–21* (1935), *Collectivism...*(1937), *Japan over Asia* (1937).

**Cham'bers** (chām'bẽrz), **Charles Haddon.** 1860–1921. Australian playwright, b. in New South Wales; settled in England (1882). His plays include *One of Them* (1886), *The Open Gate* (1887), *Captain Swift, The Tyranny of Tears, The Impossible Woman.*

**Chambers,** Sir **Edmund Kerchever.** 1866–1954. English scholar and educator, b. in Berkshire: educ. Oxford; member of national education department (1892). Author of *The Medieval Stage* (1903), *The Elizabethan Stage* (1923), and *William Shakespeare* (1930), *A Sheaf of Studies* (1942), etc.

**Chambers, Ephraim.** d. 1740. English encyclopedist and translator; published his *Cyclopaedia*, or *Universal Dictionary of Arts and Sciences* (2 vols., 1728), which served as basis for *Encyclopédie* of Diderot and d'Alembert. Cf. Robert CHAMBERS.

**Chambers, Ernest John.** 1862–1925. Canadian author, b. in Staffordshire, Eng.; to Canada as child. Educ. Montreal; on staff of Montreal *Star* (1885); coproprietor and editor, *Canada Military Gazette* (1893–96); gentleman usher of the Black Rod in Canadian parliament (1904–25). Author of *The Book of Canada* (1905), *The History of the Royal Northwest Mounted Police* (1906), *Canada's Fertile Northland* (1908), etc.

**Chambers, John Graham.** 1843–1883. English athlete. B.A., Cantab. (1865); formulator of definitions of *ama-*

*teur* and of rules for athletic competitions; under supervision of 8th marquis of Queensberry (see under DOUGLAS family), founded amateur athletic club to encourage boxing and drew up Marquis of Queensberry rules (1867).

**Chambers, Raymond Wilson.** 1874–1942. English scholar and educator. B.A., University Coll., London (1894). Librarian, University Coll. (1901–22), and professor of English language and literature (from 1922). Author of studies of Beowulf and Bede, and *England before the Norman Conquest* (1926), etc.

**Chambers, Robert.** 1802–1871. Scottish publisher and author. Founded (soon after 1832), with his brother **William**, publishing firm (W. & R. Chambers) in Edinburgh, which issued multitude of cheap educational works, *Chambers's Cyclopaedia of English Literature* (compiled jointly by Robert and Robert Carruthers, 1844), and *Chambers's Encyclopaedia* (10 vols., 1859–68). Cf. Ephraim CHAMBERS. Author of works on biography and Scottish history, geological works, and of *Book of Days*, an antiquarian miscellany (1862–64), and *Vestiges of the Natural History of Creation* (1844), proposing a theory of evolution of species and preparing way for Darwin's theories. His brother **William** (1800–1883), bookseller and printer; financial expert of the firm; started *Chambers's Edinburgh Journal* (1832); as lord provost of Edinburgh (1865–69), secured reconstruction of old town; restored St. Giles Church; author of notes of travel, tales, etc., and, with Robert, *A Gazetteer of Scotland.* Robert's son **Robert** (1832–1888), head of firm (1883), conducted the *Journal* until his death.

**Chambers, Robert.** 1881–1957. American biologist, b. in Turkey of Canadian parents; educ. in Turkey, Canada, and Germany (Ph.D., Munich, 1908); research professor, N.Y.U. (1928–48); known for his researches on the nature of protoplasm and the constituents of the living cell.

**Chambers, Robert William.** 1865–1933. American artist and author, b. Brooklyn, N.Y. Studied in Académie Julian, Paris (1886–93); illustrator for *Life, Vogue, Truth,* and other magazines; devoted himself chiefly to writing (from 1893). Author of *A King and a Few Dukes* (1894), *Ashes of Empire* (1897), *Cardigan* (1901), *Iole* (1905), *Japonette* (1912), *Athalie* (1915), *Barbarians* (1917), *The Crimson Tide* (1919), *The Man They Hanged* (1925), *The Rogue's Moon* (1927), etc.

**Chambers,** Sir **William.** 1726–1796. British architect; settled in London (1755); employed at Kew Gardens (1757–62); designed Somerset House (1775). Author of *Treatise of Civil Architecture* (1759).

**Cham'bon'nières'** (shäɴ'bô'nyâr'), **Jacques Cham'pion'** (shäɴ'pyôɴ') **de.** 17th-century French musician, player on the harpsichord.

**Cham'bord'** (shäɴ'bôr'), Comte **de. Henri Charles Ferdinand Marie Dieu'don'né' d'Ar'tois'** (dyû'dô'nā' dȧr'twȧ'). Duc **de Bor'deaux'** (bôr'dō'). 1820–1883. Bourbon claimant to throne of France; son of Charles Ferdinand de Bourbon, Duc de Berry. Chosen by Charles X on abdication (1830) to succeed him; on death of Charles (1836), proclaimed king (Henri V) by Legitimists; last representative of elder Bourbon branch; after death (1844) of his uncle, duc d'Angoulême (*q.v.*), compelled to live abroad, in later years in Lower Austria.

**Cham'brun'** (shäɴ'brûɴ'), Comte **René de.** 1906– . French soldier and writer; direct descendant of marquis de Lafayette and, by virtue of this fact, honorary American citizen. Captain of infantry in war against Germany (1939–40); sent to U.S. (June, 1940) in effort to get speedy aid for France. Author of *I Saw France Fall* (Oct., 1940).

**Cham'fort'** (shäɴ'fôr'), **Sébastien Roch Nicolas.** 1741–1794. French writer and wit. At outbreak of Revolution, joined Jacobins, took part in storming of Bastille, bitterly attacked National Convention. Mortally wounded himself when about to be arrested by order of Convention. Best known for his *Maximes*, published posthumously; author also of comedies, literary criticisms, letters, and verse.

**Cham'ier** (shăm'yẽr), **Frederick.** 1796–1870. English novelist; served in navy (1809–56). Author of sea stories, including *Tom Bowling* (1841).

**Cha'mil'ly'** (shȧ'mē'yē'), Comte **de. Noël Bou'ton'** (bōō'tôɴ'). 1636–1715. French soldier; served in Portugal, Candia, Holland; governor of Grave, distinguished himself in its defense (1672). Known in literature as person addressed by a Portuguese nun, Marianna Alcoforado (*q.v.*), in short series of letters published under title *Portuguese Letters*, deprecating his desertion.

**Cha'mi'nade'** (shȧ'mē'nȧd'), **Cécile Louise Stéphanie.** 1861–1944. French composer and pianist, b. Paris; toured Europe and U.S. (1908) as concert pianist. Compositions include *Concertstück* for piano and orchestra, lyric symphony *Les Amazones* for chorus and orchestra (1888), ballet symphony *Callirhoë* (1888), and many piano pieces and songs.

**Cha·mis'so** (shä·mĭs'ō), **Adelbert von.** *Orig.* **Louis Charles Adélaïde de Cha'mis'so'** (dē shȧ'mē'sō'). 1781–1838. German romantic writer and naturalist; b. in Champagne, France, of French family forced by Revolution to flee from France. Served in Prussian army (1798–1807). Member of literary coterie near Geneva centering about Mme. de Staël (1811–12). Botanist on the *Rurik* on Otto von Kotzebue's (*q.v.*) scientific voyage around the world (1815–18). Curator, Berlin botanical gardens (1818). Editor, *Deutscher Musenalmanach* (from 1832), in which he published much of his verse. Best-known work the prose tale *Peter Schlemihls Wunderbare Geschichte* (1814), treating realistically and humorously story of a man who sold his shadow; best-known verse the cycle of lyrics *Frauenliebe und -leben* (1831; set to music by Schumann).

**Cha·mor'ro Var'gas** (chä·môr'rō vär'gäs), **Emiliano.** 1871–1966. Nicaraguan general and politician. President of Nicaragua (1917–20); with A. Díaz seized power by coup d'état (Oct. 25, 1925); again elected president (Jan., 1926); refused recognition by U.S., which ordered gunboats to Nicaragua; resigned (Oct., 1926) and left country.

**Cham'pa'gny'** (shäɴ'pȧ'nyē'), **Jean Baptiste Nom'père'** (nôɴ'pâr') **de.** Duc **de Ca·do're** (kä·dō'rā). 1756–1834. French statesman; served in navy (1774–87); during French revolutionary excesses (1791–1800) lived in retirement, from which he was called by Napoleon; ambassador to Austria (1801–04); minister of the interior (1804–07), of foreign affairs (1807–11); senator (1813); peer of France (1819).

**Cham'paigne'** (shäɴ'pȧn'y') *or* **Cham'pagne'** (-pȧn'y'), **Philippe de.** 1602–1674. Belgian painter of Flemish school; aided in decorating the Luxembourg; commissioned by Richelieu to adorn his palace and paint murals for dome of the Sorbonne; also favorably regarded as a portraitist.

**Champeaux.** See GUILLAUME DE CHAMPEAUX.

**Champ'fleu'ry'** (shäɴ'flû'rē'). *Real name* **Jules Fleu'ry'-Hus'son'** (flû'rē'ü'sôɴ') *or* **Husson.** 1821–1889. French novelist, a leader of the realistic school; among his novels are *Chien-Caillou* (1847), *Les Bourgeois de Molinchart* (1855), *Les Amoureux de Sainte Périne* (1859), *Monsieur Tringle* (1866), *Fanny Minoret* (1882). Interested in ceramics; director of factory of Sèvres.

**Cham'pion'net'** (shäN'pyô'nĕ'), **Jean Antoine Étienne.** 1762–1800. French soldier in revolutionary armies; engaged at Fleurus (1794), in Holland (1797); commanded army of Rome (1798), captured Naples, organized Parthenopean Republic; commanded army of Alps (1799) against Austrians; died of plague.

**Cham·plain'** (shăm·plān'; *Fr.* shäN'plăN'), **Samuel de.** 1567?–1635. French explorer in America, b. near Rochefort, France. As commander of a Spanish vessel (1599–1601), visited West Indies, Mexico, Cartagena, and Panama. Under orders of Henry IV of France, accompanied exploring and fur-trading expedition to Gulf of St. Lawrence (1603); ascended St. Lawrence River to Lachine Rapids. Accompanied expedition of settlers to Port Royal; explored coast from Nova Scotia down as far as Vineyard Haven (1604–07). With commission as lieutenant governor, headed group of settlers (1608) who founded Quebec. With Quebec as base, explored northern New York, down to lake that bears his name (1609), Ottawa River (1613), Great Lakes (1615). Governor of the colony (1633–35). Author of *The Savages* (1603), *The Travels of Sieur de Champlain* (1613), *Travels and Discoveries in New France* (1619), *Travels in New France, called Canada, 1603–1629* (1632).

**Champ'mes'lé'** (shäN'mĕ'lā'), **Marie,** *nee* **Des'mares'** (dā'mȧr'). 1642–1698. French actress; m. (1666) comedian and playwright **Charles Che·vil'let'** (shē-vē'yĕ'), *called* **Champmeslé** (1645–1701); long intimate with Racine; created roles of Hermione, Berenice, Monimia, and Phèdre in his plays, Racine himself training her in interpretation of these parts. La Fontaine dedicated *Belphégor* to her and Boileau immortalized her in his poetry.

**Champ'neys** (chămp'nĭz), **Basil.** 1842–1935. English architect; B.A., Cantab. (1864). Among his works are buildings at Oxford U. and Cambridge U., Bedford Coll. in London, and many churches, schools, and residences. Author of *A Quiet Corner of England* (1875), *Coventry Patmore* (1900), etc.

**Cham'pol'lion'** (shäN'pô'lyôN'), *known as* **Cham'-pol'lion'-Fi'geac'** (-fē'zhȧk'), **Jean Jacques.** 1778–1867. French archaeologist; librarian and professor at Grenoble; curator of manuscripts, Bibliothèque Royale; dismissed by Republican government (1848), but later appointed librarian at Château of Fontainebleau; author of *L'Égypte Ancienne* (1839), *Le Palais de Fontainebleau* (1866), etc. His brother **Jean François Champollion** (1790–1832), Egyptologist; founded Egyptian museum of the Louvre and was appointed its curator; from study of Rosetta stone, obtained clue for deciphering Egyptian hieroglyphics; author of *Précis du Système Hiéroglyphique des Anciens Égyptiens.* Jean Jacques's son **Aimé Louis Champollion-Figeac** (1813–1894), director in charge of departmental archives, Bibliothèque Royale; author of *Louis et Charles, Ducs d'Orléans, et leur Influence sur leur Siècle* (1844), *La Captivité du Roi François Ier* (1847), *Manuel de l'Archiviste* (1860), etc.

**Cham'son'** (shäN'sôN'), **André.** 1900– . French novelist and essayist, b. Nîmes.

**Chan'ca** (chäng'kä), **Diego Álvarez.** Spanish physician, b. Seville; accompanied Columbus on second voyage (1493); known esp. for his letter to cathedral chapter of Seville describing flora, fauna, and ethnography of America, one of principal documents for history of voyage.

**Chancel, Joseph de Lagrange-.** See LAGRANGE-CHANCEL.

**Chan'cel·lor** (chȧn'sĕ·lẽr), **Richard.** d. 1556. English navigator; commander of a ship in Sir Hugh Willoughby's expedition into White Sea in search of northeast passage to India; reached Archangel; visited Moscow and laid foundations of English trade with Russia.

**Chand' Bar·da'i** (chŭnd' bȧr·dä'ē) *or* **Chund' Bar-da'i.** fl. 1200 A.D. Hindu poet, b. Lahore; court poet of Prithiraj, last king of Delhi. Composed epic, *Chand Rāisā*, orig. in about 5000 verses, enlarged to more than 100,000 verses by reciters.

**Chan'dler** (chȧn'dlẽr), **Charles Frederick.** 1836–1925. American chemist, b. Lancaster, Mass. President, New York City board of health (1867–84); authority on water supply, sanitation, oil refining, assaying; fought against milk adulteration and for pure food, compulsory vaccination, compulsory sanitary plumbing.

**Chandler, Frank Wadleigh.** 1873–1947. American educator, b. Brooklyn. A.B., Brooklyn Polytech. Inst. (1894), Ph.D., Columbia (1899); professor of English, U. of Cincinnati (from 1910). Author of *Romances of Roguery...*(1899), *The Literature of Roguery* (1907), *Aspects of Modern Drama* (1914), *Modern Continental Playwrights* (1931), etc.

**Chandler, Richard.** 1738–1810. English classical antiquary; M.A., Oxon. (1761); published *Marmora Oxoniensia* (1763), description of the Arundel marbles, and works on antiquities of Ionia and Greece (1769).

**Chandler, Seth Carlo.** 1846–1913. American astronomer, b. Boston. Grad. Harvard (1861); with U.S. Coast Survey (1864–70); insurance actuary (1871–81); at Harvard Observatory (1881–85); editor, *Astronomical Journal* (from 1896). Discovered several variable stars; compiled catalogues of variable stars; wrote papers on general laws of stellar variation; demonstrated variation of terrestrial latitude.

**Chandler, William Eaton.** 1835–1917. American lawyer, b. Concord, N.H. Asst. secretary, U.S. Treasury (1865–67); directed Republican tactics in Hayes-Tilden disputed election; secretary of navy (1882–85); U.S. senator (1887–1901).

**Chandler, Zachariah.** 1813–1879. American politician, b. Bedford, N.H.; U.S. senator from Michigan (1857–75; 1879); U.S. secretary of interior (1875–77).

**Chan'dos** (shăn'dŏs; chăn'-), Marquises of. See *Richard Grenville* (1797–1861; 1823–1889), under GRENVILLE.

**Chandos,** Viscount of. See Oliver LYTTELTON.

**Chandos,** Barons and dukes of. Titles in English peerage borne by members of **Brydg'es** (brĭj'ĕz; -ĭz) family, including: **John** (1490?–1556), 1st Baron **Chandos of Sude'ley** (sūd'lĭ), soldier, whose mother was in direct descent from Sir John Chandos (*q.v.*); Roman Catholic companion of Henry VIII and supporter of Edward VI and Mary; lieutenant of Tower of London (1553–54); aided (1554) in suppression of Wyatt's rebellion; had custody of Lady Jane Grey and of Wyatt. **James** (1673–1744), 1st duke (cr. 1719), son and heir of 7th baron; paymaster general of forces abroad in War of Spanish Succession (1705–13); created earl (1714), marquis (1719) of Carnarvon; patron of Handel during composition of oratorio *Esther;* complimented in Pope's *Moral Essays.*

**Chandos,** Sir **John.** d. 1370. English soldier. Fought at siege of Cambrai (1337), at Crécy (1346); at Poitiers saved life of Black Prince; with Black Prince on expedition to restore Pedro the Cruel to throne of Castile, won victory of Navarete (1367); mortally wounded near Poitiers.

**Chandra, Bankim.** See Bankim Chandra CHATTERJI.

**Chan'dra·gup'ta** *or* **Chan'dra·gup'ta Maur'ya** (chŭn'drȧ·gŏŏp'tȧ mä'ŏŏr·yȧ). *Known in Greek as* **San'dro·cot'tus** (săn'drō·kŏt'ŭs) *or* **San'dra·cot'tus** (săn'drȧ-). d. 286? B.C. First king of Magadha (Hindu India) of the Maurya dynasty (322?–298 B.C.). In his youth met Alexander (326 or 325); led in revolution establishing Maurya dynasty; destroyed Macedonian garrisons left in India; ruled empire extending across northern India and including Afghanistan; defeated invading army of Seleucus in Punjab (305); received Megasthenes as Greek ambassador (302). According to tradition, abdicated (298), journeyed to south of India, and committed suicide.

**Chandragupta.** Name of two kings of India of the Gupta dynasty. **Chandragupta I,** a raja of Magadha; founded Gupta dynasty (320 A.D.); reigned (320–?330); by conquest and marriage extended his dominion over Oudh. His grandson **Chandragupta II,** son of Samudragupta; king (375? or 383?–413); conquered Malwa, Gujarat, and other countries of western India (395); assumed additional title, *Vikramaditya* (*q.v.*); his country visited and described by famous Chinese pilgrim Fa-Hsien; his reign a part of the Gupta golden age of Hindu literature and art.

**Cha'nel'** (shȧ'nĕl'), **Gabrielle "Coco."** 1883–1971. French dress designer; opened establishment in Paris (c. 1920), originally for designing hats and sweaters, and later for gowns; later included an accessory and perfume shop. Subject of Broadway musical *Coco* (1969).

**Cha'ney** (chā'nĭ), **Lon.** 1883–1930. American motion-picture actor, b. Colorado Springs, Colo. Known especially for his ability, by means of make-up and otherwise, to distort his face and body; greatest success in role of hunchback Quasimodo in *The Hunchback of Notre Dame.*

**Chang** (chăng) and **Eng** (ĕng). 1811–1874. The original Siamese twins, joined at the waist; b. Meklong, Siam, of Chinese parentage. Exhibited in U.S. and abroad (from 1829); became naturalized American citizens; married (1843) two sisters.

**Chan'gar'nier'** (shäɴ'gȧr'nyā'), **Nicolas Anne Théodule.** 1793–1877. French soldier. Served in Algeria (1830–48) and was appointed its governor. Commanded troops in Paris (1848–51); banished (1852) for opposition to Napoleon III; returned after amnesty (1859). In Franco-Prussian War, with Bazaine in Metz at its capitulation (Oct., 1870). Deputy (1871–75); elected senator for life (1875).

**Chang Ch'ien** (jäng' chyĕn'). Minister of Wu Ti of Han dynasty of China. Sent (138 B.C.) to the Yuechi in Bactria to secure help against the Hiung-Nu; captured by the Hiung-Nu and detained ten years; escaped; lived with the Yuechi one year; returned (126) to China unsuccessful. Negotiated treaties with kingdoms in the west (126–115).

**Ch'ang Ch'un.** See CH'IU CH'U-CHI.

**Chang Heng** (jäng' hŭng'). 78–139 A.D. Chinese scholar and poet; inventor of an early form of seismoscope.

**Chang Hsueh-liang** (jäng' shü·ĕ'lyäng'). 1898– . Chinese general; called "the Young Marshal." Son of Chang Tso-lin. Grad. Mukden Military Academy; succeeded father as commander in chief in Manchuria (1928); head of northeastern frontier defense (1929–31) subservient to Nationalist regime; driven out of Manchuria by Japanese (1933); visited Europe (1933–34). General under Chiang Kai-shek, strongly anti-Japanese; in command of Tungpei army; ordered to engage communist forces in North China (1936); instead fraternized with them in endeavor to unite country against Japan; kidnaped Chiang Kai-shek (Dec., 1936), holding him prisoner for two weeks; deprived of his command, held under guard in Taipei (1946–61).

**Chang Shan-tse** (jäng' shän'dzŭ'). 1881?–1940. Chinese painter; best known for depiction of tigers.

**Chang Tao-ling** (jäng' dou'lĭng'). fl. 1st century A.D. Chinese scholar living under Han dynasty; sometimes called the first Taoist pope. Devoted life to study of alchemy and magic; held to be founder of Taoist system of magic (corrupted Taoism); reputed to have succeeded in discovering elixir of life and to have lived 123 years. His descendants hold title "Celestial Teacher," or "Heavenly Preceptor."

**Chang Tso-lin** (jäng' tsō'lĭn'). 1873–1928. Chinese military leader; b. in Fengtien province. Common laborer; became (1904) leader of band of Manchurian brigands; joined Chinese army (1905); rapidly promoted; military governor of Fengtien (1911); loyal to young republic. Secured control (1918) of three Manchurian provinces; his autocratic rule (1918–28) generally beneficial to people. Attempted several times to reform administration at Peking; defeated (1922) by Gen. Wu P'ei-fu; declared independence of Manchuria; succeeded in occupying northeastern provinces of China (1926); formed cabinet (1927); withdrew from Peking (1928) on advance of Southern Nationalist army; killed on Mukden train by bomb. Succeeded by his son Chang Hsueh-liang (*q.v.*).

**Chan'ning** (chăn'ĭng), **Walter.** 1786–1876. Bro. of William Ellery Channing (1780–1842). American obstetrician, b. Newport, R.I. Educ. Harvard, U. of Pennsylvania, and abroad. Professor (1815–54) and dean (1819–47), Harvard Medical School. Introduced use of ether to lessen pain of labor. His son **William Ellery** (1818–1901), poet, b. Boston; associate of Emerson, Thoreau, and Hawthorne. The latter's son **Edward** (1856–1931), historian, b. Dorchester, Mass.; A.B. (1878), Ph.D. (1880), Harvard; taught history at Harvard (1883–1931; professor from 1897); author of *The Navigation Laws* (1890), *The United States of America, 1765–1865* (1896), *History of the United States* (6 vols., *1905–1925;* vol. VI, 1925, awarded Pulitzer prize).

**Channing, William Ellery.** 1780–1842. American clergyman, b. Newport, R.I.; known as the "Apostle of Unitarianism." Grad. Harvard (1798). Pastor, Federal Street Church, Boston (1803–42); liberal Congregationalist; became leader of Unitarian group (from 1819); an organizer of American Unitarian Association (1825). Intellectual leader among his contemporaries; exercised wide influence by sermons and writings on social and philanthropic issues of his time. Elected to American Hall of Fame (1900). Author of *Negro Slavery* (1835), *Self Culture* (1838), etc. His son **William Francis** (1820–1901), b. Boston, collaborated with Moses G. Farmer in inventing electric fire-alarm telegraph (pat. 1857). The latter's daughter **Grace Ellery** (1862–1937), b. Providence, R.I.; m. the painter Charles Walter Stetson (1894; d. 1911) and hence often known as **Grace Ellery Chan'ning-Stet'son** (-stĕt's'n); author of *The Sister of a Saint* (1895), *The Fortune of a Day* (1900), and a book of verse, *Sea Drift* (1899).

**Channing, William Henry.** 1810–1884. American Unitarian clergyman, b. Boston; nephew of William Ellery Channing (1780–1842). Interested in social reform; resident for a time at Brook Farm; edited (1843–44) *The Present,* Socialist periodical; during Civil War, served in camps and hospitals; chaplain, U.S. House of Representatives (1863–64); to England (1866).

**Chan'tal'** (shäɴ'tȧl'), Baronne **de.** *Known as* Sainte (săɴt) **Chantal. Jeanne Françoise Fré'miot'** (frā'myō'). 1572–1641. Grandmother of Mme. de Sévigné. French religious; m. baron de Chantal (1592); after husband's death devoted herself to prayer and works of charity; founded (1610) Congregation of the Visitation of Our Lady; superior (1618–22) of house of the order established in Paris. Canonized (1767).

**Chan'ta'voine'** (shäN'tȧ'vwȧn'), **Henri.** 1850–1918. French poet and historian; author of *Poèmes Sincères* (1877), *Satires Contemporaines* (1880), *Ad Memoriam* (1884), and of histories including *Histoire de Pinchu* (1906), *Les Principes de 1789* (1908). His son **Jean** (1877–1952), music critic for *La Revue Hebdomadaire*, *Ménestrel*, and *Excelsior;* author of *Beethoven* (1907), *Liszt* (1910), *Musiciens et Poètes* (1912).

**Chan'te·lauze'** (shäN'tlōz'), **François Régis.** 1821–1888. French historian.

**Chan'tre** (shäN'tr'), **Ernest.** 1843–1924. French archaeologist; teacher and museum curator at Lyon.

**Chan'trey** (chȧn'trĭ), Sir **Francis Legatt.** 1781–? 1841. English sculptor and portrait painter (exhibiting 1802–07); executed statues, a few equestrian statues, but at his best with busts.

**Cha·nute'** (shȧ·no͞ot'), **Oc·tave'** (ŏk·tāv'). 1832–1910. Civil engineer and aviation pioneer, b. Paris, France; to U.S. (1838); railroad engineer (1853–73); consulting engineer, esp. in bridge building (1873–83). Studied Lilienthal's experiments with gliders; experimented with gliders and scientifically tabulated results (1896–97); designed biplane glider of exceptional stability in flight. Wright Brothers acknowledged value of his experiments and designs. Author of *Aerial Navigation* (1891), *Progress in Flying Machines* (1894).

**Chan'zy'** (shäN'zē'), **Antoine Eugène Alfred** 1823–1883. French soldier. Served in Algeria; general of brigade (1868); commanded 16th corps, and later army of the Loire, in Franco-Prussian War; defeated at Le Mans (Jan., 1871). Governor of Algeria (1873); senator (1875); candidate for president of France (1879).

**Chao K'uang-yin** (jou' kwäng'yĭn'). *Known also as* **Kao Tsu** (gou' dzo͞o'). d. 976 A.D. Chinese emperor (960–976); founder of the Sung dynasty (960–1127).

**Cha·pa'ev** *or* **Cha·pa'yev** (chŭ·pä'yĕf), **Vasili I.** 1887–1919. Russian military hero; Red army leader during civil war (1918), commanding 25th division around Samara (Kuibyshev); surrounded and wounded while in pursuit of Kolchak's routed army, and drowned in Ural River when attempting to escape.

**Cha'pais'** (shȧ'pĕ'), Sir **Tho'mas'** (tô'mä'). 1858–1946. Canadian lawyer and politician. Educ. Laval U.; called to bar (1879); editor, *Le Courrier du Canada* (1884–1901). Professor of history, Laval U. Author of *Cours d'Histoire du Canada* (8 vols., 1919–35), and literary and historical studies.

**Cha'pe·lain'** (shȧ'plăN'), **Jean.** 1595–1674. French poet and man of letters, b. Paris. An organizer and original member of the Académie Française; author of *La Pucelle* (1656), an epic ridiculed by Boileau in his satires.

**Cha'pin** (chā'pĭn), **Chester William.** 1798–1883. American businessman and railroad promoter, b. Ludlow, Mass. Developed Connecticut River Valley transportation facilities; president, Connecticut River Railroad (1850–54) and Boston and Albany Railroad (1854–77). Member of U.S. House of Representatives (1875–77).

**Chapin, James.** 1887–1975. American landscape and portrait painter, b. West Orange, N.J.; studied at Art Students' League in New York, Royal Academy of Art in Antwerp; studio in New York.

**Chapin, Roy Dikeman.** 1880–1936. American industrialist, b. Lansing, Mich. Educ. U. of Michigan (1899–1901). In automobile manufacturing business (from 1901); president (1910–23), board chairman (1923–33), again president (1933–36), Hudson Motor Car Co.; U.S. secretary of commerce (1932–33).

**Chapin, Samuel.** 1598–1675. Known as Deacon Samuel Chapin. American colonial pioneer; settled in Springfield, Mass. (1642). Often stated to have been original of Augustus St.-Gaudens's statue *The Puritan* (in Springfield, Mass.), which, however, is not intended to represent any individual but a composite of the Chapin family type.

**Cha·pí' y Lo·ren'te** (chä·pē' ē lō·rān'tā), **Ruperto.** 1851–1909. Spanish composer, esp. of zarzuelas.

**Cha'plain'** (shȧ'plăN'), **Jules Clément.** 1839–1909. French sculptor and medallionist.

**Chap'lin** (chăp'lĭn). Sir **Charles Spencer.** 1889–1977. Motion-picture actor, b. London, Eng. On stage from childhood; to U.S. with vaudeville act (1910). Made motion-picture debut (1914); achieved world-wide renown as comedian; organized own company (1918); produced and starred in *A Dog's Life, The Kid, The Circus, The Gold Rush, City Lights, Modern Times, The Great Dictator,* etc. Knighted (1975).

**Chaplin,** Sir **Drummond,** *in full* **Francis Drummond Percy.** 1866–1933. British businessman and politician in South Africa; administrator of Southern Rhodesia (1914–23), Northern Rhodesia (1921–23).

**Chap'man** (chăp'măn), **Charles Edward.** 1880–1941. American historian, b. Franklin, N.H. A.B., Tufts (1902), LL.B., Harvard (1905), Ph.D., California (1915). Teacher of history, U. of California (from 1914; professor from 1927). Author of *The Founding of Spanish California* (1916), *Colonial Hispanic America...*(1933), *Republican Hispanic America...*(1937), etc.

**Chapman, Frank Michler.** 1864–1945. American ornithologist, b. Englewood, N.J. Curator (from 1908), American Museum of Natural History. Founder and editor of *Bird-Lore.* Author of *Handbook of Birds of Eastern North America* (1895), *Bird-Life, a Guide to the Study of our Common Birds* (1897), *Bird Studies with a Camera* (1900), *Key to North American Birds* (1903), *The Warblers of North America* (1907), *Our Winter Birds* (1918), *What Bird is That?* (1920), *My Tropical Air Castle* (1929), *Life in an Air Castle* (1939), etc.

**Chapman, George.** 1559?–1634. English poet and dramatist. Playwright in London; wrote poems, *The Shadow of Night* (1594), and completed Marlowe's *Hero and Leander* (1598); wrote his first play, *The Blind Beggar of Alexandria* (acted 1596); said to have been imprisoned (1605) for satirizing James I's Scottish followers in *Eastward Hoe*, a comedy written in collaboration with Ben Jonson and John Marston; aided by Prince Henry, patronized by Robert Carr, Earl of Somerset; published chief tragedies and comedies (1606–12), including *Bussy d'Ambois, The Gentleman Usher, The Widow's Tears.* Owes his place in literature to his rhyming verse translations of Homer (*Iliad*, 1598–1611; *Odyssey*, 1614–15; the *Hymns*, 1624), inspiration of a famous sonnet by John Keats.

**Chapman, John.** *Nicknamed* **Johnny Ap'ple·seed'** (ăp''l·sēd'). 1774–1845. American pioneer, b. in New England; settled in Ohio River valley, between 1800 and 1810, where he ranged widely over the country planting apple seeds and pruning the growing trees. Subject of many legends; celebrated in literature, as in Vachel Lindsay's *In Praise of Johnny Appleseed.*

**Chapman, John.** 1822–1894. English publisher, editor, and physician; grad. in medicine at St. Andrews; editor and proprietor, *Westminster Review* (from 1851); publisher and bookseller in London. Friend of Emerson, Dickens, George Eliot. His diaries published in *George Eliot and John Chapman. With Chapman's Diaries* (ed. G. S. Haight; 1940).

**Chapman, John Gadsby.** 1808–1889. American painter and etcher, b. Alexandria, Va. His *Baptism of Pocahontas* is in rotunda of Capitol, Washington, D.C.

**Chapman, John Jay.** 1862–1933. American writer, b. New York City. A.B., Harvard (1884); practiced law (1888–98); devoted himself to writing (from 1898); best known for his essays. Author of *Emerson and Other Essays* (1898), *Causes and Consequences* (1898), *Practical Agitation* (1900), *Four Plays for Children* (1908), *The Maid's Forgiveness* (play in verse; 1908), *A Sausage from Bologna* (comedy in verse; 1909), *Benedict Arnold* (play; 1911), *Learning and Other Essays* (1911), *Neptune's Isle* (1912), *William Lloyd Garrison* (1913), *Memories and Milestones* (1915), *Green Genius and Other Essays* (1915), *Songs and Poems* (1919), *Letters and Religion* (1923), *Dante* (1927), etc.

**Chapman, John Stanton Higham.** 1891– . Author, b. London, Eng.; to U.S. (1917); naturalized (1926). Aeronautical engineer by training; in British Army Reserve Air Service (1914–17) and U.S. Signal Corps (1917). Married (1917) **Mary Hamilton Ils′ley** [ĭlz′lĭ] (1895– ) coauthor with him under joint pen name **Mar′i·stan** (mâr′ĭ·stăn′) **Chapman** of works of fiction: *Happy Mountain* (1928), *Imperial Brother* (1931), *Timber Trail* (1933), *Eagle Cliff* (1934), *Rogues on Red Hill* (1937), etc.

**Chapman, Nathaniel.** 1780–1853. American physician, b. Summer Hill, Va. Pupil of Dr. Benjamin Rush of Philadelphia (1797); grad. U. of Pennsylvania med. school (1801); practiced in Philadelphia (from 1804); on staff of U. of Pennsylvania med. school (1810–50). Founder of Medical Institute of Philadelphia, first postgraduate medical school in U.S. (1817); editor, *Journal of Medical and Physical Sciences* (1820); first president of American Medical Association (1848); author of *Elements of Therapeutics and Materia Medica* (1817).

**Chapman,** Sir **Sydney John.** 1871–1951. English economist; educ. Cambridge. Professor, Owens Coll., Manchester (1901–17); permanent secretary of board of trade (1920–27); chief economic adviser to the government (1927–32); member, import duties advisory committee (1932–39). Author of *The Cotton Industry and Trade* (1905), *Outlines of Political Economy* (1911), etc.

**Cha·pone′** (shȧ·pōn′), **Hester,** *nee* **Mul′so** (mŭl′sō). 1727–1801. English essayist; one of the learned women gathered round Mrs. Elizabeth Montagu; known for her *Letters on the Improvement of the Mind* (1772).

**Chappe** (shȧp), **Claude** (1763–1805) and his brother **Ignace Urbain Jean** (1760–1828). French engineers; invented an extensively used telegraph employing visual signals. Their uncle **Jean Chappe d'Au′te·roche′** [dō′trôsh′] (1722–1769), priest and astronomer, observed transits of Venus in Siberia (1761) and in California (1769), where he died.

**Chap′pell** (chăp′ĕl; -′l), **William.** 1809–1888. English musical antiquary. Collected English airs in *Popular Music of the Olden Time* (1855–59); one of founders of Percy Society and Musical Antiquarian Society.

**Chap′tal′** (shȧp′tȧl′), **Jean Antoine.** Comte **de Chan′te·loup′** (shäɴ′tlōō′). 1756–1832. French chemist and statesman. Grad. in medicine from Montpellier, where he became professor of chemistry (1781); established factory for production of sulphuric acid, alum, etc.; head of powder works at Grenelle (1793). Councilor of state, then minister of interior (1800–04); appointed senator by Napoleon and, later, director-general of commerce and manufactures and a minister of state. Author of works on applied chemistry, esp. dyeing, agriculture, viticulture, and wine making.

**Cha′pu′** (shȧ′pü′), **Henri Michel Antoine.** 1833–1891. French sculptor; studied under Pradier, Duret, and Léon Cogniet. Among his works are: *Mercure Inventant la Caducée; Jeanne d'Arc Écoutant ses Voix;* a statue, *La Jeunesse*, in the École des Beaux-Arts (Paris) to the memory of Henri Regnault; a number of portrait busts.

**Cha′ra·ka** (chŭ′rȧ·kȧ). fl. 2d century A.D. Hindu writer on medical science; his works, translated (8th century) into Arabic, later became important source of medical knowledge in Europe.

**Char′cot′** (shȧr′kō′), **Jean Martin.** 1825–1893. French neurologist; M.D., Paris (1853); professor of pathological anatomy, Paris (1860); physician at the Salpêtrière (from 1862), where he established neurological clinic; known for work on hysteria and hypnotism, sclerosis (hence name *Charcot's disease* for cerebrospinal sclerosis), locomotor ataxia, senile diseases, etc.
His son **Jean Baptiste Étienne Auguste** (1867–1936), Antarctic explorer; educ. as physician; turned to exploration; headed two expeditions to Antarctic (1903–05, 1908–10); mapped Graham Land and its islands; discovered Charcot Land, naming it after his father; drowned with 38 of his men when the *Pourquoi-Pas?* was wrecked off western Iceland.

**Chard** (chärd), **John Rouse Merriott.** 1847–1897. English officer in Royal Engineers; heroic defender of Rorke's Drift, with 139 men against 3000 Zulus (1879), saving Natal from invasion.

**Char′din′** (shȧr′dăɴ′; *Angl.* shär′dĭn), **Jean,** *later* Sir **John.** 1643–1713. French traveler; made journeys to Persia and India, acquiring wealth by trade in jewels; a Protestant, settled in London (1681).

**Char′din′** (shȧr′dăɴ′), **Jean Baptiste Siméon.** 1699–1779. French genre painter; his notable paintings include *Le Buffet, L'Enfant au Toton, Le Jeune Violiniste, Le Bénédicité, Les Tours de Carte, La Toilette du Matin.*

**Chardin, Pierre Teilhard de.** See TEILHARD DE CHARDIN.

**Char′don′net′** (shȧr′dô′nĕ′), Comte **Hilaire Bernigaud de.** 1839–1924. French chemist and physicist; studied at École Polytechnique under Pasteur, who was then investigating silk-worm disease; patented (1884–85) an artificial silk made from cotton.

**Cha′res** (kā′rēz; kâr′ēz). Athenian general. Associate of Chabrias (*q.v.*) at outbreak of Social War (357 B.C.); after death of Chabrias held joint command with Iphicrates and Timotheus (*qq.v.*). Operated against Philip II of Macedon (from 349), and was disastrously defeated at Amphissa (338) and Chaeronea (338). Entered (332) service of Darius III of Persia.

**Chares.** Greek sculptor, of Lindos in Rhodes; carved (c. 280 B.C.) the famous Colossus of Rhodes (about 120 ft. high; considered one of seven wonders of ancient world) to commemorate defense of Rhodes against Macedonian King Demetrius Poliorcetes (305–304 B.C.).

**Cha′rette′ de la Con′trie′** (shȧ′rĕt′ dē lȧ kôɴ′trē′), **François Athanase.** 1763–1796. French Royalist leader in Vendean revolt (1793 ff.) against newly established French Republic; executed at Nantes (Mar. 29, 1796).

**Char′i·ton** (kăr′ĭ·tŏn). Greek romance writer, of Aphrodisias in Caria, in 2d century A.D. (or earlier); author of *The Loves of Chaereas and Callirrhoë.*

**Char′le·magne** (shär′lē·mān; *Fr.* shȧr′lē·mȧn′y′) *or* **Charles the Great** *or* **Charles I.** *Ger.* **Karl′ der Gros′se** (kärl′ dēr grō′sē). *Lat.* **Car′o·lus Mag′nus** (kăr′ō·lŭs măg′nŭs). 742–814. King of the Franks (768–814) and emperor of the West (800–814). Birthplace unknown. Son of Pepin the Short, at whose death (768) he became king of Neustria (western Franks), Austrasia, etc.; at death of his brother Carloman (771), became king of all the Franks; m. (771) Hildegarde, of Swabia. Fought with and subjugated the Saxons (772–785). Destroyed kingdom of Lombardy (773–774); crowned king of the Lombards (773). Led expedition

(778) into northeastern Spain against the Arabs, a campaign not historically important but which, through death at Roncesvalles of his paladin Roland, gave rise to a great body of medieval literature (the "matter of France," or Carlovingian cycle, including the epic *Chanson de Roland*). Established boundaries, or marks, for all his dominions; crowned Carolus Augustus, Emperor of the Romans (Christmas Day, 800), by Pope Leo III; subdued the Avars (791–796, 804). Organized administration of his realm, which at end of his conquests was beginning of Holy Roman Empire; retained its ancient national assemblies, strengthened Christianity, founded schools (see ALCUIN); patron of literature, science, and art. Buried at Aix-la-Chapelle.

**Charles I** (chärlz). *In full* **Charles Francis Joseph.** *Ger.* **Karl Franz Josef.** 1887–1922. Emperor of Austria (1916–18). Nephew of Francis Ferdinand; grandnephew of Emperor Francis Joseph; m. (1911) Zita (*q.v.*), Princess of Bourbon and Parma. Proclaimed himself emperor and, as Charles IV, king of Hungary (1916); abdicated (1918); formally deposed by Austrian Parliament (1919); lived in Switzerland (1919–21); made two attempts by visits to Hungary to regain throne (1921); deported by Allies to Madeira (1921); died at Funchal.

**Charles.** Name of two kings of Great Britain and Ireland, of house of Stuart (*q.v.*):

**Charles I.** 1600–1649. King (1625–49). Second son of James VI of Scotland (James I of England) and Anne of Denmark; backward and sickly child; created duke of Albany (1600), duke of York (1605); prince of Wales (1616) on death of older brother, Prince Henry. Went incognito to Madrid with his favorite, duke of Buckingham, to urge his suit with Infanta Maria of Spain (1623); failed, on refusal to turn Roman Catholic; despite promise to Parliament of no concessions, pledged to Princess Henrietta Maria of France, on betrothal, free exercise of Roman Catholic religion, toleration of Catholics, and Catholic upbringing of children. Succeeded James I (1625); married Henrietta Maria by proxy; at end of year, expelled her retinue. A tool in hands of prime minister, duke of Buckingham, for whose warlike schemes he demanded supplies of parliament; dissolved three parliaments in four years for noncompliance; with Laud and Wentworth (later created earl of Strafford) as advisers, ruled for eleven years without parliament, through subservient judges and courts; suffered shameful defeat in France (1627); had recourse to forced loans, poundage, tonnage, and ship money from seaports (1634) and from inland counties (1635) to raise funds, thus arousing John Hampden's resistance; attempted to impose episcopacy upon Church of Scotland, which resisted and restored Presbyterianism, adopting National Covenant (1638); invaded Scotland but, lacking funds, had to sign treaty of Berwick (1639). Summoned Short Parliament (Apr., 1640) to obtain money for expedition against Scots; met refusal and demand under leadership of John Pym for redress of grievances. Defied by Long Parliament (Nov., 1640), which impeached Laud and Strafford; sacrificed life of Strafford in fear for queen's safety (1641); yielded pledge that Long Parliament would be dissolved only by its own vote; in Edinburgh endeavored to win Scots by concessions to demands of Scottish Parliament (1641); was suspected of plotting deaths of covenanting lords and of being privy to Ulster massacre (1641). Attempted (1642) to arrest the Five Members, leaders in passing of Grand Remonstrance in House of Commons, in order to avert impeachment of the queen, who had sought assistance from Rome; declared war on Parliamentarians at Nottingham (1642), beginning civil war that ended in annihilation of royal army at Naseby (1645); took refuge at Oxford (Royalist headquarters from Oct., 1642); surrendered to Scots (1645); was handed over to Parliament (1647). Tried to make separate terms with Scots and with Parliament; continued his intrigues and opposition to constitutional procedure; escaped to Isle of Wight, where held captive at Carisbrooke Castle where he made secret treaty (the Engagement) with Scots by which he received aid of Scots forces for his consent to establish Presbyterianism in England for three years (1647); removed to London (Jan., 1648) and tried at Westminster, where he refused to plead before court constituted by House of Commons; condemned by court of 67 judges as tyrant and enemy of nation; behaved bravely; beheaded at Whitehall; buried in Henry VIII's vault, Windsor.

**Charles II.** 1630–1685. King (1660–1685); called the "Merry Monarch." Son of Charles I and Henrietta Maria. Prince of Wales from birth; took seat in House of Lords (1640). Present at battle of Edge Hill; withdrew to Scilly, to Jersey, then to Paris, with Hobbes as mathematical tutor (1646–48); with naval expedition reached Thames, took prizes, issued proclamation (1648), returned to Holland; sent blank sheet with his signature for any terms Parliament might set, in attempt to save his father's life (1649); came to terms with Scots, accepted Covenant, pledged himself to support Presbyterianism in Scotland and England (1651); later, as king, permitted persecution of Covenanters by his advocate, Mackenzie (1679 ff.); routed by Cromwell at Worcester (1651); escaped (after adventures including concealment in the Royal Oak) to Continent; at Cologne, Bruges, Brussels, The Hague (1654–60) held court noted for dissoluteness; journeyed to southern France in futile attempt to unite French and Spanish crowns in expedition against England (Sept., 1659). After fall of Protectorate, negotiated with General Monck and English Presbyterians; issued Declaration of Breda (1660), promising amnesty and liberty of conscience and providing restoration of parliamentary government; proclaimed king. Entrusted steps of reconstruction (1660–67) to earl of Clarendon; urged lenity in Indemnity bill; dissolved Convention Parliament (Dec., 1660); formally crowned (1661); m. (1662) Catherine of Braganza (*q.v.*). Endeavored to secure toleration for English Catholics and Puritans by Declaration of Indulgence (1662), thereby provoking strongly Anglican parliament to severe acts of repression, including Act of Uniformity (1662), Conventicle Act (1664), Five-mile Act (1665). Secretly accepted large subsidy (1661) from Louis XIV to attack Spain; sold Dunkirk to France (1662); tried by war with Dutch (1664–67) to gain stadholdership for his nephew, William of Orange; forced to conclude Peace of Breda (1667); had to exile Clarendon to appease parliament. Employed Clifford, Arlington, Buckingham, Ashley, and Lauderdale (making up the Cabal, from which the modern cabinet developed) to conduct affairs but carried on important negotiations himself (1667–74); accepted large subsidies from Louis XIV to favor French queen's claims to Spanish succession and French designs on Netherlands; used Triple Alliance (1668) with Holland and Sweden to gain popularity in England and raise Louis's offers; but reversed policy when he negotiated with Louis secret Treaty of Dover (1670), by which he was to declare himself Roman Catholic and join in war on Dutch; forced by parliamentary agitation to cancel his Declaration of Indulgence in favor of Catholics and to pass Test Act (1673), driving Catholics from office; obliged (1674) to conclude Dutch war (begun 1672);

forced by popular feeling to consent to marriage of his niece Princess Mary with William of Orange (1677). Placed earl of Danby in charge of foreign policy (1674–78) but with encouragement of duchess of Portsmouth himself made disgraceful secret engagements with Louis XIV (1676, 1678); intervened against persecution occasioned by Titus Oates's trumped-up Popish Plot only when queen was accused (1678); dissolved parliament in attempt to save Danby from impeachment after disclosure by Louis XIV of correspondence upon subsidies paid to Charles (1679); through Hyde negotiated subsidy treaty with Louis (1681); dissolved parliament that enacted Habeas Corpus Act (1679) and tried to thwart exclusion of his brother James, Duke of York, from succession by declaring James, Duke of Monmouth (his natural son by Lucy Walter) illegitimate; enforced penal laws against nonconformists; threatened with assassination by Rye House Plot (1683); reappointed duke of York lord high admiral (1684); forced to abandon Tangier (1683), let navy decay, let French seize Strasbourg; suffered apoplectic stroke; made profession of Catholic faith; buried in Westminster. Died without legitimate children; had numerous mistresses, thirteen known by name, including Lucy Walter, the duchesses of Cleveland and Portsmouth, and Nell Gwyn, and many illegitimate children, most of whom he acknowledged and ennobled. Patron of theater; encouraged science; praised by Pepys for knowledge of naval architecture.

**Charles** (chärlz; *Fr.* shȧrl). Name of ten (or eleven) kings of France:

CAROLINGIAN DYNASTY (*q.v.*):

**Charles the Great** (742–814). King of the Franks (768–814); not included in numbering of kings named Charles. See CHARLEMAGNE.

**Charles I** (823–877). See CHARLES II, Holy Roman Emperor.

**Charles II** (839–888). See CHARLES III, Holy Roman Emperor.

**Charles III.** *Called* **Charles the Simple.** *Fr.* **Charles le Sim′ple** (lẽ săɴ′pl′). 879–929. Son of Louis II. King, in opposition to Eudes (893–898); sole king (898–923); ceded (911) Normandy to Rollo, but became king of Lorraine; driven out by Robert, Count of Paris (922); captured and imprisoned (923).

CAPETIAN DYNASTY (*q.v.*):

**Charles IV.** *Called* **Charles the Fair.** *Fr.* **Charles le Bel** (lẽ bĕl′). 1294–1328. Son of Philip IV. King (1322–28), last of direct line of Capetian kings; also, as Charles I, king of Navarre. Sought to strengthen royal power by increasing taxes, exacting fines and duties, debasing coinage, and by confiscations and other questionable methods; secured Agenais from England.

HOUSE OF VALOIS (*q.v.*), CAPETIAN BRANCH:

**Charles V.** *Called* **Charles the Wise.** *Fr.* **Charles le Sage** (lẽ sȧzh′). 1337–1380. Son of John II; b. in Vincennes. Became regent when father made prisoner by English at Poitiers (1356); royal prerogatives strengthened by failure of the Jacquerie, or peasants' revolt (1358); treaty of Bretigny (1360) with England. King (1364–80); most of territory held by England regained (1369–75); greatly aided by Bertrand Du Guesclin in suppression of free companies and in wars against Navarre (1365) and England; increased taxes, but rule generally wise and economical; patron of art and literature; collected large and valuable library at the Louvre.

**Charles VI.** *Called* **Charles the Well-Beloved.** *Fr.* **Charles le Bien′-Ai′mé′** (lẽ byăɴ′-nĕ′mā′). 1368–1422. Son of Charles V; b. Paris. King (1380–1422). During minority (1380–88) under guardianship of four uncles, one (Louis, Duke of Anjou) acting as regent (1380–82); m. Isabeau, or Isabella, of Bavaria (1385); assumed government (1388); ruled well until subject to attacks of insanity (1392). Struggle for regency led to civil wars between houses of Orléans (Armagnacs) and Burgundy; affairs of realm disrupted; at times English aid invited by each party; French severely defeated by Henry V at Agincourt (1415); Peace of Troyes (1420).

**Charles VII.** 1403–1461. Fifth son of Charles VI; b. Paris. King (1422–61). Began reign with all northern France and part in southwest in English possession (1422); raised siege of Orléans with aid of Joan of Arc (1429); crowned at Reims (1429); made peace with Philip of Burgundy (1435); entered Paris (1436) after English had been gradually driven back (1429–36); recovered from English all French lands except Calais (1437–53); issued Pragmatic Sanction (1438); put down (1440) conspiracy of nobles, including the dauphin; made truce with England (1444–49); regained Normandy (1450). Last part of reign marked by reforms, establishment of a permanent tax, increased power of king, beginning of standing army, etc. For many years influenced by advice of his mistress Agnès Sorel.

**Charles VIII.** 1470–1498. Son of Louis XI; b. in Amboise. King (1483–98; from 1483–91, France ably governed by his sister Anne de Beaujeu); m. Anne de Bretagne (1491). Ambitious to revive rights of house of Anjou to Naples (see ANJOU); made concessions to England and the emperor, neglecting France; aided by Sforza in Milan, entered Naples in great pomp (1495); later driven out (1495) by Holy League forces of Ferdinand II of Naples and Gonzalo de Córdoba; died childless, Orléans line succeeding (Louis XII).

HOUSE OF VALOIS (*q.v.*), ANGOULÊME BRANCH:

**Charles IX.** 1550–1574. Second son of Henry II and Catherine de Médicis; b. Saint-Germain-en-Laye. King (1560–74); during minority, kingdom ruled by his mother; later (1563–74), completely under her domination. Reign marked by fierce civil wars—Catholics (followers of Guise) v. Huguenots (followers of Condé). Had one natural son, Charles, Duc d'Angoulême (*q.v.*).

HOUSE OF BOURBON (*q.v.*), RESTORED:

**Charles X.** 1757–1836. King (1824–30). Grandson of Louis XV; younger brother of Louis XVI and Louis XVIII; b. Versailles; known until accession as Charles Philippe, Comte d'Artois; m. Maria Theresa of Savoy (1773). After Revolution became leader of émigrés (1789–95); joined English expedition to Brittany (1795) but abandoned Vendeans; lived in England and Scotland (1795–1814). After Restoration became leader (1815) of ultraroyalists, party of extreme reaction. After accession (1824) attempted to restore absolutism of the monarch; became increasingly unpopular; dissolved Chamber of Deputies (May, 1830); ordered new elections; promulgated "four ordinances" (July 25) terminating freedom of press, decreeing new method of elections, dissolving the chamber; overthrown by ensuing revolution (July 27–29); abdicated (Aug. 2); fled to England; lived in Scotland and Prague.

**Charles.** *Called* **Charles the Bold.** *Fr.* **Charles le Té′mé′raire′** (lẽ tā′mā′râr′). 1433–1477. Last duke of Burgundy (see BURGUNDY); son of Duke Philip the Good; b. Dijon. Comte **de Cha′ro′lais′** [shȧ′rô′lĕ′] (1452–67); bitter enemy of Louis XI of France, his nominal feudal superior; joined with other nobles and defeated the king (1465). Duke (1467–77); m. (1468) Margaret, sister of Edward IV of England; almost continuously at war with France (1467–77); conquered Lorraine (1475); badly defeated twice by Swiss (1476). His death ended Burgundian resistance to France. See MARY OF BURGUNDY.

**Charles.** *Called* **Charles the Good.** *Fr.* **Charles le Bon** (shȧrl′ lẽ bôɴ′). 1083?–1127. Count of Flanders (1119–27). Son of Canute, King of Denmark; inherited through his mother, who was daughter of Robert I the Frisian; sought to rule justly and promote welfare of subjects; murdered at Bruges.

**Charles.** Name of five dukes of Lorraine:

**Charles I.** 950?–?992. Younger son of Frankish king Louis IV, of Carolingian line; received Lower Lorraine as duchy from Emperor Otto II (977); aided Otto against Lothair; defeated by Hugh Capet in attempt to secure Frankish crown (987); died in prison at Orléans.

**Charles II** (*or* **I**). *Called* **Charles the Bold.** 1365–1431. Duke of Lorraine (1391–1431); son of Duke John; neglected his duchy; his daughter Isabella married René I of Anjou (see ANJOU).

**Charles III** (*or* **II**). *Called* **Charles the Great.** 1543–1608. Duke (1545–1608); son of Duke Francis I; brought up at court of Henry II of France; m. Henry's daughter Claude (1559); took part in religious wars of France (1562–98); member of Holy League.

**Charles IV** (*or* **III**). 1604–1675. Duke (1624–34, 1659–69); son of Duke Francis II. One of the most eccentric characters in French history, chivalrous and brave, but incompetent and entirely untrustworthy, spent whole life in intrigues against France or as a wandering soldier of fortune; fought in wars of the Empire, Austria, and Spain; forced to abdicate by Richelieu (1634) but restored (1659). Much Lorraine territory lost during his rule.

**Charles V** (*or* **IV**). *Also known as* **Charles Leopold.** 1643–1690. Nephew of Duke Charles IV. Titular duke of Lorraine; kept out of duchy by Louis XIV. Served in Imperial army against Turks and later against French; twice unsuccessful candidate for crown of Poland; commanded weak Imperial army at Vienna during siege by Turks; with John Sobieski defeated Turks (1683); won great victory at Mohács against Turks (1687).

**Charles.** *Ger.* **Karl Alexander.** 1712–1780. Prince of Lorraine. Youngest son of Duke Leopold of Lorraine, grandson of Charles V of Lorraine, and brother of Emperor Francis I; b. in Lunéville. Officer in Austrian army; fought against Turks (1738–39); in War of Austrian Succession (1740–48) made field marshal by his sister-in-law Maria Theresa; often in command against Frederick the Great in Silesian Wars; sometimes successful, but severely defeated at Hohenfriedeberg (1745) and (1746) at Rocourt by Marshal Saxe; governor of Austrian Netherlands (1749–56); again given supreme command of Austrian armies by Maria Theresa at beginning of Seven Years' War (1756–63); shut up in Prague by Frederick (1757); victor at Breslau, but completely defeated by Frederick at Leuthen (1757); military adviser at court in Vienna (1757–63); governor at Brussels (1763–80).

**Charles.** *Ger.* **Karl.** Kings of Germany. = CHARLES, Holy Roman Emperors.

**Charles.** *Ger.* **Karl.** 1786–1818. Grand duke of **Ba′den** [bä′dĕn] (1811–18). Grandson of Charles Frederick (*q.v.*); m. (1806) Stéphanie de Beauharnais, adopted daughter of Napoleon; at first sided with French; after defeat of Napoleon (1813), shifted allegiance to Allies; had Baden join Germanic confederation (1815); having no direct heirs, last years of reign marked by controversy over succession; granted new liberal constitution (1818).

**Charles.** *Ger.* **Karl.** 1741–1816. Duke of Mecklenburg-Strelitz (1794–1816); grand duke (from 1815); governor of Hanover (1776–86); fought against Napoleon. His son **Charles** (1785–1837), half brother of Queen Louise of Prussia, served in Prussian army (from 1804); general of infantry (1825); president, council of state (1827); succeeded as duke.

**Charles.** *Ger.* **Karl.** Name of two dukes of Württemberg: **Charles (I) Alexander** (1684–1737), b. Stuttgart; entered service of Austria and served many years as soldier, esp. (1705–13) in War of Spanish Succession under Prince Eugene of Savoy, and (1716–18) against Turks; duke (1733–37). His son **Charles (II) Eugene** (1728–1793), b. Brussels; duke (1737–93; completed minority rule in 1744); founded Stuttgart University.

**Charles I.** *Full German name* **Karl Friedrich Alexander.** 1823–1891. King of Württemberg (1864–91). Son of King William I; b. Stuttgart; m. (1846) Grand Duchess Olga, daughter of Nicholas I of Russia; supported Austria against Prussia (1866); joined other German states in war against France (1870–71); introduced liberal reforms. Succeeded by his nephew William II.

**Charles.** *Ger.* **Karl.** Name of seven Holy Roman emperors:

**Charles I.** See CHARLEMAGNE.

**Charles II.** *Called* **Charles the Bald.** *Fr.* **Charles le Chauve** (lẽ shōv′). 823–877. Son of Louis I and Judith of Bavaria; b. Frankfurt. King of France (840–877), as Charles I; Holy Roman emperor (875–877). Joined his half brother Louis the German against Lothair, defeating him at Fontenoy (841); by Treaty of Verdun (843), became king of the West Franks (beginning of modern France); in continual strife with Louis the German (after 855). On death of Emperor Louis II (875), invaded Italy; crowned emperor (875) and made king of Italy. During his reign, France ravaged by Normans; Bordeaux, Rouen, Orléans, and part of Paris sacked.

**Charles III.** *Called* **Charles the Fat.** *Fr.* **Charles le Gros** (lẽ grō′). 839–888. Son of Louis the German. King of part of Germany (876–887); on death of Carloman (884), became king of all France (884–887), as Charles II; Holy Roman emperor (881–887; crowned 881); made humiliating treaty with Northmen at Paris (886). His deposition by Arnulf (887) marked dismemberment of empire of Charlemagne.

**Charles IV.** *Known also as* **Charles of Luxemburg.** 1316–1378. Son of John of Luxemburg, King of Bohemia. King of Germany and Bohemia and Holy Roman emperor (1347–78; crowned 1355); helped found the U. of Prague (1348); issued Golden Bull (1356), establishing new rule for the imperial election.

**Charles V.** 1500–1558. Holy Roman emperor (1519–56), and king of Spain as Charles I (1516–56). Son of Philip of Burgundy (Philip I of Spain) and grandson of Emperor Maximilian I and of Ferdinand and Isabella; inherited Burgundy and Netherlands (1506); crowned emperor (1520); m. (1525) Isabella of Portugal. *Attitude toward Reformation:* Tolerant of Protestants in Germany, for political reasons, but persecuted heretics in Spain. Summoned Diet of Worms and presided in person over it (1521); Diet of Augsburg (1530) failed to settle religious controversy; Council of Trent (1545–63) and Augsburg Interim (1548) failed to unite Catholics and Protestants. Won Schmalkaldic War (1546–47); faced armed resistance of Lutheran states (1551–52); made Peace of Augsburg (1555) with Protestants. *Wars with France* (1521–44): Defeated Francis I at Pavia (1525) and made him prisoner; Peace of Cambrai (1529); wars renewed; finally terminated by Treaty of Crépy (1544), favorable to Empire; in war (1552–56) with Henry II failed to capture Metz. *Activities in Italy and other countries:* Took Rome and made pope prisoner (1527); crowned king of Lombardy (1530). Successful in campaign against Turks under Suleiman (1532); conquered pirates of Tunis (1535). *As ruler of Spain and Spanish dominions:* Repressed revolt in Castile (1520–21); extended New World possessions through conquests of Mexico by Cortes (1519–21) and of Peru by Pizarro (1531–35), and through expeditions and other conquests in Central and South America. *Closing years:* Relinquished kingdom of Naples (1554) and Netherlands (1555) to his son Philip; resigned control of Spain and the Indies to son Philip (1556) and imperial crown to his brother Ferdinand (1556; formal abdication, 1558); retired to monastery of Yuste in western Spain (1557).

**Charles VI.** 1685–1740. Holy Roman emperor (1711–40); and (as Charles III) king of Hungary. Son of Leopold I; m. (1708) Elisabeth Christine of Brunswick-Wolfenbüttel. Assigned by his father as heir (as Charles III) to throne of Spain (1700); brought on (1701–14) War of Spanish Succession (see CHARLES II of Spain); by Peace of Rastatt (1714) ceded Spanish Netherlands to Austria and gave up all claim of the Empire to Spain. Successful in war against Turks, concluded by Treaty of Passarowitz (1718). Issued Pragmatic Sanction (1713) in order to secure Austrian throne to his daughter Maria Theresa. Unsuccessful in War of Polish Succession (1733–35), and in second war with Turks, terminated by Treaty of Belgrade (1739). Last of male line of house of Hapsburg (*q.v.*).

**Charles VII** *or* **Charles Albert.** *Ger.* **Karl Albrecht.** *Known also as* **Charles of Bavaria.** 1697–1745. Holy Roman emperor (1742–45; crowned 1742). Son of Maximilian Emanuel, Elector of Bavaria; succeeded to electorate (1726); claimant of Austrian inheritance; took part in War of Austrian Succession (1740–48) against Maria Theresa but died before its end. See WITTELSBACH.

**Charles.** Name of four kings of Hungary:

**Charles I** *or* **Charles Robert of An'jou** (ăn'jōō; *Fr.* äN'zhōō'). *Also* **Ca'ro'bert'** (kȧ'rô'bâr'). 1288–1342. Grandson of Charles II of Naples. King (1308–42); elected by the diet (1308) and crowned (1310); founder of Anjou line of Hungary; imposed direct taxes, encouraged trade, and increased privileges of towns; secured royal power on feudal basis; m. daughter of Ladislas of Poland and (1339) secured succession of Polish throne for his son Louis I (*q.v.*).

**Charles II.** *Known as* **Charles of Durazzo.** See CHARLES III of Naples.

**Charles III.** See CHARLES VI, Holy Roman Emperor.

**Charles IV** (1887–1922). See CHARLES I, Emperor of Austria and King of Hungary.

**Charles.** Name of four kings of Naples or of Two Sicilies, three of the house of Anjou (*q.v.*), one of house of Bourbon:

**Charles I.** 1226–1285. Son of Louis VIII of France. Count of Anjou and of Provence (1246–85); accompanied Louis IX on Sixth Crusade (1248–50). King of Two Sicilies (1266–85); defeated Manfred at Benevento (1266) and Conradin at Tagliacozzo (1268); became one of most powerful rulers in Europe; his harsh rule caused uprising known as Sicilian Vespers (1282); driven from Sicily by Spanish (1284).

**Charles II.** 1246–1309. Son of Charles I. Held prisoner by Spanish (1284–88). King of Naples (1285–1309); with help of pope attempted to win back Sicily, but was defeated in war with Frederick II (1296–1302). See ANJOU family.

**Charles III.** *Known as* **Charles of Du·raz'zo** (dōō·rät'tsō). 1345–1386. Great-grandson of Charles II. King of Naples (1381–86) and king of Hungary as Charles II (1385–86). Adopted by Queen Joanna I of Naples, but abandoned in favor of Louis I of Anjou; seized crown of Naples (1381); caused Joanna's death (1382); waged war with Louis I (1382–84); crowned king of Hungary as Charles II (1385), but imprisoned as result of a revolt and poisoned.

**Charles IV.** See CHARLES III of Spain.

**Charles.** Name of three dukes of Parma of Italian Bourbon line:

**Charles I.** = CHARLES III, King of Spain.

**Charles II.** *In full* **Charles Louis Ferdinand de Bour'bon'** (dē bōōr'bôN'). 1799–1883. Son of Louis de Bourbon, King of Etruria and María Luisa of Spain; duke (1803–07, 1847–49); forced to abdicate by Napoleon (1807); left duchy of Lucca by Congress of Vienna (1815); forced to abdicate again as duke of Parma by revolutionary movement of 1848.

**Charles III.** *In full* **Charles Ferdinand de Bourbon.** 1823–1854. Son of Charles II; duke (1849–54); assassinated.

**Charles I.** Duke of Savoy. See SAVOY.

**Charles III.** Prince of Monaco. See MONACO.

**Charles I.** King of Portugal. See CARLOS I.

**Charles I** and **II.** Kings of Rumania. See CAROL.

**Charles.** Name of three kings of Navarre:

**Charles I.** See CHARLES IV, King of France.

**Charles II.** *Called* **Charles the Bad.** *Fr.* **Charles le Mau'vais'** (shȧrl' lē mō'vĕ'). 1332–1387. Son of Queen Joanna. King (1349–87); count of Evreux; m. (1352) Jeanne, dau. of John II of France; in dispute with father-in-law over lands in Angoulême and Normandy; held prisoner by John (1356–57); captain general of Paris (1358); at strife with dauphin (1358–60); spent rest of life making trouble in Spain and France (hence his nickname); made and broke alliances and treaties; accused of other crimes.

**Charles III.** *Called* **Charles the Noble.** 1361–1425. King (1387–1425). Son of Charles II; m. (1375) Leonora, dau. of Henry II of Castile; recovered (1393) Cherbourg (given by his father to Richard II of England); long reign of peace and progress; created duke of Nemours; succeeded by his daughter Blanche, mother of Charles, Prince of Viana (*q.v.*).

**Charles.** *Span.* Don **Car'los** (dŏn kär'lŏs; *Span.* dôn kär'lōs). Prince of **Via'na** (vyä'nä). 1421–1461. Sometimes known as Charles IV, King of Navarre; son of John II of Aragon and Blanche of Navarre; driven out of Navarre by his father (1441); civil war. Known as poet and writer; author of a history of the kings of Navarre.

**Charles.** Name of four kings of Spain, first two Hapsburgs, last two Bourbons (see HAPSBURG; BOURBON):

**Charles I.** See CHARLES V, Holy Roman Emperor.

**Charles II.** 1661–1700. King (1665–1700). Son of Philip IV; during minority, under regency of queen mother, Mariana de Austria; assumed government (1675), with kingdom in weak and demoralized condition; took as adviser (1677–79) Don Juan, the younger (see JOHN OF AUSTRIA); m. (1) Marie Louise d'Orléans (1679); (2) Maria Anna of Bavaria-Neuburg (1689); joined Grand Alliance in war against Louis XIV, terminated by Peace of Ryswick (1697); having no offspring, was prevailed upon to choose as successor Philip of Anjou, grandson of Louis XIV. His death (Nov. 1, 1700) was signal for beginning of War of Spanish Succession. See PHILIP V of Spain.

**Charles III.** *In youth known as* Don **Carlos of Bourbon.** 1716–1788. King (1759–88). Son of Philip V and Elizabeth Farnese; great-grandson of Louis XIV of France. Given control of Parma and Piacenza (1731); conquered Two Sicilies (*i.e.* Naples and Sicily) and became king as Charles IV, first of the Neapolitan Bourbons (1734–59). Became king of Spain (1759) on death of his brother Ferdinand VI, leaving Two Sicilies to his son Ferdinand I; strengthened kingdom by reforming finances, aiding agriculture and commerce, and establishing military schools; signed Family Compact (1761) with France against England; suffered losses in Seven Years' War (1756–63); expelled Jesuits (1767).

**Charles IV.** 1748–1819. King (1788–1808). Second son of Charles III; b. Naples; m. Maria Louisa of Parma, whose complete influence over him caused vacillating policy; made Manuel de Godoy, a favorite of queen, prime minister (1792); long period of trouble with Revolutionary France, subservience to Napoleon, war with Portugal and England; Louisiana retroceded to France (1800); Spanish fleet destroyed at Trafalgar (1805); made secret treaty with Napoleon (1807); Spain invaded by French armies (1807); forced to abdicate (1808); died in Rome.

**Charles.** *Swed.* **Karl.** Name of 15 kings of Sweden, the first six being of doubtful authenticity:

**Charles VII.** d. 1167. Son of Sverker. King (1161–67); took title of "king of Swedes and Goths"; fought Russians (1164); assassinated.

**Charles VIII.** *Known as* **Karl Knuts'son** (kärl k'nōōts'sôn). 1408?–1470. King of Sweden (1448–57, 1464–65, 1467–70) and of Norway (1449–50). Elected regent by nobles (1436–40); fought long war with Denmark (1463–70); forced to flee to Germany (1457); succeeded by Christian I (1457–64); temporarily in power (1464–65); recalled to be king (1467–70).

**Charles IX.** 1550–1611. Regent of Sweden (1599–1604); king (1604–11). Third son of Gustavus Vasa; b. Stockholm. Duke of **Sö'der·man·land'** [sû'dĕr·mȧn·lȧnd'] (1560). Acted as regent during absence of his nephew King Sigismund (1592–94) and restored Protestant faith (1593–99); forced Sigismund to retire to Poland (1594); defeated Sigismund in battle at Stångebro (1598); made hereditary prince of Sweden (1599); began long war with Poland (1600); began war with Denmark (1611).

**Charles X Gustavus.** 1622–1660. King (1654–60). Son of John Casimir, Count Palatine, and Catherine, daughter of Charles IX; nephew of Gustavus Adolphus; b. Nyköping. Fought in Thirty Years' War (1642–48); became king on abdication of his cousin Christina; invaded and conquered Poland (1655–56); won great battle at Warsaw (1656); made war against Denmark (1657–58); led army across the ice; won back lands of south Sweden (Scania) by Treaty of Roskilde (1658). See VASA.

**Charles XI.** 1655–1697. King (1660–97). Son of Charles X Gustavus. King under regency of corrupt aristocrats (1660–72); assumed control (1672); defeated by coalition of Holy Roman Empire, Denmark, and Netherlands (1675–76), but more successful during latter part of war (1676–79); won favorable terms at Peace of Nijmegen (1678–79); aided by statesmen Johan Gyllenstierna and Bengt Gabrielsson Oxenstierna; m. (1680) Danish princess Ulrika Eleonora; began reorganization of Sweden (1680); forced estates of greater nobles to revert to crown; was granted (1682) practically absolute power; improved army and fleet and economic condition.

**Charles XII.** *Called* "The Alexander of the North" *and* "Madman of the North." 1682–1718. King (1697–1718). Son of Charles XI. Declared of age at fifteen; confronted by alliance of Poland, Denmark, and Russia (1699); invaded Denmark and forced peace of Travendal (1700); attacked Russians, winning great victory on the Narva (1700); defeated Saxons and Poles at Klissow (1702), dethroned Augustus II and made Stanislas Leszczyński king (1704); forced Peace of Altranstädt (1706); after remaining in Saxony a year, invaded Russia a second time (1707–08); defeated Peter the Great, but on attempt to reach Moscow met with repeated disasters; with small army, laid siege to Poltava; completely defeated in ensuing battle (1709); became fugitive with Mazepa, hetman of Dnieper Cossacks, and fled to Turkish territory; persuaded sultan to declare war on Russia (1711–12); held prisoner (1712–14) at Bender and Dimotika; fled back to Sweden (1714); escaped siege at Stralsund; found Sweden in deplorable state; raised another army that kept Russians at bay; made vast plans for recovery; invaded Norway; killed by cannon shot at siege of Fredrikshald.

**Charles XIII.** 1748–1818. King (1809–18). Second son of Adolphus Frederick and younger brother of Gustavus III. Commanded Swedish fleet against Russia (1788–90); duke of Södermanland; made regent after assassination of Gustavus III (1792–96); again regent on deposition of Gustavus IV (1809); made king (1809); signed new constitution, restoring limited monarchy; compelled by peace with Russia (1809) to give up Finland and Åland Islands; made peace with Denmark (1809) and France (1810); during reign, Norway united with Sweden (1814); much material progress made.

**Charles XIV John.** *Orig. name* **Jean Baptiste Jules Bernadotte** (see BERNADOTTE). 1763?–1844. King of Sweden and Norway (1818–44). French soldier, b. Pau; entered army (1780), served in French Revolution; in diplomatic service for Napoleon (1798–99); rose from ranks to become one of Napoleon's marshals (1804); named prince of **Pon'te·cor'vo** [pōn'tȧ·kôr'vô] (1805). Elected crown prince (1810) of Sweden, taking name of Charles John; allied with Czar Alexander of Russia (1812); commanded an allied army against Napoleon (1813); aided in winning battle of Leipzig; succeeded Charles XIII as king (1818); his reign peaceful and profitable to both kingdoms, although he was criticized and at times opposed for ultraconservative views.

**Charles XV.** 1826–1872. King of Sweden and Norway (1859–72). Son of Oscar I. Instituted legal reforms, esp. of the estates (1865); promulgated decree (1866) by which two-chamber parliament (one electoral) was established; popular in both kingdoms; writer, poet, and artist of ability.

**Charles** (chärlz), **Elizabeth,** *nee* **Run'dle** (rŭn'd'l). 1828–1896. English author of semireligious books, including *The Chronicles of the Schönberg-Cotta Family* (1862), a story about Luther.

**Charles, Enid.** See under Lancelot HOGBEN.

**Charles** (shȧrl; *Angl.* chärlz), **Jacques Alexandre César.** 1746–1823. French physicist, chemist, and inventor. Popularized in France Franklin's discoveries concerning electricity; made several balloon ascents, being first to use hydrogen for balloon inflation (1783); anticipated Gay-Lussac in study of expansion of gases (hence alternative names *Charles's law* or *Gay-Lussac's law* for law stating effect of changes in temperature on volume of a gas); invented a thermometric hydrometer; improved on the Gravesande heliostat. Became professor of physics, Conservatoire des Arts et Métiers, Paris.

**Charles** (chärlz), **James.** 1851–1906. English portrait and landscape painter; excelled in painting sunlight; best-known works: *Christening Sunday* (1887), *Will it Rain?*, *Milking Time* (1896).

**Charles, Robert Henry.** 1855–1931. Church of England clergyman, b. in County Tyrone, Ireland; B.A., Queen's U. (1877). Ordained (1883); professor of Biblical Greek,

Trinity Coll., Dublin (1898–1906); lecturer at Oxford (1905–14). Canon of Westminster (from 1913) and archdeacon (from 1919). Author of religious works, including studies of apocryphal books of the Bible.

**Charles, Thomas.** 1755–1814. Welsh preacher. B.A., Oxon. (1779); joined Calvinistic Methodists (1784); established system of Welsh circulating schools; organized distribution of Bibles; organized Welsh Calvinistic Methodists (1810–11); compiled Biblical dictionary (4 vols., 1805–08).

**Charles Albert.** *Ital.* **Carlo Alberto.** 1798–1849. King of Sardinia. Son of Prince Charles Emmanuel of Savoy-Carignan line (see SAVOY); b. Turin. Succeeded to father's title (1800) as prince of Savoy and Piedmont; at Piedmontese uprising (1821) and abdication of Victor Emmanuel I, made regent for short time, but displeased new king, Charles Felix, and became unpopular; exiled to Florence. Appointed viceroy of Sardinia (1829); succeeded to throne (1831) on death of Charles Felix, last of main Savoy line; attempted to introduce order in kingdom; reorganized finances, granted new constitution, and created an army. Strong supporter of Italian unity; declared war against Austria (1848); defeated at Custozza (1848) and Novara (1849); resigned (1849) in favor of his son Victor Emmanuel (II); retired to monastery in Oporto, Portugal.

**Charles Alexander.** *Ger.* **Karl Alexander.** (1) = CHARLES, Prince of Lorraine. (2) = CHARLES I, Duke of Württemberg. (3) 1818–1901. Grand duke of Saxe-Weimar (1853–1901). Son of Charles Frederick and Maria Paulovna; b. in Weimar and brought up there while it was still under influence of Goethe; liberal patron of arts and literature; traveled widely; made Weimar a center of culture; m. (1842) Sophia Louise, daughter of William II of the Netherlands.

**Charles Anthony.** *Ger.* **Karl Anton.** 1811–1885. Prince of Hohenzollern-Sigmaringen. Relinquished principality to king of Prussia (1849). As Prussian general, prominent in army reorganization dispute (1853–62); military governor of Rhineland region of Westphalia (1863–71); took part (1870) in controversy with France over candidature of his son Leopold for throne of Spain (see LEOPOLD, Prince of Hohenzollern-Sigmaringen). His second son became King Carol (Charles) I of Rumania.

**Charles Augustus.** *Ger.* **Karl August.** 1757–1828. Duke of Saxe-Weimar (1758–1815); grand duke (1815–28). Educ. by his mother, Amalia, during regency (1758–75). Made acquaintance of Goethe (1774) and remained his lifelong friend; his court the center of German literary leaders Goethe, Schiller, Herder, Wieland, etc. Joined Prussian army (1786); remained until Jena (1806); joined coalition against French (1813–15); influential at Congress of Vienna (1815). Advanced liberal in political opinions.

**Charles de Blois** *or* **de Châtillon.** Duke of Brittany. See Charles de BLOIS.

**Charles de Lorraine.** See under GUISE family.

**Charles' de Va'lois'** (shärl' dẽ vá'lwá'). 1270–1325. Third son of King Philip III of France; granted countship of Valois by his father (1285); m. Margaret, daughter of Charles II, King of Naples (see ANJOU, 4); thus became count of Anjou and of Maine. His eldest son, Philip, was chosen (1328) king of France as Philip VI, first of the House of Valois (see VALOIS). His second son, **Charles de Valois,** better known as duc **d'A'len'çon'** (dá'läN'sôN'), was killed at Crécy (1346). See also ANGOULÊME.

**Charles d'Orléans.** *Eng.* **Charles of Orleans.** See ORLÉANS, 2.

**Charles Edward.** = Charles Edward STUART.

**Charles Edward.** *Ger.* **Karl Eduard.** 1884–1954. Duke of Saxe-Coburg-Gotha (1900–18). Son of Prince Leopold, duke of Albany, and grandson of Queen Victoria. Succeeded to duchy on death of his uncle Alfred (1900); resigned position of officer in British regiment (1914); abdicated (1918). Supported Nationalist movement in Germany (from 1922); joined the Stahlhelm (1928) and became officer in Hitler's forces (1933); president of German Red Cross (1934).

**Charles Emmanuel.** *Ital.* **Carlo Emanuele.** (1) Name of four dukes of Savoy: **Charles Emmanuel I** (1562–1630); son of Emmanuel Philibert; b. Rivoli; became duke (1580); spent entire life fluctuating between alliances with France and Spain; gained and lost new territories. His fourth son, Thomas Francis (Tommasco Francesco), founded Savoy-Carignan line (see SAVOY). **Charles Emmanuel II** (1634–1675); son of Victor Amadeus I; duke (1638–75); reign troubled by civil dissension but marked by progress in arts, esp. in Turin. **Charles Emmanuel III** (1701–1773); son of Victor Amadeus II; b. Turin; duke of Savoy and, as Charles Emmanuel I, 2d king of Sardinia (1730–73); territory increased; long reign a period of prosperity. **Charles Emmanuel IV** (1751–1819); son of Victor Amadeus III; duke of Savoy (1796–98) and, as Charles Emmanuel II, 4th king of Sardinia (1796–1802); lost to French republic (1798) possessions on mainland (Savoy and Piedmont); abdicated (1802) in favor of his brother Victor Emmanuel I; became a Jesuit (1815).
(2) **Charles Emmanuel** (d. 1800), 6th prince of Savoy-Carignan line; father of Charles Albert (*q.v.*).

**Charles Eugene.** = CHARLES II, Duke of Württemberg.

**Charles Felix.** *Ital.* **Carlo Felice.** 1756–1831. King of Sardinia (1821–31). Son of Victor Amadeus III, Duke of Savoy; viceroy of Sardinia (1799–1806, 1817–21); became king on abdication of his brother Victor Emmanuel I; last ruler of main Savoy line; secured succession for Charles Albert (*q.v.*). See SAVOY.

**Charles Francis Joseph.** = CHARLES I of Austria.

**Charles Frederick.** *Ger.* **Karl Friedrich.** 1728–1811. Ruler of Baden, as margrave (1738–1803), elector (1803–06), grand duke (1806–11); b. Karlsruhe. Ruled under regency (1738–46); inherited lands of Baden-Baden line (1771); increased territory and influence of his state, with aid of Austria and later of Napoleon. Grandfather of Grand Duke Charles (*q.v.*).

**Charles Frederick.** *Ger.* **Karl Friedrich.** 1783–1853. Grand duke of **Saxe'-Wei'mar** [săks'vī'mär] (1828–53); son of Charles Augustus; m. Maria Paulovna (1804), daughter of Czar Paul of Russia. Their daughter Augusta was wife of William I of Prussia. See also CHARLES ALEXANDER.

**Charles John.** *Swed.* **Karl Johan.** = CHARLES XIV of Sweden.

**Charles Leopold.** = CHARLES V, Duke of Lorraine.

**Charles Leopold.** *Ger.* **Karl Leopold.** 1679–1747. Duke of Mecklenburg-Schwerin (1713–28); deposed by Emperor Charles VI; m. Catherine, daughter of Ivan V of Russia. Their daughter Anna Leopoldovna (*q.v.*) m. Anthony Ulrich of Brunswick.

**Charles Louis.** *Ger.* **Karl Ludwig.** Name of archdukes of Austria:
**Charles Louis** (1771–1847), archduke of Austria and duke of **Te'schen** (tĕsh'ĕn); b. Florence; son of Emperor Leopold II. Austrian general and field marshal; first saw action at Jemappes (1792); showed brilliant generalship in campaign against Jourdan and Moreau (1796); successful against Napoleon's generals (1799–1800); de-

feated by Masséna in Italy (1805); long the most formidable opponent of Napoleon; won battle of Aspern (1809) but lost at Wagram (1809); retired from military life (1809). Wrote several books on the theory and art of war.

**Charles Louis** (1833–1896), archduke of Austria; younger brother of Emperor Francis Joseph of Austria and of Maximilian of Mexico; governor of Tirol (1855–61); m. (1862), as 2d wife, Princess Maria Annunziata of Sicily (d. 1871), by whom he had four children, including Archduke Francis Ferdinand (assassinated 1914 at Sarajevo), Otto (1865–1906; m., 1886, Princess Maria Josepha of Saxony), and Ferdinand (1868–1915; who renounced his title); m. (1873), as 3d wife, Princess Maria Theresa (1855–1944), daughter of King Miguel of Portugal.

**Charles Louis.** *Ger.* **Karl Ludwig.** 1617–1680. Elector palatine (1648–80); son of Elector Frederick V; in Thirty Years' War, lost ancestral lands; imprisoned by Richelieu (1639–40); lands restored by Peace of Westphalia (1648).

**Charles' Mar·tel'** (chärlz' mär·tĕl'; *Fr.* shȧrl' mȧr'tĕl'), *i.e.* the Hammer [Fr. *martel*]. *Ger.* **Karl' Mar·tell'** (kärl' mär·tĕl'). 689?–741. Succeeded his father, Pepin of Herstal, as Frankish ruler of Austrasia (715–741); overcame Neustrians and made himself mayor of the palace (716–717); after Arab invasion of southern France (begun 719), totally defeated caliph's army under Abd-er-Rahman at Tours, near Poitiers (732), overthrowing Moslem menace to France. Grandfather of Charlemagne.

**Charles of Anjou.** = CHARLES I, II, and III of Naples.

**Charles of Bavaria.** = CHARLES VII, Holy Roman Emperor.

**Charles of Durazzo.** = CHARLES III of Naples.

**Charles of Hohenzollern.** = CAROL I of Rumania.

**Charles of Lorraine, Valois, Orleans.** = CHARLES DE LORRAINE, DE VALOIS, D'ORLÉANS.

**Charles of Luxemburg.** = CHARLES IV, Holy Roman Emperor.

**Charles Robert of Anjou.** = CHARLES I of Hungary.

**Charles the Bad** and **Charles the Noble.** = CHARLES II and III, kings of Navarre.

**Charles the Bald** and **Charles the Fat.** = CHARLES II and III, Holy Roman emperors.

**Charles the Bold.** (1) = CHARLES, Duke of Burgundy. (2) = CHARLES II, Duke of Lorraine.

**Charles the Good.** = CHARLES, Count of Flanders.

**Charles the Great.** (1) = CHARLEMAGNE. (2) = CHARLES III, Duke of Lorraine.

**Charles the Simple, the Fair, the Wise, the Well-Beloved.** = CHARLES III, IV, V, VI, kings of France.

**Charles Theodore.** *Ger.* **Karl Theodor.** 1724–1799. Elector of Palatinate branch of house of Wittelsbach, son of count palatine John Christian Joseph. Elector (1733–77); inherited duchy of Bavaria on death (1777) of elector Maximilian III Joseph; elector of united Palatine lands (1777–99); his dispute with his heir, Charles of Zweibrücken, caused War of Bavarian Succession (1778–79), a war without any battles; supported Austria; his sovereignty recognized by Treaty of Teschen (1779); patron of art and literature.

**Char'let'** (shȧr'lĕ'), **Nicolas Toussaint.** 1792–1845. French designer, b. Paris; best known for military subjects, as in a series of lithographs celebrating glorious events of Napoleonic era, and in paintings, as *Épisode de la Retraite de Russie* and *Convoi de Blessés Faisant Halte dans un Ravin.*

**Char'le·voix'** (shȧr'lĕ·vwȧ'; *Angl.* shär'lē·voi), **Pierre François Xavier de.** 1682–1761. Jesuit traveler in America, b. St. Quentin, France. Sent by regent of France to find new route from Acadia westward (1719); traveled up St. Lawrence River, through Great Lakes, down Illinois and Mississippi rivers to New Orleans (1720–22); returned to France, and a life of teaching and writing. Most valuable work: *History and General Description of New France with the Historical Journal of a Voyage Made in Northern America* (1744).

**Charlier, Jean.** See Jean de GERSON.

**Char'lot** (shär'lō; *Fr.* shȧr'lō'), **André Eugene Maurice.** 1882–1956. British theatrical manager and producer, b. Paris, France; known especially for revues.

**Char'lot'** (shȧr'lō'), **Jean.** 1898– . Painter, lithographer, and illustrator, b. Paris. Served in French army (1917–18); studied art; identified for a time (c. 1922) with Mexican radical group led by Siqueiros; artist on staff of director of Carnegie explorations and excavations in Yucatán (1926–29); instructor in art, Florence Cane School, New York (from 1934). Painted frescoes in public buildings in Mexico City; his *Leopard Hunter* hangs in Phillips Memorial Gallery, Washington, D.C.

**Charlot, Louis.** 1878–1951. French painter; studied under Bonnat, but strongly influenced by impressionist movement.

**Char'lotte'** (shȧr'lôt'; *Angl.* shär'lŏt). *In full* **Charlotte Aldegonde Élise Marie Wilhelmine.** 1896– . Grand duchess of Luxemburg (1919–64). Dau. of Grand Duke William IV; m. (1919) Prince Felix of Bourbon-Parma; won referendum vote (1919) for reigning grand duchess by large majority; in exile (1940–45).

**Char'lotte** (shär'lŏt). Empress of Mexico. See CARLOTA.

**Charlotte.** Queen of Portugal. See CARLOTA.

**Char'lotte E·lis'a·beth** (shär'lŏt ē·lĭz'ȧ·bĕth) of Bavaria. 1652–1722. Daughter of Charles Louis, Elector Palatine; duchess of Orléans; 2d wife (m. 1671) of Philippe d'Orléans, brother of Louis XIV (see ORLÉANS); unpopular because of her manners, brusqueness, and German sympathies. Her *Letters* (trans. 1855, 1880) give much intimate information on court of Louis XIV.

**Char'lotte So·phi'a** (shär'lŏt sō·fī'ȧ). 1744–1818. Queen (m. 1761) of George III of England; niece of duke of Mecklenburg-Strelitz.

**Charmes** (shȧrm), **Francis,** *in full* **Marie Julien Joseph François.** 1848–1916. French journalist; served in Franco-Prussian War (1870–71); editor, *Revue des Deux Mondes* (1907 ff.); member of Chamber of Deputies (1881–85, 1889–98).

**Char'mi·des** (kär'mĭ·dēz). 450?–404 B.C. Greek philosopher and politician; a cousin of Critias, disciple of Socrates, and uncle of Plato, who introduces him in one of the dialogues (*Charmides*). He was one of the Thirty Tyrants; killed in a struggle against Thrasybulus (*q.v.*).

**Char'nay'** (shȧr'nā'), **Claude Joseph Désiré.** 1828–1915. French archaeologist; excavated among ruins of ancient cities of Mexico; author of *Les Anciennes Villes du Nouveau Monde* (1884).

**Char'nock** (chär'nŏk), **Job.** d. 1693. English founder of Calcutta; removed East India Company factory from besieged Hooghly to island at mouth of Ganges (1686). His tombstone made of charnockite, which was named for him.

**Charnock** *or* **Cher'nock** (chär'-), **Robert.** 1663?–1696. English Jacobite conspirator. Roman Catholic priest; James II's agent in oppression of Magdalen Coll.; implicated in Barclay's plot to assassinate William III (1696), hanged.

**Charn'wood** (chärn'wŏŏd), 1st Baron. **Godfrey Rathbone Ben'son** (bĕn's'n). 1864–1945. Brother of Sir F. R. Benson. English biographer; educ. Oxford. Author of *Abraham Lincoln* (1916), *Theodore Roosevelt* (1923),

*According to St. John* (1926), *Tracks in the Snow* (1927), etc.

**Charolais,** Count of. See CHARLES (THE BOLD), Duke of Burgundy.

**Cha·ron′das** (kȧ·rŏn′dȧs). Jurist of 6th century B.C., of Catana in Sicily.

**Char′pen′tier′** (shȧr′päɴ′tyā′), **Alexandre Louis Marie.** 1856–1909. French sculptor; carved plaques and portrait medallions, and in his later career, decorative pieces (vases, etc.) and furniture.

**Charpentier, François Philippe.** 1734–1817. French engraver; discovered aquatint or nitric acid process in engraving and sold his discovery to Comte de Caylus (*q.v.*).

**Charpentier, Gustave.** 1860–1956. French composer, b. in Lorraine. Studied under Massenet. Composer of the orchestral suite *Impressions d'Italie*, symphonic drama *La Vie du Poète*, opera *Louise* (1900), symphonic poem *Le Couronnement de la Muse*, and choral and piano works.

**Charpentier, Marc Antoine.** 1634–1704. French organist and composer, b. Paris; studied in Italy under Carissimi; Kapellmeister of the Sainte Chapelle. Composer of operas, including *Circé* and *Amours d'Acis et Galatée*, but best known for his religious music.

**Char′ras′** (shȧ′rȧs′), **Jean Baptiste Adolphe.** 1810–1865. French soldier and historian, b. in Lorraine. Served in Algeria; undersecretary of state for war (1848); opposed policies of Louis Napoleon; banished after coup d'état (Dec. 2, 1851). Author of *Histoire de la Campagne de 1815. Waterloo* (1857).

**Char′rière′** (shȧ′ryâr′), **I′sa′belle′** (ē′zȧ′bĕl′) **de.** *Nee* **I′sa·bel′la** (ē′sȧ·bĕl′ȧ) **van Tuyll** (toil). *Pseudonyms* **Zé′lide′** (zā′lēd′) *and* **Ab′bé′ de La Tour′** (ȧ′bā′ dẽ lȧ to͞or′). 1740–1805. Author, b. Utrecht, of good family; rejected several admirers, including James Boswell; m. her brother's Swiss tutor, St. Hyacinthe de Charrière (1771), and settled near Lausanne; intimate friend of Benjamin Constant (1787–96). Author of *Lettres Neuchâteloises* (1784) and *Caliste, ou Lettres Écrites de Lausanne* (2 vols., 1785–88), also of several novels and plays.

**Char′ron′** (shȧ′rôɴ′), **Pierre.** 1541–1603. French Roman Catholic theologian and philosopher, b. Paris; renowned as pulpit orator; friend of Montaigne; author of *Les Trois Vérités* (1594), *Traité de la Sagesse* (1601).

**Char′ter′is** (chär′tẽr·ĭs; chär′tẽrz). Conventional family name of earls of WEMYSS.

**Char′ter·is** (chär′tẽr·ĭs), Sir **Evan.** 1864–1940. English lawyer and art connoisseur; served in World War (1914–18). Chairman of trustees, National Portrait Gallery (from 1928); chairman of Tate Gallery (1934–40); trustee of National Gallery (1932–39). Author of *John Sargent* (1927), *The Life and Letters of Sir Edmund Gosse* (1931), etc.

**Charteris, Leslie.** 1907– . English fiction writer; educ. Cambridge. Worked variously as seaman, rubber planter, tin miner, prospector. Author of adventure stories (many later made into motion pictures) about an attractive fictional criminal known as "the Saint," as *Enter the Saint* and *The Saint Goes On.*

**Char′tier′** (shȧr′tyā′), **Alain.** 1385?–after 1433. French writer and diplomat. In service of dauphin (later Charles VII). His prose works, chiefly written to inspire loyalty among the people to their legitimate sovereign, include *Quadrilogue Invectif* (1422) and *Traité de l'Espérance* (1428). Now remembered chiefly for his poetry, which includes *La Belle Dame Sans Merci* (a title later also used by Keats). *Lai de Plaisance. Bréviaire des Nobles.*

**Chartier, Émile Auguste.** *Pseudonym* **A′lain′** (ȧ′lăɴ′). 1868–1951. French philosopher and essayist; editor of *Libres-Propos;* professor at Lycée Henri IV. Among his many books are *Les Propos d'Alain* (1920), *Les Idées et les Âges* (1927), *Propos de Littérature* (1933), *Les Dieux* (1934), *Histoire de mes Pensées* (1936), *Mars ou la Guerre Jugée* (1936), *Les Saisons de l'Esprit* (1937).

**Char′ton′** (shȧr′tôɴ′), **Édouard Thomas.** 1807–1890. French writer and politician, b. Sens. Member of Chamber of Deputies (1871); senator (from 1878). Helped found various journals, including *Magasin Pittoresque* (1833), *L'Illustration* (1843), *Le Tour du Monde* (1860). Author of *Voyages Anciens et Modernes* (1854–57), etc.

**Char′tran′** (shȧr′träɴ′), **Théobald.** 1849–1907. French painter, b. Besançon; studied under Cabanel; best known as religious and portrait painter.

**Char′tres** (shȧr′tr′), Duc **de.** Title held by members of Orléans (*q.v.*) family (from 1661). **Robert Philippe Louis Eugène Ferdinand d'Orléans.** 1840–1910. French nobleman; 2d son of the duc d'Orléans (d. 1842). Driven into exile by Revolution of 1848; lived in Germany and England (1848–58); in America (1861–62) on Gen. McClellan's staff; served (1870–71) in French army under a pseudonym; later in active service as officer (until 1883); expelled from army by law forbidding service of princes of former reigning families.

**Chase** (chās), **Caleb.** 1831–1908. American merchant; organized (1878) firm of Chase and Sanborn, tea and coffee merchants, with home offices in Boston, Mass.

**Chase, Frederic Henry.** 1853–1925. Church of England prelate; educ. Cambridge; professor of divinity (1901–05) and president of Queen's Coll., Cambridge (1901–06); bishop of Ely (from 1905); author of theological treatises.

**Chase, Frederick Lincoln.** 1865–1933. American astronomer, b. Boulder, Colo.; Ph.D., Yale (1891); on staff of Yale Observatory (1890–1913). Author of parallax investigations of a number of stars.

**Chase, Harry Woodburn.** 1883–1955. American educator, b. Groveland, Mass. A.B., Dartmouth (1904), Ph.D., Clark (1910). Professor of psychology, U. of North Carolina (1910–14), and president (1919–30). President, U. of Illinois (1930–33). Chancellor, New York University (1933–51).

**Chase, Mary Ellen.** 1887–1973. American educator, b. Blue Hill, Me. B.A., Maine (1909), Ph.D., Minnesota (1922). Teacher of English, Smith Coll. (1918–29; professor 1929–55). Author of essays, books on writing, and novels, including *His Birthday* (1915), *Uplands* (1927), *A Goodly Heritage* (autobiographical; 1932), *Mary Peters* (1934), *Silas Crockett* (1935), *This England* 1936), *A Goodly Fellowship* (1939), *Windswept* (1941), *The Edge of Darkness* (1957), etc.

**Chase, Philander.** 1775–1852. American Episcopal clergyman, b. Cornish, N.H. In Ohio region (1817–19) organizing parishes; bishop of diocese of Ohio (1819–31); founded Kenyon College (1824). Elected bishop of Illinois (1835). Presiding bishop of Episcopal Church (1843–52).

**Chase, Salmon Portland.** 1808–1873. American lawyer and statesman, b. Cornish, N.H. Grad. Dartmouth (1826). Prominent in defending fugitive slaves; active in free-soil movement (1848); U.S. senator (1849–55; 1860); governor of Ohio (1855–59). U.S. secretary of the treasury (1861–64); originated national banking system (1863); supported prosecution of the war. Put forward by a political group as presidential candidate in place of Lincoln; resigned (1864) because of strained relations with the president. Chief justice, U.S. Supreme Court (1864–73).

**Chase, Samuel.** 1741–1811. American jurist and Revolutionary leader, b. in Somerset Co., Md. Member, committee of correspondence (1774); delegate to Continental Congress (1774–78, 1784, 1785); signer of Declaration of Independence; opposed adoption of Constitution. Associate justice, U.S. Supreme Court (1796–1811); impeached (1804) because of high-handed conduct in a trial five years before; acquitted (1805).

**Chase, Stuart.** 1888– . American writer, b. Somersworth, N.H. S.B., Harvard (1910). U.S. Federal Trade Commission investigator (1917–22); associated with Labor Bureau, Inc. (from 1922). Author of *The Tragedy of Waste* (1925), *Your Money's Worth* (with F. J. Schlink; 1927), *Men and Machines* (1929), *A New Deal* (1932), *The Economy of Abundance* (1934), *Rich Land, Poor Land* (1936), *The Tyranny of Words* (1938), *The New Western Front* (1939), etc.

**Chase, William Merritt.** 1849–1916. American painter, b. Williamsburg, Ind.; studied in Munich and Venice (1872–1877); studio in New York (from 1878). Painter of landscapes, portraits, and still-life objects.

**Cha′sins** (chā′sĭnz), **Abram.** 1903– . American pianist and composer; composer of *Concerto in F Minor, The Parade, Rush-Hour in Hong Kong*, chamber music, and piano pieces.

**Chasles** (shäl), **Michel.** 1793–1880. French mathematician, b. Épernon. Studied at École Polytechnique, Paris; took part in defense of Paris (1814); professor of geodesy and applied mechanics, École Polytechnique (1841); professor of advanced geometry, Sorbonne (1846). Author of valuable technical articles and of *Traité de Géométrie Supérieure* (1852), *Traité des Sections Coniques* (1865), etc.

**Chasles, Philarète.** 1798–1873. French scholar and writer; professor, Collège de France; later, curator of Bibliothèque Mazarine; best known for his essays, collected under title *Études de Littérature Comparée* (11 vols.); author also of *Histoire Humoristique des Humoristes* (1846), *Galileo Galilei* (1862), *L'Arétin, sa Vie et ses Écrits* (1873).

**Chas′sai′gnac′** (shȧ′sĕ′nyȧk′), **Pierre Marie Édouard.** 1804–1879. French surgeon; inventor of the linear écraseur, an instrument used in place of a knife in some operations; responsible for introduction of drainage into surgery.

**Chas′sé′** (shȧ′sā′), Baron **David Hendrik.** 1765–1849. Dutch general. Served in French army in Spain (1808–13) and as general of division against allies in defense of France (1814). Joined Dutch army after abdication of Napoleon (1814); at Waterloo (1815). Conducted defense of citadel at Antwerp against Belgians in revolution of 1830 and, later, against French (1832).

**Chasse′loup′-Lau′bat′** (shȧs′lo͞o′lō′bȧ′), **François de.** 1754–1833. French soldier and military engineer; served in armies of the republic and under Napoleon (to 1812); directed operations at siege of Danzig (1807); raised to peerage by Louis XVIII. His son **Justin Prosper Chasseloup-Laubat** (1805–1873), was minister of marine under Napoleon III (1851, 1859–67); president of council of state (1869); member of National Assembly (1871); opposed establishment of a republic.

**Chasse′pot′** (shȧs′pō′), **Antoine Alphonse.** 1833–1905. French inventor, b. in Bas-Rhin; invented musket called after him *chassepot*, adopted for use by French army (1866).

**Chas′sé′riau′** (shȧ′sā′ryō′), **Théodore.** 1819–1856. French painter, b. in Dominican Republic; studied under Ingres. Best known for decorative murals in Église Saint Merri, Église Saint Roch, and above staircase in Cour des Comptes in Palais d'Orsay.

**Chas′te·lard′** (shä′tlȧr′), **Pierre de Bos′co′sel′** (bôs′kô′zĕl′) **de.** 1540–1564. French poet, at court of Francis II; conceived hopeless passion for Mary, Queen of Scots, and followed her to Scotland after death of her husband (1561); arrested after series of indiscretions and executed in Edinburgh.

**Chas′te·let′** (shä′tlĕ′). = CHÂTELET.

**Chas′tel·lain′** *or* **Chas′te·lain′** (shä′tläɴ′), **Georges.** 1404–1475. Flemish-born Burgundian chronicler and poet; historiographer of Burgundian house (1455); author of *Chronique des Ducs de Bourgogne*, covering history of Burgundian house from 1419 to 1474. His poetry includes epitaphs, epistles, and panegyrics.

**Chas′tel·lux′** (shä′tlü′), Marquis **François Jean de.** 1734–1788. French soldier; major general in Rochambeau's army in America (1780–82).

**Cha′teau′bri′and′** (shȧ′tō′brē′äɴ′), Vicomte **François René de.** 1768–1848. French writer and statesman, b. Saint-Malo, Brittany. Served in French army (1786); traveled in U.S. (1791–92); returned to France and fought in Royalist army defeated at Thionville (Sept., 1792); émigré in England (1792–1800). Returned to France (1800); served under Napoleon as minister to Republic of Valais (1803–04); resigned after execution of duc d'Enghien (1804) and again went into exile, traveling in Holy Land, Greece, and northern Africa. Supported Bourbon cause (1814); created peer of France (1815); ambassador to Great Britain (1822); minister of foreign affairs (1823–24). Author of *Essai Historique, Politique et Moral sur les Révolutions Anciennes et Modernes*...(1797), *Atala* (1801), *Génie du Christianisme* (1802), *René* (1802), *Les Martyrs* (1809), *Itinéraire de Paris à Jérusalem* (1811), *Les Natchez* (1826), *Les Adventures du Dernier des Abencérages* (1826), *Mémoires d'Outre-tombe* (1849–50). His *Atala* and *René* are said to mark beginning of romantic movement in French literature.

**Cha′teau′bri′ant′** (shȧ′tō′brē′äɴ′), **Alphonse de.** 1877–1951. French novelist, b. Rennes; awarded Goncourt prize (1911) for *Monsieur des Lourdines*, and French Academy grand prize (1923) for *La Brière*.

**Châteauguay,** Sieur **de. Antoine Lemoyne.** See under Charles LEMOYNE.

**Châ′teau′re·nault′** *or* **Châ′teau′re·naut′** (shä′tōr′nō′) *or* **Châ′teau′re·gnaud′** (shä′tōr′nyō′), Marquis **de. François Louis Rous′se·let′** (ro͞os′lĕ′). 1637–1716. French naval officer; succeeded Tourville (*q.v.*) as vice-admiral of France (1701); during War of Spanish Succession, was disastrously defeated in Bay of Vigo by British and allied fleet under Sir George Rooke (Oct., 1702); marshal of France (1703) and, later, lieutenant general of Brittany.

**Châ′tel′** (shä′tĕl′), **Jean.** 1575?–1594. French fanatic who attempted to assassinate Henry IV (Dec. 27, 1594); executed at Paris (Dec. 29, 1594). Because of a belief that his attempt had been inspired by Jesuit influence, the Jesuits were banished from France.

**Châ′te·lain′** (shä′tläɴ′). = CHASTELLAIN.

**Châ′te·let′** (shä′tlĕ′), Marquise **du. Gabrielle Émilie Le Ton′ne·lier′ de Bre·teuil′** (lĕ tô′nĕ·lyā′ dĕ brĕ-tû′y′). 1706–1749. French writer; wife of marquis du Châtelet-Lomont, and mistress of Voltaire, residing with Voltaire at Montjeu and later at Château de Cirey (in Lorraine); author of *Traité sur la Bonheur, Lettres*, and *Traduction des Principes de Newton*.

**Châtelherault,** Duke of. See (1) *James Hamilton* (d. 1575), under HAMILTON family; (2) *James Hamilton*, 2d Earl of ABERCORN.

**Chat′field** (chăt′fēld), **Alfred Ernle Mon′ta·cute** (mŏn′tȧ·kūt). 1st Baron **Chatfield.** 1873–1967. British naval commander; entered naval service (1886); captain

(1909); rear admiral (1920); admiral (1930); admiral of the fleet (1935). Engaged as flag captain under Beatty in action off Helgoland (1914), Dogger Bank (1915), and Jutland (1916). First sea lord and chief of naval staff (1933–38). Minister for co-ordination of defense (1939–40).

**Chat′field–Tay′lor** (-tā′lēr), **Hobart C.** 1865–1945. American writer, b. Chicago; B.S., Cornell; author of *With Edge-Tools* (1891), *An American Peeress* (1893), *The Vice of Fools* (1898), *The Idle Born* (1900), *Molière* (1906), *Goldoni* (1913), *Tawny Spain* (1927), *Charmed Circles* (1935), etc.

**Chatham,** Earls of. See William PITT (1708–1778).

**Châ′til′lon′** (shä′tē′yôN′). French countship. See BLOIS.

**Châtillon, Auguste de.** 1813–1881. French painter, sculptor, and poet.

**Châtillon, Gautier de.** See GAUTIER DE LILLE.

**Châtillon** *or* **Châteillon, Sébastien.** See CASTELLIO.

**Chatrian, Alexandre.** See ERCKMANN-CHATRIAN.

**Chat′ter·ji** (chä′tēr·jē), **Ban′kim** (bông′kĭm) **Chan′dra** (chŏn′drô). *Also called* **Bankim Chandra.** 1838–1894. Indian novelist, b. in Bengal. In civil service (1858–91); granted title of C.I.E. (1891). Created Indian school of fiction on European model; wrote many novels, his most famous, *Ananda Math* (1882), a story of the sannyasi rebellion of 1772, in which occurred the song *Bande Mataram,* used in recent years in India as hymn of extremist party. Increased literary value of Bengali; influenced later writers, as Rabindranath Tagore.

**Chat′ter·ton** (chăt′ēr·t′n; -tŭn), **Edward Keble.** 1878–1944. English journalist and writer, b. Sheffield; educ. Oxford; served in World War (1914–18). Author of *Sailing Ships...*(1909), *The Story of the British Navy* (1911), *The Romance of Piracy* (1914), *Ship Models* (1923), *Whalers and Whaling* (1925), *The Sea Raiders* (1931), *Sea Spy* (novel; 1937), *Secret Ship* (novel; 1939), *The Epic of Dunkirk* (1940), etc.

**Chatterton, Thomas.** 1752–1770. English poet. Posthumous son of Bristol schoolmaster; from early years fascinated by antiquities; began to represent his imitations of ancient authors as antiques (1764) and to fabricate a romance in prose and verse of Thomas Rowley, an imaginary 15th-century monk (1765). Submitted to Horace Walpole (1769) a purported transcript of a 1469 treatise on painting in England by T. Rowley, declared a forgery by Gray and Mason; contributed political diatribes in manner of Junius to London periodicals. Lived abstemiously in London, turning out poems, burlettas, satires, political tirades, assuming style of Junius, Smollett, Churchill, Macpherson's "Ossian," Pope, Gray, Collins; wrote *Excelente Balade of Charitie* as if from parchment of priest Rowley; desperate after rejection of this poem by *Town and Country Magazine,* drank arsenic in his Holborn attic; buried in pauper's grave. Subject of 80-year controversy over genuineness of Rowley poems, shown by Prof. W. W. Skeat to have been Chatterton's own invention perversely archaized with help of John Kersey's *Dictionarium Anglo-Britannicum;* these writings now acknowledged to include poetry of a high order of originality, dramatic and imaginative power, of lyric beauty, as in his *Songe of Aella.*

**Chau′cer** (chô′sēr), **Geoffrey.** 1340?–1400. English poet, b. London, son of a vintner. Page to wife of Lionel, Duke of Clarence (1357). Served in campaign in France (1359), captured, ransomed (1360); m. (1366) Philippa Roet, sister of John of Gaunt's 3d wife; employed for ten years on diplomatic missions to Italy, Flanders, France, Lombardy, meeting Boccaccio and perhaps Petrarch. Comptroller of the customs and subsidy of wools, London (1374); received pensions from Edward III and John of Gaunt (1374); benefited by two guardianships of rich Kentish heirs; resided (1374–86) above gate of Aldgate, London; comptroller of petty customs, London (1382), and allowed (1385) a deputy, enabling him to devote time to writing; elected to parliament from Kent (1386). Suffered period of misfortune during absence of his patron, John of Gaunt; dismissed from both comptrollerships (1386); lost his wife; sold his pensions to raise money; on John of Gaunt's return, became clerk of works at royal palaces (1389–91) and held small sinecures; twice robbed (1390) of king's money by highwaymen; fell again into poverty until rescued by pensions from Richard II and Henry IV (1394, 1399); buried in Poets' Corner in Westminster Abbey. His writings fall into three periods: (1) French influence (c. 1359–72), marked by use of octosyllabic couplet: translation of *Roman de la Rose* (perhaps only first 1700 lines of extant English fragment his); a lost translation, *Book of the Lyon; The Book of the Duchess,* a poem in honor of John of Gaunt's first wife (1369), imitating machinery of French conventions and passages from Guillaume de Machaut; and minor poems. (2) Italian influence (c. 1372–86), marked by use of rhyme royal, heroic stanza of seven lines: the poems *The House of Fame* and *The Parlement of Foules;* prose translation of *Consolation* of Boethius; the story of Palamon and Arcite, from Boccaccio's *Teseide,* later incorporated in *Canterbury Tales* as the *Knight's Tale;* the unfinished *Legend of Good Women,* verse prologue and series of prose narratives of women faithful to love; *Troilus and Criseyde,* long narrative poem modeled on Boccaccio's *Filostrato.* (3) English period (1386–1400), marked by use of heroic couplet: *The Canterbury Tales,* representing 23 stories of pilgrims assembled at the Tabard Inn in Southwark, a splendid fragment of the projected scheme of two stories from each of 29 pilgrims; a prose treatise on the astrolabe written for "Litel Lowis my son" (c. 1391); and a "Complaint to his Empty Purse."

His putative son **Thomas Chaucer** (1367?–1434), chief butler to Richard II, Henry IV, Henry V, Henry VI; M.P. (in most parliaments, 1400–31); speaker of House of Commons (1407, 1410, 1411, 1414); fought at Agincourt.

**Chau′chat′** (shō′shȧ′), **Jacques Louis Henri.** 1863–1927. French army officer; inventor of a rapid-fire automatic rifle and machine gun used by French army in World War (1914–18).

**Chau′det′** (shō′dĕ′), **Antoine Denis.** 1763–1810. French sculptor and painter; his *L'Amour Séduisant l'Âme* is in the Louvre; carved colossal statue of Napoleon I which surmounted Vendôme column in Paris until destroyed at the Restoration.

**Chau′liac′** (shō′lyȧk′), **Guy de.** *Lat.* **Gui′do de Cau·li′a·co** (gĭ′dō dē kô·lī′ȧ·kō). c. 1300–c. 1370. French surgeon; physician to three popes at Avignon (1342–70); author of *Inventorium sive Collectorium Partis Chirurgicalis Medicinae* (1343), which was translated into French under title *Grande Chirurgie* (1592) and served as a manual for physicians for three centuries.

**Chau′lieu′** (shō′lyû′), Abbé **de. Guillaume Am′frye′** (äN′frē′). 1639–1720. French abbé, poet, and wit, called the "Anacreon of the Temple"; author of *Ode sur l'Inconstance, La Retraite, La Goutte,* and *La Solitude de Fontenay.*

**Chau′meix′** (shō′mĕks′), **Jean Henri André.** 1874–1955. French editor of *Le Figaro* (1926–30); director of *Revue de Paris* (1920–26), *Revue des Deux Mondes* (from 1937).

**Chau′mette′** (shō′mĕt′), **Pierre Gaspard.** 1763–1794.

French revolutionary, b. Nevers. Member of Cordeliers' Club (1790); contributed to revolutionary journals; extreme radical and leader in Commune of Paris (1792–94); active against Girondists; one of the founders of the worship of reason; guillotined by order of Robespierre.

**Chau'mo'not'** (shō'mô'nō'), **Pierre Joseph Marie.** 1611–1693. Jesuit missionary in America, b. in Burgundy, France. In Quebec (1639) for work among Indians; lived among Hurons (1639–48); on mission to Iroquois (1655–58); with Hurons (1663–92).

**Chaun'cey** (chôn'sĭ; chän'-), **Isaac.** 1772–1840. American naval officer, b. Black Rock, Conn. Lieutenant, U.S. navy (1799); served against Tripoli (1802–05); during War of 1812, commander of naval forces on Lakes Ontario and Erie; navy commissioner, Washington (1821–24; 1832–40).

**Chaun'cy** (chôn'sĭ; chän'-), **Charles.** 1592–1672. Clergyman and educator, b. in Herts, England. B.A. (1613), B.D. (1624), Cantab.; held pastorates in England (1626–37); twice summoned before ecclesiastical commissions for investigation and discipline. Fled to America (1638); lived in Plymouth, Mass. (1638–40), Scituate (1641–54), in both places his openly expressed beliefs causing dispute and schism; second president of Harvard College (1654–72), under agreement not to disseminate certain of his doctrinal views.

**Chauncy, Charles.** 1705–1787. American clergyman, b. Boston. Grad. Harvard (1721); pastor, First Church, Boston (1727–87); liberal leader; opposed Whitefield revival movement and attempt by English bishops to impose Church of England service and system on the colonies.

**Chaussée, Nivelle de La.** See LA CHAUSSÉE.

**Chaus'son'** (shō'sôɴ'), **Ernest.** 1855–1899. French composer, b. Paris. Studied at Paris conservatory in classes under Massenet and César Franck. Among his compositions are lyric dramas, symphonic poems (*Viviane*, etc.), choral works, songs, etc.

**Chau'temps'** (shō'täɴ'), **Camille.** 1885–1963. French lawyer and politician; minister of interior (1924) and of justice (1925–26); premier of France (1930); minister of public instruction (1931), of interior (1932–33); again premier of France (1933–34); minister of public works (1936); minister of state in Blum government (1936–37); again premier (1937–38); minister of co-ordination (1938–39), of state (1939).

**Chau'veau'** (shō'vō'), **Pierre Joseph Olivier.** 1820–1890. Canadian politician and novelist; premier of Quebec (1867–73); author of *Charles Guérin, Roman de Mœurs Canadiennes* (1853).

**Chau'veau'-La'garde'** (-là'gàrd'), **Claude François.** 1756–1841. French lawyer; appeared before Revolutionary Tribunal to defend Brissot, Charlotte Corday, Marie Antoinette, and others; imprisoned for a time during Reign of Terror; appointed counselor to the Court of Cassation (1828).

**Chau·vel'** (shô·vĕl'), Sir **Henry George.** 1865–1945. Australian soldier, b. in New South Wales. Adjutant general to military forces of Australia (1911–14). Commanded 1st Australian Light Horse Brigade in Egypt and Gallipoli (1914–15), 1st Australian division in Gallipoli and Egypt (1915–16), Australian and New Zealand mounted division in Sinai campaign (1916–17), Desert Mounted Corps in Palestine and Syrian campaigns including capture of Damascus (1917–19). Inspector general to Australian military forces (1919–30) and chief of general staff (1923–30).

**Chau've·lin'** (shō'vläɴ'), **François Bernard.** 1766–1832. French politician; accepted principles of French Revolution; served as ambassador to Great Britain (1792) and with Talleyrand's aid contrived to keep British government neutral; under the Restoration, became member of Chamber of Deputies, where he continued to defend liberal policies.

**Chau've·net** (shō'vĕ·nā), **William.** 1820–1870. American educator, b. Milford, Pa. Grad. Yale (1840). Professor of mathematics, U.S. navy (1841); instrumental (1842–45) in inducing secretary of navy to establish naval school, later called U.S. Naval Academy; head of department of astronomy and navigation, U.S. Naval Academy (1853). Professor, Washington U., St. Louis, Mo. (1855–62); chancellor (1862–69).

**Chau'vin'** (shō'văɴ'), **Nicolas.** French soldier of Revolutionary and Napoleonic armies; after showing great courage and being severely wounded, he received from Napoleon a sword, a red ribbon, and a pension; his enthusiasm for Napoleon and his professions of militant patriotism were so exaggerated that his comrades finally turned him to ridicule. From his name the word *chauvin* and its derivatives are said to come.

**Cha'vannes'** (shà'vàn'), **Édouard.** 1865–1918. French Sinologue, b. Lyon. Educ. École Normale Supérieure; on mission in China (to 1893; also in 1907); professor of Chinese and Tatar languages and literatures, Collège de France (from 1893); director of studies, École des Hautes Études (1908).

**Chavannes, Puvis de.** See PUVIS DE CHAVANNES.

**Cha·vasse'** (shȧ·văs'), **Francis James.** 1846–1928. Church of England prelate; educ. Oxford; bishop of Liverpool (1900–23); remembered as real founder of Liverpool Cathedral, construction of which was begun during his episcopate.

**Chá'vez** (chä'vās), **Carlos.** 1899–1978. Mexican orchestra conductor and composer; director, National Conservatory of Music, Mexico City (1928); organized (1928) and conducted Mexican Symphony Orchestra; guest conductor, Boston Symphony Orchestra (1936), New York Philharmonic Symphony Orchestra (1937). Composer of operatic ballet *H.P.* (presented in Philadelphia with Leopold Stokowski conducting; first U.S. presentation of a work of this class by a Mexican composer), *Sinfonía India*, *Sinfonía de Antígona*, etc.

**Chávez Fran'co** (fräng'kō), **Modesto.** 1872– Ecuadorian jurist, journalist, and historian; professor, Guayaquil (1902–03, 1906–12, 1932–33), and director of municipal museum and library (1925–31). Founder and editor, *El Obrero* (1892), *El Cíclope* (1893), *El Cáustico.*

**Chay'tor** (chā'tôr), Sir **Edward Walter Cler'vaux** (klâr'vō). 1868–1939. New Zealand soldier; served in South Africa (1900–02) and World War (1914–18). Commanded Australian and New Zealand mounted division of the Mediterranean expeditionary force which captured Jerusalem. Commanded New Zealand defense force (1919–24); major general, New Zealand Officers' Reserve (1924–31); retired (1931).

**Cheat'ham** (chēt'ăm), **Kitty,** *in full* **Catharine Smiley Bugge** (bŭg). 1864?–1946. American singer, b. Nashville, Tenn.; interpreter of the literature and songs of childhood. Author of *Kitty Cheatham—Her Book*, of *A Nursery Garland*, of *Children and the Bible*, and of several songs and anthems.

**Che·by·shëv'** (chĕ·bĭ·shôf'), **Pafnuti Lvovich.** 1821–1894. Russian mathematician; professor, St. Petersburg (to 1880). Author of treatises on theory of numbers, theory of probabilities, quadratic forms, theory of integrals, gearings, map making, etc. Devised a straight-line motion; proved Bertrand's postulate.

**Chee'ver** (chē'vẽr), **Ezekiel.** 1615–1708. Educator, b. London, Eng.; educ. Cambridge; to America (1637);

master of Boston Latin School (1670–1708). His textbook *Accidence, a Short Introduction to the Latin Tongue* was used in the colonies for a hundred years.

**Cheilon.** See CHILON.

**Cheke** (chēk), Sir **John.** 1514–1557. English classical scholar. M.A., Cantab. (1533); adopted principles of Reformation; regius professor of Greek, Cambridge (1540–51); with Sir Thomas Smith, introduced Erasmian pronunciation of Greek in Cambridge in opposition to Reuchlinian; tutor to Prince of Wales (1544); provost of King's Coll., Cambridge (1548); imprisoned (1553–54) by Queen Mary for serving as secretary of state for Lady Jane Grey; released; taught Greek on Continent; treacherously seized in Belgium and forced by Cardinal Pole to make public recantations and join Roman Catholic Church (1556).

**Che'khov** (chā'kôf), **Anton Pavlovich.** *Surname also spelled* **Che'kov** *or* **Tche'khov.** 1860–1904. Russian playwright and fiction writer. Studied medicine, Moscow (grad. 1884), but practiced little; resided near Moscow (1891–97), and in the Crimea and abroad (after 1897); m. actress Olga Knipper (1901). His stories include *The Chorus Girl* (1884), *A Dreary Story* (1889), *The Duel, Ward No. 6* (1892), *The Teacher of Literature* (1894), *Peasants* (1897), *The New Villa* (1899), *The Bishop* (1902). His plays include *Ivanov* (1887), *The Sea Gull* (1896), *Uncle Vanya* (1899), *The Three Sisters* (1901), *The Cherry Orchard* (1904).

**Che·lard'** (shlår), **Hippolyte André Jean Baptiste.** 1789–1861. French composer of religious music and several operas.

**Che'li·shev** (chā'lyĭ·shĕf), **Pavel.** 1898–1957. Russian painter and theatrical designer, b. Moscow. Commissioned by Diaghilev to do settings for his ballet (1928). Identified with neoromantic school.

**Chel·miń'ski** (kĕl·mēn'y'·skē), **Jan.** 1851–1925. Polish painter; in U.S.A. (1884–87); in London and Paris until return to U.S. (1914). Best known for genre and historical paintings.

**Chelms'ford** (chĕms'fērd), 1st Baron. **Frederick Thes'i·ger** (thĕs'ĭ·jēr). 1794–1878. English lawyer and lord chancellor; grandson of Saxon immigrant. Served as midshipman in navy; succeeded to estate in West Indies which was destroyed by volcano; called to bar (1818); at Chelmsford assizes, won (1832) an ejection case after three trials (hence choice of this title as a peer); solicitor general (1844); attorney general (1845, 1852); lord chancellor (1858–59, 1866–68).

His eldest son, **Frederic Augustus** (1827–1905), 2d baron; served through Crimean War, Sepoy Mutiny, and Abyssinian campaign (1868); commanded troops in Kaffir war (1878) and Zulu war (1879); lieutenant general (1882); general (1888); lieutenant of Tower of London (1884–89).

**Frederic John Na'pi·er** [nā'pĭ·ēr] (1868–1933), 1st Viscount Chelmsford; eldest son of 2d baron; M.A., Oxon. (1892); governor of Queensland (1905–09), of New South Wales (1909–13); as viceroy of India (1916–21), formulated, with Edwin S. Montagu, secretary for India, and put into effect (1920–21) system of dyarchy and other reforms, which were rejected by followers of Gandhi; defeated Mohammedan agitation supported by Afghan army; first lord of admiralty in Labor ministry (1924); agent-general for New South Wales (1926–28).

**Chem'nitz** (kĕm'nĭts) *or* **Kem'nitz, Martin.** 1522–1586. German Lutheran theologian; superintendent, Brunswick (1567); author of *Examen Concilii Tridentini* (4 vols., 1565–73), *Loci Theologici* (1591), etc. His grandson **Bogislaw Philipp von Chemnitz** (1605–1678), historian, wrote *Der Königliche Schwedische in Deutschland Geführte Krieg* (1648–53), and, under pseudonym **Hip·pol'y·tus a Lap'i·de** (*as Lat.*, hĭ-pŏl'ĭ·tŭs ā lăp'ĭ·dē), a political treatise on the German system of government.

**Chem·ni'tzer** *or* **Khem·ni'tser** (kyĕm·nyĭ'tsēr), **Ivan Ivanovich.** 1745–1784. Russian fabulist, of German descent; among his fables are *The Metaphysician, The Peasant and his Load, The Rich Man and the Poor Man.*

**Ch'ên** *or* **Chen** (chŭn). *Also known as* **Southern Ch'ên.** A Chinese dynasty (557–589), succeeded by the Sui.

**Chen** (chŭn), **Eugene.** *Orig.* **Ch'en Yu-jen.** 1878–1944. Chinese politician, b. in Trinidad, B.W.I., of mixed blood. Studied in London; practiced as solicitor in West Indies. Editor and proprietor of *Peking Gazette* (1914–16); imprisoned for alleged anti-Japanese articles (1916–17); in editorial work in northern China (1918–19 and 1925); acting minister for foreign affairs at Canton (1926); active in Kuomintang; foreign minister at Hankow (1927); in Europe (1927–30); foreign minister for several terms (between 1931 and 1938) but at other times out of favor with Nationalist government; reinstated in Kuomintang (1938).

**Che·na'vard'** (shnȧ'vȧr'), **Paul Joseph.** 1808–1895. French painter; studied under Hersent and Ingres. Commissioned (1848) to redecorate the Panthéon at Paris; planned a series to illustrate *Histoire de l'Humanité*, not executed, because of political events; completed eighteen cartoons for the paintings (now in museum at Lyon).

**Chen Cheng** (chŭn' chŭng'). 1898–1965. Chinese military leader, b. Chekiang province; educ. Paoting military college; friend and associate of Chiang Kai-shek (from 1924), and commander under him in northern campaign of 1926; commander of 18th Nationalist army (1930); field commander of Northern Route, Communist Suppression Forces (1934); a leader in the northern punitive expeditions; held administrative military posts (1936–39), resigned when blamed for fall of Ichang to Japanese (1939); in command of 6th war area; chief of staff (1946); premier (1950–54, 1958–63); vice-president (1954–65) of the Republic of China.

**Chen Chiung-ming** (chŭn' jyo͝ong'mĭng'). 1875–1933. Chinese military leader, b. in Kwangtung. In control of Kwangtung (1913); strong supporter (1916–21) of Sun Yat-sen; overthrew Kwangsi militarists (1920); civil governor of Kwangtung (1921); turned against Sun Yat-sen (1922) and drove him out of Canton; badly defeated by Chiang Kai-shek (1923).

**Chêne'dol'lé'** (shân'dô'lā'), **Charles Julien Lioult de** (lyo͞ot' dē). 1769–1833. French poet; an émigré (1789–99); author of *Le Génie de l'Homme* (1807), *L'Esprit de Rivarol* (1810), *Études Poétiques* (1820).

**Che'ner·y** (?chē'nēr·ĭ), **Thomas.** 1826–1884. British publicist and Orientalist, b. in Barbados; M.A., Cantab. Editorial writer and editor (1877–84) of *The Times.* Professor of Arabic, Oxford (1868–77); one of revisers of Old Testament.

**Che'ney** (chē'nĭ), **Charles Edward.** 1836–1916. American Episcopal clergyman, b. Canandaigua, N.Y. Grad. Hobart (1857); chief pastorate, Christ Church, Chicago (1860–1916); tried for heresy (1869 ff.), convicted, and deposed, but proceedings later (1874) declared legally null and void. Collaborated with Bishop George D. Cummins (*q.v.*) in organizing Reformed Episcopal Church (1873); consecrated bishop of Chicago in the new church (1878).

**Cheney, John Vance.** 1848–1922. American writer, b. Groveland, N.Y.; librarian, San Francisco Public Library (1887–94), Newberry Library, Chicago (1894–1909).

**Cheney, Oren Burbank.** 1816–1903. American Baptist clergyman and educator, b. in New Hampshire; grad. Dartmouth (1839); founded Maine State Seminary, Lewiston, Me. (1857), which became Bates College (1863); president (1857–94).

**Cheney, Seth Wells.** 1810–1856. American engraver and crayon artist, b. South Manchester, Conn.; m. **Edna Dow Lit′tle·hale** [lĭt′'l·hāl] (1824–1904), abolitionist, woman suffragist, and author. His brother **John** (1801–1885) was also an engraver. See Ward CHENEY.

**Cheney, Sheldon Warren.** 1886– . American dramatic and art critic, b. Berkeley, Calif.; A.B., California (1908); founder (1916) and editor (1916–21), *Theatre Arts Magazine.* Author of *The New Movement in the Theatre* (1914), *Modern Art and the Theatre* (1921), *The Art Theatre* (1925), *Stage Decoration* (1927), *A World History of Art* (1937), etc.

**Cheney, Ward.** 1813–1876. American pioneer silk manufacturer, b. South Manchester, Conn. With brothers Seth and John, organized (1838) company, incorporated as Cheney Brothers Silk Manufacturing Co. (1854); president of company (1854–76).

**Cheng Ch'eng-kung.** See KOXINGA.

**Cheng Ho** (jŭng′ hŭ′). Chinese admiral, native of Yünnan. A eunuch at court of Emperor Yung Lo of Ming dynasty; sent (1405–07) to Philippines, Brunei, Java, and Sumatra; again (1408–11) as far as Ceylon, whose king was brought back to China as prisoner; led four other expeditions (between 1412 and 1424) to Malay countries, chiefly with peaceful aim of trade; led seventh and final expedition (1430–34) as far as Strait of Hormuz.

**Ché′nier′** (shā′nyā′), **Louis de.** 1722–1795. French diplomat and historian; long resident in Constantinople as a businessman and as French consul general; consul general in Morocco (1767–82).

**André Marie de Chénier** (1762–1794), his son; poet; published during his lifetime only two poetical works, *Le Jeu du Paume à David Peintre* and *Hymne aux Soldats de Châteauvieux;* protested against excesses of Reign of Terror; guillotined in Paris (July 25, 1794). Works published by his friends and his family after his death include *La Jeune Captive* (1795), *La Jeune Tarentine* (1801); a complete edition of his works was published (1819) and a critical edition (1862); regarded by some as foremost poet in French classic verse since Racine and Boileau.

**Marie Joseph de Chénier** (1764–1811), brother of André; politician and poet; member of National Convention, Council of Five Hundred, and the Tribunate; author of the tragedies *Charles IX*, *Henri VIII*, *Fénelon*, *Tibère*, and the words of the song *Chant du Départ.*

**Chen·nault′** (shĕ·nôlt′), **Claire Lee.** 1890–1958. American aviator, b. in Texas; joined U.S. Army Air Corps (1917); as commandant of 19th pursuit group, Hawaii (1925), began intensive study of aerial tactics; demonstrated use of parachute troops (1926); resigned from U.S. army (1937). Following Japanese invasion of China (1937), became air adviser to Chiang Kai-shek; formed a volunteer air corps, the "Flying Tigers," to aid China; widely acclaimed for protecting the Burma Road against superior Japanese air forces (1941). Named brigadier general (1942) commanding U.S. army air forces in China; major general (1943); resigned (1945).

**Ch'ên Tu-hsiu** (chŭn′ dōō′shyōō′). 1879–1942. Chinese scholar and Communist leader, b. in Anhwei. Educ. in Japan and France; dean of department of literature, Peking National U.; editor of magazine *New Youth;* began movement for adoption of vernacular Chinese (the *pai-hua*) as national language. Chief founder of Communist party in China (1924); member, Central Executive Committee of Kuomintang (1925–28); expelled from committee (1928); arrested (1932); later exiled.

**Che·nu′** (shnü), **Jean Charles.** 1808–1879. French naturalist and army physician; coauthor of *Encyclopédie d'Histoire Naturelle* (31 vols., 1850–61).

**Cheops.** See KHUFU.

**Chephren.** See KHAFRE.

**Che′ra** (chā′rȧ) *or* **Ke′ra·la** (kā′rȧ·lȧ). An early Hindu (Tamil) dynasty ruling in southern India on the west coast (modern Travancore); existed from before Christian Era but generally overshadowed by the Pallavas and later (after 990) by the Cholas.

**Ché′ra′dame′** (shā′rȧ′dȧm′), **André.** 1871–1948. French writer on Pan-Germanism (from 1901), as in *The Pan-German Plot Unmasked* (1917), *The United States and Pan-Germania* (1918), *Defense of the Americas* (1941).

**Ché′rau′** (shā′rō′), **Gaston.** 1874–1937. French novelist.

**Cher′bu′liez′** (shĕr′bü′lyā′), **Antoine Élisée.** 1797–1869. Swiss economist; author of *Richesse ou Pauvreté* (1840), *Études sur les Causes de la Misère* (1853), etc. His nephew **Victor** (1829–1899), novelist and critic (often under pseudonym **G. Val′bert′** [vȧl′bâr′]); naturalized French citizen (1880). His novels include *Miss Rovel* (1875), *Le Comte Kostia* (1863), *Le Prince Vitale* (1864), *Jacquine Vanesse* (1898); his critical works, *Études de Littérature et d'Art* (1873), *Profils Étrangers* (1889), *L'Art et la Nature* (1892), etc.

**Che·ren′kov** (chĕ·rĕng′kŏf), **Pavel Alekseevich.** 1904– . Soviet physicist. Awarded Nobel prize in physics (1958) with I. Tamm and I. Frank.

**Che·rep·nin′** (chĕ·ryĕp·nyēn′), **Nikolai Nikolaevich.** 1873–1945. Russian composer, b. St. Petersburg; conductor in St. Petersburg (1905–18); director of conservatory in Tiflis (1918–21); resident in Paris (from 1921). His son **Aleksandr Nikolaevich** (1899– ), pianist and composer; conductor in Tiflis (1918-21); to Paris (1921); composer of operas, ballets, chamber music, and orchestral works.

**Ché′ret′** (shā′rĕ′), **Jules.** 1836–1932. French painter and lithographer, b. Paris. Excelled in poster design.

**Cherle, Johann Kaspar von.** See KERLL.

**Cher·nov′** (chĕr·nôf′), **Viktor Mikhailovich.** 1876–1952. Russian journalist; a founder and leader of Russian Social Revolutionary party. Joined revolutionary movement (1893); took part in Zimmerwald Conference (1915); after Revolution (Feb., 1917) fought in White army; president of All-Russian Constituent Assembly (1918); editor of *Revolutionary Russia.*

**Chernowitz.** Variant of TCHERNOWITZ.

**Cher·nya′iev** (chĕr·nyȧ′yĕf), **Mikhail Grigorievich.** 1828–1898. Russian general; served in Crimean War (1854–56); captured Tashkent (1864); resigned from army (1867); practiced law in Moscow. Entered Serbian army (1876); was defeated by Turks.

**Cher·ny·shëv′** (chĕr·nĭ·shôf′), Prince **Aleksandr Ivanovich.** 1786–1857. Russian general. Fought against Napoleon at Austerlitz (1805) and Friedland (1807), and in support of Napoleon at Aspern (1809) and Wagram (1809); served against Napoleon (1813–14). Minister of war (1828–52); chairman, Imperial Council (1848).

**Chernyshëv,** Count **Grigori Petrovich.** 1672–1745. Russian general, of Polish descent. In service of Peter the Great and Catherine I; distinguished himself at Poltava and (1710) at Viborg and Helsingfors; created by Catherine commissary general, lieutenant general, and governor of Livonia (1726), and by Empress Anna a senator and commander in chief of Russian army (1730); created count (1742).

**Cher·ny·shev′ski** (chĕr·nĭ·shĕf′skû·ĭ; *Angl.* -skĭ), **Nikolai Gavrilovich.** 1828?–1889. Russian writer and politician; began as literary critic; became leader of radical groups; arrested (1862) and exiled for 24 years to Siberia (1864); wrote during imprisonment a classic of the Russian revolutionary movement, *What Is to Be Done?* (1863).

**Ché'ron'** (shā'rôN'), **Elisabeth Sophie.** 1648–1711. French painter and writer; her paintings include *Fuite en Egypte, Le Christ au Tombeau,* and a portrait of Mme. Deshoulières; her writings include the poem *Les Cerises Renversées* and *Livre de Principes à Dessiner* (illustrated with engravings).

**Cher'si·phron** (kûr'sĭ·frŏn). Cretan architect, of 6th century B.C.; traditionally regarded as the architect, with his son Metagenes, of the Artemision (temple of Artemis) at Ephesus.

**Che'ru·bi'ni** (kā'rōō·bē'nē), **Maria Luigi Carlo Zenobio Salvatore.** 1760–1842. Italian composer; resident (from 1788) in Paris; studied under Sarti in Bologna; appointed superintendent of music and Kapellmeister to king (1816); director of Paris conservatory of music (1821–41). Composer of many masses, motets, requiems, cantatas, and choral works, and of a number of Italian operas in traditionally light style, including *Armida* (1782), *Ifigenia in Aulide* (1787), and French operas of dramatic quality with original instrumentation, as *Médée* (1797), *Les Deux Journées* (1800), *Faniska* (1806), *Ali Baba* (1833).

**Ché'ruel'** (shā'rü·ĕl'), **Pierre Adolphe.** 1809–1891. French historian; rector of academy at Strasbourg, then at Poitiers. His works include *Dictionnaire Historique des Institutions, Mœurs et Coutumes de la France* (1855), and *Histoire de France sous le Ministère de Mazarin* (1883).

**Cher'ville'** (shĕr'vēl'), Marquis **de. Gaspard Georges Pes'cow'** (pĕs'kôv'). 1819–1898. French writer; in early life, a collaborator with Alexandre Dumas, père.

**Ché'ry'** (shā'rē'), **Philippe.** 1759–1838. French painter. His paintings include *David devant Saül, Mort d'Alcibiade, Toilette de Vénus.*

**Ches'el·den** (chĕz''l·dĕn), **William.** 1688–1752. English surgeon and writer; originated operation of lateral lithotomy and operation of iridectomy for treatment of blindness; author of *The Anatomy of the Human Body* (1713).

**Chesneus, Andreas.** = André DUCHESNE.

**Ches'ney** (chĕs'nĭ; chĕz'nĭ), **Francis Rawdon.** 1789–1872. British soldier and explorer, b. in Ireland, of Scottish ancestry; surveyed Isthmus of Suez, showing canal feasible (1830); explored Euphrates valley, proving Euphrates navigable for trade route from Syrian coast; surveyed and negotiated for railway from Antioch to Euphrates; general (1868).

**Charles Cornwallis Chesney** (1826–1876), his nephew, b. in Ireland; professor of military history at Sandhurst (1858); known for his *Waterloo Lectures* (1868), criticizing strategy and tactics of Napoleon and Wellington, giving due credit to Prussians; member of royal commission on military education.

Sir **George Tomkyns** (1830–1895), brother of C. C. Chesney; Indian army officer, wounded in assault on Delhi (1857); originated Royal Indian Civil Engineering Coll. and was its first president (1871–80); created sensation with *The Battle of Dorking* (in *Blackwoods Magazine,* 1871), portraying a supposed German invasion of England (cf. Robert Erskine CHILDERS); general (1892); author of novels, including *The Dilemma* (1876), *The Private Secretary* (1881), *The Lesters* (1893).

**Ches'nut** (chĕs'nŭt), **Victor King.** 1867–1938. American chemist and botanist, b. Nevada City, Calif.; B.S., California (1890); on staff of U.S. Department of Agriculture (as botanist, 1894–1904, and chemist, 1907–33). Author of *Principal Poisonous Plants of the United States* (1898), *The Nonvolatile Constituents of the Cotton Plant* (1926), etc.

**Ches'nutt** (chĕs'nŭt), **Charles Waddell.** 1858–1932. American Negro educator and lawyer, b. Cleveland, Ohio. Principal, State Normal School, Fayetteville, N.C. (1881); adm. to bar in Ohio (1887); practiced law in Cleveland. Author of *The Conjure Woman* (1899), *Life of Frederick Douglass* (1899), *The Colonel's Dream* (1905).

**Ches'ter** (chĕs'tĕr), Earl of. Title in English peerage first held by a Fleming named Gherbod (c. 1070), granted with palatine powers to Hugh of Avranches (d. 1101) and held by members of his family until 1232 (see below), annexed to English crown (1246), and held since 1254 (when bestowed on Prince Edward, later Edward I) by heirs apparent to English crown, since 1399 by prince of Wales.

**Hugh of A'vranches'** (ȧ'vränsh'), Earl of Chester. d. 1101. Anglo-Norman leader. Contributed sixty ships to invasion of England by William the Conqueror; fought in Normandy in support of Henry I of England, whose chief adviser he became; waged savage wars against Welsh.

**Ran'dulf de Ger'nons'** (răn'dŭlf dē zhĕr'nôN'), Earl of Chester. d. 1153. Anglo-Norman leader in civil wars under King Stephen. Grandnephew of Hugh of Avranches. With help of father-in-law, Robert, Earl of Gloucester, defeated Stephen (1141); won over by extensive grants by Stephen; won over to Duke Henry by larger grants; thought to have been poisoned by supporter of Stephen.

**Hugh of Cy·vei'liog** *or* **Ke·ve'lioc** (kû·vī'lyōg), Earl of Chester. 1147–1181. Anglo-Norman rebel against Henry II (1173); son of Randulf de Gernons. Defeated at Dol (1173), imprisoned (till 1177).

**Ra'nulf** *or* **Ran'dulf de Blun'de·vill** (rā'nŭlf [răn'dŭlf] dē blŭn'dē·vĭl), Earl of Chester. d. 1232. English feudal leader; son of Hugh of Cyveiliog; m. widow of Henry II's son; led armies in wars against Welsh (from 1210); sided with John, and later Henry III, against barons; fought for Henry III against French invaders; went on crusade to Holy Land (1218), taking part in capture of Damietta (1219). Linked in *Vision of Piers Plowman* with Robin Hood.

**Chester, Colby Mitchell.** 1844–1932. American naval officer, b. New London, Conn. Grad. U.S.N.A., Annapolis (1863). Engaged in battle of Mobile Bay and capture of Fort Morgan (Aug., 1864) and Mobile (Apr., 1865). On naval coast survey work (1877–85); commandant at U.S.N.A. (1891–94); commander of South Atlantic squadron (1897–98); superintendent of naval observatory (1902–06); rear admiral (1903); retired (1906).

**Chester, George Randolph.** 1869–1924. American writer, b. in Ohio; author of *Get-Rich-Quick Wallingford* (1908), *Wallingford and Blackie Daw* (1913), *Wallingford in His Prime* (1913), etc.

**Chester, Joseph Lemuel.** 1821–1882. American genealogist and antiquarian, b. Norwich, Conn. Journalist in Philadelphia; resident in London, Eng. (from 1858); founded Harleian Society (1869). Made voluminous extracts from parish registers, wills, etc., esp. for tracing English ancestry of New England colonists.

**Ches'ter·field** (chĕs'tĕr·fēld), 4th Earl of. **Philip Dormer Stan'hope** (stăn'ŭp). 1694–1773. English statesman and man of letters. Grandson of **Philip,** 2d earl, chamberlain to Catherine of Braganza, patron of Dryden. Great-great-grandson of **Philip,** 1st earl (created 1628). Cared for by grandmother, marchioness of

Halifax; studied one year at Cambridge; made grand tour (1714); Whig M.P. (1716–26); effective orator in House of Lords; ambassador to The Hague (1728–32); lord high steward (1730); formed intimacy with Mlle. de Bouchet, by whom he had a son, **Philip** (1732–1768); dismissed (1733) from stewardship for opposing a favorite excise bill of Walpole's; joined and led opposition in House of Lords; offended George II by marrying (1733) countess of Walsingham, daughter of George I and duchess of Kendal; visited Voltaire at Brussels and associated with French men of letters (1741); waged energetic campaign against George II and his government, attacking ministry in letters signed **Gef′fer·y Broad′bot′tom** [jĕf′ẽr·ĭ brôd′bŏt′ŭm] (1743), and received legacy of £20,000 left in gratitude by duchess of Marlborough; entered Pelham ministry (1744); as ambassador to The Hague (1744), successful in inducing Dutch to join War of Austrian Succession; as lord lieutenant of Ireland (1745–46), established schools, encouraged manufactures, checked and conciliated Orangemen and Roman Catholics; one of principal secretaries of state (1746–48); effected passage of bill for reform of calendar (1751); repudiated by Dr. Johnson in famous reply to his belated eulogizing of Johnson's *Dictionary* (1755), the prospectus of which he had ignored (since 1747); intimate with Pope, Swift, Bolingbroke; corresponded with Voltaire; withdrew gradually from politics and society as deafness increased; overwhelmed with grief and disappointment on death of his natural son (1768), for whom he had secured a seat in parliament and diplomatic posts; adopted as heir presumptive his godson, a distant cousin, **Philip Stanhope** (1755–1815). Author of political tracts and contributions to *The World* (1753–56); distinguished as a conversationalist, essayist, epigrammatist; holder of a permanent place in 18th-century literature by reason of his brilliant *Letters to his Son* (first pub. by widow, 1774), written for inculcation in his natural son of the manners and standards of a man of the world, shrewd and exquisitely phrased observations, witty, elegant, cynical; followed by similar *Letters to his Godson* (236 extant, ed. 1890).

**Ches′ter·ton** (chĕs′tẽr·t′n; -tŭn), **Ada Elizabeth,** *nee* **Jones.** 1888-1962. English writer; m. (1917) Cecil Edward Chesterton (1879–1918), brother of G. K. Correspondent for London *Daily Express* in Poland, Russia, China, and Japan. Interested herself in aid for homeless women; founded Cecil Houses, public lodginghouses for homeless women; also founded Cecil Residential Club for Working Girls, in London. Author of *In Darkest London* (1926), *Women of the Underworld* (1930), *My Russian Venture* (1931), *Young China and New Japan* (1933), *What Price Youth* (1939), and the plays *The Man who was Thursday* (dramatized from G. K. Chesterton's novel) and *The Love Game* (both with Ralph Neale collaborating).

**Chesterton, Gilbert Keith.** 1874–1936. English journalist and writer, b. Kensington. Studied art at Slade School, and began literary work by reviewing art books for *The Bookman;* later contributed regularly to a number of English and American journals; became Roman Catholic (1922) and thereafter wrote many works in defense of Catholicism. His many books include *Browning, The Napoleon of Notting Hill* (1904), *Heretics* (1905), *The Man who was Thursday* (1908), *George Bernard Shaw* (1909), *The Innocence of Father Brown* (1911), *Magic*, a play (1913), *The Flying Inn* (1914), *The Wisdom of Father Brown* (1914), *The Uses of Diversity* (1921), *Incredulity of Father Brown* (1926), *Generally Speaking* (1928), *The Resurrection of Rome* (1930), *Chaucer* (1932), *All I Survey* (1933), *The Scandal of Father Brown* (1935).

**Chet′tle** (chĕt′'l), **Henry.** 1560?–?1607. English dramatist; reputed author of thirteen plays, including *The Tragedy of Hoffman* (1602), story of a Danish pirate, and joint author of 35 plays; also, author of elegy on Queen Elizabeth, *Englande's Mourning Garment* (1603).

**Chet′wode** (chĕt′wo͝od), **Philip Walhouse.** 1st baron. 1869–1950. English soldier; brig. general (1914); major general (1916); lieutenant general (1919); general (1926); field marshal (1933). Served in Burma (1892–93), South Africa (1899–1902), and World War (1914–18). Chief of general staff in India (1928–30); commander in chief of army in India (1930–35).

**Chevalier** *or* **Chev′a·lier′ de St. George** (shĕv′ȧ·lēr′ dĕ sånt jôrj′), **the.** Name assumed by James Francis Edward STUART, the Old Pretender, whose son Charles Edward STUART, the Young Pretender, was called **the Young Chevalier.**

**Chev′a·lier′** (shĕv′ȧ·lēr′; shē·văl′yẽr, -yā), **Albert.** 1861–1923. English comedian and music-hall artist, of French descent; b. Notting Hill. Made music-hall success (1891–98), introducing many popular songs, as *The Coster's Serenade, It's the Nasty Way 'e Sez It, The Future Mrs. 'Awkins, My Old Dutch.*

**Che·va′lier′** (shē·vȧ′lyā′; *Angl.* shē·văl′yā), **Maurice Auguste.** 1888–1972. French actor and singer in variety and motion pictures. Served in World War I; prisoner in Germany (1915–18). American-made motion pictures in which he appeared include *Innocents of Paris, The Big Pond, The Smiling Lieutenant, The Merry Widow, The Beloved Vagabond, Gigi, Fanny.*

**Chevalier, Michel.** 1806–1879. French economist, follower of Saint-Simon and advocate of free trade; professor, Collège de France; also, under Napoleon III, a councilor of state and senator.

**Chevalier, Sulpice Guillaume.** See GAVARNI.

**Chevalier, Ulysse.** 1841–1923. French Roman Catholic priest and scholar; professor of ecclesiastical history, Lyon (1887). Published important bibliographies.

**Che·ve·rus′** (shē·vrüs′), **Jean Louis Le·feb′vre de** (lē fâ′vrē dē). 1768–1836. French Roman Catholic prelate; during French Revolution, fled to U.S.; consecrated first Roman Catholic bishop of Boston (1810); returned to France (1823); archbishop of Bordeaux (1826); cardinal (1836).

**Chev′es** (chĭv′ĭs), **Langdon.** 1776–1857. American banker, b. in Abbeville District, S.C.; member, U.S. House of Representatives (1810–15); speaker (1814–15); president, United States Bank (1819–22); built up resources and saved bank; known as "the Hercules of the United States Bank."

**Che·vil′lard′** (shē·vē′yȧr′), **Pierre Alexandre François.** 1811–1877. French violoncellist; professor at Paris Conservatory. His son **Camille,** *in full* **Pierre Alexandre Camille** (1859–1923), composer and orchestra leader; succeeded his father-in-law, Lamoureux, as conductor of the "Concerts Lamoureux"; compositions include a symphonic poem, a symphonic ballad, and a symphonic fantasia.

**Che·vreul′** (shē·vrûl′), **Michel Eugène.** 1786–1889. French chemist. Professor, Lycée Charlemagne (1813); director, Gobelins tapestry works, where he experimented in color contrasts (1824); professor (1830), director (1864–79), natural history museum, Jardin des Plantes. Known esp. for researches on animal fats which led to improvements in the candle and soap industry; discovered margarine, oleine, and stearine.

**Che·vreuse′** (shē·vrûz′), Duchesse **de. Marie de Ro′han′-Mont′ba′zon′** (dē rô′äN′môN′bȧ′zôN′). 1600–1679. French intriguer in royal court; m. duc de Luynes (1617; d. 1621), then (1622) Claude de Lorraine, Duc de

Chevreuse; intrigued against Richelieu; forced to leave France; returned after death of Louis XIII; intrigued with Cardinal de Retz against Mazarin; again sent into exile.

**Chev'ro·let'** (shĕv'rō·lā'), **Louis.** 1879–1941. American automobile racer, designer, and manufacturer, b. in Switzerland; to U.S. (1901); participated in automobile races; associate of W. C. Durant in founding Chevrolet Motor Co. (1911–15), later incorporated into General Motors (1915).

**Chevtchenko.** Variant of SHEVCHENKO.

**Chew, Ng Poon.** See NG POON CHEW.

**Chew** (chōō), **Samuel Claggett.** 1888–1960. American educator, b. Baltimore; A.B. (1909), Ph.D. (1913), Johns Hopkins; teacher of English, Bryn Mawr (from 1914; professor from 1920). Author of *The Dramas of Lord Byron* (1915), *Thomas Hardy* (1921), *Byron in England* (1924), *Swinburne* (1929), *The Crescent and the Rose—Islam and England During the Renaissance* (1937).

**Cheyne** (chān; chēn), **John.** 1777–1836. Scottish physician and medical writer in Dublin; physician general to forces in Ireland (1820).

**Cheyne, Thomas Kelly.** 1841–1915. English Biblical scholar. Educ. Oxford and Göttingen; disciple of Georg Heinrich Ewald; introduced German critical scholarship in England by lectures, articles, and works; member of board of revision of Old Testament (1884); Oriel professor of interpretation of Scripture, Oxford (1885–1908).

**Cheyne,** Sir **William Watson.** 1852–1932. British surgeon; educ. Edinburgh; professor (1888–90), president (1914–17), Royal Coll. of Surgeons; temporary surgeon general, British navy (from 1915); prof. of clinical surgery, King's Coll., London; author of medical works.

**Chey'ney** (chā'nĭ), **Edward Potts.** 1861–1947. American historian, b. Wallingford, Pa.; A.B., Pennsylvania (1883); professor of history, U. of Pennsylvania. Author of *Social and Industrial History of England* (1901), *European Background of American History* (1904), etc.

**Ché'zy'** (shā'zē'), **Antoine de.** 1718–1798. French engineer and mathematician; director of École des Ponts et Chaussées. His son **Antoine Leonard** (1773–1832), Orientalist, translated various classics from Persian and Sanskrit, including notably the *Sakuntala* (1830). Antoine Léonard's wife, **Wilhelmine Christine,** *called* **Helmine,** *nee* **von Klenck'e** [fōn klĕng'kĕ] (1783–1855), was famous for her memoirs and poems; wrote the text for Weber's *Euryanthe.* See Anna Luise KARSCH.

**Ch'i** *or* **Tsi** (chē). *Also known as* **Southern Ch'i.** A Chinese dynasty (479–502 A.D.), succeeded by the Liang.

**Chia·bre'ra** (kyä·brâ'rä), **Gabriello.** 1552–1637. Italian lyric poet, sometimes called "the Italian Pindar." Introduced innovations in metrical form adopted by later poets and influencing Parini and Carducci. His work includes epics, odes, pastorals, satires, and lyrics.

**Chia Ching** (jē·ä' jĭng'). d. 1566. Chinese emperor (1522–1566), of the Ming dynasty; made more extensive contacts with Europeans; granted Macao (1557) to Portuguese.

**Chia Ch'ing** (jē·ä' chĭng'). 1760–1820. Chinese emperor (1796–1820), fifth of the Ch'ing dynasty. Son of Ch'ien Lung. Refused to receive British mission under Lord Amherst (1816).

**Chiang** (jē·äng'), **Yee** (ē). 1903– . Chinese writer in England; curator, Chinese section, Welcome Historical Medical Museum, London (from 1938). His books in English (often illustrated by him) include *The Chinese Eye* (1935), *The Silent Traveller in Lakeland* (1937), *The Silent Traveller in London* (1938), *Birds and Beasts* (1939), *A Chinese Childhood* (1940), *The Silent Traveller in Yorkshire* (1940).

**Chiang Kai-shek** (jē·äng' kī'shĕk'). *In Peking dialect* **Chiang Chieh-shih** (jē·äng' jē·ĕ'shĭr'). *Real name* **Chiang Chung-cheng.** 1887–1975. Chinese general and statesman, b. near Ningpo. Graduated Tokyo Military Staff Coll.; joined Revolutionary party of Sun Yat-sen (1911); engaged in minor civil wars and insurrections (1911–16); resigned (1917) to go into business; worked with Sun Yat-sen in Canton (1921–22); sent by him to Russia (1923); developed Kuomintang army (1923–25); head of Whampoa Military Academy (1924). After Sun's death (1925) chosen generalissimo of southern army; led expedition to north (1926), establishing Kuomintang government at Wuchang; after break with Communist extremists transferred seat of government to Nanking (1927); resigned all government posts (1927); persuaded to resume command (1928); led Nanking army northward and occupied Peking (1928); president of Chinese Nationalist government (1928–31); again resigned (1931). Commander in chief of all military forces (1932); chairman of Executive Yuan of National Government (1935–38; 1939–45); adopted policy of civil war against Communists (1927–36); ordered Chang Hsueh-liang to fight the Communists (1936); kidnaped on visit at Chang's headquarters at Sian (Dec., 1936) and held prisoner for two weeks; after release, changed policy of appeasement toward Japanese to one of opposition in alliance with Communists. Assumed entire command on outbreak of hostilities with Japan (1937); retreated to Hankow, set up National Government at Chungking; as generalissimo conducted war against Japan (1937–41); appointed (Jan., 1942) supreme commander of allied air and land forces in Chinese war theater; succeeded Lin Sên as president of National Government (1943–49). Resumed presidency on Taiwan (1950–75) after Communists won control of mainland China (1949). His second wife (m. 1927), **Mei-ling,** *or* **Mayling, Soong** [mā'lĭng' sōōng'] (1898– ), youngest daughter of C. J. Soong (see SOONG family); educ. Shanghai and Wellesley Coll., U.S.A. (1917). Active and effective worker for betterment of Chinese people, especially in education and social matters; made secretary-general of Chinese Commission on Aeronautical Affairs (1936); took active part in securing release of Chiang when kidnaped at Sian (1936); of great assistance to her husband in national defense work (from 1937). Author of *China in Peace and War* and *This is Our China* (both 1940), *China Shall Rise Again* (1941), the folk tale *Little Sister Su* (1942).

**Chiappe** (kyȧp; shyȧp), **Jean.** 1878–1940. French politician; director of Sûreté Générale (1924–28) and prefect of police in Paris (1928–34); member of Chamber of Deputies (1936); appointed high commissioner in Syria (1940).

**Chia·rel'li** (kyä·rĕl'lē), **Luigi.** 1884–1947. Italian playwright and novelist; founder of Teatro del Grottesco. Among his plays are *La Maschera e il Volto* (1916), *La Scala di Seta* (1917), *Jolly* (1928), *Ninon* (1934), *Moneta Falsa* (1938); among his novels, *La Mano di Venere* (1935), *La Figlia dell'Aria* (1939).

**Chia·ri'ni** (kyä·rē'nē), **Giuseppe.** 1833–1908. Italian critic, poet, and educator. Superintendent of secondary education (1892); known esp. as friend and supporter of Carducci and as writer on Foscolo. His works include verse, a translation of Heine's *Atta Troll* (1880), and critical studies.

**Chich'e·le** *or* **Chich'e·ley** (chĭch'ĕ·lē), **Henry.** 1364–1443. English prelate and diplomat. B.A., Oxon. (1392); envoy to Pope Innocent VII (1405) and Gregory XII (1407); bishop of St. David's (1408); envoy to Pisa (1409), to France (1410); archbishop of Canterbury

(1414); erroneously blamed in Shakespeare's *Henry V* for urging conquest of France to divert Parliament from disendowment of the Church. Founder of two colleges at Oxford, St. Bernard's (1437, for Cistercians) and All Souls' (1437).

**Chi·che′rin** (chĭ·chā′ryĭn), **Boris Nikolaevich.** 1830–1904. Russian philosopher; author of *Russia at the Close of the 20th Century,* in which he declared that autocracy had finished its allotted span in Russia and a liberal regime should be inaugurated.

**Chicherin, Georgi Vasilievich.** 1872–1936. Russian statesman. Educ. St. Petersburg. In Czarist diplomatic service (to 1904); resigned because of sympathy with revolutionary agitation; after Revolution (1917), returned to Russia and served as People's Commissar for Foreign Affairs (1918–30).

**Chich′es·ter** (chĭch′ĭs·tẽr), Earls of. See PELHAM family.

**Chichester, Arthur.** Baron **Chichester of Bel′fast** (bĕl′fást; bĕl·fást′). 1563–1625. English administrator in Ireland. Educ. Oxford; commanded ship against Spanish Armada (1588). Lord deputy of Ireland (1604–14); encouraged Scottish colonization in Ulster; obtained relaxation (1607) of repressive measures of James I against Roman Catholics; recalled (1614). Lord treasurer of Ireland (1616–25).

**Chichibu,** Prince. *In full* **Ya·su·hi·to Chi·chi·bu-no–mi·ya** (yä·sōō·hē·tō chē·chē·bōō·nō·mē·yä). 1902–1953. Second son of Yoshihito (Taisho) and brother of Emperor Hirohito of Japan. Entered army (1922); studied in England (1925–27); m. (1928) Setsuko Matsudaira; visited Europe (1937).

**Chich·kov′** (chĭch·kôf′), **Aleksandr Semënovich.** 1754–1841. Russian statesman and man of letters; admiral in Russian navy; minister of public instruction (1824–28); a founder of Society of Friends of the Russian Language; author of *Treatise on Old and New Style Russian* (1802).

**Chick′er·ing** (chĭk′ẽr·ĭng), **Jonas.** 1798–1853. American piano manufacturer, b. Mason Village, N.H.

**Ch'ien Lung** *or* **Kien Lung** (chē·ĕn′lŏŏng′). *Dynastic name* **Kao Tsung.** 1711–1799. Chinese emperor (1736–96), fourth of the Ch'ing dynasty. Son of Yung Chêng and grandson of K'ang-hsi. One of ablest of Manchu rulers; during his reign, territory of empire increased: control of Tibet established (1751), Ili Valley region and Kashgaria conquered (1755–60); enjoyed friendly relations with Western powers; sanctioned establishment of trade relations (1784) with United States at Canton; received Lord Macartney's British mission (1793); invaded Burma (1765–69) and Nepal (1792); abdicated in favor of his son Chia Ch'ing. Patron of literature and art, esp. of pottery; under his authority, catalogue of Imperial Library issued (1789).

**Chi′gi** (kē′jē). Italian family, noted esp. for its protection of the arts. **Agostino Chigi** (1465?–1520), banker, b. Siena; used his great wealth to encourage leading artists, as Peruzzi, Perugino, Sebastiano del Piombo, and esp. Raphael; built (1509–11) the Villa Farnese at Rome (see FARNESE), famous for its works of art, esp. frescoes. **Fabio Chigi** (1599–1667), see Pope ALEXANDER VII. **Flavio Chigi** (1810–1885), papal diplomat and cardinal; represented papacy at coronation of Emperor Alexander II of Russia (1856); papal nuncio at Paris (1861–73); cardinal (1873).

**Chikamatsu.** *In full* **Chi·ka·ma·tsu Mon·za·e·mon** (chē·kä·mä·tsōō mōn·zä·ĕ·mōn). 1653–?1724. Japanese romantic dramatist; created new type of drama; composed nearly 100 five-act plays, about half of them still produced or read. Sometimes called "the Shakespeare of Japan."

**Chi·kha·chëv′** (chĭ·kŭ·chôf′), **Pëtr Aleksandrovich.** 1808–1890. Russian traveler and naturalist; traveled widely in Asia Minor and northern Africa. Author (in French) of *Voyage Scientifique dans l'Altaï Oriental* (1844–45), *L'Asie Mineure* (8 vols., 1852–69), etc.

**Child** (chīld), **Charles Manning.** 1869–1954. American biologist. b. Ypsilanti, Mich. Ph.B., Wesleyan (1890), Ph.D., Leipzig (1894). On teaching staff (from 1896), professor (from 1916), U. of Chicago. Author of *Senescence and Rejuvenescence* (1915), *Physiological Foundations of Behavior* (1924), etc.

**Child, Edwin Burrage.** 1868–1937. American painter, b. Gouverneur, N.Y. A.B., Amherst (1890); studied under John La Farge; portraits of John Bassett Moore, John Dewey, Dwight W. Morrow, Lyman Abbott.

**Child, Francis James.** 1825–1896. American philologist, b. Boston. Grad. Harvard (1846); professor, Harvard (1851–96). Authority on the ballad; works: *English and Scottish Ballads* (8 vols., 1857–58); *English and Scottish Popular Ballads* (5 vols., 1883–98).

**Child, Frank Samuel.** 1854–1922. American Congregational clergyman, b. Exeter, N.Y.; author of studies of colonial New England, as *An Old New England Town, i.e.* Fairfield, Conn. (1895), *A Colonial Witch* (1897), *A Puritan Wooing* (1898), etc.

**Child,** Sir **John.** d. 1690. English governor of Bombay. Chief of East India Company's affairs at Surat and Bombay (1682); charged with tyranny over natives; selected for expulsion by peace terms after war with Aurangzeb. His brother Sir **Josiah** (1630–1699), merchant and economist; despotic governor of East India Company; credited with change from unarmed to armed traffic, though actual change made under Gov. Sir Joseph Ash; author of *A New Discourse of Trade* (1668, 1690).

**Child, Lydia Maria,** *nee* **Fran′cis** (från′sĭs). 1802–1880. American abolitionist and author, b. Medford, Mass.; m. (1828) David Lee Child (d. 1874); editor, *National Anti-Slavery Standard* (1841–49); author of *An Appeal in Favor of That Class of Americans Called Africans* (1833), etc.

**Child, Richard Washburn.** 1881–1935. American lawyer, author, and diplomat, b. Worcester, Mass. A.B. (1903), LL.B. (1906), Harvard; adm. to bar (1906). Editor, *Collier's Weekly* (1919); U.S. ambassador to Italy (1921–24). Author of *Jim Hands* (1910), *The Man in the Shadow* (1911), *The Blue Wall* (1912), *Potential Russia* (1916), *Bodbank* (1916), *Vanishing Men* (1919), *Velvet Black* (1920), *Fresh Waters* (1924), *A Diplomat Looks at Europe* (1925), *Pitcher of Romance* (1930), etc.

**Childe** (chīld), **Vere Gordon.** 1892–1957. British archaeologist, b. Sidney, Australia. To Eng. (1914). Taught at Edinburgh Univ. (1927–46); Univ. of London (1946–56). Author of *The Dawn of European Civilization* (1925), *Man Makes Himself* (1936), etc.

**Chil′de·bert** (chĭl′dĕ·bĕrt; kĭl′-; *Fr.* shēl′dē·bâr′; *Ger.* kĭl′dĕ·bĕrt). Name of three Frankish kings of the Merovingian dynasty: **Childebert I,** son of Clovis, reigned 511–558. **Childebert II,** reigned 575–596. **Childebert III,** reigned 695–711. See MEROVINGIAN.

**Chil′der·ic** (chĭl′dẽr·ĭk; kĭl′-). *Fr.* **Chil′dé′ric′** (shēl′-dā′rēk′). *Ger.* **Chil′de·rich** (kĭl′dĕ·rĭk). Name of three Frankish kings: **Childeric I** (437?–481); father of Clovis; king of the Salian Franks (458?–481) with capital at Tournai. **Childeric II** (653?–673), Merovingian king of Austrasia (660–673). **Childeric III,** last of the Merovingians (741–751); deposed by Pepin (751) and forced to enter a monastery. See MEROVINGIAN.

**Chil′ders** (chĭl′dẽrz), **Hugh Culling Eardley.** 1827–1896. British political leader. B.A., Cantab. (1850). Inspector of schools, Melbourne (1851); first vice-chancellor of U.

of Melbourne; agent-general for Victoria in England (1857). First lord of admiralty (1868–71); as war secretary under Gladstone (1880–82), introduced territorial system and other administrative reforms in army; as chancellor of exchequer (1882–85), introduced into budget beer and spirit duty that caused government's fall; home secretary (1886); supported Gladstone's home-rule bill.

**Childers, Robert Caesar.** 1838–1876. English Orientalist; civil servant in Ceylon (1860–64); published first Pali text printed in England (1869); compiled Pali dictionary (1872–75); first professor of Pali and Buddhist literature, University Coll., London.

His son **Robert Erskine** (1870–1922), Anglo-Irish author and political leader; served in Boer War and as naval intelligence officer in World War; won D.S.C.; devoted himself (from 1908) to cause of full dominion status for Ireland, and (from 1919) to complete independence as a republic; member of Dail Eireann (1921); opposed Anglo-Irish treaty of 1922; joined Republican army; captured by Free State soldiers, court-martialed, and shot; author of *The Times History of the South African War*, of *The Riddle of the Sands* (1903), an imaginary account of a German raid on England (cf. George Tomkyns CHESNEY), and of *The Framework of Home Rule* (1911).

**Childs** (chīldz). Family of American restaurateurs, including the brothers **Samuel Shannon** (1863–1925), **William** (1865?–1938), and **Ellsworth** (1869–1929), founders (1889) and executives of chain of restaurants (Childs Restaurants); lost control of the business (1929).

**Childs, George William.** 1829–1894. American publisher, b. Baltimore; in bookselling business, Childs and Peterson (1854–60); co-owner with Anthony J. Drexel, Philadelphia *Public Ledger* (from 1864); author of *Recollections of General Grant* (1885).

**Childs, Marquis William.** 1903– . American journalist, b. Clinton, Iowa; on staff of St. Louis *Post-Dispatch* (from 1926); author of *Sweden—The Middle Way* (1936), *Washington Calling* (1937), *I Write from Washington* (1942), etc.

**Chil'ling·worth** (chĭl'ĭng·wûrth), **William.** 1602–1644. English theologian and controversialist. M.A., Oxon. (1624); embraced Roman Catholicism and studied at Jesuit college at Douai (1630–31); abjured Roman Catholicism (1634); vindicated sole authority of the Bible in matters of salvation, and individual's right to interpret it, in his book *The Religion of Protestants a Safe Way to Salvation* (1637); served in king's army in Civil War; invented a siege engine.

**Chi'lon** *or* **Chei'lon** (kī'lŏn) *or* **Chi'lo** (kī'lō). Spartan ephor (560 or 556 B.C.); ranked as one of the Seven Sages, or Seven Wise Men of Greece.

**Chil'per·ic** (chĭl'pẽr·ĭk; kĭl'-). *Fr.* **Chil'pé'ric'** (shēl'pā'rēk'). *Ger.* **Chil'pe·rich** (kĭl'pĕ·rĭκ). (1) King of Burgundy; father of Clotilda. (2) **Chilperic I** and **II.** Merovingian kings of the Franks (561–584 and 715–720), the former being king of Neustria, the latter king of Neustria (715–720) and of Austrasia (719–720). See BRUNHILDE.

**Chil'ton** (chĭl't'n; -tŭn), **Eleanor Carroll.** 1898–1949. American writer, b. Charleston, W.Va.; B.A., Smith (1922); m. Herbert Agar (1933). Author of *Shadows Waiting* (1927), *Fire and Sleet and Candlelight* (with Herbert Agar and Willis Fisher, 1928), *The Garment of Praise* (with H. Agar, 1929), *Follow the Furies* (1935).

**Chimay,** Princesse **de.** See Jeanne M. I. T. TALLIEN.

**Chin** *or* **Tsin** (jĭn). Name of several Chinese dynasties. **Western Chin** (265–317 A.D.), founded by Ssŭ-ma Yen, united all China for brief period, terminating period of the three kingdoms (see *Shu Han*, under HAN; also WEI and WU); broken up by internal dissension and foreign invasions (Tatars, Hiung-Nu, Tibetans). **Eastern Chin** (317–419 A.D.), with capital at Nanking, restricted to central and southern regions. One of the Five Dynasties (*q.v.*) is known as the **Later Chin** (936–941 A.D.).

**Ch'in** *or* **Ts'in** (chĭn). An early dynasty of China (255–206 B.C.); its great ruler (247–210 B.C.) was Shih Huang Ti (*q.v.*).

**Chin·chón'** (chēn·chôn'), Conde **de. Luis Gerónimo Fer·nán'dez de Ca·bre'ra Bo'ba·dil'la Cer'da y Men·do'za** (fĕr·nän'dāth thā kä·brā'rä bō'bä·thē'lyä thĕr'thä ē män·dō'thä). c. 1590–1647. Spanish administrator, b. Madrid; viceroy of Peru (1628–39). His first wife, Condesa **Ana de Osorio** (d. 1625) was long erroneously credited with introducing cinchona bark to Spain. Linnaeus named the genus *Cinchona* in her honor.

**Chin·da** (chēn·dä), Count **Sutemi.** 1856–1929. Japanese diplomat, b. Hirosaki. Educ. in U.S.; entered Japanese foreign office (1886); consul general at Shanghai (1895); later held diplomatic offices in Brazil, Netherlands, and Russia; vice-minister for foreign affairs during Russo-Japanese War; ambassador at Berlin (1908–11), Washington (1911–16), and London (1916–20). Created count (1920); adviser to emperor; grand chamberlain (1927).

**Ch'ing** *or* **Ta Ch'ing** (dä' chĭng') *or* **Man'chu** (măn'chōō). Last dynasty (Manchus) of Chinese empire (1644–1912), succeeding the Ming dynasty; ten rulers; overthrown by founding of Chinese Republic (1911–12). See *Table*, for CHINA.

**Chinghiz Khan** *or* **Chingiz Khan.** Variant of GENGHIS KHAN.

**Chini, Eusebio Francisco.** See KINO.

**Ch'in Shih Huang Ti.** = SHIH HUANG TI.

**Chip'pen·dale** (chĭp'ĕn·dāl), **Thomas.** 1718?–1779. English cabinetmaker; son of a Yorkshire carver and maker of picture frames; established factory in London (1749); published *The Gentleman and Cabinet Maker's Director* (1754). Succeeded by his son **Thomas** (d. 1822?).

**Chi'ri·co** (?kē'rē·kō), **Giorgio de.** 1888–1978. Italian painter; identified with ultramodern school; one of the founders of surrealism; executed stage decorations for Pirandello's *La Giarra* (Paris, 1925) and Alberto Savinio's *Morte di Niobe* (Rome, 1926).

**Chi'ri·kov** (chē'ryĭ·kôf), **Evgeni Nikolaevich.** 1864–1932. Russian playwright and novelist.

**Chir'ol** (chĭr'ŭl), Sir **Ignatius Valentine.** 1852–1929. British journalist. Educ. chiefly in France (grad. Sorbonne); clerk in Foreign Office (1872–76); traveled widely in Near East, Persia, India, Australia (1876–92). Berlin correspondent of London *Times* (1892–96); in charge of foreign department of *Times* (1899–1912) and member of board of Times Publishing Co. (1908–12). Author of *'Twixt Greek and Turk* (1881), *The Far Eastern Question* (1896), *The Middle Eastern Question* (1903), *Indian Unrest* (1910), *The Egyptian Problem* (1920), *The Occident and the Orient* (1924).

**Chis'holm** (chĭz'ŭm), **Hugh.** 1866–1924. English journalist and editor, b. London. Educ. Oxford; called to bar (1892). Editor, *St. James's Gazette* (1897–99), *Encyclopaedia Britannica, Eleventh Edition* (1903–11), the 1913 issue of the *Britannica Year Book*, and three supplementary volumes of the *Encyclopaedia Britannica* (pub. 1922). City editor, London *Times* (1913–20).

**Chisholm, Shirley Anita St. Hill.** 1924– Amer. reformer and congresswoman, b. Brooklyn, N.Y. First Negro woman popularly elected to U.S. Congress (1968).

**Chi-tsĕ.** Variant of KI TSE.

**Chit'ten·den** (chĭt''n·dĕn), **Kate Sara.** 1856–1949. American organist and music teacher, b. of American parentage in Hamilton, Canada. Organist and choir director in Calvary Baptist Church, New York City (1879–1906); head of piano department, Vassar College (1899–1930).

**Chittenden, Russell Henry.** 1856–1943. American chemist and educator, b. New Haven, Conn. Ph.B. (1875), Ph.D. (1880), Yale. Professor of physiological chemistry (1882–1922) and director of Sheffield Scientific School (1898–1922), Yale. Author of *Physiological Economy in Nutrition* (1905), *The Nutrition of Man* (1907), and *History of the Sheffield Scientific School* (2 vols., 1928).

**Chittenden, Thomas.** 1730–1797. American politician, b. East Guilford, Conn.; moved to Williston, Vt. (1774); governor of Vermont (1778–79; 1790–97). His son **Martin** (1763–1840) was governor of Vermont (1813–15).

**Chit'ty** (chĭt'ĭ), **Joseph.** 1776–1841. English lawyer and legal writer; barrister (1816); author of law manuals. His three sons, likewise lawyers: **Joseph** (d. 1838), author of *Chitty on Contracts* (1841); **Thomas** (1802–1878), special pleader, editor of standard law books; **Edward** (1804–1863), legal reporter, published bankruptcy cases. Thomas's son Sir **Joseph William** (1828–1899), justice of high court, chancery division (1881); lord justice of appeal (1897).

**Chi–tzŭ.** Variant of Ki Tse.

**Ch'iu Ch'u–chi** (chyōō' chōō'jē'). *Monastic name* **Ch'ang Ch'un** (chäng' chŏŏn'). 1148–1227. Chinese Taoist monk and traveler. Invited by Genghis Khan to visit him (1219); made long journey (1221–24) from Peking to Mongol emperor's camp near the Hindu Kush; after his return dictated story of journey and peoples visited, one of best extant medieval accounts of western Asia.

**Chiv'ers** (chĭv'ẽrz), **Thomas Holley.** 1809–1858. American poet, b. near Washington, Ga. Associated with Edgar Allan Poe (1845–49); accused (1850) of plagiarism from Poe; retorted by charging Poe plagiarized from him. Verse contains unusual experiments in meters.

**Chka'lov** (ch'kȧ'lôf), **Valeri Pavlovich.** 1904–1938. Soviet aviator; received Order of Lenin (1935) for exploits as test pilot; piloted nonstop flight from Moscow, via Franz Josef Land, the Siberian coast, and Yakut, to Nikolaevsk on the Amur River (1936); piloted nonstop flight from Moscow, over the North Pole, to Vancouver, Wash., U.S.A., a flight of 5400 miles, 3100 over ice fields (1937).

**Chlad'ni** (kläd'nē), **Ernst Florens Friedrich.** 1756–1827. German physicist, authority on acoustics; studied vibration of strings and rods, and of plates, by means of sand figures (Chladni's figures); measured velocity of sound in gases other than air; invented the euphonium.

**Chlodoald,** Saint. See Cloud.

**Chlodowech** *or* **Chlodwig.** See Clovis.

**Chlo·pic'ki** (klô·pēts'kē), **Józef.** 1771–1854. Polish general. In French service under Napoleon, and in Russian army (1815–18). Dictator of Poland (Dec., 1830–Jan., 1831); resigned in face of opposition to his policies and joined Polish army fighting against Russians; wounded and forced into retirement (Feb., 1831).

**Chlothar.** See Clotaire.

**Chlothilde.** See Clotilda.

**Chmiel·nic'ki** (*Pol.* kmyĕl·nēts'kē), *Russ.* **Khmel·nits'ki** (kmyāl·y'·nyēts'kû·ĭ; *Angl.* -kĭ), **Bogdan.** 1593?–1657. Cossack hetman; led revolts against Poles (1648) and won recognition as semi-independent sovereign of the Ukraine; defeated by Poles at Beresteczko (July 1, 1651); asked Russia for alliance (1652) and took oath of allegiance to czar (1654), thus ending Ukrainian aspirations for independence.

**Chmie·low'ski** (kmyĕ·lôf'skē), **Piotr.** 1848–1904. Polish writer; educ. Warsaw and Leipzig; lecturer on Polish literature, Warsaw (1880); editor of *Ateneum*, monthly literary review (1881–97). Author of *Rousseau* (1878), *Goethe* (1878), *Adam Mickiewicz* (2 vols., 1886), and *Nasza Literatura Dramatyczna* (1897).

**Choate** (chōt), **Joseph Hodges.** 1832–1917. American lawyer and diplomat, b. Salem, Mass.; second cousin of Rufus Choate. Grad. Harvard (1852), Harvard Law School (1854); adm. to bar (1855). Practiced in New York City; of counsel in cases of great importance, as the Tweed Ring prosecution, the Tilden will contest, Standard Oil antitrust cases, income tax cases. U.S. ambassador to Britain (1899–1905); head of U.S. delegation to second International Peace Conference at The Hague (1907).

**Choate, Rufus.** 1799–1859. American lawyer, b. Essex, Mass. Grad. Dartmouth (1819); practiced law, Boston (from 1834); eminent jury lawyer and orator. Member, U.S. House of Representatives (1831–34); U.S. senator (1841–45). Elected to Amer. Hall of Fame (1915).

**Cho·ca'no** (chō·kä'nō), **José Santos.** 1875–1934. Peruvian poet; author of *Iras Santas* (1895), *En la Aldea* (1895), *Azaleares* (1896), *El Canto del Siglo* (1900), *Fiat-Lux* (1908), *El Hombre-sol* (1924), etc.

**Cho Den·su** (chō dĕn·sōō). *Real name* **Min·cho** (mēn-chō). 1352–1431. Japanese painter of Ashikaga period. Much influenced by Chinese artists of Sung and Yuan periods; drew admirable Buddhist and Taoist figures; founded school, with many followers.

**Chod·kie'wicz** (kôt·kyĕ'vēch). Ruthenian family, including: **Jan** [yän] (d. 1482), who commanded joint Lithuanian-Ruthenian army which defeated Russians (1457). His son **A'lek·san'der** [ä'lĕk·sän'dĕr] (1470–1549), signer of treaty that united Lithuania with Poland (1501). Aleksander's son **Jerome** [*pron. as Eng.*] (d. 1561), commander in chief of Lithuanian armies. Jerome's son **Jan** (d. 1579), grand marshal of Lithuania; fought successfully Russian and Swedish armies. Jan's son **Jan Ka'rol** [kä'rôl] (1560–1621), distinguished himself in campaign (1600) against the Turks; chosen hetman of Lithuania; won battle of Kirchholm on the Dvina against Charles IX of Sweden (1605); fought the Turks at Chocim (1621).

**Cho'do·wiec'ki** (kō'dô·vyĕts'kē), **Daniel Nikolaus.** 1726–1801. German painter, etcher, and illustrator; director, Berlin Academy of Art (1797). His works include a set of miniatures *History of the Life of Jesus Christ*, a painting *Jean Calas and his Family*, and over 2000 vignettes and illustrations for books.

**Chodź'ko** (kôj'kô). Family of Polish scholars, including: **Jan** (1777–1851), a writer; **Le·o'nard** (lĕ·ô'närt) **Jakób** (1800–1871), historian who settled in Paris, author of *La Pologne Historique, Littéraire...;* Jan's son **Aleksander** (1804?–1891), poet, Orientalist, and Slavic scholar, professor at Collège de France.

**Choe'ri·lus** (kĕr'ĭ·lŭs; kĕr'-). fl. 6th–5th cent. B.C. Athenian playwright; author of tragedies (none extant) said to have been played in competition with works of Aeschylus and Pratinas.

**Choerilus of Sa'mos** (sā'mŏs). fl. late 5th century B.C. Epic poet, of Samos; long resident in court of Archelaus, king of Macedonia. Author of the *Perseïs*, an epic based on the Greco-Persian wars.

**Choi'seul'** (shwȧ'zûl'), Duc **César de.** 1598–1675. French soldier. Distinguished himself at siege of La Rochelle (1628); commanded Royal army before Paris at time of the Fronde; defeated Turenne and Spaniards at Rethel (1650).

**Choiseul,** Duc **Étienne François de.** *In early life* Comte **de Stain'ville'** (stăɴ'vēl'). 1719–1785. French statesman. Fought with distinction in War of Austrian Succession (1740–48); won favor of Mme. de Pompadour; lieutenant general (1748); ambassador at Rome (1754–57) and Vienna (1757–58). Minister of foreign affairs (1758–61), of war and marine (1761–66), of war and foreign affairs (1766–70); directed French policy (1758–63) through Seven Years' War; obtained best possible terms of peace for France at Treaty of Paris (1763); negotiated Family Compact (1761); instrumental in suppression of Jesuits in France (1764); a leader in European diplomacy (1764–70); dismissed through influence of Mme. du Barry (1770). Lived in retirement at Chanteloupe (1770–74) and Paris (1774–85).

**Choi'sy'** (shwȧ'zē'), **François Auguste.** 1841–1909. French archaeologist; author of works on history of architecture, esp. Roman, Greek, Byzantine, Egyptian.

**Cho'la** (chō'lȧ). An early Hindu (Tamil) dynasty ruling in southern India on Coromandel Coast (first mentioned c. 4th century B.C.); for a time, with the Cheras, ruled in south, superseding the Pandyas (*q.v.*); conquered (c. A.D. 300) by the Pallavas (*q.v.*); gradually regained power and in combination with the Chalukyas (*q.v.*) defeated the Pallavas (8th century A.D.); established powerful kingdom with center at Tanjore (888–1267) with hegemony over most of the Deccan; extinguished (1310) by Mohammedan army from Delhi. Its greatest rulers were **Ra'ja·ra'ja I** (rä'jȧ·rä'jȧ) the Great (985–1014), who invaded Ceylon (1001–04), and his son **Ra·jen'dra Cho'la·de'va I** [rä·jān'drȧ chō'lȧ·dā'vȧ] (1014–35).

**Cholmon'deley** (chŭm'lĭ), **Mary.** d. 1925. English novelist, b. in Shropshire; author of *The Danvers Jewels* (under pseudonym **Pax** [păks]; 1887), *Diana Tempest* (1893), *Red Pottage* (1899), *Prisoners* (1906), *The Lowest Rung* (1908), *Notwithstanding* (1913), *Under One Roof* (1918).

**Cho'part'** (shô'pȧr'), **François.** 1743–1795. French surgeon, noted for work in amputation of the foot.

**Cho'pin'** (shô'păɴ'; *Angl.* shō'păn), **Frédéric François.** 1810–1849. Composer and pianist, b. near Warsaw of French father and Polish mother. Professional debut as piano virtuoso, Vienna (1829); settled in Paris (1831). Long the intimate friend of George Sand (Mme. Dudevant), who during his illness took him to Majorca, nursed him back to health (1838), but later broke with him, depicting him in her novel *Lucrezia Floriani* as Prince Karol, a "high-flown, consumptive, and exasperating nuisance." Noted for his lyric compositions for piano, including (with posthumous works) 55 mazurkas, 13 polonaises, 24 preludes, 27 études, 19 nocturnes, 4 ballades, 4 scherzos; also wrote a number of songs. Among earlier works in classical style are: for piano, two concertos (with orchestra), three rondos, and three sonatas; for piano and cello, a sonata, duo concertante, and *Introduction and Polonaise;* for piano, violin, and cello, a trio.

**Chopinel, Jean** *or* **Jehan.** See JEAN DE MEUNG.

**Cho·ri'ci·us** (kô·rĭsh'ĭ·ŭs). *Known as* **Choricius of Ga'za** (gā'zȧ). fl. 491–518. Greek sophist and rhetorician.

**Chor'ley** (chôr'lĭ), **Henry Fothergill.** 1808–1872. English journalist and music critic; contributed literary and music reviews to London *Athenaeum* (1830–68).

**Cho'ron'** (shô'rôɴ'), **Alexandre Étienne.** 1772–1834. French musician and writer on music; director of the Opéra (1816–17); founder and director of a school of classical and religious music (1817–30), which in concerts introduced to Paris audiences many works of German and Italian masters, as Bach, Handel, Palestrina. Author of *Principes de Composition des Écoles d'Italie* (1808), *Dictionnaire Historique des Musiciens* (with F. J. M. Fayolle, 1810–11), etc.

**Chosroes.** Variant of KHOSRAU.

**Chotek, Sophie.** See Duchess of HOHENBERG.

**Chot'zi·noff** (shŏt'sĭ·nôf), **Samuel.** 1889–1964. Pianist and music critic, b. in Russia; to U.S. at age of 6. Educ. Columbia. Accompanist for Zimbalist, Alma Gluck, Heifetz, and others. Critic on staff of New York *World* (1925–30) and New York *Post* (1934 ff.).

**Chou** *or* **Chow** (jō). An early dynasty (1122–255 B.C.) of China, longest of all in Chinese history. Its rulers took title *Wang* ("king"); its founder, Wu Wang (son of Wên Wang), overthrew (1122) Chou Hsin, last of Shang dynasty. Empire enlarged beyond the Yangtze valley; three great philosophers of China, Lao-tzu, Confucius, and Mencius (*qq.v.*), lived during latter part of dynasty. See also CHOU KUNG.

An ephemeral dynasty, **Northern Chou** (557–581 A.D.), existed in western China, and the **Later Chou** (951–960 A.D.) was one of the Five Dynasties (*q.v.*).

**Chouan.** See COTTEREAU.

**Chouart, Médart.** See Sieur de GROSEILLIERS.

**Chou En-lai** (jō' ĕn'lī'. 1898–1976. Chinese Communist leader, b. in Szechwan of Mandarin family. Influenced by Revolution (1911–12) and by Japan's "twenty-one demands" (1915); studied in Paris (1921–22) and Germany (1923). A founder of Chinese Communist party; joined Sun Yat-sen (1924); organized Communist strikes in north China under direction of Kuomintang (1925–27); driven out of Shanghai and Nationalist party (1927); became active in Chinese Red army (1931); its political leader, second only to Mao Tse-tung; Communist representative at kidnaping of Chiang Kai-shek (1936); Communist premier (1949–76).

**Chou Hsin** (jō' shĭn'). Last ruler of Shang dynasty (*q.v.*).

**Chou Kung** (jō' go͝ong'). d. 1105 B.C. Chinese author and statesman, known as the "Duke of Chou." Son of Wên Wang and brother of Wu Wang. Regent during minority of second emperor of Chou dynasty. Supposed author of the *Chou Li,* code of rules for officials of the state.

**Chou'teau'** (sho͞o'tō'). Family of American fur traders and pioneers, including: **René Auguste** (1749–1829), who was associated with his stepfather Pierre Laclède (*q.v.*) in founding St. Louis, Mo.; his brother, **Jean Pierre** (1758–1849), who established (1796) first permanent white settlement in Oklahoma, on site of present Salina; the latter's sons **Auguste Pierre** (1786–1838) and **Pierre** (1789–1865).

**Chow.** = CHOU (dynasty).

**Chré'tien' de Troyes'.** *Also* **Chres'tien' de Troyes'** (krā'tyăɴ' dē trwȧ'). *Anglicized* **Christian of Troyes.** French poet of latter half of 12th century; a trouvère, one of first to compose after models established by troubadours of southern France. His Arthurian romances include *Perceval le Gallois* (in which legend of Holy Grail is introduced), *Erec et Enide, Yvain, ou Le Chevalier au Lyon, Le Chevalier à la Charette* (introducing Lancelot du Lac), and *Le Roman de Cligès.*

**Chris'man** (krĭs'măn), **Arthur Bow'ie** (bo͞o'ĭ). 1889–1953. American teacher and writer of books for children; author of *Shen of the Sea* (1925; awarded John Newbery Medal), *The Wind That Wouldn't Blow* (1927).

**Christ** (krīst), **Jesus.** See JESUS.

**Christ** (krĭst), **Wilhelm.** 1831–1906. German classical philologist; professor, Munich (1861). Author of *Metrik der Griechen und Römer* (1879), *Griechische Literaturgeschichte* (1888), etc.

**Chris'tian** (krĭs'chăn; krĭst'yăn). Name of ten kings of Denmark, eight of whom were kings of Norway also and two of whom were kings of Sweden.

**Christian I.** 1426–1481. King of Denmark (1448–81) and of Norway (1450–81). Son of Theodoric, Count of Oldenburg, and Hedwig, heiress of Schleswig and Holstein, and a descendant of Eric V. Founder of house of Oldenburg (*q.v.*). Union of Kalmar practically dissolved, although not officially until later (1523); Norway and Denmark united (1450–1814); seized Sweden (1457–64) but forced to give it up by defeat at Brunkeberg (1471); made duke of Slesvig and count of Holstein (1460); with his queen, founded U. of Copenhagen (1479).

**Christian II.** *Called* "the Cruel." 1481–1559. King of Denmark and Norway (1513–23) and of Sweden (1520–23); m. Isabella (1515), sister of Emperor Charles V; conquered Sweden (1520); showed extreme cruelty against Swedes, esp. in massacre of nobility at Stockholm (1520); driven out of Sweden by Gustavus Vasa (1521); deposed and driven out of Denmark (1523); attempted to seize Norway (1531–32) but captured and imprisoned for remainder of life.

**Christian III.** 1503–1559. King of Denmark and Norway (1534–59); called "father of the People." Son of Frederick I; became king at time of civil war (1533–36); ardent Lutheran, introduced the Reformation (1536); unsuccessfully attempted to make Norway a province; his rule strengthened Denmark.

**Christian IV.** 1577–1648. King of Denmark and Norway (1588–1648). Son of Frederick II; b. Frederiksborg. Ruled under regents (1588–96); strengthened Danish navy and army; Kalmar War with Sweden (1611–13) terminated successfully for Denmark by Treaty of Knærod (1613); increased influence along Baltic coast of Germany (1613–21); Christiania in Norway founded (1624) and named after him; joined Protestant cause in Thirty Years' War (1625–29); defeated severely at Lutter am Barenberge by Tilly and Wallenstein (1626); formed alliance with Gustavus Adolphus of Sweden (1628–29); his policies irritated Sweden, which declared war (1643–45), defeating Denmark; forced to yield power to nobles.

**Christian V.** 1646–1699. King of Denmark and Norway (1670–99). Son of Frederick III; b. Flensburg; tried to establish new nobility from lower orders; guided (1670–76) by his chancellor, Griffenfeld, who was imprisoned (1676); financial condition became worse; waged unsuccessful war with Sweden (1675–79); drew up new code (*Christian Code*) for Norway (1683).

**Christian VI.** 1699–1746. King of Denmark and Norway (1730–46). Son of Frederick IV; b. Copenhagen; weak and narrow-minded sovereign; showed much extravagance in new buildings following whims of wife, Sophie Magdalene of Brandenburg-Kulmbach.

**Christian VII.** 1749–1808. King of Denmark and Norway (1766–1808). Son of Frederick V; b. Copenhagen. Neglected in childhood; brought up by cruel tutor; early became depraved and imbecile; m. (1766) Caroline Matilda (*q.v.*), sister of George III of England; dismissed Count Bernstoff as minister (1770); appointed Struensee (*q.v.*), but after two years (1770–72), had him arrested and beheaded; marriage with Caroline Matilda dissolved (1772); became hopelessly insane and relinquished control to Crown Prince Frederick, who ruled as regent (1784–1808); battle of Copenhagen (1801); Danish fleet seized by English (1807).

**Christian VIII.** 1786–1848. King of Denmark (1839–48) Son of Frederick (d. 1805), stepbrother of Christian VII. Appointed viceroy of Norway (1813) and elected king (1814); refused dynastic union of Norway and Sweden (1814); driven out of Norway during brief war (1814); with second wife, lived in retirement (1815–31); member of council of state (1831–39); as king, opposed liberal projects; tried to appease Germans in Schleswig and Holstein (1846–48); raised Schleswig-Holstein question that later brought about war (1848).

**Christian IX.** 1818–1906. King of Denmark (1863–1906). Son of William, Duke of Schleswig-Holstein-Sönderborg and (from 1825) of Glücksborg (1785–1831), and Princess Louise of Hesse-Cassel (1789–1836), a direct descendant of King Christian III of Denmark. Brought up by King Frederick VI as guardian; entered army (1835); m. (1842) Louise (1817–1898), dau. of William, Prince of Hesse-Cassel. Since male line of Frederick III became extinct in Frederick VII, confirmed (1852) by council of great powers in London as crown prince ("protocol king"); succeeded to throne (1863) on death of Frederick VII; denial by duchies of Schleswig and Holstein of Danish claims to sovereignty and demand for withdrawal of November Constitutions (1863) which had incorporated Holstein (see FREDERICK VIII, 1829–1880) led to war with Prussia and Austria (1864); Jutland occupied; Denmark forced by Treaty of Vienna to renounce Schleswig, Holstein, and Lauenburg; new constitution promulgated (1866); long struggle of parties of Left and Right for supremacy of Folketing (1872–1905); generally supported the Conservatives; with their decline, finally consented to formation of Left ministry. Father of Frederick VIII of Denmark, George, King of the Hellenes (1863–1913), Waldemar (b. 1858; m. Marie d'Orléans, daughter of Robert, Duc de Chartres), and of Alexandra (m. Edward VII of Great Britain), Dagmar (Marie Feodorovna; m. heir to Russian throne, later Czar Alexander III), and Thyra (m. Ernest Augustus, 1845–1923, Duke of Cumberland).

**Christian X.** 1870–1947. Son of Frederick VIII. King of Denmark (1912–47) and Iceland (1918–44), b. Charlottenlund Castle near Copenhagen; m. (1898) Alexandrine Augustine, Duchess of Mecklenburg-Schwerin. Studied for military career; during World War, established closer relations with other Scandinavian countries; new constitution (1915) enfranchising women; Act of Union (1918) with Iceland, whereby Iceland became independent with only personal connection with Denmark through single sovereign; enthusiastically received by people of North Slesvig, former region of Denmark restored by plebiscite under Treaty of Versailles (1920); succeeded by his son **Frederik IX** (1899–1972), diplomat and rear admiral, m. (1935) Ingrid (1910–    ), granddaughter of Gustav V of Sweden.

**Chris'tian** (krĭs'chăn; krĭst'yăn), **Fletcher.** fl. 1789. English naval mutineer. Master's mate and leader of mutiny against Captain William Bligh (*q.v.*) aboard exploring ship *Bounty* (April, 1789); founder of isolated colony on Pitcairn Island.

**Chris'tian Au·gus'tus** (krĭs'chăn ô·gŭs'tŭs; krĭst'-yăn). 1798–1869. Duke of **Schles'wig–Hol'stein–Son'der·burg–Au·gu'sten·burg** [shlās'vĭκ·hôl'shtīn-zôn'dẽr·bŏŏrκ·ou·gōōs'tĕn·bŏŏrκ; shlĕs'vĭκ] (1814–69). On accession (1848) of Frederick VII of Denmark, forced to relinquish his claims under Salic law to Danish throne (protocol and treaty of London, 1850 and 1852), a renunciation later (on death of Frederick VII, 1863) repudiated by his son Frederick—main cause of war (1866) between Prussia and Austria.

**Christian of Bruns'wick** (brŭnz'wĭk). Prince of **Bruns'wick–Wol'fen·büt'tel** (-vôl'fĕn·büt'ĕl). 1599–1626. German Lutheran soldier; sometimes called "the Madman of Halberstadt." Administrator of bishopric of Halberstadt (1616); led (1621–22) army defeated by Tilly at Höchst (1622); accepted command under Prince Maurice of United Provinces and fought Spaniards; returned to Lower Saxony; again defeated by Tilly (1623);

took command again of Protestant forces under Christian IV of Denmark (1625); died without gaining important successes.

**Christian of Schles'wig-Hol'stein** (shlās'vĭк [shlĕs'-]-hôl'shtīn; *Angl.* hōl'stīn), Prince. *In full* **Frederick Christian Charles Augustus.** 1831–1917. German prince; m. (1866) Helena, 3d daughter of Queen Victoria; Prussian officer in World War.

**Christian of Troyes.** = CHRÉTIEN DE TROYES.

**Christianus Demokritus.** Pseudonym of J. K. DIPPEL.

**Chris'tie** (krĭs'tĭ), Dame **Agatha Mary Clarissa,** *nee* **Miller.** 1891–1976. English writer of mystery and detective fiction; m. 1st, Archibald Christie (1914; divorced, 1928), 2d, Max Edgar Lucien Mallowan (1930). Creator of the fictional detectives Hercule Poirot and Jane Marple.

**Christie, James.** 1730–1803. English auctioneer, founder (1766) of line of London auctioneers. His sons **James** (1773–1831), auctioneer, antiquary, writer on Etruscan and Greek vases, and **Samuel Hunter** (1784–1865), mathematician, student of magnetism, professor of mathematics at Woolwich (1806–54). S. H. Christie's son Sir **William Henry Mahoney** (1845–1922), astronomer royal (1881–1910); undertook observations of sunspots (c. 1880); erected 30-inch reflector and 26-inch photographic refractor (1890–98); designed new altazimuth; author of papers on solar eclipses.

**Christie, Richard Copley.** 1830–1901. English scholar and bibliophile. M.A., Oxon. (1855); professor, Owens Coll., Manchester; benefactor of Owens Coll., to which he bequeathed about 75,000 volumes.

**Chris·ti'na** (krĭs·tē'nȧ). 1626–1689. Queen of Sweden (1632–54), b. Stockholm; daughter of Gustavus Adolphus. Ruled (1632–44) under regency of five crown officers, affairs being actually managed by Axel Oxenstierna; came of age and crowned (1644); reign disturbed by final years of Thirty Years' War (1644–48), by dissensions in Swedish Diet, by attempted revolts; proclaimed her cousin Charles X Gustavus as successor; abdicated (1654); embraced Roman Catholicism (1655); lived in Paris; tried twice (1660, 1667) to regain Swedish throne; died in Rome. See Giovanni MONALDESCHI.

**Chris'tine' de Pi'san'** (krēs'tēn' dē pē'zäɴ'). 1363?–1431. French poet of Italian descent; m. Étienne Castel (c. 1378; d. c. 1388). Author of *Livre des Faits et Bonnes Mœurs du Roi Charles V*, *Livre de Paix*, and some ballads, verse letters, etc.

**Chris'ti·son** (krĭs'tĭ·s'n), Sir **Robert.** 1797–1882. Scottish toxicologist and physician; M.D. Edinburgh (1819); professor at Edinburgh; authority on pathology of kidneys; author of *Treatise on Poisons* (1829).

**Chri·stof'fel** (krĭ·stôf'ĕl), **Elwin Bruno.** 1829–1900. Swiss mathematician; professor, Strassburg (from 1872); known for work in higher analysis, geometry, mathematical physics, and geodesy.

**Chris'tophe'** (krēs'tôf'), **Henri.** 1767–1820. Negro king of Haiti (1811–20), b. a slave in Grenada. Able lieutenant to Toussaint L'Ouverture in revolution (1791) against French; fought against Leclerc (1802); joined uprising of Dessalines (1803–04); after killing Dessalines (1806), became king, as Henri I, in the north; proclaimed king of all Haiti (1811); crowned (1812); his cruelty and avarice caused rebellion (1818); shot himself with a silver bullet.

**Chris'to·pher** (krĭs'tô·fẽr), Saint. Christian martyr, probably of 3d century. According to tradition, devoted himself after conversion to charitable work of carrying wayfarers across a river where there was no bridge; on one occasion, undertook to carry over a small child, whose weight grew heavier and heavier until the bearer was scarcely able to reach the other shore; once there, the supposed child revealed himself as Christ—hence the name *Christophorus, i.e.* "Christ-bearer." Patron saint of ferrymen, travelers, etc.

**Christopher** *or* **Chris·toph'o·rus** (krĭs·tŏf'ô·rŭs). d. 904. Pope (903–904); b. Rome. By some, considered an antipope.

**Christopher.** d. 931. Coruler (921–931) of Eastern Roman Empire with his father, Romanus I Lecapenus.

**Christopher.** Name of three kings of Denmark. **Christopher I** (1219–1259), king (1252–59); brother of Eric and Abel; reign a period of continuous strife with archbishop of Lund (1253–59). **Christopher II** (1276–1332), king (1320–26, 1330–32); treacherous, incompetent ruler; Denmark divided. **Christopher III** (1418–1448), *known as* **Christopher of Bavaria;** nephew of Eric; king of Sweden (1440–48) and of Norway (1442–48); oppressed peasantry; made Copenhagen permanent royal residence (1443).

**Chri·sto'pou·los** (krē·stô'pōō·lôs), **Athanasios.** 1772–1847. Greek poet, author esp. of popular drinking songs and love lyrics; translated Homer and Herodotus into modern Greek.

**Chris'tus** *or* **Cris'tus** (krĭs'tŭs), **Pe'trus** (pē'trŭs). 1420?–1473. Flemish painter.

**Chris'ty** (krĭs'tĭ), **Edwin P.** 1815–1862. American actor and singer, b. Philadelphia; founder and interlocutor of a well-known blackface minstrel troupe.

**Christy, Howard Chandler.** 1873–1952. American illustrator and painter, b. in Morgan Co., Ohio. Illustrator on staff of various New York periodicals esp. (from 1910) *Cosmopolitan* and Hearst magazines; illustrated books, including three by James Whitcomb Riley and three of his own. His paintings include many portraits, as of Will H. Hays, George Harvey, Warren G. Harding, President and Mrs. Calvin Coolidge, Charles E. Hughes, Benito Mussolini, John Nance Garner, Amelia Earhart, and Mary Roberts Rinehart, and the large historical painting *Signing the Constitution* in Capitol building, Washington, D.C.

**Chro'de·gang** (krō'dĕ·găng) *or* **Go'de·grand** (gō'dĕ-grănd), Saint. d. 766. Bishop of Metz (from 742); author of *Vita Canonica.*

**Chrypffs, Nikolaus.** = NICHOLAS OF CUSA.

**Chry·san'der** (krü·zän'dẽr), **Friedrich.** 1826–1901. German music scholar. Founded Handel Society, and through it published first complete edition of Handel's works (100 vols., 1859–94). Author of a life of Handel (3 vols., 1858–67), left uncompleted at his death.

**Chry·sip'pus** (krī·sĭp'ŭs; krĭ-). Greek Stoic philosopher of 3d century B.C., b. at Soli in Cilicia; disciple of Cleanthes.

**Chrys'ler** (krīs'lẽr), **Walter Percy.** 1875–1940. American automobile manufacturer, b. Wamego, Kans.; works manager (1912–16), president and general manager (1916–19), Buick Motor Co.; organized and headed Chrysler Corporation, manufacturing automobiles.

**Chrysologus,** Saint **Peter.** See PETER CHRYSOLOGUS.

**Chrys'o·lo'ras** (krĭs'ô·lō'răs), **Man'u·el** (măn'ū·ĕl). 1355?–1415. Greek scholar, b. prob. in Constantinople. To Italy (1393) on mission from Emperor Manuel II Palaeologus to obtain aid against Turks; professor of Greek in Florence (1395–98); translated Plato's *Republic* into Latin. Later, went on mission to Paris (1408) and to Germany (1413). Author of *Erotemata sive Quaestiones*, first Greek grammar used in western Europe.

**Chrysorrhoas.** See JOHN OF DAMASCUS.

**Chrys'os·tom** (krĭs'ŭs·tŭm; krĭ·sŏs'tŭm), Saint **John.** 345?–407. Called soon after his death *Chrysostom* (from

Greek *chrysostomos*, literally "goldenmouthed"), because of his eloquence. One of the Fathers of the Greek Church, b. in Antioch. Patriarch of Constantinople (398–404). Baptized and ordained a reader (368?); practiced asceticism, esp. in desert near Antioch (375?–381); ordained deacon (381) and priest (386) in Antioch; won fame for his eloquence. Appointed bishop (patriarch) of Constantinople (398). Became popular with common people; deposed at a synod near Constantinople and banished by Empress Eudoxia and patriarch of Alexandria (403); recalled because of wrath of people, but banished again (404), to Armenia. Author of homilies, commentaries, and letters, that had great influence.

**Chtchédrine.** French spelling of SHCHEDRIN.

**Chuang'-tzu'** (jŏŏ·äng'dzŭ'). fl. 4th century B.C. Chinese philosopher and teacher, exponent of the doctrines of Lao-tzu. Writings valued during T'ang dynasty.

**Chubb** (chŭb), **Percival.** 1860–1960. Educator, b. Devonport, Eng.; to U.S.; settled in St. Louis and served as leader of Ethical Society (1911–32). Author of *Festivals and Plays in Schools and Elsewhere* (with others, 1912), *Recollections of Havelock Ellis* (1929), *On the Religious Frontier* (1931).

**Chubb, Thomas.** 1679–1746. English deist. Worked as tallow chandler most of his life; author of *The Supremacy of the Father Asserted* (1715), a defense of William Whiston's argument for Arian view of supremacy of God the Father over the other persons of the Trinity, and of deistical tracts (1734–46).

**Chudleigh, Elizabeth.** Countess of **Bristol.** See under PIERREPONT family.

**Chu Hsi** *or* **Chu Hi** (jōō' shē'). 1130–1200. Chinese philosopher, living under Southern Sung dynasty. Commentator and expounder of Confucianism; wrote many works, esp. on Confucian classics. In his teaching accepted doctrine of Mencius.

**Chu'i·kov** (chōō'ĭ·kôf), **Vasili Ivanovich.** 1900– . Soviet army officer; in Russo-Finnish War (1939–40); adviser to Chiang Kai-shek (1940–41); in command of World War II army; defended Stalingrad (1942). Author of *The Beginning of the Road* (1962).

**Chu'-ko' Liang'** (jōō'gŭ' lē·äng'). 181–234 A.D. Chinese soldier, b. Shantung; regarded by Chinese as a favorite hero. Aided Liu Pei in founding Shu or Minor Han dynasty (221–264); chief minister (221–234); known as a strategist.

**Chulalongkorn.** = RAMA V, King of Siam (Thailand).

**Ch'un** (chōōn), Prince. Name of two members of Chinese nobility of the Ch'ing dynasty. (1) *Personal name* **I Huan** (ē' hwän'). 1840–1891. Seventh son of Emperor Tao Kuang, and younger brother of Emperor Hsien Fêng; father of Emperor Kuang Hsü and grandfather of Emperor Hsüan T'ung. Adviser of empress dowager; as her favorite held several high offices. (2) His fifth son, *personal name* **Tsai Feng** (dzī' fŭng'). 1882– . Brother of Emperor Kuang Hsu and father of last Manchu emperor, Hsüan T'ung; regent for his son (1908–11); deposed by Revolution (1911); special envoy to Germany (1901); councilor to the throne (1907–08).

**Chund Bardai.** See CHAND BARDAI.

**Chunder Sen, Keshub.** See KESHUB CHUNDER SEN.

**Chung Shan.** See SUN YAT-SEN.

**Ch'ung Te.** See under SHUN CHIH.

**Chu'quet'** (shü'kĕ'), **Nicolas.** c. 1445–c. 1500. French mathematician.

**Church** (chûrch), **Alfred John.** 1829–1912. English clergyman and author. Author of classical stories retold for young people from Homer, Vergil, Livy, Herodotus, and others.

**Church, Frederick Edwin.** 1826–1900. American landscape painter, b. Hartford, Conn.; known for his *Horseshoe and American Falls, Niagara* (in Corcoran Gallery, Washington, D.C.) and Andean views.

**Church, Frederick Stuart.** 1842–1924. American illustrator and painter, b. Grand Rapids, Mich.

**Church,** Sir **Richard.** 1784–1873. British military officer and commander in the Greek service; b. in Cork of Quaker parentage; disowned by Society of Friends when he enlisted as soldier at age of 16; advocated British retention of Ionian Islands, in report to Congress of Vienna (1809); fought in service of King Ferdinand of Naples (1817–20); commander in chief of Greek insurgent army (1827) engaged in expelling Turks; led Greek revolution (1843); Greek general (1854). His nephew **Richard William Church** (1815–1890), clergyman, b. Lisbon; B.A., Oxon. (1836); fellow of Oriel Coll. and friend of Newman; one of originators of *The Guardian* magazine (1846); contributor to *The Saturday Review* and *English Men of Letters* series; dean of St. Paul's (1871–90).

**Church, Richard.** 1893–1972. English writer, b. London. His books of verse include *Flood of Life* (1917), *Hurricane* (1919), *Philip* (1923), *Twelve Noon* (1936); his prose works, *Mary Shelley* (1928), *The Prodigal Father* (1933), *The Porch* (1937), *The Stronghold* (1939), *Calling for a Spade* (1939), and three volumes of autobiography: *Over the Bridge* (1955), *The Golden Sovereign* (1957), *The Voyage Home* (1964).

**Church, William** 1778?–1863. American inventor of an early typesetting machine (casting and composing automatically; justification by hand), patented in England (1822).

**Church, William Conant.** 1836–1917. American editor, b. Rochester, N.Y.; served in Civil War; founder, with his brother **Francis P.**, of the *Army and Navy Journal* (1863).

**Church'ill** (chûrch'(h)ĭl), **Charles. 1731–1764.** English poet and satirist; son of a Westminster curate. Ordained priest (1756); won fame with his *Rosciad* (anonymous, 1761), a clever satire on London actors and actresses, and the *Apology* (1761), a ruthless attack upon his critics; indulged in dissipation, defended his way of life in poem, *Night* (1761), and gave up church offices (1763); became ally of John Wilkes, and assistant editor of *North Briton;* exercised his gift for invective in contributions to political campaign of rhymed satires on authors and politicians; died on visit to Wilkes in exile at Boulogne. Author of *The Ghost* (1763), ridiculing Dr. Johnson over his account of the Cock Lane ghost, *The Prophecy of Famine* (1763), attacking Lord Bute and the Scots, *The Duellist* (1763), assailing an unsuccessful assassin of Wilkes, *The Candidate* (1764), exposing "Jemmy Twitcher" (Lord Sandwich, an enemy of Wilkes).

**Churchill, John.** 1st Duke of **Marl'bor·ough** (märl'bŭ·rŭ; -brŭ; môl'-). 1650–1722. English military commander; called "Corporal John." Son of Sir **Winston** (1620?–1688), impoverished Royalist. Studied at St. Paul's (1663–65); page to duke of York (1665) and favorite of duchess of Cleveland; assisted in advancing fortunes by sister **Arabella** (1648–1730), mistress of duke of York (later James II). Attracted attention at Nijmegen (1672); saved life of duke of Monmouth at Maastricht (1673); as reward for successful execution of mission to Louis XIV, created (1685) Baron **Churchill of San'dridge** (săn'drĭj); second in command in crushing at Sedgemoor Monmouth's rebellion in western counties (1685). One of first to send overtures to William of Orange (1687); went over to William of Orange with 5000 troops (1688); privy councilor and earl of Marlborough (1689); sent by William, somewhat in distrust, to fight in Netherlands (1689), in Ireland (1690); imprisoned on accusation of plotting (1692); carried on negotiations with exiled King James II; restored to command (1698). Under Queen Anne, commander in chief over armies of England and Holland in War of Spanish Succession; impeded by jealousy among allies and difference of aims; by brilliant exploits at Kaiserswerth, Venlo, and Liége, drove French out of Spanish Gelderland (1702); created 1st duke of Marlborough (for later dukes, see SPENCER family). Virtually regent in England, controlling prime minister Godolphin, as his wife (see below) controlled Queen Anne. Had to abandon attack on Antwerp (1703) because of Dutch incapacity; thwarted French in attempt to join Bavarians by bloody victory of Blenheim (1704); rewarded with manor of Woodstock; held in check by jealousies (1705); routed French at Ramillies (1706), entered Brussels, Antwerp, Ostend; deserted by emperor and involved in quarrel of Whigs and Tories (1708); defeated French at Oudenarde (1708), keeping Flanders from allegiance to French; captured Lille and Ghent (1708); met Villars in protracted, rather indecisive battle of Malplaquet (1709); took Mons and other French towns, obtaining Treaty of Utrecht (1713). Undermined by political intrigue at home and dismissal of Godolphin and Sunderland, and by duchess of Marlborough's alienation of Queen Anne and defection to Whig cause; following dismissal of duchess, dismissed from offices on charge of embezzlement of public money (Dec. 31, 1711); on accession of George I returned to his military post (1714); died of apoplexy.

His wife (m. 1678), **Sarah,** ***nee*** **Jennings** (1660–1744), Duchess of Marlborough; often alluded to as **A·tos′sa** (*ȧ·tŏs′ȧ*). Became (before 1676) trusted friend of Princess Anne, the two companions adopting, soon after Anne's marriage, the nicknames Mrs. Morley (Anne) and Mrs. Freeman; helped Anne to escape (1688); gained ascendancy over her on her accession as queen; as mistress of robes and keeper of privy purse, controlled Whig ministry, dispensed offices at will, deducted pension for herself; finally by imperious and tactless behavior alienated Queen Anne; succeeded (1711) by her cousin Abigail Hill (Mrs. Masham); lived in retirement and left large fortune.

**Churchill, Randolph Henry Spencer.** *Known as* Lord **Randolph Churchill.** 1849–1895. British statesman. Third son of 7th duke of Marlborough (see under SPENCER family); m. (1874) Jennie Jerome of New York; father of Winston L. S. Churchill (*q.v.*). B.A., Oxon. (1870). As M.P. (from 1874) led a group (nicknamed the "Fourth Party") in fearless, aggressive Toryism; assailed both Gladstone and Conservative front bench; opposed government in Egyptian imbroglio; favored conciliation in Irish affairs; developed a progressive conservatism, called Tory democracy, in challenge to Liberals for part in reform; promoter and first member of Primrose League; secretary of state for India (1885–86); contested John Bright's seat (1885); chancellor of exchequer and leader of House of Commons (1886); resigned (Dec., 1886) in resistance to demands of army and navy upon exchequer; traveled for health and described travels in *Men, Mines, and Animals in South Africa* (1892); returned to parliament (1892) and attacked Gladstone's second Irish home-rule bill.

**Churchill, William.** 1859–1920. American ethnologist, b. Brooklyn, N.Y.; studied and wrote on Polynesian customs and languages.

**Churchill, Winston.** 1871–1947. American novelist, b. St. Louis. Grad. U.S.N.A., Annapolis (1894); on editorial staff, *Army and Navy Journal* (1894) and *Cosmopolitan Magazine* (1895); resident in Cornish, N.H.; prominent in New Hampshire politics (from 1906). Esp. known for his historical novels, including *Richard Carvel* (1899), *The Crisis* (1901), *The Crossing* (1904), *Coniston* (1906), *Mr. Crewe's Career* (1908), *A Modern Chronicle* (1910), *The Inside of the Cup* (1913), *A Far Country* (1915), *The Dwelling Place of Light* (1917).

**Churchill,** Sir **Winston Leonard Spencer.** 1874–1965. British statesman and author; elder son of Lord Randolph Churchill. Educ. Harrow and Sandhurst; served in Cuba with Spanish forces (1895), in India (1897), in Sudan (1898), present at Khartoum (1898); as war correspondent, captured by Boers but escaped (1899), and engaged in battles up to capture of Pretoria. M.P. (1901); joined free traders in opposition to Chamberlain's tariff proposals; undersecretary (1905–08) for colonies under Campbell-Bannerman, whose policy of self-government for Transvaal and Orange River Colony he advanced with skill and vigor. Entered cabinet as president of Board of Trade (1908–10); as home secretary (1910–11), carried Trade Boards Act providing organization of unorganized trades; first lord of admiralty (1911–15); advocate of accelerated naval program; given task of creating naval war staff for co-ordination of strategy with war office; as leader of minority in strategy, directed Antwerp expedition and Dardanelles campaign, after failure of which he was succeeded by Balfour (1915). Colonel in France (1916); minister of munitions (1917); secretary for war and air (1919–21), for colonies and air (1921), for colonies (1921–22); as chancellor of exchequer (1924–29) accomplished adjustment of war-debt questions, duties on industry, and national finance. First lord of admiralty in Neville Chamberlain's government (Sept. 3, 1939) upon entry into war against Germany. Prime minister (May 10, 1940) after debacle in Norway. Met at sea with President Roosevelt (Aug., 1941) to draw up the joint statement of American-British international policy known as the Atlantic Charter. Visited U.S. (Dec., 1941); addressed a joint session of Congress. Conferred on war strategy and international affairs with President Roosevelt at Washington (June, 1942 and May, 1943), Casablanca, Morocco (Jan., 1943), and Quebec (Aug., 1943 and Sept., 1944), with Roosevelt and Chiang Kai-shek at Cairo (Nov., 1943), with Roosevelt and Stalin at Tehran (Dec., 1943) and again at Yalta, Crimea (Feb., 1945), with Truman and Stalin at Potsdam (July, 1945). Resigned as prime minister (July, 1945) after Labor victory in elections; again prime minister (1951–1955). Author of *Lord Randolph Churchill* (1906), *My African Journey* (1908), *Liberalism and the Social Problem* (1909), *The World Crisis* (4 vols., 1923–29; rev. ed. in 1 vol., 1942), *Marlborough, his Life and Times* (6 vols., 1933–38), selected speeches, as in *While England Slept* (1938), *Step by Step* (1939), *Into Battle* (1941), *The Unrelenting Struggle* (1942), *The End of the Beginning* (1943), *The Second World War* (6 vols., 1948–53). Awarded Nobel prize in literature (1953).

**Church′yard** (chûrch′ẽrd), **Thomas.** 1520?–1604. English soldier of fortune and writer. Fought in Scotland, Ireland, Low Countries, in service of England, the emperor, and the prince of Orange. Gave offense to Queen Elizabeth in *Churchyarde's Choise* (1579). Author of poems *Shore's Wife* (1563; in *Mirror for Magistrates*) and *The Worthines of Wales* (1587), etc.

**Chur′ri·gue′ra** (cho͝or′rē·gā′rä), **José.** 1650–1723. Spanish architect; created baroquelike style, now called *churrigueresque*, long dominant in Spain.

**Chu Teh** (jo͞o′ dŭ′). 1886–1976. Chinese Communist leader, b. in Szechwan of a wealthy family; studied at Göttingen and (1925) Moscow; joined Communists (1927); elected (1931) commander in chief of Chinese

Red army; at head of Eighth Route Army when it joined with Chiang Kai-shek (1936–37); in war against Japan (1937); associated with Mao Tse-tung (*q.v.*).

**Chu' Yüan'-chang'** (jōō' yü·än' jäng'). *Better known by his reign title* **Hung Wu** (hŏŏng' wōō'). 1328–1398. Chinese emperor (1368–98), founder of the Ming dynasty; b. in Anhwei province. In youth joined a monastery; became leader of insurgent force which (1356–64) gradually secured control of region north of the Yangtze; proclaimed prince of Wu (1364–68); drove out Mongols and established new dynasty; made Nanking the capital.

**Chwol'son** (kvôl'y'·sŭn), **Daniel Abramovich.** 1819–1911. Russian archaeologist; authority on history of Oriental religions; educ. Breslau, Vienna, and St. Petersburg; gave up Jewish religion, became Christian; professor of Oriental languages at U. of St. Petersburg (1855), of Hebrew and Biblical archaeology at ecclesiastical academy in St. Petersburg (1858).

**Cial·di'ni** (chäl·dē'nē), **Enrico.** Duca **di Ga·e'ta** (gä·ā'tä). 1811–1892. Italian soldier and diplomat. Commanded regiment of Piedmontese infantry (1848); in Crimean War (1854–56); organized the "Cacciatori delle Alpi" at beginning of Italian War (1859); defeated papal army under Lamoricière at Castelfidardo (1860); conquered Gaeta (1861). Elected senator (1864); succeeded La Marmora as chief of general staff (1866); ambassador to France (1876–79, 1880–81).

**Cia'mi·cian'** (chä'mē·chän'), **Giacomo Luigi.** 1857–1922. Italian chemist, b. Trieste. Professor, Bologna (1889). Known for research in organic and photochemistry.

**Ciam'pi** (chäm'pē), **Ignazio.** 1824–1880. Italian poet and historian; professor of modern history, U. of Rome (1874–80). Author of poems, as *Serena* (1857), *Poesie Varie* (1857), the verse narrative *Stella* (1858), plays after Goldoni, as *Il Segretario e la Contessa* and *Momolo e Giorgio*, historical works, as *Storia Moderna della Scoporta dell'America alla Pace di Westfalia* (2 vols., 1881–83).

**Ciampi, Lorenzio Vincenzo.** b. 1719. Italian composer; considered by some to be one of creators of musical comedy. His operas include *Bertoldo in Corte* and *L'Arcadia in Brenta.*

**Ciampi, Sebastiano.** 1769–1847. Italian writer; professor, U. of Pisa (1803–18), U. of Warsaw (1818–22); aided in furthering study of history of art.

**Ciano,** *in full* **Cia'no di Cor'tel·laz'zo** (chä'nō dē kōr'tāl·lät'tsō), Conte **Galeazzo.** 1903–1944. Italian statesman; educ. U. of Rome; entered diplomatic service (1925); secretary of legation, Rio de Janeiro, then Buenos Aires; consul general, Shanghai; m. (1930) Edda, daughter of Benito Mussolini. Secretary of state for press and propaganda (1935); in Ethiopian war (1935–36); minister of foreign affairs (1936–43); member, Fascist Supreme Council; ambassador to Holy See (1943). His father, Conte **Costanzo** (1876–1939), naval officer and statesman; admiral of fleet during World War I; member, Chamber of Deputies (1921; president, 1934); minister of communications (1924–34); head, Chamber of Fasces and Guilds (1939).

**Ciar'di** (chär'dē), **Guglielmo.** 1844–1917. Italian painter; leader of Venetian plein-airists.

**Ciardi, John Anthony.** 1916– . Am. poet, b. Boston Mass. Taught at Harvard U. (1946–53) and Rutgers U. (1953–61). Poetry editor for the *Saturday Review* (1956). Translated *The Inferno of Dante* (1954); wrote *How Does a Poem Mean?* (1959), and poems, etc.

**Cib'ber** (sĭb'ẽr), **Colley.** 1671–1757. English actor and dramatist. Enrolled in Betterton's company of actors, Theatre Royal, Drury Lane (1690), and succeeded in comedy; played Sir Novelty Fashion in first production of his *Love's Last Shift, or the Fool in Fashion* (1696), and other eccentric characters (1697–1732); brought out thirty dramatic pieces (1697–1748), including *She Wou'd and She Wou'd Not* (1702), *The Careless Husband* (1704; for himself and Mrs. Oldfield), and *Nonjuror* (1717); expressed his Whig principles in the comedy *The Provoked Husband* (1728), an adaptation of Molière's *Tartuffe*, left unfinished by John Vanbrugh. Assailed by Jeremy Collier in his *Short View of the English Stage* (1698); with Wilks and Doggett, took management of Drury Lane (c. 1711–32). Appointed poet laureate (1730); depreciated by Pope and Johnson as composer of odes; made "hero" (in place of Theobald) of Pope's *Dunciad* (1742); attacked by Fielding on ground of style and language and for his mutilation of Shakespeare; his adaptation of Shakespeare's *Richard III* retained as the acting version (till 1821). Made last appearance on stage as Pandulph in his *Papal Tyranny in Reign of King John* (1745). Author also of *Apology for the Life of Colley Cibber, Comedian* (1740).

His father, **Caius Gabriel Cibber** *or* **Cib'ert** [sĭb'ẽrt] (1630–1700), Danish sculptor in England; employed by 4th earl of Devonshire; carver to king's closet; m. for second wife (1670) June Colley, mother of Colley Cibber; known for statues *Melancholy* and *Raving Madness.*

Colley's son **Theophilus** (1703–1758), actor and playwright; appeared first on stage (1721); impersonated Pistol and fine gentlemen with success; wrote *The Lover* (1730), *The Auction* (1757), and other plays; involved in intrigues and unsavory practices; abandoned by his wife, **Susannah Maria** (1714–1766), sister of Thomas Arne (*q.v.*), actress, who won reputation chiefly for singing in opera and oratorio, succeeded in tragedy after debut as Zarah in Aaron Hill's version of Voltaire's *Zaïre* (1736).

**Ci·bra'rio** (chē·brä'ryō), Conte **Giovanni Antonio Luigi.** 1802–1870. Italian statesman and historian. Friend and protégé of Charles Albert of Sardinia; royal commissioner to Venice to procure its union to Piedmont (1848); senator (1848); minister of finance (1852), public instruction (1852–55), foreign affairs (1855–56). His historical works include *Storia di Torino* (1847), and *Della Schiavitù e del Servaggio*. . .(1868–69).

**Cic'er·o** (sĭs'ẽr·ō), **Marcus Tullius.** 106–43 B.C. Roman orator, statesman, and philosopher, b. in Arpinum, Italy. To Rome as a youth for study of law, oratory, and Greek literature and philosophy. Quaestor in Sicily (75 B.C.); obtained impeachment of the governor, Verres, for corruption in office (70). Praetor (66); as consul (63), foiled conspiracy of Catiline (*q.v.*), arousing the people to their danger by his famous orations against Catiline, and executed some of the conspirators. Banished (58) but soon recalled (57); proconsul in Cilicia (51–50). Sided with Pompey in Civil War, but became reconciled with Caesar after battle of Pharsalus (48). After assassination of Caesar, attacked Antony in orations known as *Philippics;* proscribed by Second Triumvirate, and slain (43). In addition to his orations (57 extant) and his letters (many to his friend Titus Pomponius Atticus), extant works include *Rhetorica, De Oratore, De Republica, De Legibus, De Finibus Bonorum et Malorum, Tusculanae Disputationes, De Natura Deorum, De Divinatione, De Officiis, De Amicitia*, etc.

His brother **Quintus Tullius Cicero** (c. 102–43 B.C.) distinguished himself as a general in Gaul (54); proscribed and slain (43).

A son of Marcus, **Marcus Tullius Cicero** (65–after 30 B.C.), sided with Brutus after murder of Caesar; fled to Sicily after battle of Philippi (42); returned to Rome on proclamation of amnesty (39); honored by Octavius; consul (30); later a proconsul in Asia (or Syria).

**Ci'co·gna'ra** (chē'kō·nyä'rä), Conte **Leopoldo.** 1767–

1834. Italian antiquarian, art historian, and diplomat; accumulated valuable collection of art objects. His works include *Storia della Scultura dal Suo Risorgimento in Italia sino al Secolo di Napoleone* (3 vols., 1813–18), *Le Fabbriche Più Conspicue di Venezia* (10 vols., 1815–20).

**Cid′, the** (thē sĭd′). *Span.* **el Cid′ Cam′pe·a·dor′** (ĕl thēth′ käm′pȧ·ä·thôr′), *i.e.* the Lord Champion. *Arab.* **Say′yid** (sī′yĭd). *Real name* **Rodrigo** (*or* **Ruy**) **Dí′az de Bi·var′** (thē′äth thȧ bē·vär′). 1040?–1099. Spanish soldier, b. near Burgos; ideal hero, esp. in Spanish literature. Fought in war between Sancho II of Castile and Sancho IV of Navarre, at that time winning his sobriquet "Campeador"; served Sancho II's successor, Alfonso VI; m. Ximena, daughter of count of Oviedo; incurred Alfonso's enmity, banished (c. 1081), and became soldier of fortune; had many adventures and won great success under Arab kings of Saragossa; captured Valencia (1094); ruled Valencia and Murcia (1094–99) until overthrown and killed by Almoravides. His deeds, much romanticized, first recounted in anonymous *Poema del Cid* (c. 1140), oldest extant Spanish epic; story told also in *Crónica del Cid* (c. 1284) and used in Guillén de Castro y Bellvis's drama *Las Mocedades del Cid* (c. 1612–13), Corneille's *Le Cid* (1636), and in Massenet's opera (1885).

**Cidiè.** See SARFATTI.

**Cien·fue′gos** (thyān·fwā′gōs), **Nicasio Álvarez de.** 1764–1809. Spanish poet, b. Madrid; educ. U. of Salamanca; editor, *El Mercurio* and *La Gaceta* (1798 ff.); exiled to France (1808 ff.) as participant in anti-French demonstration; among works are the plays *Idomeneo*, and *La Condesa de Castilla*, and *Obras Poéticas* (2 vols., 1798, 1816).

**Cien·fue′gos y Jo′vel·la′nos** (thyān·fwā′gōs [syān-] ē hō′vȧ·(l)yä′nōs), **José.** 1768–1825. Spanish general; served in French wars; captain general of Cuba (1816–19); returned to Spain; minister of war (1822). Cienfuegas, Cuba, is named in his honor.

**Cier′va** (thyĕr′vä), **Juan de la.** 1896–1936. Spanish aeronautical engineer; inventor of type of aircraft trademarked "Autogiro" (first model exhibited and tested, 1928); killed in airplane accident at Croydon Aerodrome, London (Dec. 9, 1936).

**Cie′za de Le·ón′** (thyā′thä thȧ lā·ōn′), **Pedro de.** 1518–1560. Spanish soldier and historian, b. Llerena; to America (1532?–52) with Spanish armies. Author of *Crónica del Perú* (4 parts), *Historia de la Nueva España*, etc.

**Ci·gna′ni** (chē·nyä′nē), Conte **Carlo.** 1628–1719. Italian painter of Bolognese school; representative of later baroque style; pupil of Francesco Albani; known esp. for his fresco *Assumption of the Virgin* in cathedral of Forlì.

**Ci′gna·ro′li** (chē′nyä·rô′lē), **Giovanni Bettino.** 1706–1770. Venetian painter; founded Academy of Verona (1764), director (1769); known chiefly for his mythological and religious works.

**Ci′go·li** (chē′gô·lē), **Lodovico Car′di da** (kär′dē dä). 1559–1613. Italian painter and architect, b. Castelvecchio; originated baroque painting in Florence. His paintings include *Martyrdom of St. Stephen, St. Francis Receiving the Stigmata, Ecce Homo, Joseph and Potiphar's Wife*, and frescoes *Cupid and Psyche*.

**Cil′i·an** (kĭl′ĭ·ăn) *or* **Kil′i·an,** Saint. d. 697. Irish bishop, known as the apostle of Franconia; martyred at Würzburg.

**Ci′ma** (chē′mä), **Giovanni Battista.** *Called* **Ci′ma da Co′ne·glia′no** (dä kō′nā·lyä′nō). c. 1459–1517 or 1518. Venetian painter, b. Conegliano. His works include studies of Madonna with saints, *Healing of Ananias, Annunciation, Adoration of the Shepherds, Tobias with the Angels, The Glorification of St. Peter, Martyr, Madonna*, and *Pietà*.

**Ci′ma·bu′e** (chē′mä·bōō′ā), **Giovanni.** *Properly* **Cen′ni di Pe′po** (chān′nē dē pā′pō). c. 1240–c. 1302. Florentine painter and mosaicist. Regenerated Florentine art by breaking with Byzantine tradition; forerunner of Florentine school. His works include a mosaic of St. John (in Pisa Cathedral), paintings as *Madonna of Santa Trinità* (in Florence Academy) and *Crucifix of Santa Croce*, and frescoes in church of St. Francis of Assisi, as scenes from the life of the Virgin, scenes from the Apocalypse, the Crucifixion (all in upper church), and *Madonna with Angels and St. Francis* (in lower church).

**Ci′ma·ro′sa** (chē′mä·rô′zä), **Domenico.** 1749–1801. Neapolitan composer; called to St. Petersburg by Catherine II as composer and conductor (1789–92); exiled from Naples (1799) for complicity in revolutionary movement. His works include operas, oratorios, masses, dramatic cantatas, and vocal pieces.

**Ci′mon** (sī′mŏn). 507?–449 B.C. Athenian general and statesman; son of Miltiades (*q.v.*). Commander of Athenian contingent in allied fleet which continued (477 B.C.) war against Persia; defeated and scattered Persian fleet at mouth of Eurymedon River (466). Advocated alliance with Sparta to present united Greek front against Persians, and induced Athens to aid in suppressing revolt of the Helots against Sparta (464); after failure of Athenian expedition on this occasion, attacked by democratic faction led by Pericles and ostracized (c. 459–454). After recall to Athens, had important part in negotiating armistice with Sparta, and contributed liberally to the rebuilding of Athens.

**Cinamus.** Variant of CINNAMUS.

**Cin′cin·na′tus** (sĭn′sĭ·nā′tŭs; -năt′ŭs), **Lucius Quinctius.** b. about 519 B.C. Roman general and statesman. According to legend, consul (c. 460 B.C.) and supporter of patricians in struggle with plebeians (462–454). Appointed dictator (458) by Senate when a Roman army was in danger of being destroyed by Aequians. Found cultivating small farm when Senate delegation told him of appointment, he gathered troops, attacked and defeated Aequians, and resigned dictatorship, all within 16 days. Again appointed dictator (439), defeated and slew traitor Spurius Melius. In later generations, regarded as model of old-fashioned simplicity, ability, and virtue.

**Cin′ci·us Al′i·men′tus** (sĭn′shĭ·ŭs ăl′ĭ·mĕn′tŭs), **Lucius.** fl. late 3d century B.C. Roman annalist; wrote in Greek a history of Rome down to his own times, *Annales*.

**Cin′e·as** (sĭn′ē·ăs). Politician of late 4th and early 3d centuries B.C., orig. from Thessaly; minister of Pyrrhus, King of Epirus; sent to Rome to negotiate a peace after Pyrrhus's defeat of the Romans at Heraclea (280 B.C.).

**Cin′na** (sĭn′ȧ), **Gaius Helvius.** Roman poet; friend of Catullus; killed by the mob at Caesar's funeral (44 B.C.), when mistaken for Lucius Cornelius Cinna (*q.v.*).

**Cinna, Lucius Cornelius.** d. 84 B.C. Roman general and statesman; consul (87 B.C.); with Marius suppressed uprising in Rome and proscribed many leaders of Sulla's party; after Marius's death (Jan., 86), leader of the popular party; killed in a mutiny of his troops while preparing to attack Sulla. His daughter **Cornelia** was 1st wife of Julius Caesar. His son **Lucius Cornelius**, praetor (44 B.C.), sided with the assassins of Caesar.

**Cin′na·mus** (sĭn′ȧ·mŭs) *or* **Cin′a·mus** *or* **Sin′na·mus, Jo·an′nes** (jō·ăn′ēz; -ĕs). 12th-century Byzantine historian; secretary to Emperor Manuel I Comnenus; author of a history of period from 1118 to 1176 A.D.

**Ci′no da Pi·sto′ia** (chē′nō dä pēs·tō′yä). *Properly*

Guittoncino **de' Si'ni·bal'di** (dā sē'nē·bäl'dē). 1270–1336. Italian jurist and poet; friend of Dante; Ghibelline partisan; taught jurisprudence at Treviso, Siena, Florence, Naples, etc. Mentioned by Dante (*De Vulgari Eloquentia*, I xiii 33–40) as stylist in the vulgar tongue and celebrated by Petrarch in a sonnet.

**Cinq'-Mars'** (săN'mȧr'), Marquis **de. Henri Coif'fier' de Ru'zé'** (kwȧ'fyā' dē rü'zā'). 1620–1642. French nobleman and conspirator. Introduced to court of Louis XIII as protégé of Richelieu (1635); advanced to high office; a favorite of the king. Ambitious for high military command; joined Orléans faction. His conspiracy against Richelieu betrayed by Gaston d'Orléans; executed (Sept. 12, 1642). A historical novel by Alfred de Vigny (1826) and an opera by Gounod (1877) are based upon the plot.

**Cinthio** *or* **Cintio** *or* **Cinzio.** See CYNTHIUS.

**Cio'łek** (chô'lĕk), **Erazm.** *Lat.* **Erasmus Vi·tel'lo** (vĭ·tĕl'ō) *or* **Vi·tel'li·o** (-ĭ·ō). c. 1210–c. 1285. Polish scholar and mathematician.

**Cione, Andrea di.** See ORCAGNA.

**Cione, Andrea di Michele.** See Andrea del VERROCCHIO.

**Ci'pri·a'ni** (chē'prē·ä'nē), **Amilcare.** 1845–1918. Italian revolutionist, b. Rimini. Fought for Italian liberation, at Solferino and under Garibaldi; worked diplomatically under Mazzini for same end. Served in French army in Franco-Prussian War (1870–71), and was among the French revolutionist leaders in the Commune of Paris. Condemned to imprisonment at hard labor; elected to Italian Chamber of Deputies eleven times in popular protest against the sentence; finally pardoned (1888); lived in France (1888–91). On return to Italy, again imprisoned for revolutionary activity (1891–94). On outbreak of Greco-Turkish War, raised battalion and fought on Greek side; at outbreak of World War, worked vigorously for Italian participation on Allied side.

**Cipriani, Giovanni Battista.** 1727–1785. Italian historical painter and engraver in England; to London (1755); painted ceilings and decorations in Somerset House, London; an original member of Royal Academy (1768).

**Cirencester, Richard of.** See RICHARD OF CIRENCESTER.

**Ciriaco de' Pizzicolli.** *Lat.* **Ciriacus Anconitanus.** See CYRIACUS OF ANCONA.

**Cisneros,** Cardinal. See Francisco JIMÉNEZ DE CISNEROS.

**Cis'sey'** (sē'sā'), **Ernest Louis Octave Cour'tot'** (ko͞or'tō') **de.** 1810–1882. French soldier and politician; general of division in Franco-Prussian War (1870–71); aided in suppressing Commune of Paris (1871); minister of war three times (between 1871 and 1876).

**Ci·trine'** (sĭ·trēn') **of Wembley,** 1st Baron. 1887– . *Orig.* **Walter McLennan Citrine.** English trade-union leader, b. Liverpool. Trade-union official (1914); general secretary, Trades Union Congress (1926); president, International Federation of Trade Unions (1928); member, government economic advisory council (1930–33); visited U.S. to gather information on armament production (1940). Author of *The British Trade Union Movement, I Search for Truth in Russia, My American Diary* (1941), *In Russia Now* (1942).

**Ci'tro'en'** (sē'trô'ĕn'), **André Gustave.** 1878–1935. French automobile manufacturer; engaged in making munitions during World War (1914–18); after war, devoted his plant to production of low-priced automobiles. Aided in financing motor caravan expedition over 8000-mile route from Beyrouth to Peiping (1932), and similar expedition through central Africa to open new trade route. Lost control of automobile company after its bankruptcy (1934) and reorganization (1935).

**Ci'viale'** (sē'vyȧl'), **Jean.** 1792–1867. French surgeon; reputed originator of lithotrity.

**Ci·vi'lis** (sĭ·vī'lĭs), **Julius,** *erroneously* **Claudius.** Germanic leader of the Batavians in their war against Rome (69–70 A.D.); defeated by Petillius Cerealis at Trier.

**Ci'vi·ta'li** (chē'vē·tä'lē), **Matteo.** 1436–1501. Italian sculptor and architect, b. Lucca. Known esp. for his sculptural works in Lucca Cathedral.

**Cla'del'** (klȧ'dĕl'), **Léon Alpinien.** 1835–1892. French symbolist writer; author of short stories and the novel *Juive Errante* (pub. 1897).

**Claf'lin** (klăf'lĭn), **Victoria** (1838–1927) and **Tennessee Celeste** (1846–1923). American sisters, b. in Ohio. Victoria married Dr. Canning Woodhull (1853), James H. Blood (c. 1866; divorced 1876), John Biddulph Martin (1883); Tennessee married Francis Cook (1885), who later succeeded to a baronetcy and ownership of a Portuguese estate which brought him the title of Viscount de Montserrat. As mere children, the sisters gave spiritualistic séances; also, traveled with a medicine show peddling an "elixir of life." In New York (1868); gained confidence of Cornelius Vanderbilt, opened brokerage office, and profited greatly by his advice on transactions; founded (1870) and edited *Woodhull and Claflin's Weekly*, advocating equal rights for women, a single standard of morality, free love, and campaigning against prostitution and abortion; first published in their *Weekly* (Nov. 2, 1872) the story of the alleged intimacy of Henry Ward Beecher with Mrs. Theodore Tilton, one of his parishioners. Lived chiefly in England (from 1877).

**Clai'borne** (klā'bērn), **William.** 1587?–?1677. Colonist in America (from 1621), b. in Westmorland, Eng.; established (1631) trading station on Kent Island, in Chesapeake Bay, later claimed as part of Maryland grant; incited insurrection and held control of Maryland (1644–46).

**Claiborne, William Charles Coles.** 1775–1817. American lawyer, b. in Sussex Co., Va.; governor of Mississippi Territory (1801–03); governor of Territory of Orleans (1804–12); first governor of Louisiana (1812–16); U.S. senator (1817).

**Clair** (klâr), **René.** *Professional name of* **René Cho'mette'** (shô'mĕt'). 1898– . French journalist and motion-picture director and producer.

**Clai'raut'** (klĕ'rō') *or* **Clai'rault'** (-rō'), **Alexis Claude.** 1713–1765. French mathematician. Accompanied Maupertius on expedition to Lapland to measure a degree of the meridian. Promulgated "Clairaut's theorem" in his *Théorie de la Figure de la Terre* (1743); studied curves and differential equations; explained motion of the moon; predicted return of Halley's comet.

**Claire** (klâr), **Ina,** *nee* **Fa'gan** (fā'găn). 1892– . American actress, b. Washington, D.C.; m. James Whitaker (divorced), John Gilbert (1929; divorced), William Ross Wallace (1939). On stage (from 1912) and in motion pictures (briefly, from 1928); starred in *The Gold Diggers* (1919), *Bluebeard's Eighth Wife* (1922), *The Awful Truth* (1923), *The Last of Mrs. Cheyney* (1925), *Our Betters* (1928), *Biography* (1932–34), *Once is Enough* (1938), etc.

**Clairfayt.** Variant of CLERFAYT.

**Clair'mont** (klâr'mŏnt; -mŭnt), **Clara Mary Jane,** *often* **Claire** (klâr). 1798–1879. Stepdaughter of William Godwin and mother of Byron's daughter Allegra.

**Clai'ron'** (klĕ'rôN'), Mlle. *Professional name of* **Claire Josèphe Lé'ris'** (lā'rēs'). 1723–1803. French tragedienne; prominent in a number of Voltaire's tragedies, including *Zulime, Sémiramis, Olympie, Tancrède, Oreste.*

**Clair'ville'** (klĕr'vēl'), **Louis François.** *Real surname* **Ni'co'laie'** (nē'kô'lĕ'). 1811–1879. French playwright; author of, or collaborator in, more than six hundred stage presentations, including comedies, vaudeville sketches, etc.

**Clajus.** See also KLAJ.

**Cla'jus** (klä'yo͞os), **Johannes.** *Orig. surname* **Klaj** (klī). 1535–1592. German grammarian; rector in Nordhausen (1570); preacher in Bendeleben (1573); author of *Grammatica Germanicae Linguae* (1578).

**Clam'-Gal'las** (kläm'gäl'äs), Count **Eduard von.** 1805–1891. Austrian general; distinguished himself in Italy and Hungary (1848–49); engaged at Magenta and Solferino (1859); in Austro-Prussian War (1866), suffered defeats at Hühnerwasser, Podol, Münchengrätz and Gitschin; relieved of his command and retired.

**Clam'-Mar'ti·nic** (kläm'mär'tē·nĭts) *or* **Clam'-Mar'ti·nitz,** Count **Heinrich Jaroslaw von.** 1826–1887. Austrian politician; played leading role in Reichsrat (1860); joined Palacký and Rieger in demanding autonomy for Bohemia and crowning of emperor at Prague. His nephew **Heinrich** (1863–1932) was prime minister of Austria (1916–17).

**Clana, Heinrich von der.** Pseudonym of Albert Maria WEISS.

**Clanconnell,** Earl of. = *Turlough O'Neill,* under O'NEILL family.

**Claneboye,** Viscounts. See under HAMILTON family.

**Clan·ric'arde** (klăn·rĭk'ẽrd), Earls and marquises of. Titles in Irish peerage held by members of the **de Burgh** (dĕ bûrg') *or* **de Bourke** (bûrk) *or* **de Burke** (bûrk) family of Galway in Connaught. The earldom passed in 1916 to a kinsman, George Ulick Browne, marquis of **Sli'go** (slī'gō). Holders of the titles include: **Ulick de Burgh** (d. 1544), 1st Earl of **Clanricarde,** head of clan, possessor of quasi-royal authority and vast estates, who surrendered his territory to Henry VIII and undertook to introduce English customs, receiving his estates back to hold as 1st earl (1543). **Richard** (1568?–1635), 4th earl, stanch adherent of Queen Elizabeth in O'Neill's Rebellion; created earl of **St. Al'bans** [sånt ôl'bănz] (English peerage); m. Frances Walsingham, widow of Sir Philip Sidney; received harsh treatment from Wentworth, Earl of Strafford. His son **Ulick** (1604–?1657), 1st marquis and 5th earl; called the "great earl"; served with Charles I against Scots (1639); sole member of Irish Roman Catholic nobility on king's side; commissioner to urge cessation of resistance upon Irish confederates (1643); tried again (1646) to reconcile Irish to Charles I; subdued Galway (1648); forced to capitulate to Parliamentary forces (1652). **John,** 9th earl, by supporting James II, forfeited estates, not recovered till 1702. **Ulick John,** 14th earl, lord privy seal, for whom marquisate was revived (1825); created Baron **Som'er·hill** [sŭm'ẽr·hĭl] (1826). His son **Hubert George de Burgh Can'ning** [kăn'ĭng] (1832–1916), 2d marquis and 15th earl, resisted attempts to limit power of landlords, losing estates to Congested Districts Board (1915).

**Clap** (klăp), **Thomas.** 1703–1767. American Congregational clergyman and educator, b. Scituate, Mass.; grad. Harvard (1722); rector, Yale College (1739–66).

**Cla'pa'rède'** (klå'på'rĕd'), **Édouard,** *in full* **Jean Louis René Antoine Édouard.** 1832–1870. Swiss naturalist; professor at Geneva; author of studies on Infusoria, rhizopods, spiders, oligochaetes, and annelids.

**Clap'ham** (klăp'ăm; -'m), **John Harold.** 1873–1946. English economist. Professor of economic history, Cambridge (1928–38). Author of *The Woollen and Worsted Industries* (1907), *The Economic Development of France and Germany, 1815–1915* (1921), *An Economic History of Modern Britain* (3 vols., 1926–38).

**Cla'pis'son'** (klå'pē'sôɴ'), **Antonin Louis.** 1808–1866. French composer, esp. of romances and operas.

**Clapp** (klăp), **Frederick Mortimer.** 1879–1969. American poet and art connoisseur, b. New York City. B.A., Yale (1901). Head of department of fine arts, U. of Pittsburgh (1926–36); director of Frick Collection, New York (from 1936). Author of *On the Overland and Other Poems* (1916), *Jacopo Carucci...*(1916), *New York and Other Verses* (1918), *New Poems* (1936), *Said before Sunset,* poems (1938).

**Clapp,** Sir **Harold Winthrop.** 1875–1952. Australian electrical engineer; expert on railway electrification in California (1908), Brisbane, N.Y. City, and with N.Y. Central and Pennsylvania Railroads and street-railway systems in Ohio and Illinois. General manager of aircraft construction for Australian govt. (1939–42).

**Clap'per·ton** (klăp'ẽr·t'n; -tŭn), **Hugh.** 1788–1827. Scottish explorer of Africa; in Nigeria (1822–27); first European to report observation of Hausa.

**Cla'rac'** (klå'råk'), Comte **Charles Othon Frédéric Jean Baptiste de.** 1777–1847. French archaeologist; an émigré, served in Condé's army and in Russian army. Tutor to children of Murat, King of Naples (1808). Curator of museum of antiquities at the Louvre (1818). Author of *Fouilles Faites à Pompéi* (1818), *Musée de Sculpture Antique et Moderne* (1826–55), *Manuel de l'Histoire de l'Art chez les Anciens* (1830–47).

**Clare,** Earls of. See (1) de CLARE family; (2) John FITZGIBBON; (3) PELHAM family.

**Clare, de** (dĕ klâr'; dē). Name of English family in Suffolk founded by **Richard de Clare** (d. 1090), 1st Earl of Clare, a Norman known as **Richard Fitz-Gil'bert** (fĭts·gĭl'bẽrt) who followed William the Conqueror to England (1080–81); from his son **Gilbert Fitz-Rich'ard** [fĭts·rĭch'ẽrd] (d. 1115?), conqueror of Cardigan in Wales, descended (through elder son, **Richard,** 3d Earl of Clare, d. ?1136) earls of Clare and **Hert'ford** (här'fẽrd; härt'-) and (through younger son, **Gilbert,** created earl 1138, d. 1148) earls of **Pem'broke** (pĕm'bro͝ok) and **Strig'ul** (?strĭg'ŭl). The family includes: **Roger de Clare** (d. 1173), 5th Earl of Clare and 3d Earl of Hertford; son of Richard (d. 1136?); fought the Welsh; twice defeated by Rhys ap Gruffudd, Prince of South Wales; quarreled with Archbishop Becket. **Richard** (d. 1176), 2d Earl of Pembroke and Strigul, called **Richard Strong'bow'** (strông'bō'); son of Gilbert (d. 1148); took strong force to Ireland (1170) to intervene on side of dethroned king of Leinster, whose daughter Eva he married; captured Waterford and Dublin but yielded conquests to appease jealousy of Henry II, whom he aided in Normandy (1173). See MARSHAL family. **Gilbert** (d. 1230), 7th Earl of Clare, 5th Earl of Hertford, 6th Earl of Gloucester; inherited earldom of Gloucester through his mother; m. daughter of William Marshal, 2d Earl of Pembroke, bringing house to its highest fortunes; one of 25 barons entrusted with carrying out Magna Charta (1215). **Richard** (1222–1262), 8th Earl of Clare, 6th Earl of Hertford, 7th Earl of Gloucester; son of Gilbert (d. 1230); envoy to Scotland (1255) and to Germany (1256); defeated by Welsh (1244, 1257); joined Simon de Montfort (1258) but quarreled with him. Richard's son **Gilbert** (1243–1295), 9th Earl of Clare, 7th Earl of Hertford, 8th Earl of Gloucester; m. niece of Henry III (1253); joined de Montfort (1263); joined Prince Edward in repelling de Montfort (1265); took London (1267), but became reconciled to Henry III; obtained restoration of lands to disinherited barons (1271); fought Welsh (1276–83);

m. Joan, daughter of Edward I (1290). His son **Gilbert** (1291–1314), 10th Earl of Clare, 8th Earl of Hertford, 9th Earl of Gloucester; mediator between Edward II and Lancaster (1313); killed at Bannockburn. **Elizabeth** (1291?–1360), sister of 10th earl; endowed (1336) and (1359) gave a body of statutes to Clare College, Cambridge.

**Clare, John.** 1793–1864. English poet; known as the "Northamptonshire peasant poet." Herd boy, gardener, militiaman, lime burner, vagrant; published *Poems Descriptive of Rural Life and Scenery* (1820); failed as farmer (1827, 1831); confined in lunatic asylum; profited little by other poetical works, *Village Minstrel* (1821), *The Shepherd's Calendar* (1827), *Rural Muse* (1835).

**Clare** (klâr) *or* **Clar'a** (klăr'ȧ; klâr'ȧ; *Ital.* klä'rä) **of As·si'si** (äs·sē'zē), Saint. 1194–1253. Italian nun; founder with St. Francis of Assisi of order of Franciscan nuns, often called Order of the Poor Clares (1212). Canonized in 1255.

**Clar'ence** (klăr'ĕns), Dukes of. 1st, 2d, and 3d creations in house of Plantagenet. (1) **Lionel** of Antwerp (1338–1368), 3d son of Edward III. (2) **Thomas** (1388?–1421); second son of Henry IV by Mary de Bohun. Ravaged coast of Normandy (1405); made raid into Leinster (1408); commanded at siege of Harfleur (1415); took part in Henry V's victorious expedition in France (1417–20); killed in cavalry attack at Beaugé. (3) **George** (1449–1478); brother of Edward IV and Richard III, and 3d surviving son of Richard (1411–1460), 3d duke of York. Lord lieutenant of Ireland (1462); with father-in-law, earl of Warwick, invaded England (1469) and made Edward IV prisoner at Edgcott; again with Warwick invaded England and restored Henry VI to throne (1470); in disapproval of restoration of Henry VI, deserted to his brother Edward IV and aided in reestablishing York dynasty (1471); charged with causing king's death through necromancy, attainted, sentenced, and secretly put to death in Tower of London; a character in Shakespeare's *Henry VI*, part III, and *Richard III.* His eldest son, **Edward** (1475–1499), Earl of **War'wick** (wŏr'ĭk), was imprisoned in Tower by Henry VII (1485); in consequence of his personation by Simnel in Ireland, exhibited in the streets one day by Henry (1487); beheaded on pretense of conspiracy after planning escape. (4) See WILLIAM IV, of England. (5) Dukedom revived (1890) as Clarence and Avondale (*q.v.*).

**Clarence and A'von·dale'** (ā'vŭn·dāl'; ăv'ŭn-), Duke of. **Albert Victor Christian Edward.** 1864–1892. Eldest son of Edward VII. Entered training ship *Britannia* (1877); aide-de-camp to Queen Victoria (1889); betrothed (1891) to Princess Mary of Teck (later Queen Mary, consort of George V) but died before marriage.

**Clarendon,** Earls of. See under Edward HYDE and George William Frederick VILLIERS.

**Cla're'tie'** (klȧ'rĕ'tē'), **Jules,** *orig.* **Arsène Arnaud.** 1840–1913. French journalist and writer; director, Comédie Française (1885). Among his novels are *Une Drôlesse* (1862), *Un Assassin* (later entitled *Robert Burat*, 1866), *Monsieur le Ministre* (1881), *Le Prince Zilah* (1884), *La Cigarette* (1890), *Brichanteau Célèbre* (1902); among his plays, *Les Mirabeau* (1879), *Monsieur le Ministre* (1883); among his historical works, *Les Derniers Montagnards* (1867), *Histoire de la Révolution de 1870–1871* (1875–76), *Le Drapeau* (1879); among his literary studies, *La Vie Moderne au Théâtre* (1869–75), *Victor Hugo* (1902).

**Cla·ret' y Cla'ra** (klä·rĕt' ē klä'rä), Saint. *Orig. name* **Antonio María.** *Known in English as* **Anthony Claret.** 1807–1870. Spanish Roman Catholic priest; founded (1849) Congregation of the Missionary Sons of the Immaculate Heart of Mary, whose members are commonly called Claretians; canonized (1950).

**Cla'ri** (klä'rē), **Giovanni Carlo Maria.** 1669–?1745. Italian composer; pupil of Colonna; known esp. for his vocal duets and trios.

**Cla·rín'** (klä·rēn'). Pseudonym of Leopoldo ALAS.

**Clark** (klärk). See also CLARKE; CLERK; CLERKE.

**Clark, Abraham.** 1726–1794. American political leader; known as "Congress Abraham"; b. Elizabethtown, N.J.; member, Continental Congress (1776–78, 1779–83); signer of the Declaration of Independence.

**Clark, Allan.** 1896–1950. American sculptor, b. Missoula, Mont. Associated with Fogg Museum Expedition in Orient (1924–27) and made color drawings of cave chapels near Turkestan border. Among his sculptures are a bust of James Russell Lowell (American Hall of Fame), *Study for a Garden Pool* (Whitney Museum of American Art, N.Y.), *Mei Kwei* (Metropolitan Museum, N.Y.), *Javanese Actor* (museum at Honolulu).

**Clark, Alvan.** 1804–1887. American lens maker and astronomer, b. Ashfield, Mass. Engraver and painter (1824–44). His firm, Alvan Clark & Sons, made 26-inch telescopes for U.S. Naval Observatory and U. of Virginia, 30-inch telescope for Pulkovo Observatory, Russia, 36-inch for Lick Observatory. His son **Alvan Graham** (1832–1897), lens maker and astronomer, discovered 16 double stars; made 40-inch lens for the Yerkes telescope.

**Clark, Austin Hobart.** 1880–1954. American biologist, b. Wellesley, Mass.; A.B., Harvard (1903); on staff of Smithsonian Institution (1908–1950); author of *Animals of Land and Sea* (1925), *Nature Narratives* (2 vols., 1929, 1931), *The New Evolution* (1930).

**Clark, Badger,** *in full* **Charles Badger.** 1883–1957. American poet, b. Albia, Iowa; author of *Sun and Saddle Leather* (1915), *Grass Grown Trails* (1917), *Sky Lines and Wood Smoke* (1935), and a novel, *Spike* (1923).

**Clark, Barrett H.** 1890–1953. Dramatic teacher and editor, b. Toronto, Can. Educ., U. of Chicago and U. of Paris. Executive director, Dramatists Play Service, New York City (from 1936). Author of books on modern and contemporary drama.

**Clark, Champ** (chămp), *in full* **James Beauchamp.** 1850–1921. American political leader, b. near Lawrenceburg, Ky. Grad. Cincinnati Law School (1875); moved to Missouri (1876). Member, U.S. House of Representatives (1893–95, 1897–1921); speaker (1911–19). Prominent candidate for Democratic presidential nomination (1912); defeated when W. J. Bryan turned his influence to support Woodrow Wilson. His son **Bennett Champ** (1890–1954), b. Bowling Green, Mo.; A.B., U. of Mo. (1913), LL.B., George Washington U. (1914); practiced law in St. Louis (1919–33); U.S. senator from Missouri (1933–45).

**Clark, Charles Edgar.** 1843–1922. American naval officer, b. Bradford, Vt. In command of battleship *Oregon* at outbreak of Spanish-American War; made trip (Mar. 19–May 25, 1898) from San Francisco around Cape Horn in time to join Sampson in annihilation of Cervera's fleet off Santiago de Cuba (July 3, 1898).

**Clark, Francis Edward.** 1851–1927. Congregational clergyman, b. of American parentage at Aylmer, Que., Canada. Grad. Dartmouth (1873). Organized first Christian Endeavor society (1881; incorporated 1885). Edited *Golden Rule* and made it organ of the movement (1887–97), with name *Christian Endeavor World* from 1897. President, World's Christian Endeavor Union (from 1895, date of organization).

**Clark, George Lindenberg.** 1892–1969. American chemist, b. Anderson, Ind. B.A., DePauw (1914); M.S.

(1914), Ph.D. (1918), Chicago. Associate professor, Vanderbilt (1919–21), M.I.T. (1924–27; installed first industrial X-ray research laboratory); professor, Illinois (from 1927). Special editor for physical chemistry, *Webster's New International Dictionary, Second Edition.* Author of *Applied X-rays* (1927).

**Clark, George Rogers.** 1752–1818. American Revolutionary frontier leader, b. near Charlottesville, Va.; brother of William Clark (*q.v.*). Surveyor in Kentucky; organized and led frontiersmen in defense against Indian raids (1776–77). Gained approval of Patrick Henry, governor of Virginia, for expedition to conquer Illinois country (the Northwest); captured key points of Kaskaskia (1778), Vincennes (1779), saving Illinois and Kentucky region for the Colonies. Engaged in fighting British and Indians to hold this territory (1779–83).

**Clark, Howard Walton.** 1870–1941. American ichthyologist, b. in Allen Co., Indiana; grad. Indiana U. (1896); collaborator with David Starr Jordan and Barton W. Evermann on *Check List of the Fishes...of North and Middle America* (1928).

**Clark, Hubert Lyman.** 1870–1947. American zoologist, b. Amherst, Mass. A.B., Amherst (1892), Ph.D., Johns Hopkins (1897). On staff of Museum of Comparative Zoology, Harvard (from 1905), and associate professor of zoology (from 1927).

**Clark, Joe,** *in full* **Joseph.** 1939– . Canadian politician, b. High River, Alberta. In parliament (1973– ); leader of Progressive Conservative party (1976– ); prime minister of Canada (1979– ).

**Clark, John Bates.** 1847–1938. American economist, b. Providence, R.I.; A.B. (1872), Ph.D. (1890), Amherst; professor, Carleton Coll. (1877–81), Smith Coll. (1882–93), Amherst (1892–95), Columbia (1895–1923). Editor, *Political Science Quarterly* (1895–1911). Author of *The Philosophy of Wealth* (1885), *The Distribution of Wealth* (1899), *Essentials of Economic Theory* (1907), etc.

**Clark, Jonas Gilman.** 1815–1900. b. Hubbardston, Mass. Founder of Clark University, Worcester, Mass. (1887).

**Clark, Josiah Latimer.** 1822–1898. English engineer; patented a pneumatic tube for conveying letters or parcels; invented a cell (Clark cell) used as standard of electromotive force; worked on submarine cables, devising improvements in their insulation.

**Clark, Kenneth Bancroft.** 1914– . Am. educator and social psychologist, b. Panama Canal Zone. On staff of City College of New York (1942– ); studies on ghetto life, including *Youth in the Ghetto, Prejudice and Your Child, Dark Ghetto,* etc.

**Clark,** Sir **Kenneth McKenzie.** 1903– . English art connoisseur; educ. Oxford; director of National Gallery, London (1934–45). Author of *The Gothic Revival* (1929), *Leonardo da Vinci* (1939), *Civilisation* (1970).

**Clark, Lewis Gaylord.** 1808–1873. American editor, twin brother of Willis Gaylord Clark (*q.v.*); editor of *Knickerbocker Magazine,* New York (1834–61).

**Clark, Mark Wayne.** 1896– . American army officer; grad. (1917) U.S.M.A. (West Point); served in World War I; commander (1942) of U.S. ground forces in Europe; on secret mission to French North Africa (1942); commander in North Africa and Italy (1943–44); chief, U.S. f[illegible] in Austria (1945–47).

**Clark, Thomas Campbell.** 1899–1977. American lawyer, b. Dallas, Texas; A.B. (1921), LL.B. (1922), U. of Texas; practiced in Dallas; U.S. attorney general (1945–49); assoc. justice, U.S. Supreme Court (1949–67).

**Clark, William.** 1770–1838. American explorer; bro. of George Rogers Clark (*q.v.*); b. in Caroline County, Va.; moved to Louisville, Ky. (1784–85). Lieutenant, U.S. army (1792); engaged in frontier service against Indians (1791–96). Invited (1803) by Capt. Meriwether Lewis to join with him in leading exploring expedition to find route to Pacific Ocean (Lewis and Clark expedition), which left St. Louis May 14, 1804, crossed continent, reached mouth of Columbia River November, 1805, returned by land, reached St. Louis Sept. 23, 1806; resigned from army (1807); governor of Missouri Territory (1813–21). Diary of Lewis and Clark, *History of the Expedition under the Commands of Captains Lewis and Clark* published (1814).

**Clark, William Andrews.** 1839–1925. American businessman and politician, b. Fayette Co., Pa.; fought long political struggle against Marcus Daly (1888–1900); U.S. senator from Montana (1899–1900); accused of fraud in gaining election; resigned when Senate committee reported him "not duly and legally elected"; U.S. senator (1901–07).

**Clark, William George.** 1821–1878. English classical and Shakespearean scholar. Fellow of Trinity Coll., Cambridge (1844–78); established Cambridge *Journal of Philology* (1868); edited, with John Glover (vol. 1) and William Aldis Wright, librarians of Trinity, the *Cambridge Shakespeare* (9 vols., 1863–66); edited, with William Aldis Wright, the *Globe Shakespeare* (1864). Author of *Gazpacho* (1853), *Vacation Tourists* (1861–64). Cf. Charles Cowden CLARKE.

**Clark, William Tierney.** 1783–1852. English civil engineer; built suspension bridge over Thames at Hammersmith and one across Danube at Budapest.

**Clark, Willis Gaylord.** 1808–1841. Twin brother of Lewis Gaylord Clark (*q.v.*); American poet.

**Clarke** (klärk). See also CLARK; CLERK; CLERKE.

**Clarke, Adam.** 1762?–1832. Irish Wesleyan minister. Preached in Channel Islands, Shetland, and, mostly, in London; published *Bibliographical Dictionary* (6 vols., 1802), and *Commentary on the Holy Scriptures* (1810–26).

**Clarke, Alexander Ross.** 1828–1914. English geodesist; reduced and published observations on the figure of the earth (1858), on standards of length (1866); wrote a standard text *Geodesy* (1880), proposing as bases of reference ellipsoids (with compression 1/280.4, 1/295, 1/293.5) named after him.

**Clarke,** Sir **Andrew.** 1824–1902. British colonial administrator and engineer. Joined Royal Engineers (1844); transferred to New Zealand, where he served in Maori war; governor of Straits Settlements (1873–75), suppressed piracy; agent-general for Victoria (1891–94, 1897–1902).

**Clarke, Austin.** 1896–1974. Irish poet; educ. University Coll., Dublin; received national award for poetry at Tailtean Games (1932). Author of verse, as in *The Vengeance of Fionn* (1917), *The Fires of Baal* (1920), *The Sword of the West* (1921), *The Cattledrive in Connaught* (1925), *Pilgrimage* (1929), *Night and Morning* (1938), verse plays *The Flame* (1930) and *Sister Eucharia* (1939), novels *The Bright Temptation* (1932) and *The Singing-Men at Cashel* (1936).

**Clarke,** Sir **Caspar Purdon.** 1846–1911. Architect and art expert, b. Richmond, Ireland; associated with South Kensington Museum (1867–1905; director 1896–1905); director, Metropolitan Museum of Art, New York (1905–10).

**Clarke, Charles Baron.** 1832–1906. English botanist. M.A., Cantab. (1859); while inspector of schools in India, collected specimens of native plants (from 1865); presented 25,000 specimens to Kew herbarium (1877); described botanical families for Joseph Hooker's *Flora of British India.*

**Clarke, Charles Cowden.** 1787–1877. English Shakespearean scholar, son of a schoolmaster; taught Keats his letters; friend of Leigh Hunt, Shelley, Hazlitt, Charles and Mary Lamb; music publisher in partnership with Alfred Novello, whose sister he married (1828); published lectures (delivered 1834–56) on Shakespeare and European literature; collaborated with his wife **Mary Victoria Cowden-Clarke** (1809–1898) on *The Shakespeare Key* (1879) and *Recollections of Writers* (1898); resided with wife in Italy (from 1856). His wife also compiled *The Complete Concordance to Shakespeare* (monthly, 1844–45). Cf. William George CLARK.

**Clarke, Edward Daniel.** 1769–1822. English mineralogist and traveler. M.A., Cantab. (1794); collected statues and sarcophagi, manuscripts, and coins in Egypt and Palestine; professor of mineralogy, Cambridge (1808); university librarian (1817).

**Clarke,** Sir **Edward George.** 1841–1931. English lawyer, politician, and writer, b. London. Called to bar (1864); M.P. (1880–1900); solicitor general (1886–92); won renown as counsel in a number of notable cases; retired (1914). Author of *Treatise on the Law of Extradition* (1866), *The Epistles of St. Paul* (1912), *The National Church* (1916), *Benjamin Disraeli...* (1926).

**Clarke, Frank Wigglesworth.** 1847–1931. American chemist, b. Boston; S.B., Harvard (1867); professor, U. of Cincinnati (1874–83); chief chemist, U.S. Geological Survey (1883–1925); known esp. for geochemical research. Author of *Data of Geochemistry*, and Geological Survey bulletins.

**Clarke, George Herbert.** 1873–1953. Educator and poet, b. Gravesend, Eng.; to Canada (1881). B.A., McMaster U., Toronto (1895). Professor of English, U. of Tennessee (1912–19), U. of the South (1919–25), Queens U., Canada (from 1925). Author of *At the Shrine and Other Poems* (1914), *Halt and Parley, and Other Poems* (1934), *Ode on the Burial of King George the Fifth* (1936).

**Clarke, George Syd′en·ham** (sĭd′'n·ăm; sĭd′năm). 1st Baron **Sydenham of Combe** (ko͞om). 1848–1933. English soldier and colonial administrator. Entered Royal Engineers (1868); served Egyptian and Sudan expeditions, in intelligence department, Suakin; employed at War Office (till 1892); sent on special missions to Continent and America; governor of Victoria, Australia (1901–04), of Bombay (1907–13); chairman of various royal commissions (1913–16), and of executive committee of British Empire League (1915–21). Author of *Studies of an Imperialist* (1928); *Fortification, Past, Present, and Future; Imperial Defence.*

**Clarke, Helen Archibald.** 1860–1926. American editor and author, b. Philadelphia. She was cofounder (1888) and editor (1888–1903) of *Poet Lore.*

**Clarke** (klȧrk), **Henri Jacques Guillaume.** Duc **de Fel′tre** (fāl′trȧ). 1765–1818. French soldier, of Irish descent. Grad. École Militaire, Paris; general of brigade (1793); private secretary to Napoleon during Consulate (1799–1804); minister of war (1807–14); after abdication of Napoleon (1814), remained loyal to Louis XVIII and was appointed minister of war, and created marshal of France.

**Clarke** (klärk), **Jacob Augustus Lockhart.** 1817–1880. English physician; interested in microscopic anatomy; devoted himself to research on the brain and nervous system.

**Clarke, James Freeman.** 1810–1888. American Unitarian clergyman, b. Hanover, N.H.; grad. Harvard (1829); pastor in Boston (1841–50; 1854–88). Author of *Ten Great Religions* (2 parts, 1871, 1883), *Common Sense in Religion* (1874), *Self-Culture* (1882), etc.

**Clarke, John.** 1609–1676. Baptist clergyman and physician, b. Westhorpe, Eng.; to America (1637); one of founders of Rhode Island (1638); in England (1651–64), upholding the interests of Rhode Island colony; instrumental, with Roger Williams, in maintaining liberal democratic character of Rhode Island institutions.

**Clarke, John Hessin.** 1857–1945. American jurist, b. Lisbon, Ohio. A.B., Western Reserve (1877). Adm. to bar in Ohio (1878); practiced at Lisbon (1878–80), Youngstown (1880–97), Cleveland (1897–1914). Associate justice, U.S. Supreme Court (1916–22).

**Clarke, John Mason.** 1857–1925. American paleontologist, b. Canandaigua, N.Y.; grad. Amherst (1877); state paleontologist of New York (1898–1925). Author of *New Devonian Crustacea* (1882), *Early Devonic History of New York and Eastern North America* (1908), etc.

**Clarke, McDonald.** 1798–1842. American poet, b. Bath, Me.; known as "the Mad Poet."

**Clarke, Marcus Andrew His′lop** (hĭz′lŏp). 1846–1881. Australian author, b. London; emigrated (c. 1863); member of staff of Melbourne *Argus.* Author of *For the Term of his Natural Life*, concerning Australian penal settlement, also of plays and pantomimes.

**Clarke, Mary Anne.** 1776–1852. Mistress (1803–07) of Frederick Augustus, Duke of York and Albany, 2d son of George III of England. Received bribes to secure army promotions through services of duke of York, then commander in chief, causing his resignation; imprisoned for libel (1813).

**Clarke, Mary Victoria Cowden-.** See under Charles Cowden CLARKE.

**Clarke, Rebecca Sophia.** *Pseudonym* **Sophie May** (mā). 1833–1906. American writer, b. Norridgewock, Me.; author of *Dotty Dimple Stories* (1867–69) and other juveniles.

**Clarke, Samuel.** 1675–1729. English metaphysician. B.A., Cantab. (1695); disciple of Isaac Newton; expounded Newtonian views of the universe, in refutation of prevalent Cartesian views, in notes to his translation of Jacques Rohault's *Physics* (1697). Chaplain to bishop of Norwich and to Queen Anne; opposed deists, materialists, empiricists, and freethinkers; in Boyle lectures (1704–05), answered Hobbes, Spinoza, and Blount with his famous demonstration of the existence and attributes of God; carried on controversy (1712) over the Trinity with Daniel Waterland, denying that the doctrine was held by early church; corresponded with Leibnitz (1715–16) on space and time as attributes of an infinite being.

**Clarke, Thomas Shields.** 1860–1920. American sculptor and painter, b. Pittsburgh, Pa.; educ. Princeton, École des Beaux-Arts, Paris, and in Rome and Florence. His paintings include *A Fool's Fool* (in Pennsylvania Acad.), *Night Market, Morocco* (Philadelphia Art Club); his sculpture, caryatids representing *Four Seasons* (in Appellate Court Building, New York City), *Alma Mater* (at Princeton).

**Clarke, Walter.** 1638?–1714. American colonial administrator, b. Newport, R.I.; governor of Rhode Island (1676–77; 1686, when charter was suspended by Andros; 1696–98).

**Clarke, William Branwhite.** 1798–1878. English geologist. M.A., Cantab. (1824); took sea voyage to New South Wales (1839) and remained; discovered gold (1841), tin (1849), diamonds (1859); first to determine age of Australian coal measures; discovered remains of specimen of *Dinornis* (1869).

**Clarke, William Eagle.** 1853–1938. British ornithologist, b. Leeds; keeper of natural history department, Royal Scottish Museum, Edinburgh (1906–21). Author of *Studies in Bird Migration* (2 vols., 1912); editor of 3d edition of *Saunders' British Birds* (1927).

**Clark′son** (klärk′s'n), **Matthew.** 1758–1825. American Revolutionary officer; aide-de-camp to Benedict Arnold (1778–79); on staff of Gen. Lincoln (1779–83).

**Clarkson, Thomas.** 1760–1846. English abolitionist. B.A., Cantab. (1783); led crusade against African slave trade; urged French (1789–90) and czar (1818) to abolish traffic; wrote (from 1794) pamphlets on suppression of slavery, a history of its abolition, and a memoir of William Penn.

**Claude** (klōd), **Albert.** 1899–      . Belgian biologist. At Rockefeller Institute for Medical Research (1929–49); U.S. citizen (1941); director of Institut Jules Bordet (1949–71); awarded (with Christian de Duve and George E. Palade) Nobel prize for physiology or medicine (1974).

**Claude** (klōd), **Georges.** 1870–1960. French chemist and physicist, b. Paris. Educ. École de Physique et de Chimie. Showed that acetylene dissolved in acetone can be safely transported (1897), thus giving impetus to acetylene industry; produced liquid air by expansion method (1902) and separated from it the various gases of the air; pointed out uses of neon lamps for lighting (1910), as detectors, as means for measuring the length of electromagnetic waves, etc.; invented new method for synthesis of ammonia (1917); sentenced (1945) to life imprisonment for Nazi collaboration.

**Claude, Jean.** 1619–1687. French Protestant clergyman; pastor in Paris (1666); engaged in controversy with Boussuet, Nicole, Arnaud, and others to maintain Edict of Nantes; expelled from France after revocation of Edict (1685); settled in Holland.

**Claude de France** (dē fräɴs′). *Also* **Clau′di·a** (klô′dĭ·*ȧ*). 1499–1524. Oldest daughter of Louis XII and Anne de Bretagne; m. (1514) Francis, Duc d'Angoulême, later (1515) king of France.

**Claude Lorrain** *or* **Claude Gellée** (*or* **Gelée**). See LORRAIN.

**Clau′del′** (klō′dĕl′), **Paul Louis Charles.** 1868–1955. French diplomat, poet, and dramatist. Entered diplomatic service (1892); minister to Brazil (1916), Denmark (1919); ambassador to Japan (1921), U.S. (1927). Associated with symbolist school; author of poetry, as in *Cinq Grandes Odes Suivies d'un Processionnal pour Saluer le Siècle Nouveau* (1911), *Deux Poèmes d'Été: la Cantate à Troix Voix* (1914), *Poèmes de Guerre* (1914–15), plays, as *Tête d'Or* (1890), *La Ville* (1892), *L'Otage* (1911), *Le Pain Dur* (1918), *Le Père Humilié* (1920), and the lyrical drama *Christophe Colomb* (1928; music by Milhaud).

**Clau′det′** (klō′dĕ′), **Antoine François Jean.** 1797–1867. French daguerreotypist in England. First to adopt collodion process; invented photographometer (1848), the focimeter for securing perfect focus (1849), and the stereomonoscope (1858).

**Clau′di·an** (klô′dĭ·*ă*n). *Full Latin name* **Claudius Clau′di·a′nus** (klô′dĭ·ā′n*ŭ*s). Latin poet, b. probably in Alexandria, Egypt; to Rome (c. 395 A.D.). Gained recognition by panegyrics celebrating deeds of Theodosius, Honorius, Stilicho, and others.

**Clau′di·us** (klô′dĭ·*ŭ*s). Name of two Roman emperors. **Claudius I.** *Full name* **Tiberius Claudius Drusus Nero Ger·man′i·cus** (jûr·măn′ĭ·k*ŭ*s). 10 B.C.–54 A.D. Emperor (41–54 A.D.). Second son of Drusus (Nero Claudius Drusus) and Antonia and stepgrandson of Augustus; neglected by Augustus and Tiberius. Proclaimed emperor by soldiers on death of Caligula. Married four times: third wife, at the time of his accession, Valeria Messalina, influenced him to cruelty; fourth wife (m. 49 A.D.), his niece Agrippina (*q.v.*), prevailed upon him to set aside his own son Britannicus and adopt her son Nero as heir. Carried on wars, through his generals, in Britain, Germany, Syria, and Mauretania; made the last a province (42 A.D.); built harbor at mouth of Tiber, and the Claudian aqueduct. Poisoned by Agrippina.

**Claudius II.** *Full name* **Marcus Aurelius Claudius,** *surnamed* **Goth′i·cus** (gŏth′ĭ·k*ŭ*s). 214–270. Emperor (268–270). Of an obscure Illyrian family; performed distinguished military service under Decius, Valerian, and Gallienus; as emperor won two great battles; defeated Alamanni in northern Italy (268) and the Goths near Naissus, Moesia (269); died at Sirmium.

**Claudius.** Name of a distinguished Roman gens, including: **Appius Sabinus In′reg′il·len′sis** (ĭn′rĕj′ĭ·lĕn′sĭs), *or* **Reg′il·len′sis** (rĕj′ĭ·lĕn′sĭs), **Claudius,** founder of the Claudian gens; settled in Rome (c. 504 B.C.); consul (495 B.C.); by his enforcement of laws of debt caused secession of the plebeians from Rome (494). **Appius Claudius,** *surnamed* **Cras′sus** (krăs′*ŭ*s), consul (471 B.C. and 451 B.C.); decemvir (451–450 B.C.); instituted reign of terror during which, according to a legend, he attempted to obtain for himself, by adjudging her as a slave to one of his clients, Virginia, daughter of a plebeian centurion, Virginius; forced to resign because of public resentment when Virginius stabbed his daughter to death rather than see her disgraced; imprisoned; died in prison. Subject of John Webster's play *Appius and Virginia.* **Appius Claudius,** *surnamed* **Cae′cus** (sē′k*ŭ*s), censor (312–307 B.C.); consul (307 B.C.); interrex (298); consul (296); praetor (295); and dictator; famed for many reforms giving more privileges to the plebeians; as an orator and author, credited with founding Latin prose and oratory. **Publius Claudius,** *surnamed* **Pul′cher** (pŭl′kēr), consul (249 B.C.); commanded Roman fleet against Carthaginians; disastrously defeated in harbor of Drepanum (Trapani); accused of treason and heavily fined. **Appius Claudius,** *surnamed* **Pulcher,** praetor (57 B.C.); consul (54); governor of Cilicia (53); censor (50); took Pompey's side in Civil War and was appointed to a command in Greece; died before battle of Pharsalus (48); brother of P. Clodius Pulcher (see CLODIUS).

**Clau′di·us, Mat·thi′as** (mä·tē′äs klou′dē·ōōs; *Angl.* mă·thī′ăs klô′dĭ·*ŭ*s). *Pseudonym* **As′mus** (äs′mōōs). 1740–1815. German poet; best known as lyric poet; some of his songs have become German folk songs. His great-grandson **Hermann** (1878–      ), author of verse, including *Mank Muern* (1912; in low-German dialect), *Lieder der Unruh* (1919), *Heimkehr* (1925), and novels, including *Das Silberschiff* (1922) and *Meister Bertram* (1927).

**Claudius Nero, Gaius.** See Gaius Claudius NERO.

**Claudius Tiberius Germanicus.** See BRITANNICUS.

**Claus** (klous), **Émile.** 1849–1924. Flemish impressionist painter.

**Claus** (klous), **Karl Friedrich Wilhelm.** 1835–1899. German zoologist, in Vienna and Trieste; conducted researches on invertebrates, esp. crustaceans and coelenterates.

**Clau′sel′** *or* **Clau′zel′** (klō′zĕl′), Comte **Bertrand.** 1772–1842. French soldier; a volunteer (1791), rose to general of division (1802); distinguished himself in Peninsular War (1809–12); aided Napoleon during the Hundred Days; in exile (1815–20); governor of Algeria (1830); marshal of France (1831).

**Clau′sen** (klou′s'n), Sir **George.** 1852–1944. English figure and landscape painter; professor, Royal Acad. of Art, London. His well-known paintings include *The Ploughboy, The Mowers, The Gleaners Returning,* and *Twilight.*

**Clau′se·witz** (klou′zĕ·vĭts), **Karl von.** 1780–1831.

Prussian army officer, b. in Burg. Served with Russian army (1812); staff officer with Blücher (1813); chief of staff to general Thielmann (1814–18); major general, director of Allgemeine Kriegsschule (1818). Best remembered for his books on the science of war, especially his *Vom Kriege* (3 vols., 1833).

**Clau'si·us** (klou'zē·ōōs), **Rudolf Julius Emanuel.** 1822–1888. German mathematical physicist, one of the founders of thermodynamics. Professor at Zurich (1855–67), Würzburg (1867–69), Bonn (from 1869). Enunciated second law of thermodynamics (1850); contributed to kinetic theory of gases and to theory of electrolysis.

**Claus'sen** (klou's'n), **Sophus.** 1865–1931. Danish lyric poet and novelist.

**Clauss'–Szár'va·dy** (klous'sär'vŏ·dĭ), **Wil'hel·mi'ne** (vĭl'hĕl·mē'nĕ). 1834–1907. Bohemian piano virtuoso; known for her interpretation of Chopin, Bach, and Beethoven.

**Clauzel,** Comte **Bertrand.** See CLAUSEL.

**Claver,** Saint **Peter,** *Span.* San **Pedro.** See PETER CLAVER.

**Claverhouse, John Graham of.** See John GRAHAM.

**Clavers,** Mrs. **Mary.** Pseudonym of Caroline Matilda KIRKLAND.

**Cla'vière'** (klȧ'vyâr'), **Étienne.** 1735–1793. Swiss-born French revolutionist; identified with the Girondists in the legislative assembly (1791); minister of finance (1792); on fall of the Gironde (1793), brought before Revolutionary Tribunal; committed suicide in prison.

**Cla'vi·je'ro** *or* **Cla'vi·ge'ro** (klä'vē·hā'rō), **Francisco Javier.** 1731–1787. Mexican historian, b. Vera Cruz. Lived among Mexican Indians as missionary; to Italy on expulsion of Jesuits from Mexico (1767); settled at Ferrara, later at Bologna; founded academy, Bologna. His works, published in Italian, later widely translated, include *Storia Antica del Messico* (1780) and *Storia della California* (pub. 1789).

**Cla·vi'jo** (klä·vē'hō), **Ruy González de.** See GONZÁLEZ DE CLAVIJO.

**Clavijo y Fa·jar'do** (ē fä·här'thō), **José.** 1726–1806. Spanish writer, b. in Canary Islands; published *Mercurio Histórico y Político* (1773–1806); translated Buffon's *Histoire Naturelle* (16 vols., 1791–1802). Known for his quarrel (1764) with Beaumarchais over his love affair with latter's sister; subject of Goethe's drama *Clavigo.*

**Cla'vi·us** (klä'vē·ōōs), **Christopher.** 1537–1612. Bavarian Jesuit astronomer and mathematician; carried on mathematical researches at Coimbra, Portugal; professor at Rome; appointed by Pope Gregory XIII to reform the calendar; introduced the decimal point (1593).

**Clax'ton** (klăks'tŭn), **Kate,** *nee* **Cone** (kōn). 1848–1924. American actress, b. Somerville, N.J.; m. Isadore Lyon (1865), Charles A. Stevenson (1878); best known for role of Louise, the blind girl, in *The Two Orphans.*

**Claxton, Philander Priestley.** 1862–1957. American educator, b. in Bedford Co., Tenn.; professor of education, U. of Tennessee (1902–11); U.S. commissioner of education (1911–21).

**Claxton, Thomas Folkes.** 1874–1952. English astronomer, b. London. On staff of Royal Observatory, Greenwich (1890–95); asst. director (1895–96), director (1896–1912), Royal Alfred Observatory, Mauritius; director, Royal Observatory, Hong Kong (1912–32). Published annual *Magnetic and Meteorological Observations, Mauritius* (1896–1910), and studies of climate and winds at Hong Kong.

**Clay** (klā), **Albert Tobias.** 1866–1925. American archaeologist, b. Hanover, Pa. Professor of Assyriology, Yale (1910–25). Editor of cuneiform texts.

**Clay, Bertha M.** Pseudonym under which the English author **Charlotte Monica Braeme** [brām] (1836–1884) originated a long series of novels. See Nick CARTER.

**Clay, Cassius Marcellus.** 1810–1903. American abolitionist and political campaigner, b. in Madison Co., Ky.; joined new Republican party and supported Frémont in 1856, Lincoln in 1860; U.S. minister to Russia (1861–62, 1863–69). Son of **Green Clay** (1757–1826), b. Powhatan County, Va., who raised siege of Fort Meigs (1813).

**Clay, Cassius Marcellus.** 1942– . See Muhammad ALI.

**Clay, Frederick.** 1838–1889. English musical composer, b. Paris, son of **James Clay** (1805–1873; a celebrated whist authority); wrote compositions for stage, including two with librettos by W. S. Gilbert, *Ages Ago* (1869) and *Princess Toto* (1875); friend of Sir Arthur Sullivan; composer of two cantatas, *The Knights of the Cross* (1866) and *Lalla Rookh* (1877), the latter containing "I'll sing thee songs of Araby" and quartet "Morn wanes, we must away"; last works, *The Merry Duchess* (1883) and *The Golden Ring* (1883).

**Clay, Henry.** 1777–1852. American lawyer and statesman, b. in Hanover Co., Va. Self-educated. Practiced law, Lexington, Ky. (from 1797). U.S. senator (1806–07; 1810–11). Member, U.S. House of Representatives (1811–14, 1815–21, 1823–25); speaker (same years, except 1821). Urged moderately protective tariff (1816), recognition of South American republics (1817), Missouri Compromise (1820) from which he gained nickname "Great Pacificator"; supported John Quincy Adams in presidential election of 1824, gaining nickname of "President Maker." U.S. secretary of state (1825–29). U.S. senator (1831–42); in nullification crisis, presented compromise of 1833, which prevented conflict. Whig candidate for president (1832, 1844); defeated. U.S. senator (1849–52); reached height of statesmanship by series of resolutions, known as the Compromise of 1850, by which he sought to avoid forever a civil war. Elected to American Hall of Fame (1900).

**Clay, Lucius DuBi'gnon'** (dü'bē'nyôɴ'). 1897–1978. American army officer, b. Marietta, Ga.; director of matériel, Army Service Forces (1942–44); administrator of U. S.-occupied Germany (1945–49). Wrote *Decision in Germany* (1950).

**Cla'ys** (klȧ'ĭs), **Paul Jean.** 1819–1900. Belgian painter.

**Clay'ton** (klā't'n), Sir **Gilbert Falkingham.** 1875–1929. English soldier; educ. Royal Military Acad., Woolwich. Served with Egyptian army (1900–10), Sudan government (1910–19); director of intelligence in Egypt (1914–17); chief political officer with Egyptian expeditionary force (1917–19); adviser to ministry of interior, Egypt (1919–22); chief secretary, government of Palestine (1922–25); British high commissioner in Iraq (1929).

**Clayton, Henry De Lamar.** 1857–1929. American jurist and legislator, b. in Barbour Co., Ala. A.B. (1877) and LL.B. (1878), Alabama. Practiced law, Eufaula, Ala. (1880–1914). Member, U.S. House of Representatives (1897–1915); chairman of its judiciary committee (1911–15); antitrust legislation (Clayton Antitrust Act, passed Oct. 14, 1914, to supplement Sherman Antitrust Act of 1890). U.S. district judge (1914–29).

**Clayton, Henry Helm.** 1861–1946. American meteorologist, b. Murfreesboro, Tenn. On staff of Blue Hill Meteorological Observatory (1886–91; 1894–1909); weather forecaster, Oficina Meteorologica Argentina (1913–22). Originator (1918) of forecasting based on solar heat changes. Author of *World Weather* (1923), *Solar Relations to Weather and Life* (1943), etc.

**Clayton, John.** 1685?–1773. Botanist, b. Fulham, Eng.; to Va. (1705); supplied specimens used by Gronovius in *Flora Virginica.*

**Clayton, John Middleton.** 1796–1856. American jurist,

b. Dagsborough, Del. Grad. Yale (1815). U.S. senator from Delaware (1829–36). Opposed Jackson's United States Bank policy; supported Jackson in nullification crisis; aided Clay in passing compromise tariff of 1833. Chief justice of Delaware (1837–39). U.S. senator (1845–49). U.S. secretary of state (1849–50); negotiated Clayton-Bulwer treaty with Great Britain, providing for a neutralized interoceanic canal across the American isthmus (1850). U.S. senator (1853–56). See John M. HAY.

**Clayton, Joshua.** 1744–1798. American politician, b. in Cecil County, Md. President of Delaware (1789–92); first governor of Delaware (1792–96).

**Clayton, Powell.** 1833–1914. American politician, b. in Bethel, Pa. Republican "carpetbag" governor of Arkansas (1868–71); U.S. senator (1871–77); U.S. ambassador to Mexico (1897–1905).

**Cle·an′thes** (klē·ăn′thēz). Greek Stoic philosopher, of 3d century B.C.; succeeded Zeno as head of Stoic school. Only fragments of his works extant.

**Cle·ar′chus** (klē·är′kŭs). Spartan-born professional soldier. Governor of Byzantium (408 B.C.), where his severe administration caused the people during his temporary absence to surrender the city to the Athenians. Commanded contingent of Greek mercenaries in expedition of Cyrus the Younger against Artaxerxes; handed over to Artaxerxes after battle of Cunaxa (401), and executed.

**Cleave′land** (klēv′lănd). See also CLEVELAND.

**Cleaveland, Moses.** 1754–1806. American pioneer, b. Canterbury, Conn. As official of Connecticut Land Company, sent to Western Reserve to survey and settle land bought by company; founded (1796) Cleveland, Ohio, first called Cleaveland.

**Cleaveland, Parker.** 1780–1858. American mineralogist, b. Byfield, Mass. His *Elementary Treatise on Mineralogy and Geology* (1816) first American book on this subject.

**Clebsch** (klāpsh), **Alfred,** *in full* **Rudolf Friedrich Alfred.** 1833–1872. German mathematician; professor at Giessen (1863), Göttingen (1868); contributed to theory of invariants; made applications of theory of elliptic and Abelian functions to geometry and to the study of rational and elliptic curves.

**Cle′burne** (klē′bērn), **Patrick Ronayne.** 1828–1864. Army officer, b. in County Cork, Ireland. Served in British army (1846–49); emigrated to America (1849). In Confederate army in Civil War; at Murfreesboro earned nickname of "Stonewall of the West"; framed letter, disapproved by Jefferson Davis, advising slaves be freed and enlisted as soldiers in Confederate army; killed in action.

**Cleef, Joos van.** See CLEVE.

**Cleg′horn** (klĕg′hôrn), **Sarah Norcliffe.** 1876–1959. American writer, b. Norfolk, Va.; educ. Radcliffe (1895–96); author of *A Turnpike Lady* (1907), *The Spinster* (1916), etc.

**Cleis′the·nes** (klīs′thē·nēz) *or* **Clis′the·nes** (klĭs′-). (1) **Cleisthenes of Sic′y·on** (sĭsh′ĭ·ŏn; sĭs′ĭ-), Greek tyrant of Sicyon; emphasized superiority of Ionian over Dorian elements in the people; championed Delphian oracle against city of Crisa in first Sacred War (c. 590 B.C.); founded Pythian games at Sicyon and built a Sicyonian treasury at Delphi.
(2) His grandson **Cleisthenes,** Athenian statesman, headed a democratic party which, against opposition of great landowners, put into effect reforms of Solon; expelled (507 B.C.) by Isagoras, leader of aristocratic party, but soon recalled; reputed to have established system of ostracism.

**Cleitarchus, Cleitomachus, Cleitus.** Variants of CLITARCHUS, CLITOMACHUS, CLITUS.

**Clel′and** (klĕl′ănd), **Robert Glass.** 1885–1957. American historian, b. Shelbyville, Ky.; A.B., Occidental Coll. (1907) and Princeton (1909), Ph.D., Princeton (1912); professor of history, Occidental Coll. (1912–1943). Author of *History of California, The American Period* (1922), *One Hundred Years of the Monroe Doctrine* (1923), *California Pathfinders* (1928), *The History of Occidental College* (1937). Prepared *Mexican Year Book* (1922 and 1924).

**Cleland, William.** 1661?–1689. Scottish Covenanter and poet.

**Clémanges, Nicolas de.** *Also* **Nicolas Clé′man′gis′** *or* **Clé′men′gis′** (klā′mäN′zhēs′). = NICHOLAS OF CLÉMANGES.

**Cle′men′ceau′** (klā′mäN′sō′), **Georges.** 1841–1929. French statesman; known as "the Tiger." War correspondent in U.S. with Grant's army (1865); member of Chamber of Deputies (1876–93); senator (from 1902). Premier of France (1906–09); carried out law separating church and state; used military force to end a miners' strike. Again premier (1917); led France through critical days of World War I; headed French delegation to Peace Conference at Paris (1919); retired (1920).

**Clem′ens** (klĕm′ĕnz), **Samuel Langhorne.** *Pseudonym* **Mark Twain** (märk twān). 1835–1910. American humorist, b. Florida, Mo. Resident, Hannibal, Mo. (1839–53), on Mississippi River; journeyman printer (1847–55); river pilot on Mississippi (1857–61). In Carson City, Nev., as a prospector (1861); in Virginia City, Nev., as newspaper reporter (1862), using as pseudonym *Mark Twain* (term meaning two fathoms deep, used by leadsmen taking soundings on Mississippi). Encouraged in his writing by Charles Farrar Browne ("Artemus Ward"); went to California (1864). Published first great success *The Jumping Frog of Calaveras County* (1865) and first book *The Celebrated Jumping Frog of Calaveras County, and Other Sketches* (1867); successful also on lecture platform. From an excursion to Mediterranean and Holy Land obtained material for *The Innocents Abroad* (1869). At height of powers during next twenty years, wrote: *Roughing It* (1872), *The Gilded Age* (with Charles Dudley Warner; 1873), *The Adventures of Tom Sawyer* (1876), *A Tramp Abroad* (1880), *The Stolen White Elephant* (1882), *The Prince and the Pauper* (1882), *Life on the Mississippi* (1883), *Adventures of Huckleberry Finn* (1885), *A Connecticut Yankee At King Arthur's Court* (1889). From peak reached in *Tom Sawyer* and *Huckleberry Finn* his later works show a decline. Involved in failure of publishing house of Charles L. Webster & Co. (1896), took to lecture stage to clear his obligations, and continued writing. In some of his later works, *What is Man?* (1906), and *The Mysterious Stranger* (not publ. until 1916), showed vein of bitterness not evident theretofore. Other works: *The American Claimant* (1892), *The £1,000,000 Bank Note* (1893), *The Tragedy of Pudd'nhead Wilson* (1894), *Tom Sawyer Abroad* (1894), *Tom Sawyer, Detective* (1896), *Personal Recollections of Joan of Arc* (1896), *Following the Equator* (1897), *The Man That Corrupted Hadleyburg* (1900), *Eve's Diary* (1906), *The $30,000 Bequest* (1906). Elected to American Hall of Fame (1920). See Isaiah SELLERS; Ossip GABRILÓWITSCH.

**Clem′ens Al′ex·an·dri′nus** (klĕm′ĕnz [klē′mĕnz] ăl′ĕg·zăn·drī′nŭs [ăl′ĭg-]). = CLEMENT OF ALEXANDRIA.

**Clem′ent** (klĕm′ĕnt). Name of fourteen popes (see *Table of Popes*, Nos. 4, 149, 174, 183, 195, 198, 221, 233, 240, 241, 245, 248, 250, 251) and three antipopes, especially:

**Clement I.** Saint. *Also* **Clem'ens Ro·ma'nus** (klĕm'ĕnz [klē'mĕnz] rō·mā'nŭs). 30?–?100. Pope (bishop of Rome; 90?–?99; according to some, 88?–?97); first of the Apostolic Fathers; author of *Epistle to the Corinthians* (95 or 96), one of the most valuable works of the early church; probably died in exile.

**Clement III.** *Real name* **Paolo Sco·la'ri** (skō·lä'rē). d. 1191. Pope (1187–91). Preached Third Crusade; made Scottish church dependent on Rome.

**Clement IV.** *Real name* **Guy Foulques** (gē fōōlk) *or* **Gui'do le Gros** (gwē'dō lẽ grō'). d. 1268. Pope (1265–68), b. Saint-Gilles, France; held office at court of Louis IX; cardinal (1262); papal legate to England when elected pope; favored Charles of Anjou against Manfred in struggle for Naples; befriended Roger Bacon; died at Viterbo.

**Clement V.** *Real name* **Bertrand de Got** (dẽ gō). 1264–1314. Pope (1305–14), b. near Bordeaux, France; friend of King Philip the Fair, at whose request papal residence removed from Rome to Avignon (1309); suppressed Order of Templars (1312).

**Clement VI.** *Real name* **Pierre Ro'ger'** (rō'zhā'). 1291–1352. Pope (1342–52), b. near Limoges, France; as pope, resided at Avignon and refused to return to Rome; purchased (1348) Avignon for papacy; excommunicated Emperor Louis of Bavaria.

**Clement VII.** *Real name* **Giulio de' Me'di·ci** (dā mā'dē·chē; *Angl.* mĕd'ĭ-, mā'dē-). 1478–1534. Pope (1523–34), b. Florence; natural son of Giuliano de' Medici (see MEDICI); cousin of Pope Leo X. Cardinal (1513); entered league (Holy League of Cognac; 1526) with France, Venice, and Milan against Charles V; taken prisoner on sack of Rome by Constable Bourbon and imperial troops (1527); fled to Orvieto on release, but returned to Rome (1528); made peace with Charles and crowned him emperor at Bologna (1530); quarreled with England and refused (1534) to sanction divorce of Henry VIII from Catherine of Aragon.

**Clement VIII.** *Real name* **Ippolito Al'do·bran·di'ni** (äl'dō·brän·dē'nē). 1536–1605. Pope (1592–1605), b. Fano, Italy. Pious and scholarly; ordered revisions of the Vulgate, breviary, and liturgical books; revision of Vulgate (called the *Clementine;* issued 1592) has been standard Bible text of Roman Catholic Church for more than 300 years; annexed lands of house of Este to States of the Church; occupied in last years with controversy between Jesuits and Dominicans on question of grace.

**Clement IX.** *Real name* **Giulio Ro'spi·glio'si** (rō'spē·lyō'sē). 1600–1669. Pope (1667–69), b. Pistoia; mediated (1668) peace of Aix-la-Chapelle between Louis XIV and Spain; suppressed Jesuate order (1668); temporarily closed Jansenist controversy.

**Clement XI.** *Real name* **Giovanni Francesco Al·ba'ni** (äl·bä'nē). 1649–1721. Pope (1700–1721), b. Urbino; involved (1701–13) in European political disputes in connection with War of Spanish Succession, esp. (1708–09) with Emperor Joseph I; published bulls against Jansenist writings, as *Vineam Domini* (1705) and *Unigenitus* (1713).

**Clement XIII.** *Real name* **Carlo del'la Tor're Rez·zo'ni·co** (dāl'lä tōr'rā rād·dzō'nē·kō). 1693–1769. Pope (1758–69), b. Venice; elected through influence of Jesuits; issued bulls opposing demands for suppression of Society of Jesus.

**Clement XIV.** *Real name* **Giovanni Vincenzo Antonio Gan'ga·nel'li** (gäng'gä·nĕl'lē). 1705–1774. Pope (1769–74), b. at Sant' Arcangelo di Romagna; cardinal (1759); tried to keep peace with Roman Catholic princes; issued (1773) apostolic brief suppressing Jesuit order; founded Clementine Museum at the Vatican.

*Antipopes:* **Clement III;** *real name* **Gui'bert'** (gē'bâr') **of Ravenna** (1030?–1100); antipope (1080, 1084–1100) in time of Popes Gregory VII, Victor III, Urban II, and Paschal II; elected through influence of Emperor Henry IV. **Clement VII;** *real name* **Robert of Geneva** (1342?–1394); antipope (1378–94); elected in opposition to Urban VI; resided at Avignon; first antipope of the Western Schism. **Clement VIII;** *real name* **Gil Sán'chez Mu·ñoz'** [hēl sän'chāth mōō-nyōth'] (1380?–1446); antipope (1424?–29) in opposition to Martin V.

**Clé'ment'** (klā'mäN'), **Frédéric Jean Edmond.** 1867–1928. French tenor in light opera, at Opéra Comique in Paris and Théâtre de la Monnaie in Brussels.

**Clément, Jacques.** *Latin nickname* **Clem'ens non Pa'pa** (klĕm'ĕnz [klē'mĕnz] nŏn pā'pȧ), *i.e.* "Clement not pope": *to distinguish him from Pope Clement VII.* c. 1510–before 1556. Flemish composer of masses, motets, psalms, and songs; known as master of counterpoint.

**Clément, Jacques.** 1567?–1589. Fanatic Jacobin monk (a Dominican friar), murderer of King Henry III of France (1589).

**Clément, Jacques Alfred Félix.** 1822–1885. French musician; organist, church of the Sorbonne, Paris. Author of many treatises on music.

**Clem'ent** (klĕm'ĕnt) **of Alexandria.** *Full name* **Titus Flavius Clem'ens** (klĕm'ĕnz; klē'mĕnz). 150?–?220 A.D. Greek theologian of early Christian church; a father of the church; b. probably in Athens. Studied in Christian school in Alexandria; entered church; head of catechetical school in Alexandria (190–203 A.D.), which, by his teaching and that of his pupil Origen, became one of famous contemporary centers of learning; left Alexandria during persecutions of Christians (c. 203 A.D.). Regarded as a founder of the Alexandrian school of theology. His works include *Exhortation to the Greeks, The Tutor* (3 books), *The Stromateis* (transl. as *Miscellanies,* 8 books), *Who Is the Rich Man That Shall Be Saved?*

**Clé'men'tel'** (klā'mäN'tĕl'), **Étienne.** 1864–1936. French statesman; minister of colonies (1905; 1906), agriculture (1913), finance (1914; 1924), commerce and national economy (1916–20); elected senator (1920).

**Cle·men'ti** (klā·mĕn'tē), **Muzio.** 1752–1832. Italian pianist and composer; resident in England most of life; made many concert tours to the Continent; a leader in modern school of piano technique. Composer of symphonies, sonatas, and a series of piano studies under title *Gradus ad Parnassum* (1817).

**Clem'ents** (klĕm'ĕnts), **Frederic Edward.** 1874–1945. American plant ecologist, b. Lincoln, Nebraska. B.S. (1894), Ph.D. (1898), Nebraska. Professor and head of department of botany, Minnesota (1907–17); associate in charge of ecological research, Carnegie Institution, Washington (from 1917); collaborator, U.S. soil-conservation service (from 1934).

His wife (m. 1899) **Edith,** *nee* **Schwartz** (shwôrts), b. Albany, N.Y.; B.A. (1898), Ph.D. (1906), Nebraska; instructor in botany, Minnesota (1909–13); investigator and illustrator, Carnegie Institution, Washington, D.C. (from 1918).

**Clemmer, Mary.** See Mary Clemmer AMES.

**Clem'son** (klĕm's'n), **Thomas Green.** 1807–1888. American mining engineer, b. Philadelphia; left fortune to State of South Carolina for founding of college (Clemson College; chartered 1889, opened 1893).

**Clen·den'ing** (klĕn·dĕn'ĭng), **Logan.** 1884–1945. American physician and author, b. Kansas City, Mo. M.D., Kansas (1907); began practice in Kansas City. Author of *Modern Methods of Treatment* (1924), *The Human Body* (1927), *The Care and Feeding of Adults* (1931), *Behind the Doctor* (1933).

**Cle'o·bu'lus** (klē'ō·bū'lŭs). Greek sage of 6th century B.C., one of the Seven Wise Men of Greece.

**Cle·om'bro·tus** (klē·ŏm'brō·tŭs). Name of two kings of Sparta: **Cleombrotus I,** king (380–371 B.C.); waged war against Thebes; defeated and killed at battle of Leuctra. **Cleombrotus II,** king (242–240 B.C.).

**Cle'o·me'des** (klē'ō·mē'dēz). Greek astronomer of 1st century A.D. (or later); author of *The Circular Theory of the Heavenly Bodies.*

**Cle·om'e·nes** (klē·ŏm'ē·nēz). Name of three kings of Sparta: **Cleomenes I,** king (c. 519–491 B.C.); defeated the Argives and won for Sparta undisputed domination of Peloponnesus; aided aristocratic party in Athens in expelling Cleisthenes (*q.v.*) but failed to make Isagoras tyrant of city; forced to flee from Sparta (491 B.C.) when his bribery of Delphian priestesses discovered; committed suicide (c. 488). **Cleomenes II,** king (370–309 B.C.). **Cleomenes III,** king (235–219 B.C.); tried to institute social reforms, including redistribution of land, remission of debts, restoration of earlier training system, and admission of selected Perioeci to Spartan citizenship; warred successfully against the Achaeans, but finally defeated at Sellasia (222 or 221 B.C.) by an alliance including Macedonia; fled to Alexandria; committed suicide.

**Cleomenes.** Athenian sculptor whose signature carved on the base of the Venus de' Medici is regarded as a modern forgery.

**Cle'on** (klē'ŏn). Athenian demagogue; became leader of democratic party, opposed Nicias, and demanded continuation of Peloponnesian War; led successful expedition against Sparta (425 B.C.); defeated and killed in battle of Amphipolis (422).

**Cle'o·pa'tra** (klē'ō·pā'trȧ; -pä'trȧ; -păt'rȧ). Name of several queens and princesses of the Ptolemies of Egypt. For Queens **Cleopatra I–VI,** see PTOLEMY V–XII. **Cleopatra VII** (*or* **VI**). 69–30 B.C. Daughter of Ptolemy XII Auletes. Queen (51–49, 48–30 B.C.). By will of her father, became joint ruler (51–49) with her brother Ptolemy XIII (who was also her husband); driven out by him (49); supported by Julius Caesar, who defeated Ptolemy (who drowned during flight). Relinquished actual government of kingdom to younger brother, Ptolemy XIV (whom she had married); became Caesar's mistress; lived with him in Rome (46–44). Returned to Egypt (44); murdered Ptolemy XIV to make room for her son Cesarion as her associate on the throne. After Philippi (42), met Antony in Cilicia, appearing as Aphrodite in a vessel magnificently adorned and with a splendid retinue; won Antony's love; bore him twin children, Alexander Helios and Cleopatra Selene (*q.v.*); deserted by Antony (40) but joined him at Antioch (36–34) where he was in command against the Parthians; lived with Antony in Egypt (32–31); with him at Actium (31), but withdrew her fleet and fled to Alexandria; could not influence Octavianus and killed herself, probably with poison (legend says by an asp), on learning that he intended to exhibit her in his triumph at Rome.

**Cleopatra Se·le'ne** (sē·lē'nē). (1) = CLEOPATRA V (see under PTOLEMY IX). (2) Daughter of Cleopatra VII and Antony (b. 40 B.C.); m. Juba II, King of Numidia; their son Ptolemy (*q.v.*), last of dynastic line, slain by Caligula.

**Cleopatra The'a** (thē'ȧ). d. 121 B.C. Queen of Syria. Daughter of Ptolemy VI Philometor; m. 1st (?150 B.C.) Alexander Balas, by whom she was mother of Antiochus VI; m. 2d Demetrius II Nicator, by whom she was mother of Seleucus V and Antiochus VIII Grypus; administered kingdom during campaign of Demetrius in Parthia; after his capture and marriage with Rodogune, daughter of Mithridates I of Parthia, m. as third husband Antiochus VII Euergetes; joint ruler as regent for her son Antiochus VIII (125–121 B.C.), by whom, according to legend, she was poisoned.

**Cle'o·phon** (klē'ō·fŏn). d. 405 B.C. Athenian politician; leader of democratic party after Cleon following Cleon's policy of demanding continued prosecution of war against Sparta; executed (405 B.C.) by Athenian council while Athens was besieged by Lysander.

**Cle·os'tra·tus** (klē·ŏs'trȧ·tŭs). Greek astronomer of 5th century B.C.; reputed to have arranged the signs of the zodiac.

**Clerc** (klâr), **Laurent.** 1785–1869. Educator of the deaf, b. near Lyons, France; deaf from infancy; educ. at deaf and dumb institute, Paris; to America (1816) with Dr. T. H. Gallaudet; founded (1817), at Hartford, Conn., school now called American School for the Deaf; taught there (1817–58).

**Cler'fayt'** *or* **Clair'fayt'** (klĕr'fĕ'), Count **von. Charles de Croix** (dē krwä'). 1733–1798. Austrian general; served in Seven Years' War (1756–63), Turkish War (1788–91); defeated Jourdan at Höchst and Mainz (1795), concluding armistice with the French.

**Cler'get'** (klĕr'zhĕ'), **Pierre.** 1875–1943. French engineer; pioneer in designing light motors for airplanes (from 1895); best-known invention the rotary motor (1910); later, constructed successful Diesel engines for airplanes.

**Clericus, Johannes.** See Jean LE CLERC.

**Clérigo, El.** See Juan de las ROELAS.

**Clerk** (klärk), Sir **Dugald.** 1854–1932. Scottish engineer; authority on internal-combustion engines; inventor of Clerk cycle gas engine (1877); author of *The Gas and Oil Engine,* etc.

**Clerk, John.** d. 1541. English prelate; chaplain and agent of Wolsey; bishop of Bath and Wells (1523); tried to get papacy for Wolsey (1523).

**Clerk** of Pen'i·cuik (pĕn'ĭ·kŏŏk), Sir **John.** 1684–1755. Scottish antiquary; left memoirs of historical value. His seventh son, **John Clerk** of El'din [ĕl'dĭn] (1728–1812), merchant in Edinburgh; practiced etching; studied geology; devised a new maneuver in naval tactics for breaking an enemy line; wrote *Essay on Naval Tactics* (1790, 1797).

**Clerke** (klärk), **Agnes Mary.** 1842–1907. British astronomer, b. in Ireland; lived in Italy (1867–77); won Actonian prize (1893). Author of *A Popular History of Astronomy in the 19th Century* (1885), *The System of the Stars* (1890), *Problems in Astrophysics* (1903).

**Clerke, Charles.** 1741–1779. British navigator and naval officer; master's mate and lieutenant of *Endeavour* on Captain Cook's first voyage (1768–71); second lieutenant of *Resolution* on Cook's second voyage (1772–75); appointed (1776) captain of *Discovery* on Cook's third voyage; succeeded at Cook's death to command of expedition, but died shortly thereafter.

**Clerk-Maxwell, James.** = James Clerk MAXWELL.

**Cler'mont'** (klĕr'môN'), Count of. **Robert de France.** See BOURBON.

**Cler'mont'-Gan'neau'** (-gȧ'nō'), **Charles.** 1846–1923. French Orientalist; most of his work appeared in volumes of *Études d'Archéologie Orientale.* Exposed a number of archaeological frauds, including the forgeries of Hebrew texts offered (1883) to British Museum by M. W. Shapira, and the supposedly antique "tiara of Saïtapharnes."

**Cler′mont′-Ton′nerre′** (-tô′nâr′), Comte **Stanislas Marie Adélaïde de.** 1757–1792. French nobleman and politician; deputy of nobility in States-General (1789).

**Cléron.** See Comte d'HAUSSONVILLE.

**Cle′ry** (klēr′ĭ), Sir **Cornelius Francis.** 1838–1926. British soldier, b. Cork, Ireland. Author of *Minor Tactics* (1875), long used as military textbook. Major general (1894); commanded 2d division in Boer War (1899–1900) through campaign ending in relief of Ladysmith.

**Clé′sin′ger′** (klā′zăN′zhâr′), **Jean Baptiste.** 1814–1883. French sculptor.

**Cletus.** See Saint ANACLETUS.

**Cle′ve** (klā′vĕ) *or* **Cleef** (klāf), **Joos van.** *Also* **Joos van der Be′ke** (vän dēr bā′kĕ). d. 1540. Flemish painter; worked in Antwerp (from c. 1511); generally identified with "the master of the death of Mary," painter of two pictures on this subject in Cologne and Munich museums. His son **Cornelis** (1520–1567), portrait painter, died insane in England.

**Cle′ve** (klā′vĕ), **Per Teodor.** 1840–1905. Swedish chemist; known esp. for work on metallic ammonium compounds and rare-earth metals; discovered the element holmium (1879).

**Cleve′land** (klēv′lănd), Duchess of. See Barbara VILLIERS.

**Cleve′land** *or* **Cleive′land** (klēv′lănd), **John.** 1613–1658. English cavalier poet. Author of mostly satirical poems valued by contemporaries above Milton's, including: *Smectymnuus, or the Club Divines; Rupertismus;* and *The Rebel Scot.*

**Cleveland, Stephen Grover.** 1837–1908. Twenty-second and twenty-fourth president of the United States, b. Caldwell, N.J. Practiced law, Buffalo, N.Y. (from 1859). Mayor of Buffalo (1881–82); reformed city administration. Governor of New York (1883–85). Democratic president of the United States (1885–89); supported civil service reform and a lower tariff; blocked undeserved Civil War pensions. Democratic candidate for presidency (1888); defeated by Benjamin Harrison. Elected president (1892); served (1893–97); opposed currency inflation and caused repeal of Sherman Silver Purchase Act of 1890; favored tariff reduction; when Pullman strikers in Chicago interfered with movement of mail, sent U.S. troops to intervene; took strong stand against use of force by British in their boundary dispute with Venezuela. Lived in Princeton, N.J. (1897–1908). Elected to American Hall of Fame (1935).

**Clev′en·ger** (klĕv′ĕn·jēr), **Shobal Vail.** 1812–1843. American sculptor, b. near Middletown, Ohio; executed busts of Henry Clay, Edward Everett, Daniel Webster, etc. His son **Shobal Vail** (1843–1920) was a psychiatrist.

**Cleves** (klēvz). *Fr.* **Clèves** (klâv). *Ger.* **Kle′ve** (klā′vĕ). A medieval German duchy and its ruling house. Members include: (1) **Mary of Cleves,** *Fr.* **Marie de Clèves** (1426–1487); grandniece of Philip the Good, of Burgundy; m. (1441) Charles, Duc d'Orléans (see ORLÉANS). (2) Anne of Cleves (*q.v.*).

**Clews** (klōōz), **Henry.** 1834–1923. Banker, b. in Staffordshire, Eng.; to New York (c. 1850); in banking and brokerage business (from c. 1858); one of agents of U.S. government in marketing of bonds to finance Civil War.

**Cli′burn** (klī′bērn), **Van.** *In Full* **Harvey Lavan Cliburn, Jr.** 1934– . Am. pianist, b. La. Winner, International Tschaikovsky Piano Competition (1958).

**Clic′quot′** (klē′kō′), **François Henri.** 1728–1791. French organ manufacturer.

**Clif′ford** (klĭf′ērd). *Orig.* **de Clifford.** Name of an English family and barony comprising descendants of **Walter de Clifford** (d. 1190?), who acquired estates in western Herefordshire, taking his surname from Clifford Castle, and whose daughter **Rosamund Clifford** (d. 1176?), known as "Fair Rosamund," was mistress of Henry II. Members of the family include:

BARONS OF WEST′MOR·LAND (wĕs(t)′mēr·lănd):

**Robert de Clifford** (1273–1314), 5th Baron Clifford, 1st Baron of Westmorland; soldier and judge; warden of marches (1297); fought Scots, distinguished himself at siege of Caerlaverock Castle (1300); fought against Piers Gaveston; killed at Bannockburn.

**John de Clifford** (1435?–1461), 9th Baron of Westmorland; called "the Butcher" because of his cruelty in fighting for Henry VI in Wars of the Roses; murdered Edmund, son of 3d duke of York, as mentioned in Shakespeare's *King Henry VI;* killed at Ferrybridge.

**Henry de Clifford** (1455?–1523), 10th Baron of Westmorland, 1st Baron **Ves′ci** (vĕs′ĭ); called "the Shepherd Lord" from living in disguise as a shepherd before restoration (1485) to titles and estates of his father, 9th baron; subject of Wordsworth's poems *The White Doe of Rylstone* and *Brougham Castle.*

EARLS OF CUM′BER·LAND (kŭm′bēr·lănd):

**Henry de Clifford** (1493–1542), 1st Earl of Cumberland (cr. 1525), 11th Baron of Westmorland; son of 10th baron; in constant service against Scots; remained loyal and was besieged by insurgents in Skipton Castle (1536).

**George de Clifford** (1558–1605), 3d earl; grandson of 1st earl; M.A., Cantab. (1576); wasted estates in gambling; commanded ship against Spanish Armada (1588); fitted out ten privateering expeditions against Spanish (1586–98). His daughter **Anne Clifford** (1590–1676), Countess of Dorset, Pembroke, and Montgomery; engaged in lawsuit over estates of her father (to 1617); educ. by poet Samuel Daniel; m. (1609) Richard Sackville, Earl of Dorset; m. (1630) Philip Herbert, Earl of Pembroke and Montgomery (see HERBERT family); restored or rebuilt several castles and churches.

**Henry Clifford** (1591–1643), 5th earl; B.A., Oxon. (1609); supported Charles I through wars with Scots and in Yorkshire in civil war (1642–43).

BARONS CLIFFORD OF CHUD′LEIGH [chŭd′lĭ] (cadet branch in Devonshire):

**Thomas Clifford** (1630–1673), 1st baron (cr. 1672); educ. Oxford; commissioner for care of wounded and sick prisoners in Dutch war (1664); confidant of Arlington and member of the Cabal; served with fleet (1665–66); an ardent Roman Catholic, favored Charles II's design to establish Romanism and absolute government in England (1669); intrigued in France against Triple Alliance; as acting principal secretary of state (1672), chiefly responsible for stop of exchequer payments and Declaration of Indulgence (1672); lord treasurer.

**William Hugh Clifford** (1858–1943), 10th baron; lived in New Zealand (1876–90) and Tasmania (till 1916); authority on radiology; made visible ultraviolet and infrared rays; author of *The Portal of Evolution* (1922), *Light Rays: What They Are and How They Cure.*

Sir **Bede Edmund Hugh Clifford** (1890–1969), colonial governor; youngest son of 10th baron; military secretary to governor general of Australia (1919–20) and to governor general of South Africa (1921–24); imperial secretary, Union of South Africa; governor of Bahamas (1932–37), of Mauritius (1937–42), of Trinidad (1942–47).

Sir **Hugh Clifford** (1866–1941), colonial administrator; grandson of 7th baron; entered Malay Straits civil service (1883); governor's agent, afterwards resident, at Pahang (1887–99, 1901); colonial secretary at Trinidad (1903), Ceylon (1907); governor of Gold Coast (1912), Nigeria (1919), Ceylon (1925–27), Straits Settlements (1927–29). Author of stories of Malayan Peninsula, including *Studies in Brown Humanity* (1898), *Bush-*

*Whacking* (1901), *Malayan Monochromes* (1913), *A Prince of Malaya* (1926); joint author with Sir Frank Swettenham of *Dictionary of the Malay Language*. See also Lady CLIFFORD.

**Clifford, Clark McAdams.** 1906– American lawyer; b. Fort Scott, Kansas; U.S. secretary of defense (1968–69).

**Clifford,** Lady. *Nee* **Elizabeth Lydia Rosabelle Bon′ham** (bŏn′ăm). d. 1945. Mrs. **de la Pas·ture** (dĕ lăp′ȧ·tẽr). English novelist and playwright; m. 1st Henry de la Pasture (d. 1908), 2d (1910) Sir Hugh Clifford (*q.v.*, under CLIFFORD family); mother of Elizabeth Dashwood (*q.v.*). Author of *The Little Squire* (1894), *The Lonely Lady of Grosvenor Square* (1907), *Erica* (1912), *Michael Ferrys* (1913); her plays, *The Lonely Millionaires* (1906), *Her Grace the Reformer* (1907), etc.

**Clifford, John.** 1836–1923. English Baptist clergyman, b. in Derbyshire. Pastor of Praed Street Baptist Church, Paddington, London (from 1858). Exercised wide influence in directing church thought toward contemporary social problems. First president, Baptist World Alliance (1905–11).

**Clifford, Nathan.** 1803–1881. American jurist, b. Rumney, N.H. Member, U.S. House of Representatives (1839–43); U.S. attorney general (1846–48); associate justice, U.S. Supreme Court (1858–81).

**Clifford, William Kingdon.** 1845–1879. English mathematician and metaphysician. Fellow, Trinity Coll., Cambridge (1868); professor of applied mathematics, University Coll., London (1871–79); in his lectures and treatises, including *Elements of Dynamic* (1879–87), explained consciousness as built of "mind-stuff," and conscience and moral law as development in each individual of a "self," hence the "tribal self." His wife (m. 1875), **Lucy,** *nee* **Lane** (d. 1929), a Barbadian; novelist and dramatist; author of *Mrs. Keith's Crime* (1885), *Aunt Anne* (1893), *Woodside Farm* (1902), *The House in Marylebone* (1917), *Miss Fingal* (1919); her plays, *A Long Duel* (1901), *A Woman Alone* (1914), etc.

**Cline′dinst** (klīn′dĭnst), **Benjamin West.** 1860–1931. American genre and portrait painter, and illustrator, b. Woodstock, Va. Studied under Cabanel and Bonnat. Painted portraits of Theodore Roosevelt, Admiral Peary; illustrated books of Hawthorne, Stevenson, Cable, Bret Harte, Mark Twain, etc.

**Clin′ton** (klĭn′t'n; -tŭn). Family name of earls of LINCOLN (from 1572) and (from 1756) of dukes of NEWCASTLE.

**Clinton, DeWitt.** 1769–1828. American lawyer and statesman, b. Little Britain, N.Y. Grad. Columbia (1786). Secretary to his uncle, Governor George Clinton (1790–95). Member, New York Assembly (1798); New York Senate (1798–1802; 1806–11). U.S. senator (1802–03). Mayor of New York City (1803–07, 1810, 1811, 1813, 1814–15). Candidate of Peace party for president of the United States (1812); defeated by Madison. Governor of New York (1817–21; 1825–28). His father, **James** (1733–1812), b. Little Britain, N.Y.; brigadier general in Revolutionary army (from 1776); with Gen. John Sullivan led successful punitive expedition against Indians in Pennsylvania and New York (1779). James's brother **George** (1739–1812), lawyer and statesman; member, Continental Congress (1775–76); brigadier general (1777); governor of New York (1777–95; 1801–04); vice-president of the United States (1805–12).

**Clinton, George.** 1686?–1761. Colonial governor in America, b. in England; son of 6th earl of Lincoln. In British navy, from 1708, rising to rank of admiral; governor of Newfoundland (1732–41), of New York (appointed 1741; served 1743–53). Father of Sir Henry Clinton (*q.v.*).

**Clinton,** Sir **Henry.** 1738?–1795. English soldier, b. in Newfoundland, of which his father, Admiral George Clinton (*q.v.*), was governor. Served in New York militia, Coldstream Guards, as aide-de-camp in Germany in Seven Years' War (1760–62); fought in battles of Bunker Hill and Long Island; succeeded Sir William Howe as commander in chief in North America (1778); captured Charleston (1780); quarreled with Cornwallis, second in command; resigned (1781); general (1793); died while governor of Gibraltar. His elder son, Sir **William Henry** (1769–1846), became a general (1830). His younger son, Sir **Henry,** the younger (1771–1829), fought with Prussians in Holland (1789); major general (1810); divisional commander under Wellington in Peninsular War (1811–14) and at Waterloo (1815); lieutenant general.

**Clinton, Henry Fynes.** 1781–1852. English chronologist. M.A., Oxon. (1805); M.P. (1806–26); published civil and literary chronologies of Greece (1824–34) and Rome (1845–50).

**Clis′son′** (klē′sôɴ′), **Olivier de.** 1336–1407. French soldier; in service of Du Guesclin (from 1370); constable of France (1380); after death (1399) of Duke John IV of Brittany, became protector of the duchy and guardian of the young princes.

**Clisthenes.** Variant of CLEISTHENES.

**Cli·tar′chus** (klī·tär′kŭs). Greek historian, of late 4th century B.C.; author of a history of Alexander the Great, extant in fragments.

**Cli·tom′a·chus** (klī·tŏm′ȧ·kŭs). Greek philosopher, orig. from Carthage; settled in Athens, and studied under Carneades, whom he succeeded (129 B.C.) as head of the New, or Third, Academy. Little of his work is extant.

**Cli′tus** (klī′tŭs). Name of two of Alexander's commanders. (1) **Clitus,** known as "the Black"; saved Alexander's life at the passage of the Granicus (334 B.C.); killed by Alexander in a drunken rage, when at a banquet (328) he criticized Alexander and extolled the simplicity and accomplishments of Philip of Macedon. (2) **Clitus,** known as "the White"; accompanied Alexander in his expedition to the East, but sent back to a Macedonian command (324); commanded Macedonian fleet in successful war against Lamia (322 B.C.); defeated by Antigonus and killed (318 B.C.).

**Clive** (klīv), **Caroline,** *nee* **Mey′sey-Wig′ley** (?mā′zĭ-wĭg′lĭ). 1801–1873. English writer of verses and novels (1840–72), including *Paul Ferroll* (1855) and *Why Paul Ferroll Killed his Wife* (1860).

**Clive, Kitty,** *properly* **Catherine,** *nee* **Raf′tor** (răf′tẽr). 1711–1785. British actress of Irish extraction. Played under manager Colley Cibber at Drury Lane, London (1728–41); m. (1731?) George Clive, barrister, relative of Robert Clive; won recognition as comedy actress (1731) in *The Devil to Pay;* an original member of Garrick's company, Drury Lane (1746–69).

**Clive, Robert.** Baron **Clive of Plas′sey** (plăs′ĭ). 1725–1774. British soldier and founder of the empire of British India. Son of a Shropshire squire; sent to Madras (1743) as a writer in East India Company; captured by French, escaped to Fort St. David (1746); took part in fruitless siege of Pondichéry (1748); allowed to make his proposed daring dash to seize Arcot, capital of the Carnatic (1751); held citadel eleven weeks with small force of Englishmen and Sepoys until relieved; captured other French strongholds. Married (1753) Margaret Maskelyne, sister of Nevil Maskelyne, astronomer; returned to England. Again in India (1755) as governor of Fort

St. David; reduced pirate stronghold of Gheriah (1756); sent to avenge atrocity of Black Hole of Calcutta; recovered Calcutta; took French settlement Chandernagor; tricked Hindu merchant Omichund, go-between in negotiations with Mir Jafar; after great victory over treacherous nawab of Bengal at Plassey (1757), installed Mir Jafar as nawab, accepting from him a large present and the quit-rent of the company's territory; virtual ruler of Bengal; repulsed Dutch colonizing attempt (1759). Returned to England (1760); entered Parliament (1760–74); raised to Irish peerage as Baron Clive of Plassey (1762). Sent out (1764) as governor and commander in chief of Bengal to right the disorder and corruption grown up in his absence; reformed civil service; restored military discipline; obtained for East India Company sovereignty over whole province, founding empire of British India; from legacy left him by Mir Jafar, set up pension fund for disabled soldiers. Returned to England (1767) in shattered health to meet storm of obloquy, parliamentary inquiries; victim of opium, committed suicide.

**Clodd** (klŏd), **Edward.** 1840–1930. English banker and miscellaneous writer, b. Margate; on staff of London Joint-Stock Bank, Ltd. (1862–1915). Author of *The Childhood of the World* (1872), *Jesus of Nazareth* (1880), *Myths and Dreams* (1885), *Animism: or the Seed of Religion* (1906), *Magic in Names* (1920), etc.

**Clo′dion′** (klô′dyôN′). *Real name* **Claude Mi′chel′** (mē′shĕl′). 1738–1814. French sculptor; known esp. for statuettes and small bas-reliefs, in marble or terra cotta, of nymphs, fauns, children dancing etc.

**Clo′di·us** (klō′dĭ·ŭs). Variant of CLAUDIUS.

**Clodius** *or less often* **Clau′di·us** (klô′dĭ·ŭs), **Publius.** *Surnamed* **Pul′cher** (pŭl′kẽr). 93?–52 B.C. Roman politician; brother of Appius Claudius Pulcher (see CLAUDIUS). Quaestor in Sicily (61 B.C.); tribune of the people in Rome (59); m. Fulvia. As bitter opponent of Cicero, exiled and his property confiscated; pandered to wishes of the mob in Rome and for a time was master of the city. Killed (Jan. 20, 52) in a street brawl during an election.

**Clodoald,** Saint. See CLOUD.

**Clodt′-Jür′gens·burg** (klōt′yür′gĕns·bŏŏrk), Baron **Pëtr Karlovich.** 1805–1867. Russian sculptor; known esp. as sculptor of horses, as in quadriga group on triumphal arch in St. Petersburg.

**Cloe′te** (klōō′tē), **Stuart,** *in full* **Edward Fairly Stuart Graham.** 1897– . South African novelist, b. Paris, France; served in World War (1914–18); farmer in South Africa (1925–35). Author of *The Turning Wheels* (1937), *Watch for the Dawn* (1939), *The Hill of Doves* (1941), etc.

**Cloots** (klōts), Baron **de. Jean Baptiste du Val′-de-Grâce′** (dü vȧl′dĕ·gräs′). *Known as* **An′a·char′sis** (ăn′ȧ·kär′sĭs; *Fr.* ȧ′nȧ′kȧr′sēs′) **Cloots.** 1755–1794. Revolutionary fanatic of Prussian extraction; settled in Paris (1776); published, under pseudonym of **Ali Gier-Ber,** *La Certitude des Preuves du Mahométisme* (1780). Elected to National Convention; styled himself "Orator of the Human Race"; one of initiators of "Worship of Reason"; guillotined with followers of Hébert (Mar. 24, 1794).

**Clopinel, Jean** *or* **Jehan.** See JEAN DE MEUNG.

**Clop′ton** (klŏp′tŭn), Sir **Hugh.** d. 1496. Lord Mayor of London (1492) and builder (1483) at Stratford-on-Avon of "New Place," later bought by Shakespeare.

**Close, Upton.** Pseudonym of Josef Washington HALL.

**Closse** (klôs; *in Eng., also* klŏs), **Raphael Lambert.** 1620?–1662. French soldier in Canada, b. Tours, France; to Canada (1642); acting governor of Montreal (1655); invested with the fief of St. Lambert (1658); killed in skirmish with Indians (Feb. 6, 1662).

**Clo′ster·man** (klō′stẽr·măn), **John.** *Ger.* **Johann Klo′ster·mann** (klō′stẽr·män). 1656–1713. Portrait painter, b. in Hanover; to England (1681); painted Blenheim group of duke of Marlborough and family.

**Clot** (klō), **Antoine Barthélemy.** *Called also* **Clot′ Bey′** (bā′). 1793–1868. French physician. Chief surgeon (1822–49) to Mehemet Ali, viceroy of Egypt; head of Egyptian medical administration (1836).

**Clo·taire′** (klô·târ′; *Fr.* klô′-) *or* **Clo·thaire′** (klô·thâr′; -târ′). *Ger.* **Chlo·thar′** (klô·tär′; klō′tär). Also **Lo·thar′** (lô·tär′; lō′tär) *and* **Lo·thaire′** (lô·thâr′; -târ′; *Fr.* lô′târ′). Name of four Merovingian kings: **Clotaire I,** king of Soissons (511–558) and of all the Franks (558–561). **Clotaire II,** king of all the Franks (584–628; civil wars). **Clotaire III,** king of Neustria (658–670). **Clotaire IV,** king of Neustria (717–719). See MEROVINGIAN.

**Clo·til′da** (klô·tĭl′dȧ), Saint. *Fr.* **Clo′tilde′** (klô′tēld′). *Ger.* **Chlo·thil′de** (klô·tĭl′dĕ). 475?–?545. Daughter of Chilperic, King of the Burgundians. Queen of the Franks, as wife of Clovis (493). Educated in Christian faith; converted Clovis; after death of Clovis (511) retired to monastery at Tours. Her daughter **Clotilda** (497?–531) married Amalaric, king of the Visigoths.

**Cloud** (klōō), Saint (*Fr.* săN). *Also* **Clo′do·ald** *or* **Chlo′do·ald** (klō′dô·ăld; -ōld; *Ger.* -ält). 520?–560. Grandson of King Clovis I. Brought up by his grandmother Clotilda; escaped death from his uncles Clotaire (I) and Childebert (I); lived in solitude as a monk in Provence; returned to neighborhood of Paris where he built abbey at Nogent (later named Saint-Cloud).

**Clou′et′** (klōō′ĕ′). Family of Flemish-French painters, including: **Jean,** *or* **Jehan, Clouet,** 15th-century painter attached to house of duke of Burgundy; his son **Jean** (1485?–1545), painter in ordinary to King Francis I, and painter of portraits of the king and members of the court; and the latter's son **François** (1510?–?1572), who succeeded his father as painter to the king (1545).

**Clough** (klŭf), **Arthur Hugh.** 1819–1861. English poet, b. Liverpool, son of cotton merchant. Spent childhood in Charleston, S.C.; educ. Rugby (1829–36) under Dr. Arnold; B.A., Oxon. (1841); fellow of Oriel (1841–48), tutor (1843–48); resigned because of skepticism, and traveled, visiting Emerson (1852). Examiner in education office, London (1853); secretary to commission for study of military education abroad (1856); sought recovery from failing health in southern Europe; died of paralysis in Florence. Subject of Matthew Arnold's elegy *Thyrsis.* Author of a pastoral in hexameters, *The Bothie of Toper-na-Fuosich,* revised to *Tober-na-Vuolich* (1848), *Amours de Voyage,* a rhymed novelette (1849), *Dipsychus,* a serious satire (1850), *Mari Magno,* idylls (1861), and a prose revision of a 17th-century translation of Plutarch's *Lives* (1859). His sister **Anne Jemima** (1820–1892) opened a school (1841), another (1852); helped found North of England council for promoting higher education of women; first principal (1871) of house for women students, later Newnham Coll., Cambridge.

**Clo′vio** (klô′vyô), **Giulio.** 1498–1578. Croatian-born Italian miniaturist and book illuminator; took orders and was assigned as canon to house of Cardinal Alexander Farnese. Twelve of his miniatures, depicting victories of Emperor Charles V, are in British Museum; books containing his illuminations are in Bibliothèque Nationale, Vatican library, J. P. Morgan library, and New York Public Library.

**Clo′vis I** (klō′vĭs; *Fr.* klô′vēs′). *Ger.* **Chlod′wig** (klōt′-

vĭĸ). *Also* **Chlo′dō·wech** (klō′dō·vĕĸ). 466?–511. King of the Salian Franks and one of earliest rulers of Merovingian dynasty of the Franks (481–511). Son of Childeric I; m. Clotilda, a Christian Burgundian princess, niece of Gundobad, who converted him to Christianity (496). Overthrew Gallo-Roman colony governed by Syagrius, near Soissons (486); defeated the Alamanni at Tolbiacum (Zülpich), near the Rhine (496); fixed his court at Paris (507); defeated West Goths (507); endeavored to unite all Frankish people in one kingdom, but just before his death (511) redivided his newly organized realm among four sons.

**Clovis II** (632–657) and **Clovis III** (682–695) were descendants of Clovis I in the Merovingian dynasty and kings of Neustria (638–657 and 691–695, respectively). See MEROVINGIAN; Saint CLOUD.

**Clowes** (klōōz), Sir **William Laird**. 1856–1905. English naval writer, using pen name *Nauticus;* founded and edited *Naval Pocket Book;* collaborated on *The Royal Navy* (7 vols., 1897–1903).

**Clu′ett** (klōō′ĕt; -ĭt). Family of shirt and collar manufacturers, of Troy, N.Y., including **George B. Cluett** orig. of England, founder of business. **Robert** (1846–1927), b. Birmingham, Eng.; member (from 1866) of firm George B. Cluett Bro. & Co., incorporated (1901) as Cluett, Peabody & Co.; president of Cluett, Peabody & Co. (1902–07). **George Alfred** (1873–1955), b. Troy, N.Y.; with Cluett, Peabody & Co. (from 1896); president (from 1919). **Ernest Harold** (1874–1954), b. Troy; treasurer, Cluett, Peabody & Co. (1900–16); vice-president (1916–29); chairman of the board (1929–37). **Sanford Lockwood Cluett** (1874-1968), b. Troy; director of engineering and research, Cluett, Peabody & Co. (from 1919); later, vice-president; inventor of patented process of Sanforizing, named for him.

**Cluny, Hugh** (*or* **Hugo**) **of.** = HUGH THE GREAT.

**Clu′se·ret′** (klüz′rĕ′), **Gustave Paul**. 1823–1900. French soldier and politician; served (colonel) in Garibaldi's expedition against Kingdom of the Two Sicilies (1860), and in Union army (1862) during the American Civil War. Member of Commune of Paris, and minister of war (Apr. 4–30, 1871); in exile from France (1871–84); member of Chamber of Deputies (1888).

**Clusius, Carolus**. See Charles de LÉCLUSE.

**Clute** (klōōt), **Willard Nelson**. 1869–1950. American botanist, b. Painted Post, N.Y. Founder of *Plant World* and *Bryologist;* founder and editor of *Fern Bulletin* and *American Botanist;* author of *Our Ferns in Their Haunts* (1901), *Useful Plants of the World* (1927), *Our Ferns—Their Haunts, Habits, and Folklore* (1938), etc.

**Clut′ton-Brock′** (klŭt′'n·brŏk′), **Arthur**. 1868–1924. English essayist and critic. Grad. Oxford; practiced law; art critic *The Times* (1908). Author of *Shelley, the Man and the Poet* (1909), *Essays on Religion* (1926), etc.

**Clu′ver** (klōō′vĕr) *or* **Clü′ver** (klü′vĕr), **Philipp**. *Lat.* **Clu·ve′ri·us** (klōō·vĕr′ĭ·ŭs). 1580–1622. German antiquarian and geographer; regarded as founder of historical geography. Author of *Germania Antiqua* (1616), *Italia Antiqua* (1624), etc.

**Clyde** (klīd), Baron. See Sir Colin CAMPBELL.

**Clyde, William Pancoast**. 1839–1923. American shipowner, b. Claymont, Del.; founder and head of William P. Clyde & Co., later Clyde Steamship Co.

**Cly′mer** (klī′mĕr), **George**. 1739–1813. American politician, b. Philadelphia; merchant in Philadelphia; member, Continental Congress (1776–78; 1780–83); signer of Declaration of Independence.

**Clymer, George E.** 1754–1834. American inventor of an improved printing press, known as the "Columbian."

**Clynes** (klīnz), **John Robert**. 1869–1949. English labor leader and politician, b. Oldham. M.P. (1906–31; 1935 ff.); food controller (1918–19). Chairman, Parliamentary Labor party (1921–22); lord privy seal, and deputy leader of House of Commons (1924) in first British Labor cabinet. Secretary of state for home affairs (1929–31).

**Cnut**. See CANUTE.

**Coates** (kōts), **Albert**. 1882–1953. English conductor and composer, b. St. Petersburg, Russia, of English parentage. Studied under Nikisch. Chief conductor, Imperial Opera House, St. Petersburg (1910–17); to London (1919); conductor at Covent Garden; guest conductor, New York Symphony Orchestra (1920, 1921); director, Philharmonic Orchestra, Rochester, N.Y. (1923–25). Composer of the operas *Samuel Pepys* (1929), *Pickwick* (1936).

**Coates, Eric**. 1886–1957. English viola player and composer, b. Hucknall. Principal viola player, Queen's Hall Orchestra. Composer of orchestral works, fantasies, rhapsodies, ballets, and many songs, including *The Mill o' Dreams, The Green Hills o' Somerset, A Song Remembered.*

**Coates, Florence**, *nee* **Earle** (ûrl). 1850–1927. American lyric poet, b. Philadelphia.

**Coates, George James**. 1869–1930. British painter of portraits and murals, b. Melbourne, Australia. Official artist to the Australian government (1919). His *Motherhood* hangs in National Gallery at Melbourne.

**Coates, John**. 1865–1941. English tenor, chiefly in light opera and musical comedy.

**Coates, Joseph Gordon**. 1878–1943. New Zealand statesman, b. Matakohe. Served with New Zealand troops in France during World War. Minister of justice (1919–20); postmaster general and minister of telegraphs (1919–25); minister of public works (1920–26); prime minister of New Zealand (1925–28); minister of railways (1923–28), of native affairs (1921–28), of external affairs (1928). Leader of the opposition (1928–31). Minister of public works, employment, and transport (1931–33), of finance, customs, and transport (1933–35); member of N.Z. war cabinet (1940–43).

**Coats** (kōts), **James**. 1774–1857. Scottish founder of thread manufactory; son of Paisley weaver who built factory (1826) for manufacture of sewing cotton; organized business that in hands of his sons became (1890) J. & P. Coats, Ltd., whose Ferguslie threadworks became largest in the world. His sons engaged in the business were **James**, Sir **Peter** (1808–1890), and **Thomas** (1809–1883), philanthropist and collector of Scottish coins.

**Coats′worth** (kōts′wûrth; -wĕrth), **Elizabeth**. 1893– American poet and author of children's books, b. Buffalo, N.Y.; A.B., Vassar (1915); m. Henry Beston (1929). Author of volumes of verse *Fox Footprints* (1923), *Compass Rose* (1929), a novel, *Here I Stay* (1938), and books for children, including *The Cat and the Captain* (1927), *The Cat Who Went to Heaven* (1930; awarded Newbery prize), *Away Goes Sally* (1934), *Alice-All-by-Herself* (1937), *Dancing Tom* (1938).

**Cobb** (kŏb), **Frank Irving**. 1869–1923. American journalist, b. Shawnee County, Kansas; editor in chief, New York *World* (1911–23).

**Cobb, Henry Ives**. 1859–1931. American architect, b. Brookline, Mass. Educ. M.I.T. and Harvard (S.B., 1880). Practiced in Chicago (from 1881). Designed Newberry Library, university buildings, and Church of the Atonement in Chicago, Pennsylvania State capitol at Harrisburg, American University buildings at Washington, D.C. Special architect for U.S. government (1893–1903).

**Cobb, Howell.** 1815–1868. American lawyer, b. in Jefferson Co., Ga. Grad. U. of Georgia (1834). Member, U.S. House of Representatives (1843–51; 1855–57); speaker (1849–51). Governor of Georgia (1851–53). U.S. secretary of the treasury (1857–60). Advocated immediate secession of Georgia after Lincoln's election. Confederate brigadier general (1862); major general (1863).

**Cobb, Irvin Shrewsbury.** 1876–1944. American journalist, humorist, and dramatic writer, b. Paducah, Ky. Staff correspondent and columnist, Louisville (Ky.) *Evening Post* (1898–1901); managing editor, Paducah *News Democrat* (1901–04); editor of humor section, New York *Evening Sun* (1904–05); on staff of New York *World* (1905–11), *Saturday Evening Post* (1911–22), *Cosmopolitan Magazine* (1922–32). Among his many humorous books and collections of short stories are: *Back Home* (1912), *Old Judge Priest* (1915), *Speaking of Operations—* (1917), *The Life of the Party* (1919), *Jeff Poindexter* (1922), *Alias Ben Alibi* (1924), *Ladies and Gentlemen* (1927), *Judge Priest Turns Detective* (1936). Author of and collaborator in many plays, including *Funabashi* (musical comedy, 1907), *Mr. Buoybody* (musical sketch, 1908), *Back Home* (comedy, with Bayard Veiller, 1915), *Under Sentence* (drama, with Roi Megrue, 1916). Also author of motion-picture scenarios, and actor in motion-picture productions. Wrote autobiography *Exit Laughing* (1941).

**Cobb, Ty** (tī), *in full* **Ty'rus** (tī'rŭs) **Raymond.** 1886–1961. American professional baseball player; with Detroit (1904–26) and Philadelphia (1926–30), in American League.

**Cobbe** (kŏb), **Frances Power.** 1822–1904. British philanthropist and writer on religious and social subjects, b. in Ireland; great-granddaughter of **Charles Cobbe** (1687–1765), Archbishop of Dublin. Edited works of Theodore Parker (14 vols., 1863–71); published anonymously *The Theory of Intuitive Morals* (1855); associated with Mary Carpenter in ragged schools (1858); preached in Unitarian chapels. Author of *Broken Lights* (1864), *Darwinism in Morals* (1872), *The Duties of Women* (1881), and an autobiography (2 vols., 1904).

**Cob'bett** (kŏb'ĕt; -ĭt), **William.** *Pseudonym* **Peter Por'cu·pine** (pôr'kû·pīn). 1763–1835. English political journalist and essayist. Son of small farmer in Surrey; during service in British army (1783–91), taught himself grammar and composition; obtained court martial of his former officers for peculation. Sailed for Philadelphia (1792) to avoid prosecution for pamphlet on army abuses; published pamphlets attacking French Revolution and any form of radicalism, and vituperative criticism of American democracy; published newspaper *Porcupine's Gazette;* fined for libel. Returned to England (1800); edited with aid of John Wright (*q.v.*) works on parliamentary history; edited (from 1802) weekly *Political Register*, at first a Tory journal but (from 1804) champion of radicalism, demanding parliamentary and social reform; farmed in Hampshire (1804–17); took up cause of dispossessed rural laborers; imprisoned in Newgate (1810–12) for denouncing flogging of militiamen by German mercenaries; bankrupt; as leader of discontented working classes after ending of war (1815), had to flee to Long Island farm (1817–19); espoused cause of Queen Caroline (1820); developed successful seed farm in Kensington; urged cultivation of Indian corn; defended himself against charge of sedition (1831); M.P. (1832), leader of handful of extreme radicals; died of influenza. Author of a *Grammar of the English Language* for working-class students (1818), *Rural Rides* (1830), *Advice to Young Men* (1830), *The English Gardener* (1829), and forty to fifty other vigorous prose works.

**Cob'bold** (kŏb'ōld; -'ld), **Thomas Spencer.** 1828–1886. English biologist; M.D., Edinburgh (1851); professor of botany, Royal Veterinary Coll., later professor of helminthology; specialist on worms parasitic in man and animals. His father, **Richard** (1797–1877), wrote *History of Margaret Catchpole.*

**Cob'den** (kŏb'dĕn), **Richard.** 1804–1865. English statesman and economist; known as "Apostle of Free Trade." Son of a Sussex farmer; clerk (1819) and traveler for his uncle, London calico merchant; as partner in calico-printing factory in Lancashire (1831), gained independent fortune; studied economic and financial systems in U.S., Near East, Germany (1835–38); published pamphlets *England, Ireland, and America*, opposing defense of Turkey against Russia (1835), and *Russia*, attacking doctrine of balance of power (1836). With John Bright, a leader of national Anti-Corn-Law League (1838–46); campaigned in country and in Parliament; succeeded in forcing repeal of corn laws; financially ruined by neglect of his business; traveled in Europe urging international arbitration and disarmament (1846–47); organized series of international congresses to forward peace (1848–51); shared unpopularity with John Bright for opposition to Crimean War; successfully opposed Palmerston's Chinese war policy (1857); declined office in cabinet; negotiated (1859–60) commercial treaty with France providing mutual reduction of tariffs; opposed intervention in favor of Denmark (1864); declared for the North in American Civil War; with John Bright, led the Manchester school; believer in minimum of government at home and minimum of intervention abroad.

**Cob'den-San'der·son** (-săn'dẽr·s'n), **Thomas James.** 1840–1922. English bookbinder and printer. Educ. Owens College (Manchester) and Cambridge U.; practiced law in London (1871–82); under influence of William Morris, withdrew from practice to devote himself to some form of handicraft. Studied bookbinding and established workshop (1884) in London, succeeded (in 1893) by the Doves bindery at Hammersmith (1893–1921); later (c. 1900), associated with Emery Walker in establishing the Doves Press, at Hammersmith, and in designing a new font of type; among books printed on this press were an English Bible (1903–05) and an edition of Milton (1905).

**Co'bet'** (kô'bĕ'), **Ca'rel'** (kȧ'rĕl') **Ga'bri'el'** (gȧ'brē'ĕl'). 1813–1889. Dutch classical scholar; professor, Leiden (c. 1847). Founded philological review *Mnemosyne* (1856). Published editions of classics.

**Cobham,** Lord. See Sir John Oldcastle.

**Co'bo** (kō'bō), **Bernabé.** 1582–1657. Spanish naturalist. To America (1596); became Jesuit in Peru (1601); wrote history of New World including information on natural features and inhabitants of Spanish America.

**Co'burn** (kō'bẽrn), **Charles Douville.** 1877–1961. American actor and manager, b. Savannah, Ga. On stage in stock companies (to 1906); m. (1906) **Ivah Wills** (d. 1937); with her organized the Coburn Players (1906), a producing company in which they were leading actors.

**Coccaius, Merlinus.** *Or* **Merlino Coccaio.** See Teofilo Folengo.

**Coc·ce'ius** *or* **Coc·ce'jus** (*as Lat.*, kŏk·sē'yŭs; *as Ger.*, kôk·tsā'yo͝os), **Johannes.** *Orig. surname* **Koch** (kôk). 1603–1669. Protestant theologian, b. Bremen; professor, Bremen (1629), Franeker (1636), Leiden (1650).

**Coc·ce'ius** (kŏk·sē'yŭs), **Nerva.** See Nerva.

**Coc·ce'ji** (kôk·tsā'yē), Baron **Heinrich von.** 1644–1719. German jurist; professor, Heidelberg (1671), Utrecht (1688), Frankfort on the Oder (1690). Author of

*Juris Publici Prudentia* (1695). His son Baron **Samuel** (1679–1755), jurist; professor, Frankfort on the Oder (1702); Prussian minister of state and war (1727); chief of Prussian judiciary (1738), which he reformed; chancellor of Prussia (1747).

**Coc′cia** (kôt′chä), **Carlo.** 1782–1873. Italian composer of operas, cantatas, and religious music.

**Coc′ci·us** (kŏk′tsē·ōōs), **Ernst Adolf.** 1825–1890. German ophthalmologist; devised a new ophthalmometer used in diagnosis of astigmatism.

**Co′chet′** (kô′shĕ′), **Henri.** 1901– . French lawn tennis player; member of Davis Cup team (1925–33) that won cup (1927–32); turned professional (1933).

**Cochet, Jean Benoît Désiré.** 1812–1875. French abbé and archaeologist.

**Co′chin′** (kô′shăN′). Family of French engravers, including: **Charles Nicolas** (1688–1754), who engraved esp. after painters of French school, as Coypel, Watteau, etc. His son **Charles Nicolas** (1715–1790), most famous of family; engraved frontispiece of the *Encyclopédie* and vignettes for editions of Ariosto, Tasso, and Boileau; ornamented lettering for titles, etc., influencing development of decorative type; also wrote and illustrated *Voyage d'Italie* and *Observations sur les Antiquités d'Herculanum.*

**Cochin.** Family of French men of affairs and authors, including: **Jean Denis Marie** (1789–1841), jurist and philanthropist. His son **Pierre Suzanne Augustin** (1823–1872), student of social conditions; author of *Les Ouvriers Européens* (1856), *Abolition de l'Esclavage* (1861), *La Révolution Sociale en France* (1865), etc. Pierre's son **Denys** (1851–1922), municipal councilor in Paris (from 1881); member of Chamber of Deputies (from 1893); author of *L'Évolution et la Vie* (1886), *Le Monde Extérieur* (1895), *L'Esprit Nouveau* (1900). Denys's brother **Henry** (1854–1926), member of Chamber of Deputies (1893–1914); translator of Dante's *Vita Nuova;* author of *Boccace, Études Italiennes* (1890), *Un Ami de Pétrarque: J. Nell* (1892), *La Chronologie du Canzoniere de Pétrarque* (1897), etc. Denys's son **Augustin Denys Marie** (1876–1916), historian, esp. of French Revolution.

**Coch·lae′us** (kŏk·lē′ŭs; *as Ger.*, kôĸ·lā′ōōs), **Johannes.** *Orig. name* **Johann Do′be·nek** (dō′bĕ·nĕk) *or* **Dob′neck** (dôb′nĕk). 1479–1552. German Roman Catholic controversialist; prominent opponent of Luther (from 1521). Author of *Commentaria de Actis et Scriptis Lutheri* (1549).

**Coch′ran** (kŏk′răn), **Alexander Smith.** 1874–1929. American manufacturer, book collector, and philanthropist; b. Yonkers, N.Y.

**Cochran, Charles Blake.** 1872–1951. English theatrical manager and producer.

**Cochran, Jacqueline.** American businesswoman and aviator; m. (1936) Floyd Bostwick Odlum. Manufacturer of cosmetics and head of chain of beauty parlors. Winner of Bendix Transcontinental Air Race (1938), and holder of a number of national and international speed records.

**Coch′rane** (kŏk′răn), **Thomas.** 10th Earl of **Dun·don′ald** (dŭn·dŏn′'ld). *Called* Lord **Cochrane.** 1775–1860. British naval commander, of an old Scottish family. Entered navy (1793); as commander of sloop *Speedy* took over fifty prizes (1800–01), including a 32-gun Spanish frigate; returned to prize-taking off Azores (1805) and Bay of Biscay (1806); in Parliament, exposed naval abuses; on account of jealousy of superiors, only partly successful in burning French fleet in Aix Roads (1809); accused of connivance in speculative fraud, fined, imprisoned, and expelled from navy (1814–16). In command of Chile's navy in war for freedom by Chile and Peru, neutralized Spanish squadron, took Valdivia, contributed to capture of Lima (1819–22); in command of Brazilian navy, secured Brazilian independence (1823–25); commanded Greek navy (1827–28); first to use steam-propelled ships of war; advocated adoption of screw propellers. Received free pardon, reinstated in British navy, and promoted rear admiral (1832); commander in chief on North American station (1848–51); admiral (1851); proposed for second time his secret war plan to overcome fleets with sulphur fumes, for use against Russia (1854). His uncle Sir **Alexander Forrester Inglis Cochrane** (1758–1832), admiral; blockaded Ferrol (1804); held command in West Indies (1805–14) and on American station (1814–15), directing naval operations in unsuccessful attacks on Baltimore and New Orleans.

**Douglas Mackinnon Baillie Hamilton** (1852–1935), 12th earl; grandson of 10th earl; soldier; entered 2d Life Guards (1870) and rose through grades to major general (1900); lieut. general (1907); served in Nile expedition (1884–85), Stewart's expedition to relieve Khartoum (1885), Boer War (1899–1902), and World War I (1914–18); author of *My Army Life* (1926).

**Cock·ain′** (kŏ·kān′), Sir **Aston.** = Sir Aston Cokayne.

**Cock′burn** (kō′bẽrn), Sir **Alexander James Edmund.** 1802–1880. British judge, of ancient Scottish stock; LL.B., Cantab. (1829); M.P. (1847); defended Palmerston's foreign policy (1850); attorney general (1851–56); chief justice of common pleas (1856); lord chief justice of England (1859); British representative in arbitration of *Alabama* case at Geneva (1872). His uncle Sir **George** (1772–1853), naval officer; aided in reduction of Martinique (1809); sent to harass American coast (1812–15); took part in capture of Washington (1814); conveyed Napoleon to St. Helena; governor of St. Helena (1815–16); admiral of fleet (1851).

**Cockburn, Alicia** *or* **Alison,** *nee* **Ruth′er·ford** (rŭth′ẽr·fẽrd). 1713–1794. Scottish poet and leader of Edinburgh society; author of Scottish ballad *Flowers of the Forest* (pub. 1765) beginning "I've seen the smiling of Fortune beguiling."

**Cockburn, Henry Thomas.** *Known as* Lord **Cockburn.** 1779–1854. Scottish judge. Solicitor general for Scotland (1830); a lord of justiciary (1837). Author of a biography of Lord Jeffrey (1852).

**Cock′croft** (kŏk′rôft), Sir **John Douglas.** 1897–1967. British nuclear physicist. Awarded Nobel prize in physics (1951) with E. T. S. Walton for being first to split an atom by artificial means (1932).

**Cocke** (kŏk), **John Hartwell.** 1780–1866. American planter and publicist, b. in Surry Co., Va.; prominent in opposition to slavery, dueling, intemperance, and tobacco; co-operated with Thomas Jefferson in planning and founding University of Virginia.

**Cock′er** (kŏk′ẽr), **Edward.** 1631–1675. English engraver and teacher; published manuals of penmanship, and an arithmetic (1678) that went through a hundred editions —hence the expression "according to Cocker."

**Cock′er·am** (kŏk′ẽr·ăm; kŏk′răm), **Henry.** fl. 1650. English lexicographer; author of earliest published dictionary of English, *The English Dictionaries, or a New Interpreter of Hard English Words* (1623).

**Cock′er·ell** (kŏk′ẽr·ĕl; kŏk′rĕl), **Charles Robert.** 1788–1863. English architect; conducted excavations in the Levant; R.A. (1827); professor of architecture to Royal Academy (1840–57); designed chiefly in classic models, including buildings at Oxford and Cambridge and banks, also Gothic chapels at Lampeter and Harrow.

**Cockerell, Theodore Dru Alison.** 1866–1948. Zoologist, b. Norwood, England. To U.S.; entomologist, N.Mex.

Agric. Experiment Station (1893–1901); professor of zoology (1906–34), Colorado. Known esp. for work on mollusks, insects, fishes, paleontology, and evolution.

**Cock'er·ill** (kŏk'ẽr·ĭl; kŏk'rĭl), **William.** 1759–1832. English inventor in Belgium; constructed (1799) at Verviers first wool-carding and wool-spinning machines on Continent and established (1807) factory for making these machines. His youngest son, **John** (1790–1840), developed the business and built foundry and machine factory at Seraing, Belgium (1817).

**Cock Lane Ghost.** See Elizabeth PARSONS.

**Cock'le** (kŏk''l), Sir **James.** 1819–1895. English lawyer and mathematician; M.A., Cantab. (1845); first chief justice of Queensland, Australia (1863–79); made contributions to theory of differential equations.

**Cock'ran** (kŏk'răn), **William Bourke.** 1854–1923. Lawyer, politician, and orator, b. in County Sligo, Ireland; to New York (1871); member, U.S. House of Representatives (1887–89; 1891–95; 1904–09; 1921–23).

**Cock'ton** (kŏk'tŭn), **Henry.** 1807–1853. English author of humorous novels, *Valentine Vox, the Ventriloquist* (1840) and *Sylvester Sound, the Somnambulist* (1844).

**Cocles, Horatius.** See HORATIUS COCLES.

**Coc'teau'** (kôk'tō'), **Jean.** 1889–1963. French poet, novelist, playwright, and miscellaneous writer; author of *Poésie, Thomas l'Imposteur, Notes Autour de la Musique, Carte Blanche, Picasso,* the plays *Les Mariés de la Tour Eiffel, Le Bœuf sur le Toit, Antigone,* etc.

**Cocx, Gonzales.** See COQUES.

**Co·daz'zi** (kô·dät'tsē), **Agostino.** 1792–1859. Italian engineer, explorer, and geographer, b. Lugo, Emilia. Explored deserts of Guiana (1831–38). His works include *Atlas Físico y Político de la República de Venezuela* (1840), *Resumen de la Geografía de Venezuela* (1841), *Geografía Física y Política de los Estados Unidos de Colombia* (2 vols., 1862–63).

**Cod'de** (kŏd'ĕ), **Pieter.** 1599–1678. Dutch genre painter.

**Cod'ding·ton** (kŏd'ĭng·tŭn), **Henry.** d. 1845. English mathematician and writer on optics; recommended (1830) use in microscopes of grooved-sphere lens first described by Brewster (1820) but named *Coddington lens.*

**Coddington, William.** 1601–1678. Colonial governor in America, b. Boston, Eng. To Massachusetts (c. 1630); protested the prosecution of Anne Hutchinson (1637); withdrew (1638) to Aquidneck (Rhode Island); a founder of Newport (1639). Governor of Aquidneck (1640); governor of Rhode Island and Providence Plantations (1674, 1675, 1678).

**Codomannus.** See DARIUS III.

**Codreanu, Corneliu Zelea-.** See ZELEA-CODREANU.

**Cod'ring·ton** (kŏd'rĭng·tŭn), **Christopher.** 1668–1710. British soldier, b. in Barbados; served in Flanders (1694); governor of Leeward Islands (1697–1703); founder, through bequest of his Barbados estates, of Codrington College (built 1714–42).

**Codrington,** Sir **Edward.** 1770–1851. British naval commander, of Gloucestershire family; commanded ship at Trafalgar (1805); served under Sir Alexander Cochrane on North American station (1814); vice-admiral (1821); commanded British, French, and Russian fleet in destroying Turkish fleet at Navarino (1827); admiral (1837). His second son, Sir **William John** (1804–1884), was commander in chief at Sevastopol (1855–56); his third son, Sir **Henry John** (1808–1877), wounded at Navarino, became admiral of the fleet (1877).

**Cod'rus** (kŏd'rŭs). Last king of Athens, who according to legend, reigned about 1068 B.C. and sacrificed himself during a Dorian invasion of the Peloponnesus to fulfill a prophecy and insure Athenian success.

**Co'dy** (kō'dĭ), **Henry John.** 1868–1951. Canadian Anglican clergyman and educator, b. in Ontario. Educ. Toronto U.; professor, Wycliffe Coll., Toronto (1894–99); rector of St. Paul's Church, Toronto (1899–1932); canon of St. James' Cathedral, Toronto. President; U. of Toronto (1932–45); chancellor (1945).

**Cody, John Patrick.** 1907– . Amer. Roman Catholic cardinal, b. St. Louis, Mo. Ordained (1931); archbishop of New Orleans (1964–65), of Chicago (1965– ).

**Cody, William Frederick.** *Known as* **Buf'fa·lo Bill** (bŭf'ȧ·lō bĭl'); *so called by E. Z. C. Judson.* 1846–1917. American scout and showman, b. Scott Co., Iowa. Rider for the Pony Express (1860); scout for Kansas cavalry outfit against Indians (1863); in army (1863–65); furnished buffalo meat for train construction crews (1867–68); scout, 5th U.S. cavalry (1868–72). On stage as actor (1872–83). Organized and managed Buffalo Bill's Wild West Show (from 1883). Settled on land granted to him in Wyoming; town of Cody is named in his honor.

**Coe'hoorn** (kōō'hōrn) *or* **Coe'horn** (kōō'hôrn; kō'-) *or* **Co'horn** (kō'hôrn), Baron **Menno van.** 1641–1704. Dutch soldier and military engineer. Invented small bronze mortar (*coehorn*) first used at siege of Grave; authority on fortifications, esp. in Low Countries.

**Co·e'lho** (kōō·ā'lyōō), **Francisco Adolpho.** 1847–1921. Portuguese philologist; professor, Lisbon; author of treatise on historical development of Portuguese language and of *Diccionario Manual Etymologico da Lingua Portugueza;* editor of a collection of Portuguese folk tales.

**Coelho Net'to** (nĕ'tōō), **Henrique.** 1864–1934. Brazilian writer; director, Municipal School of the Drama, Rio de Janeiro; author of verse, plays, and prose works.

**Coelho Pe·rei'ra** (pĕ·rā'ē·rȧ), **Duarte.** 1485?–1554. Portuguese soldier; granted captaincy of Pernambuco (1534), which he developed into most flourishing colony in Brazil. His son **Duarte Coelho de Al'bu·quer'que** [thē äl'bōō·kĕr'kĕ] (1537–?1579) inherited captaincy of Pernambuco (1554) and governed it (1560–72); returned to Portugal; went to Africa; captured by Muslims. Another son, **Jorge de Albuquerque Coelho** (1539–after 1596), inherited captaincy of Pernambuco (1579).

**Co·el'lo** (kô·ā'lyō), **Alonzo Sánchez.** See SÁNCHEZ COELLO.

**Coello, Claudio.** c. 1630–1693. Spanish painter, b. Madrid, of Portuguese descent; pupil of Carreño de Miranda; court painter (1684); considered last leading painter of Madrid school; known particularly for his canvas altar panel *La Sagrada Forma.*

**Coen** (kōōn), **Jan Pieterszoon.** 1587–1629. Dutch colonial governor; governor general of Dutch East Indies (1618–23; 1627–29); founded Batavia (1619). Regarded as founder of Dutch East Indian colonial empire.

**Coer'ne** (?kōōr'nĕ), **Louis Adolphe.** 1870–1922. American musician and director, b. Newark, N.J. Composer of *Zenobia,* first grand opera by an American composer to be played before European audiences (1905–07), *Hiawatha* (symphonic poem), *Beloved America* (cantata), *Mass in D Minor,* etc.

**Cœur** (kûr), **Jacques.** 1395?–1456. French merchant; inaugurated extensive trade with the Levant; in charge of French royal finances (from c. 1436); falsely accused of traitorous conduct, condemned, and deprived of his property (c. 1450); in exile in Rome.

**Cœur de Lion.** See (1) RICHARD I of England; (2) LOUIS VIII of France.

**Cof'fin** (kŏf'ĭn), **Charles Albert.** 1844–1926. American businessman, b. in Somerset Co., Me.; head of General Electric Co. (from its organization, 1892, to 1913); chairman, board of directors (1913–22).

**Coffin, Henry Sloane.** 1877–1954. American clergyman,

b. New York City. B.A., Yale (1897), B.D., Union Theol. Sem. (1900); ordained in Presbyterian ministry (1900); pastor of Madison Avenue Church, New York City (1905–26); president, Union Theol. Sem. (1926–45).

**Coffin,** Sir **Isaac.** 1759–1839. British admiral, b. Boston, Mass. In British navy (from 1773; commander, 1781; admiral, 1814). Founded (1827) Coffin School, Nantucket, Mass.

**Coffin, Robert Peter Tristram.** 1892–1955. American poet, essayist, and biographer, b. Brunswick, Me. A.B., Bowdoin (1915), A.B., Oxon. (1920); served in A.E.F. (1918–19); teacher of English, Wells College, Aurora, N.Y. (1921–34; professor from 1926); professor of English, Bowdoin (from 1934). Author of books of verse, as *Christchurch* (1924), *Golden Falcon* (1929), *Strange Holiness* (1935; awarded Pulitzer prize), *Saltwater Farm* (1937), of books of essays, as *Book of Crowns and Cottages* (1925), *An Attic Room* (1929), of biographies, as *Laud* (1930), *The Dukes of Buckingham* (1931), *Portrait of an American* (1931), *Captain Abby and Captain John* (1939), of novels, as *Red Sky in the Morning* (1935) and *John Dawn* (1936), and of *Kennebec: Cradle of Americans* (1937) in "Rivers of America" series.

**Coff'man** (kôf'măn), **Lotus Delta.** 1875–1938. American educator, b. Salem, Ind. A.B., Indiana (1906), Ph.D., Columbia (1911); president, U. of Minnesota (1920–38).

**Cogălniceanu.** Variant of Kogălniceanu.

**Co·ghet'ti** (kō·gāt'tē), **Francesco.** 1804–1875. Italian painter; his works include *Assumption of the Virgin* (at Bergamo), and frescoes in Villa Torlonia, Rome.

**Cog'hill** (kŏg'hĭl), **George Ellett.** 1872–1941. American anatomist; professor, Wistar Institute of Anatomy, Philadelphia (1925–35); known for his researches on the nervous system of Amphibia and on the correlation of structure and function in the development of the nervous system in relation to the development of behavior.

**Cogh'lan** (kŏg'lăn), Sir **Charles Patrick John.** 1863–1927. South African statesman, b. in Cape Colony. Practiced law at Bulawayo in Southern Rhodesia (1900); became prominent in political life of Southern Rhodesia; first premier (1923–27) of territory when it was granted self-government.

**Coghlan, Rose.** 1853–1932. Actress, b. Peterborough, Eng.; to U.S. (1872); naturalized (1902). Leading lady in Wallack's company (1880–89); acted Countess Zicka in first American presentation of *Diplomacy* (1878); made great success as Stephanie in *Forget-Me-Not* (1880).

**Coghlan,** Sir **Timothy Augustine.** 1856–1926. Australian statistician and public official, b. Sydney; government statistician for New South Wales (1886–1905). Author of *Wealth and Progress of New South Wales*, *Statistical Account of Australia and New Zealand*, etc.

**Co'gnacq'** (kô'nyàk'), **Théodore Ernest** (1839–1928) and his wife **Marie Louise,** *nee* **Jay** [zhā] (1838–1925). French merchants, founders (1870) and proprietors of the Parisian department store À la Samaritaine; widely known for their philanthropies, esp. for their joint bequest, the Cognacq-Jay Foundation, of 100 million francs, the income of which was to be distributed among French families with a large number of children.

**Co'gniard'** (kô'nyàr'), **Charles Théodore** (1806–1872) and his brother **Jean Hippolyte** (1807–1882). French theater directors, and collaborators in many comedies, farces, operettas, etc.

**Co'gniet'** (kô'nyĕ'), **Léon.** 1794–1880. French painter; professor, École des Beaux-Arts, Paris; among his works are *Marius sur les Ruines de Carthage, Massacre des Innocents, Monsieur de Crillon.*

**Cogs'well** (kŏgz'wĕl; -wĕl), **Joseph Green.** 1786–1871. American librarian and bibliographer, b. Ipswich, Mass. Grad. Harvard (1806); librarian, Harvard (1820–23); superintendent and bibliographer of Astor collection (1848–61).

**Co·han'** (kō·hăn'), **George Michael.** 1878–1942. American actor, playwright, and producer, b. Providence, R.I. On stage from childhood; appeared in *Peck's Bad Boy* (1890); in vaudeville as one of "The Four Cohans"; starred in *Little Johnny Jones* (1904) and other stage productions including *I'd Rather Be Right* (1937–38). Associated with Sam Harris in firm Cohan & Harris (1904–20). Among the many plays that he wrote, produced, and acted in are: *The Wise Guy, The Governor's Son, Little Johnny Jones, Forty-five Minutes from Broadway, The Talk of New York, The Yankee Prince, Get-Rich-Quick Wallingford, The Little Millionaire, Seven Keys to Baldpate, The Song and Dance Man, The Merry Malones, Gambling.* Author also of many popular songs, including *Mary's a Grand Old Name; So Long, Mary; I'm a Yankee Doodle Dandy; You're a Grand Old Flag; Give My Regards to Broadway;* and *Over There.*

**Co'hen** (kō'ĕn), **Alfred Morton.** 1859–1949. American lawyer, b. Cincinnati; LL.B., Cincinnati Law School, (1880); practiced in Cincinnati. International president, B'nai B'rith.

**Cohen, Arthur.** 1829–1914. English lawyer; B.A., Cantab., first man of Jewish faith to graduate at Cambridge; junior counsel for Great Britain in arbitration of Alabama claims (1872); M.P. (1880); counsel for Great Britain in Venezuela arbitration at The Hague (1903).

**Cohen, Benjamin Victor.** 1894– . American lawyer, b. Muncie, Ind. Ph.B. (1914) and J.D. (1915), Chicago; S.J.D., Harvard (1916). Practiced in Chicago and (1922–33) New York; assisted in drafting Securities Act (1933), Securities Exchange Act (1934), Public Utility Holding Company Act (1935).

**Co'hen** (kō'ĕn), **Emil.** 1842–1905. German mineralogist and geologist; professor, Heidelberg, Strassburg (1878), and Greifswald (1885); wrote on the microscopic structure of minerals and rocks, also on meteors.

**Co·hen'** (kō·hĕn'), **Ernst Julius.** 1869–1944. Dutch chemist; assistant to van't Hoff at U. of Amsterdam (1893); professor of physical chemistry, Utrecht (1902); known for studies on the allotropy of metals and piezo-chemical phenomena.

**Co'hen'** (kô'ĕn'), **Henri.** 1808–1880. French musician and numismatist; director of Lille conservatory of music; composer of a short opera, *L'Impegnatrice;* author of several treatises on music, and of *Description Générale des Monnaies de la République Romaine* (1857), etc.

**Co'hen** (kō'ĕn), **Hermann.** 1842–1918. German philosopher; professor, Marburg (1876–1912); founder of so-called Marburg school of Neo-Kantianism.

**Co'hen'** (kô'ĕn'), **Jules Émile David.** 1830–1901. French composer, esp. of church music and chamber music.

**Co'hen** (kō'ĕn), **Louis.** 1876–1948. American physicist, b. Kiev, Russia. B.S., Armour Inst. of Tech., Chicago (1901); Ph.D., Columbia. Professor of electrical engineering, George Washington U. (from 1916). Investigated alternating current problems and theory of the electrical circuit; invented devices in radio and cable telegraphy.

**Cohen, Morris Raphael.** 1880–1947. Philosopher and educator, b. Minsk, Russia; to U.S. (1892); B.S., C.C.N.Y. (1900), Ph.D., Harvard (1906); professor of philosophy, C.C.N.Y. (1912–38), and U. of Chicago (from 1938). Author of *Reason and Nature* (1931), *Law and the Social Order* (1933), *Faith of a Liberal* (1946).

**Cohen, Oc·tav′us** (ŏk·tăv′ŭs) **Roy.** 1891–1959. American fiction writer, b. Charleston, S.C.; B.S., Clemson (1911); adm. to bar (1913), but devoted time to writing (from 1915). Well known as author of series of Negro stories (from 1918); his books include *The Crimson Alibi* (1919), *Polished Ebony* (1919), *Come Seven* (1920), *Jim Hanvey, Detective* (1923), *Detours* (1927), *Florian Slappey Goes Abroad* (1928), *Epic Peters, Pullman Porter* (1930), *The Townsend Murder Mystery* (1933), *Child of Evil* (1936).

**Cohen, Solomon Solis.** 1857–1948. American physician, b. Philadelphia. M.D., Jefferson Med. Coll. (1883), where he became professor (from 1902). Author of *Therapeutics of Tuberculosis* (1891), *When Love Passed By and Other Verses* (1929), etc.

**Co′hen–Port′heim** (kō′ĕn·pôrt′hīm), **Paul.** 1880–1932. Austrian painter and writer, b. Berlin; spent boyhood in Austria; studied art in Paris; interned in England (1914–18) where he was painting at outbreak of World War. Author of *The Discovery of Europe; England the Unknown Isle; Time Stood Still, My Internment in England 1914–1918; The Spirit of London; The Spirit of France;* etc.

**Cohn** (kōn), **Ferdinand Julius.** 1828–1898. German botanist, often called the founder of bacteriology, b. Breslau. Educ. Breslau and Berlin. Professor, Breslau (from 1859); founder (1866) and director (from 1872) of inst. of plant physiology. Worked on morphology and life history of lower algae and fungi; demonstrated that bacteria are plants; discovered nature of zoogloea and of true spores; studied insect-killing fungi and microscopic analysis of water; aided Koch in publishing paper on anthrax.

**Cohn′heim** (kōn′hīm), **Julius Friedrich.** 1839–1884. German pathologist. Professor in Kiel (1868), Breslau (1872), Leipzig (1878). Known esp. for studies of inflammation and pus formation.

**Cohorn,** Baron **Menno van.** See COEHOORN.

**Coi′gny′** (kwȧ′nyē′). Family of Normandy, including: **Robert Jean Antoine** (1630–1704), founder of family; commander of the army in Flanders (1701). His son **François** (1670–1759), French soldier; maintained his position on Rhine against Prince Eugène. François's grandson **Marie François Henri** (1737–1821), marshal of France, distinguished himself in conquest of Hanover; deputy in States-General (1789); an émigré, fighting in army of Condé (from 1789). His daughter **Anne Françoise Aimée** (1769–1820), inspiration of André Chénier's elegy *La Jeune Captive.* M. F. H. Coigny's grandson **Augustin Louis Joseph Casimir Gustave** (1780–1865) engaged in campaigns in Spain (1808–11) and in Russia (1812); commissioned colonel of cavalry (1814); member of Chamber of Peers (1821); created field marshal (1830).

**Coissi, Graman.** See QUASSI.

**Coit** (koit), **Henry Le′ber** (lē′bẽr). 1854–1917. American physician, b. Peapack, N.J.; specialist in hygiene and diseases of children; instrumental in raising standards of cleanliness in milk handling; coined phrase "certified milk."

**Coit, Stanton.** 1857–1944. Ethical culture leader, b. Columbus, Ohio. Educ. Amherst and Columbia; Ph.D., Berlin. Assistant to Felix Adler in the Society for Ethical Culture. To England (1888); ethical culture minister in London; president, West London Ethical Society; organized many ethical culture societies throughout England. Author of books on ethical culture.

**Coi′ter** (koi′tẽr), **Volcher.** 1534–1590. Dutch anatomist, one of the founders of pathological anatomy.

**Co·kayne′** (kŏ·kān′), Sir **Aston.** 1608–1684. English poet; educ. Cambridge; author of comedies *The Obstinate Lady* (1657) and *Trappolin,* also *The Tragedy of Ovid* (1662), and poems, valued for genealogical purposes. His father, **Thomas** (1587–1638), lexicographer, compiled an English-Greek lexicon (1658) of words in New Testament.

**Coke** (ko͝ok), Sir **Edward.** *Commonly called* Lord **Coke** *or* **Cooke.** 1552–1634. English jurist. Educ. Cambridge; gained reputation by enunciation of common-law rule in Shelley's case. Solicitor general (1592); speaker of House of Commons (1593); attorney general (1594), to disappointment of Francis Bacon; m. (1598) Lady Elizabeth Hatton, granddaughter of Burghley, again thwarting Bacon. Began his law reports (1600); prosecuted Essex and Southampton (1600), Raleigh (1603), and Gunpowder Plot conspirators (1605). Chief justice of Court of Common Pleas (1606); implacable adherent of common law, initiated series of conflicts with James I, abetted by Bacon; decided (1610) that king's proclamation cannot change the law; contested church's attempt to have ecclesiastical causes decided by court of high commission; made chief justice of King's Bench (1613; first to be called lord chief justice of England) to render him less troublesome; sustained common-law courts in attempt to curtail chancellor's right to interfere in decisions (1615); defied James I's order to stay proceedings in case of commendams (holding of livings in plurality); too zealous to ascertain the truth in Sir Thomas Overbury case (1615); dismissed from judicial functions, partly through Bacon's efforts, on trivial charges (1616) and ordered to expunge from his reports opinions detrimental to king's prerogative. M.P. (1620), leader of popular party; opposed Spanish marriage proposals; attacked monopolies; denounced interference with liberties of Parliament; imprisoned nine months (1622). Served on committee to impeach Bacon; instrumental in framing and passing the Petition of Right; opposed Charles I's demand for subsidies; denounced duke of Buckingham in Parliament as a dangerous adviser to king; d. at Stoke Poges; his papers and will seized by Charles I. Made an epoch in the history of the law with his *Reports* (1600–15), compendia of law bearing on cases (trans. from French and Latin, 6 vols., 1826). Now best known for his four *Institutes* (1628–44), the first of which is known as *Coke upon Littleton.*

**Coke** (?kōk; ko͝ok), **Thomas.** 1747–1814. Methodist bishop, b. Brecon, Wales. Grad. Oxford (1768); Anglican clergyman (1770–76). Joined Wesley movement (1777); appointed by John Wesley superintendent of Methodist Church in America (1784); later assumed title of bishop; made frequent visits to America (1784–1803).

**Coke, Thomas William.** Earl of **Leices′ter** (lĕs′tẽr) **of Holk′ham** (hōl′kăm). 1752–1842. English agriculturist; son of Thomas Wenman; assumed name Coke on succession (1776) to estate of maternal uncle Thomas Coke, Earl of Leicester; M.P. (1776), protectionist, advocate of parliamentary reform; bred Southdown sheep, Devon cattle; improved Suffolk breed of pigs.

**Cola di Rienzi.** See RIENZI.

**Col′bert′** (kôl′bâr′), **Jean Baptiste.** 1619–1683. French statesman, b. Reims. Secretary in war office (1639). Entered employ of Cardinal Mazarin (1651). Made controller general of finance by Louis XIV (1665); instituted council of finance to purify service; greatly increased state revenues; developed industry; made minister of marine (1669); soon controlled colonies and extended French trade; imposed a protective tariff; built roads and canals; created French navy (1669–72) and mercantile marine; revised civil code; introduced marine code and "code noir" (colonial code); driven to levy oppressive taxes to meet expenses of Louis's wars. A great financial reformer and organizer, but cold (hence Mme. de Sévigné's nickname, **le Nord** [lē nôr'], "the North"), strict, and unpopular. Patron of writers, scientists, and academies. His brother **Charles** (1625–1696), Marquis **de Crois'sy'** (krwä'sē'), plenipotentiary at Congress of Aix-la-Chapelle (1668), aided in drafting Treaty of Nijmegen (1678); secretary of state for foreign affairs (1679–96). J. B. Colbert's son **Jean Baptiste** (1651–1690), Marquis **de Sei'gne·lay'** (sĕ'nyē·lā'), minister of marine (1683–89) and minister of state (1689–90).

**Col'borne** (kōl'bĕrn), Sir **John**. 1st Baron **Sea'ton** (sē't'n). 1778–1863. British general. Served in Egypt (1801), Sicily (1806); officer in Peninsular War and at Waterloo; major general (1825). Lieutenant governor of Upper Canada (1830); crushed revolt of 1838. Governor of Ionian Islands (1843–49). General (1854); field marshal (1860).

**Col'burn** (kōl'bĕrn), **Warren**. 1793–1833. American educator, b. Dedham, Mass.; author of *First Lessons in Arithmetic, on the Plan of Pestalozzi* (1821), long a standard textbook.

**Col'by** (kōl'bĭ), **Bainbridge**. 1869–1950. American lawyer, b. St. Louis, Mo. A.B., Williams (1890), LL.B., New York Law School; practiced in New York City. Associated with candidacy of Theodore Roosevelt for presidential nomination (1912) and a founder of Progressive party (1912). U.S. secretary of state (1920–21). Partner with Woodrow Wilson in practice of law (1921–23). Author of *The Close of Woodrow Wilson's Administration and the Final Years.*

**Colby, Frank Moore**. 1865–1925. American editor, b. Washington, D.C.; grad. Columbia Univ. (1888); editor, *International* (later *New International) Year Book* (from 1898), *New International Encyclopaedia* (1900–03 and 2d ed. 1913–15).

**Colby, Gardner**. 1810–1879. American woolen manufacturer and railroad builder, b. Bowdoinham, Me.; benefactor of Waterville Literary College, renamed Colby College in his honor.

**Col'cord** (?kŏl'kĕrd), **Lincoln Ross**. 1883–1947. American writer, b. at sea, off Cape Horn. Educ. Maine (1900–06). Civil engineer with Bangor and Aroostook Railroad (1906–09); devoted himself to writing (from 1909); assoc. editor, *The Nation*, New York (1919–20). Author of sea stories in *The Drifting Diamond* (1912) and *The Game of Life and Death* (1914), and verse in *Vision of War* (1915) and *An Instrument of the Gods* (1922); collaborator with O. E. Rölvaag in translating the latter's *Giants in the Earth* (1927).

**Col'den** (kōl'dĕn), **Cadwallader**. 1688–1776. Colonial administrator in America, b. in Ireland, of Scottish parents. Grad. U. of Edinburgh (1705); to Philadelphia (1710); practiced medicine; moved to New York (1718); lieutenant governor of New York (1761–76); upheld British policy. Noted for scientific interests; classified American plants in his neighborhood according to Linnaean system; submitted work to Linnaeus, who published it. Author of *The History of the Five Indian Nations* (1727). His daughter **Jane** (1724–1766), wife of Dr. William Farquhar (m. 1759), was a botanist. His grandson **Cadwallader David** (1769–1834), lawyer; mayor of New York (1818–20); member, U.S. House of Representatives (1821–23).

**Cole** (kōl). Name of an old Devonshire and Cornwall family, descended from Sir **William Cole** (d. 1653), who settled in Ireland in County Fermanagh (before 1607). His descendant **William Willoughby Cole** (1736–1803), created (1789) 1st earl of **En'nis·kil'len** (ĕn'ĭs·kĭl'ĕn). Sir **Galbraith Lowry** (1772–1842), son of 1st earl; officer in famous cavalry regiment the Enniskilleners; commanded fourth division in Peninsular War (1809–14); general (1830). **William Willoughby** (1807–1886), 3d earl; paleontologist; educ. Oxford; gathered collection of fossil fishes now in British Museum.

**Cole, George Douglas Howard**. 1889–1959. English economist and novelist; educ. Oxford. Author of *The World of Labour* (1913), *Social Theory* (1920), *Organized Labour* (1924), *Gold, Credit and Unemployment* (1930), *What Marx Really Meant* (1934), *Principles of Economic Planning* (1935), *Socialism in Evolution* (1938). Collaborator with his wife (m. 1918) **Margaret Isabel**, *nee* **Post'gate** [pōst'gāt] (1893– ), in a number of detective stories and novels, including *The Brooklyn Murders* (1923), *A Lesson in Crime* (1933), *Last Will and Testament* (1936), *Greek Tragedy* (1939).

**Cole, George Watson**. 1850–1939. American bibliographer and librarian, b. Warren, Conn. Practiced law (1876–85). Librarian, Henry E. Huntington Library and Art Gallery, San Marino, Calif. (1915–24). Author of bibliographies, and books on libraries and library science.

**Cole**, Sir **Henry**. 1808–1882. English civil servant. Virtual director (1853–73) of science and art department, Victoria and Albert Museum; painted, etched, engraved book illustrations; edited works of Thomas Love Peacock.

**Cole, Rossetter Gleason**. 1866–1952. American musician and composer, b. Clyde, Mich. Ph.B., Michigan (1888). Professor of music, Grinnell College, Iowa (1894–1901), U. of Wisconsin (1907–09); at Cosmopolitan School of Music (1915–52). Composer of cantatas, sonatas, symphonic prelude, orchestral overtures and suites, and choral pieces.

**Cole, Thomas**. 1801–1848. Landscape painter, b. in Lancashire, Eng.; to America (1819); founder of Hudson River school, a school of painters who found their early inspiration in scenery of the Hudson River Valley.

**Cole, Timothy**. 1852–1931. Wood engraver, b. London, Eng.; to U.S. (1857). In employ of *Scribner's* (from 1875) and its successor, *Century Magazine;* sent to Europe to engrave old masters (1883); finished Italian series (1892), Dutch and Flemish series (1896), English series (1900), Spanish series (1907), French series (1910); engaged thereafter in engraving old masters in American public and private collections.

**Cole, Vicat**. 1833–1895. English painter of Surrey and Sussex landscapes; R.A. (1880); known for *The Pool of London.* Son of **George Cole** (1810–83), landscape painter.

**Cole, William**. 1714–1782. English antiquary, friend of Horace Walpole; bequeathed mss. to British Museum.

**Cole'brooke** (kōl'bro͝ok), **Henry Thomas**. 1765–1837. English Orientalist. Civilian in India (1782–1814); member council of India (1807–14); completed translation of *Digest of Hindu Laws* begun by Sir William Jones (4 vols., 1798). Author of a Sanskrit grammar (1805) and lexicon (1808), works on Hindu mathematics and philosophy, and *Essay on the Vedas* (1805).

**Cole'man** (kōl'măn), **Charles**. d. 1664. English composer. Member of band of Charles I and of Charles II; chamber musician to Charles I; composed part of music for Davenant's *Siege of Rhodes* (1656). His son **Edward** (d. 1669), composed music for James Shirley's dirge beginning "The glories of our blood and state."

**Coleman, Charles Caryl**. 1840–1928. American landscape painter, b. Buffalo, N.Y.

**Cole'man, D'Alton Cor'ry** (kôr'ĭ). 1879–1956. Canadian railway official, b. Carleton Place, Ontario; president, Canadian Pacific Railway (1942–47).

**Coleman, William Tell**. 1824–1893. American pioneer in California, b. in Harrison Co., Ky.; associated with

Francis M. Smith (*q.v.*) in manufacture of borax. The mineral colemanite is named for him.

**Co·len′so** (kō·lĕn′zō), **John William.** 1814–1883. English bishop of Natal, b. in Cornwall; educ. Cambridge. Bishop of Natal (1853); compiled grammar and dictionary of Zulu and translated New Testament into Zulu; provoked controversy (1862) by liberality in not requiring polygamous Zulu converts to divorce their wives, by combating doctrine of eternal punishment, by declaring Pentateuch a post-exile forgery; deposed and excommunicated by bishop of Cape Town (1863); confirmed in his episcopal income by courts (1866); championed natives against Boer oppression (1875).

**Coleoni, Bartolommeo.** See COLLEONI.

**Cole′pep′er** (kŭl′pĕp′ẽr). See also CULPEPER.

**Colepeper, John.** 1st Baron **Colepeper of Thores′way** [thōrz′wā] (cr. 1644). d. 1660. English Royalist leader. Member of Long Parliament (1640); denounced monopolies and Strafford (1641), but defended episcopacy, opposed Grand Remonstrance (1641); chancellor of exchequer (1642–43); master of the rolls (1643); urged Charles I to make terms, first with Parliament, later with Scots, and Charles II with Scots; accompanied prince of Wales (later Charles II) in flight and in naval expedition to Thames (1648); received loan of 20,000 rubles from czar (1650); accompanied Charles II to southern France (1659) to conclude treaty of the Pyrenees. His eldest son, **Thomas Colepeper** *or* **Culpeper** (1635–1689), 2d baron, colonial administrator in America; jointly with Lord Arlington received from Charles II grant of all Virginia; commissioned governor (1675); to Virginia (1680); taxed and punished tobacco growers with intolerable severity; dissolved assembly; returned to England (1683).

**Co′ler** (kō′lẽr), **Alwin Gustav Edmund von.** 1831–1901. Prussian military surgeon; instrumental in improving army hygiene and hospital service; introduced antiseptics into military surgery.

**Cole′ridge** (kōl′rĭj), **Samuel Taylor.** 1772–1834. English poet and critic; youngest child of **John Coleridge** (1719–1781), schoolmaster and vicar at Ottery St. Mary, Devonshire. Scholar, Jesus Coll., Cambridge, read desultorily, adopted extreme views in politics and religion; enlisted (1793) in dragoons, and bought out by brother; took up with enthusiasm Robert Southey's scheme of pantisocracy and helped form quixotic plan for community on the Susquehanna, Pa., U.S.A.; wrote act one, Southey, acts two and three, of *The Fall of Robespierre* (1794); m. (1795) Sara Fricker, sister-in-law of Southey. Published first volume of poems (1796); in Bristol, started the weekly *Watchman*, which failed; preached in Unitarian chapels; practically supported by a tanner, Thomas Poole; began use of laudanum (c. 1796). Formed intimate association with William and Dorothy Wordsworth (1797); joined with Wordsworth (*q.v.*) in producing the *Lyrical Ballads* (1798 ff.), contributing *The Ancient Mariner, The Nightingale*, two scenes from *Osorio*, and (in 2d ed.) *Love;* wrote first part of *Christabel*, tragedy of *Osorio* (acted as *Remorse* at Drury Lane, 1813), and *Kubla Khan;* granted annuity by Wedgewood brothers on condition of devoting himself to literature. Visited Germany (1798–99); translated Schiller's *Wallenstein* (1800); a slave to opium (from 1803). Lectured unsuccessfully (1810–13); dependent on Wordsworth (1809), on James Gillman, a surgeon (1816–34), leaving his family dependent on friends; started *The Friend*, a philosophical magazine, which ran eight months. Published earlier works and *Biographia Literaria* and *Sibylline Leaves* (1817), *Aids to Reflection* (1825), the latter his most popular prose work. Returned to Trinitarianism; pensioner of Society of Literature (1824–30); his *Table Talk* (1835) and his original *Confessions of an Inquiring Spirit* (1840) posthumously published. Creator in England of the higher criticism well advanced in Germany; father of modern Shakespearean studies; introducer to England of German idealistic philosophy.

His eldest son, **David Hartley** (1796–1849), poet and man of letters; brought up by Southey; B.A., Oxon. (1819), forfeited Oriel fellowship by intemperance; did hack work for a Leeds publisher (1830–36); schoolmaster (1837–38); edited Massinger and Ford (1839); author of unfinished lyric drama *Prometheus* and graceful sonnets. His daughter **Sara** (1802–1852) m. her cousin Henry Nelson Coleridge (see below); wrote popular *Pretty Lessons in Verse* (1834) and *Phantasmion, A Fairy Tale* (1837), and annotated and edited her father's writings.

NEPHEWS OF S. T. COLERIDGE: (1) Sir **John Taylor Coleridge** (1790–1876); M.A., Oxon. (1817); contributor and editor of *Quarterly Review;* editor of Blackstone's *Commentaries* (1825); justice of King's Bench (1835–58). (2) **Henry Nelson Coleridge** (1798–1843), lawyer; m. Sara Coleridge (see above); literary editor of Samuel Taylor Coleridge; published his uncle's *Table Talk* and edited works. (3) **William Hart Coleridge** (1789–1849), bishop of Barbados (1824–41).

Sir **John Duke Coleridge** (1820–1894), 1st Baron **Coleridge;** eldest son of Sir John Taylor Coleridge; M.A., Oxon. (1846); bencher (1861); Liberal M.P. (1865–73); attorney general (1871); chief justice of Common Pleas (1873–80); chief justice of Queen's Bench (1880–94). His son **Bernard John Seymour** (1851–1927), 2d baron; educ. Oxford; called to bar (1877); queen's counsel (1892); M.P. (1885–94); judge, King's Bench division (1907–23).

**Henry James Coleridge** (1822–1893), brother of 1st baron; M.A., Oxon. (1847), entered Roman Catholic Church (1852), priest (1855); editor of Jesuit periodical (1865–81).

**Herbert Coleridge** (1830–1861), lawyer and philologist; son of Henry Nelson and Sara Coleridge; won double first in classics and mathematics at Oxford (1852); one of original promoters of project for standard English dictionary that later developed into *New English Dictionary* (begun 1884).

**Ernest Hartley Coleridge** (1846–1920), author; son of S. T. Coleridge's second son, Derwent; grad. Oxford (1870); secretary to lord chief justice of England (1894); edited letters (1895) and complete works (2 vols., 1912) of his grandfather, works of Byron (1898–1903), letters of 1st baron Coleridge, *Anima Poetae* (1895), and selections from unpublished notebooks of his grandfather's.

**Mary Elizabeth Coleridge** (1861–1907), poet and novelist; great-granddaughter of S. T. Coleridge's older brother; published first novel, *The Seven Sleepers of Ephesus* (1893); author of *Poems Old and New* (1907) and *Gathered Leaves* (1910).

**Cole′ridge–Tay′lor** (-tā′lẽr), **Samuel.** 1875–1912. English composer; son of Dr. Paul Taylor, native of Sierra Leone, West Africa, and English mother; studied violin and composition at Royal Coll. of Music. Won reputation with melodious choral work in trilogy, *Hiawatha's Wedding Feast* (1898), *Death of Minnehaha* (1899), and in *A Tale of Old Japan* (1911). Wrote incidental music for plays of Stephen Phillips.

**Co·le′rus** (kō·lā′rōōs), **Egmont.** 1888–1939. Austrian writer, b. Linz; statistician in Austrian government; known esp. for historical works extolling Faustian spirit of action. Author of novels, as *Antarktis* (1920), *Sodom* (1920), *Pythagoras* (1924), etc.

**Coles** (kōlz), **Abraham.** 1813–1891. American poet, remembered chiefly as author of *My Native Land.*

**Coles, Elisha.** 1640?–1680. English schoolmaster and lexicographer; published treatise on shorthand, primers of English and Latin (1674–75); compiled an English dictionary (1676) and a Latin dictionary (1677).

**Col′et** (kŏl′ĕt; -ĭt), **John.** 1467?–1519. English classical scholar and theologian; one of leaders of Renaissance in England. M.A., Oxon. (c. 1490); studied canon and civil law, patristics, and Greek in Paris and Italy (1493–96); met Budé and Erasmus; influenced by teachings of Savonarola. Lectured in Oxford (1496–1504) on New Testament, opposing interpretations of scholastic theologians; dean of St. Paul's (1504–19); preached against sale of bishoprics, custom of pluralities, church lawyers; devoted large fortune inherited from his father to founding and endowing (1509–12) St. Paul's School, first example of nonclerical education; accused of heresy for liberal opinions but protected by Archbishop William Warham; made Canterbury pilgrimage with Erasmus (1514); preached at Wolsey's installation as cardinal (1515).

**Co′let′** (kô′lĕ′), **Louise,** *nee* **Re·voil′** (rē·vwȧl′). 1810–1870. French writer; m. Hippolyte Colet (1834). Close friend of Mme. Récamier, Cousin, Alfred de Musset, Flaubert, Villemain. Author of verse, as in *Fleurs du Midi* (1836) and *Penserosa* (1839), and prose, as *La Jeunesse de Mirabeau* (1841), *Les Cœurs Brisés* (1843), *Lui* (1859), *L'Italie des Italiens* (1862–64).

**Co′lette′** (kô′lĕt′), Saint. 1381–1447. Flemish religious; entered Franciscan order of St. Clare (Poor Clares); instituted reforms in its rules and administration.

**Colette.** *Pen name of* **Sidonie Gabrielle Claudine Colette.** 1873–1954. French writer; m. Henry Gauthier-Villars (1893; divorced, 1906), Henry de Jouvenel (1910; divorced, 1924). Her works include a series of stories about an autobiographical character, Claudine (*Claudine à l'École,* 1900; *Claudine à Paris,* 1901; *Claudine en Ménage,* 1902; etc.), novels, as *La Retraite Sentimentale* (1907), *La Vagabonde* (1910), *L'Entrave* (1914), *Chéri* (1920), *La Fin de Chéri* (1926), and *La Chatte* (1933), short stories, essays, and a few plays.

**Co′ley** (kō′lĭ), **William Bradley.** 1862–1936. American surgeon, b. Westport, Conn. B.A., Yale (1884), M.D., Harvard (1888). Known for research on cancer and for radical cure of hernia.

**Col′fax** (kōl′făks), **Schuyler.** 1823–1885. American politician, b. New York City. Moved to Indiana (1836). Member, U.S. House of Representatives (1855–69); speaker (1863–69). Vice-president of the United States (1869–73). Involved in Crédit Mobilier scandal, and political career terminated.

**Col′gate** (kōl′gāt), **William.** 1783–1857. Soap manufacturer, b. in Kent, Eng., brought to U.S. as a child. Founded tallow chandlery and soap manufacturing business (1806), later expanded to include various toilet preparations. Benefactor of Madison U., Hamilton, N.Y., renamed (1890) Colgate U. in his honor. His son **James Boorman** (1818–1904), broker and banker; benefactor of Colgate U. Another son, **Samuel** (1822–1897), continued soap business, expanding plant in Jersey City, N.J., until it became one of largest establishments of its kind in world; trustee and benefactor of Colgate U. Samuel's son **Sidney Morse** (1862–1930), continued in soap business, becoming chairman of board of consolidated Colgate-Palmolive-Peet Co., in which company his brother **Gilbert** (1858–1933) became a director.

**Co′li′gny′** *or* **Co′li′gni′** (kô′lē′nyē′), **Gaspard (II) de.** 1519–1572. Admiral and leader of the Huguenots. Of a noble family, b. Châtillon-sur-Loing; third son of Gaspard (I) de Coligny (1470?–1522), marshal of France. Served under duc d'Enghien in Italy (1544); won renown for skill and bravery as a leader; colonel general of infantry (1547); admiral of France (1552); defended St.-Quentin with small force (1557) but defeated and held as prisoner in Spain (1557–59). Converted to Protestantism during imprisonment; became joint leader of Huguenots with Louis I, Prince of Condé (1560); opposed by Guise and Montmorency; aided Huguenots by sending colonies to New World (1562, 1564); at battles of Dreux (1562), Jarnac, and Moncontour (1569), but failed to take Poitiers; joined (1569) by Henry of Navarre as leader of Huguenots. Gained much influence over King Charles IX, thus arousing Guise and Catholics; killed at Massacre of St. Bartholomew (1572).

**Odet de Coligny** (1517–1571), his older brother; cardinal (1533) and archbishop (1534); convert to Calvinism; fled to England. A younger brother, **François** (1521–1569), soldier; also a convert to Protestantism; fought at Dreux, St.-Denis, and Jarnac.

**Louise** (1555–1620), daughter of Gaspard II; lost first husband in Massacre of St. Bartholomew; m. 2d (1583), William, Prince of Orange (assassinated 1584); both she and her brother **François** (1557–1591) were devoted followers of Henry IV in establishing Protestant faith. **Gaspard (III)** (1584–1646), son of François and grandson of Gaspard II; marshal of France under Louis XIII.

**Co·lijn′** (kô·līn′), **Hendrik.** 1869–1944. Dutch statesman; minister of war (1911–13); finance minister (1923); premier (1925–26); member of upper chamber (from 1926); again premier of the Netherlands (1933–39); forced to resign (July 8, 1939) because of his policy of retrenchment; most prominent leader of anti-Fascists.

**Co·lin′** (kŏ·lēn′) *or* **Co·lins′** *or* **Co·lyns′** (kŏ·lēns′), **A′lex′an′dre** (ȧ′lĕk′säɴ′dr′). 1527 (or 1529)–1612. Flemish sculptor; modeled decorations on castle of Heidelberg, and reliefs on tomb of Maximilian I and Hans Fugger at Innsbruck.

**Co·lin′dres** (kô·lēn′drās), **Vicente Me·jí′a** (mĕ·hē′ä). President of Honduras (1929–33).

**Co′lines′** (kô′lēn′), **Simon de.** 1480–1546. French printer; first to use italics in France; founded printing establishment at Meaux (1522).

**Col′la·mer** (kŏl′ȧ·mẽr), **Jacob.** 1791–1865. American lawyer, b. Troy, N.Y.; member (from Vermont), U.S. House of Representatives (1843–49); U.S. postmaster general (1849); U.S. senator (1855–65).

**Col′la·ti′nus** (kŏl′ȧ·tī′nŭs), **Lucius Tarquinius.** *Sometimes Anglicized* **Col′la·tine** (kŏl′ȧ·tīn). Husband of Lucretia (*q.v.*).

**Col′lé′** (kô′lā′), **Charles.** 1709–1783. French playwright and song writer.

**Col′le** (kôl′lā), **Raffaello dal.** *Known also as* **Raf′fa·el·li′no** (räf′fä·āl·lē′nō). c. 1490–c. 1540. Tuscan painter; pupil and associate of Raphael; collaborated with Giulio Romano at Rome and Mantua; founded and directed academy at Borgo San Sepolcro.

**Col′le·o′ni** (kōl′lā·ō′nē) *or* **Co′le·o′ni** (kō′lā-), **Bartolommeo.** 1400–1475. Italian soldier; general in chief of armies of Venice (1454); gained reputation as foremost tactician and disciplinarian of 15th century.

**Col′le·rye′** (kôl′rē′), **Roger de.** *Pseudonym* **Roger Bon′temps′** (bôɴ′täɴ′). 1470?–?1540. French poet; organized (under pseudonym) society of bons vivants, whose president was titled "Abbé des Fous." Béranger, in one of his songs, has popularized Collerye's pseudonym. Author of many lyrics (pub. 1536).

**Col′les** (kŏl′ĕs; -ĭs), **Henry Cope.** 1879–1943. English music critic; B.A., Oxon. (1902). Music critic, London *Times* (from 1911). Author of *Brahms* (1908), *The*

*Growth of Music* (3 parts, 1912–16), vol. vii of *Oxford History of Music* (1934). Editor of third and fourth editions of *Grove's Dictionary of Music and Musicians* (1927, 1940).

**Col'lett** (kŏl'lĕt), **Camilla,** *nee* **Wer'ge·land** (văr'gĕ-län). 1813–1895. Norwegian novelist; sister of Henrik Wergeland (*q.v.*); m. P. J. Collett (1841). A leader of feminist movement in Norway, reflected in her novels.

**Col·let'ta** (kôl·lāt'tä), **Pietro.** 1775–1831. Neapolitan general and historian. Served under Mack von Leiberich against the French (1798) but supported the Parthenopean Republic when organized (1799) and later served under Joseph Napoleon and under Murat; involved in revolution (1820) and exiled to Florence.

**Col'ley** (kŏl'ĭ) *or* **Cow'ley** (kou'lĭ). Original name of the Wellesley family (*q.v.*).

**Colley,** Sir **George Pomeroy.** 1835–1881. Irish general in British army. Served in South Africa (1854–60), China (1860); chief of staff in Zulu war (1879); governor and commander in chief of Natal (1880); defeated and killed by Boers.

**Col'lier** (kŏl'yẽr; kŏl'ĭ·ẽr), **Arthur.** 1680–1732. English philosopher; educ. Oxford; devoted himself to study of Descartes and Malebranche; anticipated in *Clavis Universalis* (written 1703, pub. 1713) views of Berkeley on the impossibility of an external world.

**Collier, Constance.** *Family name* **Har'die** (här'dĭ). 1880–1955. English actress; m. Julian L'Estrange. In Beerbohm Tree's company at His Majesty's Theatre (1901–07); on New York stage (1908, 1909, 1911, 1912). Author of *Harlequinade: The Story of my Life* (1929).

**Collier, Jeremy.** 1650–1726. English clergyman. M.A., Cantab. (1676); refused oath of allegiance to William and Mary; outlawed for absolving on the scaffold two would-be assassins of William (1696). Published his famous *Short View of the Immorality and Profaneness of the English Stage* (1698) and defended himself against angry replies by Congreve, Vanbrugh, and others (till 1708). Published (1701–21) his *Historical Dictionary*, founded on Louis Moreri's dictionary, and *Ecclesiastical History of Great Britain* (1708–14). Was ordained a nonjuring bishop (1713).

**Collier, John.** 1850–1934. English portrait painter, b. London; studied at Slade School (London) and in Paris and Munich.

**Collier, John Payne.** 1789–1883. English Shakespearean critic. Journalist (1809–47); barrister (1829); issued new editions of Dodsley's *Old Plays* (1825–27, 1833, 1851); published *History of English Dramatic Poetry* (1831). In *New Facts, New Particulars and Further Particulars* (1835–39), about Shakespeare, and in *Perkins Folio* (1852), introduced forged marginal corrections in texts; brought out texts of Shakespeare based on these forgeries; exposed (1859–61). Edited Spenser's works (1862); compiled critical account of rarest books in English language (1865).

**Collier, Peter Fenelon.** 1849–1909. Publisher, b. in County Carlow, Ireland; to U.S. (1866); in publishing business (from 1877); founded *Collier's Weekly* (1896). His son **Robert Joseph** (1876–1918) succeeded to the presidency of the firm and editorship of *Collier's Weekly* (from 1909).

**Collier, Price,** *in full* **Hiram Price.** 1860–1913. American writer, b. Davenport, Iowa. Grad. Harvard Divinity School (1882) and served in Unitarian ministry (1882–91). Devoted himself to writing (from 1891). Author of *England and the English from an American Point of View* (1909), *The West in the East from an American Point of View* (1911), *Germany and the Germans from an American Point of View* (1913), etc.

**Collier, Robert Porrett.** See Baron MONKSWELL.

**Collier, William.** 1866–1944. American comedian and playwright. Member of Daly Theatre Company (1883–88); starred in *On the Quiet* (1901–02) and *The Dictator* (1905–06); also appeared in *A Lucky Star* (1909), *Bunty Pulls the Strings* (1912–13); coauthor of, and actor in, *I'll be Hanged if I Do* (1910), *Take My Advice* (1911), *Never Say Die* (1912); author of *Caught in the Rain* (1906) and *The Patriot* (1908).

**Collier, William Miller.** 1867–1956. American lawyer and diplomat, b. Lodi, N.Y. A.B., Hamilton (1889). Adm. to bar (1892) and practiced in New York. U.S. ambassador to Spain (1905–09), and Chile (1921–28). Lecturer on international law, New York Law School (1912–18). President, George Washington U. (1918–21). Author of *Collier on Bankruptcy* (1898), *Collier on Civil Service Law* (1901), *The Trusts* (1900), *The Influence of Lawyers in the Past and in the Future* (1921), etc.

**Col'lin** (kôl'ēn), **Heinrich Josef von.** 1771–1811. Austrian poet and playwright.

**Col'lin' d'Har'le·ville'** (kô'lăɴ' där'lē·vēl'), **Jean François.** 1755–1806. French playwright; author of *L'Inconstant* (1786), *Le Vieillard et les Jeunes Hommes* (1804), etc.

**Col'lings** (kŏl'ĭngz), **Jesse.** 1831–1920. English leader of land reform; M.P. (1880–1908); took part in Joseph Chamberlain's municipal reform from Joseph Arch's land-reform movement; used slogan "Three acres and a cow"; undersecretary to home department (1895–1902).

**Col'ling·wood** (kŏl'ĭng·wŏŏd), **Cuthbert.** Baron **Collingwood.** 1750–1810. English naval commander. Served in naval brigade at Bunker Hill (1775); lieutenant under Nelson; blockaded Cádiz (1797–98), Brest (1799–1805); vice-admiral (1804); took command on Nelson's death at Trafalgar (1805); missed chance of destroying Toulon fleet (1808).

**Col'lins** (kŏl'ĭnz), **Anthony.** 1676–1729. English deist; intimate of John Locke. Author of an essay on *Use of Reason* (1707), *Discourse of Free Thinking* (1713; which called forth replies from Hoadly, Bentley, Swift), *Inquiry concerning Human Liberty* (1715), defending necessitarianism.

**Collins, Charles Allston.** See under Wilkie COLLINS.

**Collins, Dale.** 1897–1956. Australian writer, b. Sydney. Author of *Seatracks of the Speejacks, the Story of the First Motor-Boat Voyage around the World*, the novels *Ordeal, Vanity Under the Sun, Idolaters*, and the plays *Ordeal* (1924) and *Romantic Ladies* (1935).

**Collins, Edward Trowbridge.** 1887–1951. American professional baseball player, b. Millerton, N.Y.; with Chicago and Philadelphia, American League (1906–30).

**Collins, Frank Shipley.** 1848–1920. American algologist, b. Boston; author of *The Green Algae of North America* (1909), etc.

**Collins,** Sir **Godfrey P.** 1875–1936. British soldier and politician; M.P. (1910–36). During World War (1914–18), served in Egypt, Gallipoli, and Mesopotamia (1915–17; lieutenant colonel, 1916). Chief Liberal whip in House of Commons (1924–26). Secretary of state for Scotland (1932–36).

**Collins, John Churton.** 1848–1908. English literary critic. B.A., Oxon. (1872); author of *Study of English Literature* (1891); professor, Birmingham (1904–08). Author of *Ephemera Critica* (1901), *Studies in Shakespeare* (1904), etc.

**Collins, Joseph.** 1866–1950. American neurologist, b. Brookfield, Conn. M.D., N.Y.U. (1888). Professor, New York Post-Graduate Med. School (1897–1909). Author of *The Faculty of Speech* (1900), *Pathology of Nervous Diseases* (1901), *Sleep and the Sleepless* (1912), *The*

*Doctor Looks at Literature* (1923), *The Doctor Looks at Love and Life* (1926), *The Doctor Looks at Life and Death* (1931), etc.

**Collins, Michael.** 1890–1922. Irish revolutionary leader and soldier, b. in County Cork; at work in London (1906–16). Participated in the Easter Rebellion (1916) and was one of party that seized the general post-office building in Dublin; was arrested and held prisoner in an internment camp (to Christmas, 1916). When released, rose rapidly to leadership in the Sinn Fein movement and in the military body known as the Irish Volunteers. Arrested (Apr., 1918), tried, convicted of seditious speech, and confined in jail at Sligo. Aided in adoption of declaration of independence and a provisional constitution (Jan., 1919), and in planning and carrying through escape of de Valera from Lincoln jail (Feb., 1919); became minister of finance in the Sinn Fein ministry (1919–22), and retained this office after conclusion of a treaty of peace with Great Britain; also, was appointed commander in chief of the military forces of the Irish Free State. Mortally wounded (Aug. 22, 1922) in repelling an attack by a party of irregulars.

**Collins, Mortimer.** 1827–1876. English writer; mathematics master in Guernsey (1850–56); author of poem *The British Birds, a Communication from the Ghost of Aristophanes* (1872) and a number of novels, including *Sweet Anne Page* (1868).

**Collins, Norman Richard.** 1907– . English writer of fiction; deputy chairman, Victor Gollancz, Ltd., publishers. Author of *Penang Appointment* (1934), *The Three Friends* (1935), *Trinity Town* (1936), *Love in our Time* (1938), *I shall not want* (1939), *Anna* (1942), etc.

**Collins, Wilkie,** *in full* **William Wilkie.** 1824–1889. English novelist. Articled to firm of tea merchants; called to bar (1851); began literary career with biography of his father (1848). His first novel a historical romance, *Antonina* (1850); contributed two novels to Dickens's *Household Words* (from 1855); collaborated with Dickens in *No Thoroughfare* (1867). Author of novels of mystery with skillful and complex plots (influencing technique of Dickens's later novels), including *The Woman in White* (1860), in which he created the character Count Fosco, *The Moonstone* (1868), *The New Magdalen* (1873). His father, **William Collins** (1788–1847), landscape and figure painter and etcher, made a specialty of portraying child life; remembered for *Blackberry Gatherers, The Bird Catchers* (1814), *Happy as a King* (1836), *Cromer Sands* (1845). Wilkie's brother **Charles Allston** (1828–1873), painter of Pre-Raphaelite school, married younger dau. of Charles Dickens.

**Collins, William.** 1721–1759. English lyric poet; son of a hatter at Chichester. B.A., Oxon. (1743); friend of Warton and Gilbert White; at 17, wrote *Persian Eclogues* (1742; changed 1759 to *Oriental Eclogues*), his only poems valued by contemporaries. Composed his memorable *Odes* (12 in number, 1747), including *To Evening, The Passions, To Simplicity*, which attracted no notice. Intimate with James Thomson, on whose death he wrote the exquisite *Elegy on Thomson* (pub. 1749); dedicated *Ode on Popular Superstitions of the Highlands* (written 1750) to John Home.

**Col'lin·son** (kŏl'ĭn·s'n), **James.** 1825?–1881. English painter; an original member of Pre-Raphaelite Brotherhood.

**Collinson,** Sir **Richard.** 1811–1883. English naval officer. Arctic navigator through Bering Strait in search for Sir John Franklin (1850–54); admiral (1875); edited *Three Voyages of Martin Frobisher* (1867).

**Col'lip** (kŏl'ĭp), **James Bertram.** 1892–1965. Canadian biochemist. B.A. (1912) and Ph.D. (1916), U. of Toronto. Professor, McGill U. (from 1928); head of the Research Inst. of Endocrinology, McGill (from 1941). Known for work on internal secretions, esp. of the parathyroid and pituitary glands. See Frederick Grant BANTING.

**Col'li·shaw** (kŏl'ĭ·shô), **Raymond.** 1893– . British military aviator, b. in Canada. Served in Royal Canadian navy (1908–14), entering the air service (1915), and commanding squadrons in France (1916–18); recorded as having destroyed 60 enemy aircraft. Commanded Royal Air Force detachments in South Russia (1919–20), Iraq (1921–23), the Sudan (1935–36), Heliopolis (1936–38), and Egypt (from 1939).

**Col'li·son** (kŏl'ĭ·s'n), **Wilson.** 1893–1941. American playwright and novelist, b. Glouster, Ohio. Author of the plays *The Girl with Carmine Lips* (1922), *A Bachelor's Night* (1923), *Desert Sands* (1924), *The Vagabond* (1927), *Red Dust* (1927); collaborated with Otto Harbach in *Up in Mabel's Room* (1919) and with Avery Hopwood in *The Girl in the Limousine* (1919) and in *Getting Gertie's Garter* (1921). Author of a number of murder mysteries and novels.

**Col'litz** (kŏl'ĭts; *Angl.* kŏl'-), **Her'mann** (hĕr'män; *Angl.* hûr'măn). 1855–1935. Philologist, b. in Germany; to U.S. (1886); assoc. professor (1886–97), and professor (1897–1907), of comparative philology and German, Bryn Mawr College; professor of Germanic philology, Johns Hopkins (1907–27). Author of *Die Neueste Sprachforschung* (1886), *Das Schwache Praeteritum und seine Vorgeschichte* (1912). He married (1904) **Kla'ra** (klä'rä; *Angl.* klâr'*ă*) **Hech'ten·burg** [hĕk'tĕn·bŏŏrk] (1863–1944), Ph.D., Heidelberg (1901), author of *Das Fremdwort bei Grimmelshausen* (1901), *Fremdwörterbuch des 17. Jahrhunderts* (1904), *Verbs of Motion in their Semantic Divergence* (1931).

**Collodi.** See Carlo LORENZINI.

**Col'lo·re'do, von** (fôn kôl'ō·rā'dō). Austrian noble family of soldiers, including: **Hieronymus** (1582–1638), who commanded a regiment at Lützen (1632). His brother **Rudolf** (1585–1657), a trusted adviser to Ferdinand III, field marshal, succeeding Wallenstein in command of the army in Bohemia. **Joseph Maria, Count von Mels'-Wald'see'** [mĕls'vält'zā'] (1735–1818), field marshal in the Seven Years' War and director-general of artillery. **Hieronymus, Count von Colloredo-Mans'feld** [-mäns'fĕlt] (1775–1822), field marshal during the French Revolutionary and Napoleonic wars.

**Col'lot' d'Her'bois'** (kô'lō' dĕr'bwȧ'), **Jean Marie.** 1750–1796. French revolutionist; an actor by profession; member of the Convention (1792), joined the Mountain. Notorious for his cruelty in hunting down and judging suspected Royalists at Lyon (1793–94); involved in conspiracy against Robespierre (1794); expelled from the Convention (Apr., 1795); transported to French Guiana, where he died.

**Colluthus.** Variant of COLUTHUS.

**Coll'yer** (kŏl'yẽr), **Robert.** 1823–1912. Unitarian clergyman, b. in Keighley, England; to U.S. (1850). Blacksmith and Methodist lay preacher at Shoemakertown, near Philadelphia. Entered Unitarian ministry (1859); pastorates in Chicago (1859–79) and in Church of the Messiah, New York City (1879–1903).

**Col'man** (kōl'mŏn), Saint. d. 676. Irish monk at Iona; bishop of Lindisfarne (661); supporter of Celtic usages against the Roman at Whitby (664).

**Col'man** (kōl'măn), **Benjamin.** 1673–1747. American clergyman, b. Boston. Grad. Harvard (1692). Pastor, Brattle Street Church, Boston (1699–1747).

**Colman, George,** the elder. 1732–1794. English dramatist, b. Florence, Tuscany, son of British envoy. Educ. by his uncle William Pulteney, later Earl of Bath; M.A., Oxon. (1758); joint editor of *The Connoisseur* (1754–56). In first play, *Polly Honeycomb* (1760), mocked sentimental novels; won fame with *The Jealous Wife* (1761), based in part on Fielding's *Tom Jones;* produced *The Clandestine Marriage* jointly with David Garrick (1766); as acting manager of Covent Garden, produced plays of his own and adaptations from Shakespeare (1767–74); manager of Haymarket (1777–89). Edited plays of Beaumont & Fletcher (1778); author of a version of Horace's *Ars Poetica* (1783). His son **George**, the younger (1762–1836), was also a dramatist; educ. at Oxford and Aberdeen; his first play, *The Female Dramatist*, based in part upon *Roderick Random*, produced (1782) at the Haymarket, roundly condemned; wrote or adapted (1784–1822) about twenty-five comedies, musical comedies, operas, of which best were the comedies *John Bull, or an Englishman's Fireside* (1803) and *The Heir at Law* (1808), introducing in the latter the avaricious pedant Dr. Pangloss. Manager of Haymarket (1789–1813).

**Colman, Norman Jay.** 1827–1911. American agriculturist, b. near Richfield Springs, N.Y. Edited *Colman's Rural World* (1865–1911). U.S. commissioner of agriculture (1885–89); first U.S. secretary of agriculture (1889).

**Colman, Samuel.** 1832–1920. American landscape painter, b. Portland, Me.; a founder and first president (1866) of American Water-color Society.

**Cöln** (kûln), **Franz.** 1873– . Educator, b. Linz, Germany. To U.S.; naturalized citizen; professor of sacred scripture, Catholic U., Washington, D.C. Defined Eastern Church terms for *Webster's New International Dictionary, Second Edition.*

**Col·na′ghi** (kŏl·nä′gĭ), **Martin Henry.** 1821–1908. English picture dealer and collector; authority on Dutch and Flemish pictures; discoverer of van Goyen.

**Co·lo′ma** (kō·lō′mä), **Luis.** 1851–1915. Spanish writer, b. at Jerez; Jesuit (1874 ff.); known esp. for his satirical novel of Madrid society *Pequeñeces* (1891).

**Coloman.** See Koloman.

**Col′omb** (kŏl′ŭm), **Philip Howard.** 1831–1899. British naval officer and historian, b. in Scotland; served in Burmese war (1852); engaged in suppressing slave trade (1868–70); flag captain to Vice-Admiral Alfred P. Ryder in China (1874–77); rear admiral (1887). Devised new system of night signaling for steam vessels, "Colomb's flashing signals" (1858), a new system of tactics, and new signal book for British navy. Working independently of Admiral Mahan, wrote *Naval Warfare* (1891), demonstrating prime importance of sea supremacy for military offensive. His brother Sir **John Charles Ready** (1838–1909), captain in Royal Marine Artillery, was a high authority on imperial defense; author of *Imperial Federation* (1887).

**Co′lombe′** (kô′lôɴb′) *or* **Co′lomb′** (kô′lôɴ′) *or* **Co′lumb′** (kô′lôɴ′), **Michel.** 1430?–1512. French sculptor; studio at Tours. Regarded as one of the masters of the early French Renaissance period. Most important work, tomb of Francis II, Duc de Bretagne, and his wife Marguerite, now in the cathedral at Nantes.

**Co′lom·bi′ni** (kō′lōm·bē′nē), **John.** 1300–1367. Italian founder of the Jesuate order, confirmed by Pope Urban V (1367) but suppressed by Clement IX (1668) because of its extensive manufacture and sale of distilled liquors.

**Co·lom′bo** (kō·lōm′bō), **Matteo Realdo.** 1516?–?1559. Italian anatomist; professor at Padua, Pisa, and Rome; credited with discovery of pulmonary circulation; used animals to demonstrate movements of heart and lungs.

**Co·lon′na** (kō·lōn′nä). Noble Roman family; originated probably with **Pietro**, Lord of Colonna (c. 1100); held great fiefs in the Campagna; in medieval times, often at feud with the Orsini and Caetani; members include one pope, 30 cardinals, and many distinguished generals and senators; most prominent members include:
**Egidio** (1247–1316), Augustinian theologian at Paris; preceptor of King Philip IV; general of Augustinian order (1292); archbishop of Bourges (1296); author of political treatise *De Regimine Principum.* **Sciarra** (d. 1329), bitter enemy of Pope Boniface VIII; lost his possessions at Palestrina (1298); excommunicated; returned with French aid and took pope prisoner (1303); supported Louis the Bavarian and crowned him emperor at Rome (1328). **Stefano** (d. 1347), Count of **Ro·ma′gna** (rō·mä′nyä); brother of Sciarra; friend of Petrarch; governor of Bologna (1289); involved in struggle with papacy; defeated by Cola di Rienzi. **Ottone**; see Pope Martin V. **Fabrizio** (d. 1520), Grand Constable of Naples, **Prospero** (1452–1523), grandnephew of Pope Martin V, and **Pompeo** (d. 1532), cardinal, nephew of Prospero; all three able generals in wars of 16th century of Italian states against France. **Vittoria** (1492?–1547), poet; daughter of Fabrizio; b. Castello di Marino, near Rome; m. Fernando Francisco de Ávalos (*q.v.*), Marqués de Pescara; gradually estranged from him; after his death at Pavia (1525), wrote many poems of which he was the inspiration; knew leading literary persons of her time; much admired by Michelangelo, who addressed sonnets to her; her poetry deeply religious. **Marc Antonio** (d. 1584), Duke of **Pa·lia′no** (pä·lyä′nō); general and viceroy; exiled from Rome by Pope Pius IV; entered military service of Spain; led Spanish army successfully against Papal States (1556); recalled and commanded papal galleys at Lepanto (1571) against Turks; viceroy of Sicily. **Fabio** (1567–?1650), botanist, b. Naples; wrote compilation of then-known botanical knowledge, valuable to later classifiers of botanical species; discovered about eighty new plants. **Fabrizio** (1840–1923), Duke of **Paliano** (1912); general and senator, head of modern Colonna family; served in World War (1914–19); many years a senator; vice-president of Italian Senate.

**Colonna, Giovanni Paolo.** 1637–1695. Italian composer, b. Bologna. Composer of church music, oratorios, and operas.

**Co′lonne′** (kô′lôn′), **Édouard.** *Real name* **Jules Édouard Ju′da′** (zhü′dȧ′). 1838–1910. French violinist and orchestra conductor, b. Bordeaux. Founded (c. 1874), and for many years conducted, the "Concerts Colonne"; brought out for first time in Paris new works of famous composers, as Dubois, Franck, Saint-Saëns, Brahms, Wagner, Grieg, Tchaikovsky, Rimski-Korsakov, and Berlioz.

**Co·lon′ne** (kō·lōn′nā), **Guido delle.** Also **Guido da Colonna.** See Guido delle Colonne.

**Colqu·houn′** (kō·hōōn′), **Archibald Ross.** 1848–1914. British journalist and traveler; b. off Cape of Good Hope, son of Scottish doctor. Administrator of Mashonaland, South Africa (1890); examined Nicaragua and Panama canal routes (1895). Author of travel books.

**Colquhoun, Patrick.** 1745–1820. Scottish writer on economic subjects. Merchant in Virginia and (1766–89) in Glasgow; founded (1782) Glasgow Chamber of Commerce, oldest of its kind in Great Britain; police magistrate in London (1792); advocated reform of police system. His great-grandson Sir **Patrick MacChombaich de Colquhoun** (1815–1891), British lawyer and diplomat, was amateur champion oarsman (1837); M.A., Cantab. (1844); councilor of legation in Saxony (till

1866); chief justice of supreme court of Ionian Islands (1861).

**Col'quitt** (kŏl'kwĭt), **Walter Terry.** 1799–1855. American lawyer, b. in Halifax County, Va.; educ. College of New Jersey (Princeton). Member, U.S. House of Representatives (1839–40; 1842–43); U.S. senator (1843–48). His son **Alfred Holt** (1824–1894), b. in Walton County, Ga., was governor of Georgia (1876–82) and U.S. senator (1883–94).

**Cols'man** (kōls'män), **Alfred.** 1873–1955. German Zeppelin builder; founder of first German commercial air-transport company and cofounder of Lufthansa (German air-transport company).

**Colt** (kōlt), **Samuel.** 1814–1862. American inventor, b. Hartford, Conn. Invented revolver (U.S. patent issued 1836, on improved models 1839 and 1850).

**Col'ton** (kōl't'n; -tŭn), **Arthur Willis.** 1868–1943. American writer, b. Washington, Conn. A.B. (1890) and Ph.D. (1893), Yale. Librarian, University Club, New York City (1906–29). Author of *Bennie Ben Cree* (1900), *The Delectable Mountains* (1901), *The Debatable Land* (1901), *Tioba* (1903), *The Belted Seas* (1905), *The Cruise of the Violetta* (1906), *Harps Hung Up in Babylon* (1907).

**Colton, Charles Caleb.** 1780?–1832. English clergyman, sportsman, wine merchant; author of *Lacon* (1820–22), two volumes of aphorisms.

**Colton, Walter.** 1797–1851. American Congregational clergyman and author, b. in Rutland County, Vt. Chaplain, U.S. navy (1831–51). Founded *The Californian*, first newspaper published in California. Author of *Ship and Shore* (1835), *Deck and Port* (1850), etc. His brother **Gardner Quincy** (1814–1898) conducted demonstration of effects of nitrous oxide (laughing gas) which inspired the dentist Horace Wells to use this as an anesthetic.

**Col'um** (kŏl'ŭm), **Padraic.** 1881–1972. Poet and playwright, b. Longford, Ireland; to U.S. (1914). Formerly, editor of *Irish Review*, Dublin, and a founder of Irish Theatre. Author of verse, *Wild Earth* (1907), *Dramatic Legends* (1922), *Creatures* (1927), *Poems* (1932), *The Story of Lowry Maen* (1937); plays, *Three Plays* (1916), *Mogu, the Wanderer* (1917), *The Miracle of the Corn* (1917), *The Betrayal* (1920), *Balloon* (1929); juveniles, *The Boy Who Knew What the Bird Said* (1918), *The Girl Who Sat by the Ashes* (1919), *The Children Who Followed the Piper* (1922), etc. Also, compiler of *An Anthology of Irish Poetry* (1921). m. (1912) **Mary Gunning Ma·guire'** (mȧ·gwīr') (1887?–1957), lit. critic and short-story writer; author of *From These Roots* (1937).

**Columb, Michel.** See COLOMBE.

**Co·lum'ba** (kō·lŭm'bȧ), Saint. *Irish* **Col'um** (kŭl'ŭm) *or* **Col'um·cille** (kŭl'ŭm·kĭl). 521–597. Irish missionary; called "Apostle of Caledonia"; b. Donegal, son of Ulster chief. Ordained priest (c. 551); with 12 disciples established (563) monastery on island of Iona; converted northern Picts; gave benediction to Aidan as king of Scots (574); held sway over Columban churches in Ireland and north of England, largely independent of papal supervision; author of three hymns.

**Co·lum'ban** (kō·lŭm'băn) *or* **Col'um·ba'nus** (kŏl'ŭm·bā'nŭs), Saint. 543–615. Irish missionary, b. in Leinster; with twelve monks left Ireland and settled in the Vosges (c. 585); built abbey of Luxeuil, Haute-Saône, for which he drew up a monastic rule; involved in controversy with French bishops over the tonsure and over keeping Easter according to Celtic usage; expelled; founded Monastery of Bobbio in the Appennines (613).

**Co·lum'bus** (kō·lŭm'bŭs), **Christopher.** *Ital.* **Cristoforo Co·lom'bo** (kō·lōm'bō). *Span.* **Cristóbal Co·lón'** (kō·lōn'). 1451–1506. Discoverer of America, b. at or near Genoa, Italy. To sea at early age; settled in Lisbon, Portugal (c. 1477), where he married and had a son, Diego. Believing in theory that earth is round, conceived idea of reaching Asia by sailing due west and submitted proposals to king of Portugal suggesting that he equip an expedition for this purpose. Meeting with no success, went to Spain (c. 1484) and submitted proposals to Ferdinand and Isabella, who, after many refusals, agreed to requests (April 17, 1492). Fitted out three vessels, *Santa María* (which he commanded, with Juan de la Cosa as his pilot), *Niña* (Vicente Pinzón, captain), and *Pinta* (Martín Pinzón, captain); sailed from Palos (Aug. 3, 1492) and sighted land (Oct. 12, 1492), one of the Bahamas (island of Guanahani, renamed by Columbus San Salvador and now generally identified with Watlings Island). Continued voyage, sailing along north coast of Cuba and Haiti (Hispaniola); left colony of 40 men on Haitian coast building a fort, La Navidad; started home (Jan. 4, 1493) and reached Palos (March 15, 1493). Sailed on 2d voyage (Sept. 25, 1493) with seventeen ships and 1500 men; discovered Dominica (Nov. 3, 1493); reached La Navidad and found colony destroyed by hostile Indians; made new settlement at Isabela, island of Haiti (Dec., 1493), first European town in New World; sailed westward, discovered Jamaica; returned to Isabela; fought Indians, defeating them on the Vega Real (April 25, 1495). Returned to Spain (March, 1496) with Juan de Aguado, royal commissioner sent out by Spanish authorities, at instance of Columbus's opponents, to investigate his dealings with natives; presented his case to the king, favorably heard, and charges dismissed. Left Spain on 3d voyage (May 30, 1498); discovered Trinidad (July 31, 1498) and land at mouth of Orinoco River (Aug. 1, 1498), probably first discovery of mainland of South America. Further complaints of trouble in the new lands brought (Aug. 24, 1500) a new official investigator, Francisco de Bobadilla, who arrested Columbus and his brothers and sent them back to Spain in chains; released in Spain but could not obtain reinstatement in his honors and dignities. Left Spain on 4th voyage (March, 1502); discovered Honduras (July 30, 1502) and coasted down to Isthmus of Panama, seeking westward passage in apparent effort to sail around world; failing to find passage, returned to Jamaica (Feb., 1503); after many difficulties there, returned to Spain (Nov. 7, 1504). Failed to gain reinstatement in his honors and died in Valladolid in poverty and neglect (May 20 or 21, 1506), still believing that he had discovered coast of Asia.

His brothers: (1) **Bartholomew,** *Span.* **Bartolomé** (1445?–?1514), captain of Spanish supply fleet to New World (1493); governed Haiti (1496–98) during Christopher's absence; founded Santo Domingo (1496); accompanied Christopher on 4th voyage (1502–04); accompanied his nephew Diego (in 1509) to Haiti and held office in government at Santo Domingo. (2) **Diego** (1450?–?1515), accompanied Christopher on 2d voyage (1493) and governed at intervals in Isabela and in Santo Domingo; became a priest; again in Santo Domingo (1509).

Christopher's son **Diego** (1480?–1526) was created admiral of the Indies and governor of Hispaniola (1509); after much trouble, recalled by Council of the Indies (1523) to defend himself from charges brought against him; never convicted, but failed to obtain redress for grievances. His son **Luis** (1521?–1572) was granted island of Jamaica in fief, a pension, territories in Veragua, and titles of duke of **Ve·ra'gua** (vā·rä'gwä) and marquis of **Ja·mai'ca** (jȧ·mā'kȧ); governed Hispaniola as captain general (1540–51); banished to Oran, Africa (1565), where he died. The title duke of Veragua passed to his son **Diego**, who died childless (1578), then to descendants of Luis's sister **Isabel**, and on failure of that line (1733), to descendants of Luis's daughter **Francisca**. **Ferdinand**, *Span.* **Fernando** (1488–1539), natural son of Christopher Columbus and Beatriz Enríquez of Córdoba; accompanied his father on 4th voyage (1502–04); received large royal grants; amassed great library; wrote biography (now lost) of his father, used by historian Las Casas.

**Col'u·mel'la** (kŏl'ū·mĕl'ȧ), **Lucius Junius Moderatus.** Roman writer on agriculture, of 1st century A.D.; b. at Gades (Cádiz), Spain; author of *De Re Rustica.*

**Co·lu'thus** (kō·lū'thŭs) *or* **Col·lu'thus** (kŏ-). Greek epic poet of 5th century A.D.; little of his work is extant.

**Col'vin** (kŏl'vĭn), **John Russell.** 1807–1857. Anglo-Indian administrator; b. Calcutta; lieutenant governor of North-West Provinces during Sepoy Mutiny. His son Sir **Auckland** (1838–1908), b. Calcutta, entered Indian civil service (1858); English comptroller general in Egypt (1880–82), financial adviser to khedive (1883–87); lieutenant governor of North-West Provinces (1887–92); author of *The Making of Modern Egypt* (1906), and a biography of his father.

**Col'vin** (kŏl'vĭn), Sir **Sidney.** 1845–1927. English literary and art critic, b. at Norwood. Educ. Cambridge U. Slade professor of fine art, Cambridge (1873–85); also, director, Fitzwilliam Museum (1876–84); keeper of department of prints and drawings, British Museum (1884–1912). Intimate friend of Robert Louis Stevenson; editor of Edinburgh edition of Stevenson's works, and publisher of *Vailima Letters* (1895), letters written to him by Stevenson from Samoa. Author also of *John Keats, His Life and Poetry* (1917), and autobiographical fragments *Memories and Notes* (1921).

**Combe** (ko͞om), **George.** 1788–1858. Scottish phrenologist; educ. Edinburgh; practiced law; visited Spurzheim in Paris (1817) and became disciple; founded Phrenological Society (1820) and *Phrenological Journal* (1823); m. (1833) dau. of Mrs. Siddons; lectured on Continent and in America and studied treatment of criminal classes; author of *The Constitution of Man* (1828). Cf. F. J. GALL. His brother **Andrew** (1797–1847), physiologist and phrenologist, became disciple of Spurzheim (1818); practiced medicine in Edinburgh (1823–32, 1836–40); physician to Queen Victoria (1838); author of *Principles of Physiology* (1834).

**Combe, William.** 1741–1823. English adventurer and creator of "Dr. Syntax." Nicknamed "Count Combe" for extravagance in spending his patrimony. Private soldier, cook and waiter, law student, London bookseller's hack; made success with a bitter satire, *The Diaboliad* (1776); spent much of life (from 1780) in King's Bench debtors' prison. Wrote political pamphlets and letterpress for illustrated books; wrote in descriptive and moralizing verse the three *Tours of Dr. Syntax,* in search of the picturesque, in search of consolation, and in search of a wife (1812, 1820, 1821), with illustrations by Thomas Rowlandson; wrote letterpress for Rowlandson's *Dance of Death* (1815–16) and *Dance of Life* (1816).

**Com'ber·mere** (kŭm'bẽr·mẹr), Viscount. Sir **Stapleton Cot'ton** (kŏt''n). 1773–1865. British military commander, b. in Wales; served at Cape of Good Hope (1796), against Tipu Sahib (1799), in Ireland (1800); commanded cavalry in Peninsular War (1808–12); fought at Salamanca (1812); commander in chief in Ireland (1822–25), in India (1825–30); field marshal (1855).

**Combes** (kôɴb), **Justin Louis Émile.** 1835–1921. French politician. Senator (from 1885); vice-president of Senate (1894–95); premier of France (1902–05); followed strong anticlerical policy.

**Co·me'ni·us** (kō·mē'nĭ·ŭs), **John Amos.** *Czech* **Jan Amos Ko'men·ský** (kô'mĕn·skē). 1592–1670. Czech theologian and educator. Studied in Heidelberg; taught in Přerov and Fulnek; driven by Spanish into Poland (1621); rector (1636) of gymnasium at Leszno (Lissa); gained fame by innovations in methods of teaching, esp. of languages; author of *Pansophiae Prodromus* (1630) and *Janua Linguarum Reserata* (1631). Called to Sweden (1642) to improve the educational system. Last bishop (elected 1648) of the Unitas Fratrum at Leszno; after burning of Leszno by the Poles (1656), settled at Amsterdam. Author also of *Orbis Sensualium Pictus* (Latin, 1654; Hungarian, 1658), first textbook with pictures adapted for teaching children.

**Com'fort** (kŭm'fẽrt), **George Fisk.** 1833–1910. American educator, b. Berkshire, N.Y. Grad. Wesleyan (1857). Professor of modern languages and aesthetics, Syracuse U. (1872–87), and founder and first dean of its college of fine arts (1873–93). Organizer (1896) and director of the Syracuse Museum of Fine Arts.

**Comfort, Will Levington.** 1878–1932. American novelist, b. Kalamazoo, Mich. War correspondent (1899–1904) in Philippines, China, Russia, Japan. Author of *Routledge Rides Alone* (1910), *Fate Knocks at the Door* (1912), *Midstream* (1914), *The Hive* (1918), *This Man's World* (1921), *Somewhere South in Sonora* (1925), etc.

**Comfort, William Wistar.** 1874–1955. American educator, b. Germantown, Pa. Ph.D., Harvard (1902). Professor of Romance languages, Haverford (1901–09) and Cornell (1909–17). President, Haverford (1917–40).

**Co'mines'** *or* **Com'mines'** *or* **Com'mynes'** *or* **Co'mynes'** (kô'mēn'), **Philippe de.** Sire **d'Ar'gen'ton'** (dȧr'zhäɴ'tôɴ'). 1447?–?1511. French chronicler; in service successively of Charles the Bold, Louis XI, Charles VIII; member of the council of regency during minority of Charles VIII. Wrote his *Mémoires,* regarded as one of the classics of medieval history.

**Co·mis'key** (kō·mĭs'kĭ), **Charles A.** 1858–1931. American baseball executive, b. Chicago; active as professional player (from age of 17); manager, captain, and player, St. Louis Browns; owner and president of Chicago club in American League from its organization (1900).

**Com'ma·ger** (kŏm'ȧ·jẽr), **Henry Steele.** 1902– Amer. educator and historian, b. Pittsburgh, Pa. Taught at New York U. (1926–38), Columbia U. (1938–56), and Amherst Coll. (1956– ). Author of *The Blue and the Gray* (1950), *The Era of Reform* (1960), etc. Editor of *Documents of American History* (2 vols., 1969), etc.

**Com'mer** (kôm'ẽr), **Franz.** 1813–1887. German composer and music scholar; composer of masses, cantatas, and other choral works.

**Commines.** See COMINES.

**Com·mo'di·a'nus** (kŏ·mō'dĭ·ā'nŭs). Christian Latin poet of 3d century A.D. (or, perhaps, later). His *Instructiones LXXX adversus Gentium Deos* and *Carmen Apologeticum* are extant.

**Com'mo·dus** (kŏm'ō·dŭs), **Lucius Aelius Aurelius.** 161–192 A.D. Roman emperor (180–192). Son of Marcus Aurelius Antoninus. On death of Aurelius made disgraceful peace with Marcomanni and Quadi; his reign marked by his violence, prodigality, and unrestrained indulgence; proud of his physical strength which he exhibited in gladiatorial combats.

**Com'mons** (kŏm'ŭnz), **John Rogers.** 1862–1945. American economist, b. Hollandsburg, Ohio. A.B., Oberlin (1888). Professor, Oberlin (1892), Indiana U. (1893–95), Syracuse U. (1895–99), Wisconsin (1904–32). Author of *The Distribution of Wealth, Proportional Representation, Trade Unionism and Labor Problems, Races and Immigrants in America, Labor and Administration,* and an autobiography.

**Commynes.** See COMINES.
**Comnena, Anna.** See ANNA COMNENA.
**Com·ne′nus** (kŏm·nē′nŭs). *Plural* **Com·ne′ni** (-nī). Name of a Byzantine noble family, originating in Paphlagonia, that furnished several rulers of the Eastern Roman Empire (1057–1204) and of Trebizond (1204–1461). **Man′u·el (E·rot′i·cus)** [măn′ū·ĕl ē·rŏt′ĭ·kŭs] **Comnenus** was a general under Emperor Basil II and father of Isaac I, first emperor of the Comneni (1057–59). Isaac's nephew Alexius was emperor (1081–1118), followed by other members of the family: John II, Manuel I, Alexius II, and Andronicus I (d. 1185). See individual biographies; see also ANNA COMNENA. The empire of Trebizond was founded by Alexius I of the younger line (1204) and lasted until conquered by Mohammed II (1461).
**Co′mon·fort′** (kō′mŏn·fôrt′), **Ignacio.** 1812–1863. Mexican liberal political leader, b. Puebla. A leader with Álvarez in revolution of Ayutla which overthrew Santa Anna (1855); minister of war under Álvarez (1855); provisional president of Mexico (1855–57); elected president (Dec., 1857). Forced to flee to U.S. (1858); returned to fight French invaders (1861–63); killed in ambush.
**Com·pa′gni** (kôm·pä′nyē), **Dino.** d. 1324. Florentine historian; gonfalonier of justice (1293). Author of *Cronaca delle Cose Occorrenti ne' Tempi Suoi* (written 1310–12), a chronicle of Florentine history from 1280, with special emphasis on events of 1300.
**Com′pa·ret′ti** (kōm′pä·rāt′tē), **Domenico.** 1835–1927. Italian philologist. Professor of Greek, U. of Pisa (1859 ff.), Florence, and Rome; known esp. for his epigraphical, papyrological, and dialect studies; known also as a Romance philologist and student of medieval culture.
**Com′pay′ré′** (kôɴ′pĕ′rā′), **Gabriel.** 1843–1913. French educator; professor of philosophy, Toulouse (1874). Author of *Histoire Critique des Doctrines de l'Education en France depuis le XVI^e Siècle* (1879) and textbooks.
**Com′père′** (kôɴ′pâr′), **Louis** *or* **Loyset.** d. 1518. French musician; famed for mastery of counterpoint.
**Comp′ton** (kŏmp′tŭn), **Arthur Holly.** 1892–1962. American physicist, b. Wooster, Ohio; brother of K. T. Compton. B.S., Wooster (1913); Ph.D., Princeton (1916); studied at Cambridge, England (1919–20). Professor and head of department, Washington U. (1920–23); professor, Chicago (1923–45). Investigated the earth's rotation; discovered change in wave length of scattered X rays, known as the *Compton effect*, for which he was awarded 1927 Nobel prize for physics (jointly with C. T. R. Wilson); discovered total reflection of X rays; collaborated in the polarization of X rays and in the production of X-ray spectra by ruled gratings; investigated cosmic rays, discovering their electrical nature; director, Metallurgical Project (1942–45); chancellor, Washington U., St. Louis (from 1945).
**Comp′ton** (kŏmp′tŭn; kŭmp′-), **Henry.** 1632–1713. English prelate and leader of Revolution of 1688. Youngest son of Spencer Compton, 2d Earl of Northampton (*q.v.*); educ. Oxford; bishop of Oxford (1674); bishop of London (1675). Religious instructor of James II's daughters Mary and Anne; helped French Protestants; liberal toward dissenters; suspended from episcopal functions for refusing to suspend John Sharp, antipapal writer; reinstated (1688). Protested James II's illegal acts; voted for declaring throne vacant; crowned William and Mary (1689); one of commissioners for revising the liturgy; one of commissioners for arranging union of Scotland and England. Collector of exotic and rare botanical specimens; myricaceous genus *Comptonia* named for him. His brother Sir **William** (1625–1663) was Royalist governor of Banbury; stood siege of 13 weeks (1644).
**Comp′ton** (kŏmp′tŭn), **Karl Taylor.** 1887–1954. American physicist, b. Wooster, Ohio; brother of A. H. Compton. Ph.B., Wooster (1908); Ph.D., Princeton (1912). Asst. professor (1915–19), professor (1919–30), Princeton; president, M.I.T. (1930–48). Conducted researches on the contact difference of potential and the Peltier effect, the structure of crystals by X-ray photography, photoelectric effect, ionization, thermionic emission, etc.
**Comp′ton** (kŏmp′tŭn; kŭmp′-), **Spencer.** 2d Earl of **North·amp′ton** (nôr·thămp′tŭn). 1601–1643. English partisan of Charles I in struggle with Parliament; arrayed Warwickshire for king (1642); commanded Royalist forces at Hopton Heath, where he was killed; father of Henry Compton (*q.v.*), Bishop of London. His grandson **Spencer Compton** (1673?–1743), Earl of **Wil′ming·ton** (wĭl′mĭng·tŭn), was speaker of the House of Commons (1715–27); paymaster general (1722–30); lord privy seal (1730); first lord of treasury (1742–43).
**Com′stock** (kŭm′stŏk), **Ada Louise.** 1876–1973. American educator, b. Moorhead, Minn. B.L., Smith Coll. (1897). Dean, Smith College (1912–23). President, Radcliffe College (1923–43); m. (1943) Wallace Notestein.
**Com′stock** (kŏm′stŏk), **Anna Botsford.** See under John Henry COMSTOCK.
**Com′stock** (kŭm′stŏk), **Anthony.** 1844–1915. American reformer, b. New Canaan, Conn. Served in Union army during Civil War. Secretary, Society for the Suppression of Vice, in New York (1873–1915); conducted spectacular raids on publishers and vendors. Author of *Frauds Exposed* (1880), *Traps for the Young* (1883), *Morals Versus Art* (1887), etc.
**Com′stock** (kŏm′stŏk), **George Cary.** 1855–1934. American astronomer, b. Madison, Wis. Ph.B., Michigan (1877); LL.B., Wisconsin (1883). Professor, Wisconsin (1887–1922), and director of Washburn Observatory (1889–1922). Known esp. for work on double stars.
**Com′stock** (kŭm′stŏk), **Henry Tompkins Paige.** 1820–1870. American prospector, b. Trenton, Ont., Canada. In Nevada (1856–62); located on the ground where "Comstock lode" was discovered (1859), but sold his claim for a small amount.
**Com′stock** (kŏm′stŏk), **John Henry.** 1849–1931. American entomologist, b. Janesville, Wis.; B.S., Cornell U. (1874); studied at Yale and Leipzig. Professor, Cornell U. (from 1882). Author of *Introduction to Entomology* (1888), *Insect Life* (1897), *How to Know the Butterflies* (with his wife, 1904), *The Spider Book* (1912), and *The Wings of Insects* (1918). His wife, **Anna,** *nee* **Bots′ford** [bŏts′fērd] (1854–1930; m. 1878), was a naturalist and wood engraver, b. Otto, N.Y.; grad. Cornell U. (1878); studied art at Cooper Union, N.Y. City; taught nature study at Cornell U. (from 1913; professor from 1920). Author of *Ways of the Six-Footed* (1903), *Handbook of Nature Study* (1911), *The Pet Book* (1914), and *Bird, Animal, Tree and Plant Notebooks* (1914); editor, *Nature Study Review* (1917–23).
**Comte** (kôɴt), **Auguste,** *in full* **Isidore Auguste Marie François.** 1798–1857. French mathematician and philosopher, b. Montpellier; founder of positivism. Educ. École Polytechnique, Paris; disciple of Saint-Simon (to 1824); lectured at his home on his philosophical system; on staff, École Polytechnique, Paris (1833–51); subsisted on financial aid secured by J. S. Mill and Littré; died insane (Sept. 5, 1857). Author of *Cours de Philosophie Positive* (6 vols., 1830–42), *Traité Élémentaire de Géométrie Analytique* (1843), *Traité d'Astronomie Populaire* (1845), *Système de Politique Positive* (4 vols., 1851–54),

*Catéchisme Positiviste, ou Sommaire Exposition de la Religion Universelle* (1852).

**Com'yn** (kŭm'ĭn). Family name of earls of BUCHAN (first creation).

**Comyn.** Name of a once eminent Scottish family (from town Comines on Franco-Belgian border), founded by Robert de Comyn, made earl of Northumberland (1068); and including: **Alexander Comyn,** 2d Earl of **Buch'an** [bŭK'ăn; bŭk'ăn] (d. 1289), constable of Scotland (1270), regent (1286). **John** the elder (d. 1300?), grandnephew of Alexander, one of regents (1286–92), claimant for throne (1291) but supported brother-in-law John de Baliol's claim; submitted to Edward I (1296). **John** the younger (d. 1306), called "the Red," son of John the elder, supported Baliol's claim; led resistance to English king; submitted to Edward I (1304); after quarrel with Robert the Bruce, was stabbed to death at Dumfries. **John** (d. 1313?), 3d earl, son of Alexander Comyn, 2d earl, was defeated by Bruce near Inveraray (1308) in feud for murder of John Comyn, the younger; fled to England, losing family possessions in Scotland and England to king.

**Comynes.** See COMINES.

**Conan Doyle,** Sir **Arthur.** See DOYLE.

**Co'nant** (kō'nănt), **Charles Arthur.** 1861–1915. American banking expert, b. Winchester, Mass. Financial reporter, Boston *Post,* New York *Journal of Commerce* (to 1901). Appointed by McKinley to report on Philippine monetary system (1901). Assisted Nicaragua (1911–12) and Cuba (1914–15) in currency reform. Author of *A History of Modern Banks of Issue* (1896); *Principles of Money and Banking* (2 vols., 1905); etc.

**Conant, James Bryant.** 1893–1978. Am. educator, b. Dorchester, Mass. A.B. (1913), Ph.D. (1916), Harvard. Taught chemistry, Harvard (1916–33); prof., (1927–33). Pres., Harvard (1933–53). U.S. high commissioner for Ger. (1953–55); amb. to W. Ger. (1955–57). Author of works on organic chemistry and education.

**Conant, Roger.** 1592?–1679. Pioneer in America, b. East Budleigh, Eng. Emigrated to Massachusetts (1623). A founder and governor of colony at Naumkeag (Salem), 1626–28.

**Conant, Thomas Jefferson.** 1802–1891. American Biblical scholar, b. Brandon, Vt. Grad. Middlebury College (1823). Member (1873–81) American revision committee, co-operating in producing the Revised Version of the Bible (1881). His wife, **Hannah O'Brien,** *nee* **Chap'lin** [chăp'lĭn] (1809–1865), was author of *The English Bible,* a popular history of its translation into English (1856).

**Concha, José Gutiérrez de la.** See GUTIÉRREZ DE LA CONCHA.

**Concini, Concino.** Marquis **d'Ancre.** See ANCRE.

**Con·co'ne** (kông·kō'nā), **Giuseppe.** 1810–1861. Italian composer and singing teacher: studio in Paris (1837–48); organist, chapel royal, Turin (1848 ff.).

**Condamine, Charles Marie de la.** See LA CONDAMINE.

**Con'dé'** (kôN'dā'). Name of a great family of French nobility, bearing title Prince **de Condé,** derived from the town of Condé (-sur-l'Escaut) on the Scheldt, in northeastern France. See CONTI. The family formed a branch of the house of **Bourbon** (*q.v.*); became extinct (1830); it included:

**Louis I de Bour'bon'** (dĕ bo͞or'bôN'). 1530–1569. Youngest son of Charles de Bourbon, Duc de Vendôme. First to bear title of Prince de Condé. A soldier, active at Metz (1552) and St.-Quentin (1557). As a Protestant, joined Huguenots and took part in conspiracy of Amboise (1559); imprisoned, but released. Made governor of Picardy by Catherine de Médicis (1561). Fought Guise faction (1562), was defeated and made prisoner, but again liberated (1563). Joined Huguenots again and slain at Jarnac. His son **Henry I** (1552–1588) joined Huguenot cause, but had to renounce it at the Massacre of St. Bartholomew (1572); fled to Germany and later died of wounds received fighting against the Holy League at Coutras (1587). Henry's son **Henry II** (1588–1646), posthumous and possibly illegitimate, was brought up a Catholic; spent most of his life in intrigues at court; a partisan of Richelieu. Henry II's son **Louis II** (1621–1686), called "the Great Condé," b. Paris, bore title of duc **d'En'ghien'** (dăN'găN') during his father's life. Entered military service, won battle of Rocroi (1643) against the Spanish, and, partly in co-operation with Turenne, won victories (1643–46) against Imperialists, especially Nördlingen (1645). Became head of Condé family (1646). After victory of Lens (1648), recalled to Paris to put down the Fronde. Had trouble with Mazarin; fought on the side of the Fronde against Turenne, later also as ally of Spain. Defeated at battle of the Dunes by Turenne and the English (1658). Pardoned (1659) and again commanded armies of France (1673–75); retired to Chantilly. Friend of Molière, Racine, Boileau, Boussuet, and La Bruyère. His only son, **Henri Jules** (1643–1709), took part in many campaigns. **Louis Joseph de Bourbon.** 1736–1818. Great-grandson of Louis II; distinguished soldier in Seven Years' War. Strong supporter of monarchy at time of Revolution; fled (1789) to Germany and organized "army of Condé" (émigrés and Austrians), but unsuccessful (1792–97). Entered Russian service (1797) and English (1801). Spent last years at Chantilly. Wrote a life of the Great Condé. His son **Louis Henri Joseph** (1756–1830) was the last of the Condé princes. Wounded at Gibraltar (1782); later served under his father against France. Supposed to have committed suicide. His only son was the duc d'Enghien, 1772–1804 (see ENGHIEN).

**Con'de** (kôn'dā), **José Antonio.** 1765?–1820. Spanish Orientalist, d. Peraleja, Cuenca; educ. U. of Alcalá. Author of *Historia de la Dominación de los Árabes en España* (1820–21), now generally discredited by scholars.

**Con'dell** *or* **Cun'dell** (kŭn'd'l), **Henry.** d. 1627. English actor. Member of lord chamberlain's company, along with Shakespeare and Burbage; partner with Burbage in Globe Theatre (1599); received mourning ring by will from Shakespeare (1616); with John Heming, edited first folio of Shakespeare's plays (1623).

**Con'der** (kŏn'dẽr), **Claude Reignier.** 1848–1910. English Palestinian explorer and Hittite and Altaic scholar; grandson of **Josiah Conder** (1789–1855), London bookseller, editor of *Modern Traveller* (30 vols., 1825–29). Officer in Royal Engineers; commanded survey of Palestine (1872–78, 1881–82); discovered city of Kadesh; served in Egypt (1882), in Bechuanaland (1884), on ordnance survey (1887–94), on Irish ordnance survey (1900–05). Contributor to William Smith's *Dictionary of the Bible;* author of *Tell Amarna Tablets* (1893), works on Palestinian geography, on the Hittites and their language, and Altaic inscriptions. His cousin **Charles** (1868–1909), artist, while in government service in Australia (1884–90) attracted attention with painting *The Hot Wind* (1890); developed unique decorative style, esp. in water colors on panels of white silk.

**Con'dil'lac'** (kôN'dē'yȧk'), **Étienne Bonnot de.** 1715–1780. French philosopher; associate of Diderot, J. J. Rousseau, and Duclos; modern exponent of doctrine of sensationalism.

**Con'don** (kŏn'dŭn), **Edward Uhler.** 1902–1974. American physicist, b. Alamogordo, N.Mex. A.B. (1924) and

Ph.D. (1926), California. Assoc. professor, Princeton (1930–37); assoc. director, Westinghouse research laboratories (1937–45); on govt. uranium committees (1941–43); director, U.S. Bureau of Standards (1945–51).

**Condorcanqui, José Gabriel.** See TUPAC AMARU.

**Con'dor'cet'** (kôN'dôr'sĕ'), Marquis **de. Marie Jean Antoine Nicholas de Ca'ri'tat'** (dĕ kȧ'rē'tȧ'). 1743–1794. French philosopher, mathematician, and politician. Member of Legislative Assembly (1791) and president thereof (1792). Member of the National Convention, and of the Girondists (1793). Arrested with others of the Girondist group; died in prison (Mar. 28, 1794).

**Cone** (kōn), **Helen Gray.** 1859–1934. American educator and poet, b. New York City. Professor of English, Hunter College (1899–1926). Author of *Oberon and Puck, Verses Grave and Gay* (1885), *A Chant of Love for England, and Other Poems* (1915), etc.

**Cone, Hutchinson Ingham.** 1871–1941. American naval officer, b. Brooklyn, N.Y.; grad. U.S.N.A., Annapolis (1894). Served on *Baltimore* in battle of Manila Bay (May 1, 1898); rear admiral (1909); commanded U.S. naval aviation forces in foreign service (Aug., 1917–Oct., 1918); wounded on board *Leinster* when it was sunk in Irish Sea by German submarine. Retired (1922). Commissioner, U.S. Shipping Board (1928).

**Cone, Spencer Houghton.** 1785–1855. American Baptist clergyman, b. Princeton, N.J.; a founder and president, American and Foreign Bible Society (1837–50); president, American Bible Union (1850).

**Conegliano, Cima da.** See CIMA.

**Con'fa·lo·nie'ri** (kōn'fä·lō·nyâ'rē), Conte **Federico.** 1785–1846. Italian patriot, b. Milan; ardent nationalist; pleaded cause of Lombard independence in Paris and London. Arrested by Austrians after outbreak of Piedmontese revolt (1821); after celebrated trial, sentenced to life imprisonment in fortress of Spielberg (Jan., 1824); pardoned and exiled to America (1836); returned to Europe (1838) and Milan (1840).

**Con·fu'cius** (kŏn·fū'shŭs; -shĭ·ŭs). *Latinized form of Chinese* **K'ung Fu-tzŭ** *or* **Kung Fu-tse** (ko͝ong' fo͞o'dzŭ'), *i.e., literally,* "Philosopher Kung." *Also* **K'ung Ch'iu** (ko͝ong' chyo͞o'). c. 551–479 B.C. Chinese philosopher, b. in the state of Lu, now the province of Shantung, where at the small town of Küfow (or Ch'ü-fou) descendants in the 76th generation still live. At early age devoted himself to study of ancient writings; gained reputation for scholarship; made prime minister of Lu; resigned (c. 495 B.C.) when ruler gave himself up to pleasure; wandered for 12 or 13 years from state to state teaching. Not a religious teacher, his precepts (*Confucianism*) dealt with morals, the family system, social reforms, statecraft; his maxims, still taught as a guide for daily life of people, are of practical value as a utilitarian philosophy; called himself "a transmitter, not an originator"; his writings consisted chiefly of comments on the Chinese classics; has had many disciples who have added much to Confucian literature. The *Analects*, brief record of his teachings on various subjects, is one of the Five Books of Chinese classics.

**Con'greve** (kŏn'grēv; kŏng'grēv), **Richard.** 1818–1899. English Positivist and essayist. M.A., Oxon. (1843); upon meeting Barthélemy St.-Hilaire and Auguste Comte in Paris adopted Positivism and devoted life to its propagation.

**Congreve,** Sir **Walter Norris.** 1862–1927. English soldier, b. at Chatham. Educ. Oxford U., and Royal Military Coll. at Sandhurst. Served in India (1885–89, 1893–95), in South Africa (1899–1902; awarded Victoria Cross for gallantry in action, Dec., 1899), and France in World War I (1914–18). Brigadier general commanding eighteenth infantry brigade (1911–15); major general commanding sixth division (1915); lieutenant general commanding thirteenth army corps (1915–17); lost left hand in action at Vimy Ridge; commanded seventh corps resisting German attack (Jan.–Mar., 1918); held command in Egypt, Palestine, and Syria (1919). Promoted general (1922); aide-de-camp general to the king (1923). Governor of Malta (1924–27).

**Congreve, William.** 1670–1729. English dramatist, master of comedy of manners. Educ. in Ireland, fellow student of Jonathan Swift; published a weak novel of cross-purposes and disguises, *Incognita* (1691); contributed to Dryden's *Juvenal* (1692); won fame with series of brilliant comedies, *Old Bachelor* (1693), *Double Dealer* (1693), *Love for Love* (1695), *The Way of the World* (1700), remarkable for wit and grace of dialogue; made ambitious attempt at tragedy in blank verse, *The Mourning Bride* (1697), which opens with line "Music hath charms to soothe the savage breast"; abandoned theater after comparative failure of *The Way of the World;* defended morality of stage in reply to Jeremy Collier's *Short View.*

**Congreve,** Sir **William.** 1772–1828. English artillerist; inventor of Congreve rocket (used as late as 1860); designed new gun for frigates (1813).

**Coningh.** See KONINCK.

**Con'ing·ton** (kŏn'ĭng·tŭn), **John.** 1825–1869. English classical scholar. Professor of Latin, Oxford (1854–69); edited Aeschylus's *Agamemnon* (1848) and *Choëphoroi* (1857); translated *Odes* of Horace (1863); translated Vergil's *Aeneid* in octosyllabic meter of Scott.

**Co'ninx·loo** (kō'nĭngks·lō), **Gillis van.** 1544–1607. Flemish landscape painter.

**Conk'lin** (kŏngk'lĭn), **Edwin Grant.** 1863–1952. American biologist, b. Waldo, Ohio. S.B., Ohio Wesleyan (1885), Ph.D., Johns Hopkins (1891). Professor of zoology, Pennsylvania (1896–1908), Princeton (from 1908). Author of *Heredity and Environment, Mechanism of Evolution, Freedom and Responsibility,* etc.

**Conk'ling** (kŏngk'lĭng), **Grace Walcott,** *nee* **Haz'ard** (hăz'ẽrd). 1878–1958. American poet, b. New York City; m. Roscoe Platt Conkling (1905). B.L., Smith College (1899). Teacher of English, Smith College (from 1914). Author of *Afternoons of April* (1915), *Wilderness Songs* (1920), *Ship's Log and Other Poems* (1924), *Flying Fish* (1926), *Witch and Other Poems* (1929). Her daughter **Hilda** (1910– ) wrote *Poems by a Little Girl* (1920) and *Shoes of the Wind* (1922).

**Conkling, Roscoe.** 1829–1888. American lawyer, b. Albany, N.Y. Member, U.S. House of Representatives (1859–63; 1865–67); U.S. senator (1867–81); rival of Blaine for Republican presidential nomination (1876), when Hayes was finally nominated. Opposed Hayes and his policies; also opposed Garfield; resigned his senate seat (1881) in protest against Garfield's policies; sought but failed of re-election.

**Con'naught** (kŏn'ôt), Duke of. Prince **Arthur William Patrick Albert.** 1850–1942. 3d son and 7th child of Queen Victoria; m. (1879) Princess Louise Marguerite of Prussia (1860–1917); gazetted to Royal Engineers (1868); held command in India (1886–90); general (1893); commander in chief in Ireland (1900), in Mediterranean (1907–09); governor general of Canada (1911–16). His son Prince **Arthur Frederick Patrick Albert** (1883–1938); m. (1913) duchess of Fife; personal aide to Edward VII and George V; aide-de-camp to Field Marshal French in B.E.F. (1914–15); governor general of Union of South Africa (1920–23). Princess **Patricia** (1886– ), known as **Princess Pat** (păt); daughter of duke of Connaught; m. (1919) Rear Admiral

Sir Alexander Robert Maule Ramsay, 3d son of 13th earl of Dalhousie; honorary colonel in chief of Princess Patricia's Canadian Light Infantry Battalion (from 1918).

**Con'neau'** (kô'nō'), **Jean.** 1880–1937. French aviator under name of **André Beau'mont'** (bō'môN'); in a Blériot monoplane won (June 18, 1911) European Circuit Race, Paris-Brussels-London-Paris, 1073 miles, in 58 hours, 38 minutes; also, winner (July 22, 1911) of Circuit of Britain Race, 1010 miles, in 22 hours, 28 minutes, 19 seconds.

**Connell, Norreys.** Pseudonym of Conal O'RIORDAN.

**Con'nel·ly** (kŏn''l·ĭ), **Marc,** *in full* **Marcus Cook.** 1890– . American playwright, b. McKeesport, Pa. Coauthor, with George Kaufman, of *Dulcy* (1921), dramatization of *Merton of the Movies* (1922), *Beggar on Horseback* (1924) and, with Frank Ball Elser, of *The Farmer Takes a Wife* (1934). Sole author of *The Wisdom Tooth* (1926), *The Green Pastures* (based on Roark Bradford's *Old Man Adam an' His Chillun;* awarded Pulitzer prize, 1930). Assoc. professor of playwriting, Yale (from 1947).

**Connelly, Pierce Francis.** 1841–? American sculptor, b. Grand Coteau, La. His *Honor Arresting the Triumph of Death* is now in Pennsylvania Academy of Fine Arts; his *Thetis,* in Metropolitan Museum of Art, New York.

**Con'ne·ly** (kŏn''l·ĭ), **Willard.** 1888–1967. American educator, b. Atlantic City, N.J. B.S., Dartmouth (1911); B.A., Oxon. (1927); taught English, Harvard (1920–25); director, American University Union, London (from 1930). Author of *Brawny Wycherley* (1930), *Sir Richard Steele* (1934), *Addison and Steele* (1937).

**Con'ner** (kŏn'ẽr), **David.** 1792–1856. American naval officer, b. Harrisburg, Pa. Served through War of 1812; awarded two Congressional medals for valor. Led attack on Vera Cruz and landed Scott's army (Mar. 9, 1847).

**Con'ners** (kŏn'ẽrz), **William James.** 1857–1929. American shipowner and newspaper publisher, b. Buffalo, N.Y. Proprietor, Buffalo *Enquirer* (from 1895) and Buffalo *Courier* (from 1897). Organized Great Lakes Transit Corp. (1916) and controlled steamships on the Great Lakes. Established Conners Foundation (1925) with endowment of $1,000,000 for relief of poor in Buffalo. His newspaper and shipping interests passed to his son **William James** (1895–1951); grad. Yale (1918); publisher and president, Buffalo *Courier-Express* (from 1919).

**Connington, John Jervis.** See Alfred Walter STEWART.

**Con'nol·ly** (kŏn''l·ĭ), **James.** 1870–1916. Irish socialist, b. in Ulster; joined Sinn Fein; commander in chief in Easter week rebellion; executed (1916).

**Connolly, James Brendan.** 1868–1957. American writer, b. South Boston, Mass. A champion at first modern Olympic games (1896). Served in Spanish-American War; at Santiago (1898); in U.S. navy (1907–08). War correspondent for *Collier's* in Mexico (1914) and in European waters (1917–18). Author of *Out of Gloucester* (1902), *The Seiners* (1904), *An Olympic Victor* (1908), *Open Water* (1910), *The Trawler* (1914), *The U-Boat Hunters* (1918), *Tide Rips* (1922), *Gloucestermen* (1930), etc.

**Connolly, Walter.** 1887–1940. American actor; with Sothern-Marlowe Shakespearean company (1911–14); on stage at Cohan Theatre in New York (1916), Garrick in Philadelphia (1934), Cort in New York (1935), etc.; in motion pictures (from 1932).

**Connor, Ralph.** Pseudonym of Charles William GORDON.

**Con'ol·ly** (kŏn''l·ĭ), **John.** 1794–1866. English physician of Irish extraction. M.D., Edinburgh (1821); professor, University Coll., London (1828–30); as physician to Hanwell Asylum (1839–52) introduced principle of nonrestraint in treatment of insane.

**Co'non** (kō'nŏn). d. 687. Pope (686–687).

**Conon.** Athenian commander of late 5th and early 4th centuries B.C.; defeated Spartan fleet off Cnidus (394 B.C.); restored the long walls and fortifications of the Peiraeus, at Athens; died, probably in Cyprus (c. 390).

**Conon of Sa'mos** (sā'mŏs). Greek astronomer and mathematician of 3d century B.C.; author of a work on astronomy (7 books) and of a treatise on conic sections. Discovered constellation Coma Berenices (*i.e.* "the hair of Berenice").

**Conrad.** See also KONRAD.

**Con'rad** (kŏn'răd). *Ger.* **Kon'rad** (kôn'rät). Name of four kings of Germany:

**Conrad I.** d. 918. Duke of Franconia. King of Germany (911–918). Reckoned in the line of Holy Roman emperors, but never crowned. Continually at war with Danes, Slavs, and Magyars, and with Henry, Duke of Saxony, who succeeded him as Henry I.

**Conrad II.** = CONRAD II, Holy Roman Emperor.

**Conrad III.** 1093–1152. Son of Frederick of Swabia. King of Germany (1138–52). Founder of the Hohenstaufen dynasty of the Holy Roman emperors, but never himself crowned emperor. Fought with Lothair (II) of Saxony for Italy (1128–35), but unsuccessful. Began (1138) conflict with Henry the Proud, Duke of Bavaria and Saxony, which led to the long struggle between Guelphs and Ghibellines (see WAIBLINGEN). Leader, with Louis VII of France, of the disastrous Second Crusade to Palestine (1147–49).

**Conrad IV.** 1228–1254. Son of Frederick II. King of Germany and Sicily (1250–54); never crowned as emperor. Engaged in petty wars in Germany in absence of the emperor (1240–50). Opposed for imperial crown by William of Holland. Led expedition into southern Italy (1251–54) to enforce his right of succession. Last of the Hohenstaufen dynasty to rule as emperor. Death followed by the Great Interregnum in the Holy Roman Empire (1254–73). See HOHENSTAUFEN.

**Conrad II.** *Called* **the Sa'li·an** (sā'lĭ·ăn). 990?–1039. Holy Roman emperor (1024–39; crowned 1027). King of Germany and founder of the Franconian or Salian dynasty. Descendant of Otto the Great by female line. Subdued rebellious cities of Milan and Pavia (1026); in Germany, put down formidable revolt in Swabia (1025–30); added Lusatia (1031) and Burgundy (1033–34) to the Empire; only partly successful in overcoming opposition in northern Italy (1036–37). See FRANCONIAN.

**Conrad.** *Called* **Conrad the Red.** *Ger.* **Kon'rad der Ro'te** (kôn'rät dẽr rō'tĕ). d. 955. Duke of Lorraine (944–953); m. (947) Otto I's daughter Liutgard; joined brother-in-law Liudolf, Duke of Swabia, in revolt (953) against Otto; defeated and deprived of duchy; called in Magyars but became reconciled with Otto and fought with him against Magyars at Lechfeld, losing life there. Ancestor of Salian branch of Holy Roman emperors (see FRANCONIAN).

**Conrad III** (*or* **I**). 1208–1261. Burgrave of Nuremberg and founder of the Franconian branch of Hohenzollern (*q.v.*).

**Conrad.** Marquis of **Mont'fer'rat'** (môN'fĕ'rȧ'). d. 1192. Italian crusader. Successfully defended Tyre (1187) against Saladin (hence his title Lord of **Tyre** [tīr]); largely responsible for Third Crusade; m. (1190) Isabella, daughter of King Amalric I of Jerusalem; elected king of Jerusalem but slain soon after by an emissary of the Assassins.

**Conrad, Charles Magill.** 1804–1878. American politician, b. Winchester, Va. U.S. secretary of war (1850–53).

**Conrad, Con** (kŏn). *Real name* **Conrad K. Do'ber** (dō'bẽr). 1893–1938. American song writer, b. New York City. Vaudeville actor (1914). His songs include *Margie, Barney Google, The Continental* (with Herbert Magidson; Motion Picture Academy award for best song of 1934).

**Conrad, Frank.** 1874–1941. American electrical engineer and inventor, pioneer in radio, esp. in short-wave and frequency-modulation experimentation and in broadcasting, b. Pittsburgh, Pa. Made experimental radio broadcasts using phonograph records (1919); built radio transmitter for Westinghouse company (fall of 1920); instrumental in developing station KDKA, Pittsburgh, from which was made (November 2, 1920) the broadcast regarded as the birth of public broadcasting.

**Con'rad** (kôn'rät), **George.** Pseudonym of GEORGE, Prince of Prussia.

**Conrad, Johannes.** 1839–1915. German economist; professor, Halle (from 1872).

**Con'rad** (kŏn'răd), **Joseph.** *Orig. name* **Teodor Józef Konrad Kor'ze·niow'ski** (kôr'zĕ·nyôf'skē). 1857–1924. Novelist, b. Berdichev, in the Ukraine. Became naturalized British subject under name of **Joseph Conrad** (1886). Seaman in French merchant marine (1874–78) and in British merchant marine (1878–94); qualified as third mate (1880), second mate (1881), first mate (1883), and master (1886). Left merchant marine (1894) to devote himself to writing; gained recognition as a master of English prose in a series of brilliant tales, many of them written against the background of his intimate knowledge of the sea. Among his novels are *Almayer's Folly* (1895), *An Outcast of the Islands* (1896), *The Nigger of the 'Narcissus'* (1897), *Lord Jim* (1900), *Youth* (short stories; 1902), *Typhoon* (short stories; 1903), *Nostromo* (1904), *The Mirror of the Sea* (reminiscences; 1906), *The Secret Agent* (1907; dramatized 1922), *Under Western Eyes* (1911), *Chance* (1913), *Victory* (1915; dramatized 1919), *The Shadow-Line* (1917), *The Arrow of Gold* (1919), *The Rescue* (1920), *The Rover* (1922), *Tales of Hearsay* (short stories; 1925).

**Con'rad** (kôn'rät), **Michael Georg.** 1846–1927. German writer; founder of journal *Die Gesellschaft* (1885); author of the novels *Madame Lutetia* (1882), *In Purpurner Finsternis* (1895), *Majestät* (1902), etc.

**Con'rad von Höt'zen·dorf** (kôn'rät fôn hût'sĕn·dôrf), Count **Franz.** 1852–1925. Austrian field marshal in World War; chief of staff of Austro-Hungarian army (1914–17), and commander in chief of southwest front in Tirol (1917–18).

**Con·ra'di** (kôn·rä'dē), **August.** 1821–1873. German conductor and composer of operas, symphonies, and medleys.

**Conradi, Hermann.** 1862–1890. German author of verse, novels, and prose sketches.

**Con'ra·din** (kŏn'rȧ·dēn; *Ger.* kôn'rä·dēn) *or* **Conrad the Younger.** 1252–1268. Son of Conrad IV, b. Wolfstein, Bavaria. King of Jerusalem and Sicily (1266–68). Duke of Swabia (1262). On death of Manfred (1266), began struggle with Charles of Anjou; defeated and captured (1268); beheaded. Last of the Hohenstaufens (*q.v.*).

**Con·ra'dy** (kôn·rä'dē), **August.** 1864–1925. German Oriental scholar; professor, Leipzig (from 1897).

**Con'rart'** (kôɴ'rȧr'), **Valentin.** 1603–1675. French man of letters; a founder (1634) of Académie Française; elected (1635) its first secretary for life.

**Con'ried** (kŏn'rēt), **Heinrich.** 1855–1909. Actor and theatrical manager, b. Bielitz, Austria. To U.S. (about 1878); leased Irving Place Theater (1892) and presented German stock company in German classics and modern comedy. Manager, Metropolitan Opera House, New York (1903–08).

**Con'ring** (kôn'rĭng), **Herman.** 1606–1681. German scholar, physician, and writer on the history of German jurisprudence. Opponent of alchemy; advocate of Harvey's theory of the circulation of the blood; recognized the value of chemistry to pharmacy.

**Con·sal'vi** (kôn·säl'vē), **Ercole.** 1757–1824. Italian ecclesiastical diplomat; chamberlain to Pius VI (1783); auditor of Sacra Romana Rota (1792). Secretary of Venice conclave (1799); created cardinal and secretary of state by Pius VII (1800); concluded concordat with France (1801); removed from office through Napoleon (1806). Secured restoration of Papal States at Congress of Vienna (1815); again papal secretary of state (1815–23); effected reforms and suppressed administrative abuses.

**Con·scien'ce** (kŏn·syän'sĕ), **Hendrik.** 1812–1883. Flemish writer of more than 100 novels and short stories in Flemish; regarded as founder of modern Flemish literature.

**Con'si'dé'rant'** (kôɴ'sē'dā'räɴ'), **Victor Prosper.** 1809–1893. Social reformer, b. Salins, France. Disciple of Fourier and leader of Fourierists (from 1837). Unsuccessfully tried to establish Fourierist colony near Dallas, Tex. (1855–57).

**Con'sta·ble** (kŭn'stȧ·b'l; kŏn'-), **Archibald.** 1774–1827. Scottish publisher. Founded *Edinburgh Review* (1802); joint publisher, with Longman & Co., of Scott's *Lay of the Last Minstrel* (1805) and *Marmion* (1807); purchased copyright of *Encyclopaedia Britannica* (1812) and added supplement (6 vols., 1816–24); purchased copyright of *Waverley* (1814); failed in crisis of 1826 (see Sir Walter SCOTT); began (1827) *Constable's Miscellany.*

**Constable, Henry.** 1562–1613. English poet. B.A., Cantab. (1580); embraced Roman Catholicism; in secret service of English government, in Paris (1584–85); papal envoy to Scotland (1598). Author of *Diana* (volume of sonnets; 1592); contributed four poems to *England's Helicon* (1600).

**Constable, John.** 1776–1837. English landscape painter. Through encouragement of Sir George Beaumont studied art in London (1795–97); exhibited his first landscape (1802). Produced realistic English landscapes and studies of English rustic life (1803–37) which won scant recognition at home; received awards in France (1824, 1825) where his work exerted notable influence upon landscape painting; m. Maria Bicknell (d. 1828). Notable among his landscapes are *The White Horse* (1819), *Hay Wain* (1821), *Bridge of the Stour* (1822), *The Leaping Horse* (1825), *The Cornfield* (1826), *Dedham Vale* (1828), *Salisbury Cathedral* (1831), *Valley Farm* (1835), *Arundel Mill and Castle* (1837).

**Constable,** Sir **Marmaduke.** 1455?–1518. English soldier; fought in France with Edward IV (1475) and with Henry VII (1492); commanded left wing at Flodden (1513). His son Sir **Marmaduke** (1480?–1545), knighted for service at Flodden, attended Henry VIII on Field of the Cloth of Gold (1520). Another member of the family, Sir **William** (d. 1655), regicide, fought with Parliamentary forces; joint jailer of Charles I at Carisbrooke (1648); one of king's judges (1649).

**Con'stance** (kŏn'stȧns) of Sicily. *Ger.* **Kon'stanz** (kôn'stänts). 1152–1198. Wife of Holy Roman Emperor Henry VI and mother of Emperor Frederick II.

**Constance.** *Span.* **Con·stan'cia** (kôn·stän'thyä). Daughter of Peter the Cruel, King of Castile; m. John of Gaunt, causing him to assume (1372) kingship of Castile against Henry II of Trastamara; mother of Catherine, wife of Henry III of Castile.

**Con'stans II** (kŏn'stănz), **Flavius Heraclius.** 630–668. Son of Constantine III; emperor of the Eastern Roman Empire (641–668). During reign Saracens completed conquest of Egypt (643) and Syria (646), seized Rhodes (651), and ravaged Asia Minor. Reorganized provinces of empire. Tried unsuccessfully to drive Lombards out of Italy (662–663). Issued the Type (648), an edict forbidding religious discussion. Assassinated at Syracuse.

**Constans, Flavius Julius.** 323?–350. Roman emperor (337–350). Youngest of three sons of Constantine the Great and Fausta. On division of empire (337) received Italy, Africa, and Illyricum; in war between the brothers (340) defeated Constantine at Aquileia; slain by soldiers of Magnentius.

**Cons'tans'** (kôns'tän'), **Jean Antoine Ernest.** 1833–1913. French statesman. French minister to China (1886), governor general of Indo-China (1886–88). Elected senator (1889). French ambassador at Constantinople (1898–1907).

**Cons'tant'** (kôns'tän'), Baron **d'Estournelles de. Paul Henri Benjamin Balluat.** See ESTOURNELLES DE CONSTANT.

**Cons·tant'** (kōns·tănnt'), **Benjamin.** See BOTELHO DE MAGALHÃES.

**Cons'tant'** (kôns'tän'), **Benjamin.** 1845–1902. French painter, b. Paris. Studied at École des Beaux-Arts (Paris) and under Cabanel. Among his notable paintings are *Prisonniers Marocains, Entrée de Mahomet II à Constantinople, Les Chérifas*, and many portraits, as *Mon Fils André, Jusserand, Queen Victoria, Leconte de Lisle.*

**Con·stant'** (kŏn·stänt'), **W.** Pseudonym of Constant WURZBACH.

**Cons'tant' de Re·becque'** (kôns'tän' dẽ rē·běk'), **Benjamin.** 1767–1830. French writer and politician; protégé of Mme. de Staël (from 1794). Member of the Tribunate (1799–1802); joined opposition to Napoleon and was banished (1802); returned to France (1814); accepted office under Napoleon during the Hundred Days; banished by Louis XVIII (1815–16); member of Chamber of Deputies (1819–30). Author of the psychological novel *Adolphe;* a historical study, *De la Religion...; Mémoires sur les Cent-Jours; Journal Intime;* etc.

**Con·stan'ti·a** (kŏn·stăn'shĭ·ȧ) *or* **Con'stan·ti'na** (kŏn'stăn·tī'nȧ). *Full name* **Flavia Valeria Constantia.** d. about 330. Daughter of Constantius Chlorus and half sister of Constantine the Great. Married (313) Licinius, Emperor of the East.

**Con'stan·tine** (kŏn'stăn·tīn; -tēn). Name of a pope and an antipope:

**Constantine (I).** d. 715. Pope (708–715), b. in Syria. Received submission of Felix, Archbishop of Ravenna; journeyed to Constantinople (710) on invitation of Justinian II to confirm certain decrees.

**Constantine (II).** d. 769. Antipope (767–768) in opposition to Saint Paul I; by some, considered a true pope. Forced to accept pontificate by his brother; not elected from College of Cardinals; sought Frankish protection, but was overwhelmed and imprisoned by Lombards.

**Constantine.** *Full name* **Flavius Claudius Con'stan·ti'nus** (kŏn'stăn·tī'nŭs). d. 411. Usurper; proclaimed himself emperor, gained control in Britain, Gaul, and Spain (407–411); defeated by Constantius, general of Honorius, taken prisoner, and put to death at Ravenna.

**Constantine.** Name of two Roman emperors:

**Constantine I.** *Called* "the Great." *Full name* **Flavius Valerius Aurelius Con'stan·ti'nus** (kŏn'stăn·tī'nŭs). 280?–337. Roman emperor (306–337), b. at Naissus (Nish) in Moesia; eldest son of Constantius Chlorus. Accompanied Diocletian in expedition to Egypt (296); served under Galerius in Persian War, and later under his father, then emperor of the West. Proclaimed successor (caesar) by his father at York, Britain (306); at the time five other claimants to throne of Roman Empire; caused death (310) of Maximian for conspiracy; defeated Maxentius in three battles, the last at the Milvian Bridge (312) at Rome; on this occasion legend states that a cross and the words, *in hoc signo vinces* ("by this sign thou shalt conquer"), appeared in the heavens; persuaded to adopt Christianity (Edict of Milan, 313). Became sole emperor of the West (312); defeated Licinius (314); devoted next nine years (314–323) to administration, correction of abuses, strengthening of frontiers, and restraining barbarians; built Arch of Constantine (315) at Rome; again at war with Licinius (323) who was defeated and put to death (324). Thus became sole emperor of the Roman world; called the great Council of Nicaea (325) at which Nicene Creed was adopted; chose Byzantium as his new capital (323), inaugurating and renaming it (330) after himself "Constantinople" (City of Constantine). Married twice; had son, Flavius Julius Crispus (*q.v.*), by first wife; as second wife m. (307) Fausta (*q.v.*).

**Constantine II** (*or* **Junior**). *Full name* **Flavius Claudius Constantinus.** 317?–340. Eldest son of Constantine the Great, b. at Arelate (Arles), Gaul. Roman emperor (337–340). On his father's death became joint emperor with his brothers Constantius and Constans; received Gaul, Britain, Spain, etc.; invaded dominions of Constans (340); killed at Aquileia.

**Constantine.** Name of nine rulers of the Eastern Roman Empire (see also CONSTANTINE I and II, Roman emperors before the division):

**Constantine III.** 612?–641. Son of Heraclius; joint emperor with half brother Heracleonas (641); supposed to have been poisoned.

**Constantine IV.** *Called* **Po'go·na'tus** (pō'gō·nā'tŭs; pŏg'ō-), *i.e.* the Bearded. 648–685. Son of Constans II; emperor (668–685); besieged six years (672–677) in Constantinople by Arabs under Caliph Muawiyah, who were, however, compelled to make peace; fleet saved by invention of Greek fire; Thessalonica saved from attacks of Slavs and Avars, but Bulgars established (679) across the Danube within the empire; summoned ecumenical council at Constantinople (680).

**Constantine V.** *Called* **Cop·ron'y·mus** (kŏp·rŏn'ĭ·mŭs). 719–775. Son of Leo III; emperor (741–775); overcame usurper Artavasdus, his brother-in-law (741–742); won military victories over Arabs (745–746, 751), Slavs (758), and Bulgars (759, 762, 772); an iconoclast, vigorously suppressed monasticism, convoked council on image worship (753); restored aqueducts, repeopled Constantinople, revived commerce.

**Constantine VI.** 771–?797. Son of Leo IV; emperor (780–797), last of the Isaurian emperors; under guardianship of his mother Irene (780–790); quarreled with his mother, who had him put to death, and herself usurped throne.

**Constantine VII.** *Called* **Por'phy·ro·gen'i·tus** (pôr'fĭ·rō·jěn'ĭ·tŭs), *i.e.* "born in the purple." 905–959. Son of Leo VI; emperor (912–959), under regency of Alexander (912–913) and his mother Zoë (913–919); joint ruler with stepfather, Romanus I Lecapenus (919–944), practically excluded from actual administration of government; made successful campaign against Arabs in

Syria; poisoned by son and successor, Romanus II; liberal patron of arts and literature; author of a life of Basil I (959?), and political treatises as *On the Themes* (*De Thematibus*) (935), *On the Ceremonies at the Court of Constantinople* (*De Cerimoniis aulae Byzantinae*) (953?), and *On the Administration of the Empire* (*De Administrando Imperio*) (953?); caused many works to be written that included excerpts from the classics, scientific collections, and collections of laws.

**Constantine VIII.** 960?–1028. Son of Romanus II; nominal joint ruler with his brother Basil II (976–1025); sole ruler (1025–28) on Basil's death.

**Constantine IX.** *Called* **Mo·nom'a·chus** (mō-nŏm'ȧ·kŭs), *i.e.* "who fights in single combat." 1000?–1055. Emperor (1042–55); married Empress Zoë (1042); coruler with Zoë and Theodora. During reign, defenses of empire weakened, great sums of money spent on luxuries and public buildings, Italy lost to empire when Normans conquered Benevento (1053), revolts at home, arrival of Seljuk Turks in Armenia.

**Constantine X Du'cas** (dū'kȧs). 1007?–1067. Emperor (1059–67); able minister under preceding emperors, but incapable as a ruler. During reign, army reduced, Armenia conquered (1064) by Seljuk Turks under Alp Arslan, Belgrade seized by Magyars, Thrace and Macedonia invaded by Turks.

**Constantine XI Pa'lae·ol'o·gus** (pā'lē·ŏl'ō·gŭs). *Called* **Dra·ga'ses** (drȧ·gā'sēz). 1404–1453. Son of Manuel II; emperor (1448–53; crowned 1449), last emperor of the Eastern Roman Empire; before accession, general and ruler in the Morea (1441–46), where defeated (1446) by Murad II; brave and resolute leader, but cause hopeless before Turkish armies, which besieged and captured Constantinople (1453); killed in last fighting at one of gates of city.

**Constantine XIII.** = CONSTANTINE XI; so called by some early historians.

**Constantine I.** 1868–1923. King of the Hellenes (1913–17, 1920–22). Eldest son of George I of Greece, b. Athens. Received military education in Germany; m. (1889) Princess Sophie, sister of German emperor, William II. Commanded Greek forces in disastrous Turkish War (1897); because of this defeat, forced to leave Greece for time; in Balkan War (1912–13), led Greek forces to remarkable success. Became king on assassination of father; by treaties of London and Bucharest (1913), ruled over enlarged Greece; in first part of World War, advocated neutrality; opposed by Venizelos and majority of Greek people and by Allied pressure, forced to resign (1917); lived in Switzerland (1917–20); recalled by plebiscite (1920); in spite of British and French protests, continued former policy against Turks, leading to disastrous campaign in Asia Minor; abdicated (1922) in favor of his son George II. His grandson **Constantine** 1940– . King (from 1964).

**Constantine A·sen'** (ȧ·sān') *or* **Constantine Tych** (tĭK). d. 1277. Czar of Bulgaria (1258–77), of Serbian origin. Chosen by nobles as successor to last of the Asen dynasty (*q.v.*); m. daughter of Nicaean emperor, Theodore II Lascaris, who was of the Asen family, and assumed the name; involved in conflict with Hungary and with Michael VIII Palaeologus of restored Greek Empire; killed by usurping peasant.

**Constantine** (*Russ.* **Kon·stan·tin'** [kŭn·stŭn·tyēn']) **Ni·ko·la'e·vich** (nyĭ·kŭ·lȧ'yĕ·vyĭch). 1827–1892. Russian grand duke; son of Czar Nicholas I and brother of Czar Alexander II. Commanded Russian fleet in Baltic during Crimean War (1854–55); governor of Poland (1862–63); president of Council of the Empire (1865).

**Constantine** (*Russ.* **Konstantin**) **Pa·vlo'vich** (pŭ-vlô'vyĭch). 1779–1831. Russian grand duke; 2d son of Czar Paul I and brother of Czars Alexander I and Nicholas I; renounced (1822) his right to succession to throne in event of brother Alexander's death. Governor general of Poland (1815–1831), where severity of his administration led to Polish rebellion (1830–31).

**Con'stan·tine the Af'ri·can** (kŏn'stăn·tīn [-tēn] thē ăf'rĭ·kăn). *Lat.* **Con'stan·ti'nus Af'ri·ca'nus** (kŏn'-stăn·tī'nŭs ăf'rĭ·kā'nŭs). c. 1020–c. 1087. Translator, said to have been born at Carthage; spent most of life in Benedictine monastery of Monte Cassino. Translated (into Latin) Arabic works of Jewish writers of North Africa on philosophy, Aristotelian physics, and esp. Greek medicine.

**Cons'tan'tin'-We'yer'** (kôɴs'tăɴ'tăɴ'vā'yâr'), **Maurice.** 1881–1964. French writer; to Canada (1902) and worked as farmer, cowboy, trapper, fur trader, and journalist (to 1914). Served in World War (1914–18). Author of *Vers l'Ouest* (1922), *Cavelier de la Salle* (1927), *Un Homme se Penche sur son Passé* (1928; awarded Goncourt prize), etc.

**Con·stan'ti·us** (kŏn·stăn'shĭ·ŭs). Name of three Roman emperors:

**Constantius I.** *Full name* **Flavius Valerius Constantius.** *Surnamed* **Chlo'rus** (klō'rŭs), *i.e.* "the Pale." 250?–306. Emperor (305–306); son-in-law of Maximian; father of Constantine the Great. Adopted as caesar by Maximian (292); given government of Gaul; on abdication of Diocletian and Maximian (305) became emperor of the West; died at Eboracum (York) in Britain.

**Constantius II.** *Full name* **Flavius Julius Constantius.** 317–361. Emperor (337–361); second son of Constantine the Great and Fausta, b. at Sirmium. Made caesar (333); appointed ruler in the East (335); emperor of the East (337); had many conflicts with Persians; disastrously defeated by them (348); after defeat of Magnentius (351–353) became sole ruler; appointed Julian as caesar in Gaul (355); died on march to punish Julian, who had been proclaimed emperor by his soldiers.

**Constantius III.** d. 421. Emperor (421). Roman general, b. in Illyria; m. (417) Galla Placidia, sister of Emperor Honorius. Successful in campaigns in Gaul and Spain; defeated usurper Constantine (411); made coemperor of the West by Honorius; died at Ravenna after reign of seven months.

**Con'tades'** (kôɴ'tȧd'), Duc **Louis Georges Érasme de.** 1704–1795. French soldier; marshal of France (1758); commanded army defeated at Minden (1759).

**Con'ta·ri'ni** (kōn'tä·rē'nē). Noted Venetian family, including: **Domenico**, doge of Venice from 1043–1071; **Giacomo**, doge from 1275–1280; **Andrea**, doge from 1367–1382; **Gasparo** (1483–1542), cardinal (1535) and diplomat who attempted to effect a reconciliation between Protestants and Catholics at the Diet of Ratisbon (1541); **Simone** (1563–1633), a diplomat; **Niccolò**, doge from 1630–31; **Lodovico** (d. 1653), diplomat; **Domenico II**, doge from 1659–1674, signed cession of Candia to the Turks; **Luigi**, doge from 1676–1684.

**Con'té'** (kôɴ'tā'), **Nicolas Jacques.** 1755–1805. French chemist; invented substitute for plumbago, used by painters and for making Conté crayons or pencils; conducted experiments for inflation of military balloons; devised a metal-covered barometer for measuring heights.

**Con'ti'** (*Fr.* kôɴ'tē'; *Ital.* kōn'tē), House of. (1) Collateral branch of French Bourbons whose members bore title Prince **de Conti.**

**Armand de Bour'bon'** (dē bo͝or'bôɴ'). 1629–1666. Founder of the family; French soldier; brother of the

Great Condé. Engaged in wars of the Fronde; m. niece of Cardinal Mazarin; engaged in war with Spain and captured Villafranca and Puigcerdá (1654); held command in Italy (1657). His son **Louis Armand** (1661–1685) married Marie Anne (1680), daughter of Louis XIV and Louise de La Vallière; served in Flanders (1683) and aided Imperialists to defeat Turks (1683) at Gran (Esztergom). Another son, **François Louis** (1664–1709), also aided Imperialists in Hungary (1683); m. (1688) Marie Thérèse de Bourbon, granddaughter of the Great Condé; served with great distinction in battles of Fleurus, Steenkerke, and Neerwinden; elected king of Poland (1697) but on arrival there found Augustus II, Elector of Saxony, already holding crown; appointed commander of French troops in Italy during War of the Spanish Succession, but died (Feb. 9, 1709) before taking the field.

**Louis François de Bourbon.** 1717–1776. Grandson of François Louis de Bourbon; commanded army in Italy and won battle of Coni (1744); served in Germany (1745) and Netherlands (1746–47); unsuccessful candidate for throne of Poland (1747); when he was not given command of army of the Rhine at outbreak of Seven Years' War (1756), he became opponent of government of Louis XV. His son **Louis François Joseph** (1734–1814) distinguished himself during Seven Years' War (1756–63); left France as an émigré (1789); returned (1790); arrested as a noble (1793) and tried, but acquitted; estates confiscated; banished from France; lived in retirement at Barcelona; with his death (1814) house of Conti became extinct.

(2) An illustrious Italian family dating from 11th century, which attained dukedom of **Po'li** (pô'lē) and was represented by several cardinals, numerous officers of the church, and a pope, **Michelangelo Conti** (see INNOCENT XIII).

**Con'ti** (kōn'tē), **Augusto.** 1822–1905. Italian philosopher. Professor of philosophy, San Miniato, Lucca (1855), Pisa (1863), Florence (1864). Works include *Storia della Filosofia* (1864), *Il Vero nell'Ordine* (2 vols., 1876), *Il Bello nel Vero* (2 vols., 1884), etc.

**Conti, Niccolò de'.** Venetian traveler and writer, of noble family. Left Venice (c. 1419); visited Damascus and Baghdad; thence by water to Cambay on west coast of India; later visited Sumatra, Java, Indo-China, and Burma as far north as Ava; traversed Ganges valley; returned to Venice (1444) by way of Socotra, Mecca, and Egypt. As penance for compulsory renunciation of Christianity, ordered by Pope Eugenius IV to relate to papal secretary Poggio Bracciolini the story of his wanderings, published (1723) as *Historiae de Varietate Fortunae.*

**Con·ti'no** (kôn·tē'nô), **Antonio.** Italian architect; known esp. as architect (c. 1595–1605) of Bridge of Sighs at Venice.

**Contucci, Andrea.** See Andrea SANSOVINO.

**Con'verse** (kŏn'vûrs; -vẽrs), **Charles Crozat.** 1832–1918. American composer, b. Warren, Mass.; best-known hymn, *What a Friend We Have in Jesus.*

**Converse, Florence.** 1871– . American writer, b. New Orleans. B.S., Wellesley (1893). Author of *Diana Victrix* (1897), *The Burden of Christopher* (1900), *The House of Prayer* (1908), *Garments of Praise* (1921), *Into the Void* (1926), *Sphinx* (1931), *Collected Poems* (1937).

**Converse, Frederick Shepherd.** 1871–1940. American musician and composer, b. Newton, Mass. A.B., Harvard (1893). Professor, New England Conservatory of Music, and dean (from 1931) of the faculty. Composer of symphonic poems (*The Festival of Pan, Ormazd, Night and Day*), a fantasy (*The Mystic Trumpeter*), an overture (*Youth*), an oratorio (*Job*), operas (*The Pipe of Desire, The Sacrifice, The Immigrants*), a cantata (*The Peace Pipe*), symphonies, choral works, and songs.

**Con'way** (kŏn'wā), **Francis Seymour–** and **Francis Charles Seymour–.** See SEYMOUR family.

**Conway, Henry Seymour.** 1721–1795. English soldier and statesman. M.P. (1741–84). At Fontenoy (1745); at Culloden Moor (1746) as aide-de-camp to duke of Cumberland; major general (1756); discredited by failure of expedition against Rochefort (1757); dismissed for opposing George III's views on Wilkes case. Secretary of state in Rockingham ministry (1765–68), and leader of House of Commons; carried repeal of Stamp Act (1766); governor of Jersey (1772–95). Opposed Lord North's American policy and brought about his resignation (1782); commander in chief with cabinet seat (1782–83); supported Fox in opposition to Pitt (1784); field marshal (1793).

**Conway, Moncure Daniel.** 1832–1907. American clergyman, b. in Stafford County, Va. Grad. Dickinson College (1849); Harvard Divinity School (1854). Vigorous abolitionist; edited *The Dial*, Cincinnati (1860–61), *Commonwealth*, Boston (1862); pastor in London, Eng. (1864–84; 1892–97). Author of *Demonology and Devil Lore* (1878), *The Wandering Jew* (1881), *Life of Thomas Paine* (1892), *Autobiography* (1904), etc.

**Conway, Robert Seymour.** 1864–1933. English classical philologist; educ. Cambridge U. Professor of Latin, University Coll., Cardiff (1893–1903), Victoria U., Manchester (1903–29). Among his many books are *The Restored Pronunciation of Greek and Latin* (1896), *Limen, a first Latin Book* (1908), *Deigma, a first Greek Book* (in collaboration with C. F. Walters, 1916), *New Studies of a Great Inheritance* (1921), *The Portrait of a Roman Gentleman from Livy* (1922).

**Conway, Thomas.** 1735–?1800. Soldier of fortune, b. in Ireland. Educ. in France. Served in French army (1749–76). To America (1777); appointed major general, against Washington's recommendation (Dec. 14, 1777). In conspiracy, known as the Conway Cabal, to supplant Washington by Gen. Horatio Gates (1778); on discovery of conspiracy, resigned his commission. Rejoined French army (1779); served in India (1781–87); governor general, French possessions in India (1787).

**Conway of Al'ling·ton** (ăl'ĭng·tŭn), 1st Baron. **William Martin Conway.** 1856–1937. English explorer, art historian, and writer, b. at Rochester. Educ. Cambridge U. Professor of art, University College, Liverpool (1885–88), Cambridge (1901–04); trustee of the Wallace Collection (1916–24). M.P. (1918–31). Explored Spitsbergen (1896–97), Bolivian Andes (1898), and Tierra del Fuego. Author of books on mountain climbing and art.

**Con'well** (kŏn'wĕl; -wĕl), **Russell Herman.** 1843–1925. American clergyman, b. South Worthington, Mass. A lawyer (1865–79); Baptist clergyman, in Philadelphia (1881–91); founder (1888) and first president, Temple Univ. His lecture *Acres of Diamonds* delivered over 6000 times.

**Con'y·beare** (kŏn'ĭ·bẽr; kŭn'-), **John.** 1692–1755. English clergyman. M.A., Oxon. (1716); dean of Christ Church, Oxford (1733–55); bishop of Bristol (1750); author of *A Defence of Revealed Religion*, a reply to Matthew Tindal. His grandson **John Josias Conybeare** (1779–1824), M.A., Oxon. (1804), was Oxford professor of Anglo-Saxon (1807–12), of poetry (1812–21), contributor to geological and chemical literature. Another grandson, **William Daniel Conybeare** (1787–1857), M.A., Oxon. (1811), dean of Llandaff (1845–57), first described genus *Ichthyosaurus;* author, with William Phillips, of first widely used treatise on geology in English. **Frederick Cornwallis Conybeare** (1856–1924), descendant of William Daniel Conybeare, M.A., Oxon. (1883), was an Armenian scholar; made discoveries important to history of Christianity and Biblical literature; author of *The Historical Christ* (1914) and *The Dreyfus Case* (1898), defending Dreyfus.

**Con′ze** (kŏn′tsĕ), **Alexander Christian Leopold.** 1831–1914. German archaeologist.

**Cook** (ko͝ok), **Albert Stanburrough.** 1853–1927. American philologist, b. Montville, N.J. Grad. Rutgers (1872). Professor of English, Yale (1889–1921). Author of *The Phonological Investigation of Old English* (1888), *The Art of Poetry* (1892), *First Book in Old English* (1894); translator of Sievers's *Angelsächsische Grammatik* (*Old English Grammar*).

**Cook, Arthur Bernard.** 1868–1952. English classical scholar and archaeologist; educ. Cambridge. Professor of Greek, London (1892–1907); reader in classical archaeology (1908–31), and professor (1931–34), Cambridge.

**Cook, Arthur James.** 1885–1931. English labor leader, b. in Somersetshire. Secretary of Miners' Federation of Great Britain (1924). Influential in bringing on the coal miners' strike and the general strike (1926).

**Cook, Eliza.** 1818–1889. English poetess. Published *Lays of a Wild Harp* (1835); conducted *Eliza Cook's Journal* for family reading (1849–54); author of poem *The Old Arm Chair* (1837).

**Cook, Flavius Josephus.** See Joseph Cook.

**Cook, Frederick Albert.** 1865–1940. American physician and arctic explorer, b. at Callicoon Depot, N.Y. M.D., N.Y.U. (1890). Surgeon in Peary Arctic Expedition (1891–92) and Belgian Antarctic Expedition (1897–99). Led expeditions to climb Mt. McKinley (1903–06); announced he had succeeded (1906). On arctic exploration trip (1907–09) in effort to reach North Pole; on his return, announced he had reached the pole April 21, 1908; claim denounced by Peary and rejected, on grounds of insufficient evidence, by scientists at Copenhagen after study of data submitted by Cook. Author of *Through the First Antarctic Night* (1900), *To the Top of the Continent* (1908), *My Attainment of the Pole* (1909).

**Cook, George Cram.** 1873–1924. American novelist, playwright, and dramatic director, b. Davenport, Iowa. Educ. U. of Iowa, Harvard, Heidelberg. Organized and directed (1915) the Provincetown Players, Provincetown, Mass.; established Playwrights' Theater, New York City, first of the "little theaters" (1915). See Susan Glaspell.

**Cook, James.** *Known as* Captain **Cook.** 1728–1779. English mariner and explorer. Common seaman in British navy (1755); master (1759); surveyed St. Lawrence Channel (1759), coast of Newfoundland and Labrador (1763–67). Conducted, in the *Endeavour*, expedition (1768) to South Pacific Ocean; at Tahiti observed the transit of Venus (1769); charted coasts of New Zealand, Australia, and New Guinea; returned by way of Cape of Good Hope (1771). Conducted, with the *Resolution* and the *Adventure*, an expedition (1772–75) in search of the great southern continent then believed to exist; skirted Antarctic ice fields, visited Tahiti, New Hebrides, and discovered New Caledonia; by enforcement of strict hygienic and dietary rules, he conquered fever and scurvy and completed three-year voyage with the loss of but one man; awarded Copley gold medal. Conducted, with the *Resolution* and the *Discovery*, his last expedition, to discover a passage round North America from the Pacific (1776); rediscovered Sandwich Islands (1778), charted Pacific coast of North America (1778) as far as Bering Strait; visited Hawaii, where he was killed in scuffle with natives over a stolen boat.

**Cook, John Mason.** See under Thomas Cook.

**Cook, Joseph,** *orig.* **Flavius Josephus.** 1838–1901. American lecturer, b. Ticonderoga, N.Y. Grad. Harvard (1865) and Andover Sem. (1868). Among volumes of his lectures are *Biology* (1877), *Heredity* (1878), *Socialism* (1880), *Current Religious Perils* (1888).

**Cook,** Sir **Joseph.** 1860–1947. English-born Australian statesman; to Australia (1885). Postmaster general (1894–98); minister for mines and agriculture (1898–99); minister for defense (1909–10); prime minister of Australia (1913–14). Minister for the navy (1917–20), and Australian representative at the Versailles Peace Conference (1919); commonwealth treasurer (1920–21); high commissioner for Australia, in London (1921–27).

**Cook, Melville Thurston.** 1869–1952. American botanist, b. Coffeen, Ill. A.B., Stanford (1894); Ph.D., Ohio State (1904). Plant pathologist in Santiago, Cuba (1904–06), Newark, N.J. (1907–11), State of New Jersey (1911–23), Puerto Rico (from 1923). Also, professor of plant pathology, Rutgers (1911–23). Editor, *Journal of Department of Agriculture of Puerto Rico* (from 1928). Author of *Diseases of Tropical Plants* (1912), *Applied Economic Botany* (1919), etc.

**Cook, Or′a·tor** (ŏr′ȧ·tẽr) **Fuller.** 1867–1949. American botanist, b. Clyde, N.Y. Ph.B., Syracuse (1890). Agent investigating conditions in Liberia (1891–97). On staff of U.S. National Museum, Washington, D.C. (from 1898). On various expeditions collecting botanical specimens, as to Peru (1915), Haiti (1917), China (1919), Central America (1922–31).

**Cook, Robert Johnson.** 1849–1922. American crew coach, b. near Cookstown, Pa. Grad. Yale (1876). Business manager, Philadelphia *Press* (1882–97). Coach of thirteen Yale crews between 1876 and 1897; inventor of the "Bob Cook stroke."

**Cook, Stanley Arthur.** 1873–1949. English Orientalist, b. at King's Lynn. Educ. Cambridge U. On editorial staff of *Encyclopaedia Biblica* (1896–1903), and adviser on Old Testament and Semitic subjects for eleventh edition of *Encyclopaedia Britannica;* editor for Palestine Exploration Fund (1902–32). Professor of Hebrew, Cambridge (1932–38). Joint editor, *Cambridge Ancient History.* Among his many books are *Religion of Ancient Palestine* (1908), *Ethical Monotheism* (1932), *The Old Testament; a Reinterpretation* (1936), *The "Truth" of the Bible* (1938).

**Cook,** Lady **Tennessee Celeste,** *nee* **Claflin.** See under Victoria Claflin.

**Cook, Thomas.** 1808–1892. English tourist agent, founder of Thomas Cook & Son. Woodturner; printer; Baptist missionary for Rutland (c. 1828–29). Aided visitors to reach the Great Exhibition of 1851, the Paris Exhibition (1855), to make circular tour of Europe (1856); initiated system of providing hotel accommodations (1866); commissioned to convey General Gordon to the Sudan (1884). His son **John Mason** (1834–1899), in partnership with him (from 1864), extended services of company to America and Continent.

**Cooke** (ko͝ok), **Elisha.** 1637–1715. American colonial political leader, b. Boston. Grad. Harvard (1657). Practicing physician, Boston. Leader in movement overthrowing and imprisoning Andros and Dudley (1689); agent of Massachusetts Colony in London (1690–92); insisted on retention of old charter. Instrumental in preventing Increase Mather from getting new charter for Harvard College; forced Mather to resign as president of Harvard (1700–01). Judge, Massachusetts superior court (1694–1702). Elected member governor's council (1715). His son **Elisha** (1678–1737), b. Boston, grad. Harvard (1697), was also a practicing physician in Boston, deputy in Mass. General Court (1715–33), member of governor's council (1717, 1724–26, 1728), and a leader in upholding colonists' rights to a share in their own government.

**Cooke, Henry.** d. 1672. English composer and choirmaster.

**Cooke, Henry.** 1788–1868. Irish Presbyterian leader. Minister, Belfast (1829–68); as leader of orthodox party, succeeded in excluding Arian ministers from Presbyterian Church; opposed disestablishment of Protestantism in Ireland.

**Cooke, Hesiod.** See Thomas COOKE.

**Cooke, James Francis.** 1875–1960. American music educator and author, b. Bay City, Mich. Author of *Standard History of Music* (1909), *Great Men and Famous Musicians* (1925), *Musical Travelogues* (1934), etc.

**Cooke, Jay.** 1821–1905. American banker, b. Sandusky, Ohio. Jay Cooke & Co. (1861) marketed government bonds for financing Civil War; fiscal agent, U.S. Treasury (1862–64, 1865). After war, financed construction of western railroads, esp. Northern Pacific; failed (1873), precipitating financial panic. Recouped fortune by mining investments in Utah.

**Cooke, John Esten.** 1830–1886. American novelist, b. Winchester, Va. Author of *Leather Stocking and Silk* (1854), *The Virginia Comedians* (1854), *Wearing of the Gray* (1867), *My Lady Pokahontas* (1885), etc. His brother **Philip Pendleton** (1816–1850) wrote romances.

**Cooke, Josiah Parsons.** 1827–1894. American chemist, b. Boston. Grad. Harvard (1848). Professor, Harvard (1850–94); investigated atomic weights of elements.

**Cooke, Mordecai Cubitt.** 1825–1913. English mycologist. Author of botanical manuals and works on British and American fungi.

**Cooke, Rose,** *nee* **Terry.** 1827–1892. American author of verse and stories of New England life, b. West Hartford, Conn.

**Cooke, Rupert Croft–.** See CROFT-COOKE.

**Cooke, Terence James.** 1921– . American Roman Catholic clergyman; consecrated bishop (1965); archbishop of New York (1968); cardinal (1969).

**Cooke, Thomas.** 1703–1756. English poet, journalist, and pamphleteer. Known as "Hesiod Cooke," from his translation of Hesiod. Translated Terence and other authors; author of a poem, *The Battle of the Poets*, containing criticism of Pope's Greek which won him a place in the *Dunciad*.

**Cooke, Thomas Simpson.** 1782–1848. Singer and composer, b. Dublin; principal tenor (1815), and musical director (1821–42), Drury Lane Theatre, London.

**Cooke, Sir William Fothergill.** 1806–1879. English electrical engineer. Educ. Edinburgh, Paris, and Heidelberg. Collaborated with Charles Wheatstone in invention of electric telegraphs, the two finally patenting a workable single-needle apparatus (1845); quarreled with Wheatstone, each claiming chief credit for invention.

**Cook'wor'thy** (ko͝ok'wûr'thĭ), **William.** 1705–1780. English potter. Quaker; druggist at Plymouth; discoverer of kaolin and China stone near St. Austell (1756), the foundation of English porcelain and fine earthenware.

**Cool'brith** (ko͞ol'brĭth), **I'na** (ī'nȧ) **Donna.** 1842–1928. American poet, b. near Springfield, Ill. Associated with Bret Harte in editing the *Overland Monthly* (1868). Librarian (1873–1906). Crowned poet laureate of California (1915).

**Coo'ley** (ko͞o'lĭ), **Thomas McIntyre.** 1824–1898. American jurist, b. near Attica, N.Y. Judge, Michigan supreme court (1864–85). Professor of law, U. of Michigan (1859–84). Member, Interstate Commerce Commission (1887–91). Author of legal treatises, esp. on constitutional law.

**Coo'lidge** (ko͞o'lĭj), **Archibald Cary.** 1866–1928. American historian, b. Boston. Nephew of Thomas Jefferson Coolidge (*q.v.*). Grad. Harvard (1887); Ph.D., Freiburg (1892). Taught at Harvard (1893–1928; professor from 1908). Editor, *Foreign Affairs* (1922–27). Author of *The United States as a World Power* (1908), *Origins of the Triple Alliance* (1917), *Ten Years of War and Peace* (1927).

**Coolidge, Calvin,** *in full* **John Calvin.** 1872–1933. Thirtieth president of the U.S., b. Plymouth, Vt. A.B., Amherst (1895). Practiced law in Northampton, Mass. (from 1897). Mayor of Northampton (1910–11). Member of Massachusetts State Senate (1912–15). Lieutenant governor of Massachusetts (1916, 1917, 1918); governor (1919, 1920). Attracted nationwide attention by firm stand during Boston police strike (1919). Vice-president of the U.S. (Mar. 4, 1921–Aug. 2, 1923); succeeded to presidency on death of Harding, and was sworn in at his father's home in Plymouth, Vt., early in the morning of Aug. 3, 1923. Elected (1924) president of the U.S. and served full term (1925–29).

**Coolidge, Charles Allerton.** 1858–1936. American architect, b. Boston. A.B., Harvard (1881). Practiced in Boston. Among buildings designed by him are Stanford U., Harvard Med. School in Boston, public library and art institute in Chicago, Rockefeller Institute in New York, medical school and hospital group for Vanderbilt U. in Nashville, Tenn., medical school for Western Reserve U. in Cleveland, Ohio.

**Coolidge, Dane.** 1873–1940. American naturalist and novelist, b. Natick, Mass. A.B., Stanford (1898). Author of many western stories, including *Hidden Water* (1910), *The Desert Trail* (1915), *Silver and Gold* (1918), *Gun Smoke* (1927), *Silver Hat* (1934), *Rawhide Johnny* (1936), *Ranger Two-Rifles* (1937), etc. His wife, **Mary Elizabeth Burroughs,** *nee* **Roberts** (1860–1945), writer; Ph.B. (1880) and M.S. (1882), Cornell; Ph.D., Stanford (1896); m. Albert W. Smith (1890) and Dane Coolidge (1906); professor of sociology in Mills College (1918–27); author of *Chinese Immigration* (1909), *Why Women Are So* (1912), *The Rain Makers* (1929), *The Navajo Indians* (with Dane Coolidge, 1930).

**Coolidge, Julian Lowell.** 1873–1954. Bro. of Archibald Cary Coolidge. American mathematician, b. Brookline, Mass. A.B., Harvard (1895); B.Sc, Oxon. (1897); Ph.D., Bonn (1904). Teacher of mathematics, Harvard (from 1900); professor (from 1918). Author of *Elements of Non-Euclidean Geometry* (1909), *Treatise on the Circle and the Sphere* (1916), *Geometry of the Complex Domain* (1924), *Algebraic Plane Curves* (1931).

**Coolidge, Susan.** Pseudonym of Sarah Chauncey Woolsey (see under Theodore Dwight WOOLSEY).

**Coolidge, Thomas Jefferson.** 1831–1920. American diplomat, b. Boston. Grad. Harvard (1850). U.S. minister to France (1892–93).

**Coolidge, William Augustus Brevoort.** 1850–1926. Mountaineer and historian, b. near New York City. Educ. Oxford U., England. Ordained deacon (1882) and priest (1883), in the Anglican ministry. Resident chiefly in Switzerland (from 1885), and a student of Swiss geography and history; widely known as mountain climber, making about 1750 ascents among the Alps (1865–1900). Editor of *Alpine Journal* (1880–89).

**Coolidge, William David.** 1873–1975. American physical chemist, b. Hudson, Mass. B.S., M.I.T. (1896); Ph.D., U. of Leipzig (1899). Engaged in research at General Electric Co., Schenectady, N.Y. (from 1905); director of research laboratory (1932). Invented and made applications of ductile tungsten; devised a tube (Coolidge tube) for the production of X rays.

**Coo′lus′** (kō′lüs′), **Romain.** *Pseudonym of* **René Weill** (vīl). 1868–1952. French playwright.

**Coo·ma′ra·swa′my** (ko͞o·mä′rȧ·swä′mĭ), **A′nan·da′** (ä′nȧn·dŭ′) **Kent′ish** (kĕn′tĭsh). 1877–1947. East Indian scholar in U.S., b. Colombo, Ceylon. D.Sc., U. of London, Eng. (1904). Director of mineral survey of Ceylon (1906). Inaugurated movement in India for national education. Research fellow in Indian, Persian, and Mohammedan art, Museum of Fine Arts in Boston (from 1917). Author of books on Buddhism and the art and literature of India, including *Indian Drawings* (2 vols., 1910–12), *Buddha and the Gospel of Buddhism* (1916), *The Dance of Siva* (1918), *A New Approach to the Vedas* (1933), *Is Art a Superstition or a Way of Life?* (1937). Editor of East Indian terms for *Webster's New International Dictionary, Second Edition.*

**Coombe, William.** = William COMBE.

**Coo′per** (ko͞o′pẽr; ko͝op′ẽr), **Alexander.** See under Samuel COOPER.

**Cooper, Alfred Duff** (dŭf). 1890–1954. English political leader; educ. Oxford U. Served in World War (1914–18). M.P. (1924–29, 1931–45); financial secretary, War Office (1928–29, 1931–34), Treasury (1934–35); secretary of state for war (1935–37); first lord of the admiralty (1937–38); minister of information (1940–41); amb. to France (1944–47). Author of *Talleyrand* (1932), *Haig* (2 vols., 1935–36). His wife (m. 1919), **Lady Diana Man′ners** (măn′ẽrz) (1892– ), daughter of the 8th duke of Rutland, was on the stage, appearing as the Madonna in *The Miracle.*

**Cooper, Anthony Ashley.** See earls of SHAFTESBURY.

**Cooper,** Sir **Astley Paston.** 1768–1841. English surgeon. Studied in London, Edinburgh, and in Paris. Surgeon to Guy's Hospital, London (1800); professor of comparative anatomy, Royal Coll. of Surgeons (1813); surgeon to the king (1828). First to attempt to tie the aorta in treatment of aneurysm (1817).

**Cooper, Charles Henry.** 1808–1866. English antiquary, of Cambridge.

**Cooper, Colin Campbell.** 1856–1937. American painter, b. Philadelphia. Studied at Pennsylvania Academy of Fine Arts and at Paris. Best known for his paintings of scenes in American and European cities.

**Cooper, Courtney Ryley.** 1886–1940. American writer, b. Kansas City, Mo. Ran away as a boy (1901) to become clown in a circus; variously thereafter, newsboy, trucker, glove salesman, journalist, circus press agent, actor, monologuist, vaudeville dancer, and circus manager. Author of many stories of circuses and of jungle animal life, also of photoplays, as *Weary River, Wild Cargo, The Plainsman.*

**Cooper, Edith Emma.** See Michael FIELD.

**Cooper,** Sir **Edwin.** 1873–1942. English architect; designed many public and private buildings in London, college and school buildings in Oxford and elsewhere, etc.

**Cooper, Henry Ernest.** 1857–1929. American-Hawaiian lawyer and statesman, b. New Albany, Ind. Grad. Boston Univ. (1878). Resident of Hawaii from 1891. Instrumental in organizing revolution that deposed queen and established provisional government. Successively, minister of foreign affairs, Republic of Hawaii, minister of public instruction, acting president (1898), and attorney general. Advocate of annexation to United States. Secretary of the Territory of Hawaii (1900–03).

**Cooper, Hugh Lincoln.** 1865–1937. American hydraulic engineer, b. near Winona, Minn. Began in bridge engineering (1883); specialized in hydraulic engineering as applied to electric power development (from 1891). Among plants designed and built under his supervision are water-power project at Muscle Shoals, Ala.; Dnieper dam in the Soviet Union.

**Cooper, James Fenimore.** 1789–1851. American novelist, b. Burlington, N.J. Educ. Yale (1803–05). Went to sea (1806); midshipman, U.S. navy (1808); resigned (1811). Lived life of a country gentleman (1811–22). Fiction writing begun by chance challenge from his wife to make good his boast that he could write a better novel than the one they were reading together. First story, *Precaution* (1820), a failure; but second, *The Spy* (1821), a great success; followed by *The Pioneers,* first of the so-called Leatherstocking series (1823), and *The Pilot* (1823). To New York (1822), and continued his novels: *The Last of the Mohicans* (1826), *The Prairie* (1827), *The Red Rover* (1828), *The Wept of Wish-ton-Wish* (1829), *The Water Witch* (1831). Traveled abroad much of time between 1826 and 1833; returned critical of Americans and their culture; wrote several books expressing his criticism, and suffered sharp loss of popularity (1838). Victorious in several libel suits against newspapers. Continued writing with two books, *The Pathfinder* (1840) and *The Deerslayer* (1841), that completed the Leatherstocking series. Later works, *History of the Navy of the United States* (1839), *The Wing-and-Wing* (1842), *Satanstoe* (1845). Elected to American Hall of Fame (1910). His daughter **Susan Fenimore Cooper** (1813–1894) was author of *Rural Hours* (1850), etc.

**Cooper, Lane.** 1875–1959. American educator, b. New Brunswick, N.J. Ph.D., Leipzig (1901). Teacher of English, Cornell (from 1902). Compiler of a *Concordance to the Poems of William Wordsworth* (1911).

**Cooper, Leon N.** 1930– . Physicist, b. New York City. Ph.D., Columbia, 1953. Shared 1972 Nobel prize in physics with John Bardeen and John R. Schrieffer for work on superconductivity of metals.

**Cooper, Merian C.** 1893–1973. American writer and motion-picture producer, b. Jacksonville, Fla. Author of *Grass* (1925); coproducer of *Grass* (1925), *Chang* (1927), *King Kong* (1933), *Last Days of Pompeii* (1935), *She Wore a Yellow Ribbon* (1949), *The Quiet Man* (1952).

**Cooper, Peter.** 1791–1883. American manufacturer and philanthropist, b. New York City. Proprietor of ironworks in Baltimore (from 1828); designed and built first American locomotive, for Baltimore and Ohio Railroad (1830); promoter and financial backer of the laying of Atlantic cable. Founded (1857–59) Cooper Union, New York City, for the "advancement of science and art," giving free courses in science, chemistry, electricity, engineering, and art. Elected to American Hall of Fame (1900). His son **Edward** (1824–1905), iron and steel manufacturer, New York City; with A. S. Hewitt (*q.v.*) formed Cooper, Hewitt & Co.

**Cooper, Samuel.** 1609–1672. English miniature painter. Painted portraits of Mrs. Pepys, Cromwell, Milton, Prince Rupert, George Monck, as well as portraits of royalty. His brother **Alexander** (d. 1660) was miniature painter to Queen Christina of Sweden (1646–54).

**Coo′per** *or* **Cou′per** (ko͞o′pẽr), **Thomas.** 1517?–1594. English bishop; B.A., Oxon. (1539); issued *Thesaurus Linguae Romanae et Britannicae* (1565), known as *Cooper's Dictionary;* bishop of Lincoln (1570), of Winchester (1584–94); against Martin Marprelate writings.

**Coo′per** (ko͞o′pẽr; ko͝op′ẽr), **Thomas.** 1805–1892. English Chartist. Apprentice to shoemaker; taught himself Greek, Latin, and Hebrew; schoolmaster; journalist; became Chartist and edited Chartist paper, took part in general strike of 1842; imprisoned.

**Cooper, Thomas Sidney.** 1803–1902. English painter; exhibited pictures of cattle and sheep (1833–1902).

**Coorn'hert** (kōrn'hĕrt), **Dirck Volckertszoon.** 1522–1590. Dutch scholar; copper engraver; secretary of Holland, in service of William of Orange (1572). Chief prose work is *Ethics, that is the Art of Well Living* (1586). Author of translations from Cicero, Seneca, Erasmus, and the Odyssey. Credited with great influence in establishing the literary language of Holland.

**Coote** (ko͞ot), Sir **Eyre.** 1726–1783. British soldier, b. in Ireland. Captain in first British regiment sent to India (1754); led a division at Plassey (1757); gained victory of Wandewash (1760); took Pondichéry (1761); commander in chief in India (1777); routed Haidar Ali at Porto Novo (1781). His nephew Sir **Eyre Coote** (1762–1823), soldier, served in America (1775–81), West Indies (1793, 1795), in Egypt (1801); governor of Jamaica (1805–08); general (1814).

**Coote, Richard.** 1st Earl of **Bel'la·mont** (bĕl'ȧ·mŏnt) *or* **Bel'lo·mont** (bĕl'ô·mŏnt). 1636–1701. British colonial administrator in America. M.P. (1688–95); supporter of William of Orange, who created him earl in Irish peerage (1689). Governor of N.Y., Mass., and N.H. (1697–1701); commissioned to suppress illegal trade and piracy; sent out Captain William Kidd to combat freebooters; had to arrest Kidd for piracy (1699).

**Cope** (kōp), **Charles West.** 1811–1890. English historical and genre painter. Executed frescoes for Houses of Parliament (1843).

**Cope, Edward Drinker.** 1840–1897. American naturalist, b. Philadelphia. Owner and editor, *American Naturalist* (1878–97). Made contributions in field of extinct vertebrates, herpetology, and ichthyology.

**Cope, Walter.** 1860–1902. American architect, b. Philadelphia. Especially known as designer of college buildings.

**Co'peau'** (kô'pō'), **Jacques.** 1879–1949. French actor and theater director; founder (1913) of Théâtre du Vieux Colombier, where he developed new stage technique with simplification of setting.

**Cope'land** (kōp'lănd), **Charles Townsend.** 1860–1952. American educator, b. Calais, Me. A.B., Harvard (1882). Teacher of English, Harvard (from 1893; professor from 1925); known esp. for his classroom and public readings of English literary classics.

**Copeland, Edwin Bingham.** 1873–?1965. American botanist, b. Monroe, Wis. A.B., Stanford (1895); Ph.D., Halle (1896). Botanist of Philippine government (1903–08); dean of college of agriculture, and professor, U. of the Philippines (1909–17). Curator of herbarium, U. of California (1928–32). Author of *The Coco-nut* (1914), *The Ferns of Borneo* (1917), *Rice* (1924), *Fiji Ferns* (1929), etc.

**Copeland, Ralph.** 1837–1905. British astronomer and explorer, b. in Lancashire; educ. Göttingen; coauthor of *First Göttingen Catalogue of Stars* (1869); with German Arctic expedition to explore east coast of Greenland (1869). Accompanied Lord Lindsay to Mauritius to observe transit of Venus; discovered a great tree fern at Trinidad (1874); in charge of observatory of Lord Lindsay at Aberdeen (1876); astronomer royal for Scotland and professor in Edinburgh (1889).

**Copeland, Royal Samuel.** 1868–1938. American physician and politician, b. Dexter, Mich. M.D., Michigan (1889). Professor of ophthalmology, U. of Michigan (1895–1908). Dean, Flower Hospital Medical College, New York (1908–18). President, New York City Board of Health (1918–23). U.S. senator from New York (1923–38); sponsored legislation to guarantee pure foods and drugs.

**Co·pel'lo** (kô·pā'lō), **Santiago Luis.** 1880-1967. Argentine prelate, b. San Isidro. Educ. Buenos Aires and Rome. Archbishop (from 1932) of Buenos Aires; cardinal (1935); primate of Argentina (1936).

**Co·per'ni·cus** (kô·pûr'nĭ·kŭs), **Nic'o·la'us** (nĭk'ô·lā'ŭs). *Latinized form of* **Mikołaj Ko·per'nik** (kô·pĕr'nēk) *or* **Ni'klas** (nē'kläs) **Kop'per·nigk** (kŏp'ẽr·nĭk). 1473–1543. Polish (or Prussian) astronomer, b. Thorn (Toruń), then in Prussian Poland. Educ. Cracow and (1496–1500) Bologna. Canon of cathedral at Frauenburg (1497). Lectured on astronomy at Rome (1500). Received doctor's degree in canon law at Ferrara (1503) and continued studies in medical school at Padua (to 1506). Physician to his uncle and patron, Lucas Watzelrode, Bishop of Ermeland (to 1512); occupied thereafter with his duties at cathedral at Frauenburg. Probably began consideration of his theory of the solar system as early as 1507; had his great work, *De Revolutionibus Orbium Coelestium,* practically completed (c. 1530), but delayed printing it because of political and religious conditions; printing completed (1543) just in time to reach Copernicus on his deathbed. Regarded as founder of modern astronomy in establishing theory that earth rotates daily on its axis and that planets revolve in orbits around the sun.

**Cop'land** (kōp'lănd), **Aaron.** 1900– . American composer, b. Brooklyn, N.Y.; his works include *El Salon Mexico, Billy the Kid, The Second Hurricane, Appalachian Spring,* symphonies, chamber music, a concerto for piano and orchestra, etc.

**Cop'land** (kŏp'lănd; kōp'lănd), **James.** 1791–1870. English physician; compiler of a *Dictionary of Practical Medicine* (1832).

**Copland, Robert.** fl. 1508–1547. English printer; issued books with his imprint (1515–47); author of *The Hye Way to the Spyttel Hous, Jyl of Breyntford's Testament* (in verse); translator of French romances.

**Cop'le·ston** (kŏp''l·stŭn), **Edward.** 1776–1849. English prelate; B.A., Oxon. (1795). Bishop of Llandaff and dean of St. Paul's (1828–49); author of pamphlets on economic subjects.

**Cop'ley** (kŏp'lĭ), Sir **Godfrey.** d. 1709. English founder of the Copley Medal, awarded annually by the Royal Society to the author of the best work on experimental philosophy.

**Copley, John Singleton.** 1738–1815. American portrait painter, b. Boston. Studio in Boston from about 1757. Settled (ab. 1775) in London. Examples of his work: *John Hancock, Samuel Adams,* and *The Copley Family,* in Boston Art Museum; *Mrs. Thomas Boylston,* in Memorial Hall, Harvard; *Lady Wentworth* and *Mrs. Robert Harper,* in New York Public Library; *Lord Cornwallis,* in Corporation Art Gallery, London; *Earl of Mansfield,* in National Gallery, London. His son **John Singleton** (1772–1863), Baron **Lynd'hurst** (lĭnd'hûrst), b. Boston, to England (1775), a jurist, was lord chancellor of England (1827–30, 1834–35, 1841–46).

**Cop'pard** (kŏp'ẽrd), **Alfred Edgar.** 1878–1957. English poet and short-story writer, b. at Folkestone. Among his volumes of verse are *Hips and Haws* (1922), *Pelagea and Other Poems* (1926), *Cherry Ripe* (1935); among his books of stories, *Adam and Eve and Pinch Me* (1921), *Fishmonger's Fiddle* (1925), *The Field of Mustard* (1926), *Pink Furniture* (1930), *Tapster's Tapestry* (1938), *You Never Know, Do You?* (1939).

**Cop'pée'** (kô'pā'), **François Édouard Joachim.** 1842–1908. French writer, b. Paris. Gained repute as one of the Parnassian group with his early poetry, *Le Reliquaire* (1866), *Intimités* (1868), *Les Humbles* (1872), *Le Cahier Rouge* (1874). Among his plays are *Le Passant* (verse comedy, 1869), *Le Luthier de Crémone* (1876), *Les Jacobites* (1885), *Pour la Couronne* (1895). Among his prose works are *Contes, Toute une Jeunesse, Le Coupable.*

**Coppet, Edward J. de.** See DE COPPET.

**Co'quard'** (kô'kȧr'), **Arthur.** 1846–1910. French composer of operas and orchestral and choral works.

**Co'que·lin'** (kô'klăN'), **Benoît Constant.** *Known as* **Coquelin Aî'né'** (ā'nā'). 1841–1909. French actor; debut at Comédie Française (1860); created roles in *Gringoire, Tabarin, L'Étrangère, Le Monde où l'on s'Ennuie,* etc.; actor-manager of the Porte Saint Martin theater (1897) where he created his most successful role, Cyrano in *Cyrano de Bergerac.* Author of *L'Art et le Comédien* (1880), *Les Comédiens, par un Comédien* (1882), etc. His brother **Ernest** (1848–1909), known as **Coquelin Ca'det'** (kȧ'dĕ'), comedian, played at the Odéon, Comédie Française, and Variétés; author of *Le Monologue Moderne* (1881), *Le Rire* (1887), *Pirouettes* (1888), etc. Benoît's son **Jean** (1865–1944), began his stage career with his father, most notably as Ragueneau in *Cyrano de Bergerac* and the Dog in *Chantecler.*

**Co'que·rel'** (kô'krĕl'). Family of French clergymen active in the cause of liberalism, including: **Athanase Laurent Charles** (1795–1868), pastor in Paris (1830), aided in founding (1853) *Alliance Chrétienne Universelle;* author of *L'Orthodoxie Moderne* (1842), *Le Christianisme Expérimental* (1847), etc. His brother **Charles Augustin** (1797–1851), a founder (1825) of *Revue Britannique,* author of *L'Histoire des Églises du Désert* (1841). Athanase's sons **Athanase Josué** (1820–1875), who opened a free liberal church in Paris, author of *Jean Calas et sa Famille* (1857), *Histoire de l'Église Réformée de Paris* (1860), *Histoire du Credo* (1868), etc., and **Jean Étienne** (1829–1901), author of *Libéraux et Orthodoxes* (1864), *M. Guizot et l'Orthodoxie Protestante* (1864), etc.

**Coques** *or* **Cocx** (kŏks), **Gonzales.** 1614–1684. Flemish portrait painter, esp. of family groups on small canvases.

**Coquillett, Daniel William.** 1856–1911. American entomologist, b. near Woodstock, Ill.; acclimatized Australian ladybird beetle in California to destroy the cottony-cushion scale, thus saving the California citrus industry (1887).

**Coraës.** See CORAY.

**Co'ram** (kō'răm), **Thomas.** 1668–1751. English philanthropist, b. Lyme Regis, Eng. Shipwright by trade. In Massachusetts colony (1693–1704); merchant in London (from 1720). Projected and founded Foundling Hospital (chartered 1739).

**Co'rax of Syr'a·cuse** (kō'răks ŭv sĭr'ȧ·kūs; -kūz; *esp. Brit.,* sī'rȧ·kūz). Rhetorician of 5th century B.C.; regarded as a founder of Greek teaching of rhetoric.

**Co'ra'y'** (kô'rȧ'ē'). *Fr. form of surname of* **A'da·man'-tios** (ä'thä·män'tyôs) **Co'ra·ës'** *or* **Ko'ra·ës'** *or* **Ko'ra·ïs'** (kô'rä·ēs'). 1748–1833. Greek scholar and patriot; resident of Paris (1788–1833). Devoted himself to inspiring Greek people with the thought of their inheritance from Greek civilization of ancient times; did much to purify language of Greek contemporary literature; published editions of Greek classical authors.

**Cor'beil'** (kôr'bĕ'y') *or* **Cur'buil'** (kôr'bü'y') *or* **Cor'-beuil'** (kôr'bû'y'), **William of.** d. 1136. English prelate, b. in Normandy. Chosen archbishop of Canterbury (1123), received pallium only after protracted dispute with Thurstan, Archbishop of York; appointed papal legate in England and Scotland in place of Cardinal John of Crema; despite oath to support claim of Matilda to English throne, crowned Stephen (1135); finished Canterbury Cathedral.

**Cor'bet** (kôr'bĕt; -bĭt), **Richard.** 1582–1635. English prelate and poet. M.A., Oxon. (1605); bishop of Oxford (1628), translated to Norwich (1632); friend of Ben Jonson.

**Cor'bett** (kôr'bĕt; -bĭt), **Harvey Wiley.** 1873–1954. American architect, b. San Francisco. B.Sc., California (1895); grad. École des Beaux-Arts (Paris; 1900). Among buildings designed by him are Springfield (Mass.) Municipal Group, Bush Terminal Office Building in New York City, Holy Innocents Church in Brooklyn, Bushnell Memorial Hall in Hartford, Conn.; collaborated with Raymond Hood in planning Rockefeller Center's Radio City; married (1905) **Gail Sherman,** (d. 1952), sculptor, among whose works are Hamilton S. White Memorial in Syracuse, the bronze doors of the Municipal Group in Springfield, Mass., George Washington Masonic Memorial in Alexandria, Va., Constance Witherby Memorial in Providence, R.I.

**Corbett, James J.** 1866–1933. American professional pugilist, b. San Francisco, Calif. Won over Joe Choynski (June 5, 1889); drew 61-round fight with Peter Jackson (May 21, 1891); won world's championship by knocking out John L. Sullivan in the 21st round (Sept. 7, 1892); lost title to Robert Fitzsimmons in 14th round (Mar. 17, 1897); failed to regain title in fights with James J. Jeffries (1900 and 1903). Appeared on the stage, in motion pictures, and on the radio. Often called "Gentleman Jim" from his natty appearance and gentlemanly bearing.

**Corbett,** Sir **Julian Stafford.** 1854–1922. English lawyer and naval historian; educ. Cambridge. Called to the bar (1879), but practiced only a few years. After writing a few novels (*For God and Gold,* 1887; *Kophetua the Thirteenth,* 1889), devoted himself to naval history. Among his books are *Drake and the Tudor Navy* (1898), *The Successors of Drake* (1900), *The Campaign of Trafalgar* (1910), *Naval Operations* (3 vols. completed, 1920, 1921, 1923).

**Cor'bière'** (kôr'byâr'), **Jean Antoine René Édouard.** 1793–1875. French naval officer. Writer of verse and of sea tales. His son **Édouard Joachim,** *known as* **Tristan** (1845–1875), symbolist poet; author of *Les Amours Jaunes* (1873).

**Cor'bin** (kôr'bĭn), **Alice.** See Alice Corbin HENDERSON.

**Corbin, John.** 1870–1959. American author and critic, b. Chicago. A.B., Harvard (1892). Dramatic critic for New York *Times* (1917–19) and editorial writer (1919–26). Author of *The Elizabethan Hamlet* (1895), *An American at Oxford* (1902), *The First Loves of Perilla* (1903), *The Cave Man* (1907), *The Return of the Middle Class* (1922), *The Unknown Washington* (1930), etc.

**Corbin, Margaret,** *nee* **Coch'ran** (kŏk'răn). 1751–1800. American Revolutionary heroine, b. in Franklin County, Pa.; replaced her husband at his cannon when he was killed at battle of Fort Washington (1776).

**Cor·bi'no** (kôr·bē'nō), **Jon** (jŏn). 1905–1964. Painter, b. in Sicily; to U.S. (1913) and settled in New York City. Studied at Art Students' League; awarded Guggenheim Fellowships (1936, 1937); work represented in Pennsylvania Academy of Art, Toledo Museum of Art.

**Cor'bould** (kôr'bōld), **Edward Henry.** 1815–1905. English water-color painter.

**Cor'bu·lo** (kôr'bû·lō), **Gnaeus Domitius.** Roman general of 1st century A.D.; distinguished himself against Parthians and in conquest of Armenia (58–63 A.D.); recalled by Nero (67), apparently on suspicion of conspiracy; committed suicide.

**Cor'co·ran** (kôr'kō·răn), **Thomas Gardiner.** 1900– . American lawyer and politician, b. Pawtucket, R.I. B.A., Brown (1921); LL.B., Harvard (1925). Practiced law in New York City (1927–32). Special assistant to the attorney general of the United States (1932–35); special counsel to Reconstruction Finance Corporation (from 1932); assistant to secretary of the treasury (1933).

Close friend and adviser of President Franklin D. Roosevelt. Collaborated with partner Benjamin V. Cohen in drafting important New Deal legislation, including Securities Act (1933), Securities Exchange Act (1934), Public Utility Holding Company Act (1935), etc.

**Corcoran, William Wilson.** 1798–1888. American financier and philanthropist, b. Georgetown, D.C. Founder of the Corcoran Art Gallery, Washington, D.C., to which he gave his own art collection and liberal sums for maintenance.

**Cor′da** (kôr′dä), **August Karl Joseph.** 1809–1849. Botanist, b. in Bohemia; one of the first to investigate fossil plant anatomy.

**Cor′day′** (kôr′dā′), **Charlotte.** *In full* **Marie Anne Charlotte Corday d'Ar′mont′** (dȧr′môɴ′). 1768–1793. French patriot; believed in principles of French Revolution, but horrified at excesses of Reign of Terror; gained entrance to the room of Marat, leader among the Terrorists, and stabbed him to death (1793).

**Cor·dei′ro** (ko͞or·dā′ē·ro͞o), **Luciano.** 1844–1901. Portuguese geographer; published *Viagems, Explorações e Conquistas dos Portuguezes* (1881).

**Cor′der** (kôr′dẽr), **Frederick.** 1852–1932. English musician and conductor, b. London; conductor at a number of music festivals; author of English translations of Wagner's music dramas (1880–82); composer of many songs. His son **Paul Walford** (1879–1942), musician and composer; professor, Royal Academy of Music (from 1907); composer of two operas, a violin concerto, a ballet, and orchestral and choral works.

**Corderius.** See Mathurin CORDIER.

**Cor·dia′ni** (kôr·dyä′nē), **Antonio.** = Antonio da SANGALLO (1483?–1546).

**Cor′dier′** (kôr′dyā′), **Henri.** 1849–1925. Orientalist, b. in New Orleans; educ. in Paris and London. Professor in Paris; editor of *Revue d'Extrême-Orient* (1883–87) and *T'oung Pao* (1890–1925). Works include *Bibliotheca Sinica* (1881–85), *Histoire Générale de la Chine* (1920–21).

**Cordier, Mathurin.** *Lat.* **Cor·de′ri·us** (kôr·dẹ̄r′ĭ·ŭs). 1479–1564. French teacher; converted to Protestantism and settled (1537) in Geneva; published books on pedagogy, including a beginner's Latin manual *Colloquiorum Scholasticorum Libri Quatuor* (1563), translated into English as *The Colloquies of Corderius* and known as the *Cor′der·y* [kôr′dẽr·ĭ] in English schools.

**Cordière, La Belle.** See Louise LABÉ.

**Córdoba, Fernández de.** See FERNÁNDEZ DE CÓRDOBA.

**Cór′do·ba** (kôr′thō·bä) *or* **Cór′do·va** (kôr′thō·vä; *Angl.* kôr′dō·vȧ), **Francisco Fernández** (*or* **Hernández**) **de.** d. 1518. Spanish soldier and explorer. In Cuba with Velásquez (1511–17); fitted out expedition, and sailed westward (1517), discovered Yucatán; first Spaniard to find traces of Maya civilization.

**Córdoba** *or* **Córdova, Francisco Fernández** (*or* **Hernández**) **de.** 1475?–1526. Spanish soldier and explorer. Went with Pedrarias to Panama (1514); sent by him to take possession of Nicaragua (1522); founded Granada and León (1523); threw off allegiance to Pedrarias (1525), but was surprised and killed.

**Córdoba, Hernández Gonzalo de.** See GONZALO DE CÓRDOBA.

**Córdoba, José María.** 1800?–1830. Colombian soldier, b. Ríonegro, Antioquia. Distinguished himself under Bolívar and Sucre; became general at twenty-two; took part in victory over Spaniards at Ayacucho (1824).

**Córdova.** Variant of CÓRDOBA.

**Cor′dus** (kôr′dŭs), **Aulus Cremutius.** Roman historian of late 1st century B.C. and early 1st century A.D.; author of a history of the Roman civil wars and the reign of Augustus. Only fragments of his work are extant.

**Cor′dus** (kôr′dŭs; *Ger.* kôr′do͝os), **Eu·ri′ci·us** (ū·rĭsh′ĭ·ŭs; *Ger.* oi·rē′tsē·o͝os). 1486–1535. German physician and humanist; disciple of Luther; professor, Marburg (1527); city physician, Bremen (1534). Author of Latin epigrammatic poems; showed satirical vein in medical work *Liber de Urinis* (1543) in which he opposed medical superstitions; his *Botanologicon* (1534) is first to attempt to establish botany on a scientific basis in Germany. His son **Va·le′ri·us** [vȧ·lẹ̄r′ĭ·ŭs; *Ger.* vä·lā′rē·o͝os] (1515–1544), author of first pharmacopoeia (1535) used in Germany; first to produce sulphuric ether.

**Co·rel′li** (kō·rĕl′lē), **Arcangelo.** 1653–1713. Italian violin virtuoso and composer; resident in Rome under patronage of Cardinal Pietro Ottoboni. Considered creator of the concerto grosso.

**Co·rel′li** (kō·rĕl′ĭ), **Mar′ie** (mär′ĭ). *Pseudonym of* **Mary Mac·kay′** (mȧ·kī′). 1855–1924. English novelist, b. London. Author of *The Romance of Two Worlds* (1886), *Thelma* (1887), *The Sorrows of Satan* (1895), *The Master Christian* (1900), *Holy Orders* (1908), *The Secret Power* (1921), etc.

**Co·ren′zio** (kō·rĕn′tsyō), **Belisario.** 1558?–?1643. Italian mannerist painter, b. in Greece; reputed pupil of Tintoretto at Venice; court painter to Don Pedro de Toledo, Viceroy of Naples; known chiefly for his frescoes.

**Co′rey** (kō′rĭ), **William Ellis.** 1866–1934. American industrialist, b. Braddock, Pa. President, Carnegie Steel Co. (1901–03), and U.S. Steel Corp. (1903–11).

**Co′ri** (kō′rĭ), **Carl Ferdinand.** 1896– . Amer. biochemist, b. Czechoslovakia. To U.S. (1922). Awarded Nobel prize (1947) with his wife, **Gerty Theresa Cori** (1896–1957), and B. A. Houssay.

**Co·rin′na** (kō·rĭn′ȧ). Greek lyric poet of 5th century B.C., b. at Tanagra, in Boeotia; resident in Thebes; instructor of Pindar, and victor over him in five poetical contests. Only a few fragments of her verse are extant.

**Co·rinth′** (kō·rĭnt′), **Lovis.** 1858–1925. German painter. Studio in Munich (1890–1900) and Berlin (from 1900); a leader in Berlin of modernist movement in German art.

**Cor′i·o·la′nus** (kŏr′ĭ·ō·lā′nŭs; kō·rī′ō·lăn′ŭs), **Gaius** (*or* **Gnaeus**) **Marcius.** Legendary Roman hero of 5th century B.C.; gained name *Coriolanus* because of his courage against the Volsci at the siege of Corioli (493 B.C). Later exiled from Rome, took refuge among the Volsci, and campaigned successfully as commander of the Volscian army against Rome, retiring finally in answer to pleas from his mother, **Ve·tu′ri·a** (vē·tū′rĭ·ȧ), and his wife, **Vo·lum′ni·a** (vō·lŭm′nĭ·ȧ). Subject of Shakespeare's tragedy *Coriolanus.*

**Co′rio′lis′** (kō′ryō′lēs′; *Angl.* kôr′ĭ·ō′lĭs), **Gaspard Gustave de.** 1792–1843. French mathematician.

**Co·rip′pus** (kō·rĭp′ŭs), **Flavius Cresconius.** Latin epic poet of 6th century A.D., a native of Africa; resident in Byzantium (from c. 565 A.D.). Author of *Johannis,* or *De Bellis Libycis,* and *In Laudem Justini Minoris.*

**Cork,** Earls of. See BOYLE family.

**Cork and Orrery,** Countess of. See Mary MONCKTON.

**Cor′ker·y** (kôr′kẽr·ĭ), **Daniel.** 1878–1964. Irish writer. Among his plays are *The Labour Leader, The Yellow Bittern, Fohnam the Sculptor;* among his volumes of short stories, *A Munster Twilight, The Hounds of Banba;* author also of a novel, *The Threshold of Quiet,* and of literary studies.

**Cor′ley** (kôr′lĭ), **Donald.** d. 1955. Amer. writer, b. Corrington, Ga.; educ. Emory College; charter member of Provincetown Players. Author and illustrator of *The House of Lost Identity* (1927), *The Haunted Jester* (1931); also wrote *The Fifth Son of the Shoemaker* (1929).

**Cor′liss** (kôr′lĭs), Mrs. **Charles Albert.** Married name of Anne PARRISH.

**Corliss, George Henry.** 1817–1888. American inventor and manufacturer of the Corliss engine; b. Easton, N.Y.

**Cor'me·nin'** (kôr'mẽ·năN'), Vicomte **de. Louis Marie de La'haye'** (dē lȧ'ā'). 1788–1868. French lawyer and political writer; member of Chamber of Deputies (1830–46; 1848); opposed to Louis Philippe; appointed councilor of state (after 1848). Author of *Droit Administratif* (1821), *Les Entretiens de Village* (1846), etc.

**Cor'mon'** (kôr'môN'). *Pseudonym of* **Fernand Anne Pies'tre** (pyĕ'tr'). 1845–1924. French painter; studied under Cabanel; works include *Les Noces des Nibelungen, La Mort de Ravana, Caïn, Les Vainqueurs de Salamine.*

**Cor·na'ro** (kôr·nä'rō). Noble Venetian family reputedly descended from the Gracchi, including: Several doges, as **Marco** (1284?–1367; in office in 1365), **Giovanni** (in office 1624–29), **Giovanni II** (1647–1722; in office from 1709). **Caterina** (1454–1510), queen of Cyprus; succeeded her husband, James II of Lusignan, on throne (1473); abdicated in favor of Venetian republic (1489); set up court at Asolo, Treviso; patroness of art and literature, celebrated in paintings by Paolo Veronese, Pordenone, Titian, etc., in operas by Halévy, Lachner, and Donizetti, and in *Gli Asolani* by her cousin Cardinal Pietro Bembo (*q.v.*). **Elena Lucrezia Piscopia** (1646–1684), writer and scholar; granted doctorate at U. of Padua (1678). **Flaminio** (1693–1778), historian and statesman.

**Cornbury,** Viscounts. See 2d and 3d *earls of Clarendon,* under Edward HYDE.

**Cor'neille'** (kôr'nâ'y'; *Angl.* -nā', -nāl'), **Pierre.** 1606–1684. French playwright, b. Rouen. Studied law; adm. to bar (1624). Made dramatic debut with a series of comedies: *Mélite* (1629), *Clitandre* (c. 1631), *La Veuve* (1633), *La Galerie du Palais* (1633), *La Suivante* (1634), *La Place Royale* (1634), *L'Illusion Comique* (1636). Made his supreme success with his tragedies, including *Médée* (1635), *Le Cid* (1636 or 1637), *Horace* (1640), *Cinna* (1640), *Polyeucte* (?1642), *La Mort de Pompée* (1643), *Rodogune* (1644 or 1645), *Héraclius* (1647), *Andromède* (1650). Meanwhile, he produced one fine comedy, *Le Menteur* (1643). Returned to field of tragedy and wrote *Œdipe* (1859), *Sertorius* (1662), *Sophonisbe* (1663), *Othon* (1664). Regarded as creator of French tragedy and one of France's greatest tragic poets.

**Corneille, Thomas.** 1625–1709. Younger bro. of Pierre Corneille (*q.v.*). French playwright and miscellaneous writer; among his plays are *Bertrand de Cigaral* (comedy, 1650), *Timocrate* (tragedy, 1656), *Bellérophon* (opera, 1679).

**Cor·ne'jo** (kôr·nĕ'hō), **Mariano Har'lan** (är'län). 1863-1942. Peruvian statesman and jurist. President, House of Representatives (1901–03); senator (1911–20); member, Hague Tribunal (1916 ff.); author of Code of Criminal Procedure (1916; adopted by Peru, 1920); president of constituent assembly (1919–20) and author of constitution adopted by it; member, Council of League of Nations (1929).

**Cor·nel'ia** (kôr·nēl'yȧ; -nē'lĭ·ȧ). Roman matron of 2d century B.C.; daughter of Scipio Africanus the elder, and mother of the Gracchi (see Tiberius and Gaius GRACCHUS), leaders of the democratic faction in Rome. Famed for her remark to a visiting lady who wanted to see her jewels, "These [her children] are my jewels." A statue erected to her memory after her death bore the simple inscription, "Cornelia, the mother of the Gracchi."

**Cornelia.** d. 67? B.C. Daughter of Lucius Cornelius Cinna; m. Julius Caesar (83 B.C.); mother of Julia, wife of Pompey.

**Cor·ne'lisz** (kôr·nā'lĭs), **Cornelis.** *Called* **Cornelisz van Haar'lem** (vän här'lĕm). 1562–1638. Dutch historical and portrait painter; among his canvases are the *Banquet of the Archer's Guild* (1583; Haarlem Museum), *Massacre of the Innocents* (1590; Amsterdam).

**Cornelisz, Jakob.** *Known also as* **Cornelisz van Am'ster·dam'** (vän äm'stẽr·däm'; *Angl.* ăm'stẽr·dăm) *or* **Jakob van Oost·sa'nen** (ōst·sȧ'nĕn). Before 1470–before 1533. Dutch painter, d. Oostsanen (Oostzaan). Works represented in museums at The Hague, Antwerp, Berlin, Vienna, and Kassel.

**Cor·nel'ius** (kôr·nēl'yŭs; -nē'lĭ·ŭs), Saint. Pope (bishop of Rome, 251–253). Opposed (251) by Antipope Novatian; exiled to Centum Cellae (Civitavecchia); friend of St. Cyprian.

**Cor·ne'li·us** (kôr·nā'lē·ōōs), **Hans.** 1863–1947. German philosopher, b. Munich; professor, Frankfurt (1910 ff.); advanced an empirical theory of perception; developed psychological interpretation and extension of Neo-Kantianism.

**Cornelius, Peter von.** 1783–1867. German painter; studied and painted in Rome (1811–19) where he became associated with J. F. Overbeck (*q.v.*), Munich (1825–41), and Berlin (from 1841). His notable works include frescoes in the Glyptothek, Old Pinakothek, and Ludwigskirche, in Munich, and cartoons for frescoes to adorn the Campo Santo in Berlin. Credited with establishing, by his work, a national German school of painting and reviving interest in murals. His nephew **Karl Adolf Cornelius** (1819–1903), historian; professor, Bonn (1854), Munich (1856); member of first German National Assembly (1848–49). Author of *Geschichte des Münsterischen Aufruhrs der Wiedertäufer* (2 vols., 1855–60), *Die Gründung der Calvinischen Kirchenverfassung in Genf* (1892). Karl's brother **Peter** (1824–1874), composer and poet; admirer of Liszt and champion of Wagner; professor, royal music school, Munich (1864); composer of many song cycles, and of the operas *Der Barbier von Bagdad* (produced in Weimar by Liszt; 1858), *Der Cid* (1865).

**Cor·nel'ius Nepos** (kôr·nēl'yŭs; -nē'lĭ·ŭs). See NEPOS.

**Cor·nell'** (kôr·nĕl'), **Ezra.** 1807–1874. American financier and philanthropist, b. Westchester Landing, N.Y. Associated with Morse in devising method of insulating wire on poles for telegraph transmission; one of organizers of Magnetic Telegraph Co. to connect New York and Washington. Organized Western Union Telegraph Co. (chartered 1856). Founded (with Andrew D. White), and contributed heavily to endowment of, Cornell U. (incorporated 1865, opened 1868).

**Cornell, Katharine.** 1893–1974. Actress, b. Berlin, Ger. of American parentage; m. (1921) Guthrie McClintic. Stage debut, with Washington Square Players, New York City (1917). Prominent roles in *Bill of Divorcement, Casanova, The Green Hat, The Age of Innocence, The Barretts of Wimpole Street, Romeo and Juliet, Saint Joan, The Wingless Victory.*

**Corn'ford** (kôrn'fẽrd), **Francis Macdonald.** 1874–1943. English philosopher; educ. Cambridge. Professor, Cambridge U. Author of *From Religion to Philosophy* (1912), *Before and After Socrates* (1932), *Plato's Cosmology* (1937), etc. His wife, **Frances Crofts,** *nee* **Dar'win** [där'wĭn] (1886–1960), poet; among her books of verse are *Spring Morning* and *Mountains and Molehills.*

**Corn'forth** (kôrn'fẽrth; -fōrth', -fôrth'), **John Warcup.** 1917– . British chemist, b. Australia. With Medical Research Council (1946–62); Milstead Laboratory of Chemical Enzymology (1962–75); at the U. of Sussex (1975– ); awarded (with Vladimir Prelog) Nobel prize for chemistry (1975).

**Cor·nia'ni** (kôr·nyä'nē), Count **Giambattista.** 1742–1813. Italian literary historian; author of *I Secoli della*

*Letteratura Italiana* (1804–13), a history of Italian literature from the 11th century to the middle of the 18th.

**Cor'ning** (kôr'nĭng), **James Leonard.** 1855–1923. American neurologist, b. Stamford, Conn.; educ. Heidelberg and Würzburg (M.D., 1878). Discovered spinal anesthesia; demonstrated that action of certain medicinal substances is increased while subject remains in compressed air; first to inject liquid paraffin into the tissues and solidify it there.

**Cor'nu'** (kôr'nü'), **Marie Alfred.** 1841–1902. French physicist. Professor, École Polytechnique, Paris (from 1867). Known for work in optics and spectroscopy.

**Cornu, Sébastien Melchior.** 1804–1870. French painter; studied under Ingras; his *Le Christ sur la Croix* is at Poitiers, *Les Bacchanales* at Grenoble, *La Vision d'un Turc* at Valenciennes, *Le Combat d'Oued-Halleg* at Versailles.

**Cor·nu'tus** (kôr·nū'tŭs), **Lucius Annaeus.** Roman Stoic philosopher of 1st century A.D.; teacher and friend of Persius.

**Corn'wall** (kôrn'wăl; -wôl), Duke of. Hereditary title of the Prince of Wales, created for Black Prince (1337).

**Cornwall,** Earls of. See (1) RICHARD (1209–1272); (2) Piers GAVESTON.

**Cornwall, Barry.** Pseudonym of Bryan Waller PROCTER.

**Corn·wal'lis** (kôrn·wŏl'ĭs), **Charles.** 1st Marquis **Cornwallis.** 1738–1805. English soldier, son of 1st Earl Cornwallis. Educ. Cambridge; M.P. (1760); fought in Germany (1761–62). Major general in American War of Independence (1776); defeated Greene at Guilford Court House (1781), but was besieged at Yorktown by French and American armies, and forced to capitulate (1781). Governor general and commander in chief in India (1786); interrupted in civil and military reforms by outbreak under Tipu Sahib, whom he defeated near Seringapatam (1791) and deprived of half his realm. Created marquis (1792); endeavored to make zamindars owners of soil in Bengal (1793); general (1793). Viceroy of Ireland (1798–1801); thwarted threatened rebellion and forced French under Gen. Jean R. M. Humbert to surrender; resigned because of king's refusal to grant Roman Catholic emancipation. Negotiated Treaty of Amiens (1802); again governor general of India (1805); died at Ghazipur on way to assume command of the troops. His brother Sir **William** (1744–1819), naval officer, was in constant service (1755–87) in British West Indies; commodore in East Indies (1789–93); vice-admiral (1794); brought off his squadron with small damage in brush with French fleet off Brest (1795); admiral (1799).

**Corn'well** (kôrn'wĕl; -wĕl), **Dean.** 1892–1960. American illustrator and mural painter, b. Louisville, Ky. Illustrated books by Blasco Ibáñez, W. Somerset Maugham, and others. Mural paintings in Los Angeles Public Library, U.S. Post Office at Morgantown, N.C., and General Motors Building at New York's 1939 World's Fair.

**Co'rom·bo'na** (kō'rŏm·bō'nȧ), **Vit·to'ri·a** (vĭ·tō'rĭ·ȧ; -tōr'yȧ). = Vittoria ACCORAMBONI.

**Co'ro·na'do** (kō'rō·nä'thō), **Carolina.** 1823–1909. Spanish poet and novelist; author of *Poesías* (1843) and the novels *Paquita, Jarilla, Sigea,* etc.

**Co'ro·na'do** (kō'rō·nä'thō; *Angl.* kŏr'ō·nä'dō), **Francisco Vásquez de.** 1510–54. Span. explorer in America, b. Salamanca, Spain; to Mexico (1535). Commander of exploring expedition northward (1540) in search of famed Quivira, a town reputed to be fabulously rich; ascended Colorado River and discovered the Grand Canyon; explored the California peninsula; followed course of the Rio Grande, and pushed north across what is now the Texas Panhandle and Oklahoma into eastern Kansas (1540–42).

**Co'ro·na'do** (kō'rō·nä'thō), **Juan Vásquez de.** 1525?–1565. Spanish conquistador, b. Salamanca. To Guatemala (1550); active as explorer in various parts of Central America (1550–64); founded Cartago (1563).

**Co'ro·nel'li** (kō'rō·nĕl'lē), **Marco Vincenzo.** 1650–1718. Venetian monk and geographer; professor, Venice; general of Minorite order; cosmographer of Venetian republic (1702 ff.). His writings include *Atlante Veneto* (1690), and *Roma Antica e Moderna* (1716).

**Co'rot'** (kô'rō'), **Jean Baptiste Camille.** 1796–1875. French landscape painter, b. Paris. Identified with Barbizon school. Among his canvases are *La Campagne de Rome, Vue d'Italie, Souvenir des Environs de Florence, La Danse des Nymphes, Soleil Couchant dans le Tyrol, Matin Soirée, Orphée, Le Repos, La Solitude, Pastorale, Paysage.*

**Cor'ra·di'ni** (kōr'rä·dē'nē), **Enrico.** 1865–1931. Italian journalist, novelist, and playwright.

**Cor·re'a da Ser'ra** (kōōr·rā'ȧ thȧ sĕr'rȧ), **José Francisco.** 1750–1823. Portuguese statesman, scholar, and botanist, b. Serpa. Founded Portuguese Academy of Sciences at Lisbon; to France to escape Inquisition. Secretary to Portuguese embassy in England; minister at Washington (1816–20); deputy to Portuguese Cortes (after 1820). Known esp. for his *Colecção de Livros Inéditos da História Portuguesa* (4 vols., 1790–1816).

**Cor·re'a Gar·ção'** (gĕr·souN'), **Pedro Antônio Joaquim.** *Academic name* **Co·ry·don' E'ri·man·the'o** (kōō·rē·thōN' ē'rē·măN·tā'ōō). 1724–1772. Portuguese poet; studied law, U. of Coimbra; a founder (1756) of Arcadia Lusitana, academy devoted to literary reform; author of sonnets, odes, epistles, and hendecasyllabic verse comedies.

**Cor·reg'gio** (kôr·rād'jō; *Angl.* kŏ·rĕj'ō, -rĕj'ĭ·ō). *Real name* **Antonio Al·le'gri da Correggio** (äl·lā'grē dä). 1494–1534. Italian painter of Lombard school; one of great artists of Italy; founded school of painting at Parma; influenced by Andrea Mantegna and Leonardo da Vinci; studied under uncle Lorenzo Allegri and probably under Lorenzo Costa; employed at Correggio, Modena, and Parma. Works include *Holy Family* (Malaspina Gallery, Pavia), *Madonna* (Museo Civico, Milan), *Madonna* (Uffizi Gallery), *Zingarella* (Naples Gallery), altarpiece *Madonna Blessing St. Francis* (Dresden), frescoes in Convent of San Paolo at Parma, frescoes in cupola of Church of San Giovanni at Parma, the series of frescoes entitled *Ascension of the Virgin* (in cupola of Parma Cathedral), *Marriage of St. Catherine* (Louvre), *Holy Night* (Dresden), *Jupiter and Antiope* (Louvre), and *Danaë* (Borghese Gallery, Rome). His son **Pomponio Allegri** (1521–c. 1593) was a minor Italian painter.

**Correia-Botelho,** Visconde **de.** See CASTELLO-BRANCO.

**Cor'rens** (kôr'ĕns), **Karl Erich.** 1864–1933. German botanist. Professor, Leipzig (1903), Münster (1909); director, Kaiser Wilhelm Inst. of Biology, Berlin (from 1914); professor of philosophy, Berlin (1920–24). Conducted experiments in genetics that led to his rediscovery of Mendel's law of inheritance (1900; almost simultaneously with De Vries of Holland and Tschermak von Seysenegg of Austria). Author of works on heredity and the determination of sex in plants.

**Cor·ren'ti** (kôr·rĕn'tē), **Cesare.** 1815–1888. Italian statesman and writer, b. Milan. Ardent nationalist; councilor of war and secretary general of Milanese provisional government (1848). Councilor of state (1860), deputy from Milan (1865); minister of education (1866, 1869–72); senator (1886).

**Cor'ri·gan** (kŏr'ĭ·găn), **Mairead.** 1944– Irish peace activist. Awarded (with Betty Williams) Nobel prize for peace (1977, for 1976).

**Cor'ry** (kŏr'ĭ), **Montagu William Lowry.** Baron **Row'·ton** (rou't'n; rô'-). 1838–1903. English political leader and philanthropist. B.A., Cantab. (1860). Private secretary to Disraeli (1866–81); originator of scheme of Rowton houses, hotels with good accommodations at low prices for poor men.

**Corse** (kôrs), **John Murray.** 1835–1893. American army officer, b. Pittsburgh, Pa. Hero of defense of Allatoona Pass (Oct. 5, 1864), which inspired Philip P. Bliss's hymn *Hold the Fort.*

**Cor·si'ni** (kôr·sē'nē). Noble family of Florence and later of Rome, including: Saint **Andrea** (1302–1373), bishop of Fiesole (1362), canonized by Urban VIII (1629); **Lorenzo** (1652–1740) = Pope CLEMENT XII; Cardinal **Neri Maria** (1685–1770); **Neri** (1805–1859), marchese **di La·ja'·ti·co** (lä·yä'tē·kō), a leader of the Liberal party in Florence.

**Cor'son** (kôr's'n), **Hiram.** 1828–1911. American educator, b. Philadelphia. Professor of English, Cornell (1870–1903). Author of *Handbook of Anglo-Saxon and Early English* (1871), *Introduction to the Study of Robert Browning's Poetry* (1886), *Introduction to the Study of Shakespeare* (1889), *Primer of English Verse* (1892), etc.

**Corson, Juliet.** 1842–1897. American educator, b. Roxbury, Mass. Opened New York School of Cookery (1876). Author of *Cooking Manual* (1877), *Dietary for Schools* (1878).

**Cors'sen** (kôr'sĕn), **Wilhelm Paul.** 1820–1875. German philologist; professor, Schulpforte (1846–66).

**Cort** (kôrt), **Cornelis.** 1533 (or 1536)–1578. Dutch engraver and painter; to Venice (1566) and Rome (1571) where he founded a school; engraved after Raphael, Titian, Michelangelo, Correggio, Michiel van Coxie, Heemskerck, Rogier van der Weyden, and others.

**Cort, Frans de.** 1834–1878. Flemish journalist and poet.

**Cort** (kôrt), **Henry.** 1740–1800. English ironmaster; invented process for purifying iron by puddling (1783–84).

**Cor'tel·you** (kôr't'l·yōō), **George Bruce.** 1862–1940. American lawyer and politician, b. New York City. LL.B., Georgetown (1895). Secretary to President McKinley (1900–01) and to President Theodore Roosevelt (1901–03). First secretary, U.S. Department of Commerce and Labor (1903–04); U.S. postmaster general (1905–07); U.S. secretary of the treasury (1907–09). President of Consolidated Gas Co. of N.Y. (1909–35).

**Cor'te–Re·al'** *or* **Cor'ter·re·al'** (kōr'tĕ·rē·äl'), **Gaspar.** 1450?–?1501. Portuguese navigator. Explored coast of Labrador and Newfoundland (1500); on second voyage (1501) sent back two vessels, but did not return himself. His brother **Miguel** visited North America (1502) in search for him, but also failed to return.

**Cor'tes** (kôr'tĕz) *or* **Cor'tez, Her·nan'do** (hĕr·năn'dō). *Span.* **Her·nán'** (ĕr·nän') **Cor·tés'** (kôr·tās'). 1485–1547. Spanish conqueror of Mexico, b. at Medellín, Estremadura. Sailed to Santo Domingo (1504); officer on expedition of Diego Velásquez to Cuba (1511). Given command of expedition of discovery to mainland (1518–19); coasted along Yucatán and Mexico (battle of Tabasco) to San Juan de Ulúa (1519); founded Veracruz; destroyed his fleet. On march inland defeated and made alliance with Tlascalans; entered Mexico City (Nov. 8, 1519); held Montezuma as hostage; made quick march to coast, captured Narváez, who had been sent to arrest him; returned to find Aztecs aroused to revolt (1520). On death of Montezuma, led (June 30, 1520) Spaniards and allies out of city after severe fighting (*la noche triste*); engaged in battle of Otumba and retreat to Tlaxcala; resumed (April, 1521) assault of Mexico City and captured it (Aug., 1521); made governor (1523). Undertook long journey to Honduras (1524–26). Deposed (1526); called back to Spain (1528); granted honors and created Marquis of the Valley of Oaxaca; married daughter of Count of Aguilar. Returned to Mexico (1530); discovered Lower California (1536). Went back to Spain (1540); took part in expedition to Algiers (1541); shipwrecked. Died on estate near Seville. See MARINA. His son **Martín** (1532–1589), b. Mexico, went to Spain (1540); lived at court of Philip II; inherited title of Marqués del Valle; lived in great splendor in Mexico (1562–66); accused of conspiracy, but freed after some years.

**Cor·tés'** (kôr·tās'), **José Domingo.** 1830?–1884. Chilean writer, b. Coquimbo; journalist; librarian in Bolivia; author of biographical and historical works.

**Cortés, Juan Francisco María de la Salud Donoso–.** See DONOSO-CORTÉS.

**Cor·tés' Cas'tro** (kôr·tās' käs'trō), **León.** 1882–1946. Costa Rican political leader, b. Alajuela. President of Costa Rica (1936–40).

**Cor'ti** (kôr'tē), **Alfonso.** 1822–1876. Italian anatomist; studied in Vienna; discovered the complex organ of the ear (organ of Corti) by which sound is directly perceived.

**Corti, Bonaventura.** 1729–1813. Italian priest and botanist; professor of metaphysics and geometry, Reggio Emilia; director, Modena Botanical Garden; investigated flow of protoplasm in plants.

**Cor·ti'na y Gar·cí'a** (kôr·tē'nä ē gär·sē'ä), **José Manuel.** 1880– . Cuban lawyer and writer; member of Cuban legislature; president of Cuban delegation to League of Nations.

**Cor·tis'soz** (kôr·tē'sŭz), **Royal.** 1869–1948. American art critic, b. Brooklyn, N.Y. Art editor of New York *Tribune* and its successor, the *Herald-Tribune* (from 1891). Author of *Augustus St. Gaudens* (1907), *John La Farge* (1911), *Art and Common Sense* (1913), *American Artists* (1923), *The Painter's Craft* (1930), etc. His wife, **Ellen Mac·kay'** (mȧ·kā'), *nee* **Hutch'in·son** [hŭch'·ĭn·s'n] (d. 1933), was a poet and editor; author of *Songs and Lyrics;* editor, with E. C. Stedman, of *The Library of American Literature* (11 vols., 1889–90).

**Cor·to'na** (kôr·tō'nä), **Luca da.** See Luca SIGNORELLI.

**Cortona, Pietro da.** *Orig. name* **Pietro Ber'ret·ti'ni** (bār'rât·tē'nē). 1596–1669. Italian painter and architect, b. at Cortona; known esp. as creator of individualistic style of painting in Rome. His paintings include frescoes in Barberini Palace, in church of Santa Maria in Vallicella, and in Palazzo Pamfili (all in Rome), decorations in Pitti Palace (Florence). As architect, designed church of Santa Martina, façade of Santa Maria in Via Lata, and portico of Santa Maria della Pace (all in Rome).

**Cor'tot'** (kôr'tō'), **Alfred.** 1877–1962. French pianist and conductor; an interpreter of Wagner.

**Corvinus, Jakob.** Pseudonym of Wilhelm RAABE.

**Corvinus, Johannes** and **Matthias.** See MATTHIAS CORVINUS.

**Corvinus, Marcus Valerius Messala.** See MESSALA CORVINUS.

**Cor'vi'sart' des Ma'rets'** (kôr'vē'zȧr' dā mȧ'rĕ'), **Jean Nicolas.** 1755–1821. French physician; physician to Napoleon (1807). Regarded as a founder of pathological anatomy; developed method of percussion for diagnosing diseases of the chest, esp. heart diseases.

**Cor'win** (kôr'wĭn), **Thomas.** 1794–1865. American lawyer, b. in Bourbon County, Ky. Member, U.S. House of Representatives (1831–40 and 1859–61). Governor of

Ohio (1840–42); U.S. senator (1845–50). U.S. secretary of the treasury (1850–53). U.S. minister to Mexico (1861–64).

**Co'ry** (kō'rĭ), **Charles Barney.** *Pseudonym* **Owen Nox** (nŏks). 1857–1921. American ornithologist, b. Boston. With Field Museum, Chicago (from 1906).

**Cory, William Johnson.** *Orig. surname* **Johnson.** 1823–1892. English schoolmaster and lyric poet. Educ. Cambridge; assumed name Cory on receipt of an estate (1872). Author of *Ionica* (1858; a volume of verse containing "Mimnermus in Church"), *Lucretilis* (1871; on writing Latin verse), and a *Guide to Modern History from 1815 to 1835.*

**Cor'y·ate** (kŏr'ĭ·ăt; kôr'yăt) *or* **Cor'y·at, Thomas.** 1577?–1617. English traveler; educ. Oxford. Became a buffoon at court and entered household of Prince Henry. Traveled mostly on foot to Venice, and back through Switzerland, Germany, and Holland (1608); published narrative of travels, *Coryate's Crudities,* with two appendices, *Coryate's Crambe* and *The Odcombian Banquet* (1611).

**Coryell, John R.** See Nick CARTER.

**Co'sa** (kō'sä), **Juan de la.** 1460?–1510. Spanish navigator and geographer. Master of the *Santa María* on first voyage of Columbus (1492–93) and with him on second voyage (1493). Pilot of expeditions to north coast of South America (1499–1500, 1500–02, 1504–07, 1507–08); killed by Indians near Cartagena. Made first large map of New World (1500; now in Madrid), of great value to cartographers.

**Co·senz'** (kō·zĕnts'), **Enrico.** 1812–1898. Italian soldier, b. at Gaeta. Colonel in Garibaldi's "Cacciatori delle Alpi" (1859); led third Garibaldian expedition to Sicily (1860); after Garibaldi's seizure of Naples, appointed minister of war; deputy (1860 ff.). Commanded division in Italian army (from 1861); senator (1872 ff.); chief of general staff (1881–93).

**Cos'grave** (kŏz'grāv), **William Thomas.** 1880–1965. Irish statesman, b. Dublin. Identified with Sinn Fein, and a member of the Dail Eireann from its beginning (1917). Chairman of the provisional government, and president of Dail Eireann (1922); president of the executive council of the Irish Free State (1922–32).

**Cosimo.** See PIERO DI COSIMO.

**Cos'in** (kŭz''n), **John.** 1594–1672. English clergyman of school of Laud, and Anglican bishop. Educ. Cambridge; prepared, by command of Charles I, a *Collection of Private Devotions* (1627); introduced ornate chapel ornaments and services in Durham Cathedral; obtained ejection of Peter Smart, Puritan prebendary of Durham (1628); ejected from mastership of Peterhouse, Cambridge (1642); chaplain to royal household in Paris (1642–60). Bishop of Durham (1660); one of revisers of the Book of Common Prayer (1661); used militia to coerce nonconformists into church attendance; repressed both Puritan and Roman Catholic recusancy; exacted levies to pay for his two castles, Durham Cathedral, library at Durham, and for general benevolence.

**Co'sio** (kō'syō), **Pedro.** 1873– . Uruguayan economist and diplomat; minister to Spain (1917), Great Britain (1917, 1932–36), U.S. (1918), and Germany (1927); delegate to League of Nations (1928, 1930, 1931).

**Cos'mas** (kŏz'măs) and **Da'mi·an** (dā'mĭ·ăn), Saints. Third-century Christian martyrs, brothers, physicians and missionaries; martyred in Cilicia in reign of Diocletian. Justinian I built a church in their honor in Byzantium, and Pope Felix IV one in Rome. Patron saints of physicians and apothecaries.

**Cosmas.** *Surnamed* **In'di·co·pleus'tes** (ĭn'dĭ·kō-plōōs'tēz). Sixth-century traveler, of Alexandria, Egypt; traveled as far as western India and Ceylon; later became monk and wrote *Topographia Christiana,* intended to vindicate Biblical account of the world.

**Cosmas of Prague** (präg; prăg). 1039?–1125. Earliest Bohemian chronicler, whose *Chronica Bohemorum* carries the history of Bohemia almost up to the year of his death.

**Cos·ma'ti** (kōz·mä'tē). Name of a family of Roman architects, sculptors, and mosaic workers of the 13th century, including: **Jacopo** (fl. 1205–10), **Cosimo** (fl. 1210–35), **Luca** (fl. 1231–35), **Jacopo** (fl. 1231–93), **Adeodato** (fl. 1294), **Giovanni** (fl. 1296–1303).

**Cos'sa** (kôs'sä), **Baldassare.** 1360?–1419. Pope (1410–15) but deposed and considered an antipope.

**Cossa, Francesco.** 1438?–?1480. Italian painter; regarded as one of the founders of the Bolognese school.

**Cossa, Pietro.** 1830–1881. Italian playwright; known as a romantic treating classic subject matter.

**Cos'sé'** (kô'sā'), **Charles de.** Comte **de Bris'sac'** (brē'sȧk'). 1505?–1563. French soldier; engaged in campaigns against the English and Imperialists (1544–46); grand master of the artillery (1547); marshal of France (1550). His brother **Artus** (1512?–1582), Comte **de Se·con'di'gny'** (sē·gôɴ'dē'nyē'), soldier, aided in defense of Metz (1552); campaigned against Spanish in Italy (1554); marshal of France (1567).

**Cos·su'ti·us** (kŏ·sū'shĭ·ŭs). Roman architect of 2d century B.C.; designed most of the temple of Zeus at Athens.

**Cos'ta** (kôsh'tȧ), **Afonso Augusto da.** 1871–1937. Portuguese statesman, b. at Ceia, Beira; professor of law, Lisbon (1896 ff.); republican deputy to the Cortes Gerais (1900); engaged in revolutionary activities (1910); minister of justice (1910–11); premier and minister of finance (1913).

**Cos'ta** (kôs'tȧ), **Cláudio Manuel da.** 1729–?1790. Brazilian poet, b. Marianna, Minas Gerais; studied law, U. of Coimbra. His works, considered classics by the Portuguese, include sonnets, songs, and the epic *Villarica* (1773; pub. 1841).

**Cos'ta** (kŏs'tȧ), **Izaak Da.** See DA COSTA.

**Co'sta** (kôs'tä), **Lorenzo.** c. 1460–1535. Italian painter; painted frescoes in chapel of San Giacomo Maggiore, at Bologna; to Mantua (1506) and worked under the patronage of Marchese Francesco Gonzaga; one of his canvases, *Madonna and Child Enthroned,* hangs in the National Gallery in London.

**Cos'ta** (kŏs'tȧ), Sir **Michael Andrew Ag'nus** (ăg'nŭs). 1808–1884. Italian conductor and composer in England (from 1829). Conducted opera at Her Majesty's Theatre, London (1832–46); conductor at Covent Garden (from 1846); composed oratorios, operas, and ballets.

**Cos'ta** (kôsh'tȧ), **Uriel da.** See Gabriel ACOSTA.

**Cos'ta Ca·bral'** (kôsh'tȧ kȧ·bräl'), **Antônio Bernardo da.** Conde **de Tho·mar'** (tōō·mär'). 1803–1889. Portuguese statesman, b. Fornos de Algodres, Beira. Judge of supreme court, Oporto and Lisbon; radical (later royalist) deputy (1835 ff.); governor of Lisbon (1838); minister of justice (1839–42); fomented insurrection (1842), assuming dictatorial control of government; restored Dom Pedro's constitution of 1824; deposed (1846). Again prime minister (1849–51); deposed by revolution led by Saldanha (April, 1851); ambassador to Brazil (1859–61); president, superior administrative court (1862 ff.).

**Co·stan'zo** (kō·stän'tsō), **Angelo di.** Signore **di Can'ta·lu'po** (kän'tä·lōō'pō). 1507–1591. Italian poet and historian; known esp. for his *Rime,* chiefly sonnets.

**Coste** (kōst), **Dieudonné.** 1892–1973. French aviator; with Maurice Bellonte, made first nonstop flight from Paris to New York (Sept. 1–2, 1930), 4100 miles in 37 hours, 18 mins., 30 secs.

**Cos·tel'lo** (kŏs·tĕl'ō), **Louisa Stuart.** 1799–1870. Irish miniature painter in Paris and London, and author of verse, notes of travel, novels, etc.

**Cos'ter** (kŏs'tẽr), **Charles de.** 1827–1879. Belgian writer; chief work, *La Légende de Thyl Ulenspiegel et de Lamme Goedzak* (in old Flemish; 1868); author also of *Légendes Flamandes* (1858).

**Cos'ter** *or* **Kos'ter** (kŏs'tẽr), **Laurens Janszoon.** fl. 1440. A Dutchman, native of Haarlem, credited by some (esp. Dutch) scholars with the European invention of the art of printing and by some with the invention of movable type. These claims have been much disputed; some scholars maintain that he has been confused with a Laurens Janszoon (d. about 1439), a sacristan of Haarlem (*koster* is Dutch for *sacristan*). Cf. GUTENBERG.

**Coster** *or* **Koster, Samuel.** 1579–?1665. Dutch physician and playwright; among his comedies are *Rural Diversion*...(1612), *Mattheus van der Schilde* (1613); among his tragedies, *The Rich Man* (1615), *Isabella* (1618), *Polyxena* (1619).

**Cos'ti·gan** (kŏs'tĭ·găn), **John Edward.** 1888–1972. American painter, b. Providence, R.I. Work represented in Art Institute of Chicago, Brooklyn Museum of Art, Metropolitan Museum of Art in New York City, and Library of Congress in Washington, D.C.

**Cos'way** (kŏz'wā), **Richard.** 1742?–1821. English miniature painter. Gained prince of Wales as patron through clever portraiture of Mrs. Fitzherbert; painted Lady Beechy, Mme. du Barry, members of royal family; made effective use of ivory background in miniatures; m. (1781) **Maria Cecilia Louisa Had'field** [hăd'fēld] (1759–1838), Irish-Italian painter and musician, subject of one of his finest engravings.

**Co'ta de Ma·gua'que** (kō'tä thā mä·gwä'kā), **Rodrigo.** d. about 1495. Spanish poet, b. Toledo; author of *Diálogo entre el Amor y un Caballero Viejo.*

**Co'té'** (kō'tā'), **Aurèle Suzor.** 1870–1937. Canadian painter, b. in Arthabaska, Quebec. His painting *The Death of Archimedes* won grand prize at Salon, Paris (1898). Executed panel decorations for Canadian parliament buildings at Ottawa, and a portrait of Sir Wilfrid Laurier.

**Cotes** (kōts), **Everard.** 1862–1944. English journalist; London correspondent of *Christian Science Monitor* (1922–39); wrote *Signs and Portents in the Far East*, etc. His first wife, **Sara Jeannette,** *nee* **Duncan** (1862–1922), was a journalist and novelist, b. Brantford, Canada; correspondent in Japan and the Far East for the Montreal *Star;* author of *An American Girl in London* (1891), *Those Delightful Americans* (1902), *Cousin Cinderella* (1908), etc.

**Cotes, Roger.** 1682–1716. English mathematician and philosopher. M.A., Cantab. (1706), and professor of astronomy and experimental philosophy (1706); aided Newton in 1713 edition of *Principia* and wrote the preface; published *Logometria* (1713), treatise on ratios.

**Cot'grave** (kŏt'grāv), **Randle.** d. 1634? English lexicographer; educ. Cambridge; compiled French-English dictionary (1611).

**Cotignola,** Baron **von.** See A. G. JOCHMUS.

**Co'tin'** (kô'tăN'), **Charles.** 1604–1682. French abbé and poetaster; councilor and almoner to the king; ridiculed by Boileau, and by Molière, who represented him in the character of Trissotin in *Les Femmes Savantes.*

**Cot'man** (kŏt'măn), **John Sell.** 1782–1842. English landscape painter and etcher, b. Norwich. Executed water colors of Wales and Yorkshire; drawing master, Norwich (1807–34), King's Coll., London (1834–42); best-known among his oil paintings, *Waterfall* and *Silver Birches.*

**Cots'worth** (kŏts'wûrth; -wẽrth), **Moses Bru'ines** (brōō'ĭnz). 1859–1943. English advocate of calendar reform; originator and director of International Fixed Calendar League, organized to promote establishment of a year of 13 months of 28 days each, plus the last day of June in each year as the yearday; author of many pamphlets on calendar reform; appointed expert to League of Nations' committee on calendar reform (1922–31).

**Cot'ta** (kŏt'ä). Name of a family of German publishers, proprietors of J. G. Cottasche Buchhandlung, founded in Tübingen by **Johann Georg Cotta** (1631–1692). His great-grandson **Johann Friedrich** (1764–1832), Baron **Cotta von Cot'ten·dorf** (fôn kŏt'ĕn·dôrf), took over business (1787); opened Stuttgart branch (1811); with Schiller founded literary journal *Horen* (1795); printed works of Schiller, Goethe, Fichte, and others; founded *Allgemeine Zeitung* (1798). His son **Johann Georg** (1796–1863), Baron **Cotta von Cottendorf,** bought the G. J. Göschen business in Leipzig (1839) and the Vogel business in Landshut (1845), thus greatly extending the scope of the Cotta house. Business sold (1889) to Adolf and Paul Kröner, Stuttgart publishers.

**Cotta, Heinrich von.** 1763–1844. German forester; founded (1795) near Eisenach, Thuringia, a school of forestry, later (1811) removed to Tharandt, Saxony, and incorporated (1817) as a state forestry academy. His son **Bernhard** (1808–1879), geologist; professor of geology, school of mining, Freiberg, Saxony; published, with Naumann (*q.v.*), geological map of Saxony; author of *Geologie der Gegenwart* (1866), etc.

**Cotte** (kôt), **de.** Family of French architects, including: **Fresnin,** architect to the king (1630). His grandson **Robert** (1656–1735) built dome of the Invalides, Hôtel de Ville at Lyon, chapel of the château at Versailles, episcopal palace at Verdun, and many châteaux.

**Cot'te·reau'** (kô'trō'). Family name of four brothers, known as the "Chou·an' Brothers (shwäN')," leaders of Royalist insurgents (Chouans) in western France (1794): **Pierre** (1756–1794), guillotined at Laval; **Jean** (1757–1794), surprised and killed in flight; **François** (1762?–1794), died of wounds; **René** (1764–1846), survived the revolt, awarded small pension at Restoration.

**Cot'tet'** (kô'tĕ'), **Charles.** 1863–1925. French landscape painter and etcher; studied under Puvis de Chavannes and Roll.

**Cot'ti·us** (kŏt'ĭ·ŭs). Ligurian chieftain of early 1st century A.D.; established kingdom in the Alps, long independent, but finally subject to Rome. The Cottian Alps derive their name from him.

**Cot'tle** (kŏt''l), **Joseph.** 1770–1853. English bookseller and poet; publisher of some of first works of Southey, Coleridge, and Wordsworth (1796–98). His poems ridiculed by Byron. Author of *Recollections* (1837) of the Lake poets.

**Cot'ton'** (kô'tôN'), **Aimé Auguste.** 1869–1951. French physicist, b. Bourg. Educ. École Normale Supérieure. Professor and director of laboratory of physical research, Sorbonne. Studied anomalous dispersion and dichroism. With H. Mouton, devised simple apparatus for observing ultramicroscopic objects, and discovered double refraction of liquids in a magnetic field. With Pierre Weiss, studied the Zeeman effect, deduced the ratio $\frac{e}{m}$ of the charge of the electron to its mass.

**Cot'ton** (kŏt''n), **Charles.** 1630–1687. English poet. Author of burlesques of Vergil (1664) and Lucian (1675), a humorous *Voyage to Ireland* (1670), a second part to Walton's *Compleat Angler* (1676), a standard translation of Montaigne's *Essays* (1685).

**Cotton, George Edward Lynch.** 1813–1866. English educator; B.A., Cantab. (1836). Bishop of Calcutta (1858); founded schools for British and Eurasian children. Figures as the young master in *Tom Brown's School Days.*

**Cotton, John.** 1584–1652. Known as "The Patriarch of New England." Puritan clergyman, b. Derby, Eng. Grad. Cambridge (1603). Ordained in Church of England ministry (1610); pastorate, Boston, Lincolnshire, Eng. (1612–33). Emigrated to Boston, Massachusetts (1633); teacher of First Church, Boston (1633–52); became head of Congregationalism in America. Engaged in controversy with Roger Williams; opposed to democratic institutions; upheld authority of the magistrates over religious as well as secular affairs of citizens. Author of *The Keyes of the Kingdom of Heaven* (1644), *The Way of the Churches of Christ in New England* (1645), *Spiritual Milk for Babes* (1646).

**Cotton, Nathaniel.** 1705–1788. English physician and poet; treated mental diseases in his asylum at St. Albans. Author of *Visions in Verse* (1751) and short poems still included in anthologies, as *The Fireside* and *To a Child Five Years Old.*

**Cotton,** Sir **Robert Bruce.** 1571–1631. English antiquary and founder of Cottonian library in British Museum; B.A., Cantab. (1585). Collected ancient records scattered after dissolution of the monasteries, also books, manuscripts, and coins. Probably supervised writing of Camden's *History of Elizabeth,* esp. the account of Mary, Queen of Scots, in James I's interest. M.P. (1624); turned from court to intimacy with Sir John Eliot, John Selden, Pym, and Coke; wrote tracts against debasement of the currency and criticizing kingcraft, deemed dangerous by Charles I and the Star Chamber. Excluded from his library (1629–31), which was increased by his son Sir **Thomas** (1594–1662) and transferred (1700) to the nation by his great-grandson Sir **John** (1679–1731).

**Cotton,** Sir **Stapleton.** See Viscount COMBERMERE.

**Cotton, William H.** 1880–1958. American portrait and mural painter, b. Newport, R.I. Studied in Boston and at Académie Julian in Paris; painted murals for several New York theaters.

**Cot'trell** (kŏt'rĕl), **Frederick Gardner.** 1877–1948. American physical chemist, b. Oakland, Calif. B.S., California (1896); Ph.D., Leipzig (1902). On staff of U.S. Department of Agriculture (from 1922); president, Research Associates, Inc. (from 1935). Inventor of the Cottrell process in which dust and suspended particles are removed from gases by an electrostatic apparatus (Cottrell precipitator).

**Co·tu'gno** (kô·tōō'nyô), **Domenico.** *Lat.* **Co·tun'ni·us** (kô·tŭn'ĭ·ŭs). 1736–1822. Italian anatomist and physician; professor, Naples (from 1766); known for work on the internal ear; described sciatica; eponym of *liquor Cotunnii, nerve of Cotunnius, cotunnite.*

**Co'ty'** (kô'tē'), **François.** *Real name* **Francesco Giuseppe Spo·tur'no** (spô·tōōr'nô). 1874–1934. Corsican-born French industrialist and newspaper owner; successful manufacturer of perfumes; bought *Figaro* (1924); financed royalist journal *Action Française;* edited (1928) *Ami du Peuple.*

**Coty, René Jules Gustave.** 1882–1962. French lawyer; second president of the Fourth Republic (1954–59).

**Cou'ber'tin'** (kōō'bĕr'tăN'), Baron **de. Charles Louis de Fré'dy'** (dē frā'dē'). 1822–1908. French painter, chiefly of genre and religious-historical subjects. His son **Pierre** (1863–1937), educator and sportsman, revived the Olympic games in Greece (1894) and was president of International Olympic Committee (1894–1925); published treatises on education.

**Couch,** Sir **Arthur Quiller-.** See QUILLER-COUCH.

**Cou'cy'** (kōō'sē'), **Châ'te·lain'** (shä'tlăN') **de.** French trouvère (variously identified) of the late 12th and early 13th centuries. The legend of the love of the châtelain for the Dame de Fayel dates from a late 13th-century verse romance by Jakemon Sakesep (probably a pseudonym) and lacks historical basis. The theme of the romance, a jealous husband forcing his wife to eat the heart of her deceased lover, is common in various literatures. Cf. Guillaume de CABESTAING.

**Cou'der'** (kōō'dâr'), **Louis Charles Auguste.** 1790–1873. French painter; studied under Regnault and David; known esp. for his historical and religious paintings. His brother **Jean Baptiste Amédée** (1797–1865) was employed in industrial designing, and in promoting expositions of art as applied to industry.

**Cou·dert'** (kōō·dâr'), **Amalia,** *nee* **Küss'ner** (küs'nẽr). 1876–1932. American painter, b. Terre Haute, Ind.; m. Charles D. Coudert (1900); studio in London (1896–99); painted duchess of Marlborough, Lady Warwick, and prince of Wales; on trip to Russia, painted members of the imperial family; to South Africa (1899) to paint Cecil Rhodes. Studio in New York (from 1900).

**Cou·dert'** (kōō·dâr'), **Frederic Re·né'** (rē·nā'). 1832–1903. American lawyer, b. New York City. Grad. Columbia (1850). Counsel for U.S. in Bering Sea fur-seal arbitration (1893–95). Member, U.S. commission to report on Venezuelan boundary dispute. Expert in international law.

**Cou'dreau'** (kōō'drō'), **Henri Anatole.** 1859–1899. French explorer in South America.

**Cou·é'** (kwā; *Angl.* kōō·ā'), **Émile.** 1857–1926. French exponent of autosuggestion, b. Troyes. Pharmacist in Troyes (1882–1910); studied hypnotism and suggestion (from 1901); developed and introduced system of psychotherapy known as Couéism.

**Coues** (kouz), **Elliott.** 1842–1899. American ornithologist, b. Portsmouth, N.H. Author of *Key to North American Birds* (1872), *Birds of the Northwest* (1874), *Birds of the Colorado Valley* (1878). One of committee which prepared the *Check List of North American Birds* (1886).

**Cou'langes'** (kōō'läNzh'), Marquis **Philippe Emmanuel de.** 1633–1716. French courtier; relative of Mme. de Sévigné, with whom he corresponded; his *Lettres* appeared with those of Mme. de Sévigné. His wife, **Marie Angélique,** *nee* **du Gué** [dü gā'] (1641–1723), was author of about 50 letters.

**Cou'le·vain'** (kōōl'văN'), **Augustine Favre de.** *Pen name* **Pierre de Coulevain.** 1838–1913. French novelist; author of *Noblesse Américaine* (1898), *Eve Victorieuse* (1901), *Au Cœur de la Vie* (1908), etc.

**Cou'lomb'** (kōō'lôN'; *Angl.* kōō·lŏm'), **Charles Augustin de.** 1736–1806. French physicist, b. at Angoulême. Served as military engineer in early life. Known for work on friction and, esp., on electricity and magnetism; invented a torsion balance for measuring force of magnetic and electric attraction; formulated Coulomb's law; showed that the electrical charge is on the surface of a conductor. The coulomb, an electrical unit, is named after him.

**Coul'ter** (kōl'tẽr), **Ernest Kent.** 1871?–1952. American lawyer and humanitarian, b. Columbus, Ohio. Grad. Ohio State (1893); LL.B., N.Y. Law School (1904). Practiced in New York City. One of organizers of Children's Court of New York (1902–12); founder (1904) of Big Brother Movement. General manager and assistant to president, New York S.P.C.C. (1914–36). Served in A.E.F. (1917–19); engaged (major and lieut. colonel) in Aisne-Marne, Oise-Aisne, and Meuse-Argonne operations. Author of *The Children in Shadow* and *The History of Child Protection.*

**Coulter, John Merle.** 1851–1928. American botanist, b. Ningpo, China, of missionary parents. Professor, U. of Chicago (1896–1925). Founder and editor, *Botanical Gazette* (1875). Author of *Manual of the Botany of the Rocky Mountain Region* (1885), *Plant Relations* (1899), *Plant Genetics* (1918), etc.

**Coul'ton** (kōl′t'n; -tŭn), **George Gordon.** 1858–1947. English historian, b. at King's Lynn. Educ. Cambridge and Heidelberg. Rhind lecturer at Edinburgh (1931). Among his many books are *The Medieval Village* (1925), *Art and the Reformation* (1928), *Life in the Middle Ages* (4 vols., 1928–29), *Medieval Thought* (1939).

**Counts** (kounts), **George Sylvester.** 1889–1974. American educator, b. near Baldwin City, Kans. A.B., Baker U. (1911); Ph.D., Chicago (1916); professor of education, Teachers Coll., Columbia (1927–56). Author of *The American Road to Culture* (1930), *The Social Foundations of Education* (1934), etc.

**Cou'per** (kōō′pẽr). See also COOPER and COWPER.

**Couper, William.** 1853–1942. American sculptor, b. Norfolk, Va.; studio in Italy and in New York; carved portrait busts (Thomas Eggleston, President McKinley), bas-reliefs, and ideal figures.

**Cou'pe·rin'** (kōō′prăN′). Family of French musicians, identified with the Church of Saint Gervais, in Paris, where each one served in turn as organist, including: **Louis** (1630–1665); his brother **François** (1631–?1701); another brother, **Charles** (1638–1669); a son of Charles, **François** (1668–1733), most renowned of the line, first great composer exclusively for the harpsichord and author of a book on the subject; a son of the first François Couperin, **Nicolas** (1680–1748); Nicolas's son **Armand Louis** (1725?–1789); and Armand's son **François Gervais** (1759–1826), last of the Couperin organists at Saint Gervais.

**Cou·pe'rus** (kōō·pā′rûs), **Louis.** 1863–1923. Dutch fiction writer; resided in Batavia (1873–78); novels include *The Small Souls, The Later Life, Old People and the Things that Pass,* and *Iskander.*

**Cou'rant** (kōōr′änt), **Richard.** 1888–1972. Mathematician; professor, Gottingen (1920–33); to U.S. (1934), naturalized (1940); professor, New York U. (1934–58); emeritus (1958). See David HILBERT.

**Cou'ray'er'** (kōō′rā′yā′), **Pierre François le.** 1681–1776. French Roman Catholic theologian. Received (1727) Oxford degree of D.D. for dissertation (1723) demonstrating the apostolic succession of English clergy; forced to spend rest of life in England.

**Cour'bet'** (kōōr′bĕ′), **Amédée Anatole Prosper.** 1827–1885. French naval officer; in campaign at Tonkin (1883); after violation by Chinese of the treaty of Tientsin, destroyed Chinese fleet (1884).

**Courbet, Gustave.** 1819–1877. French painter, known as a leader among the realists; studied under Steuben. Associated himself with the Commune (1871) and took charge of the destruction of the column in Place Vendôme; in prison for 6 months, and condemned (1875) to pay cost of erecting the column again. Among his notable canvases are *L'Après-dîner à Ornans, La Vallée de la Loue, Enterrement à Ornans, Casseurs de Pierres, Paysans de Flagey, Baigneuses, Fileuse.*

**Courcillon, Philippe de.** See DANGEAU.

**Courde de Montaiglon, Anatole de.** See MONTAIGLON.

**Cou'rier'** (kōō′ryā′), **Paul Louis.** 1772–1825. French writer, b. Paris. Engaged in political pamphleteering (from 1817) in France: murdered (Apr. 10, 1825) Hellenist, edited pastoral by Longus, *Daphnis and Chloë.*

**Cour'nand** (kōōr′nänd; kōōr′näN′), **André Frédéric.** 1895– . Am. (French-born) physiologist, b. Paris. To U.S. (1930). At Columbia U. (1935– ). Awarded Nobel prize in physiology and medicine (1956) with W. Forssmann and D. W. Richards, Jr.

**Cournos, John.** 1881–1966. Writer, b. Kiev, Russia; to U.S. (1891). In newspaper work, Philadelphia (to 1912), London (1912–c. 1916). Author of *The Mask* (1919), *The Wall* (1921), *Babel* (1922), *The New Candide* (1924), *Wandering Women* (1930), *The Devil Is an English Gentleman* (1932), and translations from Russian; also collaborated with his wife, Helen (pen name **Sybil Norton**), in writing children's books.

**Cour'not'** (kōōr′nō′), **Antoine Augustin.** 1801–1877. French economist and mathematician. Professor, Lyons (1834); rector of academy at Grenoble (1835), Dijon (1854). Conducted researches in the calculus of probabilities; attempted to apply mathematics to solution of economic problems.

**Court** (kōōr), **Antoine.** 1696–1760. French Protestant clergyman; founded and directed seminary at Lausanne (1729–60); credited with being leading factor in restoring the Reformed Church in France. His son **Antoine Court de Gé'be·lin'** [dẽ gā′blăN′] (1725–1784) was a scholar, resident in Paris (from 1763); author of *Le Monde Primitif...* (1773–84), *Affaires de l'Angleterre et de l'Amérique* (1776 ff.), etc.

**Cour'tauld** (*Eng.* kôr′tōld; *Fr.* kōōr′tō′). Family of 18th-century London goldsmiths and silversmiths, descended from **Augustine Courtauld** (1686–1751), son of Huguenot refugee.

**Cour'te·line'** (kōōr′tĕ·lēn′), **Georges.** *Pseudonym of* **Georges Moi'neaux'** (mwá′nō′). 1860–1929. French humorist, sometimes called "the Mark Twain of France"; author of *Les Gaîtés de l'Escadron* (1886), *Boubouroche* (1893), *Ah Jeunesse!* (1894), *Monsieur Badin* (1897), *Les Linottes* (1913), etc.

**Courte'nay** (kōrt′nĭ). See also COURTNEY.

**Courtenay.** Name of an illustrious English feudal family that probably sprang from a younger branch of a royal line of Courtenay, France, including descendants from **Re·naud'** (rĕ·nō′) **de Courtenay,** a favorite of Henry II, among them the earls of **Dev'on** or **Dev'on·shire** (dĕv′ŭn·shĭr; -shẽr) and the following:

**William Courtenay** (1342?–1396), prelate; 4th son of Hugh, 2d Earl of Devon; chancellor of Oxford U. (1367); bishop of Hereford (1370), of London (1375); archbishop of Canterbury (1381); opposed John of Gaunt, Duke of Lancaster; strove to crush Lollards, prosecuted Wycliffe; chancellor of England (1381). **Richard** (d. 1415), prelate; grandson of 2d earl; educ. at Oxford; chancellor of university (1407, 1411–12), resisted unsuccessfully (1411) attempted intrusion by Archbishop Arundel, supported by Henry IV and Pope John XXIII, upon the independence of the university; bishop of Norwich (1413). **Peter** (d. 1492), prelate; grandnephew of Richard; educ. at Oxford; bishop of Exeter (1478), of Winchester (1487); was attainted by Richard III for attempted rebellion (1483); restored by Henry VII.

**Henry** (1496?–1538), Marquis of **Ex'e·ter** (ĕk′sĕ·tẽr) and Earl of **Devonshire;** courtier and diplomat; envoy to France (1525); supported his cousin Henry VIII's divorce proceedings (1529–33); commissioner to try Anne Boleyn (1536); commissioned to suppress Pilgrimage of Grace; beheaded as aspirant to crown. His son **Edward** (1526?–1556), his successor as earl, was released from Tower of London, where imprisoned (1538–53) because of his father's aspiration to crown.

**Cour'te·nay'** (kōōr′tĕ·nā′). Name of feudal French family originating about 11th century. **Renaud,** an early magnate of the elder branch, went to Palestine. His daughter **Elizabeth** brought Courtenay (near Sens) to her husband Peter (*Fr.* Pierre), youngest son of King Louis VI of France. A descendant, **Peter of Courtenay** (d. 1217), married Yolande (*q.v.*), sister of Baldwin I and Henry of Flanders, first two Latin emperors of Eastern Empire, and, on Henry's death (1216), became emperor (1217); succeeded by his wife as regent (1217–19) and sons **Robert of Courtenay** (ruled 1221–28) and **Baldwin II** (ruled 1228–61). This branch became extinct with **Roger de Courtenay,** an abbé (d. 1733). The younger branch derived from a cousin of Renaud, **Josselin,** a son of whom was founder of the English family (see COURTENAY, English branch).

**Cour'teys'** (ko͞or'tĕs') *or* **Cour'tois'** (ko͞or'twȧ'), **de.** Family of French enamelers, including **Jean** (1511–1586) and **Pierre** (1520–1586), both with productions preserved at the Louvre and in museums at Dresden, Vienna, Munich, Angers, etc.

**Court'hope** (kōrt'ŭp; kōrt'(h)ōp), **William John.** 1842–1917. English critic and literary historian. B.A., Oxon.; professor of poetry, Oxford (1895–1901); gave promise as poet in *Ludibria Lunæ* (1869) and *The Paradise of Birds* (1870); biographer of Addison; author of *History of English Poetry* (6 vols., 1895–1909); editor of concluding five volumes of standard edition of Pope (10 vols., 1871–89). See Whitwell ELWIN.

**Courths'-Mah'ler** (ko͝orts'mä'lẽr), **Hedwig.** 1867–1950. German author of light fiction.

**Court'ney** (kōrt'nĭ). See also COURTENAY.

**Courtney, Charles Edward.** 1849–1920. American amateur single sculler (1868–77), b. Union Springs, N.Y.; professional (1877–85). Crew coach, Cornell (1885–1916).

**Courtney,** Sir **Christopher Lloyd.** 1890– . English aviator; served in World War (1914–18). Director of training, Air Ministry (1933–34); director of operations and intelligence, and deputy chief of air staff (1935–36); commander of British air forces in Iraq (1937–38), of R.A.F. reserves (1939–40); member of air council (1940–45); air chief marshal.

**Courtney, Leonard Henry.** 1st Baron **Courtney.** 1832–1918. English journalist and statesman. B.A., Cantab.; editorial writer, *The Times* (1865–81); professor of political economy, University Coll., London (1872–75). M.P. (1876); secretary of treasury (1882–84). Zealous advocate of proportional representation; opponent of Gladstone's home-rule policy and of Boer War.

**Courtney, William Leonard.** 1850–1928. English philosopher and journalist, b. in India. Educ. Oxford U. On faculty of New College, Oxford (1876–90). Among his books are *The Metaphysics of John Stuart Mill* (1879), *Studies in Philosophy* (1882), *Constructive Ethics* (1886).

**Cour'tois'** (ko͞or'twȧ'). See COURTEYS family.

**Courtois, Bernard.** 1777–1838. French chemist; discovered iodine while studying products of mother liquors obtained in leaching ashes of burnt seaweed (1811).

**Courtois, Gustave Claude Étienne.** 1852–1923. French painter; studied at École des Beaux-Arts (Paris) under Gérôme.

**Courtois, Jacques.** *Known as* **Le Bour'gui'gnon'** (lẽ bo͞or'gē'nyôɴ'). *Ital.* **Il Bor'go·gno'ne** (ēl bōr'gō-nyō'nā). 1621–1676. French war painter, chiefly at Bologna, Italy. Best known for his paintings of cavalry.

**Cou'sin'** (ko͞o'zăɴ'), **Jean** (1490?–1560) and his son **Jean** (1522?–1590). French painters, famous for their work in stained glass.

**Cousin, Victor.** 1792–1867. French philosopher, b. Paris. Studied under Royer-Collard and Maine de Biran. Lecturer at the Sorbonne (1815–17 and from 1828). Traveled in Germany, interesting himself in study of German philosophy, and meeting Hegel, Jacobi, and Schelling. Created (1830) councilor of state, peer of France, director of École Normale, and (1840) minister of public instruction. Retired from public life (1851). Regarded as leader of the Eclectic school, and first to formulate eclecticism as a method. Among his notable works are *Fragments Philosophiques* (1826), *Histoire de la Philosophie du XVIII$^e$ Siècle* (1826), *Cours d'Histoire de la Philosophie Morale au XVIII$^e$ Siècle* (1841), *Études sur Pascal* (1842), *Philosophie de Kant* (1842), *Du Vrai, Du Bien et Du Beau* (1858), *Histoire Générale de la Philosophie* (1863).

**Cousin Jacques.** Pseudonym of BEFFROY DE REIGNY.

**Cou'sin'-Mon'tau'ban'** (ko͞o'zăɴ'môɴ'tō'băɴ'), **Charles Guillaume Marie Apollinaire Antoine.** Comte **de Pa'li'ka'o'** (pȧ'lē'kȧ'ō'). 1796–1878. French general; commanded expeditionary force in China, and captured Peking (1860). Headed a 24-day ministry (Aug. 9–Sept. 2, 1870) putting Paris in state of defense during Franco-Prussian War; was offered dictatorship after fall of Sedan (Sept. 2, 1870) but refused.

**Cous'ins** (kŭz''nz), **Norman.** 1912– . Amer. editor, b. Union Hill, N.J. Editor of the *Saturday Review* (1940–71); wrote *Talks with Nehru* (1951), etc.

**Cousins, Samuel.** 1801–1887. English mezzotint engraver. Won reputation with transcripts of Sir Thomas Lawrence.

**Cous'se·ma'ker'** (ko͞os'mȧ'kâr'), **Charles Edmond Henri de.** 1805–1876. French scholar, jurist, and musicographer.

**Cousser, Johann Siegmund.** See KUSSER.

**Cous'tou'** (ko͞os'to͞o'). Family of French sculptors, including: **Nicolas** (1658–1733), whose *Descente de Croix* is at Notre Dame in Paris, *Tritons* in Versailles, bas-relief *Le Passage du Rhin* in the Louvre. His brother **Guillaume** (1677–1746), sculptor of famous *Chevaux de Marly* at the entrance of the Champs Elysées in Paris; *L'Océan et la Méditerranée* at Marly; *Le Rhône* at Lyon; *La Mort d'Hercule, Louis XIII,* and *Marie Leczinska* in the Louvre. Guillaume's son **Guillaume II** (1716–1777), sculptor of statue *Saint Roch,* formerly in the Church of Saint Roch in Paris; bronze bas-relief *Visitation* in the Château at Versailles; the mausoleum of the dauphin, father of Louis XVI, in cathedral at Sens.

**Cou'tances'** (ko͞o'täɴs'), **Walter of.** d. 1207. English prelate, diplomat, and administrator. Envoy to Flanders (1177), to France (1186, 1188); bishop of Lincoln (1182), archbishop of Rouen (1184); set out with Richard on Third Crusade (1189); sent back to take over government of England, as chief justiciar (1191–93), driving out William Longchamp; managed Richard's release by ransom and became hostage for him in Germany (1194); accepted John on death of Richard.

**Cou'tard'** (ko͞o'tȧr'), **Henri.** 1876–1950. French roentgenologist; known for work on therapeutic use of radium and radioactive substances, esp. in treatment of cancer.

**Cou'thon'** (ko͞o'tôɴ'), **Georges.** 1755–1794. French revolutionist; member of Legislative Assembly (1791) and National Convention (1792); associate and follower of Robespierre; guillotined with him (July 28, 1794).

**Coutinho, Manoel de Sousa.** See Frei Luiz de SOUSA.

**Coutts** (ko͞ots), **Thomas.** 1735–1822. Banker; founder of London banking firm of Coutts & Co.; banker of George III; 4th son of **John Coutts** (1699–1751), grain merchant and lord provost of Edinburgh (1742–44). His daughter Sophia was mother of the philanthropist Angela Georgina Burdett-Coutts (*q.v.*).

**Cou'ture'** (ko͞o'tür'), **Thomas.** 1815–1879. French painter; studied under Gros and Delaroche.

**Couvreur, Adrienne Le.** See Adrienne LECOUVREUR.

**Couza, Alexandru Ioan.** = CUZA.

**Couz'ens** (kŭz'ʼnz), **James.** 1872–1936. Industrialist and politician, b. Chatham, Ontario, Can.; to U.S. while young. Accumulated fortune by association with Henry Ford in automobile manufacture (from 1903); mayor of Detroit (1919–22); U.S. senator from Mich. (1922–36).

**Co'var·ru'bias** (kō'vär·rōō'byäs), **Miguel.** 1904–1957. Mexican artist and illustrator; best known for his grotesque drawings in book illustrations, current magazines (as *Vanity Fair*), etc.

**Co·vel'li** (kō·vĕl'lē), **Niccolò.** 1790–1829. Italian chemist; known for work in mineralogy, esp. on lava. The mineral covellite is named after him.

**Cov'en·try** (kŏv'ĕn·trĭ; kŭv'-), **Thomas.** 1st Baron **Coventry.** 1578–1640. English judge. Educ. Oxford; barrister; attorney general (1621); M.P. (1621); lord chancellor (1625); moderate in presenting king's policy to Parliament; restrained Star Chamber from tyrannical actions. Lady Dorothy Pakington was his daughter. His son Sir **William** (1628?–1686), political leader, educ. Oxford; sought assistance in France for Royalists during Civil War; secretary to duke of York (1660–67); commissioner for navy (1662–67) and friend of Samuel Pepys; privy councilor (1665–69); forced Clarendon's resignation (1667); dismissed (1669) to make way for Buckingham and the Cabal.

Sir **John Coventry** (d. 1682), nephew of Sir William, Royalist, had his nose slit to the bone by Sir Thomas Sandys and his ruffians for a jest in House of Commons on Charles II's relations with actresses.

**Cov'er·dale** (kŭv'ẽr:dāl), **Miles.** 1488–1568. English translator of the Bible. Studied at Cambridge; joined Augustinian hermits, Cambridge (1514–26), from whose prior, Robert Barnes, he imbibed Lutheran doctrines. Left convent and preached against confession and veneration of images; lived abroad (1528–34); published translations of two theological tracts (1534). Published (1535, Zurich) first translation into English of whole Bible with Apocrypha, using probably the Vulgate, the Latin version of the Italian Hebraist Paginus (Santes Pagnino), Luther's translation, and the Zurich version, with aid of Tyndale's Pentateuch and New Testament; employed by Thomas Cromwell to superintend printing of the Great Bible (1539), begun at Paris, completed in London, which version was presented to Henry VIII and ordered to be placed in all English churches; edited second Great Bible, called *Cranmer's Bible* (1540); left England on fall of Cromwell. m. Elizabeth Macheson (1542); pastor and schoolmaster in Rhenish Bavaria (1543–47); returned to England (1548), preached against Anabaptists; bishop of Exeter (1551–53); deprived on accession of Mary because of his marriage. Allowed to leave England on intercession of king of Denmark; returned to England (1559); held but resigned living near London Bridge on account of Puritan scruples about the liturgy (1566); continued preaching to large following.

**Co·vi·lhão'** (kōō·vē·lyouN'), **Pedro de.** *Older Port.* **Co·vi·lham'** (-lyouN') *or* **Co·vi·lhã'** (-lyăN'). 1450?–?1545. Portuguese explorer, b. Covilhã, Beira; sent (1487) by John II to Levant in search of spices and the land of Prester John (*q.v.*); to Aden, Cannanore, Calicut, Goa, Hormuz, Red Sea, Sofala (Madagascar), Cairo; met José de Lamego, the king's messenger, at Cairo and reported his findings (later reputedly utilized by Vasco da Gama); visited eastern Africa and Abyssinia (1490) where he remained till his death.

**Cow'ard** (kou'ẽrd), Sir **Noel.** 1899–1973. English actor, playwright, composer; on stage from childhood. Among his productions are *The Vortex, Fallen Angels, The Marquise* (1927), *On with the Dance* (a revue), *Bitter Sweet* (operetta, 1929), *Private Lives* (1930), *Cavalcade* (1931), *Words and Music* (revue, 1932), *Conversation Piece* (1934), *To-Night at Eight-Thirty* (group of one-act plays; 1936), *Operette* (1938), *Blithe Spirit* (1942). His films include *In Which We Serve* (1942) and *Brief Encounter* (1946). Author of *Collected Sketches and Lyrics* (1931), *Present Indicative* (autobiography, 1937), *To Step Aside* (1939).

**Cow'den–Clarke'** (kou'd'n-). See Charles Cowden CLARKE.

**Cow'dray** (kou'drā; -drĭ), 1st Viscount. **Weetman Dickinson Pear'son** (pẽr's'n). 1856–1927. English contractor and philanthropist, b. in Yorkshire; gained profitable contracts in Mexico and valuable oil-bearing properties. Among large construction works carried through by his firm were the Blackwell tunnel under the Thames, four tunnels for the Pennsylvania Railroad under the East River at New York, the dam across the Blue Nile above Khartoum, Egypt.

**Cow'ell** (kou'ĕl), **Edward Byles.** 1826–1903. English Sanskrit scholar. B.A., Oxon. (1854); professor of English history, Presidency Coll., Calcutta (1856–64); principal of Sanskrit Coll., Calcutta (1858); edited part of *Black Yajur Veda* (1858–64), edited and translated the *Kusumāñjali* (1864) and other texts; first professor of Sanskrit, Cambridge (1867–1903).

**Cowell, John.** 1554–1611. English jurist. Regius professor of Civil law, Cambridge (1594–1610). His law dictionary, *The Interpreter* (1607), upholding king's absolute power, was burned by order of House of Commons.

**Cow'en** (kou'ĕn), Sir **Frederic Hymen.** 1852–1935. British composer and conductor, b. Kingston, Jamaica, B.W.I. Conductor of philharmonic concerts (1888–92), the Handel Festival (1903, 1906, 1909, 1912, 1920, 1923), Cardiff Festival (1902, 1904, 1907, 1910). Among his compositions are cantatas, operas, and many orchestral works, piano pieces, and songs.

**Cowen, Joseph.** 1831–1900. English orator and journalist. Educ. at Edinburgh; supported movements in behalf of democracy and liberty; champion of Kossuth, Mazzini, Garibaldi (1848); M.P. (1874–85); early advocate of imperial federation and home rule for Ireland; editor of *Newcastle Daily Chronicle.*

**Cowl** (koul), **Jane.** *Orig. surname* **Cowles** (koulz). 1884–1950. American actress, b. Boston; m. (1908) Adolph Klauber (*q.v.*); starred in *Within the Law, Common Clay, Lilac Time, Smilin' Through, Romeo and Juliet, Antony and Cleopatra, The Road to Rome,* etc.

**Cowles** (kōlz), **Alfred Hutchinson.** 1858–1929. American engineer and metallurgist, b. Cleveland, Ohio. Educ. Ohio State and Cornell U. Pioneer (with his brother **Eugene H.**) in electric smelting; with his brother, organized the Electric Smelting and Aluminum Co. (1885), of which he was president (from 1895).

**Cowles, Henry Chandler.** 1869–1939. American botanist, b. Kensington, Conn. A.B., Oberlin (1893); Ph.D., Chicago (1898). Taught at Chicago (1902–34); professor (from 1915); chairman of botany department (1925–34).

**Cow'ley** (kou'lĭ), Earls and barons. See WELLESLEY family.

**Cowley, Abraham.** 1618–1667. English poet of the metaphysical school, b. London, son of a stationer. M.A., Cantab. (1642). Joined Royalists; followed queen to Paris (1646); carried on her correspondence in cipher with the king. At Restoration, received through Henry Jermyn, Lord St. Albans, a competency near Chertsey in Surrey, where he devoted himself to botany and experimental science; buried in Westminster Abbey. Author of *Davideis* (1656, unfinished), an epic on life of

David; *Pindarique Odes* (1656), weighty with Alexandrines; *The Mistress* (1647), affected amatory verse; elegies, odes, and graceful essays with verses interspersed, his most enduring work.

**Cowley, Hannah,** *nee* **Park'house** (pärk'hous). 1743–1809. English dramatist. Author of *The Belle's Stratagem* (1780), *A Bold Stroke for a Husband* (1783); under pseudonym of "Anna Matilda," contributed sentimental verse to the *World.*

**Cowley, Malcolm.** 1898– . American editor and writer, b. Belsano, Pa. A.B., Harvard (1920); literary editor of *The New Republic* (from 1929); author of *Blue Juniata* (1929), *Exile's Return* (1934), and several translations from French authors.

**Cow'per** (?kōō'pẽr; kou'-), **Francis Thomas de Grey.** 7th Earl **Cowper.** 1834–1905. English political leader; educ. Oxford; pioneer of volunteer army movement; lord lieutenant of Ireland (1880) during agitation and suppression of Land League; active opponent of Gladstone's home rule (1886); president of royal commission on working of Irish land acts (1881, 1885, 1886–87).

**Cow'per** (kōō'pẽr), **Frank Cadogan.** 1877–1958. English painter, b. in Northamptonshire. Among his canvases are *The Good Samaritan, Hamlet, St. Francis of Assisi, St. Agnes,* decorative panels in the houses of parliament, and portraits.

**Cow'per** (kōō'pẽr) *or* **Coo'per, William.** 1666–1709. English surgeon and anatomist in London; author of *The Anatomy of Humane Bodies* (1698), a description (1702) of Cowper's gland (discovered by him), etc.

**Cow'per** (?kōō'pẽr; kou'-), **William.** 1st Earl **Cowper.** 1665?–1723. English judge; gave allegiance to prince of Orange (1688); parliamentary orator; lord keeper of great seal (1705); conducted negotiations for union with Scotland (1706); first lord chancellor of Great Britain (1707–10; 1714–18). Presided at trial of Dr. Sacheverell (1710); presided (1716) as lord high steward at trials of Earl Winton and other peers involved in Jacobite uprising (1715). His brother **Spencer** (1669–1728), justice of Court of Common Pleas (1727), was grandfather of the poet William Cowper.

**Cow'per** (kōō'pẽr), **William.** 1731–1800. English poet; grandson of Spencer Cowper (see under William COWPER, 1st earl). Called to bar (1754); began to show symptoms of mental disorder; a commissioner of bankrupts (1759–64). Obsessed with fear of opposition to his appointment to a clerkship in House of Lords, lost his reason temporarily and tried to commit suicide (1763). Collaborated with the evangelical curate John Newton on the *Olney Hymns* (1779), composing 67 of them; occupied himself with gardening and writing verses, among them *The Progress of Error, Truth, Expostulation, Hope, Charity, Conversation, Retirement;* at suggestion of a neighbor, Lady Austen, turned story of John Gilpin into a famous ballad (1782) and wrote *The Task* (1783; pub. 1785) in blank verse, an immediate success. Began his translation of Homer (1784), which he completed, with help of friends the Throckmortons, at Weston Underwood (1791), despite period of insanity (1787); attempted to fight off increasing melancholy by translating Latin and Italian poems and editing Milton; wrote his last poem, *The Castaway,* in 1798. Led the way in freeing English verse of artificiality of Pope's classicism. Known also as a letter writer of idiomatic purity.

**Cox** (kŏks), **David.** 1783–1859. English landscape painter, esp. in water color; by many regarded as greatest English water-colorist. Son of a Birmingham blacksmith; drawing master in London (1814–26); published *A Treatise on Landscape Painting* (1814). Secured fame in London (1835–40); executed about a hundred works in oil (from 1839), including scenes from his favorite sketching ground, North Wales. His son **David** (1809–1885) was also a notable water-colorist.

**Cox,** Sir **George William.** 1827–1902. English historical writer, b. Benares, India. M.A., Oxon. (1859); ordained (1850); defended theological views of Bishop Colenso. Author of *Aryan Mythology* (1870) and *Introduction to the Science of Comparative Mythology* (1881).

**Cox, Jacob Dolson.** 1828–1900. American lawyer and army officer, b. Montreal, Canada, of American parentage. In Union army through Civil War. Governor of Ohio (1866–68). U.S. secretary of the interior (1869–70). Dean, Cincinnati Law School (1881–97); president, U. of Cincinnati (1885–89).

**Cox, James Middleton.** 1870–1957. American newspaper publisher and politician, b. Jacksonburg, Ohio. On editorial staff, Cincinnati *Enquirer;* bought Dayton *Daily News* (1898), Springfield (Ohio) *Press-Republic* (1903) and *Sun* (1928). Member, U.S. House of Representatives (1909–13). Governor of Ohio (1913–15, 1917–21). Democratic nominee for president of U.S. (1920).

**Cox, Kenyon.** 1856–1919. Son of Jacob Dolson Cox. American painter and author, b. Warren, Ohio. Studied at Pennsylvania Academy of Fine Arts (1876), École des Beaux-Arts, Paris (1877–82). Examples of his work: *The Hunting Nymph,* now in the Lotos Club, New York; *Harp Player* and portrait of Saint Gaudens, in Metropolitan Museum of Art, New York; murals in Walker Art Building, Bowdoin College, Me., Library of Congress, Minnesota State Capitol. Author of *The Fine Arts* (1911), *Concerning Painting* (1917), etc. He married (1892) **Louise Howland King** (1865–1945), known for murals and paintings of children, including *Lucile, Goldilocks, My Children.*

**Cox, Palmer.** 1840–1924. Illustrator and author, b. Granby, Canada. In California (1863–75); New York City (from 1875). About 1880, began illustrating for *St. Nicholas Magazine.* Wrote and illustrated series of "Brownie" books for children.

**Cox,** Sir **Percy Zachariah.** 1864–1937. English soldier and administrator; consul and political agent, Muscat, Arabia (1899–1904); chief political officer, Indian Expeditionary Force "D" (1914–18). British high commissioner in Mesopotamia (1920–23).

**Cox, Richard.** 1500?–1581. English prelate and promoter of Reformation. B.A., Cantab. (1524); headmaster of Eton. In Edward VI's reign became active Protestant of the Reformation; as chancellor of Oxford U. (1547–52), eradicated books, mss., statues savoring of Romanism. A refugee in Frankfort (1555–58) where he led opposition to John Knox and Calvinistic doctrine. Bishop of Norwich (1559), of Ely (1559–80); resigned on intervention of Queen Elizabeth in favor of courtiers coveting episcopal lands. Translated Gospels, Acts, Romans for *Bishops' Bible;* was consulted on compilation of first and second Books of Common Prayer.

**Cox, Samuel Sullivan.** 1824–1889. Known as "Sunset Cox." American lawyer, b. Zanesville, Ohio. Member, U.S. House of Representatives, from Ohio (1857–65), from New York (1869–73; 1873–85; 1886–89). Advocated tariff reform and civil-service reform.

**Coxcie, Michiel van.** See COXIE.

**Coxe** (kŏks), **Arthur Cleveland.** 1818–1896. Son of Samuel Hanson Cox. American Episcopal bishop of Western New York (1865), b. Mendham, N.J.

**Coxe, Henry Octavius.** 1811–1881. English librarian and paleographer. M.A., Oxon. (1836); head librarian of Bodleian (1860–81); sent to Levant to examine monastic libraries (1857); devoted himself to compiling colossal catalogue of Bodleian (1859–80).

**Coxe, William.** 1747–1828. English historian. M.A., Cantab. (1772); clergyman (from 1788). Compiler of memoirs of house of Austria (1807), Spanish Bourbons (1813), Walpole (1798), Marlborough (1818–19).

**Cox′ey** (kŏk′sĭ), **Jacob Sech′ler** (sĕk′lēr). 1854–1951. American businessman and politician, b. Selinsgrove, Pa. Employed in silica sandstone quarrying (1881–1929). Led groups of unemployed (Coxey's Army) to Washington, D.C. (1894 and 1914), to demonstrate in favor of legislation to furnish funds to all communities, without interest, to pay unemployed for work on public improvements. Candidate for various public offices (from 1894), from mayor to president of U.S.; mayor of Massillon, Ohio (1931–33).

**Cox′ie** *or* **Cox′cie** (kŏk′sē), **Michiel van.** 1499–1592. Flemish painter; court painter to Philip II. His son **Raphael** (1540–1616) was also a painter, teacher of Caspar de Crayer.

**Cox′well** (kŏks′wĕl; -wĕl), **Henry Tracey.** 1819–1900. English aeronaut. Surgeon-dentist in London; made his first balloon ascent (1844); attained (1862), with Dr. James Glaisher, height of seven miles; managed war balloons for Germans (1870).

**Coyle** (koil), **Kathleen.** Irish novelist, b. in northwestern Ireland; author of *Piccadilly* (1923), *Liv* (1929), *There Is a Door* (1931), *Immortal Ease* (1939), *The Magical Realm* (1943; autobiography), etc.; d. 1952.

**Coy′pel′** (kwȧ′pĕl′). Family of French painters, including: **Noël** (1628–1707), director of Académie de France at Rome (1672). His sons **Antoine** (1661–1722), who was appointed first painter to the king (1716), decorated the altar in the château of Meudon for the dauphin, the grand gallery of the Palais Royal for the duc d'Orléans, and the chapel at Versailles, and **Noël Nicolas** (1690–1734), who painted esp. mythological scenes. Antoine's son **Charles Antoine** (1694–1752); known esp. for genre scenes; first painter to the king (1747).

**Coy′se·vox′** (kwȧz′vôks′), **Antoine.** 1640–1720. French sculptor, b. Lyon. Employed under Charles LeBrun in carving decorations for Versailles; best known for his portrait busts of his contemporaries, including Louis XIV, Richelieu, Mazarin, Bossuet, Condé.

**Coz′ens** (kŭz′′nz), **John Robert.** 1752?–1797. English landscape painter in water colors; son of **Alexander Cozens** (d. 1786), water-color painter, reputed son of Peter the Great. Known esp. for his *Hannibal Crossing the Alps* (1776).

**Coz′zens** (kŭz′′nz), **Frederick Swart′wout** (swôrt′out). *Pseud.* **Richard Hay′warde** (hā′wẽrd). 1818–1869. American humorist, b. New York City; author of *Sparrowgrass Papers* (1856), etc.

**Cozzens, James Gould.** 1903–1978. American novelist, b. Chicago. Educ. Harvard (1922–24). Author of *Confusion* (1924), *Michael Scarlett* (1925), *Cockpit* (1928), *The Son of Perdition* (1929), *S.S. San Pedro* (1931), *The Last Adam* (1933), *The Just and the Unjust* (1942), etc.

**C. R.** See Chakravarti RAJAGOPALACHARIA.

**Crabb** (krăb), **George.** 1778–1851. English lawyer and author. M.A., Oxon. (1822); compiled a history of English law (1829) and a *Dictionary of English Synonymes* (1816).

**Crabbe** (krăb), **George.** 1754–1832. English poet, b. Aldeburgh, Suffolk, where he practiced surgery. Published first poem, *Inebriety*, in Ipswich (1775), *The Candidate* in London (1780); befriended by Edmund Burke, who helped him with publication of *The Library* (1781) and *The Village* (1783) and in entering church and obtaining livings in Dorsetshire. Published *The Parish Register* (1807), *The Borough* (1810), *Tales in Verse* (1812), *Tales of the Hall* (1819); addicted in later years to opium. His son **George** (1785–1857) was his biographer (1834).

**Cra·beth′** (krȧ·bĕt′), **Dirck Pietersz** (1501–1577) and his brother **Wouter Pietersz** (1509–c. 1590). Dutch stained-glass painters; collaborated in painting windows for churches in Belgium, France, and Italy.

**Crab′tree′** (krăb′trē′), **Lotta.** 1847–1924. American actress, b. New York City. Comedienne, excelling in burlesque; retired (1891) and lived in California.

**Craddock, Charles Egbert.** Pseudonym of Mary Noailles MURFREE.

**Crad′ock** (krăd′ŭk), Sir **Christopher George Francis Maurice.** 1862–1914. British naval officer. Led vanguard at storming of Taku forts (1900); rear admiral (1910); responsible for keeping North and South Atlantic free for British trade (1914); defeated in battle with squadron under Admiral von Spee off Coronel, and went down with his flagship, the *Good Hope*. Author of *Whispers from the Fleet* (1907).

**Craes′beeck** (krȧs′bāk), **Joos van.** 1605?–?1661. Flemish painter; works represented in the Louvre and museums at Munich, Berlin, Antwerp, and Brussels.

**Crafts** (krȧfts), **James Mason.** 1839–1917. American organic chemist, b. Boston. Grad. Lawrence Scientific School, Harvard (1858). Studied in Germany and France (1860–65); research work in France (1874–91). Professor, M.I.T. (1892–98); president (1898–1900). Codiscoverer (with a French chemist, Charles Friedel) of Friedel-Crafts reaction, a synthetic reaction in which anhydrous aluminum chloride acts as a catalytic agent, responsible for bringing into existence hundreds of new carbon compounds.

**Craig** (krāg), **Charles Franklin.** 1872–1950. American bacteriologist, b. Danbury, Conn. M.D., Yale (1894). 1st lieutenant (1903), colonel (1918), U.S. army. Commandant and director of clinical pathology and preventive medicine, Army Medical School, Washington, D.C. (1926–30); professor of tropical medicine, Tulane (from 1931). Author of *The Aestivo-Autumnal Malarial Fevers* (1901), *The Parasitic Amoebae of Man* (1911), *The Wassermann Test* (1918), *Amebiasis and Amebic Dysentery* (1935), etc.

**Craig, Edward Gordon.** 1872–1966. Son of Ellen Terry (*q.v.*). English actor, stage designer, and producer. Founded *The Mask* (1908), a journal devoted to the art of the theater; founded school in Florence (1913). Among plays produced by him, with sets of his design, are Alfred de Musset's *On ne Badine pas avec l'Amour*, *The Masque of Love* (1901), Handel's opera *Acis and Galatea* (1902), Housman's *Bethlehem* (1903), Ibsen's *Vikings* (1903), *Much Ado About Nothing* (1903), Ibsen's *Rosmersholm* (in Florence, 1906), *Hamlet* (in Moscow, 1912). Author of *The Art of the Theatre* (1905), *Ellen Terry and Her Secret Self* (1931), etc.

**Craig, James.** See 1st Viscount CRAIGAVON.

**Craig,** Sir **James Henry.** 1748–1812. English soldier, b. Gibraltar; wounded at Bunker Hill; took part in capturing Ticonderoga (1777); governor general of Canada (1807–11); general (1812).

**Craig, John.** 1512?–1600. Scottish reformer; colleague of John Knox. Educ. St. Andrews; became a Dominican friar. His Protestant tenets strengthened on reading Calvin's *Institutes;* sentenced to death by Inquisition in Rome but escaped (1559). Published banns of marriage between Mary and Bothwell.

**Craig, Malin.** 1875–1945. American army officer, b. Saint Joseph, Mo. Grad. U.S.M.A., West Point (1898). Brigadier general (1921); major general (1924); general (1935). Served in Santiago campaign (1898), Boxer Rebellion (1900), and in France (1917–19). Chief of staff, U.S. army (1935–39); retired (1939); recalled (1941).

**Craig,** Sir **Thomas.** 1538?–1608. Scottish jurist. B.A., St. Andrews (1555); justice deputy of Scotland, presided over criminal trials (1564–73); commissioner for union with England (1604). Author of an epithalamium on marriage of Mary, Queen of Scots, and Darnley (1565), and other Latin poems, and of *Ius Feudale* (1603) on feudal law of England and Scotland.

**Craig, William James.** 1843–1906. British Shakespearean editor, b. in Ireland; B.A. (1865) and M.A. (1870), Dublin; professor of English, Aberystwyth (1876–79). Edited *Oxford Shakespeare* (1 vol., 1894), *Little Quarto Shakespeare* (40 vols., 1901–04), the *Arden Shakespeare* (40 vols.).

**Craig·av'on** (krāg·ăv'ŭn), 1st Viscount. **James Craig.** 1871–1940. Statesman of Northern Ireland. Served in British army, in South Africa (1900–02), and during part of World War. Member of parliament (1906–21); member of House of Commons of Northern Ireland (from 1921). First prime minister of Northern Ireland (1921–40). Created viscount (1927).

**Crai'gie** (krā'gĭ), **Pearl Mary Teresa,** *nee* **Richards.** *Pseudonym* **John Oliver Hobbes** (hŏbz). 1867–1906. American-born English novelist and dramatist, b. Boston; m. (1887) Reginald Walpole Craigie (divorced, 1895); joined Roman Catholic Church (1892). Author of novels, including *The Sinner's Comedy* (1892), *The Herb Moon* (1896), and of plays, including *The Ambassador* (1892; produced 1898).

**Craigie,** Sir **Robert Leslie.** 1883–1959. British diplomat; entered Foreign Office (1907); held diplomatic posts at Berne (1916–20), Sofia (1920), Washington (1920–23); in Foreign Office (1923–37; assistant undersecretary of state from 1934); ambassador to Japan (1937–41, until declaration of war).

**Craigie,** Sir **William A.** 1867–1957. British philologist and lexicographer, b. in Dundee, Scotland. Educ. St. Andrews U. (1883–88); studied Scandinavian languages, in Copenhagen (1892–93). On faculty of St. Andrews (1893–97), Oxford U. (from 1905). On editorial staff of *Oxford English Dictionary* (from 1897), and joint editor (1901–33). Author of *Icelandic Sagas* (1913), *The Pronunciation of English* (1917), *Easy Readings in Anglo-Saxon* (1923), *The Poetry of Iceland* (1925), *The Study of American English* (1927), etc. Editor of *A Dictionary of the Older Scottish Tongue* (1931 ff.), *A Historical Dictionary of American English* (1936 ff.).

**Craik** (krāk), **Dinah Maria,** *nee* **Mu'lock** (mū'lŏk). 1826–1887. English novelist, of Irish extraction; m. (1864) George Lillie Craik, publisher. Author of *John Halifax, Gentleman* (1857; a picture of English middle-class life), *A Life for a Life* (1859), and children's stories, poems, and essays.

**Craik, George Lillie.** 1798–1866. Scottish man of letters. Studied divinity at St. Andrews; went to London (1824), where he wrote for Society for Diffusion of Useful Knowledge. Professor of English literature and history, Belfast (1849–66). Author of *The History of English Literature and the English Language* (1861).

**Craik,** Sir **Henry.** 1846–1927. Scottish educator and politician, b. in Glasgow. Educ. Glasgow U. and Oxford. Secretary of a committee of the privy council having control of Scottish education (1885–1904). Member of parliament (1906–27). Among his books are *Life of Swift* (1882), *The State and Education* (1883), *A Century of Scottish History* (1901), *Life of Edward, First Earl of Clarendon* (1911).

**Craik, James.** 1730–1814. Physician, b. near Dumfries, Scotland. Educ. at Edinburgh U. Came to Virginia and was commissioned surgeon in the army (1754); chief physician and surgeon of the army (1781–83). Attended Washington in his last illness (1799).

**Craik, Robert.** 1829–1906. Canadian physician and surgeon, b. Montreal, of Scottish family; grad. McGill (1854); professor of clinical surgery (1860), professor of chemistry (1867–79), dean of medical faculty (1889), McGill. Early made a name for himself in resection of joints and as ovariotomist.

**Cram** (krăm), **Ralph Adams.** 1863–1942. American architect, b. Hampton Falls, N.H. Supervising architect for Princeton U. (1907–29); consulting architect for Bryn Mawr and Wellesley colleges. As member of firm of Cram, Goodhue and Ferguson, New York City, shared in plans of Rice Inst. at Houston, Tex., buildings for Williams Coll. and Phillips Exeter Acad., St. Thomas's Church in New York, and buildings for U.S.M.A., West Point. Appointed professor, M.I.T. (1914). Author of many books on architecture.

**Cra'mer** (krä'mẽr), **Gabriel.** 1704–1752. Swiss mathematician; professor of mathematics and philosophy at Geneva.

**Cramer, Johann Andreas.** 1723–1788. German Protestant theologian and poet; professor (from 1774) and chancellor, U. of Kiel; author of odes and hymns, including *Er ist gekommen her*, *Der Herr ist Gott und Keiner mehr*, etc. His son **Karl Friedrich** (1752–1807), professor of Greek and Oriental languages at Kiel (1775–94); founded publishing house in Paris (1795); wrote two notable studies, on Klopstock and on musical history.

**Cra'mer** (krä'mẽr; *Angl.* krā'mẽr), **Johann Baptist.** 1771–1858. English pianist and composer, b. Mannheim, Germany; to London (1772), studied under Clementi; foremost professional performer of his time, esteemed by Beethoven; composer of classic *Études*. His brother **Franz** (1772–1848), violinist, was one of first professors of Royal Academy of Music. Their father, **Wilhelm** (1745?–1799), was a noted violinist and conductor.

**Cramp** (krămp), **William.** 1807–1879. American shipbuilder, b. Philadelphia. Established the William Cramp Shipbuilding Co. (1830); president (1830–79). His son **Charles Henry** (1828–1913), a naval architect of distinction, was president of the company (1879–1903), and developed it into the largest and best known in U.S.

**Cram'pel'** (krän'pĕl'), **Paul.** 1864–1891. French explorer in Africa; explored northern part of French Congo (1888–89); slain on expedition to Lake Chad to unite French Sudan with French Congo.

**Cramp'ton** (krămp'tŭn), **Henry Edward.** 1875–1956. American zoologist, b. New York City; A.B. (1893) and Ph.D. (1899), Columbia; on teaching staff there (from 1896), professor (from 1904); known for work on evolution, heredity, and embryology.

**Crampton, Thomas Russell.** 1816–1888. English engineer. Designed and patented Crampton locomotive (1843); laid telegraphic cable from Dover to Calais (1851); constructed Smyrna railway, and Varna railway (in Bulgaria).

**Cra'nach** *or* **Kra'nach** (krä'näk) *or* **Kro'nach** (krō'näk), **Lucas.** 1472–1553. German painter, engraver, and woodcut designer, b. Kronach, near Bamberg; court painter (1504) to Elector Frederick the Wise of Saxony, and his brother. His works include altarpieces, many portraits of his friends Luther and Melanchthon, and a number of Biblical paintings. His son **Lucas** (1515–1586) was also a portrait and historical painter.

**Cranborne,** Viscount. See CECIL family.

**Cranbrook,** Earl of. See Gathorne GATHORNE-HARDY.

**Cranch** (krănch), **Christopher Pearse.** 1813–1892.

American clergyman, painter, and poet, b. Alexandria, Va. Unitarian clergyman (1832–42); devoted time to art and poetry (from 1843). Author of *The Last of the Huggermuggers* (1856), *Kobboltozo* (1857), *The Bird and the Bell* (1875), *Ariel and Caliban* (1887). His father, **William** (1769–1855), was chief justice of the U.S. circuit court of the District of Columbia (1805–55), and compiler of collections of legal reports.

**Cran′dall** (krăn′d'l), **Prudence.** 1803–1890. American schoolteacher, b. Hopkinton, R.I. Opened school (1831) in Canterbury, Conn., for Negro girls; prosecuted (1833) in famous case which intensified the conflict between abolitionists and southern sympathizers in the North. Married Rev. Calvin Philleo, Baptist clergyman (1834); moved to Illinois.

**Crane** (krān), **Bruce,** *in full* **Robert Bruce.** 1857–1937. American landscape painter, b. New York City. Among his paintings are *Autumn Uplands* (Metropolitan Museum of Art, New York), *Autumn* (National Gallery of Art, Washington, D.C.), *Grey Morning,* and *Golden Afternoon.*

**Crane, Charles Richard.** 1858–1939. American industrialist and diplomat, b. Chicago. With Crane Co., manufacturers of valves, fittings, etc., president (1912–14). Member of special diplomatic mission to Russia (1917). U.S. minister to China (1920–21). Aided in developing Marine Biological Laboratory, Woods Hole, Mass. His son **Richard** (1882– ), businessman and diplomat, b. Denver; in employ of Crane Co. (from 1904); U.S. minister to Czechoslovakia (1919–21).

**Crane, Frank.** 1861–1928. American clergyman, b. Urbana, Ill. Methodist clergyman (1882–1903); Congregationalist (1903–09). Syndicate writer of daily inspirational columns for newspapers (1909–28).

**Crane, Hart,** *in full* **Harold Hart.** 1899–1932. American poet, b. Garrettsville, Ohio. Author of *White Buildings* (1926), *The Bridge* (1930).

**Crane, Leo.** 1881– . American Indian-agent and author, b. Baltimore. On staff of Indian bureau (1903–25). Author of *Indians of the Enchanted Desert* (1925), *Desert Drums* (1928), and many short stories.

**Crane, Na·thal′ia** (nȧ·thäl′yȧ) **Clara Ruth A·bar′ba·nel′** (ȧ·bär′bȧ·nĕl′). 1913– . American writer, b. New York City. Educ. Madrid, and Barnard Coll., Columbia (1931–35). Teacher, Pratt Inst.; m. (1945) Vete George Black. Began writing at the age of nine. Author of verse, *The Janitor's Boy* (1924), *The Singing Crow* (1926), *Pocahontas* (1930), *Swear by the Night* (1936); novels, *The Sunken Garden* (1926), and *The Alien from Heaven* (1929).

**Crane, Stephen.** 1871–1900. American writer, b. Newark, N.J. Free-lance writer, New York (1890–95). First novel, *Maggie: A Girl of the Streets* (1893), a failure; second *The Red Badge of Courage* (1895), a realistic story of the heroism of the common man under fire in battle. War correspondent in Cuba and Greece (1896–98).

**Crane, Walter.** 1845–1915. English painter and illustrator. As wood engraver, studied works of Pre-Raphaelites; influenced by Botticelli; leader with William Morris in romantic movement in British decorative art. Best known for imaginative and humorous illustrations in antique style, esp. of juvenile books; his *Goose Girl,* from illustrations of *Stories from Grimm* (1882), was woven in tapestry by Morris; his finest illustration, Spencer's *Faerie Queene* (1894–96). Associated with Morris in Socialist movement. His father, **Thomas** (1808–1859), was a portrait painter and miniaturist.

**Crane, William Henry.** 1845–1928. American actor, chiefly in comedy; b. Leicester, Mass.

**Crane, Winthrop Murray.** 1853–1920. American manufacturer, b. Dalton, Mass. In family paper-manufacturing business (from 1870). Governor of Massachusetts (1900, 1901, 1902); U.S. senator (1904–13).

**Cran′mer** (krăn′mẽr), **Thomas.** 1489–1556. English reformer; archbishop of Canterbury. M.A., Cantab. (1515). Gained favor of Henry VIII by suggesting that establishment of Catherine of Aragon's prior marriage to Prince Arthur would nullify her marriage to Henry; dispatched to Rome and to Charles V to argue the case (1530–32). At Nuremberg, found Osiander in agreement on the new religious order, and was married to Osiander's niece. Archbishop of Canterbury (1533); declared Henry's marriage with Catherine null and void; pronounced marriage of Henry and Anne Boleyn; crowned Anne queen; stood godfather to future Queen Elizabeth. Supported the king's claim to supremacy over Church of England, maintaining divine right of kings as against divine right of popes, the joint sovereignty of church and state. Annulled Henry's marriage with Anne Boleyn (1536); was instrument for divorce of Anne of Cleves (1540); informed king of prenuptial frailty of Catherine Howard (1541) and sought to persuade her to confess. Made ineffectual attempt to oppose the Six Articles for abolishing diversity of opinions (1539); took part in persecution of Frith, Lambert, and others. Promoted translation of the Bible into the vernacular; procured order requiring a copy in each church; repudiated doctrine of transubstantiation (1538); twice saved by Henry VIII from enemy plots (1543–45). One of regents during absence of Henry VIII (1541) and on death of Henry (1547); prepared church formularies; edited *Homilies* (1547), four of his own writing; compiled (1548) Edward VI's first Prayer Book (sanctioned 1549) and its revision (1552), the latter of which converted the Mass into the Communion. Sought through Melanchthon to promote union of reformed churches; chief composer of 42 articles of religion (1552; later reduced to 39; hence called the Thirty-nine Articles); gave to Prayer Book its stately and rhythmical language. Perjured himself by signing Edward VI's devise of the crown to Lady Jane Grey, the queen of nine days (1553). On accession of Queen Mary, condemned for treason, convicted by papal commission (1555), excommunicated, degraded from archbishopric, condemned for heresy by Cardinal Pole; signed seven recantations, admitting papal supremacy, but at the last renounced all of them. Burned at the stake, holding his offending right hand in fire to be burned first.

**Cran′mer-Byng′** (krăn′mẽr·bĭng′), **Launcelot A.** 1872–1945. English writer; educ. Cambridge. Editor of *Wisdom of the East* series, designed to popularize study of Oriental literatures. Author of *A Feast of Lanterns, The Odes of Confucius, Tomorrow's Star,* etc.

**Cran′tor** (krăn′tôr). Greek philosopher of late 4th century B.C., b. at Soli in Cilicia. Known as the first commentator on Plato.

**Cranworth,** Baron. See Robert Monsey ROLFE.

**Crap′sey** (krăp′sĭ), **Algernon Sidney.** 1847–1927. American Episcopal clergyman, b. Fairmount, Ohio. Rector, St. Andrew's Church, Rochester, N.Y. (1879–1906). Tried and convicted of heresy (1906); deposed from the ministry. Author of *The Greater Love* (1902, a novel); *Religion and Politics* (1905); *The Last of the Heretics* (1924); etc. His daughter **Adelaide** (1878–1914) wrote a volume of poems (publ. 1915), many being in an original verse form called the cinquain.

**Crash′aw** (krăsh′ô), **Richard.** 1613?–1649. English poet of the metaphysical school, son of a Puritan poet and clergyman, **William Crashaw** (1572–1626). M.A.,

Cantab. (1638); expelled from fellowship for refusal to accept Solemn League and Covenant (1643); embraced Roman Catholicism; through Queen Henrietta Maria became subcanon at Loreto (1649), where he died soon after. Author of *Steps to the Temple* (1646), religious poems abounding in conceits in the manner of Herbert and in lyric felicities, and of *The Delights of the Muses* (1646), secular poems.

**Cras′sus** (krăs′ŭs), **Lucius Licinius.** 140–91 B.C. Roman orator and politician; consul (95 B.C.); censor (92). Introduced by Cicero as a speaker in his *De Oratore.*

**Crassus, Marcus Licinius.** *Surnamed* **Di′ves** (dī′vēz), *i.e.* "the Rich." 115?–53 B.C. Roman financier and politician; sided with Sulla against Marius, and laid basis of vast fortune by speculation in confiscated property during the period of Sulla's proscriptions in Rome. Praetor (71 B.C.), crushed revolt led by Spartacus; consul (with Pompey, 70); censor (65). Joined Pompey and Caesar in organizing First Triumvirate, being its financial backer (60); again consul with Pompey (55). Governor of Syria (54); undertook campaign against the Parthians; disastrously defeated at Carrhae (Haran), captured, and executed (53).

**Crat′er·us** (krăt′ẽr·ŭs). d. 321 B.C. Macedonian general in army of Alexander the Great; associated with Antipater in ruling Macedonia after Alexander's death (323 B.C.); defeated and killed by Eumenes in Cappadocia (321).

**Cra′tes** (krā′tēz). Athenian comedist of 5th century B.C.; few fragments of his works extant.

**Crates of Mal′lus** (măl′ŭs). Greek Stoic philosopher and scholar of 2d century B.C. Ambassador of King Attalus II of Pergamum to Rome (c. 159 B.C.); lectured in Rome, and inspired scholarly study among his pupils.

**Crates of Thebes** (thēbz). Cynic philosopher of late 4th century B.C.; disciple of Diogenes; gave up his fortune to devote himself to attaining virtue and self-control. Zeno of Citium was one of his pupils.

**Cra·ti′nus** (kră·tī′nŭs). 520?–?423 B.C. Greek playwright; author of 21 comedies, and winner of the prize for comedy 9 times, triumphing once over Aristophanes; only fragments of his works extant.

**Cra·tip′pus** (kră·tĭp′ŭs). Greek historian of 4th century B.C.; continued the history of Thucydides down to battle of Cnidus (394 B.C); only fragments of his work extant.

**Cratippus of Myt′i·le′ne** (mĭt′ĭ·lē′nē). Greek Peripatetic philosopher of 1st century B.C., in Athens; tutor of Cicero's son; praised by Cicero in his *De Officiis.*

**Crat′y·lus** (krăt′ĭ·lŭs). Greek philosopher of 5th and 4th centuries B.C.; a disciple of Heraclitus (*q.v.*); introduced by Plato as chief speaker in one of his dialogues (*Cratylus*).

**Crau′furd** (krô′fẽrd), **Quintin.** 1743–1819. Scottish author. Served East India Company (till 1780); gathered a library at Paris; friend of Marie Antoinette and royal family; helped arrange their flight to Varennes. Author of history of the Bastille (1798) and researches on Hindu civilization (1817).

**Crauk** (krōk), **Gustave Adolphe Désiré.** 1827–1905. French sculptor; studied under Pradier. Among his works are monuments to Coligny and Cardinal Lavigerie, many portrait busts, including Niel and MacMahon, and statues of Marshal MacMahon, General Chanzy.

**Cra′ven** (krā′vĕn), **Alfred.** 1846–1926. American civil engineer, b. Bound Brook, N.J. Grad. U.S.N.A., Annapolis (1867). In geological surveying, irrigation work and mining engineering in California and Nevada (1871–84). Engaged on New York City projects: Croton Aqueduct (1884–95), Jerome Park Reservoir (1895–1900), part of Broadway subway system, dual system of subways (chief engineer in charge of construction); consulting engineer, Transit Construction Commission, New York City (from 1916).

**Craven, Frank.** 1880–1945. American actor and playwright, b. Boston; author of *Two Many Cooks;* appeared on stage in *Bought and Paid For, Two Many Cooks, This Way Out, New Brooms, Our Town,* etc.; also in motion pictures.

**Craven, Pau′line′** (pô′lēn′). 1808–1891. French author, dau. of Comte Auguste Marie de la Ferronays, diplomat; m. (1834) **Augustus Craven** (d. 1884), British diplomat, grandson of margravine of Anspach. Author of *Récit d'une Sœur* (1866), a record of the slow passing of her family, crowned by French Academy.

**Craven, Thomas.** 1889–1969. American author and art critic, b. Salina, Kans. A.B. Kansas Wesleyan (1908). Author of *Men of Art* (1931) and *Modern Art* (1934); editor of *Life of Benvenuto Cellini* (1937), *A Treasury of Art Masterpieces* (1939), and *A Treasury of American Prints* (1939).

**Craven, William.** Earl of **Craven.** 1606–1697. English Royalist, son of Sir **William Craven** (1548?–1618), lord mayor of London (1610). Served under princes of Orange (from 1623), under Gustavus Adolphus (1631); aided Frederick, exiled king of Bohemia, and his son Charles Louis in attempt to recover the Palatinate (1632, 1637), and afterwards served Elizabeth of Bohemia; supplied Charles I and II with financial aid; privy councilor (1666, 1681); patron of letters.

**Craw′ford** (krô′fẽrd), Earls of. See LINDSAY family.

**Crawford, Francis Marion.** 1854–1909. Son of Thomas Crawford (*q.v.*). American novelist, b. in Bagni di Lucca, Italy. After education in U.S. and Europe, traveled in India (1879–80); returned to New York and wrote his first novel, *Mr. Isaacs* (1882). Settled in Sorrento, Italy (1885) and spent rest of life in writing. Other works: *Dr. Claudius* (1883), *Zoroaster* (1885), *A Cigarette Maker's Romance* (1890), *The Ralstons* (1895), *Via Crucis* (1898), *Marietta* (1901), *The Heart of Rome* (1903), *Soradella* (1909), *Wandering Ghosts* (1911), etc.

**Crawford, Isabella Valancy.** 1850–1887. Canadian poet, b. Dublin; to Ontario (1858); journalist in Toronto. Author of *Old Spookeses Pass* and *Malcolm's Katie* (1884).

**Crawford,** Mrs. **Louisa Macartney.** See Frederick Nicholls CROUCH.

**Crawford, Mary Caroline.** 1874–1932. American writer, b. Boston. Author of *The Romance of Old New England Rooftrees* (1902), *...Old New England Churches* (1903), *Among Old New England Inns* (1907), *St. Botolph's Town* (1908), *Social Life in Old New England* (1914), etc.

**Crawford, Nelson Antrim.** 1888–1963. American editor and author, b. Miller, S.Dak. Editor in chief of *The Household Magazine* (from 1928). Author of *The Carrying of the Ghost* (verse, 1923), *A Man of Learning* (fiction, 1928), *Unhappy Wind* (novel, 1930), *We Liberals* (1936), *Your Child Faces War* (1937), etc. Awarded Kansas poetry prize (1920) and Betty Earle lyric prize (1923).

**Crawford, Thomas.** 1813?–1857. American sculptor, b. New York City. Studied in Rome, with Thorvaldsen (1835); resident in Rome most of his life. Examples of his work: *Beethoven,* in Symphony Hall, Boston; *Orpheus,* in Boston Art Museum; *Dancing Girl, Dying Indian Maiden, Flora,* in Metropolitan Museum of Art, New York; *Peri,* in Corcoran Art Gallery, Washington, D.C. The *Washington* statue in Richmond, Va., and some of the sculptural decorations for the capitol at Washington, D.C. (notably the armed figure of Liberty on its dome) were executed from his designs.

**Crawford, William Harris.** 1772–1834. American lawyer, b. in Amherst County, Va. U.S. senator from Georgia (1807–13). U.S. minister to France (1813–15). U.S. secretary of war (1815–16); secretary of the treasury (1816–25). Candidate for president of the U.S. (1824).

**Craw′furd** (krô′fẽrd), **John.** 1783–1868. Scottish Orientalist. East Indian army doctor; envoy to Siam; administrator of Singapore (1823). Author of *History of the Indian Archipelago* (1820) and a Malay grammar and dictionary (1852).

**Cra′yer** (krȧ′yẽr), **Caspar de.** c. 1584–1669. Flemish painter; studied under Raphael van Coxie.

**Crayon, Geoffrey.** *Also* **Geoffrey Crayon, Gent.** (Gentleman). Pseudonyms of Washington Irving.

**Cra′zy Horse′** (krā′zĭ hôrs′). *Indian name* **Tashunca-Uitco.** 1849?–1877. American Indian chief, of the Oglala tribe of the Sioux, in battle of Little Big Horn, in which Custer was killed (1876); surrendered; killed while resisting imprisonment (Sept. 5, 1877).

**Creagh** (krā), Sir **Garrett O'Moore.** 1848–1923. British soldier, b. in County Clare, Ireland. Educ. Royal Military Coll., Sandhurst. Served in India, in Afghan War (1879–80) where he won the Victoria Cross; brigadier general (1899), major general (1903), lieutenant general (1904), and general (1907). Commanded second brigade in China Expedition (1900), and the entire British expeditionary force in China (1901). Succeeded Lord Kitchener as commander in chief in India (1909–14).

**Crea′sy** (krē′sĭ), Sir **Edward Shepherd.** 1812–1878. English historian. Educ. Cambridge; barrister; professor, London U. (1840); chief justice of Ceylon (1860). Known esp. for his *Fifteen Decisive Battles of the World* (1851).

**Cré′bil′lon′** (krā′bē′yôɴ′). *Pen name of* **Prosper Jo′lyot′** (zhô′lyō′). Sieur **de Crais′-Bil′lon′** (krĕ′bē′yôɴ′). 1674–1762. French tragic poet; among his important tragedies are *Idoménée* (1705), *Atrée et Thyeste* (1707), *Électre* (1708), *Rhadamiste et Zénobie* (1711), *Xerxès* (1714), *Sémiramis* (1717), *Pyrrhus* (1726), *Catilina* (1748), *Le Triumvirat* (1754). His son **Claude Prosper Jolyot de Crébillon** (1707–1777), novelist, depicted corruption in high society of the period.

**Cre·dé′** (krē·dā′), **Karl Sigismund Franz.** 1819–1892. German gynecologist; professor of obstetrics in Leipzig (1856). The Credé method of dropping silver-nitrate solution in the eyes of a newborn infant as a preventive treatment, and the Credé method of expression of the placenta after birth of the child, are named after him.

**Cre′di** (krā′dē), **Lorenzo di.** 1459–1537. Florentine painter; pupil of Andrea del Verrocchio. His paintings include *Nativity* and *Adoration of the Shepherds* (both in Florentine Academy), *Annunciation*, *Venus* (both in the Uffizi), studies of the Madonna and Child (in the Louvre, National Gallery at London, in galleries at Dresden, Turin, etc.).

**Cred′ner** (krād′nẽr), **Heinrich,** *in full* **Karl Friedrich Heinrich.** 1809–1876. German geologist for whom the mineral crednerite was named; privy councilor and director of mining in the Halle region (1868). His son **Karl Hermann** (1841–1913) was professor of geology and paleontology at Leipzig (from 1870); director of the geological survey of Saxony; author of the textbook *Elemente der Geologie* (1872). Another son, **Rudolf** (1850–1908), was professor of geography at Greifswald (from 1881).

**Creech** (krēch), **Thomas.** 1659–1700. English classical scholar. M.A., Oxon. (1683); hanged himself (1700). Translator of Lucretius into rhymed heroic couplets (1682), of Horace (1684), Theocritus (1684), and others.

**Creech, William.** 1745–1815. Scottish publisher. On withdrawal of his partner Kincaid, became foremost publisher in Scotland; brought out first Edinburgh editions of Burns, Blair, Beattie, Mackenzie; lord provost of Edinburgh (1811–13).

**Creel** (krēl), **George.** 1876–1953. American journalist and publicity director, b. in Lafayette County, Mo. Editor, Kansas City *Independent* (1899–1909), Denver *Post* (1909–10), *Rocky Mountain News* (1911–13). Chairman, Committee on Public Information (1917–19); chairman, national advisory board, Works Progress Administration (1935). Author of *Quatrains of Christ* (1907), *Wilson and the Issues* (1916), *The People Next Door* (1926), *Tom Paine—Liberty Bell* (1931), etc.

**Creel′man** (krēl′măn), **James.** 1859–1915. American journalist and war correspondent, b. Montreal, Canada; to New York as a boy; covered Chinese-Japanese War (1894), Greco-Turkish War (1897), Spanish-American War (1898).

**Cree′vey** (krē′vĭ), **Thomas.** 1768–1838. English diarist. Educ. at Cambridge; Whig M.P. (1802); secretary to board of control (1806); treasurer of ordnance (1830); treasurer of Greenwich Hospital. Known for *Creevey Papers* (pub. 1903), consisting of journals and correspondence covering 36 years and depicting political and social life of late Georgian era.

**Creigh′ton** (krā′t'n), **Edward** (1802–1874) and his brother **John Andrew** (1831–1907). American businessmen; benefactors of Creighton University.

**Creighton, James Edwin.** 1861–1924. Educator, b. Pictou, Nova Scotia. Grad. Dalhousie College, Halifax (1887); studied in Germany (1887–89). Professor, Cornell (1895–1924). Editor in chief, *Philosophical Review* (1902–24). Leading exponent in America of idealistic or speculative philosophy.

**Creigh′ton** (krī′t'n), **Man′dell** (măn′d'l). 1843–1901. English Anglican prelate and historian. B.A., Oxon (1867). Professor of ecclesiastical history, Cambridge (1884); first editor of *English Historical Review* (1886–91). Bishop of Peterborough (1891), of London (1897); condemned as unhistorical, and strove to eradicate, extravagances of ultraritualists. Author of *History of the Papacy* (1882–97), *Age of Elizabeth* (1876), *Cardinal Wolsey* (1888).

**Crei′ze·nach** (krī′tsĕ·näκ), **Theodor.** 1818–1877. German poet, of Jewish birth; adopted Christian faith (1854); published *Dichtungen* (1839) and *Gedichte* (1848). His son **Wilhelm** (1851–1919) was historian of literature; professor, Cracow (1883–1913).

**Crell** *or* **Krell** (krĕl), **Nikolaus.** 1551?–1601. Saxon statesman; councilor of Christian, Elector of Saxony (from 1586); chancellor of Saxony (1589). Endeavored to supplant Lutheranism in Saxony with his own faith, a form of Calvinism. On death of Elector Christian (1591), condemned to death and executed (Oct. 9, 1601).

**Crel′le** (krĕl′ĕ), **August Leopold.** 1780–1855. German road-building engineer. Constructed most of Prussian highroads built 1816–26; planned Berlin-Potsdam railway; publisher of Legendre's geometry (1823) and Lagrange's mathematical work (1823–24); founder of the mathematical periodical known today as *Crelle's Journal.*

**Cré′ma′zie′** (krā′mȧ′zē′), **Octave.** 1822–1879. French-Canadian poet; his *Le Vieux Soldat Canadien* (1855) won for him title as official poet of Canada; resident in France (from 1863).

**Cre′mer** (krā′mẽr), **Jacobus Jan.** 1827–1880. Dutch novelist; author of *De Lelie van's Gravenhage* (1851), *Daniël Sils* (1856), *Dokter Helmond en zijnn Vrouw* (1870), *Tooneelspelers* (1875), and short stories.

**Cre′mer** (krē′mẽr), Sir **William Randal.** 1838–1908. English pacifist. One of founders of carpenters' and joiners' union (1860). Resigned as secretary of British section of First International (1866). As secretary of

Workman's Peace Association (1871–1908), advocated international arbitration in America and Europe; Radical M.P. (1885). Edited peace journal *Arbitrator* (from 1889). Awarded Nobel peace prize for 1903.

**Cré'mieux'** (krā'myû'), **Adolphe.** *Real name* **Isaac Mo'ïse'** (mô'ēz'). 1796–1880. French lawyer and politician. Member of Chamber of Deputies (1842–48; 1849–51; 1869–70; 1871–75); minister of justice (1848; 1870–71); appointed senator for life (1875).

**Cre·mo'na** (krâ·mō'nä), **Luigi.** 1830–1903. Italian mathematician. Professor, Bologna (1860), Milan (1866), and Rome (1873), where he reorganized and directed the engineering college; minister of education (1898); known esp. for work in projective geometry and graphical statics, and for reorganization of the technical schools.

**Cremutius Cordus, Aulus.** See CORDUS.

**Cré'qui'** (krā'kē'). Name of a French family, originally from Créquy, including: **Henri Créqui,** who followed Saint Louis on his crusade and was killed at Damietta (1240). **Jacques de Créqui,** killed at Agincourt (1415). **Antoine de Créqui,** killed at siege of Hesdin (1523). **Charles I de Créqui de Blanche'fort' de Ca'na'ples** [dē bläNsh'fôr' dē kȧ'nȧ'pl'] (1567?–1638), marshal of France (1622), killed in action before Crema, Italy (1638). Duc **Charles III de Créqui** (1623–1687), soldier; engaged at Rocroi and Nördlingen; French ambassador at Rome (1662); governor of Paris (1676). Charles III's brother **François de Bonne** (bôn), Marquis **de Créqui** (1624?–1687), known as **Ma'ré'chal'** (mȧ'rā'shȧl') **de Créqui,** distinguished himself in fighting in Flanders and Catalonia; marshal of France (1668); refused to serve under Turenne and was disgraced; defeated forces of the elector of Brandenburg (1679) and had a part in preparing the Peace of Nijmegen. **Renée Caroline,** *nee* **de Froul'lay'** (dē frōō'lā'), Marquise **de Créqui** (1714–1803), society leader in Paris; m. Marquis **Louis Marie de Créqui** (1737).

**Cre'rar** (krē'rär), **Henry Duncan Graham.** 1888–1965. Canadian soldier; educ. Royal Military Coll., Kingston. Served in World War (1914–18); chief of Canadian general staff (1940–41); general (1944); retired (1945).

**Crerar, John.** 1827–1889. American businessman and philanthropist, b. New York City; endowed John Crerar Library in Chicago.

**Cre'scen·ti'ni** (krā'shân·tē'nē), **Girolamo.** 1766–1846. Italian mezzo-soprano; engaged in Italy, London, Vienna, Paris, returning to Naples (c. 1816) to become professor in conservatory there.

**Cre·scen'ti·us** (krĕ·sĕn'shĭ·ŭs). Name of a family of leaders of Roman aristocracy in 10th century, including: **Crescentius** the Elder (d. 984 A.D.); overthrew Pope Benedict VI (974) and installed Antipope Boniface VII; later became monk. His son **Johannes** *or* **John Crescentius,** *surnamed* **No'men·ta'nus** (nō'mĕn·tā'nŭs), *known as* "the Younger" (d. 998 A.D.), assumed title of patrician and dominated Rome and the papacy; opposed Emperor Otto III and Pope Gregory V and raised John XVI as antipope; defeated by Otto III at castle of Sant'Angelo (April, 998) and executed. **Johannes** *or* **John Crescentius** (d. 1011), son of Crescentius the Younger and his successor as head of the government in Rome.

**Cre·scen'zi** (krâ·shĕn'tsē), **Pietro.** *Latinized* **Petrus de Cre·scen'ti·is** (krĕ·sĕn'shĭ·ĭs). 1230?–?1310. Italian writer on agriculture; author of *Opus Ruralium Commodorum.*

**Cre'scim·be'ni** (krā'shēm·bâ'nē), **Giovanni Maria.** 1663–1728. Italian poet and literary historian, b. at Macerata; one of founders and first president (1690–1728) of Academy of Arcadians. His works include *Rime* (1695), *Storia della Volgar Poesia* (1698), and *Commentario intorno alla Volgar Poesia* (5 vols., 1702–11).

**Cres'i·las** (krĕs'ĭ·lăs). Greek sculptor, of Crete, in 5th century B.C.

**Cre'spi** (krās'pē), **Giovanni Battista** (1557–1633), *known as* **il Ce·ra'no** (ēl châ·rä'nō), and his nephew **Daniele** (c. 1590–1630). Italian painters of religious subjects.

**Cre'spi** (krās'pē), **Giuseppe Maria.** *Known as* **lo Spa·gnuo'lo** (lō spä·nywô'lō). 1665–1747. Italian painter, of Bologna; among his canvases are *La Cène* and *The Seven Sacraments* (Dresden gallery).

**Cres'pi** (krās'pē), **Juan.** 1721–1782. Spanish Roman Catholic missionary and explorer in America. With Portolá, a discoverer of San Francisco Bay; explored route around the bay (1772).

**Cres'po** (krās'pō), **Joaquín.** 1845–1898. Venezuelan soldier and political leader, b. San Francisco, Cuba. Supporter of Guzmán Blanco, serving as figurehead president under Blanco's dominance (1884–86). Led revolution deposing President Andueza Palacio (1892) and set up dictatorship (1892–94); elected president (1894–98); boundary dispute with Great Britain led to crisis between Great Britain and U.S. (1895–97); killed in unsuccessful defense of his successor, Ignacio Andrade.

**Cress'well** (krĕz'wĕl; -wĕl; krĕs'-), Sir **Cresswell.** 1794–1863. English judge. M.A., Cantab. (1818); first judge of probate and divorce court (1858).

**Cres'sy** (krĕs'ĭ), **Hugh Paulinus de.** 1605?–1674. English Benedictine monk and ecclesiastical historian.

**Cres'well** (krĕs'wĕl; -wĕl), **John Angel James.** 1828–1891. U.S. postmaster general (1869–74), b. Port Deposit, Md.; instituted great improvements in postal service.

**Cres'wick** (krĕz'ĭk), **Thomas.** 1811–1869. English landscape painter and book illustrator.

**Cret** (krĕ; *Angl.* krā), **Paul Philippe.** 1876–1945. Architect, b. Lyon, France. To U.S., and became professor of design, U. of Pennsylvania (1903–37). Designed Valley Forge Memorial Arch in Philadelphia, Folger Shakespeare Library in Washington, D.C., Federal Reserve Board building in Washington, D.C., and building at U.S.M.A., West Point.

**Creutz** (krûêts), Count **Gustav Philip.** 1731–1785. Swedish diplomat and poet. Ambassador in Madrid (1763) and Paris (1766–83); concluded (Apr. 3, 1783) with Franklin commercial treaty between Sweden and U.S. Poetical works include the idyl *Atis och Camilla* (1761) and the verse narrative *Daphne.*

**Creu'zer** (kroi'tsēr), **Friedrich.** 1771–1858. German classical philologist; professor, Marburg (1802) and Heidelberg (1807–45).

**Creuziger** *or* **Creutzinger, Kaspar.** See CRUCIGER.

**Cre·vaux'** (krē·vō'), **Jules Nicolas.** 1847–1882. French surgeon and explorer in South America.

**Crève'cœur'** (krĕv'kûr'), **Michel Guillaume Jean de.** *Pseudonym* **J. Hector St. John** (sânt jŏn'). 1735–1813. Writer, b. near Caen, Normandy, France. In New York (from 1759); naturalized citizen (1765). Returned to France (1780–83; 1790–1813). Fame rests on his *Letters from an American Farmer* (1782), a series of essays giving a farmer's reactions to the life and issues of the times.

**Crew** (krōō), **Henry.** 1859–1953. American physicist, b. Richmond, Ohio; A.B., Princeton (1882); Ph.D., Johns Hopkins (1887); professor, Northwestern (1892–1930); worked in spectroscopy.

**Crewe** (krōō), 1st Marquis of. **Robert Offley Ashburton Crewe'–Milnes'** (-mĭlz'). 1858–1945. English statesman and diplomat, b. London. Educ. Cambridge. Lord lieutenant of Ireland (1892–95); lord president of the council (1905–08, 1915–16); lord privy seal (1908, 1912–15); secretary of state for the colonies (1908–10) and for India (1910–15); president, Board of Education (1916). Ambassador to France (1922–28). Secretary of state for war (1931). Created marquis (1911).

**Crews** (krōōz), **Laura Hope.** 1880–1942. American actress, b. San Francisco. Supported Eleanor Robson in *Merely Mary Ann*, Henry Miller in *Joseph Entangled.* Created role of Polly Jordan in *The Great Divide* (1906). In motion pictures (from 1929).

**Creyton, Paul.** Pseudonym of John Townsend TROWBRIDGE.

**Cribb** (krĭb), **Tom.** 1781–1848. English champion pugilist; b. Bristol; defeated Jem Belcher for championship (1807) and again (1809); retired (1821).

**Crich'ton** (krī't'n), **James.** 1560?–1582. Scottish prodigy of learning and athletic accomplishments; known as "the Admirable Crichton," an epithet from the Scottish poet John Johnston's *Heroes Scoti* (1603). M.A., St. Andrews (1575). In Paris (1577), said to have disputed on scientific questions in twelve languages; served in French army two years; in Genoa (1579), made Latin address to doge; in Venice (1580), introduced to learned world by Aldus Manutius, vanquished all disputants except Mazzoni; in Padua (1581), disputed with university professors their interpretations of Aristotle and exposed their faulty mathematics.

**Crich'ton–Browne'** (-broun'), Sir **James.** 1840–1938. British physician; educ. Edinburgh U. and Paris. Specialist in mental and nervous diseases; lord chancellor's visitor in lunacy (1875–1922). Author of *What the Doctor Thought* (1930), *The Doctor's After-Thoughts* (1932). His oldest son, **Harold William Alexander Francis** (1866–1937), educ. Cambridge U., entered army, served in Boer War (1900–02); commanded King's Own Scottish Borderers (1911–18), colonel (1918); explored Atlas Mountains with Joseph Thomson's expedition (1888); author of *In the Heart of the Atlas*, etc.

**Crichton–Stuart.** Family name of marquis of Bute (see under STEWART family).

**Crick** (krĭk), **Francis Harry Compton.** 1916– British biologist. Awarded Nobel prize in physiology and medicine (1962) with J. Watson and M. Wilkins.

**Crile** (krīl), **George Washington.** 1864–1943. American surgeon, b. Chilo, Ohio. A.B., Ohio Northern (1884); M.D. (1887), Western Reserve; studied in Vienna, London, Paris. Professor, Western Reserve (1893–1924); one of founders and director (1921), Cleveland Clinic Foundation; surgeon, Cleveland Clinic Hospital (1924). Author of *Surgical Shock* (1897), *Origin and Nature of the Emotions* (1915), *A Mechanistic View of War and Peace* (1915), *A Bipolar Theory of Living Processes* (1925), *The Phenomena of Life* (1936), etc.

**Cril'lon'** (krē'yôN'). Family of French soldiers, including: **Louis des Balbes de Ber'ton' de Crillon** (dā bȧlb' dẽ bĕr'tôN' dẽ), Duc **de Ma'hon'** [mȧ'ôN'] (1717–1796); distinguished himself at Fontenoy and in the Seven Years' War; lieutenant general (1758); passed into Spanish service (1762) and forced capitulation of Minorca by the English (1782). His son **François Félix Dorothée des Balbes de Berton de Quiers** (kyâr), Duc **de Crillon** (1748–1820), member of States-General (1789); joined the Third Estate, became suspect, fled to Spain; returned to France under the Directory; appointed to Chamber of Peers (1815). François's half brother **Louis Antoine François de Paule des Balbes de Berton de Quiers de Crillon,** Duc **de Mahon** (1775–1832), lieutenant general in the Spanish army, submitted to Joseph Bonaparte and was appointed viceroy of Navarre; proscribed by Ferdinand VII (1814) and returned to France. François's son **Marie Gérard Louis Félix Rodrigue des Balbes de Berton,** Duc **de Crillon** (1782–1870), émigré from France, inherited title of duc and dignity of a peer of France; appointed field marshal after the campaign in Spain (1823).

**Crillon, Louis Bal'bis' de Ber'ton' de** (bȧl'bē' dẽ bĕr'tôN' dẽ). *Known as* **L'Homme' sans Peur'** (lôm' säN pûr'). 1541–1615. Served against the Huguenots in the French civil wars; engaged as a knight of Malta under Don John of Austria at battle of Lepanto (1571); served in army of Henry III during war against the Holy League (1580–89); fought under Henry IV at Ivry-La-Bataille (1590); with Sully, commanded army of Savoy (1600).

**Cri·nag'o·ras** (krĭ·năg'ō·răs). Greek epigrammatist, of Mytilene, in 1st century B.C.

**Cripps** (krĭps), **Charles Alfred.** 1st Baron **Par'moor** (pär'mŏŏr). 1852–1941. English lawyer and statesman. Grad. Oxford; queen's counsel (1890); Conservative M.P. (1895–1914); prominent High-Church layman; raised to peerage (1914); stanch peace advocate; joined Labor party, and was lord president of council (1924, 1929–31) in Labor governments, and British representative on council of League of Nations and delegate to assembly. His youngest son, **Sir Richard Stafford** (1889–1952), lawyer and socialist, was educ. University Coll., London; king's counsel (1927); solicitor general (1930–31); Labor M.P. (1931); champion of united front with left-wing parties (1936); executive officer of Labor party (1937); ambassador to Russia (1940); named lord privy seal and leader of House of Commons (Feb., 1942); special envoy to India (Mar.–Apr., 1942); minister of aircraft production (1942–45); president of Board of Trade (1945–47); chancellor of exchequer (1947–50).

**Crisp** (krĭsp), **Arthur.** 1881– . Painter, b. Hamilton, Ontario, Can. Studied at Art Students' League, New York. Teacher of mural painting at National Acad. of Design. Best known for murals.

**Crisp, Charles Frederick.** 1845–1896. American lawyer, b. of American parentage at Sheffield, Eng. Member, U.S. House of Representatives (1883–96); speaker (1891–95).

**Cri'spi** (krēs'pē), **Francesco.** 1819–1901. Italian statesman, b. at Ribera, Sicily. Aided Garibaldi in expedition to Sicily (1860); first representative from Palermo to Italian parliament (1861); leader of radical Left; president, Chamber of Deputies (1876); minister of interior (1877–78). Premier (1887–91, 1893–96); advocate of Triple Alliance (Germany, Italy, Austria); sought Italian protectorate over Abyssinia; deposed after Italian defeat at Aduwa (1896).

**Cris'pin** (krĭs'pĭn) and **Cris·pin'i·an** (krĭs·pĭn'ĭ·ăn; -pĭn'yăn), Saints. Christian martyrs of 3d century; brothers, shoemakers by trade; did missionary work in Gaul; beheaded by order of Emperor Maximian (c. 287). Patron saints of shoemakers, saddlers, and tanners.

**Cris'pus** (krĭs'pŭs), **Flavius Julius.** d. 326 A.D. Son of Constantine the Great (*q.v.*). Won naval victory (323 A.D.) over Licinius, in the Hellespont (Dardanelles). Executed by his father on charge of high treason (326). See FAUSTA.

**Cri·sto'fo·ri** (krēs·tô'fō·rē), **Bartolommeo.** 1655–1731. Italian maker of harpsichords; credited with inventing the hammer action characteristic of the modern piano (c. 1710–11).

**Cristus, Petrus.** See CHRISTUS.

**Cri'ti·as** (krĭsh'ĭ·ăs; krĭt'ĭ·ăs). Athenian orator and politician of late 5th century B.C.; a pupil of Socrates. Aided in overcoming the Four Hundred (411 B.C.); banished (c. 407). One of the Thirty Tyrants appointed by the

Spartans to govern Athens at end of Peloponnesian War (404). Killed in war against Thrasybulus (403). Introduced by Plato in one of his dialogues (*Critias*).

**Cri'ti·us** (krĭsh'ĭ·ŭs; krĭt'ĭ·ŭs) and **Nes'i·o'tes** (nĕs'ĭ-ō'tēz). Greek sculptors of 5th century B.C.; commissioned to carve duplicates of Antenor's statues of Harmodius and Aristogiton, the Tyrannicides, when the originals were carried off to Persia by Xerxes.

**Cri'to** (krī'tō). fl. late 5th century B.C. Athenian, friend and disciple of Socrates, whose escape he tried to arrange; introduced by Plato in one of his dialogues (*Crito*).

**Crit'o·la'us** (krĭt'ō·lā'ŭs). Greek Peripatetic philosopher of 2d century B.C.; lectured in Rome on philosophy; dismissed from the city by Cato the Elder.

**Crit'ten·den** (krĭt''n·dĕn), **John Jordan.** 1787–1863. American lawyer, b. near Versailles, Ky. U.S. senator (1817–19; 1835–41; 1842–48; 1855–61). U.S. attorney general (1841; 1850–53). Governor of Kentucky (1848–50). Introduced "Crittenden Compromise" in senate (Dec., 1860) as measure of conciliation between North and South, but compromise was defeated in committee. His son **George Bibb** (1812–1880), a Confederate officer in Civil War, was defeated at Mill Springs, Ky. (1862). Another son, **Thomas Leonidas** (1819–1893), a major general in Union army in Civil War, was relieved of his command after a repulse at Chickamauga but honorably acquitted by a court of inquiry. A nephew, **Thomas Theodore Crittenden** (1832–1909), an officer in Union army in Civil War, was governor of Missouri (1881–85) and consul general in Mexico City (1893–97).

**Crit'ten·ton** (krĭt''n·tŭn), **Charles Nelson.** 1833–1909. American businessman and philanthropist, b. Henderson, N.Y. In memory of daughter Florence, who died (1882) at age of four, established and endowed Florence Crittenton Homes for homeless and unfortunate women; incorporated as National Florence Crittenton Mission (1895).

**Cri·vel'li** (krē·vĕl'lē), **Carlo.** 1430?–?1494. Venetian painter; worked in Venice (to 1457), in The Marches (from 1468). His works include Madonnas (in Verona museum and the Vatican), *Pietà* (in Berlin Gallery and the Boston Art Museum), *Annunciation* (in National Gallery, London), *Crucifixion, Coronation of the Virgin, Madonna della Candeletta* (all in the Brera).

**Cro'ce** (krō'chā), **Benedetto.** 1866–1952. Italian philosopher, statesman, literary critic, and historian, b. at Pescasseroli, Aquila. Educ. U. of Rome. Senator (1910 ff.); minister of public instruction (1920–21); founded (1903) and edited (1903–37) *La Critica Rivista di Letteratura, Storia, e Filosofia.* Author of *Filosofia Come Scienza dello Spirito, Saggio Sull'Hegel* (1906), *La Filosofia di G. B. Vico* (1911), a long series *I Scrittori d'Italia* (1911– ), *La Letteratura della Nuova Italia* (4 vols., 1914–15), an autobiography *Contributo alla Critica di Me Stesso* (1918), *Goethe* (1919), *Ariosto, Shakespeare, e Corneille* (1920), *La Poesia di Dante* (1920), *Storia d'Europa nel Seculo Decimonono* (1932), *La Poesia*...(1936), *La Storia Come Pensiero e Come Azione* (1938), etc.

**Crock'er** (krŏk'ẽr), **Charles.** 1822–1888. American financier, b. Troy, N.Y. Went overland to California (1850); settled in Sacramento (1852). In charge of construction, Central Pacific Railroad (1863–69). President, Southern Pacific Railroad of California (from 1871); merged Southern Pacific and Central Pacific railroads (1884).

**Crocker, Francis Bacon.** 1861–1921. American electrical engineer, b. New York City. Instrumental in establishing American electrical standards. Author of *Practical Management of Dynamos and Motors* (with S. S. Wheeler; 1894), *Electric Lighting* (2 vols., 1896–1901), *Electric Motors* (1910). See Schuyler S. WHEELER.

**Crocker, William.** 1876–1950. American botanist, b. Medina, Ohio. A.B., Illinois (1902); Ph.D., Chicago (1906). Taught at Chicago (1909–21); director, Boyce Thompson Inst., Yonkers, N.Y. (from 1921). Known for work on the germination of seeds, on plant hormones, on tropisms, and on the effect of toxic gases on plants.

**Crock'ett** (krŏk'ĕt; -ĭt), **David,** *known as* **Davy.** 1786–1836. American frontiersman, b. in Greene County, Tenn. Served under Jackson in Creek War (1813–14). Active on frontier in western Tenn.; known as humorist and expert shot. Member, U.S. House of Representatives, from Tenn. (1827–31; 1833–35). Joined Texan forces (1836); killed at the Alamo (Mar. 6, 1836).

**Crockett, Samuel Rutherford.** 1860–1914. Scottish novelist. M.A., Edinburgh; abandoned Free Church ministry for novel-writing (1895); joined kailyard school with *The Stickit Minister* (1893); participated in romantic revival with novels including *The Raiders* and *Mad Sir Uchtred* (1894), *Man of the Mountain* (1909).

**Croe'sus** (krē'sŭs). d. 546 B.C. Last king of Lydia, of house of Mermnadae; reigned (560–546 B.C.). Conquered regions of western Asia Minor; extended kingdom to the Halys on the east and the Taurus on the south; invaded Cappadocia; surprised at Sardis by Cyrus and overcome (546 B.C.). Acquired great wealth through trade; subject of many legends.

**Croft** (krôft), Sir **Herbert.** 1751–1816. English scholar and linguist. Known esp. for his life of poet Young in Johnson's *Lives of the Poets,* written in Johnson's style.

**Croft, William.** 1678–1727. English composer of sacred music. Organist of chapel royal (1707), Westminster Abbey (1708); published *Musica Sacra* (2 vols., 1724), his choral works, including his masterly burial service.

**Croft'-Cooke'** (krôft'kŏŏk'), **Rupert.** 1904– . English writer; author of novels, a play, and a few volumes of verse.

**Crof'ton** (krôf'tŭn), Sir **Walter.** 1815–1897. Irish penologist; originated the Irish, or Crofton, system of prison administration.

**Crofts** (krôfts), **Ernest.** 1847–1911. English historical painter; one of chief English battle painters.

**Crofts, Freeman Wills.** 1879–1957. Irish civil engineer and detective-story writer, b. Dublin. Among his stories are *Inspector French's Greatest Case, Inspector French and the Cheyne Mystery, The Box Office Murders, Fatal Venture.*

**Croi'set'** (krwä'zĕ'), **Marie Joseph Alfred.** 1845–1923. French Hellenist; dean of the faculty of letters, Paris (1898–1919); author of *Xénophon*...(1873), *La Poésie de Pindare et les Lois du Lyrisme Grec* (1880), *Démocraties de l'Antiquité* (1909). His brother **Maurice** (1846–1935) was also a Hellenic scholar; professor at Montpellier (1876) and Collège de France (1893); author of *La Civilisation Hellénique* and coauthor with his brother of *Histoire de la Littérature Grecque* (1887–93).

**Crois'set'** (krwä'sĕ'), **Francis de.** *Orig. surname* **Wie'-ner** (vē'nẽr). 1877–1937. Belgian-born French playwright; his many plays include *Chérubin* (1902; set to music by Massenet, 1905), *Qui Trop Embrasse* (1903), *Le Tour de Main* (1906), *Arsène Lupin* (with Leblanc, 1908), *Le Cœur Dispose* (1912), *Le Docteur Miracle* (1926), *Pierre et Jack* (1931), *Le Vol Nuptial* (1933); author also of works on the theater, novels, and travel sketches.

**Croissy,** Marquis **de.** See Charles COLBERT.

**Croix** (krwä), Marqués **Carlos Francisco de.** 1699–1786. Spanish soldier, b. in Flanders; viceroy of Mexico (1766–71) and captain general of Valencia (1771–86).

**Croix, Charles de.** See CLERFAYT.

**Croix, Teodoro de.** 1730–1792. Spanish administrator in America, b. in Flanders. In New Spain (1765–71). Commandant general of a province including Coahuila, Texas, New Mexico, Sinaloa, Sonora, and California (1776–83). Viceroy of Peru (1784–89).

**Cro′ker** (krō′kẽr), **John Wilson.** 1780–1857. British Tory leader and essayist, b. in Galway, Ireland; B.A., Trinity Coll., Dublin (1800). Secretary to admiralty (1810–30), exposed defalcations; determined opponent of Reform Bill. Contributor to *Quarterly Review* from its foundation; responsible for scathing *Quarterly* article on Keats's *Endymion;* edited Boswell's *Life of Johnson* (1831); began an annotated edition of Pope's works, completed by Elwin and Courthope. The supposed original of Rigby in Disraeli's *Coningsby.*

**Croker, Richard.** 1841–1922. Known as "Boss Croker." American politician, b. in Ireland; to New York City as a child. Identified with Tammany Hall (from 1862); joined faction opposed to Boss Tweed (1868). Leader of Tammany Hall and managed Democratic politics in New York City (1886–1902). To England (1903), and later to Ireland, living as a country gentleman.

**Croker, Thomas Crofton.** 1798–1854. Irish antiquary. Clerk in admiralty, London (1818–50). Friend of Tom Moore, to whom he sent ancient Irish poetry; one of founders of Camden Society, Percy Society, and British Archaeological Association. Author of *The Fairy Legends and Traditions of the South of Ireland* (1825), and of humorous works.

**Croll** (krōl), **James.** 1821–1890. Scottish geologist and climatologist. Largely self-educated. Keeper of maps and correspondence, Geological Survey of Scotland (1867–80); author of *Climate and Time* (1875) and *Philosophic Basis of Evolution* (1890), etc.

**Cro′ly** (krō′lĭ), **David Goodman.** 1829–1889. Journalist, b. in County Cork, Ireland; to U.S. as a child. Managing editor, New York *World* (1862–72); editor, *Daily Graphic* (1873–78). His wife, **Jane,** *nee* **Cun′ning·ham** (kŭn′ĭng·ăm), *pseudonym* **Jennie June** [jo͞on] (1829–1901), b. in Leicestershire, Eng., was editor of *Demorest's Illustrated Monthly* (1860–87); founded "Sorosis," a woman's club (1868), and the Woman's Press Club, New York (1889). Their son **Herbert** (1869–1930), journalist and political philosopher, was editor of the *Architectural Record* (1900–06), and founder (1914) and editor (1914–30) of *The New Republic;* author of *The Promise of American Life* (1909), *Marcus Alonzo Hanna* (1912), *Progressive Democracy* (1914).

**Croly, George.** 1780–1860. Irish author and Anglican clergyman. Settled in London (1810) as journalist. Author of poems, dramas, and novels, including a romance *Salathiel* (1829), founded on the legend of the Wandering Jew.

**Crome** (krōm), **John.** 1768–1821. English landscape painter; founded (1803) Norwich school of painting; exhibited scenes from rural Norfolk (from 1806), notable for fidelity to nature. His son and pupil **John Bernay** (1794–1842), called "Young Crome," painted usually coast and river scenes of England and the Continent.

**Cro′me** (krō′mĕ), **Karl.** 1859–1931. German jurist; professor, Berlin (1895), Bonn (1898–1923).

**Cro′mek** (?krō′mĕk), **Robert Hartley.** 1770–1812. English engraver. Student of Bartolozzi; published edition of Blair's *Grave* with illustrations by William Blake (1808); compiled *Reliques of Burns* (1808).

**Cromer,** 1st Earl of. See BARING family.

**Cromp′ton** (krŭmp′tŭn), **Richmal.** Pen name of Richmal Crompton LAMBURN.

**Crompton, Samuel.** 1753–1827. English inventor of the spinning mule (1779), the rights to which he sold for about £60 because he was too poor to patent it; finally granted £5000 by House of Commons (1812); died in Bolton.

**Crompton, William** (1806–1891) and his son **George** (1829–1886). English textile workers, b. Lancashire, Eng.; to U.S. in 1836. Inventors of improved weaving loom.

**Crom′well** (krŏm′wĕl; -wĕl; krŭm′-), **Oliver.** 1599–1658. Lord protector of England (1653–58). Nicknamed **Old Noll** (nŏl) by Cavaliers. Great-great-grandson of Morgan Williams, a Welshman who married sister of Thomas Cromwell (*q.v.*), and whose son Richard took the name Cromwell. Left Cambridge to take up support of mother (1617); m. Elizabeth Bourchier, London merchant's daughter (1620). M.P. (1628); espoused Puritanism as an enthusiast (1638); moved second reading of bill for annual parliaments (1640); carried resolution putting kingdom in posture of defense (1642). At outbreak of first part of the Civil War, captain of troop of horse at Edge Hill (1642); formed his unconquerable Ironsides, combining strict discipline and religious enthusiasm; in eastern counties, upheld firmly Parliamentary cause which was wavering elsewhere; decided with cavalry charge fortunes of day at Marston Moor (1644). Assumed leadership of the Independents, made up largely of religious sects in the army demanding religious toleration and vigorous prosecution of the war, as against the Presbyterians, comprising the aristocratic generals and the majority in Parliament, seeking to make terms with Charles; secured remodeling of the army and passing of Self-denying Ordinance (1645); under Fairfax, led army to victory at Naseby (1645); probably ordered abduction of king from Holmby (1647); recognizing grievances of the army against Parliament, marched on London and coerced Parliament into ceasing further addresses to king (1648). In second part of Civil War, routed Scots under Hamilton at Preston (1648); active in prosecution of Charles up to execution and abolition of the monarchy. As commander in chief and lord lieutenant of Ireland, stormed Drogheda and Wexford, massacred garrisons (1649); left reduction of rest of the island to successors. Commander in chief (1650); defeated one army of Scots at Dunbar (1650) and other in command of Charles II at Worcester (1651); united the three kingdoms; dissolved Rump Parliament (1653); called Puritan convention, nicknamed Barebones Parliament, or Little Parliament, which proved ineffective and was dissolved by the moderates. Installed as "Lord Protector" on adoption of the "Instrument of Government," constitution designed to establish balance of power between Parliament and the protector, or chief executive, with his council of state (1653); used power to rule by ordinances until meeting of Parliament, providing judicial administration in Scotland, Irish representation in British Parliament, and reorganization of Church of England (1653–54); forced by attempts of Parliament to perpetuate itself in control of both army and the protector, to exclude all who refused to agree not to alter the "four fundamentals" of the Instrument; dissolved Parliament (1655). Placed ten major generals over ten districts of England; called a Parliament (1656) which drafted new constitution (1657); refused to take title of king (1657); on outbreak of conspiracies against his life, dissolved his last Parliament (1658). Brought war against Dutch States-General to successful conclusion (1654); made commercial treaties with Sweden and Denmark; ended war with Portugal by treaty (1653), which was renewed (1656); made treaty with France against Spain in interests of religious liberty and commerce (1655), another (1657) providing for joint attack on Spanish Netherlands; humbled Spanish at Dunkirk (1658); failed in endeavor to form European Protestant league. Denounced in pamphlet *Killing No Murder* (1657); died of tertian ague; buried in Westminster Abbey; attainted (1660), with other regicides; disinterred and hung on gallows (1661). His daughter **Bridget** married Henry Ireton (*q.v.*).

His eldest surviving son, **Richard** (1626–1712), Lord Protector of England (1658–1659), was trained by him as his successor; M.P. (1654); member of committee of trade and navigation (1655); member of council of state (1657); proclaimed protector (Sept. 3, 1658); victim of jealousy between army officers and Parliament; refused to make any attempt to retain power and allowed himself to be dismissed (May, 1659); lived in seclusion in France as **John Clarke** (until 1680).

Oliver's fourth son, **Henry** (1628–1674), served under him in latter part of Civil War; was an Irish representative in the Little Parliament (1653); lord deputy of Ireland (1657), rigorous in transplantation of native Irish but remonstrated against oath of abjuration required of Roman Catholics; governor general of Ireland (1658); returned to England to live in retirement (1659).

**Cromwell, Thomas.** Earl of **Es'sex** (ĕs'ĕks; -ĭks). 1485?–1540. English statesman, son of a brewer, smith, and fuller of Putney. Served in French army; trader in Antwerp; m. (c. 1512) Elizabeth Wykes of Putney; engaged in cloth dressing and moneylending. Legal adviser to nobles and to Cardinal Wolsey; collector of revenues of see of York, employed by Wolsey (1514); M.P. (1523); harsh and venal as Wolsey's agent in dissolution of smaller monasteries (1525), and a secretary in arranging for Wolsey's colleges at Oxford and Ipswich; pleaded successfully in House of Commons for quashing bill of attainder against Wolsey (1529). Privy councilor (1531); master of the jewels (1532); chancellor of exchequer (1533); king's secretary (1534); drafted most of the Reformation acts (1532–39); as vicar-general (1535), carried into effect the Act of Supremacy and suppression of monasteries (1536–39) and confiscation of their properties; exerted himself to Protestantize English church, chiefly as a means of supporting absolute monarchy in behalf of Henry VIII; lord privy seal (1536) and Baron Cromwell (1536); lord great chamberlain (1539); rewarded with confiscated lands of monasteries; earl of Essex (1540). Alienated Henry VIII by negotiating marriage with Anne of Cleves (1539); accused of treason by Norfolk; attainted by Parliament; beheaded; died in Catholic faith.

**Cronaca, il.** = Simone POLLAIUOLO.

**Cro'nin** (krō'nĭn), **Archibald Joseph.** 1896– . English physician and novelist; educ. Glasgow U. Served in World War. In general practice in South Wales (1921–24), and in London (1926–30); withdrew from practice to devote himself to writing. Author of *Hatter's Castle* (1931), *Three Loves* (1932), *Grand Canary* (1933), *The Stars Look Down* (1935), *The Citadel* (1937), *The Keys of the Kingdom* (1941), and the play *Jupiter Laughs* (1940).

**Cron·jé'** (krôn·yā'), **Piet Arnoldus.** 1840?–1911. Boer leader. Distinguished himself at Doornkop and Majuba Hill in Transvaal insurrection (1881); forced surrender of Jameson raiders (1896). In Boer War of 1899, commanded western frontier and by victory over Lord Methuen at Magersfontein checked British column advancing to relief of Kimberley until Lord Roberts's invasion (1900). Surrounded near Paardeberg, forced to surrender by failure of food and ammunition; prisoner at St. Helena until end of war (1902).

**Cron'stedt** (kro͞on'stĕt), Baron **Axel Fredric.** 1722–1765. Swedish mineralogist and chemist; first to isolate nickel in impure condition (1751); introduced use of blowpipe for study of minerals; made chemical composition basis of his classification of minerals. The mineral cronstedtite is named for him.

**Cronwright-Schreiner.** See under Olive SCHREINER.

**Crook** (kro͝ok), **George.** 1829–1890. American army officer, b. near Dayton, Ohio. Grad. U.S.M.A., West Point (1852). Served through Civil War. Indian fighting in far northwest (1866–72); in Sioux War (1876); served against Apaches under Geronimo (1882–85). Promoted major general (1888).

**Crookes** (kro͝oks), Sir **William.** 1832–1919. English physicist and chemist, b. London. Educ. Royal Coll. of Chemistry. On staff of Radcliffe Observatory, Oxford (1854); lecturer in chemistry, Chester Training Coll. (1855); worked in own London laboratory. Discovered thallium (1861); invented radiometer; investigated passage of electrical discharge through highly rarefied gases; invented Crookes tube, a highly exhausted vacuum tube; studied rare earths; produced minute diamonds artificially; studied radium; invented spinthariscope; produced special glass to protect workers from injurious rays emitted by molten glass; also, engaged in psychical research. O.M. (1910). Founder and editor of *Chemical News;* author of *Select Methods in Chemical Analysis* (1871), etc.

**Crooks** (kro͝oks), **Richard,** *in full* **Alexander Richard.** 1900–1972. American operatic tenor, b. Trenton, N.J. With Metropolitan Opera Co.

**Crop'sey** (krŏp'sĭ), **Jaspar Francis. 1823–1900.** American landscape painter, b. Rossville, N.Y. Examples of his work: *Niagara Falls,* now in Brooklyn Museum of Art; *Landscape,* in Metropolitan Museum of Art, New York; *Sunset, Lake George,* in New York Public Library.

**Cros'by** (krŏz'bĭ), **Frances Jane,** *known as* **Fanny.** 1820–1915. American hymn writer, b. Southeast, N.Y. Blind from infancy; educ. New York Institution for the Blind; teacher there (1847–58); m. Alexander Van Alstyne, a blind organist (1858); resided Brooklyn, N.Y. Composed about 6000 hymns (from 1864) including *Safe in the Arms of Jesus; Pass me not, O gentle Saviour; Jesus is Calling.* Other works, collections of verse: *The Blind Girl and Other Poems* (1844); *Bells at Evening and Other Poems* (1897).

**Crosby, Howard.** 1826–1891. American Presbyterian clergyman and author, b. New York City. Pastor, Fourth Avenue Presbyterian Church, New York City (1863–91). Founder, Society for the Prevention of Crime (1877). His son **Ernest Howard** (1856–1907), b. New York City, was a social reformer and author, founder and first president of Social Reform Club, a vegetarian, single taxer, and antimilitarist.

**Cros'key** (krŏs'kĭ), **John Welsh.** 1858–1951. American ophthalmologist, b. Philadelphia, Pa. M.D., Medico-Chirurgical Coll., Philadelphia (1889).

**Cros'ley** (krŏz'lĭ), **Powel.** 1886–1961. American manufacturer, b. Cincinnati, Ohio. Organizer of Crosley Radio Corp. (1921); president of Crosley Corp., manufacturer of radios, refrigerators, washing machines, etc. President of Cincinnati Baseball Club Co. (from 1934).

**Cros'man** (krŏz'măn), **Henrietta.** 1870–1944. American actress, b. Wheeling, W.Va.; m. Maurice Campbell (1897). Leading woman in Charles Frohman's company (1892–94); later starred in *One of Our Girls, Mistress Nell, The Real Thing,* etc.

**Cross** (krŏs), **Ada.** Mrs. **George Frederick Cross.** See Ada CAMBRIDGE.

**Cross, Charles Frederick.** 1855–1935. English industrial chemist. Educ. King's Coll., London, Zurich U., and U. of London. With collaborators E. J. Bevan and

C. Beadle, discovered and patented viscose (1892).

**Cross, Henri Edmond.** See Henri Edmond DELACROIX.

**Cross,** Mrs. **John W.** *Nee* **Mary Ann Evans.** See George ELIOT.

**Cross, Richard Assheton.** 1st Viscount **Cross.** 1823–1914. English political leader; grad. Cambridge (1846). Conservative M.P. (1857); home secretary (1874–80, 1885–86); introduced legislation relating to workers' dwellings and factory conditions; secretary for India (1886–92); lord privy seal (1895–1900).

**Cross, Roy.** 1884–1947. American chemist, b. Ellis, Kans. A.B. (1906) and M.D. (1908), Kansas. Coinventor of a petroleum-cracking process; designer of gasoline-refining plants.

**Cross, Whitman,** *in full* **Charles Whitman.** 1854–1949. American geologist, b. Amherst, Mass. B.S., Amherst (1875); Ph.D., Leipzig (1880). With U.S. Geological Survey (from 1880), geologist (1888–1925). Author (with Pirsson, Iddings, and Washington, 1903) of *Quantitative Classification of Igneous Rocks*, a system of petrography. The mineral crossite is named for him.

**Cross, Wilbur Lucius.** 1862–1948. American educator and politician, b. Mansfield, Conn. A.B. (1885) and Ph.D. (1889), Yale. Teacher of English at Yale (from 1894), and professor (from 1902); also, dean of Yale Graduate School (1916–30). Governor of Connecticut (1931–39). Author of *Development of the English Novel* (1899), *Life and Times of Laurence Sterne* (1909), *History of Henry Fielding* (1918), *Connecticut Yankee, an Autobiography* (1943), etc. Editor of *Yale Review*.

**Cross'ley** (krŏs'lĭ), **Ada.** 1874–1929. Australian contralto singer; best known for her rendition of oratorios, classical song recitals, and ballad programs.

**Crotch** (krŏch), **William.** 1775–1847. English composer; musical prodigy, performed in London at age of four; professor of music at Oxford (1797–1806); first principal, Royal Academy of Music (1822–32).

**Croth'ers** (krŭth'ẽrz), **Rachel.** 1878–1958. American playwright, b. Bloomington, Ill. Grad. Illinois State Normal U. (1892). Author of *The Three of Us, A Man's World, The Heart of Paddy-Whack, Once Upon a Time, Nice People, Everyday, A Lady's Virtue, Let us Be Gay, When Ladies Meet, Susan and God*, etc.

**Crothers, Samuel McChord.** 1857–1927. American Unitarian clergyman and essayist, b. Oswego, Ill. Minister of The First Parish, Cambridge, Mass. (1894–1927). Author of *The Understanding Heart* (1903), *The Gentle Reader* (1903), *The Pardoner's Wallet* (1905), *By the Christmas Fire* (1908), *Among Friends* (1910), *Humanly Speaking* (1912), *The Pleasures of an Absentee Landlord* (1916), *The Cheerful Giver* (1923).

**Cro'tus Ru'bi·a'nus** (krō'tŭs rōō'bĭ·ā'nŭs). *Real name* **Johannes Jä'ger** (yâ'gẽr). 1480?–after 1539. German humanist. Head of the monastery school at Fulda (1510); to Bologna and Rome (1517–19). Accepted principles of Reformation; received Luther at Erfurt (1521), where he was rector of the university. Re-entered Roman Catholic Church (c. 1530); canon in Halle. Contributed (c. 1515) satirical letters on scholasticism and monasticism to first part of *Epistolae Obscurorum Virorum*.

**Crouch** (krouch), **Frederick Nicholls.** 1808–1896. Musician and composer, b. London, Eng.; member of Queen Adelaide's private band (until 1832); taught singing at Plymouth; lectured on songs and legends of Ireland. To U.S. (1849); settled in Baltimore as teacher of singing. Wrote two operas and many songs; best remembered as composer of *Kathleen Mavourneen*, with words by a little-known English poet Mrs. **Louisa,** *nee* **Ma·cart'ney** (mȧ·kärt'nĭ), **Crawford** (1790–1858), sometimes ascribed to Mrs. **Anne B. Crawford** or to Mrs. **Julia Crawford.**

**Crouse** (krous), **Russel.** 1893–1966. American journalist and writer, b. Findlay, Ohio. On staff of Kansas City *Star* (1911–16), New York *Evening Post* (columnist, 1925–31). Author of *Mr. Currier and Mr. Ives* (1930), *It Seems Like Yesterday* (1931), *Murder Won't Out* (1932), and libretto for the musical comedy *The Gang's All Here;* collaborated with Howard Lindsay (q.v.) in dramatization of Clarence Day's *Life with Father* (1939) and of motion-picture scenarios (from 1937).

**Crow** (krō), **Carl,** *in full* **Herbert Carl.** 1883–1945. American journalist, b. Highland, Mo. Educ. U. of Missouri. To China (1911) as editor of *China Press*, an American daily newspaper in Shanghai; to Japan (1913) as business manager of *Japan Advertiser*. Founded and edited Shanghai *Post*. Author of *Four Hundred Million Customers*, a book on sales methods adapted to Chinese conditions and of other books on China.

**Crow, Martha,** *nee* **Foote** (fŏŏt). 1854–1924. American writer, b. Sackets Harbor, N.Y. Ph.B., Syracuse (1876) and Ph.D. (1885); m. John M. Crow (1884; d. 1891). Teacher of English literature (from 1876); asst. professor, U. of Chicago (1892–1900), Northwestern U. (1900–05). Author of *Elizabethan Sonnet-Cycles* (4 vols., 1896), *The World Above* (1905), *Harriet Beecher Stowe* (a biography, 1913), *The American Country Girl* (1915), *Lafayette* (1916), etc.

**Crow'der** (krou'dẽr), **Enoch Herbert.** 1859–1932. American army officer, b. in Missouri. Grad. U.S.M.A., West Point (1881); LL.B., Missouri (1886). Served in judge advocate's department; major general and judge advocate general (1917–23); retired (1923). U.S. ambassador to Cuba (1923–27).

**Crowe** (krō), **Catherine,** *nee* **Stevens.** 1800?–1876. English novelist; author of *Susan Hopley* (1841), *Lilly Dawson* (1847), *Night Side of Nature* (1848).

**Crowe,** Sir **Joseph Archer.** 1825–1896. English journalist and art critic; son of the historian and novelist **Eyre Evans Crowe** (1799–1868). War correspondent in Crimea and during Sepoy Mutiny; held consular posts in Europe (1860–82); collaborator with Italian critic Cavalcaselle on *Early Flemish Painters* and other classic histories of art. His brother **Eyre** (1824–1910) was an artist; student of Paul Delaroche (1839–44); Thackeray's secretary (1851–53); inspector under science and art department, South Kensington Museum; known for his *Brick Court, Middle Temple* (1863), *The Queen of the May* (1879).

Sir **Eyre Alexander Barby Wichart Crowe** (1864–1925), diplomat, son of Sir Joseph Archer Crowe and a German wife, was educ. at Düsseldorf, Berlin, Paris; delegate, second International Peace Conference (1907); submitted before World War comprehensive memorandum on German foreign policy and proposed seizure of German ships in English ports at the crisis; one of six drafters of a convention for League of Nations; participated in Paris Peace Conference (1919); permanent undersecretary for foreign affairs.

**Crow'ell** (krō'ĕl), **Grace,** *nee* **Noll** (nōl). 1877–1969. American poet, b. Inland, Cedar Co., Iowa; m. Norman H. Crowell (1901). Poet laureate of Texas (1935–37). Among her books of verse are *White Fire* (1925), *Flame in the Wind* (1930), *Bright Destiny* (1936), *This Golden Summit* (1937).

**Crowell, John Franklin.** 1857–1931. American economist, b. York, Pa. A.B., Yale (1883); Ph.D., Columbia (1897). On editorial staff of Wall Street *Journal* (1906–15); director of World Market Inst. of New York (from 1919).

**Crowell, Luther Childs.** 1840–1903. American inventor, b. Cape Cod, Mass.; invented the square-bottomed paper bag and machinery for manufacturing it, and improvements in printing presses.

**Crow'field** (krō'fēld), **Christopher.** Pseudonym sometimes used by Harriet Beecher STOWE.

**Crow'foot** (krō'fo͝ot) **Hodgkin, Dorothy.** See Dorothy Crowfoot HODGKIN.

**Crow'ley** (krou'lĭ), **Patrick Edward.** 1864–1953. American railway executive, b. Cattaraugus, N.Y.; with New York Central R.R. (from 1889); president of New York Central Lines (1924–32).

**Crow'ley** (krō'lĭ), **Robert.** 1518–1588. English printer and reformer; B.A., Oxon. (1542). Set up printing office; as typographer noted for his three impressions of *Vision of Pierce Plowman* (1550) and early printing of Welsh books. Returning from exile on accession of Queen Elizabeth, became archdeacon of Hereford; resisted use of surplice in what has been pointed out as first clear expression of Nonconformity. Author of *Way to Wealth* (1550) and *Pleasure and Pain* (1551).

**Crowne** (kroun), **John.** 1640?–?1703. British Restoration dramatist, b. in Nova Scotia. To England and began career with romance *Pandion and Amphigenia* (1665) and a tragicomedy *Juliana, or the Princess of Poland* (1671); won favor of Charles II with masque *Calisto;* at request of king, adapted Spanish play into *Sir Courtly Nice, or It Cannot Be* (1685); other comedies, *The English Friar* (1690), *The Married Beau* (1694).

**Crown'in·shield** (kroun'ĭn·shēld), **Francis Welch.** *Pseudonym* **Arthur Loring Bruce.** 1872–1947. American editor, b. Paris, of American parentage. Publisher of *The Bookman* (1895–1900) and *Metropolitan Magazine* (1900–02); asst. editor, *Munsey's Magazine* (1903–07), art editor, *Century Magazine* (1910–13), editor, *Vanity Fair* (1914–35).

**Crowninshield, Frederic.** 1845–1918. American painter and author, b. Boston; painter esp. of murals and stained-glass windows.

**Crowquill, Alfred.** Pseudonym of Alfred Henry and Charles Robert FORRESTER.

**Crow'ther** (krou'thẽr), **Samuel Ad'jai** (ăj'ī). 1809?–1891. African Negro missionary, b. in Yoruba country, West Africa. Rescued from slavery by British (1821); ordained in England (1843); missionary in Yoruba country; prepared schoolbooks and translations of Bible into Yoruba; bishop of Niger territories (1864).

**Cro'zat'** (krô'zȧ'), **Pierre.** 1665–1740. French art collector. Uncle of **Joseph Antoine Crozat** (1696–1751), also art collector, & **Louis François Crozat** (1691–1750), Marquis **du Châ'tel' et de Moy'** (dü shä'tĕl' ā dē mwȧ'), general in the French army, who served under Prince Eugène against Turks (1717), and in campaigns in Spain, Germany, Italy, and the Low Countries.

**Cro'zier** (krō'zhẽr), **William.** 1855–1942. American army officer, b. Carrollton, Ohio. Grad. U.S.M.A., West Point (1876). Coinventor with Gen. Buffington of Buffington-Crozier disappearing gun carriage; inventor of Crozier wire-wound gun. Chief of ordnance, U.S. army (1901–17); member of supreme war council (1917–18) and served in France and Italy; retired (1919).

**Cru·cha'ga To'cor·nal'** (kro͞o·chä'gä tō'kôr·näl'), **Miguel.** 1869–1949. Chilean diplomat and statesman. Minister of finance (1904–05); prime minister (1905–06); minister to Argentina and Uruguay (1909–13), Germany and Netherlands (1913–20); ambassador to Brazil (1923–25), U.S. (1926–27, 1931–38); president of senate (1938).

**Cru'ci·ger** (*as Lat.*, kro͞o'sĭ·jẽr; *as Ger.*, kro͞o'tsĭ·gẽr) *or* **Creu'zi·ger** (kroi'tsĭ·gẽr) *or* **Creut'zing·er** (kroi'tsĭng·ẽr), **Kaspar.** 1504–1548. German Protestant theologian; professor of theology, Wittenberg (from 1533); collaborated with Luther in translating the Bible.

**Cru'den** (kro͞o'd'n), **Alexander.** 1701–1770. Scottish bookseller in London and compiler of a well-known Biblical concordance (1737).

**Crü'ger** (krü'gẽr), **Johann.** 1598–1662. German composer of choral music for Protestant church use; organist of St. Nicholas Church in Berlin (from 1622). His best-known tunes include those for *Nun danket alle Gott, Jesus meine Zuversicht;* author of treatises on musical theory.

**Cruik'shank** (kro͝ok'shăngk), **George.** 1792–1878. English caricaturist and illustrator; son of a caricaturist and water-colorist, **Isaac Cruikshank** (1756?–?1811). Caricaturist in colors of political leaders, enemies of England, court, church, great persons, commoners. As book illustrator, produced colored etchings for *The Humorist* (1819–21), *Peter Schlemihl* (1823), Grimm's *German Popular Stories* (1824–26), Bentley's *Miscellany* (14 vols., 1837–43; including *Oliver Twist, Jack Sheppard, Guy Fawkes, Ingoldsby Legends*); engraved for Dickens's *Sketches by Boz* (1836, 1837); illustrated works for W. Harrison Ainsworth, Charles Lever, and William Hamilton Maxwell's *History of Irish Rebellion in 1798* (1845); started magazine *Table Book* (1845). Supported cause of abstinence in his pictures *The Bottle* (series of 8 plates, 1847), and its sequel, *The Drunkard's Children* (1848), and his magnum opus, the cartoon *Worship of Bacchus* (1862). His elder brother **Isaac Robert** (1789–1856), caricaturist and miniature painter, satirized social extravagances and London life.

**Crum** (krŭm), **Walter Ewing.** 1865–1944. English Coptic scholar; compiler of Coptic dictionary (6 parts, 1929–39).

**Crummus** *or* **Crumn.** See KRUM.

**Cru'sen·stol'pe** (kro͞o'sĕn·stôl'pĕ), **Magnus Jakob.** 1795–1865. Swedish writer of historical novels and histories.

**Cru'si·us** (kro͞o'zē·o͝os), **Christian August.** 1715–1775. German theologian and philosopher; professor, Leipzig (1750); opponent of Wolffian philosophy.

**Crus'sol'** (krü'sôl'). Prominent French family originally from Crussol and including: **Antoine de Crussol,** Duc **d'U'zès'** [dü'zâs'] (1528–1573), originally a Catholic and political agent of Catherine de Médicis in the Midi; became converted and a leader of the Protestants in the religious wars, and was killed at the siege of La Rochelle (1573). His brother **Jacques de Crussol,** Seigneur **d'As'sier'** [dȧ'syā'] (1540–1594), courageous auxiliary of the prince de Condé, governor of Nîmes and later of Cognac, served under François, Duc d'Alençon, at the siege of La Rochelle (1573); became a Catholic and fought vigorously against the Protestants.

**Cru'veil'hier'** (krü'vĕ'yā'), **Jean.** 1791–1874. French anatomist; professor, Paris (from 1835); first to describe disseminated sclerosis; gave an account of progressive muscular atrophy (sometimes called *Cruveilhier's atrophy* or *paralysis*).

**Cru·vel'li** (kro͞o·vĕl'ē), **Johanne Sophie Charlotte.** *Orig. surname* **Crü·well'** (krü·vĕl'). 1826–1907. German-Italian contralto; sang in Paris in Verdi's *Les Vêpres Siciliennes,* written especially for her (1855); m. Vicomte Vigier (1856) and retired.

**Cruz** (kro͞os), **José María de la.** 1801–1875. Chilean soldier and statesman.

**Cruz** (kro͞oth), San **Juan de la.** See Saint JOHN OF THE CROSS.

**Cruz** (kro͞os), **Juana Inés de La.** 1651–1695. Spanish nun and poet, b. in Mexico; for many years lady in waiting to wife of viceroy of New Spain; entered convent of San Jerónimo, in Mexico. Author of many poems, chiefly on subjects drawn from the Scriptures.

**Cruz** (krōōs), **Oswaldo.** 1872–1917. Brazilian hygienist responsible for freeing Rio de Janeiro from yellow fever.

**Cruz** (krōōth), **Ramón de la.** *In full* **Ramón Francisco de la Cruz Ca'no y Ol'me·dil'la** (kä'nō ē ôl'mā·thē'-lyä). 1731–1794. Spanish dramatist, b. Madrid; author of over 500 plays, chiefly *sainetes* (one-act representations of scenes from everyday life), which genre he developed from the older *pasos* and *entremeses;* author of first Spanish translation of *Hamlet.*

**Cruz e Sil'va** (krōōz' ē sĭl'vȧ), **Antônio Diniz da.** See DINIZ DA CRUZ E SILVA.

**Cruz y Go'ye·ne'che** (krōōs' ē gō'yā·nā'chā), **Luis de la.** 1768–1828. Chilean caudillo and statesman, b. Concepción; explored Andes (1806); commanded division in revolutionary army (1810); prisoner of war (to 1817); acting president of Chile in absence of O'Higgins; minister of marine (1828).

**Csá'ky** (chä'kĭ), Count **István.** 1894?–1941. Hungarian diplomat and statesman; foreign minister (from 1938); advocated co-operation with Germany.

**Csi'ky** (chĭ'kĭ), **Gergely.** 1842–1891. Hungarian playwright; author of *The Proletariat, The Irresistible, Two Loves, The Bashful,* etc.

**Cso'ko·nai Vi'téz** (chô'kô·noi vĭ'tāz), **Mihály.** 1773–1805. Hungarian poet; author of a philosophical poem *On the Immortality of the Soul,* a mock-heroic epic *Dorothy* (1804), odes, elegies, etc.

**Csoma de Kőrös.** See KŐRÖSI CSOMA.

**Cte'si·as** (tē'zĭ·ăs). Greek physician and historian, of 5th century B.C.; physician at court of Artaxerxes Mnemon. Author of *Persica* (only fragments of which are extant), a history of Persia from Persian sources, intended to discredit the history of Herodotus.

**Cte·sib'i·us** (tē·sĭb'ĭ·ŭs) of Alexandria. fl. 2d century B.C. Greek physicist and inventor. Credited with inventing a clepsydra and a hydraulic organ, and several devices which operate by air pressure, as an air gun, fire engine, and force pump.

**Ctes'i·phon** (tĕs'ĭ·fŏn; tē'sĭ-). Athenian citizen of 4th century B.C., prosecuted by Aeschines (*q.v.*) for proposing that Demosthenes receive a crown for his distinguished services; his defense was conducted by Demosthenes (*q.v.*).

**Cuauhtémoc.** See GUATEMOTZIN.

**Cu'bitt** (kū'bĭt), Sir **William.** 1785–1861. English civil engineer. Constructed canals, docks at Cardiff, South-Eastern railway, waterworks in Berlin.

**Cud'a·hy** (kŭd'ȧ·hĭ), **Michael.** 1841–1910. American meat packer, b. in County Kilkenny, Ireland; to U.S. as a child. Partner, Armour & Co. (1875–90). Formed Cudahy Packing Co. (1890); president (1890–1910).

**Cud'worth** (kŭd'wûrth; -wẽrth), **Ralph.** 1617–1688. English philosopher, chief of the Cambridge Platonists. Professor of Hebrew (1645–88), master of Christ's Coll. (1654), Cambridge. Sought in his magnum opus, *The True Intellectual System of the Universe* (1678), to establish a supreme divine intelligence, to refute determinism, or materialistic atheism, to justify moral ideas, and to establish freewill; replied to Hobbes in a *Treatise concerning Eternal and Immutable Morality* (1731) from point of view of Platonism.

**Cuer'vo** (kwĕr'vō), **Rufino José.** 1844–1911. Colombian philologist and author, b. Bogotá; wrote dictionary of Spanish and a Latin grammar for Spanish-speaking people.

**Cues'tas** (kwās'täs), **Juan Lindolfo.** 1837–1905. Uruguayan political leader, b. Paysandú. President of Uruguay (1897–1903).

**Cue'va** (kwā'vä), **Alfonso de la.** See Marqués de BEDMAR.

**Cueva, Beltrán de la.** d. 1492. Spanish nobleman; supposed to have been father of Juana la Beltraneja (see JUANA OF PORTUGAL).

**Cueva de la Ga·ro'za** (thā lä gä·rō'thä), **Juan de la.** 1550?–?1610. Spanish dramatist and poet, b. Seville; known esp. for his innovations in Spanish drama, as use of new metrical forms, introduction of historical material, and dramatic adaptation of old romances.

**Cueva y del Rí'o** (ē thĕl rē'ō), **Roberto de la.** 1908– . Mexican painter; commissioned to adorn Mexican embassy in Washington, D.C., with frescoes depicting life and history of Mexico (1933).

**Cu'gnot'** (kü'nyō'), **Nicolas Joseph.** 1725–1804. French engineer. Invented (c. 1770) a three-wheeled carriage propelled by a steam engine, believed to be earliest predecessor of the automobile.

**Cui** (*Fr.* kü·ē'), **César Antonovitch.** *Russ.* **Tsezar Antonovich Kyui** (kyōō·ē'). 1835–1918. Russian military engineer and composer, of French descent; author of textbooks on fortification. Best known as composer of symphonies, piano works, songs, and operas.

**Cu·ja'ci·us** (kû·yā'shĭ·ŭs). *Orig.* **Jacques Cu'jas'** (kü'zhäs'). 1522–1590. French jurist, b. at Toulouse. Chief representative of the historical school in the teaching of law.

**Cul'bert·son** (kŭl'bẽrt·s'n), **Ely.** 1891–1955. American authority on contract bridge, b. in Rumania, of American parentage. Editor, *The Bridge World Magazine.* Captain of American team in international bridge matches (1933–34, 1937).

**Culbertson, William Smith.** 1884–1966. American lawyer and diplomat, b. Greensburg, Pa. A.B. (1908) and Ph.D. (1911), Yale. Practiced law, Washington, D.C. (from 1912). Member (1917–25) and vice-chairman (1922–25), U.S. Tariff Commission. U.S. ambassador to Rumania (1925–28) and Chile (1928–33).

**Cul'len** (kŭl'ĕn), **Coun·tee'** (koun·tā'). 1903–1946. American Negro poet, b. New York City. A.B., N.Y.U. (1925). Author of *Color* (1925), *Caroling Dusk* (1927), *The Ballad of the Brown Girl* (1928), *The Black Christ...* (1929), *One Way to Heaven* (1931, a novel), etc.

**Cullen, Paul.** 1803–1878. Irish prelate. Archbishop of Armagh (1849–52), of Dublin (1852); distrusted national movement and opposed Fenian Brotherhood; first Irish cardinal (1866).

**Cullen, Thomas Stephen.** 1868–1953. Surgeon, b. Bridgewater, Ontario, Canada. M.B., Toronto (1890). Gynecologist, Johns Hopkins Hospital (from 1892); authority on cancer and tumors of the uterus.

**Cullen, William.** 1710–1790. Scottish physician. M.D., Glasgow U. (1740). Professor, Glasgow (1751–55), Edinburgh (1756 ff.).

**Cul'lum** (kŭl'ŭm), **George Washington.** 1809–1892. American army officer, b. New York City. Grad. U.S.M.A., West Point (1833). Served through Civil War; brigadier general (1861). Retired (1874). Bequeathed money for erection of Memorial Hall at West Point.

**Cul'mann** (kōōl'män), **Karl.** 1821–1881. German engineer; professor, Zurich (1855). Credited with founding science of graphical statics for determining strength of structures by means of diagrams (Culmann's diagrams, or funicular polygons). Author of *Die Graphische Statik* (1865).

**Culmbach.** Variant of KULMBACH.

**Culp** (kûlp), **Julia.** 1881– . Dutch contralto concert singer, known esp. as lieder singer.

**Cul'pep'er** (kŭl'pĕp'ẽr). See also COLEPEPER.

**Culpeper, John.** English surveyor and political leader in the Carolinas. Surveyor general of colony (1671); fomented Culpeper's insurrection in protest against British trade laws in northern Carolina (1677) and, upon deposition of the proprietaries' deputies, aided in formation of a new popular government, acting as governor (1677–79); made rough plan for laying out city of Charleston (1680).

**Cul'ver·wel** (kŭl'vẽr·wĕl; -wĕl), **Nathanael.** d. 1651? English clergyman; one of the Cambridge Platonists; author of *Light of Nature* (1652).

**Cum'ber·land** (kŭm'bẽr·lănd), Duke of. Title of English nobility created and re-created five times in favor of the following: (1644) Prince Rupert (*q.v.*), Count Palatine; (1689) George (*q.v.*), Prince of Denmark, husband of Queen Anne; (1726) William Augustus (*q.v.*), son of George II; (1766) Henry Frederick (1745–1790), brother of George III; (1799) Ernest Augustus (*q.v.*), son of George III and King of Hanover, whose descendants continued to hold the title.

**Cumberland,** Earls of. See CLIFFORD family.

**Cumberland, Richard.** 1631–1718. English philosopher. M.A., Cantab. (1656); bishop of Peterborough (1691). Author of *De Legibus Naturae* (1672), written in reply to Hobbes, presenting principle of universal benevolence as antithesis of Hobbes's egoism and setting up the greatest good of universe of rational beings as foundation of ethical theory; hence often regarded as founder of English utilitarianism. Great-grandfather of **Richard Cumberland** (1732–1811), dramatist; b. Cambridge; secretary to board of trade (c. 1776–82); undertook secret mission to Spain to arrange separate peace (1780); retired to write farces, tragedies, comedies, essays, and two novels; ridiculed in Sheridan's *Critic* as Sir Fretful Plagiary.

**Cum'mings** (kŭm'ĭngz), **Bruce Frederick.** *Pseudonym* **W. N. P. Bar·bel'lion** (bär·bĕl'yŭn). 1889–1919. Biologist in Natural History Museum, South Kensington; published extracts from his diaries as *The Journal of a Disappointed Man* (1919).

**Cummings, Byron.** 1861–1957. American archaeologist, b. Westville, N.Y. B.A. (1889), Rutgers; studied at Chicago (1896), Berlin (1910–11). Professor of archaeology and director of museum (1915–37; dean, 1917–21), U. of Arizona. Known for investigations of prehistoric man in Utah, Arizona, and Mexico.

**Cummings, Edward Estlin.** 1894–1962. American poet and painter, b. Cambridge, Mass. A.B. (1915) and M.A. (1916), Harvard. Studio in New York City.

**Cummings, Homer Stil'lé** (stĭl'ā). 1870–1956. American lawyer and politician, b. Chicago. Ph.B. (1891) and LL.B. (1893), Yale. Adm. to bar (1893); practiced in Stamford, Conn. Mayor of Stamford (1900–02; 1904–06). U.S. attorney general (1933–39). Author of *Liberty Under Law and Administration* (1934).

**Cum'mins** (kŭm'ĭnz), **Albert Baird.** 1850–1926. American lawyer and statesman, b. Carmichaels, Pa. Governor of Iowa (1902–08); U.S. senator (1908–26). Joint author with Esch of the Esch-Cummins Transportation Act (1920).

**Cummins, George David.** 1822–1876. American clergyman, b. near Smyrna, Del. In Protestant Episcopal ministry (1845–74); withdrew because of opposition to emphasis on ritualism. Organized the Reformed Episcopal Church (1873).

**Cummins, Maria Susanna.** 1827–1866. American novelist, b. Salem, Mass.; author of *The Lamplighter* (1854), a great popular success.

**Cu'mont'** (kü'môɴ'), **Franz Valéry Marie.** 1868–1947. Belgian historian of religion; professor, Ghent (1892–1910); curator, royal museum, Brussels (1899–1912). Chief work, *Textes et Monuments Figurés Relatifs aux Mystères de Mithra* (1894–1901).

**Cu·nard'** (kū·närd'), Sir **Samuel.** 1787–1865. British shipowner; founder of the Cunard Line; b. in Halifax, Nova Scotia. Joined George and James Burns of Glasgow and David M'Iver of Liverpool in founding (1839) Royal Mail Steam Packet Company; introduced iron steamers (1855) and screws in place of paddle wheels (1862).

**Cundell, Henry.** See CONDELL.

**Cu'nha** (kōō'nyȧ), **Tristão da.** 1460?–?1540. Portuguese navigator. Led expedition to Africa; discovered Tristan da Cunha Islands (1506); accompanied Albuquerque to India; won fame for work in the East; special emissary to Pope Leo X (1514); member of king's special council. His son **Nunho** (1487–1539) first went to East Indies (1506); consolidated Portuguese possessions in Indies (1528) by conquest of Diu; died on voyage home.

**Cun'liffe** (kŭn'lĭf), 1st Baron. **Walter Cunliffe.** 1855–1920. English banker; educ. Cambridge U. Director, Bank of England (from 1895), and governor (1913–18). Associated with British government in handling British finances throughout the World War; member of financial mission to U.S. (1917).

**Cunliffe, John William.** 1865–1946. Educator and author, b. Bolton, Eng. B.A., London (1884). Taught English, McGill, Montreal (1899–1906); professor of English, Wisconsin (1906–12), Columbia (1912–20); director, school of journalism, Columbia (1920–31). Editor of many English texts, and of *Century Readings in English Literature* (1910, 5th ed. 1940), *Shakespeare's Principal Plays* (1914), etc. Author of books on English literature.

**Cunliffe–Lister, Philip.** See 1st Viscount SWINTON.

**Cun'ning·ham** (kŭn'ĭng·ăm; *in U.S., also* -hăm), **Alexander.** 5th Earl of **Glen·cairn'** (glĕn·kârn'). d. 1574. Scottish promoter of Reformation. Signer of invitation to Knox to return from Geneva (1557); stopped queen regent's advance against reformers at Perth with 2500 volunteers (1559), and applied to Queen Elizabeth for aid; demolished monasteries in western Scotland (1561); privy councilor, Scotland (1561); commanded insurgents against Mary, Queen of Scots, and led a division at Langside (1568).

**Cunningham, Alexander.** 1655?–1730. Scottish classical scholar and critic.

**Cunningham, Allan.** 1784–1842. Scottish poet and man of letters. Friend of James Hogg, the Ettrick shepherd; contributed imitations of old Scottish ballads to Cromek's *Remains of Nithsdale and Galloway Song* (1810), which gained him friendship of Scott. Edited Burns's works (1834). Author of three novels, a life of Sir D. Wilkie (3 vols., 1843), *Lives of the Most Eminent British Painters, Sculptors, and Architects* (6 vols., 1829–33), and many songs, including *A Wet Sheet and a Flowing Sea* (1825). Father of: **Joseph Davey** (1812–1851), who served in Bengal Engineers (from 1831) and wrote *History of the Sikhs* (1849). Sir **Alexander** (1814–1893), who also served in Bengal Engineers, retired as major general (1861); was director-general of Indian Archaeological Survey (1870–85); wrote *Ancient Geography of India* (1871) and *Coins of Mediaeval India* (1894). **Peter** (1816–1869), who wrote *Handbook to London* (1849) and *The Life of Drummond of Hawthornden* (1833) and other biographical studies. **Francis** (1820–1875), field engineer in Indian army, who edited Marlowe (1870), Massinger (1871), Ben Jonson (1871).

**Cunningham, Allan.** 1791–1839. English botanist.

**Cunningham,** **Andrew Browne.** 1st Viscount **Cunningham of Hynd'hope** (hĭnd'hōp). 1883–1963. British admiral. Entered navy (1898); served in World War I; rear admiral (1933); vice-admiral commanding battle-cruiser squadron (1937–38); admiral and commander in chief of British naval forces in Mediterranean (1939–42): executed brilliant raid against Italian fleet at anchor in Gulf of Taranto (Nov., 1940), won victory in Ionian Sea (Mar., 1941); chief of allied naval operations in Northwest African campaign (Nov., 1942); admiral of the fleet; allied naval commander in chief, under Eisenhower (*q.v.*), in Mediterranean theater (Feb., 1943); British first sea lord and chief of naval staff (Oct., 1943–46). His brother Sir **Alan Gordon** (1887– ) commanded British forces in Ethiopian campaign and in Libya (1941); high commissioner for Palestine and Trans-Jordan (1945–48).

**Cunningham,** **Merce.** 1922?– . American choreographer and dancer, b. Centralia, Washington.

**Cunningham,** **William.** 1805–1861. Scottish theologian; one of founders of the Free Church.

**Cunningham,** **William.** 1849–1919. British economist; b. Edinburgh; educ. Edinburgh, Tübingen, Cambridge; professor of economics, King's Coll., London (1891–97); archdeacon of Ely (1907–19). Author of *The Growth of English Industry and Commerce* (7 editions, 1882–1910).

**Cun'ning·hame–Gra'ham** (kŭn'ĭng·ăm[-hăm]·grā'-ăm [-grâ'ăm]), **Robert.** d. about 1797. See GRAHAM.

**Cunninghame Graham,** **Robert Bontine.** 1852–1936. Scottish writer; traveled in South America, Mexico, Spain, Morocco; M.P. (1886–92, 1918). Among his books are *Mograb el Acksa* (1898), *A Vanished Arcadia* (1901), *Success* (1902), *Hernando de Soto* (1903), *Progress* (1905), *Faith* (1909), *Hope* (1910), *Charity* (1912), *Life of Bernal Diaz del Castillo* (1915), *The Conquest of New Granada* (1922), *The Conquest of the River Plate* (1924), *Conqueror of Chile* (1926), *Writ in Sand* (1932), *Portrait of a Dictator* (1933).

**Cu'no** (kōō'nō), **Wilhelm.** 1876–1933. German statesman and business man. Entered government service; during World War I in charge of grain office (1914–16), then assistant to food department (1916–17). With Hamburg-American Steamship Line (1917). Chancellor of republican Germany (1922–23).

**Cu'no·be·li'nus** (kū'nō·bē·lī'nŭs) *or* **Cym'be·line** (sĭm'bĕ·lēn). d. about 43 A.D. British king; ally of Augustus and chief ruler in Britain. Shakespeare's Cymbeline, named for him, is not historical.

**Cup'py** (kŭp'ĭ), **Will,** *in full* **William Jacob.** 1884–1949. American critic and humorist, b. Auburn, Ind. Ph.B., Chicago (1907). Officer (1917–18) in World War. On staff, N.Y. *Herald Tribune.* Author of *How to be a Hermit* (1929), *How to Tell Your Friends from the Apes* (1931).

**Curchod,** **Suzanne.** See under Jacques NECKER.

**Cur'ci** (kōōr'chē), **Carlo Maria.** 1810–1891. Italian prelate and writer. Entered Society of Jesus (1826); cofounder (1850) and editor (1850–53, 1856–63) of Jesuit publication *Civiltà Cattolica;* expelled from Jesuit order because of opposition to Vatican political policy (1877); reinstated shortly before death.

**Cu'rel'** (kü'rĕl'), **François de.** 1854–1928. French playwright, b. Metz. Among his dramas are *L'Envers d'une Sainte* (1892), *La Fille Sauvage* (1902), *L'Ivresse du Sage* (1922), *Orage Mystique* (1927).

**Curé of Ars.** See Saint Jean Baptiste Marie VIANNEY.

**Cure'ton** (kūr't'n), **William.** 1808–1864. English Syriac scholar. M.A., Oxon. (1833); on staff of British Museum; discovered epistles of St. Ignatius among Syriac mss. from the Nitrian monasteries, also the Curetonian Gospels; canon of Westminster (1849–64).

**Cu'rie'** (kü'rē'; *Angl.* kū·rē'), **Pierre.** 1859–1906. French chemist; educ. at the Sorbonne; conducted researches on piezoelectricity, the magnetic properties of bodies at various temperatures, etc.; professor at the School of Physics and Chemistry at Paris (1895), at the Sorbonne (1904); known esp. for work with his wife on radioactivity leading to their discovery of polonium and radium, for which they were awarded (with A. H. Becquerel) 1903 Nobel prize for physics; m. (1895) **Marja Skło·dow'ska** [sklô·dôf'skä] (1867–1934), physical chemist, b. Warsaw; studied in Warsaw under her father, teacher in a high school; began studies at the Sorbonne (1891), receiving doctorate (1904); with husband, at the School of Physics and Chemistry in Paris, investigated radioactivity (see above); succeeded husband as professor of general physics at the Sorbonne (1906); awarded 1911 Nobel prize for chemistry for work on radium and its compounds; director of research department of Radium Inst. of U. of Paris; organizer of radiological service for hospitals during World War. Their daughter **Irène** (1897–1956), physicist, b. Paris; m. (1926) Frédéric Joliot (later Joliot-Curie, *q.v.*); shared with him 1935 Nobel prize for chemistry for their synthesis of new radioactive elements. Another daughter, **Ève** (âv) **Curie** (1904– ), musician and playwright, wrote *Madame Curie* (1937), a biography of her mother, *Journey Among Warriors* (1943), etc.

**Curie-Joliot.** See JOLIOT-CURIE.

**Cu'ri·o** (kū'rĭ·ō), **Gaius Scribonius.** Roman politician and soldier of 1st century B.C. Tribune (90 B.C.); served in Sulla's army in Greece against army of Mithridates, and as Sulla's representative in Asia. Consul (76); governor of Macedonia (75–73), where he defeated the Dardani and extended his conquests to the Danube River; pontifex maximus (57); died (53). His son **Gaius Scribonius Curio** supported cause of Caesar in Civil War (from 50 B.C.); defeated and killed in Africa in battle against Juba I, King of Numidia (49).

**Curius Dentatus,** **Manius.** See DENTATUS.

**Curle** (kûrl), **Richard Henry Par·nell'** (pär·nĕl'). 1883–1968. English writer and traveler; friend of Joseph Conrad; author of books on Joseph Conrad's life, also of *Wanderings*, *Oriental Trail*, *The Echo of Voices*, etc.

**Cur'ley** (kûr'lĭ), **Michael Joseph.** 1879–1947. Roman Catholic prelate, b. in County Athlone, Ireland. Archbishop of Baltimore (from 1921).

**Curll** (kûrl), **Edmund.** 1675–1747. English bookseller. Ascribed to Pope authorship of *Court Poems* (1716); lampooned in Pope's *Dunciad;* convicted of printing obscene books and fined (1728) for publishing *A Nun in her Smock* and *De Usu Flagrorum*, giving rise to term "Curlicism" for literary indecency.

**Curme** (kûrm), **George Oliver.** 1860–1948. American philologist and grammarian. b. Richmond, Ind. A.B., Michigan (1882), Ph.D., Heidelberg (1926). Professor, Cornell Coll., Iowa (1887–96), Northwestern U. (1896–1933). Author of *A Grammar of the German Language* (1905), *College English Grammar* (1925), *A Grammar of the English Language* (vol. 3, *Syntax*, 1931; vol. 2, *Parts of Speech and Accidence*, 1935).

**Cur'ran** (kûr'ăn), **Charles Courtney.** 1861–1942. American painter, b. Hartford, Ky. Studio in New York City. Among his paintings are *Perfume of the Roses*, *The Breezy Day*, and *Mountain Laurel.*

**Curran,** **John Philpot.** 1750–1817. Irish orator and judge. M.A., Dublin (1773); called to Irish bar (1775). A Protestant, gained verdict for Roman Catholic priest against nobleman on charge of assault (1780). Member of Irish parliament (1783); spoke for Catholic emancipation, attacked ministerial bribery. Known chiefly for defense of leaders of insurrection of 1798; acquitted of implication in Robert Emmet's insurrection of 1803.

**Cur·rel′ly** (kŭ·rĕl′ĭ), **Charles Trick.** 1876–1957. Canadian archaeologist, b. in Exeter, Ontario. Educ. U. of Toronto. On staff of Egypt Exploration Fund (1902–09), and shared in important discoveries in the Sinai peninsula, including the tombs of Ahmose and Mentuhotep III. Director, Royal Ontario Museum of Archaeology, Toronto (from 1908), and professor of archaeology at U. of Toronto. Coauthor with Flinders Petrie of *Researches in Sinai;* author of *Abydos III.*

**Cur′rie** (kûr′ĭ), Sir **Arthur William.** 1875–1933. Canadian soldier and educator. Served in World War; commanded second Canadian infantry brigade (1914–15), first Canadian division (1915–17); general (1917) commanding the Canadian corps in France (1917–19). Principal of McGill U. (1920–33).

**Currie,** Sir **Donald.** 1825–1909. Scottish shipowner. Joined Cunard Line (1844–62); founded Castle line of sailing ships between Liverpool and Calcutta (1862), line between England and South Africa (1872); M.P. (1880), disagreed with Gladstone on home rule.

**Currie, James.** 1756–1805. Scottish physician and editor. Graduated in medicine at Glasgow (1780); practiced in Liverpool. Wrote pamphlet *Reports on the Effects of Water in Fever and Febrile Diseases* (1797); edited collected works of the poet Robert Burns for the benefit of Burns's family (1800).

**Currie, Mary Montgomerie,** *nee* **Lamb** (lăm). Baroness **Currie.** *Pseudonym* **Violet Fane** (fān). 1843–1905. English author; m. 1st (1864) Henry Sydenham Singleton; 2d (1894) Sir **Philip Henry Wodehouse Currie** (1834–1906), Baron **Currie,** diplomat, ambassador at Constantinople (1893), Rome (1898–1903). She wrote *Denzil Place; a Story in Verse* (1875) and verse, essays, and novels.

**Cur′ri·er** (kûr′ĭ·ẽr), **Nathaniel.** 1813–1888. American lithographer, b. Roxbury, Mass. Set up business in New York (about 1834). Issued (1835) lithograph drawn by one J. H. Bufford showing the *Ruins of the Merchants' Exchange,* first of series (now known as Currier and Ives prints) giving vivid picture of manners, outstanding events, and persons of the U.S. J. Merritt Ives was admitted to partnership (1857); all prints published by firm bore imprint Currier & Ives, after 1857.

**Cur′ry** (kûr′ĭ), **Arthur Mansfield.** 1866–1953. American musician, b. Chelsea, Mass. Choral and orchestral conductor in Boston; teacher, New England Conservatory of Music. Composer of an overture, symphonic poem (*Atala*), and choral works.

**Curry, Jabez Lamar Monroe.** 1825–1903. American educator, b. in Lincoln County, Ga. Grad. U. of Georgia (1843). Member, U.S. House of Representatives (1857–61); Confederate congress (1861–63; 1864). In Confederate army (1864–65). President, Howard College, Ala. (1865–68). U.S. minister to Spain (1885–88; 1902). Agent of the Peabody Fund, donated for public education through the South (from 1881); also, agent of the Slater Fund, for establishment of Negro schools through the South (from 1890). Supervising director, Southern Education Board (from 1901).

**Curry, John Steuart.** 1897–1946. American painter, b. Dunavant, Kans. Artist in residence, Coll. of Agric., U. of Wisconsin (from 1936). Painted murals for U.S. Department of Justice building and U.S. Department of Interior building in Washington, D.C.; commissioned to do series of murals for the State Capitol, Topeka, Kans.

**Cur′tin** (kûr′tĭn), **Jeremiah.** 1840?–1906. American folklorist, b. Greenfield, Wis. Grad. Harvard (1863). Studied in Russia and eastern Europe (1864–70). With Smithsonian Institution, Washington, D.C. (1883–91); investigated North American Indian tongues. Author of *Myths and Folk-Tales of the Russians, Western Slavs and Magyars* (1890), *Creation Myths of Primitive America* (1898), *Myths of the Modocs* (1912), and translations of Tolstoi, Sienkiewicz, and others.

**Curtin, John.** 1885–1945. Australian politician, b. Creswick, Victoria; editor, *Westralian Worker* (1917–28); Australian delegate to International Labor Conference, Geneva (1924); member (1923–31; 1934–41), and leader of opposition (1935–41), Commonwealth Parliament; prime minister of Australia (1941–45).

**Cur′tis** (kûr′tĭs), **Benjamin Robbins.** 1809–1874. Bro. of George Ticknor Curtis. American jurist, b. Watertown, Mass. Grad. Harvard (1829). Associate justice, U.S. Supreme Court (1851–57). One of Andrew Johnson's counsel during impeachment trial (1868).

**Curtis, Charles.** 1860–1936. Thirty-first vice-president of the United States, b. in N. Topeka, Kans. Adm. to bar (1881) and practiced in Topeka. Member, U.S. House of Representatives (1893–1907), U.S. Senate (1907–13, 1915–29). Vice-president of United States (1929–33).

**Curtis, Charles Gordon.** 1860–1953. American inventor, b. Boston, Mass. C.E. (1881) and LL.B. (1883), Columbia. Patent lawyer for eight years; invented a steam turbine widely used in electric power plants and in marine propulsion.

**Curtis, Cyrus Hermann Kotzsch′mar** (kŏch′mär). 1850–1933. American publisher, b. Portland, Me. Moved to Philadelphia (1876) and established *Ladies' Home Journal;* head of Curtis Publishing Co., publishers of *Ladies' Home Journal, The Country Gentleman, Saturday Evening Post;* succeeded by son-in-law Edward William Bok (*q.v.*). Bought Philadelphia *Public Ledger* (1913) and New York *Evening Post* (1923).

**Curtis, Edward S.** 1868–1952. American photographer and writer on Indians, b. Madison, Wis. Author of *North American Indian* (1907–11), *Indian Days of the Long Ago* (1914), and *In the Land of the Head Hunters* (1915).

**Curtis, George Carroll.** 1872–1926. American geographic sculptor, b. Abington, Mass. B.S. (1896) and graduate student of physiography and geographic modeling, Harvard. First to apply aerial perspective to topographical models; made model of Washington, D.C. (1902). Represented National Geographic Society on Dixie expedition to West Indian eruptions; first to reach crater of La Soufrière; discovered new summit of Mt. Pelée; made relief landscape paintings of Yosemite, Grand Canyon, etc.

**Curtis, George Ticknor.** 1812–1894. Bro. of Benjamin R. Curtis. American lawyer, b. Watertown, Mass. Grad. Harvard (1832). In addition to legal works, he published *History of the Origin, Formation, and Adoption of the Constitution of the United States* (2 vols., 1854–58), *Life of Daniel Webster* (2 vols., 1870), *Life of James Buchanan* (2 vols., 1883), etc.

**Curtis, George William.** 1824–1892. American man of letters, b. Providence, R.I. In Brook Farm community (1842–43). As editorial writer in *Harper's Magazine* (*The Easy Chair*), as editor of *Harper's Weekly* (from 1863), and as lecturer, strongly influenced opinions of his day. Author of *Nile Notes of a Howadji* (1851), *Lotus-Eating* (1852), *Potiphar Papers* (1853), *Prue and I* (1857), *Trumps* (1861), *Orations and Addresses* (edited by Charles Eliot Norton; 3 vols., 1893–94).

**Curtis, Heber Doust.** 1872–1942. American astrophysicist, b. Muskegon, Mich. A.B., Michigan (1892); Ph.D., Virginia (1902). Astronomer (1909–20), Lick Observatory, U. of California; in charge of D. O. Mills expedition to the Southern Hemisphere (1906–09); director, Allegheny Observatory, U. of Pittsburgh (1920–30); director, U. of Michigan observatories (from 1930). Special editor for astrophysics, *Webster's New International Dictionary, Second Edition.*

**Curtis, William.** 1746–1799. English botanist and entomologist.

**Cur'tiss** (kûr'tĭs), **Glenn Hammond.** 1878–1930. American inventor and aviator, b. Hammondsport, N.Y. Educ. in public schools. Established motorcycle factory, Hammondsport (1902); set motorcycle speed records (1905, 1907); designed motors for dirigibles (1907–09); won trophy for first public airplane flight of a mile in U.S. (1908); won cup at international aviation meet, Reims, France (1909) with airplane and motor of his own design; won New York *World's* $10,000 prize for flight from Albany to New York in 2 hours, 51 minutes (1910); after several years of experiment, demonstrated hydroplane (1911) and flying boat (1912). Established aviation schools at Hammondsport, San Diego, Buffalo, Miami, etc. (1909–19); expanded his factories to supply U.S., British, and Russian demands in World War; developed the "Wasp," Navy-Curtiss (NC) flying boat that made the first Atlantic crossing (1919), and other aircraft, motors, scooters, speedboats, etc.

**Cur'ti·us** (ko͝or'tsē·o͝os), **Ernst.** 1814–1896. German classical philologist and archaeologist. In Greece (1836–40); professor, Berlin (1844), Göttingen (1856), again Berlin (1868); directed German excavation of Olympia, Greece (1875–81) and, with Adler, published official report of work. His brother **Georg** (1820–1885), also a classical philologist; professor, Prague (1849), Kiel (1854), Leipzig (1862).

**Curtius, Ernst Robert.** 1886–1956. German historian of literature, b. in Alsace. Professor of French, Bonn (1919, from 1929), Marburg (1920), Heidelberg (1924). Author of *Balzac* (1923), *Französischer Geist im Neuen Europa* (1925), *James Joyce* (1929), etc.

**Curtius, Julius.** 1877–1948. German statesman. Army officer on western front during World War (1914–18). Elected to Reichstag (1920–32) as representative of German People's party; minister of economic affairs (1926–29); invited by von Hindenburg to form a ministry (Jan., 1927), but failed; on Stresemann's death (Oct., 1929), succeeded him as minister of foreign affairs, and represented Germany at Hague conference (1929–30); retired (1932).

**Cur'ti·us** (kûr'shĭ·ŭs), **Marcus** *or* **Mettus.** Legendary Roman hero of 4th century B.C. According to the story, when a great crack was opened through the Forum by an earthquake and a soothsayer proclaimed it could be closed only by sacrifice of Rome's greatest treasure, Curtius, believing the city possessed no greater treasure than a brave man, leaped on his horse and in full armor rode into the chasm, which thereupon closed.

**Cur'ti·us** (ko͝or'tsē·o͝os), **Theodor.** 1857–1928. German chemist; professor, Heidelberg (from 1897); known for organic syntheses from diazo derivatives of the fatty series; discovered hydrazine (1887).

**Cur'ti·us Ru'fus** (kûr'shĭ·ŭs ro͞o'fŭs), **Quintus.** fl. 1st century A.D. Latin biographer of Alexander the Great, in ten books, of which the first two have been lost, and the remaining eight are incomplete.

**Cur'wen** (kûr'wĕn), **John.** 1816–1880. English founder of tonic sol-fa system of musical teaching, adapted from system devised by Sarah Ann Glover. His son **John Spencer** (1847–1916), principal of Tonic Sol-Fa Coll., continued to promulgate the system.

**Cur'wood** (kûr'wo͝od), **James Oliver.** 1878–1927. American novelist, b. Owosso, Mich. Author esp. of stories of adventure in the American northwest, as *The Courage of Captain Plum* (1908), *Kazan* (1914), *The Grizzly King* (1916), *Nomads of the North* (1919), *A Gentleman of Courage* (1924), *The Black Hunter* (1926).

**Cur'zon** (kûr'z'n), **George Nathaniel.** 1st Baron and 1st Marquis **Curzon of Ked'le·ston** (kĕd''l·stŭn; kĕl'stŭn). 1859–1925. English statesman. Grad. and fellow of Oxford; Conservative M.P. (1885); traveled widely in Asia; undersecretary of state for India (1891–92), for foreign affairs (1895–98). Viceroy and governor general of India (1899–1905); stabilized financial relations between provinces and the government, reduced salt tax, executed reforms; resigned as result of disagreement with Lord Kitchener. As chancellor of Oxford U. (1907), inaugurated constitutional reforms; member House of Lords (1908); created earl (1911), marquis (1921). Lord privy seal in Asquith's cabinet (1915); president of air board (1916); one of four ministers composing the war cabinet. Secretary of state for foreign affairs (1919–24); submitted to dominance of diplomacy by Lloyd George (till 1922); obtained suspension of Russian anti-British action and propaganda in Asia (1923); condemned French expedition into Ruhr (1922–23) and gained approval of advisory committee of experts (later the Dawes committee); leader of House of Lords (1916–24). Received gold medal of Royal Geographical Society (1925). Author of *Russia in Central Asia* (1889), *Problems of the Far East* (1894), *Lord Curzon in India* (1906), etc.

**Cush'en·dun** (ko͝osh'ĕn·dŭn), 1st Baron. **Ronald John McNeill.** 1861–1934. British editor and statesman, b. in County Antrim, Ireland. Educ. Oxford U. Called to the bar (1887). Editor (1900–04), *St. James's Gazette;* assistant editor, eleventh edition of *Encyclopaedia Britannica* (1906–11). M.P. (1911–27); financial secretary to the treasury (1925–27); chancellor of the duchy of Lancaster (1927–29); acting secretary of state for foreign affairs (1928). Author of *Home Rule...* (1907), *Socialism* (1908), *Ulster's Stand for Union* (1922), etc. Created baron (1927).

**Cush'ing** (ko͝osh'ĭng), **Caleb.** 1800–1879. American lawyer and diplomat, b. Salisbury, Mass. Grad. Harvard (1817). Member, U.S. House of Representatives (1835–43). Special U.S. envoy to China (1843–45); negotiated Treaty of Wanghsia (1844) opening five Chinese ports to American trade. U.S. attorney general (1853–57). Chairman, committee to codify U.S. statutes (1866–70). Senior counsel for the U.S. before the tribunal of arbitration to settle Alabama claims (1872). Nominated chief justice, U.S. Supreme Court, but not confirmed by U.S. Senate. U.S. minister to Spain (1874–77).

**Cushing, Frank Hamilton.** 1857–1900. American ethnologist, b. North East, Pa. In Bureau of American Ethnology (from 1879). Studied, and lived for five years among, the Zuñi Pueblo Indians of New Mexico. Author of *Zuñi Creation Myths* (1896), *Zuñi Folk Tales* (1901).

**Cushing, Harvey.** 1869–1939. American surgeon, b. Cleveland, Ohio. A.B., Yale (1891); M.D., Harvard (1895). Practiced in Boston; eminent as specialist in brain surgery. Served in army medical corps in World War. Author of *The Pituitary Body and Its Disorders* (1912), *The Life of Sir William Osler* (awarded Pulitzer prize; 1925), *Consecratio Medici and other Essays* (1928), *Intracranial Tumours* (1932), *From a Surgeon's Journal, 1915–1918* (1936), etc.

**Cushing, Luther Stearns.** 1803–1856. American jurist, b. Lunenburg, Mass. Grad. Harvard (1826). Author of *A Manual of Parliamentary Practice* (1844), commonly called *Cushing's Manual.*

**Cushing, Richard James.** 1895–1970. Amer. Roman Catholic churchman, cardinal, b. Boston, Mass. Ordained (1921); archbishop of Boston (1944–70).

**Cushing, Thomas.** 1725–1788. American political leader, b. Boston. Grad. Harvard (1744). Member, Mass. General Court (1761–74). Member, Boston Committee of Correspondence (1773), Committee of Safety (1774), Continental Congress (1774–76).

**Cushing, William.** 1732–1810. American jurist, b. Scituate, Mass. Grad. Harvard (1751). Chief justice, Mass. Supreme Court (1777). Associate justice, U.S. Supreme Court (1789–1810)

**Cushing, William Barker.** 1842–1874. American naval officer, b. Delafield, Wis. Noted for daring exploits, culminating in torpedoing of the Confederate ram *Albemarle* in the Roanoke River (Oct. 27, 1864).

**Cush′man** (kŏŏsh′măn), **Allerton Seward.** 1867–1930. American chemist. b. Rome, Italy. Founder and director (1910–24), Inst. of Industrial Research, Washington, D.C. Known for work on preparation of potash from feldspathic rocks, use of ground rock as fertilizer, and corrosion and preservation of iron and steel.

**Cushman, Charlotte Saunders.** 1816–1876. American actress, b. Boston, Mass. On stage from 1835–1858. In England (1845–49). On tour in U.S. (1849–52). Elected to American Hall of Fame (1915).

**Cushman, Robert.** 1579?–1625. English agent of the Plymouth colony, b. Canterbury, Eng. In Holland (about 1609) joined Pilgrim church at Leiden. Made financial arrangements with English merchants for prospective colony; organized group sailing direct from England on the *Mayflower*. Served in England as agent of the Pilgrims (1620–25).

**Cush′ny** (kŭsh′nĭ), **Arthur Robertson.** 1866–1926. Physician and pharmacologist, b. Moray, Scotland. Professor, U. of Michigan (1893–1905), London, Eng. (1905–18), Edinburgh (1918–26).

**Cu′sins** (kū′zĭnz), Sir **William George.** 1833–1893. English composer of *Royal Wedding Serenata* (1863), the oratorio *Gideon* (1871), and instrumental and chamber music.

**Cust** (kŭst), Sir **Edward.** 1794–1878. English military historian. 6th son of Sir **Brownlow Cust** (1744–1807), 1st Baron **Brown′low** (broun′lō). Brother of **John Cust,** 1st Earl Brownlow. Grandson of Sir **John Cust** (1718–1770), speaker of House of Commons (1761, 1768–70). Fought through Peninsular War; master of ceremonies to Queen Victoria (1847); general (1866); author of *Annals of the Wars of the Eighteenth Century.* His nephew **Robert Needham Cust** (1821–1909), Orientalist and Africanist; Indian civil servant, served in Sikh wars and pacification of Punjab after Sepoy Mutiny of 1858, retiring 1867; author of sixty-odd volumes on philology of the East Indies (1878) of Africa (1882), of Oceania, also seven series of linguistic essays (1880–1904). Robert's son **Robert Henry Hobart** (1861–1940), M.A., Cantab. (1887), alderman (from 1935) of Hampstead Borough, wrote studies in Italian painting, translated Cellini's autobiography. **Henry John Cockayne Cust** (1861–1917), journalist; nephew of Robert Needham and great-grandson of 1st Baron Brownlow; B.A., Cantab.; Unionist M.P. (1890); editor of *Pall Mall Gazette* (1892–96); founder of Central Committee for National Patriotic Organizations (1914). Sir **Lionel Henry Cust** (1859–1929), art critic; first cousin of Henry J. C. Cust; as assistant in department of prints and drawings in British Museum (1884), prepared invaluable indexes; director of National Portrait Gallery (1895–1909); surveyor of king's pictures (1901–27); author of studies of Van Dyck and Dürer, Eton College, and royal collections.

**Cus′ter** (kŭs′tẽr), **George Armstrong.** 1839–1876. American army officer, b. New Rumley, Ohio. Grad. U.S.M.A., West Point (1861). Served through Civil War. Engaged on western patrol duty and in Indian fighting (1867–76), esp. in expedition to Black Hills (1874); killed with all his immediate command in battle of Little Big Horn (June 25, 1876).

**Cus′tine′** (küs′tēn′), Comte **Adam Philippe de.** 1740–1793. French army officer; quartermaster general of the French troops in America (1780–83). Member of the States-General (1789). Commanded one of the Revolutionary armies (1792); captured Speyer (Sept. 29, 1792) and Mainz (Oct. 21, 1792); failed in campaign to relieve Mainz (1793) which had been recaptured by forces of the foreign coalition against France. Charged with conspiring with the enemy to bring about a counterrevolution; convicted; guillotined at Paris (Aug. 28, 1793).

**Cus′tis** (kŭs′tĭs). Family name of descendants of Martha Washington (*q.v.*) by her first husband, Daniel Parke Custis; esp. **George Washington Parke Custis** (1781–1857), playwright, b. Mount Airy, Md., and his daughter **Mary,** wife of Robert E. Lee.

**Cuth′bert** (kŭth′bẽrt), Saint. 635?–687. English monk. Entered monastery of Melrose (651); prior (661); retired (676) to a hermit's cell on island of Farne. Bishop of Hexham (684), of Lindisfarne (685) in exchange; retired to Farne to his cell (687). His body, believed to work miracles, was transferred to Durham Cathedral (1104).

**Cut′ler** (kŭt′lẽr), **Manasseh.** 1742–1823. American Congregational clergyman, botanist, and pioneer, b. Killingly, Conn. Grad. Yale (1765). Pastor at Ipswich Hamlet (now Hamilton), Mass. (1771–1823). Prepared account of flora of New England, classified by Linnaean method. One of organizers of Ohio Company, for colonizing lands in Ohio River Valley (1786); assisted in drafting the ordinance of 1787 for government of Northwest Territory; obtained grant of area near what is now Marietta.

**Cutler, Timothy.** 1684–1765. American clergyman, b. Charlestown, Mass. Grad. Harvard (1701). Rector, Yale College (1719–22). Ordained in Church of England (1723); rector, Christ Church, Boston (1723–65).

**Cutpurse, Moll.** See Mary FRITH.

**Cut′ten** (kŭt′'n), **George Barton.** 1874–1962. Educator, b. Amherst, Nova Scotia. B.A. (1897), Ph.D. (1902), B.D. (1903), Yale. President of Acadia U., Nova Scotia (1910–22), and Colgate (1922–42).

**Cut′ter** (kŭt′ẽr), **Charles Ammi.** 1837–1903. American librarian, b. Boston. Grad. Harvard (1855). Librarian, Boston Athenaeum (1868–93). Interested in development of new Forbes Library, Northampton, Mass. (from 1894). Originated system of labeling books by initial letters and numbers to represent authors' names. Published *Catalogue of the Library of the Boston Athenaeum* (5 vols., 1874–82), *Rules for a Printed Dictionary Catalogue* (1875), *Expansive Classification* (1891–1904).

**Cutter, George Washington.** 1801–1865. American poet, b. Quebec, Canada. Author of *Buena Vista and Other Poems* (1848), etc.

**Cutts** (kŭts), **John.** Baron **Cutts** of Gowran, in Ireland. 1661–1707. English soldier; fought for William III in Revolution of 1688, and distinguished himself at the Boyne (1690); hero of siege of Namur (1695); served under Marlborough in Low Countries (1701); third in command at Blenheim (1704); commander in chief in Ireland (1705).

**Cu′vier′** (kü′vyā′; *Angl.* kū′vĭ·ā, kōō′vĭ·ā), Baron **Georges Léopold Chrétien Frédéric Dagobert.** 1769–1832. French naturalist, b. Montbéliard. Called founder of comparative anatomy and, sometimes, of paleontology. Educ. at home and at the academy of Stuttgart. Tutor in family of comte d'Héricy, near Caen; assistant at Jardin des Plantes, Paris (1795); lecturer, École Centrale du Panthéon (1796); professor of natural history, Collège de France (1799); titular professor, Jardin des Plantes (1802). Originated natural system of animal classification (recognizing four distinct branches or phyla), introduced in his *Tableau Élémentaire de l'Histoire Naturelle des Animaux* (1798); investigated comparative anatomy of fishes and osteology of mammals; published *Leçons d'Anatomie Comparée* (5 vols., 1800–05; assisted by A. M. C. Duméril in first two and by G. L. Duvernoy in last three); studied fossil mammals and reptiles; published his first work on paleontology, *Mémoires sur les Espèces d'Éléphants Vivants et Fossiles* (1800). Inspector of education (1802); appointed to council of Imperial U. by Napoleon (1808); councilor of state (1814); chancellor of U. of Paris; president, committee of the interior (1819); also held other positions with the government and with U. of Paris. His brother **Frédéric** (1773–1838), also a naturalist, was professor at the Jardin des Plantes.

**Cu'vil'les'** (kü'vē'yā') *or* **Cu'vil'liés'** (kü'vē'yā'), **François de.** 1698–1767. French architect to elector of Bavaria (1738), and later to Emperor Charles VII at Munich, where he was succeeded by his son **François** (1731–1777).

**Cuyp** *or* **Kuyp** (koip), **Jacob Gerritsz.** 1594–?1651. Dutch portrait painter. His son **Albert** (1620?–1691), also a painter, esp. of landscapes with figures, as in *Riders with the Boy and Herdsman* (in National Gallery, London) and *Piper with Cows* (in the Louvre).

**Cuy'pers** (koi'pērs), **Petrus Josephus Hubertus.** 1827–1921. Dutch architect; designed churches in early Gothic style, and the Rijks Museum in Amsterdam; restored Mainz cathedral.

**Cu'za** (kōō'zä), **Alexandru Ioan.** 1820–1873. Prince of Rumania (1859–66), b. Huşi. Took part in revolution at Jassy (1848); arrested but later made prefect of Galatz (1850). Elected prince of Moldavia and Walachia; recognized by Turkey as ruler of united principalities; took title of Prince Alexandru Ioan I; failed as administrator; forced to abdicate; succeeded by Carol I (*q.v.*).

**Cvi'jić** (tsvē'yĕt·y'; *Angl.* -yĭch), **Jovan.** 1865–1927. Serbian geographer; professor, Belgrade (from 1893). Founder and head of Serbian Geographic Society.

**Cy·ax'a·res** (sī·ăk'sȧ·rēz). d. about 585 B.C. King of Media (625–585 B.C.). Son of Phraortes and grandson of Deïoces. Established Median independence; defeated by Scythians; subject to them for many years. Joined with Nabopolassar of Chaldea and destroyed Nineveh (612); subdued countries of northern Mesopotamia (Armenia); moved boundaries westward to the Halys (Kizil Irmak); engaged in long war with Lydia (590–585), date determined by eclipse visible on the Halys (585). Father of Astyages (*q.v.*).

**Cyg·nä'us** (*Finn.* süg·nä'ōōs; *Swed.* süng·nā'ŭs), **Fredrik.** 1807–1881. Finnish writer in Swedish; professor of aesthetics and modern literature, Helsingfors (1854–67); his verse was collected in six volumes, *Samlade Dikter* (1851–70). His brother **U'no** [ōō'nŏ] (1810–1888), clergyman and educator; chief inspector, Finnish public-school system (1861); introduced manual training for first time in a public-school system.

**Cy'lon** (sī'lŏn). Athenian statesman of 7th century B.C.; m. daughter of Theagenes, tyrant of Megara; in an attempt to make himself tyrant of Athens, raised a revolt, which was crushed.

**Cymbeline.** See CUNOBELINUS.

**Cyn'e·wulf** (kĭn'ĕ·wōōlf; *A.-S.* kün'ĕ-) *or* **Cyn'wulf** (kĭn'wōōlf) *or* **Kyn'e·wulf.** fl. 750. Anglo-Saxon poet. Probably a Northumbrian minstrel; Latin scholar, familiar with religious literature. Author of four poems preserved in Exeter codex and Vercelli codex (both of 11th century), namely *Juliana, Elene, The Ascension, The Fates of the Apostles,* into the epilogues of which the poet wove "Cynewulf" or "Cynwulf" in runic characters. By some credited with authorship of various other poems, including three poems known as the *Christ,* two poems on *St. Guthlac, Andreas,* and *The Dream of the Rood.*

**Cynewulf.** d. 785. King of West Saxons (from 757). Warred against Welsh; defeated by Offa (779); slain by Cyneheard (brother of Sigebert, King of the West Saxons, whom Cynewulf had deposed) and his followers.

**Cyn'thi·us** (sĭn'thĭ·ŭs). *Ital.* **Cin'zio** (chēn'tsyō), *older* **Cin'tio** (chēn'tyō) *or* **Cin'thio** (chēn'tyō). *Academic name of* **Giovanni Battista Gi·ral'di** (jē·räl'dē). 1504–1573. Italian writer; professor of natural philosophy, U. of Ferrara (1525 ff.); secretary of state under Ercole d'Este II and Alfonso II of Ferrara. Among his works are tragedies, and a collection of tales, *Gli Hecatommithi* (1565), known esp. as source material for Shakespeare's *Othello* and *Measure for Measure,* and for several of the plays of Beaumont and Fletcher.

**Cyon** (syôN), **Élie de.** 1843–1912. Russian physiologist. Professor at St. Petersburg Acad. of Medicine (1870); to Paris (1877). Known esp. for work on the vasomotor nerves of the heart.

**Cyp'ri·an** (sĭp'rĭ·ăn), Saint. *In full* **Thascius Caecilius Cyp'ri·a'nus** (sĭp'rĭ·ā'nŭs). Christian martyr of 3d century; bishop of Carthage (from 248 A.D.); beheaded at Carthage (258).

**Cyp'se·lus** (sĭp'sē·lŭs). Greek politician of 7th century B.C.; tyrant of Corinth (655?–625 B.C.).

**Cy'ra'no' de Ber'ge·rac'** (sē'rȧ'nō' dē bĕr'zhē·rȧk'), **Savinien de.** 1619–1655. French poet and soldier; served in the army (1637–40) but was forced to end his military career after being severely wounded; joined the household of the duc d'Arpajon (1653); famous as a duelist. Reputed pupil of Gassendi; influenced by him in direction of free-thinking. Author of *Le Pédant Joué* (a comedy, 1654), *La Mort d'Agrippine* (a tragedy, 1654), *Histoire Comique des États et Empires de la Lune* (1656), *Histoire Comique des États et Empires du Soleil* (1662). Rostand's tragedy *Cyrano de Bergerac* takes its name from this 17th-century soldier-poet, though the plot has little foundation in Cyrano's life.

**Cyrenius.** See QUIRINUS.

**Cy·ri'a·cus of An·co'na** (sĭ·rĭ'ȧ·kŭs, ăng·kō'nȧ). *Lat.* **Ci·ri'a·cus An·co'ni·ta'nus** (sĭ·rĭ'ȧ·kŭs ăng·kō'nĭ-tā'nŭs). *Real name* **Ci·ri'a·co de' Piz'zi·col'li** (chē·rē'ä·kō dā pēt'tsē·kôl'lē). 1391–after 1449. Italian humanist and antiquarian; in guise of itinerant trader, traveled in Egypt, Syria, Aegean Islands, and Greece, collecting manuscripts, coins, works of art, making copies of inscriptions, and noting all evidences of the life of ancient Greece, thus accumulating in diaries and commentaries a vast amount of material of great value to later scholars.

**Cyr'il** (sĭr'ĭl) of Jerusalem, Saint. 315?–386 A.D. Roman Catholic ecclesiastic; a doctor of the church. Bishop of Jerusalem (350 A.D.); opposed Arian heresy, and was deposed from his bishopric (357). Continued to defend orthodoxy, and was restored to his see (c. 379).

**Cyr'il** (sĭr'ĭl) of Alexandria, Saint. 376–444 A.D. Early Roman Catholic ecclesiastic; a doctor of the church; archbishop of Alexandria (412 A.D.). Vigorously defended orthodoxy; persecuted Novatians; expelled Jews from Alexandria; opposed the Nestorians; presided over the Council of Ephesus (431) at which Nestorius was condemned as a heretic.

**Cyril,** Saint. *Secular name* **Constantine.** 827–869 A.D. Apostle to the Slavs, b. in Thessalonica. With his brother Saint **Me·tho'di·us** [mē·thō'dĭ·ŭs] (826–885), preached the gospel to the Khazar and later to the Moravians; reputed to have invented the Cyrillic alphabet and translated the gospels and liturgical books into Old Slavonic.

**Cyril.** *Russ.* **Ki·rill' Vla·di'mi·ro·vich** (kyĭ·ryēl' vlŭ·dyē'myĭ·rŭ·vyĭch). 1876–1938. Russian grand duke; nephew of Czar Alexander III and cousin of Nicholas II. After Russian Revolution (1917), forced to flee from Russia; lived an exile in Paris; recognized as head of house of Romanov and claimant to Russian throne.

**Cyrinus.** See QUIRINUS.

**Cy'rus** (sī'rŭs). *Called* "the Great" *or* "the Elder." 600?–529 B.C. King of Persia (550–529 B.C.) and founder of Persian Empire. Son of Cambyses (I) and father of Cambyses (II). One of the Achaemenidae; king of Anshan (from 558), of the Medes and Persians (from 550), and of Babylon (from 539). Led expedition of Persians against Astyages, King of Media; took him prisoner (550); strengthened kingdom with Susa as capital (550–547); overthrew Croesus and his kingdom of Lydia (547–546); successful in conquest of Babylon (540–539) and seized its king, Nabonidus (*q.v.*); delivered Jews from their captivity and allowed them to return to Palestine; killed in fighting the Massagetae, a savage tribe east of the Caspian. See HARPAGUS.

**Cyrus** the Younger. 424?–401 B.C. Persian prince and satrap. Younger son of Darius Nothus and brother of Artaxerxes II. Satrap of Asia Minor (407); conspired (401) against his brother, the king; led great army of Asiatics and about 13,000 Greek mercenaries from Sardis to Babylonia; met at Cunaxa by Artaxerxes, defeated, and killed; battle resulted in famous retreat (401–399) of 10,000 Greeks under Xenophon (*q.v.*), described in Xenophon's *Anabasis.*

**Cyzicenus.** See ANTIOCHUS IX of Syria.

**Czaj·kow'ski** (chī·kôf'skē), **Michał.** 1808–1886. Polish revolutionist, adventurer, and writer, b. in Ukraine. Involved in rebellion against Russia, fled to Paris (1831). On mission to Turkey (1840 ff.); adopted Mohammedan faith (1851) and, as **Sa·dyk' Pa·sha'** (sä·dĭk' pä·shä'), commanded a force of Turks in war against Russia (1853–54). Converted to Greek Church, and granted amnesty by Russia (1873); settled in Kiev. Author of tales of Cossack and Ukrainian life.

**Czar'to·rys'ki** (chär'tô·rĭs'kē). Polish-Lithuanian noble family, including: Prince **Fryderyk Michał** (1696–1775), Polish statesman under Stanisław Poniatowski; exercised determining influence on Polish policy during reign of Augustus III of Saxony (1734–63). Prince **Adam Kazimierz** (1734–1823), unsuccessful candidate for Polish throne at death of Augustus III of Saxony (1763). Adam's daughter Princess **Marya** (1768–1854), Duchess of **Würt'tem·berg** (vür'tĕm·bĕrк), novelist; author of *Malvina, or the Heart Guesses Quickly.* Adam's son Prince **Adam Jerzy** (1770–1861), Polish general and statesman; president of Polish provisional government (1830) and national government (1831); forced to take refuge in France after Russia crushed Polish state.

**Czer'mak** (chĕr'mäk), **Johann Ne'po·muk** (nā'pô·mo͝ok). 1828–1873. Bohemian physiologist; professor, Budapest (1858), Jena (1865), Leipzig (1869); at own expense, built laboratory and auditorium adapted for experimental physiology demonstrations; improved upon the laryngoscope; did pioneer work in rhinoscopy. His brother **Ja'ro·slaw** [yä'rô·släf] (1831–1878), painter, esp. of scenes from Bohemian history, pictures of Slavic life, and north Balkan landscapes.

**Czer'nin von und zu Chu'de·nitz** (chĕr'nēn fôn o͝ont tso͞o ко͞o'dĕ·nĭts), Count **Ottokar.** 1872–1932. Austro-Hungarian statesman, of noble Bohemian descent. Member of Bohemian diet (1903) and of Austrian upper chamber (from 1912). As Austro-Hungarian minister to Rumania (1913), endeavored to prevent Rumania entering World War I; on return to Vienna, served as minister of foreign affairs (1916–18); delegate of democratic party to Austrian legislature (1920–23). Author of *Im Weltkriege* (1919).

**Czer'ny** (chĕr'nē), **Karl.** 1791–1857. Austrian pianist and composer; noted piano teacher, master of Liszt, Thalberg, Kullak, and others. His best-known works are his piano exercises, as in *The School of Fingering, The School of Velocity, The School of Virtuosity.*

**Czer'ny** (chĕr'nē), **Vin'cenz** (vĭn'tsĕnts). 1842–1916. Bohemian surgeon; professor, Heidelberg (1877); director of institute for cancer research (1906).

**Czerny Djordje.** See KARAGEORGE.

**Czol'gosz** (chôl'gôsh), **Leon.** 1873–1901. Assassin of William McKinley (*q.v.*).

**Czu'czor** (tso͞o'tsôr), **Gergely.** 1800–1866. Hungarian poet.

# D

☞ **d', da, dal, de, de', degli, dei, del, de l', de la, de las, dell', della, delle, de los, der, des, di, di', do, du.** Many names containing one of these elements will be found at that part of the name following the element.

**D'Ab'er·non** (dăb'ĕr·nŭn), 1st Viscount. **Edgar Vin'·cent** (vĭn's'nt). 1857–1941. English financier. Financial adviser to Egyptian government (1883–89); governor, Imperial Ottoman Bank, Constantinople (1889–97). Head of British economic mission to Argentina and Brazil (1929).

**Da'blon'** (dȧ'blôɴ'), **Claude.** 1618–1697. French Jesuit missionary in America; superior of Canadian missions (1671–80; 1686–93); named Marquette to accompany Jolliet on his exploration of the Mississippi.

**Dab'ney** (dăb'nĭ), **Charles William.** 1855–1945. American educator, b. Hampden Sydney, Va. Director, North Carolina Agricultural Experiment Station (1880–87). President, U. of Tennessee (1887–1904), U. of Cincinnati (1904–20). Discoverer of phosphate deposits and tin ore in North Carolina.

**Da'bo** (dä'bō), **Leon.** 1868–1960. American muralist and landscape painter, b. Detroit, Mich.; studio in Paris; executed murals (*The Ascension, The Life of Christ*) for church of St. John the Baptist in Brooklyn and friezes in history rooms of Flower Memorial Library in Watertown, N.Y.

**Dąbrowski, Jan Henryk.** See DOMBROWSKI.

**Dach** (däκ), **Simon.** 1605–1659. German lyric poet; member of the Königsberg group of poets, including Heinrich Albert.

**Da'cier'** (dȧ'syā'), **André.** 1651–1722. French classical scholar; translator of Horace, Aristotle, Plato, Epictetus, Plutarch, Sophocles. His wife (m. 1683), **Anne,** *nee* **Le·feb'vre** [lĕ·fâ'vr'] (1654–1720), was also a classical scholar; translated the *Iliad* and the *Odyssey.*

**Da Cos'ta** (dȧ kŏs'tȧ), **Izaak.** 1798–1860. Dutch Protestant theologian and poet; author of *Prometheus* (1820), *Feestliederen* (1828), *Hagar* (1840), etc.

**Da'cres** (dā'kẽrz), **James Richard.** 1788–1853. British naval officer; surrendered the *Guerrière* after fight with the U.S.S. *Constitution* (1811).

**D'A·cu'nha** *or* **da Cu'nha** (dȧ·kōō'nyȧ), **Tristão.** = Tristão da CUNHA.

**Da'du** (dä'dōō). 1544–1603. Hindu religious reformer and poet, b. Ahmadabad. Founder of the Dadupanthis, a Vaishnava sect, specially numerous in Rajputana; author of a long devotional poem.

**Daen'dels** (dän'dĕls), **Herman Willem.** 1762–1818. Dutch soldier; joined French Revolutionary army (1793). Lieutenant general in Batavian Republic army, opposed Anglo-Russian invasion (1799). Entered service of king of Holland (1806); created marshal (1806) and governor general of Dutch East Indies; governor of Dutch possessions on African Gold Coast (1814).

**Da'foe** (dā'fō), **Allan Roy.** 1883–1943. Canadian physician; M.D., Toronto (1907); practiced in Callander, Ontario, where he successfully delivered the Dionne quintuplets (May 28, 1934); author of *Dr. Dafoe's Guide Book for Mothers* (1936).

**Dafoe, John Wesley.** 1866–1944. Canadian journalist; editor in chief, Winnipeg *Free Press* (from 1901). Chancellor, U. of Manitoba (from 1934).

**Da'fydd** (dȧ'vĭth). Welsh form of DAVID.

**Da'gnan'-Bou've·ret'** (dȧ'nyäN'bōō'vrĕ'), **Pascal Adolphe Jean.** 1852–1929. French painter; among his canvases are *Un Accident, Le Pain Bénit, La Cène.*

**Dag'o·bert** (dăg'ō·bẽrt). Name of three Merovingian kings: **Dagobert I,** King of all the Franks (629–639); **Dagobert II,** King of Austrasia (656–659, 676–679); **Dagobert III,** King of Neustria (711–715). See MEROVINGIAN.

**Dagonet.** Pseudonym of George Robert SIMS.

**Da'guerre'** (dȧ'gâr'), **Louis Jacques Mandé.** 1787–1851. French painter, inventor of the daguerreotype. Scene painter for the opera. With Bouton, founded the Diorama in Paris (1822); worked on the obtaining of permanent pictures on metal plates by the action of sunlight, collaborating with J. N. Niepce (*q.v.*) from 1829 until Niepce's death in 1833; continued alone, his work leading to the discovery of the daguerreotype process, communicated to the Academy of Sciences in 1839. Cf. William H. F. TALBOT.

**Daguesseau, Henri François.** See AGUESSEAU.

**Dahl** (däl), **Anders.** 18th-century Swedish botanist for whom the genus *Dahlia* is named; a pupil of Linnaeus.

**Dahl** (däl), **Hans.** 1849–1919. Norwegian-born landscape and genre painter in Germany.

**Dahl** (däl), **Johan Christian.** 1788–1857. Norwegian painter; best known for Norwegian landscapes.

**Dahl** (däl), **Michael.** 1656–1743. Swedish portrait painter in London (from 1688).

**Dahl** (*Dan.* dȧl) *or* **Dal** (*Russ.* dȧl'y'), **Vladimir Ivanovich.** 1801–1872. Russian physician and writer, of Danish origin; wrote short stories, essays, and a number of textbooks in botany, zoology, and biology; chief work, *Dictionary of the Living Russian Tongues* (1861–68).

**Dahl'berg** *or* **Dahl'bergh** (däl'bâr·y'), Count **Erik Jönsson.** 1625–1703. Swedish military engineer; director-general of fortifications (from 1676); gained title of "Vauban of Sweden."

**Dahl'gren** (däl'grān), **Fredrik August.** 1816–1895. Swedish poet; author of dialect songs and ballads and a few plays. His son **Erik Wilhelm** (1848–1934), director (1903–16) of royal library in Stockholm, published bibliographies and works on the history of geography.

**Dahl'gren** (dăl'grĕn), **John Adolphus Bernard.** 1809–1870. American naval officer, b. Philadelphia. On ordnance duty, Washington, D.C. (1847–63); reorganized and equipped navy ordnance yard, at Washington; devised (1851) a new 11-inch gun, known as Dahlgren gun. Chief of Bureau of Ordnance in addition to duties as commandant of ordnance yard (1862); rear admiral in Union navy (1862). On sea duty during Civil War (1862–65). Works include *The System of Boat Armament in the United States Navy* (1852), *Shells and Shell Guns* (1856).

**Dahl'gren** (däl'grān), **Karl Fredrik.** 1791–1844. Swedish clergyman; in Stockholm (from 1815). Author of nature lyrics, humorous verse, mock-heroic poems, etc.

**Dahl'mann** (däl'män), **Friedrich Christoph.** 1785–1860. German politician and historian; member of National Assembly at Frankfurt (1848–49) and of its committee designated to draw up a constitution. Among his works are *Geschichte von Dänemark* (3 vols., 1840–43) and *Geschichte der Französischen Revolution* (1845).

**Dahl'stier'na** (däl'shâr'nȧ), **Gunno.** *Orig. surname* **Eu·re'li·us** (ā·ōō·rā'lĭ·ŭs). 1661–1709. Swedish author of patriotic verse, including *Kungaskald* (1697), elegy on death of Charles XI, and *The Goth's Battle Song, concerning the King and Master Peter* (1701).

**Dahn** (dän), **Felix,** *in full* **Julius Sophus Felix.** 1834–1912. German historian, legal scholar, and poet; author of verse, novels, plays, and opera librettos; of legal works and historical works, including his masterpiece *Die Könige der Germanen* (20 vols., 1861–1911).

**Daigo II.** *Also* **Go-Dai·go** [gō·dī·gō] (see Go). 1287–1339. Japanese emperor (1318–39). Threw off domination of the court by retired emperors (1322); plotted against Hojos (1324); unsuccessful in civil war (1331–32); captured and exiled (1332–33); escaped and returned to throne; at first supported by Takauji; ruled briefly (1333–36); driven out of Kyoto by Takauji (1336); set up rival government south of Nara.

**Daim'ler** (dīm'lẽr), **Gottlieb.** 1834–1900. German engineer, inventor, and pioneer automobile manufacturer, b. in Württemberg. With Maybach (*q.v.*), established automobile research laboratory at Cannstatt; founded Daimler Motor Co. (1890) which produced the Mercedes automobile and which joined with Firma Benz & Co. to form Daimler-Benz & Co. (1926). Patented small high-speed internal combustion engine (Daimler engine) important in development of automobile (1887).

**Dain'ger·field** (dān'jẽr·fēld), **Elliott.** 1859–1932. American landscape and religious painter, b. Harpers Ferry, W.Va.; studio in New York.

**Da·ki'ki** *or* **Da·qī'qī** (dä·kē'kē), **Abu Mansur.** fl. c. 1000 A.D. Persian poet; author of odes and sonnets; predecessor of Firdausi.

**Da'kin** (dā'kĭn), **Henry Drysdale.** 1880–1952. English chemist; engaged in research at Herter Laboratory, New York City (1905–20); during World War, developed Dakin's solution for treating wounds; known for researches in biochemistry, esp. on enzymes; awarded Davy medal by Royal Society (1941). Coauthor of *Handbook of Chemical Antiseptics* (1917). See Alexis CARREL.

**Dal, Vladimir Ivanovich.** See DAHL.

**Da'la'dier'** (dȧ'lȧ'dyā'), **Édouard.** 1884–1970. French statesman, b. in southern France, son of a baker. Served in World War I (1914–18). Member, chamber of deputies (from 1919); friend and associate of Édouard Herriot; identified with Radical Socialists. After being member of several cabinets, became premier of France (1933; 1934, for only 11 days; 1938–40). Arrested after collapse of French defense (1940); liberated (1945).

**Da'lay'rac'** *or* **d'A'lay'rac'** (dȧ'lā'rȧk'), **Nicolas.** 1753–1809. French composer, esp. of light operas, as *Le Petit Souper* (1781), *Le Corsaire* (1783), *La Soirée Orageuse* (1790), *Maison à Vendre* (1800).

**d'Albe, Edmund Edward Fournier.** See FOURNIER D'ALBE.

**Dal'berg** (däl'bĕrk). Name of an ancient German noble family holding under Holy Roman Empire dignity of First Knight of the Empire, and including: **Karl Theodor Anton Maria von Dalberg** (1744–1817), last archbishop-elector of Mainz (from 1802); sought by alliance with Napoleon to save Germany from dissolution; on dissolution of empire, made grand duke of Frankfurt with increased territories (1810); on fall of Napoleon, stripped of all but archbishopric of Regensburg; patron of letters; friend of Goethe, Schiller, Wieland. His brother **Wolfgang Heribert von Dalberg** (1750–1806); first to stage Schiller's early plays; wrote plays and adaptations of Shakespeare. The latter's son Duc **Emmerich Joseph de Dalberg** (1773–1833); entered service of Napoleon, who made him duke and councilor of state (1810); attended Congress of Vienna with Talleyrand; state minister and peer of France (1815); ambassador to Turin (1816). See also 1st Baron ACTON.

**Dalberg-Acton, J. E. E.** See 1st Baron ACTON.

**D'Al'bert** (*Ger.* däl'bĕrt; *Eng.* dăl'bẽrt), **Eu·gen'** (oi·gān'). 1864–1932. Pianist and composer, b. Glasgow; court pianist to king of Saxony; gave concerts on the Continent and in U.S. (from 1883). Composer of operas, string quartets, and symphonies.

**Dal·bo'no** (däl·bô'nō), **Edoardo.** 1843–1915. Neapolitan painter; known esp. for Neapolitan scenes.

**Dalcroze, Émile Jaques-.** See JAQUES-DALCROZE.

**Dale** (dāl), **David.** 1739–1806. Scottish industrialist and philanthropist. Erected mill at New Lanark (1785), at first in partnership with Arkwright; sold mills to Robert Owen (1799), who married his daughter (1799); organized religious community of which he was chief minister.

**Dale,** Sir **Henry Hallett.** 1875–1968. English physiologist, b. London. Educ. Cambridge U., St. Bartholomew's Hospital, and University Coll., London. Director, Wellcome Physiological Research Laboratories (1904–14); director, National Institute for Medical Research, London. Awarded, with Otto Loewi, the 1936 Nobel prize in physiology and medicine for work relating to chemical transmission of nerve impulses. Secretary of Royal Society (1925–35), president (from 1940).

**Dale, Richard.** 1756–1826. American naval officer, b. in Norfolk County, Va. Joined British navy at outbreak of American Revolution, but quickly switched to colonial cause. On the *Bon Homme Richard* under John Paul Jones in battle with the *Serapis*. In merchant fleet (1783–94). Captain, U.S. navy (1794); retired (1802).

**Dale, Robert William.** 1829–1895. English Congregational minister and educational reformer; advocated disestablishment and secular education as only outcome of nonconformist principles.

**Dale,** Sir **Thomas.** d. 1619. Colonial administrator in America. Appointed marshal of Va.; arrived Va. (1611); found colonists lazy and insubordinate; placed them under martial law; published rigorous code (*Dale's Code*) and enforced its provisions, causing the years 1611–16 to be known as "five years of slavery"; acting governor of colony (1614–16). Returned to England (1616).

**d'Alembert, Jean Le Rond.** See ALEMBERT.

**Da·lén'** (dȧ·lān'), **Nils Gustaf.** 1869–1937. Swedish inventor; devised improvements in hot-air turbines, air compressors, and milking machines; invented method of dissolving acetylene in acetone and perfected a sun valve used for lighting unmanned beacons at sunset. Awarded 1912 Nobel prize in physics. Blinded as the result of an explosion during an experiment (1913).

**Dal·gar'no** (dăl·gär'nō), **George.** 1626?–1687. Scottish educator. Author of *Ars Signorum* (1661), an attempt at a philosophical language in which letters of the alphabet stand for ideas, and of *Didascalocophus* (1680), presenting a two-hand deaf-and-dumb alphabet.

**Dalhousie,** Earls and marquises of. See RAMSAY family.

**Da'li** (dä'lē), **Salvador.** 1904–   . Spanish painter, b. in Figueras, Catalonia. Associated with ultramodern schools, notably futurism, constructivism, cubism, abstract irrationalism, and surrealism; a leader of the surrealist school. His painting *Persistence of Memory*, a landscape with limp watches hanging over various objects in the picture, attracted much attention. Collaborator in scenarios of two surrealist motion pictures, *Le Chien Andalou* and *L'Âge d'Or;* author of *Babaoua*.

**Dalila.** See DELILAH.

**Da·lin'** (dȧ·lēn'), **Olof von.** 1708–1763. Swedish poet and historian; tutor (1751) to Crown Prince Gustav, who became King Gustav III; royal historiographer (1755). Among his works are the verse tragedy *Brynilda* (1738), comedy *Den Afundsjuke* (1738), epic *Swenska Friheten* (1742), various satires, fables, and lyrics; chief historical work was *Svea Rikes Historia* (3 vols., 1747–62). See Hedvig NORDENFLYCHT.

**Dall** (dôl), **William Healey.** 1845–1927. American naturalist, b. Boston. Studied under Louis Agassiz. Accompanied telegraph expedition to Alaska (1865–68); gathered zoological specimens; published *Alaska and Its Resources* (1870). With U.S. Coast Survey (1871–84); on survey of Aleutian Islands. Transferred to U.S. Geological Survey (1884); worked in Smithsonian Institution; became authority on mollusks, esp. those of the Pacific coast.

**Dal'las** (dăl'ăs), **Alexander James.** 1759–1817. Brother of Robert Charles Dallas (*q.v.*). American administrator, b. in Jamaica, West Indies. To U.S. (1783); settled in Philadelphia; became naturalized. Adm. to bar (1785). U.S. secretary of the treasury (1814–16), at critical period in government finance; restored public credit, advocated a national banking institution (passed 1816), urged protective tariff. Served also as acting secretary of war (1815). His son **George Mifflin** (1792–1864) was U.S. senator (1831–33), U.S. minister to Russia (1837–39), vice-president of the U.S. (1845–49), U.S. minister to Great Britain (1856–61).

**Dallas, Robert Charles.** 1754–1824. English writer of tales, poems, and ethical treatises. Brother of Alexander James Dallas. Friend of Lord Byron; acted as Byron's agent in dealing with publishers; published *Recollections of Byron*.

**Dal'lin** (dăl'ĭn), **Cyrus Edwin.** 1861–1944. American sculptor, b. in Utah. Known esp. for success in interpreting American Indian life and scenes. Among his works are *Signal of Peace*, Lincoln Park, Chicago; *Pioneer Monument*, Salt Lake City; *Medicine Man*, Fairmount Park, Philadelphia; *The Scout*, Kansas City; *Sir Isaac Newton*, Congressional Library, Washington, D.C.

**Dalling and Bulwer,** Baron. See William Henry Lytton Earle BULWER.

**Dall'mey'er** (däl'mī'ēr), **John Henry.** 1830–1883. Optician, b. in Germany; to London (1851); made improvements in portrait and landscape photographic lenses, also in microscope object glasses; made photoheliographs for Harvard observatory (1864), and British government (1873).

**Dall'On'ga·ro** (däl·lông'gä·rō), **Francesco.** 1808–1873. Italian writer; founded revolutionary journal *La Favilla* (Trieste, 1836); organized first Italian legion for Garibaldi (1848); in exile (to 1859); professor of literature, Florence (1859) and Naples (1869). Author esp. of political lyrics.

**Dal'man** (däl'män), **Gustaf.** 1855–1941. German Protestant theologian.

**Dalmatia,** Duke of. See SOULT.

**Da'lou'** (dá'lōō'), **Jules.** 1838–1902. French sculptor, b. Paris. Involved in the Commune (1871); spent two years in exile in London (1871–73). Among his works are *Dame Romaine Jouant aux Osselets, Le Triomphe de Silène, Victor Moir, Blanqui, Triomphe de la République,* and many portrait busts.

**Dal·rym'ple** (dăl·rĭm'p'l; dăl'rĭm'p'l). Name of a Scottish family sprung from one of the Lollards of Kyle summoned before James IV (1494), and possessing the viscountcy and earldom of **Stair** (stâr), including:

Sir **James Dalrymple** (1619–1695), 1st Viscount Stair (cr. 1690), lawyer and judge; judge of reformed court of session (1657–60) on recommendation of Monck; allowed by Charles II to take declaration under the Solemn League and Covenant under an implied reservation; president of court of session (1671); M.P. (1672); privy councilor of Scotland (1674); on enforcing of Test Act, retired (1679) to country and worked on *The Institutions of the Law of Scotland* (1681); repaired to Holland on account of hostility of duke of York and Claverhouse (1682); returned with William of Orange (1688) and was restored to presidency of court of session (1689); his daughter Janet's luckless marriage (1669) suggested to Scott the *Bride of Lammermoor.*

*His sons:* His eldest son, Sir **John Dalrymple** (1648–1707), 1st Earl of Stair, lawyer; imprisoned because of hostility of Claverhouse (1682–84); king's advocate (1686–88); under William III, lord advocate; conciliated Presbyterians; joint secretary of state (1691) with chief management of Scottish affairs; culpable, with Breadalbane and king, for the massacre of the Macdonald clan of Glencoe (1692); privy councilor (1702); created earl (1703); supported Act of Union (1707). Sir **James Dalrymple** of Borth'wick [bôrth'wĭk] (fl. 1714), antiquary; second son of 1st Viscount Stair; principal clerk of court of session; author of *Collections concerning Scottish History preceding 1153* (1705). Sir **Hew Dalrymple** (1652–1737), Lord **North Ber'wick** (bĕr'ĭk); 3d son of 1st viscount; succeeded his father as president in court of session (1698–1737). Sir **David Dalrymple** of Hailes [hālz] (d. 1721); 5th son of 1st viscount; solicitor general to Queen Anne; British M.P. (1708–21); auditor to Scottish exchequer (1720).

**John Dalrymple** (1673–1747), 2d Earl of Stair, known as Marshal Stair, military leader and diplomat; son of 1st earl; distinguished himself in Marlborough's campaigns (1701–11), esp. at Oudenarde and Malplaquet; general (1712); as ambassador to France (1715–20), counteracted schemes for reinstatement of James Edward, the Old Pretender; field marshal (1742), commanded army until George II's assumption of command; fought at Detingen (1743); general of marines (1746).

Sir **David Dalrymple** (1726–1792), Lord **Hailes,** judge and antiquary; grandson of Sir David Dalrymple of Hailes; judge of court of session (1766); judge of the justiciary or criminal court (1776), with record of humanitarianism; author of *Annals of Scotland* (1776). His younger brother **Alexander** (1737–1808), hydrographer; in East India Company's service, negotiated commercial treaty with sultan of Sulu (1758); first hydrographer to British admiralty (1795–1808); author of accounts of discoveries in South Pacific.

**John Dalrymple** (1720–89), 5th Earl of Stair; son of 5th son of 1st earl; opposed in House of Lords measures leading to American Revolution and presented petition in favor of Massachusetts (1774). His son **John** (1749–1821), 6th earl; served under Sir Henry Clinton in American Revolution; minister to Poland (1782), to Berlin (1785–88).

**Dals'gaard** (dáls'gôr), **Christen.** 1824–1907. Danish genre painter.

**Dal'ton** (dôl't'n; -tŭn), Baron **Hugh.** 1887–1962. Brit. lawyer and politician, b. in Wales; educ. Cambridge; M.P. (1924–57); president of Board of Trade (1942–45); chancellor of the exchequer (1945–47).

**Dal'ton** (dôl't'n; -tŭn), **John.** 1766–1844. English chemist and physicist, b. near Cockermouth in Cumberland. Teacher of mathematics and physics in New Coll., Manchester (1793–99); lecturer and private teacher. Kept meteorological diary (from 1787); published *Meteorological Observations and Essays,* in which he maintained electrical origin of aurora borealis (1793); gave first detailed description of color blindness, or Daltonism, from which he and his brother suffered (1794); read paper (1803; pub. 1805) on the *Absorption of Gases by Water and Other Liquids* containing statement of law of partial pressures (Dalton's law); arranged table of atomic weights (1803); first to give clear statement of atomic theory (1803–07); discovered law of multiple proportions; investigated force of steam and expansion of gases by heat. Published *A New System of Chemical Philosophy* (3 parts, 1808–27).

**Dalton, John Call.** 1825–1889. American physiologist, b. Chelmsford, Mass. Professor, College of Physicians and Surgeons, New York (1855–83).

**Da'ly** (dā'lĭ), **Arnold,** *in full* **Peter Christopher Arnold.** 1875–1927. American actor, b. Brooklyn, N.Y. Introduced with *Candida* (1903) plays of Bernard Shaw to American stage. *Mrs. Warren's Profession* (1905) was banned by police after one performance; Daly arrested, tried, and acquitted in famous case.

**Daly, Augustin,** *in full* **John Augustin.** 1838–1899. American playwright and theatrical manager, b. Plymouth, N.C. Newspaper dramatic critic, New York City (1859–69). After some success in adaptations of French and German plays (as *Leah the Forsaken,* 1862), wrote popular original melodramas, *Under the Gaslight* (1867), *A Flash of Lightning* (1868), and *The Red Scarf* (1869). Leased Fifth Avenue Theater (1869–77); organized own company; presented successfully revivals of old English comedies, also his own plays *Divorce* (1871), *Roughing It* (1873), *Pique* (1875), and *The Dark City* (1877). Turned old Broadway Theater into Daly's Theater (1879); assembled a new company including John Drew, Ada Rehan, and Otis Skinner, and presented again adaptations of French and German dramatic successes. Chosen by Tennyson to adapt *The Foresters* to the stage (1891). Opened theater in London (1893); presented Shakespearean comedies with marked success. From 1894, produced Shakespearean comedies in his New York theater also.

**Daly, Marcus.** 1841–1900. American mineowner, b. in Ireland; to America (1856). To California; rose from pick-and-shovel man to one of the wealthiest mineowners of the West; prominent in developing copper mines (*Anaconda*) in Butte, Montana, district; organized

Amalgamated Copper Co. Long political feud between Daly and William A. Clark (1888–1900).

**Daly, Reginald Aldworth.** 1871–1957. American geologist, b. in Canada. Professor, M.I.T. (1907–12), Harvard (1912–1957). Authority on origin of rocks and glaciers.

**Daly, Thomas Augustine.** 1871–1948. American journalist and poet, b. Philadelphia. On staff of Philadelphia *Record* (1891–98; 1918–29); columnist on Philadelphia *Evening Bulletin* (from 1929). Author of *Canzoni* (1906), *Carmina* (1909), *Madrigali* (1912), *McAroni Ballads* (1919), *McAroni Medleys* (1931).

**Dal'yell** (dăl'yĕl; dē·ĕl') *or* **Dal'zell** (dăl'yĕl; dē·ĕl') of Binns (bĭnz), **Thomas.** 1599?–1685. Scottish Royalist soldier, known as "the Muscovy general." Served in Rochelle military expedition of duke of Buckingham (1627) and in Ireland; taken prisoner at Worcester (1651); escaped and took part in Highland rebellion (1654); in service of Russian czar, fought against Turks and Tatars; as commander in chief in Scotland subdued Covenanters (1666); privy councilor (1667); M.P. in Scottish parliament (1678–85); commissioned to punish rebels of Bothwell Bridge (1679).

**Dal'zi·el** (dăl'zĭ·ĕl; dăl'yĕl; dē·ĕl'), **Davison Alexander.** Baron **Dalziel.** 1854–1928. English newspaper proprietor, b. in London. One of founders of Dalziel's News Agency, London; purchased control (1910) of London *Standard* and *Evening Standard.* Sold newspaper interests (1916); chairman, Pullman Car Co. (from 1915); manipulated controlling interest in International Sleeping Car Co. (1927), and negotiated purchase by this company of Thomas Cook & Son Tourist Agency (1928).

**Dalziel of Kirk·cal'dy** (kûr·kô(l)'dĭ), 1st Baron. **James Henry Dalziel.** 1868–1935. British newspaper proprietor; acquired control of *Pall Mall Gazette;* founded *Sunday Evening Telegram;* also published the *Era* and *Country World.* M.P. (1892–1921); chairman of committee in charge of German prisoners (1914–18).

**Dam** (dȧm), **Carl Peter Henrik.** 1895– . Danish biochemist, b. Copenhagen; professor, Polytechnic Inst., Copenhagen (1941–65); at U. of Rochester (1942–45); for work on vitamin K, shared with E. A. Doisy (*q.v.*) 1943 Nobel prize for medicine.

**Damascene, John.** See John of Damascus.

**Da·mas'ci·us** (dȧ·măsh'ĭ·ŭs). Greek Neoplatonist philosopher, b. Damascus (c. 480 A.D.); after his Athens school was closed (529) by Justinian, went to court of Khosrau I.

**Dam'a·sus** (dăm'ȧ·sŭs). Name of two popes (see *Table of Popes*, Nos. 37, 150):

**Damasus I,** Saint. 304?–384. Pope (bishop of Rome; 366–384). Election contested, but recognized by Valentinian I; opposed Arianism; received favor for interest in the tombs of the martyrs, for his inscriptions composed for them, and for restoration of the catacombs; commissioned Jerome to revise the Bible (version later known as the Vulgate).

**Damasus II.** Pope for 23 days only (1048).

**Da'mer** (dā'mẽr), **Anne Seymour.** 1748–1828. English sculptress, daughter of Field Marshal Conway; friend of Nelson, Walpole, Napoleon; executed statue of George III, and bust of Nelson.

**Da'me·ron'** (dȧm'rôɴ'), **Émile Charles.** 1848–1908. French landscape painter.

**Damian,** Saint. See Saints Cosmas and Damian.

**Da·mia'ni** (dä·myä'nē), San **Pietro.** *English* Saint **Peter Da'mi·an** (dā'mĭ·ăn). 1007–1072. Italian Roman Catholic ecclesiastic; entered hermitage near Gubbio, in Umbria (c. 1035). Advocated reforms; denounced vices of clergy; trusted adviser to several popes. Cardinal bishop of Ostia (1057); presided at Council of Milan (1059); papal legate to Germany (1069), where he induced Emperor Henry IV to give up idea of divorcing his wife, Bertha.

**Da'mien' de Veus'ter'** (dȧ'myăɴ' dẽ vûs'târ'; *Angl.* dā'mĭ·ĕn), **Joseph.** *Known as* **Father Damien.** 1840–1889. Belgian Roman Catholic missionary; devoted life (from 1873) to caring for lepers isolated in a government hospital on Molokai Island, Hawaiian Islands; contracted the disease and died. An article by a Presbyterian minister impugning character of Father Damien elicited Robert Louis Stevenson's famous response *Father Damien: An Open Letter to the Rev. Dr. Hyde* (1890).

**Da'miens'** (dȧ'myăɴ'), **Robert François.** 1715–1757. French fanatic who attempted to assassinate King Louis XV at Versailles (Jan. 5, 1757); tortured and executed.

**Da·mi'ri, al-** (ăd'dă·mē'rē). *Arab.* **Kamāl al-Dīn Muḥammad ibn-Mūsa al-Damīri.** 1344?–1405. Arab jurist in Egypt and writer on natural history; chief work, *Ḥayāt al- Ḥayawān* (*Life of Animals*).

**Da'mi'ron'** (dȧ'mē'rôɴ'), **Jean Philibert.** 1794–1862. French philosopher; professor, Sorbonne, Paris.

**Dam'ja·nich** (dŏm'yŏ·nĭch), **János.** 1804–1849. Hungarian general and patriot, of Serbian origin; served in Hungarian war for independence (1848–49); after battle at Világos, surrendered to Russians, was handed over to Austrians and executed.

**Dam'o·cles** (dăm'ŏ·klēz). Courtier of 4th century B.C., in retinue of Dionysius the Elder of Syracuse. According to story related by Cicero, Damocles, having commented on the good fortune of Dionysius, was invited by Dionysius to a banquet, at which he was seated under a naked sword suspended by a single hair.

**Da'mon** (dā'mŭn) of Athens. Greek musician and philosopher of 5th century B.C.; a teacher of Socrates and Pericles; as a friend of Pericles, accepted ostracism.

**Damon** and **Pyth'i·as** (pĭth'ĭ·ăs) *or, more correctly,* **Phin'ti·as** (fĭn'tĭ·ăs). Pythagorean philosophers, of 4th century B.C., noted for their mutual devotion. According to the story, when Pythias, condemned to death for plotting against Dionysius of Syracuse, desired time to arrange his affairs before his execution, Damon placed himself in the hands of Dionysius as a substitute for him and was willing to die if Pythias failed to return; Pythias returned at the last moment and Dionysius, struck by the strength of their friendship, pardoned Pythias.

**Da'mon** (dā'mŭn), **Samuel Foster.** 1893–1971. American educator and poet, b. Newton, Mass.; author of critical studies on William Blake and Amy Lowell.

**Dam'o·phon** (dăm'ŏ·fŏn). Greek sculptor of 2d century B.C. in Messene.

**Dam'pi·er** (dăm'pĭ·ẽr; dămp'yẽr), **William.** 1652–1715. English buccaneer and circumnavigator. With band of buccaneers crossed Isthmus of Darien (1679), plundered Peruvian coast. Engaged (1683) in buccaneering expedition along coasts of Chile, Peru, and Mexico. Made expedition with a Captain Swan along Mexican coast, to East Indies, Philippines, marooned Captain Swan in Mindanao, was marooned himself at his own request in Nicobar Islands (1688), made way back to England (1691). Sent out by admiralty (1699) on exploration trip along coasts of Australia, New Guinea, New Britain, his second circumnavigation of globe; gave his name to Dampier Archipelago and Dampier Strait. Commanded unsuccessful privateering expedition to South Seas (1703–07); pilot under Captain Woodes Rogers on privateering expedition (1708–11) which rescued Alexander Selkirk, prototype of Robinson Crusoe, from uninhabited island (1709) and made profit of nearly £200,000.

Author of accounts of his voyages, including *A New Voyage round the World* (1697).

**Dam'pierre'** (däN'pyâr'), Marquis **de. Auguste Henri Marie Pi'cot'** (pē'kō'). 1756–1793. French soldier; commanded a division at Valmy and Jemappes (1792) and at Neerwinden (1793); succeeded to command of the army of Belgium after the desertion of Dumouriez; mortally wounded in action (May 8, 1793).

**Dam'rosch** (dăm'rŏsh; *Ger.* däm'rôsh), **Le'o·pold** (lē'ō-pōld; *Ger.* lā'ô·pôlt). 1832–1885. Musical conductor, b. Posen, Poland; conductor, Breslau Philharmonic Orchestra (1858); organizer, Breslau Orchestra Society (1862). Accepted invitation to be conductor, Arion Society, New York (1871); organized New York Oratorio Society (1873) and New York Symphony Society (1878); conducted chief Wagnerian operas at Metropolitan Opera House, New York City (1884–85).

His sons **Frank Hei'no Dam'rosch** [frăngk hī'nō dăm'-rŏsh] (1859–1937) and **Wal'ter Jo·han'nes Dam'rosch** [wôl'tẽr jō·hăn'ĕs dăm'rŏsh] (1862–1950), both musical directors, b. in Breslau, Germany. Frank was chorus master, Metropolitan Opera House, New York City (1885–91); conductor, People's Choral Union and Singing Classes (1892–1912), Musical Art Society, New York (1893–1920), Orpheus Club, Philadelphia (1897–1905), Symphony Concerts for Young People (1898–1912), Mendelssohn Glee Club (1904–09). Walter Damrosch came to U.S. in 1871; assistant director (1885) under Anton Seidl of German opera at the Metropolitan Opera Company and of the Oratorio and Symphony societies; presented Wagner's *Parsifal* first time in U.S. (1896); founded Damrosch Opera Company (1894) for production of Wagnerian operas; director, New York Symphony Orchestra (1903–27); musical counsel, National Broadcasting Company (from 1928); founder and conductor of orchestral radio concerts for public schools and colleges; composer of *Manila Te Deum*, the operas *Cyrano* and *The Man Without a Country* (1937; libretto by Arthur Guiterman), and incidental music. Leopold's daughter **Clara** married David Mannes (*q.v.*).

**Dan** (dăn). In Bible, Jacob's fifth son (*Genesis* xxx. 1–6), ancestor of one of twelve tribes of Israel.

**Da'na** (dā'nȧ), **Charles Anderson.** 1819–1897. American newspaper editor, b. Hinsdale, N.H. At Brook Farm (1841–46). Editorial work, New York *Tribune* (1847–62). Assistant secretary of war (1863–64). Coeditor with George Ripley of the *New American Cyclopaedia* (16 vols., 1858–63). Owner and editor, New York *Sun* (1868–97). His son **Paul** (1852–1930) succeeded him as editor (1897–1903).

**Dana, James Dwight.** 1813–1895. American geologist, b. Utica, N.Y. Geologist on Wilkes Exploring Expedition sent by U.S. government into southern Pacific (1838–42). Published reports under titles *Zoophytes* (1846), *Geology* (1849), and *Crustacea* (1852–54). Editor, *American Journal of Science* (from 1840). Professor of natural history, Yale (1849–64); of geology and mineralogy (1864–90). Other works include *Manual of Geology* (1862), *Textbook of Geology* (1864), *Corals and Coral Islands* (1872), *Characteristics of Volcanoes* (1890). His son **Edward Salisbury** (1849–1935) was best known as a mineralogist; professor of physics (1890–1917), and curator of mineral collection (1874–1922), Yale; author of *Textbook of Mineralogy* (1877, new ed. 1898), *Minerals and How to Study Them* (1895), etc.

**Dana, John Cotton.** 1856–1929. Cousin of James Dwight Dana. American librarian, b. Woodstock, Vt.; librarian, Denver (Colo.) Public Library (1889–98); Springfield (Mass.) City Library (1898–1902); Newark (N.J.) Public Library (1902–29).

**Dana, Richard.** 1700–1772. American jurist, b. Cambridge, Mass. Grad. Harvard (1718). Adm. to bar; practiced, Marblehead, Charlestown, Boston. Identified with colonial cause in years preceding American Revolution. His son **Francis** (1743–1811) was a jurist; in England, attempting to adjust differences between Great Britain and the colonies (1774–75); member, Continental Congress (1776–78); a signer, Articles of Confederation (1778); in France as secretary to John Adams (1780); designated minister to Russia, but not officially received as such in Russia (1780–83); associate justice, Mass. Supreme Court (1785–91); chief justice (1791–1806). Francis's son **Richard Henry** (1787–1879) was a lawyer and miscellaneous writer; author of *The Buccaneer and Other Poems* (1827), etc. Richard Henry's son **Richard Henry** (1815–1882) was sailor, author, and lawyer; sailed on a brig from Boston around Cape Horn to California (1834–36); embodied his experiences in *Two Years Before the Mast* (1840), which has become an American classic of sea adventure; adm. to bar (1840); specialized in admiralty law. The latter's son **Richard Henry** (1851–1931) was a lawyer; organized Associated Charities of Boston (1878–79); drafted Massachusetts Civil Service Reform Act (1884); lectured on civil service reform, municipal government reform, electoral reform, and better housing for workingmen.

**Dana, Samuel Luther.** 1795–1868. American chemist, b. Amherst, N.H. Applied his knowledge of chemistry to industrial processes; devised new system of bleaching cotton cloth; also, devised new ways of printing calicoes. Published two books on agricultural chemistry.

**Dana, William Parsons Winchester.** 1833–1927. American painter, b. Boston; lived abroad (from 1870); best known for marines and figure paintings.

**Dan'by** (dăn'bĭ), Earl of. See Thomas OSBORNE.

**Danby, Francis.** 1793–1861. Irish historical and landscape painter. Lived near Lake of Geneva (1829–41), in England (1841–61); known for ideal and poetic landscapes.

**Dance** (dȧns), **George.** 1700–1768. English architect; designer of Mansion House, London (1739). His son **George** (1741–1825), architect and artist, rebuilt Newgate Prison (1770) and designed front of Guildhall. Another son, Sir **Nathaniel Dance–Hol'land** [-hŏl'ănd] (1735–1811), painter, was associated with his brother in founding the Royal Academy.

**Dan'cla'** (däN'klȧ'), **Jean Charles.** 1818–1907. French violinist and composer; author of chamber music and compositions for the violin. One brother, **Arnaud** (1820–1862), was a noted violoncellist, and another, **Léopold** (1822–1895), a violin virtuoso.

**d'Ancona, Alessandro.** See ANCONA.

**Dan'court'** (däN'ko͞or'), **Florent Carton.** Sieur **d'An'-court'** (däN'ko͞or'). 1661–1725. French actor and playwright; successful as comedian at Comédie Française (1685–1718). Among his many comedies are *Le Chevalier à la Mode, La Maison de Campagne, Les Bourgeoises de Qualité.*

**Dan'din** (dŭn'dĭn). fl. 6th century A.D. Sanskrit author and poet. Wrote a manual of poetics and *Daśakumāracharita* ("Adventures of the Ten Princes"), a collection of stories of common life.

**Dan'do·lo** (dän'dô·lō). Patrician family of Venice, including: **Enrico** (1108?–1205), doge (1192–1205); leader of Venetians and crusaders who captured Constantinople (1203, 1204); ambassador in Constantinople (1173); blinded by order of Emperor Manuel. **Andrea** (1310–1354), doge (1343–54); on crusade (1343–46), winning from Turks advantageous peace for Venice; led hostilities against Genoa almost continually (1348–54).

**Dan'du'rand'** (däN'dü'räN'), **Raoul.** 1861–1942. Canadian lawyer and statesman, b. Montreal. Rose to leadership of Liberal party in Canada. Member of Canadian senate (from 1898); speaker of senate (1905–09); member of privy council (1909). Minister without portfolio in dominion cabinet (1921–26, 1926–30). President, 6th Assembly of League of Nations (1925).

**Dane** (dān), **Clemence**. *Pseudonym of* **Winifred Ash′ton** (ăsh′tŭn). 1888–1965. English writer of novels: *Regiment of Women* (1917), *Legend* (1919), *Wandering Stars* (1924), *The Babyons* (1928), *Broome Stages* (1931), *The Moon is Feminine* (1938), *The Arrogant History of White Ben* (1939); plays, as *A Bill of Divorcement* (1921), *Will Shakespeare* (1921), *The Way Things Happen* (1923), *Naboth's Vineyard* (1925), *Granite* (1926), *Mariners* (1926), *Moonlight is Silver* (1934); essays, as *The Women's Side* (1927), *Tradition and Hugh Walpole* (1930).

**Dane, Nathan.** 1752–1835. American jurist, b. Ipswich, Mass. Member, Continental Congress (1785–87); shared with Manasseh Cutler the drafting of the ordinance for the government of the Northwest Territory (1787). Author of *General Abridgment and Digest of American Law* (8 vols., 1823; supplementary vol., 1829). The Dane professorship of law in Harvard Law School is named in his honor.

**Danei, Paolo Francesco.** See Saint PAUL OF THE CROSS.

**Dan′en·how′er** (dăn′ĕn·hou′ẽr), **John Wilson.** 1849–1887. American Arctic explorer, b. Chicago. Grad. U.S.N.A., Annapolis (1870). Member, the De Long arctic exploring expedition (1879–81). Ship *Jeannette* was crushed in ice; Danenhower among those saved. *Lieutenant Danenhower's Narrative of the Jeannette* (1882) gives vivid story of the trip and the disaster.

**Da′nev** (dä′nĕf), **Stoyan.** 1858–1940. Bulgarian statesman; minister of foreign affairs (1901) and premier (1902–03); president of Sobranje (1911); again premier for about a month (1913) at outbreak of Second Balkan War; finance minister (1918–19, 1919–21).

**Dan′forth** (dăn′fōrth), **Moseley Isaac.** 1800–1862. American engraver, b. Hartford, Conn.; interested in engraving of bank notes; formed firm for this work (1850); firm merged with American Bank Note Co. (1858), of which he became vice-president.

**Dangan,** Viscount. See under WELLESLEY family.

**Dan′geau′** (däN′zhō′), Marquis **de. Philippe de Cour′cil′lon′** (dĕ kōōr′sē′yôN′). 1638–1720. French courtier; aide-de-camp and favorite of Louis XIV; governor of Touraine (1667); left *Mémoires* covering years 1684–1720, valuable as source book for that period.

**Dan′hau′ser** (dän′hou′zẽr), **Joseph.** 1805–1845. Austrian historical and genre painter.

**Danican** family. See PHILIDOR.

**Dan′iel** (dăn′yĕl). A Hebrew prophet captive in Babylon who, according to Old Testament book of *Daniel*, interpreted dreams of Nebuchadnezzar and handwriting on the wall for Belshazzar, and who was delivered by God from the lions into whose den he had been thrown for refusing to obey a decree of Darius. Other stories of Daniel are recorded in Apocryphal books of *Susanna* (see SUSANNA) and *Bel and the Dragon*. Cf. SHADRACH.

**Dan′iel** (dăn′yĕl). *Called* "the Pilgrim." Russian ecclesiastic; pilgrim to the Holy Land (c. 1106–07); author of *The Pilgrim*, popular in the Middle Ages.

**Da′niel′** (dȧ′nyĕl′; *Angl.* dăn′yĕl), **Anthony.** 1601–1648. French Jesuit missionary in America; accompanied Samuel de Champlain to Quebec (1633); labored among Huron Indians; slain by hostile Iroquois. Canonized 1930.

**Da′niel′** (dȧ′nyĕl′), **Arnaud** *or* **Arnaut** *or* **Arnault.** 12th-century Provençal poet; called by Petrarch "the great master of love"; inventor of verse form known as sestina, later used by Dante and Petrarch.

**Daniel, Gabriel.** 1649–1728. French Jesuit and historian; author of a history of France.

**Da′ni·el** (dä′nē·ĕl), **Hermann Adalbert.** 1812–1871. German geographer and theologian; author of the collection *Thesaurus Hymnologicus* (4 parts, 1841–53) and of geographical textbooks, etc.

**Dan′iel** (dăn′yĕl), **John Moncure.** 1825–1865. American editor, b. in Stafford County, Va. Editor, Richmond (Va.) *Examiner* (1847–53; 1861–65); urged secession; advocated military conscription; distrusted Jefferson Davis's administration.

**Daniel, Lewis C.** 1901–1952. American painter, etcher, and illustrator, b. New York City. Illustrated an edition of Whitman's *Song of the Open Road*, James Joyce's *Ulysses*.

**Daniel, Peter Vivian.** 1784–1860. American jurist, b. in Stafford County, Va. Associate justice, U.S. Supreme Court (1841–60).

**Daniel, Samuel.** 1562–1619. English poet; tutor to William Herbert (who became earl of Pembroke), later, to daughter of countess of Cumberland. Got into difficulties when Philotas in his tragedy was taken to represent Essex (1605); master of queen's revels, composed pastoral tragicomedies and two masques, *Tethys Festival* (1610) and *Hymen's Triumph* (1615); inspector of children of queen's revels (1615–18); retired. Author of sonnets, *Delia* (1592); *The Complaint of Rosamond* (a soliloquy; 1592); *Books of Civil Wars between York and Lancaster* (8 books in ottava rima; 1595); *Musophilus* (a dialogue in defense of learning, 1599); *Defence of Rime* (a prose reply to Thomas Campion, 1602); a prose history of England (1612–17). Official evidence is wanting for the statement that he received, prior to Ben Jonson, the title of poet laureate.

**Dan′iell** (dăn′yĕl), **John Frederic.** 1790–1845. English chemist and physicist; invented Daniell's hygrometer (1820); published *Meteorological Essays* (1823); emphasized importance of proper moisture for hothouses; invented Daniell's cell.

**Daniell, Thomas.** 1749–1840. English landscape painter of topographical subjects; with his nephew **William Daniell** (1769–1837), painted Eastern subjects in India (1784–94).

**Dan′iels** (dăn′yĕlz), **Frank.** 1860–1935. American comedian, b. Dayton, Ohio; appeared in *The Pink Lady*, *The Tattooed Man*, *Wizard of the Nile*, etc.

**Daniels, Josephus.** 1862–1948. American journalist and statesman, b. Washington, N.C. Editor of Raleigh (N.C.) *State Chronicle* (1885–94) and *News and Observer* (1894–1933). U.S. secretary of the navy (1913–21); U.S. ambassador to Mexico (1933–41). Succeeded (1933) as editor of *News and Observer* by his son **Jonathan Worth** (1902–     ), b. Raleigh, N.C.; A.B. (1921) and M.A. (1922), North Carolina; author of *Clash of Angels* (novel, 1930), *A Southerner Discovers the South* (1938), *A Southerner Discovers New England* (1940), *Tar Heels: A Portrait of North Carolina* (1941).

**Daniels, Winthrop More.** 1867–1944. American transportation authority, b. Dayton, Ohio; professor of political economy, Princeton (1892–1911); member (1914–23) and chairman (1918–19), Interstate Commerce Commission; professor of transportation, Yale (1923–40).

**Da·ni′lo** (dä·nē′lō). *In full* **Danilo Pe′tro·vić** (pĕ′trō·vēt′y′; *Angl.* -vĭch) **of Nje′goš** (nyĕ′gōsh). Name of two ruling princes of Montenegro: **Danilo** (1677–1737); first hereditary prince-bishop (*vladika;* 1711); nearly put to death by Turks (1702); instigated massacre of Mohammedans (1702); at war with Turks (1711–15).

**Danilo I** (1826–1860); succeeded Peter II as prince-bishop (1851) and reigning prince (1852–60); discontinued hereditary office of bishop; at war with Turkey (1852–53) and again (1856–58); defeated Turks at Grahovo (1858); established independence of Montenegro; succeeded by Nicholas I.

**Da·ni′lo·va** (dȧ·nē′lŭ·vȧ), **Alexandra.** 1906– . Amer. ballet dancer and choreographer, b. Russia. To U.S. (1934). Choreographer at Metropolitan Opera Co.

**Da′ni·łow′ski** (dä′nē·lôf′skē), **Gustaw.** 1871–1927. Polish poet and novelist; served with Piłsudski's Polish Legion during World War I; author of the poem *In an Island* (1901) and novels *Past Days* (1902), *The Swallow* (1907), *Marie-Madeleine* (1912), *Lilli* (1917).

**Dan′kl** (däng′k'l), Baron **Viktor von.** 1854–1941. Austrian general; at outbreak of World War I, commanded 1st army; defeated Russians at Krasnik (Aug. 23–24, 1914); commanded Austrian defense in Tirol against Italians (1915–16).

**Danks** (dăngks), **Hart Pease.** 1834–1903. American composer of hymns and songs, b. New Haven, Conn. Best-known song, *Silver Threads Among the Gold.*

**Dan′nat** (dăn′ăt), **William T.** 1853–1929. American painter, b. New York City; best known for portraits and figure paintings.

**Dannay, Frederic.** 1905– . See Ellery QUEEN.

**Dan′neck·er** (dän′ĕk·ẽr), **Johann Heinrich von.** 1758–1841. German sculptor; court sculptor at Württemberg; friend of Schiller, Goethe, Herder, Canova. His best-known works are busts of Schiller and Gluck.

**Dann′reu′ther** (dän′roi′tẽr; *Eng.* dăn′-), **Edward.** 1844–1905. German pianist and writer; in London (from 1863); founded London Wagner Society (1872) and devoted himself to advancing understanding of Wagner's music in England.

**D'An·nun′zi·o** (dän·no͞on′tsyô), **Gabriele.** 1863–1938. Italian author and soldier, b. Francavilla al Mare, Pescara. Educ. in Florence and at U. of Rome; on staff of *Tribuna,* Rome, writing under pseudonym **Du′ca Mi′ni·mo** (do͞o′kä mē′nē·mō); lived in Arcachon, France (1908–15). Ardent advocate of Italian entry into World War; returned to Italy (May, 1915); served in army, navy, and finally as aviator, winning reputation for sensational exploits, including reconnaissance flight over Vienna (Aug., 1918); lost eye in aerial combat. During controversy between Italy and Yugoslavia over status of Fiume, headed force of Italian soldiers and, without orders from Italian government, occupied city (Sept., 1919), holding it until Italian government sent force against him (Dec., 1920); lived thereafter in villa at Gardone on Lago di Garda; created (1924) Prince of **Mon′te Ne·vo′so** (mōn′tā nā·vō′sō). His works include poetry: *Primo Vere* (1879), *Canto Novo* (1881), *L'Intermezzo di Rime* (1884), *La Chimera* (1888), *Il Poema Paradisiaco* (1891), *Odi Navali* (1893), *Laudi del Cielo, del Mare, della Terra, e degli Eroi* (1903), *Gli Inni Sacri della Guerra Giusta* (1914 ff.), *Laus Mortis* (1927); short stories (written chiefly 1882–86) later collected in *Le Novelle della Pescara;* dramatic works: *La Gioconda* (1898), *Francesca da Rimini* (1902), *La Figlia di Jorio* (1904), *La Nave* (1908); novels: *Il Piacere* (1889), *L'Innocente* (1892), *Il Trionfo della Morte* (1894), *Le Vergini delle Rocce* (1895), *Il Fuoco* (1900), *Forse che Sì, Forse che No* (1910), *La Leda senza Cigno* (1916), and *Notturno,* describing sensations of his blindness (1921); political and patriotic writings and addresses: *Per la Più Grande Italia* (1915), *Contro Uno è contro Tutti,* powerful invective against Allies and President Wilson over Fiume controversy (1919), *Per l'Italia degli Italiani* (1923). Italian government undertook publication of his works (1927).

☞ Evidence does not support often-made statement that **Ra′pa·gnet′ta** (rä′pä·nyāt′tä), not **D'Annunzio,** was his real name.

**Dan′tan′** (däɴ′täɴ′), **Antoine Louis.** 1798–1878. French sculptor; studied under Bosio; carved statues of Villars, the dauphin of France, the Dauphine Marie Josèphe of Saxony, Duquesne, and portrait busts of Rachel, Baron Mounier, etc. His brother **Jean Pierre** (1800–1869), known as "Dantan the Younger," was also a sculptor, esp. of caricatured figures and grotesques; alleged to have originated modern caricature in sculpture. Jean's son **Joseph Édouard** (1848–1897) was a painter, esp. of historical, religious, and genre pictures.

**Dan′tas** (dăɴn′tȧsh), **Júlio.** 1876–1962. Portuguese writer; author of plays, lyrics, short stories, translations of Shakespeare, Wilde, and Rostand.

**Dan′te** (dăn′tē; *Ital.* dän′tā). *In full* **Dante,** *orig.* **Du·ran′te** (do͞o·rän′tā), **A′li·ghie′ri** (ä′lē·gyâ′rē). 1265–1321. Italian poet, b. Florence. Spent youth at Florence; met (reputedly c. 1273) Beatrice Portinari (*q.v.*); friend of Guido Cavalcanti, Cino da Pistoia, Brunetto Latini, and Giotto; reputed to have studied at Bologna, Padua, Paris, and probably Oxford; fought on side of Guelphs against Ghibellines (Campaldino, 1289) and Pisans (1290); entered political life (c. 1295); m. Gemma Donati (c. 1297); as Guelph partisan and member of the Bianchi (the Whites), entrusted with various diplomatic missions; elected prior of Florence (1300); banished from Florence (c. 1302); led wandering life, living at Verona (c. 1303, 1314), Bologna (1304?), Lunigiana (1306), Casentino (1307), Paris (1309), Pisa (1313), and Ravenna (c. 1315–21). Known esp. for *Commedia,* later called *Divina Commedia* (begun c. 1307), a philosophico-political poem in terza rima, consisting of 100 cantos, and recounting an imaginary journey of the author through Hell, Purgatory, and Paradise (*Inferno, Purgatorio, Paradiso*), guided through first two by Vergil and through last by Beatrice; considered a masterpiece of world literature. Wrote in Italian *La Vita Nuova,* collection of 31 love poems, chiefly sonnets, in the dolce stil nuovo (lit., sweet new style), with prose commentaries; *Il Convivio* or *Il Convito,* prose commentary on three canzoni (4 books); *Il Canzoniere;* and perhaps *Il Fiore,* series of sonnets paraphrasing *Roman de la Rose.* Wrote in Latin *De Vulgari Eloquentia,* a defense of a hypothetical universalized Italian language as a literary and philosophical medium; *De Monarchia; Epistolae* (esp. the *Epistola ad Canem Grandem*); *Eclogae; Quaestio de Aqua et Terra.*

**Dan′ti** (dän′tē), **Vincenzo.** 1530–1576. Italian sculptor, architect, and painter; known chiefly as sculptor.

**Dan′ton′** (däɴ′tôɴ′), **Georges Jacques.** 1759–1794. French revolutionary leader; practiced law (1785–91) before Parliament of Paris. A founder of the Cordelier (1790); advocated extreme action; fled to England (1791) but returned and incited Tuileries riots (Aug., 1792). Assumed leadership of revolutionaries; minister of justice. In face of foreign dangers, urged action (speech of Sept. 2, 1792: "De l'audace, encore de l'audace, et toujours de l'audace!"). Elected to National Convention (Sept., 1792); voted for death of king (Jan., 1793); elected president of Jacobin Club (Mar., 1793), aim of which was unity of the country and a stable republican government; member of the Committee of Public Safety (April–Sept., 1793); approved of expulsion and death of Girondists (May–Oct., 1793). With Desmoulins and followers overcome by more radical Robespierre and leaders of the Reign of Terror; seized and imprisoned; defiant in farcical trial; condemned and guillotined (Apr. 5, 1794).

**Dantzig, Duc de.** See François Joseph LEFEBVRE.

**d'Anville, Jean Baptiste Bourguignon.** See ANVILLE.

**Dan'zel** (dän'tsĕl), **Theodor Wilhelm.** 1818–1850. German aesthetician and historian of literature.

**Dan'zi** (dän'tsē), **Franz.** 1763–1826. German composer of operas, church music, symphonies, and chamber music.

**Da Pon'te** (dä pōn'tā), **Lo·ren'zo** (lô·rĕn'tsô). *Orig. name* **E'ma·nue'le** (ā'mä·nwâ'lā) **Co'ne·glia'no** (kō'nâ·lyä'nô). 1749–1838. A Jew, son of Geremia Conegliano; converted to Roman Catholic faith, baptized by Monsignor Lorenzo Da Ponte, bishop of Ceneda, whose name he took in accordance with the custom of the time. Appointed (c. 1780) by Austrian government "Poet to the Italian Theater"; wrote librettos for Mozart's *Le Nozze di Figaro* (1786), *Don Giovanni* (1787), *Così fan Tutte* (1790). In London (1793–1805); wrote for Drury Lane Theater *La Capricciosa Correto, L'Isola del Piacere, La Scuola de' Maritati.* To U.S. (1805); established a class in Italian in New York City; professor of Italian literature, Columbia (from 1825); inspired interest in Italian culture and esp. in study of Dante.

**Daqīqī.** See DAKIKI.

**Da'quin'** *or* **d'A'quin'** (dȧ'kăN'), **Louis Claude.** 1694–1772. French organist; composer of organ pieces, carols, motets, and cantatas.

**Da'rá·nyi** (dŏ'rä·nyĭ), **Kálmán de** (dē). 1886–1939. Hungarian pro-Nazi politician; premier (1936–38); speaker of lower chamber (1938–39).

**Da·ra·zi', al-** (ăd'dă·rä·zē'). *Arab.* **Muḥammad ibn-Ismā'īl al-Darazi.** d. 1019. Mohammedan religious leader; a founder and first missionary of the sect of the Druses (named after him). See al-HAKIM.

**d'Arblay,** Madame. See Fanny BURNEY.

**Dar'boux'** (dȧr'bōō'), **Jean Gaston.** 1842–1917. French mathematician; author of works on geometry, esp. on orthogonal surfaces and on infinitesimal geometry; also on approximation to functions of large numbers, discontinuous functions, etc.

**Dar'boy'** (dȧr'bwȧ'), **Georges.** 1813–1871. Archbishop of Paris (1863–71); arrested and shot by Communards.

**Dar'by** (där'bĭ), **John Nelson.** 1800–1882. English theological writer. Chief founder of the Plymouth Brethren (c. 1830) and of an exclusive section of this sect, the *Darbyites* (1847).

**Darc** *or* **d'Arc, Jeanne.** See JOAN OF ARC.

**Dar'cet'** (dȧr'sĕ'), **Jean.** 1725–1801. French chemist and physician; applied chemistry to art and industry, improving manufacture of coins, tapestries, and porcelain; produced an alloy of bismuth, lead, and tin, fusible in boiling water; investigated the action of fire on diamonds, etc. His son **Jean Pierre Joseph** (1777–1844), industrial chemist, made improvements in manufacture of alloys of copper and of tin for cymbals, and in manufacture of bicarbonate of soda, sulphuric acid, soap, etc.

**Dare** (dâr), **Virginia.** 1587–? First child born in America of English parents, b. on Roanoke Island, Va. (now North Carolina); granddaughter of Gov. John White, founder and governor of the colony. Nine days after her birth, Governor White sailed to England for supplies. The Spanish war prevented his return. In 1591, aid was sent from England, but all trace of the colony on Roanoke Island had vanished. Its fate has remained undetermined.

**Dar'es Phryg'i·us** (dâr'ēz [dā'rēz] frĭj'ĭ·ŭs); *Eng.* **Dares the Phrygian.** Legendary author of *De Excidio Trojae Historia,* a chief source of medieval stories of the Trojan War. Cf. DICTYS CRETENSIS.

**Da'reste' de La Cha'vanne'** (dȧ'rĕst' dē lȧ shȧ'vȧn'), **Antoine Élisabeth Cléophas.** 1820–1882. French historian; author of *Histoire de France* (9 vols., 1865–79), etc. His brother **Rodolphe** (1824–1911) was a magistrate and a scholar; author of *Études d'Histoire de Droit* (1889), etc.

**d'Arezzo, Guido** and **Guittone.** See GUIDO D'AREZZO and GUITTONE D'AREZZO.

**Dar'gan** (där'găn), **Edwin Preston.** 1879–1940. American professor of French literature, Chicago (from 1918). Author of *Honoré de Balzac—A Force of Nature* (1932) and *Anatole France* (1937); collaborator with W. A. Nitze in *A History of French Literature* (1922).

**Dargan, Olive,** *nee* **Til'ford** (tĭl'fērd). 1869–1968. American poet and novelist, b. Grayson County, Ky.; m. Pegram Dargan; her works include poetic dramas *Semiramis* (1904), *Lords and Lovers* (1906), *The Mortal Gods* (1912) and, under pseudonym **Fielding Burke,** the novels *Call Home the Heart* (1932) and *A Stone Came Rolling* (1935).

**Dar·go·myzh'ski** (dŭr·gŭ·mĭsh'skû·ĭ; *Angl.* -skĭ), **Aleksandr Sergeevich.** 1813–1869. Russian composer, esp. of operas.

**Da·rí'o** (dä·rē'ō), **Rubén.** *Pen name of* **Félix Rubén Gar·cí'a–Sar·mien'to** (gär·sē'ä·sär·myān'tō). 1867–1916. Nicaraguan poet, b. Metapa; Nicaraguan minister to Brazil (1904), Madrid (1908–11). Known esp. for his lyrics; experimented with metrical innovations. His works include *Abrojos* (1887), *Azul* (a collection of prose and verse, 1888), *Los Raros* (studies of leading representatives of modernism, 1893), *Prosas Profanas* (a collection of poems, 1896), *Cantos de Vida y Esperanza* (1905), *El Canto Errante* (1907), an autobiography (1916), and other prose works.

**Da·ri'us** (dȧ·rī'ŭs). Name of three kings of Persia:

**Darius I.** *Surnamed* **Hys·tas'pis** (hĭs·tăs'pĭs), *i.e.* [son] of Hystaspes. *Called* **Darius the Great.** 558?–486 B.C. King (521–486 B.C.). Married Atossa, daughter of Cyrus the Great; defeated the usurper Gaumata (see SMERDIS); chosen by nobles as king (521), probably because he was an Achaemenid (of the younger line, fourth in descent from Teispes). At first troubled by revolts in various parts of empire, esp. in Babylon; restored order and reorganized administration; divided land into 20 satrapies; introduced reforms in taxation, built roads, established a postal system; built Persepolis; liberal in policy toward Jews, allowing them to rebuild temple (520). Failed in great expedition against Scythians (516); annexed a province of India along the Indus; began great struggle with Greece, caused first by revolt of Ionian cities (499–494); raised two armies to punish Greece—first (492), under his son-in-law Mardonius, only partly successful: second, under Artaphernes and Datis, defeated at Marathon (490); faced by revolt of Egypt (486); died while preparing third expedition against Greece. Events of reign recorded in many inscriptions, esp. that of Behistun. Succeeded by his son Xerxes I.

**Darius II.** *Orig.* **O'chus** (ō'kŭs). *Surnamed in Greek* **No'thus** (nō'thŭs), *i.e.* bastard. d. 404 B.C. Natural son of Artaxerxes I. King (423–404 B.C.). A weak sovereign, dominated by his half sister and wife, Parysatis; reign marked by revolts in Asia Minor and Egypt; appointed (407) his younger son, Cyrus the Younger, satrap in supreme command in Asia Minor. Succeeded by his son Artaxerxes II (*q.v.*).

**Darius III.** *Surnamed* **Cod'o·man'nus** (kŏd'ō·măn'ŭs). d. 330 B.C. King (336–330 B.C.). Great-grandson of Darius II. Raised to throne through murder of Artaxerxes III and his son Arses by eunuch Bagoas; his satraps defeated (334) at Granicus by Greeks under Alexander; himself defeated and his family captured at Issus (333); overwhelmed (331) at Arbela or Erbil (Gaugamela); fled to Ecbatana and Bactria (Balkh); murdered by his satrap Bessus.

**Darius the Mede** (mēd). According to Biblical narrative (*Daniel* vi. 28; ix. 1), son of Ahasuerus (*q.v.*) and conqueror of Babylon; succeeded Belshazzar on the throne (*Daniel* v. 31). There is no historical record of a king of the Medes named *Darius.*

**Dar'lan'** (dár'läɴ'), **Jean Louis Xavier François.** 1881–1942. French naval officer and politician; entered navy (1902); rear admiral (1929); vice-admiral (1932); chief of naval staff (1936); commander in chief of naval forces (1939). During Vichy regime: admiral of the fleet, vice-premier (Feb., 1941), and minister of defense (Aug., 1941) in charge of all armed forces; upon Anglo-American invasion of North Africa (Nov., 1942), surrendered Algiers, ordered cessation of French resistance, arranged to co-operate with Gen. Eisenhower, and assumed authority as chief of state in French Africa; assassinated (Dec. 24, 1942).

**Dar'ley** (där'lĭ), **Felix Octavius Carr.** 1822–1888. American illustrator, b. Philadelphia; in New York (from 1848). Illustrated Irving's *Rip Van Winkle* (1849) and *Legend of Sleepy Hollow* (1850), Ik Marvel's *Lorgnette* (1851), also an edition of the works of James Fenimore Cooper, Dickens, etc.

**Darley, George.** 1795–1846. Irish poet. Author of fairy opera *Sylvia* (1827), poem *Nepenthe* (1839), etc.

**Dar'ling** (där'lĭng), **Charles John.** 1st Baron **Darling.** 1849–1936. English jurist and writer. Author of *Scintillae Juris, Meditations in the Tea Room, Seria Ludo, On the Oxford Circuit, A Pensioner's Garden* (1926), *Reconsidered Rimes* (1930), *Autumnal Leaves* (1933).

**Darling, Grace Horsley.** 1815–1842. English heroine; with her father, lighthouse keeper on one of Farne Islands, rescued nine survivors of the *Forfarshire* (1838).

**Darling, Jay Norwood.** *Known by his signature* **Ding** (dĭng). 1876–1962. American cartoonist, b. Norwood, Mich. Ph.B., Beloit (1900). On staff of Des Moines *Register* (1906–11; 1913–17), New York *Tribune* and Des Moines *Register* (from 1917). Also interested in preservation of wild life; served as chief of biological survey, U.S. Department of Agriculture (1934–36).

**Darling, Samuel Taylor.** 1872–1925. American physician, b. Harrison, N.J.; associated with General Gorgas in Isthmian Canal Commission; chief of laboratories, Panama Canal Zone (1906–15); on staff, International Health Board, investigating anemia in Fiji, Java, and Malaya (1915–18); professor of hygiene at medical school in São Paulo, Brazil (1918–21); director, field laboratory for research into nature and causes of malaria, under Rockefeller Foundation (1921–25).

**Dar'ling·ton** (där'lĭng·tŭn), **James Henry.** 1856–1930. American Protestant Episcopal clergyman, b. Brooklyn, N.Y.; rector of Christ Church, Brooklyn, N.Y. (1883–1905). Consecrated first bishop of Harrisburg, Pa. (1905). His son **Henry** (1889–1955), rector of Church of the Heavenly Rest, New York City (1922–50).

**Dar'mes'te'ter'** (dár'mĕs'tā'târ'), **Arsène.** 1846–1888. French philologist; with collaboration of Adolphe Hatzfeld and Antoine Thomas, compiled *Dictionnaire Général de la Langue Française*, published posthumously (1890–1900). His brother **James** (1849–1894) was an Oriental scholar. James's wife, **Mary,** *in full* **Agnes Mary Frances,** *nee* **Robinson** (1857–1944), b. Leamington, England; after his death, m. Pierre Émile Duclaux (1901); author of *A Handful of Honeysuckles* (verse; 1878), *The Crowned Hippolytus* (novel; 1881), *Arden* (1883), *The End of the Middle Ages* (1888), *Madame de Sévigné* (1914), *A Portrait of Pascal* (1926), etc.

**Darn'ley** (därn'lĭ), Lord. **Henry Stewart** *or* **Stuart.** 1545–1567. Scottish nobleman; second husband of Mary, Queen of Scots. Son of Matthew Stewart (1516–1571), Earl of Lennox (see under STEWART family), and, through his mother, great-grandson of English king Henry VII. Educ. in England; skillful penman and lutanist; allowed by Queen Elizabeth to go to Scotland at Mary's request (1565); created duke of Albany and married to Mary (1565). Jealous of David Rizzio's political influence; joined nobles' conspiracy (1566) for murder of Rizzio, with promise of establishing Protestantism for crown matrimonial; betrayed his companions to Mary. Refused to attend baptism of his son, James VI (through whom he was ancestor of English sovereigns from 1603). Murdered at Kirk o'Field, Edinburgh, possibly through Mary's complicity (see MARY, QUEEN OF SCOTS).

**d'Arrest, Heinrich Ludwig.** See ARREST.

**Dar'row** (dăr'ō), **Clarence Seward.** 1857–1938. American lawyer, b. Kinsman, Ohio. Adm. to bar (1878) and practiced in Chicago (from 1888). Prominent as member of counsel for Eugene V. Debs, Socialist leader indicted (1894) for conspiracy in the Railroad Union case; chief counsel for labor interests in anthracite strike arbitration proceedings at Scranton, Pa. (1902–03). Defense counsel in several widely publicized trials, including those of Nathan Leopold and Richard Loeb charged with killing Bobbie Franks (1924), John Thomas Scopes of Dayton, Tenn., charged with violating state law forbidding teaching of evolution in publicly supported schools and colleges (1925), and the Negroes in the Scottsboro case (1932). Retired from regular practice (1927) and devoted himself to lecturing and writing. Among his books are *Farmington* (novel), *Crime, its Cause and Treatment,* and *The Story of My Life* (1932).

**d'Arsonval, Jacques Arsène.** See ARSONVAL.

**Dar'ti'gue·nave'** (dár'tēg'náv'), **Philippe Sudre.** President of Haiti (1915–22); named president under American supervision. By treaty U.S. established political and financial control for 10 years; new constitution introduced (1918); revolt directed against U.S. suppressed (1918–19).

**Dartmouth,** Barons and earls of. See LEGGE family.

**Da'ru'** (dá'rü'), Comte. **Pierre Antoine Noël Mathieu Bru'no'** (brü'nō'). 1767–1829. French statesman and writer. On military service (1783–99); member of the Tribunate (1802); councilor of state (1805); intendant general of the army in Austria (1805; 1809) and Prussia (1806–07); secretary of state (1811); member of the Chamber of Peers (1819). Author of *Histoire de la République de Venise* (1819).

**D'Arusmont** *or* **Darusmont,** Mme. **Frances.** See Frances WRIGHT.

**Dar'win** (där'wĭn), **Charles Galton.** 1887–1962. Son of Sir G. H. Darwin. English physicist; author of *The New Conceptions of Matter* (1931), etc.

**Darwin, Erasmus.** 1731–1802. English physiologist and poet. Grandfather of Charles Robert Darwin (see below) and of Francis Galton. B.A. (1754) and M.B. (1755), Cantab., physician at Lichfield (1757), where he cultivated an 8-acre botanical garden (1778), and at Derby (from 1781), where he founded Philosophical Society (1784). Author of *The Loves of the Plants* (1789) and *Economy of Vegetation* (1792), which were parts of his poetic work, *Botanic Garden; The Temple of Nature* (1803); also prose works anticipating views on evolution later expounded by Lamarck, including *Zoonomia* (1794–96).

**Charles Robert Darwin** (1809–1882), the great naturalist, b. Shrewsbury, was son of **Robert Waring** (1766–

1848), physician, 3d son of Erasmus. Charles was educated for the ministry, at Edinburgh and Cambridge; at Cambridge met Adam Sedgwick, geologist, and John Stevens Henslow, botanist. Sailed as naturalist on the *Beagle* on surveying expedition to southern islands, South American coasts, and Australasia (Dec., 1831–Oct., 1836); gathered data on flora, fauna, and geology of many lands and islands, made special study of fossils and species on Galapagos Archipelago; published *Zoology of the Voyage of the Beagle* (1840). m. (1839) his cousin Emma Wedgwood. Secretary of Geological Society (1838–41), associated with Sir Charles Lyell, who induced him to write out (1856) results of his experiments in inbreeding and his theory of evolution by natural selection (first given written shape, 1844); received (June, 1858) manuscript from Alfred Russel Wallace from the Moluccas presenting an abstract of an identical theory of natural selection; published Wallace's essay along with his own 1844 essay and his letter with an outline of his theory sent to Asa Gray in 1857. Published *On the Origin of Species by Means of Natural Selection* (1859), arousing a storm of controversy; *The Variation of Animals and Plants under Domestication*, setting up provisional hypothesis of pangenesis (1868); *The Descent of Man*, deriving the human race from an animal of the anthropoid group (1871); a series of supplemental treatises on cross-fertilization and self-fertilization and his theory of circumnutation, and a biography of Erasmus Darwin (1879). Buried in Westminster Abbey.

Of his five sons four were prominent scientists: Sir **George Howard** (1845–1912), mathematician and astronomer; authority on tidal friction, geodesy, and dynamical meteorology. Sir **Francis** (1848–1925), botanist; made researches in vegetable physiology, esp. plant movements and response to stimuli and transpiration through stomata; his father's editor and biographer. **Leonard** (1850–1943), engineer, economist, and eugenist; author of *Bimetallism* (1898) and *The Need for Eugenic Reform* (1926). Sir **Horace** (1851–1928), civil engineer.

**Das** (däs), **Chitta Ranjan.** 1870–1925. Indian politician, b. Calcutta; leader of Swaraj party in Bengal. Called to English bar (1894); ardent nationalist; at first (1918) supported Gandhi in non-co-operation movement, but later led modified form of opposition; with M. Nehru organized Swaraj party (1922); twice elected president of Indian National Congress; elected first mayor of Calcutta (1924). Opposed to Western methods; often advocated measures bordering on violence; in later years gradually lost to Gandhi in influence. Author of several volumes of verse and of political speeches, especially *The Way to Swaraj* (1923).

**Da'sent** (dā's'nt), Sir **George Webbe.** 1817–1896. English Scandinavian scholar; asst. editor of *Times* (1845–70); published translation of Norse popular tales.

**Dash·ko'va** (dŭsh·kô'vŭ), Princess **Ekaterina Romanovna.** 1743–1810. Daughter of Count Roman Vorontsov. Russian woman of letters; m. Prince Mikhail Dashkov (c. 1759). Director, Academy of Arts and Sciences, St. Petersburg (1782); planned Russian dictionary to be published by academy, and did some work on it. Author of plays and the memoirs *Mon Histoire* (written in French).

**Dash'wood** (dăsh'wo͝od), **Elizabeth Monica,** *nee* **de la Pas·ture** (dĕ·lăp'ȧ·tēr). *Pen name* **E. M. Del'a·field** (dĕl'ȧ·fēld). 1890–1943. English novelist; dau. of Mrs. Henry de la Pasture, Lady Clifford (*q.v.*); m. Arthur Paul Dashwood (1919). Among her many books are *Humbug; Jill* (1926); and a series beginning with *Diary of a Provincial Lady* (1931).

**Dashwood, Francis.** 15th Baron **le Des·pen'cer** (lĕ dĕs·pĕn'sēr). 1708–1781. English profligate. Member of household of prince of Wales; M.P. (1741); founder of Hell-fire Club, or the secret society of "Mad Monks of Medmenham" (c. 1755), meeting summer nights in ruins of Medmenham Abbey to indulge in obscene parodies upon Roman Catholic ritual, the ringleaders including Lord Sandwich, John Wilkes, and George Bubb Dodington. Chancellor of exchequer (1762–63); joint postmaster general (1770–81).

**Daskam, Josephine Dodge.** See Josephine Dodge Daskam BACON.

**Dass** (däs), **Petter.** 1647–1708. Norwegian clergyman and poet; chief work, *Nordlands Trompet;* author also of lyric, epic, and religious verse. Regarded as "Father of Modern Norwegian Poetry."

**Da·szyń'ski** (dä·shĭn'y'·skē), **Ignacy.** 1866–1936. Polish Socialist politician. On invitation from Marshal Piłsudski, aided in setting up government for Poland; leader of Socialist party in Polish parliament (1919); deputy prime minister (1920) and chairman of lower chamber (1928–30).

**Da'ti** (dä'tē), **Carlo Roberto.** 1619–1675. Italian scholar and writer; crusader for classical linguistic purity in Italian; collaborated in editing *Vocabolario della Crusca.*

**Da'tis** (dā'tĭs). A Mede, joint commander with Artaphernes of Persian army sent to Greece by Darius I and defeated in battle of Marathon (490 B.C.).

**Da'to I'ra·dier'** (dä'tō ē'rä·thyĕr'), **Eduardo.** 1856–1921. Spanish statesman and jurist, minister of interior (1899–1900), justice (1902–03), foreign affairs (1918); mayor of Madrid (1907 ff.); president, chamber of deputies; premier (1913–15, 1917, 1920–21); assassinated by anarchist (March 8, 1921).

**Dau'ban'** (dō'bäN'), **Jules Joseph.** 1822–1908. French painter; among his canvases are *La Mort du Trappiste, Mme Roland se Rendant au Tribunal Revolutionnaire.*

**Dau'ben'ton'** *or* **d'Au'ben'ton'** (dō'bäN'tôN'), **Louis Jean Marie.** 1716–?1800. French naturalist. Assistant to Buffon at Jardin des Plantes, Paris (1742); provided anatomical descriptions of mammals for Buffon's *Histoire Naturelle.* Conducted experiments in agriculture; introduced Merino sheep into France.

**Dau'be·ny** (dô'bĕ·nĭ; dôb'nĭ), **Charles Giles Bridle.** 1795–1867. English chemist and naturalist; author of *An Introduction to the Atomic Theory* (1831), etc.

**d'Aubignac.** See AUBIGNAC.

**d'Aubigné, Jean Henri Merle.** See MERLE D'AUBIGNÉ.

**d'Aubigné, Théodore Agrippa.** See AUBIGNÉ.

**Dau'bi'gny'** (dō'bē'nyē'), **Charles François.** 1817–1878. French landscape painter, b. Paris; a leader in the Barbizon school. Among his notable paintings are *Soleil Couché, Les Îles Vierges de Bezons, Champs au Printemps, Lever de Lune, Les Bords de l'Oise,* etc. His son **Karl** (kárl) **Pierre** (1846–1886) also painted landscapes.

**Däu'bler** (doi'blēr), **Theodor.** 1876–1934. German writer; author of the epic *Das Nordlicht* (1910 ff.), collections of lyric verse, art criticism, a *Symphonie* in prose, and a novel; regarded as a leader of expressionist school in German literature.

**Dau'brée'** (dō'brā'), **Gabriel Auguste.** 1814–1896. French geologist and mineralogist; known for investigations on the formation and structure of rocks and minerals.

**Dau'det'** (dō'dĕ'), **Alphonse.** 1840–1897. French novelist, b. at Nîmes. Settled in Paris (1857); wrote books of verse *Les Amoureuses* (1858), *La Double Conversion* (1859). Made first striking success with *Lettres de mon Moulin* (1866); thereafter published *Le Petit Chose* (1868), *Tartarin de Tarascon* (1872), *Fromont Jeune et*

*Risler Aîné* (1874), *Jack* (1876), *Les Rois en Exil* (1879), *Sapho* (1884, later made into a play), *Tartarin sur les Alpes* (1885), *L'Immortel* (1888), *Port-Tarascon* (1890), *Soutien de Famille* (1898), etc. His wife, **Julie Rosalie Céleste,** *nee* **Al'lard'** [á'lár'] (1847–1940), often collaborated with him; also published independently books of verse and memoirs. See also Ernest Louis Marie DAUDET and Léon DAUDET.

**Daudet, Ernest Louis Marie.** 1837–1921. Brother of Alphonse Daudet (*q.v.*). French historian and novelist, b. at Nîmes. Editor of *Journal Officiel* (1873), *Petit Moniteur* (1876); among his histories are *La Terreur Blanche* (1887), *Soixante Années du Règne des Romanoff* (1919); among his novels are *Thérèse* (1859), *Fils d'Émigré* (1890), *Drapeaux Ennemis* (1896), etc.

**Daudet, Léon.** 1867–1942. Son of Alphonse Daudet (*q.v.*). French journalist and writer, b. Paris. On staff of *Figaro, Gaulois, Soleil, La Libre Parole;* founded, with Charles Maurras, *L'Action Française* (1907), a royalist journal. Member of Chamber of Deputies (1919–24). Author of many books, including: novels, *Haeres* (1892), *L'Astre Noir* (1893), *Les Morticoles* (1894), *Sylla et son Destin* (1925), etc.; books on psychology and medicine, as *Le Monde des Images* (1919); political works, as *Une Campagne d'Action Française* (1910), *L'Avant-Guerre* (1913), *L'Agonie du Régime* (1925); books of literary criticism, as *Le Stupide XIXe Siècle* (1922); and volumes of reminiscences.

**Dau'gan'** (dō'gäN'), **Albert Joseph Marie.** 1866–1952. French general in the World War (1914–18).

**Daugh'er·ty** (dô'ĕr·tĭ), **Harry Micajah.** 1860–1941. American lawyer and politician, b. Washington Court House, Ohio. U.S. attorney general (1921–24). Tried and acquitted (1927) on charges of conspiracy to defraud U.S. government. Author of *The Inside Story of the Harding Tragedy* (1932; with Thomas Dixon, *q.v.*).

**Dau'gher·ty** (dô'hĕr·tĭ), **James Henry.** 1889–1974. American painter and illustrator, b. Asheville, N.C.; illustrator of Irving's *History of New York...by Diedrich Knickerbocker*, Sandburg's *Abe Lincoln Grows Up*, Stewart Edward White's *Daniel Boone*, etc.

**Dau'mas'** (dō'má'), **Melchior Joseph Eugène.** 1803–1871. French general who distinguished himself in Algeria. Author of *Mœurs et Coutumes de l'Algérie* (1857), *Les Chevaux du Sahara* (1858), etc. See Ausone de CHANCEL.

**Daumat, Jean.** See DOMAT.

**Dau'mer** (dou'mĕr), **Georg Friedrich.** 1800–1875. German writer; author of various anti-Christian works, but later changed his attitude and adopted the Roman Catholic faith, explaining his act in *Meine Konversion* (1859). Published poetry under pseudonym **Eu·se'bi·us Em'me·ran** (oi·zā'bē·o͝os ĕm'ē·rän). See Kaspar HAUSER.

**Dau'mier'** (dō'myā'), **Honoré.** 1808–1879. French caricaturist; on staff of *La Caricature* (1832) when one of his political caricatures caused his arrest and a six months' prison term. Later, joined staff of *Charivari* where he caricatured bourgeois society. Known also as a serious painter, with works in leading art museums.

**Daun** *or* **Dhaun** (doun), Count **Leopold von.** 1705–1766. Austrian soldier. Commissioned field marshal (1754); defeated Frederick the Great at Kolín (June 18, 1757) and at Hochkirch (Oct. 14, 1758); received surrender of General Finck at Maxen (Nov. 21, 1759); defeated by Frederick the Great at Torgau (Nov. 3, 1760).

**Dau'nou'** (dō'no͞o'), **Pierre Claude François.** 1761–1840. French politician and historian; member of the Convention (1792), Council of the Five Hundred (1795), the Tribunate (1800). Author of *Cours d'Études Historiques* (20 vols., lectures delivered at Collège de France).

**Daurat, Jean.** See DORAT.

**Dau'then·dey** (dou'tĕn·dī), **Max.** 1867–1918. German poet and playwright.

**Daut'zen·berg** (dou'tsĕn·bĕrK), **Johan Michiel.** 1808–1869. Flemish poet; champion of Flemish movement in literature.

**Dau'zat'** (dō'zá'), **Albert.** 1877–1955. French linguistic scholar; author of *La Philosophie du Langage* (1912), etc.

**Da'vaine'** (dá'vĕn'), **Casimir Joseph.** 1812–1882. French physician; first to produce experimental infection in animals with blood containing the anthrax bacillus and to suggest that the bacillus caused the disease (1863).

**Da'vel'** (dá'vĕl'), **Jean Daniel Abraham.** 1670–1723. Swiss patriot of Vaud; led uprising to overthrow Bernese domination; captured and executed near Lausanne.

**Dav'e·nant** *or* **D'Av'e·nant** (dăv'ē·nănt), Sir **William.** 1606–1668. English poet and dramatist. Son of a vintner at Oxford, keeper of inn at which Shakespeare is said to have stopped; educ. Oxford; entered household of Fulke Greville, on whose death he turned to writing plays and masques, including the tragedy *Albovine, King of the Lombards* (1629) and his comic masterpiece, *The Wits* (acted 1633); became poet laureate following Ben Jonson (1638). Royalist, fought for Charles; captured on mission to Virginia for Henrietta Maria (1650); while imprisoned in Tower (1650–52), wrote his epic *Gondibert;* released through influence of Milton. Presented semi-private dramatic productions at Rutland House in evasion of Puritan prohibition of plays (from 1656); founded English opera with his *Siege of Rhodes* (1656); opened the Cockpit, a theater in Drury Lane (1658); imprisoned for complicity in insurrection of Sir George Booth (1659). At Restoration, set up company, the Duke of York's Players, at Lincoln's Inn Fields; produced many adaptations of plays by Shakespeare, Jonson, and Fletcher. His son **Charles** (1656–1714) wrote tracts on political economy.

**Dav'en·port** (dăv'ĕn·pōrt), **Charles Benedict.** 1866–1944. American zoologist, b. Stamford, Conn. Director, Carnegie Institution Station for Experimental Evolution (1904–34) and Eugenics Record Office (1910–34), Cold Springs Harbor, N.Y.; director, biological laboratory, Brooklyn Institute of Arts and Sciences (1898–1923). Author of *Experimental Morphology* (1897–99), *Elements of Zoology* (1911), *Heredity in Relation to Eugenics* (1911), *Body Build and Its Inheritance* (1923), *How We Came By Our Bodies* (1936), etc.

**Davenport, Edward Loomis.** 1815–1877. American actor, b. Boston. Leading actor on American stage (1854–74). Chief roles: Benedick, Othello, Iago, Shylock, Hamlet, Lear, Brutus, Richelieu, Wolsey, Bill Sykes, Giles Overreach in Massinger's *A New Way to Pay Old Debts.* His daughter **Fanny Lily Gypsy** (1850–1898), b. London, Eng., was an actress in Augustin Daly's company (1869–77).

**Davenport, George.** 1783–1845. American fur trader, b. in Lincolnshire, Eng.; to New York (1804); on frontier as settler and trader (1814–26); agent, American Fur Co. (from 1826); one of the founders of Davenport, Iowa, named in his honor (1835).

**Davenport, Homer Calvin.** 1867–1912. American caricaturist, b. Silverton, Ore. Cartoonist, New York *Evening Journal*, New York *Evening Mail*, New York *American.*

**Davenport, Ira Erastus** (1839–1911) and his brother **William Henry Harrison** (1841–1877). American spiritualistic mediums; prominent in Europe and U.S.

(c. 1860–77); investigated and exposed as sleight-of-hand experts by Houdini.

**Davenport, John.** 1597–1670. Clergyman, b. Coventry, Eng. Pastorates in England (1615–25). Developed Puritan sympathies; aided in procuring charter for Massachusetts Company (1629); fled from England to Holland (1633); sailed to Boston (1637). Founded New Haven colony (1638); with Theophilus Eaton (*q.v.*) drew up code of laws for the colony. Gave refuge to the regicide judges Whalley and Goffe (1661). Opposed union of New Haven and Connecticut colonies (1665). Accepted call to First Church in Boston (1668).

**Dav'en·port, Marcia,** *nee* **Gluck** (glo͝ok). 1903– American author and music critic, b. New York City; daughter of Alma Gluck (*q.v.*); m. Russell W. Davenport (1929); author of *Mozart* (1932) and novels *Of Lena Geyer* (1936), *The Valley of Decision* (1942).

**Davenport, Robert.** fl. 1623–1639. English dramatist; said to have collaborated with Shakespeare.

**Da'vey** (dā'vĭ), **John.** 1846–1923. Tree surgeon, b. Eng.; to U.S. (1872); specialized in care of ornamental trees. His son **Martin L.** (1884–1946) was governor of Ohio (1935–39).

**Da'vid** (dā'vĭd) *or* **De'wi** (dā'wĭ), **Saint. c. 500–600.** Patron saint of Wales. Said to have presided over so-called Synod of Victory at Caerleon-on-Usk; as primate of South Wales, moved seat of ecclesiastical government to Mynyw or Menevia (now St. David's); founder of churches; canonized (1120).

**Da'vid** (dā'vĭd). d. about 973 B.C. King of Judah and Israel (1013?–?973 B.C.). Youngest son of Jesse of Bethlehem. One of greatest figures in Hebrew history and literature, subject of many narratives in Old Testament, with some repetition (*1 Samuel* xvii. 12 to *1 Kings* ii. 12; also *1 Chronicles* xi–xxix); anointed by Samuel as Saul's successor; served in Saul's court; slew Philistine giant, Goliath (*1 Samuel* xvii. 1 to xviii. 5); m. Michal, Saul's daughter; by his successes, became object of Saul's enmity; won friendship of Jonathan (*1 Samuel* xx); outlawed for years by Saul; after Saul's death, ruled in Hebron seven years, then became king of all Israel, conquering Jerusalem and making it his capital ("the City of David"); broke power of Philistines and defeated Moabites, Ammonites, and Edomites; reign troubled by revolt and death of Absalom (*q.v.*); m. Bathsheba (*q.v.*), wife of Uriah the Hittite; succeeded by Solomon, Bath-sheba's son, instead of by his son, Adonijah; reputed author of many Psalms. See JOAB.

**David.** Name of two kings of Scotland:

**David I.** 1084–1153. Called "the Scotch Justinian." Son of Malcolm III Canmore. Gained by marriage earldom of Huntingdon; on death of King Edgar (1107), received southern Scotland and succeeded (1124) on death of brother Alexander to whole of Scotland and the crown; supported claim of Matilda, daughter of Henry I, to English crown as against Stephen, but was defeated at Battle of the Standard (1138); unsuccessfully invaded England (1149); founded bishoprics and monasteries; furthered process of feudalizing Scotland; initiated the chancellery. Succeeded by grandson Malcolm IV.

**David II.** 1324–1371. See under BRUCE, Scottish family.

**Da'vid.** *Welsh* **Da'fydd ap Gwi'lym** (dā'vĭd [dȧ'vĭth] ȧp gwĭ'lĭm). c. 1340–1400. Welsh poet, b. in Cardiganshire; elected chief bard of Glamorganshire; attempted to elope with Morfudd of Anglesey. Author of love odes, satires, and nature poems, including *The Lark, The Wind,* and *The Mist.*

**Da'vid'** (dä'vēd'), **Armand.** 1826–1900. French missionary and naturalist; traveled especially in China.

**Da'vid** (dā'vĭd), Sir **Edgeworth,** *in full* **Tannatt William Edgeworth.** 1858–1934. Australian geologist; scientific officer with Shackleton Antarctic expedition (1907–09); led party reaching South Magnetic Pole (Jan., 1909). Author of *The Geology of Australia* (1932).

**Da'vid'** (dä'vēd'), **Félicien César.** 1810–1876. French composer of the symphonic ode *Le Désert* (1844), *La Perle du Brésil* (an opera, 1851), *Herculanum* (1859), *Lalla-Roukh* (1862), and *Le Saphir* (1865). His use of quaint and weird Oriental melodies introduced a new movement in French music.

**Da'vid** (dä'vēt; -vĭt; -fēt; -fĭt), **Ferdinand.** 1810–1873. German violin virtuoso, teacher, and composer of violin concertos, symphonies, an opera, and miscellaneous works.

**Da'vid** (dȧ'vĭt), **Gerard** *or* **Gheerardt** *or* **Gheeraert.** 1450? or 1460?–1523. Dutch painter of religious subjects; regarded as one of most important among Flemish primitives.

**Da'vid'** (dä'vēd'), **Jacques Louis.** 1748–1825. French painter, b. Paris; regarded as founder of French classical school of painting; court painter to Louis XVI. Sympathized with principles of the Revolution, and became associate of Robespierre; after establishment of the Empire, was appointed court painter by Napoleon (1804); at the Restoration (1815), was exiled.

**David d'An'gers'** (däɴ'zhā'), **Pierre Jean.** 1788–1856. French sculptor; studio at Paris (after 1816); executed large number of works, as statues of the great Condé, Cuvier, Talma, and Jean Bart, portrait busts of Goethe, Jeremy Bentham, Chateaubriand, Lamartine, and Victor Hugo, medallions of Bonaparte, Ney, Jacques Louis David, Gérard, Rossini, Paganini, Théophile Gautier, Alfred de Vigny, Mme. Récamier, Alfred de Musset, etc.

**Da'vid of Di'nant'** (dā'vĭd, dē'näɴ'). fl. 1200. Belgian scholastic philosopher; his followers were known as Davidists.

**David the Philosopher.** *Also* **Dawith Anjalth.** 6th-century Armenian philosopher and religious writer.

**Da·vi'dov** (dŭ·vyē'dôf), **Karl.** 1838–1889. Russian violoncellist. Solo violoncellist to czar of Russia (1862); director, Conservatory of Music, St. Petersburg (1876–87); made successful concert tours in Europe.

**Da·vi'do·vić** (dä·vē'dô·vēt'y'; *Angl.* -vĭch), **Ljubomir.** 1863–1940. Yugoslav statesman; a founder of Independent Radical party in Serbia (1902). President of the Skupshtina (1905). Prime minister of Yugoslavia (1919–20, 1924).

**Da'vids** (dā'vĭdz), **Thomas William Rhys.** 1843–1922. English Orientalist, b. at Colchester. Joined Ceylon civil service (1866); interested himself in study of Pali and early Buddhism. Among his books are *Buddhism* (1878), *Buddhist Suttas from the Pali* (1881), *Buddhist India* (1903), *Early Buddhism* (1908). Compiler, with William Stede, of a Pali dictionary. Married (1894) **Caroline Augusta Fo'ley** (fō'lĭ), also an authority on Buddhism, who collaborated with him in parts of his work, esp. in translations from Pali texts; d. 1942.

**Da'vid·son** (dā'vĭd·s'n), **Andrew Bruce.** 1831–1902. Scottish Biblical scholar; member of Old Testament revision committee (1870–84); made life work of language research and historical exegesis of Old Testament; his commentary on one third of Book of Job (1862) the first scientific Old Testament commentary in English.

**Davidson, Donald Grady.** 1893–1968. American writer, b. Campbellsville, Tenn.; teacher of English, Vanderbilt U. (from 1920; professor from 1937); advocate of regionalism and agrarianism; a founder of periodical *The Fugitive;* author of *The Tall Men* (1927; blank-verse poem on Tennessee).

**Davidson, George.** 1825–1911. Geographer and astronomer, b. Nottingham, Eng.; to U.S. as a child. With U.S. Coast Survey (1845–95); prepared a mariner's *Directory for the Pacific Coast of the U.S.* (1858), and a survey of the Alaskan coast (1868). Directed observations of the transit of Venus, in Japan (1874) and in New Mexico (1882); published catalogues of star positions; aided in determining site of Lick observatory.

**Da′vid·son** (dā′vĭd·s'n), **Israel.** *Real surname* **Mov·sho′vitz** (mōv·shō′vĭts). 1870–1939. Hebrew scholar, b. in Russia; to U.S. (1888). Professor of medieval Hebrew literature, Jewish Theol. Sem. of America (1915–1939). Compiler of *Thesaurus of Mediaeval Hebrew Poetry* (4 vols., 1924–33).

**Davidson, Jo.** 1883–1952. American sculptor, b. New York City. Among his notable sculptures are *Woodrow Wilson* and *Anatole France*, in the Luxembourg, Paris; *Robert M. La Follette*, in the rotunda of the Capitol, Washington, D.C.; *Marshal Foch; General Pershing; Will Rogers; Walt Whitman;* and portrait busts *Clemenceau, Rabindranath Tagore, Zangwill, Chaliapin,* etc.

**Davidson, John.** 1857–1909. Scottish poet and playwright. Published highly individual plays, *Bruce* (1886), *Smith; a tragic Farce* (1888), *Scaramouch in Naxos* (1889). Gained reputation as gifted, if unconventional, lyric poet with *Fleet Street Eclogues* and several volumes of *Ballads;* expressed materialistic and pessimistic philosophy in series of *Testaments* (1901–08).

**Davidson, Samuel.** 1807–1898. Irish Biblical scholar; his advanced ideas in *The Text of the Old Testament* were objected to on doctrinal grounds.

**Davidson, Thomas.** 1817–1885. British paleontologist; author of *Monograph of British Fossil Brachiopoda* (6 vols., 1850–86).

**Davidson of Lam′beth** (lăm′bĕth; -bĕth), Baron. **Randall Thomas Davidson.** 1848–1930. Anglican prelate, b. at Edinburgh. Dean of Windsor (1883) and domestic chaplain to the queen. Consecrated archbishop of Canterbury (1903); resigned on account of ill health (1928).

**Da′vie** (dā′vĭ), **William Richardson.** 1756–1820. American lawyer, b. in Cumberland, Eng.; to America as a child. Served brilliantly in latter years of Revolutionary War. In North Carolina legislature (1786–98); instrumental in securing codification of the laws, the cession of Tennessee to the Union, the founding of the U. of North Carolina. Governor of North Carolina (1798–99).

**Da′viel′** (dȧ′vyĕl′), **Jacques.** 1693–1762. French oculist; originated surgical treatment of cataract by removal of the lens of the eye.

**Da′vies** (dā′vēz; *esp. Brit.*, -vĭs), **Arthur Bowen.** 1862–1928. American painter, b. Utica, N.Y. Studio in New York (from 1894). Examples of his work: *Four o'Clock Ladies*, now in Phillips Memorial Gallery, Washington, D.C.; *The Girdle of Ares*, in Metropolitan Museum of Art, New York; *Leda and the Dioscuri, Maya, Mirror of Illusions*, in Chicago Art Institute; *Children of Yesteryear*, in Brooklyn Museum of Art.

**Davies, Ben,** *in full* **Benjamin Grey.** 1858–1943. Welsh operatic and concert tenor.

**Davies, Clara Novello,** *nee* **Davies.** 1861–1943. British singing instructor and choral conductor, b. Cardiff, Wales. Daughter of Jacob Davies, professional musician; m. David Davies (d. 1931). Founder and conductor of Royal Welsh Ladies' Choir. Performed by royal command before Queen Victoria (1894) and George V and Queen Mary (1928). Mother of Ivor Novello (*q.v.*).

**Davies, David.** 1818–1890. Welsh industrialist; railway builder in mid-Wales; pioneer exploiter of coal in Rhondda Valley; proponent of trades-unions; creator of dock at Barry; Liberal M.P., opponent of home rule. His grandson **David Davies** (1880–1944), 1st Baron **Davies** of Llandinam, served in Royal Welsh Fusiliers (1914–16); private secretary to Lloyd George; M.P. (1906–29); president of University Coll. of Wales, Aberystwyth; author of *Suicide or Sanity* (1932), *Nearing the Abyss* (1936).

**Davies,** Sir **Henry Walford.** 1869–1941. English organist, director, and composer, b. in Shropshire. Organist of St. George's Chapel, Windsor (1927–32); master of the king's music (from 1934). Composer of religious music, esp. oratorios and cantatas; compiler of songbooks and hymnbooks.

**Davies, Hubert Henry.** 1876–1917. English playwright, b. in Cheshire. Journalistic and vaudeville experience in San Francisco (1893 ff.); returned to England (1901) and wrote *Cousin Kate* (1903), *Cynthia* (1904), *The Mollusc* (1907), *Mrs. Gorringe's Necklace* (1910), *Doormats* (1913).

**Davies** of Her′e·ford (hĕr′ĕ·fẽrd), **John.** 1565?–1618. English poet, writing on theological and philosophical themes, as *Mirum in Modum* (1602), *Microcosmos* (1603), *The Picture of a Happy Man* (1612), *Wit's Bedlam* (1617).

**Davies,** Sir **John.** 1569–1626. English jurist and poet. Attorney general for Ireland (1606–19); sought to establish Protestantism in Ulster. Speaker of Irish parliament (1613–19); sat in English Parliament (1621). Appointed lord chief justice (1626) but died before entering office. Known for his poems, *Orchestra* (1594), *Nosce Teipsum* (1599; a set of quatrains on immortality of the soul), and *Hymns to Astraea* (1599).

**Davies, John Langdon–.** See LANGDON-DAVIES.

**Davies, Joseph Edward.** 1876–1958. American lawyer and diplomat, b. Watertown, Wis. U.S. commissioner of corporations (1913–15); chairman (1915–16) and vice-chairman (1916–18), Federal Trade Commission. U.S. ambassador to Russia (1936–38), Belgium (1938–39). Author of *Mission to Moscow* (1941).

**Davies,** Sir **Louis Henry.** 1845–1924. Canadian jurist, b. Charlottetown, Prince Edward Island. Premier and attorney general, Prince Edward Island (1876). Member of Dominion House of Commons (1882–1901) and minister of marine and fisheries (1896). Knighted (1897); appointed judge of Supreme Court of Canada (1901).

**Davies,** Mrs. **Mary.** 1855–1930. Welsh operatic and concert soprano, b. in London; m. W. Cadwaladr Davies (1888; d. 1905). Principal soprano at London ballad concerts for 15 years.

**Davies, Mary Carolyn.** American writer; author of verse (*Drums in Our Street*, 1918; *Youth Riding*, 1919; *Penny Show*, 1927) and a novel, *The Husband Test* (1921).

**Davies, Rhys.** 1903– . Welsh writer; author of *Withered Root* (1928), *Rings on her Fingers* (1930), *Arfon* (1931), *Red Hills* (1932), *Daisy Matthews* (1932), *Honey and Bread* (1935), *Time to Laugh* (1937), *Jubilee Blues* (1938).

**Davies, Richard.** 1505?–1581. Welsh Biblical scholar; bishop of St. David's (1561); aided in translation of New Testament and Book of Common Prayer into Welsh; revised *Deuteronomy* and *2 Samuel* for Bishops' Bible (1568).

**Davies, Samuel.** 1723–1761. American educator; ordained in Presbyterian ministry (1747); sent to Eng. (1753) to raise funds for The College of New Jersey (Princeton); president of the college (1759–61).

**Davies, Thomas.** 1712?–1785. Scottish bookseller in London; introduced Boswell to Dr. Johnson (1763); biographer of Garrick (1780).

**Davies, William Henry.** 1871–1940. Welsh-born English poet; lived the life of a tramp in England and U.S. (to c. 1905); then devoted himself to writing, esp. verse. Among his books of poetry are *Nature Poems, Songs of Joy, A Song of Life, The Hour of Magic, Secrets, The Song of Love, Ambition.* Among his prose works are *The Autobiography of a Super-tramp, Beggars, The Adventures of Johnny Walker, Dancing Mad,* etc.

**Dá'vi·la** (dä'vē·lä), **Carlos Guillermo.** 1887–1955. Chilean diplomat and political leader; ambassador to U.S. (1927–31); member of junta that overthrew President Montero (1932); acting president of Chile (July–Sept., 1932); advocate of state socialism.

**Da'vi·la** (dä'vē·lä), **Enrico Caterino.** 1576–1631. Italian soldier and historian; fought in civil wars under Henry IV (1594–99); served Venice as governor of Candia, Friuli, Dalmatia, and Crema; known esp. for his *Storia delle Guerre Civili di Francia* (1630; Eng. trans., *History of French Civil Wars,* 1647).

**Dá'vi·la** (dä'vē·lä), **Gil González.** c. 1578–1658. = Gil González de ÁVILA.

**Dávila, Miguel R.** d. 1927. Provisional president of Honduras (1907–08) placed in power by Zelaya of Nicaragua; elected president (1908–11); after Zelaya's downfall (1909), he was overthrown (1911).

**Dávila, Pedrarias.** See PEDRARIAS.

**Dávila y Pa·dil'la** (ē pä·thē'(l)yä), **Agustín.** 1562–1604. Mexican historian, called "Chronicler of the Indies"; b. Mexico City. Entered Dominican order (1579); Dominican representative to Rome and Madrid (1596); court preacher at Madrid (1598); zealous officer of the Inquisition; bishop of Santo Domingo (1599–1604). His chief work, commissioned by the government, is *Historia de la Fundación de la Provincia de Santiago de Méjico de la Orden de Predicadores* (1596, 1624), published later as *Varia Historia de la Nueva España y Florida* (1634).

**Da'vioud'** (dá'vyōō'), **Gabriel Jean Antoine.** 1823–1881. French architect; collaborated in building Palais du Trocadéro.

**Da'vis** (dā'vĭs), **Alexander Jackson.** 1803–1892. American architect, b. New York City. In firm of Town & Davis (1829–43); practicing alone (1843–80). Examples of his work: with Ithiel Town, Indiana State capitol and Patent Office, Washington, D.C.; independently, Assembly Hall, U. of North Carolina; buildings for Virginia Military Institute.

**Da'vis, Benjamin Oliver.** 1877–1970. American Negro army officer, b. Washington, D.C.; lieutenant of volunteers (1898–99); enlisted in army (1899); military attaché in Liberia (1911–12); professor of military science at Wilberforce U. and Tuskegee Inst.; assistant to the inspector general of army (1941), to England (1942).

**Davis, Charles Harold.** 1856–1933. American landscape painter, b. Amesbury, Mass.

**Davis, Charles Henry.** 1807–1877. American naval officer, b. Boston. In Civil War, commanded Union gunboat flotilla on Mississippi (1862). Chief, Bureau of Navigation (1862). His son **Charles Henry** (1845–1921) graduated U.S.N.A., Annapolis (1864); served through Spanish-American War.

**Davis, Cushman Kellogg.** 1838–1900. American lawyer, b. Henderson, N.Y. Served in Civil War (1862–64). Governor of Minnesota (1874, 1875). U.S. senator (1887–1900).

**Davis, David.** 1815–1886. American jurist, b. in Cecil County, Md.; friend of Abraham Lincoln; active in campaign securing Lincoln's nomination for presidency (1860). Associate justice, U.S. Supreme Court (1862–77). U.S. senator (1877–83). When Chester A. Arthur became president of the U.S., Davis succeeded him as presiding officer of U.S. Senate (1881–83).

**Davis, Dwight Filley.** 1879–1945. American public official, b. Saint Louis, Mo.; served in World War (captain, May, 1917; major, Nov., 1917; lieut. col., Oct., 1918); awarded D.S.C. (1923). U.S. secretary of war (1925–29); governor general of the Philippines (1929–32); appointed director general of U.S. Army Specialists Corps (1942). Donor (1900) of the Davis Cup, an international lawn tennis challenge cup now signifying world team championship.

**Davis, Edwin Hamilton.** 1811–1888. American archaeologist, b. Hillsboro, Ohio. Collaborator with E. G. Squier in study of earthworks of the Mound Builders, and in book *Ancient Monuments of the Mississippi Valley,* first book issued by the Smithsonian Institution (1847).

**Davis, Elmer Holmes.** 1890–1958. American writer and radio news commentator, b. Aurora, Ind.; Rhodes scholar at Oxford (1912–14); on staff of New York *Times* (from 1914); radio news commentator (from 1939); appointed head of Office of War Information (1942).

**Davis, Fannie Stearns.** See Fannie Stearns Davis GIFFORD.

**Davis, George Breckenridge.** 1847–1914. American army officer, b. Ware, Mass. Judge advocate general, U.S. army (1901). Retired, major general (1911). Author of *Outlines of International Law* (1887), *The Elements of Law...Constitutional and Military* (1897), *A Treatise in the Military Law of the United States* (1898).

**Davis, George Whitefield.** 1839–1918. American army officer, b. Thompson, Conn. Major general (1902); retired (1903). Member, Isthmian Canal Commission (1904); governor, Canal Zone (1904–05); chairman, board of engineers to recommend type of canal to be built; favored sea-level canal.

**Davis, Harold Le·noir'** (lĕ·nôr'). 1896–1960. American writer, b. Yoncalla, Ore. Variously, compositor, rancher, surveyor, deputy sheriff, and newspaper editor. Served in World War. Awarded Levison poetry prize by *Poetry Magazine,* Chicago (1919), and a Guggenheim fellowship (1932). Author of *Honey in the Horn* (1935; Harper prize novel, later awarded Pulitzer prize).

**Davis, Henry Gassaway.** 1823–1916. American businessman and political leader, b. Woodstock, Md. U.S. senator (1871–83). Unsuccessful candidate for vice-president of the U.S. on the Alton B. Parker ticket (1904).

**Davis, Henry Gassett.** 1807–1896. American pioneer in orthopedic surgery, b. Trenton, Me.

**Davis, Henry William Banks.** 1833–1914. English animal painter, b. in Finchley. Also, carved a number of portrait busts and statues.

**Davis, Henry William Carless.** 1874–1928. English historian; regius professor of modern history, Oxford (1925–28), and curator of the Bodleian Library (1926–28). Director of *Dictionary of National Biography* (from 1902). Authority on medieval history; among his books are *England under the Normans and Angevins* (1905), *Medieval Europe* (1911).

**Davis, Henry Winter.** 1817–1865. American lawyer and political leader, b. Annapolis, Md. Practiced law, Alexandria, Va., and Baltimore. Member, U.S. House of Representatives (1855–61; 1863–65). Instrumental in preventing Maryland from joining the Confederacy. Later opposed Lincoln and criticized his reconstruction program; succeeded (1864) in substituting reconstruction plan of his own (known as the congressional plan), vetoed by Lincoln; participated in conference of leading Republicans in New York and issued "the Wade-Davis Manifesto," ridiculing Lincoln's reconstruction plan

(1864). Political peace patched up between Davis and Lincoln for elections of 1864. Opposed President Johnson and again put forward his own (congressional) plan of reconstruction.

**Davis, Herbert John.** 1893–1967. English educator, b. in Northamptonshire, Eng. Professor of English, Cornell (1937), and chairman of department (1938–40). President of Smith College (1940–49); professor emeritus, Oxford (from 1960). Authority on Jonathan Swift; editor of *Complete Prose Works of Jonathan Swift.*

**Davis, James Cox.** 1857–1937. American lawyer, b. Keokuk, Iowa; general counsel for U.S. railroad administration (1920); director-general of railroads (1921–26).

**Davis, James John.** 1873–1947. Steel worker and politician, b. in South Wales; to U.S. (1881). Director-general of Loyal Order of Moose (from 1906), building up membership to over 600,000. U.S. secretary of labor (1921–30); U.S. senator from Pennsylvania (1930–44).

**Davis, Jefferson.** 1808–1889. President of the Confederate States of America, b. in Christian (now Todd) County, Ky.; taken to Mississippi as a child. Grad. U.S.M.A., West Point (1828). Frontier army service (1828–35); resigned from army (1835). Mississippi planter (1835–45). Member, U.S. House of Representatives (1845–46); resigned to serve in Mexican War. U.S. senator from Mississippi (1847–51). U.S. secretary of war in Pierce's cabinet (1853–57). U.S. senator (1857–61); conspicuous as defender of South and institution of slavery. Withdrew from senate when Mississippi seceded. Chosen by the provisional congress President of the Confederacy (Feb. 18, 1861); elected by popular vote president for six years and inaugurated at Richmond, Va. (Feb. 22, 1862). Policies aroused serious opposition within the Confederacy; failed to gain foreign recognition and aid; constant conflict between extreme States' rights advocates and the president; unable to solve financial stringency; as fortune of war turned against South after Gettysburg, criticism of Davis increased in intensity; suspected of planning emancipation of slaves; strong group favored negotiations for peace; forced Hampton Roads Conference (Feb. 3, 1865); Davis failed to realize desperate military plight and determined to demand independence for the Confederacy. Fled from Richmond (April 3, 1865); captured at Irwinville, Ga. (May 10, 1865). Imprisoned at Fortress Monroe, Va. (1865–67); indicted for treason (May 8, 1866); released on bond (May 14, 1867); government entered a nolle prosequi (Dec., 1868). Last years of life spent in retirement at estate "Beauvoir," on Gulf of Mexico, near Biloxi, Mississippi. Wrote: *The Rise and Fall of the Confederate Government* (1878–81). His wife, **Va·ri′na** (vȧ·rē′nȧ), *nee* **How′ell** [hou′ĕl] (1826–1906), wrote *Jefferson Davis, Ex-President of the Confederate States of America* (2 vols., 1890). His daughter **Varina Anne Jefferson Davis** (1864–1898), known as "the Daughter of the Confederacy," was a novelist, author of *The Veiled Doctor* (1895), *A Romance of Summer Seas* (1899), etc.

**Davis, John.** English explorer. See Davys.

**Davis, John Chandler Bancroft.** 1822–1907. American diplomat and jurist, b. Worcester, Mass. Asst. secretary of state (1869–71; 1873–74). U.S. minister to Germany (1874–77). Judge, U.S. court of claims (1878–81; 1881–83). Reporter, U.S. Supreme Court (1883–1902), editing vols. 108–186 of *United States Reports.* His father, **John Davis** (1787–1854), known as "Honest John," b. Northboro, Mass., was governor of Mass. (1834, 1835, 1841–43) and U.S. senator (1835–41, 1845–53).

**Davis, John William.** 1873–1955. American lawyer and politician, b. Clarksburg, W.Va. Member, U.S. House of Representatives (1911–13). U.S. solicitor general (1913–18). U.S. ambassador to Great Britain (1918–21). Democratic candidate for president of U.S. (1924).

**Davis, Nathan Smith.** 1817–1904. American physician, b. Greene, N.Y. Practiced Binghamton, N.Y. (1838–47); New York City (1847–49). Instrumental in organization of American Medical Association. Professor, Rush Medical College, Chicago (1849–59). Founded Lind Univ. medical department (1859), which later became medical department of Northwestern U.; professor (1859–86).

**Davis, Norman H.** 1878–1944. American financier and diplomat, b. in Bedford County, Tenn. Organized and headed The Trust Company of Cuba (1905–17). Finance commissioner of U.S. to Europe (1919). Asst. secretary, U.S. treasury (1919–20); undersecretary of state (1920–21). Member, League of Nations financial committee; U.S. delegate to disarmament conference at Geneva, Switzerland (1932); head of American delegation to international sugar conference (1937).

**Davis, Owen.** 1874–1956. American playwright, b. Portland, Me. Author of *Icebound* (1923; awarded Pulitzer prize), *The Nervous Wreck* (1923), *The Detour* (1923), *Lazybones* (1924), *Beware of Widows* (1925), and a large number of farces and melodramas, as *Nellie the Beautiful Cloak Model, The Convict's Sweetheart,* etc.

**Davis, Richard Harding.** 1864–1916. American newspaperman, war correspondent, and novelist, b. Philadelphia. Joined staff of New York *Sun* (1889). Managing editor, *Harper's Weekly* (1890). War correspondent in six wars; wrote travel books, popular fiction, and plays: fiction, *Gallegher and Other Stories* (1891), *Van Bibber and Others* (1892), *Soldiers of Fortune* (1897), *The King's Jackal* (1898), *Captain Macklin* (1902), *Ranson's Folly* (1902), *The Bar Sinister* (1903), *Vera the Medium* (1908), *The White Mice* (1909); plays, *Ranson's Folly* (1904), *The Dictator* (1904), *Miss Civilization* (1906). His mother, **Rebecca Blaine,** *nee* **Harding** (1831–1910), b. Washington, Pa., was also a novelist, author of *Margaret Howth* (1862), *A Law unto Herself* (1878), *Dr. Warrick's Daughters* (1896), etc.

**Davis, Thomas Osborne.** 1814–1845. Irish poet; with John Blake Dillon and Charles Gavan Duffy, founded *The Nation* (1842), to which he contributed lyrics; one of leaders of extremist Young Ireland party, dissatisfied with O'Connell's methods.

**Davis, Varina.** See under Jefferson Davis.

**Davis, William.** 1812–1868. American inventor, b. Pittsburgh, Pa. Invented improved refrigerating freight car for transporting fresh meats, fish, and fruits (patented 1868).

**Davis, William Augustine.** 1809–1875. American postal authority, b. in Barren County, Ky. Postmaster at St. Joseph, Mo.; devised system of sorting mail on trains to expedite handling at junction points, thus originating railway post-office service (1862).

**Davis, William Morris.** 1850–1934. American geographer and geologist; authority on physiography; b. Philadelphia, Pa. Professor of geology, Harvard (from 1899). Physiographer to Pumpelly's Carnegie Institution expedition to Turkestan (1903). Author of *Elementary Meteorology* (1894), *Geographical Essays* (1909), *Coral Reef Problem* (1928), etc.

**Davis, William Stearns.** 1877–1930. American educator and writer, b. Amherst, Mass. Professor of history, Minnesota (1909–27). Author of *A Friend of Caesar* (1900), *A Day in Old Athens* (1914), *The Roots of the*

*War* (1918), *Life on a Mediaeval Barony* (1923), *Europe Since Waterloo* (1926), etc.

**Da′vi·son** (dā′vĭ·s'n), **Henry Pom′er·oy** (pŏm′ẽr·oi). 1867–1922. American financier, b. Troy, Pa. Partner, J. P. Morgan & Co., bankers, New York City. Chairman, American Red Cross Council during World War.

**Davison, William.** 1541?–1608. Scottish secretary to Queen Elizabeth (1586–87); member of commission for trial of Mary, Queen of Scots; imprisoned on Elizabeth's false charge of undue haste in securing her signature to Mary's death warrant.

**Da′vis·son** (dā′vĭ·s'n), **Clinton Joseph.** 1881–1958. American physicist; known for researches in electricity, magnetism, and radiant energy; discovered (with L. H. Germer) the diffraction of electrons by crystals (1927). Shared with George Paget Thomson the **1937** Nobel prize in physics.

**Dav′itt** (dăv′ĭt), **Michael.** 1846–1906. Irish Nationalist leader and founder of Irish Land League. Joined Fenian brotherhood (1865); served seven years penal servitude for attempt to send firearms into Ireland. Met Henry George in America; organized Land League (1879) in order to link up independence with agrarian unrest; imprisoned for seditious speeches. Elected M.P. (1882); conducted campaign for land nationalization; repudiated by Parnell (1882–85); spoke five days in defense against charge of plotting independence of Ireland by violence (1889). M.P. as anti-Parnellite; helped William O'Brien found United Irish League to reconcile factions (1898). Author of *Leaves from a Prison Diary* (1884) and *The Fall of Feudalism in Ireland* (1904).

**Da′vout′** (då′vōō′), **Louis Nicolas.** Duc **d'Au′er′stædt′** (då′wĕr′ståt′). Prince **d'Eck′mühl′** (dĕk′mül′). 1770–1823. French soldier in Revolutionary and Napoleonic armies; general of division (1800); marshal of France (1804); fought at Austerlitz (1805), Auerstedt (1806), Eggmühl and Wagram (1809), and in Russian campaign (1812). Minister of war during Hundred Days.

**Da′vy** (dā′vĭ), Sir **Humphry.** 1778–1829. English chemist, b. Penzance, Cornwall. Professor of chemistry (1802–12), Royal Institution, London; on Continental tour (1813–15) with wife and Michael Faraday, his assistant in Royal Institution laboratory; president of Royal Society (1820). Discovered exhilarating effect of nitrous oxide when inhaled (1799); experimented also on inhalation of carbureted hydrogen, nitrogen, and other gases; first prepared potassium (1807), sodium (1807), and calcium (1808), by electrolytic means; demonstrated that chlorine is an element, that the diamond is carbon, that the rare earths are not elements but oxides of elements (1808), that some acids are free from oxygen, suggesting that hydrogen gives the acid character to acids (1810–15); advanced electrical theory of chemical affinity in *On Some Chemical Agencies of Electricity* (1807); invented miner's safety lamp (1815). Published *Elements of Chemical Philosophy* (1812), *Elements of Agricultural Chemistry* (based on his lectures; 1813), *Salmonia, or Days of Fly Fishing* (1827), *Consolations in Travel* (1830).

**Da′vys** *or* **Da′vis** (dā′vĭs), **John.** 1550?–1605. English navigator and Arctic explorer. Made voyages with Adrian Gilbert; started (1585) on first expedition to find northwestern passage; pushed through strait named for him (Davis Strait) into Baffin Bay (1587); accompanied Thomas Cavendish to South Seas and continued alone to discover Falkland Islands. Killed by Japanese pirates off Singapore. Inventor of backstaff and double quadrant, called *Davis's quadrant.*

**Dawe** (dô), **George.** 1781–1829. English portrait painter and mezzotint engraver.

**Dawes** (dôz), **Charles Gates.** 1865–1951. American lawyer, financier, and politician, b. Marietta, Ohio. U.S. comptroller of the currency (1897–1901). To Chicago, and organized (1902) Central Union Trust Co., its president (1902–21) and chairman of board of directors (1921–25); chairman of board of City National Bank and Trust Co., Chicago (from 1932). Served in A.E.F., in France (1917–19; brigadier general). First director, U.S. Bureau of the Budget (1921). President of commission to investigate possibilities of German budget and German payments of reparations (1923); commission evolved so-called Dawes plan, put in effect (Sept. 1, 1924). Vice-president of the United States (1925–29). U.S. ambassador to Great Britain (1929–32). President, Reconstruction Finance Corp. (1932). Corecipient, with Sir Austen Chamberlain of England, of Nobel peace prize (1925). Author of *A Journal of the Great War* (1921), *Notes as Vice-President* (1935), *A Journal of Reparations* (1939), etc. His brother **Rufus Cutler** (1867–1940), public utility executive, served as adviser to commission that evolved the Dawes plan (1923–24) and as assistant to Owen D. Young, first agent-general of reparations; president, Century of Progress Exposition, Chicago.

**Dawes, Henry Laurens.** 1816–1903. American political leader, b. Cummington, Mass. Member, U.S. House of Representatives (1857–75); U.S. Senate (1875–93); author of Dawes Act, conferring citizenship on all civilized Indians.

**Dawes, William.** 1745–1799. American patriot, b. Boston; rode with Paul Revere (April 18, 1775) from Lexington toward Concord, warning people of coming of British.

**Da′wi·son** (dä′vē·sôn), **Bogumił.** 1818–1872. Polish actor; successful in Germany and U.S.; important roles were Shylock, King Lear, Richard III, Mephisto, Othello.

**Dawith Anjalth.** See DAVID THE PHILOSOPHER.

**Daw′kins** (dô′kĭnz), Sir **William Boyd.** 1837–1929. British geologist and archaeologist, b. in Wales. First professor of geology, Owens Coll. (now Victoria U.), Manchester (1874–1908). Investigated prehistoric cave dwellers.

**Daw′son** (dô′s'n), **A. J.** 1872–1951. English soldier and novelist, b. London. Officer in World War (1914–18). Among his books are *God's Foundling, Bismillah, Finn the Wolfhound, Son of Finn, A Temporary Gentleman in France, Peter of Monks-lease, The Case Books of X 37.*

**Dawson, Bul′ly** (bŏŏl′ĭ). Notorious London sharper of 17th century.

**Dawson, Con′ings·by** (kŏn′ĭngz·bĭ) **William.** 1883–1959. Writer, b. High Wycombe, Buckinghamshire, Eng.; to U.S. (1905). Served with Canadian contingent in World War, in France (1916–18). Lectured throughout U.S. on results of the war and on reconstruction problems. Among his many books are *The Worker and Other Poems* (1906), *The Garden Without Walls* (1913), *Living Bayonets* (1919), *Pilgrims of the Impossible* (1928), *Inspiration Valley* (1935), etc.

**Dawson, Geoffrey.** 1874–1944. English journalist; editor, Johannesburg *Star* (1905–10) and London *Times* (1912–19; 1923–41).

**Dawson, Henry.** 1811–1878. English landscape painter; praised as colorist by Ruskin.

**Dawson, James.** 1717?–1746. English volunteer officer in service of the Young Pretender (1745); hanged, drawn, and quartered on Kensington Green, his betrothed dying of grief in her coach the same day (1746); subject of Shenstone's ballad *Jemmy Dawson.*

**Dawson,** Sir **John William.** 1820–1899. Canadian geologist; specialist in natural history and geology of Nova Scotia and New Brunswick. Professor of geology and principal (1855–93), McGill U., Montreal; associated with controversy over eozoon; opponent of Darwinian explanation of origin of life forms. His son **George Mercer** (1849–1901) was also a geologist; member (1875), asst. director (1883), director (1895) of geological survey of Canada; in charge of Yukon expedition (1887); member, Bering Sea Commission (1891).

**Dawson, William Harbutt.** 1860–1948. English publicist; best known for books interpreting for English readers German thought, manners, history, and institutions.

**Dawson, William James.** 1854–1928. Clergyman, poet, and miscellaneous writer, b. in Northampton, Eng.; ordained Wesleyan minister (1875); to U.S. (1905). Author of *A Vision of Souls* (verse, 1884), *Makers of English Poetry* (1890), *Makers of English Prose* (1899), *The Book of Courage* (1911), *Robert Shenstone* (novel, 1917), *The Autobiography of a Mind* (1925), etc.

**Dawson of Penn** (pĕn), 1st Viscount. **Bertrand Edward Dawson.** 1864–1945. English physician, b. Croydon. Physician in ordinary to royal family (from 1907); member of privy council (from 1929); president, Royal College of Physicians (1931–38), British Medical Association (1943–44).

**Day** (dā), **Benjamin Henry.** 1810–1889. American newspaperman, b. West Springfield, Mass.; founded first one-cent daily paper, New York *Sun* (1833). His son **Benjamin** (1838–1916), New York printer, invented the Ben Day process for shading in printing illustrations. Benjamin Henry's grandson **Clarence Shepard Day, Jr.** (1874–1935), writer, b. New York City; author of *This Simian World* (1920), *The Crow's Nest* (1921), *Thoughts Without Words* (1928), *God and My Father* (1932), *In the Green Mountain Country* (1934), *Life with Father* (1935; dramatized by Howard Lindsay and Russel Crouse, 1939), *Life with Mother* (pub. 1937), etc.

**Day, Clive.** 1871–1951. American economist; professor, Yale (1907–36). Author of *History of Commerce* (1907), *Economic Development in Modern Europe* (1933), etc.

**Day, Edmund Ezra.** 1883–1951. American educator, b. Manchester, N.H. Teacher of economics, Michigan (1923–27), where he organized, and was first dean (1924–27) of, school of business administration. President, Cornell U. (1937–51).

**Day, Frank Miles.** 1861–1918. American architect, b. Philadelphia. Examples of work: Philadelphia Art Club; Prudence Risley Hall, Cornell U.; dormitory and dining-hall group, Princeton U.; Liberal Arts building, Wellesley College.

**Day, Holman Francis.** 1865–1935. American writer; managing editor, Lewiston (Me.) *Daily Sun.* Author of *Up in Maine* (verse, 1900), *Pine Tree Ballads* (1902), *Squire Phin* (novel, 1905), *Along Came Ruth* (play, 1914), *Leadbetter's Luck* (1923), *Starwagons* (1928), *Ships of Joy* (1932), etc.

**Day, James Roscoe.** 1845–1923. American Methodist clergyman and educator; b. Whitneyville, Me.; chancellor, U. of Syracuse (1894–1922).

**Day, Jeremiah.** 1773–1867. American educator, b. New Preston, Conn. Professor of mathematics and natural philosophy (1803–17), president (1817–46), Yale.

**Day, John.** 1574–?1640. English playwright; collaborator with Henry Chettle, Thomas Dekker, and others. Author of *The Ile of Guls* (1606), *Law Trickes* and *Humour out of Breath* (1608), and *The Parliament of Bees* (a satirically allegorical masque; 1607?).

**Day, John Godfrey Fitzmaurice.** 1874–1938. Bishop of Ossory, Ferns, and Leighlin (1920–38). Primate of all Ireland (Church of Ireland) and archbishop of Armagh (1938).

**Day** *or* **Daye** (dā), **Stephen.** 1594?–1668. Printer, b. in England; to America (1638); first printer in English colonies in America, with press in Cambridge, Mass. The *Bay Psalm Book*, printed by him (1640), was the first book in English printed in America.

**Day, Thomas.** 1748–1789. English author; admirer of Rousseau's doctrines; attempted philanthropic schemes of moral and social reform. Author of *The Dying Negro* (poem; 1773) and *History of Sandford and Merton* (3 vols., 1783, 1787, 1789), an attempt in fiction to reconcile Rousseauistic naturalism with conventional morality.

**Day, William Rufus.** 1849–1923. American statesman and jurist, b. Ravenna, Ohio. U.S. secretary of state (1898). Chairman, U.S. commission to arrange peace with Spain (1898–99). Associate justice, U.S. Supreme Court (1903–22).

**Da·yan′** (dä·yän′), **Moshe.** 1915– . Israeli army officer and statesman, b. Palestine. Israeli chief of staff (1953–58), minister of agriculture (1959–64), of defense (1967– ).

**Daye, Stephen.** See Stephen DAY.

**Day–Lewis, Cecil.** See Cecil Day LEWIS.

**Day′ton** (dā′t'n), **Elias.** 1737–1807. American Revolutionary officer, b. Elizabeth, N.J. Promoted brigadier general (1783) on direct recommendation of Washington. Member, U.S. House of Representatives (1787–88). His son **Jonathan** (1760–1824) was captain in Revolutionary army (1783); member, Continental Congress (1787–89), U.S. House of Representatives (1791–99; speaker, 1795–99); U.S. senator (1799–1805). Jonathan's nephew **William Lewis Dayton** (1807–1864) was unsuccessful candidate for vice-president of the U.S. (1856); U.S. minister to France (1861–64).

**Dayukku.** See DEÏOCES.

**Da′za** (dä′sä), **Hilarión.** *Real surname* **Gro′so·lé′** (grō′sô·lā′). 1840–1894. Bolivian general, b. Sucre. President of Bolivia (1876–80); joined Peru in war against Chile (1879–80); defeated; overthrown by revolution (1880); returned from exile (1894); killed by a mob.

**d'Azeglio,** Marchese. See AZEGLIO.

**Da′zey** (dā′zĭ), **Charles Turner.** 1855–1938. American playwright and scenarist, b. Lima, Ill.; author of successful melodrama *In Old Kentucky.*

**Dead′wood′ Dick** (dĕd′wŏŏd′ dĭk′). *Sobriquet of* **Richard W. Clarke.** 1845–1930. English-born frontiersman in South Dakota.

**De′ák** (dĕ′äk), **Ferencz.** 1803–1876. Hungarian lawyer and statesman. Member of Hungarian legislature (1833–36, 1839–40); rose to leadership in Liberal Reform party. Minister of justice (1848); opposed Kossuth and radical policies, while standing firmly for restoration of Hungarian constitution. Became generally acknowledged leader of Hungary (from c. 1861); gained from Austrian emperor restoration of Hungarian constitution (Feb. 18, 1867) and established the dual monarchy of Austria-Hungary.

**Dea′kin** (dē′kĭn), **Alfred.** 1856–1919. Australian statesman, b. Melbourne. Solicitor general of Victoria (1883); promoted federation movement in Victoria (1891–98); first attorney general under commonwealth (1901); premier (1903–04, 1905–08, 1909–10).

**Dea′ley** (dē′lĭ), **James Quayle.** 1861–1937. Political scientist, b. Manchester, Eng.; to U.S. Professor, Brown (1895–1928). Author of *Textbook of Sociology* (with Lester F. Ward; 1905), *The Development of the State* (1909), *Foreign Policies of the United States* (1927), etc.

**De A·mi′cis** (dā ä·mē′chēs), **Edmondo.** 1846–1908. Italian traveler and author of sketches of army life

(1867), travel books, impressions of writers (*Ritratti Letterari*, 1881), historical novelettes, socialistic novels.

**Dean** (dēn), **Bashford.** 1867–1928. American zoologist, b. New York. Curator of reptiles and fishes, American Museum of Natural History (1903–10); also, curator of arms and armor, Metropolitan Museum of Art (1906–27). Author of *Bibliography of Fishes* (3 vols., 1916–23).

**Dean,** Sir **Patrick Henry.** 1909– . British diplomat, b. Germany. Permanent Brit. representative to UN (1960–64); Ambassador to U.S. (1965–69).

**Deane** (dēn), **Anthony Charles.** 1870–1946. English Anglican clergyman and writer; chaplain to the king (from 1934). Best known for his volumes of light verse, including *Frivolous Verses* (1892), *Leaves in the Wind* (1896), *A Little Book of Light Verse* (1902). Author also of a number of religious books, as *The Reformation* (1907), *Jesus Christ* (1927), *Sixth-Form Religion* (1936).

**Deane, Charles.** 1813–1889. American historical scholar, b. Biddeford, Me. Edited Gov. Bradford's *History of Plymouth Plantation* (1856).

**Deane, Richard.** 1610–1653. English military and naval commander and regicide. Commander of Parliamentary artillery (1644–47); commander of right wing at Preston (1648); commissioner for trial of Charles I and signed death warrant. Commander as a general at sea (1649); fought as major general at Worcester (1651); as commander in chief in Scotland, pacified Highlands (1652).

**Deane, Silas.** 1737–1789. American lawyer and diplomat, b. Groton, Conn. Leader of revolutionary agitation in Conn.; member, Continental Congress (1774–76). Sent to France as American confidential agent to secure supplies and aid (1776); succeeded in purchasing shiploads of supplies and enlisting the aid of a number of military men, including Lafayette, Steuben, Pulaski (1776–77). Joined by Benjamin Franklin and Arthur Lee (*q.v.*) to form commission of three; ordered back to America (1778); required to give detailed statement of his transactions in France; failed to satisfy Congress; returned to France to hasten auditing of accounts and obtain vouchers (1780). From Europe wrote pessimistic letters on American chances of success, and urged reconciliation with England (1781); publication of letters turned Americans against him; accused of being traitor and embezzler; character vindicated by Congress (1842).

**De An'ge·lis** (dē ăn'jĕ·lĭs), **Jefferson.** 1859–1933. American comedian, b. San Francisco; among plays in which he starred were *The Great White Way*, *Mikado*, *Revelry*, *School for Scandal*, and *Apron Strings*.

**Dear'born** (dēr'bẽrn; -bôrn), **George Van Ness.** 1869–1938. American neuropsychiatrist, b. Nashua, N.H.; professor of psychology and education, Sargent Normal School, Cambridge (1906–21); with U.S. Veterans' Administration (from 1921). Author of *A Textbook of Human Physiology* (1908), *Relations of Mind and Body* (1914), *The Physiology of Exercise* (1918), etc.

**Dearborn, Henry.** 1751–1829. American political leader; U.S. secretary of war (1801–09). Commanded forces on Canadian border; campaign mismanaged and Dearborn recalled (1813); placed in command at New York (1813–15); resigned commission (1815). U.S. minister to Portugal (1822–24).

**Dear'den** (dēr'd'n), **Harold.** 1882– . English physician and writer; served in World War (1914–18). Specialist in psychological medicine. Author of *The Doctor Looks at Life* (1924), *The Science of Happiness* (1925), *Queer People* (1933), etc. Author also of the plays *Collision*, *Interference*, *The Siren*, *Frail Purposes*, *To Kill a Cat* (with R. Pertwee, 1939).

**Dear'mer** (dēr'mẽr), **Percy.** 1867–1936. English ecclesiastic and writer; canon of Westminster (from 1931). Author of *Highways and Byways in Normandy* (1900), *The English Liturgy* (1903), *False Gods* (1914), *Our National Church* (1934), *Christianity as a New Religion* (1935).

**Dearth** (dûrth), **Henry Golden.** 1864–1918. American landscape painter, b. Bristol, R.I. Examples of work: *Boulogne Harbor*, now in Metropolitan Museum of Art, New York City; *An Old Church at Montreuil*, in National Gallery, Washington, D.C.; *Dreamland* and *Golden Sunset*, both in Brooklyn Museum of Art.

**De Bar'de·le'ben** (dĕ bär'dĕ·lā'bĕn), **Henry Fairchild.** 1840–1910. American industrialist, b. Alabama; developed coal resources and steel industry in Birmingham area.

**De Ba·ry'** (dĕ bä·rē'), **Heinrich Anton.** 1831–1888. German botanist; founder of science of mycology; first to work out life histories of many of the fungi, esp. parasitic fungi; also worked on the conjugate algae and on apogamy in ferns.

**Debbora.** See DEBORAH.

**De·be·ney'** (dē·bē·nā'), **Marie Eugène.** 1864–1943. French general in the World War (1914–18); engaged before Verdun (1916); commanding 7th army in Alsace and armies of the north and northeast (1917); commanded 1st army on northeastern front (1918).

**De·ber'ly'** (dē·bĕr'lē'), **Henri.** 1882–1947. French novelist; author of *Le Supplice de Phèdre* (awarded Goncourt prize, 1927).

**De·bi'dour'** (dē·bē'do͞or'), **Antonin,** *in full* **Élie Louis Marc Marie Antoine.** 1847–1917. French historian.

**De·bierne'** (dē·byĕrn'), **André Louis.** 1874–1949. French chemist; discovered element actinium in pitchblende (1899); collaborating with Marja Curie, isolated pure radium.

**Deb'o·rah** (dĕb'ō·rȧ). *In Douay Version* **Deb'bo·ra** (dĕb'ō·rȧ). In Bible, a prophetess and judge of Israel, at whose command Barak (*q.v.*) led Israelites to victory against Canaanites (*Judges* iv). Her song (*Judges* v) of triumph for the victory is apparently oldest piece of Hebrew literature.

**De Bow** (dĕ bō'), **James Dunwoody Brownson.** 1820–1867. American editor; founded and edited *Commercial Review of the South and Southwest* (known as *De Bow's Review*), in New Orleans (from 1846). Superintendent, U.S. census; prepared census of 1850, and *Statistical View of the United States* (pub. 1854).

**De·brett'** (dĕ·brĕt'), **John.** d. 1822. English publisher; compiler of a *Peerage of England, Scotland, and Ireland* (1802) and a *Baronetage of England* (1808).

**de Broglie.** See BROGLIE.

**de Brosses, Charles.** See BROSSES.

**Debs** (dĕbz), **Eugene Victor.** 1855–1926. American Socialist, b. Terre Haute, Ind. Locomotive fireman (1870–74); grocery clerk (1874–79). National secretary and treasurer, Brotherhood of Locomotive Firemen (1880). Leader in Pullman strike, Chicago (1894); arrested and sentenced to six months' imprisonment for contempt of court. Organized Social Democratic Party of America (1897); candidate of Socialists for president of the U.S. (1900, 1904, 1908, 1912, 1920). Indicted for violation of Espionage Act (1918); convicted and sentenced to ten years' imprisonment; released by order of President Harding (1921). See P. S. GROSSCUP.

**De·bu'court'** (dē·bü'ko͞or'), **Philibert Louis.** 1755–1832. French painter and engraver; best known for his genre paintings.

**de Burgh** *or* **Bourke** *or* **Burke.** Family name of earls and marquises of CLANRICARDE.

**De·bus'sy'** (dē·bü'sē'; *Angl.* dē·bū'sĭ), **Claude Achille.** 1862–1918. French composer; regarded as a leader of the ultramodern school of music in France. Among his most important works are *L'Enfant Prodigue* (cantata, 1884), *Printemps* (symphonic suite), *L'Après-midi d'un Faune* (symphonic poem, 1902), *Pelléas et Mélisande* (opera, 1902), nocturnes and other orchestral works, piano compositions, and songs.

**De·bye'** (dĕ·bī'), **Peter Joseph Wilhelm.** 1884–1966. Physicist, b. Holland; director, Kaiser Wilhelm Institute for Physics, Berlin (from 1935). Known especially for studies of molecular structure through investigations on dipole moments and on diffraction of X rays and electrons in gases. Awarded 1936 Nobel prize in chemistry. Professor of chemistry and department chairman, Cornell U. (from 1940).

**De·caen'** (dē·kän'), Comte **Charles Mathieu Isidore.** 1769–1832. French general in Revolutionary and Napoleonic armies; engaged at Hohenlinden (1800). Sent by Napoleon to command French possessions in East Indies (1803); made headquarters at Mauritius (1803–11) and harassed British trade. His son **Claude Théodore** (1811–1870) was also a French general; promoted general of division at Magenta (1859); mortally wounded (1870) in battle of Borny (Courcelles).

**De·caisne'** (dē·kân'), **Joseph.** 1807–1882. French botanist; author of *Jardin Fruitier du Muséum*, etc. His brother **Henri** (1799–1852), Belgian painter, known for historical and genre paintings.

**De Camp** (dĕ kămp'; dē), **Joseph Ro'de·fer** (rō'dĕ·fēr). 1858–1923. American painter, b. Cincinnati, Ohio; studio in Boston (from 1880). Examples of work: *Woman Drying Her Hair*, now in Cincinnati Museum of Art; *Horace Howard Furness*, in Pennsylvania Academy of Art, Philadelphia.

**De·camps'** (dē·käN'), **Alexandre Gabriel.** 1803–1860. French painter; traveled in Italy and Near East (1827–28) and thereafter devoted himself esp. to painting Oriental subjects; associated with Delacroix in laying foundations of Orientalism in French art.

**de Candolle.** See CANDOLLE.

**De Cas'ser·es** (dĕ kăs'ĕr·ĕs; -ĭs), **Benjamin.** 1873–1945. American journalist and poet, b. Philadelphia; conductor of column *On the Nail* in New York *American* and allied Hearst papers (from 1934). Author of *The Shadow-Eater* (verse, 1915), *Black Suns* (verse, 1936), *Broken Images* (essays, 1936), *Sir Galahad* (1938), etc.

**De·ca'tur** (dē·kā'tēr), **Stephen.** 1779–1820. American naval officer, b. Sinepuxent, Md. Commanded schooner *Enterprise* in Tripolitan waters (1803). Performed daring exploit in burning a frigate captured and held by Tripolitans (Feb. 16, 1804); promoted to captain; commanded one division of gunboats in attacks on Tripoli (August, 1804). In War of 1812, commanded the *United States* in victory over the British ship *Macedonian* (Oct. 25, 1812) and the *President* in victory over *Endymion* (Jan. 15, 1815). Commanded squadron which sailed to Algeria and forced a peace on American terms (1815). In a banquet on his return, he gave the famous toast: "Our country! In her intercourse with foreign nations may she always be in the right; but our country, right or wrong!" Killed by James Barron, a naval officer in a duel (Mar. 22, 1820). His father, **Stephen Decatur** (1752–1808), b. Newport, R.I., was also an American naval officer.

**De·cau'ville'** (dē·kō'vēl'), **Paul.** 1846–1922. French industrialist; inventor of, and manufacturer of equipment for, a narrow-gauge railroad (named after him) with demountable and transportable track.

**De·cazes'** (dē·käz'), Duc **Élie.** 1780–1860. French jurist and statesman; minister of police (1815) and minister of the interior and premier (1819–20). Created Duc Decazes and peer of France (1820); ambassador to Great Britain (1820). His son **Louis Charles Amadieu Decazes,** Duc **de Glücks'berg'** [glüks'bĕrg'] (1819–1886), was minister of foreign affairs (1873–77).

**De·ceb'a·lus** (dē·sĕb'ȧ·lŭs). d. about 107 A.D. King of the Dacians. Received tribute from Roman emperor Domitian; defeated by Trajan (103) and again in second campaign (104–106) when Dacia became Roman province.

**De Celles** (dē sĕl'), **Alfred Duclos.** 1843–1925. Canadian journalist, librarian, and historian; author of *Cartier et son Temps* (1907), etc.

**De·cem'bri·o** (dā·chĕm'brē·ō), **Pier Candido.** 1399–1477. Italian Humanist; apostolic secretary to Nicholas V; author of biographies of Visconti and Francesco Sforza.

**De Ce'sa·re** (dā chā'zä·rā), **Carlo.** 1824–1882. Italian political economist and statesman; secretary-general of agriculture, industry, and commerce (1868). Author of *Della Scienza Statistica*...(1857), *Del Potere Temporale del Papa* (2d ed., 1861), *Manuale Popolare di Economia Pubblica* (2 vols., 1862), etc.

**De Chair** (dĕ shâr'), Sir **Dudley Rawson Stratford.** 1864–1958. British naval officer; in World War, commanded 10th cruiser squadron organizing and maintaining North Sea blockade (1914–16); commanded 3d battle squadron (1917–18); vice-admiral (1917). Admiral (1920); retired (1923). Governor of New South Wales (1923–30).

**De·champs'** (dē·shäN'), **Adolphe.** 1807–1875. Belgian statesman; a leader of the Catholic party; minister of public works (1843) and of foreign affairs (1845). His brother **Victor Auguste** (1810–1883) was a Roman Catholic prelate; archbishop of Malines (1867), cardinal (1874).

**Dé'che·lette'** (dāsh'lĕt'), **Joseph.** 1862–1914. French archaeologist, authority on Gallo-Roman and Celtic coins. Author of *Manuel d'Archéologie Préhistorique, Celtique, et Gallo-Romaine* (4 vols., 1908–14), etc.

**De'chen** (dĕK'ĕn), **Heinrich von.** 1800–1889. German geologist and mineralogist; authority on the coal formations of Westphalia and northern Europe and the mineralogy of the Rhineland.

**De'ci·us** (dē'shĭ·ŭs; -shŭs). *Full name* **Gaius Messius Quintus Tra·ja'nus Decius** (trȧ·jā'nŭs). 201–251. Roman emperor (249–251), b. in Pannonia. Commanded troops of Emperor Philip on the Danube; his soldiers revolted (249); proclaimed emperor against his will; defeated and killed Philip at Verona; conducted cruel persecution of Christians; killed in Thrace in battle with Goths.

**Decius Mus** (mŭs), **Publius.** Name of three Roman consuls, father, son, and grandson, who sacrificed themselves to assure Roman victory in the Samnite War (340 B.C.), at battle of Sentinum (295 B.C.), and at battle of Ausculum (279 B.C.), respectively.

**Deck** (dĕk), **Théodore,** *in full* **Joseph Théodore.** 1823–1891. French ceramist; created imitations of Persian and Chinese ware, also new colors for porcelain, including turquoise blue; director of Sèvres factory (1887).

**Deck'en** (dĕk'ĕn), **Karl Klaus von der.** 1833–1865. German explorer in East Africa (1860–65); murdered by natives.

**Deck'er** (dĕk'ēr), **Cornelis Gerrits.** d. 1678. Dutch landscape painter.

**Deck'er** *or* **Dek'ker** (dĕk'ēr), **Jeremias de.** 1609–1666. Dutch poet; author of *Rijm-Oefeningen* (1656), *Lof der Geldzucht* (1667), etc.

**Decker, Thomas.** See DEKKER.

**de Cop'pet'** (dē kô'pā'), **Edward J.** 1855–1916. American banker and music patron. Founder of banking and brokerage firm of De Coppet & Doremus. Organizer of the Flonzaley Quartet (1904), a string quartet renowned for its performances of chamber music.

**De Cort** *or* **Decort, Frans.** See CORT.

**de Coster, Charles.** See COSTER.

**De·cour'celle'** (dē·kōōr'sĕl'), **Pierre Henri Adrien.** 1821–1892. French author or coauthor of many plays, including the verse comedy *Une Soirée à la Bastille* and the drama *Jenny l'Ouvrière.* His son **Pierre** (1856–1926) was playwright and novelist.

**De'de·kind** (dā'dĕ·kĭnt), **Friedrich.** 1525?–1598. German poet and playwright.

**Dedekind, Julius Wilhelm Richard.** 1831–1916. German mathematician; known for work on algebraic numbers and functions; originated a theory of irrational numbers.

**De Du've** (dĕ dōō'vĕ), **Christian René Marie Joseph.** 1917– . Belgian biochemist. At Catholic U. of Louvain (1947– ); also at Rockefeller U. (1962– ); awarded (with Albert Claude and George E. Palade) Nobel prize for physiology or medicine (1974).

**Dee** (dē), **John.** 1527–1608. English mathematician and astrologer; acquitted by Star Chamber on charge of practicing sorcery against Queen Mary (1555); enjoyed favor of Queen Elizabeth, for whom he drew up hydrographical and geographical accounts of newly discovered territories; advocated adoption of Gregorian calendar in England, and made preparatory calculations (1583); collaborated with the knave Edward Kelley (*q.v.*) in Poland and Bohemia in chicanery of crystal gazing and magic (1583–89). Author of Latin treatises on logic, mathematics, navigation, alchemy, etc., including *Monas Hieroglyphica* (1564).

**Deems** (dēmz), **Charles Force.** 1820–1893. American Methodist clergyman; founded undenominational Church of the Strangers, New York City (1868); served as its pastor (1868–93). Author of *Life of Jesus* (1872), *A Scotch Verdict in Evolution* (1885), etc.

**Deep'ing** (dēp'ĭng), **George Warwick.** 1877–1950. English novelist, b. Southend, Essex. Studied medicine, but withdrew from practice to devote himself to writing. Served during World War in Gallipoli, Egypt, and France. Among his many novels are *Unrest* (1916), *Valour* (1918), *Sorrell and Son* (1925), *Old Pybus* (1928), *Old Wine and New* (1932), *Blind Man's Year* (1937), *The Man who went Back* (1940).

**Deere** (dēr), **John.** 1804–1886. American industrialist, b. Rutland, Vt. Manufacturer of steel plows; firm incorporated as Deere & Co. (1868). Cf. John LANE.

**Deer'ing** (dēr'ĭng), **William.** 1826–1913. American industrialist, b. South Paris, Me. Established harvester manufacturing business at Plano, Ill. (1873); incorporated as William Deering & Co. (1883); merged with International Harvester Co., Chicago (1902).

**De·fauw'** (dĕ·fou'), **Dé'si'ré'** (dā'zē'rā'). 1885–1960. Belgian violinist and orchestra conductor; musical director of Belgium's Institut National de Radiodiffusion, and conductor of 84-piece orchestra for radio broadcasting; in U.S. as guest conductor of National Broadcasting Co. (1939).

**de Ferranti, Sebastian Ziani.** See FERRANTI.

**Def'fand'** (dĕ'fäɴ'), Marquise **du.** *Nee* **Marie de Vi'chy'-Cham'rond'** (dē vē'shē'shäɴ'rôɴ'). 1697–1780. French noblewoman; m. Marquis du Deffand (1719); a leader in social life of the period. Remembered chiefly for her friendship and correspondence with noted men, including Voltaire, Hénault, Montesquieu, Horace Walpole.

**De·foe'** (dĕ·fō'; dē-), **Daniel.** 1659?–1731. English journalist and novelist, b. London. Employed by government as writer, produced his *Essay on Projects* (1698), making commercial and social proposals in advance of his time; *The True-Born Englishman* (1701), a satire in verse upon purity of blood in a nation; pamphlets on William III's war policy. Fined, imprisoned, pilloried for his *Shortest Way with Dissenters* (1702), and composed *Hymn to the Pillory* (1704). Sent as secret agent of government to Scotland (1706–07) to promote union; showed his skill as a reporter in the *True Relation of the Apparition of one Mrs. Veal* (1706). Supported Whig policies of Marlborough and Godolphin (1708–10); on Harley's return to power, supported Tory war policy; shared Harley's downfall; generally discredited, published apologia, *An Appeal to Honour and Justice* (1715); convicted of libel against Lord Annesley but released on condition of serving as government secret agent in subediting the Jacobite *Mist's Journal* (1717–24) and High Church organs; published *The Wars of Charles XII* (1715). Turned to fiction when nearly sixty years old and, with background from Dampier's *Voyage round the World* (1697) and from accounts by Woodes Rogers, Captain Edward Cooke, and Richard Steele, narrated adventures of Alexander Selkirk (*q.v.*) in *Robinson Crusoe* (1719) and sequel, *Serious Reflections* (1720). During next five years, produced prolifically fiction and fictitious histories: *Life of Mr. Duncan Campbell* (1720), the deaf and dumb fortune teller; *Captain Singleton* (1720), brilliant record of journey across Africa, anticipating discoveries; *Moll Flanders, The Journal of the Plague Year,* and *The History of Colonel Jack* (1721); a series of stories of criminals, *Jack Sheppard* (1724), *Jonathan Wild* (1725), *The Highland Rogue* (*Rob Roy;* 1723); also a three-volume guidebook of Great Britain (1724–27), *A New Voyage round the World* (1725), and the romance *Roxana* (1724). In closing years, published pamphlets showing social and economic farsightedness, such as *A Plan of the English Commerce* (1728), didactic works, such as *Everybody's Business is Nobody's Business* (1725), and a series of demonological works, including an *Essay on the History of Apparitions* (1728). Lived in hiding, probably on discovery of his service as secret agent; adopted pseudonym **Andrew More'ton** (mōr't'n). His youngest daughter, **Sophia,** married (1729) Henry Baker, naturalist and poet (*q.v.*).

**De' Forciglioni, Antonio.** See Saint ANTONINUS.

**De For'est** (dĕ fŏr'ĕst; -ĭst), **John William.** 1826–1906. American writer, b. Seymour, Conn. Author of *Miss Ravenel's Conversion* (1866), *The Wetherel Affair* (1873), *Honest John Vane* (1875), *A Lover's Revolt* (1889), etc.

**De Forest, Lee.** 1873–1961. American inventor, b. Council Bluffs, Iowa. Pioneer in wireless telegraphy and radiotelephony in America; sometimes called "the father of radio." Patented over 300 inventions in wireless telegraphy, radio telephony, sound-on-film talking pictures, high-speed facsimile transmission, television, radiotherapy, etc.; added third electrode to the electron tube, making possible its use as radio detector, radio and telephone amplifier, and as oscillator; also invented glow-lamp recording of sound on film for motion pictures, etc. Designed and installed first high-power radio stations for U.S. navy; broadcast Caruso's voice by radio (1910), first news by radio (1916); established radio station (1916). Exhibited sound-on-film motion pictures at Rivoli Theater, New York City (1923).

**De Forest, Robert Weeks.** 1848–1931. American lawyer, b. New York City. Trustee, Metropolitan Museum of Art (from 1889), and president (from 1913). First tenement house commissioner of New York City (1902–

03). President, Municipal Art Commission (1905–29). His brother **Lockwood** (1850–1932), artist, traveled and worked in Egypt and Near East (1875–78) and in India (1881–82); founded workshops at Ahmadabad, India, for revival of art of woodcarving (1881).

**De′freg′ger** (dā′frĕg′ẽr), **Franz von.** 1835–1921. Austrian painter; famed for genre pictures of scenes from Tirolese peasant life.

**De Gar′mo** (dĕ gär′mō), **Charles.** 1849–1934. American educator; president, Swarthmore Coll. (1891–98); professor of science and art of education, Cornell U. (1898–1914). Author of *Herbart and the Herbartians* (1898), *Interest and Education* (1903), etc.

**De·gas′** (dē·gä′), **Hilaire Germain Edgar.** 1834–1917. French impressionist painter, b. Paris. One of leaders of impressionist school, and associate of Manet, Monet, Renoir, and Fantin-Latour. Known esp. for his scenes from the theater.

**de Gaspé, Philippe Aubert.** See GASPÉ.

**de Gaulle′** (dē gōl′), **Charles André Joseph Marie.** 1890–1970. French soldier, b. Lille. Grad. St.-Cyr; served in World War I (1914–18); entered l'École Supérieure de Guerre (1924). Made himself known for his advocacy of a highly mechanized French army; urged construction of tanks and training of men for tank corps; wrote, on subject of mechanized warfare, *Le Fil de l'Épée* (1932), *Vers l'Armée de Métier* (1934), *La France et son Armée* (1938). Promoted general of brigade soon after beginning of war with Germany (1939) and then general of division; sent by Marshal Pétain to England (1940) to confer on military aid. Refused to accept France's capitulation; became head of provisional Free French national committee in England; gained adherence of several French colonies; co-operated with British in conquest of Syria (1941); assumed control of Madagascar (Dec., 1942); copresident with Giraud (June–Nov., 1943), then sole head, of French Committee of National Liberation; returned to France after liberation of Paris (1944); interim president of France (1945–46); president of the Fifth Republic (1959–69).

**de Geer,** Baron **Louis Gerhard.** See GEER.

**de Gérando** *or* **Degérando.** See GÉRANDO.

**de'Gianuzzi, Giulio.** See Giulio ROMANO.

**de Girardin, Émile** and **Delphine Gay.** See GIRARDIN.

**degli.** See note under letter D.

**de Goeje, Jan.** See GOEJE.

**De Go′gor·za′** (dā gō′gôr·thä′), **E·mi′lio** (ā·mē′lyō) **E·duar′do** (ā·thwär′thō). 1874–1949. American operatic baritone, b. Brooklyn, N.Y.; m. (1911) Emma Eames (*q.v.*); debut with Metropolitan Opera Company (1897); also a concert and recital singer.

**De·goutte′** (dē·goot′), **Jean Marie Joseph.** 1866–1938. French general in the World War; commanded Allied forces of occupation in the Ruhr region (1923–25).

**de Grasse.** See GRASSE.

**De·grelle′** (dē·grĕl′), **Léon.** 1906– . Belgian lawyer and political agitator; organized (1935) in the Catholic party, ostensibly to purify it, the Rex (orig. Christus Rex) movement, which gained 21 seats in 1936 general elections, probably with Nazi support. In order to test political strength, opposed Premier van Zeeland in special election (1937); defeated by vote of 275,840 to 69,242. Nazi puppet governor of Belgium (1944); fled to Spain; interned (1945).

**de Grey** *or* **de Gray.** See GREY.

**de Grey and Ripon,** Earl. = George Frederick Samuel ROBINSON.

**de Groot.** See GROOT and GROTIUS.

**de Gubernatis,** Conte **Angelo.** See GUBERNATIS.

**De Haas, Jacob** and **Maurice.** See HAAS.

**Dehan, Richard.** See Clotilde GRAVES.

**de Hav′il·land** (dĕ hăv′ĭ·lănd), Sir **Geoffrey.** 1882–1965. British aeronautical engineer; designer and manufacturer of de Havilland airplanes.

**Deh′mel** (dā′mĕl), **Richard.** 1863–1920. German poet and playwright.

**Dehn** (dān), **Ad′olf** (ăd′ŏlf) **Arthur.** 1895–1968. American etcher, b. Waterville, Minn.

**Dehn** (dān), **Siegfried Wilhelm.** 1799–1858. German writer on theory of music. Author of *Theoretisch-Praktische Harmonielehre* (1840) and *Lehre vom Kontrapunkt, dem Canon und der Fuge* (1859).

**De·ho′dencq′** (dē·ô′dăɴk′), **Edme Alfred Alexis.** 1822–1882. French painter, esp. of Spanish and North African scenes.

**de Hondt, Joos.** See Jodocus HONDIUS.

**dei.** See note under letter D.

**Deim′ling** (dīm′lĭng), **Berthold von.** 1853–1944. German soldier; during World War (1914–18), commanded 15th army corps on Western Front (1914–17).

**Deinarchus.** = DINARCHUS.

**Dein′hard·stein′** (dīn′härt·shtīn′), **Johann Ludwig.** 1794–1859. Austrian playwright; vice-director, Hofburgtheater, Vienna (1832–41).

**Deinocrates.** = DINOCRATES.

**Deinostratus.** = DINOSTRATUS.

**De′ïo·ces** (dē′yō·sēz). Legendary first king of the Medes (according to Herodotus); reigned (c. 699–647 B.C). Supposed to have united Median tribes and built their capital city of Ecbatana; historically, probably a tribal chieftain, **Da·yuk′ku** (dä·yŏŏk′ōō), a subject of the Assyrians. See PHRAORTES, his son.

**De·ïot′a·rus** (dē·yŏt′ȧ·rŭs). Galatian sovereign, ally of Rome. Received from Pompey title of king (c. 62 B.C.); sided with Pompey in civil war and, after Pharsalus (48), fled to Asia; pardoned by Caesar (47); later accused of attempt to assassinate Caesar, his defense being conducted by Cicero (45–44), but trial ended by Caesar's murder (Mar. 15, 44); supported cause of Brutus and Cassius but, after Philippi, switched to side of triumvirs and retained his kingdom.

**Deitz′ler** (dēts′lẽr), **George Washington.** 1826–1884. American abolitionist, b. Pine Grove, Pa.; emigrated to Kansas (1855). Leader of Free State forces in Kansas (1855–61); commanded Kansas militia in repelling Price's Confederate raid into eastern Kansas (1864).

**Dé′ja′zet′** (dā′zhȧ′zĕ′), **Pauline Virginie.** 1797–1875. French actress; on stage from childhood; excelled as comedienne, esp. in soubrette and "boy" roles. Her son **Eugène** (1820–1880) was a composer and theater director; author of comic opera *Un Mariage en l'Air;* director of Théâtre des Folies-Nouvelles, renamed Théâtre Déjazet.

**De·jean′** (dē·zhäɴ′), Comte **Jean François Aimé.** 1749–1824. French general in the Revolutionary armies; minister of war (1802–09) under Napoleon; peer of France at the Restoration. His son **Pierre François** (1780–1845) was an entomologist as well as a soldier; served under Napoleon, as general of brigade (1810) and of division (1813); exiled (1815–19); created peer of France (1824); author of a history and description of the Coleoptera.

**Dé′je·rine′** (dāzh′rēn′), **Joseph Jules.** 1849–1917. French neurologist; coauthor of *Traité des Maladies de la Moelle Épinière,* with A. Thomas, and *Anatomie du Système Nerveux,* with his wife, **Au·gus′ta** (ô·gŭs′tȧ), *nee* **Klump′ke** [klŭm(p)′kē] (1859–1927), specialist in nervous pathology.

**De·joux′** (dē·zhōō′), **Claude.** 1732–1816. French sculptor; studied under Pigalle.

**de Kalb,** Baron. See Johann Kalb.

**de Kay** (dĕ kā′), **Charles.** 1848–1935. American editor and writer, b. Washington, D.C. Literary and art editor, New York *Times* (1876–94); art editor, New York *Evening Post* (1907). Author of *The Bohemian* (1878), *Hesperus and Other Poems* (1880), *Vision of Esther* (dramatic poem, 1882), *Bird Gods* (1898), etc.

**De′ken** (dā′kĕn), **Aagje.** 1741–1804. Dutch poetess and novelist; frequently collaborated with Elizabeth Bekker in realistic novels of Dutch life.

**Dek′ker** (dĕk′ẽr), **Eduard Douwes.** *Pseudonym* **Mul′ta·tu′li** (mûl′tä·tü′lē; *as Lat.*, mŭl′tȧ·tū′lī). 1820–1887. Dutch writer; in Dutch colonial civil service in Dutch East Indies (1838–57); protested against abuses in Dutch colonial system. Wrote a romance to expose evils of Dutch administration in Java.

**Dekker, Jeremias de.** See Decker.

**Dek′ker** *or* **Deck′er** (dĕk′ẽr), **Thomas.** 1572?–?1632. English dramatist. Engaged (c. 1598) by Philip Henslowe to write plays in collaboration with Ben Jonson and others; published (1600) *Old Fortunatus* (played 1599), based on a German tale of a beggar, and *The Shoemaker's Holiday;* depicted London life and manners of citizens, apprentices, and aristocrats; with Marston held up to ridicule by Jonson, retaliated with *Satiromastix* (1602); collaborated with Chettle and William Haughton in *Patient Grissel* (played 1600); collaborated in *The Honest Whore* and *Westward Hoe* (1604); collaborated with Middleton in *The Roaring Girle* (1611), with Massinger in *The Virgin Martyr* (1621), with Ford and Rowley in *The Witch of Edmonton* (pub. 1658); probable sole author of *If it be not Good the Devil is in It* (c. 1610) and the tragicomedy *Match Me in London.* As a pamphleteer, published *The Gull's Hornbook* (1609), *The Wonderful Year* (1603; that is, the plague year) and *The Seven Deadly Sins of London* (1606). Author of charming lyrics, including "Art thou poor, yet hast thou golden slumbers?"

**de Koo′ning** (dĕ kō′nĭng), **Willem.** 1904– . American artist, b. Holland. An abstract expressionist style is dominant in his work, including *The Woman I,* etc.

**De Ko′ven** (dĕ kō′vĕn), **Reginald,** *in full* **Henry Louis Reginald.** 1859–1920. American composer, b. Middletown, Conn. Organized and led Washington Philharmonic Orchestra (1902–05). Works: light operas, *The Begum* (1887), *Robin Hood* (1890), *The Fencing Master* (1892), *Rob Roy* (1894), *The Highwayman* (1897), *The Three Dragoons* (1899), *Happy Land* (1905), *Student King* (1906); grand opera, *The Canterbury Pilgrims* (1917), with libretto by Percy Mackaye; songs, *O Promise Me;* musical setting for Kipling's *Recessional;* and more than one hundred others.

**de Kruif** (dĕ krīf′), **Paul Henry.** 1890–1971. American bacteriologist and writer, b. Zeeland, Mich. Bacteriologist for Rockefeller Institute (1920–22). Author of *Our Medicine Men* (1922), *Microbe Hunters* (1926), *Hunger Fighters* (1928), *Seven Iron Men* (1929), *Men Against Death* (1932), *Why Keep Them Alive?* (1936), *The Fight for Life* (1939).

**De la Bar′ra** (dā lä bär′rä), **Francisco León.** 1863–1939. Mexican Catholic leader and diplomat; minister for foreign affairs under Díaz (March, 1911); provisional president after abdication of Díaz (May to Nov., 1911); cabinet member under Huerta (1913). To Europe (1914); professor of international law at Sorbonne and arbitral commissioner of World Court at the Hague.

**De la Beche** (dĕl′ȧ·bĕsh), Sir **Henry Thomas.** 1796–1855. English geologist. Appointed (1832) to conduct government geological survey; influential in establishing Jermyn Street Museum in London (1851).

**Delaborde.** See Laborde.

**De·la′borde′** (dẽ·lȧ′bôrd′), Vicomte **Henri.** 1812–1899. French painter and art critic; author of *La Gravure* (1882), *L'Académie des Beaux Arts* (1891), etc. His son Comte **Bénigne Marie Henri François** (1854–1927) was author of *Jean Froissart et son Temps* (1895), etc., and editor of medieval texts.

**De·la′croix′** (dẽ·lȧ′krwä′), **Ferdinand Victor Eugène.** 1798–1863. French painter; leader of the romantic school in painting. Among his notable canvases are *Dante et Virgile...*, *Milton Aveugle Dictant le "Paradis Perdu," Christ en Croix, Le Prisonnier de Chillon, Médée, Noce Juive dans le Maroc.* Also painted great murals in the library of the Chamber of Deputies, in the Galerie d'Apollon in the Louvre, in the library of the Luxembourg, and in the Salon de la Paix of the Hôtel de Ville de Paris.

**Delacroix, Henri Edmond.** *Known as* **Henri Edmond Cross** (krŏs). 1856–1910. French painter; a leader of the divisionists.

**Delacroix, Léon.** 1865–1929. Belgian lawyer and statesman; premier (1919–21); member of Reparations Commission (1921) and of commission to organize Bank for International Settlements.

**de Lacy.** See Lacy.

**Del′a·field** (dĕl′ȧ·fēld), **E. M.** Pen name of E. M. Dashwood.

**Delafield, Edward.** 1794–1875. American specialist in diseases of the eye; founder and first president (1864) of American Ophthalmological Society. His son **Francis** (1841–1915), authority in pathology and clinical diagnosis, was founder and first president (1886), Association of American Physicians; author of *Text-book of Pathology* (1911; with T. M. Prudden). Edward's brother **Richard** (1798–1873) was a military engineer; grad. U.S.M.A., West Point (1818); chief of engineers, U.S. army (1864–66).

**De·lage′** (dẽ·lȧzh′), **Yves.** 1854–1920. French zoologist; known esp. for studies on reproduction, hybridism, heredity; also wrote on evolution, sponges, etc.

**Delaharpe.** See Laharpe.

**de la Mare** (dẽ lȧ mâr′), **Walter John.** 1873–1956. English poet and novelist, b. Charlton, Kent, of Huguenot descent. Among his many books are *Songs of Childhood* (1902), *Poems* (1906), *The Listeners and Other Poems* (1912), *Peacock Pie* (1913), *Crossings* (play), *Memoirs of a Midget* (1921), *The Riddle, and other Stories* (1923), *Broomsticks, and other Tales* (1925), *Stuff and Nonsense* (1927), *Poems for Children* (1930), *The Wind Blows Over* (1936), *Memory, and other Poems* (1938), *Behold, This Dreamer* (1939), *Bells and Grass* (1941).

**Delamater, Cornelius Henry.** 1821–1889. American mechanical engineer; built for John Ericsson first iron boats and first steam fire engines used in America, and engines for the *Monitor;* built Holland's first successful submarine (1881).

**De·lambre′** (dẽ·läɴ′br′), **Jean Baptiste Joseph.** 1749–1822. French astronomer. Computed tables of the motions of Uranus, Jupiter, and Saturn; with Méchain, measured arc of the meridian between Dunkirk and Barcelona for French government; discovered four formulas (Delambre's analogies) in spherical trigonometry (1807).

**Delamere** *or* **de la Mer,** Barons. See George Booth.

**de la Motte–Guyon, Jeanne Marie Bouvier.** See Guyon.

**De Lan′cey** (dĕ lăn′sĭ), **James.** 1703–1760. American colonial administrator, b. New York City. Judge, New York supreme court (1731–33); chief justice (1733–60). Opposed Governor Clinton's policies (1744–53). Served as lieutenant governor (1753–55; 1757–60). His brother

**Oliver** (1718–1785) was a loyalist during the American Revolution, a brigadier general in the British army in America. Their nephew **James** (1746–1804) was a loyalist during the Revolution, commanded De Lancey's Horse, a raiding cavalry troop operating outside New York City, and fled to Nova Scotia (1782). Oliver's son **Oliver** (1749–1822) was a British adjutant general in America during the Revolution.

**De·land′** (dĕ·lănd′), **Margaret,** *in full* **Margaretta Wade,** *nee* **Campbell.** 1857–1945. American novelist, b. Allegheny, Pa.; m. Lorin F. Deland (1880). Best known for tales of "Old Chester," grouped about the character "Dr. Lavendar," as in *Old Chester Tales, Dr. Lavendar's People;* other works include *John Ward, Preacher* (1888), *The Old Garden and Other Verses, The Story of a Child, The Wisdom of Fools, The Awakening of Helena Richie* (1906), *The Iron Woman* (1911), *The Rising Tide* (1916), *The Kays* (1926), etc.

**De·lane′** (dĕ·lān′), **John Thadeus.** 1817–1879. English newspaper editor; editor of *The Times* (1841–77); attacked government's neglect of commissariat in Crimean War; influenced foreign policy.

**Del′a·no** (dĕl′ȧ·nō), **Columbus.** 1809–1896. American lawyer, b. Shoreham, Vt. U.S. secretary of the interior (1870–75); charges of fraud in Bureau of Indian Affairs brought congressional investigation and findings of neglect and incompetence; resigned (1875).

**Delano, Edith,** *nee* **Bar′nard** (bär′nẽrd). 1875–1946. American writer, b. Washington, D.C.; m. James Delano (1908). Among her tales are *Zebedee V* (1912), *June* (1916), *The Way of All Earth* (1925).

**Delano, Jane Arminda.** 1862–1919. American nurse, b. Townsend, N.Y. Organized Red Cross nursing service (1911–18); director, Department of Nursing, American Red Cross (1918–19).

**De·la′ny** (dĕ·lā′nĭ), **Martin Robinson.** 1812–1885. Amer. physician, social reformer, and soldier, b. W. Va. Founded and edited (1847–49) the *North Star* with F. Douglass (*q.v.*). First Negro to become a major in the U.S. army (1865).

**Delany, Mary,** *nee* **Gran′ville** (grăn′vĭl). 1700–1788. English literary correspondent of Swift. Niece of 1st Baron Lansdowne; m. (1718) Alexander Pendarves (d. 1724); m. (1743) friend of Dean Swift, **Patrick Delany** (1685?–1768), Irish preacher, dean of Down. Introduced Fanny Burney at court; author of six volumes of autobiography and correspondence.

**Delany, Patrick Bernard.** 1845–1924. Electrical engineer, b. Ireland; to U.S. as a child. Telegraph operator (1863–76). Invented a multiplex telegraph, by which six messages could be sent at the same time over one wire; a rapid machine telegraph system, capable of recording three thousand words a minute over a single wire.

**de la Pasture.** See (1) Lady CLIFFORD; (2) E. M. DASHWOOD.

**De·la′planche′** (dẽ·lȧ′plänsh′), **Eugène.** 1836–1891. French sculptor, whose *Ève avant le Péché* stands in the garden of the Tuileries, and *L'Aurore* in the garden of the Luxembourg.

**de la Pole.** See POLE.

**De·la′porte′** (dẽ·lȧ′pôrt′), **Louis Joseph.** 1874–1944. French Orientalist; director of archaeological excavations in Asiatic Turkey (1931 ff.).

**de la Ramée, Marie Louise.** See RAMÉE.

**De La Rey** (dĕ lȧ rī′), **Jacobus Hercules.** 1847–1914. Boer general, b. in western Transvaal, of French Huguenot descent. Distinguished himself at battle of Magersfontein (1899) and in conduct of retreat before Lord Roberts's superior army; made record as brilliant commander in subsequent guerilla warfare. At end of war (1902), aided in negotiating peace with Great Britain. Member of legislative assembly in new Transvaal parliament (1907).

**de la Rive, Auguste** and **Charles.** See LA RIVE.

**de la Roche** (dẽ lȧ rôsh′), **Ma′zo** (mā′zō). 1879–1961. Canadian novelist; awarded Atlantic Monthly's $10,000 prize for her *Jalna* (1927), first of a series of works dealing with Whiteoak family, including *Whiteoaks of Jalna* (1929; dramatized, 1936), *The Master of Jalna* (1933), *Young Renny* (1935), *Whiteoak Harvest* (1936), *The Sacred Bullock* (short stories, 1939), *Whiteoak Heritage* (1940); author also of *Portrait of a Dog* (1930), *Growth of a Man* (1938).

**De·la′roche′** (dẽ·lȧ′rôsh′), **Paul,** *in full* **Hippolyte Paul.** 1797–1856. French painter; known as founder of the Eclectic school in painting, with ideal of uniting the drawing of the Classic school with the coloring and subject matter of the Romantic school. Known esp. as a portrait, historical, and mural painter.

**De·la′rue′** (dẽ·lȧ′rü′), **Gervais.** 1751–1835. French abbé and scholar; émigré during French revolutionary period (1793 ff.); author of *Essais Historiques sur les Bardes, les Jongleurs et les Trouvères Normands et Anglo-Normands* (1834).

**de la Rue** (dĕl′ȧ·rōō′; dĕl′ȧ·rōō′), **Warren.** 1815–1889. English astronomer and inventor, b. in Guernsey. Invented envelope-making machine (1851); constructed 13-inch reflecting telescope, mounted finally at Cranford, Middlesex; took lunar photographs; devised heliograph for photographing the sun daily (1858); by photographs of eclipse of the sun taken in Spain proved that the prominences observed during eclipses belong to the sun (1860); made chemical researches on glyceric acid and on electric discharges through gases.

**de las.** See note under letter D.

**De·lat′tre** (dẽ·lȧ′tr′), **Alfred Louis.** 1850–1932. French archaeologist; known for investigations of the ruins of ancient Carthage.

**Delattre** *or* **de Lattre, Roland.** Original name of Orlando di LASSO.

**de Launay.** See Baronne de STAAL DE LAUNAY.

**de Launay** *or* **Delaunay,** Vicomte **Charles.** Pseudonym of Delphine Gay de Girardin (see under Émile de GIRARDIN).

**De·lau′nay′** (dẽ·lō′nā′), **Charles Eugène.** 1816–1872. French astronomer; known for work on lunar theory and on tides.

**Delaunay, Jules Élie.** 1828–1891. French painter; executed frescoes for the opera house at Paris and for the hall of the Conseil d'État in the Palais Royal.

**Delaunay, Louis Arsène.** 1826–1903. French actor; debut in *Tartuffe* (1845); esp. known for his interpretation of young-lover roles.

**De Laval, Carl Gustaf Patrik.** See LAVAL.

**De·la′vigne′** (dẽ·lȧ′vēn′y'), **Casimir.** 1793–1843. French poet and playwright, b. Havre; published three elegies (*Les Messéniennes*) after Napoleon's fall (1815); ranked with Béranger as a national poet. Among his plays are *Les Vêpres Siciliennes, Paria, École des Vieillards, La Princesse Aurélie, Marino Faliero.* Composed song *La Parisienne* (1830). His brother **Germain** (1790–1868) wrote opera librettos, comedies, and vaudeville sketches.

**De La Warr** (dĕl′ȧ·wẽr), 5th Earl. See under SACKVILLE-WEST family.

**De La Warr,** 3d (*or* 12th) Baron. **Thomas West.** *Known as* **Lord Del′a·ware** (dĕl′ȧ·wâr). 1577–1618. Colonial administrator in America, b. in England. Member of the council, Virginia Company, London (1609); governor and captain general, Colony of Virginia (1610); arrived at Jamestown just in time to prevent colonists from deserting the settlement (1610). Returned to England to obtain aid for colony (1611).

**Del'bœuf'** (dĕl'bûf'), **Joseph Rémy Léopold.** 1831–1896. Belgian philosopher and psychologist; known for work in logic and on hypnotism.

**Del'brück** (dĕl'brük), **Clemens von.** 1856–1921. German government official. Prussian minister of commerce (1905). Directed economic mobilization (1914–16); chief of Emperor William II's civil cabinet (1918).

**Delbrück, Hans.** 1848–1929. German historian, esp. of art of war, as in *Geschichte der Kriegskunst im Rahmen der Politischen Geschichte* (5 parts, 1900–27), *Weltgeschichte* (3 vols., 1923–26), *Vor und Nach dem Weltkriege* (1926).

**Delbrück, Max.** 1906– American biologist, b. Germany. To U.S. (1937); at Calif. Institute of Tech. (1947– ). Awarded Nobel prize in physiology and medicine (1969) with A. Hershey and S. Luria.

**Delbrück, Rudolf von.** 1817–1903. Prussian statesman; in ministry of commerce (1848); influential in expanding the Zollverein. First president of the chancery of North German Confederation (1867–70); president of newly organized imperial chancery (1871–76). His nephew **Berthold Delbrück** (1842–1922) was a philologist; author of *Vergleichende Syntax der Indogermanischen Sprachen*, etc.

**Del'cas'sé'** (dĕl'kȧ'sā'), **Théophile.** 1852–1923. French statesman; minister of colonies (1893–95) and minister of foreign affairs (1898–1905). During ministry, negotiated settlement of Fashoda incident and agreement with Great Britain on the Nile Valley and Central Africa, preparing ground for Anglo-French agreement (1904) leading to the Entente Cordiale. Forced out of office (1905) as result of Moroccan dispute with Germany. Minister of foreign affairs in the Ministry of National Defense (1914–15).

**De·lé'cluze'** (dē·lā'klüz'), **Étienne Jean.** 1781–1863. French painter and art critic.

**De·led'da** (dâ·lĕd'dä), **Grazia.** 1871–1936. Italian writer, b. Nuoro; m. Palmerino Madesani, attaché of Italian War Ministry (1900); awarded Nobel prize for literature (1926); member, Italian Acad. of Immortals. Known esp. for her novels on Sardinian peasantry; author of *Racconti Sardi* (1893), *Anime Oneste* (1899), *Il Vecchio della Montagna* (1900), *Elias Portolu* (1902), *Cenere* (1903), *L'Edera* (1907), *L'Ombra del Passato* (1908), *Il Nonno* (1909), *Nel Deserto* (1911), *Canne al Vento* (1913), *Le Colpe Altrui* (1914), *La Via del Male* (1916), *La Madre* (1920), *Il Segreto dell' Uomo Solitario* (1921), *Il Dio dei Viventi* (1922), *La Danza della Collana* (1924), *La Fuga in Egitto* (1926), and *Annalena Bilsini* (1928).

**De Lee** (dĕ lē'), **Joseph Bolivar.** 1869–1942. American obstetrician, b. Cold Spring, N.Y.; professor, Northwestern U. (1897–1929), U. of Chicago (from 1929); founder, Chicago Lying-in Hospital and Dispensary (1895), Chicago Maternity Center (1932).

**De·les'cluze'** (dē·lā'klüz'), **Louis Charles.** 1809–1871. French politician; active in revolutionary agitation (1830, 1848, 1870); leader of Paris Commune (1871).

**De·lesse'** (dē·lĕs'), **Achille Ernest Oscar Joseph.** 1817–1881. French geologist and mineralogist.

**de Lesseps,** Vicomte **Ferdinand Marie.** See LESSEPS.

**De·les'sert'** (dē·lĕ'sâr'), **Étienne.** 1735–1816. French banker; founded (1782) first fire-insurance company in France. His son **Benjamin** (1773–1847), industrialist, financier, and philanthropist, regent of Bank of Fr.; founded Société d'Encouragement pour l'Industrie; instrumental in introduction of savings banks into Fr.

**Delharpe.** See LAHARPE.

**De·libes'** (dē·lēb'), **Léo.** 1836–1891. French composer, esp. of operettas and ballets, including *Sylvia ou la Nymphe de Diane* (1876), *Lakmé* (libretto by Gille, 1883).

**Delijannis, Theodoros.** = DELIYIANNES.

**De·li'lah** (dē·lī'lȧ). *In Douay Version* **Da·li'la** (dȧ·lī'lȧ). In Bible, Philistine woman who lured from Samson secret of his strength and brought about his capture by Philistines (*Judges* xvi).

**De·lille'** (dē·lēl'), **Jacques.** 1738–1813. French abbé and poet; author of a verse translation of Vergil's *Georgics*, also *Les Jardins*, a series of descriptive poems, and translations of Vergil's *Aeneid* and Milton's *Paradise Lost.*

**Delisle** *or* **de Lisle** *or* **de l'Isle.** See (1) LECONTE DE LISLE; (2) ROMÉ DE LISLE; (3) ROUGET DE LISLE; (4) VILLIERS DE L'ISLE-ADAM.

**de Lisle** (dĕ līl'), Sir **Beau'voir** (bē'vẽr). 1864–1955. English soldier; major general (1915), lieutenant general (1919), and general (1926); in World War (1914–18), served in France, Flanders, and Gallipoli.

**De·lisle'** (dē·lēl'), **Guillaume.** 1675–1726. French geographer; royal geographer (1718); published maps showing voyages of discovery and exploration; regarded as a founder of modern geography. See Joseph Nicolas DELISLE.

**Delisle, Jacques.** = Jacques DELILLE.

**Delisle, Joseph Nicolas.** 1688–1768. French astronomer. Brother of Guillaume Delisle. In St. Petersburg (1725–47), where he founded school of astronomy; geographical astronomer to French navy (1747). Proposed "diffraction theory" of the corona of the sun (1715); originated method for observing transits of Venus and Mercury, first proposed in letter to J. Cassini (1743); proposed first method for determining the heliocentric co-ordinates of sunspots.

**Delisle, Léopold Victor.** 1826–1910. French scholar, b. Valognes. Curator (1871) and administrator (1874), Bibliothèque Nationale, Paris. Published papers on French medieval history, esp. on Normandy; responsible for printing of *Catalogue Générale* (begun in 1897) of the Bibliothèque Nationale.

**De'litzsch** (dā'lĭch), **Franz.** 1813–1890. German Protestant theologian; works include commentaries on books of the Old Testament. His son **Friedrich** (1850–1922), Assyriologist, is author of an Assyrian dictionary, an Assyrian grammar, and books on Assyrian literary remains.

**De'li·us** (dē'lĭ·ŭs; dēl'yŭs), **Frederick.** 1862–1934. English composer, of German descent, b. Bradford, Yorkshire. His works include operas, orchestral works, choral works (*A Mass of Life, Requiem, Sea Drift*), a piano concerto, violin concerto, chamber music, and songs.

**De'li·us** (dā'lē·o͝os), **Nikolaus.** 1813–1888. German Shakespearean scholar; published first critical edition of Shakespeare's works in Germany (7 vols., 1854–61).

**De'li·yian'nes, De'li·jan'nis** (thā'lyē·yän'ēs), *or* **Del·yan'nis** (*Angl.* dĕl·yăn'ĭs), **Theodoros.** 1826–1905. Greek statesman; prime minister (1885–86, 1890–92, 1895–97, 1902–03, 1904–05); assassinated.

**dell', della, delle.** See note under letter D.

**Dell** (dĕl), **Ethel M.** d. 1939. English writer of romantic fiction; m. G. T. Savage (1922). Among her many novels are *The Way of an Eagle* (1912), *The Lamp in the Desert* (1919), *The Prison Wall* (1932), *Sown Among Thorns* (1939).

**Dell, Floyd.** 1887–1969. American editor, novelist, and playwright, b. Barry, Ill. Assoc. editor, *The Masses*, New York (1914–17), and *The Liberator* (1918–24). Among his novels are *Moon-Calf* (1920), *Runaway* (1925), *Souvenir* (1929), *Diana Stair* (1932), *The Golden Spike* (1934); among his plays, *Little Accident* (with

Thomas Mitchell, 1928), *Cloudy with Showers* (with Thomas Mitchell, 1931).

**della Robbia.** See ROBBIA.

**delle Grazie, Marie Eugenie.** See GRAZIE.

**Del'len·baugh** (dĕl'ĕn·bô), **Frederick Samuel.** 1853–1935. American painter, explorer, and writer; with Powell expedition down Colorado River (1871–73); with Harriman expedition to Alaska and Siberia (1899). Author of *The North Americans of Yesterday* (1900), *A Canyon Voyage* (1908), *Frémont and '49* (1913), etc.

**Del'lin·ger** (dĕl'ĭn·jẽr), **John Howard.** 1886–1962. American radio engineer, b. Cleveland, Ohio. Physicist (1907), chief of radio section (1918–46), U.S. Bureau of Standards; chief engineer, Federal Radio Commission (1928–29); chief of radio section of research division, aeronautics branch, Department of Commerce (1926–34). Author of articles on radio and electricity; special editor, *Webster's New International Dictionary, Second Edition.*

**Del'ling·er** (dĕl'ĭng·ẽr), **Rudolf.** 1857–1910. German composer of operas *Don Cesar* (1885), *Die Chansonette* (1895), *Jadwiga* (1901), *Der Letzte Jonas* (1910), etc.

**Del Mar** (dĕl'mär), **Alexander.** 1836–1926. American economist and mining engineer, b. New York City. Author of *A History of the Precious Metals* (1880), *The Science of Money* (1885), *Money and Civilization* (1886), etc.

**Del'mar** (dĕl'mär), **Vi'ña** (vē'nyȧ), *nee* **Cro'ter** (krō'tẽr). 1905– . American writer, b. New York City; m. Eugene Delmar (1921); author of *Bad Girl* (1928), *Kept Woman* (1930), *Marriage Racket* (1933), etc.

**Del·mon'i·co** (dĕl·mŏn'ĭ·kō), **Lo·ren'zo** (lô·rĕn'zō). 1813–1881. Restaurateur, b. Marengo, Switzerland; to U.S. (1832). With uncles John and Peter, established restaurant (Delmonico's) in New York City (about 1834). Moved to Broadway and Twenty-sixth Street (1876).

**De·lolme'** (dẽ·lôlm'), **Jean Louis.** 1740–1806. Swiss jurist and writer on English constitution.

**De·lo'ney** *or* **De·lo'ne** (dĕ·lō'nĭ), **Thomas.** 1543?–?1607. English writer of broadsides, three on coming of Spanish Armada (1588), and historical ballads, in *The Royal Garland of Love and Delight* and *The Garland of Good Will* (1604).

**De Long** (dĕ lŏng'), **George Washington.** 1844–1881. American naval officer and explorer; grad., U.S.N.A., Annapolis (1865). Financially aided by James Gordon Bennett, prepared expedition on ship *Jeannette* for Arctic exploration; sailed from San Francisco (July 8, 1879). Ship crushed in ice north of Siberia (June 12, 1881); party set out for Siberia, dividing into three groups. Of the group led by De Long, all died of starvation; bodies found by searching party (1882). De Long's journal, *The Voyage of the Jeannette,* published by his widow (1883).

**De·lord'** (dẽ·lôr'), **Taxile.** 1815–1877. French journalist; editor of *Charivari* (1848–58); author of *Physiologie de la Parisienne* (1841), etc.

**De·lorme'** *or* **de Lorme** (dẽ·lôrm'), **Marion.** 1611–?1650. French courtesan; mistress of Marquis de Cinq-Mars (beheaded 1642); reputedly mistress thereafter of Saint-Évremond, Buckingham, Gramont, Condé, and others; found dead by officers sent to carry out Cardinal Mazarin's orders to arrest her for complicity in the Fronde uprising (1650). Subject of many legends, notably one that she escaped to London and lived to a great age. Subject of Victor Hugo's drama *Marion Delorme* and a conspicuous figure in Alfred de Vigny's novel *Cinq-Mars.*

**De·lorme'** *or* **de l'Orme** (dẽ·lôrm'), **Philibert.** 1515?–1570. French architect; royal architect to Henri II; directed work at Fontainebleau (1543–59) and built châteaux of Muette, Saint-Germain, Saint-Maur, Meudon, and gallery at the château of Chenonceaux; built Tuileries for Catherine de Médicis.

**de los.** See note under letter D.

**de Loutherbourg, Philippe Jacques.** See LOUTHERBOURG.

**Del'sarte'** (dĕl'sȧrt'), **François Alexandre Nicolas Chéri.** 1811–1871. French inventor of system of calisthenics (Delsarte, or Delsarte system) designed to develop coordination, power, and grace.

**Del'teil'** (dĕl'tâ'y'), **Joseph.** 1894– . French poet and novelist; author of *Le Cœur Grec* (verse, 1918), *Le Jonque de Porcelaine* (verse, 1928), and the novels *Choléra* (1923), *Jeanne d'Arc* (1925), *Les Poilus* (1926), *Le Vert Galant* (1931), etc.

**De·luc'** (dẽ·lük'), **Jean André.** 1727–1817. Swiss geologist and meteorologist; to England (1773). Attempted to reconcile science with the account of creation in *Genesis,* interpreting the six "days" as six "epochs"; conducted experiments on the atmosphere; one of first to notice disappearance of heat when ice melts; proved that water is densest at about 39° F.; invented a hygrometer; published first correct rules for determining heights of mountains by the barometer; credited with invention of the dry pile later improved by one Zamboni.

**De Lu'ca** (dā lōō'kä), **Giuseppe.** 1876–1950. Operatic baritone, b. Rome, Italy. After eight seasons at La Scala, Milan, joined Metropolitan Opera Company, New York (1915); debut as Figaro in *Barber of Seville.* Leading roles in *Rigoletto, Don Giovanni, Otello, Damnation of Faust, Tannhäuser, Parsifal, Pagliacci,* etc.

**Del'vaux'** (dĕl'vō'), **Lau'rent'** (lō'räN'). 1695–1778. Flemish sculptor; lived in London (1717–26) where he executed works in bronze and marble for Westminster Abbey; court sculptor to Charles, Duke of Lorraine (1750–78).

**Delyannis, Theodoros.** See DELIYIANNES.

**De·ma'des** (dē·mā'dēz). 380–319 B.C. Athenian orator and politician. Supported cause of Philip of Macedon and Alexander the Great; secured lenient treatment of Athens after Alexander destroyed Thebes. Negotiated peace with Antipater (322 B.C.); executed (319) by order of Cassander when he learned Demades had intrigued with Perdiccas.

**De·man'geon'** (dẽ·mäN'zhôN'), **Albert.** 1872–1940. French geographer; specialist in study of regional and economic geography; author of *Le Déclin de l'Europe* (1920), *L'Empire Britannique* (1923), *Les Îles Britanniques* (1928), etc.

**Dem'a·ra'tus** (dĕm'ȧ·rā'tŭs). fl. 500 B.C. King of Sparta (c. 510–491 B.C.). Colleague of Cleomenes I; quarreled with Cleomenes; deposed (491) by him in favor of Leotychides; fled to Persian court; given Pergamum and other cities to rule; accompanied Xerxes on his expedition to Greece (481–480).

**De·mar'çay'** (dẽ·mȧr'sā'), **Eugène.** 1852–1903. French chemist; discovered spectroscopically (1896), element europium.

**Dem·biń'ski** (dĕm·bēn'y'·skē), **Bronisław.** 1857–1940. Polish historian.

**Dembiński, Henryk.** 1791–1864. Polish soldier; in Polish Revolution (1830–31), conducted retreat of Polish army through Lithuania (1831). Commanded Hungarian army (1849) and was defeated at Temesvár (Timişoara); forced to take refuge in Turkey and, later, in France.

**De·me'tri·us** (dē·mē'trĭ·ŭs). fl. about 206–175 B.C. King of Bactria (c. 190–175 B.C.). Invaded India and conquered the Punjab and valley of the Indus.

**Demetrius.** Name of two kings of Macedonia:

**Demetrius I.** *Surnamed* **Pol'i·or·ce'tes** (pŏl'ĭ·ôr·sē'tēz), *i.e.* "besieger." 337?–283 B.C. King (294–283 B.C.). Son of Antigonus Cyclops, whom he aided in wars with generals of Alexander; defeated (312) by Ptolemy (later Ptolemy I) at Gaza; freed Athens (307) from Cassander and Ptolemy; destroyed naval power of Egypt in battle at Cyprus (306), a victory commemorated by the statue of Nike of Samothrace; besieged Rhodes (305–304) but failed to take it; defeated with his father at Ipsus (301) by Seleucus and Lysimachus; lost power for a time, but recovered Athens (295), Aegina, and Salamis; seized throne of Macedonia (294); driven out by Pyrrhus (288) and taken prisoner by Seleucus I (285). Succeeded by his son Antigonus Gonatas.

**Demetrius II.** 278?–229 B.C. Son of Antigonus Gonatas. King (239–229 B.C.). Engaged continuously in wars with Aetolian and Achaean leagues and with wild tribes on northern borders. Succeeded by his cousin Antigonus Doson.

**Demetrius.** *Russ.* **Dmitri** *or* **Dimitri.** Name borne by several Russian rulers, including: **Demetrius,** *Russ.* **Dmitri Ivanovich** (1581–1591), czarevitch; youngest son of Ivan the Terrible; last representative of Rurik line; died at age of ten, believed murdered by regent Boris Godunov (*q.v.*); placed among martyrs of Russian Church. Four usurpers: **Demetrius I,** *usually called* **Pseudo–Demetrius,** who held power for about a year (1605–06) and was murdered; **Demetrius II,** who held power for about three years (1607–10) and was killed; and two who claimed to be sons of Demetrius II and who both died by violence, **Demetrius III** (d. about 1610) and **Demetrius IV** (executed 1613).

**Demetrius.** Name of three kings of Syria:

**Demetrius I.** *Surnamed* **So'ter** (sō'tẽr), *i.e.* "preserver." d. 150 B.C. King (162–150 B.C.). Son of Seleucus IV Philopator and father of Demetrius II and Antiochus VII. Lived as hostage at Rome (c. 187–163); escaped (163); overthrew his cousin Antiochus V Eupator (162); delivered Babylonians from tyranny of satrap Timarchus (c. 160); fought with Maccabees; fell in battle against usurper Alexander Balas.

**Demetrius II.** *Surnamed* **Ni·ca'tor** (nī·kā'tôr; -tẽr). d. about 125 B.C. King (145–139 and 129–125 B.C.). Son of Demetrius I and brother of Antiochus VII. Aided by Ptolemy VI Philometor, secured throne, defeating and killing Alexander Balas (145); m. (150?) Alexander Balas's widow, Cleopatra Thea (*q.v.*), by whom he was father of Seleucus V and Antiochus VIII; opposed (145–142) by boy king, Antiochus VI, at Antioch; in expedition against Parthians, defeated and held prisoner; m. Rodogune (*q.v.*), daughter of Mithridates I; regained throne (129); killed in civil war and succeeded by his sons Seleucus V (killed after a very short reign) and Antiochus VIII Grypus.

**Demetrius III.** *Surnamed* **Eu·kai'ros** (ū·kī'rŏs) *and* **Phil'o·me'tor** (fĭl'ō·mē'tôr). d. 88? B.C. King (95–88 B.C.). Son of Antiochus VIII Grypus. Seized Damascus (95), ruling in opposition (95–93) to his cousin Antiochus X; ruled jointly (93–88) with his brother Philip, but during part of time engaged in civil war with him; defeated by Arabs and Parthians; died prisoner among Parthians.

**Demetrius.** Greek sculptor of early 4th century B.C.

**Demetrius Don·skoi'** (dŭn·skoi'). *Russ.* **Dimitri Donskoi.** 1350–1389. Russian nobleman; son of Ivan II and father of Basil I; grand duke of Vladimir and Moscow (1359–89). Built the Kremlin; organized Russian princes to fight Tatars; won great victory (1380); defeated (1381) by Toktamish, a lieutenant of Tamerlane.

**Demetrius Pha·le'reus** (fȧ·lē'rōōs; fȧ·lẹr'ē·ŭs). 345?–283 B.C. Athenian orator and statesman, b. Phalerum, Attica. Appointed by Cassander to govern Athens (317–307 B.C.); when democratic government was restored under Demetrius Poliorcetes (307), fled to Alexandria to escape execution and lived at court of Ptolemy I Soter.

**Demetrius the Cynic.** Greek Cynic philosopher of 1st century A.D., whose criticisms caused his banishment from Rome by Nero and, later, by Vespasian.

**De·metz'** (dē·mĕts'), **Frédéric Auguste.** 1796–1873. French jurist; interested in prison reform; established farm colony for training offenders in useful occupations.

**De·mi'dov** (dyĕ·myē'dôf). Distinguished Russian family, descended from **Nikita Demidov** (1665?–after 1720), ironworker and armorer, favorite of Peter the Great, and including: Nikita's son **Akinfi Nikitich** (d. about 1740); discovered and operated gold, silver, and copper mines. Akinfi's nephew **Pavel Grigorievich** (1738–1821), traveler, patron of scientists, founder of botanical garden in Moscow. Pavel's nephew Count **Nikolai Nikitich** (1774–1828); raised and commanded regiment to fight Napoleon (1812); patron of scientific education in Moscow. Nikolai's son **Pavel Nikolaevich** (1798–1840), patron of Petersburg Acad. of Science. Nikolai's son Prince **Anatoli Nikolaevich** (1813–1870), traveler, philanthropist, and art patron; m. Princess Matilde Bonaparte, daughter of Jérôme Bonaparte.

**De Mille** (dĕ mĭl'), **Agnes George.** 1905– Am. dancer and choreographer, b. New York City. Dau. of William C. De Mille. Choreographed *Rodeo, Fall River Legend*, etc.; and musicals *Oklahoma!*, etc.

**De Mille, Henry Churchill.** 1853–1893. American playwright, b. Washington, N.C. Grad. Columbia (1875). Collaborated with David Belasco in producing *The Wife* (1887), *Lord Chumley* (1887), *The Charity Ball* (1889), *Men and Women* (1890). He was father of (1) **William Churchill** (1878–1955), playwright, author of *Strongheart, The Warrens of Virginia, The Land of the Free, The Woman, Hollywood Saga* (1939), and collaborator on *The Royal Mounted* and *Classmates;* and (2) **Cec'il** (sĕs''l) **Blount** [blŭnt] (1881–1959), motion-picture producer, president of Cecil B. De Mille Productions, Inc., producing *Ten Commandments, The King of Kings, The Sign of the Cross, Cleopatra, The Crusades, The Plainsman, The Buccaneer*, etc.

**Dem'me** (dĕm'ĕ), **Hermann Christoph Gottfried.** *Pseudonym* **Karl Stil'le** (shtĭl'ĕ). 1760–1822. German novelist and lyric poet.

**Dem'o·ce'des** (dĕm'ō·sē'dēz). Greek physician of late 6th century B.C., b. Crotone, Magna Graecia; practiced successively in Aegina, Athens, Samos; captured by Persians and practiced in court of Darius I.

**De·moch'a·res** (dē·mŏk'ȧ·rēz). Athenian orator and politician, nephew of Demosthenes. Orator of anti-Macedonian party (after 322 B.C.) and leader of the popular party after restoration of democratic government by Demetrius Poliorcetes (307); ambassador to Lysimachus (c. 282).

**De·moc'ri·tus** (dē·mŏk'rĭ·tŭs). Greek philosopher of late 5th and early 4th century B.C.; known as "the Ab'de·rite" [ăb'dĕ·rīt] (because a native of Abdera, in Thrace) and as "the Laughing Philosopher" (because of his cheerful disposition). Regarded as greatest among Greek physical philosophers. Adopted and extended atomistic theory of Leucippus.

**Democritus Junior.** Pseudonym of Robert BURTON.

**De·mo'geot'** (dē·mô'zhō'), **Jacques Claude.** 1808–1894. French scholar; author of *Histoire de la Littérature Française*...(1851), etc.

**De·moi'vre** (*Fr.* dē·mwȧ'vr'; *Angl.* -moi'vẽr), **Abraham.**

1667–1754. French mathematician in England (from 1688); chosen by Royal Society to arbitrate on claims of Newton and Leibnitz to invention of infinitesimal calculus (1712); author of works on fluxions (1695), doctrine of chances (1711, 1718), and life annuities (1725); created imaginary trigonometry.

**De·mo′nax** (dē·mō′năks). Greek Cynic philosopher of 2d century A.D.; taught in Athens.

**De Mor′gan** (dĕ môr′găn), **Augustus.** 1806–1871. English mathematician and logician; professor, University Coll., London (1828–31, 1836–66); author of *Essay on Probabilities* (1838), *Trigonometry and Double Algebra* (1849), and treatises on calculus; published *Formal Logic* (1847); one of the independent discoverers of the principle of quantification of the predicate; in series of memoirs (1850–63) on the syllogism, developed a new logic of relations and a new system of nomenclature for logical expression; gave name to *De Morgan's theorem;* contributed commutation columns to calculation of insurance; advocated decimal coinage.
His son **William Frend** (1839–1917), artist and novelist, in association with Pre-Raphaelite circle, experimented with stained glass and other decorative arts (1864–71); devoted himself to ceramics (1871–1905); rediscovered process of making brilliant blue and green glazes; manufactured tiles and other pottery commercially (1888); on retiring from business, wrote novels *Joseph Vance* (1906), *Alice-for-Short* (1907), *Somehow Good* (1908), *It Never Can Happen Again* (1909), *When Ghost Meets Ghost* (1914).

**De·mos′the·nes** (dē·mŏs′thē·nēz). d. 413 B.C. Athenian commander of expedition (426 B.C.) which destroyed power of Corinth over northwestern Greece; defended Pylos (425) against attacks from Sparta and Corcyra (Corfu); captured in attack on Syracuse (413) and executed under orders from the Syracuse government.

**Demosthenes.** 385?–322 B.C. Athenian orator and statesman; regarded as greatest of Greek orators. Attacked Philip of Macedon in a series of orations, *Philippics* (from 352); leader of patriotic party opposing Philip; caused Athenian fleet to be sent to relief of Byzantium (340), besieged by Philip; advocated Athenian alliance with Thebes against Philip, the allied army being defeated by Philip at Chaeronea (338). Exiled by pro-Macedonian party (324) but recalled after Alexander's death (323). Fled from Athens when city was captured by Antipater and Craterus (322) and took poison to avoid capture. Among his great orations, in addition to the *Philippics*, are three *Olynthiacs*, *On the Peace*, *On the Embassy*, *On the Affairs of the Chersonese*, *On the Crown*. See AESCHINES and CTESIPHON.

**Demp′sey** (dĕm(p)′sĭ), **William Harrison,** *known as* **Jack.** 1895– . American heavyweight pugilist, b. Manassa, Colo.; won heavyweight championship by defeating Jess Willard at Toledo (July 4, 1919); lost title to Gene Tunney at Philadelphia (Sept. 23, 1926).

**Demp′ster** (dĕm(p)′stẽr), **Thomas.** 1570–1625. Scottish scholar and historian. Blocked from preferment in England by his Roman Catholicism. Professor of Pandects, Pisa; professor of humanities, Bologna, then foremost European university. Known as Latin poet; compiled biographical dictionary of illustrious Scots (1627).

**De·muth′** (dĕ·mōōth′), **Charles.** 1883–1935. American painter and illustrator, b. Lancaster, Pa., known esp. for his water-color studies of flowers.

**Denbigh,** Earls of. See William FEILDING.

**Den′by** (dĕn′bĭ), **Charles.** 1830–1904. American lawyer and diplomat, b. Mount Joy, Va. U.S. minister to China (1885–98); member, U.S. Philippines Commission (1899). His son **Edwin** (1870–1929) was member of U.S. House of Representatives (1905–11); U.S. secretary of the navy (1921–24); criticized for allowing transfer of administration of naval oil reserves from navy department to department of interior (May 31, 1921); his signature on leases of Teapot Dome oil lands involved him in the scandal, but he was not accused of corruption; resigned (effective Mar. 10, 1924) to lessen embarrassment to President Coolidge.

**Denck, Johannes.** See DENK.

**Den′fert′-Ro′che·reau′** (dăɴ′fâr′rôsh′rō′), **Pierre Marie Philippe Aristide.** 1823–1878. French defender of fortress of Belfort (1870).

**Dengyo Daishi.** See SAICHO.

**Den′ham** (dĕn′ăm), **Dixon.** 1786–1828. English traveler in Africa; explored central Sudan with Dr. Walter Oudney and Hugh Clapperton; explored west and south shore of Lake Chad.

**Denham,** Sir **John.** 1615–1669. English poet; b. in Ireland, son of Sir **John Denham** (1559–1639), lord chief justice of King's Bench in Ireland. Made reputation with *The Sophy* (historical tragedy, 1642); published best-known poem, *Cooper's Hill* (1642), poetical description of scenery. Royalist, performed secret service for Charles I in Holland; architect by profession, surveyor general of works (1660); wrote elegy on Abraham Cowley (1667).

**Den′hardt** (dĕn′härt), **Clemens** (1852–1929) and his brother **Gustav** (1856–1917). German explorers; with physician Gustav Fischer, explored Tana River region in East Africa (1878–79); later acquired possession of coastal territory north of mouth of Tana River. Part of the territory was transferred to German colonial society, Deutsche Witugesellschaft, and later (1890) traded to England for Helgoland.

**Den′i·fle′** (dĕn′ē·flĕ′), **Heinrich Seuse.** 1844–1905. Austrian Roman Catholic theologian and historian; entered Dominican order (1861); summoned to Rome as German representative of his order (1880). Asst. archivist at Vatican (1883). Made special study of Middle Ages.

**De·nijn′** *or* **De·nyn′** (dĕ·nīn′), **Jef.** 1862–1941. Belgian carillonneur, b. Malines. Succeeded his father, **Adolphe,** as municipal carillonneur of Malines (1881).

**De′ni′ker′** (dā′nē′kâr′), **Joseph.** 1852–1918. French anthropologist, b. in Astrakhan, Russia, of French parents. Educ. St. Petersburg; traveled as engineer in petroleum fields of Caucasia, central Europe, etc. Librarian of the Museum of Natural History, Paris (1888). His ethnologic classification of Europeans according to stature, cranial index, and color of hair, set forth in *Les Races de l'Europe* (1908), is the basis of the common modern classification.

**De·ni′kin** (dyĭ·nyē′kyĭn), **Anton Ivanovich.** 1872–1947. Russian soldier; lieutenant general during World War. After Russian Revolution (1917), fled to Caucasus and joined Alekseev and Kornilov in raising force to fight the Bolsheviks; succeeded to supreme command after death of Kornilov (Mar. 31, 1918) and Alekseev (Sept. 25, 1918); established himself for a time in southern Russia and set up a South Russian government (1919); failed to win popular support; defeated by Bolshevik troops under Budënny (1920). Fled to Constantinople; lived in France (from 1926).

**De·ni′na** (dā·nē′nä), **Giacomo Maria Carlo.** 1731–1813. Italian historian; university librarian, Turin (1800); imperial librarian, Paris (1804–13). Known particularly for *Storia delle Rivoluzioni d'Italia* (3 vols., 1768–72).

**Den′is** *or* **Den′ys,** Saint (sănt dĕn′ĭs; *Fr.* săɴ′ dē·nē′). The apostle to the Gauls, first bishop of Paris, and patron saint of France, martyred by decapitation at Paris in the 3d century. He is represented in art as raising himself to carry his severed head and was in popular belief identified with Dionysius the Areopagite (*Acts* xvii. 34).

**Den′is** (dĕn′ĭs). King of Portugal. See DINIZ.

**De·nis′** (dē·nē′), **Armand.** 1896–1971. Belgian photographer; consulting engineer in motion-picture industry (1929); invented automatic film-printing machine, sold to Eastman Co. In collaboration with his wife, **Leila,** *nee* **Roosevelt,** made motion picture in Bali; scored success with *Dark Rapture* (1935), a picture of Congo native life and customs.

**De·nis′** *or* **De·nys′** (dē·nē′), **Jean Baptiste.** d. 1704. French physician; consultant to Louis XIV; credited with performing first successful blood transfusion on man (c. 1667).

**De·nis′** (dē·nē′), **Maurice.** 1870–1943. French painter; admirer of Gauguin, and one of the original symbolists; painted many religious pictures; best known for his murals, as in the Théâtre des Champs Élysées at Paris, church of Le Vésinet at Geneva.

**Denis le Flamand.** See Denis CALVAERT.

**Den′i·son** (dĕn′ĭ·s'n), **George Taylor.** 1839–1925. Canadian soldier and historical writer; served in militia, repelling Fenian raids (1866) and suppressing 2d Riel Rebellion (1885); author of *The Fenian Raid at Fort Erie, History of Cavalry, The Struggle for Imperial Unity,* etc.

**Denk** *or* **Denck** (dĕngk), **Johannes.** 1495?–1527. German Anabaptist. With Ludwig Hetzer (*q.v.*), translated Old Testament prophets; published theological treatises.

**Den′man** (dĕn′măn), **Thomas.** 1st Baron **Denman.** 1779–1854. English judge; son of **Thomas Denman** (1733–1815), physician, navy surgeon, obstetrician. Solicitor general to Queen Caroline (1820), whose innocence he maintained before bar of House of Lords (1820); attorney general (1830); prosecuted reform rioters (1832); lord chief justice (1832–50); speaker of House of Lords (1835); condemned Moxon, publisher of Shelley's complete works, for blasphemy (1841). His seventh son, **George** (1819–1896), was judge in Court of Common Pleas (1872), judge of high court of justice, queen's bench division (1881–92); privy councilor (1893). The 1st baron's great-grandson **Thomas Denman** (1874–1954), 3d baron, served in Boer and World Wars; was governor general of Australia (1911–14); deputy speaker of House of Lords.

**Den′ner** (dĕn′ẽr), **Balthasar.** 1685–1749. German portrait painter.

**Denner, Johann Christoph.** 1655–1707. German manufacturer of wood-wind instruments; inventor of the clarinet (c. 1700).

**Den′ne·ry′** (dĕn′rē′), **Adolphe Philippe.** *Name legally changed to* **d'En′ne·ry′** (1858). 1811–1899. French playwright; author or coauthor of *Gaspard Hauser* (1838), *Don César de Bazan* (1844), *Les Deux Orphelines* (1874), *Michel Strogoff* (1880), and librettos of *Si J'Étais Roi, Le Tribut de Zamora* (music by Gounod), *Le Cid* (music by Massenet).

**Den′nett** (dĕn′ĕt; -ĭt), **Richard Edward.** 1857–1921. English writer; employed by British firm for service in African trade (1875–79). Called attention to atrocities in Congo Free State (1886); his agitation largely responsible for formation of Congo Reform Assoc.

**Dennett, Tyler.** 1883–1949. American historian and educator; president, Williams Coll. (1934–37). Author of *The Democratic Movement in Asia* (1918), *Biography of John Hay* (1933; awarded Pulitzer prize), etc.

**Den′nie** (dĕn′ĭ), **Joseph.** 1768–1812. Known as "The American Addison." American editor, b. Boston. Founded (1801) and edited *The Port Folio,* Philadelphia (1801–12).

**Den′ning** (dĕn′ĭng), **William Frederick.** 1848–1931. English amateur astronomer; accountant by profession. Discovered five comets, some nebulae, and a new star in Cygnus (Aug. 20, 1920); studied surface markings and rotation periods of Mars, Jupiter, and Saturn; authority on meteors.

**Den′nis** (dĕn′ĭs), **Geoffrey Pomeroy.** 1892–1964. English writer; member of League of Nations staff (1920–37), rising to chief editor and chief of document services. Among his books are *Mary Lee* (1922), *The End of the World* (1930; awarded Hawthornden prize), *Sale by Auction* (1932), *Bloody Mary's* (1934).

**Dennis, John.** 1657–1734. English critic and dramatist; gained scant success with nine plays, including *A Plot and No Plot* (1697; a satire on Jacobites), *Liberty Asserted* (1704), *Appius and Virginia* (produced 1709). Satirized by Pope for bombast, replied in *Reflections, Critical and Satirical* (1711); defended stage against Law and Collier; best known for *The Advancement and Reformation of Modern Poetry* (1701) and writings on genius of Shakespeare.

**Den′ni·son** (dĕn′ĭ·s'n), **Aaron Lufkin.** 1812–1895. American watch manufacturer, b. Freeport, Me. Devised machine-made interchangeable parts in manufacturing watches, increasing accuracy and lowering cost; known as "the Father of American Watchmaking."

**Dennison, William.** 1815–1882. American lawyer, b. Cincinnati, Ohio. Governor of Ohio (1860–62). U.S. postmaster general (1864–66).

**Den′ny** (dĕn′ĭ), **George Hutcheson.** 1870–1955. American educator, b. in Hanover County, Va. Professor of Latin (1899–1911) and president (1902–11), Washington and Lee U. President, U. of Alabama (1912–37, 1942), and chancellor (1937–42, 1943–55).

**De·non′** (dē·nôN′), Baron **Dominique Vivant.** 1747–1825. French illustrator and government official; accompanied Napoleon on Egyptian campaign; director-general of French museums; first administrator to organize the collections in the Louvre.

**Dent** (dĕnt), **Joseph Malaby.** 1849–1926. English publisher; to London (1867), worked as bookbinder; opened bookbinding shop (1872). Started publishing business (1888) with issuance of Lamb's *Essays of Elia* and *The Last Essays of Elia,* edited by Augustine Birrell; published pocket-size "Temple" edition of Shakespeare, (1893) and "Temple Classics" series (1896 ff.); made great success with "Everyman's Library" series (see E. P. DUTTON); succeeded as head of firm of J. M. Dent and Sons by his son **Hugh Rail′ton** [rāl′tŭn; -t'n] (1874–1938).

**Den·ta′tus** (dĕn·tā′tŭs), **Manius Curius.** fl. 290–272 B.C. Roman general; consul (290 and 275 B.C.); vanquished Samnites, Bruttians, Lucanians, Sabines, and Pyrrhus (at battle of Beneventum, 275). Famed for simplicity, frugality, and incorruptible patriotism.

**Den′ver** (dĕn′vẽr), **James William.** 1817–1892. American government official, b. Winchester, Va. Secretary of state, California (1853); member, U.S. House of Representatives (1855–57). Governor of Territory of Kansas (1857–58); restored law and order in the territory. In Civil War, Union brigadier general of volunteers (1861–63). The city of Denver, Colo., is named in his honor.

**Denyn, Jef.** See DENIJN.

**Denys.** Variant of DENIS.

**Den′za** (dĕn′tsä), **Luigi.** 1846–1922. Italian musician; settled in London (1879 ff.); professor of singing, Royal Acad. of Music, London (1898 ff.); composer chiefly of songs and an opera, *Wallenstein* (1876); known particularly for his Neapolitan song *Funiculì Funiculà* (1880).

**Den'zing·er** (dĕn'tsĭng·ẽr), **Franz Joseph.** 1821–1894. German architect.

**d'Éon de Beaumont.** Chevalier **d'Éon.** See ÉON DE BEAUMONT.

**De·par'cieux'** (dē·pȧr'syû'), **Antoine.** 1703–1768. French mathematician and statistician; known esp. for compilation of mortality tables.

**De·Pauw'** (dē̆·pô'), **Washington Charles.** 1822–1887. American banker and industrialist; b. Salem, Ind.; benefactor of Indiana Asbury U. (est. 1839), which changed its name (1884) to DePauw University in his honor.

**De·pew'** (dē̆·pū'), **Chauncey Mitchell.** 1834–1928. American lawyer, b. Peekskill, N.Y. Secretary of state, New York (1863). Attorney for Vanderbilt railroad interests (from 1866); president, New York Central Railroad (1885–99). U.S. senator (1899–1911). Renowned after-dinner speaker and wit.

**De Peys'ter** (dē̆ pīs'tẽr), **Abraham.** 1657–1728. Son of **Johannes De Peyster** (1600–1685), a burgomaster and early settler in New York. American merchant and shipowner, b. New Amsterdam (New York). Mayor of New Amsterdam (1691–94); member, governor's council (1698–1702, 1709, 1710–22); justice, supreme court (1698–1702); treasurer of the province (1706–21). His grandson **Ar'ent** (ăr'ĕnt) **Schuyler de Peyster** (1736–1832) was a royalist officer in the American Revolution and commanded at Detroit and in various positions in Upper Canada.

**De·près'** (dē·prĕ') *or* **des Prés'** (dā prā'), **Josquin** *or* **Josse.** *Latinized* **Jodocus** *or* **Josquinus Pra·ten'sis** (prȧ·tĕn'sĭs) *or* **a Pra'to** (ā prā'tō) *or* **a Pra'tis** (ā prā'tĭs). *Ital.* **del Pra'to** (dâl prä'tō). 1450?–1521. Flemish composer, b. probably at Condé in Hennegau (Hainaut); master of Netherlands school; composed chiefly masses (3 vols., 1502–14), many motets, French chansons, and hymns and psalms.

**De·pre'tis** (dâ·prâ'tēs), **Agostino.** 1813–1887. Italian statesman; supporter of Mazzini; founded journal *Il Progresso* (Turin, 1848). Premier (1876–78, 1878–79, 1881–87); minister of interior (1879–81); known for political policy of transformism; his premiership marked by reforms and ameliorations; active in organizing Triple Alliance (1882).

**De·prez'** (dē·prā'), **Marcel.** 1843–1918. French engineer and pioneer electrician. Said to have effected first long-distance transmission of electric power, through a distance of about 35 miles over telegraph wires between Munich and Miesbach (1882); also worked on friction, regulation of speed of electric motors, etc.

**De Quin'cey** (dē̆ kwĭn'sĭ; -zĭ), **Thomas.** 1785–1859. English author, b. Manchester, son of a linen merchant. Ran away from school to Wales, then to Bohemian life in London; in second year at Oxford began use of opium; left Oxford (1808); through Coleridge made acquaintance of Wordsworth and Southey at the Lake District and settled (1809) at Grasmere, explored German metaphysics and literature; m. (1816) Margaret Simpson, by whom he had five sons and three daughters. Contributed to *Blackwood's*, the *Quarterly*, etc.; published (1821), in *London Magazine*, the *Confessions of an English Opium Eater*, which made him famous. On wife's death (1837), placed children at Lasswade and wandered from lodging to lodging; in magazines issued *Murder considered as one of the Fine Arts* (1827), *Suspiria De Profundis* (1845), *The Spanish Military Nun* (1847), *The English Mail-coach, and Vision of Sudden Death* (1849); published, outside of periodicals, only two books, *Klosterheim* (1832) and *The Logic of Political Economy* (1844).

**De·rain'** (dē·răN'), **André.** 1880–1954. French painter, a leader in the postimpressionist school, and one of the Fauvists.

**Der'by** (*Brit. usu.* där'bĭ), Countesses of. See (1) Elizabeth FARREN; (2) *Charlotte de la Trémoille*, under STANLEY family.

**Derby,** Earls of. See (1) FERRERS family; (2) STANLEY family. The earldom of Derby is one of three existent English earldoms, with Shrewsbury and Huntingdon, created prior to 17th century.

**Der'by** (dûr'bĭ), **George Horatio.** *Pseudonym* **John Phoe'nix** (fē'nĭks). *Nickname* **Squi'bob** (skwī'bŏb). 1823–1861. American humorist, b. Dedham, Mass.; resident California (from 1853); author of *Phoenixiana* (1855), *The Squibob Papers* (1859), etc.

**Der'cum** (dûr'kŭm), **Francis Xavier.** 1856–1931. American neurologist, b. Philadelphia. Professor of nervous and mental diseases, Jefferson Medical Coll. (1892–1925). Described (1892) adiposis dolorosa (Dercum's disease). Author of *A Clinical Manual of Mental Diseases* (1913), *The Physiology of the Mind* (1925), etc.

**Der·cyl'li·das** (dûr·sĭl'ĭ·dȧs). Spartan general and diplomat of late 5th and early 4th century B.C.

**De·rème'** (dē·râm'), **Tristan.** *Pseudonym of* **Philippe Huc** (ük). 1889–1941. French poet; author of *Le Renard et le Corbeau* (1905), *Le Parfum des Roses Fanées* (1908), *La Flûte Fleurie* (1913), *L'Enlèvement sans Clair de Lune* (1924), etc.

**De·ren'bourg'** (dē·räN'bōōr'), **Joseph.** 1811–1895. German-born Oriental scholar in France. His son **Hart'wig'** [ȧrt'vēg'] (1844–1908), professor of Arabic at École des Hautes-Études, collaborated with him in editing (1893) Saadia (*q.v.*), and prepared editions of other Arabic writers.

**De·rennes'** (dē·rĕn'), **Charles.** 1882–1930. French novelist and poet.

**Derf'fling·er** (dĕr'flĭng·ẽr), Baron **Georg von.** 1606–1695. Brandenburg soldier; commissioned general field marshal (1670); engaged at battles of Warsaw (July, 1656), Fehrbellin (June 28, 1675), and in campaign against Sweden (1678–79).

**Der'in·ger** (dĕr'ĭn·jẽr), **Henry.** Early 19th-century manufacturer of small arms, of Philadelphia; invented a short-barreled pocket pistol, known as a "derringer."

**der Kürenberger.** See KÜRENBERG.

**d'Er'lan'ger'** (dĕr'läN'zhā'), Baron **Frederic A.** 1868–1943. Composer, b. Paris, of a German father and American mother; to London (c. 1889) and became naturalized British citizen. Composer esp. of operas, chamber music, symphonic and choral works, etc.

**Der'leth** (dûr'lĕth), **August William.** 1909–1971. American writer, b. Sauk City, Wis.; B.A., Wisconsin (1930); author of prose and poetical works about Wisconsin.

**Dermot Mac Murrough.** See MAC MURROUGH.

**Dern** (dûrn), **George Henry.** 1872–1936. American mining executive and politician, b. in Dodge County, Nebr. Invented, with Theodore P. Holt, Holt-Dern ore roaster. Governor of Utah (1925–32); author of Workmen's Compensation Law, Corrupt Practices Act, and State Mineral Land Leasing law. U.S. secretary of war (1933–36).

**Dern'burg** (dĕrn'bōōrK), **Heinrich.** 1829–1907. German jurist. His brother **Friedrich** (1833–1911), editor of Berlin *Nationalzeitung* and coeditor of *Berliner Tageblatt*, wrote travel sketches, plays, novels, etc. Friedrich's son **Bernhard** (1865–1937) was director of colonial office (1906–10); member of Prussian house of lords (1913); propaganda minister in U.S. during World War; minister of finance (1919–March, 1920).

**de Ro'beck** (dē̆ rō'bĕk), Sir **John Michael.** 1862–1928. British naval officer, b. in County Kildare, Ireland; rear admiral (1911); commander of naval force in Dardanelles

(1915); vice-admiral (1917); commander in chief of Mediterranean fleet (1919–22), of Atlantic fleet (1922–24); admiral of fleet (1925).

**De·rôme′** (dĕ·rōm′). Name of a French family of bookbinders of the 18th century, the most important being **Nicolas Denis** (1731–1788), known for his dentelle borders resembling those of Padeloup but with small birds interspersed among the arabesques.

**de Roos** (dĕ rōs′), **Sjoerd H.** 1877– . Dutch type designer; curator of typographic museum, Amsterdam. Author of *Modern Book Education* (1928).

**Dé′rou′lède′** (dā′rōō′lĕd′), **Paul.** 1846–1914. French writer and politician; author of patriotic verse, *Chants du Soldat* (1872), and a verse drama, *L'Hetman.* One of organizers (1882) of La Ligue des Patriotes; supported General Boulanger (1887); involved in intrigues to overturn the government (1899 and 1900), and banished for 10 years; returned to France after amnesty (1905). Others of his works are *Avant la Bataille* (1886), *Chants du Paysan* (1894), and the plays *Messire Du Guesclin* (1895), *La Mort de Hoche* (1897).

**de Ruyter** *or* **de Ruiter,** Admiral **M. A.** See RUYTER.

**Der·vish′ Pa·sha′** (dĕr·vēsh′ pä·shä′), **Ibrahim.** 1817–1896. Turkish general in Russo-Turkish war (1877–78); suppressed Albanian revolt (1880); served in Egypt (1882); aide-de-camp to sultan of Turkey (1888).

**der von Kürenberg.** See KÜRENBERG.

**Derwentwater,** Earls of. See Sir James RADCLIFFE.

**Der·zha′vin** (dyĕr·zhá′vyĭn), **Gavriil Romanovich.** 1743–1816. Russian lyric poet. Notable poems include *Ode to God, Monody on Prince Mestcherski,* and *The Taking of Warsaw.* Regarded as greatest Russian poet before Pushkin.

**De·sa′i** (dā·sä′ĭ), **Bhulabhai J.** 1877–1946. Hindu lawyer, b. in Gujarat. A Brahman, follower of Gandhi; active in Indian politics (from 1932); leader of opposition in Legislative Assembly (1936–43).

**De·saix′ de Vey′goux′** (dĕ·zĕ′ dĕ vā′gōō′), **Louis Charles Antoine.** 1768–1800. French general; commanded advance guard of army in Egypt (1798); took part in battle of the Pyramids (1798) and conquered Upper Egypt (1798–99); commanded reserves and with them decided the issue in the battle of Marengo (June 14, 1800), but was killed in the battle.

**De Sanc′tis** (dā sängk′tēs), **Francesco.** 1817–1883. Italian critic; professor of comparative literature, U. of Naples (1871 ff.); known particularly as founder of modern literary criticism in Italy. Author of *Petrarca* (1869), *Saggi Critici* (1881), *La Letteratura Italiana nel Secolo XIX* (pub. 1897), etc.

**De′sargues′** (dā′zárg′), **Gérard.** 1593–1662. French mathematician, a founder of modern geometry. With Pascal, introduced the method of perspective; treated conic sections as projections of circles, formulated the so-called Arguesian transformation; developed the theory of involution and of transversals; defined parallels as lines that intersect at infinity.

**Dé′sau′giers′** (dā′zō′zhyā′), **Marc Antoine.** 1742–1793. French composer, esp. of operas, as *Le Médecin Malgré Lui* (1792; an adaptation of Molière's play, into which he introduced the air of *Ça Ira*). His son **Marc Antoine Madeleine** (1772–1827), singer and vaudeville actor, émigré (1789–97), director of the Théâtre du Vaudeville, Paris (1815), wrote songs and vaudeville sketches.

**De·sault′** (dĕ·sō′), **Pierre Joseph.** 1744–1795. French surgeon; instituted the first clinical school of surgery in France; made improvements in surgical technique and instruments.

**Des·barres′** (dā·bär′), **Joseph Frederick Walsh** *or* **Wallet.** 1722–1824. English military engineer and hydrographer, of Huguenot parentage; aide to Wolfe at Quebec; made surveys in Nova Scotia and Newfoundland (1763–73); charted North American coast; lieutenant governor of Cape Breton (1784–1805), of Prince Edward Island (1805–13).

**Des′bordes′-Val′more′** (dā′bôrd′vál′môr′), Mme. **Marceline Félicité Josèphe,** *nee* **Desbordes.** 1785–1859. French poet; m. François Lanchantin, an actor whose stage name was Valmore (1817). Among her books of verse are *Élégies et Romances* (1818), *Les Pleurs* (1833), *Pauvres Fleurs* (1839), *Bouquets et Prières* (1843).

**Des′bo·rough** *or* **Des′bo·row** (dĕz′bŭ·rŭ; dĕz′brŭ) *or* **Dis′browe** (dĭz′brō; -brŭ), **John.** 1608–1680. English soldier. Fought on Parliamentary side; nearly captured Charles II after battle of Worcester. Instigated hostility of army against Richard Cromwell's administration; member of council of state and Rump Parliament. Imprisoned (1666–67) for republican intrigue. Caricatured in Butler's *Hudibras.*

**Des′brosses′** (dā′brôs′), **Jean Alfred.** 1835–1906. French painter, esp. of rural scenes.

**Des′camps′** (dā′käN′), Baron **Édouard Eugène François.** 1847–1933. Belgian jurist; member of Hague Tribunal; minister of arts and sciences (1907).

**Des·cartes′** (dā·kärt′; *Fr.* dā′kárt′), **René.** *Lat.* **Renatus Car·te′si·us** (kär·tē′zhĭ·ŭs; -zhŭs). 1596–1650. French scientist and philosopher, b. La Haye, in Touraine. Resident in Holland (1629–49). Noted as mathematician as well as philosopher; fame based on treatise *Discours de la Méthode* (1637), with its supporting essays *La Dioptrique, Les Météores, La Géométrie.* The Cartesian system (Cartesianism) established the ideal of mathematical certitude in metaphysical demonstrations and, by brushing aside the then familiar scholastic subtleties, introduced modern philosophy and science of thought. Others of his works are *Meditationes de Prima Philosophia* (1641), *Principia Philosophiae* (1644), and the posthumous publications *De l'Homme* (1664) and *Opuscula Posthuma, Physica et Mathematica* (1701).

**Des′caves′** (dā′káv′), **Lucien.** 1861–1949. French journalist and writer of novels and plays.

**Des′champs′** (dā′shäN′), **Émile.** *In full* **Émile Deschamps de Saint′ A′mand′** (dĕ säN′-tá′mäN′). 1791–1871. French poet of the romantic school; with Victor Hugo, founded (1824) *La Muse Française;* author of *Études Françaises et Étrangères* (1828), including translations from other languages, and a preface constituting a manifesto of the romanticists. His brother **An′to′ny′** (äN′tô′nē′), *in full* **Antoine François Marie** (1800–1869), also a poet of the romantic school, translated Dante's *Divina Commedia.*

**Deschamps, Eustache.** 1340?–?1407. French poet; author of over a thousand ballades; wrote also a long poem *Le Miroir de Mariage* (a satire on women, containing over 12,000 verses), rondeaux, virelays, etc.

**Deschamps, Gaston.** 1861–1931. French journalist; editor of *Journal des Débats* (to 1893); literary critic of *Le Temps,* succeeding Anatole France (1893).

**Deschamps, Louis Henri.** 1846–1902. French painter.

**Des′cha′nel′** (dā′shá′nĕl′), **Émile Auguste Étienne Martin.** 1819–1904. French critic and author; professor of modern literature at Collège de France (1881); senator (1881–1904). Works include critical studies of Aristophanes, Racine, Voltaire, Lamartine, and Benjamin Franklin, and the important *Romantisme des Classiques* (1882). His son **Paul Eugène Louis** (1856–1922), statesman and author, was 10th president of French Republic; leader of progressive Republicans; president of Chamber of Deputies (1898–1902, 1912–20); president of France (Feb.–Sept., 1920); resigned because of ill health.

**Des Cloi′zeaux′** (dā klwȧ′zō′), **Alfred Louis Olivier Legrand.** 1817–1897. French mineralogist; known for work on pseudomorphism, use of the microscope, and optical properties of crystals.

**Des·clot′** (dās·klôt′), **Bernat.** fl. 1285. Catalan historian; author of a history of Peter III of Aragon, earliest important composition in Catalan.

**de Selincourt.** See SELINCOURT.

**De Sélincourt,** Mrs. **Aubrey.** See Irene Rutherford MCLEOD.

**de Se·ver′sky** (dyĕ syĕ·vyĕr′skû·ĭ; *Angl.* dĕ sĕ·vĕr′skĭ), **Alexander Procofieff.** 1894–1974. Aviator and aeronautical engineer, b. Tiflis, Russia; to U.S. (1918); naturalized (1927); president, Seversky Aircraft Corp. (1931–39), manufacturing pursuit planes. Inventor of various airplane devices including a bombsight (sold to U.S. government); interested in air-pollution control; author of *Victory Through Air Power* (1942).

**Des′fon′taines′** (dā′fôɴ′tĕn′), **René Louiche.** 1750–1833. French botanist. Author of *Flora Atlantica* (1798), in which plants collected during his two-year travels in the Barbary States are described.

**Des′hayes′** (dā′ā′), **Gérard Paul.** 1795–1875. French naturalist; authority on fossil conchology.

**Des′hou′lières′** (dā′zo͞o′lyâr′), **Antoinette,** *nee* **du Li′gier′ de la Garde** (dü lē′zhyā′ dĕ lȧ gȧrd′). 1638–1694. French poet; author of idyls, eclogues, odes, madrigals, elegies, etc. Her poetry was edited and published (1695) by her daughter **Antoinette Thérèse** (1662–1718).

**De′si·de′rio da Set′ti·gna′no** (dā′sē·dâ′ryō dä sāt′tē-nyä′nō). 1428–1464. Florentine sculptor; one of leading early Renaissance sculptors.

**Desiderius.** See Pope VICTOR III.

**Des′i·de′ri·us** (dĕs′ĭ·dēr′ĭ·ŭs). Last king of theLombards (756–774 A.D.). Duke of Tuscany; after becoming Lombard king, attacked papacy, who sought aid (c. 772) from the Franks; his territory invaded (773) by Charlemagne and his capital, Ticinum (Pavia), captured; taken as prisoner to France.

**Dé′si′rée′** (dā′zē′rā′), **Ber′nar′dine′ Eu′gé′nie′** (bĕr′nȧr′-dēn′ û′zhā′nē′; ü′zhā′nē′). 1777–1860. Queen of Sweden (1818–44), b. Marseille; m. (1798) Gen. Jean Bernadotte (later King Charles XIV John of Sweden); visited Sweden (1810–11) after Bernadotte's selection as heir to throne, but did not live there until 1823.

**de Sitter, Willem.** See SITTER.

**Des′jar′dins′** (dā′zhär′dăɴ′), **Ernest Émile Antoine.** 1823–1886. French historian.

**Desjardins, Marie Catherine.** *Pseudonym* Mme. **de Ville′dieu′** (vēl′dyû′). 1640?–1683. French writer; author of *Les Désordres de l'Amour, Les Amours des Grands Hommes, Annales Galantes,* etc.

**Desjardins, Martin.** *Orig. surname* **van den Bo′gaert** (vän dĕn bō′gȧrt). d. 1694. Dutch sculptor; studio in Paris; one of the chief decorators of Versailles.

**Des′landres′** (dā′läɴ′dr′), **Henri Alexandre.** 1853–1948. French astrophysicist. Director of observatory at Meudon (from 1907), also of observatory at Paris (from 1927). Known esp. for work on spectral analysis of the sun and on band spectra. See G. E. HALE.

**Des′ma′rets′** (dā′mȧ′rā′), **Nicolas.** = Nicolas DES MARETS.

**Desmarets de Saint′-Sor′lin′** (dĕ săɴ′sôr′lăɴ′), **Jean.** 1596–1676. French writer of plays, verse, and essays; protégé of Richelieu, and recipient of political preferment from the cardinal.

**De Smet** (dĕ smĕt′), **Pierre Jean.** 1801–1873. Jesuit missionary in America, b. Termonde, Belgium. To U.S. (1821). Missionary to Indians along western frontier (from 1838). Called "Blackrobe" by Indians.

**de Smet de Naeyer.** See SMET DE NAEYER.

**Des′mond** (dĕz′mŭnd), Earls of. See FITZGERALD family.

**Desmond, Shaw.** 1877–1960. Irish journalist, novelist, and poet. Founder of International Inst. for Psychical Research (1934). Among his books are *Democracy* (1919), *Passion* (1920), *The Drama of Sinn Fein* (1923), *The Isle of Ghosts* (1925), *Ragnarok* (1926), *Windjammer: the Book of the Horn* (1932), *We do not Die* (1934), *World-Birth* (1937), *Reincarnation for Everyman* (1939).

**Des′mou′lins′** (dā′mo͞o′lăɴ′), **Camille,** *in full* **Lucie Simplice Camille Benoît.** 1760–1794. Called **Pro′cu′-reur′ de la lan′terne′** (prô′kü′rûr′ dĕ lȧ läɴ′tĕrn′), *i.e.* agent of the lantern, from his pamphlet against aristocrats *Le Discours de la Lanterne aux Parisiens.* French journalist and revolutionary leader, b. in Guise. Educ. at college of Louis-le-Grand, Paris; studied law, advocate in Paris (1785–88); not successful; m. (1790) **Lucile Duplessis** (1771–1794). Excited by dismissal of Necker (July 11, 1789), harangued crowds (July 12), urging revolt—actual beginning of Revolution, the Bastille being taken two days later. Wrote pamphlet *La France Libre* (1789) supporting Revolution; won friendship of Mirabeau; published *La Tribune des Patriotes,* organ of Cordeliers; also wrote a bitter attack on Girondists; deputy for Paris to National Convention (Sept., 1793). Later, joined Danton in calling for more moderation; antagonism with ultra-Jacobins increased; arrested by Robespierre; given only mock trial; executed with Danton (Apr. 5, 1794), his wife being guillotined fortnight later. Author of *La Philosophie du Peuple Français* (1788), *Histoire des Brissotins* (1793).

**Des′noires′terres′** (dā′nwȧr′tĕr′), **Gustave Le Brisoys.** 1817–1892. French writer; author of books on 18th-century life in France.

**Des′noy′ers′** (dā′nwȧ′yā′), Baron. **Auguste Gaspard Louis Bou′cher′** (bo͞o′shā′). *Known as* **Boucher-Desnoyers.** 1779–1857. French engraver; best known for his engravings after Raphael.

**Desnoyers, Louis Claude Joseph Florence.** 1802–1868. French author of classics in the literature of education, as *Mésaventures de Jean-Paul Choppart* (1836).

**de So′to** (dē sō′tō; *Span.* dā), **Hernando** *or* **Fernando.** 1500?–1542. Spanish explorer in America, b. Barcarrota, Spain. Served in Central America and Peru before receiving (1537) from Charles V of Spain approval of an expedition to conquer Florida. Landed in Florida (May 30, 1539); for three years his force explored the country, pushing northward and westward in the search for gold and treasure, in constant conflict with hostile Indians; discovered and crossed the Mississippi River (1541). Discouraged, turned back in spring of 1542; de Soto died on the banks of the Mississippi and his body was sunk in the river to prevent its being desecrated by Indians. His companions floated down river to Gulf of Mexico.

**Des′pard** (dĕs′pērd; -pärd), **Edward Marcus.** 1751–1803. Irish conspirator; entered British navy (1766); commanded expedition against Spanish possessions in West Indies (1782); superintended colony in Yucatán (1784–90); devised plot to assassinate George III; last man sentenced to be hanged, drawn, and quartered in England.

**Des·pen′ser** (dĕs·pĕn′sēr), **Hugh le** (lĕ). d. 1265. Last of the justiciaries of England (1260, reappointed 1263); leader of baronial side in Mad Parliament of Oxford (1258); joined de Montfort party (1264); one of four arbitrators for arranging terms between de Montfort and earl of Gloucester; killed at Evesham. His son **Hugh** (1262–1326), Earl of **Win′ches′ter** (wĭn′chĕs′tēr; -chĭs-tēr), secured from Pope Clement V, King Edward I's release from oaths to observe charters (1305); succeeded Piers Gaveston as chief adviser; expelled by barons (1321); restored by Edward II and created earl (1322); with his son, virtually ruled the country; captured by barons under Roger de Mortimer (*q.v.*) and Queen Isabella (1326), whom he had induced king to outlaw; hanged. His son **Hugh** (d. 1326) was king's chamberlain (1313); banished with his father (1321) by barons, who hated him for his wealth and rapacity; recalled by king (1322); negotiator of truce with Scotland (1323); taken with king (1326) by barons under Queen Isabella and hanged. **Edward** (d. 1375), grandson of Hugh the younger, fought at Poitiers and under Pope Urban V in 1369 and was patron of Froissart. **Thomas** (1373–1400), son of Edward, supported Richard II against duke of Gloucester and other lords appellant (1397); implicated in Gloucester's death; joined conspiracy against Henry IV and was betrayed; beheaded. **Henry** (1341?–1406), brother of Edward, became bishop of Norwich (1370); defeated insurgent Norfolk peasants (1381); led crusade in Flanders for Pope Urban VI against antipope adherents (1383); denounced as a fighting prelate by Wycliffe; persecuted the Lollards; imprisoned (1399) for loyalty to Richard II, but reconciled with Henry IV (1401). Cf. SPENCER family.

**Des'pi'au'** (dĕs'pē'ō'), **Charles.** 1874–1946. French sculptor; best known for portrait busts; also carved *Bacchante Assise, Jeune Faune, Ève, Monument aux Morts.*

**Des'portes'** (dā'pôrt'), **Alexandre François.** 1661–1743. French painter, esp. of portraits and hunting scenes.

**Desportes, Philippe.** 1546–1606. French poet, disciple of Ronsard; author of elegies, psalms, songs, and collections of love sonnets.

**des Prés.** See DEPRÈS.

**Des'prés'** (dā'prā'), **Suzanne.** 1875–1951. French actress; m. Aurélien Lugné-Poë; played at Théâtre Antoine and (from 1902) Comédie Française.

**Des'pretz'** (dā'prā'), **César Mansuète.** 1791?–1863. French physicist, b. in Belgium. Studied expansion of liquids, action of the galvanic pile, conduction, latent heat of various gases, etc.

**Des'saix'** (dā'sĕ'), Comte **Joseph Marie.** 1764–1834. French general in Napoleon's armies; dubbed **l'In'tré'pide'** (lăN'trā'pēd') by Napoleon after battle of Wagram (1809).

**Des'sa'lines'** (dā'sȧ'lēn'), **Jean Jacques.** 1758–1806. Negro leader in Haiti and emperor (1804–06), b. a slave, at Grande Rivière; took name of French master. Joined insurrection (1791) and aided Toussaint L'Ouverture (1797); finally compelled to submit to French under Leclerc (1802); helped by British, drove out French (1803); established republic (1804) with himself as head; declared himself emperor as Jacques I (1804–06); assassinated by Christophe and Pétion.

**Des'sau'er** (dĕs'ou'ĕr), **Jo'seph** (yō'zĕf). 1794–1876. Czech composer of comic operas and esp. songs.

**Des·soir'** (dĕ·swär'), **Ludwig.** 1810–1874. German actor; chief roles included Hamlet, Othello, Richard III, Narcissus.

**De Ste'fa·ni** (dȧ stā'fä·nē; stâ'-), **Alberto.** 1879–1969. Italian economist; elected deputy (1921); minister of finance (1922–25); member, Fascist Grand Council. Author of *La Legislazione Economica della Guerra* (1927), *Garanzie di Potenza* (1936), etc.

**De'stinn** (dĕs'tĭn), **Em'my** (ĕm'ē). *Orig. surname* **Kit'tl** (kĭt''l). 1878–1930. Bohemian operatic soprano; created leading role in Puccini's *Madame Butterfly* in London (1905) and Richard Strauss's *Salome* in Paris and Berlin (1907); member of Metropolitan Opera Co., New York (1908–16); m. Captain Naisbach (1923).

**Des'touches'** (dā'tōōsh'), **André Cardinal.** 1662–1749. French composer; superintendent of music for king (1728). Among his operas are *Amadis de Grèce* (1699), *Omphale* (1701), *Callirhoë* (1712), *Sémiramis* (1718).

**Des'touches'** (dā'tōōsh'), **Franz Seraph von.** 1772–1844. German composer of operas, operettas, and theater music for plays by Schiller and Kotzebue.

**Destouches, Louis Fuch.** *Pseudonym* **Louis-Ferdinand Cé'line'** (sā'lēn'). 1894–1961. French physician and novelist; author of *Journey to the End of the Night* and *Death on the Installment Plan.*

**Destouches, Philippe.** *Real surname* **Né'ri'cault'** (nā'rē'kō'). 1680–1754. French playwright; master of the sentimental comedy (*comédie larmoyante*); author of 17 comedies, including *Le Curieux Impertinent, Le Médisant* (1715), *Le Philosophe Marié* (1727), *Le Glorieux* (1732), *Le Dissipateur* (1736), *L'Ambitieux* (1737).

**Des'tutt' de Tra'cy'** (dĕs'tüt' dē trȧ'sē'), Comte **Antoine Louis Claude.** 1754–1836. French philosopher; member of States-General (1789); appointed by the Directory member of the Committee of Public Instruction; under the Consulate, member of the Senate; regarded by Napoleon as chief of the ideologists; appointed peer of France after the Restoration.

**Des'val'lières'** (dā'vȧ'lyâr'), **Georges Olivier.** 1861–1950. French landscape and genre painter.

**De Swert** (dĕ svĕrt'), **Jules.** 1843–1891. Belgian violoncellist and composer of two operas, three concertos, and many piano pieces.

**de Tabley,** Baron. See John Byrne Leicester WARREN.

**De·taille'** (dē·tä'y'), **Édouard,** *in full* **Jean Baptiste Édouard.** 1848–1912. French painter; best known for his battle scenes and paintings of soldiers.

**De'ter·ding** (dā'tĕr·dĭng), Sir **Henri.** 1865–1939. Dutch oil magnate, b. Amsterdam. Joined Royal Dutch Oil Co. (1896) and became its director-general (1902). Merged with other oil interests to form Asiatic Petroleum Co. (1903); entered American field, and expanded operations to include Mexico, Egypt, the Near East and the Far East, and the Argentine. His claim to Russian oil properties of the Rothschild interests (bought 1903) was denied by Russian Soviet government (after 1920) and he became a supporter of the Hitler Nazi movement in Germany. Retired (1937), but continued as member of various boards.

**Dett** (dĕt), **Robert Nathaniel.** 1882–1943. Conductor and composer, b. in Province of Ontario, Can. Director of music, Hampton Inst. (from 1913); conductor of Hampton Inst. choir which toured U.S., Canada, and Europe. First American to utilize Negro folk tunes for classic development. Among his many compositions are *America the Beautiful* (chorus), *The Ordering of Moses* (oratorio). Author and editor of *The Dett Collection of Negro Spirituals* (4 books, 1937).

**Dett'mann** (dĕt'män), **Ludwig.** 1865–1944. German landscape and (1914–18) battle painter.

**Dett'wei'ler** (dĕt'vī'lĕr), **Peter.** 1837–1904. German physician; specialist in tuberculosis.

**Deu'bler** (doi'blĕr), **Konrad.** 1814–1884. Austrian philosopher; known as "the Peasant Philosopher."

**Deu'cher** (doi'kĕr), **Adolf.** 1831–1912. Swiss statesman; president of Swiss Confederation (1886, 1897, 1903, 1909).

**De'us·ded'it** (dē'ŭs·dĕd'ĭt; -dē'dĭt), Saint. *Sometimes called* **Adeodatus I.** Pope (615–618). Cf. ADEODATUS.

**Deus Ra'mos** (dā'ōōsh rä'mōōsh), **João de.** 1830–1896. Portuguese poet; newspaper editor (from 1862); deputy to Cortes (1869); devoted himself to improving educational conditions in Portugal. Foremost Portuguese poet of his time; known particularly for love poems.

**Deus′sen** (doi′sĕn), **Paul.** 1845–1919. German philosopher and Sanskrit scholar. Among his works are *Elementen der Metaphysik* (1877), *Das System des Vedânta* (1883), *Die Sûtras des Vedânta* (1887), etc.

**Deutsch** (doich), **Babette.** See under Avrahm YARMOLINSKY.

**Deutsch** (doich), **Emanuel Oscar Me′na·hem** (mā′nä·hĕm; mȧ·nä′hĕm). 1829–1873. Semitic scholar, b. in Silesia, of Jewish extraction; assistant in British Museum (1855–70); deciphered Phoenician inscriptions; known for his essay on the Talmud in *Quarterly Review* (1867).

**Deutsch, Nikolaus.** See Nikolaus MANUEL.

**de Va·le′ra** (dĕv′ȧ·lâr′ȧ), **Ea′mon** (ā′mŭn). 1882– . Irish political leader, b. New York City of Spanish father and Irish mother. Educated Blackrock College and Royal U., Dublin. Led party of insurgents in Irish nationalist uprising (1916); president of Sinn Fein (1917–26); chosen president of an Irish republican government for which he obtained funds in America (1919); member Dail Eireann (1919–22) and leader of opposition to Anglo-Irish treaty (Dec., 1921–Jan., 1922), signed by colleagues Arthur Griffith and Michael Collins (*qq.v.*); resigned presidency; established and presided over Fianna Fail (1924), comprising extreme republicans; took oath of allegiance to king and led Fianna Fail into Free State parliament (1927); pres. of executive council and minister for external affairs (1932–37); prime min. (1937–48; 1951–54; 1957–59); pres. of Ireland (from 1959).

**De·vam′bez′** (dē·väN′bâz′), **André Victor Édouard.** 1867–1944. French landscape and figure painter.

**De·vaux′** (dē·vō′), **Paul.** 1801–1880. Belgian statesman. A founder (1824) of opposition journal *Politique*, influential in agitation leading to independence of Belgium from Netherlands. Advocated choice of Leopold of Saxe-Coburg as king.

**Dé′vay** *or* **Dé′vai** (dā′voi), **Mâtyâs Birô.** 1500?–?1545. Hungarian church reformer. Entered Roman Catholic priesthood; adopted (1529) principles of Reformation and studied at Wittenberg with Luther. Preached Lutheranism, later Calvinism, in Hungary; regarded as founder of Reformed Church of Hungary.

**De Vec′chi di Val Cis·mon′** (dâ vĕk′kē dē väl chēz·mōn′), Count **Cesare Maria.** 1884–1959. Italian politician and administrator; president of Fascist group in parliament (1921–22); governor of Somaliland (1923–28); permanent member of Fascist Council. Ambassador to the Vatican (1929–34); minister of national education (1935–36); governor of Rhodes (1936–40).

**Dev′ens** (dĕv′ĕnz), **Charles.** 1820–1891. American political leader, b. Charlestown, Mass. Served through Civil War. U.S. attorney general (1877–81). Justice, Mass. supreme court (1881–91). Camp Devens, the New England army camp, was named in his honor.

**De′ven·ter** (dā′vĕn·tĕr), Sir **Jacob Louis van.** 1874–1922. South African soldier, b. in Orange Free State. Second in command to Gen. Smuts, Boer War (1899–1902). Served in German South-West Africa (1914–15); as temporary lieutenant general, commanded Allied forces in successful campaign in East Africa (1917).

**de Vere** (dĕ vēr′), **Aubrey Thomas.** 1814–1902. Irish poet; intimate with Browning and Tennyson. First work *The Waldenses and Other Poems* (1842); sympathized with Irish moderates in public questions, as in his *English Misrule and Irish Misdeeds* (1848); joined Church of Rome (1851); wrote devotional verse and hymns; turned to Irish bardic lore and ecclesiastical medievalism, as in *Inisfail* (1862), *Irish Odes* (1869), *Legends of St. Patrick* (1872); wrote literary and critical essays and recollections of Wordsworth, Newman, and others. His father, **Sir Aubrey de Vere** (1788–1846), a son of Sir Vere Hunt, was a poet, author of *Julian The Apostate* (1822) and *Mary Tudor* (1847).

**de Vere, Maximilian Schele.** See SCHELE DE VERE.

**Dev′er·eux** (dĕv′ĕr·ōō; -ōōks). Name of an English family bearing the title earl of Essex, including:

**Walter Devereux** (1541?–1576), 1st Earl of **Es′sex** (ĕs′ĕks; -ĭks) of 6th creation and 2d Viscount of **Her′e·ford** (hĕr′ē·fẽrd); grandson of **Walter Devereux** (d. 1558; 1st Viscount and 3d Baron **Fer′rers** [fĕr′ĕrz], chief justice of South Wales); aided in suppression of northern rebellion (1569); attempted to subdue rebel O'Neills and Scots under Sorley Boy MacDonnell in Ulster (1573); treacherously captured and executed Irish chief Sir Brian MacPhelim (1574); made earl marshal of Ireland by Queen Elizabeth; massacred hundreds of followers of Sorley Boy (1575).

His eldest son, **Robert** (1566–1601), 2d earl; M.A., Cantab. (1581); distinguished himself at Zutphen (1586); became chief favorite of Elizabeth I on the death of Leicester; joined expedition against Spain (1589); offended Elizabeth by secret marriage with widow of Sir Philip Sidney (1590); commanded fruitless campaign in aid of Henry of Navarre (1591–92); gained glory in successful expedition against Cádiz (1596); during quarrel with queen, was counseled and aided by Francis Bacon; on expedition to Azores failed to capture Spanish treasure fleet (1597–98); earl marshal of England (1597); as lieutenant and governor general of Ireland, met defeat at Arklow (1599), made truce with Tyrone, left post to vindicate himself before the queen; deprived of his offices and his liberty; induced by Mountjoy, Southampton, and others to form plot for removing queen's counselors (1601), but failed in attempt to raise citizens of London; prosecuted for treason by old friend Bacon and executed; a patron of literature and author of sonnets.

**Robert** (1591–1646), 3d earl, son of 2d earl; educ. Oxford; restored to his father's titles by Parliament (1604); lived in household with prince of Wales; served in wars of the Palatinate (1620–23); vice-admiral in futile expedition to capture Cádiz (1625); supported Petition of Right (1628); voted for death of Strafford (1640); commanded Parliamentary army, held the field at Edge Hill (1642), took Reading (1643), relieved Gloucester (1643); nearly lost army in Cornwall, partly because of disease and financial trouble, partly through incompetence (1644); after passing of Self-denying Ordinance, resigned (1645). His first wife Frances Howard married (1613) Robert Carr (*q.v.*), Earl of Rochester.

**Penelope** (1562?–1607), daughter of 1st earl of Essex, who intended her to marry her admirer Sir Philip Sidney (*q.v.*); m. (1581) Robert Rich, 3d Baron Rich, afterwards earl of Warwick; dissatisfied with marriage, welcomed attentions and love sonnets of Sir Philip Sidney, collected under title *Astrophel and Stella* (1591); after Sidney's death, became Lord Mountjoy's mistress; divorced by Lord Rich (1605), married Mountjoy, Earl of Devonshire (see Charles BLOUNT).

**Dev′ers** (dĕv′ĕrz), **Jacob Loucks.** 1887– . American army officer, b. York, Pa.; grad. U.S.M.A., West Point (1909); advanced through the grades to brigadier general (1940), general (1945); chief of staff, Panama department (1939–40); chief of armored forces (1941–43), of allied invasion forces in southern France (1944–45); permanent major general (1946).

**Deville, Henri Étienne Sainte-Claire** and **Charles Sainte-Claire.** See SAINTE-CLAIRE DEVILLE.

**De Vil′liers** (dĕ vĭl′yĕrz), **Jacob.** 1868–1931. South African judge, b. in Orange Free State. Served in Boer

War; wounded at Bothaville. On granting of responsible government, became attorney general and minister of mines; chief justice of South Africa.

**De Villiers, John Henry.** 1st Baron **De Villiers.** 1842–1914. South African judge, b. Paarl, Cape of Good Hope. First chief justice of Union of South Africa (1910); acting governor general (1912, 1914).

**De·vine′** (dĕ·vīn′; dē-), **Edward Thomas.** 1867–1948. American sociologist and social-service worker, b. Union, Iowa. Editor of *Survey* (1897–1912); professor of social economy at Columbia (1905–19) and American U. in Washington, D.C. (1926–28); director of New York School of Philanthropy (1904–07, 1912–17). Author of *Economics* (1898), *Misery and Its Causes* (1909), *Progressive Social Action* (1933), etc.

**De Vin′ne** (dĕ vĭn′ē), **Theodore Low.** 1828–1914. American printer, b. Stamford, Conn. With Francis Hart's printing shop in New York (1850–58); partner (1858–77); took over business as Theo. L. De Vinne & Co., on Hart's death (1877); incorporated as The De Vinne Press (1908). Brought about great improvements in American typography. Author of *The Invention of Printing* (1876), *The Practice of Typography* (4 vols., 1900, 1901, 1902, 1904), etc.

**Devizes, Richard of.** See RICHARD OF DEVIZES.

**Dev′lin** (dĕv′lĭn), **Joseph.** 1872–1934. Irish politician, b. Belfast. Agitator for Irish home rule; member of Parliament (1902–22, 1929 ff.); also, member of parliament of Northern Ireland (from 1921). Influence waned with rise of Sinn Fein and founding of Irish Free State.

**Dev′on** (dĕv′ŭn) *or occasionally* **Dev′on·shire** (-shĭr; -shẽr), Earl of. A title borne (till 1262) by members of REDVERS family, by Humphrey STAFFORD, and (c. 1300–1462, 1485–1556, 1831 ff.) by Courtenay family (*q.v.*).

**Dev′on·port** (dĕv′ŭn·pōrt), 1st Viscount. **Hudson Ewbanke Kear′ley** (kẽr′lĭ). 1856–1934. English merchant and politician; M.P. (1892–1910); chairman, Port of London Authority (1909–25). Appointed food controller (1916) and chairman of royal commission in sugar supplies (1917).

**Dev′on·shire** (dĕv′ŭn·shĭr; -shẽr), Dukes of. See CAVENDISH family.

**Devonshire,** Earl of. An English title held by Charles BLOUNT and (from 1618) by members of Cavendish family (see William CAVENDISH), the fourth earl being created duke (1694). See also earl of DEVON.

**De Vo′to** (dĕ vō′tō), **Bernard Augustine.** 1897–1955. American writer, b. Ogden, Utah. On English teaching staff, Harvard (1929–36). Editor of "The Easy Chair" in *Harper's Magazine* (from 1935); editor, *Saturday Review of Literature* (1936–38). Author of *The Crooked Mile* (1924), *The Chariot of Fire* (1926), *Mark Twain's America* (1932), *Forays and Rebuttals* (1936), *Minority Report* (1940), *Mark Twain at Work* (1942), etc.

**de Vriendt, Frans.** See Frans FLORIS.

**De·vri′ent′** (dē·vrē′äN′; dĕ·vrēnt′). Family of German actors, including: **Ludwig** (1784–1832), noted in the roles of Shylock, Lear, Richard III, Falstaff, Mercutio; his three nephews, **Karl August** (1797–1872), **Philipp Eduard** (1801–1877), and **Gustav Emil** (1803–1872); Philipp Eduard's son **Otto** (1838–1894); Gustav Emil's son **Max** (1857–1929).

**De Vries** (dĕ vrēs′), **David Pietersen.** 1592?–?1655. Dutch colonizer in America, b. La Rochelle, France. Voyaged to America (1631, 1632–33, 1634–36, 1638–44). Established a colony on Staten Island and another near what is now Tappan, both destroyed by Indians (1643). Wrote account of his travels (pub. 1655).

**De Vries, Hugo.** 1848–1935. Dutch botanist, b. Haarlem; professor, U. of Amsterdam (1878–1918). One of those to discover and reveal (1900) the importance of Mendel's publications; developed the experimental method of studying evolution through observing mutations instead of the results of natural selection; conducted researches on osmosis and plasmolysis. Author of *Eine Methode zur Analyse der Turgorkraft* (1884), *Die Mutationstheorie* (2 vols., 1900–03), *Plant Breeding* (1907), etc.

**Dew′ar** (dū′ẽr), Sir **James.** 1842–1923. Scottish chemist and physicist; professor of natural experimental philosophy, Cambridge (1875–1923), and of chemistry, Royal Institution, London (1877–1923). Investigated specific heat of hydrogen and physiological action of light on the eye; made spectroscopic studies; first to produce liquid hydrogen (1898), later (1899) obtaining it as a solid; invented Dewar vessel, forerunner of the vacuum bottle; discovered that the absorbent power of charcoal for gases is increased by cold (1902); studied properties of matter at low temperatures; with Frederick Augustus Abel invented cordite.

**Dewar, Thomas Robert.** 1st Baron **Dewar** of Homestall. 1864–1930. British distiller, sportsman, and raconteur, b. Perth, Scotland. Became London agent of distillery founded by his father, **John Dewar;** largely expanded business and succeeded father as head of John Dewar & Sons. Created baron (1919). Author of *Toasts and Maxims and Wisdom Compressed, A Ramble Around the Globe,* etc.

**de Wentworth, Cecile.** See Cecile de WENTWORTH.

**D'Ewes** (dūz), Sir **Simonds.** 1602–1650. English antiquarian; collected journals of all parliaments during reign of Elizabeth (pub. 1682); his transcripts from ancient records and his diaries (1621–24, 1643–47) are valuable, often the only, authority for incidents.

**De Wet** (dĕ vĕt′), **Christiaan Rudolph.** 1854–1922. Boer soldier and politician, b. in Orange Free State. Served in Boer War (1899–1902) as general under Cronjé in western area; became commander in chief of Orange Free State forces after British captured Cronjé (Feb. 27, 1900); esp. successful as guerilla leader. Supported Hertzog in separatist policy (1912–13); aided in organizing Nationalist party; rebelled against South African government (1914) and imprisoned; released (Dec., 1915) on pledge to cease political agitation.

**De Wet′te** (dā vĕt′ĕ), **Wilhelm Martin Leberecht.** 1780–1849. German Protestant theologian and Bible scholar.

**Dew′ey** (dū′ĭ), **Charles Melville.** 1849–1937. American landscape painter, b. Lowville, N.Y.

**Dewey, Davis Rich.** 1858–1942. Brother of John Dewey. American economist, b. Burlington, Vt. Author of *Financial History of the United States* (1902), *Banking and Credit* (with M. J. Shugrue; 1922), etc.

**Dewey, George.** 1837–1917. American naval officer, b. Montpelier, Vt.; grad. U.S.N.A., Annapolis (1858). During Civil War, served under Farragut. Commanding officer of Asiatic squadron (Jan. 3, 1898); took squadron to Hong Kong where (Apr. 26) he received news of declaration of war against Spain; immediately steered for Manila, Philippine Islands; destroyed Spanish squadron in battle of Manila Bay (May 1, 1898) and supported army in capture of city of Manila (Aug. 13). Admiral, U.S. navy (from 1899); president, general board, U.S. Navy Department, Washington, D.C. (1900–17).

**Dewey, John.** 1859–1952. Brother of Davis Rich Dewey. American philosopher and educator, b. Burlington, Vt. Professor, Minnesota (1888–89), Michigan (1889–94), Chicago (1894–1904), Columbia (from 1904); adherent of pragmatism as formulated by C. S. Peirce and William James. Among his many books are *Leibnitz* (1888), *School and Society* (1899), *How We Think* (1909),

*Democracy and Education* (1916), *Reconstruction in Philosophy* (1920), *The Quest for Certainty* (1929), *Art as Experience* (1934), *Liberalism and Social Action* (1935), *Logic: The Theory of Inquiry* (1938).

**Dewey, Melvil.** 1851–1931. American librarian, b. Adams Center, N.Y. Chief librarian and professor of library economy, Columbia (1883–88); director New York State Library (1889–1906); also, founder and director, New York State Library School (1887–1906). A founder of American Library Assoc., Spelling Reform Assoc.; founder and editor, *Library Journal* (1876–81) and *Library Notes* (1886–98). Originated decimal classification system and published *Decimal Classification and Relativ Index* (1876–1929).

**Dewey, Thomas Edmund.** 1902–1971. American lawyer, b. Owosso, Mich.; A.B., Michigan (1923), LL.B., Columbia (1925); U.S. attorney, southern district of N.Y. (1933); special prosecutor in investigation of organized crime, N.Y. (1935–37); district attorney of New York county (1937–38); governor of N.Y. (1942–54). Republican candidate for president of U.S. (1944, 1948).

**Dewi,** Saint. See Saint DAVID.

**De Windt** (dĕ wĭnt′), **Harry.** 1856–1933. English explorer. Made trip from Peking to France by land (1887), Russia to India via Persia (1889), New York to Paris by land (crossing Bering Straits; 1896), Paris to New York by land (1901–02). Author of travel books.

**Dew′ing** (dū′ĭng), **Thomas Wilmer.** 1851–1938. American figure and portrait painter, b. Boston. His wife, **Maria Richards,** *nee* **Oa′key** [ō′kĭ] (1845–1927), was also a painter, esp. of flower pictures.

**de Wint** (dĕ wĭnt′), **Peter.** 1784–1849. English landscape painter, b. in Staffordshire, of Dutch descent; chiefly a water-colorist, illustrator of landscape, architecture, and country life of England.

**De Win′ter** (dĕ vĭn′tĕr), **Jan Willem.** 1750–1812. Dutch admiral; entered French army at outbreak of French Revolution (1789); engaged in campaigns of 1792, 1793, and (against Holland) 1795; rose to rank of brigadier general. Assigned by States-General of France to reorganize Dutch fleet; defeated by British off Camperdown (Oct. 11, 1797). Ambassador to France (1798–1802). Commanded Dutch fleet which sailed to Mediterranean and negotiated peace with pirates of Tripoli (1802 ff.).

**De Witt** (dĕ vĭt′), **Jan.** 1625–1672. Dutch statesman; pensionary for Dordrecht in the states of Holland (1650); advocate of authority of states in opposition to princes of house of Orange. Grand pensionary of Holland (1653–72); concluded peace with England (1654); restored national finances and strengthened Dutch commercial supremacy in East; opposed recognizing prince of Orange as stadholder; helped Denmark against Sweden (1658–59); conducted war against England (1665–67), terminated by favorable Treaty of Breda (1667); secured passage of perpetual edict against house of Orange (1667); concluded Triple Alliance (1668) with Sweden and England against France; forced to resign as pensionary when Louis XIV invaded United Provinces (1672) and Dutch people called William III to leadership. Killed by angry mob along with brother **Cornelis** (1623–1672), who had held various state offices, and had accompanied Admiral de Ruyter in naval battles against England.

**de Witte, Emanuel.** See WITTE.

**Dex·ip′pus** (dĕk·sĭp′ŭs), **Publius Herennius.** Greek general and historian; checked invasion of Greece by the Heruli (269 A.D.). Author of a history of Rome's wars with the Scythians in 3d century and of a chronicle of world history. Only fragments of his works are extant.

**Dex′ter** (dĕks′tĕr), **Samuel.** 1761–1816. American lawyer, b. Boston. Member, U.S. House of Representatives (1793–95); U.S. Senate (1799–1800). U.S. secretary of war (1800); U.S. secretary of the treasury (1801).

**de Young** (dĕ yŭng′), **Michel Harry.** 1849–1925. American journalist, b. St. Louis, Mo.; taken to San Francisco as a child. With his brother **Charles** (1847–1880) founded (1865) a newspaper that later became the San Francisco *Chronicle;* sole owner and editor in chief (from 1880).

**Dha′nis′** (dȧ′nēs′), Baron **François.** 1861–1909. Belgian soldier and colonial administrator in the **Congo.**

**Dhaun, Leopold von.** See DAUN.

**d'Hé′relle′** (dā′rĕl′), **Félix Hubert. 1873–1949. Bac**teriologist, b. Montreal, Canada. Director, bacteriological laboratory, Guatemala (1902–06), Mérida, Mexico (1907–08); asst. (1908–14), chief of laboratory (1914–21), Pasteur Inst., Paris; professor, Yale (1928–34); professor, U. of Tiflis, U.S.S.R. (from 1934). Discovered bacteriophage **(1917).** Author of *Le Bactériophage* (1921).

**Dhorme** (dôrm), **Édouard.** *Religious name* Father **Paul** (pôl). 1881– . French Dominican monk and Oriental scholar.

**Dhuleep Singh.** See under RANJIT SINGH.

**Di′a·bel′li** (dē′ä·bĕl′ē), **An·to′ni·o** (än·tō′nē·ō). 1781–1858. Austrian composer and music publisher; founded (1824) music publishing house Diabelli & Co. Composer of piano pieces, songs, masses, and an operetta. On one of his waltz themes, Beethoven wrote his *Thirty-Three Variations* (Opus 120).

**Dia′ghi·lev** (dyȧ′gyĭ·lyĕf), **Sergei Pavlovich.** 1872–1929. Russian ballet producer and art critic, b. Novgorod. Grad. St. Petersburg Conservatory of Music (1892). Founded art journal (1899). Joined staff of Imperial Russian Theater, Moscow (1899); collaborated with its director, Michel Fokine, and with the painter Léon Bakst in developing Russian ballet by careful co-ordination of dancing, costumes, stage sets, lighting, and music; successfully introduced ballets adapted to well-known orchestral works, as Rimski-Korsakov's *Schéhérazade,* Debussy's *L'Après-midi d'un Faune,* etc. Collaborated with Stravinsky, who wrote the music for *The Firebird* (*L'Oiseau de Feu*) and *Petrouchka.* Organized own company, the Ballet Russe (Paris, 1909), in which Nijinsky (*q.v.*) appeared; visited New York with his company (1916); presented his work chiefly in Paris and London (after 1921).

**Di·ag′o·ras** (dī·ăg′ō·răs). *Surnamed* **the Atheist.** fl. late 5th century B.C. Greek sophist and poet, b. Melos; writer of hymns and dithyrambs; long resident in Athens; took refuge in Corinth when condemned to death by the Athenians for impiety.

**Diagoras of Rhodes** (rōdz). Greek athlete; four times victor in Olympic games. His victory in boxing at 7th Olympian games (464 B.C.) was celebrated in a poem by Pindar.

**Dia·man′te** (dyä·män′tā), **Juan Bautista.** 1626?–?1687. Spanish dramatist; author of *El Honrador de Su Padre,* based on Corneille's *Le Cid* (1658).

**Diane de France** (dyȧn dē fräNs). Duchesse **de Mont′mo′ren′cy′ et An′gou′lême′** (dē môN′mô′räN′sē′ ā äN′gōō′lâm′). 1538–1619. Natural daughter (legitimized) of King Henry II of France; m. 1st Orazio Farnese, son of duke of Parma (1553), 2d François de Montmorency (1559); politically influential in court of Henry III and Henry IV of France.

**Diane de Poi′tiers′** (dē pwȧ′tyā′). Duchesse **de Va′len′ti′nois′** (dē vȧ′läN′tē′nwȧ′). 1499–1566. Mistress of Henry II of France. Married Comte de Maulevrier, grand seneschal of Normandy; widow (1533). Became mistress of Henry while he was still dauphin (1536); had great influence over him during entire reign (1547–59).

**Di'as** (dē'ȧs), **Antônio Gonçalves.** See GONÇALVES DIAS.

**Di'as** *or* **Di'az** (dē'ȧsh), **Bartholomeu.** 1450?–1500. Portuguese navigator. Chosen by King John II (1486) to lead a voyage around Africa, continuing previous Portuguese discoveries; with two vessels sailed south (1487–88) beyond farthest point reached by Diogo Cam and beyond south end of Africa (1488); turned back and entered Mossel Bay and Algoa Bay, then steered westward passing Cape Agulhas and discovering Table Mountain and the cape which he called Cabo Tormentoso ("Cape of Storms"), later renamed by King John Cabo da Bōa Esperança ("Cape of Good Hope"); first to double south end of Africa and to open way to the East. Engaged in African trade (1490–95); accompanied Vasco da Gama as far as Cape Verde Islands (1497); commanded a ship (1500) in Cabral's fleet to Brazil; perished in a storm.

**Di'as** (dē'ȧs), **Henrique.** 1600?–?1662. Brazilian Negro soldier, b. Pernambuco; fought with Portuguese against Dutch (1633); promoted commander in chief of Negro forces; led rebellion against Spaniards (1645); aided in recovery of Recife (1654). His name still given to Brazilian regiment under Negro command.

**Diavolo,** Fra. See FRA DIAVOLO.

**Dí'az** (dē'äs), **Adolfo.** 1874–1964. Nicaraguan politician; provisional president (May–Oct., 1911); suppressed President Luis Mena's revolt; elected president (1913–16); with General Emiliano Chamorro Vargas seized power by coup d'état (1925); again president (1926–28) after Chamorro's resignation and flight; appealed for aid (against revolution) to U.S., which sent marines who defeated rebels under Sandino (1927).

**Díaz, Alberto Cabero.** See CABERO DÍAZ.

**Dí'az** (dē'äts), **Armando.** 1861–1928. Italian major general (1914) and lieutenant general (1916); succeeded General Cadorna (Nov. 6, 1917) in command after the disaster at Caporetto (Oct. 24, 1917); won victory over the Austrians on the Piave (June 15–20, 1918); led victorious campaign (Oct.–Nov., 1918) which led to capitulation of Austria; created (1920) marshal of Italy and **Du'ca del'la Vit·to'ria** (dōō'kä dāl'lä vēt·tô'ryä), *i.e.* Duke of Victory.

**Dí'az** (dē'äth), **Juan Martín.** See EMPECINADO.

**Dí'az** (dē'äs), **Porfirio,** *in full* **José de la Cruz Porfirio.** 1830–1915. Mexican general and statesman, a mestizo, b. Oaxaca. Distinguished as soldier in war with U.S. (1846–48), War of the Reform (1858–60) in support of Juárez, and struggle against French (1863–67). Unsuccessful candidate for presidency (1867 and 1871); plotted continually against government and (1876) finally overthrew Lerdo de Tejada; provisional president of Mexico (1876 and 1877). Elected president (1877–80); again president (1884–1911; seven terms; constitution amended to allow for his continuance in office); his administrations marked by peace, material prosperity, and foreign investments, but also by dictatorial methods, with little improvement in the condition of the masses; finally forced to abdicate (May, 1911) and leave Mexico; died in exile in Paris (July 2, 1915).

**Dí'az de Bivar** (dē'äth), **Rodrigo** *or* **Ruy.** See the CID.

**Diaz de La Pe'ña'** (dyȧz' dē lȧ pā'nyȧ'), **Narcisse Virgile.** 1807?–1876. French landscape painter, of Spanish descent; member of Barbizon school. Known esp. for his scenes from forest of Fontainebleau, and for a series of nymphs, Venuses, Cupids, etc. His son **Eugène** (1837–1901) was a composer; works include comic opera *Le Roi Candaule* and lyric drama *Benvenuto.*

**Dí'az del Cas·til'lo** (dē'äth thĕl käs·tē'lyō), **Bernal.** c. 1492–?1581. Spanish soldier and historian; to Darien (1514) under Pedrarias; to Yucatán with Córdoba (1517); with Cortes during conquest of Mexico (1519–21). Known esp. for *Historia Verdadera de la Conquista de la Nueva España* (3 vols., 1632), an eyewitness account of the conquest of Mexico and an attack on the history of Francisco López de Gómara, chaplain to Cortes.

**Dib'din** (dĭb'dĭn), **Charles.** 1745–1814. English dramatist, actor, and composer of stage music, Drury Lane Theatre; produced *The Waterman* (1774) and *The Quaker* (1775); satirized Garrick and contemporaries in *The Comic Mirror*, a puppet play. Wrote first of his sea songs, "Blow high, blow low," for the *Seraglio* (1776); introduced popular songs " 'Twas in the good ship Rover" and "Tom Bowling" into a variety show; said to have written upwards of 1400 songs and 30 dramatic pieces; retired (1805). His elder son, **Charles** (1768–1833), was an acting manager of Sadler's Wells Theatre and a dramatist and composer of songs. His younger son, **Thomas John** (1771–1841), had his *Jew and the Doctor* produced at Covent Garden (1798–99); wrote *The British Raft*, containing "The Snug Little Island" (1797); produced his best opera, *The Cabinet* (1801–02); wrote pantomimes, including *Mother Goose* (1807); said to have written 2000 songs and 200 operas and plays.

**Thomas Frognall Dibdin** (1776–1847), bibliographer, was nephew of the elder Charles Dibdin; took orders (1804); with *Introduction to the Knowledge of Editions of the Classics* (1802) gained attention of third earl of Spencer, who employed him to catalogue library at Althorp and sent him to Continent to buy books, an expedition described in *A Bibliographical, Antiquarian, and Picturesque Tour* (1821). Pseudonym **Reginald Wolfe** (wŏŏlf).

**Di·be'li·us** (dē·bā'lē·ŏŏs), **Martin. 1883–1947.** German theologian; professor, Heidelberg **(from 1915)**; specialized in literature and history of early Christianity and other religions; author of *Die Formgeschichte des Evangeliums* (1919), *Geschichte der Urchristlichen Literatur* (1926), *Die Botschaft von Jesus Christus* (1935), etc.

**Dibich-Zabalkanski,** Count **Ivan.** See Count Hans DIEBITSCH.

**Di'cae·ar'chus** (dī'sē·är'kŭs). Greek peripatetic philosopher of 4th century B.C., historian, and geographer; disciple of Aristotle. Only titles and a few fragments of his works are extant.

**Di'cey** (dī'sĭ), **Edward James Stephen.** 1832–1911. English journalist; editor of London *Observer* (1870–89). Author of *England and Egypt* (1884) and *Bulgaria, the Peasant State* (1895). His brother **Albert Venn** (1835–1922), jurist, wrote *The Law of the Constitution* (1885; a standard work).

**Dick** (dĭk), **George Frederick. 1881–1967.** American physician, b. Fort Wayne, Ind.; professor and head of medical dept., Rush Medical Coll. (until 1933), Chicago (from 1933). With his wife, isolated the germ of, and originated a serum for, scarlet fever; also devised a test (Dick test) to determine susceptibility to scarlet fever. His wife (m. 1914), **Gladys,** *nee* **Hen'ry** [hĕn'rĭ] (1881–1963), b. Pawnee City, Nebr.; B.S., Nebraska (1900), M.D. Johns Hopkins (1907); connected with McCormick Institute for Infectious Diseases (1914–?36).

**Dick'ens** (dĭk'ĕnz; -ĭnz), **Charles John Huffam.** 1812–1870. English novelist, b. Portsmouth, Hants. Passed childhood of hardships, including work as drudge at a blacking factory (c. 1823), and humiliations, including father's imprisonment for debt (c. 1824); little formal education; shorthand reporter of House of Commons debates for the *True Sun*, the *Mirror of Parliament*, and (1835) *Morning Chronicle.* Under pen name **Boz** (bŏz), first used Aug., 1834, contributed to periodicals fictional sketches (first sketch pub. Dec., 1833) which were collected and published as *Sketches by Boz* (1836); first editor of *Bentley's Miscellany* (1837); pub. other works in steady succession till his death. Toured America (1842); advocated international copyright and abolition of slavery; pub. *American Notes* (Oct., 1842); assisted Miss Coutts (later Baroness Burdett-Coutts) in philanthropic work (1843); lived in Italy (1844–45) and Switzerland (1846); managed theatrical company which toured English provinces (1847–52); started weekly journal *Household Words* (1849), succeeded by *All the Year Round* (1859); began giving public readings from his works (1858); reading tour in America (1867–68). Chief works: *Posthumous Papers of the Pickwick Club*, usually called *Pickwick Papers* (1836–37), *Oliver Twist* (1837–39), *Nicholas Nickleby* (1838–39), *Old Curiosity Shop* (1840–41), *Barnaby Rudge* (1841), *Martin Chuzzlewit* (1843–44), *A Christmas Carol* (1843), *The Chimes* (1844), *The Cricket on the Hearth* (1845), *Dombey and Son* (1846–48), *David Copperfield* (1849–50), *Bleak House* (1852–53), *Hard Times* (1854), *Little Dorrit* (1855–57), *A Tale of Two Cities* (1859), *Great Expectations* (1860–61), *Our Mutual Friend* (1864–65), *Mystery of Edwin Drood* (incomplete, 1870). Chief illustrators of his works: George Cruikshank (*Sketches by Boz, Oliver Twist*); Hablot Knight Browne, called "Phiz" (*Pickwick, Chuzzlewit, Copperfield, Bleak House*, and others); John Leech; Marcus Stone (*Great Expectations, Our Mutual Friend*). Of his ten children, his eldest son, **Charles** (1837–1896), was subeditor of *All the Year Round* (1869), partner in a printing firm, compiler of a series of dictionary guides (1879–84); his next to youngest son, Sir **Henry Fielding** (1849–1933), was author of *Memories of my Father* (1929) and *Recollections* (1934). His great-granddaughter **Monica Enid** (1915– ), author of fiction, radio scripts, etc., including *One Pair of Hands* (1939) and *One Pair of Feet* (1942), both autobiographical.

**Dick'er·son** (dĭk'ẽr·s'n), **Mahlon.** 1770–1853. American lawyer and manufacturer, b. Hanover Neck, N.J. Governor of New Jersey (1815–17); U.S. senator (1817–33); U.S. secretary of the navy (1834–38).

**Dick'ey** (dĭk'ĭ), **Robert.** 1840–1912. American trapper and scout, reputed original of "Deadwood Dick," scout and Indian fighter of dime-novel romances.

**Dick'ins** (dĭk'ĭnz), **John.** 1747–1798. Clergyman, b. London, Eng. To America (before 1776); a pioneer in establishing the Methodist Episcopal Church in America.

**Dick'in·son** (dĭk'ĭn·s'n), **Anna Elizabeth.** 1842–1932. American reformer and lecturer, b. Philadelphia. Lectured for woman suffrage, labor reform, etc.

**Dickinson, Charles Monroe.** 1842–1924. American diplomat, b. near Lowville, N.Y. U.S. consul general to Turkey (1897–1906) and (from 1901) diplomatic agent to Bulgaria; procured release of American missionary, Ellen M. Stone, held by Bulgarian bandits; consul general at large to the Near East (1906–08).

**Dickinson, Clarence.** 1873–1969. American organist and composer, b. Lafayette, Ind. Author of *Sacred Choruses, Sacred Solos*, a symphony (*Storm King*, 1919), a comic opera (*The Medicine Man*), etc.

**Dickinson, Donald McDonald.** 1846–1917. American lawyer; U.S. postmaster general (1888–89).

**Dickinson, Emily Elizabeth.** 1830–1886. American poet, b. Amherst, Mass., where she lived a quiet, retired life. Began writing poetry, according to her own statement, in winter of 1861–62; works not published during her lifetime. Six volumes of her poems were published after her death, in 1890, 1891, 1896, 1914, 1929, and 1936.

**Dickinson, Goldsworthy Lowes.** 1862–1932. English essayist; author of *From King to King, The Greek View of Life, The Meaning of Good, Justice and Liberty, Religion and Immortality, Appearances, The European Anarchy* (1916), *War: its Nature, Cause, and Cure* (1923), etc.

**Dickinson, Jacob McGavock.** 1851–1928. American lawyer; U.S. secretary of war (1909–11).

**Dickinson, John.** 1732–1808. American statesman, b. in Talbot County, Md. Adm. to bar (1757); practiced, Philadelphia. Member, Continental Congress (1774–76); advocated conciliation with England; opposed separation; voted against Declaration of Independence, but served for a time in Continental army. Member, Continental Congress (1776, 1777, 1779, 1780). Member from Delaware to convention that framed the Constitution (1787); published a series of letters, signed "Fabius," urging adoption of Constitution. His brother **Philemon** (1739–1809) was an officer (major general and commander in chief from June, 1777) of the New Jersey militia in the Revolutionary War, defeating raiding expedition by Cornwallis's troops (Jan., 1777), retarding British retreat toward New York before battle of Monmouth (1778), and conducting an attack at battle of Springfield (1780). He was a member, from Delaware, of the Continental Congress (1782–83).

**Dickinson, Jonathan.** 1688–1747. American clergyman and educator, b. Hatfield, Mass.; leading defender of Presbyterianism. Obtained charter for College of New Jersey, now Princeton (1746); served as its first president (May–Oct., 1747).

**Dickinson, Sidney Edward.** 1890– . American portrait painter, b. Wallingford, Conn.

**Dick'man** (dĭk'măn), **Joseph Theodore.** 1857–1927. American army officer, b. Dayton, Ohio; grad. U.S.M.A., West Point (1881); major general (Aug. 5, 1917). In World War, commanded Third Division in France (to Aug. 18, 1918), Fourth Corps (Aug. 18–Oct. 12), First Corps (Oct. 12–Nov. 15), taking part in straightening the Saint Mihiel salient and in Meuse-Argonne advance; organized Third Army for occupation of Germany and commanded it (Nov. 15, 1918–Apr. 28, 1919). Retired (1921).

**Dick'see** (dĭk'sē), Sir **Francis Bernard**, *known as* **Frank.** 1853–1928. English painter. His *Harmony* hangs in Tate Gallery, London; among other canvases are *A Love Story, Romeo and Juliet, Paolo and Francesca, A Reverie, The Two Crowns, This for Remembrance.* Among his portraits are *Duchess of Buckingham and Chandos, Lady Hillingdon, Marchioness of Ailesbury.* Knighted (1925).

**Dick'son** (dĭk's'n), **Leonard Eugene.** 1874–1954. American mathematician, b. Independence, Iowa. Teacher (from 1900) and professor (from 1910), Chicago. Author of *Linear Groups, and Exposition of the Galois Field Theory* (1901), *Linear Algebras* (1914), *History of the Theory of Numbers* (3 vols., 1919–23), *Studies in the Theory of Numbers* (1930), etc.

**Dickson, Samuel Henry.** 1798–1872. American physician, b. Charleston, S.C. Founder (1833) and professor (1833–47, 1851–58), Medical College of South Carolina; professor, Jefferson Medical College, Philadelphia (1858–72).

**Dic'tys Cre·ten'sis** (dĭk'tĭs krē·tĕn'sĭs), *i.e.* the Cretan. Supposed author of a diary of the Trojan War (*Ephemeris Belli Trojani*), one of chief sources in medieval times for story of the Trojan War. The diary appears in a 4th-century A.D. Latin version of a Greek original. Cf. DARES PHRYGIUS.

**Di'day'** (dē'dā'), **François.** 1802–1877. Swiss landscape painter, best known for Alpine scenes.

**Di'de·rot'** (dē'drō'), **Denis.** *Nicknamed* **Pan'to'phile'** (päN'tô'fēl') **Diderot.** 1713–1784. French encyclopedist and philosopher, b. Langres. Educated by Jesuits; published first philosophic work of importance, *Lettre sur les Aveugles* (1749); thrown into prison because of parts of this work. Released to work with d'Alembert on the *Encyclopédie* (see Ephraim CHAMBERS); labored 20 years (1751–72) at this task; aided by Voltaire, Montesquieu, Rousseau, Buffon, Turgot, Quesnay and others; work published as *Encyclopédie, ou Dictionnaire Raisonné des Sciences, des Arts et des Métiers* (in 28 volumes, increased by a 6-volume supplement, 1776–77, and by 2 volumes of tables, 1780), a work of practical value, and an active force during the period of the Enlightenment. Simultaneously aided friends (see Melchior GRIMM) in literary work, composed two plays, *Le Fils Naturel* (1757) and *Le Père de Famille* (1758), and wrote *Les Salons* (1759–79), in which criticism of pictorial art was elevated and given greater scope. Sold library (1773) to Catherine II of Russia to raise dowry for his daughter; visited St. Petersburg (1773–74); spent last years in literary pursuits. Several works, including *Jacques le Fataliste* and *Le Neveu de Rameau*, were published posthumously.

**Did'i·us Ju'li·a'nus** (dĭd'ĭ·ŭs jo͞o'lĭ·ā'nŭs) *or* **Didius Sal'vi·us** (săl'vĭ·ŭs) **Julianus.** *Later known as* **Marcus Didius Se·ve'rus** (sė·vẹr'ŭs) **Julianus.** 133–193. Roman emperor (193). On death of Emperor Pertinax purchased imperial dignity from Praetorian Guard.

**Di'don'** (dē'dôɴ'), **Henri Gabriel.** 1840–1900. French Dominican preacher and educator.

**Di'dot'** (dē'dō'). Family of French printers and publishers, including: **François** (1689–1757), founder of family. His two sons, **François Ambroise** (1730–1804), noted for many improvements in type founding and printing, and **Pierre François** (1732–1793), founder of paper factory at Essonnes. Two sons of François Ambroise, **Pierre** (1761–1853) and **Firmin** (1764–1836), the latter renowned as printer, engraver, type founder, and introducer of stereotype in publishing less expensive editions. Pierre François's son **Henri** (1765–1852), who published editions in microscopic types.

**Did'y·mus** (dĭd'ĭ·mŭs). See THOMAS (the apostle).

**Didymus.** *Surnamed* **Chal·cen'ter·us** (kăl·sĕn'tẽr·ŭs). 63 B.C.?–10 A.D. Greek scholar; taught in Alexandria and Rome; author of commentaries (only fragments extant) on Greek writers.

**Didymus** of Alexandria. *Surnamed* **the Blind.** Ecclesiastical writer of 4th century A.D.; blind from age of 4; became head of the catechetical school in Alexandria; extant works include *De Trinitate, De Spiritu Sancto, Adversus Manichaeos.*

**Die'bitsch** (dē'bĭch), Count **Hans Karl Friedrich Anton von.** *Russ. name* Count **Ivan Ivanovich Di'bich-Za·bal·kan'ski** (dyē'byĭch·zŭ·bŭl·kán'skû·ĭ; *Angl.* -skĭ). 1785–1831. German-born soldier in Russian service; fought with distinction at Leipzig (1813). Captured Varna (1828) and Silistra (1829); held command against Poles at Grochów and Ostrołęnka (1831).

**Die'fen·bach** (dē'fĕn·bäĸ), **Lorenz.** 1806–1883. German Catholic clergyman, philologist and ethnologist.

**Die'fen·ba'ker** (dē'fĕn·bā'kẽr), **John George.** 1895–1979. Canadian lawyer and statesman, b. Ontario. Member of conservative party; prime minister (1957–63).

**Dief'fen·bach** (dē'fĕn·bäĸ), **Anton.** 1831–1914. German painter of genre scenes.

**Dieffenbach, Johann Friedrich.** 1795–1847. German surgeon; known for improvements in surgical technique, esp. in plastic surgery, tenotomy, and blood transfusion.

**Diel'man** (dēl'măn), **Frederick.** 1847–1935. Figure painter and illustrator, b. Hanover, Ger.; to U.S. in childhood. Designed mosaic panels *Law* and *History* in Congressional Library in Washington, D.C.

**Diels** (dēls), **Hermann.** 1848–1922. German classical philologist.

**Diels, Otto Paul Hermann.** 1876–1954. German chemist; awarded Nobel prize in chemistry (1950) with K. Adler.

**Diemen, Anton Van.** See VAN DIEMEN.

**Die'pen·beeck** (dē'pĕn·bāk), **Abraham van.** 1596?–1675. Flemish painter and stained-glass artist.

**Dierx** (dyĕrks), **Léon.** 1838–1912. French poet; one of most distinguished of the Parnassians.

**Dies** (dīz), **Martin.** 1900–1972. American lawyer and legislator, b. in Texas. Member, U.S. Congress (1931–45, 1953–59). Appointed (1938) chairman of house committee investigating un-American activities.

**Die'sel** (dē'zĕl), **Rudolf.** 1858–1913. German mechanical engineer, b. in Paris. Patented a type of internal-combustion engine (later known as the *Diesel engine*) having autoignition of the fuel (1892); elaborated on this type in *Theorie und Konstruktion eines Rationellen Wärmemotors* (1893); devoted himself to developing the engine and, in association with the firm of Friedrich Krupp in Essen and the Augsburg-Nuremberg machine factory, built the first successful Diesel engine (1893–97).

**Dies'kau** (dēs'kou), **Ludwig August.** 1701–1767. General in the French service, b. in Saxony. Commanded French troops against the British in Canada (1755).

**Die'ster·weg** (dē'stẽr·vāĸ), **Friedrich Adolf Wilhelm.** 1790–1866. German educator; introduced Pestalozzi's ideas and methods into Germany, revolutionizing its school system.

**Die'te·ri'ci** (dē'tĕ·rĭ'tsē), **Friedrich Heinrich.** 1821–1903. German philosopher and Arabic scholar; edited and translated Arab texts.

**Dietmar.** See THIETMAR.

**Die'trich** (dē'trĭĸ) *or* **Dietrich von Bern.** See THEODORIC the Great.

**Dietrich, Adam.** 1711–1782. German peasant known for his knowledge of botany and his correspondence with Linnaeus; called "the botanist of Zie'gen·hain" (tsē'gĕn·hīn).

**Dietrich, Albert Hermann.** 1829–1908. German composer of an opera *Robin Hood*, a symphony in D minor, *Normannenfahrt*, chamber music, and choral works.

**Die'trich** (dē'trĭĸ) *or* **Die·tri'ci** (dė·trĭ'tsē) *or* **Die·tri'cy** (dė·trĭ'tsē), **Christian Wilhelm Ernst.** 1712–1774. German landscape painter and engraver.

**Dietrich von Niem** (*or* **Nieheim** *or* **Nyem**). See NIEM.

**Die'trich·son** (dē'trĕk·sôn), **Lorentz Henrik Segelcke.** 1834–1917. Norwegian historian of art and literature; works include *Outline of the History of Norwegian Poetry* (1866–69), *Antinoos*...(1884), *The Norwegian Wood-carving Art* (with Munthe; 1893).

**Dietz** (dēts), **Feodor.** 1813–1870. German painter of historical and battle pictures.

**Dietz, Howard.** 1896– American writer; best known as librettist for comic operas, as *Dear Sir* (with Jerome Kern; 1924), *Merry-Go-Round* (with Morris Ryskind; 1927), etc.

**Dietz, Johann Christian.** 1778–1845. German manufacturer of musical instruments; inventor of melodion and claviharp.

**Diet'zen·schmidt** (dē'tsĕn·shmĭt). *Professional name of* **Anton Franz Schmidt.** 1893–1955. German playwright, novelist, and critic; dramatic critic on staff of *Berliner Tageblatt.* Author of *König Tod, Christopher, Verfolgung, Volkskomödie vom Lieben Augustin, Närrische Liebe.*

**Dieu'la'foy'** (dyû'lȧ'fwä'), **Marcel Auguste.** 1844–1920. French archaeologist and engineer of roads and bridges; in Persia, explored remains of palaces of Darius I and of

Artaxerxes, bringing back (1886) architectural specimens now in the Louvre; author of *L'Art Antique de la Perse* (5 vols., 1884–89), *L'Acropole de Suse* (1890–93), etc. His wife, **Jeanne Paule Henriette Rachel**, *nee* **Ma′gre** [mȧ′gr'] (1851–1916), accompanied him on his expeditions; discovered ruins of a 12th-century mosque at Hassân in Morocco; author of works on archaeological expeditions, including *La Perse, la Chaldée et la Susiane* (1887), also of novels and plays. His brother **Georges** (1839–1911), physician, investigated Bright's disease, appendicitis, and tuberculosis; invented an aspirator.

**Diez** (dēts), **Friedrich Christian.** 1794–1876. German philologist; founder of Romance philology; professor, Bonn (1823). Notable works include *Die Poesie der Troubadours* (1826), *Grammatik der Romanischen Sprachen* (3 vols., 1838–42), *Etymologisches Wörterbuch der Romanischen Sprachen* (1853).

**Diez, Wilhelm von.** 1839–1907. German painter; illustrated Schiller's *History of the Thirty Years' War.*

**Dig′by** (dĭg′bĭ), **John.** 1st Earl of **Bris′tol** (brĭs′t'l). 1580–1653. English diplomat. Ambassador of James I in negotiations (1611–24) for a Spanish marriage, first for James's son Henry, and after Henry's death, for Charles (later Charles I); offended Prince Charles and Buckingham in Madrid (1623); censured for his conduct of Spanish negotiations; confined in Tower (1626–28); charge against him dismissed; restored to seat in House of Lords; favored acceptance by king of Petition of Right (1628); commissioner to treat with rebellious Scots (1640); distrusted by parliamentary party, dismissed from public office (1643); went into exile at Caen, France (1644). His son **George** (1612–1677), 2d earl; M.A., Oxon. (1636); attacked Roman Catholicism in letters to Sir Kenelm Digby (1638–39), fled to Holland after urging arrest of Pym and four fellow members of parliament (Jan., 1642); as lieut. general of king's forces north of Trent, was defeated at Sherburn (1645); fled to France; forced to resign (1657) as secretary of state to Charles II at Bruges because of turning Catholic; welcomed at court only on expulsion of Clarendon (1667).

**Digby,** Sir **Kenelm.** 1603–1665. English author of religious and quasi-scientific works; naval commander and diplomat. Bred a Roman Catholic; educ. at Oxford. Secretly married (1625) Venetia Stanley, a beauty celebrated by Ben Jonson in *Eupheme.* Made privateering expedition, defeating French and Venetian ships in Scanderoon harbor (1628); professed Protestantism (from 1630). After his wife's death, retired to Gresham Coll., London, to experiment with chemistry; announced reconversion to Catholicism (1636); solicited money for support of king's Scottish expedition (1641); supported king's cause in Civil War and pleaded Charles's cause with Pope Innocent X; banished for a time; engaged by Cromwell in diplomatic business (1656). At Restoration retained office of Queen Henrietta Maria's chancellor; one of first members of Royal Society (1663); discovered necessity of oxygen to plant life. Author of a criticism (1643) of Sir Thomas Browne's *Religio Medici, Of Bodies* and *Of the Immortality of Man's Soul* (1644), and highly fantastic and bombastic *Memoirs* (1827).
His father, Sir **Everard Digby** (1578–1606), came into a large estate (1592), turned Roman Catholic (1599); joining conspirators in the Gunpowder Plot (1605), accepted assignment of inciting a rising in Midlands; deserted his companions in flight; executed.

**Digby, Kenelm Henry.** 1800–1880. English writer on medieval theology; author of *The Broadstone of Honour* (1822), a survey of medieval customs, enlarged (1826–27) and published in 4 vols., entitled *Godefridus, Tancredus, Morus,* and *Orlandus.*

**Digges** (dĭgz), **Leonard.** d. 1571? English mathematician; experimented with magnifying effects from combinations of lenses, and was said to have anticipated invention of the telescope (1579). His son **Thomas** (d. 1595) was also a mathematician; mustermaster general of English forces in Netherlands (1586–94); author of works on applied mathematics and military engineering. Sir **Dudley** (1583–1639), son of Thomas, was a diplomat and judge; ambassador in Russia (1618); opened case for impeachment of Buckingham (1626); master of the rolls (1636); joint author with his father of *Four Paradoxes or Politique Discourses* (1604).

**di Giacomo, Salvatore.** See GIACOMO.

**Dilke** (dĭlk), **Charles Wentworth.** 1789–1864. English critic and antiquary; continued Dodsley's *Old Plays* (6 vols., 1814–16); edited *Athenaeum* (1830–46). His son Sir **Charles Wentworth** (1810–1869) was one of proposers and one of executive committee of the (London) International Exhibition of 1851.
The latter's son Sir **Charles Wentworth** (1843–1911) wrote of his travels round the world in *Greater Britain* (1868); M.P. (1868–86), saw no incompatibility between his imperialism and extreme radicalism; undersecretary for foreign affairs (1880–82); president of local-government board under Gladstone (1882–85); chairman of royal commission on housing of working classes; supported acts legalizing position of trades-unions and shortening hours of labor; sought legislation to secure a minimum wage and representation of labor in House of Commons; instrumental in passage of Redistribution bill (1885); wrote with authority on foreign affairs and colonial questions.
His second wife, **Emilia Frances,** *nee* **Strong** (1840–1904), historian of French art, m. 1st (1861) Mark Pattison (*q.v.*), was author of studies of architects and sculptors, furniture and decoration, engravers and draftsmen of 18th century, including *French Painters of the Eighteenth Century* (1899); strove for amelioration of social and industrial condition of working women.

**Dill** (dĭl), Sir **John Greer.** 1881–1944. British soldier; m. 1st Ada Maud Le Mottée; 2d (1941) Mrs. N. Furlong. Entered army (1901); promoted through grades to rank of general (1939); served in South Africa (1901–02), in World War (1914–18); commandant, Staff College, Camberley (1931–34); director of military operations and intelligence, War Office (1934–36); commander, 1st army corps, France (1939–40); chief of imperial general staff (1940–41); to Washington with Churchill (Dec., 1941), remaining in U.S. as member of joint Anglo-American board of strategy.

**Dill** (dĭl), **Ludwig.** 1848–1940. German painter, esp. of coastal landscapes and marines.

**Dill,** Sir **Samuel.** 1844–1924. British classical scholar, b. in County Down, Ireland; among his books are *Roman Society in the Last Century of the Western Empire* (1898), *Roman Society from Nero to Marcus Aurelius* (1904), *Roman Society in Gaul in the Merovingian Age* (1926).

**Dil·le′ni·us** (*Ger.* dĭ·lā′nē·ŏŏs; *Eng.* dĭ·lē′nĭ·ŭs) *or* **Dil′len** (*Ger. & Eng.* dĭl′ĕn), **Johann Jakob.** 1687–1747. German botanist in England (from 1721); first professor of botany at Oxford (1728–47); author of *Historia Muscorum* (1741).

**Dil′lens** (dĭl′ĕns), **Julien.** 1849–1904. Belgian sculptor.

**Dil′ling·ham** (dĭl′ĭng·hăm; -ăm), **Charles Bancroft.** 1868–1934. American theatrical manager and producer, esp. of musical plays; b. Hartford, Conn. Manager of Globe Theatre in New York and partner of A. L. Erlanger in twenty other theaters.

**Dillingham, William Paul.** 1843–1923. American

lawyer, b. Waterbury, Vt. Governor of Vermont (1888–90). U.S. senator (1900–23); favored quota system in limiting immigration, embodied in Dillingham Bill (enacted May 19, 1921).

**Dill'mann** (dĭl'män), **August.** 1823–1894. German Protestant theologian and Oriental scholar; chief work was in study of Ethiopian language.

**Dil'lon** (dĭl'ŭn). Name of an Irish family of royalists and Jacobites that provided a number of military officers in foreign service: Sir **James Dillon** (fl. 1667), 8th son of Theobald, 1st Viscount Dillon, was governor of Athlone and Connaught, participant in Leinster revolt (1652), brigadier general in service of Spain and the Fronde. **Arthur** (1670–1733), son of 7th Viscount Dillon, who raised a Jacobite regiment, served in his father's regiment in service of Louis XIV through siege of Barcelona, was Old Pretender's agent in Paris. His youngest son, **Arthur Richard** (1721–1806), was bishop of Évreux (1753), archbishop of Toulouse (1758), archbishop of Narbonne and primate of the Gauls (1763); migrated to Coblenz (1790). **Arthur Richard** (1750–1794), son of 11th Viscount Dillon and grandson of Arthur Dillon (1670–1733), was in service of Louis XV, deputy for Martinique in National Assembly, Jacobin general in Argonne (1792); guillotined.

**Dillon, E'mile'** (ā'mēl') **Joseph.** 1854–1933. British journalist, b. in Ireland; special correspondent of London *Daily Telegraph*, from Armenia, Spain, Crete, France, China. Author of *Maxim Gorky* (1902), *A Scrap of Paper* (1914), *Ourselves and Germany* (1916), *The Peace Conference* (1920), *President Obregón, a World Reformer* (1923), *Russia Today and Yesterday* (1929).

**Dillon, George.** 1906–1968. American writer, b. Jacksonville, Fla.; awarded Guggenheim fellowship (1932, 1933). Editor of magazine *Poetry*. Author of *Boy in the Wind* (1927), *The Flowering Stone* (1931; awarded Pulitzer prize for poetry; with Edna Millay did verse translation of Baudelaire's *Les Fleurs du Mal* (1935).

**Dillon, John.** 1851–1927. Irish Nationalist politician, b. near Dublin. Educ. Catholic U. and Catholic U. Med. School; qualified as surgeon. Supporter of Parnell (1879–c. 1890); member of Parliament (1880–83, 1885–1918); violence of his attacks on government caused his imprisonment on several occasions. Chairman, Irish Nationalist Federation (1896); associated with Redmond (1900–18) in direction of policies of Irish Nationalist party and, on Redmond's death (1918), succeeded to the chairmanship; vigorously supported government during World War I, aided recruiting, but opposed extension of conscription to Ireland. With rise of Sinn Fein, he was defeated in parliamentary elections (1918).
His father, **John Blake Dillon** (1816–1866), also a politician, founded, with T. O. Davis and C. G. Duffy, of *The Nation* (1842), organ of the Young Ireland party.

**Dillon, Wentworth.** = Earl of ROSCOMMON.

**Dil'ly** (dĭl'ĭ), **Charles.** 1739–1807. English bookseller; liberal entertainer of writers; publisher of Boswell's *Tour to the Hebrides* (1780), *Life of Johnson* (1791).

**Dil'they** (dĭl'tī), **Wilhelm.** 1833–1911. German philosopher; works include *Weltanschauung und Analyse des Menschen seit Renaissance und Reformation* (1913), *Weltanschauungslehre* (1931), and *Pädagogik* (1934).

**Di·Mag'gi·o** (dĭ·măj'ĭ·ō), **Joseph Paul.** 1914– . Amer. baseball player, b. Martinez, Calif. Outfielder for New York Yankees (1936–51), with career batting average of .325.

**Di'mier'** (dē'myā'), **Louis.** 1865–1943. French historian, esp. of art.

**Dimitri.** See DEMETRIUS.

**Dimitri Donskoi.** See DEMETRIUS DONSKOI.

**Di·mi'tri·ev** (dyĭ·myē'tryĭ·yĕf). Variant of DMITRIEV.

**Di·mi'tri'je·vić** (dē·mē'trē'yĕ·vēt'y'; *Angl.* -vĭch), **Dragutin.** *Known as* **A·pis'** (ä·pēs'). 1876–1917. Serbian soldier and intriguer; one of plotters of assassination of King Alexander Obrenovich (1903). Founded secret society, commonly known as the Black Hand, to strive for union of all southern Slavs; engaged in irregular warfare in Macedonia and in anti-Austrian movement in Bosnia. Chief of intelligence, Serbian general staff (1913); planned murder of Archduke Francis Ferdinand at Sarajevo (1914); arrested at Salonika (Dec. 15, 1916); condemned and shot (June, 1917).

**Dim'net'** (dēm'nĕ'), **Ernest.** 1866–1954. French abbé, lecturer, and writer; canon of Cambray Cathedral. Authority on the Brontës. Among his books, many written in English, are *Les Sœurs Brontë* (1910; trans. 1928), *France Herself Again* (1914), *From a Paris Balcony* (1924), *The Art of Thinking* (1928), *What We Live By* (1932), *My Old World* (1935), *My New World* (1938).

**Dimpna,** Saint. See DYMPNA.

**Di'nah** (dī'nȧ). *In Douay Version* **Di'na.** In Bible, daughter of Jacob and Leah; seduced by a prince of the Hivites, on whom her brothers Simeon and Levi took revenge (*Genesis* xxx. 21; xxxiv).

**Dinant, David of.** See DAVID OF DINANT.

**Di·nar'chus** *or* **Dei·nar'chus** (dī·när'kŭs). 361?–?291 B.C. Greek orator and statesman, b. Corinth; moved to Athens as a young man. Favored pro-Macedonian policy and, on restoration of democratic government in Athens by Demetrius Poliorcetes (307 B.C.), was condemned to death; took refuge at Chalkis in Euboea. Only a few of his many speeches are extant.

**Din'dorf** (dĭn'dôrf), **Wilhelm.** 1802–1883. German classical philologist; collaborator in revision (9 vols., 1831–65) of Henry Estienne's *Thesaurus Linguae Graecae;* editor of a number of Greek texts.

**d'Indy.** See INDY.

**Dines** (dīnz), **William Henry.** 1855–1927. English meteorologist, exponent of experimental meteorology. Known for studies of the upper air, wind force, and solar and terrestrial radiation; developed an anemometer.

**Di'ne·sen** (dē'nĕ·s'n), **Isak.** *Pen name of* Baroness **Karen Blix'en** (blĕk's'n), *nee* **Dinesen.** 1885–1962. Danish writer; m. Baron Bror von Blixen (later divorced). Resided many years in Kenya Colony, Africa; managed farm there. Author of *Seven Gothic Tales* (1934), *Out of Africa* (1938), *Winter's Tales* (1943), etc.

**Ding.** See Jay Norwood DARLING.

**Din'gaan** (dĭng'gȧn). *Dutch spelling of Zulu* **Di'nga'ne** (dĭ'ngȧ'nĕ). fl. 1838. Zulu chieftain. Succeeded his half brother Chaka as king after doing away with another half brother (sometime after 1828); admitted Boers (1837); entered pact (1838) with Boer colonists in Natal under Pieter Retief (*q.v.*) and treacherously massacred them; defeated by Andries Pretorius (Dec. 16, 1838, now a South African legal holiday, Dingaan's Day); overthrown (1840) by his brother Umpanda with help of Boers.

**Ding'el·stedt** (dĭng'ĕl·shtĕt), Baron **Franz von.** 1814–1881. German writer and theater director; director, Court Opera Theater (1867), Hofburg Theater (1871), Vienna. Author of tragedy *Das Haus der Barneveldt* (1850), several volumes of verse, and the novels *Unter der Erde* (2 parts, 1840), *Die Amazone* (1868), *Künstlergeschichten* (1877).

**Din'gle** (dĭng'g'l), **Herbert.** 1890– . English astrophysicist; author of *Relativity for All* (1922), *Modern Astrophysics* (1924), etc.

**Ding'ley** (dĭng'lĭ), **Nelson.** 1832–1899. American political leader, b. Durham, Me. Governor of Maine (1874–

75). Member, U.S. House of Representatives (1881–99); championed protective tariff; chairman, committee on ways and means (from 1896); sponsor of tariff law (known as the Dingley Act) passed in 1897, and in effect until 1909.

**Ding'ling·er** (dĭng'lĭng·ẽr). Name of family of German goldsmiths and jewelers, including: **Johann Melchior** (1664–1731), court goldsmith (1698) to August the Strong of Saxony. His brothers **Georg Friedrich** (1666–1720) and **Georg Christoph** (1668–1728) and his son **Johann Friedrich** (1702–1767).

**Di·niz'** (dḗ·nēsh'). *Eng.* **Den'is** (dĕn'ĭs). 1261–1325. King of Portugal (1279–1325). Son of Alfonso III and father of Alfonso IV; led rebellion against father (1277–79); m. (1283) Saint Isabel (*q.v.*), daughter of Peter III of Aragon; encouraged agriculture and commerce, earning sobriquet of Ré Lavrador ("farmer, or laborer, king").

**Di·niz' da Cruz' e Sil'va** (dḗ·nēzh' thȧ krōōz' ḗ sĭl'vȧ), **Antônio.** 1731–1799. Portuguese poet, b. Lisbon; one of revivers of poetry of Portugal; associated in founding *Arcadia Ulysipponense* or *Arcádia Lusitana;* known esp. for his heroicomic epic *O Hissope;* author also of lyric poems *Odes Pindáricas.* Called "the Portuguese Pindar."

**Di·noc'ra·tes** *or* **Dei·noc'ra·tes** (dī·nŏk'rȧ·tēz). Greek architect of late 4th century B.C.; designed for Alexander the Great the new city of Alexandria, in Egypt, and built the funeral pyre of Hephaestion.

**Di·nos'tra·tus** *or* **Dei·nos'tra·tus** (dī·nŏs'trȧ·tŭs). Greek mathematician of 4th century B.C.; contributed to development of geometry.

**Dins'moor** (dĭnz'mōr; -mōōr) *or* **Dins'more** (-mōr), **Robert.** 1757–1836. American poet, b. Windham, N.H.; friend of Whittier and subject of an essay by him.

**Dins'more** (dĭnz'mōr), **Charles Allen.** 1860–1941. American Congregational clergyman and Dante scholar; author of *The Teachings of Dante* (1901), *Aids to the Study of Dante* (1903), *Life of Dante* (1919), etc.

**Din'ter** (dĭn'tẽr), **Gustav Friedrich.** 1760–1831. German theologian and educator.

**Din·wid'die** (dĭn·wĭd'ĭ; dĭn'wĭd'ĭ), **Robert.** 1693–1770. Colonial administrator in America, b. near Glasgow, Scotland. Lieutenant governor of Virginia (1751); sent out George Washington with detachment to protect Ohio region from seizure by French (1754); supplied Braddock's force with provisions for its campaign (1755); defended frontier as best he could after Braddock's defeat; attempted to get co-operation from other colonies, Pennsylvania, Maryland, and the Carolinas, but failed. Left Virginia (1758); died at Bristol, England (July 27, 1770).

**Di'o Cas'si·us** (dī'ō kăsh'ĭ·ŭs; kăsh'ŭs; kăs'ĭ·ŭs) *or* **Di'on Cassius** (dī'ŏn). *Surnamed* **Coc'ce·ia'nus** (kŏk'sḗ·yā'nŭs). 155?–after 230 A.D. Roman politician and historian, of Bithynia; consul (c. 220, and again 229 A.D.). Chief work, a history of Rome, written in Greek (80 books).

**Dio Chrysostomus.** See DION CHRYSOSTOMUS.

**Di'o·cles** (dī'ō·klēz). Syracusan democratic statesman; reputed drafter of new code of laws for Syracuse (411 B.C.).

**Diocles.** Greek mathematician of 2d century A.D. (or earlier); invented the cissoid in order to solve the Delian problem.

**Diocles of Ca·rys'tus** (kȧ·rĭs'tŭs). Greek physician of 3d century B.C. (or earlier).

**Di'o·cle'tian** (dī'ō·klē'shăn). *Full name* **Gaius Aurelius Valerius Di'o·cle'ti·a'nus** (dī'ō·klē'shĭ·ā'nŭs). *Surnamed* **Jo'vi·us** (jō'vĭ·ŭs). 245–313. Roman emperor (284–305), b. at Dioclea in Dalmatia (whence his name). Held command under Probus, Aurelian, and Carus. Proclaimed emperor (284) on death of Numerianus; fought Carinus in Moesia (285); adopted (286) as colleague Maximian who ruled in Gaul, the joint emperors (known as *Augusti*) later (292), because of invasions and revolts in the empire, choosing other associates, Galerius and Constantius Chlorus (known as *Caesars*); acknowledged as chief of the four rulers; kept Asia and Egypt as his administrative unit, with Nicomedia as capital. Subdued revolt in Egypt (296); issued edict (301) in attempt to fix prices, especially in interest of soldiers; although previously friendly to Christians, suddenly issued edict (303) against them, probably persuaded by false accusations of Galerius, beginning terrible persecutions which raged for 10 years (303–313). Abdicated (305); retired to Salona, Dalmatia, and engaged in gardening; with Maximian built Baths of Diocletian in Rome (opened 306).

**Di'o·da'ti** (dē'ō·dä'tḗ), **Charles.** 1608?–1638. English classical scholar, friend of Milton. Nephew of Giovanni Diodati, Genevan Calvinist. Celebrated by Milton in two Latin elegies and an Italian sonnet, and lamented in *Epitaphium Damonis* (1645). His father, **Theodore** (1574?–1651), physician, emigrated to England as a youth; aided Florio with translation of Montaigne.

**Diodati, Giovanni.** 1576–1649. Swiss Protestant theologian; published Italian translation of Bible (1607), and French translation (1644).

**Di'o·do'rus Cro'nus** (dī'ō·dō'rŭs krō'nŭs). Greek philosopher of Megarian school in 4th century B.C.

**Diodorus of Tyre** (tīr). Greek philosopher of 2d century B.C.; studied under Critolaus and succeeded him as head of the Peripatetic school in Athens.

**Diodorus Sic'u·lus** (sĭk'ū·lŭs). Greek historian of late 1st century B.C., b. Agyrium (Agira) in Sicily. Author of *Historical Library* (40 books) of which only books I–V and XI–XX are extant.

**Di·od'o·tus** (dī·ŏd'ō·tŭs). Name of two rulers of Bactria: **Diodotus I** (d. 239? B.C.), Seleucid satrap of Bactria; rebelled (c. 255) against Antiochus II and founded (c. 250) Greco-Bactrian kingdom. Succeeded by his son **Diodotus II** (d. 230? B.C.); made peace with Parthians but was slain by usurper Euthydemus.

**Di·og'e·nes** (dī·ŏj'ḗ·nēz). 412?–323 B.C. Greek Cynic philosopher, b. Sinope in Asia Minor. Studied at Athens under Antisthenes. Rejected social conventions; lived in a tub; according to tradition, once went through streets holding up a lantern, "looking for an honest man." On a voyage from Athens to Aegina, captured by pirates and sold as a slave to a rich citizen of Corinth, who gave him back his freedom. According to legend, he was visited at Corinth by Alexander the Great who asked if he could oblige the philosopher in any way: "Yes," answered Diogenes, "stand from between me and the sun."

**Diogenes La·ër'ti·us** (lȧ·ûr'shĭ·ŭs). Biographer of 3d century A.D.; author of work on lives of Greek philosophers (10 books), sole source of information about many of the philosophers it treats.

**Diogenes of Ap'ol·lo'ni·a** (ăp'ŏ·lō'nĭ·ȧ). Greek philosopher of 5th century B.C., b. Apollonia, in Crete; studied and taught in Athens.

**Diogenes of Babylonia** *or* **of Se·leu'ci·a** (sḗ·lū'shĭ·ȧ). Stoic philosopher of 2d century B.C.; regarded as one of chief philosophers of Stoic school.

**Di'o·ge'ni·a'nus** (dī'ō·jē'nĭ·ā'nŭs). Greek scholar of 2d century A.D., in Heraclea; author of a lexicon, a collection of proverbs, an anthology of epigrams, and geographical works. See PAMPHILUS.

**Di′o·me′des** (dī′ō·mē′dēz). Latin scholar of late 4th century A.D. His *Ars Grammatica* (3 books) is extant.

**Di′on** (dī′ŏn). 408?–353 B.C. Syracusan philosopher and politician; regent for his nephew Dionysius the Younger; made himself master of Syracuse (355 B.C.); assassinated.

**Dion Cassius.** See DIO CASSIUS.

**Dion** (*or* **Di′o** [dī′ō]) **Chry·sos′to·mus** (krĭ·sŏs′tō·mŭs) *or* **Chrys′os·tom** (krĭs′ŭs·tŭm; krĭ·sŏs′tŭm). 40?–?115 A.D. Greek sophist and scholar, b. in Bithynia; migrated to Rome; banished from Rome by Domitian, but enjoyed the favor of Nerva and Trajan; in late life became a convert to stoicism. Eighty of his orations are extant.

**Dionne** (dyôn, dzyôn; *Angl.* dē·ŏn′, dē·ōn′), **Cé′cile′** (*Can. Fr.* sā′sīl′), **Yvonne, Annette, Émilie** d. 1954 **Marie** d. 1970. Canadian quintuplets, b. May 28, 1934 to Elzire, wife of Oliva Dionne, of Callander, Northern Ontario. See Dr. Allan DAFOE.

**Di′o·ny′si·us** (dī′ō·nĭsh′ĭ·ŭs; -nĭsh′ŭs; -nĭs′ĭ·ŭs; -nī′sĭ·ŭs), Saint. = Saint DENIS.

**Dionysius,** Saint. Pope (bishop of Rome; 259–268); reorganized the church after the Decian persecutions (250–251).

**Dionysius.** Name of two tyrants of Syracuse:

**Dionysius the Elder.** c. 430–367 B.C. Tyrant (405–367 B.C.); of humble origin; gained influence by supporting poorer classes; fought with distinction against Carthaginians; usurped power (405); strengthened position by a political marriage, by making peace with Carthage (404), and by employing mercenaries. Engaged in war with Carthage (398–392) and made advantageous peace; conducted successful campaign in southern Italy (390–379); captured Rhegium (Reggio di Calabria) after long siege (386); his last two wars against Carthage (383–378, 368) disastrous. Exerted wide influence over Greek cities; encouraged letters and won first prize (367) at the Lenaea (Athens) with a tragedy.

**Dionysius the Younger.** Son of Dionysius the Elder; tyrant (367–356 and 347–344 B.C.); at first, under regency of his uncle Dion; Plato was invited to Syracuse as his tutor, but was dismissed; driven out (366) and fled to Locris; returned (347), but his despotic rule caused citizens to invite Timoleon to their assistance; defeated and taken to Corinth (344 or 343).

**Dionysius.** King of Portugal. = DINIZ.

**Dionysius Ex·ig′u·us** (ĕg·zĭg′ū·ŭs; ĕks·ĭg′-). Christian monk and scholar of 6th century, b. in Scythia. In his *Cyclus Paschalis,* introduced method of reckoning the Christian era (Dionysian period) which is still used, making the birth of Christ the starting point of modern chronology. Cf. VICTORINUS.

**Dionysius of Alexandria,** Saint. Roman Catholic theologian of 3d century; head of catechetical school in Alexandria (231); bishop of Alexandria (247); fled (251) to avoid persecution under Decius; banished (257) in reign of Valerian; returned to his see (260). Only fragments of his works are extant.

**Dionysius of Hal′i·car·nas′sus** (hăl′ĭ·kär·năs′ŭs). d. about 7 B.C. Greek scholar; settled in Rome (c. 29 B.C.) and devoted himself to writing history of Rome. Much of this work, *Roman Antiquities* (20 books), is extant.

**Dionysius Per′i·e·ge′tes** (pĕr′ĭ·ē·jē′tēz). Greek geographer and poet of 4th century A.D. (or earlier), perhaps of Alexandria; author of geographical description (periegesis) of the habitable earth, written in Greek hexameters.

**Dionysius the Ar′e·op′a·gite** (ăr′ē·ŏp′ȧ·jīt; -gīt). (1) An Athenian of the 1st century converted by St. Paul (*Acts* xvii. 34). See Saint DENIS. (2) An unknown author (c. A.D. 500), for centuries identified with St. Paul's convert, whose works of mystical and speculative theology (*The Celestial Hierarchy, The Divine Names,* etc.) exercised vast influence on medieval thought. Called also *Pseudo-Dionysius* and *Pseudo-Areopagite.*

**Dionysius Thrax** (thrăks), *i.e.* of Thrace. fl. 100 B.C. Greek grammarian, of Alexandria; author of the first Greek grammar.

**Dionysus.** See ANTIOCHUS VI and ANTIOCHUS XII of Syria.

**Di′o·phan′tus** (dī′ō·făn′tŭs). Greek mathematician of 3d century A.D. (or later), in Alexandria; reputed inventor of algebra. Chief work, *Arithmetica* (13 books, of which 6 are extant).

**Di′os·cor′i·des** (dī′ŏs·kŏr′ĭ·dēz), **Pedanius.** Greek physician of 1st century A.D.; author of *De Materia Medica* (5 books), which remained for 1500 years the authority in botany and materia medica.

**Di·os′po·lite** (dī·ŏs′pō·līt). Name sometimes given to XVIIIth, XIXth, and XXth dynasties of Egyptian kings of the New Kingdom, reigning c. 1580–1090 B.C., derived from Diospolis ("City of God"), a name of Thebes, its capital. See *Table (in Appendix)* for EGYPT.

**Diph′i·lus** (dĭf′ĭ·lŭs). Athenian writer of comedies of late 4th century B.C., b. Sinope; contemporary of Menander; only fragments of his works extant.

**Dipoenus.** See SCYLLIS.

**Dip′pel** (dĭp′ĕl), **Johann Andreas.** 1866–1933. German operatic tenor; joint director, with Gatti-Casazza, Metropolitan Opera House in New York (1908–10); organized (1910) and directed (1910–13) Chicago Opera Company; impresario of a comic-opera company (1914 ff.).

**Dippel, Johann Konrad.** 1673–1734. German Pietist theologian, physician, and alchemist. As chemist in Berlin, distilled animal bones in preparing curative mixture known as Dippel's oil. Practiced medicine in Netherlands, at Altona, and in Sweden. Published collected writings under title *Eröffneter Weg zum Frieden mit Gott und mit allen Creaturen* (1709) under pseudonym **Chri′sti·a′nus De·mo′kri·tus** (krĭs′tē·ä′no͝os dā·mō′krē·to͝os).

**Di·rac′** (dĭ·răk′), **Paul A′dri·en** (ā′drĭ·ĕn) **Mau′rice** (mô′rĭs). 1902– . English physicist, b. Bristol. Professor of mathematics, Cambridge (from 1932). Known for work in quantum mechanics; developed theory of the spinning electron. Shared 1933 Nobel prize for physics with Erwin Schrödinger. Author of *Principles of Quantum Mechanics* (1930).

**Dirceu.** Pseudonym of Tomaz Antônio GONZAGA.

**Di′ri·chlet′** (dē′rē·klā′), **Peter Gustav Le·jeune′** (lĕ·zhûn′). 1805–1859. German mathematician; known esp. for work on theory of numbers, which he furthered by application of higher analysis, as well as work on definite integrals.

**Disbrowe, John.** See DESBOROUGH.

**Dis′ney** (dĭz′nĭ), **Walt,** *in full* **Walter E.** 1901–1966. American producer of animated motion-picture cartoons, b. Chicago. Creator of *Oswald, Donald Duck, Mickey Mouse, Silly Symphonies.* Made great success with full-length animated films *Snow White and the Seven Dwarfs* (1938), *Pinocchio* (1940), *Fantasia* (1940), *Dumbo* (1941).

**Dis·rae′li** (dĭz·rā′lĭ), **Benjamin.** 1st Earl of **Bea′cons·field** (bē′kŭnz·fēld; bĕk′ŭnz-; *the former appears to have been the earl's own pron.; the latter is the local pron. for the town in Buckinghamshire from which the title comes*). *Nicknamed* **Diz′zy** (dĭz′ĭ). 1804–1881. Prime minister of Great Britain, and author, b. London; son of Isaac

D'Israeli (*q.v.*). M.P. (1837–80); first speech a failure; member of Young England party; supported corn laws; attacked Peel for repealing them (1846); championed protection (1845–50). Chancellor of exchequer under Lord Derby (1852, 1858–59, 1866–68); also leader of commons (1858–59); introduced, but lost, reform bill (1859); attacked Gladstone's financial system (1860, 1862) and Russell's foreign policy (yearly till 1865); carried Reform Act enfranchising all ratepayers (1867). Succeeded Lord Derby as prime minister (1868); resigned after general election (1868); criticized Gladstone's Irish and foreign policy; prime minister (1874–80); borrowed money and purchased for British government, on own responsibility, khedive's interest in Suez Canal (1875); had Queen Victoria assume title of Empress of India (1876); created earl of Beaconsfield (1876); became intimate friend of Queen Victoria; English plenipotentiary at Congress of Berlin (1878). Author of *Vindication of the British Constitution* (1835), and the novels *Vivian Grey* (1826), *The Young Duke* (1831), *Henrietta Temple* (1837), *Coningsby* (1844), *Sybil* (1845), *Tancred* (1847), *Lothair* (1870), *Endymion* (1880).

**D'Is·rae'li** *or* **Dis·rae'li** (dĭz·rā'lĭ), **Isaac.** 1766–1848. English man of letters, b. London. Son of Benjamin D'Israeli, a Jewish merchant, descended from a family of Spanish refugees in Venice, who went to England (1748), became British subject (1801). Studied in Amsterdam; became disciple of Rousseau; published anonymously *Curiosities of Literature* (6 vols., 1791–1834), a collection of literary and historical anecdotes; m. (1802) Maria Basevi (1775–1847), by whom he had four sons, the eldest, Benjamin, later becoming earl of Beaconsfield; had his children baptized into Anglican Church. Author also of *Calamities of Authors* (1812–13), *Quarrels of Authors* (1814), *Amenities of Literature* (3 vols., 1841), and three novels and two historical works.

**Di'ste·li** (dĭs'tȧ·lē), **Martin.** 1802–1844. Swiss caricaturist and painter; illustrated Fröhlich's *Fabeln, Münchhausens Abenteuern*, etc.

**Dithmar.** See THIETMAR.

**Dit'mars** (dĭt'märz), **Raymond Lee.** 1876–1942. American naturalist, b. Newark, N.J. Curator of reptiles, New York Zoological Park (from 1899), and in charge of department of mammals (from 1910). Authority on snakes. Author of *The Reptile Book* (1907), *Strange Animals I Have Known* (1931), *The Book of Living Reptiles* (1936), *The Book of Insect Oddities* (1938), etc.

**Di'trich·stein** (dē'trĭk·stīn), **Le'o** (lē'ō). 1865–1928. Actor and playwright, b. Temesvár, Hungary; to U.S. (1890). Great success in part of Zou Zou in stage version of du Maurier's *Trilby* (1895). Adapted many plays from German and French successes. Wrote popular farce comedies, *All on Account of Eliza* (1900) and *Are You a Mason?* (1901).

**Dit'ten·ber'ger** (dĭt'ĕn·bĕr'gẽr), **Wilhelm.** 1840–1906. German classical scholar.

**Dit'ters von Dit'ters·dorf** (dĭt'ẽrs fŏn dĭt'ẽrs·dôrf), **Karl.** 1739–1799. Austrian violin virtuoso and composer; Kapellmeister for bishop of Grosswardein (1765) and for prince-bishop of Breslau (1770). Composer of 44 operas, over 100 symphonies, including 12 program symphonies on Ovid's *Metamorphoses*, chamber music, two oratorios (*Esther* and *Hiob*), and many piano and violin pieces.

**Ditzen, Rudolf.** Real name of Hans FALLADA.

**Divino, El.** See Luis de MORALES.

**Div'i·ti'a·cus** (dĭv'ĭ·tĭ'ȧ·kŭs). Chieftain of the Aedui in 1st century B.C.; brother of Dumnorix, personal friend of Julius Caesar, and guest of Cicero on a visit to Rome. Ally of Caesar against Ariovistus and against the Belgae.

**Di'voire'** (dē'vwȧr'), **Fernand.** 1883–1951. French poet and critic, b. Brussels. Editor in chief of *Intransigeant.*

**Dix** (dĭks), **Beulah Marie.** See Beulah Marie Dix FLEBBE.

**Dix, Dorothea Lynde,** *orig.* **Dorothy.** 1802–1887. American philanthropist and reformer, b. Hampden, Me. Established and headed a school for girls, Boston (1820?–35). Secured reforms in treatment of the insane in prisons, almshouses, and houses of correction in Mass., and later in other states (from 1841); served through Civil War as superintendent of women nurses. Wrote a number of books for children.

**Dix, Dorothy.** Pseudonym of Elizabeth Meriwether GILMER.

**Dix, John Adams.** 1798–1879. American army officer and political leader, b. Boscawen, N.H. Served in War of 1812. Secretary of state of New York (1833–39). U.S. senator (1845–49). U.S. secretary of the treasury (1861). Served as major general during Civil War. U.S. minister to France (1866–69). Governor of New York (1873–75). His son **Morgan** (1827–1908), a Protestant Episcopal clergyman, was rector of Trinity Church, New York (1862–1908).

**Dix** (dĭks), **Otto.** 1891–1969. German painter; served in World War (1914–18) and painted series of scenes of stark realism revealing his abhorrence of war. Later, took subjects from contemporary peasant and bourgeois life, becoming leader of contemporary movement (*Neue Sachlichkeit*, "new realism"; from c. 1922) towards objective representation in art and literature.

**Dix'on** (dĭk's'n), **Charles.** 1858–1926. English ornithologist and author; studied migration of birds and the geographical distribution of species, setting forth new theories. Author of *Annals of Bird Life* (1890), *The Migration of Birds* (1892), *British Sea Birds* (1896), etc.

**Dixon, Frank Haigh** (hăg). 1869–1944. American transportation economist; chief statistician for bureau of railway economics (1910–18); special expert for U.S. Shipping Board (1918); professor, Princeton (from 1919). Author of *Railroads and Government, Their Relations in the United States* (1922), etc.

**Dixon, George.** 1755?–1800. English navigator; sailed with Captain Cook on third expedition; exploring shores of present British Columbia, discovered (1787) Queen Charlotte Islands.

**Dixon, Henry Hall.** *Pen name* **The Dru'id** (drōō'ĭd). 1822–1870. English sporting writer; author of three novels, *Post and Paddock* (1856), *Silk and Scarlet* (1859), *Scott and Sebright* (1862).

**Dixon, James Main.** 1856–1933. Educator, b. Paisley, Scotland; professor of Oriental studies and comparative literature, Southern California (from 1911). Compiler of *A Dictionary of Idiomatic English Phrases* (1890).

**Dixon, Jeremiah.** fl. 1763–1767. English surveyor who, with Charles Mason (*q.v.*), determined southern boundary of Pennsylvania, which became known as Mason and Dixon's line and was considered as being in part the boundary between free and slave states before the Civil War.

**Dixon, Richard Watson.** 1833–1900. English poet. At Oxford one of "Birmingham group," joining with William Morris and Burne-Jones in Pre-Raphaelite movement; vicar of Warkworth (1883–1900). Author of seven volumes of poetry and *A History of the Church of England* (1877–1900).

**Dixon, Roland Burrage.** 1875–1934. American anthropologist, b. Worcester, Mass. Professor, Harvard (from 1916). Author of *Oceanic Mythology* (1916), *Racial*

*History of Man* (1923), *The Building of Cultures* (1928), etc.

**Dixon, Thomas.** 1864–1946. American Baptist clergyman and writer, b. Shelby, N.C.; chief pastorate in New York City (1889–99). Author of *Leopard's Spots* (1902), *The Clansman* (1905), *The Southerner* (1913), *The Birth of a Nation* (photoplay, 1915), *A Man of the People* (1920), *The Inside Story of the Harding Tragedy* (1932; with Harry M. Daugherty, *q.v.*), etc.

**Dixon, William Hepworth.** 1821–1879. English historian and traveler; editor of the *Athenaeum* (1853–69). Author of biographies, including *William Penn* (1851; in defense of Penn against charges made in Macaulay's *History of England*), *Admiral Blake* (1852) and *Lord Bacon* (1862), travel books, and historical works, including one on Catherine of Aragon and Anne Boleyn, *History of Two Queens* (1873).

**Diya–al–Din.** See under IBN-AL-ATHIR.

**Di'zen·goff** (dĭ'zĕn·gōf), **Mei'er** (mī'ẽr). 1861–1936. Zionist leader, b. in Bessarabia. Settled in Palestine (1905); laid foundations of city of Tel Aviv (1906). Mayor of Tel Aviv, first Palestinian Jewish city (1920–25).

**Djal'ski** (dyäl'skē), **Ksaver Šandor.** *Real name* **Ljubomir Ba'bić** (bä'bēt·y'; *Angl.* -bĭch). 1854–1935. Yugoslav writer and patriot; vigorous advocate of Yugoslav unity.

**Djem.** See JEM.

**Dje·mal' Pa·sha'** (jĕ·mäl' pä·shä'), **Ahmed.** 1872?–1922. Turkish general and statesman; commanded division during Balkan wars (1912–13); instrumental in influencing Turkey to join Central Powers in World War (1914–18); commanded armies against Allenby. Fled from Turkey (1918); assassinated.

**Djerjinsky** *or* **Djerzinsky.** Variants of DZERZHINSKI.

**Djez·zar'** (jĕz·zär'), *i.e.* butcher. *Nickname of* **Ah·med' Pa·sha'** (ä·mĕt' pä·shä'). 1735?–1804. Turkish official, b. in Bosnia, of Christian parents. Turned Moslem; entered service of Ali Bey (*q.v.*); made pasha of Acre; defended it successfully (1799) against Napoleon.

**Djugashvili.** Variant of *Dzhugashvili* (see Joseph STALIN).

**Dłu'gosz** (dlōō'gôsh), **Jan.** *Lat.* **Johannes Lon·gi'nus** (lŏn·jī'nŭs). 1415–1480. Polish historian; archbishop of Lemberg (1478). Author of *Historia Polonica* (13 vols., pub. 1614).

**Dmitri.** See DEMETRIUS.

**Dmi'tri·ev** (d'myē'tryĭ·yĕf), **Ivan Ivanovich.** 1760–1837. Russian statesman and poet; minister of justice (1810–14) under Emperor Alexander I; author of fables, odes, satires, songs, and a short dramatic poem on Yermak Timofeiev, Cossack conqueror of Siberia.

**Dmi'tri·ev, Radko.** *Bulg.* **Di·mi'tri·ev** (dē·mē'trē·yĕf). 1859–1919. Bulgarian-born general in Russian army; commanded 3d Russian army at outbreak of World War (1914–15); captured Przemyśl and defended Riga-Dünamünde front; died (1919), probably murdered by Bolsheviks.

**Dmow'ski** (d'môf'skē), **Roman.** 1864–1939. Polish statesman; founded Polish National Democratic Party (1893); headed Polish representatives in Russian Duma (1903); after World War (1914–18), headed Paris committee recognized as temporary government of Poland, and signed Treaty of Versailles (1919); minister of foreign affairs (1923); opposed Piłsudski, and soon thereafter retired from politics.

**Doak** (dōk), **William Nuckles.** 1882–1933. American labor leader and politician, b. Rural Retreat, Va. Official of Brotherhood of Railroad Trainmen (from 1908). U.S. secretary of labor (1930–33).

**Doane** (dōn), **George Washington.** 1799–1859. American Protestant Episcopal bishop, b. Trenton, N.J. Bishop of New Jersey (from 1832); a leader of the High-Church party in America. Author of many hymns, including: *Softly now the light of day; Thou art the way, to Thee alone; Father of mercies, hear, Thy pardon we implore; Fling out the banner, let it float.* His son **William Croswell** (1832–1913) was the first Protestant Episcopal bishop of Albany (from 1869), and author of the hymn *Ancient of Days.*

**Dob'bie** (dŏb'ĭ), Sir **William George Shedden.** 1879–1964. British army officer; lieutenant general (1941); governor of Malta (1940–42).

**Dob'bin** (dŏb'ĭn), **James Cochran.** 1814–1857. American lawyer, b. Fayetteville, N.C. U.S. secretary of the navy (1853–57); instrumental in enlarging and reorganizing the navy.

**Dobbs** (dŏbz), **Arthur.** 1689–1765. Colonial administrator in America, b. in County Antrim, Ireland. Purchased a 400,000-acre estate in North Carolina (1745); appointed governor of North Carolina (1754).

**Do·bell'** (dō·bĕl'), **Bertram.** 1842–1914. English bookseller and man of letters; befriended James Thomson (from 1876) and arranged publication of *The City of Dreadful Night* (1880); recovered, identified, and edited, poetical works of Thomas Traherne.

**Dobell,** Sir **Charles Macpherson.** 1869–1954. British soldier, b. in Quebec. Served in Boer War (1899–1900), Boxer Rebellion (1900), and World War; commanded Allied troops in the Cameroons (1914–16), Egyptian expeditionary force (1916–17), and a division in India (1917–19).

**Dobell, Horace Benge.** 1828–1917. English physician; had R. L. Stevenson as one of his patients at Bournemouth; wrote *Bacillary Consumption* and *Medical Aspects of Bournemouth.* Dobell's solution is named after him.

**Dobell, Sydney Thompson.** *Pseudonym* **Sydney Yen'dys** (yĕn'dĭs). 1824–1874. English poet and critic, b. in Cranbrook, Kent. Ardent liberalist and advocate of cause of oppressed nationalities and cause of Italian unity; wrote with Alexander Smith sonnets on Crimean War (1855). Author of the dramatic poem *The Roman* (1850), *Balder* (part I, 1854), *England in Time of War* (1856). Member, with George Gilfillan, Philip James Bailey, John Stanyan Bigg, and Alexander Smith (*q.v.*), of the "spasmodic school," so named by Professor W. E. Aytoun, who parodied in *Firmilian* (1854) their style and attitude of skeptical unrest.

**Dober, Conrad K.** Real name of Con CONRAD.

**Dö'be·rei'ner** (dû'bĕ·rī'nẽr), **Johann Wolfgang.** 1780–1849. German chemist; discovered catalytic action of platinum sponge on hydrogen, an action utilized in his lamp (Döbereiner's lamp) for instantaneous production of a flame; discovered furfural; recognized (before 1829) relationship between the properties of elements and their atomic weights, upon which the periodic table of elements is based; classed closely related elements in groups of three (known as Döbereiner's triads).

**Do'bie** (dō'bĭ), **Charles Caldwell.** 1881–1943. American fiction writer and playwright; author of the plays *Doubling in Brass, Retribution, Believe It or Not,* etc.

**Dobie, James Frank.** 1888–1964. American educator, writer, and folklorist, b. in Live Oak County, Tex. Professor of English, U. of Texas (1933–47). Author of *A Vaquero of the Brush Country* (1929), *Coronado's Children* (1931), *Apache Gold and Yaqui Silver* (1939), *The Longhorns* (1941), etc.

**Dö'blin** (dû'blēn), **Alfred.** 1878–1957. German physician and writer; nerve specialist in Berlin (from 1912–

33); in exile (from 1934). Author of novels, plays, an epic, *Manas* (1926), and essays.

**Do'brée** (dō'brē), **Bonamy.** 1891– . English literary scholar and editor; served in World War I and II; lieut. colonel; authority on Restoration drama; author of *Restoration Comedy* (1924), *Restoration Tragedy* (1929); collaborated in *The Victorians and After* (1938). His wife, **Valentine Gladys,** *nee* **Brooke'–Pe'chell** (pē'chĕl) (1884– ), is author of *Your Cuckoo Sings by Kind* (1927), *Emperor's Tigers* (1929), *To Blush Unseen* (1935).

**Do'bree** (dō'brē), **Peter Paul.** 1782–1825. English classical scholar, b. in Guernsey.

**Dö'bren·te'i** (dû'brĕn·tĕ'ĭ), **Gábor.** 1786–1851. Hungarian philologist; editor of *Ancient Monuments of the Magyar Language* (1838 ff.).

**Do'briz·hof'fer** (dō'brĭts·hôf'ẽr), **Martin.** 1717–1791. Austrian Jesuit missionary in South America; in Paraguay (1749–67), working seven years among Abipon Indians. Author of a valuable ethnological work, *Historia de Abiponibus, Equestri Bellicosaque Paraguariae Natione* (3 vols., 1783).

**Do·bro·lyu'bov** (dŭ·brŭ·lyōō'bôf), **Nikolai Aleksandrovich.** 1836–1861. Russian journalist and critic; regarded by some as an originator of revolutionary activity in Russia.

**Do'brov·ský** (dô'brôf·skē), **Josef.** 1753–1829. Czech Jesuit and philologist; regarded as founder of Slavic philology. Chief work, *Institutiones Linguae Slavicae Dialecti Veteris* (1822), first scientific grammar of Old Slav.

**Dob'son** (dŏb's'n), **Austin,** *in full* **Henry Austin.** 1840–1921. English poet and man of letters. Clerk (from 1856), principal clerk (1884–1901) in marine department of Board of Trade. Author of *Vignettes in Rhyme* (1873) and *At the Sign of the Lyre* (collection of light verse; 1885), and of prose works including critical essays and biographies.

**Dobson, Frank.** 1888–1963. English sculptor, b. London. Among his notable sculptures are *The Man Child, Susanna, Morning,* bronze bust of earl of Oxford and Asquith, and brass head of Osbert Sitwell.

**Dobson, William.** 1610–1646. English portrait painter; succeeded Vandyke (1641) as court painter to Charles I; painted portraits of Charles I, Prince of Wales, and Prince Rupert.

**Dock'wra** (dŏk'rȧ) *or* **Dock'wray** (-rā), **William.** d. 1716. London merchant who established a penny postal system in the metropolis (1683).

**Dó'czi** (dō'tsĭ), Baron **Ludwig von.** 1845–1919. Hungarian playwright. Among his plays are *The Kiss* (1871; Hungarian Acad. award) and *Marie Szecsy* (1885).

**Dodd** (dŏd), **Frank Howard.** 1844–1916. American publisher, b. Bloomfield, N.J. Son of Moses Woodruff Dodd. Joined father's publishing business (1860); became head of firm (1870); later took in as partners Edward S. Mead and Bleecker Van Wagenen, forming firm of Dodd, Mead, & Co.

**Dodd, Lee Wilson.** 1879–1933. American writer, b. Franklin, Pa. Author of plays *The Return of Eve* (1909), *Speed* (1911), *His Majesty Bunker Bean* (1915), *The Changelings* (1923); novels, *The Book of Susan* (1920) and *The Girl Next Door* (1923); verse, *The Middle Miles* (1915), *The Great Enlightenment* (1928), etc.

**Dodd, Moses Woodruff.** 1813–1899. American publisher, b. Bloomfield, N.J. Formed partnership in publishing business with John S. Taylor (1839), and after Taylor's withdrawal (1840) continued the business until his retirement (1870). See Frank Howard DODD.

**Dodd, Robert.** 1748–1816? English marine painter, known for his storm effects.

**Dodd, William.** 1729–1777. English preacher; forced to flee England because of wife's attempt to bribe wife of lord chancellor to gain preferment for him (1774); forged a bond in name of earl of Chesterfield; hanged despite petitions for his pardon, one by Dr. Johnson. Author of *The Beauties of Shakespeare* (1752), *Reflections on Death* (1763), etc.

**Dodd, William Edward.** 1869–1940. American historian, b. Clayton, N.C. Professor of American history, Chicago (1908–33). U.S. ambassador to Germany (1933–37). Author of *Life of Jefferson Davis* (1907), *Statesmen of the Old South* (1911), *Expansion and Conflict* (1915), *Woodrow Wilson and His Work* (1920), *Ambassador Dodd's Diary* (pub. 1941; covering period 1933–37). Joint editor, with Ray Stannard Baker, of *The Public Papers of Woodrow Wilson* (1924–26).

**Dodd'ridge** (dŏd'rĭj), **Philip.** 1702–1751. English nonconformist clergyman and religious writer. Author of several hymns, including "O God of Bethel [Jacob], by whose hand."

**Dodds** (dŏdz), **Harold Willis.** 1889– . American political scientist, b. Utica, Pa. Editor, *National Municipal Review* (1920–33). Electoral adviser to government of Nicaragua (1922–24, 1928). Professor of politics (1927–34) and president (1933–57), Princeton.

**Dode' de La Bru'ne·rie'** (dôd' dẽ lȧ brün'rē'), Vicomte **Guillaume.** 1775–1851. French general; noted for his defense of Glogau (1813–14).

**Dö'der·lein** (dû'dẽr·līn), **Ludwig.** 1791–1863. German classical scholar.

**Dodge** (dŏj), **Augustus Caesar.** See under Henry DODGE.

**Dodge, Bayard.** 1888–1972. American educator, b. New York City; president (1923–48), U. of Beirut, Syria.

**Dodge, David Low.** 1774–1852. American merchant and pacifist, b. Brooklyn, Conn.; founder of New York Peace Society (1815). His son **William Earl** (1805–1883), merchant and philanthropist, was an organizer of the Young Men's Christian Association in America. David's great-granddaughter **Grace Hoadley Dodge** (1856–1914) was a social worker, organized a working girls' club from which developed the Associations of Working Girls' Societies; member of the New York City Board of Education (1886), and prominent in the organization (1889) and early activity of Teachers College, Columbia U.; helped found the New York Travelers Aid Society (1907).

**Dodge, Grenville Mellen.** 1831–1916. American army officer and civil engineer, b. Danvers, Mass. Served through Civil War; major general of volunteers (1864). Chief engineer, Union Pacific Railroad (1866–70). Associated with Jay Gould in railroad development in the Southwest (1873–83). Organized and built railroad in Cuba (1899–1903).

**Dodge, Henry.** 1782–1867. American political leader, b. Vincennes, Ind.; governor of Territory of Wisconsin (1836–41). Member, U.S. House of Representatives, as delegate from Territory of Wisconsin (1841–45); again governor (1845–48). U.S. senator from Wisconsin (1848–57). His son **Augustus Caesar** (1812–1883) was first U.S. senator from Iowa (1848–55), and U.S. minister to Spain (1855–59).

**Dodge, Mabel.** See Mabel LUHAN.

**Dodge, Mary Abigail.** *Pseudonym* **Gail Hamilton.** 1833–1896. American writer, b. Hamilton, Mass. Author of *Gala Days* (1863), *A New Atmosphere* (1865), *Woman's Worth and Worthlessness* (1872), *James G. Blaine* (1895), etc.

**Dodge, Mary Elizabeth,** *nee* **Mapes** (māps). 1831–1905. American writer, b. New York City; m. (1851) William

Dodge (d. 1858). Editor, *St. Nicholas Magazine* (1873–1905). Successful esp. in books for children, as *Hans Brinker, or the Silver Skates* (1865), *Donald and Dorothy* (1883), *When Life is Young* (poetry, 1894), *The Land of Pluck* (1894).

**Dodge, Raymond.** 1871–1942. American psychologist and editor; professor, Yale (1924–36).

**Dodge, Theodore Ay′rault** (ī′rôlt). 1842–1909. American army officer and military historian, b. Pittsfield, Mass. Served in Civil War; lost leg at Gettysburg. Author of *A Bird's-Eye View of Our Civil War* (1883), *Alexander* (1890), *Hannibal* (1891), *Caesar* (1892), *Riders of Many Lands* (1894), *Gustavus Adolphus* (1895), *Napoleon* (4 vols., 1904–07), etc.

**Dodge, William Earl.** See under David Low DODGE.

**Dodg′son** (dŏj′s′n), **Charles Lutwidge.** *Pseudonym* **Lewis Car′roll** (kăr′ŭl). 1832–1898. English mathematician and writer. Son of clergyman; educ. at Rugby and Oxford (B.A., 1854); took orders (1861). Mathematical lecturer at Oxford (1855–81); published mathematical treatises, including *Euclid and his Modern Rivals* (1879). Author of the household classics *Alice's Adventures in Wonderland* (1865) and *Through the Looking Glass* (1872), written for Alice Liddell, second daughter of Henry George Liddell (*q.v.*), and illustrated by Sir John Tenniel (*q.v.*); author also of *Phantasmagoria* (1869), *Hunting of the Snark* (1876), *Sylvie and Bruno* (1889).

**Dod′ing·ton** (dŏd′ĭng·tŭn), **George Bubb.** Baron **Mel′combe** (mĕl′kŭm). 1691–1762. English politician. Son of Jeremias Bubb, an Irishman; adopted name Dodington on inheriting uncle's estate (1720). Bartered his votes in parliament first to one side then to the other; a lord of treasury (1724–40); one of the "mad monks of Medmenham Abbey" (see Sir Francis DASHWOOD); treasurer of navy (1744, 1755); reached his ambition, a peerage (1761); spoke against execution of Admiral Byng (1757). Patron of Young, Thomson, Fielding.

**Do·doens′** (dô·dōōns′), **Rembert.** *Lat.* **Rembertus Do′do·nae′us** (dō′dô·nē′ŭs). 1517–1585. Dutch botanist; author of *Cruydeboek* (1554 and 1563) on domestic and foreign plants.

**Dods′ley** (dŏdz′lĭ), **Robert.** 1703–1764. English poet, playwright, and bookseller. Set up as bookseller (1735); published Dr. Johnson's *London* (1738) and works by Pope, Young, Akenside, Chesterfield, Walpole, Goldsmith; helped to finance Johnson's dictionary; founded several literary periodicals, among them the *Annual Register*, with Edmund Burke as editor (1758). Wrote plays, collected as *Trifles* (1745), also *The Blind Beggar of Bethnal Green* (1741); closed career as dramatist with tragedy *Cleone* (1758). Best known as editor of two collections, *Old Plays* (12 vols., 1744), and *A Collection of Poems by Several Hands* (3 vols., 1748).

**Dod′well** (dŏd′wĕl; -wĕl), **Edward.** 1767–1832. English archaeologist in Greece (1801–06), in Rome (1807–32); procured the Dodwell Vase from Corinth and many antiquities from Attica.

**Dodwell, Henry.** 1641–1711. Irish theologian and historian; Camden professor of history, Oxford (1688–91); deprived for refusing oath of allegiance to William and Mary; champion of nonjurors; advanced eccentric theological theories, such as the natural mortality of the soul.

**Do′eg** (dō′ĕg). In the Bible, an Edomite who reported to Saul the befriending of David by Ahimelech and who afterward executed Saul's command to kill the priests and destroy the village of Nob (*1 Samuel* xxi–xxii).

**Doe′nitz** (dû′nĭts), **Karl.** 1891– . German naval commander; in submarine service (from 1916); planned and commanded U-boat fleet; grand admiral (1943); as Nazi supreme commander, surrendered (May 7, 1945); sentenced as war criminal to ten years' imprisonment.

**Does** (dōōs), **Jacob van der.** 1623–1673. Dutch painter.

**Does, Jan van der.** See Janus DOUSA.

**Does′burg** (dōōs′bûrk), **Theo van.** 1883–1931. Dutch painter; founder of the de Stijl school of painting; his paintings in later years became pure abstractions. See Georges van TONGERLOO.

**Dog′gett** (dŏg′ĕt; -ĭt), **Thomas.** d. 1721. Irish actor, b. Dublin. Made first London appearance as Nincompoop in D'Urfey's *Love for Money* (1691); created part of Ben, written for him, in Congreve's *Love for Love* (1695); author of *The Country Wake*, in which he played Young Hobb (1696). Founded (1715) a sculling prize, "Doggett's Coat and Badge," for Thames watermen, still rowed for annually on August 1.

**Do·he′ny** (dô·hē′nĭ), **Edward Laurence.** 1856–1935. American oil producer, b. Fond du Lac, Wis. Organized Mexican Petroleum Co. (1900), reorganized as Mexican Petroleum Co., Ltd., of Delaware (1907). Also founded Pan American Petroleum Co. (1916). Involved in Teapot Dome oil scandals; accused (1924) of bribing Albert B. Fall (*q.v.*) in order to obtain preferred treatment in distribution of oil leases, esp. of leases of Elk Hills naval oil reserves; leases canceled (1924) and Doheny indicted with Fall on charges of conspiracy and bribery; acquitted.

**Do′her·ty** (dō′ẽr·tĭ), **Charles Joseph.** 1855–1931. Canadian jurist and statesman; professor at McGill U.; puisne judge, superior court, Quebec (1891–1906); minister of justice (1911–21); Canadian representative at Paris Peace Conference (1919), and in Assembly of the League of Nations (1920–21).

**Doherty, Henry Latham.** 1870–1939. American oil and utilities magnate, b. Columbus, Ohio. Organized Henry L. Doherty & Co., bankers and public utility operators, New York (1905), and Cities Service Co., holding company for public utility and petroleum properties (1910); president, Cities Service Co. (1910–39).

**Doherty, Reginald Frank** (1872–1911) and his brother **Hugh Lawrence** (1875–1919). English lawn-tennis players. All-England singles champions at Wimbledon (Reginald 1897–1900 and Hugh 1902–06), and doubles champions (1897–1905); Hugh was also American national champion (1903). Joint authors of the classic *On Lawn Tennis* (1903).

**Doherty, Robert Ernest.** 1885–1950. American educator, b. Clay City, Ill. Professor of electrical engineering, Yale (1931–36), and dean of Yale School of Engineering (1933–36). President, Carnegie Tech. (from 1936).

**Dohm** (dōm), **Ernst.** 1819–1883. German writer; co-editor of humorous periodical *Kladderadatsch* (from 1849); translator of La Fontaine's *Fables* into German.

**Doh′na** (dō′nä). Distinguished German family, including Burgrave **Fabian von Dohna** (1550–1622), soldier in Polish service who later aided Henry IV of France against Catholic League, and the following, all bearing title Burgrave and Count **zu Dohna-Schlo′bit′ten** (-shlō′bĭt′ĕn): **Alexander** (1661–1728), field marshal in Prussian service; his brother **Christoph** (1665–1733), colonel of regiment of French émigrés after revocation of Edict of Nantes, ambassador to London (1698–99), general of infantry (1713), ambassador to Vienna (1714–16); **Friedrich Ferdinand Alexander** (1771–1831), Prussian minister of interior (1808–10), determined opponent of Napoleon, an organizer of Prussian Landwehr; his brother **Friedrich** (1784–1859), Prussian general, who resisted French domination in Prussia (1806–11), served in Russian army (1812–15), and returned to Prussian service in time to fight in battle of Waterloo (1815).

**Doh'ná·nyi** (dō'nä·nyĭ), **Ernö.** 1877–1960. Hungarian musician and composer of an opera *Ivas Turm* (1922), comic operas *Tante Simona* (1912) and *The Tenor* (1929), a pantomime, orchestral rhapsody, piano concerto, violin concerto, string quartets, and piano works. Known esp. for his suite for orchestra (opus 19).

**Dohrn** (dōrn), **Anton.** 1840–1909. German zoologist. Son of **Karl August Dohrn** (1806–1892), coleopterist.

**Do·i·ha·ra** (dō·ē·hä·rä), **Kenji.** 1883–1948. Japanese soldier; intelligence officer and Japanese propagandist in northern China (1931 ff.); commander in chief of Japanese air force (1942); hanged as war criminal.

**Doi'sy** (doi'zĭ), **Edward Adelbert.** 1893– . American biochemist; known for work on blood buffers, sex hormones (notably, isolation of theelin, 1929), and vitamin K. Corecipient of 1943 Nobel physiology prize.

**Dol'a·bel'la** (dŏl'ȧ·bĕl'ȧ), **Publius Cornelius.** 70?–43 B.C. Roman general; son-in-law of Cicero. In the civil war, joined Caesar; was engaged at battle of Pharsala (48 B.C.) and accompanied Caesar to Africa and Spain. After assassination of Caesar (Mar. 15, 44), seized consulship and, by favor of Brutus, was allowed to hold it. Deserted Brutus's cause to accept from Antony command of an expedition against the Parthians and governorship of Syria. His extortions and crimes caused him to be declared a public enemy; attacked and defeated at Laodicea and, to escape capture, ordered one of his soldiers to kill him.

**Dol'ce** (dōl'châ), **Lodovico.** 1508–1568. Italian writer and scholar, b. Venice; among his works are translations, as of Horace, Homer, and Vergil; *Osservazioni nella Volgar Lingua* (1550); *Commedie* (1560); *Tragedie* (1560), including *Marianna.*

**Dol'ci** (dōl'chē) *or* **Dol'ce** (-châ), **Carlo** *or* **Carlino.** 1616–1686. Florentine painter; known chiefly for small religious canvases and for portraits.

**Dole** (dōl), **Charles Fletcher.** 1845–1927. American Unitarian clergyman, b. Brewer, Me. Pastorate, Jamaica Plain, Mass. (1876–1916). Among his many books are *The Citizen and the Neighbor* (1884), *The Golden Rule in Business* (1895), *The Coming Religion* (1910), *A Religion for the New Day* (1920). His brother **Nathan Haskell** (1852–1935) was on editorial staff of Philadelphia *Press* (1881–87) and T. Y. Crowell & Co. (1887–1901); author of poems, essays, and biographical sketches, and translator and editor of works from Russian, Spanish, French, and Italian literature.

**Dole, Sanford Ballard.** 1844–1926. American lawyer and political leader in Hawaii, b. Honolulu. Adm. to bar, Massachusetts (1868); practiced, Honolulu; associate justice, Hawaii supreme court (1887–93). Head of revolutionary provisional government (1893); president, Republic of Hawaii (1894–98); first governor, Territory of Hawaii (1900–03); judge, U.S. district court for Hawaii (1904–15).

**Dolega-Kamieński.** Pen name of Lucian KAMIEŃSKI.

**Do'les** (dō'lĕs), **Johann Friedrich.** 1715–1797. German church composer; studied under Johann Sebastian Bach.

**Do'let'** (dô'lĕ'), **Étienne.** 1509–1546. French printer and philologist; a leading representative of early 16th-century intellectual renaissance in France. Convicted of heresy and executed at Paris (Aug. 3, 1546).

**Dol·go·ru'ki** (dŭl·gŭ·rōō'kû·ĭ; *Angl.* dŏl'gō·rōō'kĭ) *or* **Dol·go·ru'kov** (-kôf). *Fem.* **Dol·go·ru'ka·ya** (dŭl·gŭ·rōō'kŭ·yŭ) *or* **Dol·go·ru'ko·va** (dŭl·gŭ·rōō'kŭ·vŭ). Princely Russian family, including notably: **Vasili Lukich** (1670–1739), diplomat; became member of supreme privy council (c. 1727); vainly endeavored to control Empress Anna Ivanovna; executed at Novgorod (Nov. 8, 1739). **Vasili Mikhailovich** (1722–1782), surnamed **Krym'ski** (krĭm'skû·ĭ; *Angl.* -skĭ) because in 15 days he conquered the Crimea (1771). **Ivan Mikhailovich** (1764–1823), governor of Samara (1802–12) and poet. **Pëtr Vladimirovich** (1817–1868), genealogist and author, exiled because of his book *The Truth about Russia* (1860). **Ekaterina Mikhailovna** (1846–1922), 2d wife (1880) of Czar Alexander II and author of *Alexander II.: détails inédits sur sa vie intime et sa mort* (1882).

**d'O'lier** (dōl'yā), **Franklin.** 1877–1953. American insurance executive; officer in A.E.F., in France (1917–19); elected first national commander of American Legion (Nov. 12, 1919).

**Dol'lar** (dŏl'ẽr), **Robert.** 1844–1932. Shipping magnate, b. Falkirk, Scotland; to U.S. (1856), naturalized (1888). Settled in San Francisco, Calif.; founder and president, Dollar Steamship Co., Robert Dollar Co., Dollar Portland Lumber Co., Canadian Robert Dollar Co. Author of *Memoirs.*

**Doll'fuss** (dôl'fōōs), **Engelbert.** 1892–1934. Austrian statesman. Minister of agriculture and forestry (1931) and chancellor (1932), Austria. Came into conflict with Nazi interests because of plans to maintain Austrian independence; proclaimed dictatorship (Mar. 7, 1933) and, soon after, dissolved Bundesversammlung, abolished freedom of speech, press, and assemblage, and use of Nazi distinctive uniform. Shot and killed by Austrian Nazi rebels, who seized the chancellery (July 25, 1934).

**Dol'ling** (dŏl'ĭng), **Robert William Radclyffe.** 1851–1902. British social reformer, known as "Father Dolling"; b. in County Down; engaged in social work, Dublin (1870–78); head of mission in London (1883–85), of Winchester Coll. mission at Landport (1885–95). Author of *Ten Years in a Portsmouth Slum* (1896), recounting experiences at Landport.

**Döl'ling·er** (dûl'ĭng·ẽr), **Ignaz.** 1770–1841. German physician. His son **Johann Joseph Ignaz von Döllinger** (1799–1890), theologian, was a leader in Old Catholic movement; excommunicated from Roman Catholic Church (1871); author of *Kirche und Kirchen, Papsttum und Kirchenstaat* (1861), *Papstfabeln des Mittelalters* (1863), *Beiträge zur Politisch-Kirchlichen Kulturgeschichte der Letzten 6 Jahrhunderte* (3 vols., 1862–82), *Geschichte der Moralstreitigkeiten in der Römisch-Katholischen Kirche seit dem 16. Jahrhundert* (2 vols., 1889).

**Dol'lond** (dŏl'ŭnd), **John.** 1706–1761. English optician. Son of Huguenot refugee, a silk weaver, whose trade he followed while he studied classical languages, mathematics, science. Joined his eldest son, **Peter** (1730–1820), in making optical instruments (1752); read before Royal Society (1758) paper on refrangibility of light and how he discovered means of constructing achromatic lenses by combination of crown and flint glasses, improving telescopic lenses; invented modern heliometer (1754); his son Peter invented improved triple achromatic object glasses; and his nephew **George** (1774–1852) invented an improved altazimuth (1821) and an atmospheric recorder.

**Do'lo'mieu'** (dô'lô'myû'), **Déodat Guy Silvain Tancrède Gratet de.** 1750–1801. French geologist and mineralogist; visited Spain, Sicily, the Pyrenees, Calabria, and the Alps; described (1791) the mineral named after him "dolomite"; professor, École des Mines (1796). Scientist on Bonaparte's expedition to Egypt (1798); on return trip, was captured and imprisoned at Messina for 21 months; while in prison, made pen of wood and, using soot from lamp, wrote on the margins of his Bible *Traité de Philosophie Minéralogique* and *Memoire sur* *l'Espèce Minérale;* after release, professor of mineralogy, Museum of Natural History, Paris.

**Do'magk** (dō'mäk), **Gerhard.** 1895–1964. German chemist. Teacher at universities of Greifswald and Münster; director of I. G. Farbenindustrie research institute, Elberfeld (from 1927). Known for discovery of, and experimental work with, "prontosil," forerunner of sulphanilamide. Declined 1939 Nobel prize for physiology and medicine in accordance with instructions of German government.

**Do'mas y Val'le** (dō'mäs ē vä'lyā), **José.** 1717?–1803. Spanish naval commander; commanded *Asís* in campaign against British in West Indies (1779–80); active in capture of Pensacola (1781) and in siege of Gibraltar (1783); governor of Panama (1786–94); captain general of Guatemala (1794–1801).

**Do'ma·szew'ski** (dō'mä·shĕf'skē), **Alfred von.** 1856–1927. German historian of ancient Roman life and institutions.

**Do'mat'** (dô'mȧ') *or* **Dau'mat'** (dō'mȧ'), **Jean.** 1625–1696. French jurist; author of *Les Lois Civiles dans leur Ordre Naturel* (1689–94), etc.

**Dom'basle'** (dôɴ'bäl'), **Mathieu de,** *in full* **Christophe Joseph Alexandre Mathieu de.** 1777–1843. French agriculturist; invented a plow; founded school of agriculture near Nancy (1822).

**Dom·brow'ski** (dôɴm·brôf'skē) *or, more correctly,* **Dą·brow'ski** (dôɴm-), **Jan Henryk.** 1755–1818. Polish soldier; served against Russians (1792) and in defense of Warsaw (1794). Organized Polish legion to fight in service of France and commanded it in Italy (1798–1801). Served as general of Polish troops under Napoleon; engaged at Friedland (1807), against Austrians (1809), in Russian campaign (1812), and at battle of Leipzig (1813). To Poland (1813) and designated by czar to reorganize Polish army; appointed general of cavalry (1815) and senator palatine of kingdom of Poland.

**Do'me·ni·chi'no, Il** (ēl dō'mā·nē·kē'nō). *Real name* **Domenico Zam·pie'ri** (tsäm·pyâ'rē). 1581–1641. Bolognese painter; with Guido Reni, leader of Eclectic school after the Carracci; at Rome (1603–17), Bologna (1617–21); chief Vatican architect (1621–23); at Naples (1630–34, 1635–38). Works include *Communion of St. Jerome* (the Vatican), *Diana and Nymphs Hunting* (Borghese Palace, Rome), *Madonna of the Rosary* (Bologna gallery), *Life of St. Januarius* (Cappella del Tesoro in Naples Cathedral), landscapes, and portraits.

**Domenico.** See El GRECO.

**Domenico Fiorentino.** See Domenico del BARBIERE.

**Dom'ett** (dŏm'ĕt; -ĭt), **Alfred.** 1811–1887. English poet and colonial administrator, b. in Camberwell; intimate of Robert Browning; subject of Browning's poem *Waring.* Emigrated to New Zealand (1842), where he was prime minister (1862–63), registrar-general of land (1865–71). Author of *Ranolf and Amohia, a South Sea Day Dream* (1872), *Flotsam and Jetsam* (1877).

**Do·mey'ko** (dô·mĕ'ē·kō), **Ignacio.** *Pol.* **Ignacy Do·mey'ko** (dô·mĕ'ĭ·kô). 1802–1889. Polish mineralogist in Chile; founded school of chemistry and mineralogy at Coquimbo; professor (1839 ff.) and rector (1867 ff.), U. of Santiago; responsible for speeding development of Chilean resources.

**Dom'i·nic** (dŏm'ĭ·nĭk), Saint. 1170–1221. Spanish-born Roman Catholic priest; founder of Dominican order (confirmed by pope, 1216). Canon of cathedral at Osma (1195). In Languedoc (1205), where he attacked the Albigenses and first organized Dominican order (1215), whose official name was Fratres Praedicatores, or Preaching Friars.

**Do'mi·nis** (dô'mē·nēs), **Marco Antonio de.** 1566–1624. Italian ecclesiastic; archbishop of Spalato (1600) and primate of Dalmatia and Croatia. Involved in quarrel between papacy and Venice, crossed to England (1616); became convert to Anglicanism and dean of Windsor (1619); attacked the papacy in *De Republica Ecclesiasticâ* (1617). Recanted in his *Consilium Reditus* (1623); imprisoned by the Inquisition.

**Do·mi'tian** (dô·mĭsh'ăn; -ĭ·ăn). *Full name* **Titus Flavius Do·mi'ti·a'nus Au·gus'tus** (dô·mĭsh'ĭ·ā'nŭs ô·gŭs'tŭs). 51–96 A.D. Third of the Flavian emperors of Rome (81–96). Second son of Vespasian and Flavia Domitila, and brother of Titus. Triumphed over the Chatti (83) but unsuccessful in campaign against the Dacians under Decebalus (86–90); aroused by jealousy, recalled (84) Agricola from his victories in Britain (78–84); murdered by a freedman, as the result of a conspiracy by the empress Domitia and officers of the court.

**Domitius Ahenobarbus** *or* **Enobarbus.** See AHENOBARBUS.

**Domnus.** See DONUS.

**Don'ald** (dŏn'ʼld), **William Henry.** 1875–1946. Australian journalist and economist in China; on Hong Kong paper for several years (after 1904); joined Chinese Revolution as adviser to Sun Yat-sen (1911); later, adviser to several governments in China; first revealed Japan's Twenty-one Demands (1915); helped defeat monarchical designs of Yüan Shih-k'ai (1916). Editor of *Far Eastern Review;* adviser (1928–33) to Marshal Chang Hsueh-liang in Manchuria; adviser to Chiang Kai-shek (1934 ff.); exerted great influence on events at time of Chiang's capture (1936).

**Don'ald·son** (dŏn'ʼld·s'n), Sir **James.** 1831–1915. Scottish classical and patristic scholar.

**Donaldson, John William.** 1811–1861. English philologist and Biblical critic. Attempted in the *New Cratylus* (1839) to apply to Greek scientific principles of comparative philology introduced from Germany; in *Varronianus* (1844) undertook application of same method to Latin, Umbrian, and Oscan.

**Don'a·li'ti·us** (dŏn'ȧ·lĭsh'ĭ·ŭs), **Chris'tian** (krĭs'chăn; krĭst'yăn). *Lith.* **Kristijonas Do'ne·lai'tis** (dô'nă·lī'tĭs) *or* **Duo'ne·lai'tis** (dwô'-). 1714–1780. Lithuanian poet.

**Don'a·tel'lo** (dŏn'ȧ·tĕl'ō; *Ital.* dō'nä·tĕl'lô). *Real name* **Donato di Nic'co·lò' di Bet'to Bar'di** (dē nēk'kô·lô' dē bāt'tô bär'dē). 1386?–1466. Italian sculptor, b. Florence; leading sculptor of early Renaissance; considered founder of modern sculpture. Broke with classicism, substituting realism, stressing dramatic action and character delineation; associate of Ghiberti, Brunelleschi, and Michelozzo. To Rome (c. 1403 and again, 1433); to Padua (1443–53), Florence (1457 ff.). His works in Florence include *St. George, John the Evangelist, David, Poggio, Zuccone, Habakuk, St. Louis, Magdalen,* and *Judith and Holofernes* (Loggia dei Lanzi); other sculptures by him are in Padua, Naples, and Siena.

**Do·na'ti** (dô·nä'tē), **Corso.** ?–1308. Florentine political leader; member of Guelph party; became popular through victory at Campaldino over Arezzo (1289); formed Neri faction against bourgeois Bianchi; exiled (1300); repatriated (1301) by Charles of Valois; dictator of Florence (1301–08).

**Do·na'ti** (dô·nä'tē), **Giovanni Battista.** 1826–1873. Italian astronomer, b. at Pisa. Director of Florence observatory (1864); discovered six comets, one of which is named after him; by spectroscopic means, discovered the gaseous composition of comets.

**Donato d'Agnolo** *or* **d'Angelo.** See BRAMANTE.

**Do·na'tus** (dô·nā'tŭs). Bishop of Casae Nigrae, in

North Africa, in early 4th century; fanatically courted martyrdom during Diocletian persecutions and opposed policy of traditor ecclesiastics who chose to surrender their sacred books in order to escape persecution. His stand (c. 311 A.D.) really started the Donatist schism in North Africa, though the rigoristic party was named from Donatus the Great (*q.v.*).

**Donatus.** *Known as* **the Great.** Bishop of Carthage (315 A.D.); elected by the rigoristic party among Christians of North Africa. This party (Donatists) had gone into a schism (311) as a protest against the consecration of Caecilian, Primate of Carthage, by Felix, a traditor bishop. The Donatists held that the validity of the sacraments depends on the spiritual state of the minister, that sanctity is essential for church membership, and that those who joined their sect should be rebaptized. The schism continued for over a century.

**Donatus, Aelius.** Roman grammarian of middle 4th century A.D.; author of an *Ars Grammatica* so widely used as an elementary textbook in western Europe in the Middle Ages that the term *Do'nat* (dō'năt) or *Do'net* (dō'nĕt) came to be synonymous with grammar or with any textbook treating elementary principles of a subject.

**Don'ders** (dôn'dẽrs), **Frans Cornelis.** 1818–1889. Dutch ophthalmologist and physiologist; investigated physiology and pathology of the eye; introduced use of prismatic and cylindrical lenses for eyeglasses.

**Do'neau'** (dô'nō'), **Hugues.** *Lat.* **Do·nel'lus** (dō̇-nĕl'ŭs). 1527–1591. French jurist; author of *Commentarii de Jure Civili* (pub. in 16 vols., 1801–34).

**Donelaitis, Kristijonas.** See Christian DONALITIUS.

**Don'el·son** (dŏn''l·s'n), **Andrew Jackson.** 1799–1871. American army officer and diplomat, b. near Nashville, Tenn.; reared by Andrew Jackson at "The Hermitage." Aide-de-camp to Jackson in Seminole War. Adm. to bar (1823); practiced, Nashville. Secretary to Jackson (1829–37). Negotiated treaty of annexation with Republic of Texas (1844–45); U.S. minister to Prussia (1846–49). Unsuccessful candidate for vice-presidency of the United States (1856).

**Don'gan** (dŏng'găn), **Thomas.** Earl of **Lim'er·ick** (lĭm'ẽr·ĭk). 1634–1715. Colonial administrator in America, b. in County Kildare, Ireland. Governor of New York (1682–88).

**Don'ham** (dŏn'ăm), **Wallace Brett.** 1877–1954. American educator; dean, graduate school of business administration, Harvard (1919–42).

**Do'ni** (dō'nē̇), **Anton Francesco.** 1513?–1574. Italian miscellaneous writer; led wandering life as author and editor; founder of Italian bibliography.

**Doni, Giovanni Battista.** 1593–1647. Italian scholar; protégé of Cardinal Barberini (1622 ff.). Known particularly for researches on ancient music; invented type of double lyre called, after his patron, Lyra Barberina.

**Do'niol'** (dô'nyôl'), **Jean Henri Antoine.** 1818–1906. French administrator and author of *Histoire de la Participation de la France à l'Établissement des États-Unis d'Amérique* (5 vols., 1886–90), etc.

**Don'i·zet'ti** (dŏn'ĭ·zĕt'ĭ; *Ital.* dō'nē̇·dzāt'tē̇), **Gaetano.** 1797–1848. Italian operatic composer; after death of Bellini, was leading dramatic composer of Italy; settled at Paris (1835). His works include *L'Elisir d'Amore* (1832), *Lucrezia Borgia* (1833), *Lucia di Lammermoor* (1835), *La Fille du Régiment* (1840), *Linda di Chamounix* (1842), *Don Pasquale* (comic opera; 1843).

**Don'kin** (dŏng'kĭn), **Bryan.** 1768–1855. English civil engineer and inventor. Developed practical working machines for making paper (from 1804); had part in developing Fourdrinier machine; invented an early high-speed printing machine (1813) and composition printing roller; devised (1812) method of preserving meat and vegetables in tin.

**Don'nan** (dŏn'ăn), **Frederick George.** 1870–1956. British chemist, b. at Colombo, Ceylon; professor of chemistry (1913–37) and director of chemical laboratories (1928–37), University Coll., London.

**Don'nay'** (dô'nā'), **Charles Maurice.** 1859–1945. French playwright; author of *Lysistrata* (1893), *Amants* (1896), *L'Affranchie* (1898), *La Clairière* (1900), *Oiseaux de Passage* (1904), *La Chasse à l'Homme* (1919), etc.

**Donn'-Byrne'** (dŏn'bûrn'), **Brian Oswald.** *Known as* **Donn Byrne.** 1889–1928. Novelist and short-story writer, b. New York; author of *Messer Marco Polo* (1921), *Blind Raftery* (1924), *Hangman's House* (1926).

**Donn'dorf** (dôn'dôrf), **Adolf von.** 1835–1916. German sculptor.

**Donne** (dŭn; dŏn), **John.** 1573–1631. English poet, chief of the metaphysical poets; b. London, son of wealthy ironmonger. Brought up as Roman Catholic; studied law; joined Anglican Church. Sailed in Essex's expedition to Cádiz (1596); dismissed from private secretaryship to Sir Thomas Egerton, keeper of great seal, because of clandestine marriage with his patron's niece. Published extravagant elegy on daughter of his host Sir Robert Drury, *An Anatomy of the World* (1611); contended in *Biathanatos* (pub. 1644) that suicide was not essentially sinful. Having won approval of James I with *Pseudo-Martyr* (1610), assuring Roman Catholics of freedom from inconsistency in taking oath of allegiance to James I, followed king's suggestion that he take holy orders (1614); preached sermons unexcelled in 17th century; executed mission to Bohemia and preached before Princess Elizabeth at Heidelberg (1619); dean of St. Paul's (1621–31); preached often before Charles I. Among his poetical works are *Of the Progress of the Soul* (begun 1601; pub. 1633; a satire setting up a hypothetical metempsychosis of the soul), *Divine Poems* (1607), *Epithalamium* (1613; on marriage of count palatine and Princess Elizabeth), *Cycle of Holy Sonnets* (1618). Biographized by Izaak Walton; works edited by an eccentric son, **John** (1604–1662).

**Don'nel·ly** (dŏn''l·ĭ), **Ignatius.** 1831–1901. American politician and author, b. Philadelphia. Moved to Minnesota (1857). Member, U.S. House of Representatives (1863–69). Editor, *Anti-Monopolist* (1874–79), an independent weekly journal. Author of *Atlantis, the Antediluvian World* (1882), *Ragnarok, The Age of Fire and Gravel* (1883), *The Great Cryptogram* (1888; a book intended to prove by a cipher that Francis Bacon was writer of plays attributed to Shakespeare), *Caesar's Column* (1891).

**Don'ner** (dôn'ẽr), **Georg Raphael.** 1693–1741. Austrian sculptor; studio in Salzburg (1725–28), Pressburg (1728–38), and Vienna (1738–41).

**Dön'ni·ges** (dûn'ĭ·gĕs), **Wilhelm von.** 1814–1872. German diplomat and historian. His daughter **Helene** (1845–1911) was wife successively of the Rumanian boyar Racowiţa, the actor Siegwart Friedmann, and the writer Serge von Schewitsch; known esp. for her affair with Ferdinand Lassalle, who picked quarrel with Racowiţa and was killed in resulting duel (1864); author of *Meine Beziehungen zu Ferdinand Lassalle* (1879) and *Von Andern und Mir* (1909).

**Dono, Paolo di.** See Paolo UCCELLO.

**Do·no'so** (dō̇·nō'sō), **Justo.** 1800–1868. Chilean prelate, writer, and jurist; judge of ecclesiastical court; one of founders of *Revista Católica;* bishop of Ancud (1844–55), Serena (1855–68). His works include *Instituciones de Derecho Canónico Americano* (1849, 1863; a standard authority), etc.

**Do·no'so–Cor·tés'** (-kôr·tās'), **Juan Francisco María de la Sa·lud'** (sä·lōōth'). Marqués **de Val'de·ga'mas** (väl'dā·gä'mäs). 1809–1853. Spanish orator, writer, statesman, and diplomat; supported Isabella against Don Carlos (1833); defended interests of Maria Christina; ambassador to Berlin (1848), Paris.

**Don'o·van** (dŏn'ō·văn), **William Joseph**. *Nicknamed* "Wild Bill Donovan." 1883–1959. American lawyer, b. Buffalo; served in World War I (Congressional Medal of Honor); asst. to U.S. attorney general (1925–29); U.S. co-ordinator of information (1941–42); World War II head of office of strategic services (1942–45).

**Dont** (dônt), **Jakob**. 1815–1888. Austrian violin virtuoso; author of *Gradus ad Parnassum.*

**Do'nus** (dō'nŭs) *or* **Dom'nus** (dŏm'nŭs). d. 678. Pope (676–678).

**Dooley,** Mr. See Finley Peter DUNNE.

**Doo'lit'tle** (dōō'lĭt''l), **Charles Leander.** 1843–1919. American astronomer; professor, Lehigh U. (1875–95), U. of Pennsylvania (1895–1912). His son **Eric** (1869–1920), authority on double stars, taught astronomy in U. of Pennsylvania (from 1896).

**Doolittle, Hilda.** *Pen name* **H. D.** 1886–1961. Imagist poet, b. Bethlehem, Pa.; educ. Bryn Mawr; m. (1913) English poet and novelist Richard Aldington (*q.v.*). Author of *Oread, Pear Tree, Heat, Lethe, Heliodora and other Poems* (1924), *Palimpsest* (1926), *Hippolytus Temporizes* (play; 1927), *Hedylus* (1928), *Red Roses for Bronze* (1931), *Hedgehog* (1937).

**Doolittle, James Harold.** 1896– . American aviator and army officer, b. Alameda, Calif.; flight and gunnery instructor during World War I (1917–18); stunt flyer (1918); commissioned in air service, U.S. army (1920); made cross-country flight, from Paola Beach, Fla., to San Diego, Calif., in 21 hrs., 19 min. (1922). Engaged in aviation research and testing (1924 ff.); resigned from U.S. army (1930); won Bendix trophy for coast-to-coast flight (1931); set world's speed record for land planes (1932). Recalled to army duty (1940); led bombing raid over Tokyo (1942); in command of U.S. air forces in North African invasion (1942), of 8th Air Force, Europe (1944).

**Dopp'ler** (dŏp'lĕr), **Christian Johann.** 1803–1853. Austrian physicist and mathematician; published paper *Über das Farbige Licht der Doppelsterne* (1842) in which he enunciated the principle (now known as *Doppler's principle*) that, if the distance is changing between an observer and a source of constant vibrations, as of sound or light, the wave number appears to be greater or less than the true value according as the distance is being diminished or lengthened. The application of this principle to the light coming from a star was explained by Fizeau (1848), and the term *Doppler shift* is applied to the phenomenon of the shifting of the lines in the spectrum of a luminous body towards violet as the distance decreases and towards red as the distance increases.

**Do'ra** (dō'rȧ), Sister. See under Mark PATTISON.

**Do'ra d'I'stri·a** (*Ital.* dô'rä dēs'trē·ä). *Pseudonym of* Princess **He'lene' Ghi'ca** (ā'lĕn' gē'kä). 1828–1888. Rumanian writer, b. Bucharest; author of *La Vie Monastique dans l'Église Orientale* (1855), *Les Femmes en Orient* (2 vols., 1859–60), *Des Femmes par une Femme* (2 vols., 1864), etc.

**Do'ran** (dō'răn), **George H.** 1869–1956. Publisher, b. in Canada; established George H. Doran Co. (in Toronto, 1907; moved to N.Y. 1908); joined with F. N. Doubleday to form Doubleday, Doran & Co. (1927).

**Doran, John.** 1807–1878. British journalist and historian of the stage, of Irish parentage. Editor of *Notes and Queries* (1870–78). Author of *Their Majesties' Servants* (1860), *In and About Drury Lane* (1885; an account of English stage from Betterton to Kean), and an account of Mrs. Elizabeth Montagu and the bluestockings in *A Lady of the Last Century* (1873).

**Do'rat'** (dô'rȧ'), **Claude Joseph.** 1734–1780. French poet and writer of romances and plays.

**Dorat** *or* **Dau'rat'** (dō'rȧ'), **Jean.** 1508–1588. French poet; member of the Pleiad; director, Collège de Coqueret where Ronsard was his pupil; professor of Greek, Collège de France (1560); appointed poet royal by Charles IX.

**Dor'cas** (dôr'kăs) *or* **Tab'i·tha** (tăb'ĭ·thȧ). In Bible (*Acts* ix. 36–42), Christian woman of Joppa known for "good works," including making garments for the poor; hence name "Dorcas societies" applied to church sewing circles.

**Dorchester,** 1st Baron. See Sir Guy CARLETON.

**Dorchester,** Marquises of. See PIERREPONT family.

**Do'ré'** (dô'rā'), **Paul Gustave.** 1833–1883. French illustrator and painter; among books illustrated by him are *Œuvres de Rabelais, Légende du Juif Errant, Contes Drolatiques de Balzac, Divina Commedia de Dante, Don Quichotte, Fables de La Fontaine;* among his paintings are *Paolo et Francesca da Rimini, Dante dans les Cercles Glacés, Le Néophyte.*

**Do·re'mus** (dô·rē'mŭs), **Sarah Platt,** *nee* **Haines** (hānz). 1802–1877. American philanthropist, b. New York City; m. Thomas C. Doremus (1821). Instrumental in founding New York Woman's Hospital, Woman's Union Missionary Society, and shelters and homes for unfortunates. Her son **Robert Ogden** (1824–1906) was professor of chemistry at the College of the City of New York (1852–1903) and at Bellevue Hospital (from 1862).

**Do'rer** (dō'rĕr), **Ro'bert** (rō'bĕrt). 1830–1893. Swiss sculptor.

**Dor'gan** (dôr'găn), **Thomas Aloysius.** *Pseudonym* **Tad** (tăd). 1877–1929. American cartoonist and sports commentator, b. San Francisco. On San Francisco *Bulletin* (1892–1902) and New York *Journal* (from 1902).

**Dor'ge·lès'** (dôr'zhĕ·lĕs'), **Roland.** *Orig. name* **Roland Lé'ca've·lé** (lā'kȧv'lā'). 1886–1973. French novelist, author of *Les Croix de Bois* (1918).

**Do'ria** (dô'ryä), **Andrea.** 1468?–1560. Genoese admiral and statesman; called "Father of Peace" and "Liberator of Genoa." Captain general of galleys (c. 1513 ff.); as high admiral of the Levant, commanded French fleet against Charles V (1524–28); transferred allegiance from Francis I to Charles V (1528); took Genoa and set up new form of government (1528); victorious over Turks at Patras (1532); achieved conquest of Tunis (1535); in service of Charles V against Algiers (1541); granted principality of Melfi by Charles V. See Giovanni FIESCO.

**Do'ri'gny'** (dô'rē'nyē'), **Michel.** 1617–1666. French painter and engraver. His son Sir **Nicholas** (1658–1746) spent 28 years in Italy engraving pictures and Raphael's tapestries in Vatican; to England (1711–19) to engrave Raphael's cartoons at Hampton Court.

**Do'rion'** (dô'ryôɴ'), Sir **Antoine Aimé.** 1818–1891. Canadian judge; leader of French-Canadian liberals in assembly (1863–64); minister of justice (1873); chief justice of court of Queen's Bench, Quebec (1874–91).

**Dor'is·laus** (dŏr'ĭs·lôs), **Isaac.** 1595–1649. Anglo-Dutch diplomatist, b. in Alkmaar; lecturer on history, Cambridge, England (1627); defended Dutch revolt against Spain; acting judge advocate, Bishops' War (1640), army of Essex (1642); a judge of admiralty court (1648).

**Dör'mann** (dûr'män), **Felix.** *Real name* **Felix Bie'der·mann** (bē'dĕr·män). 1876–1928. Austrian writer of verse, dramas, short stories, and operetta librettos.

**Dorn** (dôrn), **Bernhard,** *in full* **Johann Albrecht Bernhard.** 1805–1881. German Oriental scholar.

**Dorn, Heinrich.** 1804–1892. German composer of 8 operas, an operetta, a ballet, piano pieces, and songs. Best-known opera is *Die Nibelungen* (1854).

**Dor'ner** (dôr'nẽr), **Isaak August.** 1809–1884. German Protestant theologian. His son **August** (1846–1920), also a theologian. August's son **Hermann** (1882–1963), airplane designer and manufacturer.

**Dor·nier'** (dôr·nyā'), **Claude** (klōd). 1884–1969. German airplane builder; entered service of Count Zeppelin (1910); began construction of all-metal airplanes (1914); owner of aircraft manufacturing company at Friedrichshafen. Builder of "DO-X," largest passenger airplane of its time (1929); later, of fast bombers, reconnaissance flying boats, and torpedo-carrying airplanes.

**Do·roth'e·us** (dō·rŏth'ē·ŭs). Jurist of 6th century A.D., in Syria; commissioned, with Tribonian and Theophilus, by Emperor Justinian to draw up a book of institutes as an introduction to the *Digest*, an integral part of the Corpus Juris Civilis.

**Dörp'feld** (dûrp'fĕlt), **Friedrich Wilhelm.** 1824–1893. German educator; opposed influence of church over schools. His son **Wilhelm** (1853–1940), archaeologist and architect, engaged in excavations in various regions of ancient Greek world.

**Dorr** (dôr), **John Van Nos'trand** (văn nōs'trănd). 1872–1962. American metallurgical engineer, b. Newark, N.J. Inventor of Dorr classifier, Dorr thickener, and Dorr agitator, used in ore dressing.

**Dorr, Julia Caroline,** *nee* **Rip'ley** (rĭp'lĭ). 1825–1913. American writer, b. Charleston, S.C. Best known for her poems, of which some ten volumes were published between 1872 and 1913.

**Dorr, Thomas Wilson.** 1805–1854. American lawyer and politician, leader of "Dorr's Rebellion," b. Providence, R.I. Agitator for widening the suffrage in Rhode Island (from 1834); organizer and leader of People's party, which submitted (1840) a new liberal constitution that was almost unanimously approved by electorate. Action declared illegal by state authorities, who submitted (1842) a constitution of their own that failed to gain popular approval. People's party elected an entire state ticket, with Dorr as governor, thus giving Rhode Island two governments. Little violence occurred; Dorr was arrested, tried, convicted, and sentenced (1844) to life imprisonment and hard labor but released a year later under an act of general amnesty. State authorities drew up new liberal constitution which was accepted by people.

**Dor're·ga·ray' y Ro'min·gue'ra** (dôr'rā·gä·rä'ē ē rō'mēng·gā'rä), **Antonio.** 1820–1882. Spanish Carlist general; active in Carlist campaigns (1836–39, 1872–76) and in Morocco (1859).

**Dor·re'go** (dôr·rā'gō), **Manuel.** 1787–1828. Argentine statesman, b. Buenos Aires. On outbreak of separatist movements, saw military service in Chile, Bolivia, Uruguay, and Argentina; exiled to U.S.; on return (1820) acted as provisional governor of Buenos Aires; prominent in constituent assembly (1826); elected governor of Buenos Aires (1827); terminated war with Brazil (1828); as provisional president attempted to put down a revolt; captured and put to death by rebel leaders.

**Dorrien,** Sir **Horace Lockwood Smith–.** See SMITH-DORRIEN.

**d'Orsay.** See ORSAY.

**Dor'set** (dôr'sĕt; -sĭt), Countess of. See *Anne Clifford*, under CLIFFORD family.

**Dorset.** (1) Earls of: see BEAUFORT and SACKVILLE families, also Thomas SACKVILLE. (2) Dukes of: see SACKVILLE family. (3) Marquises of: see BEAUFORT and GREY families.

**Dorset, Marion.** 1872–1935. American chemist; known for his work on the chemistry and biology of the tubercle bacillus and on the chemistry and bacteriology of meats; codiscoverer of hog-cholera serum.

**Dor'sey** (dôr'sĭ), **George Amos.** 1868–1931. American anthropologist, b. Hebron, Ohio. Curator of anthropology, Field Museum of Natural History, Chicago (1898–1915); lecturer, New School for Social Research, New York (from 1925). Author of *Why We Behave Like Human Beings* (1925), *The Nature of Man* (1927), *Hows and Whys of Human Behavior* (1929), etc. His brother **Herbert Grove** (1876– ), physicist, on staff of U.S. Coast and Geodetic Survey (from 1926); inventor of various acoustic devices, including the Dorsey Phonelescope, a dynamic loudspeaker, a Fathometer.

**Dorsey, James Owen.** 1848–1895. American anthropologist and philologist, b. Baltimore. Deacon, Protestant Episcopal Church (1871); missionary among Pawnee Indians, Dakota Territory (1871–80). Sent by U.S. Bureau of American Ethnology to study Omaha Indians (1880). Author of *Of the Comparative Phonology of Four Siouan Languages* (1883), *The Cegiha Language* (1890), and *A Dictionary of the Biloxi and Ofo Languages* (with John Reed Swanton; pub. 1912).

**Do·sith'e·us** (dō·sĭth'ē·ŭs). 1st-century Jewish heretic, whose followers, known as Dositheans, believed him to be the Messiah.

**Dositheus.** Patriarch of Jerusalem (1669–1707); called synod at Jerusalem (1672) which adopted so-called Confession of Dositheus, directed against Calvinism, last official statement of doctrine issued by the Orthodox Church.

**Dositheus Ma·gis'ter** (mȧ·jĭs'tẽr). Greek grammarian of 4th century A.D., teacher in Rome; published Greek translation of Latin grammar, for use as textbook.

**Dos Pas'sos** (dŭs păs'ŭs), **John Rod·er·i'go** (rŏd·rē'gō). 1896–1970. American writer, b. Chicago. A.B., Harvard (1916). Among his many books are *A Pushcart at the Curb* (verse, 1922), *Manhattan Transfer* (1925), *The Garbage Man* (play, 1926), *Airways, Inc.* (play, 1929), *The 42d Parallel* (1930), *Nineteen Nineteen* (1931), *The Big Money* (1936), *Adventures of a Young Man* (1939), *The Ground We Stand On* (1941), *Number One* (1943).

**Dos'so Dos'si** (dôs'sō dôs'sē). *Real name* **Giovanni di Lu·te'ro** (lōō·tā'rō). 1479?–1542. Italian painter of Ferrarese school; in service of dukes of Ferrara. Works include frescoes (with his brother Battista) in Castello del Buon Conciglio at Trent and in Villa Imperiale at Pesaro, and canvases, as *Madonna with Saints Michael and George*, *St. Sebastian*, and *Apollo and Daphne* (Borghese Gallery). His brother **Battista Dossi,** *real name* **di Lutero** (d. 1548?), collaborated with him on chief artistic commissions.

**Dost Mo·ham'med Khan** (dōst mō·hŭm'mĕd kän). 1793–1863. Ruler of Afghanistan (1826–63); founder of dynasty ruling to 1929. As khan of Kabul, secured control of Afghanistan (1826); assumed title of amir (1835); failed to win friendship of Anglo-Indian government; opposed attempt of Shah Shuja, backed by British, to gain throne—cause of first Afghan War (1838–42); held prisoner (1839) but allowed to return (1842); assisted Sikhs in their war (1845) against British; concluded treaty with India (1855); remained neutral during the Sepoy Mutiny (1857); acquired province of Herat (1863). See AKBAR KHAN and SHERE ALI.

**Do·sto·ev'ski** (dŭ·stŭ·yăf'skû·ĭ; *Angl.* dŏs'tŭ·yĕv'skĭ), **Fëdor Mikhailovich.** 1821–1881. Russian novelist, b. Moscow. In army (1841–44); resigned to take up writing. Arrested (April 23, 1849) and tried for conspiracy against the government; convicted and sentenced to be shot; reprieved at last moment and sent to prison settlement at Omsk, Siberia (1849–54). Resumed literary work (1856); founded a review *The Times* (suppressed by government, 1863), and its successor (failed, c. 1865). Spent some years abroad to escape financial troubles; returned to Russia (1871) and again founded a review, *An Author's Diary* (1876 ff.), which proved successful. His novels include *Poor Folk* (1846), *Netochka Nezvanova* (1849), *The House of Death* (1861), *Letters from the Underworld* (1864), *Crime and Punishment* (1866), *The Idiot* (1868–69), *The Demons* (or *The Possessed;* 1871), *The Brothers Karamazov* (1880).

**Dot'zau'er** (dô'tsou'ẽr), **Justus Johann Friedrich.** 1783–1860. German violoncello virtuoso.

**Dou** *or* **Dow** *or* **Douw** (dou), **Gerard.** 1613–1675. Dutch painter; studied under Rembrandt; painted portraits of Rembrandt's father and mother; best known for genre scenes.

**Dou·ay'** (dwā), **Charles Abel.** 1809–1870. French general; distinguished himself at Malakoff (1855) and at Solferino (1859); killed at battle of Wissembourg (Aug. 4, 1870). His brother **Félix Charles** (1816–1879), also a general (from 1863), distinguished himself at Sedan (1870) and in commanding troops entering Paris during Commune of Paris (May 21, 1871).

**Dou'ble·day** (dŭb''l·dā), **Abner.** 1819–1893. American army officer, b. Ballston Spa, N.Y. He is credited with the creation and naming, while attending school in Cooperstown, N.Y., of the modern game of baseball, the adoption of the diamond-shaped field and the assignment of definite playing positions being ascribed to him. Grad. U.S.M.A., West Point (1842). Served through Mexican War, on routine duty, and through Civil War; retired (1873). Author of *Reminiscences of Forts Sumter and Moultrie in 1860–61* (1876), *Chancellorsville and Gettysburg* (1882).

**Doubleday, Frank Nelson.** 1862–1934. American publisher, b. Brooklyn, N.Y. With Charles Scribner's Sons (1877–1895); member of firm of Doubleday & McClure Co. (1897–1900); president, Doubleday, Page & Co. (1900–27); chairman of board, Doubleday, Doran & Co. (1927–34); m. (1886) **Nelt'je de Graff'** [nĕlt'yĕ dĕ grȧf'] (1865–1918), b. Chicago, who wrote under pseudonym **Neltje Blan'chan** (blăn'chăn) many books on nature subjects, including *Bird Neighbors* (1896), *Nature's Garden* (1900), *Birds Worth Knowing* (1917).

**Douce** (dous), **Francis.** 1757–1834. English antiquary. Author of *Illustrations of Shakespeare* (1807), *The Dance of Death* (1833).

**Dou'cet'** (do͞o'sĕ'), **Charles Camille.** 1812–1895. French playwright; author of *Un Jeune Homme* (1841), *Les Ennemis de la Maison* (1851), *Le Fruit Défendu* (1858), *La Considération* (1860), etc.

**Doucet, Henry Lucien.** 1856–1896. French portrait painter.

**Doud'ney** (dŭd'nĭ), **Sarah.** 1843–?1926. English author of verse, including *Psalms of Life* (1871) and *Drifting Leaves* (1889), and many novels.

**Douf'fet'** (do͞o'fĕ'), **Gerard.** 1594–1660. Dutch painter; studied under Rubens.

**Dou'gher·ty** (dô'hẽr·tĭ), **Denis J.** 1865–1951. American Roman Catholic prelate, b. Girardville, Pa.; archbishop of Philadelphia (1918); cardinal (1921).

**Dough'er·ty** (dŏκ'ẽr·tĭ), **Paul.** 1877–1947. American painter, b. Brooklyn, N.Y. Brother of Walter Hampden (*q.v.*).

**Dough'ton** (dou't'n), **Robert Lee.** 1863–1954. American politician; representative from North Carolina (1911–1953) and chairman of the committee on ways and means (from 1933), U.S. House of Representatives.

**Dough'ty** (dou'tĭ), **Charles Montagu.** 1843–1926. English poet and traveler, b. in Suffolk. Conceived idea of purifying English style by reviving the English of Chaucer, Spenser, and the Elizabethan age; devoted himself to linguistic and antiquarian study. His wide travels included journey through Arabia disguised as an Arab (1876–78), on which he learned many new facts about Arab life and customs and about the geography and geology of northwestern Arabia. Author of *Travels in Arabia Deserta* (1888), now recognized as masterpiece of graphic narration and description, and of a number of long poems and poetic dramas, including *The Dawn in Britain* (6 vols., 1906–07), *Adam Cast Forth* (1908), *The Cliffs* (1909), *The Clouds* (1912), *The Titans* (1916), *Mansoul* (1920).

**Doughty, Thomas.** 1793–1856. American landscape painter, b. Philadelphia. Member of Hudson River school.

**Dough'ty–Wy'lie** (-wī'lĭ), **Charles Hotham Montagu.** 1868–1915. English soldier and consul. Nephew of Charles Montagu Doughty. Saw active service in India, Egyptian campaign (1898), Boer War, and China (1901); killed leading charge at Gallipoli.

**Doug'las** (dŭg'lȧs). Name of a powerful Scottish family having its home in the dale of Douglas in Lanarkshire, represented by the earls of Douglas (created 1358), of Angus (cr. 1389), of Morton (cr. 1458), marquises of Douglas (cr. 1633), dukes of Hamilton (cr. 1660), of Queensberry (cr. 1684), and many lesser dignities. Members of the family include the following:

**William** of Douglas or Dufglas, whose name appears on charters (1175–1213), said to have been of same stock as the house of Murray; Sir **Archibald** *or* **Erkenbald** (d. 1240?), his eldest son, who succeeded him, and **Bricie** *or* **Brice** (d. 1222), his second son, who was bishop of Moray.

Sir **William** of Douglas, called "the Hardy" (d. 1298), 1st Lord of Douglas; grandson of Sir Archibald; swore fealty to Edward I (1291), but commanded Baliol forces at Berwick Castle; surrendered to English (1296); on renewal of homage to Edward I, restored to possessions in seven Scottish counties; joined Wallace's rising (1297).

Sir **James Douglas,** called "the Good" (1286–?1330), Lord of Douglas, son of 1st lord; educ. Paris; escaped with Bruce from battle of Methven; three times destroyed English garrisons in his castle of Douglas; by raids into England earned dreaded name of "the Black Douglas"; took Teviotdale; commanded left wing at Bannockburn (1314); invaded Yorkshire; defeated army of archbishop of York and bishop of Ely at Mitton (1319); surprised English at Weardale (1327), nearly capturing Edward III; during peace that followed, carrying embalmed heart of Bruce to Holy Land according to dying king's wish, fell fighting Moors in Andalusia. His son **William** was killed at Halidon Hill (1333), as was his half brother, the youngest son of Sir William the Hardy, Sir **Archibald** (1296?–1333), who conquered Edward de Baliol (1332) and was regent (1333).

Sir **William Douglas** (1300?–1353), Knight of **Liddes'dale** (lĭdz'dāl); probably great-grandson of Sir Archibald (d. 1240?); sided with David II, killing Edward de Baliol's lieutenant in Scotland (1337); ambassador to France; killed on hunting trip by his kinsman William, later 1st earl of Douglas.

EARLS OF DOUGLAS (distinguished as the Black Douglases):

**William Douglas** (1327?–1384), 1st Earl of Douglas

(cr. 1358) and, by marriage, Earl of **Mar** (mär); son of Sir Archibald (1296?–1333); returned from training in France (1348) and recovered Ettrick Forest to Scottish allegiance; present at battle of Poitiers (1356); warden of east marches; rebelled against David II (1363) in consequence of royal misappropriation of funds raised for ransom; reconciled, swore allegiance to Robert II (1371); justiciar of southern Scotland (from 1371).

His son **James** (1358?–1388), 2d Earl of Douglas and Mar; m. (1373) Isabel, daughter of Robert II; made war on English with aid of French under Jean de Vienne (1385); defeated two sons of earl of Northumberland in battle of Otterburn, in which he was killed and Hotspur captured (celebrated in Scottish ballad *The Battle of Otterburn* and English ballad *Chevy Chase*).

**Archibald** (1328?–?1400), 3d Earl of Douglas, Lord of **Gal′lo·way** (găl′ō·wā); natural son of Sir James Douglas the Good; called "the Grim"; nicknamed (like his father) "the Black Douglas"; warden of western marches (1364, 1368); twice sent on missions to French court (1369, 1371); invaded England (1389); codified laws of marches; married his daughter Marjory to heir apparent of Scottish crown.

**Archibald** (1372–1424), 4th Earl of Douglas and 1st Duke of **Tou′raine′** [tōō′rān′; *Fr.* -rân′] (cr. 1423), called **Tine′man** (tīn′măn), *i.e.* Loser; son of Archibald the Grim; m. (1390) Margaret, eldest daughter of Robert III; allied himself with ambitious 1st duke of Albany (1402); defeated and taken prisoner by George Dunbar, earl of March, and Hotspur (at Humbledon Hill; 1402), by English (1403–08); formed personal alliance with John the Fearless, Duke of Burgundy (1412); led Scottish contingent to aid Charles VII of France (1423); defeated and slain at Verneuil.

**Archibald** (1391?–1439), 5th Earl of Douglas and 2d Duke of Touraine; son of 4th earl and 1st duke; fought against English at Beaugé (1421); carried James I home from English captivity; his two sons, **William** (1423?–1440), 6th earl, and **David**, were beheaded after mock trial before James II, after which the family's power was broken, the earldom passing to **James Douglas** (1371?–1443), 7th Earl of Douglas and Earl of **Av′on·dale** (ăv′ŭn·dāl), called "the Gross" or "the Fat," younger son of 3d earl.

**William** (1425?–1452), 8th Earl of Douglas; son of 7th earl; recovered estates by marriage with the Fair Maid of Galloway, sister of 6th earl; stood high in favor of James II (until 1452); on refusal to break up league with earl of Crawford, was attacked and killed by king and followers.

His brother **James** (1426–1488), 9th and last Earl of Douglas; forced, by failure of allies, to desist from denunciation of James II as murderer and traitor; married his brother's widow, the Maid of Galloway, and held family estates intact; rebelled again (1455); his forces under his three brothers routed by a kinsman, the Red Douglas, 4th Earl of Angus (see below); his lands forfeited; fled to England; employed by Edward IV to negotiate league with western highlanders; died a monk. For restoration of title of Douglas see *marquises of Douglas* below.

EARLS OF AN′GUS [ăng′gŭs] (distinguished as the Red Douglases):

**George Douglas** (1380?–1403), 1st Earl of Angus (created by grant of his mother's earldom of Angus, 1389); illegitimate son of William, 1st Earl of Douglas, and his wife's sister-in-law, Margaret Stewart, Countess of Angus (third creation) and of Mar (by marriage); held seat in shire of Forfar (or Angus); taken prisoner at Humbledon Hill (1402); died of plague in England.

**George** (1412?–1462), 4th Earl of Angus; grandson of 1st earl; led forces of James II against his kinsmen the Black Douglases under James, 9th Earl of Douglas (1455); defeated Douglas and Percy (1458); granted inheritance of Douglasdale on forfeiture by earl of Douglas.

His son **Archibald** (1450?–?1514), 5th Earl of Angus, known as "the Great Earl"; nicknamed "Bell-the-Cat" for his capture of Robert Cochrane, Earl of Mar, hated favorite of James III; joined duke of Albany (see under STEWART family) in intrigue with Edward IV (1482); one of leaders in rebellion against James III (1487–88); chancellor of kingdom under James IV (1493–98); lost two sons at Flodden. (For his son Gawin, or Gavin, Douglas, poet and bishop, see separate entry.)

**Archibald** (1489?–1557), 6th Earl of Angus; grandson of 5th earl; m. (1514) queen dowager Margaret Tudor, sister of Henry VIII and widow of James IV of Scotland, thereby arousing jealousy of nobles; made peace (1515) with duke of Albany, regent and leader of French party in Scotland, who besieged Queen Margaret and took possession of her son, the young king, James V; in absence of Albany, gained supreme power by defeating Arran; charged with high treason by Albany, who was joined, on her return from seeking help in England, by Margaret because of her husband's liaison with daughter of laird of Traquair; sent to France (1520); returning with help of Henry VIII (1525), took charge of his stepson, whose majority he declared (1526); gained as chancellor (1526) supreme power in Scotland; killed his rival Lennox; on divorce (1528) by Margaret and escape of James V to his mother's side, forced to flee to England, while forfeiture was passed against him and his kinsmen and his sister Janet was burned at the stake by James V; returned (after 1542) to Scotland and joined regent Arran in resisting English. His daughter by Margaret Tudor, Lady **Margaret Douglas** (1515–1578), Countess of **Len′nox** (lĕn′ŭks), m. Matthew Stewart, 4th Earl of Lennox, and was mother of Lord Darnley; barred from English succession by Roman Catholicism (1546); grandmother of James VI (James I of England).

**Archibald** (1555–1588), 8th Earl of Angus, called "the Good Earl"; grandson of 6th earl; warden of west marches (1577); appealed to England for aid to rescue his uncle, 4th earl of Morton (see below), who was removed from regency (1578) and subsequently executed; welcomed by Queen Elizabeth; joined unsuccessful insurrection of earl of Mar (see John ERSKINE) and Glamis (1584); invaded Scotland and secured restoration of estates from James (1585); warden of marches (1586). Succeeded in turn by a cousin, William of Glenbervie, 9th earl, by his son William, 10th earl, a convert to Roman Catholicism and conspirator against the government, and by his son William, 11th earl, afterwards 1st marquis of Douglas (see next ¶).

MARQUISES AND DUKE OF DOUGLAS AND BARONS DOUGLAS OF DOUGLAS:

**William Douglas** (1589–1660), 11th Earl of Angus and 1st Marquis of Douglas (cr. 1633); son of 10th earl; joined Montrose at Philiphaugh (1645); imprisoned, and released only on signing Solemn League and Covenant. His son William became 3d duke of Hamilton (see marquises and dukes of HAMILTON), whose descendants became heirs male of house of Douglas.

**Archibald** (1694–1761), 3d Marquis and 1st (and only) Duke of Douglas (cr. 1703); great-grandson of 1st marquis; a Hanoverian supporter; fought at Sheriffmuir. His sister Lady **Jane Douglas** (1698–1753) secretly married (1746) Colonel John Stewart, or Steuart, of Grandtully, by whom she had twin sons in Paris, one surviving, **Archibald James Edward Stewart,** *or*

**Steuart** (1748–1827), 1st Baron **Douglas of Douglas** (cr. 1790) in British peerage, who won inheritance of Douglas estates in lawsuit brought by the Hamiltons (1769); his sons leaving no male issue let estates pass (1857) to earls of Home, representing Douglas line on female side.

MARQUISES AND DUKES OF HAMILTON (from 1660): see marquises and dukes of HAMILTON.

EARLS OF MOR′TON (môr′t'n):

Sir **James Douglas of Dal·keith′** (dăl·kēth′), 1st Earl of Morton (cr. 1458), Lord Dalkeith and **Ab′er·dour′** [ăb′ẽr·dour′] (cr. 1458); grandson of Sir **James Douglas** of Dalkeith, entertainer of Froissart and a nephew of Sir William Douglas (1300?–1353), Knight of Liddesdale (see above); m. daughter of James I. On death of his grandson, 3d earl (d. 1553), without male issue, earldom passed to daughter's husband as 4th earl.

**James Douglas** (1525?–1581), 4th Earl of Morton; statesman; son of a younger brother of Archibald, 6th Earl of Angus (see above); privy councilor on return of Mary, Queen of Scots, to Scotland (1561); lord high chancellor of Scotland (1563); prime mover in assassination of Rizzio, Mary's favorite (1566); led army that defeated queen's forces at Langside (1568) and secured her abdication at Loch Leven; regent (1572); temporarily ousted by Argyll and Atholl, who brought about assumption of government by James VI (Mar.–June, 1578); condemned on charge by Esmé Stuart, Earl of Lennox, with connivance of James VI, of complicity in death of Darnley; executed.

Sir **William Douglas of Loch·le′ven** [lŏκ·lē′vĕn] (d. 1606), 6th or 7th Earl of Morton (from 1588); descendant of Sir John of Dalkeith, ancestor of 1st earl of Morton; implicated in assassination of Rizzio (1566); custodian in charge of Mary, Queen of Scots, after surrender at Carberry Hill (1567); commanded rear guard at Langside (1568); signed bond to support James VI (1582); banished (1583–85); as one of leaders of Presbyterian party, a commissioner for executing acts against Jesuits (1587); influential at court.

His grandson **William** (1582–1650), 7th or 8th Earl of Morton; title contested unsuccessfully by John Maxwell; commanded Scots regiment in Rochelle expedition (1627); lord high treasurer of Scotland (1630–35); privy councilor of England (1635); in return for advances of money to Charles I, received grant of Orkney and Shetland Islands (1643).

**James** (1702–1768), 14th Earl of Morton; M.A., Cantab. (1722); student of physics and astronomy; a representative peer of Scotland (1739); made outright owner of Orkney and Shetland Islands by act of Parliament (1742); lord clerk register of Scotland (from 1760); fellow of London Royal Society (1733); its president (1764); devoted himself to scientific investigation and promotion of Royal Society.

**Sholto George Watson Douglas** (1844–1935), 20th Earl of Morton; a representative peer of Scotland (from 1886).

EARLS, MARQUISES, AND DUKES OF QUEENS′BER′RY (kwēnz′bĕr′ĭ; -bĕr·ĭ; -brĭ):

Sir **William Douglas** (d. 1640), 1st Earl of Queensberry; eldest son of Sir James Douglas of Drumlanrig (d. 1616), a descendant of an illegitimate son of James, 2d Earl of Douglas and Mar (see above); created viscount of **Drum·lan′rig** [drŭm·lăn′rĭg] (1617) and earl of Queensberry (1633).

His grandson **William** (1637–1695), 3d Earl and 1st Marquis (cr. 1682) and 1st Duke (cr. 1684) of Queensberry; lord justice general of Scotland (1680–86); lord high treasurer (1682–86); president of council (1686); one of lords of privy council of both kingdoms (1687).

**James** (1662–1711), 2d Duke of Queensberry and 1st Duke of **Do′ver** (dō′vẽr); eldest son of 1st duke; educ. Glasgow; lord high treasurer (1693); royal commissioner to famous Scottish parliament of 1700; one of secretaries of state (1702); unintentionally implicated in Jacobite designs of Simon Fraser, Lord Lovat, and temporarily deprived of office (1703–05); as commissioner to Scottish parliament (1706), carried through treaty of union despite Scottish opposition; third secretary of state (1709).

**Charles** (1698–1778), 3d Duke of Queensberry and 2d Duke of Dover; son of 2d duke and 1st duke; created (1706) earl of **Sol′way** (sŏl′wā); lord justice general of Scotland (1763–78); m. (1720) **Catherine Hyde** (1703?–1777), daughter of Henry Hyde, 4th Earl of Clarendon, eccentric woman of fashion, friend of wits and writers, including Swift, Congreve, Gay, Pope, Prior, Walpole.

**William** (1724–1810), 3d Earl of **March** (märch) and 4th Duke of Queensberry; latterly known as "Old Q"; notorious for his escapades and extravagances; developed horse racing; a representative peer for Scotland (1761); vice-admiral of Scotland (1767–76); succeeded his cousin Charles, 3d Duke of Queensberry (1778); lord of bedchamber (1760–89); satirized by Burns, portrayed by Wordsworth, and in Thackeray's *Virginians.* His title of duke of Queensberry passed to Henry Scott, Duke of Buccleuch (*q.v.*); his title of earl of March passed to earls of Wemyss (see Francis WEMYSS-CHARTERIS-DOUGLAS); the marquisate passed to Sir Charles Douglas of Kelhead (1777–1837) and his descendants, including 8th marquis (see next name).

Sir **John Sholto Douglas** (1844–1900), 8th Marquis of Queensberry, Earl of Queensberry; served in navy (1859–64); a representative peer for Scotland (1872–80); best known as a patron of boxing who supervised formulation by John Graham Chambers (*q.v.*) of Marquis of Queensberry Rules (1867).

His eldest surviving son, Lord **Alfred Bruce Douglas** (1870–1945); educ. Oxford; founder and editor of *Plain English* and *Plain Speech;* friend of Oscar Wilde (*q.v.*), whose *Salomé* he translated into English (1894); author of *The City of the Soul* (1899), *Sonnets and Lyrics* (1935), volumes of light verse, including *The Pongo Papers,* autobiography (1929), and *The True History of Shakespeare's Sonnets* (1933); m. (1902) **Olive Custance Douglas,** author of *Opals* (1897), *Rainbows* (1902), *The Inn of Dreams* (1910).

EARLS OF SEL′KIRK (sĕl′kûrk). Descendants of Lord **William Douglas,** third son of 1st marquis of Douglas (see above), who was created earl of Selkirk (1646), including: **Thomas Douglas** (1771–1820), 5th Earl of Selkirk; colonizer; educ. Edinburgh; settled 800 emigrants from highlands of Scotland in Prince Edward Island (1803) and about a hundred (1811) in Red River Valley (now Manitoba and Minnesota); latter colonists twice evicted by soldiers of Northwest Fur Co. (1815, 1816); re-established his colony after attack on chief post of Northwest Fur Co. (1817).

**Douglas,** Earls, marquises, and duke of and barons **Douglas of.** See DOUGLAS family.

**Douglas,** Lord **Alfred Bruce**. See under *marquises of Queensberry,* under DOUGLAS family.

**Douglas, Amanda Minnie**. 1831–1916. American writer, b. New York City; lived Newark, N.J. (from 1853). Author of juvenile stories, esp. of the Kathie series, the Little Girl series, and the Helen Grant series.

**Douglas,** Sir **Archibald Lucius**. 1842–1913. British admiral, b. Quebec. Director of Imperial Japanese Naval College (1873–75) and in large measure creator of modern Japanese navy. Commander in chief in East Indies

(1898); second sea lord of admiralty (1899–1902); commander in chief (1902–07) in North America and West Indies as vice-admiral, and later at Portsmouth; admiral (1905).

**Douglas, Charles Winfred.** 1867–1944. American Protestant Episcopal clergyman and musician, b. Oswego, N.Y. Editor or compiler of many books of or about church music.

**Douglas, Clifford Hugh.** 1879–1952. English civil engineer and social economist; chief reconstruction adviser to government of Alberta, Canada (1935); attempted to introduce his plan for social credit in that province. Author of *Economic Democracy, Social Credit, The Monopoly of Credit,* etc.

**Douglas, David.** 1798–1834. Scottish botanist in America. Collector in U.S. for Royal Horticultural Society (1823) and on later expeditions in America and the Pacific; discovered the Douglas fir (1825); the Douglas squirrel named for him.

**Douglas, David Charles.** 1898– . English historian; professor of medieval history, Leeds (from 1939). Author of *The Norman Conquest* (1926), *The Development of Medieval Europe* (1935), *English Scholars* (1939; awarded James Tait Black memorial prize), etc.

**Douglas, Ga'win** (gä'wĭn; gä'ĕn) *or* **Gav'in** (găv'ĭn). 1474?–1522. Scottish poet and ecclesiastic. Son of 5th earl of Angus (see DOUGLAS family). Studied at St. Andrews (1489–94); occupied until battle of Flodden with ecclesiastical duties, classical translation, and writing poetry; ousted by John Hepburn, the prior, from archbishopric of St. Andrews, to which he was appointed after marriage of his nephew, 6th earl of Angus, to James IV's widowed queen (1514); as member of English party in Scotland, imprisoned by duke of Albany, leader of French party; ultimately obtained bishopric of Dunkeld (1516–20); deprived of see for appealing to English court on fall of earl of Angus; died of plague in London. Author of poems *The Palice of Honour* (allegory in tradition of the courts of love), *King Hart* (allegory), *Conscience.* Best known for translation of the *Aeneid* in ten-syllabled meter, earliest translation of a classical work into any English dialect.

**Douglas, George.** Pen name of George Douglas BROWN.

**Douglas,** Sir **Howard.** 1776–1861. British naval and artillery expert. Commanded regiment at Quebec (1795); served in Peninsular War (1808–09, 1812); governor of New Brunswick (1823–31); founder of U. of Fredericton; lord high commissioner of Ionian Islands (1835–40), for which he drew up the Douglas code; general (1851). Author of works on military bridge construction (1816), on errors of Carnot's system of fortification (1819), and a *Treatise on Naval Gunnery* (1820).

**Douglas,** Sir **James.** 1803–1877. Canadian businessman and government official, b. at Demerara, British Guiana. Fur trader in upper Canada (1819–24) and western Canada (after 1824); instrumental in founding British Columbia. Governor of Vancouver Island (1851) while it was still a property of the Hudson's Bay Company, and of the crown colony of British Columbia (1858–63).

**Douglas, James.** 1837–1918. Metallurgist and mining engineer, b. Quebec city. Moved to Arizona (1880); president of Copper Queen Consolidated Mining Co.; brought about reforms in mining and metallurgical industry. Author of technical papers and historical books such as *New England and New France* (1913). The town of Douglas, Ariz., is named for him. His grandson **Lewis Williams Douglas** (1894–1974), b. Bisbee, Ariz., was engaged in mining and citrus ranching in Arizona (1921–27); member U.S. House of Representatives (1927–33); U.S. director of the budget (1933–34); principal and vice-chancellor, McGill U. (1938–39); deputy administrator, war shipping board (1942–44); U.S. ambassador to Gt. Britain (1947–50).

**Douglas,** Lady **Jane.** See *marquises of Douglas*, above.

**Douglas, John.** 1721–1807. British prelate, b. in Fife, Scotland. Dean of Windsor (1788); bishop of Salisbury (1791–1807). Author of a defense of Milton (1750), exposing William Lauder's forgeries, and *Letter on the Criterion of Miracles* (1754), attacking Hume.

**Douglas, Lloyd Cas'sel** (kăs''l). 1877–1951. American Lutheran clergyman and novelist, b. Columbia City, Ind.; author of *Magnificent Obsession* (1929), *Green Light* (1935), *White Banners* (1936), *Dr. Hudson's Secret Journal* (1939), *Invitation to Live* (1940), *The Robe* (1942), etc.

**Douglas, Norman.** 1868–1952. English writer; author of *Siren Land* (1911), *South Wind* (1917), *Old Calabria* (1928), *Goodbye to Western Culture* (1930), *Paneros* (1931), *Looking Back* (2 vols., 1933), etc.

**Douglas, Olive Custance.** See under *marquises of Queensberry,* under DOUGLAS family.

**Douglas,** Sir **Robert Kennaway.** 1838–1913. English Orientalist; professor of Chinese, King's Coll., London; author of works on language, literature, religions, and history of China.

**Douglas, Robert Langton.** 1864–1951. English art critic, lecturer, writer; authority on Italian Renaissance.

**Douglas, William Sholto.** 1st Baron **Douglas of Kirtleside.** 1893–1969. British air officer, son of Robert Langton Douglas; air marshal, Royal Air Force.

**Douglas, Stephen Arnold.** 1813–1861. American political leader, b. Brandon, Vt. Adm. to Illinois bar (1834); practiced, Jacksonville, Ill.; judge, Illinois supreme court (1841). Member, U.S. House of Representatives (1843–47); U.S. senator (1847–61); drafted Kansas-Nebraska Bill (1854), which left decision as to slavery to the territories themselves and thus caused bitter struggles there. Defeated by Buchanan for Democratic nomination to presidency (1856); withdrew support from Buchanan (1858) upon learning he would approve a pro-slavery constitution for Kansas. In campaign of 1858, engaged with Abraham Lincoln in series of platform debates on slavery, from which Lincoln emerged as a figure of national prominence. Nominated for president by northern wing of Democratic party (1860); defeated by Lincoln; was second in the popular vote; loyally supported Lincoln's administration.

**Douglas** of Kirk·cud'bright (kûr·kōō'brĭ), **William.** 1672?–1748. Scottish poet. Author of *Annie Laurie,* written (c. 1700) to Anne, daughter of Sir Robert Laurie of the Maxwellton family.

**Douglas,** Sir **William Fettes.** 1822–1891. Scottish landscape and figure painter.

**Douglas, William Lewis.** 1845–1924. American shoe manufacturer; governor of Massachusetts (1905–06).

**Douglas, William Orville.** 1898– . American jurist, b. Maine, Minn. Professor of law, Yale (1931–39); also, collaborator with U.S. Department of Commerce in bankruptcy studies (1929–32), and member (1934–36) and chairman (1936–39), Securities and Exchange Commission. Assoc. justice, U.S. Supreme Court (1939–75).

**Doug'lass** (dŭg'lăs), **Andrew Ellicott.** 1867–1962. American astronomer, b. Windsor, Vt. Best known for researches in dating prehistoric ruins by tree rings. Photographer of shadow bands and zodiacal light on Mars. Author of *Climatic Cycles and Tree Growth* (3 vols., 1919, 1928, 1936).

**Douglass, Frederick.** *Real name* **Frederick Augustus Washington Bai'ley** (bā'lĭ). 1817?–1895. American

Negro lecturer and writer, b. Tuckahoe, Md., illegitimate son of a white man and a Negro slave, Harriet Bailey. Escaped from slavery (1838); settled in New Bedford, Mass., changing his name to Frederick Douglass. Addressed antislavery convention, Nantucket (1841); engaged as agent of Massachusetts Antislavery Society; published his autobiography, *Narrative of the Life of Frederick Douglass* (1845). Lectured in Britain and Ireland (1845–47); with proceeds from lectures, bought his freedom; settled at Rochester, N.Y.; founded and edited (1847–60), with M. D. Delany (*q.v.*), the *North Star*, an abolitionist paper. At outbreak of Civil War, helped recruit Negro regiments; consulted by Lincoln. U.S. marshal for District of Columbia (1877–81); recorder of deeds, District of Columbia (1881–86); U.S. minister to Haiti (1889–91).

**Dou·het′** (do͞o·ĕ′), **Giulio.** 1869–1930. Italian military officer; committed to prison by military tribunal (1916) for critical analysis of operations of war; justified in criticisms by debacle at Caporetto, recalled to army (1918) as head of central direction of aviation; general (1921); advocate of establishment of independent air unit having autonomy equal to that of army and navy; credited witn first expounding the technique of the Blitzkrieg.

**Doul′ton** (dōl′t′n; -tŭn), Sir **Henry.** 1820–1897. English potter; introduced (1846) stoneware drainpipes and appliances that made name of Doulton firm famous; began (1870) manufacture of art pottery, a revival in modified form of sgraffito ware of the 17th century.

**Dou′mer′** (do͞o′mâr′), **Paul.** 1857–1932. French statesman and 13th president of the republic, b. Aurillac. Deputy (1888–95); minister of finance (1895–96); governor general of French Indo-China (1897–1902); deputy (1902–12) and president of Chamber of Deputies (1905–06); senator representing Corsica (1912); cabinet minister (1917, 1921–22, 1925–26); president of the Senate (1927–31); president of France (1931–32); assassinated (May 7, 1932) by Paul Gorgoulov, a Russian.

**Dou′mergue′** (do͞o′mĕrg′), **Gaston.** 1863–1937. French statesman and 12th president of the republic, b. near Nûnes. Colonial judge in Cochin China (1890–92) and in Algeria (1893). Radical-Socialist deputy from Nûnes (1893–1910); secretary to the Chamber of Deputies (1895–96); its vice-president (1905–06); held various cabinet offices (1902–10); elected senator (1910); re-elected (1912); prime minister (1913–14). During World War, colonial minister in Viviani-Briand ministries (1914–17); special agent to Russia (1917); re-entered Senate (1917); president of Left Democratic group in Senate (1919–23); president of the Senate (1923–24). President of France (1924–31); retired but recalled to act as premier during Stavisky scandal (Feb.–Nov., 1934).

**Dou′mic′** (do͞o′mēk′), **René.** 1860–1937. French writer and critic; editor of *La Revue des Deux Mondes* (1916). Author of *Éléments d'Histoire Littéraire* (1888), *De Scribe à Ibsen* (1893), *Le Théâtre Nouveau* (1908), *Saint Simon* (1920), etc.

**Dou′ris** (do͞o′rĭs). Greek potter and vase painter of 5th century B.C.

**Douris of Samos.** See DURIS.

**Dou′sa** (do͞o′sȧ), **Ja′nus** (jā′nŭs). *Latinized form of* **Jan van der Does** (do͞os). 1545–1604. Dutch scholar and statesman; leader among nobles who organized League of the Gueux (Beggars) against Philip II of Spain (1566); defended Leiden against Spaniards (1574–75). First curator, U. of Leiden (1575–1604). Author of commentaries on Latin classics and of *Annals of Holland* (1599).

**Douw, Gerard.** See Gerard DOU.

**Do′ve** (dō′vĕ), **Heinrich Wilhelm.** 1803–1879. German physicist and meteorologist; formulated meteorological law of gyration, which states that the wind generally shifts in its direction with the sun; investigated climatology, induced electricity, and circularly polarized light. His son **Alfred** (1844–1916), historian, essayist, and journalist, was editor of *Grenzboten* (1870), and of *Allgemeine Zeitung*, Munich (1891–97); published posthumous manuscripts of Ranke (1890); edited last volumes of Bismarck's parliamentary speeches (1891). An older son, **Richard Wilhelm** (1833–1907), jurist and politician, helped found (1860) and contributed to *Zeitschrift für Kirchenrecht;* revised Richter's *Lehrbuch...des Kirchenrechts* (8th ed., 1877–86).

**Do′ver** (dō′vẽr), Dukes of. See *dukes of Queensberry*, under DOUGLAS family.

**Dover, Thomas.** 1660–1742. English physician. Captain of privateer *Duke* on expedition commanded by Captain Woodes Rogers, sacked Guayaquil in Peru (now in Ecuador); cured 172 of his sailors of plague (1709); returning on a Spanish prize, rescued Alexander Selkirk from one of Juan Fernández Islands (1709). Invented Dover's powder, an anodyne diaphoretic.

**d'Ovidio, Francesco.** See OVIDIO.

**Dow** (dou), **Charles H.** 1851–1902. Am. financial statistician, b. in Conn. With Edward D. Jones (1856–1920), founded *Wall Street Journal* (1882), and inaugurated publication of an average calculated from the daily market prices of a group of carefully selected representative securities, these Dow-Jones averages being widely accepted as indicating security market trends.

**Dow, Gerard.** See Gerard DOU.

**Dow, Herbert Henry.** 1866–1930. American chemist and manufacturer, b. Belleville, Ont., Canada. President, Dow Chemical Co., Midland, Mich. Developed and patented over 100 chemical processes.

**Dow, Neal.** 1804–1897. Known as "Father of the Maine Law." American temperance advocate, b. Portland, Me. Mayor of Portland (1851); drafted prohibition law, submitted it to legislature, and saw it passed; cleaned up liquor traffic in Portland and gained nationwide reputation. Candidate of Prohibition party for president of the United States (1880).

**Dow′den** (dou′d′n), **Edward.** 1843–1913. Irish Shakespearean critic. Gained wide reputation with *Shakspere, his Mind and Art* (1875); edited Hamlet and other plays; author also of *Shakspere Primer* (1877), *New Studies in Literature* (1895), and a *Life of Shelley* (1886). His brother **John** (1840–1910), theologian and antiquary, was Episcopal bishop of Edinburgh (1886–1910); author of works on the Book of Common Prayer, the Celtic church, and the medieval church in Scotland.

**Dow′ding** (dou′dĭng), Sir **Hugh Caswall Tre′men·heere** (trē′mĕn·hẹ̄r). 1st Baron **Dowding** (1943). 1882–1970. British soldier; educ. Royal Military Acad., Woolwich; served in air forces through World War (1914–18). Air chief marshal, head of R.A.F. fighter command (1936–40); on special mission in U.S. (1940–42; retired).

**Dow′ie** (dou′ĭ), **John Alexander.** 1847–1907. Religious leader, b. Edinburgh, Scotland. Emigrated to South Australia (1860); ordained Congregational pastor, Alma, S. Australia. To U.S. (1888); in Chicago (1890–96); organized (Feb. 22, 1896) new church, Christian Catholic Church in Zion. Became fanatical megalomaniac; identified himself (1899) with the messenger of the Covenant (prophesied by Malachi); proclaimed himself Elijah the Restorer (1901); built up Zion City, 42 miles from Chicago, inhabited by his followers but wholly owned by him. Invaded New York City (1903); ridiculed by New Yorkers. Deposed from leadership and membership in his own church (1906) by revolt of his followers led by Wilbur Glenn Voliva (*q.v.*).

**Dow'land** (dou'lănd), **John** (1563?-?1626) and his son **Robert** (1585?-?1641). English lutists.

**Downes** (dounz), **Andrew**. 1549?-1628. English classical scholar. One of seven translators of Apocrypha for the Authorized Version, and one of six revisers.

**Downes, Edwin Olin**. 1886-1955. American music critic, b. Evanston, Ill.; on staff of Boston *Post* (1906-24) and New York *Times* (from 1924); author of *The Lure of Music* (1918), *Symphonic Broadcasts* (1932).

**Dow'ney** (dou'nĭ), **Fairfax Davis**. 1893- . American writer, b. Salt Lake City, Utah; author of *When We Were Rather Older* (1926), *Burton, Arabian Nights Adventurer* (1931), *Portrait of an Era, as Drawn by C. D. Gibson* (1936), etc.

**Dow'ning** (dou'nĭng), **Andrew Jackson**. 1815-1852. American horticulturist, nurseryman, and landscape architect, b. Newburgh, N.Y. Editor, *The Horticulturist* (1846-52). With his brother **Charles** (1802-1885), horticulturist and pomologist, wrote *The Fruits and Fruit Trees of America* (1845), long a standard work.

**Downing,** Sir **George**. 1623-1684. Diplomat, b. Dublin, Ireland. To America (1638); second graduate of Harvard College (1642). Returned to England (1645); M.P. (1654-56); British resident minister at The Hague (1657). In favor with the Stuarts after the Restoration. Downing Street, London, is named in his honor. His grandson Sir **George Downing** (1684?-1749) left a bequest to found Downing College, Cambridge.

**Downing,** Major **Jack**. See Seba SMITH.

**Downshire,** Marquis of. See Wills HILL.

**Dowse** (dous), **Thomas**. 1772-1856. American bibliophile, b. Charlestown, Mass.; his books now form the Dowse collection of the Massachusetts Historical Society.

**Dow'son** (dou's'n), **Ernest Christopher**. 1867-1900. English lyric poet; coauthor of two novels, and author of exquisite lyrics, including "I have been faithful to thee, Cynara, in my fashion."

**Dox·ia'dis** (dôk·syä'thēs), **Constantinos Apostolos**. 1913-1975. Greek architect and city planner. Author of *Urban Renewal and the Future of the American City* (1966).

**Doy'en'** (dwȧ'yăN'), **Gabriel François**. 1726-1806. French historical painter; among his works are murals in the imperial palace at St. Petersburg.

**Doyle** (doil), **Alexander**. 1857-1922. American sculptor, b. Steubenville, Ohio. Designed bronze statue of *Horace Greeley*, New York City; *National Revolutionary Monument*, Yorktown, Va.; *Gen. Garfield*, Cleveland, Ohio; *Benjamin H. Hill*, Atlanta, Ga.; *Thomas H. Benton*, *Francis P. Blair*, and *John E. Kenna*, Washington, D.C.

**Doyle,** Sir **Arthur Co'nan** (kō'năn). 1859-1930. British physician, novelist, and detective-story writer, b. Edinburgh. Practiced medicine, Southsea (1882-90). Among his novels are *Micah Clarke* (1888), *The White Company* (1890), *The Refugees* (1891), *The Great Shadow* (1892), *Rodney Stone* (1896), and *Sir Nigel* (1906). Best known for his detective stories centering about fictional character Sherlock Holmes of Baker Street, London, and his friend Dr. Watson, as *The Sign of the Four* (1889), *Adventures of Sherlock Holmes* (1891), *The Memoirs of Sherlock Holmes* (1893), *The Hound of the Baskervilles* (1902), *Return of Sherlock Holmes* (1904). Author also of historical works, as *The Great Boer War* (1900) and *History of the British Campaign in France and Flanders* (6 vols., 1915-20). In later years, champion of and writer of books on spiritualism, including *History of Spiritualism* (2 vols., 1926). Cf. William GILLETTE.

**Doyle,** Sir **Francis Hastings Charles**. 1810-1888. English poet, b. in Yorkshire. Receiver-general of customs (1846-69), commissioner (1869-83). Professor of poetry, Oxford (1867-77); published several volumes of poetry; remembered esp. for the pieces *The Loss of the Birkenhead* and *The Private of the Buffs*.

**Doyle, John Andrew**. 1844-1907. English historian; author of *The English Colonies in America* (5 vols., 1882-1907), etc.

**Doyle, Lynn**. *Pseudonym of* **Leslie Alexander Montgomery**. 1873-1961. Irish writer; among his plays are *Love and Land* (1913; produced 1925 under title *Persevering Pat*), *The Lilac Ribbon* (1919), *Turncoats* (1922), *Revenge* (1926); among his novels and short stories are *Mr. Wildridge of the Bank—a novel* (1916), *Lobster Salad—Irish short stories* (1922), *Dear Ducks* (short stories, 1925), *Me and Mr. Murphy* (short stories, 1930), *Fiddling Farmer* (a novel, 1937).

**Doyle, Richard**. 1824-1883. English caricaturist and water-color painter. Contributor to *Punch* (1843-50), the cover of which is his design. Illustrated three of Dickens's *Christmas Books*, Thackeray's *Newcomes*, Ruskin's *King of the Golden River*, and Leigh Hunt's *Jar of Honey;* author of stories told in pictures, including *Adventures of Brown, Jones, and Robinson*.

**D'Oyly Carte.** See Richard D'Oyly CARTE.

**Dó'zsa** (dō'zhŏ), **György**. d. 1514. Hungarian soldier of fortune and rebel; raised force from peasantry and rabble to fight Turks and remained as their leader when they turned against nobles and government; defeated at Timişoara, captured and grilled alive upon a glowing throne of red-hot iron.

**Do'zy** (dō'zē), **Reinhart**. 1820-1883. Dutch Oriental scholar and historian, esp. of the Moors in Spain.

**Drach'man** (drăk'măn), **Ber·nard'** (bẽr·närd'). 1861-1945. American rabbi, b. New York City. Adherent of orthodox faith of Judaism. Rabbi of New York congregation (from 1889). Author of *From the Heart of Israel* (1905), *Looking at America* (1935), etc.

**Drach'mann** (dräK'män), **Holger Henrik Herholdt**. 1846-1908. Danish writer; orig. a painter, esp. of marines. Among his poetical works are *Poems* (1872), *Muffled Melodies* (1875), *Songs by the Sea* (1877), *Youth in Poetry and Song* (1879), and *East of the Sun and West of the Moon* (1880); among his prose works are *From the Frontier* (1871), *Young Blood* (1876), *Tannhäuser* (1877), *On a Sailor's Word* (1878), *With a Broad Brush* (1887), *Forskrevet* (1890), *The Sacred Fire* (1899), and *Dädalus* (1900); among his plays are *Once Upon a Time* (1886), *Wayland the Smith* (1897), *Brav-Karl* (1897), *Gurre* (1899), *Hallfred Vandraadeskjald* (1900), etc.

**Dra'co** (drā'kō). Athenian lawgiver; prepared first written code of laws for Athens (c. 621 B.C.), prescribing death for nearly all offenses; whence the word *Draconian*, meaning "barbarously severe; harsh; cruel."

**Dra·con'ti·us** (drȧ·kŏn'shĭ·ŭs), **Blossius Aemilius**. Christian poet of late 5th century A.D.; practiced law in Carthage. Works include *De Laudibus Dei*, a number of short epics, an elegy, and two epithalamiums.

**Drae'se·ke** (drâ'zĕ·kĕ), **Felix**. 1835-1913. German composer of operas, symphonies, symphonic overtures, string quartets, string quintets, a piano quintet, songs, and a number of great choral works.

**Dra'ga** (drä'gä): 1867-1903. Queen of Serbia (1900-03). An adventuress, widow of a Czech engineer named Mashin; m. (1900) King Alexander I Obrenovich (*q.v.*).

**Dra'go** (drä'gō), **Luis María**. 1859-1921. Argentine jurist; minister of foreign affairs (1902-03); member, Hague Tribunal; prominent supporter of doctrine (known as *Drago doctrine*, though originally proposed by Carlos Calvo of Argentina) that public debt could not be used as excuse for armed intervention or territorial occupation in American nations by a European power.

**Dra·go·ma'nov** (drŭ·gŭ·mȧ'nôf), **Mikhail Petrovich.** 1841–1895. Russian scholar; professor of general history, Kiev (to 1876); exiled from Little Russia; professor of history, Sofia (1888 ff.). Published *The Historical Songs of Little Russia* (with Antonovich, 1874), *La Pologne Historique et la Démocratie Moscovite* (1881), etc.

**Dra·go·mi'rov** (drŭ·gŭ·myē'rôf), **Mikhail Ivanovich.** 1830–1905. Russian soldier; commanded Russian advance guard against Turks (1877–78); wounded at Shipka Pass. Governor general of Kiev (1898–1903).

**Dra'go·net'ti** (drä'gô·nāt'tē), **Domenico.** 1763–1846. Italian double-bass player, b. Venice; played with fellow virtuoso, Robert Lindley, violoncellist; friend of Beethoven and Haydn; composed sonatas.

**Dra·gou'mes** *or* **Dra·gou'mis** (thrä·gōō'mēs), **Stephanos.** 1842–1923. Greek statesman; minister of foreign affairs (1886–90, 1892–93); prime minister of Greece (1910); governor of Crete (1912).

**Drake** (drāk), **Alexander Wilson.** 1843–1916. American artist and critic, b. Westfield, N.J. As art director of *Century Magazine* and *St. Nicholas Magazine* (1881–1913), a leading figure in development of American illustrative art.

**Drake, Daniel.** 1785–1852. American physician, b. near Plainfield, N.J. Practiced medicine, Cincinnati, Ohio (from 1807). Founder (1827) and editor (1827–48), *Western Journal of the Medical and Physical Sciences.* His brother **Benjamin** (1795–1841) was a lawyer, editor of the *Cincinnati Chronicle* (1826–34), and author of *The Life and Adventures of Blackhawk* (1838), etc. Daniel's son **Charles Daniel** (1811–1892) was U.S. senator from Missouri (1867–70) and chief justice, U.S. court of claims (1870–85).

**Drake, Edwin Laurentine.** 1819–1880. American pioneer in oil industry, b. Greenville, N.Y. First to tap petroleum at its source by drilling, at Titusville, Pa. (Aug., 1859).

**Drake,** Sir **Francis.** 1540?–1596. English navigator; educ. under care of Sir John Hawkins, a kinsman, on whose expedition (1567) to Gulf of Mexico he commanded the *Judith.* Commissioned as privateer by Elizabeth I (1570); then made three expeditions (1570, 1571, 1572) to West Indies, plundering Spanish towns and shipping; crossed Isthmus of Panama, first English commander to see Pacific (1572); returned and served as volunteer under earl of Essex in Ireland. Started out (1577) to explore Strait of Magellan; sailed through straits for 16 days, became separated by storm from other ships; renamed his ship *Golden Hind,* continued to Mocha Islands, plundered coast of Chile and Peru, named Californian coast New Albion and claimed it for Queen Elizabeth. Failing to find passage into Atlantic, reached Moluccas (1579), Celebes, Java, doubled Cape of Good Hope, touched at Sierra Leone, and returned to Plymouth (1580), having made first circumnavigation of globe by an Englishman. Knighted by queen in face of Spanish protests. Mayor of Plymouth (1581); on reopening of hostilities with Spain, sailed with 25 ships against Spanish Indies, took Santiago (in Cape Verde Islands), Santo Domingo, Cartagena, and St. Augustine; after great suffering from sickness, returned home (1586), carrying back first colonists of Virginia with potatoes and the material and implements of tobacco smoking. With fleet of thirty sail destroyed 33 ships in bay of Cádiz and escaped unscathed (1587); seized off Azores (1587) Portuguese carrack said to be worth £100,000. Urged queen to ward off Spanish invasion by attacking Spain; appointed vice-admiral under Lord Howard and at approach of Spanish Armada was stationed off Ushant with one of three divisions of fleet; defeated Armada off Gravelines and pursued it to north of Scotland (1588); captured off Portland the Spanish galleon *Rosario* and quarreled with Sir Martin Frobisher over the spoil (1588). Commander of fleet sent with land forces under Sir John Norris (1589) to aid Don Antônio, claimant to Portuguese throne, plundered La Coruña, burned Vigo, but failed in mission. Brought the Meavy River into Plymouth to assure water supply. With Sir John Hawkins, commanded an ill-fated expedition to West Indies (1595) on which he died aboard his own ship.

**Drake, Francis Samuel.** See under Samuel Gardner DRAKE.

**Dra'ke** (drä'kĕ), **Friedrich.** 1805–1882. German sculptor; studied under Rauch.

**Drake** (drāk), **Joseph Rodman.** 1795–1820. American poet, b. New York City. His best-known poems, including "The Culprit Fay" and "The American Flag" were published in *The Culprit Fay and Other Poems* (1835). He was eulogized by his friend Fitz-Greene Halleck in poem, "Green be the turf above thee."

**Drake, Nathan.** 1766–1836. English essayist and physician; M.D., Edinburgh (1789); author of *Shakespeare and his Times* (1817), bringing together work of Tyrwhitt, Benjamin Heath, and Ritson, and of *Memorials of Shakespeare* (1828).

**Drake, Samuel Gardner.** 1798–1875. American antiquarian and historian, b. Pittsfield, N.H. Bookseller in Boston (from 1830). Editor of first 15 vols. of *New England Historical and Genealogical Register* (1847–72). Author esp. of books on the American Indians, and *The Witchcraft Delusion in New England* (3 vols., 1866). Two of his sons were also historical writers: **Francis Samuel** (1828–1885), author of a one-volume *Dictionary of American Biography* (1872), *Indian History for Young Folks* (1885), etc.; **Samuel Adams** (1833–1905), author of *The Making of New England* (1886), *The Making of the Great West* (1887), etc.

**Dra'per** (drā'pẽr), **Andrew Sloan.** 1848–1913. American educator, b. Westford, N.Y. N.Y. State superintendent of public instruction (1886–92); president, U. of Illinois (1894–1904); N.Y. State commissioner of education (1904–13).

**Draper, Henry.** 1837–1882. Son of John William Draper. American astronomer, b. Prince Edward County, Va. Professor of natural science (1860–66), and of physiology (1866–73), U. of City of New York. Interested in astronomy (from 1860); built for himself an observatory with 15½-inch speculum, and devised methods for photographing the skies; built and mounted a 28-inch speculum (1869), with which he did unique work in stellar spectroscopy. Chosen to organize photographic work of U.S. expedition to observe the transit of Venus (1874). The standard Draper Catalogue (begun 1885, completed 1924) of stellar magnitudes and spectral types was undertaken by the Harvard Observatory as a memorial to him.

**Draper, John.** 1702–1762. American printer and journalist; succeeded (1732) his father-in-law, Bartholomew Green, as publisher of the *Boston News-Letter.* Succeeded by his son **Richard** (1727–1774), whose wife **Margaret,** *nee* **Green** (fl. 1750–1807), continued the publication until the Revolution caused its suspension (Feb. 22, 1776).

**Draper, John William.** 1811–1882. Scientist and author, b. near Liverpool, Eng. To U.S. (1831), M.D., U. of Pennsylvania (1836). President, medical school, U. of the City of New York (1850). Made important scientific contributions in fields of radiant energy, photochemistry, photography, and electric telegraph. Author of *Human*

*Physiology, Statical and Dynamical* (1856), *History of the American Civil War* (3 vols., 1867–70), *History of the Conflict between Religion and Science* (1874), etc. A son, **John Christopher** (1835–1885), was professor of natural science, College of the City of New York (1863–85), and of chemistry, medical dept. of New York U. (1866–85). Another son was the astronomer Henry Draper (*q.v.*).

**Draper, Lyman Copeland.** 1815–1891. American historical research scholar, b. Hamburg (now Evans), N.Y. Secretary, Wisconsin State Historical Society (1854–86); edited first ten volumes of *Wisconsin Historical Collections;* author of *King's Mountain and its Heroes* (1881).

**Draper, Ruth.** 1884–1956. American monologuist.

**Dra′pi·er** (drā′pĭ·ẽr; drăp′yẽr), **M. B.** Pseudonym of Jonathan SWIFT in *Drapier Letters.*

**Draw′baugh** (drô′bô), **Daniel.** 19th-century American inventor whose claim to invention of the telephone precipitated eight years of litigation before United States Supreme Court decided in favor of Alexander Graham Bell.

**Drax, Reginald Aylmer Ranfurly Plunkett-Ernle-Erle-.** See under Sir Horace Curzon PLUNKETT.

**Dray′ton** (drā′t'n), **Michael.** 1563–1631. English poet, b. in Warwickshire; settled in London (1590). His earliest volume of poems, *The Harmony of the Church* (1591), burned by public order. Published volume of 9 eclogues, *Idea; The Shepherd's Garland* (1593); a cycle of 64 sonnets in honor of a Warwickshire lady; three historical poems, *Piers Gaveston* (1593), *Matilda* (1594), *Robert, Duke of Normandy* (1596). His *Mortimeriados* (1596) was recast (1603) as *The Barons' Wars;* collaborated in dramatic work with Henry Chettle, Thomas Dekker, and John Webster; included in *Poems Lyric and Pastoral* (c. 1605) the spirited *Ballad of Agincourt.* Finished his magnum opus, *Polyolbion* (1622), a topographical description of England in 12-syllabled verse; published miscellaneous volume (1627), including his most graceful poem, *Nymphidia* (an epic of fairyland), and *The Battle of Agincourt* (a historical poem in ottava rima, not to be confused with the ballad); his last work, *The Muses' Elizium* (1630), contains pastorals.

**Drayton, William.** 1732–1790. American jurist, b. in S. Carolina; first judge of U.S. court for District of South Carolina (1789–90). His son **William** (1776–1846) practiced law in Charleston, S.C.; member, U.S. House of Representatives (1825–33), opposing tariff and nullification; as president (1841), wound up affairs of Bank of the United States. Of the latter's sons, one, **Thomas Fenwick** (1808–1891), was a Confederate army officer in the Civil War; another, **Percival** (1812–1865), was a Federal naval officer, serving under Du Pont against Port Royal (whose defense his brother directed) and Fort Sumter, and under Farragut in Mobile Bay.

**Drayton, William Henry.** 1742–1779. Cousin of William Drayton (1732–1790). American Revolutionary political leader, b. near Charleston, S.C. Member, governor's council, South Carolina (1772–75); suspended for protesting system of filling government places with appointees from England; devoted himself thereafter to colonial cause. President, provincial congress (1775); advocated aggressive measures leading to war. Chief justice of South Carolina (1776). Member, Continental Congress (1778–79). Manuscripts left by him formed basis of the valuable two-volume *Memoirs of the American Revolution... as Relating to South Carolina* published (1821) by his son **John** (1766–1822).

**Drd′la** (dûrd′lȧ), **Franz.** 1868–1944. Austrian violinist and composer of operettas and works for violin and piano. His *Serenade in A Major* was dedicated to, and played by, Kubelik.

**Dreb′bel** (drĕb′ĕl), **Cornelis.** 1572–1634. Dutch inventor. To England (c. 1604), where James I became his patron; invented a machine designed to produce perpetual motion; sometimes credited with invention of the microscope, telescope, and thermometer, but probably introduced them into England; discovered method for dyeing wool scarlet with tin and cochineal.

**Drei′ser** (drī′sẽr; -zẽr; *the first is his own pron.*), **Theodore.** 1871–1945. American editor and writer, b. Terre Haute, Ind.; editor of *Smith's Magazine* (1905–06), *Broadway Magazine* (1906–07), and Butterick publications (1907–10). To Russia (1927). Editor of *American Spectator* (to 1934). Author of *Sister Carrie* (1900), *The Financier* (1912), *The Titan* (1914), *The Genius* (1915), *The Hand of the Potter* (tragedy, 1918), *An American Tragedy* (1925), *Moods* (verse, 1926), *Dreiser Looks at Russia* (1928), *Dawn* (1931), *Tragic America* (1932), etc. His brother, **Paul Dresser** (1857–1911), songwriter; composed "On the Banks of the Wabash," etc.

**Dren′nan** (drĕn′ăn), **William.** 1754–1820. Irish poet, son of Presbyterian minister at Belfast. Formulator of original prospectus of Society of United Irishmen (1791), and chairman (1792, 1793). Author of patriotic lyrics; first Irish poet to call Ireland "the Emerald Isle."

**Dress′ler** (drĕs′lẽr), **Marie.** *Orig. surname* **Koer′ber** (kûr′bẽr). 1873–1934. Actress; b. Cobourg, Canada; joined Weber company in New York as leading comedienne (1906); made success as star in *Tillie's Nightmare* and *Tillie's Punctured Romance;* followed stage career with success in motion pictures, as in *Min and Bill, Tugboat Annie, The Late Christopher Bean.*

**Dre·vet′** (drẽ·vĕ′). Family of French copper engravers, including: **Pierre** (1664–1738), engraver of portraits of Louis XIV, Louis XV, Prince de Conti, Boileau, Villars, Cardinal de Fleury, Duchesse de Nemours; a son and pupil of Pierre, **Pierre Louis** (1697–1739), also engraver; a nephew of Pierre, **Claude** (1705–1782).

**Drew** (drōō), **Charles Richard.** 1904–1950. American physician, b. Washington, D.C. Developed efficient way to store blood plasma in blood banks (1940).

**Drew, Daniel.** 1797–1879. American financier, b. Carmel, N.Y. Cattle drover and horse trader (1815–34). Resident, New York City (from 1829). In steamboat business, competing with Cornelius Vanderbilt (1834). Wall Street broker (from 1844). Forced himself on board of directors, Erie Railroad (1857); manipulated stock to his own advantage; victorious in bitter stock-market fight (the "Erie War") with Vanderbilt (1866–68). Later operations made him bankrupt (1876). His benefactions made possible founding (1866) of Drew Theological Seminary, Madison, N.J. See James FISK.

**Drew, John.** 1827–1862. Actor, b. Dublin, Ireland. On American stage (from c. 1842). Gained success as portrayer of Irish roles in comedies, as Sir Lucius O'Trigger in Sheridan's *Rivals.* His wife, **Louisa,** *nee* **Lane** (1820–1897), b. London, Eng., to U.S. (1827), was on the stage from childhood; after her third marriage, to John Drew (1850), concentrated on comedy roles, as Peg Woffington, Lady Teazle, and Mrs. Malaprop; assisted husband in management of Arch Street Theatre; sole manager as well as leading actress (1861–93). Their son **John** (1853–1927), b. Philadelphia, was a noted actor, in Augustin Daly's company, New York (1875); supported Jefferson in *Rip Van Winkle;* on barnstorming tour with brother-in-law, Maurice Barrymore; again with Daly's company (1879–92), playing opposite Ada Rehan, one of their chief successes being in *The Taming of the Shrew;* first appeared as a star under Charles Frohman's management (1892), in Clyde Fitch's *Masked Ball,* with Maude Adams as leading lady; remained under Frohman's management until latter's death (1915), starring esp. in contemporary plays; last appearance in revival of Pinero's *Trelawney of the Wells*, shortly before his death. His sister **Georgiana Emma** married Maurice Barrymore (*q.v.*).

**Drews** (drāvs), **Arthur.** 1865–1935. German philosopher; professor; works include *Die Deutsche Spekulation seit Kant* (2 vols., 1893), *Plotin* (1908), *Psychologie des Unbewussten* (1924), *Lehrbuch der Logik* (1928).

**Drex'el** (drĕk's'l), **Francis Martin.** 1792–1863. Banker, b. Dornbirn, Austrian Tirol. To U.S. (1817); portrait painter in Philadelphia; established in Philadelphia (1838) a brokerage office, originally for dealing in foreign currencies and securities, which developed into banking house of Drexel & Co. His son **Anthony Joseph** (1826–1893) became member of the firm (1847) and the dominating influence during its period of expansion (after 1863); senior partner after death of his older brother **Francis** (1885). Co-owner, with George W. Childs, of Philadelphia *Public Ledger* (from 1864). Founder (1892) and benefactor of Drexel Institute, Philadelphia.

**Drey'er** (drī'ẽr), **Johan Ludwig Emil.** 1852–1926. Danish astronomer, b. Copenhagen; director of observatory at Armagh (1882–1916). Known for work on nebulae and on motions of stars, and on the history of astronomy.

**Drey'er** (drī'ẽr), **Max.** 1862–1946. German journalist, playwright, and novelist; editor, *Täglicher Rundschau* (1888–98). His plays include *Drei* (1894), *Winterschlaf* (1895), *Die Siebzehnjährigen* (1904), *Der Grünende Zweig* (1913); novels, *Der Deutsche Morgen* (1915), *Nachwuchs* (1917), *Tapfere Kleine Renate* (1932).

**Drey'fus** (drā'fŭs; drī'fŭs; *Fr.* drā'füs'), **Alfred.** 1859–1935. French army officer, of Jewish blood, b. in Alsace; convicted (1894) of treason and imprisoned (1895) on Devil's Island; later investigation, forced (1898) largely by Émile Zola (*q.v.*), proved that the papers on which he had been convicted were forged by Major Esterhazy and Lieut. Col. Henry (*qq.v.*); defended also by Georges Picquart (*q.v.*); tried a second time at Rennes (1899); original conviction was set aside (1906), and Dreyfus was restored to rank in the army and given the decoration of the Legion of Honor.

**Drey'schock** (drī'shŏk), **A'le·xan'der** (ä'lĕ·ksän'dẽr). 1818–1869. Bohemian piano virtuoso. Composed over 100 works for piano.

**Drey'se** (drī'zĕ), **Johann Nikolaus von.** 1787–1867. German inventor of muzzle-loading (1827) and breech-loading (1836) needle guns, adopted by the Prussian army (1840).

**Driesch** (drēsh), **Hans Adolf Eduard.** 1867–1941. German biologist and philosopher; advocate of vitalism. Professor, Heidelberg (1911), Cologne (1920), Leipzig (1921). Author of *Analytische Theorie der Organischen Entwicklung* (1894), *Geschichte des Vitalismus* (1905), *Leib und Seele* (1916), *Parapsychologie* (1932), etc.

**Drink'wa'ter** (drĭngk'wô'tẽr; -wŏt'ẽr), **John.** 1882–1937. English poet and playwright; originally employee in assurance companies for twelve years. A founder of The Pilgrim Players, now The Birmingham Repertory Theatre. His works include *Poems, 1908–1914*, *Swords and Ploughshares* (1915), *Tides* (1917), *Preludes* (1922), *Mr. Charles, King of England* (1926), *Pepys* (1930), *Shakespeare* (1933), *John Hampden's England* (1933), the autobiographical volumes *Inheritance* (1931) and *Discovery* (1932), and many plays, including *Rebellion* (in verse; 1914), *Abraham Lincoln* (1918), *Loyalties* (1919), *Mary Stuart* (1919), *Oliver Cromwell* (1921), *Robert E. Lee* (1923), *Robert Burns* (1925), *Bird-in Hand* (1928), *Midsummer Eve* (1932), *Laying the Devil* (1933), *A Man's House* (1934).

**Dri'o'ton'** (drē'ô'tôɴ'), **Étienne Marie.** **1889–1961.** French ecclesiastic and Egyptologist. Director-general of antiquities, Egypt (1936 ff.). Author of *L'Art Égyptien* (1930), *L'Égypte* (1938), etc.

**Dris'ler** (drĭz'lẽr), **Henry.** **1818–1897.** American classical scholar.

**Dri'ver** (drī'vẽr), **Samuel Rolles.** **1846–1914.** English Biblical scholar; at Oxford, regius professor of Hebrew and canon of Christ Church; member of Old Testament revision committee (1876–84).

**Dro'bisch** (drō'bĭsh), **Moritz Wilhelm.** 1802–1896. German mathematician and philosopher; professor, Leipzig. Author of *Neue Darstellung der Logik* (1836), *Grundlehren der Religionsphilosophie* (1840), etc.

**Droes'hout** (dro͞os'hout), **Mar'tin** (mär'tĭn). b. 1601. Flemish engraver, b. London; known chiefly for his engraved portrait of William Shakespeare prefixed to the First Folio (1623).

**Drol'ling'** (drô'lăɴg'), **Martin.** 1752–1817. French genre painter. His son **Michel** (1786–1851), historical painter.

**Drop'sie** (drŏp'sĭ), **Moses Aaron.** 1821–1905. American lawyer; bequeathed his estate for founding of Dropsie College for Hebrew and Cognate Learning.

**Dro·si'nes** *or* **Dro·si'nis** (thrô·sē'nyēs), **Georgios.** 1859–1950. Greek writer, b. Athens. Among his volumes of verse are *Spun Webs* (1880), *Idylls* (1885), *Light of Love* (1894); among prose works, *Rural Letters* (1882), *Fables* (1889).

**Dro'ste-Hüls'hoff** (drôs'tĕ·hüls'hôf), Baroness **Annette Elisabeth von.** 1797–1848. German poet; author of *Gedichte* (1838) and a volume of religious verse.

**Droste zu Vi'sche·ring** (tso͞o fĭsh'ĕ·rĭng), Baron **Klemens August von.** 1773–1845. German Roman Catholic prelate; archbishop of Cologne (1835–42); imprisoned (1837–39) following dispute with Prussian government over question of mixed marriages.

**Drou'ais'** (dro͞o'ĕ'). Family of French artists, including: **Hubert** (1699–1767), painter of portraits and miniatures; his son **François Hubert** (1727–1775), painter of portraits of Louis XV, Mme. du Barry, Mme. de Pompadour; the latter's son **Jean Germain** (1763–1788), painter of *La Chananéenne aux Pieds de Jésus* and *Marius à Minturnes*, both in the Louvre.

**Drou'et'** (dro͞o'ĕ'), **Jean Baptiste.** 1763–1824. French revolutionist who recognized Louis XVI at Sainte-Menehould, when the king was attempting to flee France, and caused his arrest at Varennes. Member of National Convention (1792) and Council of Five Hundred (1795); involved in the Babeuf plot (see François Émile BABEUF) and imprisoned, but escaped.

**Drouet d'Er'lon'** (dĕr'lôɴ'), Comte **Jean Baptiste.** 1765–1844. French soldier in the Napoleonic armies; general of division (1803); distinguished himself at Jena (1806), Friedland (1807), Waterloo (1815); governor general of Algeria (1834); created marshal of France (1843).

**Drou'ot'** (dro͞o'ō'), Comte **Antoine.** 1774–1847. French general; general of division and aide-de-camp to Napoleon (1813); accompanied Napoleon to Elba (1814). Called by Napoleon *le Sage de la Grande Armée.*

**Drou'yn' de Lhu·ys'** (dro͞o'ăɴ' dē lü·ēs'), **Édouard.** 1805–1881. French statesman; minister of foreign affairs (1848–49; 1851; 1852–55; 1862–66).

**Drown** (droun), **Thomas Messinger.** 1842–1904. American chemist, b. Philadelphia. Professor, M.I.T. (1885–95); president, Lehigh U. (1895–1904). As director of analytical laboratories (1887) and adviser to project as a whole, he is largely responsible for the pioneer work of Massachusetts in examining and protecting state water supplies.

**Droy'sen** (droi'zĕn), **Johann Gustav.** 1808–1884. German historian; professor, Kiel (1840), Jena (1851), Berlin (1859); author of *Geschichte des Hellenismus* (2 vols., 1836–43), *Geschichte der Preussischen Politik* (14 vols., 1855–86), etc.

**Droz** (drôz). Family of French artists, of Swiss origin, including: **Jean Pierre** (1746–1823), engraver of money and medals; his son **Jules Antoine** (1807–1872), a sculptor; Jules's son **Antoine Gustave** (1832–1895), painter, and author of *Monsieur, Madame et Bébé* (1866), *Entre Nous* (1867), *Une Femme Gênante* (1875), etc.

**Droz, François Xavier Joseph.** 1773–1850. French moral philosopher and historian; author of *Essai sur l'Art d'être Heureux, Histoire du Règne de Louis XVI*...(1839–42), etc.

**Droz, Numa.** 1844–1899. Swiss journalist and statesman; editor, *National Suisse* (1864); president of the Swiss Confederation (1881, 1887).

**Dru'de** (drōō'dĕ), **Karl Georg Oskar.** 1852–1933. German botanist; professor, Technische Hochschule, and director of botanical gardens, Dresden (1879–1920). His stepbrother **Paul Karl Ludwig** (1863–1906), physicist, investigated relationship between optical and electrical phenomena; developed theory of the physics of metals based on electronic theory; studied electric waves.

**Druf'fel** (drōōf'ĕl), **August von.** 1841–1891. German historian.

**Drum** (drŭm), **Hugh Aloysius.** 1879–1951. American army officer, b. Fort Brady, Mich. Brigadier general (1922), major general (1931), lieutenant general (1939). Engaged in Philippines (1899–1901, 1908–10) and on Mexican border (1912–14). Asst. chief of staff to Gen. Pershing in France (1917); chief of staff of 1st army, A.E.F. (1918–19). Asst. chief of staff (1923–26), inspector general (1930), deputy chief of staff (1933), U.S. army. In command of Hawaiian department (1935–37). Lieutenant general (1939), in command of 1st army.

**Drumcairn,** Lord. See *Thomas Hamilton* (1563–1637), under earls of HADDINGTON.

**Drum'mond** (drŭm'ŭnd). Name of an old Scottish family bearing (from 1605 to 1760) the title of earl of **Perth** (pûrth), raised by James II to duke of Perth, and including:

**James Drummond** (1648–1716), 4th Earl and 1st titular Duke of Perth; supported Lauderdale in permitting highland raids (1677); joined Scottish nobles in opposition to Lauderdale (1678); associated with William Penn in settlement of New Jersey (1681); justice general (1682), lord chancellor of Scotland (1684); retained in office by James II as chief Roman Catholic agent in Scotland. His son **James** (1675–1720), 5th earl and 2d titular duke; took part in the Jacobite uprising of 1715–16, led cavalry at battle of Sheriffmuir, escaped with James Edward, the Old Pretender, to the Continent (1716); father of **James** (1713–1747), 6th earl and 3d titular duke (self-styled despite the attainting of his father), who commanded Young Pretender's left wing at Culloden Moor (1746), and of **John** (d. 1747), 4th duke who was sent from France to join Prince Charles Edward (1745), was instrumental in gaining Jacobite victory at Falkirk (1746), fought at Culloden Moor (1746).

Sir **Eric Drummond** (1876–1951), 16th Earl of Perth, 12th Viscount **Strath·al'lan** (străth·ăl'ăn); diplomat; educ. Eton; entered foreign office (1900); précis writer to foreign secretary (1908, 1910–11); one of private secretaries to prime minister (1912–15); private secretary to foreign secretary (1915–19); with Balfour at first months of peace conference in Paris; first secretary general of League of Nations (1919–33); organized secretariat of about 600 persons of forty nationalities on plan of an international civil service; ambassador to Italy (1933–39); succeeded his half brother, 15th earl of Perth (1937); in charge of foreign publicity department of foreign office and chief adviser on foreign publicity to ministry of information (since 1939).

**Drummond, Henry.** 1786–1860. English banker and Irvingite apostle; opposed Socinian tendencies at Geneva; one of founders and propagators of the Catholic Apostolic or Irvingite Church, of which he was an apostle, evangelist, and prophet.

**Drummond, Henry.** 1851–1897. Scottish evangelical writer and lecturer. Educ. at Edinburgh; joined (1873) evangelical movement led by Dwight L. Moody and Ira D. Sankey; lecturer on natural science, Free Church School, Glasgow (1877); sought to reconcile evangelical Christianity with evolution in *Natural Law in the Spiritual World* (1883); professor of theology in the New Jerusalem Church (1884). Reported explorations in tropical Africa (1888); emphasized altruistic actions of animals toward each other in scheme of natural selection, in *Ascent of Man* (1894), given as Lowell Lectures in Boston; toured Australian and American colleges; published address *The Greatest Thing in the World* (1890).

**Drummond, James.** 1835–1918. British Unitarian theologian, b. Dublin; advocated doctrinal freedom, rejected the Resurrection and nature miracles.

**Drummond, Roy Maxwell.** 1894– . British air officer, b. Perth, Australia; served in Australian forces (1914–15) and in R.A.F. (1916–20) in Middle East. Air vice-marshal, deputy commander in chief of R.A.F. in Middle East (from 1941); directed air attack on Rommel's army (Nov., 1942).

**Drummond, Thomas.** 1797–1840. British engineer and administrator, b. Edinburgh. Entered Royal Engineers (1815); joined trigonometrical survey of Great Britain (1820), facilitated by his limelight apparatus, the Drummond light; devised an improved heliostat. Undersecretary of state for Ireland (1835–40).

**Drummond** of Haw'thorn'den (hô'thôrn'dĕn), **William.** 1585–1649. Scottish poet. Son of **John Drummond** (1553–1610), 1st Laird of Hawthornden, related to Scottish royal house. Royalist and Episcopalian. Wrote elegy on Prince Henry Frederick (1613); wrote sonnets and songs to memory of Mary Cunningham of Barns, who died on eve of their marriage (1615); made contributions to Petrarchan sonnet. Friend and correspondent of Sir William Alexander, Earl of Stirling (from c. 1613), and of Michael Drayton; recorded notes of conversations during memorable visit of Ben Jonson (1618–19). Had to subscribe to Solemn League and Covenant but protested in sarcastic verses (1643); wrote in favor of negotiations with Charles I (1646). Author of *Flowers of Zion* (1623, religious verse), *The Cypresse Grove* (1623, a meditation on death), *History of Scotland 1423–1542* (1655).

**Drummond, William.** 1st Viscount of **Strath·al'lan** (străth·ăl'ăn). 1617?–1688. Scottish soldier. Royalist commander at battle of Worcester (1651) and in Highlands (1653); held command in Russian service (1655–65). Major general of forces in Scotland (1666); popularly supposed to have introduced torture by thumbscrew from Russia.

**Drummond, William Henry.** 1854–1907. Canadian poet, b. in Ireland; emigrated to Canada (1865); graduate in medicine, Bishop's Coll., Lennoxville (1884). Portrayed the French-Canadian habitant in numerous poems, mostly in patois, collected in *The Habitant* (1897), *Johnny Courteau* (1901), *The Voyageur* (1905), *The Great Fight* (1908), etc.

**Dru·sil'la** (drōō·sĭl'ȧ). 15–38 A.D. Daughter of Germanicus Caesar and Agrippina; sister and mistress of Caligula.

**Drusilla.** b. 38 A.D. Younger daughter of Herod Agrippa I and sister of Herod Agrippa II and Berenice; in defiance of Jewish law, m. as second husband Antonius Felix, Roman procurator of Judea (*Acts* xxiv. 24).

**Dru'sus** (drōō'sŭs). Roman plebeian family of the gens Livius, including:

**Marcus Livius Drusus** (d. 109? B.C.), tribune of the people with Gaius Gracchus (122 B.C.); opposed reforms of his colleague; made more extreme democratic proposals than did Gracchus but refused to carry them out when they were accepted; granted consulship (112) by senatorial party; received Macedonia; advanced to the Danube.

His son **Marcus Livius Drusus** (d. 91 B.C.), tribune of the people (91 B.C.); proposed measures to restore judicial functions from equites to senate; to win popular votes proposed also establishment of colonies, lower price of grain, and extension of citizenship to Italians; these measures passed, but aroused senate abrogated them; assassinated at beginning of civil war (Social War).

**Livia Drusilla** (*q.v.*); adopted into this family; third wife of Augustus; by her first husband, Tiberius Claudius Nero, mother of **Nero Claudius Drusus Ger·man'i·cus** [jûr·măn'ĭ·kŭs] (38 B.C.–9 B.C.), *called* **Drusus Senior;** Roman general; with his older brother Tiberius (later emperor), subdued Rhaeti and Vindelici (15 B.C.); governor of Gaul (13–10); made several campaigns from Gaul against German tribes beyond Rhine; returned to Rome and was elected consul (9); defeated Chatti, Suevi, Marcomanni, and others, penetrating as far north as the Elbe (9 B.C.); died after being thrown from his horse. Father by his wife Antonia (daughter of Marcus Antonius, the triumvir) of Germanicus Caesar, the emperor Claudius, and a daughter Livilla or Livia (wife of Drusus Caesar).

His nephew **Drusus Caesar** (15? B.C.–23 A.D.), *called* **Drusus Junior;** son of Emperor Tiberius and Vipsania Agrippina; sent to Pannonia (15 A.D.); governor of Illyricum (17); consul with his father (21); incurred enmity of Sejanus (*q.v.*), who seduced his wife Livilla (daughter of Drusus Senior); poisoned by Sejanus and Livilla.

**Drusus.** d. 33 A.D. Son of Germanicus Caesar and Agrippina; kept imprisoned and starved to death by Emperor Tiberius, who was jealous of the favor in which Drusus stood with the populace.

**Dryander.** See ENZINAS.

**Dry'an·der'** (drü'än·dûr'), **Jonas.** 1748–1810. Swedish botanist in England; librarian to Royal Society; one of founders of Linnaean Society and (1788) its vice-president.

**Dry'den** (drī'd'n), **John.** 1631–1700. English poet, b. in Northamptonshire. Clerk to his cousin Sir Gilbert Pickering, Cromwell's chamberlain; panegyrist in *Heroic Stanzas on the Death of Oliver Cromwell* (pub. with two poems by Thomas Sprat and Edmund Waller, 1659) and in *Astræa Redux* (1660) and *Panegyric* on the Restoration (1661); m. (1663) Lady Elizabeth Howard, sister of his patron Sir Robert Howard (*q.v.*). Established reputation with *The Rival Ladies* (1663, a tragicomedy using the rhymed couplet); produced *The Indian Queen* (1664), *The Indian Emperor or the Conquest of Mexico by the Spaniards* (1665), *Amboyna*, designed to excite hatred of the Dutch (1673), *Tyrannic Love* (1669), *Almanzor and Almahide or the Conquest of Granada* (1670), *Marriage-a-la-mode* (his best comedy, 1673), *Aurengzebe* (a rhymed tragedy, 1676), *All for Love* (a version of the story of Antony and Cleopatra in blank verse, 1678), and *The Spanish Fryar* (1681), besides adaptations of Shakespeare's tragedies. Published *Annus Mirabilis*, treating of the great fire and the Dutch war (1667). Poet laureate and historiographer (1670). Had controversy with Elkanah Settle, author of bombastic plays (from 1673); was beaten by masked bravoes of John Wilmot, Earl of Rochester, for an attributed derogatory passage in an anonymous essay (1679; see John SHEFFIELD). Partly in retaliation for Buckingham's ridicule of heroic drama in *The Rehearsal*, launched in *Absalom and Achitophel* (1681) a crushing satire upon Monmouth, Shaftesbury, Buckingham, Charles II, Titus Oates, and others involved in conspiracy to exclude duke of York in favor of duke of Monmouth; satirized the ignoramus of grand jury at Shaftesbury's trial in *The Medal* (1682), and Thomas Shadwell in *Mac Flecknoe* (1682); defended Anglicanism in *Religio Laici* (1682); justified his conversion to Roman Catholicism in *The Hind and the Panther* (1687); declining to take oaths at the English Revolution, lost his places and pensions (1689). Turned again to playwriting, without much success, in *Don Sebastian* (tragicomedy, 1690), *Amphitryon* (comedy, 1690), and *Love Triumphant* (tragicomedy, 1694). Produced translations in verse of Perseus, satires of Juvenal, and the whole of Vergil (1697); produced adaptations from Chaucer and Boccaccio, including the ode for St. Cecilia's day entitled *Alexander's Feast* (1697) and *Fables, Ancient and Modern* (1699), his last great work.

**Dryden, John Fairfield.** 1839–1911. American pioneer in industrial insurance; established (1875) at Newark, N.J., Prudential Friendly Society, which developed into The Prudential Insurance Co. (so called from 1878); president of the company (from 1881). U.S. senator (1902–07). His son **Forrest Fairchild** (1864–1932) succeeded him as president (1912–22).

**Dry·gal'ski** (drē·gäl'skē), **Erich von.** 1865–1949. German geophysicist, geographer, and explorer; led scientific expedition to West Greenland (1891; 1892–93), South Polar region (1901–03).

**Du·ane'** (dū̇·ān'), **James.** 1733–1797. American jurist; practiced, New York. Member, Continental Congress (1774–84); assisted in draft of Articles of Confederation; mayor of New York City (1784–89); U.S. district judge, District of New York (1789–94). His grandson **James Chatham Duane** (1824–1897) was a military engineer; chief engineer under McClellan and (from 1863) of the Army of the Potomac; chief of engineers (1886–88). His son **Alexander** (1858–1926) was an ophthalmologist and medical writer, contributor of medical definitions to *Webster's International Dictionary* and *Oxford English Dictionary.*

**Duane, William.** 1760–1835. American journalist, b. near Lake Champlain, N.Y. To Ireland as a child; learned printer's trade; to India (1787); established *Indian World*, Calcutta; deported to England for criticizing authorities. Returned to U.S. (1795); associated with B. F. Bache in editing the *Aurora*, Philadelphia; sole editor after Bache's death (1798); made the *Aurora* powerful organ of Jeffersonian party; arrested (1799) on charge of inciting riot; acquitted; indicted under Sedition Law (1799); charge dismissed when Jefferson became president. Political influence waned after transfer of seat of government from Philadelphia to Washington; sold the *Aurora* (1822). His son **William John** (1780–1865) was on staff of the *Aurora* (1798–1806); practiced law (from 1815); U.S. secretary of the treasury (1833); removed for refusing to withdraw government deposits from United States Bank before meeting of Congress.

**Duane, William.** 1872–1935. American physicist, b. Philadelphia, Pa. Professor of biophysics, Harvard (from 1917). Developed methods and apparatus for utilizing X rays and radium in medicine, esp. in the treatment of cancer; investigated the structure of matter, mechanism of radiations, etc.

**Duarte.** Portuguese form of EDWARD.

**Du'bail'** (dü'bá'y'), **Auguste Yvon Edmond.** 1851–1934. French general in the World War.

**Du'ban'** (dü'bäN'), **Félix Louis Jacques.** 1797–1870. French architect; studied at École des Beaux-Arts (Paris); designed reconstruction and enlargement of École des Beaux-Arts (from 1834), restoration of Château de Blois, and improvements at Fontainebleau and Chantilly; architect of the Louvre (1848–54).

**Du Bar'ry** (dŏŏ băr'ĭ; *Fr.* dü bá'rē'), Comtesse. **Marie Jeanne Bé'cu'** (bā'kü'). 1746 (or 1743?)–1793. Adventuress and mistress of Louis XV, Vaucouleurs; natural daughter of Anne Bécu. Mistress (1764–68) of Chevalier Jean du Barry (1723–1794); presided over his gambling house. Became mistress of king (1768); m. Comte Guillaume du Barry, brother of Jean; ruled king and court (1769–74), aided by her confidant, duc d'Aiguillon; patron of artists and men of letters; dismissed duc de Choiseul (1770); retired from court on death of Louis (1774). Arrested by Robespierre (1793); tried by Revolutionary Tribunal, condemned, and guillotined (Dec. 7).

**du Bartas.** See BARTAS.

**du Bellay.** See BELLAY.

**Du'boc'** (dü'bôk'), **É'douard'** (ā'dwȧr'). *Pseudonym* **Ro'bert Wald'mül'ler** (rō'bĕrt vält'mül'ẽr). 1822–1910. German writer of French descent, b. Hamburg; settled in Dresden (1859). Author of lyrics, *Brunhild* (tragedy; 1873), *Leid und Lust* (novel; 1874), etc. His brother **Julius** (1829–1903), philosopher and publicist, wrote *Die Psychologie der Liebe* (1874), *Die Lust als Sozial-Esthisches Entwicklungsprinzip* (1900), etc.

**Duboccage, Marie Anne.** See BOCCAGE.

**Du'bois'** (dü'bwä'; -bwȧ'), **Eugène**, *in full* **Marie Eugène François Thomas.** 1858–1940. Dutch anatomist and paleontologist. While serving as military surgeon in the Dutch East Indies (1887–95), discovered in Java the bones of an animal, apparently intermediate between man and the existing anthropoid apes, which he named *Pithecanthropus erectus* (1891–92).

**Du'bois'** (dü'bwä'; -bwȧ'), **Guillaume.** 1656–1723. Cardinal and prime minister of France; tutor of Philippe, Duke of Orléans, at that time duc de Chartres; private secretary of the duke, at that time regent (1715); virtual ruler of France; determined regent's foreign policy; formed Triple Alliance against Spain (1717). Became archbishop of Cambrai (1720), cardinal (1721), prime minister (1722).

**du'Bois'** (dü'bwä'; -bwȧ'), **Guy** (gē) **Pène** (pân). 1884–1958. American painter, b. Brooklyn, N.Y.; studio in Paris (1924–30) and New York.

**Dubois, Jean Antoine.** 1765–1848. French Roman Catholic missionary in India; author of *Mœurs, Institutions et Cérémonies des Peuples de l'Inde* (1825).

**Dubois, Louis Ernest.** 1856–1929. French Roman Catholic prelate; created cardinal (1916), and cardinal-archbishop of Paris (1920).

**Dubois, Paul.** 1829–1905. French sculptor; regarded as one of chief representatives of the Academical school. Among his works are portrait busts of Paul Baudry, Pasteur, and Charles Gounod, and equestrian statues of Constable Anne de Montmorency, and Joan of Arc.

**Dubois, Pierre Joseph Louis Alfred.** 1852?–1925. French general in the World War (1914–18).

**Dubois, Théodore**, *in full* **Clément François Théodore.** 1837–1924. French composer; organist at the Madeleine, Paris (1877); professor (from 1871) and director (1896–1905), Paris Conservatory of Music. Composer of operas, oratorios, masses, motets, chamber music, symphonic poems, organ and piano pieces, and songs.

**Du Bois** (dōō bois'), **William Edward Burg'hardt** (bûrg'härd). 1868–1963. American educator, editor, and writer, b. Great Barrington, Mass., of Negro ancestry. A.B. (1890) and Ph.D. (1895), Harvard. Professor of economics and history, Atlanta (1897–1910). Editor of *Crisis* (1910–32). Professor of sociology, Atlanta (from 1932). Editor of Atlanta U. *Studies of the Negro Problem* (1897–1911). Author of *The Souls of Black Folk* (1903), *John Brown* (1909), *The Negro* (1915), *Darkwater* (1920), *Black Reconstruction* (1935), etc.

**Du'bois' de Cran'cé'** (dü'bwä' [-bwȧ'] dē kräN'sā'), **Edmond Louis Alexis de.** 1747–1814. French revolutionary politician; member of the States-General (1789), the National Convention (1792); voted for execution of Louis XVI; member of Council of Five Hundred (1795); minister of war (1799). Retired (1799).

**Du Bois'-Rey'mond'** (dü bwä'rā'môN'; dü bwȧ'-), **Emil.** 1818–1896. German physiologist, pioneer in experimental physiology; known esp. for investigations in animal electricity, physiology of muscles and nerves, and metabolic processes. His brother **Paul** (1831–1889), mathematician, wrote *Die Allgemeine Funktionentheorie* (1882) and *Grundlagen der Erkenntnis in den Exakten Wissenschaften* (1890).

**Du'bos'** *or* **Du Bos** (dü'bôs'), **Jean Baptiste.** 1670–1742. French abbé, diplomat, and historian.

**Dubos, René Jules.** 1901– . Bacteriologist, b. in France. B.S., Institut National Agronomique, Paris (1921); Ph.D., Rutgers (1927); naturalized U.S. citizen (1938). With Rockefeller Institute for Medical Research (from 1927). Known for work in internal medicine, especially discovery of a substance produced by certain soil bacteria, used in treating bacterial infections.

**Du'brun'faut'** (dü'brûN'fō'), **Auguste Pierre.** 1797–1881. French industrialist and chemist; author of works relating to the alcohol-distilling industry; devised a method permitting further crystallization of sugar from exhausted beet molasses (1850).

**Dubs** (dōōps), **Jakob.** 1822–1879. Swiss jurist and statesman; president of Swiss Confederation (1864, 1868, 1870).

**Du'bufe'** (dü'büf'). Family of French painters, including **Claude Marie** (1790–1864), genre and portrait painter; his son **Louis Édouard** (1820–1883), whose works include portraits of Empress Eugénie, Charles Gounod, Dumas fils, Philippe Rousseau; the latter's son **Édouard Marie Guillaume** (1853–1909), painter esp. of murals and allegorical compositions.

**Du'buf'fet'** (dü'bü'bĕ'), **Jean.** 1901– . French artist; uses experimental material such as sand, tar, glass, sponges, and nails in his works.

**Du·buque'** (dŭ·būk'; *Fr.* dü'bük'), **Jul'ien** (jōōl'yĕn; *Fr.* zhü'lyăN'). 1762–1810. Pioneer in Iowa, b. in Province of Quebec. Negotiated agreement with Fox Indians for right to work lead mines in Iowa region (1788); first white settler near what is now Dubuque, Iowa.

**Duc** (dük), **Joseph Louis.** 1802–1879. French architect; aided in rebuilding and enlarging the Palais de Justice.

**Du Camp** (dü käN'), **Maxime.** 1822–1894. French journalist and traveler; on editorial staff of *La Revue de Paris, La Revue des Deux Mondes, Journal des Débats.* Among his books are *Souvenirs et Paysages d'Orient* (1848), *Le Nil* (1854), *Les Chants Modernes* (1855).

**Du Cange** (dü käNzh'), Sieur. **Charles du Fresne** (dü frân'). 1610–1688. French scholar; author of *Histoire de L'Empire de Constantinople sous les Empereurs Français* (1657); compiler of *Glossarium Mediae et Infimae Latinitatis* (1678), *Glossarium ad Scriptores Mediae et Infimae Graecitatis* (1688).

**Du'cange'** (dü'käNzh'), **Victor Henri Joseph Brahain.**

1783–1833. French novelist and playwright; author of the novels *Agathe*. . .(1819), *Léonide*. . .(1823), *Marco Loricot*. . .(1836), and the melodramas *Calas* (1819), *Le Jésuite* (1830), etc.

**Du'cas** (dū'kăs). Name of a noble Byzantine family that furnished rulers of the Eastern Roman Empire: **Constantine X** (reigned 1059–67), **Michael VII** (1071–78), **Alexius V** (1204), **John III** (1222–54), **Theodore II** (1254–58), and **John IV** (1258–61). The last three were also connected with the Lascaris family. **Michael Ducas** (fl. middle of 15th cent.), probably of this family, was a Byzantine historian; lived at Constantinople and Lesbos; author of a trustworthy history of Eastern Greek Empire for the period 1341–1462, first published in Paris (1649).

**Du Casse** (dü kȧs'), Baron **Pierre Emmanuel Albert.** 1813–1893. French army officer and writer on military subjects; took part in Italian campaign (1859).

**Du'casse'** (dü'kȧs'), **Roger,** *in full* **Jean Jules Amable Roger.** *Also known as* **Ro'ger'–Du'casse'** (rô'zhā'-). 1873–1954. French composer of symphonies and symphonic poems, choral works, motets, and piano pieces.

**Duc'cio di Buo'nin·se'gna** (do͞ot'chō dē bwô'nēn·sā'-nyä). 1255?–?1319. Italian painter; first leading representative of Sienese school; marks perfection of Italo-Byzantine art; known esp. for altarpiece (1308–11) for Cathedral of Siena, including large panel *Madonna Enthroned, with Angels and Saints* (now in cathedral museum, Siena) and scenes from the life of the Virgin Mary and of Christ.

**Du Cerceau, Androuet.** See ANDROUET DU CERCEAU.

**Du Chail'lu'** (dü shȧ'yü'), **Paul Bel'lo'ni'** (bĕ'lô'nē'). 1831–1903. African explorer, b. in France. To U.S. (1852); on exploring expedition in Central Africa (1856–59); brought back specimens of birds and animals, and first gorillas ever seen in America; made second trip to Africa (1863–65). Author of *Explorations and Adventures in Equatorial Africa* (1861), *Stories of the Gorilla Country* (1868), *Wild Life Under the Equator* (1869), *Lost in the Jungle* (1869), *The Country of the Dwarfs* (1871), etc.

**Du'champ'–Vil'lon'** (dü'shäɴ'vē'yôɴ'), **Raymond.** 1876–1918. French sculptor, identified with cubist school. His brother **Marcel Duchamp** (1887–1968). Fr.-born Amer. painter, pioneer member of Dadaist school.

**Du·ché'** (do͞o·shā'), **Jacob.** 1738–1798. Anglican clergyman, b. Philadelphia; chaplain of first Continental Congress (1774); turned loyalist (1775); lived in England (1777–92); again in Philadelphia (1792–98).

**Du'chenne'** (dü'shĕn'), **Guillaume Benjamin Amand.** *Called* **Duchenne de Bou'logne'** (dē bo͞o'lôn'y'). 1806–1875. French physician; pioneer in use of electricity for diagnosis and treatment of disease; credited with first description of locomotor ataxia, progressive muscular paralysis, etc.; studied physiology of the emotions; regarded as one of founders of neuropathology.

**Du'chesne'** (dü'shân'), **André.** *Lat.* **Andreas Ches'ne·us** (kĕs'nē·ŭs) *or* **Quer'ce·ta'nus** (kwûr'sē·tā'nŭs). 1584–1640. French historian; appointed historiographer to king; known as the "father of French history." Author of *Antiquitez et Recherches de la Grandeur et Majesté des Rois de France* (1609), etc.

**Duchesne, Louis Marie Olivier.** 1843–1922. French Roman Catholic prelate and scholar; author of treatises on church history.

**Duchesne, Père.** Sobriquet of Jacques René HÉBERT.

**Du·chesne'** (do͞o·shān'; *Fr.* dü'shân'), **Rose** (rōz) **Phil'ip·pine** (fĭl'ĭ·pēn; *Fr.* fē'lē'pēn'). 1769–1852. Roman Catholic religious, of the Society of the Sacred Heart, b. Grenoble, France. Sent to America (1818) as missionary and teacher in the St. Louis region, where she established schools and convents; voted (1918) by Historical Society of Missouri the greatest benefactress of the region.

**Du'ches'nois'** (dü'shĕ'nwȧ'), Mlle. *Stage name of* **Catherine Joséphine Ra'fin'** (rȧ'făɴ'). 1777–1835. French tragedienne; rival of Mlle. George (*q.v.*) for several years; retired (1833).

**Duchess, The.** Pseudonym of Margaret Wolfe HUNGERFORD.

**Du'cis'** (dü'sēs'), **Jean François.** 1733–1816. French playwright; best known for his adaptations of Shakespeare's plays for the French stage.

**Duck'worth** (dŭk'wûrth), Sir **John Thomas.** 1748–1817. English naval commander. Took part in defeat of Brest fleet off Ushant (1794); reduced Swedish and Danish possessions in West Indies (1801); defeated French fleet off Santo Domingo (1806); admiral (1810).

**Du'claux'** (dü'klō'), **Pierre Émile.** 1840–1904. French biochemist. Professor, Sorbonne (1885); director, Pasteur Inst. in Paris (1895). For wife, **Mary,** see under Arsène DARMESTETER.

**Du'clerc'** (dü'klâr'), **Charles Théodore Eugène.** 1812–1888. French politician and journalist; minister of foreign affairs and premier (1882–83).

**Du'clos'** (dü'klō'), **Charles Pinot.** 1704–?1772. French writer of fiction, essays, and history, as *Histoire de Mlle de Luz* (novel, 1741), *Essai de Grammaire Française* (1754), *Mémoires pour Servir à l'Histoire des Mœurs du XVIII^e Siècle* (1751), etc.

**Du'com'mun'** (dü'kô'mûɴ'), **Élie.** 1833–1906. Swiss journalist; editor, *Revue de Genève* (1855); contributor to *Progrès, Helvétie, États-Unis d'Europe;* organizer (1891) of International Bureau of Peace, Bern. With Charles Albert Gobat, awarded Nobel peace prize (1902).

**Du'cor'net'** (dü'kôr'nĕ'), **Louis César Joseph.** 1806–1856. French historical and portrait painter of the romantic school; born armless, painted with feet.

**Du'cos'** (dü'kō'), **Pierre Roger.** 1747–1816. French politician; member of National Convention (1792), and Council of Five Hundred (1795); Third Consul (with Bonaparte and Sieyès) at the beginning of the Consulate (1799); vice-president of the Senate. Exiled after Restoration.

**Ducos du Hau'ron'** (dü ō'rôɴ'), **Louis.** 1837–1920. French physicist; pioneer in color photography; inventor of a trichrome process for printing colored pictures.

**Du'crot'** (dü'krō'), **Auguste Alexandre.** 1817–1882. French general; in command of army corps at Wörth and Sedan (1870); captured, but escaped and commanded France's second army in Paris; attempted vainly to break Prussian siege (Sept. 19, Oct. 21, Nov. 30, 1870, and Jan. 19, 1871). Commanded 8th army corps (1872–78); relieved of his command for demonstrations against the republican regime.

**Ducrotay de Blainville, Henri Marie.** See BLAINVILLE.

**Dud·dell'** (dŭ·dĕl'; dŭ-), **William du Bois.** 1872–1917. English electrical engineer; invented an oscillograph; discovered the singing arc; designed a high-frequency generator and a thermoammeter.

**Du'den** (do͞o'dĕn), **Konrad.** 1829–1911. German philologist.

**Dude'ney** (do͞od'nĭ), Mrs. **Henry.** 1866–1945. English novelist; m. Henry Ernest Dudeney (d. 1930). Author of *The Maternity of Harriott Wicken, The Secret Son, The House in the High Street, Petty Cash,* etc.

**Dudevant, Aurore** and **Maurice.** See George SAND.

**Dud'ley** (dŭd'lĭ), **Benjamin Winslow.** 1785–1870. American surgeon, b. in Spotsylvania County, Va.; practiced,

Lexington, Ky. (1814–53); professor, Transylvania U. (1817–50); regarded as the outstanding American lithotomist of his time.

**Dudley, Charles Benjamin.** 1842–1909. American chemist; made revolutionary applications of chemistry in increasing efficiency and safety on railroads.

**Dudley, Charles Edward.** 1780–1841. American politician, b. Staffordshire, England; to U.S. (1794). New York State senator (1820–25); mayor of Albany (1821–24, 1828, 1829); member of the "Albany regency," political group headed by Martin Van Buren; succeeded Van Buren as U.S. senator (1829–33). His widow donated (1856) funds to build Dudley Observatory, Albany.

**Dudley, Dud.** 1599–1684. English ironmaster in Worcestershire; first to smelt iron ore with coal, and probably coke, rather than charcoal (1619); author of *Metallum Martis* (1665).

**Dudley,** Lady **Jane.** = Lady *Jane Grey,* under GREY family.

**Dudley, John.** Duke of **North·um'ber·land** (nôr-thŭm'bẽr·lănd) and Earl of **War'wick** (wŏr'ĭk). 1502?–1553. English soldier and conspirator for enthroning Lady Jane Grey. Son of **Edmund Dudley** (1462?–1510, lawyer, colleague in carrying out Henry VII's extortionate tax policy, speaker of House of Commons [1504], executed for constructive treason). Restored in blood on repeal of father's attainder (1512–13); deputy governor of Calais (1538); warden of Scottish marches (1542); raised to peerage as Viscount **Lisle** (1542); joint regent and high chamberlain of England (1547); defeated Scots at Pinkie (1547); brought about execution of Somerset (1552); married his fourth son, **Guildford** (d. 1554), to Lady Jane Grey and induced Edward VI to sign letters patent altering succession of crown to fall to Lady Jane Grey (see GREY family); executed for resisting Mary's succession (1553). His third son, **Ambrose** (1528?–1590), Earl of **Warwick,** was pardoned for supporting claim of Lady Jane Grey; aided forces of Philip II of Spain at siege of Saint-Quentin (1557); besieged in Havre while aiding Protestants there and forced to surrender (1563); took part in trial of Mary, Queen of Scots (1586). See also Robert DUDLEY.

**Dudley, Plimmon Henry.** 1843–1924. American civil and metallurgical engineer; invented a dynamometer (1874), track indicator (1880), and stremmatograph; announced that fungi caused decay in wood (1884).

**Dudley, Robert.** 1st Earl of **Leices'ter** (lĕs'tẽr) of 4th creation (1564). 1532?–1588. English courtier, favorite of Elizabeth I. Fifth son of John Dudley, Duke of Northumberland (*q.v.*); m. (1550) **Amy Rob'sart** [rŏb'-särt] (1532?–1560), who was found dead at foot of staircase in Cumnor Hall, Oxfordshire, probably a suicide. Sentenced to death with his father for supporting Lady Jane Grey (1554), but pardoned; advanced, as Queen Elizabeth's favorite, to privy council (1559); intrigued with queen's consent, but unsuccessfully, to gain Spanish and Catholic support to projected marriage with Elizabeth (1561); offended queen by presumptuousness (1563); failed to displace Cecil; secretly married the Dowager Lady Douglas Sheffield (1573); entertained queen in great magnificence, with masques, at Kenilworth castle (1575); m. (1578) **Lettice,** *nee* **Knollys** [nōlz] (1541?–1634), widow of Walter Devereux, 1st Earl of Essex; commanded expedition into Low Countries to aid States-General against Spaniards (1585), in which campaign his nephew Sir Philip Sidney was killed; recalled (1587) after an indecisive campaign; restored to favor and appointed to command armies to resist Spanish Armada.

His son by Lady Sheffield, Sir **Robert Dudley** (1574–1649), titular Duke of **Northumberland** and Earl of **Warwick,** engineer, studied at Oxford (1587); inherited properties of earl of Leicester and of Ambrose Dudley, Earl of Warwick; explored Guiana (1594); took part in expedition to Cádiz (1596); when refused titles of his father and uncle by Star Chamber, deserted family and traveled to Italy, avowing himself a Roman Catholic; employed by duke of Tuscany draining marshes behind Leghorn; invented scheme of a navy with an added fifth class of war vessel; author of *Dell'Arcano del Mare* (3 vols., 1645–46), a collection of items of naval knowledge.

**Dudley, Samuel William.** 1879–1963. American mechanical engineer, b. New Haven, Conn.; Ph.B. (1900) and M.E. (1903), Yale; on staff of Westinghouse Air Brake Co. (1905–21); professor of mechanical engineering (from 1921) and dean (from 1936), Yale School of Engineering. Special editor for mechanical engineering, *Webster's New International Dictionary, Second Edition.*

**Dudley, Thomas.** 1576–1653. Colonial administrator in America, b. Northampton, England. Steward to the earl of Lincoln (1616–29). Emigrated to Massachusetts Bay Colony (1630), where he was governor (1634, 1640, 1645, 1650) and thirteen times deputy governor. Member of committee (1637) considering founding of college at Cambridge; one of first overseers of Harvard. His son **Joseph** (1647–1720) was also an administrator in the colony; member, Mass. general court (1673–76); upper house (1676–83); president of the council and governor of Massachusetts, New Hampshire, and mainland of Rhode Island west of Narragansett Bay (May 17, 1686); superseded by Andros (Dec. 19, 1686); member of Andros's council and chief justice of superior court (1686–89); detested by colonials for his share in Andros's administration; imprisoned when Andros government overthrown (1689); sent to England for trial; acquitted; chief of the council of New York (1691–92); deputy governor, Isle of Wight (1693–1701); governor of Massachusetts (1702–15); his administration a constant conflict with the general court. His son **Paul** (1675–1751) was attorney general of Massachusetts Bay Province (1702–18); judge, superior court (1718–45); chief justice (1745–51).

**Dudley, William Russel.** 1849–1911. American botanist; professor, Stanford U. (1892–1911). His botanical collection forms nucleus of the Dudley Herbarium at Stanford.

**Duellius, Gaius.** See Gaius DUILIUS.

**Du'er** (dū'ẽr), **William.** 1747–1799. American Revolutionary leader, b. in Devon, England. To America (1768); settled in province of New York. Delegate to Provincial Congress (1775), New York Constitutional Convention (1776), and Continental Congress (1777–78); a signer of the Articles of Confederation. U.S. assistant secretary of the treasury under Hamilton (1789). Heavily involved in land speculation and government contracts; sued by government for financial irregularities in his official position; arrested for debt and imprisoned, causing financial panic (1792); died in prison. One son, **William Alexander** (1780–1858), b. Rhinebeck, N.Y., was a judge, N.Y. supreme court (1822–29), and president of Columbia College (1829–42). Another son, **John** (1782–1858), b. Albany, N.Y., was a judge (1849–57), then chief justice (1857), N.Y. City superior court.

**Due'sen·berg** (dōō'z'n·bûrg), **Frederick S.** 1876–1932. German-born American manufacturer of automobiles, esp. racing cars.

**Du·ez'** (dü·ĕz'), **Ernest Ange.** 1843–1896. French portrait, landscape, and genre painter.

**Du'faure'** (dü'fōr'), **Armand Jules Stanislas.** 1798–1881. French lawyer and statesman; member of various cabinets (at intervals, from 1839); premier of France (Mar. 9–Dec. 2, 1876; and Sept. 14, 1877–Feb. 1, 1879).

**Du Fay** (dü fā'), **Charles François de Cis'ter'nay'** (dẽ sēs'tĕr'nā'). 1698–1739. French chemist; credited with discovery that there are two kinds of electricity, positive and negative; pursued researches including work on phosphorescence, caustic lime, the magnetic needle, and double refraction in crystals.

**Du'fay'** (dü'fā'), **Guillaume.** 1400?–1474. Composer of the Flemish school; ordained priest in Paris and assigned as canon of Cambrai. Regarded as an early master of counterpoint; developed four-part music; credited with improvements in musical notation. Compositions include masses, motets, Magnificats, songs, etc.

**Duff** (dŭf), **Alexander.** 1806–1878. Scottish missionary in India. Opened mission college in Calcutta (1830) combining religious teaching with western science; changed over allegiance from Church of Scotland to Free Church (1843); gave up his college on governor general's adoption of compromise between Orientalist and European policy, and began building anew; founded *Calcutta Review* (1844); one of founders of U. of Calcutta.

**Duff, Mountstuart Elphinstone Grant.** 1829–1906. Scottish man of letters and British administrator in India; son of **James Grant Duff** (1789–1858; historian of India). Undersecretary of state for India (1868–74), for colonies (1880); governor of Madras (1881–86); author of *Notes from a Diary 1851–1901* (14 vols., 1897–1905), valuable as social history.

**Duff Cooper, Alfred.** See Alfred Duff COOPER.

**Dufferin,** Countess of. See under Frederick BLACKWOOD.

**Dufferin and Ava,** Marquis of. See Frederick BLACKWOOD.

**Duff'-Gor'don** (dŭf'gôr'd'n), Lady **Lucie** *or* **Lucy.** 1821–1869. English woman of letters, daughter of John Austin, jurist (*q.v.*); playmate of John Stuart Mill; m. (1840) Sir Alexander Cornewall Duff-Gordon (1811–72). Gathered about her brilliant circle of celebrities; lived in Egypt (from 1862); died in Cairo. Known for translations from the German, as well as historical works. Remembered chiefly for her *Letters from the Cape* (1862–63), *Letters from Egypt* (1863), and *Last Letters from Egypt* (1875). Her daughter **Janet Anne Duff-Gordon Ross** [rŏs] (1842–1927); m. (1860) Henry Ross, banker in Egypt and traveler, described her life in Egypt in *Reminiscences* (1912); correspondent of *The Times* (1863–67); died in Florence; author of *Three Generations of English Women* (2 vols., 1888) and *Lives of the Early Medici* (1910); the original of Rose Jocelyn in George Meredith's *Evan Harrington.*

**Duf'field** (dŭf'ēld), **George.** 1794–1868. American Presbyterian clergyman; grad. U. of Pennsylvania (1811); pastor, Carlisle, Pa. (1816–35). His *Spiritual Life, or, Regeneration* (pub. 1832), made him center of a doctrinal dispute; he was charged with heresy, his book was condemned by the presbytery, and he was dismissed from his church. As pastor, Detroit (1838–68), he continued active in New School theology and was moderator of New School general assembly (1862). His grandson **Samuel Augustus Willoughby Duffield** (1843–1887), b. Brooklyn, N.Y., was a Presbyterian clergyman and hymn writer; author of *English Hymns, Their Authors and History* (1886).

**Duf'fy** (dŭf'ĭ), Sir **Charles Gavan.** 1816–1903. Irish Nationalist and Australian political leader, b. in County Monaghan. Journalist in Dublin; a founder with T. O. Davis and John Blake Dillon of *The Nation* (1842), the organ of Young Ireland party; stimulated taste in Ireland for national history and literature; started *Library of Ireland*, shilling series of biography, poetry, etc. Engaged in nationalist agitation for twelve years; tried for treason-felony (1848); unable to agree with O'Connell; joined Irish Tenant League for fixed tenure, fair rents, and free sale; unable to unite Roman Catholics and Protestants on land question, emigrated to Australia (1856). Minister of public works, Victoria (1857–59, 1862–65); prime minister (1871–72); speaker of house of assembly (1877–80). Spent remainder of life in southern Europe in literary work. Author of *Young Ireland 1840–50* (2 vols., 1880–83), *Conversations with Thomas Carlyle* (1892), and an autobiography (1898). His son Sir **Frank Gavan** (1852–1936), Australian jurist, b. Dublin, Ireland; justice of high court of Australia (1913–31); chief justice of Commonwealth of Australia (1931–34).

**Duffy, Edmund.** 1899–1962. American cartoonist, b. Jersey City, N.J. On staff of Baltimore *Sun* (from 1924); awarded Pulitzer prize for cartoons (1930; 1933; 1939).

**Duffy, Francis Patrick.** 1871–1932. Canadian-born American Roman Catholic clergyman; organizer and rector, Church of Our Saviour, South Fordham, New York City (1912 ff.). Chaplain of 69th regiment of N.Y. National Guard, which became 165th infantry in national army during World War; accompanied regiment to Mexican border (1916) and overseas (1917–18). Awarded Distinguished Service Cross, Distinguished Service Medal, Croix de Guerre with palm; created chevalier of the French Legion of Honor. Author of *Father Duffy's Story* (1919). Pastor, Holy Cross Church, New York City (1920 ff.).

**Du'four'** (dü'fo͝or'), **Guillaume Henri.** 1787–1875. Swiss soldier; general of federal army (1847); suppressed rebellious Roman Catholic cantons in Sonderbund War (1847); represented Switzerland in diplomatic negotiations in Paris (1856 and 1859). Author of *La Campagne du Sonderbund et les Événements de 1856* (1875), etc.

**Dufour, Pierre.** Pseudonym of Paul LACROIX.

**Dufour, Valentin Charles.** 1826–1896. French Roman Catholic ecclesiastic and archaeologist.

**du Four'net'** (dü fo͝or'nĕ'), **Louis René Marie Charles Dar'tige'** (dȧr'tēzh'). 1856–1940. French vice-admiral during World War.

**Du'fré'noy'** (dü'frā'nwȧ'), **Ours Pierre Armand Pe·tit'-** (pẽ·tē'-). 1792–1857. French geologist and mineralogist. With Élie de Beaumont, published (1841) geological map of France.

**du Fresne, Charles.** See DU CANGE.

**Du'fres'ny'** (dü'frĕ'nē'), **Charles Rivière.** 1648–1724. French author of a number of comedies, including *La Noce Interrompue, Le Dédit, Le Chevalier Joueur, Le Mariage Fait et Rompu.*

**Du'fy'** (dü'fē'), **Raoul.** 1877–1953. French painter and decorator; associated with the Fauvist group.

**Du Gard** (dü gȧr'), **Roger Martin.** 1881–1958. French novelist, b. Paris. Awarded Nobel prize for literature (1937) for his series of novels under the general title *Les Thibaults* (1921 ff.).

**Du'ga'zon'** (dü'gä'zôɴ'), **Jean Baptiste Henri.** *Orig. surname* **Gour'gaud'** (go͞or'gō'). 1746–1809. French comedian at Comédie Française (from 1771); m. **Rose Lefèvre** (1755–1821), actress, esp. in roles of young mothers or of women past their first youth. Their son **Gustave** (1782–1826) was a composer, esp. of ballets.

**Dug'dale** (dŭg'dāl), **Richard Louis.** 1841–1883. American sociologist, b. Paris, France, of English parentage; to U.S. (1851); settled in New York City. Member, executive committee, New York Prison Association (from 1868); published (1875), in a report of the Association, *The Jukes, a Study in Crime, Pauperism, Disease,* *and Heredity*, republished (1877) with *Further Studies of Criminals*. See Henry H. GODDARD.

**Dugdale**, Sir **William**. 1605–1686. English antiquary, garter king-of-arms. Rouge Croix pursuivant in ordinary (1639); accompanied Charles I to Oxford; present at Edge Hill, made survey of battlefield; collaborated with the antiquary Roger Dodsworth in *Monasticon Anglicanum* (1655, 1664, 1673), an account of English monastic houses; at Restoration, Norroy king-of-arms; garter principal king-of-arms (1677). Author of *Antiquities of Warwickshire* (1656), *History of St. Paul's Cathedral* (1658), *Imbanking and Drayning* (1662), and *Baronage of England* (3 vols., 1675–76).

**Dug'gan** (dŭg'ăn), **Eileen**. New Zealand poet, author of *New Zealand Bird Songs*, *Poems* (1938), etc.

**Dug'gar** (dŭg'ĕr), **Benjamin Minge**. 1872–1956. American botanist, b. Gallion, Ala. Research professor, Missouri Botanical Garden and Washington U., St. Louis (1912–27); professor, Wisconsin (1927–43). Author of *Plant Physiology* (1911), etc.

**Du'ghet'** (dü'gĕ'), **Gaspard**. *Known as* **Le Guas'pre** (lẽ gȧs'pr') *and* **Gas'pard'-Pous'sin'** (gȧs'pȧr'po͞o'săɴ'). 1613–1675. Painter, b. in Rome of French parentage; brother-in-law of Nicolas Poussin; best known for his landscapes.

**Dug'more** (dŭg'mōr), **Arthur Radclyffe**. 1870–1955. English naturalist and animal photographer; exhibited animal paintings in England and U.S. Author of *Bird Homes* (1900), *Nature and the Camera* (1902), *Camera Adventures in the African Wilds* (1910), *Through the Sudan* (1938), etc.

**Du'go·nics** (do͝o'gō·nĭch), **András**. 1740–1818. Hungarian Piarist and novelist; a leader in so-called popular school of Hungarian literature.

**Du'guay'-Trou'in'** or **Du Guay'-Trou'in'** (dü'gā'-tro͞o'ăɴ'), **René**. 1673–1736. French naval commander. Among his exploits were capture of a British convoy (1707) and capture and sack of Rio de Janiero (1711).

**Du'gué'** (dü'gā'), **Charles Oscar**. 1821–1872. American Creole poet, b. New Orleans.

**Du Gues'clin'** (dü gĕ'klăɴ'), **Bertrand**. 1320?–1380. Called "the Eagle of Brittany." Constable of France, b. near Dinan, Brittany. Entered service of Charles de Blois (1342); relieved Rennes (1356–57). Under Kings John II and Charles V did great service for France; made count of Longueville (1364); taken prisoner at Auray (1364) and ransomed; led grand companies into Spain (1367) to aid Henry of Trastamara against Peter the Cruel; taken prisoner by the Black Prince (1367) and again ransomed; won battle of Montiel (1369); created duke of Molinas by Henry for his services (1369); constable of France (1370); for ten years active in driving out English from south and west of France; died at siege of Châteauneuf-de-Randon.

**Du'guit'** (dü'gē'), **Léon**. 1859–1928. French jurist; author of *Des Fonctions de l'État Moderne* (1894), *Traité de Droit Constitutionnel* (1911), etc.

**Du'ha'mel'** (dü'ȧ'mĕl'), **Georges**. *Pseudonym* **Denis Thé've·nin'** (tāv'năɴ'). 1884–1966. French writer; a physician by profession; published, first, volumes of verse, *Des Légendes, des Batailles* (1907), *L'Homme en Tête* (1909), *Selon ma Loi* (1910), *Les Compagnons* (1912); also, *La Lumière* (play, 1911), *Dans l'Ombre des Statues* (play, 1912), *Combat* (play, 1913), *Civilisation* (book inspired by his experiences in army in World War, 1918; awarded Goncourt prize), *Les Hommes Abandonnés* (1923), *Deux Hommes* (1925), *Le Voyage de Moscou* (1927), *Chronique des Pasquier* (1936), etc.

**Du'ha'mel'-Du'mon'ceau'** (-dü'môɴ'sō'), **Henri Louis**. 1700–1782. French engineer and agriculturist. Experimented in plant and animal physiology and chemistry; author of works on trees and shrubs.

**Du'hem'** (dü'ĕm'), **Pierre Maurice Marie**. 1861–1916. French physicist and mathematician.

**Duhm** (do͞om), **Bernhard**. 1847–1928. German Protestant theologian; author of commentaries on prophetic books of the Old Testament; proposed the Trito-Isaiah theory of authorship of Isaiah lvi–lxvi.

**Düh'ring** (dü'rĭng), **Karl Eugen**. 1833–1921. German positivist philosopher and economist; author of *Kritische Geschichte der Philosophie* (1869), *Die Judenfrage* (1881), *Wirklichkeitsphilosophie* (1895), etc.

**Du·if'fo·prug'gar** (do͞o·ē'fō·pro͝og'är). Variant of TIEFFENBRUCKER.

**Du·il'i·us** *or* **Du·il'i·us Ne'pos** (dū·ĭl'ĭ·ŭs nē'pŏs), **Gaius**. fl. 3d century B.C. Roman general. Consul (260 B.C.) with Gnaeus Cornelius Scipio; after defeat of Scipio by Carthaginians off Lipara, took command of Roman fleet; won decisive victory (260) over larger fleet off Mylae; first to use device of grappling irons and boarding bridges; victory of great importance to Romans in First Punic War and in establishing beginning of Rome's sea power; in his honor, Duilian Column was erected in Forum at Rome.

**Du'jar'din'** (dü'zhȧr'dăɴ'), **Édouard**. 1861–1949. French journalist and writer; associated with symbolists. Among his works are *Les Lauriers sont Coupés* (novel, 1887), *Le Délassement du Guerrier* (verse, 1904), *La Comédie des Amours* (verse, 1913), *Le Mystère du Dieu Mort et Ressuscité* (play, 1923), etc.

**Dujardin, Félix**. 1801–1860. French zoologist; distinguished the protoplasm of the body of a unicellular animal, calling it *sarcode* (1835); author of a natural history of the Infusoria (1841).

**Dujardin, Karel**. 1622?–1678. Dutch painter of landscapes, portraits, etchings, and genre pictures.

**Du'kas'** (dü'kȧ'), **Paul Abraham**. 1865–1935. French composer; professor, Paris Conservatory of Music. Compositions include cantata *Velléda*, symphonic poem *L'Apprenti-Sorcier*, music for Maeterlinck's lyrical opera *Ariane et Barbe Bleue* (1907), ballet *La Péri* (1912), part of orchestration for Guiraud's unfinished opera *Frédégonde*, and a number of piano works.

**Duke** (dūk), **Benjamin Newton** (1855–1929) and his brother **James Buchanan** (1856–1925). American industrialists, b. near Durham, N.C. Established their first tobacco factory at Durham (1874), and branch factory in New York (1884); engaged in "cigarette war" that resulted in joining of rival companies in the American Tobacco Company with J. B. Duke as president (1890). Acquired control of other branches of tobacco industry by means of other combinations, and invaded English market, with result that English manufacturers formed Imperial Tobacco Company to fight them; made agreement restricting Consolidated to American market and Imperial to English market and forming British-American Tobacco Company (with Duke interests owning two thirds of stock) for other markets of world. In 1911. U.S. Supreme Court ordered dissolution of American Tobacco Company as a combination in restraint of trade; J. B. Duke chiefly responsible for necessary resultant company reorganization. Both brothers were large benefactors of Trinity College, Durham, which was renamed Duke University in their honor.

**Duke**, Sir **Frederick William**. 1863–1924. British administrator in India; chief secretary to government of Bengal (1909); acting lieutenant governor (1911–12); retired (1914) and was appointed member of Council of India; aided in formulating Montagu-Chelmsford reforms of Indian political system (1918–19); appointed permanent undersecretary of state at India Office (1920–24).

**Dukes** (dūks), **Ashley.** 1885–1959. English dramatic critic, playwright, and theater manager; director of Mercury Theatre (from 1933). Author of *Modern Dramatists* (1911), *The Youngest Drama* (1923), *Drama* (1926), and a number of plays, including *Matchmaker's Arms* (1930), *Mandragola* (from Machiavelli; 1939), etc.

**Du'lac'** (dü'lȧk'), **Edmund.** 1882–1953. Artist, illustrator, and stage designer, b. Toulouse, France; naturalized British citizen (1912). Best known for his illustrated editions of many classics, including *The Arabian Nights* (1907), *The Tempest* (1908), *The Rubaiyat of Omar Khayyam* (1909), *Hans Andersen's Snow Queen and other tales* (1912), *Sindbad the Sailor* (1914), *Tanglewood Tales* (1918). Designed the coronation stamp (1937) and King George VI's cameo portrait on stamps of his early reign.

**Du·la'ny** (dů·lā'nĭ), **Daniel.** 1685–1753. Lawyer, b. in Queen's County, Ireland; to America (about 1703). Member, Maryland legislature (1722–42); upheld colonial cause in pamphlet *The Rights of the Inhabitants of Maryland to the Benefit of English Laws* (1728). Member, governor's council (1742–53). His son **Daniel** (1722–1797) was also a lawyer; member, governor's council (from 1757); commissary general of Maryland (1759–61); secretary of Maryland (1761–74). Author (1765) of powerful pamphlet against Stamp Act, *Considerations on the Propriety of Imposing Taxes in the British Colonies, for the Purpose of Raising a Revenue, by Act of Parliament;* he later opposed radical policies of the colonial leaders, disapproved revolution, and had his estates confiscated (1781).

**Dul·bec'co** (dŭl·bĕk·ō), **Renato.** 1914– . American virologist, b. Italy. At California Institute of Technology (1949–63), Salk Institute for Biological Studies (1963–72; 1977– ), Imperial Cancer Research Fund (1972–77); awarded (with David Baltimore and Howard Temin) Nobel prize for physiology or medicine (1975).

**Dul'ce y Ga·ray'** (dōōl'thā [-sā] ē gä·rä'ē), **Domingo.** Marqués **de Cas·tel'flo·ri'te** (käs·tĕl'flô·rē'tā). 1808–1869. Spanish general; took part in Carlist war and in revolution of 1854 as captain general of Catalonia; twice governor of Cuba (1862–66, and 1869).

**Dul·ci'no of No·va'ra** (dōōl·chē'nô, nô·vä'rä). d. 1307. Italian sectarian, a leader of the Apostolic Brothers; burned at the stake (1308).

**Dulhut** *or* **Du Lhut.** Variants of DULUTH.

**Dulk** (dŏŏlk), **Albert.** 1819–1884. German writer; took anti-Christian stand in philosophical works. Among his plays are *Orla* (1844), *Lea* (1848), *Simson* (1859), *Jesus der Christ* (1865), *Konrad II* (1867).

**Dul'ler** (dŏŏl'ēr), **Eduard.** 1809–1853. German writer; active in German Catholic movement (1836).

**Dul'les** (dŭl'ĕs), **John Foster.** 1888–1959. American lawyer, b. Washington, D.C.; practiced, New York City (from 1911). Counsel to American commission to negotiate peace (1918–19); member of reparations commission and supreme economic council (1919). American representative at Berlin debt conferences (1933). U.S. secretary of state (1953–59).

**Du'long'** (dü'lôɴ'), **Pierre Louis.** 1785–1838. French chemist and physicist. Discovered nitrogen chloride (1811); collaborated with Alexis Thérèse Petit in research on heat; with Petit, enunciated the principle (law of Dulong and Petit) that the elements in the solid state have nearly the same atomic heat (1819); investigated the specific heats of gases, the elasticity of steam at high temperatures, etc.; devised empirical formula (Dulong's formula) for calculating the heat value of fuels from their chemical composition.

**Du·luth'** (dů·lōōth'; *Fr.* dü'lüt') *or* **Du'lhut'** (dü'lüt'), Sieur. **Daniel Grey'so'lon'** (grā'sô'lôɴ'). 1636–1710. French explorer; in Montreal, Canada (from about 1675); on expedition to explore Lake Superior region (1678); reached head of Lake Superior (July, 1679); negotiated peace with Sioux and penetrated into what is now northern Minnesota (1680). Made other trips into Lake Superior region (1684 and 1687). In command at Fort Frontenac (1690). Largely responsible for establishing French control over the northwest country.

**Du'ma'noir'** (dü'mȧ'nwȧr'), **Philippe François Pinel.** 1806–1865. French playwright, b. on island of Guadeloupe; author of *Don César de Bazan* (1844) and a number of vaudeville sketches.

**Du'mas'** (dü'mȧ'; *Angl.* dōō·mä', dōō'mä), **Adolphe.** 1806–1861. French Félibriste poet; published collection of Provençal verse, and *La Cité des Hommes* (1835), *Provence* (1840), etc.

**Dumas, Alexandre.** *Real name* **Alexandre Da'vy' de La Pail'le·te·rie'** (dȧ'vē' dē lȧ pä'y'·trē'). 1762–1806. Father of Alexandre Dumas père (*q.v.*) and grandfather of Alexandre Dumas fils (*q.v.*). French soldier, b. in Santo Domingo; natural son of a French colonist and a Negress. Served in the Revolutionary and Napoleonic armies; general of division (1793); accompanied Napoleon to Italy (1797); distinguished himself at Bressanone in the Tyrol by his singlehanded defense of a bridge, and was called by Napoleon **Ho'ra'ti·us' Co'clès' du Ty'rol'** (ô'rä'syüs' kô'klâs' dü tē'rôl'). Commanded French cavalry in the Egyptian expedition (1798).

**Dumas, Alexandre.** *Known as* **Dumas père** (pâr). 1802–1870. Son of Alexandre Davy de La Pailleterie, called Dumas (*q.v.*). French novelist and playwright, b. Villers-Cotterets, France. Started as clerical worker; soon turned to writing, using many collaborators, esp. Auguste Maquet, who collected facts for historical backgrounds for his novels. Among his outstanding novels are *Le Chevalier d'Harmental* (1849), *Les Trois Mousquetaires* (1844) and its sequels *Vingt Ans Après* (1845) and *Le Vicomte de Bragelonne* (1848; parts of which have been issued separately as *Louise de la Vallière* and *The Man in the Iron Mask*), *Le Comte de Monte Cristo* (1844), *La Reine Margot* (1845), *La Dame de Monsoreau* (1846) and its sequel *Les Quarante-cinq* (1848), *Le Chevalier de Maison Rouge* (1846), *Mémoires d'un Médecin* (1848) and its sequels *Ange Pitou* (1853) and *La Comtesse de Charny* (1855). Among his plays are *Henri III et sa Cour* (romantic drama; 1829), *Antony* (psychological study of a romantic hero; 1831), *Richard Darlington* (1831), *Kean* (1836), *Mademoiselle de Belle-Isle* (1839).

**Dumas, Alexandre.** *Known as* **Dumas fils** (fēs). 1824–1895. Natural son of Alexandre Dumas père (*q.v.*). French playwright and novelist, b. Paris. Published volume of verse *Péchés de Jeunesse* (1847); achieved success as novelist but, after successful adaptation of two of his novels for the stage, devoted himself chiefly to playwriting. His works include *La Dame aux Camélias* (novel, 1848; play, 1852), *Diane de Lys* (novel, 1851; play, 1853); the novels *Tristan le Roux* (1849), *Henri de Navarre* (1850), *La Dame aux Perles* (1854), *L'Affaire Clémenceau* (1866); the plays *Le Demi-Monde* (1855), *La Question d'Argent* (1857), *Le Fils Naturel* (1858), *Un Père Prodigue* (1859), *L'Ami des Femmes* (1864), *Monsieur Alphonse* (1873), *La Princesse de Bagdad* (1881), *Francillon* (1887).

**Dumas,** Comte **Guillaume Mathieu.** 1753–1837. French soldier and historian; aide-de-camp to Rochambeau in America, and to Lafayette (1789); took Louis XVI back to Paris after the king was arrested at Varennes. Minister of war under King Joseph at Naples and later at Madrid. Author of *Essai Historique sur les Campagnes de 1799 à 1814* (1816–26) and translator of Napier's *History of the Peninsular War.* His brother **René François** (1757–1794) was president of the Revolutionary Tribunal during the Reign of Terror; guillotined (1794).

**Dumas, Jean Baptiste André.** 1800–1884. French chemist. Professor, École Centrale des Arts et Manufactures, Paris (which he founded in 1829). Master of the French mint. Known for researches on vapor density of the elements, the formulas of alcohols and ethers, the composition of water and of the atmosphere, atomic weights, the law of substitution in organic compounds, the theory of chemical types, etc. Author of *Traité de Chimie Appliquée aux Arts* (8 vols., 1828–45), etc. See Pierre BOULLAY.

**du Mau′ri·er** (dŭ mô′rĭ·ā; *Fr.* dü mô′ryā′), **George Louis Pal·mel′la** (păl·mĕl′ȧ) **Bus′son′** (bü′sôN′). 1834–1896. British artist and novelist, b. Paris, grandson of émigrés who left France to settle in London during Reign of Terror. Adopted art as profession (1856); illustrated new editions of Thackeray's *Henry Esmond*, Foxe's *Book of Martyrs*, and stories for *Cornhill Magazine* (1863–83); prompted by *Punch's Almanack*, set out (c. 1859) to be graphic humorist; successor to John Leech on staff of *Punch*, satirized fashionable upper-class and middle-class life; wrote and illustrated three novels, *Peter Ibbetson* (1891) and *Trilby* (1894), both recording incidents in his own life, and *The Martian* (1896). His elder son, **Guy Louis Busson du Maurier** (1865–1915), lieutenant colonel in Royal Fusiliers, was widely known for military play, *An Englishman's Home* (1909). His younger son, Sir **Gerald du Maurier** (1873–1934), was a well-known actor-manager. Gerald's 2d daughter, **Daphne du Maurier,** Lady **Browning.** (1907– ), novelist, b. London, m. (1932) Sir Frederick A. M. Browning of Grenadier Guards; author of *Gerald, a Portrait* (1934), of *The du Mauriers* (1937), and of novels, including *The Loving Spirit* (1931), *Jamaica Inn* (1936), *Rebecca* (1938), *Frenchman's Creek* (1942).

**Du′mé′ril′** (dü′mā′rēl′), **André Marie Constant.** 1774–1860. French physician and naturalist; authority on herpetology and ichthyology. His son **Henri André** (1812–1870) was professor of zoology, author of *Histoire Naturelle des Poissons* (1865–70), etc.

**Duméril, Edelestand Pon′tas′** (pôN′tȧs′). 1801–1871. French student of the literary history of the Middle Ages; author of *Essai Philosophique sur la Formation de la Langue Française* (1852), *Histoire de la Comédie: Période Primitive* (1864–69), etc.

**Du′mes′nil′** (dü′mĕ′nēl′), **Marie Françoise.** *Stage name of* **Marie Françoise Mar′chand′** (mår′shäN′). 1711–1803. French tragedienne.

**Du·Mez′** (dü·mā′), **Andrew Grover.** 1885–1948. American pharmaceutical chemist, b. Horicon, Wis. With U.S. Public Health Service (1917–26); dean of school of pharmacy, U. of Maryland (from 1926); editor of technical publications, incl. (from 1935) *Pharmaceutical Abstracts;* special editor for pharmacy, *Webster's New International Dictionary, Second Edition.*

**Dü′mi·chen** (dü′mē·kĕn), **Johannes.** 1833–1894. German Egyptologist; author of *Geographische Inschriften Altägyptischer Denkmäler* (3 vols., 1866), etc.

**Dum′mer** (dŭm′ẽr), **Jeremiah.** 1645–1718. American silversmith, b. Newbury, Mass. His son **Jeremiah** (1679?–1739), b. Boston, Mass., practiced law in England (from about 1704); was appointed agent for Massachusetts (1710) and for Connecticut (1712); influenced Elihu Yale to contribute for establishment of college in New England, and himself sent (1714) several hundred books to Yale College. Dismissed as agent by Massachusetts assembly (1721) and by Connecticut (1730), apparently for failure to support colonial radical demands. Author of *Defence of the New England Charters* (1715).

**Dümm′ler** (düm′lẽr), **Ernst.** 1830–1902. German historian; member of committee directing the *Monumenta Germaniae Historica* (1875); collaborator with Wattenbach in completing Jaffé's *Monumenta Alcuiniana.*

**Dum′no·rix** (dŭm′nô·rĭks). A chief of the Aedui; brother of Divitiacus (*q.v.*). Killed in Gaul (54 B.C.).

**Du′mon′ceau′** (dü′môN′sō′), **Jean Baptiste.** Comte **de Ber′gen·dael** (bĕr′gĕn·dȧl). 1760–1821. Belgian soldier; involved in rebellion of Brabant against Austria (1789–90), took refuge in France (1790); distinguished himself in battle of Jemappes (1792) and in conquest of Low Countries by French; lieutenant general of Batavian Republic (1795). Appointed (by Louis Bonaparte, King of Holland) marshal of Holland, councilor of state, and minister to Paris.

**Du′mont′** (dü′môN′). Family of French sculptors, including: **Pierre** (1660–1737); his son **François** (1687–1726); François's son **Edme** (1720–1775); Edme's son **Jacques Edme** (1761–1844); Jacques's son **Augustin Alexandre** (1801–1884).

**Dumont, Alberto Santos-.** See SANTOS-DUMONT.

**Dumont, Henri.** 1610–1684. Belgian organist and composer; organist at St. Paul's Church, Paris (from 1639). Among his compositions are religious works, esp. masses (known as *Messes Royales*), of which *Mass of Dumont* is still used on solemn feast days.

**Dumont, Jean.** 1666–1726. French publicist and historian; opposed Louis XIV and absolute monarchy; moved to Vienna, and received appointment as historiographer to the emperor. Author of *Cours Universel et Diplomatique du Droit des Gens* (1726), etc.

**Dumont, Pierre Étienne Louis.** 1759–1829. Swiss publicist; ordained in ministry (1781); secretary to Jeremy Bentham (*q.v.*) and associate of Mirabeau; author of *Souvenirs sur Mirabeau...* (1832) and editor of books on Bentham's philosophy.

**Dumont d'Ur′ville′** (dür′vēl′), **Jules Sébastien César.** 1790–1842. French naval commander and explorer; on expedition to Grecian Archipelago (1819–20) recognized importance of a statue of Venus dug up on Island of Melos; in report to French consul urged preservation of statue, now in Louvre and known as Venus of Milo. Commanded frigate *Astrolabe* on a voyage to Polynesia in search of remains of La Pérouse (1826–29); commanded the *Zélée* on a voyage of discovery in South Seas (1837–40); wrote accounts of his expeditions.

**Du′mou′lin′** (dü′mo͞o′lăN′), **Charles.** 1500–1566. French jurist, b. Paris. Author of *De Feudis* (1539), *Sommaire du Livre Analytique des Contrats, Usures, Rentes Constituées, Intérêts et Monnoyes* (1547–1556), *Extricatio Labyrinthi Dividui et Individui*, etc.

**Du′mou′riez′** (dü′mo͞o′ryā′), **Charles François.** 1739–1823. French general; under Louis XVI, commandant of Cherbourg (1778–88); major general (1788). At outbreak of Revolution joined Jacobin Club; minister of foreign affairs (1792); lieutenant general of Army of the North (1792); conducted campaign that checked duke of Brunswick at Valmy (Sept., 1792); defeated Austrians at Jemappes (Nov., 1792); was defeated at Neerwinden (1793); was denounced by National Assembly and deserted to Austrians. Wandered through Europe; lived in exile (1804–23) in England.

**Dun** (dŭn), **Robert Graham.** 1826–1900. American authority on mercantile credit, b. Chillicothe, Ohio. Entered mercantile agency, New York (1850); rose to head concern, organized (1859) as R. G. Dun & Co. and merged (1933) with Bradstreet Co. to form Dun & Bradstreet, Inc.; published (from 1893) *Dun's Review*, weekly report of business conditions.

**Du′nant′** (dü′näɴ′), **Jean Henri.** 1828–1910. Swiss philanthropist, b. Geneva; founder of Red Cross. Inspired by compassion at sight of wounded on battlefield of Solferino (1859), he labored for creation of an organization to aid wounded soldiers; succeeded in bringing about conference at Geneva (1863) from which came the Geneva Convention (1864) and establishment of International Red Cross. With Frédéric Passy, shared first Nobel peace prize (1901). Devoted entire fortune to charity.

**Dun·bar′** (dŭn·bär′), **Agnes.** Countess of **Dunbar and March** (märch). 1312?–1369. Known as "Black Agnes," from her swarthy complexion. Daughter of Sir Thomas Randolph, Earl of Moray; m. **Patrick Dunbar** (1285–1369), 10th Earl of Dunbar and 2d Earl of March, who at first protected Edward II, later renounced allegiance and fought against the English. In absence of her husband, defended Dunbar Castle (1338) against earls of Salisbury and Arundel.

**Dun′bar** (dŭn′bär), **Charles Franklin.** 1830–1900. American economist and educator; first professor of political economy, Harvard (1870–1900). Editor, *Quarterly Journal of Economics* (1886–96).

**Dunbar, Paul Laurence.** 1872–1906. American poet, b. Dayton, Ohio, son of an escaped Negro slave. Elevator boy, Dayton (1891–95). Volume of poems, *Majors and Minors* (1895), received favorable notice by William Dean Howells; a second volume, *Lyrics of Lowly Life* (1896), with an introduction by Howells, established his literary reputation. Other works: *Poems of Cabin and Field* (1899), *Lyrics of the Hearthside* (1899), *Candle-Lightin' Time* (1902), *Lyrics of Love and Laughter* (1903), *Lyrics of Sunshine and Shadow* (1905), and four novels, *The Uncalled* (1896), *The Love of Landry* (1900), *The Fanatics* (1901), *The Sport of the Gods* (1902).

**Dun·bar′** (dŭn·bär′), **William.** 1460?–?1520. Scottish poet. Traveled over England as Franciscan friar; visited England with embassy to negotiate marriage of James IV and Margaret Tudor (1501). Composed in honor of queen's arrival a political allegory *The Thrissill and the Rois* (1503); described Queen Margaret's visit (1511) to north of Scotland in *The Quenis Progress at Aberdeen;* disappeared altogether after battle of Flodden. Author of satires, including *The Dance of the Sevin Deidly Synnis* (between 1503 and 1508), of an allegorical poem, *The Goldyn Targe*, and an elegy, *The Lament for the Makaris* (poets). Cf. Walter KENNEDY.

**Dun′can I** (dŭng′kăn). d. 1040. King of Scotland. Succeeded his maternal grandfather, Malcolm II, as king (1034); defeated and killed (perhaps murdered, as in Shakespeare's *Macbeth*) by Maelbaethe or Macbeth, Mormaor of Moray. His son and lawful successor, Malcolm III, father of **Duncan II** (d. 1094), lived for a time as hostage in Normandy; gained English and Norman help to drive out his father's brother Donald Bane (1093), by whose agents he was treacherously slain.

**Duncan, Adam.** 1st Viscount **Duncan of Cam′per·down** (kăm′pẽr·doun). 1731–1804. British naval commander, b. in Forfarshire, Scotland. Commanded the *Valiant* in reduction of Havana (1762); admiral (1795); commander in chief of North Sea fleet (1795–1801); defeated De Winter, Dutch admiral, off Camperdown (1797), capturing eleven ships.

**Duncan,** Sir **Andrew Rae.** 1884–1952. British government official. Chairman, executive committee of British Iron and Steel Federation; M.P. (1940–50). President of Board of Trade (1940; 1941–42); minister of supply (1940–41; 1942–45).

**Duncan, Isadora.** 1878–1927. American dancer, b. San Francisco. Under patronage of Mrs. Patrick Campbell, aroused enthusiasm in London and Paris. Joined Loie Fuller's company and toured Germany; acclaimed in Vienna and Budapest. Established school of dancing, for children, at Grünewald, near Berlin (1904). Invited to Russia (1921); opened school in Moscow; m. (1922) Sergei Esenin (*q.v.*). Wrote autobiography, *My Life* (1926–27). Killed in automobile accident. Among her dances were renditions of the *Marseillaise*, Tchaikovsky's *Marche Slave*, and Chopin's *Marche Funèbre*.

**Duncan, James.** 1857–1928. American labor leader, b. in Kincardine County, Scotland; to U.S. in 1880. Associate of Samuel Gompers; active in development of American Federation of Labor (vice-pres., 1900–28).

**Duncan,** Sir **Patrick.** 1870–1943. South African lawyer and politician. Colonial secretary of the Transvaal (1903–06); acting lieutenant governor (1906); minister of the interior, public health, and education, Union of South Africa (1921–24); minister of mines (1933–36); governor general, Union of South Africa (from 1937).

**Duncan, Robert Kennedy.** 1868–1914. Chemist and educator, b. Brantford, Ontario, Canada. Professor, U. of Pittsburgh (1910–14). Author of *The New Knowledge* (1905), *The Chemistry of Commerce* (1907), and *Some Chemical Problems of Today* (1911). His interest in application of chemical research to practical needs of industry led to idea of establishing industrial fellowships to that end; success of his early fellowships attracted the Mellons' notice and resulted in founding (1913) of Mellon Institute of Industrial Research, U. of Pittsburgh.

**Duncan, Thomas.** 1807–1845. Scottish portrait, genre, and historical painter. Best known for his *Prince Charles Edward and the Highlanders entering Edinburgh* (1840) and *Charles Edward asleep after Culloden, protected by Flora MacDonald* (1843).

**Duncannon,** Viscounts. See PONSONBY family.

**Dunck′er** (dŏŏng′kẽr), **Max,** *in full* **Maximilian Wolfgang.** 1811–1886. German historian; chief work *Geschichte des Altertums* (1852–57).

**Dun′combe** (dŭn′kŭm; dŭng′-), **Thomas Slingsby.** 1796–1861. English radical leader. M.P. (1826); assisted in passing Reform Bill (1832); presented to Parliament (1842) the Chartist petition; took part in letting Prince Louis Napoleon escape from Ham (1846); member of council of Friends of Italy (1851) at request of Mazzini; interested himself on behalf of Kossuth in matter of Hungarian notes (1861).

**Dun·das′** (dŭn·dăs′; dŭn′dăs) of Ar′nis·ton (är′nĭs·tŭn). Name of a Scottish noble family, including: Sir **James Dundas,** Lord Arniston (d. 1679); lord of session (1662–63); deprived on refusal to renounce Solemn League and Covenant. His grandson **Robert Dundas** (1685–1753), Lord Arniston the elder; solicitor general for Scotland (1717–20); lord advocate (1720); dean of Faculty of Advocates (1721); M.P. (1722); lord president of session (1748–53); reintroduced "guilty" or "not guilty" as possible findings by juries. The latter's son **Robert** (1713–1787), Lord Arniston the younger; studied Roman law at Utrecht and Paris; solicitor general (1742–46); lord advocate (1754); M.P. (1754); lord president of session (1760); gave his casting vote against Archibald (Stewart) Douglas in Douglas peerage case (1767).

VISCOUNTS MELVILLE: **Henry Dundas** (1742–1811), 1st Viscount **Mel′ville** (mĕl′vĭl) and Baron **Dun·i′ra** (dŭn·ẽr′ȧ); 4th son of Robert Dundas, Lord Arniston the elder; educ. Edinburgh; solicitor general (1766); M.P. (1774–1802); lord advocate (1775–83); strenuously supported Lord North and war with America; privy councilor and treasurer of navy (1782–83, 1784–1800); initiated movement leading to recall from India and impeachment of Warren Hastings; transferred support to Pitt, becoming home secretary (1791–94), president of board of control (1793–1801), and secretary of war (1794–1801); carried through successful Egyptian campaign (1801) contrary to advice of Pitt and king; raised to peerage (1802) under Addington administration; first lord of the admiralty in Pitt's second ministry; erased from roll of privy council (1805) and impeached (1806) for gross malversation as treasurer of navy; acquitted of all except negligence (1806); sometimes called "Starvation Dundas" because of his use of the word in a speech (1775) upholding restrictive trade measures on New England colonies.

**Robert Saunders Dundas** (1771–1851), 2d viscount; son of 1st viscount; privy councilor (1807); president of board of control (1807, 1809); Irish secretary (1809); first lord of the admiralty (1812–27); received recognition of his interest in arctic exploration by naming of Melville Sound. His eldest son, **Henry** (1801–1876), 3d viscount, took part in suppression of Canadian rebellion (1837); held second command at capture of Multan (1847); general (1868). The 2d viscount's 2d son, Sir **Richard Saunders** (1802–1861), distinguished himself in naval service in Opium War (1841); commander in chief of Baltic fleet (1855–61).

**Henry Charles Clement Dundas** (1873–1935), 7th viscount; eldest son of 6th viscount; spent his life in British consular service, largely in central and east Africa and South America; after service as commandant of prisoners in World War, continued as consul at Ajaccio, Corsica (1909–22). **Kenneth Robert** (1882–1915), 4th son of 6th viscount; educ. in Germany and Norway; engaged in colonial civil service; district commissioner in British East Africa (1908); contributed material to Sir James G. Frazer and anthropological articles.

The marquises of **Zetland** (see Lawrence DUNDAS) belong to another line of the Dundas family.

**Dundas,** Sir **David.** 1735–1820. British army officer, b. Edinburgh; commander in chief (1809–11); devised new system for British army from Prussian code of tactics of Frederick the Great's school.

**Dundas, Lawrence.** 1st Marquis of **Zet′land** [zĕt′lănd] (cr. 1892). Earl of **Ron′ald·shay** [rŏn′'ld·shā] (cr. 1892). 3d Earl of **Zetland** (cr. 1838). 1844–1929. Scottish grandson of 1st earl of Zetland and nephew of 2d earl (d. 1873). M.A., Cantab.; privy councilor of Great Britain, lord lieutenant of Ireland (1889–92), vice-lieutenant of North Riding (1920). His eldest surviving son, **Lawrence John Lumley** (1876–1961), 2d marquis, governor of Bengal (1917–22); secretary of state for India (1935–1940), for Burma (1937–1940); author of books on Asia and of biographies of Lord Curzon (1928) and Lord Cromer (1932). Cf. DUNDAS family.

**Dundee,** Viscount. See John GRAHAM (of Claverhouse).

**Dundonald,** Earls of. See Thomas COCHRANE.

**Du·nér′** (dōō·nār′), **Nils Christofer.** 1839–1914. Swedish astronomer; director of the observatory, Uppsala (1888–1909). His works deal chiefly with double stars, variable stars, and spectroscopic observations of fixed stars and the sun.

**Dunfermline,** 1st Baron. See James ABERCROMBY.

**Dunfermline,** Earls of. See SETON family.

**Dun′gi** (dōŏn′gē). Incorrect form of SHULGI.

**Dun′gli·son** (dŭng′glĭ·s'n), **Robley.** 1798–1869. Physician, b. Keswick, England. Professor of medicine, U. of Virginia (1825–33), U. of Maryland (1833–36), Jefferson Medical College, Philadelphia (1836–68). Author of *Human Physiology* (1832), *A New Dictionary of Medical Science and Literature* (1833), etc.

**Dun′ham** (dŭn′ăm), **Katherine.** 1910– . Anthropologist, dancer, choreographer, b. Chicago. Educated U. of Chicago (B.A.,M.A.). Studied dance of Caribbean, Brazil, etc. Major works include *Bahiana, Bal Negre;* choreography for New York theater and opera and for films. Wrote *Journey to Accompong* (1946), *Touch of Innocence* (1959).

**Dun′hill** (dŭn′hĭl), **Thomas Frederick.** 1877–1946. English composer of comic operas (*Happy Families* and *Tantivy Towers*), an opera (*The Enchanted Garden;* received Carnegie award, 1925), ballets, songs, etc.

**Du′ni** (dōō′nē), **Egidio Romoaldo.** 1709–1775. Italian opera composer; resident in Paris (from 1757), where he was one of originators of opéra comique.

**Dunk, George Montagu.** 2d Earl of **Halifax.** See under Charles MONTAGU.

**Dün′kel·berg** (düng′kĕl·bĕrK), **Friedrich Wilhelm.** 1819–1912. German agricultural engineer; author of *Enzyklopädie und Methodologie der Kulturtechnik* (2 vols., 1883), etc.

**Dun′lap** (dŭn′lăp; -lăp), **John.** 1747–1812. American printer, b. in County Tyrone, Ireland; to America (c. 1757). Apprenticed to his uncle, a printer; took over uncle's business (1768); published (from 1771) *The Pennsylvania Packet, or The General Advertiser,* at first a weekly but from Sept. 21, 1784, a daily, the first daily newspaper published in U.S.

**Dunlap, William.** 1766–1839. American painter, playwright, and historian, b. Perth Amboy, N.J. Studied painting in London under Benjamin West (1784). On return to America (about 1787), wrote plays (the first American playwright, sometimes called "Father of American Drama"); bought (1796) interest in New York theatrical company; bankrupt (1805). Returned to painting (1816); a founder of National Academy of Design (1826). His plays include *The Father of an Only Child* (1789), *Leicester* (1794), *Fontainville Abbey* (1795), *André* (1798). Other works, *History of the American Theatre* (1832), *History of the Rise and Progress of the Arts of Design in the United States* (1834).

**Dun·lop′** (dŭn·lŏp′; dŭn′lŏp), **John Boyd.** 1840–1921. Scottish inventor; commonly credited with invention of the pneumatic tire. Patented pneumatic tire (1888) and began marketing tricycles equipped with pneumatic tires; sold patent to William Harvey Du Cros, a manufacturer The principle of the pneumatic tire had been patented in 1846 (see Robert William THOMSON) but the company, which eventually became the Dunlop Rubber Co., was enabled because of accessory patents to establish rights to the invention.

**Dunlop, John Colin.** 1785–1842. Scottish advocate and man of letters. Sheriff of Renfrewshire (1816–42). Author of *History of Prose Fiction* (1814), a learned work criticized by Hazlitt. His father, **John Dunlop** (1755–1820), was author of the lyrics "Oh dinna ask me gin I lo'e ye" and "Here's to the year that's awa."

**Dun·more′** (dŭn·mōr′), 4th Earl of. **John Murray.** 1732–1809. Grandson of Lord **Charles Murray** (1660–1710), 1st earl, Scottish soldier and privy councilor, who was son of John Murray, 1st Marquis of Atholl (see ATHOLL). Scottish colonial administrator in America; appointed governor of New York (1770); governor of Virginia (1771–75); attempted to suppress revolutionary agitation in the colony; forced to flee to British warship (June 1, 1775); returned to England (1776). Governor of the Bahamas (1787–96).

**Charles Adolphus Murray** (1841–1907), 7th earl, explorer, was lord in waiting to Queen Victoria (1874–80);

explored Kashmir and Tibet (1892); author of *The Pamirs* (1893) and a novel, *Ormisdale* (1893). His son **Alexander Edward** (1871–1962), 8th earl, soldier, was aide to viceroy of India (1895–97); won Victoria Cross in Afghanistan (1897), dispatches and medal in Boer War, and Distinguished Service Cross (1914–16).

**Dunn** (dŭn), **Beverly Wyly.** 1860–1936. American soldier and ordnance expert, b. Clinton Parish, La. Grad. U.S.M.A., West Point (1883). Left army (1911) to continue work in Bureau of Explosives which he had organized for the American Railway Association. Invented high explosive named after him *explosive D* or *dunnite;* investigated Black Tom explosion (Jersey City, N.J., July, 1916); re-entered U.S. army and served during World War; returned to Bureau of Explosives after the war.

**Dunn, Ga·no′** (gä·nō′; gā′nō). 1870–1953. American electrical engineer, b. New York City. Known for designs of motors and dynamos, work on distribution of power in factories, hydroelectric developments, etc.

**Dunn, Joseph.** 1872–1951. American educator, b. New Haven, Conn. A.B. (1895) and Ph.D. (1898), Yale. Professor of Celtic languages and literatures, Catholic U. of America (from 1904). Author of *A Grammar of the Modern Portuguese Language* (1927); translator of old Irish epic *Táin Bó Cuailnge* (1913); special editor for Celtic terms, *Webster's New International Dictionary, Second Edition.*

**Dunn, Samuel Orace.** 1877–1958. American editor and transportation authority, b. Bloomfield, Iowa. Editor, *Railway Age Gazette* and *Railway Age* (from 1908). Author of *American Transportation Question* (1912), *Government Ownership of Railways* (1913), etc.

**Dunne** (dŭn), **Finley Peter.** 1867–1936. American humorist, b. Chicago. On editorial staff, Chicago *Evening Post* and Chicago *Times-Herald* (1892–97); editor, Chicago *Journal* (1897–1900). Creator of Irish saloonkeeper-philosopher character "Mr. Dooley (dōō′lĭ)," as in *Mr. Dooley in Peace and War* (1898), *Mr. Dooley's Philosophy* (1900), *Dissertations by Mr. Dooley* (1906), *Mr. Dooley Says* (1910), etc.

**Dunne, John William.** 1875–1949. British soldier, airplane designer, and philosopher. Designed and built first British military airplane (1906–07). His philosophical works present an introduction to a new ontology and include *An Experiment with Time* (1927), *The Serial Universe* (1934), *The New Immortality* (1938).

**Dun′ning** (dŭn′ĭng), **John.** See Baron ASHBURTON.

**Dunning, William Archibald.** 1857–1922. American historian, b. Plainfield, N.J. Teacher of history at Columbia (1886–1922, professor from 1904); managing editor, *Political Science Quarterly* (1894–1903). Author of *Essays on the Civil War and Reconstruction* (1898), *A History of Political Theories: Ancient and Mediaeval* (1902), *The British Empire and the United States* (1914), etc.

**Du′nois′** (dü′nwȧ′), **Jean.** Comte **de Dunois.** *Called* **the Bastard of Orléans.** 1403?–1468. French general, b. Paris; natural son of Louis, Duc d'Orléans. Attached (1421) to the person of the dauphin, Charles. Defended Orléans (1428–29) until siege raised by Joan of Arc; aided Joan in other campaigns and made triumphant entry into Paris (1436); drove English northward, conquering Normandy and Guienne (1436–51). Made count (1439); given added title of comte de Longueville (1450). Joined League of the Public Good (1465).

**Du′noy′er′ de Se·gon′zac′** (dü′nwȧ′yā′ dē sē·gôɴ′zȧk′), **André** 1884–1974. French painter and engraver; known for landscapes and figure paintings.

**Dun·ra′ven** (dŭn·rā′vĕn), Earl of. *In full* Earl of **Dunraven and Mount′-Earl′** (mount′ûrl′) and Viscount **A·dare′** (ȧ·dâr′). A title in peerage of Ireland created (1822) for members of Irish family of **Quin** [kwĭn] (2d earl added wife's name Wyndham), including: Sir **Edwin Richard Windham Wynd′ham–Quin′** [wĭn′dăm-] (1812–1871), 3d Earl of Dunraven and Mount-Earl, 1st Baron **Ken′ry** [?kĕn′rĭ] (united kingdom); B.A., Dublin (1833); Conservative M.P. (1837–51); a distinguished scholar in literature and archaeology; author of an architectural history.

His only son, **Windham Thomas Wyndham–Quin** (1841–1926), 4th earl; educ. Oxford; served as war correspondent in Abyssinia and during Franco-Prussian War; undersecretary of state for colonies (1885–86, 1886–87), resigned in protest against unfairness to Newfoundland on fisheries question and against ultra-Toryism; chairman of House of Lords committee on sweated labor (1888–90); competed unsuccessfully for the America's cup in international yacht races in specially built yachts, Valkyrie II and III (1893, 1895); achieved the success of his life as chairman of Irish Land Conference (1902–03), winning settlement upon general policy that Irish landlords should be bought out; advocated policy known as devolution; urged at Irish convention (1917) conciliation among Irish factions and settlement along federal lines; bought and operated steam yacht as hospital ship in English Channel and in Mediterranean in World War; Irish Free State senator (from 1921). Author of *The Great Divide* (consisting of American observations, 1874), *The Irish Question* (1880), *Self-instruction in Navigation* (1900), *Past Times and Pastimes* (1922).

**Dun·sa′ny** (dŭn·sā′nĭ), 18th Baron. **Edward John Moreton Drax Plun′kett** (plŭng′kĕt; -kĭt). *Known as* Lord **Dunsany.** 1878–1957. Irish poet and dramatist; nephew of Sir Horace Plunkett (*q.v.*). Joined Coldstream Guards, served in Boer War, wounded in World War. Author of poems and tales, including *The Gods of Pegana* (1905), *Evil Kettle* (1926), *Fifty Poems* (1929), *Travel Tales of Mr. Joseph Jorkens* (1931), *Patches of Sunlight* (1938); won reputation as playwright with *The Glittering Gate* (produced by W. B. Yeats in Abbey Theatre, Dublin, 1909); other plays, *The Gods of the Mountain* (1911), *The Laughter of the Gods, A Night at an Inn* (1916), *If* (1921), etc.

**Duns Sco′tus** (dŭnz skō′tŭs), **John.** 1265?–?1308. Scottish scholastic theologian, b. Duns, Scotland. Known as **Doc′tor Sub·ti′lis** (dŏk′tẽr [-tôr] sŭb·tī′lĭs) on account of his dialectical skill and his refined distinctions. Joined Franciscan order; studied and lectured at Oxford, in Paris, and in Cologne. Author of a philosophic grammar and commentaries on the Bible, Aristotle, and the *Sententiae* of Peter Lombard (12 vols., pub. 1639 by Luke Wadding). Founder of a scholastic system called Scotism; critic of preceding scholastic systems of Christian theology worked out by St. Thomas Aquinas, Henry of Ghent, and Godfrey of Fontaine; upholder of the separability and independence of the rational soul from the body, provoker of a long controversy between Scotists and Thomists; a voluntarist, contended against Aquinas's subordination, following Aristotle, of the practical to the theoretical in Christianity and emphasis upon speculation to the detriment of practice, arguing that faith, upon which theology rests, is not speculative but an act of will; a conceptualist in logic, followed ibn-Gabirol in the theory of universal matter, basis of all existences, with some positive entity of its own; zealous defender of the doctrine of the Immaculate Conception. Stubborn opposition of Scotists to classical studies of Renaissance and their obstructionist and caviling practices gave rise to the use of *dunce* for a sophist, pedant, or blockhead.

**Dun'sta·ble** (dŭn'stă·b'l) *or, formerly,* **Dun'sta·ple** (-stȧ·p'l), **John.** 1370?–1453. English mathematician, and earliest of old English composers, probably b. at Dunstable. Composer of six manuscript volumes of motets, masses, antiphons, and songs including a three-part chanson, *O Rosa bella.*

**Dun'stan** (dŭn'stăn), Saint. c. 925 (or c. 910)–988. English prelate, b. near Glastonbury. Son of a West Saxon noble; educ. by Irish pilgrims; accused of practicing black arts, expelled from King Athelstan's court; took monastic vows; made abbot of Glastonbury by King Edmund (c. 943). Rebuilt the abbey; introduced stricter Continental form of Benedictine rule, establishing thriving center of religious teaching. As treasurer and chief adviser of King Edred, virtual ruler of realm; outlawed and driven to Flanders by Edwy (955–957); recalled by Edgar, created bishop of Worcester, bishop of London (959), archbishop of Canterbury (961); as primate again virtual ruler of kingdom. Sought to make Danes integral part of nation, promoted education, urged respect for law, obliged landowners to pay tithes; on murder of Edward and accession of Ethelred II, retired to Canterbury (978).

**Dun'ster** (dŭn'stẽr), **Henry.** 1609?–1659. Clergyman and educator, b. in Lancashire, England. Emigrated to Massachusetts Colony (1640). First president of Harvard College (1640–54); forced to resign because of his views on infant baptism. Indicted, tried, convicted, and publicly admonished for opposing the church ordinance on infant baptism (1655); pastor in Scituate till his death. See Samuel GREEN.

**Dun'ton** (dŭn't'n; -tŭn), **John.** 1659–1733. English bookseller in London; published weekly *Athenian Gazette* (1690–96; later *Athenian Mercury*); attacked Oxford and Bolingbroke in political satires; became mentally unbalanced.

**Dünt'zer** (dün'tsẽr), **Heinrich,** *in full* **Johann Heinrich Joseph.** 1813–1901. German philologist and historian of literature; published works on Greek and Latin philology, and biographical studies of Goethe.

**Duonelaitis, Kristijonas.** See Christian DONALITIUS.

**Du'pan'loup'** (dü'päɴ'lo͞o'), **Félix Antoine Philibert.** 1802–1878. French Roman Catholic prelate and political leader; bishop of Orléans (1849); member, National Assembly (1871); elected senator for life (1876).

**Du'parc'** (dü'pȧrk'), **Marie Eugène Henri Fouques'–** (fo͞ok'-). 1848–1933. French composer; compositions include symphonic poem *Lenore,* nocturne for orchestra *Aux Étoiles,* motet for three voices, and many songs which have stimulated development of French chanson.

**Du'per'ré'** (dü'pĕ'rā'), Baron **Victor Guy.** 1775–1846. French naval commander; distinguished himself (1808) in fight with British vessels; commanded France's fleet in Adriatic and defended Venice against Austrians (1813–14); commanded fleet before Algiers (1830); created admiral and peer of France; member of three French ministries (between 1834 and 1843).

**Du'per'rey'** (dü'pĕ'rā'), **Louis Isidore.** 1786–1865. French naval officer and scientist; accompanied de Freycinet on the *Uranie* around world (1817–20); commanded *Coquille* on trip to Oceania and South America (1822–25); by his investigations, determined positions of the magnetic poles and the magnetic equator.

**Duperron, Anquetil-.** See ANQUETIL-DUPERRON.

**Du Per'ron'** (dü pĕ'rôɴ'), **Jacques Da'vy'** (dȧ'vē'). 1556–1618. French Roman Catholic prelate; supported cause of Henry IV and is credited with converting him to the Catholic faith; bishop of Évreux (1591); created cardinal (1604) and archbishop of Sens (1606); member of the Council of Regency (1610).

**Du'pe·tit'-Thou'ars'** (düp'tē'twȧr'), **Louis Marie Au'bert'** (ō'bâr'). 1758–1831. French botanist; visited Madagascar and neighboring islands (1792–1802); author of *Histoire des Végétaux Recueillis dans les Îles de France, de Bourbon et de Madagascar.* His nephew **Abel Aubert** (1793–1864), vice-admiral (1846); completed voyage around world (1839); brought (1842) Marquesas and (1843) Society Islands under French protection.

**Du'pin'** (dü'păɴ'), **Amandine Aurore Lucie.** See George SAND.

**Dupin, André Marie Jean Jacques.** 1783–1865. French lawyer and politician; as lawyer, defended Marshal Ney, Béranger, Jouy, and General Alix; took part in Revolution of 1830; procureur général to Court of Cassation; president of Chamber of Deputies (1832–40) and of Legislative Assembly (1849–51). A brother, Baron **François Pierre Charles** (1784–1873), was an economist and engineer; councilor of state (1831); minister of marine (1833); member of the Constituent Assembly and the Legislative Assembly (1848); senator (1852); author of mathematical and economic treatises, as *Développement de Géométrie pour Faire Suite à la "Géométrie Pratique" de Monge* (1813; a treatise containing the theorem known as *Dupin's indicatrix*) and *Forces Productives des Nations de 1800 à 1851* (1851). Another member of the family, **Jean Henri Dupin** (1787–1887), playwright, was author or coauthor of over 200 comedies and vaudeville sketches.

**Du Pin** *or* **Du'pin'** (dü'păɴ'), **Louis Ellies.** 1657–1719. French Roman Catholic clergyman and church historian.

**Du'pleix'** (dü'plĕks'; *Angl.* dū̍·plĕks', -plāks'), Marquis **Joseph François.** 1697–1763. French colonial administrator; governor general of all French possessions in India (1742–54). Engaged in long struggle with the British in India. Recalled (1754), his work unfinished, the value of his services unrecognized, and his fortune swept away.

**Duplessis-Mornay.** See Philippe de MORNAY.

**Du'ploy'é'** (dü'plwȧ'yā'), **Émile.** 1833–1912. French inventor of the Duployé method of stenography.

**Du Pon'ceau'** *or* **Du'pon'ceau'** (dü'pôɴ'sō'; *Angl.* dū̍·pŏn'sō), **Pierre Étienne,** *known in America as* **Peter Stephen.** 1760–1844. Lawyer and writer, b. St.-Martin, Île de Ré, France. Accompanied Baron von Steuben to America as secretary (1777); aide-de-camp to Steuben (1777–79). Became naturalized citizen, Pennsylvania (1781). Adm. to bar (1785); practiced, Philadelphia. His writings include legal and historical works and treatises on philology, including original studies of various North American Indian languages.

**Du Pont** family. See DU PONT DE NEMOURS.

**Du'pont'** (dü'pôɴ'), **Pierre.** 1821–1870. French lyric poet; author of *Les Deux Anges* (1842; awarded prize by French Academy), *Les Bœufs* (1846), *Le Chant du Blé, La Chanson du Pain, Le Chant des Ouvriers, Le Chant des Nations,* etc.

**Dupont de l'É'tang'** (dẽ lā'täɴ'), Comte **Pierre Antoine.** 1765–1840. French general; distinguished himself at Valmy, Marengo, Ulm, Friedland; forced to surrender at Bailén (1808). Appointed minister of war by Louis XVIII (1814), member of privy council (1815).

**Dupont de l'Eure'** (dẽ lûr'), **Jacques Charles.** 1767–1855. French lawyer and politician; member of Council of Five Hundred (1795), Chamber of Deputies (1814). Took part in Revolution of 1830; minister of justice (1830). President of provisional government (1848).

**Du Pont' de Ne·mours'** (dü pôɴ' dẽ nẽ·mo͞or'; *Eng.* dū̍ pŏnt' dẽ nẽ·mo͝or'), **Pierre Samuel.** 1739–1817. French economist, b. Paris. Friend and disciple of

François Quesnay; expounded economic doctrines of Quesnay's school (the physiocrats) in his *Physiocratie* (1768). Collaborator of Turgot (1774–76); shared his disgrace; recalled by Vergennes to assist in negotiating with England treaty to accord independence to United States (1783). Member of States-General (1789); his reactionary views led to his imprisonment (1792) and later (1799) to his emigration to United States. Prepared at Jefferson's request a scheme for national education in U.S., never adopted in U.S. but used in part in French code of education. Returned to France (1802); secretary to provisional government (1814); again emigrated (1815) to U.S., where he died. His two sons, Victor Marie and Éleuthère Irénée (see below), founded the two American branches of the family.

**Victor Marie Du Pont** (1767–1827), diplomat and industrialist, b. Paris, France, was in U.S. (from 1787) as attaché of French legation (1787–89), aide-de-camp to Lafayette (1789–91), second secretary of French legation (1791–92), and first secretary (1795–96). Settled in U.S. (1800); naturalized. His mercantile importing business in New York (1802–05), V. du Pont de Nemours & Co., failed, as did a land development project (1806–09); became manager of his brother Irénée's woolen mills near Wilmington, Del., but was unsuccessful. Became a director, Bank of the United States, Philadelphia. His son **Samuel Francis** (1803–1865), b. Bergen Point, N.J., was a naval officer; midshipman, U.S. navy (1815). Served through Mexican War. Member of board appointed to draw up curriculum and regulations for a naval academy (1850). Served through Civil War; in command of squadron that captured Port Royal, S.C. (Nov., 1861); rank of rear admiral (1862); captured islands and forts along Georgia and Florida coasts and established 14 blockading stations; commanded fleet of monitors repulsed in attack on defenses of Charleston (Apr., 1863); relieved of his command; retired from active duty.

**Éleuthère Irénée Du Pont** (1771–1834), industrialist, b. Paris, France, was in father's printing plant, Paris (1791–97), until it was closed by French radicals; to U.S. (1799). Established near Wilmington, Del. (1802–04), plant for manufacturing gunpowder, the successful beginning of E. I. Du Pont de Nemours & Co. Among his successors in the presidency of the company have been his sons **Alfred Victor** (1798–1856) and **Henry** (1812–1889), grandson **Eugene**, and great-grandsons **Thomas Coleman** (1863–1930), **Pierre** (pyâr) **Samuel** (1870–1954), **I'ré·née** [ĭr'ĕ·nā] (1876–1963), **Lam·mot'** [lă·mŏt'] (1880–1952). Henry's son **Henry Algernon** (1838–1926), a U.S. army officer (1861–75) serving through Civil War and a member of the family firm (1878–1902), was opponent of John Edward Addicks in struggle (1889–1906) for seat in U.S. Senate, Du Pont being finally seated and serving two terms (1906–17).

**Du·port'** (dŭ·pōrt'; -pôrt'), **James.** 1606–1679. English classical scholar. Regius professor of Greek, Cambridge (1639–54, 1660); master of Magdalen Coll. (1668). Best known for his *Homeri Gnomologia* (1660), a collection of aphorisms in *Iliad* and *Odyssey*.

**Du'port'** (dü'pôr'), **Jean Pierre** (1741–1818) and his brother **Jean Louis** (1749–1819). French violoncellists and composers, esp. of music for violoncello.

**Du'prat'** (dü'prȧ'), **Antoine.** 1463–1535. French Roman Catholic prelate and statesman; chancellor of France (1515). Consecrated archbishop of Sens (1525); created cardinal (1527). Chief minister of Louise of Savoy during the second regency (1525). Unsuccessful candidate for the papacy after death of Clement VII.

**Du'pray'** (dü'prā'), **Henri Louis.** 1841–1909. French painter of military scenes.

**Du'pré'** (dü'prā'), **Ernest Pierre.** 1862–1921. French physician; specialist in neuropathology and psychiatry.

**Du'pré'** (dü'prā'), **Giovanni.** 1817–1882. Italian sculptor, b. Siena. Among his works are *Abel, Cain,* bas-relief *Triumph of the Cross* in Church of Santa Croce (Florence), and monument to Cavour (Turin).

**Dupré, Guillaume.** 1574?–1647. French sculptor and medallionist.

**Dupré, Jules.** 1811–1889. French landscape painter; identified with Barbizon school; regarded as one of founders of modern French school of landscape painting. Among his notable canvases are *Vue des Environs d'Abbeville, Forêt de Compiègne, Souvenir des Landes, Les Bords du Ruisseau, Clair de Lune.*

**Du'prez'** (dü'prā'), **Gilbert Louis.** 1806–1896. French operatic tenor; sang roles in *La Reine de Chypre, Charles VI,* and *Othello.* Composed oratorio *Le Jugement Dernier* and several light operas.

**Du'puis'** (dü'pü·ē'), **Charles Alfred Marie.** 1867–1938. French publicist; author of *Principe d'Équilibre et Concert Européen* (1909), etc.

**Dupuis, Charles François.** 1742–1809. French scholar; professor, Collège de France (1787). Member of National Convention (1792) and Council of Five Hundred (1795). Author of *L'Origine de Tous les Cultes ou Religion Universelle* (1795).

**Du'puy'** (dü'pü·ē'), **Charles Alexandre.** 1851–1923. French educator and statesman; member of Chamber of Deputies (1885–1900), Senate (from 1900). Premier of France (1893; 1894–95; 1898–99).

**Dupuy, Jean.** 1844–1919. French journalist and politician; member of Chamber of Deputies and (1891) of the Senate. During World War, was minister of state and member of war council.

**Dupuy, Pierre.** 1582–1651. French historian and librarian; curator (1645), with his brother **Jacques** (1586–1656), of royal library, Paris, to which Jacques bequeathed his own valuable collection of books.

**Dupuy de Lôme'** (dē lōm'), **Stanislas Charles Henri Laurent.** 1816–1885. French naval engineer; in charge of building first French screw steamships and first armored vessels (*Gloire, Invincible, Normandie*). Senator for life (1877).

**Du'puy'tren'** (dü'pü·ē'trăN'), Baron **Guillaume.** 1777–1835. French surgeon and anatomist; improved operating techniques and invented surgical instruments.

**Du'quesne'** (dü'kān'; *Angl.* dŭ·kān'), Marquis **Abraham.** 1610–1688. French naval commander; distinguished himself in the Coruña expedition (1639) and in battles at Tarragona (1641), Barcelona (1643), and Cabo-de-Gata. In Swedish service (1643–45), defeated combined Danish and Dutch fleets. Returned to French service (1645); captured Bordeaux, which had revolted and was receiving Spanish aid (1650). Defeated combined fleets of Spain and Holland, under Admiral de Ruyter, near Catania (April 20, 1676), de Ruyter being mortally wounded.

**Du'ques'noy'** (dü'kĕ'nwȧ'), **François.** *Known as* **François Fla'mand'** (flȧ'mäN'). 1594?–1642. Belgian sculptor; among his works are *La Justice* on Brussels chancellery, *Deux Anges* for door of Jesuit church in Brussels, *Silène Endormi et Entouré de Jeunes Garçons,* sculpture of the baldachin at St. Peter's in Rome, marble tomb of Gaspard de Wischer in Naples.

**Du·rán'** (dōō·rän'), **Agustín.** 1789–1862. Spanish critic and poet, b. Madrid; author of *Discurso sobre...la Decadencia del Teatro Antiguo* (1828), *Romancero General* (collection of Spanish ballad literature; 5 vols., 1828–32), and the poem *Leyenda de las Tres Toronjas del Vergel de Amor* (1856).

**Du'ran'** (dü'räɴ'), **Ca'ro'lus'** (kȧ'rô'lüs'). *Professional name of* **Charles Auguste Émile Du'rand'** (dü'räɴ'). 1837–1917. French painter of portraits, landscapes, and genre pictures; studio in Paris (from 1873).

**Du'rand'** (dü'räɴ'), **Alice Fleury.** See Henry GRÉVILLE.

**Du·rand'** (dû·rănd'), **Asher Brown.** 1796–1886. American engraver and painter, b. near Newark, N.J. Established reputation with *The Signing of the Declaration of Independence*, after Trumbull (1823); mastery of steel engraving shown by a series of more than 50 engraved portraits of eminent contemporaries. In 1836 he turned to painting, at first chiefly of portraits and figure pieces; later, turned to landscape painting, drawing inspiration from scenery of Hudson River Valley and New England; regarded as a founder (with Thomas Cole) of Hudson River school of landscape.

**Durand, Edward Dana.** 1871–1960. American economist and statistician, b. Romeo, Mich. Director, U.S. census (1909–13). Professor, Minnesota (1913–17). On staff of U.S. food administration, in Europe (1917–19). Chief economist of U.S. Tariff Commission (1930–35), and member of commission (from 1935). Author of *The Trust Problem* (1915), *Industry and Commerce of the United States* (1930), etc.

**Du'rand'** (dü'räɴ'), **Guillaume.** See Gulielmus DURANDUS.

**Du·rand'** (dû·rănd'), **William Frederick.** 1859–1958. American mechanical engineer, b. Bethany, Conn. In engineering corps, U.S. navy (1880–87); professor, Michigan State (1887–91), Cornell (1891–1904), Stanford (1904–24). Author of *Fundamental Principles of Mechanics* (1889), *Practical Marine Engineering* (1901), etc.

**Du·ran'do** (dōō·rän'dō), **Giacomo.** 1807–1894. Italian soldier and statesman; served in constitutional armies of Portugal and Spain. Joined Sardinian army as general (1848); checked Austrians at Caffaro; aide-de-camp to Charles Albert at battle of Novara (1849). Senator, minister of war (1855); ambassador to Constantinople (1856–61); minister of foreign affairs under Rattazzi; senate president (1884–87). His brother **Giovanni** (1804–1869), also a soldier, commissioned by Antonelli to organize troops in Romagna (1848); defeated by Austrians at Vicenza; under Charles Albert, commanded division at battles of Mortara and Novara (1849); took part in Crimean expedition (1854–56); commanded division at battle of Solferino (1859); senator (1860).

**Du·ran'dus** (dû·răn'dŭs), **Gulielmus.** *Fr.* **Guillaume Du'rand'** (dü'räɴ'). *Ital.* **Du·ran'ti** (dōō·rän'tē) *or* **Du·ran'tis** (dōō·rän'tēs). 1237?–1296. French prelate and jurist; appointed by Pope Gregory X governor of patrimony of Saint Peter; bishop of Mende (1287); author of *Speculum Judiciale* and *Rationale Divinorum Officiorum*. His nephew **Gulielmus Durandus,** *Fr.* **Guillaume Durand** (d. 1330), also a canonist, succeeded him as bishop of Mende (1296).

**Durandus de Sanc'to Por'ci·a'no** (dē săngk'tō pôr'sĭ·ā'nō), **Gulielmus.** *Lat. form of Fr.* **Guillaume Du'rand' de Saint'-Pour'çain'** (dü'räɴ' dē săɴ'-pōōr'săɴ'). *Known as* **Doc'tor Res'o·lu·tis'si·mus** (dŏk'tēr [-tôr] rĕz'ō·lū·tĭs'ĭ·mŭs). d. 1332. French scholastic Dominican monk; summoned to Avignon by Pope John XXII as master of the sacred palace; successively, bishop of Limoux (1317), Le Puy (1318), Meaux (1326). Author of *De Jurisdictione Ecclesiastica et de Legibus* and *De Statu Animarum Sanctarum.*

**Du·rant'** (dû·rănt'), **Henry.** 1802–1875. American Congregational clergyman, b. Acton, Mass. To California (1853); instrumental in securing charter for College of California (1855), succeeded by U. of California (1868); first president, U. of California (1870–72).

**Durant, Henry Fowle.** *Orig. name* **Henry Welles Smith.** 1822–1881. American lawyer, b. Hanover, N.H.; changed name because of number of other Smiths. Practiced, Lowell, Mass. (1843–48), Boston (1848–63). Affected by death of his young son, gave up law, became a lay preacher, and conducted revival meetings in Massachusetts and New Hampshire (1864–75). Founder (1870) and treasurer (1870–81) of Wellesley College.

**Durant, Thomas Clark.** 1820–1885. Vice-president, Union Pacific Railroad Co. (1863), b. Lee, Mass. Started building of road; secured charter of Crédit Mobilier and became its president (1863–67); during long-drawn factional struggle in Union Pacific directorate for control of road, he pushed building of road to completion (May 10, 1869); ousted from directorate (May 25, 1869).

**Durant, Will,** *in full* **William James.** 1885– . American educator and writer, b. North Adams, Mass. Director of Labor Temple School, New York City (1914–27). Professor of philosophy, U.C.L.A. (1935). Author of *The Story of Philosophy* (1926), *Adventures in Genius* (1931), *On the Meaning of Life* (1932), *The Story of Civilization* (1st volume, 1935), *The Life of Greece* (1939).

**Durant, William Crapo.** 1861–1947. American industrialist, b. Boston. Organized Durant-Dort Carriage Co., Flint, Mich. (1886), Buick Motor Car Co. (1905), General Motors Co. (1908), Chevrolet Motor Co. (1911–15; with Louis Chevrolet, *q.v.*). Lost control of General Motors Co. and Chevrolet Motor Co. (1920). Organized Durant Motors, Inc. (1921). Later, interested himself in manufacture of rayon.

**Du·ran'te** (dōō·rän'tā), **Francesco.** 1684–1755. Italian composer; reputed successor of Scarlatti at Sant'Onofrio (1718–42); head of Conservatorio di Santa Maria di Loreto, Naples (1742–55). Works include masses, requiems, and *Lamentations* of Jeremiah.

**Duranti** *or* **Durantis.** See Gulielmus DURANDUS.

**Du·ran'ty** (dû·răn'tĭ), **Walter.** 1884–1957. Journalist and author, b. Liverpool, Eng. On staff of New York *Times* (from 1913); its Moscow correspondent (1921–35); awarded Pulitzer prize for reporting (1932). Won O. Henry short-story award (1928) with *The Parrot*, a tale of Russia. Author also of *I Write as I Please* (1935), *One Life, One Kopek* (1937), *The Gold Train* (1938), etc.

**Durão, José de Santa Ritta.** See SANTA RITTA DURÃO.

**Duras,** Ducs **de.** See DURFORT family.

**D'Ur'ban** (dûr'băn), Sir **Benjamin.** 1777–1849. British military commander and colonial administrator. Took part in Peninsular War (1808–15); lieutenant general (1837). Governor of Antigua (1820), Barbados (1825–29); first governor of British Guiana (1831); governor of Cape of Good Hope (1834–38); attempted to extend eastern boundaries to include Xosa Kaffirs but was overruled (1835) by colonial secretary, whereupon the great trek of Dutch farmers began (1836); died in Montreal, in command of troops in Canada (from 1847). Port Natal was renamed Durban in his honor.

**Dü'rer** (dü'rēr), **Albrecht.** 1471–1528. German painter and engraver, b. Nürnberg; regarded as leader of German Renaissance school of painting. Studied under Wohlgemuth and worked in his studio (to c. 1497); studio in Venice (1505–07), then in Nürnberg. Court painter for emperors Maximilian I and Charles V. Regarded as inventor of etching and famed as engraver and woodcut artist. Woodcuts include *The Apocalypse* (16 subjects), *The Greater Passion* (12 subjects), and *The Lesser Passion* (37 subjects); engravings include *Death and the Devil* and *St. Jerome in his Study;* paintings include *Adoration of the Trinity*, *Adam and Eve*, and *Four Apostles.*

**Du'ret'** (dü'rĕ'), **François Joseph.** 1732–1816. French sculptor, whose works include *L'Empereur Napoléon, Sapho Inspirée par l'Amour, Esculape Rendant Hippolyte à la Vie.* Among the sculptures of his son and pupil, **François,** *called* **Francisque Joseph** (1804–1865), are *Jeune Pêcheur Dansant la Tarentelle, Le Danseur Napolitain, La France Protégeant ses Enfants,* and statues of Philippe de France, Cardinal de Richelieu, and Dunois.

**Du'rey'** (dü'rā'), **Louis Edmond.** 1888– . French composer of impressionistic school; member of "The Six" (see A. HONEGGER); works include *Pastorale* for orchestra, the choral work *Éloges,* string quartet and string trio, and many songs.

**D'Ur'fey** (dûr'fĭ), **Thomas.** *Known as* **Tom Dur'fey** (dûr'fĭ). 1653–1723. English song writer and dramatist; descendant of French Huguenots; nephew of Honoré d'Urfé (see URFÉ). After his first play, *The Siege of Memphis,* a bombastic tragedy (produced 1676), became successful with comedies, including *The Fond Husband* (1676), *Madame Fickle* (1677), *The Virtuous Wife* (1680), *Campaigners* (1698), and a comic opera, *Wonders in the Sun.* His songs were collected as *Wit and Mirth or Pills to Purge Melancholy* (6 vols., 1719–20).

**Dur'fort'** (dür'fôr'). Name of an old French family taking its name from village of Durfort in southwestern France and tracing descent from **Arnaud de Durfort** (fl. 1305), who acquired fief of Duras by marriage with niece of Pope Clement V; the family includes:

**Jacques Henri de Durfort** (1625–1704), Duc **de Du'ras'** (dü'räs'), governor of Franche-Comté, which he helped to conquer, and marshal of France (1675); at head of English army, took Philippsburg and Mannheim (1688). His brother **Guy Aldonce de Durfort de Duras** (1630–1702), Comte **de Lorges** (lôrzh) and Duc **de Quin'tin'** (kăN'tăN'), became a marshal of France (1676); led an army into Germany and captured Heidelberg (1693). His youngest brother, **Louis de Durfort de Duras** (1640?–1709), Marquis **de Blan'que·fort'** [bläNk'fôr'] (in French peerage), Earl of **Fev'er·sham** [fĕv'ẽr·shăm] (in English peerage), accompanied duke of York to England and was naturalized (1663); created Baron **Duras of Hol'den·by** [hōm'bĭ] (1673); succeeded to his father-in-law's title of earl of Feversham (1677); English ambassador to peace of Nijmegen (1675); under James II was privy councilor, chief commander against rebels under Monmouth at battle of Sedgemoor (1685), commander of James II's army (1686); made peace with William III on intercession of queen dowager.

**Jean Baptiste de Durfort** (1684–1770), Duc de Duras, son of Marshal Jacques Henri de Durfort, served with distinction in England, Flanders, and Spain, became marshal of France (1751). His son **Emmanuel Félicité de Durfort** (1715–1789), Duc de Duras, took part in wars of Louis XV; was ambassador to Spain (1752), marshal of France (1775), without having commanded an army, an academician (1775), having written nothing. Duc **Amédée Bretagne Malo de Duras** (1771–1838), grandson of Emmanuel Félicité de Durfort, was loyal to Louis XVI, made field marshal by Louis XVIII; his wife, **Claire de Ker'saint'** [dĕ kĕr'săN'] (1778–1828), daughter of Armand Kersaint (*q.v.*), presided over a brilliant salon; author of two novels, *Ourika* (1823) and *Édouard* (1825); an admirer of Chateaubriand.

The family of Durfort is represented by the branch **Dur'fort'–Ci'vrac'** (-sē'vräk'), dating from the 16th century.

**Durham,** Earl of. See John George LAMBTON.

**Dü'rings·feld** (dü'rĭngs·fĕlt), **Ida von.** 1815–1876. German writer; m. Baron Otto von Reinsberg (1845). Author of verse, novels, and travel sketches.

**Du'ris** (dū'rĭs) *or* **Dou'ris** (dōō'rĭs) of Samos. Greek historian of late 4th and early 3d century B.C. Author of history of Greece from battle of Leuctra (371 B.C.) to death of Lysimachus (281), annals of Samos, a life of Agathocles, and literary and artistic essays.

**Durk'heim'** (dür'kĕm'), **Émile.** 1858–1917. French sociologist; author of *De la Division du Travail Social* (1893), *Règles de la Méthode Sociologique* (1894), etc.

**Du'roc'** (dü'rôk'), **Géraud Christophe Michel.** Duke of **Fri'u·li** (frē'ōō·lē; frē·ōō'lē). 1772–1813. French general under Napoleon; served in Italian and Egyptian campaigns. Engaged at Austerlitz, Essling, Wagram.

**Dur'rell** (dûr'ĕl), **Lawrence George.** 1912– . British author and poet. Author of the *Alexandria Quartet* (1957–60), *Collected Poems* (1960; 1968), etc.

**Durst** (dûrst), **Alan.** 1883–1970. English sculptor, b. Alverstoke; studio in London. Carved sculptures on Royal Acad. of Dramatic Art building and Merchant Taylor's School, both in London.

**Dur'tain'** (dür'tăN'), **Luc.** *Pseudonym of* **André Nep·veu'** (nĕ·vû'). 1881–1959. French writer; author of *Douze Cent Mille* (1922), *L'Autre Europe, Moscou et sa Foi* (1927), *Hollywood Dépassé* (1928), *Captain O. K.* (1931), *Frank et Marjorie* (1934), *Quatre Continents* (verse; 1936), *Le Mari Singulier* (comedy; 1937), *La Guerre n'existe pas...* (1939).

**Du'ruy'** (dü'rü·ē'), **Victor.** 1811–1894. French historian; professor at Reims, and later at Paris. Author of many school histories, and of *Histoire du Peuple Romain* (7 vols.), *Histoire Grecque* (3 vols.), etc.

**Dur'yea** (dŏŏr'yā), **Charles Edgar.** 1861–1938. American inventor and manufacturer, b. near Canton, Ill. Reputed "father of the automobile." Organized Duryea Motor Wagon Co., Springfield, Mass. (1895); sold first car (1896); also organized Duryea Power Co., Reading, Pa., for making automobiles (1900). Inventor of spray carburetor (1892) and first to use pneumatic tires on cars (1893). Assisted by his brother **J. Frank,** who drove in and won first automobile race (Chicago, 1895). Cf. Elwood HAYNES and George B. SELDEN.

**Dur'yée** (dŏŏr'yā), **Abram.** 1815–1890. American army officer, b. New York City. Raised a regiment of volunteers, known as Duryée's Zouaves (1861), for Civil War service; brigadier general (1861); brevet major general (1865). Police commissioner, New York City (1873).

**Du'sart** (dü'särt), **Cornelis.** 1660–1704. Dutch painter, esp. of scenes of Dutch peasant life.

**Du'se** (dōō'zā), **Eleonora.** 1859–1924. Italian actress. Began stage career at 13 in itinerant companies; established reputation at Naples (1878) and Milan (1885); m. (1885) Tebaldo Checchi (later separated). Toured Europe; American debut, New York (1893). Close friend of Gabriele D'Annunzio (to 1899); left stage (1909–21). Known esp. for interpretation of heroines of Dumas, Sardou, Ibsen, Sudermann, D'Annunzio, and Maeterlinck; chief roles include Francesca da Rimini, Juliet, Camille, Magda, and Fernande.

**Dushan, Stephen.** See *Stephen Nemanya IX,* under STEPHEN of Serbia.

**Dush'man** (dōōsh'măn), **Saul** (sôl). 1883–1954. Physical chemist, b. Rostov, Russia; to America (1891); naturalized (1917). Author of *High Vacuum* (1923), *Elements of Quantum Mechanics* (1937), etc.

**Du Som'me·rard'** (dü sôm'rär'), **Alexandre.** 1779–1842. French archaeologist. Traveled through France and Italy, making collections of medieval art objects and other relics, which, with his mansion, were bought by the government (1843) to form the Musée de Cluny.

**Dus'sek** (dŏŏ'sĕk) *or* **Du'šík** (dŏŏ'sēk), **Jan Ladislav.** 1760–1812. Bohemian pianist and composer of 12 concertos, 80 violin sonatas, over 60 two-hand and four-hand piano sonatas.

**Dus'tin** (dŭs'tĭn), **Hannah,** *nee prob.* **Emerson.** b. 1659, American heroine, b. Haverhill, Mass.; m. (1677) Thomas Dustin (or Duston or Durston). Captured by Indians (1697); escaped and returned home, after killing and scalping her captors while they slept.

**Du'tens'** (dü'tăɴs'), **Louis.** 1730–1812. Man of letters and diplomat, b. Tours, France. Huguenot refugee in England; historiographer to the king of England.

**Du'tra** (dŏŏ'trȧ), **Eu·ri'co** (ā·ŏŏ·rē'kŏŏ) **Gaspar.** 1885–1974. Brazilian soldier, b. Cuiabá, Mato Grosso; enlisted (1902); commissioned (1910); general (1935); war minister (1936–45); president of Brazil (1946–51).

**Du'treuil' de Rhins'** (dü'trû'y' dē răɴs'), **Jules Léon.** 1846–1894. French mariner and explorer; explored region of the Ogowe in equatorial Africa (1883); explored Chinese Turkestan and Tibet (1891–94); murdered by natives in eastern Tibet.

**Du'tro'chet'** (dü'trô'shĕ'), **René Joachim Henri.** 1776–1847. French physiologist and natural philosopher; studied development of eggs of birds, structure of feathers, etc.

**Dutt** (dôt), **Mi'chael** (mī'kĕl; -k'l) **Madhu Sudan.** 1824–1873. Bengali poet; abandoned Hinduism for Christianity (1843); studied law in England (after 1862) and barrister in Calcutta (from 1867); author of the dramas *Ratnavali* (1858), *Sarmishtha* (1859), *Krishna Kumari* (1858–61), and the epic poem *Meghanad-Badha* (1861).

**Dut'ton** (dŭt''n), **Clarence Edward.** 1841–1912. American geologist, b. Wallingford, Conn. Served through Civil War; remained in U.S. army until 1901. Detailed to U.S. Geological and Geographical Survey (1875–90); made study of plateau region of Utah and Arizona. Author of *Report on the Geology of the High Plateau of Utah* (1879–80), *Hawaiian Volcanoes* (1884), *Earthquakes in the Light of the New Seismology* (1904), etc.

**Dutton, Edward Payson.** 1831–1923. American publisher, b. Keene, N.H. In employ of booksellers Ide & Dutton, Boston (1852); bought out Ide's interest and organized as E. P. Dutton & Co., with himself as president (1858). Bought Ticknor & Fields retail business in Boston (1864) and bookselling business of General Protestant Episcopal Sunday School Union and Church Book Society of New York. Associated with J. M. Dent (*q.v.*), English publisher, in publication and sale of "Everyman's Library" series of inexpensive reprints of English classics.

**Duun** (dōōn), **Olav.** 1876–1939. Norwegian writer; public school teacher (1904–26). Works include series of six novels (1918–23) called *Juvikfolke* (*The People of Juvik*), tracing story of four generations of Norwegian 19th-century peasant landholders.

**Du'val'** (dü'vȧl'). *Orig.* **Pi'neux'–Du'val'** (pē'nû'-). French family including the brothers: **Amaury,** *in full* **Charles Alexandre Amaury** (1760–1838), archaeologist, author of *Des Sépultures* (1801), *Paris et ses Monuments* (1803), etc. **Alexandre Vincent** (1767–1842), playwright, at one time manager of Théâtre Louvois (1808) and the Odéon, author of a number of comedies of manners, and a critical study *Le Théâtre Français Depuis Cinquante Ans* (1838). **Henri Charles** (1770–1847), writer, father of the painter Amaury-Duval (*q.v.*).

**Duval, Amaury–.** See AMAURY-DUVAL.

**Duval, Claude.** 1643–1670. French domestic servant and highwayman in England, noted for daring and for gallantry to women; accompanied duke of Richmond to England at Restoration; hanged at Tyburn.

**Duval, Paul.** *Pseudonym* **Jean Lor'rain'** (lô'răɴ'). 1850?–1906. French man of letters; on staff of *Courrier Français*, *Écho de Paris*, etc. Among his books of verse are *Le Sang des Dieux* (1882), *Modernités* (1885), *Les Griseries* (1887), *Songeuse* (1891), *Sensations et Souvenirs* (1895); among his plays, *Yanthis* (1894), *Une Nuit de Grenelle* (1903), etc.

**Du·veen'** (dů·vēn'), **Joseph.** Baron **Duveen of Mil'-bank** (mĭl'băngk). 1869–1939. English art connoisseur and art dealer, b. Hull. Employed first in father's antique shop; later joined his uncle in U.S. and developed business as art dealer. Benefactor of National Gallery, London, and donor of gallery to house the Elgin marbles.

**Du've·neck** (dōō'vĕ·nĕk), **Frank.** *Orig.* **Frank Deck'er** (dĕk'ẽr); *took name* Duveneck *from stepfather.* 1848–1919. American painter, sculptor, and etcher, b. Covington, Ky. Studied and painted in Munich (from 1870), where he started (1878) a school, among his pupils being John W. Alexander, W. M. Chase, and others of note, on whom he exerted great influence; moved his school to Italy (1879); produced (1880–85) notable series of etchings of Venetian scenes. On death of his wife (1888), carved magnificent memorial now over her grave in Florence. Returned to Cincinnati (1888); devoted himself chiefly to teaching. Bequeathed his collection of paintings, etchings, sketches, etc., to Cincinnati Museum of Art.

**Du Ver'gier' de Hau'ranne'** (dü vĕr'zhyā' dē ō'rȧn'), **Jean.** 1581–1643. French theologian; abbé de Saint Cyran (1620) and director of Port Royal (1636); lifelong friend and associate of Jansen, and with him a critic of contemporary Roman Catholic doctrine and practice; arrested and imprisoned by Richelieu's orders (1638–42); now regarded, with Jansen, as founder of, and strongest force in spreading doctrines of, Jansenism.

**Du'ver'gier' de Hau'ranne'** (dü'vĕr'zhyā' dē ō'rȧn'), **Prosper.** 1798–1881. French journalist and politician; royalist in sympathy; opposed coup d'état (1851) by which Louis Napoleon later became emperor as Napoleon III (1852), and was arrested and for a time exiled from France; author of *Histoire du Gouvernement Parlementaire en France de 1814 à 1848* (1857–72).

**Du'ver'ney'** (dü'vĕr'nā'), **Guichard Joseph.** 1648–1730. French anatomist; known esp. for researches on the eye and ear.

**Du'ver'nois'** (dü'vĕr'nwȧ'), **Henri.** 1875–1937. French novelist and playwright.

**Du'ver'noy'** (dü'vĕr'nwȧ'), **Georges Louis.** 1777–1855. French anatomist and zoologist. Grandfather of Charles Friedel (*q.v.*). Assisted Cuvier in editing *Leçons d'Anatomie Comparée;* professor of natural history at Strasbourg (1827) and at Collège de France (1837).

**Du'vey'rier'** (dü'vā'ryā'), **Anne Honoré Joseph.** *Pseudonym* **Mé'les'ville'** (mā'lĕs'vēl'). 1787–1865. French playwright; often collaborator with Scribe and others; among the many plays in which he collaborated were *Les Deux Précepteurs*, *L'Espionne Russe*, *Une Affaire d'Honneur*, *Zoé*, *Zampa*, *Le Fruit Défendu*. His brother **Charles** (1803–1866) was a lawyer and writer; a disciple of Saint Simon, whose economic theories he accepted; founded journal *Le Crédit;* author also of comedies, opera librettos, plays, and vaudeville sketches, many in collaboration with his brother, or with Scribe or others. A son of Charles, **Henri** (1840–1892), was an explorer, chiefly in the Sahara region.

**du Vi'gneaud** (dů vēn'yō), **Vincent.** 1901–1978. American biochemist, b. Chicago. B.S., Illinois (1923), Ph.D., Rochester (1927); professor, school of medicine, George Washington U. (1932–38), Cornell U. medical college

(1938–67). His researches include work on hormones, insulin, amino acids, proteins, and vitamins, and on the role of sulphur in bodily chemistry.

**Duyc'kinck** (dī'kĭngk), **Evert Augustus.** 1816–1878. American editor, b. New York City. Editor of weekly *Literary World* (1848–53), and a two-volume *Cyclopaedia of American Literature* (1855), in both of which his brother **George Long** (1823–1863) was an associate.

**Duy'se** (doi'sĕ), **Prudens van.** 1804–1859. Flemish writer; municipal archivist at Ghent (from 1838); his volumes of verse include *Vaderlandsche Poëzij* (*Patriotic Poetry*, 3 vols., 1840) and *Het Klaverblad* (*The Cloverleaf*, 1848). His son **Florimond** (1843–1910), student of old Dutch folk songs, composed 11 operas.

**Dvo'řák** (dvôr'zhäk), **Anton.** 1841–1904. Czech composer; director, National Conservatory of Music, New York City (1892–95); returned to Prague (1895); head of conservatory there (1901). His operas include *Der König und der Köhler* (1874), *Wanda* (1876), *Der Bauer, ein Schelm* (1878), *Der Dickschädel* (1881), *Dimitri* (1882), *Jacobin* (1889), *Der Teufel und die Wilde Käte* (1899), *Rusalka* (1901), *Armida* (1904). Orchestral works include symphonies (notably, the *New World Symphony*), symphonic poems, overtures, rhapsodies, nocturnes, scherzos, and concertos. Choral works include *Stabat Mater*, oratorio *Die Heilige Ludmila*, cantata *The Specter's Bride*, a mass, requiem, and *Te Deum*. Piano music includes the well-known *Humoresque*.

**Dvorsky.** See Josef Casimir HOFMANN.

**Dwig'gins** (dwĭg'ĭnz), **William Addison.** 1880–1956. American type designer, b. Martinsville, Ohio. Author of books and essays on typography.

**Dwight** (dwīt), **Harrison Gray Otis.** 1803–1862. American Congregational missionary, b. Conway, Mass. Missionary to the Armenians. Explored Armenia with Eli Smith (*q.v.*). Made headquarters in Constantinople (1834–62). His son **Henry Otis** (1843–1917), b. Constantinople, was a missionary in Turkey (1867–99) and special correspondent for N.Y. *Tribune* (1875–92); author of *Turkish Life in War Time* (1881), *Constantinople and its Problems* (1901), *A Muslim Sir Galahad* (1913); editor of *Turkish and English Lexicon* (1890), *Encyclopaedia of Missions* (1904), etc.

**Dwight, Harrison Griswold.** 1875–1959. American writer, b. Constantinople, Turkey. On staff of consultants for the peace commission in Paris (1918–19); special assistant in U.S. Department of State (1920–25). Author of *Stamboul Nights* (1916), *Persian Miniatures* (1917), *The Emperor of Elam and Other Stories* (1920), etc.

**Dwight, John.** 1637 or 1640?–1703. Earliest English potter of note; patentee (1671, 1684) for manufacture of porcelain or china and of Cologne ware; produced ware resembling Oriental porcelain; executed statuettes of mythological and contemporary characters in a fine red stoneware later developed by John and David Elers.

**Dwight, John Sullivan.** 1813–1893. American music critic, b. Boston. Joined Brook Farm community (1841–47). Contributed musical criticism to various periodicals (1847–52); founded and edited *Dwight's Journal of Music* (1852–81, discontinued). Instrumental in organizing Boston Philharmonic Society (1865), and in establishing professorship of music at Harvard (1876).

**Dwight, Mabel.** 1876–1955. American artist, b. Cincinnati; best known for aquarelles and lithographic work.

**Dwight, Theodore.** 1764–1846. Bro. of Timothy Dwight (1752–1817). American lawyer and author; practiced, Hartford (1791–1815). One of group known as "Hartford Wits"; frequent contributor to *Connecticut Courant* and *Connecticut Mirror*. Founded and edited *Daily Advertiser*, Albany, N.Y. (1815–16), *New York Daily Advertiser* (1817–35). His son **Theodore** (1796–1866), b. Hartford, was a journalist in New York (from 1833); author of *Tour in Italy* (1821), *Sketches of Scenery and Manners in the United States* (1829), *Life of General Garibaldi* (1861), etc.

**Dwight, Thomas.** 1843–1911. American surgeon and anatomist, b. Boston. Succeeded Oliver Wendell Holmes as professor, Harvard (1883–1911). Author of *Intercranial Circulation* (1867), *Anatomy of the Head* (1876), *Thoughts of a Catholic Anatomist* (1911), etc.

**Dwight, Timothy.** 1752–1817. Grandson of Jonathan Edwards. American Congregational clergyman and educator, b. Northampton, Mass. Grad. Yale (1769). Headmaster, Hopkins Grammar School, New Haven (1769–71); tutor, Yale (1771–77). Licensed to preach; chaplain, American Revolutionary army, at West Point (1777–79). Clergyman, teacher, and farm manager, Northampton, Mass. (1779–83); pastor, Greenfield Hill, Conn. (1783–95); one of the "Hartford Wits." President, Yale (1795–1817). Author of *The Triumph of Infidelity, a Poem* (1788), *Greenfield Hill* (1794), *Theology, Explained and Defended* (5 vols., 1818–19), *Travels in New England and New York* (4 vols., 1821–22). One of his sons, **Sereno Edwards Dwight** (1786–1850), edited the writings of Jonathan Edwards. A grandson, **Theodore William Dwight** (1822–1892), was professor of municipal law, Columbia Law School (1858–91). Another grandson, **Timothy Dwight** (1828–1916), b. Norwich, Conn., was a Congregational clergyman and educator; grad. Yale (1849); tutor, Yale (1851–55); studied in Germany (1856–58); asst. professor of sacred literature, Yale Divinity School (1858–61); professor (from 1861); ordained (1861); president of Yale (1886–98).

**Dwyfor,** Earl of. See David LLOYD GEORGE.

**Dy'ar** (dī'ẽr), **Harrison Gray.** 1866–1929. American entomologist, b. New York City. Custodian of Lepidoptera, U.S. National Museum, Washington, D.C. (1897–1929). Works: with Frederick Knab and L. O. Howard, *The Mosquitoes of North and Central America and the West Indies* (4 vols., 1912–17), *The Mosquitoes of the Americas* (1928).

**Dyce** (dīs), **Alexander.** 1798–1869. Scottish dramatic editor; edited Collins's poems (1827), works of Peele (1828, 1839), Webster (1830), Greene (1831), Shirley (1833), Middleton (1840), Beaumont and Fletcher (1843–46), Marlowe (1850), and Richard Bentley (1836–38); known chiefly for his edition of Shakespeare (1857, 1866) and notes on Shakespeare and on Collier's edition of Shakespeare; author of *Recollections of the Table Talk of Samuel Rogers* (1856).

His cousin **William Dyce** (1806–1864), historical and portrait painter, was master of school of design, Edinburgh (1837); professor of fine arts, King's Coll., London (1844); showed in his *Madonna and Child* (1828) tendency toward what became Pre-Raphaelite school of painting in England; executed frescoes of allegorical and sacred figures and scenes from Arthurian legend, some in houses of Parliament.

**Dyche** (dīch), **Thomas.** d. 1735? English schoolmaster, grammarian, and lexicographer. Master of Bow School. Compiled English and Latin grammars and lexicons, including *The Spelling Dictionary* (2d ed., 1725) and *A New General English Dictionary* (3d ed., 1740).

**Dyck** (dīk), Sir **Anthony Van.** See VANDYKE.

**Dyck** (dīk) *or* **Dijk** (dīk), **Philip van.** 1680?–1752. Known as "the little van Dyck." Dutch painter; works represented at the Louvre and The Hague.

**Dyck'mans** (dīk'mäns), **Joseph Lau'rent'** (lō'räɴ'). 1811–1888. Belgian painter; best known for small genre scenes.

**Dy'er** (dī'ẽr), Sir **Edward**. d. 1607. English courtier and poet. Friend of Sir Philip Sidney, whose books he shared with Fulke Greville under Sidney's will; sent on diplomatic missions to Low Countries (1584), to Denmark (1589); reputed Rosicrucian; cited by Puttenham as a master of elegy.

**Dyer, Eliphalet**. 1721–1807. American jurist, b. Windham, Conn. Member, governor's council (1762–84). Judge, Connecticut Superior Court (1766–93), chief justice (1789–93). Connecticut delegate, Continental Congress (1774–79, 1780–83). Member, Committee of Public Safety (1775). An organizer (1753) of Susquehanna Company, to establish settlement in Wyoming Valley, west of New York province; counsel for Connecticut before board of commissioners that awarded to Connecticut title to the territory (1782).

**Dyer, George**. 1755–1841. English author and eccentric; clergyman, converted to Unitarianism; bibliographer; hack writer. Simple, kindly, slovenly, humorless; source of amusement to his friend Charles Lamb, who describes in *Amicus Redivivus* Dyer's absent-minded plunge into the New River. Author of poems and essays, a history of Cambridge University (1814); contributed "all that was original" to Abraham J. Valpy's edition of the Delphin classics (141 vols., 1819–30).

**Dyer, Isadore**. 1865–1920. American dermatologist, b. Galveston, Tex. Specialized in study of leprosy; founded (1894) Louisiana Leper Home (which became National Leprosarium).

**Dyer, John**. 1700?–1758. British poet, b. in Wales. Itinerant artist in South Wales; author of *Grongar Hill* (1726), *Ruins of Rome* (1740), *The Fleece* (1757), notable for natural description and precision of phrase.

**Dyer, Mary**. d. 1660. Quaker martyr; emigrated with husband, William, from England to Massachusetts (c. 1635); followed Anne Hutchinson to Rhode Island (1637–38); to England (1650); became Quaker; to Boston (1657), where she was arrested and banished; after twice (1659, 1660) returning to Boston to visit imprisoned Quakers, condemned for sedition and hanged.

**Dyer, Nehemiah Mayo**. 1839–1910. American naval officer, b. Provincetown, Mass.; took part in battle of Mobile Bay (1864); commanded the *Baltimore* in battle of Manila Bay (1898).

**Dyer, Reginald Edward Harry**. 1864–1927. British soldier, b. in the Punjab. During World War, commanded operations in southeastern Persia (1916–17). In command in the Punjab at time of Amritsar affair (April 13, 1919) when he marched a detachment to a square crowded with natives assembled in defiance of his orders and opened fire on them, killing nearly 400 and wounding many more; after official investigation (Oct., 1919), was forced to resign from service (March, 1920).

**Dyer, Samuel**. 1725–1772. English translator; an original member of Dr. Johnson's Ivy Lane club (1749); translated lives of Pericles and Demetrius for Tonson's edition of *Plutarch's Lives* (1758); in the opinion of Sir Joshua Reynolds and Edmund Malone, author of *Letters of Junius*. Cf. Sir Philip FRANCIS.

**Dyer, Thomas Henry**. 1804–1888. English historian. Author of *Life of Calvin* (1850), *History of the City of Rome* (1865), *History of the Kings of Rome* (1868), etc.

**Dyk** (dĭk), **Viktor**. 1877–1931. Czech writer; author of lyrical and satirical verse, plays, and novels.

**Dy'ke·ma** (dī'kĕ·mȧ), **Peter William**. 1873–1951. American music director; professor, Wisconsin (1913–24), Teachers Coll., Columbia (from 1924). Active in promoting community singing.

**Dykes** (dīks), **John Bacchus**. 1823–1876. English clergyman and composer of hymn tunes. Joint editor of *Hymns Ancient and Modern;* composed *Lead, Kindly Light; Nearer, my God, to Thee; Jesus, Lover of my Soul,* and other hymn tunes.

**Dyk'stra** (dīk'strȧ), **Clarence Addison**. 1883–1950. American educator, b. Cleveland, Ohio. Professor of political science, Kansas (1909–18). Commissioner, department of water and power, Los Angeles (1923–26); director of personnel and efficiency in this department (1926–30). City manager, Cincinnati, Ohio (1930–37). President, U. of Wisconsin (1937–45). On leave from Wisconsin (1940–41) to serve as director of selective service; provost, U. of California, 1945–50.

**Dym'oke** (dĭm'ŭk). Name of an English family of Lincolnshire holding (since 1377) the office of king's champion, whose function was to challenge all comers to deny the king's title at the coronation banquet. Sir **John** (d. 1381), lord of Scrivelsby, Lincolnshire, by marriage with Margaret de Ludlow, heiress of the Marmions, was the first to perform the office, at coronation of Richard II. Sir **Thomas** (1428?–1471) joined his brother-in-law in a Lancastrian rising (1469); beheaded by Edward IV; his son **Robert** (d. 1546) was champion at coronations of Richard III, Henry VII, and Henry VIII, fought with distinction at siege of Tournai. Sir **Henry** (1801–1865) was champion at coronation of George IV, after which the ceremony was allowed to lapse. Members of a collateral branch of the family bore the standard of England at coronation of Edward VII and George V.

**Dy'mond** (dī'mŭnd), **John**. 1836–1922. Sugar planter, b. in Canada; successful broker in New York, dealing in Louisiana sugar and molasses (1863–68). Settled on sugar plantation below New Orleans (from about 1868); introduced new and more efficient methods in sugar manufacturing.

**Dymond, Jonathan**. 1796–1828. English linen draper and Quaker moralist. Author of anonymous pamphlet showing war contrary to Christianity (1823), and *Essays on the Principles of Morality* (1829).

**Dymp'na** *or* **Dimp'na** (dĭmp'nȧ), Saint. Irish princess and Christian martyr of 7th century. Overtaken and slain at Gheel in Belgium in flight from incestuous designs of her pagan father.

**Dy'son** (dī's'n), Sir **Frank Watson**. 1868–1939. British astronomer, b. in Ashby de la Zouch. Astronomer royal of Scotland (1905–10), of England (1910–33).

**Dyson, William Henry**. 1883–1938. British etcher and cartoonist, b. Ballarat, Australia; long on staff of London *Daily Herald*.

**Dy've·ke** (dü'vĕ·kĕ) *or, Dutch,* **Dui've·ke** (doi'vĕ·kĕ), *i.e.* "Little Dove." 1491?–1517. Daughter of Dutch innkeeper at Bergen and mistress of Christian II of Denmark; died suddenly, perhaps by poison (1517).

**Dzer·zhin'ski** (dyẽr·zhēn'skû·ĭ; *Angl.* -skĭ), **Feliks Edmundovich**. 1877–1926. Russian Soviet politician and administrator, of Polish descent. Banished to Siberia for political agitation (1897); escaped (1899); took part in revolution of 1905; again banished (1905–12); arrested in Warsaw and sentenced to nine years' hard labor (c. 1912). Released after the Russian Revolution (1917) and became organizer and head (1917–21) of the Russian secret police (the Cheka, later known as the Ogpu); commissar of transport (1921); reorganized and improved the railway system; transferred to head of the supreme economic council (1924).

**Dzhugashvili, Iosif Vissarionovich**. See Joseph STALIN.

**Dzier'zon** (dzyẽr'zhôn), **Johann**. 1811–1906. German apiculturist; devoted himself to apiculture; constructed beehive with detachable cells; discovered parthenogenesis in bees, in which drones develop from unfertilized eggs of queens.

# E

**Ea'chard** (ā'chẽrd), **John.** 1636?–1697. English clergyman and author of satirical attacks upon the clergy (1670) and upon the philosophy of Thomas Hobbes (1672, 1673).

**Ead'bald** (ĕd'bôld; *A.-S.* â'ȧd·bäld) *or* **Æth'el·bald** (ăth'ĕl·bôld; *A.-S.* ă'thĕl·bäld). d. 640. King of Kent. On conversion by Laurentius, Archbishop of Canterbury, recalled Christians he had persecuted and built church at Canterbury.

**Ead'frid** (ĕd'frĭd) *or* **Ead'frith** (â'ȧd·frĭth). d. 721. Bishop of Lindisfarne (Holy Island), Northumbria (from 698); began compilation of what is known as *the Lindisfarne Book*, containing a text of the Gospels in Latin.

**Eadgar, Eadmer, Eadmund, Eadred, Eadric, Eadward, Eadwig,** etc. See EDGAR, EDMER, EDMUND, EDRED, EDRIC, EDWARD, EDWY, etc.

**Ea'die** (ē'dĭ), **John.** 1810–1876. Scottish Presbyterian theologian and Biblical scholar.

**Eads** (ēdz), **James Buchanan.** 1820–1887. American engineer and inventor, b. Lawrenceburg, Ind. Invented diving bell; organized partnership to use diving bell for salvaging from steamboats sunk in river and made fortune (1848–57). Suggested fleet of armor-plated gunboats for controlling Mississippi River (1861); contracted to deliver them, ready for armament, in sixty-five days; completed contract on time. Built bridge (Eads Bridge, 1867–74) across Mississippi at St. Louis. Proposed to Congress (1874) to open a mouth of Mississippi into Gulf of Mexico and keep channel at proper depth for navigation; succeeded by using a jetty system (1879). At time of his death, was projecting a ship railway across Tehuantepec Isthmus, to provide a route 2000 miles shorter than that afforded by the Panama Canal. Elected to American Hall of Fame (1920).

**Eagle, Solomon.** Pseudonym of John Collings SQUIRE.

**Ea'ker** (ā'kẽr), **Ira Clarence.** 1896– . American aviator and army officer; member of U.S. army air force from 1917; pilot of army plane *Question Mark*, which set world's endurance record (1929); made first transcontinental blind flight (1936); head of U.S. bomber command in Europe (July, 1942); lieut. general (1943); chief, Mediterranean allied air forces (1944).

**Ea'kins** (ā'kĭnz), **Thomas.** 1844–1916. American painter and sculptor, b. Philadelphia. Studio in Philadelphia (from 1870); paintings include *Clinic of Dr. Gross*, *Clinic of Dr. Agnew*, *The Chess Players* and *Max Schmitt in a Single Scull;* his sculptures include reliefs on the battle monument in Trenton, N.J.

**Ealdred.** See ALDRED.

**Ealhwine.** Anglo-Saxon name of ALCUIN.

**Eames** (āmz), **Emma.** 1865–1952. American operatic soprano, b. Shanghai, China, of American parentage; m. Julian Story, portrait painter (1891; divorced 1907), Emilio De Gogorza, operatic baritone (1911). Operatic debut as Juliette, Paris (1889); appeared thereafter in London and New York during operatic seasons.

**Eames** (ēmz), **Henry Pur·mort'** (pûr·môrt'). 1872–1950. American musician, b. Chicago. Professor of musical art and aesthetics, Scripps Coll. (1928–1941). On frequent tours in Europe and U.S. as concert pianist.

**Eames** (ēmz), **Wilberforce.** 1855–1937. American librarian and bibliographer.

**Eanes, Gil.** See GILIANES.

**Ear'hart** (âr'härt), **Amelia.** 1897–1937. American aviatrix, b. Atchison, Kans., m. George Palmer Putnam (1931). First woman to cross Atlantic Ocean in airplane, Newfoundland to Burry Port, Wales (June 17, 1928). Lost on Pacific flight (July, 1937). Author of *Last Flight* (edited by her husband; 1938).

**Earle** (ûrl), **Alice,** *nee* **Morse.** 1853–1911. American author; m. (1874) Henry Earle. Her books, which deal chiefly with American colonial history, include *The Sabbath in Puritan New England* (1891), *Customs and Fashions in Old New England* (1893), *Stage Coach and Tavern Days* (1900), *Two Centuries of Costume in America* (2 vols., 1903).

**Earle, John.** 1601?–1665. English prelate; tutor (1641) to Prince Charles (later Charles II); chaplain to Charles in France. At Restoration, dean of Westminster (1660); bishop of Worcester (1662–63), of Salisbury (1663–65). Author of *Microcosmographie* (1628).

**Earle, John.** 1824–1903. English philologist. M.A., Oxon. (1849); professor of Anglo-Saxon, Oxford (1849–54, 1876–1903); rector of Swanswick, near Bath (1857–1903). Author of *The Philology of the English Tongue* (1866), *Anglo-Saxon Literature* (1884), etc.

**Earle, Pliny.** 1762–1832. American inventor (of a machine for pricking leather for cards) and manufacturer of cotton-carding and wool-carding machinery. One of his sons, **Thomas** (1796–1849), was a lawyer and editor in Philadelphia; candidate of Liberty party for vice-president of the U.S. (1840); dropped from ticket because of opposition of abolitionists. Another son, **Pliny** (1809–1892), was a psychiatrist; studied abroad, specializing in investigation of institutions for the insane.

**Earle, Ralph.** 1874–1939. American naval officer and educator; chief, bureau of ordnance (1916–19; retired 1925); president, Worcester Tech. (1925–39).

**Ear'lom** (ûr'lŭm), **Richard.** 1743–1822. English mezzotint engraver.

**Ear'ly** (ûr'lĭ), **Jubal Anderson.** 1816–1894. American army officer, b. in Franklin County, Va. Grad. U.S.M.A., West Point (1837); resigned from army (1838) to study law; practiced, Rocky Mount, Va. Opposed secession, but was loyal to Virginia when it seceded, and entered Confederate army; brigadier general (1861); major general (1863); lieutenant general in charge of great raid (1864) down Shenandoah Valley toward Washington; defeated by Sheridan at Winchester, Fisher's Hill, and Cedar Creek, and his army almost destroyed at Waynesboro (1865). Relieved of command; fled to Mexico, thence to Canada (1866). Returned (1869) to practice law, Lynchburg, Va. Remained an "unreconstructed rebel" all his life; never took oath of allegiance to U.S. after the Civil War.

**Early, Stephen Ty·ree'** (tī·rē'). 1889–1951. American journalist, b. Crozet, Va.; asst. secretary to President Roosevelt (1933–37), secretary (1937–45).

**Earp** (ûrp), **Wyatt.** 1848–1929. American lawman.

**East** (ēst), Sir **Alfred.** 1849–1913. English landscape painter and etcher.

**East, Edward Murray.** 1879–1938. American biologist; on teaching staff, Harvard (from 1909); author of *Heterozygosis in Evolution and Plant Breeding* (1912), *Mankind at the Crossroads* (1923), *Heredity and Human Affairs* (1927), etc.

**East'lake'** (ēst'lāk'), Sir **Charles Lock.** 1793–1865. English painter and art critic. From a small boat in Plymouth harbor, made sketches of Napoleon (then a prisoner aboard H.M.S. *Bellerophon*) from which he produced two full-length portraits, on proceeds of which he visited Italy (1816–30); keeper of National Gallery

(1843–47), director (1855); knighted (1850). Known esp. for banditti pictures, and for *Pilgrims in Sight of Rome* (1828), *Christ Blessing Little Children* (1839), *Christ weeping over Jerusalem* (1841). His wife (m. 1849), Lady **Elizabeth** *nee* **Rig′by** [rĭg′bĭ] (1809–1893), woman of letters and art critic; after traveling in Germany and Russia, published *A Residence on the Shores of the Baltic* (1841); edited her husband's works; author of works on art criticism.

**East′man** (ēst′măn), **Charles Alexander.** *Indian name* **O·hi′ye·sa′** (ō·hē′yȧ·sä′). 1858–1939. American physician, of Sioux Indian parentage. U.S. government physician at Pine Ridge agency (1890–93), at Crow Creek, S.Dak. (1900–03). Member of national council, Boy Scouts of America (from 1922). Author of *Indian Boyhood* (1902), *Old Indian Days* (1907), *The Soul of the Indian* (1911), *The Indian Today* (1915), *Indian Heroes and Great Chieftains* (1918), etc. See Elaine GOODALE.

**Eastman, Charles Gamage.** 1816–1860. American journalist and poet.

**Eastman, George.** 1854–1932. American inventor and industrialist; perfected process for making photographic dry plates (1880) and flexible film (patented 1884), and invented the Kodak (1888). Treasurer and general manager, Eastman Kodak Co., Rochester, N.Y. Founder, Eastman School of Music, Rochester, N.Y.

**Eastman, John Robie.** 1836–1913. American astronomer. His *Second Washington Catalogue of Stars* (1898) embodies results of some 80,000 observations (1866–91).

**Eastman, Joseph Bartlett.** 1882–1944. American government official; member, Massachusetts Public Service Commission (1915–19), and U.S. Interstate Commerce Commission (from 1919); federal co-ordinator of transportation (1933–36); director, Office of Defense Transportation (Dec., 1941–44).

**Eastman, Max Forrester.** 1883–1969. American editor and writer; editor of *The Masses* (1913–17) and *The Liberator* (1918–22). Author of *Enjoyment of Poetry* (1913), *Colors of Life* (verse, 1918), *Marx and Lenin, the Science of Revolution* (1926), *Kinds of Love* (verse, 1931), *Enjoyment of Laughter* (1936), *The End of Socialism in Russia* (1937), *Marxism: is it Science* (1940), *Lot's Wife* (poem, 1942). Translator of Russian authors, esp. Trotsky. Editor of Marx's *Capital and Other Writings* (1932).

**Eas′ton** (ēs′tŭn), **Nicholas.** 1593–1675. Colonial administrator in America. In Rhode Island (from 1638); "president" of the colony (1650–51, 1654); deputy governor (1666–69; 1670–71); governor (1672–74). His son **John** (1625?–1705) was deputy governor of R.I. (1674–76) and governor (1690–95).

**East′wick** (ēst′(w)ĭk), **Edward Backhouse.** 1814–1883. English Orientalist and diplomat.

**Ea′ton** (ē′t'n). Name of family of New England stencilers, including: **Moses** (1753–1833), who used wall stencils, and his two sons, **Moses** (1796–1886), whose wall stencils were in demand until use of wallpaper became general, and **William Page** (1819–1904), known as best stenciler of his time and an expert chair painter.

**Eaton, Amos.** 1776–1842. American scientist; author of *A Manual of Botany for the Northern States* (1817). His grandson **Daniel Cady Eaton** (1834–1895) studied under Asa Gray (1857–60); professor of botany, Yale (1864–95); author of *The Ferns of North America* (2 vols., 1877–80).

**Eaton, Arthur Wentworth Hamilton.** 1849–1937. Protestant Episcopal clergyman and poet, b. Kentville, Nova Scotia. Author of *Acadian Legends and Lyrics* (1889), *Poems of the Christian Year* (1905), *Acadian Ballads and Lyrics in Many Moods* (1930), and books on Nova Scotia.

**Eaton, Charles Warren.** 1857–1937. American painter; best known for landscapes.

**Eaton, Dorman Bridgman.** 1823–1899. American lawyer and civil service reformer; practiced law, New York City (1850–70). Strong champion of merit system in local and national government; chairman, national Civil Service Commission (1873–75); drafted National Civil Service Act (known as Pendleton Act) passed in 1883; head of Civil Service Commission (1883–86). Bequeathed funds for Eaton professorship of the science of government at Harvard, and for Eaton professorship of municipal science at Columbia.

**Eaton, John Henry.** 1790–1856. American lawyer and politician; personal friend of Andrew Jackson; practiced law, Franklin, Tenn.; m. 1st Myra Lewis, a ward of Andrew Jackson. U.S. senator (1818–29). U.S. secretary of war (1829–31). Appointed governor of Florida (1834–36); U.S. minister to Spain (1836–40). His 2d wife (m. 1829), **Margaret,** *known as* **Peggy,** *nee* **O'Neale′** *or* **O'Neill′** [ō·nēl′] (1799–1879), was daughter of a Washington innkeeper; m. 1st John B. Timberlake (d. 1828). On Eaton's elevation to the cabinet (1829), the wives of the other cabinet members refused to accept her socially, and forced her husband to resign (1831), despite President Jackson's intervention.

**Eaton, Theophilus.** 1590–1658. Colonist and administrator in America, b. Stony Stratford, England. One of original patentees of Massachusetts Bay Company; emigrated to Massachusetts (1637). Established new colony at New Haven (1638) and was chosen governor; reelected annually till his death. Drew up, with help of John Davenport, code of laws for the colony (printed in London, 1656). A brother, **Nathaniel** (1609?–1674), who also emigrated to Massachusetts in 1637, was appointed the first head (but not entitled president) of Harvard College (1638–39); removed from office for cruelty and financial irregularity; fined and excommunicated from Anglican Church; escaped to Virginia and later returned to England; vicar in Shropshire (1661); rector of Bideford, Devon (1668); died in debtor's prison. Another brother, **Samuel** (1596?–1665), Anglican clergyman, was for a short time colleague of John Davenport in New Haven, but returned to England (1640).

**Eaton, Timothy.** 1834–1907. Canadian merchant, b. Clogher, Ireland; to Canada (1857). Founded, at Toronto, T. Eaton Co., Ltd., which developed into one of largest department stores in America, with branches in Winnipeg and Montreal. Succeeded (1907) as head of the business by his son Sir **John Craig** (1876–1922), donor of Timothy Eaton Memorial Wing to Toronto General Hospital and of Timothy Eaton Memorial Church at Toronto.

**Eaton, Walter Prichard.** 1878–1957. American author, critic, and educator; assoc. professor of playwrighting, Yale (1933–47). Author of *American Stage of Today* (1908), *The Man Who Found Christmas* (1913), *Plays and Players* (1916), *Green Trails and Upland Pastures* (1917), *Echoes and Realities* (verse, 1918), *Queen Victoria* (a play, with David Carb, 1923), *Ten Years of the Theatre Guild* (1929), *The Drama in English* (1930), *Wild Gardens of New England* (1935), etc.

**Eaton, William.** 1764–1811. American army officer and adventurer; captain, U.S. army (1792). U.S. consul at Tunis (1798); engaged in involved negotiations in Tunis and Tripoli, ending in proposal to restore exiled pasha (Hamet) to throne of Tripoli usurped by his brother; as "navy agent to the Barbary States" (1804), found Hamet in Upper Egypt, gathered force of Greeks, Italians, and Arabs, and succeeded in bringing Hamet to Derna, a seaport of Tripoli which he captured (Apr. 27,

1805). Ordered to vacate Tripoli because of new negotiations leading to recognition of the usurping pasha. Returned to U.S.; withdrew from service.

**Eaton, Wyatt.** 1849–1896. Portrait and figure painter, b. Phillipsburg, Canada, of American parentage. A founder of the Society of American Artists (1877); its first secretary and later its president. His portraits of Americans include Bishop Horatio Potter, President Garfield, John Burroughs, and Mrs. R. W. Gilder; of Canadians, Sir William and Lady Van Horne, Sir Donald and Lady Smith.

**Eb'bing·haus'** (ĕb'ĭng·hous'), **Hermann.** 1850–1909. German experimental psychologist; known esp. for study of the memory.

**Ebco von Repgow.** See EIKE VON REPGOW.

**E'be** (ā'bĕ), **Gustav.** 1834–1916. German architect.

**E'bel** (ā'bĕl), **Johann Gottfried.** 1764–1830. German physician and writer on geography; naturalized Swiss (1801), settling in Zurich. Author of first good guidebook to Switzerland.

**Ebel, Johann Wilhelm.** 1784–1861. German Lutheran clergyman and teacher; pastor in Königsberg (1816), where he founded the mystic and theosophic Mucker society, dissolved (1839) following charges of gross immorality and sectarianism; declared innocent at end of 6 years' trial (1835–41), but removed from office on charge of "neglect."

**E'be·ling** (ā'bĕ·lĭng), **Christoph Daniel.** 1741–1817. German geographer and scholar; author of works on music, translations into German of Burney's travel diaries and of the English text of Handel's *Messiah* (with Klopstock), etc.

**E'ber** (ā'bẽr), **Paul.** 1511–1569. German Protestant theologian, b. in Franconia; at first disciple and secretary of Melanchthon, then follower of Luther. Author of a revision of the Old Testament in the Wittenberg German-Latin edition of the Bible, a postexilic history of the Jews (in Latin), church songs, etc.

**E'ber·hard** (ā'bẽr·härt). See WÜRTTEMBERG.

**Eberhard.** d. 939. Duke of the Franks; supported his brother Conrad I against Henry the Fowler of Saxony (915), but after Conrad's death (918), conveyed German crown and scepter to Henry. Rebelled (938 and 939) against Henry's successor, Otto the Great, and was killed in action.

**Eberhard, Christian August Gottlob.** 1769–1845. German writer and poet; author of stories, the idyl *Hannchen und die Küchlein* (1822), the didactic poem *Der Erste Mensch und die Erde* (1828), etc.

**Eberhard, Johann August.** 1739–1809. German Leibnitzian philosopher, theologian, and writer; author of *Neue Apologie des Sokrates*, a criticism of Kantian philosophy (2 vols., 1772–78), *Handbuch der Ästhetik* (4 vols., 1803–05), essays on musical subjects, etc.

**Eberhard, Konrad.** 1768–1859. German sculptor; associated with Nazarene group in Rome (1806–19, 1821–26).

**E'berl** (ā'bẽrl), **Anton.** 1766?–1807. Viennese pianist and composer; friend of Mozart and Gluck.

**Eb'er·le** (ĕb'ẽr·lē), **Abastenia St. Leg'er** (sânt lĕj'ẽr). 1878–1942. American sculptor.

**Eberle, Edward Walter.** 1864–1929. American naval officer; on *Oregon* in dash around the Horn, and in battle of Santiago, Spanish-American War. Chief of naval operations (1923–27).

**Eberle, John.** 1787–1838. American physician and medical writer, b. Hagerstown, Md.

**E'ber·le** (ā'bẽr·lĕ), **Robert.** 1815–1860. German animal and landscape painter. His son **Adolph** (1843–1914) was a genre and animal painter.

**E'ber·lein** (ā'bẽr·līn), **Gustav.** 1847–1926. German sculptor; produced decorative works including a long frieze with 50 life-size figures for Berlin Ministry of Public Instruction, also statues, many public monuments, etc.

**E'ber·lin** (ā'bẽr·lēn), **Johann Ernst.** 1702–1762. German organist and composer, esp. of church music.

**E'ber·may'er** (ā'bẽr·mī'ẽr), **Ludwig.** 1858–1933. German jurist; authority on criminal jurisprudence; had important part in reform of German penal law. His son **Erich** (1900– ), playwright and novelist.

**E'bers** (ā'bẽrs), **Emil.** 1807–1884. German painter of humorous military scenes and of scenes from the life of smugglers, fishermen, and sailors.

**Ebers, Georg Moritz.** 1837–1898. German Egyptologist and novelist; acquired (1873) the famous 16th-century B.C. Egyptian medical papyrus called *Papyrus Ebers* (pub. 1875). Author of *Egypt and the Books of Moses* (1868), and of historical novels of Egypt, as *An Egyptian Princess* (3 vols., 1864), and of other novels, as *The Burgomaster's Wife* (1882).

**Ebers, Karl Friedrich.** 1770–1836. German composer of four operas, symphonies, cantatas, sonatas and other piano pieces, the drinking song *Wir Sind die Könige der Welt*, etc.

**E'bert** (ā'bẽrt), **Adolf.** 1820–1890. German Romance scholar, philologist, and literary historian; author of *Allgemeine Geschichte der Literatur des Mittelalters im Abendlande* (3 vols., 1874–87), etc.

**Ebert, Friedrich.** 1871–1925. German Social Democratic leader and first president of the German Reich (1919–25), b. Heidelberg. Practiced trade of saddle maker; elected to Reichstag (1912); president of party (1913). Worked for government during World War (1914–19); joined party demand for peace and abdication of kaiser (1918); on downfall of government, was appointed chancellor in place of Prince Max of Baden; member of temporary government; opposed by Spartacists; elected president by National Assembly at Weimar (Feb., 1919); suppressed Kapp Putsch (1920) and attempt of Hitler and Ludendorff to establish dictatorship in Bavaria (1923).

**Ebert, Friedrich Adolf.** 1791–1834. German librarian and bibliographer; author of *Allgemeines Bibliographisches Lexikon* (2 vols., 1821–30).

**Ebert, Karl Egon von.** 1801–1882. Poet, b. in Prague. Author in German of many dramatic works, and of lyric poetry and ballads and romances, the Bohemian national heroic poem and epic *Wlasta* (1829), a collection of sonnets (1855), etc.

**E'berth** (ā'bẽrt), **Karl Joseph.** 1835–1926. German anatomist and bacteriologist. Known for work on lung epithelium, the relationship of fetal rachitis to cretinism, etc., and esp. for identification, simultaneously with Koch, of the bacillus of typhoid fever (1880) named *Eberthella typhi* after him.

**E'ber·wein** (ā'bẽr·vīn), **Traugott Maximilian.** 1775–1831. German composer and conductor. His brother **Karl** (1786–1868), violinist and composer, was leader of Goethe's private orchestra, and composer of music to Goethe's *Faust* and *Proserpina* and to Holtei's *Lenore.*

**Eb'ner–E'schen·bach** (āb'nẽr·ĕsh'ĕn·bäκ), Baroness **Marie von.** *Nee* Countess **Dub'sky** (dŏŏp'skē). 1830–1916. Austrian novelist and poet, b. in Moravia. Author of the drama *Maria von Schottland* (1860), and of humorous and psychological stories and novels chiefly of life in Bohemia and among the Austrian aristocracy.

**É'bo·li** (ā'bō·lē), Princesa **de. Ana de Men·do'za** (thā mān·dō'thä). 1540–1592. Mistress of King Philip II of Spain; involved in Spanish court intrigue and betrayed by secret agent of Don John of Austria;

a character in Schiller's *Don Carlos.*

**É'boué'** (ā'bwā'), **Félix Adolphe**. 1884–1944. French colonial administrator, b. in Martinique; governor of Chad (1939–41); first colonial governor to adhere to Free French cause; governor general of Equatorial Africa (1941–44).

**E'brard** (ā'brärt), **August**. 1818–1888. German Reformed theologian and writer.

**E'bro·ïn** (ā'brō·ēn). d. 681. Frankish mayor of the palace; defeated Burgundians and Austrasians (678), establishing himself as sole ruler of Franks.

**E'ça de Quei·roz'** (ā'sȧ thĕ kâ·ē·rôsh'), **José Maria**. 1843–1900. Portuguese novelist.

**Ec'card** (ĕk'ärt). See ECKHART.

**Eccard, Johannes**. 1553–1611. German composer of Protestant church music.

**Eccelino da Romano**. See EZZELINO DA ROMANO.

**Ec'chel·len'sis** *or* **Ech'el·len'sis** (ĕk'ĕ·lĕn'sĭs), **A'braham** (ā'brȧ·hăm). d. 1664. Arabic scholar; educ. in Rome; professor of Arabic and Syriac in College of Propagandists; professor, Collège Royal, Paris (1646); helped in preparation of Arabic Bible (pub. 1671).

**Ec'cles** (ĕk''lz), Sir **John Carew**. 1903– . Australian physiologist. Awarded Nobel prize in physiology and medicine (1963) with A. Hodgkin and A. Huxley for discoveries concerning the nervous system.

**Eccles, Marriner Stoddard**. 1890–1977. American economist, b. Logan, Utah; governor, Federal Reserve Board (1934–36); chairman, board of governors of Federal Reserve System (1936–48).

**Ecco von Repgow**. See EIKE VON REPGOW.

**Ecgberht** *or* **Ecgbryht**. See EGBERT.

**E'che·ga·ray' y Ei'za·guir're** (ā'chā·gä·rä'ē ē ĕ'ē·thä·gēr'rā), **José**. 1832–1916. Spanish dramatist, b. Madrid. Engineer; professor of mathematics and physics, Madrid (1854–68). Corecipient with Frédéric Mistral of Nobel prize in literature (1904). His plays include *La Esposa del Vengador* (1874), *O Locura o Santidad* (1876; Eng. trans. *Madman or Saint*), *El Gran Galeoto* (1881; produced in U.S. as *The World and His Wife*), *Mariana* (1892), *El Estigma* (1895), *La Duda* (1898), *El Loco Diós* (1900), *La Desequilibrada* (1903), and *A Fuerza de Arrastrarse* (1905).

**E'che·ver·rí'a** (ā'chā·vĕr·rē'ä), **Esteban**. 1809–1851. Argentine poet; credited with introducing into Spanish America the literary conceptions of the European romantics; banished by the dictator Rosas. Author of *Consuelos* (1834), *Rimas; La Cautiva* (1837).

**Ech'ter** (ĕκ'tēr), **Michael**. 1812–1879. German mural and historical painter.

**Ech'ter·mey'er** (ĕκ'tēr·mī'ēr), **Ernst Theodor**. 1805–1844. German writer and literary critic.

**Eck** (ĕk), **Johann**. *Orig. surname* **May'er** (mī'ēr). 1486–1543. German Roman Catholic theologian and leading opponent of Luther and the Reformation, b. in Eck (now Egg), Swabia. Professor of theology, Ingolstadt (1510); disputed at Leipzig with Karlstadt and Luther (1519), against whom he was influential in procuring the papal bull from Rome (1520). Attended Augsburg Diet (1530); took part in religious convocations at Worms (1540) and Ratisbon (1541). Author of *Obelisci* (1518) and *Operum Johannis Eckii contra Lutherum* (5 vols., 1530–35).

**Eck, Johann Friedrich**. 1766–?1809. German violinist.

**Eck'ardt** (ĕk'ärt), **Julius von**. 1836–1908. Russo-German journalist, writer, and diplomat, b. in Livonia. A champion of the German Constitutional party in Estonia, Livonia, and Kurland; to Germany (1867); edited newspaper *Die Grenzboten* at Leipzig (1867–70; with Gustav Freytag) and *Der Hamburger Correspondent* (1870–74). Author of works on Russian politics.

**Eckart** *or* **Eckardt**. See ECKHART.

**Eck'e·ner** (ĕk'ĕ·nēr), **Hugo**. 1868–1954. German aeronaut. Entered Zeppelin factory (1908); director of German Aerial Navigation Co. (1911); president of the Zeppelin Co. (1924); builder of the *Graf Zeppelin* in which he circled the earth (1929).

**Eck'er·mann** (ĕk'ēr·män), **Johann Peter**. 1792–1854. German writer; friend and literary assistant to Goethe. Became acquainted with Goethe (1822), who helped bring about publication of his *Beiträge zur Poesie mit Besonderer Hinweisung auf Goethe* (1823); became Goethe's literary assistant and helped him prepare final edition of his works. Author of *Gespräche mit Goethe* (Eng. *Conversations with Goethe*, 3 vols., 1836–48); editor of Goethe's *Nachgelassene Schriften* (1832–33) and of *Sämtliche Werke* (with Riemer; 40 vols., 1839–40).

**Eck'ers·berg** (ĕk'ērs·bĕrg), **Kristoffer Vilhelm**. 1783–1853. Danish painter, b. in Slesvig; founder of the national Danish school of painting. His works include esp. historical and religious subjects.

**Eck'ers·ley** (ĕk'ērz·lĭ), **Peter Pendleton**. 1892– English radio engineer, b. Mexico; chief engineer, British Broadcasting Corp. (1923–29); first regular broadcaster in Britain (1921–22); first to propose and operate high-power long-wave broadcasting station (1925); author of *The Power Behind the Microphone* (1941), etc.

**Eck'ert** (ĕk'ērt), **Christian**. 1874– . German political economist; professor, Bonn (1904) and Cologne (1919).

**Eckert, Karl Anton Florian**. 1820–1879. German violinist, pianist, conductor, and composer. Composed the opera *Das Fischermädchen* (1830), the oratorio *Ruth* (1833), chamber music, songs, etc.

**Eck'ford** (ĕk'fērd), **Henry**. 1775–1832. Shipbuilder, b. Scotland; to New York City (1796). Built the *Robert Fulton*, which made first successful voyage by steam from New York to New Orleans and Havana (1822).

**Eck'hart** (ĕk'härt) *or* **Eck'art** (ĕk'ärt) *or* **Eck'ardt** (ĕk'ärt) *or* **Ec'card** (ĕk'ärt) *or* **Eck'e·hart** (ĕk'ĕ·härt), **Johannes**. *Usually called* **Mei'ster Eckhart** (mī'stēr), *i.e.* Master Eckart. 1260?–?1327. German Dominican theologian, mystic, and preacher; founder of German mysticism and father of German philosophical language. Magister in theology, Paris (1302); provincial of his order for Saxony (1303–11) and vicar-general of Bohemia (1307); accused of heresy (1327) but declared his orthodoxy to the pope, who condemned 28 of his propositions after his death (1329); championed a kind of pantheistic philosophy influenced by scholasticism, Neoplatonism, and Arabic and Jewish conceptions.

**Eckhart**, *orig.* **Ec'card** (ĕk'ärt), **Johann Georg von**. 1664–1730. German historian. Assisted Leibnitz (1694–1716) and completed the latter's *Annales Imperii* and *Origines Guelficae*. Professor, Helmstedt (1706); historiographer, Hanover (1714), and court librarian and historiographer (1716–23); court and university librarian, Würzburg (1724).

**Eck'hel** (ĕk'ĕl), **Joseph Hilarius**. 1737–1798. Austrian numismatist; founder of modern numismatics. Author of the scientific work *Doctrina Numorum Veterum* (8 vols., 1792–98; addenda by Steinbüchel, 1826), etc.

**Eckhof, Konrad**. See EKHOF.

**Eckmühl**, Prince **d'**. See Louis Nicolas DAVOUT.

**Eck'stein** (ĕk'shtīn), **Ernst**. 1845–1900. German humorist, novelist, and poet, b. in Giessen. On staff of *Neue Freie Presse* in Vienna (1872–74); in Leipzig (1874–84), editor of literary journal *Deutsche Dichterhalle* (1875–82) and comic weekly *Schalk* (1879–82); in Dresden (from 1885). Author of humorous epics, travel sketches, satirical school sketches, historical novels, modern novels and stories, and lyrics and translations.

**Ed'di** (ĕd'ĭ) *or* **Æd'de** (ăd'dĕ) *or* **Ed'di·us** (ĕd'ĭ·ŭs). c. 634–c. 709. Kentish choirmaster brought to Northumbria by Wilfrid, Bishop of York, to teach Roman method of chanting (669); his *Life of Wilfrid* earliest extant work of an Anglo-Saxon author.

**Ed'ding·ton** (ĕd'ĭng·tŭn), Sir **Arthur Stanley.** 1882–1944. English astronomer, b. Kendal. Educ. Trinity Coll., Cambridge. Chief assistant, Royal Observatory, Greenwich (1906–13); professor, Cambridge (from 1913) and director of the observatory (1914). Known esp. for researches on the motion, internal constitution, and evolution of stars, and elucidation of the theory of relativity. Recipient of many scientific awards; civil member of Order of Merit (1939). Author of *Stellar Movements and the Structure of the Universe* (1914), *Space, Time, and Gravitation* (1920), *The Nature of the Physical World* (1928), *Science and the Unseen World* (1929), *The Expanding Universe* (1933), *New Pathways in Science* (1935), *Relativity Theory of Protons and Electrons* (1936), *The Philosophy of Physical Science* (1939), etc.

**Ed'dy** (ĕd'ĭ), **Clarence.** 1851–1937. American organist and composer, b. Greenfield, Mass. Organist and choirmaster in Chicago (1874–93). Author of *The Church and Concert Organist* (3 vols.), *Pipe Organ Method* (6 vols.).

**Eddy, Mary Morse,** *nee* **Baker.** 1821–1910. Founder of the Christian Science Church, b. Bow, N.H. m. (1843) George Washington Glover (d. 1844), then (1853) Daniel Patterson (divorced 1873), Asa Gilbert Eddy (1877; d. 1882). As an invalid, she sought many types of healing; after exhaustive trial of physical methods she investigated mental healing, but it was not until she had turned to the Bible during her recovery from the effects of a severe fall that she discovered the spiritual and metaphysical system known as Christian Science. Completed *Science and Health* (1875) explaining this system; chartered (1879) "Church of Christ, Scientist." Author also of works in both prose and verse and of the *Church Manual* (1895). Founded *The Christian Science Journal* (1st issue, 1883) and The Christian Science Publishing Society (1898), publishers of *The Christian Science Quarterly, The Christian Science Monitor* (1908), etc.

**Eddy, Sherwood.** 1871–1963. American Y.M.C.A. official and writer. Author of *India Awakening* (1911), *The New Era in Asia* (1913), *With Our Soldiers in France* (1917), *Religion and Social Justice* (1928), *A Pilgrimage of Ideas* (1935), etc.

**Eddy, William Abner.** 1858–1909. American meteorologist; studied air currents and layers by means of kites (the Eddy kite, a quadrilateral tailless kite, being named for him); photographed the earth with a camera attached to a kite (1896).

**E'del·felt'** (ā'dĕl·fĕlt'), **Albert.** 1854–1905. Finnish portrait, genre, and landscape painter.

**E'de·linck** (ā'dĕ·lĭngk), **Gérard.** 1640–1707. Flemish copperplate engraver in France; pioneer in use of lozenge shape and in representing objects realistically as to color and texture. He produced over 300 engravings, including portraits of Philippe de Champaigne, Le Brun, Louis XIV, and *The Holy Family* (after Raphael), etc.

**E'del·man** (ĕd''l-măn), **Gerald Maurice.** 1929– . Biochemist, b. New York City. M.D., U. of Penna., 1954; Ph.D., Rockefeller U., 1960. Shared 1972 Nobel prize for physiology and medicine with R.R. Porter for work on immunology.

**E'del·mann** (ed''l·man), **Johann Christian.** 1698–1767. German freethinker and opponent of positive religion; persecuted as freethinker esp. in Hamburg and Frankfurt, where his writings were publicly burned; fled to Altona and lived one year in hiding; permitted by Frederick III to return to Berlin (1749), but forbidden to publish further.

**E·dén'** (ĕ·dān'), **Nils.** 1871–1945. Swedish statesman and historian; prime minister of Sweden (1917–20).

**E'den** (ē'd'n), **William.** 1st Baron **Auck'land** (ôk'lănd). 1744–1814. English statesman. M.A. Oxon. (1768). Undersecretary of state (1772); commissioner to American colonies (1778); chief secretary for Ireland (1780); negotiated Pitt's commercial treaty with France (1786–87); ambassador to Spain (1788), Holland (1790–93); president of board of trade under Grenville (1806). His son **George** (1784–1849), Earl of **Auckland,** educ. Oxford, was member of Lord Grey's reform cabinet (1830–34); governor general of India (1835–41); first lord of the admiralty (1846). George's sister **Emily** (1797–1869) accompanied him to India; published *Portraits of the People and Princes of India* (1844), *Up the Country* (1866), and two novels.

Sir **Ashley Eden** (1831–1887), Indian official, grandson of 1st Baron Auckland; secretary to governor of Bengal (1860–71); as envoy to Bhutan, was driven to accepting a disadvantageous treaty (1863); first civilian governor of British Burma (1871); lieutenant governor of Bengal (1877–82); member of council of secretary of state for India (1882–87).

**Sir Anthony,** *in full* **Robert Anthony** (1897–1977), Earl of **Avon,** 2d surviving son of 7th baronet of Windlestone Hall, Durham, descended from the father of Willian Eden, 1st Baron Auckland, received a first class in Oriental languages, Oxford (1922); served as captain in King's Royal Rifle Corps and as general staff officer in World War (1915–19); won Military Cross; M.P. (1923); parliamentary private secretary to foreign secretary Sir Austen Chamberlain (1926–29); undersecretary, foreign office (1931–33); lord privy seal and privy councilor (1934–35); minister without portfolio for League of Nations affairs (1935); secretary of state for foreign affairs (1935–38); concluded "gentlemen's agreement" with Count Ciano concerning Mediterranean (1937); represented Great Britain at Nine Power Conference regarding Chinese-Japanese conflict (Nov., 1937); resigned in disagreement with policy of Chamberlain government after the Munich conference; secretary of state for dominions (1939–40); war secretary (1940); secretary of state for foreign affairs (1940–45; 1951–55); prime minister (1955–57).

**E'der** (ā'dẽr), **Joseph Maria.** 1855–1946. Austrian photochemist and historian of photography; director of research institute for photography, Vienna (1888); investigated chemical effects produced by light.

**E'der·le** (ā'dẽr·lē), **Gertrude Caroline.** 1906– American swimmer, b. New York City. Swam the English channel from France to England (Aug. 6, 1926) in 14 hrs. 31 min., first woman to accomplish this feat.

**Ed'gar** (ĕd'gẽr) *or* **Ead'gar** (ā'ȧd·gär). *Called* **the Peaceful.** 944–975. King of the English. Younger son of Edmund the Magnificent. Father of Edward the Martyr. Made king of Northumbria and Mercia (957) by nobles discontented with rule of his elder brother, Edwy, on whose death (959) he succeeded as king of united England; recalled Dunstan from exile and made him chief adviser; pacified Northumbria (966); said to have ceded Lothian (northern Bernicia) to Kenneth of Scotland for sake of his good will; allowed northern Danes a degree of self-government; received his deferred coronation (973) and, soon after, homage of eight British princes, including kings of Scotland and Strathclyde; restored monastic houses to Benedictine monks, expelling secular clergy; improved judiciary system; organized fleet for defense against northern pirates.

**Edgar** *or* **Eadgar.** *Called* **the Æ'the·ling** (ă'thĕ·lĭng). 1050?–?1130. English prince, b. probably in Hungary; grandson of Edmund Ironside. His sister Margaret was wife of Malcolm III. After defeat of Harold (1066), chosen king by Morcar and his brother Edwin but forced by defections to submit to William I; led two unsuccessful risings (1068, 1069); went to William's Norman court and made peace (1074); led expedition to Scotland (1097); went on First Crusade (1099).

**Edge** (ĕj), **Walter Evans.** 1873–1956. American journalist and diplomat, b. Philadelphia. Proprietor, Atlantic City *Daily Press* and Atlantic City *Evening Union.* Governor of New Jersey (1917–19); U.S. senator from New Jersey (1919–29); U.S. ambassador to France (1929–33); governor of N.J. (1944–47).

**Edg'er·ton** (ĕj'ĕr·t'n; -tŭn), **Harold Eugene.** 1903– . American electrical engineer, b. Fremont, Nebraska. B.S., Nebraska (1925), Sc.D., M.I.T. (1931). Associate professor of electrical measurements, M.I.T. Known for stroboscopic motion pictures.

**Edge'worth** (ĕj'wûrth; -wĕrth), **Francis Ysidro.** 1845–1926. British economist; first editor of *Economic Journal* (from 1891).

**Edgeworth, Richard Lovell.** 1744–1817. British writer on education and mechanics; invented plan for telegraphic communication between Dublin and Galway (accepted by government, 1804) and many mechanical inventions, including a semaphore, a velocipede, a pedometer, a new land-measuring machine. Formed friendship with Thomas Day, to whom he suggested writing of *History of Sandford and Merton,* and with Dr. Erasmus Darwin; visited Rousseau, according to whose system he educated his eldest son. Collaborated with his daughter Maria in *Practical Education* (1798) and in *Essay on Irish Bulls* (1802).

His eldest daughter, **Maria** (1767–1849), novelist, b. in Oxfordshire, accompanied her father to Ireland (1782) and was his inseparable companion and assistant; completed her father's memoirs on his death (1817); visited Scott at Abbotsford (1823); rendered practical aid to peasants during Irish famine (1846). Author of twenty-odd volumes, including *The Absentee* (1812) and *Ormond* (1817), masterpieces of Irish life, like *Castle Rackrent, Belinda* (1801), *Leonora* (1806), *Tales from Fashionable Life* (1809, 1812), *Helen* (1834), her last novel. See Thomas BEDDOES.

**Edgeworth,** Sir **Tannatt William.** = Sir Edgeworth DAVID.

**Edge'worth de Fir'mont'** (ĕj'wûrth [-wĕrth] dē fēr'-môN'), **Henry Essex.** 1745–1807. Irish confessor to Louis XVI. Confessor to Princess Élisabeth, sister of Louis XVI (1791), and to Louis XVI, whom he attended on scaffold (1793); escaped to England (1796) carrying Élisabeth's last message to her brother, future King Charles X; chaplain to Louis XVIII, whom he accompanied to Russia.

**Ed'gren** (ĕd'grĕn), **Anne Charlotte,** *nee* **Leff'ler** (lĕf'lĕr). Duchess **di Ca'ja·nel'lo** (dē kä'yä·nĕl'lō). 1849–1892. Swedish novelist and playwright; m. 1st, G. Edgren (1872; divorced 1889); 2d, Duke di Cajanello (1890). Author of short stories, a series of sketches of upper Swedish society, the comedies *True Women* (1883) and *An Angel of Deliverance* (1883), the dramas *The Actress* (1873; anon.), *How to do Good* (1885), and *The Struggle for Happiness* (1887; with Sonya Kovalevski), etc.

**Ed·hem' Pa·sha'** (ĕt·hĕm' pä·shä'; ĕ·tĕm'). 1813?–1893. Turkish general and statesman, b. on island of Chios of Greek parentage. Aide on staff of Sultan (1849); rose to rank of general of division. Turkish ambassador in Berlin (1876); grand vizier (1877); ambassador in Vienna (1879–83); minister of interior (1883–85).

**Edhem Pasha.** 1851–1909. Turkish soldier; brigade commander at siege of Pleven (1877); general in chief in Greco-Turkish War (1897); minister of war (1909).

**Edinburgh,** Duke of. See Prince ALFRED (1844–1900).

**Edinburgh,** Duke of. See Prince PHILIP (1921– ).

**Ed'i·son** (ĕd'ĭ·s'n), **Charles.** 1890–1969. Son of Thomas Alva Edison. American scientist and politician, b. West Orange, N.J. Educ., M.I.T. President and director, Thomas A. Edison, Inc.; engaged in manufacture of war materials during World War I. Secretary of the navy (1939–40); governor of New Jersey (1941–44).

**Edison, Thomas Alva.** 1847–1931. American inventor, b. in Milan, Ohio; passed childhood in Port Huron, Mich. At 12, newsboy on Grand Trunk Railway running into Detroit; as reward for saving life of child of stationmaster was given lessons in telegraph operation at Mount Clemens, Mich.; became operator in various cities in U.S. and Canada (until c. 1869); sale of inventions, including telegraphic devices, enabled him to establish own workshop at Newark, N.J., which was removed to Menlo Park, N.J. (1876), and to West Orange, N.J. (1887). Among his inventions, of which he patented over a thousand, are a vote recorder, automatic telegraph repeater, quadruplex telegraph, printing telegraph, electric pen, mimeograph, carbon telephone transmitter, the microphone, the phonograph, the Ediphone, the incandescent electric lamp, the electric valve, a system of telegraphy for communicating with moving trains, kinetoscope, alkaline storage battery (Edison storage battery). Produced talking motion pictures (1913); improved dynamos and motors; worked on magnetic method of concentrating iron ores, and on war problems for the government during World War I, also on the production of carbolic acid and other chemicals. See E. S. PORTER. Elected to Am. Hall of Fame (1960).

**Ed·lén'** (ĕd·lān'), **Bengt.** 1906– . Swedish astrophysicist; professor of physics, Uppsala U.; known esp. for investigations of the spectrum of the solar corona and explanation of coronium as "broken atoms" of iron, calcium, and nickel.

**Ed'lund** (ĕd'lo͝ond), **Erik.** 1819–1888. Swedish physicist; conducted researches on the theory of electricity, atmospheric electricity, etc.

**Ed'man** (ĕd'măn), **Irwin.** 1896–1954. American philosopher; on teaching staff at Columbia (from 1920; professor from 1935). Author of *Human Traits and Their Social Significance* (1920), *Poems* (1925), *Adam, the Baby and the Man from Mars* (1929), *The Contemporary and His Soul* (1932), *Philosopher's Holiday* (1938), etc.

**Ed'mands** (ĕd'măndz), **John.** 1820–1915. American librarian; prepared booklet from which W. F. Poole later developed the *Index to Periodical Literature.* Devised a system of library classification.

**Ed'mer** *or* **Ead'mer** (ĕd'mĕr). 1060?–1124. English ecclesiastic and historian. Chronicler of contemporary (1066–1122), chiefly ecclesiastical, events in *Historia Novorum.*

**Ed'monds** (ĕd'măndz), **Walter Du·maux'** (dū·mō'). 1903– . American fiction writer; author of *Rome Haul* (1929), *The Big Barn* (1930), *Erie Water* (1933), *Mostly Canallers* (1934), *Drums Along the Mohawk* (1936), *The Matchlock Gun* (1941).

**Ed'mund** (ĕd'mŭnd) *or* **Ead'mund** (*A.-S.* â'ȧd-mo͝ond), Saint. *Known as* **the Martyr.** 841?–870. King of East Anglia. According to tradition, b. Nuremberg, son of King Alkmund; succeeded as king (855); as outcome of Danish invasion of 866–870, defeated at Hoxne (870). Ultimately interred at Bury St. Edmunds.

**Edmund** *or* **Eadmund I.** *Called* **the Deed–doer** *and*

**the Magnificent.** 922?–946. King of the English. Son of Edward the Elder. Succeeded his half brother Athelstan (940), with whom he had fought at Brunanburh. Made truce with Olaf Sitricson by which the five Danish boroughs were protected from raids by Norwegian kings of Northumbria; on breaking of truce drove Olaf from Northumbria (944); entrusted Cumbria to Malcolm I of Scotland as ally (945); stabbed by an exiled robber at Pucklechurch. Succeeded by his brother Edred.

**Edmund** *or* **Eadmund II.** *Called* **I'ron·side'** (ī'ẽrn-sīd'). 980?–1016. King of the English. Son of Ethelred the Unready. On invasion of Canute (1015), was deserted by Edric, his brother-in-law, who was incensed by his marriage to the widow of a Danish earl and receipt of submission of Five Boroughs of Danish confederacy; on death of father (1016) chosen king by Londoners, while Canute was chosen by witan at Southampton; defeated Canute at Pen and Sherston, gaining Wessex; after two more victories was rejoined by Edric, who by treachery caused rout of English at Assandun (Ashingdon in Essex); by compromise with Canute received south of England (1016), which at his death was also taken by Canute.

**Ed'mund** (ĕd'mŭnd). *Called* **Crouchback.** Earl of **Lancaster** (1245–1296). See LANCASTER.

**Edmund of Langley.** 1st Duke of York. See YORK.

**Edmund Rich** (rĭch), Saint. 1175?–1240. English prelate. Grad. Paris; divinity lecturer, Oxford; appointed by Gregory IX to preach the Sixth Crusade throughout England (c. 1227). Archbishop of Canterbury (1234); rebuked Henry III for following foreign counselors and as responsible for murder of Richard Marshal, leader of National party; threatened excommunication; got favorites dismissed; thwarted in every move by papal legate sent at king's request (1237); retired (1240) to abbey of Pontigny, France. Canonized (c. 1249).

**Ed'munds** (ĕd'mŭndz), **Albert Joseph.** 1857–1941. Librarian, b. Tottenham, Eng.; to U.S. (1885). Authority on Buddhism, and author of *Marvelous Birth of the Buddhas* (1899), *A Dialogue Between Two Saviors*, etc.

**Edmunds, George Franklin.** 1828–1919. American lawyer and senator; U.S. senator from Vermont (1866–91); regarded as authority on constitutional law. Instrumental in passage of act (1877) providing for appointment of federal electoral commission; name attached to an act (1882) aimed at suppressing polygamy in the territories; author of greater part of the Sherman Antitrust Act (1890). President pro tempore of senate at death of President Garfield. Candidate for Republican nomination for president of U.S. (1880, and, against Blaine, 1884).

**Edom.** = ESAU.

**Ed'red** (ĕd'rĕd; -rĭd) *or* **Ead'red** (â'ȧd·rād). d. 955. King of the English. Youngest son of Edward the Elder. Succeeded his brother Edmund I (946); ravaged Northumbria to suppress insurrection headed by Wulfstan, Archbishop of York, and Eric Bloodaxe, Norwegian king of Northumbria; took over Northumbria on Eric's death (954), granting limited autonomy to Danes on Dunstan's advice. Succeeded by his nephew Edwy.

**Ed'ric** (ĕd'rĭk) *or* **Ead'ric Streo'na** (â'ȧd·rēch strā'ō·nä). d. 1017. Alderman of Mercians (from 1007). Advanced by Ethelred II, whose daughter he married; dissuaded Ethelred from attacking the Danes; had Sigeferth and Morkere, chief thegns of Danish confederacy, slain through treachery (1015); deserted his brother-in-law Edmund Ironside for Canute (1015) and helped Canute take Wessex and Mercia; returned to Edmund; by treachery at Assandun (Ashingdon in Essex) brought about English defeat at hands of Danes; restored to earldom by Canute but executed as untrustworthy. His nephew **Edric Sil·vat'i·cus** [sĭl·văt'ĭ·kŭs] (fl. 1067–1072) of Herefordshire and Shropshire, submitted to William I and accompanied him on expedition to Scotland (1072).

**Edrisi.** See IDRISI.

**Ed'schmid** (āt'shmĭt), **Kasimir.** *Pseudonym of* Eduard **Schmidt.** 1890–1966. German writer; leader in expressionist movement in Germany.

**Ed'strom** (ĕd'strŭm; *Swed.* ād'strûm), **David.** 1873–1938. Sculptor, b. in Sweden; to U.S. (1880). Among his portrait busts are the crown prince and princess of Sweden, Princess Patricia of Connaught, and Ellen Key; among his psychological sculptures are *Fear, Pride, Envy, Caliban*, and *The Cry of Poverty.*

**Ed'ward** (ĕd'wẽrd) *or* **Ead'ward** (*A.-S.* â'ȧd·wärd). Name of three pre-Norman kings of the English:

**Edward** *or* **Eadward** *or* **Ead'weard** (*A.-S.* â'ȧd·wă'ĕrd). *Called* **the Elder.** 870?–924. King of the Angles and Saxons. Son of Alfred the Great, whom he succeeded (899); defeated attempt of his cousin Ethelwold, helped by revolting East Anglican Danes, to take the throne (905); won victories (909, 910) over invading Danes; took over from Mercia government of London and Oxford on death of his sister Ethelfleda's husband (912); continued to capture and fortify towns of Essex; received submission of East Anglian Danes (918); annexed Mercia on death of Ethelfleda (918?); subdued kings of North Welsh (921), and successively Scottish king, Norwegian king of Northumbria, the Strathclyde Welsh.

**Edward** *or* **Eadward.** *Called* **the Martyr.** 963?–978. Son of Edgar the Peaceful; crowned (975). Following counsels of Dunstan, defended church and monasteries against growing antimonastic reaction; assassinated at Corfe Castle at instigation of his stepmother Elfrida (Aelfthryth), ambitious for her son Ethelred II.

**Edward** *or* **Eadward.** *Called* **the Confessor.** 1002?–1066. Last of Anglo-Saxon line. Son of Ethelred the Unready, b. in Oxfordshire. Cousin of William the Conqueror (*q.v.*). Lived in court of his uncle, duke of Normandy, during Danish supremacy; developed ecclesiastical interests; took vow of chastity. Recalled by Hardecanute and on his death (1042) placed on throne through influence of the great Earl Godwin of Wessex, whose daughter Edith he married (1045). Crowned (1043); throughout reign, entrusted more of administration of government to foreign favorites of Norman or court party than to the national party of Godwin and his son Harold; rejected the archbishop-elect (one Ælfric, kinsman of Godwin canonically elected) in favor of Robert of Jumièges for archbishop of Canterbury (1051); quarreled with Godwin over latter's refusal to punish Dover; after flight of foreign favorites before rebellion of the outlawed Godwin, became reconciled and restored Godwin and Harold, whose influence (after 1052) was supreme; forced to give up his favorite, Tostig, Earl of Northumbria, against whose government the Danish population rebelled (1065); mortified at this humiliation, fell ill and was unable to attend consecration of the new Westminster Abbey he had founded and in which he was buried. Enfranchised the Cinque Ports, remitted the Danegeld, favored monasticism, was first English king to employ royal touch for alleged cure of scrofulous taint. Canonized (1161). Anglo-Saxon legal uses codified (1070) as *Laws of Edward the Confessor.*

**Edward.** Name of eight post-Norman English (British) kings:

**Edward I.** *Called* **Long'shanks'** (lŏng'shăngks'). 1239–1307. King of England (1272–1307) of the house of

Anjou or Plantagenet (see PLANTAGENET). Eldest son of Henry III and Eleanor of Provence. Married Eleanor of Castile (1254), half sister of Spanish king. Granted by his father the duchy of Gascony, earldom of Chester, king's lands in Ireland and Wales; waged ineffective campaign against Llewelyn, Prince of Wales (1256); dispelled unpopularity by supporting barons in insistence upon reform, co-operating with Simon de Montfort, Earl of Leicester, in formulating Provisions of Westminster (1259). By rashness in pursuit, contributed to his father's defeat at Lewes (1264); held as hostage, but escaped and with Welsh aid defeated and killed Montfort at Evesham (1265). Joined Seventh Crusade (1270); relieved Acre; won victory at Haifa. Succeeded to English crown (1272); received homage of Alexander III of Scotland but had to wage war on Prince Llewelyn to obtain his submission (1276). Carried through legislation (1275–90) eliminating feudalism and establishing the parliamentary system; refused tribute to Rome and ended papal overlordship; punished corrupt judges (1289); summoned (1295) a parliament representing the three estates, later called the Model Parliament. Defeated and killed Llewelyn in Radnorshire (1282); had Llewelyn's brother hanged and quartered (1283); assimilated future administration in Wales to English pattern (1284). Remained abroad improving administration in Gascony and mediating between houses of Anjou and Aragon (1286–89). Banished 16,000 Jews on charge of extortionate usury (1290). On death of Margaret, Maid of Norway (1290), undertook to arbitrate among claimants for Scottish throne; adjudged throne to John de Baliol (1292), who did homage; in order to put down revolt by Scots, exasperated by this claim of jurisdiction over Scotland, stormed Berwick, penetrated to Aberdeen, Banff, and Elgin, accepted Baliol's surrender of crown, and carried Coronation Stone back to England (1296). Turning to recovery of Gascony, temporarily yielded (1293) to Philip the Fair, met opposition of clergy to fresh subsidies and of barons to proposed campaign in Gascony (1297); made compromise with clergy, to obtain grants, and obtained temporary illegal grants from nobles and commons, but at Ghent had to confirm the charters safeguarding people against arbitrary taxation; made truce with France (1299), married French king's sister Margaret, gaining restitution of Gascony by deserting his ally, count of Flanders. Free (1303) to turn to conquest of Scotland; captured Stirling Castle (1304); beheaded Wallace (1305); gave Scotland new constitution and representation in English Parliament. Crushed clerical opposition when Pope Clement V allowed him (1306) to suspend Archbishop Robert de Winchelsea, who had denounced him as a marauder; made concessions to baronial opposition until death of Humphrey de Bohun, Earl of Hereford; died at Burgh-by-Sands en route to Scotland to crush new revolt by Robert Bruce; buried in Westminster Abbey.

**Edward II** of Carnarvon. 1284–1327. King of England (1307–27), of the house of Anjou or Plantagenet (see PLANTAGENET); b. Caernarvon, Wales, 4th son of Edward I and Eleanor of Castile. Created (1301) prince of Wales, first heir apparent to bear the title; took part in Scottish campaigns (1301, 1303, 1304). On accession to throne (1307), abandoned his father's cherished ambition, subjugation of Scotland, and recalled his Gascon favorite, Piers Gaveston, who had been banished by Edward I, and created him earl of Cornwall; m. Isabella, daughter of Philip the Fair, King of France (1308). Forced by threatened withdrawal of allegiance to consent to government of the realm by baronial committee of 21 lords ordainers (1311); required by barons to banish Gaveston, later twice recalled but kidnaped (1312) by Guy de Beauchamp, Earl of Warwick and executed; forced to submit to his kinsman, Thomas, Earl of Lancaster, leader of barons. Led army to relief of Stirling, the only Scottish fortress not occupied by Robert Bruce; defeated by Bruce at Bannockburn (1314); lost Berwick to Bruce (1318). With aid of new favorites, the Despensers, and a faction of the opposition under Aymer de Valence, Earl of Pembroke, overthrew and beheaded Lancaster at Boroughbridge (1322). Made futile attempt to invade Scotland (1322); concluded truce with Bruce for 13 years; alienated his wife Isabella by favors heaped upon the Despensers; sent Isabella to king of France, her brother, to do homage for Aquitaine and Ponthieu (1325); forced to flee when Isabella, having formed criminal connection with Roger de Mortimer, 1st Earl of March, led a force of baronial exiles in invasion, captured Bristol, executed the Despensers; was captured, imprisoned, forced to resign throne (1327); brutally treated in Berkeley Castle and murdered.

**Edward III** of Windsor. 1312–1377. King of England (1327–77), of the house of Anjou or Plantagenet (see PLANTAGENET). Eldest son of Edward II; b. Windsor. Earl of Chester (1320); duke of Aquitaine (1325); made abortive campaign against Scots (1327); by treaty of Northampton recognized independence of Scotland (1328). m. Philippa of Hainaut (1328). Took government into his own hands (1330), executing Mortimer and placing Isabella, his mother, under restraint; invaded Scotland and, assisting Edward de Baliol, claimant to throne of David Bruce, defeated Scots at Halidon Hill (1333); twice vainly restored Baliol to throne. Laid claim (previously made, 1328) to crown of France in right of his mother, Isabella, sister of Charles, a groundless claim in view of exclusion of females from throne, and became involved in the Hundred Years' War. Declared war against Philip, and made alliance with Emperor Louis the Bavarian; won brilliant sea victory over French fleet at Sluis (1340); accompanied by his son Edward, the Black Prince, sacked cities of Normandy, won decisive victory at Crécy (1346), effected reduction of Calais (1347); in want of money made truce, returned to England. Held magnificent tournaments and revels; established Order of the Garter (1349). Renewed war on large scale (1355); despite Black Prince's victory at Poitiers (1356), failed in attempt to assume crown of France at Reims (1359) and in attack on Paris; renounced all claim to French crown in exchange for Aquitaine (1360). Made agreement with David II of Scotland providing, in the absence of male issue, union with England (1363); passed antipapal and anticlerical legislation, repudiated feudal claims of papacy growing out of King John's submission and promise of tribute thirty years earlier, and forbade payment of Peter's pence (1366). In a second war with France lost Aquitaine, lost command of the sea, made truce, retaining little except four posts in France. With public finances ruined and Parliament recalcitrant, gave himself into hands of a greedy mistress, Alice Perrers, letting her and his son, John of Gaunt, dominate the government. Credited with enlightened commercial policy, introduced Flemish weavers to England; devoted himself to naval administration. Father of: Edward, the Black Prince, Lionel of Antwerp (Duke of Clarence), John of Gaunt, Edmund of Langley, and Thomas of Woodstock. Succeeded by his grandson Richard II.

**Edward IV.** 1442–1483. King of England (1461–70; 1471–83), of the house of York. Earl of March, heir to the Mortimer estates (see MORTIMER family). b. Rouen, son of Richard, Duke of York, and Cecily Neville, dau.

of 1st earl of Westmorland. Driven from England and attainted by Lancastrian king HenryVI, at Ludlow field (1459); with his uncle and cousin, the Nevilles, invaded England, defeated Lancastrians at Northampton (1460); after his father's defeat and death at Wakefield, defeated Lancastrians at Mortimer's Cross (1461), proclaimed himself king, clinched the throne by victory at Towton, and was crowned (June, 1461). Guided by the Nevilles, crushed resistance of Lancastrian queen Margaret, in the north; by privately marrying (1464) Elizabeth, daughter of Richard Woodville (*q.v.*), lost his early popularity and offended Richard Neville, Earl of Warwick, who had projected a match with French princess; thwarted Warwick's proposed alliance with France by alliance with Burgundy; by heaping honors on the Woodvilles, provoked Warwick and his own brother George, Duke of Clarence, to unite with Queen Margaret and Lancastrian exiles in driving him from the throne and elevating the helpless Henry VI (1470). Furnished with money by his brother-in-law, Charles of Burgundy, landed with his brother Richard, Duke of Gloucester, at Ravenspur, was rejoined by duke of Clarence, defeated and slew Warwick at Barnet (1471), captured Queen Margaret at Tewkesbury, and caused murder of her son Prince Edward and probably murder of Henry VI in Tower (1471); re-established York dynasty (1471); settled rivalry between his brothers for share in Neville estates by judicial murder of Clarence in the Tower (1478). Deserted his ally the duke of Burgundy in return for an annual subsidy from Louis XI and stipulated marriage of his daughter to the dauphin, secured by treaty of Picquigny (1475); relieved by this subsidy from necessity of heavy taxation and responsibility to Parliament, built up autocratic rule preparing way for absolute monarchy of the Tudors. Patron of the new culture in England; his reign saw introduction of printing and silk manufacture. His brother Richard, Duke of Gloucester, deposed his son Edward V and became king as Richard III.

**Edward V.** 1470–1483. King of England (April–June, 1483), of the house of York. Eldest son of Edward IV and Elizabeth Woodville; b. in Westminster sanctuary. Created prince of Wales (1471). Seized from his maternal uncle, Earl Rivers, by his paternal uncle Richard, Duke of Gloucester, at Northampton on death of Edward IV, brought to London; thrown into Tower, along with his brother, the young duke of York (1483); deposed by an assembly of lords and commons under direction of Gloucester on ground of illegitimacy because of Edward IV's betrothal to Lady Eleanor Butler previous to his marriage to Elizabeth Woodville; murdered, with the duke of York, in Tower by smothering, probably by command of Gloucester, who had assumed the crown as Richard III.

**Edward VI.** 1537–1553. King of England and Ireland (1547–53), of the house of Tudor. Only child of King Henry VIII by his third wife, Jane Seymour; b. at Hampton Court. Educated under guidance of Sir John Cheke and Roger Ascham. Succeeded to throne and headship of the church (1547) under regency of his uncle Edward Seymour, Duke of Somerset, who set up project to marry him to Mary, Queen of Scots, as pretext for invading Scotland (1549). Consented (1552) to execution of Somerset on charges of overambition made by John Dudley, Duke of Northumberland, who assumed complete dominion over him and induced him to sign a will excluding his half sisters Mary and Elizabeth and devising the succession to Lady Jane Grey (see GREY family), to whom Northumberland had married his own son. Attacked by consumption (1553). Favored principles of the Reformation and establishment of Protestantism; authorized publication of Forty-Two Articles of the Church of England in Latin and English (1553) and the First Prayer Book, compiled by Thomas Cranmer (1549).

**Edward VII. Albert Edward.** *Called* **the Peacemaker.** 1841–1910. King of Great Britain and Ireland (1901–10), of house of Saxe-Coburg. Eldest son of Queen Victoria; created prince of Wales (1841). Studied at Edinburgh, Oxford, and Cambridge; colonel in army (1858). Paid first visit by a royal prince to a British colony (Canada; 1860); traveled with Dean Stanley in the East (1862); privy councilor and took seat in House of Lords as duke of Cornwall (1863). m. (1863) Alexandra, eldest daughter of Christian IX of Denmark. Created sensation and gave rise to scandalous insinuations on appearing as witness in a divorce suit (1870); opened International Exhibition at South Kensington (1871); victim of typhoid (1871–72); paid official visits to India (1875–76), Ireland (1885); strictly excluded from foreign negotiations by Queen Victoria because of his indiscretion, reluctantly allowed to share in official intelligence in Gladstone's last ministry (1892–94). First chancellor of U. of Wales; carried responsibility for large part of arrangements of queen's jubilees (1887, 1897); assisted in promoting Royal Coll. of Music; won Derby (three times: 1896, 1900, 1909) and Grand National (1900). Succeeded to throne on death (1901) of Queen Victoria; sustained position as constitutional monarch established by Victoria; instituted Order of Merit (1902); his coronation (Aug., 1902) proclaimed in India in durbar at Delhi (1903). Promoted international amity by visits to European capitals, always with undersecretary of foreign office in attendance (1903–04), and prepared way for treaties of arbitration and Anglo-French and Anglo-Russian ententes; visited Berlin (1909) to dispel suspicions of Anglo-German rivalry; disturbed by constitutional crisis over rejection of Lloyd George's budget by House of Lords and Liberals' demand for abolition of peers' veto power, but abstained from interference. After bronchial attack at Biarritz (spring, 1910), died of heart failure. Brought crown into active participation in public life and into touch with all sections of the empire. Succeeded by his 2d son, as George V (*q.v.*).

**Edward VIII.** *Full name* **Edward Albert Christian George Andrew Patrick David.** *After abdication, known as* Duke of **Wind'sor** (wĭn'zẽr). 1894–1972. King of Great Britain and Ireland (Jan. 20–Dec. 11, 1936; abdicated), of the house of Windsor. Eldest son of George V and Queen Mary. Prepared for navy at Osborne and at Dartmouth (1909–11); created prince of Wales and earl of Chester (1911); at investiture in Carnarvon Castle was first English prince to address Welsh in their own tongue; midshipman on H.M.S. *Hindostan;* in World War, served with B.E.F. in Flanders and France and on Italian front, on staff of commander of Mediterranean Expeditionary Force in Egypt, and with Canadian Corps. Taking up public duties, toured Canada, visited U.S. (1919); paid state visits to Australia and West Indies (1920), India (1921–22); president of British Empire Exhibition at Wembley (1924); visited British South Africa and South America (1925), and Canada, with Stanley Baldwin, for centenary celebration of Canadian confederation; toured Latin and South America in interests of British trade (1931). Succeeded his father (1936), first bachelor king in 176 years; raised storm of official protest by his proposal to marry and elevate as queen Mrs. Wallis Simpson, *nee* Warfield, an American whose second divorce was pending; met by unyielding opposition of his ministers, chose to abdicate and took up residence in Austria; m. Mrs. Simpson at Château de Candé, near Tours (June, 1937); visited

Germany to study social and housing conditions and met Hitler, Goebbels, and Göring (1937); major general attached to staff of B.E.F., assigned to liaison work in France (1939); governor of the Bahama Islands (Aug., 1940–Mar., 1945).

**Edward.** Prince of **Wales.** *Called sometimes* **Edward IV** *or* **Edward of Wood'stock** (wŏŏd'stŏk). 1330–1376. Eldest son of Edward III. Duke of **Corn'wall** (kôrn'wăl; -wôl), first duke created in England (1337); known as "the Black Prince." Began career with Edward III's Norman campaign (1346); commanded right wing at Crécy; at siege of Calais and on Calais expedition (1349); one of original Knights of the Garter. As lieutenant in Gascony, led foray through Armagnac and Languedoc and plundered Narbonne (1355); on marauding expedition (1356), routed French and took King John prisoner at Poitiers; had share in negotiating Treaty of Bretigny (1360). m. (1361) Joan, Fair Maid of Kent. As prince of **Aq'ui·taine'** (ăk'wĭ·tān') and **Gas'co·ny** (găs'kō·nĭ), received all English kingdom in southern France from his father (1362); won favor of towns by fostering trade but was looked on with suspicion by nobles; after peace of six years, restored Pedro (Peter the Cruel) to throne of Castile by expedition into Spain and victory at Nájera (1367), last of his great victories. Needing funds badly, obtained hearth tax for five years, which was made pretext by barons for revolt (1368) that spread throughout Aquitania; at war with Charles V (1369); captured Limoges and massacred defenders (1370); stricken with mortal disease contracted in Spain, returned to England; resigned his principality in Aquitaine and Gascony (1372); led commons in attack on Lancastrian administration.

**Edward.** Prince of **Wales** (created 1454). 1453–1471. Only son of Henry VI; carried for safety by Queen Margaret to Scotland, thence to France and Lorraine, during strife with Yorkists. After his father's restoration by earl of Warwick and duke of Clarence (1470) returned to England, but was defeated at Tewkesbury and killed by Edward IV.

**Edward.** Earl of **Warwick.** 1475–1499. See under George, Duke of CLARENCE.

**Edward.** *Port.* **Duarte.** 1391–1438. King of Portugal (1433–38). Son of John I and father of Alfonso V. Took part in capture of Ceuta from Moors (1415); led unsuccessful expedition against Tangier (1437); wrote two prose works: *Leal conselheiro* ("The Faithful Councilor") and a book of instruction in horsemanship.

**Edward Augustus** (1767–1820). See duke of KENT.

**Edward of Norwich.** 2d Duke of York. See YORK.

**Ed'wardes** (ĕd'wẽrdz), Sir **Herbert Benjamin.** 1819–1868. British soldier and official in India. Urdu, Hindi, and Persian interpreter to his regiment. Aide-de-camp to commander in chief in India through Sikh war, wounded at Mudki (1845), fought at Sobraon (1846); twice routed rebel Mulraj, Prince of Multan (1848–49). As commissioner of Peshawar (1853–59), during Sepoy Mutiny effected reconciliation with emir of Afghanistan and raised mixed force for use against mutineers at Delhi; commissioner of Ambala (1862); major general (1868).

**Ed'wards** (ĕd'wẽrdz), **Agustín.** 1878–1941. Chilean banker and diplomat; vice-president of Chile (1901–02). Minister for foreign affairs (1903, 1905, 1909, 1910); minister to Italy, Spain, and Switzerland (1905–06) and to Great Britain (1910–25); ambassador to Great Britain (1935–38). President, League of Nations Assembly (1922), and of 5th Pan-American conference (1923).

**Ed'wards** (ĕd'wẽrdz), **Alfred George.** 1848–1937. Anglican prelate; bishop of St. Asaph (1889–1934); first archbishop of Wales (1920–34). Author of books on Welsh church history.

**Edwards, Amelia Ann Blanford.** 1831–1892. English novelist and Egyptologist. Among her novels were *Debenham's Vow* (1870) and *Lord Brackenbury* (1880); founded Egyptian Exploration Fund (1882) and published papers on Egyptology. Her cousin **Matilda Barbara Be'tham–Ed'wards** [bē'thăm-] (1836–1919) was novelist and writer on French life; author of *The White House by the Sea* (1857), *Dr. Jacob* (1864), *Kitty* (1869), *The Dream-Charlotte* (1896), etc.

**Edwards, Bryan.** 1743–1800. English West Indian merchant, in Jamaica for thirty years and in England. M.P. (1796); antiabolitionist. Author of *History of the British Colonies in the West Indies* (1793).

**Edwards, Clarence Ransom.** 1860–1931. American army officer, b. Cleveland, Ohio. Grad. U.S.M.A., West Point (1883). Commander, U.S. troops in Panama Canal Zone (1915–17). Major general, national army (1917); organized 26th division and commanded it in France (1917–18). Major general, U.S. army (1921); retired (1922).

**Edwards, George.** 1693–1773. English naturalist; author of *A History of Birds* (4 vols., 1743–51) and *Elements of Fossilology* (1776).

**Edwards, George Wharton.** 1859–1950. American portrait and mural painter; well known as illustrator; illustrated many books of his travels, as *Thumbnail Sketches* (1886), *Belgium Old and New* (1920), *Constantinople* (1929–30).

**Edwards, Harry Stillwell.** 1855–1938. American journalist and writer; author of *Sons and Fathers* (awarded Chicago *Record* $10,000 prize, 1896), *Fifth Dimension* (1912), *Æneas Africanus* (1919), *Little Legends of the Land* (verse, 1930), etc.

**Edwards, John.** 1748–1837. American planter, b. in Stafford Co., Va.; moved (1780) to Kentucky section; prominent in activities leading to Kentucky's becoming a State; one of Kentucky's first two U.S. senators. His nephew **Ninian Edwards** (1775–1833) was chief justice, Kentucky court of appeals (1807); governor of Illinois Territory (1809–18); U.S. senator from Illinois (1818–24); governor of Illinois (1826–30). Ninian's son **Ninian Wirt** (1809–1889) was first superintendent of public instruction in Illinois (1854–57); secured passage (1855) of law that laid foundation of state's school system; friend of Lincoln; at his house Lincoln first met Mary Todd, sister of Edwards's wife, and in his house they were married.

**Edwards, Jonathan.** 1703–1758. American Congregational clergyman and theologian, b. East Windsor, Conn. Grad. Yale (1720). Became colleague and (1729) successor of his grandfather Solomon Stoddard in Northampton, Mass.; accepted central Calvinistic doctrine of absolute divine sovereignty and supreme right to bestow eternal salvation or damnation, and ardently opposed Arminian theology; became widely known as powerful preacher. Led a revival (1734–35) that spread throughout the county and into parts of Connecticut and resulted in morbid impulses toward suicide on the part of some converts; turned in his sermons to theme of Christian love, as in the series *Charity and Its Fruits* (1738; pub. 1751). Published (1737) *A Faithful Narrative of the Surprising Work of God in the Conversion of Many Hundred Souls in Northampton, and the Neighboring Towns and Villages*, which prepared way for great social response to tour of George Whitefield (1740–42). After revival of 1740 had produced social and church divisions, Edwards preached a series of sermons (1742–43) setting forth his psychology of religion. Dismissed

(July, 1750) after long dispute with his congregation over the terms of admission to full membership in the church, on which Edwards held scrupulously to his theological views. Accepted (1751) pastorate, as missionary to the Indians, at Stockbridge, Mass., where he wrote and published (1754) his treatise on the *Freedom of the Will.* President (1757–58) of the College of New Jersey (now Princeton U.). Elected to American Hall of Fame (1900). His second son, **Jonathan** (1745–1801), b. Northampton, grad. Princeton (1765), was pastor of White Haven Church, New Haven, Conn. (1769–95), and president of Union College, Schenectady (1799–1801). Another son, **Pierpont** (1750–1826), b. Northampton, was a delegate from Connecticut to Continental Congress (1787–88), judge of district court of Conn. (1806–26), and member of constitutional convention (1818) that drafted new constitution for Conn. Pierpont's son **Henry Waggaman** (1779–1847), b. New Haven, was governor of Conn. (1833, 1835–38).

**Edwards, Lewis.** 1809–1887. Welsh Calvinistic Methodist; principal of Bala Coll. (1837–87), North Wales, and lecturer on classics, ethics, metaphysics, and theology; one of outstanding educators of modern Wales.

**Edwards, Milne.** See MILNE-EDWARDS.

**Edwards, Ninian** *and* **Ninian Wirt.** See under John EDWARDS.

**Edwards, Richard.** 1523?–1566. English playwright and poet; M.A., Oxon. (1547); master of the children of Chapel Royal (1561). Author of *Palamon and Arcite,* performed before Queen Elizabeth (1566), and one extant play, *Damon and Pithias* (1571).

**Ed'win** (ĕd'wĭn) *or* **Ead'wi'ne** (â'ȧd·wĭ'nĕ). *Lat.* **Ae'du·i'nus** (ē'dū̇·ī'nŭs; ĕd'ū̇-). 585?–633. King of Northumbria. Son of Ælla, King of Deira (559–588). Expelled by Æthelfrith of Bernicia; with help of Redwald, King of East Anglia, defeated Æthelfrith (617) and formed a united Northumbria extending as far north as Edinburgh; m. (625) Æthelburh, sister of Eadbald, King of Kent; converted to Christianity by Paulinus, whom he made archbishop of York; defeated and slain by Caedwalla of North Wales and Penda of Mercia.

**Ed'wy** (ĕd'wĭ) *or* **Ead'wig** (â'ȧd·wē'y'). *Called* **the Fair.** d. 959. King of the English (955–959). Eldest son of Edmund the Magnificent. Succeeded his uncle Edred; resenting interference of Dunstan in his proposed marriage with Ælfgifu, daughter of his reputed foster mother, Æthelgifu, exiled Dunstan; forced to yield up country north of Thames to his brother Edgar (957).

**Eeck'hout** (āk'hout), **Gerbrand van den.** 1621–1674. Dutch portrait, genre, and Biblical painter in Amsterdam. Pupil and imitator of Rembrandt (1635–40).

**Ee'den** (ā'dĕn), **Frederik van.** 1860–1932. Dutch poet, writer, and neurologist. Cofounder of the organ of the younger group of writers *De Nieuwe Gids* (1885); author of *Little Johannes* (story of animal life; 3 parts, 1886–1906), *The Deeps of Deliverance* (psychological novel, 1900), *Ellen* (cycle of elegies, 1891), the historical drama *Lioba* (1897), and of lyric poetry, sociological and satirical plays, etc.

**Eek'houd** (āk'hout), **Georges** (zhôrzh). 1854–1927. Belgian novelist and poet, b. Amsterdam. Cofounder of literary journal *La Jeune Belgique* (1881); author of collections of romantic poems, and of realistic and historical novels and short stories of Flemish life.

**Ef'fiat'** (ā'fyā'), Marquis **d'. Antoine Coif'fier'** (kwȧ'fyā'). *Known as* **Ru'zé'** (rü'zā'). 1581–1632. Father of Cinq-Mars. French diplomat and soldier; negotiated marriage of Charles I of England with Princess Henrietta Maria. Took part in siege of La Rochelle; created marshal of France (1631).

**Ef'fing·ham** (ĕf'ĭng·ăm), Earl of. See *Kenneth Alexander Howard,* under HOWARD family.

**Ef'ros** (ĕf'rŏs), **Israel Isaac.** 1891– . Jewish Semitic scholar, theologian, and poet, b. in Volhynia, Poland; to U.S. (1906). Founder and dean, Baltimore Hebrew College (1917–28); professor of Semitics, Buffalo U. (1928–40); assoc. professor, Hunter Coll. (from 1940); collaborator on *English-Hebrew Dictionary* (1929).

**Égalité, Philippe-.** See ORLÉANS, 4.

**E'gan** (ē'găn), **Maurice Francis.** 1852–1924. American writer and diplomat, b. Philadelphia. Journalist and editor in Philadelphia and New York (till 1888); professor of English, Notre Dame U. (1888–96), Catholic U., Washington (1896–1907). Minister to Denmark (1907); instrumental in negotiating purchase by U.S. of Danish West Indies, now American Virgin Islands (1916). Author of a series of stories about an Irish-American character, Sexton Maginnis (1902–05).

**Egan, Patrick.** 1841–1919. Politician and diplomat, b. Ballymahon, Co. Longford, Ireland. One of organizers of Home Rule League; migrated to U.S. (1883); U.S. citizen (1888). One of three who called the Irish convention at Philadelphia (1883) which organized Irish National League of America; president of league (1884–86). U.S. minister to Chile (1888 ff.).

**Egan, Pierce.** 1772–1849. English sports writer. Wrote, set, and printed *The Mistress of Royalty* (1814), concerning the prince regent and Perdita (Mary) Robinson; author of *Boxiana, or Sketches of Modern Pugilism* (1818–24), *Tom and Jerry, or Life in London* (1821), *Book of Sports* (1832); provided slang phrases for Grose's *Dictionary of the Vulgar Tongue* (1823). His son **Pierce** (1814–1880) executed etchings for his father's *The Pilgrims of the Thames* (1837), and wrote many novels of the type of *Eve, or the Angel of Innocence* (1867) and *The Poor Girl* (1862–63).

**E·ga'ña** (ā·gä'nyä), **Juan.** 1769–1836. Spanish American jurist, statesman, and writer, b. Lima, Peru. To Santiago, Chile, to practice law; one of leaders of Chilean revolution (1810); president, constituent congress of Chile (1823); planned Chilean constitution. His works, collected in 10 vols., include poems, educational textbooks, and essays.

**Egbert** *or* **Ecg'berht** (ĕj'bĕrKt) *or* **Ecg'bryht** (ĕj'brüKt). 775?–839. King of West Saxons (802–839). Son of an underking of Kent, whose ancestors were early kings of Wessex. Forced into exile by Offa of Mercia and his son-in-law, spent youth at court of Charlemagne; became king (802), regained kingdom of Kent, conquered Cornish, gained submission of Mercia (828), was recognized as Bretwalda; first to bring all English peoples under one overlord; repelled Scandinavian invasion by victory at Hingston Down (837).

**E'ge·de** (ā'gĕ·dĕ), **Hans.** 1686–1758. Norwegian missionary to Eskimos of Greenland; stationed among Eskimos of Danish Greenland (1721–36); to Copenhagen (1736), where he founded a seminary for training missionaries to Greenland, and became superintendent of Greenland mission (1740). His son **Paul** (1708–1789) succeeded him in the Greenland mission, and as director of the seminary.

**E'gel·haaf** (ā'gĕl·häf), **Gottlob.** 1848–1934. German literary historian.

**Eg'er·ton** (ĕj'ĕr·t'n; -tŭn). Name of English family including earls and dukes of Bridgewater, earls of Ellesmere, and their descendants, among them the following: Sir **Thomas Egerton** (1540?–1617), Baron **Elles'mere** (ĕlz'mēr) and Viscount **Brack'ley** (brăk'lĭ); statesman and judge; educ. Oxford; solicitor general (1581); friend of Francis Bacon and Essex; took a leading role in trial of Mary, Queen of Scots (1586); adjured Essex to desist from rebellion (1601); lord chancellor (1603–17); gained victory for chancellor's court of equity over Sir Edward Coke, proponent of the common law (1616); left legal treatises in manuscript. His son **John** (1579–1649), created (1617) 1st earl of **Bridge'wa'ter** (brĭj'wô'tẽr; -wŏt'ẽr); privy councilor (1626); his induction as lord lieutenant of Wales occasion for which Milton's *Comus* was written and first acted at Ludlow Castle (1634), with earl's son **John** (1622–1686), 2nd earl, as the elder brother. **John** (1646–1701), 3d earl; son of 2d earl; first lord of the admiralty (1699); lord justice of the kingdom (1699). **Francis** (1736–1803), 3d Duke of Bridgewater; pioneer in British inland navigation; employed James Brindley to construct first canal in England entirely independent of a natural stream (1760), from Worsley to Manchester for transport of coal from his collieries. **Francis Henry** (1756–1829), 8th earl; clergyman and antiquarian; son and grandson of bishops; left £8000 for best work on "Goodness of God as manifested in the Creation," which was allotted eventually to authors of eight separate treatises (Bridgewater Treatises) republished in Bohn Scientific Library. **Francis** (1800–1857), 1st Earl of Ellesmere (cr. 1846) and Viscount Brackley; orig. surname **Leveson-Gower;** 2d son of George Granville Leveson-Gower (*q.v.*), 1st Duke of Sutherland; hence, grandnephew of 3d duke of Bridgewater and second beneficiary of Bridgewater estates; educ. Oxford; spoke in Parliament for free trade (1822–46); Irish secretary (1828–30); secretary for war (1830); took name Egerton (1833); author of graceful poems; translator of *Faust* (1823); munificent patron of artists, adding to Bridgewater galleries; left personal reminiscences of duke of Wellington (pub. 1904). **Hugh Edward** (1855–1927); historian; descendant of 2d earl of Bridgewater; occupied Beit chair of colonial history, Oxford (1905–20).

**Egerton, George.** *Pseudonym of* **Mary Chavelita Dunne.** 1859–1945. Australian writer, b. Melbourne; daughter of Capt. John J. Dunne; m. 1st (1888) H. H. Melville (d. 1889); 2d (1891) Egerton Clairmonte (d. 1901), author of *The Africander;* 3d (1901) Reginald Golding Bright (d. 1941). Author of *Keynotes* (1893), *The Wheel of God* (1898), *Flies in Amber* (1905), and of plays and adaptations of plays.

**Egestorff, Georg.** Pseudonym of Baron Georg von OMPTEDA.

**Egg** (ĕg), **Augustus Leopold.** 1816–1863. English genre painter; traveled with Dickens and Wilkie Collins (1853); actor in Dickens's company of amateurs.

**Eg'ge** (ăg'gĕ), **Peter.** 1869–1959. Norwegian realistic writer, representative of modern Norwegian literature; author of novels, folk stories, and plays.

**Eg'gen·berg** (ĕg'ĕn·bĕrK), Prince **Hans Ulrich von.** 1568–1634. Austrian statesman; chancellor to Emperor Ferdinand II, and director of imperial policy during earlier part of Thirty Years' War.

**Eg'ger'** (ā'gâr'), **Émile.** 1813–1885. French philologist and Hellenist; author of *Essai sur l'Histoire de la Critique chez les Grecs* (1849), etc.

**Eg'gers** (ĕg'ẽrz), **George William.** 1883–1958. American art teacher, at Chicago Normal Coll. (1906–16), Art Institute of Chicago (1917–21), Denver Art Museum (1921–26), Worcester, Mass., Art Museum (1926–30). Professor of art, C.C.N.Y. (from 1930). Art editor, *Webster's New International Dictionary, Second Edition.*

**Eg'ge·stein** (ĕg'ĕ·shtīn), **Heinrich.** d. about 1483. Printer in Strasbourg, b. in Alsace; printed *Decretum Gratiani* (1471).

**Eg'gle·ston** (ĕg''l·stŭn), **Edward.** 1837–1902. American author, b. Vevay, Ind. Bible agent and Methodist pastor, in Minnesota (1858–66). *The Hoosier Schoolmaster* (pub. in *Hearth and Home*, 1871) first of a long list of works of fiction, including: *The End of the World* (1872), *The Circuit Rider* (1873–74), *Roxy* (1877–78), *The Hoosier Schoolboy* (1881–82), *The Graysons* (1887–88), *The Faith Doctor* (1891), and short stories. His brother **George Cary** (1839–1911), b. Vevay, Ind., was a journalist and novelist; taught school in Indiana; served in Confederate army; pursued journalistic career in New York (1870–1900). Author of: (1) boys' books: *Big Brother Series* (1875–82), *Strange Stories from History* (1886); (2) novels: *A Man of Honor* (1873), *Dorothy South* (1902), *The Master of Warlock* (1903), *Evelyn Byrd* (1904); (3) biography and history: *A Rebel's Recollections* (1874), *The First of the Hoosiers: Reminiscences of Edward Eggleston* (1903), *Recollections of a Varied Life* (1910), *The History of the Confederate War* (2 vols., 1910).

**E'gill Skall'a·gríms'son** (ā'gĭd·'l skäd''l·ä·grēms'sŏn). 900?–?980. Icelandic scald and adventurer. Forced to emigrate after Harold Fairhair's victory; fought in service of English king Athelstan (925 ff.); returned to Norway and sought revenge by killing son of Eric Bloodaxe, successor to Harold (934); taken prisoner, but regained liberty by poem in praise of the king *Höfudhlauson* (*the Redemption of the Head*); became blind; retired to Mosfell (978). Author of the sagas *Sonatorrek*, on the death of his own son, *Arinbjarnardrápa* (975), and *Skjaldardrápa*. His experiences are described in the Icelandic poem *Egill's Saga.*

**E'gils·son** (ā'gĭls·sŏn), **Sveinbjörn.** 1791–1852. Icelandic philologist and poet. Compiler of the dictionary of Norse poetry *Lexicon Poeticum Antiquae Linguae Septentrionalis* (1854–60).

**Eginhard.** See EINHARD.

**Eg'le·ston** (ĕg''l·stŭn), **Thomas.** 1832–1900. American mineralogist, b. New York City. Founded (1864) School of Mines of Columbia College, first school of its kind in U.S.

**Eg'li** (ĕg'lē), **Henry.** 1824–1890. Mennonite leader, b. in Baden, Ger.; to U.S. (1837); ordained Amish-Mennonite minister (1854) and bishop (1858). Withdrew from Amish-Mennonite connection (1866) and formed a church known as the "Defenseless Mennonites."

**Egli, Johann Heinrich.** 1742–1810. Swiss composer of sacred and secular songs.

**Eglinton** *or* **Eglintoun,** Earls of. See MONTGOMERIE family.

**Eglinton, John.** Pseudonym of William Kirkpatrick MAGEE.

**Eg'loff** (ĕg'lŏf), **Gustav.** 1886–1955. American chemist, b. New York City; expert in petroleum chemistry; devised multiple-coil process for cracking crude oil that increases the yield of high-octane gasoline; discovered a way of making rubber from butane gas.

**Eg'mont** (*Du.* ĕK'mônt; *Angl.* ĕg'mŏnt, -mŭnt) *or* **Eg'mond** (*Du.* ĕK'mônt; *Angl.* ĕg'mŏnd, -mŭnd). Name of family prominent in history of the Netherlands during the 15th and 16th centuries, including: (1) **John II** (d. 1452). (2) His grandson **John III**, 1st Count of **Egmont** (1486). (3) His great-grandson **Charles** (1470–1538), Duke of **Guel'dre** (gĕl'dr'); spent life trying to regain duchy of Gueldre that had been lost to Charles the Bold of Burgundy; at first, leagued with France; later (1537), forced to yield to Emperor Charles V. (4) In direct descent from **Frederick**, brother of John III, **Anna van Bu'ren** [vän bü'rĕn] (d. 1558), first wife (m. 1551) of William, Count of Nassau. (5) **John IV** (d. 1528), son of John III; acquired county of **Ga'vre** (gȧ'vr'), later (1540) erected into a principality; one of his children was Lamoral (see entry below); another, **Marguerite**

(m. Nicolas de Lorraine, Comte de Vaudémont), was mother of Louis de Lorraine (1553–1601), wife of King Henry III of France.

**Eg′mont** (ĕg′mŏnt; -mŭnt), Earls of. See under Sir John PERCEVAL.

**Eg′mont** (ĕκ′mônt; *Angl.* ĕg′mŏnt, -mŭnt), **Joost van.** 1602–1674. Dutch portrait and historical painter; court painter to Louis XIII and Louis XIV and one of first members of Academy of Painting and Sculpture (1648).

**Egmont, Lamoral,** Comte **d'.** 1522–1568. Flemish general and statesman, b. in Hainaut. Prince of **Ga′vre** (gȧ′vr′); son of John IV of Egmont. Conducted negotiations (1554) for marriage of Philip of Spain with Mary Tudor; served brilliantly in war between Spain and France (1557–59), esp. at battles of St. Quentin and Gravelines. Became an enemy of the duke of Alva, but was looked upon by his countrymen as a leader; refused to march against the Flemings; stadholder of Flanders and Artois (1559–67); joined William of Orange in protests to Spain (1561–64); on special mission to Spain (1565) to inform Philip of affairs in Netherlands. Arrested by Alva and condemned to death (1567) by Council of Blood; with Count Horn, executed at Brussels, their deaths leading to revolt of Netherlands; event made theme of Goethe's drama *Egmont* (1788).

**Egremont,** Earls of. See WYNDHAM.

**E′he·berg** (ā′ĕ·bĕrκ), **Karl Theodor von.** 1855–1941. German political economist; professor, Erlangen (from 1882); author of *Finanzwissenschaft* (1901), etc.

**Eh′ren·berg** (ā′rĕn·bĕrκ), **Christian Gottfried.** 1795–1876. German naturalist; known esp. for investigations and publications dealing with infusoria.

**Ehrenberg, Richard.** 1857–1921. German political economist.

**Eh′ren·burg** (ā′rĕn·bŏŏrκ), **Ilya Grigorievich.** 1891–1967. Russian writer, b. Kiev. Joined Bolshevist party (1906); arrested (1908), but escaped to Paris (1909–17). Returned to Russia after Bolshevik revolution, but later (after 1921) again resided in Paris. Among his works are *Poems* (1921),...*Nicholas Kourbov* (1922), *Street in Moscow* (1927), *Michael Lykow* (1929), *Factory of Dreams* (1931), and many short stories.

**Ehrencron-Kidde, Astrid.** See under Harald KIDDE.

**Eh′ren·fels** (ā′rĕn·fĕls), Baron **Christian von.** 1859–1932. German philosopher; introduced the term *Gestalt* into psychology; chief work, *System der Werttheorie* (2 vols., 1897–98).

**Eh′ren·svärd′** (â′rĕn·svârd′). Name of a Swedish family of German origin including: Count **Augustin Ehrensvärd** (1710–1772), field marshal and military engineer; built fortifications of Sveaborg (1749) and created Swedish coast fleet (1756); commanded briefly in Seven Years' War (1761–62). His son Count **Karl August** (1745–1800), admiral and art critic; commanded in 1st naval battle of Russian war at Svensksund (1789) and was dismissed following defeat; chief commander of navy (1792–94) following death of Gustavus III; resigned to devote life to science and the arts. Augustin's grandson Count **Albert Karl August Lars** (1821–1901), statesman, champion of free trade and liberalism; foreign minister (1885–89).

**Eh′ret** (ā′rĕt), **George Dionysius.** 1710–1770. German botanical illustrator in England; friend of Linnaeus, whose *Hortus Cliffortianus* he illustrated.

**Ehr′hard** (âr′härt), **Albert.** 1862–1940. German Roman Catholic theologian.

**Ehr′le** (âr′lĕ), **Franz.** 1845–1934. German Jesuit scholar, cardinal, and historian.

**Ehr′lich** (âr′lĭκ), **Ar′nold** (är′n'ld) **Bo·gu′mil** (bô·gōō′-mēl). 1848–1919. Bible scholar, b. Włodawa, Poland; to U.S. (1878). Author of important works in field of Old Testament exegesis.

**Ehr′lich** (âr′lĭκ), **Heinrich.** 1822–1899. Austrian pianist, critic, and writer.

**Ehrlich, Paul.** 1854–1915. German bacteriologist; pioneer in modern immunology and chemotherapy; b. in Silesia. Conducted researches in histology of the blood and in immunity; proposed the side-chain theory as a chemical explanation of immunity; developed methods for staining the tubercle bacillus, living nerves, etc.; worked on standardization of diphtheria antitoxin; discovered "606" (Salvarsan, or arsphenamine), a specific remedy for syphilis (1909). Awarded, jointly with E. Metchnikoff, 1908 Nobel prize for physiology and medicine. See Kiyoshi SHIGA and Sahachiro HATA.

**Eich′berg** (īκ′bĕrκ), **Julius.** 1824–1893. Musician and composer, b. Düsseldorf, Germany; to U.S. (1857); musical leader at Boston Museum (1859–67); established Boston Conservatory of Music (1867); its director (1870–72). Composer of works for violin and piano, of songs and vocal pieces, and of operettas.

**Ei′chel·ber′ger** (ī′kĕl·bûr′gẽr), **William Snyder.** 1865–1951. American astronomer, b. Baltimore. Known esp. for work on the positions and proper motions of standard stars. See F. B. LITTELL.

**Ei′chen·dorff** (ī′κĕn·dôrf), Baron **Joseph von.** 1788–1857. German Roman Catholic lyric poet, novelist, and critic; joined religious Romanticist group of Friedrich and Dorothea Schlegel; government councilor on Roman Catholic affairs in Prussian ministry of public worship and education, Berlin (1831–44); settled in Neisse (1855). Author of romances and tales, lyric and narrative poems, and romantic tragedies and comedies.

**Eich′horn** (īκ′hôrn), **Johann Albrecht Friedrich.** 1779–1856. Prussian statesman; entered central government after battle of Leipzig (1813); member of state council (1817); director in foreign ministry (1831), where he helped develop the Zollverein; championed religious orthodoxy as minister of culture (1840–48). His grandson **Hermann von Eichhorn** (1848–1918), field marshal, led 10th army against Russia in World War I (1915); commanded the Eichhorn military group in Kurland (1916–18), later the Kiev group.

**Eichhorn, Johann Gottfried.** 1752–1827. German Protestant theologian, Orientalist, and historian; author of first purely literary historical treatment of the Biblical writings, and of works on Oriental philology, literary history, world history, etc. His son **Karl Friedrich** (1781–1854) was a jurist, founder of the historical school of German law.

**Eich′ler** (īκ′lẽr), **August Wilhelm.** 1839–1887. German botanist; known for descriptions of Brazilian plants and for comparative studies of the structure of flowers.

**Eich′mann** (īκ′män), **Karl Adolf.** 1906–1962. German Nazi leader. Convicted (1961) and executed in Israel for crimes committed during World War II.

**Eich′rodt** (īκ′rōt), **Ludwig.** *Pseudonym* **Rudolf Rodt** (rōt). 1827–1892. German humorous poet and jurist; author of the cycle *Wanderlust* in *Fliegende Blätter* (1848), and of *Gedichte in Allerlei Humoren* (1853).

**Eichstätt,** Prince of. See Eugène de BEAUHARNAIS.

**Eich′wald** (īκ′vält), **Karl Eduard.** 1795–1876. Russian naturalist and traveler; professor of zoology, mineralogy, and medicine, St. Petersburg (1838).

**Eick′e·mey′er** (ī′kĕ·mī′ẽr), **Rudolf.** 1831–1895. Inventor, b. Altenbamberg, Bavaria; to U.S. (1850). Patented about 150 inventions, including hat-manufacturing machinery that helped revolutionize this industry, differential gear for mowing and reaping machine (1870), many electrical machines and devices (first symmetrical drum armature, iron-clad dynamo, direct-connected railway motor, etc.). Discovered and was first employer of Charles P. Steinmetz.

**Eid'litz** (īd'lĭts), **Leopold.** 1823–1908. Architect, b. Prague; to New York (1843). Exponent of "Gothic revival"; built many churches and houses in Gothic style; redesigned State Capitol at Albany, N.Y. His son **Cyrus Lazelle Warner** (1853–1921) was architect of Dearborn Station in Chicago, public library in Buffalo, and New York Times building in New York City.

**Ei'el·sen** (ī'ĕl·sĕn), **Elling.** 1804–1883. Religious leader, b. Voss, Norway; to U.S. (1839); settled at Fox River, Ill. Conducted religious services in his own house; also preached at new settlements in northern Middle West and Texas, and did missionary work among Indians; organized (1846) the Evangelical Lutheran Church of America.

**Eif'fel'** (ĕ'fĕl'; *Angl.* ī'fĕl), **Alexandre Gustave.** 1832–1923. French engineer; one of the founders of aerodynamics. Constructed iron bridge over the Garonne (1858), the railway bridge over the Douro at Oporto, etc.; also, the framework for Bartholdi's Statue of Liberty and the Eiffel tower in Paris (1887–89) for which he is chiefly known. Designed locks for Panama Canal; founded first laboratory of aerodynamics, at Auteuil (1912); investigated effects of air currents on airplanes.

**Ei'gen** (ī'gĕn), **Manfred.** 1927– . German physical chemist. Awarded Nobel prize in chemistry (1967) with R. Norrish and G. Porter.

**Ei'gen·mann** (ī'gĕn·män), **Carl H.** 1863–1927. Ichthyologist, b. Flehingen, Germany; to U.S. (1877); m. (1887) Rosa Smith, his collaborator in studies of South American catfishes (1888) and of California fishes.

**Eijk'man** (īk'män), **Christiaan.** 1858–1930. Dutch hygienist; army surgeon on expedition to Netherlands Indies to investigate beriberi (1886); director of pathological laboratory in Batavia (1888–96); first person to produce a dietary deficiency disease experimentally, when by feeding fowl a diet consisting exclusively of polished rice, he produced a disease resembling beriberi in human beings; recognized that the disease in fowl was caused by lack of essential food factor (later called antineuritic vitamin). Awarded, with Sir F. G. Hopkins, 1929 Nobel prize for physiology and medicine.

**Ei'ke von Rep'gow** (ī'kĕ fōn rĕp'gō) *or* **Rep'kow** (-kō). *Variant spellings* **Ey'ke** (ī'kĕ), **Ei'ko** (ī'kō), **Ec'co** (ĕk'ō), **Eb'ko** (ĕp'kō). 13th-century Saxon nobleman, jurist, and writer; author in Latin of *Sachsenspiegel*, a treatise on the law of the Saxons, the beginning of German law writing (1220); reputed author of *Sächsische Weltchronik* (pub. 1877).

**Eil'hart von O'ber'ge** (īl'härt fōn ō'bĕr'gĕ). fl. late 12th and early 13th century. Middle High German poet; author (from French sources) of the romantic epic *Tristrant und Isalde* (c. 1180), first German version of *Tristan and Isolde*.

**Eil·she'mi·us** (īl·shē'mĭ·ŭs), **Louis Michel.** 1864–1941. American painter.

**Ei'nem** (ī'nĕm), **Karl von.** *Called also* **Karl von Roth'ma'ler** (rōt'mä'lĕr). 1853–1934. German colonel general; Prussian minister of war (1903–09); built up Prussian army. Commander in World War I (1914).

**Ein'hard** (īn'härt). Incorrectly **E'gin·hard** (ā'gĭn-härt). 770?–840. Frankish secretary and biographer of Charlemagne, and architect. Minister of public works to Charlemagne; retained favor under Louis the Pious (until 830) and became abbot of various monasteries.

**Ein'horn** (īn'hôrn), **David.** 1809–1879. Rabbi, b. Dispeck, Bavaria; to U.S. (1855). A leading theologian of reform Judaism in U.S.

**Ein'stein** (īn'shtīn; *Angl.* -stīn), **Albert.** 1879–1955. Theoretical physicist, b. Ulm, Germany; naturalized Swiss at age of 15. Professor, Zurich (1909–11), Deutsche U., Prague (1911–12), invited to Berlin by Prussian Academy of Sciences, adopted German citizenship, and became professor, U. of Berlin (1914). Director, Kaiser Wilhelm Physical Institute, Berlin (1914). To U.S. (1933); member, Institute for Advanced Study, Princeton (1933–45). Deprived of German citizenship and property confiscated by the Nazi government (1934); became naturalized American citizen. Enunciated theory of relativity, publishing account of special theory of relativity (1905) and of general theory (1916), papers on a unified field theory which seeks to include in a single mathematical formula the laws of electromagnetism and gravitation (1929); explained Brownian movement and gave formula for it; deduced influence of gravity on propagation of light; developed law of photoelectric effect to explain transformation of light quanta. Awarded 1921 Nobel prize for physics (1922). Author of *The Meaning of Relativity* (1923), *Builders of the Universe* (1932), *On the Method of Theoretical Physics* (1933), *Why War?* (with Freud, 1933), *The World As I See It* (1934), *The Evolution of Physics* (with L. Infeld, 1938), etc.

**Einstein, Alfred.** 1880–1952. German music scholar, critic, and editor; became American citizen (1945).

**Eint'ho'ven** (īnt'hō'vĕn), **Willem.** 1860–1927. Dutch physiologist; professor, Leiden (from 1886). Invented a string galvanometer that served as the basis for the electrocardiograph; awarded the 1924 Nobel prize for physiology and medicine.

**Ei'se·len** (ī'zĕ·lĕn), **Ernst Wilhelm Bernhard.** 1793–1846. German promoter of gymnastics.

**Ei'sen·how'er** (ī'z'n·hou'ēr), **Dwight David.** 1890–1969. Thirty-fourth president of the U.S., b. Denison, Texas; grad. U.S.M.A., West Point (1915); member, American military mission to Philippine Islands (1935–39); brigadier general (1941); chief of war plans division, U.S. general staff (Feb., 1942); lieutenant general (July, 1942), commander in chief of U.S. forces in European theater; commander of allied forces in Northwest Africa (1942); general, supreme allied commander in North Africa (1943) and in western Mediterranean (1943); commander in chief of allied forces in western Europe (from Dec., 1943); general of the army (1944); U.S. member of Allied Control Commission for Germany; chief of staff of U.S. Army (1945–48); president of Columbia Univ. (1948–53); supreme commander, Western European Defense Force (1951–52). President of the U.S. (1953–61). Author of *Mandate for Change* (1963).

**Ei'sen·stein** (ī'zĕn·shtīn), **Ferdinand Gottfried Max.** 1823–1852. German mathematician; known esp. for work on theory of functions and theory of numbers.

**Ei'sen·stein** (ī'zyĭn·shtūĭn), **Sergei Mikhailovich.** 1898–1948. Russian theater director and motion-picture producer, in Paris and Hollywood (1931).

**Eis'ler** (īs'lĕr), **Rudolf.** 1873–1926. Austrian writer on philosophy; disciple of Wundt and Kant.

**Eis'ner** (īs'nĕr), **Kurt.** 1867–1919. German journalist, politician, and Socialist leader in Bavaria, b. in Berlin of Jewish parents; educ. Marburg. On staff of *Frankfurter Zeitung* (1892–93); editor of *Vorwärts*, Berlin (1899); editor in chief of Socialist *Fränkische Tagespost*, Nuremberg (1907–10); Social Democratic writer in Munich. In World War supported government at first, but later (1917) supported Independents; organized Munich revolution which overthrew monarchy (1918) and became first minister president of Bavarian republic; championed separatism; publicly admitted German war guilt; assassinated by Count Arco-Valley.

**Ei'tel·ber'ger von E'del·berg** (ī'tĕl·bĕr'gĕr fōn ā'dĕl-bĕrk), **Rudolf.** 1817–1885. Austrian art historian; founder and director, Austrian Museum of Art and Industry (1864).

**Eit'ner** (īt'nĕr), **Robert.** 1832–1905. German music historian and composer; composed Biblical opera *Judith*, a cantata, piano works, songs, etc.

**Eitoku.** See KANO.

**Ekaterina.** Russian form of CATHERINE.

**E'ke·lund'** (ā'kĕ·lŭnd'), **Vilhelm.** 1880–1949. Swedish poet and essayist.

**Ek'hof** *or* **Eck'hof** (ĕk'hōf), **Konrad.** 1720–1778. German actor; a founder of modern German theater and exponent of realistic school of acting.

**Ekkehard von Aura.** See under FRUTOLF.

**Elagabalus.** = HELIOGABALUS.

**E'lah** (ē'lȧ). *In Douay Bible* **E'la.** King of Israel (c. 888–887 B.C.); son of Baasha; slain by Zimri, one of his generals (*1 Kings* xvi. 6–10).

**El'bo'gen** (ĕl'bō'gĕn), **Ismar.** 1874–1943. German Jewish scholar; professor (1919–33), Jewish Inst., Berlin. Assoc. editor, *Encyclopaedia Judaica* and *Germania Judaica.*

**El Cano** *or* **Elcano, Juan Sebastián de.** See CANO.

**Elcho,** Lord. See earl of WEMYSS.

**El'der** (ĕl'dĕr), **John.** 1824–1869. Scottish marine engineer and shipbuilder; inventor of the compound reciprocating steam engine.

**El'der'** (ĕl'dâr'), **Marc.** Pseudonym of Marcel TENDRON.

**El'der** (ĕl'dĕr), Sir **Thomas.** 1818–1897. Scottish merchant in Australia; to Adelaide, S. Australia (1854) to take over management of business of Elder & Co., founded (c. 1840) by his older brother **Alexander** (1815–1885). Admitted brother-in-law Robert Barr Smith to partnership, and reorganized firm as Elder, Smith & Co. Benefactor of U. of Adelaide, the Adelaide museum, the zoological gardens, the National Gallery.

**El'don** (ĕl'dŭn), 1st Earl of. **John Scott.** 1751–1838. English justice. M.P. (1782); supporter of Pitt and object of Sheridan's ridicule. Solicitor general (1788), attorney general (1793); prosecuted Horne Tooke. Chief justice of common pleas (1799); lord high chancellor of England (1801, almost continuously till 1827), the dominant member of the cabinet, resisting innovation, opponent of Roman Catholic emancipation and parliamentary reform; adopted vigorous policy against Napoleon. See Percy Bysshe SHELLEY and William SCOTT.

**El'ea·nor** (ĕl'ȧ·nĕr) **of Aq'ui·taine'** (ăk'wĭ·tān') *or* **of Gui'enne'** (gü·ē'yĕn'; gē'yĕn'). *Also* **A'li'e'nor'** (ȧ'lē'ā'nôr'). 1122?–1204. Queen of Louis VII of France (1137–52), and of Henry II of England. Known as "Damsel of Brittany." Succeeded her father, William X, as duchess of Aquitaine (1137); married by her father to Louis VII of France (1137); divorced on pretext of consanguinity (1152). m. (1152) Henry of Anjou, bringing to England part of Aquitaine, of which she was heiress, thereby setting up strife between England and France lasting some 400 years. Supported her sons in rebellion against her unfaithful husband (1173); held in honorable confinement (1173–85); secured succession of Richard I; frustrated John's attempted treacherous conspiracy with France during Richard's absence (1193); reconciled Richard and John on Richard's return; crushed an uprising in Anjou in favor of her grandson Arthur against her son King John (1199). Published compilation of maritime laws, *Laws of Oléron.* See LOUIS VII of France and HENRY II of England.

**Eleanor of Cas·tile'** (kăs·tēl'). d. 1290. Queen of Edward I of England. Daughter of Ferdinand III of Castile and Juana; m. Prince Edward (1254), bringing to English crown her mother's provinces of Ponthieu and Montreuil and a claim on Gascony; accompanied Edward I on Seventh Crusade (1270).

**Eleanor of Pro'vence'** (prô'väɴs'). d. 1291. Queen of Henry III of England. Daughter of Raymond Berenger IV, Count of Provence; m. Henry III (1236); accompanied him on expedition to Gascony (1242); joint governor of England with king's brother (1253); collected mercenaries to support Henry in Barons' War (1264).

**El'e·a'zar** (ĕl'ē·ā'zĕr). In Bible, third son of Aaron, whom he succeeded as high priest (*Num.* xx. 25–28); assisted Joshua in distributing Canaan among the tribes (*Josh.* xiv. 1); succeeded by his son Phinehas.

**Eleazar.** In the Apocrypha, son of Mattathias, and brother of Judas Maccabaeus (*1 Macc.* ii. 5). See MACCABEES.

**Éléonore.** French form of ELEANOR.

**El'ers** (*Angl.* ĕl'ĕrz; *Ger.* ā'lĕrs), **John Philip** and his brother **David.** fl. 1690–1730. English ceramists, of Saxon origin, who produced in Staffordshire a hard, red, unglazed earthenware (Elers ware).

**El'eu·the'ri·us** (ĕl'ū·thē̆r'ĭ·ŭs), Saint. Pope (bishop of Rome; 174–189).

**El'gar** (ĕl'gĕr; -gär), Sir **Edward.** 1857–1934. English composer; succeeded his father, **W. H. Elgar** (d. 1885), as organist of St. George's Roman Catholic Church in Worcester (1885; resigned 1890); settled in Malvern and devoted himself to composition. Notable compositions include oratorios *Dream of Gerontius* (1900) and *The Apostles* (1903), *Pomp and Circumstance* (march; 1902), *In the South* (concert overture; 1904), *The Kingdom* (oratorio; 1906), *Falstaff* (1913), symphonies, songs, sonatas, etc.

**Elgin,** Earls of. See BRUCE, English family.

**E'li** (ē'lī). *In Douay Version* **He'li** (hē'lī). In Bible, high priest of Israel (first of the line of Ithamar, youngest son of Aaron) and judge; dealt too leniently with his sons Hophni and Phinehas when they behaved scandalously; died after hearing of defeat of Israelites, death of his sons, and capture of the ark by the Philistines (*1 Sam.* i. 9 – iv. 18). Cf. SAMUEL.

**E'li·a** (ē'lĭ·ȧ). Pseudonym of Charles LAMB in *Essays of Elia.*

**E·li'a·kim** (ē·lī'ȧ·kĭm). = JEHOIAKIM (*2 Kings* xxiii. 34).

**Elias.** See ELIJAH.

**Elias ben Solomon** *or* **Elias** (*or* **Elijah**) **Wilna.** See WILNA.

**Elias Levita.** See LEVITA.

**El'i·bank** (ĕl'ĭ·băngk), Baron of. Title held by members of Scottish family, the Murrays of Blackbarony, Peeblesshire. See James MURRAY (1719–1794).

**Élie de Beaumont, Jean B. A. L. L.** See BEAUMONT.

**Eligius.** See ÉLOI.

**E·li'jah** (ē·lī'jȧ). *In Douay Version and in Authorized Version of New Testament* **E·li'as** (-ăs). A Hebrew prophet of 9th century B.C. Biblical account of his career (*1 Kings* xvii – *2 Kings* ii. 15) points to his era as one of great social and religious change, centering in continual struggle of Elijah against worship of Phoenician god Baal, supported by King Ahab and his wife Jezebel.

**Elijah Levita.** See LEVITA.

**el Inca.** See GARCILASO DE LA VEGA (1539?–1616).

**E·lí'o** (ā·lē'ō), **Francisco Javier.** 1767–1822. Spanish soldier; to Plata River (1805) as commander against English; recaptured Montevideo (1807); viceroy of Buenos Aires (1810). To Spain and commanded Catalonian and Valencian army (1812); governor of Murcia and Valencia (1813); deposed by Liberal insurgents (1822); executed (Sept. 4, 1822).

**El'i·ot** (ĕl'ĭ·ŭt; ĕl'yŭt). See also ELIOTT, ELLIOT, ELLIOTT, ELYOT.

**Eliot,** Sir **Charles Norton Edgcumbe.** 1862–1931. British diplomat and scholar; ambassador to Japan (1919–26). Author of *Letters from the Far East* (1907), *Hinduism and Buddhism* (1921), etc.

**Eliot, Charles William.** 1834–1926. American educator, b. Boston, Mass. Educ. Harvard. Assistant prof. of mathematics and chemistry, Harvard (1858–63); professor of chemistry, M.I.T. (1865–69); wrote articles on "The New Education: Its Organization" in *Atlantic Monthly* (1869). President of Harvard (1869–1909); promoted plan to embrace all undergraduate studies in Harvard College and gather about it complete group of graduate and professional schools; established exchange professorships with France and Germany; developed, though he did not inaugurate, "elective system" of undergraduate courses; reformed administration of athletics and helped introduce stricter intercollegiate eligibility rules. Organized graduate school of arts and sciences (1890); made divinity school nonsectarian; appointed C. C. Langdell to law-school faculty and co-operated with him in working out reforms in administration and instruction; raised medical-school standards. Co-operated in various steps leading to establishment of Radcliffe College (1894). Author of *The Happy Life* (1896), *Educational Reform* (1898), *The Religion of the Future* (1909), *The Durable Satisfactions of Life* (1910), *A Late Harvest* (posthumous, 1924); editor of the *Harvard Classics* ("five-foot shelf"). See F. H. STORER.

**Eliot, Edward Granville.** 3d Earl of **St. Ger'mans** (sănt jûr'mănz). 1798–1877. British diplomat. Descendant of Sir John Eliot (1592–1632). As envoy extraordinary to Spain, induced Carlists and Royalists to adopt Eliot convention providing for better treatment of prisoners of war (1834); chief secretary for Ireland (1841–45); postmaster general; lord lieutenant of Ireland (1852–55); confidential adviser of Queen Victoria.

**Eliot, George.** *Pseudonym of* **Mary Ann** *or* **Marian Evans.** 1819–1880. English novelist, b. in Warwickshire. Studied German, Italian, and music. After trip abroad, became asst. editor of *Westminster Review* (1851–53); acquainted with Herbert Spencer, Carlyle, Harriet Martineau. Formed (1854) with George Henry Lewes (*q.v.*) irregular relationship which she regarded as a marriage. Published in *Blackwood's Magazine* (1857), under name George Eliot, her first story, *The Sad Fortunes of the Rev. Amos Barton*, first of the *Scenes from Clerical Life* (2 vols., 1858); won success with *Adam Bede* (1859); continued success with *The Mill on the Floss* (1860) and *Silas Marner* (1861). After trip to Florence, published historical novel *Romola* (1863) and *Felix Holt the Radical* (1866); turned to poetry (1868–71) in the *Spanish Gypsy* (1868), *Agatha* (1869), and others; returned to fiction with *Middlemarch* (1872), and her last novel, *Daniel Deronda* (1874–76); after a collection of essays, *The Impressions of Theophrastus Such* (1878), followed by death of Lewes (1878), wrote no more; m. John W. Cross, New York banker (1880).

**Eliot, George Fielding.** 1894–1971. Army officer, author, and radio commentator, b. Brooklyn, N.Y. To Melbourne, Australia (1902); served with Australian contingent in World War I; engaged at the Dardanelles, Egypt, the Somme, Arras, Passchendaele, Amiens, and in piercing Hindenburg line. To U.S. and became reserve officer (major) in military intelligence division (1922–30). Author of *The Ramparts We Watch* (1938), *Bombs Bursting in Air* (1939), etc.

**Eliot,** Sir **John.** 1592–1632. English parliamentary statesman and orator. Supporter of Buckingham; urged enforcement of laws against Roman Catholics. As leader of House of Commons (1626), was alienated by Buckingham's bad faith; demanded inquiry into disaster at Cádiz; obtained deferment of grant of subsidies; carried Buckingham's impeachment to House of Lords, comparing him to Sejanus; imprisoned (1627) for refusing to pay a forced loan; insisted on acceptance of the Petition of Right (1628). Presented resolutions in House of Commons against king's right to levy tonnage and poundage and the king's innovations in religion (1629); imprisoned and fined £2000 (1630); died in prison. See John PYM.

**Eliot, John.** 1604–1690. "Apostle of the Indians," b. Widford, Hertfordshire, Eng. Migrated to Massachusetts (1631), and was teacher of the church at Roxbury for 60 years. Devoted himself also to work among the Indians; many of its results destroyed by King Philip's War. Author of *A Primer or Catechism, in the Massachusetts Indian Language* (1654), Indian translation of Bible (N.T. 1661, O.T. 1663–first Bible printed in North America), *Up-Bookum Psalmes* (1663), etc.

**Eliot, Thomas Stearns.** 1888–1965. Poet and critic, b. St. Louis, Mo.; resident, London, Eng. (from 1914); naturalized British citizen (1927); adopted Anglo-Catholicism. Author of *Prufrock and Other Observations* (1917), *Poems* (1919; containing 24 poems including *Portrait of a Lady* and *Sweeney Among the Nightingales*), *Ara Vos Prec* (verse; 1919), *The Sacred Wood* (critical essays; 1920), *The Waste Land* (poem, 1922; awarded the Dial prize in poetry), *An Essay of Poetic Drama* (1928), *Dante* (1929), *Ash Wednesday* (short series of poems; 1930), *Selected Essays* (1932), *After Strange Gods* (1934), *The Rock* (1934), *Elizabethan Essays* (1934), *Murder in the Cathedral* (play in blank verse; 1935), *Essays Ancient and Modern* (1936), *Four Quartets* (1943), etc. Awarded Nobel prize in literature (1948).

**El'i·ott** (ĕl'ĭ·ŭt; ĕl'yŭt), **George Augustus.** 1st Baron **Heath'field** (hēth'fēld). 1717–1790. Scottish soldier; governor of Gibraltar (1775), defended it heroically against Spaniards and French (1779–83).

**E'li·pan'do** (ā'lē·pän'dō). *Lat.* **El'i·pan'dus** (ĕl'ĭ·păn'dŭs). 717–?808. Archbishop of Toledo. His doctrine that Christ was son of God not by nature but by adoption (adoptionism) was condemned as heresy at the Council of Frankfort (794).

**E·lis'a·beth** *or* **E·liz'a·beth** (ē·lĭz'ȧ·bĕth). In Bible, mother of John the Baptist (*Luke* i. 5 ff.). A saint of Roman Catholic Church.

**Elisabeth.** 1876–1965. Queen of the Belgians (1909–34); dau. of Duke Charles Theodore of Bavaria; m. (1900) Prince Albert (later Albert I) of Belgium; devoted to charities; patriotic and of great aid to the king during World War I; lived in France (1914–18).

**Elisabeth Charlotte.** = CHARLOTTE ELISABETH.

**E·lis'a·beth Chris·tine' of Bruns'wick–Wol'fen·büt'tel** (ē·lĭz'ȧ·bĕth krĭs·tēn' [krĭs'tēn] ŭv brŭnz'wĭk-vŏl'fĕn·büt'ĕl; *Ger.* ā·lē'zä·bĕt krĭ·stē'nĕ). (1) 1691–1750. Empress of Germany as wife (m. 1708) of Emperor Charles VI; mother of Maria Theresa. (2) 1715–1797. Wife (m. 1733) of Frederick the Great of Prussia.

**É'li'sa'beth' de France'** (ā'lē'zȧ'bĕt' dē fräNs'), Madame. **Élisabeth Philippine Marie Hélène.** 1764–1794. Sister of King Louis XVI of France. Accompanied Louis XVI on attempted flight from France; captured with him at Varennes (June, 1791); executed (May 10, 1794). See EDGEWORTH DE FIRMONT.

**E·li'sha** (ē·lī'shȧ). *In Douay Version* **El'i·se'us** (ĕl'ĭ-sē'ŭs). In Bible, a Hebrew prophet, disciple and successor of Elijah (*1 Kings* xix. 16 ff.; *2 Kings* ii–xiii).

**E·liz'a·beth** (ē·lĭz'ȧ·bĕth). Saint. 1207–1231. Daughter

of Andrew II, King of Hungary (d. 1235), b. in Pressburg. Married (1221) Louis IV, Landgrave of Thuringia; devoted herself to religion and charitable works; on death of Louis driven from Thuringia (1227) by Henry Raspe (*q.v.*); found refuge with her uncle the bishop of Bamberg; later lived in seclusion at Marburg; believed to have performed miracles; canonized by Pope Gregory IX (1235). See also SOPHIA, Landgravine of Hesse.

**Elizabeth** Saint. See Saint ISABEL.

**Elizabeth.** *Full Ger. name* **Elisabeth Amalie Eugenie.** 1837–1898. Empress of Austria (1854–98), b. Munich. Daughter of Duke Maximilian Joseph of Bavaria; m. (1854) her cousin Emperor Francis Joseph I of Austria; became queen of Hungary (1867); popular with her people because of her beauty and charm and her philanthropies; assassinated by an Italian anarchist.

**Elizabeth.** *Also* **Elizabeth Stu′art** (stū′ẽrt). 1596–1662. Queen of Frederick V of Bohemia. Called "Queen of Hearts." Eldest daughter of James I of England; b. in Scotland; m. (1613) Frederick V, Elector Palatine, chosen king (1619); her marriage commemorated in *Epithalamium* by John Donne. On routing of Frederick V by the Catholic League (1620), took refuge at The Hague; lost her eldest son (1629) and her husband (1632); levied (1633) small army in behalf of her son Charles Louis, to whom was restored a portion of the Rhenish Palatinate by the Treaty of Westphalia (1648), and by whom she was deserted and forced to live on the generosity of Holland; returned to England (1661), despite opposition of her nephew Charles II, and was pensioned. Honored as a martyr to Protestantism; celebrated in poem by Sir Henry Wotton. Mother of thirteen children, including Sophia, mother of George I, King of Great Britain and Ireland. See John HARINGTON (d. 1613).

**Elizabeth.** *Sometimes known as* **Elizabeth of Bohemia.** 1618–1680. Princess palatine; daughter of Elector Palatine Frederick V, who was for a short time king of Bohemia. Abbess of Herford (from 1667). Descartes dedicated his *Principia Philosophiae* to her.

**Elizabeth.** 1437?–1492. Queen of Edward IV of England. Daughter of Sir Richard Woodville, 1st Earl Rivers; m. Sir John Grey (killed 1461); privately m. (1464) to Edward IV; crowned (1465). Withdrew into sanctuary at Westminster on Edward's flight (1470); her sons Edward V and Richard, Duke of York, murdered in the Tower (1483); put in possession of her rights as queen dowager by Henry VII (1486). Her daughter **Elizabeth** (1465–1503) was queen of Henry VII, marrying him (1486) in pursuance of petition presented to the king by Parliament; subject of an elegy by Sir Thomas More; mother of Henry VIII.

**Elizabeth I.** 1533–1603. Queen of England and Ireland (1558–1603), of house of Tudor. Only child of Henry VIII and Anne Boleyn; declared illegitimate by Parliament in favor of son of Jane Seymour (1536). Studied under exponents of the New Learning and adherents of the Reformation; rejected suit of Sir Thomas Seymour (*q.v.*); sided with her half sister Mary against Lady Jane Grey (1553), refused to participate in Wyatt's Rebellion (1554); imprisoned in Tower and at Woodstock. Succeeded Mary on the throne (1558); crowned by bishop of Carlisle, most of other bishops refusing to recognize her as head of church (1559); issued proclamation that the English litany be read in London churches and elevation of the host discontinued (1559); sent help to Condé and French Protestants against duke of Guise; aided Protestants in Scotland and Low Countries; promulgated the Thirty-nine Articles and obtained from Parliament (1563) extension of provisions of the Act of Supremacy, rendering Protestantism and patriotism synonymous in England. Found her rival, the Roman Catholic Mary Stuart, Queen of Scots, in her power after the defeat at Langside by the "Regent Murray" (1568); imprisoned her in Carlisle, thus giving rise to plots for liberating her. Increased severity of persecution of Roman Catholics; finally yielded to demand of Cecil, Walsingham, and other ministers and to popular outcry for removing Mary, Queen of Scots, as a menace to public safety and peace, and consented to sign the death warrant (1587). By persecutions of Mary's adherents incurred wrath of Roman Catholic powers, among them Philip of Spain, who (1588) sent out from the Tagus the Spanish Armada for invasion of England; prepared to meet the assault, disregarded advice of Walsingham and her council to precipitate an attack on the armada, which was finally defeated (July, 1588) by Howard, Drake, Hawkins, Frobisher, with the aid of a storm. Sent Drake and Hawkins on an expedition to the West Indies (1595); suffered defeat in Ireland by an insurrection prompted by maladministration (1598); sent Robert Devereux, Earl of Essex, as governor general in Ireland to quell revolt of earl of Tyrone, but he failed and was executed (1601). Avoided conflict with Parliament and attempted to curb monopolies and curtail expenditures.

**Elizabeth II.** *In full* **Elizabeth Alexandra Mary.** 1926– . Queen of Great Britain and Northern Ireland (1952– ). Dau. of George VI; m. (1947) Prince Philip, Duke of Edinburgh; mother of Prince Charles (b. 1948), created prince of Wales (1969).

**Elizabeth.** *In full* **Elizabeth Angela Marguerite Bowes′–Ly′on** (bōz′lī′ŭn). 1900– . Queen of George VI, King of Great Britain and Ireland; b. in Hertfordshire; daughter of **Claud George Bowes–Lyon** (1855–1944), 14th Earl of **Strath·more′ and King′horne** [străth·mōr′, kĭng′hôrn] (cr. 1677; in peerage of United Kingdom, 1937), lord lieutenant of Forfarshire, a descendant of Robert II of Scotland; m. (1923) George, Duke of York, with whom she succeeded to the throne (Dec. 11, 1936) and was crowned (May 12, 1937). With him visited Canada and U.S. (1939). See GEORGE VI.

**Elizabeth.** *Nee* **Pau·li′ne E·li′sa·beth Ot·ti′li·e Lu·i′se** (pou·lē′nĕ ā·lē′zä·bĕt ŏ·tē′lē·ĕ lōō·ē′zĕ). Princess of **Wied** (vēt). 1843–1916. Queen of Rumania, and writer under pseudonym **Car′men Syl′va** (*Rum.* kär′mĕn sēl′vä; *Ger.* kär′mĕn zül′vä; *Angl.* kär′mĕn sĭl′vȧ); m. (1869) Prince Carol (later Carol I) of Rumania. Author of about 20 books (mostly in German) including *The Thoughts of a Queen* (*Pensées d'une Reine;* 1882), *Pelesch Märchen* (1883), *Astra* (1886), *The Bard of Dimbovitza* (*Lieder aus dem Dimbovitzathal;* 1889), *Defizit* (1890), *Geflüsterte Worte* (1903), and several novels in collaboration with Mme. Mite Kremnitz (*q.v.*), under the pseudonym **Di′to und I′dem** (dē′tō ŏŏnt ē′dĕm).

**Elizabeth.** *Span.* **Isabel.** 1602–1644. Queen of Spain. Daughter of Henry IV of France; m. Philip IV of Spain; mother of Infante Baltasar Carlos and of María Theresa, wife of Louis XIV of France (see MARIE THÉRÈSE).

**Elizabeth.** Pen name of Countess Elizabeth Mary RUSSELL.

**Elizabeth Farnese.** See House of FARNESE.

**Elizabeth of Aragon.** Queen of Portugal. See Saint ISABEL.

**Elizabeth of Bavaria.** See ISABEAU.

**Elizabeth of Va′lois′** (vȧ′lwȧ′). *Fr.* **É′li′sa′beth′ de France′** (ā′lē′zȧ′bĕt′ dē fräɴs′). *Span.* **Isabel.** 1545–1568. Daughter of Henry II of France and Catherine de Médicis; married (1560) Philip II of Spain; marriage not a success politically, but queen much beloved.

**Elizabeth Pe·trov′na** (pyĭ·trôv′nŭ). *Russ.* **Elizaveta**

**Petrovna.** 1709–1762. Empress of Russia (1741–62). Younger daughter of Peter the Great and Catherine I. Gained throne by overthrowing government of Anna Leopoldovna, acting regent for Ivan VI; took part in wars against Frederick the Great; in Seven Years' War allied Russia with Austria and France against Prussia; freed Russia from German dominance, aided by her chancellor Bestuzhev-Ryumin; founded University of Moscow, and Academy of Fine Arts at St. Petersburg.

**El'kan** (ĕl'kän), **Sophie,** *nee* **Salomon.** *Pseudonym* **Rust Roest.** 1853–1921. Swedish novelist.

**El'kin** (ĕl'kĭn), **William Lewis.** 1855–1933. American astronomer; at Yale Observatory (from 1884), director (1896–1910); determined parallaxes of numerous stars.

**El'kins** (ĕl'kĭnz), **Stephen Benton.** 1841–1911. American lawyer, industrialist, and political leader. Served in Union army; to New Mexico (1864); practiced law. Member, U.S. House of Representatives (1872–77); active in railroad, coal mining, and financial affairs in N.Mex. and W.Va.; founded town of Elkins, W.Va., moving there about 1890. U.S. secretary of war (1891–93); U.S. senator from W.Va. (1895–1911). See J. R. MANN.

**Ellenborough,** Baron and earl of. See Edward LAW.

**El'ler** (ĕl'ẽr), **Elias.** 1690–1750. German visionary; founder of Ronsdorfer sect of millenarians.

**El·le'ro** (äl·lâ'rô), **Pietro.** b. 1833. Italian criminologist and politician.

**El'ler·y** (ĕl'ẽr·ĭ), **William.** 1727–1820. American political leader, b. Newport, R.I. Member, Continental Congress (1776–81, 1783–85); a signer of the Declaration of Independence. Chief Justice, Rhode Island (1785).

**Ellesmere,** Barons and earls of. See EGERTON family.

**El'let** (ĕl'ĕt; -ĭt), **Charles.** 1810–1862. Called "the Brunel of America." American civil engineer; built suspension bridges, notably one over the Schuylkill at Fairmount (1842) and one over the Ohio at Wheeling, W.Va. (1849). In charge of fleet of ram boats to clear Mississippi of Confederate vessels (1862).

**El'li·cott** (ĕl'ĭ·kŭt), **Andrew.** 1754–1820. American surveyor; served in Revolutionary War. Published *The United States Almanack* (earliest of the series, 1782). Member of survey that continued Mason and Dixon's line; on Pennsylvania commissions that surveyed western and northern boundaries of state (1785–86); on federal commission that fixed southwestern New York State boundary (1789); surveyed the site of Washington, D.C. (1791–93); made (1792) redrawing of L'Enfant's plan for city of Washington, known as the Ellicott plan; surveyed boundary between U.S. and Florida (1796–1800), and between Georgia and South Carolina (1811).

**Ellicott, Charles John.** 1819–1905. English Biblical commentator. M.A., Cantab. (1844), and Hulsean professor of divinity (1860); bishop of Gloucester and Bristol (1863–97), of Gloucester (1897–1905); chairman of New Testament Revision Committee for eleven years.

**El'ling·ton** (ĕl'ĭng·tŭn), **Edward Kennedy.** *Known as* **Duke Ellington.** 1899–1974. Amer. bandleader and composer, b. Washington, D.C. Composed many suites, including *Black, Brown, and Beige;* motion picture scores; and songs, including *Mood Indigo,* etc.

**El'li·ot** (ĕl'ĭ·ŭt; ĕl'yŭt). See also ELLIOTT, ELIOT, ELIOTT.

**Elliot** of Craig'end' (krāg'ĕnd'). Name of a Scottish family of Roxburgh holding the baronetcy, barony, and the earldom of Minto, and including among its members: Sir **Gilbert Elliot** (1651–1718), Lord **Min'to** (mĭn'tō); writer in Edinburgh; condemned for participation in earl of Argyll's rising (1685); pardoned; judge of session (1705). His son Sir **Gilbert** (1693–1766), lord of justiciary (1733–66), barely escaped Prince Charles Edward's Highlanders (1745) through quick wit of his daughter **Jane** or **Jean** (1727–1805), authoress of the ballad *Flowers of the Forest* (1756).

Sir **Gilbert Elliot** (1722–1777), 3d Baronet of **Minto;** statesman and poet; studied at Edinburgh and Leiden; M.P. (1754); treasurer of navy (1770); brought to bear George III's influence to defeat conciliatory motion to allow American colonies to tax themselves (1775); because of his disapprobation of skeptical philosophy dissuaded Hume from publishing *Dialogues of Natural Religion* during his lifetime; a song writer remembered for his *Amynta,* a pastoral, and *'Twas at the hour of dark midnight* (1745).

Sir **Gilbert Elliot-Murray-Kyn·yn'mond** [-kĭn·ĭn'-mŭnd] (1751–1814), 1st Earl of **Minto;** eldest son of 3d baronet; diplomat and Indian administrator; schoolfellow, with his brother **Hugh** (1752–1830), diplomatist, of Mirabeau at Fontainebleau; studied at Oxford; Whig M.P. (1776); aided Burke in attack on Warren Hastings; viceroy of Corsica (1794–96); envoy to Vienna (1799–1801); as governor general of India (1807–13), annexed Amboina, the Molucca Islands, and (1811) Java.

His eldest son, **Gilbert Elliot-Murray-Kynynmond** (1782–1859), 2d earl; ambassador to Berlin (1832–34); first lord of admiralty (1835–41), lord privy seal (1846).

Sir **George Elliot** (1784–1863), British naval commander, 2d son of 1st earl, served at reduction of Java (1811); commander in chief at Cape of Good Hope (1837–40); in China (1840); admiral (1853). Sir **Charles Elliot** (1801–1875), British naval commander; son of Hugh (1752–1830); in charge of hostilities in China, ransomed Canton (1840); governor of Bermuda (1846–54) and of St. Helena (1863–69); admiral (1865).

Sir **Henry George Elliot** (1817–1907), diplomat; son of 2d earl of Minto; sent on special missions to Naples (1859) and to Greece (1862); envoy at Turin (1863); ambassador at Vienna (1877–84).

**Gilbert John Elliot-Murray-Kynynmond** (1845–1914), 4th earl; grandson of 2d earl; colonial administrator; served in wars in various parts of world (1870–82); governor general of Canada (1898–1904); viceroy of India (1905–10); co-operated with Morley in founding new policy of gradual extension of self-government in India (1909).

**Elliot, Daniel Gi·raud'** (jē·rō'). 1835–1915. American zoologist, b. New York City; published (1865 ff.) folio monographs with his own illustrations on various bird families. Curator of zoology, Field Museum of Natural History, Chicago (1894–1906).

**El'li·ot·son** (ĕl'ĭ·ŭt·s'n; ĕl'yŭt-), **John.** 1791–1868. English physician and physiologist; founded a mesmeric hospital (1849); founder and president of the Phrenological Society.

**El'li·ott** (ĕl'ĭ·ŭt; ĕl'yŭt). See also ELIOT, ELIOTT, ELLIOT.

**Elliott, Aaron Marshall.** 1844–1910. American philologist.

**Elliott,** Sir **Charles Alfred.** 1835–1911. British administrator in India. Served in Sepoy Mutiny; directed famine relief in Mysore, issuing famous report (1878); lieutenant governor of Bengal (1890–95). His father's sister **Charlotte** (1789–1871) was author of religious poems and hymns, including "Just as I am."

**Elliott, Charles Loring.** 1812–1868. American portrait painter.

**Elliott, Ebenezer.** 1781–1849. English poet, called the "Corn-Law Rhymer." Began with romantic poetry in *The Vernal Walk, Night* (1818), and *The Village Patriarch* (1829); active chartist until chartists dissented from corn-law agitation; attributed all national misfortunes to the "bread tax," which he denounced bitterly in *Corn-Law Rhymes* (1831) and *The Splendid Village* (1833–35).

**Elliott, Jesse Duncan.** 1782–1845. American naval officer, b. Hagerstown, Md. Captured British brigs *Detroit* and *Caledonia* on Lake Erie, first American success in War of 1812; ranking officer under Commodore Perry; his conduct in support of Perry during battle of Lake Erie (1813) formed subject of a bitter controversy lasting more than 30 years.

**Elliott, John.** 1858–1925. American mural and portrait painter, b. in Lincolnshire, England. His *War Portrait*, red-chalk drawing of members of Lafayette Escadrille and other young Americans killed in World War, is in National Museum, Washington.

**Elliott, Maud,** *nee* **Howe.** 1854–1948. American writer, b. Boston; m. John Elliott (1887). Author of *Mammon, Roma Beata, The Story of an Artist;* collaborated with her sister Laura E. Richards (*q.v.*) in *The Life of Julia Ward Howe* (1916).

**Elliott, Maxine.** *Real name* **Jessie Der′mot** (dûr′mŭt). 1871–1940. American actress; m. George A. McDermott (divorced 1896) and Nathaniel C. Goodwin (1898; divorced 1908). Member of Augustin Daly's company (1895–97) and appeared in Shakespeare repertory; co-star with Nat Goodwin (1898–1903). Owner and manager of Maxine Elliott's Theatre, N.Y. (1908).

**Elliott, Stephen.** 1771–1830. American botanist and man of affairs, b. Beaufort, S.C. Served in state senate (1808–12); president of Bank of the State of South Carolina (1812–30). Cofounder of the quarterly *Southern Review* (1828). His granddaughter **Sarah Barnwell Elliott** (1848–1928) lived chiefly at Sewanee, Tenn., and wrote many Tennessee stories.

**El′lis** (ĕl′ĭs) *or* **Sharpe** (shärp), **Alexander John.** 1814–1890. English philologist and mathematician. Took name Ellis on receipt of bequest from a relative of that name to finance his life of research. First in England to reduce study of phonetics to a science; aided Isaac Pitman in devising system of printing English called phonotypy and in attempts at spelling reform; devised phonetic system (palaeotype, used by Henry Sweet as basis of Romic), and a popular system (glossic); spent large part of his life on *Early English Pronunciation* (1869–89).

**El′lis** (ĕl′ĭs), **Augustine ap.** See AP ELLIS.

**Ellis, Edward Sylvester.** 1840–1916. American author of juveniles and dime novels, as *Seth Jones, or the Captive of the Frontier* (1860).

**Ellis, George.** 1753–1815. English author. Son of West Indian planter. Won reputation with *Poetical Tales by Sir Gregory Gander* (1778); edited specimens of *Early English Poets* (1790), *Specimens of Early English Metrical Romances* (1805); friend of Sir Walter Scott.

**Ellis, Havelock,** *in full* **Henry Havelock.** 1859–1939. English scientist and man of letters, b. Croydon, Surrey. Studied medicine; gave up practice to devote himself to scientific and literary work. Conducted researches in psychology and sociology of sex, results of which appeared in seven volumes under separate titles (1897–1928), constituting his monumental *Studies in the Psychology of Sex.* Author of *The World of Dreams* (1911), *Essays in War-time* (1916), *Little Essays of Love and Virtue* (1922), *The Dance of Life* (1923), *George Chapman* (1934), and *My Confessional* (1934).

**Ellis, Job Bicknell.** 1829–1905. American mycologist; coauthor of *The North American Pyrenomycetes* (1892).

**Ellis, Robinson.** 1834–1913. English classical scholar. Corpus Christi professor of Latin, Oxford (from 1893). Chief work, *Commentary on Catullus* (1876).

**Ellis, William.** 1794–1872. English missionary; in South Sea Islands (1816–24), acclimatized tropical fruits and plants and set up first printing press in South Seas. Author of *Polynesian Researches* (1829) and three books on Madagascar.

**El′lis–Fer′mor** (-fûr′môr), **Una Mary.** 1894–1958. English lecturer and literary critic; author of *Christopher Marlowe* (1926), *Jacobean Drama* (1936), *The Irish Dramatic Movement* (1939), etc.

**El′li·son** (ĕl′ĭ·s′n), **Ralph Waldo.** 1914– . Amer. author, b. Oklahoma City, Okla. Wrote *Invisible Man* (1952); also short stories, essays, etc.

**El′lis·ton** (ĕl′ĭs·tŭn), **Robert William.** 1774–1831. English actor and manager. Praised by Charles Lamb and Leigh Hunt; first comedian of his day, esp. in parts of Doricourt, Charles Surface, Rover, and Ranger.

**Ells′berg** (ĕlz′bûrg), **Edward.** 1891– . American engineer, inventor, and writer; grad. U.S.N.A., Annapolis (1914); on naval duty, promoted through grades to captain. Invented underwater torch for cutting steel. Chief engineer, Tide Water Oil Co. (1926–35); invented improved methods of dehydrating and dewaxing lubricating oils, and of cracking crude oil for manufacturing antiknock gasoline. Author of *Salvage Operations on S-51* (1927), *On the Bottom* (1929), *Thirty Fathoms Deep* (1930), *Pigboats* (1931), *Ocean Gold* (1935), *Spanish Ingots* (1936), *Hell on Ice* (1938), *Captain Paul* (1941), *I Have Just Begun to Fight* (1942), etc.

**Ells′worth** (ĕlz′wûrth; -wẽrth), **Lincoln.** 1880–1951. American polar explorer, b. Chicago. Organized, for Johns Hopkins U., expedition to make geological cross section of Andes Mountains (1924). Turned to polar exploration, participating in seaplane flight from Spitsbergen to 88° N. Lat. (with Roald Amundsen, 1925), transpolar flight in airship *Norge* from Spitsbergen to Teller, Alaska (with Amundsen and Umberto Nobile, May 11–13, 1926), transarctic submarine expedition (with Hubert Wilkins, 1931), 2300-mile airplane flight across Antarctic (Nov., 1935), claiming 300,000 sq. miles of new land for U.S. Author of *The Last Wild Buffalo Hunt* (1915), *Search* (1932), *Beyond Horizons* (1938); collaborated with Amundsen in *Our Polar Flight* (1925) and *First Crossing of the Polar Sea* (1927).

**Ellsworth, Oliver.** 1745–1807. American jurist and statesman, b. Windsor, Conn.; to Hartford (1775); superior court judge (1785–89). Took prominent part in Connecticut's activities in Revolutionary War; delegate to Continental Congress (1777–84), and Constitutional Convention (1787). U.S. senator from Conn. (1789–96); chairman of committee that drew up bill organizing federal judiciary. Chief justice of the U.S. (1796–99). One of commissioners to France who negotiated agreement with Napoleon (1800). His son **Henry Leavitt** (1791–1858), b. Windsor, Conn., grad. Yale (1810), was first U.S. commissioner of patents (1835–45); helped secure first government appropriation for agriculture, hence sometimes called "father of the Department of Agriculture." His twin brother, **William Wolcott** (1791–1868), son-in-law of Noah Webster, grad. Yale (1810), was governor of Connecticut (1838–42) and associate judge, Conn. supreme court (1847–61).

**Ell′wood** (ĕl′wo͝od), **Charles Abram.** 1873–1946. American sociologist.

**Ellwood, Thomas.** 1639–1714. English Quaker and friend of Milton. Latin reader to Milton; professed to have suggested idea of *Paradise Regained* (1665). Author of polemical works on Quakerism, poems, and an autobiography with information about Milton.

**El′man** (ĕl′măn), **Mischa.** 1891–1967. Russian Jewish violinist, b. Talnoye, Russia; to U.S. (naturalized 1923).

**Elms'ley** (ĕlmz'lĭ), **Peter.** 1773–1825. English classical scholar; chiefly famous for work on manuscripts of Sophocles and Euripides.

**É'loi'** (ā'lwȧ') *or* **E·lig'i·us** (ė·lĭj'ĭ·ŭs), Saint. 588?–659. French ecclesiastic; learned goldsmith's trade and gained favor of Clotaire II by skill in making a throne; chief councilor to Dagobert I; bishop of Noyon (639); patron saint of goldsmiths.

**El'phin·stone** (ĕl'fĭn·stōn; *Brit.* -stŭn). Name of a Scottish family including: **Alexander** (1552–?1648), 4th Baron Elphinstone; lord high treasurer of Scotland (1599); lord of the articles (1604, 1607); commissioner for the union with England (1604).

Barons Bal·mer'i·no (băl·mĕr'ĭ·nō): Alexander's brother **James** (1553?–1612), 1st Baron Balmerino; one of the Octavians (1595); secretary of state in Scotland (1598); commissioner for the union (1604); disgraced and attainted for a compromising letter to Pope Clement VIII, to which he had surreptitiously obtained James VI's signature. **John** (d. 1649), 2d baron; son of 1st baron; restored to blood and peerage (1613); imprisoned for opposition to Charles I; sentenced to death for handling a petition against Charles I's ecclesiastical measures; pardoned through intercession of poet Drummond of Hawthornden and others (1635); privy councilor and extraordinary lord of session (1641). **Arthur** (1688–1746), 6th baron; joined Jacobites after Sheriffmuir (1715); one of first to join Charles Edward (1745); fought at Falkirk; captured at Culloden Moor and beheaded.

**George Keith Elphinstone** (1746–1823), Viscount **Keith** [kēth] (in peerage of United Kingdom); British naval commander; 5th son of 10th Baron Elphinstone; entered navy (1761); served on shore at reduction of Charleston (1780); rear admiral (1794); forced Dutch squadron directed at Cape Town to surrender in Saldanha Bay (1796); pursued a French fleet from Mediterranean to Brest (1799); took Malta and Genoa (1800); co-operated with Abercromby in operations in Egypt; landed Abercromby's army in Abukir Bay (1801); admiral (1801). His wife (m. 1808), **Hester Maria** (1762–1857), daughter of Henry and Hester Thrale (see Hester L. Piozzi); educ. under direction of Dr. Johnson; gave herself to study of Hebrew and mathematics.

**Mountstuart** (1779–1859); statesman in India; 4th son of 11th baron Elphinstone; appointed to Bengal civil service (1796); diplomatist on Wellesley's mission to Marathas; military attaché to Wellesley at battle of Assaye (1803); envoy to Shah Shuja at Kabul (1808); resident at Poona (1810–16); put end to Maratha war (1817) and organized the annexed territory of Poona; as governor of Bombay (1819–27), compiled code of laws that lasted forty years and founded system of state education; twice declined governor-generalship of India; author of a history of India (1841) and of the incomplete *Rise of the British Power in the East* (1858).

**Elphinstone, William.** 1431–1514. Scottish prelate and statesman; bishop of Ross (1481), of Aberdeen (1483–1514); lord high chancellor (1488). Sent by James IV to England, France, and to Emperor Maximilian I; keeper of privy seal (1492–1514); made treaty with Holland (1493); opposed policy of hostility to England. Founded U. of Aberdeen, built King's Coll. (1506), and rebuilt choir of Aberdeen Cathedral. Made possible introduction of first printing press into Scotland (1507), on which he had *Aberdeen Breviary* printed.

**El'ser** (ĕl'sẽr), **Frank Ball.** 1885–1935. American journalist and playwright; author of novel *The Keen Desire* (1926) and successful play *The Farmer Takes a Wife* (with Marc Connelly, 1934), later presented as motion picture.

**Elsevier.** See Elzevir.

**Els'hei'mer** (ĕls'hī'mẽr), **Adam.** *Called* **Il Te·de'sco** (ēl tā·dās'kō). 1578–1610. German painter and etcher, b. Frankfurt; a founder of modern landscape painting, and forerunner of Rembrandt; settled in Rome (1598) and was friend of Rubens, Pieter Lastman, and Paul Bril. His works include chiefly Biblical and mythological paintings, often on copper, with landscapes.

**Els'kamp** (ĕls'kämp), **Max.** 1862–1931. Belgian poet; identified with the symbolists, and with the literary and Catholic renaissance in Belgium.

**El'son** (ĕl's'n), **Henry William.** 1857–1954. American historian; lecturer, N.Y.U. (from 1927). Author of *History of the United States* (5 vols., 1906), *Modern Times and the Living Past* (1921), *United States—Its Past and Present* (1925), etc.

**Elson, Louis Charles.** 1848–1920. American music critic and lecturer, b. Boston, Mass. Music critic, Boston *Advertiser* (from 1886). Author of *Great Composers and Their Work* (1898), *The History of American Music* (1904), *Elson's Music Dictionary* (1905). His son **Arthur** (1873–1940), music critic for Boston *Advertiser;* author of *The Musician's Guide* (1913), *The Book of Musical Knowledge* (1915), etc.

**Elss'ler** (ĕls'lẽr), **Therese** (1808–1878) and her sister **Fanny** (1810–1884). Austrian ballet dancers. Therese retired from the stage (1850), became morganatic wife of Prince Adalbert of Prussia, and was made baroness von Barnim by Frederick William IV. Fanny amassed a fortune and retired from the stage in 1851.

**El'ster** (ĕl'stẽr), **Julius.** 1854–1920. German physicist; with **Hans Friedrich Gei'tel** [gī'tĕl] (1855–1923), credited with constructing the first practical photoelectric cell, first photoelectric photometer, and a Tesla transformer.

**El'ton** (ĕl't'n; -tŭn), **Oliver.** 1861–1945. English educator and literary historian; professor of English literature, Liverpool (1900–25). Among his books are *The Augustan Ages* (1899), *Survey of English Literature from 1780–1830* (1912), *...from 1830 to 1880* (1920), *...from 1730 to 1780* (1928).

**É'luard'** (ā'lü·ȧr'), **Paul.** 1895–1952. French poet, identified with the surrealist movement.

**El've·stad** (ăl'vĕ·stä), **Sven.** *Pseudonym* **Stein Ri'ver·ton** (rē'vẽr·tôn). 1884–1934. Norwegian novelist.

**El'vey** (ĕl'vĭ), Sir **George Job.** 1816–1893. English organist and composer. Organist, St. George's Chapel, Windsor (1835–82); composed two oratorios, anthems, and services. His brother **Stephen** (1805–1860) was organist at New Coll. and St. John's, Oxford (from 1830); composed church services.

**El'well** (ĕl'wĕl; -wĕl), **Frank Edwin.** 1858–1922. American sculptor, b. Concord, Mass. Studio in New York (1885).

**El'win** (ĕl'wĭn), **Whitwell.** 1816–1900. English critic and editor. B.A., Cantab. (1839); rector of Booton, Norfolk; editor of *Quarterly Review* (1853–60); completed five volumes of standard edition of Pope, finished by W. J. Courthope (*q.v.*).

**E'ly** (ē'lĭ), **Richard Theodore.** 1854–1943. American economist; head of dept. of political economy, Johns Hopkins (1881–92); professor, U. of Wisconsin (1892–1925), Northwestern U. (1925–33).

**El'y·mas** (ĕl'ĭ·măs). *Known also as* **Bar'–Je'sus** (bär'jē'zŭs). In the Bible, a Jewish sorcerer (*Acts* xiii. 6–12).

**El'yot** (ĕl'yŭt), Sir **Thomas.** 1490?–1546. English diplomat and scholar. Son of **Richard Elyot** (1450?–1522), judge of common pleas. On publication of his *Boke Called the Governour* (1531; treatise on education of princes, dedicated to Henry VIII), was appointed ambassador to Emperor Charles V with instructions to gain emperor's consent to Henry VIII's divorce from Catherine of Aragon and to procure arrest of William Tyndale. Translator of *The Doctrine of Princes* (1534; from Isocrates), and of Platonic dialogues. Friend of Sir Thomas More but not a Roman Catholic; influenced by Erasmus and Italian Humanists. Author of *The Castel of Helth* (a popular medical treatise, 1534), and *Defence of Good Women* (1545). Compiler of first Latin-English dictionary (1538). See George PUTTENHAM.

**Elysio, Filinto.** Pseudonym of Francisco Manuel do NASCIMENTO.

**El'ze** (ĕl'tsĕ), **Karl.** 1821–1889. German Anglicist; prepared critical editions of Shakespeare's *Hamlet* (1857), *Alphonsus* (1867; a tragedy attributed to Chapman), and Rowley's *When You See Me* (1874); author of biographies of Scott (2 vols., 1864), Byron (1870), and Shakespeare (1876), and of *Essays on Shakespeare, Notes on Elizabethan Dramatists* (3 vols., 1880–86), etc.

**El'ze·vir** (ĕl'zĕ·vĭr; -vẽr) *or* **El'ze·vier** (ĕl'zĕ·vẽr). *Sometimes* **El'se·vier** (ĕl'zĕ·vẽr). Family of Dutch publishers and printers, including: **Louis I** (1540?–1617), who founded the business at Leiden (c. 1580); his five sons, **Matthieu** (1564?–1640), **Louis II** (1566?–1621), **Gilles** (1570?–1651), **Joost** (1575?–?1617), **Bonaventure** (1583–1652), who was in partnership with Matthieu (1617–22) and later with Matthieu's son **Abraham** (1592?–1652); another son of Matthieu, **Isaac** (1596–1651); a son of Abraham, **Jean** (1622–1661); a son of Bonaventure, **Daniel** (1626?–1680); a son of Joost, **Louis III** (1604–1670); and a son of Jean, **Abraham II** (1653–1712), who was university printer at Leiden (1681–1712). A style of type has been named *Elzevir* after this family.

**E'mants** (ā'mänts), **Marcellus.** 1848–1923. Dutch poet, playwright, and novelist.

**E·man'u·el** (ē·măn'ū·ĕl). *Port.* **Manuel** *or* **Manoel.** *Sometimes known as* **Manuel I.** *Called* **the Great** *and* **the Fortunate.** 1469–1521. Duke of Beja, and king of Portugal (1495–1521). Cousin of John II; m. (1) Isabella, daughter of Ferdinand and Isabella of Spain; (2) Maria, her sister; and (3) Leonora of Austria, sister of Charles V. His reign the golden era of Portuguese history and an era of exploration and discovery. Sent out Vasco da Gama, Corte-Real, Cabral, Albuquerque, Tristão da Cunha, etc.; promulgated new code of laws; expelled Jews (1497–98).

**Em'bick** (ĕm'bĭk), **Stanley Dun·bar'** (dŭn·bär'). 1877–1957. American army officer; b. in Franklin County, Pa.; grad. U.S.M.A., West Point (1899); promoted through the grades to brigadier general (1930), major general (1936), lieutenant general (1939); chief of staff of American section, Supreme War Council at Versailles, France (1917–18); member of American delegation to Peace Conference at Paris (1918–19); commander, 4th corps area (1938–40); named permanent chairman of Inter-American Defense Board (1942).

**Em'bur·y** (ĕm'bẽr·ĭ), **Philip.** 1728–1773. Reputed first Methodist preacher in America, b. prob. in Ballingrane, Ireland, of German descent. To New York (1760). Founded (1768) Wesley Chapel (the first John Street Church, New York); established (1770) at Ashgrove, N.Y., the first Methodist congregation north of New York City. Cf. Barbara HECK.

**Em'den** (ĕm'dĕn), **Robert.** 1862–1940. German astrophysicist.

**E'me·lé'** (ĕ'mā·lā'), **Wilhelm.** 1830–1905. German painter of battle and military scenes.

**É'me·ric'–Da'vid'** (ĕm'rēk'dä'vēd'), **Toussaint Bernard.** 1755–1839. French archaeologist.

**Em'er·son** (ĕm'ẽr·s'n), **Charles Phillips.** 1872–1938. American physician; author of *Pneumothorax* (1904), *Clinical Diagnosis* (1906), *Essentials of Medicine* (1908).

**Emerson, Oliver Farrar.** 1860–1927. American philologist; author of works on the history of the English language and a *Middle English Reader* (1905).

**Emerson, Ralph Waldo.** 1803–1882. American essayist and poet, b. Boston, Mass. Grad. Harvard (1821); taught school. Studied for ministry; licensed to preach (1826); minister of Second Church of Boston, Unitarian (1829–32); resigned because of doctrinal differences. Visited Europe, meeting Wordsworth, Coleridge, and Carlyle, with last of whom he maintained friendship and correspondence for over forty years. Settled in Concord, Mass. (from 1834); formed circle of friends, including A. B. Alcott, Margaret Fuller, Thoreau, Jones Very, and Hawthorne. Preached in various churches during next several years; meantime began delivering public lectures, material for which he drew from the *Journals* he had been keeping for many years. First published work, *Nature* (1836), contained gist of his transcendental philosophy, which views the world of phenomena as a sort of symbol of the inner life and emphasizes individual freedom and self-reliance. His address to the Phi Beta Kappa society of Harvard on "the American scholar" (1837) and another address to the graduating class of the Cambridge Divinity College (1838) applied his doctrine to the scholar and the clergyman, the second address provoking sharp controversy. Edited *The Dial* (1842–44). His two volumes of *Essays* (1841, 1844) made his reputation international. Lectured in England (1847). Slowly drawn into participation in national issues and delivered many antislavery speeches; welcomed beginning of Civil War. After 1866 did little new writing; gradually declined in mental powers. Other works: *Poems* (1846, but dated 1847), *Representative Men* (1850), *English Traits* (1856), *The Conduct of Life* (1860), *May-Day and Other Pieces* (poems, 1867), *Society and Solitude* (1870), *Letters and Social Aims* (essays, 1876), *Natural History of Intellect* (1893). Elected to American Hall of Fame (1900). The centenary edition of his works was edited by his son **Edward Waldo** (1844–1930), who also edited his *Journals* and his correspondence with John Sterling, and who wrote *Emerson in Concord* (1889).

**E'mich** (ā'mĭκ), **Friedrich.** 1860–1940. Austrian chemist, founder of microchemistry; developed microanalytical methods in inorganic and organic chemistry.

**E·mi'lio** (ā·mē'lyō), **Paolo.** *Lat.* **Paulus Ae·mil'i·us** (ē·mĭl'ĭ·ŭs; ē·mĭl'yŭs). d. 1529. Italian historian, b. Verona; invited to France to write history of kings of France, wrote *De Rebus Gestis Francorum* (in Latin; French tr., 1581).

**E'mi·ne'scu** (ĕ'mē·nĕ'skōō), **Mihail.** 1850–1889. Rumanian poet.

**E·min' Pa·sha'** (ē·mēn' pä·shä'), **Mehmed.** *Real name* **Eduard Schnit'zer** (shnĭt'sẽr). 1840–1892. German traveler and explorer in Africa. District physician to Turkish government in Antivari, Montenegro (1865). To Khartoum (1875), where as Emin Effendi he became government medical officer in Egyptian service under "Chinese" Gordon (1876). Named governor of equatorial province, with title of bey (1878); added to geographical knowledge of Central Africa, and extended explorations over eastern Sudan. Isolated by Mahdi revolt (1883 ff.); made pasha by Egyptian government (1887); rescued at Kavalli by H. M. Stanley (1888); returned to his province, but was deposed and imprisoned during revolt (1888), and failed to regain authority following release (1889). Entered service of German East

Africa Company (1890) and undertook expedition to Central Africa; hoisted German flag at Tabora, and founded station of Bukoba (1890); murdered by Arabs near Stanley Falls.

**Em'lyn** (ĕm'lĭn), **Thomas.** 1663–1741. English nonconformist minister, the first self-declared Unitarian minister in England.

**Em'ma** (ĕm'ȧ) of Normandy. d. 1052. Queen of Ethelred the Unready, King of England. Daughter of Richard the Fearless, Duke of the Normans; m. Ethelred (1002) and adopted English name **Ælf'gi'fu** (ălf'yĭ'vo͞o). After Ethelred's death (1016), married to Canute (1017), on whose death (1035) she made attempt, thwarted by stepson Harold, to set her son Hardecanute on throne; banished by Harold (1037), fled to court of Baldwin V, Count of Flanders; influential during reign of Hardecanute (1040–41); her wealth seized (1043) by Edward the Confessor, who was her son by Ethelred, probably because of her favor to partisans of Danish line.

**Em'ma** (ĕm'ȧ; *Ger.* ĕm'ä; *Du.* ĕm'ȧ). *In full* **Emma A'del·heid Wil'hel·mi'ne The·re'se** (*Ger.* ä'dĕl·hīt vĭl'hĕl·mē'nĕ tā·rā'zĕ). 1858–1934. Daughter of Prince George Victor of Waldeck-Pyrmont. Queen of the Netherlands (1879–90), as second wife (m. 1879) of King William III. As dowager queen, acted as regent (1890–98) until accession of her daughter Wilhelmina (b. 1880).

**Em'ma'nuel' Phi'li'bert'** (ĕ'mȧ'nü·ĕl' fē'lē'bâr'). 1528–1580. Tenth duke of Savoy (1553–80), b. Chambéry. Son of Charles III of Savoy. Sided with Spain in war with France (1556–59) and won great victory at Saint-Quentin (1557); results of peace (1559) restored Savoy but on difficult terms; m. (1559) Margaret of France; lost Geneva and districts in Vaud. See SAVOY.

**Em'me·rich** (ĕm'ĕ·rĭĸ) *or* **Em'me·rick** (-rĭk), **Anna Katharina.** *Called* **the Nun of Dül'men** (dül'mĕn). 1774–1824. German nun and visionary. Her visions described by the poet Clemens Brentano (*q.v.*).

**Em'met** (ĕm'ĕt; -ĭt), **Thomas Addis.** 1764–1827. Irish lawyer and patriot, b. Cork. Practiced medicine, London and Dublin. Studied law; adm. to Irish bar (1790). Joined United Irishmen; arrested (1798) for political activity; imprisoned in Scotland till 1802; released on condition he leave British Empire. To U.S. (1804); practiced law in New York till his death. His younger brother **Robert** (1778–1803) was also an Irish nationalist; interviewed (1802) Napoleon and Talleyrand trying to secure support for Irish independence; returned to Dublin (Oct., 1802) and led a small body of followers in a rising (July 23, 1803), one purpose of which was to capture the viceroy; fled into hiding when rioters were dispersed after a few acts of violence, including two murders; captured (Aug. 25), tried by special court, and hanged (Sept. 20). T. A. Emmet's grandson **Thomas Addis Emmet** (1828–1919), b. near Charlottesville, Va., was an American gynecologist.

**Em'mett** (ĕm'ĕt; -ĭt), **Daniel Decatur.** 1815–1904. American minstrel and song writer. In winter of 1842–43 organized first "Negro minstrel" troupe (the "Virginia Minstrels"); played in New York, Boston, and England. Composed *Dixie*, later adopted as war song of the South; other songs, *Old Dan Tucker; The Road to Richmond; Walk along, John; Here We Are, or Cross Ober Jordan.*

**Em'mich** (ĕm'ĭĸ), **Otto von.** 1848–1915. German general; commanded army which invaded Belgium (1914).

**Em'mons** (ĕm'ŭnz), **De·los'** (dĕ·lŏs') **Carleton.** 1888–1965. American soldier; grad. U.S.M.A., West Point (1909). Brigadier general (1936); major general in air corps (1939); lieutenant general commanding air corps (1940); commander of Hawaiian department of U.S. army (Dec., 1941–May, 1943).

**Em'pe·ci·na'do, El** (ĕl ām'pā·thē·nä'thō). *Real name* **Juan Martín Dí'az** (dē'äth). 1775–1825. Spanish patriot; led guerrilla bands against French in Peninsular War; in revolution of 1820 as Constitutionalist; captured (1823) and exposed publicly in an iron cage.

**Em·ped'o·cles** (ĕm·pĕd'ō·klēz). Greek philosopher and statesman, of 5th century B.C. Disciple of Pythagoras and Parmenides. According to tradition, hurled himself into crater of Mt. Etna in order that his sudden disappearance might convince people he was a god.

**Em'ser** (ĕm'zĕr; ām'-), **Hieronymus.** 1477?–1527. German theologian; antagonist of Luther.

**Énambuc, Pierre Belain d'.** See BELAIN.

**En·ci'na** *or* **En·zi'na** (ān·thē'nä), **Juan del.** 1469?–?1529. Spanish dramatist. Known esp. for his plays (*églogas, representaciones,* and *autos*) which mark transition in Spain from religious to secular drama; author also of lyrics, many with his own musical settings.

**Encinas.** = ENZINAS.

**Enciso, Martín Fernández de.** See FERNÁNDEZ DE ENCISO.

**Enck'e** (ĕng'kĕ), **Erdmann.** 1843–1896. German sculptor.

**Encke, Johann Franz.** 1791–1865. German astronomer. Determined orbit of the comet of 1680 and period of the comet (Encke's comet) discovered by Pons (1818); deduced a solar parallax long accepted as correct.

**En'de·cott** *or* **En'di·cott** (ĕn'dĭ·kŭt), **John.** 1589?–1665. Colonial governor of Massachusetts, b. Chagford, Devon, England. One of six persons who bought patent from Plymouth Council in England for territory on Massachusetts Bay; sailed (1628); acted as first governor of colony till arrival of main body of colonists (1630), when Winthrop (appointed governor in England, Oct., 1629) took charge; continued in public service of colony, as assistant governor (1630–34, 1636–40, 1645–48), deputy governor (1641–43, '50, '54), and governor (1644, '49, '51–53, '55–64).

**En'ders** (ĕn'dĕrz), **John Franklin.** 1897– . Amer. bacteriologist, b. W. Hartford, Conn. Awarded Nobel prize in physiology and medicine (1954) with T. Weller and F. Robbins for discoveries concerning the virus of poliomyelitis.

**End'li·cher** (ĕnt'lĭ·ĸĕr), **Stephan Ladislaus.** 1804–1849. Hungarian botanist and philologist, b. Pressburg; a founder of the Vienna Academy of Sciences. Author of *Genera Plantarum* (18 parts and 5 suppl., 1836–50) and *Enchiridion Botanicum* (1841), an elaboration of the natural system of classification of plants; also of *Anfangsgründe der Chinesischen Grammatik* (1845).

**E·ne'sco** (ĕ·nĕ'skō) *or* **E·ne'scu** (-sko͞o), **Georges** (zhôrzh). 1881–1955. Rumanian violinist, composer, and conductor; court violinist to Queen of Rumania; teacher of Yehudi Menuhin.

**En'fan'tin'** (äɴ'fäɴ'tăɴ'), **Barthélemy Prosper.** *Known as* **Le Père Enfantin** (lĕ pâr). 1796–1864. French Socialist; a leader of Saint-Simonianism; founded model Socialist community at Ménilmontant, with forty disciples, but was arrested and imprisoned for a short time.

**Eng.** See CHANG AND ENG.

**Eng'el** (ĕng'ĕl), **Ernst.** 1821–1896. German statistician and economist. Formulated generalization (Engel's law) on relation between increased family income and expenditures for food, clothing, rent, etc.

**Engel, Johann Jakob.** 1741–1802. German writer, dramatist, and philosopher. Author of works on popular philosophy, art, and aesthetics, and of the novel *Herr Lorenz Starke* (1795; first published in Schiller's *Horen*, 1801).

**Eng'el·bert I** (ĕng'ĕl·bĕrt), Saint. 1185?–1225. Archbishop of Cologne (from 1216); re-established law and order, brought about improvements in life of his people. Aroused antagonism of his cousin Count Frederick of Isenburg, who caused him to be murdered (1225); honored as martyr.

**Engelbert I** *or* **Eng′el·brecht I** (ĕng′ĕl·brĕKt). See NASSAU, 2a.

**Eng′el·brecht′sen** (ăng′ĕl·brĕKt′sĕn), **Cornelis.** 1468–1533. Dutch religious painter of Leiden, a pioneer of the Dutch Renaissance school.

**Eng′el·hard** (ĕng′ĕl·härt), **Wilhelm.** 1813–1902. German sculptor and painter.

**Eng′el·mann** (ĕng′(g)ĕl·măn; *Ger.* ĕng′ĕl·män), **George.** 1809–1884. Meteorologist, physician, and botanist, b. Frankfurt am Main; to U.S. (1832); practiced medicine in St. Louis (from 1835). Made meteorological observations and botanical investigations during rest of life.

**Eng′el·mann** (ĕng′ĕl·män), **Theodor Wilhelm.** 1843–1909. German physiologist.

**Eng′els** (ĕng′ĕls), **Friedrich.** 1820–1895. German Socialist; collaborator with Karl Marx (*q.v.*) in the *Communist Manifesto* (1847); involved in revolutionary agitation in Baden (1848–49); fled to England, where he was a manufacturer at Manchester (1850–69); to London (1870–95). Associated with Marx in spreading Socialist propaganda; edited and published Marx's works. Author of *Die Lage der Arbeitenden Klassen in England* (1845), *Entwickelung des Sozialismus von der Utopie zur Wissenschaft* (c. 1880), etc. See also Moses HESS.

**Eng′erth** (ĕng′ērt), Baron **Wilhelm von.** 1814–1884. Austrian engineer; invented Engerth system of gearing for freight locomotives; took active part in regulating Danube at Vienna; supervising architect of buildings of Vienna Exposition of 1873 and chief of engineering department. His brother **Eduard** (1818–1897) was historical and portrait painter.

**En′ghien′** (*Fr.* äN′găN′; *Belg.* -gyăN′), Duc **d′.** A title borne by the eldest son of the prince of Condé (see CONDÉ), especially by: (1) **Louis II de Bourbon,** during his father's life (1621–46). (2) **Louis Antoine Henri de Bourbon-Condé** (1772–1804), only son of the last Condé prince; at outbreak of war (1792) held a command in the army of émigrés; m. (1801) Princess Charlotte, niece of cardinal de Rohan; lived at Ettenheim, Baden; falsely accused of plotting against France; secretly seized (1804) by French gendarmes under Napoleon's orders, condemned by military tribunal and shot.

**Eng′land** (ĭng′glănd), **John.** 1786–1842. Roman Catholic bishop of Charleston, S.C., b. Cork, Ireland. Brought about reforms in transportation of convicts to Australia and got British government to permit non-Anglican clergymen in Australian penal settlements; has been termed "founder of the Catholic Church in Australia." Consecrated (1820) bishop of new apostolic see of Charleston (the Carolinas and Georgia); instituted many educational activities in his see.

**Engländer, Richard.** See Peter ALTENBERG.

**En′gle** (ĕng′g′l), **Paul Hamilton.** 1908– . American poet, b. Cedar Rapids, Iowa; A.B., Coe (1931) and Oxford (as Rhodes scholar, 1936); author of *American Song* (1934), *Break the Heart's Anger* (1936), *Corn* (1939), *Always the Land* (novel; 1941).

**Eng′ler** (ĕng′lẽr), **Adolf,** *in full* **Heinrich Gustav Adolf.** 1844–1930. German botanist. Worked out a natural system of classification of plants; also known for work in plant geography.

**Engler, Karl.** 1842–1925. German chemist.

**Eng′lish** (ĭng′glĭsh), **Thomas Dunn.** 1819–1902. American physician, lawyer, and writer; author of the song *Ben Bolt,* and numerous novels, plays, and poems.

**En′na** (ĕn′ȧ), **August.** 1860–1939. Danish composer of Italian and German descent.

**En′ne·king** (ĕn′ĕ·kĭng), **John Joseph.** 1841–1916. American landscape and figure painter.

**En′ne·mo′ser** (ĕn′ĕ·mō′zẽr), **Joseph.** 1787–1854. Austrian physician, b. in the Tirol; to Munich (1841) and gained reputation by application of hypnotism (then called *magnetism*) as a cure.

**Ennery, Adolphe Philippe d′.** See DENNERY.

**En′ne·ver** (ĕn′ĕ·vẽr), **William Joseph.** 1869–1947. English journalist, and originator of mnemonic training system known as Pelmanism, b. London. Established first Pelman Inst. in London (1898).

**En′nis** (ĕn′ĭs), **George Pearse.** 1884–1936. American painter, b. St. Louis; studio in New York; best known for landscapes, murals, and stained-glass work.

**Enniskillen,** Earls of. See COLE family.

**En′ni·us** (ĕn′ĭ·ŭs), **Quintus.** 239–?169 B.C. Roman poet, b. Rudiae in Calabria. Taught Greek and translated Greek plays, Rome (from c. 204 B.C.); made Roman citizen (184). Regarded as one of founders of Latin literature; author of a number of tragedies and, notably, of the epic poem *Annales* (18 books), in which the hexameter is introduced into Latin. Only fragments of his works are extant.

**En·no′di·us** (ĕ·nō′dĭ·ŭs), **Magnus Felix.** 473?–521. Roman Catholic prelate and writer; bishop of Pavia (c. 515).

**E′no·bar′bus** (ē′nō·bär′bŭs; ĕn′ō-). Variant of AHENOBARBUS.

**E·no·mo·to** (ĕ·nō·mō·tō), Viscount **Buyo.** 1839?–1909. Japanese vice-admiral (1874); minister to Russia; negotiated treaty with Russia (1874) exchanging southern half of Sakhalin for Kuril Islands; minister to China (1882).

**Enotrio Romano.** See Giosuè CARDUCCI.

**Enrique.** Spanish form of HENRY.

**Enríquez Acevedo de Toledo, Pedro.** See Conde de FUENTES.

**En·rí′quez Gó′mez** (ān·rē′kāth gō′māth), **Antonio.** *Orig. surname* **Enríquez de Paz** (thȧ päth′). 1602–?1662. Spanish writer, b. Segovia, of Portuguese Jewish origin; to France (1636) to escape Inquisition; majordomo to Louis XIII; to Amsterdam (1660), openly professing Judaism. Author of comedies, a mystic poem *La Culpa del Primer Peregrino* (1644), an epic *El Sansón Nazareno* (1656).

**En′sche·dé′** (ĕn′sKĕ·dā′). Name of a Dutch family of printers and type founders, including **Isaak** (1681–1761), founder of a press in Haarlem (1703) to which he added a type foundry; and his son and successor **Johannes** (1708–1780), collector of dies and matrices of the 15th–17th centuries.

**En′se·na′da** (ān′sȧ·nä′thä), Marqués **de la. Ze·nón′** *or* **Ce·nón′ de So′mo·de·vil′la** (thȧ·nôn′ dȧ sō′mō·thȧ·vē′lyä). 1702–1781. Spanish naval officer and statesman; prime minister (1743–54); administered vigorous policy of internal reform; exiled from court (1754–59).

**En′sor** (ĕn′sôr), Baron **James** (jāmz). 1860–1949. Belgian painter and etcher.

**En′ters** (ĕn′tẽrs), **Ang′na** (änzh′nä). 1907– . American dancer, painter, and author, b. New York City. Awarded Guggenheim fellowship (1934–35). She has created new theater form combining arts of dance, pantomime, music, and costume.

**En′tragues′** (äN′trȧg′), **Catherine Henriette de Bal′zac′** (dē bȧl′zȧk′) **d′.** Marquise **de Ver′neuil′** (dē vĕr′nû′y′). Mistress of Henry IV of France and a central figure in plots and counterplots in the French court.

**En′tre·cas′teaux′** (äN′trē·kȧs′tō′), Chevalier **d′.** Antoine Raymond Joseph **de Bru'ni'** (brü'nē'). 1737–1793. French naval officer and explorer; in command of French fleet in East Indies (1785). Governor of Mauritius (1787–89); rear admiral (1791) and sent to find La Pérouse; explored coasts of New Caledonia, New Holland, Tasmania.

**En·ver' Pa·sha'** (ĕn·vĕr' pä·shä'). *In earlier years known as* **Enver Bey** (bā'). 1881?–1922. Turkish soldier and leader of Young Turks. Raised revolt in Macedonia (1908) forcing Sultan Abdul-Hamid to restore constitution of 1876. During negotiations (1913) after Balkan war, led group which assassinated minister of war, Nazim Pasha, turned out of office grand vizier, Kiamil Pasha, and forced sultan to fill governmental offices with Young Turk leaders; on murder (June, 1913) of Young Turk grand vizier, Mahmud Shevket, effected dismissal of officers not in sympathy with Young Turk policies; assumed post of minister of war (Jan. 3, 1914). Held command during World War, but without notable success; in internal affairs, elevated himself to position of absolute ruler. Fled after collapse of Turkey.

**Enzina, Juan del.** See ENCINA.

**En·zi'nas** (ān·thē'näs), **Francisco de.** *Also known as* **Dry'an·der'** (drē'än·dĕr'). 1520?–?1552. Spanish Protestant theologian; translated New Testament into Spanish and dedicated it to Emperor Charles V, who turned him over to the Inquisition; escaped to Wittenberg; wrote account of his imprisonment.

**En'zio** (ĕn'tsyō) *or* **En'zo** (ĕn'tsō). *Eng. also* **Henry.** 1225?–1272. Titular king of Sardinia. Natural son of Emperor Frederick II of Germany; m. (1238) Adelasia, a Sardinian heiress and took (1243) title of king of Sardinia, but never exercised sovereignty; defeated and captured (1249) by Bolognese; imprisoned (1249–72).

**Eobanus Hessus.** See HESSUS.

**É'on' de Beau'mont'** (ā'ôN' dē bō'môN'), **Charles Geneviève Louis Auguste André Timothée d'.** *Known as* Chevalier **d'Éon.** 1728–1810. French political adventurer. Sent as secret agent to Russia by Louis XV (1755); adopted woman's dress; agent, then minister plenipotentiary, in London (1762–74); in order to receive pension from France, forced by Louis XVI's decree to wear woman's dress to end of his life.

**Eormenric.** See ERMANARIC.

**Eöt'vös** (ût'vûsh), **József.** Baron **von Vá'sá·ros·ne'mény** (vä'shä·rōsh·nĕ'mān·y'). 1813–1871. Hungarian statesman and writer; leader of Hungarian reform movement (1840 ff.); champion of centralists; minister of education in Batthyány's cabinet (1848); in Munich (1848–51). Re-entered political life in Hungary (1861) and supported Deák in diets of 1861, 1865, 1867; again minister of education in Andrássy's cabinet (1867–71); established modern system of national education in Hungary. Author of social and political novels, political writings, dramas, etc. His son Baron **Roland** (1848–1919), physicist, was professor at the U. of Budapest (from 1873); minister of education (1894–95); studied gravitation and the earth's field of gravity; constructed a torsion balance (Eötvös balance) for measurement of the density of underlying rocks by means of variations in gravity, used in geological prospecting.

**E·pam'i·non'das** (ē·păm'ĭ·nŏn'dăs). 418?–362 B.C. Theban general and statesman. Defeated Spartan army at Leuctra (371 B.C.); invaded Peloponnesus (370–369). Defeated Spartans again at Mantineia (362), but mortally wounded in the battle.

**É'pée'** (ā'pā'), Abbé **Charles Michel de l'.** 1712–1789. French abbé; perfected one-hand sign alphabet for use of deaf and dumb; founded (1770) institution for deaf and dumb, in Paris.

**É'per'non'** (ā'pĕr'nôN'), Duc **d'. Jean Louis de No'ga'ret' de La Va'lette'** (dē nō'gà'rĕ' dē là vȧ'lĕt'). 1554–1642. French courtier and politician; appointed governor of Limousin (1596) by King Henry IV; transferred to Guienne (1622). Opposed policies of Cardinal Richelieu and was removed from office (1641). His son **Bernard** (1592–1662) was governor successively of Burgundy and Guienne, where his greed and cruelty made his administration unpopular.

**Eph'i·al'tes** (ĕf'ĭ·ăl'tēz). d. 469 B.C. Traitor who guided Persian detachment up mountain paths to rear of Greek force under Leonidas defending pass of Thermopylae (480 B.C.).

**Ephialtes.** d. about 456 B.C. Athenian general and statesman; sponsor of law curbing power of the Areopagus and instituting democratic government in Athens.

**Eph'o·rus** (ĕf'ō·rŭs). Greek historian of 4th century B.C., of Cyme in Asia Minor. Author of universal history (29 books) of which fragments remain.

**E'phra·em** (ē'frȧ·ĕm; -frĭ·ĕm) *or* **E'phra·im** (ē'frȧ·ĭm; -frĭ·ŭm) *or* **Eph·rem'** (ĕf·răm'), Saint. *Called* **Ephraem Sy'rus** (sī'rŭs), *i.e.* the Syrian. 306?–?373. Syrian churchman and writer, b. Nisibin, Mesopotamia. Author of commentaries on the Holy Scriptures, theological treatises, homilies, and hymns. Given title of Doctor of the Church (1920).

**E'phra·im** (ē'frȧ·ĭm; ē'frĭ·ŭm). In Bible, Joseph's younger son (*Gen.* xli. 50–52), ancestor of a tribe of Israelites (*Joshua* xvi). See JOSEPH.

**Ep'i·char'mus** (ĕp'ĭ·kär'mŭs). Greek writer of comedies in late 6th and early 5th century B.C.; b. on island of Cos. Only fragments of his plays are extant.

**Ep'ic·te'tus** (ĕp'ĭk·tē'tŭs). Greek Stoic philosopher, prob. native of Hierapolis in Phrygia. Originally a slave, he was freed by his master and taught philosophy in Rome (until 90 A.D.); expelled from Rome with other philosophers by Emperor Domitian (90). Left no writings; his philosophy known through the *Discourses* and the *Enchiridion* of his pupil Flavius Arrian.

**Ep'i·cu'rus** (ĕp'ĭ·kū'rŭs). 342?–270 B.C. Greek philosopher, b. in Samos; founder of Epicureanism. Taught in Athens (from 306 B.C.), emphasizing that pleasure is the only good and the end of all morality, but that the genuine life of pleasure must be a life of prudence, honor, and justice; in field of physics, he adopted atomistic theory of school of Democritus. Only fragments of his many works are extant.

**Ep'i·men'i·des** (ĕp'ĭ·mĕn'ĭ·dēz). Cretan philosopher, prophet, and poet, of 7th century B.C. According to legend, he fell asleep as a lad in a cave and awoke after 57 years to find that his soul, freed from the burden of the flesh, had studied philosophy and medicine and made him a great scholar in the new world about him. He sometimes replaces Periander (*q.v.*) as one of the Seven Wise Men of Greece. Goethe makes the legend subject of his poem *Des Epimenides Erwachen.*

**É'pi'nay'** (ā'pē'nā'), **Louise Florence Pétronille de la Live** (dē là lēv') **d'.** *Nee* **Tar'dieu' d'Es'cla'velles'** (tȧr'dyû' dĕs'klȧ'vĕl'). 1726–1783. French author, b. Valenciennes. Friend of Diderot, d'Alembert, Holbach, and esp. of Rousseau and Melchior Grimm (*qq.v.*); visited Geneva where she was guest of Voltaire (1757–59); aided Melchior Grimm with his *Correspondance;* wrote *Les Conversations d'Émilie* (1774; later crowned by the Academy), also *Mémoires et Correspondances* (3 vols., pub. 1818; genuine letters of Rousseau, Grimm, Diderot, etc., in the form of an autobiographical romance).

**Epiphanes.** See ANTIOCHUS IV of Syria; PTOLEMY V.

**Epiphanes Dionysus.** See ANTIOCHUS VI of Syria.

**Epiphanes Nicator.** See SELEUCUS VI.

**Epiphanes Philadelphus.** See ANTIOCHUS XI of Syria.

**Ep'i·pha'ni·us** (ĕp'ĭ·fā'nĭ·ŭs), Saint. 315?–403. Eastern church father and writer, b. in Palestine, of Jewish parents. Disciple of Hilarion; embraced Christianity and was ordained priest; founded (335) and directed (30 years) a monastery near Eleutheropolis; bishop of Constantia (formerly Salamis) in Cyprus (from 367). Champion of traditionalistic orthodoxy and zealous opponent of Origen and his school. Author of the treatise, directed against 80 heresies, entitled *Panarion*, of the anti-Arian work *Ancoratus*, etc.

**Ep'i·sco'pi·us** (ĕp'ĭ·skō'pĭ·ŭs), **Si'mon** (sī'mŭn). *Surname Latinized from* **Bis'cop, Bis'chop,** *or* **Biss'chop** (bĭs'kŏp). 1583–1643. Dutch theologian and leader of the Arminians. Studied under Arminius at Leiden; professor of theology, Leiden (1612–18); represented Remonstrants at The Hague (1611), Delft (1613), and Synod of Dort (1618); expelled from church by Synod of Dort and banished from Holland (1618); lived in exile (1618–26) in Antwerp, Paris, and Rouen; director of Remonstrant seminary, Amsterdam (from 1634), and successor to Arminius as head of Arminian, or Remonstrant, movement. Author of Remonstrant confession of faith *Confessio* (1622), *Apologia* (1629), *Institutiones Theologiae* (pub. 1650 ff.), etc.

**Epp** (ĕp), **Franz Xaver von.** 1868–1947. German general. Commanded Royal Bavarian infantry regiment in World War (1914–18); led anti-Communist campaign in Munich (1919); entered Reichswehr (1919) and retired as lieutenant general (1923); organizer of Nazi Storm Troops (1919–33) and one of its group leaders; general (1935); governor of Bavaria (1933–45).

**É'pré'mes'nil'** (ā'prā'mĕ'nēl'), **Jean Jacques Du'val'** (dü'vȧl') **d'.** 1746–1794. French jurist and politician; at beginning of French Revolution advocated establishment of constitutional monarchy; defended Parliament of Paris (1788) against royal infringement of its powers; elected to States-General (1789); defended royal cause; as member of the National Assembly, protested (1791) against new constitution; sent to guillotine by Revolutionary Tribunal (1794). His wife, **Françoise Augustine,** *nee* **de Sanc'tua'ry'** [dē säNk'tü·ȧ'rē'] (1754–1794), called **Mère' des Pau'vres** (mâr' dā pō'vr') because of her many charities, was guillotined at the same time.

**Ep'stein** (ĕp'stīn), Sir **Jacob.** 1880–1959. British sculptor of Russo-Polish descent, b. New York City. Settled in London (1905); worked in New York and other American cities (1927 ff.); author of *The Sculptor Speaks* (1931). His works include 18 symbolical figures decorating British Medical Association Building, London (1907–08); tomb of Oscar Wilde (1909); a marble Venus (exhibited 1917); life-size bronze Christ (c. 1920); bronze *Visitation* (1926; Tate Gallery); marble *Genesis* (1931); life-size statue in Subiaco stone *Ecce Homo* (1933); huge alabaster statue *Adam* (1939); and many bronze portraits.

**É'rard'** (ā'rȧr'), **Sébastien.** 1752–1831. French manufacturer of musical instruments; best known for invention of a double-action harp (exhibited in London, 1811) and improvements in pianos and organs. His nephew **Pierre Érard** (1796–1855) succeeded him in the business.

**Er'a·sis'tra·tus** (ĕr'ȧ·sĭs'trȧ·tŭs). Greek physician and anatomist of 3d century B.C.; founded school of anatomy at Alexandria. Credited with being first to distinguish between motor and sensory nerves; traced veins and arteries to the heart; invented a catheter; rejected humoral theory of disease, originating theory of pneuma.

**E·ras'mus** (ē·răz'mŭs), **Des'i·de'ri·us** (dĕs'ĭ·dēr'ĭ·ŭs). *Orig.* **Gerhard Ge'rhards** (gā'rärts; gĕr'härts) *or* **Geert Geerts** (gārts). 1466?–1536. Dutch scholar, b. Rotterdam. Traveled widely; in England (1498–99), met Colet, Grocyn, Linacre, and More at Oxford; again in England (1510–14), taught Greek at Cambridge; settled in Basel (1521) and Freiburg im Breisgau (1529). At first favored Reformation, but later opposed it and endeavored to promote reform within Roman Catholic Church. Edited New Testament in Greek, with a Latin translation (1516); also wrote *Colloquies* and *Encomium Moriae* (*Praise of Folly*). Regarded as leader in renaissance of learning in northern Europe.

**E·ras'tus** (ē·răs'tŭs; *Ger.* ā·räs'tōōs), **Thomas.** *Real surname* **Lie'ber** (lē'bēr) *or* **Lie'bler** (lē'blēr). 1524–1583. German-Swiss Zwinglian theologian, physician, and natural philosopher. Took part in theological conferences at Heidelberg (1560) and Maulbronn (1564), upheld Zwinglian doctrine of the Lord's Supper, and denied right of excommunication as a divine ordinance in controversy with Olevianus and others; excommunicated on charge of Socinianism (1570–75). Professor of medicine (1580) and of ethics (1583) in Basel, where he established the Erastian Foundation for poor medical students. Author of a collection of theses on excommunication *Explicatio...* (1568; pub. 1589). The doctrine known as Erastianism, which upholds state supremacy in ecclesiastical affairs, goes by his name, but was not directly expressed by him in its broad sense and application.

**Er'a·tos'the·nes** (ĕr'ȧ·tŏs'thē·nēz). Greek astronomer and geographer of 3d century B.C., b. in Cyrene in Africa; called by Ptolemy Euergetes to Alexandria to head the library there. Among his achievements were the establishment of a scientific chronology whereby dates were reckoned from the conquest of Troy, the measurement of the obliquity of the ecliptic, and the measurement of the circumference of the earth. Fragments of his *Geographica* have been preserved.

**Erb** (ĕrb), **Joseph Marie.** 1860–1944. French organist and composer of a series of religious compositions, piano pieces, symphonic poems, operas, etc.

**Erb** (ĕrp), **Wilhelm Heinrich.** 1840–1921. German physician; specialist in diseases of the nervous system and in electrotherapy.

**Er'ben** (ĕr'bĕn), **Karel Jaromir.** 1811–1870. Czech scholar, poet, and ethnologist; author of a volume of ballads (1853) from which Dvořák and other musicians have drawn for subject matter; published collections of Czech folk songs (3 vols., 1842–45) and folk tales (1865), editions of old texts, etc.

**Er'cel·doune** (ûr's'l·dōōn), **Thomas of.** *Called also* **Thomas the Rhymer** *and* **Thomas Lear'mont** (lēr'mŏnt). fl. 1220–1297. Scottish seer and poet. Reputed to have predicted death of Alexander III and battle of Bannockburn; reputed author of metrical romance on Tristram story, prob. from French 12th-century source.

**Er·cil'la y Zú'ñi·ga** (ĕr·thē'lyä ē thōō'nyē·gä), **Alonso de.** 1533–?1596. Spanish epic poet and soldier, b. Madrid. To Chile (1554) to aid in quelling revolt of Araucanians whose heroic resistance inspired him to write his epic *La Araucana* (37 cantos; 1569–1590), considered the first work of literary distinction in the Americas.

**Erck'mann'–Cha'tri'an'** (ĕrk'mȧn'shȧ'trē'äN'). *Joint pen name of* **Émile Erckmann** (1822–1899) *and* **Alexandre Chatrian** (1826–1890). French authors, collaborators (from 1847); achieved success with *L'Illustre Docteur Mathéus* (1859). Their fame rests on their novels, including *Le Fou Yégof* (1862), *Madame Thérèse* (1863), *Histoire d'un Conscrit de 1813* (1864), *L'Ami Fritz* (1864), *Waterloo* (1865), etc. Authors also of several plays.

**Er'dé·lyi** (ĕr'dā·lyĭ), **János.** 1814–1868. Hungarian philosopher and man of letters; published collections of Hungarian folk songs and folk tales (3 vols., 1846–48) and Hungarian proverbs (1851).

**Erd'mann** (ärt'män), **Benno.** 1851–1921. German philosopher and psychologist. Author of works on history of philosophy, esp. Kantian philosophy, and on psychology, logic, and the perception theory.

**Erdmann, Johann Eduard.** 1805–1892. German philosopher and historian of philosophy.

**Erdmann, Otto Lin'né** (lĭn'ā). 1804–1869. German chemist; known for researches on nickel, indigo, and illuminating gas, and determinations of atomic weights.

**Erd'manns·dör'fer** (ärt'mäns·dûr'fẽr), **Max von.** 1848–1905. German conductor and composer.

**E·re·men'ko.** Variant of YEREMENKO.

**Er'hard** (ĕr'härt, *Ger.*ār'-) **Ludwig.** 1897–1977. German economist and politician; chancellor of West Germany (1963–66).

**Er'ic** (ĕr'ĭk; ẹr'-; *Dan.* ẹ'rĕk) *or* **Er'ik** *or* **Er'ick.** Name of several kings of Denmark, including:

**Eric I.** *Called* **Ev'er·good'** (ĕv'ẽr·go͝od'). 1056–1103. King (1095–1103); first European king to go on pilgrimage to Palestine; died in Cyprus.

**Eric II.** *Called* **the Memorable.** d. 1137. King (1134–37); son of Eric I; reign marked by civil war.

**Eric III.** *Called* **the Lamb.** d. 1147. King (1137–47); abdicated.

**Eric IV** (*or* **VI**). *Called* **Plough'pen'ny** (plou'pĕn'ĭ). 1216–1250. King (1241–50); son of Waldemar II; civil war during reign; killed by his brother Abel.

**Eric V** (*or* **VII**). *Called* **Klip'ping** (klē'pĕng). 1249?–1286. King (1259–86); son of Christopher I; during minority, kingdom under queen mother, Margaret; reign marked by continual struggle with church, new constitution (1282), charters granted to towns.

**Eric VI** (*or* **VIII**). *Called* **Mœnd'ved** *or* **Men'ved** (mĕn'vĭth). 1274–1319. King (1286–1319); son of Eric V; fought war with Norway; imprisoned archbishop and suffered papal interdict.

**Eric VII** of Pomerania. 1382–1459. Grandnephew of Margaret; recognized as heir to throne; king of Norway (1389–1439); nominally sole ruler under Union of Kalmar (1397–1412), but affairs controlled by Margaret; succeeded to throne (1412–39) as Eric VII of Denmark and Eric XIII of Sweden; reign a period of dissension; made pilgrimage to Palestine (1423–25); driven out of Sweden by uprising of the Dalecarlians (1434–36); deposed in both countries (1439); fled to Gotland living as a pirate (1439–49); in Pomerania (1449–59).

**Eric** (*Norw.* ā'rĕk). *Also known as* **Eric I.** d. 1024? Natural son of Earl Haakon. Ruler of Norway (1000–15). Divided Norway with his brother Earl Sweyn (1000); took eastern shires; his rule never complete; abdicated (1015) and sailed to England, where he assisted Canute in his conquest.

**Eric** (*Swed.* ā'rĭk'). Name of fourteen kings of Sweden, especially:

**Eric IX.** *Called* **the Saint.** d. 1160. King (1150–60). Zealous Christian; led crusade to Finland (1157); forced defeated Finns to be baptized; patron saint of Swedes.

**Eric X** *or* **Eric Cnuts'son** (k'no͞ot'sôn). d. 1216. King (1208–16). Grandson of Eric IX.

**Eric XI.** *Called* **the Lisping** *and* **the Lame.** d. 1250. King (1222–50). Sought aid of powerful Earl Birger, who established Folkung dynasty (1250).

**Eric XII.** 1339–1359. King (1356–59). Son of Magnus II Eriksson. At first supported Magnus in Sweden; later, ruled in Sweden alone.

**Eric XIII.** = ERIC VII of Denmark.

**Eric XIV.** 1533–1577. King (1560–68). Son of Gustavus Vasa, b. Stockholm. Imprisoned his brother John (1563); fought seven years' war with Denmark (1563–70); for seven years (1558–65), wrote love letters to, and unsuccessfully sought marriage with, Queen Elizabeth of England; proposed also to Mary, Queen of Scots and other royal princesses; finally m. (1568) Catherine Karin, a corporal's daughter; became mentally deranged; his brother John proclaimed king (1568); formally deposed (1569); imprisoned and probably finally poisoned (1569–77).

**Eric Blood'axe'** (blŭd'ăks') *or* **Bloody Axe.** *Norw.* **Blod'öx'** (blōd'ûks'). d. 954? King of Norway (930–934). Son of Harold I, at whose abdication he became king; killed several of his brothers to secure his throne; unpopular because of his cruelty; defeated by his half brother Haakon (934), who became king (935); fled to England; ruled Northumbria; killed in battle. His son Harold became king of Norway (961).

**E'ric Mag'nus·son** (*Norw.* ā'rĕk mäng'no͞o·sôn). *Also known as* **Eric II.** *Called* **Priest–Hater.** 1268–1299. King of Norway (1280–99). Neutral in conflict between barons and church (1280–82); continued war against Denmark begun by his father Magnus VI (1280–95); made peace with Hanseatic cities (1285); m. 1st (1282) Margaret of Scotland; their daughter Margaret (*q.v.*) known as "Maid of Norway"; m. 2d (1293) Isabella Bruce, sister of Robert Bruce, later king of Scotland.

**Eric the Red.** fl. 10th century. Norwegian navigator. Left Iceland (982) and spent three years exploring southwest coast of Greenland (982–985); named new land "Greenland" to make it attractive to colonists; planted colony (986) near present Julianehaab. Subject of Icelandic *Saga of Eric the Red.* See Leif ERICSON.

**Er'ich·sen** (ĕr'ĭk·s'n), Sir **John Eric.** 1818–1896. British surgeon, b. Copenhagen. Professor of surgery (1850–75), University Coll.; surgeon extraordinary to Queen Victoria.

**Erichsen, Ludvig Mylius–.** See MYLIUS-ERICHSEN.

**Er'ic·son** *or* **Er'ics·son** (ĕr'ĭk·s'n), **Leif** (lāv). *Also* **Er'ik·sen, Er'ik·son, Er'iks·son.** Son of Eric the Red (*q.v.*). Norse mariner and adventurer who, according to Icelandic sagas, sailed westward and discovered (c. 1000) land which he named Vinland because of grapevines found there. His Vinland has been variously identified as the coast of Labrador, of Newfoundland, and of New England.

**Er'ics·son** (ĕr'ĭk·s'n; *Swed.* ā'rĭk·sôn'), **John.** 1803–1889. Engineer and inventor, b. in Värmland Province, Sweden. To London (1826), then to U.S. (1839); naturalized. Reputation as engineer established while in England, esp. by his introduction of the screw propeller on a commercial vessel. In U.S. his name associated with ironclad *Monitor* (launched 1862), whose construction and equipment (propelled by steam only, using screw propeller, having guns mounted in revolving armored turret) inaugurated new era in naval engineering. Also effected improvements in design of heavy guns and mountings, and many improvements in steam machinery. See T. R. TIMBY. His elder brother **Nils** (1802–1870) was a Swedish army engineer, built docks at Stockholm, and first of important series of canals in Finland, joining Lake Saima with Gulf of Finland.

**E·rig'e·na** (ĕ·rĭj'ĕ·nȧ), **Johannes Scotus.** *Later (16th century ff.) designation of* **Johannes Sco'tus** (skō'tŭs), *i.e.* John the Scot. *Literary pseudonym* **Johannes Ie·ru'ge·na** (yĕ·ro͞o'jĕ·nȧ) *or* **Er'i·u'ge·na** (ĕr'ĭ·ū'jĕ·nȧ), *meaning perhaps* "Irish-born." 815?–?877. Medieval philosopher and theologian, doubtless native of Ireland, perhaps of Scottish parentage. Invited to

France by Charles the Bald and made head of court school (c. 847); in his first work, sometimes confused with a treatise by an Aquitanian monk **Ra·tram′nus** [rȧ·trăm′nŭs] (d. about 868), advanced doctrine that the eucharist is symbolical or commemorative; went to aid of Hincmar, Archbishop of Reims, in predestination controversy, with treatise *De Divina Praedestinatione* (c. 851), defending liberty of the will, denying any necessity in God or in man, which was condemned by councils of Valence (855), Langres (859), and Vercelli (1050); translated into Latin works of Dionysius the Areopagite (c. 858) at request of Charles the Bald with his own commentary on the original. Author of *De Divisione Naturae* (c. 865–870), maintaining a monism merging God and the world in the higher unity of nature, presenting the universe as ultimate unity working out in rational system of the world, and hence attempting to reconcile authority with reason, a position condemned by council at Sens and by Pope Honorius III (1225).

**Erik.** See ERIC.

**Eriksen** *or* **Erikson** *or* **Eriksson, Leif.** See ERICSON.

**E′riks·son′** (ā′rĭk·sôn′), **Christian.** 1858–1935. Swedish sculptor.

**E·rin′na** (ē·rĭn′ȧ). Greek poet regarded by some authorities as contemporary and friend of Sappho (6th century B.C.), by others as of 4th century B.C. Only slight fragments of her works are extant.

**Erk** (ĕrk), **Ludwig Christian.** 1807–1883. German singing teacher and editor; helped collect and foster German "popular," or folk, songs; in Berlin, founded the Erk male choral society (1845) and Erk mixed chorus (1852).

**Er′kel** (ĕr′kĕl), **Franz** *or* **Ferencz.** 1810–1893. Hungarian conductor and composer, creator of Hungarian national opera. Composer of Hungarian national hymn (1845) and of 9 operas.

**Er′lach′, d′** (dĕr′lȧk′). Swiss family of soldiers and diplomats, including: **Jean Louis** (1595–1650), who passed into French service, was naturalized, and distinguished himself in campaigns in Germany and at the battle of Lens (1648); **Jean** (1628–1694), who also entered French service, distinguished himself at Gravelines and Maastricht; **Jean Louis** (1648–1680), who served in the Dutch navy under Admiral Tromp and became vice-admiral (1678); **Jérôme** (1667–1748), who served in France, and later in Austria, and returned to become chief magistrate at Bern (1721–47); **Charles Louis** (1746–1798), who served France and then was appointed (1798) general in chief of the Bernese army to resist French invasion, was defeated at Fraubrunnen and slain by his own troops; **Rodolphe Louis** (1749–1810), who led a rebellion of Bernese against the French (1802).

**Er′lang′er** (ûr′lăng′ẽr), **Abraham Lincoln.** 1860–1930. American theatrical manager and producer, b. Buffalo, N.Y.; helped form (1896) Theatrical Syndicate which for years had virtual monopoly of American theatrical business; his firm (Klaw & Erlanger) also did independent producing.

**Er′lan′ger′** (ĕr′läɴ′zhā′), **Camille.** 1863–1919. French composer, b. Paris. Author of the dramatic legend *Saint Jean l'Hospitalier*, and operas.

**Erlanger,** Baron **Frederic A. d′.** See D'ERLANGER.

**Er′lang′er** (ûr′lăng′ẽr), **Joseph.** 1874–1965. American physiologist, b. San Francisco; professor, Washington U., St. Louis (from 1910); shared with H. S. Gasser (*q.v.*) 1944 Nobel prize for medicine, for work on nerve fibers.

**Er′len·mey′er** (ĕr′lĕn·mī′ẽr), **Emil.** 1825–1909. German organic chemist; proposed the commonly accepted formula for naphthalene (1866); originated the flat-bottomed, cone-shaped, thin glass flask named after him.

**Erlon, Jean Baptiste Drouet d′.** See DROUET D'ERLON.

**Er·mak′ Ti·mo·fe′ev** (yĭr·mȧk′ tyĭ·mŭ·fyā′yĕf). d. 1584. Hetman of Don Cossacks and conqueror of Siberia; his exploits are themes of Russian folk songs; hero of Khomyakov's verse drama *Ermak.*

**Er′man** (ĕr′män), **Adolf.** 1854–1937. German Egyptologist and lexicographer, founder of scientific study of the ancient Egyptian language.

**Er′man** (ĕr′män), **Paul.** 1764–1851. German physicist. His son **Georg Adolf** (1806–1877), also a physicist, made measurements of the earth's magnetism on a journey through northern Asia and around the world (1828–30), these data being used by Gauss in constructing his theory of terrestrial magnetism.

**Er·man′a·ric** (ûr·măn′ȧ·rĭk). fl. 350–376 A.D. King of the Ostrogoths, first of the Amalings. Built up an empire in eastern Europe on Dnieper River; overthrown by invasion of the Huns. Called "the Gothic Alexander"; in German legend the type of the cruel tyrant. In Anglo-Saxon poetry appears as **Eor′men·ric** (ĕ′ôr-mĕn·rēch), in Norse literature as **Jor′mun·rek** (yôr′mo͞on·rāk).

**Er′ma·ting′er** (ĕr′mä·tĭng′ẽr), **Emil.** 1873–1953. Swiss literary historian.

**Ermenegild.** See under LEOVIGILD.

**Er′men′gem′** (ĕr′mäɴ′gĕm′), **Frédéric van** (vȧn). *Pseudonym* **Franz Hel′lens′** (fräɴts ā′lĕns′). 1881– . Belgian writer; author of *Les Clartés Latentes* (awarded Picard prize, 1912), *Fraîcheur de la Mer* (Grand Prix de Littérature, 1935), etc.

**Er′nest** (ûr′nĕst; -nĭst). *Ger.* **Ernst.** 1441–1486. Elector of Saxony. Elder son of Frederick the Gentle. Founder of the Ernestine line (*q.v.*). Joint ruler of Saxony (1464–85) with his brother Albert III (*q.v.*); received central portions of Thuringia in division of dominions (1485). See also ALBERTINE LINE.

**Ernest.** *Ger.* **Ernst.** 1497–1546. Duke of Brunswick-Lü′ne·burg [-lü′nĕ·bo͝orᴋ] (1521–46); called "the Confessor." Introduced Lutheranism into duchy (1527); signed protest against edict of Diet of Spires (1529); signed Augsburg Confession (1530); member of League of Schmalkalden (1531).

**Ernest I.** *Ger.* **Ernst.** *Called* **der From′me** (dĕr frôm′ĕ), *i.e.* the Pious. 1601–1675. Duke of Saxe′-Wei′mar [săks′vī′mär] (1620–40) and of Saxe-Gotha (1640–75). Son of John, Duke of Weimar, of the Ernestine line; founded ducal house which through his sons became houses of Saxe-Coburg-Gotha, Saxe-Meiningen, etc. (*q.v.*). Fought in Thirty Years' War under Gustavus Adolphus and his own younger brother, Bernhard of Saxe-Weimar; signed Peace of Prague (1635); received (1644) half of Eisenach and (1672) the greater part of Altenburg and Coburg. His eldest son, Frederick, inherited the duchy of Saxe-Gotha; his second son, Albert, founded (1680) the new line of Saxe-Coburg; his sixth son, **Ernest,** established (1683) the minor duchy of Saxe-Hildburghausen (*q.v.*).

**Ernest.** *Ger.* **Ernst.** Name of two dukes of Saxe-Coburg-Gotha (*q.v.*):

**Ernest I.** 1784–1844. Duke of Saxe-Coburg-Saal′feld [-zäl′fĕlt] (as Ernest III, 1806–26) and of Saxe-Coburg-Gotha (1826–44). Son of Francis Frederick, Duke of Saxe-Coburg-Saalfeld. On extinction (1825) of Saxe-Gotha-Al′ten·burg (-äl′tĕn·bo͝orᴋ) line, exchanged Saalfeld for Gotha and assumed title of Ernest I (1826). Fought against Napoleon (1806) and lost his lands, recovered by Treaty of Tilsit (1807); again joined Allies against France (1813); awarded principality of Lichtenberg by Congress of Vienna (1816); acquired Gotha (1826); sold Lichtenberg to Prussia (1834). His younger son, Albert, m. (1840) Queen Victoria of England.

**Ernest II.** 1818–1893. Duke (1844–93); older son of Ernest I; b. Coburg; educ. at Bonn and traveled extensively. Fought successfully in war against Denmark (1849); by his liberal policies prevented disturbances in his duchy during revolutionary crisis (1848–49); a nationalist, but favored Austrian leadership and long opposed Bismarck; later sided with Prussia in Seven Weeks' War (1866) and took part in Franco-Prussian War (1870–71). Known as an excellent musician; wrote several operas.

**Ernest I.** *Ger.* **Ernst.** 1826–1908. Duke of Saxe'-Al'ten·burg [săks'äl'tĕn·bŏŏrk] (1853–1908); son of Duke George; b. at Hildburghausen; officer in Prussian army (1851–53); took part in Franco-Prussian War (1870–71); left no heir, succession passing to his nephew **Ernest II** (1871–1955), general in Prussian army, duke (1908–18; abdicated).

**Ernest Au·gus'tus** (ô·gŭs'tŭs). *Ger.* **Ernst August.** Name of rulers of Hanover. (1) 1629–1698. First elector (1692–98) of Hanover; m. (1658) **Sophia** (1630–1714), daughter of elector Frederick V of the Palatinate and of Elizabeth, daughter of James I of England. Their son became king of England as George I, first of the house of Hanover (see HANOVER).

(2) 1771–1851. First king (1837–51) of Hanover. Son of George III of England; created (1799) duke of **Cum'ber·land** (kŭm'bēr·lănd); became king of Hanover on separation (1837) of English and Hanoverian crowns at accession of Victoria as queen of England. Succeeded as king by his son George V, who ruled until annexation of Hanover by Prussia (1866).

(3) 1845–1923. Son and successor of George V, and duke of Brunswick-Lüneburg (from 1884, at extinction of elder Brunswick line; see BRUNSWICK), but not allowed by Hohenzollerns to rule.

(4) 1887–1953. Son of the preceding; m. (1913) Victoria Louise, daughter of William II of Germany; succeeded to duchy of Brunswick (1913–18; abdicated).

**Er·ne'sti** (ĕr·nĕs'tē), **Johann August.** 1707–1781. German Protestant theologian and classical philologist.

**Er'nes·tine line** (ûr'nĕs·tĭn; -nĭs-; -tēn). *Also known as* **Lau'en·burg line** (lou'ĕn·bŏŏrk). Elder line of Wettin family (*q.v.*), established (1485) with division of electoral duchy of Saxony between Ernest and Albert III (*qq.v.;* see also ALBERTINE LINE), sons of Frederick the Gentle. At division received central part of region that is now Thuringia (see FREDERICK the Wise and JOHN); but lost (1547) electoral dignity and much territory to Albertine line (see JOHN FREDERICK the Magnanimous and MAURICE); remaining lands broken up into Ernestine duchies (see SAXE-ALTENBURG, SAXE-COBURG-GOTHA, SAXE-GOTHA, SAXE-MEININGEN, SAXE-WEIMAR-EISENACH), thus becoming actually the secondary line.

**Ernle,** 1st Baron. See Rowland Edmund PROTHERO.

**Ernst** (ĕrnst). German form of ERNEST.

**Ernst** (ûrnst), **Edwin Charles.** 1885– . American radiologist; known for diagnosis and treatment by means of X-ray and radium applications and for researches in X-ray unit measurement.

**Ernst, Harold Clarence.** 1856–1922. American bacteriologist; studied under Koch. Taught bacteriology at Harvard Medical School (from 1885), professor (1895–1922); in Boston, established first diphtheria-antitoxin laboratory.

**Ernst** (ĕrnst), **Heinrich Wilhelm.** 1814–1865. Violin virtuoso and composer, b. Brünn, Moravia; lived chiefly in Paris and London.

**Ernst, Max.** 1891– . German surrealist painter, cofounder in Cologne of a Dadaist group (1919) which collaborated on the Fatagaga collages.

**Ernst, Otto.** Pseudonym of Otto Ernst SCHMIDT.

**Ernst, Paul.** 1866–1933. German writer, dramatist, and critic. Author of translations of old Italian tales (1902), original short stories and narrative poems modeled in part after Boccaccio and other Italian writers; the historical epic in verse *Das Kaiserbuch* (1923–38), critical essays, works on sociological and economic questions, novels, plays, autobiographical writings, etc.

**Er·pe'ni·us** (ûr·pē'nĭ·ŭs; -pēn'yŭs), *orig.* **van Er'pe** (văn ĕr'pĕ), **Thomas.** 1584–1624. Dutch Orientalist, b. in Gorinchem; friend of Scaliger and Casaubon. Author of an Arabic grammar (1613), a Hebrew grammar (1621), a Chaldean and Syrian grammar (1628), etc.

**Ersch** (ĕrsh), **Johann Samuel.** 1766–1828. German bibliographer and encyclopedist; founder of modern German bibliography.

**Er'skine** (ûr'skĭn). Family name of earls of BUCHAN (after 1617).

**Erskine, David Steuart.** 11th Earl of **Buch'an** (bŭk'ăn; bŭk'ăn). 1742–1829. Called Lord **Card'ross** (kärd'rŏs) until death of his father, the 10th earl. Instrumental in freeing election of Scottish representative peers of governmental interference; presented George Washington (1792) with snuffbox made from tree that sheltered Wallace.

His brother **Henry** (1746–1817) was lord advocate of Scotland (1783, 1806); dean of Faculty of Advocates (1785–95), not re-elected on account of his condemnation of government's sedition and treason bills as unconstitutional; remembered as eloquent and witty orator at Scottish bar; author of *The Emigrant, an Eclogue* (1773) and other poems.

**Thomas** (1750–1823), 1st Baron **Erskine of Res·tor'mel** (rĕs·tôr'mĕl), another brother, eminent advocate before English bar, was called to bar (1778); won instant success with defense of Captain Baillie of Greenwich Hospital, accused of libel; made successful defenses of Admiral Lord Keppel and of Lord George Gordon, demolishing the doctrine of constructive treason (1781); M.P. (1783); attorney general to prince of Wales (1783); contributed to passing of Fox's Libel Act (1792); sympathizing with French Revolution, procured acquittal for Tom Paine, Frost, Hardy, and Horne Tooke; attacked current theory of criminal responsibility in defense of Hadfield, who was charged with shooting at George III (1800); lord chancellor in Grenville's All-the-Talents Administration (1806), despite his ignorance of equity; resigned (1807); advocated Negro emancipation; made last speech in House of Lords (1820), in defense of Queen Caroline, with impassioned eloquence; worked for cause of Greek independence (1822–23).

**Erskine, Ebenezer.** 1680–1754. Scottish clergyman. Grandson of a cadet of family of earl of Mar. Refused oath of abjuration; defended heterodox views of *Marrow of Modern Divinity* in the Marrow controversy (1720); censured prevalent doctrinal errors and advocated right of people to choose their pastors (1733); deposed. With his son-in-law James Fisher, compiler of Fisher's *Catechism*, William Wilson and Alexander Moncrieff (three fellow ministers of Church of Scotland), at Gairney Bridge near Kinross (1733), formed an Associate Presbytery, setting up the Secession Church or Marrowkirk, earliest dissenters from the national church, whence they were called the Secession Fathers; headed (1747) the Burghers in the split of the Seceders into Burghers and Antiburghers. His brother **Ralph** (1685–1752), clergyman and poet, joined the Associate Presbytery (1737), took side of Burghers; author of *Gospel Sonnets* (1732) and the odd conceit *Smoking Spiritualized.*

**Erskine, John.** 6th Baron **Erskine,** 1st *or* 6th Earl of

**Mar** (mär) of Erskine line. d. 1572. Son of John, 5th Lord Erskine (d. 1552), who was guardian of King James V, later of Mary, Queen of Scots. Like his father, keeper of Edinburgh Castle (1554); member of council of Mary Stuart (1561) and favored her marriage with Darnley; fought at Langside; guardian of James, later King James VI, saved young prince from clutches of Bothwell (1569); joined nobles against Mary and Bothwell; regent of Scotland (1571), but a tool of Morton.

His only son, **John** (1558?–1634), 2d or 7th Earl of Mar, guardian of young King James VI (1578), but a puppet of earl of Morton; foiled plot to carry off king (1580); took part in seizure of king through raid of Ruthven (1582) and on king's escape, fled to England. Conspired (1584) with Sir Thomas Lyon, master of Glamis, captured Stirling, and on flight of Arran made terms with Elizabeth and became privy councilor of Scotland (1585) and guardian of Prince Henry (1595); helped to thwart Gowrie conspiracy (1600); envoy to London to negotiate James VI's accession to English throne (1601); lord high treasurer of Scotland (1616–30).

**John** (1675–1732), 6th or 11th Earl of Mar, Jacobite leader, eldest son of 5th earl, was one of commissioners for union (1705); English secretary of state for Scotland (1713), deprived (1714); placed himself at head of adherents of James Edward, the Old Pretender (1715), proclaimed James VIII king; defeated at Sheriffmuir by Archibald Campbell, Duke of Argyll, escaped with Pretender to Gravelines; later, was distrusted by Jacobites, accepted pension from George I (1721); attainted (1716), leaving earldom under forfeiture for 108 years. His grandson **John Francis Erskine** (1741–1825) was restored earl by act of Parliament (1824) and was succeeded by his grandson (1828), who inherited (1835) earldom of Kellie.

**Erskine** of Dun (dŭn), **John.** 1509–1591. Scottish Reformer. Son of 5th laird of Dun, of branch of Erskine family later honored with earldom of Mar. Brought back from abroad first teacher of Greek in Scotland; supported George Wishart and John Knox, Reform preachers, acting as conciliator between Knox and the queen; superintendent of Reformed Church of Scotland for Angus and Mearns (1560–89); one of compilers of *Second Book of Discipline* (1578).

**Erskine** of Car′nock (kär′nŏk), **John.** 1695–1768. Scottish jurist. Presented connected treatment of Scots law in *Principles of the Law of Scotland* (1754); author of *Institutes of the Law of Scotland* (1773). His son **John** (1721–1803), theologian, friend of Whitefield and Jonathan Edwards, was leader of evangelical party of the church. His grandson **Thomas Erskine** of Lin·la′then [lĭn·lā′thĕn] (1788–1870), theological writer, became member of Edinburgh Faculty of Advocates (1810) and belonged to brilliant legal circle; upheld Calvinism, interpreting its mystical side; developed unorthodox doctrine of universal atonement advanced by John McLeod Campbell; author of Christian apologetics.

**Erskine, John.** 1879–1951. American educator and writer, b. New York City. Taught English at Columbia (1909–37). Author of many books on English literature, and of *The Private Life of Helen of Troy* (1925), *Galahad* (1926), *Adam and Eve* (1927), *Penelope's Man* (1928), *Tristan and Isolde* (1932), *Solomon, My Son!* (1935), *Brief Hour of François Villon* (1937), etc.

**Ertz** (?ûrts), **Susan.** Novelist, b. in England, of American parentage; m. J. Ronald McCrindle (1932). Author of *Madame Claire* (1922), *Nina* (1924), *The Galaxy* (1929), *Woman Alive* (1935), *Black, White, and Caroline* (1938), and volumes of short stories.

**Er′vine** (ûr′vĭn), **St. John Greer.** 1883–1971. Irish playwright and novelist, b. Belfast. Manager of Abbey Theatre, Dublin (1915); professor of dramatic literature, Royal Society of Literature (1933–36). Author of plays, including *Mixed Marriage* (1910), *Jane Clegg* (1911), *John Ferguson* (1914), *The First Mrs. Fraser* (1928), *People of our Class* (1934), *Robert's Wife* (1937), *The Christies* (1939); of novels, including *Mrs. Martin's Man, Alice and a Family, Changing Winds, The Foolish Lovers, The Wayward Man, Sophia;* of miscellaneous prose works, as *If I Were Dictator.*

**Er′win** (ĕr′vēn). *After 17th century often called* **Er′win von Stein′bach** (fôn shtīn′bäκ). 1244?–1318. German architect, engaged (with his son, namesake, and successor, **Erwin**) in construction of part of Strasbourg Cathedral (1277–1339).

**Erx′le′ben** (ĕrks′lā′bĕn), **Johann Christian Polycarp.** 1744–1777. German physician and naturalist; author of *Systema Regni Animalis* (1776), etc.

**Erz′ber′ger** (ĕrts′bĕr′gẽr), **Matthias.** 1875–1921. German statesman; in Reichstag (1903); leader of left wing of Center party. Sought to enlighten neutral opinion during World War I and worked for international relationship, primarily of Roman Catholic clergy; opposed German war policy (1917) and advocated peace by agreement; took active part in coalition of Centrists, Progressives, and Social Democrats, and fathered July Resolution in Reichstag in favor of peace without annexations (1917). Secretary of state without portfolio under Maximilian, Prince of Baden (1918); chairman of armistice commission and signed Compiègne armistice (1918); minister without portfolio under Scheidemann (1919); favored acceptance of Versailles treaty at Weimar National Assembly; minister of finance and, briefly, vice-chancellor under Bauer (1919); carried through Erzberger system of imperial finance and tax reforms; charged with questionable private transactions and financial misdemeanors while in office by Helfferich, whom he sued for libel (1920); resigned (1920). Headed Württemberg Center party in Reichstag (1920); shot and killed by former officers (1921).

**Esaias.** See ISAIAH.

**Es·a′ki** (ĕ·säk′ē), **Leo.** 1925–    Japanese physicist. With International Business Machines Co. in U.S. (1960–  ); awarded (with Ivar Giaever and Brian Josephson) Nobel prize for physics (1973).

**E′sar·had′don** (ē′sär·hăd′′n) *or* **Es′sar·had′don** (ĕs′är·hăd′′n). d. 669 B.C. A Sargonid king of Assyria (681–669 B.C.). Son of Sennacherib. Quelled civil war that broke out as result of murder of Sennacherib by one of his sons; rebuilt Babylon; made conquests in east and north; many Asiatic kings became subject to him, including Jewish rulers in Palestine; destroyed Sidon (677); led two great armies into Egypt (675–669); at first turned back by Taharka (*q.v.*), but later (671) defeated him; plundered Memphis; one of most powerful kings of Assyria; a great builder, erected palace in Nineveh. Father of Shamash-shum-ukin and of Ashurbanipal (*qq.v.*).

**E′sau** (ē′sô) *or* **E′dom** (ē′dŭm). In Bible, son of Isaac and Rebekah, and twin brother of Jacob, to whom he sold his birthright (*Gen.* xxv. 21–34; xxvii); ancestor of the Edomites (*Gen.* xxxvi).

**Es′bach′** (ĕz′bȧk′), **Georges Hubert.** 1843–1890. French physician.

**Es′björn** (ĕs′byûrn), **Lars Paul.** 1808–1870. Lutheran clergyman and educator, b. in Sweden; to U.S. (1849). Leader of secession of Swedish Lutherans and of organization of independent Augustana Synod (1860).

**Es′ca·lan′te** (äs′kä·län′tā), **Juan de.** d. 1519. Spanish soldier and explorer; to Mexico with Hernando Cortes; killed in battle with Aztecs.

**Esch** (ĕsh), **John Jacob.** 1861–1941. American lawyer and politician; member, U.S. House of Representatives (1899–1921). Member of U.S. Interstate Commerce Commission (1921–28). Author with Senator Cummins of Iowa of Esch-Cummins Transportation Act (1920).

**Eschenbach, Wolfram von.** See WOLFRAM VON ESCHENBACH.

**E'schen·burg** (ĕsh'ĕn·bŏŏrk), **Johann Joachim.** 1743–1820. German critic, literary historian, and translator. Translated works of English writers on aesthetics, Italian and English opera and oratorio texts, and, for the first time, the complete dramatic works of Shakespeare (13 vols., 1775–82).

**E'schen·may'er** (ĕsh'ĕn·mī'ēr), **Adam Karl August.** 1768–1852. German metaphysician; agreed with Schelling and opposed Hegel; placed faith above philosophical speculation.

**E'scher** (ĕsh'ēr), **Johann Heinrich Alfred.** 1819–1882. Swiss statesman. President of national council (1849–50). Advocated reform of federal system, and favored private ownership of Swiss railroads.

**E'sche·rich** (ĕsh'ĕ·rĭk), **Karl.** 1871–1951. German entomologist.

**E'scher von der Linth** (ĕsh'ēr fôn dēr lĭnt'), **Hans Konrad.** 1767–1823. Swiss statesman. Member of grand council of Helvetic Republic (1798–1802); as president of board of inspection, devoted himself to canalization of the Linth, upper course of the Limmat (Escher Canal; 1807–22). He and his family were officially granted honorary surname "von der Linth" by grand council of Zurich (1823).

**Esch'scholtz** (ĕsh'shōlts), **Johann Friedrich.** 1793–1831. German naturalist and traveler. See Otto von KOTZEBUE.

**Es'co·bar' y Men·do'za** (ās'kō·bär' ē mān·dō'thä), **Antonio.** 1589–1669. Spanish Jesuit and casuist, b. Valladolid. Known esp. for his doctrine that the sole determinant of the moral value of actions is the moral intent of the agent, the actions being in themselves amoral.

**Es'co·be'do** (ās'kō·bā'thō), **Mariano.** 1827–1902. Mexican soldier; as brigadier general, resisted French invasion (1861–63); to San Antonio, Texas; organized Republican army. Re-entered Mexico (1865), taking Monterey; defeated Miramón at San Jacinto (1867); promoted commander in chief of Republican forces; defeated and captured Maximilian at Querétaro (May 15, 1867); signed order for Maximilian's execution (June 16, 1867).

**Es'cof'fier'** (ĕs'kô'fyā'), **Georges Auguste.** 1846–1935. Famous Parisian chef.

**Es·cói'quiz** (ās·koi'kēth), **Juan.** 1762–1820. Spanish statesman and ecclesiastic; tutor to prince of Asturias (later Ferdinand VII); appointed counselor of state on Ferdinand's accession (1808); accompanied Ferdinand to Bayonne (1808), remaining with him during his imprisonment by Napoleon (to 1814); minister of state (1815); exiled (1815 ff.). Translated Young's *Night Thoughts* and Milton's *Paradise Lost.*

**Es'co·su'ra** (ās'kō·sōō'rä), **Patricio de la.** 1807–1878. Spanish statesman and writer, b. Madrid; minister of interior; ambassador to Germany (1872). Author of many novels and plays.

**Esdras.** See EZRA.

**Esek, Uncle.** Pseudonym of Henry Wheeler SHAW.

**E·se'nin** (yĭ·syā'nyĭn), **Sergei Aleksandrovich.** 1895–1925. Russian poet; founded imagist group in Russia (1919); known as "poet laureate of the Revolution"; m. 1st Isadora Duncan (*q.v.*), and 2d, a granddaughter of Tolstoi; became insane, committed suicide.

**E'sher** (ē'shēr), 1st Viscount. **William Baliol Brett** (brĕt). 1817–1899. English judge. M.P. (1866); solicitor general (1868); justice, Court of Common Pleas (1868); lord justice of appeal (1877–83); master of the rolls (1883); retired and was created Viscount Esher (1897). His son **Reginald Baliol** (1852–1930), 2d viscount; counselor to prime ministers; chairman of committee that created a general staff for army, with a chief charged with war operations and training of staff officers in war and peace (1904); parliamentary committeeman on imperial defense (from 1905–30); deputy governor, and governor, of Windsor Castle (1901–30); chosen one of editors of *Correspondence of Queen Victoria* (1907); wrote *The Girlhood of Queen Victoria* (1912), *The Tragedy of Lord Kitchener* (1921), *Cloud-capt Towers* (1927).

**Esh·kol'** (**Shkol'nik**) [ĕsh·kôl' (shkôl'nĕk)], **Le'vi** (lē'vē). 1895–1969. Israeli politician; minister of finance (1952–63); prime minister (1963–69).

**Es·la'va y E'li·zon'da** (ās·lä'vä ē ā'lē·thôn'dä), **Miguel Hilarión.** 1807–1878. Spanish composer. His works include operas, religious music, and collections of Spanish church music of the 16th–19th centuries.

**Es'march** (ĕs'märk), **Johannes Friedrich August von.** 1823–1908. German surgeon; authority on military surgery; inventor of a method for keeping a limb nearly bloodless during amputation.

**Esnambuc, Pierre Belain d'.** See BELAIN.

**Es'pa'gnat'** (ĕs'pȧ'nyȧ'), **Georges d'.** 1870–1950. French painter; identified with neoimpressionism.

**Es'par·te'ro** (ās'pär·tā'rō), **Baldomero.** Conde **de Lu·cha'na** (lōō·chä'nä). 1792–1879. Spanish general and statesman; to South America and fought against colonists (1815–23); taken prisoner at Ayacucho (1824). On return to Spain supported Isabella II; fought in Carlist war (1834–40); commander in chief of government forces (1836); defeated Carlists; regent (virtually dictator) of Spain after resignation of queen regent Maria Christina (1841–43). After Isabella was declared of age, was driven out of Spain by rebels under Narváez (1843); regained honors by royal decree (1848); prime minister (1854–56); made prince of **Ver·ga'ra** (vĕr·gä'rä) by King Amadeus. See Leopoldo O'DÓNNELL.

**Es·pe'jo** (ās·pĕ'hō), **Antonio de.** fl. 1581–83. Spanish merchant in Mexico; explored New Mexico region.

**Esperey, Franchet d'.** See FRANCHET D'ESPEREY.

**Es·pi'na de Ser'na** (ās·pē'nä thā sĕr'nä), **Concha.** 1877–1955. Spanish novelist.

**Es'pi'nasse'** (ĕs'pē'nȧs'), **Charles Marie Esprit.** 1815–1859. French general; killed at Magenta.

**Espinasse, Julie de l'.** See LESPINASSE.

**Es'pi·nel'** (ās'pē·nĕl'), **Vicente Martínez.** 1551?–1624. Spanish writer and musician. Revived the *décima* (stanza of ten octosyllabic lines), now called after him the *espinela;* credited by some with having introduced fifth string on the guitar. Known esp. for his picaresque novel *Vida del Escudero Marcos de Obregón* (1618), a source for Lesage's *Gil Blas.*

**Es'pi·no'sa** (ās'pē·nō'sä), **Gaspar de.** 1484?–1537. Spanish soldier and lawyer. To Darien with Pedrarias' expedition (1514); appointed chief justice; tried Balboa, later (1517) condemning him to death on order of governor.

**Espinosa y Tel'lo** (ē tā'lyō), **José de.** 1763–1815. Spanish mariner and hydrographer.

**Es'pron·ce'da** (ās'prôn·thā'thä), **José de.** 1808–1842. Spanish poet; often called "the Spanish Byron." Involved from early youth (1822) in revolutionary struggles and plots, living mostly in exile (Lisbon, London, Paris). A leading exponent of Spanish Romanticism.

**Es'py** (ĕs'pĭ), **James Pollard.** 1785–1860. American

meteorologist; called "Storm King," for his theory of storms (announced 1835), attributing precipitation to upward movement, with consequent expansion and cooling, of moist air. As meteorologist to War Dept. (from 1842) and Navy Dept. (from 1848), laid foundation for weather forecasting by system of telegraphic weather bulletins from one locality to another.

**Es·que'me·ling** (ĕs·kwā'mĕ·lĭng) *or* **Ex·que'me·ling** (ĕks·kwā'-) *or* **Oex'me·lin'** (ĕks'mē·lăN'), **Alexander Olivier.** 1645?–1707. Dutch buccaneer, traveler, and writer; author of *De Americaenshe Zeerovers* (*The Buccaneers of America*, 1678), an important source book for the history of piracy.

**Es'qui·la'che** (ās'kē·lä'chā), Príncipe **de. Francisco de Bor'ja y A'ra·gón'** (thā bôr'hä ē ä'rä·gôn') *or* **A'ce·ve'do** (ä'thā·vā'thō). 1581–1658. Spanish poet; viceroy of Peru (1614–21).

**Es'qui'rol'** (ĕs'kü·ē'rôl'), **Jean Étienne Dominique.** 1772–1840. French alienist; one of founders of modern psychiatry; effected reforms in treatment of insane.

**Es'qui'ros'** (ĕs'kü·ē'rôs'), **Henri Alphonse.** 1814–1876. French writer and politician; member of Legislative Assembly (1849), but exiled (1851) because he opposed the Second Empire; again in Legislative Assembly (1869); senator (1876). Author of verse and several histories.

**Ess** (ĕs), **Leander van** *baptized* **Johann Heinrich van.** 1772–1847. German Roman Catholic theologian and Benedictine monk of the liberal school; translated into German, with his cousin **Karl van Ess** (1770–1824), the New Testament (1807) and the Old Testament (1822–36; complete joint edition, 1839 ff.).

**Es·sad' Pa·sha'** (ĕ·sät' pä·shä'). 1863?–1920. Albanian-born Turkish general and politician. Joined Turkish revolutionary movement (1908); commanded defense of Scutari; attacked by Montenegrins (1912–13), secretly intrigued with them and surrendered city. Instrumental in seating Prince William of Wied on Albanian throne (1914); minister of war and minister of interior in Albanian cabinet. During World War (1914–18), headed Albanian delegation in Paris. After war, proclaimed by so-called National Assembly king of Albania; assassinated by an Albanian in Paris (June 13, 1920) before he could establish himself on throne.

**Es'sen** (ĕs'ĕn), Count **Hans Henrik von.** 1755–1824. Swedish field marshal and statesman. Favorite and aide-de-camp of King Gustavus III; defended Stralsund against French (1807). Became count and member of council of state (1809), and concluded peace between Sweden and France at Paris (1810); field marshal (1811). Commanded Swedish army sent against Norway (1813); governor of Norway (1814–16) and field marshal after its union with Sweden; marshal of Sweden (1816); governor general of Skåne (1817).

**Es'sen** (ĕs'ĕn), Admiral **Nicholas Otto von.** 1860–1915. Russian naval commander; served with distinction in Russo-Japanese War (1904–05); promoted commander in chief of Russian navy.

**Es'sen·wein** (ĕs'ĕn·vīn), **August von.** 1831–1892. German architect, archaeologist, and art historian; director of Germanic Museum, Nuremberg (1866–92).

**Es'ser** (ĕs'ĕr), **Heinrich.** 1818–1872. German orchestra conductor and composer.

**Es'sex** (ĕs'ĕks; -ĭks), Earl of. An English title borne chiefly by the following: Geoffrey and William de MANDEVILLE; Geoffrey FITZPETER; members of BOHUN family, also earls of Hereford (see Humphrey de BOHUN); Thomas CROMWELL; members of DEVEREUX family (including 2d earl of Essex, favorite of Queen Elizabeth); Arthur CAPEL and his descendants.

**Essling,** Prince **d'.** See André MASSÉNA.

**Es'taing'** (ĕs'tăN'), Comte **Jean Baptiste Charles Henri Hector d'.** 1729–1794. French naval commander; commanded squadron aiding Americans during American Revolution. Appointed admiral of France (1792). Guillotined in Paris (Apr. 28, 1794).

**Es'tau'nié'** (ĕs'tō'nyā'), **Édouard.** 1862–1942. French novelist; author of *Le Ferment* (1899), *L'Épave* (1902), *Le Labyrinthe* (1924), *Tels qu'ils Furent* (1927), etc.

**E'ste** (ĕs'tā). Distinguished Italian princely family, including: **Alberto Azzo II** (996–1097), who was invested by Emperor Henry VII with Este and other Italian fiefs, and first adopted name Este; his older son, **Guelph IV** (gwĕlf), is ancestor of the noble houses of Brunswick and Hanover; through his younger son, **Folco I** (1060–1135), was descended the Italian branch of the family which played prominent role in medieval and renaissance Italy. Folco's son **Obizzo I** (d. 1194) was first to bear title of marquis of Este. Obizzo's son **Azzo V** (d. 1201?) married into Guelph family of Ferrara. His son **Azzo VI** (1170–1212) became head of Guelph party and (1208) first lord of Ferrara. Azzo's successor, **Azzo VII** (1205–1264), was leagued with Pope Gregory IX against the Ghibellines and succeeded in establishing himself in full control of Ferrara. Among later descendants of note were: **Nicholas III** (1384–1441), who ruled Ferrara, Modena, Parma, Reggio, and, in his last years, Milan. Nicholas III's sons **Borso** (1413–1471), patron of learning; and **Ercole I** (1431–1505), patron of Ariosto; and Ercole's children **Beatrice d'Este** (1475–1497), Duchess of Milan, a noted beauty, patron of learning, and wise politician; m. (1491) Lodovico Sforza (*q.v.*). **Isabella d'Este** (1474–1539), Marchioness of Mantua, was also a beauty, patron of learning, and skilled diplomat; m. (1490) Giovanni Francesco Gonzaga (*q.v.*); **Ippolito I** (1479–1520), Cardinal d'Este and Archbishop of Milan; patron of Ariosto; and **Alfonso I** (1486–1534), husband of Lucrezia Borgia (*q.v.*) and successful military commander. Alfonso I's sons **Ercole II** (1508–59), patron of arts, husband of Renée, daughter of Louis XII of France; and **Ippolito II** (1509–72), Cardinal d'Este and Archbishop of Milan, who built Villa d'Este at Tivoli. Ercole II's son **Alfonso II** (1533–1597), duke of Terrara, patron of Torquato Tasso. **Alfonso IV** (1634–1662), father of Mary Beatrice, who became wife of King James II of England. Alfonso IV's son **Francis II** (1660–1694), who started Este library at Modena and founded the university there. The Este line came to an end with death of **Ercole III Rinaldo** (1727–1803).

**Es·té'ba·nez Cal'de·rón'** (ās·tā'bä·nāth käl'dā·rôn'), **Serafín.** *Pseudonym* **El So'li·ta'rio** (ĕl sō'lē·tä'ryō). 1779–1867. Spanish writer; political leader of Logroño (1836) and Seville (1838); member of council of state (1856 ff.). Author of volume of poetry (1831), *Cristianos y Moriscos* (1838; series of sketches of Andalusian life and manners), *Escenas Andaluzas* (1847), etc.

**Es'ter·há'zy.** *Hung.* **Esz'ter·há'zy** (ĕs'tĕr·hä'zĭ). Noble Magyar family, including: **Ferenc Zer'há'zy** [zĕr'hä'zĭ] (1563–1594), who first took name Esterházy when created baron of **Ga'lán·ta** (gŏ'län·tŏ); his son **Miklós** (1582–1645), elected palatine of Hungary (1625); victor over Turks (1623) and strong supporter of plans for consolidating Hapsburg dynasty in order to free Hungary from Turkish dominance; Miklós's son **Pál** (1635–1713), who established princely branch of family; elected palatine (1681); fought Turks, aiding in freeing Vienna from siege (1683) and capturing Buda (1686); strong supporter of Hapsburg monarchy; created prince of the empire (1687); instrumental in curtailing powers of great Magyar nobles. Later members of family include: Prince **Miklós József** (1714–1790), art patron, builder of Schloss Esterházy in renaissance style; employed Haydn for thirty years as his musical director and conductor of his private orchestra; Prince **Miklós** (1765–1833), amassed great collection of paintings and engravings, fought Napoleon (1797); Prince **Pál Antal** (1786–1866), Austrian diplomat under Metternich; Count **Moritz** (1807–1890), Austrian diplomat, minister in Rome (to 1856), where he conducted negotiations for a concordat, and minister without portfolio (1861–66).

**Es'ter'ha'zy'** (ĕs'tĕr'á'zē'), **Marie Charles Ferdinand Wal'sin'** (vál'săN'). 1847–1923. French army officer; notorious because of his connection with the Dreyfus case; confessed (1899) that he had forged the document which constituted the chief evidence against Dreyfus. Spent rest of his life (from 1899) in exile in England. See Émile ZOLA.

**Es'ther** (ĕs'tĕr). *In Douay version* **E·dis'sa** (ė·dĭs'ȧ), *i.e.* "myrtle." *Orig. name said to be* **Ha·das'sah** (hȧ·dăs'ȧ). In Bible, a Jewish heroine, an orphan brought up by her cousin Mordecai (*Esther* ii. 7); chosen to replace the banished Vashti as wife of Ahasuerus of Persia. When the royal favorite Haman, angered at Mordecai, obtained an edict against the Jews, Esther interceded with Ahasuerus and brought about their deliverance and the death of Haman. Commemorated on the Jewish festival Purim.

**Es'tienne'** (ĕs'tyĕn') *or* **É'tienne'** (ā'tyĕn'). *Lat.* **Steph'a·nus** (stĕf'ȧ·nŭs). French family of printers and bookdealers, including: **Henri I** (d. 1520), founder of the business; his three sons, **François** (1502–50), **Robert I** (1503–1559), who was appointed royal printer to Francis I (1539) and moved to Geneva (c. 1552), and published many editions of Greek and Latin classics, a Latin-French dictionary, and various editions of the Bible, and **Charles** (1504–1564), who first studied medicine and later succeeded his brother Robert as royal printer (1551) and published a great book on anatomy, *De Dissectione Partium Corporis Humani* (1545); and three sons of Robert, **Henri II** (1528?–1598), who succeeded Robert in charge of printing establishment at Geneva (1559) and printed and edited many editions of Greek and Latin classics and compiled *Thesaurus Linguae Graecae* (1572), **Robert II** (1530–1570), who remained Roman Catholic when father joined the Reformed Church and succeeded his uncle Charles as royal printer (1564), and **François II** (1536–?), who founded at Geneva (1562) a studio of typography (1562–82).

**Es'tienne'** (ĕs'tyĕn'), **Jean Baptiste Eugène.** 1860–1936. French soldier; commanded artillery in the Vaux and Douaumont sectors in front of Verdun (1915); general of brigade (1916) and of division (1918).

**Es'ti·gar·ri'bia** (ās'tē·gär·rē'byä), **José Félix.** 1888–1940. Paraguayan general; inspector general of army (1931) when Chaco war broke out; as commander in chief won victories during early part of contest (1932–35). Minister to U.S. (1938–39); instrumental in arranging peace between Bolivia and Chile (1938); president of Paraguay (1939–40); officially proclaimed himself dictator (1940). Killed in airplane crash.

**Es'tour'nelles' de Cons'tant'** (ĕs'tōōr'nĕl' dē kôNs'-täN'), Baron **de Constant de Re·becque'** (rē·bĕk') **d'. Paul Henri Benjamin Bal'luat'** (bá'lü·á'). 1852–1924. French diplomat and politician. Member of Chamber of Deputies (1895–1904) and of the Senate (from 1904). Devoted himself to furthering international conciliation; French delegate at The Hague conference (1907). Received, with Auguste Beernaert, Nobel peace prize (1909).

**Es·tra'da Ca·bre'ra** (ās·trä'thä kä·brā'rä), **Manuel.** 1857–1924. Guatemalan politician; secretary of state (1892). On assassination of President Barrios, made provisional president (Feb., 1898); constitutional president (1898–1905); ruled as military despot until 1920, regularly elected but with no opposing candidates; driven from power by revolution under Carlos Herrera.

**Estrada Palma, Tomás.** See PALMA.

**Es'trades'** (ĕs'trȧd'), Comte **Godefroi Louis d'.** 1607–1686. French marshal and diplomat; campaigned in Italy (1648), Catalonia (1655), the Low Countries (1672); marshal of France (1675). Ambassador to Holland (1646); negotiated Treaty of Breda with Denmark (1667) and Treaty of Nijmegen with Holland (1678).

**Es'trées'** (ĕs'trā'). Noble French family originally of Picardy, including: **Antoine d'Estrées** (d. 1530), called **le Jeune** (lē zhûn'), founder of the line. **Gabrielle d'Estrées** (1573–1599), mistress of Henry IV; created Marquise **de Mon'ceaux'** (dē môN'sō') and Duchesse **de Beau'fort'** (bō'fôr'). Duc **François Annibal d'Estrées** (1573–1670), Marquis **de Cœu'vres** (kû'vr'), brother of Gabrielle, lieutenant general in the French army, created marshal of France (1626), French ambassador in Rome (1636), governor of Île de France (1654), author of *Mémoires* of the regencies of Marie de Médicis and Anne of Austria. His son Comte **Jean d'Estrées** (1624–1707); distinguished himself at Gravelines, at the battle of Lens, and during the Fronde; accompanied Louis XIV and Turenne in Spanish Netherlands (1667), entered naval service and became vice-admiral (1669); engaged against the Dutch at Southwold Bay (1672) and Schooneveldt and Texel (1673), and in the Antilles (1677), where his squadron was shipwrecked; created marshal of France (1681); appointed governor of Brittany. Jean's son Duc **Victor Marie d'Estrées** (1660–1737), Marquis **de Cœuvres,** lieutenant general (1688); entered naval service and commanded advance guard of the fleet of de Tourville; created marshal of France (1703); distinguished himself in naval campaign ending with battle of Málaga (1704), appointed minister of state. **Louis Charles César Le Tel'lier'** (lē tĕ'lyā'), Marquis **de Cour'tan'vaux'** (dē kōōr'täN'vō'), Duc **d'Estrées** (1695–1771), field marshal (1735), lieutenant general (1748) and engaged at battle of Fontenoy; created marshal of France (1757) and duc d'Estrées (1763).

**Es'trith** (ĕs'trĕth). A dynasty of Denmark (1047–1375); began with **Sweyn Es'trith·son** [-sôn] (ruled 1047–75), son of Earl Ulf and of Estrith, daughter of Sweyn Forkbeard (ruled 985–1014). Sweyn Estrithson succeeded Magnus the Good of Norway and Denmark (d. 1047) and was followed by five of his sons (1075–1134); dynasty also included: Waldemar I the Great (ruled 1157–82), Canute VI (1182–1202), Waldemar II the Victorious (1202–41), Eric Mœndved (1286–1319), and Waldemar IV Atterdag (1340–75), last of the line; dynasty interrupted by several periods of civil war. Waldemar IV was succeeded by his daughter Margaret, who procured election (1376) of her five-year-old son, Olaf. See individual biographies.

**Es'trup** (ĕs'trōōp), **Jacob Brönnum Scavenius.** 1825–1913. Danish statesman; leader of Agrarians in Landsting (1864–98; 1900 ff.); minister-president and finance minister (1875–94).

**É'tampes'** (ā'täNp'), Duchesse **d'.** *Nee* **Anne de Pis'se·leu'** (dē pēs'lû'). 1508–1580. Mistress of Francis I of France.

**É'tex'** (ā'tĕks'), **Antoine.** 1808–1888. French sculptor, painter, and architect; among his architectural works are the tomb of Napoleon I in the Hôtel des Invalides and a monument to the revolution of 1848.

**Eth'el·bald** (ĕth'ĕl·bôld) *or* **Æth'el·bald** (ăth'ĕl·bôld; *A.-S.* ä'thĕl·bäld). d. 757. King of Mercia (716); invaded Wessex (733); defeated by rebel overlord of Wessex (752).

**Ethelbald** *or* **Æthelbald.** d. 860. King of West Saxons (858–860).

**Eth′el·bert** (ĕth′ĕl·bẽrt) *or* **Æ′thel·berht** (ă′thĕl-bĕrkt) *or* **Æ′gel·briht** (ă′yĕl·brĭkt) *or* **Al′bert** (ăl′-bẽrt), Saint. d. 794. King of East Angles; beheaded by order of Offa, king of Mercians; venerated at Hereford as patron of cathedral.

**Eth′el·bert** (ĕth′ĕl·bẽrt) *or* **Æth′el·bert** (ăth′ĕl·bẽrt) *or* **Æ′dil·berct** (ă′dĭl·bĕrkt). 552?–616. King of Kent (560); defeated by West Saxons (568); baptized by St. Augustine (597); promulgated legal code after the Roman.

**Ethelbert.** d. 866. King of West Saxons (860–866).

**Eth′el·dre′da** (ĕth′ĕl·drē′dȧ), Saint. 630?–679. Queen of Northumbria. Married but disowned marriage duties; founded abbey at Ely; consecrated Abbess of Ely (673).

**Eth′el·fle′da** (ĕth′ĕl·flē′dȧ) *or* **Æ′thel·flæd′** (ă′thĕl-flâd′) *or* **Æl′fled** (ăl′flĕd). d. 918? Called Lady of the Mercians after husband's death (912). Dau. of Alfred the Great; m. Ethelred, Mercian ealdorman. Built fortresses against Danes and Norwegians; defeated Welsh at Brecknock (916) and Danes at Derby (917), to control Mercia north to Humber. See Edward the Elder.

**Eth′el·red** (ĕth′ĕl·rĕd) *or* **Æ′thel·red′** (ă′thĕl·rād′) *or* **Ail′red** (āl′rĕd) *or* **Ael′red** (āl′rĕd), Saint. 1109?–1166. English historical writer. Abbot of Rievaulx (rĭv′ĭs; -ŭz), Yorkshire (1146–66). As missionary to Galloway Picts, persuaded chief to become monk; canonized (1191). Wrote biography of Edward the Confessor and chronicles.

**Ethelred** *or* **Æthelred I.** d. 871. King (866–871) of West Saxons and Kentishmen; repelled Danish invasions (868, 871).

**Ethelred** *or* **Æthelred II.** 968?–1016. King of England. Called "the Unready." Became king (978) on assassination of his brother Edward the Martyr (*q.v.*). Bought off Norwegian invaders Olaf Tryggvesson and Sweyn (994); m. Emma, dau. of Richard, Duke of Normandy; promulgated police and military codes; bought off the Danes (1012); fled to Rouen when Sweyn was declared king of England; returned and expelled Canute (1014).

**Eth′el·werd** (ĕth′ĕl·wẽrd) *or* **Æ′thel·weard** (ă′thĕl-wă′ẽrd). d. about 998. English chronicler; compiled a history of world to 973 A.D. (ed. 1596 by Savile).

**Eth′el·wold** (ĕth′ĕl·wōld; -wôld) *or* **Æ′thel·wold′** (ă′thĕl·wŏld′) *or* **Ad′el·wold** (ăd′′l·wōld; -wôld), Saint. 908?–984. English ecclesiastical leader. Re-established monastic house at Abingdon and introduced strict Benedictine rule (c. 954); bishop of Winchester (963); built cathedral at Winchester.

**Eth′el·wulf** (ĕth′ĕl·wŏŏlf) *or* **Æ′thel·wulf′** (ă′thĕl-wŏŏlf′) *or* **Ad′el·wlf** (ăd′′l·wŏŏlf) *or* **Ath′ulf** (ăth′ŏŏlf). d. 858. King of West Saxons and Kentishmen and bishop of Winchester. Father of Alfred the Great. Defeated by Danes in naval engagement (842); routed Danes at Ockley (852). Made grants of one tenth of his land for benefactions; made pilgrimage to Rome. m. Judith, daughter of Charles the Bald (856). Gave up kingdom of West Saxons to rebellious son Ethelbald.

**Eth′er·ege** (ĕth′ẽr·ĭj), Sir **George.** 1635?–?1691. English dramatist. Began period of Restoration comedy with *Love in a Tub* (1664), partly in rhymed heroic verse, partly in realistic scenes of lively comedy; continued to picture life of the day in *She would if she could* (1667) and *The Man of Mode* (1676); invented comedy of intrigue; paved way for comedy of manners of Congreve and Sheridan.

**E′thi·o′pi·an** (ē′thĭ·ō′pĭ·ăn). Name, according to Manetho, of XXVth dynasty of Egypt (712–663 B.C.).

**É′tienne′** (ā′tyĕn′). See also Estienne.

**Étienne, Charles Guillaume.** 1777–1845. French journalist and dramatist.

**Ett** (ĕt), **Kaspar.** 1788–1847. German composer; helped revive Roman Catholic church music of 16th–18th centuries, esp. polyphonic a cappella music, after which he patterned his original masses, requiems, and offertories.

**Et′tings·hau′sen** (ĕt′ĭngs·hou′zĕn), Baron **Konstantin von.** 1826–1897. Austrian paleontologist.

**Ett′mül′ler** (ĕt′mül′ẽr), **Ernst Moritz Ludwig.** 1802–1877. German philologist; edited many Middle High German and Low German texts, an Anglo-Saxon chrestomathy (1850) and lexicon (1851).

**Ettrick Shepherd, The.** See James Hogg.

**Et′ty** (ĕt′ĭ), **William.** 1787–1849. English figure painter; pupil of Sir Thomas Lawrence.

**Etzel.** See Attila.

**Eu** (û), Comte **d′.** Prince **Louis Philippe Marie Ferdinand Gaston d′Or′lé′ans′** (dôr′lā′äN′). 1842–1922. Eldest son of duke of Nemours; entered Brazilian army; commander in chief (1869–70) of allied forces in war with Paraguay; unpopular because of extreme clerical views; forced to leave Brazil on downfall of empire (1889). See Isabella of Brazil.

**Eu·bu′li·des** (ū·bŭ′lĭ·dēz). Greek philosopher of 4th century B.C.; succeeded Euclid of Megara (*q.v.*) as head of the Megarian school.

**Euck′en** (oi′kĕn), **Rudolf Christoph.** 1846–1926. German philosopher, b. in Aurich, Ostfriesland. Professor, Jena (1874–1920); received Nobel prize in literature (1908); exchange professor at Harvard (1912–13). Championed Germany during World War and signed manifesto of German intellectuals in her defense (1914). Author of works on historical philosophy, religion, and on his own philosophy of ethical activism, a metaphysical-idealistic philosophy of life.

**Eu′clid** (ū′klĭd) *or* **Eu·cli′des** (ū·klī′dēz) of **Meg′a·ra** (mĕg′ȧ·rȧ). 450?–374 B.C. Greek philosopher; disciple of Socrates; founder of the Megarian school. Only titles of his works are extant.

**Euclid.** fl. about 300 B.C. Greek geometer; founded a school in Alexandria. His chief work, *Elements* (13 books), is basis of many later works in geometry.

**Eu·de′mus of Rhodes** (ū·dē′mŭs, rōdz). Greek philosopher of 4th century B.C.; pupil and friend of Aristotle; supposed editor of *Eudemian Ethics*, one of three treatises in which ethical works of Aristotle are known to us.

**Eudes** *or* **Odo.** Count of Paris. See Capetian dynasty.

**Eudes** (ûd) *or* **Eu′don′** (û′dôN′) *or* **O′do** (ō′dō). 665–?735 A.D. Duke of Aquitaine. Defeated invading Arabs (721); when threatened later by Arab commander Abd-er-Rahman, was aided by Charles Martel, who defeated Arabs at Tours, near Poitiers (732).

**Eudes** *or* **Odo.** Name of four dukes of Burgundy. **Eudes III** (ruled 1193–1218), son of Hugh III, took part in the Albigensian crusade (1209–18) and commanded part of army at Bouvines (1214). **Eudes IV** (ruled 1315–1350), son of Robert II, inherited Franche-Comté and Artois; fought for Philip of Valois in Flanders.

**Eudes,** Saint **Jean.** 1601–1680. French priest; famed as a preacher; founded (1643) Congregation of Jesus and Mary, whose members became known as *Eudists;* also founded, at Caen, Daughters of Our Lady of Charity.

**Eudes de Mézeray, François.** See Mézeray.

**Eudes of Bayeux.** See Odo of Bayeux.

**Eu·do′ci·a** (ū·dō′shĭ·ȧ). Name of three empresses of the Eastern Roman Empire:

**Eudocia.** *Earlier name* **Ath'e·na'ïs** (ăth'ē·nā'ĭs). 401?–?460. Wife of Theodosius II (m. 421); daughter of Athenian philosopher Leontius; became rival of Pulcheria, sister of the emperor; exiled to Jerusalem (441?).

**Eudocia In'ge·ri'na** (ĭn'jĕ·rī'nȧ). d. 882. Wife of Basil I and mistress of Michael III; mother of Leo VI.

**Eudocia Mac'rem·bol'i·tis'sa** (măk'rĕm·bŏl'ĭ·tĭs'ȧ). 1021?–1096. Wife of Constantine X Ducas; after his death (1067) married Romanus IV Diogenes, making him coregent emperor with her during minority of her son Michael VII Ducas (1067–71); banished on defeat of Romanus by the Turks (1071); wrongly regarded as author of the *Ionia.*

**Eudon.** See EUDES.

**Eu·dox'i·a** (ū·dŏk'sĭ·ȧ). d. 404. Empress of the Eastern Roman Empire; daughter of Bauto, a Frank. Married Arcadius (395), whom she completely controlled; sent the patriarch John Chrysostom into exile (403) for preaching against her wickedness.

**Eu·dox'i·a** (ū·dŏk'sĭ·ȧ). *Full Russian name* **Evdokiya Fëdorovna Lo·pu'khi·na** (lŭ·po͞o'kyĭ·nŭ). 1669?–1731. Czarina of Russia, first wife of Peter the Great. Daughter of Boyar Fëdor Lopukhin; m. Peter (1689) at command of his mother; bored Peter by her piety; sent to monastery (1698) for refusing divorce; spent most of remaining life in cloisters. Mother of Czarevitch Alexis and grandmother of Czar Peter II (1727–30).

**Eu·dox'us** (ū·dŏk'sŭs). Greek scholar of Cnidus, in early 4th century B.C. Studied at Athens under Plato and in Egypt with the priests at Heliopolis. Founded a school in Cyzicus; later, went to Athens. Known chiefly for work in astronomy and mathematics; corrected length of solar year; attempted an early explanation of the paths of planets; discovered the part of geometry now included in 5th book of Euclid.

**Eudoxus of Cyz'i·cus** (sĭz'ĭ·kŭs). Greek navigator of late 2d century B.C.; commissioned by Ptolemy Euergetes to explore the Arabian Sea; said later to have sailed south along the west coast of Africa.

**Euemerus.** = EUHEMERUS.

**Euergetes.** See ANTIOCHUS VII of Syria; PTOLEMY III and VII.

**Eu·gen'** (oi·gān'). *Russ.* **Evgeni.** Duke of **Würt'tem·berg** (vür'tĕm·bĕrk). 1788–1857. Russian general, b. Oels, Prussia. Nephew of wife of Czar Paul. Distinguished himself in battles against Napoleon in Russia and Germany (1812–13); commanded Seventh Russian Army Corps (1828) in Russo-Turkish War. Retired (after 1829) for study; composed music (symphonies, lieder, and an opera) and wrote memoirs (pub. 1826).

**Eu·gene'** (ū·jēn'; ū'jēn). Archduke of **Austria.** 1863–1954. Austro-Hungarian field marshal; held command on Italian front during World War (1914–18).

**Eugene** *or* **Eu'gène'** (û'zhân'; ü'-). Prince of **Savoy.** *Full French name* **François Eugène de Savoie–Carignan** (see SAVOY). 1663–1736. Austrian general. Son of Eugène Maurice de Savoie-Carignan, Count of Soissons, b. Paris. Because of banishment of his mother from France by Louis XIV, renounced his country and entered service of Austrian Emperor Leopold I. Fought against Turks at Vienna (1683); active in coalition against Louis XIV (1689–97), esp. in Italy; field marshal (1693); defeated Turks in battle of Senta (1697). In War of Spanish Succession (1701–14), in command in Italy (1701–03); president of imperial council of war (1703–14); with Marlborough won battle of Blenheim (1704); saved Turin and expelled French from Italy (1706); with Marlborough victorious at Oudenarde (1708) and Malplaquet (1709); defeated at Denain (1712). Again in command against Turks (1716), won battles of Peterwardein (1716) and Belgrade (1717); in new war with France (1733–35).

**Eugène de Beauharnais.** See BEAUHARNAIS and LEUCHTENBERG.

**Eu'gé'nie'** (û'zhā'nē'; ü'-). *In full* **Eugénie Marie de Mon·ti'jo de Guz·mán'** (thā môn·tē'hō thā go͞oth·män'). Comtesse **de Te'ba** (thā tā'bä). 1826–1920. Empress of the French (1853–71), b. Granada; daughter of a Spanish grandee, the count of Montijo, and of Maria Manuela Kirkpatrick, whose father (William Kirkpatrick, a Scotsman by birth and an American by residence) had been U.S. consul at Málaga. Educ. in Paris; m. Napoleon III (Jan., 1853) soon after he became emperor (Dec., 1852). Leader in fashions of Europe, contributed much to brilliancy of French court (1853–70); had marked influence over Napoleon in many of his policies; strong advocate of church; opposed liberal and democratic ideas; advised sending Maximilian to Mexico (1863); probably urged emperor to enter upon war with Prussia (1870); three times acted as regent during absence of emperor (1859, 1865, 1870). On downfall of Empire fled to England. Befriended by Queen Victoria. Her one son, the Prince Napoleon, was killed in Zululand at age of 23.

**Eu·ge'ni·us** (ū·jē'nĭ·ŭs; -jēn'yŭs) *or* **Eu·gene'** (ū·jēn'; ū'jēn). Name of four popes (see *Table of Popes*, Nos. 75, 99, 167, 209), especially:

**Eugenius II.** d. 827. Pope (824–827), b. Rome. Under Frankish influence, but supported reforms and advanced cause of learning.

**Eugenius III.** *Real name* **Bernardo Pa'ga·nel'li** (pä'gä·nĕl'lē) *or* **Pi'gna·tel'li** (pē'nyä·tĕl'lē). d. 1153. Pope (1145–53). Native of Pisa; pupil of St. Bernard of Clairvaux. Refused to renounce temporal power; expelled from Rome (1145) by Roman mob; journeyed to France (1147) where he made preparations for Second Crusade; held synods at Paris, Reims, and Trier; made treaty (1153) with Frederick Barbarossa, newly elected emperor.

**Eugenius IV.** *Real name* **Gabriele Con'dol·mie'ri** (kōn'dôl·myâ'rē) *or* Gabriel **Con'dul·mer** (kŏn'dŭl·mĕr). 1383–1447. Pope (1431–47), b. Venice; nephew of Gregory XII. Engaged in long struggle (1431–47) with Council of Basel; dissolved council (1431), which refused to dissolve; resided for ten years at Florence (1434–43); convened Council of Ferrara (1438); was deposed (1439) by Council of Basel which elected Felix V (*q.v.*); schism remained during pontificate; returned to Rome (1443).

**Eugenius.** d. 394 A.D. Roman emperor (392–394). Gallic rhetorician, set up by Arbogast as emperor; both defeated and slain in battle near Aquileia.

**Eu·gip'pi·us** *or* **Eu·gyp'pi·us** (ū·jĭp'ĭ·ŭs). 455?–?538. Latin scholar and monk. Author of *Vita Sancti Severini* (511; important source for early German church history), and compiler of *Thesaurus Augustinianeus.*

**Eu·he'mer·us** (ū·hē'mĕr·ŭs; ū·hĕm'ĕr·ŭs) *or* **Eu·e'mer·us** (ū·ē'mĕr·ŭs; ū·ĕm'ĕr·ŭs) *or* **E·ve'mer·us** (ē·vē'mĕr·ŭs; ē·vĕm'ĕr·ŭs). Greek mythographer of late 4th century B.C., b. in Sicily. Chief work, *Sacred History,* a philosophical romance in which he rationalized the Greek myths, depicting the gods as originally human heroes and warriors, and asserting that the myths were distorted representations of historical events.

**Eu·la'li·a of Bar'ce·lo'na** (ū·lā'lĭ·ȧ [-lāl'yȧ], bär'sĕ·lō'nȧ), Saint. Spanish virgin martyred under Diocletian (Barcelona, 304); patroness of Barcelona and of sailors. Often identified with Saint **Eulalia of Mé'ri·da** [mā'rē·thä] (c. 291–304), also a virgin said to have been martyred under Diocletian, and patroness of Oviedo and Mérida.

**Eu·la′li·us** (ū·lā′lĭ·ŭs; -lāl′yŭs). d. 423. Antipope (418–419).

**Eu′len·berg** (oi′lĕn·bĕrk), **Herbert.** 1876–1949. German dramatist and novelist.

**Eu′len·burg** (oi′lĕn·bŏŏrk), Counts **zu.** Members of an old noble Prussian family including: **Botho Heinrich zu Eulenburg–Wick′en** [-vĭk′ĕn] (1804–1879), government official; president, Prussian House of Representatives (1855–58); member of Prussian House of Lords (1864) and of Reichstag (1867–78); headed Prussian national debt administration (1874). His son **Botho zu Eulenburg** (1831–1912), statesman and administrator; member of Prussian House of Representatives (1863–70) and conservative member of North German Reichstag (1867); chief councilor in ministry of interior (1867); succeeded Friedrich (see below) as minister of interior (1878); formulated Socialist law and worked for administrative reforms; resigned following differences with Bismarck (1881); succeeded Caprivi as Prussian minister president (1892); opposed Caprivi in controversy over amendment of criminal code and was dismissed with him (1894); member of House of Lords (1899). The latter's younger brother **August zu Eulenburg** (1838–1921), Prussian courtier and army officer; personal adjutant (1865) and chamberlain and court marshal to the crown prince (1868); chief court and house marshal to the emperor (1890); minister of imperial house (1907–13). Botho Heinrich's cousin **Friedrich (Fritz) Albrecht zu Eulenburg** (1815–1881), statesman; consul general in Antwerp (1852) and Warsaw (1858); headed Prussian Eastern Asiatic expedition (1859) and effected trade and maritime agreements with China and Japan; minister of interior (1862); supported Bismarck in constitutional conflicts (1863); sought to develop self-administration, was opposed by Bismarck, and resigned (1878); member of Prussian Chamber of Deputies (1866–77); author of *Zehn Jahre Innere Politik 1862–72* (1872) and of the letters *Ostasien 1860–62.*

**Philipp zu Eulenburg und Her′te·feld** [hĕr′tĕ·fĕlt] (1847–1921), diplomat and writer; intimate friend of William II; German ambassador at Vienna (1894–1902); raised to rank of prince (1900) and made hereditary member of House of Lords; charged with homosexuality and involved in scandalous revelations of Maximilian Harden; author of poems and musical compositions including *Rosenlieder* and *Skaldengesänge* (1892), a volume of reminiscences and letters *Aus 50 Jahren* (pub. 1923), etc.

**Eulenburg, Albert.** 1840–1917. German physician.

**Eulenburg, Franz.** 1867–1943. German economist.

**Eu′len·spie′gel** (oi′lĕn·shpē′gĕl) *or* **U′len·spie′gel** (ōō′-), **Till.** *English* **Owl′glass′** (oul′glȧs′). German traditional figure and hero of a chapbook of early 16th century, supposedly born at Kneitlingen in Brunswick at end of 13th century, died near Lübeck (1350); a wily peasant and wandering Jack-of-all-trades who exercised his wit and played jokes on tradespeople, priests, nobles, and esp. innkeepers; figures in Chaucer's *Somnours Tale;* referred to as "Howleglass" and "Ulenspiegel" in Ben Jonson's *Masque of the Fortunate Isles*, *Poetaster*, *Alchemist*, and *Sad Shepherd.*

**Eu′ler** (oi′lẽr), **Leonhard.** 1707–1783. Swiss mathematician and physicist; one of the founders of the science of pure mathematics. Called to St. Petersburg by Catherine I (1727) where he became professor of physics (1730) and of mathematics (1733); called to Berlin by Frederick the Great (1741) becoming director of mathematics at the Academy of Science (1744); recalled to St. Petersburg (1766). Lost sight of one eye in 1735 and of the other in 1766 but continued working. Founder of the calculus of variation, on which he published the first textbook; author of works on analytic mathematics, algebra, and other mathematical subjects, also on analytic mechanics, hydrodynamics, astronomy, optics, and acoustics; devised a system of logarithms (binary logarithms) to facilitate musical calculations. Cf. J. L. LAGRANGE.

**Eu′ler** (ĕ′ŏŏ·lẽr), **Ulf Svante von.** 1905– . Swedish physiologist. Awarded Nobel prize in physiology and medicine (1970) with B. Katz and J. Axelrod.

**Eu′ler–Chel′pin** (oi′lẽr·kĕl′pĭn, ĕ′ŏŏ·lẽr-), **Hans August Simon von.** 1873–1964. Chemist, b. Germany; to Sweden in 1897. Conducted researches on the fermentation of sugars and enzyme action. Awarded, jointly with Sir Arthur Harden, 1929 Nobel prize for chemistry.

**Eumathius.** See EUSTATHIUS.

**Eu′me·nes** (ū′mē·nēz). Name of two rulers of Pergamum:

**Eumenes I.** d. 241 B.C. Ruler (263–241 B.C.), but never recognized as king; defeated Antiochus I (262).

**Eumenes II.** d. ?160 B.C. King (197–?160 B.C.). Son of Attalus I. An ally of the Romans; took important part (190) in battle of Magnesia (Manisa) in which Antiochus the Great was defeated; received large part of Asia Minor from Romans for his services; made Pergamum a center of learning; founded great library. Succeeded by his brother Attalus II.

**Eumenes.** 360?–316 B.C. Macedonian general; secretary on staff of Philip of Macedon and Alexander the Great; at Alexander's death (323 B.C.), allotted Cappadocia and Paphlagonia; fought to maintain power; defeated (321) Craterus and Neoptolemus, generals of Alexander the Great, but was betrayed to Antigonus.

**Eunan,** Saint. See ADAMNAN.

**Eu·no′mi·us** (ū·nō′mĭ·ŭs). d. about 393. Roman Catholic ecclesiastic; bishop of Cyzicus (360); deposed (361) because of extreme Arian views; became, with Aëtius of Antioch, recognized leader of the Anomoeans, or Eunomians. Chief work, *Apologia.*

**Eupator.** See ANTIOCHUS V of Syria.

**Eu·pho′ri·on** (ū·fō′rĭ·ŏn). Greek scholar and poet; lived in Athens (to c. 221 B.C.) and then went to Antioch to serve as librarian of royal library there. Author of epics about mythological heroes, elegies, and satirical verse.

**Eu·phra′nor** (ū·frā′nôr). Greek sculptor and painter of middle 4th century B.C.

**Eu·phro′ni·us** (ū·frō′nĭ·ŭs). Athenian potter and vase painter of late 6th and early 5th century B.C.

**Eu′po·lis** (ū′pō·lĭs). Greek writer of comedies in 5th century B.C.; rival of Aristophanes. Winner of first prize for comedy seven times.

**Eu·pom′pus** (ū·pŏm′pŭs). Greek painter of 4th century B.C.; founder of the Sicyonian school.

**Eu′ric** (ū′rĭk) *or* **Ev′a·ric** (ĕv′ȧ·rĭk). d. about 484 A.D. King of the Visigoths (466–484); ruled at height of Gothic power in Spain, with capital at Toulouse. See THEODORIC II.

**Eu·rip′i·des** (ū·rĭp′ĭ·dēz). Greek playwright of 5th century B.C. Ranked with Aeschylus and Sophocles as greatest of Greek dramatists; said to have won first prize in five dramatic contests. Lived in Athens (to c. 408 B.C.) and at court of Archelaus, King of Macedonia (from c. 408). Of plays attributed to him, 18 are extant: *Alcestis, Medea, Hippolytus, Hecuba, Andromache, Ion, The Suppliants, Heracleidae, Mad Heracles, Iphigenia among the Tauri, Troades* (or *The Trojan Women*), *Helen, Phoenissae* (or *The Phoenician Women*), *Electra, Orestes, Iphigenia at Aulis, Bacchae, Cyclops.*

**Eu′ry·bi′a·des** (ū′rĭ·bī′ȧ·dēz). Spartan fleet commander, and nominal commander of allied Greek fleets, in victories against Persians at Artemisium and Salamis (480 B.C.).

**Eu·rym′e·don** (ū·rĭm′ē·dŏn). d. 413 B.C. Athenian general in Peloponnesian War; slain in attempting to reinforce Athenian troops at Syracuse.

**Eus′den** (ūz′dĕn), **Laurence.** 1688–1730. English poet. M.A., Cantab. (1712); made poet laureate (1718) by duke of Newcastle, whose marriage he had celebrated (1717); remembered as object of Pope's satire and as the "L. E." of Pope and Swift's treatise on bathos.

**Eusebes.** See ANTIOCHUS X of Syria.

**Eu·se′bi·us** (ū·sē′bĭ·ŭs), Saint. Pope (bishop of Rome; 309, or 310?); banished by Emperor Maxentius.

**Eusebius of Caes′a·re′a** (sĕs′ȧ·rē′ȧ; sĕz′ȧ-; sē′zȧ-). *Surnamed* **Pam′phi·li** (păm′fĭ·lī) *after his friend and teacher Pamphilus.* 260?–?340. Theologian, church historian, and scholar, b. in Palestine; called "father of ecclesiastical history." Became bishop of Caesarea (c. 314) and stood in favor with Emperor Constantine; attended Council of Nicaea (325) as leader of Origenist middle party of moderates in Arian conflict, but later yielded to Athanasians and voted to repudiate position of extreme Arians; attended synods of Antioch (330) and Tyre (335). Author of *Historia Ecclesiastica* (on Christian church history to 324; 10 books) and *Chronicon* (universal history to 325), etc.

**Eusebius of Dor′y·lae′um** (dŏr′ĭ·lē′ŭm). d. about 452. Greek theologian. Opposed heresy of Nestorius, Bishop of Constantinople (428); bishop of Dorylaeum (448); denounced heresy of his friend Eutyches (448); deposed (449) and imprisoned; escaped to Rome and was reinstated by Council of Chalcedon (451).

**Eusebius of Em′e·sa** (ĕm′ē·sȧ). 300?–?359. Semi-Arian bishop and ecclesiastic writer of the Alexandrian school; favorite of Constantine. Bishop of Emesa (now Homs) in Phoenicia.

**Eusebius of Nic′o·me·di′a** (nĭk′ō·mē·dī′ȧ). d. about 342. Arian leader and bishop. Held successively sees of Beyrouth and Nicomedia; head of Arians (sometimes called *Eusebians*), and patriarch of Constantinople (339).

**Eusebius of Sa·mos′a·ta** (sȧ·mŏs′ȧ·tȧ), Saint. d. about 379. Bishop of Samosata and martyr; opponent of Arianism.

**Eusebius of Ver·cel′li** (vâr·chĕl′lē), Saint. 283–371. Bishop of Vercelli and martyr, b. in Sardinia. Consecrated bishop of Vercelli (340); became first western bishop to unite monastic with clerical life; sought to end dissensions between Arians and the orthodox; visited churches in East in attempt to restore peace in interest of orthodox faith; a leading opponent of Arianism.

**Eus′tace** (ūs′tĭs). Name of four counts of Bou·logne′ (bōō·lōn′; *Fr.* bōō′lôn′y'), especially: **Eustace II** (d. 1093), m. Goda, daughter of King Ethelred the Unready; accompanied William the Conqueror to England and fought at Hastings (1066); quarreled with William (1067); his confiscated fiefs later returned to him. His grandson **Eustace IV** (d. 1153), son of Matilda and Stephen (later king of England), became heir apparent to English throne; his death made possible a peaceful settlement between Stephen and Henry of Anjou.

**Eu·sta′chio** (ā·ōō·stä′kyō), **Bartolommeo.** *Latin* **Eu·sta′chi·us** (ū·stā′kĭ·ŭs). 1524?–1574. Italian anatomist; one of the founders of modern anatomy. Described the Eustachian tube in the ear and the Eustachian valve of the heart, also the stapes, the thoracic duct, the uterus, the kidney, and the teeth.

**Eu·sta′chi·us** (ū·stā′kĭ·ŭs) *or* **Eu·sta′thi·us** (-thĭ·ŭs), Saint. Roman saint and martyr of 2d century, patron of the chase, and one of 14 saints called "Helpers in Need" because often invoked by those in need, sickness, or danger. According to legend, he was a Roman general named Placidus, who was converted by an apparition of Christ between the antlers of a stag, and who suffered martyrdom under Hadrian (c. 118).

**Eu·sta′thi·us** (ū·stā′thĭ·ŭs) *or* **Eu·ma′thi·us** (ū·mā′thĭ·ŭs). *Surnamed* **Mac′rem·bo·li′tes** (măk′rĕm·bō·lī′tēz). fl. 2d half of 12th cent. Byzantine novelist, last of Greek romance writers; author of the sensual novel *The Story of Hysmine and Hysminias* (11 books).

**Eustathius of An′ti·och** (ăn′tĭ·ŏk). d. about 360. Bishop of Antioch, b. in Side, Pamphylia. Became (c. 320) bishop of Beroea (now Aleppo) and patriarch of Antioch in Syria; strongly opposed Arians at Council of Nicaea (325); deposed (331) and banished. His deposition resulted in a schism (lasting till 413), the party protesting it being known as *Eustathians.*

**Eustathius of Se·bas′te** (sē·băs′tē). d. about 380. Semi-Arian bishop of Sebaste (Sebustiye) in Armenia (c. 355), where he introduced monasticism; founded the party of ascetics and celibates called Eustathians, condemned by Synod of Gangra (340); deposed by Synod of Militene (358).

**Eustathius of Thes′sa·lo·ni′ca** (thĕs′ȧ·lō·nī′kȧ). d. about 1193. Byzantine classical scholar and religious reformer. Archbishop (from 1175) of Thessalonica (Salonika). Author of commentaries on Homer, on the geographical epic of Dionysius Periegetes, and on Pindar.

**Eus′tis** (ūs′tĭs), **William.** 1753–1825. American politician; served as surgeon in Revolutionary War; practiced medicine in Boston. Secretary of war (1809–13), resigning under criticism. Minister to Holland (1814–18). Governor of Massachusetts (1823–25).

**Eu·thym′i·us** (ū·thĭm′ĭ·ŭs). d. about 1393. Bulgarian patriarch and hagiographer; patriarch of Trnovo (1375); opposed Bogomiles and other heretics.

**Euthymius Zig′a·be′nus** (zĭg′ȧ·bē′nŭs). d. after 1118. Greek monk and theologian.

**Eu′ting** (oi′tĭng), **Julius.** 1839–1913. German Semitic scholar and epigraphist.

**Eu·tro′pi·us** (ū·trō′pĭ·ŭs) *or* **Fla′vi·us** (flā′vĭ·ŭs) **Eutropius.** Roman historian of 4th century A.D.; author of compendium of Roman history, *Breviarium ab Urbe Condita.*

**Eu′ty·ches** (ū′tĭ·kēz). 375?–?454. Heresiarch, presbyter, and archimandrite of Eastern Church in Constantinople; founder of Eutychian sect and representative of Monophysitism, or belief in a single composite human and divine nature in Christ. Condemned for heresy and deposed by Synod of Constantinople under Bishop Flavian (448); reinstated (449) by Council of Ephesus ("Robber Synod"); again condemned by Council of Chalcedon (451), excommunicated, and banished.

**Eu·tych′i·a′nus** (ū·tĭk′ĭ·ā′nŭs) *or* **Eu·tych′i·an** (ū·tĭk′ĭ·ăn), Saint. Pope (bishop of Rome; 275–283).

**E·vag′o·ras I** (ē·văg′ō·rȧs). d. 374 B.C. King of Salamis in Cyprus (410?–374 B.C.); pursued policy friendly to Athens and hostile to Persia; after Peace of Antalcidas (387), deserted by Athens and subjugated by Persia.

**E·vag′ri·us** (ē·văg′rĭ·ŭs). *Surnamed* **Scho·las′ti·cus** (skō·lăs′tĭ·kŭs). 536?–?600. Byzantine church historian and advocate; legal adviser of Gregory, patriarch of Antioch; author of an ecclesiastical history for the period 431–594, a continuation of the work of Eusebius, Socrates, Sozomen, and Theodoret of Cyrrhus.

**Evald.** See EWALD.

**Ev′ans** (ĕv′ănz), Sir **Arthur John.** 1851–1941. English archaeologist; conducted excavations in Crete and discovered pre-Phoenician script (1893 ff.); excavated prehistoric palace of Knossos (1900–08), seat of early Minoan culture.

**Evans, Augusta Jane.** 1835–1909. American novelist, b. Columbus, Ga.; m. (1868) Lorenzo Madison Wilson. Author of *St. Elmo* (1866), etc.

**Evans, Ca·ra'doc** (kä·rä'dŏg). 1883?–1945. Welsh novelist, playwright, and journalist; m. Oliver Sandys (*q.v.*); author esp. of books of short stories bitterly satirizing the Welsh.

**Evans, David.** 1874–1948. Welsh musician and composer.

**Evans,** Sir **Edward Ratcliffe Garth Russell.** 1881–1957. British explorer, admiral, and author; second in command of British Antarctic expedition (1909); in command of *Mohawk* in bombardment of German army at the Belgian coast (1914); commander of H.M.S. *Broke* in defeat of six German destroyers (1917); rear admiral commanding Royal Australian navy (1929–31); commander in chief, African station (1933–35); commander in chief, The Nore (1935–39). Author of *Keeping the Seas* (1920), *South with Scott* (1921), and books for boys.

**Evans,** Sir **George de Lacy.** 1787–1870. British military commander; served against French on Iberian Peninsula, against Americans at Baltimore, Washington, and New Orleans (1814–15); asst. quartermaster general in Waterloo campaign (1815); commanded British Legion in Carlist insurrection (1835–37); commanded a division in Crimean War, repulsing sortie from Sevastopol (1854); general (1861).

**Evans, Herbert McLean.** 1882–1971. American anatomist and embryologist. Demonstrated origin of vascular trunk from capillaries (1909); discovered 48 chromosomes in man (1918) and vitamin E (1922); first produced gigantism experimentally by parenteral administration of anterior hypophyseal hormone (1922); also did work on action of vital dyes of the benzidine series, physiology of reproduction, and relation between fertility and nutrition.

**Evans,** Sir **John.** 1823–1908. English archaeologist and numismatist. Son of **Arthur Benoni Evans** (1781–1854), schoolmaster and writer. Collected stone and bronze implements, fossils, and British coins; author of *The Coins of the Ancient Britons* (1864) and treatises on ancient stone and bronze implements of Great Britain.

**Evans, Mary Ann** *or* **Marian.** See George ELIOT.

**Evans, Maurice.** 1901– . English actor, b. in Dorsetshire, Eng. First marked success as Second Lieutenant Raleigh in *Journey's End* (1929). Played Shakespearean roles in stock company (1934–35). To U.S.; appeared with Katharine Cornell in *Romeo and Juliet* (1935–36), Shaw's *St. Joan* (1936–37). Played Shakespeare's *Richard II* (1937), Falstaff in *Henry IV* (part I; 1937–38), and *Hamlet* (1938–39), with great success.

**Evans, Oliver.** 1755–1819. American inventor, b. near Newport, Del. Constructed first high-pressure steam engine in America (before 1802) and specialized in construction of such engines. He has been called the "Watt of America."

**Evans, Robley Dunglison.** 1846–1912. Known as "Fighting Bob Evans." American naval officer, b. in Virginia. Perfected long-distance signal lamp (1876). Regarded as expert on steelmaking; influential in navy's decision to build steel warships; chief inspector of steel (1886–87). To Chile in charge of gunboat *Yorktown* (1891); to Bering Sea, in command of flotilla, to stop abuses in seal fisheries (1892). His ship fired first gun at Cervera's fleet, at Santiago (1898). Rear admiral (1901); commanding officer, Asiatic fleet (1902); appointed commander in chief of U.S. fleet on its voyage round the world (1907), but retired during voyage, because of illness. Author of *A Sailor's Log* (1901), *An Admiral's Log* (1910).

**Evans, Rudulph.** 1878–1960. American sculptor, b. Washington, D.C. Sculptor of busts of Whittier, Longfellow, George Bancroft, Grover Cleveland in American Hall of Fame, bronze statue of Gen. Robert E. Lee in state capitol at Richmond, Va., William Jennings Bryan at Washington, D.C., etc.

**Evans, T. Hopkin.** 1879–1940. Welsh conductor and composer; conductor of American Song Festival at Cleveland, Ohio (1934), and of International Eisteddfod at World's Fair, New York (1939). Composer of many choral works.

**Evans, Thomas.** 1798–1868. American Quaker minister, b. Philadelphia, Pa.; author of works (chiefly compilations) on Quaker history and doctrine.

**Evans, Thomas Wiltberger.** 1823–1897. American dentist and philanthropist. In Paris, France (from about 1847); through friendship with Napoleon III, built up dental practice and established American dental prestige in Europe. Helped Empress Eugénie escape from Paris (1870).

**Ev'an–Thom'as** (ĕv'ăn·tŏm'ăs), Sir **Hugh.** 1862–1928. British admiral; second in command of first battle squadron (1913–15); commander of fifth battle squadron, and engaged in battle of Jutland (1916); vice-admiral (1917) and admiral (1920).

**Evaric.** See EURIC.

**Ev'a·ris'tus** (ĕv'ȧ·rĭs'tŭs), Saint. Pope (bishop of Rome; 99?–?107).

**Ev'arts** (ĕv'ẽrts), **Hal G.** 1887–1934. American writer of adventure stories, b. Topeka, Kans. Author of *The Cross Pull* (1920), *Passing of the Old West* (1921), *Tumbleweeds* (1923), *Shortgrass* (1932), etc.

**Evarts, William Maxwell.** 1818–1901. American lawyer and statesman, b. Boston, Mass. During Civil War was secretary of Union defense committee; sent by Lincoln on diplomatic missions to England (1863–64). Chief counsel for President Johnson in impeachment proceedings and largely responsible for his acquittal (1868). Attorney general of the U.S. (1868–69). Counsel for U.S. before Geneva court of arbitration (1871–72). As president (1870–80) of Association of the Bar of the City of New York led movements for law reform and against "Tweed Ring." Chief counsel for Republican party in Hayes-Tilden electoral votes dispute before electoral commission (1877). U.S. secretary of state (1877–81). U.S. delegate to Paris monetary conference (1881). U.S. senator from New York (1885–91).

**Ev'att** (ĕv'ăt), **Herbert Vere.** 1894–1965. Australian lawyer and statesman; king's counsel (1929); justice, federal high court (1930–40); M.P. (from 1940); member, commonwealth advisory war council (1941); attorney general and minister for external affairs (from 1942); delegate to UN (from 1946).

**Evdokiya.** Russian form for EUDOXIA.

**Eve** (ēv), **Arthur Stewart.** 1862–1948. British physicist; teacher of physics at McGill U., Montreal (from 1903), head of department (1919–35). Authority on ionization and radioactivity.

**Ève** (âv), **Nicolas** and **Clovis.** French bookbinders of the 16th and 17th centuries, both bearing the title of binder to the king of France (Nicolas, to Henry III; Clovis, to Henry IV and Louis XIII).

**Eve** (ēv), **Paul Fitzsimons.** 1806–1877. American surgeon; leading surgeon and teacher of surgery in southern states. Credited with being first American surgeon to perform hysterectomy.

**Eve'lyn** (ēv'lĭn), **John.** 1620–1706. English Royalist, minor government official, and diarist. After Restoration, served in minor offices, such as commissioner of the mint; treasurer of Greenwich Hospital (1695–1703);

prominent member of Royal Society, and its secretary (1672). Author of over 30 works on numismatics, architecture, landscape gardening, upon which he was an authority; also on painting, engraving, politics, education, commerce, including *Fumifugium* (1661), *Sculptura* (1662), *Sylva*, a book on practical arboriculture (1664). Chronicled his travels and contemporary events in his *Diary* (1640–1706), a record of historical value. Cf. Samuel PEPYS.

**Evemerus.** = EUHEMERUS.

**E've·ne·poel'** (ā'vĕ·nĕ·po͞ol'), **Henri Jacques Édouard.** 1872–1899. Belgian painter.

**E·ven'e·tus** (ē·vĕn'ē·tŭs). Syracusan engraver of coins, of late 5th and early 4th century B.C.

**Everaerts, Jan Nicolai.** See Johannes SECUNDUS.

**E'ver·ding'en** (ā'vĕr·dĭng'ĕn), **Allart** *or* **Aldert van.** 1621–1675. Dutch landscape and marine painter and engraver.

**Ev'er·est** (ĕv'ĕr·ĕst; -ĭst), Sir **George.** 1790–1866. British military engineer; superintendent of trigonometrical survey of India (1823) and surveyor general of India (1830–43), in whose honor Mount Everest was named.

**Ev'er·ett** (ĕv'ĕr·ĕt; -ĭt), **Alexander Hill.** 1790–1847. Bro. of Edward Everett. American diplomat, b. Boston, Mass. Chargé d'affaires (1818–24) at The Hague; minister to Spain (1825–29); first U.S. commissioner to China under new treaty (1845).

**Everett, Charles Carroll.** 1829–1900. American theologian, b. Brunswick, Me. Unitarian pastor at Bangor, Me. (1859–69). Professor (from 1869) and dean (from 1878) in Harvard Divinity School.

**Everett, Edward.** 1794–1865. American Unitarian clergyman, orator, and statesman, b. Dorchester, Mass. Pastor of Brattle Street Church, Boston (1814). Accepted newly established chair of Greek at Harvard; studied in Europe (1815–19); received from Göttingen (1817) first Ph.D. given an American. Member, U.S. House of Representatives (1825–35). Governor of Massachusetts (1836–40). U.S. minister to Great Britain (1841–45). President of Harvard (1846–49). U.S. secretary of state for four months (1852–53). U.S. senator (1853–54). When Civil War broke out, abandoned compromise and campaigned for the Union; best-known wartime oration delivered at dedication of national cemetery at Gettysburg (Nov. 19, 1863), on the same occasion as that on which Lincoln made his celebrated address.

**Ev'er·mann** (ĕv'ĕr·măn), **Barton Warren.** 1853–1932. American ichthyologist; ichthyologist (1891–1914), U.S. Bureau of Fisheries. Director, Museum of California Academy of Sciences (1914–32) and Steinhart Aquarium (1922–32). Author of *Studies of the Pacific Coast Salmon* (1894–97), *The Fishes of North and Middle America* (with David Starr Jordan; 4 vols., 1896–1900), *American Food and Game Fishes* (with Jordan; 1902), *The Fishes of Peru* (1915), *Check List of the Fishes...of North and Middle America* (with Jordan and H. Walton Clark; 1928), etc.

**Eversley,** Baron and Viscount. See SHAW-LEFEVRE.

**Eves** (ēvz), **Reginald Grenville.** 1876–1941. English portrait painter; R.A. (1939); official war artist (1940–41).

**E'vil-Me·ro'dach** (ē'vĭl·mē·rō'dăk; -mĕr'ō·dăk). *Bab.* **A'mel-Mar'duk** (ä'mĕl·mär'do͝ok). d. 560 B.C. King of Babylonia (562–560 B.C.). Son of Nebuchadnezzar II. Released Jehoiachin, King of Judah, from prison in the 37th year of his captivity (*2 Kings* xxv. 27–30); dethroned by a conspiracy.

**Evoe.** Pseudonym of Edmund G. V. KNOX.

**Évremond.** See SAINT-ÉVREMOND.

**E'wald** (ā'vält), **Georg Heinrich August.** 1803–1875. German Semitic scholar and Biblical critic, b. Göttingen. Professor, Göttingen (1831–37), Tübingen (1838–48), Göttingen (1848–67); retired for refusal to take oath of allegiance to king of Prussia. Took active part in movement for Protestant reform in Germany (from 1862). Author of *Ausführliches Lehrbuch der Hebräischen Sprache*, *Grammatica Critica Linguae Arabicae* (2 vols., 1831–33), *Geschichte des Volkes Israel* (1843–48) and its sequel, *Die Johanneischen Schriften* (1861–62), etc.

**E'wald** (ĭ'väl), **Herman Frederik.** 1821–1908. Danish historical novelist.

**E'wald** *or* **E'vald** (ĭ'väl), **Johannes.** 1743–1781. Danish national lyric poet and dramatist; author of *Elegies* on the death of Frederick V (1766), the Biblical drama *Adam and Eve* (1769), the first original Danish tragedy *Rolf Krage* (1770), the heroic drama in iambic pentameter *Balder's Death* (1773), the national festival drama *The Fishers* (1779) containing the Danish national song *King Christian Stood by the Lofty Mast*, an uncompleted autobiography, etc.

**Ew'bank** (ū'băngk), **Thomas.** 1792–1870. Inventor and manufacturer, b. Durham, England; to New York (1819). His *Descriptive Account of Hydraulic and Other Machines for Raising Water* (1842) was long a standard work. As U.S. commissioner of patents (1849–52) laid foundation for present rules of practice in patent office.

**Ew'ell** (ū'ĕl), **Arthur Woolsey.** 1873– . American physicist.

**Ewell, Richard Stoddert.** 1817–1872. Grandson of Benjamin Stoddert. American soldier; grad. U.S.M.A., West Point (1840). Resigned from U.S. army to join Confederate cause (1861); brigadier general (June, 1861); major general (Oct., 1861). Led division under "Stonewall" Jackson in Shenandoah Valley campaign; lieutenant general (May, 1863); succeeded to command of Jackson's corps after Chancellorsville; cleared Union forces from the valley; led advance into Pennsylvania; took part in battle of Gettysburg and the Wilderness; in charge of Richmond defenses; captured after evacuation of city and imprisoned at Fort Warren. After war, lived in retirement in Tennessee. His brother **Benjamin Stoddert** (1810–1894), grad. U.S.M.A., West Point (1832), was acting president of William and Mary College (1848–54), then its president till 1861 (when it closed because of Civil War) and again from 1869–81. During the war he was chief of staff to General Joseph E. Johnston.

**Ew'ing** (ū'ĭng), Sir **Alfred,** *in full* **James Alfred.** 1855–1935. Scottish physicist and engineer. Principal and vice-chancellor, U. of Edinburgh (1916–29). Investigated magnetic properties of iron, steel, etc.; proposed the theory of magnetization now generally accepted; observed and named the phenomenon of hysteresis; investigated the crystalline structure of several metals; studied earthquakes in Japan; invented several apparatus used in testing iron used for dynamo construction.

**Ewing, Finis.** 1773–1841. American clergyman, b. Bedford Co., Va. One of three clergymen who founded the Cumberland Presbyterian Church (1810).

**Ewing, James.** 1866–1943. American pathologist; authority on tumors; professor, Cornell (from 1899).

**Ewing, James Caruthers Rhea.** 1854–1925. American Presbyterian missionary, b. Rural Valley, Pa.; to India (1879); principal of Forman Christian College, Lahore (1888–1918), raising it to high rank; also dean (1890–1907) and vice-chancellor (1910–17) of Punjab U.

**Ewing, John.** 1732–1802. American Presbyterian clergyman; pastor in Philadelphia (1759–1802). First provost, U. of Pennsylvania (1791–1802).

**Ewing, Juliana Horatia,** *nee* **Gat'ty** (găt'ĭ). 1841–1885. English writer of stories for children. Daughter of **Alfred Gatty** (1813–1903), Vicar of Ecclesfield and author of *The Bell, its Origin and History* (1847), and **Margaret Gatty** (1807–1873), originator of *Aunt Judy's Magazine* (1866) and author of *Aunt Judy's Tales* (1859) and *Aunt Judy's Letters.* Juliana, as one of a large family, composed nursery plays and served as nursery storyteller, published stories in *Aunt Judy's Magazine;* m. (1867) **Alexander Ewing** (1830–1895), composer of *Jerusalem the Golden.* Her stories include *Melchior's Dream* (1862), *The Brownies* (1870), *Lob-lie-by-the-Fire* (1873), *Jackanapes* (1884), *Jan of the Windmill* (1884), *The Story of a Short Life* (1885). Her brother **Alfred Scott Scott-Gatty** (1847–1919) composed operettas, wrote *Rumpelstiltskin.*

**Ewing, Thomas.** 1789–1871. American lawyer, b. near West Liberty, Va. (now W.Va.). U.S. senator from Ohio (1831–37, 1850–51). U.S. secretary of the treasury (1841). U.S. secretary of the interior (1849–50).

**Ex'el'mans'** (ĕg'zĕl'mäɴs'), Comte **Remi Joseph Isidore.** 1775–1852. Marshal of France; colonel at Austerlitz (1805), general of brigade at Eylau (1807), general of division after Moscow (1812). Exiled after the Restoration (1815–19). Created marshal (1851).

**Ex'e·ter** (ĕk'sē·tẽr). (1) Dukes of. See John Holland; Sir Thomas Beaufort. (2) Earls and marquises of. See Cecil family. (3) Marquis of. See Henry Courtenay.

**Ex'mouth** (ĕks'mouth), 1st Viscount. Sir **Edward Pel·lew'** (pĕ·lū'). 1757–1833. English naval officer. Took part in battle on Lake Champlain (1776); captured first frigate in French war (1793), and destroyed a French 74-gun ship (1797); in parliament supported admiralty against hostile critics. Rear admiral (1804); destroyed Dutch fleet in East Indies (1807); vice-admiral (1808); bombarded Algiers and forced dey to abolish Christian slavery (1816); vice-admiral of United Kingdom (1832).

**Ex'ner** (ĕks'nẽr), **Franz.** 1802–1853. Austrian Herbartian philosopher and pedagogue.

**Exner, Siegmund.** 1846–1926. Austrian authority on nervous physiology, esp. of the cerebral cortex.

**Ex'pert'** (ĕks'pâr'), **Henry,** *in full* **Norbert Isidore Henry.** 1863–1952. French musicologist; cofounder of Société d'Études Musicales (1903); librarian, Paris Conservatory (1909); teacher at École de Musique Classique and at École des Hautes Études Sociales. Edited collection of Franco-Flemish music of 15th–16th centuries, also six volumes of new collection *Monuments de la Musique Française au Temps de la Renaissance* (1924 ff.), etc.

**Exquemeling.** See Esquemeling.

**Eyb** (īp), **Albrecht von.** 1420–1475. German writer and humanist; author of work on marriage *Ehebüchlein* (1472) and of *Spiegel der Sitten* with translations from Plautus (pub. 1511).

**Ey'bler** (ī'blẽr), **Joseph von.** 1764–1846. Austrian composer, esp. of church music.

**Eyck** (īk), **Hubert** *or* **Huybrecht van** (1366?–1426) and his brother **Jan van** (1370?–?1440). Flemish painters, b. at Maeseyck. Founders of Flemish school of painting; reputed originators of process of oil painting with a drying varnish; studio chiefly at Bruges and Ghent. Only existing known work of Hubert is an altarpiece at Ghent, on which he collaborated with Jan. Among Jan's notable paintings are *Vierge Glorieuse Adorée par le Chanoine Van der Pale* (Bruges); *Vierge Glorieuse Adorée par le Chancelier Rollin* (Louvre); *Saint François Recevant les Stigmates, La Vierge à l'Enfant,* and portraits.

**Ey'e** (ī'ĕ), **August von.** 1825–1896. German art and culture historian and critic; carried on colonization work and researches in history of culture in Brazil (1879–89).

**Eyke von Repgow.** See Eike von Repgow.

**Eyk'man** (īk'män). = Eijkman.

**Ey'me·ri'co** (ĕ'ē·mä·rē'kō), **Nicolás.** *Lat.* **Ey'me·ri'cus** (ī'mĕ·rĭ'kŭs). 1320–1399. Spanish theologian; Dominican (1334 ff.); grand inquisitor (1356–99); author of *Directorium Inquisitorum* (pub. 1503).

**Eyre** (âr), **Edward John.** 1815–1901. English explorer and colonial governor, b. in Yorkshire. Emigrated to Australia and engaged in sheep farming (1833); explored deserts of interior of Australia and King George Sound; published *Discoveries in Central Australia* (1845). Lieutenant governor of New Zealand (1846–53), governor of St. Vincent (1854–60), governor of Jamaica (1864); condemned for rigor in suppressing rebellion of Morant Bay natives; recalled (1866).

**Eyre, Laurence.** American actor and playwright; played Shakespearean roles as member of Ben Greet company.

**Eyre, Wilson.** 1858–1944. American architect.

**Ey'stein** (ûü'stĕin). Name of two kings of Norway:

**Eystein Mag'nus·son** (mäng'nōō·sŏn). 1089–1122. King (1103–22). With his brothers Olaf IV and Sigurd I (*qq.v.*) ruled subdivisions of Norway; brought peace, encouraged building and trade.

**Eystein Ha'ralds·son** (här'räl·sŏn). d. 1157. King (1142–57). Brought up in Scotland; his reign a period of civil war; was deserted and assassinated.

**Ey'tel·wein** (ī'tĕl·vīn), **Johann Albert.** 1764–1848. German hydraulic engineer.

**Ey'vind Finn'son** (ûü'vĕnd fĕn'sŏn). *Nicknamed* **Skal'da·spil'lir** (skäl'dä·spēl'lẽr). Norwegian scald of the 10th century; adviser to Haakon the Good, whom he celebrated in his *Hakonarmal;* author of *Haleygjatal,* in praise of Jarl Haakon, and of *Islendingadrapa,* dealing with the Icelanders.

**Ezechias** *or* **Ezekias.** See Hezekiah.

**E·zech'iel** *or* **E·zek'iel** (ē·zĕk'yĕl; ē·zē'kĭ·ĕl). Jewish playwright of Alexandria in 2d century A.D.; wrote in Greek. Only fragments of his plays are extant.

**E·zek'iel.** *In Douay Bible* **E·zech'iel** (ē·zĕk'yĕl; ē·zē'kĭ·ĕl). fl. 6th cent. B.C. One of the major Hebrew prophets. The Old Testament book of *Ezekiel* records his visions and prophecies of judgment on apostate Israel (chaps. i–xxiv) and on her enemies (xxv–xxxii), and of her final redemption.

**Ezekiel, Moses Jacob.** *Known as* Sir **Moses Ezekiel** *after receiving German and Italian knighthood honors.* 1844–1917. American sculptor, b. Richmond, Va. Examples of his work (in U.S.): *Virginia Mourning her Dead,* Lexington, Va.; Stonewall Jackson statue, Charleston, W.Va.; Thomas Jefferson monument, Louisville, Ky.; monument to the Confederate dead, Arlington National Cemetery; *Religious Liberty,* Philadelphia; *Christ,* Baltimore; *Judith,* Cincinnati Museum.

**E·zhov'** (yĕ·zhôf'). Variant of Yezhov.

**Ez'ra** (ĕz'rȧ). Hebrew scribe and priest, of 5th century B.C. The book of *Ezra* in the Old Testament, part of which at least is attributed to him, forms with *Nehemiah* a continuous account of postexilic Jewish history. The Greek form of his name, **Es'dras** (ĕz'drȧs), is attached to two books in the Protestant Apocrypha. In Roman Catholic use these two are regarded as uncanonical and are numbered *3* and *4 Esdras;* the canonical books corresponding to the A.V. books of *Ezra* and *Nehemiah* are designated *1 Esdras* and *2 Esdras, alias Nehemias.*

**Ez'ze·li'no** (äd'dzȧ·lē'nō) *or* **Ec'ce·li'no** (ät'chȧ-) **da Ro·ma'no** (dä rō·mä'nō). Prominent Ghibelline family of Italy, including: **Ezzelino I,** German knight who settled in Italy in early 11th century and received castle of Romano. **Ezzelino IV** (1194–1259), powerful opponent of the papacy; conquered and wasted all northeast Italy; finally conquered and imprisoned, starved himself to death (1259); mentioned in Dante's *Inferno.*

# F

**Fabbroni.** Variant of FABRONI.

**Fa′ber** (fā′bẽr), **Frederick William.** 1814–1863. English Roman Catholic clergyman and hymn writer, b. Calverley, Yorkshire. B.A., Oxon. (1836). Anglican clergyman; joined Roman Catholic Church (1845) and formed Catholic community, Brothers of the Will of God (1845); joined Oratory of St. Philip Neri (1848) and established London Oratory (1849). Best known for hymns, as *The Pilgrims of the Night, The Land Beyond the Sea.*

**Faber, Geoffrey Cust.** 1889–1961. English publisher and writer; chairman (from 1924), Faber and Faber, Ltd., publishers.

**Fa′ber** (fā′bẽr) *or* **Fa′bri** (fā′brī), **Jacobus.** See Jacques LEFÈVRE D'ÉTAPLES.

**Fa′ber** (fä′bẽr), **Johann Lothar von.** 1817–1896. German manufacturer of lead pencils, b. in Stein near Nuremberg, Bavaria. Took over (1839) family business of present A. W. Faber Co. (founded 1761 by his great-grandfather **Kaspar** and named for the founder's son **Anton Wilhelm**) in Stein; established branches and additional manufactories (including mills at Cedar Keys, Fla.) and agencies; added manufacture of other writing, drawing, and painting materials; received patent of nobility (1881); councilor of state for services to German industry. A brother, **Eb′er·hard Fa′ber** [*in English,* ĕb′ẽr·härd fā′bẽr] (1823–1879), b. Stein, representative of firm in U.S. (1848); became naturalized; established in N.Y. (1849) independent business, now Eberhard Faber Pencil Co., carried on by his sons; first manufacturer to put rubber tips on pencils.

**Fa′ber** (fä′bẽr), **Johannes.** *Orig. family name* **Hei′ger·lin** (hī′gẽr·lĭn). *Called* **Mal′le·us Hae·ret′i·co′rum** (măl′ē·ŭs hē·rĕt′ĭ·kō′rŭm), *i.e.* the Hammer of Heretics. 1478–1541. German Roman Catholic bishop and opponent of Reformation, b. Swabia. Dominican monk, then vicar-general of bishop of Constance (1518); friend of Erasmus and sympathizer with Zwingli and Melanchthon; later, strong opponent of Lutherans; court preacher to Emperor Ferdinand (1526); envoy to Spain and England (1527–28); worked zealously against Turkish invasion; bishop of Vienna (1531). Author of *Malleus in Haeresin Lutheranam* (1524).

**Fa′ber** (fā′bẽr), **John** (1660?–1721) and his son **John** (1695?–1756). English mezzotint engravers.

**Fa′ber** (fä′bẽr), **Knud.** 1862–1956. Danish physician.

**Fa′ber** (fā′bẽr), **Petrus.** See Pierre FAVRE.

**Fa′bert′** (fȧ′bâr′), **Abraham de.** 1599–1662. French soldier; governor of Sedan (1642); marshal of France (1650).

**Fa′bi·an** (fā′bĭ·ăn; făb′yăn), **Saint.** Pope (bishop of Rome; 236–250).

**Fa′bi·us** (fā′bĭ·ŭs; făb′yŭs). Name of a number of prominent Romans of one of oldest and most distinguished patrician families, including: **Quintus Fabius Vib′u·la′nus** (vĭb′ū·lā′nŭs), consul for seven successive years (485–479 B.C.), and his brothers **Caeso** and **Marcus. Marcus Fabius An·bus′tus** (ăn·bŭs′tŭs), pontifex maximus the year that the Gauls captured Rome (390 B.C.). **Caius Fabius Pic′tor** (pĭk′tẽr; -tôr) of late 4th century B.C., first Roman patrician to devote himself to painting. **Quintus Fabius Pictor** of late 3d century B.C., wrote a history of Rome (now lost) including Second Punic War, in which he personally served. **Quintus Fabius Max′i·mus** (măk′sĭ·mŭs), *surnamed* **Rul′li·a′nus** [rŭl′ĭ·ā′nŭs] (d. about 290 B.C.), was six times consul; dictator (315 B.C.); distinguished himself in Third Samnite War, winning battle of Sentinum (295). His grandson **Quintus Fabius Maximus Ver′ru·co′sus** [vĕr′ū·kō′sŭs; vĕr′ōō-] (d. 203), *surnamed* **Cunc·ta′tor** (kŭngk·tā′tẽr; -tôr), *i.e.* the Delayer, because of his military strategy; consul (233 B.C.); censor (230); again consul (228); emissary to Carthage (218); dictator and army commander (217); again consul (215, 214, 209); in Second Punic War withstood Hannibal's military strength by his strategy (hence termed "Fabian") of conducting harassing operations while avoiding decisive conflicts.

**Fa′bre** (fȧ′br′), **Émile.** 1870–1955. French playwright.

**Fabre, Ferdinand.** 1827–1898. French novelist.

**Fabre,** Baron **François Xavier Pascal.** 1766–1837. French historical painter.

**Fabre, Jean Henri.** 1823–1915. French entomologist. b. St. Leon, Aveyron; educ. Normal School of Vaucluse; teacher, Carpentras, College of Ajaccio (Corsica), and Lycée of Avignon; retired; at Sérignan devoted himself to direct observational study of habits of insects, esp. hymenoptera, coleoptera, and orthoptera, and spiders. Author of *Souvenirs Entomologiques* (10 vols., 1879–1907), parts of which have appeared in English under such titles as *The Life and Love of the Insect* (tr. by A. Teixeira de Mattos, 1911) and *Social Life in the Insect World* (tr. by Bernard Miall, 1913); also author of *Histoire de la Bûche* (1866), *Notions Préliminaires de Physique* (1867–70), etc.

**Fabre, Lucien.** 1889–1952. French novelist; author of *Rabevel* (1923; awarded Goncourt prize), *Le Taramagnon* (1925), and a treatise on Einstein's theory of relativity.

**Fa′bre d′É′glan′tine′** (fȧ′br′ dā′gläɴ′tēn′). *Real name* **Philippe François Nazaire Fabre.** 1750–1794. French playwright and revolutionary politician. His plays include the well-known comedy *Le Philinte de Molière ou la Suite du Misanthrope* (1790). Friend of Danton and Desmoulins, and prominent in the Cordeliers; member of National Convention (1792); author of names of months and days in Revolutionary calendar; suspected of moderacy by Robespierre (1794); guillotined at Paris same day as Danton and Desmoulins (Apr. 5, 1794).

**Fa·bret′ti** (fä·brāt′tē), **Raffaele.** 1618–1700. Italian antiquary; papal archivist at Castel Sant'Angelo under Innocent XII.

**Fabri, Jacobus.** See Jacques LEFÈVRE D'ÉTAPLES.

**Fabriano, Gentile da.** See GENTILE DA FABRIANO.

**Fa·brice′** (fä·brēs′), Count **Georg Friedrich Alfred von.** 1818–1891. German general and statesman, b. in France. Commander of Saxon forces in Bohemia in war against Prussia (1866); after the war became Saxon minister of war; represented chancellor in France during Franco-German truce (1871), conducted preliminary peace negotiations, commanded German army of occupation; again Saxon minister of war (1871); prime minister (1876); minister of foreign affairs (1882); created count (1884).

**Fabrici, Geronimo** *or* **Girolamo.** See FABRICIUS AB AQUAPENDENTE.

**Fa·bri′ci·us** (fȧ·brĭsh′ĭ·ŭs; -brĭsh′ŭs). *In full* **Gaius Fabricius Lus·ci′nus** (lŭ·sī′nŭs). d. after 275 B.C. Roman general and statesman; consul (282 B.C.). After Roman defeat at Heraclea (280), sent to negotiate with Pyrrhus for ransom and exchange of prisoners; established reputation for honesty when he rejected all attempts to bribe him. Again consul (278); negotiated peace with Pyrrhus; defeated Samnites, Lucanians, and Bruttians; awarded triumph on return to Rome.

**Fa·bri'ci·us** (fä·brē'tsē·o͝os), **David**. 1564–1617. German theologian and astronomer; his observations utilized by Kepler in researches on planet Mars; discovered variable star Mira in constellation Cetus (1596). His son **Johannes** (1587–1615), astronomer, is credited with discovery of sunspots (1610) and detection, by means of their movements, of rotation of sun on its axis.

**Fabricius, Ernst**. 1857–1942. German archaeologist.

**Fabricius, Georg**. *Orig. surname* **Gold'schmied** (gôlt'-shmēt). 1516–1571. German classical scholar, philologist, and Latin poet.

**Fa·bri'ci·us** (fȧ·brē'sē·ûs), **Jan**. 1871–1964. Dutch playwright.

**Fabricius, Johan Christian**. 1743–1808. Danish entomologist; studied under Linnaeus; developed system of classification of insects based on mouth structure.

**Fa·bri'ci·us** (fä·brē'tsē·o͝os), **Johann Albert**. 1668–1736. German classical scholar, philologist, and bibliographer. Professor at Hamburg (from 1699) and rector of the Johanneum.

**Fa·bri'ci·us ab Aq'ua·pen·den'te** (fȧ·brĭsh'ĭ·ŭs [-brĭsh'ŭs] ăb ăk'wȧ·pĕn·dĕn'tē), **Hieronymus**. *Italian* **Geronimo** *or* **Girolamo Fa·bri'zi·o** (fä·brē'tsyō) *or* **Fa·bri'ci** (fä·brē'chē). 1537–1619. Italian anatomist and surgeon; pupil of Fallopius; professor, Padua (from 1562); teacher of William Harvey; known esp. for work in comparative anatomy and embryology; described valves in veins; made improvements in surgery.

**Fa·bri'ci·us Hil·da'nus** (fȧ·brĭsh'ĭ·ŭs [-brĭsh'ŭs] hĭl-dā'nŭs). *Ger.* **Wilhelm Fa'bry** (fä'brē). 1560–1634. Eminent German surgeon.

**Fa·bri'ti·us** (fȧ·brē'tsē·ûs), **Carel**. 1624?–1654. Dutch painter. Pupil of Rembrandt and teacher of Jan Vermeer van Delft; lived in Amsterdam and (1652–54) in Delft. His works include a portrait of Abraham de Notte, *The Goldfinch, The Sentinel* and *Family Group* (destroyed by fire in Rotterdam museum).

**Fabrizio, Geronimo** *or* **Girolamo**. See FABRICIUS AB AQUAPENDENTE.

**Fa·bro'ni** (fä·brō'nē) *or* **Fab·bro'ni** (fäb·brō'nē), **Angelo**. 1732–1803. Tuscan biographer; author of *Vitae Italorum Doctrina Excellentium Qui Saeculis XVII. et XVIII. Floruerunt* (20 vols., 1778–99, 1804–05).

**Fabroni** *or* **Fabbroni, Giovanni Valentino Matteo**. 1752–1822. Italian naturalist, chemist, and engineer; built Col de Genèvre (pass) and started Corniche road from Genoa to Nice.

**Fa'bry'** (fȧ'brē'), **Charles**. 1867–1945. French physicist; known for work in optics, esp. in spectroscopy and photometry, and applications of phenomenon of interference.

**Fa'bry** (fä'brē), **Wilhelm**. See FABRICIUS HILDANUS.

**Fab'vier'** (fȧ'vyā'), Baron **Charles Nicolas**. 1782–1855. French general; served in Napoleonic armies, notably at Borodino. Remained loyal to Louis XVIII during the Hundred Days; later involved in intrigue against Bourbons; fled from France; aided Greece in struggle with Turkey. Returned to France (1830); lieutenant general (1839); peer of France (1845).

**Fa'by·an** (fā'bĭ·ăn; făb'yăn), **Robert**. d. 1513. English chronicler; author of chronicle of England *The Concordance of Histories*, pub. (1516) under title *The New Chronicles of England and France.*

**Fac'cio·la'ti** (fät'chō·lä'tē), **Jacopo**. 1682–1769. Italian philologist and lexicographer; professor, Padua; collaborated with Forcellini (*q.v.*) in editing Calepino's *Dictionarium Undecim Linguarum* (1718); wrote *Fasti Gymnasii Patavini* (1757).

**Fac'ta** (fäk'tä), **Luigi**. 1861–1930. Italian statesman; premier of Italy (1922); senator (1924).

**Fad'den** (făd''n), Sir **Arthur William**. 1895–1973. Australian politician; leader of Country party; prime minister (Aug.–Oct., 1941); leader of opposition in parliament (1941–43); member of advisory war council.

**Fa·de'ev** (fŭ·dyā'yĕf), **Aleksandr Aleksandrovich**. 1901–1956. Russian novelist; joined Communist party (1918) and fought in civil war; member of Praesidium, Union of Soviet Writers (1932–38) and its secretary (1938 ff.); among his novels are *The Flood* (1924), *Defeat* (1927).

**Fad'i·man** (făd'ĭ·măn), **Clifton Paul**. 1904– . Am. writer and editor, b. Brooklyn, N.Y. Book editor for the *New Yorker* (1933–43); master of ceremonies, *Information Please* radio program (1938–48).

**Faed** (fād), **John**. 1819–1902. Scottish painter; painted miniature portraits, historical scenes, and genre pictures. His brother **Thomas** (1826–1900) was also a painter, esp. of genre scenes from Scottish life.

**Fae'si** (fâ'zē), **Robert**. 1883– Swiss poet, playwright, and miscellaneous writer.

**Fa'gel** (fä'gĕl), **Kaspar**. 1629–1688. Dutch statesman. Brought about choice of William III of Orange as hereditary stadholder of Netherlands (1672) and supported his expedition to England (1688).

**Fa'ger·lin'** (fä'gēr·lēn'), **Ferdinand Julius**. 1825–1907. Swedish genre painter; known esp. for paintings of Dutch fishermen's and seamen's life.

**Fa'gniez'** (fȧ'nyā'), **Gustave**. 1842–1927. French historian; authority esp. on economic history.

**Fa'guet'** (fȧ'gĕ'), **Émile**. 1847–1916. French literary critic; professor at the Sorbonne (1890); author of *La Tragédie Française au XVI$^{e}$ Siècle* (1883), *Corneille* (1885), *La Fontaine* (1889), *Voltaire* (1894), *Flaubert* (1899), *Histoire de la Littérature Française* (1900), *L'Art de Lire* (1912)

**Fahl'crantz** (fäl'krȧns), **Christian Erik**. 1790–1866. Swedish theologian, poet, and writer; bishop of Västerås (1849); author of *Noah's Ark* (2 parts, 1825–26), *Ansgarius* (11 parts, 1835–46), etc. His brother **Karl Johan** (1774–1861) was a landscape painter.

**Fah'ren·heit** (fä'rĕn·hīt; *Angl.* făr'ĕn-), **Gabriel Daniel**. 1686–1736. German physicist, b. Danzig. Lived most of life in Holland and England; improved thermometer by using mercury instead of alcohol (1714); introduced scale (Fahrenheit scale) commonly used for thermometers in the U.S. and England.

**Fa–Hsien** *or* **Fa–Hien** (fä'shē·ĕn'). fl. 399–414 A.D. Chinese Buddhist priest, traveler, and author, b. Shansi. Studied Buddhism; journeyed by land to India (399); spent about ten years (401?–?412) during reign of Chandragupta II visiting scenes of Buddha's life, copying Buddhist texts, etc.; wrote account of travels, and translated Buddhist texts.

**Fai'dherbe'** (fĕ'dĕrb'), **Louis Léon César**. 1818–1889. French soldier; as governor of Senegal (1854), extended French territorial possessions and successfully reorganized administration. In Franco-Prussian War, offered services to Gambetta; commander of Army of the North; defeated at St.-Quentin (1871). Senator (1879).

**Fai'dit'** (fĕ'dē'), **Gau'cel'me** (gō'sĕl'mĕ). Provençal troubadour of end of 12th and beginning of 13th century.

**Fail'ly'** (fȧ'yē'), **Pierre Louis Charles de**. 1810–1892. French soldier; served in Crimea (1854–55); general of division (1855). Engaged at Solferino (1859). Defeated by Prussians near Beaumont (1870) and replaced by General de Wimpffen on day of battle of Sedan (1870).

**Fain** (făN), Baron **Agathon Jean François**. 1778–1837. French historian; secretary to Napoleon (1806–15).

**Fair'bairn** (fâr'bârn), **Andrew Martin**. 1838–1912. Scottish nonconformist theologian.

**Fairbairn, Patrick**. 1805–1874. Scottish clergyman.

**Fairbairn,** Sir **William.** 1789–1874. Scottish engineer; established shipbuilding works in London (1835–49); patented principle of wrought-iron girders for use in bridge construction, etc.

**Fair'banks** (fâr'băngks), **Arthur.** 1864–1944. American educator, b. Hanover, N.H. Professor of Greek, Iowa (1900–06) and Michigan (1906–07); director, Boston Museum of Fine Arts (1907–25); professor of fine arts, Dartmouth (1928–33).

**Fairbanks, Charles Warren.** 1852–1918. American lawyer and political leader; U.S. senator from Indiana (1897–1905); vice-president of U.S. (1905–09).

**Fairbanks, Douglas.** 1883–1939. American actor, b. Denver, Colo.; played leading parts in *Frenzied Finance, A Gentleman from Mississippi, Henrietta, Show Shop.* Starred in motion pictures. Headed own company from 1916; productions included *The Mollycoddle, The Nut, The Three Musketeers, Robin Hood, The Thief of Bagdad, The Iron Mask.* See also Mary PICKFORD. His son **Douglas Elton** (1908– ), also an actor.

**Fairbanks, Thaddeus.** 1796–1886. American inventor of platform scale, b. Brimfield, Mass.; devised first platform scale, obtaining basic patent (1831); thereafter E. & T. Fairbanks & Company (incorporated as Fairbanks Scale Company, 1874) made manufacturing of platform scales for all purposes their chief business. His brother **Erastus** (1792–1864) was associated with him in business; governor of Vermont (1852–53, 1860–61). A son of Thaddeus, **Henry** (1830–1918), b. St. Johnsbury, Vt., was a clergyman, inventor, and manufacturer; grad. Dartmouth (1853) and Andover Sem. (1857); in Congregational ministry (1857–60); professor, Dartmouth (1860–69); in scale-manufacturing business (from 1869).

**Fair'child** (fâr'chīld), **Charles Stebbins.** 1842–1924. American lawyer and financier; U.S. secretary of the treasury (1887–89).

**Fairchild, David Grandison.** 1869–1954. American botanist, b. East Lansing, Mich. Botanist (from 1889), agricultural explorer (from 1898), U.S. Department of Agriculture; research for economic plants (from 1895) in Dutch East Indies, South Seas, Australia, South America, Egypt, Japan, China, Persian Gulf.

**Fairchild, Henry Pratt.** 1880–1956. American social scientist, b. Dundee, Ill. Ph.D., Yale (1909). Professor, N.Y.U. (from 1919). Author of *Immigration* (1913), *Elements of Social Science* (1924), *General Sociology* (1934), *Economics for the Millions* (1940).

**Fairchild, James Harris.** 1817–1902. American educator, b. Stockbridge, Mass. Educ. Oberlin. Taught, Oberlin (till 1898); president (1866–1889). Author of *Moral Philosophy or the Science of Obligation* (1869), *Elements of Theology* (1892), etc. His brother **George Thompson** (1838–1901), b. Brownhelm, Ohio, also an educator; grad. Oberlin; professor, Michigan State (1865–79); president, Kansas State (1879–97); author of *Rural Wealth and Welfare* (1900).

**Fair'fax** (fâr'făks), **Thomas.** 1st Baron **Fairfax** of Cam'er·on (kăm'ĕr·ŭn), in Scottish peerage (cr. 1627). 1560–1640. Scottish diplomat used by Queen Elizabeth in communication with James VI of Scotland. One son, **Edward** (d. 1635), poet, translated Tasso's *Gerusalemme Liberata.* Another son, **Ferdinando** (1584–1648), 2d baron; M.P. (1622; 1624–27; Long Parliament, 1640); commanded Parliamentary forces in Yorkshire in Civil War; defended Hull (1643); stationed on right of Parliamentary line in battle of Marston Moor (July 2, 1644). Ferdinando's son **Thomas** (1612–1671), 3d baron; commander in chief of Parliamentary army (1645), defeated Charles I at Naseby (1645); sat in judgment on the king (1649); resigned from military command because of unwillingness to invade Scotland (1650); headed commission dispatched to Charles II at The Hague (1660). **Thomas** (1692–1782), 6th baron; b. Yorkshire; grad. Oxford; said to have been intimate with Bolingbroke, Addison, and Steele; visited maternal estates of the Northern Neck of Virginia (1735–37), and settled there as proprietor (1747); acquainted with Washington family; entrusted to George Washington surveying and mapping of the Fairfax estates in Shenandoah Valley (1748); steadfast loyalist.

**Fairfield, Cicily Isabel.** See Rebecca WEST.

**Fair'holt** (fâr'hōlt), **Frederick William.** 1814–1866. English engraver and antiquarian, b. London. Illustrated Halliwell's *Sir John Maundeville* and *Life of Shakespeare;* published illustrated antiquarian study *Costume in England* (1846); edited *A Dictionary of Terms in Art* (1854).

**Fair'lie** (fâr'lĭ), **John Archibald.** 1872–1947. Political scientist, b. Glasgow, Scotland; to U.S. in youth. Author of texts upon municipal and national administration in U.S. and Great Britian.

**Fai'sal** (fī'zăl; -săl). *In full* **Faisal Ibn Abdul-Aziz al Saud.** 1906?–1975. Saudi Arabian monarch. Declared Crown Prince (1953); prime minister and minister of foreign affairs (1953–60); defense minister (1958–64); king of Saudi Arabia (1964–75); assassinated; succeeded by his brother, Khalid.

**Fai'sal I** (fī'săl). *Also* **Fei'sal** (fī'săl) *or* **Fei'sul** (-s'l). 1885–1933. King of Syria (1920), and Iraq (1921–33). Third son of Husein ibn-Ali (*q.v.*); b. Mecca (Arabia); reared among Bedouins; educ. later in Constantinople; trained in Turkish army; active in Young Turk movement (1908–09). In World War, posted first in Syria under charge of Turkish governor; escaped (1916) to the Hejaz and took command of Arab rebels at Medina; co-operated with Colonel Lawrence and General Allenby in campaign which captured Jerusalem (Dec. 9, 1917) and Damascus (Oct. 3, 1918). After war, proclaimed (Mar., 1920) king of Syria by a Syrian national congress, but deposed by French under General Gouraud (July, 1920). Placed by British (1921) on throne of Iraq (formerly Mesopotamia), this country being administered as British mandate until admitted into League of Nations as independent state (1932). Succeeded by his son **Ghazi** (1912–1939), who in turn was succeeded by his son **Faisal II** (1935–58); king (1939–58).

**Faith'full** (fāth'fo͝ol; -f'l), **Emily.** 1835–1895. English philanthropist, businesswoman, and lecturer; interested in providing opportunities for women in industry.

**Fai'thorne** (fā'thôrn), **William.** 1616–1691. English engraver; engraved map of London and Westminster and of Virginia and Maryland; also a portrait painter. His son **William** (1656–?1701) engraved portraits of Queen Anne, Charles I, Charles II, and John Dryden.

**Faizi.** See FEISI.

**Fa'jans** (fä'yäns), **Ka'si·mir** (kä'zē·mēr). 1887– . Chemist, b. Warsaw, Poland. Educ. Leipzig, Heidelberg, Manchester. Professor, Munich (1917–35), Michigan (from 1936). Author of *Radioactivity and Latest Developments in the Study of Chemical Elements* (1919; English tr., 1922), *Radioelements and Isotopes* (1931).

**Fajardo, Diego Saavedra y.** See SAAVEDRA Y FAJARDO.

**Fakhr' al-Din'** (fäκ'-ro͞od·dēn'). *Arab.* **Fakhr al-Dīn al-Rāzi.** 1149–1209. Arab historian and theologian; defender of orthodox Mohammedanism; his chief work, *Mafātīh al-Ghaib* (*i.e.* The Keys of Mystery), a commentary on the Koran.

**Falb** (fälp), **Rudolf.** 1838–1903. Austrian astronomer and meteorologist. Held that sun and moon by their effect on atmosphere and on fluid interior of earth are responsible for the weather, earthquakes, and other phenomena.

**Falckenstein, Eduard Vogel von.** See VOGEL VON FALCKENSTEIN.

**Fal·cón'** (fäl·kōn'), **Juan Crisóstomo.** 1820–1870. Venezuelan soldier and political leader, b. Paraguaná; president of Venezuela (1863–68); overthrown by revolution.

**Falconberg, Thomas.** See FAUCONBERG.

**Fal·co'ne** (fäl·kō'nā), **Aniello.** *Called* **l'O·ra'co·lo del'le Bat·ta'glie** (lō·rä'kō·lō dāl'lā bät·tä'lyā). 1607–1656. Italian painter; pupil of Ribera; known esp. for battle scenes (in the Prado, the Louvre, and Naples museum).

**Fal'con·er** (fôk'nẽr; fô(l)'kŭn·ẽr), **Hugh.** 1808–1865. Scottish paleontologist and botanist; M.A., Aberdeen (1826); M.D., Edinburgh (1829). Asst. surgeon on East India Co.'s Bengal establishment (1830); discoverer of fossil mammals and reptiles in Siwalik Hills (1832); made earliest experiments in manufacture of Indian tea; superintended arrangement of East Indian fossils of British Museum for exhibition (1844); professor of botany, Calcutta Medical Coll. (1848–55).

**Fal'con·er** (fôk'nẽr), Sir **Robert Alexander.** 1867–1943. Canadian clergyman and educator, b. Charlottetown, Prince Edward Island. Ordained Presbyterian minister (1892). Taught New Testament Greek (1892–1907), president (1904–07), Pine Hill Coll., Halifax, N.S. President, U. of Toronto (1907–32).

**Fal'con·er** (fôk'nẽr; fô(l)'kŭn·ẽr), **William.** 1732–1769. English poet; chief work, *The Shipwreck* (1762).

**Fal'co'net'** (fàl'kô'nĕ'), **Étienne Maurice.** 1716–1791. French sculptor; among his works are *Pygmalion*, *La Baigneuse*, *L'Amour Menaçant*, and equestrian statue of Peter the Great at St. Petersburg carved on commission from Catherine II.

**Fal'co·net'to** (fäl'kō·nāt'tō), **Giovanni Maria.** 1458?–?1534. Veronese painter and architect.

**Fal'guière'** (fàl'gyâr'), **Jean Alexandre Joseph.** 1831–1900. French sculptor and painter; professor at École des Beaux Arts (Paris; 1882); among his notable sculptures are *Danseuse Égyptienne*, *Bacchantes*, and many portrait busts; among his canvases, *Lutteurs*, *Incendiaire.*

**Fa·lie'ri** (fä·lyâ'rē) *or* **Fa·lie'ro** (-rō) *or sometimes* **Fa·lier'** (fä·lyĕr'), **Marino.** 1278?–1355. Doge of Venice. Commanded Venetian army at siege of Zara (1346); elected doge (Sept., 1354); convicted of conspiracy to murder Venetian patricians and have himself proclaimed prince, executed (April 17, 1355). Subject of tragedies by Byron and Casimir Delavigne and of novel by Hoffmann.

**Falk** (fälk), **Adalbert.** 1827–1900. German statesman and jurist, b. Silesia. Old Liberal member, Prussian House of Representatives (1858); member of supreme court, Berlin (1861) and of court of appeal, Glogau (1862); Prussian plenipotentiary in Federal Council (1871); as minister of public worship and education (1872), worked for system of national education under state legislation; assisted Bismarck in Kulturkampf and helped work out May laws aimed at Roman Catholics (1873–75); member of Prussian House of Representatives and of Reichstag (1873–82), where he opposed modification of his laws; president of superior provincial court in Hamm (1882).

**Falk, Johannes Daniel.** 1768–1826. German writer and philanthropist, b. Danzig. Settled in Weimar (1797), became friend of Goethe; founded Falksches Institut for care and education of neglected children at Weimar (1813). Author of satirical works, as *Der Mensch* (1795), the dramatic poem *Prometheus* (1803), and *Goethe aus Näherem Persönlichen Umgange Dargestellt* (pub. 1832).

**Falk** (fŏlk), **Max.** 1828–1908. Hungarian publicist and politician. Editor in chief of the *Pester Lloyd* (1868–1906); conservative Liberal member of Hungarian parliament (1869–1906).

**Falk'ber'get** (fälk'bĕr'gĕ), **Johan.** 1879–1967. Norwegian novelist and short-story writer.

**Fal'ke** (fäl'kĕ), **Johannes Friedrich Gottlieb.** 1823–1876. German historian; author of *Geschichte des Deutschen Handels* (2 vols., 1859–60), *Die Hansa* (1862), and *Geschichte des Deutschen Zollwesens* (1869). His brother **Jakob von Falke** (1825–1897), historian of art and culture, was custodian (1864), vice-director (1872), and director (from 1885) of Austrian Museum, Vienna; author of *Kostümgeschichte der Kulturvölker* (1882), *Geschichte des Geschmacks im Mittelalter* (1892). Their nephew **Gustav Falke** (1853–1916), lyric poet and novelist, was author of volumes of verse, novels, and juveniles. Jakob's son **Otto von Falke** (1862–1942), art historian, b. Vienna, was director-general of government museum, Berlin (1920–28), and author of *Majolika* (1896), *Geschichte des Kunstgewerbes* (with others, 1907), *Deutsche Möbel...* (1924).

**Falke, Konrad.** *Pseudonym* **Karl Frey** (frī). 1880–1942. Swiss writer of novels, plays, and verse.

**Fal'ken·hau'sen** (fäl'kĕn·hou'zĕn), Baron **Ludwig von.** 1844–1936. German soldier; served in Austro-Prussian War (1866) and Franco-Prussian War (1870–71); recalled from retirement to service in World War (1914–18); succeeded von Bissing as governor of Belgium (Mar., 1917–Nov., 1918).

**Fal'ken·hayn** (fäl'kĕn·hīn), **Erich von.** 1861–1922. Prussian general, b. near Graudenz. Took part in China expedition (1899–1903); general (1913); Prussian war minister (1913–15); chief of general staff of German army (1914–16); active in planning offensives against Russia, Serbia, and Verdun; severely blamed for failure at Verdun; succeeded by von Hindenburg (1916); commanded army in Rumania (1916) and in the Caucasus (1917).

**Fal'ken·horst** (fäl'kĕn·hôrst), **Nikolaus von.** 1885–1968. German soldier in World War (1914–18); lieutenant general commanding 21st army corps in Polish campaign (1939); promoted general of infantry; commanded forces which occupied Norway and drove out the British (May, 1940); commander in White Sea region, Russian campaign (July, 1941).

**Falk'land** (fôk'lănd; fôlk'-), 2d Viscount (Scottish peerage). **Lucius Cary.** 1610?–1643. English writer. Son of 1st viscount, who was lord deputy of Ireland (1622–29). Educ. Dublin; vainly sought service in young republic of Holland; inherited fortune (1629) and devoted himself to literature; M.P. (1640); opposed Laud; eloquent for constitutional liberty; sided against Strafford; secretary of state (1642); took king's side reluctantly, courted death and was killed at Newbury.

**Falk'land** (fälk'länt), **Samuel.** See Herman HEIJERMANS.

**Falk'ner** (fôk'nẽr), **Thomas.** 1707–1784. English Jesuit missionary in Paraguay and Tucumán (to 1768); expelled from South America as a Jesuit (1768); author of treatises on medicine and natural history of South America.

**Falkner, William** See FAULKNER.

**Fall** (fôl), **Albert Bacon.** 1861–1944. American lawyer and politician, b. Frankfort, Ky. Practiced law in New Mexico (from 1889). U.S. senator from New Mexico (1912–21). U.S. secretary of the interior (1921–23; resigned); disclosed by investigation to have secretly transferred government oil lands (Teapot Dome) to Doheny and Sinclair, receiving $100,000 as a "loan" from Doheny and a lucrative position in Sinclair organization after retirement; eventually convicted (1929) for accepting bribe and imprisoned (1931–32).

**Fall** (fäl), **Leo.** 1873–1925. Austrian composer.

**Fal'la** (fä'lyä), **Manuel de.** **1876–1946.** Spanish composer. His compositions, showing nationalistic and impressionistic tendencies, include opera *Life is Short* (*La Vida Breve;* 1905), ballets *Wedded by Witchcraft* (1915) and *The Three-Cornered Hat* (1919), marionette play *Master Peter's Puppet Show* (1923), and piano and orchestral pieces.

**Fal'la·da** (fä'lä·dä), **Hans.** *Pen name of* **Rudolf Dit'zen** (dĭt'sĕn). 1893–1947. German novelist; author of *Anton und Gerda* (1923), *Little Man, What Now?* (1932; on post-war Germany), *The World Outside* (1934), *Wolf Among Wolves* (1937), etc.

**Fallersleben, Hoffmann von.** See August Heinrich HOFFMANN.

**Fal'lières'** (fá'lyâr'), **Clément Armand.** 1841–1931. French statesman and 8th president of the Republic, b. Mézin, Lot-et-Garonne. Educ. for law; member, Chamber of Deputies (1876–80); undersecretary and secretary of the interior (1880–83); cabinet officer (1883–92); elected to Senate (1890–99), its president (1899–1906). President of France, elected by Republican Left (1906–13).

**Fall'me·ray'er** (fäl'mĕ·rī'ēr), **Jakob Philipp.** 1790–1861. German historian and traveler in East (1831, 1840, 1847) and in France and Italy (1836); professor, Munich (1848–49) and member of Frankfurt Parliament. Author of a work on Slavic origin of modern Greek people, *Das Albanische Element in Griechenland* (3 parts, 1857–60), which aroused much controversy.

**Fal·lo'pi·us** (fă·lō'pĭ·ŭs), **Gabriel.** *Lat. form of* **Gabriello Fal·lo'pio** (fäl·lô'pyô) *or* **Fal·lo'pia** (fäl·lô'pyä). 1523–1562. Italian anatomist, b. Modena. Discovered function of oviducts (Fallopian tubes); described other anatomical structures, including chorda tympani, sphenoid and ethmoid bones, and opening of oviducts into abdominal cavity.

**Fal'loux'** (fá'lōō'), Comte **Frédéric Alfred Pierre de.** 1811–1886. French politician; minister of public instruction (1848–49); introduced law, known as *Loi Falloux*, providing for freedom of instruction (passed 1850).

**Falls** (fôlz), **Cyril Bentham.** 1888–1971. English military historian; served in World War I; member of historical section, Committee of Imperial Defence (from 1923). Engaged in preparation of official military histories of British campaigns in World War II.

**Fal'sen** (fäl'sĕn), **Christian Magnus.** 1782–1830. Norwegian statesman, jurist, and writer; attorney general of kingdom (1822); president of Supreme Court of Norway (1827).

**Fa·min'tsyn** (fŭ·myēn'tsĭn), **Andrei Sergeevich.** 1835–1921. Russian botanist; investigator of development of embryos of seed plants. His brother **Aleksandr Sergeevich** (1841–1896) composed operas, orchestral works, chamber music, and songs.

**Fane** (fān), **John.** 11th Earl of **West'mor·land** (wĕs(t)'mẽr·lănd). 1784–1859. English soldier and diplomat; served in Peninsular War (1808–10); commissioned general (1854). Minister to Florence (1814) and Berlin (1841–51). Founder of Royal Acad. of Music (1823).

**Fane, Violet.** Pseudonym of Mary Montgomerie CURRIE.

**Fan'euil** (făn''l; -yĕl; -ū·ĭl; *old-fashioned*, fŭn''l), **Peter.** 1700–1743. American merchant, b. New Rochelle, N.Y. Built up large fortune in Boston; gave to city building since known as Faneuil Hall.

**Fan·fa'ni** (fän·fä'nē), **Pietro.** 1815–1879. Italian philologist and lexicographer.

**Fank'hau'ser** (fängk'hou'zẽr), **Alfred.** 1890– . Swiss poet, novelist, and essayist.

**Fan'ning** (făn'ĭng), **John Thomas.** 1837–1911. American hydraulic engineer, b. Norwich, Conn. Served through Civil War; constructed water-supply system for Manchester, N.H. His *Practical Treatise on Water Supply Engineering* (1877; 16th ed. 1906) was long the standard work on this subject. Continued work of planning city water-supply systems, including those of Minneapolis, Des Moines, Omaha, Birmingham.

**Fanning, Nathaniel.** 1755–1805. Privateersman under Franco-American auspices (1778–83) and naval officer in French and U.S. navies. Midshipman and private secretary to John Paul Jones (1779); distinguished himself for bravery in action against the *Serapis*.

**Fan'ni·us** (făn'ĭ·ŭs). *In full* **Gaius Fannius Stra'bo** (strā'bō). Roman soldier and historian; campaigned in Africa (146 B.C.) and in Spain (142); wrote *Annals* (now lost).

**Fanny,** Lord. See John HERVEY.

**Fan·sa'ga** (fän·sä'gä), **Cosimo.** 1591–1678. Italian architect and sculptor; pupil of Bernini.

**Fan'shawe** (făn'shô), Sir **Richard.** 1608–1666. English diplomat; fought in Royalist army in Civil War; captured at battle of Worcester (1651). Master of requests and Latin secretary to Prince Charles, The Hague (1660). British ambassador to Portugal (1662–63) and Spain (1664–66). Translator of Guarini's *Pastor Fido* and Camoëns's *Lusiad*.

**Fan'ti** (fän'tē), **Manfredo.** 1808–1865. Italian soldier, b. Carpi; in Italian service against Austrians (1849); general of brigade in Crimean War (1854–56); commanded forces of Tuscany, Parma, Modena, and Romagna in war of 1859. Minister of war under Cavour (1860–61); commander in chief of military department, Florence; senator (1860 ff.).

**Fan'tin'-La'tour'** (fäɴ'tăɴ'lá'tōōr'), **Ignace Henri Joseph Théodore.** 1836–1904. French painter; studied under Courbet. Best known for portraits, still-life studies, and paintings of intimate familiar scenes.

**Fa·ra'bi, al-** (ăl'fä·rä'bĭ). *Lat.* **Al'fa·ra'bi·us** (ăl'fá·rā'bĭ·ŭs). *Arab.* **Muḥammad ibn-Muḥammad ibn-Ṭarhkān abu-Naṣr al-Fārābi.** 870?–950 A.D. Arab philosopher, b. Transoxiana, of Turkish descent; lived in Aleppo. One of first Moslem scholars to introduce a knowledge of Aristotle and Plato among the Arabs; credited with continuing harmonization of Greek philosophy with Islam, and with influencing the thought of Avicenna and Averroës.

**Far'a·day** (făr'á·dā; -dĭ), **Michael.** 1791–1867. English chemist and physicist, b. Newington, Surrey. Apprentice to bookbinder; assistant in laboratory of Royal Institution; accompanied Sir Humphry Davy on Continental tour (1813–15); director of the laboratory (1825), professor of chemistry (1833), Royal Institution. Discovered two chlorides of carbon, and benzene; liquefied several gases; produced new kinds of optical glass. His discoveries relating to electricity include that of the revolution of a magnetic needle around an electric current (1821), method of producing continuous rotation of a wire around a magnet and of a magnet around a wire, and induction of electric currents (1841). Established identity of electricity generated in different ways; in electrolysis, discovered that the amount of liquid decomposed is proportional to the current passing through the solution; discovered rotation of the plane of polarized light by a magnetic field (1845); described properties of a diamagnetic substance (1845). His publications include

*Chemical Manipulation, being Instructions to Students in Chemistry* (1827), *Experimental Researches in Electricity* (1844–55), *Experimental Researches in Chemistry and Physics* (1859), *Lectures on the Chemical History of a Candle* (1861), *On the Various Forces in Nature.* See Joseph HENRY.

**Fa·ra′goh** (fȧ·rä′gō), **Francis Edwards.** 1898–1966. Playwright and stage director in U.S., b. Budapest. Managing director, New Playwrights Theatre, New York City. Author of *Pinwheel, Ritornelle.* Wrote, adapted, or collaborated in writing scenarios, including *Little Caesar, Frankenstein, Ann of Green Gables, Becky Sharp.*

**Fa·raz′daq, al-** (ăl′fȧ·răz′dăk) *or* **al-Fe·raz′daq.** *Orig.* **Hammām.** 640?–?732 A.D. Moslem Arabic poet, b. Basra. One of three great poets of Ommiad period (see al-AKHTAL and JARIR) noted for their style and technique; poet laureate of reign of Abd-al-Malik and his successors; wrote satires, panegyrics, and lampoons.

**Fa′rel′** (fȧ′rĕl′), **Guillaume.** 1489–1565. French leader in Reformation; settled at Geneva, Switzerland (1532) and succeeded in having the Reformation established there by vote of Genevan Great Council (1535). Persuaded Calvin to settle in Geneva (1536); banished with Calvin (1538). Pastor at Neuchâtel (from 1538), from which center he continued to spread Reformation doctrines.

**Far·gha′ni, al-** (ăl′făr·gä′nĭ). *Latinized* **Al′fra·ga′nus** (ăl′frȧ·gā′nŭs). *Arab.* **abu-al-‘Abbās Aḥmad al-Farghāni.** fl. 9th century A.D. Arab astronomer of Transoxiana. Author of astronomical treatise widely used in Middle Ages (tr. into Latin by Johannes Hispalensis and Gerard of Cremona, 1135); superintended erection (861) of Nilometer for Abbasside caliph.

**Far′go** (fär′gō), **William George.** 1818–1881. American express owner, b. Pompey, N.Y. Part owner of Wells & Company, first express concern west of Buffalo (1844), which merged with two others (1850) to form American Express Company, with Fargo as secretary; president, after larger merger (1868–81). Organized Wells, Fargo & Company, to handle express business between New York and California (1852); consolidated with rival companies (1866).

**Fa·ri′a e Sou′sa** (fȧ·rē′ȧ ē sō′zȧ), **Manuel de.** 1590–1649. Portuguese historian and poet; to Madrid (c. 1613); wrote in both Spanish and Portuguese.

**Far′i·bault** (făr′ĭ·bō; *Fr.* fȧ′rē′bō′), **Jean Baptiste.** 1775–1860. American pioneer and fur trader, b. Berthier, Quebec, Canada. Faribault County, Minn., is named after him, and the city after his son **Alexander.**

**Farid ud-din Attar.** See ATTAR.

**Farigoule, Louis.** Real name of Jules ROMAINS.

**Fa·ri′na** (fä·rē′nä), **Giuseppe La.** See LA FARINA.

**Farina, Salvatore.** 1846–1918. Italian novelist; called "the Italian Dickens." Works include *Amore Bendato* (1873), *Mio Figlio* (1879–80), *Il Signor Io* (1880), *Più Forte dell'Amore* (1890), *I Due Desideri* (1904), and *Verso il Tramonto* (1913).

**Fa′ri·nac′ci** (fä′rē·nät′chē), **Roberto.** 1892–1945. Italian politician, b. Isernia. Founded daily paper *Cremona Nuova* (later *Regime Fascista*); agitated for Italian intervention in World War II. Organized Fascist movement in Cremona; secretary-general of Fascist party (1925–26); opposed Mussolini's rapprochement with Vatican; returned to professional life in Cremona (1926); member, Fascist Grand Council (1935–43); captured and executed by partisans.

**Fa′ri·na′ta de′gli U·ber′ti** (fä′rē·nä′tä dā′lyē ōō·bĕr′tē). Florentine Ghibelline leader; banished to Siena (1258); with Manfred, King of Sicily, recaptured Florence from Guelphs (1260); immortalized by Dante in his *Divina Commedia* (Inferno X, 22–51).

**Fa′ri·na′to** (fä′rē·nä′tō) *or* **Fa′ri·na′ti** (-tē), **Paolo.** c. 1525–1606. Veronese painter, architect, and engraver. Known chiefly for frescoes in Verona churches. His sons **Orazio** and **Giovanni Battista** and his daughter **Vittoria** were painters.

**Fa′ri·nel′li** (fä′rē·nĕl′lē), **Arturo.** 1867–1948. Italian historian of literature.

**Fa′ri·nel′li** (fä′rē·nĕl′lē), **Carlo.** *Orig. surname* **Bro′schi** (brōs′kē). *Called* **"Il Ra·gaz′zo"** (ēl rä·gät′tsō). 1705–1782. Italian male soprano; famous throughout Europe for extraordinary compass of voice; outdone in contest only once, by rival castrato Bernacchi. At Spanish court (1737–59) had power approaching that of a prime minister under Philip V and Ferdinand VI; retired to castle near Bologna (1761).

**Fa·ri′ni** (fä·rē′nē), **Gilarmi A.** *Known as* **Farini the Great.** 1839–1929. Tightrope walker; crossed Niagara Falls on a tightrope (1864). See Charles BLONDIN.

**Farini, Luigi Carlo.** 1812–1866. Italian physician, historian, and statesman, b. Russi, Emilia. Dictator of Modena (1859); secured union of Parma, Bologna, and Florence under Piedmont; minister of interior, Cavour cabinet (1860); viceroy of Naples (Nov., 1860–Jan., 1861); prime minister (Dec., 1862–March, 1863).

**Far′is** (făr′ĭs), **John Thomson.** 1871–1949. American Presbyterian clergyman and editor, b. Cape Girardeau, Mo. On editorial staff, Presbyterian board of publication and Sunday School work (1908–23) and board of Christian education (1923–37).

**Far′jeon** (fär′jŭn), **Benjamin Leopold.** 1838–1903. English novelist; for several years, journalist in Australia and New Zealand; author of novels *Joshua Marvel, In a Silver Sea,* and *Toilers of Babylon.*

**Farjeon, Eleanor.** 1881–1965. Granddaughter of Joseph Jefferson. English writer; author of juveniles and short stories, and collaborator with brother **Herbert** (1887–1945) in plays, including *Kings and Queens* (1932), *An Elephant in Arcady* (1938). Other brothers: **Joseph Jefferson** (1883–1955), playwright, author of *No. 17* (1925), *After Dark* (1926), *The Green Dragon* (1929), *Philomel* (1932); and **Harry** (1878–1948), composer and music critic, author of an opera, a concerto, and piano pieces.

**Far′ley** (fär′lĭ), **James Aloysius.** 1888–1976. American politician, b. Grassy Point, N.Y. Grad. Packard Commercial School, New York City (1906). In building-supply business, New York City; organized James A. Farley & Co. (1926), which was merged with other firms (1929) to form General Building Supply Corp., of which he was president (1929–33). Chairman, N.Y. State Athletic Commission (1925–33). Chairman, Democratic National Committee (1932–40). U.S. postmaster general (1933–40).

**Farley, James Lewis.** 1823–1885. British financier and publicist, b. Dublin. On staff of Ottoman bank, Beirut; later, accountant general of state bank of Turkey, Constantinople (1860). Consul for sultan at Bristol, Eng. (1870–84). Author of *Resources of Turkey* (1862), *Turks and Christians* (1876).

**Farley, John Murphy.** 1842–1918. American cardinal, b. Ireland; to U.S. (1864). Auxiliary bishop of New York; archbishop of New York (1902); cardinal (1911).

**Far′low** (fär′lō), **William Gilson.** 1844–1919. American botanist, b. Boston, Mass. Assistant to Asa Gray, at Harvard; taught botany at Harvard (from 1874).

**Far′man** (fär′măn), **Elbert Eli.** 1831–1911. American diplomat, b. New Haven, N.Y.; diplomatic agent and consul general at Cairo, Egypt (1876–81), and judge on Mixed Tribunal (1881–84); secured gift (1879) from khedive of obelisk (Cleopatra's Needle) now in New York City; U.S. member of international commissions on Egyptian matters (1880, 1883); collector of Egyptian antiquities. Author of *Egypt and Its Betrayal* (1908).

**Far'man'** (fär'mäN'), **Henri**. 1874–1958. French pioneer in aviation and airplane manufacture, b. Paris; with a Voisin biplane made first airplane flight of one kilometer in a complete circle (1908); flew from Bouy to Reims (1908), first flight from city to city; with brother **Maurice** (1877–1964), developed the Farman biplane; established airplane factory at Boulogne Billancourt; constructed the *Goliath*, which flew to Dakar (1919); held distance, altitude, and duration records for flights.

**Far'mer** (fär'mẽr), **Fannie Merritt**. 1857–1915. American cookery expert, b. Boston, Mass. Established Miss Farmer's School of Cookery (1902), with courses designed to train housewives rather than teachers of cookery; also specialized in invalid cookery. Editor of *The Boston Cooking School Cook Book* (1896; 21 editions before her death); author of *Chafing Dish Possibilities* (1898), *A New Book of Cookery* (1912), etc.

**Farmer, James Leonard**. 1920– . Amer. social reformer, b. Marshall, Tex. A founder of the Congress of Racial Equality (CORE; 1942), national chairman (1942–44; 1950), national director (1961–66).

**Farmer, John**. fl. 1591–1601. English composer of madrigals.

**Farmer, John**. 1789–1838. American antiquarian and genealogist, b. Chelmsford, Mass. Author of *A Genealogical Register of the First Settlers of New England* (1829).

**Farmer, John S**. English lexicographer; compiler of *Americanisms Old and New* (1889) and *Slang and its Analogues* (with W. E. Henley; 1890–1904).

**Farmer, Moses Gerrish**. 1820–1893. American inventor and pioneer electrician, b. Boscawen, N.H. Coinventor (with William F. Channing) of electric fire-alarm system adopted by city of Boston (1851); discovered means for duplex and quadruplex telegraphy (1855); devised an incandescent electric lamp with platinum filament, supplied by wet-cell battery (1859); patented self-exciting dynamo (1866); installed electric lighting in a Cambridge, Mass., residence, using one of his dynamos and 40 of his lamps arranged in multiple (1868); as electrician at U.S. Torpedo Station, Newport, R.I., effected improvements in torpedo warfare (1872–81).

**Farmer, Richard**. 1735–1797. English scholar and educator; educ. Cambridge. Master of Emmanuel Coll., Cambridge (from 1775); author of *Essay on the Learning of Shakespeare* (1767), in which he maintained that Shakespeare knew the classics only through translations.

**Far'na·by** (fär'nȧ·bĭ), **Thomas**. 1575?–1647. English schoolmaster; educ. at Jesuit college in Spain; founder and a master of a school in London; commissioned by Charles I to prepare new Latin grammar for school use (1641); edited Latin classics.

**Farnborough**, Baron. See Thomas Erskine MAY.

**Far·ne'se** (fär·nā'sā), House of. An Italian family, originating about the 12th century, named from a castle near Lake Bolsena. Founded as ducal family of Parma (1545–1731) by **Alessandro** (= Pope PAUL III), when he secured consent of sacred college to erect states of Parma and Piacenza into duchy for his natural son, the vicious and debauched **Pier Luigi** or **Pierluigi** (1503–1547), who was assassinated by nobles of Piacenza. **Ottavio** (1520–1586), son of Pier Luigi, recovered duchy from imperialists (1551); sought protection of France (1551–56); subject to Philip II and a Spanish garrison (1556–85); m. (1538) Margaret of Parma. **Alessandro** (1545–1592), son of Ottavio; general and diplomat; m. Maria of Portugal (1565); brought up in Spain; fought at Lepanto (1571); in service of Philip II in Netherlands (1577–86); besieged and captured Antwerp (1584–85); duke of Parma (1586–92) but never took possession of throne; head of Spanish armies in Netherlands (1586–92); mortally wounded at Caudebec. **Ranuccio** (1569–1622), son and successor of Alessandro. **Antonio** (1679–1731), last of male line.

**Elizabeth** (1692–1766), granddaughter of Ranuccio; m. Philip V of Spain (1714) by proxy, arranged by Cardinal Alberoni; at once secured great influence over the weak king; formed policy of expansion for Spain, but thwarted (1720) by Triple Alliance (formed 1717); forced to dismiss Alberoni; lost Sicily; after death of Louis I (1724) sought to get thrones in Italy for her two sons (Don Carlos and Philip), of whom Don Carlos (king of Spain as CHARLES III, *q.v.*; first of Bourbon-Farnese branch) secured Parma (1732) and conquered Two Sicilies (1736).

**Farn'ham** (fär'năm), **Eliza Woodson**, *nee* **Burhans**. 1815–1864. American philanthropist and author, b. Rensselaerville, N.Y.; m. 1st (1836) **Thomas Jefferson Farnham** (1804–1848), author of *Travels in the Great Western Prairies* (1841); m. 2d William Fitzpatrick. Matron, women's department, Sing Sing prison (1844–48). Author of *Life in Prairie Land* (1846), *Woman and Her Era* (2 vols., 1864).

**Far'nol** (fär'n'l), **John Jeffery**. 1878–1952. English novelist; author of *The Broad Highway*, *The Amateur Gentleman*, *Beltane the Smith* (1915), *Peregrine's Progress* (1922), *The Quest of Youth* (1927), *The Way Beyond* (1933), *The Lonely Road* (1938), *Murder by Nail* (1942).

**Farns'worth** (färnz'wûrth; -wẽrth), **Jerry**. 1895– . American painter, b. Dalton, Ga. Among his paintings are *The Dancer*, *Helen*, *Three Churches*.

**Farnsworth, Philo Taylor**. 1906–1971. American radio research engineer, b. Beaver, Utah; conducted important experiments in television.

**Far'num** (fär'năm), **Dustin Lancy**. 1874–1929. American actor, b. Hampton Beach, N.H.; established reputation as romantic hero of melodrama; in motion pictures (1913–25). His brother **William** (1876–1953), b. in Boston, also an actor, starred in *Ben Hur*, *Prince of India*, and *The Littlest Rebel*.

**Farouk I**. See FARUK I.

**Far'quhar** (fär'kwẽr; -kẽr), **George**. 1678–1707. British dramatist, b. in Ireland. Educ. Trinity Coll., Dublin. To London (c. 1697); his first play, a comedy, *Love and a Bottle* (1699), was followed by *The Constant Couple* (1700), *Sir Harry Wildair* (1701), *The Recruiting Officer* (1706), and *The Beaux' Stratagem* (1707).

**Farquharson, Martha**. See Martha Farquharson FINLEY.

**Farr** (fär), **William**. 1807–1883. English statistician, b. Shropshire; commissioner for the census (1871); prepared mortality table based on observations of population of England (pub. 1864).

**Far'ra·gut** (făr'ȧ·gŭt), **David Glasgow**. 1801–1870. American admiral, b. near Knoxville, Tenn. Adopted by Commander (later Commodore) Porter (1808). Midshipman (1810); routine naval duty (1810–47); commanded sloop *Saratoga* during Mexican War; stationed at Norfolk, Va. (1860–61). When Virginia seceded, moved to Hastings-on-Hudson, N.Y., and offered services to Federal government; put in command of the West Gulf Blockading Squadron (flagship *Hartford*, Dec., 1861), with orders to take New Orleans. Bombarded Fort Jackson (Apr. 18, 1862); ran ships past Forts Jackson and St. Philip (Apr. 24); engaged Confederate flotilla and captured New Orleans without bloodshed; spent rest of 1862 chiefly in blockade duty along Gulf Coast. Ran

*Hartford* and one other vessel past Port Hudson defenses (Mar., 1863) and controlled Mississippi between Port Hudson and Vicksburg. Again in Gulf (Jan., 1864), with orders to capture Forts Morgan and Gaines, defenses of Mobile Bay; attacked (Aug. 5), silencing Fort Morgan, running blockade of "torpedoes" (*i.e.* mines) across mouth of Bay, dispersing Confederate fleet in the Bay, and obtaining surrender of Forts Gaines and Morgan (Aug. 7 and 23). Vice-admiral (Dec., 1864) and admiral (July, 1866), two grades specially created for him by Congress. Elected to American Hall of Fame (1900). His father **George** (1755–1817) was a naval and army officer, b. Ciudadela, Minorca (at that time a British possession); joined cause of American colonists, serving at defense of Savannah and siege of Charleston; transferred to army and commanded company of volunteer cavalry against Cornwallis.

**Far'rand** (făr'ănd), **Livingston.** 1867–1939. American educator, b. Newark, N.J. A.B., Princeton (1888), M.D., Coll. of Phys. & Surg., N.Y. (1891); teacher of psychology, Columbia (1893–1903); professor of anthropology, Columbia (1903–14); president, U. of Colorado (1914–19); president of Cornell (1921–37). His brother **Max** (1869–1945), historian, A.B. (1892) and Ph.D. (1896), Princeton; taught history at Wesleyan (1896–1901); professor of history, Stanford (1901–08), and Yale (1908–25); on staff of Commonwealth Fund (1919–27); director of research at Henry E. Huntington Library and Art Gallery (1927–41); author of *Development of the United States* (1918), *Fathers of the Constitution* (1921), etc.

**Far'rant** (făr'ănt), **Richard.** fl. 1564–1580. English organist, and composer of church music, including a service in G minor and anthems. Adapted (1576) an old Blackfriars monastery in London for a theater to present performances by children of the chapel, the theater being used later (from 1596) by Shakespeare's company.

**Far'rar** (făr'ẽr), **Frederic William.** 1831–1903. Anglican clergyman and writer, b. Bombay, India. Educ. King's Coll. in London, and Cambridge. Master at Harrow (1855–70); headmaster of Marlborough (1871–76). Canon (1876–83) and archdeacon (1883–95) of Westminster; dean of Canterbury (1895–1903). Author of the school stories *Eric* (1858), *Julian Home* (1859), and *St. Winifred's* (1862); of *An Essay on the Origin of Language* (1860), *Life of Christ* (1874), *Life of St. Paul* (1879), *Lives of the Fathers* (1889), etc.

**Far·rar'** (fȧ·rär'), **Geraldine.** 1882–1967. American dramatic soprano, b. Melrose, Mass.; m. Lou Tellegen (1916; divorced 1923). Debut as Marguerite in *Faust*, at Berlin (1901); member of Metropolitan Opera, New York City (1906–22). Chief roles include Madame Butterfly, Manon, Mignon, Tosca, Juliet, Gilda.

**Far'rar** (făr'ẽr), **John Chipman.** 1896–1974. American publisher, editor, poet, b. Burlington, Vt. Editor of *The Bookman* (1921–27); editor for George H. Doran Co. (1925); with Farrar and Rinehart (1929–44); lecturer, Columbia U. (1945–47). Author of *Forgotten Shrines* (1919), *Songs for Parents* (1921), *The Magic Sea Shell* (1923), *The Middle Twenties* (1924), *Songs for Johnny Jump-Up* (1930).

**Far'rell** (făr'ĕl), **James Augustine.** 1863–1943. American steel manufacturer, b. New Haven, Conn.; began work in steel factory at age of 16 (1879); rose to presidency of U.S. Steel Corp. (1911–32).

**Farrell, James Thomas.** 1904– . American journalist and novelist, b. Chicago, Ill.; author of *Gas House McGinty* (1933), *Studs Lonigan* (trilogy; 1935), *No Star is Lost* (1938), *Father and Son* (1940), *$1,000 a Week, and Other Stories* (1942).

**Farrell, M. J.** Pseudonym of Mary Nesta SKRINE.

**Far'ren** (făr'ĕn), **Elizabeth.** Countess of **Der'by** (där'bĭ). 1759?–1829. English actress; succeeded Mrs. Abington on stage at Drury Lane (1782–97); m. Edward Stanley, 12th Earl of Derby, and retired from stage (1797).

**Farren, Ellen,** *called* **Nellie.** 1848–1904. English actress; m. (1867) Robert Soutar (1827–1908). Excelled in comedy roles, as Lydia Languish in *The Rivals* and Maria in *Twelfth Night.*

**Farren, William.** 1786–1861. English actor and theater manager; played Sir Peter Teazle at Covent Garden (1818); excelled in interpreting roles of elderly men; manager of Strand and Olympic theaters. His son **Henry** (1826?–1860), also an actor, played Charles Surface at Haymarket Theatre (c. 1847); manager of Brighton Theatre, and later of a theater in St. Louis, U.S.A.

**Far'rer** (făr'ẽr), **Thomas Henry.** 1st Baron **Farrer** (cr. 1893). 1819–1899. English lawyer, economist, and statistician, b. London. B.A., Oxon. (1840). Called to bar (1844); permanent secretary, Board of Trade (1865–86); member, London County Council (1889–98). Author of *Free Trade versus Fair Trade* (1886), *Studies in Currency* (1898).

**Far'rère'** (fȧ'râr'), **Claude.** *Pseudonym of* **Frédéric Charles Bar'gone'** (bȧr'gōn'). 1876–1957. French naval officer and writer; in naval service (1899–1919); author of *Fumée d'Opium* (1904), *Les Civilisés* (1905; awarded Goncourt prize), *La Bataille* (1909), *Les Hommes Nouveaux* (1923), *La Marche Funèbre* (1929), etc.

**Far'son** (fär's'n), **James Negley.** 1890–1960. American writer, b. Plainfield, N.J. Foreign correspondent, Chicago *Daily News* (1924–35). Author of *Sailing Across Europe* (1926), *Seeing Red* (1930), *The Way of a Transgressor* (1936), *Behind God's Back* (1940).

**Fa·ruk' I** *or* **Fa·rouk' I** (fȧ·rōōk'). 1920–1965. King of Egypt (1936–52; abdicated); son of King Fuad I; educ. in England; citizen of Monaco (1959).

**Far'well** (fär'wĕl; -wĕl), **Arthur.** 1872–1952. American musician, b. St. Paul, Minn.; best known for American Indian songs and melodies; also composed incidental music for *Joseph and His Brethren* and *The Gods of the Mountain*, symphonic music, and string quartets.

**Farwell, Charles Benjamin.** 1823–1903. American businessman, b. Steuben Co., N.Y. To Chicago (1844); in real estate, then dry-goods business. Member, U.S. House of Representatives (1871–76, 81–83); U.S. senator from Illinois (1887–91). His brother **John Villiers** (1825–1908), dry-goods merchant in Chicago, partner (1851) in firm that became (1865) John V. Farwell & Co., long Chicago's leading wholesale dry-goods house; friend of Dwight L. Moody and visited England (1867) to study results of Moody's mission work; gave land for first Y.M.C.A. building in U.S., at Chicago.

**Fasch** (fäsh), **Johann Friedrich.** 1688–1758. German conductor and composer of orchestral overtures and suites, church cantatas, masses, sonata trios, instrumental concerto, etc. His son **Karl Friedrich Christian** (1736–1800), music teacher in Berlin and (1774–76) Kapellmeister at Royal Opera, founded (1792) and conducted (until 1800) choral society Berliner Singakademie; composed church music including a mass for 16 voices.

**Fas'sett** (făs'ĕt; -ĭt), **Cornelia Adèle,** *nee* **Strong.** 1831–1898. American portrait and figure painter.

**Fa'sten·rath** (fäs'tĕn·rät), **Johannes.** 1839–1908. German poet and translator; traveled in Spain (1864 ff.); wrote in German and Spanish works chiefly on Spain.

**Fas'tolf** (făs'tŏlf), **Sir John.** 1378?–1459. English soldier; distinguished himself in battle of Agincourt (1415).

King Henry VI's lieutenant and regent in Normandy (1423), and governor of Anjou and Maine (1423–26). Captured John II, Duke of Alençon, at battle of Verneuil (1424); defeated French near Orléans (1429), but was defeated at Patay (1429). Retired to the Tower at outbreak of Cade's Rebellion (1450). Friend of John Paston; many of his private papers preserved among Paston letters. A character in Shakespeare's *Henry VI*, and supposed by some to be the original of Falstaff in *Henry IV* on account of a few coincidences in their careers that are probably accidental. Cf. John OLDCASTLE.

**Fath A·li'** *or* **Fatḥ 'A·lī'** (făt' ȧ·lē'). 1762?–1835. Shah of Persia (1797–1835) of Kajar dynasty. Nephew and successor of Agha Mohammed Khan. Subdued rebellious tribes in Khurasan; forced to surrender Derbent and other districts to Russia (1797); lost Georgia (1802); established Persian order (1808) of the Sun and Lion; involved in two other wars with Russia (1811–13, 1826–28); by Treaty of Gulistan (1813), ceded Dagestan, Baku, etc., to Russia, and by Treaty of Turkmanchai (1828), most of Persian Armenia. See ABBAS MIRZA.

**Fat'i·ma** (*Angl.* făt'ĭ·mȧ *or, erroneously,* fȧ·tē'mȧ). *Arab.* **Fāṭimah.** 606–632 A.D. Daughter of Mohammed by his first wife, Khadija; m. Ali, cousin of Mohammed. From them the Fatimid (*q.v.*) dynasty of northern Africa claimed descent.

**Fat'i·mid** (făt'ĭ·mĭd) *or* **Fat'i·mite** (făt'ĭ·mīt). A powerful Mohammedan (Shiite) dynasty ruling (909–1171) in North Africa and Egypt; claimed descent from Fatima and Ali through Ismail. Founded by Ubaydullah (head of Syrian Shiites, among Berber tribes), with capital at Mahdia (c. 920). Its 14 caliphs include Ubaydullah (909–934), al-Qaim (934–946), al-Mansur (946–952), al-Aziz (975–996), and al-Hakim (996–1021). In 10th century its boundaries greatly extended, Sicily conquered (c. 945), Egypt overrun and new capital established at Cairo (969–973); western part of North Africa (El Maghreb el Aqsa) gradually lost (after 1000); driven out of Syria by Seljuks (1076); disappeared with last caliph, al-Adid, when Saladin conquered Egypt (1171).

**Fattore, Il.** See Gianfrancesco PENNI.

**Fau'cher'** (fō'shā'), **Léon.** 1804–1854. French economist and politician; minister of public works (1848) and of the interior (1851).

**Fau'chet'** (fō'shĕ'), **Claude.** 1744–1793. French priest and revolutionist; member of Legislative Assembly (1791) and National Convention (1792); constitutional bishop of Calvados; joined the Girondists (May, 1792); executed with Girondist leaders (Oct., 1793).

**Fau'chois'** (fō'shwȧ'), **René.** 1882–1962. French playwright.

**Fau'cit** (fô'sĭt), **Helen,** *properly* **Helena Saville.** Lady **Mar'tin** (mär'tĭn). 1817–1898. English actress; m. (1851) Sir Theodore Martin (*q.v.*). Member of Covent Garden company (1836), Haymarket Theatre company (1839–41); played opposite Macready in such roles as Desdemona, Cordelia, Portia, Lady Macbeth, Rosalind. Author of *On Some of Shakespeare's Female Characters* (1885).

**Fau'con·berg** *or* **Fal'con·berg** (fô'kŭn·bûrg), **Thomas.** *Sometimes called* **Thomas the Bastard.** d. 1471. English rebel soldier; raised county of Kent to support Warwick and Henry VI, and burned a section of London (1471); his fleet destroyed, he was captured and beheaded.

**Fau'con'nier'** (fo'ko'nya'). **Henri.** 1879–c. 1955. French novelist; took law degree at Bordeaux; to Singapore (c. 1903) as manager of rubber plantation; served as machine gunner in French army in World War I; winner of Goncourt prize (1930) with his *Malaisie.*

**Fau'jas' de Saint'-Fond'** (fō'zhȧs' dẽ săN'fôN'), **Barthélemy.** 1741–1819. French geologist and traveler; developed a theory of origin of volcanoes.

**Faul'ha'ber** (foul'hä'bẽr), **Michael von.** 1869–1952. German cardinal and archbishop. Archbishop of Munich and Freising (1917); cardinal (1921); author of concordat between Bavaria and papal throne (1925).

**Faulk'ner** (fôk'nẽr), **Barry.** 1881–1966. American painter, best known for murals.

**Faulkner, John.** 1901–1963. American novelist, b. Ripley, Miss.; brother of William Faulkner; author of *Men Working* (1941), *Dollar Cotton* (1942).

**Faulk'ner, William Cuthbert,** *orig.* **Falk'ner** (fôk'nẽr). 1897–1962. American novelist, b. New Albany, Miss.; educ. U. of Mississippi (1919–21); served with British Royal Air Force (1918). Author of *The Marble Faun* (1924), *Soldier's Pay* (1926), *Mosquitoes* (1927), *Sartoris* (1929), *The Sound and the Fury* (1929), *As I Lay Dying* (1930), *Sanctuary* (1931), *Light in August* (1932), *Pylon* (1935), *Absalom, Absalom!* (1936), *The Unvanquished* (1938), *The Wild Palms* (1939), *The Hamlet* (1940), *Go Down, Moses and Other Stories* (1942), *Intruder in the Dust* (1948), *Requiem for a Nun* (1951), *A Fable* (1954), *The Town* (1957), *The Mansion* (1959), *The Reivers* (1962); received Nobel prize for literature (1949), Pulitzer prizes (1955, and 1963 posthumously).

**Faunce** (fôns), **William Herbert Perry.** 1859–1930. American Baptist clergyman and educator, b. Worcester, Mass. Grad. Brown (1880), Newton Theological Institution (1884). Pastor in Springfield, Mass. (1884–89), and New York City (1889–97); resident preacher, Harvard U. (1898–99). President, Brown U. (1899–1929). Author of *What Does Christianity Mean?* (1912), etc.

**Fau'quier'** (fô'kẽr'), **Francis.** 1704?–1768. English colonial administrator; lieutenant governor of Virginia (1758).

**Faure** (fôr), **Élie.** 1873–1937. French art historian.

**Faure, François Félix.** 1841–1899. French statesman and 6th president of the republic, b. Paris. Cabinet officer in department of commerce and colonies (1882, 1883–85, 1888); minister of marine under President Casimir-Périer (1894–95), whom he succeeded as president (1895–99).

**Fau'ré'** (fô'rā'), **Gabriel Urbain.** 1845–1924. French composer; professor (1896), director (1905–20), Conservatory of Music, Paris. Composer esp. of melodies, piano pieces, chamber music, sonatas, concertos, and incidental music for various plays, as *Pelléas et Mélisande;* credited, with Debussy, with freeing modern French music from German influence.

**Faure** (fôr), **Jean Baptiste.** 1830–1914. French baritone singer; his grand opera roles included *Don Juan, Hamlet, Faust;* composer esp. of sacred songs, as *Les Rameaux, Le Crucifix.* m. (1859) **Constance Caroline Le·feb'vre** [lẽ·fâ'vr'] (1828–1905), singer at Opéra Comique and Théâtre Lyrique.

**Fau'riel'** (fô'ryĕl'), **Claude.** 1772–1844. French historian and scholar; compiler of *Chants Populaires de la Grèce Moderne* (1824–25); author of *Histoire de la Gaule Méridionale sous la Domination des Conquérants Germains* (1836).

**Fau'set** (fô'sĕt; -sĭt), **Arthur Huff.** 1899– . American Negro educator and writer, b. Flemington, N.J.; teacher in Philadelphia; author of *For Freedom, Sojourner Truth* (1938). His sister **Jessie** (1882–1961), writer and teacher; A.B., Cornell; m. Herbert Harris (1929); author of *Gift of Laughter, There is a Confusion.*

**Faus'set** (fô'sĕt; -sĭt), **Hugh I'Anson.** 1895–1965. English poet and literary critic; educ. Cambridge. Author of *The Lady Alcuin and other Poems* (1918), *The Spirit of*

*Love: a Sonnet Sequence* (1921), *Keats* (1922), *Tennyson* (1923), *John Donne* (1924), *A Modern Prelude* (1933), *Walt Whitman: Poet of Democracy* (1942).

**Faust** (foust), **Albert Bern′hardt** (bûrn′härt). 1870–1951. American Germanic scholar; professor, Cornell U. (from 1910). Author of *The German Element in the United States* (1909; received prize awards), etc.

**Faust, Bernard Christoph.** 1755–1842. German physician and writer on hygiene.

**Faust, Johann.** Gutenberg's partner. See FUST.

**Faust** (foust), Dr. **Johann.** *Lat.* **Johannes Faus′tus** (fôs′tŭs). *Real name prob.* **Georg Faust.** 1480?–?1540. Magician, astrologer, and soothsayer, b. Knittlingen, Württemberg. Began to practice magic art (1506); school teacher in university cities; won favor of archbishop of Cologne (1532) and subsequently gained prominence and respect. The legend of his performing miracles with help of devil (Mephistopheles), and being carried off by him after death, has been frequently treated in literature and music, as in *Historia von Dr. Johann Fausten* (pub. by Johann Spiess, or Spies, 1587), dramatized by Christopher Marlowe (*q.v.*); subject of verse drama by Goethe, opera by Gounod, overture by Wagner, symphony by Liszt.

**Faus′ta** (fôs′tȧ). *In full* **Flavia Maximiana Fausta.** 289–326 A.D. Roman empress; daughter of Emperor Maximianus Herculius; wife (m. 307 A.D.) of Constantine the Great. Mother of emperors Constantine II, Constantius II, and Constans. Said to have induced Constantine to execute Crispus, his eldest son by a former marriage; suffocated in heated bath by order of Constantine, according to one account, because her accusations against Crispus were proved false.

**Faus′tin′ I** (fōs′tăN′). See SOULOUQUE.

**Faus·ti′na** (fôs·tī′nȧ). *In full* **Annia Galeria Faustina.** Name of two Roman empresses, mother and daughter, both notorious for their profligacy: the elder (c. 104–141 A.D.), wife (m. 138) of Antoninus Pius; the younger (c. 125–c. 175 A.D.), wife (c. 145) of Marcus Aurelius.

**Faus′tus Byz′an·ti′nus** (fôs′tŭs bĭz′ăn·tī′nŭs). Armenian historian of 4th century A.D.; wrote in Greek a history of Armenia from 344 to 392 A.D.

**Faustus of Riez** (ryĕz). 400?–after 485. Semi-Pelagian leader in S. France, b. prob. in Great Britain. Bishop of Regium (Riez) in Provence (452); championed Semi-Pelagian doctrine of free will and divine grace at synod of Arles (471); opposed the Arians and was exiled by Euric, king of Visigoths (477–485).

**Fa′vart′** (fȧ′vȧr′), **Charles Simon.** 1710–1792. French playwright; known as creator of the musical comedy, or comic opera; m. (1745) the singer **Marie Justine Benoîte Du′ron′ce·ray′** [dü′rôNs′rā′] (1727–1772).

**Fav′er·sham** (făv′ẽr·shăm; -shăm), **William.** 1868–1940. Actor, b. in England; to U.S. (1888); leading man in Charles Frohman's company (6 years). Created role of Jim Carson in *The Squaw Man* (1905–06); appeared in *The World and his Wife* (1908), Stephen Phillips's *Herod* (1909), *Julius Caesar* (1912), and *Othello* (1914). His 2d wife, **Julie,** *nee* **Opp** [ŏp] (1871–1921; m. 1902), b. New York City, also member of Frohman company, played in his support.

**Fav′o·ri′nus** (făv′ō·rī′nŭs; fā′vō-). Greek Sophist and skeptic philosopher of 2d century A.D.

**Fa′vo′ry′** (fȧ′vô′rē′), **André.** 1889–1937. French painter, esp. of landscapes and nudes.

**Fa′vras′** (fȧ′vrȧs′), Marquis **de. Thomas de Ma′hy′** (dẽ mȧ′ē′). 1744–1790. French army officer; royalist at outbreak of French Revolution; planned escape of royal family from Paris (1789); captured and hanged.

**Fa′vre** (fȧ′vr′), **Jules,** *in full* **Gabriel Claude Jules.** 1809–1880. French lawyer and statesman; leader of opposition to the Second Empire (1863–68); minister of foreign affairs, and vice-president of the Government of National Defense (1870–71); member of the Senate (1876–80).

**Favre, Louis.** 1826–1879. Swiss engineer who built the St. Gotthard Tunnel.

**Favre** *or* **Le·fè′vre** (lẽ·fȧ′vr′), **Pierre.** *Also* **Petrus Fa′ber** (fā′bẽr). 1506–1546. French Jesuit theologian, cofounder of Society of Jesus, b. near Geneva. Tutor and friend of Loyola at Paris and one of his six coadjutors in establishing Jesuit order at Montmartre (1534); named professor of theology at Rome by Pope Paul III (1537); founded Jesuit colleges at Cologne (1544) and in Spain; delegate to Council of Trent.

**Faw′cett** (fô′sĕt; -sĭt), **Edgar.** 1847–1904. American author, b. New York City. Author of verse, novels, and plays, chiefly satirizing New York high society.

**Fawcett, Henry.** 1833–1884. English economist and statesman; B.A., Cantab. (1856). Accidentally blinded (1858). Professor, Cambridge (1863–84). M.P. (1865–84); contributed actively to passage of Reform Act (1867); postmaster general (1880), and inaugurator of parcel post (1882). His wife (m. 1867), **Millicent,** *nee* **Gar′rett** [găr′ĕt] (1847–1929), prominent woman-suffrage leader, collaborated with him in his economic studies.

**Fawkes** (fôks), **Francis.** 1720–1777. Anglican clergyman, classical scholar, and poet; educ. Cambridge. Translator of Anacreon, Sappho, Theocritus, Apollonius. Author of comic song *The Brown Jug.*

**Fawkes** (fôks; *Brit. also* fŏks), **Guy.** 1570–1606. English conspirator, b. at York. Turned Roman Catholic and enlisted in the Spanish army in Flanders (1593). Returned to England (1603) and became involved with Catesby, Thomas Percy, Thomas Winter, and others in Gunpowder Plot (1604–05) to blow up the Houses of Parliament in revenge for penal laws against Catholics. Plot discovered; Fawkes arrested when entering the gunpowder-filled cellar under the Houses of Parliament (night of Nov. 4–5, 1605); under torture revealed names of fellow conspirators (Nov. 9, 1605); tried, convicted, and executed (Jan. 31, 1606). November 5th is celebrated in England and parts of British Empire as Guy Fawkes Day.

**Fawk′ner** (fôk′nẽr), **John Pascoe.** 1792–1869. Australian settler, journalist, and politician; settled on site of Melbourne (1835); founded Melbourne *Advertiser* (1838), Port Phillip *Patriot* (1839); instrumental in effecting separation of Victoria from New South Wales (1850).

**Fa·xar′do** (fä·här′thō). Variant of *Fajardo* (see SAAVEDRA Y FAJARDO).

**Fá′y** (fä′ĭ), **Andras.** 1786–1864. Hungarian writer; author of poems, plays, romances, and tales, including the first Hungarian society novel *The House of the Béltekys* (1832), the humorous novel *Dr. Jávor* (1855), and more than 600 fables (1820 ff.).

**Faÿ** (fȧ′y′), **Bernard.** 1893– . French historian and biographer; author esp. of books on American history, including as translated, *Revolutionary Spirit in France and America* (1927), *Franklin, the Apostle of Modern Times* (1929), *George Washington, Republican Aristocrat* (1931).

**Fay** (fā), **Charles Alexandre.** 1827–1903. French general; served in Crimean War and Franco-Prussian War; general of brigade (1879) and of division (1885). Author of *Journal d'un Officier de l'Armée du Rhin* (1871), etc.

**Fay** (fā), **Edward Allen.** 1843–1923. American teacher of the deaf, b. Morristown, N.J.

**Fay, Sidney Bradshaw.** 1876–1967. American historian, b. Washington, D.C. A.B. (1896) and Ph.D. (1900), Harvard. Professor, Dartmouth (1902–14), Smith (1914–29), Harvard (from 1929; emeritus from 1946). Author of *Origins of the World War* (2 vols., 1928), *Guide to Historical Literature* (1931), *Rise of Brandenburg-Prussia to 1786* (1937), etc.

**Fay, Theodore Sedgwick.** 1807–1898. American writer and diplomat, b. New York City. Studied law; secretary, U.S. legation, Berlin (1837–53); resident minister to Switzerland (1853–61). Author of the novels *Norman Leslie* (1835), *The Countess Ida* (1840), *Hoboken* (1843), the narrative poem *Ulric* (1851), and a popular political history of Germany, *The Three Germanys* (1889).

**Fa'yard'** (fá'yàr'), **Jean.** 1902– . French novelist; awarded Goncourt prize for his novel *Mal d'Amour* (1931).

**Faye** (fā), **Hervé Auguste Étienne Albans.** 1814–1902. French astronomer. Discovered the periodic comet named for him (1843); president of the Bureau of Longitudes (1876); minister of public education (1878). Author of works on the parallaxes of stars and planets, on the formation of clouds and hail, on sunspots, the origin of the earth, etc.

**Fa'yolle'** (fá'yôl'), **Marie Émile.** 1852–1928. French general; commanded 6th army in battle of the Somme (1916); commanded French divisions sent to Italian aid after Caporetto (1917–18); commanded reserve army which saved Compiègne and took part in final successful offensive in France (1918); marshal of France (1921).

**Fay'rer** (fâr'ēr), Sir **Joseph.** 1824–1907. English surgeon and writer, b. Plymouth. Surgeon at Lucknow during Sepoy Mutiny (1857). President of medical board of India Office (1873–95). His chief work was *The Thanatophidia of India* (1872); also wrote on clinical surgery in India and on tropical diseases.

**Fa'zio de'gli U·ber'ti** (fä'tsyô dā'lyē ōō·bĕr'tē). d. about 1367. Florentine poet; Ghibelline. Known esp. for his geographical epic in terza rima, *Dittamondo* ("Discourse of the World"), in imitation of Dante.

**Fazl.** See Barmecides.

**Fa'zy'** (fá'zē'), **Jean Jacques,** *called* **James.** 1794–1878. Swiss statesman, journalist, and writer; championed freedom of the press (1830); fined and imprisoned for radical republican principles. Returned to Geneva (1833); a leader of opposition in favor of democratic constitution (1841); head of Geneva government (1846–53; 1855–61) and an author of constitution of 1848; completely modernized Geneva; deposed (1862). Fled to Paris; edited journal *La France Nouvelle* (1870); returned to Geneva (1871); became professor of international law. His grandnephew **Henri** (1842–1920), statesman and historian, was active as Radical in Genevese politics (from 1868); member of Swiss National Council and professor, U. of Geneva (1896–99; 1902 ff.).

**Fe'a** (fâ'ä), **Carlo.** 1753–1834. Italian ecclesiastic and archaeologist; director of excavations, Rome (1800–34); one of founders of modern study of Roman topography.

**Fear'ing** (fēr'ĭng), **Kenneth.** 1902–1961. American journalist and poet, b. Chicago. Author of *Angel Arms* (1929), *Poems* (1935), *Dead Reckoning* (1938), *The Hospital* (novel; 1939).

**Fearn** (fûrn), **Anne,** *nee* **Wal'ter** (wôl'tēr). 1868?–1939. American physician, b. in Mississippi. M.D., Women's Medical College of Pennsylvania (1893). To China (1893); practiced in Soochow; m. Dr. John B. Fearn (1894); later, practiced in Shanghai. Founded a coeducational medical school in Soochow, and the Fearn Sanitarium in Shanghai.

**Fearn'ley** (fûrn'lĭ), **Thomas.** 1802–1842. Norwegian landscape painter.

**Febronius, Justinus.** Pseudonym of Johann Nikolaus von Hontheim.

**Feb'vre** (fâ'vr'), **Alexandre Frédéric.** 1835–1916. French actor; excelled in comedy roles.

**Fech'ner** (fĕk'nēr), **Gustav Theodor.** 1801–1887. German physicist, philosopher, and experimental psychologist, b. in Lower Lusatia; a founder of psychophysics. Professor of physics, Leipzig (1834–40), where he worked mainly on galvanism, electrochemistry, and theory of color; subsequently devoted himself to psychophysics, natural philosophy, anthropology, and aesthetics; formulated Fechner's law (or the Weber-Fechner law, deduced from Weber's law) that the intensity of sensation increases as the logarithm of the stimulus. Author of *Über die Physikalische und Philosophische Atomlehre* (1855), *Elemente der Psychophysik* (on the relations between physiology and psychology; 2 parts, 1860), and, under the pseudonym **Dr. Mi'ses** (dôk'tôr [*Ger.*] mē'zĕs), of poems, and humorous and satirical essays.

**Fech'ner** (fĕk'nēr), **Robert.** 1876–1939. American labor leader and government official; director, U.S. Civilian Conservation Corps (1933–39).

**Fech'ter** (fĕk'tēr), **Charles Albert.** 1824–1879. Actor, b. London, England. His interpretation of Hamlet as a man of action aroused a critical debate and has influenced later interpretations of the character.

**Feck'en·ham** (fĕk'ĕn·ăm), **John de.** *Orig.* **John How'man** (hou'măn). 1518?–1585. English Roman Catholic clergyman; chaplain and confessor to Queen Mary I (1553); abbot, abbey of St. Peter's, Westminster (1556–59); removed from the abbey (1559) for maintaining his religious faith and complaining of changes inaugurated under Queen Elizabeth's reign.

**Fed'chen·ko** (fyät'chĕn·kô), **Aleksei Pavlovich.** 1844–1873. Russian naturalist and traveler in Turkestan, lower Syr Darya valley, and Samarkand. Author of *Journeys in Turkistan* (1874), etc.

**Fed'der·sen** (fĕd'ēr·zĕn), **Berend Wilhelm.** 1832–1918. German physicist.

**Fe·de'le** (fâ·dā'lâ), **Pietro.** 1873–1943. Italian historian, educator, and statesman; minister of public instruction (1925–35). Compiler of *Grande Dizionario Enciclopedico* (1935).

**Fe'de·rer** (fā'dĕ·rēr), **Heinrich.** 1866–1928. Swiss author of novels of Switzerland and of central Italy.

**Fe'der·mann** (fā'dēr·män), **Nikolaus.** 1501?–?1543. German adventurer and explorer in South America.

**Fe'der·zo'ni** (fā'dâr·tsō'nē), **Luigi.** 1878–1967. Italian journalist and statesman, b. at Bologna. Editor of the organ of Nationalist party *Idea Nazionale* (from 1913); editor of periodical *Nuova Antologia* (from 1931). Leader of Nationalist movement; supported Mussolini (1922). Minister of colonies (1922–24, 1926–28), of interior (1924–26); senator (1928); senate president (from 1929); member, Fascist Grand Council.

**Fe'din** (fyā'dyĭn), **Konstantin Aleksandrovich.** 1892– . Russian novelist.

**Fë'dor** (fyô'dēr) *or* **Fe·o'dor** (fyĭ·ô'dēr). *Eng.* **Theodore.** Name of three Russian czars: **Fëdor I I·va'no·vich** [ĭ·vá'nŭ·vyĭch] (1557–1598), czar (1584–98); last of the Rurik dynasty (*q.v.*); son of Ivan IV (the Terrible); actual government in hands of boyars, esp. of Boris Godunov, his brother-in-law; in his reign Russian patriarchate established (1589). **Fëdor II** (1589–1605), czar (April–June, 1605); son of Boris Godunov; succeeded in disturbed period after death of his father; murdered by boyars. **Fëdor III A·le·kse'e·vich** [ŭ·lyĭ·ksā'yĕ·vyĭch] (1656–1682), czar (1676–82), of Romanov house;

son of Alexis; fought first of many wars against Turks; succeeded by Ivan V. See ROMANOV.

**Fedra.** See INGHIRAMI.

**Fee'han** (fē'ăn), **Patrick Augustine.** 1829–1902. Roman Catholic prelate, b. in County Tipperary, Ireland; to U.S. (1852). Archbishop of Chicago (1880).

**Feh'ling** (fā'lĭng), **Hermann.** 1812–1885. German chemist. Known for researches in analytical and industrial chemistry; introduced a method for the determination of reducing sugars by the use of a solution of Rochelle salt and blue vitriol (Fehling solution).

**Feh'ren·bach** (fā'rĕn·bäκ), **Konstantin.** 1852–1926. German statesman; leader of Catholic Center party. Member (from 1903) and president (1918) of Reichstag; president of Weimar National Assembly (1919–20); chancellor, at head of minority government of Center, Democratic, and German People's parties (1920–21); took part in conferences with allies at Spa (1920) and London (1921); chairman of Reichstag group of Left Center party (from 1924).

**Fei·jó'** *or* **Fei·joo'** (fā·ē·zhō'), **Diogo Antônio.** 1784–1843. Brazilian statesman, b. São Paulo; ordained Roman Catholic priest (1807); Brazilian deputy to Cortes at Lisbon (1822), resigning on proclamation of Brazilian independence (Sept., 1822); deputy to Brazilian Cortes (1823–33); senator (1833 ff.); regent of Brazil (1835–37).

**Fei·jo'o y Mon'te·ne'gro** (fĕ·ē·hō'ō ē môn'tā·nā'grō), **Benito Jeronimo.** 1676–1764. Spanish Benedictine monk, critic, and scholar; considered one of dominant forces leading to educational reawakening of Spain.

**Feil'ding** (fēl'dĭng), **William.** 1st Earl of **Den'bigh** (dĕn'bĭ). d. 1643. English naval and military officer. Educ. Cambridge; m. Susan Villiers, sister of George Villiers, future duke of Buckingham, and rose with the favorite; attended Prince Charles on Spanish adventure (1623); commanded disastrous attempt to relieve La Rochelle (1628); member of council of Wales (1633); served under Prince Rupert and died of wounds received in attack on Birmingham. His eldest son, **Basil** (1608?–1675), 2d earl, educ. Cambridge, was member of House of Lords (1628); ambassador to Venice (1634–39); commander in chief of Parliamentary forces in Midlands; resigned after passing of Self-denying Ordinance; supported army against Parliament but refused any part in trial of Charles I (1648); member of council of state but turned to Royalist side.

A relative of the family, **Robert Feilding** (1651?–1712), known as "Beau Feilding," notorious rake, followed James II to Ireland in command of a regiment; sat in Irish parliament (1689); m. duchess of Cleveland, former mistress of Charles II; described by Steele as Orlando in the *Tatler* (nos. 50 & 51, 1709).

**Fei'ning·er** (fī'nĭng·ẽr), **Lyonel.** 1871–1956. German-American painter, b. New York City; caricaturist and political cartoonist (1895–1910); devoted himself to painting (from 1907) and adopted an individual style somewhat influenced by cubism.

**Feisal** *or* **Feisul.** See FAISAL.

**Fei'si** *or* **Fei'ya·si** *or* **Fai'zi** (fī'zē), **A·bul' Feis ibn Mu·ba'rak** (ă·bo͝ol' fīs' ĭb'n mo͝o·bä'răk). 1547–1595. Indo-Persian poet and scholar; court poet of Emperor Akbar (1572); wrote lyrics, a commentary on the Koran, mathematical and philosophical works, and translations into Persian of episodes of the *Mahabharata.*

**Feith** (fīt), **Rhijnvis.** 1753–1824. Dutch poet, dramatist, and writer; works influenced by Goethe's *Werther* and Klopstock's *Odes.*

**Fe'jér** (fĕ'yār), **György.** 1766–1851. Hungarian historian and writer; professor of theology (1808) and librarian (1824), U. of Pest.

**Fe'jér·vá'ry de Kom'lós–Ke'resz·tes** (fĕ'yār·vä'rĭ dĕ kôm'lōsh·kĕ'rĕs·tĕsh), Baron **Géza.** 1833–1914. Hungarian statesman and army officer; secretary of state in ministry of national defense (1872–84); minister of national defense (1884–1903); minister president at head of provisional neutral cabinet following Tisza's fall (1905).

**Feke** (fēk), **Robert.** 1705?–?1750. American portrait painter, b. Oyster Bay, Long Island, N.Y.

**Fé'li'bien'** (fā'lē'byăN'), **André.** Sieur **des A'vaux' et de Ja'ver'cy'** (dā·zȧ'vō' ā dĕ zhȧ'vĕr'sē'). 1619–1695. French architect and writer; author esp. of books on painting, sculpture, and architecture.

**Felipe.** Spanish form of PHILIP.

**Fe'lix** (fē'lĭks). Name of three popes (see *Table of Popes*, Numbers 26, 48, 54) and two antipopes, especially:

**Felix II.** d. 365. Antipope (355–358), by some held to be a pope; b. Rome. Chosen by Arian party after Liberius had been banished by the emperor; deposed (358) when Liberius was reinstated.

**Felix II** (or **III**), Saint. d. 492. Pope (483–492). Repudiated the Henoticon and excommunicated (484?) bishops of Eastern Church; began schism of 34 years between Eastern and Western churches.

**Felix III** (or **IV**), Saint. d. 530. Pope (526–530), b. Samnium, Italy. Chosen pope through influence of Theodoric, King of the East Goths.

**Felix V.** *Real name* **Am'a·de'us** (ăm'ȧ·dē'ŭs). 1383–1451. Antipope (1439–49), b. Chambéry, France. Became count of Savoy as Amadeus VIII (1391); made duke (1416) by Emperor Sigismund; resigned duchy (1434); formed semimonastic order on Lake of Geneva; chosen pope by schismatical Council of Basel (1439); crowned (1440); excommunicated by Pope Eugenius IV; renounced claim in favor of Nicholas V (1449); made a cardinal; last of the antipopes. See SAVOY.

**Felix, Antonius.** Greek freedman of the emperor Claudius; procurator of Judaea (c. 52–60 A.D.), under whom (according to *Acts* xxiv) St. Paul was tried and kept prisoner; succeeded by Festus (*q.v.*).

**Fé'lix'** (fā'lĕks'), **Élisa.** See Mlle. RACHEL.

**Fe'lix** (fē'lĭks), **M. Minucius.** See MINUCIUS FELIX.

**Fé'lix of Ur·gel'** (fā'lĕks ŭv o͞or·gĕl'). 750?–816. Spanish bishop; bishop of Seo de Urgel and a champion of the adoptionist heresy. See ELIPANDO.

**Fé'lix' of Va'lois'** (fā'lĕks' ŭv vȧ'lwȧ'), Saint. 1127–1212. French monk; a founder of the Order of the Holy Trinity, for the Redemption of Captives, whose members were known as Trinitarians or Redemptionists. See Saint JEAN DE MATHA.

**Fel'kin** (fĕl'kĭn), **Ellen Thorneycroft,** *nee* **Fowler.** 1860–1929. English novelist, b. at Wolverhampton; m. Alfred Laurence Felkin (1903). After three volumes of verse, published successful novel *Concerning Isabel Carnaby* (1898), and followed it with *A Double Thread* (1899), *Fuel of Fire* (1902), *The Wisdom of Folly* (1910), *The Lower Pool* (1923), *Signs and Wonders* (1926), etc.

**Fell** (fĕl), **John.** 1625–1686. Anglican clergyman; dean of Christ Church, Oxford, and chaplain to the king (1660); vice-chancellor of Oxford (1666–69); bishop of Oxford (1675). Subject of Tom Brown's doggerel verse beginning "I do not love thee, Dr. Fell."

**Fel'len·berg** (fĕl'ĕn·bĕrκ), **Philipp Emanuel von.** 1771–1844. Swiss educator and agriculturist; bought estate near Bern (1799), where he founded experimental educational institution and sought to advance agriculture and improve Swiss education through training of lower and upper classes. Established several industrial and agricultural schools. Member of cantonal grand council (1820); magistrate, Bern (1833).

**Fel'ler'** (fā'lâr'), **François Xavier de.** 1735–1802. Belgian priest and writer; entered Jesuit order (1754); after suppression of the order, edited *Journal Historique et Littéraire* (1774–94); compiled *Dictionnaire Historique* (1781–84), often re-edited under title *Biographie Universelle.*

**Fel'lowes** (fĕl'ōz), **Edmund Horace.** 1870–1951. Anglican clergyman and authority on English madrigals.

**Fel'lows** (fĕl'ōz), Sir **Charles.** 1799–1860. English archaeologist; explored Asia Minor (1838 ff.); discovered ruins of ancient Xanthus and Tlos, and other cities of Lycia; gave archaeological collection to British Museum.

**Fell'tham** *or* **Fel'tham** (fĕl'thăm), **Owen.** 1602?–1668. English writer; secretary or chaplain to the earl of Thomond. Author of *Resolves, Divine, Morall, Politicall* (c. 1620), a collection of short moral essays. Royalist in sympathy; author of poem *Epitaph to the Eternal Memory of Charles the First...*, in which he refers to Charles as "Christ the Second."

**Fel'sen·thal** (fĕl'zĕn·täl), **Bern'hard** (bĕrn'härt). 1822–1908. Rabbi, b. in Bavaria; to U.S. (1854). Rabbi of Zion Congregation, Chicago (1864–87). A leading advocate of Reformed Judaism and Zionism.

**Fel'sing** (fĕl'zĭng). A family of German copper engravers in Darmstadt, including **Johann Heinrich** (1800–75), who studied under his father **Johann Konrad** (1766–1819) and in Paris; perfected the galvanoplastic method. His brother **Jakob** (1802–1883), pupil of his father, and of Longhi in Milan; engraved Correggio's *Marriage of St. Catherine*, Raphael's *Violin Player*, etc.

**Felt** (fĕlt), **Dorr Eugene.** 1862–1930. American inventor, b. Beloit, Wis. Invented the comptometer.

**Feltham, Owen.** See FELLTHAM.

**Fel'ton** (fĕl't'n; -tŭn), **Cornelius Conway.** 1807–1862. American classical scholar, b. Newbury, Mass. Grad. Harvard (1827). Professor of Greek literature (from 1834), president (1860–62), Harvard.

**Felton, John.** 1595?–1628. English lieutenant at Cádiz (1625); assassinated (Aug. 23, 1628) duke of Buckingham, who had rejected his application for captain's commission; hanged at Tyburn.

**Felton, Rebecca,** *nee* **Latimer.** 1835–1930. First woman to become United States senator; b. near Decatur, Ga.; m. Dr. William Harrell Felton (1853). Regular contributor of political comment to Atlanta (Ga.) *Journal.* Appointed U.S. senator by Gov. Hardwick of Georgia (Oct. 3, 1922), and served until her elected successor took his seat (Nov. 22, 1922).

**Felton, William Harrell.** 1823–1909. American Methodist clergyman and politician. Member, U.S. House of Representatives (1875–81). See Rebecca FELTON.

**Feltre, Vittorino da.** See VITTORINO DA FELTRE.

**Fé'ne·lon'** (fān'lôɴ'), **François de Sa'li'gnac' de La Mothe-** (dē sȧ'lē'nyȧk' dē lȧ môt'-). 1651–1715. French prelate and writer; appointed by Louis XIV as tutor to his grandson, the duc de Bourgogne (1689); composed for instruction of his pupil *Fables, Dialogues des Morts, Abrégé des Vies des Anciens Philosophes, Télémaque.* Consecrated archbishop of Cambrai (1695). Involved in development of semiquietism in France; wrote *Maximes des Saints*, which in part was condemned by the pope; submitted wholeheartedly to the papal decision. Fell into disgrace at the court upon publication of *Télémaque*, which was construed as satirizing the king and his policies.

**Fen'es·tel'la** (fĕn'ĕs·tĕl'ȧ). Roman historian of late 1st century B.C. and early 1st century A.D.

**Feng'er** (fĕng'ĕr), **Christian.** 1840–1902. Pathologist, b. in Denmark. To U.S.; settled in Chicago (1877); chief pathologist, Cook County Hospital (1878–93); professor of surgery, Coll. Phys. & Surg., N.Y. (1884), Northwestern U. (1893), Rush Med. Coll. (1899).

**Fêng Kuo-chang** (fŭng' gwô'jäng'). 1858–1920. Chinese general and politician; vice-president with Li Yüan-hung (1916–17); acting president (1917–18); resigned.

**Fêng Tao** (fŭng' dä'ō). 882–954 A.D. Chinese administrator. Prime minister under seven emperors and four of the Five Dynasties of central China (c. 929–954). Conquered Shu (929), where he learned about block printing; caused the Confucian classics and their commentaries to be printed (932–953; in 130 volumes, none extant) from wood blocks at Lo-yang (Honanfu), capital of the Later T'ang dynasty. The printing of this work ushered in the renaissance of the Sung era (960–1127) and demonstrated the practical value of printing.

**Fêng Yü-hsiang** *or* **Feng Yu-hsiang** (fŭng' yü'shē-äng'). 1880–1948. Chinese general, called the "Christian General"; b. in Anhwei province. Received military education; saw service in Tibet (1909) and at Sian (1912). Organized famous 11th Division; received independent command (1921) in Shensi; here, and later (1922) in Honan, gave excellent administration; transferred to Peking (1922); made field marshal (1923); by a coup d'état (1924) drove out Wu P'ei-fu and Hsüan T'ung and with help of Chang Tso-lin installed Tuan Ch'i-jui as president; retired to northwest provinces (1926). Visited Moscow (1926–27); for next six years (1928–33) led varied career of official in Nationalist government; opponent of Chiang Kai-shek, several times a member of the Kuomintang and as many times expelled; always anti-Japanese; active in Nationalist government (1940).

**Fenn** (fĕn), **George Manville.** 1831–1909. English novelist; author of many books for boys; wrote also dramatic criticism and farces.

**Fen'ner** (fĕn'ĕr), **Thomas.** d. 1590? English naval officer; probably a rear admiral under Drake in expedition against Cádiz (1587), and a vice-admiral in English fleet opposing Spanish Armada (1588).

**Fen'no** (fĕn'ō), **John.** 1751–1798. American editor, b. Boston. Published *Gazette of the United States* (New York, Apr. 11, 1789–Apr. 13, 1790; Philadelphia, from Apr. 14, 1790), a Federalist organ under special favor of Alexander Hamilton.

**Fen'ol·lo'sa** (fĕn'ŭ·lō'sȧ), **Ernest Fran·cis'co** (frăn-sĭs'kō). 1853–1908. American Orientalist; grad. Harvard (1874). Taught in U. of Tokyo, Japan (1878–86). Manager, Tokyo Fine Arts Academy, and Imperial Museum (1888). Became professing Buddhist; baptized in that faith; decorated by emperor of Japan. Curator, department of Oriental art, Boston Museum of Fine Arts (1890–97). Professor, Imperial Normal School, Tokyo, Japan (1897–1900). See Ezra POUND.

**Fen'ton** (fĕn't'n; -tŭn), **Edward.** d. 1603. English mariner; sailed with Frobisher on his second and third voyages (1577 and 1578) to discover Northwest Passage to China; commanded trading expedition (1582) to Moluccas and China by way of Cape of Good Hope; served against Spanish Armada (1588).

**Fenton, Elijah.** 1683–1730. English poet; B.A., Cantab. (1704). Edited works of Milton and Waller; translated 1st, 4th, 19th, and 20th books of the *Odyssey* for Alexander Pope; author of the tragedy *Mariamne* (1723).

**Fenton,** Sir **Geoffrey.** 1539?–1608. English politician and writer. Principal secretary of state in Ireland (1580 ff.), and under James I, joint secretary (to 1608). Best-known literary work is a collection (1567) of Bandello's novels freely translated from *Histoires Tragiques*, French versions by Pierre Boaisteau and François de Belleforest, which contained the stories of Hamlet and Romeo and Juliet.

**Fenton, Lavinia.** Duchess of **Bol′ton** (bōl′t'n; -tŭn). 1708–1760. English actress; m. (1751) Charles Paulet, 3d Duke of Bolton. Greatest success as Polly Peachum in Gay's *Beggar's Opera* (1728 ff.).

**Fenton, Reuben Eaton.** 1819–1885. American politician, b. Carroll, N.Y. A founder of Republican party in New York; governor of New York (1865–68); accused (1868) of corruption in signing bill that legalized acts of directorate of the Erie Railroad, but investigation did not support charges. U.S. senator (1869–75).

**Fen′wick** (fĕn′(w)ĭk), **Benedict Joseph.** 1782–1846. American Roman Catholic prelate; consecrated bishop of Boston (Nov. 1, 1825).

**Fenwick, Charles G.** 1880–1973. U.S. political scientist, b. Baltimore, Md. Ph.D., Johns Hopkins, 1912. Specialist in international law; author of text, *International Law* (1924; fourth ed. 1965); *The Organization of American States* (1963).

**Fenwick, Edward Dominic.** 1768–1832. American Roman Catholic prelate; bishop of Cincinnati (1822).

**Fenwick, Ethel Gordon,** *nee* **Man′son** (măn′s'n). 1857–1947. British nurse, b. in Scotland; m. Dr. Bedford Fenwick (1887). Founder and first member of British Nurses' Association (1887); instrumental in procuring an act of parliament (1919) to provide for registration of nurses; became a registered nurse (1921).

**Fenwick, George.** 1603–1657. English colonist in America. One of group granted territory west of Narragansett River, in America (1632). Visited Saybrook settlement (1636); settled there (1639). Transferred land interests to Connecticut Colony (1644–45). Magistrate, Connecticut Colony (1644, 1645, 1647, 1648). Returned to England (about 1645); member, the Long Parliament (1645); colonel in Parliamentary army; governor of Tynemouth (1648); governor of Berwick (1649); governor of Edinburgh and Leith (1650). Member of parliament (1654, 1656).

**Fenwick, John.** 1618–1683. English colonist in America, b. Binfield, England. An officer in Cromwell's army; became a Quaker; conceived idea of a Quaker colony in America; with others, bought half of New Jersey (West New Jersey). Settled first Quaker colony on Delaware River (1675).

**Fenwick,** Sir **John.** 1645?–1697. English soldier and conspirator; involved in plot to assassinate William III (1695); associated in plot with Barclay and Charnock (1696); upon arrest (1696), accused Whig leaders, including Marlborough, Godolphin, and Shrewsbury, of treasonable negotiations with the Jacobites; beheaded.

**Feodor.** Variant of FËDOR.

**Ferabosco.** See FERRABOSCO family.

**Fer′ber** (fûr′bẽr), **Edna.** 1887–1968. American author, b. Kalamazoo, Mich. Author of novels and short stories, including *Dawn O'Hara* (1911), *Emma McChesney & Co.* (1915), *Gigolo* (1922), *So Big* (1924; awarded Pulitzer prize), *Show Boat* (1926), *Cimarron* (1929), *American Beauty* (1931), *Come and Get It* (1935), *Saratoga Trunk* (1941), and her autobiography, *Peculiar Treasure* (1939). Coauthor of plays, chiefly comedies.

**Fer′di·nand I** (fûr′dĭ·nănd; *Ger.* fĕr′dē·nänt). 1793–1875. Emperor of Austria (1835–48). Son of Francis I. King of Hungary (1830–48). A weak sovereign, leaving control of the government to Metternich; forced to abdicate (Dec., 1848) after revolution overthrew Metternich; named Francis Joseph as successor; retired to Prague.

**Ferdinand,** Archduke. = FRANCIS FERDINAND, of Austria.

**Ferdinand I.** *Full name* **Maximilian Karl Leopold Maria.** 1861–1948. King of Bulgaria (1908–18), b. Vienna. A prince of Saxe-Coburg, son of Prince August of Saxe-Coburg-Gotha and Clémentine, daughter of Louis Philippe of France (see ORLÉANS), and grandson of Duke Francis Frederick (see SAXE-COBURG-GOTHA). Elected to throne of Bulgaria (1887) as prince to succeed Alexander; first part of reign (1887–96) made difficult by disturbed condition of country and refusal of powers to recognize him; recognized by Russia (1896). Declared independence and assumed title (1908) of king, or czar; his new title recognized by Turkey and the powers (1909). Joined other Balkan states in First Balkan War (1912–13) against Turkey; badly defeated in Second Balkan War (1913); took Bulgaria into World War I on side of Central Powers (1915); abdicated (1918) in favor of his son Boris; retired to Coburg. m. first (1893) Marie Louise (1870–1899), daughter of Duke Robert of Parma, second (1908) Eleonor of Reuss (1860–1917).

**Ferdinand.** Name of three Holy Roman emperors:

**Ferdinand I.** 1503–1564. Younger brother of Charles V. Holy Roman emperor (1556–64). Chosen by Charles to administer Germany (1521); m. (1521) Anne of Bohemia and Hungary. On death of Louis II, elected king of Hungary and Bohemia (1526). Title to Hungary disputed by John Zápolya; long war (1526–38) against Zápolya and the Turks, only partly successful. Elected king of Germany (1531–64). Mediator (1552) between Charles and Maurice of Saxony, leader of the Protestants. Failed to accomplish much in settling religious disputes. Continued struggle against the Turks. Effected institutional reforms, esp. the definite organization of the Aulic Council (1559; first begun 1501).

**Ferdinand II.** 1578–1637. Cousin of Emp. Matthias and grandson of Ferdinand I. King of Bohemia (1617–19, 1620–37), of Hungary (1621–37). Holy Roman emperor (1619–37). Educated by Jesuits who taught him bitter hatred of Protestantism. Deposed in Bohemia by Protestant estates (1619). Allied with Catholic League and Spain, overthrew Elector Palatine Frederick V of Bohemia in battle of White Mountain (1620). Drove Protestantism out of Bohemia. Edict of Restitution (1629). Entire reign occupied in war against Protestants (first part of Thirty Years' War); emperor and Catholic League at first victorious, led by Tilly and Wallenstein, but final success prevented by opposition of Richelieu and skill of Gustavus Adolphus and Swedish generals.

**Ferdinand III.** 1608–1657. King of Hungary (1625–57) and Holy Roman emperor (1637–57). Son of Ferdinand II. After the death of Wallenstein (1634), appointed to command of imperial armies. Nominal leader in victory over the Swedes at Nördlingen (1634). Made king of Germany (1636) and succeeded to the Empire (1637). Continued struggle against Protestants, but signed the Peace of Westphalia (1648) which terminated the Thirty Years' War. Sent army into Italy to help Spain (1656) and concluded alliance with Poland (1657) against Sweden. A scholar and excellent composer of music.

**Ferdinand.** 1721–1792. Duke of Brunswick and Prussian field marshal, b. Wolfenbüttel. Son of Ferdinand Albert II. Entered Prussian service (1740); fought under Frederick the Great and was for many years his close companion; rendered distinguished service at Hohenfriedeberg (1745); one of ablest commanders of Seven Years' War (victories over French at Crefeld (1758) and Minden (1759) ); governor of Magdeburg (1755–57 and 1763–66); estranged from Frederick (1766).

**Ferdinand.** *Ital.* **Ferrante.** Name of four kings of Naples:

**Ferdinand I.** 1423–1494. King (1458–94); natural son of Alfonso I, King of Naples; opposed by Pope Calixtus III, who supported John of Anjou, son of René the Good; defeated by John at Sarno (1460); with help of Alessandro Sforza and Scanderbeg completely defeated John (1462); during his reign, Turks occupied Otranto (1480–81), nobles revolted (1485), printing press established at Naples (1474); involved in struggle (1489–92) with Innocent VIII.

**Ferdinand II.** 1469–1496. King (1495–96), last of Anjou line in Italy (see ANJOU), grandson of Ferdinand I and son of Alfonso II. Driven out by Charles VIII of France, but with help of Spanish general Gonzalo de Córdoba, defeated invaders (1495).

**Ferdinand III.** See FERDINAND V of Castile.

**Ferdinand IV.** See FERDINAND I of the Two Sicilies.

**Ferdinand.** Name of two kings of the Two Sicilies:

**Ferdinand I.** 1751–1825. Third son of Don Carlos of Bourbon (later Charles III of Spain). King of Naples (1759–1806, 1815–25) as Ferdinand IV; under regent Bernardo Tanucci (1759–67); expelled Jesuits (1767); m. Maria Carolina of Austria (1768); under influence of wife and prime minister Sir John Acton; joined coalition against France (1793); remained hostile to Napoleon; fled to Palermo while French established short-lived Parthenopean Republic at Naples (1799); again fled to Sicily (1806) where he ruled as Ferdinand III while Naples was ruled by Joseph Bonaparte and Murat (1806–15); restored to Naples (1815). Made king of the Two Sicilies (1816) as Ferdinand I; ruthlessly repressed liberal opinion; tyranny brought on revolution (1820); his last years an era of cruel vengeance and persecution.

**Ferdinand II.** *Known as* King **Bom′ba** (bŏm′bä). 1810–1859. Son of Francis I; b. Palermo. King (1830–59). Promised reforms but soon became subservient to Austria; entire reign a series of conspiracies, revolts (1837, 1841, 1844, 1847, and esp., 1848), cruel repressions, and political prosecutions; bombarded cities in Sicily during insurrection (1848–49), hence, his nickname; died on eve of war with Austria.

**Ferdinand.** Name of four grand dukes of Tuscany:

**Ferdinand I** and **II.** See MEDICI.

**Ferdinand III.** 1769–1824. Grand duke (1790–99, 1814–24) and archduke of Austria; son of Emperor Leopold II and brother of Emperor Francis II; remained neutral in first coalition against France; first ruler to recognize French Republic (1792); forced to side against Bonaparte (1793–95); made disadvantageous treaty with Bonaparte (1797); because of alliance with Austria driven out of Tuscany (1799), and by Treaty of Lunéville (1801) forced to relinquish all claims to his duchy; lived in Austria (1799–1814); a member prince of the Confederation of the Rhine; reinstated in grand duchy (1814); ruled (1814–24) as benevolent despot; succeeded by his son Leopold II.

**Ferdinand IV.** 1835–1908. Son of Leopold II; succeeded (1859) on abdication of his father; protested against incorporation of Tuscany into Sardinia; deposed (1860); lived at castle of Salzburg in Austria (1860–1908).

**Ferdinand.** *Port.* **Fernando.** Name of two rulers of Portugual:

**Ferdinand I.** 1345–1383. King of Portugual (1367–83), called "the Handsome." Son of Pedro I; b. at Coimbra; one of claimants to throne of Castile and León on death of Pedro el Cruel (1369); waged disastrous war (1370–82) with Henry of Trastamara and his successor; made alliance with England (1372); forced to make peace (1383); m. Leonora Telles, who became very unpopular and who, at his death, assumed regency, but was soon driven out; last of the House of Burgundy (*q.v.*); interregnum (1383–85) followed. See JOHN I of Portugal.

**Ferdinand II.** 1816–1885. Titular king of Portugal. Son of duke of Saxe-Coburg-Gotha and nephew of Leopold, King of Belgium; m. Queen Maria da Gloria of Portugal (1836); king consort (1836–53); regent (1853–55) and again for a short period (1861) after death of his son King Pedro V.

**Ferdinand.** 1402–1443. Infante of Portugal, called "the Constant Prince." Son of John I and younger brother of King Edward and of Prince Henry the Navigator, b. at Santarem. Grand master of Order of Aviz; an ardent crusader, urged expedition against Tangier (1437); on its failure sacrificed himself as hostage; died in captivity in Fez after long and cruel imprisonment; beatified (1470).

**Ferdinand I.** 1865–1927. King of Rumania (1914–27), b. at Sigmaringen. Son of Leopold (*q.v.*) of Hohenzollern-Sigmaringen and nephew of Carol I of Rumania. Declared heir presumptive to throne (1889); m. (1893; see MARIE, Queen of Rumania); lived in Rumania (1889–1914), devoting himself chiefly to study of science; called to throne (1914) on death of Carol I; although a Hohenzollern, endeavored to rule impartially; on promises of Allies took Rumania into World War (1916); defeated by Central Powers (1917); remained in Rumania and by courage won with queen affection of people; returned in triumph to Bucharest (1918); crowned king of Greater Rumania (1922); last years of reign marked by reforms, but also by serious political difficulties and domestic troubles; succeeded by his grandson Michael, his son Carol having renounced his right. Children: Carol II (*q.v.*), Elizabeth (m. Prince George of Greece, 1921; divorced, 1935), Maria (m. Alexander of Yugoslavia, 1922; assassinated, 1934), Ileana (m. Archduke Anton of Austria-Tuscany, 1931), Nicholas (b. 1903).

**Ferdinand.** *Span.* **Fernando.** Name of two kings of Aragon:

**Ferdinand I.** *Called* **the Just.** 1379?–1416. King (1412–16).

**Ferdinand II.** 1452–1516. See FERDINAND V, king of Castile.

**Ferdinand.** *Span.* **Fernando.** Name of five kings of Castile and León:

**Ferdinand I.** *Called* **el Mag′no** (ĕl mäg′nō), *i.e.* the Great. d. 1065. Second son of Sancho the Great of Navarre; king (1037–65); made king of Castile (1033) by Sancho; married sister of Bermudo III of León; secured León by defeat of Bermudo (1037); reformed church abuses; assumed title of Emperor of Spain (1056); won territory back from Moors (1058–65), beginning period of reconquest by Spaniards.

**Ferdinand II.** d. 1188. Second son of Alfonso VII; king of León only (1157–88); at war with Alfonso VIII of Castile and with Portugal.

**Ferdinand III.** *Called* **el San′to** (ĕl sän′tō), *i.e.* the Saint. 1199–1252. Son of Alfonso IX (of León) and Berengaria; king of Castile (1217–52); succeeded also to León (1230) on death of his father; Castile and León permanently united; m. (1st) Beatrice of Swabia (1219), daughter of the Hohenstaufen emperor Philip; waged successful war against Moors (1230–48); took Córdoba (1236), and Seville (1248); began codification of Spanish law, later completed by his son Alfonso X as *Las Siete Partidas;* persecuted Albigenses; refounded University of Salamanca (1242); m. (2d) Juana (Joanna) of Ponthieu, their daughter Eleanor becoming wife of Edward I of England; canonized by Pope Clement X (1671).

**Ferdinand IV.** *Called* **el Em′pla·za′do** (ĕl ām′plä-thä′thō), *i.e.* the Summoned. 1286?–1312. Son of Sancho IV; king of Castile and León (1295–1312); his minority a period of anarchy; continued wars against the Moors (1305–12).

**Ferdinand V** of Castile *or* **Ferdinand II** of Aragon. *Called* **the Catholic.** 1452–1516. Son of John II of Aragon, b. at Sos, Aragon. King of Sicily (1468–1516); m. (1st) Isabella of Castile (1469), (2d) Germaine de Foix (1505). King of Castile as Ferdinand V, joint sovereign with Isabella (1474–1504); king of Aragon (1479–1516) as Ferdinand II, uniting the two kingdoms. Organized the Santa Hermandad (1476) and the Inquisition (1480); final war with Moors (1482–92); conquest of Granada (1492); Jews expelled (1492). At first aided Columbus in voyages of discovery but after 1499 turned against him. King of Naples (1504–16) as Ferdinand III. Regent of Castile for his daughter Juana (*q.v.*), because of her insanity (1506–16). Joined League of Cambrai (1508) against Venice. Conquest of Navarre (1512). Fought with France for supremacy in Italy (1511–13). With Isabella, granted title of **los re'yes ca·tó'li·cos** (lōs rā'-yās kä·tō'lē·kōs), *i.e.* "the Catholic Kings."

**Ferdinand.** Name of two Bourbon kings of Spain (see BOURBON):

**Ferdinand VI.** *Called* **el Sa'bio** (ĕl sä'byō), *i.e.* the Learned. 1713–1759. Second son of Philip V and Maria Louisa of Savoy, b. Madrid; m. (1729) Maria Magdalena Barbara, daughter of John V of Portugal. King (1746–59); took part in Treaty of Aix-la-Chapelle (1748); kept Spain neutral during first part of Seven Years' War (1756–59); government generally administered by ministers José de Carvajal and Ensenada; during last year suffered from extreme melancholy which developed into insanity.

**Ferdinand VII.** 1784–1833. Son of Charles IV, b. at San Ildefonso. King (1808, and 1814–33). Prince of Asturias (1789–1808); encouraged to oppose Godoy (1806), arrested and confined in Escorial (1807); proclaimed king after forced abdication of Charles IV (1808); invited by Napoleon to conference at Bayonne; made prisoner and kept under strict guard at château of Valençay, central France (1808–13); reinstated by Napoleon (1814); all acts promulgated during French occupation abrogated, including constitution of 1812; cruel and tyrannical rule (1814–20); many insurrections; Constitutionalists victorious (1820–23) but Holy Alliance using French troops restored absolutism (1823); returned to Madrid (1823); reactionary rule complete (1823–33); m., as fourth wife, Maria Christina of Naples (1829); abolished Salic law in Spain by a pragmatic sanction (1830); led to formation of Carlist party (see Don CARLOS); reign disastrous to Spain, which not only lost all colonies in North and South America except Cuba, but lost position as European power.

**Ferdinand Albert.** Name of two dukes of Brunswick: **Ferdinand Albert I** (1638–1687), first duke of Brunswick-Bevern. His son **Ferdinand Albert II** (1680–1735), German general, fought in War of Spanish Succession; lieutenant general (1711); fought under Prince Eugene of Savoy in Turkish wars; field marshal of empire (1733); became duke (1735); father of Anthony Ulrich who married Anna Leopoldovna, Ferdinand, duke of Brunswick (see FERDINAND), and of Elisabeth Christine, wife of Frederick the Great. See BRUNSWICK.

**Fer'gus** (fûr'gŭs), **John F.** 1865–1943. Scottish physician and writer of books on medical history, of verse, and of a comedy *Healing Waters* (1928).

**Fer'gu·son** (fûr'gŭ·s'n), **Adam.** 1723–1816. Scottish philosopher; professor of natural philosophy (1759), of pneumatics (psychology) and moral philosophy (1764–85), and mathematics (1785), at U. of Edinburgh. Author of *Institutes of Moral Philosophy* (1772), etc.

**Ferguson, Elsie.** 1883–1961. American actress, b. New York City; m. Fred Hoey (1907); Thomas Benedict Clarke, Jr. (1916). Starred in *Such a Little Queen*, *The First Lady of the Land*, *Outcast*, *Margaret Schiller*, and *Shirley Kaye;* in motion pictures (from 1917).

**Ferguson, James.** 1710–1776. Scottish astronomer; built an orrery; invented a tide dial and an eclipsareon; observed transit of Venus with a six-foot reflector (c. 1763).

**Ferguson, James Edward.** 1871–1944. American politician; governor of Texas (1915–17); impeached and removed from office (1917); m. (1899) **Miriam A. Wallace** (1875–1961), popularly known as "Ma Ferguson," governor of Texas (1925–27; 1933–35).

**Ferguson, John Calvin.** 1866–1945. Authority on Chinese affairs, b. in Ontario, Can.; A.B., Boston U. (1886). President, Nanking U. (1888–97) and Nanyang Coll. in Shanghai (1897–1902). Chief secretary, Imperial Chinese Ry. Administration (1903–07). Foreign adviser to viceroys of Nanking (1898–1911) and Wuchang (1900–10) and to president of Republic of China (1917–28).

**Ferguson, Patrick.** 1744–1780. British soldier; inventor of first breech-loading rifle used in British army (1776); served in America; killed at battle of Kings Mountain (1780).

**Ferguson, Robert.** d. 1714. Scottish conspirator, called "the Plotter." Involved in Rye House Plot to assassinate Charles II (1683), and in plot on life of William III (1696); committed to Newgate for treason (1704), but admitted to bail and never tried.

**Ferguson,** Sir **Samuel.** 1810–1886. Irish antiquary and poet; published *Lays of the Western Gael* (1865), *Congal, an Epic Poem* (1872).

**Ferguson, William Jason.** 1844–1930. Callboy at Ford's Theater, Washington, D.C. (1863–65), and sole witness of the shooting of Abraham Lincoln (Apr. 14, 1865). On stage (from 1872); excelled in comedy roles.

**Fer'gus·son** (fûr'gŭ·s'n), **Harvey.** 1890–1971. American writer, b. Alberquerque, N.Mex.; author of *The Blood of the Conquerors* (1921), *Women and Wives* (1924), *Rio Grande* (1933), *The Life of Riley* (1937), etc.

**Fergusson, James.** 1808–1886. Scottish industrialist and student of architecture; amassed fortune in India manufacturing indigo; retired from business to write on architecture. Author of *An Historical Enquiry into the True Principles of Beauty in Art* (1849), *A History of Architecture...* (1865–67), etc.

**Fergusson,** Sir **James.** 1832–1907. British colonial administrator. Governor of South Australia (1868–73), New Zealand (1873–74), Bombay (1880–85). Postmaster general (1891–92). His son Sir **Charles** (1865–1951), soldier and colonial administrator; in World War I (1914–18), commanded successively fifth division, second army corps, seventeenth army corps; military governor of occupied German territory (1918–19); governor general of New Zealand (1924–30).

**Fergusson, Robert.** 1750–1774. Scottish poet, b. Edinburgh.

**Fergusson,** Sir **William.** 1808–1877. Scottish surgeon. Author of *System of Practical Surgery* (1842).

**Ferid Eddin Attar.** See ATTAR.

**Fe·rid' Pa·sha'** (fĕ·rēd' pä·shä'). 1850–1923. Turkish statesman, of Albanian descent. Son-in-law (hence entitled *da·mad'* [dä·mäd']) of the sultan. Grand vizier (1903); minister of the interior in Hilmi Pasha's cabinet (1909); and grand vizier again (1919–20). Constantly under attack by Mustafa Kemal, he resigned as grand vizier (Oct., 1920).

**Fe·rish·tah'** (fĭ·rĭsh·tă') *or* **Fi·rish·ta', Mohammed Kasim.** 1550?–?1626. Persian historian, b. in Asterabad, on the Caspian. To Bijapur (1589), where the shah commissioned him to write a history of the Mohammedan dynasties of India. His work has been translated and published (4 vols., 1829) by General J. Briggs under title *The History of the Rise of the Mahometan Power in India.*

**Fer'land'** (fĕr'läN'), **Jean Baptiste Antoine.** 1805–1865. French-Canadian Roman Catholic clergyman and historian.

**Ferland, Joseph Auge Albert.** 1872–1943. French-Canadian poet, b. in Montreal.

**Fer'mat'** (fĕr'mȧ'), **Pierre de.** 1601–1665. French mathematician. Known chiefly by his notations and correspondence published by his son under the title of *Varia Opera Mathematica* (1679); called founder of modern theory of numbers; regarded by d'Alembert, Lagrange, and Laplace as inventor of the differential calculus and by Laplace as inventor (with Pascal) of the calculus of probabilities.

**Fer'mi** (fār'mē), **Enrico.** 1901–1954. Italian physicist. Conducted investigations in theoretical and mathematical physics, esp. in the fields of quantum theory and atomic structure and behavior; demonstrated that the bombardment of elements by neutrons causes transmutations; synthesized transuranium, element number 93, by bombarding uranium with neutrons. Awarded 1938 Nobel prize for physics. Fermi Award given in his honor.

**Fer'mor** (fûr'môr; -mẽr), Count **William of.** 1704–1771. Russian general, b. in Pskov of English origin. Distinguished himself at Danzig (1734) and against Turks (1736); lieutenant general (1746); commanded Russian army against Prussia at Gross-Jägersdorf (1758); defeated by Frederick the Great at Zorndorf (1758) and relinquished command to Gen. Saltykov (1759); governor general of Smolensk (1762–68).

**Fern, Fanny.** Pseudonym of Sara Payson Willis PARTON.

**Fer'nald** (fûr'n'ld), **Charles Henry.** 1838–1921. American zoologist, b. Mount Desert Island, Me. Professor, Maine State College (1871–86), Mass. State (1886–1910). Specialized in study of small moths.

**Fernald, Chester Bailey.** 1869–1938. American writer, b. Boston; author of *The Cat and the Cherub* (1896; afterwards adapted for stage and as opera libretto of *L'Oracolo*), *Chinatown Stories* (1899), *John Kendry's Idea* (1907), and a number of plays, including *The Ghetto, The Jest, The Love Thief.*

**Fernald, James Champlin.** 1838–1918. American Baptist clergyman and editor, b. Portland, Me. On editorial staff, *Standard Dictionary* (1893–1913). Author of *English Synonyms and Antonyms* (1896), *Connectives of English Speech* (1904).

**Fernald, Merritt Lyndon.** 1873–1950. American botanist, b. Orono, Me. B.S., Harvard (1897). Curator (1915–36), director (from 1937), Gray Herbarium, Harvard; taught at Harvard (1905–49).

**Fer·nan'des** (fĕr·năNn'dĕsh), **Álvaro.** 15th-century Portuguese explorer.

**Fernandes, João.** 15th-century Portuguese navigator; penetrated into interior of Africa by way of Río de Oro (1445); explored parts of West Africa (1446, 1447).

**Fer·nan'des Pi·nhei'ro** (fĕr·năNn'dēs pē·nyā'rōō), **José Feliciano.** Visconde **de São' Le·o·pol'do** (souN' lē·ōō·pôl'dōō). 1774–1847. Brazilian statesman and writer, b. Santos. First president of Rio Grande do Sul (1823–25); organized first German colony, São Leopoldo; minister of justice (1825–27); senator (1827 ff.).

**Fer·nán'dez** (fĕr·nän'dāth; -dās). See also HERNÁNDEZ.

**Fer·nán'dez, Juan** (*Span.* hwän fĕr·nän'dāth; *Angl.* jōō'ăn fẽr·năn'dĕz). 1536–?1602. Spanish navigator; plied southern Pacific between Panama and settlements in Peru and Chile (c. 1550–c. 1590); discovered several islands, including the group (discovered c. 1563) named for him.

**Fer·nán'dez** (fĕr·nän'dāth), **Lucas.** 1474?–1542. Spanish dramatist; imitator of Encina. Known esp. for his *Farsas y Églogas al Modo y Estilo Pastoril y Castellano,* a collection of six short plays, including his best-known piece, *Auto de la Pasión* (1514).

**Fer·nán'dez** (fĕr·nän'dās), **Próspero.** 1834–1885. Costa Rican soldier; president of Costa Rica (1882–85).

**Fer·nán'dez Ar·bós'** (fĕr·nän'dāth är·bōs'), **Enrique.** See ARBÓS.

**Fernández de A'vel·la·ne'da** (thā ä'vā·lyä·nā'thä), **Alonso.** Pseudonym of unidentified author of spurious second part (1614) of *Don Quixote.* The genuine second part (by Cervantes) appeared in 1615.

**Fernández de Cas'tro** (käs'trō), **Manuel.** 1825–1895. Spanish geologist; government mining engineer and geologist in Cuba and Santo Domingo (1859–69); director, commission of geological map of Spain (1873 ff.).

**Fernández de Cór'do·ba** (kôr'thō·bä), **Diego.** Marqués **de Gua'dal·cá'zar** (thā gwä'thäl·kä'thär) *and* Conde **de Po·sa'das** (pō·sä'thäs). Spanish administrator; viceroy of Mexico (1612–21); founded Lerma (1613), Córdoba (1618), and Guadalcázar (1620); viceroy of Peru (1622–29).

**Fernández de Córdoba, Francisco.** See CÓRDOBA.

**Fernández de Córdoba, Gonzalo.** See CÓRDOBA.

**Fernández de Córdoba y Val·cár'cel** (ē väl·kär'thĕl), **Fernando.** 1809–1883. Spanish soldier and statesman; field marshal (1844); minister of war (1847). Commander in chief of army sent to Rome to liberate pope (1849); captain general of Cuba (1850, 1870). Promoted general in chief of cavalry (1853); fled to France (1854) as supporter of Isabella II; minister of war under Narváez (1864). Participated in Prim y Prats revolution against Isabella (1868); minister of state ad interim (1871); on proclamation of republic (1873), minister of war.

**Fer·nán'dez de En·ci'so** (fĕr·nän'dāth [-dās] thā än·thē'sō [-sē'sō]), **Martín.** 1470?–?1528. Spanish colonizer, b. Seville; to America (1500); settled as lawyer at Santo Domingo. Founded Santa María la Antigua, Darien (1510). Author of *Suma de Geografía,* first account in Spanish of discoveries in New World (1519).

**Fernández de la Cue'va** (lä kwā'vä), **Francisco.** Duque **de Al'bu·quer'que** (thā äl'bōō·kĕr'kā). Spanish administrator; viceroy of Mexico (1653–60), of Sicily (1660 ff.). His grandson **Francisco Fernández de la Cueva Hen·rí'quez** (ān·rē'kāth; -kās), Duque **de Albuquerque,** was viceroy of Mexico (1702–11). Albuquerque, New Mexico, founded at this time, was named in his honor.

**Fer·nán'dez de Li·zar'di** (fĕr·nän'dās thā lē·sär'thē), **José Joaquín.** 1776–1827. Mexican novelist, known esp. for the picaresque novel *El Periquillo Sarniento* (1816; Eng. translation *The Itching Parrot,* 1941).

**Fer·nán'dez de Na'var·re'te** (fĕr·nän'dāth thā nä'vär·rĕ'tā), **Martín.** See NAVARRETE.

**Fernández de Pa·len'cia** (pä·lān'thyä), **Diego.** 1520?–?1581. Spanish soldier and historian; historiographer of Peru (1556). Known esp. for his *Primera y Segunda Parte de la Historia del Perú,* account of the conquest of Peru, covering period 1544–64 (pub. 1571).

**Fernández Guer'ra y Or'be** (gĕr'rä ē ôr'bā), **Aureliano.** 1816–1891. Spanish dramatist and scholar.

**Fer·nán'dez Ma·drid'** (fĕr·nän'dās mä·thrē(th)'), **José.** 1789–1830. South American physician, statesman, and writer, b. Cartagena, Colombia. Educ. at Bogotá; participated in Colombian revolt for independence (1810); elected president of Colombia (1816). Captured by Spaniards and interned (1816–25) at Havana, Cuba; Colombian minister to England (1825 ff.). His works include poems (considered his best work), the tragedies *Atala* (1822) and *Guatimozín* (1827), and scientific works.

**Fer·nán'dez Na'var·re'te** (fĕr·nän'dāth nä'vär·rĕ'tā), **Juan.** *Called* **El Mu'do** (ĕl mōō'thō), *i.e.* the Mute. 1526–1579. Spanish painter; pupil of Titian; court painter to Philip II (1568 ff.); employed on decoration of the Escorial.

**Fernando.** Portuguese and Spanish form of FERDINAND.

**Fer·nán' Gon·zá'lez** (fĕr·nän' gôn·thä'lāth). 910–970. Count of Castile; continually in rebellion against León; ruled as first king of Castile (932–970); fought Moors.

**Fer'nel'** (fĕr'nĕl'), **Jean.** *Lat.* **Fer·ne'li·us** (fēr·nē'lĭ·ŭs; -nēl'yŭs). 1497–1558. Called "the modern Galen." French physician, astronomer, and mathematician.

**Fern'korn** (fĕrn'kôrn), **Anton Dominik von.** 1813–1878. German sculptor and bronze founder; settled in Vienna (1840); director of imperial bronze foundry.

**Fer'now** (fĕr'nō), **Bern'hard** (bĕrn'härt) **E'du·ard** (ā'dōō·ärt). 1851–1923. Forester, b. Inowrazlaw, Posen, Germany; to U.S. (1876). Chief, Division of Forestry, U.S. Department of Agriculture (1886–98); organized forestry school in Cornell U. (1898–1903); head of forestry department, U. of Toronto (1907–19).

**Fernow, Karl Ludwig.** 1763–1808. German writer on art; at Weimar, member of Goethe's circle.

**Fé'ron'** (fā'rôN'), **Firmin Éloi.** 1802–1876. French painter.

**Fer'ra·bo'sco** (fār'rä·bôs'kō) *or* **Fe'ra·bo'sco** (fā'rä-). Family of musicians of Italian origin, settled in England in 16th century, including: **Alfonso** (fl. 1544–1587), composer esp. of madrigals, pensioned by Queen Elizabeth (1567); his son **Alfonso** (d. 1628), lutanist and composer, musical instructor to Prince Henry (1605), and composer in ordinary to Charles I (1626); and his son **Alfonso** (d. 1661), musician in ordinary to Charles I (1628).

**Fer·rán'** (fĕr·rän'), **Jaime.** 1852–1929. Spanish bacteriologist; credited with the discovery of an anticholera serum.

**Fer'rand'** (fĕ'räN'), **Marie Louis.** 1753–1807. French soldier; with Rochambeau in American Revolution.

**Ferrante.** Ital. form of FERDINAND (kings of Naples).

**Fer·ran'ti** (fĕ·răn'tĭ), **Sebastian Zia'ni de** (dzyä'nĭ dā). 1864–1930. English electrical engineer; known esp. for work on generating and distributing high-potential electrical current; patented 176 inventions, including the Ferranti alternator (1882) and Ferranti cables.

**Fer'rar** (fĕr'ēr), **Nicholas.** 1592–1637. English theologian; B.A., Cantab. (1610). Purchased manor in Huntingdonshire, and established religious Utopian community largely composed of members of his own family; introduced bookbinding as industry of the community; community broken up by Parliament (1647).

**Fer·ra'ra** (fār·rä'rä), **Andrea.** 16th-century Italian broadswordmaker; armorer at Belluno (1585).

**Fer·ra'ri** (fār·rä'rē), **Bartolommeo.** 1497–1544. Italian ecclesiastic; a founder (1530) of the Barnabites, or order of Regular Clerks of Saint Paul.

**Ferrari, Benedetto.** 1597–1681. Italian poet and composer; theorbo virtuoso; wrote libretto of and produced *Andromeda*, said to have been first publicly performed opera (Venice, 1637).

**Ferrari, Gaudenzio.** 1484?–1546. Lombard painter.

**Ferrari, Giuseppe.** 1812–1876. Italian philosopher, historian, and statesman. Disciple of Romagnosi and Vico. Elected deputy (1859); opposed Cavour's single monarchy; professor, Turin, Milan, Rome; senator (1876).

**Ferrari, Luigi.** 1810–1894. Italian sculptor.

**Ferrari, Paolo.** 1822–1889. Italian dramatist and critic.

**Fer·ra'ri–Fon·ta'na** (fār·rä'rē·fôn·tä'nä), **Edoardo.** 1878–1936. Italian operatic tenor; m. Margarete Matzenauer (1912); joined Metropolitan Opera Co., New York (1913); member of Chicago Grand Opera Co. (1915–16).

**Fer·ra'ris** (fār·rä'rēs), **Galileo.** 1847–1897. Italian physicist and electrical engineer. Discovered principle of the rotary magnetic field (1885) which led to the development of polyphase motors and of the hydroelectric industry in Italy; devised transformers for alternating current. Established first electrical engineering school in Italy (1886–87).

**Fer'ré'** (fĕ'rā'), **Charles Théophile.** 1845–1871. A leader of the Commune of Paris (1871); prefect of police (May 14–24, 1871); captured and shot (Nov. 28, 1871).

**Fer·rei'ra** (fĕr·rā'ē·rȧ), **Antônio.** 1528–1569. Portuguese poet; follower of Sá de Miranda, and a founder of Portuguese classicism, imitating Italian and Latin verse forms. Author of the earliest known Portuguese tragedy, *Inês de Castro* (pub. 1587), of the comedies *Bristo* and *O Cioso*, and of sonnets, odes, epigrams, and epithalamiums.

**Ferreira, Tomas Antônio Ribeiro–.** See RIBEIRO-FERREIRA.

**Fer'rel** (fĕr'ĕl), **William.** 1817–1891. American meteorologist; with U.S. Coast and Geodetic Survey (1867–1882) and Signal Service (1882–86).

**Ferrer,** Saint **Vincent,** *or Span.* San **Vicente.** See Saint VINCENT FERRER.

**Fer·re'ras** (fĕr·rĕ'räs), **Juan de.** 1652–1735. Spanish historian; author of *Sinopsis Histórica Cronológica de España* (16 vols., 1700–16).

**Fer·rer' Guar'dia** (fĕr·rĕr' gwär'thyä), **Francisco.** 1859–1909. Spanish freethinker, revolutionary, and educator, b. Alella. Was bequeathed legacy by Catholic woman for purpose of founding a school; French ecclesiastical authorities unsuccessfully sought to utilize legacy in founding church school; in Barcelona (1901), founded Escuela Moderna, devoted to antireligious and anarchistic doctrine. Acquitted (1907) on charges of complicity in attempt to assassinate king and queen of Spain (1906); to England (1909). Returned on hearing of uprising in Barcelona; arrested on charges of complicity in uprising, convicted, and executed (Oct. 13, 1909); his trial caused downfall of Maura ministry and created violent antagonism abroad against Spain and Catholicism.

**Fer·re'ro** (fĕ·rā'rō), **Edward.** 1831–1899. American army officer, b. Granada, Spain; to U.S. as a child. Engaged at Second Bull Run, Antietam, Fredericksburg; served under Grant in Vicksburg campaign; criticized for handling of division at Petersburg and Knoxville; mustered out (1865).

**Fer·re'ro** (fār·râ'rō), **Guglielmo.** 1871–1942. Italian historian and author; ardent advocate of Italian intervention in World War. Among his works translated into English are *The Female Offender* (with Cesare Lombroso, 1895), *Greatness and Decline of Rome* (1907–09), *Ancient Rome and Modern America* (1914), *Short History of Rome* (with Corrado Barbagallo, 1918), *Four Years of Fascism* (1924).

**Fer'rers** (fĕr'ērz). Name, taken from Ferrières-St.-Hilaire, Normandy, of an old Norman-English feudal house possessing, after the Conquest (1066), great fief in the Midlands and the earldom of Derby (1138–?1279). The Ferrers barony passed to the Devereux family (1450) and thence to the Shirleys. **Laurence Shir'ley** (shûr'lĭ), 4th Earl **Ferrers** (1720–1760), who killed his land steward in paroxysm of rage, was the last English nobleman to be hanged as a felon.

**Ferrers, George.** 1500?–1579. English politician and

poet; M.P. (1542, 1545, 1553, 1554, 1555, 1571); master of the king's pastimes (1551, 1552); lord of misrule to Queen Mary I (1553); aided in suppressing Wyatt's rebellion (1554). One of the authors of the series of historical poems entitled *A Mirror for Magistrates.*

**Ferrers of Groby,** Baron. See *John Grey,* under GREY family.

**Fer'ri** (fĕr'rē), **Ciro.** 1634–1689. Italian painter; pupil and successor of Pietro da Cortona.

**Ferri, Enrico.** 1856–1929. Italian criminologist and politician; adherent of Fascism (1926 ff.); senator (1929). Edited socialist organ *Avanti* (1898 ff.).

**Ferri, Luigi.** 1826–1895. Italian philosopher; educ. in France; professor in France (1850–55), at Florence (1863), Rome (1871 ff.); editor, *Rivista Italiana di Filosofia.*

**Fer'rié'** (fĕ'ryā'), **Gustave Auguste.** 1868–1932. French general and wireless expert. Made improvements in wireless telegraphy, esp. in military use during World War; equipped Eiffel Tower as a wireless station; pioneered in television and wireless transmission of photographs.

**Fer'ri·er** (fĕr'ĭ·ẽr), Sir **David.** 1843–1928. Scottish cerebral anatomist and neurologist. Known for research on physiology of the brain, esp. on localization of cerebral functions.

**Fer'rier'** (fĕ'ryā'), **Gabriel Joseph Marie Augustin.** 1847–1914. French painter; professor, Académie des Beaux-Arts (from 1906).

**Fer'ri·er** (fĕr'ĭ·ẽr), **James Frederick.** 1808–1864. Scottish philosopher; wrote *Institutes of Metaphysic* (1854).

**Fer'rier'** (fĕ'ryā'), **Paul.** 1843–1920. French playwright; author of comedies, comic operas, and lyrical dramas.

**Fer'ri·er** (fĕr'ĭ·ẽr), **Susan Edmonstone.** 1782–1854. Scottish novelist; author of *Marriage* (1818), *The Inheritance* (1824), *Destiny* (1831).

**Fer'ris** (fĕr'ĭs), **George Washington Gale.** 1859–1896. American engineer; in railroad and bridge engineering (from 1881); built the Ferris wheel for the World's Columbian Exposition, Chicago (1893).

**Ferris, Jean** (zhän) **Lé'on'** (lā'ôɴ') **Gé'rôme'** (zhā'rōm'). 1863–1930. American painter. He was named for the French painter Jean Léon Gérôme (*q.v.*).

**Ferris, Woodbridge Nathan.** 1853–1928. American educator and political leader, b. near Spencer, N.Y. Founded and headed Ferris Institute, Big Rapids, Mich. (from 1884). Governor of Michigan (1913–16); U.S. senator (1923–28).

**Fer·ruc'ci** (fâr·rōōt'chē), **Andrea.** 1465–1526. Tuscan sculptor and architect; known esp. for marble baptismal font in cathedral of Pistoia.

**Fer'ry'** (fĕ'rē'), **Gabriel.** *Pseudonym of* **Eugène Louis Gabriel de Belle'mare'** (bĕl'mȧr'). 1809–1852. French writer; spent seven years in Mexico; contributed studies of Mexican life and customs to *Revue des Deux Mondes.* His son **Gabriel de Bellemare,** also known as **Gabriel Ferry** (1846– ? ), was author of plays and novels.

**Ferry, Jules François Camille.** 1832–1893. French lawyer and statesman; member of Government of National Defense (1870–71); premier of France (1880–81; 1883–85); pursued vigorous colonial policy extending French possessions in Africa and Asia.

**Fer'sen** (fĕr'sĕn), Count **Fredrik Axel von.** 1719–1794. Swedish politician; an army officer, rose to rank of field marshal; in politics, a vigorous defender of the rights of the nobility against encroachments by the sovereign. His son Count **Hans Axel** (1755–1810) was a soldier; aide-de-camp to Rochambeau in American Revolution; resident at French court at Versailles, and known as an admirer of Marie Antoinette; disguised as coachman, aided royal family in attempt to flee from France (1791) when they were arrested at Varennes; returned to Sweden; murdered in a popular uprising.

**Fers'man** (fyārs'mŭn), **Aleksandr Evgenievich.** 1883–1945. Russian mineralogist.

**Fer'stel** (fĕr'stĕl), Baron **Heinrich von.** 1828–1883. Austrian architect.

**Fes'ca** (fĕs'kä), **Friedrich Ernst.** 1789–1826. German violinist and composer of chamber music, 3 symphonies, 4 overtures, 2 operas, and sacred music. His son **Alexander Ernst** (1820–1849) was a pianist; composer of 4 operas, chamber music, and songs.

**Fesch** (fĕsh), **Joseph.** 1763–1839. Half brother of Letizia Buonaparte, mother of Napoleon. French Roman Catholic prelate; archbishop of Lyon (1802); created cardinal (1803). Arranged for consecration of Napoleon as emperor by the pope at Paris (1804). Opposed certain of Napoleon's policies (from 1810). Banished by Bourbons (1815) and retired to Rome (1815–39).

**Fess** (fĕs), **Simeon D.** 1861–1936. American educator and politician, b. in Allen County, Ohio. President, Antioch Coll. (1907–17); member, U.S. House of Representatives (1913–23) and U.S. Senate (1923–35).

**Fes'sen·den** (fĕs''n·dĕn), **Reginald Aubrey.** 1866–1932. Physicist and radio technician, b. Milton, Canada, of American parentage. Professor, U. of Pittsburgh (1893–1900). Consulting engineer, Submarine Signal Co. (1910–32).

**Fessenden, Thomas Green.** 1771–1837. American satirist, b. Walpole, N.H.; published *Democracy Unveiled, or Tyranny Stripped of the Garb of Patriotism* (1805), a long, bitter, poetic attack on Jefferson and other Democratic leaders. In Vermont (1809–22); practiced law and edited Brattleboro *Reporter* (1815–16), and Bellows Falls *Advertiser* (1817–22). Moved to Boston (1822); established and edited *New England Farmer* (1822–37). Further indulged his gift for satire in *Pills, Poetical, Political, and Philosophical*...(1809).

**Fessenden, William Pitt.** 1806–1869. American political leader, b. Boscawen, N.H. Member, U.S. House of Representatives (1841–43); U.S. Senate (1854–64); opposed Kansas-Nebraska bill (1854); member, senate finance committee (1857–64); opposed Buchanan administration; supported Lincoln's administration. U.S. secretary of the treasury in Lincoln's cabinet (1864–65). U.S. senator (1865–69).

**Fess'ler** (fĕs'lẽr), **I·gnaz'** (ĭ·gnäts'; ĭg'näts) **Au·re'li·us** (ou·rā'lē·ŏŏs). 1756–1839. Hungarian ecclesiastic and historian. Entered Capuchin order (1773; dismissed 1781); converted to Lutheranism (1791); in Berlin (1796–1808); joined Royal York lodge of Freemasons (1796) which he and Fichte converted into the Grand Royal York Lodge of Prussia (1798). Consistorial president of evangelical communities (1820) and superintendent (1833) and ecclesiastical adviser of Lutheran communities in St. Petersburg.

**Fe'sta** (fĕs'tä), **Costanzo.** d. 1545. Italian singer and composer; forerunner of Palestrina.

**Fes'tus** (fĕs'tŭs), **Porcius.** d. about 62 A.D. Successor of Felix (*q.v.*) as Roman procurator of Judea (58 or 60–62 A.D.); before him St. Paul made his famous "appeal unto Caesar" (*Acts* xxv. 12).

**Festus, Sextus Pompeius.** Roman grammarian and lexicographer of 2d century A.D.; compiled an epitome of Marcus Verrius Flaccus's *De Verborum Significatu.*

**Fet** (fyāt), **Afanasi Afanasievich.** *Orig. Ger. family name* **Foeth** (fût). *Surname legally changed* (1876) *to* **Shen·shin'** (shyĕn·shĭn'). 1820?–1892. Russian poet; friend of Tolstoi and Turgenev. Best known for his nature poetry and love lyrics.

**Feth Ali.** Variant of FATH ALI.

**Feti, Domenico.** See Domenico FETTI.

**Fé'tis'** (fā'tēs'), **François Joseph.** 1784–1871. Belgian composer and writer on music; founded and edited in Paris (1827–33) *Revue Musicale*, first paper devoted to musical criticism; director of Brussels Conservatory and court Kapellmeister in Brussels (from 1833); composed operas, symphonies, church and chamber music, piano and organ pieces, and songs. His son **Édouard Louis François** (1812–1909), librarian and writer on music and art, was long librarian of Royal Library in Brussels, and professor of aesthetics at Academy of Fine Arts. Another son, **Adolphe Louis Eugène** (1820–1873), was a pianist, teacher, and composer, in Brussels and Antwerp, and (from 1856) in Paris.

**Fet'ter·man** (fĕt'ẽr·măn), **William Judd.** 1833?–1866. American army officer; ambushed and killed by Indians, "Fetterman massacre" (Dec. 21, 1866).

**Fet'tes** (fĕt'ĭs), Sir **William.** 1750–1836. Scottish merchant; created endowment for education of orphaned or needy children (1830), which later developed into Fettes College, at Edinburgh.

**Fet'ti** (fāt'tē) *or* **Fe'ti** (fā'tē), **Domenico.** 1589–1624. Italian painter of Roman school.

**Feuch'ters·le'ben** (foiκ'tẽrs·lā'bĕn), Baron **Ernst von.** 1806–1849. Viennese physician, poet, and philosopher.

**Feucht'wang'er** (foiκt'văng'ẽr), **Lion.** 1884–1958. German novelist and dramatist, b. in Munich of Jewish origin; expatriate in London and France; to U.S. (1940). Author of adaptations of old plays, original dramas, as *Warren Hastings* (1916) and *The Oil Islands* (1927), a volume of satirical poems, and historical and modern novels, as *The Ugly Duchess* (1923), *Jud Süss* (1925; Amer. title *Power*), *Success* (1930), *Josephus* (1932), *The Oppermanns* (1933; against the Hitler regime), *The Jew of Rome* (1935), *The False Nero* (1937), *Paris Gazette* (1939), *The Day Will Come* (1942), etc.

**Feu'er·bach** (foi'ẽr·bäκ). Name of a German family including: **Paul Johann Anselm von Feuerbach** (1775–1833), jurist and philosopher; specialist in criminology and penal reform; entered department of justice at Munich (1805) and became privy councilor. Originated new theory of psychological coercion or intimidation in criminal law, favored abolition of torture, and championed rigorist application of penal law by judges and exemplary rather than vindictive punishment. His reforms in penal legislation influenced other European states.

His sons: (1) **Anselm** (1798–1851), archaeologist, professor of philology at Freiburg (from 1836), author of *Der Vatikanische Apollo* (1833) and a history of Greek plastic art, etc. Anselm's 2d wife, **Henriette,** *nee* **Hey'den·reich** [hī'dĕn·rīκ] (1812–1892), helped edit his works, furthered the artistic studies of her stepson Anselm (see next ¶) and edited his memoirs under the title *Ein Vermächtnis* (1882). (2) **Karl Wilhelm** (1800–1834), mathematician and professor at Erlangen, after whom the Feuerbach (9-point) circle is named. (3) **Ludwig Andreas** (1804–1872), philosopher, pupil of Hegel in Berlin; abandoned Hegelian idealism for a naturalistic materialism, subsequently attacked orthodox religion and immortality, concluded that God is the outward projection of man's inward nature; author of *Das Wesen des Christentums* (1840), *Das Wesen der Religion* (1845), etc.

Anselm's son **Anselm** (1829–1880), historical and portrait painter; pupil of Schadow in Düsseldorf (1846) and Rahl in Munich (1848); worked in Paris, Karlsruhe, and (1856–72) Rome; professor at Vienna Academy (1873–76); resident thereafter chiefly in Venice.

**Feuil'let'** (fû'yĕ'), **Octave.** 1821–1890. French novelist and playwright; among his novels are *La Petite Comtesse* (1857), *Le Roman d'un Jeune Homme Pauvre* (1858), *Monsieur de Camors* (1867), *Histoire d'une Parisienne* (1881), *La Morte* (1886); among his plays are *Le Pour et le Contre* (1853), *Le Village* (1856), *Dalila* (1857), *Le Cheveu Blanc* (1860), *Montjoie* (1863), *Le Sphinx* (1874), *Chamillac* (1886).

**Feul'ner** (foil'nẽr), **Adolph.** 1884–1945. German art scholar; regarded as authority on medieval art and baroque sculpture and painting.

**Feurial, Le.** See FEVRIAL.

**Fé'val'** (fā'väl'), **Paul Henri Corentin.** 1817–1887. French novelist and playwright; among his fictional works were *Les Mystères de Londres* (11 vols., 1844), *Le Bossu* (1858), *L'Hôtel Carnavalet* (1877); among his plays, *Belles de Nuit* and the very popular *Le Bossu.*

**Feversham,** Earl of. See *Louis de Durfort de Duras,* under DURFORT family.

**Fe'vret' de Saint'–Mes'min'** (fā'vrĕ' dẽ săɴ'mā'măɴ'), **Charles Balthasar Julien.** = Charles Balthazar Julien Fevret de SAINT-MÉMIN.

**Fe'vri'al'** (fā'vrē'äl') *or* **Le Feu'rial'** (lẽ fû'ryäl'). d. 1525 or 1528. Court fool of Louis XII and Francis I of France. Appears, under name **Tri'bou'let'** (trē'bōō'lĕ'), in Rabelais and in Hugo's *Le Roi s'Amuse.*

**Few** (fū), **William Preston.** 1867–1940. American educator, b. Greenville, S.C.; first president, Duke U., including Trinity College (1924–40).

**Fewkes** (fūks), **Jesse Walter.** 1850–1930. American ethnologist; in Bureau of American Ethnology (1895–1918); chief of bureau (1918–28). Noted esp. for investigations of Hopi Indian culture and history.

**Fey** (fī), **Emil.** 1888–1938. Austrian soldier and politician; in World War I; took active part (1930) in organizing in Vienna units of Heimwehr, anti-Socialist military force. Vice-chancellor in Dollfuss cabinet (1933); commanded government and Heimwehr forces that crushed Socialist uprising (1934). Minister of interior in Schuschnigg's cabinet (1934–35). Committed suicide after Nazis annexed Austria.

**Fey'deau'** (fā'dō'), **Ernest Aimé.** 1821–1873. French novelist and poet. His son **Georges** (1862–1921) was a playwright; author of the popular *Le Tailleur pour Dames* (1887), and vaudeville sketches, comedies, and one-act humorous pieces.

**Feyjoo.** Variant of FEIJÓ or FEIJOO.

**Feyn'man** (fīn'măn), **Richard Phillips.** 1918– . Amer. physicist, b. New York City. Awarded Nobel prize in physics (1965) with J. Schwinger and S. Tomonaga for work on quantum electrodynamics.

**ff.** Modern representation of an early method of indicating capital F.

**ffoulkes** (fouks), **Charles John.** 1868–1947. English museum curator and authority on armor.

**Ffrang'con–Da'vies** (frăng'kŭn·dā'vēz; -vĭs), **David Thomas.** 1858?–1918. Welsh clergyman of the Established Church of Wales; known as oratorio singer; sang role of Jesus in Sir Edward Elgar's oratorio *The Apostles.* His biography written by his daughter **Marjorie** (1938). Another daughter, **Gwen,** actress, created role of Eve in Shaw's *Back to Methuselah.*

**Fi'a·cre** (fē'ȧ·kẽr; *Fr.* fyȧ'kr') *or* **Fi'a·chrach** (fē'ȧ·kräκ), Saint. d. about 670. Irish nobleman; founder of a monastery at Breuil, near Paris; famous for reputed miraculous cure of a tumor. His name was adopted by Hôtel St. Fiacre, an inn at Paris where small hackney coaches (hence called *fiacres*) are said to have been first offered for hire (c. 1640).

**Fi·a'la** (fī·ä'lȧ), **Anthony.** 1869–1950. American explorer, b. Jersey City Heights, N.J. Trooper and war correspondent in Spanish-American War (1898); photographer with Baldwin-Ziegler polar expedition (1901–02); commander, Ziegler polar expedition (1903–05); with Theodore Roosevelt on trip through Brazil (1914).

**Fialin, Jean Gilbert Victor.** See duc de PERSIGNY.

**Fiam·met'ta** (fyäm·măt'tä). Name under which Boccaccio celebrated Princess **Maria de'i Con'ti d'A·qui'no** (dä'ē kōn'tē dä·kwē'nō), believed to have been daughter of Robert d'Anjou, King of Naples.

**Fiammingo, Pietro.** See Pierre Antoine VERSCHAFFELT.

**Fi'bich** (fĭ'bĭκ), **Zdenko.** 1850–1900. Czech composer of operas, as *Bukovín* (1874), *Blaník* (1881), *Šárka* (1898), the melodramatic trilogy *Hippodamia* (1890–91), about 400 piano pieces, symphonic poems, overtures, symphonies, chamber music, choral works, songs, etc.

**Fi'bi·ger** (fē'bē·gẽr), **Johannes.** 1867–1928. Danish pathologist; credited with first producing cancer experimentally (in rats); awarded 1926 Nobel prize for physiology and medicine (1927).

**Fi'bo·nac'ci** (fē'bō·nät'chē), **Leonardo.** *Also known as* **Leonardo Pi·sa'no** (pē·sä'nō). 1180?–?1250. Italian mathematician; author of *Liber Abaci*, first work of a European on Indian and Arabian mathematics.

**Fi'chet'** (fē'shĕ'), **Guillaume.** 1433?–?1480. French scholar; installed at the Sorbonne the first printing press in France. See Ulrich GERING.

**Fich'te** (fĭκ'tĕ), **Johann Gottlieb.** 1762–1814. German philosopher and metaphysician, b. Rammenau, Upper Lusatia; exponent of a system of transcendental idealism emphasizing self-activity of reason and setting forth a perfected Kantian system, or science of knowledge, in which he connected practical reason with pure reason. At first an ardent disciple of Kant (1790), visiting him at Königsberg (1791); resident in Berlin as member of Romantic circle and private lecturer (1799); delivered his famous patriotic lectures *Reden an die Deutsche Nation* (1807–08); professor and first rector of newly-founded U. of Berlin (1810–14). Author of *Versuch einer Kritik aller Offenbarung*, first attributed to Kant (1792), *Über den Begriff der Wissenschaftslehre* (1794), *Die Bestimmung des Menschen* (1800), *Die Anweisung zum Seligen Leben* (1806), etc.

His son **Immanuel Hermann von Fichte** (1796–1879), philosopher, exponent of an ethical or speculative theism; professor, Bonn (1836) and Tübingen (1842–63); founded (1837) *Zeitschrift für Philosophie und Spekulative Theologie;* called first German philosophical congress at Gotha (1841); ennobled (1867). Author of *System der Ethik* (2 vols., 1850–53), *Anthropologie* (1856), *Die Theistische Weltanschauung* (1873), etc.

**Fi·ci'no** (fē·chē'nō), **Marsilio.** 1433–1499. Italian philosopher; known chiefly as Platonist; commissioned by the elder Cosimo de' Medici to translate (into Latin) works of Plato and several Neo-Platonists.

**Fick** (fĭk), **Adolf Eugen.** 1829–1901. German physiologist.

**Fick, August.** 1833–1916. German philologist; professor, Göttingen (1876–87) and Breslau (1887–91).

**Fick, Rudolf Armin.** 1866–1939. German anatomist.

**Fick'e** (fĭk'ĕ; -ē), **Arthur Davison.** 1883–1945. American poet; author of *From the Isles* (1907), *Sonnets of a Portrait Painter* (1914), *Out of Silence* (1924), *The Secret* (1936), *Tumultuous Shore* (1942), etc.

**Fick'er** (fĭk'ẽr), **Heinrich von.** 1881–1957. German meteorologist.

**Ficker, Johannes.** 1861–1944. German Protestant theologian.

**Ficker, Julius von.** 1826–1902. German jurist and historian; author of *Forschungen zur Reichs- und Rechtsgeschichte Italiens* (4 vols., 1868–74), etc.

**Fic'quel'mont'** (fē'kĕl'môɴ'), Count **Karl Ludwig von.** 1777–1857. Austrian general and statesman; took part in campaigns against France (until 1814); ambassador to Stockholm, Florence, and Naples (1815 ff.); minister in St. Petersburg (1829–39) and confidant of Metternich; minister of foreign affairs and minister president (briefly, 1848).

**Fie'dler** (fē'dlẽr), **Max,** *in full* **August Max.** 1859–1939. German orchestra conductor and pianist. Conductor of Boston Symphony Orchestra (1908–12); municipal director of music, Essen (from 1916). His compositions include a symphony, an overture, chamber music, piano pieces, and songs.

**Fieh'ler** (fē'lẽr), **Karl.** 1895– . German politician; joined Sturmabteilung (Storm Troops) and took part in attempted coup d'état (1923); arrested and imprisoned for fifteen months. Deputy chief of National Socialist party and leader of Sturmabteilung group.

**Field** (fēld), **Cyrus West.** 1819–1892. American financier, b. Stockbridge, Mass.; son of David Dudley Field (1781–1867), *q.v.* Amassed fortune in paper business (1841–53). Promoted first submarine telegraph cable between America and Europe (from 1854; cable laying begun 1857); despite loss of personal fortune in depression of 1857, continued to find capital and finally succeeded (1858; messages interchanged between Queen Victoria and President Buchanan Aug. 16); following cessation of operation after a few weeks, resumed project, new cable embodying technical improvements being laid (1866), a great success. Interested himself in building of New York's elevated railway (from 1877). Through serious business reverses again lost fortune in his later years.

**Field, David Dudley.** 1781–1867. American Congregational clergyman, b. East Guilford (now Madison), Conn.; grad. Yale (1802); pastor at Haddam, Conn. (1804–18; 1837–44), Stockbridge, Mass. (1819–37), Higganum, Conn. (1844–51). For his sons Cyrus West, David Dudley, Henry Martyn, and Stephen Johnson, and his grandson Stephen Dudley, see separate biographies.

**Field, David Dudley.** 1805–1894. American lawyer, b. Haddam, Conn.; son of David Dudley Field (*q.v.*). Practiced, New York City; counsel in important cases, many involving constitutional issues. Interested in codification of law; instrumental in obtaining adoption of Code of Civil Procedure (now in force in whole or in part in 24 States); also instrumental in drafting of New York codes (completed 1865); attempted an international code, collaborating in preparation (1872) of *Draft Outline of an International Code.*

**Field, Eugene.** 1850–1895. American poet and journalist, b. St. Louis, Mo. Educ. Williams, Knox, and Missouri. Traveled abroad, on staff of St. Joseph (Mo.) *Gazette*, St. Louis *Journal*, Kansas City *Times*, and Denver *Tribune;* on staff of Chicago *Morning News* (later named the *Record*), as editor of column *Sharps and Flats* (1883–95), in which first appeared most of his work, a mixture of whimsical narrative, children's verse, wit and humor. Author of *The Tribune Primer* (1882), *A Little Book of Western Verse* (1889), *A Little Book of Profitable Tales* (1889–90), *With Trumpet and Drum* (1892), *Second Book of Verse* (1892), *Echoes from the Sabine Farm* (1892). Best known as a poet of childhood, good examples of his children's verse being *Wynken, Blynken, and Nod; Little Boy Blue; The Little Peach.*

**Field, Henry Martyn.** 1822–1907. American clergyman, b. Stockbridge, Mass.; son of David Dudley Field (1781–1867), *q.v.* Pastor of Third Presbyterian Church, St. Louis, Mo. (1842–47), Congregational Church, West

Springfield, Mass. (1851–54); moved to New York City and edited the *Evangelist* (1854–90).

**Field, John.** 1782–1837. British pianist and composer, b. Dublin; best known for his *Nocturnes*, which are said to have inspired Chopin.

**Field, Joseph M.** 1810–1856. Actor, b. probably in Dublin; to U.S. as a child. Well known as tragedian, later as comedian, in theaters of New Orleans, St. Louis, Mobile, and Cincinnati. His daughter **Mary Katherine Keem'le** (?kēm'lē), *known as* **Kate** (1838–1896), b. St. Louis, Mo., journalist, actress, lecturer, author; edited her own journal, *Kate Field's Washington* (from 1891); author of *Adelaide Ristori* (1867), *Mad on Purpose, a Comedy* (1868), *Hap-Hazard* (1873), *Ten Days in Spain* (1875), etc.

**Field, Marshall.** 1834–1906. American merchant, b. near Conway, Mass. Clerk in dry-goods store, Pittsfield, Mass. (1851–56). Moved to Chicago (1856); became clerk in dry-goods firm, Cooley, Wadsworth & Co.; general manager (1861); partner (1862); continued expansion and change of firm names until organization became Marshall Field & Co. (1881); remained head of business as it grew to be largest wholesale and retail dry-goods establishment in world (1881–1906). Gave ground for U. of Chicago site; gave funds for Columbian Museum at Chicago World's Fair (1893), later developed into Field Museum of Natural History.

**Field, Michael.** Pseudonym of **Katharine Harris Bradley** (1846–1914) and **Edith Emma Cooper** (1862–1913). English collaborating authors of lyric poetry and poetic dramas (1884–1913).

**Field, Nathaniel,** *orig.* **Nathan.** 1587–1633. English actor and playwright; comedian with Children of the Queen's Revels, who performed Ben Jonson's *Cynthia's Revels* (1600). Author of *A Woman's a Weathercock* (1612), *Amends for Ladies* (1618), *The Fatal Dowry* (with Massinger; 1632).

**Field, Rachel Lyman.** 1894–1942. American writer, b. New York City; m. Arthur S. Pederson (1935). Author of many one-act plays, juveniles, verse, and novels.

**Field, Stephen Dudley.** 1846–1913. American inventor, b. Stockbridge, Mass.; grandson of David Dudley Field (1781–1867). Inventor of a multiple-call district telegraph box (1874), a dynamo quadruplex telegraph (1879–80), a rapid-speed stock ticker (1884), an electric locomotive (with Rudolf Eickemeyer; 1887).

**Field, Stephen Johnson.** 1816–1899. American jurist, b. Haddam, Conn.; son of David Dudley Field (1781–1867), *q.v.* Associate justice, U.S. Supreme Court (1863–97); resigned. His decisions important in development of constitutional law.

**Fiel'ding** (fēl'dĭng), **Copley,** *in full* **Antony Vandyke Copley.** 1787–1855. English water-color painter, esp. of landscapes and marines.

**Fielding, Henry.** 1707–1754. Half brother of Sir John Fielding. English novelist and playwright, b. near Glastonbury, Somersetshire. Called to bar (1740); justice of the peace for Westminster (1748); chairman of quarter sessions at Hicks's Hall (1749). Began literary career with comedies for the stage, including *The Temple Beau* (1730), *The Modern Husband* (1732), adaptations from Molière, and *Tom Thumb* (1730), a burlesque on the popular playwrights of the day; reached his height in series of realistic novels including *Joseph Andrews* (1742), *Jonathan Wild* (1743), *Tom Jones* (1749), and *Amelia* (1751); author also of a *Journal of a Voyage to Lisbon* (pub. 1755). His sister **Sarah** (1710–1768), also a writer, translated Xenophon's *Memorabilia*, and wrote romances including *The Adventures of David Simple in Search of a Faithful Friend* (1744).

**Fielding,** Sir **John.** d. 1780. Half brother of Henry Fielding. English jurist.

**Fields** (fēldz), **Gracie.** *Maiden name* **Grace Stans'field** (stănz'fēld). 1898– . English comedienne, b. at Rochdale, Lancashire; m. Archie Pitt (divorced, 1940); m. (1940) film director Monty Banks (Mario Bianchi). Appeared in London with great success in *Mr. Tower of London* (over 4000 performances, 1918–25); became popular motion-picture actress.

**Fields, James Thomas.** 1817–1881. American author and publisher, b. Portsmouth, N.H. Partner in firm of Ticknor, Reed & Fields (in Boston, Mass.; 1838–54), known as Ticknor & Fields (1854–64). Succeeded James Russell Lowell as editor, *Atlantic Monthly* (1861–70). Author of *Poems* (1849), *Yesterdays with Authors* (1872), *In and Out of Doors with Charles Dickens* (1876). See W. D. TICKNOR.

**Fields, Lew.** See at Joseph M. WEBER.

**Fields, W. C.** *Orig. name* **William Claude Dukenfield.** 1880–1946. Amer. entertainer, b. Philadelphia, Pa. Appeared in the motion pictures *Mississippi, You Can't Cheat an Honest Man, My Little Chickadee,* etc.

**Fie'litz** (fē'lĭts), **Alexander von.** 1860–1930. German composer of songs, including the *Mädchenlieder* cycle, the operas *Vendetta* (1891) and *Das Stille Dorf* (1900), and chamber music.

**Fie'ne** (fē'nĕ), **Ernest.** 1894–1965. German-born American portrait and landscape painter, and etcher and lithograph artist.

**Fiennes** (fīnz), **William.** 1st Viscount **Saye' and Sele'** (sā' ăn(d) sēl'). 1582–1662. English parliamentary leader. Son of Richard Fiennes, 7th Baron Saye and Sele, descended from **James Fiennes** (d. 1450), Baron Saye and Sele, lord chamberlain and treasurer to Henry VI. Possessed land on Connecticut River (1632) and in New Hampshire (1633); proposed hereditary aristocracy in New England. Refused military oath to king (1639); privy councilor, master of court of wards, commissioner of treasury (1641); lord lieutenant of three counties and member of committee of safety (1642); turned scale in favor of Self-denying Ordinance in House of Lords; privy councilor and lord privy seal (1660). Saybrooke, Conn., named after Viscount Saye and Lord Brooke.

His son **Nathaniel** (1608?–1669) was a parliamentary leader; member of Long Parliament; member of committee of safety (1642); governor of Bristol; sentenced to death for surrendering Bristol to Prince Rupert (1643), but exonerated by Cromwell; member of House of Lords (1658); urged Cromwell to accept crown.

**Fierabrace.** See GUILLAUME D'ORANGE.

**Fie'schi** (fyĕs'kē), **Giuseppe Maria,** *Fr.* **Joseph Marie.** 1790–1836. Corsican conspirator; made unsuccessful attempt on life of Louis Philippe (July 28, 1835) with infernal machine, killing 18 people.

**Fie'sco** (fyĕs'kō) *or* **de' Fie'schi** (dā fyĕs'kē), **Giovanni Luigi.** Conte **di La·va'gna** (dē lä·vä'nyä). 1524?–1547. Genoese conspirator; plotted with Francis I of France, Pope Paul III, and Pier Luigi Farnese, Duke of Parma, the overthrow of Andrea Doria, Doge of Genoa, and Gianettino Doria, his nephew and appointed successor. Popularized by Cardinal de Retz, Jean Jacques Rousseau, and Schiller (in his tragedy *Fiesco,* 1783).

**Fie'so·le** (fyâ'zō·lā), **Giovanni da.** *Known as* Fra **An·ge'li·co** (än·jâ'lē·kō). *Orig. name* **Guido di Pie'tro** (dē pyâ'trō). 1387–1455. Italian Dominican friar and painter of religious subjects. Among his most famous works are frescoes at Orvieto.

**Fiesole, Mino da.** 1431?–?1481. Italian sculptor of the early Renaissance. Carved many monuments, portrait busts, altars, reliefs, tabernacles, madonnas, etc.

**Fife** (fīf), 1st Duke of. **Alexander William George Duff** (dŭf). 1849–1912. British nobleman; created duke of Fife on marriage (1889) to Princess Louise Victoria, eldest daughter of Edward VII. Their daughter **Alexandra** (1891–1959), duchess of Fife, married (1913) Prince Arthur of Connaught.

**Fígaro.** Pseudonym of Mariano José de LARRA.

**Figg** (fĭg), **James.** d. 1734. English pugilist, b. in Oxfordshire; won championship (1719).

**Fig′gis** (fĭg′ĭs), **Darrell.** *Pseudonym* **Michael Ire′land** (īr′lănd). 1882–1925. Irish poet and miscellaneous writer.

**Fig′ner** (fyĕg′nyẽr), **Vera Nikolaevna.** 1852–1942. Russian Soviet revolutionist; involved in assassination of Czar Alexander II (1881); imprisoned in Shlisselburg fortress for twenty years (1884–1904) and, on her release, exiled to province of Archangel until Revolution of 1917. Published *The Prisoners of Shlisselburg, After Shlisselburg,* and *Memoirs of a Revolutionary* (7 vols.).

**Fi·gue′ras y Mo·ra′gas** (fē·gā′räs ē mō·rä′gäs), **Estanislao.** 1818–1882. Spanish lawyer and statesman; sought establishment of republic after revolution of 1868; opposed Amadeus of Savoy during latter's reign (1870–73); president of provisional council of ministers on establishment of republic (1873); retired on restoration of monarchy (Dec., 1874).

**Fi′gue·ro′a** (fē′gā·rō′ä), **Francisco de.** 1536?–1620. Spanish poet; master of blank verse; his works include an eclogue *Tirsi,* sonnets, elegies, and canzoni.

**Figueroa, Francisco A·cu′ña de** (ä·kōō′nyä thā). 1790–1862. Uruguayan poet; author of *Mosáico Poético* (pub. 1857), a classic collection of poems, including a diary in verse describing siege of Montevideo in 1812–14.

**Figueroa y de Torres, Álvaro de.** See Conde de ROMANONES.

**Fi′guier′** (fē′gyā′), **Guillaume Louis.** 1819–1894. French writer; popularizer of science.

**Fi′lan·gie′ri** (fē′län·jâ′rē), **Gaetano.** 1752–1788. Italian jurist; author of *Scienza della Legislazione* (1780–85). His son **Carlo** (1784–1867), Principe **di Sa·tria′no** (sä·tryä′nō), Neapolitan general, was premier of the Two Sicilies (1859–60).

**Fi′la·re′te** (fē′lä·râ′tā). *Real name* **Antonio di Pie′tro A′ver·li′no** (dē pyâ′trō ä′vâr·lē′nō) *or* **A′ve·ru·li′no** (ä′vâ·rōō·lē′nō). 1400?–?1470. Florentine architect and sculptor; built bronze doors of St. Peter's (Rome) and Porta Giova of Sforzesco Castle (Milan); began Cathedral of Bergamo.

**Filch′ner** (fĭlk′nẽr), **Wilhelm.** 1877–1957. German traveler and explorer in Russia, the Balkans, Asia Minor, and (1900) over the Pamir region; explored East Tibet with his wife and Albert Tafel (1903–05); conducted 2d German Antarctic expedition on *Deutschland* into Weddell Sea (1911–12) and discovered southwestern continuation of Coats Land; established many magnetic stations and made maps of region traversed in Central Asiatic expedition (1925–28).

**Fildes** (fīldz), Sir **Luke,** *in full* **Samuel Luke.** 1844–1927. English genre and portrait painter, b. at Liverpool.

**Fi·lel′fo** (fē·lĕl′fō), **Francesco.** *Lat. surname* **Phi·lel′phus** (fĭ·lĕl′fŭs). 1398–1481. Italian humanist.

**Fi·lene′** (fĭ·lēn′; fī-; *the first is the usual pron. in the family*), **Edward Albert.** 1860–1937. American merchant; entered father's dry goods and clothing store in Boston; after father's death, became president of company, Wm. Filene & Sons. Successful in applying principles of scientific management in business; active in promoting employees' welfare. Student also of world economics. Succeeded (1937) as president of Wm. Filene & Sons by his brother **Lincoln** (1865–1957).

**Fi′li·ca′ia** (fē′lē·kä′yä), **Vincenzo da.** 1642–1707. Italian lyric poet. Known for his *Poesie Toscane* (1707), containing canzoni on Turkish wars (1684) and sonnets to Italy.

**Fi′li·pe′scu** (fē′lē·pĕ′skōō), **Nich′o·las** (nĭk′ō·lăs). 1862–1916. Rumanian politician; head of Young Conservative party (1910) and strong opponent of Ionescu; reorganized Rumanian army as minister of war (1910); zealously opposed pro-German party leader Marghiloman (from 1914) and supported Rumania's entry into World War on side of allies.

**Fi·lip′pi** (fē·lēp′pē), **Filippo de.** 1814–1867. Italian naturalist.

**Filippi, Filippo de.** 1869–1938. Italian Alpinist and explorer. On duke of the Abruzzi's Alaskan expedition when Mt. St. Elias was first ascended; also on the duke's African expedition exploring Ruwenzori (1906); to Kashmir on mountain-climbing expedition (1911) and on geological expedition (1914); author of accounts of the expeditions.

**Filippino Lippi.** See under Fra Filippo LIPPI.

**Filippo Lippi** *or* **Filippo del Carmine,** Fra. See LIPPI.

**Fill′more** (fĭl′mōr), **John Comfort.** 1843–1898. American musician, b. near Franklin, Conn. An authority on American Indian music, and collaborator in writing *A Study of Omaha Indian Music* (1893).

**Fillmore, Millard.** 1800–1874. Thirteenth president of the United States, b. Locke, N.Y. Adm. to bar, Erie County, N.Y. (1823); practiced, Buffalo (from 1830). Member, U.S. House of Representatives (1833–35; 1837–43). Vice-president of the United States (1849–50); succeeded to presidency on death of Taylor (July 9, 1850). Supported compromise policy in slavery issue; signed Fugitive Slave Law, thus alienating abolitionist support. Unsuccessful Whig candidate for president (1852) and National American ("Know-Nothing") candidate (1856).

**Fil′mer** (fĭl′mẽr), Sir **Robert.** d. 1653. English political writer. Royalist in sympathy. Author of *Patriarcha, or the Natural Power of Kings Asserted* (1680), upholding theory of divine right of kings.

**Fi′lon′** (fē′lôɴ′), **Charles Auguste Désiré.** 1800–1875. French historian; author of *Histoire de l'Europe au XVI*[e] *Siècle* (1838), *Histoire de la Démocratie Athénienne* (1854), etc. His son **Pierre Marie Augustin** (1841–1916) was a writer; tutor of the prince imperial (1867); author of many literary studies.

**Fi′lov** (fĭ′lôf), **Bogdan.** 1883–1945. Bulgarian scholar and politician; professor of archaeology and history of art, Sofia U. Minister of education (1938–40); premier of Bulgaria (1940).

**Fim′bri·a** (fĭm′brĭ·ȧ), **Gaius Flavius.** d. 84 B.C. Roman general; partisan of Marius. Assigned to command in Asia (86 B.C.), where he warred against Mithridates, and persecuted partisans of Sulla. Committed suicide (84) when attacked by Sulla.

**Finch** (fĭnch). Name of English family descended from Sir **William Finch,** knighted for service at siege of Terouenne (1513), and his son Sir **Thomas** (d. 1563), knighted for his share in suppression of Wyatt's rebellion in Kent (1554), and including among its members earls of **Win′chil·sea** (wĭn′chĭl·sē), **Not′ting·ham** (nŏt′ĭng·ăm), and **Ayles′ford** (ālz′fẽrd; āls′-).

Sir **Henry** (1558–1625), legal expert; 2d son of Sir Thomas; sergeant-at-law (1616) employed on codification of statute laws; author of a valuable treatise on common law, in legal French (1613 ff.). Henry's son Sir **John** (1584–1660), Baron **Finch of Ford′wich** (fōrd′(w)ĭch); judge; king's counsel (1626); speaker of House of Commons (1628–29), held in his chair by Holles while Sir John Eliot presented resolution on tonnage and poundage; chief justice of Court of Common Pleas (1634), brutal in treatment of William Prynne and John Langton, a subordinate of the exchequer, and considered chiefly responsible, in trial of John Hampden, for decision that king's policy in ship-money issue was constitutional (1637); lord keeper (1640); impeached by Long Parliament (1640).

John's first cousin **Thomas Finch,** grandson of Sir Thomas, became 1st earl of Winchilsea through his mother, **Elizabeth,** *nee* **Hen′eage** (hĕn′ĭj), created countess of Winchilsea (1628). **Heneage** (d. 1631), youngest brother of 1st earl; defended royal prerogative in parliamentary debate on impositions (1610); speaker of House of Commons (1626). Sir Heneage's eldest son, **Heneage** (1621–1682), 1st Earl of Nottingham (cr. 1681); judge; expert on municipal law; solicitor general (1660); attorney general (1670); lord keeper of the seals (1673); Baron Finch and Lord Chancellor (1674); the original of Amri in Dryden's *Absalom and Achitophel*. Heneage's son **Daniel** (1647–1730), 2d Earl of Nottingham; statesman; became also 6th earl of Winchilsea (1729) on death of his cousin the 5th earl, great-grandson of 1st earl; first lord of admiralty (1681–84); secretary for war (1688–93); secretary of state (1702–04); headed High Church Tories under Queen Anne; carried act forbidding occasional conformance of dissenters; dismissed from presidency of council for leniency to Jacobite peers. Daniel's brother **Heneage** (1647?–1719), 1st Earl of Aylesford (cr. 1714); king's counsel (1677) and solicitor general (1679–86); leading counsel for the Seven Bishops (1688); privy councilor (1703).

**Edward Finch-Hat′ton** [-hăt′'n] (d. 1771), diplomat; 5th son of Daniel Finch, 2d Earl of Nottingham; assumed name Hatton (1764) under will of his aunt, daughter of Viscount Hatton; instituted prize for Latin essay at Cambridge; ambassador in Sweden, Holland, Poland, and Russia. Edward's grandson **George William Finch-Hatton** (1791–1858), 9th Earl of Winchilsea and 5th Earl of Nottingham; opposed in House of Lords every liberal measure; favored Orange party in Ireland; fought duel with duke of Wellington over his hostility to Catholic relief bill (1829); opposed Reform bill (1832).

**Harold Heneage Finch-Hatton** (1856–1904), son of 10th earl of Winchilsea, cattle raiser and gold prospector in Queensland, wrote *Advance Australia* (1885) and founded Imperial Federation League.

**Anne Finch** (1666–1720), Countess of Winchilsea; poet; wife of Heneage Finch, 4th Earl of Winchilsea; maid of honor to duke of York's second wife; friend of Pope and Rowe; author of occasional verse, including a long poem *The Spleen* (1701), containing a couplet echoed in Pope's *Essay on Man* and in Shelley's *Epipsychidion*.

**Finch, Francis Miles.** 1827–1907. American poet and jurist, b. Ithaca, N.Y. Associate judge, New York court of appeals (1880–95). Professor, Cornell Law School (1895–1901). Author of *The Blue and the Gray* (1867).

**Finch-Hatton.** See under FINCH family.

**Finck** (fĭngk), **Friedrich August von.** 1718–1766. Prussian general; attempted to cut off enemy retreat at Maxen on orders of Frederick the Great, but was attacked and forced to surrender (1759); court-martialed, dismissed from army, and imprisoned in fortress.

**Finck, Heinrich.** 1445–1527. German composer, of Bavarian origin; composed part songs, hymns, and motets. His grandnephew **Hermann** (1527–1558) composed part songs, and wrote *Practica Musica* (5 books, 1556; in Latin).

**Finck, Henry Theophilus.** *Middle name orig.* **Gott′lob** (gôt′lōp). 1854–1926. American musical critic; on staff of *The Nation* (1881–1924). Noted champion of Wagner's music.

**Finckh** (fĭngk), **Ludwig.** 1876–1964. German poet and short-story writer.

**Finck von Finck′en·stein** (fĭngk′ fôn fĭngk′ĕn·shtīn), Count **Karl Wilhelm.** 1714–1800. Prussian statesman; friend and adviser of Frederick the Great. Ambassador (until 1749) successively at Stockholm, Copenhagen, London, again Stockholm, and St. Petersburg; Prussian cabinet minister (1749); conducted foreign affairs of kingdom alone (1760–63); continued in office under Frederick William II and Frederick William III.

**Fin′den** (fĭn′dĕn), **William** (1787–1852) and his brother **Edward Francis** (1791–1857). English engravers who engraved the Elgin marbles (for the British Museum), the Royal Gallery of British Art, etc.

**Find′la′ter** (fĭn(d)′lă′tẽr), **Andrew.** 1810–1885. Scottish editor; editor of *Chambers's Encyclopaedia* (1861–68) and *Information for the People* (1857).

**Findlater, Jane Helen.** 1866–1946. Scottish novelist; author of *Green Graves of Balgowrie, The Ladder to the Stars* (with Kate Douglas Wiggin), *A Green Grass Widow and other Stories* (1921). Collaborator with her sister **Mary** (1865–1963) in *The Affair at the Inn, Tales that are Told, Penny Monypenny* (1911), *Beneath the Visiting Moon.* Mary wrote independently the novels *Over the Hills, Betty Musgrave, The Rose of Joy,* etc.

**Find′lay** (fĭn(d)′lā; -lĭ), **John Ritchie.** 1824–1898. Scottish newspaper proprietor and philanthropist; chief proprietor of the *Scotsman* (from 1870); presented to the nation the Scottish National Portrait Gallery, at Edinburgh (opened 1889).

**Fine** (fīn), **Henry Burchard.** 1858–1928. American mathematician, b. Chambersburg, Pa. Teacher, Princeton (1885–1928); professor (from 1891); dean of the faculty (1903–12); dean of the scientific departments (1909–28).

**Fine** (fēn), **Oronce.** *Latin* **O·ron′ti·us Fi′ne·us** (ō·rŏn′shĭ·ŭs fĭ′nē·ŭs). 1494–1555. French mathematician; constructed mathematical and astronomical instruments; drew first map of France printed in that country (1525); published editions of Euclid and other mathematical treatises.

**Fine′man** (fīn′măn), **Irving.** 1893– . American novelist, b. New York City. Taught English literature at Bennington College, Vt. (from 1932). Author of *This Pure Young Man* (1930), *Lovers Must Learn* (1932), *Hear, Ye Sons* (1933), *Doctor Addams* (1939).

**Fin′ger** (fĭng′gẽr), **Charles Joseph.** 1869–1941. American writer of juveniles; his many works include *Tales from Silver Lands* (awarded Newbery Medal, 1924), and *Courageous Companions* (awarded Longmans Green juvenile fiction prize, 1929).

**Fi′ni·guer′ra** (fē′nē·gwĕr′rä), **Maso,** *in full* **Tommaso di Antonio.** 1426–1464. Florentine goldsmith, niellist, and engraver; introduced copperplate engraving into Italy; known esp. for his nielli.

**Fink** (fĭngk), **Albert.** 1827–1897. Engineer and statistician, b. in Germany; to U.S. (1849). Invented special form of truss and used it in iron railroad bridges. Also, analyzed and standardized freight rates; applied a knowledge of statistics to determine scientifically costs of transportation, thus virtually founding the science of railroad economics.

**Fin′ke** (fĭng′kĕ), **Fidelio.** 1891– . Czech composer.

**Finke, Heinrich.** 1855–1938. German historian; authority on Renaissance, church, and Spanish history.

**Fin′kel·stein** (fĭng′kĕl·stīn), **Louis.** 1895– . American rabbi and educator, b. Cincinnati. Rabbi, N.Y. City

(1919–31); taught at Jewish Theol. Sem. of America (from 1920), professor (1931), assistant to the president (1934), and provost (1937); succeeded Dr. Cyrus Adler as president (1940).

**Fin·lay′** (*Span.* fēn·lī′), **Carlos Juan.** 1833–1915. Cuban physician and biologist of Scottish-French parentage. Investigated yellow fever; wrote paper (1881) suggesting mosquito as agent of transmission; his later contention that stegomyia mosquito is agent proved correct by Reed Commission (1900). Chairman, commission on infectious diseases, Havana (1899–1902); chief sanitary officer of Cuba (1902–09). Made notable contributions to etiology and pathology of yellow fever.

**Fin′lay** (fĭn′lā; -lĭ), **George.** 1799–1875. English historian, b. at Faversham, Kent. Joined Byron in Greece and served with him in Greek war for independence (1823); settled on estate in Attica, devoted himself to study of Greek history. Author of *History of Greece.*

**Finlay, Robert Bannatyne.** 1st Viscount **Finlay.** 1842–1929. British jurist, b. near Edinburgh. Called to bar (1867); queen's counsel (1882); solicitor general (1895–1900); attorney general (1900–06); lord chancellor (1916–18). Member of Hague Tribunal (1920), and one of first judges of Permanent Court of International Justice, at The Hague (1921).

**Fin′ley** (fĭn′lĭ), **John Hus′ton** (hŭs′tŭn). 1863–1940. American educator and editor, b. Grand Ridge, Ill. A.B., Knox (1887); studied at Johns Hopkins (1887–89). President, Knox Coll. (1892–99). Professor of politics, Princeton (1900–03). President, C.C.N.Y. (1903–13). Commissioner of education of state of New York (1913–21). Associate editor (1921–37) and editor in chief (1937–38), New York *Times.*

**Finley, Martha Farquharson.** *Pen name* **Martha Far′quhar·son** (fär′k(w)ẽr·s′n). 1828–1909. American author of popular juveniles, including the *Elsie Series* (heroine, *Elsie Dinsmore*, 26 vols.), the *Mildred Series* (7 vols.), and *Pewit's Nest Series* (12 vols.).

**Finley, Robert.** 1772–1817. American Presbyterian clergyman; organizer of American Colonization Society (1816), formed to plan a colony on African soil to which American Negroes could be sent as a means of solving or ending slavery problem. President, U. of Georgia (1817).

**Finley, Samuel.** 1715–1766. American Presbyterian clergyman and educator; b. in Ireland; to America (1734). Inspired by Whitefield, engaged in evangelistic work; arrested when called to preach at a Separatist congregation in New Haven and expelled from the colony as a "vagrant" (1744). President, Princeton (1761–66).

**Finn** (fĭn), **Francis James.** 1859–1928. American Jesuit and writer of juveniles, including *Percy Wynn* (1889), *Tom Playfair* (1892), *Lucky Bob* (1917), *Sunshine and Freckles* (1925).

**Fin′ne** (fĕn′nĕ), **Gabriel.** 1866–1899. Norwegian journalist and author of plays and novels.

**Fin′ney** (fĭn′ĭ), **Charles Grandison.** 1792–1875. American clergyman and educator; conducted revivalist meetings (1824–32), and continued evangelistic meetings throughout his life. Pastor, the Broadway Tabernacle (Congregational), organized especially for him (1834–37); withdrew from Presbyterian Church (1836). Professor, Oberlin College (1837–75), president (1851–66).

**Finney, John Miller Turpin.** 1863–1942. American surgeon; professor, Johns Hopkins; author of *A Surgeon's Life* (1940).

**Finn Mac Cool** (fĭn′ măk kōōl′). Irish legendary leader of the Fianna, in 2d and 3d centuries A.D. Legends of the exploits of the Fianna make up the Fenian cycle of Irish romance.

**Finn Magnusen** *or* **Magnussen** *or* **Finnur Magnúsen** *or* **Magnússen.** = Finnur MAGNÚSSON.

**Finsch** (fĭnsh), **Otto,** *in full* **Friedrich Hermann Otto.** 1839–1917. German traveler, ethnologist, and ornithologist. Undertook expeditions to Turkestan, western Siberia (1876), the South Seas (1879–82), Bismark Archipelago and New Guinea (1884), etc.

**Fin′sen** (fĭn′s'n), **Niels Ryberg.** 1860–1904. Danish physician. Studied physiological effects of light, demonstrating that they are due to the violet and ultraviolet rays of the spectrum; excluded light containing these rays from smallpox patients and prevented suppuration and scar formation; discovered therapeutic value of the actinic rays in the blues and violets of the spectrum; developed method of treating skin diseases, esp. lupus, by exposure to light. Awarded 1903 Nobel prize for physiology and medicine.

**Fio′re** (fyō′rā), **Pasquale.** 1837–1914. Italian jurist; author esp. of treatises on international law.

**Fiore della Neve.** Pseudonym of Martinus van LOGHEM.

**Fio·rel′li** (fyō·rĕl′lē), **Giuseppe.** 1823–1896. Italian archaeologist; superintended excavations at Pompeii (1845–49); director-general of antiquities and fine arts in museums at Rome (1881).

**Fiorelli, Tiberio.** d. 1694. Italian creator of the boastful stock character Scaramuccio (Scaramouch) in the commedia dell' arte (c. 1640).

**Fio′ren·ti′no** (fyō′rān·tē′nō), **Francesco.** 1834–1884. Italian Hegelian philosopher.

**Fiorentino, Pier Angelo.** 1806–1864. Italian writer and critic.

**Fiorenzo di Lorenzo.** See LORENZO.

**Fio·ril′lo** (fyō·rēl′lō), **Ignazio.** 1715–1787. Italian composer of operas, religious music, symphonies, and sonatas. His son **Federigo** (1753–after 1823), violinist and composer, is known esp. for his 36 études, or caprices.

**Fi′o·ril′lo** (fē′ō·rĭl′ō), **Johann Dominik.** 1748–1821. German painter and art historian; professor of philosophy (1799), and occupied first chair of art history, Göttingen U.

**Fir′bank** (fûr′băngk), **Ronald,** *in full* **Arthur Annesley Ronald.** 1886–1926. English writer, b. London. Author of *A Study in Temperament* (1905), *Caprice* (1917), *The Flower Beneath the Foot* (1922), *Sorrow in Sunlight* (American title *Prancing Nigger;* 1924), etc.

**Fir·dau′si** (fĭr·dou′sē) *or* **Fir·du′si** (-dōō′sē) *or* **Fir·dou′si** (-dōō′sē). *Real name* **Abul Qasim Mansur** *or* **Hasan.** 940?–?1020. Persian epic poet, b. near Tūs, in Khurasan. Spent about 35 years (from c. 976) writing his great epic, *Shah Namah* (*Book of Kings*); published first edition (1010); its 60,000 rhyming couplets recounted story of Persian kings, legendary and historical, down to Moslem conquest (641), a work highly patriotic and dignified in style, one of the great world epics, the most ancient in modern Persian. Dedicated poem to Mahmud of Ghazni; received meager reward; in revenge, wrote bitter satire on Mahmud; fled to Herat, later to Mazanderan and Bagdad; composed there a long poem, *Yūsuf and Zuleikha*, on a theme borrowed from the Koran, the Arabic version of the Biblical story of Joseph and Potiphar's wife; just before death, received forgiveness of Mahmud.

**Fi′ren·zuo′la** (fē′rān·tswô′lä), **Agnolo.** 1493–?1545. Italian poet; known chiefly for translation of Apuleius's *Golden Ass.*

**Fire′stone** (fīr′stōn), **Harvey Samuel.** 1868–1938. American industrialist; organized Firestone Tire & Rubber Co. (1900), its president (1903–32) and board chairman (1932–38). Active in promoting development of rubber-growing in Philippines and South American countries; opened up leased lands in Liberia (1926) and planted 60,000 acres in rubber trees (by 1936). His son **Harvey Samuel** (1898–1973) also in rubber business.

**Firishta.** See FERISHTAH.

**Fir·ko'vich** (fyĭr·kô'vyĭch), **Abraham ben Samuel.** 1786–1874. Jewish Karaite scholar and archaeologist.

**Fir'mi·an** (fĭr'mē·än), Count **Karl Joseph von.** 1716–1782. Austrian statesman; patron of arts and sciences. Ambassador to Naples (1753); governor of Lombardy (1759).

**Firmianus Lactantius.** See LACTANTIUS FIRMIANUS.

**Fir'mi·cus Ma·ter'nus** (fûr'mĭ·kŭs mȧ·tûr'nŭs), **Julius.** Latin writer of 4th century A.D.; author of attack upon paganism, *De Erroribus Profanarum Religionum* (c. 346 A.D.). Identified by some authorities as author also of *Matheseos Libri VIII* (c. 354), and introduction to astrology according to Egyptian and Babylonian lore.

**Firth** (fûrth), Sir **Charles Harding.** 1857–1936. English historian; regius professor of modern history, Oxford (1904–25).

**Fi·ruz'** (fē·rōōz'). Name of three kings of Persia. **Firuz I,** *also known as* **Ar'sa·ces XXIV** [är'sȧ·sēz] (reigned 78–103 A.D.), one of the Arsacids. **Firuz II** *or* **Pe·roz'** [pā·rōz'] (reigned 457–484), one of the Sassanidae; overcome in war with the Ephthalites. **Firuz III** (d. 679), last of the Sassanidae; driven out of Persia after defeat of his father, Yazdegerd III, at Nehavend (c. 641) by the Mohammedans; took refuge with emperor of China.

**Fi·ru'za·ba'di** (fē·rōō'zä·bä'dē). *Arab.* **Abū'l-Ṭāhir Majd al-Dīn al-Fīrūzābādī.** 1329–1414. Arab lexicographer, b. near Shiraz; educ. Baghdad and Damascus; engaged in literary work and teaching in Jerusalem (1349–59); traveled in western Asia and Egypt; lived chiefly in Mecca (from 1368). Prepared many-volumed dictionary, consolidating dictionaries of ibn-Sida and Sajani, which served as basis of later European dictionaries of classic Arabic.

**Fi·ruz' Shah** (fē·rōōz' shä') *or* **Fi·roz' Shah** (fē·rōz'). Name of three kings of Delhi, especially: **Firuz Shah II** (d. 1295), better known as **Ja·lal'-ud-din'** (jă·lä'-lŏŏd·dēn'), founder of the Khilji (*q.v.*) dynasty. **Firuz Shah III** (1308?–1388), 3d king of the Tughlak dynasty (1351–88); cousin of Mohammed Tughlak; waged wars with Bengal (1353–54, 1360), resulting in Bengal's independence; won only nominal success in attacks on Sind (1360–62); built Jumna Canal.

**Fi'schart** (fĭsh'ärt), **Johann.** *Called* **Ment'zer** (mĕn'-tsēr) *or* **Main'zer** (mīn'tsēr). 1546?–?1590. German poet, jurist, and satirist. Lived as writer (1575–80); advocate to supreme court, Speyer (1580–83); magistrate, Forbach (1583). Author of the anti-Catholic polemical writings *Bienenkorb des Heiligen Römischen Immenschwarms* (1579) and the rhymed *Jesuitenhütlein* (1580); *Geschichtschrift* or *Geschichtsklitterung* in imitation of Rabelais's *Gargantua* (1575); the humorous *Flöhhaz* (1573) and *Podagrammisch Trostbüchlein* (1575); *Philosophisch Ehzuchtbüchlein,* in praise of marriage and family life (1578); also serious paraphrases of various psalms, original hymns, etc.

**Fischer.** See also FISHER.

**Fi'scher** (fĭsh'ēr), **Aloys.** 1880–1937. German educator.

**Fischer, Emil.** 1852–1919. German chemist. Synthesized simple sugars, purine derivatives and peptides; awarded 1902 Nobel prize for chemistry.

**Fischer, Emil Friedrich August.** 1838–1914. Operatic basso, b. in Brunswick, Germany. With Metropolitan Opera Company, New York City (1885–98). Chief roles, Landgrave in *Tannhäuser;* King Henry in *Lohengrin;* King Mark in *Tristan;* Wotan in *Die Walküre;* Hagen in *Siegfried;* and Hans Sachs in *Die Meistersinger.*

**Fischer, Ernst Otto.** 1918– . German chemist. At U. of Munich (1957–64), Technical U., Munich, (1964– ); awarded (with Geoffrey Wilkinson) Nobel prize for chemistry (1973).

**Fischer, Eugen.** 1874–1967. German anthropologist.

**Fischer, Franz.** 1877–1947. German chemist; discoverer of process for obtaining fuel and oil from coal.

**Fischer, Gustav Adolf.** 1848–1886. German explorer in Africa, and physician. Author of *Mehr Licht im Dunkeln Weltteil* (1885).

**Fischer, Hans.** 1881–1945. German chemist. Known for work on the composition of the coloring matter of leaves and of blood; synthesized hemin (1928). Awarded 1930 Nobel prize for chemistry.

**Fi'scher** (fĭsh'ēr; *Fr.* fē'shâr'), **Jean Chrétien.** d. 1762. German soldier in French service; brigadier general (1759). Under authority of Marshal de Belle-Isle, organized (1743) a company which he called chasseurs, origin of the branch of chasseurs in the French army.

**Fischer, Kuno,** *in full* **Ernst Kuno Berthold.** 1824–1907. German historian of philosophy and literary critic, b. in Silesia. Professor, Jena (1856) and Heidelberg (1872–1906). Author of *Geschichte der Neueren Philosophie* (6 vols., 1852–77), the Hegelian *System der Logik und Metaphysik oder Wissenschaftslehre* (1852), *Kants Leben und die Grundlagen seiner Lehre* (1860), *Über die Entstehung und Entwicklungsformen des Witzes* (1871); studies of Shakespeare, Lessing, Goethe, and Schiller, etc.

**Fisch'er** (fĭsh'ēr), **Louis.** 1896–1970. American journalist, b. Philadelphia. European correspondent of *The Nation* magazine, New York (from 1922), serving chiefly in Russia. Author of *Oil Imperialism* (1926), *The Soviet in World Affairs* (1930), *Soviet Journey* (1935), *Why Spain Fights On* (1937), *Men and Politics* (autobiography; 1941), etc.

**Fi'scher** (fĭsh'ēr), **Ludwig.** 1745–1825. German bass singer. Composed the bass song *Im Tiefen Keller Sitz' Ich Hier* (1802). Mozart wrote for him the role of Osmin in *Entführung aus dem Serail.*

**Fi'scher'** (fē'shâr'), **Max** (1880– ) and **Alex** (1881– ). French fiction writers; brothers who collaborated in writing *Après vous, mon Général* (1904), *Camembert-sur-Ourcq* (1908), etc.

**Fi'scher** (fĭsh'ēr), **Samuel.** 1859–1934. German publisher; founder (1886) of the publishing house S. Fischer, publisher of books of Hauptmann, Ibsen, etc.

**Fischer, Theobald.** 1846–1910. German geographer and Mediterranean explorer; undertook many explorations to North Africa.

**Fischer von Er'lach** (fôn ĕr'läκ), **Johann Bernhard.** 1656–1723. Austrian architect, b. Graz. Designed various religious edifices, the Clam-Gallas Palace in Prague (1707 ff.) and the palace of Prince Eugene in Vienna (1705); made original plans for Castle Schönbrunn (1695–1700) and the Royal Library (begun 1722) in Vienna. His son and associate **Joseph Emanuel** (1693–1742) completed many of his father's architectural works and plans.

**Fischer von Wald'heim** (fôn vält'hīm), **Gotthelf.** 1771–1853. Naturalist, b. in Germany; director of the Museum of Natural History, Moscow.

**Fi'set'** (fē'zĕ'), Sir **Eugene,** *in full* **Joseph Eugene.** 1874–1951. Canadian physician, soldier (major general), and public official. Served in Boer War (1899–1900); director-general of medical services of Canada (1903–06); deputy minister of militia and defense (1906), of national defense (1923–24); M.P. (from 1920).

**Fiset, Louis Joseph Cyprien.** 1827–1898. Canadian poet, b. at Quebec.

**Fish** (fĭsh), **Carl Russell.** 1876–1932. American historian; author of *Development of American Nationality* (1913), *American Diplomacy* (1915), *History of America* (1925), etc.

**Fish, Hamilton.** 1808–1893. American statesman, b. New York City. Adm. to bar (1830); practiced, New York City. Member, U.S. House of Representatives (1843–45); governor of New York (1849–50); U.S. senator (1851–57). U.S. secretary of state (1869–77); negotiated settlement of "Alabama Claims" with Great Britain by arbitration, and settlement of northwestern boundary dispute; also, obtained satisfactory settlement from Spain for the seizure of the ship *Virginius* and the execution of its master, crew, and passengers. His father, **Nicholas** (1758–1833), b. New York City, was a soldier and politician; brevetted lieutenant colonel (1783) for his services in American Revolution. Hamilton Fish's son **Stuyvesant** (1851–1923), b. New York City, was a railroad, insurance, and bank executive. Another son, **Hamilton** (1849–1936), b. Albany, N.Y., was a lawyer and politician; assistant treasurer of the United States (1903–08); member, U.S. House of Representatives (1909–11). The latter's son **Hamilton** (1888–     ), politician; member, from 26th N.Y. district, U.S. House of Representatives (1919–45).

**Fish'back** (fĭsh'băk), **Margaret.** 1904–     . American poet; m. Alberto G. Antolini (1935). Author of light verse, as *I Feel Better Now, Out of My Head, I Take It Back, One to a Customer.*

**Fish'bein** (fĭsh'bīn), **Morris.** 1889–1976. American physician, medical writer, and editor, b. St. Louis, Mo. B.Sc., Chicago (1910), M.D., Rush Medical College (1912). Assistant editor (1913–24), editor (1924–49), *Journal of the American Medical Association.* Author of *Medical Follies* (1925), *The Human Body and Its Care* (1929), *Shattering Health Superstitions* (1930), *Fads and Quackery in Healing* (1933), *Frontiers of Medicine* (1933), *Do You Want to Become a Doctor?* (1939), etc.

**Fish'er** (fĭsh'ẽr). See also FISCHER.

**Fisher, Albert Kendrick.** 1856–1948. American biologist; member of Death Valley expedition (1891) which made biological surveys in California, Nevada, etc., for U.S. Department of Agriculture; on Harriman expedition to Alaska (1899) and Pinchot South Sea expedition (1929); in charge of economic investigations of U.S. Department of Agriculture (1906–31).

**Fisher, Alvan.** See under John Dix FISHER.

**Fisher, Andrew.** 1862–1928. Australian statesman, b. near Kilmarnock, Scotland; to Queensland, Australia (1885). Laborite member of Queensland parliament (1893–96; 1899). Founded Labor newspaper *Gympie Truth.* Member of first parliament of Commonwealth of Australia (1901–15); minister of trade and customs (1904); prime minister of Australia (1908–09, 1910–13, 1914–15); high commissioner for the Commonwealth of Australia, in London (1916–21).

**Fisher, Clara.** 1811–1898. Actress, b. London, Eng.; to New York (1827); m. James Gaspard Maeder (1834). Chief roles, Ophelia in *Hamlet,* Viola in *Twelfth Night,* Lady Teazle in *School for Scandal.*

**Fisher, Dorothy,** *in full* **Dorothea Frances,** *nee* **Can'field** (kăn'fēld). 1879–1958. American novelist and essayist, b. Lawrence, Kans.; m. John Redwood Fisher (1907). Author of *The Squirrel-Cage* (1912), *Hillsboro People* (1915), *The Bent Twig* (1915), *The Day of Glory* (1919), *The Brimming Cup* (1921), *Raw Material* (1923), *Her Son's Wife* (1926), *The Deepening Stream* (1930), *Bonfire* (1933), *Seasoned Timber* (1939), etc. Translator of Papini's life of Christ, from the Italian.

**Fisher, Edward.** fl. 1627–1655. See Thomas BOSTON.

**Fisher, Frederick Bohn.** 1882–1938. American Methodist Episcopal clergyman; bishop, in residence at Calcutta, India (1920–30); pastorate in Detroit (1934–38). Author of *That Strange Little Brown Man Gandhi* (1932), etc.

**Fisher, George Park.** 1827–1909. American Congregational clergyman; professor of divinity and college pastor, Yale (1854–61); professor of ecclesiastical history, Yale Divinity School (1861–1901); dean of the school (1895–1901). Author of *The Christian Religion* (1882), *Outlines of Universal History* (1885), *The Colonial Era* (1892), *Brief History of the Nations* (1896), etc.

**Fisher, Harrison.** 1877–1934. American illustrator, b. Brooklyn, N.Y. Illustrator of books, including *Three Men on Wheels* by Jerome K. Jerome, *The Eagle's Heart* by Hamlin Garland. Illustrations appeared in *Saturday Evening Post, Life, Puck,* and other magazines. Widely known for his type of the "American girl."

**Fisher, Herbert Albert Laurens.** 1865–1940. English historian, b. London. President, Board of Education (1916–22); M.P. (1916–26), instrumental in passage of act (Fisher Act, 1918) reorganizing system of public education in England; warden of New College, Oxford (from 1925). Author of *The Mediaeval Empire* (1898), *Bonapartism* (1908), *Napoleon Bonaparte* (1913), *Life of Lord Bryce* (1926), *A History of Europe* (3 vols., 1935), *England and Europe* (1936). O.M. (1937).

**Fisher, Irving.** 1867–1947. American economist, b. Saugerties, N.Y. A.B. (1888), Ph.D. (1891), Yale; studied in Berlin and Paris. Professor of political economy, Yale (from 1898). Author of *The Nature of Capital and Income* (1906), *The Purchasing Power of Money* (1911), *Stabilizing the Dollar* (1920), *The Money Illusion* (1928), *The Theory of Interest* (1930), *Booms and Depressions* (1932), *Inflation* (1933), *100% Money* (1935), etc.

**Fisher, James.** 1697–1775. See under Ebenezer ERSKINE.

**Fisher,** Saint **John.** 1459–1535. English Roman Catholic prelate and martyr; M.A., Cantab. (1491). Professor of divinity (1503), chancellor (1504), president of Queen's Coll. (1505–08), Cambridge; promoted the New Learning. Bishop of Rochester (from 1504). Author of treatises against Luther (1523–25); opponent of church reform (1529); committed to Tower of London (1534) for refusing to recognize validity of Henry's marriage with Anne Boleyn; beheaded (1535) for refusing to acknowledge the king as supreme head of the church under the Act of Supremacy. Made cardinal by Pope Paul III (1535). Canonized (1935).

**Fisher, John Arbuthnot.** 1st Baron **Fisher of Kil'verstone** (kĭl'vẽr·stŭn). 1841–1920. British admiral. Served at capture of Canton and Pei forts (1859–60); in Egyptian war (1882); a lord of the admiralty (1892–97); commander in chief on North American and West Indies station (1897–99) and Mediterranean station (1899–1902). First sea lord of the admiralty (1904–10, 1914–15); largely responsible for preparing British navy for efficient action in World War; disapproved Dardanelles enterprise (1915) and resigned in protest against it. O.M. (1905). His brother Sir **Frederic William** (1851–1943) was also naval officer; in Mediterranean service (1887–91), Australian (1894–98); admiral (1907); president, Royal Naval Coll., Greenwich (1911–14).

**Fisher, John Dix.** 1797–1850. American physician, b. Needham, Mass. Introduced into America a movement for educating the blind and is responsible for establishment of the Perkins Institution and Massachusetts School for the Blind (1829). His brother **Alvan** (1792–1863) was a portrait painter; studio in Boston.

**Fisher, Mahlon Leonard.** 1874–1947. American poet,

b. Williamsport, Pa. Founder and editor of *The Sonnet* (from 1917); author of *Sonnets...*(1917), *Lyrics between the Years* (1928), etc.

**Fisher,** Sir **Norman Fenwick Warren**. 1879–1948. English government official. Permanent secretary to the treasury, and official head of civil service (1919–39). Treasury notes (first issued Oct., 1919) bearing his signature sometimes called *Fishers*. Cf. J. S. BRADBURY.

**Fisher, Sydney Arthur**. 1850–1921. Canadian statesman, b. Montreal.

**Fisher, Sydney George**. 1856–1927. American lawyer and historian; author of *The Evolution of the Constitution of the United States* (1897), *The True Benjamin Franklin* (1899), *The True William Penn* (1900), *The True Daniel Webster* (1911), *The Quaker Colonies* (1919), etc.

**Fisher, Theodore Willis**. 1837–1914. American psychiatrist.

**Fisher, Vardis**. 1895–1968. American writer; author of *Sonnets to an Imaginary Madonna* (1927), *Toilers of the Hills* (1928), *The Neurotic Nightingale* (1935), *Odyssey of a Hero* (1937), *Children of God* (1939; story of the Mormons), *Darkness and the Deep* (1943), etc.

**Fisher, Walter Kenrick**. 1878–1953. American zoologist; author of *Starfishes and Holothurians of Hawaii* (1906), *Starfishes of Philippine Waters...*(1919), etc.

**Fisher, Walter Lowrie**. 1862–1935. American lawyer and politician; practiced in Chicago. U.S. secretary of the interior (1911–13).

**Fish′ta** (físh′tȧ), **Gjergj** (gyĕrg′y′). 1871–1941. Albanian poet; author of *The Sounds of the Mountains* (epic song cycle; 2 vols., 1905–07), *Dewdrops* (lyrics; 1909), etc.

**Fisk** (fĭsk). See also FISKE.

**Fisk, Clinton Bowen**. 1828–1890. American Civil War officer; brigadier general (1862); brevetted major general (1865). Founded Fisk U. for Negroes (chartered 1867).

**Fisk, James**. 1834–1872. American stock-market speculator, b. Bennington, Vt. Aided by Daniel Drew, founded brokerage house Fisk & Belden, New York (1866). Drawn into Erie affairs, he made fortune in wrecking the Erie Railroad; co-operated with Drew and Jay Gould to raise price of gold (1868), reaping a fortune for themselves but causing countrywide depression and loss of millions to others; attempted to corner the gold market (Black Friday, September, 1869) and failed when Grant released government gold; repudiated his partner's contracts for which he was in honor liable. In quarrel with Edward S. Stokes over a woman, was shot (Jan. 6, 1872) and died the next day.

**Fisk, Wilbur**. 1792–1839. American Methodist Episcopal clergyman; first president, Wesleyan U., Middletown, Conn. (1830–39).

**Fiske** (fĭsk). See also FISK.

**Fiske, Amos Kidder**. 1842–1921. American journalist; on staff of New York *Times* (1869–71; 1878–97), New York *Journal of Commerce* (1902–19). Author of *The Myths of Israel* (1897), *The West Indies* (1899), *The Modern Bank* (1904), *The Great Epic of Israel* (1911), *Honest Business* (1914), etc.

**Fiske, Bradley Allen**. 1854–1942. American naval officer and inventor, b. Lyons, N.Y. Grad. U.S.N.A., Annapolis (1874). Navigator of the *Petrel* in battle of Manila Bay (1898). Rear admiral (1911); retired (1916). Invented system of electric communication for interiors of warships, an electric range finder, an electric ammunition hoist, a naval telescope sight, a system of wireless control of moving vessels, and a torpedoplane.

**Fiske, John**. *Orig.* **Edmund Fisk Green**. *Name legally changed* (*1855*) *to* **John Fisk**. *Adopted form* **Fiske** *about 1860*. 1842–1901. American philosopher and historian, b. Hartford, Conn.; grad. Harvard (1863). Adm. to bar (1864), but decided to devote himself to literature. Assistant librarian, Harvard (1872–79). Took to lecture platform, with great success (from 1879). A leading interpreter and supporter of the new doctrine of evolution. Professor of American history, Washington U., St. Louis (from 1884). Author of *Myths and Myth-Makers* (1872), *Outlines of Cosmic Philosophy* (2 vols., 1874), *Darwinism and Other Essays* (1879), *Excursions of an Evolutionist* (1884), *The Idea of God as Affected by Modern Knowledge* (1886), *The Beginnings of New England* (1889), *Civil Government in the United States* (1890), *The American Revolution* (2 vols., 1891), *The Discovery of America* (2 vols., 1892), *Dutch and Quaker Colonies* (2 vols., 1899), *The Origin of Evil* (1899), *A Century of Science and Other Essays* (1899), *Through Nature to God* (1899), *How the United States Became a Nation* (1904), etc.

**Fiske, Minnie Maddern**, *nee* **Da′vey** (dā′vĭ). 1865–1932. American actress, b. New Orleans. Under her husband's management appeared in *Hester Crewe*, *A Doll's House*, *Tess of the D' Urbervilles*, *Frou Frou*, *Rosmersholm*, *The Pillars of Society*, *Ghosts*, *The School for Scandal*, etc. Did much to popularize Ibsen's plays in America. Married (1890) **Harrison Grey Fiske** (1861–1942), b. Harrison, N.Y., theatrical manager and director; also playwright, author of *Hester Crewe*, *The District Attorney* (with Charles Klein), *The Dice of the Gods*, etc.

**Fiske, Stephen Ryder**. 1840–1916. American dramatic critic and theater manager; dramatic critic, New York *Herald* (1862–66). Managed St. James's Theater and Royal English Opera Co., London (about 1872–76); succeeded Augustin Daly in managing Fifth Avenue Theater, New York (1877); introduced Mary Anderson and Madame Modjeska to New York stage. Founded *New York Dramatic Mirror* (1879). Works: plays, *Corporal Cartouche*, *Martin Chuzzlewit* (from Dickens's novel); sketches, *English Photographs* (1869), *Off-Hand Portraits of Prominent New Yorkers* (1884). His brother **Haley** (1852–1929) was president, Metropolitan Life Insurance Co., New York (1919–29).

**Fiske, Thomas Scott**. 1865–1944. American mathematician; author of *Theory of Functions of a Complex Variable* (1906).

**Fitch** (fĭch), **Albert Parker**. 1877–1944. American Congregational clergyman and educator. Author of *Can the Church Survive in the Changing Order?* (1920), *None So Blind* (1924), etc.

**Fitch, Clyde**, *in full* **William Clyde**. 1865–1909. American playwright, b. Elmira, N.Y.; grad. Amherst (1886). On order, wrote for Richard Mansfield a play around character of Beau Brummell. Thereafter, produced large number of plays, excelling in society drama, as *The Moth and the Flame* (1898), *Nathan Hale* (1898), *Barbara Frietchie* (1898), *The Climbers* (1901), *The Girl with the Green Eyes* (1902), *The Woman in the Case* (1905), *The Truth* (1907).

**Fitch, Ebenezer**. 1756–1833. American clergyman and educator, b. Norwich, Conn.; first president of Williams Coll. (1793–1815).

**Fitch, John**. 1743–1798. American inventor, b. Windsor, Conn. Established brass and silversmith business, Trenton, N.J., but failed at outbreak of American Revolution. Served in a New Jersey regiment and later as sutler to the Continental army; used profits to buy lands in Ohio River Valley (1780); captured by Indians (1782); imprisoned by British in Canada (1782–83). Organized company to purchase and develop land in Northwest Territory (1783); project unsuccessful. Became interested in invention of steamboat (1785); obtained from New Jersey (1786) and Pennsylvania, New York, Delaware, and Virginia (1787) exclusive privileges for fourteen years of building and operating steamboats on their waters; interested Philadelphians in financing his experiment. Successfully launched his first vessel (Aug. 22, 1787) on Delaware River, a second and larger vessel (in July, 1788), and a third and still larger one (in 1790); received U.S. patent (Aug. 26, 1791). Wrecking of fourth boat by a storm (1792) discouraged financial backers; moved to Kentucky to claim lands there; died Bardstown, Ky. (July 2, 1798).

**Fitch,** Sir **Joshua Girling.** 1824–1903. English educator; B.A., London U. (1850); author of *Lectures on Teaching* (1881), *Educational Aims and Methods* (1900).

**Fitch, Ralph.** fl. 1583–1606. English merchant and traveler; made overland trip to India (1583), and was first to visit Burma and Siam (1586–87).

**Fi'tel·berg** (fē'tĕl·bĕrk), **Grze'gorz** (gzhĕ'gôsh). 1879–1953. Polish conductor and composer, b. in Livonia; champion of a modern national Polish music. Director of Diaghilev's Russian ballet in western Europe; Kapellmeister, Warsaw Philharmonic Concerts (1923 ff.). Composer of a symphony, symphonic poems, a Polish rhapsody, songs, and chamber music.

**Fit'ger** (fĭt'gẽr), **Arthur.** 1840–1909. German painter and poet; painted large decorative pictures and friezes for public and private buildings, chiefly in Bremen and Hamburg; wrote plays, and lyric and epic poems.

**Fit'tig** (fĭt'ĭk), **Rudolf.** 1835–1910. German organic chemist. Professor, Tübingen (1870), Strasbourg (1876). First determined the chemical constitution of lactones; discovered phenanthrene in coal tar; effected the synthesis of important aromatic hydrocarbons; introduced the Wurtz-Fittig reaction or synthesis, a reaction for inducing the synthesis of two organic halogen compounds.

**Fit'ting** (fĭt'ĭng), **Hans.** 1877– . German botanist; known for work on rubber-producing plants, orchids, and mimosa, and on geotropism, phototropism, the retention of water by desert plants, the assimilation of salts and other substances by living cells, the streaming of protoplasm, etc.

**Fit'ton** (fĭt''n), **Mary.** fl. 1600. English maid of honor at court of Queen Elizabeth. Mistress of William Herbert, 3d Earl of Pembroke. Identified by some Shakespearean commentators with the "dark lady" of the sonnets.

**Fitz** (fĭts), **Reginald Heber.** 1843–1913. American physician, b. Chelsea, Mass. Grad. Harvard Med. School (1868). In his paper *Perforating Inflammation of the Vermiform Appendix* (1886), he named the disease now called appendicitis and proposed surgery for its cure.

**Fitz·al'an** (fĭts·ăl'ăn). Family name of earls of ARUNDEL (1267–1580).

**Fitzalan–Howard.** See under HOWARD family.

**Fitz·ball'** (fĭts·bôl'), **Edward.** *Orig. surname* **Ball.** 1792–1873. English playwright; author of adaptations from Scott and Cooper including *Peveril of the Peak* (1823), *Waverley* (1824), *The Pilot* (1825); a triumphant melodrama *Jonathan Bradford* (1833); *Nitocris* (1855); wrote also romances, librettos, and songs, including *The Bloom is on the Rye.*

**Fitz·boo'dle** (fĭts·bōō'd'l), **George Savage.** Pseudonym of William Makepeace THACKERAY.

**Fitz·ger'ald** (fĭts·jĕr'ăld). Name of an ancient Irish house descending from **Walter**, son of Other, Norman tenant in chief in five counties in Domesday Survey (1086), and whose son **Gerald** of Windsor, steward of Pembroke Castle, m. (c. 1095) Nesta, sister of prince of South Wales, and was father of **David** (d. 1176), Bishop of St. David's (1147–76), who was uncle of Giraldus Cambrensis. Members of the family include:

**Maurice Fitzgerald** (d. 1176), 3d son of Gerald and Nesta; invited to Ireland by King Dermot (1169); led English contingent of Dermot's attack on Dublin; founded fortunes of Geraldine family in Ireland with grants of land in Kildare. His son **Gerald** (d. 1204), Baron of **Of'fa·ly** (ŏf'ȧ·lĭ); received property from Strongbow in Kildare; built Maynooth. **Maurice** (1194?–1257), 2d baron; son of 1st baron; justiciar (*i.e.* viceroy) of Ireland (1232–45); defeated his earl marshal, earl of Pembroke (1234); fought Irish and Welsh; was ancestor of both earls of Kildare and earls of Desmond.

EARLS OF KIL·DARE' (kĭl·dâr'): His grandson **John Fitz·thom'as** [fĭts·tŏm'ăs] (d. 1316), 1st Earl of Kildare and 6th Baron of Offaly; fought Irish to retain his territories; captured Richard de Burgh, Earl of Ulster (1294), to whose daughter Joan he married his son Thomas; served Edward I in Scotland. **Thomas Fitzgerald** (d. 1328), 2d earl, son of 1st earl; justiciar of Ireland (1320, 1327); led large army against Edward Bruce (1316). His younger son, **Maurice** (1318–1390), 4th earl, known as **Maurice Fitzthomas,** justiciar (1356–57, 1361, 1371, 1376), was great-grandfather of **Thomas Fitzgerald** (1427–1477), 7th earl, repeatedly in charge of government of Ireland as deputy for dukes of York and Clarence, lord chancellor (1463). **Gerald Fitzgerald** (d. 1513), 8th earl, called "More (mōr; môr), the Great," son of 7th earl, his son **Gerald** (1487–1534), 9th earl, and his grandson **Thomas** (1513–1537), 10th earl, known as "Silken Thomas," were deputy governors of Ireland, fighting the Irish and their hereditary rival, Ormonde, until open revolt against the government (1534) brought death to the survivors, attainder (repealed 1569) and ruin to family. Lady **Elizabeth Fitzgerald** (1528?–1589), daughter of 9th earl, was the "Fair Geraldine" to whom Henry Howard, Earl of Surrey, addressed famous sonnets published in *Tottel's Miscellany* (1557), and whom Michael Drayton and Sir Walter Scott celebrated in verse.

**James Fitzgerald** (1722–1773), 1st Duke of **Lein'ster** (lĕn'stẽr), succeeded (1744) as 20th earl of Kildare, was lord deputy of Ireland (1756). His fifth son, Lord **Edward Fitzgerald** (1763–1798), served in American Revolution, wounded at battle of Eutaw Springs (1781); M.P. in Irish parliament; journeyed from Fredericton, N.B., to Quebec, to New Orleans, fraternizing with Indians; cashiered for attending revolutionary banquet in Paris, where he repudiated his own title (1792); joined United Irishmen (1796), who were committed to establishment of independent Irish republic, accompanied Arthur O'Connor to the Continent to negotiate for French invasion; seized with other conspirators (1798) on disclosure of hiding place by an informer. His wife, **Pamela** (1776?–1831), protégé of Mme. de Genlis and commonly believed to be her daughter by Philippe, Duc d'Orléans, went to England (1791); m. Fitzgerald (1792), with Louis Philippe as witness; accompanied her husband to Ireland; later m. American consul at Hamburg.

EARLS OF DES'MOND (dĕz'mŭnd): **Maurice Fitzthomas** *or* **Fitzgerald** (d. 1356), 1st Earl of Desmond (cr. 1329); great-great-grandson of a younger son of Maurice Fitzgerald (d. 1176); inherited vast estates in Munster; m. (1312) Catherine de Burgh, daughter of earl of Ulster; received grant of palatine county of Kerry (1329); took lead of Anglo-Irish party against the English policy of viceroys (1341–46); eventually gained favor of English and ruled as viceroy (1355–56). His younger son, **Gerald Fitzgerald** (1359–1398), 3d earl; justiciar (*i.e.* viceroy) of Ireland (1367–69); carried on policy of amalgamation with natives. **Thomas** (d. 1477), 8th earl; lord deputy of

Ireland (1463–67); executed at Drogheda on charge of alliance with Irish. **James Fitzgerald** (d. 1558), *called* **Fitz·john′** (fĭts·jŏn′), 14th earl, played prudent part by submitting to Lord Deputy St. Leger; received by Henry VIII (1542); made lord treasurer of Ireland by Edward VI, continued by Mary; kept Munster quiet and in order. Succeeded by a son by his second wife, **Gerald Fitzgerald** (d. 1583), 15th earl, who allied himself with 11th earl of Kildare in opposition to Thomas Butler, 10th Earl of Ormonde; summoned to London and confined for misdeeds of his clans (1562–64); taken prisoner in open war and imprisoned in Tower (1567–73); after return to Ireland (1573) carried on war in Munster; rebelled (1579–80) against Elizabeth, sacked Youghal; declared traitor and outlaw; driven into woods by successes of Ormonde and Pelham; finally seized and murdered at Glanaginty in Kerry mountains. **James Fitzgerald** (1570?–1601), the "Tower Earl" or the "Queen's Earl of Desmond," son of 15th earl, spent most of his life in Tower; failed in attempt (1600) to bring Geraldines back to allegiance; earldom became extinct with his death.

**Fitzgerald, Barry.** 1888–1961. Irish actor; with Abbey Theatre Company; created part of the "Paycock" in Sean O'Casey's *Juno and the Paycock.*

**FitzGerald, Edward.** 1809–1883. English poet and translator, b. near Woodbridge, Suffolk. Son of John Purcell, who assumed wife's maiden name FitzGerald (1818). Educ. Cambridge. Best known for his translation in rhymed verse (quatrains) of the *Rubáiyát of Omar Khayyám* (pub. 1859). Author also of English versions of the *Agamemnon,* two plays of Sophocles, and six dramas of Calderon, and of *Euphranor: a Dialogue on Youth* (1851), and *Polonius: a Collection of Wise Saws and Modern Instances* (1852); known also as a letter writer.

**Fitzgerald, Francis Scott Key.** 1896–1940. American fiction writer, b. St. Paul, Minn. Educ. Princeton (1913–17). Officer in World War. Author of *This Side of Paradise* (1920), *The Beautiful and Damned* (1921), *The Great Gatsby* (1925), *Taps at Reveille* (1935), etc.

**FitzGerald, George Francis.** 1851–1901. Irish physicist; B.A., Trinity Coll., Dublin (1871). Professor, Dublin (1881–1901). Conducted research work in electric waves and electrolysis; developed electromagnetic theory of radiation. Formulated, following the Michelson-Morley experiment, theory of the change of shape of a body (known as the *Lorentz-FitzGerald contraction*) due to its motion through the ether.

**Fitzgerald, Percy Hetherington.** 1834–1925. Irish sculptor and writer; executed busts of Carlyle and Dickens, and bronze statues of Dr. Johnson and Boswell; author of biographical studies of Lamb, Garrick, the Kembles, Sterne, George IV, William IV, Queen Charlotte, and of several novels and plays.

**Fitz·gib′bon** (fĭts·gĭb′ŭn), **Catherine.** See Sister IRENE.

**Fitzgibbon, John.** 1st Earl of **Clare** (klâr). 1749–1802. Irish jurist and political administrator. Attorney general (1783); opposed attempts to remove disabilities of Roman Catholics; supported commercial treaty with England (1785); fought duel with John Philpot Curran; began policy of repression with stringent measures against Whiteboy raids (1787); first Irishman since the Revolution to become lord chancellor of Ireland (1789–1802); kept Irish legislature in subjection to English executive; urged passage of Act of Union (1800), only to find after passage that Pitt and Castlereagh had promised Catholics that union would prepare way for emancipation.

**Fitz–Gilbert, Richard** (d. 1090). See family de CLARE.

**Fitz·her′bert** (fĭts·hûr′bẽrt), Sir **Anthony.** 1470–1538. English jurist and legal writer; judge of court of common pleas (1522); signer of articles of impeachment against Wolsey (1529) and member of courts which tried Fisher and More. Author of *La Graunde Abridgement* (1514), first important effort to systematize the entire law. His grandson **Thomas** (1552–1640), Roman Catholic priest; entered Jesuit order (1613); served as agent for English clergy (1613–25), and rector of English college at Rome (1618–39); author of treatises on political aspects of Roman Catholicism.

**Fitzherbert, Maria Anne,** *nee* **Smythe** (smĭth; smĭth). 1756–1837. Commonly referred to as "Mrs. Fitzherbert." Wife of King George IV of England; m. 1st, Edward Weld (1775; d. 1775); 2d, Thomas Fitzherbert (1778; d. 1781); 3d, George, Prince of Wales (1785). Marriage to George was made illegal under the Royal Marriage Act and the Act of Settlement, since George was under age at the time and Mrs. Fitzherbert was a Roman Catholic, but she was recognized by the royal family, lived with prince of Wales (to 1803), and maintained relations with him even after his official marriage with Caroline of Brunswick.

**Fitzherbert,** Saint **William.** d. 1154. English Roman Catholic prelate; archbishop of York (1142), but was refused pallium by Pope Eugenius III; formally deposed at council of Reims (1147), but restored and given the pallium (1153); died suddenly, perhaps from poison; canonized (1227).

**Fitzjames, James.** Duke of **Berwick.** See BERWICK.

**Fitz·mau′rice** (fĭts·mô′rĭs; -mŏr′ĭs). Original family name of marquises of LANSDOWNE.

**Fitzmaurice, James.** See under Hermann KÖHL.

**Fitzmaurice,** Sir **Maurice.** 1861–1924. British civil engineer, b. County Kerry, Ireland. Chief resident engineer to Egyptian government, engaged on Assuan dam (1898–1901); chief engineer in London County Council (1901–12); engineer of design and construction of Rotherhithe tunnel under the Thames (1904–08), of Vauxhall bridge, of Kingsway and tramway subway.

**Fitzmaurice,** Sir **Maurice Swynfen.** 1870–1927. British naval officer. Naval transport officer, Dardanelles and Salonika (1915–16); chief of staff, Eastern Mediterranean (1916–17); director of naval intelligence, admiralty (1921–24); vice-admiral (1926); commander in chief, Africa station (from 1924).

**Fitz·mau′rice–Kel′ly** (-kĕl′ĭ), **James.** 1857–1923. English Spanish scholar; professor, U. of Liverpool (1909–16), and U. of London (1916–23). Author of *Life of Cervantes* (1892), *A History of Spanish Literature* (1898), *Cervantes and Shakespeare* (1916); editor of *The Oxford Book of Spanish Verse* (1913), *Complete Works of Miguel de Cervantes Saavedra.*

**Fitz·neale′** (fĭts·nēl′) *or* **Fitz·ni′gel** (-nī′jĕl), **Richard.** d. 1198. English cleric and statesman; treasurer of England (1169); dean of Lincoln (1184) and bishop of London (1189); remained loyal to Richard I against Prince John.

**Fitz·os′bern** (fĭts·ŏz′bẽrn), **William.** Earl of **Her′e·ford** (hĕr′ē·fẽrd). d. 1071. Norman nobleman; urged William of Normandy to conquest of England, and commanded Norman right at battle of Hastings (1066); joint viceroy of England during William's absence (1067); as earl of Hereford, defended border against Welsh attacks.

**Fitz·pat′rick** (fĭts·păt′rĭk), Sir **Charles.** 1853–1942. Canadian jurist and statesman, b. at Quebec; chief justice of Canada, and deputy governor general (1906–18); lieutenant governor, province of Quebec (1918–23).

**Fitzpatrick, Daniel Robert.** 1891–1969. American

cartoonist, b. Superior, Wis. On staff of St. Louis *Post-Dispatch* (from 1913).

**Fitzpatrick,** Sir **James Percy.** 1862–1931. South African merchant and writer; author of *The Transvaal from Within, Jock of the Bushveld* (1907).

**Fitzpatrick, Richard.** 1747–1813. British soldier and politician; served in America (1777–78). Intimate friend of Charles James Fox. M.P. (1774, 1807–12); chief secretary for Ireland (1782); secretary of war (1783, 1806–07). One of authors of the *Rolliad*, a series of Whig satires directed against Pitt and others.

**Fitzpatrick, Thomas.** 1799?–1854. Fur trader, guide, and Indian agent, b. in County Cavan, Ireland; to U.S. as a youth. Trader, trapper, and scout (1823–30); guide for first emigrant train bound for Pacific through northwestern Montana (1841); guide for Frémont's second expedition (1843–44); and for Kearny's expeditions (1845 and 1846); Indian agent (1846–50; 1851–54).

**Fitz·pe′ter** (fĭts·pē′tẽr), **Geoffrey.** Earl of **Es′sex** (ĕs′ĕks; -ĭks). d. 1213. English statesman. During Richard I's absence, one of five justices standing next in authority to Longchamp, the regent; succeeded to earldom of Essex through marriage (1190) with descendant of Geoffrey de Mandeville; aided baronial expulsion of Longchamp; chief justiciar (1198), succeeding Hubert Walter; maintained bureaucracy of Henry I and II; supported John in extortions.

**Fitz–Richard, Gilbert** (d. 1115?). See family de CLARE.

**Fitz·roy′** (fĭts·roi′). Name of descendants of Charles II by Barbara Villiers (*q.v.*), among whom were included dukes of **Graf′ton** (grăf′tŭn):

**Henry** (1663–1690), 1st Duke of Grafton; 2d son of Charles II by Barbara Villiers; married while still a child to daughter of earl of Arlington; lord high constable at James II's coronation; commanded royal troops in Monmouth rebellion; seceded to William of Orange; distinguished himself in battle of Beachy Head (1690); mortally wounded at siege of Cork under Marlborough.

His grandson **Augustus Henry** (1735–1811), 3d duke; statesman; M.A., Cantab. (1753); came into notice through opposition to Bute; secretary of state for northern department in Rockingham's first ministry (1765–66); first lord of treasury, but only nominally prime minister in Pitt (Lord Chatham) ministry (1766); actual first minister (1768); outvoted in his own cabinet on American tea duty; resigned under attacks of Junius; privy seal under Lord North (1771–75) and in new Rockingham cabinet (1782–83); a prominent Unitarian; appointed poet Gray professor of modern history at Cambridge.

His grandson **Robert** (1805–1865), naval commander and meteorologist; in command of the *Beagle*, surveyed coasts of Patagonia and Strait of Magellan and circumnavigated globe (1828–36); accompanied by Darwin as naturalist (1831–36); collaborated with Darwin in writing *Narrative of the Surveying Voyages of H. M. Ships Adventure and Beagle* (3 vols., 1839). Governor of New Zealand (1843–45); chief of meteorological department (1854), where he inaugurated a system of storm warnings, the first weather forecasts; invented Fitzroy barometer. The genus *Fitzroya* (of evergreen timber trees) is named for him.

For Charles (1662–1730), Duke of Southampton and Cleveland, see under Barbara VILLIERS.

**Fitz·sim′mons** (fĭt(s)·sĭm′ŭnz), **Robert Prometheus.** 1862–1917. Pugilist, b. in Cornwall, England. Reared in New Zealand. To U.S. (1890); won world's middleweight championship from Jack Dempsey at New Orleans (Jan. 14, 1891); world's heavyweight championship from James J. Corbett at Carson City, Nev. (Mar. 17, 1897); lost championship to James J. Jeffries at Coney Island (June 9, 1899).

**Fitzthomas, John** and **Maurice.** See FITZGERALD family.

**Fitz·urse′** (fĭts·ûrs′; fĭt·zûrs′), **Reginald.** fl. 1170. One of the murderers of Thomas à Becket.

**Fitz·wal′ter** (fĭts·wôl′tẽr), **Robert.** d. 1235. English leader of the barons in their opposition to King John; commanded army which forced John to grant the Magna Charta (1215); later, went on crusade under King Andrew of Hungary and took part in the siege of Damietta (1219–20).

**Fitz·wil′liam** (fĭts·wĭl′yăm), **William Wentworth.** 2d Earl **Fitzwilliam.** 1748–1833. English statesman; nephew of Charles Watson-Wentworth, 2d Marquis of Rockingham (*q.v.*); educ. Cambridge. Associated with Pitt in Old Whig group; president of the council (1794); lord lieutenant of Ireland (1795), but recalled in three months because of expression of sympathy for Catholic emancipation; fought duel with John Beresford; president of the council in Grenville's All-the-Talents administration (1806–07).

**Five Dynasties.** Name given to five short dynasties of China (907–960 A.D.) between the T'ang and the Sung dynasties: the Later Liang (907–923), the Later T'ang (923–936), the Later Chin (936–947), the Later Han (947–950), and the Later Chou (951–960). There were many rulers, mostly Turkish or Uigur adventurers. Cf. LIANG, T'ANG, CHIN, HAN, and CHOU.

**Fi′zeau′** (fē′zō′), **Armand Hippolyte Louis.** 1819–1896. French physicist, b. in Paris. Made improvements in the daguerreotype; worked with Foucault on heat and light; made determination of the velocity of light; gave correct explanation of Doppler's principle; conducted experiments to detect ether drift.

**Flac′cus** (flăk′ŭs), **Gaius Valerius.** See VALERIUS FLACCUS.

**Flaccus, Marcus Verrius.** Roman scholar of early 1st century A.D.; a freedman, and tutor of the grandson of Augustus; author of *De Verborum Significatu*, later abridged by Festus (*q.v.*).

**Flaccus, Quintus Fulvius.** Roman statesman of 3d century B.C.; consul (237 B.C.); censor (231); again consul (224); pontifex maximus (216); praetor (215); again consul (212 and 209); defeated Hanno near Beneventum (212), and successfully besieged Capua. His grandnephew **Marcus** (fl. 2d century B.C.), consul (125 B.C.), was supporter of the Gracchi; proposed conferring Roman citizenship on the allies; killed at same time as Gaius Sempronius Gracchus (*q.v.*).

**Flach** (flȧsh), **Jacques Geoffroi.** 1846–1919. French jurist and historian; professor at Collège de France (1879). Author of *Les Origines de l'Ancienne France* (1886–93), *Mirabeau* (1891), etc.

**Fla′chat′** (flȧ′shȧ′), **Eugène.** 1802–1873. French civil engineer; associated with his half brother **Stéphane Mo′ny′** [mô′nē′] (1800–1884) in building the first railroad in France, from Paris to Saint-Germain-en-Laye.

**Fla′ci·us Il·lyr′i·cus** (flā′shĭ·ŭs ĭ·lĭr′ĭ·kŭs), **Matthias.** *Known in Croatian literature as* **Matija Vla′čić I′lir** (vlä′chĕt·y′ [*Angl.* -chĭch] ē′lĕr). *In Serbian* **Matija Fran′ko·vić Ilir** (frän′kô·vēt′y′; *Angl.* -vĭch). 1520–1575. German Protestant theologian and leader of strict Lutherans, b. Albona, Istria. Pupil of Luther in Wittenberg; professor, Jena (1557); dismissed for opposition to synergism (1561); subsequently in Regensburg, Antwerp, Frankfurt, Strasbourg. First representative of verbal inspiration among Lutheran theologians, and champion of orthodoxy in various religious controversies.

**Fla′court′** (flȧ′ko͞or′), **Étienne de.** 1607–1660. French colonizer; served in Madagascar (1648–55). Author of *Histoire de la Grande Isle de Madagascar* (1658); compiler of a dictionary of the Madagascan language.

**Flad** (flăd; *Ger.* flät), **Henry**. 1824–1898. Engineer, b. in Baden, Germany. After Revolution of 1848, fled to U.S. Associated with James B. Eads in building of "Eads Bridge" at St. Louis (1867–74). Member, Mississippi River Commission (1890–98). Invented water filter, water meter, street sprinkler, electromagnetic air brake, etc.

**Flagg** (flăg), **Ernest**. 1857–1947. American architect, b. Brooklyn, N.Y. Designer of St. Luke's Hospital and Singer building in New York, buildings of U.S.N.A., Annapolis, Md., Corcoran Gallery in Washington, D.C.

**Flagg, George Whiting**. 1816–1897. American historical painter, b. New Haven, Conn. His brother **Jared Bradley** (1820–1899) was a painter and a Protestant Episcopal clergyman; studio in New York (after 1849); pastor of Grace Church, Brooklyn Heights, N.Y. (1855–63); his portraits of William M. Evarts and Chief Justice Church hang in the capitol at Albany, N.Y.

**Flagg, James Montgomery**. 1877–1960. American painter, illustrator, and author, b. Pelham Manor, N.Y. Contributed to *St. Nicholas* (from 1890), *Judge* and *Life* (from 1892). Author of *Yankee Girls Abroad* (1900), *Tomfoolery* (1904), *City People* (1909), *The Adventures of Kitty Cobb* (1912), *All the Way—Maybe* (1925), etc.

**Flagg, Thomas Wilson**. 1805–1884. American naturalist; author of *The Birds and Seasons of New England* (1875); etc.

**Flag'ler** (flăg'lẽr), **Henry Morrison**. 1830–1913. American oil magnate and promoter, b. Hopewell, N.Y. Associated with John D. Rockefeller in development of Standard Oil Co. (from 1865). Organized Florida East Coast Railway (1886); extended line to Miami and built great hotels at shore resorts (1892–96); extended line to Key West (opened 1913). His son **Harry Harkness** (1870–1952), b. Cleveland, Ohio; A.B., Columbia (1897); president, The Philharmonic-Symphony Society, New York (1928–34).

**Flag'stad** (fläg'stä), **Kirsten**. 1895-1962. Norwegian operatic soprano; m. Sigurd Hall (1919), and 2d, Henry Johansen (1930). U.S. debut in New York as Sieglinde in *Die Walküre* (1935); member of Metropolitan Opera Company, New York (from 1935); best known for interpretation of Wagnerian roles.

**Fla'haut' de la Bil'lar'de·rie'** (flȧ'ō' dē lȧ bē'yȧr'-drē'), Comte **Auguste Charles Joseph de**. 1785–1870. French general and diplomat; general of brigade (1813) and of division (1814) under Napoleon, and engaged at Leipzig, Hanau, and Waterloo; minister to Berlin (1831) and ambassador to England (1842).

**Fla'her·ty** (flă'ẽr·tĭ), **Robert Joseph**. 1884–1951. Explorer, motion-picture director, and writer, b. Iron Mt.; Michigan; educ. Upper Canada Coll., Toronto, Canada. Explored subarctic eastern Canada (1910–16). Directed motion pictures *Nanook of the North* (1920–22), *Moana* (1923–25), *Tabu* (1929–31), *Man of Aran* (1932–34), *Elephant Boy* (1935). Author of *The Captain's Chair* (1938) and *White Master* (1939), novels, and *A Film-Maker's Odyssey* (1939).

**Flaisch'len** (flīsh'lĕn), **Cäsar**. 1864–1920. German writer of the naturalistic school; author of the plays *Toni Stürmer* (1891) and *Martin Lehnhardt* (1895), prose poems *Von Alltag und Sonne* (1898), and the autobiographical novel *Jost Seyfried* (1905).

**Flamand, François**. See François DUQUESNOY.

**Flam'bard** (flăm'bärd; -bẽrd), **Rannulf**. d. 1128. Norman ecclesiastic in England; chief adviser of King William II; bishop of Durham (1099).

**Fla'meng'** (flȧ'mäN'), **Léopold**. 1834–1911. French engraver; engraved after Rembrandt, Rubens, Watteau, Ingres, and others. His son **François** (1856–1923) was a painter, esp. of historical scenes.

**Flam'i·ni'nus** (flăm'ĭ·nī'nŭs), **Titus Quinctius** *or* **Quintius**. 230?–?174 B.C. Roman general and statesman; quaestor (199 B.C.); consul (198). Conducted campaign in Macedonia against Philip V, culminating in victory at Cynoscephalae (197), where Roman legions met Macedonian phalanx for first time; at Isthmian games, in Corinth, proclaimed independence of Greek states (196). His brother **Lucius Quinctius** (d. 170 B.C.) commanded Roman fleet during war with Philip V of Macedonia (197); consul (192); proconsul in Gaul (191).

**Fla·min'i·us** (flȧ·mĭn'ĭ·ŭs), **Gaius**. d. 217 B.C. Roman general and statesman, of plebeian family; tribune of the plebs (232 B.C.); consul (223); censor (220); and again consul (217). In military operations, pacified the Insubrians (223). While censor, built two great public works, the Circus Flaminius, and a continuation (known as *Via Flaminia*) of military road from Rome to Ariminum (Rimini). Defeated by Hannibal and killed at Lago di Trasimeno (217). His son **Gaius**, praetor (193 B.C.) and governor of Hispania Citerior, used his soldiers to build a military road from Bononia (Bologna) to Arretium (Arezzo).

**Flam'ma'rion'** (flȧ'mȧ'ryôN'), **Camille**, *in full* **Nicolas Camille**. 1842–1925. French astronomer. Connected with the Paris observatory (1858–62; 1867), Bureau of Longitudes (1862–65); established private observatory at Juvisy (1882); studied the moon, Mars, and double stars; founded the French Astronomical Society (1887); edited astronomic reviews; popularized study of astronomy in his writings. Author of *Astronomie Populaire* (1879), *L'Atmosphère* (1871), *Le Monde avant la Création de l'Homme* (1885), *Les Phénomènes de la Foudre* (1905), *La Mort et son Mystère* (1920–21), etc.

**Flam'steed** (flăm'stēd), **John**. 1646–1719. English astronomer; first astronomer royal (1675); ascertained absolute right ascensions through simultaneous observations of the sun and a star near both equinoxes; furnished data to Sir Isaac Newton; published (1707 ff.) results of his observations (made 1676–89) of stars in *Historia Coelestis Britannica*, completed (1725) by his assistant Joseph Crosthwait.

**Flan'a·gan** (flăn'ȧ·găn; -ĭ·găn), **Edward Joseph**. 1886–1948. Roman Catholic clergyman, b. in Roscommon, Ireland. Pastorate in Omaha, Nebr. (1913–17). Founded Father Flanagan's Home for Boys, in Omaha (1917), moved to larger quarters west of Omaha, the farm becoming an incorporated village known as Boys Town, where the boys elect their own village executives and council, and direct their own affairs.

**Flanagan, John**. 1863?–1952. American sculptor, b. Newark, N.J. Studied under St. Gaudens in New York, and Chapu and Falguière at École des Beaux-Arts (Paris). Among his works are the monumental clock in the Library of Congress, Washington, D.C., bronze portrait bust of Samuel P. Langley in Smithsonian Institution, Washington, D.C., Bulkeley Memorial at Aetna Life Insurance Co., Hartford, Conn., bust of Joseph Henry in American Hall of Fame.

**Flanders**, Counts of. See ROBERT; *William Clito*, under WILLIAM, dukes of Normandy.

**Flanders, Henry of**. See HENRY OF FLANDERS.

**Flan'din'** (fläN'dăN'), **Eugène Napoléon**. 1809–1876. French painter and archaeologist.

**Flandin, Pierre Étienne**. 1889–1958. French politician and lawyer; minister of commerce, in François-Marsal's cabinet (1924) and in Tardieu's cabinet (1929–30); minister of finance, in Laval's cabinet (1931–32) and in Tardieu's cabinet (Feb.–May, 1932); minister of public works in Doumergue's cabinet (Feb.–Nov., 1934); premier of France (Nov., 1934–June, 1935); minister without portfolio in Laval's cabinet (1935–36); minister of foreign affairs (1936; 1940–41, in Vichy regime); sentenced (1946) to five years' loss of civil rights; reprieved.

**Flan′drin′** (flän′drän′). Family of French painters, including: **Auguste** (1804–1843); his brother **Hippolyte** (1809–1864); another brother, **Jean Paul** (1811–1902), landscape painter; and Hippolyte's son **Paul Hippolyte** (1856–1921), painter esp. of religious scenes.

**Flas′san′** (flȧ′sän′), **Jean Baptiste Gaëtan de Rax′is′** (dē ràk′sēs′) **de.** 1760–1845. French diplomat; author of *Histoire...de la Diplomatie Française...*(1808).

**Flat′man** (flăt′măn), **Thomas.** 1637–1688. English poet and miniature painter.

**Flau′bert′** (flō′bâr′), **Gustave.** 1821–1880. French novelist, b. Rouen. Studied medicine, but abandoned that to devote himself to writing; regarded as leader of the naturalist school. His first novel, *Madame Bovary* (1857), brought legal prosecution on the ground of immorality, but he was acquitted. Among his works, all characterized by distinction of style, are *Salammbô* (1862), *L'Éducation Sentimentale* (1874), *La Tentation de Saint Antoine* (1874), *Trois Contes: La Légende de Saint Julien l'Hospitalier, Hérodias, Un Cœur Simple* (1877).

**Flav′el** (flăv′ĕl), **John.** 1630?–1691. English Presbyterian clergyman; educ. Oxford. Formally ejected from pastorate at Dartmouth (1662), but continued secretly as pastor; author of *Husbandry Spiritualized* (1669).

**Fla′vi·an** (flā′vĭ·ăn), Saint. 390?–449. Patriarch of Constantinople (447–449). Condemned Eutychian heresy (448), but was himself deposed and excommunicated by the Council of Ephesus, or "Robber Synod" (449), and is said to have died from bodily injuries received from theological opponents; canonized as martyr by Council of Chalcedon (451).

**Flavian.** Name of two bishops of Antioch:

**Flavian I.** 320?–?404 A.D. Bishop (381–404 A.D.), whose appointment, since it was not recognized by the bishop of Rome and the bishops of Egypt, continued a schism in the orthodox church at Antioch.

**Flavian II.** d. 518 A.D. Bishop (c. 498–512 A.D.); accepted decree of union issued (482) by Emperor Zeno; anathematized by patriarch of Constantinople; deposed by Emperor Anastasius.

**Fla′vin** (flā′vĭn), **Martin.** 1883–1967. American playwright and novelist, b. San Francisco. Author of *Children of the Moon* (1923), *Service for Two* (1926), *Crossroads* (1929), *Spindrift* (1930), *Sunday* (1933), *Blue Jeans* (1937), etc.; awarded 1943 Pulitzer prize for his novel, *Journey in the Dark.*

**Fla′vio Bion′do** (flä′vyō byōn′dō). *Lat.* **Flavius Blon′dus** (blŏn′dŭs). 1388–1463. Italian historian and antiquary, b. Forlì; papal secretary under Eugene IV, Nicholas V, Calixtus III, Pius II; by his *Decades* set standard for historical writings in 15th century.

**Fla′vi·us** (flā′vĭ·ŭs). Name borne by members of the Roman Flavian gens. The Flavian emperors were Vespasian and his sons Titus and Domitian.

**Flavius Eutropius.** See EUTROPIUS.

**Flavius Fimbria, Gaius.** See FIMBRIA.

**Flax′man** (flăks′măn), **John.** 1755–1826. English sculptor and draftsman, b. York. Executed drawings for the *Iliad* and the *Odyssey*, Dante's *Divina Commedia*, and tragedies of Aeschylus. First professor of sculpture at Royal Academy of Art (1810); his sculptures include statues of Burns and Kemble in Westminster Abbey, and *Shield of Achilles.*

**Fleay** (flā), **Frederick Gard.** 1831–1909. English Shakespearean scholar. B.A., Cantab. (1853); ordained priest (1857), relinquished orders (1884); educator (1856–76). Author of *A Chronicle History of the Life and Work of William Shakespeare* (1886), *A Chronicle History of the London Stage 1559–1642* (1890), *A Biographical Chronicle of the English Drama 1559–1642* (2 vols., 1891).

**Fleb′be** (flĕb′ē; -ĕ), **Beulah Marie,** *née* **Dix** (dĭks). 1876– . American novelist, b. Kingston, Mass. A.B., Radcliffe (1897); m. George H. Flebbe (1910). Author of *Hugh Gwyeth* (1899), *Fighting Blade* (1912), *Pity of God* (1932).

**Flé′chier′** (flā′shyā′), **Valentin Esprit.** 1632–1710. French Roman Catholic prelate; bishop of Lavaur (1685) and of Nîmes (1687); best known for his funeral orations.

**Fleck′er** (flĕk′ẽr), **Herman James Elroy.** 1884–1915. English poet and playwright; educ. Oxford. In British consular service (1908–15). His collected poems published posthumously (1916), and two plays, *Hassan* (1922) and *Don Juan* (1925).

**Fleck′noe** (flĕk′nō), **Richard.** d. about 1678. Irish poet, said to have been a priest, whose name Dryden used in the title of his poem *Mac Flecknoe*, lampooning the poet Thomas Shadwell.

**Fleet′wood** (flēt′wŏŏd), **Charles.** d. 1692. English Parliamentarian general. Commanded regiment of horse at Naseby (1645); lieutenant general of horse at Dunbar (1650); commander of English forces before Worcester (1651); m. (1652) Bridget Ireton, eldest daughter of Oliver Cromwell and widow of Henry Ireton; lord deputy and commander in chief in Ireland (1654–57). After Oliver Cromwell's death (1658), supported cause of Richard Cromwell; headed army opposition to Parliament; became commander in chief of army (1659), but failed to come to terms with Gen. Monck. At Restoration, incapacitated for life from holding public office.

**Fleetwood, William.** 1656–1723. Anglican prelate, b. London; educ. Cambridge; canon of Windsor (1702); bishop of St. Asaph (1708–14), of Ely (1714–23).

**Fle′gel** (flā′gĕl), **Robert.** 1855–1886. German explorer in Africa; b. in Vilna, Russia. Ascended and surveyed Niger and Benue rivers; visited present Nigeria several times (1880 ff.), explored Sokoto in northwest and reached Yola and Ngaundere in east. Author of *Vom Niger-Benue* (pub. 1890) and of accounts of his travels.

**Flei′scher** (flī′shẽr), **Heinrich Leberecht.** 1801–1888. German Orientalist; professor, Leipzig (from 1835); edited Abulfeda's *Historia Ante-Islamica* (1831), al-Baidawi's commentary on the Koran (2 vols., 1844–48), and other Persian, Arabic, and Turkish works.

**Fleischer, Oskar.** 1856–1933. German musicologist. Professor, Berlin U. (1895–1925); founder and president, Internationale Musikgesellschaft (1899), and coeditor of its publications (until 1904).

**Fleisch′mann** (flīsh′măn), **Charles Louis.** 1834–1897. American yeast manufacturer, b. near Budapest, Hungary.

**Fleisch′mann** (flīsh′män), **Max.** 1872–1944. German jurist.

**Flé′mal′** (flā′màl′) *or* **Fle·mael′** (flȧ·màl′) *or* **Flé′malle′** (flā′màl′), **Bertholet.** 1614–1675. Flemish historical and portrait painter, b. in Liége; representative of later Flemish school and pioneer of classicist movement.

**Flé′malle′** (flā′màl′) *or* **Mé′rode′** (mā′rôd′), **Le Maî′tre de** (lē mâ′trĕ dē), *i.e.* Master of. Name given to a 15th-century Flemish painter so called after the Abbey of Flémalle near Liége, whence are said to have come his 3 panels of an altarpiece representing a Madonna, St. Veronica, and the Trinity; also painted *The Bad Thief* (in Frankfurt) and is identified by some with Rogier van der Weyden, but more often with their teacher **Robert Cam′pin** [kăm′pĭn] (1375?–1444), painter of the Tournai school.

**Flem′ing** (flĕm′ĭng), **Sir Alexander.** 1881–1955. British bacteriologist, b. Lochfield, Ayrshire; professor, London U.; discovered lysozyme (1929); shared with Sir Howard Florey (*q.v.*) and Ernest B. Chain 1945 Nobel prize for medicine, for discovery (1928) and development of penicillin.

**Fleming, George.** Pseudonym of Constance FLETCHER.

**Fleming,** Sir **John Ambrose.** 1849–1945. English electrical engineer, b. Lancaster. Professor of electrical engineering, University College, London (1885–1926). Known for many applications of electricity; contributed to development of telephony, electric lighting, and wireless telegraphy; devised the first electron tube (1904). An editor of and contributor to the *Encyclopaedia Britannica* (10th & 11th eds.). Author of *The Principles of Electric Wave Telegraphy and Telephony* (1906), *Fifty Years of Electricity* (1921), etc.

**Fleming, Peter.** 1907–1971. English writer; educ. Oxford; traveled widely; wrote *Brazilian Adventure* (1933), *News from Tartary* (1936), *The Flying Visit* (1940), *The Siege at Peking* (1959), etc.

**Fleming, Philip Bracken.** 1887–1955. American army officer, b. Burlington, Iowa; grad. U.S.M.A. (1911); colonel in World War I. Administrator of wages and hours division in U.S. Department of Labor (1939–41).

**Fleming** *or* **Flem′ming** *or* **Flem′mynge** (flĕm′ĭng), **Richard.** d. 1431. English prelate, b. Crofton, Yorkshire. Bishop of Lincoln (1420–31); represented England at councils of Pavia and Siena (1428–29); founder of Lincoln Coll., Oxford (1427). His nephew **Robert Flemming** (d. 1483) was dean of Lincoln (1451), a benefactor of Lincoln Coll., prothonotary to Pope Sixtus IV, and author of Latin poems.

**Fleming,** Sir **Sandford.** 1827–1915. Scottish-born Canadian engineer; chief engineer of railways to government of Nova Scotia (1864); chief engineer of Inter-Colonial Railway (1867–76) and Canadian Pacific Railway (1872–80).

**Fleming, Wil′lia·mi′na** (wĭl′yȧ·mī′nȧ) **Paton,** *nee* **Stevens.** 1857–1911. Astronomer, b. Dundee, Scotland; m. James Orr Fleming (1877). To U.S. (1878); on staff, Harvard observatory (1879–98); noted as discoverer of new stars and variables and as investigator of stellar spectra.

**Flem′ming** (flĕm′ĭng). See also FLEMING.

**Flem′ming** (flĕm′ĭng) *or* **Fle′ming** (flā′mĭng), **Paul.** 1609–1640. German lyric poet and physician.

**Flemming, Willi.** 1888– . German literary historian; author of *Epik und Dramatik* (1925), *Das Deutsche Barockdrama* (1931–34), *Deutsche Kultur im Zeitalter des Barock* (1937–39).

**Flem′mynge** (flĕm′ĭng). See also FLEMING, FLEMMING.

**Flers** (flâr), Marquis **de. Robert Pel′le·vé′ de la Motte′-An′go′** (pĕl′vā′ dē lȧ mōt′äɴ′gō′). 1872–1927. French playwright; collaborator with G. A. de Caillavet; wrote gay, sparkling fantasies and comedies of manners.

**Flesch** (flĕsh), **Karl.** 1873–1944. Hungarian violinist and teacher. Studied at Vienna (1886–89) and Paris (1890–94). Professor, Bucharest (1897–1902), Amsterdam (1903–08); to Berlin (1908); head of violin department at Curtis Inst., Philadelphia (1924) and founder of Curtis String Quartet (1925); settled in Baden-Baden (1926). Author of *Urstudien* for violin (1911) and *Die Kunst des Violinspiels* (2 vols., 1923–28).

**Fletch′er** (flĕch′ẽr), **Alice Cunningham.** 1838–1923. American ethnologist, b. in Cuba of American parentage. Lived among Plains Indians, studying their culture and their needs; pioneer in study of Indian music.

**Fletcher** of Sal′toun (sôl′t′n; -tŭn), **Andrew.** 1655–1716. Scottish politician; adviser of Monmouth in London and later in Holland, and accompanied Monmouth on his expedition to England (1685); opposed English rule in Scotland and union of Scotland with England.

**Fletcher, Banister.** 1833–1899. English architect; coauthor, with his son the architect Sir **Banister Flight** (1866–1953), of *A History of Architecture on the Comparative Method* (1896).

**Fletcher, Constance.** *Pseudonym* **George Flem′ing** (flĕm′ĭng). 1858–1938. Novelist and playwright, of American parentage, long resident in Venice; among her novels are *A Nile Novel* (1877), *Vestigia* (1882), *The Truth about Clement Ker* (1889); among her plays, *Mrs. Lessingham* (1894), *The Canary* (1899), *The Fantasticks* (1900; English version of Rostand's *Romanesques*).

**Fletcher, Giles** the elder. 1549?–1611. English diplomat and writer, b. Hertfordshire; educ. Cambridge. Envoy to Russia (1588); author of book *Of the Russe Common Wealth* (1591), parts of which were printed in Hakluyt's *Voyages* and reprinted in *Purchas, his Pilgrimage* (the whole book not printed until 1856). Author also of a series of sonnets, *Licia, or Poemes of Love* (1593). He was uncle of the playwright John Fletcher (*q.v.*) and father of the poets Giles and Phineas Fletcher, disciples of Edmund Spenser: **Giles** the younger (1588?–1623), B.A., Cantab. (1606), rector of Alderton in Suffolk, author of *Christ's Victorie and Triumph in Heaven and Earth* (poem; 1610); **Phineas** (1582–1650), educ. Cambridge, author of a pastoral play, eclogues, and *The Purple Island, or the Isle of Man* (1633), his chief work, an allegory of the human anatomy.

**Richard** (d. 1596), prelate; brother of Giles the elder; B.A., Cantab. (1566); prebendary of St. Paul's (1572); chaplain to Queen Elizabeth (1581); dean of Peterborough (1583); chaplain at execution of Mary, Queen of Scots; bishop of Bristol (1589), Worcester (1593), London (1594); suspended by Elizabeth because of his second marriage. His son was the playwright John Fletcher (*q.v.*).

**Fletcher, Henry Prath′er** (prăth′ẽr). 1873–1959. American diplomat, b. Greencastle, Pa. U.S. minister to Chile (1909); ambassador to Chile (1914), Mexico (1916–20), Belgium (1922–24), Italy (1924–29). Chairman, U.S. Tariff Commission (1930–31) and Republican National Committee (1934–36).

**Fletcher, Horace.** 1849–1919. American nutritionist, b. Lawrence, Mass. After active and varied business life, turned attention to researches in field of human nutrition (from 1895); attributed his own health to thorough mastication of his food; wrote and lectured widely on nutrition, popularizing his ideas until *Fletcherism* and *to fletcherize* became part of American language.

**Fletcher, Jefferson Butler.** 1865–1946. American educator and author, b. Chicago. A.B. (1887), A.M. (1889), Harvard. Teacher of English (1890–1902) and comparative literature (1902–04), Harvard; professor of comparative literature, Columbia (1904–39). Author of *The Religion of Beauty in Woman* (1911), *Dante* (1916); translator of Dante's *Divina Commedia* (1931).

**Fletcher, John.** 1579–1625. English dramatist. Son of Richard Fletcher (see under Giles FLETCHER). Educ. Cambridge. Collaborated with Francis Beaumont (from c. 1606) till the latter's death (1616) on about fifty comedies and tragedies (see Francis BEAUMONT). Collaborated with Philip Massinger on *The Honest Man's*

*Fortune*, *Thierry and Theodoret*, *The Knight of Malta*, *The Spanish Curate*, *The Prophetess*, and many others; and with Shakespeare on *Henry VIII* and *Two Noble Kinsmen*. Sole author of *The Faithful Shepherdess*, the romantic tragedies *Bonduca* and *Valentinian*, the comedies *Women Pleased*, *The Pilgrim*, *The Wild Goose-Chase*.

**Fletcher, John Gould.** 1886–1950. American poet and critic, b. Little Rock, Ark. Educ. Harvard (1903–07). Identified with the imagist group of poets (from 1914). His volumes of verse include *Fire and Wine* (1913), *Irradiations—Sand and Spray* (1915), *Goblins and Pagodas* (1916), *Japanese Prints* (1918), *The Tree of Life* (1918), *Breakers and Granite* (1921), *Parables* (1925), *Branches of Adam* (1926), *The Black Rock* (1928), *XXIV Elegies* (1935), *The Epic of Arkansas* (1936); his critical works include *Paul Gauguin...*(1921), *John Smith—also Pocahontas* (1928), *The Two Frontiers* (1930).

**Fletcher, John William.** *Orig. surname* **de la Flé′chère′** (dē lȧ flā′shâr′). 1729–1785. English clergyman, b. Nyon, Switzerland. To England (c. 1752); ordained (1757); intimate friend of John and Charles Wesley; vicar at Madeley (1760–85); superintendent, Countess of Huntington's College, Trevecca, Wales (1768–71). Author of theological works, including a defense of his Arminian beliefs against Calvinists.

**Fletcher, Joseph Smith.** 1863–1935. English journalist and novelist; under pseudonym "A Son of the Soil" contributed articles on rural life to newspapers. Wrote histories and historical romances (1892–1920), and detective fiction thereafter; works include *When Charles the First was King* (1892), *The Builders* (1897), *Daniel Quayne* (1907), *The Stolen Budget* (1926), *Murder at Wrides Park* (1931), *The Ebony Box* (1934).

**Fletcher, Percy E.** 1879–1932. English composer.

**Fletcher, Richard.** See under Giles FLETCHER.

**Fletcher, Robert.** 1823–1912. Surgeon and bibliographer, b. Bristol, England. To U.S. (1847); practiced, Cincinnati, Ohio. Served in medical corps in Civil War. Assistant to John Shaw Billings in library of surgeon general's office (1876); aided Billings in preparing *Index-Catalogue of the Library of the Surgeon General's Office* (1880–95); on Billings's retirement, continued the work.

**Flett′ner** (flĕt′nẽr), **Anton.** 1885–1961. German engineer and inventor. Interested in remote control by radio waves; invented an army tank operated by remote control (1915); served with German air force in World War; invented the rotor ship (1924).

**Fleuranges,** Seigneur **de.** See *Robert III de La Marck*, under BOUILLON family.

**Fleu′riais′** (flû′ryĕ′), **Georges Ernest.** 1840–1895. French naval officer; perfected the gyroscopic horizon used in navigation.

**Fleu′rieu′** (flû′ryû′), Comte **de. Charles Pierre Cla′ret′** (klȧ′rĕ′). 1738–1810. French naval officer; assisted Berthoud in the invention of a marine chronometer.

**Fleu′ry′** (flû′rē′), **André Hercule de.** 1653–1743. French cardinal and statesman, b. Lodève. Educ. Paris; canon at Montpellier. Almoner to Queen Marie Thérèse (1679–83); royal almoner (1683); bishop of Fréjus (1698). Tutor of young Louis XV (1715); had great influence over Louis XV during first part of reign (1715–43); made member of Council of State (1723), virtually prime minister (1726–43) after dismissal of Louis Henri, Duc de Bourbon. Cardinal (1726).

**Fleury, Claude.** 1640–1723. French Roman Catholic clergyman and ecclesiastical historian.

**Fleury,** Comte **Émile Félix.** 1815–1884. French soldier; ordnance officer to Prince Louis Napoleon (1848) and active in furthering the coup d'état (Dec. 2, 1851); brigadier general and aide-de-camp to Napoleon III (1856); ambassador at St. Petersburg (1867). His son Comte **Maurice** (1856–1921), historian, wrote *Louis XV* (1899), *Carrier* (1897), *La Société du Second Empire* (1911), etc.

**Fleury, Joseph Nicolas Robert.** See ROBERT-FLEURY.

**Fleury-Husson, Jules.** See CHAMPFLEURY.

**Flex′ner** (flĕks′nẽr), **Simon.** 1863–1946. American pathologist, b. Louisville, Ky. M.D., Louisville (1889). Professor, U. of Pennsylvania (1899–1903); director of laboratories, Rockefeller Institute of Medical Research (1903–35); author of treatises on bacteriology and pathology. His brother **Abraham** (1866–1959), educator, A.B., Johns Hopkins (1886), A.M., Harvard (1906), was on staff of Carnegie Foundation for the Advancement of Teaching (1908–12); secretary (1917–25), and director of division of studies and medical education (1925–28), General Education Board; director of Institute for Advanced Study, Princeton (1930–39); author of *The American College* (1908), *Medical Education in the United States and Canada* (1910), *Medical Education in Europe* (1912), *A Modern College* (1923), *Universities—American, English, German* (1930), etc. Abraham's wife (m. 1898), **Anne,** *nee* **Craw′ford** (1874–1955), playwright, A.B., Vassar (1895), author of *Miranda of the Balcony* (1901), dramatization of *Mrs. Wiggs of the Cabbage Patch* (1903), *The Marriage Game* (1913), *The Blue Pearl* (1918), *All Souls' Eve* (1919).

**Flick′el** (flĭk′ĕl), **Paul.** 1852–1903. German painter of Italian and north German scenes, esp. German forests with sunlight effects.

**Flied′ner** (flēd′nẽr), **Theodor.** 1800–1864. German Protestant theologian and philanthropist. Devoted himself to prison reform and founded first society for prison reform of Germany (1826); opened refuge for discharged female convicts at Kaiserswerth (1833) and first Protestant deaconesses' home devoted to works of religion and charity (1836); also a hospital, infant school (1835), orphanage (1842), asylum for female lunatics (1847), and similar institutions.

**Flinck** (flĭngk), **Govaert.** 1615–1660. Dutch Biblical, genre, and portrait painter, b. in Cleves. Pupil and imitator of Rembrandt; obtained patronage of elector of Brandenburg and stadholder of Cleves; citizen of Amsterdam (1652). His works include *Isaac Blessing Jacob*, *Celebration of the Peace of Westphalia*, *Man with a Gray Beard*, *Angels Telling the Shepherds of Christ's Birth*.

**Flin′ders** (flĭn′dẽrz), **Matthew.** 1774–1814. Grandfather of Flinders Petrie (*q.v.*). English mariner and hydrographer, b. Lincolnshire; with George Bass explored and surveyed coast of New South Wales (1795–1800) and circumnavigated Tasmania (1798); made first survey of a large section of west coast of Australia (1801–03); detained at Mauritius by French governor six and a half years; author of *Voyage to Terra Australis* (1814); first to correct for deflection of compass caused by iron in ship.

**Flint** (flĭnt), **Austin.** 1812–1886. American physician, b. Petersham, Mass.; grad. Harvard (1833). Practiced, Northampton, Boston, Buffalo; moved to New York (1859). Founded Buffalo Med. Coll. (1847), and professor there (1847–61); also professor, U. of Louisville (1852–56), and New Orleans Med. Coll. (1859–61). In New York, founded Bellevue Hospital Med. Coll. (1861); professor there (1861–86); also, professor of pathology and practical medicine, Long Island Coll. Hospital (1861–68). His son **Austin** (1836–1915), b. Northampton, Mass., was also a physician; educ. Harvard; M.D., Jefferson Med. Coll. (1857); professor of physiology, Bellevue Hospital Med. Coll. (1861–98) and Cornell

(1898–1906); also specialized in treatment of mental disease.

**Flint, Charles Wesley.** 1878–1964. Methodist Episcopal clergyman and educator, b. Stouffville, Ontario, Canada. B.A., Toronto (1900); entered ministry (1900); B.D., Drew Theol. Sem. (1906). Pastorates, Brooklyn (1906–08, 1913–15) and Middletown, Conn. (1908–13). Chancellor, Syracuse U. (1922–36). Bishop in Methodist Episcopal Church (from 1936).

**Flint, Francis Stewart.** 1885–1960. British imagist poet and translator.

**Flint, Joseph Marshall.** 1872–1944. American surgeon, b. Chicago. B.S., Chicago (1895); M.D., Johns Hopkins (1900). Professor, California (1901–07) and Yale (1907–21). Served with Allied army and in A.E.F., in France (1915–19); organized first mobile hospital of A.E.F.; lieutenant colonel, U.S. army Medical Corps (July, 1918). Awarded D.S.M. (Mar. 1, 1919).

**Flint, Robert.** 1838–1910. Scottish philosopher and theologian; author of *Theism* (1877), *Antitheistic Theories* (1879), *Socialism* (1894), *Agnosticism* (1903).

**Flint, Timothy.** 1780–1840. American Congregational clergyman and author, b. near North Reading, Mass.; grad. Harvard (1800). Author of *Francis Berrian, or, The Mexican Patriot* (2 vols., 1826), *Life and Adventures of Arthur Clenning* (1828), *The Shoshonee Valley* (2 vols., 1830), *Daniel Boone* (1833), etc.

**Flo′bert′** (flô′bâr′). 1819–1894. French manufacturer of firearms, esp. light breech-loading firearms; the Flobert rifle is named after him.

**Flo′do′ard′** (flô′dô′år′) *or* **Fro′do′ard′** (frô′-). 894?–966. French chronicler; author of *Annales*, covering history of France from 919 to 966.

**Flood** (flŭd), **Henry.** 1732–1791. Irish politician, b. County Kilkenny; member of Irish parliament (1759 ff.), leader of opposition; vice-treasurer of Ireland (1775–81); co-operated with Grattan in obtaining independence of Irish parliament (1782), but quarreled with Grattan over later policies. British M.P. (1783 ff.); opposed commercial treaty with France (1787); proposed a reform bill based on household suffrage in counties (1790).

**Flood, William Henry Grattan.** 1859–1928. Irish musicologist; composer of Masses, motets, hymns, etc. Editor of *Moore's Irish Melodies* and of the *Catholic Hymnal* for Ireland; author of *History of Irish Music* (1895), etc.

**Flo′quet′** (flô′kĕ′), **Charles Thomas.** 1828–1896. French politician and lawyer. Opposed second empire and was active in government of national defense (1870); attempted reconciliation between revolutionary leaders and Versailles government during Commune, but was briefly imprisoned at Paris for radical sentiments (1871). Entered Chamber of Deputies (1876); prefect of the Seine (1882); president of Chamber of Deputies (1885–88); president of council and minister of interior (1888–89); combated Boulangism and wounded Boulanger in duel (1888). Again president of chamber (1889–93); implicated in Panama scandal (1892–93) and failed of re-election; senator (1894).

**Flor** (flôr), **Rog′er** (rŏj′ẽr) **di** (dē) *or* **de** (dē). 1280–1307. Military adventurer of German origin, b. in Brindisi. Joined Templar order and fought in Palestine. Later in service of Frederick of Aragon, King of Sicily; headed Catalan Grand Company (composed largely of Frederick's discharged mercenaries) in service of Byzantine emperor Andronicus II against Turks; arrived at Constantinople (1303) and married into imperial family; entered Asia (1304); plundered country; created Caesar (1306); assassinated by order of emperor.

**Flor′ence** (flŏr′ĕns), **William Jermyn.** *Stage name of* **Bernard Con′lin** (kŏn′lĭn). 1831–1891. American comedian, b. Albany, N.Y.; excelled in dialect impersonation.

**Florence of Worces′ter** (wo͝os′tẽr). d. 1118. English monk and chronicler.

**Flo·renz′** (flô·rĕnts′), **Karl.** 1865–1939. German Japanese scholar; professor, Hamburg (1914–35).

**Flo′res** (flō′rās), **Juan José.** 1800–1864. Ecuadorian soldier and statesman, b. Puerto Cabello, Venezuela. Served under Bolívar in War of Independence; won victory of Tarqui (1829); proclaimed Ecuador independent of Greater Colombia (1830) and became its first president (1830–35). After administration of Rocafuerte, again president (1839–45); deposed by revolution and passed many years in exile; recalled (1863).

**Flores, Venancio.** 1809–1868. Uruguayan soldier and politician, b. Paysandú. Following the civil war (1842–51), leader of the Colorados in revolt against government; had himself elected president (1854–55), but was overthrown. Retired to Argentina; entered Argentine military service. Later, returned to Uruguay, aided by Brazil and Argentina (1864); proclaimed provisional president (1865); president (1866–68); assassinated.

**Florestan I.** Prince of **Monaco.** See MONACO.

**Flo′rey** (flō′rĭ), **Sir Howard Walter.** 1898–1968. British pathologist, b. Australia; professor, Sheffield U. (1931–35), Oxford (from 1935); corecipient (see Sir Alexander FLEMING) of 1945 Nobel prize for medicine, for work on penicillin.

**Fló′rez** (flō′rāth), **Enrique.** 1702–1773. Spanish Augustinian monk, b. Valladolid. Author of *España Sagrada* (a history of the church in Spain, 53 vols., 27 of which publ. during his life; most of later vols. written by others) and *Memorias de las Reinas Católicas* (1761).

**Flo′ri·an** (flō′rē·än), *Lat.* **Flo′ri·a′nus** (flō′rĭ·ā′nŭs), Saint. d. about 303. Martyr and patron saint of Upper Austria.

**Flo′ri·an** (flō′rĭ·ăn). *Lat.* **Marcus Annius Flo′ri·a′nus** (flō′rĭ·ā′nŭs). Half brother of the Roman emperor Tacitus; proclaimed emperor a few weeks before being killed at Tarsus (276 A.D.).

**Flo′rian′** (flô′ryäN′), **Jean Pierre Cla′ris′** (klȧ′rēs′) **de.** 1755–1794. French writer of fables, romances (including *Gonzalve de Cordone*, *Galatée*), and plays.

**Flo·ri′da·blan′ca** (flô·rē′thä·bläng′kä), Conde **de. José Mo·ñi′no y Re·don′do** (mō·nyē′nō ē rā·thôn′dō). 1728–1808. Spanish statesman, b. Murcia. Procurator general to council of Castile; drew up decree for expulsion of Jesuits (1767); to Rome (1772) as ambassador to court of Pope Clement XIV. Minister of foreign affairs and prime minister (1777–92); his ministry very successful; deposed by court intrigue (1792). President of Central Junta of Spanish government during uprising against Napoleonic invasion (1808).

**Floridor.** See Josias de SOULAS.

**Flo′ri·mo** (flô′rē·mō), **Francesco.** 1800–1888. Italian composer and musical scholar.

**Flo′ri·o** (flô′rē·ō; *in Eng., also* flō′-), **John.** 1553?–1625. English lexicographer, son of an Italian Protestant refugee in London. Protégé of earls of Leicester, Southampton, and Pembroke. Compiled Italian-English dictionary entitled *A Worlde of Wordes*...(1598), revised and enlarged under title *Queen Anna's New World of Words*...(1611); translated Montaigne's *Essays* (3 books, 1603).

**Flo′ris** (flō′rĭs), **Frans.** *Real name* **Frans de Vriendt** (dĕ vrēnt′). 1517?–1570. Flemish painter, etcher, and designer of woodcuts, b. in Antwerp; under patronage of William of Orange. His works include decorations for receptions of Charles V and Philip II in Antwerp (1549, 1556) and for houses of many Spanish nobles and Antwerp dignitaries.

**Flo'rus** (flō'rŭs), **Lucius Annaeus.** Roman historian of early 2d century A.D.; compiled outline of the history of Rome, drawn chiefly from the work of Livy. Identified by some with **Publius Annius Florus,** Roman poet and rhetorician.

**Flo'ry** (flō'rē), **Paul John.** 1910– . American chemist. At Cornell U. (1948–56), Mellon Institute (1956–61), Stanford U. (1961–75); awarded Nobel prize for chemistry (1974).

**Flo'tow** (flō'tō), Baron **Friedrich von.** 1812–1883. German composer of light opera, b. in Mecklenburg-Schwerin. Composed operas *Alessandro Stradella* (1844), *Martha* (which interpolates Moore's *Last Rose of Summer;* 1847), *Indra* (1853), and *L'Ombre* (1869); also ballets and songs.

**Flou'rens'** (flōō'räNs'), **Pierre Jean Marie.** 1794–1867. French physiologist; professor in Collège de France. Among his notable works are *De l'Instinct et de l'Intelligence des Animaux* (1841), *Psychologie Comparée* (1864). His son **Gustave** (1838–1871) was a revolutionist; member of the Commune of Paris (1871); killed by a gendarme. Another son, **Léopold Émile** (1841–1920), was a politician; councilor of state (1879); minister of foreign affairs (1886–88).

**Flow'er** (flou'ẽr), **Benjamin Orange.** 1858–1918. American editor, b. Albion, Ill. Founded the *American Spectator,* Boston (1886); merged it with the *Arena* (1889); editor of these (1886–96, 1904–09). Founded and edited *Twentieth Century Magazine,* Boston (1909–11). Author of *Civilization's Inferno* (1893), *Gerald Massey* (1895), *Whittier* (1896), *Persons, Places, and Ideas* (1896), *The Patriot's Manual* (1915).

**Flower,** Sir **William Henry.** 1831–1899. English zoologist, b. Stratford upon Avon; served in Crimean War. Curator of Hunterian Museum, Royal Coll. of Surgeons (1861–84), and Hunterian professor of anatomy and physiology (1870–84); director of Natural History Museum, London (1884–98). President, Zoological Society (1879–99). Author, with Richard Lydekker (*q.v.*), of *An Introduction to the Study of Mammals* (1891).

**Floyd** (floid), **John Buchanan.** 1806–1863. American politician, b. Smithfield, Va. Governor of Virginia (1849–52). U.S. secretary of war in Buchanan's cabinet (1857–60), resigned at request of president. Entered Confederate service as brigadier of volunteers; removed from his command by Jefferson Davis.

**Floyd, William.** 1734–1821. American Revolutionary leader, b. Brookhaven, Long Island, N.Y. Member, Continental Congress (1774–77, 1778–83); a signer of Declaration of Independence. Member, U.S. House of Representatives (1789–91).

**Fludd** *or* **Flud** (flŭd), **Robert.** 1574–1637. English physician and Rosicrucian; M.A., Oxon. (1598), M.D. (1605). Practiced in London. Wrote treatises defending the Rosicrucians.

**Flü'gel** (flü'gĕl), **Ewald.** 1863–1914. Philologist, b. Leipzig. Educ. Freiburg, Leipzig (grad. 1885). Professor of English philology, Stanford (from 1892). Chief work, a Chaucerian dictionary, about one half completed at time of his death.

**Flügel, Gustav Lebrecht.** 1802–1870. German Arabic scholar; catalogued Oriental manuscripts at Vienna court library. Author of editions of the encyclopedic and bibliographical dictionary of Hajji Khalfah, with Latin translations (7 vols., 1835–58), and of the Koran (1838).

**Flügel, Johann Gottfried.** 1788–1855. German lexicographer; compiled *Vollständiges Englisch-Deutsches und Deutsch-Englisches Wörterbuch* (2 vols., 1830).

**Flüg'ge** (flüg'ĕ), **Karl.** 1847–1923. German hygienist and bacteriologist.

**Flür'scheim** (flür'shīm), **Michael.** 1844–1912. German economist; advocate of government control of land to advance social justice and to counteract socialism.

**Flygare** *or* **Fly'ga·re'–Car·lén'** (flü'gȧ·rĕ'kȧr·lān'), **Emilie.** = Emilie CARLÉN.

**Flynn** (flĭn), **John Thomas.** 1882–1964. American journalist, b. Bladensburg, Md. Educ. Georgetown. Columnist for *New Republic* magazine (1931–40). Author of *Investment Trusts Gone Wrong* (1930), *Graft in Business* (1931), *God's Gold* (1932), *The Fifteen Decisive Fortunes of the World* (1940), etc.

**Flynn, William James.** 1867–1928. American detective, b. New York City. On staff (1897–1917) and chief (1912–17), U.S. Secret Service. Director, bureau of investigation, U.S. Department of Justice (1919–21).

**Flynt, Josiah.** Pen name of Josiah Flynt WILLARD.

**Fo'a'** (fô'ȧ'), **Eugénie,** *nee* **Ro'drigues'–Gra'dis'** (rô'drēg'grȧ'dēs'). 1798?–1853. French novelist; author of *La Juive*...(1835), etc.

**Foakes'–Jack'son** (fōks'jăk's'n), **Frederick John.** *Orig. surname* **Jackson.** 1855–1941. Theologian, b. Ipswich, Eng.; B.A. (1879), M.A. (1882), B.D. (1903), Cantab.; to U.S. (1916); professor of Christian institutions, Union Theol. Sem. (1916–34). Author of *History of the Christian Church* (1891), *Rise of Gentile Christianity* (1927), *The Church in the Middle Ages* (1934), etc.

**Foch** (fôsh), **Ferdinand.** 1851–1929. French soldier, b. Tarbes. Grad. École Polytechnique (1873); entered artillery corps; professor of strategy, École Supérieure de la Guerre (1898); general of brigade and commandant of the school (1907). At outbreak of World War, commanded 20th army corps; checked German drive toward Calais; planned strategy by which Joffre defeated Germans on Marne (1914); commanded group of armies of the north (1915), directing spring and autumn offensives in Artois; directed action in battle of the Somme (1916); technical adviser to French government, and president of inter-Allied Council at Versailles (1917); appointed to supreme command of all Allied armies (Mar. 26, 1918); marshal of France (Aug., 1918); carried 1918 offensive to triumphant conclusion.

**Fock** (fŏk), **Dirk.** 1858–1941. Dutch statesman; governor general, Dutch East Indies (1921–26); minister of state (1928 ff.) and member of First Chamber (1929–35).

**Fock** (fôk), **Gorch.** *Real name* **Johann Ki'nau** (kē'nou). 1880–1916. German writer (in Low German) of novels and short stories.

**Fock'e** (fŏk'ĕ), **Henrich.** 1890–1979. German aeronautical engineer.

**Fo·dor'** (fô·dôr'). Family of Dutch musicians including: **Joseph** (1752–1828), violinist and composer; his brother **Anton** (1759–1849), pianist and composer; said to have written music and words to *Numa Pompilius,* first Dutch national opera; Joseph's daughter **Josephine** (1793–1870), operatic soprano; m. (1812) the actor Mainvielle.

**Foer'ster** (fûr'stẽr). See also FÖRSTER.

**Foerster, Norman.** 1887–1972. American educator, b. Pittsburgh, Pa.; A.B., Harvard (1910); professor of English, North Carolina (1919–30), Iowa (1930–44); author of *Nature in American Literature* (1923), *The American Scholar* (1929), *Toward Standards* (1931), etc.

**Foerster, Wendelin.** 1844–1915. German Romance philologist; established Breton origin of Arthurian legend; edited collected writings of Chrétien de Troyes (4 vols., 1884–99) and other old French texts.

**Foerster, Wilhelm.** 1832–1921. German astronomer; director of Berlin observatory (from 1865). His son **Friedrich Wilhelm** (1869–1966), philosopher, pedagogue, and pacifist; professor of pedagogy, Munich (1914–20), resigning because of pacifist opinions; returned to Zurich and became Bavarian minister in Switzerland after the revolution; advocate of education based on spirit of a positive Catholic Christianity, and opponent of German militarism and governmental policy; exiled from Germany (1933).

**Foeth, Afanasi.** See FET.

**Fo'gaz·za'ro** (fō'gät·tsä'rō), **Antonio.** 1842–1911. Italian novelist; representative of Liberal Catholic movement in Italian literature; attempted reconciliation of traditional dogma with modern science.

**Fo'gel·berg'** (fōō'gĕl·băr'y'), **Bengt Erland.** 1786–1854. Swedish sculptor of classical school; settled in Rome (1820). His works include sculptures of Venus and Cupid, colossal plastic sculptures of Odin, Thor, and Balder, statues of Gustavus Adolphus, Charles XIV John, etc.

**Foix** (fwä). Name of a French family flourishing from 11th to 15th century; the first count was **Roger Bernard I,** created comte **de Foix** (1012–35) by his father, Count Roger of Carcassonne. Members of family include: **Gaston III,** *surnamed* **Phoe'bus'** [fā'büs'] (1331–1391); became count 1343; in early life supported French king but later fought two years against Charles VI before being deprived of governorship of Languedoc (1380–82). **François Phoebus,** Comte **de Foix** (1473–83); inherited kingdom of Navarre (1479) and passed it on to his sister Catherine. **Catherine de Foix** (1470?–1517); queen of Navarre (1491–1517); m. (1484) Jean d'Albret (see ALBRET), the Foix and Albret families becoming merged in Bourbon family through Henry of Navarre when (1589) he became king of France (see BOURBON). **Gaston de Foix** (1489–1512), Duc **de Ne·mours'** (nē·mōōr'), called "the Thunderbolt of Italy"; French soldier, nephew of Louis XII; commanded French army in Italy; noted for the rapidity of his maneuvers; killed at Ravenna. Gaston's sister **Germaine de Foix** (1488–1538); queen of Aragon and Naples; niece of Louis XII of France; m., as 2d wife (1505), her great-uncle Ferdinand (V) the Catholic, of Spain; granted by Louis all claims to kingdom of Naples as dowry; only son, Juan, died in infancy, leaving Charles (later Emperor Charles V), son of Philip and Juana, as only heir to Spanish kingdom.

**Foix, Paul de.** 1528–1584. French diplomat and prelate; ambassador at court of Queen Elizabeth (1561–65) and at Rome (1579–84); archbishop of Toulouse (1576–84).

**Fo'kine** (fô'kyĭn; *Fr.* fô'kēn'), **Michel.** 1880–1942. Choreographer, b. St. Petersburg; credited with creation of modern ballet. Director of Diaghilev's Russian ballet (1909–14), of own ballet company in U.S. (from 1925); influenced by Isadora Duncan; became American citizen (1932). His notable ballets include *Acis et Galatée, Le Cygne* (composed for Pavlova), *Schéhérazade, Petrouchka, Les Sylphides, L'Oiseau de Feu, Cleopâtre, Papillons, Le Coq d'Or, Paganini, Blue Beard.*

**Fok'ker** (fŏk'ēr), **Anthony Herman Gerard.** 1890–1939. Aircraft designer and builder, b. Kediri, Java; educ. Haarlem, the Netherlands; established airplane factory at Johannesthal, Germany (1912), and another at Schwerin (1913); manufactured German pursuit planes during World War; invented apparatus making it possible to shoot through the field of an airplane propeller. Founded aircraft works at Amsterdam after the war. To U.S. (1922); naturalized; president, Fokker Aircraft Corporation of America, Hasbrouck Heights, N.J.

**Fo'lard'** (fô'lär'), Chevalier **Jean Charles de.** 1669–1752. French soldier; aide-de-camp to duc de Vendôme; wounded at Cassano d'Adda, and again at Malplaquet; after Treaty of Utrecht (1713) served with Knights of Malta against Turks, and with Swedish army under Charles XII.

**Föl'des** (fûl'dĕsh), **Jolán.** 1903– . Hungarian novelist; author of *The Street of the Fishing Cat* (1936; awarded All-Nations prize) and *I'm Getting Married* (1938).

**Fo·len'go** (fō·lĕng'gō), **Teofilo.** *Pseudonym* **Mer·li'nus Coc·ca'ius** (mûr·lī'nŭs kŏ·kā'yŭs) *or* **Mer·li'no Coc·ca'io** (mâr·lē'nō kôk·kä'yō). 1496?–1544. Italian macaronic poet; Benedictine monk (c. 1512–24, 1534–44); known esp. for his mock epic *Baldus* (1517, 1521, 1534–35) in macaronic verse; influenced Rabelais.

**Fo'ley** (fō'lĭ), **John Henry.** 1818–1874. Irish sculptor, b. Dublin. His notable works include: equestrian statues of Sir James Outram, Lord Canning, and Lord Hardinge, in Calcutta; statues of O'Connell, Goldsmith, and Burke, in Dublin; Lord Clyde, in Glasgow; Clive, in Shrewsbury; John Stuart Mill and Sir Charles Barry, in London; Stonewall Jackson, in Richmond, Va.; and a group (*Asia*) and statue of Prince Albert, in the Albert Memorial in London. Designed seal of the Confederate States of America.

**Foley, Martha.** See under Whit BURNETT.

**Foley,** Sir **Thomas.** 1757–1833. British naval officer; commanded the *Goliath*, leading English into battle of the Nile (1798); flag captain on the *Elephant* in support of Nelson at Copenhagen (1801).

**Fol'ger** (fōl'jēr), **Charles James.** 1818–1884. American jurist and politician, b. Nantucket, Mass. U.S. secretary of the treasury (1881–84).

**Folger, Henry Clay.** 1857–1930. American oil magnate and collector of Shakespeareana, b. New York City. With Standard Oil interests (from 1879); president (1911–23), chairman of board (1923–28), Standard Oil Co. of N.Y. Collected great Shakespearean library, to house which he erected special building in Washington, D.C., leaving his fortune as an endowment for it.

**Fol'ins·bee** (fŏl'ĭnz·bē), **John Fulton.** 1892–1972. American landscape painter.

**Foljambe.** Family name of earls of LIVERPOOL.

**Folk** (fōk), **Joseph Wingate.** 1869–1923. American lawyer and politician, b. Brownsville, Tenn. Circuit attorney at St. Louis (1900–04); exposed municipal political corruption, prosecuting those responsible. Governor of Missouri (1905–09); solicitor, U.S. Department of State (1913–14); counsel, Interstate Commerce Commission (1914–18); in law practice, Washington, D.C. (from 1918).

**Folkes** (fōlks), **Martin.** 1690–1754. English antiquary; educ. Cambridge. President of the Royal Society (1741–53). Aided Theobald in preparation of notes on Shakespeare.

**Folkmar, Daniel.** 1861–1932. American statistician and anthropologist, b. Roxbury, Wis. Anthropologist and lieutenant governor, Philippine Civil Service (1903–07); special agent, Immigration Commission of the U.S. (1908–09); with U.S. census bureau (1910–14; 1919–31). Author of *Dictionary of Races* (1911), etc.

**Folks** (fōks), **Homer.** 1867–1963. American social-service worker, b. Hanover, Mich. A.B., Harvard (1890). Secretary, State Charities Aid Assoc. of New York (1893–1902; from 1904); adviser to American Red Cross in Europe (1921). Author of *Care of Destitute, Neglected and Delinquent Children* (1902), *The Human Costs of the War* (1920).

**Fol'kung** dynasty (fôl'kōōng) *or* **Fol'kung'ar** (fôl'kōōng'är). Name of Scandinavian dynastic house, powerful in Sweden (1250–1365) and Norway (1319–1387). It came to Swedish throne through Earl Birger of Bjälbo who ruled as regent (1250–66); succeeded by Waldemar (ruled 1250–75), Magnus I (1275–90),

Birger II (1290–1318), and Magnus (II) Eriksson (1319–65); terminated (1365) with defeat and capture of Magnus by Albert of Mecklenburg. In Norway its rulers were Magnus Eriksson (1319–55), his son Haakon, (1355–80), and grandson Olaf (1380–87). See individual biographies and *Table* (*in Appendix*) for SWEDEN.

**Fol'len** (fŏl'ĕn), **August**, *later called* **Adolf Ludwig.** *Lat. surname* **Fol·le'ni·us** (fô·lā'nē·ŏŏs; *Angl.* fŏ·lē'nĭ·ŭs). 1794–1855. German poet and politician. Imprisoned at Berlin for demagogic agitation (1819–21); lived thereafter in Switzerland, taught in Aarau, and was member of Grand Council at Zurich. His brother **Charles,** *Ger.* **Karl, Fol'len** [*Angl.* fŏl'ĕn] (1795–1840), poet, clergyman, and reformer; lecturer, U. of Giessen (1818); driven from Germany to France and Switzerland for radical political activities, and finally from Switzerland (1824) to America (naturalized 1830); taught German at Harvard (1825–35); dismissed for abolitionist sympathies. Author of patriotic liberal songs including *Brause, die Freiheitssang.*

**Fol'lett** (fŏl'ĕt; -ĭt), **Wilson.** 1887–1963. American writer; educ. Harvard. Author of *The Modern Novel* (1918), *Some Modern Novelists* (with Helen Thomas Follett, 1918), *Zona Gale, an Artist in Fiction* (1923), *No More Sea* (1933).

**Fol'mer** (fōl'mẽr), **William F.** 1862–1936. American inventor and manufacturer, b. Covington, Kentucky. B.S., Kentucky. His more than 300 inventions include the first high-speed multiple-slit focal-plane shutter for cameras (1898), a camera (trade name *Graflex*), and one of the first aerial cameras.

**Fol'quet' de Mar'seille'** (fôl'kĕ' dē mȧr'sâ'y'). 1160?–1231. Provençal troubadour, composer of delicate love lyrics; entered holy orders (c. 1195) and became (1205) bishop of Toulouse.

**Fol'som** (fōl'sŭm), **Charles.** 1794–1872. American teacher and librarian, b. Exeter, N.H. Grad. Harvard (1813). Librarian, Boston Athenaeum (1846–56).

**Folsom, Nathaniel.** 1726–1790. American Revolutionary leader, b. Exeter, N.H.; member, Continental Congress (1774, 1775, 1777–80); major general, commanding New Hampshire State militia (1775); executive councilor (1778); president, N.H. constitutional convention (1783).

**Foltz** (fôlts), **Philipp von.** 1805–1877. German painter; works include decorations for Schiller room of New Royal Palace in Munich and other murals and ceiling decorations.

**Folz** (fôlts), **Hans.** 1478?–?1515. Meistersinger, b. prob. in Worms, Ger.; worked as barber-surgeon in Nuremberg; author of tales, festival plays, Meistersinger songs, riddles, etc.

**Fon·blanque'** (fŏn·blăngk'; fŏn'blăngk), **Albany.** 1793–1872. English journalist; editorial writer for London *Examiner* (1826), editor (1830–47); statistical officer in the Board of Trade (1847).

**Fon'cin'** (fôɴ'săɴ'), **Pierre.** 1841–1916. French scholar and educator; founder of l'Alliance Française for furthering knowledge of French language.

**Fonck** (fôɴk), **René.** 1894–1953. French aviator in World War, credited with destruction of 75 enemy planes.

**Fön'hus** (fûn'hōōs), **Mikkjel.** 1894– . Norwegian author of novels and stories, chiefly of Norwegian forest and animal life.

**Fon·se'ca** (fôn·sâ'kä), Marchesa **di.** *Nee* **Eleonora Pi·men·tel'** (pē·mān·tĕl'). 1768–1799. Italian patriot, b. Naples; author of sonnets and plays; adherent of popular party in Naples; founder and editor of antiroyalist journal *Monitore Napoletano* (1798–99); condemned and executed on restoration of Ferdinand IV to throne of Naples (1799).

**Fon·se'ca** (fōɴ·sā'kȧ), **Antônio Manuel da.** 1795–1893. Portuguese historical and portrait painter.

**Fon·se'ca** (fôn·sā'kä), **Juan Rodríguez de.** See RODRÍGUEZ DE FONSECA.

**Fon·se'ca** (fōɴ·sā'kȧ), **Manuel Deodoro da.** 1827–1892. Brazilian general, b. Alagoas. Active in war with Paraguay (1868–70); governor of Rio Grande do Sul (1887–89); leader in movement against Dom Pedro; head of provisional government (1889–91); president of Brazil (Feb. 24 to Nov. 23, 1891; resigned). His nephew **Hermes da Fonseca** (1855–1923) was president of Brazil (1910–14).

**Fonseca e Vasconcellos, Joaquim da.** See VASCONCELLOS.

**Fon'tai'nas'** (fôɴ'tā'nȧs'), **André.** 1865–1948. French writer, b. Brussels; to France; naturalized French citizen. Associated with the symbolists. Author of verse, novels, as *L'Indécis* (1903), *Les Étangs Noirs* (1912), a comedy, and critical studies, essays, translations from English authors, etc.

**Fon'taine'** (fôɴ'tĕn'), **Jean de la.** See LA FONTAINE.

**Fontaine, Pierre François Léonard.** 1762–1853. French architect; collaborator with Percier in restoring Malmaison by order of Napoleon and in planning the joining of the Louvre and the Tuileries; chief architect of the emperor (1813); retained favor of Louis XVIII and Louis Philippe.

**Fon'tan'** (fôɴ'täɴ'), **Louis Marie.** 1801–1839. French writer; journalist in Paris; wrote *Le Mouton Enragé,* directed against Charles X, and was sentenced to five years' imprisonment (1829) but was released at the Revolution (1830); author of plays *Perkins Warbec* and *Jeanne la Folle.*

**Fon·ta'na** (fôn·tä'nä), **Carlo.** 1634–1714. Italian architect; pupil of Bernini; built façade of San Marcello, fountain in Piazza di San Pietro, tomb of Queen Christina in St. Peter's, library of Minervan convent (all in Rome).

**Fontana, Domenico.** 1543–1607. Italian architect and engineer, b. Mili, near Lake Como. Protégé of Cardinal Peretti (later Pope Sixtus V). Chief architect of Sixtus V (1585–90); completed dome and lantern of St. Peter's after Michelangelo's plans, modified by della Porta (1588–90); built Lateran Palace, Vatican library (1587–90), etc.; with his brother **Giovanni** (1540–1614), also an architect, constructed Acqua Felice aqueduct and Acqua Paola fountain.

**Fontana, Felice.** 1720–1805. Italian physiologist and naturalist; court physiologist under grand duke of Tuscany, for whom he organized a museum of natural history and physiology.

**Fontana, Gaetano.** 1645–1719. Italian astronomer.

**Fontana, Prospero.** 1512–1597. Bolognese painter; employed at Vatican under Julius III. His daughter and pupil **Lavinia** (1552–1602) was also a painter; m. Paolo Zappi, amateur painter; known esp. as fashionable portraitist.

**Fon'tane'** (fôɴ'tȧn'), **Marius.** 1838–1914. French writer; author of *Le Canal Maritime de Suez* (1869), *Essais de Poésie Védique* (1876), etc.

**Fon·ta'ne** (fôn·tä'nĕ), **Theodor.** 1819–1898. German poet, novelist, and essayist, of French descent. Editor of *Kreuzzeitung,* Berlin (1860–70). Followed Prussian armies in campaigns of 1864, 1866, 1870; imprisoned at Domremy during war of 1870. Dramatic critic for *Vossische Zeitung* (1870–89). Author of ballad collections *Männer und Helden* (1850) and *Balladen* (1861); *Ein Sommer in London* (1854), *Jenseits des Tweed* (1860);

novels and stories chiefly of contemporary life; and reminiscences.

**Fon'tanes'** (fôN'tàn'), **Louis de.** 1757–1821. French writer and statesman; member of Corps Législatif (1802) and its president (1804); senator (1810); created marquis by Louis XVIII, and member of the privy council.

**Fon'tanges'** (fôN'täNzh'), Duchesse **de.** *Nee* **Marie Angélique de Scor'raille' de Rous'silles'** (dẽ skô'rà'y' dẽ ro͞o'sē'y'). 1661–1681. Mistress of Louis XIV, who created her duchesse de Fontanges.

**Fon'tanne'** (fôN'tàn'; *Angl.* fŏn·tăn'), **Lynn.** 1887?– . Actress; b. London, Eng.; m. (1922) Alfred Lunt (*q.v.*). Acted in London in support of Beerbohm Tree, and others; in U.S., acted as lead, usually as costar with her husband, in *The Guardsman, Strange Interlude, Pygmalion, Design for Living, Taming of the Shrew, Elizabeth and Essex, Idiot's Delight, Amphytrion 38,* etc.

**Fon'te·nelle'** (fôNt'nĕl'), **Bernard Le Bo'vier' de** (lẽ bô'vyā' dẽ). 1657–1757. French man of letters. Author of *Entretiens sur la Pluralité des Mondes* (an attempt to popularize new astronomical theory, 1686), *Dialogues des Morts* (an imitation of Lucian, 1693), etc.

**Fon·vi'zin** (fŭn·vyē'zyĭn), **Denis Ivanovich.** 1745–1792. Russian playwright; author esp. of satirical comedies, as *The Brigadier* (1766), *The Minor* (1782), etc.

**Foote** (fo͝ot), **Andrew Hull.** 1806–1863. American naval officer, b. New Haven, Conn. Ardent temperance advocate; made his vessel first temperance ship in U.S. navy; active in abolishing the liquor ration throughout navy, put in effect in 1862. When in command off African coast, active in capturing slavers and trying to break up slave trade (1849–51). At Canton, China, in return for insult to American flag, stormed and destroyed four forts below the city (1856). In command of naval operations on upper Mississippi (1861–62); co-operated with army in breaking Confederate defenses along the river in northern Tennessee; promoted rear admiral (1862).

**Foote, Arthur.** 1853–1937. American composer, b. Salem, Mass. A.B. (1874), Harvard. Organist, First Unitarian Church, Boston (1878–1910). Composer of church music, songs, organ and piano pieces, an overture (*In the Mountains*), chamber music, and cantatas.

**Foote, Henry Stuart.** 1804–1880. American political leader, b. in Fauquier County, Va. Governor of Mississippi (1852–54). Member, Confederate Congress; criticized Jefferson Davis for not accepting Lincoln's peace proposals; resigned from Congress and was imprisoned by Confederates; when released, went over to Union lines and sailed for Europe. After war, practiced law, Washington, D.C. Superintendent, U.S. mint at New Orleans (1878–80).

**Foote, Mary,** *nee* **Hal'lock** (hăl'ŭk). 1847–1938. American author, b. Milton, N.Y.; m. Arthur De Wint Foote (1876). After her marriage lived in Colorado, California, and Idaho (to 1928), and in Boston (1928–38). Her novels, illustrated by her own drawings, are laid in the Far West.

**Foote, Samuel.** 1720–1777. English actor and playwright, b. Truro. Educ. Oxford. Played comedy roles at Drury Lane (1745); made success esp. as mimic of prominent persons; had leg amputated as result of hunting accident (1766); made capital of lost leg in *The Devil upon Two Sticks* (1768) and *The Lame Lover* (1770); built and managed (1767–77) new Haymarket Theatre; indicted for libel because of his caricature of the duchess of Kingston as Kitty Crocodile in *The Trip to Calais* (1776; altered to *The Capuchin*). His plays include *The Knights,* ridiculing Italian opera (1749), *The Englishman in Paris* (1753), *The Mayor of Garratt* (1763), *The Commissary* (1765), *The Nabob,* satirizing East India Company servants (1772).

**Foote, Will Howe.** 1874–1965. American landscape painter, b. Grand Rapids, Mich.

**Fop'pa** (fôp'pä), **Vincenzo.** 15th-century Italian painter; settled in Pavia (c. 1456) and headed Lombard school.

**Fo'rain'** (fô'răN'), **Jean Louis.** 1852–1931. French painter and illustrator, b. Reims. On staff of *Monde Parisien, La Revue Illustrée, Courrier Français, La Vie Parisienne, Figaro, L'Écho de Paris.*

**For'a·ker** (fŏr'ȧ·kẽr), **Joseph Benson.** 1846–1917. American political leader, b. near Rainsboro, Ohio. Served through Civil War. Adm. to bar (1869); practiced, Cincinnati, Ohio. Governor of Ohio (1885–89). U.S. senator (1897–1909).

**Forbes** (fôrbz; *Scot.* fôr'bĭs), **Alexander Penrose.** 1817–1875. Scottish clergyman, b. Edinburgh. Bishop of Brechin (1848); censured for High-Church views, esp. for promulgating doctrine of the real presence (1860); friend of Döllinger and Pusey. Author of *Explanation of the Thirty-Nine Articles* (1867–68), etc.

**Forbes, Archibald.** 1838–1900. British journalist, b. Morayshire, Scotland. War correspondent for London *Morning Advertiser,* and later London *Daily News,* during Franco-Prussian War (1870–71), Russo-Turkish War (1877), Afghan War (1878–79), Zulu War (1880).

**Forbes, Bertie Charles.** 1880–1954. Journalist, b. in Scotland; to U.S. (1904), naturalized (1917). Founder and editor of *Forbes Magazine;* author of popular books on finance and business.

**Forbes, David.** 1828–1876. British geologist; surveyor for nickel and cobalt deposits in Bolivia and Peru (1857–60); student of volcanic phenomena in the southern Pacific; one of first scientists to apply microscope to study of rocks. His brother **Edward** (1815–1854) was professor of botany, King's College, London (1842) and professor of natural history, Edinburgh (1854).

**Forbes** of **Cul·lod'en** (kŭ·lŏd''n), **Duncan.** 1685–1747. Scottish jurist and patriot, b. near Inverness. Lord advocate (1725); lord president of the court of session (1737). Aided government during Jacobite uprising of 1745, and after battle of Culloden Moor (1746) endeavored to mitigate punishment inflicted on rebels.

**Forbes, Edwin.** 1839–1895. American landscape painter and etcher, b. New York City. Accompanied Army of the Potomac in Civil War and made war sketches published in *Frank Leslie's Illustrated Newspaper.*

**Forbes, Elizabeth Armstrong.** See under Stanhope A. FORBES.

**Forbes, Esther.** 1894–1967. American novelist, b. Westboro, Mass.; m. Albert L. Hoskins, Jr. (1926; divorced 1933). Author of *Miss Marvel* (1935), *Paradise* (1937), *The General's Daughter* (1939), *Paul Revere and the World He Lived In* (1942; awarded Pulitzer prize), etc.

**Forbes, George William.** 1869–1947. New Zealand statesman, b. Lyttelton, N.Z.; prime minister of New Zealand (1930–35).

**Forbes, Henry Ogg.** 1851–1932. Scottish naturalist and explorer; carried on extensive explorations in Cocos Islands, Java, Sumatra, Timor (1878–84), in New Guinea (1885–86), Chatham Islands (1893), island of Socotra (1898–99); commissioned by Peru to report upon birds of so-called Guano Islands (1911–13).

**Forbes, James.** 1871–1938. Playwright, b. Salem, Ontario, Canada; to U.S. (1884) and naturalized (1892). Author of *The Chorus Lady* (1906), *The Traveling Salesman* (1908), *The Famous Mrs. Fair* (1919), etc.

**Forbes, James David.** 1809–1868. Scottish scientist, b. Edinburgh. First scientist to specialize on study of phenomena of glaciers.

**Forbes, John.** 1710–1759. British officer in America, b. Dunfermline, Scotland. In command of expedition that captured French stronghold at Fort Duquesne (Nov. 25, 1758); renamed it Pittsburgh.

**Forbes,** Sir **John.** 1787–1861. Scottish physician; a founder of *British and Foreign Medical Review* (1836–47); coeditor of *Cyclopaedia of Practical Medicine* (1832–35).

**Forbes, John Colin.** 1846–1925. Canadian portrait and landscape painter; studio in London (from 1911). Painted portraits of Gladstone, King Edward VII, Queen Alexandra, etc.

**Forbes, Rosita,** *in full* **Joan Rosita,** *nee* **Torr** (tôr). 1893–1967. English traveler, lecturer, and writer.

**Forbes, Stanhope Alexander.** 1857–1947. Irish genre painter, b. Dublin. His first wife (m. 1889; d. 1912), **Elizabeth Adela,** *nee* **Armstrong,** was also a painter.

**Forbes, Stephen Alfred.** 1844–1930. American entomologist, b. Silver Creek, Ill. Professor, U. of Illinois (1884–1921).

**Forbes** of **Pit·sli′go** (pĭt·slī′gō), Sir **William.** 1739–1806. Scottish banker; member of Dr. Johnson's literary club; author of *Memoirs of a Banking House* (1803).

**Forbes, William Cameron.** 1870–1959. American diplomat, b. Milton, Mass.; A.B., Harvard (1892). Member of Philippine commission (1904–08); governor general of the Philippines (1909–13); U.S. ambassador to Japan (1930–32).

**Forbes′–Rob′ert·son** (-rŏb′ẽrt·s′n), Sir **Johnston.** 1853–1937. English actor, b. London. Member of leading English companies; appeared with Mrs. Patrick Campbell in *The Notorious Mrs. Ebbsmith* and in *Romeo and Juliet* (1895); achieved success in *Othello* and *Hamlet* (1898); other plays in which he appeared include *As You Like It* (1885), Shaw's *Caesar and Cleopatra* (1906), *The Passing of the Third Floor Back* (1909–11). His daughter **Jean** (1905–1962), actress; stage debut in London (1925); plays in which she has appeared include *Berkeley Square, Romeo and Juliet, Twelfth Night, Peter Pan, The Constant Nymph, St. Joan;* appeared under her own management (1934–35) in *The Lady of the Camellias, Mary Rose, As You Desire Me,* etc. His daughter **Diana** (1914– ) married (1935) Vincent Sheean (*q.v.*).

**For′bin′** (fôr′băɴ′), **Claude de.** 1656–1733. French naval commander; preyed on British, Dutch, and Austrian shipping in Mediterranean and North Sea (1690–1707); commodore in French navy (1702–10).

**Forbin,** Comte **Louis Nicolas Philippe Auguste de.** 1777–1841. French painter and archaeologist; director of royal museums (1815); reorganized the Louvre, and founded the Luxembourg for living artists.

**For′bush** (fôr′bo͝osh), **Edward Howe.** 1858–1929. American ornithologist, b. Quincy, Mass. Author of *Birds of Massachusetts and Other New England States* (3 vols., 1925, 1927, 1929, with illustrations by Louis Agassiz Fuertes and Allan Brooks), etc.

**Force** (fōrs), **Peter.** 1790–1868. American historian, b. near Passaic Falls, N.J. A printer, Washington, D.C. (1815). Chief historical work, *American Archives,* planned to present original source material of American history (9 vols., pub. 1837–53; covering years 1774–76). Force's library of Americana bought by government (1867) for Library of Congress.

**For′cel·li′ni** (fōr′chăl·lē′nē), **Egidio.** 1688–1768. Italian philologist and lexicographer; pupil and collaborator of Jacopo Facciolati (*q.v.*), known esp. for his *Totius Latinitatis Lexicon* (1771). See Ambrogio CALEPINO.

**Forch′ham′mer** (fŏrk′ăm′ẽr), **Johann Georg.** 1794–1865. Geologist, b. at Husum, Schleswig. Professor of mineralogy (1831), U. of Copenhagen; wrote on the geology of Denmark, crystallography, etc. His brother **Peter Wilhelm** (1801–1894), classical archaeologist, was professor of philology, Kiel (1843); author of works on topography and ancient Greek mythology, which he regarded as arising from personifications of the phenomena of nature.

**Forck′en·beck** (fôr′kĕn·bĕk), **Max von.** 1821–1892. German politician and jurist. Member (1858) and president (1866–73) of Prussian House of Representatives, and cofounder of Progressive (1861) and National Liberal parties (1866). Member (1867) and president (1874–79) of Reichstag; opposed Bismarck's protective tariff policy and, with National Liberal secessionists, founded the Liberal Union (1881), which joined the German Liberal party (1884). Member of Prussian House of Lords (from 1873).

**Ford** (fōrd), **Edward Onslow.** 1852–1901. English sculptor, b. London; best known for his portrait busts.

**Ford, Ford Madox.** *Orig. surname* **Huef′fer** (hŭf′ẽr). 1873–1939. English writer, of German descent, b. at Merton, Eng. Collaborated with Joseph Conrad in the novels *The Inheritors* (1901) and *Romance* (1903). Author of *Poems for Pictures* (1897), *The Fifth Queen* (1906), *Collected Poems* (1914), *Joseph Conrad* (1924), *No More Parades* (1925), *The Last Post* (1928), *The English Novel* (1930), etc.

**Ford, Gerald Rudolph.** 1913– . Thirty-eighth president of the U.S., b. Omaha, Nebr. Member, U.S. House of Representatives (1948–73), minority leader (1965–73); U.S. vice-president (1973–74); became U.S. president (1974–77) upon resignation of Richard M. Nixon August 9, 1974.

**Ford, Henry.** 1863–1947. American automobile manufacturer, b. Greenfield, Mich. Machinist by trade; resident of Detroit, Mich. (from 1887). Chief engineer, Edison Illuminating Co., Detroit. Organizer and president, Ford Motor Co. (1903–19, 1943–45), world's largest manufacturer of automobiles, with over 100,000 employees; introduced profit sharing in Ford Motor Co. (1914). During World War, chartered ship (Peace Ship) and at own expense took party to Europe in futile attempt to organize a peace conference and end the war (1915–16). Built Henry Ford Hospital, Detroit. His son **Edsel Bryant** (1893–1943), b. Detroit, president of Ford Motor Co. (1919–43). Edsel's son, **Henry (1917– ),** president (from 1945).

**Ford, Henry Jones.** 1851–1925. American political scientist, b. Baltimore, Md.

**Ford, Jeremiah Denis Mathias.** 1873–1958. American educator, b. Cambridge, Mass. A.B. (1894) and Ph.D. (1897), Harvard. Professor of French and Spanish, Harvard and Radcliffe (from 1907). Author of *Main Currents of Spanish Literature* (1919), *Portuguese Grammar* (1925), *Spanish Grammar for Colleges* (1928), etc.

**Ford, John.** 1586?–after 1638. English playwright, b. Ilsington, Devonshire. His plays include *The Lovers Melancholy* (1629), *'Tis Pity Shee's a Whore* (1633), *The Broken Heart* (1633), *Chronicle Historie of Perkin Warbeck* (1634), *The Ladies Triall* (1638); coauthor with Dekker and Rowley of *Witch of Edmonton* (publ. 1658).

**Ford, John.** *Orig. name* **Sean O'Fee′ney** (ō·fē′nĭ). 1895–1973. American motion-picture director, b. Cape Elizabeth, Me.; director of *The Iron Horse* (1924), *The Informer* (1935), *Stagecoach* (1939), *The Grapes of Wrath* (1940), *Tobacco Road* (1941), *How Green Was My Valley* (1941), *The Quiet Man* (1952); received directorial award of Academy of Motion Picture Arts and Sciences (1935, 1940, 1941, 1953).

**Ford, John Thomson.** 1829–1894. American theater manager, b. Baltimore. In one of his theaters, known as

Ford's Theater, in Washington, D.C., President Lincoln was shot by John Wilkes Booth (1865).

**Ford, Leslie.** Pseudonym of Zenith Jones BROWN.

**Ford, Paul Leicester.** 1865–1902. Bro. of Worthington Chauncey Ford. American historian and novelist, b. Brooklyn, N.Y. Edited: *The Writings of Thomas Jefferson* (10 vols., from 1892), *The Writings of John Dickinson* (2 vols., 1893). Author of *The True George Washington* (1896), *The Many-Sided Franklin* (1899), and the novels *The Honorable Peter Stirling* (1894), *Janice Meredith* (1899).

**Ford, Richard.** 1796–1858. English traveler and writer; toured Spain on horseback; author of *Handbook for Travellers in Spain* (1845), *Gatherings from Spain* (1846).

**Ford, Stanley Hamer.** 1877– . American army officer, b. Columbus, Ohio. B.Ph., Ohio State (1898). Served in Cuba (1898–99), Philippines (1900–02), China (1914–17), France (1918). Asst. chief of staff (1927–30).

**Ford, Worthington Chauncey.** 1858–1941. Bro. of Paul Leicester Ford. American statistician and educator, b. Brooklyn, N.Y. Chief of bureau of statistics in U.S. State Department (1885–89) and Treasury Department (1893–98). On staff of Boston Public Library (1897–1902) and Library of Congress (1902–09). Author of *American Citizen's Manual* (1883), *The Standard Silver Dollar* (1884), *George Washington* (1899), etc.

**Forde** (fōrd), **Francis Michael.** 1890– . Australian politician; schoolteacher; electrical engineer; M.P. (1922); minister for trade and customs (1931–32); deputy prime minister, and minister for the army (1941–46); high commissioner in Canada (1946–53).

**Ford'ney** (fōrd'nĭ), **Joseph Warren.** 1853–1932. American legislator, b. in Blackford County, Ind. Member, U.S. House of Representatives (1899–1923). Best known as cosponsor of Fordney-McCumber Tariff Act (1922).

**For'dun** (fōr'd'n), **John of.** d. about 1384. Scottish chronicler; probably a priest at Aberdeen; author of *Chronica Gentis Scotorum* (a history of Scotland).

**Fo'rel'** (fô'rĕl'), **Auguste Henri.** 1848–1931. Swiss psychiatrist and entomologist; known for work on the anatomy of the brain, and in hypnotism and forensic psychiatry; authority on insects, esp. the psychology of ants; pioneer in sex hygiene. His cousin **François Alphonse Forel** (1841–1912), naturalist, conducted limnological investigations on lakes Geneva and Constance; also investigated Swiss glaciers and earthquakes.

**Fore'paugh** (fōr'pô), **Adam** (1831–1890) and his brother **Charles** (1838–1929). American circus proprietors.

**Forest.** See also DE FOREST.

**For'es·ter** (fŏr'ĕs·tẽr; -ĭs·tẽr), **Cecil Scott.** 1899-1966. English writer, b. Cairo, Egypt; son of a British army officer. First novel, *Payment Deferred*, a murder story (1924; later adapted by him for stage and screen), followed by biographical works including studies of Napoleon (1924), Josephine (1925), Victor Emmanuel (1927), Louis XIV (1928), Nelson (1929). Other novels include *The Gun* (1933), *The General* (1936), the trilogy *Captain Horatio Hornblower* (1939: originally published as *Beat to Quarters*, 1937, *Ship of the Line*, 1938, and *Flying Colours*, 1939), *To the Indies* (1940), *The Captain from Connecticut* (1941), *The Ship* (1943).

**Forester, Frank.** See *Henry William Herbert* (1807–1858), under HERBERT family.

**Fo'rey'** (fô'rā'), **Élie Frédéric.** 1804–1872. French soldier; aided coup d'état (1851) by which Louis Napoleon seized power in France; in Crimean War (1854–55) and war in Italy (1859). Commanded French force in Mexico (1862–63). Created marshal of France.

**For'gan** (fôr'găn), **James Berwick.** 1852–1924. American banker, b. St. Andrews, Scotland; to U.S. (1885); naturalized. Vice-president (1892–1900), president (1900–24), First National Bank, Chicago, Ill.; director, Chicago Federal Reserve Bank (1914–20).

**For'kel** (fôr'kĕl), **Johann Nikolaus.** 1749–1818. German musicologist; director of music, Göttingen (from 1778). Author of *Allgemeine Literatur der Musik* (1792), the first biography of Bach (1802), etc.

**For'man** (fôr'măn), **Justus Miles.** 1875–1915. American novelist, b. Le Roy, N.Y.

**Forman, Simon.** 1552–1611. English astrologer and quack doctor; in London as an astrologer (1583), and later (1588) resorted to necromancy; granted by Cambridge U. a license to practice medicine. His love philters are referred to in Ben Jonson's *Epicoene.* At his death, left manuscript of *The Booke of Plaies*, which came into possession of Ashmole and was found to contain earliest account of performances of Shakespeare's *Macbeth, Winter's Tale*, and *Cymbeline.*

**For'mes** (fôr'mĕs), **Karl Johann.** 1810–1889. German operatic basso. His brother **Theodor** (1826–1874) was an operatic tenor.

**For'mi'gé'** (fôr'mē'zhā'), **Jean Camille.** 1845–1926. French architect.

**For·mo'sus** (fôr·mō'sŭs). 816?–896. Pope (891–896). Bishop of Porto; sent on an embassy to the Bulgarians (c. 866) and later to France; excommunicated by Pope John VIII but restored by Marinus; as pope, crowned Arnulf as emperor (896); much dispute over his legitimacy as pope.

**For·ner'** (fôr·nĕr'), **Juan Pablo.** 1756–1797. Spanish writer, b. at Mérida; author of *Exequias de la Lengua Castellana*, etc.

**For'rest** (fŏr'ĕst; -ĭst), **Edwin.** 1806–1872. American actor, b. Philadelphia. First New York success, at Park Theater, as Othello (June 23, 1826). Appeared at Drury Lane as Spartacus (1834). After years of success, began a feud with Macready; tragic result May 10, 1849, when a mob attacked Astor Place Opera House where Macready was appearing, attempted to wreck the building, and were fired on by the militia with loss of 22 and wounding of 36 persons. Forrest given (from 1850) to long spells of brooding and melancholy; last stage appearance (1872). Established a home (Forrest Home, Philadelphia) for aged actors. Chief roles, Lear, Coriolanus, Richard III, Virginius, Damon.

**Forrest, John.** 1st Baron **Forrest.** 1847–1918. Australian explorer, b. in Western Australia. Conducted coastal explorations from Perth to Adelaide (1870), Central Australian explorations (1874). First premier of Western Australia (1890–1901). Created baron (1918), first Australian statesman raised to the peerage.

**Forrest, Nathan Bedford.** 1821–1877. American army officer, b. in Bedford County, Tenn. Joined Confederate service at outbreak of Civil War. Became head of famous cavalry raiding force.

**For'res·tal** (for'ĕs·t'l), **James Vincent.** 1892–1949. American investment banker, b. Beacon, N.Y.; A.B., Princeton (1915); undersecretary of the navy (1940–44), secretary (1944–47); first secretary of defense (1947–49).

**For'res·ter** (fŏr'ĕs·tẽr; -ĭs·tẽr), **Alfred Henry.** 1804–1872. English artist; contributed sketches to *Punch* and *Illustrated London News;* wrote and illustrated humorous and juvenile books. Collaborated as artist with his elder brother, **Charles Robert** (1803–1850), in novels and *Absurdities in Prose and Verse* (1827) under joint pseudonym **Alfred Crow'quill'** (krō'kwĭl'); illustrator of *Beauty and the Beast* (1843), ballads, and fairy tales.

**For'skål'** (fŏŏr'skōl'), **Peter.** 1736?–1763. Swedish naturalist and traveler; pupil of Linnaeus; died of plague in Arabia on Niebuhr's Danish expedition to Egypt and

Arabia; author of *Flora Aegyptiaco-Arabica* (publ. 1775).

**Fors′man** (*Swed.* fôrs′mån), **Georg Zachris.** *Known as* **Yrjö Sakari Yr′jö–Kos′ki·nen** (*Finn.* ür′yû·kŏs′kĭ·nĕn). 1830–1903. Finnish historian; author of a history of the Finnish people. His brother **Jaakko Oskar** (1839–1899) was an educator; author of several works on Finnish law.

**Fors·sell′** (fôr·sĕl′), **Hans Ludvig.** 1843–1901. Swedish historian and statesman. Minister of finance (1875–80); member of upper house in Diet (1879–97); president of treasury board (1888); helped establish gold standard in Sweden. Author of *History of Sweden after Gustavus I* (2 vols., 1869–75), *Sweden in 1571* (2 parts, 1872–83), etc.

**Forss′mann** (fôrs′män), **Werner Theodor Otto.** 1904–1979. German physician. Awarded Nobel prize in physiology and medicine (1956) with A. Cournand and D. Richards.

**För′ster** (fûr′stĕr). See also FOERSTER.

**For′ster** (fôr′stĕr), **Edward Morgan.** 1879–1970. British novelist; author of *Where Angels Fear to Tread, A Room with a View, Howards End, The Celestial Omnibus, A Passage to India, The Eternal Moment,* etc.

**För′ster** (fûr′stĕr), **Erich.** 1865– . German Protestant theologian.

**Fors′ter′** (fôrs′târ′), **François.** 1790–1872. French engraver.

**För′ster** (fûr′stĕr), **Friedrich Christoph.** 1791–1868. German historian and poet. On staff of literary journals (1821–26); curator, Royal Museum, Berlin (from 1829). Author of spirited war songs, the historical drama *Gustav Adolf* (1833), the historical works *Albrecht von Wallenstein* (1834), *Geschichte Friedrich Wilhelm I* (3 vols., 1835), and *Preussens Helden in Krieg und Frieden* (1846). His brother **Ernst** (1800–1889), painter and art historian, painted frescoes in the Aula at Bonn and in the Glyptothek, Munich (until 1826); discovered and restored frescoes by Jacopo Avanzo at Padua (1837); edited several works of his father-in-law Jean Paul Richter.

**For′ster** (fôr′stĕr), **Georg,** *in full* **Johann Georg Adam.** 1754–1794. German traveler and writer; accompanied Captain Cook in his voyage around world (1772). Author of *A Voyage Around the World* (1777), *Ansichten vom Niederrhein, Brabant,*... (3 vols., 1791–94). His father, **Johann Reinhold Forster** (1729–1798), also on the voyage with Cook (1772), wrote *Observations Made During a Voyage Round the World* (1778).

**För′ster** (fûr′stĕr), **Heinrich.** 1800–1881. German Roman Catholic bishop, and pulpit orator. Princely bishop of Breslau (1853). Opposed dogma of infallibility at Vatican Council (1870); deposed from see by German court for opposition to May laws in Kulturkampf (1875).

**For′ster** (fôr′stĕr), **Henry William.** 1st Baron **Forster.** 1866–1936. English financier, and governor general of Australia (1920–25).

**Forster, John.** 1812–1876. English historian and biographer, b. at Newcastle. Edited *Foreign Quarterly Review* (1842–43), London *Daily News* (1846), London *Examiner* (1847–55). Author of biographies of Landor, Goldsmith, and Dickens.

**För′ster** (fûr′stĕr), **Josef Bohuslav.** 1859–1951. Czech composer, b. near Prague. Professor of composition (1920) and rector (1922–23) at Prague Conservatory. Composer of operas, symphonies, symphonic poems, and other orchestral works, a Stabat Mater, choral works with orchestra, chamber music, piano pieces, and songs.

**Förster, Max.** 1869–1954. German Old English scholar; professor, Würzburg (1898), Halle (1909), Leipzig (1910), Munich (1925–34). Published *Beowulf-Materialien* (1900), *Altenglisches Lesebuch* (1913), *Das Elisabethanische Sprichwort* (1918), *Die Beowulf-Handschrift* (1919), *The Exeter Book of Old English Poetry* (1933), etc.

**For′ster** (fôr′stĕr), **William.** 1784–1854. Brother-in-law of Elizabeth Fry. English Quaker minister; visited U.S. (1820–25) and was influential in checking spread of Unitarian views among the Quakers.

**För′ster–Nietz′sche** (fûr′stĕr·nē′chĕ), **Elisabeth.** 1846–1935. German writer; m. Bernhard Förster (1885); after his death (1889), acted as companion, secretary, and nurse (until his death, 1900) to her brother Friedrich Nietzsche, about whom she wrote a number of books.

**For·syth′** (fôr·sīth′), **Alexander John.** 1769–1843. Scottish clergyman and inventor; invented the percussion lock for firearms, and was pensioned by the British government after refusing an offer from Napoleon of £20,000 for the secret.

**Forsyth, Andrew Russell.** 1858–1942. Scottish mathematician. Author of *Treatise on the Theory of Functions* (1893), *Calculus of Variations* (1927), *Intrinsic Geometry of Ideal Space* (1935), etc.

**Forsyth, John.** 1780–1841. American political leader, b. Fredericksburg, Va. Grad. Princeton (1799). Adm. to bar (1802). Member, U.S. House of Representatives (1813–18); U.S. Senate (1818–19). U.S. minister to Spain (1819–23); gained Spanish king's ratification of treaty of 1819, ceding Florida to United States. Member, U.S. House of Representatives (1823–27). Governor of Georgia (1827–29). U.S. senator (1829–34). Secretary of state (1834–41).

**Forsyth, William.** 1737–1804. British botanist and gardener; superintendent of the Royal Gardens at St. James's and Kensington (1784). The genus of shrubs *Forsythia,* introduced from China, is named in his honor.

**For·sythe′** (fôr·sīth′). Variant of FORSYTH.

**Fort** (fôr), **Paul.** 1872–1960. French poet of the symbolist group; founded Théâtre des Arts (1890); edited the magazine *Vers et Prose* (1905–14); most notable poetical work is included in his more than 30 volumes of *Ballades Françaises.*

**For′tas** (fôr′tăs), **Abe.** 1910– . Amer. jurist, b. Memphis, Tenn. Associate justice, U.S. Supreme Court (1965–69).

**For′te·guer′ri** (fōr′tâ·gwĕr′rē) *or* **For′ti·guer′ra** (fōr′tē·gwĕr′rä), **Niccolò.** *Pseudonym* **Car′te·ro′ma·co** (kär′tâ·rô′mä·kō). 1674–1735. Italian prelate and poet; among his literary works are a blank-verse translation of Terence (1736); *Capitoli; Epistole Poetiche;* and a comic epic, *Il Ricciardetto* (1738), parodying works of Pulci, Boiardo, Ariosto.

**For′tes·cue** (fôr′tĕs·kū; -tĭs-), *afterwards* **Par′kin·son–For′tes·cue** (pär′kĭn·s′n-), **Chichester Samuel.** Baron **Car′ling·ford** (kär′lĭng·fērd). 1823–1898. British political administrator, b. in County Louth, Ireland. M.A., Oxon. (1847); assumed name Parkinson (1862); chief secretary for Ireland (1865–66, 1868–70), under Gladstone; aided with Irish Land Act of 1870; president of Board of Trade (1871–74); lord privy seal (1881–85); ceasing to support Gladstone's Irish policy (1885), rejected home-rule cause.

**Fortescue,** Sir **John.** 1394?–?1476. English jurist. Lord chief justice of the King's Bench (1442–61); attainted (1461) by Edward IV as a Lancastrian, followed Queen Margaret to Flanders (1463); fought at Tewkesbury, was captured (1471), and accepted a pardon granted by Edward IV; recognized Edward as rightful king (1471). Known as one of the earliest of English constitutional lawyers; author of *De Laudibus Legum Angliae,* etc.

**Fortescue,** Sir **John.** 1531?–1607. English statesman, a cousin of Queen Elizabeth. M.P. (from 1572). Chancellor of the exchequer (1589); chancellor of the duchy of Lancaster (1601). His defeat by Sir Francis Goodwin in parliamentary election (1604) raised a constitutional question when the clerk of the crown refused to receive the return of Goodwin because he was an outlaw, whereas the House of Commons recognized Goodwin's election as legal; as a result of the dispute, the House of Commons established its right to decide upon legality of election returns.

**Forth,** Earl of. See Patrick RUTHVEN.

**For'tier'** (fôr'tyā'), **Alcée**. 1856–1914. American scholar b. in St. James Parish, La. Professor at Tulane; esp. interested in Creole history and customs. Author of *Lousiana Folk Tales* (1895), *History of Louisiana* (1904), etc.

**For'tin'** (fôr'tăN'), **Jean**. 1750–1831. French physicist and engineer; invented a cup barometer (Fortin's barometer) used for scientific purposes.

**Fort'la'ge** (fôrt'lä'gĕ), **Karl**. 1806–1881. German philosopher. Professor, Jena (from 1846); followed teachings of Hegel, then of Beneke and Fichte, and considered psychology the basis of philosophy.

**For'tu·na'tus** (fôr'tū·nā'tŭs), **Venantius Honorius Clementianus**. 530?–?610 A.D. Latin poet, b. Ceneda, Italy. At court of Sigebert, King of Austrasia (565); wrote epithalamium on marriage of Sigebert and Brunhilde (566). Protégé and chaplain of Queen Radegunde, wife of Clotaire I, at Poitiers; bishop of Poitiers (599). Among his works are eleven books of short poems, hymns, verse epistles, etc., a poem in four cantos on St. Martin of Tours, and prose lives of saints.

**For'tune** (fôr'tūn; -tūn), **Robert**. 1813–1880. Scottish traveler and botanist; visited China (1842 and 1848), whence he introduced into England a double yellow rose and a Japanese anemone; also visited Formosa and Japan (1853). The genus *Fortunella* (containing the kumquat) derives its name from him.

**For·tuny' y Car·bó'** (fôr·tōōn'y' ē kär·bō'), **Mariano**. 1838–1874. Spanish painter, b. at Reus, Catalonia; dominant influence in Spanish art before rise of impressionism. Son-in-law of Madrazo. Resided chiefly in Rome. Known esp. for his rococo pictures.

**For'ward** (fôr'wẽrd), **Walter**. 1786–1852. American political leader, b. East Granby, Conn.; to Ohio as a boy. Adm. to bar (1806); practiced, Pittsburgh. U.S. secretary of the treasury (1841–43).

**Fo'sca·ri** (fôs'kä·rē), **Francesco**. 1372?–1457. Doge of Venice (1423–1457). Waged successful wars extending Venice's power in northern Italy (1426–54). Later life embittered by political activities of his only surviving son, **Giacopo** (c. 1457), who was tried, and banished (1445) for receiving bribes to use his influence in distributing state offices, was again tried, and banished (1450) for being involved in a political assassination, and was a third time punished the same way (1456) for alleged treasonable correspondence with enemies of Venice. Francesco was deposed (Oct. 24, 1457) and died a week later. Subject of Byron's tragedy *The Two Foscari*.

**Fo'sca·ri'ni** (fōs'kä·rē'nē), **Marco**. 1696–1763. Doge of Venice (1762–63) and author of the unfinished literary history *Della Letteratura Veneziana* (1752).

**Fo'sco·lo** (fôs'kō·lō), **Ugo**, *orig.* **Niccolò**. 1778–1827. Italian writer, b. on island of Zante. Served in Napoleonic armies; émigré (1815) to Switzerland, then England, to escape Austrian rule in Italy; continually involved in romantic intrigues. Author of the epistolary novel *Ultime Lettere di Jacopo Ortis* (1802), sonnets, odes, tragedies, a long philosophic poem, and critical essays.

**Fos'dick** (fŏz'dĭk), **Charles Austin**. *Pseudonym* **Harry Cas'tle·mon** (kás''l·mŭn). 1842–1915. American writer of juveniles, including *Frank on the Lower Mississippi* (1869), *The Buried Treasure* (1877), *The Boy Trapper* (1878), *Oscar in Africa* (1894), *Carl the Trailer* (1900), *The Floating Treasure* (1901), *Frank Nelson in the Forecastle* (1904).

**Fosdick, Harry Emerson**. 1878–1969. American clergyman, b. Buffalo, N.Y. A.B., Colgate (1900), B.D., Union Theol. Sem. (1904). Ordained in Baptist ministry (1903); pastor, Montclair, N.J. (1904–15); professor of practical theology, Union Theol. Sem. (1915–46); pastor, Riverside Church, N.Y. City. Author of *The Second Mile* (1908), *The Manhood of the Master* (1913), *The Assurance of Immortality* (1913), *The Meaning of Prayer* (1915), *Twelve Tests of Character* (1923), *As I See Religion* (1932), *A Guide to Understanding the Bible* (1938), *On Being a Real Person* (1943), etc. His brother **Raymond Blaine** (1883–1972), lawyer; A.B., Princeton (1905); LL.B., New York Law School (1908); special representative of U.S. War Department, in France (1918–19); undersecretary general of League of Nations (1919–20); president, Rockefeller Foundation (1936–48); author of *European Police Systems* (1915), *American Police Systems* (1920), *The Old Savage in the New Civilization* (1928), etc.

**Foss** (fŏs), **Cyrus David**. 1834–1910. American Methodist Episcopal bishop and educator.

**Foss, Sam Walter**. 1858–1911. American editor and humorist, b. Candia, N.H.; grad. Brown (1882). Editor, *Yankee Blade*, Boston, and writer for Boston *Globe* (1887–94). Contributor, esp. of light verse, to various magazines. Author of *Back Country Poems* (1892), *Dreams in Homespun* (1897), *Songs of War and Peace* (1899), *Songs of the Average Man* (1907).

**Fosse, Charles de La.** See Charles de LAFOSSE.

**Fos'ter** (fŏs'tẽr), **Abby** (*or* **Abigail**) **Kelley**. See under Stephen Symonds FOSTER.

**Foster, Benjamin**. 1852–1926. American landscape painter, b. North Anson, Me. Studied under Abbott Thayer in New York and Merson and Morot in Paris.

**Foster, Birket**. See Myles Birket FOSTER.

**Foster, Charles**. 1828–1904. American political leader, b. Fostoria, Ohio. Governor of Ohio (1880–84); U.S. secretary of the treasury (1891–93).

**Foster, Edward P.** 1853–1937. American clergyman; resident of Marietta, Ohio. Inventor (c. 1906) of a world language, "Ro," based on the classification of ideas.

**Foster, Fay**. 1886–1960. American musician and composer of chamber music, choral and piano pieces, and more than one hundred songs; winner of many prizes for her compositions.

**Foster, Frank Pierce**. 1841–1911. American physician, b. Concord, N.H. Grad. Coll. Phys. & Surg., N.Y. (1862). Advocated use of animal lymph in vaccination; operated a vaccine farm at Cos Cob, N.Y. Compiled *Illustrated Encyclopedic Medical Dictionary* (4 vols., 1888–94), etc.

**Foster, George Burman**. 1858–1918. American Baptist theologian, b. Alderson, W.Va.; professor, U. of Chicago (1895–1918). Debated publicly with Clarence Darrow on subjects *Is Life Worth Living?* and *Resolved, That the Human Will is Free* (1917 and 1918).

**Foster,** Sir **George Eulas**. 1847–1931. Canadian educator and statesman, b. in New Brunswick. Professor of classics, U. of New Brunswick (1872–79). Member of Canadian House of Commons (from 1882); senator (1921). Canadian representative at Peace Conference in Paris (1919), and at first, seventh, and ninth assemblies, League of Nations (1921, 1926, 1929); vice-president of league (1921).

**Foster, Henry**. 1796–1831. English navigator; served as

astronomer on Parry's polar expeditions (1824–25; 1827). Commanded government sloop *Chanticleer*, sent out (1828–29) to determine specific ellipticity of the earth by pendulum experiments in the South Seas, and to record observations on meteorology, magnetism, direction of ocean currents, etc.

**Foster, John.** 1770–1843. English Baptist clergyman (1792–1806) and essayist; republican in political sympathy, and a critic of existing system of ecclesiastical institutions.

**Foster, John Watson.** 1836–1917. American statesman, b. in Pike County, Ind.; grad. Indiana (1855). Adm. to bar (1857); practiced, Evansville, Ind. Served through Civil War. U.S. minister to Mexico (1873–80), Russia (1880–81), Spain (1883–85). U.S. secretary of state (1892–93). Invited by China, joined Chinese commissioners in negotiating peace with Japan (1894); represented China at Second Hague Conference (1907). U.S. agent in arbitration to fix Alaska-Canadian boundary (1903). Author of *A Century of American Diplomacy, 1776–1876* (1900), etc.

**Foster, John Wells.** 1815–1873. American geologist and paleontologist, b. Brimfield, Mass. Assisted on geological survey of Ohio (1837), studying coal beds and limestone deposits near Columbus; assisted on survey of Lake Superior region, reporting on mineral resources. Conducted paleontological and ethnological investigations in the Mississippi Valley.

**Foster,** Mrs. **Laurence.** *Pseudonym* **Ru'mer God'den** (rōō'mẽr gŏd''n). 1909– . English novelist; author of *Black Narcissus* (1939), *Breakfast with the Nikolides* (1941); m. (1949) James Haynes-Dixon.

**Foster,** Sir **Michael.** 1836–1907. English physiologist; lecturer (1870–83) and professor (1883–1903), Cambridge U.; co-operated with Huxley in devising method of practical laboratory work; a founder and editor (to 1894) of the *Journal of Physiology.* Joint editor of Huxley's *Scientific Memoirs* (1898–1902).

**Foster, Myles Birket.** 1825–1899. English illustrator of editions of English and American poets and prose authors (1846–58), and painter, esp. of water-color studies of roadside and woodland landscapes.

**Foster, Randolph Sinks.** 1820–1903. American Methodist Episcopal clergyman and educator; president of Northwestern U. (1857–60); professor, Drew Theol. Sem. (1868–72); president of the seminary (1870–72). Consecrated bishop (1872).

**Foster, Robert Frederick.** 1853–1945. Authority on card games, b. Edinburgh, Scotland. Civil engineer and architect by profession; retired (1893) to specialize on games of cards. Card editor, New York *Sun* (from 1895). Author of *Whist Manual* (1890), *Foster's Hoyle* (1897), *Foster's Complete Bridge* (1906). Special editor for card games and gambling, *Webster's New International Dictionary, Second Edition.*

**Foster, Stephen Collins.** 1826–1864. American song writer, b. near Pittsburgh, Pa. Musical genius developed early; contributed many songs for the then popular Negro minstrel troupes. Resident of Pittsburgh (until 1860), New York City (from 1860). Improvident and intemperate by nature, died in charity ward of Bellevue Hospital in spite of large sums realized from his songs. Best-known songs: *Open thy Lattice, Love; Louisiana Belle; My Old Kentucky Home; Massa's in the Cold, Cold Ground; Old Folks at Home; Come Where My Love Lies Dreaming; Nelly was a Lady; O Susanna; Away down South; Old Dog Tray; Old Black Joe.* Elected to American Hall of Fame (1940).

**Foster, Stephen Symonds.** 1809–1881. American abolitionist, b. Canterbury, N.H.; grad. Dartmouth (1838). Antislavery lecturer and agitator, associate of Garrison; later, advocated woman suffrage, temperance, world peace, and reform in conditions of labor. His wife, **Abigail,** *better known as* **Abby,** *nee* **Kel'ley** [kĕl'ĭ] (1810–1887), b. Pelham, Mass., supported his abolitionist agitation and was herself a pioneer in woman suffrage.

**Foster, William Trufant.** 1879–1950. American economist; collaborator in writing *Money* (1923), *Profits* (1925), *The Road to Plenty* (1927), and *Progress and Plenty* (1930).

**Foster, William Zebulon.** 1881–1961. American labor leader, b. Taunton, Mass.; educ. Phila. Joined Socialist party (1900), I.W.W. (1909), and Communist party (c. 1921). Active in organizing steelworkers for the great strike (1919). Communist party candidate for president of the United States (1924, 1928, 1932) and for governor of New York (1930). Author of *Towards Soviet America, From Bryan to Stalin* (1937).

**Foth'er·gill** (fŏth'ẽr·gĭl), **Jessie.** 1851–1891. English novelist, b. Manchester; author of novels depicting Lancashire and Yorkshire factory life. Her best-known novel is *The First Violin* (1878).

**Fothergill, John.** 1712–1780. British physician, of Quaker family; M.D., Edinburgh (1736); practiced in London (from 1740); maintained botanical garden known through Europe. His *Account of the Sore Throat Attended with Ulcers* (1748) contains first recognition of diphtheria in England. Aided Benjamin Franklin (1774) in drafting scheme of reconciliation between England and American colonies.

**Fou'cault'** (fōō'kō'), **Jean Bernard Léon.** 1819–1868. French physicist, b. Paris. Studied medicine, then turned to experimental physics. With A. H. L. Fizeau, conducted experiments on light and heat; demonstrated that the velocity of light varies in different media (1850); independently measured the velocity of light in air; demonstrated the axial rotation of the earth by the apparent clockwise motion of a pendulum's plane of oscillation (1851); invented the gyroscope (1852); appointed physicist at Paris observatory (1855); discovered the eddy, or Foucault, induced electric current; invented the Foucault prism, a variety of Nicol prism (1857); devised method of giving to the mirrors of reflecting telescopes the form of a spheroid or paraboloid of revolution (1858).

**Fou'ché'** (fōō'shā'), **Edmond.** French inventor; credited with devising (c. 1903) first practical and safe oxyacetylene torch for metallic welding.

**Fouché, Joseph.** Duc **d'O'trante'** (dô'träɴt'). 1763–1820. French statesman; member of the National Convention (1792–95). Minister of police (1799–1802; 1804–10; and 1815). Famous for unfeeling efficiency, his system of spies, and various political intrigues designed to save or benefit himself in any contingency. Advised Napoleon to abdicate after Waterloo, and assumed leadership of the provisional government formed hastily to negotiate with the allies. Exiled from France (1816) and lived in retirement at Trieste (1816–20).

**Fou'cher' de Ca'reil'** (fōō'shā' dẽ kȧ'rā'y'), Comte **Louis Alexandre.** 1826–1891. French writer and politician; member of the Senate (1876); ambassador at Vienna (1883–86). Author of *Leibnitz, Descartes et Spinoza* (1863), *Dante* (1864), *Goethe et son Œuvre* (1865), etc.

**Foucher de Char'tres** (shȧr'tr'). 1058–after 1127. French priest and historian; chaplain of Baldwin, King of Jerusalem. His *Historia Hierosolymitana* tells story of First Crusade.

**Foucquet.** Variant of FOUQUET.

**Fouil'lée'** (fōō'yā'), **Alfred Jules Émile.** 1838–1912. French philosopher and educator; professor successively at Douai, Montpellier, Bordeaux, Paris.

**Fould** (fōōld), **Achille.** 1800–1867. French statesman and financier; minister of finance (1849–52; 1861–67); senator and minister of state (1852).

**Foulis** (foulz), **Robert** (1707–1776) and his brother **Andrew** (1712–1775). Scottish booksellers and printers; in partnership at Glasgow (from c. 1741); best known for their editions of the classics, and quarto editions of works of Thomas Gray (1768) and Milton's *Paradise Lost* (1770).

**Foulke** (fōlk), **William Dudley.** 1848–1935. American lawyer and writer; member of U.S. Civil Service Commission (1901–03) and president of National Civil Service Reform League (1923–24). Author of *Slav or Saxon* (1887), *Maya...* (1900), *Lyrics of War and Peace* (1916), *Roosevelt and the Spoilsmen* (1925), *Songs of Eventide* (1928), *Earth's Generations Pass* (verse, 1930), etc.

**Foul'lon'** (fōō'lôN'), **Joseph François.** 1717–1789. French government official; intendant general of the French army during the Seven Years' War (1756–63), and intendant of finance (1771). After fall of the Bastille (July 14, 1789), he went into hiding, but was caught and hanged from a lamppost by the mob.

**Foulques** (fōōlk). See ANJOU family.

**Foulques** (fōōlk) *or* **Fulk** (fŏŏlk). 840?–900. French ecclesiastic; archbishop of Reims (883); played important political rule, esp. in crowning Charles the Simple (893) to contest the claims of Eudes, Count of Paris, to the throne; created chancellor of France (898); assassinated by order of Count Baldwin of Flanders.

**Foulques de Neuil'ly'** (dē nû'yē'). d. 1202. French ecclesiastic, famed as a pulpit orator; under instructions from Pope Innocent III, aroused people to undertake the Fourth Crusade (1198).

**Fouqué.** See LA MOTTE-FOUQUÉ.

**Fou'qué'** (fōō'kā'), **Ferdinand André.** 1828–1904. French geologist and petrologist; studied the volatile products of volcanic eruptions and the formation of volcanic craters; introduced into France the use of the microscope for petrographic study; reproduced rocks and minerals artificially.

**Fou'quet'** *or* **Fouc'quet'** (fōō'kĕ'), **Jean.** 1416?–1480. French painter; court painter of Louis XI; known esp. for his illumination of *Livres d'Heures*, one for Étienne Chevalier, one for Marie de Clèves, widow of the duke of Orléans, and one for Philippe de Comines.

**Fouquet** *or* **Foucquet, Nicolas.** 1615–1680. French government official; confidential agent of Cardinal Mazarin, and appointed superintendent of finance (1653); arrested (1661), tried for embezzlement, convicted after trial lasting most of four years, and imprisoned for rest of his life; identified by some, probably erroneously, as the Man in the Iron Mask. See duc de BELLE-ISLE.

**Fou'quier'-Tin'ville'** (fōō'kyā'tăN'vēl'), **Antoine Quentin.** 1746–1795. French Revolutionary politician; public accuser before the Revolutionary Tribunal (March, 1793–July, 1794); guillotined (May 7, 1795).

**Four'croy'** (fōōr'krwȧ'), Count **Antoine François de.** 1755–1809. French chemist, b. Paris. M.D. (1780); professor, Jardin des Plantes (from 1784); one of earliest converts to theories of Lavoisier. Author of *Méthode de Nomenclature Chimique* (with Lavoisier, Berthollet, and Guyton de Morveau, 1787), etc. See LAVOISIER.

**Four·drin'i·er** (fōōr·drĭn'ĭ·ẽr), **Henry** (1766–1854) and his brother **Sealy** (d. 1847). English papermakers and inventors; invented (with aid of Bryan Donkin) and patented (1807) improved papermaking machine capable of producing a continuous sheet of paper of any desired size from the wood pulp; received parliamentary grant (1840) to compensate them for outlays in the course of their experiments.

**Fou'reau'** (fōō'rō'), **Fernand.** 1850–1914. French explorer in Africa; made special study of Sahara region.

**Fou'ri'chon'** (fōō'rē'shôN'), **Martin.** 1809–1884. French naval officer.

**Fou'rier'** (fōō'ryā'), **François Marie Charles.** 1772–1837. French social scientist and reformer, b. at Besançon. Devoted himself to study of society and methods of improving social and economic conditions; published (1808) *Théorie des Quatre Mouvements et des Destinées Générales*, advocating a co-operative organization of society into phalansteries, each one large enough to allow for industrial and social needs of the group. Author also of *Traité de l'Association Domestique et Agricole* (1822), *La Fausse Industrie Morcelée* (1835–36). Fourierism, as his proposed system was called, made a strong appeal to many thoughtful people and a number of attempts were made to organize as he suggested; Brook Farm in the U.S. was a famous example of a Fourieristic experiment.

**Fourier,** Baron **Jean Baptiste Joseph.** 1768–1830. French geometrician and physicist, b. Auxerre. Known for researches in the theory of heat and of numerical equations. Accompanied Bonaparte to Egypt (1798) where he became perpetual secretary of the Institute of Cairo; returned to France (1801); prefect of Isère (1802–15); created baron by Napoleon (1808).

**Fourier, Pierre.** 1565–1640. French Roman Catholic priest; founder (1597) of the religious order School Sisters of Notre Dame.

**Four'mont'** (fōōr'môN'), **Étienne.** 1683–1745. French Oriental scholar; a student of Chinese language.

**Four'neau'** (fōōr'nō'), **Ernest François Auguste. 1872–1949.** French chemist; chief of staff at Pasteur Institute; known esp. for studies on local anesthetics.

**Fournet, Louis René Marie Charles Dartige du.** See DU FOURNET.

**Four'ney'ron'** (fōōr'nā'rôN'), **Benoît.** 1802–1867. French engineer; inventor of a hydraulic turbine.

**Four'nier'** (fōōr'nyā'), **Édouard.** 1819–1880. French writer; editor of *Le Théâtre* (1853–55); author of *L'Esprit dans l'Histoire* (1857), *Le Théâtre Français au XVI^e^ et au XVII^e^ Siècle* (1871), *Histoire des Enseignes de Paris* (1884), etc.

**Fournier, Henri Alain.** See ALAIN-FOURNIER.

**Fournier, Pierre Simon.** 1712–1768. French type founder; author of *Manuel des Caractères de l'Imprimerie* (1742), etc.

**Fournier, Télesphore.** 1824–1896. Canadian jurist and politician; postmaster general (1875); puisne judge, Supreme Court of Canada (1875–96).

**Four'nier d'Albe'** (fōōr'nyā dălb'), **Edmund Edward.** 1868–1933. English physicist and lexicographer, b. in London. Assistant in physical laboratory of Royal College of Science for Ireland and Trinity Coll., Dublin; active in Pan-Celtic movement; published an English-Irish dictionary (1903). Invented optophone, an instrument by which light energy is converted into sound energy (1912), developing it so that blind persons can read printed matter by ear (1914); transmitted by radio first photographic portrait broadcast from London (1923); invented system of wireless telewriting and telephotography based upon acoustic resonance (1925). Author of *The Electron Theory* (1906), *Contemporary Chemistry* (1912), *The Moon-Element* (1924), *Hephaestus, or the Soul of the Machine* (1925), etc.

**Fowl'er** (foul'ẽr), **Alfred.** 1868–1940. English astrophysicist; author of papers relating to the spectra of comets, the sun, and stars, and the structure of spectra.

**Fowler, Ellen Thorneycroft.** See Ellen Thorneycroft FELKIN.

**Fowler, Frank.** 1852–1910. American portrait painter, b. Brooklyn, N.Y.; studio, New York City (from 1880).

**Fowler, Gene.** 1890–1960. American journalist, playwright, and scenarist, b. Denver, Colo. Author of *The Great McGoo* (1931; play, with Ben Hecht), *Timberline* (1933), *Mighty Barnum* (with Bess Meredyth, 1935), etc.

**Fowler, Harold North.** 1859–1955. American educator, b. Westfield, Mass. A.B., Harvard (1880); Ph.D., Bonn (1885). Professor of Greek, Coll. for Women, Western Reserve (1893–1929). Editor and translator of many Greek and Latin classics. Author of *Ancient Greek Literature* (1902), *Roman Literature* (1903), *Sculpture* (1916).

**Fowler, Henry Hartley.** 1st Viscount **Wol'ver·hamp'-ton** (wo͝ol'vẽr·hăm(p)'tŭn). 1830–1911. British cabinet minister. President of Board of Trade (1892); secretary for India (1894); supported Boer War and opposed tariff reform; chancellor of duchy of Lancaster (1905); lord president of council (1908).

**Fowler, Henry Watson.** 1858–1933. English lexicographer; educ. Oxford. Coauthor with his brother **F. G. Fowler** (d. 1918) of *The King's English* (1906). Published *The Concise Oxford Dictionary of Current English* (1911), *The Pocket Oxford Dictionary* (1924), both being drawn from the great *Oxford English Dictionary.* Compiled *A Dictionary of Modern English Usage* (1926), and wrote *On Grammatical Inversions* (1922), *Some Comparative Values* (1929), *If Wishes Were Horses* (1929), *Rhymes of Darby to Joan* (1931).

**Fowler,** Sir **John.** 1817–1898. English engineer, b. near Sheffield; designed Pimlico railway bridge (1860), Forth bridge (with his partner, Sir Benjamin Baker; 1882–90). Engineer of London Metropolitan railway (from 1853), pioneer of underground railways; engineering adviser in Egypt to khedive Ismail Pasha (1871–79).

**Fowler, Sydney.** See Sydney Fowler WRIGHT.

**Fowler, Thomas.** 1832–1904. English philosopher; professor of logic (1873), president of Corpus Christi College (1881), and vice-chancellor of the university (1899–1901), Oxford. Author of *The Elements of Deductive Logic* (1867), *The Elements of Inductive Logic* (1870), etc.

**Fox** (fŏks). See also FOXE.

**Fox, Caroline.** 1819–1871. English diarist; friend of John Stuart Mill, John Sterling, Thomas Carlyle, and other prominent persons. Extracts from her diary (1835–71) were edited and published by Horace N. Pym (1882) under the title *Memories of Old Friends, Being Extracts from the Journal and Letters of Caroline Fox.*

**Fox,** Sir **Charles.** 1810–1874. English engineer. Constructing engineer, London and Birmingham railway; introduced the switch into railway use; engaged in railway construction in Ireland, Denmark, France, Canada, India, Cape Colony, Queensland. Also, designed buildings in Hyde Park for the exhibition (1851), and built the Berlin waterworks. His son Sir **Francis** (1844–1927), civil engineer, engaged esp. in railroad and tunnel engineering, and in later years in preserving cathedrals and ancient buildings. Served as engineer in building the Great Northern and City tube railway, and the bridge over Zambezi River at Victoria Falls, etc. Directed preservation work at Winchester Cathedral, Canterbury Cathedral, Lincoln Cathedral, and others.

**Fox, Charles James.** 1749–1806. English statesman and orator; 3d son of Henry Fox (*q.v.*), 1st Baron Holland. Tory M.P. (1768); member of North's cabinet as a lord of admiralty (1770–72) and of treasury (1772–74); dismissed because of independence of action and dislike on part of George III. Went over to Whig opposition and with brilliant oratory led opposition to North's coercive measures against American colonies, including tea duty (1774); attacked admiralty, advocated triennial parliaments and Roman Catholic relief; on fall of North (1782), became foreign secretary in Rockingham's ministry, despite king's objections, but was thwarted by Shelburne, the other secretary of state; resigned. Became foreign secretary, with North as home secretary, in coalition ministry of duke of Portland (1783), which was defeated on Fox's India reform bill through personal influence of king (Dec., 1783); kept out of office by king (till 1806), joined opposition to Pitt, objected to wars with France, favored French Revolution; moved impeachment of Warren Hastings; opened charge of Hastings's tyrannical rule at Benares in five-hour speech (1788). Urged abolition of slavery; urged removal of disabilities of Dissenters and Roman Catholics; opposed treason and sedition bills (1795–96); carried measure giving juries full powers in libel actions (1792). Remained mostly away from Parliament for five years, engaged in historical and literary work; gave toast "Our Sovereign, the people," for which name erased from privy council (1798). Excluded by king (1804) from proposed coalition ministry with Grenville; on death of Pitt (1806), again foreign secretary in All-the-Talents ministry, started negotiations for peace with France and revealed plot to assassinate Napoleon; moved abolition of slave trade just before his death; buried in Westminster Abbey. Author of a *History of Reign of James II*, left incomplete.

**Fox, Dixon Ryan.** 1887–1945. American historian and educator, b. Potsdam, N.Y.; teacher of history, Columbia (1912–34; professor, 1927–34); president, Union Coll., and chancellor, Union U. (1934–45); coauthor with A. M. Schlesinger of *A History of American Life* (a cultural, economic, and social analysis; 12 vols., 1927).

**Fox, Edward.** 1496?–1538. English prelate; strong supporter of Henry VIII; sent by the king on various political and ecclesiastical missions.

**Fox, George.** 1624–1691. English religious leader, b. in Leicestershire. Founder of the Society of Friends (nicknamed *Quakers* by Justice Gervase Bennet, 1650). Began preaching in his home neighborhood (1647–48), calling his society the "Friends of Truth"; his teaching, chiefly developed as a protest against the Presbyterian system, drew many recruits from the lower middle classes. Extended his preaching by making missionary journeys to Scotland (1657), Ireland (1669; the year in which first annual meeting of the society was held), North America and West Indies (1671–72), Holland (1677, 1684); frequently persecuted and imprisoned, but continued his preaching until his death. His *Journal*, revised by a committee directed by William Penn, appeared in 1694; he also wrote *A Collection of... Epistles* (publ. 1698) and *Gospel Truth* (publ. 1706).

**Fox, Henry.** 1st Baron **Hol'land** (hŏl'ănd). 1705–1774. British statesman. Son of Sir **Stephen Fox** (1627–1716; Royalist, who after battle of Worcester accompanied Charles II to Holland; managed Charles's household; was intermediary between king and General Monck; M.P., 1661; a commissioner of treasury, 1679–1702). M.P. (1738), attached himself to Walpole; a lord of treasury (1743); secretary at war (1746–54); secretary of state with seat in cabinet and leader of House of Commons (1755–56); amassed fortune as paymaster general; again leader of House of Commons, in Bute's cabinet; by bribery and intimidation, carried Treaty of Paris (1763) and was rewarded by elevation to peerage; created social sensation by secret marriage to Lady Caroline Georgiana Lennox (1744). Two of their sons were Charles James Fox (*q.v.*) and **Henry Edward** (1755–1811), military commander who served in America at Concord, Bunker Hill, Long Island, White Plains, Brandywine, repulsed French army at Pont-à-Chin (1794), was commander in chief in Ireland during rising of Robert Emmet (1803), ambassador to court of Naples (1806), general (1808).

**Henry Richard Vassall Fox** (1773–1840), 3d Baron Holland; grandson of 1st baron; M.A., Oxon. (1792); trained for public life by his uncle Charles James Fox; a Whig in House of Lords; with Lord Auckland, concluded unratified treaty with American commissioners Monroe and Pinckney (1806); lord privy seal in Grenville ministry (1806–07); sought in Parliament to mitigate severity of criminal code, introduced bill for abolition of death penalty for stealing (1809); advocated abolition of slave trade, though himself a West Indian planter; sought repeal of corn laws; opposed union with Ireland; urged rescission of order in council prohibiting trade with France (1812); opposed Sidmouth's coercive measures and foreign enlistment bill (1817–19); proposed intervention in Portugal (1828–30); chancellor of duchy of Lancaster (1830–34, 1835–40). Author of biographies of Guillén de Castro y Bellvis and Lope de Vega, translations of Spanish comedies, and a biography of his uncle. His wife **Elizabeth**, *nee* **Vas′sall** [văs′'l] (1770–1845), Lady Holland, b. Jamaica, was divorced by Sir Godfrey Webster for adultery with Lord Holland (1797); beautiful and vivacious hostess, presiding over brilliant circle of wits and statesmen at Holland House; attacked by Byron in *English Bards and Scotch Reviewers;* sent message and books to Napoleon and received bequest of gold snuffbox given him by Pius VI.

**Fox, John William.** *Known as* **John Fox, Jr.** 1863–1919. American novelist, b. Stony Point, Ky. Grad. Harvard (1883). Rough rider in Cuba in Spanish-American War; also, correspondent for *Harper's Weekly* (1898); m. (1908; later divorced) Fritzi Scheff (*q.v.*). Author of *A Mountain Europa* (1894), *The Kentuckians* (1897), *The Little Shepherd of Kingdom Come* (1903), *The Trail of the Lonesome Pine* (1908), *The Heart of the Hills* (1913), etc.

**Fox, Luke.** 1586–1635. English navigator; commanded expedition seeking the Northwest Passage (1631), and wrote an account of his trip.

**Fox, Margaret.** 1833–1893. American spiritualist medium, b. Bath, Canada, brought as a child to a farm in Wayne County, N.Y. Claimed by means of spirit rappings to have established communication with supernatural world; with sisters Leah and Catharine as aids, toured U.S. and Europe as a "medium"; her success responsible for widespread investigation of spiritualistic phenomena. Confessed imposture (1888); later retracted this confession. Claimed to be common-law wife of Dr. Elisha Kent Kane and assumed his name; published his letters to her, *The Love Life of Dr. Kane* (1866).

**Fox,** Sir **William.** 1812–1893. New Zealand statesman, b. in England; to New Zealand (1842); prime minister of New Zealand (1856, 1861–62, 1869–72, 1873).

**Fox, William Johnson.** 1786–1864. English Unitarian preacher and politician; noted for eloquence of sermons. M.P. (1847–63).

**Fox, Williams Carlton.** 1855–1924. American diplomat, b. St. Louis, Mo. U.S. consul, Brunswick, Germany (1876–88). Director of Pan-American Union (1905–07); U.S. minister to Ecuador (1907–11).

**Foxe** (fŏks). See also Fox.

**Foxe, John.** 1516–1587. English martyrologist, b. at Boston, in Lincolnshire; B.A., Oxon. (1537). Tutor to children of Henry Howard, Earl of Surrey (1548–53). Ordained deacon (1550), and priest (1560); prebendary in Salisbury Cathedral (1563). Author of *Rerum in Ecclesia Gestarum...Commentarii* (1559), which was translated into English and printed under the title *Actes and Monuments* (1563), or, popularly, *The Book of Martyrs.*

**Foxe** *or* **Fox, Richard.** 1448?–1528. English prelate and statesman, b. in Lincolnshire. Educ. Oxford U. and in Paris. Entered service of Henry, Earl of Richmond, in Paris; appointed by Henry, after his accession to English throne as Henry VII (1485), secretary of state, lord privy seal, and bishop of Exeter (1487), of Bath and Wells (1492–94), of Durham (1494–1501), of Winchester (1501 ff.). Negotiated marriages of Margaret Tudor with James IV of Scotland and Prince Arthur with Catherine of Aragon. With accession of Henry VIII, continued as one of chief advisers to the king; negotiated treaty with Louis XII of France (1510) and was a commissioner at the treaty of 1514; retired from politics (1516). Founded Corpus Christi Coll., Oxford, for the secular clergy.

**Foy** (fwȧ), **Maximilien Sébastien.** 1775–1825. French general; served in Napoleon's armies in Spain; general of brigade (1809) and of division (1811). Member of Chamber of Deputies (1819–25), where he defended freedom of the individual and freedom of the press.

**Foy′a′tier′** (fwȧ′yȧ′tyā′), **Denis.** 1793–1863. French sculptor.

**F. P. A.** See Franklin Pierce ADAMS.

**Fra Angelico.** See Giovanni da FIESOLE.

**Fra′ca·sto′ro** (frä′kä·stô′rō), **Girolamo.** 1483–1553. Italian physician, astronomer, and poet, b. at Verona. Known esp. for his poem *Syphilis sive Morbus Gallicus* (1530) from which the disease syphilis takes its name.

**Fra Dia′vo·lo** (frä dyä′vō·lō). *Sobriquet of* **Michele Pez′za** (pĕt′tsä). 1771?–1806. Italian brigand, b. in Calabria; reputed to have been formerly a monk called **Fra An′ge·lo** (än′jā·lō); leader of band of robbers; employed by Cardinal Ruffo (*q.v.*) against Parthenopean republic (1799) and by English against French at Naples (1806); captured by French and hanged at Naples (Nov. 10, 1806); celebrated in Auber's opera *Fra Diavolo* (1830).

**Fraen′kel** (frĕng′kĕl), **Karl.** *Surname changed in 1912 to* **Fraen′ken** (frĕng′kĕn). 1861–1916. German bacteriologist.

**Fra′go′nard′** (frȧ′gô′nȧr′), **Jean Honoré.** 1732–1806. French painter and engraver; studied under Chardin, Vanloo, and Boucher. Among his paintings are *Instant Désiré, Heure du Berger, Serment d'Amour, Billet Doux,* and a series ordered by Mme. du Barry to decorate a pavilion and now known as *Romance of Love and Youth.* His son **Alexandre Évariste** (1780–1850) was a historical painter.

**Frähn** (frân), **Christian Martin Joachim.** 1782–1851. German Orientalist, numismatist, and historian; authority on Asiatic coins. Professor of Oriental languages, Kazan, Russia (1807); librarian and director of Asiatic Museum, St. Petersburg (1815).

**Frai′kin′** (frĕ′kăɴ′), **Charles Auguste.** 1817–1893. Belgian sculptor.

**Frak′nó·i** (frŏk′nō·ĭ), **Vilmos.** *Orig.* **Wilhelm Fran′kl** (fräng′k'l). 1843–1924. Hungarian historian and prelate; chief inspector of Hungarian museums and libraries (1897); founder and inspector (1900) of Hungarian Historical Institute at Rome. Author of *Péter Pázmány and his Time* (3 vols., 1868–69), *Hungary before the Battle of Mohács* (1884), etc.

**Framp′ton** (frăm(p)′tŭn), Sir **George James.** 1860–1928. English sculptor, b. London. His notable sculptures include *An Act of Mercy, Angel of Death,* the Edith

Cavell Memorial, portrait busts of King George V and Queen Mary, statue of Edward VI.

**Fran′çais′** (fräN′sĕ′), **François Louis.** 1814–1897. French painter of landscapes.

**Francavilla, Pietro.** See Pierre de FRANCHEVILLE.

**France** (fräNs; *Angl.* fråns), **Anatole.** *Pseudonym of* **Jacques Anatole François Thi′bault′** (tē′bō′). 1844–1924. French novelist, critic, poet, and playwright, b. Paris. Regarded as eminent satirist and humorist, and master of literary style. Among his notable works are *Poèmes Dorés* (1873); *Les Noces Corinthiennes* (a play in verse, 1876); the novels *Le Crime de Sylvestre Bonnard* (1881), *Thaïs* (1890), *La Rôtisserie de la Reine Pédauque* (1893), *La Révolte des Anges* (1914); a *Histoire Contemporaine* including the volumes *L'Orme du Mail* (1897), *Le Mannequin d'Osier* (1897), *L'Anneau d'Améthyste* (1899), and *Monsieur Bergeret à Paris* (1901); *Les Dieux ont Soif* (1912); *La Vie en Fleur* (1922). Awarded Nobel prize in literature (1921).

**Fran·ce′sca** (frän·chās′kä), **Piero della.** *Real name* **Piero de′i Fran·ce′schi** (dā′ē frän·chās′kē). 1420?–1492. Italian painter of Umbrian school, b. at Borgo San Sepolcro. Leading realist of his time; theorist and mathematician. Known esp. for series of frescoes *Story of the True Cross* in choir of San Francesco, Arezzo; wrote treatise on geometry *De Quinque Corporibus*, and manual on perspective.

**Francesca da Ri′mi·ni** (dä rē′mē·nē). d. 1285? Italian lady; daughter of Guido da Polenta, lord of Ravenna; m. Giovanni, son of Malatesta da Rimini (see MALATESTA); carried on illicit romance with brother-in-law Paolo; slain together with Paolo by her husband as an adulteress. Immortalized by Dante in his *Inferno* (canto V); subject of dramas by Silvio Pellico, Paul Heyse, D'Annunzio, Stephen Phillips, et al., and of paintings by Ingres, Cabanel, Watts, et al., and of operas by Hermann Götz, Ambroise Thomas, symphonic poem by Tchaikovsky, poem by Leigh Hunt.

**Fran′ce·schi′ni** (frän′chās·kē′nē), **Baldassare.** 1611–1689. Florentine painter, b. at Volterra; hence sometimes called **il Vol′ter·ra′no** (ēl vōl′târ·rä′nō).

**Franceschini, Marcantonio.** 1648–1729. Italian painter, b. at Bologna. Pupil and associate of Carlo Cignani; last leader of Bolognese school; director, Accademia Clementina (Bologna); known esp. for frescoes and altarpieces.

**Fran·ce′sco** (frän·chās′kō). Italian form of FRANCIS.

**Francesco di Gior′gio** (dē jōr′jō; jôr′jō). *Full name* **Francesco Maurizio di Giorgio Mar·ti′ni** (mär·tē′nē), *or* **di Mar·ti′no** (mär·tē′nō), **Pol′lai·uo′lo** (pōl′lī·wô′lō). 1439–1502. Italian engineer, architect, sculptor, and painter, b. Siena. Known esp. for his military constructions; military architect under duke of Urbino (1478 ff.); reputed inventor of mines at siege of Naples (1495); built Madonna del Calcinaio church (near Cortona), municipal buildings at Ancona and at Iesi; appointed chief architect, cathedral of Siena (1498).

**Fran′ces of Rome** (från′sĕs [-sĭs] ŭv rōm′), Saint. *Nee* **Francesca Bus′sa di Le·o′ni** (bōōs′sä dē lā·ō′nē). 1384–1440. Roman matron; m. Lorenzo Ponziani (1395; d. 1436); founded (1425) the Benedictine Oblate Congregation of Tor di Specchi.

**Fran′chet′ d'Es′pe·rey′** (fräN′shĕ′ dĕs′prā′), **Louis Félix Marie François.** 1856–1942. French army commander; general of brigade (1908) and of division (1912). In the World War (1914–18), engaged on the Marne and Meuse rivers (1914), commanded allied army which defeated Bulgars and Germans on the Vardar River in the Balkans (Aug., 1918). Created marshal of France (1921).

**Fran·chet′ti** (fräng·kāt′tē), Baron **Alberto.** 1860–1942. Italian composer of operas, chamber music, overtures, and a symphony in E minor.

**Fran′che·ville′** (fräNsh′vēl′) *or* **Fran′que·ville′** (fräNk′vēl′), **Pierre de.** *Ital.* **Pietro Fran′ca·vil′la** (fräng′kä·vēl′lä). 1548–1618. French sculptor, painter, and architect, long resident in Italy. Recalled to France by Henry IV; executed *Le Temps qui Enlève la Vérité*, now in the garden of the Tuileries. Appointed sculptor to King Louis XIII.

**Fran′chi** (fräng′kē), **Ausonio.** *Real name* **Cristoforo Bo′na·vi′no** (bô′nä·vē′nō). 1821–1895. Italian philosopher; ordained (1844); left priesthood to crusade for liberalism (1849); professor, Pavia (1860) and Milan (1863); turned to Thomism; retired to monastery (1891).

**Fran′cia** (frän′chä). *Real name* **Francesco di Mar′co di Gia′co·mo Rai′bo·li′ni** (dē mär′kō dē jä′kō·mō rī′bō·lē′nē). 1450?–?1517. Italian painter and goldsmith, b. at Bologna. First known as medalist and niellist; master of Bolognese mint.

**Fran′cia** (frän′syä), **José Gaspar Rodríguez.** *Known as* **Dr. Francia.** 1761?–1840. Paraguayan lawyer and dictator, b. Asunción. Active in junta following declaration of Paraguayan independence (1811 ff.); designated by legislature (1813) one of two consuls to govern Paraguay and (1814) dictator of Paraguay for three years (1814–17); made dictator for life (1817). See Carlos Antonio LÓPEZ.

**Fran′cia·bi′gio** (frän′chä·bē′jō). *Real name* **Francesco di Cri·sto′fa·no Bi′gi** (dē krēs·tô′fä·nō bē′jē). 1482?–1525. Florentine painter; pupil and associate of Andrea del Sarto.

**Fran′cis I** (från′sĭs). Emperor of Austria. See FRANCIS II, Holy Roman Emperor.

**Francis II.** 1435–1488. Last duke of Brittany (1459–88). His daughter Anne married Charles VIII of France, thus uniting duchy of Brittany with kingdom of France.

**Francis.** *Fr.* **François.** Name of two kings of France of Angoulême branch of house of Valois (*q.v.*):

**Francis I.** 1494–1547. King (1515–47); son of Charles, Count of Angoulême, and Louise of Savoy; b. Cognac; m. Claude de France, daughter of Louis XII (1514). Continued war against Holy League; victorious in Marignano campaign (1515) in northern Italy, gaining possession of Lombardy; made concordat with Pope Leo X (1516); defeated in election to imperial throne (1519), Charles I of Spain becoming emperor as Charles V; entertained Henry VIII of England at Field of the Cloth of Gold, near Guines (1520); by lack of tact drove constable Bourbon to side with enemies (1522–23). Began long series of wars against Empire; in first war (1521–25), defeated by Charles and taken prisoner at Pavia (1525); released (Treaty of Madrid, 1526) after giving up Burgundy and making other extreme concessions; broke pledges; waged second war with Charles (1527–29), losing Italy by treaty of peace signed for him by his mother (Paix des Dames; at Cambrai, 1529); conducted third war (1536–38), renewed (1542) with victory over Imperial forces at Ceresole Alba (1544). Possessed a love for letters and arts; his reign marked by Renaissance in France. See MARGARET OF NAVARRE, his sister.

**Francis II.** 1544–1560. King (1559–60); eldest son of Henry II and Catherine de Médicis; b. Fontainebleau; m. Mary Stuart (1558). Sickly and weak-minded; the tool of his uncles François de Lorraine, Duc de Guise, and Charles, Cardinal of Lorraine, who actually governed; conspiracy formed by certain nobles against him and the Guises was defeated (1560).

**Francis.** *Ger.* **Franz.** Name of two Holy Roman emperors:

**Francis I.** *Orig.* **Francis Ste′phen** (stē′vĕn). 1708–1765. Holy Roman emperor (1745–65); son of Leopold, Duke of Lorraine. Succeeded to duchy (1729), but ceded it (1737) to Stanislas Leszczyński, King of Poland; m. Maria Theresa of Austria (1736), with whom he was coregent as ruler of Austria (1740–45). Chosen emperor (1745); did not concern himself much with wars (1740–48) of Frederick against Maria Theresa nor with Seven Years' War (1756–63).

**Francis II.** 1768–1835. The last Holy Roman emperor (1792–1806); emperor of Austria (1804–35) as Francis I. Son of Leopold II. Joined all coalitions against France except fourth and was defeated by Napoleon in all wars resulting from them except last. Proclaimed himself hereditary emperor of Austria (1804) and abdicated crown of Holy Roman Empire (1806); acquired much territory by Congress of Vienna (1814–15); joined Holy Alliance (1815); followed policy of reaction under guidance of Metternich (1815–35). His daughter Maria Louisa (Marie Louise) married Napoleon (1810).

**Francis.** Name of dukes of **Mo′de·na** (mô′dā·nä):

**Francis IV d'E′ste–Lor·raine′** (dĕs′tā·lŏ·rān′; -lō-rān′). 1779–1846. Took possession of duchy after fall of Napoleon (1814–15); posed as champion of absolutism; governed despotically, suppressing ruthlessly all liberal movements; crushed revolts (1831) with Austrian aid.

**Francis V.** 1819–1875. Duke (1846–59), son of Francis IV; continued father's reactionary policies; had to rely on Austrian assistance after revolution of 1848 to secure him in power; lost throne after victory of Piedmontese army over Austrians at Magenta (1859); passed remainder of life (1860–75) in retirement in Austria.

**Francis.** *Ital.* **Francesco.** Name of two kings of the Two Sicilies:

**Francis I.** 1777–1830. Son of Ferdinand I; appointed regent of Sicily (1812); granted a constitution which was suppressed by Ferdinand on his restoration (1816); created duke of Calabria (1817–25); succeeded father as king (1825–30).

**Francis II.** 1836–1894. Son of Ferdinand II; last of Bourbon kings of Naples (1859–61); m. (1859) Maria Sophia Amalia, sister of Empress Elizabeth of Austria; attempted to keep Naples neutral in war with Austria; driven out of Naples (1860) by revolutionaries under Garibaldi; on capitulation of Gaeta (1861), forced to abdicate; spent rest of life in exile in Rome, France, and Austria.

**Fran′cis** (frȧn′sĭs), **David Rowland.** 1850–1927. American politician, b. Richmond, Ky.; governor of Missouri (1889–93); U.S. secretary of the interior (1896–97); U.S. ambassador to Russia (1916–18).

**Francis, Edward.** 1872–1957. American bacteriologist, b. Shandon, Ohio; B.S., Ohio State (1894), M.D., U. of Cincinnati (1897); with U.S. Public Health Service (from 1900), surgeon (1913–30), medical director (from 1930); known especially for work on tularemia in rabbits and men.

**Francis, James Bich′e·no** (bĭsh′ĕ·nō). 1815–1892. Hydraulic engineer, b. Southleigh, England; to U.S. (1833). Employed in construction of locomotives for a firm at Lowell, Mass. (1834); chief engineer (from 1837); in charge (from 1845) of development of water power in Merrimac River at Lowell; often called "father of modern hydraulic engineering." Author of *Lowell Hydraulic Experiments* (1855).

**Francis, John Wakefield.** 1789–1861. American physician, b. New York City; eminent obstetrician; taught in Coll. Phys. & Surg. and in Rutgers Med. Coll.; founded (1846) New York Academy of Medicine.

**Francis,** Sir **Philip.** 1740–1818. British government official and writer, b. Dublin. One of commission of four councilors of the governor general of India (1774); charged Warren Hastings with official corruption; wounded in resulting duel (1779); M.P. (1784 ff.); aided managers of impeachment of Hastings (1787); quarreled with Charles James Fox when refused appointment as viceroy of India (1806). Reputed author of the *Letters of Junius*, a series of 69 political letters published in the *Public Advertiser* (Nov. 21, 1768–Jan. 21, 1772) attacking public characters of the day connected with the government. Cf. Samuel DYER. His father, **Philip** (1708?–1773), schoolteacher, clergyman, and translator; B.A., Trinity Coll., Dublin (1728); rector of Barrow, in Suffolk (1762–73); translator of works of Horace.

**Francis Charles.** *Ger.* **Franz Karl.** 1802–1878. Archduke of Austria; m. (1824) Sophie, Austrian duchess, daughter of King Maximilian I; father of Emperor Francis Joseph of Austria and of Archduke Charles Louis.

**Francis Ferdinand.** *Ger.* **Franz Ferdinand.** 1863–1914. Archduke of Austria, b. Graz. Son of Archduke Charles Louis and nephew of Emperor Francis Joseph; uncle of Charles I of Austria. Inherited title of archduke of **Aus′tri·a–E′ste** [-ĕs′tā; -tĕ] (1875). Became heir apparent to crown by deaths of Crown Prince Rudolf (1889) and of his own father (1896); m. (1900) Countess Sophie Chotek, Duchess of Hohenberg (1868–1914) but renounced right of succession for their children. With his wife, was assassinated (June 28, 1914) by Serbians in a political plot at Sarajevo, Bosnia; this assassination was the immediate cause of the World War.

**Francis Frederick.** *Ger.* **Franz Friedrich.** 1750–1806. Duke of Saxe-Coburg-Saalfeld (1800–06); lost possession of duchy during Napoleonic wars. See SAXE-COBURG-GOTHA.

**Francis Joseph I.** *Ger.* **Franz Josef.** 1830–1916. Emperor of Austria (1848–1916). Son of Archduke Francis Charles and nephew of Emperor Ferdinand I; m. (1854) his cousin Elizabeth, dau. of Duke Maximilian Joseph of Bavaria. At accession, empire in state of revolution; pacified Italy (battle of Novara) and subdued Hungary (1849); defeated in Italian War of Liberation (1859). In alliance with Prussia, waged successful war against Denmark (1864), but quarreled with Prussia concerning disposition of seized districts, bringing on Seven Weeks' War (June–July, 1866); overwhelmed at Sadowa; lost Venetia to Italy (1866) and was expelled from the German Confederation; effected compromise with Hungarians by Ausgleich (1867); became king of Hungary (1867–1916); adhered to Dreikaiserbund (1872–78); concluded Triple Alliance with Germany and Italy (1883); saw Austria involved in World War following assassination of his nephew and heir Archduke Francis Ferdinand (*q.v.*) at Sarajevo (June 28, 1914). His rule at first entirely absolutist; after 1867, unsympathetically constitutionalist.

**Francis of As·si′si** (äs·sē′zē), Saint. *Lay name* **Giovanni Francesco Ber′nar·do′ne** (bär′när·dō′nā). 1182–1226. Italian friar and preacher, founder of the Franciscan order. Consecrated himself to poverty and religion (from c. 1206); gathered a few companions and drew up for their administration a rule approved by Pope Innocent III (1209), replaced by later rules (1221 and 1223), the order being confirmed by Pope Honorius III (1223). Retired as a hermit to Monte Alverno where, according to legend, he experienced (1224) the miracle of the stigmata. Canonized by Pope Gregory IX (1228).

**Francis of Pa′o·la** (pä′ō·lä) *or* **Pa′u·la** (pä′o͞o·lä), Saint. 1416–1507. Calabrian Franciscan monk; founder of Order of Minims (1436; statutes confirmed by Sixtus IV, 1474); canonized (1519) by Leo X.

**Francis of Sales** (sālz; *Fr.* sȧl), Saint. *Fr.* **François de Sales.** 1567–1622. Savoyard nobleman and ecclesiastic. Doctor of Laws, Padua (1591); ordained (1593). Successfully completed mission to Chablais, Savoy (1594 ff.) to convert Calvinists; coadjutor (1599), bishop of Geneva (1602). Aided St. Jeanne Françoise de Chantal in founding Order of the Visitation of Our Lady (1610). Canonized (1665) by Alexander VII; declared doctor of the church (1877) by Pius IX; patron saint of Catholic writers (since 1922). Among his works are *Introduction to the Devout Life, The Love of God.*

**Francis of Vitoria.** = FRANCISCO DE VITORIA.

**Francis Xavier,** Saint. See XAVIER.

**Fran·cis′co de A·sís′** (frän·thēs′kō thā ä·sēs′), **María Fernando.** 1822–1902. Nephew of Ferdinand VII of Spain, b. at Aranjuez; m. (1846) his cousin Queen Isabella II; granted no part in administration of affairs; left Spain (1868) when queen was driven out; granted separation (1870).

**Francisco de Vi·to′ria** (vē·tō′ryä). 1480?–1546. Spanish Dominican theologian; professor, U. of Salamanca (1524–44); influenced 16th-century theological thought and writing; author of *Relectiones XII Theologicae in Duo Libros Distinctae* (1604).

**Francisque.** See Jean François MILLET (1642?–1679).

**Franck.** See also FRANK.

**Franck** (fräɴk), **Adolphe.** 1809–1893. French philosopher; professor, Collège de France (1856–86).

**Franck, César Auguste.** 1822–1890. Belgian-French organist and composer, b. Liége; called founder of modern French instrumental school. Studied at Liége (until 1837) and Paris (until 1842); settled in Paris as teacher (1844); became organist at St. Clotilde (1858); professor of organ at Paris Conservatory (1872); naturalized (1873). His compositions include the oratorios *Ruth* (1846), *Rédemption* (1872), *Les Béatitudes* (1880), and *Rébecca* (1881), the symphonic poems *Les Éolides* (1876), *Le Chasseur Maudit* (1883), and *Les Djinns* (1884), the operas *Hulda* (1895) and *Ghisèle* (1896), *La Procession*, for soprano and orchestra (1888), symphony in D minor (1889), piano trios and other piano pieces, organ music, a violin sonata (1886), a string quartet (1889), a Mass (1860) and other church music, etc.

**Franck** (frängk), **Hans.** 1879–1964. German playwright, fiction writer, and poet.

**Franck** (frăngk), **Harry Alverson.** 1881–1962. American writer of travel books, b. Munger, Mich. Author of *Vagabonding Down the Andes* (1917), *A Vagabond in Sovietland* (1935), etc.

**Franck** (frängk), **James.** 1882–1964. American (German-born) physicist. Professor, Berlin (1915), Göttingen (1920). Known for researches with Gustav Hertz on effects of impact of electrons on atoms, proving value of quantum theory; awarded, jointly with Hertz, 1925 Nobel prize for physics.

**Franck, Melchior.** 1573?–1639. German composer.

**Franck, Philipp.** 1860–1944. German painter.

**Franck** *or* **Frank** (frängk), **Sebastian.** *Known as* **Franck von Wörd** (fôn vûrt′). *Lat. surname* **Fran′cus** (frăng′kŭs). 1499–?1543. German freethinker, reformer, and writer on popular religion and history, b. Donauwörth. Roman Catholic priest (1524); joined Lutheran Church, but later separated from it (1528); writer in Nuremberg and in Strasbourg (1529–31); driven out by authorities; expelled from Ulm; settled in Basel. Author of religious writings, historical works, the collection of German proverbs *Sprichwörter* (2 vols., 1541), etc.

**Franck′e** (fräng′kĕ), **August Hermann.** 1663–1727. German pietistic preacher, educator, and philanthropist; founder of Pietism. Lectured on philosophy at Leipzig (1684); was professor of philosophy and (from 1698) of theology, U. of Halle. Founded at Halle (1695) a charity school, to which were added an orphanage (1698), a training school, a Latin school, a boarding school, etc., later combined into the Francke Institutions.

**Francke, Kuno.** 1855–1930. Historian and educator, b. Kiel, Germany; naturalized American citizen (1891). Educ. Kiel, Berlin, Jena, Munich (Ph.D., 1878); teacher at Harvard (from 1884); professor of the history of German culture (1896–1917); founder and curator, Germanic Museum, Harvard. Author of *Social Forces in German Literature* (1896), *A German-American's Confession of Faith* (1915), *Kant and Art* (1925), *German After-War Problems* (1927), etc.

**Franck′en** (fräng′kĕn). Family of Flemish painters, including: **Hieronymus** *or* **Jeroen** (1540–1610); his brother **Frans** (1542–1616); another brother, **Ambrosius** (1544–1618); and Frans's son **Frans** (1581–1642).

**Franck′en·stein** (fräng′kĕn·shtīn), Baron **Clemens von.** 1875–1942. German composer and music director. Composer of operas *Griseldis* (1898), *Rahab* (1911), and *Li Tai Pe* (1920), of orchestral works, songs, etc.

**Franckenstein,** Baron **Georg Arbogast von und zu.** 1825–1890. German politician. Member (1872) and leader of Centrist party in Reichstag, of which he was first vice-president (1879–87); drafted Franckenstein Clause, incorporated in protective tariff law of 1879.

**Fran′co** (frăɴng′ko͞o), **Afranio de Mello.** See MELLO FRANCO.

**Fran′co** (fräng′kô), **Battista.** *Called* **Il Se′mo·le′i** (ēl sā′mô·lā′ē). 1510–1561. Italian painter.

**Fran′co** (fräng′kō), **Francisco.** *In full* **Francisco Paulino Hermenegildo Teódulo Franco–Ba′ha·mon′de** (-bä′ä·môn′dā). 1892–1975. Spanish soldier and dictator, b. El Ferrol, Galicia; son of naval officer. Educ. in military academy at the Alcazar, Toledo. Served against Riffs in Morocco; credited with planning and carrying out battle which finally defeated Abd-el-Krim's army (1926). Studied at L'École Militaire in Paris (1926). Appointed chief of staff of Spanish army (1935); governor of Canary Islands (Feb., 1936). At outbreak of civil war in Spain, flew to Tetuán, in Spanish Morocco (July, 1936), and organized transport of foreign legionnaires and Moorish troops into Spain; after deaths of generals José Sanjurjo and Goded, became military leader of insurgents; invested at Burgos (Oct. 1, 1936) with titles commander in chief of Spanish army and chief of Spanish state; in civil war (1936–39), received substantial aid from Nazi Germany and Fascist Italy, and, indirectly, from Great Britain and the U.S. through their "nonintervention" policy, enabling the insurgents, but not the Spanish government, to buy war supplies; captured Madrid (Mar. 28, 1939); assumed powers of dictator; signed concordat with the Vatican (May, 1941), empowering him to designate Spanish bishops, subject to ratification by the Holy See; sent Spanish troops to help Germany against Russia (1941).

**Fran′co** (frăɴng′ko͞o), **João.** 1855–1929. Portuguese politician, b. near Lisbon. Prime minister (1906–07); when not supported by elections, assumed virtual dictatorship (1907–08); an able administrator, but opposed to movement for republic; on assassination of King Carlos and crown prince (1908), resigned and left country.

**Fran′co** (fräng′kō), **Modesto Chávez.** See CHÁVEZ FRANCO.

**Fran′çois′** (fräɴ′swȧ′). French form of FRANCIS.

**François, Jean Charles.** 1717–1769. French engraver;

appointed engraver to King Louis XV of France, and King Stanislas of Poland.

**Fran'çois'** (fräN'sô·ä'), **Kurt von.** 1853–1931. German explorer and colonial officer in Africa, b. Luxemburg. On Wissmann's Kasai expedition (1883); explored tributaries of Congo with Grenfell (1885); penetrated to Togo hinterland (1888); captain in command of protectorate troops in German Southwest Africa (1889); acting imperial commissioner (1891); led expedition to Okavango, besieged chief fortress of native chieftain (1893) but subsequently failed in complete subjugation of Hottentots, and was released from commission (1894); settled in German Southwest Africa (1901). Prepared maps of Southwest Africa; wrote *Deutsch-Südwestafrika* (1899), *Staat oder Gesellschaft in Unsern Kolonien?* (1901), etc. His brother **Hermann** (1856–1933), Prussian general; as commanding general of 1st army corps in Königsberg, distinguished himself at beginning of World War.

**François, Luise von.** 1817–1893. German writer; author of novels chiefly of the 18th and 19th centuries.

**Fran'çois'** (fräN'swå'), **Nicolas Louis.** *Called* **François de Neuf'châ'teau'** (dẽ nû'shä'tō'). 1750–1828. French statesman; minister of interior (1797); member of the Directory (1797–98); president of the Senate (1804–06); created comte under the Empire. His works include the comedy *Paméla ou la Vertu Récompensée* (1793), *Fables en Contes en Vers* (1814), translations, and anthologies.

**Fran'cois'–Mar'sal'** (-mår'sål'), **Frédéric.** 1874–1958. French financier; minister of finance (1920–24); premier of France for a short time (1924).

**Fran'çois'-Pon'cet'** (-pôN'sĕ'), **André.** 1887–1978. French diplomat; ambassador to Germany (1931–38), Italy (1938–40), West Germany (1955).

**Fran·co'ni·an** (frăng·kō'nĭ·ăn) *or* **Sa'li·an** (sā'lĭ·ăn) house. From *Franconia, Ger. Franken,* old duchy of southern Germany; or from *Sala* (now Ijssel) River. (1) Name of house of German emperors, usually called the Salian emperors, founded by Conrad II (duke of Franconia (1024–39) and ruling from 1024 to 1125. Conrad's successors were Henry III (1039–56), Henry IV (1056–1106), and Henry V (1106–25; died without heir). Agnes, sister of Henry V, m. (1079) Frederick of Swabia, ancestor of house of Hohenstaufen (*q.v.*). (2) Name of branch of Hohenzollern family founded by Conrad III (or I; d. 1261), burgrave of Nuremberg, son of Burgrave Frederick III (or I; d. 1201). See HOHENZOLLERN (2).

**Fran·cuc'ci** (fräng·ko͞ot'chē), **Innocenzo di Pie'tro** (dē pyâ'trō). *Known as* **Innocenzo da I'mo·la** (dä ē'mô·lä). 1494–c. 1550. Bolognese painter; pupil of Francia in Bologna and Albertinelli in Florence.

**Fran'gi·pa'ni** (frän'jē·pä'nē; *Angl.* frăn'jĭ·păn'ĭ). Noble Roman family, including: **Leo** (fl. 1014), founder of family. **Cenzio** (fl. early 12th century), head of Imperialist party in Rome; after death of Pope Pascal II (1118), refused to recognize his successor Gelasius II and, with aid of Emperor Henry V, secured election of an antipope, Gregory VIII, thus causing a schism in the church.

**Frank.** See also FRANCK.

**Frank** (frängk), **Adolf.** 1834–1916. German industrial chemist; founder of potash industry in Germany; worked on production of paper pulp by sulphite process, production of hydrogen from water gas, etc.; with Nikodem Caro, discovered reaction used in cyanamide process for utilization of atmospheric nitrogen.

**Frank, Bruno.** 1887–1945. German writer and poet; author of verse, fiction, and plays.

**Frank, Ernst.** 1847–1889. German composer and orchestra conductor; composed operas, choruses, and songs, and completed Götz's opera *Francesca da Rimini* (1877).

**Frank** (frăngk), **Florence,** *nee* **Ki'per** (?kī'pẽr). 1886?–1976. American poet and playwright; m. (1914) Jerome N. Frank (*q.v.*); author of *Three Plays for a Children's Theatre* (1926, including *Over the Hills and Far Away, Return of Proserpine, Three Spinners*), etc.

**Frank** (frängk), **Franz Hermann Reinhold von.** 1827–1894. German Lutheran theologian, of Erlangen school; professor, Erlangen (from 1857). Author of *System der Christlichen Gewissheit* (2 vols., 1870–73), *System der Christlichen Sittlichkeit* (2 vols., 1884–87), *Geschichte und Kritik der Neueren Theologie* (1894), etc.

**Frank** (frăngk), **Glenn.** 1887–1940. American educator, b. Queen City, Mo. B.A., Northwestern (1912); associate editor (1919–21) and editor in chief (1921–25) of *Century Magazine;* president, U. of Wisconsin (1925–37); editor of *Rural Progress Magazine* (from 1937). Author of *An American Looks at His World* (1923), *America's Hour of Decision* (1934), etc.

**Frank** (frängk), **Hans.** 1900–1946. German jurist; member of Reichstag (1930 ff.), and head of legal department of National Socialist party; Reich commissioner for justice (1933–35); appointed head of civil administration in Polish territory (1939).

**Frank** (frăngk), **Ilya Mikhailovich.** 1908– . Soviet physicist. Awarded Nobel prize in physics (1958) with P. Cherenkov and I. Tamm.

**Frank** (frăngk; frängk), **Ja'cob** (jā'kŭb; yä'kôp). *Real name* **Jankiew Lei·bo'wicz** (lā·bô'vēch). 1726?–1791. Polish-Jewish mystic, sectarian, and adventurer, b. in Podolia; founder of semi-Christian Frankist, or Zoharist, sect among Jews. Joined Sabbatai Zebi sect in Salonika; with hundreds of followers feigned conversion to Roman Catholicism as transition stage toward Messianic religion (1756), then to Islamism (1758), and again to Christianity (1759); chose 12 apostles and posed as Messiah; settled in Brünn and posed as "holy master" among neighboring Poles; won favor of Maria Theresa of Austria who believed him disseminator of Christianity; succeeded by daughter Eve as head of sect and "holy mistress." The Frankists eventually became real Roman Catholics.

**Frank** (frăngk), **Jerome New.** 1889–1957. American lawyer and government administrator, b. New York City. Ph.B. (1909) and J.D. (1912), Chicago. General counsel, Agricultural Adjustment Administration (1933–35), and Federal Surplus Relief Administration (1933–35); member (1937–41), chairman (1939–41), Securities and Exchange Commission. Author of *Law and The Modern Mind* (1930), *Save America First* (1938), *If Men Were Angels* (1942). See Florence FRANK.

**Frank** (frängk), **Johann Peter.** 1745–1821. German physician, one of chief founders of science of public health. Physician to Czar Alexander I (1805–08).

**Frank, Leonhard.** 1882–1961. German novelist, b. Würzburg; resident in Berlin, then in exile.

**Frank, Reinhard von.** 1860–1934. German jurist and legal writer; authority on criminal law.

**Frank** (frăngk), **Tenney.** 1876–1939. American classical scholar; professor, Johns Hopkins (from 1919). Author of *Roman Imperialism* (1914), *Life and Literature of the Roman Republic* (1930); editor (and author of 2 vols.) of *An Economic Survey of Ancient Rome* (5 vols., 1933–40).

**Frank, Waldo David.** 1889–1967. American writer, b. Long Branch, N.J.; B.A., Yale (1911); on staff of New York *Evening Post* and New York *Times* (1911–13); a founder and an editor of *The Seven Arts* (1916–17). Author of *The Unwelcome Man* (1917), *The Art of the Vieux Colombier* (1918), *Our America* (1919), *Rahab* (1922), *Salvos* (1924), *Dawn in Russia* (1932), *In the American Jungle* (1937), collaborator in *The American*

*Caravan* (1928), *Man and His World* (1929), and *Sex in Civilization* (1929).

**Frank, Walter Hale.** 1886– . American army officer, b. Humphrey, N.Y.; grad. U.S.M.A., West Point (1910); chief of staff, G.H.Q., air force (1938); major general commanding 3d air force (Oct., 1941); retired (1945).

**Fran'kau** (frăng'kou), **Gilbert.** 1884–1952. English writer; in World War I. Wrote *One of Us* (1912), *The City of Fear* (1917), *The Love-Story of Aliette Brunton* (1922), *Men, Maids, and Mustard-Pot* (1923), *Life—and Erica* (1925), *Wine, Women, and Waiters* (1932), *Farewell Romance* (1936), *The Dangerous Years* (1937), *Self-Portrait* (1939), *World Without End* (1943).

**Fran'ke** (fräng'kĕ), **Otto.** 1863–1946. German Chinese scholar; in consular service in China (1888–1901); professor of Chinese, Hamburg (1910) and Berlin (1923).

**Frän'kel** (frĕng'kĕl), **Bernhard.** 1836–1911. German laryngologist in Berlin.

**Fran'kel** (fräng'kĕl), **Zacharias.** 1801–1875. German rabbi, b. Prague; a founder of Breslau school of historical Judaism. Chief rabbi, Dresden and Leipzig (1836–54); director of new Jewish Theol. Sem., Breslau (from 1854).

**Fran'ken** (frăng'kĕn), **Rose.** 1898– . American writer, b. in Texas; m. S.W.A. Franken, 2d William Brown Meloney; author of novels including *Pattern* (1925), *Twice Born* (1935), *Claudia* (1939), *Claudia and David* (1940), *Another Claudia* (1943), and plays including *Another Language* (1934), *Claudia* (1941).

**Frank'furt·er** (frăngk'fẽr·tẽr), **Felix.** 1882–1965. Jurist, b. Vienna, Austria; to U.S. (1894). LL.B., Harvard (1906). Professor, Harvard Law School (1914–39). Assoc. justice, U.S. Supreme Court (1939–1962).

**Fran'kl** (fräng'k'l), **Ludwig August.** Ritter **von Hoch'wart** (hōκ'värt). 1810–1894. Austrian poet and philanthropist, b. in Bohemia. Professor of aesthetics, Conservatory of Vienna Music Society (1851); established first Jewish school in Jerusalem (1856). Author of epics and ballads, satirical poems, travel books, biographies, and works on Jewish subjects.

**Frankl, Paul.** 1878–1962. German art critic and historian.

**Frankl, Wilhelm.** See Vilmos FRAKNÓI.

**Frank'land** (frăngk'lănd), Sir **Edward.** 1825–1899. English chemist, b. in Lancashire; professor, Royal Institution (1863–68), Royal Coll. of Chemistry (1865); president of Chemical Society (1871–72, 1872–73) and Institute of Chemistry (1877–80); author of *Experimental Researches in Pure, Applied, and Physical Chemistry* (1877), etc. His son **Percy Faraday** (1858–1946), chemist; lecturer, Royal School of Mines (1880–88); professor, Birmingham U. (from 1900); known for work on fermentation and stereochemistry, and the purification of water and the bacterial treatment of sewage; m. **Grace Coolidge Toynbee** (1858–1946), bacteriologist; educ. Bedford Coll., London; author of technical articles and, with her husband, *Micro-organisms in Water* (1894) and *Life of Pasteur* (1897). Their son **Edward Percy** (1884–1958), educ. Cambridge; because of health gave up chemistry for writing; author of fiction with background of life in dales of Westmorland.

**Frank'lin** (frăngk'lĭn), **Benjamin.** 1706–1790. American statesman, scientist, and philosopher, b. Boston. Apprenticed (1718) to his brother **James** (1697–1735), printer; after disagreements with James, left Boston (1723). Settled in Philadelphia; obtained employment as printer; proprietor of printing business and publisher of *The Pennsylvania Gazette* (1730–48); gained wide circle of readers by *Poor Richard's Almanack* (1732–57), published under pseudonym of **Richard Saunders** and containing store of witty aphorisms and moral precepts that influenced the thought of the time; formed discussion club the "Junto" (c. 1727), which (1743) developed into American Philosophical Society; laid foundations of library (1731) for use of public, which developed into Philadelphia Library (chartered 1742); instrumental in improving care and lighting of city streets; deputy postmaster at Philadelphia (1737–53); deputy postmaster general for the colonies (1753–74); invented improved heating stove (about 1744); interested in natural philosophy; sold business to his foreman and retired (1748). Began experiments with electricity (about 1746); tried famous kite experiment (1752). In public life from 1754; Pennsylvania's delegate to Albany Congress (1754); to England to represent Pennsylvania Assembly in efforts to enforce taxes on proprietary estates (1757–62); again in England (1766), called before House of Commons to explain colonial opposition to the Stamp Tax and made remarkably successful plea; appointed Pennsylvania's agent in England, remaining there through years preceding Revolution, trying for conciliation but realizing drift toward war; returned to Philadelphia as war became inevitable (1775). Member, Second Continental Congress (1775); on committee to draft Declaration of Independence, and one of its signers. Sent by Congress as one of committee of three to negotiate treaty with France (1776); welcomed (unofficially) by leaders of the French and became immensely popular during his stay (1776–85); after signing (Feb. 6, 1778) of a treaty of commerce and a treaty of defensive alliance, appointed sole plenipotentiary to France (Sept. 14, 1778); appointed (June 8, 1781) commissioner, with Jay and Adams, to negotiate peace with Great Britain (preliminary negotiations successfully completed Nov. 30, 1781; final peace signed Sept. 3, 1783). Returned to Philadelphia (Sept. 14, 1785); president, Pennsylvania executive council (1785–87); member, Constitutional Convention (1787); signed a memorial to Congress asking for the abolition of slavery (Feb. 12, 1790). His *Autobiography* was first published in complete and accurate form in 1868, after partial or inaccurate versions in 1791 and 1817. Elected to American Hall of Fame (1900). His only daughter, **Sarah**, married Richard Bache (*q.v.*). See also William FRANKLIN (his son).

**Franklin, Edward Curtis.** 1862–1937. American chemist, b. Geary City, Kans.; B.S., Kansas (1888), Ph.D., Johns Hopkins (1894); professor of physical chemistry, Kansas (1899–1903) and of organic chemistry, Stanford (from 1906); authority on the ammonia system of compounds and liquid ammonia as an electrolytic solvent. His brother **William Suddards** (1863–1930), physicist, b. Geary City; B.S., Kansas (1887), D.Sc., Cornell (1901); assistant professor, Kansas (1887–90); professor, Iowa State College (1892–97), Lehigh U. (1897–1915), M.I.T. (1917–29), Rollins Coll. (from 1929); joint author of *Elements of Physics* (3 vols.), etc.

**Franklin, Fabian.** 1853–1939. American mathematician and writer, b. Eger, Hungary. Ph.B., George Washington (1869). Associate professor and professor, Johns Hopkins (1879–95). Editor, Baltimore *News* (1895–1908); associate editor, New York *Evening Post* (1909–17); editor, *The Weekly Review* (1919–23). Author of *People and Problems* (1908), *Plain Talks on Economics* (1924), etc. See Christine LADD-FRANKLIN.

**Franklin,** Sir **John.** 1786–1847. English arctic explorer; entered Royal Navy (1801) and served at Trafalgar (1805) and in expedition against New Orleans (1814–15). Headed expeditions into arctic (1818, 1819–22, 1825–27, 1845–47); all members lost (1847). His second wife (m. 1828), **Jane,** *nee* **Grif'fin** [grĭf'ĭn] (1792–1875), fitted out five ships (between 1850 and

1857) to search for him, and was awarded the gold medal of the Royal Geographical Society (1860) in recognition of her services.

**Franklin, William.** 1731–1813. American colonial administrator, b. Philadelphia. Son of Benjamin Franklin (*q.v.*). Appointed by his father comptroller of the general post office (1754–56); accompanied father to England (1757); adm. to bar in London; appointed governor of New Jersey (1763); upheld royal authority and was in conflict with colonists; estranged from his father who declared him "a thorough government man"; his arrest ordered by Provincial Congress of New Jersey (June 15, 1776); returned to England (c. 1782).

**Franklin, William Buel.** 1823–1903. American army officer, b. York, Pa.; grad. U.S.M.A., West Point (1843); served in Mexican War and in Civil War; held by Gen. Burnside partly responsible for defeat at Fredericksburg (1862) and relieved of his command; served in Louisiana (1863), in Department of the Gulf (1864); resigned from army (1866).

**Frank'lin'–Bouil'lon'** (fräɴk'lăɴ' bōō'yôɴ'), **Henry.** 1872–1937. French journalist and politician; minister of propaganda (1917); French representative named to negotiate with Kemal Atatürk (1921–22), a preliminary step to the Treaty of Lausanne (1923).

**Fran'ko** (från'kō), **Ivan.** 1856–1916. Ukrainian poet and nationalist. Author of lyric and epic poems, and stories of the peasant and working classes, works on Ukrainian literature and folklore and Rutheno-Galician proverbs.

**Franks** (frăngks), Baron **Oliver Shewell.** 1905– British diplomat and educator. Taught at U. of Glasgow (1937–45); permanent secy. of ministry of supply (1945–46); ambassador to U.S. (1948–52).

**Franqueville, Pierre de.** See FRANCHEVILLE.

**Fran'secky** (fräns'kĕ), **Eduard Friedrich von.** 1807–1890. Prussian general. Served under Wrangel against Denmark (1848); commanded infantry division at Königgrätz (1866); during Franco-Prussian War (1870–71), led 2d army corps to battlefield of Gravelotte, repelled Gen. Ducrot's attempts to break through lines at Champigny (1870), took part in Manteuffel's campaign against Bourbaki's army of the East (1871) and forced French retreat into Switzerland; commanding general of 15th army corps in Strassburg (1871–79); governor of Berlin (1879–82).

**Franz** (fränts). German form of FRANCIS.

**Franz, Robert.** *Orig. surname* **Knauth** (k'nout). 1815–1892. German song composer. In Halle as organist and director of singing school later named after him, and director of university music; resigned (1868). Author of works on Bach and Handel; composed over 350 songs, esp. love lyrics, also the 117th psalm for double choir, chorals, a Kyrie, etc.

**Fran·zén'** (från·sān'), **Frans Mikael.** 1772–1847. Poet, b. in Oulu, Finland. Professor, Åbo, now Turku (1798); clergyman in Sweden following Russia's annexation of Finland (1809); bishop of Härnösand (from 1831). Author of *Selma and Fanny* (lyrical cycle; 1824), epic poems, as *Christopher Columbus* (1831) and *Gustavus Adolphus in Germany* (unfinished), didactic poems, prose biographies of prominent Swedes, etc.

**Fran'zos** (frän'tsōs; frän·tsōs'), **Karl Emil.** 1848–1904. German novelist and journalist, b. in Russian Podolia of Jewish parentage. Author of sketches on life in Galicia, Rumania, and southern Russia, and of novels and tales, chiefly of life in southeastern Europe.

**Fra'pan–A'ku·nian'** (frä'pän·ä'kōō·nyän'; frä·pän'-), **Ilse.** *Pen name of* **Ilse Le·vien'** (lā·vēn'). 1852–1908. German novelist, b. Hamburg; m. Armenian writer Akunian (1898). Her works include *Hamburger Novellen* (1886), *Zwischen Elbe und Alster* (1890), ***Arbeit*** (1903), *Erich Hetebrink* (1907).

**Fra Paolo.** See Paolo SARPI.

**Fra'pié'** (frȧ'pyā'), **Léon.** 1863–1950. French novelist; author of *La Maternelle* (1904), *La Divinisée* (1927), etc.

**Frare, Il.** See Francesco BIANCHI-FERRARI.

**Frar'y** (frâr'ĭ), **Francis Cowles.** 1884–1970. American chemist, b. Minneapolis, Minn.

**Fras, Jacob.** = Stanko VRAZ.

**Frasch** (fräsh), **Herman.** 1851?–1914. Chemist and inventor, b. Gaildorf, Württemberg. To U.S. (1868); studied methods of refining petroleum. To London, Ontario; organized Empire Oil Co. (1885); devised processes for desulphurizing crude oils, thus making Canadian and Ohio oils commercially valuable; his patents and Empire Oil Co. acquired by Standard Oil Co. (1888). Devised hot-water melting process of extracting sulphur (1891); headed Union Sulphur Co.; founded great American sulphur-mining industry.

**Fra'ser** (frā'zẽr). See also FRAZER.

**Fraser, Alexander Campbell.** 1819–1914. Scottish philosopher; educ. Edinburgh U. Professor, Edinburgh U. (1856–91). Edited Berkeley's works, Locke's *Essay Concerning Human Understanding*, etc.; author of ***Philosophy of Theism*** (1898), etc.

**Fraser, Claud Lovat.** 1890–1921. British artist. His works influenced Br. stage design; also illustrated books and did designs for *The Beggar's Opera* (1920), *As You Like It* (1920), etc.

**Fraser, Hugh.** See William MAGINN.

**Fraser, James Baillie.** 1783–1856. Scottish traveler and writer; with his brother **William** (1784?–1835), explored Nepal (1815). Author of travel books, and tales based on Persian life and customs.

**Fraser, James Earle.** 1876–1953. American sculptor, b. Winona, Minn. Executed portrait busts of Ulysses Grant and Augustus Saint-Gaudens and Theodore Roosevelt and Elihu Root, monuments of Bishop Potter, John Hay, John Ericsson, Lincoln; designed U.S. five-cent piece having an Indian head and a buffalo (1913), and Victory Medal (1919). His wife (m. 1913), **Laura,** *nee* **Gar'din** [gär'dĭn] (1889–1966), b. Chicago; designer of many medals and coins; sculptor of busts of Gilbert Stuart and Mary Lyon.

**Fraser, Mary,** *nee* **Crawford.** d. 1922. English writer, b. Rome; sister of F. Marion Crawford (*q.v.*); m. Hugh Fraser; entered Roman Catholic Church (1884); lived in Far East. Author of *A Diplomat's Wife in Japan* (1899), *Letters from Japan* (1904).

**Fraser, Peter.** 1884–1950. New Zealand statesman, b. in Ross, Scotland; to New Zealand (1910); prime minister of New Zealand (1940–49).

**Fraser, Simon.** 12th Baron **Lov'at** (lŭv'ăt). 1667?–1747. Scottish Jacobite intriguer. M.A., Aberdeen; joined regiment of Lord Murray (later duke of Atholl) on assurance of intended treachery to William III; after assumption by his father of title Lord Lovat on death of his grandnephew, attempted to abduct latter's nine-year-old daughter and heiress; baffled, forcibly married the child's mother, for which he was outlawed; succeeded his father as Lord Lovat (1699); attempted minor rebellions until Atholl family's rise to power on Queen Anne's accession forced his flight to France. Returning secretly, formed Queensberry plot, professing to reveal Jacobite plans, but fled on discovery of his duplicity; recalled by his clan, took government side with his clan in order to obtain his cousin's estates, as result of her husband's joining rebellion of 1715; received pardon and life rent of Lovat estates (1716) and, after litigation, recognition of his title (1733). Sent his son with clan to fight for the Pretender (1745), protesting his loyalty; captured after Culloden, impeached, and beheaded. His eldest son, **Simon** (1726–1782), sometime master of Lovat; headed clan in support of Pretender (1745); pardoned (1750); raised Highlanders and commanded them in America (1757–61); served at Louisburg; wounded during siege of Quebec (1759); major general in Portuguese army and (1771) in British army; raised 71st Highlanders for service in American Revolution.

**Fraser, Simon.** 1729?–1777. Scottish soldier in British army. Served with Scots brigade in Dutch army, with 78th Highlanders at Louisburg (1758), and at Quebec; served in Germany, at Gibraltar, and in Ireland; accompanied Burgoyne, won victory at Hubbardton (1777); mortally wounded at Bemis Heights.

**Frauenlob.** See HEINRICH VON MEISSEN.

**Frau′en·städt** (frou′ĕn·shtĕt), **Julius**, *in full* **Christian Martin Julius**. 1813–1879. German philosopher, disciple and expounder of Schopenhauer.

**Fraunce** (frôns; fräns), **Abraham**. fl. 1587–1633. English poet; educ. Cambridge. Author of *The Countesse of Pembrokes Yuychurch* (in 2 parts, 1591), and songs contributed to Sidney's *Astrophel and Stella*. Referred to as "Corydon" in Spenser's *Colin Clouts come home againe*.

**Fraun′ces** (frôn′sĕs; -sĭs; frän′-), **Samuel**. 1722?–1795. West Indian Negro, keeper of Fraunces Tavern, New York City, famous resort (1762–65; 1770–89); household steward (1789–94) to George Washington.

**Fraun′ho′fer** (froun′hō′fẽr), **Joseph von.** 1787–1826. Bavarian optician and physicist. While investigating refractive index of various kinds of glass, observed dark lines (Fraunhofer lines) in solar spectrum; investigated spectra of planets and fixed stars; invented a heliometer, a micrometer, and a diffraction grating he used to measure wave lengths of light (1814); made improvements in telescopes and other optical instruments.

**Fravartish.** See PHRAORTES.

**Frayne** (frān), **Hugh**. 1869–1934. American labor union official, b. Scranton, Pa.; general organizer (1901–10) and in charge of New York office (from 1910), American Federation of Labor; representative of labor on War Industries Board (1917–19).

**Frays′si′nous′** (frā′sē′nōōs′), Comte **Denis de.** 1765–1841. French Roman Catholic prelate; conducted religious lectures for young people at Paris churches until prohibited by Napoleon (1809); resumed these lectures (1814–22) and published them (1825) under title *Défense du Christianisme*, almoner of the king (1821); titular bishop of Hermoupolis (1822); minister of ecclesiastical affairs (1824–28).

**Fra′zee** (?frā′zē; frā·zē′), **John**. 1790–1852. Pioneer American sculptor, b. Rahway, N.J.; carved busts of Daniel Webster, Nathaniel Bowditch, John Marshall, William Prescott, John Lovell, Thomas H. Perkins for Boston Athenaeum.

**Fra′zer** (frā′zẽr). See also FRASER.

**Frazer,** Sir **James George**. 1854–1941. Scottish anthropologist, b. Glasgow. Educ. Glasgow and Cambridge U.; professor of social anthropology, U. of Liverpool (1907); member of Order of Merit (1925). His great work *The Golden Bough*, a study of cults, myths, rites, etc., their origins and their importance in the historical development of religions, originally published in 1890, revised in 1900, was expanded by revision and addition of related studies into a series of twelve volumes, including a volume of bibliography and index (1915); a one-volume abridgment, *The Golden Bough*, appeared in 1922, and a supplementary volume, *Aftermath*, in 1936. Other works include: *Questions on the Customs, Beliefs, and Languages of Savages* (1907), *Totemism and Exogamy* (1910; reissued 1935; supplementary volume, *Totemica*, 1937), *The Belief in Immortality and the Worship of the Dead* (3 vols.: 1913, 1922, 1924), *Folk-lore in the Old Testament* (1918; abridged ed., 1923), *Man, God, and Immortality* (1927), *Myths of the Origin of Fire* (1930), *The Fear of the Dead in Primitive Religion* (3 vols.: 1933, 1934, 1936), *Creation and Evolution in Primitive Cosmogonies* (1935), etc.

**Frazer, John Fries.** 1812–1872. American scientist, b. Philadelphia; grad. Pennsylvania (1830); professor of chemistry and natural philosophy, U. of Pennsylvania (1844–72); a founder, National Academy of Sciences (1863). See Persifor FRAZER.

**Frazer, Persifor.** 1844–1909. American scientist, b. Philadelphia; son of John Fries Frazer (*q.v.*). Grad. Pennsylvania (1862); served in Union army in Civil War; mineralogist and metallurgist, U.S. Geological Survey (1869–70); instructor (1870–72), professor (1872–74), U. of Pennsylvania; with Second Geological Survey of Pennsylvania (1874–82); professor of chemistry, Franklin Institute (1882); a founder and editor, *American Geologist* (1888–1905). Noted also as handwriting expert.

**Fra′zier** (frā′zhẽr), **Edward Franklin.** 1894–1962. Sociologist, b. Baltimore, Md. Ph.D., Chicago, 1931. Author of *The Negro Family in the United States* (1939); *Race and Culture Contacts in the Modern World* (1957); *The Negro Church in America* (1963); etc.

**Frear** (frḗr), **Walter Francis**. 1863–1948. American jurist and politician in Hawaii, b. Grass Valley, Calif. A.B. (1885) and LL.B. (1890), Yale. Second assoc. justice of supreme court, provisional government of Hawaii (1893); first assoc. justice of supreme court, Republic of Hawaii (1896); chief justice (1900–07). Governor of Territory of Hawaii (1907–13).

**Fré′chette′** (frā′shĕt′), **Louis Honoré**. 1839–1908. Canadian journalist and poet, b. near Quebec. Editor of *Journal de Québec;* clerk of legislative council (1889–1908). Author of poems in French, including *Mes Loisirs* (1863), *Les Fleurs Boréales* (1881; crowned by the French Academy), *La Légende d'un Peuple* (1887). Author also of a collection of prose tales and dramas, *Le Noël au Canada*.

**Fred′e·gar** (frĕd′ē·gär; *Ger.* frā′dĕ·gär) *or* **Fred′e·gar′i·us** (frĕd′ē·gâr′ĭ·ŭs). *Surnamed* **Scho·las′ti·cus** (skō·lăs′tĭ·kŭs). Name assigned to the alleged 7th-century compiler (of whom there were really 3) of the "Fredegar" chronicle *Historia Francorum*, a large work in corrupt Latin on general and early Frankish history to the year 642 (continued by others during 8th century in *Gesta Francorum*).

**Fred′e·gund** (frĕd′ĕ·gŭnd). *Fr.* **Fré′dé′gonde′** (frā′dā′gôɴd′). d. 597 A.D. Frankish queen; wife of Chilperic I of Neustria. Caused assassination of Galeswintha, previous wife of Chilperic and sister of Brunhilde, wife of Sigebert, King of Austrasia; after Sigebert's victory in war that followed, had him murdered (575) by her agents; ruled as regent for her son Clotaire and defeated Brunhilde in war (596).

**Fredeman de Vries.** See VREDEMAN DE VRIES.

**Fred′er·ic** (frĕd′ẽr·ĭk; frĕd′rĭk), **Harold**. 1856–1898. American novelist, b. Utica, N.Y.; author of *The Lawton Girl* (1890), *The Copperhead* (1893), *The Damnation of Theron Ware* (1896), *Gloria Mundi* (1898), *The Market Place* (1899), etc.

**Fré′dé′ric′** (frā′dā′rēk′), **Léon.** 1856–1940. Belgian painter.

**Fred′er·ick** (frĕd′ẽr·ĭk; frĕd′rĭk). *Ger.* **Friedrich.** Name of several dukes and archdukes of Austria, including:

**Frederick II.** Duke (1230–46). See BABENBERG family.

**Frederick of Austria.** Duke (1306–30). = FREDERICK III, king of Germany.

**Frederick V.** Archduke. = FREDERICK III, Holy Roman emperor.

**Frederick Maria Albert William Charles.** 1856–1936. Archduke and general, b. Gross-Seelowitz (Židlochovice), Moravia; son of Archduke Charles Ferdinand; his training and career almost entirely military; commander in chief of Austro-Hungarian armies (1914) after death of Archduke Francis Ferdinand; as field marshal commanded during first part of World War I (1914–16); not a successful leader.

**Frederick.** *Dan.* **Frederik.** Name of nine kings of Denmark, the first six of whom were also kings of Norway:

**Frederick I.** 1471?–1533. King (1523–33). Son of Christian I and brother of John I. Duke of Holstein; chosen king when Christian II dethroned; strengthened nobility.

**Frederick II.** 1534–1588. King (1559–88). Son of Christian III. Subdued Dithmarschen (1559); waged war with Sweden (1563–70); made peace at Stettin; rest of reign (1570–88) years of peace; suppressed pirates; built fortress of Kronborg at Helsingör; able and popular ruler.

**Frederick III.** 1609–1670. King (1648–70). Son of Christian IV, b. Haderslev. Held several positions in the church (1623–34); m. (1643) Sophie Amalie of Brunswick-Lüneburg; engaged in war with Sweden (1657–60); forced by Charles X to sign Treaty of Roskilde (1658); compelled Swedes to raise siege of Copenhagen (1659); finally defeated in war and forced to sign unfavorable peace terms (1660); with aid of commons and clergy, reduced power of nobles; became hereditary monarch (1660) with absolute power; raised Peder Schumacher, his secretary, to high position (1662–70).

**Frederick IV.** 1671–1730. King (1699–1730). Son of Christian V. Allied himself with Poland and Russia against Sweden (1700) but forced by Charles XII to make peace; freed peasants from serfdom (1702); again declared war on Sweden after Charles's defeat at Poltava (1709) but Danes defeated at Hålsingborg (1710); made peace (1720) by which possessions in Germany were given up.

**Frederick V.** 1723–1766. King (1746–66). Son of Christian VI; m. (1744) Louisa, dau. of George II of England; took little interest in affairs of state; made Count Bernstorff chief minister (1750–66); saved from Russian attack (1762) by death of Peter III; increased commerce and manufacture, established Asiatic Company; patronized literature, fostered education in Norway.

**Frederick VI.** 1768–1839. King of Denmark (1808–39) and of Norway (1808–14). Son of Christian VII. Called to head of state council (1784) when his father became insane; ruled as regent (1784–1808); greatly assisted by his minister A. P. Bernstorff (*q.v.*); aided in abolishing serfdom and slave trade; with his council, caused Denmark to join (1800) armed neutrality of the North; as a result, saw Danish fleet destroyed by British (1801) and Copenhagen bombarded (1807); became ally of Napoleon (1807); lost Norway to Sweden (1814); ruled wisely during period of recovery and reform (1814–39), although conservative and somewhat narrow-minded.

**Frederick VII.** 1808–1863. King of Denmark (1848–63). Son of Christian VIII. Promulgated new constitution (1849) which deprived him of absolute power; involved during much of reign in disputes with Germany and Austria over duchies of Schleswig and Holstein; died childless as last of the Oldenburg line (*q.v.*).

**Frederick VIII.** 1843–1912. King of Denmark (1906–12). Son of Christian IX; m. (1869) Princess Louise of Sweden; father of Haakon VII of Norway.

**Frederick IX** 1899–1972. King of Denmark (1947–72). Son of Christian X; m. (1935) Princess Ingrid of Sweden. Succeeded by his daughter Margrethe.

**Frederick.** *Ger.* **Friedrich.** Kings of Germany:

**Frederick I, II, IV.** = FREDERICK I, II, III, Holy Roman emperors.

**Frederick III.** 1286?–1330. *Known also as* **Frederick of Austria.** *Called* **Frederick the Fair** *or* **the Handsome.** Duke of Austria (1306–30); king of Germany (1314–22), chosen by a minority of electors (1314); waged long war with Louis of Bavaria (1314–22); defeated at Mühldorf (1322) and imprisoned (1322–25); acknowledged Louis as emperor; joint ruler (1325–26).

**Frederick.** *Ger.* **Friedrich.** Name of three Holy Roman emperors:

**Frederick I.** *Called* **Frederick Bar'ba·ros'sa** (bär'-bȧ·rŏs'ȧ). 1123?–1190. Holy Roman emperor (1152–90; crowned 1155). Duke of Swabia as Frederick III; son of Frederick II, Duke of Swabia; nephew of Conrad III (see FREDERICK, dukes of Swabia). King of Germany (1152–90) and of Italy (1155–90). Engaged in long struggle with cities of northern Italy (1155–83); made six expeditions (1154–84); at first successful; after formation of Lombard League (1167) and his defeat at Legnano (1176), Peace of Constance (1183) granted independence to Lombard cities. Opposed by Pope Alexander III in Italian struggle (1159–77). Overcame Guelphs, led by Henry the Lion, in Germany (1180–81). Set out on Third Crusade (1189); drowned (June, 1190) in the Calycadnus (Göksu), river of Cilicia. Esteemed by Germans as one of greatest of their race. Empire enlarged, learning advanced, internal peace maintained, and town and city development encouraged.

**Frederick II.** 1194–1250. King of Sicily as Frederick I (1198–1250). Holy Roman emperor (1215–50; crowned 1220). Son of Henry VI. Because of privileges granted by his mother, came (1198) under guardianship of pope. After battle of Bouvines, king of Germany (1215–50). Attempted to bring about union of Italy and Germany but opposed by popes and by revived Lombard League (1226–50). Three times excommunicated (1227, 1239, 1245). Married (1225), as 2d wife, Yolande, daughter of John of Brienne; became titular king of Jerusalem (1227) and assumed crown (1229). Led Fifth Crusade (1228–29); captured Jerusalem and made 10-year truce with sultan of Egypt. Married (1235), as 3d wife, Isabella, daughter of John of England. Noted for his varied talents and learning; patron of literature and science. Germany declined as result of neglect.

**Frederick III.** 1415–1493. Descendant of Albert I, Hapsburg king of Germany. King of Germany as Frederick IV and Holy Roman emperor (1440–93; crowned 1452). Archduke of Austria as Frederick V. Concordat of Vienna concluded (1448) between emperor and Pope Nicholas V. Sought to increase Empire but in general failed. His reign marked by almost continual conflict.

**Frederick.** Name of two grand dukes of Baden (*q.v.*):

**Frederick I.** *Ger.* **Friedrich Wilhelm Ludwig.** 1826–1907. Son of Grand Duke Leopold and Princess Sophia of Sweden; b. Karlsruhe; prince regent for his brother (1852–56); grand duke (1856–1907); m. (1856) Louise, daughter of William I of Prussia; sided with Austria in Seven Weeks' War (1866); labored for economic and educational progress of duchy.

His son and successor, **Frederick II.** 1857–1928. Soldier (1892–1907); grand duke (1907; abdicated 1918).

**Frederick.** Name of three rulers of Brandenburg:
**Frederick I.** 1372–1440. Prince (as Frederick VI) of the house of Hohenzollern (*q.v.*); served in Hungarian army; saved life of King Sigismund at Nicopolis (1396); burgrave of Nuremberg (1398); supported Sigismund for Imperial crown (1409); secured control of Brandenburg (1415); made elector and margrave of Brandenburg (1417), thus becoming founder of royal Prussian line (see house of PRUSSIA); quarreled with Sigismund (1423); unsuccessful candidate for throne of Germany (1438).
**Frederick II.** *Called* **Frederick the Iron.** 1413–1471. Son of Frederick I; in conflict with towns (1431–47); elector (1440–70); strict in internal affairs, conciliatory in dealing with neighboring states; waged war with Pomerania; abdicated (1470).
**Frederick III.** See FREDERICK I of Prussia.
**Frederick.** Name of two landgraves of Hesse-Cassel:
**Frederick I.** 1676–1751. = FREDERICK I of Sweden.
**Frederick II.** 1720–1785. Son of Landgrave William VIII; fought in War of Austrian Succession and (1745) against the Young Pretender in Scotland; did much to improve Kassel, esp. its fine buildings; to provide funds sold an army of 12,000 Hessians to British to employ in the American Revolution.
**Frederick II.** *Known as* Prince of **Hom'burg** (hŏm'bûrg; *Ger.* hôm'bŏŏrk). 1633–1708. German general, and landgrave (1681–1708) of Hesse-Homburg (*q.v.*). Son of Landgrave Frederick I. Served in Swedish army (1654–59) under Charles X Gustavus; lost left leg at Copenhagen (1659); general of cavalry (1670–78) under Frederick William, elector of Brandenburg; active in defeat of Swedes at Fehrbellin (1675); succeeded his brother George Christian as landgrave (1681); spent entire rule in improving and beautifying Homburg. Subject of Kleist's drama *Prinz Friedrich von Homburg* (1821).
**Frederick.** *Called* **the Stern.** 1332–1381. Margrave of Meissen (1349–81).
**Frederick.** Name of five electors of the Palatinate:
**Frederick I.** *Called* **the Victorious.** 1425–1476. Received appointment of elector for life (1451); opposed Emperor Frederick III; increased Palatinate territory.
**Frederick II.** *Called* **the Wise.** 1482–1556. Elector (1544–56); commanded Imperial army when Sultan Suleiman besieged Vienna (1529); influenced by Melanchthon, accepted Protestant faith.
**Frederick III.** *Called* **the Pious.** 1515–1576. Elector (1559–76); embraced Lutheranism (1546), Calvinism (1561); had Heidelberg Catechism drawn up (1563).
**Frederick IV.** *Called* **the Upright.** 1574–1610. Elector (1592–1610); founded Evangelical Union (1608); strongly devoted to Protestant cause.
**Frederick V.** 1596–1632. Known as "the Winter King"; son of Frederick IV; elector (1610–23); chosen king of Bohemia (1619); completely defeated at battle of White Mountain (1620); deprived of electorate (1623) and in exile until his death. Married (1613) Elizabeth, daughter of James I of England; their daughter Sophia, wife of Ernest Augustus, first elector of Hanover, was mother of George I, first English king of the house of Hanover (see HANOVER).
**Frederick.** Names of three kings of Prussia:
**Frederick I.** 1657–1713. Son of Frederick William, elector of Brandenburg; b. Königsberg; m., as 2d wife, Sophia Charlotte (*q.v.*). Elector of Brandenburg (1688–1701) as Frederick III. For aid to Emperor Leopold I in War of Spanish Succession (1701–14), granted royal title to Prussia; king of Prussia (1701–13); received only small reward at Peace of Utrecht (1713). Patron of scholars, esp. Leibnitz; founder of Order of the Black Eagle (1701–1919) and of the U. of Halle (1694).
**Frederick II.** *Known as* **Frederick the Great.** 1712–1786. King of Prussia (1740–86). Son of King Frederick William I and Sophia Dorothea; grandson of Frederick I; b. Berlin. Tried to escape from father's control (1730); arrested, tried as deserter, and made to believe he would receive severe punishment, but pardoned; m. (1733) Elisabeth Christine, daughter of Ferdinand Albert II of Brunswick; engaged in literary and social pursuits (1732–40). Became king (May, 1740); on death of Emperor Charles VI (Oct., 1740) and accession of his daughter Maria Theresa (*q.v.*), made claims to Silesia for Prussia; began War of Austrian Succession (1740–48); formed alliance with France and Bavaria; won battles at Mollwitz (1741) and Chotusitz (1742), invaded Bohemia (1744), and by Peace of Dresden (1745) secured possession of Silesia; built (1745–47) palace of Sans Souci, near Potsdam, for royal residence. Formed new alliance (1756) with England against Maria Theresa, France, Russia, Sweden, and Saxony, which marked beginning of Seven Years' War (1756–63); displayed great military genius and perseverance in face of great odds; won many battles but was badly defeated in some; emerged after Peace of Hubertusburg (1763) enjoying great military prestige and with Prussia a much strengthened state. Joined Russia in first partition of Poland (1772); took part in War of Bavarian Succession (1778); formed (1785) Fürstenbund, a league of German princes to defend imperial constitution against Austria. Notable patron of literature (esp. 1745–55); invited Voltaire to live at his court (1750–53); favored French culture but indifferent to German writers. Skillful administrator of national economy, encouraging agricultural and industrial improvements; began codification of new Prussian code; instituted many social reforms; took special interest in improvement of Prussian army; greatly interested in American Revolution and an admirer of Washington. Voluminous writer; important works include *Memoirs of the House of Brandenburg*, and a history of the Seven Years' War, and *Anti-Macchiavel* (1740), an exposition of the duties of sovereigns; complete works published in 30 volumes (1846–57).
**Frederick III.** 1831–1888. Son of William I of Prussia, b. Potsdam. King and German emperor (March 9–June 15, 1888). Educ. Bonn (1849–50); engaged in military duties and travel (1851–58); m. Victoria Adelaide Mary Louise (1858), eldest daughter of Queen Victoria of England. As **Frederick William,** *nicknamed* **Un'ser Fritz** (ŏŏn'zĕr frĭts'), crown prince of Prussia (1861–88); strongly opposed to Bismarck's policies for strengthening Prussia (1861–66) and to war with Austria (1866), but took part in war, commanding division that secured victory at Königgrätz (1866); in command of armies of southern states in Franco-Prussian War (1870–71); took part in battles of Wörth and Sedan and in siege of Paris. Patron of literature and science. Attacked by cancer in the throat (1887); lived at San Remo (1887–88); called to throne on death of father but reigned only three months. Left two sons: William, who succeeded him, and Prince Henry, admiral in German navy.
**Frederick.** Name of three electors of Saxony:
**Frederick I.** *Called* **the Warlike.** 1370–1428. Son of Frederick of Meissen; duke of Saxony (1382–1428); vigorously opposed Hussites (1420–26); made elector of Saxony by Emperor Sigismund (1423); defeated (1426) by Hussites at Aussig (Ústí). U. of Leipzig founded during his reign.
**Frederick II.** *Called* **the Gentle** *or* **Mild.** 1412?–1464. Son of Frederick I; succeeded to electorate (1428); in long conflict (1445–51) with his brother William, mar-

grave of Meissen, over partition of lands. See ALBERTINE LINE; ERNESTINE LINE.

**Frederick III.** *Called* **the Wise.** 1463–1525. Grandson of Frederick II; duke and elector (1486–1525); founded U. of Wittenberg (1502); called Luther and Melanchthon to its faculty; did not become a follower of Luther but was tolerant of reform; protected Luther at Worms (1519), refused to execute papal ban against him, and (1521) caused him to be conveyed to the castle of Wartburg under his protection.

**Frederick VIII.** Duke of **Schles′wig–Hol′stein–Son′der·burg–Au·gu′sten·burg** (shlās′vĭκ·hô̇l′shtīn-zô̇n′dẽr·bo͝orκ·ou·go͝os′tĕ̇n·bo͝orκ; shlĕs′vĭκ-). 1829–1880. Son of Christian Augustus. On death of King Frederick VII of Denmark (1863) without heirs, claimed succession in Schleswig-Holstein, bringing about contest (1864) between Denmark on one hand and Prussia and Austria on other, and Seven Weeks' War (1866) between Prussia and Austria, and incorporation of Schleswig-Holstein in Prussia; his claim to dukedom not acknowledged by Prussia (1867); on death of father (1869), became duke of Schleswig-Holstein and successor in Augustenburg line. His eldest daughter, Augusta Victoria, married Emperor William II of Germany.

**Frederick.** Name of five dukes of Swabia:

**Frederick I.** d. 1105. Created duke of Swabia (1079) on marriage with Agnes, daughter of Holy Roman Emperor Henry IV; father of Conrad III, founder of Hohenstaufen dynasty (*q.v.*).

**Frederick II.** 1090–1147. Duke (1105–47), son of Duke Frederick I; m. Judith, daughter of Henry, Duke of Bavaria (d. 1126), thus uniting Welf and Hohenstaufen families; active in wars of Emperor Henry V.

**Frederick III.** 1123?–1190. Duke (1147–52; 1167–68), son of Duke Frederick II. Holy Roman emperor (1152–90) as Frederick I (*q.v.*), commonly called Barbarossa.

**Frederick IV.** 1146–1167. Son of Conrad III; held dukedom (1152–67) under Emperor Frederick I (Barbarossa).

**Frederick V.** 1168–1191. Duke (1168–91); second son of Emperor Frederick I (Barbarossa).

**Frederick I.** *In full* **Frederick William Charles.** 1754–1816. Duke of Württemberg (*q.v.*) as Frederick II (1797–1805); king as Frederick I (1806–16). Son of Duke Frederick (I) Eugene (1732–1797) and Sophia Dorothea, niece of Frederick the Great; b. Treptow, Pomerania. Served in Prussian and Russian armies; as duke, joined second coalition against France; lost some of possessions (1801) but received title of elector (1803); sided with Napoleon, and had his duchy raised to a kingdom (1805); joined Confederation of the Rhine (1806); after defeat of Napoleon at Leipzig (1813), joined Allies. His daughter Catherine married (1807) Jérôme Bonaparte, King of Westphalia.

**Frederick.** Name of three kings of Sicily:

**Frederick I.** = FREDERICK II, Holy Roman emperor; in his minority, king of Sicily (1198–1212).

**Frederick II.** 1272–1337. Also called by himself Frederick III, because he was third son of King Pedro III of Aragon. Governor of Sicily (1291), on death of brother Alfonso; supported by Sicilians, refused to give up Sicily to the church (1295); king of Sicily (1296–1337); waged war with Charles II of Naples (1296–1302), renewed (1313–17) against Charles's successor; island put under interdict by pope (1321–35); war with Angevins continued (1325 ff.).

**Frederick III.** *Called* **the Simple.** 1341–1377. King (1355–77), last of Aragonese line; continued war with Naples; held Sicily as fief of Joanna I of Naples (1372–77).

**Frederick.** 1452–1504. King of the Two Sicilies (1496–1501) of the Aragonese line; son of Ferdinand I of Naples; succeeded his nephew Ferdinand II; forced to yield Naples to Louis XII of France.

**Frederick.** Name of six kings of Norway: = FREDERICK I–VI of Denmark.

**Frederick I.** 1676–1751. King of Sweden (1720–51), b. in Kassel. As landgrave of Hesse-Cassel, married Ulrika Eleonora (*q.v.*); elected king on her abdication; deprived of power by new constitution; during rest of reign affairs of state controlled largely by House of Nobles; much strife between political parties (Caps and Hats); foreign policy dominated (1720–38) by Count Arvid Horn; war fought (1741–43) with Russia in Finland.

**Frederick, Pauline.** *Real surname* **Lib′by** (lĭb′ĭ). 1885–1938. American actress, b. Boston; debut on New York stage (1902); starred in *The Little Gray Lady*, *The Fourth Estate*, *Innocent*, etc.; appeared also in motion pictures *The Eternal City*, *Zaza*, and *Madame X*.

**Frederick Augustus.** See Duke of YORK AND ALBANY.

**Frederick Augustus.** *Ger.* **Friedrich August.** (1) Name of three electors of Saxony: see AUGUSTUS II and III of Poland; FREDERICK AUGUSTUS I of Saxony, below. (2) Name of three kings of Saxony:

**Frederick Augustus I.** *Called* **the Just.** 1750–1827. Son of Frederick Christian; elector of Saxony as Frederick Augustus III (1768–1806); first king (1806–27); aided Frederick the Great against Austria (1778–79); joined League of the German Princes; refused crown of Poland (1791); fought against France (1792–1806); after defeat of Jena, made by Napoleon nominal ruler of new duchy of Warsaw (1807); ally of Napoleon (1807–15); deprived of half of kingdom by Congress of Vienna (1815).

**Frederick Augustus II.** 1797–1854. Nephew of Frederick Augustus I; joint regent with Anthony (1830–36); king (1836–54); suppressed insurrection in Dresden (1849); rest of reign tranquil.

**Frederick Augustus III.** 1865–1932. Son of George; entered army (1883); general in Prussian service (1902); king (1904–18); constitutional struggle continued from preceding reign; abdicated (1918); formed mercantile corporation.

**Frederick Charles.** *In full* **Frederick Charles Nicholas.** 1828–1885. Prussian general, b. Berlin; called "the Red Prince." Nephew of Emperor William I of Prussia. Educ. Bonn; served in army in first Schleswig-Holstein war (1848–49); became commander of 3d army corps (1860); fought with distinction in war against Denmark (1864); commanded first army in Six Weeks' War (1866) against Austria and led 2d army in Franco-Prussian War (1870–71), entering Metz and Orléans (1870) and Le Mans (1871).

**Frederick Francis.** *Ger.* **Friedrich Franz.** Name of four grand dukes of Mecklenburg-Schwerin (*q.v.*), esp.:

**Frederick Francis II** (1823–1883), German general; grand duke (1842–83); in Prussian military service (1842–71); in wars against Denmark (1864) and Austria (1866); took important part in Franco-Prussian War (1870–71).

**Frederick Henry.** 1584–1647. Prince of Orange-Nassau and stadholder of the Dutch Republic (1625–47). Son of William the Silent; b. Delft; received military training from his brother Maurice; as stadholder took many cities from Spaniards including 's Hertogenbosch (1629), Maastricht (1632), Breda (1637), Hulst (1645); concluded alliances with Denmark, Sweden, and France; negotiated favorable treaty with Spain (1647).

**Frederick Louis.** Prince of Wales. 1707–1751. Eldest son of George II and Queen Caroline; b. Hanover, Germany. Bitter against father for vetoing his marriage to Wilhelmina, Princess Royal of Prussia, and for refusal of adequate allowance; wrote or inspired *Histoire du Prince Titi*, a caricature of his parents (1735); m. Princess Augusta of Saxe-Gotha (1736); refused permission by father to command British army against Jacobites (1745). His eldest son became George III of England.

**Frederick William.** Former crown prince of Germany. See WILLIAM.

**Frederick William.** *Ger.* **Friedrich Wilhelm.** 1620–1688. Elector of Brandenburg (1640–88); called "the Great Elector." Son of Elector George William; b. Berlin. On accession found his dominions devastated by armies of Thirty Years' War, then still in progress; by neutral policy, reorganized finances, restored towns and cities, and built up an army; accorded recognition in Treaty of Westphalia (1648); joined Sweden against Poland (1656); granted by Poland (1657) suzerainty over duchy of Prussia; entered league against France (1672); at first unsuccessful, Brandenburg being ravaged by Swedes at instigation of Louis XIV; defeated Swedes at Fehrbellin (1675), but forced by Treaty of Saint-Germain (1679) to return conquests made from Sweden; spent last years in improving condition of electorate: greatly aided education, improved finances, and developed strong army.

**Frederick William.** 1771–1815. Duke of Brunswick. See BRUNSWICK.

**Frederick William.** 1802–1875. Elector of Hesse-Cassel (1847–66), b. near Hanau. Son of Elector William II. Coregent of the electorate (1831–47); made elector (1847); sided with Austria during Seven Weeks' War (1866); refused to make terms with Prussia; arrested and imprisoned at Stettin and his territories annexed to Prussia (1866); died at Prague.

**Frederick William.** Name of FREDERICK III of Prussia, when crown prince.

**Frederick William.** *Ger.* **Friedrich Wilhelm.** Name of four kings of Prussia (see HOHENZOLLERN):

**Frederick William I.** 1688–1740. Son of King Frederick I; m. Sophia Dorothea of Hanover (1706). King (1713–40); involved in war with Sweden over Pomerania (1713–20); received greater part of Pomerania by Treaty of Stockholm (1720); most of reign spent in improving kingdom internally; personally attended to minute details of administration; rigidly economical; keenly interested in military matters; left Prussia a strongly established power; illiterate and unfriendly to culture.

**Frederick William II.** 1744–1797. Grandson of Frederick William I; son of Prince Augustus William and nephew of Frederick the Great. King (1786–97), his lack of administrative ability causing Prussia to decline; joined Austria in support of French royalty during French Revolution, which involved him in war (1792–95); compelled by Treaty of Basel (1795) to give up Prussian territories west of Rhine; took part in second and third partitions of Poland (1793, 1795).

**Frederick William III.** 1770–1840. Son of Frederick William II; king (1797–1840), b. Potsdam; received military training; took part in French campaigns (1792–94); m. Louise (1793), daughter of Prince Charles of Mecklenburg-Strelitz. Unable to strengthen kingdom or solve difficulties of Napoleonic Wars; after complete subjection of Prussia to Napoleon (1801–05), forced by urging of queen and by aroused spirit of nation to oppose French, resulting in Prussian defeats at Jena and Auerstedt (1806) and dismemberment of kingdom by Treaty of Tilsit (1807); under Stein, Hardenberg, Scharnhorst, and Gneisenau, army slowly reorganized (1807–12), victory at Leipzig (1813) liberating Germany and Blücher's successes in French campaigns and at Waterloo re-establishing Prussia's position (1814–15). After Waterloo, disappointed hopes of German people by joining Holy Alliance (1815); duped by Metternich; at later congresses (1818–22), and esp. after Revolution of 1830, sympathized with repressive policy; despite lack of liberal government, Prussian internal improvement advanced, Zollverein established (1834).

**Frederick William IV.** 1795–1861. Son of Frederick William III; king (1840–61). Failed to carry out promises of liberal reforms; forced by Revolution of 1848 to grant a constitution; refused imperial crown offered by Parliament of Frankfort (1849); soon after, reactionary regime again in control; rendered incompetent to rule by attacks of insanity; government administered by his brother (afterwards William I) as regent (1858–61).

**Frederick William Charles.** 1797–1881. Prince of the Netherlands; second son of King William I; served in Dutch army; took part in Belgian Revolution (1830); m. (1825) Princess Louise (d. 1870), daughter of Frederick William III of Prussia.

**Fre'de·ricq'** (frā'dȧ·rēk'), **Paul.** 1850–1920. Flemish historian, b. Ghent. Professor, Liége (1879), Ghent (1883); championed extension of Flemish language, customs, and laws; deported from Belgium by German government during World War for attempts to strengthen morale of Belgians; rector of Ghent U. (1919).

**Frederik.** Danish form of FREDERICK.

**Fredeswitha.** See FRIDESWIDE.

**Fredrik.** Swedish and Norwegian form of FREDERICK.

**Fre'dro** (frĕ'drô), Count **Alexander.** 1793–1876. Polish playwright, b. in Galicia; called "the Polish Molière." Author of many comedies, including *Ladies and Hussars, Pan* [*Mr.*] *Geldhab, Revenge*, etc.

**Free'den** (frā'dĕn), **Wilhelm Ihno Adolf von.** 1822–1894. German expert on navigation. Founder and director (1867–75) of naval observatory at Hamburg.

**Free'man** (frē'măn), **Douglas Sou'thall** (sou'thôl). 1886–1953. American editor, b. Lynchburg, Va. A.B., Richmond (1904), Ph.D., Johns Hopkins (1908). Editor, Richmond *News Leader* (from 1915). Author of *Virginia—A Gentle Dominion* (1924), *R. E. Lee* (4 vols., 1934; awarded Pulitzer prize), *The South to Posterity* (1939), *Lee's Lieutenants* (3 vols., 1942–44).

**Freeman, Edward Augustus.** 1823–1892. English historian, b. in Staffordshire. B.A., Oxon. (1845). Succeeded Stubbs as regius professor of modern history at Oxford (1884–92). His many notable works include *The History and Conquests of the Saracens* (1856), *The History of the Norman Conquest* (1867–79), *Growth of the English Constitution* (1872), *Chief Periods of European History* (1886), etc.

**Freeman, Harold Webber.** 1899– . English novelist; author of *Joseph and His Brethren* (1928), *Hester and Her Family* (1936), *Andrew to the Lions* (1938), etc.

**Freeman, James.** 1759–1835. American Unitarian clergyman, b. Charlestown, Mass. Grad. Harvard (1777). Reader, King's Chapel, Boston (1782); proposed revision of the liturgy to omit certain Trinitarian parts; revision accepted by proprietors of King's Chapel (1785). Ordination having been refused by the Episcopal bishop, Freeman was ordained by the senior warden of the church, and by this act the first Episcopal church in New England was transformed into the first Unitarian church in America (Nov. 18, 1787). Continued in this pastorate (1787–1826); retired (1826).

**Freeman, James Edward.** 1866–1943. American Protestant Episcopal clergyman, b. New York City. Consecrated bishop of Washington, D.C. (1923).

**Freeman, James Edwards.** 1808–1884. American painter, b. in Nova Scotia; to U.S. as a child. Best known for his genre paintings.

**Freeman, John.** 1880–1929. English poet and critic, b. London. His books of verse include *Twenty Poems* (1909), *Stone Trees, and Other Poems* (1916), *Memories of Childhood* (1919), *Poems New and Old* (1920; awarded Hawthornden prize), *Collected Poems* (1928). His prose works include *The Moderns* (1916), *English Portraits* (1924), *Herman Melville* (1926).

**Freeman, John Ripley.** 1855–1932. American civil and mechanical engineer, b. W. Bridgton, Me. B.S., M.I.T. (1876). Connected with water-power construction for manufacturing corporations and water-supply projects for numerous cities including New York, Los Angeles, Baltimore, and Mexico City; consultant on Isthmian Canal locks and dams, and on water-power conservation to Canadian government.

**Freeman, Joseph.** 1897–1965. American (Russ.-born) journalist. To U.S. (1904); naturalized (1920). Cofounder of *New Masses* (1926), editor (1931–33; 1936–37); works include *Voices of October* (1930), *The Soviet Worker* (1932), *An American Testament* (1936).

**Freeman, Mary Eleanor,** *nee* **Wilkins.** 1852–1930. American writer, b. Randolph, Mass. Educ. Mount Holyoke (1870–71). m. Dr. Charles M. Freeman (1902); lived thereafter in Metuchen, N.J. Author of *A Humble Romance* (1887), *A New England Nun* (1891), *Jane Field* (1893), *Giles Corey* (1893), *Pembroke* (1894), *Jerome, a Poor Man* (1897), *Silence and Other Stories* (1898), *The Love of Parson Lord* (1900), *The Debtor* (1905), *Butterfly House* (1912).

**Freeman, Orville Lothrop.** 1918– . Amer. government official, b. Minneapolis, Minn. Governor of Minnesota (1955–61); Secretary of Agriculture (1961–69).

**Freeman, Richard Austin.** 1862–1943. English physician and detective-story writer. In World War I. Among his many detective novels are *The Red Thumb Mark* (1907), which introduced the fictional scientific detective Dr. John Thorndyke, *Dr. Thorndyke's Case Book* (1923), *Pontifex, Son and Thorndyke* (1931), *The Penrose Mystery* (1936), *Mr. Polton Explains* (1940).

**Freeman–Mitford, Algernon Bertram** and **John.** Barons **Redesdale.** See under William MITFORD.

**Freeman–Thomas, Freeman.** See marquis of WILLINGDON.

**Freer** (frēr), **Charles Lang.** 1856–1919. American art collector, b. Kingston, N.Y. In railroad and car manufacturing business (1873–99); instrumental in forming American Car and Foundry Co. (1899). Great art collection included masterpieces of Whistler, of Chinese and Japanese painters, and of ancient glazed pottery of all regions. Presented collection, with funds for erection of Freer Gallery of Art at Washington, D.C., to the Smithsonian Institution (1906).

**Frei'dank** (frī'dängk). Name (or pseudonym) of a Middle High German didactic poet of the early 13th century; wrote *Bescheidenheit*, a collection of proverbs, aphorisms, and satirical observations.

**Frei'lig·rath** (frī'lĭk·rät), **Ferdinand.** 1810–1876. German poet. His works include lyric and political poems, as *Glaubensbekenntnis* (1844), *Ça Ira!* (1846); the volume *Zwischen den Garben* (1849; containing *Der Löwenritt*) and *Neuere Politische und Soziale Gedichte* (1849–51); patriotic war songs, and translations from Victor Hugo, Burns, Shakespeare, etc.

**Frei're** (frĕ'ē·rā), **Ramón.** 1787–1851. Chilean soldier and statesman, b. Santiago, Chile; grandson of Gomes Freire de Andrade. Served in Chilean war for independence (1811–20); leader of Liberal party; dictator after fall of O'Higgins (1823); ended Spanish domination of Chile; re-elected dictator (1827); forced to resign by accession of Conservative party. Led army revolt against government; defeated by Prieto (1830) and banished to Peru (until 1842).

**Frei're de An·dra'de** (frā'ē·rĕ thē ăNn·drȧ'thĕ), **Gomes.** 1685?–?1763. Portuguese general and administrator, b. Coimbra. Governor and captain general of Rio de Janeiro (1733–63). Celebrated in da Gama's epic poem *Épicos Brasileiros.* See Ramón FREIRE.

**Fre'ling·huy'sen** (frē'lĭng·hī'z'n), **Frederick.** 1753–1804. American Revolutionary leader, b. near Somerville, N.J. Grad. Princeton (1770). Adm. to bar (1774); practiced in Somerset County, N.J. Identified with colonial cause; served in Continental army. Member, Continental Congress (1778, 1779, 1782, 1783); U.S. senator (1793–96); resigned. His son **Theodore** (1787–1862) was a politician and educator; grad. Princeton (1804); adm. to bar (1808) and practiced in Newark, N.J.; attorney general of New Jersey (1817–29); U.S. senator (1829–35); chancellor, N.Y.U. (1839–50); president, Rutgers (1850–62). Theodore's nephew and adopted son **Frederick Theodore** (1817–1885) was also a politician; grad. Rutgers (1836); practiced law in Newark; attorney general of New Jersey (1861–66); U.S. senator (1866–69, 1871–77); U.S. secretary of state (1881–85).

**Fre'man'tle** (frē'măn't'l), Sir **Edmund Robert.** 1836–1929. English naval officer, b. London. Rear admiral (1885), admiral (1896). Served in Burmese War (1852), New Zealand War (1864–66), Ashanti War (1873–74), Witu punitive expedition (1890).

**Fremantle, William Henry.** 1831–1916. English clergyman; canon of Canterbury (1882–95); dean of Ripon (1895 ff.). Author of *The Gospel of Secular Life* (1882), *Natural Christianity* (1911), etc.

**Fré'miet'** (frā'myĕ'), **Emmanuel.** 1824–1910. French sculptor; ranked among leading modern sculptors of animals.

**Fré'mont** (frē'mŏnt), **John Charles.** 1813–1890. American explorer and army officer (known as "the pathfinder"), b. Savannah, Ga. Lieutenant, U.S. army; member, Nicollet's expedition to explore region between upper Mississippi and Missouri rivers (1838–39); under congressional authority, led three expeditions into Oregon territory, on first expedition (summer 1842) mapped Oregon Trail, on second penetrated northern Colorado, Nevada, and crossed Rocky Mountains to California (1843–44), on third reached California (Dec., 1845). Played prominent part in conquering California during Mexican War; appointed by R. F. Stockton Civil governor of California; became involved in Stockton-Kearny (see Stephen W. KEARNY) quarrel; refused to obey orders of Kearny, who arrested him for mutiny and insubordination; court-martialed at Washington, and convicted (Jan., 1848); penalty remitted by President Polk; Frémont resigned from army. Led midwinter expedition to locate passes for railroad line from upper Rio Grande into California (1848–49). Elected one of first two U.S. senators from California (1850); served 1850–51. Again led winter expedition to locate southern railway route to Pacific (1853–54). Nominated for president of the United States by new Republican party (1856); defeated by Buchanan. At outbreak of Civil War, appointed major general commanding department of the West, headquarters at St. Louis (1861); severity of measures aroused protests; relieved of command and appointed to command mountain department in western Virginia (1862); placed under Pope and asked to be relieved; resigned (1864). Nominated for president by faction of Republican party (1864), but withdrew before elections.

Lost fortune in railroad ventures (1870). Saved from dire poverty by wife's writings and by appointment as governor of Territory of Arizona (1878–83), and by restoration of rank as major general, U.S. army, with retired pay (1890).
His wife (m. 1841), **Jessie,** *nee* **Benton** (1824–1902), daughter of U.S. senator Thomas H. Benton, was a writer; author of *The Story of the Guard, a Chronicle of the War* (1863), *Far West Sketches* (1890), *The Will and the Way Stories* (1891), etc.

**Frem′stad** (frĕm′städ), **Anna Olivia,** *known as* **Olive.** 1872–1951. Dramatic soprano, b. Stockholm, Sweden; to U.S. as a child (c. 1882). With Metropolitan Opera, New York City (from 1903); widely known as interpreter of Wagnerian roles.

**Fré′my′** (frā′mē′), **Edmond.** 1814–1894. French chemist, b. Versailles. Professor, École Polytechnique, Paris (1846), Muséum d'Histoire Naturelle (1850). Studied ferric acid, osmic acid, palmitic acid, cellulose, chlorophyll, the composition of bone and other organic substances, etc.; contributed to the manufacture of iron and steel, sulphuric acid, etc.; worked on the saponification of fats with sulphuric acid; discovered a process for making artificial rubies; disagreed with Pasteur concerning fermentation. Author of *Traité de Chimie Générale* (with Pelouze, 1854–57), *Encyclopédie Chimique* (with others, 1882–94), etc.

**French** (frĕnch), **Aaron.** 1823–1902. American inventor, b. Wadsworth, Ohio. Invented coil and elliptic railroad-car springs which revolutionized railroad industry.

**French, Alice.** *Pseudonym* **Oc′tave Than′et** (ŏk′tāv thăn′ĕt; -ĭt). 1850–1934. American fiction writer, b. Andover, Mass. Resident chiefly in Arkansas and Iowa, which supply the background of her early stories. Among her books are *Knitters in the Sun* (1887), *Stories of a Western Town* (1893), *Man of the Hour* (1905), *The Lion's Share* (1907), *By Inheritance* (1910), *And the Captain Answered* (1917), etc.

**French, Anne Warner.** See Anne Richmond WARNER.

**French, Daniel Chester.** 1850–1931. American sculptor, b. Exeter, N.H. Studied in Boston and in Florence, Italy. Studio in Washington (1876–78), Boston and Concord, Mass. (1878–87), and New York (from 1887). Among his best-known works are *The Minute Man of Concord* at Concord, *John Harvard* in Harvard University yard, *Statue of The Republic* at Chicago Exposition of 1893, the bronze doors of Boston Public Library, groups representing *Europe, Asia, Africa,* and *America* in front of New York Custom House, statues of General Cass, Rufus Choate, Thomas Starr King, George F. Hoar, Governor James Oglethorpe, Abraham Lincoln, and portrait busts (in the Hall of Fame) of Poe, Emerson, Hawthorne, and Phillips Brooks.

**French, John Denton Pinkstone.** 1st Earl of **Y′pres** (ē′pr′). 1852–1925. British field marshal, b. in Kent. Served in navy (1866–70) and army (from 1874). Distinguished himself in Nile expedition (1884–85) and by success as cavalry commander in Boer War (1899–1901) in relieving Kimberley and advanced into Transvaal; promoted general (1907). Chief of imperial general staff (1912–14) and field marshal (1913); placed in supreme command of British army on Western Front. In battle of Ypres, prevented Germans from reaching Calais; failed to work in harmony with Kitchener and, under criticism for costly advances, resigned (Dec., 1915). Commander in chief in United Kingdom; lord lieutenant of Ireland (May, 1918). Member, Order of Merit (1914). Author of *1914*.

**Fre·neau′** (frē·nō′; frē′nō), **Philip Mo′rin′** (mô′răN′). 1752–1832. Known as "the Poet of the American Revolution." American poet, b. New York City. Grad. Princeton (1771). At outbreak of American Revolution, wrote bitter satires directed against British. In West Indies (1776–79). Took out privateer; captured by British; held on prison ship until exchanged (1780); wrote verse account of experience in *The British Prison-Ship, a Poem in Four Cantoes* (1781). Employed in Philadelphia post office (1781–84); contributor of many poems to *Freeman's Journal.* Again at sea (1784–89). On newspaper editorial work (1789–95); appointed translating clerk in U.S. Department of State by Thomas Jefferson (1791); founded and edited *National Gazette,* a democratic paper rivaling Fenno's *Gazette of the United States* (1791–93). Retired from newspaper work and politics (1793); remainder of life spent on his New Jersey estate and at sea. Individual poems: *The Indian Burying Ground, The Wild Honeysuckle, Eutaw Springs, The House of Night, Santa Cruz, The Jamaica Funeral.* Collections of his works: *The Poems of Philip Freneau* (1786), *Poems Written between the Years 1768 and 1794* (1795), *Poems Written and Published During the American Revolutionary War* (2 vols., 1809).

**Frens′sen** (frĕn′sĕn), **Gustav.** 1863–1945. German writer and clergyman. Author of novels and stories chiefly of peasant life in north Germany, as *Joern Uhl* (1901); also wrote the epic poem *Bismarck* (1914) and plays.

**Fren′zel** (frĕn′tsĕl), **Karl.** 1827–1914. German novelist and dramatic and literary critic.

**Frep′pel′** (frā′pĕl′), **Charles Émile.** 1827–1891. French Roman Catholic prelate; pulpit orator and hagiographer; bishop of Angers (1870) and founder of the Catholic university there (1875); leader of Clerical party in Chamber of Deputies (from 1881).

**Frère** (frâr). Family of French painters, including: **Charles Théodore** (1814–1888), genre and landscape painter and aquarellist; **Pierre Édouard** (1819–1886), genre painter; Pierre Édouard's son **Charles Édouard** (1837–1894), genre painter.

**Frere** (frēr), **John Hookham.** 1769–1846. English diplomat, b. London. Educ. Cambridge. M.P. (1799–1802). British envoy at Lisbon (1800–02), Madrid (1802–04); British minister with the Spanish Junta (1808–09). Lived in retirement at Malta (1818–46). A founder of *Quarterly Review.*
His nephew Sir **Henry Bartle Edward Frere** (1815–1884), colonial administrator; entered Bombay civil service (1834); chief commissioner of Sind (1850–59); governor of Bombay (1862–67); in England as member of the Council of India (1867); governor of the Cape, and first high commissioner of South Africa (1877); his demands on Cetewayo precipitated the Zulu War (1879), and he was recalled (1880).

**Frère′-Or′ban′** (frâr′ôr′bäN′), **Hubert Joseph Walther.** 1812–1896. Belgian statesman and lawyer. Leading Liberal member of lower house (1847–94); minister of public works (1847), of finance (1848–52, 1857–70), of state (1861). Minister president (1867–70, 1878–84) and foreign minister.

**Fré′ret′** (frā′rĕ′), **Nicolas.** 1688–1749. French historian, archaeologist, and philologist.

**Fré′ron′** (frā′rôN′), **Élie Catherine.** 1719–1776. French journalist and critic; founded (1754) and edited (1754–76) *L'Année Littéraire,* a journal in which he assailed Voltaire and the Encyclopedists, esp. for their irreligion, and by his attacks evoked from Voltaire famous rejoinders, as *Le Pauvre Diable* and *L'Écossaise.* His son **Louis Marie Stanislas** (1754–1802), Revolutionary politician, founded (1790) a journal, *L'Orateur du Peuple,* in which he opposed Mirabeau.

**Fre′sco·bal′di** (frās′kō·bäl′dē), **Girolamo.** 1583–1643.

Italian organist, and composer of canzoni, madrigals, hymns, toccatas, motets, caprices, etc.

**Fre·se'ni·us** (frā·zā'nē·o͝os), **Carl Remigius.** 1818–1897. German chemist; assistant in Liebig's laboratory, Giessen; professor at the Agricultural Institute (1845) and founder (1848) of a laboratory for teaching and research, Wiesbaden; known for work in, and textbooks on, analytical chemistry.

**Fresh'field** (frĕsh'fēld), **Douglas William.** 1845–1934. English mountain climber and geographer; educ. Oxford. His explorations extended to mountain regions of northern India, Uganda, Syria, Algeria, the Caucasus, the Apennines, and the Alpine region. Author of *The Italian Alps* (1875); editor of *Alpine Journal* (1872–80).

**Fres'nel'** (frā'nĕl'), **Augustin Jean.** 1788–1827. French physicist. Known for work in optics: by investigations of interference, was instrumental in establishing the wave theory of light; studied double refraction; with Arago investigated polarized light; produced circularly polarized light by means of a rhomb of glass; pioneered in use of compound lenses in lighthouses.

**Freud** (froit; *Angl.* froid), **Sig'mund** (zēk'mo͝ont; *Angl.* sĭg'mŭnd). 1856–1939. Austrian neurologist, founder of psychoanalysis, b. Freiberg, Moravia, of Jewish extraction. M.D., U. of Vienna (1881). Privatdocent (1883), professor of neuropathology (1902–38), U. of Vienna; forced to leave Vienna by Nazi regime (1938), thereafter living in London. Studied in Paris under Charcot (1885–86); worked with Breuer on the treatment of hysteria by hypnosis; later developed a method of treatment (which served as basis of his psychoanalysis) in which he replaced hypnosis by free association of ideas, or the calling up of one idea by another previously linked with it. Believed that a complex of repressed and forgotten impressions underlies all abnormal mental states such as hysteria, and that mere revelation of these impressions often effects a cure; regarded infantile mental processes of particular importance in later development; developed a theory that dreams are an unconscious representation of repressed desires, especially of sexual desires. Author of *Studien über Hysterie* (with Breuer, 1895), *Traumdeutung* (1900), *Zur Psychopathologie des Alltagslebens* (1901), *Über Psychoanalyse* (1910), *Vorlesungen zur Einführung in die Psychoanalyse* (1917), *Das Ich und das Es* (1923), *Die Zukunft einer Illusion* (1927), *Das Unbehagen in der Kultur* (1930), *Neue Folge der Vorlesungen zur Einführung* (1932), *Der Mann Moses und die Monotheistische Religion* (1939).

**Freund** (froint), **Wilhelm.** 1806–1894. German classical philologist; compiled Latin lexicon *Wörterbuch der Lateinischen Sprache* (4 vols., 1834–45), on which many Latin-English dictionaries are based.

**Freund'lich** (froint'lĭκ), **Emmy.** 1878–1948. Austrian Socialist politician and leader of women workers' movement, b. in Czechoslovakia.

**Frey** (frī), **Emil.** 1838–1922. Swiss politician; served in Union army in American Civil War, and was prisoner of war in Libby prison. Returned to Switzerland; member of National Council (1872); Swiss minister to United States (1882–88); president of Swiss Confederation (1893).

**Frey, Jakob.** 1824–1875. Swiss writer; author of tales of Swiss life. His son **Adolf** (1855–1920), poet and literary historian, was author of many biographical works, and of historical novels, lyrics and dialect poems, dramas, etc.

**Frey, Karl.** Pseudonym of Konrad FALKE.

**Frey'berg** (frī'bûrg), 1st Baron. **Bernard Cyril Freyberg.** 1889–1963. New Zealand general, b. in London, Eng. Educ. Wellington Coll., N.Z. Served in World War (1914–18); engaged at Gallipoli; V.C. (1916); commanded 2d New Zealand Expeditionary Force (1939–45); engaged in Greece, Crete, North Africa, Italy; lieutenant general (1943); governor general of New Zealand (1946–52).

**Frey'ci'net'** (frā'sē'nĕ'), Baron **de. Louis Henri de Saulces** (dē sōls). 1777–1840. French naval officer; rear admiral (1826), major general of marine at Toulon (1830), maritime prefect at Rochefort (1834). His brother **Louis Claude de Saulces de Freycinet** (1779–1842) was also a naval officer; directed an expedition around the world (1817–20) studying meteorology and terrestrial magnetism, and published *Voyage Autour du Monde* (13 vols., 4 maps, 1824 ff.). His nephew **Charles Louis de Saulces de Freycinet** (1828–1923) was a civil engineer and politician; senator (1876); minister of public works (1877–79); premier of France (1879–80; 1882; 1886; 1890–92); minister of state (1915–16).

**Frey'er** (frī'ẽr), **Hans.** 1887– . German sociologist.

**Frey'ling·hau'sen** (frī'lĭng·hou'zĕn), **Johann Anastasius.** 1670–1739. German religious poet and Pietist theologian; published two collections of sacred songs (1704, 1714) containing about 1500 hymns.

**Frey'tag** (frī'täκ), **Georg Wilhelm.** 1788–1861. German Arabic scholar; compiled *Lexicon Arabico-Latinum* (4 vols., 1830–37); edited Arabic songs and Arabic proverbs.

**Freytag, Gustav.** 1816–1895. German novelist, playwright, and critic, b. in Silesia. Educ. Breslau and Berlin; coeditor of *Die Grenzboten* at Leipzig (1848–70); champion of German liberalism and German middle classes. Won support of duke of Saxe-Coburg-Gotha; represented Erfurt at North German Reichstag (1867–70); attached to headquarters of crown prince during part of 1870 campaign; lived chiefly at Wiesbaden (from 1879). Author of plays, including the comedies *Die Brautfahrt* (1844) and *Die Journalisten* (1854), of *Soll und Haben* (realistic novel of German commercial life, 1855), *Die Verlorene Handschrift* (novel of Leipzig society and university life, 1864), and a series of six historical novels entitled *Die Ahnen* (1872–80).

**Frey'tag–Lo'ring·ho'ven** (frī'täκ·lō'rĭng·hō'fĕn), Baron **Hugo von.** 1855–1924. German general and military author, b. in Copenhagen of Russian parentage. Became naturalized German (c. 1876); served in Prussian army (from 1878). In World War, quartermaster general of German army in the field (1915); chief of general staff after von Moltke's death (1916).

**Fri'ant'** (frē'äɴ'), Comte **Louis.** 1758–1829. French soldier; general of brigade (1794), of division (1800); engaged at Austerlitz, Auerstedt, Eggmühl, Wagram, and Moscow; commanded a division of the guard at Waterloo.

**Frí'as** (frē'äs), **Tomás.** 1804–1882. Bolivian statesman and diplomat, b. Potosí. In exile (1861–71); acting president of Bolivia (1872–73); president (1874–76; overthrown).

**Frick** (frĭk), **Henry Clay.** 1849–1919. American industrialist, b. West Overton, Pa. Organized Frick & Co. to build and operate coke ovens in Connellsville coal district of Pennsylvania (1871); rose to control of two thirds of capacity of that area (1889). Chairman, Carnegie Steel Co. (1889–1900); managing head of company during Homestead labor strike (1892); played important part in consolidation forming United States Steel Corp. (1901). Bequeathed his home in New York, with its art treasures and a large endowment, to the public to be used as a museum.

**Frick** (frĭk), **Wilhelm.** 1877–1946. German politician; minister of interior (1933–43); hanged as war criminal.

**Fri'da** (frĭ'dȧ), **Emil.** *Pseudonym* **Jaroslav Vrch'lic·ký** (vûrκ'lĭts·kē). 1853–1912. Czech poet, dramatist, and translator.

**Fri'de·ri'cia** (frē'thĕ·rē'shä), **Julius Albert.** 1849–1912. Danish historian.

**Fri'de·swi'de** (frĭ'dĕ·swē'dĕ; frĭ'thĕ·swē'thĕ) *or* **Fri'the·swith** (frĭ'thĕ·swĭth; -thĕ·swēth) *or* **Fre'de·swi'tha** (frĕ'dĕ·swē'thȧ), Saint. d. 735? An English princess; reputed founder of a monastery at Oxford.

**Fridigern.** See FRITIGERN.

**Fri'do·lin** (frē'dō·lēn), Saint. Christian missionary of the 6th century; founded a monastery and church on island of Säckingen in the Rhine. Patron saint of the canton of Glarus, Switzerland.

**Fried** (frēt), **Alfred Hermann.** 1864–1921. Austrian pacifist and publicist, b. in Vienna. Settled in Berlin (1883) as bookseller and author; founded (1891) and edited first and leading German pacifist paper *Die Waffen Nieder!* (called *Die Friedenswarte* from 1899); founded German peace society (1892); took leading part in all international peace movements; co-winner of Nobel peace prize (1911).

**Fried, Oskar.** 1871–1941. German composer and choral and orchestral director.

**Fried'berg** (frēt'bĕrk), **Emil.** 1837–1910. German legal scholar; took part in Kulturkampf legislation (1872); championed state supremacy in ecclesiastical affairs.

**Frie'del'** (frē'dĕl'), **Charles.** 1832–1899. French chemist and mineralogist, b. Strasbourg. Worked on the artificial production of minerals; studied pyroelectric properties of crystals, crystallographic constants, and ketones and aldehydes; with James Mason Crafts, prepared various compounds of silicon and described a synthetic reaction (Friedel-Crafts reaction) for producing aromatic homologues; with R. D. da Silva, synthesized glycerine. See Georges L. DUVERNOY.

**Frie'de·ri'ci** (frē'dĕ·rĭ'tsē), **Georg.** 1866–1947. German ethnologist.

**Fried'heim** (frēt'hīm), **Arthur.** 1859–1932. Piano virtuoso and interpreter of Liszt, b. St. Petersburg, Russia, of German parentage.

**Fried'jung** (frēt'yŏŏng), **Heinrich.** 1851–1920. Austrian historian and political writer, b. in Moravia; champion of German nationalism. Author of *Der Kampf um die Vorherrschaft in Deutschland 1859–66* (2 vols., 1897–98), *Österreich 1848–60* (2 vols., 1908–12), *Das Zeitalter des Imperialismus 1884–1914* (3 vols., 1919–22; finished by Pribram), etc.

**Fried'laen'der** (frēt'lĕn'dēr), **Julius.** 1813–1884. German numismatist; author of works on late Roman coins.

**Friedland, Valentin.** See Valentin TROTZENDORF.

**Fried'län'der** (frēt'lĕn'dēr), **David.** 1750–1834. German writer and Hebrew scholar. Settled in Berlin (1771); devoted himself to emancipation of Jews and improvement of their condition in Berlin.

**Friedländer, Friedrich.** 1825–1901. Austrian genre and historical painter, esp. of scenes from Austrian life and among war wounded.

**Friedländer, Ludwig.** 1824–1909. German classical philologist and archaeologist.

**Friedländer, Max.** 1852–1934. German musicologist and singer, b. in Silesia. Engaged in musical research in Berlin under Spitta's direction (from 1883); professor, U. of Berlin (1903); exchange professor, Harvard U. (1911) and lecturer at other American universities. Edited songs of Schubert, Schumann, and Mendelssohn, Beethoven's Scottish songs, Brahms's folk songs, etc.

**Friedländer, Max J.** 1867–1958. German art scholar.

**Fried'man** (frēt'män), **I'gnaz** (ĭg'näts; ĭg·näts'). 1882–1948. Polish pianist and composer; interpreter of Chopin.

**Fried'man** (frēd'mȧn), **Milton.** 1912– . American economist. At U. of Chicago (1946– ); awarded Nobel prize for economics (1976).

**Fried'mann** (frēt'män), **Me'ir ben Je're·mi'ah** (mā'ĭr bĕn yā'rā·mē'ä). 1831–1908. Hungarian Jewish scholar and teacher.

**Frie'dreich** (frē'drīk), **Nikolaus.** 1825–1882. German physician; authority on diseases of the heart and the vascular and nervous systems.

**Frie'drich** (frē'drĭk). German form of FREDERICK.

**Friedrich, Johannes.** 1836–1917. German theologian and historian. Ordained Roman Catholic priest (1859); professor of church history, Munich (1865–1905); assisted at Vatican Council in Rome (1870); excommunicated with his teacher Döllinger for opposing dogma of papal infallibility (1871); became a leader in Old Catholic movement and helped establish Old Catholic theological faculty at U. of Bern (1874).

**Friedrich, Kaspar** (*or* **Caspar**) **David.** 1774–1840. German landscape painter. His importance in German Romanticism was rediscovered and fully recognized at German Centenary Exhibition in Berlin (1906).

**Friedrich, Stephan.** 1883– Hungarian politician. Supported Károlyi in October revolution of 1918; subsequently went over to conservatives; overthrew Julius Peidl's socialist government (1919) and became minister president (Aug.–Nov., 1919) under Archduke Joseph's regency; then war minister in Huszár's cabinet (Nov., 1919–March, 1920); took leading part in Christian national movement as member of extreme legitimistic group.

**Friedrich, Woldemar.** 1846–1910. German painter and illustrator; his works include murals in Booksellers' Exchange at Leipzig; illustrations for editions of Schiller; landscapes and genre pictures in water colors, etc.

**Friedrich Wilhelm.** Duke of **Brunswick.** See BRUNSWICK.

**Fries** (frēs), **Adriaen de.** See VRIES.

**Fries, Elias Magnus.** 1794–1878. Swedish botanist; authority on classification of cryptogams, esp. fungi. The genus *Freesia* is named for him.

**Fries, Ernst** (1801–1833) and his brother **Bernhard** (1820–1879). German landscape painters.

**Fries, Jakob Friedrich.** 1773–1843. German philosopher; attempted to find by psychological method a new basis for critical philosophy of Kant and to reconcile criticism of Kant to Jacobi's religious philosophy.

**Fries, John.** 1750?–1818. American insurgent, b. in Montgomery County, Pa. Opposed federal property tax levied in anticipation of war with France (1798); led armed force of Pennsylvania Germans against assessors (1799). Federal troops ordered into area by President Adams; Fries arrested, tried, sentenced to death for treason; pardoned by the president (1800).

**Frie'se** (frē'zĕ), **Richard.** 1854–1918. German painter of animals (esp. lions and tigers) and landscapes.

**Frie'sen** (frē'zĕn), **Karl Friedrich.** 1785–1814. German mathematician, architect, and cartographer; cofounder of German gymnastics. Assisted Jahn in establishing first German athletic grounds. Asst. organizer and adjutant of Adolf von Lützow's volunteer corps (1813); captured and shot by French (1814).

**Fri'esz'** (frē'ĕs'), **Émile Othon.** 1879–1949. French painter; studied under Bonnat; associated with Fauvists.

**Fri·gan'za** (frĭ·găn'zȧ), **Trixie.** *Professional name of* **Delia O'Cal'la·han** (ō·kăl'ȧ·hăn). 1870–1955. American actress and singer, b. Grenola, Kans.; m. (1st) Dr. W. J. M. Barry; (2d) Charles A. Goettler. Played Lady Saphir in *Patience*, Celia in *Iolanthe*, and leading roles in *Sally in our Alley*, *The Sho-Gun*, *Prince of Pilsen*.

**Friis** (frēs), **Aage.** 1870–1949. Danish historian.

**Friml** (frĭm''l), **Ru'dolf** (rōō'dŏlf), *in full* **Charles** (chärlz) **Rudolf.** 1879–1972. Bohemian pianist and composer; studied in Prague; accompanist for Kubelik on tours in U.S. (1901, 1906); resident in New York City (1906). Known for his light operas, including *The Firefly*, *High Jinks*, *Katinka*, *You're in Love*, *Rose Marie;* composer of many piano compositions and songs.

**Fri·mont'** (frē·môN'), Count **Johann Maria Philipp von.** Prince of **An'tro·doc'co** (än'trô·dôk'ō). 1759–1831. Austrian general; commander in chief of Austrian troops in Italy (1815) and besieged Lyons; suppressed revolution at Naples (1821); received Italian title of prince (1821) and rank of cavalry general. Governor general of Lombardo-Venetian kingdom (1825); suppressed uprisings in Modena, Parma, and the papal territory (1831). President of Aulic Council (1831).

**Frisch** (frĭsh), **Johann Leonhard.** 1666–1743. German philologist and naturalist; works include *Teutsch-Lateinisches Wörter-Buch*, first scientific work of its kind (2 vols., 1741).

**Frisch, Karl von.** 1886– . Austrian zoologist. At U. of Munich (1910–21; 1925; 1950–58); awarded (with Konrad Lorenz and Nikolaas Tinbergen) Nobel prize for physiology or medicine (1973).

**Frisch** (frēsh), **Otto Robert.** 1904– . British (Austrian-born) physicist; known for work on the uranium atom.

**Frisch, Ragnar.** 1895–1973. Norwegian economist. Awarded the first Nobel prize in economic science (1968) with J. Tinbergen.

**Frisch'lin** (frĭsh'lēn), **Nikodemus.** 1547–1590. German philologist and poet. Professor of history and poetry, Tübingen (1568–82); forced to leave for satirical writings on nobility. Author esp. of Latin comedies including *Julius Redivivus* (pub. 1585), *Priscianus Vapulans* (a satire on grammar, 1571); the Reformation drama *Phasma* (1580); a Latin grammar (1585), etc.

**Fri'si** (frē'zē), **Paolo.** 1728–1784. Italian mathematician and astronomer, b. Milan. Author of *Disquisitio Mathematica* (on physical causes of shape and size of the earth, 1751), *Cosmographia Physica et Mathematica* (1774–75), etc.

**Fri'so** (frē'sō). Name given to several members of the house of Nassau, including John William Friso (see NASSAU, ORANGE, and WILLIAM IV, Count of Nassau) and Charles Henry Friso (= WILLIAM IV).

**Fritch'ie** (frĭch'ĭ), **Barbara.** American woman, resident of Frederick, Md., who, according to legend, waved a Union flag defiantly at Stonewall Jackson when he ordered his troops to fire on it in her window (Sept., 1862). Subsequent investigation has cast doubt on the accuracy of the story. Subject of a poem, *Barbara Frietchie* [frē'chĭ] (1864), by Whittier and of a play (1898) by Clyde Fitch.

**Frith** (frĭth), **John.** 1503–1533. English Protestant clergyman and martyr, b. in Kent; B.A., Cantab. (1525). Aided Tyndale in translating the New Testament; forced to reside abroad (1528–32) to escape religious persecution; on return to England (1532) imprisoned for heresy, and burned at the stake (July 4, 1533).

**Frith, Mary.** *Nickname* **Moll** (mŏl), *or* **Mall** (môl), **Cut'purse'** (kŭt'pûrs'). 1584?–1659. English pickpocket; chief personage in Middleton and Dekker's play *The Roaring Girle.*

**Frith, William Powell.** 1819–1909. English artist; studied at Royal Academy schools. Among his notable canvases are *Derby Day* (in Tate Gallery, London), *Charles II's Last Whitehall Sunday*, *Charles Dickens*, *Uncle Toby and the Widow Wadman* (in Tate Gallery).

**Fritheswith.** See FRIDESWIDE.

**Frit'i·gern** (frĭt'ĭ·gûrn) *or* **Frid'i·gern** (frĭd'ĭ·gûrn). d. after 382. Visigoth chieftain and Arian Christian; forced from Dacia by Huns, and with band of Christian Visigoths sought refuge in Moesia by permission of Emperor Valens (376); rebelled at ill treatment by Roman officials and ultimately defeated Romans and killed Valens at Adrianople (378).

**Fritsch,** Baron **Werner von.** 1880–1939. German army officer; during World War (1914–18), served as major on general staff. Promoted lieutenant general (1932) and chief of staff with rank of general of artillery (1933). Apparently lost favor of Chancellor Hitler and was relieved of command (1938). Killed in action before Warsaw (Sept. 22, 1939) while leading reconnoitering party.

**Fritz** (frĭts), **John.** 1822–1913. American authority on iron and steel manufacture, b. in Chester County, Pa. With Bethlehem Iron Co. (from 1860); among the first to introduce the Bessemer process in U.S., open-hearth furnaces, and other improvements.

**Fröbel.** = FROEBEL.

**Fro'ben** (frō'bĕn), **Johann.** *Lat.* **Fro·be'ni·us** (frô·bā'nē·o͝os; *Angl.* frô·bē'nĭ·ŭs). 1460?–1527. German printer and publisher, b. in Franconia. Founded (1491) printing press at Basel, Switz., famous for accuracy and artistic taste. Published a Latin Bible (1491), works of Tertullian, St. Ambrose, and other Latin church fathers and Roman authors; works written or edited by his friend Erasmus, including the Greek New Testament (1516), etc.

**Fro·be'ni·us** (frô·bā'nē·o͝os; *Angl.* frô·bē'nĭ·ŭs), **Leo.** 1873–1938. German ethnologist and explorer; authority on prehistoric African art; b. Berlin. Propounded theory that civilization undergoes an organic development similar to that of plants, animals, and man.

**Fro'ber'ger** (frō'bĕr'gēr), **Johann Jakob.** 1616–1667. German organist and composer; pioneer in early development of instrumental composition.

**Fro'bish·er** (frō'bĭsh·ēr; frŏb'ĭsh-), Sir **Martin.** 1535?–1594. English mariner; commanded expedition in search for Northwest Passage (1576), and discovered bay in Canada since known as Frobisher Bay; returned to same region in search for gold (1577; 1578). Vice-admiral under Drake in the West Indian expedition (1586); commanded the *Triumph* against the Spanish Armada (1588); vice-admiral under Hawkins (1590). Knighted (1588).

**Frö'ding'** (frû'dĭng'), **Gustaf.** 1860–1911. Swedish poet; wrote lyric and, later, religious verse.

**Frodoard.** See FLODOARD.

**Froe'bel** *or* **Frö'bel** (frû'bĕl), **Friedrich.** 1782–1852. German educator and founder of the kindergarten system, b. in Oberweissbach, Schwarzburg-Rudolstadt. Forester's apprentice (1797); studied architecture; studied and worked under Pestalozzi at Yverdon, Switz. (1808–10); served in Lützow corps during anti-French campaign (1813–14); assistant in mineralogical museum, Berlin. Founded school at Griesheim (1816); moved to Keilhau near Rudolstadt (1817); devoted himself exclusively to study of preschool children (from 1836) and devised series of educational games and employments for children; founded a kindergarten at Blankenburg, Thuringia (1837); established training courses for kindergartners and introduced kindergartens throughout Germany; schools condemned in Prussia for alleged atheistic and Socialistic teachings (1851–60); took active part in political and educational reform movements (1848). Author of *Die Menschenerziehung* (1826), *Mutter- und Koselieder* (1844), etc. His nephew **Julius** (1805–1893) taught mineralogy in Zurich schools (1833–44); founded radical *Literarisches Comptoir*, Zurich (1842); to Germany (1846); a leader of radical Democrats in revolutionary movement of 1848 and member of Frankfurt

National Assembly. Traveled and edited papers in North and Central America (1849–57); championed Austro-German reform policy in Vienna (1862–66); edited conservative liberal *Süddeutsche Presse*, Munich (1867–73); German consul at Smyrna (1873–76) and Algiers (1876–89). Author of *Theorie der Politik* (2 vols., 1861–64), *Aus Amerika* (2 vols., 1857–58), etc.

**Fröh'lich** (frû'lĭκ), **Abraham Emanuel.** 1796–1865. Swiss poet; author of *Fabeln* (satires in verse, 1825), of satirical attacks on freethinking and revolutionary ideas, *Ulrich Zwingli* (1840) and *Ulrich von Hutten* (1845).

**Froh'man** (frō'măn), **Charles.** 1860–1915. American theatrical manager, b. Sandusky, Ohio. Gradually built up Empire Stock Company, with such actors as Maude Adams, Julia Marlowe, Margaret Anglin, Elsie de Wolfe, and William Faversham. Produced plays by leading dramatists of the day. Became known as "the Napoleon of the Drama"; leading figure in the group of theatrical managers known as The Theatrical Syndicate. Died in the *Lusitania* disaster (May 7, 1915). His brother **Daniel** (1851–1940), a theatrical manager, managed Fifth Avenue Theater and Madison Square Theater, New York City (1879–85), Lyceum Theater, New York City (from 1885), and was president of Lyceum Theater co.

**Frohman, Philip Hubert.** 1887–1972. American architect, b. New York; practiced in Pasadena, Boston, Washington; specialist in ecclesiastical architecture.

**Froh'scham'mer** (frō'shäm'ĕr), **Jakob.** 1821–1893. German theologian and philosopher. Roman Catholic priest (1847); professor of philosophy (from 1855), Munich; wrote radical works on theology placed on Index Expurgatorius and was suspended from office as preacher (1862). Founded and edited (1862–64) liberal Catholic organ *Athenäum*, and engaged in controversy with Catholic theologians; excommunicated (1871).

**Froíla.** See FRUELA.

**Frois'sart'** (frwȧ'sȧr'; *Angl.* froi'särt), **Jean.** 1333?–?1400. French chronicler; visited England (1360), Scotland (1365), and Milan (with Chaucer and Petrarch, 1368); entered the church (c. 1372). His classic work, *Chronique de France, d'Angleterre, d'Écosse et d'Espagne*, covers history between 1325 and about 1400.

**Frome, David.** Pseudonym of Zenith Jones BROWN.

**Fro'men'tin'** (frô'mäɴ'tăɴ'), **Eugène.** 1820–1876. French genre painter, esp. of Algerian scenes.

**Fromm** (frŏm), **Erich.** 1900– . Amer. (German-born) psychoanalyst. At Bennington Coll. (1941–50), Mich. State U. (1957–61), N. Y. U. (1962– ). Wrote *Psychoanalysis and Religion* (1950), *Marx's Concept of Man* (1961), *Beyond the Chains of Illusion* (1962), etc.

**Fron·di'zi** (frôn·dē'sē), **Arturo.** 1908– . Argentine statesman. President of Argentina (1958–62).

**Frondsberg** *or* **Fronsperg, Georg von.** See FRUNDSBERG.

**Fron'te·nac'** (frôɴt'nȧk'; *Angl.* frŏn'tʼn·ăk), Comte **de Pal'lu·au' et de** (dē pȧ'lü·ō' ā dē). **Louis de Bu·ade'** (dē bü·ȧd'). 1620–1698. French soldier and colonial governor; served in Flanders, Germany, and Italy (to 1672); governor of New France (Canada, 1672–82 and 1689–98). In New France, encouraged explorations, forced English to lift the siege of Quebec (1690), and fought against the Iroquois.

**Fron·ti'nus** (frŏn·tī'nŭs), **Sextus Julius.** Roman soldier and writer of 1st century A.D.; governor of Britain (75–78 A.D.); superintendent of the water-supply system at Rome (97).

**Fron'to** (frŏn'tō), **Marcus Cornelius.** Roman lawyer and scholar of 2d century A.D., b. in Numidia; practiced in Rome. Tutor to Marcus Aurelius and Lucius Verus. Consul (143 A.D.). Strove to revive interest in early Roman literature and to restore the simplicity and force of the old Latin language.

**Fro'riep** (frō'rēp), **August von.** 1849–1917. German anatomist.

**Fros'sard'** (frô'sȧr'), **Charles Auguste.** 1807–1875. French general; served in Crimean War (1854–55); general of brigade (1855), aide-de-camp to Napoleon III (1857). Commanded 2d corps of Army of the Rhine (1870); was defeated, driven back into Metz.

**Frost** (frŏst), **Arthur Burdett.** 1851–1928. American illustrator, b. Philadelphia. On staff of New York *Graphic* (1875), *Harper's* (1876). Illustrated Joel Chandler Harris's *Uncle Remus* books. Independent collections of humorous sketches: *Stuff and Nonsense* (1884), *The Bull Calf and Other Tales* (1892).

**Frost, Edwin Brant.** 1866–1935. American astronomer, b. Brattleboro, Vt. A.B. (1886), Dartmouth. Professor, Dartmouth (1895–98), Chicago (1898–1935); director of Yerkes Observatory (1905–32). Made special study of stellar velocities in the line of sight, stellar spectroscopy, sunspots, and sun thermal radiation.

**Frost, Frances.** 1905–1959. American novelist and poet; her novels include *Innocent Summer* (1936), *Yoke of Stars* (1939), *Kate Trimingham* (1940).

**Frost, Robert Lee.** 1874–1963. American poet, b. San Francisco. Educ. Dartmouth (1892) and Harvard (1897–99). Professor of English, Amherst (1916–20; 1923–25; 1926–38); professor of poetry, Harvard (from 1936). Awarded Pulitzer prizes for **1923, 1930, 1936, 1942.** Author of *A Boy's Will* (1913), *North of Boston* (1914), *Mountain Interval* (1916), *New Hampshire* (1923), *West-running Brook* (1928), *A Further Range* (1936), *From Snow to Snow* (1936), *A Witness Tree* (1942), etc.

**Frost, William Edward.** 1810–1877. English painter.

**Froth'ing·ham** (frŏth'ĭng·hăm; -ăm), **Arthur Lincoln.** 1859–1923. American archaeologist, b. Boston. Professor, Princeton (1886–1905). Founded and edited *American Journal of Archaeology* (1885–96).

**Frothingham, Nathaniel Langdon.** 1793–1870. American Unitarian clergyman, b. Boston; grad. Harvard (1811); pastor, First Church of Boston (1815–50). His son **Octavius Brooks** (1822–1895) was also a clergyman; grad. Harvard (1843) and Harvard Divinity School (1846); in Unitarian ministry (to 1867); separated from orthodox Unitarianism and became independent minister (after 1867).

**Frothingham, Richard.** 1812–1880. American historian, b. Charlestown, Mass. Author of *The Rise of the Republic of the United States* (1872), etc.

**Froude** (frōōd), **James Anthony.** 1818–1894. English historian, b. at Dartington, Devonshire. B.A., Oxon. (1842). Ordained deacon (1844); resigned (1872) because of change of religious convictions. Met Thomas Carlyle (1849) and became his close friend and admirer; named by Carlyle his literary executor, and as such published Carlyle's *Reminiscences* (1881), *Letters and Memorials of Jane Welsh Carlyle* (1883), *History of the First Forty Years of Carlyle's Life* (1882), *History of Carlyle's Life in London* (1884). Regius professor of modern history at Oxford (1892–94). Among his works are *History of England...* (12 vols., 1856–70), *The English in Ireland in the Eighteenth Century* (1872–74), *The English in the West Indies* (1888).

His older brother **Richard Hurrell** (1803–1836), clergyman; educ. Oxford; close friend of John Henry Newman; exercised important influence on Tractarian movement, writing three of the *Tracts for the Times;* collaborated with Newman in Rome (1833) in writing poems contained in *Lyra Apostolica.*

Another brother, **William** (1810–1879), was an engineer

and naval architect; educ. Oxford; introduced bilge keels to lessen rolling of ships; conducted for the admiralty experiments on resistance and propulsion of ships; built dynamometer to measure power of marine engines.

**Frowde** (froud), **Henry**. 1841–1927. English publisher, b. at Southsea. Publisher of Clarendon Press books, and official publisher to the U. of Oxford (1883–1913).

**Fru·e'la** (frōō·ā'lä) *or* **Fro·í'la** (frô·ē'lä). Name of two kings of Asturias and León: **Fruela I** (722–768); king (757–768); reign marked by civil rebellions; founded Oviedo. **Fruela II** (d. 925); governor of Asturias (910–923); king of León and Asturias (923–925).

**Frug** (frōōk), **Semën Grigorievich**. 1860–1916. Russian-Jewish poet, b. in government of Kherson. Among his volumes of verse are *Stikhotvoleniya* (1885), *Dumy i Poesii* (1887), *Lieder und Gedanken* (Yiddish poems; 1886), and *Zionidy* (Zionistic songs; 1902).

**Fru·go'ni** (frōō·gō'nē), **Carlo Innocenzo**. 1692–1768. Italian poet; protégé at court of duke of Parma; composed light lyric poetry.

**Fruin** (froin), **Robert Jacobus**. 1823–1899. Dutch historian and political writer; authority on Dutch history.

**Fru·men'ti·us** (frōō·mĕn'shĭ·ŭs), Saint. d. about 380. Christian apostle of the Abyssinians and founder of the Abyssinian Church, b. in Tyre, Phoenicia. Taken as slave with brother Aedisius to court of Aksum following shipwreck on Red Sea (c. 326); gained favor of king and propagated Christianity throughout kingdom. Consecrated bishop of Aksum by Athanasius in Alexandria (c. 328); assumed titles "Abba Salamah" (father of peace) and "Abuna" (our father).

**Frunds'berg** (frōōnts'bĕrk) *or* **Fronds'berg** (frŏnts'-bĕrk) *or* **Frons'perg** (frŏns'pĕrk), **Georg von**. 1473–1528. German general, b. in Swabia. Called "father of the German Lands'knech'te" (länts'k'nĕk'tĕ). Fought for Maximilian I against Swiss (1499); helped Maximilian organize and develop Landsknechte; took part in campaign between League of Cambria and Venice, and commanded infantry troops of Swabian League against Ulrich von Württemberg (1519); met Luther at Diet of Worms (1521). Received command against French from Charles V; took part in invasion of Picardy, gained victory at La Bicocca (1522), and won distinction at battle of Pavia (1525).

**Frun'ze** (frōōn'zyĕ), **Mikhail Vasilievich**. 1885–1925. Russian Soviet army commander, b. Pishpek (now Frunze). Banished to Siberia (1914), but escaped in time to take part in Bolshevist revolution (1917). Commanded Soviet armies operating against Admiral Kolchak (1919–20) and General Wrangel (1920). People's commissar for military and naval affairs (Jan., 1925).

**Fru'tolf** (frōō'tôlf). d. 1103. German chronicler; prior of Michelsberg Cloister near Bamberg. His world chronicle of the years 1057–1103, dealing esp. with the history of Henry IV, was ascribed until 1896 to the Benedictine abbot **Ek'ke·hard von Au'ra** [ĕk'ĕ·härt fôn ou'rä] (d. about 1125), who revised it several times and brought it down to 1125.

**Fry** (frī), **Christopher**. 1907– British dramatist. Wrote *The Lady's Not for Burning* (1949), etc.; participated in writing the film scripts *Ben Hur, Barabbas, The Bible*, etc. Translated Ibsen's *Peer Gynt* (1970).

**Fry** (frī), **Elizabeth**, *nee* **Gur'ney** (gûr'nĭ). 1780–1845. English Quaker philanthropist, b. in Norfolk; m. Joseph Fry (1820). A Quaker minister (from 1809); interested in prison reform; founded order of nursing sisters.

**Fry, Joseph**. 1728–1787. English businessman and type founder; orig. a physician, practicing in Bristol; founded at Bristol firm of J. S. Fry & Sons, chocolate manufacturers. Later, associated with the printer William Pine in type founding; settled in London and published an edition of the Bible (5 vols., 1774–76), and *Specimen of Printing Types made by Joseph Fry & Sons* (1785). His grandson **Francis** (1803–1886) was businessman and bibliographer; partner in chocolate-manufacturing firm of J. S. Fry & Sons; member of Quaker delegation to monarchs of Europe to advance the cause of abolition of slavery (1850); amassed large collection of early English Bibles, and printed facsimile of Tyndale's *New Testament* (1862), *Souldier's Pocket Bible* (1862), and a *Description of the Great Bible of 1539...Cranmer's Bible...and editions in large folio of the Authorized Version* (1865). Joseph's great-grandson Sir **Edward** (1827–1918) was a jurist; practiced in London; judge, Court of Appeal (1883–92); judge on the Hague Tribunal (1900); arbitrator in important international cases, as in the dispute between U.S. and Mexico over the Pious Fund (1902–03), and the controversy between France and Germany over the Casablanca incident (1908–09).

**Fry, Roger Eliot**. 1866–1934. English painter and critic; educ. Cambridge. Author of *Sir Joshua Reynold's Discourses* (1905), *Vision and Design* (1920), *Transformations* (1926), *Henri Matisse* (1930), *Reflections on British Painting* (1934), *Last Lectures* (publ. 1939).

**Fry, Sherry Edmundson**. 1879– . American sculptor, b. Creston, Iowa. Among his notable works are reliefs on Grant Memorial in Washington, D.C., pediment for the Labor and Interstate Commerce building in Washington, D.C.

**Fry, William Henry**. 1815–1864. American composer and music critic; his opera *Leonora* (presented 1845) was first publicly performed grand opera written by native American.

**Fry'att** (frī'ăt), **Charles Algernon**. 1872–1916. British captain in the merchant marine; master of the ship *Brussels* (1916); captured by Germans, accused of having attempted (Mar. 28, 1916) to ram a German submarine.

**Frye** (frī), **Alexis Everett**. 1859–1936. American educator; author and compiler of many geography textbooks.

**Frye, William Pierce**. 1831–1911. American political leader, b. Lewiston, Me.; member, U.S. House of Representatives (1871–81); U.S. Senate (1881–1911); member of conservative "old guard" group; favored protective tariff; opposed government regulation of industry; an expansionist, supported McKinley's war policies; president pro tempore of the Senate (from 1896).

**Fryth** (frĭth). See also FRITH.

**Fryx·ell'** (frük·sĕl'), **Anders**. 1795–1881. Swedish historian and Protestant theologian. Author of a Swedish grammar (1824) and of *Narratives from Swedish History* (46 vols., 1823–79), etc.

**Fu·ad' I** (fōō·äd'). *Orig.* **Ah'med Fu·ad' Pa'sha** (ă'măd, pä'shä). 1868–1936. Sultan (1917–22) and king (1922–36) of Egypt; b. Cairo. Son of Ismail Pasha (*q.v.*); youngest of twelve children. Educ. Italy; general in Egyptian army (1892–95); became interested in educational matters; founded (1908) Egyptian U. (later known as Fuad I University) at Giza; succeeded his brother Hussein Kamil as sultan (1917); when native unrest forced British to end protectorate (1922), took title of king; opposed all British attempts at control; dissolved parliament twice (1928, 1930), but each time compelled to relinquish autocratic rule; founded Arab Acad. at Cairo (1932); twice married; succeeded by his son Faruk I.

**Fu·ad' Pa·sha'** (fōō·ät' pä·shä'), **Mehmet**. 1814–1869. Turkish statesman; educated for medicine, and served for a time as army surgeon. Minister of foreign affairs (1852–53; 1853–55; 1858; 1867–68); grand vizier (1861–66). Credited with introducing many western European methods into Turkey, but blamed for adding to Turkey's financial difficulties by the cost of his reforms. Wrote verse, a Turkish grammar, etc.

**Fuchs** (fo͝oks; füks), **Emil.** 1866–1929. Painter and sculptor, b. Vienna, Austria; to U.S. (1905).

**Fuchs** (fo͝oks), **Ernst.** 1851–1930. Austrian ophthalmologist.

**Fuchs, Ernst.** 1859–1929. German jurist.

**Fuchs, Immanuel Lazarus.** 1833–1902. German mathematician. Known for works on the theory of numbers and the theory of functions.

**Fuchs, Johann Nepomuk von.** 1774–1856. German mineralogist and chemist; credited with discovery of water glass (1823) and its application in stereochromy.

**Fuchs, Johann Nepomuk.** 1842–1899. Austrian conductor. Composed opera *Zingara* (1872) and arranged operas of Handel, Gluck, and Schubert. His brother **Robert** (1847–1927) composed the operas *Die Königsbraut* (1889) and *Die Teufelsglocken* (1892), and symphonies, serenades, Masses, chamber music, piano pieces, choruses, and songs.

**Fuchs, Karl Dorius Johannes.** 1838–1922. German musician, choral conductor, organist, and (from 1887) writer on music.

**Fuchs, Karl Johannes.** 1865–1934. German economist.

**Fuchs, Leonhard.** 1501–1566. German botanist. The genus *Fuchsia* is named for him.

**Fu·ci′ni** (fo͞o·chē′nē), **Renato.** *Anagrammatic pseudonym* **Ne′ri Tan·fu′cio** (nā′rē tän·fo͞o′chō). 1843–1921. Italian dialect poet and writer; engineer by profession. Author of *Cento Sonetti in Dialetto Pisano* (1872), *Le Veglie di Neri* (1884), *Napoli a Occhio Nudo* (1878).

**Fuen′tes** (fwān′tās), Conde **de. Pedro En·rí′quez A′ce·ve′do de To·le′do** (ān·rē′kāth ä′thā·vā′thō thā tō·lā′thō). c. 1535–1610. Spanish soldier and statesman; served in defense of Lisbon against English (1589); fought in Netherlands (1591 ff.); governor general of Netherlands (1595–96); governor of Milan (c. 1600 ff.).

**Fuer′tes** (fwĕr′tās), **Louis Agassiz.** 1874–1927. American naturalist illustrator, b. Troy, N.Y.; grad. Cornell (1897). His bird illustrations are found in *Song Birds and Water Fowl* (1897), *The Woodpeckers* (1901), *Second Book of Birds* (1901), *Birds of the Rockies* (1902), *Handbook of Birds of the Western United States* (1902), *Handbook of Birds of the Eastern United States* (1902), *Waterfowl* (1903), *Birds of New York* (1910).

**Fuess** (fēz), **Claude Moore.** 1885-1963. American educator; teacher of English (1908–33) and headmaster (1933–47), Phillips Acad., Andover, Mass.

**Füessli.** See FÜSSLI.

**Fu′e·ter** (fo͞o′ĕ·tẽr), **Eduard.** 1876–1928. Swiss historian.

**Fueter, Rudolf.** 1880–1950. Swiss mathematician.

**Fu′ga** (fo͞o′gä), **Ferdinando.** 1699–1780. Florentine architect.

**Fü′ger** (fü′gẽr), **Heinrich Friedrich.** 1751–1818. German painter. Works include historical paintings, miniature portraits of leading noblemen, artists, and scholars, illustrations to Klopstock's *Messiah*, and India-ink sketches in late baroque style.

**Fug′ger** (fo͝og′ẽr). Name of a family of financiers and merchants in Bavarian Swabia descended from the weaver **Johannes Fugger** (1348–1409) of Augsburg and including: His sons **Andreas** (d. 1457), founder of the **Fugger vom Reh** (fōm rā′) branch, and **Jakob I** (d. 1469), founder of the main branch of the family and of the Fugger firm. Jakob's sons (all ennobled) **Ulrich** (1441–1510), **Georg** (1453–1506), and **Jakob II** "the Rich" (1459–1525), who carried on and extended the business; Jakob II leased mines in Spain, Tirol, Carinthia, and Hungary, traded in spices over the new sea passage to India, acted as papal banker, made loans to Maximilian I (who mortgaged to him the county of Kirchberg and the lordship of Weissenhorn, ennobled him as count, 1514, and appointed him imperial adviser), financed election of Charles V (1519), and erected the Fuggerei, a settlement of low-rent dwellings near Augsburg for poor Catholics. His heirs, Georg's sons **Raymund** (1489–1535) and **Anton** (1493–1560), founders of two of the chief and still flourishing lines of the Fugger house, zealous Roman Catholic supporters of Eck against Luther, patrons of art and science, created counts by Charles V (1530), admitted to Swabian bench of counts, and given rights of princes, and later (1535) given right to coin gold and silver. Raymund's sons **Hans Jakob** (1516–1579), art patron and family chronicler, **Ulrich** (1526–1584), Protestant, publisher of classics and collector of valuable manuscripts bequeathed to U. of Heidelberg, and **Georg** (d. 1569), mathematician, founder of the branch of counts **Fugger von Kirch′berg** (kĭrk′-bĕrk) **und Weis′sen·horn** (vī′sĕn·hôrn).

**Füh′rich** (fü′rĭk), **Joseph von.** 1800–1876. Austrian religious and historical painter; his works include frescoes, designs for woodcuts and steel engravings including the series of illustrations to the Psalter, the Book of Ruth, and Thomas a Kempis, and original etchings, as the cycle *Triumph of Christ* (1839), etc.

**Fu Hsi** (fo͞o′ shē′). fl. c. 2800 B.C. A legendary emperor of China, reputed inventor of the Eight Diagrams (later the basis of the *I Ching*, one of the Five Classics); also reputed to have invented writing, devised a calendar, and formulated laws of marriage. Cf. WÊN WANG.

**Fu·ji·wa·ra** (fo͞o·jē·wä·rä). A Japanese noble family, or clan, dating from 7th century (**Ka·ma·ta·ri** [kä·mä·tä·rē], earliest prominent representative, d. 669 A.D.) and at first known by name **Na·ka·to·mi** [nä·kä·tō·mē]; grew in power until **Yo·shi·fu·sa** [yō·shē·fo͞o·sä] (804–872) achieved for it complete domination over imperial family (858); thereafter (to c. 1156) members of clan (most famous, Michinaga, *q.v.*) ruled as regents or dictators, while most of emperors were mere puppets; power of clan broken in civil wars (1156–60) by Minamoto and Taira leaders, esp. Taira Kiyomori.

**Fu·ku·shi·ma** (fo͞o·ko͞o·shē·mä), Baron **Yasumasa.** 1853–1919. Japanese general, b. Matsumoto. In command of Japanese force in Boxer rebellion (1900). On general staff (1904–05) in Russo-Japanese War.

**Fu·ku·za·wa** (fo͞o·ko͞o·zä·wä), **Yukichi.** 1834–1901. Japanese educator, journalist, and author, b. Nakatsu. Founded at Tokyo (1867) Keio Gijuku, which became one of Japan's great universities; established (1882) the influential daily paper *Jiji Shimpo.* Father of **Ichitaro Fukuzawa** (1863–1938), educ. at Keio and Yale, chancellor of Keio U., and **Sutejiro Fukuzawa** (1865–1926), educ. at Keio and in Boston, manager of *Jiji Shimpo* (1894 ff.) and of Osaka *Jiji* (founded 1909).

**Ful′bert′ de Char′tres** (fül′bâr′ dẽ shår′tr′). 960?–1028. French Roman Catholic priest; director of the school at Chartres; bishop of Chartres (1006); with aid of donations from friends began rebuilding Chartres Cathedral; his *Lettres* are a valuable source for the history of his times.

**Ful′bright** (fo͝ol′brīt), **James William.** 1905– . Amer. statesman, b. Sumner, Mo. Taught at George Washington U. (1935–36), U. of Arkansas (1936–39; president 1939–41). Member, U.S. Congress (1943–45); U.S. Senator from Arkansas (1945– ).

**Fulc** (fo͝olk). Variant of FULK (see ANJOU family).

**Fulc** (fo͝olk) *or* **Ful′co** (fŭl′kō) **of Neuilly.** = FOULQUES DE NEUILLY.

**Ful′cher of Char′tres** (fo͝ol′chẽr ŭv shår′tr′). = FOUCHER DE CHARTRES.

**Ful′da** (fo͝ol′dä), **Ludwig.** 1862–1939. German author, b. in Frankfurt. Received cross of French Legion of Honor for translations of French plays (1933); forced to retire during Hitler regime. His works include the comedies *Der Talisman* (1892), *Jugendfreunde* (1897), and *Die Zwillingsschwester* (1900); the symbolical drama *Der Sohn des Kalifen; Sinngedichte* (verse; 1888), etc.

**Ful′ford** (fo͝ol′fẽrd), **Francis.** 1803–1868. Anglican prelate; educ. Oxford. First bishop of Montreal, Canada (1850–60), and metropolitan of Canada (1860).

**Ful·gen′ti·us** (fŭl·jĕn′shĭ·ŭs), **Fabius Planciades.** Latin scholar of 5th and 6th centuries A.D.; a native of northern Africa, and perhaps a relative of Saint Fulgentius.

**Fulgentius of Rus′pe** (rŭs′pē), Saint. 468–533 A.D. Early Christian prelate, regarded as one of the "fathers of the church." Bishop of Ruspe, in northern Africa (508 A.D.); retired to a monastery (532). Author of works against Arianism and Pelagianism.

**Fulk.** See FOULQUES.

**Fulk.** *Fr.* **Foulques.** Name of five counts of Anjou. See ANJOU family.

**Ful′ler** (fo͝ol′ẽr), **Andrew.** 1754–1815. English Baptist clergyman.

**Fuller, Andrew S.** 1828–1896. American horticulturist, b. Utica, N.Y.

**Fuller, Buckminster** *in full* **Richard Buckminster.** 1895– . Builder and designer, b. Milton, Mass. Developed geodesic dome, constructed of adjoining tetrahedrons. Author of *Ideas and Integrities: A Spontaneous Autobiographical Disclosure* (1963); *I Seem to Be a Verb* (1970).

**Fuller, George.** 1822–1884. American painter, b. Deerfield, Mass.; studio in Boston. Examples of his work: *Winifred Dysart* (now in Worcester, Mass.), *She Was a Witch, Quadroon,* and *Nydia* (in Metropolitan Museum, New York), *Arethusa* (in Boston).

**Fuller, Henry Blake.** 1857–1929. American novelist, b. Chicago. Author of *The Chevalier of Pensieri-Vani* (under pseudonym **Stanton Page,** 1890), *The Chatelaine of La Trinité* (1892), *The Cliff Dwellers* (1893), *With the Procession* (1895), *Under the Skylights* (1901), *Waldo Trench, and Others* (1908), *Gardens of This World* (1929), *Not on the Screen* (1930).

**Fuller, John Frederick Charles.** 1878–1966. British soldier; served in Boer War (1899–1902) and World War I (1914–18); major general (1930). Author of *Tanks in the Great War, 1914–18* (1920), *War and Western Civilization, 1832–1932* (1932), *The Last of the Gentlemen's Wars* (1937), *Decisive Battles of the U.S.A.* (1942), etc.

**Fuller, Loie.** 1862–1928. American dancer, b. in Du Page County, Ill. Inventor of serpentine dance (about 1890); head of a school of dancing, in Paris (from about 1920); wrote *Fifteen Years of a Dancer's Life* (1913).

**Fuller, Margaret,** *in full* **Sarah Margaret.** Marchioness **Os′so·li** (ôs′sō·lē). 1810–1850. American critic and social reformer, b. Cambridgeport, Mass. Conducted "conversations" with a group of ladies in Boston as a means of general cultural education (1839–44); associated with, though not a part of, the Brook Farm experiment; with Ralph Waldo Emerson and George Ripley, an editor of the *Dial*, organ of the transcendentalists (1840–42). On staff, New York *Tribune*, as literary critic (1844–46); established reputation as one of ablest critics in America. Visited Europe (1846); m. Marquis Angelo Ossoli, in Rome (1847); took part with Ossoli in Revolution of 1848. Lost with husband and child in wreck off Fire Island, N.Y. (July 19, 1850). Author of *Summer on the Lakes, in 1843* (1844), *Woman in the Nineteenth Century* (1845), *Papers on Literature and Art* (1846). Said to have been in part the original of the character Zenobia in Hawthorne's *Blithedale Romance.*

**Fuller, Melville Weston.** 1833–1910. American jurist, b. Augusta, Me.; grad. Bowdoin (1853). Chief justice, U.S. Supreme Court (1888–1910); also, member, Permanent Court of Arbitration, The Hague (1900–10).

**Fuller, Richard.** 1804–1876. American Baptist clergyman, b. Beaufort, S.C. Defender of institution of slavery.

**Fuller, Thomas.** 1608–1661. English clergyman; educ. Cambridge. Curate of the Savoy, at London (1642), preached sermons advocating maintenance of peace between king and parliament; rector of Cranford (1658). After Restoration (1660), became "chaplain in extraordinary" to Charles II. Author of *History of the Holy Warre* (*i.e.* the Crusades; 1643), *The Holy State and the Profane State* (1642), *History of the Worthies of England* (publ. 1662), etc.

**Ful′ler–Mait′land** (-māt′lănd), **John Alexander.** 1856–1936. English writer on music; educ. Cambridge. Music critic of the London *Times* (1889–1911).

**Ful′ler·ton** (fo͝ol′ẽr·t'n; -tŭn), Lady **Georgiana Charlotte.** See LEVESON-GOWER family.

**Fü′löp–Mil′ler** (fü′lûp·mĭl′ẽr), **Re·né′** (rē·nā′). 1891–1963. Writer, translator, and journalist, b. in the Banat region, Austria-Hungary. Journalist in Berlin, Paris, Vienna, and elsewhere; resident in Vienna. Author of *Lenin and Gandhi* (1927), *Rasputin, the Holy Devil* (1927), *The Power and Secret of the Jesuit* (1929), and works on Bolshevism (1926) and the Russian and American theater.

**Ful′ton** (fo͝ol′t'n; -tŭn), **Robert.** 1765–1815. American engineer and inventor, b. in Lancaster County, Pa. Painted portraits in Philadelphia (1782–86). In England (1786–97); painting, student of Benjamin West, until about 1793; devoted himself thereafter to mechanics and engineering study and experiments. Patented: machine for sawing marble; machine for spinning flax; machine for twisting hemp into rope. Interested himself in canals; published *A Treatise on the Improvement of Canal Navigation* (1796). In Paris (1797–1806) invented submarine, but could not interest governments in it. Commissioned by Robert R. Livingston, U.S. minister to France, to build a steamboat (1802); after successful experiments on the Seine, returned to U.S. (1806); succeeded with the *Clermont*, which steamed up to Albany and back (Aug. 17–22, 1807). *Clermont* was not the first steamboat, but was the first one built and operated at a cost which promised fair profits to its owners; it was the first of a "line" of commercial steamboats. Designed thereafter seventeen steamboats, a torpedo boat, and a ferry; under authority of Congress, built steam frigate (launched 1815). Elected to Am. Hall of Fame (1900).

**Fultz** (fo͝olts), **Abraham.** American farmer who discovered (1862) on his Pennsylvania farm three spikes of awnless wheat growing in a field of awned wheat, and bred from these spikes a fine new variety of winter wheat, known as Fultz.

**Ful′vi·a** (fŭl′vĭ·ȧ). d. 40 B.C. Roman matron; wife successively of Clodius, Curio, and Mark Antony. Instigated a revolt (41 B.C.) against Octavius in the hope of drawing Antony away from Egypt and Cleopatra.

**Fulvius Flaccus.** See Quintus Fulvius FLACCUS.

**Funck′–Bren′ta′no′** (fûɴk′brăɴ′tá′nō′), **Théodore.** 1830–1906. French philosopher and sociologist, b. in Luxemburg; naturalized (after 1870) and settled in Paris. Author of *Les Sciences Humaines* (1868), *La Science Sociale* (1897), *Les Sophistes Français* (1905), etc. His son **Frantz** (1862–1947), historian, author of *Études sur la Société du XVII^e Siècle* (1900), *La Régence 1715–23* (1909), *L'Ancien Régime* (1926), etc.

**Fu′nes** (fo͞o′nās), **Gregorio.** 1749–1830. Argentine historian, b. Córdoba; ordained priest; rector, U. of

Córdoba; known as lecturer, preacher, and orator; dean, cathedral of Córdoba. Known esp. for his *Ensayo de la Historia Civil del Paraguay, Buenos Aires, y Tucumán* (3 vols., 1816).

**Funk** (fŏŏngk), **Cas'i·mir** (kăz'ĭ·mĭr). 1884–1967. Biochemist credited with discovery of vitamins, b. Warsaw, Poland. Ph.D., Bern (1904). Engaged in research at Pasteur Institute, Paris (1904–06); assistant to Abderhalden in Berlin (1906–10); engaged in research at Lister Institute of Preventive Medicine, London; head of biochemical department, Cancer Hospital Research Institute, London (1913–15); engaged in research at Cornell Medical College (1915–16); head of research department, H. A. Metz and Co., New York (1917–23); biochemist, Columbia (1921–23); head of the department of biochemistry, State School of Hygiene, Warsaw, Poland (1923–27); founded Casa Biochemica, Rueil-Malmaison, near Paris; research consultant, U.S. Vitamin Corp., New York City (from 1936).

**Funk, Franz Xaver von.** 1840–1907. German Roman Catholic theologian; professor, Tübingen (1870).

**Funk** (fŭngk), **Isaac Kauffman.** 1839–1912. American clergyman, editor, and publisher, b. Clifton, Ohio. In Lutheran ministry (1861–72). In book business (from 1876); with Wagnalls, formed I. K. Funk & Co. (1877), which became Funk & Wagnalls Co. (1891). Editor, *Literary Digest* (1890), *Standard Dictionary of the English Language* (1890–93); assisted in bringing out *The Jewish Encyclopedia* (12 vols., 1901–06). Interested in prohibition, psychical research, and simplified spelling.

**Funk** (fŏŏnk), **Walther.** 1890–1960. German journalist and economist; chief, Press Bureau (1933); minister of economics (1938); president, Reichsbank (1939–45); sentenced (1946) as war criminal to life imprisonment.

**Fun'ston** (fŭn'stŭn), **Frederick.** 1865–1917. American army officer, b. New Carlisle, Ohio. Served with Cuban insurrectionists in Cuba (1896–98). Appointed to command Kansas regiment in Spanish War; sent to Philippines (Nov., 1898); aided in suppressing rebellion under Aguinaldo; promoted brigadier general and awarded Medal of Honor. Brilliant exploit was capture of Aguinaldo (Mar. 14–25, 1901). Transferred to regular army with rank of brigadier general; in command at San Francisco at time of earthquake (1906); in command of force that seized Vera Cruz (1914); promoted major general (Nov. 17, 1914).

**Fu're·tière'** (fü'rĕ·tyâr'), **Antoine.** 1619–1688. French lexicographer; compiler of *Dictionnaire Universel*, on which he labored for some forty years only to have its publication prohibited by a royal edict (1674) forbidding printing of any dictionary until that of the French Academy appeared; the *Dictionnaire Universel* was published in Rotterdam (1690) after his death.

**Fu'ri·us** (fū'rĭ·ŭs). *In full* **Marcus Furius Bi·bac'u·lus** (bĭ·băk'ū·lŭs). Latin poet of 1st century B.C. Author of satires directed against Julius Caesar and Augustus.

**Fur'man** (fûr'măn), **Lucy.** 1869?–1958. Am. writer and settlement worker, b. Henderson, Ky. Author of *The Quare Women* (1923), *The Lonesome Road* (1927), etc.

**Furman, Richard.** 1755–1825. American Baptist clergyman, b. Esopus, N.Y. Pastor of Baptist church, Charleston, S.C. (1787–1822); became leading Baptist personality in the South. Furman U., Greenville, S.C., of which his son **James Clement** (1809–1891) was president (1852–79), was named in his honor.

**Fur'ness** (fûr'nĕs; -nĭs), **Christopher.** 1st Baron **Furness of Grant'ley** (grănt'lĭ). 1852–1912. English shipowner (from 1877); founder of Furness line of steamships; partner also in shipbuilding works, Furness, Withy & Co. (from 1891), and South Durham Steel and Iron Co. (from 1898). M.P. (1891–95; 1900–10); created baron (1910).

**Furness, William Henry.** 1802–1896. American Unitarian clergyman and abolitionist, b. Boston; pastor of Unitarian church in Philadelphia (1825–75). His son **Horace Howard** (1833–1912) was a Shakespearean scholar; b. Philadelphia; grad. Harvard (1854); adm. to bar (1859); from 1866, devoted himself to preparation and publication of the *Variorum Shakespeare*, the first volume, *Romeo and Juliet*, appearing 1871, and the work being carried to completion by his son **Horace Howard** (1865–1930). Another son of the elder H. H. Furness, **William Henry** (1866–1920), was a physician and ethnologist; b. Wallingford, Pa.; A.B., Harvard (1888); M.D., Pennsylvania (1891); curator, museum of science and arts at U. of Pennsylvania (1904–20); author of *Home Life of the Borneo Head Hunters*...(1902), *Uap, the Island of Stone Money* (1910).

**Fur'niss** (fûr'nĭs), **Harry.** 1854–1925. British illustrator and caricaturist; on staff of *Illustrated London News* (1876), *Punch* (1880–94). Also, illustrated *Sylvie and Bruno* by Lewis Carroll (C. L. Dodgson), and editions of Dickens (1910) and Thackeray (1911).

**Fur'ni·vall** (fûr'nĭ·văl), **Frederick James.** 1825–1910. English philologist, b. at Egham, Surrey. Educ. Cambridge. Studied law; called to bar (1849). Interested himself in Christian Socialist group and in social reform work; met Ruskin (1849) and aided in founding Working Men's College in London. Member of Philological Society (1847–1910), its secretary (1862–1910); undertook editorship of society's proposed English dictionary (1861), which developed into the *Oxford English Dictionary.* Founder of Early English Text Society (1864), Chaucer Society (1868), New Shakespeare Society (1873), Wycliffe Society (1881), Browning Society (1881), Shelley Society (1886). Editor of Chaucer's works and (with J. W. Hales) of *Percy Ballads*, and many early English texts. Enthusiastic oarsman all his life.

**Fur'rer** (fŏŏr'ĕr), **Jonas.** 1805–1861. Swiss statesman and lawyer. Member (1834–39, 1843) and president (1837, 1846) of grand council; member and president of diet council (1848) and first president of Swiss Federation.

**Furse** (fûrz), **Charles Wellington.** 1868–1904. English painter; studied under Alphonse Legros in London, and at Académie Julian in Paris; his paintings include *Return from the Ride* and *Diana of the Uplands* (both in Tate Gallery, London), and many portraits. His wife (m. 1900) Dame **Katharine,** *nee* **Symonds** (1875–1952), daughter of John Addington Symonds (*q.v.*), went to France with a staff of nurses (1914) who formed the nucleus of what became recognized as the Voluntary Aid Detachment (V.A.D.), a branch of the Red Cross; director, Women's Royal Naval Service (1917–19); created dame of the British Empire (1917) in recognition of her services.

**Fürst** (fürst), **Julius.** 1805–1873. German Orientalist, b. in Posen of Jewish parentage. Author of works on Hebrew and Aramaic linguistics, Jewish history and bibliography, and Biblical literature.

**Für'sten·au** (für'stĕn·ou). Name of a family of German musicians including: **Kaspar** (1772–1819), flutist and composer for the flute; court musician in Oldenburg. His son **Anton Bernard** (1792–1852), flutist, member of royal chapel in Dresden (from 1820). **Moritz** (1824–1889), son of Anton and his successor as flutist of royal chapel at Dresden (1842); custodian of royal music collection (1852) and teacher at Dresden Conservatory (1858).

**Für'sten·berg** (für'stĕn·bĕrK). Name of two German families of the nobility:

(1) *Swabian line:* ruled in a principality of the Black

Forest region, with parts of its domain in Baden, Württemberg, and Sigmaringen; named from the ancestral castle (built 1218) in south Baden; originated probably in time of Charlemagne but traceable definitely to 12th century only; its territories changed many times in extent; its princes have been strong supporters of the Hapsburgs. Has existed in two branches since middle of 19th century. Notable members of the family are: **Franz Egon** (1625–1682), began (after 1650) ecclesiastical career at Cologne; bishop of Strasbourg (1663–74); deprived of office and fled to France. His brother **Wilhelm Egon** (1629–1704), soldier in French service; seized and imprisoned at Vienna (1672–79); appointed bishop of Strasbourg (1682) by Louis XIV; cardinal (1686); deprived of office and retired to France. **Karl Egon** (1796–1854), inherited Swabian principality (1804); lost much of his estate to Baden (1806); his palace a center of culture. Succeeded by his son **Karl Egon II** (1820–1892) and grandson **Karl Egon III** (1852–1896).

(2) *Westphalian line:* ruled in Westphalia and the Rhineland; named from the ancestral castle of Fürstenberg on the Ruhr; originated in the 13th century.

**Furt′wäng′ler** (fo͝ort′vĕng′lẽr), **Adolf.** 1853–1907. German classical archaeologist and art critic. Took part in archaeological excavations at Olympia (1878–79); professor, Munich (1894) and director of collection of antiques; accompanied expeditions to Aegina, Amyclae, and Orchomenus (1901–07). His works are chiefly on art history of early Greece and on ancient vases and gems. His son **Wilhelm** (1886–1954) was opera conductor in Lübeck (1911–15), Mannheim (1915–19), and Vienna (1919); succeeded Nikisch as conductor of Leipzig Gewandhaus concerts (1922–28) and of Berlin Philharmonic (1922 ff.); director of Philharmonic concerts in New York (1925–27) and of Berlin Philharmonic in Paris (1928); opera conductor in Vienna, Berlin, and Mannheim (from 1928); municipal music director (1929–34) and first director of State opera (1933–34) in Berlin.

**Fu′ru·seth** (fū′ro͝o·sĕth), **Andrew.** 1854–1938. Labor leader, b. in Norway; to U.S. (1880). President of International Seamen's Union of America (1908–38); authority on American merchant marine; instrumental in raising standards of employment and working conditions for American sailors.

**Fu·shi·mi** (fo͝o·shē·mē), Prince **Sadanaru.** 1858–1923. Japanese soldier and diplomat; uncle of Emperor Yoshihito. Served in war with China (1894–95) and in Russo-Japanese War (1904–05); rose to rank of general; the emperor's personal representative in U.S. (1904); lord keeper of privy seal at time of death.

**Füss′li** *or* **Füess′li** (füs′lē). Family of artists, orig. from Zurich, Switzerland, including: **Matthias** (1598–1665), battle painter; **Johann Kaspar** (1707–1782), portrait painter; his son **Hans Rudolf** (1737–1806), painter, illustrator, and engraver; **Johann Rudolf** (1709–1793), miniaturist, and his son **Johann Heinrich** (1742–1825), illustrator and engraver as well as painter, settled in London and illustrated Shakespeare's plays and Milton's *Paradise Lost;* **Wilhelm** (1830–?), portrait painter.

**Fust** (fo͞ost) *or* **Faust** (foust), **Johann.** 1400?–?1466. German printer, bookdealer, and moneylender, said also to have been a goldsmith. Partner (1450?–55) of Gutenberg, whom he financed in completing invention of printing and in printing the Gutenberg Bible; obtained possession of Gutenberg's apparatus on dissolution of partnership (1455), established a new printing business with his future son-in-law Peter Schöffer as assistant, and published a Psalter (first printed book with a complete date, 1457). Sometimes erroneously identified with the magician Doctor Johann Faust (*q.v.*).

**Fus′tel′ de Cou′langes′** (füs′tĕl′ dē ko͞o′läNzh′), **Numa Denis.** 1830–1889. French historian; made special study of ancient and medieval history.

**Fux** (fo͝oks), **Johann Joseph.** 1660–1741. Austrian composer and music theorist. Author of theoretical work on counterpoint *Gradus ad Parnassum* (in Latin, 1725); composer of operas, Masses, requiems, psalms and vespers, oratorios, suites, sonata trios, etc.

**Fu·zu·li′** (fo͝o·zo͝o·lĭ′). *Real name* **Mehmet Suleiman O·glou′** (ō·glo͞o′). d. about 1572. Turkish poet, b. in Azerbaijan. Wrote in Turkish, Arabic, and Persian; author of love lyrics, gazels, and a poem which provided theme for first Mohammedan opera, *Leili-ve-Medjnon,* presented at Baku (1908).

**Fyfe** (fīf), **Henry Hamilton.** 1869–1951. British journalist and writer; educ. Edinburgh U. Editor, London *Daily Herald* (1922–26). Author of *A Player's Tragedy* (1894), *A Modern Aspasia* (play; 1909), *The Borstal Boy* (play; 1913), *The Widow's Cruse* (1920), *The Religion of an Optimist* (1927), *What Communism Means To-day* (1937), *The Illusion of National Character* (1940), etc. His brother Sir **William Hamilton** (1878–1965), educator; educ. Oxford. On teaching staff at Oxford (1904–19); headmaster of Christ's Hospital (1919–30); principal and vice-chancellor of Queen's University, Kingston, Ontario (1930–36); principal and vice-chancellor, Aberdeen U. (1936–48).

**Fyffe** (fĭf), **Charles Alan.** 1845–1892. English historian; educ. Oxford. Author of *History of Modern Europe* (3 vols., 1880–90).

**Fyle′man** (fīl′măn), **Rose.** 1877–1957. English writer; best known as author of children's books.

**Fyt** (fīt), **Jan.** 1611–1661. Flemish animal and still-life painter and etcher, b. in Antwerp.

# G

**Gabb** (găb), **William More.** 1839–1878. American paleontologist, b. Philadelphia. Student of American Cretaceous and Tertiary paleontology.

**Gab·bia′ni** (gäb·byä′nē), **Antonio Domenico.** 1652–1726. Florentine painter; founded academy at Florence.

**Ga′be·lentz** (gä′bĕ·lĕnts), **Hans Co′non** (kō′nôn) **von der.** 1807–1874. German philologist; made special study of little-known languages, including those of Asiatic, African, and Pacific Island peoples. His son **Hans Georg** (1840–1893) specialized in East Asian philology. Hans Georg's son **Georg** (1868–1940) was a writer of psychological novels.

**Ga′bels·ber′ger** (gä′bĕls·bĕr′gẽr), **Franz Xaver.** 1789–1849. German stenographer; founded system of German shorthand.

**Ga·bin′i·us** (gȧ·bĭn′ĭ·ŭs), **Aulus.** d. 48 (or 47) B.C. Roman statesman and general; partisan of Pompey. Tribune of the people (67 B.C.); sponsored law giving Pompey command against pirates together with control over Mediterranean Sea and its coasts. Consul (58); proconsul in Syria (57–54). Entered Caesar's service (49).

**Ga'blenz** (gä'blĕnts), Baron **Ludwig von.** 1814–1874. Austrian soldier; commanded Austrian forces in joint Austro-Prussian attack upon Denmark (1864); commanded army corps at battle of Königgrätz (1866).

**Ga'bler** (gä'blẽr), **Georg Andreas.** 1786–1853. German philosopher; disciple of Hegel.

**Ga'bo** (gȧ'bŏŏ), **Na·um** (nȧ'ŏŏm). *Orig.* **Naum Pevsner.** 1890–1977. Am. (Russ.-born) sculptor; to U.S. (1946), naturalized (1952); leader of Constructivist school.

**Ga'bor** (gäb'ôr), **Dennis** 1900–1979. British (Hungarian-born) physicist. Inventor of the holograph. Awarded Nobel prize in physics (1971) for work in three dimensional photography (holography).

**Ga'bo'riau'** (gȧ'bô'ryō'), **Émile.** 1835–1873. French writer of detective fiction; creator of fictional detectives "Monsieur Lecoq" and "Père Tabaret." Author of *L'Affaire Lerouge* (1866), *Monsieur Lecoq* (1869), etc.

**Ga'bri'el'** (gȧ'brē'ĕl'). Family of French architects, including: **Jacques** (1630–1686), architect of the king and builder of the Pont Royal and, with Mansart, the Château de Choisy-le-Roi; his son and successor as royal architect **Jacques** (1667–1742), designer of hôtels de ville at Rennes and Dijon; and the latter's son **Jacques Ange** (1698–1782), who designed restoration of the Louvre (from 1755), and built the École Militaire, Hôtel Crillon, and Château du Petit Trianon.

**Ga'bri·el** (gā'brĭ·ĕl), **Gilbert Wolf.** 1890–1952. American music and dramatic critic.

**Ga'bri·e'li** (gä'brē·ā'lē) *or* **Ga'bri·el'li** (-ĕl'lē), **Andrea.** 1510?–1586. Italian organist and composer; organist at Saint Mark's, Venice. His nephew and pupil **Giovanni Gabrieli** (1557–1612) was also organist at Saint Mark's.

**Ga'bri·el'li** (gä'brē·ĕl'lē), **Catarina.** 1730–1796. Italian singer, in Vienna, Paris, Russia, Venice, and Milan.

**Ga'bri·ló'witsch** (*Angl.* gä'brĭ·lŭ'vĭch; *Russ.* gŭ·vryĭ-lô'vyĭch), **Ossip.** 1878–1936. Russian pianist and conductor; m. Clara Clemens (1909), dau. of S. L. Clemens (*q.v.*). Director, Detroit Symphony Orchestra (1918–36).

**Ga'chard'** (gȧ'shȧr'), **Louis Prosper.** 1800–1885. Belgian historian, b. Paris; to Belgium (1826) and became naturalized. Keeper of royal archives, at Brussels.

**Ga'con'** (gȧ'kôɴ'), **François.** 1667–1725. French satirical poet; author of attacks upon Boileau-Despréaux, J. B. Rousseau, Fontenelle, and others in his *Poète sans Fard* (1697) and later works.

**Gad** (găd). In Bible, Jacob's seventh son (*Gen.* xxx. 9–11), ancestor of one of the twelve tribes of Israel.

**Gad'di** (gäd'dē). Family of Florentine artists, including: **Gaddo** (1260–1332); his son **Taddeo** (1300?–1366), architect, student of Giotto, continued the work of Giotto on the campanile at Florence; Taddeo's son **Agnolo** (1333?–1396), painter of frescoes in the style of Giotto.

**Gaddi, Dario.** See Domenico GNOLI.

**Ga'de** (gȧ'thĕ), **Niels Wilhelm.** 1817–1890. Danish composer and conductor; successor to Mendelssohn as conductor of concerts of the Gewandhaus. Returned to Copenhagen (1848) and became court Kapellmeister. Composer of eight symphonies, a number of overtures, cantatas, choral works, chamber music, and songs.

**Ga'dow** (gä'dō), **Hans Friedrich.** 1855–1928. Zoologist, b. in Pomerania; curator and lecturer on morphology of vertebrates, Cambridge U., England (from 1884). Author of *A Classification of Vertebrata* (1898), *The Wanderings of Animals*, etc.

**Gads'den** (gădz'dĕn), **Christopher.** 1724–1805. American Revolutionary leader, b. Charleston, S.C.; leader of South Carolina radicals. Delegate to Continental Congress (1774–76). Colonel of South Carolina troops (1776); brigadier general, Continental army (Sept., 1776); resigned (1778). In convention of 1788, voted for ratification of United States Constitution. See James GADSDEN.

**Gadsden, James.** 1788–1858. Grandson of Christopher Gadsden. American army officer and diplomat, b. Charleston, S.C. In U.S. army (to 1821); in Florida (1821–39); U.S. commissioner to move Seminoles to reservations (1823). Projected southern transcontinental railroad; believed purchase of land from Mexico necessary; appointed U.S. minister to Mexico (1853–54); negotiated treaty for purchase of strip (Gadsden Purchase) in what is now New Mexico and Arizona, total of 45,535 square miles.

**Gad'ski** (gät'skē), **Johanna.** 1872–1932. German concert and operatic soprano; m. Hans Tauscher (1892), Austrian army officer. Member of Metropolitan Opera Co. (1898), alternating appearances in New York and in London; interpreter of Wagnerian roles.

**Gaeta,** Duca **di.** See Enrico CIALDINI.

**Gaetani.** Variant of CAETANI.

**Gaetano.** See CAJETAN.

**Gaff'ky** (gäf'kē), **Georg Theodor August.** 1850–1918. German bacteriologist. Credited with obtaining first pure culture of typhoid bacillus (1884).

**Ga·fo'ri** (gä·fô'rē) *or* **Ga·fo'rio** (gä·fô'ryō), **Franchino.** 1451–1522. Italian priest, musician, and writer on music.

**Gág** (gäg), **Wanda.** 1893–1946. American painter, author, and illustrator; widely known as author and illustrator of children's books, as *Millions of Cats* (1928).

**Ga·ga'rin** (gŭ·gȧ'ryĭn). Name of Russian princely family, including: **Matvei Petrovich** (d. 1721), governor of Siberia (1711–21); accused by Peter the Great of attempting to make Siberia an independent state. **Aleksandr Ivanovich** (d. 1857), soldier; distinguished service in the Caucasus and Crimean War; governor of Kutais. **Pavel Pavlovich** (d. 1872), member of ministry at time of emancipation of serfs (1864–65). **Ivan Sergeevich** (1814–1882), diplomat and Jesuit writer; in diplomatic service in Vienna and Paris (1837–43); converted to Roman Catholicism and joined Jesuit order (1843).

**Gagarin, Yuri Alekseyevich.** 1934–1968. Soviet cosmonaut; first man to travel in space (1961).

**Gage** (gāj), **Lyman Judson.** 1836–1927. American banker and political leader. President, First National Bank of Chicago (1891). President, board of directors, World's Columbian Exposition, Chicago (1893); largely responsible for its success. U.S. secretary of the treasury (1897–1902). President, United States Trust Co., New York City (1902–06).

**Gage, Simon Henry.** 1851–1944. American biologist.

**Gage, Thomas.** 1721–1787. British general and colonial governor in America, b. Firle, Sussex, England. To America under Gen. Braddock (1754); served under Abercrombie in Ticonderoga expedition (1758). Brigadier general under Amherst in conquest of Canada (1760); major general (1761). Commander in chief in North America, headquarters at New York (1763–73). Appointed governor of Massachusetts (1774); used troops to seize military stores; precipitated battle of Lexington (Apr. 19, 1775) and battle of Bunker Hill (June 17, 1775); resigned and sailed from Boston (Oct. 10, 1775), the last royal governor of Massachusetts. In England, commissioned general (1782).

**Ga'ger** (gā'jẽr), **Charles Stuart.** 1872–1943. American botanist, b. Norwich, N.Y. Director, Brooklyn Botanic Garden (from 1910).

**Ga'gern, von** (fôn gä'gẽrn). German noble family, including: Baron **Hans Christoph Ernst von Gagern** (1766–1852), prime minister of the Netherlands (1814–

15), Luxemburg envoy at German Diet (1816–18). His three sons: Baron **Friedrich Balduin** (1794–1848); served in Austrian army at Dresden, Kulm (Chełmno), and Leipzig, and in Dutch army during 1815 campaign; governor at The Hague (1847). Baron **Heinrich** (1799–1880); fought at Waterloo in Nassau army; studied law; took part in liberal movements in Germany and became first president of German national parliament (1848) and head of imperial ministry (1848–49) after Austrian representatives withdrew from that parliament. Baron **Maximilian** (1810–1889); member of German national parliament (1848); in service of duchy of Nassau (after 1848) and of Austria (from 1855); became life member of Austrian Herrenhaus (1881). Baron **Friedrich** (1882–1947); grandson of Hans Christoph Ernst; novelist.

**Ga·glia'no** (gä·lyä'nō). Family of Italian violinmakers, in Naples, including: **Alessandro** (1660?–1725); his two sons, **Nicola** (1695?–1780) and **Gennaro** (1700?–1770); Nicola's four sons, **Fernando** (1724–1781), **Giuseppe** (1725–1793), **Antonio** (1728?–1795), and **Giovanni** (1740?–1806).

**Gagliano, Marco da.** 1575?–1642. Italian priest and composer, esp. of church music and madrigals; known also for his opera *La Dafne* (1607).

**Ga·gliar'di** (gä·lyär'dē), **Ernst.** 1882–1940. Swiss historian; professor, Zurich (1919–40).

**Ga'gneur'** (gȧ'nyûr'), **Louise,** *nee* **Mi'gne·rot'** (mēn'-y'·rō'). 1832–1902. French novelist.

**Ga'guin'** (gȧ'găN'), **Robert.** 1433?–1501. French priest and scholar; best known for his chronicle *Compendium de Origine et Gestis Francorum* (1495).

**Gahn** (gän), **Johan Gottlieb.** 1745–1818. Swedish mineralogist and chemist; first to isolate manganese. The mineral gahnite is named after him.

**Gai** (gī), **Ljudevit.** = Ljudevit GAJ.

**Gai'doz'** (gā'dō'), **Henri.** 1842–1932. French archaeologist and Celtic scholar.

**Gail** (gȧ'y'), **Jean Baptiste.** 1755–1829. French Hellenic scholar. His wife, **Edmée Sophie,** *nee* **Garre** [gȧr] (1775–1819), was a musician and composer of comic operas. Their son **Jean François** (1795–1845) was also a Hellenist.

**Gail'lard'** (gȧ'yȧr'), **Claude Ferdinand.** 1834–1887. French painter and engraver.

**Gail·lard'** (gĭl·yärd'), **David Du Bose.** 1859–1913. American army officer and engineer; selected by Gen. Goethals as head of department of dredging and excavating, Panama Canal (1907); later (1908) in charge of excavation at Culebra Cut (renamed Gaillard Cut).

**Gai'nas** (gī'năs). d. 400. Visigoth general in Roman army; caused murder of Rufinus in Constantinople (395); turned traitor and headed revolt (399); his Gothic army defeated; killed by the Huns.

**Gaines** (gānz), **Edmund Pendleton.** 1777–1849. American army officer. In War of 1812, commanded defense of Fort Erie; served in Seminole War, Black Hawk War, Florida War, Mexican War.

**Gains'bor'ough** (gānz'bûr'ō; *esp. Brit.*, -bŭ·rŭ, -brŭ), **Thomas.** 1727–1788. English painter. Studied under Gravelot in London; one of original 36 members of Royal Acad. (1768). Excelled in portraits and landscapes. Among notable canvases are *The Blue Boy, Duchess of Devonshire, Mrs. Siddons, George III* (several portraits), *The Shepherd's Boy, Garrick, Quin, Lord Camden, Richardson, Sterne, Chatterton, The Harvest Waggon, Colonel St. Leger,* and *Girl with Pigs.*

**Gaird'ner** (gȧrd'nẽr; gärd'-), **James.** 1828–1912. British historian. Edited *Paston Letters* and collaborated in editing *Calendar of Letters and Papers of the Reign of Henry VIII.* Author of *Houses of Lancaster and York* (1874), *Life and Reign of Richard III* (1878), etc.

**Gaiseric.** See GENSERIC.

**Gais'ford** (gāz'fẽrd; gās'-), **Thomas.** 1779–1855. English classical scholar. Regius professor of Greek, Oxford (1812); dean of Christ Church, Oxford (1831–55).

**Gait'skell** (gāt'skĕl), **Hugh Todd Naylor.** 1906–1963. British statesman. Chancellor of the Exchequer (1950–51); Labor party leader (1955–63).

**Ga'ius** (gā'yŭs; gī'ŭs) *or* **Ca'ius** (kā'yŭs; kī'ŭs). Roman jurist of 2d century A.D.; chief work, the Institutes of Gaius, an exposition of the elements of Roman law, later used as a basis for the famous Institutes of Justinian.

**Gaius** *or* **Caius,** Saint. Pope (bishop of Rome; 283–296).

**Gaius Caesar.** See CALIGULA.

**Gaj** (gī), **Ljudevit,** *Eng.* **Louis.** 1809–1872. Croatian writer; exerted influence in uniting Croats and Serbs in opposition to Magyars in Hungary.

**Gaj'du·sek'** (gī'dŭ·shĕk'), **D. Carleton,** *in full* **Daniel Carleton.** 1923– . American virologist. With National Institutes of Health (1958– ); awarded (with Baruch S. Blumberg) Nobel prize for physiology or medicine (1976).

**Gal** *or* **Gall** (gȧl), Saint. 487–551. French ecclesiastic; bishop of Clermont (from 527).

**Gál** (gäl), **Hans.** 1890– . Austrian composer of operas, choral works, chamber music, piano pieces, etc.

**Gal'ba** (găl'bȧ; gôl'bȧ), **Servius Sulpicius.** 5 B.C.?–69 A.D. Roman emperor (68–69). Of a patrician family; praetor (20 A.D.); consul (33); served as governor under several emperors in Aquitania, Germany, Africa, and Spain (39–68). Joined insurrection of Julius Vindex (68) against Nero; on Nero's death made emperor by praetorians; adopted Piso Licinianus as Caesar.

**Gal'braith** (găl'brāth), **John Kenneth.** 1908– . Amer. economist, b. Ontario, Canada. Editor of *Fortune* magazine (1943–48); ambassador to India (1961–63); author of *American Capitalism* (1952), *The Great Crash: 1929* (1955), *The Affluent Society* (1958), *The New Industrial State* (1967), etc.

**Galdós, Benito Pérez.** See PÉREZ GALDÓS.

**Gale, Norman.** 1862–1942. English poet; author of *A Country Muse* (2 vols., 1892), *Orchard Songs* (1893), *Cricket Songs* (1894), *A Book of Quatrains* (1909), *Verse in Bloom* (1925), *Love-in-a-Mist* (1939), etc.

**Gale, Zona.** 1874–1938. American writer, b. Portage, Wis.; m. William Llywelyn Breese (1928). Author of *Romance Island* (1906), *The Loves of Pelleas and Etarre* (1907), *Friendship Village* (1908), *Mothers to Men* (1911), *Birth* (1918), *Miss Lulu Bett* (1920), *Papa La Fleur* (1933), *Light Woman* (1937).

**Galecki, Tadeusz.** See Andrzej STRUG.

**Ga'len** (gā'lĕn). fl. 2d century A.D. Greek physician, b. in Pergamum, Asia Minor; settled in Rome (164 A.D.). Of his many treatises, about 100 are extant. His works were accepted for many centuries as authoritative in Greek, Roman, and Arabic medical practice.

**Ga'len** (gä'lĕn), Baron **Christoph Bernhard von.** 1606–1678. German Roman Catholic prelate and soldier; prince-bishop of Münster (1650).

**Galen, Philipp.** Pseudonym of Ernst Philipp Karl LANGE.

**Ga·le'ri·us** (gȧ·lēr'ĭ·ŭs). *Full name* **Gaius Galerius Va·le'ri·us Max·im'i·a'nus** (vȧ·lēr'ĭ·ŭs măk·sĭm'ĭ-ā'nŭs). d. 311. Roman emperor (305–311), b. in Dacia. Made Caesar by Diocletian (292; see DIOCLETIAN); was defeated by Persians (296) but later severely defeated them (297); on abdication of Diocletian (305) became emperor (Augustus) in the East; made Licinius his successor (308). Hostile to the Christians; probably persuaded Diocletian to issue his edict of persecution.

**Gales** (gālz), **Joseph.** 1761–1841. Printer and journalist,

b. Eckington, England. Founded Sheffield (Eng.) *Register* (1787), a weekly journal; champion of liberal reforms; forced to flee to Continent (1794) and to America (1795). Founded and edited Raleigh (N.C.) *Register* (1799), a Jeffersonian weekly paper. His son **Joseph** (1786–1860) was also a journalist; newspaper reporter of U.S. Senate proceedings (1807–20) for the *National Intelligencer;* his reports are source material for congressional debates of the period. See William W. SEATON.

**Gal'e·swin'tha** (găl'ē·swĭn'thȧ). See BRUNHILDE.

**Gal'ga·cus** (găl'gȧ·kŭs) *or* **Cal'ga·cus** (kăl'-). fl. 84 A.D. Caledonian chieftain; commanded tribes defeated at Mt. Graupius by Agricola.

**Galgario,** Fra. See Fra Vittore GHISLANDI.

**Ga'li** (gä'lē), **Francisco.** 1539–1591. Spanish navigator; discovered coast of California; entered San Francisco Bay (1584).

**Ga·lia'ni** (gä·lyä'nē), **Fernando.** 1728–1787. Italian political economist and student of philosophy, history, archaeology.

**Ga'li·gna'ni** (gä'lē·nyä'nē). Name of family of publishers in Paris: **Giovanni Antonio** (1752–1821), b. Brescia, Italy, settled in England, where his sons **John Anthony** (1796–1873) and **William** (1798–1882) were born; to Paris (c. 1799), where he established publishing business and founded (1814) *Galignani's Messenger.* His sons carried on the business, publishing many reprints of English books. John Anthony remained British subject; William became French citizen (1832).

**Ga'li·le'i** (gä'lē·lâ'ē), **Ga'li·le'o** (gä'lē·lâ'ō; *Angl.* găl'ĭ·lē'ō). *Commonly known as* **Galileo.** 1564–1642. Italian astronomer and physicist, b. Pisa. Discovered isochronism of the pendulum; invented the hydrostatic balance; demonstrated from leaning tower of Pisa that bodies of different weights fall with same velocity; conceived the three laws of motion later formulated by Sir Isaac Newton; demonstrated that the path of a projectile is a parabola. Professor of mathematics at Padua (1592–1610); devised a simple open-air thermometer (c. 1593); constructed (1609) and improved refracting telescope for astronomical use, later making many because of demand for them; discovered that the moon shines with reflected light and that its surface is mountainous, that the Milky Way is made up of countless stars, and that Jupiter has four large satellites; observed phases of Venus; discovered sunspots and noticed that they move across surface of sun; discovered moon's libration (1637). As result of astronomical work, appointed professor for life at U. of Florence; also appointed philosopher and mathematician extraordinary to grand duke of Tuscany. Denounced for propounding heretical views in his *Letters on the Solar Spots* (pub. 1613), in which he advocated the Copernican system; attempted to show that there was scriptural confirmation for Copernican system, but the system was condemned and he was admonished by the pope not to defend it (1616); published *Dialogo dei due Massimi Sistemi del Mondo* (1632), for which he was again summoned to Rome, tried by the Inquisition, and forced to abjure belief that the sun is the central body around which earth and planets revolve; allowed to retire for rest of life to villa at Arcetri, near Florence; blind after 1637.

**Ga'li'mard'** (gȧ'lē'mȧr'), **Nicolas Auguste.** 1813–1880. French painter, esp. of religious canvases.

**Ga'lim·ber'ti** (gä'lēm·bĕr'tē), **Luigi.** 1836–1896. Roman Catholic prelate and diplomat; canon of St. Peter's; archbishop of Nicaea. Effected papal arbitration in Spanish-German controversy over sovereignty of Caroline Islands; effected final abrogation (1887) of German May laws (passed May, 1873), ending Bismarck's Kulturkampf (1872–87). Cardinal, prefect of papal archives (1893).

**Ga·li'tzin** (gŭ·lyē'tsĭn). Variant of GOLITSYN.

**Gall** (gȧl). See GAL.

**Gall** (gôl), Saint. *Orig. name* **Cellach** *or* **Caillech.** 550?–?645. Irish missionary, disciple of Saint Columbanus. Known as apostle to the Suevi and Alamanni. Built (c. 613) cell on Steinach River, Switzerland, around which was later developed monastery of Saint Gall.

**Gall** (gôl). 1840?–1894. American Sioux Indian chieftain, b. in South Dakota; a leader in battle of Little Big Horn (June 25, 1876) where Custer and his command were slain; friendly to the whites (from 1881); a judge at the Indian Agency's Court of Indian Offenses (from 1889).

**Gall** (gäl), **Franz Joseph.** 1758–1828. German physician and founder of phrenology. Studied brains and skulls of men and animals and sought to establish relationship between mental faculties and shape of brain and skull; took up residence in Paris (1807); his hypothesis developed by Spurzheim and George Combe (*qq.v.*). Chief publication, *Anatomie et Physiologie du Système Nerveux en Général* (1810–19).

**Gal'la·gher** (găl'ȧ·gẽr; găl'ĭ-), **Ed.** See under Al SHEAN.

**Gallagher, Michael James.** 1866–1937. American Roman Catholic clergyman; bishop of Detroit (1918–37).

**Gal'lait'** (gȧ'lĕ'), **Louis.** 1810–1887. Belgian painter; best known for historical paintings.

**Gal'land'** (gȧ'läɴ'), **Antoine.** 1646–1715. French Oriental scholar; best known for his translation of the *Arabian Nights,* its first translation into a European language (12 vols., 1704–17).

**Galland, Pierre Victor.** 1822–1892. French muralist and designer of some Gobelin tapestries.

**Gal'la Pla·cid'i·a** (găl'ȧ plȧ·sĭd'ĭ·ȧ). 388–450 A.D. Roman empress of the West. Daughter of Theodosius the Great by his second wife, Galla, and half sister of Honorius. Taken prisoner by Alaric (410); held as hostage (410–414); m. Ataulphus (414), successor of Alaric; upon Ataulphus's death (415), restored to Honorius; m. (417) Constantius (III); mother of Valentinian III and regent for him during his minority (425–c. 440).

**Gal'las** (gäl'äs), **Matthias.** Count of **Cam'po** (käm'pō) *and* Duke of **Lu·ce'ra** (lōō·châ'rä). 1584–1647. Austrian soldier; joined army of Catholic League and distinguished himself at Stadtlohn (1623). Served in Italy (1628–31). Fought against Gustavus Adolphus of Sweden; lieutenant general. Conspired against Wallenstein and succeeded him in command of Imperial army (1634); defeated Swedes at Nördlingen (Aug. 23, 1634).

**Gal'la·tin** (găl'ȧ·tĭn), **Albert,** *in full* **Abraham Alfonse Albert.** 1761–1849. Financier and statesman, b. Geneva, Switzerland; to America (1780). Elected U.S. senator (1793) but unseated on ground that he had not been citizen for required nine years (1794). Member, U.S. House of Representatives (1795–1801); leader of Republican minority (from 1797); revealed himself as having genius for finance. U.S. secretary of the treasury (1801–14). A negotiator of peace (Dec. 24, 1814) with Great Britain after War of 1812; U.S. minister to France (1816–23), to Great Britain (1826–27). President National (later Gallatin) Bank, New York (1831–39). His great grandson **Albert Eugene** (1881–1952), painter, art collector, writer on art, esp. modern painters and painting.

**Gal'lau·det'** (găl'ŏ·dĕt'), **Thomas Hopkins.** 1787–1851. American teacher of the deaf and dumb, b. Philadelphia. Studied in France (1815–16); brought back to U.S. Laurent Clerc, teacher of the deaf in a Paris school (1816); established first free American school for the deaf (known as Connecticut Asylum, and later as American

Asylum), Hartford, Conn. (1817); principal of this school (1817–30). Gallaudet College, Washington, D.C., is named in his honor. His son **Thomas** (1822–1902) was a Protestant Episcopal clergyman; established church in New York for deaf-mutes (1859); founded Gallaudet Home, near Poughkeepsie, N.Y. for aged and infirm deaf-mutes (1885). Another son, **Edward Miner** (1837–1917), was a teacher of the deaf and dumb in the American Asylum at Hartford; then became head (1857) of Columbia Institution for the Deaf and Dumb, Washington, D.C., the senior department of which became Gallaudet College.

**Gal'le** (gäl'ĕ). Family of Dutch engravers; best known is **Cornelis** (1576–1656), who engraved *Charles I* and *Henrietta Maria* (of England), after Van Dyck, and *The Virgin Crowned with Flowers*, after Rubens.

**Gal'lé'** (gȧ'lā'), **Émile.** 1846–1904. French artist in glass manufacturing and furniture designing.

**Gal'le** (gäl'ĕ), **Johann Gottfried.** 1812–1910. German astronomer; first to observe planet Neptune (Sept. 23, 1846), whose existence had been proved by Leverrier's calculations.

**Gal·le'go** (gä·lyā'gō), **Juan Nicasio.** 1777–1853. Spanish poet; known esp. for his patriotic ode *El Dos de Mayo*, inspired by the uprising of 1808.

**Gal·len'ga** (gäl·lĕng'gä), **Antonio Carlo Napoleone.** 1810–1895. Italian educator, journalist, and politician; involved in political agitation and exiled from Italy (1830); adopted name **Luigi Ma'ri·ot'ti** (mä'rē·ôt'tē). Became naturalized British subject (1846); professor of Italian, University Coll., London (1848–59). Returned to Italy and sat in Chamber of Deputies (1859–64).

**Gal·lén'–Kal'le·la** (gȧl·lān'kȧl'lĕ·lȧ), **Aksel.** 1865–1931. Finnish painter; to Paris (1889), and made success with fantastic symbolic paintings interpreting Finnish folk epic *Kalevala;* also portrait and landscape painter.

**Gal·let'ti** (gä·lĕt'ē), **Johann Georg.** 1750–1828. German historian.

**Gal'li·co** (găl'ĭ·kō), **Paul.** 1897– . American journalist and short-story writer; exposed professionalism in supposedly amateur sports in his book *Farewell to Sport* (1938).

**Gal'li–Cur'ci** (gäl'lē·kōōr'chē), **Amelita,** *nee* **Galli.** 1889–1963. Operatic soprano, b. Milan, Italy; m., 1st, Marquis Luigi Curci (1910; divorced 1920), 2d, Homer Samuels (1921). Joined Metropolitan Opera Co., New York (1920). Roles include Lakmé in *Lakmé*, Violetta in *La Traviata*, Gilda in *Rigoletto*, Juliette in *Roméo et Juliette*, Lucia in *Lucia di Lammermoor*, Mimi in *La Bohème*, and Elvira in *I Puritani.*

**Galli da Bibiena** *or* **Bibbiena.** See BIBIENA.

**Gal'lie'ni'** (gȧ'lyā'nē'), **Joseph Simon.** 1849–1916. French soldier; governor general of Madagascar (1896–1905). Military governor of Paris (1914); rushed 80,000 reserves in automobiles to strengthen General Maunoury's army, thus enabling Maunoury to repulse von Kluck; called "the Savior of Paris."

**Gal'li·e'nus** (găl'ĭ·ē'nŭs), **Publius Licinius Valerianus Egnatius.** d. 268. Roman emperor (253–268). Son of the emperor Valerian; made emperor and colleague to his father (253–260); on capture of Valerian by Persians, became sole emperor (260–268).

**Gal'lif'fet'** (gȧ'lē'fĕ'), Marquis **Gaston Alexandre Auguste de.** 1830–1909. French army commander; led cavalry charge at Sedan; general of division (1875). As president of the cavalry board, reformed cavalry regulations and tactics.

**Gal'li·o** (găl'ĭ·ō). *In full* **Junius Annaeus Gallio.** *Orig. name* **Marcus An·nae'us No·va'tus** (ă·nē'ŭs nō·vā'tŭs). Roman proconsul of Achaia; brother of Seneca; refused (according to *Acts* xviii. 12–17) to try cases arising out of religious disputes and dismissed the Jews' accusation against Paul.

**Gal·li'tzin** (*Russ.* gŭ·lyē'tsĭn). Variant of GOLITSYN.

**Gal·li'tzin** (gă·lĭt'sĭn), **De·me'tri·us** (dē·mē'trĭ·ŭs) **Au·gus'tine** (ô·gŭs'tĭn). 1770–1840. Roman Catholic priest and missionary in America, b. The Hague, where his father, Prince Dmitri Alekseevich Golitsyn (*q.v.*) was Russian ambassador to the Netherlands. Entered Roman Catholic Church (1787); under name of **Augustine Smith** (or **Schmet**), came to U.S. (1792); studied for priesthood in Baltimore. Established Roman Catholic settlement on Pennsylvania frontier; founded town of Loretto (1799). Became naturalized citizen (1802); after his father's death (1803), resumed his family name. Gallitzin, Pa., is named in his honor.

**Gal'lo·way** (găl'ō·wā), **Fair Maid of.** See *8th earl of Douglas*, under DOUGLAS family.

**Galloway, Joseph.** 1729?–1803. American lawyer and loyalist; practiced in Philadelphia; member, Pennsylvania colonial legislature (1756–64; 1765–75), Continental Congress (1774–75); opposed independence of colonies.

**Gal'lup** (găl'ŭp), **George Horace.** 1901– . American statistician; founder (1935) of American Inst. of Public Opinion to conduct polls (Gallup polls) to measure public interest in news or advertising features, or to determine public opinion on issues.

**Gal·lup'pi** (gäl·lōōp'pē), **Pasquale.** 1770–1846. Italian philosopher; professor, Naples.

**Gal'lus** (găl'ŭs), **Gaius Cornelius.** d. 26 B.C. Roman soldier and politician; supported Octavius and fought at Actium (31 B.C.). First prefect of Egypt (30); incurred hostility of Octavius; removed from prefecture and exiled by Roman senate.

**Gallus, Gaius Sulpicius.** Roman general, statesman, and scholar; commanded legion at battle of Pydna (168 B.C.); ambassador in Greece and Asia (164), where, at Sardis, he investigated charges brought by cities of Asia Minor against Eumenes of Pergamum.

**Gallus, Gaius Vibius Trebonianus.** 205?–?253. Roman emperor (251–253). Served under Decius in campaign against Goths (251); elected emperor after defeat and death of Decius; killed by his own soldiers.

**Gallus, Jacobus.** See Jakob HANDL.

**Gallus, Udalricus.** See Ulrich HAN.

**Gall'witz** (gäl'vĭts), **Max von.** 1852–1937. German soldier; in World War, commanding general of armies in Poland, Serbia, and on the Somme River in France; commanded 5th army on the Meuse; driven back by American armies (1918).

**Ga'lois'** (gȧ'lwȧ'), **Évariste.** 1811–1832. French mathematician; considered founder of theory of groups and a founder of modern theory of functions.

**Gals'wor'thy** (gôlz'wûr'thĭ), **John.** *Pseudonym in early works* **John Sin'john** (sĭn'jŭn). 1867–1933. English novelist and playwright, b. Coombe, Surrey. Educ. Oxford. Called to bar (1890), but did not practice. Fiction includes *Jocelyn* (1898), *A Man of Devon* (1901), *The Patrician* (1911), *The Dark Flower* (1913), *The Forsyte Saga* (1922; trilogy: *The Man of Property*, 1906; *In Chancery*, 1920; *To Let*, 1921), *A Modern Comedy* (1929; trilogy: *The White Monkey*, 1924; *The Silver Spoon*, 1926; *Swan Song*, 1928), and *Caravan* (1927; collected short stories). Plays include *Joy* (1907), *Strife* (1909), *Justice* (1910), *The Pigeon* (1912), *The Eldest Son* (1912), *The Fugitive* (1913), *The Mob* (1914), *The Skin Game* (1920), *A Family Man* (1921), *Loyalties* (1922), *Old English* (1924), *Escape* (1926), *Exiled* (1929), and *The Roof* (1929). Member of Order of Merit (1929). Awarded Nobel prize for literature (1932).

**Galt** (gôlt), **John.** 1779–1839. Scottish writer of novels depicting Scottish life and character. His son Sir **Alexander Tilloch** (1817–1893) emigrated to Canada (1835); first minister of finance of Dominion of Canada (1867–72) and Canadian high commissioner in England (1880–83).

**Gal'ton** (gôl't'n; -tŭn), Sir **Francis.** 1822–1911. English scientist, b. near Birmingham; grad. Cambridge (1844). Entered British civil service; made study of meteorology; published *Meteorographica* (1863), basis of modern weather maps. Best known for his work in anthropology and the study of heredity; founder of the science of eugenics; devised system of fingerprint identification. Among his works are *Hereditary Genius* (1869), *Inquiries into Human Faculty...* (1883), *Record of Family Faculties ...* (1883), *Natural Inheritance* (1889), *Finger Prints, Essays on Eugenics.* See Erasmus DARWIN.

**Ga·lup'pi** (gä·lōōp'pē), **Baldassare.** *Called* **Il Bu'ra·nel'lo** (ēl bōō'rä·nĕl'lō). 1706–1785. Italian composer of many comic operas.

**Gal·va'ni** (gäl·vä'nē), **Luigi** *or* **Aloisio.** 1737–1798. Italian physician and physicist. Known as founder of galvanism because of researches on twitchings of muscles in frogs' legs caused by current of electricity; he attributed the movements to animal electricity (1791), but Volta later gave correct explanation.

**Gál'vez** (gäl'vāth; -vās), **Bernardo de.** 1746?–1786. Spanish administrator in America; governor of Louisiana (1777). In war against Great Britain (declared 1779), captured Baton Rouge and Natchez (1779), Mobile (1780), and Pensacola (1781); made possible Spanish acquisition of Florida in peace settlement (1783). Captain general of Cuba (1784); viceroy of New Spain (1785).

**Gál'vez** (gäl'vās), **Delfina Bunge de.** See under Agusto BUNGE.

**Gál'vez** (gäl'vāth; -vās), **José.** Marqués **de la So·no'ra** (thā lä sō·nō'rä). 1729–1787. Spanish jurist and statesman. To Mexico (1761) as visitador general; introduced beneficial reforms; to Sonora (1767) in same capacity; fitted out expeditions (1769) which made first settlements in Upper California. To Spain (1774); president, Council of the Indies; minister of the Indies (1776); effected administrative reforms and expanded commerce. Considered Spain's greatest colonial administrator.

**Gál'vez** (gäl'vās), **Manuel.** 1882– . Argentine author of novels and stories of life in Brazil and Argentina.

**Gál'vez de Mon·tal'vo** (gäl'vāth thā môn·täl'vō), **Luis.** 1549?–?1591. Spanish poet; author of the pastoral romance *El Pastor de Filida.*

**Gal'way** (gôl'wā), Earl of. English title (cr. 1697) of Henri de MASSUE (1648–1720).

**Galway,** 8th Viscount. **George Vere Arundell Monck'-ton–Ar'un·dell** (mŭngk'tŭn·ăr'ŭn·dĕl). 1882–1943. British soldier and colonial governor; served in World War (1914–18); quartermaster general (1917–19); governor general of New Zealand (1935–41).

**Ga'ma** (gä'mä), **Antonio de Le·ón' y** (thā lā·ōn' ē). 1735–1802. Mexican scholar; known esp. for studies relating to Aztec calendar stone.

**Ga'ma** (gă'mȧ), **José Basílio da.** 1740–1795. Brazilian poet; settled at Lisbon as protégé of Pombal; known esp. for his epic *O Uruguay*, an anti-Jesuit account of Portuguese-Spanish campaign against Guarani Indians (1769).

**Ga'ma** (gă'mȧ), **Vasco da.** 1469?–1524. Portuguese navigator; commissioned by King Emanuel I to make journey by sea to India; sailed from Lisbon (July 8, 1497) with four vessels; rounded Cape of Good Hope, reached Malindi on east coast of Africa, thence sailed directly across Indian Ocean, arriving at Calicut (May 19, 1498)—the first voyage from western Europe around Africa to the East. On second journey (1502–03), planted Portuguese colonies at Mozambique and Sofala. Forced raja of Calicut to make peace. Viceroy of Portuguese Asia (1524). His first voyage the subject of Camoëns's *Lusiad.*

**Gam'age** (găm'ĭj), **Albert Walter.** 1855–1930. English merchant; founded A. W. Gamage, Ltd. (1878), which under his management developed into one of largest department stores in London.

**Ga·ma'li·el** (gȧ·mā'lĭ·ĕl; gȧ·māl'yĕl). Name of several Jewish rabbis, especially: (1) **Gamaliel** the elder (d. about 50 A.D.); teacher of St. Paul (*Acts* xxii. 3); as member of Sanhedrin, advised against persecuting the apostles (*Acts* v. 34 ff.); according to the Talmud, a grandson of Hillel (*q.v.*); first to be given title of "rabban." (2) **Gamaliel** of Jabneh, or the younger (d. 115?); grandson of Gamaliel the elder; leader of Jewish people in difficult period after destruction of Jerusalem (70); a noted scholar, of liberal views; made innovations in Jewish ritual.

**Ga·mar'ra** (gä·mär'rä), **Agustín.** 1785–1841. Peruvian general and political leader; native Inca. President of Peru (1829–33). Led insurrection against his successor Luis José Orbegoso. In war between Chile and Peru-Bolivian Confederation (1839), commanded Chilean reserve division; after Chilean victory at Yungay, became president of Peru for second time (1839–41); killed in battle of Ingaví (Yngaví) in war against Bolivia (1841).

**Gam'ba** (gäm'bä), **Bartolommeo.** 1776–1841. Italian bibliographer; on library staff, St. Mark's, Venice; known esp. for his *Serie dell'Edizioni dei Testi di Lingua Italiana* (1812–28).

**Gambarelli.** See ROSSELLINO.

**Gam·bet'ta** (găm·bĕt'ȧ; *Fr.* gäN'bĕ'tȧ'), **Léon.** 1838–1882. French lawyer and statesman. Leader of opposition to government of Napoleon III. Member of the Government of National Defense (1870). Made spectacular escape from Prussian-besieged Paris by balloon (Oct. 8, 1870), and attempted to organize France for defense. Resigned as minister; member of the National Assembly and (1876) of the Chamber of Deputies; president of the Chamber of Deputies (1879–81); premier of France (1881–82).

**Gam'bier** (găm'bēr), **James.** 1st Baron **Gambier.** 1756–1833. British naval commander, b. Nassau, Bahamas; vice-admiral (1799); admiral (1805). Led British fleet in bombardment of Copenhagen and capture of Danish fleet (1807); commander of Channel fleet (1808–11); blockaded and partly fired French fleet in Basque roads. Admiral of the fleet (1830). Commissioner to negotiate peace with U.S. (1814).

**Gam·bo'a** (gäm·bō'ä), **Federico.** 1864–1939. Mexican diplomat, novelist, and playwright. Minister of foreign affairs (1908–09) and during the Huerta regime (1913–14). Among his notable works are *Del Natural* (1888), *La Última Campaña* (a play, 1894), *Metamorfosis* (1899), *Santa* (1900) and *La Llaga* (both dramatized for motion-picture presentation).

**Ga'me·lin'** (gȧm'lăN'), **Maurice Gustave.** 1872–1958. French soldier; promoted general of brigade during World War (1914–18). Assistant to General Sarrail in Syria (1925) and promoted general of division. Chief of the French general staff (1931); succeeded Weygand as inspector general of the French army and vice-president of the Higher Council of War (1935); on defeat of French armies by Germans (1940), imprisoned; liberated (1945).

**Ga'mill·scheg'** (gä'mĭl·shĕK'), **Ernst.** 1887–1971. German Romance language scholar.

**Ga'mow** (gā'mou), **George.** 1904–1968. Physicist, b. Odessa, Russia; professor, George Washington U.

(1934 ff.); known for researches in nuclear physics and its applications to stellar evolution.

**Gán'da·ra y Na·var'ro** (gän'dä·rä ē nä·vär'rō), **José de la.** 1820–1885. Spanish general; governor general of Philippines (1865).

**Gandhi, Indira Nehru.** See NEHRU.

**Gan'dhi** (gän'dē; *Angl.* -dĭ), **Mohandas Karamchand.** *Called* **Ma·hat'ma** (mȧ·hät'mȧ; *Angl.* mȧ·hăt'mȧ) [*i.e.* "great-souled"] **Gandhi.** 1869–1948. Hindu nationalist and spiritual leader, b. Porbandar, India. To London to study law (1888); practiced in India (1893). To South Africa (1893); because of his mistreatment there by whites for his defense of Asiatic immigrants, instituted a campaign of "passive resistance"; organized ambulance corps in Boer War (1899–1902). Returned to India (1914); active in recruiting campaign during World War. After passage of Rowlatt Acts (1919), organized Satyagraha, a politico-religious movement of non-co-operation with the British government in India; advocated revival of home industries and political independence (swaraj); given title of *Mahatma* by common people (c. 1920); his policies went beyond his control and resulted in general boycott of British goods (1920), the Mopla rebellion (1921–22) and other riots and disturbances; sentenced to prison for six years (1922) but released (1924) because of serious illness; resumed control of Swaraj party; president of Indian National Congress (1925). Renewed campaign of civil disobedience (1929–30) which resulted in rioting and a second imprisonment; made truce (1931) and attended Round Table Conference in London. Again urged boycott (1932) and advocated social reforms; began "fast unto death" (1932) in protest against government's treatment of "untouchables"; after six days' fast won pact in their favor; again arrested and again released (1933). Resigned presidency of Indian National Congress (1934); from 1937 less active against government, though still recognized as a leader in India's struggle for independence; again arrested (1942) for activities against Great Britain. Author of *Indian Home Rule, Universal Dawn, Young India,* etc.

**Ga·ne'sha Dat'ta Shas'tri** (gȧ·nā'shȧ dŭt'ȧ shäs'trē), Shri **Jagadguru.** 1861–1940. East Indian philosopher and Sanskrit scholar.

**Ganga Singhji** (*or* **Singh**) **Bahadur.** See Maharaja of BIKANER.

**Gang'ho'fer** (gäng'hō'fẽr), **Ludwig.** 1855–1920. German playwright and novelist.

**Ga'ni·vet'** (gä'nē·vĕt'), **Ángel.** 1865–1898. Spanish writer; known esp. for his *Idearium Español,* a study of Spanish genius and character (1897).

**Gann** (găn), **Thomas William Francis.** 1868–1938. English archaeologist; discovered ancient Maya city of Cobā, northern Yucatán, also cities of Tzibanchē and Ichpaatum; named and first described Maya city of Xumuchȧ (1928). In charge of British Museum expedition to British Honduras (1928) and Minanhȧ (1929). Author of works on Mexico and Central America.

**Gan·nett'** (gă·nĕt'; gȧ-), **Frank Ernest.** 1876–1957. American editor and publisher of a chain of newspapers.

**Gan'nett** (găn'ĕt; -ĭt), **Henry.** 1846–1914. American cartographer. Topographer, Hayden Survey (1872–79), mapping in Colorado and Wyoming. Chief geographer, U.S. Geological Survey (from 1882). A founder and a president, National Geographic Society. Known as "father of American map making."

**Gans** (gäns), **Eduard.** 1798–1839. German jurist and legal philosopher.

**Gäns'ba'cher** (gĕns'bä'kẽr), **Johann Baptist.** 1778–1844. Austrian composer, chiefly of church music; associated with Weber and Meyerbeer.

**Ganse'voort** (gănz'vōrt; -vôrt), **Peter.** 1749–1812. American Revolutionary officer, b. Albany, N.Y. In command of Fort George (1776) and Fort Schuyler (1777), which he defended through a siege by St. Leger at head of British and Indians. In command at Saratoga (1780); brigadier general, U.S. army (1809).

**Gansfort, Wessel.** See WESSEL.

**Gantt** (gănt), **Henry Laurence.** 1861–1919. American industrial engineer. Associated with Frederick Winslow Taylor in industrial management (1887–90; 1897–1902); consulting engineer (from 1902).

**Ganz** (gänts), **Rudolph.** 1877–1972. Swiss-born composer and conductor in America; head of piano department in Chicago Musical Coll. (1901–05); on tour (1905 ff.). Conductor, St. Louis Symphony Orchestra (1921–27); president, Chicago Musical Coll. (1933–1954).

**Ga·pon'** (gŭ·pôn'), **Georgi Apollonovich.** *Called* Father **Gapon.** 1870?–1906. Russian revolutionist, b. in Poltava government. Educ. for priesthood; began mission work among factory population of St. Petersburg; allowed by secret police to organize labor unions (1903–04); inaugurated labor strike (1905); led striking employees to palace to petition czar, the crowd being fired upon by troops (Bloody Sunday, Jan. 22, 1905); escaped to London.

**Gar'a·mond** (găr'ȧ·mŏnd; *Fr.* gȧ'rȧ'môɴ') *or* **Gar'a·mont** (găr'ȧ·mŏnt; *Fr.* gȧ'rȧ'môɴ'), **Claude.** d. 1561. French type designer and founder, b. Paris; introduced roman type to replace the Gothic then commonly used; by order of King Francis I, designed and cut the three fonts of characters used by Robert Estienne (*q.v.*) in his editions of Greek classics. The name *Garamond* is applied to several styles of type in modern use.

**Gar'and** (găr'ănd), **John Can'tius** (käɴ'tsyŭs). 1888–1974. American inventor, b. St. Remi, near Montreal, Canada. To U.S.; worked, esp. as toolmaker, chiefly in Providence, R.I. (1907–16), and New York City; naturalized (1920). Designed light machine gun and called to Washington, D.C., to work at U.S. Bureau of Standards. Ordnance engineer, U.S. Armory, Springfield, Mass. (from 1919); invented semiautomatic rifle (Garand rifle) adopted (1936) by U.S. army as standard shoulder weapon.

**Ga'rat'** (gȧ'rȧ'), Comte **Dominique Joseph.** 1749–1833. French lawyer, politician, and historian; member of States-General (1789); minister of justice (1792) and of the interior (1793). Member of the Council of Five Hundred and the Council of Ancients. Created comte by Napoleon (1808). Author of *Considérations sur la Révolution Française* (1792), etc. His nephew **Dominique Pierre Jean** (1764–1823) was a singer; known esp. for unusual range of his voice, including tenor and baritone registers.

**Garat,** Baron **Martin.** 1748–1830. French financier; one of the founders of the Bank of France (1800) and its first director-general.

**Ga'ray** (gŏ'roi), **János.** 1812–1853. Hungarian poet and playwright.

**Ga·ray'** (gä·rä'ē), **Juan de.** 1527?–?1583. Spanish soldier; to Paraguay (c. 1565); founded city of Santa Fe de la Vera Cruz (1573); governor of Paraguay (1576); captain general of La Plata territory, founded Buenos Aires (June 11, 1580) on site of abandoned (1541) settlement of Mendoza; massacred by Indians.

**Gar'be** (gär'bĕ), **Richard von.** 1857–1927. German Sanskrit scholar.

**Gar'ber** (gär'bẽr), **Daniel.** 1880–1958. American landscape painter.

**Gar'bett** (gär'bĕt; -bĭt), **Cyril Forster.** 1875–1955. English clergyman; bishop of Winchester (1932–42); archbishop of York (enthroned June, 1942).

**Gar′bo** (gär′bō), **Greta.** *Real surname* **Gus′taff·son** (gŭs′täf·sôn). 1905– . Motion-picture actress, b. Stockholm, Sweden; after success in Swedish film *Gösta Berling*, came to U.S. and starred in *Anna Christie*, *Mata Hari*, *Camille*, *Ninotchka*, etc.

**Garbo, Raffaelino del.** See RAFFAELINO DEL GARBO.

**Gar′borg** (gär′bŏrg), **Arne.** 1851–1924. Norwegian poet, novelist, and speech reformer; wrote cycle of lyric poems; in fiction, wrote novels of a religious nature. Author also of dramas, literary criticism, etc. As speech reformer, associated himself with movement for establishing Norwegian literary language based on peasant spoken dialect known as Landsmaal.

**Garção, Correa.** See CORREA GARÇÃO.

**Garcia.** *Span.* **Gar·cí′a** (gär·thē′ä). d. 914. King of León (910–914).

**García, Calixto.** See GARCÍA ÍÑIGUEZ.

**Gar·cí′a** (*Span.* gär·sē′ä, -thē′ä), **Diego.** *Port.* **Diogo Gar·ci′a** (gẽr·sē′ȧ). 1471–1529. Portuguese navigator in Spanish service, b. Lisbon. Commanded expedition to South America (1526); explored Uruguay and Paraná rivers; aided Sebastian Cabot expedition besieged by Indians on lower Paraná.

**Gar·cí′a** (gär·thē′ä), **Manuel del Pópolo Vicente.** 1775–1832. Spanish tenor, singing master, and composer, b. Seville. Created roles in several Rossini operas, Naples; sang in Paris (1819–23). Famous as singing teacher in London and Paris, introducing methods of instruction recognized as basis of modern teaching. Composer of many operas. Author of *Metodo di Canto*, book expounding his method of teaching singing. See MALIBRAN and VIARDOT. His son **Manuel** (1805–1906) was also a singing teacher; professor, Paris Conservatory of Music (1830–48), and Royal Acad. of Music, at London (1848–95); inventor of laryngoscope.

**Gar·cí′a Cal′de·rón′** (gär·sē′ä käl′dā·rôn′), **Francisco.** 1883– . Peruvian diplomat and writer. Son of President Francisco García Calderón (see CALDERÓN). Delegate to Peace Conference at Paris (1919); minister to Belgium (1918–21); ambassador to France (from 1930). His brother **Ventura** (1886–1959) is author of fiction and literary criticism.

**Gar·cí′a de la Huer′ta y Mu·ñoz′** (gär·thē′ä thā lä wĕr′tä ē mōō·nyôth′), **Vicente Antonio.** 1734–1787. Spanish dramatist. Neoclassicist in style; avowed advocate of national tradition in drama; known esp. for drama *La Raquel* (1788), imitated in Grillparzer's *Die Jüdin von Toledo*.

**Gar·ci′a de Mas′ca·re′nhas** (gẽr·sē′ȧ thĕ măsh′kȧ·rā′nyȧsh), **Braz.** 1596–1656. Portuguese poet. After Camoëns, considered by many leading poet of Portugal; known esp. for *Viriato Trágico* (epic in twenty cantos, pub. 1699).

**Gar·cí′a de Pa·re′des** (gär·thē′ä thā pä·rā′thās), **Diego.** 1466–1534. Spanish soldier; comrade-in-arms of Gonzalo de Córdoba; distinguished himself in Sicily at Cephalonia (1500), Seminara and Cerignola (1503), Pavia (1525). A leading chivalric hero of Spain, popular in Spanish legend.

**Gar·cí′a de Que·ve′do** (gär·sē′ä thā kā·vā′thō), **José Heriberto.** 1819–1871. Venezuelan poet, playwright, and novelist.

**Gar·cí′a Gu·tiér′rez** (gär·thē′ä gōō·tyĕr′rāth), **Antonio.** 1813–1884. Spanish dramatist, b. Chiclana de la Frontera; educ. Cádiz; to Madrid (1833); lived in Cuba and Mérida, Yucatán (1844–50), England (1854–57), and France; director of Archaeological Museum, Madrid (1872 ff.). A foremost representative of romantic drama in Spain; known esp. for his play *El Travador* (1836), later (1852) adapted by Verdi as opera *Il Trovatore*.

**Gar·cí′a Í′ñi·guez** (gär·sē′ä ē′nyē·gās; *Angl.* gär′shȧ, -shĭ·ȧ, -sĭ·ȧ), **Calixto.** 1836?–1898. Cuban lawyer, soldier, and revolutionist, b. Holguín, Santiago. A leader in Ten Years' War (1868–78) against Spain; led Cuban force at El Caney (1898) in Spanish-American War; appointed to represent Cuba in negotiations with U.S. for Cuban independence (1898). Known widely in U.S. through Elbert Hubbard's inspirational essay *A Message to Garcia*.

**Gar·cí′a Mo·re′no** (gär·sē′ä mô·rā′nō), **Gabriel.** 1821–1875. Ecuadorian journalist and political leader, b. Guayaquil. Son-in-law of J. J. Flores. President of Ecuador (1861–65, 1869–75); established Roman Catholic Church as state church; signed concordat with pope (1862) and promulgated two conservative constitutions (1861, 1869); assassinated (Aug. 5, 1875).

**Gar′ci·la′so de la Ve′ga** (gär′thē·lä′sō thā lä vā′gä). 1503–1536. Spanish poet and soldier; to Vienna (1531) with duke of Alva; to Naples (1532) with Don Pedro de Toledo, viceroy of Naples; killed in battle. His poems include pastorals, sonnets, canciones, elegies, and a blank verse epistle. Often called "the Spanish Petrarch."

**Gar′ci·la′so de la Ve′ga** (gär′sē·lä′sō thā lä vā′gä). *Called* **el In′ca** (ĕl ēng′kä). 1539?–1616. Peruvian historian, b. Cuzco; to Spain (1560); served as captain in Spanish army against Moors; settled at Córdoba. Works include *La Florida del Inca: Historia del Adelantado Hernando De Soto* (1605) and *Comentarios Reales Que Tratan del Origen de los Incas*, history of Incas in Peru (Part I, 1609) and of conquest of Peru (Part II, pub. 1617; Eng. trans., 2 vols., 1869–71). His father, **Sebastián Garcilaso de la Vega y Var′gas** [ē vär′gäs] (c. 1500–1559), served under Cortes in Mexico; to Peru (1534) with Alvarado, joining Pizarro's forces; governor of Cuzco.

**Gar′cin′ de Tas′sy′** (gȧr′săN′ dẽ tȧ′sē′), **Joseph Héliodore Sagesse Vertu.** 1794–1878. French Oriental scholar; student of Hindustani language and literature.

**Gard, Roger Martin Du.** See Roger Martin DU GARD.

**Gar′den** (gär′d'n), **Alexander.** 1730?–1791. Naturalist and physician, b. in Aberdeenshire, Scotland; resident in South Carolina (from c. 1754). Collected botanical, mineralogical, and zoological specimens; friend of Linnaeus. In American Revolution, remained loyal to British. The gardenia is named after him. His son **Alexander** (1757–1829) returned to America in 1780 and served in Continental army (1780–82).

**Garden, Mary.** 1874–1967. Operatic soprano, b. Aberdeen, Scotland; to U.S. as a child (1883). Debut at Opéra Comique, Paris (1900) in title role of Charpentier's *Louise;* American debut in *Thaïs* in New York (1907). With Chicago Civic Opera Company (from 1910). Chief roles Marguerite, Mélisande, Salome, Sappho, Thaïs, Louise.

**Gar′den·er** (gär′d'n·ẽr; gärd′nẽr), **Helen Hamilton.** *Nee* **Alice Chen′o·weth** (chĕn′ō·wĕth). 1853–1925. American woman suffragist and reformer, b. Winchester, Va.; m. Charles Selden Smart (1875, d. 1898), Selden Allen Day (1901). Associated with Susan B. Anthony and Elizabeth Cady Stanton in woman-suffrage movement. Member, U.S. Civil Service Commission (1920), first woman appointed to that office.

**Gar′die** (gȧr′dē), Count **Jacob de la** (dē lȧ). 1583–1652. Swedish field marshal. His son Count **Magnus Gabriel** (1622–1686), statesman, favorite of Queen Christina, ambassador to France (1646); lord chancellor and member of council of regency during minority of Charles XI; retired (1682) after unfavorable report by commission investigating regency.

**Gar′di·ner** (gärd′nẽr), **Alfred G.** 1865–1946. English

journalist; editor of the London *Daily News* (1902–19); wrote *Pillars of Society, Certain People of Importance.*

**Gardiner, John Sylvester John.** 1765–1830. Welsh-born Episcopalian clergyman in U.S.; rector of Trinity Church, Boston (from 1805). A founder of Boston Athenaeum.

**Gardiner, Lion.** 1599–1663. English colonist in America; arrived at Boston 1635. Built fort (1636) at mouth of Connecticut River (Saybrook); bought island (Gardiner's Island) from Indians (1640); bought land on Long Island (Easthampton) and moved there (1653).

**Gardiner, Samuel Rawson.** 1829–1902. English historian; B.A., Oxon. (1851). Among his chief works are *History of England...1603–1642* (10 vols., 1863–82), *History of the Great Civil War, 1642–1649* (3 vols., 1886–91), and *History of the Commonwealth and Protectorate, 1649–1660* (3 vols., 1895–1901).

**Gardiner, Stephen.** 1483?–1555. English prelate and statesman. Educ. Cambridge; master of Trinity Hall, Cambridge (1525 ff.); chancellor of Cambridge (1540–47, 1553 ff.). Employed by Henry VIII in negotiations to obtain divorce from Catherine of Aragon; after fall of Cardinal Wolsey, acted as secretary to Henry (to 1534). Bishop of Winchester (1531); member of court which invalidated marriage of Henry and Catherine (1533); signer of renunciation of obedience to Roman jurisdiction. After fall of Cromwell, wielded great influence; inspired the Six Articles (1539). Imprisoned in Tower of London during reign of Edward VI, and deprived of his see (1551); reinstated and appointed lord chancellor at accession of Mary (1553); supported persecution of Protestants during Mary's regime, but tried to save Cranmer and Northumberland; supported Mary's severe policy toward Elizabeth and procured parliamentary declaration that Elizabeth was illegitimate.

**Gard'ner** (gärd'nẽr), **Erle Stanley.** 1889–1970. American lawyer and writer of detective fiction.

**Gardner, Ernest Arthur.** 1862–1939. English archaeologist.

**Gardner, John William.** 1912– . American leader, b. Los Angeles, Calif. President, Carnegie Corp. of N.Y. (1955–65); U.S. secy. of health, education, and welfare (1965–68); chairman, Urban Coalition (1968– ).

**Gardner, Percy.** 1846–1937. English archaeologist, b. at Hackney. Professor at Cambridge (1880–87) and Oxford (1887–1925). Among his works are *Types of Greek Coins* (1883), *A Grammar of Greek Art* (1905), *History of Ancient Coinage* (1918), *New Chapters in Greek Art* (1926).

**Gardt'hau'sen** (gärt'hou'zĕn), **Viktor.** 1843–1925. German historian.

**Gar'ey** (gâr'ĭ), **Thomas Andrew.** 1830–1909. American fruitgrower, b. Cincinnati, Ohio. One of earliest growers of citrus fruit in California; town of Garey, Calif., is named in his honor.

**Gar'field** (gär'fēld), **Harry Augustus.** 1863–1942. Son of James Abram Garfield. American lawyer and educator; president, Williams Coll. (1908–34). U.S. fuel administrator during World War I (1917–19).

**Garfield, James Abram.** 1831–1881. Twentieth president of the United States, b. in Cuyahoga County, Ohio. Grad. Williams (1856). Teacher and head, Hiram College, Hiram, Ohio (1857–61). Colonel, Ohio volunteer infantry regiment (1861). Member, U.S. House of Representatives (1863–80); Republican leader (from 1876). Elected (1880), and inaugurated as president (Mar. 4, 1881). Shot by Charles J. Guiteau in Washington railroad station July 2, 1881; died Sept. 19, 1881.

**Garfield, James Rudolph.** 1865–1950. Son of James Abram Garfield. American lawyer and public official. U.S. secretary of the interior (1907–09).

**Gar'i·bal'di** (găr'ĭ·bôl'dĭ; -băl'dĭ; *Ital.* gä'rē·bäl'dē), **Giuseppe.** 1807–1882. Italian patriot, b. Nice. Associated with Mazzini in agitation for Italian freedom; forced to flee from Italy (1834); lived in Uruguay (1836–48). Returned to Italy and served in army of the Roman Republic; when that army was defeated (1849), he fled to U.S., became naturalized, and lived for a few years as a candlemaker on Staten Island. Returned to Italy (1854); commanded corps known as *Cacciatori delle Alpi* in Sardinian army (1859). Organized expedition of 1000 men (the famous Redshirts) and attacked Sicily (May, 1860), crossed to mainland of Italy and expelled Francis II from Naples, thus defeating the so-called Kingdom of the Two Sicilies. Retired peaceably to his farm on island of Caprera after union of Kingdom of the Two Sicilies with Sardinia and the proclamation (Mar. 17, 1861) of Victor Emmanuel of Sardinia as king of Italy. Organized another expedition and marched against Rome (1862) but was defeated; again attacked Rome (1867) but was again defeated. Held a command in the French army during the Franco-Prussian War (1870–71). Elected deputy for Rome in Italian parliament (1874). See also Menotti GARIBALDI, Ricciotti GARIBALDI, Giuseppe GARIBALDI (1879–1950).

**Garibaldi, Menotti.** 1840–1903. Son of Giuseppe Garibaldi (*q.v.*). Italian soldier, b. in Brazil; fought beside his father (1859–67), and in French army in Franco-Prussian War (1870–71); entered Italian parliament and joined party of the extreme left. His brother **Ricciotti** (1847–1924), b. in Montevideo, distinguished himself in French army in Franco-Prussian War (1870–71), and in Greek army fighting the Turks (1897); organized Garibaldi Legion to fight for France in World War (1914–18); after the war, received Mussolini on his estate in the island of Caprera and hailed the Black Shirts as continuing the tradition of Garibaldi's Redshirts. Ricciotti's son **Giuseppe** (1879–1950), *known as* **Peppino**, b. in Melbourne, Australia, fought in Greek army beside his father (1897), and in Boer army in Boer War (1901–02); joined insurgents who rose against President Castro of Venezuela (1904); served as general of brigade in Greek army during Balkan Wars (1913); and joined Italian army (1915) during World War, commanding the Alpine brigade (1918).

**Ga'ri·bol'di** (gä'rē·bôl'dē), **Italo.** 1879?– . Italian army commander; succeeded Marshal Rodolfo Graziani in command of Italian forces in Libya (1941).

**Gar'land** (gär'lănd), **Augustus Hill.** 1832–1899. American lawyer and politician; member, Confederate provisional congress, lower house (1861–64); senate (1864–65). Elected U.S. senator (1867) but not allowed to take seat. Governor of Arkansas (1874–76). U.S. senator (1877–85); U.S. attorney general (1885–89).

**Garland, Hamlin.** 1860–1940. American writer, b. West Salem, Wis. Author of *Main-Travelled Roads* (1891), *Her Mountain Lover* (1901), *Hesper* (1903), *The Long Trail* (1907), *A Son of the Middle Border* (1917), *A Daughter of the Middle Border* (1921, awarded Pulitzer prize), *The Book of the American Indian* (1923), *The Trail-makers* (1926), *Afternoon Neighbors* (1934), *Forty Years of Psychic Research* (1936), *Mystery of the Buried Crosses* (1939), etc.

**Gar·lan'da** (gär·län'dä), **Federigo.** 1857–?1915. Italian literary scholar; chief work, *Shakespeare, il Poeta e l'Uomo* (1891). See Ada NEGRI.

**Gar'man** (gär'măn), **Samuel.** 1843–1927. American zoologist; authority on sharks, skates, and rays.

**Gar'neau'** (gȧr'nō'), **François Xavier.** 1809–1866. Canadian historian; greffier of Quebec (1844–64); author of *Histoire du Canada* (1845–46), etc.

**Gar′ner** (gär′nẽr), **James Wilford.** 1871–1938. American political scientist; professor, Illinois (1904–38). Author of *Introduction to Political Science* (1910), *Political Science and Government* (1927), etc.

**Garner, John Nance.** 1868–1967. American politician; member, U.S. House of Representatives (1903–33), speaker (1931–33); vice-president of the U.S. (1933–41).

**Gar′ne·rin′** (gȧr′nē·răN′), **André Jacques.** 1769–1823. French aeronaut; invented a parachute in which he made first parachute descent from a balloon (1797). His brother **Jean Baptiste Olivier** (1766–1849) devised improvements in parachutes.

**Gar′net** (gär′nĕt; -nĭt), **Henry Highland.** 1815–1882. Afro-American clergyman, b. a slave in Kent County, Md. Leader of abolition movement among Negroes; in speech at Buffalo, N.Y., called upon slaves to rise and murder their masters (1843). After various pastorates appointed U.S. minister to Liberia (1881).

**Gar′nett** (gär′nĕt; -nĭt), **Edward.** 1868–1937. English writer; author of *The Breaking Point, The Feud, Turgenef* (1917), and *The Trial of Jeanne d'Arc* (a play, 1931). His wife, **Constance,** *nee* **Black** [blăk] (1862–1946), known under her married name as translator of many novels from the Russian of Turgenev, Tolstoi, Chekhov, etc. Their son **David** (1892– ), also a writer; for a time partner of Francis Meynell in Nonesuch Press; author of *Lady into Fox* (awarded Hawthornden and James Tait Black memorial prizes, 1923), *The Old Dovecote* (1928), *The Grasshoppers Come* (1931), *The Life of Pocahontas* (1931–32), *A Rabbit in the Air* (1932), *Beany-Eye* (1935), *War in the Air* (1941), etc. See Richard GARNETT (1835–1906).

**Garnett, Henry.** 1555–1606. English Jesuit; superior of the English province (1587–1606); executed on charge of complicity in Gunpowder Plot.

**Garnett, James Mercer.** 1840–1916. American educator; principal, St. John's College, Annapolis, Md. (1870–80); professor of English, U. of Virginia (1882–96). Author of metrical translations of *Beowulf, Elene,* and other Old English works.

**Gar·nett′** (gär·nĕt′), **Louise,** *nee* **Ayres** (ârz). d. 1937. American composer and writer; m. Eugene H. Garnett (1900). Author esp. of librettos set to music by Henry Hadley.

**Gar′nett** (gär′nĕt; -nĭt), **Porter.** 1871–1951. American writer and printer, b. San Francisco. Founded Laboratory Press at Carnegie Tech. (1923) and specialized in hand-press printing. Produced many plays for the Bohemian Club (1904–19). Author of *The Green Knight* (play, 1911), *A Pageant of May* (1914), etc.

**Garnett, Richard.** 1789–1850. English clergyman and philologist; on staff of British Museum (1838–50); his philological essays edited and published by his son (1859). His son **Richard** (1835–1906), on staff of British Museum (from 1857), was keeper of printed books (1890–99); published *Relics of Shelley* (1862), *The Twilight of the Gods* (1888), *History of Italian Literature* (1897), and several biographies. Father of Edward Garnett (*q.v.*).

**Gar′nier′** (gȧr′nyā′), **Adolphe.** 1801–1864. French philosopher.

**Garnier,** Saint **Charles.** 1606–1649. French Jesuit missionary in America; to New France (Canada; 1636) and established himself among the Hurons; slain by the Iroquois (1649); ranked among the Jesuit martyrs of North America. Canonized (1930).

**Garnier, Clément Joseph.** 1813–1882. French economist; a founder of the Société d'Économie Politique (1842); author of *Éléments de l'Économie Politique* (1845), *Du Principe de la Population* (1857), *Traité des Finances* (1862).

**Garnier, Francis,** *properly* **Marie Joseph François.** 1839–1873. French explorer in China. Accompanied Lagrée's expedition from Cambodia to Shanghai by way of Yünnan (1866–68), bringing party down Yangtze to coast after Lagrée's death.

**Garnier,** Marquis **Germain.** 1754–1821. French economist and politician; elected to States-General (1789) but left France as an émigré; returned to Paris (1795) and was appointed comte and senator (1804). Peer of France and minister of state under the Restoration. As an economist, identified with the physiocrats.

**Garnier, Jean Louis Charles.** 1825–1898. French architect. Designed the Paris Opéra, the Nice Conservatory, the Monte Carlo Casino, and the tombs of Bizet and Offenbach.

**Garnier, Jules Arsène.** 1847–1889. French painter; best known for his genre paintings of subjects drawn from history.

**Garnier, Robert.** 1534–1590. French playwright; author of verse tragedies *Porcie* (1568), *Cornélie* (1574), *Marc Antoine* (1578), *Antigone* (1580), *Bradamante* (1582), etc.

**Gar′nier′-Pa′gès′** (gȧr′nyā′pȧ′zhĕs′), **Étienne Joseph Louis.** 1801–1841. French lawyer and politician; one of leaders of republican party during the July monarchy (1830–41). His half brother **Louis Antoine** (1803–1878) was also a lawyer and politician; minister of finance in the provisional government (1848); member of Government of National Defense (1870–71).

**Garn′sey** (gärn′zĭ), **Elmer Ellsworth.** 1862–1946. American painter, b. Holmdel, N.J.; best known for murals, as in Boston Public Library, Library of Congress in Washington.

**Ga·ro′fa·lo** (gä·rô′fä·lō), **Benvenuto da.** *Real name* **Benvenuto Ti′si** (tē′zē) *or* **Ti′sio** (tē′zyō). 1481?–1559. Italian painter of Ferrarese school.

**Garofalo,** Baron **Raffaele.** 1851–1934. Italian jurist, statesman, and criminologist; one of founders of Italian positivist school.

**Gar·rett′** (gȧr·rĕt′), Visconde **de Almeida-.** See ALMEIDA-GARRETT.

**Gar′rett** (găr′ĕt), **Garet,** *really* **Edward Peter.** 1878–1954. American journalist and economist; author of popular books and articles on economic subjects.

**Garrett, John Work** (wûrk). 1872–1942. American banker and diplomat; U.S. minister to Venezuela (1910–11), Argentina (1911–14), the Netherlands and Luxemburg (1917–19); U.S. ambassador to Italy (1929–33).

**Gar′rett Anderson** (găr′ĕt), **Elizabeth.** See ANDERSON.

**Gar′rick** (găr′ĭk), **David.** 1717–1779. English actor, b. Hereford, of Huguenot descent. While a student at Lichfield grammar school, met Samuel Johnson and became his first pupil at Edial; accompanied Johnson to London (1737). Made reputation by his acting in *Richard III* (Oct. 19, 1741); continued success in other Shakespearean plays; became comanager of Drury Lane Theatre (1747). His marriage (1749) to a Viennese dancer, Eva Maria Violetti, resented by Quin, Macklin, Barry, and Mrs. Cibber. Successful in large repertory; amassed fortune and retired to Hampton (1776). Enjoyed friendship of Johnson and his circle and of other distinguished persons of the day. Regarded as one of the greatest actors in the history of the English stage.

**Gar′ri·son** (găr′ĭ·s′n), **Lindley Miller.** 1864–1932. American lawyer and public official; vice-chancellor of New Jersey (1904–13); U.S. secretary of war (1913–16).

**Garrison, Mabel.** 1886–1963. American soprano, b. Baltimore; m. George Siemonn (1908). Joined Metropolitan Opera Co. of New York (1914). Professor of vocal music, Smith Coll. (from 1933).

**Gar'rison, William Lloyd.** 1805–1879. American abolitionist, b. Newburyport, Mass. Founded the *Liberator* (1831), famous antislavery journal; became leader of fanatical abolitionists. A founder, American Anti-Slavery Society (1833), and its president (1843–65). Mobbed in Boston (1835); lectured with the Negro Frederick Douglass (1847); opposed Compromise of 1850; urged separation between North and South. After Civil War, campaigned against liquor, prostitution, injustice in treatment of Indians; favored woman suffrage. His son **Wendell Phillips** (1840–1907) was literary editor of the *Nation* (1865–1906); collaborated with his brother **F. J. Garrison** in writing *William Lloyd Garrison, 1805–79: The Story of His Life Told by His Children* (4 vols., 1885–89). His daughter **Helen** married Henry Villard (*q.v.*).

**Gar'rod** (găr'ŭd), Sir **Alfred Baring.** 1819–1907. English physician; professor of therapeutics, University Coll. Hospital (1851–63) and King's Coll. Hospital (1863–74); author of *Treatise on Gout and Rheumatic Gout* (1859). His son **Alfred Henry** (1846–1879), zoologist, was professor of comparative anatomy, King's Coll., London (1874–79); conducted investigations in anatomy and myology of birds and ruminants. Another son, Sir **Archibald** (1857–1936), was regius professor of medicine at Oxford (1920–28); author of *Inborn Errors of Metabolism* (2d ed., 1923) and *Inborn Factors in Disease* (1931). Sir Archibald's daughter **Dorothy Annie Elizabeth** (1892–1968), educ. Newnham Coll., Cambridge, where she became director of studies in archaeology and anthropology, was director of archaeological expeditions in Kurdistan (1928) and Palestine (1929–34); first woman to be appointed (1939) professor at Cambridge.

**Garrod, Heath'cote** (hĕth'kŭt) **William.** 1878–1960. English essayist and educator; professor of poetry, Oxford (1923–28) and Harvard (1929).

**Gar'ros'** (gȧ'rôs'), **Roland.** 1888–1918. French aviator; first to fly across the Mediterranean, Saint-Raphaël to Bizerte (Sept. 23, 1913); killed in action (1918); the Roland Garros stadium was named in his honor.

**Gar'shin** (gȧr'shĭn), **Vsevolod Mikhailovich.** 1855–1888. Russian author; fought in Turkish campaign (1876–77), which provided background for his realistic *Four Days* (1877), that made his reputation; became insane (1880) and spent two years in an asylum; on recovery, wrote *The Journal of Private Tvanov, Red Flower* (his best work), and *The Coward*, psychological studies dealing with madness, war, or moral questions.

**Gar'stang** (gär'stăng), **John.** 1876–1956. English archaeologist. Conducted excavations on Roman sites in Britain, and sites in Egypt, Asia Minor, North Syria, Sudan, Palestine (Jericho), etc.

**Garth** (gärth), Sir **Samuel.** 1661–1719. English physician and author of occasional verse, including the mock-heroic *The Dispensary* (1699).

**Gärt'ner** (gĕrt'nĕr), **August.** 1848–1934. German hygienist and bacteriologist. Discovered (1888) Gärtner's bacillus (*Salmonella enteritidis*), the cause of meat poisoning.

**Gärtner, Joseph.** 1732–1791. German botanist; professor of anatomy, Calw (in Württemberg); credited with founding morphology of fruit and seeds through his work *De Fructibus et Seminibus Plantarum* (1780–91).

**Gar'van** (gär'vă̆n), **Francis Patrick.** 1875–1937. American lawyer and public official; appointed alien property custodian (1919) and asst. attorney general of U.S. (1920). Organized and headed Chemical Foundation, Inc. (from 1919), which purchased about 4500 German patents from alien property custodian; purchase upheld by U.S. Supreme Court (1926).

**Gar've** (gär'vĕ), **Christian.** 1742–1798. German philosopher.

**Gar'vey** (gär'vĭ), **Marcus.** 1887–1940. Jamaica-born black-nationalist leader; founder of Universal Negro Improvement Association (UNIA, 1914); to U.S. 1916. In New York City held first UNIA international convention (1920). Founded several businesses; convicted of fraud (1925); sentence commuted by Pres. Coolidge (1927); deported to Jamaica on release.

**Gar'vice** (gär'vĭs), **Charles.** 1833–1920. English journalist, novelist, and playwright.

**Gar'vie** (gär'vĭ), **Alfred Ernest.** 1861–1945. British Congregational clergyman and educator; principal of New Coll., London (1907), of Hackney Coll. (1922), and of Hackney and New Coll. (1924–33). Author of books on religious subjects.

**Gar'vin** (gär'vĭn), **James Louis.** 1868–1947. English journalist and editor; editor of *Outlook* (1905–06), *Observer* (from 1908), *Pall Mall Gazette* (1912–15); editor in chief, 14th edition of *Encyclopaedia Britannica* (1926–29).

**Gar'y** (gâr'ĭ), **Elbert Henry.** 1846–1927. American lawyer and business leader; practiced law, Chicago. President, Federal Steel Co. (1898); instrumental in organizing United States Steel Corp.; chairman, executive committee, U.S. Steel Corp. (1901–03); chairman, board of directors, U.S. Steel Corp. (1903–27).

**Gary, James Albert.** 1833–1920. American industrialist; U.S. postmaster general (1897–98).

**Gas'ca** (gäs'kä), **Pedro de la.** 1485–1567. Spanish lawyer and bishop, b. near Ávila. President of audiencia of Peru (1547–50); put down rebellion of Gonzalo Pizarro (1548); bishop of Palencia (1550–61) and of Sigüenza (1561–67).

**Gas'coigne** (găs'koin), Sir **Bernard.** *Orig. name* **Bernardo** *or* **Bernardino Guas·co'ni** (gwäs·kō'nē). 1614–1687. Italian-born soldier and diplomat in English service; fought for Charles I at Colchester (1648). Returned to England after Restoration; sent as envoy to Vienna to negotiate marriage of duke of York with a daughter of archduke of Austria (1672).

**Gascoigne, George.** 1525?–1577. English poet. Educ. Cambridge; studied law in London; M.P. (1557–59). Produced at Gray's Inn (1566) *The Supposes*, prose adaptation of Ariosto's *Gli Suppositi*. Published (1575) *The Posies of George Gascoigne*, containing short poems; a blank verse tragedy, *Iocasta*, adapted from Euripides and regarded by some as earliest English translation from Greek tragedy; a prose essay, *Making of Verse or Ryme in English*, regarded as first English critical essay. Continued literary work with *A Glass of Government* ("tragical comedy"; 1575); verses and masques for Leicester's entertainment of Elizabeth, issued (1576) as *The Princely Pleasures at the Court of Kenilworth;* a blank-verse satire, *The Steel Glass* (1576); the serious prose work *The Droomme of Doomesday* (1576).

**Gascoigne,** Sir **William.** 1350?–1419. English jurist; chief justice of King's Bench (1400). According to one account (followed by Shakespeare in *Henry IV*), committed Prince Hal (later King Henry V) to prison when Hal struck him for punishing one of Hal's companions.

**Gascoigne, William.** 1612?–1644. English astronomer; inventor of the micrometer.

**Gas'kell** (găs'kĕl; -kĕl), **Elizabeth Cleghorn,** *nee* **Ste'ven·son** (stē'vĕn·s'n). 1810–1865. English novelist; m. William Gaskell (1832). Author esp. of works depicting life in manufacturing cities of the Midlands, including *Mary Barton* (1848), *Cranford* (1853), *Lizzie Leigh* (1855), *Sylvia's Lovers* (1863), *Wives and Daughters* (1865). Also wrote *Life of Charlotte Brontë* (1857).

**Gaspard-Poussin.** See Gaspard DUGHET.

**Ga·spar'ri** (gäs·pär'rē), **Pietro.** 1852–1934. Italian Roman Catholic prelate; created cardinal (1907); papal secretary of state (from 1914).

**Gas'pé'** (gȧs'pā'), **Philippe Aubert de.** 1786–1871. Canadian lawyer and writer; his *Les Anciens Canadiens* (1862), though written as fiction, gives historical descriptions of life and customs in old Quebec; his *Mémoires* constitute historical source material for the same period.

**Gas'quet'** (gȧs'kĕ'), **Amédée.** 1852–1914. French author of books on Byzantine history.

**Gasquet, Francis Aidan.** 1846–1929. English Roman Catholic prelate of French descent, b. London. Superior of the Benedictine monastery and Coll. of St. Gregory at Downside (1878–84); president of international commission for revision of the Vulgate; cardinal (1914); prefect of the Vatican archives (from 1918).

**Gasquet, Joachim.** 1873–1921. French poet.

**Gass** (gäs), **Wilhelm.** 1813–1889. German Protestant theologian and historian.

**Gas'sen'di'** (gȧ'săN'dē') *or* **Gas'send'** (gȧ'săN'), **Pierre.** 1592–1655. French philosopher and savant; advocate of empirical method; attacked Aristotelian philosophy and opposed Cartesian philosophy; revived and maintained Epicurean doctrines; friend of Galileo and Kepler.

**Gas'ser** (găs'ẽr), **Herbert Spencer.** 1888–1963. American physiologist, b. Platteville, Wis.; professor, Cornell U. (1931–35); director, Rockefeller Inst. (from 1935); shared with Joseph Erlanger (*q.v.*) 1944 Nobel prize for medicine, for work on nerve fibers.

**Gas'sion'** (gȧ'syôN'), **Jean de.** 1609–1647. French soldier; served under Gustavus Adolphus of Sweden until the Swedish king's death (1632); returned to serve in French army; promoted field marshal (1638), and marshal of France (1643); directed sieges of Thionville, Béthune, Gravelines, Saint-Venant; mortally wounded before Lens.

**Gass'ner** (gäs'nẽr), **Johann Joseph.** 1727–1779. German Roman Catholic priest; undertook to exorcise evil spirits and cure the sick; achieved fame as an exorcist; became center of bitter controversies about genuineness of his cures.

**Gas'ter** (?gäs'tẽr), **Moses.** 1856–1939. Jewish scholar, b. Bucharest, Rumania; to England, and became lecturer in Byzantine and Slavonic languages at Oxford (1886, 1891); also, principal of Montefiore Coll. (1890–96). Chief rabbi of Sephardic communities in England (from 1887).

**Gas'ton** (găs'tŭn), **William.** 1778–1844. American jurist, b. New Bern, N.C. Member, U.S. House of Representatives (1813–17); judge, North Carolina supreme court (1833–44); widely known as an orator.

**Ga·szyń'ski** (gä·shĭn'y'·skē), **Konstanty.** 1809?–1866. Polish poet; author of *Songs of a Polish Pilgrim* (1833), etc.

**Gates** (gāts), **Caleb Frank.** 1857–1946. American Congregationalist clergyman; missionary in Turkey (1881–94); president of Euphrates Coll., Harput, Turkey (1894–1902), and Robert Coll. in Constantinople (1903–32).

**Gates, Eleanor.** 1875–1951. American writer; m. (1901) Richard Walton Tully (*q.v.*), Frederick Ferdinand Moore (1914). Author of *The Biography of a Prairie Girl* (1902), *The Plow-Woman* (1906), *The Poor Little Rich Girl* (play and novel, 1913), *The Rich Little Poor Boy* (1921), *Out of the West* (play, 1924), *Fish-Bait* (play, 1928), etc.

**Gates, Frederick Taylor.** 1853–1929. American Baptist clergyman, b. Maine, N.Y. Instrumental in raising funds for establishment of U. of Chicago. Called by J. D. Rockefeller to become representative of Rockefeller interests (1893); chairman, general education board (1903), and of Rockefeller Institute for Medical Research. Instrumental in establishing Rockefeller Foundation.

**Gates, George Augustus.** 1851–1912. American educator, b. Topsham, Vt. President, Grinnell (1887–1900), Pomona (1901–09), Fisk U., Nashville, Tenn. (1909–12).

**Gates, Horatio.** 1728?–1806. American Revolutionary officer, b. Maldon, England. Entered British army; joined Braddock's army in Virginia (1755); on service in America (1755–61). Invited by Washington, took up land in Virginia (1772). Took colonial side at outbreak of Revolutionary War; adjutant general, Continental army (1775); major general (1776); in command, Fort Ticonderoga (1776–77); received credit for success in repulsing Burgoyne's army from the north, although Schuyler and Benedict Arnold were really responsible for the defense. Friends of Gates sought to put him in Washington's place as commander in chief; Conway Cabal formed for this purpose; failed. Lost disastrous battle of Camden, S.C. (Aug. 16, 1780). Relieved of his command, retired to his plantation and asked official inquiry into his conduct at battle of Camden; Congress finally (1782) without inquiry ordered him back into service under Washington; served loyally at Washington's headquarters remainder of war.

**Gates, John Warne.** 1855–1911. American promoter and daring speculator and gambler, known as "Bet-you-a-million Gates"; in New York stock-market circles. feared for his "bear" activities; in market battle with J. P. Morgan over control of Louisville & Nashville Railroad, lost fortune and forced to agree to cease activities on New York stock exchange. Retired from New York field to enter oil industry in Texas; one of organizers of Texas Company.

**Gates,** Sir **Thomas.** d. 1621. Colonial administrator in America; one of grantees named in charter to Virginia Company (1606); in Virginia (1610 and 1611–14); acted as governor of colony while there.

**Ga'thorne-Har'dy** (gā'thôrn·här'dĭ), **Gathorne.** 1st Earl of **Cran'brook** (krăn'bro͝ok). 1814–1906. English statesman. As home secretary (1867–68) took resolute measures against Fenian conspirators; secretary for war (1874–78) under Disraeli, whose pro-Turkish policy he supported; secretary for India (1878–80), promoted Lord Lytton's aggressive policy on Afghan frontier; lord president of council (1885–92).

**Gat'ley** (găt'lĭ), **Clement Carpenter.** 1881–1936. English jurist; author of *The Law and Practice of Libel and Slander in a Civil Action* (1924).

**Gat'ling** (găt'lĭng), **Richard Jordan.** 1818–1903. b. in Hertford County, N.C. American inventor of a rapid-fire gun, the "Gatling gun" (patented Nov. 4, 1862).

**Gat'schet** (găch'ĕt; -ĭt), **Albert Samuel.** 1832–1907. Ethnologist, b. in Switzerland; to U.S. (1868). Ethnologist, U.S. Geological Survey (1877); associated with U.S. Bureau of Ethnology (1879). Studied American Indian families and languages.

**Gat'ta·me·la'ta** (gät'tä·mȧ·lä'tä), **Erasmo.** *Also called* **Erasmo de' Nar'ni** (dā när'nē). 1370?–1443. Italian condottiere; in service of popes Martin V and Eugenius IV; later in service of Venice against Milan (1434–41).

**Gat'te·rer** (gät'ĕ·rẽr), **Johann Christoph.** 1727–1799. German historian.

**Gat'ti** (gät'tē), **Bernardino.** *Known as* **il So·ia'ro** (ēl sō·yä'rō). 1495?–1575. Italian painter.

**Gat'ti-Ca·saz'za** (gät'tē·kä·zät'tsä), **Giulio.** 1869–1940. Operatic manager; director of La Scala, opera house at Milan, Italy (1898–1908); general manager of Metropolitan Opera House in New York (1908–35). See Frances ALDA.

**Gat′ty** (găt′ĭ), **Alfred** and **Margaret**. See under Juliana Horatia EWING.

**Gatty, Nicholas Comyn.** 1874–1946. English composer of operas, choral and orchestral music, piano pieces, etc.

**Gau′bil′** (gō′bēl′), **Antoine.** 1689–1759. French Jesuit missionary to China; translator of a life of Genghis Khan, of the *Shu Ching* (one of the Five Classics), and of some T'ang annals.

**Gau′den** (gô′d'n), **John.** 1605–1662. English prelate; chaplain to earl of Warwick (1640), bishop of Exeter (1660–62) and Worcester (1662). Claimed, probably justly, authorship of *Eikon Basilike.*

**Gau′dens** (gô′d'nz), **E′tienne′** (?ā′tyĕn′) **Robert.** English inventor, took out in England (1840) first patent for a machine for distributing type after use. Cf. Frederick ROSENBERG.

**Gau′di′chaud′–Beau′pré′** (gō′dē′shō′bō′prā′), **Charles.** 1789–1854. French botanist.

**Gau′dier′–Brzes′ka′** (gō′dyā′bzhĕs′kȧ′), **Henri.** 1891–1915. French sculptor; identified with the ultramodernist movement in art known as vorticism.

**Gau′din′** (gō′dăN′), **Martin Michel Charles.** Duc **de Ga′ète′** (gȧ′ĕt′). 1756–1841. French financier and statesman; minister of finance (1799–1814); a founder of the Bank of France (1800) and its governor (1820); member of Chamber of Deputies (1815).

**Gau′dry′** (gō′drē′), **Albert.** 1827–1908. French paleontologist. Investigated fossil animals in Greece, southern France, Patagonia, etc.

**Gau′guin′** (gō′găN′), **Eugène Henri Paul.** 1848–1903. French painter; one of the principal founders of the symbolist school of Pont-Aven. Set up studio in Tahiti (1890) and from there sent back brilliant, decorative, and original canvases to Paris.

**Gaul** (gôl), **Harvey Bartlett.** 1881–1945. American organist and composer; organist of Calvary Church, Pittsburgh (from 1910); also, music critic of Pittsburgh *Post-Gazette* (1914–34) and conductor of local orchestras and choruses. Composer of cantatas, anthems, and organ and orchestral works.

**Gaul, William Gilbert.** 1855–1919. American painter; noted for historical pictures of Civil War.

**Gaulle, Charles de.** See DE GAULLE.

**Gaulli, Giovanni Battista.** See Il BACICCIO.

**Gault** (gôlt), **Robert Harvey.** 1874– . American psychologist.

**Gaumata.** See SMERDIS.

**Gau′mont′** (gō′môN′; *Angl.* gō′mŏnt), **Léon Ernest.** 1864–1946. French motion-picture inventor; developed (1901) method of synchronizing a motion-picture projector with a phonograph; introduced (1912–13) process of motion-picture photography in color, involving a three-color separation method and the use of special lenses and projectors.

**Gaunt, John of.** See JOHN OF GAUNT.

**Gaupp** (goup), **Robert Eugen.** 1870–1953. German psychiatrist.

**Gauss** (gous), **Christian.** 1878–1951. American educator; professor of modern languages (from 1907), and dean of the college (from 1925), Princeton. Author of *Life in College* (1930), etc.

**Gauss** (gous), **Karl Friedrich.** 1777–1855. German mathematician and astronomer; director and professor of astronomy, Göttingen observatory (from 1807). Demonstrated that a circle can be divided into seventeen equal arcs by elementary geometry (1796); published *Disquisitiones Arithmeticae* on the theory of numbers (1801); propounded method of least squares; devised solution for binomial equations. Made magnetic and electrical researches; considered founder of mathematical theory of electricity; proposed an absolute system of magnetic units (the gauss, a magnetic unit, is named after him); participated in geodetic surveys. Cf. W. E. WEBER.

**Gau′ta·ma Bud′dha** (*Skr.* gä′o͝o·tȧ·mȧ bo͝od′dȧ; *Angl.* gou′tȧ·mȧ bo͝od′ȧ) *or* **Go′ta·ma Bud′dha** (*Pali* gō′tȧ·mȧ). *Orig. name* Prince **Sid·dhar′tha** (sĭd·där′tȧ). *Called* **Sak′ya·mu′ni** (shäk′yȧ·mo͝o′nĭ), *i.e.* Sage of the Sakyas. 563?–?483 B.C. Indian philosopher, founder of Buddhism. Of noble birth, son of Suddhodana, chief of the Sakyas, b. at Kapilavastu, near border of Nepal. Married Yasodhara; had one son, Rahula. According to tradition, became weary of luxuries of life in the palace; resolved on his great renunciation (c. 533 B.C.), left home and journeyed about northern India; at Buddh Gaya, near Benares, forced himself to undergo long and severe penance; found ascetic life futile; legend says emancipation of spirit came to him under a pipal tree (the sacred Bo tree) at Buddh Gaya (hence his title, Buddha, *i.e.* Enlightened One); taught forty-five years (528–483), up and down Ganges valley; founded monastic orders and built up his teachings into the faith known as Buddhism; died at Kusinagara (in Nepal, not far from his birthplace). For romantic story of his life, see Sir Edwin Arnold's poem, *The Light of Asia* (1879).

**Gau′tier′** (gō′tyā′), **Léon.** 1832–1897. French paleographer and literary historian; authority on medieval European literature.

**Gautier, Théophile.** 1811–1872. French man of letters; a leader of the Parnassians. Art and dramatic critic for *La Presse* (1837–45); on editorial staff of *Moniteur Universel* (from 1845). Among his many notable works are *Premières Poésies* (1830), *Les Jeune-France* (1832), *Mademoiselle de Maupin* (1835), *Fortunio* (1837); a number of short stories, including *La Morte Amoureuse, Arria Marcella, Jettatura,* and *Avatar; Émaux et Camées* (collected verse of period 1850–1865); *Le Capitaine Fracasse* (2 vols., 1861, 1863); volumes of literary criticism, including *Les Grotesques* (1844), *Histoire du Romantisme* (1854), *Rapport sur le Progrès de la Poésie depuis 1830* (1868), *Histoire de l'Art Dramatique en France* (6 vols., 1858–59); travel books, as *Voyage en Espagne* (1843), *Italia* (1852), *Constantinople* (1854), *La Russie* (1866). His daughter **Judith** (1850–1917) was a poet and novelist; m. Catulle Mendès (later divorced) and Pierre Loti (1913); author of *Le Dragon Impérial* (1869), *L'Usurpateur* (1875), *Le Jeu de l'Amour et de la Mort* (1876), *Richard Wagner...* (1882), *Iskender* (1886), *Fleurs d'Orient* (1893), *Le Vieux de la Montagne* (1893), *Princesse d'Amour* (1900), and *La Fille du Ciel* (with Loti, 1911).

**Gautier d'Ar′ras′** (dȧ′räs′). 12th-century French poet; author of two verse romances, *Éracle* and *Ille et Galeron.*

**Gautier de Lille** (dē lēl′) *or* **de Châ′til′lon′** (shä′tē′yôN′). 12th-century French poet, writing in Latin; author of a 10-volume epic on Alexander the Great.

**Gautier sans avoir.** See WALTER THE PENNILESS.

**Gautsch von Fran′ken·thurn** (gouch′ fôn fräng′kĕn-to͝orn), Baron **Paul von.** 1851–1918. Austrian statesman; prime minister (1897–98; 1904–06; 1911).

**Ga′var′ni′** (gȧ′vȧr′nē′). *Pseudonym of* **Sulpice Guillaume Che·va′lier′** (shē·vȧ′lyā′). 1804–1866. French illustrator and caricaturist; on staff successively of *La Mode, L'Artiste, La Silhouette, Charivari, L'Illustration;* best known for his sketches of Parisian life and presentations (in *L'Illustration*) of social contrasts between extremes of luxury and poverty.

**Ga·vaz′zi** (gä·vät′sē), **Alessandro.** 1809–1889. Italian preacher, patriot, and reformer; ordained Roman Catholic priest; champion of liberal ideas. Left Italy (1849); joined Evangelical church (1850); organized Italian Protestants in London (1850–60). Served under Garibaldi (1860). Organized Free Church of Italy (1870); established theological school, Rome (1875).

**Gav'es·ton** (găv'ĕs·tŭn), **Piers.** Earl of **Corn'wall** (kôrn'wôl; *Brit. usu.* -wŭl). d. 1312. Gascon foster brother of Edward II of England. Companion and favorite of Edward, who, on accession, created him earl of Cornwall and, on departure for France to marry daughter of Philip IV, left him regent of kingdom; banished three times, on demand of barons, for insolence and extravagance; secretly returned (1311) and publicly restored to favor by Edward II; kidnaped by Warwick and executed in presence of barons. Cf. Thomas, Earl of LANCASTER.

**Ga'vi'niès** (gȧ'vē'nyĕs'), **Pierre.** 1726–1800. French violin virtuoso; regarded by some as founder of modern school of violin playing. Composer of a three-act comic opera, six violin concertos, nine violin sonatas, and a collection of violin studies.

**Gay** (gā), **Delphine.** See under Émile de GIRARDIN.

**Gay** (gā), **Ebenezer.** 1696–1787. American clergyman, b. Dedham, Mass.; so liberal in his Congregationalism that he is regarded by some as a forerunner of Unitarianism. His great-grandson **Sydney Howard Gay** (1814–1888), b. Hingham, Mass., was a journalist; active in abolitionist agitation; on staff, New York *Tribune* (1857–65) and managing editor (1862–65); managing editor, Chicago *Tribune* (1867–71); on New York *Evening Post* (1872–74). Sydney's brother **Winckworth Allan** (1821–1910) was a landscape painter.

**Gay, Frederick Parker.** 1874–1939. American pathologist and bacteriologist; known for work in immunology.

**Gay, John.** 1685–1732. English poet and playwright, b. Barnstaple, Devon. Apprenticed to a mercer in London, but devoted himself to writing. Author of verse, *Shepherd's Week* (satirical eclogues, 1714), *Trivia, or the Art of Walking the Streets of London* (1716), *Fables* (2 series, pub. 1727, 1738); plays, including *Three Hours after Marriage* (acted 1717), *Captives* (1724); *The Beggar's Opera*, his best known work (1728, played for two seasons), and its sequel, *Polly*, prohibited (1728) from performance, but published and widely read; opera, *Achilles* (produced at Covent Garden, 1733).

**Gay, Marie Françoise Sophie,** *nee* **Ni'chault' de La'va'lette'** (nē'shō' dĕ lȧ'vȧ'lĕt'). 1776–1852. French writer; author of a number of sentimental novels including *Laure d'Estell* (1802), *Anatole* (1815), and *La Duchesse de Châteauroux* (1834), and a successful comedy, *Le Marquis de Pomenars* (1820). See Delphine de GIRARDIN.

**Gay, Walter.** 1856–1937. American genre and figure painter.

**Ga·yan'gos y Ar'ce** (gä·yäng'gōs ē är'thā), **Pascual de.** 1809–1897. Spanish historian and Orientalist.

**Ga'yar'ré'** (*Fr.* gȧ'yȧ'rā'; *Span.* gä·yär'rā), **Charles Étienne Arthur.** 1805–1895. American historian, b. New Orleans; author of *History of Louisiana* (4 vols., 1851 ff.), *Philip II of Spain* (1866).

**Gay'da** (gä'ē·dä), **Virginio.** 1885–1944. Italian publicist; director, *Messaggero* (1921–26), *Giornale d'Italia* (1926–44).

**Gay'ley** (gā'lĭ), **Charles Mills.** 1858–1932. American educator, b. Shanghai, China, of American parentage. Professor of English, U. of California (1889–1923). Author of *Classic Myths in English Literature* (1893), *Methods and Materials of Literary Criticism* (with F. N. Scott, 1899), *The Principles and Progress of English Poetry* (with C. C. Young, 1904), etc.

**Gayley, James.** 1855–1920. American metallurgist and inventor. Managing director, Carnegie Steel Co. (1897); first vice-president, U.S. Steel Corporation (1901–09). Invented a bronze cooling plate for the walls of blast furnaces (patented 1891), auxiliary casting stand for Bessemer steel plants (patented 1896), dry-air blast (patented with improvements, 1894–1911).

**Gay'-Lus'sac'** (gā'lü'sȧk'), **Joseph Louis.** 1778–1850. French chemist and physicist. Professor of chemistry, École Polytechnique (1809), of physics, Sorbonne (1808–32), of chemistry, Jardin des Plantes (from 1832). Made balloon ascents to investigate effects of terrestrial magnetism and composition of air at high altitudes; enunciated the law of volumes (or Gay-Lussac's law) concerning combination of gases; with A. von Humboldt, investigated composition of water; with L. J. Thénard, discovered process for preparing potassium from fused potash and devised improved methods for analyzing organic compounds; isolated boron from boracic acid; proved that prussic acid contains hydrogen but not oxygen; isolated cyanogen; improved processes for manufacturing sulphuric acid, oxalic acid, etc.; invented a hydrometer. See also J. A. C. CHARLES.

**Gay'nor** (gā'nẽr), **William Jay.** 1849–1913. American jurist and politician; mayor of New York City (1909–13).

**Ga'za** (gä'dzä), **Teodoro.** *Greek* **Theodoros Ga·zes'** (gä·zēs'). 15th-century Greek scholar; a leader in revival of learning in Italy. Professor, Ferrara (1447–50); called to Rome by Pope Nicholas V to make Latin translations of Greek authors (1450–55). His Greek grammar was long used as a textbook.

**G. B. S.** = George Bernard SHAW.

**Gea'ry** (gẽr'ĭ), **John White.** 1819–1873. American political leader; mayor of San Francisco (1850). Territorial governor of Kansas (1856), then torn by factional strife; firm policy restored peace; on failure of President Pierce to support his policy, resigned (Mar., 1857). Served through Civil War; brigadier general (1862); brevetted major general (1865). Governor of Pennsylvania (1867–73).

**Ge'bau·er** (gĕ'bou·ĕr), **Jan.** 1838–1907. Czech philologist; author of historical grammar of Czech language.

**Ge'ber** (*Lat.* jē'bẽr) *or* **Ja'bir** (*Arab.* jä'bĭr). *Arab.* **Jābir ibn-Ḥayyān.** fl. 721–776. Arab scholar. Lived at Al Kufa and Baghdad; had great influence in field of medieval chemical science; held theory that baser metals could be transmuted into nobler; his works (about 22) were basic in Europe and Asia after 14th century, and were studied by Roger Bacon.

**Geb'hard** (gĕp'härt), **Heinrich.** 1878–1963. Piano virtuoso, b. Sobernheim, Ger.; to U.S. (1889) and settled in Boston.

**Geb'hardt** (gĕp'härt), **Eduard von.** 1838–1925. German painter; sought to interpret religious scenes and church history according to the contemporary mode in painting.

**Geb'hart'** (gā'bȧr'), **Émile.** 1839–1908. French scholar and art historian.

**Ge'bler** (gā'blẽr), **Otto.** 1838–1917. German painter, esp. of animals.

**Ged** (gĕd), **William.** 1690–1749. Scottish inventor of stereotyping.

**Ge·dalge'** (zhē·dȧlzh'), **André.** 1856–1927. French composer; professor, Paris Conservatory (from 1905).

**Ged'des** (gĕd'ĭs), **Alexander.** 1737–1802. Scottish Roman Catholic clergyman and writer; devoted himself chiefly to literary work; planned new translation of Bible for Roman Catholics, issuing the historical books of the Old Testament and the book of *Ruth*, with *Critical Remarks on the Hebrew Scriptures* (1800), the rationalistic nature of which caused suspension from ecclesiastical functions.

**Geddes, Andrew.** 1783–1844. Scottish painter and etcher; excelled in portraits, landscapes, and copies of old masters.

**Geddes,** Sir **Eric Campbell.** 1875–1937. English industrialist and statesman, b. in India. During World War, served as director-general of transportation (1916–17); first lord of the admiralty (1917–18); member of imperial war cabinet (1918); minister without portfolio (1919); minister of transport (1919–21). His brother Sir **Auckland** (1879–1954), scientist, public official, and diplomat, served as director of recruiting (1916–17) in War Office, minister of national service (1917–19), minister of reconstruction (1919); president of the Board of Trade (1919–20); British ambassador to the United States (1920–24); chairman of royal commission on food prices (1924–25).

**Ged′des** (gĕd′ĕz), **James.** 1858–1948. American educator; professor of Romance languages, Boston U. (1892–1937). Author of *Canadian French, the Language and Literature* (1902) and translator of *La Chanson de Roland* into French prose (1906).

**Ged′des** (gĕd′ēz), **Norman Bel.** 1893–1958. American stage designer and architect; stage designer for Metropolitan Opera Company (1918) and later for other theaters. Among sets designed by him are those for *Pélléas et Mélisande, The Miracle, Jeanne d'Arc, Dead End, Hamlet.* Entered field of industrial designing (1927), and modeled furniture, radio cabinets, airplane interiors, etc.; largely responsible for popularizing streamlining.

**Ged′des** (gĕd′ĭs), Sir **Patrick.** 1854–1932. Scottish biologist and sociologist, b. Perth. Professor (1883) of botany, University Coll.; professor of sociology and civics, U. of Bombay (1919); director of Scots Coll., Montpellier, France. Instrumental in organizing university halls at Edinburgh and Chelsea which served as laboratories of sociological enquiry; active in city planning in Great Britain and on the Continent; designed Hebrew U. building in Jerusalem; director of printing establishment of Geddes and Colleagues, issuing chiefly Celtic books.

**Gedeon.** See GIDEON.

**Ge′di·ke** (gā′dĭ·kĕ), **Friedrich.** 1754–1803. German educator; regarded as a leader of a new humanist movement in Germany.

**Gedimin.** *Pol.* **Ge·dy′min** (gĕ·dĭ′mēn). *Lith.* **Ge′di·mi′nas** (gĕ′dĭ·mĭ′näs). d. about 1340. Lithuanian prince; inherited territory including Lithuania, Samogitia, Red Russia, Polotsk, and Minsk (1316); defended these lands from the Teutonic Knights and the Livonian Knights of the Sword; built chain of forts along his borders; founded Vilna, capital of Lithuania. Credited with making Lithuania great power in Europe. Father of Olgierd (*q.v.*) and grandfather of Jagello (see LADISLAS II of Poland).

**Ge′don** (gā′dôn), **Lorenz.** 1843–1883. German architect and sculptor; best-known work, palace of Adolf Schack in Munich.

**Geefs** (gāfs), **Willem** (1806–1883) and his brother **Joseph** (1808–1885). Belgian sculptors.

**Geer** (gār), **Dirk Jan de.** 1870–1960. Dutch jurist and statesman; prime minister of the Netherlands (1926–29); prime minister and minister of finance (1939).

**Geer** (yār), Baron **Louis Gerhard de** (dē). 1818–1896. Swedish statesman; prime minister of Sweden (1876–80). Introduced numerous reforms, including religious liberty, reform of the penal code, replacement of the four orders of the Diet by two chambers.

**Geerarts, Marcus.** See GHEERAERTS.

**Geert′gen tot Sint Jans** (gārt′gĕn tŏt sĭnt yäns′). 1465?–?1495. Dutch painter; chief work, a triptych for altar of Knights of Saint John, part of which is preserved in Vienna gallery.

**Geff′cken** (gĕf′kĕn), **Heinrich.** 1830–1896. German jurist and diplomat. His son **Johannes** (1861–1935) was a classical scholar.

**Gef′frard′** (zhĕ′frȧr′), **Nicholas Fabre.** 1806–1879. Haitian general and politician; led insurrection (1858–59) that overthrew Soulouque; declared a republic and became its president (1859–67).

**Gef′froy′** (zhĕ′frwä′), **Gustave.** 1855–1926. French writer and art critic.

**Geffroy, Matthieu Auguste.** 1820–1895. French historian.

**Ge′gen·baur** (gā′gĕn·bour), **Karl.** 1826–1903. German anatomist; one of first to consider anatomy from evolutionary standpoint; authority on comparative anatomy of vertebrates.

**Gehr′cke** (gār′kĕ), **Ernst.** 1878–1960. German physicist; codiscoverer of anode rays; inventor of ray oscillographs, interference spectroscopes. See Otto LUMMER.

**Geh′rig** (gĕr′ĭg), **Henry Louis,** *called* **Lou.** 1903–1941. American professional baseball player, b. New York City. First baseman, New York Yankees (1925–39), establishing a batting average for his baseball career of .340, and a record of playing in 2130 consecutive major league games. Retired from baseball (1939); appointed parole commissioner for New York City (Jan. 2, 1940).

**Gehr′kens** (gâr′kĕns), **Karl Wilson.** 1882– . American music educator; professor of school music, Oberlin (from 1912). Editor of musical terms for *Webster's New International Dictionary, Second Edition.*

**Gei′bel** (gī′bĕl), **Emanuel.** 1815–1884. German poet.

**Gei′ger** (gī′gẽr), **Abraham.** 1810–1874. German Jewish theologian; champion of modernism. Rabbi at Wiesbaden (1832), Breslau (1840), Frankfurt (1863), Berlin (1870). His son **Ludwig** (1848–1919) was a historian of literature; professor at Berlin (from 1880).

**Geiger, Albert.** 1866–1915. German writer; author of lyrics, dramas, and stories.

**Geiger, Lazarus.** 1829–1870. German philologist.

**Geiger, Ludwig Wilhelm.** 1856–1943. German Oriental scholar. His son **Hans** (1882–1945), physicist; interested esp. in radium research.

**Geiger, Moritz.** 1880–1938. German philosopher; professor, Göttingen; conducted researches in aesthetics, psychology, and philosophy of mathematics.

**Geiger, Nikolaus.** 1849–1897. German sculptor and painter.

**Gei′jer** (yĕ′ĭ·ẽr), **Erik Gustaf.** 1783–1847. Swedish historian, poet, philosopher, and composer; professor, Uppsala (1817–46). A founder of Gothic Society and an editor of, and contributor to, its journal, *Iduna.*

**Gei′jer·stam′** (yĕ′ĭ·ẽr·shtäm′), **Gösta af.** 1888– . Norwegian novelist.

**Gei′jer·stam′** (yĕ′ĭ·ẽr·stȧm′), **Gustaf af.** 1858–1909. Swedish writer; champion of naturalism in Sweden.

**Gei′kie** (gē′kĭ), Sir **Archibald.** 1835–1924. Scottish geologist, b. Edinburgh; educ. Edinburgh; director of geological survey of Scotland (1867 ff.); director-general of geological survey of the United Kingdom and director of the Museum of Practical Geology (1882–1901). Among his many books are *The Story of a Boulder...*(1858), *Textbook of Geology* (1882), *The Ancient Volcanoes of Britain* (2 vols., 1897), *Landscape in History* (1905), and *The Love of Nature Among the Romans* (1912). His brother **James** (1839–1915), also a geologist, wrote *The Great Ice Age* (1874), *Prehistoric Europe* (1881), *Outlines of Geology* (1886), etc.

**Geikie, John Cunningham.** 1824–1906. Scottish-born clergyman; in Canada and Nova Scotia (to 1860), and in England (from 1860). Author of *The Life and Words of Christ* (2 vols., 1877), etc.

**Geilamir.** See GELIMER.

**Gei'ler von Kay'sers·berg** (gī'lẽr fōn kī'zẽrs·bĕrk), **Johann.** 1445–1510. Swiss-born German Roman Catholic priest; preacher at Cathedral of Strasbourg (1478–1510).

**Gei'nitz** (gī'nĭts), **Hanns Bruno.** 1814–1900. German geologist; author of works on Permian and Cretaceous formations of Germany.

**Gei'sel** (gī'z'l), **The'o·dor** (thē'ô·dôr) **Seuss** (sois). *Pseudonym* **Dr. Seuss.** 1904– . American writer and illustrator; b. Springfield, Mass. Author of children's books with illustrations of his own.

**Geishüsler, Oswald.** See Oswald MYCONIUS.

**Geis'sel** (gī'sĕl), **Johannes von.** 1796–1864. German Roman Catholic prelate; archbishop (1846) of Cologne; created cardinal (1850). Upheld ultramontane position in Germany; favored Jesuit order; suppressed Hermesianism.

**Geiss'ler** (gīs'lẽr), **Heinrich.** 1814–1879. German glassblower and mechanic; founded at Bonn a shop for making scientific apparatus (1854); produced the first Geissler tube and a mercury pump, the Geissler pump.

**Geitel, Hans Friedrich.** See under Julius ELSTER.

**Ge·la'si·us** (jē·lā'shĭ·ŭs; -zhĭ·ŭs; -zĭ-). Name of two popes (see *Table of Popes*, Nos. 49, 161):

**Gelasius I,** Saint. Pope (492–496), b. Rome. Attempted to heal schism between Eastern and Western churches; a notable writer of his period, esp. of letters; probably wrote part of the liturgy known as the *Gelasian Sacramentary.*

**Gelasius II.** *Real name* **Giovanni da Ga·e'ta** (dä gä·ā'tä). Pope (1118–19), b. Gaeta. In early life a Benedictine monk at Monte Cassino; as pope, was persecuted by the Frangipani; partisan of Emperor Henry V; driven out of Rome; fled to France and died in convent of Cluny.

**Gel'der** (gĕl'dẽr), **Aert de.** 1645–1727. Dutch painter.

**Geld'ner** (gĕld'nẽr), **Karl Friedrich.** 1852–1929. German Oriental scholar.

**Gelée, Claude.** See Claude LORRAIN.

**Ge'lert** (gē'lẽrt), **Johannes Sophus.** 1852–1923. Sculptor, b. in Schleswig, Denmark; to U.S. (1887), naturalized (1892). Among his works are statues of Gen. U. S. Grant at Galena, Ill., of Emperor Napoleon at St. Louis Exposition, and a statue symbolic of Denmark for U.S. Custom House, New York.

**Gel'i·mer** (gĕl'ĭ·mẽr) *or* **Gei'la·mir** (gī'lȧ·mĭr) *or* **Gil'i·mer** (gĭl'ĭ·mẽr). Last king of the Vandals in Africa (530–534 A.D.); captured (534) by Justinian's army under Belisarius (*q.v.*).

**Gell** (gĕl), Sir **William.** 1777–1836. English archaeologist; educ. Cambridge. Traveled in Greece and wrote *Geography and Antiquities of Ithaca* (1807), *Itinerary of Greece* (1810), *Itinerary of the Morea* (1817), and *Journey in the Morea* (1823). Lived in Naples and Rome (from 1820) and published *Pompeiana* (1817–19) and *Topography of Rome* (1834).

**Gellée, Claude.** See Claude LORRAIN.

**Gel'lert** (gĕl'ẽrt), **Christian Fürchtegott.** 1715–1769. German poet, b. in Saxony. Author of romance *Das Leben der Schwedischen Gräfin G.* (1746) and several comedies, but best known for songs and fables.

**Gell'horn** (gĕl'hôrn), **Martha Ellis.** 1908– . American novelist; m. (1940) as 3d wife Ernest Hemingway (*q.v.*); author of *The Trouble I've Seen* (1936), *A Stricken Field* (1940), *The Heart of Another* (short stories; 1941), *Wine of Astonishment* (1941).

**Gel'li** (jĕl'lē), **Giovanni Battista.** 1498–1563. Florentine writer; commissioned by Cosimo de'Medici to write commentaries on Dante; wrote poems, letters, and two comedies.

**Gel'li·brand** (gĕl'ĭ·brănd), **Henry.** 1597–1636. English mathematician and astronomer; completed Briggs's *Trigonometria Britannica;* wrote *Epitome of Navigation.*

**Gel'li·us** (jĕl'ĭ·ŭs), **Aulus.** Latin writer of 2d century A.D. His *Noctes Atticae* contains notes and miscellaneous information on ancient language and literature, customs, laws, philosophy, and natural science.

**Gell–Mann** (gĕl'män), **Murray.** 1929– . Amer. physicist, b. New York City. At Calif. Inst. of Tech. (1955– ). Awarded Nobel prize in physics (1969) for contributing to the classification and description of elementary particles of physics.

**Ge'lon** (jē'lŏn) *or* **Ge'lo** (jē'lō). d. 478 B.C. Syracusan soldier and politician; cavalry commander under Hippocrates, Tyrant of Gela, whom he succeeded (491 B.C.) as tyrant. Became tyrant of Syracuse (485 B.C.) and extended his power in Sicily; noted for beneficence and wisdom of administration. Defeated Carthaginians in battle of Himera (480). Another **Gelon** of Syracuse, (d. 215 B.C.). Son of King Hiero II, was associated with his father in the government.

**Gel'zer** (gĕl'tsẽr), **Johann Heinrich.** 1813–1889. Swiss historian and publicist; advocate of German unity. His son **Heinrich** (1847–1906), b. Berlin, was a philologist and historian.

**Gé'mier'** (zhā'myā'), **Firmin.** 1865–1933. French actor and theater director; friend of André Antoine (from 1892), and co-operated with him in effort to introduce realism, with natural speech and gesture, on French stage; appeared in plays by Brieux, Ibsen, Hauptmann, Shaw, and revivals of Shakespeare. Director of the Odéon (1921–30), of Théâtre National Populaire, at the Trocadero (from 1930).

**Ge'mi·nia'ni** (jā'mē·nyä'nē), **Francesco.** 1674?–?1762. Italian violin virtuoso and composer.

**Ge·mis'tus Ple'tho** (jē·mĭs'tŭs plē'thō), **Georgius.** *Also* **Georgios Gemistos Ple'thon** (plē'thŏn). 1355?–?1450. Byzantine Platonic philosopher; regarded as a pioneer in the revival of learning in western Europe.

**Gem·mei** (gĕm·mā) *or* **Gem·myo** (gĕm·myō). 653–714. Japanese empress (708–714), of Nara period; daughter of Emperor Tenchi. Transferred capital to Nara; caused the *Kojiki* (Japanese historical chronicle) to be written.

**Gen'de·bien'** (zhäɴd'byăɴ'), **Jean François.** 1753–1838. Belgian lawyer and politician. His son **Alexandre Joseph Sébastien** (1789–1869) was also a lawyer and politician; member of the provisional government (1830) and of the National Congress which effected Belgian separation from Holland.

**Gen'dron'** (zhäɴ'drôɴ'), **Auguste.** 1818–1881. French historical painter.

**Ge·née'** *or* **Ge·née'–Is'itt** (shĭ·nē̆z'ĭt), Dame **Adeline.** 1878–1970. Danish dancer; m. Frank S. N. Isitt (1910). In London (1897–1907), U.S. (1908); took own company to U.S. (1912), Australia and New Zealand (1913).

**Ge·née'** (zhē·nā'), **Richard.** 1823–1895. German composer of songs, choral works, operas, and esp. operettas. His brother **Rudolf** (1824–1914) was a writer; gave Shakespearean readings in chief cities of Germany. Their sister **Ottilie** (1836–1911), actress, founded (1869) German theater in San Francisco.

**Ge·nel'li** (jā·nĕl'ē), **Bonaventura.** 1798–1868. German painter and designer of illustrations for Homer and Dante and the books *Leben eines Wüstlings* and *Leben eines Künstlers.*

**Ge·ne'si·us** (jē·nē'shĭ·ŭs; -sĭ·ŭs; -zĭ·ŭs), **Josephus.** *Also* *known as* **Josephus Byz′an·ti′nus** (bĭz′ăn·tī′nŭs). 10th century Byzantine historian; under commission from Emperor Constantine VII, wrote *Porphyrogenitus*, history of the Eastern Empire, 813–886.

**Ge·nest′** (jĕ·nĕst′), **John.** 1764–1839. English historian of the theater; author of *Some Account of the English Stage from the Restoration in 1660 to 1830* (1832).

**Ge·nêt′** (zhē·nĕ′), **Edmond Charles Édouard.** 1763–1834. French diplomat in United States, b. Versailles, France. Appointed first French minister to United States (1792); arrived U.S. (Apr. 8, 1793). Hoped to draw U.S. into France's war against Great Britain and Spain; used his position to outfit privateers in American harbors to prey on British commerce and to intrigue against Spanish territory; attacked Washington for his policy of neutrality; Washington requested his recall; replaced (1794). Became U. S. citizen.

**Ge·net,** (zhē·nĕ′), **Jean.** 1910– . French playwright, author, and poet. Wrote the plays *The Maids* (1947), *The Balcony* (1956), *The Blacks* (1959), etc.; novels; and *The Thief's Journal* (1949).

**Ge·ne·viève′** (zhēn·vyâv′; *Angl.* jĕn′ĕ·vēv′, jĕn′ĕ·vēv), Saint. 422?–512. Patron saint of Paris; reputed to have saved Paris from the Huns by her prayers (451); supported Parisian resistance to Clovis until Clovis was converted to Christianity.

**Ge·ne·voix′** (zhēn·vwȧ′), **Maurice.** 1890– . French novelist; author of *Raboliot* (1925; awarded Goncourt prize), *Nuits de Guerre*, etc.

**Gen′ga** (jĕng′gä), **Girolamo.** 1476?–1551. Italian painter and architect. His son **Bartolommeo** (1516–1558), also an architect and painter.

**Gen′ghis Khan** (jĕng′gĭs kän′). *Also* **Jen′ghiz** (jĕng′gĭz) *or* **Jin′ghis** (jĭng′gĭs) *or* **Chin′ghiz** (chĭng′gĭz) *or* **Chin′giz** (chĭng′gĭz) **Khan.** *Original name* **Tem′u·jin** (tĕm′ŏŏ·jĭn) *or* **Tem′u·chin** (-chĭn). 1162–1227. Mongol conqueror, b. near Lake Baikal. At age of 13 succeeded his father as tribal chief; proclaimed khan of all the Mongols (1206); consolidated his authority among Mongols (1206–12); made his capital at Karakorum. Invaded northern China (1213) and conquered the Kins; subdued Korea (1218); soon embarked on wider conquests in west (1218–22), overcoming shah of Khwarazm (modern Khiva), plundering northern India, and overrunning and subduing what is now Iran, Iraq, and part of Russia; drove Turks before him, who later invaded Europe. A bold leader and military genius, but one who left few permanent institutions. Had four sons: (1) Juji, or Juchi, who died during his father's lifetime, but whose son Batu Khan (*q.v.*) was later khan; (2) Jagatai (*q.v.*), or Chagatai, founder of dynasty that later ruled in Turkestan; (3) Ogadai (*q.v.*), who succeeded his father as khan (1229–41); (4) Tului, or Tulē, whose three sons were all great Mongol leaders (see MANGU KHAN, KUBLAI KHAN, HULAGU).

**Genji.** See MINAMOTO.

**Gen′lis′** (zhäN′lēs′), Comtesse **de.** *Nee* **Stéphanie Félicité du Crest de Saint′-Au′bin′** (dü krĕst′ dē săN′-tō′băN′). 1746–1830. French writer; m. Charles Brulart de Genlis (1762; guillotined, 1793). Governess of the children of the duchesse de Chartres (1777–91). Author of *Adèle et Théodore* (1782), *Les Petits Émigrés* (1798), *Madame de Maintenon* (1806), *Mémoires* (1825).

**Gen·na′di·us II** (jĕ·nā′dĭ·ŭs). *Orig.* **Georgios Scho·la′ri·os** (skô·lä′ryôs; skô·lâr′ĭ·ŏs). Greek scholar and prelate of middle 15th century; patriarch of Constantinople (1453–59).

**Gennaro,** San. See Saint JANUARIUS.

**Ge·noude′** (zhē·nōōd′). *Pseudonym of* **Antoine Eugène Ge·noud′** (zhē·nōō′). 1792–1849. French journalist; founder, with Lamennais, of *Le Défenseur* (1820), soon succeeded by *L'Étoile*, which became the official government organ; revived *Gazette de France* (1825). Took orders after death of his wife (1835).

**Ge′no·ve′si** (jā′nô·vā′sē), **Antonio.** 1712–1769. Italian economist and philosopher.

**Gen′se·ric** (gĕn′sĕ·rĭk; jĕn′-) *or* **Gai′se·ric** (gī′zĕ·rĭk). d. 477 A.D. King of the Vandals (428–477). Invaded Africa from Spain (429) and captured Carthage, making it his capital (439). Sacked Rome (455).

**Gen′si·chen** (gĕn′zĭ·kĕn), **Otto Franz.** 1847–1933. German writer of verse, verse romances, plays and novels.

**Gen′son′né′** (zhäN′sô′nā′), **Armand.** 1758–1793. French revolutionary politician; president of the convention (March, 1793); a leader of the Girondists, guillotined with other Girondists (Oct. 31, 1793).

**Genth** (gĕnt), **Frederick Augustus,** *orig.* **Friedrich August Ludwig Karl Wilhelm.** 1820–1893. Chemist, b. near Hanau, Hesse-Cassel, Germany. To U.S. (1848); opened chemical laboratory, Philadelphia. Professor, U. of Pennsylvania (1872–88). Specialized in study of minerals; discovered 23 new kinds of minerals, one of which, genthite, is named in his honor.

**Genth** (gĕnth), **Lillian.** 1876?–1953. American painter.

**Gen′til′** (zhäN′tē′), **Émile.** 1866–1914. French explorer in French Equatorial Africa.

**Gen·ti′le** (jân·tē′lâ), **Giovanni.** 1875–1944. Italian philosopher; professor, Naples (1898–1906), Palermo (1906–14), Pisa (1914–17), Rome (1917–44). Founded *Giornale Critico della Filosofia Italiana* (1920). Minister of public instruction (1922–24); reformed Italian educational system; president, Supreme Council of Education (1926–28).

**Gentile da Fa′bri·a′no** (dä fä′brē·ä′nô). *Real name* **Gentile Mas′si** (mäs′sē). 1370?–?1427. Italian painter, b. in Fabriano; first great representative of Umbrian school and outstanding among the primitives.

**Gen′ti·le′schi** (jān′tē·lĕs′kē), **Orazio.** 1563–1647. Italian-born painter in England (from 1626); under patronage of King Charles I and duke of Buckingham. His daughter **Artemisia** (1590–?1642) accompanied him to England, where she painted a number of portraits.

**Gen·ti′li** (jân·tē′lē), **Alberico.** *Lat.* **Albericus Gen·ti′lis** (jĕn·tĭ′lĭs). 1552–1608. Italian-born jurist in England; to London as a refugee (1580) because of opinions regarded as heretical; regius professor of civil law at Oxford (1587). Regarded as one of earliest authorities on international law.

**Gen′tle·man** (jĕn′t'l·măn), **Francis.** 1728–1784. Irish actor and playwright.

**Gentz** (gĕnts), **Friedrich von.** 1764–1832. German publicist and diplomat. In Prussian government service (1786–1802); transferred to Austrian service (1802); friend and adviser of Metternich (from c. 1812). Chief secretary of important European congresses, including Vienna (1814–15), Aix-la-Chapelle (1818), Carlsbad (1819), Vienna (1819), Troppau (1820), Laibach (1821), Verona (1822). In his writings, attacked French Revolution and, later, Napoleon; was long subsidized by British government as writer against Napoleon.

**Gentz, Wilhelm.** 1822–1890. German painter, esp. of scenes against an Oriental background.

**Ge·nung′** (jĕ·nŭng′), **John Franklin.** 1850–1919. American rhetorician and Biblical scholar; ordained Baptist clergyman. Teacher, Amherst Coll. (from 1882; professor from 1889). Author of *Practical Elements of Rhetoric* (1885), *The Epic of the Inner Life* (1891), *Ecclesiastes* (1904), *A Guidebook to the Biblical Literature* (1919); edited Tennyson's *In Memoriam* (1884), with textual criticism.

**Geof'frey** (jĕf'rĭ). *Fr.* **Geoffroi.** Name of four counts of Anjou. See Anjou family.

**Geoffrey.** 1158–1186. Count of Brittany; fourth son of Henry II of England. Joined his brothers and the French king in invasion of his father's fief of Normandy (1173), but did homage to his father on latter's promise to give him half the revenues of Brittany (1175). Later (1183–84) warred against his brother Richard.

**Geoffrey.** d. 1212. English prelate. Illegitimate but acknowledged son of Henry II, King of England. Bishop of Lincoln (1173), but never consecrated; resigned (1182); chancellor of England and loyal to father in war with Richard and Philip Augustus (1188–89). Named archbishop of York by Richard (1189), consecrated (1191), enthroned (1194); quarreled with Canterbury, Chancellor William Longchamps, his half brothers Richard and John, and his canons over his demand for contributions for King Richard I's ransom. Led clergy in refusal to pay tax on church property; fled abroad (1207).

**Geoffrey of Mon'mouth** (mŏn'mŭth). 1100?–1154. English ecclesiastic and chronicler; bishop of St. Asaph (1152–54). His *Historia Britonum*, compiled from Nennius and a book of Breton legends (now lost), traced descent of British princes from the Trojans. Its publication was followed within a half century by the cycle of medieval Arthurian romances based partly upon its material. It was abridged by Alfred of Beverley as *Historia de Gestis Regum Britanniae* and translated into Anglo-Norman by Geoffrey Gaimar and Wace, Wace's version being later translated into English by Layamon and Robert of Gloucester.

**Geoffrey the Gram·mar'i·an** (gră·mâr'ĭ·ăn). *Known also as* **Geoffrey Star'key** (stär'kĭ). fl. 1440. English friar who compiled an English-Latin dictionary *Promptorium Parvulorum* (or *Promptuarium Parvulorum Clericorum*) now valued as a record of 15th-century English and East Anglian dialect, and for elucidation of the debased Latin of the period.

**Geof'frin'** (zhô'frăN'), **Marie Thérèse,** *nee* **Ro'det'** (rô'dĕ'). 1699–1777. French patroness of literature; maintained famous salon frequented by fashionable, literary, and artistic persons of the period.

**Geof'froy'** (zhô'frwä'), **Jean.** 1853–1924. French genre painter.

**Geoffroy, Julien Louis.** 1743–1814. French literary critic.

**Geoffroy Saint'-Hi'laire'** (săN'-tē'lâr'), **Étienne.** 1772–1844. French naturalist, b. Étampes; accompanied Napoleon's expedition to Egypt to collect specimens (1798); professor, Paris (1809). Propounded theory of organic unity which held that a single plan of structure prevails throughout animal kingdom; violently opposed by Georges Cuvier, who held that there were four types of structure; Cuvier opposed him also in maintaining the immutability of species. His son **Isidore** (1805–1861), zoologist, succeeded to his professorship, wrote teratological work *Histoire Générale et Particulière des Anomalies de l'Organisation chez l'Homme et les Animaux* (1832), and *Histoire Naturelle Générale des Regnes Organiques* (1854–62).

**George** (jôrj), Saint. d. about 303. Christian martyr; a native of Cappadocia; adopted in time of Edward III as patron saint of England; among legends developed about him was that of his conquest of the dragon (representing the Devil) and rescue of the king's daughter Sabra (representing the Church).

**George.** 1653–1708. Prince of Denmark; m. (1683) Queen Anne of England; deserted cause of her father, James II (1688); naturalized a British subject; created duke of Cumberland (1689). At his wife's accession to the crown (1702), he was designated generalissimo and lord high admiral of England.

**George.** Name of five electors (till 1815) and kings of Hanover. **George I** *to* **IV** = George I *to* IV, kings of Great Britain. **George V** (1819–1878), last king of Hanover (1851–66); son of Ernest Augustus (*q.v.*); a reactionary, refused to yield to Prussia's demands; sided with Austria in Seven Weeks' War (1866); forced to abdicate.

**George.** Name of two landgraves of Hesse-Darmstadt (*q.v.*):

**George I.** 1547–1596. Son of Philip the Magnanimous; landgrave (1567–96); founder of the younger line of the house of Hesse; father of Frederick I of Hesse-Homburg (see Hesse-Homburg).

**George II.** *Called* **the Learned.** 1605–1661. Son of Louis V; landgrave (1626–61); sided with Imperial forces in Thirty Years' War.

**George.** 1826–1902. Prince of Prussia; soldier and playwright; lieutenant general (1860) and general of cavalry (1866). Under pseudonym **Georg Con'rad** (kŏn'rät), wrote plays, including *Yolanthe* (1877), *Sappho* (1887).

**George II.** 1826–1914. Duke (1866–1914) of Saxe-Meiningen (*q.v.*); son of Bernhard II; called to throne on deposition of father; fought in Franco-Prussian War.

**George.** *Surnamed* **the Bearded.** 1471–1539. Duke of Saxony; son and successor of Albert the Bold (d. 1500). Opposed Reformation and debated with Martin Luther.

**George.** *Ger.* **Georg.** 1832–1904. King of Saxony (1902–04). Second son of King John; took part in Seven Weeks' War (1866) and in Franco-Prussian War (1870–71); field marshal general (1888).

**George.** Name of six kings of Great Britain, the first four of the house of Hanover (*q.v.*), the last two of the house of Windsor (*q.v.*), formerly Saxe-Coburg-Gotha:

**George I. George Louis.** 1660–1727. King of Great Britain and Ireland (1714–1727), 1st king of house of Hanover; also, elector of Hanover, as George I (1698–1727). Son of Sophia, Electress of Hanover, granddaughter of James I of England; m. (1682) Sophia Dorothea (*q.v.*), daughter of George William, Duke of Brunswick and Zell. As a Protestant, became heir to English throne by virtue of Act of Settlement (passed 1701). Succeeded to British throne on death of Queen Anne (Aug. 1, 1714); crowned at Westminster (Oct. 20, 1714). Regarding Tory party as favorable to Jacobites and Roman Catholic cause, appointed Whig ministry, with Townshend as secretary of state for northern department, and dissolved the Tory parliament (1715). Early years of reign troubled by Jacobite plots; strengthened position of his house by concluding Triple Alliance (1717) with France and Holland guaranteeing Hanoverian succession; spent many half years in Hanover. Appointed Stanhope chief minister (1717) and Sir Robert Walpole (1721).

**George II.** *In full* **George Augustus.** 1683–1760. King of Great Britain and Ireland (1727–1760); also elector of Hanover (1727–1760). Son of George I; m. (1705) Caroline of Anspach (*q.v.*). Continued father's policy of favoring Whigs for office; retained Sir Robert Walpole as prime minister (to 1742). Became involved in wars on Continent because of his anxiety to protect Hanover (1740–45); commanded in person and won battle of Dettingen (June 27, 1743); lost popular favor by subordinating British interests to Hanoverian interests. Suppressed Jacobite rebellion in Scotland under the Young Pretender (1745) when his army under his son the duke of Cumberland won battle of Culloden Moor (Apr. 27, 1746). Attack by the French upon the

English colonists in America (1754 ff.) caused him to join alliance with Frederick the Great of Prussia (1756). During last years of his reign, British arms were successful in India, Canada, and on the ocean. Quarreled with his son Frederick Louis (c. 1751), who had married Augusta, daughter of duke of Saxe-Coburg-Gotha; succeeded by his grandson George III, son of Frederick Louis.

**George III.** *In full* **George William Frederick.** 1738–1820. King of Great Britain and Ireland (1760–1820); also elector (1760–1815), then king (1815–20) of Hanover. Grandson of George II; m. Charlotte Sophia of Mecklenburg-Strelitz (1761). Early part of reign marked by struggles with ministers and attempt to abolish party system; appointed Bute secretary of state (1761) and prime minister (1762), and acted for some time under his advice; suffered first attack of mental illness (1765). Despite opposition, made North prime minister (1770); through patronage system, personally directed government for twelve years; supported policy that led to war with and loss of American colonies; blocked measures for Roman Catholic emancipation. Saved London by his conduct during Gordon Riots (1780); supported Pitt in elections of 1783 and followed his advice as prime minister; suffered second mental attack (1788–89), and third and fourth attacks (1803–04); opened parliament for last time (1805); took part for last time in forming a ministry, the feeble Perceval ministry (1809–12); became blind and (after 1811) permanently deranged, his son (later George IV) acting as regent till his death (Regency Act, 1811).

**George IV.** *In full* **George Augustus Frederick.** 1762–1830. King of Great Britain and Ireland (1820–30), and king of Hanover. Son of George III. Maintained liaison with Mrs. Fitzherbert (*q.v.*); married her (Dec., 1785; marriage illegal); deserted her (1794); failed in entreaties for her return until she gained assurance of papal approval of marriage (1800); m. (April 8, 1795) his cousin Caroline of Brunswick. Gained ill will of his father by his extravagances and dissolute habits, and by his open association with Fox and Sheridan and other leaders of the parliamentary opposition. Prince regent when his father became permanently deranged (1811–20); succeeded as king (1820). Refused to allow Queen Caroline, from whom he had long been estranged, to be present at his coronation; instituted proceedings for divorce on ground of infidelity, but had to drop the suit because of lack of evidence. During his reign Catholic Emancipation Act passed (1829). Succeeded by his brother William IV.

**George V.** *In full* **George Frederick Ernest Albert.** 1865–1936. King of Great Britain and Northern Ireland, and emperor of India (1910–36), of house of Saxe-Coburg-Gotha, later (1917) changed to house of Windsor (*q.v.*). Son of Edward VII. Became heir apparent (1892) on death of his elder brother, Albert Victor, duke of Clarence; created duke of York (1892); prince of Wales (1901; at father's accession to throne); m. Princess Victoria Mary of Teck (1893). Ascended throne on death of Edward VII (May 6, 1910); crowned king (June 22, 1911) and emperor of India (Dec. 12, 1911). Chief events of his reign, the World War (1914–18), agreement with the Irish Free State (1921).

**George VI.** *In full* **Albert Frederick Arthur George.** 1895–1952. King of Great Britain and Northern Ireland (1936–52), and emperor of India (1936–48), of house of Windsor. Son of George V; m. (April 26, 1923) Lady Elizabeth Bowes-Lyon. Served in World War I; studied at Trinity College, Cambridge (1919). Created duke of York (1920). Succeeded to the throne (Dec. 11, 1936) at abdication of his brother Edward VIII (*q.v.*); crowned (May 12, 1937). With queen, visited Canada and U.S. (1939).

**George.** Name of two kings of Greece:

**George I.** *In full* **Christian William Ferdinand Adolphus George.** 1845–1913. King (1863–1913). Second son of Christian IX of Denmark. Served some time in Danish navy; after deposition (1862) of Otto I, elected king of the Hellenes (1863) by Greek National Assembly and election approved by Great Powers; m. (1867) Grand Duchess Olga, niece of czar of Russia; during reign, greater part of Thessaly and part of Epirus incorporated (1881) in Greece; Cretan insurrection (1896–97) unsuccessful; involved in First Balkan War (1912–13); assassinated at Salonika; succeeded by son Constantine I.

**George II.** 1890–1947. Eldest son of Constantine I and grandson of George I. King (1922–23, 1935–47). m. (1921) Elizabeth, daughter of Ferdinand and Marie of Rumania (divorced (1935); ruled with no actual authority; unpopular; deposed by military junta (1923); recalled to throne as result of plebiscite (1935); overshadowed by Metaxas, who became dictator (1936); fled (1941) from Nazis to Crete and England; restored to throne by plebiscite (1946); succeeded by his brother **Paul I** (1901–1964), who married (1938) Princess **Frederika** (1917– ), dau. of Duke of Brunswick.

**George,** Prince. 1869–1957. Greek prince; high commissioner of Crete (1898–1906). Second son of George I. Commanded flotilla in war against Turkey (1897); appointed high commissioner in Crete (1898) at insistence of czar of Russia; reappointed (1901 and 1904); resigned because of disagreements with Venizelos; banished from Greece (1924); lived in France but later returned to Greece.

**George.** *Surnamed* **Syn·cel'lus** (sĭn·sĕl'ŭs). *Greek* **Gorgios Syn·kel'los** (*Angl.* sĭng·kĕl'ŏs; *mod. Gr.* sĕng'kĕ·lôs). Byzantine ecclesiastic and historian of late 8th and early 9th century A.D.; author of a *Chronicle* of world history.

**George** (zhôrzh), Mlle. *Stage name of* **Marguerite Joséphine Wei'mer'** (vā'mâr'). 1787–1867. French actress; excelled in tragedy roles; rival of Mlle. Duchesnois; member of Théâtre Français company (1802–08). Deserted Paris and played at Vienna, Moscow, and St. Petersburg (1808–13). Rejoined Théâtre Français company (1813–17); played at the Odéon (1821) and at the Porte Saint-Martin (1831); retired (1849). Created many of the roles in plays of Hugo and Dumas père.

**Ge·or'ge** (gā·ōr'gĕ), **Amara.** See under Alexander KAUFMANN.

**George** (jôrj), **David Lloyd.** See David LLOYD GEORGE.

**George,** Sir **Ernest.** 1839–1922. English architect.

**George, Grace.** See under William A. BRADY.

**George, Henry.** 1839–1897. American economist, b. Philadelphia. Sailed as foremast boy to Australia and India (1855–56). Learned printing business (1856–57); employed as typesetter, San Francisco (1859). Obtained editorial position in San Francisco (1866–68). In studying California land boom following railroad development, developed germ of single-tax theory (1868–69); published pamphlet, *Our Land and Land Policy* (1871), containing essence of his theory, namely, that land values represent monopoly power, that the entire tax burden should be laid on land, freeing industry from taxation and equalizing opportunities by destroying monopoly advantage. Expanded his pamphlet into classic work, *Progress and Poverty* (1877–79). Followed publication of book by lecturing and magazine writing; moved to New York (1880); published *The Irish Land*

*Question* (1881); spent year in Ireland and England (1881–82). Wrote series of articles for *Frank Leslie's Illustrated Newspaper*, published as *Social Problems* (1883). Lectured in England and Scotland (1883–84). Published *Protection or Free Trade* (1886). Ran for mayor of New York on social welfare platform (1886); defeated by Abram S. Hewitt, but made strong showing. Again lectured in Great Britain (1888–89), in Australia (1890). Ran again for mayor of New York (1897); stricken with apoplexy near end of speaking campaign; died Oct. 29, 1897. His son **Henry** (1862–1916), a journalist, wrote his father's biography, *Life of Henry George* (1900).

**Ge·or'ge** (gā·ôr'gĕ), **Stefan.** 1868–1933. German poet; associated with Baudelaire and Mallarmé in Paris and with Pre-Raphaelite group in London. Leader of "art for art's sake" school of poetry in Germany.

**George** (jôrj), **Walter Lionel.** 1882–1926. English writer, b. Paris, France. Educ. Paris and Germany; journalist (1907). Served in French army during World War (1914–18). Author of *A Bed of Roses* (1911), *The City of Light* (1912), *Caliban* (1920), *The Confession of Ursula Trent* (1921), *One of the Guilty* (1923), etc.

**George, William Reuben.** 1866–1936. American businessman and philanthropist; founder (1895) of George Junior Republic, self-governing industrial community near Ithaca, N.Y., planned to give an opportunity to neglected or delinquent children to get a fair start in life.

**George of Podĕbrad.** See PODĔBRAD.

**George of Treb'i·zond'** (trĕb'ĭ·zŏnd'). 1396?–?1486. Byzantine scholar; professor of Greek, Venice (1428); papal secretary (1450 ff.); ardent Aristotelian; engaged in controversy with Platonist Gemistus Pletho.

**George the Pi·sid'ian** (pĭ·sĭd'ĭ·ăn). *Greek* **Georgios Pi·si'des** (pĭ·sī'dēz). *Lat.* **Georgius Pi·si'da** (pĭ·sī'dȧ). Byzantine poet. Accompanied Emperor Heraclius in expedition against Persians (622 A.D.) and wrote an epic on this subject.

**Ge·or'ges** (gā·ôr'gĕs), **Karl Ernst.** 1806–1895. German lexicographer.

**Ger'ald de Bar'ri, Bar'ry,** *or* **Bar'y** (jĕr'ăld dĕ băr'ĭ). = GIRALDUS DE BARRI.

**Ger'al·dine** (jĕr'ăl·dēn). A member or supporter of Irish family of Fitzgerald (*q.v.*), comprising earls of Desmond and Kildare, hereditary enemies of Butler family, comprising dukes of Ormonde.

**Ge'ral·di'ni** (jā'räl·dē'nē), **Alessandro.** 1455–1525. Italian prelate; ordained priest in Spain; tutor to Spanish princesses; said to have aided Columbus in obtaining first interview with Ferdinand and Isabella. First bishop of Santo Domingo (1520). Author of account, in Latin, of his voyage to America. His brother **Antonio** (1457–1488) was a Latin poet.

**Gé'ral'dy'** (zhā'rȧl'dē'), **Paul.** 1885– . French poet and playwright.

**Gé'ramb'** (zhā'räɴ'), Baron **François Ferdinand de.** 1772–1848. French Trappist monk; procurator-general of the Trappist Order.

**Gé'ran'do'** (zhā'räɴ'dō'), Baron **Joseph Marie de.** 1772–1842. French politician and philosopher; held high administrative posts under Napoleon, and was created baron (1812); admitted to peerage (1837); among his works are *Théorie des Signes et de l'Art de Penser dans leurs Rapports Mutuels* (1800), *Histoire Comparée des Systèmes de Philosophie Relativement aux Principes des Connaissances Humaines* (1804).

**Ge·rard'** (jĕ·rärd'; *esp. Brit.*, jĕr'ärd, jĕr'ērd). *Surnamed* **the Blessed.** Ecclesiastic; guardian of a hospice for Christian pilgrims in Jerusalem (c. 1100); organized order of Knights of St. John of Jerusalem, recognized by Pope Paschal II (1113) and confirmed by Pope Calixtus II before Gerard's death (1120).

**Gerard, Alexander.** 1728–1795. Scottish philosopher; author of *Essay on Taste* (1759), *Essay on Genius* (1774), etc.

**Gé'rard'** (zhā'rȧr'), **Balthasar.** 1558–1584. Assassin of William, Prince of Orange.

**Ge·rard'** (jĕ·rärd'; *esp. Brit.*, jĕr'ärd, jĕr'ērd), **Charles.** 1st Baron **Gerard of Bran'don** (brăn'dŭn). Viscount **Brandon.** Earl of **Mac'cles·field** (măk''lz·fēld). 1618?–1694. English Royalist commander, of an old Lancashire family. Commanded brigade at Edge Hill (1642); distinguished himself at Newbury (1643) and Newark (1644); commander of Charles I's bodyguard in retreat from Cardiff to Oxford, thence to Chester (1645). At Restoration, returned with Charles II from Breda at head of Life Guards; regained estates; envoy extraordinary to Paris (1662); as adherent of Monmouth, presented by grand jury as disloyal (1684); escaped abroad; returned with William III as commander of bodyguard (1688). His son **Charles** (1659?–1701), 2d earl, b. in France, naturalized in England, participated in intrigues of Monmouth; sentenced to death (1685) for complicity in Rye House Plot (1683); pardoned (1687); envoy extraordinary to Hanover (1701).

**Gé'rard'** (zhā'rȧr'), Comte **Étienne Maurice.** 1773–1852. French soldier in the Napoleonic armies; distinguished himself at Austerlitz (1805); general of brigade (1806) and of division in the Russian campaign (1812); engaged at Waterloo (1815). Exiled from France (1815–17); minister of war under Louis Philippe (1830 and 1834), and created marshal of France; directed siege of Antwerp (1832); appointed senator by Napoleon III (1852).

**Gérard,** Baron **François Pascal.** 1770–1837. French historical and portrait painter; among his historical canvases are *Bataille d'Austerlitz*, *Entrée d'Henri IV à Paris;* among his portraits are those of Napoleon, Moreau, Mme. Récamier, Talleyrand, Emperor Alexander of Russia, Duke of Wellington, Louis XVIII, Charles X, Louis Philippe.

**Ge·rard'** (jĕ·rärd'), **James Watson.** 1867–1951. American lawyer and diplomat; U.S. ambassador to Germany (1913–17). Author of *My Four Years in Germany* (1917), *Face to Face with Kaiserism* (1918).

**Gé'rard'** (zhā'rȧr'), **Jean Ignace Isidore.** See GRANDVILLE.

**Ge·rard'** (jĕ·rärd'; *esp. Brit.*, jĕr'ärd, jĕr'ērd), **John.** 1545–1612. English botanist and barber-surgeon; became superintendent of Burghley's gardens. Published a herbal (1597), and a list of the plants growing in his own London garden. The genus *Gerardia* is named for him.

**Ge·rard'** (jĕ·rärd'), **Richard H.** 1876–1948. b. New York City. American author of words of popular song *Sweet Adeline* (1903; music by Harry Armstrong).

**Gé'rard' d'Alsace** (zhā'rȧr'). See LORRAINE family.

**Gérard de Nerval.** See NERVAL.

**Ge·rard' of Cre·mo'na** (jĕ·rärd' [*esp. Brit.*, jĕr'ärd, -ērd], krĕ·mō'nȧ). 1114?–1187. Translator, esp. from Greek and Arabic into Latin; b. Cremona, Italy; long resident in college of translators established by Archbishop Raymond in Toledo, Spain. Among his translations were works of Aristotle, Ptolemy, al-Kindi, al-Farabi, Avicenna.

**Gerardus Magnus.** See Gerhard GROOTE.

**Géraud, André.** See PERTINAX.

**Gérault, Charles.** 1878– . See PERTINAX.

**Ger'ber** (gĕr'bĕr), **Ernst Ludwig.** 1746–1819. German organist and music historian.

**Gerber, Heinrich,** *in full* **Johann Gottfried Heinrich.** 1832–1912. German engineer; pioneer in construction of cantilever bridges.

**Gerber, Karl Friedrich Wilhelm von.** 1823–1891. German jurist and statesman. Regarded as chief founder, with his friend Jhering, of younger historical school in teaching of law.

**Ger'bert'** (zhĕr'bâr'), See Pope SYLVESTER II.

**Ger'bert von Hor'nau** (gĕr'bĕrt fôn hôr'nou), **Martin.** 1720–1793. German Roman Catholic priest and writer on music.

**Ger·bran'dy** (gĕr·brän'dē), **Pieter S.** 1885–1961. Prime minister 1940–45 of the Netherlands and, after German invasion, of the Netherlands government in exile, London; minister of state (1955–61).

**Ger'gonne'** (zhĕr'gôn'), **Joseph Diez.** 1771–1859. French mathematician; known for work on principle of geometric duality.

**Ger'hard** (*Ger.* gār'härt). See also GERARD.

**Gerhard, Eduard.** 1795–1867. German archaeologist; author of treatises on antique sculpture, Etruscan glass, vases of Apulia, etc.

**Gerhard, Johann.** 1582–1637. German Lutheran theologian; leader of orthodox Lutherans.

**Ger'hard** (gĕr'ĕrd), **William Wood.** 1809–1872. American physician, b. Philadelphia; in paper (publ. 1837) distinguished typhus clearly from typhoid fever; also published paper (1863) on epidemic meningitis.

**Ger·har'die** (jĕr·här'dĭ), **William Alexander.** 1895–1977. English novelist and short-story writer, b. St. Petersburg, Russia. Military attaché at British embassy in Petrograd (1917–18); with British military mission to Siberia (1918–20).

**Gerhards, Gerhard.** See ERASMUS.

**Ger'hardt'** (zhā'rȧr'), **Charles Frédéric.** 1816–1856. French chemist. Prepared acid anhydrides; experimented on homologous series and on the type theory; proposed a classification of organic compounds.

**Ger'hardt** (gār'härt), **Dagobert von.** *Pseudonym* **Gerhard von A·myn'tor** (ä·mün'tôr). 1831–1910. German soldier and writer; best known for novels, including *Frauenlob* (2 vols., 1885), *Ein Kampf um Gott* (1902).

**Gerhardt, Elena.** 1883–1961. German concert singer; m. Dr. Fritz Kohl (1932); best known as a lieder singer.

**Gerhardt, Paul.** 1607–1676. German Lutheran clergyman and hymn writer. Made German translation (from Latin) of *O Sacred Head Now Wounded;* author of German original of *Jesus, Thy Boundless Love to Me.*

**Gé'ri'cault'** (zhā'rē'kō'), **Jean Louis André Théodore.** 1791–1824. French painter; by his unorthodox coloring and bold designs, he broke the classical tradition and had important influence in inaugurating the romantic movement in French art.

**Ge'rick·e** (gā'rĭ·kĕ), **Wilhelm.** 1845–1925. Orchestra conductor, b. Gratz, Styria, Austria. Conductor in Vienna (1880; 1889–95). In U.S., conducted Boston Symphony Orchestra (1884–89; 1898–1906).

**Ge'ring** (gā'rĭng), **Ulrich.** d. 1510. Swiss-born printer in Paris; commissioned (c. 1470) by Sorbonne professors Heynlin and Fichet to establish a printing press, the first to be set up in France.

**Gé'rin'-La'joie'** (zhā'răN'lȧ'jwä'), **Antoine.** 1824–1882. Canadian editor and writer.

**Ger'lach** (gĕr'läκ), **Hellmuth von.** 1866–1935. German politician; a founder of the National-Social Union (1896), and member of Reichstag (1903–06); a founder of the Democratic party (1918); president, League for German Rights. Editor in chief, *Welt am Montage* (1901–31), wherein he presented his pacifist convictions; exiled from Germany when Hitler gained power (1933).

**Gerlach, Leopold von.** 1790–1861. Prussian soldier; general of infantry (1859). His brother **Ernst Ludwig** (1795–1877) was a Prussian jurist and politician; founder (1848) of Conservative party in Prussia, and of its journal, *Kreuzzeitung;* later, member of center group in Prussian legislature (1870–76) and Reichstag (1877). Another brother, **Otto** (1801–1849), was a Protestant clergyman; court preacher in Berlin (1847).

**Gerlach, Walther.** 1889– . German physicist.

**Ger'lache'** (zhĕr'lȧsh'), **Adrien de.** *Also known as* **Gerlache de Go'me·ry'** (dē gôm'rē'). 1866–1934. Belgian naval officer and explorer; conducted Antarctic exploration in ship *Belgica* (1897–99) and was technical director on expedition of Louis Philippe Robert, Duc d'Orléans, in polar regions (1905).

**Gerlache,** Baron **Étienne Constantin de.** 1785–1871. Belgian jurist and statesman; successfully advocated offering crown of Belgium to Duke Leopold of Saxe-Coburg (1831). First president, Belgian court of cassation (1832–67).

**Ger'land** (gĕr'länt), **Georg Karl Cornelius.** 1833–1919. German philologist, ethnologist, and geographer.

**Ger'loff** (gĕr'lôf), **Wilhelm.** 1880–1954. German economist.

**Ger'main'** (zhĕr'măN'), Saint. *Latin* **Ger·ma'nus** (jûr·mā'nŭs). 378?–448 A.D. French ecclesiastic; bishop of Auxerre (418 A.D.). To Britain (429) and successfully controverted the Pelagian heresy; visited Britain again (447) and again defeated the Pelagians in disputation.

**Germain,** Saint. 496?–576. French ecclesiastic; bishop of Paris (555); participated in Council of Paris (557 and 573) and Council of Tours (566); consecrated Church of Saint Vincent in Paris (558); later dedicated to him under the name of Saint Germain des Prés.

**Ger'main** (jûr'măn; -mān), Lord **George** and his son **Charles Sackville.** See under SACKVILLE family.

**Ger'main'** (zhĕr'măN'), **Sophie.** 1776–1831. French mathematician; associate of Lagrange and Gauss; awarded prize by Institute of France for her treatise on vibration of elastic plates.

**Germaine de Foix.** See FOIX.

**Ger'man** (jûr'măn), Sir **Edward.** *Orig. name* **Edward German Jones.** 1862–1936. English conductor and composer; best known for his incidental music for a number of Shakespeare's plays; composed also operas, as *Merry England, Tom Jones,* and two symphonies, and chamber music.

**German, William Manley.** 1851–1933. Canadian lawyer and legislator; one of leaders of Conservative party in struggle to break U.S. power monopoly at Niagara Falls; interested in promoting St. Lawrence waterway.

**Ger·man'i·cus** (jûr·măn'ĭ·kŭs). An agnomen of: (1) Nero Claudius DRUSUS; (2) emperor CLAUDIUS I; (3) emperor NERO; (4) BRITANNICUS.

**Germanicus Cae'sar** (sē'zēr). 15 B.C.–19 A.D. Son of Nero Claudius Drusus and nephew of Emperor Tiberius. Roman general; campaigned against the Germans (11–16 A.D.), and defeated Arminius (16); received a triumph in Rome (17). Through jealousy of Tiberius was assigned command of Eastern provinces (17); died near Antioch, perhaps poisoned by orders of the emperor (19). By his wife Agrippina, granddaughter of Augustus, was father of nine children, including the emperor Caligula, and Agrippina, mother of Nero.

**Ger'ma·nos'** (yâr'mä·nôs'). 1771–1826. Greek patriot; archbishop of Patras; gave signal (Mar. 25, 1821) for outbreak of revolution which freed Greece from the Turks. March 25th is celebrated as Independence Day in Greece.

**Germanus,** Saint. See Saint GERMAIN.

**Ger'mer** (gûr'mẽr), **Lester Hal'bert** (hăl'bẽrt). 1896–1971. American physicist; discoverer (with Clinton J. Davisson) of electron diffraction in crystals (1927); made investigations in thermionics and surface chemistry.

**Ger'nez'** (zhĕr'nâz'), **Désiré Jean Baptiste.** 1834–1910. French chemist. Collaborated with Pasteur in researches on wine and on maladies of silk worms; investigated rotary power of various liquids, crystallization in supersaturated solutions, boiling, etc.

**Ge'ro** (gā'rō). d. 965. German margrave and duke of Ostmark; conquered tribes between Elbe and Oder rivers; referred to in the *Nibelungenlied*, where the "Grosse Markgraf" is called "Marcgrâve Gêre."

**Gé'rôme'** (zhā'rōm'), **Jean Léon.** 1824–1904. French painter, b. Vesoul. Studied under Paul Delaroche and in Italy (1844–45). Professor at École des Beaux-Arts (Paris; 1863). Executed also a number of sculptures.

**Ge·ron'i·mo** (jĕ·rŏn'ĭ·mō). *Indian name* **Goyathlay,** *i.e.* One Who Yawns. 1829–1909. American Apache chieftain, b. in southern Arizona; led sensational campaign (1885–86) against the whites; finally captured by Gen. Crook; escaped, and captured by Capt. Lawton; surrendered to Gen. Miles, who had relieved Crook. Finally settled with members of his tribe as farmers and stock raisers at Fort Sill, Okla.; joined Dutch Reformed Church (1903); dictated autobiography (1906).

**Ger'ould** (jĕr'ŭld), **Gordon Hall.** 1877–1953. American philologist; teacher of English at Princeton (from 1905; professor from 1916). Author of *The North English Homily Collection* (1902), *The Ballad of Tradition* (1932), *How to Read Fiction* (1937), etc., also of the novels *Peter Sanders, Retired* (1917), *Youth in Harley* (1920), *A Midsummer Mystery* (1925). He married (1910) **Katharine Ful'ler·ton** [fŏŏl'ẽr·tŭn; -t'n] (1879–1944), b. Brockton, Mass., short-story writer and essayist; author of *Vain Oblations* (1914), *A Change of Air* (1917), *Modes and Morals* (essays; 1919), *Valiant Dust* (1922), *The Light That Never Was* (1931), *Ringside Seats* (1937), etc.

**Ger'ry** (gĕr'ĭ), **Elbridge.** 1744–1814. American statesman, b. Marblehead, Mass. Member, Massachusetts Provincial Congress (1774–75); Continental Congress (1776–81, 1782–85); a signer of Declaration of Independence, and also of Articles of Confederation. Delegate to Constitutional Convention (1787); opposed the Constitution as drafted. Member, U.S. House of Representatives (1789–93). Member, famous X Y Z mission to France (1797–98); at odds with Marshall and Pinckney, his fellow negotiators; tried to negotiate separate terms with Talleyrand; recalled (1798). Governor of Massachusetts (1810, 1811). During second term the redistricting of Massachusetts in a way planned to give Republicans continued control gave rise to famous term "gerrymander." Vice-president of the United States (1813–14).

**Gerry, Elbridge Thomas.** 1837–1927. Grandson of Elbridge Gerry. American lawyer and philanthropist; practiced, New York. Counsel for Society for Prevention of Cruelty to Animals (from 1870). A founder, New York Society for Prevention of Cruelty to Children (incorporated 1875); withdrew from law work to devote his time to this charity; president (1879–1901); society became popularly known as Gerry's Society. Also, active in obtaining substitution of electric chair for hanging; in procuring more humane treatment of insane; trustee, American Museum of Natural History (1895–1902).

**Ger'shom ben Ju'dah** (gûr'shŏm bĕn jōō'dȧ). 960–1040. Rabbi, b. Metz; resident for many years at Mainz; founder of Talmudic study in France and Germany; revised text of Mishnah and Talmud, and published Biblical exegetical treatises.

**Gershon, Levi ben.** See LEVI BEN GERSHON.

**Gersh'win** (gûrsh'wĭn), **George.** 1898–1937. American composer, b. Brooklyn, N.Y. Author esp. of musical comedies and orchestral works; wrote music scores for *George White's Scandals* (1920–24); symphonic jazz compositions *Rhapsody in Blue* (1923), *Piano Concerto in F* (1925); musical comedies, *Lady Be Good* (1924), *Funny Face* (1927), *Girl Crazy* (1930), *Of Thee I Sing* (1931; awarded Pulitzer prize); the opera *Porgy and Bess*, etc. His brother **Ira** (1896– ) wrote the lyrics for many of his musical comedies.

**Ger'son'** (zhĕr'sôN'), **Jean de.** *Orig. surname* **Char'lier'** (shȧr'lyā'). 1362–?1428. French theologian; attempted to forward church unity and ecclesiastical reforms.

**Ger'son** (gĕr'sôn), **Wojciech.** 1831–1901. Polish historical painter.

**Gersonides.** See LEVI BEN GERSHON.

**Ger'stäck'er** (gĕr'stĕk'ẽr), **Friedrich.** 1816–1872. German traveler and writer; author of many novels and adventure stories.

**Ger'sten·berg** (gûr'stĕn·bûrg), **Alice.** American writer, b. Chicago. Educ. Bryn Mawr. Author of *Unquenched Fire* (novel, 1912), *Overtones* (play, 1915), and a number of one-act plays.

**Ger'sten·berg** (gĕr'stĕn·bĕrK), **Heinrich Wilhelm von.** 1737–1823. Danish poet and critic, b. in Germany. Chief work of literary criticism was *Briefe über Merkwürdigkeiten der Literatur* (vols. 1–3, 1766–71; vol. 4, 1770), which formulated critical principles of German Sturm und Drang movement.

**Ger'trude** (gûr'trōōd), Saint. 1256–1311. German saint; known as "Gertrude the Great"; famed for supernatural visions.

**Gertrude.** d. 1143. Daughter of Emperor Lothair II; m. Henry the Proud, of Bavaria (1127); mother of Henry the Lion, of Bavaria.

**Gertsen, Aleksandr Ivanovich.** See Aleksandr I. HERZEN.

**Ger'vais'** (zhĕr'vĕ'), **Paul,** *in full* **François Louis Paul.** 1816–1879. French naturalist. Known esp. for researches on Tertiary mammals.

**Ger'vaise** (jûr'vās). Variant of GERVASE.

**Ger'vase of Can'ter·bur'y** (jûr'vās ŭv kăn'tẽr·bĕr'ĭ; -bẽr·ĭ; -brĭ). *Latin* **Ger·va'si·us Do'ro·bor·nen'sis** (jẽr·vā'zhĭ·ŭs dō'rō·bôr·nĕn'sĭs). fl. 1188. English monk and chronicler; author of a history of the archbishops of Canterbury from Augustine to Hubert Walter, a Canterbury chronicle (from the accession of Stephen to the death of Richard I), and a *Gesta Regum*.

**Gervase of Til'bur·y** (tĭl'bẽr·ĭ). fl. 1211. English ecclesiastic and writer; wrote for Emperor Otto IV of Germany his *Otia Imperialia*, a medley of medieval legends and superstitions.

**Ger'vex'** (zhĕr'vĕks'), **Henri.** 1852–1929. French painter; identified with the impressionist school.

**Ger·vi'nus** (gĕr·vē'nŏŏs), **Georg Gottfried.** 1805–1871. German historian.

**Ge·sell'** (gĕ·zĕl'), **Arnold Lucius.** 1880–1961. American psychologist and pediatrician, b. Alma, Wis.; M.D., Yale (1915); on teaching staff, Yale (from 1911); founder (1911) and director, Yale Clinic of Child Development; author (with collaborators) of *An Atlas of Infant Behavior* (2 vols.; 1934), *The First Five Years* (1940), etc.

**Ge·sell'** (gĕ·zĕl'), **Silvio.** 1862–1930. German merchant and economist, b. in Belgium; lived chiefly in Buenos Aires (1887–1914) and Germany (after 1914); known esp. for his emphasis on the velocity of money circulation and advocacy of stamped paper currency as a medium of exchange. Author of *Die Verstaatlichung des Geldes* (1891), etc.

**Ge·sel'li·us** (gĕ·sĕl'ĭ·o͝os), **Herman.** **1874–1916. Finnish architect. See G. E. Saarinen.**

**Ge·sel'schap** (gĕ·zĕl'skäp), **Eduard.** 1814–1878. Dutch genre painter.

**Ge·se'ni·us** (gā·zā'nē·o͝os), **Wilhelm.** 1786–1842. German Protestant theologian and Hebrew scholar; author of a Hebrew grammar (1813) and works on the languages of the Old Testament.

**Ges'ner** (gĕs'nĕr), **Johann Matthias.** 1691–1761. German classical philologian.

**Gesner,** *incorrectly* **Gess'ner, Konrad von.** 1516–1565. Swiss naturalist; collected and described plants and animals of New and Old World, his *Historia Animalium* (1551–58) being considered basis of modern zoology.

**Ges'si** (jĕs'sē), **Romolo.** 1831–1881. Italian explorer in Africa.

**Gess'ler** (gĕs'lĕr), **Otto.** 1875–1955. German statesman; minister of reconstruction (1919–20); succeeded Noske as Reichswehr minister (1920); minister of defense (1920–28); collaborated with General von Seeckt in reorganizing Reichswehr.

**Gess'ner** (gĕs'nĕr), **Konrad von.** See Gesner.

**Gessner, Salomon.** 1730–1788. Swiss poet and artist; as artist, known for landscapes and etchings; as poet, wrote *Daphnis* (1754), *Idyllen* (1756), and *Der Tod Abels* (1758), an idyll in rhythmical prose, translated into most European languages.

**Gest** (gĕst), **Morris.** 1881–1942. Theatrical producer, b. Wilno, Russia; to U.S. (1893), and settled in Boston. Partner with F. Ray Comstock (1905–28); lessee of Manhattan Opera House in New York (1911–20) and Century Theatre in New York (1917–20). Introduced original Russian ballet in New York, Baliev's Chauve-Souris (1922), Moscow Art Theatre in repertory (1923–25), etc. Operated independently as Morris Gest, Inc. (from 1928).

**Ge'ta** (jē'tȧ), **Publius Septimius.** 189–212. Second son of Septimius Severus. Joint emperor (211–212) with his brother Caracalla, who caused his murder.

**Get'ty** (gĕt'ĭ), **George Washington.** 1819–1901. American army officer; in Civil War, brigadier general of volunteers (1862); distinguished for defense of Suffolk, Va. (1863); with Sheridan's Army of the Shenandoah (1864); with Army of the Potomac (1865).

**Geu'lincx** (gû'lĭngks), **Arnold.** 1625–1669. Cartesian philosopher, b. Antwerp; joined Protestant church and became professor at Leiden (1665); founded metaphysical theory known as occasionalism.

**Ge'vaert** (gā'vȧrt), **François Auguste.** 1828–1908. Belgian musical scholar and composer of operas, cantatas, orchestral works, choral pieces, and songs.

**Geyl** (gīl), **Pieter.** 1887-1966. Dutch historian; professor, London U. (1919–36) and Utrecht (1936 ff.).

**Gey'mül'ler** (gī'mül'ĕr), Baron **Heinrich von.** 1839–1909. Austrian art scholar and writer.

**Gey'ser** (gī'zĕr), **Josef.** 1869–1948. German philosopher; made special study of the theory of knowledge.

**Ge·zel'le** (gĕ·zĕl'ĕ), **Guido.** 1830–1899. Flemish poet; vicar (1871) at Kortrijk (Courtrai); head of cloister at Bruges (1898). A leader in movement for revival of Flemish as a literary language.

**Gfrö'rer** (g'frû'rĕr), **August Friedrich.** 1803–1861. German religious historian.

**Ghas·sa'nid** (gă·sä'nĭd). Christianized Arab dynasty originating in a South Arabian tribe and ruling (5th century to 636 A.D.) in Northern Arabia (Palestine, Trans-Jordan and region around Palmyra).

**Gha·zan' Khan** (gä·zän' kän). 1271–1304. Mongol ruler (Il-khan) of Persia (1295–1304). Extended dominions and established reforms; friendly to Christians; in alliance with Templars (1299) defeated Mohammedan sultans of Damascus and Egypt; captured Damascus and entered Jerusalem; later defeated, and abandoned Syria; made Mohammedanism established religion of Persia.

**Gha'zi I** (gä'zē). 1912–1939. Son of King Faisal of Iraq. King of Iraq (1933–39); killed in automobile accident; succeeded by his three-year-old son, Faisal II (*q.v.*).

**Ghaz'ne·vid** (gŭz'nĕ·vĭd) *or* **Ghaz'ne·vide** (-vīd). Name of Moslem dynasty (977–1186) of Turkic speech ruling in southwestern Asia with its capital at Ghazni (Afghanistan). It was founded (977) by Subuktigin and its greatest ruler was Mahmud of Ghazni (*q.v.*); overcome by sultan of Ghor (1186). See Samanid.

**Ghaz·za'li** *or* **Gha·za'li, al-** (ăl'gă(z)·zä'lē). *Lat.* **Al'ga·zel'** (ăl'gȧ·zĕl'). *Arab.* **Abu-Ḥāmid Muḥammad al-Ghazzāli.** 1058–1111. Arab philosopher; native of Khurasan; one of great figures of Moslem religious thought; by some called "Father of the Church in Islam." Taught at Baghdad (1091–95); gave up teaching to become mystical ascetic. Showed distrust of scholastic theology and of intellectualism in his writings.

**Ghee'raerts** (gā'rȧrts) *or* **Gee'rarts** (gā'rärts) *or* **Ge'rards** (gā'rärts), **Marcus.** Flemish-born painters, father (1510?–?1590) and son (1561–1635); resident in England (from 1568) as Protestant refugees.

**Ghe'rar·de'sca, del'la** (dāl'lä gā'rär·dās'kä). Italian noble family of Tuscan origin, prominent Ghibelline leaders in Pisa and enemies of the Visconti in 13th and 14th centuries. **Ugolino della Gherardesca,** Conte **di Do'no·ra'ti·co** [dē dō'nō·rä'tē·kō] (1220?–1289), also known as **Ugolino da Pi'sa** (dä pē'sä), celebrated by Dante in *Divina Commedia* (Inferno, XXXIII); conspired to seize power in Pisa; imprisoned and wealth confiscated (1274); escaped and allied himself with Florentine and Luccan Guelphs then at war with Pisa; forced restitution of his territories (1276); reputedly contrived defeat of Pisans by Genoese at battle of Meloria (1284); appointed captain general of Pisa; overthrown by conspiracy led by Ruggiero Ubaldini, Archbishop of Pisa; imprisoned (July, 1288) with two sons, Gaddo and Uguccione, and two grandsons, Ugolino and Anselmuccio, in tower of Gualandi (since called Torre di Fame), where they were starved to death.

**Ghe·rar'di del Te'sta** (gā·rär'dē dāl tĕs'tä), Count **Tommaso.** 1814–1881. Italian poet, playwright, and novelist.

**Ghib'el·line** (gĭb'ĕ·lĭn; -lēn; -līn). *Ital.* **Ghi'bel·li'no** (gē'bāl·lē'nō). Name in Italy (12th to 15th century) of supporters of the Hohenstaufen in Germany against the Welfs (see also Waiblingen). See Guelph.

**Ghi·ber'ti** (gē·bĕr'tē), **Lorenzo.** *Orig. name* **Lorenzo di Cio'ne di Ser Buo'nac·cor'so** (dē chō'nā dē sĕr bwô'näk·kōr'sō). 1378–1455. Florentine goldsmith, painter, and sculptor. Painted frescoes for palace of Carlo Malatesta at Rimini. Awarded commission (1403) to construct bronze doors of baptistery of San Giovanni (Florence); completed north portals (1424), east portals (1447).

**Ghi'ka** *or* **Ghi'ca** *or* **Ghy'ka** (gē'kä). Princely family of Moldavia and Walachia, descended from the Albanian-born **George Ghika** (1600?–1664), designated hospodar of Moldavia (1658) and of Walachia (1660). The family includes notably: **Gregory** hospodar of Walachia (1660–64; 1672–74); made prince of the Holy Roman Empire by Emperor Leopold I; **Alexander,** hospodar of Walachia (1834–42); **Gregory** (1807–1857), of Moldavia (1849–56); **Jon** (yôn) (1817–1897), premier of Walachia (1866–67; 1870–71) and ambassador to Great Britain (1881–89). See also Dora d'Istria.

**Ghil** (gēl), **René.** 1862–1925. French poet of Belgian birth; advanced (1888) a theory of basing poetry on science, and endeavored to create "scientific poetry."

**Ghir'lan·da'jo** *or* **Ghir'lan·da'io** (gēr'län·dä'yō) *or* **Gril'lan·da'jo** (grēl'län·dä'yō). *Pseudonyms of* **Domenico di Tom·ma'so Bi·gor'di** (dē tôm·mä'zō bē·gōr'dē). 1449–1494. Florentine painter and mosaicist, b. Florence. Founder of a school of painting; teacher of Michelangelo. Best known for his frescoes in the Palazzo Vecchio, the choir of Santa Maria Novella, and the church of the Innocenti, all in Florence; aided in decorating the Sistine Chapel at the Vatican (1483). His son **Ridolfo Ghirlandajo** (1483–1561) was also a painter; an admirer of Leonardo da Vinci and later of Raphael; his *Coronation of the Virgin* hangs in the Louvre.

**Ghis·lan'di** (gēz·län'dē), Fra **Vittore.** *Known also as* Fra **Pa'o·lot'to** (pä'ō·lôt'tō) *or* Fra **Gal·ga'rio** (gäl·gä'ryō). 1655–1743. Italian painter and Franciscan monk; known esp. for portraits.

**Ghis'lan·zo'ni** (gēz'län·tsō'nē), **Antonio.** 1824–1893. Italian opera singer and writer; lost voice (1854); founded comic paper *L'Uomo di Pietra* (1857); published *Gazetta Musicale* (Milan); wrote opera librettos.

**Ghiyas-ud-din Tughlak.** See TUGHLAK.

**Ghor,** House of. See GHURI.

**Ghorm'ley** (gôrm'lĭ), **Robert Lee.** 1883–1958. American naval officer, b. Portland, Ore.; grad. U.S.N.A., Annapolis (1906); advanced through the grades to vice-admiral (1941); director of war plans division, U.S. Navy Department (1938–39); assistant to chief of naval operations (1939–40); special naval observer, London, Eng. (1940–42); as commander of Allied naval forces in South Pacific (May–Oct., 1942), directed attack against the Solomon Islands (Aug., 1942).

**Ghose** (gōs), Sri **Aurobindo.** 1872–1950. Indian Yoga philosopher. Prominent in nationalist movement (1907); editor of various periodicals (1914–20); subsequently resident in Pondichéry leading life of a Yogi.

**Ghu'ri** (gōō'rē) *or* **Ghu'rides** (gōō'rīdz). *Called also* **House of Ghor** (gōr) *from a district in northwestern Afghanistan.* Moslem (Afghan) dynasty of medieval Persia (c. 1148–1215). Founded by Ala ud-Din and brothers; captured Ghazni (1148, 1155)—see GHAZNEVID; its most famous prince, Mohammed of Ghor (*q.v.*), conquered northern India (1186–1206).

**Ghyka.** See GHIKA.

**Gia'co·mo** (jä'kō·mō), **Salvatore di.** 1862–1934. Italian author of plays, dialect poems, and historical studies.

**Gia'co'mot'ti'** (*Fr.* jà'kô'mô'tē'; *Ital.* jä'kō·môt'tē), **Félix Henri.** 1828–1909. French painter of Italian descent.

**Gia·co'sa** (jä·kō'sä), **Giuseppe.** 1847–1906. Italian dramatist; attempted to free Italian stage from foreign influence. Collaborated on librettos of *La Bohème, Madame Butterfly.*

**Giae'ver** (yā'vẽr), **Ivar.** 1929– . Norwegian physicist. With General Electric Co. in Canada (1954–56) and U.S. (1956– ); awarded (with Leo Esaki and Brian Josephson) Nobel prize for physics (1973).

**Gialong.** *Orig.* **Nguyen-Anh.** d. 1820. King of Annam, Indo-China (1798–1820). Secured throne (1798) with aid of French; founded Nguyen dynasty (1801) ruling Annam, Tonkin, and Cochin China.

**Giambelli, Federigo.** See GIANIBELLI.

**Giamberti, Antonio** and **Giuliano.** See SANGALLO.

**Gia'ni·bel'li** (jä'nē·bĕl'lē) *or* **Giam·bel'li** (jäm·bĕl'lē), **Federigo.** Italian military engineer in service of Queen Elizabeth, esp. when England was threatened by Spanish Armada.

**Gian·no'ne** (jän·nō'nā), **Pietro.** 1676–1748. Italian historian; known esp. for his monumental work *Storia Civile del Regno di Napoli* (4 vols., 1723).

**Gianuzzi, Giulio de'.** See Giulio ROMANO.

**Giard** (zhyȧr), **Alfred Mathieu.** 1846–1908. French biologist; advocate of transformism; investigated parasitic castration and its effect on secondary sex characters and on the morphology of the individual.

**Giar·di'ni** (jär·dē'nē), **Felice di.** 1716–1796. Italian violinist and composer of violin pieces, chamber music, and several operas.

**Giar·di'no** (jär·dē'nō), **Gaetano.** 1864–1935. Italian soldier; commander of 48th brigade in attack on Gorizia (1916); lieutenant general (1917) and minister of war; commanded attack forcing Austrian retreat (Oct. 24–Nov. 3, 1918); promoted general (1919); took military control of Fiume (1923) until it was annexed to Italy (Jan., 1924).

**Gi·auque'** (jē·ōk'), **William Francis.** 1895– . American chemist; known for discovery (with Herrick Lee Johnston) of oxygen isotopes, and for discovery of adiabatic demagnetization method of producing temperatures below 1° absolute. Awarded Nobel prize in chemistry (1949).

**Gibb** (gĭb), Sir **Hamilton Alexander Rosskeen.** 1895–1971. English Orientalist; served in World War I; author of treatises on Arabic culture and literature.

**Gib'bon** (gĭb'ŭn), **Edward.** 1737–1794. English historian; M.P. (1774–80; 1781–83); settled in Lausanne (1783). His chief work was *The History of the Decline and Fall of the Roman Empire* (vol. I, 1776; vols. II & III, 1781; vols. IV & V, 1788). In prolonged controversy over his account of rise of Christianity defended only fidelity as historian, as in *Vindication* (1779).

**Gibbon, John.** 1827–1896. American army officer; brigadier general of volunteers (May 2, 1862); his brigade became known as the "Iron Brigade".

**Gibbon, John Murray.** 1875–1952. Canadian publicist, b. in Ceylon. General publicity agent of Canadian Pacific Railway (from 1913); instrumental in aiding Canadian authors to secure adequate copyright protection; student of Canadian history and folk literature.

**Gibbon, Perceval.** 1879–1926. British journalist and war correspondent, b. in Carmarthenshire, Wales. Author of *African Items* (verse), the novels *Souls in Bondage, Salvator, Margaret Harding,* and many short stories.

**Gib'bons** (gĭb'ŭnz), **Abigail,** *nee* **Hop'per** (hŏp'ẽr). 1801–1893. Dau. of Isaac Tatem Hopper. American abolitionist and social reformer; m. (1833) James Sloan Gibbons (*q.v.*). Resident, New York City (from 1835). Aided in establishment of Protestant Asylum for Infants; president, Women's Prison Association; a founder of Isaac T. Hopper Home for discharged prisoners.

**Gibbons, Floyd Phillips.** 1887–1939. American journalist; war correspondent for Chicago *Tribune;* with Villa in Mexican Revolution (1915), with Pershing on Mexican punitive expedition (1916). Was on torpedoed liner *Laconia* when sunk (Feb. 25, 1917) and, after his rescue, cabled account of disaster. War correspondent in France (1918); lost eye in battle of Château-Thierry.

**Gibbons, Grinling.** 1648–1720. English woodcarver and sculptor, b. Rotterdam, of Dutch origin. Employed by Sir Christopher Wren to carve the stalls in St. Paul's and other new London churches; did work for the king at Windsor, Whitehall, and Kensington.

**Gibbons, Herbert Adams.** 1880–1934. American journalist and historian; correspondent for New York *Herald* in France and Near East (1908–18); staff correspondent, *Century Magazine* (1919–21) and *Christian Science Monitor* (1922). Author of many historical books, including *The New Map of Europe* (1914), *Europe Since 1918* (1923), *Contemporary World History* (1934), etc.

**Gibbons, James.** 1834–1921. American Roman Catholic cardinal, b. Baltimore, Md. Grad. St. Charles College, near Baltimore (1858). Ordained priest (1861). In charge of St. Bridget's church, near Baltimore, and chaplain at Fort McHenry near by (1861–65). Consecrated titular bishop of Adramyttium (1868); head of the vicariate apostolic of North Carolina. Bishop of Richmond, Va. (1872); bishop of Baltimore (1877). Instrumental in establishing Catholic U., Washington, D.C. Created cardinal by Pope Leo XIII (1886). Gained respect of all classes by his judicious policies.

**Gibbons, James Sloan.** 1810–1892. American abolitionist; to New York (1835); in banking business there. Active member of American Anti-Slavery Society, but opposed Garrison's disunion policies; home sacked by mobs in antidraft riots (July 13–16, 1863). Author of the war song, *We are coming, Father Abraham, three hundred thousand strong*. See Abigail Hopper GIBBONS.

**Gibbons, Orlando.** 1583–1625. English organist and composer; best known for his sacred music, which gained him the title "English Palestrina"; published also madrigals, motets, and fantasies. His brothers **Edward** (1570?–?1653) and **Ellis** (1573–1603) and his son **Christopher** (1615–1676) were all organists and composers.

**Gibbons Stella Dorothea.** 1902– . Eng. poet and nov.; m. (1933) Allan Bourne Webb (1907–59). Her verse includes *The Mountain Beast* (1930), *The Priestess* (1934); her fiction includes *Cold Comfort Farm* (1932), *Miss Linsey and Pa* (1936), *Nightingale Wood* (1938).

**Gibbons, Thomas.** 1720–1785. English dissenting minister and poet; author of hymns.

**Gibbons, Thomas.** 1757–1826. See under Aaron OGDEN.

**Gibbs** (gĭbz), **Arthur Hamilton.** See under Sir Philip GIBBS.

**Gibbs, George.** 1815–1873. American historian and ethnologist; settled in Columbia, Ore. (1849); made study of Indians in the northwest. His brother **Oliver Wolcott** (1822–1908) was a chemist; known for investigations of vapor densities, platinum metals, and ammonia-cobalt bases. His father **George Gibbs** (1776–1833), b. Bristol, R.I., was a mineralogist.

**Gibbs, George.** 1870–1942. American fiction writer and illustrator. Among the many tales which he wrote and illustrated are *Pike and Cutlass* (1900), *The Splendid Outcast* (1920), *The Joyous Conspirator* (1927), *The Isle of Illusion* (1929), *The Vanishing Idol* (1936).

**Gibbs, Henry Hucks.** See ALDENHAM.

**Gibbs, James.** 1682–1754. British architect.

**Gibbs, James Ethan Allen.** 1829–1902. American inventor of improvements in sewing machines (patented 1856–57); in partnership with James Willcox, Philadelphia, in making Willcox & Gibbs sewing machines.

**Gibbs, Josiah Willard.** 1790–1861. American philologist; publ. translation of a German-Hebrew dictionary, *Hebrew and English Lexicon of the Old Testament including the Biblical Chaldee* (1824). His son **Josiah Willard** (1839–1903) was a physicist, b. New Haven, Conn.; Ph.D., Yale (1863). Professor of mathematical physics, Yale (1871–1903). Author of *On the Equilibrium of Heterogeneous Substances* (1876, 1878), *Elementary Principles in Statistical Mechanics* (1902), and papers on mathematical physics. His investigations established the basic theory for physical chemistry. Elected to American Hall of Fame (1950).

**Gibbs, Oliver Wolcott.** See under George GIBBS.

**Gibbs,** Sir **Philip.** 1877–1962. English journalist, editor, and novelist; war correspondent with French and Belgian armies (1914) and British armies (1915–18); editor, *Review of Reviews* (1921–22). His many novels include *The Individualist* and *Venetian Lovers* (1922), *The Unchanging Quest* (1925), *The Golden Years* (1931), *Cities of Refuge* (1936). Author also of historical studies and essays, as *The Battles of the Somme* (1916), *Now It Can Be Told* (1920), *Ordeal in England* (1937). His youngest brother, **Arthur Hamilton** (1888–1964), novelist, served in World War I (major); citizen of U.S. (from 1931); author of *Cheadle and Son* and *Soundings* (1925), *Labels* (1926), *Harness* (1928), *Chances* (1930), *Undertow* (1932), *Rivers Glide On* (1934), *The Need We Have* (1936), *A Half Inch of Candle* (1939). See also Cosmo HAMILTON (another brother).

**Gib·ran'** (jŏŏb·rän'), **Kah·lil'** (kă·lēl'). 1883–1931. Syrian symbolist poet and painter; resident in U.S. (from c. 1910); author of *Broken Wings*, *The Madman*, *The Prophet*, *The Wanderer*, etc.

**Gib'son** (gĭb's'n), **Charles Dana.** 1867–1944. American illustrator, b. Roxbury, Mass. Contributed illustrations to magazines (*Life*, *Scribner's*, *Century*, *Harper's*); master of black-and-white drawing; created so-called "Gibson girl" type. Author of *The Education of Mr. Pipp*, *The Americans*, *The Social Ladder*, etc.

**Gibson, Edmund.** 1669–1748. English prelate; educ. Oxford; bishop of Lincoln (1716–20), London (1720–48); chief work, *Codex Juris Ecclesiae Anglicanae* (1713).

**Gibson, Edward.** See Baron ASHBOURNE.

**Gibson, Hugh Simons.** 1883–1954. American diplomat; secretary of legation, Brussels, Belgium (1914–16); first U.S. minister to Poland (1919–24); U.S. minister to Switzerland (1924–27), Belgium (1927–33), Brazil (1933–37), Belgium (1937–38).

**Gibson, John.** 1740–1822. American Revolutionary officer; member, expedition that captured Fort Duquesne (renamed Fort Pitt), 1758. Fur trader (1758–74). In Washington's Continental army; colonel (1777). In command, Fort Pitt (1781–82). After Revolution, judge, court of common pleas, Allegheny County. Appointed by Jefferson secretary of Indiana Territory; settled at Vincennes (1800–16).

**Gibson, John.** 1790–1866. English sculptor; modeled statue of Queen Victoria for the houses of Parliament, and a statue of Sir Robert Peel for Westminster Abbey.

**Gibson, John Bannister.** 1780–1853. American jurist.

**Gibson, Randall Lee.** 1832–1892. American army officer and legislator; served in Confederate army through Civil War; brigadier general (1864). Member, U.S. House of Representatives (1875–83); U.S. Senate (1883–92); interested esp. in measures for improving navigation in Mississippi River. Instrumental in founding Tulane U.

**Gibson, Thomas Mil'ner-** (mĭl'nẽr-). 1806–1884. English statesman; M.P. (1837–39; 1841 ff.); president of Board of Trade (1859–66); promoted commercial treaty with France.

**Gibson, Wilfrid Wilson.** 1878–1962. English poet; author of *Stonefolds* (1907), *Daily Bread* (1910), *Fires* (1912), *Thoroughfares* (1914), *Borderlands* (1914), *Battle* (1915), *Whin* (1918), *Neighbours* (1920), *The Golden Room* (1928), *Hazards* (1930), *Islands* (1932), *Fuel* (1934), *The Alert* (1941).

**Gibson, William Hamilton.** 1850–1896. American illustrator. Best known for illustrations of nature articles in *Harper's*, *Century*, and *Scribner's*. Collected works in *Pastoral Days* (1881), *Sharp Eyes* (1892), *Eye Spy* (1897), *My Studio Neighbors* (1898), *Our Native Orchids* (1905).

**Gid'dings** (gĭd'ĭngz), **Franklin Henry.** 1855–1931. American sociologist; professor, Columbia (from 1894). Author of *The Principles of Sociology* (1896), *The Responsible State* (1918), *The Scientific Study of Human Society* (1924), etc.

**Giddings, Joshua Reed.** 1795–1864. American legislator, b. in Bradford County, Pa.; taken as a child to Ohio. Member, U.S. House of Representatives (1838–42); violent antislavery advocate; censured by house for activities (1842); resigned, but was re-elected and served (1842–59); opposed Mexican War and Compromise of 1850. U.S. consul general to Canada (1861–64).

**Gide** (zhēd), **Jean Paul Guillaume.** 1832–1880. French jurist; professor of Roman law, in Paris (1866–80). His brother **Charles** (1847–1932), economist, was professor at Collège de France. Jean Paul's son **André Paul Guillaume** (1869–1951), writer, whose works include *Le Voyage d'Urien* (1893), *Paludes* (1895), *Les Nourritures Terrestres* (1897; trans., *Fruits of the Earth*, 1948), *L'Immoraliste* (1902; trans., *The Immoralist*, 1930), *Les Faux Monnayeurs* (1926; trans., *The Counterfeiters*, 1927), *The Journals of André Gide* (4 vols., 1947–51); critical studies; and translations of English classics, as of Shakespeare. Awarded Nobel prize in literature (1947).

**Gi'del'** (zhē'dĕl'), **Charles Antoine.** 1827–1900. French literary historian.

**Gid'e·on** (gĭd'ē·ŭn). *Surnamed* **Jer'ub·ba'al** (jĕr'ŭ(b)-bā'ăl). *In Douay Version* **Ged'e·on Jer'o·ba'al** (gĕd'ē·ŭn jĕr'ō·bā'ăl). In Bible (*Judges* vi–viii), leader of the Jews who, with a band of 300 men, defeated Midianites and delivered his people from their oppression; father of Abimelech.

**Gid'e·onse** (gĭd'ē·ŭnz), **Harry David.** 1901– . Economist and educator, b. Rotterdam, Netherlands; to U.S. (1904); president of Brooklyn Coll. (from 1939).

**Gié** (zhyā). A branch of the Rohan family of France holding a seigneury. See Rohan, esp. *René de Rohan* (1550–86).

**Giel'gud** (gĭl'gŏŏd), Sir **Arthur John.** 1904– . English actor; among his prominent roles are Lewis Dodd in *Constant Nymph*, Richard II in *Richard of Bordeaux*, Romeo, and Hamlet.

**Gi·em'sa** (gē·ĕm'zä), **Gustav.** 1867–1948. German chemotherapist.

**Gier'ke** (gēr'kĕ), **Otto von.** 1841–1921. German legal scholar; professor, Breslau (1872), Heidelberg (1884), Berlin (1887). His son **Julius** (1875–1960), also a legal scholar; professor, Königsberg (1903), Halle (1919), Göttingen (1925).

**Giers, Nikolai Karlovich de.** *Russ. surname* **Girs** (gyērs). 1820–1895. Russian statesman of Swedish descent; minister to Teheran (1863), Bern (1869), and Stockholm (1872); married into family of Prince Gorchakov, whom he succeeded (1882–95) as minister of foreign affairs; exercised restraining influence in European diplomacy, esp. in negotiations with Great Britain on Afghan boundary.

**Gie'se** (gē'zĕ), **Friedrich.** 1882–1958. German legal scholar.

**Giese, Wilhelm Oskar Fritz.** 1890–1935. German psychologist; known for work in psychotechnology.

**Gie'se·brecht** (gē'zĕ·brĕKt), **Wilhelm von.** 1814–1889. German historian.

**Gie'se·king** (gē'zĕ·kĭng), **Walter Wilhelm.** 1895–1956. Pianist, b. Lyons, France, of German descent. On tours as concert pianist in Europe and America.

**Gie'sel** (gē'zĕl), **Fritz.** 1852–1927. German chemist; discovered emanium now called actinium; pioneer in preparation of pure radium compounds.

**Gif'fard** (jĭf'ērd), **Hardinge Stanley.** 1st Earl of **Hals'bur·y** (hôlz'bĕr·ĭ; -brĭ). 1823–1921. British statesman. Solicitor general (1875); lord chancellor (1885–86; 1886–92; 1895–1905). Led die-hards in House of Lords against Parliament Act (1911). Presided over preparation of digest of *Laws of England* (1905–16).

**Gif'fard'** (zhē'fȧr'), **Henri.** 1825–1882. French engineer. Constructed 5 h.p. steam engine which he used to propel an elongated balloon (1851); invented the injector for steam boilers.

**Gif'fen** (gĭf'ĕn), Sir **Robert.** 1837–1910. English economist and statistician; chief of statistical department, Board of Trade (1876–97). His many works include *Essays in Finance* (2 series, 1880–86), *The Case against Bimetallism* (1892).

**Gif'ford** (gĭf'ērd), Countess of. See under Frederick Blackwood.

**Gifford, Adam.** Lord **Gifford.** 1820–1887. Scottish jurist; bequeathed £80,000 to establish Gifford lectureship in natural theology.

**Gifford, Fannie Stearns,** *nee* **Davis.** 1884– . American writer, b. Cleveland, Ohio; m. Augustus McKinstry Gifford (1914). Author of *Myself and I* (1913), *Crack o' Dawn* (1915), and *The Ancient Beautiful Things* (verse, 1923).

**Gifford, Robert Swain.** 1840–1905. American landscape painter and etcher.

**Gifford, Sanford Robinson.** 1823–1880. American landscape painter.

**Gifford, William.** 1554–1629. English prelate. Entered Benedictine order (1608); renowned as pulpit orator throughout France. First president of English Benedictines (1617). Archbishop of Reims (1622–29).

**Gifford, William.** 1756–1826. English literary critic and poet; in his *Baviad* (1794) and *Maeviad* (1795), ridiculed the Della-Cruscans and the minor playwrights. First editor (1809–24) of *Quarterly Review;* credited with writing the magazine's attack on Keats's *Endymion* (1818). Edited Juvenal; translated Persius; edited plays of Massinger, Ben Jonson, and Ford.

**Gi'gli** (jē'lyē), **Beniamino.** 1890–1957. Operatic tenor, b. Recanati, Italy. Member, Metropolitan Opera Co., New York City (1920–32). Appeared in concert performances in Europe and South America (from 1932).

**Gi'gout'** (zhē'gōō'), **Eugène.** 1844–1925. French organist and composer.

**Gi'goux'** (zhē'gōō'), **Jean François.** 1806–1894. French painter and illustrator.

**Gil'bert** (gĭl'bērt), Sir **Alfred.** 1854–1934. English sculptor and goldsmith; among his notable works are a seated statue of Queen Victoria for Winchester, the tomb of the duke of Clarence in Albert Chapel at Windsor Castle, a memorial to Queen Alexandra in Marlborough House, and portrait busts.

**Gilbert, Anne,** *nee* **Hart'ley** (härt'lĭ). 1821–1904. Actress, b. Rochdale, England; m. George H. Gilbert (1846). To U.S. (1849); on American stage (from 1850); excelled in portraying elderly characters in comedy.

**Gilbert, Cass.** 1859–1934. American architect; among his notable works are the U.S. Custom House and the Woolworth Building in New York City, the Minnesota capitol in St. Paul, the Detroit Public Library, the St. Louis Central Public Library.

**Gilbert, Charles Henry.** 1859–1928. American ichthyologist; professor, Cincinnati (1884–89), Indiana (1889–91), Stanford (1891–1925). Author of *Synopsis of the Fishes of North America* (with David Starr Jordan; 1882), *The Deep Sea Fishes* (of Hawaii; 1905), etc.

**Gilbert, Grove Karl.** 1843–1918. American geologist; chief geologist, U.S. Geological Survey (1889–92).

**Gilbert, Henry Franklin Belknap.** 1868–1928. American composer. His *Comedy Overture* (1905) was performed by Boston Symphony Orchestra (1911), *Negro Rhapsody* (1912) at Norfolk Music Festival (1913), *Dance in Place Congo* (1906) at Metropolitan Opera

House, New York (1918); *Nocturne, from Whitman* (1925) by Philadelphia Symphony Orchestra (1928).

**Gilbert,** Sir **Humphrey**. 1539?–1583. English navigator and soldier. Half brother of Sir Walter Raleigh. Served under Sir Henry Sidney in Ireland (1566–70); served in Netherlands, but failed to capture Goes (1572). Undertook expedition for exploration and colonization in New World (1578), but failed in first attempt (1579); succeeded in second attempt (1583), establishing first British colony in North America at St. John's, Newfoundland.

**Gilbert,** Sir **John**. 1817–1897. English historical painter and book illustrator.

**Gilbert, John Gibbs**. 1810–1889. American comedian, b. Boston. With Wallack's company, New York (1862–88); in Joseph Jefferson's company (1888–89).

**Gilbert,** Sir **John Thomas**. 1829–1898. Irish historian.

**Gilbert,** Sir **Joseph Henry**. 1817–1901. English agricultural chemist; collaborated with John Bennet Lawes in experiments at Rothamsted.

**Gilbert, Linda**. 1847–1895. American philanthropist, b. Rochester, N.Y. Established the Gilbert Library (to provide books for prisons) and the Prisoner's Aid Society (1876).

**Gilbert, Marie Dolores Eliza Rosanna**. See Lola MONTEZ.

**Gil'bert'** (zhēl'bâr'), **Nicolas Joseph Laurent**. 1751–1780. French poet; known for satirical verse.

**Gil'bert** (gĭl'bērt), **Rufus Henry**. 1832–1885. American physician and inventor; patented (1870) elevated railway system; incorporated Gilbert Elevated Railway Co. (1872); railway built in New York City (1876–78).

**Gilbert, Seymour Parker**. 1892–1938. American lawyer and financier; practiced law in New York City (1915–18). Counsel to U.S. secretary of the treasury in war loan matters (1918–20); undersecretary of the treasury (1921–23). Agent-general for reparation payments in Germany (1924–30). Partner in J. P. Morgan & Co. (1931–38).

**Gilbert, William**. 1540–1603. English physician and physicist. His experiments in magnetism, and his use for the first time of terms *electric force*, *electric attraction*, and *magnetic pole* have gained him title of "father of electricity." His treatise *De Magnete, Magneticisque Corporibus* (1600) was the first great scientific work published in England. The gilbert, the C.G.S. unit of magnetomotive force, is named after him.

**Gilbert,** Sir **William Schwenck**. 1836–1911. English playwright, b. London. B.A., London U. (1857). Called to the bar (1863). First literary work, *Bab Ballads* (2 series, 1869, 1873). Began collaboration with Arthur Sullivan (Gilbert writing the librettos, Sullivan the music) with the burlesque *Thespis* (1871), and continued with the famous comic operas, performed by D'Oyly Carte's opera company, *Trial by Jury* (1875), *The Sorcerer* (1877), *H. M. S. Pinafore* (1878), *The Pirates of Penzance* (1879), *Patience* (1881), *Iolanthe* (1882), *Princess Ida* (1884), *The Mikado* (1885), *Ruddigore* (1887), *The Yeomen of the Guard* (1888), *The Gondoliers* (1889), *Utopia, Limited* (1893), *The Grand Duke* (1896). Also wrote independently *The Palace of Truth* (1870), *Pygmalion and Galatea* (1871), *The Wicked World* (1873), *The Happy Land* (1873), *Charity* (1874), *Broken Hearts* (1875), *Dan'l Druce* (1876).

**Gil'bert' de La Porrée** (zhēl'bâr'). See PORRÉE.

**Gil'bert of Sem'pring·ham** (gĭl'bērt, sĕm'prĭng·ăm). 1083?–1189. English priest; founder of the Gilbertine order. Supported Becket against Henry II, but continued to be held in high regard by Henry and Queen Eleanor. Canonized (1202).

**Gil·ber'tus Por're·ta'nus** (gĭl·bûr'tŭs pŏr'ē·tā'nŭs). See Gilbert de La PORRÉE.

**Gil'breth** (gĭl'brĕth), **Frank Bunker**. 1868–1924. American contracting engineer and efficiency expert, b. Fairfield, Me. In business in Boston (1895–1904) and New York (1904–11); consulting engineer (from 1911). Organized Society for the Promotion of the Science of Management, later called Taylor Society after Frederick Winslow Taylor (*q.v.*). Author of *Primer of Scientific Management* (1911). His wife (m. 1904), **Lillian Evelyn,** *nee* **Mol'ler** [mŏl'ēr] (1878–1972), also an engineer, took over her husband's efficiency-engineering projects at his death. Author of *Psychology of Management* (1912), *The Home-Maker and Her Job* (1927), *Living With Our Children* (1928). Collaborated with husband in *Fatigue Study* (1919), *Time Study* (1920), etc.

**Gil'christ** (gĭl'krĭst), **John Borthwick**. 1759–1841. Scottish Orientalist; studied Hindustani, Sanskrit, and Persian. Published *Hindustani Dictionary* (1787–90), *Hindustani Grammar* (1796), and Persian textbooks.

**Gilchrist, Percy Carlyle**. See Sidney G. THOMAS.

**Gilchrist, William Wallace**. 1846–1916. American composer of choral works, orchestral compositions, and chamber music.

**Gil'das** (gĭl'dăs). 516?–?570. British monk and historian; known as "Saint Gildas the Wise." Author of *De Excidio Britanniae*, a history of Britain from earliest times.

**Gil'de·mei'ster** (gĭl'dĕ·mī'stēr), **Johann**. 1812–1890. German Oriental scholar.

**Gil'der** (gĭl'dēr), **Richard Watson**. 1844–1909. American poet and editor, b. Bordentown, N.J. Assistant editor, *Scribner's Monthly* (1870–81); editor, the *Century*, which succeeded *Scribner's* (1881–1909). Contributor of verse to the magazines of the day. Wrote *Lincoln the Leader* (1909), *Grover Cleveland* (1910). His brother **William Henry** (1838–1900) was a journalist and explorer; accompanied expedition to King William Land to locate Sir John Franklin party (1878–80); proved loss of Franklin and his companions and found some records of the Franklin expedition; also with expedition to locate De Long party in the Arctic (1881–83); after ship was crushed made 2000-mile winter journey across Siberia to telegraph news of disaster. Their sister **Jeannette Leonard** (1849–1916) was a journalist; cofounder (1881) and editor (1881–1906) of the *Critic;* author of *The Autobiography of a Tomboy* (1900), *The Tomboy at Work* (1904).

**Gilder, Robert Fletcher**. 1856–1940. American journalist, landscape painter, and archaeologist; discoverer of Nebraska "loess man," oldest human remains found in America.

**Gil'der·sleeve** (gĭl'dēr·slēv), **Bas'il** (băs''l) **Lan'neau** (lăn'ō). 1831–1924. American classical scholar; professor of Greek, U. of Virginia (1856–76), Johns Hopkins (1876–1915). Served in Confederate army. Founded (1880) and edited (1880–1920) *American Journal of Philology*. Author of *A Latin Grammar* (1867).

**Gildersleeve, Virginia Cro'che·ron** (krō'shĕ·rŏn). 1877–1965. American educator; teacher of English, Barnard Coll. (from 1900), professor and dean (1911–47).

**Gil Eanes.** See GILIANES.

**Giles** (jīlz), Saint. 7th-century Grecian-born saint; a hermit in a desert region near Arles, France; became patron saint of cripples, beggars, and lepers; St. Giles's Church, Cripplegate, London, is so named in his honor.

**Giles,** Blessed. See AEGIDIUS OF ASSISI.

**Giles, Herbert Allen**. 1845–1935. English Oriental scholar; member of China consular service (1867–93); professor of Chinese, Cambridge U. (1897–1932). Compiler of a *Chinese-English Dictionary* (1892) and a *Chinese Biographical Dictionary* (1897); author of *Chinese Sketches* (1876), *Confucianism and its Rivals* (1915), *Chaos in China* (1924), etc.

**Giles, Howard Everett.** 1876–1955. American landscape painter.

**Giles, William Branch.** 1762–1830. American legislator; member, U.S. House of Representatives (1790–98; 1801–03); opposed to Hamilton; supporter of Jefferson. U.S. senator (1804–15); opposed Gallatin and Monroe; leader of malcontents opposing administration in War of 1812. Governor of Virginia (1827–30).

**Gil·fil'lan** (gĭl·fĭl'ăn), **George.** 1813–1878. Scottish Presbyterian clergyman and writer; friend of De Quincey, Carlyle, Sydney Dobell, and Alexander Smith. His overstrained literary style associated him with the spasmodic school of writers.

**Gilfillan, Robert.** 1798–1850. Scottish poet; author of the humorous satire *Peter M'Craw* (1828), praised in John Wilson's *Noctes Ambrosianae.*

**Gi·lia'nes** (zhē·lyă'nĕsh) *or* **Guil·lia'nes** (gē·lyă'nĕsh) *or* **Gil Ea'nes** (zhĭl yă'nĕsh). Portuguese navigator; first to round Cape Bojador (1433).

**Gilimer.** See GELIMER.

**Gil'kin'** (zhēl'kăN'), **I'wan'** (ē'väN'). 1858–1923. Belgian poet. A founder of *La Jeune Belgique* (1881; cf. Albert GIRAUD). Among his volumes of verse are *La Nuit* (1897), showing influence of Baudelaire, and *Le Cerisier Fleuri* (1899).

**Gill** (zhēl), **André.** *Professional name of* **Louis Alexandre Gos'set' de Guines** (gô'sĕ' dē gēn'). 1840–1885. French painter, illustrator, and caricaturist; best known for his political caricatures.

**Gill** (gĭl), **Colin Unwin.** 1892– . English painter; official war artist (1918–19); best known for his portraits and murals.

**Gill,** Sir **David.** 1843–1914. Scottish astronomer; astronomer royal at Cape of Good Hope (1879–1907). A pioneer in applying photography to astronomy; made photographic survey of southern heavens (1885–98).

**Gill, Eric.** 1882–1940. English sculptor and engraver. Author of *Sculpture...*(1917), *Christianity and Art* (1927), *Money and Morals* (1934), *25 Nudes* (a book of engravings, 1938), etc.

**Gill, Theodore Nicholas.** 1837–1914. American zoologist; member of staff, Smithsonian Institution, Washington, D.C. (from 1861). On staff of Library of Congress (1866–74). Specialist in ichthyology.

**Gill, William John.** 1843–1882. English military engineer and traveler. In India (1869–71); traveled in Persia, China, eastern Tibet, and the region between Tunis and Egypt. His map of eastern Tibet was awarded the Royal Geographical Society's gold medal.

**Gille** (zhēl), **Philippe Émile François.** 1831–1901. French playwright and literary critic. Author of, or collaborator in writing, the librettos of *Vent du Soir* (1857) and *Les Bergers* (1865), both with music by Offenbach, *Le Bœuf Apis* (1865), *Jean de Nivelle* (1880), *Lakmé,* the last three with music by Delibes.

**Gille, Valère.** 1867–1950. Belgian poet.

**Gilles de la Tou'rette'** (zhēl' dē lȧ to͞o'rĕt'), **Georges.** 1857–1904. French physician; known for work relating to hypnotism and to neuropathology.

**Gil·les'pie** (gĭ·lĕs'pĭ), **George.** 1613–1648. Scottish Presbyterian clergyman; author of theological and controversial works.

**Gillespie, Thomas.** 1708–1774. Scottish Presbyterian clergyman. Educ. Edinburgh. Deposed by general assembly of his church; preached in Dunfermline and on the open highway for over six years. He and his followers formed a presbytery and founded the Relief Church in Scotland (1761).

**Gillespie, William Mitchell.** 1816–1868. American engineer; author of *Treatise on Leveling, Topography, and Higher Surveying* (1871), etc.

**Gil'let'** (zhē'lĕ'), **Louis.** 1876–1943. French art historian.

**Gil·lett'** (jĭ·lĕt'), **Frederick Huntington.** 1851–1935. American lawyer and politician, b. Westfield, Mass. Member, U.S. House of Representatives (1893–1925), and speaker (1919–25); member, U.S. Senate (1925–31).

**Gil·lette'** (jĭ·lĕt'), **King Camp.** 1855–1932. American inventor of the safety razor; organized and headed Gillette Safety Razor Co. (1901–32). Author of *Human Drift* (1894), *Gillette's Industrial Solution* (1900), *The People's Corporation* (1924).

**Gillette, William.** 1855–1937. American actor, b. Hartford, Conn.; best known for his dramatization of Conan Doyle's *Sherlock Holmes;* also starred in *Diplomacy, The Admirable Crichton, Dear Brutus,* etc.

**Gil'lié'ron'** (zhē'lyā'rôN'), **Jules.** 1854–1926. French Romance language scholar; by his work, with collaboration of E. Edmont, in preparing *Atlas Linguistique de la France* (1902–09), he founded study of linguistic geography.

**Gil'lies** (gĭl'ĭs; -ĭz), **John.** 1747–1836. Scottish historian and classical scholar.

**Gil'liss** (gĭl'ĭs), **James Melville.** 1811–1865. American astronomer; instrumental in obtaining appropriation for new Naval Observatory in Washington (1841–44). In charge, expedition to South America to study Venus and Mars and determine solar parallax (1849–52); observed solar eclipse, in South America (1858), and in Washington Territory (1860). In charge, Naval Observatory, Washington, D.C. (1861–65).

**Gilliss, Walter.** 1855–1925. American typographer; secretary of the Grolier Club for over twenty years; typographical adviser to Doubleday, Page & Co. (1911–25).

**Gill'more** (gĭl'mōr), **Inez Haynes.** See under Will IRWIN.

**Gillmore, Quincy Adams.** 1825–1888. American military engineer, b. Black River, Ohio. Grad. U.S.M.A., West Point (1849). In Civil War, brigadier general of volunteers (1862); major general (1863); in command, Department of the South (1865). President, Mississippi River Commission (1879).

**Gil'lot'** (zhē'lō'), **Claude.** 1673–1722. French engraver, esp. of comedy scenes and burlesques.

**Gillot, Firmin.** 1820–1872. French lithographer; originator of the gillotype.

**Gil'louin'** (zhē'lwăN'), **René.** 1881– . French philosopher; student of problems of social and religious philosophy.

**Gill'ray** (gĭl'rā), **James.** 1757–1815. English caricaturist; known esp. for his political caricatures, many satirizing the royal family.

**Gil'man** (gĭl'măn), **Arthur.** 1837–1909. American educator, b. Alton, Ill. Instrumental in obtaining Harvard collegiate instruction for women (from 1879); developed Radcliffe College (incorporated 1893); regent, Radcliffe College (1893–95).

**Gilman, Arthur Delevan.** 1821–1882. American architect.

**Gilman, Caroline,** *nee* **Howard.** 1794–1888. American author, b. Boston; m. (1819) Samuel Gilman (*q.v.*); settled at Charleston, S.C. Editor of the *Southern Rosebud* (later *Southern Rose*), one of the first children's papers in U.S. (1832–39).

**Gilman, Charlotte,** *nee* **Perkins.** 1860–1935. American lecturer and writer; m. (1884; div. 1894) Charles Walter Stetson, American painter, and (1900) George H. Gilman. Lecturer on ethics, economics, and sociology (from 1890); associated with movements to improve conditions of labor and to advance the cause of women.

**Gilman, Daniel Coit.** 1831–1908. American educator; drew up plans for a scientific school at Yale (1856); librarian, secretary, and professor of geography, Sheffield Scientific School, Yale (1861–72). President, U. of California (1872–75); first president, Johns Hopkins (1875–1901); retired. First president, Carnegie Institution, Washington, D.C. (1901–04); resigned. President, National Civil Service Reform League (1901–07).

**Gil′man** (gĭl′măn), **Lawrence.** 1878–1939. American author and critic, b. Flushing, N.Y. Music critic, *Harper's Weekly* (1901–13), and managing editor (1911–13); music, dramatic, and literary critic, *North American Review* (1915–23); music critic, New York *Herald-Tribune* (1923–39).

**Gilman, Samuel.** 1791–1858. American Unitarian clergyman and poet; author of *Fair Harvard.* See Caroline GILMAN.

**Gil′mer** (gĭl′mẽr), **Elizabeth,** *nee* **Mer′i·weth′er** (mĕr′ĭ·wĕth′ẽr). *Pseudonym* **Dorothy Dix** (dĭks). 1870–1951. American journalist; m. George O. Gilmer (1888). Editor of woman's department, New Orleans *Picayune* (1896–1901); began writing her famous column of advice to the lovelorn. Joined staff of New York *Journal* (1901), Wheeler Syndicate (1917), and Ledger Syndicate (1923). Author of *How to Win and Hold a Husband* (1939), etc.

**Gilmer, Thomas Walker.** 1802–1844. American politician; governor of Virginia (1840–41); member, U.S. House of Representatives (1841–44); advocated governmental economy; opposed dictation by Henry Clay; became Tyler's administration spokesman in House. U.S. secretary of the navy (1844).

**Gil′more** (gĭl′mōr), **Eugene Allen.** 1871–1953. American educator; president, State U. of Iowa (1934–40); dean of law school, U. of Pittsburgh (1940–42); professor of law, U. of Iowa (from 1942).

**Gilmore, James Roberts.** *Pseudonym* **Edmund Kirke** (kûrk). 1822–1903. American businessman and Civil War mediator, b. Boston. Sent unofficially by Lincoln (1864) to Jefferson Davis to discuss terms for ending Civil War; conferred with Davis at Richmond, Va. (July 17, 1864); Davis's rejection of Lincoln's proposals because not recognizing independence of the Confederacy made conference futile. When account of conference was published in *Atlantic Monthly* (1864), it did much to undermine the peace party in North and aided in Lincoln's re-election. Author of *Among the Pines* (1862), *The Life of James A. Garfield* (1880), *Personal Recollections of Abraham Lincoln and the Civil War* (1898), etc.

**Gilmore, Patrick Sarsfield.** 1829–1892. American bandmaster, b. near Dublin, Ireland; to U.S. (c. 1850); author, under pseudonym **Louis Lam′bert** (lăm′bẽrt), of, *When Johnny comes marching home again.*

**Gil·pat′ric** (gĭl·păt′rĭk), **Guy.** 1896–1950. American fiction writer, b. New York City. Aviator and test pilot (1912–17); in advertising business (1918–30); devoted time to writing (from 1930). Creator of character "Mr. Glencannon," Scottish engineer.

**Gil′pin** (gĭl′pĭn), **Bernard.** 1517–1583. English clergyman; his annual journeys through neglected sections of Northumberland and Yorkshire, where he preached and ministered to the poor, gained him the title "Apostle of the North."

**Gilpin, Charles Sidney.** 1878–1930. American Negro actor, b. Richmond, Va. Appeared as William Custis, the Negro clergyman in Drinkwater's *Abraham Lincoln,* New York (1919); great success as Brutus Jones in O'Neill's *Emperor Jones* (1920–24). Received Drama League award for his outstanding performance (1921), and Spingarn medal by N.A.A.C.P. (1921).

**Gil Po′lo** (hēl pō′lō), **Gaspar.** 1535?–1591. Spanish poet, b. Valencia; author of the widely translated pastoral romance *La Diana Enamorada,* a continuation of Montemayor's *Diana* (1564).

**Gil Ro′bles Qui·ño′nes** (hēl rō′blās kē·nyō′nās), **José María.** 1898– . Spanish Catholic political leader; editor of Catholic newspaper *El Debate* (1922); leader of Catholic faction Acción Popular (1931); minister of war (1935); fled to Portugal (1936).

**Gil′son′** (zhēl′sôɴ′), **Etienne Henry.** 1884–1978. French Neo-Thomist philosopher.

**Gil y Zá′ra·te** (hēl′ ē thä′rä·tā), **Antonio.** 1793–1861. Spanish dramatist and literary historian. Works include dramas *Carlos II el Hechizado* (his best known play, 1837), *El Gran Capitán, Guzmán el Bueno, Un Monarca y su Privado;* tragedies, as *Doña Blanca de Borbón* and *Don Rodrigo;* comedies, as *Don Pedro de Portugal, Un Año después de la Boda, ¡Cuidado con las Novias!,* etc.

**Gim′bel** (gĭm′bĕl). Family of American merchants, owners of a chain of department stores, in New York City, Philadelphia, Pittsburgh, Milwaukee, and Chicago. Its members, many of whom came from Vincennes, Ind., include **Jacob** (1850–1922), founder of New York Gimbel Brothers' store; **Charles** (1861–1932), one of founders of Gimbel Brothers and a chairman of the board; **Ellis A.** (1865–1950), a vice-president and a chairman of the board of Gimbel Brothers; **Bernard F.** (1885–1966), associated with Gimbel Brothers (from 1907) and president of the firm (from 1927).

**Gin′de·ly** (gĭn′dĕ·lĭ), **Anton.** 1829–1892. Bohemian historian.

**Gin′gue·né′** (zhăɴg′nā′), **Pierre Louis.** 1748–1816. French literary historian; chief work, *Histoire Littéraire de l'Italie* (1811–19).

**Gi′nis′ty′** (zhē′nēs′tē′), **Paul.** 1858–1932. French man of letters; director of the Odéon (1896–1906); author of novels, plays, and historical works.

**Gin′kel** (gĭng′kĕl), **Godert de.** 1st Earl of **Ath·lone′** (ăth·lōn′). 1644–1703. Dutch-born general in British service. Accompanied William of Orange to England (1688); captured Athlone; won victory of Aughrim; took Limerick (1691); created earl of Athlone (1692); second in command to Marlborough (1702).

**Ginn** (gĭn), **Edwin.** 1838–1914. American publisher; opened publishing house, Boston (1867), known as Ginn & Co. (from 1885); esp. successful in textbook field.

**Gin′ne·ken** (gĭn′ĕ·kĕn), **Jacobus Johannes Antonius van.** 1877–1945. Dutch Jesuit and philologist.

**Gins′burg** (gĭnz′bûrg), **Allen.** 1926– . American poet, b. Newark, N.J. Wrote *Howl and Other Poems* (1956), *Kaddish and Other Poems* (1961), etc.

**Ginsburg, Christian David.** 1831–1914. Bible scholar, b. in Poland; adopted Christian faith (c. 1847); to England, naturalized (1858); an original member of Old Testament revision group; published an edition of *The Massorah* (1880 ff.).

**Gintl** (gĭn′t'l), **Wilhelm Julius.** 1804–1883. Austrian telegraphist. Inventions include field telegraph and first duplex system of telegraphy.

**Ginz′berg** (gĭnz′bûrg), **Asher.** See ACHAD HAAM.

**Ginzberg, Louis.** 1873–1953. Talmudic scholar, b. Kovno (Kaunas), Russia. Ph.D., Heidelberg (1898). To U.S. (1899); professor of Talmud and Rabbinics (current Jewish customs and ceremonies) at Jewish Theol. Sem., New York (from 1902).

**Gio·ber'ti** (jô·bĕr'tē), **Vincenzo.** 1801–1852. Italian philosopher and politician; premier of Sardinia (1848–49); ambassador at Paris (1849–51). Among his books are *Introduzione allo Studio della Filosofia* (1839–40), *Del Rinnovamento Civile d'Italia* (1851).

**Gio·con'do** (jô·kōn'dō), Fra **Giovanni.** 1433?–1515. Italian architect and antiquary; published editions of Latin authors and collected numerous Latin inscriptions; credited with design of Loggia del Consiglio (Verona).

**Gio'ja** (jô'yä), **Flavio.** Italian mariner of the 14th century; contributed to improvement of the compass, and was in later centuries incorrectly credited with its invention.

**Gio'ja** *or* **Gio'ia** (jô'yä), **Melchiorre.** 1767–1829. Italian economist and statistician.

**Gio·lit'ti** (jô·lēt'tē), **Giovanni.** 1842–1928. Italian statesman; minister of the treasury (1889) and of finance (1890). Prime minister of Italy (1892–93; 1903–05; 1906–09; 1911–14; 1920–21). Opposed Italy's entry into World War I.

**Gio'no'** (jô'nō'), **Jean.** 1895–1970. French novelist, depicting esp. peasant life in remote districts of the Basses-Alpes. Author of *Harvest* (trans. 1939).

**Gior·da'ni** (jôr·dä'nē), **Giuseppe.** c. 1744–1798. Italian composer of operas and songs; his song *Caro Mio Ben* achieved wide popularity. His brother **Tommaso** (c. 1740–1806) was a conductor and composer, esp. of operas.

**Giordani, Pietro.** 1774–1848. Italian writer; known chiefly as classical stylist. His works include critical essays, eulogies (as *Panegirico a Napoleone*), pamphlets, addresses, and *Epistolario* in *Opere Complete* (14 vols., 1854–65).

**Gior·da'no** (jôr·dä'nō), **Luca.** *Called* **Fa Pre'sto** (fä prĕs'tō). 1632–1705. Neapolitan painter, esp. of decorative frescoes, as in Corsini chapel (Florence) and the Escorial (Spain).

**Giordano, Umberto.** 1867–1948. Italian composer of operas.

**Giorgio, Francesco di.** See FRANCESCO DI GIORGIO.

**Gior·gio'ne, Il** (ēl jôr·jō'nā). *Also* **Gior·gio'ne da Ca'stel·fran'co** (dä käs'tĕl·fräng'kō). *Orig.* **Giorgio Bar'ba·rel'li** (bär'bä·rĕl'lē). c. 1478–1511. Venetian painter; chief master of Venetian school in his day; influenced contemporaries, including Titian; aided in decoration of façade of Fondaco dei Tedeschi (Venice); died of plague at Venice (1511). Of unquestioned authenticity are his altarpiece *Enthroned Madonna* (Castelfranco Cathedral), *Gypsy and Soldier* (Palazzo Giovanelli, Venice), and *Evander Showing Aeneas the Site of Rome* (Vienna Museum).

**Giot·ti'no** (jôt·tē'nō). Italian painter of 14th century; employed at Vatican (1369).

**Giot'to** (jôt'tō). *In full* **Giot'to di Bon·do'ne** (dē bôn·dō'nā). 1266?–1337. Florentine painter, architect, and sculptor; chief Italian pre-Renaissance painter; pupil of Cimabue; friend of Dante. Works attributed to him include series of frescoes depicting life of St. Francis and life of Christ (both in Church of St. Francis at Assisi), altarpiece for St. Peter's (now in the sacristy), fresco fragment entitled *Boniface VIII Proclaiming the Jubilee* (St. John Lateran, Rome), decorative frescoes *Life of Christ, Life of the Virgin, Last Judgment, Allegories,* etc. (Arena chapel, Padua), allegorical frescoes *Marriage of St. Francis with Poverty, Triumph of Charity, Triumph of Obedience, Glorification of St. Francis* (all in St. Francis lower church, Assisi), fresco series depicting life of John the Evangelist and life of John the Baptist (both in Peruzzi chapel, Church of Santa Croce, Florence), *Last Supper* (Munich), and *Presentation of Christ in the Temple* (Boston). As chief architect of the Duomo in Florence, designed the campanile and façade.

**Giovane, Palma.** See under Jacopo PALMA.

**Giovanna.** See JOANNA (of Naples).

**Giovanni.** Italian form of JOHN.

**Gio'vio** (jô'vyō), **Paolo.** *Latin* **Paulus Jo'vi·us** (jō'vĭ·ŭs). 1483–1552. Italian biographer and historian; distinguished as Latin stylist.

**Gipps** (gĭps), Sir **George.** 1791–1847. British colonial administrator; governor of New South Wales (1838–46), where he did much to open up the country and prevent exploitation of the native population.

**Gi·ral'di** (jē·räl'dē), **Giovanni Battista.** See CYNTHIUS.

**Gi·ral'dus** (jĭ·răl'dŭs) *or* **Ger'ald** (jĕr'ăld) **de Bar'ri** (dĕ băr'ĭ). *Best known by his literary name* **Giraldus Cam·bren'sis** (kăm·brĕn'sĭs). 1146?–?1220. Welsh ecclesiastical scholar, geographer, and historian. Son of William de Barri of a Norman family and a princess of the Welsh royal family. Elected by chapter to succeed his uncle as bishop of St. David's, but rejected by Henry II (1176); described natural history and inhabitants of Ireland in *Topographia Hibernica* after accompanying Prince John thither (1185); described Wales in *Itinerarium Cambriae* after assisting archbishop of Canterbury preach third crusade; again elected to see of St. David's (1198); excluded by archbishop of Canterbury; devoted rest of life to study.

**Gi'rard'** (zhē'rár'), Abbé **Gabriel.** 1677–1748. French grammarian; author of *La Justesse de la Langue Françoise, ou les Différentes Significations des Mots Qui Passent pour Être Synonymes* (1718), *Vrais Principes de Langue Françoise...* (1747).

**Girard, Jean Baptiste.** *Known as* **Le Père** (lẽ pâr) **Girard** *and* (*in Franciscan order*) **Le Père Gré'goire'** (grā'gwár'). 1765–1850. Swiss educator; entered Franciscan order. Principal of primary school at Fribourg (1804–23) and of free school at Lucerne (1827–34); retired (1834) to devote himself to writing on theory of education. In Switzerland, regarded as an educator second only to Pestalozzi.

**Girard, Jules Augustin.** 1825–1902. French Hellenic scholar; among his notable works are *Thucydide* (1860), *Le Sentiment Religieux en Grèce* (1868).

**Girard, Paul Frédéric.** 1852–1925. French jurist.

**Girard, Philippe Henri de.** 1775–1845. French mechanician, inventor, and industrialist; invented a flax-spinning machine.

**Gi·rard'** (jĭ·rärd'; *Fr.* zhē'rár'), **Stephen.** 1750–1831. Businessman and philanthropist, b. Bordeaux, France; merchant in Philadelphia (from 1777). Founded banking house, Bank of Stephen Girard (1812), to take over business of Bank of United States. Aided government in financing the War of 1812; aided in establishing the Second Bank of the United States (1816). Bequeathed funds used to build Girard College, Philadelphia, for "poor, white, male orphans" to be trained in the arts and trades.

**Gi'rar'din'** (zhē'rár'dăN'), **Émile de.** 1806–1881. French journalist; inaugurated low-priced journalism in France with his editorship of *La Presse* (1836–56; 1862–66) at annual subscription cost of only 40 francs; later, edited *La Liberté* (1867), *L'Union Française* (1871), *Le Petit Journal, Journal Officiel, La France;* member of Chamber of Deputies (1834–51; 1877–81). His wife, **Delphine,** *nee* **Gay** (gā) (1804–1855), *pseudonym* Vicomte **Charles de Lau'nay'** (lō'nā'), daughter of Sophie Gay, was a writer of novels, comedies, verse, and a series of *Lettres Parisiennes.*

**Girardin, Saint-Marc.** See SAINT-MARC GIRARDIN.

**Gi'rar'don'** (zhē'rȧr'dôɴ'), **François.** 1628–1715. French sculptor; employed under direction of LeBrun in decoration of Versailles and the Trianon; also, executed tomb of Cardinal Richelieu in the Sorbonne and an equestrian statue of Louis XIV in Paris.

**Gi'raud'** (zhē'rō'), **Albert.** *Pseudonym of* **Marie Émile Albert Ka'yen·bergh** (kȧ'yĕm·bĕrк). 1860–1929. Belgian poet, b. Louvain. A founder of *La Jeune Belgique* (1881; cf. Iwan GILKIN); editor of *Étoile Belge.* Author of *Héros et Pierrots* (1898), etc.

**Gi·ra'ud** (jē·rä'o͞od), Conte **Giovanni.** 1776–1834. Italian playwright, b. Rome; appointed director of theaters in Italy by Napoleon (1809).

**Gi'raud'** (zhē'rō'), **Henri Honoré.** 1879–1949. French general; served through World War I; served in Morocco against Riffs (1925–26); commanded allied defenses in northern France (1940); captured, but escaped from Germany (Apr., 1942) to unoccupied France; to Algeria (Nov., 1942) to co-operate with allies by organizing French colonial army; succeeded Darlan (Dec., 1942) as high commissioner of French North and West Africa. Commander of French forces in North Africa; joined with Free French group in organizing French Committee of National Liberation (1943).

**Gi'rau'doux'** (zhē'rō'do͞o'), **Jean.** 1882–1944. French writer; chief of propaganda (1939–40). Among his many novels are *Simon le Pathétique* (1918), *Adorable Clio* (1920), *Siegfried et le Limousin* (1922; awarded Goncourt prize, 1926), *Bella* (a roman à clef, 1926), *Églantine* (1927), *Le Sport* (1928); author also of the successful play *Amphitryon 38* (1929) and the political essay *Pleins Pouvoirs* (1939).

**Gir'ling** (gûr'lĭng), **Zo'ë** (zō'ē). Mrs. **Aleksandre Piotr Zajd'ler** (zīd'lẽr). *Pseudonym* **Martin Hare** (hâr). Writer, b. in a vicarage in Ireland; author of *Describe a Circle* (1933), *If This Be Error* (1934), *Mirror for Skylarks* (1935), *English Rue* (1938), *Polonaise* (1940).

**Gi'ro'det'–Tri'o'son'** (zhē'rô'dĕ'trē'ô'zôɴ'). *Orig.* **Anne Louis Girodet de Rou'cy'** (dē ro͞o'sē'). 1767–1824. French painter.

**Girón, Francisco Hernández.** See HERNÁNDEZ GIRÓN.

**Girón, Pedro Téllez y.** See Duke of OSUNA.

**Gir'tin** (gûr'tĭn), **Thomas.** 1775–1802. English landscape painter; regarded as founder of art of modern water-color painting. Among his notable works are *Melrose Abbey, St. Asaph, Bolton Bridge.*

**Gir'ty** (gûr'tĭ), **Simon.** 1741–1818. Known as "The Great Renegade." American soldier who turned against Americans (1778) and became leader of British and Indian raiding expeditions along the northern and western frontier; fled into Canada when the British gave up Detroit (1796).

**Gisander.** See Johann Gottfried SCHNABEL.

**Gi'se·la** (gē'zĕ·lä). d. 1043. Roman empress; m. Conrad II (1016) and was crowned with him in Rome (1027); mother of Emperor Henry III.

**Gish** (gĭsh), **Lillian.** 1896?– . American stage and motion-picture actress; appeared in *Birth of a Nation, Way Down East, Orphans of the Storm, Scarlet Letter, Camille.* Her sister **Dorothy** (1898?–1968), also an actress; m. James Rennie (1920); appeared in *Hearts of the World, Orphans of the Storm, Romola, Nell Gwyn, Madame Pompadour,* etc.

**Gis'sing** (gĭs'ĭng), **George Robert.** 1857–1903. English novelist, b. Wakefield. Became prominent for depiction of middle-class life in England, and esp. for portrayals of degrading effect of poverty on character. His novels include *The Unclassed* (1884), *Demos* (1886), *The Nether World* (1889), *New Grub Street* (1891), *The Town Traveller* (1898), *The Private Papers of Henry Ryecroft* (1903).

**Gist** (gĭst), **Christopher.** 1706?–1759. American frontiersman; accompanied George Washington on trip to Fort Duquesne (1753–54); guide in Braddock's expedition (1755).

**Giu·lia'ni** (jo͞o·lyä'nē), **Giambattista.** 1818–1884. Italian philologist; known esp. as Dante scholar.

**Giulio Romano.** See (1) Giulio CACCINI; (2) Giulio ROMANO.

**Giun'ta** (jo͞on'tä) *or* **Giun'ti** (jo͞on'tē). *Span.* **Jun'ta** (ho͞on'tä) *or* **Jun'ti** (ho͞on'tē) *or* **Zon'ta** (thôn'tä). *Fr.* **Junte** (zhôɴt). Italian family of printers and bookbinders, including: **Luca Antonio** (d. about 1537), who founded publishing house in Venice (c. 1494); his brother **Filippo** (1450–1517), who established printing house in Florence; the latter's sons **Benedetto** and **Bernardo** (d. about 1551), printers of Boccaccio's *Decameron;* **Giulio** and **Tommaso,** printers to king of Spain (1595–1624); **Giacomo,** who founded publishing house at Lyon (1520).

**Giunta Pi·sa'no** (pē·sä'nō). 1202?–1258. Italian painter.

**Giu·ria'ti** (jo͞o·ryä'tē), **Giovanni Battista.** 1876– . Italian politician; prime minister of D'Annunzio in Fiume (1919); member of Fascist legislature (from 1921) and senator (1934). Minister of public works (1925–29); president, Chamber of Deputies (1929–34); general secretary of Fascist party (1930–32).

**Giu'sti** (jo͞os'tē), **Giuseppe.** 1809–1850. Italian satirical poet.

**Giu'sti·nia'ni** (jo͞os'tē·nyä'nē). Italian family, including: **Leonardo** (1388–1446), Venetian poet, author of *Canzoni e Strambotti d'Amore;* his son **Bernardo** (1408–1489), historian and diplomat; **Agostino** (1470–1536), Orientalist, professor of Hebrew at Paris; **Vicenzo** (1519–1582), Roman Catholic prelate, general of the Dominican order (1558).

**Gjal'ski** (dyäl'skē). Variant of DJALSKI.

**Gjel'le·rup** (gĕl'lĕ·ro͝op), **Karl.** 1857–1919. Danish writer; long resident in Germany; wrote many of his later works in German. Among his works are *En Idealist* (1878), *G-Dur* (1882), *Minna* (1889), *Die Hügelmühle* (1896), *Der Pilger Kamanita* (1906; trans. as *The Pilgrim Kamenita*), *Die Weltwanderer* (1909), and *Reif für das Leben* (1915). Recipient, jointly with Henrik Pontoppidan, of the Nobel prize for literature (1917).

**Gla'ber'** (glȧ'bâr'), **Raoul.** Early 11th-century French chronicler, whose *Chronique* in five books covers the period from 900 to 1046.

**Glack'ens** (glăk'ĕnz), **William James.** 1870–1938. American painter.

**Glad'den** (glăd''n), **Washington.** *Orig.* **Solomon Washington.** 1836–1918. American Congregational clergyman; joined editorial staff of *Independent* (1871–75); pastorate at Springfield, Mass. (1875–82) and Columbus, Ohio (1882–1918). Preached the practical application of the principles of religion to current social problems. Author of *Plain Thoughts on the Art of Living* (1868), *Being a Christian* (1871), *Applied Christianity* (1886), *Ultima Veritas and Other Verses* (1912), etc.

**Glad·kov'** (glŭt·kôf'), **Fëdor Vasilievich.** 1883–1958. Russian novelist. Author of *The Fiery Steed, Cement,* etc.

**Glad'stone** (glăd'stōn; *Brit. usu.* -stŭn), **Herbert John.** Viscount **Gladstone.** 1854–1930. British statesman, b. London; youngest son of W. E. Gladstone. Educ. Oxford. M.P. (1880–1910); created viscount (1910). Chief liberal whip (1899); influential in maintaining neutrality within liberal party through Boer War (1899–1902). Secretary of state for home affairs (1905–10). First governor general and high commissioner of Union of South Africa (1910–14).

**Gladstone, John Hall.** 1827–1902. English chemist; known for work on optical refractivity and on the chemistry of the lead storage battery; used copper-zinc couple to prepare organic compounds; made spectroscopic studies of rising and setting sun.

**Gladstone, William Ewart.** 1809–1898. British statesman, b. Liverpool. B.A., Oxon. (1831). M.P. (1832–95, with a break of only a year and a half). President of Board of Trade in Sir Robert Peel's cabinet (1843–45), and secretary of state for colonies (1845–46). Chancellor of the exchequer in Aberdeen's cabinet (1852–55), again in Palmerston's cabinet and at queen's request continued in office under Lord Russell (1859–66). Succeeded Lord Russell as leader of the Liberal party (1867). Prime minister (1868–74; 1880–85; 1886; 1892–94). Among important measures and policies with which he is identified are the disestablishment of the Irish church (1869), an Irish land bill (1870), denunciation of Turkish atrocities in Bulgaria (1875), reform of Irish government by a new land bill and a home-rule bill (presented to Parliament, but defeated, 1886 and again 1893). Author of *The State in its Relations to the Church* (1838), *Studies on Homer and the Homeric Age* (1858), *Juventus Mundi* (1869), *Bulgarian Horrors* (1876–77), *Homeric Synchronism* (1876), *Gleanings of Past Years* (1879).

**Glae′ser** (glâ′zẽr), **Ernst.** 1902–1963. German novelist; author of *Class of 1902* (trans. 1929), *Last Civilian* (trans. 1935), etc.

**Glaire** (glâr), **Jean Baptiste.** 1798–1879. French theologian and Orientalist.

**Glais′-Bi′zoin′** (glĕ′bē′zwăN′), **Alexandre Olivier.** 1800–1877. French politician; opposed Louis Napoleon (1848); member of corps législatif (1863–70) and of the Government of National Defense (1870).

**Glai′sher** (glā′shẽr), **James.** 1809–1903. English astronomer and meteorologist; chief of magnetic and meteorological department at Greenwich (1838–74); balloon ascents to obtain meteorological data (1862–66). Prepared meteorological reports (1847–1902).

**Glaisher, James Whitbread Lee.** 1848–1928. English mathematician and astronomer; educ. Cambridge. On staff of Trinity Coll., Cambridge (1871–1901). President, London Mathematical Society (1884–86) and Royal Astronomical Society (1886–88, 1901–03).

**Glaize** (glâz), **Auguste Barthélemi.** 1807–1893. French painter.

**Glan′vill** (glăn′vĭl), **Joseph.** 1636–1680. English clergyman and philosopher; attacked scholastic philosophy in *The Vanity of Dogmatizing* (1661); defended pre-existence of souls in *Lux Orientalis* (1662), and belief in witchcraft in ... *Witches and Witchcraft* (1666; also known as *Sadducismus Triumphatus*).

**Glan′ville** (glăn′vĭl), **Bartholomew de.** See BARTHOLOMAEUS ANGLICUS.

**Glan′ville** *or* **Glan′vil** (glăn′vĭl), **Ranulf de.** d. 1190. English statesman and jurist. Justiciar of England (1180–89), and influential adviser of King Henry II.

**Glanville, Stephen Ran′ulph** (răn′ŭlf) **Kingdon.** 1900–1956. English Egyptologist.

**Glap′thorne** (glăp′thôrn), **Henry.** fl. 1639–42. English playwright.

**Gla′re·a′nus** (glä′rā·ä′nōōs), **Henricus.** *Real name* **Heinrich Lo′ris** (lō′rĭs). 1488–1563. Swiss Humanist; published treatises on classical Latin writers and books on music.

**Glas, John.** See John GLASS.

**Gla′se·napp** (glä′zĕ·näp), **Karl Friedrich.** 1847–1915. German writer on Wagner and Wagnerian music.

**Gla′ser** (glä′zẽr), **Christoph.** fl. 2d half 17th century. Swiss chemist; apothecary to Louis XIV of France; credited with discovery of potassium sulphate. The mineral glaserite (aphthitalite) was named after him.

**Glaser, Donald Arthur.** 1926– . Amer. physicist, b. Cleveland, Ohio. At U. of Mich. (1949–59), U. of Calif. (1959– ). Awarded Nobel prize in physics (1960) for inventing the bubble chamber.

**Glaser, Eduard.** 1855–1908. Austrian explorer in southern Arabia.

**Glaser, Julius.** 1831–1885. Austrian jurist and statesman; minister of justice (1871); general procurator to court of cassation, Vienna (1879).

**Glas′gow** (glăs′gō), **Ellen Anderson Gholson.** 1873–1945. American novelist, b. Richmond, Va. Author of *The Descendant* (1897), *The Battle-ground* (1902), *The Wheel of Life* (1906), *Life and Gabriella* (1916), *The Builders* (1919), *Barren Ground* (1925), *The Romantic Comedians* (1926), *The Sheltered Life* (1932), *Vein of Iron* (1935), *In This Our Life* (1941).

**Glas′pell** (glăs′pĕl), **Susan.** 1882–1948. American writer, b. Davenport, Iowa; m. (1913) George Cram Cook (d. 1924); Norman H. Matson (1925). Associated with Little Theater movement. Author of novels, *The Glory of the Conquered* (1909), *The Visioning* (1911), *Brook Evans* (1928), *Ambrose Holt and Family* (1931), *Norma Ashe* (1942); plays, *Trifles* (1917), *Suppressed Desires* (with George Cram Cook, 1917); *Bernice* (1920), *Inheritors* (1921), *Verge* (1922), *The Comic Artist* (with Norman H. Matson, 1927), *Alison's House* (1930).

**Glass** (glȧs), **Carter.** 1858–1946. American statesman, b. Lynchburg, Va. Acquired interest in Lynchburg newspapers *Daily News* and *Daily Advance.* Member of U.S. House of Representatives (1902–19); patron and floor manager in the House of Federal Reserve Bank Act (passed 1918). U.S. secretary of the treasury (1918–20). U.S. senator from Virginia (1920–46). See Robert L. OWEN and Henry B. STEAGALL.

**Glass** *or* **Glas, John.** 1695–1773. Scottish Presbyterian clergyman; organized at Dundee a sect of independent Presbyterians; moved to Perth (1733) and was joined by Robert Sandeman. Members of the sect were known as *Glassites*, or *Sandemanians.*

**Glass, Montague Marsden.** 1877–1934. Fiction writer and playwright, b. Manchester, Eng.; to U.S. (1890). Established himself as writer with success of *Potash and Perlmutter* (1910), successfully dramatized (1913, in collab. with Charles Klein). Other works: fiction, *Abe and Mawruss* (1911), *Worrying Won't Win* (1918), *Y' Understand* (1925), etc.; plays, *Abe and Mawruss* (with R. C. Megrue, 1915), *Business Before Pleasure* (1917), *Lucky Numbers* (1927), etc.

**Glass′bren′ner** (gläs′brĕn′ẽr), **Adolf.** *Pseudonym* **Adolf Brenn′glas′** (brĕn′gläs′). 1810–1876. German writer, b. Berlin. Best known for humorous and satirical sketches of Berlin life.

**Glasse** (glȧs), **Hannah.** fl. 1747. English writer on cooking, housekeeping, etc.

**Glas′ser** (gläs′ẽr), **Otto.** 1895–1964. Biophysicist, b. in Germany; to U.S.; head of department of biophysics, Cleveland Clinic Foundation (from 1927). Worked on biological effects of radiations, esp. of X rays and the gamma rays of radium; developed a dosimeter.

**Glass′ford** (glȧs′fẽrd), **William Alexander, II.** 1886–1958. American naval officer; grad. U.S.N.A., Annapolis (1906); in command in Southwest Pacific (1942).

**Gla′ti′gny′** (glȧ′tē′nyē′), **Joseph Albert.** 1839–1873. French strolling minstrel.

**Glau′ber** (glou′bẽr), **Johann Rudolf.** 1604–1668. German chemist and physician; investigated decomposition of common salt through action of acids and bases. Glauber's salt is named after him.

**Glau'cus** (glô'kŭs). Chian artist of 6th century B.C.; worked esp. in metals; reputed inventor of art of soldering metals.

**Glaze'brook** (glāz'brŏŏk), Sir **Richard Tetley**. 1854–1935. English physicist; director of National Physical Laboratory (1899–1919); chairman, Aeronautical Research Committee (1908–33); editor of *Dictionary of Applied Physics*.

**Gla·zu·nov'** (glŭ·zŏŏ·nôf'), **Aleksandr Konstantinovich**. 1865–1936. Russian composer; friend of Liszt; won successes with his symphonies at Weimar (1884), Paris (1889), and London (1897); a director of Russian symphony concerts at St. Petersburg (1896–97); professor of music at St. Petersburg Conservatory (1900–06) and its director (1906–17); visited U.S. (1929).

**Glea'son** (glē's'n), **Frederic Grant**. 1848–1903. American composer of *The Culprit Fay* (a cantata), symphonies, *Otho Visconti* and *Montezuma* (operas), etc.

**Gleaves** (glēvz), **Albert**. 1858–1937. American naval officer, b. Nashville, Tenn.; rear admiral (1915). Promoted vice-admiral and admiral in World War I (1917–19); retired (1922), and promoted admiral on retired list. Conducted convoy operations in Atlantic (1917–19); commanded Asiatic station (1919–21).

**Glei'chen** (glī'kĕn), Lord **Edward**, *in full* **Albert Edward Wilfred**. 1863–1937. British soldier; major general (1917); in World War I organized and directed a new intelligence bureau in the department of information; retired (1919); chairman, Permanent Committee on Geographical Names. His sister Lady **Feodora Georgina Maud** (1861–1922), b. London, was a sculptor, designed and carved Queen Victoria group for the Children's Hospital, Montreal, the Edward VII Memorial at Windsor, the Florence Nightingale Memorial at Derby, the Kitchener Memorial in Khartoum Cathedral.

**Gleim** (glīm), **Johann Wilhelm Ludwig**. 1719–1803. German poet; best work contained in *Preussische Kriegslieder* (1758).

**Gleis'pach** (glīs'päκ), Count **Wenzel**. 1876–1944. Austrian jurist.

**Gleizes** (glâz), **Albert Léon**. 1881–1953. French painter and illustrator; identified with cubist movement.

**Glé'nard'** (glā'när'), **Alexandre**. 1818–1894. French chemist. His son **Frantz** (1848–1920), physician, first described enteroptosis (Glénard's disease).

**Glencairn**, Earl of. Title held by Scottish family of Cunningham; see Alexander CUNNINGHAM (d. 1574).

**Glen'dow'er** (*Eng.* glĕn'dou'ēr; glĕn'dou'ēr), **Owen**. *Welsh* **Ow'ain ab Gruf'fydd** (ō'ĭn ȧb grĭf'ĭth). 1359?–?1416. Welsh rebel; lord of Glyn·dwr' (*Welsh* glĭn-dŏŏr') and Sycharth. Head of Welsh rebellion against Henry of Bolingbroke when he ascended English throne as Henry IV (1399). Proclaimed himself prince of Wales, and waged war until 1415, when defeated and pardoned.

**Glenn** (glĕn), **John Herschel, Jr.** 1921– . Amer. astronaut, b. Cambridge, Ohio. Entered Marine Corps (1943). First American to orbit the earth in a spacecraft (1962); U.S. senator from Ohio (1975– ).

**Gleyre** (glâr), **Charles Gabriel**. 1808–1874. Swiss painter.

**Glid'den** (glĭd''n), **Carlos**. See under Christopher Latham SHOLES.

**Glidden, Charles Jasper**. 1857–1927. American pioneer in telephone industry, b. Lowell, Mass. Organized first telephone exchange, Lowell, Mass. (1877); developed system rapidly through country under New England Telephone & Telegraph Co., and Erie Telephone & Telegraph Co.; sold out interests to Bell organization (about 1901). Presented Glidden Trophy to American Automobile Association. Interested also in aeronautics.

**Glin'ka** (glyēn'kŭ), **Fëdor Nikolaevich**. 1786–1880. Russian soldier and author, b. Smolensk. Fought in campaigns of Austerlitz (1805) and against French invasion (1812–14); became a mystic (after 1853); wrote account of his army experiences (1815–16), poem *Kareliya* (1830), and poetical translations of parts of the Bible. His nephew **Mikhail Ivanovich** (1803–1857), composer, composed *A Life for The Czar* (first Russian national opera; 1836), and a second opera, *Russlan and Ludmilla*, based on a poem of Pushkin (1842), both successful; lived in Spain (1845–47) and wrote two overtures on Spanish national themes; other works include symphonies, songs, and orchestral suites.

**Glis'son** (glĭs''n), **Francis**. 1597–1677. English physician; one of founders of Royal Society.

**Gloag** (glōg), **John Edwards**. 1896– . English architect, designer, and writer; author of books on architecture and design, a book of verse, and several novels.

**Glotz** (glôts), **Gustave**. 1862–1935. French historian.

**Glouces'ter** (glŏs'tēr; glôs'-), Dukes of. For early creations see THOMAS OF WOODSTOCK (1355–1397), HUMPHREY (1391–1447), RICHARD III. Later creations included Henry (1639–1660), 3d son of Charles I and Henrietta Maria, Frederick Louis (1707–1751), Prince of Wales, and his 3d son and grandson.

Prince **Henry William Frederick Albert** 1900–1974. Son of George V and brother of Edward VIII and George VI; m. (1935) Lady **Alice Montagu-Douglas-Scott** (1901– ), daughter of 7th duke of Buccleuch; governor general of Australia (1945–46).

**Gloucester**, Earls of. See ROBERT (d. 1147), Earl of Gloucester; de CLARE family.

**Glouvet, Jules de.** Pseudonym of Jules QUESNAY DE BEAUREPAIRE.

**Glov'er** (glŭv'ēr), **John**. 1732–1797. American Revolutionary officer; colonel of Massachusetts militia regiment (1775); joined Continental army (1776); commanded vessels that transported American troops from Long Island; manned boats and led advance on Trenton (Dec. 25, 1776). Brigadier general (1777); in campaign against Burgoyne. Succeeded Sullivan in command at Providence, R.I. (1779). On court that sentenced André to be hanged as a spy (1780). Retired (1782). Member, Massachusetts convention to ratify constitution (1788).

**Glover, John**. 1767–1849. English landscape painter; a founder of the Society of British Artists.

**Glover, Julia**, *nee* **Bet'ter·ton** (bĕt'ēr·t'n; -tŭn). 1779–1850. English actress; m. Samuel Glover (1800); excelled in comedy. Her son **William Howard** (1819–1875), music critic on London *Morning Post* (1849–65), composed *Tam o' Shanter* (cantata; 1855), *Ruy Blas* (opera; 1861), overtures, and many songs.

**Glover, Richard**. 1712–1785. English poet, b. London; author of the ballad *Hosier's Ghost* (pub. in Percy's *Reliques*), the plays *Boadicea* (1753) and *Medea* (1763), and an epic in 30 books, *Athenaid* (pub. 1787).

**Glover, Sarah Ann**. 1785–1867. English music teacher; invented (c. 1812) tonic sol-fa system of notation.

**Glover, Stephen**. 1812–1870. English composer of popular songs and ballads. His brother **Charles William** (1806–1863) was a violinist and composer of songs.

**Glover, Terrot Reaveley**. 1869–1943. English classicist; public orator, Cambridge U. (1920–39); author of many works on classical and early Christian times, including studies of Vergil (1904), Jesus (1917), Herodotus (1924), St. Paul (1925 and 1942), Horace (1932).

**Głowacki, Aleksander**. See Bolesław PRUS.

**Glox'in** (glôk'sĕn), **Benjamin Peter**. Eighteenth-century German physician and botanist for whom the genus *Gloxinia* is named.

**Gluck** (glo͝ok), **Al′ma** (ăl′mȧ). *Maiden name* **Reba Fier′sohn** (fēr′zōn). 1884–1938. Operatic soprano, b. Bucharest, Rumania; to U.S. (1890); m. 1st Bernard Gluck, 2d (1914) Efrem Zimbalist (*q.v.*). Operatic debut, in New York (1909). Widely known also as concert singer.

**Glück** (glük), **Barbara Elisabeth.** *Pseudonym* **Betty Pa′o·li** (pä′ō·lē). 1814–1894. Austrian writer of verse, fiction, and critical studies.

**Gluck** (glo͝ok), **Christoph Willibald.** 1714–1787. German composer, b. Erasbach in Bavaria; court Kapellmeister (1754) and settled at Vienna (1756). Turned to new style of opera in effort to reform this musical form; produced masterpieces, as *Orfeo ed Euridice* (1762), *Alceste* (1767), *Paride ed Elene* (1769), *Iphigénie en Aulide* (1774), *Armide* (1777), and *Iphigénie en Tauride* (1779), which revolutionized opera by the expressive power and dramatic force of the music.

**Glücksburg.** See Oldenburg, 2 b and 4 b.

**Gly′con** (glī′kŏn) of Athens. Sculptor of 1st century B.C. (or later), who carved the so-called Farnese Hercules, discovered (1540) in the baths of Caracalla in Rome and now in the National Museum at Naples.

**Glyn** (glĭn), **Elinor,** *nee* **Suth′er·land** (sŭth′ēr·lănd). 1864–1943. British novelist, b. Island of Jersey; m. Clayton Glyn (1892; d. 1915). Author of *The Visits of Elizabeth* (1900), *Three Weeks* (1907), *Halcyone* (1912), *Man and Maid* (1922), *It* (1927), *Did She?* (1934), *Romantic Adventure* (1936); author also of motion-picture scenarios.

**Gme′lin** (g′mā′lēn). Name of German family of scientists of Tübingen, including: **Johann Georg** (1709–1755); with Bering and others explored Siberia as far as the Lena (1733–43); professor of botany and chemistry in Tübingen (1749). His nephew **Samuel Gottlieb** (1744–1774), botanist and traveler; explored southeastern Russia. **Johann Friedrich** (1748–1804), another nephew of Johann Georg, was professor of medicine and chemistry in Tübingen; made mineralogical researches; wrote a history of chemistry. His son **Leopold** (1788–1853), professor of medicine and chemistry in Heidelberg (1788–1853), discovered potassium ferricyanide (hence also called Gmelin's salt). Gmelin's test is named for him. **Christian Gottlob** (1792–1860), nephew of Samuel Gottlieb, was professor of chemistry in Tübingen; one of first to prepare artificial ultramarine.

**Gne′dich** (g′nyā′dyĭch), **Nikolai Ivanovich.** 1784–1833. Russian poet; best-known work a metrical translation (1809–29) of the *Iliad;* translated many works of Shakespeare, Voltaire, Schiller, Byron, and others.

**Gnei′se·nau** (g′nī′zĕ·nou), Count **August Neit′hardt** (nīt′härt) **von.** 1760–1831. Prussian field marshal; with British mercenary force in America (1782–83); in Prussian army (1786–1806). Served in Poland (1793–95); fought against Napoleon (1806–07); after Peace of Tilsit (1807), engaged with Scharnhorst in military reorganization of Prussia (1807–09); served in War of Liberation (1813–14); played important part at Leipzig and on Blücher's staff at Ligny and Waterloo; governor of Berlin (1818); made field marshal general (1825).

**Gneist** (g′nīst), **Rudolf von.** 1816–1895. German jurist and politician, b. Berlin. Professor, Berlin (1844). Member of Prussian Abgeordnetenhaus (1858–93) and of German Reichstag (1868–84). Judge of Prussian supreme court and member of Prussian privy council (1875).

**Gno′li** (nyô′lē), **Domenico.** *Pseudonyms* **Giulio Or·si′ni** (ōr·sē′nē) *and* **Dario Gad′di** (gäd′dē). 1838–1915. Italian scholar and writer; professor of Italian literature, Turin.

**Go** (gō̇). Japanese prefix meaning "coming after"; used with names of rulers, as *Go-Daigo*, etc., equivalent to the numeral II. See Daigo II.

**Go′bat′** (gô′bȧ′), **Charles Albert.** 1843–1914. Swiss lawyer and statesman; member of Nationalrat (1890–1914). Prominent advocate of international peace and awarded, jointly with Élie Ducommun, Nobel prize for peace (1902).

**Gobbo.** See Solari.

**Go′bel′** (gô′bĕl′), **Jean Baptiste Joseph.** 1727–1794. French Roman Catholic prelate; member of States-General (1789); accepted principles of the Revolution, and favored the worship of reason and marriage of the clergy; became constitutional archbishop of Paris; joined Hébertists and was guillotined with them.

**Gob′e·lin** (gŏb′ĕ·lĭn; *Fr.* gô′blăN′). Family of 15th-century French dyers, including **Gilles** and **Jehan** (fl. 1450), who established near Paris a factory, later famous for its tapestry, which was made a royal establishment by Louis XIV and is now the Manufacture Nationale des Gobelins.

**Go′bert′** (gô′bâr′), **Jacques Nicolas.** 1760–1808. French general in the Napoleonic armies. His son Baron **Napoléon** (1807–1833) founded two prizes of 10,000 francs each to be awarded each year to outstanding works on French history.

**Go′bi′neau′** (gô′bē′nō′), Comte **Joseph Arthur de.** 1816–1882. French diplomat, Orientalist, and writer; most important work, a sociological treatise, *Essai sur l'Inégalité des Races Humaines* (1854 and 1884), in which he advanced the theory (Gobinism) that the dolichocephalic blond Aryan, or Teuton, is the superior race among the races of men.

**Go′blet′** (gô′blĕ′), **René.** 1828–1905. French lawyer and politician; premier of France (1886–87).

**Goblet d'Al′viel′la′** (dȧl′vyĕ′lȧ′), **Albert Joseph.** 1790–1873. Belgian soldier and statesman; minister of foreign affairs (1832–33); lieutenant general (1835); minister at Lisbon; again minister of foreign affairs (1843–45).

**Goblet d'Alviella,** Comte **Eugène.** 1846–1925. Belgian politician and writer on religious history.

**Go′blot′** (gô′blō′), **Edmond,** *in full* **Léonce Laurent Edmond.** 1858–1935. French philosopher.

**Go′brecht** (gō′brĕKt), **Christian.** 1785–1844. American engraver, b. Hanover, Pa. Engraver, U.S. Mint, Philadelphia; his name appears on some of the specimens of U.S. pattern coins, known as Gobrecht dollars, of series struck in 1836, 1838, and 1839.

**Gob′ry·as** (gŏb′rĭ·ăs; gō′brĭ-). Persian governor of Gutium, region east of the Tigris below Nineveh; commanded army of Cyrus the Great that captured Babylon (539 B.C.; see Nabonidus). Father of Mardonius (*q.v.*).

**Goch.** See Johannes von Goch.

**Go·cle′ni·us** (gō·klē′nĭ·ŭs). *Lat. name of* **Rudolf Goeck′el** (gûk′ĕl). 1547–1628. German logician and philosopher. In logic, the Goclenian, or regressive, sorites derives its name from him.

**Go–Daigo.** See Go.

**Go′dard′** (gô′dȧr′), **Benjamin,** *in full* **Benjamin Louis Paul.** 1849–1895. French composer of symphonic and chamber music, several operas, and piano pieces and songs.

**God′dard** (gŏd′ẽrd), **Arabella.** 1836–1922. English pianist; m. J. W. Davison (1859); best known for interpretations of Beethoven.

**Goddard, Henry Herbert.** 1866–1957. American psychologist; professor, Ohio State U. (from 1922). Author of *The Kallikak Family* (1912, a study similar to that of the "Jukes family" by R. L. Dugdale, *q.v.*, 1877), *Feeble-Mindedness* (1914), *The Criminal Imbecile* (1915).

**Goddard, John.** 1724–1785. American colonial cabinetmaker, b. Dartmouth, Mass.

**Goddard, Pliny Earle.** 1869–1928. American ethnologist; on staff of American Museum of Natural History, New York (1909–28); writer of monographs on American Indian tribes.

**Goddard, Ralph Bartlett.** 1861–1936. American sculptor, b. Meadville, Pa.; best known for portrait busts.

**Goddard, Robert Hutchings.** 1882–1945. American physicist; engaged in rocket research for reaching high altitudes, in Roswell, N.Mex. (from 1934).

**Godden, Rumer.** Pseudonym of Mrs. Laurence FOSTER.

**Go'deb'ski'** (gô'dĕb'skē'), **Cyprien.** 1835–1909. French sculptor of Polish descent; carved statues of Marshal Laudon and Marshal Peter Lacy at Vienna, the monument commemorating the Crimean War at Sevastopol, the tomb of Théophile Gautier in the Montmartre cemetery in Paris, and the marble group *La Force Brutale Étouffant le Génie.*

**Go'de·froy'** (gôd'frwä'). *Lat.* **Goth'o·fre'dus** (gŏth'ō·frē'dŭs). French family, including: **Denis** the elder (1549–1621), jurist. His two sons **Théodore** (1580–1649), historian, and **Jacques** (1587–1652), jurist. Théodore's son **Denis** the younger (1615–1681), jurist.

**Godefroy, Frédéric Eugène.** 1826–1897. French literary historian and lexicographer.

**Goderich,** Viscounts. See Frederick John ROBINSON.

**Go'det'** (gô'dĕ'), **Frédéric.** 1812–1900. Swiss Protestant theologian; tutor to Prince Frederick William (who became Frederick III); professor, Neuchâtel (1850). A founder of Evangelical Church of Neuchâtel (1873), independent of the state, and a professor on its theological faculty. His son **Philippe Ernest** (1850–1922) was a poet and historian of literature.

**Go'dey** (gō'dĭ), **Louis An'toine** (ăn'twän). 1804–1878. American publisher, b. New York City. With Charles Alexander, established in Philadelphia the *Lady's Book* (1830), later known as *Godey's Lady's Book,* the first woman's periodical in the U.S.

**God'frey** (gŏd'frĭ), Sir **Edmund Berry.** 1621–1678. English jurist; received first depositions of Titus Oates (1678); found murdered shortly thereafter, and believed by some to have been assassinated by agents of Oates.

**Godfrey, Hollis.** 1874–1936. American engineer and educator; president, Drexel Inst. (1913–21). Associated with Elihu Root and others in creating Council of National Defense. Author of *The Man Who Ended War* (1908), *Creating Wealth* (1927), *Stable Profits* (1933), etc.

**Godfrey, Thomas.** 1704–1749. American mathematician and inventor, b. Philadelphia; asserted to be inventor of the improved quadrant now known as *Hadley's Quadrant.* His son **Thomas** (1736–1763) was a poet and playwright; author of lyric and narrative verse, and the *Prince of Parthia,* first drama by a native American to be produced on professional stage.

**God'frey of Bouil'lon'** (gŏd'frĭ ŭv bōō'yôN'). *Fr.* **Go'de·froy' de Bouil'lon'** (gôd'frwä' dē bōō'yôN'). 1061?–1100. French crusade leader. Made duke of Lower Lorraine by Henry IV (1088), having Bouillon as his capital. Joined First Crusade (1096–99); after capture of Jerusalem, elected "Baron and Defender of the Holy Sepulcher" (1099); defeated sultan of Egypt at Ascalon (1099). Subject of many legends; hero of Tasso's *Jerusalem Delivered.*

**Godfrey of Vi·ter'bo** (vē·tĕr'bō). 12th-century chronicler, prob. of Italian birth; his *Gesta Friderici I* is a valuable source book for period 1155 to 1180.

**Go'din'** (gô'dăN'), **Jean Baptiste André.** 1817–1888. French industrialist and social reformer; head of ironworks at Guise; influenced by Fourierism, established the familistère among his operatives. Author of *Solutions Sociales* (1871), *Le Gouvernement et le Vrai Socialisme en Action* (1883), etc.

**Godin, Louis.** 1704–1760. French astronomer.

**Go·di'va** (gō·dī'vȧ; -dē'vȧ) *or* **God'gi'fu** (gŏd'yĭ'vŏŏ). fl. 11th century. Wife of Leofric, Earl of Mercia. According to legend, rode naked through Coventry to win from her husband relief for the people of the town from burdensome taxation. Built and endowed monasteries at Stow and Coventry.

**God'kin** (gŏd'kĭn), **Edwin Lawrence.** 1831–1902. Editor and author, b. Moyne, County Wicklow, Ireland. To U.S. (1856); founder and editor, the *Nation,* a weekly periodical (1865; merged into New York *Evening Post,* 1881); editor in chief, N.Y. *Evening Post* (1883–1900).

**God'lee** (gŏd'lē), Sir **Rickman John.** 1849–1925. Nephew of Lord Lister. English surgeon; performed first operation for removal of a tumor from the brain (Nov. 25, 1884). President, Royal Coll. of Surgeons (1911–13) and Royal Society of Medicine (1916–18).

**God'ley** (gŏd'lĭ), **Alfred Denis.** 1856–1925. British poet and scholar, b. in County Cavan, Ireland. Author of *Verses to Order* (1892), *Lyra Frivola* (1899), etc.; also of *Socrates, and Athenian Society in his Age* (1896), etc.

**God'love** (gŏd'lŭv), **Isaac Hahn.** 1892–1954. American physicist and chemist; professor, U. of Oklahoma (1921–25). Colorimetrist in dyestuffs division of E. I. Du Pont de Nemours & Co. (1935–43). Special editor for color terms, *Webster's New International Dictionary, Second Edition.*

**God'man** (gŏd'măn), **John Davidson.** 1794–1830. American physician and naturalist.

**Go·dol'phin** (gō·dŏl'fĭn), **Sidney.** 1st Earl of **Godolphin.** 1645–1712. English statesman; secretary of state (1684); chamberlain to Queen Mary of Modena (1685); loyal to James II, with whom he kept up secret correspondence after James left England (1688). Lord high treasurer of England, and ally of Marlborough (1702–10). Dismissed from office by Queen Anne (1710), but allowed a pension for life.

**Go·dow'sky** (gō·dôf'skē), **Leopold.** 1870–1938. Piano virtuoso and composer, b. Wilno, Russia. Director of piano department, Chicago Conservatory of Music (1895–1900). Settled in St. Louis, Mo. (1912), and became editor for Art Publication Society.

**Go·doy', Manuel de.** *In full* **Manuel de Go·doy' y Ál'va·rez de Fa'ria** (dā gō·thoi' ē äl'vä·rāth thā fä'ryä). 1767–1851. Spanish statesman, b. in Badajoz. Gained favor of King Charles IV and Queen Maria Louisa (1788–91). Granted title of Duke of Alcudia (1791); made minister (1792–97); declared war against France (1792–95); defeated; negotiated Treaty of Basel (1795), for which he was granted title of "Prince of the Peace." Returned to power (1801); compelled by French to lead Spain in attack on Portugal (1801); aided France in war with England (1801–05) but made very unpopular by arbitrary acts and by defeat of Spanish fleet at Trafalgar (1805). Imprisoned by king; aided by Napoleon (1808). Lived in Rome, Paris, and Madrid (1808–51); wrote *Memoirs* (pub. in English 1836).

**Godoy de Alcayaga.** See Gabriela MISTRAL.

**Go·du·nov'** (gŭ·dŏŏ·nôf'), **Boris Fëdorovich.** 1551?–1605. Czar of Russia. A favorite of Ivan IV; chief member of regency during reign (1584–98) of his brother-in-law, the young Czar Fëdor Ivanovich; said to have caused death (1591) of Czarevitch Demetrius (Dmitri); defeated the Crimean Tatars (1591), recovered territory from Sweden (1595), and recolonized Siberia. On Fëdor's death (1598), elected to throne; died in struggle with false Demetrius and boyars. His career subject of a play by Pushkin and an opera by Musorgski, based on the play.

**God'win** (gŏd'wĭn) *or* **God'wi'ne** (gŏd'wĭ'nĕ). d. 1053. Earl of the West Saxons. Instrumental in placing Edward the Confessor on the throne (1042); arranged a marriage between his daughter Edith (Eadgyth) and the king.

**God'win** (gŏd'wĭn), **Francis.** 1562–1633. English ecclesiastic; bishop of Llandaff (1601), of Hereford (1617). From his romance *Man in the Moone* (pub. 1638), John Wilkins and Cyrano de Bergerac are supposed to have borrowed their sketches of life in the moon.

**Godwin, Mary,** *nee* **Woll'stone·craft** (wo͝ol'stŭn-krȧft). 1759–1797. English author. Formed connection in Paris with Gilbert Imlay (1793–95) and on his desertion of her and their daughter Fanny, attempted suicide; m. William Godwin the elder (1797) and died on birth of daughter Mary (second wife of Shelley; see Mary Wollstonecraft SHELLEY). Author of *Vindication of the Rights of Women* (1792), plain-spoken attack on conventions.

**Godwin, Parke.** 1816–1904. American journalist and author. On staff, N.Y. *Evening Post* (1837–81); editor in chief (1878–81). Editor, *Commercial Advertiser* (from 1881). Author of *A Popular View of the Doctrine of Fourier* (1844), *Democracy, Constructive and Pacific* (1844), *Out of the Past* (1870). Compiled *Hand-Book of Universal Biography* (1852).

**Godwin, William.** 1756–1836. English philosopher, novelist, and miscellaneous writer. Dissenting minister (1777–82); became atheist and devoted himself to study and writing. Married (1797) Mary Wollstonecraft, who died same year; m. 2d (1801) Mrs. Clairmont. Later converted by Coleridge to theism. Started a publishing business (1805) which failed (1822); published Lamb's *Tales from Shakespeare* and some children's books of his own (under pseudonym **Edward Bald'win** [bôld'wĭn]). Author of *Enquiry Concerning Political Justice* (1793; which gained him a reputation as philosophical representative of English radicalism), the novels *Adventures of Caleb Williams* (1794) and *St. Leon* (1799), *Life of Chaucer* (1803), an essay *Of Population* (1820; in answer to Malthus), and a *History of the Commonwealth* (1824–28). See Mary Wollstonecraft GODWIN and Mary Wollstonecraft SHELLEY.

**God'win-Aus'ten** (-ôs'tĕn; -tĭn), **Henry Haversham.** 1834–1923. English explorer and geologist. Attached to Great Trigonometrical Survey of India (1856); carried on survey work in northern India in regions not theretofore visited by Europeans (1856–77).

**Godwin-Austen, Robert Alfred Cloyne.** 1808–1884. English geologist; B.A., Oxon. (1830); author of treatises on geological formations in England, esp. a paper (1854) *On the Possible Extension of the Coal-Measures beneath the South-Eastern Parts of England.*

**Goeb'bels** (gûb'ĕls), **Joseph Paul.** 1897–1945. German politician; district leader of Nazi party in Berlin (1926); organized party membership in northern Germany. Founder (1927) and editor of the Nazi journal *Der Angriff.* Nazi party propaganda leader (1929); minister for propaganda and national enlightenment (1933 ff.); member of Hitler's cabinet council (1938 ff.); suicide.

**Goe'bel** (gû'bĕl), **Julius.** 1857–1931. Philologian, b. Frankfort, Ger. To U.S. (1882); professor of Germanic philology and literature, Stanford (1892–1905) and Illinois (1908–26). Editor, *Journal of English and Germanic Philology* (1909–26).

**Goe'bel** (gō'bĕl), **Julius.** 1892– . American lawyer and educator; professor of law (1931), and of legal history (1937), Columbia.

**Goe'bel** (gû'bĕl), **Karl Eberhardt von.** 1855–1932. German botanist; wrote esp. on organography of plants.

**Goe'ben** (gû'bĕn), **August von.** 1816–1880. Prussian soldier; distinguished himself in battles of Spichern (Aug. 7, 1870) and Gravelotte (Aug. 18, 1870); succeeded Manteuffel in command of 1st army and won decisive battle of St.-Quentin (Jan. 18–19, 1871).

**Goeckel, Rudolf.** See GOCLENIUS.

**Goe'deck·e·mey'er** (gû'dĕ·kĕ·mī'ẽr), **Albert.** b. 1873. German philosopher.

**Goe'de·ke** (gû'dĕ·kĕ), **Karl.** *Pseudonym* **Karl Stahl** (shtäl). 1814–1887. German scholar; author of *Deutsche Dichtung im Mittelalter* (1854), and *Grundriss zur Geschichte der Deutschen Dichtung* (3 vols., 1859–81).

**Goe'je** (go͞o'yĕ), **Jan de,** *in full* **Michael Jan de.** 1836–1909. Dutch Arabic scholar; professor at Leiden (from 1866); edited many Arabic works.

**Goeppert-Mayer, Maria.** See Maria Goeppert MAYER.

**Goering.** = GÖRING.

**Go'es** (gō'ēsh), **Damião de.** 1501–1573. Portuguese Humanist, historian, and diplomat; engaged in diplomatic missions in Flanders (1523), Poland (1529), Denmark and Sweden (1533); historiographer and archivist, Lisbon (1546); arrested by Inquisition on charges of Lutheranism (1571); imprisoned in monastery at Batalha (1572). Known esp. for *Crónica do Felicíssimo Rei Dom Manuel* (4 vols., 1566–67).

**Goes** (go͞os), **Hugo van der.** 1440?–1482. Dutch painter, b. Ghent; painted great altarpiece, *The Adoration of the Shepherds,* for chapel in hospital of Santa Maria Nuova, Florence, Italy, now preserved in Ufizzi Gallery in Florence.

**Goes, Jan Antonisz van der.** *Latin* **Joannes An·to'ni·des** (ăn·tō'nĭ·dēz; *Du.* än·tō'nē·dĕs). 1647–1684. Dutch poet; chief work, *De IJstroom* (1671).

**Goe'tel** (gĕ'tĕl), **Ferdynand.** 1890–1960. Polish novelist; author of a number of exotic novels, including *Kar-Chat, The Pilgrim of Karapet, Across the Flaming Orient.*

**Goe'thals** (gō'thălz), **George Washington.** 1858–1928. American army officer and engineer, b. Brooklyn, N.Y. Grad. U.S.M.A., West Point (1880). Appointed by President Theodore Roosevelt as chief engineer on Panama Canal Commission (1907). Carried canal construction through to completion (1914). Goethals, promoted major general (1915), remained as governor of Canal Zone (until 1916). During World War I, on active duty as acting quartermaster general and director of purchase, storage, and traffic. Head of consulting engineering firm, George W. Goethals & Co. (1923–28).

**Goe'the** (gû'tĕ), **August von.** 1789–1830. Son of Johann Wolfgang von Goethe (*q.v.*). German government official; chamberlain to the grand duke of Saxe-Weimar. His wife, **Ottilie,** Baroness **von Pog'wisch** (pôk'vĭsh) (1796–1872), took care of Johann Wolfgang von Goethe during his last years, after the death (1816) of his wife. Children of August and Ottilie were **Walther Wolfgang** (1818–1885), a composer; **Wolfgang Maximilian** (1820–1883), a jurist and writer; and **Alma** (1827–1844).

**Goethe, Johann Wolfgang von.** 1749–1832. German poet, b. at Frankfurt am Main. Educ. Leipzig; studied law at Strasbourg; licensed to practice law (1771). During his year at Strasbourg, was strongly influenced by Herder. Returned to Frankfurt (1772) and published (1773) his tragedy *Götz von Berlichingen;* its success established Shakespearean form of drama on German stage, and inaugurated German literary movement known as "Sturm und Drang." A year later (1774), he published *Die Leiden des Jungen Werthers,* a romantic love story inspired by an affair with Charlotte Buff (*q.v.*). On invitation from Charles Augustus, heir apparent to duchy of Saxe-Weimar, Goethe settled in Weimar (1775), then the literary and intellectual center of Germany; became a leader in the life at Weimar, and an associate of Wieland, Herder, and later, of Schiller; formed romantic attachment for Charlotte von Stein, wife of a Weimar official. Was ennobled, created a privy councilor, and appointed to administrative posts, where he acquitted himself with credit; produced chiefly lyrics during this period. Visited Italy (1786–88; 1790), and received new inspiration; published the verse dramas *Iphigenie auf Tauris* (1787), *Egmont* (1788), *Torquato Tasso* (1790). Firm literary friendship (from 1794) with Schiller stimulated Goethe; he published *Wilhelm Meisters Lehrjahre* (1796), the epic idyll *Hermann und Dorothea* (1798), and a number of poems, including *Der Zauberlehrling, Der Gott und die Bajadere, Die Braut von Korinth, Alexis und Dora, Der Neue Pausias, Die Schöne Müllerin* (a verse cycle); wrote also first part of *Faust* (not pub. until 1808). Married Christiane Vulpius (1806), who had been a member of his household (from 1788); but even after this period formed romantic attachments with various women, including Bettina von Arnim, Minna Herzlieb, Marianne von Willemer, Ulrike von Levetzow. His later years were distinguished by completion of his novel *Die Wahlverwandtschaften* (1809), his autobiography under the title *Aus Meinem Leben, Dichtung und Wahrheit* (vol. I, 1811; II, 1812; III, 1814; IV, 1833), *Italienische Reise* (1816–17), *Westöstlicher Diwan* (a collection of lyrics, 1819), *Wilhelm Meisters Wanderjahre* (1821–29), *Trilogie der Leidenschaft* (1822), and the second part of *Faust* (1832). Exercised dominant influence on development of German literature; his *Götz von Berlichingen* inaugurated the romantic school; his *Die Leiden des Jungen Werthers*, the sentimental school; his *Faust*, the modern spirit in literature.

**Goethe–Tischbein.** See J. H. W. TISCHBEIN.

**Goe'tschi·us** (gěch'ĭ·ŭs), **Percy.** 1853–1943. American music educator; professor, New England Conservatory of Music (1892–96); on teaching staff of Inst. of Musical Art, New York (1905–25). Author of books on musical art, history, and appreciation.

**Goetz.** See GÖTZ.

**Goe'ze** (gû'tsě), **Johann Melchior.** 1717–1786. German Lutheran theologian; known esp. for long controversy with Lessing because of publication of Reimarus's *Fragmente eines Ungenannten* in Lessing's "Wolfenbüttel Fragments."

**Goff** (gŏf), **John William.** 1848–1924. American jurist, b. Ireland. Counsel for Lexow Committee investigating New York City police administration (1893–94); justice, New York State supreme court (1906–19).

**Goffe** *or* **Gough** (gŏf), **William.** d. about 1679. English regicide; one of judges at trial of Charles I; held military command under Cromwell at Dunbar (1650), Worcester (1651); major general for Sussex, Berkshire, and Hampshire (1655). At Restoration, fled to America.

**Go'ga** (gŏ'gä), **Octavian.** 1881–1938. Rumanian writer and politician; author of poems on Transylvanian life; awarded national prize for poetry. Joined Rumanian army during World War I; member of Rumanian delegation at Peace Conference in Paris (1919). Founded (1921) National Agrarian party, which was merged (1935) with League for National Christian Defense. Prime minister of Rumania (1937–38); promulgated anti-Semitic decrees.

**Go'gar·ty** (gō'gẽr·tĭ), **Oliver St. John.** 1878–1957. Irish physician and writer; senator (1922–36), Irish Free State. Author of *Poems and Plays* (1920), *An Offering of Swans* (1924), *As I was going down Sackville Street* (1937), *Tumbling in the Hay* (1939), etc.

**Gogh** (gŏκ), **Vincent van.** 1853–1890. Dutch painter, etcher, and lithographer; associated with postimpressionist school. Studio at Brussels (1880), Antwerp (1885), and Paris; settled at Arles, Provence (1888). Among his notable canvases are *The Potato Eaters, The Restaurant on Montmartre* (in the Luxembourg), *L'Arlésienne, Berceuse*, and *Mairie au 14 Juillet.*

**Go'gol** (gô'gŭl·y'), **Nikolai Vasilievich.** 1809–1852. Russian writer, b. near Mirgorod, Poltava. Left Russia (1836), living most of time in Rome; after 1835, devoted himself to literature. His first works two series of Ukrainian sketches, *Evenings on a Farm near Dikanka* (1831) and *Mirgorod* (1835), including *Taras Bulba* (rewritten and enlarged, 1842), one of the best of his historical novels, a tale of Cossack struggles with Poles and Tartars in 16th century; also wrote *Dead Souls*, a social satire (1842, first part only), *Revizor*, or *The Inspector General*, a comedy ridiculing corruption and ignorance of petty officials (1836), and *Cossack Tales* (1836); called father of realism in Russian literature.

**Go'guel'** (gô'gĕl'), **Maurice.** 1880–1955. French Protestant theologian; professor, faculty of Protestant theology, Paris (from 1910); director, École des Hautes Études, Paris (1927); author of *Jésus de Nazareth: Mythe ou Histoire* (1925), *Jésus et les Origines du Christianisme* (1934).

**Go'hier'** (gô'yā'), **Louis Jérôme.** 1746–1830. French jurist and politician.

**Gohl.** See Jacobus GOLIUS.

**Goijen, Jan van.** See Jan van GOYEN.

**Go'ing** (gō'ĭng), **Charles Buxton.** b. 1863. American writer; on staff of *Engineering Magazine* (1896–1915). Author of *Summer-Fallow* (1892), *Star-Glow and Song* (1909), *Principles of Industrial Engineering* (1911), *Adventures in Statecraft* (1940), etc.

**Go'kha·le** (gō'kȧ·lāɴ), **Gopal Krishna.** 1866–1915. Indian educator and politician; taught at Fergusson Coll., Poona (1884–1902). Became identified with Indian National Congress movement; served as its president (1905); founded Servants of India Society (1905); member of Indian Public Services Commission (1912–15); a leader of the moderate Nationalists.

**Golaw, Salomon von.** Pseudonym of Baron Friedrich von LOGAU.

**Gol'dast** (gôl'däst), **Melchior.** *Known as* **Goldast von Hai'mens·feld** (fôn hī'mĕns·fĕlt). 1578–1635. German jurist and historian.

**Gold'beck** (gōld'bĕk), **Robert.** 1839–1908. Pianist, teacher, and composer, b. Potsdam, Prussia; to U.S. (c. 1861); with Eben Lourjée founded (1867) New England Conservatory of Music.

**Gold'berg** (gōld'bûrg), **Arthur Joseph.** 1908– . Am. lawyer, b. Chicago, Ill. U.S. Secretary of Labor (1961–62); associate justice, U.S. Supreme Court (1962–65); U.S. ambassador to the United Nations (1965–68).

**Goldberg, Isaac.** 1887–1938. American writer, b. Boston. A.B. (1910) and Ph.D. (1912), Harvard. Literary editor, *American Freeman* (1923–32). Special lecturer on Hispano-American literature, Harvard; instrumental in introducing to English readers the modern literature of Spanish and Portuguese America (*Studies in Spanish-American Literature*, 1920; *Brazilian Literature*, 1922). Among his other books are *The Fine Art of Living* (1929), *What Makes You Laugh and Why* (1938), and *The Wonder of Words* (1939).

**Goldberg, Reuben Lucius,** *known as* **Rube** (ro͞ob). 1883–1970. American cartoonist and comic-strip artist, b. San Francisco. B.S., California (1904). On staff of

New York *Evening Mail* (1907–21); syndicate cartoonist (1921–64); known for cartoons of mechanical contrivances whose humor derives from the absurdly unnecessary complexity of the contrivances depicted, and as creator of comic characters "Boob McNutt," "Lala Palooza," etc.

**Gold'ber'ger** (gōld'bûr'gẽr), **Joseph.** 1874–1929. American physician, b. in Austria; to U.S. At Hygienic Laboratory, Washington, D.C. (from 1904); discoverer of nature of and remedy for pellagra (1913–25).

**Gol'den** (gōl'dĕn), **John.** 1874–1955. American playwright and producer, b. New York City. Wrote or produced *Turn to the Right, Lightnin', Three Wise Fools, When Ladies Meet, Susan and God.* Composer also of many songs, and producer of musical comedies.

**Gol'den·wei'ser** (gōl'dĕn·vī'zẽr), **Alexander A.** 1880–1940. American anthropologist and sociologist, b. Kiev, Russia. To U.S.; A.B. (1902) and Ph.D. (1910), Columbia. Lecturer, Columbia (1910–19), New School for Social Research, New York (1919–26), Rand School of Social Science (1915–29); professor of thought and culture, Oregon State System of Higher Education, Portland Extension (from 1930). Author of *Totemism* (1910), *Early Civilization* (1922), *Our Changing Morality* (1924), *Population Problems* (1925), *Sex in Civilization* (1929), *Robots or Gods* (1932), *History, Psychology and Culture* (1933), *Anthropology, An Introduction to Primitive Culture* (1937).

**Gol'die** (gōl'dĭ), Sir **George Dashwood Taub'man** (?tôb'măn). 1846–1925. English colonial administrator, b. on the Isle of Man. Visited Niger region (1877) and deliberately set out to add this region to the British Empire; accomplished his purpose by merging commercial companies trading in the Niger region and obtaining a charter from the British Parliament conferring governmental powers on officers of the combine, which became known as the Royal Niger Co. (1886); government organized with Lord Aberdare as governor (1886–95), succeeded by Goldie (1895). The Royal Niger Co. transferred its territories to the British government (1900) and they were organized into the protectorates of Northern Nigeria and Southern Nigeria.

**Gol'ding** (gōl'dĭng), **Arthur.** 1536?–?1605. English translator; translated Ovid's *Metamorphoses* (1565–67), which was known to Shakespeare.

**Golding, Louis.** 1895–1958. English writer, b. Manchester. Author of verse, as in *Sorrow of War* (1919), *Shepherd Singing Ragtime* (1921), and *Prophet and Fool* (1923), and novels, as *Forward from Babylon* (1920), *Store of Ladies* (1927), *Give up your Lovers* (1930), *Magnolia Street* (1932; dramatized 1934), *The Camberwell Beauty* (1935), *Mr. Emmanuel* (1939), etc.

**Golding, William Gerald.** 1911– . British author. Wrote *Lord of the Flies* (1954), *The Inheritors* (1955), *Pincher Martin* (1956), *Free Fall* (1959), etc.

**Gold'man** (gōld'măn), **Edwin Fran'ko** (frăng'kō). 1878–1956. American composer and band conductor.

**Goldman, Emma.** 1869–1940. Anarchist, b. in province of Kovno (Kaunas), Russia; to U.S. (1886) and soon after identified herself with anarchist party. For agitation in New York, was arrested and sentenced to a year's imprisonment in Blackwells Island (1893). Delegate to first (1899) and second (1907) anarchist congresses. Author of *Anarchism and Other Essays* (1910), *Living My Life,* autobiography (1931).

**Goldman, Solomon.** 1893-1953. Russian-born American rabbi: congregations in Brooklyn (1917–18), Cleveland (1919–29), Chicago (from 1929).

**Gold'mann** (gōld'măn), **Na'hum** (nä'hōōm). 1895– . American (Polish-born) Jewish scholar and Zionist leader.

**Gold'mark** (gôlt'märk; *Eng.* gōld'märk), **Karl.** 1830–1915. Hungarian composer of operas, symphonies, symphonic poems, overtures, violin concertos, chamber music, piano pieces, songs. His nephew **Rubin** (1872–1936), b. New York, composed symphonic poems, tone poems, sonatas, overtures, and songs.

**Gold'mark** (gōld'märk), **Peter Carl.** 1906–1977. Am. (Hungarian-born) engineer; with Columbia Broadcasting System (1936–71); president, CBS Laboratories (1954–71); credited with invention of color television (1940).

**Gol·do'ni** (gôl·dō'nē), **Carlo.** 1707–1793. Italian playwright, b. Venice. Wrote for Teatro Sant'Angelo (1748–52) and Teatro San Luca (1752 ff.) in Venice. Created modern Italian comedy in style of Molière, superseding conventional buffoonery (commedia dell'arte) typified by Harlequin and Pantaleone. Among his comedies, about 150 in all, are *La Donna di Garbo, Un Curioso Accidente, Pamela Nubile, I Rusteghi, Il Vero Amico, Todero Brontalon, La Casa Nuova, La Locandiera, Il Vecchio Bizzarro, L'Adulatore,* and *Ventaglio.*

**Gol'dring** (gōl'drĭng), **Douglas.** 1887-1960. English editor and writer; author of *Ways of Escape, A Book of London Verses, Margot's Progress, Cuckoo, The Façade, The Coast of Illusion, Pot Luck in England,* etc.

**Golds'bor'ough** (gōldz'bûr'ō), **Louis Males'herbes'** (?măl'zĕrb'). 1805–1877. American naval officer; explored California and Oregon (1849–50). In command of blockading squadron at outbreak of Civil War. Commanded fleet that captured Roanoke Island and destroyed Confederate fleet (Feb. 7–9, 1862).

**Gold'schmidt** (gôlt'shmĭt), **Adolph.** 1863–1944. German art scholar; professor, Halle (1904), Berlin (1912), Harvard (1927–28; 1930–31), New York U. (1936–37).

**Goldschmidt, Hans.** 1861–1923. German chemist; invented the aluminothermic, or Goldschmidt's, process of producing great heat for reducing certain metals from their oxides and for obtaining molten iron for welding.

**Goldschmidt, James.** 1874– . German jurist; professor, Berlin (1908–33).

**Goldschmidt, Levin.** 1829–1897. German jurist; specialist in commercial law.

**Gold'schmidt** (gôl'shmĕt), **Meyer** (*or* **Meir**) **Aaron.** 1819–1887. Danish journalist, fiction writer, and politician. Author of *En Jöde* (1845; trans. as *The Jew of Denmark*), *Hjemlös* (5 vols., 1853–57; trans. as *Homeless; or, A Poet's Inner Life*), and an autobiography *Livserindringer* (1877).

**Gold'schmidt** (gôlt'shmĭt), **Otto.** 1829–1907. German-born pianist and composer in England; toured in America with Jenny Lind (1851), and married her (1852). Settled in England (1856); pianoforte professor at Royal Academy of Music (1863). Composer esp. of piano works.

**Goldschmidt, Richard Benedikt G.** 1878–1958. German zoologist; professor, U. of California (1936 ff.). Author of *Physiological Genetics* (1938), *The Material Basis of Evolution* (1940), etc.

**Goldschmidt, Rudolph.** 1876–1950. German engineer; inventor of high-frequency generator used in wireless telegraphy.

**Goldschmied, Johann.** = Johann AURIFABER (both).

**Gold'smid** (gōld'smĭd). Prominent English Jewish family, including: **Benjamin** (1753?–1808) and his brother **Abraham** (1756?–1810), financiers. Abraham's nephew Sir **Isaac Lyon Goldsmid** (1778–1859), financier and philanthropist, England's first Jewish baronet. Isaac's son Sir **Francis Henry** (1808–1878), first English Jewish barrister; M.P. (from 1860). Benjamin's grandson Sir **Frederick John** (1818–1908), army officer in

China (1840), Crimean War (1854–55), and Sepoy Mutiny; major general. See C. J. Goldsmid-MONTEFIORE.

**Goldsmid-Montefiore, Claude Joseph.** See C. J. Goldsmid-MONTEFIORE.

**Gold′smith** (gōld′smĭth), **Oliver.** 1728–1774. British poet, playwright, and novelist, b. in County Longford, Ireland. Studied medicine in Edinburgh. After a year of roaming through Europe, tried practice of medicine in London (1756), but failed; devoted himself to literary hack work to make a living. Became acquainted with Dr. Johnson (1761) and a member of the famous club centered around Johnson. Author of *Enquiry into the Present State of Polite Learning in Europe* (1759), *The Citizen of the World* (1762; orig. contributed as "Chinese Letters" to Newbery's *Universal Chronicle*), *The Traveller* (didactic poem; 1764), *The Vicar of Wakefield* (novel; 1766), *The Goodnatured Man* (comedy; 1768), *The Deserted Village* (poem; 1770), *A History of England* (1771), *She Stoops to Conquer* (comedy; 1773), *The History of Greece* (1774), etc.

**Gold′stein** (gôlt′shtīn), **Eugen.** 1850–1930. German physicist; investigated electrical phenomena in gases; studied cathode rays; credited with discovery of canal rays (1886).

**Gold′stein** (gôlt′shtīn; *Angl.* gōld′stīn), **Kurt.** 1878–1965. German neuropsychiatrist; head of neurophysiology laboratory, Montefiore Hospital, N.Y. (1936–40); professor, Tufts Medical School (1940–45).

**Gold′stück′er** (gôlt′shtü′kẽr), **Theodor.** 1821–1872. German-born Sanskrit scholar in England (from 1850).

**Gold′wa′ter** (gōld′wô′tẽr; -wŏt′ẽr), **Barry Morris.** 1909– . Amer. politician, b. Phoenix, Ariz. Member, U.S. Senate (1953–64; 1968– ) from Arizona; Republican candidate for president of U.S. (1964).

**Gold′wyn** (gōld′wĭn), **Samuel.** *Family name orig.* **Gold′fish** (gōld′fĭsh). 1882–1974. Motion-picture producer, b. Poland; to U.S. (1896), naturalized (1902). Organized Goldwyn Pictures Corp. (1919). Instrumental in inducing eminent authors and actors to enter motion-picture field. Merged with other companies (see L. B. MAYER) to form Metro-Goldwyn-Mayer Corp.

**Gold′zi′her** (gôlt′tsē′ẽr), **Ignaz.** 1850–1921. Hungarian Arabic scholar.

**Go′ler** (?gō′lẽr), **George Washington.** 1864–1940. American physician; medical inspector (1892–96) and health officer (1896–1932), Rochester Board of Health; established first municipal milk depots in U.S. (1897); established Rochester Hospital for Infectious Diseases (1904).

**Gol′gi** (gôl′jē), **Camillo.** 1844–1926. Italian physician. First to use silver nitrate to stain nerve tissue for study; proved that there is interlacement of nerves instead of a network. The Golgi apparatus, Golgi cell, etc., are named after him; discovered three varieties of malarial parasites. Shared with Santiago Ramón y Cajal 1906 Nobel prize for physiology and medicine.

**Go·li′ath** (gō·lī′ăth). In Bible (*1 Samuel* xvii), the Philistine giant of Goth killed by David with a sling.

**Go·li′tsyn** (gŭ·lyē′tsĭn). Noble Russian family, descended from the boyar **Mikhail Ivanovich Bul·ga′kov** (bŏŏl·gá′kôf), *called* **Golitsa** (d. 1554) and including: Prince **Vasili Vasilievich Golitsyn** (1643–1714), general and statesman; reorganized Russian army; prime minister during regency of Sophia Alekseevna (to 1689); exiled to Siberia. His cousin Prince **Mikhail Mikhailovich** (1674–1730), general; served under Peter the Great in defeating Charles XII of Sweden at Poltava (1709). Mikhail's brother Prince **Dmitri Mikhailovich** (1654–1738), diplomat and statesman; ambassador to Constantinople and to Vienna (1713–19); member of High Council and supporter of charter forced upon Anna Ivanovna at her elevation to throne (1730); imprisoned by Empress Anna when she repudiated charter (1731). Prince **Boris Alekseevich** (1654–1714), minister under Peter the Great. Prince **Dmitri Alekseevich** (1738–1803), ambassador to France and at The Hague; author of scientific treatises. See also Demetrius Augustine GALLITZIN. **Nikolai Borisovich** (d. 1865), friend and patron of Beethoven, to whom Beethoven dedicated three quartets and an overture. **Boris Borisovich** (1862–1916), physicist, known for his work in seismography. **Nikolai,** successor of Aleksandr Trepov (Jan. 7, 1917) as prime minister of Russia, holding office for a month just before the Revolution.

**Go′li·us** (gō′lē·ŭs) *or* **Gohl** (gōl), **Jacobus.** 1596–1667. Dutch Oriental scholar.

**Goll** (gôl), **Friedrich.** 1829–1903. Swiss physician; first described fasciculus gracilis, or column of Goll, a tract of the spinal cord (1860).

**Goll, Jaroslav.** 1846–1929. Czech poet and historian.

**Gol′lancz** (gŏl′ănts), Sir **Hermann.** 1852–1930. Rabbi and Semitic scholar, b. Bremen; educ. University Coll., London; first Jew to obtain D.Litt. degree there; preacher at the Bayswater Synagogue (1892–1923); professor of Hebrew, University Coll., London (1902–23); knighted (1923), first British rabbi so honored; widely known as philanthropist and as founder of synagogues in working-class areas. His brother Sir **Israel** (1864–1930), educ. University Coll., London, and Cambridge, was lecturer at Cambridge (1896–1906); professor of English language and literature, University Coll., London; edited and published *Cynewulf's Christ* (1892), *Exeter Book of Anglo-Saxon Poetry* (1895), *Temple Shakespeare* (1894–96), and *The Sources of Hamlet* (1926); edited also *The Temple Classics*, and *The Caedmon Manuscript of Anglo-Saxon Biblical Poetry.*

**Go·lov·nin′** (gŭ·lŭf·nyĕn′), **Vasili Mikhailovich.** 1776–1831. Russian navigator. Served in British navy under Nelson and Cornwallis; on return to Russia (1806), given command of *Diana*, in which he surveyed coasts of Russian empire and circumnavigated globe; made second circumnavigation in *Kamchatka.*

**Golsch′mann** (gōlsh′măn), **Vla′di·mir** (vlà′dē·mẽr). 1893–1972. Conductor, b. Paris, France. Founder and director, Concerts Golschmann, Paris (1919–24); conductor, St. Louis Symphony Orchestra (1931–57).

**Gol′ter·mann** (gôl′tẽr·măn), **Georg.** 1824–1898. German violoncellist and composer.

**Gol′ther** (gôl′tẽr), **Wolfgang.** 1863–1945. German scholar; author of *Deutsche Heldensage* (1894), *Handbuch der Germanischen Mythologie* (1895), *Die Deutsche Dichtung im Mittelalter* (1913), etc.; editor of Wagner's letters and collected works (1914).

**Goltz** (gôlts), Count **August Friedrich Ferdinand von der.** 1765–1832. Prussian statesman, b. Dresden. Prussian minister at St. Petersburg (1802); minister of foreign affairs (1807); concluded Treaty of Tilsit (1807) with Napoleon and represented Prussia at Congress of Erfurt (1808); under Hardenberg's instructions, negotiated with Napoleon (1812).

**Goltz, Bogumil.** 1801–1870. German humorist and moral philosopher.

**Goltz, Friedrich Leopold.** 1834–1902. German physiologist. Authority on the physiology of the nervous system.

**Goltz,** Baron **Kolmar von der.** 1843–1916. German general; in Turkey (1883–96), reorganized Turkish army; in Germany, general of infantry (1900) and lieutenant general (1908). Again in Turkey (1908–10). Military governor of Belgium after its conquest (1914). After entry of Turkey into World War I, directed Turkish armies; died on Turkish front (Apr. 19, 1916).

**Goltz,** Count **Robert von der.** 1817–1869. Prussian diplomat; minister at Athens (1857), Constantinople (1859), St. Petersburg (1862), Paris (1863); at Paris, carried through skillfully negotiations with Napoleon III at time of Seven Weeks' War (1866).

**Goltz,** Count **Rüdiger von der.** 1865–1930. German general in the World War (1914–18); commanded a Landwehr division in battle of the Masurian Lakes (1915); commander in chief in the Baltic countries (1918).

**Gol'tzi·us** (gŏl'tsē·ŭs), **Hendrik.** 1558–1617. Dutch engraver, etcher, and painter; founded engraving school at Haarlem (1582); among his best works are engraved portraits, many of them miniatures, and prints after Italian painters.

**Go'lu·chow'ski** (gō'lo͞o·κôf'skē), Count **Agenor von.** 1812–1875. Austrian statesman of Polish descent, b. in Lwów; governor of Galicia (1848–59; 1866–68; 1871–75), and Austrian minister of the interior (1859–61). His son **Agenor** (1849–1921) was Austro-Hungarian minister of foreign affairs (1895–1906).

**Gó'ma·ra** (gō'mä·rä), **Francisco Ló'pez de** (lō'pāth thā). 1510–?1560. Spanish historian; author of early history of America, generally considered unreliable.

**Go·ma'rus** (gō·mä'rŭs), **Franciscus.** *Orig. surname* **Gom'mer** (gŏm'ēr). 1563–1641. Dutch Calvinistic theologian; leader of the opponents of Arminius. His followers were known as Gomarians, Gomarists, or Gomarites.

**Gombaud.** See GUNDOBAD.

**Gom'berg** (gŏm'bûrg), **Moses.** 1866–1947. American chemist; asst. professor (1899), professor (1904–36), Michigan. Work includes studies on free radicals and on tautomerism.

**Gom'ber'ville'** (gôN'bĕr'vēl'), **Marin Le Roy** (lē rwä') **de.** 1600–1674. French writer of romances.

**Göm'bös** (gûm'bûsh), **Gyula** (*Eng.* **Julius**) **von.** 1886–1936. Hungarian general and statesman; served in World War (1914–18), notably in Serbian and Russian campaigns. Leader (1923–28) of Race Defense party, committed to opposition to the Jews, to legitimists, and to the evils of the capitalistic system. Premier of Hungary (1932–36).

**Go'mes** (gō'mēs), **Antônio Carlos.** 1839–1896. Brazilian composer.

**Go'mes** (gō'mēsh), **Manuel Tei·xei'ra** (tā·ē·shā'ē·rȧ). 1862–1941. President of Portugal (1923–25).

**Go'mes de A·mo·rim'** (gō'mēzh thē ȧ·mo͞o·rēN'), **Francisco.** 1827–1891. Portuguese writer; to Brazil in early youth as laborer; studied natives in Brazilian forests; to Portugal (1846 ff.); in government service (1851 ff.). Works include lyrics, novels, dramas, and memoirs.

**Gó'mez** (gō'mās), **José Miguel.** 1858–1921. Cuban general and politician; president of Cuba (1909–13). His son **Miguel Mariano**, president of Cuba (May to December, 1936); in continuous struggle with Col. Fulgencio Batista, chief of staff of the army; impeached and removed on charges instituted by Batista forces; to U.S. (1936).

**Gómez, Juan Vicente.** 1857?–1935. Venezuelan soldier and political leader; supporter of Castro (1899); vice-president and commander of army (1902–08); in Castro's absence, seized government (1908); supreme dictator (1908–35): provisional president of Venezuela (1908–10); elected president (1910–15, 1922–29, 1931–35); also elected for intervening periods but declined to serve; commander in chief of army (1915–35); completely dominated two provisional presidents, V. M. Bustillos (1915–22) and Juan Bautista Pérez (1929–31).

**Gó'mez de Avellaneda y Arteaga** (gō'mās; -māth), **Gertrudis.** See AVELLANEDA Y ARTEAGA.

**Gó'mez de la Ser'na** (gō'māth thā lä sĕr'nä), **Ramón.** *Known as* **Ra·món'** (rä·môn'). 1888–1963. Spanish writer; leading exponent of expressionism in Spain; known esp. for *Greguerías*, metaphoric maxims or aphorisms in prose and verse (1917).

**Gó'mez y Bá'ez** (gō'mās ē bä'ās), **Máximo.** 1826–1905. Cuban patriot and general; served in Spanish army in Santo Domingo and Cuba; settled in Cuba as farmer. Joined insurgents during revolution of 1868–78; general in chief of Cuban forces of second Cuban revolution (1895); on American intervention, placed troops at disposal of U.S. army; deposed from supreme command (1899) by Cuban military assembly for accepting for Cuban army $3,000,000 voted by U.S. government.

**Gomme** (gŏm), Sir **George Laurence.** 1853–1916. English folklorist; founded folklore society; edited *Archaeological Review*, *Folklore Journal*, *Antiquary*.

**Gom'pers** (gŏm'pērz), **Samuel.** 1850–1924. American labor leader, b. London, England; to America as a boy. Journeyman cigarmaker (1863); in reorganization of Cigarmakers' Union (1877), Gompers became president of his local. Chairman, Committee on Constitution, newly created Federation of Organized Trades and Labor Unions (1881), which was reorganized as American Federation of Labor (1886); president, A.F. of L. (1886–1924, except 1895); chiefly responsible for determining its nature and development. Appointed by President Wilson a member, Council of National Defense (1917); member, Commission on International Labor Legislation, at Peace Conference (1919).

**Gom'pertz** (gŏm'pērts), **Benjamin.** 1779–1865. English mathematician, astronomer, and actuary. Brother-in-law of Moses Montefiore. Collaborated with Francis Baily in preparing a catalogue of stars (1822); worked out new series of mortality tables for Royal Society; propounded (1825) a law of human mortality known as *Gompertz's law.*

**Gom'perz** (gŏm'pĕrts), **Theodor.** 1832–1912. German philologist. His son **Heinrich** (1873–1942), professor of philosophy, Vienna (1920–34).

**Gon·çal'ves Di'as** (gôN·säl'vēz thē'ȧs), **Antônio.** 1823–1864. Brazilian poet; considered leading lyric poet of Brazil. His works include collections of lyric poems, as *Primeiros Cantos* (1846), *Segundos Cantos* (1848), and *Últimos Cantos* (1851), an epic, *Os Timbiras* (1857), a dictionary of Tupi (1858), and historical and ethnographical studies.

**Gon·cha·rov'** (gŭn·chŭ·rôf'), **Ivan Aleksandrovich.** 1812–1891. Russian novelist.

**Gon'court'** (gôN'ko͞or'), **Edmond Louis Antoine de** (1822–1896) and **Jules Alfred Huot de** (1830–1870). French novelists, brothers and collaborators. Their novels include *Charles Demailly* (1860), *Sœur Philomène* (1861), *Renée Mauperin* (1864), *Madame Gervaisais* (1869); authors also of works on 18th-century French history. Edmond bequeathed most of his fortune to endow the Académie des Goncourt, a group of noted literary men charged with awarding each year the Prix Goncourt of 10,000 francs to the author of an imaginative prose work of high merit, usually a novel.

**Gondebaud.** See GUNDOBAD.

**Gondemar.** See GUNDIMAR.

**Gondéric** *or* **Gondioc.** See GUNDERIC.

**Gondi, Jean François Paul de.** See Cardinal de RETZ.

**Gondicaire.** See GUNDICAR.

**Gon'di'net'** (gôN'dē'nĕ'), **Edmond.** 1828–1888. French playwright; author of vaudeville sketches and comedies.

**Gondola, Giovanni.** See Ivo GUNDULIĆ.

**Gon'do·mar'** (gôn'dō·mär'), Count of. **Diego Sar·mien'to de A·cu'ña** (sär·myān'tō thā ä·kōō'nyä). 1567–1626. Spanish diplomat; ambassador to England (1613–18 and 1619–22); sent at first to negotiate marriage between Infanta María and Charles, son of James; successful in keeping James from aiding Spain's enemies.

**Gón'go·ra y Ar·go'te** (gông'gō·rä ē är·gō'tā), **Luis de.** 1561–1627. Spanish poet. Son of Francisco de Argote, of Córdoba; adopted his mother's name (Góngora). Wrote fine lyrical poems and several dramas in early years (1585–c. 1610); later, originator in Spain of affected elegance and euphuism of style known as *Gongorism* or, in a later exaggerated form, *cultism;* this poetry obscure and often meaningless, full of conceits, artificial antitheses, extreme inversions of root meanings, exaggerated metaphors, etc.

**Gonne** (?gŏn), **Maud.** 1866–1953. Irish patriot and philanthropist; m. (1903) Major Mac·Bride' [măk·brīd'] (executed by British after Easter Rebellion, 1916). Engaged in constant political agitation against the British. Heroine of many of the lyrics and plays of William Butler Yeats.

**Gonneville, Marie de.** See Comtesse de MIRABEAU.

**Gonsalvo di Cordova.** See GONZALO DE CÓRDOBA.

**Gontaut, de.** See BIRON.

**Gon·za'ga** (gôn·dzä'gä). Italian princely family, descended from **Luigi Gonzaga** (1267–1360), who gained control of Mantua (1328) with title of captain general; the captaincy became a marquisate (1432) and a dukedom (1530). Among notable members of the family were: **Giovanni Francesco** (d. 1444). **Giovanni Francesco II** (d. 1519); m. (1490) Isabella d'Este; governed Mantua (1484–1519). **Federigo II** (d. 1540), who made Mantua during his reign (1519–40) the most magnificent court in Europe. **Guglielmo** (reigned 1550–1587), an enlightened ruler. **Vicenzo** (reigned 1587–1612), friend and patron of Tasso.

**Gon·za'ga** (gôn·dzä'gä; *Angl.* gŏn·zăg'ȧ, -zä'gȧ, -zā'gȧ), Saint **Aloysius.** 1568–1591. Italian Jesuit; died while ministering to those stricken by famine and pestilence in Rome; canonized (1726).

**Gon·za'ga** (gôɴ·zȧ'gȧ), **Tomaz Antônio.** *Pseudonym* **Dir·ceu'** (dēr·sā'ōō). 1744–1807. Portuguese poet; to Brazil (1768 ff.); judge at Villa Rica (Ouro Preto), Minas Geraes; nominated member of supreme court of Bahia; exiled to Mozambique (1792) for alleged complicity in conspiracy; died insane. Known esp. for his *Marilia de Dirceu,* collection of love poems.

**Gon·zá'lez** (gôn·sä'lās), **Manuel.** 1833–1893. Mexican general and political leader; president of Mexico (1880–84).

**Gon·zá'lez Bra'vo** (gôn·thä'lāth brä'vō), **Luis.** 1811–1871. Spanish statesman; prime minister (1843–44); ambassador to Lisbon (1844–47, 1854 ff.); minister of interior (1864–65, 1866–68); succeeded Narváez as prime minister (1868); forced to resign at deposition of Queen Isabella II after revolution of Sept., 1868; joined Carlists.

**Gon·zá'lez–Car'va·jal'** (-kär'vä·häl'), **Tomás José.** 1753–1834. Spanish poet and statesman; minister of supreme council of war (1829). Author of *Los Salmos* (1819), metrical translations of poetical books of the Bible.

**González de Ávila, Gil.** See ÁVILA.

**González de Cla·vi'jo** (thā klä·vē'hō), **Ruy.** d. 1412. Spanish diplomat; ambassador of Henry III of Castile to Tamerlane (1403); author of *Historia del Gran Tamerlane....*

**Gon·zá'lez Na·ve'ro** (gôn·sä'lās nä·vā'ro), **Emiliano.** 1861–?1938. Paraguayan statesman; vice-president of Paraguay (1908; 1928–32); president (1908–10); provisional president (1912; 1931–32); minister of war and marine (1917–18).

**González Vi·gil'** (vē·hēl'), **Francisco de Paula.** 1792–1875. Peruvian scholar and statesman; led opposition to Bolívar (1826) and Gómara (1832). Excommunicated for his *Defensa de la Autoridad de los Gobiernos contra las Pretensiones de la Curia Romana* (12 vols., 1848–56); author also of *Los Jesuitas, Diálogos sobre la Existencia de Dios,* etc.

**Gon·za'lo de Ber·ce'o** (gôn·thä'lō thā bĕr·thā'ō). 1180?–after 1246. Spanish poet, b. Berceo; earliest name known in history of Castilian poetry; author of about 13,000 verses dealing principally with lives of saints, miracles of the Virgin, and other devotional subjects.

**Gon·za'lo de Cór'do·ba** (gôn·thä'lō thā kôr'thō·bä), **Hernández.** *Ital.* **Gon·sal'vo di Cor'do·va** (gôn·säl'vō dē kôr'dō·vä). *Also* **Gonzalo Fer·nán'dez** (fĕr·nän'dāth) **de Córdoba.** *Known as* **El Gran Ca'pi·tán'** (ĕl grän kä'pē·tän'), *i.e.* the Great Captain. 1453–1515. Spanish soldier, b. Montilla; fought in Spanish wars against Portugal (1475–76) and the Moors (1486–92); negotiated surrender of Granada (1492); sent (1495) to aid king of Naples against French; won victories for Spain in southern Italy (1495–96); again victorious over Moors (1499–1500); led army into Italy (1500) and conquered kingdom of Naples (1503–04), esp. by battles of Aubigny and the Garigliano; forced to retire (1506).

**Gooch** (gōōch), Sir **Daniel.** 1816–1889. English engineer; designed important improvements in locomotive construction; interested himself also in inauguration of submarine cable telegraphic communication with U.S.

**Gooch, Frank Austin.** 1852–1929. American chemist; professor, Yale (1885–1918); developed analytical methods. The Gooch crucible or filter is named after him.

**Gooch, George Peabody.** 1873–1968. British historian; educ. Cambridge U. Among his works are *History of Our Time, History of Modern Europe, 1878–1919, Germany, Recent Revelations of European Diplomacy,* etc. See Harold W. V. TEMPERLEY.

**Gooch,** Sir **William.** 1681–1751. British colonial administrator in America; lieutenant governor of Virginia (1727–49).

**Good** (gŏŏd), **James William.** 1866–1929. American lawyer and politician; member, U.S. House of Representatives (1909–21); U.S. secretary of war (1929).

**Good, John Mason.** 1764–1827. English physician and writer; practiced (after 1793) in London. Author of *A History of Medicine* (1795), a translation of Lucretius under the title *The Nature of Things,* an annotated translation of *The Song of Songs,* etc.

**Good'ale** (gŏŏd'āl), **Elaine** (1863–1953) and her sister **Dora Read** (1866–1953). American poets, b. in Berkshire County, Mass.; collaborated in writing *Apple Blossoms* (1878), *In Berkshire with the Wildflowers* (1879), *All round the Year* (1880), *Verses from Sky Farm* (1880). Elaine became a teacher in Hampton (Va.) Institute for educating Negroes and Indians (1883); received appointment as superintendent of Indian schools in Dakota (1890); m. (1891) Dr. Charles Alexander Eastman (*q.v.*).

**Goodale, George Lincoln.** 1839–1923. American botanist; professor, Harvard (1878–1909). Also, director, Botanical Museum (1879–1909). Author of *Wild Flowers of North America* (1882), *Vegetable Physiology* (1885), *Vegetable Histology* (1885), etc.

**Good'all** (gŏŏd'ôl), **Edward.** 1795–1870. English line engraver; esp. known for his engravings of Turner's paintings. His son **Frederick** (1822–1904) was also a painter; among his canvases were *The Nubian Slave, The Flight into Egypt, Sheep Shearing in Egypt,* and many portraits and English landscapes.

**Goode** (go͝od), **George Brown.** 1851–1896. American ichthyologist; with Smithsonian Institution, Washington, D.C. (from 1877); U.S. Fish Commissioner (1887–88). Author of *Catalogue of the Fishes of the Bermudas* (1876), *Oceanic Ichthyology* (with T. H. Bean, 1895), etc.

**Good'hue** (go͝od'hū), **Bertram Grosvenor.** 1869–1924. American architect, b. Pomfret, Conn. Head draftsman with Cram & Wentworth, Boston (1889); admitted as partner (1891); firm became Cram, Goodhue, & Ferguson; office in New York (1903). In competition, designed successful plans for buildings of United States Military Academy, West Point. Work shows influence of English Gothic revival. Other examples of his work: St. Thomas's Church and St. Bartholomew's Church in New York; Trinity Church, Havana, Cuba; St. Stephen's Church, Fall River, Mass.; Academy of Sciences, Washington, D.C.; Nebraska State Capitol, Lincoln, Nebr.

**Good'man** (go͝od'măn), **Jules Eckert.** 1876–1962. American playwright.

**Goodman, Paul.** 1911–1972. Writer and social critic, b. New York City. Wrote criticism, fiction, poetry, and works on city planning and psychotherapy, including *Communitas: Means of Livelihood and Ways of Life* (w. his brother, Percival, 1947); *Growing up Absurd: Problems of Youth in the Organized System* (1960); and *Speaking and Language: Defense of Poetry* (1972).

**Good'now** (go͝od'nō), **Frank Johnson.** 1859–1939. American educator; professor of administrative law, Columbia (1891–1907). President, Johns Hopkins (1914–29). Author of *Politics and Administration* (1900), *Principles of Constitutional Government* (1916), etc.

**Good'rich** (go͝od'rĭch), **Alfred John.** 1847–1920. American composer, b. Chilo, Ohio. Taught at Grand Conservatory, New York (1866), at Fort Wayne (Ind.) Conservatory (1876), and in Chicago for nearly ten years. In Paris, France (1910–20). His works include songs, overtures, and many piano compositions.

**Goodrich, Annie Warburton.** 1866–1954. American trained nurse and educator; asst. professor of nursing and health service, Columbia (1914–23); dean of Yale U. school of nursing (1923–34).

**Goodrich, Arthur Frederick.** 1878–1941. American writer; author of the plays *So This Is London* (1922), *Caponsacchi* (1926; awarded Theatre Club Gold medal for best play of the year), *The Plutocrat* (1929), *Perfect Marriage* (1932), and *A Journey by Night* (1935).

**Goodrich, Benjamin Franklin.** 1841–1888. American industrialist, b. Ripley, N.Y.; founder of B. F. Goodrich Co., rubber manufacturers.

**Goodrich, Chauncey.** 1836–1925. American missionary, b. Hinsdale, Mass.; in China (1865–1925).

**Goodrich, Edwin Stephen.** 1868–1946. English zoologist; professor, University Museum, Oxford. Authority on morphology and on comparative anatomy.

**Goodrich, Elizur.** 1734–1797. American Congregational clergyman; pastor, Durham, Conn. (1756–97). His son **Chauncey** (1759–1815) was a lawyer and politician; practiced in Hartford; member of U.S. House of Representatives (1795–1801), U.S. Senate (1807–13); lieutenant governor of Connecticut (1813–15). Another son, **Elizur** (1761–1849), was also lawyer and politician; practiced in New Haven (from 1783); member, U.S. House of Representatives (1799–1801); U.S. collector of customs at New Haven (1801) but removed by Jefferson to make way for a Jefferson supporter (1801); member of governor's council (1803–18); professor of law, Yale (1801–10); member of Yale Corporation (from 1809) and secretary (1818–46). A son of Elizur (1761–1849), **Chauncey Allen** (1790–1860), clergyman and lexicographer, grad. Yale (1810); professor of rhetoric, Yale (1817–38); professor of pastoral theology, Yale Divinity School (1839–60); editor in chief, Webster's dictionaries (1829–60).

**Goodrich, Samuel Griswold.** *Pen name* **Peter Par'ley** (pär'lĭ). 1793–1860. American writer, b. Ridgefield, Conn. Store clerk (1808); served in War of 1812. In publishing business, Hartford, from 1816. First of Peter Parley books, *The Tales of Peter Parley about America,* appeared 1827; followed by over a hundred others of the series, written under Goodrich's direction on similar lines by members of a staff assembled for the purpose. Stories represented instructive tales told to children by a kindly old man; gained enormous popularity in their day. Founded and edited *Robert Merry's Museum* (1841–50). U.S. consul, Paris, France (1851–53). His brother **Charles Augustus** (1790–1862) was a Congregational clergyman; author of *History of the United States of America* (1822), *Lives of the Signers of the Declaration of Independence* (1829), *The Universal Traveller* (1837). Samuel's son **Frank Boott** [bo͞ot] (1826–1894), b. Boston, was a writer; in Paris (1851–55) and reported Louis Napoleon's coup d'état, marriage, and elevation to the throne in letters to New York *Times;* in New York (from 1855); author of *The Court of Napoleon* (1857), and the plays *Fascination* and *Romance after Marriage* (both with F. L. Warden, 1857), *The Dark Hour Before Dawn* (with actor John Brougham, 1859), *The Poor of New York* (with Dion Boucicault, produced 1858–59).

**Goodrich, Wallace,** *in full* **John Wallace.** 1871–1952. American organist and conductor; organist with Boston Symphony Orchestra (1897–1909); conductor, Boston Opera Co. (1909–12).

**Good'sir** (go͝od'sẽr), **John.** 1814–1867. Scottish anatomist; best known for his studies of cellular pathology.

**Good'speed** (go͝od'spēd), **Arthur Willis.** 1860–1943. American physicist; known for studies on X rays and on radioactivity.

**Goodspeed, Edgar Johnson.** 1871–1962. American Greek scholar and educator; professor of Biblical and Patristic Greek, Chicago (from 1915), and chairman of New Testament department (1923–37).

**Goodspeed, Thomas Wakefield.** 1842–1927. American Baptist clergyman; co-operated with William Rainey Harper in plans for founding the new U. of Chicago; secretary, board of trustees, U. of Chicago (1890–1912).

**Good'win** (go͝od'wĭn), **Daniel Raynes.** 1811–1890. American clergyman and educator; ordained in Protestant Episcopal Church (1848); president, Trinity College, Hartford, Conn. (1853–60); provost, U. of Pennsylvania (1860–68); dean, Philadelphia Divinity School (1868–83), and professor in this school (1865–90).

**Goodwin, Hannibal Williston.** 1822–1900. American Protestant Episcopal clergyman, and inventor of photographic film (patent applied for, May 2, 1887; patent issued, after long litigation, Sept. 13, 1898).

**Goodwin, Nat,** *in full* **Nathaniel Carll.** 1857–1919. American actor; chief successes in Henry Guy Carleton's *The Gilded Fool,* as Sir Lucius in *The Rivals,* in Clyde Fitch's *Nathan Hale,* as Fagin in *Oliver Twist.* See Maxine ELLIOTT.

**Goodwin, William Watson.** 1831–1912. American Greek scholar; author of *An Elementary Greek Grammar* (1870), *Greek Reader* (1871).

**Good'year** (go͝od'yẽr), **Charles.** 1800–1860. American inventor, b. New Haven, Conn. Began experiments in treatment of rubber (c. 1834). Purchased patent rights of N. M. Hayward to a sulphur treatment process

(1839); with this aid, developed vulcanization process (patented June 15, 1844), the basic patent of rubber manufacturing industry. A son, **Charles** (1833–1896), b. Germantown, Pa., was a pioneer in the field of machine-made shoes, associated (from c. 1880) with Gordon McKay. Another son, **William Henry** (1846–1923), b. New Haven, Conn., was an art museum curator and a historian; grad. Yale (1867); curator, Metropolitan Museum of Art, New York (1882–90) and Brooklyn Institute of Arts and Sciences (1890–1923); discovered that ancient Gothic architecture was marked by planned irregularities which enlarged the apparent size of structures and the beauty and vitality of their style.

**Googe** (gŏŏj; gōōj), **Barnabe.** 1540–1594. English poet; author of *Eglogs, Epytaphes, and Sonnetes* (1563), etc.

**Goo′kin** (gōō′kĭn), **Daniel.** 1612–1687. English colonial pioneer in America; settler in Virginia (1641); emigrated to Massachusetts (1644). Chosen assistant on the governor's council (1652–75, 1677–87); major general of Massachusetts militia troops (1681); superintendent of Indians in Massachusetts (1656, 1661).

**Goos′sens** (gōō′s'nz), **Eugene.** 1893–1962. Conductor and composer, b. London, Eng.; to U.S. (1923) as conductor of Rochester (N.Y.) Philharmonic Orchestra (1923–31). Conductor, Cincinnati Symphony Orchestra (1931–47), Sydney (Australia) Symphony Orchestra (from 1947).

**Gor.** See BAHRAM V, of Persia.

**Gor·cha·kov′** (gŭr·chŭ·kôf′). Name of a noble Russian family tracing ancestry to Vladimir the Great and Rurik, and including among its members:

Prince **Aleksandr Ivanovich** (1764–1825), soldier; served under his uncle Suvorov in Turkey and Poland; lieutenant general (1798); distinguished himself in Napoleonic Wars, esp. at Heilsberg (1807) and Friedland (1807); minister of war (1812–14); member of imperial council (1814–25).

Prince **Andrei Ivanovich** (1768–1855), soldier; brother of Aleksandr; major general under Suvorov in Italy (1799); wounded at Borodino (1812), where he commanded a division of grenadiers; fought with distinction at Leipzig and Paris; general of infantry (1819–28; retired).

Prince **Pëtr Dmitrievich** (1790–1868), soldier; fought in Napoleonic Wars (1807, 1813–14), in Caucasus, in Russo-Turkish War (1828–29); signed preliminaries of Treaty of Adrianople; governor general of Western Siberia (1843–51); retired; returned in Crimean War to serve as a commander at Alma and Inkerman (1854).

Prince **Mikhail Dmitrievich** (1795–1861), soldier; brother of Pëtr; fought in Russo-Turkish War (1828–29); distinguished himself in Polish campaign (1831), esp. at Ostrołęnka and Warsaw; military governor of Warsaw (1846); commanded Russian artillery against Hungarians (1849); chief of staff (1853); commanded Russian army on Danube in war with Turkey (1853–54); in Crimea, succeeded Menshikov as commander in chief (1855); conducted famous defense of Sevastopol; rewarded by emperor with governorship of Poland (1856–61).

Prince **Aleksandr Mikhailovich** (1798–1883). Statesman and diplomat; cousin of Mikhail. In diplomatic service at various posts (1821–41); plenipotentiary at Stuttgart (1841–50); represented Russia at Vienna (1854–56) during Crimean War. Succeeded Nesselrode (1856) as minister of foreign affairs (1856–82); restored prestige of Russia by his tact and ability; friendly with Bismarck but hostile to Austria. Chancellor of the empire (1863–83); kept Russia neutral during Seven Weeks' War (1866) and maintained neutrality in Franco-Prussian War (1870–71); guided Russian policy through war with Turkey (1877–78); in later years, suspected German attitude and established entente with France; attended Congress of Berlin (1878).

**Gor′di·a′nus** (gôr′dĭ·ā′nŭs). *Eng.* **Gor′di·an** (gôr′dĭ·ăn). Name of three Roman emperors:

**Marcus Antonius Gordianus I.** *Surnamed* **Af′ri·ca′nus** (ăf′rĭ·kā′nŭs). 158–238. Emperor (238); twice chosen consul; appointed proconsul of Africa by Alexander Severus (237); elected emperor by insurgents in his province against Emperor Maximinus (238); after a reign of a little more than a month committed suicide in grief for death of his son **Marcus Antonius Gordianus II** (192–238), who was associated with him as emperor and who was killed in battle before Carthage by Capellianus, Governor of Numidia.

**Marcus Antonius Gordianus III.** *Usually known as* **Gordianus Pi′us** (pī′ŭs). 224?–244. Grandson of Gordianus I; on death of father and grandfather, proclaimed Caesar by populace at Rome along with Pupienus Maximus and Balbinus, chosen by the Senate; made sole emperor (238–244) by the Praetorian Guard; aided by Timesitheus, his father-in-law, raised army and defeated Goths, forced Antioch, and won several victories (242) over Persians under Shapur; during further campaign in Persia, slain by Philip the Arabian, an officer in the guard who succeeded Timesitheus (*q.v.*).

**Gor′din** (gôr′dĭn; -d'n), **Jacob.** 1853–1909. Yiddish playwright, b. Mirgorod, Russia; to U.S. (1891). Became leading Yiddish playwright of New York City; produced over thirty original plays, including *Siberia, The Jewish King Lear, Kreutzer Sonata.*

**Gor′don** (gôr′d'n). Name of Scottish family having, according to genealogists, 157 main branches, taking its name from the village Gordon in Berwickshire, where a younger son of an Anglo-Norman nobleman settled in time of David I as Adam de Gordon. His descendant Sir **Adam de Gordon** (d. 1333), statesman and warrior, sided with Edward I in latter's struggle for Scottish throne (1305); justiciar of Scotland (1310–14); after Bannockburn, attached himself to Robert Bruce, who granted him lordship of Strathbogie in Aberdeenshire, on which lordship Gordon bestowed name Huntly from a village on his Berwickshire estate; killed fighting for David II in battle of Halidon Hill (1333); from him descended almost all of Gordons of eminence in Scotland. Sir Adam's great-grandson Sir **John Gordon** (d. 1394) was ancestor of earls of Aberdeen and other northern Gordon stocks; Sir Adam's other great-grandson, Sir **Adam Gordon** (d. 1402), took prominent part in raid of Roxburgh (1377) and invasion of Northumberland ending in battle of Otterburn (1388); was confirmed in lands of Strathbogie by Robert II; killed in battle of Homildon Hill (1402). His daughter Elizabeth, heiress of Gordon-Huntly estates, who married Alexander Seton (d. 1470), was ancestress of Seton-Gordons holding earldom of Huntly (see below) and of dukes of Gordon and Sutherland.

EARLS AND MARQUISES OF HUNT′LY (hŭnt′lĭ) AND DUKES OF GORDON: **Alexander Se′ton-Gordon** [sē′t'n-] (d. 1470), 1st Earl of **Huntly** (created 1449), son of Elizabeth Gordon and Alexander Seton (see SETON family), accompanied Margaret of Scotland to France on marriage with Dauphin Louis (1436); held command at siege of Roxburgh Castle (1460). His son **George Gordon** (d. 1502?), 2d earl, was lord high chancellor of Scotland (1498–1501); m. Princess Annabella, daughter of James I of Scotland; from their third son were descended the turbulent Gordons of Gight, maternal ancestors of Lord Byron. **Alexander Gordon** (d. 1524),

3d earl, eldest son of 2d earl, led Scots vanguard at Flodden (1513); supported Albany against Angus; lieutenant of Scotland and twice member of council of regency; made his house supreme in north. His grandson **George Gordon** (1514–1562), 4th earl, a regent (1536–37), supported Cardinal Beaton against Arran (1543); as lieutenant of north, crushed Camerons and Macdonalds (1544); lord chancellor (1546); received earldom of Moray (1548) but, when stripped of it through queen's jealousy of his power, joined lords of the congregation (1560) and died in revolt against royal authority. George's (1514–1562) second son, **George Gordon** (d. 1576), 5th earl, restored to his father's lands and dignities (nominally, 1565; actually, 1567), allied himself with Bothwell and Queen Mary (1566); lord chancellor; aided in murder of Darnley, divorce of his sister from Bothwell, and Mary's marriage with Bothwell; conspired for Queen Mary's deliverance from Loch Leven Castle (1567), but seceded from her cause (1572); held with Argyll north of Scotland, took Edinburgh Castle, captured Regent Lennox, and came to terms with Regent Morton. **George Gordon** (1562–1636), 1st Marquis (created 1559) and 6th Earl of **Huntly,** son of 5th earl and head of Roman Catholics of Scotland, corresponded secretly with Spain for Catholic restoration; took part in plot leading to execution of Morton (1581) and in conspiracy that delivered King James VI from Ruthven raiders (1583); raised rebellion in north (1589) but had to submit to king; in private war with Grants and Mackintoshes, who were aided by earls of Atholl and Murray both of Stewart family and hereditary enemies of his house, murdered "bonnie earl" of Murray (1592), an act commemorated in ballad *Bonnie Earl of Moray* and punished by ravaging of his lands; after interception of his Spanish letters, his attempt to imprison the king, and the destruction of his castle Strathbogie by the king, had to leave Scotland (1595), charged with treason; pardoned, received into kirk, created marquis of Huntly and joint lieutenant of the north (1599); again suspected, excommunicated (1608), and imprisoned until he signed confession of faith (1610); for private war over fishing rights (from 1630) with the Crichtons, twice summoned before privy council and imprisoned. His eldest son, **George Gordon** (d. 1649), 2d marquis (created 1632), 1st Viscount **A·boyne′** (*ȧ*·boin′), was brought up in England as Protestant; refused to subscribe covenant (1638); as lieutenant of the north, driven from Strathbogie by Montrose; in civil war, took king's side, stormed Aberdeen (1645); excepted from general pardon (1647); beheaded by order Scots parliament. George's (d. 1649) grandson **George Gordon** (1643–1716), 1st Duke of **Gordon** (created 1684) and 4th Marquis of **Huntly,** saw military service abroad; held Edinburgh Castle for James II in Revolution of 1688; his son **Alexander Gordon** (1678?–1728), 2d duke, also a Jacobite, as marquis of Huntly led 2300 men to Old Pretender at Perth (1715); Alexander's (1678?–1728) son Lord **Lewis Gordon,** Jacobite, defeated laird of Macleod (1745), died in exile (1754). Lord **George Gordon** (1751–1793), agitator, 3d son of 3d duke of Gordon, rose to rank of lieutenant in navy (1772); M.P. (1774–81); headed Protestant associations organized to secure repeal of act relieving Roman Catholics of certain disabilities (1778); headed mob of about 50,000 in march from St. George's Fields to houses of parliament with repeal petition, precipitating so-called No-Popery, or Gordon, Riots (June 2–8, 1780), which destroyed Roman Catholic chapels, broke open prisons, attacked Bank of England; acquitted of treason through Erskine's skillful defense; excommunicated (1786); convicted of libel on Marie Antoinette (1787); lived at ease in Newgate, giving dinners and dances; became proselyte to Judaism; died in Newgate. **Alexander Gordon** (1743–1827), 4th duke, grandson of 2d duke, was a Scottish representative peer (1767) and British peer (1784); author of song *There is Cauld Kail in Aberdeen;* his wife, **Jane,** *nee* **Max′well** [măks′wĕl; -wĕl] (1749?–1812), Duchess of **Gordon,** famous beauty (portrait painted by Joshua Reynolds, 1775), conducted Tory salon in Pall Mall (1787–1801). Their son **George Gordon** (1770–1836), 5th and last duke, raised Gordon Highlanders regiment and commanded it in Spain, Corsica, Ireland, Holland; general (1819); commanded division in Walcheren Expedition (1809); created Baron **Gordon Huntly** (1807); left barony and dukedom extinct at death. His cousin **George Gordon** (1761–1853), soldier, succeeded as 5th Earl of **Aboyne** (1794) and 9th Marquis of **Huntly** (1836). Lady **Charlotte Gordon,** sister of 5th duke of Gordon, m. Charles Lennox (*q.v.*), 4th Duke of Richmond, and for their grandson, Charles Henry Gordon-Lennox (see LENNOX), the dukedom of Gordon was revived (1876).

EARLS OF SUTH′ER·LAND (sŭth′ẽr·lănd): **Adam Gordon** of Aboyne (d. 1537), 2d son of George Gordon, 2d Earl of Huntly, took courtesy title earl of Sutherland in right of his wife Elizabeth, Countess of Sutherland, sister of 9th earl. Their grandson **John Gordon** (1526?–1567), 10th or 11th Earl of **Sutherland,** accompanied queen mother of Scotland to France (1550); received earldom of **Ross** [rŏs] (1555); was sent on diplomatic errands by his relative Huntly. John's (1526?–1567) great-grandson **John Gordon** (1609–1663), 13th or 14th earl, active and popular Covenanter, was one of leaders at battle of Auldearn (1645); lord privy seal in Scotland (1649); raised force against Cromwell (1650). John's (1609–1663) grandson **John Gordon** (1660?–1733), 15th or 16th earl, served under William III in Flanders; privy councilor to Queen Anne (1704); Scottish representative peer; president of board of trade (1715); his great-grandson, the 17th or 18th earl, had a daughter Elizabeth, Countess of Sutherland in her own right, who married (1785) George Granville Leveson-Gower (*q.v.*), created duke of Sutherland (1833).

VISCOUNTS KEN′MURE′ (kĕn′mūr′): Sir **John Gordon** of Loch′in·var′ [lŏk′ĭn·vär′; lŏk′-] (1599?–1634), 1st Viscount **Kenmure** (created 1633) and Baron **Lochinvar,** descendant of William Gordon, Laird of Stitchel and Lochinvar, younger son of Sir Adam de Gordon (d. 1333) and founder of Galloway branch of family. Puritan Presbyterian; friend of Samuel Rutherford, minister; brother-in-law of marquis of Argyll. **William Gordon** (d. 1716), 6th viscount; Jacobite; in rising of 1715 commanded in southern Scotland; captured at Preston and beheaded.

EARLS AND MARQUIS OF AB′ER·DEEN′ (ăb′ẽr·dēn′; ăb′ẽr·dēn): **George Gordon** (1637–1720), 1st Earl of **Aberdeen** (created 1682); Scottish statesman; great-grandson of James Gordon of Methlic and Haddo, Aberdeenshire; according to tradition descended from illegitimate brother of Sir Adam Gordon (d. 1402); professor at Aberdeen four years; practiced law in Edinburgh; member Scots parliament; chancellor of Scotland under James, Duke of York (1682–84); dismissed for leniency to nonconformists; supported treaty of union (1705–06). **George Hamilton Gordon** (1784–1860), 4th earl; British statesman, b. Edinburgh; succeeded grandfather as earl (1801); British foreign secretary under Wellington (1828–30) and Peel (1841–46). Established friendly relations with France, and with U.S. by

Ashburton and Oregon treaties. Headed coalition ministry (1852) which was forced into Crimean War; resigned (1855) upon vote of censure on mismanagement of war. His grandson **John Campbell Gordon** (1847–1934), 1st Marquis of **Aberdeen and Te·mair′** [tĕ·mâr′] (created 1915), British colonial governor, was lord lieutenant of Ireland (1886, 1905–1915); governor general of Canada (1893–98). His wife, **Ishbel Ma·ri′a** (mȧ·rī′ȧ), *nee* **Marjori′banks** [märch′băngks] (1857–1939), Marchioness of **Aberdeen and Temair,** British social worker, daughter of 1st Baron Tweedmouth and sister of Edward Marjoribanks; m. (1877); president of Canning Town women's settlement (1890–1939); founder of Victorian Order of Nurses in Canada; leader of feminist movement; author, with her husband, of *We Twa* (1925).

BARONS STAN′MORE′ (stăn′mōr′): **Arthur Charles Hamilton–Gordon** (1829–1912), 1st Baron **Stanmore** (created 1893), British colonial governor, son of 4th earl of Aberdeen; M.A., Cantab.; lieutenant governor of New Brunswick (1861); governor of Trinidad (1866–70), Mauritius (1871–74), Fiji (1875–80), New Zealand (1880–83), Ceylon (1883–90); biographer of Lord Aberdeen (1893) and Sidney Herbert (1906). His only son, **George Arthur Maurice Hamilton–Gordon** (1871–    ), 2d baron; B.A., Cantab.; M.P. (1900); treasurer, St. Bartholomew's Hospital (1921–37); chief Liberal whip in House of Lords.

**Gordon,** Dukes of. See GORDON family.

**Gordon, Adam Lindsay.** 1833–1870. Australian poet, b. in Azores, son of retired Indian officer; sent to South Australia (1853), where he joined mounted police; member, House of Assembly (1865); renowned as steeplechase rider; moved to Victoria (1867). Author of *Sea Spray and Smoke Drift* (1867), *Ashtaroth* (1867), *Bush Ballads and Galloping Rhymes* (1870).

**Gordon, Alexander.** 1692?–?1754. Scottish antiquary; the Sandy Gordon of Scott's *Antiquary;* known as "Singing Sandie."

**Gordon, Armistead Churchill.** 1855–1931. American lawyer and writer, b. in Albemarle County, Va. Rector, U. of Virginia (1897–98, 1906–18). Author of *The Ivory Gate* (verse, 1907), *Robin Aroon—A Comedy of Manners* (1908), *Maje: A Love Story* (1913), *Jefferson Davis* (1918), *The Western Front* (verse, 1928), etc.

**Gordon, Caroline.** See under Allen TATE.

**Gordon, Charles George.** *Called* **Chinese Gordon** *and* **Gordon Pa′sha** (pȧ′shä). 1833–1885. British soldier, b. Woolwich; descended from cadet branch of house of Huntly (see GORDON family). Took part in capture of Peking and destruction of Summer Palace; explored Chinese Wall (1860–62); commander of "Ever Victorious Army," a Chinese force, suppressed Taiping rebellion in thirty-three actions, took walled towns, opened rich provinces of silk district (1863–64); made mandarin of first class; C.B. (1865). Employed by Ismail Pasha, khedive of Egypt, in opening up equatorial provinces of Africa (1874–76); resigned because thwarted in suppression of slave trade; returned as governor of Sudan, equatorial provinces, and Red Sea littoral (1877–80); established communications, developed natural resources, overawed slave trader Suleiman, and suppressed slave trade, established law and justice. Visited India and China; commanded Royal Engineers in Mauritius (1881–82); spent year of quiet in Palestine (1883). On overwhelming disaster to Hicks Pasha's army at hands of the Mahdi, sent to rescue Egyptian garrisons in Sudan preparatory to its abandonment (1884); given executive powers by khedive; met refusal by British government of his requests for help from Zobeir and Turkish troops; evacuated about 2500 women, children, and wounded from Khartoum before being hemmed in by Mahdi (Mar. 12, 1884); met refusal by British government of his request that road from Suakin to Berber be opened by British; isolated by surrender of garrison at Berber; only Englishman in Khartoum after murder of two companions; repelled besieging forces for 10 months; with tardy relief expedition under Wolseley only two days' march distant, killed when Khartoum fell (Jan. 26, 1885).

**Gordon, Charles William.** *Pseudonym* **Ralph Con′nor** (kŏn′ẽr). 1860–1937. Canadian Presbyterian clergyman and novelist, b. in Glengarry, Ontario. To Canadian Northwest as missionary among miners and lumberjacks (1890–94); pastor in Winnipeg (1894–1924). Chaplain in Canadian overseas forces during World War; senior chaplain, 9th brigade (1916); served with British mission in U.S. (1917). Moderator, general assembly of Presbyterian Church of Canada (1922); influential in promoting union of Presbyterian, Methodist, and Congregational denominations into United Church of Canada. His novels, under pseudonym of Ralph Connor, written against background of Canadian Northwest, include *Black Rock* (1898), *The Sky Pilot* (1899), *The Man from Glengarry* (1901), *To Him That Hath* (1921), *The Rock and the River* (1931), *The Girl from Glengarry* (1933).

**Gordon,** Lady **Duff–.** See DUFF-GORDON.

**Gordon, George Angier.** 1853–1929. Congregational clergyman, b. in Scotland; to U.S. (1871); pastor of Old South Church, Boston (1884–1929).

**Gordon, George Byron.** 1870–1927. Archaeologist, b. on Prince Edward Island, Canada. Chief, Harvard archaeological expedition to Honduras (1894–1900). Director of the museum, U. of Pennsylvania (1910–27). Author of *The Serpent Motive in the Ancient Art of Central America and Mexico* (1906), *In the Alaska Wilderness* (1917), *Baalbek* (1919), etc.

**Gordon, George Henry.** 1823–1886. American army officer; grad. U.S.M.A., West Point (1846). Resigned from service (1854) to study law; adm. to bar (1857). Raised regiment at outbreak of Civil War; brigadier general (1862); brevetted major general (1865).

**Gordon, George Phineas.** 1810–1878. American inventor of improved job-printing presses; b. Salem, N.H.

**Gordon,** Sir **James Alexander.** 1782–1869. British naval officer; commanded the *Sea Horse* and squadron that entered the Potomac, reduced Fort Washington, captured Alexandria, Va. (1814); took part in expedition against New Orleans (1814–15); admiral (1854); admiral of the fleet (1868).

**Gor′don** (gôr′dōn), **Je·hu′da** (jē·hōō′dȧ) **Leb** (lāb). *Also known as* **Le′on** (lē′ŏn) **Gordon.** *Orig.* **Ju′dah Loeb ben Ash′er** (jōō′dȧ lûb bĕn ăsh′ẽr). 1830–1892. Russian-Jewish poet and novelist; a leader in modern renaissance of Hebrew language and literature.

**Gor′don** (gôr′d'n), **John Brown.** 1832–1904. American army officer; in Confederate army through Civil War; brigadier general (1862); major general (1864); lieutenant general (1865); led last charge at Appomattox. U.S. senator from Georgia (1873–80; 1891–97). Governor of Georgia (1886–90).

**Gordon,** Sir **John Watson–.** 1788–1864. Scottish portrait painter. Son of Captain Watson of the Royal navy; succeeded to practice of portraitist Henry Raeburn; assumed name of Gordon (1826); exhibited at Royal Academy, London (from 1827).

**Gordon, Patrick.** 1635–1699. Scottish soldier of fortune and friend of Peter the Great; took service in Russian army (1661), suppressed Cossacks in Ukraine (1670–76), fought Turks and Tatars (1677); governor of Kiev (1679); not allowed to quit Russia for English service; quartermaster general in expedition against Crim Tatars (1687, 1689); turned scale in favor of Czar Peter I against conspirators in Moscow (1689); crushed revolt of Strelitzes (1697); made general in chief; buried in Moscow.

**Gordon–Lennox.** See under LENNOX family.

**Gore** (gōr), **Catherine Grace Frances,** *nee* **Moo'dy** (mōō'dĭ). 1799–1861. English novelist and playwright.

**Gore, Charles.** 1853–1932. Anglican prelate; canon of Westminster (1894–1902); bishop of Worcester (1902–04), Birmingham (1905–11), Oxford (1911–19). Regarded as a leader of the Anglo-Catholic movement.

**Gore, Christopher.** 1758–1829. American lawyer, diplomat, and politician. Governor of Mass. (1809–10); U.S. senator (1814–17).

**Gore, John Francis.** 1885– . English journalist and biographer. Author of *A Londoner's Calendar* (1925), *King George V* (1940; undertaken at express desire of King George VI and Queen Mary), etc.

**Gore, Thomas Pryor.** 1870–1949. American lawyer and politician, b. in Webster County, Miss. Lost eyesight (1881). Began practice of law (1892); moved to Texas (1896) and Oklahoma (1901). U.S. senator from Oklahoma (1907–21, 1931–37).

**Go·rec'ki** (gô·rĕts'kē), **Antoni.** 1787–1861. Polish poet.

**Gorell,** Barons. See John Gorell BARNES.

**Go·re·my'kin** (gŭ·ryĕ·mĭ'kyĭn), **Ivan Longinovich.** 1839–1917. Russian statesman, b. Novgorod government; minister of interior (1895–99); succeeded Witte as prime minister (1906); again prime minister during World War I (1914–16); Czarist supporter; arrested after revolution (1917); imprisoned and murdered in Caucasus by Bolsheviks.

**Gor'gas** (gôr'găs), **Josiah.** 1818–1883. American army officer; chief of ordnance for the Confederacy, through Civil War; efficient in producing munitions under heavy handicaps; brigadier general (1864). President, U. of Alabama (1878–79).

His son **William Crawford** (1854–1920) was a sanitarian and army surgeon, b. near Mobile, Ala.; officer, medical corps, U.S. army (1880). In charge, yellow-fever camp in Cuba (1898); chief sanitary officer, Havana, Cuba (1898–1902); following discoveries of Walter Reed board that mosquitoes were carriers of yellow-fever germ, Gorgas applied strict measures to destroy mosquitoes; succeeded in freeing Havana from yellow fever. Chief sanitary officer, Panama Canal Commission (1904–13); did notable work again in suppressing yellow fever and thus making digging of the canal possible. Surgeon general, U.S. army, with rank of brigadier general (1914); retired (1918). Elected to Am. Hall of Fame (1950).

**Gor'ges** (gôr'jĕz; -jĭz), **Sir Ferdinando.** 1566?–1647. English soldier, mariner, and proprietor in America. With John Mason, received (1622) grant of region between Merrimac and Kennebec rivers; when new grant made to each (1629), received land between Piscataqua and Kennebec rivers; grant confirmed (1639) under title Province of Maine.

**Gör'gey** *or* **Gör'gei** (gûr'gĕĭ), **Arthur von.** 1818–1916. Hungarian general; served in war of 1848–49; appointed commander in chief (Feb., 1849) and won a series of victories, culminating in capture of Buda (May 21, 1849). Succeeded Kossuth as dictator of Hungary; was overwhelmed by Russian armies intervening to restore Austrian power; surrendered at Világos to the Russians (Aug. 13, 1849). Was interned (1849–67) by the Austrians.

**Gor'gi·as** (gôr'jĭ·ăs). 485?–?380 B.C. Greek Sophist and rhetorician, b. in Sicily. Settled in Athens and taught oratory and rhetoric. Immortalized by Plato in his dialogue *Gorgias.*

**Gor'ham** (gôr'ăm), **Jabez.** 1792–1869. American silversmith, b. Providence, R.I.; founder of Gorham Manufacturing Co.

**Gorham, Nathaniel.** 1738–1796. American statesman; member of Massachusetts board of war (1778–81) and of Continental Congress (1782, 1783, 1785–87; president 1786); as delegate to Federal Convention (1787), signed the Constitution.

**Go'ring** (gō'rĭng; gô'rĭng), **George.** Earl of **Nor'wich** (nŏr'ĭj). 1583?–1663. English Royalist. Negotiated marriage between Prince Charles and Henrietta Maria of France; fought for Charles I; after capitulation at Colchester (1648), was sentenced to death, but was respited; with Charles II on Continent (1649); pensioned (1661). His son **George** (1608–1657), Baron **Goring,** also fought for Charles I, commanding left wing at Marston Moor (1644); at end of Civil War went to Spain and commanded English regiments in Spanish service.

**Gö'ring** (gû'rĭng), **Hermann.** 1893–1946. German politician, b. in Rosenheim, Bavaria. Served in German air force in World War (1914–18); commanded Richthofen squadron. Involved in National Socialist uprising in Munich (1923), and took refuge in Italy (1923–27). Active member of the National Socialist party (the Nazis); member of the Reichstag (from 1928) and its president (1932 ff.). In Hitler's government became (1933) Reich cabinet minister for air forces, Prussian minister president and minister of the interior, and general of infantry; commissar for execution of the 4-year plan (1936); succeeded Schacht (*q.v.*) as economic dictator of Germany (Nov., 1937); field marshal (Feb., 1938); member of cabinet council (from 1938) and secret war cabinet (from 1939); president of council for war economy (from 1940); committed suicide in jail.

**Gor'ki** (*Angl.* gôr'kĭ; *Russ.* gôr'y'·kû·ĭ), **Maksim.** *Also* **Maxim Gorky.** *Pseudonym of* **Aleksei Maksimovich Pesh'kov** (pyăsh'kôf). 1868–1936. Russian writer, b. Nizhni Novgorod (renamed Gorki in his honor, 1932). Orphan at early age; had little formal education; followed various trades (1878–90); wrote first sketch (1892) for a Tiflis newspaper, using name *Gorki,* i.e. "the bitter one." Returned to Nizhni Novgorod and began journalistic career; his second tale, *Chelkash* (1895), attracted wide attention; wrote many realistic stories (1895–1900) portraying life of tramp, winning great success. Arrested and exiled as revolutionist (1901); worked with Communists; although a pacifist, fought in World War until wounded in Galicia. Gave support to Bolshevist revolution; chief of Soviet propaganda bureau (1918); member of Petrograd Soviet (1919); lived in Italy for his health (1921–32). Author of short stories, including *The Orlov Couple and Malva* (1901), *Twenty-six Men and a Girl* (1901), *My Fellow Traveller* (1901), *Tales* (1902), *The Spy* (1908); novels, including *Foma Gordeev* (1900), *Mother* (1907), *A Confession;* plays, including *The Lower Depths* (1903, his best known), *The Night Lodgings* (1905), *The Judge* (1924); several autobiographical and critical works, as *Reminiscences of My Youth* (1924) and *Fragments from My Diary* (1924); biographies of Andreev, Tolstoi, and Lenin.

**Gorm** (gôrm; *Dan.* gŏrm). *Surnamed* **the Old.** d. 940? First king of united Denmark (883?–?940).

**Gor'man** (gôr'măn), **Arthur Pue.** 1839–1906. American political leader; U.S. senator from Maryland (1881–99; 1903–06). Advocated moderate protective tariff; coauthor of the Wilson-Gorman Act (1894).

**Gorman, Herbert Sherman.** 1893–1954. American

writer; author of *The Fool of Love* (1920), *James Joyce—His First Forty Years* (1924), *A Victorian American—Henry Wadsworth Longfellow* (1926), *Hawthorne...* (1927), *The Mountain and the Plain* (1936), *James Joyce* (biography; 1940), *Brave General* (1941).

**Gör'res** (gûr'ĕs), **Joseph von.** 1776–1848. German journalist and man of letters; opposed Napoleon; after Napoleon's fall, opposed Prussian reactionary measures; founded (1814) and edited (1814–16) *Der Rheinische Merkur* (suppressed, 1816); in despair at reactionary measures throughout Germany, became ardent Ultramontane. Professor of history at Munich (1827).

**Gorria, Tobio.** See Arrigo BOITO.

**Gor'rie** (gŏr'ĭ), **John.** 1803–1855. American inventor, b. Charleston, S.C. Took out patent (May 6, 1851) on artificial refrigeration process containing basic principle of present-day mechanical refrigerators.

**Gor'ringe** (gŏr'ĭnj), Sir **George F.** 1868–1945. British soldier; aide-de-camp to Lord Kitchener (1900); served in South Africa during Boer War. Brigadier general (1909); major general (1911); served in Mesopotamia with Indian troops (1915–16). Commanded 47th division in France (1916–19), 10th division in Egypt (1919–21); promoted lieutenant general, and retired (1921).

**Gorst** (gôrst), Sir **John Eldon.** 1835–1916. English lawyer and legislator; B.A., Cantab.; M.P. (1866 ff.); solicitor general (1885); undersecretary of state for India (1886).

**Gort** (gôrt), 6th Viscount. **John Standish Surtees Prendergast Ver'e·ker** (vĕr'ĭ·kẽr). 1886–1946. English soldier; served in World War (1914–18); major general (1935); general (1937); chief of imperial general staff (1937–39); commander in chief of British Field Force in France, through the evacuation from Dunkirk (1939–40); inspector general of forces, in Britain (1940); commander at Gibraltar (1941–42), Malta (1942–44), Palestine and Trans-Jordan (1944–45).

**Gortchakov.** Variant of GORCHAKOV.

**Gor'ton** (gôr't'n), **Samuel.** 1592?–1677. Founder of a religious sect, b. Gorton, England. Emigrated to Massachusetts Colony (1637); tried for heresy, and banished (1637–38). Had similar difficulties in other settlements until he obtained a safe-conduct from the earl of Warwick (1648). Settled in Rhode Island; named town Warwick; represented Warwick in Rhode Island legislature almost continually (1649–66). His sect, the Gortonians, rejected outward religious ceremonies, held that Christ was both human and divine, and that heaven and hell exist only in the mind.

**Gö'schel** (gû'shĕl), **Karl Friedrich.** 1784–1862. German jurist and philosopher.

**Go'schen** (gō'shĕn), **George Joachim.** 1st Viscount **Goschen.** 1831–1907. British statesman, b. London. Entered father's banking firm; attracted favorable attention by his *Theory of the Foreign Exchanges* (1861). M.P. (1863–1900); member of various ministries (from 1865); chancellor of the exchequer in Salisbury's ministry (1886–92) and first lord of the admiralty (1895–1900); created viscount (1900). Vigorous supporter of Lord Hartington in forming Liberal Unionist party (1886); aided in defeating Gladstone's home-rule bill (1886); showed firmness and courage in threatened financial panic (1890); had a share in building huge British navy. His brother Sir **William Edward** (1847–1924), diplomat, was minister to Belgrade (1889–1900), Copenhagen (1900–05), Vienna (1905–08), and Germany just before outbreak of World War (1914).

**Go·shun** (gō·shōōn). 1741? or 1752?–1811. Japanese painter, of Chinese realistic school; favorite subjects, flowers and animals.

**Gos'ling** (gŏz'lĭng), **Harry.** 1861–1930. English trade-union leader.

**Gos'nold** (gŏz'nōld), **Bartholomew.** d. 1607. English navigator; in command of expedition that touched southern Maine shore and coasted southward as far as Narragansett Bay (1602); second in command of expedition that carried settlers to Jamestown, Va. (1606–07).

**Goss** (gŏs), Sir **John.** 1800–1880. English organist of St. Paul's Cathedral (1838–72), and composer of anthems, orchestral works, and glees.

**Gossaert, Jan.** *Or* **Jenni Gossart.** See Jan MABUSE.

**Gosse** (gôs), **Étienne.** 1773–1834. French journalist and playwright.

**Gosse** (gŏs), **Philip Henry.** 1810–1888. English naturalist; published *The Canadian Naturalist* (1840) and *Introduction to Zoology* (1843). To Jamaica (1844–46) to collect specimens for British Museum; published *Birds of Jamaica* (1847) and *A Naturalist's Sojourn in Jamaica* (1851).

His son Sir **Edmund William** (1849–1928), poet and man of letters. On staff of British Museum (1865–75); lecturer in English literature at Cambridge (1885–90); librarian to House of Lords (1904–14); noted for sound literary criticisms and for introducing Scandinavian literature to the English reading public. Author of several volumes of verse (*Collected Poems*, 1911), several autobiographical works, the most important being *Father and Son* (1907), and many volumes of literary criticism, surveys, and biographies, including *Seventeenth Century Studies* (1883), *A History of Eighteenth Century Literature* (1889), studies of Fielding (1898), Donne (1899), Jeremy Taylor (1904), Ibsen (1907), Swinburne (1912; 1917), and others, *French Profiles* (1905), *Leaves and Fruit* (1927).

Sir Edmund's only son, **Philip** (1879–1959), physician, served in World War (1914–18); authority on the history of piracy and collector of works on piracy; author of *The Pirates' Who's Who* (1924), *My Pirate Library* (1926), *The History of Piracy* (1932), as well as works in medicine and natural history.

**Gos'sec'** (gô'sĕk'), **François Joseph.** 1734–1829. French composer; under French Revolution, was commissioned to write revolutionary hymns and songs and published *Chant du 14-Juillet*, *Hymne à l'Être Suprème*, *Hymne à la Liberté*, *Hymne à l'Égalité*, etc. Conceived plan for École Royale de Chant (1784), nucleus for later Conservatoire; when Conservatoire was founded (1795), became an inspector and a director of a class in composition. Composer of many symphonies, overtures, oratorios, and choral and orchestral works. Credited with doing much to advance orchestral music in France.

**Gos'sen** (gŏs'ĕn; *Angl.* gŏs''n), **Herman Heinrich.** 1810–1858. German economist; expounded what has become known as "Gossen's law of satiety."

**Gos'son** (gŏs''n), **Stephen.** 1554–1624. English ecclesiastic and writer; attacked poets and players in his *Schoole of Abuse* (1579). Dedicated his works to Sir Philip Sidney without authority, calling forth from Sidney the *Apologie for Poetrie* (1595).

**Gosz·czyń'ski** (gôsh·chĭn'y'·skē), **Seweryn.** 1801–1876. Polish poet.

**Got** (gō), **François Jules Edmond.** 1822–1901. French actor; excelled in comedy roles.

**Gotama Buddha.** See GAUTAMA BUDDHA.

**Gotch** (gŏch), **John Alfred.** 1852–1942. English architect.

**Gothofredus.** See GODEFROY.

**Gothofredus.** Pseudonym of Johann Philipp ABELIN.

**Go·to** (gō·tō), Count **Shimpei.** 1856–1929. Japanese statesman; minister of foreign affairs (1916–18); mayor of Tokyo (1921–22). Created viscount (1922) and count (1926).

**Got'ter** (gôt'ẽr), **Friedrich Wilhelm.** 1746–1797. German poet and playwright; one of literary group with which Goethe was associated.

**Gott'fried von Strass'burg** (gôt'frēt fôn shträs'-bŏŏrk). Medieval German poet of late 12th and early 13th century; author of epic *Tristan und Isolde* (Celtic in origin), which in his verse gained form by which it influenced later literature and furnished Wagner the title for his opera; the poem was unfinished at Gottfried's death and two attempts were made to complete it, one by Ulrich von Türheim (c. 1236) and the other by Heinrich von Freiburg (1300).

**Gott'heil** (gôt'hīl), **Richard James Horatio.** 1862–1936. Oriental scholar, b. Manchester, Eng.; to U.S.; A.B., Columbia (1881); Ph.D., Leipzig (1904); professor of Semitic languages, Columbia (1887–1936); editor of a number of Syriac texts.

**Gotthelf, Jeremias.** Pseudonym of Albert BITZIUS.

**Got'tl-Ott·li'li·en·feld'** (gôt''l·ôt·lē'lyĕn·fĕlt'), **Friedrich von.** 1868–1958. German economist.

**Gottorp.** See OLDENBURG, 3.

**Gott'schalk** (gôt'shälk). 805?–868. German Benedictine monk; his doctrine of predestination provoked long controversy.

**Gotts'chalk** (gŏts'chôk), **Louis Mo·reau'** (mô·rō'). 1829–1869. American pianist and composer, b. New Orleans, La. Among his compositions are *Tremolo Étude*, *Bamboula*, and *Last Hope*.

**Gott'schall** (gôt'shäl), **Rudolf von.** 1823–1909. German writer; editor of *Blätter für Literarische Unterhaltung* (1864–88) and the review *Unsere Zeit;* author of lyrics, plays, historical novels, and literary treatises.

**Gott'sched** (gôt'shāt), **Johann Christoph.** 1700–1766. German scholar and writer; by works in field of literary criticism, exercised for a time (c. 1730–40) great influence over development of German literary style and thought.

**Götz** (gûts), **Hermann.** 1840–1876. German composer of operas, symphonies, choral works, chamber music, etc.

**Gou'cher** (gou'chẽr), **John Franklin.** 1845–1922. American Methodist Episcopal clergyman and educator; benefactor of Woman's College of Baltimore (renamed Goucher College, 1910), and president of the college (1890–1908).

**Goudge** (gōōj), **Elizabeth.** 1900– . British fiction writer; author of *Pedlar's Pack, Towers in the Mist, The Bird in the Tree,* etc.

**Gou'di'mel'** (gōō'dē'mĕl'), **Claude.** 1505–1572. French composer.

**Gou'dy** (gou'dĭ), **Frederic William.** 1865–1947. American printer and type designer, b. Bloomington, Ill. Established the Village Press, in Park Ridge, Ill. (1903); moved it (1906) to New York City, and (c. 1908) to his estate near Marlborough, N.Y. Designer of over 90 type faces.

**Gough** (gŏf), **Hubert de la Poer.** 1870–1963. English soldier; served in Boer War (1899–1902). Commanded 3d cavalry brigade (1914), 2d cavalry division and 7th division (1915), 1st army corps (1916), and 5th army in France and Flanders (1916–18); promoted lieutenant general; retired with rank of general (1922).

**Gough,** Sir **Hugh.** 1st Viscount **Gough.** 1779–1869. British soldier. Commanded battalion at Talavera de la Reina (1809); distinguished himself at Barrosa and Tarifa (1811); major general (1830). In command at capture of Chinese forts at Canton (1841); commander in chief in India at defeat of the Marathas (1843) and Sikhs (1845; 1848–49). General (1854); field marshal (1862).

**Gough, William.** See GOFFE.

**Gou·in'** (gwăN), Sir **Lomer.** 1861–1929. Canadian statesman, b. in Province of Quebec. Prime minister and attorney general of Province of Quebec (1905–20). Canadian minister of justice (1921). Canadian representative at imperial and economic councils in London (1924).

**Gou'jon'** (gōō'zhôN'), **Jean.** 1510?–?1568. French Renaissance sculptor; engaged (1541) in Paris with Pierre Lescot in decorating Saint Germain l'Auxerrois; and later (1544–47) in decorating Château d'Écouen for Constable Anne de Montmorency. Assisted Lescot in work on the Louvre (1547–50); decorated the château of Diane de Poitiers at Ins (1550), and then returned to his work on the Louvre (1550–62).

**Goul'burn** (gōōl'bẽrn; -bûrn), **Henry.** 1784–1856. English statesman; commissioner to negotiate peace with U.S. (1814). Chief secretary for Ireland (1821–27); chancellor of exchequer (1828–30 and 1841–46); home secretary (1834–35). His nephew **Edward Meyrick Goulburn** (1818–1897), educ. Oxford, was headmaster of Rugby (1849–57) and dean of Norwich (1866–89).

**Gould** (gōōld), **Augustus Addison.** 1805–1866. American zoologist; practicing physician in Boston. Specialized in study of mollusks. Author of *Principles of Zoology* (with Louis Agassiz, 1848), etc.

**Gould, Benjamin Apthorp.** 1787–1859. American educator, b. Lancaster, Mass. Headmaster of Boston Public Latin School (1814–28). His son **Benjamin Apthorp** (1824–1896) was an astronomer; b. Boston; grad. Harvard (1844); founded *Astronomical Journal* (1849); edited it (1849–61; 1886–96); director, longitude determinations, U.S. Coast Survey (1852–67); director, Dudley Observatory, Albany, N.Y. (1855–59); interested in study of southern celestial hemisphere (from 1865); instrumental in establishing observatory at Córdoba, Argentina (1870) and meteorological stations south to Tierra del Fuego (1872); determined magnitudes of southern stars, published in *Uranometria Argentina* (1879); prepared zone catalogues of the southern stars, published in *Resultados del Observatorio Nacional Argentino en Córdoba* (15 vols., 1879–96). See also Hannah Flagg GOULD.

**Gould, Carl Frelinghuysen.** 1873–1939. American architect; practiced in Seattle, Wash. (from 1908). Founded and headed department of architecture, U. of Washington (1914–26).

**Gould,** Sir **Francis Carruthers.** 1844–1925. English caricaturist; contributor of cartoons to *Pall Mall Gazette;* asst. editor, *Westminster Gazette;* editor and illustrator of *Picture Politics.* Published *Who Killed Cock Robin?* (1897), *Tales Told in the Zoo* (with one of his sons; 1900), and *Froissart's Modern Chronicles* (2 vols.).

**Gould, George Milbry.** 1848–1922. American physician and medical lexicographer; practiced medicine, Philadelphia; specialized in ophthalmology; invented bifocal lens eyeglasses. Compiler of medical dictionaries.

**Gould, Gerald.** 1885–1936. English poet and critic. Author of *Lyrics* (1906), *Poems* (1911), *Odes and Sonnets* (1920), and *Collected Poems* (1929); among his prose works are *Essay on the Nature of Lyric* (1909), *Essays and Parodies* (1931), and *Refuge from Nightmare, and Other Essays* (1933).

**Gould, Hannah Flagg.** 1789–1865. Sister of Benjamin Apthorp Gould (1787–1859). American poet.

**Gould, Helen Miller.** See Helen Miller Gould SHEPARD.

**Gould, Jay,** *christened* **Jason.** 1836–1892. American financier, b. Roxbury, N.Y. As a youth, was clerk in a country store, and a surveyor. In New York, a leather merchant (1859–60). Engaged in stock-market manipulation of railroad securities (from about 1860); associated with James Fisk and Daniel Drew in struggle against Cornelius Vanderbilt for control of Erie Railroad (1867–68); looted the Erie's treasury (1868). Attempted to corner gold, causing panic of Black Friday (Sept. 24, 1869). Extended railroad control to western roads, to include Missouri Pacific, Texas & Pacific, St. Louis Southwestern, International & Great Northern (by 1890). Also owned New York *World* (1879–83), New York Elevated Railways (1886), and controlled Western Union Telegraph Co. His son **George Jay** (1864–1923), b. New York City, inherited vast railway interests but lost these, one by one, to opposition financiers led by Kuhn, Loeb & Co., and Edward H. Harriman. Another son, **Edwin** (1866–1933), was a businessman and financier; head of the St. Louis Southwestern Railroad; organizer (1894) of Continental Match Co., consolidated (1899) with Diamond Match Co.; president of Bowling Green Trust Co., New York, which later was merged with Equitable Trust Co. See Helen Miller SHEPARD.

**Gould, John.** 1804–1881. English ornithologist; author of *Birds of Europe* (1832–37), *Birds of Australia* (1840–48; with supplement, 1851–69), *Birds of Asia* (1850–80), *Birds of Great Britain* (1862–73).

**Gould, Thomas Ridgeway.** 1818–1881. American sculptor; studio in Florence, Italy (from 1868).

**Gou·na′res** *or* **Gou·na′ris** (gōō·nä′rēs), **Demetrios.** 1866–1922. Greek statesman; prime minister (1915–17, 1920–22).

**Gou′nod′** (gōō′nō′; *Angl.* gōō′nō), **Charles François.** 1818–1893. French composer, b. Paris. Organist in Paris; conductor of Orphéon in Paris (1852–60). First striking success achieved by his opera *Faust* (1859); among his other operas are *Philémon et Baucis* (1860), *La Reine de Saba* (1862), *La Colombe* (1866), *Roméo et Juliette* (1867), and *Cinq-Mars* (1877). Among his church music, are *Messe de Sainte Cécile* and oratorios *La Rédemption* and *Mors et Vita.* Among his songs is the famous *Ave Maria,* based on Bach's first prelude.

**Gou′pil′** (gōō′pē′), Saint **René.** 1607?–1642. Jesuit lay brother, b. Anjou, France. Missionary in Canada (1640). Captured and tortured by Iroquois (Aug., 1642); killed (Sept. 29, 1642). Canonized (June 29, 1930).

**Gou′raud′** (gōō′rō′), **Henri Joseph Eugène.** 1867–1946. French army officer; led French expeditionary force at Dardanelles (1915) and lost an arm there; commanded 4th army in Champagne sector to end of World War I. Served as French high commissioner in Syria (1919–23); governor of Paris, and member of the supreme war council (1923–37).

**Gour′gaud′** (gōōr′gō′), Baron **Gaspard.** 1783–1852. French army officer; served in Napoleonic armies, and was chosen as one of three persons to accompany Napoleon into exile at St. Helena (1815). At Napoleon's dictation he wrote *Mémoires pour Servir à l'Histoire de France sous Napoléon* (pub. 1822–23). Returned to France (1821); promoted lieutenant general (1835); member of Legislative Assembly (1849).

**Gourgues** (gōōrg), **Dominique de.** 1530–1593. French soldier and adventurer, b. in Gascony. Learned of Spanish peacetime massacre (1565) of French Huguenot settlement at Fort Caroline, Florida; outfitted three ships, landed near mouth of St. John's River, joined forces with Indians, and avenged hanging of French Huguenots by hanging Spaniards from same trees.

**Gour′mont′** (gōōr′môɴ′), **Remy de.** 1858–1915. French writer; on staff of *Mercure de France.* Among his novels and prose works are *Merlette* (1886), *Sixtine* (1890), *Fleurs de Jadis* (1893), *Le Pèlerin du Silence* (1896), *Le Songe d'une Femme* (1899), *Un Cœur Virginal* (1907); among his critical and philosophical works are *Épilogues, Reflexions sur la Vie* (in 4 series, 1895–1912), *Livres des Masques* (2 vols., 1896 and 1898), *La Culture des Idées* (1900), *Le Problème du Style* (1902), *Promenades Littéraires* (5 series, 1904–13), *Promenades Philosophiques* (1905–09); a verse collection, *Divertissements* (1912); plays, *Lilith* (1892) and *Théodat* (1893).

**Gour′nay′** (gōōr′nā′), Seigneur **Jean Claude Marie Vincent de.** 1712–1759. French economist; intendant of commerce in France (1757); encouraged free trade and worked to suppress monopolies; reputed author of the phrase *laissez-faire,* or in full, *Laissez faire, laissez passer.*

**Gour′sat′** (gōōr′sȧ′), **Édouard Jean Baptiste.** 1858–1936. French mathematician; known esp. for work in infinitesimal analysis.

**Gour′ville′** (gōōr′vēl′), **Jean Hé′rault′** (ā′rō′) **de.** 1625–1703. French financier and diplomat.

**Gou′thière′** (gōō′tyâr′), **Pierre.** 1740–1806. French metal worker. Executed pieces for the duchesse de Mazarin, and Madame du Barry.

**Gouvion Saint-Cyr,** Marquis **de.** See SAINT-CYR.

**Gou′vy′** (gōō′vē′), **Théodore.** 1819–1898. French composer of symphonies, overtures, religious music (including *Messe Brève, Requiem, Stabat Mater,* cantata under title of *Golgotha*), choral works, piano pieces, etc.

**Gove** (gōv), **Philip Babcock.** 1902–1972. Lexicographer, b. Concord, N.H. Ph.D., Columbia, 1941. Editor in chief, *Webster's Third New International Dictionary* (1961).

**Go·vind′ Singh** (gō·vĭnd′ sĭɴ′hȧ). 1666–1708. Tenth and last guru (apostle or teacher) of the Sikhs (1675–1708). Founded Sikh military power to oppose the Mohammedans; assumed leadership with title *Singh* ("Lion"); formed strong fraternity, termed the *Khalsa* ("Pure"), with new oaths and ceremonies; waged war against Mogul power; murdered in the Deccan by an Afghan. Cf. NANAK.

**Gow** (gou), **Niel.** 1727–1807. Scottish violinist and composer, esp. of reels and strathspeys, for some of which Burns wrote words.

**Gower** (gōr; gôr), Earls. See LEVESON-GOWER family.

**Gow′er** (gou′ẽr; gōr; gôr), **John.** 1325?–1408. English poet; friend of Chaucer, who referred to him as "the moral Gower." Chief works, *Speculum Meditantis* (written in French), *Vox Clamantis* (in Latin elegiacs), *Confessio Amantis* (in English).

**Gow′ers** (gou′ẽrz), Sir **William Richard.** 1845–1915. English neurologist.

**Gowrie,** Baron and earls of. See RUTHVEN family.

**Go′yau′** (gô′yō′), **Georges,** *in full* **Pierre Louis Théophile Georges.** *Pseudonym* **Léon Gré′goire′** (grā′gwȧr′). 1869–1939. French historian; on staff of *Revue des Deux Mondes* (1894); author of treatises on religious history. His wife, **Lucie Rose Séraphine Élise,** *nee* **Fé′lix′ Faure** [fā′lēks′ fôr′] (1866–1913), daughter of François Félix Faure (president of France, 1895–99), was author of *Newman, sa Vie et son Œuvre* (1901), *Les Femmes dans l'Œuvre de Dante* (1902), *La Vie Nuancée* (verse, 1905), etc.

**Go′ya y Lu·cien′tes** (gō′yä ē lōō·thyān′tās), **Francisco José de.** 1746–1828. Spanish painter, etcher, and lithographer; chief master of Spanish school in 18th century. Employed by Raphael Mengs to design cartoons for tapestries, Madrid (intermittently, 1775–79); member (1788) and lieutenant director (1793), Acad. of San Fernando, Madrid; painter to king (1788), chief painter (1798). Supported Bonapartists during French occupation (1808–13); on accession of Ferdinand VII, was reinstated as royal painter, but left Spain because of political views (1814), settling at Bordeaux, France.

Considered foremost painter of Spanish national customs, realistically portraying battle, bullfighting, and torture scenes.

**Go'yen** (gō'ē·yĕn) *or* **Go'i·jen** (gō'ē·yĕn), **Jan van.** 1596–1656. Dutch painter; best known for landscapes.

**Go'yon'** (gô'yôN'), **Jacques.** Comte **de Ma'ti'gnon'** (dē má'tē'nyôN'). 1525–1597. Marshal of France (1576–97); friend of the Huguenots; governor of Guienne; supported Henry of Navarre. A descendant, **Jacques de Goyon-Matignon** (d. 1751), Count of **Tho'ri'gny'** (tô'rē'nyē'), married (1715) Louise Hippolyte, daughter of last member of Grimaldi line, thus inheriting Monaco. See GRIMALDI, MONACO.

**Goz'lan'** (gôz'läN'), **Léon.** 1803–1866. French journalist, novelist, and playwright; author also of familiar memoir of Balzac, whom he served for a time as secretary, *Balzac en Pantoufles* (1865).

**Goz'zi** (gōt'tsē), **Gasparo.** 1713–1786. Italian writer; founded and edited *Osservatore Veneto* on the model of the English *Spectator;* contributed to revival of interest in study of Dante. His brother Conte **Carlo** (1720–1806) was a successful playwright; author of many fairy plays.

**Goz'zo·li** (gōt'tsô·lē), **Benozzo.** *Real name* **Benozzo di Le'se di San'dro** (dē lā'sā dē sän'drō). 1420–1498. Florentine painter; as goldsmith, assisted Ghiberti on 2d bronze door of Florence baptistery (1444–47); employed also at Viterbo, Perugia (1456), Florence (c. 1458 ff.), Pisa (1469–85), etc.; notable as pictorial narrator.

**Graaf** (gráf), **Re·gnier'** (rĕ·ē·nēr') **de.** 1641–1673. Dutch physician and anatomist. Studied at Louvain, Utrecht, and Leiden, and settled at Delft. Author of works on the nature and function of the pancreatic juice and on the generative organs; discovered the Graafian follicles in the ovary.

**Gra·bar'** (grŭ·bár'y'), **Igor Emmanuilovich.** 1872–1960. Russian painter and writer on art; a leader among Moscow artists of ultramodern movement *pointillism.*

**Gra'bau** (grā'bō), **Amadeus William.** 1870–1946. American paleontologist; professor, Columbia (1905–19), and National U., Peking, China (1920 ff.); author of *Principles of Stratigraphy* (1913), *Text Book of Geology* (2 vols., 1920, 1921), *Silurian Fossils of Yunnan* (1920), etc. See Mary ANTIN.

**Grab'be** (gräb'ĕ), **Christian Dietrich.** 1801–1836. German dramatic poet; among his plays are *Don Juan und Faust* (1829), *Friedrich Barbarossa* (1829), *Heinrich VI* (1830), *Napoleon oder die Hundert Tage* (1831).

**Grab'mann** (gräp'män), **Martin.** 1875–1949. German Roman Catholic theologian.

**Grab'ski** (gräp'skē), **Władysław.** 1874–1938. Polish economist and statesman; member of Russian Duma (1905–17); prime minister of Poland (1920, 1923–25; retired).

**Gra'ça A·ra'nha** (grá'sȧ ȧ·rä'nyȧ), **José Pe·rei'ra da** (pĕ·rā'ē·rȧ thȧ). 1868–1931. Brazilian jurist, diplomat, and novelist.

**Grac'chus** (grăk'ŭs). Name of a plebeian family, Sempronian gens, of ancient Rome, including notably: **Tiberius Sem·pro'ni·us Gracchus** (sĕm·prō'nĭ·ŭs), consul (238 B.C.). **Tiberius Sempronius Gracchus,** probably son of the preceding; consul (215, 213); killed (212). **Tiberius Sempronius Gracchus** (210?–?151), husband of Cornelia (*q.v.*) and father of "the Gracchi"; praetor in Hither Spain (181); censor (169); consul (163).

**Tiberius Sempronius Gracchus** (163–133) and his brother **Gaius Sempronius Gracchus** (153–121), *known as* **the Grac'chi** (grăk'ī), Roman statesmen; Tiberius, as tribune of the people (133), sponsored proposals to restore the class of small independent farmers by restricting amount of public land a citizen might occupy and by instituting greater subdivision of lands; at end of his term of office, tried (unconstitutionally) to be re-elected and was killed in a riot; Gaius, as tribune of the people (123–122), renewed agrarian law sponsored by his brother and proposed measures leading to establishment of a democratic government in place of existing aristocracy; advocated extension of citizenship to the Latins; killed in election riot (121).

**Grace** (grās), **Eugene Gifford.** 1876–1960. American industrialist, b. Goshen, N.J. E.E., Lehigh (1899). Joined staff of Bethlehem Steel Co. (1899); president Bethlehem Steel Corporation (1913–46), chairman (from 1946).

**Grace, William Gilbert.** 1848–1915. English cricketer. Physician by profession, practicing at Bristol (1879–99). Regarded as one of greatest of cricketers and the best batsman of his day; played for England in test matches against Australia (1880, 1882). His older brother **Edward Mills** (1841–1911), also a physician (practicing at Thornbury, Gloucestershire, 1869–1911) and cricketer, played in test matches (1880).

**Grace, William Russell.** 1832–1904. Merchant and shipowner, b. Queenstown, Ireland. In New York, organized W. R. Grace & Co., to engage in South American trade (1865); organized New York and Pacific Steamship Co., and Grace Steamship Co. Elected mayor of New York (1880 and 1884).

**Gra·cián'** (grä·thyän'), **Baltasar.** *Pen name* **Lorenzo Gracián.** 1601–1658. Spanish writer; entered Jesuit order (1619); rector of Jesuit college at Tarragona. Chief representative of conceptism in Spanish literature; belonged to cult of euphuists. *El Criticón,* his best work, is a philosophical novel analyzing civilization through its effects on a savage (3 parts, 1651, 1653, 1657).

**Gra'de·ni'go** (grä'dā·nē'gō), **Pietro.** 1249–1311. Doge of Venice (1289–1311); conducted unsuccessful war against Genoese (1294–99).

**Gra'dy** (grā'dĭ), **Henry Woodfin.** 1850–1889. American editor and orator, b. Athens, Ga. Editor and part owner, Atlanta *Constitution* (1879–89); prominent as public speaker on questions involving the South.

**Grae'be** (grâ'bĕ), **Karl.** 1841–1927. German chemist. With Liebermann, produced first synthetic alizarin (1869); worked on quinone group, naphthalene, carbazole, phenanthrene, etc.

**Grae'fe** (grâ'fĕ), **Karl Ferdinand von.** 1787–1840. German surgeon; pioneer in German plastic surgery; also known as oculist. His son **Albrecht** (1828–1870), oculist; considered founder of modern ophthalmology; introduced use of Helmholtz's ophthalmoscope in diagnosis; treated glaucoma successfully. Albrecht's son **Albrecht** (1868–1933) was a politician and army major; served in World War; member of German National party in Weimar National Assembly (1919); in Reichstag (1920–28); cofounder (1922) and leader of German National Independent party.

**Grae'ner** (grâ'nĕr), **Paul.** 1872–1944. German music teacher and composer.

**Graetz** (grâts), **Heinrich.** 1817–1891. German-Jewish historian; chief work is *Geschichte der Juden von den Ältesten Zeiten* (orig. 11 vols., 1853 ff.). His son **Leo** (1856–1941), physicist, author of *Die Atomtheorie,* etc.

**Grae'vi·us** (grâ'vē·ōōs), **Johann Georg.** *Real surname* **Grä've** (grâ'vĕ) *or* **Gref'fe** (grĕf'ĕ). 1632–1703. German classical philologist; appointed historiographer by King William III of England. Edited works of many classical authors.

**Graf** (gräf), **Arturo.** 1848–1913. Italian poet and critic,

b. Athens; educ. U. of Naples; professor of Italian literature, Turin (1882 ff.).

**Grä′fe** (grâ′fĕ). See GRAEFE.

**Gräfe, Heinrich.** 1802–1868. German educator; author of *Allgemeine Pädagogik* (1845), *Die Deutsche Volkschule* (2 vols., 1847), etc.

**Graff** (gräf), **Anton.** 1736–1813. German portrait painter and etcher.

**Graff, Kasimir Romuald.** 1878–1950. German astronomer; director, Vienna observatory (1928); studied variable stars and surfaces of planets Mars, Jupiter, and Saturn.

**Gra′fi′gny′** *or* **Graf′fi′gny′** (grȧ′fē′nyē′), **Françoise**, *nee* **d'Is′sem′bourg′ d'Hap′pon′court′** (dē′säN′bōōr′ dȧ′pôN′kōōr′). 1695–1758. French writer; m. Hugues de Grafigny, from whom she soon separated; achieved fame by her *Lettres d'une Péruvienne* (an epistolary novel, 1747); wrote successful drama *Cénie* (1750). Her Paris salon was frequented by prominent literary figures of the day; her *Vie Privée de Voltaire et de Madame du Châtelet* (first pub. 1820) gives in letter form an intimate picture of Voltaire's life at Cirey, where she was guest for a few months (1738).

**Gra′fly** (grā′flĭ), **Charles.** 1862–1929. American sculptor, b. Philadelphia. Instructor, Pennsylvania Acad. of Fine Arts (from 1892), and in school of Boston Museum of Fine Arts (from 1917). His daughter **Dorothy** (1896– ), writer; art critic for Philadelphia *North American* (1920–25); art editor for Philadelphia *Public Ledger* (1925–34) and Philadelphia *Record* (from 1934); author of a number of successful one-act plays.

**Graf′ton** (grȧf′tŭn), Dukes of. See FITZROY family.

**Grafton, Charles Chapman.** 1830–1912. American Protestant Episcopal clergyman, b. Boston. In England (1865), was associated with founding Society of St. John the Evangelist, known as the Cowley Fathers. Bishop of Fond du Lac, Wis. (1889).

**Grafton, Richard.** d. about 1572. English printer and chronicler. With Edward Whitchurch, had Thomas Matthews's Bible printed in Antwerp and distributed in London (1537), published Coverdale New Testament (1538), printed Great Bible in London (1539), received exclusive patents for church service books and primers (1545); issued Book of Common Prayer, 1st edition (1549). Compiled two sets of English historical chronicles (1562, 1568).

**Gra′ham** (grā′ăm; grâ′ăm). Name of old Scottish family, settled (from 1325) at Old Montrose, near town of Montrose, which held titles of Lord **Graham** (1451) and earl, marquis, and duke of **Montrose.** See MONTROSE.

**Graham, Dougal.** 1724–1779. Scottish chapbook writer; involved in Jacobite rebellion of 1745 and wrote about it in doggerel verse.

**Graham, Ennis.** Pseudonym of Mary Louisa MOLESWORTH.

**Graham, Ernest Robert.** 1868–1936. American architect; partner in D. H. Burnham & Co., Chicago (1904–12); senior partner in Graham, Burnham & Co. (1912–17) and Graham, Anderson, Probst & White (1917–36). Among buildings designed by him are Equitable Building, Flatiron Building, and Chase National Bank, in New York City; Union Station and General Post Office in Washington, D.C.; Field Museum of Natural History, Continental-Illinois Bank, Marshall Field & Co. stores, Wrigley Building, in Chicago; Pennsylvania Station in Philadelphia; Selfridge & Co. store in London, Eng.

**Graham, Evarts Ambrose.** 1883–1957. American surgeon; known for work on origin of inflammation of gall bladder, effect of alterations of normal intrathoracic pressures on mechanics of respiration and circulation, treatment for chronic abscesses of the lung, and toxicity of chloroform and similar anesthetics.

**Graham, George.** 1673–1751. English mechanician; invented the mercurial pendulum, the deadbeat escapement, and special astronomical instruments for Halley, Bradley, and the French Academy.

**Graham, George Rex.** 1813–1894. American journalist; asst. editor, *Saturday Evening Post* (1839). Established *Graham's Magazine* (1841), and edited it (1841–53).

**Graham,** Sir **Gerald.** 1831–1899. British soldier. Major general (1881) and lieutenant general (1884). Served in Crimea (1854–56), receiving Victoria Cross (1857), in China (1860–61), in Egypt and Sudan (1882–85).

**Graham, Harry Jocelyn Clive.** 1874–1936. English poet, playwright, and miscellaneous writer; among his many works are *Ruthless Rhymes for Heartless Homes* (1899), *Ballads of the Boer War* (1902), *Deportmental Ditties* (1909), *The Perfect Gentleman* (1912), *Biffin and his Circle* (1919), *Strained Relations* (1926), *The Biffin Papers* (1933), *The Private Life of Gregory Gorm* (1936). He collaborated in a number of plays, including *Sybil, Toni, Rise and Shine.*

**Graham, Hugh.** See Baron ATHOLSTAN.

**Graham,** Sir **James Robert George.** 1792–1861. English statesman; educ. Oxford; M.P. (1818–21, 1826 ff.); first lord of the admiralty (1830–34, 1852–55); home secretary (1841–46).

**Graham,** *often* **Graham of Clav′er·house** (klăv′ẽrz; klā′vẽrz; klăv′ẽr·hous), **John.** 1st Viscount **Dun·dee′** (dŭn·dē′). *Known as* **Bloody Clav′erse** (klăv′ẽrz; klā′vẽrz) *and* **Bonny Dundee.** 1649?–1689. Scottish Royalist and Jacobite. Served in William of Orange's horse guards (1672); said to have saved William's life at Seneffe (1674); under marquis of Montrose, employed in repression of conventicles in favor of episcopacy in Scotland and in rigorous persecution of Covenanters; not responsible for Wigtown martyrdoms but executed John Brown (the Christian carrier) of Priestfield (see John BROWN); second in command of Scottish forces marching to stem revolution (1688); permitted by William III to return to Scotland with troopers; on James II's commission, collected three thousand men, met attack of Scottish commander in chief at Killiecrankie in bloody victory but fell mortally wounded.

**Graham, Martha.** 1894?– . American dancer and choreographer; b. Pittsburgh; pupil of Ruth St. Denis.

**Graham, Peter.** 1836–1921. Scottish painter; best known for Highland landscapes.

**Graham, Robert.** *Surname later* **Cun′ning·hame–Gra′ham** (kŭn′ĭng·ăm-). d. about 1797. Scottish poet; author of song *If doughty deeds my lady please.*

**Graham, Robert Bontine Cunninghame.** 1852–1936. See CUNNINGHAME GRAHAM.

**Graham, Stephen.** 1884– . English writer; long resident in Russia as a student of Russian life and customs; among his many books are *Russia and the World* (1915), *Through Russian Central Asia* (1916), *Russia in Division* (1925), *Stalin. . .*(1931), *A Life of Alexander II, Tsar of Russia* (1935).

**Graham, Sylvester.** 1794–1851. b. West Suffield, Conn. American advocate of temperance and food reform, esp. of the use of the whole of wheat unbolted and coarsely ground in making flour (hence *graham flour*).

**Graham, Thomas.** Baron **Lyne′doch** (lĭn′dŏK). 1748–1843. English soldier; commanded force blockading Malta (1799–1800); aide-de-camp to Sir John Moore in La Coruña campaign; commanded brigade in Walcheren Expedition (1809); lieutenant general (1810). Division commander under Wellington (1812–13); commanded

British contingent in Holland (1814); general (1821).

**Graham, Thomas.** 1805–1869. Scottish chemist. Formulated law (Graham's law) that the relative speeds of diffusion of gases are inversely proportional to the square roots of their densities (1834); discovered and named the process of dialysis used for separating crystalloids from colloids; made study of the three forms of phosphoric acid that led to development of the concept of polybasic acids; investigated alcoholates.

**Graham, William.** 1887–1932. British economist and leader in the Labor party.

**Graham, William Alexander.** 1804–1875. American politician; U.S. senator (1840–43); governor of North Carolina (1845–49); U.S. secretary of the navy (1850–52). Whig candidate for vice-president on the Scott ticket (1852); defeated. Leader of the moderates in North Carolina; opposed to secession, but went with his state in 1861; member, Confederate Senate (1864). Graham County, N.C., is named in his honor.

**Graham, William Franklin.** *Known as* **Billy Graham.** 1918– . Amer. evangelist, b. Charlotte, N.C. On U.S. and European evangelistic tours (1949– ). Wrote *Calling Youth to Christ* (1947), *America's Hour of Decision* (1951), *My Answer* (1960), etc.

**Gra'hame** (grā'ăm; grâ'ăm), **James.** 1765–1811. Scottish poet; author of *The Sabbath* (1804), *Birds of Scotland* (1806), etc.; satirized by Byron.

**Grahame, Kenneth.** 1859–1932. British writer, b. Edinburgh. On staff of Bank of England, secretary (1898–1908). Wrote *Pagan Papers* (1893); stories about children, *The Golden Age* (1895) and *Dream Days* (1898); children's story *The Wind in the Willows* (1908).

**Gra'hame–White'** (-hwīt'), **Claude.** 1879–1959. English aviator and aeronautical engineer. First Englishman to gain aviator's certificate of proficiency (1909); founded at Pau, France, first British school of aviation (1909); took part in numerous airplane races in Europe and America; established Grahame-White Aviation Co., later known as Grahame-White Co.

**Grain'ger** (grān'jẽr), **James.** 1721?–1766. Scottish physician and poet; friend of Dr. Johnson, Shenstone, and Bishop Percy. Published *The Sugar Cane* (verse; 1764), a translation of the *Elegies of Tibullus*, etc.

**Grainger, Percy Aldridge.** 1882–1961. Amer. pianist and composer, b. Melbourne, Australia Settled in London (c. 1899); to U.S. (1914). Composer of orchestral and choral works, chamber music, and songs.

**Gram** (gräm; *Angl.* grăm), **Hans Christian Joachim.** 1853–1938. Danish physician after whom Gram's method, Gram's stain, etc., are named.

**Gramme** (gràm), **Zénobe Théophile.** 1826–1901. Belgian electrician; invented alternating-current and direct-current machines; perfected first industrial dynamo (1872). The Gramme ring, Gramme armature, Gramme machine, etc., are all so named in his honor.

**Gra'mont'** (grà'môɴ'), **Antoine Alfred Agénor de.** Duc **de Guiche** (dē gēsh'). Prince **de Bi'dache'** (bē'dàsh'). 1819–1880. French diplomat and statesman; minister of foreign affairs (Jan.–Aug., 1870); considered responsible for precipitating Franco-Prussian War.

**Gramont,** Comte **Philibert de.** 1621?–1707. French nobleman; distinguished himself as volunteer under Condé and Turenne. A favorite in Louis XIV's court until a liaison with one of Louis's mistresses caused his banishment (1662); resident at the court of Charles II of England. The *Mémoires du Comte de Gramont* were written by Anthony Hamilton, his brother-in-law.

**Gra·nac'ci** (grä·nät'chē), **Francesco.** 1469–1544. Florentine painter; pupil and associate of Ghirlandajo; friend in youth of Michelangelo.

**Gra·na'da** (grä·nä'thä), **Luis de.** 1504–1588. Spanish prelate; famed as a preacher; provincial of the Dominican order, and confessor and counselor to Catherine, Queen Regent of Portugal.

**Gra·na'dos Cam·pi'na** (grä·nä'thōs käm·pē'nä), **Enrique.** 1867–1916. Spanish pianist and composer of operas, a symphonic poem, orchestral suites, songs, and esp. piano works.

**Gran'ber'ry** (grăn'bĕr'ĭ; -bẽr·ĭ), **Edwin Phillips.** 1897– . American writer; assoc. professor of creative literature, Rollins (from 1933). Author of *The Ancient Hunger* (1927), *Strangers and Lovers* (1928), and *The Erl King* (1930).

**Granby,** Marquises of. See MANNERS family.

**Grand** (grănd), **Sarah.** *Pseudonym of* **Frances Elizabeth M'Fall** (măk·fôl'), *nee* **Clarke** (klärk). 1862–1943. English fiction writer and feminist, b. in Ireland of English parents; m. Lieut. Col. M'Fall (1878; d. 1898); author of *The Heavenly Twins* (1893), *Babs the Impossible* (1900), *The Winged Victory* (1916), *Variety* (1922), etc.

**Grand'–Car'te·ret'** (gräɴ'kàr'trĕ'), **John** (zhôn). 1850–1927. French journalist; published many illustrated books on the customs of the day.

**Grand'gent** (grăn'jĕnt), **Charles Hall.** 1862–1939. American educator; A.B., Harvard (1883). Professor of Romance languages, Harvard (1896–1932), and head of department (1899–1911). Author of many textbooks in the fields of Italian and French; authority on Dante.

**Gran'di** (grän'dē), **Dino.** 1895– . Italian diplomat and statesman; educ. Bologna. Served in World War (1914–18; captain). Joined Fascist party and participated in march on Rome; chosen member of general council of Fascist party. Minister of foreign affairs (1929–32); ambassador to Great Britain (1932–39); minister of justice (1939–43). Sent to the Italo-Greek war front in Albania (Mar., 1941).

**Grandi, Francesco Luigi Guido.** 1671–1742. Italian religious and mathematician. Author of works relating to rectification of the cissoid and on problems of the logarithmic curve, on sound, and on conics.

**Grand'mou'gin'** (gräɴ'mōō'zhăɴ'), **Charles Jean.** 1850–1930. French poet and playwright; as poet, identified with Parnassians; as playwright, wrote several dramas in verse and a few opera librettos.

**Grand'ville'** (gräɴ'vēl'). *Professional name of* **Jean Ignace Isidore Gé'rard'** (zhā'ràr'). 1803–1847. French illustrator and caricaturist; esp. known for his political cartoons; illustrated La Fontaine's *Fables*, Swift's *Gulliver's Travels*, Béranger's chansons, etc.

**Grane** (grān), Viscount. See Lord *Leonard Grey*, under GREY family.

**Gra'net'** (grà'nĕ'), **François Marius.** 1775–1849. French painter; studied under Constantin and David, and in Italy; curator of museum at Versailles (1830–48).

**Gran'ger** (grān'jẽr), **Gideon.** 1767–1822. American political leader; U.S. postmaster general, appointed by Jefferson and continued in office under Madison (1801–14).

**Granger, Gordon.** 1822–1876. American army officer; served through Civil War, with special distinction in supporting General Thomas at Chickamauga. Brevetted major general.

**Granger, James.** 1723–1776. English biographer and print collector; educ. Oxford. Collected 14,000 engraved portraits, and used them for illustrations in his *Biographical History of England...adapted to a Methodical Catalogue of Engraved British Heads* (1769); hence the verb *grangerize* (to extra-illustrate).

**Gra'nier' de Cas'sa'gnac'** (grà'nyā' dē kà'sà'nyàk'), **Adolphe.** 1808–1880. French journalist; founded ultra-

Orleanist journal *L'Époque* (1845); became ardent Bonapartist (c. 1850) and edited *Le Pouvoir;* editor in chief of *Le Pays* (1866); author of *Histoire du Directoire* (1851–63), *Souvenirs du Second Empire* (1879 ff.), etc. His son **Paul Granier de Cassagnac,** often referred to as **Paul de Cassagnac** (1843–1904), was his colleague on *Le Pays* (1866–70) and its editor in chief (1870–84); founded Bonapartist organ *L'Autorité;* author of *Empire et Royauté* (1873), etc.

**Gra'nit** (grä'nēt), **Ragnar Arthur.** 1900– . Swedish physiologist, b. Finland. Awarded Nobel prize in physiology and medicine (1967) with H. Hartline and G. Wald for studies on visual processes in the eye.

**Gran'jon'** (grän'zhôn'), **Robert.** fl. 16th century. French type founder and engraver. Printer in Paris (1551) and Lyon (1558). In musical notation, one of first to introduce use of round notes; suppressed ligatures. Among types he designed and made were italic, roman, Greek, and Syriac. Known esp. for his *caractères de civilité,* based on French handwriting and intended to be used in France in manner comparable to use of italics in Italy.

**Grant** (grȧnt), **Albert Weston.** 1856–1930. American naval officer; World War I commander.

**Grant,** Sir **Alexander.** 1826–1884. British educator; principal, Edinburgh U. (1868–84).

**Grant, Anne,** *nee* **Mac·vic'ar** (mȧk·vĭk'ẽr). *Known as* **Mrs. Grant of Lag'gan** (lăg'ăn). 1755–1838. Scottish writer; author of *Letters from the Mountains* (1803), *Memoirs of an American Lady* (1808), *Essays on the Superstitions of the Highlands* (1811).

**Grant, Arthur James.** 1862–1948. English historian.

**Grant, Duncan James Corrowr.** 1885–1978. Scottish painter, b. Inverness; known for his decorative work.

**Grant,** Sir **Francis.** 1803–1878. Scottish portrait painter. His brother Sir **James Hope** (1808–1875), British general, distinguished himself in Sikh wars (1845–46; 1848–49) and Sepoy Mutiny (1857–58), and held command in second Chinese War (1860–61).

**Grant, George Monro.** 1835–1902. Canadian educator; educ. Glasgow U.; principal of Queen's U., Kingston (1877–1902). Author of *Ocean to Ocean* (1873), *Picturesque Canada* (1884), etc.

**Grant, Gordon.** 1875–1962. American painter and illustrator, b. San Francisco. Best known for marines and pictures of ships.

**Grant, Heber Jedediah.** 1856–1945. American Mormon, b. Salt Lake City. Elected member, Council of Twelve, Church of Latter-Day Saints (1882), and president of the church (1918–45).

**Grant, James.** 1822–1887. Scottish writer; author of historical romances.

**Grant,** Sir **James Alexander.** 1830–1920. Canadian physician, b. in Scotland; to Canada (1831). Announced discovery of serum therapy (1863); advocated electrical treatments for prolongation of life (1909).

**Grant, James Augustus.** 1827–1892. British soldier and explorer in Africa. Accompanied John Hanning Speke in African exploration from Ukuni to Karagwe (1861) and from Uganda to falls of Karuma, Faloro, and Gondokoro (1862–63).

**Grant,** Sir **James Hope.** See under Sir Francis GRANT.

**Grant, Percy Stickney.** 1860–1927. American Protestant Episcopal clergyman, b. Boston. Pastorates, Fall River, Mass. (1887–93), New York City (1893–1924). As pastor of Church of the Ascension, New York, noted for supporting socialism, and for establishing a forum for expression of views on social conditions; became radical leader among the clergy. Engaged (1923) in doctrinal dispute with Bishop Manning; resigned (1924).

**Grant, Robert.** 1814–1892. Scottish astronomer; educ. Aberdeen; professor, Glasgow (from 1859).

**Grant, Robert.** 1852–1940. American lawyer, essayist, and novelist; practiced law in Boston; judge of probate court and court of insolvency, Suffolk County (1893–1923). Member of commission that approved verdict against Sacco and Vanzetti. Author of *The Confessions of a Frivolous Girl* (1880), *The Carletons* (1886), *The Chippendales* (1909), *The Dark Horse* (1931), etc.

**Grant, Ulysses Simpson.** 1822–1885. Eighteenth president of the United States; b. Point Pleasant, Ohio. Registered at U.S.M.A., West Point, as Ulysses Hiram Grant (his baptismal names transposed); learning that his congressman had entered him as Ulysses Simpson Grant, he accepted this name; grad. U.S.M.A. (1843). Served through Mexican War; resigned from army (1854); in various business occupations without marked success (1854–61). Re-entered service at outbreak of Civil War as colonel of an Illinois volunteer regiment; appointed brigadier general (Aug., 1861); in charge of district with headquarters at Cairo, Ill., operating against Confederates based on Columbus, Ky. Led expedition which captured Fort Henry, Fort Donelson, and a Confederate force of 14,000 under General Buckner (Feb., 1862); at once appointed major general. In command at battle of Shiloh, or Pittsburg Landing (Apr. 6–7, 1862). Commanded Department of the Tennessee, headquarters at Corinth (July, 1862). Broke Confederate control of Mississippi by capturing Vicksburg with 30,000 Confederate troops under Pemberton (July 4, 1863); divided Confederacy in two. Grant's department enlarged; undertook operations against Confederate general Bragg, at Chattanooga; stormed Lookout Mountain (Nov. 24, 1863) and Missionary Ridge (Nov. 25, 1863); received Congressional vote of thanks; promoted to lieutenant general, carrying command under Lincoln of all the armies of the United States. Grant made headquarters with Army of the Potomac; co-ordinated movements of all armies to defeat Confederate forces; in spite of heavy losses in the battle of the Wilderness and at Spotsylvania, continued attack and wore the Confederates down. Received Lee's surrender at Appomattox Court House (Apr. 9, 1865). Grant promoted to rank of general (1866). Elected president of the United States (1868); re-elected (1872). Though he was personally absolutely honest, his administration was marked by serious scandals, as the Crédit Mobilier, the Whisky Ring, and the attempt of speculators to corner the gold market. On retiring from presidency, made tour of the world; received everywhere with honor. Wrote *Personal Memoirs of U. S. Grant* (2 vols., 1885–86). Elected to American Hall of Fame (1900).

**Grant, William.** 1863–1946. Scottish philologist and lexicographer; author of *Phonetic Tests for the Scottish Dialects, The Pronunciation of English in Scotland* (1913), and other works on Scottish speech; editor of *The Scottish National Dictionary.*

**Grant Duff** *or* **Grant-Duff.** See Mountstuart DUFF.

**Grantley,** 1st Baron. See Fletcher NORTON.

**Gran'velle'** (grän'vĕl'), Cardinal **de. Antoine Per're·not'** (pĕr'nō'). 1517–1586. Roman Catholic prelate and statesman, b. Besançon; secretary of state under Charles V (1550); negotiated (1553) marriage of Mary of England and Philip II of Spain; prime minister to Margaret of Parma, regent of the Netherlands (1559–64). Archbishop of Malines (1560), and cardinal (1561). Viceroy of Naples (1570). Appointed by Philip II of Spain president of the Council for Italian Affairs (1575).

**Gran'ville** (grăn'vĭl), Earls. See (1) John CARTERET; (2) LEVESON-GOWER family.

**Granville,** Sir **Bevil, George,** and Sir **Richard** (1600–1658). See under Sir Richard GRENVILLE (1541?–1591).

**Gran′ville–Bar′ker** (-bär′kẽr), **Harley Granville.** 1877–1946. English actor, manager, and playwright. Made stage debut with Ben Greet Co.; later, appeared in productions of Elizabethan Stage Society and acted in support of Mrs. Patrick Campbell. Manager of Court Theatre (1904 ff.). Among his plays are *The Marrying of Ann Leete* (1901), *The Voysey Inheritance* (1905), *Waste* (1907), *The Madras House* (1910), *Vote By Ballot* (1917), and adaptations of Schnitzler, Guitry, and Romains; author also of *A National Theater* (with William Archer; 1907), *The Exemplary Theatre* (1922), *Prefaces to Shakespeare, The Study of Drama* (1934), etc.; m. (1918) **Helen Hun′ting·ton** (hŭn′tĭng·tŭn), d. 1950, author of *Come, Julia* (1931), with whom he collaborated in translating a number of Spanish plays by G. Martínez Sierra and the Quintero brothers. See Lillah MCCARTHY.

**Gran′ville–Smith′** (-smĭth′), **Walter.** 1870–1938. American painter and illustrator, b. S. Granville, N.Y.; known for landscapes, esp. Long Island scenes.

**Gras** (grä), **Basile.** 1836–1901. French general; invented the *fusil modèle* (or Gras rifle) with which French infantry was armed (1874).

**Gras** (gräs), **Félix.** 1844–1901. French poet and fiction writer; a leader among the Félibristes, and succeeded (1891) Joseph Roumanille as head of Félibrige.

**Grass** (gräs), **Günter Wilhelm.** 1927– . German author and artist. Author of novels *The Tin Drum* (1959), *Cat and Mouse* (1961), *Dog Years* (1963), etc.

**Grasse** (gräs), **Edwin.** 1884–1954. American violin virtuoso, b. New York; blind from infancy; toured cities of Europe and U.S.

**Grasse** (gräs), Comte **François Joseph Paul de.** Marquis **de Grasse′–Til′ly′** (-tē′yē′). 1722–1788. French naval officer; commanded French fleet in Chesapeake Bay which prevented English fleet under Admiral Graves from giving aid to General Cornwallis at Yorktown (1781) and thus aided Washington in forcing the capitulation of Cornwallis; was defeated by Admiral Rodney in the West Indies (1782); wrote *Mémoire Justificatif* (1782) in justification of his defeat.

**Gras·sel′li** (grȧ·sĕl′ĭ), **Eugene Ra·mi′ro** (rȧ·mē̍r′ō). 1810–1882. Chemical manufacturer, b. in Strasbourg. To U.S. (1837); established factories for the production of sulphuric acid at Cincinnati (1839) and Cleveland (1865). His son **Caesar Augustin** (1850–1927), b. Cincinnati, moved to Cleveland (1867); established Grasselli Chemical Co. (1885); president (1885–1915) and chairman of the board (1915–27).

**Gras′set′** (grä′sĕ′), **Joseph.** 1849–1918. French physician and philosopher; authority on nervous diseases; adherent of vitalistic school of philosophy of Montpellier.

**Gras′si** (gräs′sē), **Giovanni Battista.** 1854–1925. Italian zoologist. Researches include work on life history of intestinal worms, eels, and termites.

**Grass′mann** (gräs′män), **Hermann Günther.** 1809–1877. German mathematician and Sanskritist; laid foundation of modern vector analysis; in linguistics, formulated law named after him; published Sanskrit dictionary and concordance (1875) and translation of *Rig-Veda* (1876–77).

**Gra′ti·an** (grā′shĭ·ăn; -shăn). *Lat.* **Flavius Gra′ti·a′nus** (grā′shĭ·ā′nŭs). 359–383. Roman emperor (375–383). Son of Valentinian I, b. at Sirmium, Pannonia. Made Augustus with a share in the government (367); succeeded as emperor in the West (375) with a brother, Valentinian II, as joint Augustus; after defeat of Valens at Adrianople (378) became also emperor in the East; chose Theodosius as his colleague (379); fought several campaigns against Goths, Alamanni, and others (379–381); killed at Lugdunum by rebels under usurper Maximus.

**Gratian.** *Full Latin name* **Franciscus Gratianus.** Italian ecclesiastic of early 12th century; compiler of *Concordia Discordantium Canorum* or *Decretum Gratiani*, and founder of the science of canon law.

**Gra′try′** (grȧ′trē′), **Auguste Joseph Alphonse.** 1805–1872. French Roman Catholic priest and philosopher; professor at the Sorbonne (1863).

**Grat′tan** (grăt′′n), **Clinton Hartley.** 1902– . American writer; author of *Bitter Bierce* (1929), *William J. Bryan* (with Paxton Hibben, 1929), *The Three Jameses—A Family of Minds* (1932), etc.

**Grattan, Henry.** 1746–1820. Irish orator and statesman, b. Dublin. Called to Irish bar (1772); member of Irish parliament (1775–97; 1800) and of British parliament (1805–20). Spoke and labored for Irish independence and Catholic emancipation; opposed esp. union with England (1800).

**Grattan, Thomas Colley.** 1792–1864. Irish writer. British consul at Boston (1839–46); aided in negotiating the Ashburton Treaty. Author of *Highways and Byways* (3 series, 1823–29), *Traits of Travel* (1829), etc.

**Grau** (grou), **Maurice.** 1849–1907. Operatic manager, b. Brünn, Austria; to U.S. (1854). Organized Clara Louise Kellogg English Opera Company; managed appearances of Tommaso Salvini in U.S. Associated (from 1882) with Henry Eugene Abbey and John B. Schoeffel in managing tours of Henry Irving, Ellen Terry, Sarah Bernhardt, and Mme. Réjane. Business manager, under H. E. Abbey, Metropolitan Opera House, N.Y. (1883–84; 1891–96); later (1898–1903) its managing director as head of Maurice Grau Opera Company.

**Grau** (grou), **Miguel.** 1838–1879. Peruvian naval commander; known esp. for success in holding Chilean navy at bay (1879); killed in battle off Point Augamos.

**Graun** (groun), **Karl Heinrich.** 1701–1759. German tenor singer and composer of many operas (including *Merope*), oratorios (including *Der Tod Jesu*), cantatas, concertos, motets, etc.

**Graunt** (grănt), **John.** 1620–1674. English statistician; prepared original mortality table in his *Natural and Political Observations...made upon the Bills of Mortality* (1661); an original member of the Royal Society.

**Graup′ner** (group′nẽr), **Johann Christian Gottlieb.** 1767–1836. b. in Verden, Hanover, Prussia. Musician; to Charleston, S.C. (1795) and Boston (1796); organized Philharmonic Society in Boston (c. 1810), first symphony orchestra in America; an organizer of Handel and Haydn Society (1815); gave first oratorio performance in U.S.

**Grau′ San Mar·tín′** (grou′ sän mär·tēn′), **Ramón.** 1887–1969. Cuban physician; head of provisional junta and provisional president of Cuba (Sept. 10, 1933 to Jan. 15, 1934); president (Oct., 1944–48).

**Gräve.** See GRAEVIUS.

**Gra′ve·lot′** (grȧv′lō′), **Hubert François.** *Real surname* **Bour′gui′gnon′** (bo͝or′gē′nyôɴ′). 1699–1773. French engraver; in England (from 1732); illustrated Theobald's edition of Shakespeare, Gay's *Fables*, Pope's *Dunciad*, Fielding's *Tom Jones*. In France, engraved illustrations for works of Voltaire, Racine, and Marmontel.

**Graves** (grāvz), **Alfred Perceval.** 1846–1931. Irish poet and man of letters; a leader in the Irish literary renascence; inspector of schools (1875–1910). Author of *Songs of Killarney* (1872), *Irish Songs and Ballads* (1879), *The Absentee* (an Irish play with music, 1908). His son **Robert Ran′ke** [räng′kĕ] (1895– ), poet, critic, and miscellaneous writer, author of *Poems 1914–1926*, *Poems 1926–30*, *Poems 1930–1933*, *Goodbye to All That, an Autobiography* (1929), *But It Still Goes On, a Miscellany* (1930), *T. E. Lawrence to his Biographer* (1937), *I, Claudius* (1934), *Claudius the God* (1934), *Count Belisarius* (1938), *Sergeant Lamb's America* (1940; based on memoirs of a British soldier in Revolutionary War) and its sequel, *Proceed, Sergeant Lamb* (1941), etc. See Laura RIDING.

**Graves, Charles Larcom.** 1856–1944. Irish writer. On staff of *The Spectator* (1899–1917), *Punch* (1902–36). Author of *The Hawarden Horace* (1894), *Humours of the Fray* (1907), *The Brain of the Nation* (1912), *Punch's History of Modern England* (4 vols., 1921–22), *Eulogies and Elegies* (1927); collaborated with Kipling on English version of odes of Horace, Book V (1920).

**Graves, Clo·tilde′** (klô·tēld′) **Inez Mary.** *Pseudonym* **Richard De′han** (dē′hăn). 1863–1932. Irish novelist and playwright; her novels include *The Dop Doctor* (1910), *Off Sandy Hook* (1915), *Under the Hermes* (1917), *The Sower of the Wind* (1927), *The Man in the Mask* (1931); her plays include *Nitocris* (1887), *A Matchmaker* (1896), *A Tenement Tragedy* (1907).

**Graves, Frank Pierre′pont** (pēr′pŏnt). 1869–1956. American educator; president, U. of Wyoming (1896–98) and Washington (1898–1903). President, U. of the State of New York, and N.Y. State commissioner of education (1921–40).

**Graves, Henry Solon.** 1871–1951. American forester; professor and director, Yale School of Forestry (1900–10); chief, U.S. Forest Service (1910–20). Dean, Yale School of Forestry (from 1922).

**Graves, John Temple.** 1856–1925. American journalist; editor (1907–15) of, and special writer (1915–25) for, Hearst's New York *American;* widely known as a brilliant lecturer.

**Graves, Richard.** 1715–1804. English poet and novelist. Author of *The Spiritual Quixote* (a novel ridiculing the Methodists, 1772), *The Reveries of Solitude* (1793), etc.

**Graves, Robert.** See under Alfred Perceval GRAVES.

**Graves, Robert James.** 1796–1853. Irish physician; exophthalmic goitre is sometimes referred to as Graves' disease.

**Graves, Thomas.** 1st Baron **Graves.** 1725?–1802. British admiral in command of British fleet operating against American colonies (July, 1781), and was defeated by the French fleet under de Grasse (Sept. 5, 1781).

**Graves, William Sidney.** 1865–1940. American army officer; commanded American expeditionary force in Siberia (1918–20); major general (1925); commanded in Panama Canal area (1926–28); retired (1928).

**Gra′ve·san′de** (grȧ′vĕ·sän′dĕ), **Willem Jakob.** 1688–1742. Dutch mathematician and philosopher; friend of Sir Isaac Newton; credited with invention of first heliostat; introduced Newtonian philosophy into Leiden.

**Gra·vi′na** (grä·vē′nä), Duque **Federico Carlos de.** 1756–1806. Spanish admiral; commander of Spanish fleet at Trafalgar; mortally wounded in action (1806).

**Gra·vi′na** (grä·vē′nä), **Giovanni** (*or* **Gian**) **Vincenzo.** 1664–1718. Italian jurist and writer.

**Gravina,** Conte **Manfredi.** 1883–1932. Italian statesman; served in Italian navy (1900–22). Represented Italy in League of Nations assemblies (from 1922); League's High Commissioner for Danzig (1929–32); negotiated settlement of disputes between Poland and Danzig.

**Grä′vi·us** (grâ′vē·ōōs). See GRAEVIUS.

**Grav′lund** (gräv′lōōn), **Thorkild.** 1879–1939. Danish novelist and folklorist.

**Gray** (grā). See also GREY.

**Gray,** Sir **Alexander.** 1882– . Scottish political economist; professor, Aberdeen (1921–34), Edinburgh (1935–56).

**Gray, Asa.** 1810–1888. American botanist, b. Sauquoit, N.Y. Assistant to John Torrey (1835); collaborator with him in preparing *Flora of North America* (2 vols., 1838–43). Professor of natural history, Harvard (1842–73); made Cambridge the American center of botanical study. Author of *Elements of Botany* (1836), *Botanical Text-Book* (1842; renamed, 1879, *Structural Botany*), *Manual of the Botany of the Northern United States* (1848), *First Lessons in Botany and Vegetable Physiology* (1857), *How Plants Grow* (1858), *How Plants Behave* (1872), etc. Elected to American Hall of Fame (1900).

**Gray, David.** 1838–1861. Scottish poet; to London, where he was befriended by Sydney Dobell, Lord Houghton and others; died of tuberculosis. Author of lyrical verse including a group of sonnets written in his last illness, published posthumously (1862) in a volume *The Luggie and Other Poems.*

**Gray, Elisha.** 1835–1901. American inventor of various telegraph and telephone appliances and adjuncts. With E. M. Barton (1844–1916), organized manufacturing concern Gray and Barton, from which developed the Western Electric Co. Claimed invention of telephone; long and bitter patent infringement battle was decided by U.S. Supreme Court in favor of Alexander Graham Bell. Patented telautograph (1888 and 1891).

**Gray, George.** 1840–1925. American jurist; practiced New Castle and Wilmington, Del. Attorney general of Delaware (1879–85). U.S. senator (1885–99). Member, joint high commission to adjust differences between United States and Canada (1898) and U.S. commission to negotiate peace with Spain (1898). Judge, U.S. circuit court, 3d circuit (1899–1914).

**Gray, George Buchanan.** 1865–1922. English Congregational clergyman; professor of Hebrew and the exegesis of the Old Testament, Mansfield Coll., Oxford (1900–22). Author of commentaries on certain books of the Old Testament.

**Gray, George William.** 1886–1960. American writer; on staff of Rockefeller Foundation (1937–57). Author of popular books on scientific discoveries, as *New World Picture* (1936), *Education on an International Scale* (1941).

**Gray, Henry.** 1825–1861. English anatomist; author of *Anatomy of the Human Body.*

**Gray, Henry Peters.** 1819–1877. American painter, b. New York City. Excelled in figure painting and portraits.

**Gray, Horace.** 1828–1902. American jurist; associate justice, Mass. supreme judicial court (1864–73); chief justice (1873–81). Associate justice, U.S. Supreme Court (1882–1902).

**Gray, John Edward.** 1800–1875. English zoologist; on staff of British Museum (from 1824) and keeper of its zoological collections (1840–74). His brother **George Robert** (1808–1872), zoologist and entomologist, on staff of British Museum (from 1831), is best known for his ornithological works, including *Genera of Birds* (1844–49).

**Gray, John Henry.** 1859–1946. American economist. On staff of Interstate Commerce Commission (1925–28); professor and head of department of economics, graduate school of America U. (1928–32).

**Gray, Louis Herbert.** 1875–1955. American Orientalist. Author of *Indo-Iranian Phonology* (1902), *Introduction to Semitic Comparative Linguistics* (1935), etc.

**Gray, Robert.** 1755–1806. American shipmaster and explorer, b. Tiverton, R.I. Served in American navy in American Revolution. Master of sloop *Lady Washington* which sailed from Boston in Sept., 1787, on trip around Cape Horn to load furs on the northwest coast; transferred to the *Columbia* and completed voyage around the world, arriving in Boston, Aug. 10, 1790. Commanding *Columbia*, left Boston, Sept., 1790; arrived Vancouver Island, June, 1791; discovered Grays Harbor and Columbia River (named in honor of his vessel); again completed trip around the world, landing in Boston, July 20, 1793. His trip and discoveries were foundation of American claim to Oregon country.

**Gray, Stephen.** d. 1736. English electrician. First to divide substances into electrics and nonelectrics, according as they can or can not be electrified by friction; discovered that attractive power (static electricity) can be transferred from one body to another by contact.

**Gray, Thomas.** 1716–1771. English poet, b. London. Educ. Cambridge. Accompanied Horace Walpole on Continental tour (1739–41); settled at Cambridge, where he received an appointment as professor of modern history (1768). Chief work, *Elegy Written in a Country Churchyard* (1751); other works, *Ode on a Distant Prospect of Eton College* (1747), *Progress of Poesy* (1758), *The Bard* (1758).

**Gray′son** (grā′s'n), **Cary Travers.** 1878–1938. American naval physician; physician to President Woodrow Wilson; appointed medical director, U.S. navy, with rank of rear admiral (1916); retired (1928). Chairman, American National Red Cross (from 1935).

**Grayson, David.** Pseudonym of Ray Stannard BAKER.

**Grayson, William.** 1736?–1790. American Revolutionary leader, b. in Prince William County, Va.; practiced law, Dumfries, Va. Served in Continental army; aide-de-camp to Washington (1776); commissioner of the board of war (1779–81). Member, Continental Congress (1784–87); U.S. senator (1789–90).

**Gra′zia′ni′** (grȧ′zyȧ′nē′), **Jean César.** 1859–1932. French army officer; chief of staff of French army during World War.

**Gra·zia′ni** (grä·tsyä′nē), **Rodolfo.** Marchese **di Neghel′li** (dē nā·gĕl′lē). 1882–1955. Italian marshal and administrator; commander of Italian forces in Libya (1930–34); governor of Italian Somaliland (1935–36); viceroy of Ethiopia (1936–37); governor of Libya (1940–41); minister of defense (1943–45); surrendered Ligurian army (1945).

**Gra′zi·e, Marie Eugenie del′le** (dĕl′ā grä′tsē·ā). 1864–1931. Austrian poet and playwright, of Italian descent.

**Graz·zi′ni** (grät·tsē′nē), **Antonio Francesco.** *Known as* **Il La′sca** (ēl läs′kä). 1503–1584. Italian writer, b. in Florence; an apothecary by profession. A founder (1550) of Accademia della Crusca, a literary society whose purpose was purification of the Italian language. Author of poems, stories, and plays, as *La Spiritata* (1561), and *La Gelosia* (1568).

**Grea′cen** (grē′s'n), **Edmund.** 1877–1949. American painter of portraits and landscapes.

**Great′head** (grāt′hĕd), **Henry.** 1757–1816. English inventor of the lifeboat; received grant of £1200 for his boat.

**Greathead, James Henry.** 1844–1896. British engineer, b. in South Africa. To England (1859); studied shield method of tunneling that bears his name; constructed subway under the Thames near the Tower of London (1869) and the City and South London railroad tunnels.

**Greathead, Robert.** See Robert GROSSETESTE.

**Gre·cha·ni′nov** (gryĕ·chŭ·nyē′nôf), **Aleksandr Tikhonovich.** 1864–1956. Composer, b. Moscow; to U.S. (naturalized 1946); known esp. for sacred music; composer of many songs, four symphonies, and two operas.

**Gre′co, El** (ĕl grā′kō; *Angl.* grĕk′ō, grē′kō), *i.e.* the Greek. *Also called* **Do·me′ni·co** (dō·mā′nē·kō). *Real name: Greek* **Kyriakos The′o·to·ko′pou·los** (thā′ô·tô·kô′pōō·lôs); *Spanish* **Domingo Te′o·to·có′pu·li** *or* **The′o·to·có′pu·li** (tā′ô·tô·kō′pōō·lē); *Italian* **Domenico Te′o·to·co′pu·lo** (tā′ô·tô·kô′pōō·lō) *or* **Te′o·sco′po·li** (tā′ô·skô′pô·lē) *or* **Te′o·sco′pu·li** (-pōō·lē). 1541–1614. Painter, b. prob. at Candia, Crete; to Venice; pupil of Titian (c. 1560–70); protégé of Cardinal Alessandro Farnese, Rome (1570 ff.); to Toledo (c. 1576 ff.). Foremost painter of Castilian school in 16th century; leading exponent of Spanish mysticism in painting. Works include *Christ Healing the Blind Man*, *Adoration of the Sheperds*, *Ascension*, *Christ Despoiled of His Garments*, *Baptism of Christ*, *Crucifixion*, and *The Pentecost*.

**Gré′court′** (grā′kōōr′), **Jean Baptiste Joseph Wil′lart′ de** (vē′lȧr′ dē). 1683–1743. French poet; most famous poem, *Le Solitaire et la Fortune;* composed also elegies, songs, fables in verse, etc.

**Gree′ley** (grē′lĭ), **Horace.** 1811–1872. American journalist and political leader, b. Amherst, N.H. To New York (1831). With Jonas Winchester, founded the *New Yorker*, a weekly journal (1834). Founded New York *Tribune* (1841); merged the *New Yorker* into the *Tribune* (1841); made success with the *Tribune*, and became important influence in molding thought of the people of the North. Supported Free Soil movement; encouraged antislavery sentiment. Supported administration in prosecution of Civil War. After Civil War, advocated universal amnesty and universal suffrage. Believed long imprisonment of Jefferson Davis without trial was a violation of Davis's constitutional rights, so defied public opinion in the North by signing a bail bond for Davis. Accepted nomination for presidency by a body of liberal Republicans, and was endorsed by Democrats (1872); badly beaten in election (Nov., 1872). See Josiah Bushnell GRINNELL.

**Gree′ly** (grē′lĭ), **Adolphus Washington.** 1844–1935. American army officer and arctic explorer, b. Newburyport, Mass. Volunteer at outbreak of Civil War; remained as officer in regular service after Civil War. In charge of stringing two thousand miles of military telegraph lines in Texas, the Dakotas, and Montana (1876–79). Commanded U.S. expedition (1881) to establish one of a chain of thirteen circumpolar stations; attained the most northerly point reached up to that time, 83° 24′ N., and discovered new land north of Greenland. Promoted chief signal officer with rank of brigadier general (1887) and major general (1906). In charge of building and operation of telegraph lines in Cuba, China, Philippine Islands, Alaska. In charge of relief operations in San Francisco area after the fire and earthquake (1906). Retired (1908). Author of *Three Years of Arctic Service* (2 vols., 1885), *Handbook of Polar Discoveries* (1909), *Polar Regions in the Twentieth Century* (1928), etc.

**Green** (grēn), **Alice Sophia Amelia,** *nee* **Stop′ford** (stŏp′fẽrd). *Known as* Mrs. **Stopford Green.** 1847–1929. Irish historian; to England (1874); m. (1877) John Richard Green (*q.v.*). Became zealous radical and advocate of home rule for Ireland; returned to Ireland (c. 1917) and lived in Dublin. Among her works are *The Making of Ireland and its Undoing* (1908), *A History of the Irish State to 1014* (1925).

**Green, Andrew Haswell.** 1820–1903. American lawyer, b. Worcester, Mass. Adm. to bar (1844); practiced, New York City; partner of Samuel J. Tilden. Influential in New York City affairs; member, Central Park commission (1857–70); comptroller of New York (1871–76);

member, commission to consolidate adjacent municipalities into one metropolitan area, Greater New York (1890–98); influential in uniting Astor and Lenox libraries with New York Public Library. Murdered by insane Negro (Nov. 13, 1903).

**Green, Anna Katharine.** 1846–1935. American writer, b. Brooklyn, N.Y.; m. Charles Rohlfs (1884). Known esp. for detective fiction, as *The Leavenworth Case* (her first book, 1878), *The Sword of Damocles, Dr. Izard, That Affair Next Door, The Filigree Ball, The Millionaire Baby, The Chief Legatee, The House of the Whispering Pines, The Step on the Stair*, etc.

**Green, Anne.** See under Julian GREEN.

**Green, Asa.** 1789–?1837. American physician and author, b. Ashby, Mass.; bookseller and author, New York City (from c. 1830). Works, chiefly satirical: *The Life and Adventures of Dr. Dodimus Duckworth, A.N.Q.* (1833); *Travels in America by George Fibbleton, Exbarber to His Majesty the King of Great Britain; A Glance at New York* (1837), etc.

**Green, Ashbel.** See under Jacob GREEN.

**Green, Bartholomew.** 1666–1732. Son of Samuel Green. American printer; in Boston (1692); became leading New England printer. Printed *Boston News-Letter* (1704–07; 1711 ff.) and became its publisher (1723). At his death publication was carried on by his son-in-law John Draper (*q.v.*).

**Green, Beriah.** 1795–1874. American clergyman and abolitionist; president, convention at Philadelphia that organized American Anti-Slavery Society (1833).

**Green, Duff.** 1791–1875. American journalist and politician, b. in Woodford County, Ky. Moved to Missouri (1816); studied law; adm. to bar; bought St. Louis *Enquirer* and supported Jackson (1824). Moved to Washington (1825); bought *United States Telegraph;* attacked Adams's administration in his paper; became printer to Congress (1829–33) and influential leader of Democratic party. Broke with Jackson and supported Clay for presidency (1832). Moved to Baltimore (1840); supported Harrison and Tyler (1840); in England and France as unofficial representative of United States (1840–44). U.S. consul, Galveston, Texas (1844); sent to Mexico to negotiate for U.S. purchase of Texas, New Mexico, and California, but failed. After Mexican War, served as U.S. agent for making payments to Mexico under provisions of treaty of Guadalupe Hidalgo. During Civil War, supported the Confederacy. After the war, aided in industrial recovery of the South.

**Green, George.** 1793–1841. English mathematician.

**Green, Henrietta Howland,** *nee* **Robinson.** *Known as* **Hetty Green.** 1834–1916. American financier, b. New Bedford, Mass.; m. Edward Henry Green (1867; d. 1902). Inherited fortune from father and aunt and increased it by shrewd investment and manipulation; reputed to have been the richest woman in America.

**Green, Horace.** 1802–1866. American laryngologist, b. Chittenden, Vt. Practiced in New York (from 1835); first American physician to specialize in diseases of the throat and air passages.

**Green, Jacob.** 1722–1790. American Presbyterian clergyman, b. Malden, Mass.; strongly supported colonial cause in American Revolution. His son **Ashbel** (1762–1848) was also a Presbyterian clergyman; president, Princeton (1812–22); editor, *Christian Advocate* (1822–34). Ashbel's son **Jacob** (1790–1841), b. Philadelphia, was professor of chemistry, etc., Princeton (1818–22), and Jefferson Med. Coll. (1825–41).

**Green, John Richard.** 1837–1883. English historian, b. Oxford; educ. Oxford; ordained (1860); vicar of Saint Philip's, Stepney (1866); librarian at Lambeth (1869). Author of a standard *Short History of the English People* (1874), *The Making of England* (1881), *Conquest of England* (1883). See Alice Sophia Amelia Stopford GREEN.

**Green, Joseph Andrew.** 1881–1963. American army officer; major general, and chief of U.S. Coast Artillery (from April, 1940).

**Green, Joseph Coy.** 1887– . American public official. Official, American Relief Administration in Europe (1915–19); taught history at Princeton (1920–30); on staff, U.S. Dept. of State (from 1930). Special editor for American Indian names and terms, *Webster's New International Dictionary, Second Edition.*

**Green, Julian.** 1900– . American novelist, b. in Paris, France, of American parentage. Served in World War I. Studied at U. of Virginia (1919–21). Lived thereafter in France and wrote largely in French. Elected to the French Academy (1972). Author of *Mont Cinère* (1926; trans. as *Avarice House*, 1927), *Adrienne Mésurat* (1927; trans. as *The Closed Garden*, 1928), *Léviathan* (trans. as *The Dark Journey* and awarded the Harper prize, 1929), *Épaves* (1931; trans. as *The Strange River*), *Le Visionnaire* (trans. as *The Dreamer*, 1934), *Minuit* (trans. as *Midnight*, 1936), *Varouna* (1941), etc., and of *Personal Record 1928–39* (1939; trans. from the French) and *Memories of Happy Days* (1942). His sister **Anne** (1899– ), b. Savannah, Ga., resident in France, writes in English; author of *The Selbys* (1930), *Reader, I Married Him* (1931), *That Fellow Percival* (1935), *The Silent Duchess* (1939), *Just Before Dawn* (1943), etc.

**Green, Matthew.** 1696–1737. English poet, whose poem *The Spleen* (1737) drew favorable comment from Pope and Gray.

**Green, Paul Eliot.** 1894– . American playwright, novelist, and educator; author of *The Lord's Will and Other Plays* (1925), *In Abraham's Bosom* (1927; awarded Pulitzer prize), *The Field God* (1927), *In the Valley and Other Carolina Plays* (1928), *The Laughing Pioneer* (a novel, 1932), *Roll Sweet Chariot* (1934), *This Body the Earth* (a novel, 1935), *The Lost Colony* (a play, 1937).

**Green, Samuel.** 1615–1702. American printer, b. in England; to Massachusetts (c. 1633). Settled in Cambridge. Became manager of printing press belonging to President Dunster of Harvard Coll., only printing office in American colonies until 1665; retired from business (1692). See Bartholomew GREEN.

**Green, Samuel Swett.** 1837–1918. American librarian, b. Worcester, Mass. Incorporator and (1891) president of American Library Association.

**Green, Seth.** 1817–1888. American pisciculturist; succeeded in making fish hatcheries practical and profitable.

**Green,** Mrs. **Stopford.** See Alice Sophia Amelia Stopford GREEN.

**Green, Thomas.** 1735–1812. American printer. Founded *Connecticut Courant* (now *Hartford Courant*), Hartford, Conn. (1764), *Connecticut Journal and New Haven Post Boy* (now *New Haven Journal Courier*), in New Haven (1767).

**Green, Thomas Edward.** 1857–1940. American Protestant Episcopal clergyman and lecturer, esp. in cause of international peace and the Red Cross; director of national speakers' bureau of American Red Cross (from 1918).

**Green, Thomas Hill.** 1836–1882. English idealist philosopher; professor, Oxford (1878–82). His *Prolegomena to Ethics*, left incomplete at his death, was edited by A. C. Bradley. He is the original of the character Mr. Gray in Mrs. Humphry Ward's *Robert Elsmere.*

**Green, Valentine.** 1739–1813. English mezzotint engraver; author of *Review of the Polite Arts in France* (1782).

**Green, William.** 1873–1952. American labor leader, b. Coshocton, Ohio. Employed in mines in Ohio. President, American Federation of Labor (from 1924). Member of governing board, International Labor Organization (1935–37).

**Green, William Henry.** 1825–1900. American Presbyterian clergyman and educator; noted Hebrew scholar and leader in America of ultraconservative school of Biblical criticism.

**Green'a·way** (grēn'ȧ·wā), **Catherine**, *known as* **Kate**. 1846–1901. English painter and illustrator, esp. of books for children. Published *Under the Window* (1879), *Kate Greenaway's Birthday Book* (1880), *Mother Goose* (1881), *Language of Flowers* (1884), etc.

**Green'bie** (grēn'bĭ), **Marjorie**, *nee* **Bar'stow** (bär'stō). 1891– . American writer; m. (1919) Sydney Greenbie (1889–1960). Author of *Ashes of Roses* (verse, 1924), *Wild Rose* (play, 1935), *American Saga* (1938), etc.

**Greene** (grēn), **Albert Gorton.** 1802–1868. American lawyer and poet, b. Providence, R.I. Justice of municipal court of Providence (1858–67). Writer of lyrics and humorous verse, including *Old Grimes*, *To the Weathercock on our Steeple*, *Adelheid*, *Ode on the Death of the Rev. Dr. William E. Channing*, etc.

**Greene, Francis Vinton.** 1850–1921. American army officer; grad. U.S.M.A., West Point (1870). Resigned from service (1886) and went into business. Served in Spanish-American War; in Philippines (1898); major general of volunteers (1898); resigned (1899). New York City police commissioner (1903–04). Author of *The Russian Army and Its Campaigns in Turkey in 1877–78* (1879), *The Revolutionary War* (1911), *Our First Year in the Great War* (1918).

**Greene, Frederick Stuart.** 1870–1939. American civil engineer; officer of engineers, serving in France in World War (1917–19). New York State commissioner of highways (1919–21, 1923 ff.); also, superintendent of public works of state of New York. Known also as writer of short stories.

**Greene, George Washington.** 1811–1883. American historian; grandson of Nathanael Greene. Author of *Life of Nathanael Greene* (3 vols., 1867–71), *The German Element in the War of Independence* (1876), *A Short History of Rhode Island* (1877).

**Greene, Graham.** 1904– . English writer; on staff of London *Times* (1926–30); motion-picture critic for *The Spectator* (1935–39). Author of *The Man Within* (1929), *Stamboul Train* (1932), *The Basement Room* (short stories, 1936), *The Confidential Agent* (1939), *The Power and the Glory* (1940; Hawthornden prize), etc.

**Greene, Homer.** 1853–1940. American lawyer and writer; author of *Coal and the Coal Mines* (1889), *The Tale of a Towpath* (1892), *A Lincoln Conscript* (1909), *The Guardsman* (1919), *What My Lover Said* (collected verse, 1931), etc.

**Greene, Jerome Davis.** 1874–1959. American banker and administrator, b. Yokohama, Japan. General manager, Rockefeller Inst. for Medical Research, New York (1910–12); secretary and trustee, Rockefeller Foundation (1913–17). Member of banking and brokerage firm of Lee, Higginson & Co. (1918–32). Trustee, Rockefeller Foundation (from 1928), General Education Board (from 1912), American Acad. in Rome (from 1920), etc.

**Greene, Maurice.** 1696?–1755. English organist and composer of music for Pope's *Ode on St. Cecilia's Day*, Addison's *Spacious Firmament*, Spenser's *Amoretti*, and much church music.

**Greene, Nathanael.** 1742–1786. American Revolutionary officer, b. village of Potowomut, Warwick, R.I. Commissioned brigadier general in Continental army (June 22, 1775); major general (Aug. 9, 1776). Led left wing of American force at Trenton (Dec. 26, 1776); captured Hessians. Quartermaster general of the army (Feb. 25, 1778); criticized by Congress, he resigned (1780); joined Washington. Succeeded Gates in command of the Army of the South (Oct., 1780). Conducted strategic retreat (1781) and finally turned and forced British out of Georgia and the Carolinas (1782) and back to three coastal bases. After war, lived on plantation near Savannah, Ga. See George Washington GREENE.

**Greene, Nathaniel.** 1797–1877. American journalist, b. Boscawen, N.H. Founded *American Statesman*, later called *Boston Statesman*, in Boston (1821); translated works from French, German, and Italian.

**Greene, Robert.** 1558–1592. English poet, playwright, and novelist. Chief dramatic work, *The Honorable History of Friar Bacon and Friar Bungay* (acted 1594); believed to have written part of the original Henry VI plays, rewritten by Shakespeare. His songs and eclogues are found scattered through his prose works, as in the romances *Perimedes the Blacke-Smith* (1588) and *Menaphon* (1589). Author of many tracts and pamphlets, including *Euphues, his Censure to Philautus* (a continuation of Lyly's *Euphues*, 1587), *Pandosta: the Triumph of Time* (1588), *Greene's Mourning Garment* (1590), *Farewell to Folly* (1591), *Groatsworth of Wit Bought with a Million of Repentance*, which attacks Marlowe and Peele and refers to Shakespeare (so it is thought) as an "upstart crow."

**Greene, Samuel Dana.** 1840–1884. American naval officer, b. Cumberland, Md. Executive officer of Federal ironclad *Monitor* during its duel with the *Merrimack*.

**Greene, Sarah Pratt**, *nee* **McLean.** 1856–1935. American writer; m. Franklin Lynde Greene (1887). Author of *Cape Cod Folks* (1881), *Towhead* (1883), *Last Chance Junction* (1889), *The Moral Imbeciles* (1898), *Flood-Tide* (1901), *Deacon Lysander* (1904), *Power Lot* (1906), etc.

**Greene, Ward.** 1892–1956. American journalist and writer, b. Asheville, N.C.; on staff of Atlanta (Ga.) *Journal* (1913–17, 1918–19), King Features Syndicate (from 1921). Author of *Cora Potts* (1929), *Ride the Nightmare* (1930), *Weep No More* (1932), *Death in the Deep South* (1936), and *Honey* (play, 1937).

**Greene, William.** 1696–1758. Colonial administrator in America, b. Warwick, R.I.; deputy governor of Rhode Island (1740–43); governor (1743–45; 1746–47; 1748–55). His son **William** (1731–1809) was a jurist; associate justice (1776) and chief justice (1777), Rhode Island superior court; governor of Rhode Island (1778–86).

**Green'hill** (grēn'hĭl), Sir **George.** 1847–1927. English mathematician.

**Green'leaf** (grēn'lēf), **Simon.** 1783–1853. American jurist, b. Newburyport, Mass.; practiced, Portland, Me. (from 1818). Professor of law, Harvard Law School (1833–48); associated with Story in developing efficiency of this school. Chief work, *A Treatise on the Law of Evidence* (3 vols., 1842, 1846, 1853).

**Greenock,** Lord. = 2d Earl CATHCART.

**Gree'nough** (grē'nō), **Chester Noyes.** 1874–1938. American educator; professor of English, Harvard (1915–38); also, dean of Harvard College (1921–27). Author of *A History of Literature in America* (with Barrett Wendell, 1904) and *English Composition* (with F. W. C. Hersey, 1917).

**Greenough, George Bellas.** 1778–1855. English geographer and geologist; founder (1811) and first president of the Geological Society, London; also, president of the Royal Geographical Society (1839–40).

**Greenough, Horatio.** 1805–1852. American sculptor, b. Boston. Grad. Harvard (1825). Studied in Italy

(1825–26); studio in Florence (1828–51). Examples of his work: *Washington*, a colossal statue now in Smithsonian Institution; *The Rescue*, a large group on a buttress of the portico of the capitol, Washington, D.C.; *Angel and Child*, in Boston Museum of Art; *Cupid Bound* and a portrait bust of Alexander Hamilton, in Boston Athenaeum; bust of Lafayette, in Pennsylvania Academy of Art; bust of John Quincy Adams, in New York Historical Society; *Angel Abdiel*, in Chicago Art Institute. His brother **Richard Saltonstall** (1819–1904) was also a sculptor; studied in Florence (1837–38); studio in Boston (1838–48) and in Rome (from 1848); examples of his work: bust of William H. Prescott, and *Shepherd Boy and Eagle*, in Boston Athenaeum; colossal bronze statue of Benjamin Franklin in front of Boston City Hall; *Carthaginian Maiden* in Boston Museum of Fine Arts.

**Greenough, James Bradstreet.** 1833–1901. American philologist; taught Latin at Harvard (from 1865); professor (from 1883). Author of *Analysis of the Latin Subjunctive* (1870), *Latin Grammar* (with J. H. Allen; 1872), *Words and Their Ways in English Speech* (with G. L. Kittredge; 1901).

**Green′slade** (grēn′slād), **John Wills.** 1880–1950. American naval officer, b. Bellevue, Ohio; grad. U.S.N.A., Annapolis (1899); promoted through the grades to rear admiral (1932), vice-admiral (1942); commandant, 12th naval district (1941–42); commander of western sea frontier (1942–44).

**Green′well** (grēn′wĕl; -wĕl), **Dora.** 1821–1882. English writer; author of books of verse, including *Carmina Crucis* (1869), and biographies of Lacordaire and John Woolman, and *The Patience of Hope* (1860).

**Greenwich,** Duke of. See John Campbell, 2d duke of ARGYLL.

**Green′wood** (grēn′wŏŏd), **Arthur.** 1880–1954. British politician and leader in the Labour party. M.P. (from 1922); minister of health (1929–31); minister without portfolio (1940–42); deputy leader of Labor party (from 1940); lord privy seal (from 1945).

**Greenwood, Frederick.** 1830–1909. English journalist. Succeeded Thackeray as editor of *Cornhill Magazine* (1862–68); founded (with George Smith) and edited *Pall Mall Gazette* (1865–80); founded and edited *St. James's Gazette* (1880–88).

**Greenwood, Hamar.** 1st Viscount **Greenwood.** 1870–1948. British lawyer and statesman; chief secretary for Ireland (1920–22). M.P. (1906–10; 1910–22; 1924–29); treasurer of Conservative party (1933–38).

**Greenwood, John.** d. 1593. English nonconformist clergyman; had part in organizing independent congregation in Nicholas Lane, believed by some to have been the beginning of Congregationalism; hanged at Tyburn.

**Greenwood, John.** 1760–1819. American dentist, b. Boston. Offices in New York (from c. 1785); reputed inventor of footpower drill, springs holding artificial plates in position, and use of porcelain for artificial teeth; made sets of artificial teeth for George Washington.

**Greenwood, Walter.** 1903–1974. English novelist and playwright; worked variously as office boy, stable boy, car driver, warehouseman, salesman; forced at times "on the dole." Author of novels *Love on the Dole* (1933, dramatized 1934), *Standing Room Only* (1936), *Only Mugs Work* (1938, dramatized 1938), a collection of short stories *The Cleft Stick* (1937); plays, *My Son's My Son* (1935), *Give Us This Day* (1936).

**Greer** (grēr), **David Hummell.** 1844–1919. American Protestant Episcopal bishop of New York (from 1908).

**Greet** (grēt), Sir **Ben,** *in full* **Philip Ben.** 1857–1936. English actor and manager, b. London; acted in support of Lawrence Barrett (1884), Mary Anderson, and others. Undertook management of summer open-air performances (1886 ff.); toured with own company (1890–1902) in such plays as *The Little Minister*, *Diplomacy*, *The Belle of New York;* specialized in Shakespearean productions in U.S. (1902–14) and in England (1914–24).

**Greffe.** See GRAEVIUS.

**Greg** (grĕg), Sir **Walter Wilson.** 1875–1959. English bibliographer. President of Bibliographical Society (1930–32); general editor of Malone Society (1906–39). Editor of Henslowe's diary (1904–08), and Elizabethan plays and Chester plays; author of *A List of English Plays* (1900), *Dramatic Documents from the Elizabethan Playhouses* (1931), etc.

**Gregg** (grĕg), **David McMurtrie.** 1833–1916. American army officer; brigadier general (1862); commanded cavalry on right wing of Meade's army at Gettysburg and repulsed Confederate attempt to turn Union flank (July 3, 1863); brevetted major general (Aug. 1, 1864).

**Gregh** (grĕg), **Fernand.** 1873–1960. French poet; author of *La Maison de l'Enfance* (1896), *Les Clartés Humaines* (1904), *La Chaîne Éternelle* (1910), *Couleur de la Vie* (1927), etc.

**Gré′goire′** (grā′gwȧr′), Père. See Jean Baptiste GIRARD.

**Grégoire, Henri.** 1750–1831. French Roman Catholic prelate and revolutionary; bishop of Blois; member of the States-General and Constituent Assembly (1789), the National Convention (1792), the Council of Five Hundred (1795), the Senate (1801).

**Greg′or** (grĕg′ẽr), **William.** 1761–1817. English clergyman, chemist, and mineralogist. Rector of Creed, Cornwall. Discovered titanium (in the mineral menaccanite, or ilmenite, at Manaccan in Cornwall; 1789).

**Greg′o·ras** (grĕg′ô·răs), **Nicephorus.** 14th-century Byzantine scholar and historian; chief work, a Roman history of the years 1204 to 1359 (37 books).

**Gre·go′ri·a′nus** (grĕ·gō′rĭ·ā′nŭs). Roman jurist; prepared (c. 300 A.D.) a code of law (Gregorian Code); only fragments extant.

**Gre′go·ro′vi·us** (grā′gô·rō′vē·ŏŏs), **Ferdinand.** 1821–1891. German historian; author of *Geschichte der Stadt Rom im Mittelalter* (8 vols., 1859–72), *Lucrezia Borgia* (1874), *Geschichte der Stadt Athen im Mittelalter* (1889), etc.

**Greg′o·ry** (grĕg′ô·rĭ), Saint. *Surnamed* **the Illuminator.** 257?–332. Apostle of Christianity among the Armenians; patriarch of Armenia (302 ff.); founder and patron saint of Armenian Church.

**Gregory.** Name of 16 popes (see *Table of Popes*, Nos. 64, 89, 90, 101, 140, 148, 157, 173, 178, 184, 201, 205, 228, 231, 236, 256) and one antipope, among them:

**Gregory I,** Saint. *Called* **Gregory the Great.** 540?–604. Pope (590–604); b. Rome, of a patrician family. As pope, restored monastic discipline, enforced celibacy of clergy, and was zealous in propagating Christianity; sent Augustine as missionary to Kent (597). Transformed patriarchate of Rome into the papal system that endured through the Middle Ages; exerted great influence in doctrinal matters; introduced changes in the liturgy; supposed to have arranged the Gregorian chant; wrote religious works, as dialogues, letters, homilies, and esp. the *Moralia* (morals from the Book of Job). Fourth Doctor of the Church (last of the Latin fathers).

**Gregory II,** Saint. d. 731. Pope (715–731), b. Rome. With Pope Constantine I to Constantinople (710); at first a supporter of Eastern Empire; later (726–731) opposed iconoclastic edicts of Leo the Isaurian; sent (719) Boniface as missionary to the Germans.

**Gregory III,** Saint. d. 741. Pope (731–741), b. Syria. Convoked a council in Rome (731); supported St. Boniface.

**Gregory V.** *Real name* **Bru′no** (brōō′nō) **of Carinthia.** d. 999. Pope (996–999). First German pope; nephew of Emperor Otto III. Expelled (997–998) and pontificate contested by Antipope John XVI; restored by Otto; had dispute with French king Robert, whom he excommunicated.

**Gregory VI.** *Real name* **Johannes Gra′ti·a′nus** (grā′shĭ·ā′nŭs). d. 1048? Pope (1045–46), b. Germany. Opposed by Antipope Sylvester III (1045); accused of buying pontificate from Benedict IX; deposed and banished to Germany (1046).

**Gregory VII,** Saint. *Real name* **Hil′de·brand** (hĭl′dĕ·brănd). 1020?–1085. Pope (1073–85), b. near Siena, Tuscany; Benedictine monk; as chaplain of Gregory VI (1045–47), accompanied him on exile to Germany; present at Diet of Worms (1049). On return to Rome, was created cardinal archdeacon (c. 1050); had marked influence over succeeding popes (1050–73). As pope, aimed to establish supremacy of papacy within the church and of the church over the state; issued decree (1075) against lay investitures which aroused Henry IV of Germany to anger; summoned Henry to Rome to answer charges; on his refusal, excommunicated him (1076); received Henry in penance at Canossa (1077) and granted him absolution; again resisted by Henry in continuation of quarrel (1080), and again excommunicated him; driven from Rome by Henry and displaced by Guibert as Clement III (1084); retired to Salerno, under protection of Robert Guiscard; died in exile.

**Gregory IX.** *Real name* **U′go·li′no** (ōō′gō·lē′nō), Count of **Se′gni** (sā′nyē). 1147?–1241. Pope (1227–41), b. Anagni, Italy. Incumbent of many ecclesiastical and diplomatic offices, as that of legate to Germany, before his election to papacy. Preached a crusade (1221); as pope, excommunicated Emperor Frederick II (1227) because he refused to keep his promise to go on crusade; supported by Guelphs, waged continual struggle against Frederick and Ghibellines (1235–41); again excommunicated Frederick (1239); encouraged mendicant orders and helped to develop the Holy Office of the Inquisition.

**Gregory X.** *Real name* **Teobaldo Vis·con′ti** (vēs-kōn′tē). 1210–1276. Pope (1271–76), b. Piacenza. Convoked Council of Lyon (1274), which effected temporary union between Eastern and Western churches.

**Gregory XI.** *Real name* **Pierre Roger de Beau′fort′** (dē bō′fôr′). 1331–1378. Pope (1370–78), b. near Limoges, France. Ended Babylonian captivity of popes by removing from Avignon to Rome (1377); issued bulls against Wycliffe's doctrines.

**Gregory XII.** *Real name* **Angelo Cor·ra′rio** (kôr·rä′ryō) *or* **Cor′rer** (kŏr′ĕr). 1327?–1417. Pope (1406–15), b. Venice. Elected by Roman cardinals in opposition to antipope at Avignon, Benedict XIII; deposed, along with antipope, by Council of Pisa (1409); refused to yield to new pope, Alexander V, until Council of Constance (1415); there resigned.

**Gregory XIII.** *Real name* **Ugo Buon′com·pa′gni** (bwôn′kōm·pä′nyē). 1502–1585. Pope (1572–85), b. Bologna. Held responsible offices (1539–72) under Paul III and Pius IV; vigorous in propaganda against Protestantism; aided Philip II in Netherlands and Catholic League in France; strengthened Jesuits; reformed the calendar (1582; the Gregorian calendar still in use); promoted education; built churches and many public works.

**Gregory XV.** *Real name* **Alessandro Lu′do·vi′si** (lōō′dō·vē′zē). 1554–1623. Pope (1621–23), b. Bologna. Aided Emperor Ferdinand II in the Thirty Years' War; founded (1622) Congregation of Propaganda.

**Gregory XVI.** *Real name* **Bartolommeo Alberto Cap′pel·la′ri** (käp′päl·lä′rē). 1765–1846. Pope (1831–46), b. Belluno. With aid of Austria, suppressed revolution in Papal States (1831–32); his rule disturbed by French occupation (1832–38).

*Antipope:* **Gregory VIII.** *Real name* **Maurice Bour′din′** (bōōr′dăN′). d. 1125. Antipope (1118–21). Elected in opposition to Gelasius II by Emperor Henry V; abandoned by emperor and imprisoned by Pope Calixtus II (1121).

**Gregory V.** 1739?–1821. Greek patriarch of Constantinople (1797–99; 1806–08; 1819–21). On outbreak of Greek war for independence, was believed to have given secret aid to Greeks, and was hanged at door of his own church by Turkish Janizaries on Easter Day (1821).

**Gregory,** Lady **Augusta,** *nee* **Persse** (pûrs). 1859?–1932. Irish playwright, b. in County Galway; m. Sir William Gregory (1881; d. 1892). With W. B. Yeats and others, aided in founding Irish National Theater Society; became director of the Abbey Theatre, Dublin. Among her works are *Poets and Dreamers, Gods and Fighting Men, Saints and Wonders, Irish Folk-History Plays, Our Irish Theatre, The Kiltartan History Book, The Kiltartan Poetry Book,* and *Three Last Plays.* Among her plays produced by the National Theatre Society are *Spreading the News, The Canavans, The Jackdaw, The Gaol Gate, The Full Moon, Hanrahan's Oath, The Golden Apple,* and *Sancho's Master.*

**Greg′o·ry** (grĕg′ō·rĭ), **Cas′par** (kăs′pĕr) **Re·né′** (rē·nā′). 1846–1917. German Biblical scholar, b. Philadelphia, U.S.A.; resident of Leipzig, Germany (from 1873); professor, Leipzig (from 1889); naturalized German citizen; German officer in World War I; killed in Allied bombardment of Neufchâtel-sur-Aisne (Apr. 9, 1917).

**Gregory, David.** 1661–1708. Scottish mathematician and astronomer.

**Gregory, Horace Victor.** 1898– . American poet and critic.

**Gregory, James.** 1638–1675. Scottish mathematician and inventor. Perfected earliest form of reflecting telescope, the Gregorian telescope, described in his *Optica Promota* (1663); published paper demonstrating original method of determining areas of geometrical figures, provoking controversy with Huygens; corresponded with Newton on subject of telescopes. His brother **John** (1724–1773) and John's son **James** (1753–1821) were professors of medicine at Edinburgh (1766–73 and 1776–1809, respectively).

**Gregory, John.** 1879–1958. Sculptor, b. London, Eng.; to U.S. (1893), naturalized (1912). Among his works are *Bacchante, Wood Nymph, Orpheus and Dancing Leopard,* and *Philomela.*

**Gregory, John Walter.** 1864–1932. British geologist and explorer. Headed expeditions to Lake Eyre (1901–02), Cyrenaica (1908), southern Angola (1912), alps of Chinese Tibet (1922). Works include *The Foundations of British East Africa* (1901), *The Rift Valleys and Geology of East Africa* (1921), and *Human Migration and the Future* (1928).

**Gregory,** Sir **Richard Arman.** 1864–1952. English astronomer. Editor, *Nature* (1919–39); author of *The Vault of Heaven, Religion in Science and Civilization,* etc.

**Gregory, Thomas Watt.** 1861–1933. American lawyer and politician; practiced law in Austin, Texas. Special asst. U.S. attorney general in charge of prosecuting N.Y., N.H. & H. R.R. for violation of Sherman Antitrust Act (1913). U.S. attorney general (1914–19). Practiced law in Washington, D.C. (from 1919).

**Gregory, William King.** 1876–1970. American paleontologist; research assistant to Henry Fairfield Osborn (1899–1913); curator, department of comparative anatomy (from 1921), American Museum of Natural History; professor of vertebrate paleontology, Columbia. Author of *The Orders of Mammals* (1910), *Our Face from Fish to Man* (1929), *In Quest of Gorillas* (1937), etc.

**Gregory of Naz'i·an'zus** (năz'ĭ·ăn'zŭs), Saint. *Surnamed* **The·ol'o·gus** (thē·ŏl'ō·gŭs), *i.e.* the Theologian. 329?–?389 A.D. Eastern Church ecclesiastic; known as one of the fathers of the Eastern Church. Bishop of Constantinople (380); head of the orthodox cause.

**Gregory of Nys'sa** (nĭs'ȧ), Saint. 331?–?396 A.D. Younger brother of Basil the Great (*q.v.*). Eastern Church ecclesiastic; known as one of the fathers of the Eastern Church. Bishop of Nyssa (371 or 372). A champion of orthodoxy at Council of Constantinople (381).

**Gregory of Tours** (to͝or; *Fr.* to͞or), Saint. *Real name* **Georgius Flo·ren'ti·us** (flō·rĕn'shĭ·ŭs). 538?–593 A.D. Frankish ecclesiastic and historian; bishop of Tours (573 A.D.). Chief work, *Historia Francorum*, main source of knowledge of the Merovingians to 591.

**Gregory Smith, George.** 1865–1932. British man of letters; professor and librarian, U. of Belfast (1909–30). General editor, Scottish Text Society (1899–1906); contributor to *Cambridge History of English Literature*, *Encyclopaedia Britannica*, and *Dictionary of National Biography*. Author of *The Book of Islay* (1895), *Elizabethan Critical Essays* (1904), *Ben Jonson* (1919), etc.

**Gregory Thau'ma·tur'gus** (thô'mȧ·tûr'gŭs), Saint. *Also known as* Saint **Gregory of Ne'o·caes'a·re'a** (nē'ō·sĕs'ȧ·rē'ȧ; -sĕz'ȧ-; -sē'zȧ-). 213?–?270 A.D. Eastern Church ecclesiastic; known as one of the fathers of the Eastern Church. Bishop of his native city, Neocaesarea (c. 240 A.D.).

**Gregory the Illuminator.** 257?–332. See GREGORY.

**Gré'gr** (grā'gẽr), **Eduard.** *Real surname* **Grö'ger** (grû'gẽr). 1829–1907. Czech politician; one of founders of Young Czech party, and an advocate of an independent Czech state. His brother **Julius** (1831–1896) was one of the founders of the Young Czech party; vigorously opposed German influence in Bohemia.

**Greif.** See GRYPHIUS.

**Greif'fen·ha'gen** (grī'fĕn·hä'gĕn), **Maurice.** 1862–1931. British painter and illustrator.

**Greig** (grĕg), Sir **Samuel.** 1735–1788. Scottish naval officer. Served in Russian navy (from 1764); commanded division of Russian fleet under Orlov which defeated Turks at Çeşme (July, 1770). Rear admiral (1770); vice-admiral (1773). Commanded Russian fleet against Swedes in Gulf of Finland (1788). Created modern Russian navy. His son **Aleksei Samuilovich** (1775–1845), admiral in Russian navy, distinguished himself in Russo-Turkish wars of 1807 and 1828–29.

**Grein** (?grīn), **Jacob Thomas.** 1862–1935. English dramatic critic, b. Amsterdam; to England as a young man; naturalized (1895). On staff of *Life* (1888–91), *Sunday Times* (1897–1918), *Illustrated London News* (1920–35). Founded Independent Theatre (1891) and People's Theatre (1923).

**Grein** (grīn), **Michael.** 1825–1877. German philologist; authority on Anglo-Saxon literature.

**Grell** (grĕl), **Eduard.** 1800–1886. German composer, chiefly of church choral music.

**Grel'let'** (grā'lĕ'), **Ste'phen** (stē'vĕn). *Orig.* **Étienne de Grellet du Mo'bil'lier'** (mô'bē'lyā'). 1773–1855. Quaker missionary and philanthropist, b. Limoges, France; to U.S. (c. 1795); traveling missionary minister in America and Europe, his reports on conditions in prisons and poorhouses being responsible for many reform measures.

**Grel'ling** (grĕl'ĭng), **Richard.** 1853–1929. German pacifist; a founder of German Peace Society; accused Germany of responsibility for outbreak of World War (1914) and took refuge in Switzerland; author of *J'Accuse* (1915).

**Gren'fell** (grĕn'fĕl), **Bernard Pyne.** 1869–1926. English papyrologist; professor, Oxford (1916–26). With Arthur Surridge Hunt (*q.v.*) discovered, edited, and published many Greek papyri, including collections known as the Oxyrhynchus papyri, the Amherst papyri, Tebtunis papyri, and the Greek papyri in the Cairo Museum; coauthor with A. S. Hunt of *Logia Jesu, Sayings of Our Lord*...(1897) and *New Sayings of Jesus*...(1904).

**Grenfell, Francis Wallace.** 1st Baron **Grenfell of Kil'vey** (kĭl'vĭ). 1841–1925. British soldier; engaged in Kaffir War (1878), Zulu War (1879), Egyptian expedition under Wolseley (1882), Nile expedition for relief of Gordon at Khartoum (1884). Sirdar of the Egyptian army (1885–92). Commander of forces in Egypt (1897–98). Governor of Malta (1899–1903); commander in chief in Ireland (1904–08). General (1904); field marshal (1908).

**Grenfell, George.** 1849–1906. English Baptist missionary and explorer in Africa. Surveyed Congo basin as far as the equator (1884), and affluents of the Congo (1885). As representative of King Leopold of Belgium, negotiated settlement with Portugal of boundary between Congo Free State and Angola (1893). Explored Aruwimi River (1900–02).

**Grenfell,** Sir **Wilfred Thomason.** 1865–1940. English physician and missionary. Fitted out first hospital ship to serve fishermen in the North Sea; to Labrador (1892) for missionary work, and built hospitals, established co-operative stores, introduced child welfare work; to St. John's, Newfoundland (1912), and opened King George V Seamen's Inst. Cruised annually in hospital steamer *Strathcona II* along Newfoundland and Labrador coasts, keeping in touch with mission stations. Author of *Adrift on an Ice Pan*, *Labrador Days*, and *The Romance of Labrador*.

**Gren'ville** (grĕn'vĭl). Name of an English family including earls of **Tem'ple** (tĕm'p'l) and dukes of **Buck'ing·ham** (bŭk'ĭng·ăm) **and Chan'dos** (shăn'dŏs; chăn'-):

**Richard Temple Grenville** (1711–1779), 1st Earl **Temple**, political leader. Eldest son of Richard Grenville (1678–1728) and Hester Temple, afterward Countess Temple; succeeded to mother's peerage (1752) and took name **Grenville–Temple.** M.P. (1734); first lord of admiralty (1756–57); lord privy seal (1757–61) under elder Pitt; opposed Bute; refused treasury and quarreled with Pitt (Chatham) over Stamp Act (1766); opposed conciliation of American colonies; paid Wilkes's law expenses; known to contemporaries as **Squire Gaw'key** (gô'kĭ); credited by some with authorship of *Letters of Junius* (cf. Sir Philip FRANCIS).

His brother **George Grenville** (1712–1770), statesman; educ. Oxford; barrister (1735); M.P. (1740); held subordinate office under Pelham and Newcastle; resigned treasurership of navy on dismissal of Pitt and Temple (April, 1757) but held it again (June, 1757–62); carried bill improving system of paying seamen's wages; leader of House of Commons and member of cabinet (1761); first lord of admiralty (1762–63); first lord of treasury, chancellor of exchequer, and prime minister (1763–65); resisted Bute's influence with George III, but best known for enactment of Stamp Act (1765) and early proceedings against Wilkes (1763); nicknamed "the Gentle Shepherd" in allusion to his querulous request in parliament that the gentlemen tell him *where* to lay new taxes and Pitt's mocking recitation, in the same languid tone, of the old ditty "Gentle Shepherd, tell me where!"

The eldest of George's three surviving sons, **George**

**Nu′gent-Temple-Grenville** [nū′jĕnt-] (1753–1813), 1st Marquis of **Buckingham;** educ. Oxford; M.P. (1774–79); succeeded uncle as 2d Earl **Temple** (1779); lord lieutenant of Ireland (1782–83, 1787–89); instituted order of St. Patrick (1783); instrument of George III in defeating Fox's East India bill in House of Lords (1783).

Another son, **Thomas Grenville** (1755–1846), bibliophile; educ. Oxford; M.P. (1780); adherent of Fox; later joined old Whigs; served as diplomat in negotiations with America and as envoy to Vienna and Berlin; first lord of admiralty (1806–07); best known as book collector whose bequest to British Museum contained first folio Shakespeare.

The youngest son, **William Wyndham Grenville** (1759–1834), Baron **Grenville** (created 1790), statesman; educ. Oxford; M.P. (1782); chief secretary for Ireland (1782–83); speaker of House of Commons (1789); home secretary (1789–90); foreign secretary (1791–1801), not always in agreement with Pitt; resigned because of George III's refusal of consent to any measure of Roman Catholic relief; refused office without his ally, Fox (1804); after Pitt's death, nominal head of coalition government, so-called All-the-Talents Administration (1806–07), which abolished slave trade; resigned on Catholic question.

George's (1753–1813) son **George Nugent Grenville** (1788–1850), Baron **Nugent;** educ. Oxford; M.P. (1812); promoter of the Reform Bill; lord high commissioner of Ionian Islands (1832–35); author of *Oxford and Locke* (1829), *Memorials of John Hampden* (1832), and *Lands Classical and Sacred* (1845–46).

His eldest brother, **Richard Temple Nugent Brydges Chandos Grenville** (1776–1839), 1st Duke of **Buckingham and Chandos** (cr. 1822); grad. Oxford (1791); M.P. as Earl Temple (1797–1813); m. only child of 3d duke of Chandos; on formation of ministry of his uncle William Wyndham Grenville, appointed deputy president of Board of Trade (1806–07); lord lieutenant of Buckinghamshire (1813); collector of rare prints.

**Richard Grenville** (1797–1861), 2d Duke of **Buckingham and Chandos;** only son of 1st duke; marquis of Chandos (1822–39); educ. Oxford; M.P. (1818–39); introduced tenant-at-will clause, also called "Chandos clause," in Reform Act (1832); opposed repeal of corn laws; author of memoirs of courts of George III, George IV, William IV, and Victoria; forced by unfortunate realty speculations to dispose of pictures, furniture, etc., in Stowe sale (1848), at which earl of Ellesmere purchased Chandos bust of Shakespeare.

**Richard Grenville** (1823–1889), 3d Duke of **Buckingham and Chandos;** only son of 2d duke; marquis of Chandos (1839–61); educ. Oxford; chairman of London and North Western Ry. (1853–61); president of privy council (1866–67); colonial secretary (1867–68); governor of Madras (1875–80).

**Gren′ville** (grĕn′vĭl) *or* **Greyn′ville** (grān′vĭl; grĕn′-), Sir **Richard.** 1541?–1591. British naval commander. M.P. (1571); commanded (1585) fleet for colonization of Virginia, for his cousin Sir Walter Raleigh, and captured Spanish ship on return trip; pillaged Azores (1586); organized defenses of west of England against Armada (1586–88); second in command (1591) under Lord Thomas Howard of Azores fleet sent to intercept Spanish treasure ships; mortally wounded and captured when his ship, the *Revenge*, was isolated from rest of fleet off Flores, as commemorated in Tennyson's ballad *The Revenge;* figures in Kingsley's *Westward Ho.*

His grandson Sir **Richard Grenville** *or* **Gran′ville** [grăn′vĭl] (1600–1658), Royalist soldier, served under Buckingham at Cádiz and on La Rochelle expedition; created baronet (1630); arrested and forced to join Parliamentary army but joined King Charles at Oxford (1644) and served in west of England; charged with misappropriation of war funds and insubordination (1646); lived in exile in Holland.

Another grandson, Sir **Bevil Grenville** (1596–1643), Royalist soldier; B.A., Oxon. (1614); M.P. (1621); supported Sir John Eliot, but shifted to king's side and under Sir Ralph Hopton defeated Parliamentarians at Bradock Down (1643); killed at head of Cornish infantry at Lansdowne.

Sir Bevil's grandson **George Grenville** *or* **Granville** (1667–1735), Baron **Lans′downe** (lănz′doun), poet and dramatist; M.A., Cantab. (1679); M.P. (1702); secretary of war (1710); treasurer of the household (1713); imprisoned (1715–17) on suspicion of Jacobitism; living in Paris for ten years, wrote *Vindications* of General Monck and Sir Richard Grenville; author of poems praised by Pope and plays acted at Lincoln's Inn Fields and Drury Lane, including *Heroick Love* (1698), and an opera.

**Grenville-Temple, Richard.** See GRENVILLE family.

**Gresh′am** (grĕsh′ăm), Sir **Thomas.** 1519?–1579. English financier; member of Queen Elizabeth's first council (1558). Ambassador to Netherlands (1559–61); remained there until driven home by political disturbances (1567). Crown financial agent (to 1574). Founded Royal Exchange and Gresham College, in London. Observed and commented on the tendency (called "Gresham's law"), when two coins are equal in debt-paying power but unequal in intrinsic value, for the one having the less intrinsic value to remain in circulation and for the other to be hoarded.

**Gresham, Walter Quintin.** 1832–1895. American lawyer and army officer, b. in Harrison County, Ind. Served through Civil War; brigadier general (Aug. 11, 1863); brevetted major general (Mar. 13, 1865). U.S. district judge, district of Indiana (1869–83). U.S. postmaster general (1883–84); U.S. secretary of the treasury (1884). U.S. circuit judge, 7th judicial district (1884). Opposition to protective tariff led him to leave Republican party and join Democrats. U.S. secretary of state (1893–95).

**Gres′set′** (grĕ′sĕ′), **Jean Baptiste Louis.** 1709–1777. French poet and playwright; author of *Vert Vert, Histoire d'un Perroquet de Nevers* (amusing story of a malicious and indiscreet parrot; 1734), *Édouard III* (tragedy, 1740), and the comedies *Sidney* (1745), *Les Bourgeois* (1747), *Les Parvenus* (1748).

**Gress′mann** (grĕs′män), **Hugo.** 1877–1927. German Protestant theologian.

**Gres′well** (grĕz′wĕl; -wĕl), **Edward.** 1797–1869. English chronologist.

**Gretchaninoff.** Variant of GRECHANINOV.

**Gré′try′** (grā′trē′), **André Ernest Modeste.** 1741–1813. French (Belg.-born) composer, esp. of operas.

**Greuze** (grûz), **Jean Baptiste.** 1725–1805. French portrait and genre painter.

**Grev′ille** (grĕv′ĭl; -′l), **Charles Cavendish Fulke.** 1794–1865. English diarist. Clerk to the privy council (1821–59), and thus familiar with the English statesmen of the period; for 40 years kept a diary in which he recorded his impressions and close knowledge of English politics and politicians (published as *Memoirs*, in 3 series, 1875, 1885, 1887).

**Greville,** Sir **Fulke.** 1st Baron **Brooke** (bro͝ok). 1554–1628. English poet and statesman. Friend of Sir Philip Sidney; favorite of Queen Elizabeth. Secretary for principality of Wales (1583–1628); M.P. (1592–1620); chancellor of the exchequer (1614–21). Works include sonnets, tragedies, and a life of Sidney.

**Gré′ville′** (grā′vēl′), **Henry.** *Pseudonym of* **Alice Du′rand′** (dü′räN′), *nee* **Fleu′ry′** (flû′rē′). 1842–1902. French novelist, b. Paris; resident for a time in St. Petersburg. Author of many novels, a number of them with a Russian background, as *Dosia* (1876), *Sonia* (1877), *Le Vœu de Nadia* (1882), *Nikanor* (1887), *Fidelka* (1894), *La Mamselka* (1902), etc.

**Grev′ille** (grĕv′ĭl; -'l), **Leopold Guy Francis Maynard.** 6th Earl of **War′wick** (wŏr′ĭk). *Known as* Lord **Brooke** (brŏŏk) *and* Lord **Greville** (till his succession, 1924). 1882–1928. British soldier; served in Boer War (1899–1902); war correspondent with Russian army in Russo-Japanese War (1904–05); aide-de-camp to General French at outbreak of World War (1914); brigadier general of Canadian infantry brigades (1915–18).

**Gré′vin′** (grā′văN′), **Alfred.** 1827–1892. French illustrator and caricaturist; sketched humorous scenes of Parisian life for contemporary journals.

**Grévin, Jacques.** 1538–1570. French physician, poet, and playwright.

**Gré′vy′** (grā′vē′), **François Paul Jules.** 1807–1891. Third president of the French Republic, b. Mont-sous-Vaudrey, near Dôle, Jura. Studied law in Paris; showed Republican sympathies; deputy from Jura to Constituent Assembly (1848–49); withdrew from politics (1852); president of Paris bar. Returned to politics (1868–70), holding prominent place in Republican party (1871–73); president of Chamber of Deputies (1876–79). President of France (1879–87); popularity destroyed in second term (1885–87) by scandals affecting son-in-law; not personally directly implicated, but forced to resign.

**Grew** (grōō), **Joseph Clark.** 1880–1965. American diplomat, b. Boston; A.B., Harvard (1902). Secretary of embassy, Vienna (1911–12) and Berlin (1912–16); on staff of U.S. Department of State (1917–18). U.S. minister to Denmark (1920), Switzerland (1921); negotiated treaty with Turkey (1923). Undersecretary of state (1924–27). Ambassador to Turkey (1927–32), Japan (1932–41); undersecretary of state (1944–45). Author of *Report from Tokyo* (1942), *Ten Years in Japan* (1944).

**Grew, Nehemiah.** 1641–1712. English plant physiologist; reputedly first to observe sex in plants. Author of *The Anatomy of Plants* (4 vols., 1682).

**Grey** (grā). See also GRAY.

**Grey.** Name of English family including **Greys de Wilt′on** (dĕ wĭl′t'n; -tŭn), **Greys de Ru′thin** (rōō′thĭn), **Greys of Gro′by** (grōō′bĭ), and present earls of **Stam′ford** (stăm′fẽrd) and earls Grey:

GREY DE WILTON. **John de Grey** (1268–1323), 2d Baron **Grey de Wilton,** judge; lord ordainer (1310); justice of North Wales (1315). From a younger son of his were descended barons Grey de Ruthin. From his eldest son were descended barons Grey de Wilton, including **William Grey** (d. 1562), 13th baron, who distinguished himself in French war in reign of Henry VIII and as a leader of English army at Pinkie (1547); suppressed rebellion in Oxfordshire (1549); imprisoned as supporter of duke of Somerset (1551); involved in Northumberland's attempt to set Lady Jane Grey on throne (1553); pardoned, put in charge of defense of Guînes, which he was forced to surrender (1558). His elder son, **Arthur** (1536–1593), 14th baron, helped defend Guînes; lord deputy of Ireland (1580–82), having Edmund Spenser as secretary; figures as Artegal in *Faerie Queene;* responsible for massacre of 600 Italians and Spaniards at Smerwick (1580); one of commissioners who tried Mary, Queen of Scots; author of account of defense of Guînes used by Holinshed. Arthur's son **Thomas** (d. 1614), 15th and last baron, served against Spanish Armada (1588); general of horse against Essex and Southampton (1601).

GREY DE RUTHIN. **Roger de Grey** (d. 1353), 1st Baron **Grey de Ruthin,** soldier, younger son of John de Grey, 2d Baron Grey de Wilton (see above); M.P. (1324); served in Scottish campaigns (1318, 1327, 1341). His grandson **Reginald de Grey** (1362?–1440), 3d baron, won famous lawsuit (1401–10) for right to bear Hastings arms and title earl of Pembroke, from Edward Hastings, to whom title did not belong; governor of Ireland (1398); warred on Owen Glendower (1402); continued Welsh War (1409); member of council of regency (1415). Reginald's grandson **Edmund Grey** (1420?–1489), 1st Earl of **Kent** (kĕnt), deserted Henry VI for Yorkists at battle of Northampton (1460); lord high treasurer (1463); created earl of Kent (1465). **Henry Grey** (1594–1651), 9th Earl of **Kent,** was speaker of House of Lords (1645, 1647). Henry's grandson **Henry Grey** (1664?–1740), 11th Earl of **Kent,** lord justice (1714), was created duke of Kent (1710). **Thomas Philip de Grey** (1781–1859), Earl **de Grey,** descendant of Henry, 9th Earl of Kent; succeeded as 3d Baron **Grant′ham** [grăn′tăm; grăn′thăm] (1786); first lord of admiralty (1834–35); viceroy of Ireland (1841–44); first president of Society of British Architects (1834–59); author of *Characteristics of the Duke of Wellington* (1853).

From a grandson of Reginald, 3d Baron Grey of Ruthin, by a second marriage, namely John Grey, 8th Baron Ferrers of Groby (in his mother's right), were descended marquises of Dorset and duke of Suffolk (see below) and earls of Stamford (cr. 1628), beginning with **Henry Grey** (1599–1673), 1st Earl and 2d Baron **Grey of Groby,** Parliamentary general, who declared for Charles II (1659). To a branch of these Greys of Groby belong: Sir **George Grey** (1812–1898), colonial governor; grandson of Charles, 1st Earl Grey (see below); explored Swan River, Australia (1838); governor of South Australia (1841–45), New Zealand (1845–53, 1861–68), Cape Colony (1854–60); prime minister of New Zealand (1877–79) with radical program including adult franchise, triennial parliaments, taxation of land values, and leasing instead of sale of crown lands, all of which reforms were carried by later ministries; author of *Polynesian Mythology* (1855) and topographical works on Australia and New Zealand.

DOR′SET (dôr′sĕt; -sĭt), MARQUISES OF (1475–1554). **Thomas Grey** (1451–1501), 1st Marquis of **Dorset** (cr. 1475); son of **John Grey** (1432–1461), 7th Baron **Fer′rers** (fĕr′ẽrz) **of Groby,** a Lancastrian killed at St. Albans, and of Elizabeth Woodville (dau. of Richard Woodville), later queen of Edward IV (see ELIZABETH); as stepson of Edward IV, fought at Tewkesbury; had to flee from Richard, Duke of Gloucester, after supporting his half brother Edward V; one of leaders of Buckingham insurrection; from the Continent, supported invasion (1485) by Henry, Earl of Richmond, Lancastrian claimant to throne and later Henry VII; imprisoned on suspicion (1487); pardoned, helped quell Cornish uprising (1497). His third son, **Thomas** (1477–1530), 2d marquis, styled Lord **Har′ing·ton** [hăr′ĭng·tŭn] (till 1501), spent last years of Henry VII's reign in prison; gained favor of Henry VIII, who gave him command in France (1512) and made him warden of Scottish marches (1523). Thomas's (1477–1530) brother Lord **Leonard Grey** *or* **Gray** (1490?–1541), Viscount **Grane** (grān) of Ireland; 6th son of 1st marquis; accused as lord deputy of Ireland (1536–37) of favoring Geraldines because of family connections; condemned for treason and beheaded.

**Henry Grey** (d. 1554), Duke of **Suf'folk** (sŭf'ŭk) and 3d Marquis of **Dorset;** eldest son of 2d marquis; attached himself (from 1548) to John Dudley, Duke of Northumberland; married his daughter, Lady Jane Grey, to Northumberland's son (1553); pardoned for support in Lady Jane Grey's cause; executed for taking part in Wyatt's rising against Mary Tudor's Spanish marriage.

Henry's daughter Lady **Jane Grey** (1537–1554), a great-granddaughter of Henry VII, made extraordinary progress in study of languages; married against her wish to Lord Guildford Dudley (1553) as part of plot to alter succession to her favor on death of Edward VI; proclaimed queen (July 9, 1553); on dispersal of her father-in-law's troops, imprisoned (July 19); rejected opportunity to recant Protestantism; beheaded, with her husband, after her father's participation in Wyatt's Rebellion.

EARLS GREY. **Charles Grey** (1729–1807), 1st Earl **Grey,** soldier in American Revolution; nicknamed "No Flint Grey"; younger son of Sir **Henry Grey** (d. 1749), 1st Baronet of **How'ick** (hou'ĭk), Northumberland, and Hannah, daughter of Thomas Wood of Fallodon, near Alnwick; defeated Anthony Wayne near Paoli (Sept. 20, 1777); commanded 3d brigade at Germantown (Oct., 1777); defeated Col. George Baylor's Virginia dragoons at Old Tappan, N.J. (1778); appointed major general (1778) and commander in chief in America (1782); co-operated with Jervis in capture of French West Indies (1794); appointed general and privy councilor (1795); created Baron Grey (1801), and Earl Grey and Viscount Howick (1806).

His son **Charles** (1764–1845), 2d earl, statesman, b. Fallodon; educ. Cambridge; M.P. (1786 ff.); pioneer of parliamentary reform; as lieutenant of Fox, moved impeachment of Pitt; promoted Whig secession from House of Commons in protest; first lord of the admiralty in Broad-bottomed Administration under Fox (1806) and, on Fox's death, foreign secretary (1806–07); resigned on George III's requirement of pledge not to introduce further measures for Roman Catholic emancipation; on Napoleon's return from Elba (1815), followed former policy of Fox, maintaining right of France and other nations to choose own governors; opposed renewal of war and suspension of Habeas Corpus Act (1817); opposed bill for Queen Caroline's divorce (1820); prime minister of Great Britain (1830–34); by gaining William IV's reluctant promise to create sufficient new peers to swamp opposition in House of Lords, carried Reform Bill (1832) providing reform of electoral system and suffrage, and bill abolishing slavery throughout British Empire.

Charles's (1764–1845) son **Henry George** (1802–1894), 3d earl, statesman; educ. Cambridge; M.P. (1826 ff.); secretary at war (1835–39); party leader in House of Lords (1845); secretary for colonies (1846–52); first minister to proclaim government of colonies for their own benefit, first to accord self-government in accordance with capacity for it, first to introduce free trade between Great Britain and Ireland; opposed Crimean War; opposed Gladstone's home rule policy (1885–86).

Henry's nephew **Albert Henry George** (1851–1917), 4th earl, statesman; educ. Cambridge; M.P. (1880 ff.); administrator of Rhodesia (1896–97); governor general of Canada (1904–11).

Sir **George Grey** (1799–1882), b. Gibraltar; grandson of 1st earl and nephew of 2d earl; grad. Oxford (1821) and entered law; M.P. (1832 ff.); judge advocate general (1839–41); home secretary (1846–52, 1855–58, 1861–66); outmaneuvered Chartists' leaders and kept them in order (1848); by further suspension of Habeas Corpus Act, repressed Irish discontent (1849); colonial secretary (1854–55) and chancellor of duchy of Lancaster (1841, 1859–61). Carried convict discipline bill (1846), which laid foundation for modern British prison system.

**Albert Henry George Grey** (1851–1917), 4th earl, British administrator; grandson of 2d earl and nephew of 3d earl; grad. Cambridge (1873); Liberal M.P. (1880 ff.); devoted himself to social reform and promotion of imperial unity; one of 93 dissident Liberals who defeated home rule bill (1886); administrator of Rhodesia (1896–97); successful governor general of Canada (1904–11); promoter of proportional representation.

Sir **Edward Grey** (1862–1933), Viscount **Grey of Fal'lo·don** (făl'ō·d'n; -dŭn), b. in Northumberland; grandson of Sir George Grey (1799–1882); educ. Oxford; undersecretary of state for foreign affairs (1892–95); secretary of state for foreign affairs (1905–16); consolidated Triple Entente, uniting Great Britain, France, and Russia; took important part in negotiation of Balkan problems at London Peace Conference (1912–13); resigned because of ill health (1916); served temporarily as British ambassador to U.S. in connection with peace settlement (1919); chancellor of Oxford (1928); author of *Twenty-Five Years, 1892–1916* (2 vols., 1925) and *Fallodon Papers* (1926).

Sir **William Grey** (1818–1878), colonial administrator; grandson of Charles, 1st Earl Grey, and cousin of 3d earl; secretary to government in Bengal (1854–57) and to government in India (1859); lieutenant governor of Bengal (1867–71); governor of Jamaica (1874–77).

**Grey, Zane.** 1875–1939. American novelist, b. Zanesville, Ohio. Practiced dentistry in New York (1898–1904); devoted himself to writing (from 1904). Author of adventure stories, esp. against background of American West, including *Riders of the Purple Sage* (1912), *The Lone Star Ranger* (1915), *The Mysterious Rider* (1921), *The Wanderer of the Wasteland* (1923), *The Thundering Herd* (1925), *The Vanishing American* (1926), *Code of the West* (1934), *West of the Pecos* (1937).

**Grey Owl.** *real name* **George Stansfeld Belaney** 1888–1938. Canadian (Eng.-born) writer; claimed to be Apache Indian; author of *Men of the Last Frontier* (1932), *Pilgrims of the Wild* (1935), *Adventures of Sajo and her Beaver People* (1935), *Tales of an Empty Cabin* (1936), etc.

**Gri'beau'val'** (grē'bō'vål'), **Jean Baptiste Va'quette' de** (vȧ'kĕt' dĕ). 1715–1789. French general; introduced reforms which made French artillery reputedly the best in Europe.

**Gri·bo·e'dov** (gryĭ·bŭ·yă'dôf), **Aleksandr Sergeevich.** 1795–1829. Russian poet and statesman; murdered at Teheran with members of embassy staff by a mob. Chiefly known as author of a satirical comedy in rhymed verse depicting the struggle between two generations, *Gore ot Uma* (translated under various titles in English, as *The Misfortune of Being Clever* or *Woe from Wit*).

**Grid'ley** (grĭd'lĭ), **Charles Vernon.** 1844–1898. American naval officer; commanded *Olympia,* flagship of Asiatic squadron (1897–98). To him Dewey gave famous command: "You may fire when you are ready, Gridley."

**Gridley, Richard.** 1711–1796. American military engineer; artillery officer with British army that besieged Louisburg, French fortress on Cape Breton Island (1745); also, at capture of Quebec (1759). Joined colonial forces at outbreak of American Revolution; chief engineer, rank of major general (1775); built breastworks on Breed's Hill; wounded in battle of Bunker Hill; fortified Dorchester heights (1776). Engineer general, eastern department (1777–80). His brother **Jeremiah** (1702–1767) was a lawyer; attorney general of Massachusetts Bay Province, defending (1761) legality of the Writs of Assistance; grand master of all the Masons of North America (1755–67).

**Grieg** (grĭg), **Edvard Ha'ge·rup** (hä'gĕ·rōōp). 1843–1907. Norwegian composer, b. at Bergen. Studied at Leipzig and Copenhagen under Moscheles, Hauptmann, Reinecke, Richter, Gade, and Hartmann. His compositions include *Humoresken* (for the piano), two *Peer Gynt* suites (for orchestra), *Sigurd Jorsalfar* (an opera), *Olaf Trygvason* (a choral work), a piano concerto, Norwegian dances, Norwegian folksongs, and other beautiful songs.

**Grien, Hans.** See Hans BALDUNG.

**Grie'pen·kerl** (grē'pĕn·kĕrl), **Robert.** 1810–1868. German playwright and literary critic.

**Grier** (grēr), **Robert Cooper.** 1794–1870. American jurist; practiced, Bloomsburg, Pa. (1817–18), Danville (from 1818). Associate justice, U.S. Supreme Court (1846–70).

**Grier'son** (grēr's'n), **Benjamin Henry.** 1826–1911. American army officer; led cavalry raid from La Grange, Tenn., to Baton Rouge, La., through heart of Confederacy (Apr. 17 to May 2, 1863); promoted major general (1863); brigadier general, U.S. army (1890).

**Grierson, Francis.** *Orig.* **Benjamin Henry Jesse Francis Shep'ard** (shĕp'ẽrd). 1848–1927. Musician and author, b. in Cheshire, Eng.; to U.S. in infancy. Studied in Paris (1869); under name of Jesse Shepard, gave successful piano recitals in foreign capitals. Began writing (c. 1880), changing his name to Francis Grierson. Author of *Modern Mysticism...* (1899), *The Celtic Temperament...* (1901), *Parisian Portraits* (1910), *Illusions and Realities of the War* (1918), etc.

**Grier'son** (grēr's'n), Sir **George Abraham.** 1851–1941. Irish Orientalist; author of many studies of the vernacular languages of India. O.M. (1928).

**Grierson,** Sir **Herbert John Clifford.** 1866–1960. English scholar; authority on English literature of the 17th century; author of *The First Half of the Seventeenth Century* (1906), *Metaphysical Poets, Donne to Butler* (1921), *Prophets and Poets* (1937), etc.

**Grieve, C. M.** See Hugh MACDIARMID.

**Grif'fen·feld** (grēf'ĕn·fĕlt), Count **Peder Schumacher.** 1635–1699. Danish statesman, of German descent. Librarian of new Royal Library (1662); gained favor of King Frederick III and advanced (1670–76) under Christian V; made chancellor (1673); unsuccessfully sought alliances with France and Sweden; opposed, tried for treason, and imprisoned (1676–98).

**Grif'fes** (grĭf'ĕs), **Charles Tomlinson.** 1884–1920. American pianist and composer, b. Elmira, N.Y.

**Grif'fin** (grĭf'ĭn), **Cyrus.** 1748–1810. American jurist, b. in Richmond County, Va. Member, Continental Congress (1778–81; 1787; 1788); president of the congress (1788). U.S. district judge, district of Virginia (1789–1810).

**Griffin, Gerald.** 1803–1840. Irish playwright, novelist, and poet; his novels include *The Collegians* (1829), on which Dion Boucicault based his play *The Colleen Bawn;* his plays include *Gisippus* (produced 1842).

**Griffin, Walter.** 1861–1935. American painter; studio in France (1887–1915); best known for landscapes.

**Griffin, Walter Burley.** 1876–1937. American architect; practiced in Chicago (from 1901); offices later in Sydney and Melbourne, Australia. Awarded first prize by government of Australia in international competition for designs for a federal capital at Canberra (1912); in charge of construction there (1913–21). Assumed management of Greater Sydney Development Assoc. (1921), building new harbor suburbs, etc.

**Grif'fis** (grĭf'ĭs), **William Elliot.** 1843–1928. American clergyman and author; taught in Japan (1870–74). Author of *The Mikado's Empire* (1876), *Corea, the Hermit Nation* (1882), *Matthew Calbraith Perry* (1887), *Japan, in History, Folk-Lore, and Art* (1892), *The Religions of Japan* (1895), *The Japanese Nation in Evolution* (1907), *The Mikado, Institution and Person* (1915).

**Grif'fith** (grĭf'ĭth), **Arthur.** 1872–1922. Irish political leader, b. Dublin. A printer by trade; joined Irish Republican Brotherhood (Fenians); a founder and editor of the journal *The United Irishman* (1899). Withdrew from Irish Republican Brotherhood to move for establishment of an Irish parliament united to the English Parliament only by the link of the crown; organized group (1902) to forward this movement and thus founded what became known as Sinn Fein; changed name of his journal to *Sinn Fein* (1906). Supported organization of Irish Volunteers (to oppose the Ulster Volunteers), but took no part in the Easter Rebellion (1916); was held in concentration camp (1916–17). Upon his release, reissued his journal under title *Nationality* and, when this was suppressed by the government, under the title *Eire Og.* Again seized and held in prison (1918); while in prison, was elected vice-president of the "Irish Republic." When released from prison (1919), was acting head of "Irish Republic" while the head, de Valera, was in U.S. (1919–20). Leader of delegation which negotiated (1921) treaty with England involving recognition of the Irish Free State; elected president of the Dail Eireann (Jan. 10, 1922); died suddenly (Aug. 12, 1922).

**Griffith, David Lewelyn Wark.** 1875–1948. American motion-picture producer, b. La Grange, Ky. Among pictures produced by him are *The Birth of a Nation, Intolerance, Way Down East, Broken Blossoms, Orphans of the Storm,* and *America.* Recipient (1935) of special award of Acad. of Motion Picture Arts and Sciences for achievements as producer and director.

**Griffith, Ernest Stacey.** 1896– . American political scientist; authority on municipal government and author of *Modern Development of City Government in United Kingdom and United States* (1927), *Current Municipal Problems* (1933), etc.

**Griffith, Francis Llewellyn.** 1862–1934. English Egyptologist; with Petrie and Naville in Egypt (1884–88). In charge of Oxford excavations in Nubia (1910–13; 1930 ff.).

**Griffith,** Sir **Samuel Walker.** 1845–1920. Australian lawyer and statesman; first chief justice of Australia (1903–19).

**Grif'fiths** (grĭf'ĭths), Sir **John Norton-.** 1871–1930. English engineer and contractor; executed public works projects in West Africa, America, and England. During World War I, organized companies for military mining service; planned and superintended tunneling operations under Messines Ridge, whereby this German vantage point was destroyed (June 7, 1917).

**Griffiths, John Willis.** 1809?–1882. American naval architect, b. New York City. Author of *A Treatise on Marine and Naval Architecture* (1849), etc.

**Grigg** (grĭg), Sir **James,** *in full* **Percy James.** 1890–1964. British civil servant (from 1913) and cabinet member; undersecretary for war (1939–42); secretary for war (1942–45).

**Griggs** (grĭgz), **John William.** 1849–1927. American lawyer; adm. to bar (1871); practiced, Paterson, N.J. Governor of New Jersey (1895–98). U.S. attorney general (1898–1901). Member, Permanent Court of Arbitration, The Hague (1901–12).

**Gri'gnard'** (grē'nyȧr'), **Victor.** 1871–1935. French chemist; discovered a reagent (Grignard reagent), an organometallic compound of magnesium important in organic synthesis (1900). Shared (with Paul Sabatier) 1912 Nobel prize for chemistry.

**Gri·go·ro'vich** (gryĭ·gŭ·rô'vyĭch), **Dmitri Vasilievich.** 1822–1900. Russian novelist; forerunner of Turgenev in depicting peasant life; author esp. of *The Village* (1846) and *Anton Goremyka* (1847).

**Gri·jal'va** (grē·häl'vä), **Juan de.** 1489?–1527. Spanish explorer; nephew of Diego Velásquez. Sent to follow up Córdoba's discovery of Yucatán (1518); sailed along east coast of Mexico; learned of rich Aztec empire in interior; first to give region the name of New Spain.

**Grillandajo.** See under GHIRLANDAJO.

**Grill'par'zer** (grĭl'pär'tsẽr), **Franz.** 1791–1872. Austrian playwright and poet; in Austrian government service (1813–56). His notable works include: *Die Ahnfrau* (1817); *Sappho* (1819); a trilogy, *Das Goldene Vlies* (1822), comprising *Der Gastfreund, Die Argonauten,* and *Medea; König Ottokars Glück und Ende* (1825); *Des Meeres und der Liebe Wellen* (1840); *Der Traum, ein Leben* (1840); *Weh' dem, der Lügt* (1840); *Die Jüdin von Toledo; Libussa.*

**Gri·mald'** *or* **Gri·malde'** (?grĭ·mäld') *or* **Gri·moald'** (?grĭ·mwäld'), **Nicholas.** 1519–1562. English ecclesiastic and poet, of Italian descent; contributor (1557) of verses to Tottel's poetical anthology, *Songs and Sonettes* (which was original title of first edition of *Tottel's Miscellany*); also translator of parts of Vergil and Cicero.

**Gri·mal'di** (grē·mäl'dē). A family of nobility of Genoa, prominent for several centuries (esp. 14th to 18th) in Italian history; Monaco was under their rule (968–1731). Direct male line became extinct with death of Antony I (1661–1731); his daughter, Louise Hippolyte, married (1715) Jacques de Goyon-Matignon, Count of Thorigny, who took the name Grimaldi and whose family held Monaco until driven out (1792) by the French Revolution. See GOYON, MONACO.

**Grimaldi, Francesco Maria.** 1618?–1663. Italian Jesuit and physicist; credited with discovery of diffraction of light; one of first to observe results of interference of light and dispersion of sun's rays by a prism.

**Grimaldi, Giovanni Francesco.** *Known as* **Il Bo'lo·gne'se** (ēl bō'lô·nyā'sā). 1606–1680. Italian painter and etcher; pupil of Carracci; protégé of Paul V and Innocent X (at Rome) and Cardinal Mazarin (at Paris); known esp. for landscapes.

**Grimaldi, Joseph.** 1779–1837. English comic actor, pantomimist, and clown.

**Gri·ma'ni** (grē·mä'nē), **Antonio.** 1436–1523. Venetian naval commander and statesman; admiral of the fleet sent against Bajazet (1499); doge of Venice (1521–23).

**Grimes** (grīmz), **Frances.** 1869–1963. American sculptor; among her works are: bust of Bishop Potter, Grace Church, New York; portrait busts of Charlotte Cushman and Emma Willard, American Hall of Fame, New York.

**Grimes, James Wilson.** 1816–1872. American lawyer; governor of Iowa (1854–58); U.S. senator (1859–69). Stricken by apoplexy during impeachment trial of President Johnson; carried into senate to vote for acquittal when his vote was required to prevent impeachment.

**Grim'ké** (grĭm'kē), **Archibald Henry.** 1849–1930. American Negro lawyer and writer; practiced, Boston. Editor, the *Hub* (1883–85); attacked racial discrimination. U.S. consul to Santo Domingo (1894–98). President, American Negro Academy (1903–16).

**Grimké, Sarah Moore** (1792–1873) and her sister **Angelina Emily** (1805–1879). American social reformers, b. in Charleston, S.C. Involved in Abolitionist movement (1835–38). Wrote and lectured against slavery and for women's rights. See Theodore Dwight WELD.

**Grimm** (grĭm), **Jacob** (1785–1863) and his brother **Wilhelm** (1786–1859). German philologists and mythologists. Both studied at Marburg; Jacob became librarian to Jérôme Bonaparte, King of Westphalia (1808), and was joined by Wilhelm (1814); both were professors at Kassel (1830–37), and accepted invitation of Frederick William IV of Prussia to settle in Berlin (1841). Collaborated on *Kinder- und Hausmärchen* (1812 and 1815; well known in English as *Grimm's Fairy Tales*), *Deutsche Sagen* (1816–18), *Deutsches Wörterbuch* (vol. I, 1854). Jacob's chief work is *Deutsche Grammatik* (1819–37), an exhaustive treatise, generally regarded as the foundation of Germanic philology, and containing his formulation of the philological law known as *Grimm's law;* his other works include *Über den Altdeutschen Meistergesang* (1811), *Rechtsaltertümer* (study of old Teutonic laws, 1828), *Deutsche Mythologie* (1835), *Die Geschichte der Deutschen Sprache* (2 vols., 1848). The brothers also published individually and jointly many editions and studies of early literature. A third brother, **Ludwig** (1790–1863), was a painter and etcher of portraits, landscapes, figure pieces, and animals. A son of Wilhelm, **Herman** (1828–1901), was an art critic, teacher, and novelist; professor of the history of art, Berlin (from 1873).

**Grimm** (*Ger.* grĭm; *Fr.* grēm), Baron **Melchior von,** *in full* **Friedrich Melchior von.** 1723–1807. Journalist and critic, b. Ratisbon, Ger. Studied at Leipzig; went to Paris as tutor (1748); became acquainted with Rousseau (1749); naturalized as French citizen. Noted for his *Correspondance Littéraire, Philosophique et Critique* (following example of Guillaume Raynal; written 1753–90, aided by Diderot and Mme. d'Épinay; collected and first published in 17 volumes, 1812–14), a series of private letters to princely and royal persons in Germany, Russia, Sweden, Poland, reflecting contemporary Paris, esp. happenings in intellectual world, which spread liberal ideas of the Encyclopedists through European courts. Driven out of France by Revolution; lived (1792–95) at St. Petersburg where he enjoyed favor of Catherine II; Russian minister to Hamburg (1796).

**Grimm** (grĭm), **Robert.** 1881–1958. Swiss Socialist; editor of *Berner Tagwacht* (1909–18); during World War, participated in conferences for securing revolutionary peace; head of abortive Bolshevik insurrection in Zurich (1918); defeated in election for president of National Council (1926).

**Grim'mels·hau'sen** (grĭm'ĕls·hou'zĕn), **Hans Jakob Christoffel von.** 1620?–1676. German writer; in early life a Protestant, later accepted Catholicism and entered service of the bishop of Strasbourg; was finally magistrate at Renchen. His masterpiece was *Der Abenteuerliche Simplicissimus* (1669), commonly referred to as *Simplicissimus,* but in full, with subtitle, *Der Abenteuerliche Simplicissimus Teutsch, das ist: Beschreibung des Lebens eines Seltzamen Vagantens Genannt Melchior Sternfels von Fuchshaim;* it is a picaresque novel telling the adventures of a simple youth who becomes successively soldier, jester, bourgeois, robber, pilgrim, slave, and hermit; it gives a realistic picture of the havoc wrought in Germany by Thirty Years' War (1618–48).

**Grimoald.** See GRIMALD.

**Gri'mod' de La Rey'nière'** (grē'mō' dẽ lȧ rā'nyâr'), **Alexandre Balthasar Laurent.** 1758–1838. French gastronomer and writer.

**Grimthorpe,** 1st Baron. See Edmund BECKETT.

**Grin'dal** (grĭn'd'l), **Edmund.** 1519?–1583. English Protestant prelate; archbishop of Canterbury (1576), but under suspension (1577) for refusing to carry out Elizabeth's mandate suppressing "prophesyings." Vigorous opponent of Roman Catholic Church.

**Grindal, William.** d. 1548. Tutor of Queen Elizabeth.

**Grin'gore'** (grăN'gôr') *or* **Grin'goire'** (-gwär'), **Pierre.** 1475?–?1538. French dramatic and satiric poet; author of *Folles Entreprises, Jeu du Prince des Sots,* etc.

**Grin·nell'** (grĭ·nĕl'), **George Bird.** 1849–1938. American editor and ethnologist; assistant in osteology, Peabody Museum, Yale (1874–80). Editor, *Forest and Stream* (1876–1911). Member of Custer's expedition to the Black Hills (1874), William Ludlow's expedition to Yellowstone Park (1875), and Harriman Alaska expedition (1899). Author of *Blackfoot Lodge Tales* (1892), *The Indians of Today* (1900), *By Cheyenne Campfires* (1926), and a number of books for boys (*Jack Among the Indians, Jack the Young Explorer,* etc.).

**Grinnell, Henry.** 1799–1874. American merchant, b. New Bedford, Mass. In shipping business, New York City (1818–50). Financed rescue expedition under Lieut. E. J. De Haven of U.S. navy to find Franklin in the arctic (1850) and Dr. Kane's rescue expedition for same purpose (1853). Aided in financing other arctic expeditions. Grinnell Land was so named in his honor.

**Grinnell, Joseph.** 1877–1939. American zoologist; authority on distribution and ecology of vertebrates of California.

**Grinnell, Josiah Bushnell.** 1821–1891. American Congregational clergyman; loss of his voice caused him to leave ministry. It was he whom Horace Greeley advised, "Go west, young man, go west." Moved to Iowa (1854); founded town of Grinnell; instrumental in planning institution now known as Grinnell College, of which he was a trustee for thirty years. Practiced law, Grinnell; became leading abolitionist in his section of country. Member, U.S. House of Representatives (1863–67); supported Lincoln's administration. Introduced Devon cattle and Clydesdale horses in Iowa.

**Gris** (grēs), **Juan.** 1887–1927. Spanish painter and lithographer; identified with cubist school of art; painter of portraits, still life, and figures.

**Gri'sar'** (grē'zär'), **Albert.** 1808–1869. Belgian composer of comic operas and music romances.

**Gri'sar** (grē'zär), **Hartmann.** 1845–1932. German Jesuit historian.

**Gris'com** (grĭs'kŭm), **Lloyd Carpenter.** 1872–1959. American diplomat; U.S. minister to Persia (1901–02) and Japan (1902–06); U.S. ambassador to Brazil (1906–07) and Italy (1907–09). Served in World War; with 77th division in France; liaison officer on staff of General Pershing (1918).

**Gri'se·bach** (grē'zĕ·bäK), **August.** 1814–1879. German botanist; a founder of plant geography; wrote on Oriental and South American plants.

**Grisebach, Eduard.** 1845–1906. German diplomat and writer; among his works are *Der Neue Tanhäuser* (verse, 1869), *Tanhäuser in Rom* (verse narrative, 1875), *Das Goethesche Zeitalter der Deutschen Dichtung* (1891). Wrote *Schopenhauers Leben* (1897), and edited many of Schopenhauer's works.

**Gri'si** (grē'zē), **Giuditta** (1805–1840) and her sister **Giulia** (1811?–1869). Italian operatic singers: Giuditta, a mezzo-soprano, created role of Romeo in Bellini's *I Capuleti ed i Montecchi,* esp. written for her; m. Count Barni (1833) and withdrew from the stage. Giulia, a soprano, sang in Italy, and was called to the Théâtre Italien in Paris (1832); later, sang in London and U.S.; m. Count de Melcy (1836; divorced), and her singing associate Mario, Marchese di Candia. Their cousin **Carlotta Grisi** (1819–1899), wife of the dancing master M. Perrot, was a famous dancer.

**Gris'wold** (grĭz'wŭld; -wōld; -wôld), **Alfred Whitney.** 1906–1963. American historian and educator; president of Yale (1950–63).

**Griswold, Matthew.** 1714–1799. American jurist; deputy governor of Connecticut (1769–84); governor (1784–86). Presiding officer, constitutional ratification convention (1788).

**Griswold, Rufus Wilmot.** 1815–1857. American critic and anthologist; literary executor of E. A. Poe.

**Gro'cyn** (grō'sĭn), **William.** 1446?–1519. English Greek scholar; one of the first to lecture in Greek at Oxford; friend of Linacre, More, Colet, and Erasmus.

**Groe'ner** (grû'nẽr), **Wilhelm.** 1867–1939. German soldier; promoted general (1915) and served under von Mackensen in conquest of Rumania (1916); chief of staff to General Eichhorn in the Ukrainian offensive (1917–18); replaced Ludendorff as first quartermaster general (1918); informed the kaiser that the army would no longer support him (Nov., 1918); supported Marshal von Hindenburg in his presidency of the republic and in the problem of demobilizing the army; minister of transport (1920–23); minister of defense (1928).

**Groen van Prin'ste·rer** (grōōn' vän prĭn'stĕ·rẽr), **Wilhelm.** 1801–1876. Dutch journalist, politician, and historian.

**Groes'beck** (grōs'bĕk), **William Slocum.** 1815–1897. American jurist; member of counsel for defense of President Johnson in impeachment trial.

**Groete, Gerhard.** See Gerhard GROOTE.

**Gro'gan** (grō'găn), **Ewart Scott.** 1874–1967. English zoologist and explorer in Africa.

**Grog'ger** (grŏg'ẽr), **Paula.** 1892– . Austrian-born German poet and novelist.

**Gro'lier' de Ser'vières'** (grô'lyā' dẽ sĕr'vyâr'), **Jean.** 1479–1565. French bibliophile; treasurer general of France (1537); famous for his love of books excellent in subject matter, paper, printing, and binding; designed many of his own decorations and supervised the binding of a number of his books.

**Groll** (grōl), **Albert Lor·ey'** (lôr·ā'). **1866–1952.** American landscape painter and etcher.

**Grol'man** (grōl'män), **Karl von.** 1777–1843. Prussian soldier; quartermaster general on Blücher's staff (1814); engaged at Waterloo, where he persuaded Gneisenau to go to Wellington's aid.

**Gro·my'ko** (grô·mē'kō; *Russ.* grŭ·mĭ'kô), **Andrei A.** 1909– . Russian economist and diplomat, b. Gromyki, near Gomel; ambassador to U.S. (1943–46); delegate to the UN Security Council (from 1946).

**Gron'lund** (grŏn'lŭnd; *Dan.* grûn'lōōn), **Laurence.** 1846–1899. Socialist author and lecturer, b. in Denmark; to U.S. (1867). Adm. to bar (1869); practiced, Chicago. Converted to Socialism (about 1875); gave up law practice to write and lecture on Socialism.

**Gro·no'vi·us** (grô·nō'vĭ·ŭs). Latinized name of a family of Dutch scholars, originally **Gro'nov** (grō'nou), including: **Johann Friedrich** (1611–1671), b. at Hamburg; professor, Leiden (1658–71); editor of works of Livy, Tacitus, and other classical authors; his son **Jakob** (1645–1716), also a classical scholar, professor at Leiden (from 1679) and compiler of *Thesaurus Antiquitatum Graecarum* (1697–1702); two sons of Jakob, **Johann Friedrich** (1690–1760), a botanist, author of *Flora Virginica* (2 parts, 1739, 1743) and *Flora Orientalis* (1755), and **Abraham** (1694–1775), classical scholar and librarian at U. of Leiden, editor of various Latin classics; and Johann Friedrich's son **Lorenz Theodor** (1730?–1778), a naturalist, published *Museum Ichthyologicum* (1754–56) and *Zoophylacium Gronovianum* (1763–81).

**Groom'bridge** (grōōm'brĭj), **Stephen.** 1755–1832. English West India merchant and astronomer; published (1838) *Catalogue of Circumpolar Stars,* in which was listed no. 1830, first observed by himself; a founder of the Astronomical Society.

**Groome** (grōōm), **Francis Hindes**. 1851–1902. English editor and student of Gypsy lore.

**Groos** (grōs), **Karl**. 1861-1946. German philosopher and writer on aesthetics and psychology.

**Groot, Cornelis Hofstede de.** See HOFSTEDE DE GROOT.

**Groot, Huig de.** = Hugo GROTIUS.

**Groo'te** (grō'tĕ), **Gerhard**. *Surname also* **Groot** (grōt) *or* **Groe'te** (grōō'tĕ). *Latinized name* **Gerardus Mag'nus** (măg'nŭs). 1340–1384. Dutch religious reformer, b. Deventer; itinerant preacher, opponent of scholastic theologians and advocate of reading of the scriptures; founder of an order, Brothers of the Common Life, officially sanctioned by pope (1418).

**Gro'pi·us** (grō'pĭ·ŭs; *Ger.* -pē·ōōs), **Walter**. 1883–1969. Architect, founder of Bauhaus school of architecture, b. Berlin. In private practice in Berlin (1910–14, 1928–34); founded, in Weimar, Bauhaus school of architecture having program of co-operation of art, science, and technology, and celebrated for achievement in abstract art, functionalism in architecture, and experimentation in glass, metals, and textiles as materials (1919); directed school (until 1928), which was removed (1925) to buildings in Dessau designed by him. To U.S.; professor and chairman, School of Architecture, Harvard (1938–52); in practice, in partnership with Marcel Breuer (*q.v.*), Cambridge, Mass.; adviser to New Bauhaus, American school of design opened in Chicago (1937) with program expanded upon that of original Weimar school.

**Grop'per** (grŏp'ẽr), **William**. 1897–1977. American painter and illustrator, b. New York City; began as cartoonist for N.Y. *Tribune*. Developed radical sympathies (from 1919); accompanied Theodore Dreiser to Russia as a guest of the Conference on Cultural Relations of Soviet Russia (1927). Commissioned to paint mural for U.S. Department of the Interior building in Washington, D.C. Illustrator of books by John Farrar, Jim Tully, Frank Harris, Burges Johnson.

**Gros** (grō), Baron **Antoine Jean**. 1771–1835. French historical painter; studied under David.

**Grosart, Alexander Balloch.** 1827–1899. Scottish scholar; entered Presbyterian ministry; edited reprints of rare Elizabethan and Jacobean literature.

**Grose** (grōs; grōz), **Francis**. 1731?–1791. English antiquary; published *Classical Dictionary of the Vulgar Tongue* (1785), etc.

**Grose** (grōs), **George Richmond**. 1869–1953. American Methodist Episcopal clergyman and educator; president, DePauw U. (1912–24). Bishop, Peking, China (1924–32).

**Gro'seil'liers'** (grō'zĕ'yā'), Sieur **de. Médart Chouart'** (shwȧr). 1625?–?1697. Explorer in Canada, b. in France; made expedition for British enterprisers (1668) which reached Hudson Bay and resulted in organization of Hudson's Bay Company (chartered 1670).

**Gross** (grōs), **Charles**. 1857–1909. American historian; author of *The Gild Merchant* (2 vols., 1890), etc.

**Gross** (grōs), **Hans**. 1847–1915. Austrian jurist and pioneer in criminology.

**Gross, Samuel David.** 1805–1884. American surgeon, b. near Easton, Pa. Grad. Jefferson Med. Coll. (1828); at U. of Louisville (1840), Jefferson Med. Coll. (1856). A founder of the A.M.A. Author of *Elements of Pathological Anatomy* (1839), *A System of Surgery*...(2 vols., 1859), *A Manual of Military Surgery* (1861).

**Gross'cup** (grōs'kŭp), **Peter Steng'er** (stĕng'ẽr). 1852–1921. American jurist, b. Ashland, Ohio; practiced, Chicago (from 1883). U.S. district judge, northern district of Illinois (1892–99); issued injunction to keep Debs and his union from interference with interstate commerce or the U.S. mails (1894). U.S. judge, circuit court of appeals (1899–1911); presiding judge (from 1905); reversed Judge Landis's decision in Standard Oil of Indiana case penalizing Standard Oil $29,240,000 for accepting rebates. Resigned judgeship to resume private practice in Chicago (1911).

**Gros'se** (grō'sĕ), **Ernst**. 1862–1927. German ethnologist, and student of Japanese and Chinese art.

**Grosse, Julius.** 1828–1902. German journalist, fiction writer, and poet; among his poetic works are *Gundel vom Königssee*, *Das Volkramslied;* among his comic operas, *Pesach Pardel* (1871), *Der Wasunger Not* (1872); among his plays, *Tiberius* and *Die Ynglinger;* among his fiction, *Gegen den Strom* (3 vols., 1871), *Der Getreue Eckart* (2 vols., 1885), *Am Walchensee* (1893).

**Grosse'teste** (grōs'tĕst), **Robert**. *Nicknamed* **Great'-head** (grāt'hĕd). d. 1253. English theologian and scholar. Educ. Oxford and (probably) Paris. First rector of Franciscans at Oxford (1224), and chancellor of Oxford. Bishop of Lincoln (1235–53). Vigorously defended his rights and privileges, esp. against the pope and King Henry III.

**Gros'set'ti'** (grô'sĕ'tē'), **Paul François**. 1861–1918. French soldier; general of brigade (1914) and of division (1915); distinguished himself in the battle of the Marne, the 1st battle of Ypres, and the battle of the Yser.

**Gros'si** (grôs'sē), **Tommaso**. 1790–1853. Italian poet and novelist; among his works are poems in Milanese dialect, verse novels, an heroic epic, and historical novel.

**Gross'mith** (grōs'mĭth), **George**. 1847–1912. English comedian and singer in light opera; sang in many Gilbert and Sullivan operas. His son **George** (1874–1935) achieved success in the same field, appearing in many musical comedies; entered motion-picture field (1932); reputed to have introduced the revue in England.

**Gros've·nor** (grōv'nẽr), **Edwin Augustus**. 1845–1936. American historian, b. Newburyport, Mass. Professor, Robert Coll., Constantinople (1873–90), and Amherst (1892–1914). Author of *Constantinople* (2 vols., 1895, 1900), *Contemporary History* (1899), *The Races of Europe* (1919), etc. Editor of *Reference History of the World* in *Webster's New International Dictionary* (1909). His son **Gilbert Hovey** (1875–1966), geographer, b. Constantinople; director (from 1899) and president (from 1920), National Geographic Society; editor in chief (from 1903), *National Geographic Magazine;* author of *Young Russia* (1914), *Discovery and Exploration* (1924), *A Maryland Pilgrimage* (1927), etc.

**Grosz** (grōs), **George** (jôrj). 1893-1959. German painter of ultramodern school, expressing hatred of bourgeoisie, militarism, and capitalism; a leader in school of German expressionism known as "The New Objectivity"; his paintings were among those condemned as "degenerate" by Nazi regime in Germany because they satirized World War and post-war conditions in Germany. To U.S. (1932) and established studio near New York.

**Grot** (grôt), **Yakov Karlovich**. 1812–1893. Russian philologist; private tutor to Grand Duke Alexander (later Czar Alexander III); wrote important work on philological investigations (12 vols., 1885) and revised edition (first 2 vols., 1891–92) of Russian lexicon of Academy of St. Petersburg. His son **Nikolai Yakovlevich** (1852–1898), philosopher, taught at Nezhin (1876–83), Odessa (1883–86), and Moscow (after 1886); wrote philosophical works in French and Russian.

**Grote** (grōt), **George**. 1794–1871. English historian; in banking business (to 1843); vice-chancellor, London U. (1862); chief work, *History of Greece* (8 vols., 1846–56). His wife, **Harriet**, *nee* **Lew'in** [lū'ĭn] (1792–1878), biographer, wrote *Personal Life of George Grote* (1873).

**Gro'te·fend** (grō'tĕ·fĕnt), **Georg Friedrich.** 1775–1853. German cuneiform authority; famous for success in deciphering cuneiform inscriptions. His grandson **Hermann** (1845–1931) was a historian; author of treatises on determination of medieval chronology.

**Groth** (grōt), **Klaus.** 1819–1899. German writer; author of *Quickborn* (poems in Low German depicting the simple life of common people, 1853; 2d part publ. 1871), *Hundert Blätter* (poems in High German, 1854), *Vertelln* (prose tales; 2 vols., 1855–59), *Rothgeter-Meister Lamp un sin Dochder* (an epic, 1862), etc.

**Gro'ti·us** (grō'shĭ·ŭs), **Hu'go** (hū'gō). *Latinized form of* **Huig de Groot** (hoiĸ' dĕ grōt'). 1583–1645. Dutch jurist and statesman, b. Delft. Studied for the law at Leiden; appointed historiographer by the States-General (1603); established reputation by editing works of Martianus Capella (1598), the literary remains of Aratus of Soli (1600), and by writing three dramas in Latin; created pensionary of Rotterdam (1613). As a leader of the Remonstrants, was condemned to life imprisonment (1619); escaped to France (1621). There he finished and published *De Jure Belli et Pacis* (1625), regarded as real beginning of science of international law. Swedish ambassador to France (1634–45).

**Grott'ger** (grôt'gĕr), **Artur.** 1837–1867. Polish painter and illustrator; his paintings depict scenes from the lives of the Polish people.

**Grou'chy'** (grōō'shē'), Marquis **Emmanuel de.** 1766–1847. French soldier in the Revolutionary and Napoleonic armies; general of brigade (1792) and of division (1794); commanded cavalry reserve in Waterloo campaign; defeated a detachment of Blücher's army at Ligny (June 16, 1815), but did not prevent Blücher's main force from joining Wellington and did not aid Napoleon at Waterloo, a few miles away; in exile (1815–21); created marshal of France (1831); member of Chamber of Peers (1832).

**Grove** (grōv), Sir **George.** 1820–1900. English engineer and writer on music, b. near London. Superintended construction of lighthouses in Jamaica (1842) and Bermuda (1846). Editor, *Macmillan's Magazine* (1873). Author of analytical essays on *Beethoven's Nine Symphonies* (1884; rev. ed. 1896). Edited a standard *Dictionary of Music and Musicians* (4 vols., 1878–89), subsequently revised and continued under editorship of J. A. Fuller-Maitland (4 vols., 1900; 5 vols., 1904–10) and H. C. Colles (5 vols., 1927–28), with American supplement, ed. by W. S. Pratt and C. N. Boyd (1920). First director, Royal College of Music, Kensington (1883–94).

**Grove,** Sir **William Robert.** 1811–1896. British jurist and physicist, b. in Swansea, Wales. Professor of physics, London Institution (1840–47); invented two voltaic cells, known as the Grove cell and Grove gas cell; author of *Correlation of Physical Forces* (1846), establishing theory of mutual convertibility of forces. Judge of the Court of Common Pleas (1871); judge of the Queen's Bench (1880); privy councilor (1887).

**Gro'ver** (grō'vĕr), **La Fayette.** 1823–1911. American lawyer and political leader, b. Bethel, Me. Sailed to California (1850–51); practiced law, Salem, Ore.; governor of Oregon (1870–77); U.S. senator (1877–83).

**Grover, Oliver Dennett.** 1861–1927. American painter.

**Groves** (grōvz), **Leslie Richard.** 1896–1970. American army officer, b. Albany, N.Y.; grad. U.S.M.A. (1918); major general (1944); military head of atomic bomb project (1942–47).

**Grubb** (grŭb), **Thomas.** 1800–1878. Irish optician; known for construction of fine machinery and instruments, esp. reflecting telescopes. His son Sir **Howard** (1844–1931) was an astronomer and instrument maker.

**Gru'ber** (grōō'bĕr), **Franz.** 1787–1863. German organist and choir director at Hallein; composer (1818) of *Stille Nacht, Heilige Nacht.*

**Gruber, Johann Gottfried.** 1774–1851. German writer and scholar; collaborator with J. S. Ersch in editing *Allgemeine Enzyklopädie der Wissenschaften und Künste.*

**Gruber, Max von.** 1853–1927. German hygienist and bacteriologist; discovered specific agglutination of bacteria by the serum of an organism naturally immune to a certain disease, such as typhoid fever, cholera, or cerebrospinal meningitis, or immune as result of recovery from it; this reaction was first utilized by Fernand Widal in his test (Widal test) for diagnosis of typhoid fever.

**Gru·elle'** (grōō·ĕl'), **John.** 1880–1938. American cartoonist and writer, b. Arcola, Ill.; originator of comic strip "Brutus," winner (1910) of New York *Herald* competition; author of many juveniles, including *Raggedy Ann.*

**Gru'en·berg** (grōō'ĕn·bûrg), **Louis.** 1884–1964. Pianist and composer, b. in Russia; to U.S. as a child; best known as composer of scores for operas, as for *Green Mansions, Emperor Jones,* and as composer of orchestral music, as *Jazz Suite, Enchanted Isle,* etc.

**Gruenberg, Sid'o·nie** (sĭd''n·ē), *nee* **Matz'ner** *or* **Mats'ner** (mäts'nĕr). 1881– . Educator, b. near Vienna, Austria; to U.S. (1895); m. Benjamin Charles Gruenberg (1903); on staff of Child Study Association of America (from 1906) and its director (from 1921). Lecturer, Columbia U. Teachers College (1928–36) and N.Y.U. (from 1936). Author of *Your Child Today and Tomorrow* (1913), *Sons and Daughters* (1916), *Parents, Children and Money* (with her husband, 1933), *We, the Parents* (1939), etc.

**Grue'ning** (grē'nĭng), **Ernest.** 1887–1974. American editor and public official, b. New York City. A.B. (1907) and M.D. (1912), Harvard. In newspaper editorial work (1914–34); on staff of U.S. Department of the Interior (1935–37), administering esp. Puerto Rico reconstruction (from 1935); governor of Alaska (1939–53); U.S. senator (1959–69). Author of *Mexico and Its Heritage* (1928), *The Public Pays* (1931).

**Gru'ić** (grōō'ēt·y'; *Angl.* grōō'ĭch), **Sava.** 1840–1913. Serbian general and statesman; served in war against Turks (1876); minister of war (1876–79). Prime minister of Serbia (1888; 1889–91; 1892–93; 1903–04; 1906).

**Grumb'kow Pa'sha** (grŏŏmp'kō päsh'ä), **Viktor von.** 1849–1901. German army officer who reorganized the Turkish artillery.

**Grün, Anastasius.** See A. A. von Auersperg.

**Grün, Hans.** See Hans Baldung.

**Grün'berg** (grün'bĕrĸ), **Karl.** 1861– . Rumanian-born German economist and authority on socialism.

**Grundt'vig** (grŏŏnt'vēg), **Nikolai Frederik Severin.** 1783–1872. Danish theologian and poet; priest in the church of Vartov Hospital, Copenhagen (1839); received titular rank of bishop (1861) but was not assigned to a see; advocated system of church organization under which each congregation would be virtually an independent community. As poet, published the epic *Decline of the Heroic Life in the North* (1809–11), the *Rhyme of Roskilde,* a collection of religious poems *Songs for the Danish Church* (1837–41). His son **Svend Hersleb** (1824–1883) was a philologist and folklorist; devoted himself to study of Danish folk songs and legends, and compiled and published a great collection *Danmarks Gamle Folkeviser* (1853 ff.).

**Grun'dy** (grŭn'dĭ), **Felix.** 1777–1840. American political leader, b. in Berkeley County, Va. Settled in Kentucky (1780). Member, U.S. House of Representatives

(1811–14). U.S. senator (1829–38); supported Andrew Jackson. U.S. attorney general (1838–39). Again U.S. senator (1839–40).

**Grü′ne·wald** (grü′nĕ·vält), **Matthias** *or* **Mathäus.** fl. 1500–1530. German painter, regarded as last and greatest representative of German Gothic; court painter to Albert of Brandenburg, cardinal and elector of Mainz.

**Grup′pe** (gro͝op′ĕ), **Otto Friedrich.** 1804–1876. German philosopher, antiquary, and poet; author of *Antäus* (1831), *Gegenwart und Zukunft der Philosophie in Deutschland* (1855); also, *Gedichte* (1835), *Kaiser Karl* (1852), *Firdusi* (1856), *Vaterländische Gedichte* (1866).

**Grusenberg, Mikhail Markovich.** See BORODIN.

**Gru′son** (gro͞o′zôn), **Hermann.** 1821–1895. German industrialist; founded shipyard at Buckau (1855) which became Gruson Works (1869) and later (1893) was bought by Krupp. Developed case-hardening process; manufactured armored turrets and shells, and, later, rapid-fire cannon, gun carriages, cranes, etc.

**Gruter.** See GRUYTÈRE.

**Grütz′ma′cher** (grüts′mä′kẽr). Name of a family of German violoncellists, including: **Friedrich** (1832–1903), his brother **Leopold** (1835–1900), and Leopold's son **Friedrich** (1866–1919).

**Grütz′ner** (grüts′nẽr), **Eduard.** 1846–1925. German genre painter; known esp. for depiction of humorous scenes from Shakespeare's plays (*e.g.*, Falstaff in various situations) and from monastic life.

**Gruy′tère′** (grü·ē′târ′), **Jan van.** *Surname also* **Gru′ter** (grü′tẽr). 1560–1627. Dutch humanist and archaeologist. Published *Inscriptiones Antiquæ Totius Orbis Romani* (1603), *Chronicon Chronicorum Ecclesiastico-Politicum* (1614).

**Gryph′i·us** (grĭf′ĭ·ŭs; *Ger.* grü′fē·o͞os), **Andreas.** *Latinized form of* **Greif** (grīf). 1616–1664. German poet and playwright, sometimes called "the German Shakespeare." Author of lyric poetry (odes, sonnets, hymns), but best known for his plays, including the comedies *Absurda Comica, oder Herr Peter Squentz* (1650?), *Horribilicribrifax* (1650?), *Die Geliebte Dornrose* (1660?), and the tragedies *Leo Armenius* (1646), *Katharina von Georgien* (1647), *Cardenio und Celinde* (1647), *Ermordete Majestät oder Carolus Stuardus* (1649).

**Gryphius, Sebastian.** 1493–1556. German printer and bookdealer; established press in Lyons, where he published over 300 books in Latin, Greek, and Hebrew.

**Grypus.** See ANTIOCHUS VIII of Syria.

**Gua′da·gni′ni** (gwä′dä·nyē′nē). Family of Italian violinmakers, including the brothers **Giambattista** (c. 1685–1770) and **Lorenzo** (c. 1695–1760), and a son of Lorenzo, **Giovanni Battista** (c. 1745–1790).

**Guadalupe Victoria.** See VICTORIA.

**Gua′der** (gwä′dẽr) *or* **Wa′der** (wä′dẽr), **Ralph de.** Earl of **Nor′folk** (nôr′fŭk). fl. 1070. Sole English noble to fight on William the Conqueror's side at Hastings. Forfeited earldom upon being outlawed for revolting against William (1075).

**Gua′det′** (gü·ȧ′dĕ′), **Marguerite Élie.** 1758–1794. French politician; leader among the Girondists in opposing the Montagnards; guillotined (June 15, 1794).

**Gualandi, Anselmo.** See Francesco Domenico GUERRAZZI.

**Guardati, Tommaso dei.** See MASUCCIO DI SALERNO.

**Guar′di** (gwär′dē), **Francesco.** 1712–1793. Venetian painter; pupil of Canaletto; known esp. for scenes of Venice, as of lagoons.

**Guar′dia** (gwär′thyä), **Rafael Ángel Calderón.** See CALDERÓN GUARDIA.

**Guar′dia** (gwär′thyä), **Ricardo Adolfo de la.** 1899–1969. President of Republic of Panama (1941–45), following coup d'état that overthrew President Arnulfo Arias (Oct., 1941).

**Guardia, Tomás.** 1832–1882. Costa Rican politician; elected president (1870–76); virtual dictator (1876–82).

**Guar·dio′la** (gwär·thyō′lä), **Santos.** 1812?–1862. Honduran politician and general; called "the Tiger of Central America"; b. Tegucigalpa. Led revolt that drove out president of Honduras (1855); president of Honduras (1856–58); assassinated.

**Gua·ri′ni** (gwä·rē′nē), **Giovanni Battista.** 1538–1612. Italian poet; lived at courts of Ferrara, Mantova, Florence, Urbino; known esp. for pastoral tragicomedy *Il Pastor Fido* (1590).

**Guarini, Guarino.** 1624–1683. Italian architect; developed Italian baroque to its highest degree.

**Gua·ri′no da Ve·ro′na** (gwä·rē′nō dä vā·rō′nä). *Latin* **Va·ri′nus** (vȧ·rī′nŭs). 1370–1460. Italian Humanist; studied Greek at Constantinople; professor of classics in Florence (1402), Venice (1415), Verona (1422), Ferrara (1436). Works include editions of Plautus, Livy, Pliny the Elder, and Catullus.

**Guarnerius.** See IRNERIUS.

**Guar·nie′ri** (gwär·nyâ′rē). *Lat.* **Guar·ne′ri·us** (gwär·nēr′ĭ·ŭs). Family of Italian violinmakers, including: **Andrea** (1626–1698); b. Cremona; studied under Nicolò Amati. Andrea's sons **Pietro** (1655–1728) and **Giuseppe** (1666–1739). Giuseppe's son **Pietro II** (1695–1765). Andrea's nephew **Giuseppe Antonio** (1683–1745); studied under Stradivari and became most noted of the family.

**Guarnieri, Giuseppe.** 1856–1918. Italian pathologist; discovered method of diagnosing smallpox and cowpox; described minute cell inclusions found in cases of smallpox and cowpox and named Guarnieri bodies after him (1892).

**Guaspre, Le.** See Gaspard DUGHET.

**Gua′te·mo′tzin** (gwä′tē·mō′tsĭn) *or* **Gua·tem′oc** (gwä·tĕm′ŏk) *or* **Cuauh·tem′oc** (kwou·tĕm′ŏk). 1495?–1525. Last Aztec emperor of Mexico; nephew of Montezuma II. Leader of Aztec forces opposing Spanish under Cortes; organized attack (June 30, 1520: "la Noche triste") driving Spaniards out of Mexico City; chosen emperor after Montezuma's death. Defended city against siege by Cortes (1521); captured and tortured but did not reveal location of Aztec treasure; taken as hostage by Cortes on his march to Honduras and executed on charge of treachery.

**Gub′bins** (gŭb′ĭnz), **John Harington.** 1852–1929. British diplomat in Japan. Entered Japan consular service (1871); secretary in legation (1886–1903). Author of *Dictionary of Chinese-Japanese Words in Japanese Language* (3 vols.), *The Waking of Modern Japan* (1922), and other works on Japan.

**Gu′ber·na′tis** (go͞o′bâr·nä′tēs), Conte **Angelo de.** 1840–1913. Italian Orientalist and editor; professor of Sanskrit, Florence (1863, 1867), of Italian literature, Rome (1891 ff.); founded and edited various literary periodicals (1859–87). His works include plays, Oriental studies, mythological studies, biographical compilations, and a literary history.

**Gu′bitz** (go͞o′bĭts), **Friedrich Wilhelm.** 1786–1870. German journalist and illustrator; dramatic critic on staff of *Vossische Zeitung* (1832–66).

**Guch·kov′** (go͞och·kôf′), **Aleksandr Ivanovich.** 1861?–1936. Russian politician; fought with Boers against British (1899–1900). Member of First Duma; leader of Octobrists in Third Duma (1907–12) and elected its president (1910). In revolution (March, 1917), was delegated to make formal demand of Czar Nicholas II for his abdication; a short-time minister of war under Kerenski; later (1919), emigrated to Paris.

**Gud'den** (gŏŏd'ĕn), **Bernard Aloys von.** 1824–1886. German neurologist; known for work on the histology of the brain, Gudden's commissure, a bundle of nerve fibers of the hypothalamus, being named after him.

**Gu'de** (gōō'dĕ), **Hans.** 1825–1903. Norwegian painter; best known for his landscapes.

**Gu·de'a** (gōō·dā'ä). fl. about 2350 B.C. Ruler (patesi) of Lagash, a Sumerian city-state in southern Babylonia; a temple builder and patron of arts; greatly influenced religion of Sumer; deified by later generations.

**Gu'de·hus** (gōō'dĕ·hōōs), **Heinrich.** 1845–1909. German operatic tenor.

**Gude'man** (gŏŏd'măn), **Alfred.** 1862– . American philologist; professor of Greek and Latin, Johns Hopkins (1890–93), Pennsylvania (1893–1902), Cornell U. (1902–04); asst. editor, *Thesaurus Linguae Latinae* (1904–16).

**Gu·de'ri·an** (gōō·dā'rē·än), **Heinz.** 1886–1954. German general; commander in chief of armored units, against Poland (1939), France (1940), Russia (1941).

**Gudg'er** (gŭj'ẽr), **Eugene Willis.** 1866–1956. American ichthyologist. Investigator, U.S. Bureau of Fisheries, Beaufort, N.C. (1902–11); taught biology, N.C. Coll. for Women (1905–19); on staff, American Museum of Nat. History (1919–38), assoc. curator (1935–38). Author of numerous papers on ichthyology. Special editor for ichthyology, *Webster's New International Dictionary, Second Edition.*

**Gu'din'** (gü'dăN'), **Théodore.** 1802–1880. French painter of marines.

**Gud'munds·son** (gûth'mûnts·sŏn), **Kristmann.** 1902– . Icelandic novelist, whose works, widely translated, include *Icelandic Love* (1926), *The Morning of Life* (1928; Eng. translation, 1936), *The Holy Mountain* (1931), *The Children of Earth* (1935), *Winged Citadel* (Eng. translation, 1940).

**Gué'bri'ant'** (gā'brē'äN'), Comte **Jean Baptiste Budes** (büd) **de.** 1602–1643. French soldier; served under Bernhard of Saxe-Weimar in Germany (1635–39); after Bernhard's death, negotiated transfer of Bernhard's army to France, and commanded it in the defeat and capture of the imperialist general Lamboy at Kempen (Jan. 17, 1642); created marshal of France; mortally wounded in action at Rottweil (Nov. 19, 1643).

**Gue·dal'la** (gwĕ·dăl'ȧ), **Philip.** 1889–1944. English writer; educ. Oxford. Practiced law (1913–23). Among his books are *Ignes Fatui, a Book of Parodies* (1911), *Supers and Supermen* (1920), *The Second Empire* (1922), *Palmerston* (1926), *Conquistador* (1927), *The Duke* (biography of Wellington; 1931), *Argentine Tango* (1932), *The Hundred Days* (1934), *The Hundred Years* (1936), *1936: The Hundredth Year* (1940).

**Gueldre,** Duke of. See EGMONT.

**Guelph** *or* **Guelf** (gwĕlf). *Ger.* **Welf** (vĕlf). *Ital.* **Guel'fo** (gwĕl'fō), *pl.* **Guel'fi** (gwĕl'fē). In Italy (12th to 15th century), a supporter of the Welfs (*q.v.*) against the Hohenstaufen; opponents of the Ghibellines (*q.v.*), these two becoming the great political factions of medieval Italy. The Guelphs in general supported the church and were represented by Florence, Bologna, and Milan (central Italy); the Ghibellines in general were strongest in northern Italy (Pisa, Verona, and Arezzo) and were supporters of the Holy Roman emperors. Toward the end, the contest degenerated into a mere struggle of rival factions.

**Gué'mé'née'** (gā'mā'nā'). *Later* **Gué'mé'né'.** A princely branch of the Rohan family of France, deriving its name from a village in Morbihan, Brittany. This branch originated in the 15th century with **Charles de Rohan** (d. 1425?); later (16th century) it gave rise to the Montbazon ducal branch. See Louis René Édouard, Cardinal de ROHAN; his brother **Ferdinand Maximilien Mériadec de Rohan** (1738–1813), Prince **de Guéménée,** was a prelate.

**Güé'mez de Hor'ca·si'tas** (gwā'māth thā ôr'kä·sē'täs), **Juan Francisco.** Conde **de Re·vil'la Gi·ge'do** (thā rā·vē'lyä hē·hā'thō). 1682–1768. Spanish soldier and administrator; captain general of Cuba (1734–1746); viceroy of Mexico (1746–1755). To Spain (1755); captain general of Spanish army; president, council of war. His son **Juan Vicente Güémez Pa·che'co de Pa·dil'la Horcasitas** (pä·chā'kō thā pä·thē'lyä), Conde **de Revilla Gigedo** (1740–1799), was also Spanish soldier and administrator; captain of viceregal guard, Mexico; viceroy of Mexico (1788–94); on return to Spain was appointed director-general of artillery.

**Guen'ther** (gün'tẽr), **Konrad.** 1874–1955. German zoologist; sought to reawaken a feeling for nature through stimulation of appreciation of the natural history, etc., of Germany. Author of *Das Antlitz Braziliens* (1927; English translation by Bernard Miall, *A Naturalist in Brazil,* 1931), etc.

**Gué'pratte'** (gā'prȧt'), **Émile Paul Aimable.** 1856–1939. French rear admiral in World War (1914–18); made bold attempt to force Dardanelles (Mar. 18, 1915); promoted vice-admiral.

**Gué'ran'ger'** (gā'räN'zhā'), **Prosper Louis Pascal.** 1805–1875. Benedictine monk and liturgist; restored Benedictine order in France, its rules approved by Pope Gregory XVI (1837).

**Gué'rard'** (gā'rȧr'), **Albert Léon.** 1880–1959. Educator and writer, b. Paris; in U.S. from 1906; professor of general literature, Stanford (from 1925). Author of *French Prophets of Yesterday* (1913), *The Napoleonic Legend* (1923), *Life and Death of an Ideal* (1928), *Art for Art's Sake* (1936), etc.

**Guer·ci'no** (gwâr·chē'nō). *Real name* **Giovanni Francesco Bar·bie'ri** (bär·byâ'rē). 1591–1666. Bolognese painter of Eclectic school; pupil of Lodovico Carracci; protégé of Gregory XV.

**Gue'rick·e** (gā'rĭ·kĕ), **Otto von.** 1602–1686. German physicist; invented air pump (1650); devised Magdeburg hemispheres to illustrate pressure of the air. Credited with devising first electrical generating machine, a ball of sulphur on a crank-turned shaft, the friction of the hand held against the turning ball generating static electricity.

**Gué'rin'** (gā'răN'), **Charles.** 1873–1907. French poet; author of *Fleurs de Neige* (1893), *Le Semeur de Cendres* (1901), etc.

**Guérin, Georges Maurice de.** 1810–1839. French poet; author of *Le Centaur,* published by George Sand in *Revue des Deux Mondes* (1840). His sister **Eugénie** (1805–1848), also a writer, is known esp. for her posthumously published *Journal* and *Lettres.*

**Guérin, Jean Baptiste Paulin.** 1783–1855. French painter, esp. of religious scenes.

**Gue'rin'** (gā'răN'), **Jules.** 1866–1946. American painter; studied under Benjamin Constant and Jean Paul Laurens; best known for his murals, as in Lincoln Memorial Building in Washington, D.C., Pennsylvania Railroad Station in New York City, Civic Opera Building in Chicago, etc.

**Gué'rin'** (gā'răN'), **Jules René.** 1801–1886. French surgeon; founded orthopedic institute at Muette and did valuable research work on deformations of the bones, esp. of the spine.

**Guérin,** Baron **Pierre Narcisse.** 1774–1833. French painter; studied under Regnault; professor at École des Beaux-Arts (Paris; 1814); director of Académie de France at Rome (1822–28).

**Guer'lain'** (gĕr'lăN'), **Pierre François Pascal.** 1798–1864. French perfume manufacturer of Paris.

**Guern'sey** (gûrn'zĭ), **Egbert.** 1823–1903. American physician; author of *Homoeopathic Domestic Practice* (1853); reputed memorialized in Bret Harte's story *The Man Whose Yoke Was Not Easy.*

**Gué'roult'** (gā'rōō'), **Adolphe.** 1810–1872. French journalist and politician; founder of *L'Opinion Nationale* (1859). Author of *La République en France* (1871), etc.

**Guer·raz'zi** (gwâr·rät'tsē), **Francesco Domenico.** *Pseudonym* **Anselmo Gua·lan'di** (gwä·län'dē). 1804–1873. Italian statesman and novelist, b. Livorno (Leghorn). Premier of Tuscany (1848); triumvir and dictator of Florentine republic (1849); imprisoned (1849–1853); banished to Corsica (1853–1861); member of parliament (1862, 1865).

**Guer·re'ro** (gĕr·rĕ'rō), **Francisco.** 1527?–1599. Spanish composer, esp. of church music.

**Guerrero, Manuel Amador.** See AMADOR GUERRERO.

**Guerrero, María.** 1868–1928. Spanish actress; director of Teatro Español, Madrid, where she presented and appeared in Spanish classics and the best modern plays.

**Guerrero, Vicente.** 1783?–1831. Mexican soldier and political leader; joined in war for independence under Morelos (1810); became leader of Mexican guerrilla forces. Vice-president of Mexico (1824–28); chosen president by Congress (Mar., 1829) and served until Dec., 1829, when revolution broke out against him, led by Bustamante; captured and shot (Feb., 1831).

**Guer·ri'ni** (gwâr·rē'nē), **Olindo.** *Pseudonym* **Lorenzo Stec·chet'ti** (stâk·kāt'tē). 1845–1916. Italian poet; chief representative of verism. Works include esp. lyrics and, under pseudonym **Be'pi** (bā'pē), many humorous poems in Venetian dialect.

**Guesclin, Bertrand Du.** See DU GUESCLIN.

**Guesde** (gĕd), **Jules.** *Real name* **Mathieu Ba'sile'** (bȧ'zēl'). 1845–1922. French Socialist, b. in Paris. Editor, *Les Droits de l'Homme* (1870); defended the Commune of Paris (1871) and had to flee to Switzerland. Returned to France (1876) and edited Socialist journals. Collaborated with Marx and Lafargue in preparing program adopted by national congress of the Labor party at Le Havre (1880); caused split among Socialist groups, the Guesdists rejecting all compromise with capitalistic government.

**Guess, George.** See SEQUOYA.

**Guest** (gĕst), Lady **Charlotte Elizabeth,** *nee* **Ber'tie** (bûr'tĭ; bär'-). 1812–1895. Welsh writer; m. Sir Josiah John Guest (1833; d. 1852) and Charles Schreiber (1855; d. 1884). Published *Mabinogion* (1838–49) from old Welsh manuscripts with translations.

**Guest, Edgar Albert.** 1881–1959. Writer, b. Birmingham, Eng.; to U.S. (1891). On staff of Detroit *Free Press* (from 1895); conductor of column of verse and humorous sketches. Author of many volumes of popular verse.

**Guest, Edwin.** 1800–1880. English historian; chief founder of the Philological Society (1842). Author of *History of English Rhythms* (1838), and papers on the Roman period in British history.

**Gue·va'ra** (gā·vä'rä), **Ernesto ("Che"** [chā]). *In Full* **Ernesto Guevara de la Serna.** 1928–1967. Latin American revolutionary leader, b. Argentina. Doctor of medicine (1953). Aid to Fidel Castro in Cuban revolution (1959); killed in Bolivia. Author of *Guerrilla Warfare* (1960), *Episodes of the Revolutionary War* (1963), etc.

**Guevara, Luis Vélez de.** See VÉLEZ DE GUEVARA.

**Guevara, Meraud,** *nee* **Guin'ness** (gĭn'ĭs; gĭ·nĕs'). 1910?– . English painter; m. Álvaro Guevara; excels in figure and genre painting.

**Guevara y de No·ro'ña** (ē thā nō·rō'nyä), **Antonio de.** 1480?–1545. Spanish writer, b. Treceño, Santander. Franciscan monk; court preacher and historiographer (1518); inquisitor (1523); bishop of Guadix (1527 ff.); bishop of Mondoñedo (1537 ff.). Author of popular didactic works; known esp. for rhetorical style; said to have influenced English euphuism. Works include *Relox de Príncipes con el Libro de Marco Aurelio* (idealized portrayal of the perfect prince and an imaginary life of Marcus Aurelius, source for La Fontaine's fable *Le Paysan du Danube,* 1529), *La Década de Césares* (biographies of ten Roman emperors, 1539), *Epístolas Familiares,* known as "Golden Letters" (collection of 85 letters on diverse topics: Part I, 1539; II, 1542).

**Guf'fens** (gûf'ĕns), **Godefried.** 1823–1901. Belgian painter; executed murals for Antwerp bourse, church of Notre Dame at Saint-Nicolas, near Antwerp, etc.

**Gug'gen·heim** (gŏŏg'ĕn·hīm), **Meyer.** 1828–1905. Capitalist, b. Langnau, Switzerland; to U.S. (1847). Interested himself in copper industry; with aid of his seven sons, gained dominating place in industry; controlled American Smelting and Refining Co. (from 1901). His son **Daniel** (1856–1930), b. Philadelphia, was in business in Switzerland (1873–84); joined father in copper industry in U.S.; established himself as leading figure in copper industry; extended his interests to gold mines in Alaska, rubber plantations in Africa, tin mines in Bolivia, and nitrate deposits in Chile. Noted also for philanthropy on great scale, as in establishing (1924) Daniel and Florence Guggenheim Foundation to promote "the well-being of mankind," and in establishing (1925) school of aeronautics at N.Y. Univ. and (1926–30) the Daniel Guggenheim Foundation for the Promotion of Aeronautics. Other sons, all associated with the Guggenheim business interests, were: **Isaac** (1854–1922); **Murry** (1858–1939); **Solomon R.** (1861–1949); **Benjamin** (1865–1912), lost on the *Titanic;* **Simon** (1867–1941), U.S. senator from Colorado (1907–13), who established (1925) as memorial to his son the John Simon Guggenheim Memorial Foundation; **William** (1868–1941).

**Gug·gia'ri** (gōōd·jä'rē), **José Patricio.** 1884–1957. Paraguayan lawyer and political leader; president of Paraguay (1928–Oct., 1931; Jan.–Aug., 1932).

**Gu·gliel'mi** (gōō·lyĕl'mē), **Pietro.** 1727–1804. Italian composer of operas and, later, of church music.

**Gugu.** = GYGES.

**Guiart** (gyȧr), **Guillaume.** French chronicler of 13th and early 14th century.

**Gui'bert'** (gē'bâr'), Comte **Jacques Antoine Hippolyte de.** 1743–1790. French soldier and writer; served in Seven Years' War; field marshal (1786). Author of *Essai de Tactique Générale* (1772), *Défense du Système de Guerre Moderne* (1779).

**Guibert de No'gent'** (dē nō'zhäN'). 1053–1124. French Benedictine theologian and historian; author of a history of the Crusades, regarded as best of contemporary accounts.

**Guibert of Ravenna.** See Antipope CLEMENT III.

**Guic'ciar·di'ni** (gwēt'chär·dē'nē), **Francesco.** 1483–1540. Florentine historian and statesman; papal governor of Modena and Reggio (1516–21); governor of Romagna under Clement VII (1523 ff.); in service of Alessandro de' Medici (1534–37). Author of *Storia d'Italia,* principal historical work of 16th century (16 books, pub. 1561; 4 books, 1564).

**Guic'cio·li** (gwēt'chō·lē), Countess **Teresa.** 1801?–1873. Italian noblewoman; m. Count Guiccioli (c. 1817). Known for her liaison with Lord Byron, and her book *My Recollections of Lord Byron* (orig. in French, 1868).

**Gui'chard'** *or* **Gui'schard'** (gē'shȧr'), **Karl Gottlieb.**

*Pseudonym* **Quin'tus I·ci'li·us** (kvĭn'to͝os ē·tsē'lē-o͝os). 1724–1775. German soldier and writer; served under Frederick the Great in the Seven Years' War.

**Gui'chen'** (gē'shăN'), Comte **Luc Urbain du Bouex'ic'** (dü bwĕk'sēk') **de.** 1712–1790. French naval officer; engaged against Admiral Rodney in the Antilles (1780) with indecisive results; defeated by Admiral Kempenfelt in Bay of Biscay (Dec. 12, 1781).

**Gui'di** (gwē'dē), **Carlo Alessandro.** 1650–1712. Italian poet; a founder of Accademia Arcadia; introduced canzone with free strophes, later developed by Leopardi.

**Guidi, Ignazio.** 1844–1935. Italian Orientalist; professor of Semitics, Rome (1878–1920); advanced theory that lower Euphrates was original home of Semites.

**Guidi, Tommaso.** See MASACCIO.

**Gui'dic·cio'ni** (gwē'dēt·chō'nē), **Giovanni.** 1500–1541. Italian prelate and poet, b. Lucca; in diplomatic service of Paul III; known esp. for patriotic sonnets.

**Gui'do d'A·rez'zo** (gwē'dō dä·rāt'tsō) *or* **Gui'do A're·ti'no** (ä'rā·tē'nō). *Also called* Fra **Guit·to'ne** (gwēt·tō'nā). 995?–?1050. Benedictine monk and musical reformer, b. prob. near Paris, though tradition gives Arezzo as his birthplace. Monk in monasteries of St. Maur des Fossés near Paris, of Pomposa near Ferrara, and at Arezzo; perhaps prior of Camaldolese monastery near Avellano. Reputed inventor of the medieval "great scale" or gamut, the hexachord, and hexachord solmization. Among his works on musical theory are *Micrologus de Disciplina Artis Musicae, Antiphonarium, Regulae de Ignoto Cantu, Epistolae Michaeli Monacho de Ignoto Cantu Directa.*

**Guido del'le Co·lon'ne** (dāl'lā kō·lōn'nā) *or* **da Co·lon'na** (dä kō·lōn'nä). 13th-century Sicilian poet. Chief work, *Historia Troiana* (in Latin; 1282), based on a poem by Benoît de Sainte-Maure (*q.v.*), was used as source of Trojan War material by Boccaccio, Chaucer, Shakespeare; Caxton's English version of it was first printed English book.

**Guido of Crema.** See Antipope PASCHAL III.

**Guido of Lusignan.** See GUY OF LUSIGNAN.

**Guido of Spoleto.** See GUY OF SPOLETO.

**Guido Reni.** See RENI.

**Gui'gne·bert'** (gēn'y'·bâr'), **Charles Alfred Honoré.** 1867–1940. French historian; professor of Roman history and early Christianity, Sorbonne (from 1906); author of *Le Problème de Jésus* (1914), *La Vie Cachée de Jésus* (1921), *Le Mond Juif vers le Temps de Jésus* (1935).

**Guignes** (gēn'y'), **Joseph de.** 1721–1800. French Orientalist and Chinese scholar; professor of Syriac at Collège de France (1757); wrote (1756–58) *History of the Huns, Turks, Mongols, and other Western Tatars.*

**Guil'bert'** (gēl'bâr'), **Yvette.** 1865?–1944. French singer, b. Paris; m. Dr. M. Schiller (1895). Famed as singer of topical songs, often in argot, with subjects drawn from Latin Quarter or from lower-class Parisian life; received award of Legion of Honor (1932).

**Guild** (gĭld), **Curtis.** 1827–1911. American journalist, b. Boston. Founder (1859) and editor (1859–98), Boston *Commercial Bulletin.* His son **Curtis** (1860–1915) was on staff of Boston *Commercial Bulletin* (from 1881) and its owner and editor (from 1902); governor of Massachusetts (1906–08); U.S. ambassador to Russia (1911–13).

**Guilford,** Baron and earl of. English titles borne by NORTH family.

**Guil'lain'** (gē'yăN'), **Simon.** 1581–1658. French sculptor.

**Guil'lau'mat'** (gē'yō'mȧ'), **Marie Louis Adolphe.** 1863–1940. French soldier; commanded 2d army in defense of Verdun (1916–17); commander in chief of allied armies in the East (1918); commanded 5th army in forcing passage of the Aisne River (Oct.–Nov., 1918); commander of French army on Rhine (1924).

**Guil'laume'** (gē'yōm'). French form of WILLIAM.

**Guil'laume** (gē'yōm), **Alfred.** 1888–1965. English theologian; professor of Hebrew and Oriental languages at U. of Durham (1920–30); principal of Culham Coll., Abingdon (1930–45).

**Guil'laume'** (gē'yōm'), **Charles Édouard.** 1861–1938. French physicist, b. Fleurier, Switzerland. Assistant (1883), assoc. director (1902), director (1915), Bureau of International Weights and Measures at Sèvres. Known esp. for invention of nickel-steel alloy Invar that, because of very slight expansion or contraction with changes in temperature, is used for standard measures and precision instruments; awarded 1920 Nobel prize for physics.

**Guillaume de Cham'peaux'** (shäN'pō'). 1070?–1121. French scholastic philosopher; teacher and rival of Abelard.

**Guillaume de Gellone,** Saint. See GUILLAUME D'ORANGE.

**Guillaume de Lor'ris'** (dē lō'rēs'). d. about 1235. 13th-century French poet; author of the first part of *Roman de la Rose.* See JEAN DE MEUNG.

**Guillaume de Ma'chaut'** *or* **Ma'chault'** (mȧ'shō'). 1305?–1377. French poet and composer; author of *Le Livre du Voir-dit,* best known of his verse; composer of a Mass (sung at coronation of Charles V), and lais, motets, ballads, and rondeaux.

**Guillaume de Pa'ris'** (pȧ'rē'; *Angl.* păr'ĭs). *Also known as* **Guillaume d'Au'vergne'** (dō'vĕrn'y'). 1180?–1249. French prelate and natural philosopher; consecrated bishop of Paris (1228). Author of *De Universo,* etc.

**Guillaume de Poi'tiers'** (pwȧ'tyā'). Norman chronicler of 2d half of 11th century; chronicler of William the Conqueror; author of *Gesta Willelmi.*

**Guillaume de Poitiers.** d. 1127. Duke of Aquitania. Earliest known Provençal troubadour.

**Guillaume d'O'range'** (dō'räNzh'). *Also known as* **Fie'ra'brace'** (fyĕ'rȧ'brȧs'), *as* **St. Guillaume de Gel'lone'** (zhā'lôn'), *and as* **Mar'quis' au' court' nez'** (mȧr'kē' ō' ko͞or' nā'). d. 812. Central figure of a southern cycle of French chansons de geste, in which he appears as grandson of Charles Martel and a commander under Charlemagne; fought the Moslems at Villedaigne (793) and, though defeated, caused them to retreat into Spain; captured Barcelona (803); founded monastery of Gellone (804), to which he retired (806). His exploits are probably compounded from those of a dozen or more historical personages.

**Guil'lau'met'** (gē'yō'mĕ'), **Gustave Achille.** 1840–1887. French painter, esp. of Algerian scenes.

**Guil'lau'min'** (gē'yō'măN'), **Jean Baptiste Armand.** 1841–1927. French painter of landscapes and marines.

**Guil'le·met'** (gē'y'·mĕ'), **Jean Baptiste Antoine.** 1842–1918. French landscape painter.

**Guil'le·min'** (gē'y'·măN'), **Amédée Victor.** 1826–1893. French writer of popular books on scientific subjects.

**Guillemin, Roger Charles Louis.** 1924– . American physiologist, b. France. At Baylor College of Medicine (1953–70), Salk Institute for Biological Studies (1970– ); awarded (with Andrew V. Schally and Rosalyn S. Yalow) Nobel prize for physiology or medicine (1977).

**Guillianes.** See GILIANES.

**Guil'lim** (gwĭl'ĭm), **John.** 1565–1621. English authority on heraldry.

**Guil'lo'tin'** (gē'yō'tăN'), **Joseph Ignace.** 1738–1814.

French physician; deputy to States-General (1789); first to demand doubling of Representatives of Third Estate. Defended capital punishment and proposed use of beheading machine (1789), called *guillotine* after him.

**Guil'mant'** (gēl'mäN'), **Félix Alexandre.** 1837–1911. French organist and composer; for over 30 years organist at the Church of the Trinity, Paris; also, professor of organ at the Conservatory of Music; composer of many organ works.

**Gui·ma·rães'** (gē·mȧ·rãẽNs'), **Bernardo Joa·quim' da Sil'va** (zhwȧ·kēNn' dȧ sĭl'vȧ). 1827–1884. Brazilian poet and novelist; among his books of verse are *Cantos da Solidão* (1852), *Poesias* (1865), *Fôlhas de Outono* (1883); among his novels, *O Seminarista* (1872), *Maurício* (1877).

**Gui'mard'** (gē'mȧr'), **Marie Madeleine.** 1743–1816. French dancer; star of Paris Opéra for twenty-five years; notorious for licentiousness, and for exhibition of legally prohibited plays in her private theater; retired (1789).

**Gui'me·rá'** (gē'mâ·rä'), **Ángel.** 1847–1924. Catalonian dramatist and poet, b. in Canary Islands. Works, written in Catalan, include *Judith de Welp* (1883), *Mar y Cielo* (1888), *Maria Rosa* (1894), *Tierra Baja* (considered his masterpiece, 1896).

**Gui'met'** (gē'mĕ'), **Jean Baptiste.** 1795–1871. French chemist; founded factory near Lyon for manufacture of artificial dyes; Guimet's blue, an ultramarine, is named after him. His son **Émile Étienne** (1836–1918) was an industrialist and scholar; succeeded his father in the dye factory; founded (at Lyon; moved to Paris, 1888) Musée Guimet, or Musée National des Religions, containing exhibits from Egypt and the Far Eastern countries; composer of a ballet, an oratorio, and an opera.

**Gui'ney** (gī'nĭ), **Louise Imogen.** 1861–1920. American poet and essayist, b. Boston. Resident, Oxford, England (from 1901). Her volumes of verse include *Songs at the Start* (1884), *The White Sail and Other Poems* (1887), *Happy Ending* (1909); her essays, *Goose Quill Papers* (1885), *A Little English Gallery* (1894), *Patrins* (1897).

**Gui'ni·zel'li** (gwē'nē·tsĕl'lē) *or* **Gui'ni·cel'li** (-chĕl'lē), **Guido.** 1240?–?1274. Bolognese poet; considered generally as founder of the *dolce stil nuovo;* held by Dante as father of Italian love poetry.

**Guin'ness** (gĭn'ĭs; gĭ·nĕs'). Name of a family of brewers in Ireland, including: Sir **Benjamin Lee Guinness** (1798–1868); became (1855) sole proprietor of brewing business founded by his father, Arthur; first Lord Mayor of Dublin (1851); restored St. Patrick's Cathedral in Dublin (1860–65); created baronet (1867). His sons Sir **Arthur Edward** (1840–1915), 1st Baron **Ar'di·laun'** (är'dĭ·lôn'), head of the business (1868–77), benefactor to Dublin and Church of Ireland, and **Edward Cecil** (1847–1927), 1st Earl of **I'veagh** [ī'vā] (cr. 1919), chairman of Guinness brewery at Dublin (1886–89), erected workmen's dwellings in London and Dublin, destroyed Dublin slums, endowed Lister Inst. for bacteriological research. **Rupert Edward Cecil Lee** (1874–1967), 2d Earl of Iveagh; son of 1st earl; educ. Cambridge; winner of Diamond Sculls at Henley (1895, 1896); chairman of the business; chancellor of Dublin U. (from 1927). His brother **Walter Edward** (1880–1944), 1st Baron **Moyne** (moin), politician; served in Boer War and as major in World War; M.P. (1907–31); minister of agriculture (1925–29, 1940–41); colonial secretary (1941–42); leader of House of Lords (1941–42); deputy minister of state, Cairo (1942–44); assassinated; father of **Bryan Walter** (1905– ), poet and novelist, author of *Landscape with Figures* (1934), *Johnny and Jemima* (1936), etc.

**Gui·ral'des** (gē·räl'dās), **Ricardo.** 1886–1927. Argentine writer; author of *Don Segundo Sombra* (an epic of gaucho life on the Argentine pampas, 1926).

**Gui'raud'** (gē'rō'), **Ernest.** 1837–1892. French composer; professor, Paris Conservatory. Composer of an orchestral suite, a concert overture, a caprice, and esp. of several operas.

**Guis'card'** (gēs'kȧr'), **Robert.** 1015?–1085. Norman adventurer, bro. of Roger I of Sicily; founder of the Norman state of the Two Sicilies. Confirmed by pope in his title duke of Apulia and Calabria (1059). Conquered part of Sicily from the Saracens, capturing Palermo (1072) and Salerno (1077). Defeated Alexius Comnenus at Durazzo (1081); captured Rome (1084) and delivered Pope Gregory VII from Emperor Henry IV.

**Guiscard, Roger.** See ROGER I of Sicily.

**Guischard.** See GUICHARD.

**Guise** (*Angl.* gēz *or, less often,* gwēz; *Fr.* gü·ēz' *or* gēz). Name of a powerful ducal family of Lorraine, derived from a town near Laon. Family formed branch of house of Lorraine (1528–1675); see LORRAINE. Its members included:

**Claude I.** Duc **d'Au'male'** (dō'mȧl'). 1496–1550. Son of René II, Duc de Lorraine. 1st duc de Guise (1528). Fought under Francis I in Italy (1515) and the Champagne (1523) and under Charles, Duc d'Orléans, in Flanders (1542). His daughter Mary married James V of Scotland and was mother of Mary, Queen of Scots.

**François de Lorraine.** *Known as* **le Ba'la'fré'** (lē bȧ'lȧ'frā'), *i.e.* the Scarred. 1519–1563. Son of Claude I. 2d duc de Guise, b. Barcastle. Soldier and politician. Fought at Montmédy (1542), at sieges of Landrecies (1543) and Boulogne (1545); especially efficient in defense of Metz (1552) against Charles V. Took Calais from English (1558). After death of Francis II (1560), forced to retire by Catherine de Médicis. Opposed Huguenots; assassinated by Protestant fanatic, Jean de Poltrot, Seigneur de Méré (Feb., 1563).

**Charles de Lor'raine'** (dē lô'rân'). 1524–1574. Brother of François. Archbishop of Reims (1538); created (1547) cardinal of Guise and (1550) cardinal of Lorraine. Powerful in political intrigues; zealous and intolerant Catholic; introduced Inquisition into France (1558).

**Henri I de Lorraine.** *Also known as* **le Balafré.** 1550–1588. Son of François. 3d duc de Guise. Fought against Huguenots (1567–69); forced Coligny to raise siege of Poitiers (1569). Took active part in Massacre of St. Bartholomew (1572); prime mover in establishing Holy League (1576) against Bourbons. Involved in Wars of the Three Henrys; defiance of King Henry III's order to keep away from Paris followed by Day of Barricades (May 12, 1588). Assassinated by Royal Guard (Dec., 1588).

**Louis II de Lorraine.** 1555–1588. Younger brother of Henri I de Lorraine. Archbishop of Reims; cardinal (1578). Assassinated at Blois the day after Henri's death (1588).

**Louis III de Lorraine.** 1575?–1621. Son of Louis II de Lorraine. French cardinal.

**Charles de Lorraine.** Duc **de Ma'yenne'** (dē mȧ'yĕn'). 1554–1611. Brother of Henri I. Fought in Huguenot Wars under his brother; after Henri's assassination, took command of Holy League forces. Proclaimed cardinal of Bourbon king (1588) but defeated at Arques (1589) and Ivry (1590) by Henry IV. Submitted to Henry IV (1596) and remained loyal until his death.

**Charles de Lorraine.** 1571–1640. Son of Henri I. 4th duc de Guise. Soldier under Henry IV; fought with princes against Louis XIII (1617). Exiled (1630).

**Henri II de Lorraine.** 1614–1664. Son of Charles. Trained for the church but became involved in wars against Richelieu (1641–42). Held prisoner by Spaniards (1648–52).

**François Joseph.** d. 1675. Last duc de Guise; after his death and death (1688) of his great-aunt Marie title went to Bourbon-Orléans family.

**Gui·teau'** (gĭ·tō'), **Charles J.** 1840?–1882. American lawyer; disappointed office seeker who shot President Garfield in Washington, D.C. (July 2, 1881); hanged in Washington (June 30, 1882).

**Gui·te'ras** (gê·tä'räs), **Juan.** 1852–1925. Physician, b. Matanzas, Cuba. M.D., Pennsylvania (1873). Appointed by U.S. government member of Havana Yellow Fever Commission (1879). Entered U.S. Marine Hospital service (1880–89). Professor of pathology, U. of Pennsylvania (1889–99). Served with American army in Cuba (1898). Study of yellow fever brought him into association with Major Gorgas and Major Reed; verified Reed's findings by independent experiments. Professor of pathology and tropical medicine, U. of Havana (1900–20); director of public health in Cuba (1909–21).

**Guit'er·man** (gĭt'ẽr·măn), **Arthur.** 1871–1943. American poet, b. Vienna, of American parentage. In magazine editorial work (1891–1906). Contributor of "Rhymed Reviews" to *Life* and light verse to periodicals.

**Gui'try'** (gē'trē'), **Lucien Germain.** 1860–1925. French actor at the Odéon (1891), the Théâtre de la Renaissance (1895), the Vaudeville (1898), Comédie Française (1902); manager of the Renaissance (1902–09); in his later years, appeared in a number of plays written by his son **Sacha** (1885–1957), actor and dramatist, author of *Nono* (1905), *Le Veilleur de Nuit* (1911), *Un Beau Mariage* (1911), *Pasteur* (1919), *Béranger* (1920), *Jacqueline* (1921), *Désiré* (1932), *Mon Double et Ma Moitié* (1935), and the operettas *L'Amour Masqué* (1923), *Mozart* (1925), *Mariette* (1928); writer and producer of motion pictures, as *Les Perles de la Couronne*, *Le Mot de Cambronne*.

**Guit·to'ne d'A·rez'zo** (gwēt·tō'nâ dä·rāt'tsō). d. 1294. Italian poet; author of love lyrics of the troubadour type and, later, of poems on moral, religious, and political subjects; known also as writer of earliest extant letters in the Italian language.

**Gui'zot'** (gē'zō'), **François Pierre Guillaume.** 1787–1874. French historian and statesman, b. Nîmes. Member of Chamber of Deputies (1830); premier of France (1847–48); forced into retirement by events of the Revolution of 1848. Among his many works are *Histoire de la Civilisation en Europe* (1828) and *en France* (1830), *De la Démocratie en France* (1849), *Discours sur l'Histoire de la Révolution d'Angleterre* (1850), *Histoire Parlementaire de France* (1863). His first wife, **Élisabeth Charlotte Pauline,** *nee* **de Meu'lan'** [dē mû'läɴ'] (1773–1827), was author of a few novels and *Les Enfants* (1812), *Le Journal d'une Mère* (1813), *Raoul et Victor ou l'Écolier* (1821), *Lettres de Famille sur l'Éducation Domestique* (1826). His second wife, **Marguerite Andrée Élisa,** *nee* **Dil'lon'** [dē'yôɴ'] (1804–1833), wrote *Le Maître et l'Esclave* (1828), *Madame Élisa Guizot* (1834), etc. A son of Guizot by his second wife, **Maurice Guillaume** (1833–1892), was professor of Germanic literatures at Collège de France (from 1874), translator of Macaulay's *Essays* (1882), and author of a critical study, *Montaigne* (1899).

**Gul'bran·son'** (gōōl'brăn·sôn'), **Ellen,** *nee* **Nord'gren'** (nōōrd'grān'). 1863–1947. Swedish operatic soprano; best known as interpreter of Wagnerian roles.

**Gul'brans·son** (gōōl'brän·sôn), **Olaf.** 1873–1958. Norwegian illustrator; on staff of *Simplicissimus* in Munich (from 1902); a leader among modern caricaturists.

**Guld'berg** (gōōl'băr(g)), **Cato Maximilian.** 1836–1902. Norwegian chemist and mathematician; with Peter Waage, established the law of mass action (the law of Guldberg and Waage).

**Guld'berg** (gōōl'bărg), **Ove Höegh-** (hûg'-). 1731–1808. Danish scholar and statesman; took part in overthrow (1772) of Queen Caroline Matilda and Struensee, and served as head of the administration (1772–84); when Crown Prince Frederick came to power as regent, he appointed Guldberg governor of Aarhus (1784–1802).

**Gul'din** (gōōl'dēn), **Paul.** 1577–1643. Swiss mathematician; introduced centrobaric method (called also Guldin's properties), a method of reckoning area and volume of revolutes.

**Gu'lick** (gū'lĭk), **John Thomas.** 1832–1923. American Congregational missionary and evolutionist, b. Kauai, Hawaiian Islands; missionary, Kalgan, in North China (1865–75), in Japan (1875–99). Chief work, *Evolution, Racial and Habitudinal* (1905). His brother **Luther Halsey** (1828–1891), b. Honolulu, was a missionary in the Caroline Islands, Hawaii, Japan, and China. Luther's son **Luther Halsey** (1865–1918) was a specialist in physical education; director, physical training course, Y.M.C.A. College, Springfield, Mass. (to 1903); co-operated there with James Naismith in inventing game of basketball; director, child hygiene department, Russell Sage Foundation (1907–13); an organizer of The Camp Fire Girls of America (1912). The younger Luther's brother **Sidney Lewis** (1860–1945), Congregational missionary in Japan (1887–1913) and lecturer at the Imperial U., Kyoto, Japan (1907–13); author of books in English and Japanese, esp. on the Far East. A son of Sidney Lewis Gulick, **Luther Halsey** (1892– ), b. Osaka, Japan; educator; director, New York Bureau of Municipal Research, and director of Institute of Public Administration; lecturer in political science; director of Regents Inquiry into Character and Cost of Public Education in the State of New York (1935–39).

**Gull'strand** (gŭl'strănd), **Allvar.** 1862–1930. Swedish ophthalmologist; professor in Uppsala (from 1894); investigated dioptrics of the eye; developed new conception of theory of optical images; awarded **1911** Nobel prize for physiology and medicine.

**Gum'mer·e** (gŭm'ẽr·ē), **Francis Barton.** 1855–1919. American scholar, b. Burlington, N.J. Professor of English and German, Haverford (1887–1909); professor of English literature, Haverford (1909–19). Author of *Handbook of Poetics* (1885), *Old English Ballads* (1894), *The Oldest English Epic* (1909; a translation of *Beowulf*), *Democracy and Poetry* (1911), etc.

**Gummere, John.** 1784–1845. American educator; author of *Treatise on Surveying* (1814) and *Elementary Treatise on Astronomy* (1822). His son **Samuel James** (1811–1874) was president of Haverford Coll. (1864–74).

**Gummere, Samuel René.** 1849–1920. American diplomat, b. Trenton, N.J. Consul general for Morocco (1898–1905) at time Perdicaris was kidnaped by Raisuli for ransom; transmitted John Hay's famous dispatch, "Perdicaris alive or Raisuli dead"; U.S. minister to Morocco (1905–09). See RAISULI.

**Gum·plo'wicz** (gōōm·plô'vēch), **Ludwig.** 1838–1909. Austrian economist and sociologist.

**Gu·na'ris** (gōō·nä'rēs). Var. of GOUNARES.

**Gundelfinger.** See GUNDOLF.

**Gun'de·ric** (gŭn'dē·rĭk). *Fr.* **Gon'dioc'** (gôɴ'dyôk') *or* **Gon'dé'ric'** (gôɴ'dā'rēk'). d. 473? Second king of Burgundy (436–?473); widened boundaries of kingdom; left four sons who disputed for the throne.

**Gun'di·car** (gŭn'dĭ·kär). *Fr.* **Gon'di'caire'** (gôɴ'dē'kâr'). d. 436 A.D. First king of Burgundy (413–436). Crossed Rhine (c. 413) and established new kingdom; ally of Romans (435); killed in war against Attila.

**Gun'di·mar II** (gŭn'dĭ·mär). *Fr.* **Gon'de·mar'** (gôɴd'mär'). d. 532. Second son of Gundobad. King of

Burgundy (523–532), succeeding his brother Sigismund; defeated Franks (524); made peace with Theodoric, King of the Ostrogoths; killed by sons of Clovis.

**Gun'do·bad** (gŭn'dō·băd). *Erroneously* **Gun'do·bald** (gŭn'dō·bôld) *or* **Gun'di·bald** (-dĭ-). *Fr.* **Gon'de·baud'** (gôɴd'bō') *or* **Gom'baud'** (gôɴ'bō'). d. 516. Son of Gunderic. King of Burgundy (473–516); at first shared kingdom with three brothers; later became sole ruler with capital at Vienne; defeated by Clovis (500); issued (c. 500) codification of Burgundian law (*Lex Gundobada*, Fr. *Loi Gombette*); made alliance with Clovis (506). His niece Clotilda became wife of Clovis.

**Gun'dolf** (gŏŏn'dôlf), **Friedrich**. *Pseudonym of* **Friedrich Gun'del·fing'er** (gŏŏn'dĕl·fĭng'ẽr). 1880–1931. German writer; published translation of Shakespeare's works, and studies on *Shakespeare und der Deutsche Geist* (1911), *Goethe* (1916), *Kleist* (1922), *Paracelsus* (1927), *Shakespeare* (2 vols., 1928).

**Gun'du·lić** (gōōn'dōō·lēt'y'; *Angl.* -lĭch), **Ivan Franov**. *Ital.* **Giovanni Gon'do·la** (gōn'dō·lä). 1588–1638. Croatian (or Illyrian) poet, b. Ragusa on coast of Dalmatia. Translated Tasso's *Jerusalem Delivered;* author of lyric, epic, and dramatic poems, and of dramas *Cleopatra*, *Dubravka*, *Proserpina*, which laid foundation of Slavic drama at Ragusa.

**Gunn** (gŭn), **Neil Miller**. 1891–1973. Scottish novelist; author of *Grey Coast* (1926), *Morning Tide* (1931), *Highland River* (1937), *Wild Geese Overhead* (1939), *The Silver Darlings* (1941), etc.

**Gunn, Ross**. 1897–1966. American physicist; invented electrical devices for military and naval use; investigated solar and terrestrial electricity and magnetism.

**Gun'nars·son** (gûn'närs·sŏn), **Gunnar**. 1889– . Icelandic poet and novelist; of his many works, mostly written in Danish, several have been translated into English, including *Seven Days' Darkness*, *Night and the Dream*, *Ships in the Sky*, *The Good Shepherd* (1940).

**Gun·ne'rus** (gŏŏ·nā'rŏŏs), **Johan Ernst**. 1718–1773. Norwegian botanist; bishop of Trondheim; friend of Linnaeus; authority on Norwegian botany. Gunnera, a genus of herbs, named after him.

**Gunn'laugr Orms'tung'a** (gûn'lû'ĭ·gẽr ŏrms'tŏŏng'ä). b. about 983 A.D. Icelandic scald; author of *Gunnlaugssaga*, etc.

**Gun·sau'lus** (gŭn·sô'lŭs; -sŏl'ŭs), **Frank Wakeley**. 1856–1921. American clergyman; ordained in Methodist ministry, and served until 1879; became Congregational minister (1879). Pastor, Plymouth Church, Chicago (1887–99); Central Church, Chicago (1899–1919). With aid of Philip D. Armour, established Armour Institute (opened 1893); president of the Institute (1893–1921). Widely known as preacher and lecturer.

**Gun'ter** (gŭn'tẽr), **Archibald Clavering**. 1847–1907. Novelist and playwright, b. Liverpool, Eng.; to U.S. as a child. Author of the novels *Mr. Barnes of New York* (1887), *Mr. Potter of Texas* (1888), *That Frenchman!* (1889), *Miss Nobody of Nowhere* (1890), *A Prince in the Garret* (1905); plays, *Prince Karl* (produced 1886) and *Mr. Barnes of New York*.

**Gunter, Edmund**. 1581–1626. English mathematician; professor of astronomy, Gresham Coll., London (1619–26); invented the chain, line, quadrant, and scale known by his name (Gunter's chain, Gunter's line, etc.).

**Gün'ther** (gün'tẽr; *Angl.* gĭn'tẽr), **Albert Charles Lewis Gotthilf**. 1830–1914. German-born zoologist in England; naturalized British subject (1862). On staff of British Museum; keeper of its zoological department (1875–95).

**Günther, Hans**. 1891–1968. German anthropologist; professor of social anthropology at Jena (1930), Berlin (1935).

**Günther, Johann Christian**. 1695–1723. German lyric poet.

**Gun'ther** (gŭn'thẽr), **John**. 1901–1970. American journalist, b. Chicago; European correspondent for various American newspapers (from 1924). Author of *Inside Europe* (1936), *Inside Asia* (1939), *Inside Latin America* (1941).

**Gup'ta** (gŏŏp'tȧ). A dynasty of kings (320–480) of northern India, ruling during a golden age (the Gupta period) of Hindu (Sanskrit) literature, art, and science (see KALIDASA). Its rulers were Chandragupta I (the founder), Samudragupta, Chandragupta II, Kumaragupta I, and Skandagupta. Kingdom overwhelmed by invasion of Huns (480–490); shorn of power, members of dynasty ruled in restricted area (490–647?).

**Gupta,** Sir **Krishna Govinda**. 1851–1926. East Indian statesman; one of first Indian native students to compete for Indian Civil Service; studied at London, passed examination (1873), and held several positions (1873–1904); member of Provincial Board of Revenue (1904–07); first member of Hindu race of Indian Council (1907–15); K.C.S.I. (1911).

**Gu'ra** (gōō'rä), **Eugen**. 1842–1906. German baritone; known as interpreter of Wagner, Loewe, and Schubert.

**Gurk** (gŏŏrk), **Paul**. 1880–1953. German novelist and playwright.

**Gur'ko** (gŏŏr'kô), **Osip** (*or* **Iosif**) **Vladimirovich**. 1828–1901. Russian general. Served in Crimean War (1854–56) and in Poland (1863); commanded an army in Russo-Turkish War (1877–78), defeated by Suleiman Pasha; defended Shipka Pass; occupied Sofia (1878); defeated Turks (1878) in battle of Philippopolis (Plovdiv); governor general of Poland (1882–94); retired as field marshal. His son **Vasili Iosifovich** (1864–1937) served in Russo-Japanese War (1904–05); in World War, fought under Rennenkampf (1914–16); Russian chief of staff (1916–17); commander on Rumanian front (1917).

**Gur'ley** (gûr'lĭ), **Ralph Randolph**. 1797–1872. American philanthropist; agent, and later director, American Colonization Society, formed to colonize Liberia with American Negroes (1822–72).

**Gur'litt** (gŏŏr'lĭt). Name of a German family, including: **Louis** (1812–1897), landscape painter; his brother **Cornelius** (1820–1901), a composer, esp. of piano-instruction pieces; Louis's sons **Cornelius** (1850–1938), art historian, and **Ludwig** (1855–1931), educator and writer on pedagogy; and the second Cornelius's son **Wilibald** (1889–1963), music scholar.

**Gur'ney** (gûr'nĭ), **Edmund**. 1847–1888. English philosopher and psychologist; a founder of the Society for Psychical Research (1882). Author of *Phantasms of the Living* (with F. W. H. Myers and F. Podmore, 1886), *Tertium Quid* (1887).

**Gurney,** Sir **Goldsworthy**. 1793–1875. English inventor; invented oxyhydrogen blowpipe, a high-pressure steam jet for extinguishing fires in mines, the Gurney burner and Gurney light, and a steam carriage that traveled from London to Bath and back at rate of 15 miles per hour (1829).

**Gurney, Joseph John**. 1788–1847. English Quaker philanthropist; Quaker minister (1818); visited U.S., Canada, and West Indies (1837–40); active in movements for prison reform, abolition of capital punishment, Negro emancipation.

**Gürt'ner** (gürt'nẽr), **Franz**. 1881–1941. German Nazi jurist; minister of justice (1932–41); one of those responsible for decrees (Nov., 1938) designed to destroy economic status of Jews in Germany in retaliation for murder of Ernst vom Rath, secretary of German embassy in Paris, by a young Polish Jew.

**Gur′vich** (gōōr′vyĭch), **Aleksandr Gavrilovich.** 1874–1954. Russian biologist; credited with discovery of mitogenetic rays.

**Gu′ry′** (gü′rē′), **Jean Pierre.** 1801–1866. French Jesuit theologian.

**Gus·mão′** (gōōz·mouN′), **Bartholomeu de.** 1675–1724. Brazilian Jesuit, mathematician, and inventor; regarded as pioneer in field of balloon navigation.

**Güss′feldt** (güs′fĕlt), **Paul.** 1840–1920. German explorer; led expedition to Loango (1873–75); explored Arabian Desert (1876); visited Andes of Chile and Argentina (1882–83).

**Gus′sow** (gŏŏs′ō), **Karl.** 1843–1907. German painter, esp. of genre pictures and portraits; professor in art school at Weimar (1870), Karlsruhe (1874), Berlin (1875).

**Gus·ta′vus** (gŭs·tā′vŭs; -tä′vŭs). *Swed.* **Gus′taf** (gŭs′täv). Name of six kings of Sweden, the first four of the Vasa dynasty:

**Gustavus I.** *Known as* **Gustavus Va′sa** (vä′så). *Also* **Gustavus E′riks·son′** (ā′rĭk·sôn′). 1496–1560. King (1523–60), b. Lindholmen. Son of Eric Johansson. First ruler of house of Vasa (*q.v.*). Descended on mother's side from ancient house of Sture. Educ. Uppsala (1509–14); entered service of Regent Sten Sture; fought against Christian II of Denmark; held captive as hostage in Denmark (1518–19); escaped and returned to Dalecarlia; sought by Christian (1520), who beheaded many Swedish nobles, among them his father and brother-in-law; led successful revolt of Dalecarlians (1521–23) against Danes; proclaimed administrator of Sweden (1521–23), later king (1523–60); favored Lutheran doctrine, which was legalized as state doctrine (1527–29); supported by peasantry; labored against difficulties of party strife, opposition of nobles, devastation of country by war, etc.

**Gustavus II.** *Known as* **Gustavus A·dol′phus** (*ȧ*·dŏl′fŭs). 1594–1632. Called "Lion of the North," also "Snow King." King (1611—32). Grandson of Gustavus Vasa; b. Stockholm. Brought up in Lutheran faith; declared of age soon after accession (1611); forced to wage wars with Denmark, Poland, and Russia; supported by his chancellor, Count Oxenstierna, changed policy of repressing nobility and sought co-operation of all classes; reorganized internal government; won back districts in southern Sweden from Denmark (1611–13); was victorious in war with Russia (1613–17) at peace of Stolbova; fought long defensive war (1621–29) against Sigismund (*q.v.*) of Poland, who claimed throne of Sweden; won territory and full recognition as king of Sweden; led by religious interest to support Protestant cause in Thirty Years' War (1630–32); showed brilliant generalship; secured aid of France against Holy Roman Empire (1630); left Oxenstierna in control in Sweden; defeated Tilly (1631) at Leipzig (or Breitenfeld) and again at the Lech (1632), where Tilly was mortally wounded; found road to Vienna open; confronted by Wallenstein, whom Emperor Ferdinand II had reinstated in command, at Lützen (1632); won the battle, but mortally wounded; one of greatest generals of modern times; saved Protestantism in Germany.

**Gustavus III.** 1746–1792. King (1771–92). Son of Adolphus Frederick; b. Stockholm. Became king when royal power was low and party strife intense; arrested council in a body (1772); regained power; waged useless war against Russia (1788); received new powers from Diet (1789); assassinated by J. J. Anckarström (*q.v.*), one of a conspiracy of nobles. Author of dramatic works and poems of merit.

**Gustavus IV.** *Full name* **Gustavus Adolphus.** 1778–1837. King (1792–1809). Son of Gustavus III, b. Stockholm. King under regency of his uncle, duke of Södermanland (1792–1800); crowned (1800); actuated by hatred of Napoleon, entered (1805) into coalition against him; lost Swedish Pomerania and last German possessions; received help of English, but lost Finland to Russia (1808); dethroned (1809); wandered about Europe; died in poverty at Saint Gallen, Switzerland.

**Gustavus V.** *Better known as* **Gustaf.** 1858–1950. King (1907–50), of the Bernadotte dynasty (*q.v.*). Son of Oscar II, b. Drottningholm. Educ. Uppsala (1877–78, 1880); m. (1881) Victoria, daughter of Frederick William Louis, Grand Duke of Baden; lieutenant general (1892); often acted as regent during father's absence (esp. 1899–1900); strongly favored Allies in World War but kept Sweden neutral; a popular sovereign, on 80th birthday (1938) given sum of $1,000,000 by Swedish people.

**Gustavus VI.** *Full name* **Oscar Fredrik Wilhelm Olaf Gustaf Adolf.** 1882–1973. King of Sweden (1950–73). Son of Gustavus V; m. 1st (1905) Princess Margaret of Great Britain (1882–1920), daughter of duke of Connaught, 2d (1923) Princess Louise of Battenberg (1889–1965).

**Gustavus.** See CHARLES X of Sweden.

**Gus·ta′vus A·dol′phus** (gŭs·tā′vŭs [-tä′vŭs] *ȧ*·dŏl′fŭs). *Swed.* **Gustaf Adolf.** See GUSTAVUS II and IV of Sweden.

**Gu′ten·berg** (gōō′tĕn·bĕrk; *Angl.* gōō′t'n·bûrg), **Johann.** 1400?–?1468. German inventor of printing from movable type, b. in Mainz. Father's name, Gensfleisch or Ganzfleisch; assumed mother's family name, Gutenberg. Began experiments in printing before 1439; settled in Mainz (c. 1446) and formed partnership with a goldsmith, Johann Fust, of that city to exploit his invention; Fust's demand for repayment of money advanced caused a settlement whereby Gutenberg abandoned his claims to his invention and surrendered his stock to Fust, who continued the business. Aided later by one Conrad Humery, Gutenberg again established himself in the printing business, and brought out the first printed Bible, known as the *Gutenberg Bible* (or *Mazarin Bible*, because of its discovery about 1760 in the library of Cardinal Mazarin). Archbishop Adolph of Nassau, Elector of Mainz, gave recognition to his works (1465) by presenting him with a benefice yielding him an income and various privileges.

**Guth′nick** (gōōt′nĭk), **Paul.** 1879–1947. German astronomer.

**Guth′rie** (gŭth′rĭ), **Frederick.** 1833–1886. English physicist; studied under Bunsen at Heidelberg. Author of *Elements of Heat* (1868), *Magnetism and Electricity* (1873); also, under pseudonym **Frederick Cer′ny** (?sûr′nĭ), of poems *The Jew* (1863) and *Logroño* (1877).

**Guthrie, James.** 1792–1869. American lawyer and political leader; founder and president, U. of Louisville. U.S. secretary of the treasury (1853–57). Supported Union during Civil War. U.S. senator (1865–68); supported President Johnson; opposed congressional reconstruction policies.

**Guthrie,** Sir **James.** 1859–1930. Scottish portrait painter, of the Glasgow school; painted war statesmen group for National Portrait Gallery in London.

**Guthrie, Samuel.** 1782–1848. American chemist; invented percussion priming powder, with a punch lock for exploding it, replacing flintlock muskets; discovered chloric ether (chloroform) (1831); devised a process for rapid conversion of potato starch into sugar.

**Guthrie, Thomas.** 1803–1873. Scottish clergyman and philanthropist; known as "the apostle of ragged schools" (*i.e.* schools for destitute children); platform speaker in the cause of temperance.

**Guthrie, Thomas Anstey.** *Pseudonym* **F. An′stey** (ăn′stĭ). 1856–1934. English novelist. Author of *Vice Versa* (1882), *Baboo Jabberjee, B.A.* (1897), and of plays, including adaptations from Molière.

**Guthrie, Woodrow Wilson.** *Known as* **Woody Guthrie.** 1912–1967. American folk singer and composer, b. Okemah, Okla. Wrote over 1,000 songs concerning Amer. life, including *This Land is Your Land.*

**Guth′rum** (gŏŏth′rŏŏm). *Also* **Gut′horm** *or* **Gut′torm** (gŏŏt′ŏrm). d. 890. Danish king of East Anglia. Settled in Midlands (875); defeated by Alfred at Edington in Wiltshire (878); adopted Christianity (878); reigned in peace (878–890).

**Gu·tiér′rez** (gōō·tyĕr′rāth), **Antonio García.** See Antonio GARCÍA GUTIÉRREZ.

**Gu·tiér′rez de la Con′cha** (gōō·tyĕr′rās [-rāth] thȧ lä kôn′chä), **José.** 1809–1895. Spanish general and political leader, b. Córdoba, Argentina. Captain general of Basque Provinces (1843–46); governor of Cuba three times (1850–52, 1854–59, and 1874–75); senator in Spanish Cortes (1860–62); Spanish minister to France (1862); minister of war (1863); president of the Senate (1864–68); partisan of Isabella in revolution of 1868.

**Gut′schmid** (gōōt′shmĭt), **Alfred von.** 1831–1887. German historian.

**Guts′ Muths′** (gōōts′ mōōts′), **Johann Christoph Friedrich.** 1759–1839. German pioneer in physical education.

**Gut′tin′guer′** (gü′tăN′gâr′), **Ul′rich′** (ül′rēk′). 1785–1866. French writer of the Romantic school.

**Guttorm.** See GUTHRUM.

**Gutz′kow** (gōōts′kō), **Karl.** 1811–1878. German journalist, novelist, and playwright; a leader (c. 1830–50) of Young Germany. Founded *Deutsche Revue*, at Frankfort (1835); publ. *Wally, die Zweiflerin* (1833), a satirical attack on the institution of marriage which is taken as the beginning of the revolt of Young Germany against romanticism. Others of his novels are *Die Ritter vom Geiste* (regarded as beginning the modern German social novel; 9 vols., 1850–52), *Der Zauberer von Rom* (9 vols., 1858–61), *Hohenschwangau* (1868). Among his plays are *Richard Savage* (1839), *Zopf und Schwert* (1844), *Uriel Acosta* (1846), *Der Königsleutnant* (1849).

**Guy** (gī), **John.** d. about 1628. English colonizer in America. Merchant of Bristol; governor of Newfoundland, led colonizers there (1610); returned to England. Mayor of Bristol, Eng. (1618–19); M.P. (1620–28).

**Guy, Thomas.** 1645?–1724. English bookdealer and philanthropist; one of Oxford U. printers (1769–92); M.P. (1695–1707). Founder of Guy's Hospital, London.

**Guy** (*or* **Gui′do**) **of Lu′si′gnan′** (gī, gwē′dō, lü′zē′nyäN′). *Fr.* **Gui′ de Lu′si′gnan′** (gē′dē lü′zē′nyäN′). 1140–1194. King of Jerusalem (1186–87) and of Cyprus (1192–94). Descendant of ancient ruling family in Poitou; brother of Amalric II; m. (1180; d. 1190) Sibylla, daughter of Amalric I, King of Jerusalem; succeeded Baldwin V (1186); was defeated (1187) and taken prisoner by Saladin; released (1188) on renouncing his claim to throne; laid siege to Acre (1189); supported by Richard I of England; in exchange for his claim to throne of Jerusalem was granted Cyprus by Richard I (1192).

**Guy** (*or* **Guido**) **of Spo·le′to** (spô·lā′tō). *Fr.* **Gui** (gē). *Ger.* **Wi′do** (vē′dō). d. 894. King of Italy (889–894). Duke of Spoleto (from 882); defeated his rival Berengar (889); crowned emperor of the West (891) by Pope Stephen V.

**Guy′au′** (gü·ē′yō′), **Marie Jean.** 1854–1888. French poet and philosopher; author of *Vers d'un Philosophe* (1881), *L'Irréligion de l'Avenir* (1886), etc.

**Guy′er** (gī′ĕr), **Michael Frederic.** 1874–1959. American zoologist.

**Guy′ne·mer′** (gēn′mâr′), **Georges Marie.** 1894–1917. French military aviator; in World War I, he was credited with destruction of 54 enemy planes.

**Guy′on′** (gü·ē′yôN′), Madame. *Best-known name of* **Jeanne Marie de la Motte′-Guy′on′** (dē lȧ môt′-), *nee* **Bou′vier′** (bōō′vyā′). 1648–1717. French mystic; m. Jacques de la Motte-Guyon (1664); preached and practiced semiquietism; imprisoned (1695) and later banished from Paris to Blois.

**Guyon, Jean Casimir Félix.** 1831–1920. French surgeon and urologist.

**Guy′on** (gī′ŭn; *Fr.* gü·ē′yôN′), **Richard Debaufre.** 1803–1856. English soldier of fortune; distinguished himself in command of Hungarian forces at battles of Tyrnau and Schwechat (1848). Joined Turkish service; appointed by the sultan lieutenant general (1852) with title Kurshid Pasha, the first Christian to hold a command under the Sultan; served against Russians in Anatolia (1853–55).

**Guy′ot** (gē′yō), **Arnold Henry.** 1807–1884. Geographer and geologist, b. in Switzerland. Ph.D., Berlin (1835). To U.S. (1848); professor, Princeton (1854–84); Guyot Hall, Princeton, is named in his honor.

**Guy′ot′** (gü·ē′yō′), **Yves.** 1843–1928. French economist and politician; advocate of free trade and opponent of strict government regulation and of Socialism. Minister of public works (1889–92). Author of *La Science Économique* (1881), etc.

**Guys** (gois), **Constantin,** *in full* **Ernest Adolphe Hyacinthe Constantin.** 1802–1892. Illustrator, b. in Holland; correspondent for *Illustrated London News* during Crimean War; settled in Paris (c. 1865) and sketched the life and manners of the Second Empire.

**Guy′ton′ de Mor′veau′** (gē′tôN′ dē môr′vō′), Baron **Louis Bernard.** 1737–1816. French chemist. Published *Digressions Académiques* setting forth his ideas on phlogiston and crystallization (1772); used chlorine and hydrochloric acid gas for disinfecting (1773); collaborated with Lavoisier, Berthollet, and Fourcroy in devising system of chemical nomenclature.

**Guz·mán′** (gōōth·män′), **Alonso Pé′rez de** (pā′rāth thȧ). *Called* **el Bue′no** (ĕl bwā′nō). 1256–1309. Spanish soldier, b. León; in service of sultan of Morocco, later, of Sancho IV, King of Castile; defended Tarifa (1294) against Moors led by rebel Infante Don Juan; captured Gibraltar from Moors (1308). Progenitor of dukes of Medina-Sidonia (*q.v.*).

**Guzmán, Fernán Pérez de.** 1377?–?1460. Spanish chronicler and poet.

**Guzmán, Gaspar de.** See OLIVARES.

**Guz·mán′ Blan′co** (gōōs·män′ bläng′kō), **Antonio.** 1829–1899. Venezuelan soldier and statesman, b. Caracas. Vice-president of Venezuela (1863–68); following overthrow of Falcón (1868), led successful revolution. President (1870–72, and for alternate terms of two years until 1889); practically dictator for entire period.

**Gwath′mey** (gwŏth′mĭ), **James Tayloe.** 1863–1944. American physician; anesthetist, New York Skin and Cancer Hospital and People's Hospital. Described ether-oil method of rectal anesthesia (1913); published *Anaesthesia* (1914); with Howard T. Karsner, introduced method of giving ether and oil by mouth for painful dressings; with Asa B. Davis, introduced obstetrical analgesia at Lying-in Hospital, New York (1923).

**Gwilt** (gwĭlt), **Joseph.** 1784–1863. English architect.

**Gwilym, Dafydd ap** *or* **David ap.** = DAFYDD AP GWILYM (see DAVID).

**Gwin·nett′** (gwĭ·nĕt′), **Button.** 1735–1777. American Revolutionary leader, b. in Gloucestershire, Eng.; to America before 1765. Resident, Savannah, Ga. Member, Continental Congress (1776, 1777); a signer of Declaration of Independence. President of State of Georgia (1777).

**Gwyn** *or* **Gwynne** (gwĭn), **Eleanor,** *known as* **Nell.** 1650–1687. English actress; mistress of Charles II. Excelled in gay and sprightly roles; last stage appearance (1682). Retained affection of the king until his death; bore him two sons, Charles Beauclerk (1670–1726, later duke of St. Albans) and James (b. 1671).

**Gwynn** (gwĭn), **Stephen Lucius.** 1864–1950. Irish novelist and poet; London journalist (1896–1904). Irish M.P. (1906–18); served in World War. Member of Irish Convention (1917–18); president of the Irish Literary Society (from 1932). His many works include *The Decay of Sensibility* (1900), *The Queen's Chronicler* (verse; 1901), *The Fair Hills of Ireland* (1906), *Duffer's Luck* (stories; 1924), *Irish Literature and Drama* (1936), *Fond Opinions* (essays; 1938).

**Gwynne'–Vaughan'** (gwĭn'vôn'), **Helen Charlotte Isabella,** *nee* **Fra'ser** (frā'zẽr). 1879–1967. English botanist; m. D. T. Gwynne-Vaughan (1911; d. 1915). Head of department of botany, Birkbeck Coll., London (1909–17 and from 1920). Organizer (1917) and chief controller, Women's Army Auxiliary Corps (WAAC), whose members were called for duty in France (Feb., 1917–Sept., 1918). Created Dame of the British Empire (1919). Organizer (1938) and chief controller (until 1941), Women's Auxiliary Territorial Service (WATS). Author of treatises on *Fungi* (1922 and 1927).

**Gy'ges** (jī'jēz; gī'-) *or* **Gu'gu** (gōō'gōō). King of Lydia (c. 685–652 B.C.); founder of Mermnadae dynasty. Menaced by Cimmerians; aided by Ashurbanipal (c. 663); became feudatory of Assyrian king (660); made war upon Greek Ionian cities; joined Psamtik I of Egypt in conspiracy against Ashurbanipal; defeated and slain by Cimmerians.

**Gyl·dén'** (yül·dān'), **Hugo.** 1841–1896. Swedish astronomer; known chiefly for work on the motion of celestial bodies.

**Gy·lip'pus** (jĭ·lĭp'ŭs). Spartan general of 5th century B.C. Sent to aid in defense of Syracuse (414–413 B.C.); defeated Athenians under Demosthenes and Nicias. Later, embezzled money entrusted to him by Lysander and fled into exile.

**Gyl'lem·bourg–Eh'ren·svärd** (gül'ĕn·bŏrg·ĕ'rĕn·svâr), **Thomasine,** *nee* **Bunt'zen** (bŏŏnt's'n). 1773–1856. Danish novelist; m. P. A. Heiberg (1790; divorced 1800) and Baron K. F. Ehrensvärd (1801; d. 1815), who adopted the name of Gyllembourg. Her chief work is *En Hverdags Historie* (transl., *An Everyday Story*).

**Gyl'len·borg'** (yül'lĕn·bôr'y'), Count **Carl.** 1679–1746. Swedish statesman; president of the chancellery (1739); his policies led to war with Russia (1741–43) wherein Sweden lost the province of Viborg.

**Gyl'len·stier'na** (yül'lĕn·shâr'nȧ), Count **Johan.** 1635–1680. Swedish statesman; chief counselor to the young King Charles XI; at peace congress of Lund (1679), negotiated an alliance with Denmark.

**Gyön'gyö·si** (dyûn'dyû·shĭ), **István.** 1620–1704. Hungarian poet; a founder of Hungarian poetry; author of *Murányi Venus* (epic; 1664), *Rózsa-Koszorú* ("Rose Wreath"; 1690), *Kemény-Janos* (1693), *Cupidó* (1695), and *Chariklia* (1700).

**Gyp.** Pseudonym of Comtesse de MARTEL DE JANVILLE.

**Gy'ro·wetz** (gē'rō·vĕts), **Adalbert.** 1763–1850. Austrian composer of 60 symphonies, 19 Masses, 40 ballets, 30 choral pieces, and much chamber music.

**Gy'sis** (gē'zēs), **Nikolaos.** 1842–1901. Greek painter.

**Gyu'lai** (dyŏŏ'loi), **Franz.** Count **von Ma'ros–Né'meth und Ná'das·ka** (fôn mŏ'rōsh·nā'mĕt ŏŏnt nä'dŏsh·kŏ). 1798–1868. Austrian soldier; major general (1846) and commandant in Trieste. At outbreak of revolution (1848), assumed command of Austrian naval vessels in the Adriatic and maintained strict coast defense. Minister of war (1849). Commander in chief of Austrian army in war with French and Sardinians (1859); retired after defeat in battle of Magenta.

# H

**Haag** (häg), **Carl.** 1820–1915. German-born British painter; to England (1847); naturalized; painted landscapes, and scenes in the life of the royal family at Balmoral Castle.

**Haa'kon** (hô'kŏn). *Old Norse* **Há'kon** (hä'kŏn). Name of seven kings of Norway:

**Haakon I.** *Called* **the Good.** 914?–961. King (935–961). Natural son of Harold Haarfager. Brought up in Christian religion in England by King Athelstan; provided with fleet and sailed to Norway; defeated his half brother Eric Bloodaxe, who had seized the throne; wise and popular ruler, befriended landowners; brought Christian influences to Norway; killed in battle with Eric's sons.

**Haakon II.** *Called* **Her'de·bred'** (hăr'dĕ·brā'), *i.e.* Broadshouldered. 1147–1162. King (1161–62). Son of Sigurd. Reign a period of strife; killed in surprise attack.

**Haakon III Sver'res·son** (svăr'rĕ·sŏn). King (1202–04).

**Haakon IV Haa'kons·son** (hô'kŏn·sŏn). *Called* **the Old.** 1204–1263. King (1217–63). Said to be natural son of Haakon III. In early part of reign power in hands of Earl Skule; put Earl Skule to death when openly opposed by him (1240); reign generally prosperous and quiet; united Iceland and Greenland to Norway (1262); made expedition to Hebrides and Scotland (1263).

**Haakon V Mag'nus·son** (mång'nŏŏ·sŏn). *Called* **Haa'legg** (hô'lĕg), *i.e.* Longlegs. 1270–1319. King (1299–1319). Son of Magnus VI and last male descendant of Harold Haarfager. Succeeded his brother Eric Magnusson; fought war with Denmark.

**Haakon VI Magnusson.** 1339–1380. King (1355–80). Son of Magnus VII. Nominally king during regency of father (1343–55). King of Sweden also (1362–63); waged war with Sweden (1363–71); m. (1363) Margaret, daughter of Waldemar IV of Denmark; their son Olaf named as heir to both kingdoms, which led to Union of Kalmar (see MARGARET, OLAF, of Denmark).

**Haakon VII.** *Orig.* **Carl.** 1872–1957. King (1905–57). Second son of Frederick VIII of Denmark; m. (1896) Maud (d. 1938), daughter of Edward VII of England; on separation of Norway from Sweden (1905) chosen king by Storting; crowned at Trondheim (1906). To England (1940), following German invasion; returned (1945).

**Haakon,** Earl, *Norw.* Jarl. 937?–995. Ruler of Norway

(970–995), but not generally reckoned in line of kings. Gained power over Harold Bluetooth of Denmark during latter part of his reign (970–985); asserted control over Norway (985–995); upholder of paganism.

**Haar** (här), **Bernard ter.** 1806–1880. Dutch theologian and poet.

**Haardt** (härt), **Georges Marie.** 1886–1932. Explorer, b. Naples, Italy, of Flemish parents; naturalized French citizen. First to cross Sahara Desert and to traverse length of Africa by automobile; also headed expedition that crossed Asia.

**Haar'hoff** (här'hŏf), **T. J.** 1892– . South African scholar; Rhodes scholar at Oxford (1913); professor of classics, U. of the Witwatersrand, Johannesburg (from 1922).

**Haas** (häs), **Arthur Erich.** 1884–1941. Physicist, b. Brünn, Bohemia; professor, Leipzig, Vienna, London, and (1936) Notre Dame, U.S.A.; worked on atomic theory.

**Haas** (häz), **Jacob de.** 1872–1937. English and American Jewish journalist, b. London. Editor, *Jewish World*, London (1892–1900); introduced Theodor Herzl, originator of Zionist movement, to London (1896). To U.S. (1902); became secretary of Zionist organization and editor of *Jewish Advocate*, Boston (1908–18).

**Haas** (häs), **Johannes Hubertus Leonardus de.** 1832–1908. Dutch painter, esp. of landscapes and animals.

**Haas** (häs), **Joseph.** 1879–1960. German composer of oratorios, chamber music, songs, and orchestral works, and the opera *Tobias Wunderlich.*

**Haas** (häs), **Maurice Frederick Hendrik de.** 1832–1895. Dutch marine painter; to U.S. (1858); studio in New York. Among his canvases are *Farragut Passing the Forts* and *The Rapids above Niagara.*

**Haa'se** (hä'zĕ), **Friedrich.** 1808–1867. German classical philologist.

**Haase, Friedrich.** 1825–1911. German actor; toured in U.S. (1869, 1882–83); excelled in interpretation of aristocratic roles in comedy.

**Haase, Hugo.** 1863–1919. German Socialist leader; succeeded Bebel as president, German Social Democratic Party; member of Reichstag (1897 ff.). Disagreed with majority war policy (1914–15); organized (1917) and led Independent Socialist Party, hostile to the government; spread propaganda credited with inspiring the naval mutiny (Aug., 1918); member of coalition cabinet (Nov.–Dec., 1918); assassinated.

**Haast** (häst), Sir **John Francis Julius von.** 1824–1887. German-born geologist and explorer in New Zealand; discovered coal and gold deposits (1859). Professor of geology, New Zealand U., and founder of Canterbury Museum (1866).

**Há'ba** (hä'bä), **Alois.** 1893–1972. Czech musician; champion of quarter-tone music. Wrote orchestral, string, and piano works, and opera *Die Mutter* (1931).

**Ha·bak'kuk** (hȧ·băk'ŭk; hăb'ȧ·kŭk). *In Douay Bible* **Ha·bac'uc** (hȧ·băk'ŭk; hăb'ȧ·kŭk). A minor Hebrew prophet, of unknown date. The Old Testament book of *Habakkuk* contains a dialogue between the prophet and Jehovah on the oppression of the faithful by the Chaldeans and a prayer or hymn on promised deliverance.

**Habbema, Koos.** Pseudonym of Herman HEIJERMANS.

**Hab'ber·ton** (hăb'ĕr·t'n; -tŭn), **John.** 1842–1921. American writer; on editorial staff, New York *Herald* (1876–93) and *Collier's Weekly* (1897–99). Wrote a number of stories and novels, including: *Helen's Babies* (1876), a great success; *Other People's Children* (1877), a sequel to *Helen's Babies; Budge & Toddie, or, Helen's Babies at Play* (1908); and a play, *Deacon Crankett.*

**Ha'be·neck'** (ȧb'nĕk'), **François Antoine.** 1781–1849. French conductor, and composer of violin pieces.

**Ha'ber** (hä'bĕr), **Fritz.** 1868–1934. German chemist. Professor, Karlsruhe (1898); director, Kaiser Wilhelm Inst. for Physical Chemistry, Berlin (1911). Worked in electrochemistry and on thermodynamic gas reactions; produced ammonia synthetically (1908–09); awarded 1918 Nobel prize for chemistry (1919); with Karl Bosch, invented a process (Haber process) for production of ammonia from atmospheric nitrogen.

**Ha'berl** (hä'bĕrl), **Franz Xaver.** 1840–1910. German Roman Catholic clergyman and church musician. Completed (from vol. X) edition of Palestrina's works (33 vols., 1880–1907); edited magazine *Musica Sacra* (1888 ff.), and instruction book on Gregorian chant (*Magister Choralis*); wrote on history of polyphonic church music.

**Ha'ber·landt** (hä'bĕr·länt), **Gottlieb.** 1854–1945. Austrian botanist; pioneer in physiological plant anatomy. Worked on the sensitivity of plants to external stimuli.

**Haberlandt, Michael.** 1860–1940. Austrian folklorist and Far Eastern scholar; director (1912) of Folklore Museum, Vienna; succeeded (1923) by his son **Arthur Ludwig Wolfgang** (1889–1964), ethnologist and folklorist.

**Hä'ber·lin** (hâ'bĕr·lēn), **Karl von.** 1832–1911. German painter; best known for historical works.

**Häberlin, Karl Friedrich.** 1756–1808. German jurist; authority on constitutional law.

**Häberlin, Paul.** 1878–1960. Swiss philosopher and educator; professor, Bern (1914–22) and Basel (from 1922). Author of *Wissenschaft und Philosophie* (2 vols., 1910–12), *Der Charakter* (1925), and pedagogical works.

**Ha'ber·mann** (hä'bĕr·män), Baron **Hugo von.** 1849–1929. German painter, esp. of portraits and figure pieces; identified with modern impressionist painters.

**Hab'er·sham** (hăb'ĕr·shăm), **Joseph.** 1751–1815. American political leader, b. Savannah, Ga. Colonel in Continental army. Member, Continental Congress (1785–86) and Georgia's constitutional ratification convention (1788). U.S. postmaster general (1795–1801).

**Ha·bib'ul·lah' Khan** (hȧ·bēb'ŏŏl·lä' kän). 1872–1919. Amir of Afghanistan (1901–19). Son of Abd-er-Rahman Khan. Established friendly relations with British in India; kept kingdom neutral in Anglo-Russian affairs and during World War; assassinated.

**Ha'bich** (hä'bĭk), **Ludwig.** 1872–1949. German sculptor; member of Darmstadt art colony (1900–06); professor, Stuttgart Acad. (from 1918).

**Hab'ing·ton** (hăb'ĭng·tŭn), **William.** 1605–1654. English poet; author of *Castara* (lyrical verse; 1634) and *The Queene of Arragon* (tragicomedy; 1640).

**Habsburg.** See HAPSBURG.

**Há'cha** (hä'kȧ), **Emil.** 1872–1945. Czech jurist and statesman; second president (1919–25), first president (1925–38) of high court of Czechoslovakia; judge, Permanent Court of International Justice, The Hague. Third president of Czechoslovakia (1938–39); president of the German "protectorate of Bohemia and Moravia" (1939–45); died in jail awaiting trial as war criminal.

**Ha'chette'** (ȧ'shĕt'), **Jean Nicolas Pierre.** 1769–1834. French mathematician; applied geometry to the construction of machinery.

**Hachette, Jeanne.** *Real name* **Jeanne Lais'né'** (lĕ'nā'). *Called* **Four'quet'** (fōōr'kĕ'). 15th-century French heroine who took part in the defense of Beauvais against Charles the Bold (1472).

**Hachette, Louis Christophe François.** 1800–1864. French editor and publisher; founder of publishing house Hachette et Cie. (1826).

**Hack'er** (hăk'ĕr), **Arthur.** 1858–1919. English painter of religious subjects, London street scenes, and portraits.

**Hack'ert** (hăk'ĕrt), **Philipp.** 1737–1807. German painter and etcher; friend of Goethe; best known for landscapes.

**Hack′ett** (hăk′ĕt; -ĭt), **Charles.** 1888–1942. American operatic tenor, b. Worcester, Mass.; operatic debut at Metropolitan Opera House, New York (1919); joined Chicago Civic Opera Co. (1923) and returned to Metropolitan Opera Co. (1933).

**Hackett, Francis.** 1883–1962. Writer, b. in Kilkenny, Ireland. To U.S. (1901); on staff of *The New Republic* magazine (1914–22). Author of *Ireland, a Study in Nationalism* (1918), *Horizons* (1918), *Henry the Eighth* (1929), *Francis the First* (1934), *Queen Anne Boleyn* (1938), etc.

**Hackett, James Henry.** 1800–1871. American comedian; succeeded as character impersonator. Chief roles: Falstaff, Rip Van Winkle, Nimrod Wildfire (a backwoods Kentuckian just elected to congress), Melodious Migrate (a Connecticut schoolmaster). His son **James Keteltas** (1869–1926), b. Wolfe Island, Ontario, Canada, was also an actor; member of Frohman's Lyceum stock company (1895); excelled in romantic hero roles, as in *Prisoner of Zenda, Rupert of Hentzau, The Princess and the Butterfly, The Fortunes of the King,* etc. See Mary MANNERING.

**Hack′län′der** (häk′lĕn′dẽr), **Friedrich Wilhelm von.** 1816–1877. German writer; founded, with Edmund von Zoller, journal *Über Land und Meer*, Stuttgart (c. 1857). Among his many works are *Daguerreotypen* (2 vols., 1842; later called *Reise in den Orient*), *Handel und Wandel* (2 vols., 1850), *Namenlose Geschichten* (3 vols., 1851), *Eugen Stillfried* (3 vols., 1852), *Augenblick des Glücks* (2 vols., 1857), *Verbotene Früchte* (2 vols., 1876), *Das Ende der Gräfin Patatzky* (2 vols., 1877).

**Ha′co** (hā′kō). Variant of HAAKON.

**Hadadezer.** See BENHADAD II.

**Hadad–nirari.** Variant of ADADNIRARI.

**Ha′da′mard′** (å′då′mår′), **Jacques Salomon.** 1865–1963. French mathematician. Known esp. for work on the infinitesimal calculus.

**Ha′da·mov′sky** (hä′dä·môf′skē), **Eugen.** 1904– . German radio director; member of Reich propaganda section, and a leader in Nazi mechanized corps.

**Hadassah.** See ESTHER (Bible character).

**Had′dan** (hăd′'n), **Arthur West.** 1816–1873. English church historian.

**Had′ding·ton** (hăd′ĭng·tŭn), Earl of. A Scottish title bestowed (1627) on **Thomas Hamilton** (1563–1637), Lord **Drum·cairn′** (drŭm·kârn′), Earl of **Mel′rose** (mĕl′rōz); descendant of 2d son of Walter Fitz-Gilbert (see HAMILTON family); a favorite of James VI; Lord of Session (1592); one of eight "Octavians," managers of Scottish finance (1596); secretary of state for Scotland (1612–26); lord president of the Court of Session (1616–26); lord privy seal to Charles I (1626). His son **Thomas** (1600–1640), 2d earl, Covenanter and soldier, died defending the borders. **Thomas Hamilton** (1680–1735), 6th earl, though a second son (1st son succeeded as earl of **Roth′es** [rŏth′ĭz], title from his mother's family), became representative peer (1716). **Thomas Hamilton** (1780–1858), 9th earl; M.A., Oxon. (1815); Indian commissioner (1814–22); lord lieutenant of Ireland (1834–35) under Sir Robert Peel; first lord of the admiralty (1841–46). **George Bail′lie–Ham′il·ton** [bā′lĭ-] (1802–1870), descendant of 6th earl, became 10th earl and his son **George** (1827–1917), 11th earl.

**Haddington,** Viscount. See Sir John RAMSEY.

**Haddock, Albert.** Pseudonym of Alan Patrick HERBERT.

**Had′don** (hăd′'n), **Alfred Cort.** 1855–1940. English ethnologist and anthropologist; author of *Introduction to Embryology, Evolution in Art, Study of Man, Magic and Fetishism, The Races of Man and their Distribution, History of Anthropology,* etc.

**Haddon, Walter.** 1516–1572. English educator and legal scholar; president of Magdalen Coll., Oxford (1552–53). Published *Reformatio Legum Ecclesiasticarum* (with Sir John Cheke; 1571).

**Ha′den** (hā′d'n), Sir **Francis Seymour.** 1818–1910. English surgeon and etcher; practiced successfully in London. In etching, devoted himself esp. to landscapes.

**Had′field** (hăd′fēld), Sir **Robert Abbott.** 1858–1940. English metallurgist; inventor of manganese steel, silicon steel, and other alloy steels. Author of *Metallurgy and Its Influence on Modern Progress* (1925).

**Ha′dik** (hä′dĭk), **Andreas.** Count **Hadik von Fu′tak** (fôn fo͞o′täk). 1710–1790. Austrian general; distinguished himself in Seven Years' War; commanded Austrian army in campaign against Turkey (1789).

**Ha′ding′** (å′dăɴzh′), **Jane.** *Stage name of* **Jeanne Alfrédine Tré′fou′ret′** (trā′fo͞o′rĕ′). 1859–1941. French actress; m. Victor Koning (1884; divorced 1887). Created title roles in Daudet's *Sapho* and Sardou's *Marcelle,* and role of Claire in Ohnet's *Maître de Forges;* at Gymnase in Paris (after 1885) as leading lady in high comedy.

**Had′ley** (hăd′lĭ), **Arthur Twining.** 1856–1930. American economist and educator, b. New Haven, Conn. Grad. Yale (1876). Postgraduate study, U. of Berlin (1877–79). Taught, Yale (from 1879); professor (from 1886). President, Yale (1899–1921). Author of *Railroad Transportation* (1885), *Economics* (1896), *Standards of Political Morality* (1907), *Some Influences in Modern Philosophic Thought* (1913). Special editor for economics, *Webster's New International Dictionary, Second Edition.* His father, **James** (1821–1872), was a philologist; grad. Yale (1842); taught at Yale (from 1845), professor of Greek (from 1851); author of *Greek Grammar*...(1860), and *History of the English Language,* published in introduction to *Webster's Unabridged Dictionary.*

**Hadley, Henry Kimball.** 1871–1937. American composer, b. Somerville, Mass. Conductor, San Francisco orchestra (1911–15), and Manhattan Symphony Orchestra in New York (from 1929). His symphony *The Four Seasons* won the Paderewski and New England Conservatory prizes (1902); other works include a cantata *In Musical Praise,* symphonic poems *Salome, Lucifer,* and *The Culprit Fay,* a lyric drama *Merlin and Vivian,* operas *Safie, Azora, Bianca,* and *Cleopatra's Night,* chamber music, piano pieces, and songs.

**Hadley, Herbert Spencer.** 1872–1927. American political leader; adm. to bar; practiced, Kansas City, Mo. Attorney general of Missouri (1905–09); prosecuted Standard Oil Co. Governor of Missouri (1909–13).

**Hadley, John.** 1682–1744. English mathematician and mechanician; invented first serviceable reflecting telescope (1719–20), and a reflecting quadrant (Hadley's quadrant). See Thomas GODFREY (1704–49).

**Had′ow** (hăd′ō), Sir **William Henry.** 1859–1937. English educator and writer on music. Compiler, with G. E. Hadow, of *Oxford Treasury of English Literature* (3 vols., 1906–08); author of *Studies in Modern Music* (2 vols., 1894, 1895) and *English Music* (1931); editor of *Oxford History of Music* (1901–06).

**Ha′dri·an** (hā′drĭ·ăn). Name of six popes. See ADRIAN.

**Hadrian** *or* **A′dri·an** (ā′drĭ·ăn). *Lat.* **Publius Aelius Ha′dri·a′nus** (hā′drĭ·ā′nŭs). 76–138 A.D. Roman emperor (117–138), b. Rome. Nephew of Trajan; m. Sabina, grandniece of Trajan; accompanied Trajan on many of his expeditions. On becoming emperor, established the river Euphrates as eastern boundary of Roman empire; traveled throughout all parts of the empire; visited Britain (119) and caused construction (120–123) of wall (Hadrian's Wall) from Solway Firth to mouth of

Tyne; resided in Athens (132–133); promulgated *Edictum Perpetuum* (132); suppressed revolt of Jews under Bar Cocheba (132–135); spent last years of life at Rome and Tibur. Strengthened monarchical system of Rome; rebuilt and named Hadrianopolis (modern Adrianople) and erected many fine edifices in Rome, including the mausoleum (now Castel Sant' Angelo), temple to Venus and Roma, the Aelian bridge, etc.

**Haeb'ler** (hâp'lẽr), **Konrad**. 1857–1946. German historian.

**Haeck'el** (hĕk'ĕl), **Ernst Heinrich**. 1834–1919. German biologist and philosopher, b. Potsdam. Studied medicine and natural philosophy at Würzburg, Berlin, and Vienna. Professor of zoology, Jena (1865–1908). On scientific expeditions to the Canary Islands (1866–67), Red Sea (1873), Ceylon (1881–82), Java (1900–01), etc. First German advocate of organic evolution; enunciated biogenetic law that in the development of the individual animal the stages through which the species has passed in the course of its historic evolution are repeated; first to draw up a genealogical tree relating the various orders of animals; exponent of monistic philosophy. Author of *Monographie der Radiolarien* (1862), *Generelle Morphologie der Organismen* (1866), *Natürliche Schöpfungsgeschichte* (1868), *Anthropogenie oder Entwicklungsgeschichte des Menschen* (1874), *Studien zur Gasträatheorie* (1877), *Monismus als Band zwischen Religion und Wissenschaft* (1892), *Welträtsel* (1899), etc.

**Hae'ring** (hâ'rĭng), **Theodor**. 1848–1928. German Protestant theologian; professor, Zurich (1886), Göttingen (1889), Tübingen (1895). His son **Theodor** (1884– ), philosopher; professor, Tübingen (1919); author of *Die Struktur der Weltgeschichte* (1921), *Philosophie der Naturwissenschaft* (1923), *Hegel* (1928), etc.

**Haesch'e** (hĕsh'ē), **William Edwin**. 1867–1929. American composer of symphonies, symphonic poems, choral works, and pieces for piano and violin.

**Hae'se·ler** (hâ'zĕ·lẽr), Count **Gottlieb von**. 1836–1919. German soldier; general of division (1886); field marshal (1903); during World War, military adviser to German crown prince, esp. during Verdun attack (1916).

**Haetzer**. See Ludwig HETZER.

**Haff'kine** (?hăf'kĭn), **Waldemar Mordecai Wolff**. 1860–1930. Bacteriologist, b. Odessa, Russia. Assistant to Pasteur in Paris (1889–93). Founded research laboratory in Bombay, India; discovered and used method of inoculation against cholera (1893–94), by which 42,000 persons were treated in 28 months; introduced into India a successful method of inoculation against plague (1897).

**Ha·fiz'** (hȧ·fēz'), Mulai. See ABD-AL-HAFIZ.

**Ha·fiz'** (hä·fĭz'). **Shams ud-din Mohammed**. Persian lyric poet of 14th century; studied mystic philosophy under a chief of an order of dervishes and joined order; became professor of Koranic exegesis in college which vizier of Persia founded esp. for him. Chief work, *Divan*, a collection of short odes known as gazels.

**Haf'sid** (hăf'sĭd) *or* **Haf'site** (-sīt). Name of Moslem Berber dynasty ruling in Tunis and Tripoli (1228–1574) until overthrown by Turks.

**Haf'stein** (häv'stēēn), **Hannes**. 1861–1922. Icelandic statesman and poet; leader of home rule party in Iceland. His lyric poems were collected and published (1893).

**Ha'gar** (hā'gär; -gẽr). *In Douay Version* **A'gar** (ā'gär; -gẽr). In Bible, Abraham's concubine and mother of Ishmael (*q.v.*), with whom she was driven into the wilderness because of Sarah's jealousy (*Genesis* xvi; xxi. 8–21).

**Hag'berg'** (häg'băr'y'), **Karl August**. 1810–1864. Swedish writer; translated Shakespeare (12 vols., 1847–51) and made study of Old Norse dialects.

**Ha'ge·dorn** (hä'gĕ·dôrn), **Friedrich von**. 1708–1754. German poet; author of *Fabeln und Erzählungen* (1738), *Moralische Gedichte* (1750), etc.

**Hag'e·dorn** (hăg'ĕ·dôrn), **Hermann**. 1882–1964. American poet, novelist, and critic. Author of *The Woman of Corinth* (1908), *A Troop of the Guard* (verse, 1909), *Faces in the Dawn* (novel, 1914), *Makers of Madness* (play, 1914), *Barbara Picks a Husband* (novel, 1918), *Ladders Through the Blue* (verse, 1925), biographies of Leonard Wood, E. A. Robinson, and others, *Combat at Midnight* (verse, 1940), and books on Theodore Roosevelt, including *The Bugle that Woke America* (1940).

**Hageladas**. See AGELADAS.

**Ha'ge·mann** (hä'gĕ·män), **Carl**. 1871–1945. German theater director and writer on the theater.

**Ha'gen** (hä'gĕn), **August**. 1797–1880. German writer; author of the novel *Norica* (1827), and *Künstlergeschichten* (4 vols., 1833–40).

**Hagen, Friedrich Heinrich von der**. 1780–1856. German philologist.

**Hagen, Johannes Georg**. 1847–1930. Austrian mathematician and astronomer; studied theology in England, joining Society of Jesus. Director, Georgetown U. observatory, Washington, D.C. (1888–1905), Vatican observatory, Rome (from 1906). Investigated and classified variable stars; also examined the dark nebulae.

**Hagen, Theodor**. 1842–1919. German landscapist.

**Ha'gen** (hā'gĕn), **Walter C**. 1892–1969. American professional golf player. Winner of British open championship (1922, 1924, 1928, 1929); also, twice winner of the American open championship, once of the French open championship. Captained American team in winning the Ryder cup competition against the British team, at Worcester, Mass. (1927).

**Ha'gen·bach** (hä'gĕn·bäκ), **Karl Rudolf**. 1801–1874. Swiss-German Protestant theologian.

**Ha'gen·beck** (hä'gĕn·bĕk), **Karl**. 1844–1913. German animal trainer and circus director; established (1907) zoological garden near Hamburg; toured European cities (from 1875) exhibiting animals from his collection; visited U.S. during Chicago World's Fair (1893).

**Ha'ge·rup** (hä'gĕ·rŏŏp), **Georg Francis**. 1853–1921. Norwegian jurist and statesman; minister of justice (1893); head of ministry (1895–98, 1903–05). Appointed member of Hague Tribunal (1903).

**Hag'ga·i** (hăg'â·ī). *In Douay Bible* **Ag·ge'us** (ă·gē'ŭs). One of minor Hebrew prophets; flourished during reign of Darius I (c. 520 B.C.). Old Testament book of *Haggai* contains four prophecies addressed by him to Zerubbabel and the people, urging completion of the temple.

**Hag'gard** (hăg'ẽrd), Sir **Henry Rider**. 1856–1925. English novelist, b. in Norfolk. In government service in South Africa. Best known for romantic novels written against a South African background, as *King Solomon's Mines* (1885), *Allan Quatermain* (1887), *She* (1887), *Ayesha* (1905).

**Haggard, Howard Wilcox**. 1891–1959. American physician and educator; teacher of physiology, Yale (from 1919). Author of *Are You Intelligent?* (1926), *Devils, Drugs and Doctors* (1929), *Man and His Body* (1938), etc.

**Hag'gin** (hăg'ĭn), **Ben Al'i** (ăl'ĭ). 1882–1951. American portrait painter and stage designer, b. New York City. Among his many notable portraits are those of Kitty Gordon and Mary Garden; designed sets for Beaux Arts Ball (1932) and for Ziegfeld productions.

**Hague** (hāg), **Arnold**. 1840–1917. American geologist, in U.S. geological survey service (1879–1917); special work, survey of Yellowstone National Park.

**Hague, Frank**. 1876–1956. American politician; mayor of Jersey City (1917–47).

**Hahn** (hän), **Hermann.** 1868–1945. German sculptor. Among his sculptures are the Liszt monument (Weimar), Luther monument (Speyer), Moltke monument (Bremen), Goethe monument (Chicago), and portrait busts.

**Hahn, Ludwig Albert.** 1889–1968. German banker and economist.

**Hahn, Otto.** 1879–1968. German chemist; discovered (with Lise Meitner) protoactinium; awarded 1944 Nobel prize in chemistry for work on atomic fission, and 1966 Fermi Award (with Lise Meitner and Fritz Strassman).

**Hahn** (hän), **Reynaldo.** 1874–1947. Venezuelan composer in France; composer of operas, an operetta, and songs.

**Häh′nel** (hâ′nĕl), **Ernst.** 1811–1891. German sculptor; executed bronze statue of Beethoven (Bonn), statue of King Frederick Augustus II (Dresden), equestrian statue of Prince Schwarzenberg (Vienna), and portrait busts.

**Hähnel, Jakob.** See HANDL.

**Hah′ne·mann** (hä′nĕ·män), **Samuel,** *in full* **Christian Friedrich Samuel.** 1755–1843. German physician and founder of homeopathy, b. Meissen. Docent, Leipzig (1816–22); retired to Cöthen after being driven from Leipzig by apothecaries for dispensing medicines; removed to Paris (1835). While translating Cullen's *Materia Medica* into German, noticed similarity between effects of Peruvian bark (cinchona) on a healthy person and the symptoms of disease for the cure of which the bark was used; as result of further investigation, announced the principle that a disease could be cured by a drug that would produce in a healthy person symptoms similar to those in a diseased one (1796); expounded homeopathic system of medicine in his *Organon der Rationellen Heilkunde* (1810).

**Hahn′–Hahn′** (hän′hän′), Countess **Ida von.** 1805–1880. German writer; m. her cousin Count Friedrich Wilhelm Adolf von Hahn (1826; soon separated). Adopted Roman Catholic faith (1850) and entered convent (1852); founded convent at Mainz (1854). Author of lyric verse and novels.

**Hai′dar** (*or* **Hy′der**) **A·li′** (hī′dăr [hī′dẽr] ă·lī′). 1722–1782. Mohammedan prince of India, ruler of Mysore (1759–82). Of obscure birth; joined Mysore army (1749); became virtual ruler (1761) and assumed title of maharaja (1766). Conquered neighboring states; fought against British the First Mysore War (1767–69), ended by treaty to his advantage; defeated by the Marathas (1770–71). In alliance with the French began Second Mysore War (1780–84); opposed by Warren Hastings; invaded the Carnatic (1780); defeated by Sir Eyre Coote at Porto Novo and in other battles (1781); died suddenly, leaving campaign to his son Tipu Sahib (*q.v.*).

**Hai′ding·er** (hī′dĭng·ẽr), **Wilhelm Karl von.** 1795–1871. Austrian mineralogist and geologist. Discovered Haidinger's brushes, a phenomenon by means of which plane polarized light can be detected. Edited a geognostic map of Austria.

**Haig** (hāg), **Douglas.** 1st Earl **Haig.** 1861–1928. British soldier; engaged in Sudan (1898), Boer War (1899–1902), India (1903–06); major general (1904), lieutenant general (1910), general (1914), field marshal (1917). In World War I (1914–18), commanded army (1914-15); commander in chief of expeditionary forces in France and Flanders (1915–19). After the war, commander in chief (1919–21) of the Home Forces in Great Britain. Created earl (1919).

**Haight** (hīt), **Charles Coolidge.** 1841–1917. American architect; office in New York (1867). Examples of his work: Columbia Library; Lawyer's Title Insurance Co. of New York building; New York Cancer Hospital; Vanderbilt Hall and Phelps Hall, Yale.

**Hailes, Lord.** = *David Dalrymple* (1726–1792), under DALRYMPLE family.

**Hai′le Se·las′sie** (hī′lĕ sĭl·lä′syĕ; *freq. Angl.* hī′lē sĕ·lăs′ĭ *or*-lä′·sĭ). Ras **Taffari** *or* **Tafari.** 1891–1975. Son of Ras Makonnen. Emperor of Ethiopia (1930–36); took name Haile Selassie when crowned king (1928). Driven from Ethiopia by Italian conquest and occupation (1936–41); lived in England; restored to throne (1941) after successful British campaign against Italians in East Africa (1940–41); deposed Sept. 1974.

**Hai′ley** (hā′lĭ), **Malcolm.** 1st Baron **Hailey.** 1872–1969. English colonial administrator; governor of Punjab (1924–28) and United Provinces (1928–30, 1931–34). Director of African Research Survey (1935) and author of *An African Survey* (1938).

**Hail′mann** (hīl′măn; -män), **William Nicholas.** 1836–1920. Educator, b. Glarus, Switzerland; to U.S. (1852). Leader in establishing kindergartens and in spreading the doctrines of Froebel.

**Hail′sham** (hāl′shăm), 1st Viscount. **Douglas McGarel Hogg** (hŏg). 1872–1950. British jurist. Served in Boer War. Called to bar (1902); M.P. (1922–28). Attorney general (1922–24; 1924–28); lord chancellor (1928–29); secretary of state for war (1931–35) and leader of House of Lords; lord chancellor (1935–38); lord president of the council (May–Nov., 1938).

**Haines** (hānz), **Thomas Harvey.** 1871–1951. American psychologist and psychiatrist; professor of nervous and mental diseases (1915–21), Ohio State. Worked on mental measurements, on special tests for the blind, on crime and mental deficiency, etc.

**Hai′nisch** (hī′nĭsh), **Michael.** 1858–1940. German scholar and statesman; first president of the Austrian Republic (1920–28); minister of commerce (1929–30). His mother, **Marianne Hainisch** (1839–?), was a leader of the feminist movement in Austria.

**Hajjaj, al–.** *Arab.* **al–Ḥajjāj ibn–Yūsuf.** 661–?716 A.D. Viceroy and general of Eastern caliphate during reigns of Abd-al-Malik (692–705) and Walid I (705–715). Governor of Arabia; besieged and took Mecca (692); conquered Yemen and Hejaz; made governor of Iraq (694), put down revolt with great cruelty (703); promoted irrigation and agriculture.

**Haj′ji Khal′fah** (häj′jĭ кăl′fă). *Arab.* **Ḥājji Khalfah,** *literally* "assessor who has made the pilgrimage." *Real name* **Mustafa ibn–Abdallah.** *Called also* **Ka′tib Che·le·bi′** (kä′tĭb chĕ·lĕ·bē′), *i.e.* "noble secretary." 1600?–1658. Turkish historian and bibliographer; studied at Constantinople (1633–48); appointed (1648) khalfa (assessor or lieutenant) at Imperial Coll., Constantinople. Wrote in Turkish a general history and an Oriental geography; wrote in Arabic several historical works, including *Kashf al-Ẓunūn*, an elaborate bibliographical lexicon of more than 25,000 books in Arabic, Turkish, and Persian (translated into Latin by Flügel as *Lexicon Bibliographicum et Encyclopaedicum*, Leipzig, 1835–58).

**Ha·kam′** (hă·kăm′). *Also, less correctly,* **Ha·kim′** (-kĭm′). *Arab.* **al–Ḥakam.** Name of two rulers of Córdoba. **Hakam I** (d. 822); emir (796–822); put down revolts in Córdoba (805, 814) and Toledo (814). **Hakam II** (913?–976); caliph (961–976); patron of learning; made U. of Córdoba greatest educational institution in world at that time; continued wars against Christian Spain, forcing peace (970); brought Fatimid dynasty in Morocco to end (973).

**Hake** (hāk), **Thomas Gordon.** 1809–1895. English physician and poet; practiced in London. Published several volumes of verse.

**Ha′kim, al–** (ăl·hä′kĭm). *Arab.* **abu–'Ali Manṣūr**

**al-Ḥākim.** 985–1021. Fatimid caliph (996–1021) called "the Mad Caliph." Reign marked by atrocities, destruction of Christian churches, including (1009) the Holy Sepulcher at Jerusalem, and stringent measures imposed on non-Moslems; tried to make Shiism the orthodox religion of Egypt; declared himself incarnation of the Deity and was so accepted by new sect of Druses (see al-DARAZI).

**Hakim, Hashim ibn–.** See al-MOKANNA.

**Ha'king** (hā'kĭng), Sir **Richard Cyril Byrne.** 1862–1945. British army officer; in World War I, lieutenant general (1915) commanding 11th army corps; general (1925); retired (1927).

**Hak'luyt** (hăk'lo͞ot), **Richard**. 1552?–1616. English geographer; educ. Oxford; took holy orders and became (1603) archdeacon of Westminster; member of Virginia Company of London, organized for colonizing Virginia. Chief work, the compilation *Principall Navigations, Voiages, and Discoveries of the English Nation* (1589; enlarged 3-vol. edition, 1598–1600).

**Hako** *or* **Hakon.** Variants of HAAKON.

**Hal'be** (häl'bĕ), **Max.** 1865–1945. German playwright and novelist. Among his many plays are *Freie Liebe* (1890), *Jugend* (1893), *Mutter Erde* (1897), *Der Strom* (1903); among his novels, *Die Tat des Dietrich Stobäus* (1901) and *Jo* (1916).

**Halberstadt, Madman of.** See CHRISTIAN OF BRUNSWICK.

**Hal'big** (häl'bĭĸ), **Johann.** 1814–1882. German sculptor; among his sculptures are the great sandstone Crucifixion group (Oberammergau), and an equestrian statue of William I of Württemberg (Cannstatt).

**Hal'dane** (hôl'dān). Name of distinguished Scottish family including:

**James Alexander** (1768–1851), clergyman; became (1799) first Congregational minister in Scotland. His brother **Robert** (1764–1842), evangelist and religious writer; co-operated with James in religious work in Edinburgh; carried on evangelistic work in Geneva and southern France (1816–19).

Children of James's son Robert and his wife Mary Elizabeth Burdon-Sanderson:

(1) **Richard Burdon** (1856–1928), Viscount **Haldane of Cloan** (klōn). Nephew of Sir John Scott Burdon-Sanderson (*q.v.*). British lawyer, philosopher, and statesman; called to bar (1879); queen's counsel (1890). M.P. (1885–1911); created viscount (1911); secretary of state for war (1905–12); reorganized British army, and formed the territorial reserve; lord chancellor (1912–15; 1924); head of Labor party opposition in House of Lords (1925–28). O.M. (1916). Author of *The Pathway to Reality* (1903), *The Reign of Relativity* (1921), *The Philosophy of Humanism* (1922), *Human Experience* (1926).

(2) **John Scott** (1860–1936), scientist; conducted extensive researches into mining and industrial diseases caused by poor ventilation; discovered that regulation of breathing is normally determined by tension of carbon dioxide in respiratory center of brain; served as director of a mining research laboratory (from 1912; laboratory affiliated with Birmingham U., from 1921). Author of ...*Causes of Death in Colliery Explosions* (1896), *Mechanism, Life and Personality* (1913), *Respiration* (1922), *Materialism* (1932), *The Philosophy of a Biologist* (1935), etc.

(3) **Elizabeth Sanderson** (1862–1937). Studied nursing; vice-chairman of territorial nursing service, and for some years manager of Edinburgh Royal Infirmary; took active part in public affairs; first woman justice of the peace in Scotland (1920). Author of *British Nurse in Peace and War* (1923), *George Eliot and her Times* (1927), *Mrs. Gaskell and her Friends* (1930), *From One Century to Another* (1937), etc.

Children of John Scott Haldane:

(1) **John Burdon Sanderson** (1892–1964), scientist; professor of genetics, London U. (1933–37); professor of biometry, University Coll., London (1937–1957). Author of *Possible Worlds* (1927), *Animal Biology* (with J. S. Huxley, 1927), *Science and Ethics* (1928), *Enzymes* (1930), *The Inequality of Man* (1932), *The Causes of Evolution* (1933), *Fact and Faith* (1934), *Heredity and Politics* (1938), *The Marxist Philosophy and the Sciences* (1938), *Science and Everyday Life* (1939), *New Paths in Genetics* (1941), etc.; m. (1926; dissolved 1945) **Charlotte,** *nee* **Fran'ken** (frăng'kĕn) (1894–1969), author; m. (1945) **Helen Spurway.**

(2) **Naomi.** See Naomi MITCHISON.

**Hal'de·man** (hôl'dĕ·măn), **Samuel Ste'man** (stē'măn). 1812–1880. American naturalist and philologist.

**Hal'de·man–Jul'ius** (-jo͞ol'yŭs), **Emanuel.** *Orig. surname* **Julius.** 1889–1951. American publisher and writer, b. Phila.; m. (1916) Marcet Haldeman (d. 1941), prefixed her family name to his own. Founder and head of Haldeman-Julius Publishing Co., publishers of the *Little Blue Books, Big Blue Books, The Key to Culture* and the monthly journal *The American Freeman.* Among his many books are *The Color of Life* (1920), *The Art of Reading* (1922), *An Agnostic Looks at Life* (1926), *Myths and Myth-Makers* (1927), *The Big American Parade* (1929), etc.

**Hal'der** (häl'dĕr), **Franz.** 1884–1972. German army officer; general staff officer with Bavarian infantry, World War I (1914–18); colonel general, and chief of the German General Staff (1939–42), World War II.

**Hal'di·mand** (hôl'dĭ·mănd), Sir **Frederick.** 1718–1791. Lieutenant general in British army; of Swiss birth. Served in America, at Ticonderoga (1758) and Oswego (1759), with Jeffrey Amherst's expedition against Montreal (1760). Commander in Florida (1766–78); governor and commander in chief in Canada (1778–85).

**Hale** (hāl), **Edward Everett.** 1822–1909. Son of Nathan Hale (1784–1863); nephew of Edward Everett. American Unitarian clergyman and author, b. Boston. Grad. Harvard (1839). Pastor, Church of the Unity, Worcester, Mass. (1846–56); pastor, South Congregational Church, Boston (1856–1901). Chaplain, U.S. Senate (1903–09). Identified with civic improvement and philanthropic work in Boston. His famous short story *The Man Without a Country* appeared in *The Atlantic Monthly* (Dec., 1863). Author of *In His Name* (1873), *A New England Boyhood* (1893), *James Russell Lowell and His Friends* (1899), *Memories of a Hundred Years* (2 vols., 1902), etc. His son **Edward Everett** (1863–1932), educator, was professor of English, Union College (1895–1932). Author of *Constructive Rhetoric, Lowell, Dramatists of Today.* See Lucretia P. HALE.

**Hale, Eugene.** 1836–1918. American political leader, b. Turner, Me. Republican member, U.S. House of Representatives (1869–79) and U.S. Senate (1881–1911).

**Hale, Gardner.** 1894–1932. American mural painter.

**Hale, George Ellery.** 1868–1938. American astronomer, b. Chicago. Organizer and director of Yerkes Observatory (1895–1905) and professor of astrophysics, U. of Chicago (1897–1905). Organizer and director of Mount Wilson Observatory under Carnegie Institution of Washington (1904–23). Performed important research work in solar and stellar spectroscopy; invented (simultaneously with the Frenchman Deslandres) the spectroheliograph (c. 1892). An editor of *Astronomy and Astrophysics* (1892–95) and *Astrophysical Journal* (1895–1935). Author of *The Study of Stellar Evolution, Ten*

*Years' Work of a Mountain Observatory, Beyond the Milky Way, Signals from the Stars.*

**Hale, Horatio Emmons.** See Sarah Josepha HALE.

**Hale, Irving.** 1862–1930. American brigadier general; founder of Veterans of Foreign Wars.

**Hale, John Parker.** 1806–1873. American statesman, b. Rochester, N.H. Member, U.S. House of Representatives (1843–45); U.S. senator (1847–53), first antislavery man elected to the senate; again senator (1855–65). U.S. minister to Spain (1865–69).

**Hale, Lucretia Peabody.** 1820–1900. Daughter of Nathan Hale (1784–1863). American writer, b. Boston; noted for two children's books, *The Peterkin Papers* (1880) and *The Last of the Peterkins* (1886).

**Hale,** Sir **Matthew.** 1609–1676. English jurist. Justice of common pleas (1654); M.P. (1654–60); lord chief baron of exchequer (1660); lord chief justice of King's Bench (1671). Author of *Contemplations, Moral and Divine, The Primitive Origination of Mankind Considered,* etc.

**Hale, Nathan.** 1755–1776. American Revolutionary hero, b. Coventry, Conn. Grad. Yale (1773). Taught school (1773–75). Lieutenant in Continental army (1775); captain (1776). Volunteered for hazardous spy duty behind British lines on Long Island (1776); captured by British, Sept. 21; hanged the following morning. His last words are said to have been, "I only regret that I have but one life to lose for my country."

**Hale, Nathan.** 1784–1863. Nephew of Nathan Hale (1755–1776). American journalist; owner and editor, Boston *Daily Advertiser* (1814–54); introduced editorials for first time as a newspaper feature. A founder of *North American Review* (1815) and *Christian Examiner* (1824). See Edward Everett HALE and Lucretia HALE.

**Hale, Philip.** 1854–1934. American music critic; organist in Boston (1889–1905); music critic for Boston *Post* (1890–91), Boston *Journal* (1891–1903), Boston *Herald* (1903–34).

**Hale, Philip Leslie.** 1865–1931. Son of Edward Everett Hale. American painter and art critic; studio, Boston; known esp. as a figure painter.

**Hale, Sarah Josepha,** *nee* **Bu'ell** (bū'ĕl). 1788–1879. American writer and editor; m. David Hale (1813; d. 1822). Editor, *Ladies' Magazine,* Boston (1828–37), *Godey's Lady's Book* (1837–77). Author of *Northwood* (novel, 1827), *Poems for Our Children* (containing the famous *Mary's Lamb,* 1830), *Woman's Record, or Sketches of Distinguished Women from the Creation to the Present Day* (1853). Her son **Horatio Emmons** (1817–1896) was an ethnologist; member of scientific corps of Wilkes Exploring Expedition (1838–42); made study of American Indian languages.

**Hale, William Bayard.** 1869–1924. American clergyman and journalist, b. Richmond, Ind. Episcopal clergyman (1893–1900). Editor, *Cosmopolitan Magazine* (1900), *Current Literature* (1901); on staff of New York *World* (1902); managing editor, Philadelphia *Public Ledger* (1903–07), New York *Times, Saturday Review of Books* (1907–09); on staff of *World's Work* (1909). President Wilson's confidential agent in Mexico (1913). Retained as adviser for German propaganda in U.S. (1917); paid directly from Berlin; disgraced by exposure of these facts.

**Hale, William Gardner.** 1849–1928. American classical scholar; influential in establishing American School of Classical Studies in Rome; first director of this school (1895–96).

**Hale, William Jay.** 1876–1955. American chemist; sometimes called father of chemurgy; patented processes for manufacture of phenol, aniline, acetic acid, and their derivatives.

**Há'lek** (hä'lĕk), **Vítězslav.** 1835–1874. Czech poet; best known as lyricist and founder (with Neruda) of modern school of Czech poetry.

**Hales** (hālz), **John.** 1584–1656. English clergyman; called "the Ever-Memorable." Canon of Windsor and chaplain to Laud (1639); in retirement during Commonwealth period. Published anonymously a tract on *Schism and Schismaticks* (1642); chief work, *Golden Remains* (publ. 1659).

**Hales, Stephen.** 1677–1761. English physiologist. Invented many mechanical devices, including artificial ventilators. Author of *Vegetable Staticks* (1727), credited with inaugurating the science of plant physiology.

**ha-Levi** *or* **Halevi, Judah.** See JUDAH HA-LEVI.

**Ha'lé'vy'** (hȧ'lā'vē'). *Name assumed by* **Jacques Fromental Élie Lé'vy'** (lā'vē'). 1799–1862. French composer, b. Paris. Studied under Berton and Cherubini. Professor of harmony, Paris conservatory (1827), and of composition (1833); had among his pupils Gounod and Bizet. Composer of many operas, including *La Juive* (1835), *L'Éclair* (1835), *Le Juif Errant* (1852), *La Magicienne* (1858). His brother **Léon Halévy** (1802–1883) was a poet and writer; author of books on Jewish history, a few plays, and several volumes of verse. A son of Léon, **Ludovic** (1834–1908), was a playwright and novelist; collaborator frequently with Henri Meilhac; among his many works were *La Belle Hélène* (1864), *Barbe Bleue* (1866), *La Périchole* (1868), *Froufrou* (1869), *Carmen* (from Mérimée, 1875), and the novels *Un Mariage d'Amour* (1881), *L'Abbé Constantin* (1882), *Princesse* (1886), etc. Ludovic's two sons, **Élie** (1870–1937) and **Daniel** (1872–1962), were both writers; Élie upon philosophical and historical subjects, as in his *La Formation du Radicalisme Philosophique* (3 vols., 1901–04) and *Histoire du Peuple Anglais au XIXe Siècle* (1912 ff.); Daniel upon social and philosophical subjects, as in his *Essai sur le Mouvement Ouvrier en France* (1901), *La Vie de Frédéric Nietzsche* (1909), *Jules Michelet* (1928).

**Halévy, Joseph.** 1827–1917. Orientalist, b. Adrianople, Turkey; became naturalized Frenchman. Advanced theory that the Sumerian people had never existed and that the literature ascribed to them was merely a secret writing invented by the Babylonian priesthood.

**Hal'hed** (hôl'hĕd; hăl'-), **Nathaniel Brassey.** 1751–1830. English Orientalist, in service of East India Company. Reputedly first to call attention to philological affinity between Sanskrit words and words in Persian, Arabic, and even Greek and Latin.

**Hal'i·bur'ton** (hăl'ĭ·bûr't'n), **Hugh.** Pseudonym of James Logie ROBERTSON.

**Haliburton, Thomas Chandler.** *Pseudonym* **Sam Slick** (slĭk). 1796–1865. Canadian jurist and humorist, b. Windsor, Nova Scotia. Judge of supreme court, Nova Scotia (1842–56). To England (1856); M.P. (1859–65). Created character of Sam Slick in his books *The Clockmaker, or Sayings and Doings of Sam Slick* (1st series, 1837; 2d, 1838; 3d, 1840), *The Attaché, or Sam Slick in England* (1843–44), etc.; also wrote *The Old Judge, or Life in a Colony* (1843).

**Ha·li·dé' E·dib'** (hä·lē·dā' ĕ·dēb'). 1885–1964. Turkish leader in movement for emancipation of women, b. Constantinople. First Moslem girl to graduate from American College for Girls, Constantinople (1901). m. Salih Bey (1901; divorced), Adnan Bey (1917). Supporter of the Young Turk movement (1909). Joined Nationalist party (1919) and was supporter of Mustafa Kemal; served in army in war against the Greeks, and was commissioned colonel (1922). Later, under suspicion of plotting against Kemal, was forced to flee Turkey;

resided for a time in London, and lectured in U.S. Author of several novels, and of *Memoirs of Halidé Edib* (1926), etc.

**Hal'i·fax** (hăl'ĭ·făks). (1) Earls of. See Charles MONTAGU. (2) Marquis of. See Sir George SAVILE.

**Halifax,** 1st Viscount. Sir **Charles Wood.** 1800–1885. English political leader. M.A., Oxon. (1824); chancellor of exchequer (1846); first lord of the admiralty (1855); secretary of state for India (1859–66); lord privy seal (1870–74).

**Halifax,** Earl of. **Edward Frederick Lindley Wood.** 1881-1959. English statesman, grandson of 1st Viscount Halifax. M.A., Oxon. M.P. (1910–25); undersecretary for colonies (1921–22); minister of agriculture (1924–25). Succeeded Lord Reading as governor general of India (1926–31), being raised to peerage as Baron **Ir'win** (ûr'wĭn) **of Kirk'by Un'der·dale** [kûr'bĭ ŭn'dẽr·dāl] (1925); strove to quiet widespread boycotts, riots, strikes that had prevailed from 1921, and to counteract obstruction offered by Swarajist and Liberal politicians because of noninclusion of Indians on parliamentary commission of Sir John Simon (1927); co-operated with Gandhi. Secretary for war (1935); lord privy seal (1935–37); leader of House of Lords (1935–38); lord president of the council (1937–38); foreign secretary (1938–40); ambassador to U.S. (1941–46).

**Halifax, John of.** fl. 1230. See Johannes de SACROBOSCO.

**Ha'lir** (hä'lĭr), **Karl.** 1859–1909. Bohemian violinist; studied under Joachim.

**Hal'kett** (hôl'kĕt, -kĭt; hăl'-; hăk'ĕt, -ĭt), **Hugh.** Baron **von Halkett.** 1783–1863. Hanoverian general, and colonel in the British service; distinguished himself at Copenhagen (1807), La Albuera (1811), Salamanca (1812), and during the Burgos retreat (1812); commanded two brigades of Hanoverian militia at Waterloo (1815).

**Hall** (hôl), **Abraham Oakey.** 1826–1898. American lawyer and politician; district attorney, New York (1855–58; 1862–68). Henchman of Boss Tweed (*q.v.*). Joined Tammany Hall organization (1864). Mayor of New York (1868–72) when Tweed Ring was looting the city; indicted and tried for corruption, but acquitted (1872).

**Hall, Arnold Bennett.** 1881–1936. American educator, b. Franklin, Ind. President, U. of Oregon (1926–32). Director, institute for government research, Brookings Institution, Washington, D.C. (1933–36).

**Hall, A'saph** (ā'săf). 1829–1907. American astronomer, b. Goshen, Conn. Professor of mathematics in U.S. Naval Observatory, Washington, D.C. (1862–91, retired); lectured at Harvard (1896–1901). Discovered (August, 1877) the two satellites of planet Mars, which he named Deimos and Phobos.

**Hall, Basil.** 1788–1844. Son of Sir James Hall. British naval officer and writer; interviewed Napoleon at St. Helena; chief work, *Fragments of Voyages and Travels* (1831–33).

**Hall** (häl), **Carl Christian.** 1812–1888. Danish statesman; prime minister (1857–59, 1860–63).

**Hall** (hôl), **Charles Cuthbert.** 1852–1908. American Presbyterian clergyman and educator, b. New York City. Pastor, First Presbyterian Church, Brooklyn, N.Y. (1877–97). President, Union Theol. Sem. (1897–1908).

**Hall, Charles Francis.** 1821–1871. American explorer of the Arctic; led expeditions to Arctic (1860–62, 1864–69, and 1871); on second expedition, learned from Eskimos fate of part of Franklin expedition; died in the Arctic.

**Hall, Charles Martin.** 1863–1914. American chemist and manufacturer; invented process of making aluminum inexpensively (patent issued Apr. 2, 1889). With aid of Mellon interests, formed Pittsburgh Reduction Co. to manufacture aluminum; developed into Aluminum Company of America; vice-president of this company (1890). See P. HÉROULT.

**Hall, Chester Moor.** 1703–1771. English scientist; reputed inventor of achromatic telescope (1733).

**Hall, Christopher Newman.** See under John Vine HALL.

**Hall, Edward.** d. 1547. English historian. Author of *Union of the Noble and Illustre Famelies of Lancastre and York*, commonly called *Hall's Chronicle* (1542), used as a source by Shakespeare in some of his historical plays.

**Hall, Edwin Herbert.** 1855–1938. American physicist; professor (from 1895), Harvard. Discovered (1879) the deflecting effect (Hall effect) of the magnetic field on the lines of flow in an electric circuit; investigated thermoelectric phenomena in metals, etc.

**Hall, Fitzedward.** 1825–1901. Philologist, b. Troy, N.Y. In India (1845–57, and 1860–62); professor of Sanskrit, Hindustani, and Indian jurisprudence, King's College, London (from 1862). Contributing editor, *Oxford English Dictionary* and Wright's *English Dialect Dictionary.*

**Hall, Granville Stanley.** 1846-1924. American psychologist and educator, b. Ashfield, Mass. Professor of psychology and pedagogics, Johns Hopkins (1883–88). President, Clark U. (1889–1919). Founded and edited *American Journal of Psychology* (1887). First president, American Psychological Association (1891). Author of *The Contents of Children's Minds* (1883), *Adolescence* (2 vols., 1904), *Educational Problems* (2 vols., 1911), *Jesus, the Christ, in the Light of Psychology* (2 vols., 1917), *Senescence, the Last Half of Life* (1922), *Life and Confessions of a Psychologist* (1923).

**Hall, Harry Reginald Holland.** 1873–1930. English archaeologist; on staff of British Museum, department of Egyptian and Assyrian antiquities (from 1896). In Egypt (1903–06), associated with excavation work of Egypt Exploration Fund. During World War (1914–18), served in intelligence work, esp. in Mesopotamia. After the war, directed (1919) British Museum excavation work at Ur of the Chaldees.

**Hall, Holworthy.** Pseudonym of Harold Everett PORTER.

**Hall, Isaac Hollister.** 1837–1896. American Orientalist; discovered (1876) and published (1884) Syriac manuscript of a large part of the New Testament. Member of staff, Metropolitan Museum of Art (from 1884); collaborated with Cesnola in making catalogues of Cypriote art; acknowledged authority on Syriac.

**Hall,** Sir **James.** 1761–1832. Scottish geologist and chemist; his series of experiments made to test Huttonian theories by study of Continental and Scottish geological formations is credited with inaugurating science of experimental geology.

**Hall, James.** 1793–1868. American author and jurist, b. Philadelphia. Entered army in War of 1812; court-martialed and cashiered (1817) but punishment remitted by president. Circuit judge, Illinois (1825–28). Wrote a number of books on history of, and conditions in, the West.

**Hall, James.** 1811–1898. American geologist and paleontologist, b. Hingham, Mass. State geologist of Iowa (1855–58), Wisconsin (1857–60), New York (1893). Authority on stratigraphic geology and invertebrate paleontology.

**Hall, James Norman.** 1887–1951. American writer, b. Colfax, Iowa. Ph.B., Grinnell Coll. (1910). Served in the Escadrille Lafayette (1917). Resident in Tahiti (from 1920). Coauthor with Charles Bernard Nordhoff (*q.v.*) of *The Lafayette Flying Corps* (2 vols., 1920), *Faery Lands of the South Seas* (1921), *Falcons of France* (1929), a trilogy narrating the story of the ship *Bounty* (*Mutiny on the Bounty*, 1932; *Men Against the Sea*, 1934; *Pitcairn's Island*, 1934), *The Hurricane* (1935), *The Dark River* (1936), *Botany Bay* (1941), *Men Without Country* (1942); author of *Kitchener's Mob* (1916), *Mid-Pacific* (1928), *The Tale of a Shipwreck* (1935), *The Friends* (1939), *Doctor Dogbody's Leg* (1940), *Under a Thatched Roof* (1942), etc.

**Hall,** Sir **John.** 1824–1907. New Zealand statesman; b. Hull, England; to New Zealand to engage in sheep raising (1852); prime minister of New Zealand (1879–82).

**Hall, John Vine.** 1774–1860. English bookdealer at Maidstone (1814–50); published *The Sinner's Friend*, which attained wide circulation and translation into thirty languages. His son **Christopher Newman** (1816–1902), Congregationalist clergyman in London, wrote many hymns and devotional works.

**Hall, Josef Washington.** *Pseudonym* **Upton Close** (klōs). 1894–1960. American writer and lecturer, b. Kelso, Wash.; A.B., George Washington (1915); newspaper correspondent in Far East (1917–22). Author of books on China and Japan, as *The Revolt of Asia* (1927), *Challenge—Behind the Face of Japan* (1935), etc.

**Hall, Joseph.** 1574–1656. English prelate. Bishop of Exeter (1627–41), Norwich (1641–47); impeached and imprisoned (1642) and his cathedral desecrated (1643); expelled from his palace (c. 1647). Author of verse, devotional works, satires, and controversial treatises.

**Hall, Lyman.** 1724–1790. American Revolutionary leader, b. Wallingford, Conn.; moved to Georgia; one of founders of town of Sunbury (1758); practiced medicine there. Supported colonial cause; member, Continental Congress (1775–80); a signer of Declaration of Independence. Governor of Georgia (1783).

**Hall, Marshall.** 1790–1857. English physician and physiologist; specialized in treatment of nervous diseases; discovered (1832) reflex action and published *Reflex Function of the Medulla Oblongata and Medulla Spinalis* (1833); rationalized treatment of epilepsy; introduced new method for treatment of asphyxia.

**Hall, Nathan Kelsey.** 1810–1874. American political leader; member, U.S. House of Representatives (1847–49). U.S. postmaster general (1850–52). U.S. judge, northern district of New York (1852–74).

**Hall, Radclyffe.** 1886–1943. English poet and novelist; author of *Poems of the Past and Present*, *The Forgotten Island* (verse), and the novels *The Unlit Lamp* (1924), *Adam's Breed* (1926; awarded James Tait Black prize), *The Well of Loneliness* (1928), *The Sixth Beatitude* (1936).

**Hall, Robert.** 1764–1831. English Baptist clergyman; author of *Modern Infidelity Considered with Respect to its Influence on Society* (1800), etc.

**Hall, Samuel Carter.** 1800–1889. Irish-born editor and writer in London; founded and edited *The Amulet* (1826–37); edited *Art Union Monthly*, later *Art Journal* (1839–80); published *Book of British Ballads* (1842), *Gallery of Modern Sculpture* (1849–54), etc. His wife, **Anna Maria,** *nee* **Fiel'ding** [fēl'dĭng] (1800–1881), collaborated with him; also wrote independently nine novels, including *Marian, or a Young Maid's Fortunes* (1840), *Tales of the Irish Peasantry* (1840), *Midsummer Eve, a Fairy Tale of Love* (1848).

**Hall, Samuel Read.** 1795–1877. American Congregational clergyman and educator; established training school for teachers, Concord, Vt. (incorporated 1823), first American normal school. Writer of textbooks in geology, arithmetic, grammar, history, and geography.

**Hall, Thomas Seavey.** 1827–1880. American inventor of electric automatic signal devices for use on railroads, highways, etc.

**Hall, William Edward.** 1835–1894. English legal writer; author of *International Law* (1880), etc.

**Hall, Winfield Scott.** 1861–1942. American physician and writer; professor of physiology, medical school, Northwestern (from 1895). Author of books on physiology, anatomy, sex education, sex hygiene, eugenics, marriage, etc.

**Hal'lam** (hăl'ăm), **Henry.** 1777–1859. English historian. Served for many years as commissioner of stamps; retired (1812) to devote time to historical study. Chief works, *State of Europe during the Middle Ages* (1818), *Constitutional History of England from Henry VII's Accession to the Death of George II* (1827), *Introduction to the Literature of Europe* (1837–39). His son **Arthur Henry** (1811–1833), friend of Tennyson, to whose sister he was betrothed, is subject of Tennyson's poem *In Memoriam.*

**Hal'lé** (hăl'ĕ; -ē), Sir **Charles.** *Orig.* **Karl Hal'le** (häl'ĕ). 1819–1895. German-born pianist and conductor in England (from 1848); first principal, Royal Coll. of Music at Manchester (1893).

**Hal'leck** (hăl'ĕk), **Fitz-Greene.** 1790–1867. American poet, b. Guilford, Conn. Bank clerk, New York City (1811–29); confidential clerk in John Jacob Astor's office (1832–49). Author of *Alnwick Castle, with Other Poems* (1827), *Poetical Works* (1847). Best-known poems, *Green be the turf above thee* (commemorating the death of his friend Joseph Rodman Drake) and *Marco Bozzaris* (first published in New York *Review*, June, 1825).

**Halleck, Henry Wager.** 1815–1872. American army officer; grad. U.S.M.A., West Point (1839). At outbreak of Civil War, commissioned major general; commanded Department of Missouri (1861–62); called to Washington as general in chief (1862–64); with appointment of Grant as lieutenant general, Halleck became chief of staff. After the war, commanded military division of the Pacific (1865–69) and division of the South (1869–72).

**Hal·lén'** (hȧ·lān'), **Johan Andreas.** 1846–1925. Swedish conductor and composer of operas *Harald, der Wiking*, *Hexfällen*, *Der Schatz Waldemars*, symphonic poems, chamber music, choral works, and songs.

**Hal'ler** (häl'ẽr), **Albrecht von.** 1708–1777. Swiss anatomist, physiologist, botanist, physician, and poet; studied botany of the Alps; served as professor of medicine, anatomy, surgery, and botany, Göttingen (1736–53). Author of descriptive poem *Die Alpen* (1729), the philosophical romances *Usong* (1771), *Alfred* (1773), and *Fabius and Cato* (1774), the scientific work *Elementa Physiologiae Corporis Humani* (8 vols., 1757–66) in which he enunciated the doctrine of the irritability of living tissue.

**Haller, Bertold.** 1492–1528. Swiss clergyman; pastorate at Bern (from 1519); accepted principles of Reformation (from 1522) and was influential in securing their acceptance at Bern.

**Hal'ler** (häl'lĕr), **Józef.** 1873–1960. Polish soldier; associated with Piłsudski in organizing Polish legion at outbreak of World War (1914) to oppose Russians. After treaty of Brest Litovsk (Feb. 9, 1918), left the Austrian front with 5000 men and entered the Ukraine, but was defeated by the Germans (May 15, 1918). Made his way to Paris and was put in command of Polish troops fighting with the Allies; he and his army fought the Bolsheviks in Poland (April, 1919); organized volunteer army in Poland (1920); inspector general of artillery (1923); retired (1926).

**Hal'let'** (ȧ'lĕ'), **Étienne Sulpice.** *Also* **Stephen Hallette'** (*Angl.* hă·lĕt'). 1755–1825. French architect in U.S.; submitted designs (1792) for the National Capitol at Washington, and was awarded second prize; commissioned on salary basis to revise plans of William Thornton, winner in the competition; misunderstanding led to dismissal by commissioners (June 28, 1794).

**Hal'ley** (hăl'ĭ), **Edmund.** 1656–1742. English astronomer, b. London. Made first complete observation of a transit of Mercury (1677); made observations of the comet of 1680. By his suggestions, inspired Newton to write his *Principia*, which Halley published (1687) at his own expense. Editor, Royal Society's *Transactions* (1685–93). Astronomer royal (1721). Best known for his study of comets; predicted accurately the return in 1758 of comet previously observed in 1531, 1607, and 1682 (subsequently known as Halley's comet). Also credited with originating the science of life statistics by his *Breslau Table of Mortality*.

**Hall'grīms'son** (häd''l·grēms'sŏn), **Jônas.** 1807–1844. Icelandic lyric poet; his work was influential in purifying the Icelandic language.

**Hal'li·bur'ton** (hăl'ĭ·bûr't'n), **Richard.** 1900–1939. American explorer and writer; on expedition to western Tibet (1922). Traced on foot Cortes's route in conquest of Mexico, Balboa's march across Darien; explored Yucatan, Peru, western Brazil (1928); traveled around the world in his own airplane (1931–32); traced route of first crusade, route of Alexander the Great in conquest of Asia, route of Hannibal from Carthage to Italy. Lost at sea in typhoon while sailing in a Chinese junk from Hong Kong to San Francisco (March 23–24). Also known as mountain climber and swimmer. Among his books are *The Royal Road to Romance* (1925), *The Glorious Adventure* (1927), *New Worlds to Conquer* (1929), *The Flying Carpet* (1932), *The Orient* (1937), etc.

**Halliburton, William Dobinson.** 1860–1931. English physiologist and chemist.

**Hal'li·die** (hăl'ĭ·dĭ), **Andrew Smith.** *Orig.* **Andrew Smith.** 1836–1900. Engineer and inventor, b. London, England; to California (1853); took name of his godfather. Built wire suspension bridges; invented cable railway, first introduced in San Francisco (1873).

**Hal'li·well,** *afterward* **Hal'li·well–Phil'lipps** (hăl'ĭ·wĕl[-wĕl]·fĭl'ĭps), **James Orchard.** 1820–1889. English librarian and Shakespearean scholar. Assumed wife's surname Phillipps (1872). Librarian, Jesus Coll., Cambridge; concentrated, after antiquarian studies for Camden, Percy, and Shakespeare societies, upon Shakespeare's life and editions of his works; collected Shakespearean books, mss., and rarities; published *Nursery Rhymes of England* (1845), *Dictionary of Archaic and Provincial Words* (1847), folio edition of Shakespeare (1853–65), *Outlines of Life of Shakespeare* (successive editions, 1848–87).

**Hal'lock** (hăl'ŭk), **Gerard.** 1800–1866. American journalist; one of the founders of Associated Press (1848). His Southern sympathies and advocacy of peace caused his paper, *New York Journal of Commerce*, to be barred from the mails (August, 1861) and forced his retirement. His son **Charles** (1834–1917) was founder and editor of *Forest and Stream* (1873), editor of *Nature's Realm* (1890) and *Western Field and Stream* (1896).

**Hal'lo'peau'** (ȧ'lô'pō'), **François Henri.** 1842–1919. French dermatologist; known esp. for work on leprosy and the dermatology of the extremities.

**Hal'lo·well** (hăl'ō·wĕl; -wĕl), **Robert.** 1886–1939. American painter, b. Denver, Colo. Illustrator on staff of *Century Magazine* (1910–14). A founder, and later publisher of the *New Republic* (1914–25).

**Hall–Stevenson, John.** See STEVENSON.

**Hall'ström** (hȧl'strûm), **Ivar Christian.** 1826–1901. Swedish composer of operas (*The Mountain King, Hertig Magnus*, etc.), operettas, ballet music, choral works, and Swedish folk songs.

**Hallström Per August Leonard.** 1866–1960. Swedish poet, novelist, and playwright.

**Hall'wachs** (häl'väks), **Wilhelm.** 1859–1922. German physicist; discovered Hallwachs effect, a type of photoelectric effect (1888).

**Halm** (hälm), **Friedrich.** *Pseudonym of* Baron **Eligius von Münch'–Bel'ling·hau'sen** (fôn münκ'bĕl'ĭng·hou'zĕn). 1806–1871. German poet and playwright; director of Royal Theater at Vienna (1867–70). Among his plays are *Griseldis* (1835), *Der Sohn der Wildnis* (1843), *Begum Somru* (1856), and *Wildfeuer* (1864).

**Halm, Karl von.** 1809–1882. German classical scholar.

**Ha'lo·an'der** (hä'lō·än'dẽr), **Gregor.** *Real surname* **Melt'zer** (mĕl'tsẽr). 1501–1531. German jurist.

**Hal'per** (hăl'pẽr), **Albert.** 1904– . American novelist, b. Chicago; author of *Union Square* (1933), *The Foundry* (1934), *The Chute* (1937), *Sons of the Fathers* (1940).

**Hal'pine** *or* **Hal'pin** (hăl'pĭn), **Charles Graham.** *Pseudonym* **Miles O'Reil'ly** (ō·rī'lĭ). 1829–1868. Writer, b. in Ireland; to U.S. (1851) and in journalistic work in Boston, Washington, and New York. Served in Union army during Civil War (1861–65). Author of *Life and Adventures, etc. of Private Miles O'Reilly* (1864), *Baked Meats of the Funeral...by Private M. O'Reilly* (1866).

**Hals** (häls), **Frans.** 1580?–1666. Dutch portrait and genre painter, b. Mechelen (Malines) or Antwerp. Ranked with Rembrandt, Rubens, and Vandyke as among greatest Dutch painters. Among his notable canvases are *Banquet of the Officers of St. George's Shooting Company, Governors of the Elizabeth Hospital, Laughing Cavalier, Portrait of a Lady, Jolly Trio, Herring Vender, Fool Playing a Lute, Young Married Couple.*

**Halsbury,** 1st Earl of. See Hardinge Stanley GIFFARD.

**Hal'sey** (hôl'sĭ), **John.** 1670–1716. American privateersman (1704–05); turned pirate (1705–16); operated in Red Sea and waters around Madagascar.

**Halsey,** Sir **Lionel.** 1872–1949. British naval officer; engaged at Helgoland Bight (1914) and Dogger Bank (1915); third sea lord (1917–18); commanded Australian navy (1918–20); comptroller and treasurer to prince of Wales (1920–36); vice-admiral (1921); retired (1922); admiral (1926).

**Halsey, Margaret Frances.** 1910– . American writer, b. Yonkers, N.Y.; m. Dr. Henry W. Simon (1935; div.), 2d Milton R. Stern (1944). Author of *With Malice Toward Some* (1938), *Some of My Best Friends are Soldiers* (1944).

**Halsey, William Frederick.** 1882–1959. American naval officer, b. Elizabeth, N.J.; grad. U.S.N.A., Annapolis (1904); commanded destroyer patrol force in World War I; rear admiral (1938); vice-admiral (1940); led attack on Marshall and Gilbert islands (Jan., 1942); commander of Allied naval forces in South Pacific (Oct., 1942–June, 1944); defeated Japanese in 3-day battle off Solomon Islands (Nov., 1942); admiral (Nov., 1942); commander of U.S. 3d Fleet, in Pacific (June, 1944–Nov., 1945; retired); admiral of the fleet (1945).

**Hal'sted** (hôl'stĕd; -stĭd), **William Stewart.** 1852–1922. American surgeon, b. New York City. Discovered method of anesthetizing regions of the body by injection of cocaine into certain nerves. Professor of surgery, Johns Hopkins (from 1890).

**Ham** (hăm), **Roswell Gray.** 1891– . American educator; assoc. professor of English, Yale (1920–36). President of Mt. Holyoke Coll. (1937–57).

**Ha·ma·da** (hä·mä·dä), **Kunimatsu.** 1868–1939. Japanese political leader; head of the Seiyukai, chief minority party in lower house of the legislature; speaker of house (1934–39); opposed fascism, and effected downfall of Hirota cabinet (1937).

**Ha'ma·dha'ni, al–** (ăl·hă'mă·dä'nē). *Called* **Ba·dī'' al–Za·mān'** (bă·dē' ŏŏz·ză·män'), *i.e.* Wonder of the Age. 969–1007. Moslem poet, b. Hamadan. Wrote under Persian influence; gained sobriquet from extensive knowledge of poetic forms and beauty of his style; developed new kind of poetry (magāmāt) in form of a dialogue. Poems published at Constantinople (1881).

**Ha·ma·gu·chi** (hä·mä·gōō·chē), **Yuko.** 1870–1931. Japanese statesman; vice-minister (1914–16) and minister (1924–25) of finance; minister of home affairs (1927–29); prime minister (1929–31) and head of the Minseito; supported Japan's acquiescence in London Naval Conference program (1930), arousing opposition; shot by assassin (Nov., 1930) and died six months later of wounds.

**Ha'man** (hā'măn). *In Douay Version* **A'man** (ā'măn). In Bible, chief minister of Ahasuerus and enemy of the Jews; hanged on gallows he had prepared for Mordecai (*Esther* vii. 10). Cf. ESTHER.

**Ha'mann** (hä'män), **Johann Georg.** 1730–1788. German writer, called "the Magus of the North." Translator at Königsberg (1767–77); storekeeper in mercantile house (1777–84). His writings, obscure and difficult to understand, include *Sokratische Denkwürdigkeiten* (1759) and *Kreuzzüge des Philologen* (1762).

**Ham'bidge** (hăm'bĭj), **Jay,** *orig.* **Edward John.** 1867–1924. Artist, b. Simcoe, Ontario; to U.S. (1882). Originator of theory of dynamic symmetry, a system of proportions believed to be observed in ancient Greek art; author of *Dynamic Symmetry in Composition* (1923) and *The Parthenon and Other Greek Temples: Their Dynamic Symmetry* (1924).

**Ham'bourg** (hăm'bŏŏrg), **Mark.** 1879–1960. Piano virtuoso, b. in South Russia; to England, naturalized; toured U.S. (1899–1900, 1902–03, 1907) and Canada (1910).

**Ham'bro** (häm'brô), **Carl Joachim.** 1885–1964. Norwegian statesman, b. in Bergen. Member of Norwegian Storting (1919 ff.); president of the Storting (from 1926); also, Norwegian delegate to the League of Nations (1926) and president of the League Assembly at Geneva, Switzerland (1939–46). Author of *I Saw It Happen in Norway* (1940), *How to Win the Peace* (1942).

**Ham·di' Bey** (häm·dĭ' bā'), **Osman.** 1842–1910. Turkish statesman and scholar, son of Edhem Pasha (1813?–1893). Governor of Baghdad (1868–70); director (1882) of imperial museums; founded (1882) Turkish École des Beaux-Arts; conducted archaeological work at Sidon (1887–88).

**Ha'mel'** (à'mĕl'), **Ernest.** 1826–1898. French journalist and politician; opponent of Napoleon III. Among his many historical studies are *Histoire de Saint-Just* (1859), *Histoire de Robespierre* (1864–68), *Histoire de la Seconde République* (1891).

**Ha'me·rik** (hà'mĕ·rĕk), **Asger.** *Surname properly* **Ham'me·rich** (hà'mĕ·rĕk). 1843–1923. Danish composer; director of music section of Peabody Inst., Baltimore (1871–98); composer of two operas, six symphonies, orchestral suites, choral works, chamber music, and cantatas.

**Ha'mer·ling** (hä'mĕr·lĭng), **Robert.** *Real name* **Rupert Ham'mer·ling** (häm'ĕr-). 1830–1889. Austrian poet; among his books of lyric verse are *Sinnen und Minnen* (1860), *Blätter im Winde* (1887); among his longer poems, *Venus im Exil* (1858), *Ahasverus in Rom* (1866), *Der König von Sion* (1869), *Amor und Psyche* (1882), *Homunculus* (1888). Author also of a tragedy *Danton und Robespierre* (1871) and a novel *Aspasia*...(3 vols., 1876).

**Ham'er·ton** (hăm'ĕr·t'n; -tŭn), **Philip Gilbert.** 1834–1894. English artist and essayist; a founder (1869) and editor (1869–94) of art periodical *The Portfolio.* Author of *Thoughts about Art* (1862), *Etching and Etchers* (1866), *The Intellectual Life* (1873), *The Graphic Arts* (1882), and *Human Intercourse* (1884).

**Ha·mil'car** (hȧ·mĭl'kär; hăm'ĭl·kär). Carthaginian general of 5th century B.C.; commanded expedition against Sicily; defeated by Gelon (*q.v.*).

**Hamilcar Bar'ca** (bär'kȧ) *or* **Bar'cas** (bär'kȧs). 270?–228 B.C. Father of Hannibal. Carthaginian general; commanded in Sicily (247–241); crushed revolt of troops in Carthage (241–238); led campaign to conquer Spain (237–228); killed in action (228).

**Ham'il·ton** (hăm'ĭl·tŭn; -t'n). Name of noble Scottish family of English origin descended from **Walter Fitz–Gil'bert** (fĭts·gĭl'bĕrt) of Hamilton, who swore fealty as overlord of Scotland to Edward I of England but surrendered fortress of Bothwell to Robert Bruce after Bannockburn. Surname Hamilton first assumed by his grandson Sir **David of Hamilton of Cad'zow** [kăd'zō; kăd'yōō] (d. before 1392). Members of family include the following:

Sir **James Hamilton** of Cadzow (d. 1479), 1st Baron **Hamilton;** great-grandson of Sir David; allied himself by marriage to Douglases; joined them in renunciation of allegiance to crown (1453), but deserted them (1454) in their struggle with crown and married (1469) Mary Stewart, eldest daughter of James II of Scotland.

His son **James Hamilton** (1477?–1529), 2d Baron Hamilton and 1st Earl of **Ar'ran** (ăr'ăn); during minority of James V plotted against regent Albany and became president of council of regency (1517–20); again a member (1522); joined Margaret, queen dowager, in ousting Albany and proclaiming James V (1524); rewarded on James V's escape from Angus and assumption of government.

**John Hamilton** (1511?–1571); natural son of 2d baron; archbishop of St. Andrews (1546); endowed St. Mary's College, St. Andrews; persecuted Protestants; assisted Mary, Queen of Scots, to escape from Lochleven; hanged in his pontifical vestments, under accusation of complicity in assassination of regent Murray by **James Hamilton of Both'well·haugh'** (bŏth'wĕl·häk'; bŏth'-), a kinsman.

**Patrick Hamilton** (1504?–1528); another grandson of 1st baron; early advocate of doctrines of Reformation; saw Luther and Melanchthon at Wittenberg; on return sentenced for heresy and burned at St. Andrews.

**James Hamilton** (1515?–1575), 2d Earl of Arran and Duke of **Châ'tel'he·rault'** (shä'tĕl'rō'); eldest son of 2d baron; governor of Scotland (1542) and second person in realm; regent and tutor to young queen (till 1554); went over to English party (1559); banished for opposition to Darnley marriage (1566).

**James Hamilton** (1530–1609), 3d Earl of Arran; eldest son of duke of Châtelherault; proposed by Henry VIII as husband of Princess Elizabeth but reserved by his father as husband of Mary, Queen of Scots; with Lord James Stuart (Murray), attempted to capture Bothwell; became insane (1562).

**John Hamilton** (1532?–1604), 1st Marquis of Hamilton; 2d son of duke of Châtelherault; head of house on death (1575) of his father and heir after James VI to Scottish throne; with his unscrupulous younger brother Claud, became devoted partisan of Queen Mary, aided in her delivery from Lochleven and re-establishment on throne (1568) and, forfeited by parliament, in revenge took part in assassination of Murray (1570); in danger of his life from Sir William Douglas, escaped to France (1579); reconciled (1585) with James VI; sent to negotiate marriage of king of Scots and Danish princess; one of jurors that found Huntly guilty of high treason.

**Claud Hamilton** (1543?–1622), Baron **Pais′ley** (pāz′lĭ); known as Lord Claud Hamilton; 4th son of duke of Châtelherault; fled (1579) after implication, along with brother John, in series of plots in behalf of Mary, Queen of Scots; aided Ruthven lords (1584) in Gowrie conspiracy to gain possession of person of James VI; recalled from Paris by James VI and shared leadership of Scottish Catholics; in communication with Spain, urged invasion of England by Armada. His descendants obtained titles of viscount **Stra·bane′** [strȧ·băn′] (1701), earl, marquis, and duke of Abercorn (*q.v.*). One of his grandsons, **Gustavus Hamilton** (1639–1723), Viscount **Boyne** (boin) in Irish peerage, commanded regiment at the Boyne (1690) and in Spain (1702); major general (1703); privy councilor under William III, Anne, and George I. A great-grandson of Baron Paisley's, **Anthony Hamilton** (1646?–1720), a French author, known as "Count Anthony"; a grandson of 1st earl of Abercorn (*q.v.*); as governor of Limerick (1685) openly attended Mass; commanded Jacobite dragoons at Enniskillen and Newtown Butler (1689), and engaged at battle of the Boyne (1690); spent rest of life in France; wrote memoirs of his brother-in-law comte de Gramont; also wrote some French verse and tales.

**James Hamilton** (1589?–1625), 2d Marquis of Hamilton, Earl of Arran, Earl of **Cam′bridge** (kām′brĭj) in English peerage; son of 1st marquis; secured enactment of Five Articles of Perth in Scottish Parliament (1621) and negotiated (1623) for marriage of Prince Charles to Spanish Infanta.

A natural son (legitimated 1600) of the 1st marquis, Sir **John Hamilton of Let′trick** (lĕt′rĭk), was ancestor of the barons **Bar·gen′y** (bär·gĕn′ĭ).

**James Hamilton** (1606–1649), 3d Marquis and 1st Duke of Hamilton, 2d Earl of Cambridge; commanded British force (1630–34) under Gustavus Adolphus; an advocate of compromise, persuaded Charles I (1638) to consent to election of a Scottish parliament, with promise of revocation of obnoxious prayer book and canons; opposed Strafford and Montrose; refused Covenant (1643) and joined king; attempted mediation between Charles and Scots (1646); led Scottish army; defeated at Preston (1648); condemned and executed.

**William Hamilton** (1616–1651), 2d Duke of Hamilton; brother and successor to 1st duke; secretary of state for Scotland (1640–43, 1646); signed at Carisbrooke Castle (1647) for Scots a treaty by which King Charles granted consent to Presbyterianism in England; aided in organizing second civil war. See 2d earl of ABERCORN.

Among other titles of nobility borne by descendants in different branches of Hamilton family are: (1) Barons **Bel·ha′ven** (bĕl·hā′vĕn), including **John Hamilton** (1656–1708), 2d baron, who aided settling of Scottish crown on William III, became privy councilor, and strongly opposed union of England and Scotland in famous speech called "Belhaven's Vision" (1706). (2) Viscounts **Clan′e·boye′** (klăn′ĕ·boi′) in Irish peerage, including **James Hamilton** (1559–1643), 1st viscount, who was educ. at St. Andrews, conducted Latin school in Dublin, was James VI's agent in London (1600), received large grants in Ulster (1605) and the dissolved monastery of Bangor (1630); privy councilor (1634). (3) Earls of **Haddington** (*q.v.*). (4) Earls of **Orkney**, including Lord George Hamilton (*q.v.*).

**Hamilton,** Marquises and dukes of. Titles in Scottish peerage held by descendants of Sir James Hamilton of Cadzow (see HAMILTON family) until duchy devolved (1651) on eldest daughter of 1st duke, Lady **Anne** (1636–1716). Title was transferred to her husband, **William Douglas** (1635–1694); eldest son of William Douglas, 1st Marquis of Douglas; created (1660) 3d duke of Hamilton on petition of his wife; privy councilor in Scotland (1660–76), in England (1687); royal commissioner under William III (1689, 1693). **James Douglas** (1658–1712), 4th Duke of Hamilton and Duke of **Bran′don** (brăn′dŭn); eldest son of 3d duke and brother of Lord George Hamilton (*q.v.*), Earl of Orkney; educ. at Glasgow; commanded regiment of horse against Monmouth; leader of Scottish national party but prevented armed resistance to union with England (1707); one of sixteen Scottish representative peers (1708); privy councilor (1710); ambassador extraordinary to France near conclusion of negotiations at Utrecht (1713), killed in duel with Lord Mohun, as narrated in Thackeray's *Henry Esmond;* grandfather of Sir William Hamilton (*q.v.*). **James Douglas** (1724–1758), 6th duke; grandson of 4th duke; married secretly (1752) Scottish beauty Elizabeth Gunning (1734–1790); his son **James George Douglas** (1755–1769), 7th duke, received on death of duke of Douglas (1761) the titles of marquis of Douglas and earl of **An′gus** (ăng′gŭs).

**Hamilton, Alexander.** 1755–1804. American lawyer and statesman, b. on island of Nevis, Leeward Islands. Studied at King's College (now Columbia U.). Served through American Revolution; secretary and aide-de-camp to Washington. Showed remarkable grasp of government's financial and administrative problems; pointed out defects in Articles of Confederation and necessity of strong central government (1780–81). Member, Continental Congress (1782, 1783, 1787, 1788). Practiced law, New York City (from 1783). Represented New York in Annapolis Convention (1786). Supported new constitution by contributions (with Madison and Jay) to *Federalist* (1787–88). First U.S. secretary of the treasury (1789–95); planned and initiated policies establishing a national fiscal system, strengthening central government, stimulating trade and enterprise, developing national resources, and placing public credit on sound basis. Opposition to policies led to factional divisions, from which developed political parties. Appointed inspector general of army, rank of major general (1798–1800). Instrumental in defeating Aaron Burr for presidency (1800–01) and for governorship of New York (1804). Mortally wounded, in a duel with Burr. Elected to Am. Hall of Fame (1915).

**Hamilton, Alice.** 1869–1970. Amer. toxicologist, b. New York City. Director of Ill. survey of industrial sickness (1909–10); investigator of occupational poisons, U.S. Bureau of Labor Statistics (1911–21); at Harvard medical school (1919–35); author of *Industrial Poisons in the United States* (1925), *Exploring the Dangerous Trades* (1943), etc.

**Hamilton, Allan McLane.** 1848–1919. Grandson of Alexander Hamilton. American physician, b. Brooklyn, N.Y. Pioneer neurologist in U.S.

**Hamilton, Andrew.** d. 1703. American pioneer, b. in Scotland; to American colony of East Jersey (1686); governor (1692–97). Deputy postmaster for the colonies (1692–1703); negotiated agreements with various colonies to fix uniform rates of postage.

**Hamilton, Andrew.** d. 1741. American lawyer; successfully defended John Peter Zenger, publisher of *New-York Weekly Journal*, against charge of seditious libel; decision established principle of free political press in the colonies.

**Hamilton, Clayton Meeker.** 1881–1946. American

critic, playwright, and producer, b. Brooklyn, N.Y. Dramatic critic on *The Forum* (1907–09), *Bookman* (1910–18), *Everybody's Magazine* (1911–13), *Vogue* (1912–20). Associated in dramatic production with Mrs. Fiske, William Gillette, Norman Bel Geddes, Walter Hampden. Author of the plays *The Stranger at the Inn* and (with Augustus Thomas) *The Big Idea, Thirty Days, The Better Understanding,* and of *The Theory of the Theatre* (1910), *Studies in Stagecraft* (1914), *Problems of the Playwright* (1917), and *So You're Writing a Play* (1935).

**Hamilton, Clive.** See Clive Staples LEWIS.

**Hamilton, Cosmo.** *Surname originally* **Gibbs** (gĭbz). 1879–1942. English playwright and novelist; brother of Sir Philip Gibbs; assumed mother's name by deed poll (1898). Served in World War I (1914–18). Among his plays are *The Wisdom of Folly, A Sense of Humour, The Belle of Mayfair, Mrs. Skeffington, The Blindness of Virtue, Mr. Pickwick;* among his novels, *Adam's Clay, The Miracle of Love* (1915), *The Rustle of Silk* (1922), *Caste* (1925), *The Pleasure House* (1930), *Thy Lamp, O Memory* (1939).

**Hamilton, Edith.** 1867–1963. American scholar, b. Germany. Author of *The Greek Way* (1930), *Witness to the Truth* (1948), *The Echo of Greece* (1957), etc.

**Hamilton, Emma,** *nee* **Ly′on** (lī′ŭn). 1761?–1815. Mistress of Lord Nelson. As Emma Hart, accepted protection (1780–84) of Charles Greville; mistress (from 1786), second wife (from 1791) of Greville's uncle Sir William Hamilton (*q.v.*); intimate with Queen Maria Carolina at Naples; accompanied her husband and Lord Nelson to Palermo (1800); gave birth (1801) to Horatia, later acknowledged by Lord Nelson as his daughter.

**Hamilton, Frank Hastings.** 1813–1886. American surgeon, b. Wilmington, Vt. Served in Union army in Civil War. Author of *Military Surgery and Hygiene* (1862), *Principles and Practice of Surgery* (1872).

**Hamilton, Gail.** Pseudonym of Mary Abigail DODGE.

**Hamilton,** Lord **George.** Earl of **Ork′ney** (ôrk′nĭ). 1666–1737. British soldier; brother of 4th duke of Hamilton (see marquises and dukes of HAMILTON). Captured 12,000 men and 1300 officers at Blenheim (1704); led pursuit after Ramillies (1706); opened attack at Malplaquet (1709); representative Scottish peer (1707); privy councilor (1710); governor of Virginia (1714).

**Hamilton,** Lord **George Francis.** 1845–1927. British statesman; 3d son of 1st duke of Abercorn. As first lord of admiralty (1885–92), conducted period of extensive naval reform and construction; ceded Helgoland to Germany (1890); as secretary of state for India (1895–1903), had frontier trouble (1897); chairman of royal commission on Mesopotamia campaign (1916–17).

**Hamilton, George Rostrevor.** 1888–1967. English poet; employee of inland revenue department (from 1912); special commissioner of income tax (from 1934). Works include *Escape and Fantasy* (1918), *Pieces of Eight* (1923), *The Making* (1926), *Epigrams* (1928), *Light in Six Moods* (1930), *Unknown Lovers* (1935); the prose works *Bergson and Future Philosophy* (1921), *Poetry and Contemplation* (1937).

**Hamilton,** Sir **Ian Standish Monteith.** 1853–1947. British soldier; served in Second Afghan War (1878–80), South African revolt (1881), Nile expedition (1884–85), Third Burmese War (1886–87), Tirah campaign (1897–98), Boer War (1899–1901); chief of staff to Kitchener (1901–02). With Japanese army in Manchuria (1904–05). Commanded Mediterranean expeditionary force (1915) in vain attempt to land troops in force at Gallipoli; relieved of command (Oct., 1915). Author of *The Millennium?* (1918), *Gallipoli Diary* (1920), *Jean* (a biography of his wife, Lady Hamilton; 1942).

**Hamilton, James.** 1769–1829. British language teacher; devised method of teaching foreign languages which he used with success in U.S. and Great Britain.

**Hamilton, James.** 1786–1857. American political leader; member, U.S. House of Representatives (1822–29); leader of Jackson group opposed to Adams. Governor of South Carolina (1830–32); advocated nullification policy; presided at convention that passed ordinance of nullification (1832). Appointed brigadier general commanding South Carolina troops. Not in sympathy with settlement of nullification issue. Moved to Texas (1855).

**Hamilton, James Alexander.** 1785–1845. English compiler of music-instruction works, including the often-reprinted *Pianoforte Tutor.*

**Hamilton, John.** 1761–1814. Scottish poet; assisted Scott with his *Minstrelsy of the Scottish Border;* his songs include *Up in the Mornin' Early.*

**Hamilton, John McLure.** 1853–1936. American portrait painter, b. Philadelphia. Studio in London (from 1878). Among his subjects were Gladstone (in Luxembourg Gallery), Cardinal Manning, George Meredith, Gen. Booth, Col. Edward M. House.

**Hamilton, Paul.** 1762–1816. American politician, b. in South Carolina. Served in American Revolution. U.S. secretary of the navy (1809–12).

**Hamilton, William.** 1704–1754. Scottish poet, b. Bangour; contributed lyrics to Allan Ramsay's *Tea-Table Miscellany;* composed esp. ballads, including *The Braes of Yarrow;* made earliest translation of Homer into English blank verse.

**Hamilton,** Sir **William.** 1730–1803. British diplomat and archaeologist. Grandson of 3d duke of Hamilton (see marquises and dukes of HAMILTON). British envoy to court of Naples (1764–1800); studied activities of Vesuvius (22 ascents) and Etna and Calabrian earthquakes; collector of vases, sold to British Museum (1772); took active part in excavations of Herculaneum and Pompeii; privy councilor (1791); m. (1791) Emma Hart, who became Lord Nelson's mistress (see Emma HAMILTON).

**Hamilton,** Sir **William.** 1788–1856. Scottish philosopher, b. in Glasgow; educ. Oxford. Professor of civil history, Edinburgh (1821), of logic and metaphysics (1836). Special contributions to philosophical thought include theories of the association of ideas, of unconscious mental modifications, and the inverse relation of perception and sensation. Among his published works are *Metaphysics* and *Logic* (lectures edited and pub. posthumously, 1858–60).

**Hamilton, William Gerard.** 1729–1796. English politician; educ. Oxford. M.P. (1755 ff.); gained nickname "Single-speech Hamilton" because his maiden speech so far excelled his later efforts. Chief secretary for Ireland (1761–64); chancellor of Irish exchequer (1763–84). Reputed by some of his contemporaries to have been author of *Letters of Junius.* Cf. Sir Philip FRANCIS.

**Hamilton,** Sir **William Rowan.** 1805–1865. Irish mathematician, b. Dublin. Developed theory of quaternions; discovered phenomenon of conical refraction.

**Hamilton–Gordon.** Family name of Barons Stanmore. See under GORDON family.

**Ham′ley** (hăm′lĭ), Sir **Edward Bruce.** 1824–1893. British general and writer. His *Operations of War* (1866) became a standard textbook.

**Ham′lin** (hăm′lĭn), **Cyrus.** 1811–1900. American Congregational missionary in Turkey (1839–60). With funds supplied by C. R. Robert of New York, established Robert College, first at Bebek (1863) and then at Constantinople (1871); served as its head until 1877; president, Middlebury Coll., Vt. (1881–85). His son **Alfred**

**Dwight Foster** (1855–1926), b. Constantinople, was an architect on staff of McKim, Mead & White, New York City (1881); taught at Columbia (from 1887).

**Hamlin, Emmons.** 1821–1885. American inventor and manufacturer of organs and pianos (Mason & Hamlin). See *Henry Mason* under Lowell MASON.

**Hamlin, Hannibal.** 1809–1891. American political leader, b. Paris Hill, Me. Member, U.S. House of Representatives (1843–47); U.S. Senate (1848–57). Governor of Maine (1857). Again, U.S. senator (1857–61); prominent as antislavery advocate. Vice-president of the United States (1861–65). U.S. senator (1869–81). U.S. minister to Spain (1881–82).

**Ham·mad′ al–Ra′wi·yah** (hăm·mäd′ ăr·rä′wĭ·yă). *Arab.* **Ḥammād al–Rāwiyah,** *literally* "Hammad the transmitter, or quoter." 713?–?772. Arab scholar, b. Al Kufa, of Persian descent. Noted for remarkable memory of Arabic poems; made collection preserving great part of pre-Islamic poetry and including records of legends, genealogies, and dialects.

**Ham′mann** (häm′än), **Otto.** 1852–1928. German journalist and government official; press director, German foreign office (1894–1916); adviser to von Bülow and Bethmann-Hollweg.

**Ham′mar·skjöld′** (häm′år·shûld′), **Hjalmar.** 1862–1953. Swedish statesman; prime minister of Sweden (1914–17). His son **Dag** (däg) **Hjalmar Ag′ne** (äng′nĕ) **Carl** (1905–1961), political economist; secretary-general of U. N. (1953–61). Awarded Nobel peace prize (1961).

**Hammarskjöld, Lorenzo,** *orig.* **Lars.** 1785–1827. Swedish scholar; champion of new romanticism; founded science of literary history in Sweden with book *Swedish Belles-Lettres* (1818–19).

**Ham′mer** (häm′ĕr), **Julius.** 1810–1862. German poet and novelist.

**Ham′mer** (hăm′ĕr), **William Joseph.** 1858–1934. American electrical engineer, b. Cressona, Pa. Assistant in laboratory of Thomas A. Edison, Menlo Park, N.J. (1879); chief engineer, Edison Lamp Works (1880–81). To England (1881), chief engineer for English Edison Co.; established in London first central station in the world for incandescent electric lighting. Chief engineer, German Edison Co. (1883–84). Consulting engineer in U.S. (from 1890). Invented luminous radium preparations used for watch dials, clocks, etc., and motor-driven flashing electric sign; first suggested and used radium for cancer and tumor treatment.

**Ham′me·rich** (hä′mĕ·rēk), **Peter Frederick Adolf.** 1809–1877. Danish historian.

**Hammerling.** See HAMERLING.

**Ham′mer–Purg′stall** (häm′ĕr·po͝orĸ′shtäl), **Baron Joseph von.** 1774–1856. Austrian Oriental scholar; author of *Geschichte der Goldenen Horde im Kiptschak* (1840), and *Geschichte der Chane der Krim* (1856).

**Ham′mer·stein** (hăm′ĕr·stīn), **Oscar.** 1847?–1919. Theatrical manager, b. in Germany; to U.S. (c. 1863). Worked in cigar factory; invented machine for spreading tobacco leaves; founded and edited *United States Tobacco Journal* (until 1885). Leased Stadt Theater, New York City (1870); built Harlem Opera House (1880), Columbus Theater, Olympia Music Hall (1895), Victoria Music Hall (1899), Republic Theater (1900), Manhattan Opera House (1906), Lexington Theater (1912). Competed with Metropolitan Opera (1906–10); sold out to Metropolitan (1910). Also opened theatres in Philadelphia and London. His nephew **Oscar** (1895–1960) playwright; librettist of *Show Boat* (1927) and, in collaboration, *Wildflower* (1923), *Rose Marie* (1924), *Sunny* **(1925),** ***The Desert Song*** (1926), *Music in the Air* (1932), *Oklahoma* (1943), *Carousel* (1945), *South Pacific* (1949), *The King and I* (1951), *The Sound of Music* (1959), etc. Cf. Otto A. HARBACH and Richard RODGERS.

**Ham′mett** (hăm′ĕt; -ĭt), **Dashiell.** 1894–1961. American writer of detective and mystery fiction, as *The Maltese Falcon* (1930), *The Thin Man* (1934), etc.

**Ham′mond** (hăm′ŭnd), **George Henry.** 1838–1886. American meat packer, b. Fitchburg, Mass. Pioneer in transportation of chilled meats in refrigerator cars. Hammond, Ind., is named after him.

**Hammond, Henry.** 1605–1660. English clergyman; chaplain to royal commissioners at Uxbridge (1645) and to Charles I (1647); deprived of subdeanship of Christ Church, Oxford, by parliamentary visitors and imprisoned (1648).

**Hammond, James Bartlett.** 1839–1913. American inventor, b. Boston, Mass. Invented new style of typewriter, Hammond typewriter (patent issued 1880).

**Hammond, James Henry.** 1807–1864. American political leader, b. in Newberry District, S.C. Advocated secession from beginning of nullification issue; strong believer in states' rights; member, U.S. House of Representatives (1835–36). Governor of South Carolina (1842–44). Member, U.S. Senate (1857–60). In speech (Mar. 4, 1858) he taunted northern sympathizers with: "You dare not make war on cotton—no power on earth dares make war upon it. Cotton is king."

**Hammond, John Hays.** 1855–1936. American mining engineer, b. San Francisco. On staff, U.S. Geological Survey, inspecting California gold fields (1880); associated with Cecil Rhodes in development of South African resources; a leader in Transvaal reform movement (1895–96); arrested after Jameson Raid and sentenced to death, but sentence commuted to 15 years' imprisonment; freed finally on payment of $125,000 fine. Promoter of mining properties in U.S. and Mexico (from 1900). Special representative of the president at the coronation of King George V (1911). His son **John Hays** (1888–1965), electrical and radio engineer and inventor; invented radio-controlled torpedo for coast defense, aluminothermic incendiary projectiles, a system of selective radio telegraphy by which eight messages may be transmitted simultaneously on one carrier wave, etc.

**Hammond, John Lawrence Le Breton.** 1872–1949. English journalist and historian; author of *Charles James Fox* (1903), *Gladstone and the Irish Nation* (1938); coauthor with his wife, **Lucy Barbara,** *nee* **Brad′by** [brăd′bĭ] (1873–1961), of *The Village Labourer 1760–1832* (1911), *The Town Labourer 1760–1832* (1917), *The Skilled Labourer 1760–1832* (1919), *The Rise of Modern Industry* (1925), *The Bleak Age* (1934).

**Hammond, Laurens.** 1895–1973. American manufacturer and inventor, b. Evanston, Ill. Developed an electric organ known as the Hammond electronic organ, and an electrical musical instrument, producing tones similar to orchestral instruments, known as the Hammond Novachord. Brother of Eunice Tietjens (*q.v.*).

**Hammond, Percy.** 1873–1936. American dramatic critic, b. Cadiz, Ohio; on staff of Chicago *Evening Post* (1898–1908), Chicago *Tribune* (1908–21), New York *Herald Tribune.*

**Hammond, Samuel.** 1757–1842. American Revolutionary soldier and politician, b. in Richmond County, Va.; captain (1779); lieutenant colonel (1783). Member, U.S. House of Representatives (1803–05). Military and civil commander of District of Louisiana (1805–24). Moved to S. Carolina (1824); surveyor general of S. Carolina (1827); secretary of state (1831).

**Hammond, William Alexander.** 1828–1900. American nerve specialist; surgeon general, rank of brigadier general (1862). Court-martialed and dismissed (1864), but on review of case (1878), restored to service by president and placed on retired list. Practiced, Washington, D.C. (from 1888).

**Ham'mu·ra'bi** (häm'ōō·rä'bē; hăm'-) *or* **Ham'mu-ra'pi** (-rä'pē) *or* **Kham'mu·ra'bi** (kȧm'-). Greatest king of the first dynasty of Babylon (c. 1955–1913 B.C.; or a century or two earlier, according to some). His reign was the golden age of ancient Babylonia; he built many temples and other structures, dug two great canals, conquered Elamites and Amorites, extended boundaries of empire. A block of black diorite preserving his codification of the laws and edicts was discovered in 1901, one of the most important "documents" in history of human race. See AMRAPHEL.

**Ha'mon'** (ȧ'môN'), **Jean Louis.** 1821–1874. French painter, called a Neo-Greek because of his adherence to classical style.

**Ham'or** (hăm'ẽr), **William Allen.** 1887–1961. American industrial chemist; coinventor of cellulosic foods and of processes of preserving foods and of distilling and plasticizing sulphur.

**Hamp'den** (hăm(p)'dĕn), **John.** 1594–1643. English statesman; M.P. (1621 ff.). Imprisoned (1627) for refusing to pay forced loan of 1626; resisted second ship-money writ (1635), and was defendant in case of the king vs. John Hampden (1637–38). Popular member in Short Parliament (1640), where he led opposition to king's demand for twelve subsidies in exchange for giving up ship money. Impeached by attorney general (1642) as one of Five Members in opposition to king, but escaped arrest. At outbreak of war, raised regiment of foot for Parliamentary army; mortally wounded in action (1643). See Richard HAMPDEN.

**Hampden, Richard.** 1631–1695. Son of John Hampden. English politician; M.P. (1656 ff.); chancellor of the exchequer (1690–94).

**Hamp'den** (hăm'dĕn), **Walter.** *Stage name of* **Walter Hampden Dough'er·ty** (dŏk'ẽr·tĭ). 1879–1955. American actor, b. Brooklyn, N.Y. Brother of the painter Paul Dougherty. First appeared in London (1901); on American stage (from 1907); known esp. for his work in Shakespearean roles and in *The Servant in the House, Cyrano de Bergerac, Richelieu, The Admirable Crichton.*

**Hampole, Richard Rolle de.** See ROLLE DE HAMPOLE.

**Hamp'son** (hăm(p)'s'n), **William.** 1854–1926. English inventor of self-intensive method of gas refrigeration by which air was first liquefied cheaply, the first apparatus for making surgical pencils of carbonic acid snow, and a radiometer for measuring therapeutic doses of X rays; discovered method of controlling the heart beat by electrically stimulated muscle contractions.

**Hamp'ton** (hăm(p)'tŭn), Barons. See PAKINGTON family.

**Hampton, Wade.** 1752?–1835. American political leader, b. in Halifax County, Va. Served in American Revolution; colonel (1782). Member, U.S. House of Representatives (1795–97; 1803–05). Brigadier general (1809); major general (1813); held responsible by his commanding officer (Wilkinson) for failure of expedition against Montreal (1813); resigned (1814). See Wade HAMPTON (1818–1902).

**Hampton, Wade.** 1818–1902. Grandson of Wade Hampton (1752?–1835). American politician and Confederate officer, b. Charleston, S.C. Joined Confederate army at outbreak of Civil War; engaged at Bull Run and in the Peninsular campaign; brigadier general (1862); became great cavalry commander, associated with J. E. B. Stuart in his cavalry raids; engaged at Gettysburg and in the Wilderness; led raids in upper Shenandoah Valley. Major general (1863) and commander of Confederate cavalry after Stuart's death (May 12, 1864); lieutenant general (1865). Governor of South Carolina (1876–79); U.S. senator (1879–91). Advocate of low tariffs, sound money, and conservative white control in South Carolina politics.

**Ham'sun** (häm'sōōn), **Knut.** *Pseudonym of* **Knut Pe'der·sen** (pā'dẽr·sĕn). 1859–1952. Norwegian writer, b. Lom. Variously, farmer, grade-school teacher, streetcar conductor in Chicago, coal trimmer. Best known to readers of English through his three novels *Hunger, Growth of the Soil,* and *The Woman at the Well* (or *Pump*). Awarded Nobel prize for literature (1920). Other works which have been translated into English are *Pan, Victoria, Vagabonds* (*Wanderers*), *Benoni, Rosa, August, Dreamers, Mysteries, Ring is Closed, Road Leads On, Look Back on Happiness* (1940). His wife, **Marie,** *nee* **An'der·sen** [än'nẽr·sĕn] (1881– ), also a writer; author of *Norwegian Family, Norwegian Farm,* etc.

**Ha'my'** (ȧ'mē'), **Jules Théodore Ernest.** 1842–1908. French anthropologist and ethnographer. Investigated Mexican races and South African tribes.

**Han** (hän). Name of several Chinese dynasties:

(1) A dynasty divided into two periods: **Earlier,** *or* **Western, Han** (206 or 202 B.C.–9 A.D.; founded by Liu Pang) and **Later,** *or* **Eastern, Han** (25–220 A.D.; founded by Kuang Wu-ti). The two dynasties, interrupted by the reign of the usurper Wang Mang (*q.v.*), were marked by establishment of literary civil service examination system, revival of letters, the introduction of Buddhism (see MING TI), and extension of territory; harassed by the Hiung-Nu on the north; succeeded by breakup of empire into three kingdoms. Greatest ruler, Wu Ti.

(2) **Minor Han.** *Usually called* **Shu** *or* **Shu Han** (shōō). A dynasty (221–264 A.D.), founded by Liu Pei, a descendant of the house of Han, ruling, in the west of China with capital at Chengtu, one of the three kingdoms following the downfall of the Eastern Han dynasty. It was annexed to Wei (*q.v.*).

(3) **Later Han.** One of the Five Dynasties (*q.v.*).

**Han** (hän), **Ulrich.** *Lat.* **U'dal·ri'cus Gal'lus** (ū'd'l·rī'kŭs găl'ŭs). *Also called* **Bar·ba'tus** (bär·bā'tŭs). d. 1478. Viennese printer in Italy; set up printing press in Rome, his first publication (1467) being Juan de Torquemada's *Meditationes de Vita Christi,* first illustrated book published in Italy.

**Han'a·ford** (hăn'ȧ·fẽrd), **Phoebe Ann,** *nee* **Cof'fin** (kŏf'ĭn). 1829–1921. American Universalist minister, b. on Nantucket Island; m. Joseph H. Hanaford (1849). First woman regularly ordained (1868) in New England.

**Han'by** (hăn'bĭ), **Benjamin Russel.** 1833–1867. American clergyman and writer of popular songs (*Darling Nellie Gray, Little Tillie's Grave, Ole Shady*).

**Han'cock** (hăn'kŏk), **John.** 1737–1793. American Revolutionary statesman, b. Braintree, Mass. Grad. Harvard (1754). In mercantile business (from 1754). Identified himself with colonial cause in pre-Revolutionary agitation; elected to Massachusetts legislature (1766–72). Member, Continental Congress (1775–80, 1785, 1786); president of congress (1775–77); first signer of Declaration of Independence. First governor of State of Massachusetts (1780–85); again governor (1787–93).

**Hancock, Walker Kirtland.** 1901– . American sculptor; his works include heroic groups on St. Louis Memorial building, bronze portrait bust of Stephen Foster for American Hall of Fame.

**Hancock, Winfield Scott.** 1824–1886. American army officer and political leader, b. Montgomery Square, Pa. Brigadier general (1861); major general (1862); defended key flank position (July 2, 1863) and center (July 3) in battle of Gettysburg. Democratic candidate for president of the United States (1880); defeated by Garfield.

**Hand** (hănd), **Edward.** 1744–1802. Officer in American Revolution, b. in King's County, Ireland. Settled in Lancaster, Pa., and began practice of medicine (1774). Joined Continental army at outbreak of Revolution; colonel (1776); brigadier general (1777); brevetted major general (1783). Member, Continental Congress (1784–85). Commissioned major general, U.S. army (1798); honorably discharged (1800).

**Han'del** (hăn'd'l), **George Frederick.** *German* **Georg Friedrich Hän'del** (hĕn'dĕl). 1685–1759. Composer, b. Halle, Germany; naturalized British subject (1726). Composed first opera, *Almira* (1705); to Italy (1707); presented his opera *Rodrigo* at Florence, and *Agrippina* at Venice (1708); composed oratorios *Il Trionfo del Tempo* and *La Resurrezione* at Rome. Settled in England (1712). Musical director for duke of Chandos at Canons (1718–20); director of Royal Academy of Music (1720–28); director (with Heidegger) of the King's Theatre, Covent Garden (1728–34); director of Rich's new theater in Covent Garden (1735–37). Composer of more than 40 operas, 23 oratorios, odes, songs, etc., and much church and chamber music. Best-known works are his oratorios, including *Esther* (1720), *Saul* (1739), *Israel in Egypt* (1739), *The Messiah* (1742), *Samson* (1743), *Judas Maccabaeus* (1746), *Joshua* (1748), *Jephthah* (1752).

**Han'del–Maz·zet'ti** (hän'dĕl·mä·tsĕt'ē), Baroness **Enrika von.** 1871–1955. Austrian novelist; author of *Jesse und Maria* (1906), *Die Arme Margaret* (1910), *Der Deutsche Held* (1920), *Frau Maria* (1929), etc.

**Han'dl** (hăn'd'l) *or* **Hän'dl** (hĕn'd'l) *or* **Häh'nel** (hâ'nĕl), **Jakob.** *Known as* **Jacobus Gal'lus** (*as Lat.*, găl'ŭs; *as Ger.*, gäl'o͝os). 1550–1591. German composer; chief work, *Opus Musicum*, containing motets for entire church year.

**Handley Page, Frederick.** See Frederick Handley PAGE.

**Han'dy** (hăn'dĭ), **William Christopher.** 1873–1958. American Negro musician and composer, b. Florence, Ala.; best-known work, *St. Louis Blues* (1914).

**Hä'nel** (hâ'nĕl), **Gustav Friedrich.** 1792–1878. German jurist; devoted himself to history of law. Became authority on manuscripts; published *Lex Romana Visigothorum* (1849), *Corpus Legum ab Imperatoribus Romanis ante Justiniarum Latarum* (1857–60), etc.

**Ha'ney** (hā'nĭ), **Lewis Henry.** 1882–1969. American economist; professor, U. of Texas (1912–16). Adviser to Federal Trade Commission (1916–19). Professor (from 1920), and director of bureau of business research (1920–32), New York U. Author of *History of Economic Thought* (1911), *Business Organization and Combination* (1913), *Economics in a Nut Shell* (1933), *How to Understand Money* (1935), etc.

**Han Fei** *or* **Han Fei–tzu** (hän' fā'dzŭ'). d. 233 B.C. Chinese philosopher, in time of Shih Huang Ti. Disciple of Hsün Tzŭ; influenced by Lao-tzu's doctrines; an expert in criminal law; imprisoned through jealousy of a rival official; committed suicide.

**Hanf'staengl** (hänf'shtĕng''l), **Franz.** 1804–1877. German lithographer and photographer; founder of an art printing establishment in Munich; commissioned by Saxon government to copy in lithographs canvases of Dresden gallery (work completed, 1852).

**Han Fu–chü** (hän' fo͞o'jü'). 1890–1938. Chinese general, in Shantung province. One of Feng Yu-hsiang's ablest generals, but (1929–30) sided with Nationalist government against him; appointed commander of 3d route army (1929); governor of Shantung (1930–38); on outbreak of war with Japan (1937) attempted to play a double game; captured and shot for his treachery, by Chiang Kai-shek at Hankow.

**Ha·ni·ha·ra** (hä·nē·hä·rä), **Masanao.** 1876–1934. Japanese diplomat; at Washington as attaché and secretary (1901–11); secretarial chief at Foreign Office, Tokyo; consul general at San Francisco (1916–17). Ambassador to U.S. (1923–24), recalled because of unfavorable reaction in U.S. Senate to his statement about Japanese Exclusion Act.

**Han'ka** (hàng'kà), **Václav.** 1791–1861. Czech poet and philologist.

**Han'ka·mer** (häng'kä·mẽr), **Paul.** 1891–1945. German historian of literature, esp. of 17th century.

**Han Kan** (hän' gän'). fl. middle of 8th century A.D. Chinese painter, of the T'ang dynasty, known for his paintings of horses.

**Han'kel** (häng'kĕl), **Wilhelm Gottlieb.** 1814–1899. German physicist; worked on the thermoelectric properties of crystals; invented new methods and instruments for measuring atmospheric electricity. His son **Hermann** (1839–1873), mathematician, wrote *Theorie der Komplexen Zahlensysteme* (1867), etc.

**Han'key** (hăng'kĭ), 1st Baron. **Maurice Paschal Alers Hankey.** 1877–1962. British army officer and public official; served in Royal Marine Artillery (1895–1918). Secretary, Committee of Imperial Defense (1912–38); secretary of the cabinet (1912–38); clerk of Privy Council (1923–38). British secretary at various international conferences (1919–32). In cabinet as minister without portfolio (1939), as chancellor of duchy of Lancaster (1940).

**Hanks** (hăngks), **Nancy.** 1783–1818. Mother of Abraham Lincoln; m. Thomas Lincoln (June 12, 1806).

**Han'lan** (hăn'lăn), *properly* **Han'lon, Edward.** 1855–1908. Canadian oarsman; single-sculls champion of the world (1880–84).

**Han'ley** (hăn'lĭ), **James.** 1901– . English writer; seaman (1914–24), railwayman and journalist (1924–30); author of novels and short stories.

**Hann** (hän), **Julius.** 1839–1921. Austrian meteorologist; author of works on atmospheric dynamics, climatology, etc.

**Han'na** (hăn'ȧ), **Marcus Alonzo,** *known as* **Mark.** 1837–1904. American businessman and politician, b. New Lisbon, Ohio. In father's grocery and commission business (1853–62); partner (from 1862). Served in Union army in Civil War (1864). Sponsored John Sherman in convention of 1888; supported McKinley for governor of Ohio (1891 and 1893) and for president of the United States (1896 and 1900); influential presidential adviser. U.S. senator (1897–1904). For his daughter **Ruth,** see under Robert Sanderson MCCORMICK.

**Han'nah** (hăn'ȧ). *In Douay Version* **An'na** (ăn'ȧ). In Bible, mother of prophet Samuel (*1 Sam.* i).

**Han'nay** (hăn'ā), **David.** 1853–1934. English journalist and man of letters, b. in London. Author of *Admiral Blake* (1888), *Life of Marryat* (1889), *Short History of the Royal Navy* (1898), *The Later Renaissance* (1898), etc.

**Hannay, James.** 1827–1873. British journalist and novelist; author of the naval stories *Singleton Fontenoy* (1850) and *Eustace Conyers* (1855), also of *Satire and Satirist* (1854) and *Studies on Thackeray* (1869).

**Hannay, James Owen.** *Pseudonym* **George A. Bir'ming·ham** (bûr'mĭng·ăm). 1865–1950. Irish clergyman and novelist, b. in northern Ireland. Ordained deacon (1888) and priest (1889); rector of Westport, County Mayo (1892–1913), and canon of St. Patrick's Cathedral (1912–21); rector of Mells, Frome (1924–34); vicar of Holy Trinity, Kensington Gore (from 1934).

Works include *The Spirit and Origin of Christian Monasticism, The Wisdom of the Desert*, and many novels under the pseudonym George A. Birmingham, as *The Seething Pot* (1905), *Spanish Gold* (1908), *Lalage's Lovers* (1911), *Gossamer* (1915), *The Island of Mystery* (1918), *Lady Bountiful* (1921), *The Grand Duchess* (1924), *Wild Justice* (1930), *The Search for Susie* (1941).

**Han′ne·gan** (hăn′ē·găn), **Robert Emmet.** 1903–1949. American lawyer and politician, b. St. Louis, Mo.; grad. St. Louis U. (1925); U.S. commissioner of internal revenue (1943–44); chairman of Democratic National Committee (1944); U.S. postmaster general (July, 1945–47).

**Han′ni·bal** (hăn′ĭ·băl). 247–183 B.C. Son of Hamilcar Barca. Carthaginian general; trained under father's command in Spain and sworn to eternal enmity to Rome. After father's death (228 B.C.), served under his brother-in-law Hasdrubal (*q.v.*). After Hasdrubal's assassination (221), became commander in chief of Carthaginian army in Spain. Began operations against Rome by attacking and capturing Roman-allied city of Sagunto in Spain, resulting in declaration of war by Rome (218); crossed Alps and carried war into Italy, defeating Romans at Ticino River and Trebbia River (218), at Lago di Trasimeno (217), and at Cannae (216). Wintered at Capua (216–215), and captured Tarentum (212); marched against Rome (211), but Romans held successfully to fortified positions. Defeat of Carthaginian reinforcements at Metaurus River (207) and Roman successes under Scipio Africanus in North Africa forced his recall to Carthage (203) after he had successfully maintained campaign in Italy for fifteen years. In North Africa, he was defeated by Scipio Africanus in great battle of Zama (202). Headed Carthaginian government (c. 202–196), but was accused by Romans of conspiring to break the peace; fled from Carthage (196) and joined Antiochus the Great, King of Syria, with whom he warred against the Romans; his military career ended when Antiochus, defeated (190) at Magnesia (Manisa), was forced, in treaty that followed, to promise to surrender him to Rome. Escaped to Bithynia and there, with no further hope of escape, committed suicide (183).

**Han′no** (hăn′ō). See ANNO.

**Hanno.** Carthaginian navigator of 6th century–5th century B.C. who made voyage down African west coast.

**Hanno.** *Surnamed* **the Great.** Carthaginian politician of 3d century B.C.; opponent of Hamilcar Barca and Hannibal; said to have advocated peace with Rome during Second Punic War (218–201 B.C.); after battle of Zama (202), was one of ambassadors sent to Scipio Africanus to sue for peace.

**Ha′no′taux′** (à′nô′tō′), **Gabriel,** *in full* **Albert Auguste Gabriel.** 1853–1944. French historian and statesman; minister of foreign affairs (1894–95, 1896–98). Among his notable histories are *Histoire de Richelieu* (1897 ff.), *Histoire de France Contemporaine, 1871–1892* (1903–08), *Histoire Illustrée de la Guerre de 1914* (17 vols., 1915–26).

**Ha′no′teau′** (à′nô′tō′), **Hector.** 1823–1890. French painter of genre scenes and landscapes.

**Han′o·ver** (hăn′ō·vẽr). *Ger.* **Han·no′ver** (hä·nō′vẽr; -fẽr). An electoral house of Germany and a royal family of England. The electoral house is directly descended from the Welf family (see WELF), which acquired Bavaria (1070) and Lüneburg, etc. (1120). These possessions were lost (1180) by Henry the Lion (*q.v.*), but his son William obtained Lüneburg, upper Harz, etc. (1203); William's son Otto was made first duke of Brunswick and Lüneburg (1235), thus acquiring Hanover. Many changes, divisions and reunions (1235–1546), to death of Duke Ernst (see BRUNSWICK). The younger branch, Hanover, was made an electorate (1692), Duke Ernest Augustus (*q.v.*) becoming first elector; his son, the second elector, succeeded (as George I) to English crown, establishing English royal house of Hanover (1714–1901), whose other rulers were George II, III, IV, William IV, and Victoria. Electorate, which had become a duchy, was made a kingdom by Congress of Vienna (1815). Separated from English ruling house at accession of Victoria (1837); its first independent king was Ernest Augustus (*q.v.*), Duke of Cumberland, son of George III; kingdom annexed by Prussia (1866); Ernest Augustus's grandson Ernest Augustus inherited (1884) duchy of Brunswick-Lüneburg (see BRUNSWICK), though not allowed by Hohenzollerns to rule; his son Ernest Augustus was last duke of Brunswick (1913–18; abdicated). In England the house of Hanover was succeeded by royal houses of Saxe-Coburg and Windsor (*qq.v.*). See *Table (in Appendix)* for GREAT BRITAIN.

**Hans.** King of Denmark. See JOHN I.

**Han′sard** (hăn′sẽrd; -särd), **Luke.** 1752–1828. English printer who printed the House of Commons's journals (from 1774). Official reports of parliamentary proceedings in England are still known as *Hansards.* His eldest son, **Thomas Curson** (1776–1833), also a printer, printed parliamentary debates (from 1803); patented improved hand press; published a treatise on printing, *Typographia* (1825).

**Han′sen** (hän′zĕn), **Anton.** See Anton TAMMSAARE.

**Han′sen** (hän′sĕn), **Armauer Gerhard Henrik.** 1841–1912. Norwegian physician; discovered the bacillus causing leprosy (1879).

**Han′sen** (hȧn′sĕn), **Emil Christian.** 1842–1909. Danish botanist; investigated fungi and alcoholic fermenting yeasts; proved that there are different species of yeast; collaborated in inventing ferment used in European breweries.

**Hansen, Hans Christian.** 1803–1883. Danish architect; built university at Athens, navy yard at Trieste, and municipal hospital at Copenhagen. His brother **Konstantin** (1804–1880), painter, exponent of classicism, painted architectural and genre subjects in Italy (1835–43), murals of Greek mythological subjects for the U. of Copenhagen (1844–54). Another brother, **Theophilus von Hansen** (1813–1891), architect, built the Acad. of Science and the astronomical observatory at Athens, Greece, and later, in Vienna, a Greek church and other public buildings.

**Han′sen** (hăn′s'n), **Harry.** 1884– . American editor; war correspondent, Chicago *Daily News* (1914–16) and at Peace Conference (1919); literary editor, Chicago *Daily News* (1920–26), New York *World* (1926–31), New York *World-Telegram* (from 1931); editor of O. Henry Prize stories (from 1933). Author of *Midwest Portraits* (1923), *Your Life Lies Before You* (1935), etc.

**Hansen, Marcus Lee.** 1892–1938. American historian; author of *Atlantic Migration, 1607–1680...*, *Mingling of the Canadian and American Peoples*, etc.

**Han′sen** (hän′sĕn), **Mauritz.** 1794–1842. Norwegian poet and novelist; known esp. for novels depicting life and scenes typical of small Norwegian towns.

**Han′sen** (hăn′s'n), **Niels Ebbesen.** 1866–1950. Horticulturist, b. in Denmark; to U.S. (1873). Professor, South Dakota State College and Experiment Station (1895–1937). Originated Hansen hybrid plums and a method of hybridization of alfalfas by transplanting; introduced foreign alfalfas; imported Siberian sheep from which a tailless breed was developed.

**Han′sen** (hȧn′sĕn), **Peter Andreas.** 1795–1874. Danish astronomer; assistant at Altona observatory in measuring arc of meridian (1821); director of Seeberg observatory (1825) which was removed to Gotha (1859). Known for work on theory of perturbations and on lunar theory.

**Han'si'** (äN'sē'). *Pseudonym of* **Jean Jacques Waltz** (välts). 1873–1951. Alsatian artist, satirist; author of *Le Professeur Knatschke, Mon Village, L'Alsace Heureuse, Le Voyage d'Erika en Alsace Française,* etc.

**Hans'lick** (häns'lĭk), **Eduard.** 1825–1904. Austrian music critic.

**Han'som** (hăn'sŭm), **Joseph Aloysius.** 1803–1882. English architect; designed the Birmingham town hall (1833); invented (1834) a patent safety cab named after him, the predecessor of later hansoms.

**Han'son** (hăn's'n), **Howard Harold.** 1896– . American composer, b. Wahoo, Nebr. Director, Eastman School of Music, Rochester, N.Y. (from 1924). Among his compositions are the opera *Merry Mount,* symphonies, concertos, and other orchestral and choral works.

**Han'son** (hăn's'n), **John.** 1721–1783. American Revolutionary political leader, b. in Charles County, Md. Active in colonial cause (from 1765); member, Continental Congress (1780); first president (1781–82) of the Congress after ratification of Articles of Confederation (Mar. 1, 1781). His grandson **Alexander Contee Hanson** (1786–1819) was an editor and politician; founded *Federal Republican,* Baltimore (1808), and attacked administration (1808–12); newspaper plant destroyed by mob; Hanson and associates arrested; mob broke into jail and killed one man and injured others; this incident created issue of freedom of the press and a suspicion of Republican terrorism as a political policy (1812); member, U.S. House of Representatives (1813–16) and U.S. Senate (1816–19).

**Hanson, Ole.** 1874–1940. American businessman and politician, b. in Racine County, Wis. In real estate and investment business in Seattle, Wash. (from 1902); mayor of Seattle (1918–19); gained prominence by vigorous measures taken to break general strike at Seattle (Feb., 1919). Author of *Americanism vs. Bolshevism* (1920).

**Hanson, Sir Richard Davies.** 1805–1876. Jurist, b. London, Eng.; crown prosecutor in New Zealand (1840–46). One of the founders of South Australia (1846); drafted its constitution (1851–56); chief justice of South Australia (1861–74).

**Hans'son** (hân'sôn), **Ola.** 1860–1925. Swedish writer; author of lyric verse, novels, and essays. His wife, **Laura,** *nee* **Mohr** [mōr] (1854–1928), *pseudonym* **Laura Mar'holm'** (mär'hôlm'), was also an author.

**Hansson, Per Albin.** 1885–1946. Swedish statesman; self-educated; joined Social Democratic party; elected to Riksdag (1918); minister of defense (1920–23, 1924–26); became party leader at death of Hjalmar Branting; prime minister (1932–46).

**Han'steen** (hän'stān), **Christopher.** 1784–1873. Norwegian astronomer and physicist, b. Oslo. Known esp. for researches in terrestrial magnetism; credited with discovering daily variation in horizontal magnetic intensity (1821); built astronomical observatory (1833) and magnetic observatory (1839) in Oslo.

**Han'way** (hăn'wā), **Jonas.** 1712–1786. English merchant, traveler, and philanthropist; took charge of a caravan of woolen goods down the Volga River, across the Caspian Sea, and into Persia (1743–45), returning by the same route (1745). In London (from 1750), where he occupied himself with many philanthropic measures, esp. those aiding poor children.

**Han Yü** (hän' yü'). *Better known as* **Han Wên-kung** (hän' wŭn'gŏŏng'). 768–824 A.D. Chinese poet, essayist, and philosopher, called "the Prince of Literature"; b. in Honan. An official at the court under the T'ang dynasty; for his criticism of the emperor's policy, was banished (819) to region of wild tribes in the south (modern Kwangtung); there gained fame for his rule; restored at court (820). Created the classic style for the essay and wrote poems considered by critics as perfect. Opposed Buddhism; developed a conservative philosophy.

**Hap'good** (hăp'gŏŏd), **Isabel Florence.** 1850–1928. American writer; best known for translations from Tolstoi, Gogol, Turgenev, Gorki. Also wrote *A Survey of Russian Literature* (1902).

**Hapgood, Norman.** 1868–1937. American editor and writer, b. Chicago. Editor, *Collier's Weekly* (1903–12), *Harper's Weekly* (1913–16), *Hearst's International Magazine* (1923–25). U.S. minister to Denmark (1919). Author of *Daniel Webster* (1899), *Abraham Lincoln* (1899), *George Washington* (1901), *Industry and Progress* (1911), *Up from the City Streets* (with Henry Moskowitz, 1927), *The Changing Years* (1930), etc. His brother **Hutchins** (1869–1944) wrote *The Spirit of the Ghetto* (1902), *The Autobiography of a Thief* (1903), *Types from the City Streets* (1910), *The Story of a Lover* (1919). Hutchins's wife (m. 1899), **Neith,** *nee* **Boyce** [bois] (1872–1951), wrote, over maiden name, *The Forerunner* (1903), *Eternal Spring* (1906), *The Bond* (1908), *Two Sons* (1917), *Proud Lady* (1923), *Winter's Night* (1927), etc.

**Haps'burg** (hăps'bûrg). *Ger.* **Habs'burg** (häps'bŏŏrk). A royal German family, the name of which is derived from the ancestral Castle Habsburg, in Aargau, Switzerland. Counts of Hapsburg are known as early as the 11th century; from them have sprung, besides many sovereigns of small European states, rulers of:

(1) *Germany:* Kings Rudolf I (1273–91), Albert I (1298–1308), Frederick III (1314–30), and Albert II (1438–39); Holy Roman emperors Albert II (1438–39; not crowned) and all succeeding him (except Charles VII of Bavaria, 1742–45) to Francis I; and the Hapsburg-Lorraine (*q.v.*) emperors.

(2) *Austria:* Dukes and archdukes, who from the death of Ottokar II (1278) of Bohemia and investiture of Rudolf's sons (1282) have generally also been German kings or Holy Roman emperors, down to the death of Charles VI (1740), when the male Hapsburg line became extinct (for Austrian rulers, 1740–1918, see HAPSBURG-LORRAINE).

(3) *Hungary and Bohemia:* Hereditary under rule of Hapsburgs (1526–1918) from time when Emperor Ferdinand I, who had married (1521) Anne of Bohemia and Hungary, laid claim to the two kingdoms.

(4) *Spain:* Kings (1504–1700) Philip I (1504–06; son of the Hapsburg emperor Maximilian I; married Juana, daughter of Ferdinand and Isabella of Spain), their son Charles (V as emperor and I as king of Spain), Philip II, III, IV, and Charles II (succeeded, 1700, by Philip V, first of the Bourbons).

See *Tables* (*in Appendix*) for AUSTRIA, HOLY ROMAN EMPIRE, SPAIN, and individual biographies of rulers mentioned above.

**Haps'burg-Lor·raine'** (hăps'bûrg·lŏ·rān'; -lō-). *Also* **Lorraine-Hapsburg.** The Hapsburg royal house of Austrian rulers (1740–1918) and kindred branches ruling in many German and Italian states of the 18th and 19th centuries. The Hapsburg-Lorraine line began on the extinction of the male Hapsburg line (see HAPSBURG) by the death of Emperor Charles VI (1740), and included Maria Theresa, daughter of Charles VI (m. Francis Stephen, Duke of Lorraine, later Emperor Francis I); Holy Roman emperors (1745–1806) Francis I, Joseph II, Leopold II, and Francis II; emperors of Austria (1804–48) Francis II (as Francis I) and Ferdinand I; emperors of Austria and kings of Hungary (1848–1918) Francis

Joseph I and Charles I. See *Table (in Appendix)* for Holy Roman Empire, and individual biographies of rulers mentioned above.

**Ha·ra** (hä·rä), **Takashi.** 1854–1921. Japanese statesman; an organizer (1900) of Seiyukai party; prime minister (1918–21), first Japanese without title to receive this honor; opposed too rapid absorption of western ideas; his ministry criticized for attitude toward "Twenty-one Demands" on China and for Siberian policy; assassinated by fanatic.

**Har'a·han** (hăr'ȧ·hăn), **William Johnson.** 1867–1937. American railroad executive; president, Seaboard Air Line Railway (1912–18), Hocking Valley Railway (1920–29), Chesapeake & Ohio Railway (1920–37), Pere Marquette Railway (1935–37), New York, Chicago & St. Louis Railroad Co. (1935–37).

**Ha'rald** (hä'räl). Danish and Norwegian for Harold.

**Ha'rasz·thy de Mok'csa** (hŏ'rŏs·tĭ dĕ mōk'chŏ), **Ágoston.** 1812?–1869. Hungarian pioneer in America; founded town now known as Sauk City, Wis. (c. 1841); went to California (1849); introduced Tokay, Zinfandel, and Shiras grapes into California and created grape-growing industry.

**Ha'rau'court'** (á'rō'kōōr'), **Edmond.** 1856–1941. French novelist, poet, and playwright.

**Har'bach** (här'bäk), **Otto A'bels** (ā'bĕlz). 1873–1963. American playwright and musical comedy librettist, b. Salt Lake City. Author of *Madame Sherry* (1909), *Girl of My Dreams* (1910), *The Firefly* (1912), *High Jinks* (1913), *The Silent Witness* (1915). Collaborator in *Kid Boots* (1923), *Wildflower* (1923), *No! No! Nannette* (1924), *Rose Marie* (1924), *Sunny* (1925), *The Desert Song* (1926), *Cat and the Fiddle* (1931), *Roberta* (1933), etc. Cf. Oscar Hammerstein.

**Har'baugh** (här'bô), **Henry.** 1817–1867. American German Reformed clergyman; leading exponent of Mercersburg theology. Wrote many hymns and books on religious subjects.

**Har'ben** (här'bĕn), **William Nathaniel.** 1858–1919. American novelist, b. Dalton, Ga.; most successful in stories dealing with northern Georgia.

**Har'bord** (här'bẽrd), **James Guthrie.** 1866–1947. American army officer and businessman, b. Bloomington, Ill. Enlisted in U.S. army, as private (1889); rose through grades to brigadier general (Nov. 30, 1918) and major general (Sept. 8, 1919). Chief of staff, American Expeditionary Force in France (1917–18); commanded service of supply, in France (1918–19); again, chief of staff, A.E.F. (1919). Deputy chief of staff, U.S. army (1921–22). Retired (1922). Chairman of the board, Radio Corp. of America, New York City (from 1922).

**Har'court** (här'kẽrt; -kōrt). Distinguished English family, including: **Edward Harcourt,** *surname orig.* **Ver'non** [vûr'nŭn] (1757–1847), archbishop of York (1807–47); assumed name Harcourt (1831). His son **William Vernon Harcourt** (1789–1871), canon of York (1824) and associate of Davy and Wollaston in chemical experiments. William's son Sir **William George Granville Venables Vernon Harcourt** (1827–1904), statesman; educ. Cambridge; called to bar (1854); M.P. (from 1868); solicitor general (1873–74); home secretary (1880–85); chancellor of exchequer (1886; 1892–94; 1894–95). Sir William's son **Lewis** (1863–1922), Viscount **Harcourt** (created 1917), statesman; private secretary to his father (1881–86; 1892–95; 1895–1904); M.P. (1904–17); first commissioner of works (1905–10 and 1915–17); secretary of state for colonies (1910–15).

**Har'court'** (ár'kōōr'), Duc **Henri Ier d'.** 1654–1718. French soldier and diplomat; conducted brilliant defense of Luxemburg (1692); engaged at Neerwinden (1693); ambassador at Madrid (1697); created duc (1700), marshal of France (1703), and peer (1709).

**Har'court** (här'kẽrt; -kōrt), **Simon.** Viscount **Harcourt.** 1661?–1727. English lawyer and statesman; solicitor general (1702–07); attorney general (1707–08); lord keeper of the seal (1710); lord chancellor (1713–14); created viscount (1721). Friend of Bolingbroke, Pope, Swift, Gay, and other literary men of his time. His grandson **Simon** (1714–1777), 1st Earl **Harcourt,** was ambassador to France (1768–72) and viceroy of Ireland (1772–77). Earl Harcourt's son **William** (1743–1830), 3d earl, soldier; served in America, where he commanded a regiment of dragoons and captured Gen. Charles Lee (1776); lieutenant general (1793), general (1796), and field marshal (1820).

**Hard** (härd), **William.** 1878–1962. American writer, b. at Painted Post, N.Y. On staff of Chicago *Tribune* (1901–05). Newspaper and magazine writer, headquarters in Washington, D.C. (from 1906). Author of *The Women of Tomorrow* (1911), *Raymond Robins' Story of Bolshevist Russia* (with Raymond Robins, 1919).

**Har'de·ca·nute'** *or* **Har'di·ca·nute'** (här'dĭ·kȧ·nūt'). *More correctly* **Harthacnut.** 1019?–1042. Son of Canute II and Emma of Normandy. King of Denmark (1035–42) and of England (1040–42). Subking of Denmark under his father; became king (1035) but forced to leave throne of England to half brother Harold; arrived in England with large fleet (1040); crowned king (June, 1040); unpopular with English subjects.

**Har'dee** (här'dē), **William Joseph.** 1815–1873. American army officer; grad. U.S.M.A., West Point (1838); entered Confederate service (1861). Major general (1861); lieutenant general (1862). After war, managed plantation in Alabama. His *Rifle and Light Infantry Tactics* (1855) was used as an army textbook.

**Har'den** (här'd'n), Sir **Arthur.** 1865–1940. English chemist, b. Manchester. Educ., Tettenhall Coll., Staffordshire, Owens Coll., Manchester, and Erlangen. Lecturer and demonstrator, Owens Coll. (1888–97); professor of biochemistry, London; head of biochemical department, Lister Inst. Known esp. for researches in alcoholic fermentation and the enzymatic action involved. Shared the 1929 Nobel prize for chemistry with Hans von Euler-Chelpin.

**Har'den** (här'dĕn), **Maximilian.** *Real surname* **Wit·kow'ski** (vĭt·kôf'skē). 1861–1927. German journalist, b. Berlin. Founded (1892) political weekly journal *Die Zukunft,* in which he criticized Caprivi and his policies and aroused hostility of the government; attacks finally brought charge of criminal libel, but he was exonerated, and some of the leading figures in the court camarilla were driven from public life (1906–07). During World War (1914–18), Harden retained his freedom of criticism and often attacked government policies, urging negotiated peace and stating that the government seriously underestimated the military and naval strength of the U.S. Among his works are *Apostata* (1892), *Theater und Literatur* (1896), *Köpfe* (4 vols., 1910–24), *Krieg und Friede* (2 vols., 1918), and *Deutschland, Frankreich, England* (1923).

**Har'den·berg** (här'dĕn·bĕrk), Baron **Friedrich von.** *Pseudonym* **No·va'lis** (nō·vä'lĭs). 1772–1801. German lyric poet; a leader of early romanticists in Germany. Best known as author of *Hymnen an die Nacht* (prose lyrics inspired by death of his fiancée, Sophie von Kuhn) and an unfinished novel *Heinrich von Ofterdingen.*

**Hardenberg,** Prince **Karl August von.** 1750–1822. Prussian statesman; served as councilor at Hanover (1779–82); in service of state at Brunswick (1787–90); administrator of principalities of Ansbach and Bayreuth

(1790–91). In service of Prussia in war against France (1792–95); concluded peace between Prussia and France at Basel (1795). In Prussian cabinet of Frederick William III (1798–1804); foreign minister of Prussia (1804–06); tried to preserve neutrality; kept out of office by Napoleon (1806–10); worked for reorganization of state (1807–14); chancellor of Prussia (1810–17). Made prince in recognition of part in War of Liberation (1813–14); took part in Congress of Vienna (1814–15) and in conferences at Paris; reorganized Council of State (1817); active in Holy Alliance; his policy in later years reactionary. Wrote *Memoirs, 1801–1807* (pub. 1877).

**Har′den·bergh** (här′d'n·bûrg), **Henry Janeway.** 1847–1918. American architect, b. New Brunswick, N.J. Opened own office, New York (1870). Examples of his work: Library of Rutgers Coll., New Brunswick, N.J.; Waldorf Hotel, Hotel Manhattan, Plaza Hotel, in New York City; Copley Plaza Hotel, in Boston; New Willard Hotel, and Raleigh Hotel in Washington, D.C.

**Hardenbergh, Jacob Rutsen.** 1736–1790. American Dutch Reformed clergyman and educator; upholder of Colonial cause during American Revolution. President, Queen's College, now Rutgers U. (1786–90).

**Har′der** (här′dẽr), **Johann Jakob.** 1656–1711. Swiss anatomist; discovered a lacrimal gland found in many animals (Harder's gland).

**Hardicanute.** See HARDECANUTE.

**Har′die** (här′dĭ), **Keir,** *in full* **James Keir.** 1856–1915. British Socialist and labor leader, b. in Scotland. Worked as a miner (1866–78); organized labor union among miners, and became secretary of Scottish Miners' Federation (1886). Chairman of newly organized Scottish Labor party (1888); founded and edited *Labour Leader* (1889). M.P. (1892–95; 1900–15); first leader of Labor party in parliament (1906–07).

**Har′din** (här′dĭn), **John.** 1753–1792. American army officer, b. in Fauquier County, Va. Served in Continental army through American Revolution. Moved to Kentucky (1786). Became noted Indian fighter; commissioned brigadier general (1792); murdered by Indians (May, 1792) on spot where city of Hardin, Ohio, now stands. Hardin County, Ky., and Hardin County, Ohio, are named in his honor.

**Har′ding** (här′dĭng), **Ber·ti′ta** (bẽr·tē′tȧ). *Nee* **Bertita Car′la** (kär′lȧ) **Ca·mille′** (kȧ·mēl′) **Le·o·narz′** (lē·närz′). 1907– . American writer, b. in Bavaria of Spanish and Hungarian parents. m. Jack Ellison de Harding, of Manchester, Eng. (1926); to U.S. (1926), naturalized (1927). Lecturer, and singer of Hungarian and Spanish folk songs, in U.S. and Mexico (from 1927). Author of *Phantom Crown* (1934), *Farewell 'Toinette* (1938), *Imperial Twilight* (1939), *Hungarian Rhapsody* (1940), etc.

**Harding, Chester.** 1792–1866. American portrait painter, b. Conway, Mass. Cabinetmaker, house painter, tavern keeper, sign painter, and finally, self-taught portrait painter. Studio in Springfield, Mass. (from c. 1830). His portrait of Daniel Webster hangs in Cincinnati Museum of Art; of John Randolph, in Corcoran Gallery, Washington, D.C.

**Harding, Chester.** 1866–1936. American army officer, b. Enterprise, Miss.; grad. U.S.M.A., West Point (1889). Division engineer, Gatun Locks division, Panama Canal (1907–08); engineer of maintenance, Panama Canal (1915–17). Governor of Panama Canal (1917–21).

**Harding, George.** 1882–1959. American painter and illustrator, b. Philadelphia. Appointed an official artist of A.E.F. Best known for his murals, as in U.S. Custom House in Philadelphia, Post Office buildings in Philadelphia and Washington, etc.

**Harding, James Duffield.** 1798–1863. English landscape painter and lithographer; perfected lithographic process, and invented lithotint.

**Harding,** Saint **Stephen.** 1048?–?1134. English-born cofounder (1098, with St. Robert de Molesmes) of the monastery of Cîteaux, south of Dijon, France, first abbey of the Cistercian order, and its abbot (from 1110); founded also various branches of the Cîteaux monastery. Author of *Carta Caritatis* (*Rule of Love*), the rule of the Cistercian order.

**Harding, Warren Gamaliel.** 1865–1923. Twenty-ninth president of the United States, b. in Morrow County, Ohio; bought Marion (Ohio) *Star;* edited it (from 1884); U.S. senator (1915–21); conservative Republican; favored protective tariffs, arming of American ships during World War; opposed League of Nations, high taxes on war profits. President (1921–23); administration suffered from the corruption of officials appointed by Harding, notably Daugherty and Fall. Died at San Francisco while on speaking tour (Aug. 2, 1923).

**Harding, William Procter Gould.** 1864–1930. American banker; member, Federal Reserve Board (1914); governor, Federal Reserve Board (1916–22). Managing director, War Finance Corporation (1918). Governor, Federal Reserve Bank of Boston (1923–30).

**Har′dinge** (här′dĭng), Sir **Henry.** 1st Viscount **Hardinge of La·hore′** (lȧ·hōr′). 1785–1856. British soldier; M.P. (1820–44); secretary at war (1828–30; 1841–44). Lieutenant general (1841); general (1854); field marshal (1855). Governor general of India (1844–47). His elder son, **Charles Stewart** (1822–1894), 2d viscount, was his private secretary in India (1844–47); M.P. (1851–56), and undersecretary for war (1858–59). Charles's younger son, **Charles** (1858–1944), 1st Baron **Hardinge of Pens′hurst** (pĕnz′hûrst); in diplomatic service (from 1880); ambassador to Russia (1904–06); viceroy of India (1910–16); ambassador to France (1920–23). The 1st viscount's younger son, Sir **Arthur Edward** (1828–1892), soldier, commanded Bombay army (1881–85); general (1883); governor of Gibraltar (1886–90). His son Sir **Arthur Henry** (1859–1933), diplomat; minister to Persia (1900–05), Belgium (1906–11), Portugal (1911–13); ambassador to Spain (1913–19); retired (1920); author of *A Diplomatist in Europe* (1927), etc.

**Har′douin′** (år′dwăɴ′), **Jean.** 1646–1729. French Jesuit priest and scholar; author of *Nummi Antiqui* (1684); editor of Pliny's *Historia Naturalis;* conspicuous for maintaining certain remarkable theories, as the theory that most books attributed to the ancients were actually written by 13th-century monks under the direction of one Severus Archontius, and the theory that the coins and medals supposed to be of antiquity are actually made by relatively modern artists; also, attacked authenticity of Roman Catholic church councils anterior to the Council of Trent.

**Hardouin-Mansart** *or* **-Mansard.** See MANSART.

**Hardt** (härt), **Ernst.** 1876–1947. German poet, novelist, and playwright; director, National Theater, Weimar (1919–24), State Theater, Cologne (1925), and West German Broadcasting Co., Cologne (from 1926).

**Hard′wicke** (härd′wĭk), Earls of. See Philip YORKE.

**Hardwicke,** Sir **Cedric Webster.** 1893–1964. English actor, b. in Worcestershire; served in France (1915–22). Joined Birmingham repertory company; appeared in London (1924) in Shaw's *Back to Methuselah;* roles include Caesar in *Caesar and Cleopatra*, Captain Andy in *Show Boat*, Edward Moulton-Barrett in *The Barretts of Wimpole Street*, Captain Shotover in *Heartbreak House*, and Dr. Haggett in *The Late Christopher Bean;* also appeared in motion pictures.

**Har′dy′** (år′dē′), **Alexandre.** 1570?–?1631. French

dramatic poet; credited with freeing the stage from the mannerisms of Jodelle and with introducing into French tragedy many of its characteristic features. Noteworthy among his hundreds of plays are *Didon* (1603), *Méléagre* (1604), *La Mort d'Achille* (1607), *Marianne* (1610).

**Har'dy** (här'dĭ), **Arthur Sherburne.** 1847–1930. American mathematician and writer; professor of civil engineering, Dartmouth (1874–93). U.S. minister to Persia (1897–99), to Greece, Rumania, and Serbia (1899–1901), Switzerland (1901–03), Spain (1903–05). In addition to works on advanced mathematics, he wrote *Francesca of Rimini* (verse, 1878), *But Yet a Woman* (1883), *The Wind of Destiny* (1886), *Passe Rose* (1889), *His Daughter First* (1903).

**Hardy, Godfrey Harold.** 1877–1947. English mathematician; authority on analysis and on the theory of numbers.

**Hardy, Thomas.** 1840–1928. English novelist, b. in Dorsetshire. Studied architecture, but devoted himself to literature (from 1867); O.M. (1911). Among his many novels are *Under the Greenwood Tree* (1872), *A Pair of Blue Eyes* (1873), *Far from the Madding Crowd* (1874), *The Return of the Native* (1878), *Mayor of Casterbridge* (1886), *Tess of the d'Urbervilles* (1891), *Jude the Obscure* (1895); among his poetical works are *Wessex Poems* (1898), *Poems of the Past and Present* (1901), *The Dynasts* (a poetic drama, in 3 parts, 1904–08).

**Hardy,** Sir **Thomas Masterman.** 1769–1839. British naval officer; flag captain under Nelson (1799–1805); first sea lord of the admiralty (1830).

**Har'dyng** (här'dĭng), **John.** 1378–?1465. English chronicler; in service of Sir Henry Percy (Hotspur) and later of Sir Robert de Umfreville. Received land grants in return for forged documents. His chronicle came down originally to 1436, and was extended in a later form to 1461.

**Hare** (hâr), **Augustus William.** 1792–1834. English clergyman; incumbent of Alton-Barnes (1829–34); collaborator with his brother **Julius Charles** (1795–1855), archdeacon of Lewes, in *Guesses at Truth* (1827). Their nephew **Augustus John Cuthbert Hare** (1834–1903) wrote *Memorials of a Quiet Life* (3 vols., 1872–76), *The Story of My Life* (6 vols., 1896–1900), and a series of European guidebooks.

**Hare, Hobart Amory.** 1862–1931. American physician; author of *Practical Therapeutics* (1890), *Practical Diagnosis* (1896), *Practice of Medicine* (1907), etc. His daughter **Amory** (1885–1964) was a poet and novelist; m. A. B. Cook (1908), James Pemberton Hutchinson (1927); author of the novel *Deep Country* (1933) and the books of verse *Tossed Coins* (1920), *The Swept Hearth* (1922), *The Olympians* (1925), *Sonnets* (1927).

**Hare, James H.** 1856–1946. American war correspondent and news photographer, b. London, Eng. To U.S. (1889), and covered Cuban revolution and Spanish-American War (1898), Russo-Japanese War (1904–05), Balkan War (1912), and World War (1914–18); a pioneer in aerial photography.

**Hare,** Sir **John.** *Orig. name* **John Fairs** (fârz). 1844–1921. English actor and theater manager; member of Prince of Wales's company in London (1865–74). Comanager of Court Theatre (1874–79) and St. James's Theatre (1879–88); manager of Garrick Theatre (1889–95).

**Hare, Martin.** Pseudonym of Zoë GIRLING.

**Hare, Robert.** 1781–1858. American chemist, b. Philadelphia. Invented oxyhydrogen blowpipe (1801). Specialized in study of electricity; made a number of inventions of laboratory apparatus for testing and experimenting.

**Hare, Thomas.** 1806–1891. English political reformer; a lawyer by profession. Best known for his proposed election system (Hare system), giving each class of voters in the electorate representation in proportion to its numerical strength.

**Hare, William.** fl. 1829. See William BURKE.

**Hare, William Hobart.** 1838–1909. American Protestant Episcopal bishop, b. Princeton, N.J. Served among Sioux Indians in South Dakota region; known as "the Apostle to the Sioux."

**Ha'rel'** (à'rĕl'), **Paul.** 1854–1927. French innkeeper and poet.

**Ha'ren** (hä'rĕn), **Willem van.** 1710–1768. Dutch statesman and poet. In politics, a partisan of William IV and member of States-General; in literature, author of the patriotic ode *Leonidas* (1742) calling upon his people to go to the aid of Maria Theresa in the War of the Austrian Succession. His brother **Onno Zwier** (1713–1779) was also a poet; author of the patriotic epic *De Geuzen* (1776) and several dramas.

**Harewood,** Earls of. See LASCELLES family.

**Har'grave** (här'grāv), **Lawrence.** 1850–1915. Inventor, and pioneer in aviation, b. in England; to Australia (1866). Devoted himself to solving problems of human flight; experimented with monoplane models propelled by clockwork, rubber bands in tension, compressed air, and steam (1884–92); invented a model rotary airplane engine (1889); invented the box kite (c. 1893), the first successful airplane being an arrangement of a box kite.

**Har'graves** (här'grāvz), **Edward Hammond.** 1816–1891. Australian rancher and gold prospector, b. in England; to Sydney, Australia; managed sheep ranch (1834–49); discovered gold deposits and began mining near Bathurst (1851).

**Har'greaves** (här'grēvz), **James.** d. 1778. English inventor; weaver and mechanic near Blackburn; reputed inventor of the spinning jenny (c. 1764; patented 1770).

**Hä'ring** *or* **Hae'ring** (hâ'rĭng), **Wilhelm.** *Pseudonym* **Willibald A·lex'is** (ä·lĕk'sĭs). 1798–1871. German historical novelist. Author of *Walladmor* (1824) and *Schloss Avalon* (1927), at first purported to be written by Sir Walter Scott; other works include *Cabanis* (1832), *Der Falsche Woldemar* (1842), *Isegrimm* (1854), *Dorothe* (1856), etc.

**Har'ing·ton** (hăr'ĭng·tŭn). See also HARRINGTON.

**Harington,** Sir **Charles Harington.** 1872–1940. British soldier; served in Boer War (1899–1900), World War (1914–18); commanded Black Sea army (1920–21); commanded Allied forces of occupation in Turkey (1921–23); promoted general (1927) and commanded in India (1927–31). Aide-de-camp general to the king (1930–34); governor and commander in chief at Gibraltar (1933–38).

**Harington** *or* **Harrington,** Sir **John.** 1561–1612. English writer. Godson of Queen Elizabeth. Translated Ariosto's *Orlando Furioso* by command of Elizabeth; banished from court because of certain satires, including *Metamorphosis of Ajax* (1596). Accompanied Essex to Ireland (1598); attempted vainly to reconcile Elizabeth and Essex. Author of an account of Elizabeth's last days, a *Tract on the Succession to the Crown*, and an appendix to Godwin's *De Praesulibus Angliae;* his collected epigrams were published in 1618.

**Harington, John.** 1st Baron **Harington of Ex'ton** (ĕks'tŭn). d. 1613. English nobleman, cousin of Sir John Harington (1561–1612); entrusted by James I at his coronation (1603) with guardianship of Princess Elizabeth at Combe Abbey; saved Elizabeth from Gunpowder Plot conspirators (1605), escaping with her to Coventry; accompanied her to Germany on her marriage to elector palatine (1613); died on return journey.

**Hariot, Thomas.** See Thomas HARRIOT.

**Ha·ri′ri, al–** (ăl′hä·rē′rē). *Arab.* **Abu Muḥammad al-Qāsim al-Ḥarīri.** 1054–1122. Arab scholar and poet, b. Basra; author of several philological works. Chief work, *Maqāmāt* (*i.e.* Assemblies), consisting of 50 episodes or tales in rhyme about Abu Zaid, a witty and imaginative rogue, was for centuries held as most popular and important literary composition in Arabic next to the Koran; influenced later picaresque novels of Italy and Spain.

**Har′kins** (här′kĭnz), **William Draper.** 1873–1951. American chemist, b. Titusville, Pa. Consultant to U.S. Bureau of Mines (1920–22), U.S. Air Service (1924–27) and Chemical Warfare Service (from 1927). Known esp. for work on isotopic weights and atomic structure.

**Hark′ness** (härk′nĕs; -nĭs), **Albert.** 1822–1907. American classical scholar; professor of Greek, Brown (1855–92). Published editions of classical works, and a *Latin Grammar* (1865).

**Harkness, Anna M.**, *nee* **Richardson.** 1838?–1926. American philanthropist; wife of **Stephen Vanderburg Harkness** (1818–1888), oil magnate; donor of Harkness Memorial Quadrangle (completed 1921) to Yale in memory of her son **Charles William** (d. 1916). Her gift was supplemented by a liberal contribution from her son **Edward Stephen** (1874–1940), capitalist, trustee of Metropolitan Museum of Art and the Presbyterian Hospital in New York City; also large benefactor of Harvard, donating about $12,000,000 to enable Harvard to establish a house system; his wife, **Mary**, *nee* **Stillman** (1875–1950), gave to Yale Library its copy of the Gutenberg Bible.

**Harkness, William.** 1837–1903. Astronomer, b. Ecclefechan, Scotland; to U.S. as a child. Member, Transit of Venus Commission (1871); official observer of transits of 1874 and 1882. Invented the spherometer caliper and other astronomical instruments. Astronomical director, U.S. Naval Observatory (1894).

**Har′lan** (här′lăn), **James.** 1820–1899. American political leader, b. in Clark County, Ill. U.S. senator (1855–65; 1867–73), secretary of the interior (1865–66).

**Harlan, John Marshall.** 1833–1911. American jurist, b. in Boyle County, Ky. Served in Union army in Civil War (1861–63). Attorney general of Kentucky (1863–67). Associate justice, U.S. Supreme Court (1877–1911). His grandson **John Marshall Harlan** (1899–1971), American lawyer, b. Chicago, Illinois; associate justice, U.S. Supreme Court (1955–71).

**Harlan, Otis.** 1865–1940. American actor; leading comedian, Folies Bergères Theatre, New York (1912). Acted in motion pictures (from 1920).

**Har′land** (här′lănd), **Henry.** 1861–1905. Novelist, b. St. Petersburg, Russia, of American parents. Wrote (from 1886), using pseud. **Sidney Lus′ka** (lŭs′kȧ) in earlier work. Lived in London, England (from c. 1890); associated with Aubrey Beardsley in publishing the *Yellow Book* (1894–97). Best known novels, *The Cardinal's Snuff Box* (1900), *The Lady Paramount* (1902), *My Friend Prospero* (1904).

**Harland, Marion.** Pseudonym of Mrs. Edward Payson TERHUNE.

**Har′lay′ de Champ′val′lon′** (ȧr′lā′ dē shäɴ′vȧ′lôɴ′), **François de.** 1625–1695. French Roman Catholic prelate; archbishop of Rouen (1651) and of Paris (1671); strong supporter of Louis XIV and his policies, and one of the three witnesses to the secret marriage of Louis XIV and Mme. de Maintenon.

**Harlech,** Baron. See William George Arthur ORMSBY-GORE.

**Har′ley** (här′lĭ), Sir **Edward.** 1624–1700. English Parliamentarian soldier; descended from Whig and nonconformist stock; general of horse for Herefordshire and Radnor (1645). M.P. (1646, 1656); member of council of state (1659); governor of Dunkirk (1660–61). Sat in Parliament under Charles II and in 1st, 3d, and 4th parliaments under William III.

**Harley, Robert.** 1st Earl of **Ox′ford** (ŏks′fērd). 1661–1724. English statesman. Descended from Whig and nonconformist stock; M.P. (1689–1711) as moderate Tory; speaker (1701–05), a principal secretary of state through influence of Marlborough (1704); employed Defoe and Swift as political writers; forced out of secretaryship by Godolphin and Marlborough for intriguing against them through behind-the-scenes influence with the queen (1708). Chancellor of exchequer and head of ministry (1710) but unable to organize a government; made lord treasurer (1711); corresponded with both Hanoverians and Jacobites; negotiated separate peace, independently of Allies, and by dismissal of Marlborough and creation of new peers, carried treaty of Utrecht (1713). Superseded in queen's favor by his former friend St. John (Bolingbroke) and dismissed from office; imprisoned (1715–17); his impeachment for making a peace favorable to the Old Pretender and Jacobites dismissed (1717); forbidden the court. Collected books and manuscripts. His son **Edward** (1689–1741), 2d earl, was friend and correspondent of Pope and Swift, circulated second edition of *Dunciad*, added to his father's collection of books and manuscripts.

**Har′lez′** (ȧr′lā′), **Charles de.** 1832–1899. Belgian Sanskrit scholar.

**Harmensen, Jacob.** Real name of Jacobus ARMINIUS.

**Harm′hab** (härm′hăb) *or* **Hor′em·hab** (hŏr′ĕm·hăb) *or* **Hor′em·heb** (-hĕb). First king of XIXth (Diospolite) dynasty of ancient Egypt; reigned (1350–1315 B.C.). A soldier and able ruler; restored kingdom to Amen worship; destroyed temples and remains of new religion of Ikhnaton's and Tutankhamen's reigns; reorganized administration.

**Har·mo′di·us** (här·mō′dĭ·ŭs) and **A·ris′to·gi′ton** *or* **A·ris′to·gei′ton** (ȧ·rĭs′tō·jī′tŏn; ăr′ĭs·tō-). d. 514 B.C. Two Athenian youths, devoted friends, who assassinated Hipparchus, tyrant of Athens, Harmodius being killed by guard and Aristogiton captured, tortured, and executed. Honored as heroes by Athenian people.

**Har′mon** (här′mŭn), **Judson.** 1846–1927. American politician, b. Newtown, Ohio. Practiced, Cincinnati. U.S. attorney general (1895–97). Governor of Ohio (1909–13). Prominent candidate for Democratic nomination for president (1912).

**Harmon, Millard Fillmore.** 1888–1945. American army officer; grad. (1912) U.S.M.A.; commander, 2d air force (1941–42); chief of air staff (1942); lieut. general (1943); commander, air forces in South Pacific (1942–44), in Pacific (1944–45); lost in flight.

**Harms** (härms), **Bernhard.** 1876–1939. German economist.

**Harms′worth** (härmz′wûrth; -wērth). Family of British publishers and politicians, including the brothers: **Alfred Charles William** (1865–1922), Viscount **North′cliffe** (nôrth′klĭf), b. County Dublin, Ireland; descendant of old Hampshire family. Took up free-lance journalism (1882); with his brother Harold, set up general publishing business in London (1887); started (1888) *Answers to Correspondents*, later called *Answers;* acquired and reorganized *Evening News*, Conservative party organ (1894); founded *Daily Mail*, half-penny morning newspaper with many innovations and condensed for busy men (1896); founded *Daily Mirror* (1903), altered it to half-penny illustrated morning paper; created baron

(1905); acquired *The Times* (1908); warned nation for twenty years against German threat; in World War I, became leader in British politics, advocate of vigorous conduct of war; opposed Dardanelles and Salonika campaigns; supported Lloyd George government in crisis (Dec., 1916); declined ambassadorship to U.S. but undertook mission there; director of propaganda in enemy countries (1918); contributed to defeat of Austrian armies by securing an agreement between Yugoslavs and Italian government; instrumental in bringing about Irish settlement (1921).

**Harold Sidney** (1868–1940), 1st Viscount **Roth'er·mere** (rŏth'ẽr·mẽr), joined Alfred in publishing periodicals and building up Amalgamated Press; bought Alfred's *Daily Mirror;* director-general of royal army clothing dept. (1916–17); air minister (1917–18); endowed King Edward VII chair of English literature and Vere Harmsworth chair of naval history, both at Cambridge, and Harold Vyvyan chair of American history at Oxford; author of *My Fight to Rearm Britain* (1939).

Sir **Hildebrand Aubrey** (1872–1929), editor of *New Liberal Review* (1901); joined Joseph Chamberlain's fiscal reform party (1904); proprietor of the *Globe* (1908–11).

**Cecil Bisshopp** (1869–1948), 1st Baron **Harmsworth;** Liberal M.P. (1906); undersecretary for home affairs (1915) and foreign affairs (1919–22); acting minister of blockade (1919); member of supreme economic council; member of Council, League of Nations (1922); author of *Immortals at First Hand* (1933).

Sir **Robert Leicester** (1870–1937), Liberal M.P. (1900–22); created baronet (1918).

**Har'nack** (här'näk), **Adolf von.** 1851–1930. German Protestant theologian, b. Dorpat (Tartu). His father, **Theodosius** (1817–1889), was also a Protestant theologian; author of *Luthers Theologie* (vol. I, 1862; II, 1886). Adolf's twin brother, **Axel** (1851–88), was a mathematician; author of a book on calculus. Another brother, **Otto** (1857–1914), was a historian of literature. See also Agnes von ZAHN-HARNACK.

**Harn'den** (härn'dĕn), **William Frederick.** 1812–1845. American pioneer in express business, inaugurating (1839) express carriage between Boston and New York; business finally merged into Adams Express Co.

**Har'ned** (här'nĕd; -nĭd), **Virginia.** 1868?–1946. American actress; m. E. H. Sothern (1896; divorced 1910); leading woman for E. H. Sothern under Daniel Frohman's management; created title role of *Trilby*, in Boston (1895).

**Har'nett** (här'nĕt; -nĭt), **William Michael.** 1848–1892. American painter, b. in County Cork, Ire. Known for his still-life studies, as *Emblems of Peace* (now in Springfield, Mass.)

**Ha'ro** (ä'rō), **Luis de.** Duque **de Car'pio** (thā kär'pyō). 1598–1661. Spanish diplomat, nephew of duke of Olivares. Succeeded his uncle as minister of Philip IV (1643); negotiated Peace of Pyrenees with France (1659).

**Har'old** (hăr'ŭld). *Dan.* **Ha'rald** (hä'räl). Name of three kings of Denmark:

**Harold Blue'tooth'** (blōō'tōōth'). *Dan.* **Harald Blaa'tand'** (blô'tän'). d. 985? Son of Gorm. King (940?–?985). Conquered Norway, but could not retain it; converted to Christianity (960?); killed in war against his son Sweyn.

**Harold.** d. 1018. Son of Sweyn I and brother of Canute the Great. King (1014–18).

**Harold Hen** (hĭn), *i.e.* the Gentle. *Also* **Harold Sweyn'son** (svĭn'sŏn). d. 1080. Son of Sweyn II. King (1076–80).

**Harold.** Name of two kings of the English.

**Harold I.** *Called* **Harold Hare'foot'** (hâr'fŏŏt'). d. 1040. King (1035–1040); illegitimate son of Canute; on death of Canute (1035), claimed English crown; elected king (1037) by the witan over Canute's legitimate son Hardecanute.

**Harold II.** 1022?–1066. King (Jan. 6–Oct. 14, 1066); son of Godwin, Earl of Wessex; served as chief minister of his brother-in-law, Edward the Confessor (1053–66); on Edward's death, secured his own election as king (Jan. 6, 1066); defeated his brother Tostig and Harold Haardraade, King of Norway, Tostig's ally, at Stamford Bridge (Sept. 25, 1066); hastened south to meet William, Duke of Normandy, who had just landed in England; killed in battle of Hastings or Senlac (Oct. 14, 1066).

**Harold.** *Norw.* **Harald.** Name of three kings of Norway.

**Harold I.** *Called* **the Fair'haired'** (fâr'hârd'). *Norw.* **Haar'fa'ger** (hôr'fä'gẽr). 850?–933. King (860–930). Son of Halfden the Swarthy. Norwegian earl (jarl); induced to subdue other earls and petty rulers in Norway, thence waged continual war (860–872) until last was defeated, in naval battle; forced deposed rulers to leave Norway, a memorable event in that it compelled many Norsemen to settle elsewhere—Orkneys, Hebrides, Shetlands, Faeroes, Iceland, and coast of France (Normandy: see ROLLO); established strong kingdom but power lost by dissension of sons; abdicated (930) in favor of Eric Bloodaxe.

**Harold II.** *Called* **Gray'fell'** (grā'fĕl'). 930?–?977. King (961–970). Son of Eric Bloodaxe. Overcome by Earl Haakon.

**Harold III.** *Called* **Hard'-Rul'er** (härd'rōōl'ẽr). *Norw.* **Haard'raa'de** (hôr'rô'dĕ). 1015–1066. King (1047–66). Son of Sigurd and a descendant of Harold I. Present at battle of Stiklestad (1030) when his half brother King Olaf was killed; visited courts of Novgorod, Kiev, and, later (1033), Constantinople; many adventures here and in Mediterranean regions attributed to him in Norse sagas; returned to Russia (1044) and to Norway (1046); became king at death of Magnus (1047); fought long war with Danes (1047–64); requested by Earl Tostig, brother of English king, Harold II, to aid in conquest of England (1066); sailed with large fleet; killed at battle of Stamford Bridge (Sept. 25).

**Har'old Gille** (gĭl'). 1103?–1136. Norwegian pretender, b. in Ireland. Claimed to be son of Magnus Barefoot. Appeared in Norway (1129); at death of Sigurd I (1130), chosen by one faction as king opposed to Magnus IV; civil war (1134–35); slain by another pretender; his sons in power (1137–61).

**Haroun-al-Raschid.** See HARUN AL-RASHID.

**Har'pa·gus** (här'pȧ·gŭs). Median general of 6th century B.C. According to legend, was ordered by Astyages, King of Media, to expose the infant Cyrus to die, but entrusted task to a herdsman who kept Cyrus alive and substituted for him a still-born babe. When this fact became known, Astyages punished Harpagus by serving to him at a banquet the flesh of his own son. Later, when Cyrus the Great rebelled against Astyages, Harpagus carried his army over to join Cyrus and became one of Cyrus's most trusted generals during campaigns for conquest of Asia Minor.

**Har'pa·lus** (här'pȧ·lŭs). Associate of Alexander the Great in late 4th century B.C.; entrusted by Alexander with government of conquered Babylonia and guardianship of the royal treasure; stole the treasure and fled, first to Athens and then to Crete, where he was assassinated (324 B.C.).

**Har'per** (här'pẽr), **George McLean.** 1863–1947. American educator; professor of Romance languages (1894–1900), English literature (1900–26), literature (1926–32),

Princeton. Author of *The Legend of the Holy Grail* (1893), *William Wordsworth...* (1916), *Literary Appreciations* (1937), etc.

**Harper, James.** 1795–1869. American publisher; with brother **John** (1797–1875) set up printing office, New York (1817); admitted brothers **Joseph Wesley** (1801–1870) in 1823, and **Fletcher** (1806–1877) in 1825; adopted firm name Harper & Bros. (1833).

**Harper, Robert Goodloe.** 1765–1825. American politician; member, U.S. House of Representatives (1795–1801). Served in War of 1812; major general of Maryland forces. U.S. senator (1816). An original member of American Colonization Society; suggested *Liberia* and *Monrovia* as names for the colony in Africa and its capital.

**Harper, William Rainey.** 1856–1906. American educator; first president of new U. of Chicago (1891–1906). Author of *Religion and the Higher Life* (1904), *The Trend in Higher Education* (1905), etc. His brother **Robert Francis** (1864–1914), Assyriologist, taught at Yale (1886–91) and Chicago (1892–1914; professor from 1900); published *The Code of Hammurabi* (1904).

**Har'pi'gnies'** (àr'pē'nyē'), **Henri.** 1819–1916. French painter of landscapes.

**Har'po·cra'ti·on** (här'pō·krā'shĭ·ŏn), **Valerius.** Greek scholar of Alexandria in 2d century A.D. (or later); compiler of lexicon of works of Attic orators.

**Har'ra·den** (hăr'ȧ·dĕn), **Beatrice.** 1864–1936. English novelist; author of *Ships that Pass in the Night* (1893), *The Scholar's Daughter* (1906), *Rachel* (1926), and *Search Will Find It Out* (1928), etc.

**Har'rap** (hăr'ăp), **George Godfrey.** 1867–1938. British publisher; founded (1901) George G. Harrap & Co., Ltd.

**Har'ries** (här'ēs), **Heinrich.** 1762–1802. German poet; author of the Prussian national hymn, *Heil dir im Siegerkranz.*

**Har'ri·gan** (hăr'ĭ·găn), **Edward.** 1845–1911. American actor; member of comedy team at Theatre Comique, N.Y. (1876–81) and new Theatre Comique (1881–84); wrote sketches, esp. the "Dan Mulligan" series.

**Har'ri·man** (hăr'ĭ·măn), **Edward Henry.** 1848–1909. American railroad magnate. Office boy in Wall Street (1862–69), member, stock exchange (1869); director (1883), vice-president (1887), Illinois Central; president (1903), Union Pacific; conducted scientific expedition to Alaska (1899); lost control of Northern Pacific to James J. Hill in struggle that precipitated stock market panic (1901); investigated by Interstate Commerce Comm. (1906–07). His son **William Averell** (1891– ), businessman, b. New York City; board chairman, Merchant Shipbuilding Corporation (1917–25), Union Pacific R.R. (1932–46); lend-lease coordinator (1941–43); U.S. ambassador to Russia (1943–46), to Gt. Britain (1946); secy. of commerce (1946–48); governor of N.Y. (1955–58); ambassador at large (1961; 1965–69).

**Harriman, Florence Jaffray,** *nee* **Hurst** (hûrst). 1870–1967. American diplomat, b. New York City; m. J. Borden Harriman (1889; d. 1914). Manager, New York State Reformatory for Women, Bedford, N.Y. (1906–18). Chairman, committee on women in industry, Council of National Defense (1917–19); in France, in charge of contingent of Red Cross Women's Motor Corps (1918). U.S. minister to Norway (1937–40).

**Har'ring·ton** (hăr'ĭng·tŭn). See also HARINGTON.

**Har'ring·ton** *or* **Har'ing·ton** (hăr'ĭng·tŭn), **James.** 1611–1677. English political theorist; author of *The Commonwealth of Oceana* (1656), and several tracts supporting his Utopian state.

**Harrington, Mark Walrod.** 1848–1926. American astronomer.

**Har'ri·ot** *or* **Har'i·ot** (hăr'ĭ·ŭt), **Thomas.** 1560–1621 English mathematician. His posthumously published work, *Artis Analyticae Praxis ad Aequationes Algebraicas Resolvendas* (1631), contains inventions which give algebra its modern form.

**Har'ris** (hăr'ĭs), Sir **Arthur Travers.** 1892– . British air officer; served in World War (1914–18); joined Royal Air Force (1919); air commodore (1937); air vice-marshal (1939); air marshal (1941); member, British war mission to U.S. (1941); member, combined British-American chiefs of staff (1942). Took over Bomber Command (1942–45); responsible for new British policy in bombing of Germany and German-occupied Europe.

**Harris, Benjamin.** fl. 1673–1716. Publisher and journalist in London (to 1686); to America and opened bookshop in Boston (1686). Began publication of *Publick Occurrences Both Forreign and Domestick,* first newspaper printed in America (Sept. 25, 1690); also published the famous *New England Primer* (c. 1690). Returned to London (1695); published *London Post,* a newspaper (1699–1706).

**Harris, Chapin Aaron.** 1806–1860. American dentist, b. Pompey, N.Y.; founder (1839) with Horace H. Hayden of world's first dental college, Baltimore College of Dental Surgery (chartered 1840).

**Harris, Charles Kas'sell** (?kăs''l). 1865–1930. American writer of popular songs, including *After the Ball* (1892) and *Break the News to Mother* (1897).

**Harris, Corra May,** *nee* **White.** 1869–1935. American writer; m. Lundy Howard Harris (1887; d. 1910). Author of *A Circuit Rider's Wife* (1910), *Eve's Second Husband* (1910), *As a Woman Thinks* (1925), *Happy Pilgrimage* (1927), etc.

**Harris, Frank.** 1856–1931. Author, b. Galway, Ireland; to U.S. (1870); naturalized American citizen. Editor London *Evening News* and *Fortnightly Review;* acquired control of *Saturday Review,* London. His biography of *Oscar Wilde* (1916) and the autobiographical *My Life and Loves* (1923) excited hostile criticism because of their frankness. Other works include: biographical studies, *The Man Shakespeare* (1909), *Contemporary Portraits* (4 series, 1915–23); volumes of short stories, *Elder Conklin* (1894), *Montes the Matador* (1900), *The Veils of Isis* (1915), *A Mad Love* (1920); novels, *The Bomb* (1908), *Great Days* (1914), and *Love in Youth* (1916); and plays, *Mr. and Mrs. Daventry* (1900), *Shakespeare and His Love* (1910), and *Joan la Romée* (1926).

**Harris, George.** 1st Baron **Harris.** 1746–1829. English soldier; wounded at Bunker Hill (1775); served against Tipu Sahib in India (1790–92), commanded troops in Madras (1796–1800), and captured Seringapatam and conquered Mysore (1799).

**Harris, George.** 1844–1922. See under Samuel HARRIS.

**Harris, Howel.** 1714–1773. Welsh pioneer Methodist clergyman; a founder of Welsh Calvinistic Methodism.

**Harris, James.** 1709–1780. English scholar and politician; author of *Hermes, or a Philosophical Inquiry concerning Universal Grammar* (1751). M.P. (1761–80); a lord of the treasury (1763–65); secretary to George III's queen (1774).

**Harris, James.** 1st Earl of **Malmes'bur·y** (mämz'bĕr·ĭ; -brĭ). 1746–1820. English diplomat. Minister, Berlin (1772–76); ambassador at St. Petersburg (1777–82); managed adroitly difficulties of first Armed Neutrality; minister at The Hague (1784); instrumental in overthrow of republican party in Holland in favor of house of Orange. Having seceded from Whig party, sent on futile mission to hold Prussia to first coalition against France (1793); negotiated match between prince of Wales and Princess Caroline of Brunswick; failed in last missions to negotiate peace with French Republic (1796, 1797). His grandson **James Howard Harris** (1807–1889), 3d earl; B.A., Oxon. (1827); foreign secretary in Lord Derby's first and second administrations (1852, 1858–59), recognized and established good relations with Napoleon III, aided in delaying and localizing war between France and Sardinia and Austria; lord privy seal in Lord Derby's last ministry (1866–68) and under Disraeli (1874–76).

**Harris, James Arthur.** 1880–1930. American botanist; authority on biometry.

**Harris, James Rendel.** 1852–1941. English scholar; curator of manuscripts, John Rylands Library, Manchester, Eng. (1918–25); traveled in the East looking for manuscripts. Author of treatises on Biblical literature and on Greek religion and mythology, and of *Return of the Mayflower* (1919), *The Last of the Mayflower* (1920), *The Finding of the Mayflower* (1920), *The Masts of the Mayflower* (1932), and *Who Discovered North America?* (1934).

**Harris, Joel Chandler.** 1848–1908. American writer, b. in Putnam County, Ga.; on staff, Savannah *Morning News* (1870) and Atlanta *Constitution* (1876–1900). Fame rests on his creation of Uncle Remus, as in *Uncle Remus, His Songs and His Sayings* (1880), *Nights with Uncle Remus* (1883), *Uncle Remus and His Friends* (1892), *The Tar Baby* (1904), *Uncle Remus and Brer Rabbit* (1906), *Uncle Remus Returns* (1918), etc.

**Harris, John.** 1667?–1719. English theologian and scientist; chief work, *Lexicon Technicum*, first dictionary in English of the arts and sciences (1704).

**Harris, Robert.** 1849–1919. Painter, b. Conway, North Wales. Studio in Montreal, Can.; best known as genre and portrait painter.

**Harris, Rollin Arthur.** 1863–1918. American oceanographer, b. Randolph, N.Y. Author of *Manual of Tides;* developed a wave theory of the tide.

**Harris, Roy.** 1898– . American composer of orchestral works, symphonies, including a *Folk-Song Symphony*, chamber music, and choral works.

**Harris, Sam Henry.** 1872–1941. American theatrical producer; associated with George M. Cohan (*q.v.*) in firm Cohan & Harris (1904–20); in business alone (from 1920). Produced *Music Box Revues*, *Rain*, *Animal Crackers*, *Of Thee I Sing*, *Dinner at Eight*, *You Can't Take It With You*, *Of Mice and Men*, etc.

**Harris, Samuel.** 1814–1899. American Congregational clergyman and educator; grad. Bowdoin (1833); president, Bowdoin (1867–71); professor, Yale Divinity School (1871–95). His nephew **George Harris** (1844–1922) was also a Congregational clergyman and educator; grad. Amherst (1866); president, Amherst (1899–1912).

**Harris, Thaddeus William.** 1795–1856. American entomologist; librarian, Harvard (from 1831). Author of *Insects of New England Injurious to Vegetation* (1842).

**Harris, Thomas Lake.** 1823–1906. Spiritualist, b. Fenny Stratford, England; to U.S. as a child. Became Universalist (1843); interested in spiritualism (from 1847); became medium (about 1850). Established brotherhood communities, notably at Amenia, N.Y. (about 1863), near Dunkirk, N.Y. (about 1866), and Santa Rosa, Calif. (about 1875).

**Harris, Townsend.** 1804–1878. American diplomat; first U.S. consul general to Japan (1855); first U.S. minister to Japan (1859). Negotiated commercial treaty (1858). Resigned (1861).

**Harris,** Sir **William Cornwallis.** 1807–1848. English engineer and traveler in South Africa (1835–37); published *Portraits of the Game Animals of South Africa* (1840). Discovered and described the Harris buck.

**Harris,** Sir **William Snow.** 1791–1867. English electrical expert.

**Harris, William Torrey.** 1835–1909. American philosopher and educator, b. near North Killingly, Conn. Taught school, St. Louis, Mo. (1857–80); superintendent of schools (from 1868). Founded and edited *Journal of Speculative Philosophy* (1867–93). Interested in Concord School of Philosophy (1879–89). U.S. Commissioner of Education (1889–1906). Became leading American Hegelian; interpreter of German philosophical thought to America. Assistant editor, *Johnson's New Universal Cyclopaedia;* editor in chief, *Webster's New International Dictionary*, first edition (1909). Author of *Introduction to the Study of Philosophy* (1889), *The Spiritual Sense of Dante's Divina Commedia* (1889), *The Psychologic Foundations of Education* (1898).

**Harrison, Alexander.** See Thomas Alexander HARRISON.

**Har'ri·son** (hăr'ĭ·s'n), **Benjamin.** 1726?–1791. American Revolutionary leader, b. in Charles City County, Va. Member, Virginia legislature (1749–75). Member, Continental Congress (1774–78); a signer of Declaration of Independence. Governor of Virginia (1782–84). Member, Virginia legislature (1784–91). See William Henry HARRISON.

**Harrison, Benjamin.** 1833–1901. Grandson of William Henry Harrison. Twenty-third president of the United States, b. North Bend, Ohio. Served through Civil War; brevetted brigadier general (1865). After war, resumed law practice at Indianapolis. Unsuccessful candidate for governor (1876). U.S. senator (1881–87). President of the United States (1889–93).

**Harrison, Birge.** See under Thomas Alexander HARRISON.

**Harrison, Constance,** *nee* **Car'y** (kâr'ĭ). 1843–1920. American writer, b. in Fairfax County, Va.; m. Burton Norvell Harrison (1867; d. 1904). Author of *A Daughter of the South* (1892), *Sweet Bells out of Tune* (1893), *An Errant Wooing* (1895), *The Anglomaniacs* (1899), *Latter-Day Sweethearts* (1906), etc.

**Harrison, Elizabeth.** 1849–1927. American educator; established (1887) and was president (1887–1920) of training school for teachers; author of *A Study of Child Nature* (1890), *Montessori and the Kindergarten* (1913).

**Harrison, Francis Burton.** 1873–1957. American lawyer and politician; practiced in New York. Member, U.S. House of Representatives (1903–05, 1907–13). Governor general of the Philippines (1913–21). His brother **Fairfax** (1869–1938), lawyer and railroad executive; president, Southern Railway (1913–37).

**Harrison, Frederic.** 1831–1923. English writer and positivist philosopher, b. in London. Called to bar (1858); practiced in London (1858–c. 1873). Interested himself in positivism (from c. 1856); regarded as one of the leaders in the movement in England; with his associates opened a meeting place in London (1881); founded the *Positivist Review* (1893). Among his many works are *The Meaning of History*, *Order and Progress* (1874), *Social Statics* (1875), *The Choice of Books* (1886), *Oliver Cromwell* (1888), *The Positive Evolution of Religion*, etc.

**Harrison, Gabriel.** 1818–1902. American actor; founded Brooklyn Dramatic Academy (1853); opened Park Theatre, Brooklyn (1863). Appeared as Roger Chillingworth in own dramatization of *The Scarlet Letter* (1878). Author of *Edwin Forrest, the Actor and the Man* (1889), and a number of plays.

**Harrison, George Bagshawe.** 1894– . English scholar; authority on Elizabethan and Jacobean literature; published *Elizabethan Journal* (3 series), *Elizabethan Plays and Players* (1940), *A Jacobean Journal* (1941), etc.

**Harrison, George Russell.** 1898– . American physicist; professor, M.I.T. (from 1930). Author of *Atoms in Action* (1939) and *M.I.T. Wave Length Tables* (1939).

**Harrison, Henry Sydnor.** 1880–1930. American novelist, b. Sewanee, Tenn. Served through World War; resident, New York City (from 1919). Author of *Queed* (1911), *V. V.'s Eyes* (1913), *Saint Teresa* (1922), *Andrew Bride of Paris* (1925), etc.

**Harrison, James Albert.** 1848–1911. American philologist; etymological consultant, *Century Dictionary* and *Standard Dictionary.* With W. M. Baskerville, published *Anglo-Saxon Prose Reader* (1898) and *Dictionary of Anglo-Saxon Poetry* (1900). Other works, *Greek Vignettes* (1877), *Spain in Profile* (1879); edited Virginia edition of *Works of Edgar Allan Poe* (17 vols., 1902).

**Harrison, Jane Ellen.** 1850–1928. English classical scholar; lecturer in classical archaeology, Newnham College (from 1898). Author of *The Mythology and Monuments of Ancient Athens* (1890), *Themis, a Study of the Social Origins of Greek Religion* (1912), etc.

**Harrison, John.** 1693–1776. English horologist and inventor; invented gridiron pendulum (1726) and improved chronometers for accurate determination of longitudes.

**Harrison, Joseph.** 1810–1874. American mechanical engineer; devised various improvements in manufacturing locomotives; patented (1859) Harrison steam boiler, embodying new principle in boiler construction; manufactured it in Philadelphia (from 1862).

**Harrison, Leland.** 1883–1951. American diplomat; secretary of American commission to negotiate peace (1918); assistant secretary of state (1922). U.S. minister to Sweden (1927–29), Uruguay (1929–30), Rumania (1935–37), Switzerland (1937–47).

**Harrison, Lovell Birge.** See under Thomas Alexander HARRISON.

**Harrison, Mary St. Leger.** See *Mary St. Leger Kingsley,* under Charles KINGSLEY.

**Harrison, Pat,** *in full* **Byron Patton.** 1881–1941. American politician; practiced law, Gulfport, Miss. Member, U.S. House of Representatives (1911–19); U.S. Senate (1919–41). Chairman, U.S. Senate finance committee (1933–41).

**Harrison, Peter.** 1716–1775. American architect; b. York, England; to America (1740); settled in Newport, R.I. Designer of Redwood Library, Newport, of King's Chapel, Boston, and Christ Church, Cambridge.

**Harrison, Ross Granville.** 1870–1959. American biologist; professor of comparative anatomy (1907–27), biology (from 1927), Yale. Managing editor, *Journal of Experimental Zoology* (from 1903).

**Harrison, Thomas.** 1606–1660. English Parliamentary soldier and regicide; advocated trial of Charles I, and escorted him from Hurst to London; signed king's death warrant. Held chief command in England during Cromwell's absence (1650–51); reprimanded by Cromwell for his relations with Anabaptists (1654); imprisoned (1655–56; 1658–59). At Restoration (1660), refused to flee or compromise; executed.

**Harrison, Thomas Alexander,** *known as* **Alexander.** 1853–1930. American painter, b. Philadelphia; resided in France; esp. noted for marines. His brother **Lovell Birge,** *known as* **Birge** (1854–1929), was a landscape painter; identified with Woodstock (N.Y.) art colony, esp. as director of summer school of art established by Art Students' League of New York.

**Harrison, William.** 1534–1593. English topographer and clergyman; rector of Radwinter (1559–93); author of *Description of England* (1577).

**Harrison, William Henry.** 1773–1841. Son of Benjamin Harrison (1726?–1791). Ninth president of the United States, b. in Charles City County, Va. Secretary, Northwest Territory (1798). Governor, Territory of Indiana (1801–13). Led Americans in war against Indians (1811–12); appointed to command army of the northwest, with rank of brigadier general, U.S. army (1812); promoted major general after successful campaign (1813); resigned (1814). Member, U.S. House of Representatives from Ohio (1816–19); U.S. Senate (1825–28). U.S. minister to Colombia (1828–29). Unsuccessful Whig candidate for president (1836). Elected president (1840); served as president, Mar. 4–Apr. 4, 1841; died of pneumonia. See Benjamin HARRISON (1833–1901).

**Har'risse'** (ȧ'rēs'), **Henry.** 1830–1910. Scholar, b. Paris; naturalized American citizen. Interested himself in search for documents relating to early history of the New World; published *Bibliotheca Americana Vetustissima* (1866), *John and Sebastian Cabot* (1882), *Christopher Columbus* (1884–85), *Discovery of North America* (1892), etc.

**Harrowby,** Barons and earls. See under Sir Dudley RYDER.

**Harry the Minstrel.** = HENRY THE MINSTREL.

**Har'sá·nyi** (hŏr'shä·nyĭ), **Zsolt de.** 1887–1943. Hungarian novelist, editor, and translator; author of *The Golden Raven, For Death or Life, Ecce Homo, Hungarian Rhapsody, Mathias Rex, Sacra Corona, Eppur Si Muove,* etc.

**Hars'dör'fer** (härs'dûr'fẽr), **Georg Philipp.** 1607–1658. German scholar and poet; collaborated with Johann Klaj in founding (1644) the Pegnitzorden, literary society devoted to purification of the German language.

**Har'sha** (hŭr'shȧ) *or* **Har'sha·var'dha·na** (hŭr'shȧ-vŭr'dȧ·nȧ). 590?–647. King of northern India (606–647). Reduced anarchy in the north (606–612) and established strong kingdom, with Kanauj as capital; extremely devout, a patron of art and literature, and himself a poet and author, esp. of three Sanskrit plays (best known, *Ratnāvalī,* "The Pearl Necklace"); his court made famous by the Brahman author Bana and events of his reign described by the Chinese pilgrim Hsüan Tsang.

**Hars'nett** (härs'nĕt; -nĭt), **Samuel.** 1561–1631. English prelate; archbishop of York (1629–31). Author of *A Declaration of Egregious Popish Impostures* (1603), from which Shakespeare took the names of the spirits in *King Lear.*

**Hart** (härt), **Albert Bushnell.** 1854–1943. American historian and educator, b. Clarksville, Pa. A.B., Harvard (1880); Ph.D., Freiburg (1883). Teacher of history, Harvard (from 1883); professor of history (1897–1910) and government (1910–26). Author of *Formation of the Union* (1892), *Essentials of American History* (1905), *New American History* (1917), *We and Our History* (1923), etc. Editor of several series of histories, as *Epochs of American History* (4 vols., 1891–1926) and *The American Nation* (28 vols., 1903–18). Editor in chief of *A Reference History of the World* for *Webster's New International Dictionary, Second Edition.*

**Hart, Basil Henry Liddell.** See LIDDELL HART.

**Hart, Edward.** 1854–1931. American chemist; patented a mineral wax bottle for holding hydrofluoric acid. Author of *Volumetric Analysis* (1876), *The Silica Gel Pseudomorph* (1924), etc.

**Hart, Frances Newbold,** *nee* **Noyes** (noiz). 1890–1943. American writer; m. Edward Henry Hart (1921). Author of *The Bellamy Trial* (1927), *Pigs in Clover* (1931), *The Crooked Lane* (1934), etc.

**Hart, Hastings Hornell.** 1851–1932. American social-service worker; director of department for child help

(1908–24) and consultant in delinquency and penology (from 1924), Russell Sage Foundation, New York. His son **Hornell Norris** (1888–1967), also a sociologist; professor, Duke U. (1938–57); author of *The Science of Social Relations* (1927), *Skeptic's Quest* (1938), etc.

**Hart, Heinrich** (1855–1906) and his brother **Julius** (1859–1930). German writers; collaborators in editing *Kritische Waffengänge* (1882–86), in writing dramatic criticism and in founding (1879) *Deutscher Literaturkalender*. In addition, Heinrich published the epic *Lied der Menschheit* (1887–96); and Julius, the verse *Sanfara* (1878), *Homo Sum* (1889), *Stimmen der Nacht* (1895), the dramas *Don Juan Tenorio* (1881), *Der Rächer* (1883), *Der Sumpf* (1886).

**Hart, James MacDougal.** 1828–1901. Bro. of William Hart (1823–1894). Landscape painter, b. Kilmarnock, Scotland; to U.S. as a child. Studio, Albany (1853–57) and New York City (from 1857).

**Hart, James Morgan.** 1839–1916. American philologist; author of *A Syllabus of Anglo-Saxon Literature* (1881), *Development of Standard English Speech* (1907), etc.

**Hart, Joel Tanner.** 1810–1877. American sculptor; studio, Lexington, Ky. (1831); built up reputation for marble busts of famous people of the day. Studio, Florence, Italy (from 1849). Invented and patented a measuring machine for aiding in making portrait busts.

**Hart, John.** 1711?–1779. American Revolutionary leader, b. Stonington, Conn. Member, N.J. provincial assembly (1761–71) and congress (1775–76), Continental Congress (1776). A signer of Declaration of Independence. Chairman, N.J. council of safety (1777–78).

**Hart, Liddell.** See LIDDELL HART.

**Hart, Lorenz.** 1895–1943. American lyricist; author of lyrics in *The Little Ritz Girl* (1920), *Dearest Enemy* (1925), *A Connecticut Yankee* (1927), *America's Sweetheart* (1931), *The Boys from Syracuse* (1938), etc. See Richard RODGERS.

**Hart, Moss.** 1904–1961. American librettist and playwright; collaborator with Irving Berlin in *Face the Music* (1932) and with George S. Kaufman in *Once in a Lifetime* (1930), *You Can't Take It With You* (awarded Pulitzer prize, 1936), *I'd Rather be Right* (1937), *The Fabulous Invalid* (1938), *The American Way* (1939).

**Hart,** Sir **Robert.** 1835–1911. British diplomat; entered Chinese consular service (1854); became inspector general of customs (1863–1906), and practically creator of Chinese imperial customs.

**Hart, Thomas Charles.** 1877–1971. American naval officer, b. Davidson, Mich.; grad. U.S.N.A., Annapolis (1897); rear admiral (1929); commander in chief, Asiatic fleet (1939–42); U.S. senator from Conn. (1945–47).

**Hart, William.** 1823–1894. Painter, b. Paisley, Scotland; to U.S. as a child; opened studio, New York City (c. 1852). Member of Hudson River School. See James MacDougal HART.

**Hart, William S.** 1872–1946. American actor; on legitimate stage (to 1914), starred in *Ben Hur*, *The Squaw Man*, *The Virginian*, *The Barrier*, *The Trail of the Lonesome Pine*, etc.; in motion pictures (from 1914), esp. westerns, as *Wagon Tracks*, *The Cradle of Courage*, *Travelin' On*, *Tumbleweeds*.

**Harte** (härt), **Francis Brett**, *known as* **Bret** (brĕt). 1836–1902. American writer, b. Albany, N.Y. Left school at 13 to go to work. Went to California, via Nicaragua (1854). In San Francisco, typesetter on *Golden Era;* began contribution of poems and sketches to this journal (1860); contributor to the *Californian* (1864–66). Editor, *Overland Monthly* (1868–70). Moved to New York to continue writing (1871–78). U.S. consul, Crefeld, Prussia (1878–80), and Glasgow, Scotland (1880–85). Hack writer in London, England (1885–1902). Best work done in early years, notably: *The Luck of Roaring Camp* (in *Overland Monthly*, July, 1868); *The Outcasts of Poker Flat* (in *Overland Monthly*, Jan., 1869); *Plain Language from Truthful James*, better known as *The Heathen Chinee* (1870). Books: *The Luck of Roaring Camp and Other Sketches* (1870), *Mrs. Skaggs's Husbands* (1873), *Tales of the Argonauts* (1875).

**Har'tel** (här'tĕl), **Wilhelm von.** 1839–1907. Austrian classical scholar; published *Homerische Studien* (1871–74), *Demosthenische Studien* (1877–78), *Patristische Studien* (1890–95).

**Hartenau,** Count **von.** See ALEXANDER I, of Bulgaria.

**Har'ten·stein** (här'tĕn·shtīn), **Gustav.** 1808–1890. German philosopher of Herbartian school; edited works of Herbart and Kant.

**Harthacnut.** See HARDECANUTE.

**Hartington,** Marquises of. See CAVENDISH family.

**Har'tle** (här't'l), **Russell P.** 1889–1961. American army officer, b. Chewsville, Md.; commander of U.S. army forces in the British Isles (1942).

**Hart'le'ben** (härt'lā'bĕn), **Otto Erich.** 1864–1905. German author of volumes of verse, novels, and plays.

**Hart'ley** (härt'lĭ), Sir **Alan Fleming.** 1882–1954. British army officer; commander of British forces in India (1942).

**Hartley,** Sir **Charles Augustus.** 1825–1915. English engineer; served in Crimean War (1854–56); chief engineer to European commission of Danube (1856–1907); also, member of the international technical commission of the Suez Canal (1884–1906).

**Hartley, David.** 1705–1757. English philosopher; practicing physician in Newark, Bury St. Edmunds, and London; expounded his doctrine of associationism in *Observations on Man, his Frame, his Duty, and his Expectations* (1749). His son **David** (1732–1813), diplomat; with Benjamin Franklin, drafted and signed peace treaty between U.S. and Great Britain (1783); published *Letters on the American War* (1778–79) and editions of his father's philosophical work.

**Hartley, Frank.** 1856–1913. American surgeon, b. Washington, D.C. Devised cure for trigeminal neuralgia by bisecting the ganglion of the trigeminal nerve.

**Hartley, George Inness.** 1887–1949. American artist and writer; research associate in Brazil and British Guiana for New York Zoological Society (1915–20); author of *The Boy Hunters in Demerara* (1921), *The Last Parrakeet* (1923), *The Lost Flamingos* (1924), etc.

**Hartley, Jonathan Scott.** 1845–1912. American sculptor, b. Albany, N.Y. Studio, New York City. Examples of his work: *Miles Morgan* (in Springfield, Mass.), *John Ericsson* (in Battery Park, New York City), *Rev. Thomas K. Beecher* (in Elmira, N.Y.), *Alfred the Great* (on Appellate Court Building, New York).

**Hart'lib** (härt'lĭb), **Samuel.** d. about 1670. Reformer in England; b. in Prussia of Polish father and English mother; friend of Milton. Introduced Comenius's works in England; published pamphlets on education and husbandry; praised by Milton in his treatise on education.

**Hart'line** (härt'līn), **Haldan Keffer.** 1903– . Amer. physiologist, b. Bloomsburg, Pa. Awarded Nobel prize in physiology and medicine (1967) with G. Wald and R. Granit for discoveries concerning visual processes in the eye.

**Hart'mann** (härt'măn), **Carl Sa'da·ki'chi** (sä'dä·kĭch'ĭ; -kĭch'). 1869–1944. Writer, b. in Nagasaki, Japan, of a German father and a Japanese mother; to U.S. (1882), Author of plays *Christ* (1893), *Buddha* (1897), *Confucius* (1923), *Moses* (1934); poetry, *Drifting Flowers of the Sea* (1906), *My Rubaiyat* (1926), *Tanka and Haikai* (1926); and books on art, *Japanese Art* (1901–20), etc.

**Hart′mann** (härt′män), **Eduard von,** *in full* **Karl Robert Eduard.** 1842–1906. German philosopher, b. Berlin. Known for doctrine (panpneumatism) that the world, or noumenal reality, is both unconscious will and unconscious thought, and for his pessimism with regard to the prospect of achieving happiness.

**Hart′mann** (härt′mån), **Johann Peter Emilius.** 1805–1900. Danish composer; among his notable works are the operas *The Raven* (1832), *The Corsairs* (1835), *Little Christina* (1846), a G-minor symphony, ballet and theater music, chamber music, a cantata, and piano pieces.

**Hart′mann** (härt′män), **Johannes Franz.** 1865–1936. German astronomer; authority in spectroscopy; invented a microphotometer and a spectrocomparator.

**Hartmann,** Sir **Julius von.** 1774–1856. German soldier; served under Wellington in the Peninsular campaign and at Waterloo; lieutenant general (1836); retired (1850). His son **Julius** (1817–1878) was also a soldier; commanded first cavalry division in battles around Metz and Orléans (1870) and besieged Tours (Jan., 1871); governor of Strasbourg (1871–75).

**Hartmann, Max.** 1876–1971. German protozoologist.

**Hartmann, Moritz.** 1821–1872. Bohemian-born German writer. His collected patriotic verse, *Kelch und Schwert* (1845), caused imprisonment by Austrian authorities, but he was released (1848) and sat for a time in the Frankfurt parliament. On suppression of the revolution, fled abroad. Returned to Vienna (1868) and served on staff of *Neue Freie Presse.* His son **Ludo Moritz** (1865–1924) was a historian; chief work, *Geschichte Italiens im Mittelalter* (unfinished; 4 vols., pub. 1897–1915).

**Hartmann, Nicolai.** 1882–1950. German philosopher; professor, Marburg (1920), Cologne (1926).

**Hartmann, Robert.** 1832–1893. German anatomist, anthropologist, and ethnographer.

**Hartmann von Au′e** (fôn ou′ĕ). d. between 1210 and 1220. Middle High German poet; chiefly notable for Arthurian romances *Erek* and *Iwein,* both being free versions of work of Chrétien de Troyes (*q.v.*); through his *Erek,* Arthurian legend entered German literature. Others of his poems are *Gregorius auf dem Steine* and *Der Arme Heinrich.*

**Hart′ness** (härt′nĕs; -nĭs), **James.** 1861–1934. American mechanical engineer and inventor; governor of Vermont (1920). Among his notable inventions were the flat turret lathe, automatic die, turret equatorial telescope, and screw thread comparator.

**Har′tog** (här′tŏk) *or* **Har′togs·zoon** (här′tŏk·sŭn; -sŏn; -sōn), **Dirck.** Dutch navigator along Australian coast (1616).

**Hart′ranft** (här′trănft), **John Frederick.** 1830–1889. American army officer; served through Civil War; brigadier general (1864); brevetted major general (1865). Governor of Pennsylvania (1873–79).

**Har′tree** (här′trē), **Douglas Rayner.** 1897–1958. British theoretical physicist; professor, U. of Manchester (1929–45), Cambridge U. (1946–58); known for work in atomic structure and related subjects.

**Hart′soe′ker** (härt′so͞o′kẽr), **Niklaas.** 1656–1725. Dutch physicist and histologist. Constructed a microscope and observed spermatozoa; taught Peter the Great (c. 1700). Author of works on dioptrics and principles of physics.

**Har′ty** (här′tĭ), Sir **Hamilton,** *in full* **Herbert Hamilton.** 1880–1941. Irish-born British conductor; composer of *An Irish Symphony,* violin concerto, piano concerto, orchestral works, songs, etc.

**Hart′zen·busch** (*Span.* härt′săm·bo͞och; *Ger.* här′tsĕn-bo͝osh), **Juan Eugenio.** 1806–1880. Spanish playwright, b. Madrid, of German father and Spanish mother. A leader in romantic movement in Spanish literature. Author of *Los Amantes de Teruel* (1837), *Doña Mencía* (1838), *La Madre de Pelayo* (1846), *Vida por Honra* (1858), *El Mal Apóstol y el Buen Ladrón* (1860).

**Ha·run′ al′–Ra·shid′** (*Arab.* hä·ro͞on′ ăr′ră·shēd′; *sometimes Angl.* hăr′o͞on ăl·răsh′ĭd). *Also* **Harun ar–Rashid** *or* **Haroun–al–Raschid.** *Arab.* **Hārūn al–Rashīd,** *i.e.* Aaron the Upright. 764?–809. Fifth Abbasside caliph (786–809), most famous of all caliphs of Baghdad. Son of al-Mahdi. Succeeded his brother Musa al-Hadi (caliph 785–786). Under him, Eastern caliphate attained its greatest power and covered all southwestern Asia and northern Africa; made Baghdad center of Arabic culture. Exchanged gifts with Charlemagne; had diplomatic relations with China (T'ang dynasty). Engaged in war (791–809) with Byzantines; led armies in person against Emperor Nicephorus I, who had broken peace treaty (805), defeating him at Heraclea Pontica (Eregli) and Tyana (806) and exacting extra tribute. Became jealous of Barmecides (*q.v.*), and destroyed their head (c. 803), Vizier Yahya, and his sons; faced many insurrections and toward end of reign had only nominal allegiance of much of North Africa because of rise (788) of Idrisid dynasty (*q.v.*); died on expedition to suppress uprising in Khurasan. Much of his splendor is the result of legends and of his idealization among Arabs as the caliph of *Arabian Nights.*

**Ha·ru·no·bu** (hä·ro͝o·nō·bo͝o), **Suzuki.** c. 1718–1770. Japanese painter and printer, b. Edo (Tokyo). As a painter, much influenced by Masanobu; invented true color printing in Japan; published (c. 1765) first books in polychrome printing; portrayed scenes from domestic life.

**Har′vard** (här′vẽrd), **John.** 1607–1638. Clergyman, b. London, Eng. B.A., Cantab. (1631); M.A. (1635). To America (1637); settled at Charlestown, Mass. Left his library and half his estate, valued at about £800, to the newly founded college at "New Towne" (later Cambridge). The Massachusetts General Court named the college in his honor (Mar. 13, 1639).

**Har′vey** (här′vĭ), **Edmund Newton.** 1887–1959. American physiologist; studied light production by animals, cell permeability, nerve conduction, supersonic waves, brain potentials, etc.

**Harvey, Eli.** 1860–1957. American painter and sculptor; chiefly known for his sculptures of animals of the cat family, as *Lioness* and *Maternal Caress* in Metropolitan Museum of Art, New York City; also modeled a gorilla for New York Zoological Society, eagles for the Victory Arch (1916) in New York, and a brown bear mascot for Brown U. (1923).

**Harvey, Gabriel.** 1545?–?1630. English poet and controversialist; friend of Spenser; claimed to be the father of English hexameter. His satirical verse gave offense at court (1579); attacked Robert Greene and Thomas Nash, creating a literary scandal finally quashed by the archbishop of Canterbury (1599).

**Harvey,** Sir **George.** 1806–1876. Scottish painter; known for figure paintings and landscapes.

**Harvey, George Brinton McClellan.** 1864–1928. American journalist, b. Peacham, Vt. Owner and editor, *North American Review* (1899–1926). President, Harper & Bros. (1900–15). Editor, *Harper's Weekly* (1901–13), *Harvey's Weekly* (1918–21). Instrumental in bringing about Wilson's nomination for governor of New Jersey (1910); supported Wilson for presidency (1912); turned to bitter criticism of Wilson (about 1915); opposed his re-election (1916). Also instrumental in selection of Harding as Republican candidate (1920). U.S. ambassador to Great Britain (1921–23).

**Harvey, Hayward Augustus.** 1824–1893. American steel

manufacturer; inventor of a process (Harvey process) for hardening the surface of steel, esp. for use in armor plate for battleships.

**Harvey,** Sir **John Martin.** 1863–1944. English actor and theater manager; member of Sir Henry Irving's company (1882 ff.); manager of various London theaters. Among many plays he produced are *Eugene Aram, Pelléas and Mélisande, Richard III, Œdipus, Henry V, Via Crucis, Scaramouche, The Bells.*

**Harvey, William.** 1578–1657. English physician and anatomist, discoverer of the circulation of the blood, b. Folkestone; grad. Cambridge (1597). Studied medicine under Fabricius and Galileo, at Padua, Italy (1597–1601); M.D., Cambridge (1602). Practiced in London; physician of St. Bartholomew's Hospital (1609); Lumleian lecturer at Coll. of Physicians (1615–56); physician extraordinary to James I (1618). Royalist in sympathy during Civil War; present at battle of Edge Hill; accompanied Charles I to Oxford. First expounded theory of circulation of the blood in his Lumleian lectures; published *Exercitatio de Motu Cordis et Sanguinis* (*Essay on the Motion of the Heart and the Blood,* 1628) and *Exercitationes de Generatione Animalium* (*Essays on Generation of Animals,* 1651).

**Harvey, William Henry.** 1811–1866. Irish botanist; authority on South African flora.

**Harvey, William Hope.** 1851–1936. American economist, known as "Coin Harvey"; vigorous advocate of bimetallism; candidate of Liberty party for president of the U.S. (1931). Author of *Coin's Financial School* (1894), *Coin on Money, Trusts and Imperialism* (1899), *Common Sense* (1920), etc.

**Har'wood** (här'wŏŏd), **Harold Marsh.** 1874–1959. English playwright and theater manager; m. (1918) Fryniwyd Tennyson Jesse (*q.v.*). Author or coauthor of *Interlopers* (1913), *Billeted* (1917), *The Golden Calf* (1927), *So Far and no Father* (1932), *These Mortals* (1935), *The Innocent Party* (1938), *While London Burns* (1942).

**Harwood,** Sir **Henry Harwood.** 1888–1950. British naval commander; rear admiral in command of South America division (1940); commanded British naval forces in action against German pocket battleship *Admiral Graf Spee* off the Plate River (Dec., 1939); asst. chief of staff, and member of the Admiralty Board (1940); commander of British Mediterranean fleet (May, 1942 ff.).

**Har'zer** (här'tsēr), **Paul Hermann.** 1857–1932. German astronomer.

**Hasan.** See FIRDAUSI.

**Ha·san'** *or* **Has·san'** (hă·săn') and **Hu·sain'** *or* **Ho·sein'** (hŏŏ·sīn'). *Arab.* **al-Ḥasan** (c. 624–c. 669) and **al-Ḥusayn** (c. 629–680). Two grandchildren of Mohammed, sons of Ali and Fatima. On death of Ali (661), **Hasan** was proclaimed caliph; opposed by Muawiyah, founder of Ommiad dynasty; abdicated and retired to Medina; killed in harem intrigue. **Husain,** on death of Muawiyah (680), claimed caliphate in opposition to Yazid, Muawiyah's son; slain at Karbala by Yazid on tenth of Muharram (Oct. 10, 680), a day still observed by Shiites as day of mourning. Struggles between sons of Ali and Ommiads resulted in division of Mohammedans into Shiites and Sunnites.

**Ha·san' ibn-al-Sab·bah'** (hă·săn' ĭb''n ăs'săb·bä'). *Also* **Hassan Sabbah.** *Arab.* **al-Ḥasan ibn-al-Ṣabbaḥ.** d. 1124. Persian of Ismailian branch of Mohammedans, founder of sect of Assassins. Lived short time in Egypt; returned to Persia as Fatimid missionary; seized (c. 1090) strong mountain fortess of Alamut, near Kazvin; established powerful secret organization (Assassins) not extinguished until 1256.

**Has'dai ibn-Shap·rut'** (kås'dī ĭb''n shåp·rōōt'). *Also* **Hasday ben-Shaprut** (-bĕn'-). *In full* **Hasdai Abu Yusuf ibn-Shaprut.** 915?–970 or 990. Jewish physician and scholar in Spain, b. Jaen. Minister of Caliph Abd-er-Rahman III; founded new school of culture for Spanish Jews; encouraged settlement of Jewish scholars in Andalusia; translated into Arabic the *Materia Medica* of Dioscorides.

**Hăş·deu'** (hȧsh·dyōō'), **Bogdan Petriceicu.** 1836–1907. Rumanian archivist and philologist. Compiler of *Archiva Istorică a României* (4 vols., 1865–69), in which many ancient Slavonic and Rumanian documents were first published.

**Has'dru'bal** (hăz'drōō'bȧl; hăz'drŏŏ·bȧl; hăz·drōō'bȧl). Name of several Carthaginian generals.

(1) d. 221 B.C. Son-in-law of Hamilcar Barca, whom he succeeded as commander in Spain (228); assassinated (221).

(2) d. 207 B.C. Son of Hamilcar Barca and brother of Hannibal; commanded Carthaginian army in Spain after Hannibal left for Italy (218); operated successfully against Romans under Publius and Gnaeus Scipio; crossed Alps (207) in effort to take reinforcements to Hannibal; defeated at Metaurus and fell in battle.

(3) d. about 200 B.C. Son of Gisco; associated with Mago (*q.v.*) in command of Carthaginian armies in Spain (209); recalled to Carthage (204); decisively defeated by Scipio Africanus near Utica (204).

(4) Cavalry commander in Hannibal's army; defeated Roman cavalry and charged rear of Roman infantry in battle of Cannae (216 B.C.).

(5) General in 2d century B.C.; commanded Carthaginian army against Masinissa (150); defeated and exiled; recalled at outbreak of Third Punic War (149); entrusted with defense of Carthage; forced to surrender city (146) and appear in triumph of Scipio Aemilianus.

**Ha'se** (hä'zĕ), **Karl Benedikt.** 1780–1864. German classical scholar in Paris; professor of Greek paleography, École des Langues Orientales, Paris (1816); professor of comparative grammar, U. of Paris (1852). Known esp. for his editions of works of Leo Diaconus, Valerius Maximus, and Suetonius.

**Ha·se·ga·wa** (hä·sĕ·gä·wä), Viscount **Yoshimichi.** 1850–1924. Japanese field marshal; commanded brigade in Chino-Japanese War (1894–95) and division of Imperial Guards under General Kuroki in Russo-Japanese War (1904–05); general (1904); commander in chief of Korean garrison (1905); viscount (1907).

**Haselrig,** Sir **Arthur.** See HESILRIGE.

**Ha'sel·wan'der** (hä'zĕl·vän'dēr), **Friedrich August.** 1859–1932. German engineer; inventor of the three-phase dynamo and of the compressorless Diesel motor.

**Ha'sen·au'er** (hä'zĕ·nou'ēr), Baron **Karl von.** 1833–1894. Austrian architect; among works designed by him are museums of art and of natural history in Vienna, the new Imperial theater in Vienna, and an addition to the imperial palace.

**Ha'sen·cle'ver** (hä'zĕn·klā'vēr), **Johann Peter.** 1810–1853. German painter; best known for humorous and somewhat satirical genre pictures.

**Hasenclever, Walter.** 1890–1940. German writer; author of *Das Unendliche Gespräch* (verse, 1913), *Der Jüngling* (lyric poems, 1913), *Der Sohn* (play, 1914), *Die Menschen* (drama, 1918), *Gobseck* (drama, 1921), *Mord* (drama, 1926), *Napoleon Greift Ein* (comedy, 1930), etc.

**Hash'im·ite** (hăsh'ĭm·īt). (1) Branch of Koreish to which Mohammed the Prophet, Ali, and the Abbassides belonged. (2) Modern Arab dynasty of descendants of Mohammed, founded by Husein ibn-Ali, first King of the Hejaz (1916–24). His sons were Ali ibn-Husein, King of the Hejaz (1924–25), and Abdullah ibn-Husein, ruler of Trans-Jordan (1921–51), and Faisal, King of Iraq (1921–33). See individual biographies.

**Ha·shi·mo·to** (hä·shē·mô·tô), **Kingoro.** 1890–1957. Japanese army officer and politician; involved in the February revolt (1935) and cashiered from the army, but restored to rank (colonel) at outbreak of trouble in China; said to have ordered artillery and air attack (Dec., 1937) on British gunboats *Ladybird*, *Scarab*, and *Bee*, and on American ship *Panay*. Reputed head of a Japan Youth party of 100,000 members.

**Has'kell** (hăs'kĕl), **William Nafew.** 1878–1952. American army officer, b. Albany, N.Y.; grad. U.S.M.A., West Point (1901). Served in A.E.F. in France (1918); director-general of relief in the Caucasus; chief of Relief Mission to Russia (1921–23); national director, civilian defense (1944).

**Has'kin** (hăs'kĭn), **Frederic J.** 1872–1944. American journalist, b. Shelbina, Mo. Contributor of special articles to chain of newspapers using the service of his information bureau. Author of *The American Government* (1911), *The Panama Canal* (1913), *10,000 Answers to Questions* (1937), etc.

**Has'kins** (hăs'kĭnz), **Charles Homer.** 1870–1937. American educator; professor of European History, U. of Wisconsin (1892–1902), Harvard (1902–31); also, dean of Harvard Graduate School (1908–24). Chief of division of western Europe, American commission to negotiate peace (1918–19). Author of *Norman Institutions* (1918), *The Renaissance of the Twelfth Century* (1927), *Studies in Mediaeval Culture* (1929), etc.

**Hasler, Hans Leo.** See HASSLER.

**Has'mo·nae'an** (hăz'mô·nē'ăn) *or* **As'mo·nae'an** (ăz'-). Family of the Maccabees (*q.v.*), a dynasty of independent Jewish nation (2d and 1st centuries B.C.), named probably after **Hash'mon** (hăsh'mŏn) *or* **Has'mon** (hăz'mŏn), an ancestor of Mattathias. See ANTIGONUS II.

**Has'ner** (häs'nẽr), **Leopold von Artha.** 1818–1891. Austrian lawyer, economist, and statesman; minister of education (1868–69).

**Ha'sping·er** (häs'pĭng·ẽr), **Joachim.** 1776–1858. Tyrolese patriot; fought for freedom of his country, against French (1796, 1797, 1799–1801, 1809) and Bavarians (1810).

**Has'sall** (hăs''l), **Arthur.** 1853–1930. English historian; educ. Oxford; author of *The Making of the British Empire* (1896), *The French People* (1901), *The Tudor Dynasty* (1904), *The Great Napoleon* (1911), *History of British Foreign Policy* (1912), *France, Medieval and Modern* (1918), etc.

**Hassall, Christopher Vernon.** 1912–1963. English writer: author of *Poems of Two Years* (1935), *Devil's Dyke* (play, 1936), *Christ's Comet* (play, 1937), *Penthesperon* (verse, 1938; awarded Hawthornden prize), *Crisis* (sonnet sequence, 1939).

**Has'sam** (hăs'ăm), **Childe.** 1859–1935. American painter and etcher, b. Boston. Regarded as one of foremost exponents of impressionism in America. Among his better-known individual works are *Evening Bells*, *The Little June Idyll*, *Winter*, *Manhattan's Sunset Towers*, *Aphrodite*, *Lorelei*, *Summer Sea*.

**Hassan.** Variant of HASAN.

**Has·san' II** (hă·săn'). 1929– . Son of Mohammed V; king of Morocco (from 1961).

**Has'sard** (hăs'ẽrd), **John Rose Greene.** 1836–1888. American journalist and music critic; on editorial staff, New York *Tribune* (from 1866).

**Has'se** (häs'ĕ), **Johann Adolf.** 1699–1783. German operatic tenor and composer. Composed over 80 operas, including *Sesostrate* (1726), *Attalo* (1728), *Dalisa* (1730), and *Ruggiero* (c. 1771), 14 oratorios, and church music. m. (1730) opera singer **Fau·sti'na Bor·do'ni** (fou·stē'nä bôr·dō'nē), a favorite of the elector of Saxony.

**Has'sel** (häs'ĕl), **Odd.** 1897– . Norwegian chemist. Awarded Nobel prize in chemistry (1969) with Derek H. R. Barton.

**Has'sel·quist** (hȧs'ĕl·kvĭst), **Tuve Nilsson.** 1816–1891. Swedish Lutheran clergyman in U.S.; b. in Sweden; leader in the Synod of Northern Illinois; president, Augustana Synod (1860–70); president, Augustana College and Theol. Sem. (1863–91).

**Has'selt** (häs'ĕlt), **André Henri Constant van** (vän). 1806–1874. Belgian historian and poet. Among his histories are *Les Belges aux Croisades* (1846), *Histoire des Belges* (1848); among his volumes of verse, *Primevères* (1854), *Poèmes* (1863), *Le Livre des Ballades* (1872).

**Hass'ler** (häs'lẽr), **Ferdinand Rudolph.** 1770–1843. Engineer, b. Switzerland; to U.S. (1805). Taught at West Point (1807–09), Union Coll. (1809–11). Superintendent, U.S. Coast Survey (1816–18; 1832–43).

**Hass'ler** *or* **Has'ler** (häs'lẽr), **Hans Leo.** 1564–1612. German composer. With Michael Praetorius, regarded as a master in period of German renaissance. Chief compositions are church music and songs. Two brothers, **Kaspar** (1562?–1618) and **Jacob** (1569–after 1618), were also organists.

**Has'ting** (*Angl.* hās'tĭng) *or* **Has'tings** (-tĭngz). Scandinavian viking; harried coasts of France, Spain, and England; invaded England (893–897); defeated.

**Has'tings** (hās'tĭngz). Name of an English family including among its members barons Hastings, earls of **Pem'broke** (pĕm'brŏŏk), and earls of **Hunt'ing·don** (hŭn'tĭng·dŭn).

Sir **Henry de Hastings** (d. 1268), 1st Baron Hastings (1264); baronial leader in command of Londoners at Lewes (1264) and in last stand of "disinherited" barons in island of Ely; made submission to Henry (1267). His son **John Hastings** (1262–1313), 2d baron; m. Isabella, daughter of William de Valence (1275); served against Scots and Welsh; laid claim to vacant Scottish throne (1290) on ground of descent through paternal grandmother from brother of William the Lion; fought almost continuously in France or in Scotland; signed baronial letter to Pope Boniface VIII repudiating papal interference in Scotland (1301).

**Laurence Hastings** (1318?–1348), 1st Earl of Pembroke; soldier; grandson of 2d Baron Hastings; created earl palatine (1339), inheriting estates of Valence earls of Pembroke; fought in Gascon campaigns (1345–46). **John** (1347–1375), 2d earl, son of 1st earl; soldier; served with Black Prince in France; defeated by Spanish fleet at La Rochelle (1372) and imprisoned; m. Margaret Plantagenet, daughter of King Edward III.

**William** (1430?–1483), Baron Hastings; Yorkist adherent; ambassador and deputy for Edward IV; commander of forces in France (1475); beheaded by Richard III. His grandson **George** (1488?–1545), 1st Earl of Huntingdon and 3d Baron Hastings of Hastings; one of royalist leaders during suppression of insurrection known as Pilgrimage of Grace (1536). **Francis** (1514?–1561), 2d Earl of Huntingdon; eldest son of 1st earl; chief captain of army and fleet abroad (1549); ally of John Dudley, Duke of Northumberland, with whom he was captured (1553); made lord lieutenant of Leicestershire by Queen Mary. Sir **Edward** (1520?–1572), 1st Baron Hastings of Lough'bor·ough (lŭf'bŭ·rŭ; -brŭ); brother of 2d earl; stanch Roman Catholic; master of horse and, later, lord chamberlain to Queen Mary. **Henry** (1535–1595), 3d

Earl of Huntingdon; son of 2d earl; m. (1553) Catherine, daughter of duke of Northumberland; heir presumptive to throne through his mother (Catherine Pole, great-granddaughter of duke of Clarence, brother of Edward IV); a custodian of Mary, Queen of Scots (1569); president of council of north (1572) and engaged in north until he became active in defense against Spanish Armada (1588).

Lady **Elizabeth** (1682–1739); daughter of **Theophilus Hastings** (1650–1701), 7th earl and lord lieutenant of Leicester and Derby; noted philanthropist and beauty, celebrated by Steele as Aspasia in *The Tatler* and by Congreve and William Law.

**Selina** (1707–1791), Countess of Huntingdon (wife of **Theophilus Hastings,** 9th earl, 1696–1746); religious leader, founder of Calvinistic Methodist sect known as "Countess of Huntingdon's Connexion"; joined Methodist society in London (1739); joined Wesleys (1746); supported Whitefield against Wesleys; attempted a reconciliation (1749); had Whitefield preach in her house before Chesterfield, Walpole, Bolingbroke, and bishops; supported itinerant preachers, built 64 chapels, and built a seminary in South Wales (1768); compelled to become dissenter and register her chapels as dissenting meeting houses (1779); protested against anti-Calvinistic minutes of Wesleyan conference (1770).

**Hastings, Charles Sheldon.** 1848–1932. American physicist; professor, Yale (from 1884); authority in physical optics; in astronomy, produced correcting lenses for transforming visual into photographic refractors; made improvements in the spectroscope; designed telescopes.

**Hastings, Francis Rawdon–.** 1st Marquis of **Hastings** *and* (*in Irish peerage*) 2d Earl of **Moi'ra** (moi'rȧ). 1754–1826. British soldier and colonial administrator, b. County Down, Ireland. Served against Americans (1775–82) at Bunker Hill, as adjutant general (1778), in command of left wing at Camden (1780), and at Hobkirk's Hill (1781). Championed prince of Wales on regency question (1789); assumed name of Hastings (1790); general (1803); commander in chief in Scotland (1803); attempted with Wellesley to form ministry (1812). Governor general of Bengal and commander in chief in India (1813–22); carried on successful wars against Gurkhas (1816) and Pindaris and Marathas (1817), establishing British supremacy in central India; purchased island of Singapore (1819); resigned because of imputations growing out of his permission to banking house of Palmer to lend money to Hyderabad. Governor of Malta (1824).

**Hastings, James.** 1852–1922. Scottish clergyman and editor; compiled *Dictionary of the Bible* (5 vols., 1898–1904), *Dictionary of Christ and the Gospels* (2 vols., 1906–07), *Dictionary of the Apostolic Church* (2 vols., 1915, 1918), *Encyclopaedia of Religion and Ethics* (12 vols., 1908–21).

**Hastings, Thomas.** 1860–1929. American architect; with McKim, Mead & White (1884–86); in partnership with John M. Carrère (d. 1911), Carrère & Hastings (from 1886). Examples of work: Ponce de Leon Hotel and Alcazar Hotel, St. Augustine, Fla.; New York Public Library; Senate Office Building, Washington, D.C.; Standard Oil Company building, New York City.

**Hastings, Warren.** 1732–1818. English statesman and administrator in India, b. in Oxfordshire. To Calcutta in East India Company's service (1750); member of Calcutta council (1761). Second in council at Madras (1769); governor of Bengal (1772); created governor general of India (1773). Deposed Chait Singh, zamindar of Benares (1781); confiscated (1782) part of lands and treasure of the begum of Oudh, mother of the nawab, who had aided Chait Singh. Returned to England (1785); impeached (1788) for corruption and cruelty in his administration of India; acquitted (1795) after famous trial in which Burke and Sheridan were among the prosecuting counsel. Credited with establishing political and judicial organization in India, and the method of governmental administration.

**Has'well** (hăz'wĕl; -wĕl), **Charles Haynes.** 1809–1907. American engineer; engineer in chief, U.S. navy (1844–52); consulting engineer, New York City (from 1852). Author of *Mechanic's and Engineer's Pocket Book* (1842), *Mechanics Tables* (1854), *Mensuration and Practical Geometry* (1856).

**Haswell, William Aitcheson.** 1854–1925. British zoologist, b. Edinburgh. To Australia; professor of biology (1890), Sydney U. Author of *A Text-Book of Zoölogy* (with T. Jeffery Parker, 1897) and *A Manual of Zoölogy* (1899).

**Ha·ta** (hä·tä), **Sahachiro.** 1872–1938. Japanese bacteriologist; aided Dr. Paul Ehrlich in experiments leading to discovery of Salvarsan; department chief at Keio Hospital, Tokyo (from 1911).

**Hata, Shunroku.** 1879–1962. Japanese general; minister of war (1939); commander in chief of Japanese forces in China (1941).

**Hatasu.** See HATSHEPSUT.

**Hatch** (hăch), **Carl A.** 1889–1963. American lawyer and politician; U.S. senator from New Mexico (1933 ff.). Sponsor of the Hatch Act, or Political Activity Act (1939), designed to restrict political activities of federal officials and to protect voters from compulsion.

**Hatch, Edwin.** 1835–1889. English theologian and educator; vice-principal, St. Mary Hall, Oxford (1867–85). Author of *Organisation of Early Christian Churches* (1881), *Growth of Church Institutions* (1887), etc.

**Hatch, William Henry.** 1833–1896. American legislator; served in Confederate army in Civil War. Member, U.S. House of Representatives (1879–95); active in agricultural legislation; instrumental in passing act (known as Hatch Act) granting federal aid to agricultural experiment stations in states and territories.

**Hatch, William Henry Paine.** 1875–1972. American theologian; professor, Episcopal Theol. School (from 1917). Author of theological treatises, esp. on Greek New Testament manuscripts.

**Hatch'ett** (hăch'ĕt; -ĭt), **Charles.** 1765?–1847. English chemist, for whom hatchettine (or hatchettite) and hatchettolite are named; discovered (1801) the metallic element columbium.

**Hat'field** (hăt'fēld), **William Anderson.** 1862–1930. American mountaineer of West Virginia and Kentucky region; prominent member of family engaged in long and deadly feud (with the McCoy family).

**Hath'a·way** (hăth'ȧ·wā), **Anne.** 1557?–1623. Wife of William Shakespeare (*q.v.*).

**Ha'ti·fi'** (hä'tĭ·fē'), **Abdallah.** 1460?–1521. Persian epic poet, nephew of Jami; author of *Lailā and Majnūn*, *Haft Manzar*, *Shirīn and Khusraw*, *Tīmur Nāmah* ("Book of Timur").

**Hat'schek** (hä'chĕk), **Julius.** 1876–1926. Rumanian-born jurist in Germany; authority on English law.

**Hat·shep'sut** (hăt·shĕp'so͞ot) *or* **Hat·shep'set** (-sĕt). *Also* **Ha·ta'su** (?hȧ·tä'so͞o). Queen of ancient Egypt of XVIIIth (Diospolite) dynasty. Daughter and heiress of Thutmose I, who early proclaimed her his successor; m. her half brother and ruled jointly with him (see THUTMOSE III). Preferred arts of peace to conquest; built magnificent temple, at Deir el-Bahri on west side of Nile near Thebes, which contained pictorial representations on its walls of expedition to land of Punt; erected two obelisks (1485 B.C.) at Karnak. Mother of Amenhotep II.

**Hat'to I** (hăt'ō; *Ger.* hät'ō). Archbishop of Mainz (891–913). Regent of Germany during minority of King Louis (III) the Child (899–911); sought to strengthen royal authority; became unpopular. Sometimes confused with Hatto II (*q.v.*).

**Hatto II.** d. about 970. Archbishop of Mainz (968); according to medieval legend, eaten alive by mice as punishment for burning down barn full of people caught stealing grain during a famine, whose dying shrieks he compared to the piping of mice; represented as builder of Mouse Tower on Rhine in futile attempt to escape the mice.

**Hat'ton** (hăt''n). See *Finch-Hatton*, name of earls of Winchilsea and Nottingham, under FINCH family.

**Hatton,** Sir **Christopher.** 1540–1591. English statesman; lord chancellor (1587–91); known as "the Dancing Chancellor" because he first attracted attention of Queen Elizabeth by his graceful dancing at a court masque.

**Hatton, Frank.** 1846–1894. American journalist; owned and edited Burlington (Iowa) *Daily Hawk-Eye* (from 1874). Asst. postmaster general (1881–84); U.S. postmaster general (1884–85). Editor, Chicago *Mail* (1885–88), New York *Press* (from 1888), and Washington (D.C.) *Post* (from 1889).

**Hatton, John Liptrot.** 1809–1886. English composer of operas, an oratorio, a cantata, anthems, and songs.

**Hätzer.** See Ludwig HETZER.

**Hatz'feld'** (ȧts'fĕld'), **Adolphe.** 1824–1900. French professor and author; with Arsène Darmesteter and Antoine Thomas compiled *Dictionnaire Général de la Langue Française* (1890–1900).

**Hatz'feldt, von** (fôn häts'fĕlt). Noble family of Upper Hesse, including in its various branches: **Melchior von Hatzfeldt** (1593–1658), general; distinguished himself in Thirty Years' War, leading campaigns (1639–43) in Westphalia and Rhine regions; created count (1635). **Franz Ludwig** (1750–1827), Prince **Hatzfeldt zu Tra'chen·berg** [tsōō trä'kĕn·bĕrk] (cr. 1803); general; served in Prussian army (from 1795); governor of Berlin (1806) at time of capture by Napoleon; headed conservative reaction in Prussia after fall of Napoleon (1814–15); ambassador in Vienna (1822–27). Count **Paul** (1831–1901), minister in Madrid (1874), ambassador in Constantinople (1878) and London (1885–1901). **Hermann** (1848–1933), 1st Duke of Trachenberg (cr. 1900) and 3d Prince of Hatzfeldt-Trachenberg; German legislator and statesman. **Hermann** (1867– ), 2d Prince of **Hatzfeldt-Wil'den·burg** (-vĭl'dĕn·bŏŏrk); son of Count Paul; German statesman and diplomat; ambassador in Washington (1906).

**Hauch** (houk), **Johann Carsten.** 1790–1872. Danish poet, playwright, and novelist.

**Hauck** (houk), **Albert.** 1845–1918. German Protestant theologian; chief work, *Kirchengeschichte Deutschlands* (1887–1920, unfinished).

**Hauck, Minnie.** See HAUK.

**Hauck'e** (hou'kĕ), Countess **von.** See BATTENBERG.

**Hau'er** (hou'ẽr), **Franz von.** 1822–1899. Austrian geologist; published geological map of Austro-Hungary and works on geology and paleontology of Austria. The mineral hauerite is named for him.

**Hauer, Jakob Wilhelm.** 1881–1962. German Indologist and historian of religion.

**Hauff** (houf), **Wilhelm.** 1802–1827. German novelist; author of *Lichtenstein* (3 vols., 1826), and *Phantasien im Bremer Ratskeller* (1827); wrote also a few lyrics, some of which have attained the status of folksongs, as *Steh' ich in finstrer Mitternacht* and *Morgenrot, Morgenrot.*

**Haug** (houk), **Martin.** 1827–1876. German Oriental scholar; professor of Sanskrit and comparative philology, Munich (1868). Wrote *Die Fünf Gāthas* (2 vols., 1858–60) and *Essays on the Sacred Language, Writings and Religion of the Parsees* (1862).

**Haug, Robert von.** 1857–1922. German battle painter.

**Hau'gen** (hou'gĕn), **Gilbert N.** 1859–1933. American banker and politician; member of U.S. House of Representatives (1899–1933). Chairman, committee on agriculture, and author of Haugen Packer Control and Stockyards Act. Coauthor with Senator McNary of McNary-Haugen bill designed to make effective the tariff on various agricultural products; bill was twice vetoed by President Coolidge; later (1933) in modified form passed as Farm Relief Bill.

**Haugh'ton** (hô't'n), **Percy Duncan.** 1876–1924. American football coach; grad. Harvard (1899). Coached at Cornell (1899–1900), Harvard (1908–16). Served in chemical warfare service during World War. In investment security business, New York City (1919–24).

**Haug'witz** (houk'vĭts), Count **Christian von.** 1752–1832. Prussian statesman; minister of foreign affairs (1792–1804 and 1805–06); negotiated second partition of Poland (1793), Treaty of Basel with France (1795), and Treaty of Schönbrunn (1805).

**Hauk** *or* **Hauck** (houk), **Minnie.** 1852?–1929. American operatic soprano, b. New York City; m. (1881) Baron Ernst von Hesse-Wartegg (*q.v.*). Chief roles: Juliette in Gounod's *Roméo et Juliette*, Carmen, Manon, Katharine in Götz's *Taming of the Shrew.*

**Hauks'bee** *or* **Hawks'bee** (hôks'bē), **Francis.** d. about 1713. English physicist; reputed to have invented (1706) first electrical machine; determined relative weights of air and water. Another **Francis Hauksbee** (1687–1763), perhaps his son, was a writer on scientific subjects.

**Haultain,** Sir **Frederick William Gordon.** 1857–1942. Canadian jurist and provincial government official; premier, attorney general, and commissioner of education, Northwest Territories (1891–1905); member of legislative assembly, Saskatchewan (1905–12); chief justice of supreme court, Saskatchewan (1912–38).

**Haupt** (houpt), **Herman.** 1817–1905. American engineer; grad. U.S.M.A., West Point (1835). Resigned from army to enter engineering (1835). Chief engineer, Pennsylvania Railroad (1853–56). In charge of construction of Hoosac tunnel (1856–62). In Civil War, chief of construction and transportation on military railroads (1862–63). His son **Lewis Muhlenberg** (1844–1937), civil engineer, was one of isthmian canal commissioners (1899–1902).

**Haupt, Moritz.** 1808–1874. German philologist; editor of Latin and Middle High German classics.

**Haupt, Paul.** 1858–1926. Semitic scholar, b. Görlitz, Germany. Professor of Semitic languages, Johns Hopkins (from 1883). Author of *The Sacred Books of the Old Testament* (6 vols., 1893–1904), *Purim* (1906), *Nahum* (1907), *Esther* (1908), *The Aryan Ancestry of Jesus* (1909), *Micah* (1910), etc.

**Haupt'mann** (houpt'män), **Gerhart.** 1862–1946. German writer, b. Salzbrunn, Silesia. Studied sculpture at Breslau art school and science and philosophy at Jena and Berlin. His earliest published work was the epic *Das Promethidenlos* (1885), followed by collected verse in *Das Bunte Buch* (1888). Plays began with *Vor Sonnenaufgang* (1889), followed by *Das Friedensfest* (1890), *Einsame Menschen* (1891), *Die Weber* (1892), *Fuhrmann Henschel* (1898), *Gabriel Schillings Flucht* (1912), a group of great naturalistic dramas. His romanticism found expression esp. in *Hanneles Himmelfahrt* (1892), *Die Versunkene Glocke* (1896), and *Und Pippa Tanzt* (1906). In field of fiction, wrote *Der Narr in Christo Emanuel Quint* (1910), *Atlantis* (1912), *Der Ketzer von Soana* (1918). Awarded Nobel prize in literature (1912) "in special recognition of the distinction and the wide range of his creative work in the realm of dramatic poetry." His brother **Carl** (1858–1921) was also a writer; author of dramas, poetry, and fiction.

**Hauptmann, Moritz.** 1792–1868. German composer and writer on musical theory; composer of much church music, an opera *Mathilde* and instrumental pieces. Author of *Die Natur der Harmonik und der Metrik* (1853).

**Hau'ré'au'** (ō'rā'ō'), **Jean Barthélemy.** 1812–1896. French journalist and scholar; curator of manuscripts, Bibliothèque Nationale (1848); director of Imprimerie Nationale (1871–82); edited vols. XIV–XVI of *Gallia Christiana* (1856–65); wrote *La Montagne* (1834), *Histoire de la Pologne* (1846), *Charlemagne et sa Cour* (1854), etc.

**Hau'seg'ger** (hou'zĕg'ẽr), **Friedrich von.** 1837–1899. German writer on music. His son **Siegmund** (1872–1948) was a composer and conductor; composed opera *Zinnober* (1898), symphonic works (*Barbarossa, Dyonische Phantasie,* etc.), choral pieces, and songs.

**Hau'sen** (hou'zĕn), **Max Klemens von.** 1846–1922. German soldier; at outbreak of the World War, commanded third army, which was planned to drive into France from between Aachen and Trier; was defeated by Foch (1914) and relieved of his command.

**Hau'sen·stein** (hou'zĕn·shtīn), **Wilhelm.** 1882–1957. German art scholar and critic.

**Hau'ser** (hou'zẽr), **Heinrich.** 1901–1955. German novelist; awarded Gerhart Hauptmann prize (1929) for his novel *Brackwasser* (1928); author also of the novel *Donner überm Meer* (1929).

**Hau'ser'** (ō'zâr'), **Henri.** 1866–?1946. French historian and economist; author of *Ouvriers des Temps Passés* (1898), *Les Méthodes Allemandes d'Expansion Économique* (1915), etc.

**Hau'ser** (hou'zẽr), **Kaspar.** 1812?–1833. German foundling, picked up by Nuremberg police (1828). Popular belief spread that he was of noble birth; accepted by some to be prince of Baden. Placed in custody of Professor Daumer (*q.v.*) and later adopted by Lord Stanhope, who sent him to Ansbach. Died (Dec. 17, 1833) from stab wounds which he said he had received when called to a rendezvous with the promise of information regarding his parentage. Subject of the novel *Caspar Hauser* (1909) by Jakob Wassermann.

**Hauser, Otto.** 1876– . Croatian-born poet and historian of literature, in Vienna. Author of an epic *Atlantis* (1920), a volume of lyrics, many works of literary history and criticism, and translations from more than 30 languages.

**Haus'ho'fer** (hous'hō'fẽr), **Karl.** 1869–1946. German army officer and geographer; served in World War (artillery brigade commander, 1917; divisional commander, 1918); general (1919). Editor, *Zeitschrift (für) Geopolitik* (1924 ff.); author of *Japan und die Japaner* (1923), *Macht und Erde* (1934), *Weltpolitik von Heute* (1936), *Weltmeere und Weltmachte* (1937). Credited with being political adviser to Hitler; committed suicide.

**Haus'mann** (hous'män), **Manfred.** 1898– . German author of *Lilofee* (play, 1929), *Kleine Liebe zu Amerika* (travel book, 1931), and novels.

**Hausmann, Raoul.** 1886– . Austrian painter, plastic artist, and photographer; identified with ultramodern movement in art, esp. as an early leader of Dadaism; editor of *Dada*, Berlin (1919–20).

**Haus'rath** (hous'rät), **Adolf.** 1837–1909. German Protestant theologian; author of *Der Apostel Paulus* (1865), *Peter Abälard* (1893), and *Luthers Leben* (2 vols., 1904). Under pseudonym **George Tay'lor** (tā'lẽr), published historical novels *Antinous* (1880) and *Peter Maternus* (1898).

**Häus'ser** (hois'ẽr), **Ludwig.** 1818–1867. German historian.

**Hauss'mann'** (ōs'män'), Baron **Georges Eugène.** 1809–1891. French prefect of the Seine (1853–70); inaugurated and carried through huge municipal improvements in Paris, including new water supply and sewage system, the creation of new wide boulevards (one of which was named Boulevard Haussmann in his honor), the landscape gardening of the Bois de Boulogne, the park of Vincennes, etc.

**Haus'son'ville'** (ō'sôN'vēl'), Comte **d'. Joseph Othenin Bernard de Clé'ron'** (dē klā'rôN'). 1809–1884. French politician and writer; member of Chamber of Deputies (1842–48); elected senator for life (1878); author of books on French history. His son **Gabriel Paul Othenin Bernard** (1843–1924) was also a politician and writer; a leader of Orleanist party (1891–94); author of *Socialisme et Charité* (1895), *Ombres Françaises et Visions Anglaises* (1914), etc.

**Haute'feuille'** (ōt'fû'y'), **Jean de.** 1647–1724. French ecclesiastic and mechanician; invented the spiral spring for the movement of watches, later patented by Huygens, and an engine using the explosions of gunpowder as motive power.

**Hautefeuille, Paul Gabriel.** 1836–1902. French chemist and mineralogist. The mineral hautefeuillite is named for him.

**Ha'üy'** (à'ü·ē'), Abbé **René Just.** 1743–1822. French mineralogist; a founder of the science of crystallography. Led by experiments following the accidental breaking of a crystal of calcareous spar to enunciate the geometrical law of crystallization; made observations in pyroelectricity. His brother **Valentin** (1745–1822), a teacher of the blind, invented characters embossed on paper as a means of reading for the blind; established an institute for teaching the blind at Paris (1784) and, later, one at St. Petersburg.

**Ha'vard'** (à'vàr'), **Henry.** 1838–1921. French art connoisseur; art editor of *Le Siècle;* author of *Dictionnaire de l'Ameublement et de la Décoration* (1887–90), *La France Artistique* (1892–95), etc.

**Ha'vas'** (à'väs'), **Charles.** 1785–1858. French journalist; first authorized by Napoleon to gather and forward news from armies in the field to Paris; organized news distributing agency (1835), converted into the company Havas Agency (1879), the oldest news agency in Europe.

**Hav'ell** (hăv'ĕl), **Robert.** 1793–1878. Aquatint engraver and painter, b. Reading, England; made most of plates for Audubon's *Birds of America* (1827–38); resident of U.S. (from 1839).

**Have'lock** (hăv'lŏk; -lŭk), Sir **Henry.** 1795–1857. British soldier; distinguished himself during Sepoy Mutiny (1857); major general (1857); relieved Lucknow (Sept., 1857) and held it against native siege until arrival of Sir Colin Campbell (Nov., 1857). His son Sir **Henry Marshman Havelock-Al'lan** [-ăl'ăn] (1830–1897) distinguished himself in Sepoy Mutiny (1857–59); received V.C. (1858); M.P. (1874–81; 1885; 1886–92; 1895); lieutenant general; killed on Afghan frontier.

**Have'mey'er** (hăv'mī'ẽr), **Henry Osborne.** 1847–1907. American sugar refiner, b. New York City. Entered family refineries (c. 1865). Merged refineries in New York region into Sugar Refineries Co. (1887); dissolved by court order (1890) and reorganized as American

Sugar Refining Co., under New Jersey charter (1891). Invaded coffee market in long struggle to keep John Arbuckle (*q.v.*) out of sugar industry.

**Ha'ven** (hā'vĕn), **Erastus Otis.** 1820–1881. American Methodist Episcopal bishop and educator, b. Boston. Editor, *Zion's Herald*, a Methodist weekly in Boston (1856–63). President, U. of Michigan (1863–69) and Northwestern U., Chicago (1869–72); chancellor, Syracuse U. (1874–80). Elected bishop (1880). His first cousin **Gilbert Haven** (1821–1880) was also a Methodist Episcopal bishop; editor, *Zion's Herald* (1867–72); elected bishop (1872) and stationed at Atlanta, Ga.

**Ha'ven·stein** (hä'vĕn·shtīn), **Rudolf.** 1857–1923. German financier; president of Prussian state bank (1900) and of the Reichsbank (1908); his policy of extending vast credits after the World War is said to have played a large part in the depreciation of German currency.

**Hav'er·field** (hăv'ẽr·fēld), **Francis John.** 1860–1919. English historian; author of *Roman Occupation of Britain* (1924), etc.

**Hav'er·gal** (hăv'ẽr·găl), **Frances Ridley.** 1836–1879. English author of religious verse; her work consists of *Ministry of Song* (1870), and many hymns and devotional poems.

**Hav'ers** (hăv'ẽrz; hā'vẽrz), **Clopton.** d. 1702. English physician and anatomist; chief work, *Osteologia Nova* (1691), giving first minute account of the structure of bone. Haversian canals and the Haversian system derive their names from him.

**Ha'ver·schmidt** (hä'vẽr·shmĭt), **François.** *Pseudonym* **Piet Paalt'jens** (pält'yĕns). 1835–1894. Dutch reformed church preacher and poet; author of popular *Snikken en Grimlachjes* (1867), ironically romantic verse in style of Heine and Byron.

**Ha'vet'** (à'vĕ'), **Ernest Auguste Eugène.** 1813–1889. French educator; editor of *Pensées de Pascal* (1852); author of *Le Christianisme et ses Origines* (1872–84). One son, **Pierre Louis** (1849–1925), was a philologist; another son, **Julien Pierre Eugène** (1853–1893), was on the staff of the Bibliothèque Nationale (from 1876), and joint curator (from 1890).

**Havilland, Geoffrey de.** See DE HAVILLAND.

**Ha'vlí·ček** (hä'vlē·chĕk), **Karel.** *Pseudonym* **Ha'vel Bo'rov·ský** (hä'vĕl bô'rôf·skē). 1821–1856. Czech journalist; imprisoned because of his liberal articles (1851). Author of *Tirolese Elegies*, and a ballad, a satiric poem, and many epigrams.

**Haw'eis** (hô'ĭs; hois), **Hugh Reginald.** 1838–1901. English clergyman and writer; pastorate in London (1866–1901); author of *Music and Morals* (1871), *Christ and Christianity* (5 vols., 1886–87), *Travel and Talk* (2 vols., 1896); m. (1867) **Mary Joy** [joi] (d. 1898), author of *Chaucer for Children* (1877), *Chaucer for Schools* (1880), etc.

**Hawes** (hôz), **Charles Boardman.** 1889–1923. American adventure-story writer.

**Hawes, Charles Henry.** 1867–1943. Businessman and anthropologist, b. in Middlesex, England. In mercantile business (1882–95); engaged in anthropological research in Crete and the Orient (1900–06). Professor, U. of Wisconsin (1907–09), Dartmouth (1910–17); on war service in England (1917–19); asst. director (1919–24) and assoc. director (1924–34), Boston Museum of Fine Arts. He married (1906) **Harriet Boyd** [boid] (1871–1945), anthropologist, who was engaged in archaeological explorations in Greece and Crete (from 1896); discovered and excavated citadel and tombs of the Iron Age, in Crete (1900), and town and palace of the Bronze Age, at Gournia, Crete (1901, 1903, 1904).

**Hawes, Stephen.** d. about 1523. English poet; groom of the chamber to Henry VII; author of the allegorical poem *Passetyme of Pleasure, or History of Graunde Amoure and la Bel Pucel* (printed 1509).

**Hawes, William.** 1785–1846. English singer and composer; conducted madrigal society and directed oratorios; composed songs and glees.

**Hawke** (hôk), **Edward.** 1st Baron **Hawke.** 1705–1781. English naval commander; rear admiral of the white (1747). Defeated and captured great part of French squadron protecting convoy from La Rochelle (1747). Commanded western fleet (1755–56); promoted admiral (1757). Defeated French in Quiberon Bay (1759), capturing five ships and running others ashore. First lord of the admiralty (1766–71); admiral of the fleet (1768).

**Haw'ker** (hô'kẽr), **Harry G.** 1888–1921. Australian aviator; attempted (May 18, 1919) transatlantic airplane flight from Newfoundland to Ireland but was forced down at sea.

**Hawker, Robert Stephen.** 1803–1875. English poet; vicar of Morwenstow (1834), Wellcombe (1851); accepted Roman Catholic faith in later years. Author of *Quest of the Sangraal* (1864), *Cornish Ballads and Other Poems* (1869), etc.

**Hawkes** (hôks), **Herbert Edwin.** 1872–1943. American educator; dean of Columbia Coll. (from 1918). Author of textbooks on algebra, and *College, What's the Use?* (1927).

**Hawkes'worth** (hôks'wûrth; -wẽrth), **John.** 1715?–1773. English writer; early friend and imitator of Dr. Johnson; said to have succeeded Johnson as compiler of parliamentary debates for *Gentleman's Magazine* (1744); collaborated in continuing the *Adventurer* (1752–54). Author of a play *Edgar and Emmeline* (1761), and an account of voyages in the South Seas (1773).

**Haw'kins** (hô'kĭnz), Sir **Anthony Hope.** *Pseudonym* **Anthony Hope** (hōp). 1863–1933. English novelist and playwright. Author of fiction *The Prisoner of Zenda* (1894), *The Dolly Dialogues* (1894), *Rupert of Hentzau* (1898), *The Intrusions of Peggy* (1902), *Mrs. Maxon Protests* (1911), *Little Tiger* (1925); and plays *The Adventure of Lady Ursula*, *Pilkerton's Peerage*, etc.

**Hawkins, Dexter Arnold.** 1825–1886. American lawyer and reformer; advocated free, independently controlled public schools. Drew up provisions of New York State's law to "secure to children the benefits of elementary education" (1874). Denounced political corruption; his revelations played part in overthrowing Tweed Ring.

**Hawkins,** Sir **Henry.** Baron **Bramp'ton** (brăm(p)'tŭn). 1817–1907. English judge. Counsel in several famous cases (1852–76); raised to bench (1876); gained in murder cases nickname of "Hanging Hawkins."

**Haw'kins** *or* **Haw'kyns** (hô'kĭnz), Sir **John.** 1532–1595. English naval commander. Engaged in slave trade, carrying Negroes from Africa to West Indies and Spanish Main (1562–67). Treasurer and comptroller of the navy (1573). Rear admiral in command of rear squadron in defeat of Spanish Armada (1588), and in command of center of Howard's division at Gravelines (Nov., 1588). Joint commander with Frobisher of squadron on Portuguese coast (1590); second in command to Drake on expedition to West Indies (1595), dying at sea off Puerto Rico. See Sir Richard HAWKINS.

**Hawkins,** Sir **John.** 1719–1789. English magistrate and writer; friend of Dr. Johnson and member of Johnson's club; drafted Johnson's will and served as one of his executors. Edited Johnson's works and wrote a biography of him (1787–89).

**Hawkins** *or* **Hawkyns,** Sir **Richard.** 1562?–1622. English naval officer. Son of Sir John Hawkins (*q.v.*). Served against Spanish Armada (1588) and in expedition to

Portugal (1590). Started (1593) on voyage around world; rounded Cape Horn; sailed up west coast of South America; plundered Valparaiso; was defeated and captured in San Mateo Bay, Peru (June, 1594). Sent to Spain as prisoner (1597); ransomed (1602). Vice-admiral of Devon (1604); vice-admiral on unsuccessful expedition against Algerian pirates (1620–21).

**Hawks** (hôks), **Francis Lister.** 1798–1866. American Protestant Episcopal clergyman and writer; pastorates in New York City (1831–43; 1849–62). Wrote widely on church and secular history.

**Hawks, Frank Monroe.** 1897–1938. American aviator; in U.S. air service (1917–19); established transcontinental record of 12 hrs., 25 mins., 3 secs., west to east (Aug. 13, 1930), and east to west record of 14 hrs., 50 mins., 43 secs. (Aug. 6, 1930), and nonstop transcontinental record of 13 hrs., 27 mins., 15 secs. (June 2, 1933).

**Hawksbee, Francis.** See HAUKSBEE.

**Hawk'shaw** (hôk'shô), Sir **John.** 1811–1891. English civil engineer. Among his works are bridges over the Thames, the Severn tunnel, and the East London Railway.

**Hawks'moor** (hôks'mo͝or), **Nicholas.** 1661–1736. English architect. Designed and erected library and south quadrangle of Queen's College, Oxford, and section of north quadrangle of All Souls' College.

**Hawk'wood** (hôk'wo͝od), Sir **John de.** d. 1394. English soldier of fortune; organized detachment known as the White Company; commander in chief for Florence; defeated Milan (1390–92); died in Florence.

**Hawkyns.** See also HAWKINS.

**Haw'ley** (hô'lĭ), **Gideon.** 1727–1807. American clergyman, b. Stratfield, Conn. Missionary to the Indians, with mission at Mashpee, Mass. (1758–1807).

**Hawley, Joseph.** 1723–1788. American political leader; active in colonial cause (from 1766); associate of Otis, Samuel Adams, and John Adams; urged declaration of independence and unified colonial administration.

**Hawley, Joseph Roswell.** 1826–1905. American legislator; editor, Hartford (Conn.) *Evening Press* (1857). Served through Civil War; brigadier general (1864); brevetted major general (1865). Governor of Connecticut (1866). Member, U.S. House of Representatives (1872–75; 1879–81), and U.S. Senate (1881–1905).

**Hawley, Willis Chatman.** 1864–1941. American lawyer, teacher, and legislator, b. near Monroe, Ore. Member, U.S. House of Representatives (1907–33); chairman of joint committee of Senate and House on Internal Revenue taxation; cosponsor of the Smoot-Hawley Tariff Act (1930).

**Ha'worth** (hô'ẽrth; hô'wûrth, -wẽrth; hou'ẽrth), **Adrian Hardy.** 1767–1833. English botanist and entomologist.

**Haworth** (*pron. uncertain*), **Joseph.** 1855?–1903. American actor; chief roles, Hamlet, Macbeth, Malvolio, Richelieu, Cassius, John Storm in Hall Caine's *The Christian*, Prince Dimitri in *Resurrection.*

**Ha'worth** (härth), Sir **Walter Norman.** 1883–1950. English chemist, b. in Lancashire. Prof., U. of Birmingham (from 1925). Engaged in research on carbohydrates and vitamin C; shared with Paul Karrer (*q.v.*) the 1937 Nobel prize for chemistry.

**Haw'thorne** (hô'thôrn), **Charles Webster.** 1872–1930. American painter, b. Lodi, Ill.; pupil of William M. Chase. Studio, Provincetown, Mass. (from c. 1902). Examples of his work: *The Trousseau*, now in Metropolitan Museum of Art, New York City; *The Mother*, in Boston Museum of Fine Arts; *Fisherman's Daughter*, in Corcoran Art Gallery, Washington, D.C.

**Hawthorne, Julian.** 1846–1934. Son of Nathaniel Hawthorne. American novelist and miscellaneous writer, b. Boston. Civil engineer by profession. Among his novels are *Idolatry* (1874), *Garth* (1877), *Sebastian Strome* (1880), *Noble Blood* (1884), *A Fool of Nature* (1899); other works include *Nathaniel Hawthorne and His Wife* (1885), *Hawthorne and his Circle* (1903).

**Hawthorne, Nathaniel.** 1804–1864. American novelist, b. Salem, Mass. Grad. Bowdoin (1825). Lived at Salem, devoting himself to writing (1825–37). Published stories in *Token* and *New England Magazine* (1828–42). Literary success established by *Twice-Told Tales* (1st series, 1837; 2d series, 1842), *Mosses from an Old Manse* (1846), *The Scarlet Letter* (1850), *The House of the Seven Gables* (1851), *The Snow-Image and Other Twice-Told Tales* (1851), *The Blithedale Romance* (1852), *A Wonder-Book for Girls and Boys* (1852), *Tanglewood Tales for Girls and Boys* (1853). Worked in Boston customhouse (1839–41); lived at Brook Farm for a year; resident of Concord (1842–45); neighbor of Bronson Alcott, Ellery Channing, Ralph Waldo Emerson, Henry David Thoreau; served as surveyor of the port, Salem (1845–49). U.S. consul, Liverpool, England (1853–58). Resident in Italy (1858–59) and in London (1859–60); returned to Concord, Mass. (1860). Latest works, *The Marble Faun* (1860), *Our Old Home* (1863). Elected to American Hall of Fame (1900). See Julian HAWTHORNE.

**Hawthorne, Rose.** See Mother ALPHONSA.

**Haw'trey** (hô'trĭ), Sir **Charles Henry.** 1858–1923. English actor; first success in *The Private Secretary* (1884), a play which he adapted from a German farce; best known as interpreter of comedy roles. Also known as theater manager (at the Globe, to 1887, and the Comedy, 1887–93, 1896–98) and producer.

**Hax'o'** (ȧk'sō'), **Nicolas François.** 1749–1794. French general commanding volunteers in defense of Mainz (1791). His nephew **François Nicolas Benoît** (1774–1838) was a military engineer of the Revolutionary and Napoleonic period; inspector general of fortifications under the Restoration; directed siege of the citadel of Antwerp (1832) in the Belgian Revolution.

**Haxt'hau'sen** (häkst'hou'zĕn), Baron **August von.** 1792–1866. German economist; made special studies of land laws and Prussian and Russian administration.

**Hay** (hā), **George.** 1729–1811. Scottish Roman Catholic prelate; sent from Rome on Scottish mission (1759); consecrated bishop of Daulis *in partibus* (1769); vicar-apostolic of lowland district (1778). His furniture and library burned in protestant riots at Edinburgh (1779). Founded seminary of Aquhorties, and retired there (1802).

**Hay, Ian.** Pseudonym of John Hay BEITH.

**Hay, James.** 1st Baron **Hay.** 1st Earl of **Car·lisle'** (kär·līl'; kär'līl). 1st Viscount of **Don'cas·ter** (dŏng'-kȧs·tẽr). d. 1636. Scottish courtier; accompanied King James I to England (1603); executed diplomatic missions to France, Germany, and Spain (1619–20), to Italy (1628); patentee and councilor of New England plantation; succeeded by his son by his first wife, at whose death (1660) peerage became extinct. His second wife, **Lucy Hay,** Countess of **Carlisle** (1599–1660), 2d daughter of Henry Percy, 9th Earl of Northumberland, was celebrated for her wit and beauty, and commemorated in verse by Carew, Herrick, Suckling, Waller, D'Avenant; befriended Strafford; devoted herself to Pym; disclosed king's intended arrest of the five members of the House of Commons (Jan. 4, 1642); attached herself to Presbyterian party; in second Civil War was zealous in royal cause; betrayed secrets of both sides; imprisoned in Tower (1649–50).

**Hay, John.** 2d Earl and 1st Marquis of **Tweed'dale'**

(twē(d)'dāl'). 1626–1697. Scottish soldier and civil leader. Fought for Charles I (1642), for Parliament at Marston Moor (1644), with Royalists at Preston (1648); member of Cromwell's Parliament (1656); president of Scottish council (1663); extraordinary lord of session (1664); dismissed for moderating harshness of proceedings by English against Covenanters (1674); readmitted to council (1682); lord high chancellor of Scotland (1692–96); dismissed for assenting to act supporting Darien scheme.

**Hay, John Milton.** 1838–1905. American statesman, b. Salem, Ind. Private secretary to Abraham Lincoln (1860–65). U.S. assistant secretary of state (1878). Emerged (1870–90) as important literary figure, with publication of *Pike County Ballads and Other Pieces* (1871), *Castilian Days* (1871), *The Bread-Winners* (pub. anon. 1884), *Poems* (1890), and, with John Nicolay, *Abraham Lincoln, a History* (10 vols., 1890). U.S. ambassador to Great Britain (1897–98). U.S. secretary of state (1898–1905); negotiated Hay-Pauncefote treaty (1901) providing for construction of Panama Canal and superseding Clayton-Bulwer treaty. Cf. S. R. GUMMERE.

**Ha·ya·shi** (hä·yä·shē), Baron **Gonsuke.** 1861–1939. Japanese diplomat; assigned to China, then to London embassy (1893–98), Korea (1899). Envoy extraordinary at Rome (1908–16); ambassador at Peking (1916–18); ambassador to England (1920–25; retired).

**Hayashi, Senjuro.** 1876–1943. Japanese general and premier; minister of war (1934–35); premier (Feb.–June, 1937).

**Hayashi,** Count **Tadasu.** 1850–1913. Japanese diplomat and statesman. Minister to China (1896–98), Russia (1898–99), Great Britain (1899–1906; ambassador, 1906). Created count (1907). Delegate to International Peace Conference at The Hague (1899); largely responsible for treaties of Anglo-Japanese alliance (1902, 1905).

**Hay'den** (hā'd'n), **Charles.** 1870–1937. American banker and philanthropist, b. Boston. Founded firm of Hayden, Stone & Co., bankers and brokers (1892). Gave $150,000 for apparatus of the planetarium in New York, named Hayden Planetarium in his honor.

**Hayden, Charles Henry.** 1856–1901. American landscape painter, b. Plymouth, Mass.

**Hayden, Edward Everett.** 1858-1932. American naval officer; known for his study of hurricanes.

**Hayden, Ferdinand Vandeveer.** 1829–1887. American geologist; surgeon in Union army through Civil War; with U.S. Geological Survey (1872–86); instrumental in creation of Yellowstone National Park.

**Hayden, Horace H.** 1769–1844. American dentist; with Chapin A. Harris, a founder of Baltimore Coll. of Dental Surgery, first dental college in the world (chartered 1840).

**Hay'dn** (hī'd'n; *Angl.* hā'd'n), **Joseph,** *in full* **Franz Joseph.** 1732–1809. Austrian composer. Sang in cathedral choir of St. Stephen's, Vienna (1740–49); received aid in his studies from Metastasio and Porpora. Kapellmeister in the service of the Esterházy family (1760–90), during which period he wrote some of his greatest music, operas, Masses, piano sonatas, symphonies, overtures, an oratorio, and many lesser pieces. Long friendship with Mozart (beginning 1781–82) aided in developing a fuller mastery of orchestral effects in his later symphonies. In England (1791–92) wrote and conducted six symphonies, and again (1794–95) another six symphonies. Resident in Vienna suburbs (from 1795), where he wrote his last eight Masses, his finest chamber music, the Austrian national anthem, the two great oratorios *The Creation* and *The Seasons*. Regarded as first great master of the symphony and the quartet. A brother, **Johann Michael** (1737–1806), was also a composer of over 360 works for the church, including Masses and a set of graduals, also of 3 symphonies, a string quartet in C major, and instrumental music.

**Hay'dn** (hā'd'n), **Joseph.** d. 1856. English compiler of a *Dictionary of Dates* (1841).

**Hay'don** (hā'd'n), **Benjamin Robert.** 1786–1846. English historical painter. Both Wordsworth and Keats addressed sonnets to him.

**Hay'ek** (hī'ĕk), **Friedrich August von.** 1899– . Austrian economist. At U. of London (1931–50), U. of Chicago (1950–62), U. of Freiburg (1962–69); awarded (with Gunnar Myrdal) Nobel prize for economics (1974).

**Ha'yem'** (à'yĕm'), **Georges.** 1841–1933. French physician; known esp. for work on diseases of the stomach and on composition and pathology of the blood. Hayem's corpuscle and Hayem solution are named after him.

**Hayes** (hāz), **Carlton Joseph Huntley.** 1882–1964. American historian and educator; professor, Columbia (from 1919). Author of *Political and Social History of Modern Europe* (2 vols., 1916), *Essays on Nationalism* (1926), etc. U.S. ambassador to Spain (1942–45).

**Hayes, Helen.** *Full maiden name* **Helen Hayes Brown.** 1900– . American actress; m. (1928) Charles MacArthur (*q.v.*), playwright. On stage from childhood, appearing in *Pollyanna*, *Penrod*, *Dear Brutus*, *What Every Woman Knows*, *Victoria Regina*, etc.; starred in motion pictures, as *The Sin of Madelon Claudet* and *Arrowsmith;* received Motion Picture Academy awards (1932, 1971).

**Hayes, Henry.** Pseudonym of Mrs. John Foster KIRK.

**Hayes, Isaac Israel.** 1832–1881. American explorer in the arctic. Surgeon on Kane's second arctic expedition (1853–55). Led arctic expedition, financed largely by Henry Grinnell (1860–61); explorations revealed important knowledge of polar geography. Surgeon in Union army through Civil War. On third arctic expedition, with the painter William Bradford (1869).

**Hayes, Patrick Joseph.** 1867–1938. American cardinal, b. New York City. A.B. (1888), Manhattan College, New York; S.T.D., Catholic U. (1894); D.D., Rome (1904). Chancellor of New York (1903); auxiliary bishop of New York (1914); archbishop (1919); cardinal (1924). Legate a latere to Eucharistic Conference at Cleveland, Ohio (Aug. 20, 1935).

**Hayes, Roland.** 1887–1977. American Negro tenor singer, b. Curryville, Ga. On concert state in U.S. and Europe (from 1916); gave command performances before George V of England (Apr., 1921) and Queen Mother Maria Christina of Spain (Apr., 1925). Awarded Spingarn medal (1925).

**Hayes, Rutherford Birchard.** 1822–1893. Nineteenth president of the United States, b. Delaware, Ohio. Adm. to bar (1845); practiced, Cincinnati (from 1850). In Union army through Civil War; brigadier general (1864); brevetted major general (1865). Member, U.S. House of Representatives (1865–67). Governor of Ohio (1868–72; 1876–77). Nominated for president of the U.S. (1876). Close election, with contested returns from S. Carolina, Florida, Louisiana, and Oregon; electoral commission formed to count ballots; Hayes declared victor by vote 185 to 184. President (1877–81). Cf. Samuel Jones TILDEN.

**Ha'yez** (ä'yāts), **Francesco.** 1791–1882. Italian mural, genre, and historical painter; painted murals in the Vatican.

**Hay'ford** (hā'fērd), **John Fillmore.** 1868–1925. American civil engineer; chief scientific contribution, establishment of theory of isostasy.

**Hay'ley** (hā'lĭ), **William.** 1745–1820. English poet; friend of Cowper, Romney, and Southey. Author of *Triumphs of Temper* (1781), *Triumphs of Music* (1804), *Ballads Founded on Anecdotes of Animals* (1805). Ridiculed in Byron's *English Bards and Scotch Reviewers.*

**Haym** (hīm), **Rudolf.** 1821–1901. German philosopher and literary historian.

**Hay'mer·le** (hī'mĕr·lĕ), Baron **Heinrich Karl von.** 1828–1881. Austrian statesman; ambassador to Copenhagen (1864), Constantinople (1868), Athens (1869), The Hague (1872), Rome (1877); represented Austria in the Berlin Congress (1878); foreign minister (1879–81).

**Hay'nau** (hī'nou), Baron **Julius von.** 1786–1853. Austrian general; notorious for cruelty as military dictator in Italy (1848–49) and Hungary (1849–50).

**Hayne** (hān), **Isaac.** 1745–1781. American Revolutionary soldier, b. in South Carolina. Captured by British at Charleston (1780), and paroled. Required (1781) by British authorities to return as prisoner or to take oath of allegiance to the Crown; took oath on assurance he would not be called for military service. When ordered to join British forces, he joined colonial troops and served as a colonel of South Carolina militia. Again captured by British; hanged as a spy and a traitor, his execution arousing intense indignation among Americans.

**Hayne, Paul Hamilton.** 1830–1886. American poet, b. Charleston, S.C. Published *Poems* (1855), *Sonnets and Other Poems* (1857), *Avolio* (1860), *Legends and Lyrics* (1872), *The Mountain of the Lovers* (1875), *The Broken Battalions* (1885).

**Hayne, Robert Young.** 1791–1839. American politician; adm. to bar (1812); practiced, Charleston, S.C. U.S. senator (1823–32); noted for brilliant debate with Daniel Webster on principles of the Constitution, authority of the federal government, and states' rights (1830). Governor of South Carolina (1832–34).

**Haynes** (hānz), **Elwood.** 1857–1925. American inventor; designed and built horseless carriage (1893–94), claimed to be oldest American automobile, now on exhibition at Smithsonian Institution in Washington. Discoverer of various alloys, as tungsten chrome steel (1881), alloy of chromium and nickel (1897), alloy of cobalt and chromium (1900), and alloys of cobalt, chromium, and molybdenum (1911–12); patented stainless steel (1919). Cf. Charles E. DURYEA.

**Haynes, John.** 1594–1654. Colonial administrator in America, b. Essex, England; to America (1633). Governor of Massachusetts (1635). Moved to Hartford, Conn. (1637). First governor of Connecticut under the Fundamental Laws (1639 and alternate years thereafter until his death).

**Haynes, John Henry.** 1849–1910. American archaeologist; member, archaeological expedition excavating at Assos (1881–82); expedition to Mesopotamia (1884–85); U. of Pennsylvania expedition at Nippur (1888–90; field director, 1893–95; 1896–1900).

**Hays** (hāz), **Arthur Garfield.** 1881–1954. American lawyer of German Jewish descent, b. Rochester, N.Y.; adm. to N.Y. bar (1905); known esp. for his activities in cases involving civil liberties.

**Hays, Francis.** 1870–1943. English Roman Catholic clergyman and temperance advocate; first president of World's Catholic Temperance Crusade; designated by Pope Leo XIII the Apostle of Temperance (1900).

**Hays, Will H.** 1879–1954. American lawyer and politician; chairman, Republican National Committee (1918–21). U.S. postmaster general (1921–22). President, Motion Picture Producers and Distributors of America (1922–45).

**Hays, William Jacob.** 1830–1875. American painter of animals (*The Wounded Buffalo, The Stampede, The Herd on the Move, Prairie-dog Village*).

**Hay'ter** (hā'tĕr), Sir **George.** 1792–1871. English portrait and historical painter; painter in ordinary to the queen (1841).

**Hay'ward** (hā'wĕrd), **Abraham.** 1801–1884. English essayist and miscellaneous writer. Author of *The Art of Dining* (1852), *Sketches of Eminent Statesmen and Writers* (1880), etc.

**Hayward, George.** 1791–1863. American surgeon; first surgeon to use ether anesthetic in a major operation (1846).

**Hayward,** Sir **John.** 1564?–1627. English historian; author of *First Part of the Life and Raigne of Henrie the IIII* (1599–1601), *Lives of the III Normans, Kings of England* (1613), *Life and Raigne of King Edward the Sixt* (pub. posthumously 1630).

**Hayward, Nathaniel Manley.** 1808–1865. American inventor, b. Easton, Mass. Invented process of treating rubber with sulphur to create partial vulcanization (patent issued 1839 and assigned to Charles Goodyear); also, devised a process for giving rubber shoes a polish.

**Haywood, Eliza,** *nee* **Fowler.** 1693?–1756. English novelist and playwright; satirized in Pope's *Dunciad.*

**Haywood, William Dudley,** *orig.* **William Richard.** 1869–1928. American labor leader, b. Salt Lake City; changed name to that of his father. A miner, from age of fifteen. Joined Socialist party (1901). A founder of Industrial Workers of the World (1905). Tried on charge of having a part in murder of Frank R. Steunenberg, former governor of Idaho (1907); acquitted. His advocacy of violence by workers in industrial disputes led to separation from Socialist executive board (1912). Arrested for sedition at entrance of U.S. into World War (1917); convicted (1918); released on bail pending new trial. Fled to Soviet Russia (1921–28); died in Russia.

**Haz'a·el** (hăz'ā·ĕl; hā'zā·ĕl; hȧ·zā'ĕl). fl. 841–820 B.C. King of Damascus. Killed Benhadad II and succeeded to throne (c. 841 B.C.); in Bible account (*2 Kings* viii–x) appeared as ally of Elijah in Israel; paid tribute to Shalmaneser; fought with Shalmaneser (after 839) and prevented him from taking Damascus; fought and oppressed Israel, seizing part of it; ravaged Judah (*2 Kings* xii. 17, 18; xiii. 3–7).

**Haz'ard** (hăz'ĕrd), **Caroline.** 1856–1945. American educator; president, Wellesley College (1899–1910). Author of *Narragansett Ballads* (1894), *Some Ideals in the Education of Women* (1900), *The Yosemite and Other Verse* (1917), *Anchors of Tradition* (1924), *From College Gates* (1925), *Shards and Scarabs* (1931), *Threads from the Distaff* (1934), etc.

**Ha'zard'** (à'zàr'), **Paul Gustave Marie Camille.** 1878–1944. French literary historian; professor of comparative literature, Lyon (1911–13), Sorbonne (1913–26), Collège de France (1926–44); visiting professor, Columbia U., New York City (1923–24; 1932 ff.). Elected to the French Academy (1940); his appointment as president of the Sorbonne rejected by the Nazis (Jan., 1941). Author of *La Crise de la Conscience Européenne, 1680–1715* (1935).

**Ha'zen** (hā'z'n), **Charles Downer.** 1868–1941. American historian and educator; professor, Smith (1894–1914), Columbia (from 1916). Author of *Europe since 1815* (1910), *Modern Europe* (1920), etc.

**Hazen, William Babcock.** 1830–1887. American army officer; grad. U.S.M.A., West Point (1855). Served through Civil War; major general (1864). Chief signal officer, U.S. army, rank of brigadier general (1880); in charge of organizing Greely expedition into arctic (1881); objected to secretary of war's delay in sending relief expedition (1883). Court-martialed for criticism of his superior officer (1885).

**Haz′litt** (hăz′lĭt), **Henry**. 1894– . American editor; financial writer on various New York papers (1913–23); on editorial staff, New York *Times* (from 1934). Author of *Thinking as a Science* (1916), *The Anatomy of Criticism* (1933), etc.

**Hazlitt, William**. 1778–1830. English essayist, b. in Kent. Educated for Unitarian ministry; also studied painting. Dramatic critic on *Morning Chronicle* (1814); contributed to Leigh Hunt's *Examiner;* wrote for *Edinburgh Review* (from 1814), *London Magazine*, and *Colburn's New Monthly*. Lectured widely, esp. on Shakespeare and the English drama. Author of *The Characters of Shakespeare's Plays* (1817), *Lectures on English Poets* (1818), *Lectures on the Dramatic Literature of the Reign of Queen Elizabeth* (1821), *Spirit of the Age* (1825), *Life of Napoleon Buonaparte* (4 vols., 1828–30). **William Carew Hazlitt** (1834–1913), his grandson, wrote *History of... Republic of Venice* (1858 ff.), *Handbook to Popular, Poetical, and Dramatic Literature of Great Britain* (1867), etc.

**H. D.** Pseudonym of Hilda DOOLITTLE.

**Head** (hĕd), **Barclay Vincent**. 1844–1914. English numismatist; authority on Greek coins.

**Head, Cloyd**. American poet and playwright; m. Eunice Tietjens (*q.v.*); author of *Grotesques* (verse play, 1933), *Good King Wenceslaus* (one-act Christmas play, 1937), etc.

**Head,** Sir **Edmund Walker**. 1805–1868. British colonial governor; governor of New Brunswick (1847); governor general of Canada (1854–61).

**Head,** Sir **Francis Bond**. 1793–1875. English soldier, traveler, and colonial administrator. In Royal Engineers (1811–25); engaged at Waterloo (1815); traveled in South America (1825–26); lieutenant governor of Upper Canada (1835–37).

**Head, Richard**. 1637?–?1686. English hack writer; author of part one of *The English Rogue* (1665–71) and *Life and Death of Mother Shipton* (1677).

**Head′lam** (hĕd′lăm), **Arthur Cayley**. 1862–1947. Church of England prelate, b. Durham. Educ. Oxford. Principal of King's Coll., London (1903–12); regius professor of divinity, Oxford, and Canon of Christ Church at Oxford (1918–23); bishop of Gloucester (1923–45). Author of many religious books.

**Head′lam-Mor′ley** (-môr′lĭ), Sir **James Wycliffe**. *Surname orig.* **Headlam.** 1863–1929. English historian, b. in Whorlton, Durham; brother of Arthur Cayley Headlam (*q.v.*). Changed name by royal license (1918). Professor, Queen's College, London (1894–1900); inspector of secondary schools for the board of education (1902–14); during World War (1914–18), adviser to the propaganda department, and on staff of the Foreign Office. Member of British delegation at the Peace Conference in Paris (1919). Historical adviser to the Foreign Office (1920–28). Among his works are *Bismarck and the German Empire* (1899), *The History of Twelve Days* (1915).

**Head′ley** (hĕd′lĭ), **Joel Tyler**. 1813–1897. American historian; author of *Napoleon and his Marshals* (2 vols., 1846), *Washington and his Generals* (2 vols., 1847), etc. His brother **Phineas Camp** (1819–1903) was a Presbyterian clergyman; author of a number of biographies, including *Empress Josephine* (1850), *Lafayette* (1851), *Kossuth* (1852), *General Sherman* (1865), *General Grant* (1866).

**Heald** (hēld), **Frederick De Forest**. 1872–1954. American botanist; head of department of plant pathology, Washington State College (1917–41). Author of treatises on plant pathology. Editor for terms in plant pathology and mycology for *Webster's New International Dictionary, Second Edition*.

**Hea′ly** (hē′lĭ), **George Peter Alexander**. 1813–1894. American portrait painter, b. Boston; studio in Chicago (1855), Paris (1866–67), Rome (1867–73), Paris (1873–92). Examples of his work: *Daniel Webster* and *Henry Wadsworth Longfellow*, now in Boston Museum of Fine Arts; *Chief Justice Taney*, in Capitol, Washington, D.C.; *Webster Replying to Hayne*, in Faneuil Hall, Boston; a series of the presidents of the United States, in Corcoran Art Gallery, Washington, D.C.

**Healy, Patrick Joseph**. 1871–1937. Roman Catholic clergyman and educator, b. Waterford, Ireland. S.T.B. (1898), S.T.L. (1899), S.T.D. (1903), Catholic U. Teacher of church history, Catholic U. (1903–37); professor (from 1910) and dean of the faculty. Author of *Historical Christianity and the Social Question*. Editor of Roman Catholic Church terms for *Webster's New International Dictionary, Second Edition*.

**Healy, Timothy Michael**. 1855–1931. Irish Nationalist leader and statesman, b. in County Cork. M.P. (1880); vigorously advocated home rule. Adm. to bar in Ireland (1884); queen's counsel (1899); called to English bar (1903). First governor general of Irish Free State (1922–27). Wrote esp. on Irish issues and problems.

**Heard** (hûrd), **Gerald**, *in full* **Henry Fitz Gerald**. 1889–1971. English writer; literary editor of *The Realist* (1929). Author of *The Ascent of Humanity; The Emergence of Man; This Surprising World; Pain, Sex, and Time: A New Hypothesis of Evolution* (1939), etc.

**Hearn** (hûrn), **Laf·cad′i·o** (?lăf·kăd′ĭ·ō), *in full* **Pa·tri′·ci·o** (pȧ·trĭsh′ĭ·ō) **Lafcadio Tes′si·ma** (?tĕs′ĭ·mȧ) **Carlos**. 1850–1904. Writer, b. on Greek island of Santa Maura, son of British army surgeon. To U.S. (1869). On staff, Cincinnati (Ohio) *Enquirer*, Cincinnati *Commercial* (1873–78), New Orleans *Item* (c. 1878–79), New Orleans *Times-Democrat* (1881–c. 1887). Contributor to *Century Magazine* and *Harper's Weekly*. In island of Martinique, on writing commission from *Harper's* (1887–89). Went to Japan (1890); taught English in Japanese schools (1890–1903); married Japanese woman, Setsuko Koizumi, and became Japanese citizen under name of **Ya·ku·mo Ko·i·zu·mi** (yä·kōō·mō kō·ē·zōō·mē); his chief writings an attempt to interpret Japan to English-speaking peoples. Author of *Two Years in the French West Indies* (1890), *Glimpses of Unfamiliar Japan* (1894), *Exotics and Retrospectives* (1898), *Japan, An Attempt at Interpretation* (1904).

**Hearne** (hûrn), **Samuel**. 1745–1792. English explorer in America; explored northwestern America for Hudson's Bay Company (1768–70).

**Hearst** (hûrst), **George**. 1820–1891. American mining magnate, b. in Franklin County, Mo. To California (1850); accumulated mines in western Nevada, Utah, Montana, South Dakota, and Mexico. Proprietor, San Francisco *Daily Examiner* (from 1880). U.S. senator (1886–91). His wife, **Phoebe**, *nee* **Ap′per·son** [ăp′·ẽr·s′n] (1842–1919), was noted for her philanthropies, esp. educational philanthropies in California and in Washington, D.C. See William Randolph HEARST.

**Hearst, William Randolph**. 1863–1951. Son of George Hearst. American newspaper publisher, b. San Francisco. Educ. Harvard (1882–85). Proprietor of a chain of newspapers, often cited as examples of yellow journalism, including San Francisco *Examiner*, Chicago *American*, Boston *American*, New York *American* and

New York *Mirror*, and of magazines, including *Hearst's International-Cosmopolitan, Good Housekeeping, Harper's Bazaar*, etc. Member of U.S. House of Representatives (1903–07). Defeated for New York City mayoralty (1905, 1909) and for New York governorship (1906).

**Heath** (hēth), **Edward Richard George.** 1916– . British politician; Conservative party leader (1965–75); prime minister (1969–74).

**Heath, Nicholas.** 1501?–1578. English prelate and statesman; bishop of Rochester (1539), Worcester (1543); archbishop of York (1555–59). Lord chancellor (1556–58). Opposed acts of supremacy and uniformity; deprived of his archbishopric (1559) and temporarily confined in Tower of London.

**Heath, Perry Sanford.** 1857–1927. American Newspaperman; editor, Cincinnati (Ohio) *Commercial-Gazette* (1894–96). First assistant postmaster general (1897–1900); developed rural free delivery system. Bought and edited Salt Lake *Tribune* (from 1901) and founded Salt Lake *Telegram* (1902).

**Heath, William.** 1737–1814. American Revolutionary officer, b. Roxbury, Mass. Major general in Continental army (from 1776); reprimanded by Washington for his handling of attack on Fort Independence (1777).

**Heath'coat** (hēth'kōt), **John.** 1783–1861. English inventor; invented lacemaking machine (c. 1808–09), and a rotary self-narrowing stocking frame. M.P. (1832–59).

**Heath'cote** (hēth'kōt; hĕth'kŭt), **Caleb.** 1665–1721. Merchant, b. in Derbyshire, England; to America (1692); settled in New York. Purchased about twenty square miles near Mamaroneck and had it made Manor of Scarsdale (1701), the last manor granted in British empire. Mayor of New York (1711–13).

**Heath'cote** (hĕth'kŭt), Sir **Gilbert.** 1651?–1733. English financier and politician; chief founder, new East India Company (1693); member of first board of directors, Bank of England (1794). Sheriff of London (1703); lord mayor of London (1710–11); M.P. (1700–10; 1714; 1722; 1727). Ridiculed by Alexander Pope for his parsimony.

**Heathfield,** Baron. See George Augustus ELLIOTT.

**Hea'ton** (hē't'n), **Augustus Goodyear.** 1844–1930. American painter, b. Philadelphia. Among his works are: *Washington at Fort Duquesne*, in Union League, Philadelphia; *The Recall of Columbus*, in the Capitol, Washington, D.C., and engraved (1893) on U.S. postage stamp (50-cent Columbian issue); portrait of *Paul Tulane* for Tulane U.; *Hardships of Emigration*, engraved (1898) on U.S. postage stamp (10-cent Trans-Mississippi issue). Author of *The Heart of David—The Psalmist King* (1900), *Fancies and Thoughts in Verse* (1904), etc.

**Heaton,** Sir **John Henniker.** 1848–1914. English statesman. M.P. (1885–1910). Interested himself in extending postal service; successful in campaigns for imperial penny postage (1898), Anglo-American penny postage (1908), Anglo-Australian penny postage (1905–11). Cf. Sir Rowland HILL.

**Heav'i·side** (hĕv'ĭ·sīd), **Oliver.** 1850–1925. English mathematical physicist and electrician, b. London; made suggestions for rendering duplex telegraphy practicable; suggested a new system of magnetic and electrical units; introduced "expansion theorem" and operational calculus, esp. for studying transient electrical phenomena; worked on the propagation of waves in telegraphy; suggested (1902) probable existence of the region of ionized air affecting radio-wave propagation, now known as the Heaviside, or Kennelly-Heaviside, layer or region (cf. A. E. KENNELLY). His brother **Arthur West** (1844–1923) was a pioneer in telegraphy and telephony.

**Heb'bel** (hĕb'ĕl), **Friedrich.** 1813–1863. German poet and playwright; best known for his tragedies, including *Judith* (1839; publ. 1841), *Maria Magdalena* (1844), *Julia* (1851), *Michel Angelo* (1851), *Agnes Bernauer* (1855), and a trilogy *Die Nibelungen* (1862).

**He'bel** (hā'bĕl), **Johann** (*or* **Jens**) **Peter.** 1760–1826. Swiss-born German poet; fame rests on his *Allemannische Gedichte* (1803), a collection of poems in the Alamannic dialect, favorably reviewed by Goethe.

**He'ber** (hē'bẽr), **Reginald.** 1783–1826. English prelate and hymn writer; bishop of Calcutta (1822–26). Among his best-known hymns are *From Greenland's Icy Mountains; Brightest and Best; Holy, Holy, Holy, Lord God Almighty.* His half-brother, **Richard** (1773–1833), educ. Oxford, was a book collector and classical scholar; editor of Latin classics.

**Heb'er·den** (hĕb'ẽr·d'n; -dĕn), **William.** 1710–1801. English physician and scholar; practiced in London (from 1748); first described angina pectoris; attended Johnson, Cowper, Warburton. His son **William** (1767–1845), physician in ordinary to the queen (1806) and to the king (1809), published translation of Cicero's *Letters to Atticus* (1825) and medical treatises.

**Hé'bert'** (ā'bâr'), **Antoine Auguste Ernest.** 1817–1908. French painter; among his canvases are *Le Baiser de Judas, La Perle Noire, Le Matin et le Soir de la Vie, Aux Héros sans Gloire, Le Sommeil de l'Enfant Jésus,* and many portraits.

**Hébert, Jacques René.** *Called* **Père' Du'chesne'** (pâr' dü'shân'). 1755–1794. French journalist and politician of the Revolution, b. Alençon. Lived in poverty in Paris (1780–90); published radical Republican papers, esp. *Le Père Duchesne* (whence his nickname); member of the Commune of Paris; advocated overthrow of Girondists (1793); popular, but feared by leaders for violence of his ideas; with Chaumette instituted the worship of the Goddess of Reason; arrested by Committee of Public Safety (1794); guillotined with many of his adherents (Mar. 24).

**Hébert, Louis Philippe.** 1850–1917. Canadian sculptor; carved statues of Maisonneuve and Chénier (Montreal), monument to Laval-Montmorency (Quebec), and monument to Queen Victoria (Ottawa).

**He'bra** (hā'brä), **Ferdinand von.** 1816–1880. Austrian dermatologist; a founder of modern dermatology; attributed cause of most diseases of skin to local irritation instead of to morbid condition of fluids of the body in accordance with the previously held humoral pathology.

**Hec'a·tae'us of Ab·de'ra** (hĕk'ȧ·tē'ŭs, ăb·dēr'ȧ). Greek skeptic philosopher and historian of 4th century B.C.; author of a book on the Hyperboreans and a book on Egypt.

**Hecataeus of Mi·le'tus** (mī·lē'tŭs; mĭ-). Greek traveler and historian; opposed Ionian revolt (500 B.C.) against Persia and, after Ionians were defeated, was Ionian ambassador to negotiate terms of peace with Artaphernes. Author of an account of Greek traditions and mythology; reputed author of *Travels around the Earth*, only fragments of which are extant.

**Hecht** (hĕkt), **Ben.** 1894–1964. American writer, b. New York City. On staff of Chicago *Daily News* (1914–23); founder and publisher, Chicago *Literary Times* (1923–25). Author of *Erik Dorn* (1921), *Gargoyles* (1922), *The Florentine Dagger* (1923), *1001 Afternoons in Chicago* (1923), *The Egoist* (1923), *Humpty Dumpty* (1924), *A Book of Miracles* (1939); frequent collaborator with Charles MacArthur (*q.v.*), as in the plays *The Front Page* (1928), *Twentieth Century* (1933), and the motion pictures *Crime Without Passion* and *The Scoundrel.*

**Heck** (hĕk), **Barbara,** *nee* **Ruck'le** (rŏŏk''l). 1734–1804.

b. in County Limerick, Ireland, of German parentage; m. Paul Heck. To New York (1760). With Philip Embury (*q.v.*), organized (1766) first Methodist society in New York City, regarded as beginning of Wesleyan movement in America.

**Heck'el** (hĕk'ĕl), **Erich**. 1883–1970. German painter; identified with the ultramodern school; a founder, with Schmidt-Rottluff, Kirchner, and Pechstein, of group known as "die Brücke," which rebelled against impressionism and became devoted to development of a truly German form of painting. The group tended to disregard nature and become abstract; their paintings are a transition from 19th-century German impressionism to 20th-century abstractionism.

**Heck'en·dorf** (hĕk'ĕn·dôrf), **Franz**. 1888–1962. German painter; a leader of German impressionist school.

**Heck'er** (hĕk'ẽr), **Friedrich Karl Franz**. 1811–1881. German political agitator; tried to lead revolt to establish German republic (1848); uprising suppressed; fled to Switzerland and later to America (1848). Settled in St. Clair County, Ill. (1849); served in Union army through Civil War.

**Hecker, Isaac Thomas**. 1819–1888. American Roman Catholic priest, b. New York City. Brought up a Protestant; converted to Catholicism (1844); joined Redemptorists (1845), serving as missionary priest (1851–57). Founded (1858), with four Redemptorist associates, the Congregation of the Missionary Priests of St. Paul the Apostle (known as Paulist Fathers, or Paulists), and was its first superior (1858–88); founded the *Catholic World* (1865) and the *Young Catholic* (1870), and organized (1866) Catholic Publication Society. See Augustine Francis HEWIT and Clarence Augustus WALWORTH.

**Heck'e·wel'der** (hĕk'ĕ·vĕl'dẽr), **John Gottlieb Ernestus**. 1743–1823. Pioneer Moravian Church missionary to Indians in the Ohio region; b. Bedford, England; to America as a boy.

**Hec'tor** (hĕk'tẽr), **Annie**, *nee* **French**. *Pseudonym* Mrs. **Alexander**. 1825–1902. British novelist, b. Dublin, Ireland. Author of more than 40 novels, including *The Wooing O't* (1873), *Her Dearest Foe* (1876), and *Mona's Choice* (1887).

**He'da** (hā'dȧ), **Willem Claesz**. 1594–?1681. Dutch painter; best known for his still-life paintings, esp. "breakfast" pieces, of various foods on rich plate.

**Hed'berg'** (hād'băr'y'), **Frans**. 1828–1908. Swedish writer, esp. of plays; best-known drama is *Brölloppet på Ulfåsa* (1865). His son **Tor** (1862–1931) was a novelist and playwright; author esp. of psychological novels, as *Judas* (1886) and *På Torpa Gård* (1888), and of dramas, as *Gerhard Grim* (1897), *Ett Hems Drama* (1906), *Johan Ulfstjerna* (1907), *Mikael* (1908), *Perseus* (1917), etc.

**He'de·mann** (hā'dĕ·män), **Justus Wilhelm**. 1878–1963. German jurist; associated with reform of German civil law.

**He'den·stier'na** (hā'dĕn·shâr'nȧ), Baron **Alfred**. *Pseudonym* **Si'gurd** (sē'gûrd). 1852–1906. Swedish author of humorous tales and sketches of Swedish folk life.

**Hedge** (hĕj), **Levi**. 1766–1844. American educator; grad. Harvard (1792); professor of logic and metaphysics, Harvard (1810–27), and of natural religion, moral philosophy, and civil polity (1827–32). His son **Frederic Henry** (1805–1890) was a Unitarian clergyman; pastorates, Bangor, Me. (1835–50) and Brookline, Mass. (1857–72); associated with Emerson, George Ripley, and others in what has become known as the transcendental school (1836); author of *Conservatism and Reform* (1843), *Reason in Religion* (1865), *Atheism in Philosophy* (1884), *Martin Luther and Other Essays* (1888); influential in introducing German authors to America by his translations.

**Hedg'es** (hĕj'ĕz; -ĭz), **Job Elmer**. 1862–1925. American lawyer and witty after-dinner speaker; author of *Common Sense in Politics* (1910).

**Hedges, Killingworth**. 1852–1945. English engineer; introduced electric lighting for dock work, installing dynamos at Liverpool docks (1878); designed lighting system for first steamer using incandescent lamps (1880); author of *Useful Information on Practical Electric Lighting* (1879), etc.

**He·din'** (hĕ·dēn'), **Sven Anders**. 1865–1952. Swedish geographer and explorer in Asia, b. Stockholm. Traveled through Persia and Mesopotamia (1885–86); attached to King Oscar's embassy to the shah of Persia (1890); traveled through Khurasan and Turkestan (1890–91), Asia from Orenburg to Peiping (1893–97), Gobi Desert and Tibet (1899–1902), Persia to India, through Tibet (1905–08); on Sino-Swedish expedition (1926–33). Author of *Through Asia* (1898), *From Pole to Pole* (1911), *Bagdad, Babylon, Ninive* (1917), *Jerusalem* (1917), *Mount Everest* (1922), *Jehol, City of Emperors* (1931), *The Silk Road* (1936), *Germany and World Peace* (written in German, 1937), *Chiang Kai-shek, Marshal of China* (1940), etc.

**Hé'douin'** (ā'dwăN'), **Pierre Edmond Alexandre**. 1820–1889. French painter, etcher, and engraver.

**Hed'wig** (hāt'vĭK), Saint. 1174–1243. Duchess of Silesia; m. (1186) Duke Henry I; endowed many religious houses including Cistercian convent at Trebnitz, to which she retired at husband's death (1238). Canonized (1267); patron saint of Silesia.

**Hedwig**. See JADWIGA.

**Hedwig, Johann**. 1730–1799. German botanist; a founder of muscology.

**Heem** (hām), **Jan Davidsz de** (1606–1683 or 1684) and his son and pupil **Cornelis de** (1631–1695). Dutch still-life painters, esp. of flowers and fruits.

**Heems'kerck** (hāms'kĕrk), **Egbert van** (1610–1680) and his son **Egbert van** (1645–1704). Dutch genre painters.

**Heemskerck, Johan van**. 1597–1656. Dutch poet who in his volume *Batavische Arcadia* (1637) introduced the Italian pastoral romance into Dutch literature.

**Heemskerck, Maarten van**. 1498–1574. Dutch religious painter.

**Heems'kerk** (hāms'kĕrk), **Jan van**. 1567–1607. Dutch navigator; headed expeditions (1595–97) to discover northeastern passage to China; killed in action against Spanish fleet (1607).

**Heemskerk, Theodore**. 1852–1932. Dutch statesman; prime minister (1908–13).

**Heer** (hār), **Jakob Christoph**. 1859–1925. Swiss novelist.

**Heer, Oswald**. 1809–1883. Swiss naturalist. Investigated fossil flora and fauna, esp. insects, of the Tertiary.

**Hee'ren** (hā'rĕn), **Arnold**. 1760–1842. German historian; professor, Göttingen (from 1801).

**Hee'ring·en** (hā'rĭng·ĕn), **Josias von**. 1850–1926. German soldier; in World War, commanded 7th German army and was checked by General Castelnau in the Grand Couronné (1914).

**He'fe·le** (hā'fĕ·lĕ), **Karl Joseph von**. 1809–1893. German Roman Catholic prelate and historian; chief historical work, *Conciliengeschichte* (vols. 1–7, 1855–74; vols. 8–9, 1887–90).

**Heff'ter** (hĕf'tẽr), **August Wilhelm**. 1796–1880. German jurist; chief work, *Das Europäische Völkerrecht der Gegenwart* (1844).

**Heffter, Lothar**. 1862–1962. German mathematician.

**Hef'ner–Al'te·neck** (hāf'nẽr·äl'tĕ·nĕk), **Friedrich von**.

1845–1904. German electrical engineer; invented the drum armature (1872), and the Hefner lamp, whose flame produces the Hefner candle, the official German unit of light intensity.

**He′gar** (hā′gär), **Friedrich.** 1841–1927. Swiss composer and conductor; founder and director of a music school at Zurich (1878–1914); composer of orchestral and chamber music, choral works and songs, and the oratorio *Manasse.*

**He′ge·dűs** (hĕ′gĕ·düsh), **Lóránt.** 1872– . Hungarian writer and politician; author of works on economics, esp. taxation and sociological questions, and literary subjects, including *A Banker Meets Jesus* (Eng. trans. 1937).

**He′gel** (hā′gĕl), **Georg Wilhelm Friedrich.** 1770–1831. German philosopher, b. at Stuttgart. Educ. Tübingen (1788–93), where he became a friend of Hölderlin and Schelling. Tutor at Bern, Switzerland (1793–96) and Frankfurt am Main (1797–1800). Lecturer at Jena (1801), and professor there (1807); rector of the Gymnasium at Nuremberg (1808–16); professor, Heidelberg (1816–18), and Berlin (1818–31). His system of philosophy, commonly known as *Hegelianism,* was a philosophy of the Absolute, and the leading system of metaphysics during the second quarter of the 19th century. His works include *Die Phänomenologie des Geistes* (1807), *Wissenschaft der Logik* (3 vols., 1812–16), *Enzyklopädie der Philosophischen Wissenschaften im Grundrisse* (1817), *Grundlinien der Philosophie des Rechts oder Naturrecht und Staatswissenschaft im Grundrisse* (1821). His son **Karl von Hegel** (1813–1901) was a historian; professor, Erlangen (from 1856).

**He′ge·mann** (hā′gĕ·män), **Werner.** 1881–1936. German architect; authority on city planning; his criticism of the German government caused his exile from Germany (1933); to U.S. and took out citizenship papers. On staff of Columbia school of architecture, New York City (1935).

**He·ge′mon of Tha′sos** (hē·jē′mŏn, thā′sŏs). Greek writer of comedies in late 5th century B.C., mentioned by Aristotle in his *Poetics.*

**He·ge′si·as of Mag·ne′si·a** (hē·jē′zĭ·ăs, măg·nē′zhĭ·ȧ [-zhȧ]). Greek rhetorician and historian of 4th century B.C.

**Heg′e·sip′pus** (hĕj′ē·sĭp′ŭs). Athenian orator of 4th century B.C.; in the assembly, supported anti-Macedonian policy advocated by Demosthenes.

**Hegesippus.** d. 180. Jewish convert to Christianity; author of a history of the Christian Church down to his own time, only fragments of which are extant.

**He′gi·us** (hā′gē·ōōs), **Alexander.** 1433?–1498. German Humanist; among his pupils were Erasmus and Hermann von dem Busche.

**Hehn** (hān), **Victor.** 1813–1890. German historian; teacher of German at Tartu, Russia (1846–51); librarian at St. Petersburg (1855–73); resident at Berlin (from 1873).

**Hei′berg** (hā′ĭ·băr), **Gunnar.** 1857–1929. Norwegian playwright, b. at Christiania (Oslo). Among his plays are *Kong Midas* (1890), *Kunstnere* (1893), *Balkonen* (1894), *Det Store Lod* (1895), *Folkeraadet* (1897), *Harald Svans Mor* (1899), *Kjærlighedens Tragedie* (1904), *Parade-Sengen* (1913). Author also of works of dramatic criticism.

**Hei′berg** (hī′bĕrκ), **Hermann.** 1840–1910. German novelist.

**Hei′berg** (hī′bĕrg), **Johan Ludvig.** 1854–1928. Danish classical philologist; chief works in the field of ancient mathematics, as his editions of Euclid, Apollonius of Perga, Ptolemy, Archimedes, and Hero of Alexandria.

**Heiberg, Peter Andreas.** 1758–1841. Danish writer; in comedies, songs, and pamphlets satirized the government until he was exiled (1799). To Paris; in department of foreign affairs; accompanied Talleyrand on various diplomatic journeys. His son **Johan Ludvig** (1791–1860) was a man of letters; director of the Theater Royal, Copenhagen (1849–56); creator of vaudeville in Denmark; author of comedies, dramas, vaudeville sketches, and philosophical works expounding Hegelianism. Johan's wife (m. 1831), **Johanne Luise,** *nee* **Pät′ges** (pĕt′gĕs) (1812–1890), was an actress at the Theater Royal, Copenhagen (1829–57; 1859–64); author of vaudeville sketches and a volume of reminiscences. See Thomasine GYLLEMBOURG-EHRENSVÄRD.

**Hei′deg′ger** (hī′dĕg′ēr), **Johann Heinrich.** 1633–1698. Swiss Reformed Church theologian; chief author of the *Formula Consensus Helvetica* (1675), which failed in its purpose of uniting the Swiss Reformed churches.

**Heidegger, John James.** 1659?–1749. English theater manager, prob. a native of Zurich; managed Italian opera at Haymarket for Royal Academy of Music (1720–28), in partnership with Handel (1728–34), and alone (1737–38).

**Heidegger, Martin.** 1889– . German philosopher.

**Hei′den·hain** (hī′dĕn·hīn), **Rudolf Peter Heinrich.** 1834–1897. German physiologist; worked on the mechanics, metabolism, and production of heat in muscles, and on glands. His son **Martin** (1864–1949), specialist in cytology and histology.

**Hei′den·stam** (hē′ĭ·dĕn·stȧm), **Verner von.** 1859–1940. Swedish writer; orig. a painter; passed some years in the Orient. His first volume of collected verse, *Vallfart och Vandringsår* (*Pilgrimage and Years of Wandering,* 1888), reflected his life in the Orient; in its contrast to the naturalism characteristic of Swedish literature at that period, it marked the beginning of a literary renaissance in Sweden. Other works, an oriental tale *Endymion* (1889), the epic *Hans Alienus* (1892), the prose work against the historical background of Charles XII's time *Karolinerna* (2 vols., 1897–98), the lyric collection *Nya Dikter* (1915), etc. Awarded Nobel prize for literature (1916).

**Hei′fetz** (hī′fĕts), **Ja′scha** (yä′shȧ). 1901– . American (Russian-born) violinist. Pupil of Leopold Auer at St. Petersburg. Child prodigy; played Mendelssohn's *Concerto in E* (op. 64) at age of 7 and gave public recital in St. Petersburg at age of 9. Debut in New York (1917). Has played in concerts in leading cities of the world.

**Hei′gel** (hī′gĕl), **Karl von.** 1835–1905. German writer of dramas, verse, fiction, and biography. His brother **Karl Theodor** (1842–1915) was a historian; specialized in Bavarian history.

**Hei′jer·mans** (hī′yĕr·mäns), **Herman.** 1864–1924. Dutch writer. Edited (from 1897) socialist literary journal *De Jonge Gids,* Amsterdam; on editorial staff of Social Democratic newspaper *De Nieuwe Tijd* (1899). Author of fiction, including *Trinette* (1893), *Intérieurs* (1897), *Diamantstad* (1903), *Droomkoninkje* (1924); under pseudonym **Koos Hab′be·ma** (häb′ȧ·mȧ), of a realistic novel of Jewish life *Kamertjeszonde* (1897); of plays, including *Ghetto* (1899), *Op Hoop van Zegen* (1900; English title *The Good Hope*), *Ora et Labora* (1903), *De Groote Vlucht* (1908), *Eva Bonheur* (1919), *De Dageraad* (1921); and under pseudonym **Samuel Falk′land** (fälk′länt), of a collection of sketches of Dutch small-town life, *Schetsen* (13 vols.; 1896–1909).

**Hei·ke** (hā·kĕ). The alternative Japanese name of the Taira clan.

**Heil′buth** (hīl′bōōt), **Ferdinand.** 1826–1889. Painter, b. Hamburg; naturalized Frenchman (1879).

**Hei'ler** (hī'lẽr), **Friedrich.** 1892–1967. German theologian. Orig. Roman Catholic; became Lutheran (1919); leader of German High Church Union (from 1929); editor of the *Hochkirche* (from 1930). Author of many works, esp. on Roman Catholicism and on the Evangelical Church.

**Heil'prin** (hīl'prĭn), **Michael.** 1823–1888. Scholar and writer, b. in Poland. Emigrated to Hungary (1842); took part in Hungarian Revolution of 1848; fled to France and (1856) to U.S. On staff of *New American Cyclopaedia* (from 1858); contributor to the *Nation* (from 1865). His son **An'ge·lo** [ăn'jĕ·lō] (1853–1907), b. in Hungary, was a geologist and explorer. Explored Florida Everglades (1886); in Mexico (1888); studied geology of Bermuda (1889); with Peary's exploring expedition in Arctic (1891); in Morocco, Algeria, and Tunis (1896); in Alaska (1898); ascended Mont Pelée, Martinique (1902); journeyed up Orinoco River, British Guiana (1906). Author of *The Geological Evidences of Evolution* (1888), *The Earth and Its Story* (1896), *Mont Pelée and the Tragedy of Martinique* (1903), etc.

**Heim** (hīm), **Albert.** 1849–1937. Swiss geologist; known for studies on mountain-forming processes in the Alps.

**Heim** (ĕm), **François Joseph.** 1787–1865. French historical painter.

**Heim** (hīm), **Karl.** 1874–1958. German Protestant theologian.

**Hei'mann** (hī'män), **Eduard.** 1889–1967. German economist; professor, New School for Social Research, New York (1933–58). Author of *Das Soziale System des Kapitalismus* (1929), *Communism, Fascism or Democracy* (1938), etc.

**Heim'burg** (hīm'bŏork), **Gregor.** 1400?–1472. German legal scholar and diplomat; adviser to city of Nuremberg (1435–61), and to various German and Austrian princes in their negotiations with the Papacy.

**Heim'soeth** (hīm'sût), **Heinz.** 1886– . German philosopher.

**Hein** (hīn), **Alfred.** 1894– . German author of verse and fiction.

**Hei'ne** (hī'nĕ), **Heinrich** (after 1825), *orig.* **Harry.** 1797–1856. German lyric poet and literary critic, b. at Düsseldorf of Jewish descent; adopted the Christian faith (1825). Resident in Paris (from 1831), suffering (from c. 1845) with an incurable disease of the spine which confined him to bed. His volumes of verse are *Gedichte* (1822), *Buch der Lieder* (1827), *Neue Gedichte* (1844), *Romanzero* (1851); they contain some of the best-loved German lyrics, as *Die Lorelei*, *Du Bist Wie eine Blume*, *Nach Frankreich Zogen Zwei Grenadier.* His prose works include *Reisebilder* (4 vols., 1826–31), *Geschichte der Neuren Schönen Literatur in Deutschland* (2 vols., 1833), *Der Salon* (4 vols., 1835–40), *Vermischte Schriften* (3 vols., 1854).

**Hei·nec'ci·us** (hī·nĕk'tsē·ŏŏs), **Johann Gottlieb.** 1681–1741. German jurist; regarded as most learned legal scholar of his day. Author of *Elementa Juris Civilis Secundum Ordinem Institutionum* (1725), *Elementa Juris Civilis Secundum Ordinem Pandectarum* (1727).

**Hei'ne·mann** (hī'nĕ·măn), **William.** 1863–1920. British publisher, b. at Surbiton, Eng., of German descent; established business in London (1890) and published works of Stevenson, Kipling, Galsworthy, Wells, Conrad, Pinero, Maugham, Zangwill, and others; had translations made of works of Dostoevski, Turgenev, Tolstoi, Ibsen, Björnson, Rolland; published Loeb Classical Library of translations.

**Hei'nick·e** (hī'nĭ·kĕ), **Samuel.** 1727–1790. German teacher of the deaf and dumb; founded at Leipzig (1778) first deaf and dumb institution in Germany.

**Hein'kel** (hĭng'kĕl), **Ernst.** 1888–1958. German airplane builder; founder (1922) of the Heinkel-Flugzeugwerke, in Warnemünde, producing bombers widely used by Germans in war beginning Sept., 1939.

**Hein'rich** (hīn'rĭk). German form of HENRY. **Hein'rich der Lö'we** (dĕr lû'vĕ) = HENRY the Lion. **Hein'rich der Schwar'ze** (shvär'tsĕ) = HENRY the Black. **Hein'rich der Stol'ze** (shtôl'tsĕ) = HENRY the Proud.

**Hein'rich der Glî'che·zae're** (hīn'rĭk dĕr glē'kĕ·sâ'rĕ). Middle High German poet who wrote (c. 1180) the famous beast epic *Reinecke Fuchs*, earliest German version of *Reynard the Fox.*

**Heinrich der Teich'ner** (tīk'nĕr). fl. 1350–1377. Middle High German poet; author of many didactic poems written in rhymed couplets.

**Heinrich von dem Tür'lin** (fôn dĕm tür'lēn). fl. about 1215. Middle High German poet; author of *Der Aventiure Krône*, collection of knightly adventures from the Arthurian cycle.

**Heinrich von Frei'burg** (frī'bŏork). fl. about 1300. Middle High German poet; author of *Vom Heiligen Kreuz*, *Ritterfahrt des Johann von Michelsberg*, and a continuation of Gottfried von Strassburg's *Tristan.*

**Heinrich von Meis'sen** (mī'sĕn). 1250?–1318. German poet; said to be founder of first school of "master singers," at Mainz; regarded as a transitional poet between minnesingers and meistersingers. Called **Frau'en·lob'** (frou'ĕn·lōp') [*i.e.* "praise of women"] because of his use of word *Frau* instead of *Weib* for *woman.*

**Heinrich von Mo'rung·en** (mō'rŏŏng·ĕn). Early 13th-century German minnesinger; his songs are regarded as second in quality only to those of Walther von der Vogelweide.

**Heinrich von Mü'geln** (mü'gĕln). fl. 1346–1369. Middle High German poet; translator of Valerius Maximus and of Nicholas of Lyra's *Commentary on the Psalms;* author of an allegorical poem *Der Meide Kranz*, fables, and songs (Minnelieder).

**Heinrich von Rug'ge** (rŏŏg'ĕ). fl. 1175–1178. German minnesinger.

**Heinrich von Vel'de·ke** (fĕl'dĕ·kĕ). Twelfth-century poet, b. near Maastricht in the Netherlands; author of a version of the legend of St. Servatius, patron saint of Maastricht, of an *Eneit* (in Flemish, based on a French version of the *Aeneid*), and of lyrics in the style of the minnesingers; considered one of founders of German court epic poetry.

**Heins** (?hīnz), **George Lewis.** 1860–1907. American architect; collaborated with C. G. La Farge in designing Protestant Episcopal Cathedral of Saint John the Divine, New York City.

**Hein'se** (hīn'zĕ), **Wilhelm.** 1746–1803. German writer; studied law; friend of the poet Wieland (*q.v.*). Librarian to Elector Karl Joseph (from 1787). Among his works are *Ardinghello und die Glückseligen Inseln* (1787) and *Anastasia und das Schachspiel* (1803).

**Hein'si·us** (hīn'sē·ûs), **Antonius.** 1641–1720. Dutch statesman, who, when William III of Orange succeeded to English throne (1688), became grand pensionary of Holland and determined his country's foreign policy; rose to leadership in European combinations against Louis XIV of France; finally accepted terms of peace in Treaty of Utrecht (1713).

**Heinsius, Daniel.** 1580–1655. Dutch classical philologist and poet; prepared editions of classical works; published poetry in both Latin and Dutch, tragedy *The Massacre of the Innocents* (1613), and treatise *De Politica Sapientia* (1614). His son **Nicolaas** (1620–1681) was also a classical philologist. A son of Nicolaas, **Nicolaas**

(1656–1718), was physician in ordinary to Queen Christina of Sweden and, later, to princes of the Brandenburg house; author of medical books and of the satirical picaresque novel *Den Vermakelyken Avanturier* (1695), modeled on the Spanish novel *Lazarillo de Tormes*.

**Hein'tzel·man** (hīn'tsĕl·măn), **Samuel Peter**. 1805–1880. American army officer; grad. U.S.M.A., West Point (1826). Served through Mexican War and Civil War; brigadier general (1861); major general (1862).

**Heinz** (hīnz), **Henry John**. 1844–1919. American food packer, b. Pittsburgh, Pa. With brother and cousin, founded firm F. & J. Heinz to make and sell pickles and other prepared foods (1876); firm reorganized as H. J. Heinz Co. (1888); incorporated (1905); president of company (1905–19).

**Hein'ze** (hīn'zē), **Frederick Augustus**. 1869–1914. American copper magnate; b. Brooklyn, N.Y. Owner of mines in Butte, Montana, region; engaged in long legal fight with Amalgamated Copper interests (1897–1906).

**Hein'ze** (hīn'tsĕ), **Max**. 1835–1909. German philosopher. His son **Rudolf** (1865–1928) was member of Reichstag (1907–12; from 1920); during World War, undersecretary of state in Turkish ministry of justice (1916–17); after November Revolution (1918), joined German People's party and was member of Weimar National Assembly (1919); minister of justice and vice-chancellor of Germany (1920–21; 1922–23). Another son, **Richard** (1867–1929), was a classical philologist.

**Hei'se** (hī'sĕ), **Peter**. 1830–1879. Danish composer of operas, chamber music and songs.

**Hei'sen·berg** (hī'zĕn·bĕrk), **August**. 1869–1930. German Byzantine scholar. His son **Werner** (1901–1976), physicist; professor of theoretic physics, Leipzig (from 1927); investigated atomic structure and the Zeeman effect; began work on his development of quantum mechanics (1925); announced principle of indeterminacy; awarded 1932 Nobel prize for physics (1933).

**Hei'ser** (hī'zĕr), **Victor George**. 1873–1972. American physician and public health authority, b. Johnstown, Pa. M.D., Jefferson Medical College (1897). In U.S. Marine Hospital Service (1898); chief quarantine officer, Philippine Islands (1903–15) and director of health (1905–15). Associate director, international health division of the Rockefeller Foundation (1915–34). Associated with task of eradicating plague, cholera, smallpox, malaria, hookworm, etc., in various parts of the world. Author of *An American Doctor's Odyssey* (1936), *You're the Doctor* (1939), *Toughen Up, America!* (1941).

**Hei'ster** (hī'stĕr), **Lorenz**. 1683–1758. German surgeon; wrote *Chirurgie* (1719), which was translated into almost all European languages.

**Heiter, Amalie**. Pseudonym of AMALIE MARIE FRIEDERIKE AUGUSTE.

**Hek'toen** (hĕk'tōn), **Lud'vig** (lo͝od'vĭg). 1863–1951. American pathologist, b. Westby, Wis.; professor, Coll. of Phys. and Surg., Chicago (1892–94), Rush Medical Coll. (from 1895); professor and head of department of pathology, Chicago (1901–32); director, John McCormick Inst. for Infectious Diseases, Chicago (from 1902). Author of articles on pathology, bacteriology, and immunology.

**Hel'big** (hĕl'bĭk), **Wolfgang**. 1839–1915. German archaeologist.

**Held** (hĕlt), **Adolf**. 1844–1880. German economist.

**Held** (hĕld), **Anna**. 1873?–1918. Comedienne, b. Paris, France; m. Florenz Ziegfeld (*q.v.*), theatrical producer in New York; appeared chiefly in comedies and vaudeville on American stage.

**Held, John**. 1889–1958. American illustrator, cartoonist, and writer; author of *Grim Youth* (1930), *Saga of Frankie and Johnny* (1931), *The Flesh is Weak* (1932), *A Bowl of Cherries* (1933), *Crosstown* (1934), etc.

**Hel'en** (hĕl'ĕn; -ĭn). 1896– . Princess of Greece, eldest dau. of King Constantine I, bro. of kings Alexander and George II; m. (1921) Prince Carol (later King Carol II) of Rumania; divorced 1928; mother of King Michael.

**Hel'e·na** (hĕl'ē·nȧ), Saint. d. about 330. Wife of Constantius Chlorus and mother of Constantine the Great; divorced by Constantius when he became caesar (292); made pilgrimage to Jerusalem (c. 325) and there built Church of the Holy Sepulcher and Church of the Nativity.

**Hel'fert** (hĕl'fĕrt), Baron **Joseph Alexander von**. 1820–1910. Austrian statesman and historian. Chief of education and culture section in ministry (1861–65); member of Austrian upper house (1881). Author of *Huss und Hieronymus* (1853), *Geschichte Österreichs vom Ausgang des Wiener Oktoberaufstandes 1848* (4 vols., 1869–86), etc.

**Helf'fe·rich** (hĕl'fĕ·rĭk), **Karl**. 1872–1924. German economist, banker, and politician. German minister of finance (1915–16) and of the interior (1916–18). Aided in reorganizing German trade and industry after the World War; instrumental in securing the Rentenmark currency (1923); opposed fulfillment of provisions of Treaty of Versailles.

**Hel'frich** (hĕl'frĭk), **Conrad E. L.** 1887–1962. Dutch naval officer; in Netherlands East Indies (from 1907); supreme commander of Netherlands East Indies forces (Dec., 1941); commander of Allied naval forces in southwest Pacific (1942); commander of Netherlands naval forces in Far East (1942–46).

**Heli.** See ELI.

**He'li·o·do'rus** (hē'lĭ·ō·dō'rŭs). Greek writer of 4th(?) century A.D., b. Emesa (Homs), Syria. Author of *Ethiopica*, the story of Theagenes and Chariclea, earliest of extant Greek romances.

**He'li·o·gab'a·lus** (hē'lĭ·ō·găb'ȧ·lŭs) *or* **El'a·gab'a·lus** (ĕl'ȧ·găb'ȧ·lŭs). *Orig.* **Varius A·vi'tus Bas'si·a'nus** (ȧ·vī'tŭs băs'ĭ·ā'nŭs). 204–222. Roman emperor (218–222), b. Emesa (Homs), Syria. Son of Soaemias, daughter of Julia Maesa, who was sister of the wife of Emperor Septimius Severus; by some accounts said to be natural son of Caracalla. At early age a priest in the temple of the sun god, Elagabalus, at Emesa; proclaimed emperor by soldiers (218) under name of **Marcus Aurelius An'to·ni'nus** (ăn'tō·nī'nŭs); defeated Macrinus in battle in Syria (218). Gave himself up to debauchery and extravagance; caused many senators to be put to death; killed by praetorians.

**Hel'land-Han'sen** (hāl'län·hän'sĕn), **Björn**. 1877–1957. Norwegian professor of oceanography, Bergen (1914); director, Geophysical Inst. (1917 ff.); member of exploring expeditions in northern seas.

**Hel'la·ni'cus** (hĕl'ȧ·nī'kŭs). Greek historian of 5th century B.C.; author of histories of Persia, Media, Assyria, and the Aeolians. Only fragments extant.

**Hellens, Franz**. Pseudonym of Frédéric van ERMENGEM.

**Hel'ler** (hĕl'ĕr), **Ste'phen** (shtĕf'ĕn). 1814–1888. Hungarian pianist and composer; friend of Chopin, Liszt, and Berlioz. Best known for his piano studies.

**Hell'man** (hĕl'măn), **Lillian**. 1905– . American playwright, b. New Orleans. Writer of scenarios for motion pictures (from 1935), as *The Dark Angel* (1935) and *Dead End* (1937). Author of plays *The Children's Hour* (1934), *Days to Come* (1936), *The Little Foxes* (1939), *Watch on the Rhine* (1941).

**Hell'mann** (hĕl'män), **Siegmund**. 1872–1942. German historian.

**Hel'lo'** (ĕ'lō'), **Ernest**. 1828–1885. French philosopher and critic; author of *Le Style* (1861), *L'Homme* (1872), *Philosophie et Athéisme* (1888), etc.

**Hell'pach** (hĕl'päĸ), **Willy.** 1877-1955. German physician, psychologist, and politician.

**Hell'quist** (hĕl'kvĭst), **Karl Gustaf.** 1851-1890. Swedish painter; known for folk scenes, landscapes, portraits, and historical pictures.

**Hell'rie'gel** (hĕl'rē'gĕl), **Hermann.** 1831-1895. German agricultural chemist; discovered that leguminous plants are able by means of the bacteria living in nodules on their roots to assimilate the free nitrogen of the air (1888).

**Hell'wald** (hĕl'vält), **Friedrich von.** 1842-1892. Austrian historian.

**Helm'bold** (hĕlm'bōlt), **Ludwig.** 1532-1598. German Lutheran hymn writer. Author of *Von Gott Will Ich Nicht Lassen, Es Stehn von Gottes Throne, Herr Gott, Erhalt uns Für und Für, Nun Lasst uns Gott dem Herren.*

**Hel'mers** (hĕl'mẽrs), **Jan Frederik.** 1767-1813. Dutch poet; composer esp. of intensely patriotic verse, as *Nederland in 1672 en 1678* (1793) and *Vaderlandsche Lierzang* (1799); chief work, *De Hollandsche Natie* (1812).

**Helm'holtz** (hĕlm'hōlts), **Hermann Ludwig Ferdinand von.** 1821-1894. German physicist, anatomist, and physiologist, b. Potsdam. Military physician at Potsdam (1843-48); professor of physiology, Königsberg (1849), of anatomy and physiology, Bonn (1855), of physiology, Heidelberg (1858), of physics, Berlin (1871); director of physicotechnical institute at Charlottenburg (1888). One of the founders of the principle of the conservation of energy, by virtue of his paper *Über die Erhaltung der Kraft* (1847); known for numerous other contributions to science, including determination of the velocity of nerve impulses, invention of the ophthalmoscope (1850), investigation of the mechanisms of sight, development of a theory of color vision, investigation of mechanisms of hearing, explanation of the perception of the quality of tone, study of the vortex motion of fluids, application of the principle of least action to electrodynamics, development of the theory of electricity, investigation of the motion of electricity in conductors; also worked on the theory of knowledge, the fundamentals of geometry, etc.

**Hel'mold** (hĕl'mōlt). 12th-century German historian; author of *Chronica Slavorum.*

**Hel'molt** (hĕl'mōlt), **Hans.** 1865-1929. German historian.

**Hel'mont** (hĕl'mônt), **Jan Baptista van.** 1577?-?1644. Flemish physician and chemist, b. Brussels. Invented the word *gas* (suggested by Latin and Greek *chaos*) to designate aeriform fluids; first to distinguish gases distinct from air; regarded water as prime element; believed digestion and nutrition due to action of ferments which convert food into living flesh; suggested use of alkalies to correct undue acidity of the digestive juices, and conversely. His works were published (1648) as *Ortus Medicinae, vel Opera et Opuscula Omnia* by his son **Franciscus Mercurius** (1614?-1699), naturalist and philosopher, who developed a monistic doctrine before Leibnitz, and concerned himself with the physiology of speech and the instruction of the deaf and dumb.

**Hé'lo'ïse'** (ā'lō'ēz'). See under Peter ABELARD.

**Hel'per** (hĕl'pẽr), **Hinton Row·an'** (rō·ăn'). 1829-1909. American writer, b. in Rowan (now Davie) County, N.C. In California (1850-53). Published (1857) *The Impending Crisis of the South, and How to Meet It*, a book attacking slaveholders and threatening a slave uprising; 100,000 copies were circulated in North during campaign of 1860; aroused intense antislavery feeling and contributed toward bringing on Civil War. U.S. consul, Buenos Aires, Argentina (1861-66). Other works, *The Land of Gold* (1855), *Nojoque* (1867), *Negroes in Negroland* (1868), *Oddments of Andean Diplomacy* (1879).

**Helps** (hĕlps), Sir **Arthur.** 1813-1875. English historian. Among his works are *Conquerors of the New World* (1848), *Spanish Conquest in America* (1855-61).

**Helst** (hĕlst), **Bartholomeus van der.** 1613-1670. Dutch portrait painter. Among his notable canvases are *Kompagnie des Hauptmanns Bicker, Friedensmahl der Schützen, Guitarist* (Metropolitan Museum of Art, New York), and portraits of Paul Potter, and himself.

**Hel'tai** (hĕl'toi), **Kaspar.** 1520?-?1575. Hungarian humanist, printer, and reformer; published in Hungarian translation of Bible (1551-62) and also *Chronicle of Hungary* (1572).

**Hel'vé'tius'** (ĕl'vā'syüs'), **Claude Adrien.** 1715-1771. French philosopher; appointed farmer general (1738); m. Anne Catherine de Ligniville d'Autricourt (1751) and shortly afterward retired to his country estate to devote himself to study. Author of *De l'Esprit* (1758), condemned by Sorbonne and publicly burned (1759). In it he expounds doctrine of sensationalism, or sensualism.

**Hel·vid'i·us** (hĕl·vĭd'ĭ·ŭs). Roman heretic who maintained (380 A.D.) that Mary bore children after Jesus.

**Hé'lyot'** (ā'lyō'), **Pierre.** *Known as* **Le Père Hip'po'lyte'** (lẽ pâr' ē'pô'lēt'). 1660-1716. French Franciscan monk and historian; best known for his *Histoire des Ordres Monastiques, Religieux et Militaires...* (1714 ff.; finished by P. Maximilien Bullot).

**Hem'ans** (hĕm'ănz), **Felicia Dorothea,** *nee* **Browne.** 1793-1835. English poet, b. Liverpool; m. Alfred Hemans (1812; separated 1818). Best known for lyrics, including *Casabianca, The Better Land, The Treasures of the Deep, The Lost Pleiad, The Homes of England, The Forest Sanctuary, The Vespers of Palermo.*

**He·mi'na** (hē·mī'nȧ), **Lucius Cassius.** Roman chronicler of 2d century B.C.; first annalist who wrote in Latin; author of a history of Rome to end of Third Punic War, only fragments of which are extant.

**Hem'ing** (hĕm'ĭng), **Arthur Henry Howard.** 1870-1940. Canadian artist, b. in Paris, France; best known for paintings of Canada's north country and woodlands.

**Hem'ing** *or* **Hem'minge** (hĕm'ĭng), **John.** 1556?-1630. English actor and editor. Closely associated with Shakespeare, and mentioned by Shakespeare in his will; known to have acted in Shakespeare's *Henry IV, Part I* and several of Ben Jonson's plays; a chief proprietor of Globe Theatre. Chiefly known as editor, with Henry Condell, of the first folio of Shakespeare (1623).

**Hem'ing·way** (hĕm'ĭng·wā), **Ernest.** 1899-1961. American journalist, novelist, and short-story writer, b. Oak Park, Ill. Entered World War as volunteer in American ambulance unit serving with French army, and later with the Italian Arditi. After World War I, served as European correspondent for Toronto *Star*, and later as Paris correspondent for Hearst's Syndicated News Service. Awarded Nobel prize in literature (1954). Author of *Three Stories and Ten Poems* (1923), *In Our Time* (1924), *The Torrents of Spring* (1926), *The Sun Also Rises* (1926), *Men Without Women* (1927), *A Farewell to Arms* (1929), *Death in the Afternoon* (1932), *Winner Take Nothing* (1933), *Green Hills of Africa* (1935), *To Have and Have Not* (1937), *The Fifth Column* (1938), *For Whom the Bell Tolls* (1940), *The Old Man and the Sea* (1952), etc. See Martha GELLHORN.

**Hemminge, John.** See John HEMING.

**Hé'mon'** (ā'môɴ'), **Louis.** 1880-1913. French novelist; resident in Canada (from c. 1910). His best-known work is *Maria Chapdelaine*, a story of Canadian pioneer life;

also of *La Belle que Voilà* (1923), *Journal* (Eng. trans. 1924), *Monsieur Ripois and Nemesis* (Eng., 1925), etc.

**Hem′pel** (hĕm′pĕl), **Charles Julius.** 1811–1879. Homeopathic physician, b. Germany; to U.S. (1835); translator of German and French works on homeopathy.

**Hempel, Frieda.** 1885–1955. German concert and operatic coloratura soprano; joined Metropolitan Opera Co., New York (1912); m. William B. Kahn (1918; divorced 1926). Among her chief roles are Gilda in *Rigoletto*, Susanna in *Figaro*, Eva in *Meistersinger*, Mimi in *La Bohème*, and Margaret in *Faust*.

**Hem′pl** (hĕm′p'l), *orig.* **Hem′pel, George.** 1859–1921. American philologist, b. Whitewater, Wis.; educ. Michigan and Jena; professor, English philology, U. of Michigan (1897–1906); professor, Germanic philology, Stanford U. (1906–21); known esp. for work on English etymology and phonetics and on runes and runic inscriptions; advocate of English spelling reform.

**Hem′ster·huis** (hĕm′stẽr·hois), **Tiberius.** 1685–1766. Dutch philologist; published editions of Pollux's *Onomasticon*, Lucian's *Dialogues*, and Aristophanes's *Plutus*. His son **Frans** (1721–1790) was a philosopher and writer on art.

**Hé′nault′** (ā′nō′), **Charles Jean François.** 1685–1770. French jurist and writer; counselor to the parliament of Paris (1705); president of the Chamber (1710–31); author of a few plays, and *Abrégé Chronologique de l'Histoire de France* (1744).

**Hench** (hĕnch), **Philip Showalter.** 1896–1965. Amer. physician, b. Pittsburgh, Pa. With Mayo Clinic (1923–57). Awarded Nobel prize in physiology and medicine (1950) with E. C. Kendall and T. Reichstein for research on hormones, esp. cortisone.

**Henck′ell** (hĕng′kĕl), **Karl.** 1864–1929. German writer; works include *Strophen* (1887), *Amselrufe* (1888), *Trussnachtigall* (1891), *Mein Liederbuch* (1903), and *Mein Lied* (1906).

**Hen′der·son** (hĕn′dẽr·s'n), **Alexander.** 1583?–1646. Scottish Presbyterian clergyman and diplomat. Prepared and read in Edinburgh the National Covenant (1638); drafted Solemn League and Covenant adopted by Westminster Assembly (1643). Rector, Edinburgh U. (1640–46); introduced teaching of Hebrew there. Moderator of Glasgow Assembly (1638), St. Andrews Assembly (1641). Author of *Bishop's Doom* (1638).

**Henderson, Alice,** *nee* **Cor′bin** (kôr′bĭn). 1881–1949. American poet and editor, b. St. Louis, Mo.; m. William Penhallow Henderson (1905). Assoc. editor of *Poetry* (1912–16). Author of *The Spinning Woman of the Sky* (1912), *Red Earth* (1920), *The Sun Turns West* (1933); also, a prose work, *Brothers of Light, the Penitentes of the Southwest* (1937). Compiler (with Harriet Monroe, 1917) of *The New Poetry, an Anthology*.

**Henderson, Archibald.** 1877–1963. American educator; professor of pure mathematics (from 1908) and head of mathematics department (from 1920), U. of North Carolina. Author of works on mathematics and of *George Bernard Shaw, His Life and Works* (1911), *European Dramatists* (1913), *The Conquest of the Old Southwest* (1920), *Table Talk of G.B.S.* (1925), *Is Bernard Shaw a Dramatist?* (1929), *Bernard Shaw—Playboy and Prophet* (1932), etc.

**Henderson, Arthur.** 1863–1935. British Labor party leader and statesman, b. Glasgow. Iron molder in Newcastle, Eng. Elected Labor member in Parliament (1903 ff.); at outbreak of World War, was instrumental in influencing most of Labor party to support government's war policy. In Asquith's cabinet (1915), was president of board of trade; in Lloyd George's cabinet (1916), minister without portfolio; in first Labor ministry, under MacDonald (1924), became home secretary; in second Labor ministry (1929), served as secretary for foreign affairs (1929–31). Vigorous advocate of international peace; chairman of International Disarmament Conference summoned by League of Nations (1932); awarded Nobel peace prize (1934).

**Henderson, David Bremner.** 1840–1906. American political leader, b. Old Deer, Scotland; to U.S. as a child. Served in Union army in Civil War. Practiced law, Dubuque, Iowa (from 1866). Member, U.S. House of Representatives (1883–1903) and speaker (1899–1903).

**Henderson, George Francis Robert.** 1854–1903. British army officer. Accompanied Lord Roberts to South Africa (1899); director of intelligence (1900). Author of *The Campaign of Fredericksburg* (1886), *Stonewall Jackson and the American Civil War* (2 vols., 1898).

**Henderson, James Pinckney.** 1808–1858. American political leader, b. in Lincoln County, N.C.; to Texas (1836); brigadier general in Texan army (1836); attorney general of Republic of Texas (1836). First governor of Texas (1846). U.S. senator (1858).

**Henderson, John.** 1747–1785. English actor; appeared as Hamlet in Bath (1772) and gained nickname of the "Bath Roscius." On London stage at Drury Lane and Covent Garden, his roles including Shylock, Hamlet, Falstaff, Sir Giles Overreach. Regarded by his contemporaries as second only to Garrick.

**Henderson, John Brooks.** 1826–1913. American political leader, b. Danville, Va. Adm. to bar (1844); practiced, Louisiana, Mo. Opposed secession of Missouri; instrumental in keeping state in Union (1861). U.S. senator (1862–69); supported Lincoln's policies; introduced Thirteenth Amendment to the Constitution (1864); opposed Johnson but voted "not guilty" at his impeachment trial.

**Henderson, Lawrence Joseph.** 1878–1942. American biological chemist; professor, Harvard (from 1919). Author of *The Fitness of the Environment* (1913), *The Order of Nature* (1917), *Blood* (1928), and *Pareto's Sociology: A Physiologist's Interpretation* (1935).

**Henderson, Leon.** 1895– . American economist, b. Millville, N.J.; educ. Swarthmore. Director of consumer credit research, Russell Sage Foundation (1925–34); member, National Industrial Recovery Board (1934–35); executive secretary, Temporary National Economic Committee (1938–39); member, Securities and Exchange Commission (1939–41); administrator, Office of Price Administration, and director of division of civilian supply, Office of Production Management (1941–43).

**Henderson,** Sir **Nevile Meyrick.** 1882–1942. British ambassador to Germany (1937–39); author of *Failure of a Mission* (1940).

**Henderson, Peter.** 1822–1890. Gardener and nurseryman in N.J., b. Scotland; to U.S. (1843); established (1871) seed and garden supply house.

**Henderson, Richard.** 1735–1785. American colonizer, b. in Hanover County, Va.; organized Transylvania Company to settle colony in Kentucky (1774); started colonization by sending out Daniel Boone to found Boonesborough (1775) on land bought from Indians; outbreak of Revolution caused collapse of enterprise.

**Henderson, Robert.** See Robert HENRYSON.

**Henderson, Thomas.** 1798–1844. Scottish astronomer; astronomer royal at Cape of Good Hope, where he observed transit of Mercury (1832) and Encke's and Biela's comets. First astronomer royal and professor, Edinburgh (1834–44).

**Henderson, William James.** 1855–1937. American music critic and author; on staff of New York *Times*

(1883–1902); music critic of New York *Sun* (1902–37). Associate editor, *The Standard Dictionary* (1892–94). Author of *The Story of Music* (1889), *Richard Wagner . . .* (1901), *Early History of Singing* (1921), etc.

**Henderson, Yandell.** 1873–1944. American physiologist; professor (from 1911), Yale; consulting physiologist, U.S. Bureau of Mines (1913–25). Known for work on circulation, respiration, pharmacology of gases, etc.

**Hen'drich** (hĕn'drĭĸ), **Hermann.** 1854– . German painter of scenes and figures from German legend.

**Hen'drick** (hĕn'drĭk), **Burton Jesse.** 1870–1949. American writer; in magazine and newspaper editorial work (1896–1927). Coauthor, with Admiral William S. Sims, of *The Victory at Sea* (awarded Pulitzer prize for history, 1920); author of *Life and Letters of Walter H. Page* (Pulitzer prize for biography, 1922), *The Training of an American* (Pulitzer prize for biography, 1928), *The Lees of Virginia* (1937), *Bulwark of the Republic, a Biography of the Constitution* (1937), *Statesmen of the Lost Cause* (1939).

**Hen'dricks** (hĕn'drĭks), **Thomas Andrews.** 1819–1885. American political leader; adm. to bar (1843); practiced, Shelbyville, Ind. Member, U.S. House of Representatives (1851–55). U.S. senator (1863–69). Governor of Indiana (1872). Vice-president of the U.S. (1885).

**He'ney** (hē'nĭ), **Francis Joseph.** 1859–1937. American lawyer; employed by U.S. attorney general to prosecute land-fraud cases at Portland, Ore. (1903); secured indictment of U.S. attorney John H. Hall, and others. Appointed deputy district attorney at San Francisco, secured conviction of Mayor Eugene Schmitz and political boss Abe Ruef (1906–09).

**Hen'gist** (*or* **Hen'gest**) and **Hor'sa** (hĕng'gĭst, -gĕst, hôr'sȧ). The brothers who led the band of Jutes who (c. 449 A.D.) invaded southern Britain.

**Heng'sten·berg** (hĕng'stĕn·bĕrĸ), **Ernst Wilhelm.** 1802–1869. German Protestant theologian; champion of Lutheran orthodoxy; opponent of modern Bible criticism, rationalism, and Schleiermacher.

**Henham, Ernest George.** See John TREVENA.

**Hen'ke** (hĕng'kĕ), **Heinrich Philipp Konrad.** 1752–1809. German Protestant theologian.

**Hen'le** (hĕn'lĕ), **Friedrich Gustav Jacob.** 1809–1885. German pathologist and anatomist. Investigated the anatomical structure of the hair, blood and lacteal vessels, kidney, nails, central nervous system, etc. Author of *Handbuch der Rationellen Pathologie* (2 vols., 1846–52), in which physiology and pathology were treated for the first time as branches of one science.

**Hen'lein** (hĕn'līn), **Konrad.** 1898–1945. Sudeten-German politician. Fought in Austrian army in World War (1914–18). Head of Sudetendeutsche Partei, which gained ascendancy in Czechoslovak election (May, 1935). Reichskommissar for Sudeten areas after German occupation (Oct., 1938); Gauleiter of Sudetenland (1938–39); civil commissioner for Bohemia (1939 ff.); suicide.

**Hen'ley** (hĕn'lĭ), **John.** 1692–1756. English clergyman; known as "Orator Henley"; claimed to have restored church oratory in England; widely known for his eccentricities; caricatured by Hogarth, and ridiculed by Pope in his *Dunciad.*

**Henley, Robert.** 1st Earl of **Nor'thing·ton** (nôr'thĭng·tŭn). 1708?–1772. English jurist and statesman; lord chancellor (1761); procured dismissal of Rockingham, and became president of the council (1766–67) under Grafton.

**Henley, William Ernest.** 1849–1903. English man of letters, b. in Gloucester. Cripple from childhood; to London (1877–78). Editor of weekly journal *London*, of *Magazine of Art* (1882–86), of *Scots Observer* (1889; renamed *National Observer*, 1891), *New Review* (1894–98). Author of volumes of verse, as *Book of Verses* (1888), *For England's Sake* (1900), *Hawthorn and Lavender* (1901); his best-known poem, *Invictus.* Collaborated with Robert Louis Stevenson in four plays, *Deacon Brodie, Beau Austin, Admiral Guinea, Macaire.* Collaborated with John S. Farmer in compiling *A Dictionary of Slang and its Analogues.*

**Hen'ne am Rhyn** (hĕn'ĕ äm rēn'), **Otto.** 1828–1914. Swiss historian; archivist at St. Gallen (1855–1912).

**Hen'ne·bique'** (ĕn'bēk'), **François.** 1842–1921. French structural engineer; devised a kind of reinforced concrete.

**Hen'ne·pin** (hĕn'ĕ·pĭn; *Fr.* ĕn'păɴ'), **Louis,** *baptized* **Jo·han'nes** (jō̆·hăn'ēz; *Fr.* zhô'ȧ'nĕs'). 1626–?1701. Roman Catholic friar and explorer in America, b. Ath, Hainaut. To Canada (1675); accompanied La Salle through Great Lakes (1679); with exploring party in upper Mississippi region (1680). Returned to France (1682); published *Description de la Louisiane* (1683), *Nouveau Voyage* (1696), *Nouvelle Découverte d'un Très Grand Pays Situé dans L'Amérique* (1697).

**Hen'ne·quin'** (ĕn'kăɴ'), **Philippe Augustin.** 1763–1833. French historical painter. His grandson **Alfred Néocles Hennequin** (1842–1887) was a playwright; author of a number of comedies.

**Hen'ner'** (ĕ'nâr'), **Jean Jacques.** 1829–1905. French genre painter.

**Hen'ning** (hĕn'ĭng), **Hans.** 1885– . German philosopher and psychologist; known esp. for work on the classification of odors.

**Hen'ri'** (äɴ'rē'). French form of HENRY.

**Hen'ri** (hĕn'rī), **Robert.** *Orig. name* **Robert Henry Co'zad** (ko'zad). 1865–1929. American painter, b. Cincinnati. Studio, Philadelphia (1891), New York (1899). Examples of his work: *The Equestrian,* in Carnegie Art Institute, Pittsburgh; *Laughing Girl,* in Brooklyn Institute Museum; *Spanish Gypsy,* in Metropolitan Museum of Art, New York; *Snow,* in Luxembourg Gallery, Paris. Writings collected in *The Art Spirit* (1923).

**Hen·ri'ci** (hĕn·rē'tsē), **Christian Friedrich.** 1700–1764. German poet, satirist, and playwright.

**Henricus de Gandavo.** See HENRY OF GHENT.

**Hen'ri·et'ta Anne** (hĕn'rĭ·ĕt'ȧ ăn'). Duchesse **d'Or'lé'ans'** (dôr'lā'äɴ'). 1644–1670. Fifth daughter of Charles I of England and his queen, Henrietta Maria; taken to France (1646); brought up a Roman Catholic; returned to England at Restoration (1660). Popular in her brother Charles II's court; m. Philippe, Duc d'Orléans and brother of Louis XIV (1661); became a favorite of Louis XIV and an intermediary between him and Charles II; died suddenly, possibly poisoned by agents of her husband.

**Henrietta Ma·ri'a** (mȧ·rī'ȧ). 1609–1669. Queen consort (1625–1649) of Charles I of England. Daughter of Henry IV of France and sister of Louis XIII. Attempted to influence king to aid Roman Catholics as he had promised; to the Continent to raise money and troops to aid Royalist cause (1642); led force to Oxford to join Charles (1643); forced to take refuge in France (1644); continued to plot for aid to Charles until she learned of his execution (1649). Permitted to live in England on Parliamentary grant after Restoration (1660 ff.); died in France.

**Hen'riot'** (äɴ'ryō'), **Émile.** *Pseudonym of* **Émile Mai'grot'** (mā'grō'). 1889–1961. French poet and novelist, b. Paris; on staff of *Le Temps.* Author of *Eurydice* (1907), *Valentin* (1919), *Aventures de Sylvain Dufour* (1922), *Aricie Brun* (1924; awarded Grand Prix by French Acad.), *Tout va Finir,* etc.

**Hen·ri'que** (äN·rē'kĕ). Portuguese form of Henry.

**Henriques, Robert David Quixano.** 1905–1967. English novelist; author of *Death by Moonlight* (1938), *No Arms No Armour* (1939; awarded prize in international competition), *The Voice of the Trumpet* (1942), etc.

**Hen'ri'-Ro'bert'** (äN'rē'rô'bâr'). 1863-1936. French criminal lawyer.

**Hen'ry** (hĕn'rĭ). Name of eight kings of England.

**Henry I.** *Called* **Henry Beau'clerc** (bō'klâr), *i.e.* scholar. 1068–1135. King of England (1100–35). Fourth son of William the Conqueror and Matilda. Took advantage of older brother Robert's absence from England at time of William II's death (1100) to have himself elected king by the witan; consolidated position by issuing charter (basis of later Magna Charta), by recalling Anselm, and by marrying English princess Matilda, or Maud. Conquered Normandy (1106) and captured and imprisoned Robert; defended Normandy in wars with Louis VI of France. Succeeded as king by Stephen (*q.v.*).

**Henry II.** *Sometimes known as* **Curt'man'tle** (kûrt'măn't'l) *from short Anjou mantle he wore.* 1133–1189. King (1154–89), first king of house of Anjou (*q.v.*) or Plantagenet. Son of Geoffrey Plantagenet, Count of Anjou, and Matilda, daughter of Henry I of England. Claimed English throne through his mother, who had been deprived of the succession by Stephen of Blois; adopted as successor by Stephen (1153) and acceded on Stephen's death (1154); m. (1152) Eleanor of Aquitaine. Obtained from Malcolm of Scotland restoration of northern English counties; conquered the Welsh (1158, 1163, 1165) and southeastern Ireland (1171); carried on struggle with Louis VII for provinces in France (1157–80); instituted internal reforms in judicial and financial systems. Carried on bitter controversy with Thomas à Becket, Archbishop of Canterbury, who refused to be subservient to king; after murder of Becket by four of Henry's knights (Dec. 29, 1170), did penance at archbishop's shrine (July, 1174). Died while preparing to suppress rebellion headed by his sons Richard and John aided by Philip of France. Succeeded by his son Richard I.

**Henry III.** 1207–1272. King (1216–72), of house of Anjou or Plantagenet. Son of John of England and his queen, Isabella of Angoulême. During minority, under regency of William Marshal, Earl of Pembroke (1216–19), and (1219–32) of the justiciary Hubert de Burgh, with the support of Stephen Langton, Archbishop of Canterbury; m. Eleanor of Provence (1236). Showed great favor toward foreigners, thus provoking rebellion of barons, who compelled him to accept (1258) Provisions of Oxford, a series of reforms to be carried out by a commission of barons; repudiated this agreement, causing rebellion (Barons' War) under Simon de Montfort, who defeated and took him prisoner at Lewes (May 14, 1264); rescued by his son Edward, who defeated Montfort at Evesham (Aug. 4, 1265); took little part in government thereafter. Succeeded by his son Edward I.

**Henry IV.** *Surnamed* **Bol'ing·broke** (bŏl'ĭng·brŏŏk; bō'lĭng-; *formerly* bŏŏl'ĭng-). *Often called by contemporaries* **Henry of Lan'cas·ter** (lăng'kȧs·tẽr). 1367–1413. King (1399–1413), of house of Lancaster. Son of John of Gaunt (4th son of Edward III) and Blanche (daughter of Henry, Duke of Lancaster). Distinguished himself in knightly prowess, military adventure, and travels in Prussia, Lithuania, Venice, Cyprus, and Jerusalem. Created duke of Hereford (1397). Banished from England by his cousin Richard II (1398), who confiscated estates of Lancaster on John of Gaunt's death (1399). Raised army, invaded England, and defeated and captured Richard, who forthwith abdicated. Formally acclaimed king by Parliament (1399); suppressed rebellions of Richard's sympathizers (1400), of Welsh under Owen Glendower (1399 ff.), of powerful Percy family led by Henry Percy (Hotspur) in battle of Shrewsbury (July 21, 1403), and of earl marshal Mowbray supported by Archbishop Scrope of York (1405). During his reign, persecution of Lollards was carried on. Succeeded by his son Henry V.

**Henry V.** 1387–1422. King (1413–22), of house of Lancaster. Son of Henry IV. Distinguished himself as prince of Wales in battle of Shrewsbury (1403) and as king in commanding English army which invaded France and won battle of Agincourt (Oct. 25, 1415); m. (June 2, 1420) Catherine of Valois, daughter of Charles VI of France; recognized by French as regent and heir to French throne; died (Aug. 31, 1422) while planning to secure his position against further French opposition. Succeeded by his son Henry VI.

**Henry VI.** 1421–1471. King (1422–61 and 1470–71), of house of Lancaster. Son of Henry V and Catherine of Valois. Succeeded to throne in infancy, under protectorship of his uncles John, Duke of Bedford, and Humphrey, Duke of Gloucester. Married Margaret of Anjou (1445). Crowned king of France (Dec. 16, 1431), but military successes of Joan of Arc and Charles VII expelled English forces from all of France except Calais (by 1453). Latter part of reign marked by periods of mental derangement (1454 ff.) and by economic unrest culminating in Cade's Rebellion (1450) and by struggle for power between houses of Lancaster and York leading to Wars of the Roses (1455–85); after defeat at 2d battle of St. Albans (Feb., 1461), Yorkists successful; Henry deposed (Mar. 4, 1461) and duke of York proclaimed king as Edward IV (*q.v.*); Henry imprisoned (1465–70), rescued and restored as king during uprising headed by earl of Warwick (1470), but soon recaptured and imprisoned in Tower of London, where he is said to have been murdered (May 21, 1471).

**Henry VII.** *Often referred to as* **Henry Tu'dor** (tū'dẽr) *and (until accession)* **Henry,** Earl of **Rich'mond** (rĭch'mŭnd). 1457–1509. King (1485–1509), first king of house of Tudor. Son of Edmund Tudor, Earl of Richmond, and Margaret Beaufort, direct descendant of John of Gaunt, 4th son of Edward III. During supremacy of house of York (1471–85), lived as an exile, chiefly in Brittany. Encouraged by unrest under Richard III, invaded England; defeated and killed Richard III at Bosworth Field (Aug. 22, 1485); immediately acknowledged as king. Married (Jan. 18, 1486) Elizabeth, eldest daughter of Edward IV of England, thus uniting houses of Lancaster and York. Defeated impostors Lambert Simnel (who pretended to be earl of Warwick) and Perkin Warbeck (who pretended to be duke of York); suppressed Cornish insurrection (1497). Instituted Star Chamber, by means of which he was able to restrict power of nobles; greatly increased royal power during reign; accumulated vast fortune. Succeeded by his son Henry VIII.

**Henry VIII.** 1491–1547. King (1509–47), of house of Tudor; sometimes called "Bluff King Hal." Son of Henry VII and Elizabeth of York; m. (June 11, 1509) Catherine of Aragon (*q.v.*), widow of his brother Arthur. Engaged in war on Continent, joining Holy League against France (1511); personally commanded English troops in victory of battle of the Spurs (Aug. 16, 1513); in England, his troops defeated and killed James IV of Scotland at Flodden (Sept. 9, 1513). Held interview with Francis I of France at Field of Cloth of Gold (1520). Appointed Cardinal Wolsey lord chancellor (1515); for his treatise *Assertio Septem Sacramentorum*, received from Pope Leo X (1521) title **Fi'de·i De·fen'sor** (fī'dē·ī dē·fĕn'sēr; -sôr), *i.e.* "Defender of the Faith." Involved in conflict with papal power, originating in his wish to divorce Catherine (mother of Queen Mary); dismissed Wolsey for failure to procure from pope a decree of divorce, appointing Sir Thomas More chancellor in his stead (1529); on advice of Cranmer, secured opinions declaring marriage with Catherine invalid (because she was his deceased brother's wife); thereupon secretly married Anne Boleyn (Jan. 25, 1533), by whom he became the father of Elizabeth I. Because of continued conflict with papal power, obtained from Parliament the Act of Supremacy, creating a national church separate from Roman Catholic Church and appointing the king protector and sole supreme head of church and clergy of England; executed Sir Thomas More (1535) for refusal to acknowledge royal supremacy; suppressed monasteries in England and confiscated their properties. Beheaded Anne Boleyn on charge of adultery (May 19, 1536); m. Jane Seymour (May 20, 1536; mother of Edward VI; died Oct. 24, 1537); m. Anne of Cleves (Jan. 6, 1540; divorced, 1540); m. Catherine Howard (1540; beheaded on charge of adultery, 1542); m. Catherine Parr (July 12, 1543; survived him). During reign, unified and centralized administrative power, increased scope of parliamentary powers, and improved English naval defenses. Succeeded by his son Edward VI.

**Henry IX.** Title assumed (1788) by last of Stuart royal line, Cardinal York (*q.v.*).

**Henry,** Prince. Duke of Gloucester. See GLOUCESTER.

**Henry.** *Fr.* **Henri.** Name of four kings of France:

**Henry I.** 1008–1060. King (1031–60), of Capetian (*q.v.*) line; son of Robert II. Spent first years in putting down rebellions (1031–39); aided Duke William of Normandy in subduing nobles (1035–47); later (1054, 1058) involved in war with William and defeated.

**Henry II.** 1519–1559. King (1547–59), of house of Valois (*q.v.*); second son of Francis I; b. Saint-Germain-en-Laye. With his brother the dauphin Francis, hostage in Spain (1526–30); m. Catherine de Médicis (1533); became heir apparent at death of dauphin (1536). Largely under influence of his mistress, Diane de Poitiers, and of Anne de Montmorency, Constable of France; seized three bishoprics (Toul, Metz, Verdun) from emperor (1552); in wars with England, took Boulogne (1550) and recovered Calais (1558); unsuccessful in later wars (1556–59); beaten in Italy and defeated by Spaniards in Low Countries; Peace of Cateau-Cambrésis (1559). Died of wound received in a tournament. Of his seven children three became kings of France.

**Henry III.** 1551–1589. King (1574–89). Third son of Henry II and Catherine de Médicis; b. Fontainebleau. As duke of **An'jou'** (äɴ'zhōō'; *Angl.* ăn'jōō), credited with winning battles of Jarnac and Moncontour over Condé and Coligny (1569); aided mother in plotting Massacre of St. Bartholomew (1572). Elected king of Poland (1573). On death of Charles IX (1574) became king of France; his reign marked by continuous civil conflicts between Catholics (Holy League) and Huguenots (1574–89). After death (1584) of his brother, duc d'Alençon (*q.v.*), forced to take sides with Huguenots. Fled Paris on Day of Barricades (1588); had Henry, Duke of Guise, and his brother the cardinal (Louis II of Lorraine) murdered (1588). After Catherine's death (1589), murdered by a monk, Jacques Clément; with his death Valois male line extinct.

**Henry IV.** *Often called* **Henry of Na·varre'** (nȧ·vär'). *Fr.* **Hen'ri' de Na'varre'** (äɴ'rē' dẽ nȧ'vȧr'). *Sometimes called also* **Henry the Great.** 1553–1610. Son of Anthony of Bourbon and Jeanne d'Albret (*q.v.*), b. Pau, Béarn. King of Navarre, as Henry III (1572–89); king of France (1589–1610), first of Bourbon line. In early years known as prince of Viana; brought up as a Calvinist. Joined Huguenots in religious war (1568–70); after death of Condé at Jarnac (1569) proclaimed leader, though Coligny in actual command (1569–70). Married Margaret of Valois, sister of Charles IX (1572); virtual prisoner at court (1572–76); became heir presumptive on death of François, Duc d'Alençon (1584); concluded War of Three Henrys (1585–87) by victory at Coutras. Became king at death of Henry III (1589); won battles of Arques (1589) and Ivry (1590); formally renounced Protestantism (1593) for Catholic faith; entered Paris (1594) and terminated war with Holy League (1596); signed Edict of Nantes (1598); concluded peace of Vervins with Philip II of Spain (1598); m. (1600), as second wife, Marie de Médicis (*q.v.*). His final years (1600–10) a period of recovery from wars and of prosperity for France: finances reorganized, industry encouraged, and territory increased; about to declare war on Austria (1610) but assassinated by a religious fanatic, Ravaillac (May 14, 1610).

**Henry.** *Fr.* **Henri.** Name of three kings of Navarre:

**Henry I.** *Called* **the Fat.** *Fr.* **le Gros'** (lẽ grō'). 1210?–1274. Count of **Cham'pagne'** (shäɴ'pȧn'y'; *Angl.* shăm·pān') and king of Navarre (1270–74); son of Thibaut; last of male line; succeeded by only legitimate child, Jeanne, whose marriage with Philip IV (1284) united Navarre with France.

**Henry II.** 1503–1555. Eldest son of Jean d'Albret and Catherine de Foix; on mother's death (1517) claimed Navarre, but claim disputed by Ferdinand II of Spain; titular king only (1517–55) of French Navarre; m. (1527) Marguerite d'Angoulême (see MARGARET OF NAVARRE); held court at Nérac.

**Henry III.** Son of Jeanne d'Albret, dau. of Henry II and Marguerite; king of Navarre (1572–89); became Henry IV of France (*q.v.*).

**Henry.** *Ger.* **Heinrich.** Name of kings of Germany:

**Henry I.** *Called* **Henry the Fowler.** 876?–936. Duke of Saxony (912–936); son of Otto, duke of Saxony; first of the Saxon line of kings of Germany (919–936), and reckoned as one of the emperors of the Holy Roman Empire though never crowned; fortified and strengthened the cities; reorganized the army; defeated the Wends (929), Hungarians (933), and Danes (934).

**Henry II–VII.** = HENRY II–VII, Holy Roman emperors.

**Henry.** *Ger.* **Heinrich.** Name of ten dukes of Bavaria (see also WITTELSBACH), including:

**Henry I.** d. 955. Son of German king Henry the Fowler and brother of Otto the Great; granted duchy by brother (948–955; reign disturbed).

**Henry II.** 951–995. *Called* **Henry the Wrangler** *or* **the Quarrelsome.** *Ger.* **Hein'rich der Zän'ker** (hīn'rĭk dẽr tsĕng'kẽr). Duke (955–976; 985–995); son of Duke Henry I; took part in revolt against his cousin Emperor Otto II; deposed (976), recovering duchy after death of Otto (983); father of Holy Roman Emperor Henry II (*q.v.*).

**Henry IX.** *Called* **Henry the Black.** *Ger.* **Heinrich der Schwar'ze** (dẽr shvär'tsĕ). d. 1126. Son of Welf IV (see WELF family); duke (1120–26); m. daughter of Duke Magnus of Saxony, thus uniting domains; father-in-law of Frederick, Duke of Swabia, who was brother of Conrad III, founder of Hohenstaufen line (*q.v.*) and father of Emperor Frederick I.

**Henry X.** *Called* **Henry the Proud.** *Ger.* **Heinrich**

**der Stol′ze** (dĕr shtôl′tsĕ). 1108?–1139. Duke of Bavaria (1126–38) and Saxony (1137–39); son of Henry IX; m. (1127) Gertrude, daughter of Emperor Lothair II; fought with Lothair against Hohenstaufens; opposed Conrad III as Lothair's successor; his duchies afflicted with civil wars (1138–39); lost Bavaria to Leopold IV, Margrave of Austria (1138); father of Henry the Lion (*q.v.*), Duke of Saxony.

**Henry II.** *Ger.* **Heinrich II.** Duke of **Bruns′wick-Wol′fen·büt′tel** [brŭnz′wĭk·vôl′fĕn·büt′ĕl] (1514–68). 1489–1568. Son of Duke Henry I. Kept in prison for eleven years (1514–25) before his title recognized; aided Charles V in Italy (1528); opposed Reformation; attacked by Luther; driven out of Brunswick by leaders of League of Schmalkalden (1542); after civil war, returned to Brunswick (1547); defeated Albert Alcibiades (1553); in later years, made peace with Protestant subjects.

**Henry (I).** *Called* **Henry the Child.** 1244–1308. Landgrave of Hesse (1263–1308). Grandson of St. Elizabeth of Hungary and son of Sophia. Following death of Henry Raspe (1247) and dispute over landgraviate of Thuringia, granted Hesse (*q.v.*) and became its first male ruler.

**Henry.** *Ger.* **Heinrich.** Duke of **Meck′len·burg-Schwe·rin′** (mĕk′lĕn·bŏŏrk·shvā·rēn′; mā′klĕn-). 1876–1934. Married (1901) Queen Wilhelmina (*q.v.*) of Netherlands; became naturalized Dutch subject and granted title Prince of the Netherlands.

**Henry.** *Called* **Henry the Illustrious.** *Ger.* **Heinrich der Er·lauch′te** (dĕr ĕr·louk′tĕ). 1215 or 1216–1288. Margrave of Meissen (1221–88). Supported Emperor Frederick II against pope; on death (1247) of uncle Henry Raspe, received Thuringia; division of lands among sons brought about family feuds.

**Henry.** *Ger.* **Heinrich.** Name of princes of Prussia.
(1) **Heinrich Friedrich Ludwig.** 1726–1802. Son of Frederick William I and brother of Frederick the Great. Prussian general; served with distinction in Seven Years' War (1756–63), esp. at Prague (1757) and Freiberg (1762); served as diplomat at St. Petersburg (1770), at Paris (1784), and in negotiating Treaty of Basel (1795).
(2) **Heinrich Albert Wilhelm.** 1862–1929. Son of Frederick III of Germany and brother of William II; b. Potsdam. Entered navy (1878); rear admiral (1895), admiral (1901), grand admiral (1909); on East Asiatic station (1898–99); visited United States (1882–84, 1902); general inspector of marine (1909); in command of fleet in Baltic during World War (1914–18).

**Henry.** *Ger.* **Heinrich.** Name of all rulers of both branches of house of Reuss (*q.v.*).

**Henry.** *Ger.* **Heinrich.** Dukes of Saxony.
**Henry the Lion.** *Ger.* **Heinrich der Lö′we** (dĕr lû′vĕ). 1129–1195. Duke of Saxony (1139–80) and Bavaria (1156–80). Son of Henry the Proud, b. Ravensburg. Supported Emperor Frederick I in Poland and Italy (1157–59); m., as 2d wife (1168), Matilda, daughter of Henry II of England; made pilgrimage to Jerusalem (1172–73). Quarrel with the emperor (1175–76) led to imperial ban and loss of possessions (1180); see HANOVER, electoral house; exiled twice (1182, 1189); spent most of time in England; in conflict with Emperor Henry VI, settled by Peace of Fulda (1190). Received his nickname for personal bravery. Colonized all northern Germany; his twenty-year rule beneficial.
**Henry the Pious.** 1473–1541. Duke of Saxony (1539–41); introduced Reformation into Friesland (1536).

**Henry.** *Ger.* **Heinrich.** Name of seven Holy Roman emperors:
**Henry I.** *Called* **the Fowler.** See HENRY I, King of Germany.
**Henry II.** *Called* **the Saint.** 973–1024. Duke of Bavaria (995–1024); king of Germany and Holy Roman emperor (1002–24; crowned 1014); last of the Saxon emperors. Son of Henry II, Duke of Bavaria, and great-grandson of Henry I. Made two expeditions to Italy (1004, 1013); deposed Ardoin, who had revolted; engaged in long struggle with Boleslav I of Poland (1003–18). Energetic in church reform; founded monasteries and schools.
**Henry III.** *Called* **the Black.** 1017–1056. Holy Roman emperor (1039–56; crowned 1046). Son of Conrad II. Subdued Bohemians (1041) and Hungarians (1043–45); made expedition to Rome and deposed three rival popes, appointing Clement II (1046–47); later years marked by revolts in Germany. Patron of learning; founded schools and completed cathedrals.
**Henry IV.** 1050–1106. King of Germany and Holy Roman emperor (1056–1106). Son of Henry III. During minority, Empire under regency of his mother, Agnes of Poitou. Engaged in long struggle with Hildebrand (Pope Gregory VII) on question of lay investiture; excommunicated (1076); absolved after humiliating himself at Canossa (1077). Defeated by Rudolf, Duke of Swabia (1078–80). Again excommunicated (1080); deposed Gregory (1084); crowned emperor by antipope Clement III (1084); invaded Italy (1090). Last years marked by rebellion of sons (1093–1105); dethroned and imprisoned by younger son, Henry (1105), but escaped.
**Henry V.** 1081–1125. King of Germany and Holy Roman emperor (1106–25; crowned 1111); last of Franconian dynasty (*q.v.*). Son of Henry IV. Restored peace at home; generally successful in wars against Flanders, Bohemia, Hungary, and Poland; continued controversy with papacy over lay investiture; twice invaded Italy (1110 and 1116); m. Matilda, daughter of Henry I of England (1114); accepted Concordat of Worms (1122).
**Henry VI.** 1165–1197. King of Germany (1190–97) and of Sicily (1194–97); Holy Roman emperor (1190–97; crowned 1191). Son of Frederick I; m. Constance of Sicily (1186). Endeavored to secure control of inheritances in Sicily and southern Italy, but failed in siege of Naples (1191); kept Richard I of England a prisoner (1193–94); subdued the Two Sicilies in two expeditions (1194, 1197); died as he was about to set off on a crusade to the Holy Land.
**Henry VII.** *Known also as* **Henry of Lux′em·burg** (lŭk′sĕm·bûrg; *Ger.* lŏŏk′sĕm·bŏŏrk). 1275?–1313. Count of Luxemburg (as Henry IV); king of Germany and Holy Roman emperor (1308–13; crowned 1312). Elected king on death of Albert I; confirmed charters to Swiss cantons (1300); made expedition into Italy (1310–13); opposed in southern Italy by Robert, king of Naples (1312–13).

**Henry.** Titular king of Sardinia. See ENZIO.

**Henry III.** Count of **Nassau.** See NASSAU, 2; ORANGE.

**Henry.** Prince of the Netherlands. See HENRY, Duke of Mecklenburg-Schwerin.

**Henry.** *Port.* **Henrique.** 1512–1580. King of Portugal (1578–80). Fifth son of Emanuel. Bishop of Évora and grand inquisitor (1539); made cardinal (1545); increased power of Inquisition in Portugal; regent during minority of Sebastian (1562–68); as king weak and helpless; last of house of Aviz (*q.v.*); throne seized by Philip II, Portugal becoming a dependency of Spain (1580–1640).

**Henry.** *Port.* **Henrique.** *Called* **Henry the Navigator** *or, Port.,* Dom **Hen·ri′que o Na′ve·ga·dor′** (dōn ān·rē′kyōō nä′vĕ·gȧ·thōr′). 1394–1460. Prince of Portugal; third son of John I; b. Oporto; patron of voyagers and explorers. At conquest of Ceuta (1415); took up residence (1418) at Sagres, Cape St. Vincent; established observatory and school of navigation; made no voyage himself, but spent life directing voyages of discovery along African coast; collected accounts of journeys to Africa and Asia; improved compass and shipbuilding. His pupils and captains reached Madeiras (1420), doubled Cape Bojador (1434), reached Cape Blanco (1441) and Cape Verde (1445) and the mouth of the Gambia about 15° north of the equator (1446?), these voyages leading later to circumnavigation of Africa and establishment of Portuguese colonial empire.

**Henry.** *Sp.* **Enrique.** Name of four kings of Castile:

**Henry I.** 1207?–1217. King (1214–17).

**Henry II.** 1333–1379. Natural son of Alfonso XI; count of **Tras'ta·ma'ra** (träs'tä·mä'rä); king of Castile and León (1369–79); after accession of Pedro the Cruel, fled to France (1356); attempted to drive out Pedro but defeated at Nájera, or Navarrete (1367) by the English Black Prince; with Du Guesclin overcame Pedro (1369) and killed him; made large grants to nobles and cities and remained ally of French king.

**Henry III.** 1379–1406. Son of John I; king of Castile and León (1390–1406).

**Henry IV.** 1425–1474. Son of John II; king of Castile and León (1454–74); adopted sister Isabella as heiress to throne.

**Hen'ry'** (äɴ'rē'), **Hubert Joseph.** 1846–1898. French army officer; chief of intelligence department, War Office (1896); forged papers to prove Dreyfus's guilt; finally confessed his forgery, and was arrested.

**Hen'ry** (hĕn'rĭ), **Joseph.** 1797–1878. American physicist, b. Albany, N.Y.; conducted experiments in field of electromagnetism; developed improved electromagnet; contemporaneously with Faraday, discovered method of producing induced current (hence, the name *henry* for unit of induction); invented small electromagnetic motor. Professor of natural philosophy, Princeton (1832–48); continued experiments with electricity; discovered principle underlying electromagnetic telegraph; invented low-resistance and high-resistance galvanometers; discovered oscillatory nature of electric discharge; investigated solar radiation and sunspots. Became first secretary and director, Smithsonian Institution, Washington, D.C. (1846); initiated weather report system. Elected to American Hall of Fame (1915).

**Henry, Matthew.** 1662–1714. English minister at Chester (1687–1712); left unfinished *Exposition of the Old and New Testament,* completed by thirteen of his colleagues.

**Henry, O.** Pseudonym of William Sydney PORTER.

**Henry, Patrick.** 1736–1799. American Revolutionary leader, b. in Hanover Co., Va. Storekeeper (1751–60); adm. to bar (1760), practiced in Virginia. In Virginia legislature (1765); introduced radical resolutions opposing Stamp Act, ending his speech with, "Caesar had his Brutus; Charles the First, his Cromwell; and George the Third—may profit by their example"; sprang into leadership of radical group in Virginia (from 1765). With Thomas Jefferson and Richard Henry Lee initiated intercolonial committee of correspondence (1773). Member, Continental Congress (1774–76); in provincial convention (Mar., 1775), pressed resolutions for putting colonies in state of defense with speech containing famous words, "Give me liberty, or give me death." Governor of Virginia (1776–79; 1784–86). Member, Virginia constitutional ratification convention (1788); opposed ratification; instrumental in causing adoption of first ten amendments to U.S. Constitution. Resumed practice of law. Declined offers of appointment as U.S. senator (1794), U.S. secretary of state (1795), chief justice of U.S. Supreme Court (1795). Elected to Virginia legislature (1799). Elected to American Hall of Fame (1915). See William Wirt HENRY.

**Hen'ry'** (äɴ'rē'), **Paul.** 1848–1905. French astronomer; on staff of Paris Observatory (1868); with his brother **Prosper** (1849–1903) continued preparation of ecliptic atlas of the sky begun by Chacornac, and observed (1882) the transit of Venus; improved process of astronomical photography.

**Hen'ry** (hĕn'rĭ), **Robert.** 1718–1790. Scottish Presbyterian clergyman and historian; chief work, *History of England* (5 vols., 1771–85; vol. VI, 1793).

**Hen'ry'** (äɴ'rē'), **Victor.** 1850–1907. French philologist; professor of Sanskrit and comparative grammar, Faculté des Lettres, Paris (1889).

**Hen'ry** (hĕn'rĭ), **William.** 1729–1786. American pioneer in steam propulsion, b. in Chester Co., Pa.; on business trip to England (1761) learned from James Watt about his steam engine; on return, experimented with application of steam to propulsion of boats, first person in America to do so; built (1763) a stern-wheel steamboat which, however, failed in its test.

**Henry, William.** 1774–1836. English chemist; formulated Henry's law, that the weight of a gas dissolved by a liquid is proportional to the pressure of the gas.

**Henry, William Wirt.** 1831–1900. American lawyer and historian; grandson of Patrick Henry; b. in Charlotte Co., Va.; author of *Patrick Henry, Life, Correspondence, and Speeches* (3 vols., 1891).

**Henry Benedict Maria Clement Stuart.** See Cardinal YORK.

**Henry II Ja·so'mir·gott'** (yä·zō'mēr·gôt'). 1114–1177. Margrave of Austria (from 1141), duke of Bavaria (1143–77) and first duke of Austria (1156–77) of the Babenberg family; son of Leopold III and grandfather of Leopold VI, Duke of Austria.

**Henry of Blois** (blwȧ; blwä). d. 1171. English prelate; younger brother of King Stephen. Abbot of Glastonbury (1126–71); bishop of Winchester (1129–71). Counselor to Stephen and intermediary between him and Empress Matilda. To France after Stephen's death (1154); lived at Cluny, of which he was liberal benefactor. Returned to England; consecrated Becket as archbishop of Canterbury (1162); on deathbed, rebuked Henry II for murder of Becket.

**Henry of Bur'gun·dy** (bûr'gŭn·dĭ). 1057–?1112 or 1114. Crusader knight; m. (1094) Teresa, natural daughter of Alfonso VI of León and Castile; granted Oporto and Coimbra and title of Count of Portugal by Alfonso VI (1094); continually at war with Moors and Spanish (1105–12); succeeded by his son Alfonso, who became (1139) first king of Portugal. See BURGUNDY (2).

**Henry of Cornwall** *or* **of Almaine** (1235–1271). See under RICHARD, Earl of Cornwall.

**Henry of Flan'ders** (flăn'dērz; *Brit. usu.* flän'-). 1174?–1216. Second of the Latin emperors of Eastern Roman Empire (1205–16), b. in Valenciennes. Younger son of Baldwin, Count of Flanders and Hainaut and brother of Emperor Baldwin I. Joined Fourth Crusade (c. 1201); distinguished himself at siege of Constantinople (1204). Chosen regent on his brother's capture and later emperor (1205); successful against Bulgarians and the Nicaean emperor Theodore I Lascaris.

**Henry of Ghent** (gĕnt). *Latinized* **Hen·ri'cus de Gan'da·vo** (hĕn·rī'kŭs dē găn'dȧ·vō). *Known as* **Doc'tor So·lem'nis** (dŏk'tēr [-tôr] sō·lĕm'nĭs). d. 1293. Scholastic philosopher, b. Ghent. Canon of Tournai (1267); archdeacon of Bruges (1276); master of theology and professor, Paris (from 1276). Chief work, left unfinished at death, *Summa Theologica.*

**Henry of Hun'ting·don** (hŭn'tĭng·dŭn). 1084?–1155.

English historian; archdeacon of Huntingdon (from 1109); author of *Historia Anglorum* (extending to 1154).

**Henry of Lancaster.** (1) Earl of Lancaster (1281?–1345) and (2) 1st Duke of Lancaster (1299?–1361). See LANCASTER; HENRY IV of England.

**Henry of Lau'sanne'** (lō'zän'; *Angl.* lō·zăn'). *Also known variously as* **Henry of Bru·ys'** (brü·ē'), **Henry of Clu'ny'** (klü'nē'), **Henry of Tou'louse'** (tōō'-lōōz'), *and* **Henry the Deacon.** French heresiarch of first half of 12th century; imprisoned for Petrobrusian teachings. His followers were known as Henricians.

**Henry of Luxemburg.** See HENRY VII, Holy Roman emperor.

**Henry of Navarre.** See HENRY IV, of France.

**Henry of Sal'trey** (sô(l)'trĭ). fl. 1150. Cistercian monk of Huntingdonshire, Eng. Author of *Purgatorium Sancti Patricii* (reputedly first written account of the legend of St. Patrick's Purgatory), included in Matthew Paris's *Chronica Majora.*

**Henry of Trastamara.** = HENRY II, king of Castile.

**Hen'ry Ra'spe** (hĕn'rĭ räs'pĕ). 1202?–1247. Landgrave of Thuringia (1227–39, 1241–47). Seized government of Thuringia (1227), expelling brother's widow, St. Elizabeth of Hungary, and her son Hermann; supported Emperor Frederick II (1236–37); relinquished rule of Thuringia to Hermann (1239–41); after deposition of Frederick by Pope Innocent IV (1245), elected antiking (1246–47). His niece Sophia was founder of house of Hesse (*q.v.*).

**Henry Stuart.** = Cardinal YORK.

**Henry the Black.** See (1) HENRY IX, duke of Bavaria; (2) HENRY III, Holy Roman emperor.

**Henry the Fowler.** See HENRY I, king of Germany.

**Henry the Lion** and **Henry the Pious.** See HENRY, dukes of Saxony.

**Henry the Minstrel.** *Also known as* **Blind Harry** *or* **Blind Har'y** (hăr'ĭ). fl. 1470–1492. Scottish bard; author of poem on William Wallace.

**Henry the Navigator.** = Prince HENRY of Portugal.

**Henry the Proud.** See HENRY X, duke of Bavaria.

**Hen'ry·son** (hĕn'rĭ·s'n), *or* **Hen'der·son** (hĕn'dĕr·s'n), **Robert.** 1430?–?1506. Scottish poet; chief works, *Tale of Orpheus, Testament of Cresseid* (formerly attributed to Chaucer), *Morall Fables of Esope the Phrygian.*

**Hen'schel** (hĕn'shĕl), **Georg Christian Karl.** 1759–1835. German locomotive manufacturer; founder of Henschel & Sohn, at Kassel. The business was continued by his sons, **Karl Anton** (1780–1861) and **Johann Werner** (1782–1850), who was also a sculptor, and by Karl's son **Karl** (1810–1860) and his son **Oskar** (1837–1894), and Oskar's son **Karl** (1873–1924); developed into largest European locomotive manufactory.

**Henschel,** Sir **George.** 1850–1934. Baritone singer, conductor, and composer, b. in Germany; naturalized British subject (1890). Organized and conducted London Symphony Orchestra (1884–95); founded Scottish Symphony Orchestra, Glasgow (1893). Sang frequently (from 1881) on concert stage with his wife, the soprano **Lillian,** *nee* **Bai'ley** [bā'lĭ] (d. 1901). His compositions include operas *A Sea Change* (1887) and *Nubia* (1899).

**Henschke, Alfred.** Real name of KLABUND.

**Hen'sel** (hĕn'zĕl), **Heinrich.** 1874–1935. German operatic tenor; best known as interpreter of Wagnerian roles.

**Hensel, Wilhelm.** 1794–1861. German painter of church pictures, historical pictures, and portraits. His wife, **Fanny Cäcilia,** *nee* **Men'dels·sohn–Bar·thol'dy** [mĕn'dĕls·zōn·bär·tôl'dē] (1805–1847), was an elder sister of Felix Mendelssohn (*q.v.*), and composer of a number of songs. A sister of Wilhelm, **Luise** (1798–1876), was a poet; adopted the Roman Catholic faith (1818); wrote esp. devotional verse, including the evening hymn *Müde Bin Ich, Geh' zur Ruh.*

**Hen'se·ler** (hĕn'zĕ·lĕr), **Ernst.** 1852– . German landscape, genre, and portrait painter.

**Hen'selt** (hĕn'zĕlt), **Adolf von.** 1814–1889. German pianist and composer; with Liszt, devised modern piano technique.

**Hen'sen** (hĕn'zĕn), **Viktor.** 1835–1924. German physiologist; professor, Kiel (1871–1911); known for work in embryology, in the anatomy and physiology of the organs of sense, and for studies on plankton. The cells of Hensen in the ear are named for him.

**Hen'shaw** (hĕn'shô), **Henry Wetherbee.** 1850–1930. American ornithologist and ethnologist, b. Cambridge, Mass. On staff, U.S. Bureau of Ethnology (1879); chief (1910–15), Bureau of Biological Survey, U.S. Department of Agriculture.

**Hens'low** (hĕnz'lō), **John Stevens.** 1796–1861. English botanist; compiler of *Catalogue of British Plants* (1829) and *Dictionary of Botanical Terms* (1857).

**Hens'lowe** (hĕnz'lō), **Philip.** d. 1616. English theater manager; built and managed the Rose Theatre on the Bankside, London (to 1603); associated with Edward Alleyn in management of other theaters; bought plays from Dekker, Drayton, Chapman, and others, for presentation in his theaters. Kept (from c. 1592) an account of his theatrical ventures which was edited and published by the Shakespeare Society (1845), and provides valuable source material for study of the drama of that period.

**Hen'son** (hĕn's'n), **Herbert Hensley.** 1863–1947. Church of England prelate, b. London; bishop of Durham (1920–39); author of many religious books.

**Henson, Josiah.** 1789–1883. Negro slave, b. in Charles County, Md.; escaped to Canada (1830); labored for cultural and industrial advancement of Negro race; reputed to be original of Uncle Tom in Harriet Beecher Stowe's *Uncle Tom's Cabin.*

**Hen'ty** (hĕn'tĭ), **George Alfred.** 1832–1902. English writer of books for boys, including *Out in the Pampas* (1870), *The Young Franc-Tireurs* (1872), *The Cat of Bubastes* (1889), *Redskin and Cowboy* (1892), *With Frederick the Great* (1898), *With Roberts to Pretoria* (1902).

**Hen'zen** (hĕn'tsĕn), **Johann Heinrich Wilhelm.** 1816–1887. German philologist.

**Hen'zi** (hĕn'tsē) *or* **Hent'zi** (hĕn'tsē), **Samuel.** 1701–1749. Swiss patriot; joined group (1744) petitioning the Council of Bern for a revision of the constitution, and was banished (1744–48); conspired to abolish existing constitution, and was discovered and executed (July 17, 1749).

**Hep'burn** (hĕb'ērn; -ûrn). Family name of earls of BOTHWELL.

**Hep'burn** (hĕp'bērn), **Alonzo Barton.** 1846–1922. American banker, b. Colton, N.Y. Member, New York legislature (1875–80); chairman, committee to investigate railway rate discrimination; his "Hepburn Report" (1879) was followed by "Hepburn Laws" to correct abuses. New York State superintendent of banking (1880–83). U.S. bank examiner, New York City (1889–92). U.S. comptroller of the currency (1892–93). With Chase National Bank (from 1899), president (1904–11); chairman, board of directors (1911–18); chairman, advisory board (1918–22).

**Hepburn, James Curtis.** 1815–1911. American physician and missionary in Japan (1859–92). Compiler of *English-Japanese Dictionary* (1867), *Dictionary of the Bible* (in Japanese, 1891); associated with translation of the Bible into Japanese (New Testament, 1880; Old Testament, 1887).

**Hepburn, Katharine.** 1909– . American actress, b. Hartford, Conn.; m. Ludlow Ogden Smith (later divorced). In motion pictures: *A Bill of Divorcement, Little Women, Alice Adams, Morning Glory* (for which she received award of Academy of Motion Picture Arts and Sciences, 1934), *Quality Street, Holiday;* also on legitimate stage in *The Warrior's Husband* (1931), *The Lake* (1933), *The Philadelphia Story* (1939), *Without Love* (1942).

**Hepburn, Mitchell Frederick.** 1896–1953. Canadian politician. Lieutenant in Royal Air Force; served in France in World War (1918). Elected member of House of Commons, Ottawa (1926, 1930); leader of Liberal party in Ontario (from 1930); premier of Ontario (1934–42), and minister of public works (1939).

**Hepburn, William Peters.** 1833–1916. American legislator, b. Wellsville, Ohio. Adm. to bar (1854); practiced, Iowa City, Iowa. Served in Civil War; lieutenant colonel on Sheridan's staff. Member, U.S. House of Representatives (1881–87). U.S. solicitor of the treasury (1889–93). Member, U.S. House of Representatives (1893–1909); as member of committee on Pacific railroads, dealt with transportation rate problems; Hepburn Act passed (1906); instrumental also in writing and passing Pure Food and Drug Act (1906).

**He·phaes′ti·on** (hē-fēs′tĭ·ŏn). d. 324 B.C. Macedonian general; intimate friend of Alexander the Great, who charged him with establishment of Greek colonies in conquered lands and with building of fleet for descending Indus River. On his sudden death at Ecbatana (324 B.C.), Alexander ordered erection of a vast funeral pyre and construction of temples in his honor.

**Hephaestion.** Greek scholar of 2d century A.D.; author of a treatise (extant) on Greek meters, much used as a textbook.

**Hep′ple·white** (hĕp′'l·hwīt), **George.** d. 1786. English cabinetmaker; offices in parish of St. Giles, Cripplegate, London; famed for the delicacy and beauty of furniture of his design.

**Hep′worth** (hĕp′wûrth; -wẽrth), **George Hughes.** 1833–1902. American clergyman, b. Boston. Unitarian pastorates in Boston (1858–69) and New York (1869–72); Congregationalist pastorates in New York (1872–79) and Newark (1882–85). Superintending editor, New York *Herald* (1885); editor, New York *Telegram* (1893); published popular series of weekly sermons in *Herald* (from 1892). Author of *Rocks and Shoals, Lectures to Young Men* (1870), *Hiram Golf's Religion* (1893), *Herald Sermons* (1894, 1897), *Through Armenia on Horseback* (1898), *Making the Most of Life* (1904), etc.

**He·rac′le·on** (hē·răk′lē·ŏn). Gnostic Christian of 2d century; disciple of Valentinus (*q.v.*); his followers were known as Heracleonites. Only fragments of his works are extant.

**He·rac′le·o′nas** (hē·răk′lē·ō′năs). b. 614? Son of Heraclius. Joint emperor with half brother, Constantine III (641); sole emperor on death of Constantine; dethroned after a few months' rule; exiled.

**Her′a·cle′o·pol′i·tan** (hĕr′ȧ·klē′ō·pŏl′ĭ·tăn). Name of IXth and Xth dynasties of Egyptian kings of the Middle Kingdom, c. 2445–2160 B.C.; derived from Heracleopolis, their capital city. See *Table* (*in Appendix*) for EGYPT.

**He·rac′li·an** (hē·răk′lĭ·ăn; hĕr′ȧ·klī′ăn). d. 413 A.D. Roman general; commissioned by Emperor Honorius to assassinate Stilicho (408 A.D.); appointed count of Africa; revolted (413) and was assassinated at Carthage by agents of emperor.

**Her′a·cli′des** (*or* **Her′a·clei′des**) **Pon′ti·cus** (hĕr′ȧ·klī′dēz pŏn′tĭ·kŭs). Greek philosopher of 4th century B.C.; disciple of Plato. Said to have been first to assert that the apparent rotation of the heavens is caused, not by circling of stars around the earth, but by rotation of the earth about its own axis. Only fragments of his works are extant.

**Her′a·cli′tus** (hĕr′ȧ·klī′tŭs). Greek philosopher of 6th–5th century B.C., in Ephesus; known as "the Weeping Philosopher" because of his gloomy view of life. One of the earliest metaphysicians.

**Her′a·cli′us** (hĕr′ȧ·klī′ŭs; hē·răk′lĭ·ŭs). 575?–641. Emperor of the Eastern Roman Empire (610–641), b. in Cappadocia; son of Heraclius (fl. 586–610), a general and exarch of Africa under Emperor Mauricius. With aid of father, dethroned Phocas (610); was proclaimed emperor. Defeated by Persians under Khosrau, who conquered Syria (613–614), Palestine (615), and Egypt (616), and besieged Constantinople. First campaign (622) not successful. In second (623–628) completely defeated Persians; war ended with death of Khosrau (628). Holy Cross recovered from Persians (628) and restored to Jerusalem (629). Various conflicts warded off Avars on north (619, 626). Opposed by nobles and church in reforms. Syria invaded by Saracens (629); first of Mohammedan onslaughts. Lost Damascus (635) and suffered great defeat by Saracens in the Yarmuk valley, Palestine (636); lost to them (635–641) Syria, Palestine, Mesopotamia, and Egypt. Inactive in later years; interested in theological and ecclesiastical questions. Published the Ecthesis (638).

**Hé′rault′ de Sé′chelles′** (ā′rō′ dē sā′shĕl′), **Marie Jean.** 1759–1794. French lawyer and politician; counsel to the Parliament of Paris (1785); member of the Legislative Assembly (1791), the National Convention (1792); assisted in drafting new constitution (1793); guillotined at Paris (Apr. 5, 1794).

**Her′bart** (hĕr′bärt), **Johann Friedrich.** 1776–1841. German philosopher and educator, b. at Oldenburg. Educ. Jena. Tutor in Switzerland (1797–1800), where he became interested in Pestalozzi's pedagogical methods. Among his notable works are *Allgemeine Pädagogik* (1806), *Hauptpunkte der Metaphysik* (1806), *Lehrbuch zur Psychologie* (1816), *Psychologie als Wissenschaft, neu Gegründet auf Erfahrung, Metaphysik und Mathematik* (2 vols., 1824–25), *Allgemeine Metaphysik nebst den Anfängen der Philosophischen Naturlehre* (2 vols., 1828–29). Best known for his insistence upon co-ordination of psychology and ethics in devising educational systems and methods, psychology to provide a knowledge of the human mind to be educated, and ethics to provide a knowledge of the social ends to which education should be directed.

**Her′beck** (hĕr′bĕk), **Johann von.** 1831–1877. Austrian conductor and composer of Masses, symphonies, string quartets, choral works, and songs.

**Her′be·lin′** (ĕr′bē·lăɴ′), **Jeanne Mathilde,** *nee* **Ha′bert′** (à′bâr′). 1820–1904. French painter of miniatures.

**Her′be·lot′ de Mo′lain′ville′** (ĕr′bē·lō′ dē mô′lăɴ′-vēl′), **Barthélemy de.** 1625–1695. French Orientalist; compiler of *Bibliothèque Orientale ou Dictionnaire Universel Contenant Généralement Tout ce qui Regarde la Connaissance des Peuples de l'Orient.*

**Her′be·ray′ des Es′sarts′** (ĕr′bē·rā′ dā-zā′sàr′), **Nicolas d′.** d. about 1557. French translator; by order of Francis I, translated (1540–48) first eight books of *Amadís de Gaula* and (1555) Guevara's *El Reloj de Príncipes;* compiler also of a *Cancionero.*

**Her′ber·mann** (hûr′bẽr·măn), **Charles George.** 1840–1916. Teacher and editor, b. Saerbeck, Westphalia,

Germany; to U.S. (1851). Editor in chief, *The Catholic Encyclopedia* (1905–13).

**Her'bert** (hûr'bĕrt). Name of an English family of marchmen, descendants of Jenkin ap Adam, master sergeant of a Monmouthshire lordship in time of Edward III, including holders of marquisate of Powis, earldoms of Powis, Pembroke, Montgomery, Torrington, Carnarvon, and barony of Herbert of Cherbury.

(1) Earls of Pembroke and Montgomery:

Sir **William Herbert** (d. 1469), 1st Earl of Pembroke (of 1st creation, 1468); Yorkist leader; possessor of castle, town, and lordship of Pembroke; in Wars of the Roses, effective against Jasper Tudor; chief justice of South Wales (1461), North Wales (1467); taken by northern Lancastrians and beheaded. His son **William** (1460–1491) surrendered earldom of Pembroke to crown for earldom of Huntingdon (1479).

Sir **William Herbert** (1501?–1570), 1st Earl of Pembroke (creation of 1551); courtier, soldier, and diplomat; son of an illegitimate son of Sir William (d. 1469); m. Anne Parr, sister of Henry VIII's 6th wife; one of Henry VIII's executors; member of Edward VI's council; president of Wales (1550); supported Mary Tudor against claims of Lady Jane Grey (1553); commanded forces putting down insurrection of Sir Thomas Wyatt (1554) in protest against marrying Mary to Philip of Spain; envoy to France (1555); supported Protestant party in Elizabeth's reign; lord steward (1568).

His son **Henry** (1534?–1601), 2d earl; president of Wales (1586); prominent in trial of Mary, Queen of Scots (1586); m. (1553) Lady Catherine Grey, sister of Lady Jane Grey (see Lady Catherine Seymour); m. (1577) Mary Sidney (see countess of Pembroke), sister of Sir Philip Sidney.

**William** (1580–1630), 3d earl; son of 2d earl; poet; banished from court for illicit connection with Mary Fitton (*q.v.*) and imprisoned (1601); patron of Ben Jonson, Philip Massinger, Inigo Jones, and William Browne; interested in Virginia, Northwest Passage, Bermuda, and East India companies; lord chamberlain of royal household (1615–25); lord steward (1626–30); chancellor of Oxford (from 1617), having Pembroke Coll. named after him (1624). Identified by some Shakespearean commentators with subject of Shakespeare's sonnets and with "Mr. W. H." in the dedication (1609). Object, with his brother Philip Herbert, of inscription in first folio of Shakespeare to the "incomparable pair of brothers."

**Philip** (1584–1650), 4th Earl of Pembroke and 1st Earl of Montgomery; brother of 3d earl; favorite of James I; lord chamberlain (1626–41); m. (1630) Anne Clifford (*q.v.*); strove to promote peace between Charles I and Scots (1639–40); deserted king for Parliamentary side (1641); Parliamentary governor of Isle of Wight (1642); commissioner at Oxford (1643), at Uxbridge (1645); received Charles I from the Scots (1647); vice-chancellor of Oxford (1641–50).

**Thomas** (1656–1733), 8th earl; grandson of 4th earl; first lord of admiralty (1690); lord privy seal (1692); first plenipotentiary at Treaty of Ryswick (1697); lord high admiral (1702, 1708); lord lieutenant of Ireland (1707); a lord justice (1714–15). His son **Henry** (1693–1751), 9th Earl of Pembroke and 6th Earl of Montgomery, known as "the Architect Earl," was responsible for erection of first Westminster bridge (1739–50). **Henry** (1734–1794), 10th earl, and **George Augustus** (1759–1827), 11th earl, were British generals.

**Sidney** (1810–1861), 1st Baron **Herbert of Lea** (lē); statesman; 2d son of 11th earl; B.A., Oxon. (1831); war secretary under Peel (1845–46), during Crimean War (1852–55), and under Palmerston (1859–60); his administration remarkable for invitation to Florence Nightingale to take nurses to Crimea, improvement of army sanitation and education, amalgamation of Indian forces with imperial army, and organization of volunteer movement. His eldest son, **George Robert Charles** (1850–1895), 13th Earl of Pembroke and 9th Earl of Montgomery; undersecretary for war (1874–75); author, with George Henry Kingsley, of *South Sea Bubbles* (1872), narratives of shipwreck of their yacht in Ringgold Islands.

(2) Barons, earls, marquises, dukes of Powis:

**William Herbert** (1573?–1656), 1st Baron Powis; grandson of 1st earl of Pembroke (1501?–1570). **William** (1617–1696), 1st Marquis of Powis and titular Duke of Powis; grandson of 1st baron; head of Roman Catholic aristocracy in England; arrested on suspicion of complicity in Popish Plot, imprisoned five years; privy councilor (1686); fled with James II; became James II's lord steward and chamberlain of household; created duke of Powis by dethroned king. His eldest son, **William** (d. 1745), 2d marquis; Jacobite, imprisoned on suspicion of complicity in Sir J. Fenwick's plot to assassinate William III; called Viscount Montgomery until restoration of title and estates (1722). Lady **Lucy Herbert** (1669–1744), youngest daughter of 1st marquis; prioress of English convent at Bruges (1709–44); compiler of devotional works.

**Edward Herbert** (1785–1848), 2d Earl of Powis; son of 1st earl and grandson of Baron Clive of Plassey; his mother was the daughter of **Henry Arthur Herbert** (d. 1772), Baron Powis and Earl of Powis; assumed mother's surname, Herbert (1807); active in suppression of Chartist riots (1839); brought about defeat of scheme for creating bishopric of Manchester, thereby winning gratitude of clergy and universities. Sir **Percy Egerton** (1822–1876), 2d son of 2d earl of Powis; served in Kaffir War (1851–53); quartermaster general in Crimea; held commands in campaign round Cawnpore (1858); lieutenant general (1875).

(3) Earls of Carnarvon, *descendants of Thomas Herbert, 8th Earl of Pembroke; styled viscounts Porchester until succession to earldom:*

**William Herbert** (1778–1847), 3d son of Henry Herbert, 1st Earl of Carnarvon; classical scholar, linguist, and naturalist; author of first adequate English translations from Icelandic literature, of *Attila*, an epic poem in twelve books (1838), and of botanical works. His son **Henry William** (1807–1858); writer under pseudonym **Frank For'es·ter** (fŏr'ĕs·tẽr; -ĭs·tẽr); classical tutor in New York (from 1831); author of historical romances, including *The Brothers* (1834) and *Roman Traitor* (1846), translations of Dumas and Eugène Sue, and works on outdoor sports.

**Henry John George** (1800–1849), 3d Earl of Carnarvon (creation of 1793); traveler in Barbary, Spain, Portugal, Greece; author of a tragedy, *Don Pedro*, acted by Macready and Ellen Tree (1828).

**Henry Howard Mol'y·neux** [mŏl'ĭ·nūks] (1831–1890), 4th Earl of Carnarvon; son of 3d earl; statesman; B.A., Oxon. (1852); undersecretary for colonies (1858–59); as colonial secretary (1866–67, 1874–78), brought in bill for federation of North American provinces (1867), abolished slavery on Gold Coast (1874), introduced permissive federation bill for South Africa (1877); resigned in opposition to breach of neutrality in Russo-Turkish conflict (1878); as lord lieutenant of Ireland (1885–86), favored limited self-government; resigned; opposed Gladstone's home rule and land purchase bills; urged colonial defense; published verse translations of *Agamemnon* and the *Odyssey*.

**George Edward Stanhope Molyneux** (1866–1923), 5th Earl of Carnarvon; son of 4th earl; Egyptologist; educ. Cambridge; indulged fondness for travel and horse racing; collaborated (1907–12, 1919–23) with Howard Carter in excavation near Thebes; discovered tombs of Egyptian dynasties XII and XVIII, including (1922) tomb of Tutankhamen, in Valley of the Kings; died as result of infection of mosquito bite.

(4) BRANCH INCLUDING BARONS HERBERT OF CHERBURY:

**Edward Herbert** (1583–1648), 1st Baron Herbert of Cherbury; philosopher and diplomat; educ. Oxford; fought several duels (1608–10); served in prince of Orange's army (1614); ambassador to France (1619–24); attended Charles I on Scottish expedition (1639–40); after attempt at neutrality, submitted to Parliament (1645); author of *Autobiography* (to 1624) and of *De Veritate* (1624), his chief philosophical work; advanced an antiempirical theory of knowledge like that of the Cambridge Platonists and maintained that the common articles of all religions, apprehended by instinct, include existence of God, duty of worship and repentance, future rewards and punishment (whence often called "Father of English Deism"); author of *Life of Henry VIII* (pub. 1649) and poems in Latin and English, representing the metaphysical school.

His brother **George** (1593–1633); poet; M.A., Cantab. (1616); public orator (1619–27); ordained priest (1630); author of 160 religious poems, marked by ingenious imagery, collected in *The Temple* (1633) and of prose works, including the fervently pious *A Priest to the Temple* (1652), rules for the country parson; biographized by Izaak Walton.

Another brother, Sir **Henry** (1595–1673); as master of the revels (from 1623, and again after Restoration), claimed right of licensing every kind of public entertainment throughout England, even books, a right often contested by theatrical producers, including Davenant.

The fourth brother, **Thomas** (1597–?1642), distinguished himself in naval service against Portuguese (1616) and Algerines (1620–21); wrote elegy on Strafford (1641), and pasquinades.

**Henry** (1654–1709), son of Sir Henry Herbert (1595–1673); joined William of Orange in Holland (1688); promoted Revolution in Worcestershire; created Baron Herbert of Cherbury (1694).

Sir **Edward** (1591?–1657), judge; cousin of 1st Baron Herbert of Cherbury; solicitor general (1640); attorney general (1641); under instructions by Charles I, exhibited articles of impeachment against Pym, Hampden, and four other members of Parliament for subversion of fundamental laws; impeached by House of Commons, and incapacitated; went to sea with Prince Rupert (1648).

**Arthur** (1647–1716), Earl of Torrington (cr. 1689); 2d son of Sir Edward (1591?–1657); served as naval officer against the Dutch (1666) and Algerian corsairs (1669–71, 1678–83); as admiral, relieved Tangier (1680); cashiered for refusing to support repeal of Test Act (1687); commanded fleet conducting William of Orange to England (1688); 1st lord of admiralty (1689); obliged by queen's order to engage whole French fleet off Beachy Head (1690); charged before court-martial with holding back, acquitted.

His brother Sir **Edward** (1648?–1698), titular Earl of Portland; chief justice of King's Bench (1685), of common pleas (1687); followed James II into exile.

**Henry** (d. 1691), 4th baron; grandson of 1st baron; served under Monmouth in France (1672) and supported Monmouth against duke of York.

**Herbert,** Sir **Alan Patrick.** *Pseudonym* **Albert Had'dock** (hăd'ŭk). 1890–1971. English journalist and writer; educ. Oxford. Served with Royal Naval Division (1914–17). Joined staff of *Punch* (1924). M.P. for Oxford U. (1935–1950). Among his many works are *The Bomber Gipsy, The House-by-the-River, Tinker, Tailor, The Blue Peter* (comic opera), *Plain Jane, The Trials of Topsy, The Water Gipsies, Holy Deadlock* (1934), *The Ayes Have It* (1937), *Tantivy Towers* (comic opera).

**Herbert, George.** 1593–1633. English clergyman and poet. Brother of Edward Herbert, 1st Baron Herbert of Cherbury. B.A., Cambridge (1613). Ordained priest (1630); rector of Fugglestone and Bemerton, Wiltshire. His poems published posthumously in volume entitled *The Temple; Sacred Poems and Private Ejaculations* (1633). Grouped with Donne, Cowley, and Crashaw in the metaphysical school of poets.

**Herbert, Hilary Abner.** 1834–1919. American political leader, b. Laurens, S.C. Served in Confederate army in Civil War. Member, U.S. House of Representatives (1877–93); U.S. secretary of the navy (1893–97).

**Herbert, John Rogers.** 1810–1890. English portrait and historical painter.

**Herbert, Victor.** 1859–1924. Irish-American conductor and composer, b. Dublin, Ireland. To U.S. (1886); organized and conducted his own orchestra in New York (from 1904). Success of his light opera *Prince Ananias* (produced 1894) led to other works in this field: *The Wizard of the Nile* (1895), *The Fortune Teller* (1898), *Babes in Toyland* (1903), *Mlle. Modiste* (1905), *The Red Mill* (1906), *Naughty Marietta* (1910), *Princess Pat* (1915). He also wrote two grand operas, *Natoma* (1911) and *Madeleine* (1914), musical scores for Ziegfeld Follies (1917, 1921–24), and many nondramatic compositions.

**Herbert of Cherbury,** Barons. See HERBERT family, 4.

**Herbert of Lea,** Baron. = *Sidney Herbert* (1810–1861), under HERBERT family, 1.

**Herblock.** See Herbert Lawrence BLOCK.

**Her'bort von Fritz'lar** (hĕr'bôrt fôn frĭts'lär). fl. about 1210. Middle High German poet; his *Liet von Troie* was the first German version of the Trojan War story, based on Benoît de Sainte-Maure's *Roman de Troie.*

**Herbst** (hûrpst), **Josephine Frey** (frī). 1897–1969. American writer, b. Sioux City, Iowa; A.B., U. of California (1918); m. John Hermann (1925). Author of *Pity Is Not Enough* (1933), *The Executioner Waits* (1934), *Rope of Gold* (1939), *Satan's Sergeants* (1941).

**Her'cu·la'no de Car·va'lho e A·ra·ú'jo** (ĕr'kōō·lă'-nōō thĕ kĕr·vä'lyōō ē ă·rȧ·ōō'zhōō), **Alexandre.** 1810–1877. Portuguese poet and historian, b. Lisbon; opponent of Dom Miguel; political exile at Paris (1828–30), London (1830–32); editor of *Panorama,* Lisbon (1832 ff.); director, royal library at Ajuda (1845 ff.). His works include religio-political poems, histories and novels.

**Her'der** (hĕr'dēr), **Johann Gottfried von.** 1744–1803. German philosopher and man of letters; called to Weimar (upon Goethe's recommendation) as general superintendent of the church district there (1776–1803). Among his works are *Kritische Wälder* (1769), *Abhandlung über den Ursprung der Sprache* (1772), various collections of German folksongs (the first publ. 1778; in later editions under title, *Stimmen der Völker in Liedern*), *Ideen zur Philosophie der Geschichte der Menschheit* (4 vols., 1784–91), *Briefen zur Beförderung der Humanität* (10 parts, 1793–97), and a paraphrase of the *Cid* (1803).

**Herd'man** (hûrd'măn), Sir **William Abbott.** 1858–1924. Scottish marine naturalist; founded Liverpool Marine Biology Committee (1885), which opened (1887) a research laboratory at Puffin Island, later moved to the

Isle of Man; organized a marine research laboratory in U. of Liverpool (1891); aided in establishing a fish hatchery in Barrow Strait (1897). Author of *The Founders of Oceanography* (1923), etc.

**He·re′dia** (ȧ·rā′thyä), **José María de.** 1842–1905. French poet of Spanish parentage, b. near Santiago de Cuba. To Paris (1859); one of leading representatives of French Parnassians; disciple of Leconte de Lisle; one of foremost masters of the French sonnet; known esp. for *Les Trophées*, collection of 50 sonnets (1893); notable also for his translation (1877–87) of Bernal Díaz del Castillo's *Historia Verdadera de la Conquista de la Nueva España* and for the prose romance *La Nonne Alferez* (1894). Cf. José María de HEREDIA Y CAMPUZANO.

**He·re′dia y Cam′pu·za′no** (ȧ·rā′thyä ē käm′po͞o-sä′nō), **José María de.** 1803–1839. Cuban poet, b. at Santiago de Cuba; cousin of French poet José María de Heredia. Banished from Cuba (1823) as insurrectionary; wandered in U.S. (1823–25), later settling in Mexico. Known for patriotic lyrics; considered by many Cuba's foremost lyricist. His works include the widely translated *Al Niágara*, his best-known poem; verse translations of dramas by Voltaire, Alfieri, Chénier, etc.; and *Lecciones de Historia Universal* (1830–31).

**Hereford,** Earls of. See William FITZOSBERN; BOHUN.

**He′re·mans** (hā′rĕ·mäns), **Jacob Frans Johan.** 1825–1884. Dutch philologist and historian of literature; leader of Flemish movement in the Netherlands.

**Herennius Byblius.** See PHILO BYBLIUS.

**Her′e·ward** (hĕr′ĕ·wērd). *Called* **Hereward the Wake** (wāk). fl. 1070–1071. English patriot and outlaw. Headed English rebellion at Ely (1070) against William the Conqueror; plundered Peterborough (1070); escaped when his allies surrendered to William. Subject of many legends, and of Charles Kingsley's prose romance *Hereward the Wake.*

**Her′ford** (hûr′fērd), **Charles Harold.** 1853–1931. English scholar, b. Manchester. Professor of English, U. of Manchester (1906 ff.). Author of studies of Ibsen, *The Age of Wordsworth* (1897) and other works on Wordsworth, *Robert Browning* (1904), *Goethe* (1913), several works on Shakespeare, etc.

**Herford, Oliver.** 1863–1935. Writer and illustrator, b. in England. Author of a number of whimsical works illustrated by his own drawings, as *The Bashful Earthquake...*(1898), *Rubaiyat of a Persian Kitten* (1904), *Jingle Jungles* (1915), *Cynic's Calendar* (1917), *The Herford Aesop* (1921), *Excuse It Please* (1930), *The Deb's Dictionary* (1931). His sister **Beatrice** (1868?–1952), b. Manchester, Eng., m. Sidney Willard Hayward (1897), was a noted monologuist, excelling in such monologues as *The Shop Girl* and *The Sociable Seamstress.*

**Her′gen·rö′ther** (hĕr′gĕn·rû′tēr), **Joseph.** 1824–1890. German Roman Catholic prelate and church historian; cardinal (1879).

**Her′ges·hei′mer** (hûr′gĕs·hī′mēr), **Joseph.** 1880–1954. American novelist, b. Philadelphia. Educ. at a Quaker school and at Pennsylvania Academy of Fine Arts. At first a painter with studio in Venice and later in Florence; returned to U.S. (c. 1907) and devoted himself to writing. Author of *The Lay Anthony* (1914), *Mountain Blood* (1915), *The Three Black Pennys* (1917), *Gold and Iron* (1918), *Java Head* (1919), *Linda Condon* (1919), *Cytherea* (1922), *The Bright Shawl* (1922), *Balisand* (1924), *Tampico* (1926), *Swords and Roses* (1929), *The Party Dress* (1929), *The Limestone Tree* (1931), *Tropical Winter* (1933), *The Foolscap Rose* (1934), etc.

**Hé′ri′cault′** (ā′rē′kō′), **Charles d′.** *Real name* **Charles Joseph de Ri′cault′** (dē rē′kō′). 1823–1899. French historian and novelist.

**Her′ing** (hĕr′ĭng; *Ger.* hā′rĭng), **Constantine.** 1800–1880. Homeopathic physician; b. Oschatz, Saxony, Germany; to U.S. (1833); practiced in Philadelphia. Organized first homeopathic school in the world, North American Academy of the Homeopathic Healing Art (chartered 1836); founded Homeopathic Med. Coll. of Penn. (1848) and Hahnemann Med. Coll. of Philadelphia (1867).

**He′ring** (hā′rĭng), **Ewald.** 1834–1918. German physiologist and psychologist. Professor, Leipzig (from 1895). Investigated respiration and visual space perception and opposed a nativistic theory to Helmholtz's empiristic one; regarded memory as a general function of organized matter; opposed Fechner's psychophysical principles; advanced a theory of color vision.

**Her′i·ot** (hĕr′ĭ·ŭt), **George.** 1563–1624. Scottish goldsmith and philanthropist; jeweler to James VI (James I of England); founded Heriot's Hospital at Edinburgh (opened 1659). Original of Geordic in Scott's *Fortunes of Nigel.*

**Her′ki·mer** (hûr′kĭ·mēr), **Nicholas.** 1728–1777. American Revolutionary officer, b. near present Herkimer, N.Y. Active in pre-Revolutionary agitation. Brigadier general of militia (1775); led force against Sir John Johnson (1776); mortally wounded at Oriskany, N.Y. (Aug., 1777) when, attempting to relieve Fort Schuyler, his troops were ambushed and defeated.

**Her′ko·mer** (hûr′kō·mēr; *Ger.* hār′kō′mēr), Sir **Hubert von.** 1849–1914. Bavarian-born painter, in England (from 1857); professor of fine art, Oxford (1885–94). His paintings include portraits of Wagner, Ruskin, Lord Kelvin, the Marquess of Salisbury.

**Her′lin** (hĕr′lēn), **Friedrich.** 1435–1499 or 1500. German painter, esp. of altarpieces.

**Her·mag′o·ras** (hûr·măg′ō·răs). Greek rhetorician of early 1st century B.C.; founded school in Rome for teaching of oratory.

**Her′mann I** (hĕr′män). d. 1217. Landgrave of Thuringia and count palatine of Saxony; patron of Walther von der Vogelweide and other minnesingers; promoted singing contest at the Wartburg, for which he is celebrated in opera and story.

**Hermann.** German hero. See ARMINIUS.

**Hermann, Friedrich Benedikt Wilhelm von.** 1795–1868. German economist.

**Hermann, Gottfried.** 1772–1848. German classical philologist.

**Hermann, Karl Friedrich.** 1804–1855. German classical scholar.

**Hermann of Wied** (vēt). 1477–1552. Count of Wied. Elector and archbishop of Cologne (1515–47); converted to Protestantism, instituted reforms in his diocese, and invited Martin Bucer and Melanchthon to aid him in carrying them out. Failed in reforms; deposed as elector, and excommunicated by Pope Paul III (1546); resigned his office (1547) and retired to Wied.

**Hermann von Rei′che·nau** (fôn rī′kĕ·nou). *Surnamed* **der Lah′me** (dēr lä′mĕ), *i.e.* the Lame. *Known also as* **Her·man′nus Con·trac′tus** (hûr·măn′ŭs kŏn·trăk′tŭs). 1013–1054. German monk, historian, and poet; author of a world history (*Chronicon*), down to the year 1054, continued by a pupil (Bertold) down to 1066.

**Her′man·ric** (hûr′măn·rĭk) *or* **Her′man·rich** (hûr′-măn·rĭk; *Ger.* hĕr′män·rĭK). = ERMANARIC.

**Her′mant′** (ĕr′mäN′), **Abel.** 1862–1950. French writer; author of critical essays, novels, and comedies.

**Her′mas** (hûr′măs). fl. 140 A.D. One of the Apostolic Fathers (not the Hermas of *Rom.* xvi. 14). Said to be brother of Pope Pius I; little known of his life; author of *The Shepherd of Hermas*, a description of contemporary Christian life.

**Hermenegild.** See under LEOVIGILD.

**Her'mes** (hĕr'mĕs), **Georg.** 1775–1831. German Roman Catholic theologian and philosopher. His philosophic doctrine, known as Hermesianism, was condemned by Pope Gregory XVI (1835).

**Her'me·si'a·nax** (hûr'mē·sī'ȧ·năks). Greek elegiac poet of late 4th century B.C., in Colophon, Asia Minor. Only fragments of his works are extant.

**Her·mi'ne** (hĕr·mē'nĕ). 1887–1947. Second wife (m. 1922) of Kaiser William II of Germany. Daughter of Prince Henry XXII of Reuss; m. 1st Prince Johann Georg von Schönaich-Carolath (1907; d. 1920).

**Her·mip'pus** (hûr·mĭp'ŭs). Athenian writer of comedies in 5th century B.C.; known as "the One-Eyed." Political opponent of Pericles; said to have prosecuted Aspasia for impiety and immorality. Only fragments of his works are extant.

**Her'mite'** (ĕr'mēt'), **Charles.** 1822–1901. French mathematician; known for work on elliptic functions, the theory of numbers, continued fractions, etc.; first to solve equation of the fifth degree; showed that *e*, the base of natural logarithms, is not an algebraic number.

**Her·moc'ra·tes** (hûr·mŏk'rȧ·tēz). d. about 407 B.C. Syracusan general and politician; banished (409 B.C.), and killed while trying to get control of the city.

**Her·mog'e·nes** (hûr·mŏj'ĕ·nēz). Greek rhetorician of late 2d century A.D., teaching in Rome; his rhetorical treatises widely used as textbooks.

**Her·nán'dez** (ĕr·nän'dāth; -dās). See also FERNÁNDEZ.

**Her·nán'dez** (ĕr·nän'dāth) *or* **Fer·nán'dez** (fĕr-), **Gregorio.** c. 1576–1636. Spanish sculptor, b. Santiago; launched new period in Spanish sculpture, introducing naturalism to replace classicist mannerism.

**Hernández, Mateo.** 1888–1949. Spanish sculptor.

**Her·nán'dez Gi·rón'** (ĕr·nän'dāth [-dās] hē·rôn'), **Francisco.** 1510–1554. Spanish soldier, b. Cáceres, Estremadura; to America (1535); aided in conquest of New Granada; in Peru, served in royalist army against Gonzalo Pizarro (1545–48); headed revolt against government (1553), defeating royalists under Alvarado (1554); later, captured and beheaded. Author of account of the rebellion.

**Her·nán'dez Martínez** (ĕr·nän'dās), **Maximiliano.** See MARTÍNEZ.

**Hern'don** (hûrn'dŭn), **William Henry.** 1818–1891. American lawyer, b. Greensburg, Ky. Law partner of Abraham Lincoln (from 1844); author of *Herndon's Lincoln; the True Story of a Great Life* (with Jesse W. Weik, 3 vols., 1889). His letters and papers relating to Lincoln were edited by Emanuel Hertz (*q.v.*) as *The Hidden Lincoln* (1938).

**Herne** (hûrn), **James A.** *Orig.* **James A·hern'** (ȧ·hûrn'). 1839–1901. American actor and playwright, b. Cohoes, N.Y. With David Belasco, wrote *Hearts of Oak* (produced 1879), and acted in it (1879–86); other successes include *Shore Acres* (1892), *Sag Harbor* (1899). Two daughters, **Julie** (1881-1955) and **Chrystal** (1883–1950), were also on the stage.

**He'ro** (hẹ̄r'ō) *or* **He'ron** (hẹ̄r'ŏn) of Alexandria. Greek scientist, of 3d century A.D. (or earlier), in Alexandria; author of numerous works in mathematics, physics, and mechanics; described siphons, water organs, and primitive form of steam engine. Among his extant works are *Pneumatica*, *Belopoeica*, *Mechanica*, *Geometria*, *Geodaesia*, *Mensurae*, and *On the Dioptra*.

**Her'od** (hĕr'ŭd). *Latin* **He·ro'des** (hē·rō'dēz). Name of several rulers over Palestine, forming a dynasty:

**Herod the Great.** 73?–4 B.C. King of Judea (37–4 B.C.). Son of Antipater (*q.v.*), of an Idumaean family; m. ten times, most of his children being born to his second wife, Mariamne (the Hasmonaean), fifth wife, Mariamne (dau. of High Priest Simon), sixth wife, Malthace, and seventh wife, Cleopatra. Converted to Judaism; made governor of Galilee (47); after murder of his father (43) and death (40) of Phasael, his elder brother, forced by disturbed conditions in Palestine to flee to Rome (40); there made king of Judea (39) by Antony, Octavius, and the Senate; took possession (37). Early years of reign (37–25) marked by revolts; his position strengthened by battle of Actium (31); in fit of jealousy killed (29) his second wife, Mariamne; next period (25–13) of rule prosperous, marked by building of many fortresses, theaters, hippodromes, and other public buildings; began rebuilding Great Temple at Jerusalem (20 B.C.; not completed until 64 A.D.); secured many benefits for Jewish people; his last years (13–4) marred by political and family intrigues.

**Herod Ar'che·la'us** (är'kē·lā'ŭs). *Orig.* **Archelaus.** d. before 18 A.D. Son of Herod the Great and Malthace. On father's death (4 B.C.) became ethnarch of Judea and Samaria; deposed (6 A.D.) by Augustus on complaints of the Jews and banished to Vienne in Gaul.

**Herod An'ti·pas** (ăn'tĭ·păs). *Orig.* **Antipas.** d. after 40 A.D. Ruler of Judea at time of Christ's death. Brother of Herod Archelaus. Educ. at Rome; on father's death (4 B.C.) invested with tetrarchy of Galilee and Perea (4 B.C.–40 A.D.); m. daughter of Aretas, King of Nabataeans; divorced her to marry his niece Herodias, daughter of Aristobulus (who was then wife of his brother Herod Philip), thus bringing on war with Nabataeans and making him many enemies; reproved by John the Baptist; tricked into killing John by Herodias and the dancing of her daughter, Salome (*Matt.* xiv. 3–12); driven to his ruin by ambitions of Herodias; banished (40) by Caligula to Lugdunum (modern Lyons).

**Herod Philip.** *Orig.* **Philip.** d. 34 A.D. Son of Herod the Great and his fifth wife, Mariamne. Husband of Herodias (see preceding paragraph). Called Philip in the New Testament (*Matt.* xiv. 3)—not the same as Philip the Tetrarch (*q.v.*).

**Herod A·grip'pa I** (ȧ·grĭp'ȧ) *or* **Julius Agrippa I.** *Often called* **Agrippa.** 10? B.C.–44 A.D. King of Judea (41–44 A.D.). Son of Aristobulus and grandson of Herod the Great. Educ. at Rome with Claudius and Drusus; thrown into prison for an offense against Tiberius; released by Caligula (37) and made ruler of Batanaea, Trachonitis, etc., after banishment of Herod Antipas (40); received tetrarchy of Galilee; for services to Claudius rewarded (41) with annexation of Judea and Samaria to his dominions; strongly pro-Jewish; caused death of Apostle James and imprisonment of Peter.

**Herod Agrippa II** *or* **Marcus Julius Agrippa II.** 27–?100 A.D. Son and successor of Herod Agrippa I. Educ. at Rome at court of Claudius; given Chalcis (50) with title of king after death (48) of his uncle Herod of Chalcis (see next paragraph); his domains increased (52) by what had been the tetrarchy of Philip; with Roman procurator Festus, heard defense of Paul (60); when Jewish Revolt (66–70) or war with Rome began, tried to dissuade Jews; sided with Romans; after capture of Jerusalem (70) retired to Rome with his sister Berenice (75); granted dignity of praetor; spent remainder of life (70–100?) at Rome.

**Herod of Chal'cis** (kăl'sĭs). d. 48 A.D. Brother of Herod Agrippa I. By Emperor Claudius made king of Chalcis (41), a small district (former tetrarchy) of Coele-Syria, north of Galilee.

**He·ro'das** (hē·rō'dăs) *or* **He·ron'das** (hē·rŏn'dăs). Greek poet of 3d century B.C.; author of short humorous dramatic genre sketches in choliambic verse.

**He·ro′des At′ti·cus** (hē·rō′dēz ăt′ĭ·kŭs), **Tiberius Claudius.** Greek scholar of 2d century A.D.; entrusted by Emperor Antoninus Pius with education of Marcus Aurelius and Lucius Verus. Famed for public works, including music theater at Athens, theater at Corinth, stadium at Delphi, aqueduct at Canusium (Canosa di Puglia, Italy), and restoration of many ruined cities in Greece.

**He·ro′di·an** (hē·rō′dĭ·ăn). *Latin* **He·ro′di·a′nus** (hē·rō′dĭ·ā′nŭs). fl. 3d century A.D. Greek historian in Italy; author of history of Rome for years 180 to 238 A.D.

**Herodianus, Aelius.** Greek scholar of Alexandria in 2d century A.D.; taught in Rome under patronage of Marcus Aurelius. Author of work on prosody (in 21 books).

**He·ro′di·as** (hē·rō′dĭ·ăs). 14? B.C.–after 40 A.D. Daughter of Aristobulus and sister of Herod Agrippa I; m. her uncle Herod Philip, whom she left to marry his brother Herod Antipas as second wife; mother of Salome (*Matt.* xiv. 3–12; *Mark* vi. 17–29). See HEROD.

**He·rod′o·tus** (hē·rŏd′ō·tŭs). Greek historian of 5th century B.C., b. Halicarnassus, Asia Minor. During course of his studies, traveled over most of known world of his time; lived for a while in Samos, later in Athens, and finally settled as a colonist in Thurii in Italy. His great work is a history of Greco-Persian wars from 500 to 479 B.C. His systematic treatment and mastery of style have gained for him the title "Father of History."

**Hé′ro′ët′** (ā′rô′ĕ′), **Antoine.** *Called* **la Mai′son′neuve′** (mā′zô′nûv′). d. 1568. French ecclesiastic and poet.

**He′rold′** (ā′rôld′), **Louis Joseph Ferdinand.** 1791–1833. French composer; known esp. for his comic operas, including *Les Rosières* (1816), *Le Premier Venu* (1818), *Les Troqueurs* (1819), *Le Muletier* (1823), *Marie* (1826), *L'Illusion* (1829), *Emmeline* (1830). Composed also piano pieces and ballet music. His grandson **André Ferdinand** (1865–1940), lyric and dramatic poet.

**Heron.** See HERO.

**Herondas.** See HERODAS.

**He·roph′i·lus** (hē·rŏf′ĭ·lŭs). fl. 300 B.C. Greek anatomist and surgeon; founder of school of anatomy in Alexandria. One of first to conduct post-mortem examinations, to describe the ventricles of the brain, the liver, the spleen, and genital organs, and to distinguish nerves as sensory or motor in function.

**Hé′roult′** (ā′rōō′), **Paul Louis Toussaint.** 1863–1914. French metallurgist; invented (1886) a process (Héroult process) for producing aluminum by electrolysis of alumina in cryolite (called Hall process in America where it was invented contemporaneously by C. M. Hall); also invented an electric furnace (Héroult furnace) for production of electric steel.

**Herr** (?hĕr), **Herbert Thacker.** 1876–1933. American mechanical engineer, b. Denver, Colo. Associate of George Westinghouse (1907–14); vice-president, Westinghouse Electric and Manufacturing Co. (from 1915). Invented locomotive air-brake equipment, a double-heading device for two or more locomotives, a remote control for marine steam turbines, improvements in turbines and oil and gas engines, etc.

**Herr, John.** 1781–1850. American Mennonite clergyman, b. West Lampeter, Pa.; one of founders of Reformed Mennonite Church (1812).

**Herrada, Juan de.** See Juan de RADA.

**Her·rán′** (ĕr·rän′), **Pedro Alcántara.** 1800–1872. Colombian general and statesman, b. Bogotá. Served in republican army under Sucre in Ecuador, Peru, and Bolivia (1824–26); distinguished himself at Ayacucho (1824); president (1841–45) of New Granada (Colombia).

**Her′re** (hĕr′ĕ), **Paul.** 1876–1962. German historian.

**Her·re′ra** (ĕr·rĕ′rä), **Dionisio.** 1790?–1850. President of Honduras (1824–27) and of Nicaragua (1830–33); retired (1833) to live in El Salvador.

**Herrera, Fernando de.** *Called* **el Di·vi′no** (ĕl dē·vē′nō). 1534?–1597. Spanish poet, b. Seville. Head of Sevillian school of lyric poetry; friend of Cervantes; disciple of Garcilaso de la Vega; known esp. for poems in the Italian style, particularly for his *canciones* and *sonetos;* attempted reform of Spanish poetry along classical lines.

**Herrera, Francisco de.** *Called* **el Vie′jo** (ĕl vyĕ′hō). 1576–1656. Spanish painter, b. Seville; master of Velázquez. One of principal masters of Andalusian school; a founder of national school of Spain. His son **Francisco** (1622–1685), *called* **el Mo′zo** (ĕl mō′sō; -thō), was also a painter; fled to Italy after robbing father of his money; called by the Italians **lo Spa·gnuo′lo de′i Pe′sci** (lō spä·nywô′lō dā′ē pā′shē) because of his success in painting fish; to Seville (1656); one of founders of Seville Academy (1660); to Madrid (1661); court painter to Philip IV; master of royal works under Charles II; notable also as an architect.

**Herrera, José Joaquín.** 1792–1854. Mexican general and political leader; supported Iturbide in revolution (1821); later opposed Iturbide as emperor. Opposed war with U.S. (1846–47) but was second in command under Santa Anna; twice acting president of Mexico (1844, 1844–45); president (1848–51); his attempts to establish more liberal government generally unsuccessful.

**Herrera, Juan de.** 1530–1597. Spanish architect; chief architect to Philip II (1567 ff.); known esp. for his construction (1567–84) of the Escorial, begun (1563) by Juan Bautista de Toledo.

**Herrera y Tor′de·sil′las** (ē tôr′thā·sē′lyäs), **Antonio de.** 1559–1625. Spanish historian, b. at Cuéllar; historiographer of Castile and chronicler of the Indies. Known esp. for his *Historia General de los Hechos de los Castellanos en las Islas y Tierra Firme del Mar Océano* (a history of America from 1492 to 1554; based largely on Las Casas's unpublished history) and *Descripción de las Indias Occidentales* (1601).

**Herreros, Manuel Bretón de los.** See BRETÓN DE LOS HERREROS.

**Her′res·hoff** (hĕr′ĕ·sŏf; -ĕs·hŏf), **James Brown.** 1834–1930. American inventor, b. near Bristol, R.I. Invented sliding seat for rowboats (later used in racing shells), improved process for making nitric and hydrochloric acids, a fin keel for racing yachts. His brother **John Brown** (1841–1915) was a yacht designer; blind from age of fourteen, he organized with another brother, **Nathanael Greene** (1848–1938), the Herreshoff Manufacturing Co. (1878), later famed for designing yachts to defend America's cup in international yacht races (*Vigilant*, 1892; *Defender*, 1895; *Columbia*, 1899, 1901; *Reliance*, 1903; *Resolute*, 1920). Nathanael was superintendent of Herreshoff Manufacturing Co. (1881–1915) and president (1915–24); made the first practicable application of the principle of the fin keel (1891), and was first to propose (1903) the "universal rule" of measurement for the racing of yachts.

**Her′rick** (hĕr′ĭk), **Charles Judson.** 1868–1960. American anatomist; authority on comparative neurology.

**Herrick, Christine,** *nee* **Ter·hune′** (tẽr·hūn′). 1859–1944. Daughter of Edward Payson Terhune. American author; m. James Frederick Herrick (1884; d. 1893). Writer of cookbooks and books on domestic economy.

**Herrick, Francis Hobart.** 1858–1940. American biologist; teacher (from 1888), professor (1891–1929), Western Reserve. Author of *The American Lobster* (1895), *Home Life of Wild Birds* (1902, 1905), *Audubon the Naturalist* (2 vols., 1917), *The American Eagle* (1934), etc.

**Herrick, Myron Timothy.** 1854–1929. American political leader and diplomat, b. Huntington, Ohio; active in aiding in nomination and election of McKinley as president (1896). Governor of Ohio (1903–05). U.S. ambassador to France (1912–14; 1921–29).

**Herrick, Robert.** 1591–1674. English lyric poet; vicar of Dean Prior, in Devonshire (1629–47; 1662–74); ejected for Royalist sympathies (1647); restored (1662). Published his collected verse, *Hesperides, or the Works both Human and Divine of Robert Herrick, Esq.* (1648).

**Herrick, Robert.** 1868–1938. American educator and novelist, b. Cambridge, Mass. Teacher of English, U. of Chicago (1893–1923; professor from 1905). His novels include *The Gospel of Freedom* (1898), *The Web of Life* (1900), *The Common Lot* (1904), *The Master of the Inn* (1908), *Together* (1908), *The Healer* (1911), *One Woman's Life* (1913), *The World Decision* (1916), *Homely Lilla* (1923), *Waste* (1924), *The End of Desire* (1931), *Sometime* (1933), etc.

**Her'ries** (hĕr'ĭs), Baron. See MAXWELL family.

**Herries, John Charles.** 1778–1855. English statesman; chancellor of the exchequer (1827–28); secretary at war, under Peel (1834–35); president, Board of Control, in Lord Derby's first government (1852).

**Her'ring** (hĕr'ĭng), **Augustus Moore.** 1867–1926. American experimenter with heavier-than-air flying machines; failed (1898) to obtain patents for his models. Sued by Wright Brothers (1910) for infringement of patents and defeated in lower courts, but settlement made out of court (1917) by cross-licensing agreement making all patents available on designated terms to all builders, to meet World War emergency.

**Herring, John Frederick.** 1795–1865. English painter, esp. of race horses and sporting subjects.

**Herring, Percy Theodore.** 1872–1967. British physiologist; studied reflex actions in animals and conducted experiments with dogs on which the Schafer (prone-pressure) method of artificial respiration was based.

**Her'ri·ot'** (ĕ'ryō'), **Édouard.** 1872–1957. French statesman, b. Troyes. Mayor of Lyons (1905 ff.). Member of Chamber of Deputies (from 1919), and a leader of the Radical Socialist party; premier of France (1924–25); minister of public instruction (1926–28); again premier (June–Dec., 1932); minister of state (1934–36); president of Chamber of Deputies (1936–40); Nazi prisoner (1940–45); president, National Assembly (from 1946).

**Herr'mann** (hûr'măn), **Alexander.** 1844–1896. Magician, b. Paris, France; to U.S. (1860); naturalized (1876). Author of *Herrmann's Black Art* (1898), *Herrmann's Conjuring for Amateurs* (1901), and *Herrmann's Book of Magic* (1902).

**Her'ron** (hĕr'ŭn), **Francis Jay.** 1837–1902. American army officer; brigadier general (1862); major general (Nov. 29, 1862), youngest major general who served in Civil War. Awarded Medal of Honor.

**Herron, George Davis.** 1862–1925. American Congregational clergyman; joined Socialist party (1899); instrumental with Mrs. E. D. Rand in organizing Rand School of Social Sciences, New York (1906).

**Her'schel** (hûr'shĕl), **Clemens.** 1842–1930. American hydraulic engineer; b. Boston. Inventor of Venturi tube for measuring the flow of water in pipes. Cf. G. B. VENTURI.

**Her'schel** (hûr'shĕl; *Ger.* hĕr'shĕl), Sir **William,** *orig.* **Friedrich Wilhelm.** 1738–1822. English astronomer, b. Hanover, Germany; to England (1757), where he first taught music in Leeds, Halifax, and Bath. Devoted himself to study of mathematics and astronomy; built his own telescope (c. 1773) and with it discovered planet Uranus (Mar. 13, 1781), which he named Georgium Sidus in honor of George III; appointed court astronomer (1782). Discovered (Jan. 11, 1787) two satellites of Uranus (Oberon and Titania), and (Aug. 28, 1789) a sixth satellite of Saturn, and (Sept. 17, 1789) a seventh satellite of Saturn. Regarded as virtual founder of sidereal science; discovered period of rotation of Saturn, existence of motion of binary stars, and new information about Milky Way and constitution of a nebula. Aided in observations by his sister **Caroline Lucretia** (1750–1848), who independently discovered seven comets. Sir William's son Sir **John Frederick William** (1792–1871), also an astronomer, continued Sir William's studies on double stars and nebulae; led expedition to take observations at Cape of Good Hope (1834–38); contributed further to knowledge of Milky Way, brightness and color of stars, variable stars, and Magellanic Clouds; also known for researches in light, sound, and celestial physics; discovered solvent power of sodium hyposulphite on silver salts (important for its use in photography) and was first to apply terms "positive" and "negative" to photographic images. Two of Sir John Frederick's sons, **Alexander Stewart** (1836–1907) and **John** (1837–1921), also achieved renown as astronomers.

**Her'schell** (hûr'shĕl), **Farrer.** 1st Baron **Herschell.** 1837–1899. English jurist, of Polish-Jewish descent; solicitor general (1880); lord chancellor (1886; 1892–95).

**Her'sent'** (ĕr'säɴ'), **Louis.** 1777–1860. French painter, illustrator, and lithographer.

**Her'shey** (hûr'shĭ), **Alfred Day.** 1908– . Amer. biologist, b. Owosso, Mich. Awarded Nobel prize in physiology and medicine (1969) with M. Delbruck and S. Luria for work on genetic structure of viruses.

**Her'shey, Lewis Blaine.** 1893– . American army officer; director, Selective Service System (1941–70).

**Hershey, Milton Snavely.** 1857–1945. Am. industrialist; established chocolate-manufacturing business at Lancaster, Pa. (1893); moved to new site at Hershey, Pa. Founded Hershey Industrial School, an institution for orphan boys (1905).

**Her'sko·vits** (hĕr'skō·vĭts), **Melville Jean.** 1895–1963. American anthropologist, b. Bellefontaine, Ohio; known for studies on the Negro in Africa and America, folklore, primitive economics, etc.

**Her'tel** (hĕr'tĕl), **Albert.** 1843–1912. German landscape painter.

**Her'ter** (hûr'tĕr), **Christian Archibald.** 1865–1910. Am. phys., b. Glenville, Conn. In N.Y. (from 1888); auth.: *Diagnosis of Diseases of the Nervous System* (1892), *Biological Aspects of Human Problems* (1911), etc. His bro. **Albert** (1871–1950), Am. mural painter; also, designer and weaver of artistic tapestries. Albert's son **Christian Archibald** (1895–1966), Am. diplomat; sec. of state (1959–61).

**Her'ter** (hĕr'tĕr), **Ernst.** 1846–1917. German sculptor; executed a statue of Helmholtz, a fountain in memory of Heine, an equestrian statue of Bismarck at Wiesbaden, and of Kaiser William I at Potsdam, etc.

**Hert'ford** (här'fĕrd; härt'-), Earls, countess, and marquises. See family de CLARE; Lady Catherine SEYMOUR; SEYMOUR family.

**Hert'ling** (hĕrt'lĭng), Baron (and since 1914, Count) **Georg von.** 1843–1919. German statesman and philosopher; member of Reichstag (1875–90; 1896–1912); chancellor of Germany (1917–18). Wrote *Naturrecht und Sozialpolitik* (1893), *Recht, Staat und Gesellschaft* (1906).

**Hert'wig** (hĕrt'vĭĸ), **Oskar.** 1849–1922. German embryologist; founder and director (1888–1921), Anatomical Inst., Berlin; showed that fertilization is the fusion of the nuclei of two equivalent cells; investigated malformations of vertebrate embryos, etc. His brother **Richard von Hertwig** (1850–1937), zoologist, was professor, Munich (1885–1924); with Oskar, developed the germ-layer theory; accomplished artificial fertilization of sea urchin's egg with strychnine; investigated sex differentiation in frogs, etc.

**Her'sey** (hûr'sĭ), **John Richard.** 1914– . Amer. author and journalist, b. in China of Amer. parents. Author of *A Bell for Adano* (1944), *Hiroshima* (1946), *The Algiers Motel Incident* (1968), etc.

**Her'ty** (hûr'tĭ), **Charles Holmes.** 1867–1938. American chemist, b. Milledgeville, Ga. Invented a method of turpentine orcharding and a method for determination of oil in cottonseed products; developed a process for producing white paper from young southern pines.

**Hertz** (hĕrts), **Alfred.** 1872–1942. German conductor; at Metropolitan Opera House in New York (1902–15), San Francisco (1915–29).

**Hertz** (hûrts), **Emanuel.** 1870–1940. Lawyer and writer on Abraham Lincoln, b. Butka, Austria; to U.S. (1884). Practiced law in New York (from 1895). Made special study of Lincoln's life; author of *Abraham Lincoln—A New Portrait* (1931); edited *The Hidden Lincoln* (1938) and *Lincoln Talks* (1939). Cf. William H. HERNDON.

**Hertz** (hĕrts), **Gustav.** 1887–1975. German physicist. Nephew of Heinrich Rudolph Hertz. Director, Physical Inst., Berlin Technische Hochschule (from 1928). Known for researches with James Franck on effects of impact of electrons on atoms, their results being in agreement with conclusions of modern atomic theory; awarded, with Franck, 1925 Nobel prize for physics.

**Hertz, Heinrich Rudolph.** 1857–1894. German physicist, b. Hamburg. Professor, Bonn (1889). Investigated Maxwell's electromagnetic theory of light; demonstrated (c. 1886) existence of electric or electromagnetic waves (called also "hertzian waves"), measured their length and velocity, and showed that they could be reflected, refracted, and polarized as light is; studied the discharge of electricity in rarefied gases. His discoveries led to the development of wireless telegraphy.

**Hertz** (hĕrts), **Henrik.** *Real surname* **Hey'mann** (hī'män). 1797–1870. Danish writer; author of lyrics, didactic poetry, and many plays.

**Hertz** (hûrts), **Joseph Herman.** 1872–1946. Rabbi, b. in Czechoslovakia; to U.S. in childhood. Educ., C.C.N.Y. and Columbia U. Rabbi in Johannesburg, South Africa (1898–1911); expelled temporarily during Boer War because of his pro-British sympathies. Chosen chief rabbi of the United Hebrew Congregations of the British Empire, succeeding Hermann Adler (1913).

**Hertz** (hĕrts), **Wilhelm.** 1835–1902. German poet; published *Gedichte* (1859), and adaptations of works of Middle High German poets.

**Hertz'berg** (hĕrts'bĕrk), Count **Ewald Friedrich von.** 1725–1795. Prussian statesman; prominent as publicist and diplomat during the Seven Years' War (1756–63); negotiated treaty of Hubertusburg (1763), and became cabinet minister and adviser to Frederick the Great. Continued as minister to Frederick William II (1786–91), but because of conflicting views was dismissed (1791).

**Hertzen.** See HERZEN.

**Hertz'ka** (hĕrts'kä), **Theodor.** 1845–1924. Hungarian-born Austrian economist and agrarian reformer.

**Hertz'ler** (hûrts'lĕr), **Arthur Emanuel.** 1870–1946. American surgeon and writer, b. West Point, Iowa. Investigated diseases of the peritoneum and the thyroid gland. In addition to many professional books, wrote the popular *The Horse and Buggy Doctor* (1938), *The Doctor and his Patients* (1940).

**Her'tzog** (hĕr'tsŏk), **James Barry Mun'nik** (*Du.* mûn'ŭk). 1866–1942. South African soldier and statesman, b. in Wellington, Cape Colony. A Boer general in the Boer War (1899–1902); voted against peace at Vereeniging (1902) and encouraged hostility to the British. Attorney general and minister of education, Orange River Colony (1907–10); minister of justice, Union of South Africa (1910–12). Organized party (Nationalist party) demanding complete independence from Great Britain (1913); opposed Botha-Smuts policy of South African development within the British Empire (1913–24). Prime minister of South Africa (1924–39); advocated separate peace with Germany (1939) and was forced out of office (Sept., 1939).

**Her·vás' y Pan·du'ro** (ĕr·väs' ē pän·dōō'rō), **Lorenzo.** 1735–1809. Spanish Jesuit priest and philologist. To America as missionary; to Rome (1767) on expulsion of Jesuits from Spanish America; prefect of Quirinal library (c. 1804 ff.). Works, in Spanish and Italian, include *Idea del Universo* (treatise on cosmography, 21 vols., 1778–87), *Catálogo de las Naciones Conocidas* (study in comparative philology, 6 vols., 1800–05), and *Storia della Vita dell'Uomo* (first attempt at scientific anthropology).

**Her'vé'** (ĕr'vā'). *Professional name of* **Florimond Ron'gé'** *or* **Ron'ger'** (rôN'zhā'). 1825–1892. French composer, organist, and orchestra leader; founded a theater for presentation of his own operettas, including *Fifi et Nini*, *Femme à Vendre*, etc.; achieved success with the light operas *L'Oeuil Crevé*, *Le Petit Faust*. Regarded as originator of opéra bouffe.

**Hervé, Aimé Marie Édouard.** *Pseudonym* **Raoul Val'nay'** (vȧl'nā'). 1835–1899. French journalist; founded *Le Soleil* (1873), a journal supporting principle of constitutional monarchy in France, and the authorized organ of Orleanist party (after 1879).

**Hervé, Gustave.** 1871–1944. French journalist; founded (1908) Socialist journal *La Guerre Sociale;* left Socialist party after outbreak of World War I, changed name of journal to *La Victoire*, supported Clemenceau.

**Her'vey** (här'vĭ; hûr'vĭ), **Augustus John.** 3d Earl of **Bris'tol** [brĭs't'l] (2d creation). 1724–1779. English naval officer. Served under Byng in Mediterranean, Hawke in Channel, Keppel and Rodney; M.P. (1757–75); a lord of the admiralty (1771–75); vice-admiral (1778). His brother **Frederick Augustus** (1730–1803), 4th earl, as bishop of Derry (1768–1803) advocated relaxation of Catholic penal laws and abolition of clerical tithe system; took part in Irish Volunteer movement.

**Her'vey** (hûr'vĭ), **Harry Clay.** 1900–1951. American explorer and writer, b. Beaumont, Tex.; on trip into upper Indo-China (1925), discovered additional Khmer ruins. Author of *Caravans by Night* (1922), *Where Strange Gods Call* (1924), *Travels in French Indo-China* (1933), and motion pictures, short stories, etc.

**Her'vey** (här'vĭ; hûr'-), **James.** 1714–1758. English clergyman and devotional writer.

**Hervey, John.** Baron **Hervey of Ick'worth** (ĭk'wûrth; -wĕrth). 1696–1743. English politician and writer; lord privy seal (1740–42). Author of *Memoirs of the Reign of George II.* Attacked by Pope as "Lord Fan'ny" [făn'ĭ](1733) because of his effeminate habits, and as "Spo'rus" (spō'rŭs) in *Epistle to Arbuthnot.*

**Hervey, Thomas Kibble.** 1799–1859. Scottish poet and editor; editor, the *Athenaeum* (1846–53). Chief poetical work, *Australia.*

**Her'vey' de Saint'-De·nys'** (ĕr'vā' dĕ săN'dĕ·nē'), Marquis **Marie Jean Léon d'.** 1823–1892. French Sinologue.

**Her'vieu'** (ĕr'vyû'), **Paul Ernest.** *Pseudonym* **É'lia'cin'** (ā'lyȧ'săN'). 1857–1915. French novelist and playwright. Among his novels are *L'Inconnu* (1886), *Flirt* (1890), *Peints par Eux-Mêmes* (1893), *Amitié* (1900); among his plays, *Les Paroles Restent* (1892), *Les Tenailles*

(1895), *La Loi de l'Homme* (1897), *La Course du Flambeau* (1901), *L'Énigme* (1901), *Le Dédale* (1903), *Le Réveil* (1909), *Connais-toi* (1909), *Bagatelle* (1912), etc.

**Her'vil'ly'** (ĕr'vē'yē'), **Ernest Marie d'.** 1839–1911. French writer of verse, fiction, and plays.

**Her'warth von Bit'ten·feld** (hĕr'värt fōn bĭt'ĕn-fĕlt), **Karl Eberhard.** 1796–1884. German soldier; commanded army of the Elbe in Austro-Prussian War (1866), invading Saxony and Bohemia and forming the right wing of the Prussian army at Königgrätz (1866).

**Her'wer'den** (hĕr'vĕr'dĕn), **Henricus van.** 1831–1910. Dutch classical scholar.

**Herz** (ĕrts), **Henri.** 1803–1888. Austrian-born pianist, composer, and piano manufacturer in Paris.

**Herz** (hĕrts), **Marcus.** 1747–1803. Jewish physician and philosopher in Berlin; friend of Kant and Moses Mendelssohn. His wife, **Henriette,** *nee* **de Le'mos** [dā lā'mōs] (1764–1847), was a famous beauty and society leader; adopted the Christian faith (1817).

**Herz'berg** (hûrts'bûrg), **Gerhard.** 1904– . Canadian (Ger.-born) physicist. Awarded Nobel prize in chemistry (1971) for work on the composition of molecules.

**Her'zen** *or* **Her'tzen** (hĕr'tsĕn), *Russ.* **Ger'tsen** (gār'tsĭn), **Aleksandr Ivanovich.** *Real surname* **Ya'ko·vlev** (yȧ'kô·vlyĕf). *Pseudonym* **I·skan·der'** (ĭ·skŭn-dyār'). 1812–1870. Russian writer and political agitator; left Russia (1847) and lived chiefly in Paris and London; author of the novel *Who is to Blame?* (1847), a collection of short stories, and his memoirs *My Past and My Thoughts* (1852–55).

**Herzl** (hĕr'ts'l), **Theodor.** 1860–1904. Hungarian-born Austrian Jewish writer; founder of Zionism. On staff of *Neue Freie Presse,* Vienna (1891–95), and its literary editor (from 1896). Wrote *Der Judenstaat* (1896), advocating founding of a Jewish state in Palestine; leader of Zionist movement.

**Her'zog** (hĕr'tsōĸ), **Eduard.** 1841–1924. Swiss Old Catholic prelate; first bishop of the Old Catholic Church in Switzerland (1876).

**Her'zog'** (ĕr'zôg'), **Émile Salomon Wilhelm.** See André Maurois.

**Her'zog** (*Eng.* hûr'tsŏg), **Isaac.** 1888–1959. Rabbi, b. Łomża, Poland. Chief rabbi, Dublin (1919); chief rabbi, Irish Free State (1925–36); chief rabbi, Palestine (from 1936).

**Her'zog** (hĕr'tsōĸ), **Johann Jakob.** 1805–1882. German Protestant theologian; founder and editor, *Realenzyklopädie für Protestantische Theologie und Kirche* (1854–66; Am. edition by Philip Schaff,1882–84; known as *The Schaff-Herzog Encyclopedia of Religious Knowledge*).

**Herzog, Rudolf.** 1869–1943. German writer of novels, plays, verse, and histories.

**Her'zo'gen·berg'** (hĕr'tsō'gĕn·bĕrĸ'), **Heinrich von.** 1843–1900. Austrian composer.

**He·se'ki·el** (hā·zā'kē·ĕl), **George Ludwig.** 1819–1874. German writer, esp. of poetry and historical novels. His daughter **Ludovica** (1847–1889) was also a writer; m. Wilhelm Johnsen (1887); wrote biog. sketches.

**Heseltine, Philip Arnold.** *Pseudonym* **Peter War'lock** (wôr'lŏk). 1894–1930. English composer and writer on music; edited old English airs and wrote *The English Ayre,* and many songs.

**He'sil·rige** (hā'z'l·rĭg) *or* **Ha'sel·rig** (hā'z'l·rĭg), Sir **Arthur.** d. 1661. English Parliamentarian soldier and politician. One of Five Members of Parliament impeached by Charles I (1642). Engaged at Edge Hill (1642), Lansdown and Roundway Down (1643), Cheriton (1644); accompanied Cromwell to Scotland (1648) and commanded his reserve army. Opposed Cromwell's government after dissolution of Long Parliament (1653), and intrigued with army leaders against Richard Cromwell (1658). Arrested at Restoration.

**He'si·od** (hē'sĭ·ŏd; hĕs'ĭ-). Greek poet of 8th century B.C.; known as "father of Greek didactic poetry." His poem *Works and Days* includes experiences of his daily life and work in the field, intermingled with precepts, fables, allegories; his poem *Theogony* is an account of the beginnings of the world and birth of the gods.

**Hess** (hĕs). Name of a family of German artists, including: **Karl Ernst Christoph** (1755–1828), an engraver, and his three sons, **Peter von** (1792–1871), a painter of battle pictures and genre scenes, **Heinrich von** (1798–1863), historical painter, and **Karl von** (1801–1874), painter.

**Hess,** Baron **Heinrich Hermann Josef von.** 1788–1870. Austrian soldier; chief of staff to General Radetzky in Italian campaign (1848); chief of staff to the emperor (1849); commanded Austrian army in the Crimea (1854–56); served in Italy (1859); field marshal (1860).

**Hess, Ludwig.** 1877–1944. German conductor, and composer of symphonies, choral works, chamber music, and songs.

**Hess, Moses.** 1812–1875. German Jewish Socialist; editor, with F. Engels, of *Gesellschaftsspiegel* (1845–46). After revolution (1848), broke with Marx and Engels, and became a zealous follower of Lassalle, in Paris. Known also as a champion of Zionism.

**Hess,** Dame **Myra.** 1890–1965. English pianist.

**Hess, Rudolf,** *in full* **Walther Richard Rudolf.** 1894– . German politician, b. Alexandria, Egypt. Joined Hitler political group (1921); became secretary and bodyguard to Hitler (1925); took down *Mein Kampf* from Hitler's dictation. Designated by Hitler as head of political section of National Socialist party (Dec. 9, 1932); admitted by Hitler into newly formed Cabinet Council (Feb. 4, 1934). Named by Hitler (1939) third deputy (Stellvertreter) of the Führer, second only to Göring in line of succession. Solo flight (1941) to Scotland; held as prisoner of war; sentenced (1946) as war criminal to life imprisonment.

**Hess, Victor Franz.** 1883–1964. Austrian physicist; director of research, U.S. Radium Corp. (1921–23); consultant, U.S. Bureau of Mines (1922–25); professor, Graz (1925–31, 1937–38), Innsbruck (1931–37); research associate, Carnegie Inst. of Washington (from 1940). Pioneer investigator of cosmic rays; shared with Carl D. Anderson the 1936 Nobel prize for physics.

**Hess, Walter Rudolf.** 1881– . Swiss physiologist. At U. of Zürich (1917–51); awarded Nobel prize in physiology and medicine (1949) with E. Moniz.

**Hess, Willy.** 1859–1939. German violin virtuoso; concertmeister, Manchester, Eng. (1888–95), Cologne (1895–1903), Boston, Mass. (1904–10), Berlin (1910).

**Hesse** (hĕs). *Ger.* **Hes'sen** (hĕs'ĕn). A German landgraviate, later grand duchy, in Prussia, and its ruling house, which originated with Sophia (d. 1284), niece of Henry Raspe, and her son and successor, Henry I the Child (1263–1308). House has various branches; Landgrave William II (1468–1509) in control of all Hessian territories, including Homburg (see Hesse-Homburg); his son Philip the Magnanimous (*q.v.*) divided his lands among four sons; lands later consolidated in two parts: see Hesse-Cassel and Hesse-Darmstadt.

**Hes'se** (hĕs'ĕ), **Hermann.** 1877–1962. German author, b. Calw, Swabia; to Switzerland (1919); among his novels are *Peter Camenzind* (1904), *Narziss und Goldmund* (1930), and *Das Glasperlenspiel* (1943); awarded 1946 Nobel prize for literature.

**Hesse, Ludwig Otto.** 1811–1874. German mathematician; known for contributions to analytic geometry, the theory of determinants, and the theory of invariants.

**Hesse′-Cas′sel** (hĕs′kăs′'l). *Ger.* **Hes′sen-Kas′sel** (hĕs′ĕn·käs′ĕl). Elder line of the house of Hesse (*q.v.*), founded (1567) by William IV the Wise (landgrave 1567–92), eldest son of Philip the Magnanimous; made an electorate (1803); incorporated with Prussia (1866). Rulers were: *Landgraves:* Maurice (1592–1627), William V (1627–37), William VI (1637–63), William VII (1663–70), Charles I (1670–1730), Frederick I (1730–51; also king of Sweden, 1720–51), William VIII (1751–60), Frederick II (1760–85; who sent Hessian troops as mercenaries to fight with British against American Revolutionists), William IX (1785–1803); *Electors:* William IX, as William I (1803–21), William II (1821–47), Frederick William (1847–66; last ruler; deposed). See also HESSE-DARMSTADT.

**Hesse′-Darm′stadt** (-därm′stăt). *Ger.* **Hes′sen-Darm′stadt** (hĕs′ĕn·därm′shtät). Younger line of the house of Hesse (*q.v.*), founded (1567) by George I (landgrave 1567–96), fourth son of Philip the Magnanimous; made a grand duchy (1806); forced to yield territory to Prussia (1866); became part of new German Empire (1871), since which time generally known as Hesse. Chief rulers were: *Landgraves:* Louis V (1596–1626), George II (1626–61), Louis VI (1661–78), Ernest Louis (1678–1739), Louis VIII (1739–68), Louis IX (1768–90), Louis X (1790–1806); *Grand Dukes:* Louis X as Louis I (1806–30), Louis II (1830–48), Louis III (1848–77), Louis IV (1877–92), Louis Ernest (1892–abdicated 1918). See also HESSE-CASSEL.

**Hesse′-Hom′burg** (-hŏm′bûrg). *Ger.* **Hes′sen-Hom′burg** (hĕs′ĕn·hôm′bōōrk). A German landgraviate, comprising two small districts on either side of the Rhine, a part of Hesse-Darmstadt (1567–1622); transferred (1622) to Frederick I, a younger son of George I, landgrave of Hesse-Darmstadt; one of its chief rulers was Frederick II, "Prince of Homburg"; became completely separate (1768); status changed several times (1768–1866); at last (1866) became part of Prussia; last ruler, Ferdinand (1848–66).

**Hes·se′li·us** (hĕ·sē′lĭ·ŭs; -sĕl′yŭs; *Swed.* hĕ·sā′lĭ·ŭs′), **Gustavus.** 1682–1755. Portrait painter and organ builder, b. in Sweden; to America (1711); lived in Delaware, Maryland, and Philadelphia. His son **John** (1728–1778) was also a portrait painter.

**Hes′se-War′tegg** (hĕs′ĕ·vär′tĕk), **Ernst von.** 1851–1918. Austrian traveler and writer of books of travel; m. (1881) Minnie Hauk (*q.v.*).

**Hes′sus** (hĕs′ŭs; *Ger.* hĕs′ōōs), **He′li·us** (hē′lĭ·ŭs; *Ger.* hā′lē·ōōs) **E′o·ba′nus** (ē′ō·bā′nŭs; *Ger.* ā′ō·bä′nōōs). *Real surname* **Koch** (kôk). 1488–1540. German humanist and Neo-Latin poet, b. in Hesse. Took part in political, religious, and literary quarrels of his day and favored Luther and the Reformation. Author of the poetry collection *Sylvae*, of pastoral poems, as *Bucolicon* (1509), of *Heroides Christianae* in imitation of Ovid (1514), of translations into Latin of the Psalms (1538) and the *Iliad* (1540); also, one of authors of the *Epistolae Obscurorum Virorum*.

**He·sych′i·us** (hē·sĭk′ĭ·ŭs). Greek grammarian of Alexandria in 4th century A.D. (or later); compiled Greek lexicon of unusual words, forms, and phrases. His lexicon was derived from a similar, but larger, work by Diogenianus, which in turn was derived from the dictionary (in 95 books) compiled by Pamphilus and Zopyrion (*qq.v.*).

**Hesychius** the Illustrious. Greek historian and biographer, of Miletus in Asia Minor, in 5th century A.D.

**Heth** (hēth), **Henry.** 1825–1899. American Confederate officer, b. in Chesterfield County, Va. Major general (1863); his troops unexpectedly engaged federals at Gettysburg and brought on the three days' struggle.

**Hett′ner** (hĕt′nĕr), **Hermann.** 1821–1882. German historian of art and literature. His son **Alfred** (1859–1941), geographer, conducted exploring expeditions to the Andes Mountains (1882–84; 1888–90) and to East Asia and India (1913–14). Another son, **Otto** (1875–1931), painter, designer, and sculptor; identified with the ultramodern school.

**Het′zel′** (ĕt′sĕl′), **Pierre Jules.** *Pseudonym* **P. J. Stahl** (stål). 1814–1886. French publisher; established publishing house in Paris (1862), specializing in literature for young people; published books of Jules Verne. Author of books for children.

**Het′zer** *or* **Hät′zer** *or* **Haet′zer** (hĕt′sĕr), **Ludwig.** d. 1529. Swiss leader of iconoclasts and Anabaptists; with collaboration of Johannes Denk, translated into German the Hebrew prophets, first Protestant version of the prophets in German. Imprisoned for heresy (1528); beheaded (Feb. 4, 1529).

**Heu′ber′ger** (hoi′bĕr′gĕr), **Richard.** 1850–1914. Austrian composer of operas, operettas, ballets, two orchestral suites, a symphony, choral works, and songs.

**Heug′lin** (hoik′lĭn), **Theodor von.** 1824–1876. German traveler in northeast Africa (1850–65) and in Spitsbergen and Novaya Zemlya (1870–71); wrote on his travels and on ornithology.

**Heu′mann von Teut′schen·brunn** (hoi′män fôn toi′chĕn·brōōn), **Johann.** 1711–1760. German jurist and historian; a joint founder of the science of diplomatics.

**Heu′reaux′** (û′rō′), **U·li′ses** (*Span.* ōō·lē′sās) *or* **U′lysse′** (*Fr.* ü′lēs′). 1846?–1899. Mulatto politician and dictator of the Dominican Republic; president (1882–83 and 1887–99) and in power during intervening period (1883–87); assassinated.

**Heus′ler** (hois′lĕr), **Andreas.** 1865–1940. German scholar, b. in Switzerland; specialist in ancient Germanic literature.

**Heussgen, Johannes.** See OECOLAMPADIUS.

**Heus′si** (hoi′sē), **Karl.** 1877–1961. German Protestant theologian.

**He·ve′li·us** (hē·vā′lē·ōōs), **Johannes.** *Orig. surname* **He′wel** (hā′vĕl) *or* **He′wel[c]·ke** (hā′vĕl·kĕ) *or* **Hö′wel[c]·ke** (hû′vĕl·kĕ). 1611–1687. Astronomer, b. Danzig. Built observatory in his residence (1641) and constructed the instruments for it; charted the lunar surface, catalogued many stars, observed sunspots, discovered four comets; one of first to observe transit of Mercury; studied phases of Saturn.

**He′ve·si** (hĕ′vĕ·shĭ), **Ludwig.** *Pseudonym* **On′kel Tom** (ŏng′kĕl tōm′). 1843–1910. Hungarian-born Austrian journalist and humorist. On staff of *Pester Lloyd*, Vienna (1866); art and dramatic critic, *Fremdenblatt*, Vienna (1875).

**He′ve·sy** (hĕ′vĕ·shĭ), **George de.** 1885–1966. Hungarian chemist. Codiscoverer (with the Danish physicist D. Coster) of the element hafnium (1922); worked on the separation of isotopes as indicators in chemistry and biology, etc. Awarded 1943 Nobel prize for chemistry.

**Hew′art** (hū′ĕrt), **Gordon.** 1st Baron **Hewart.** 1870–1943. English jurist. M.P. (1913–22); solicitor general (1916–19) and attorney general (1919–22). Lord chief justice of England (1922–40).

**Hewel** *or* **Hewel[c]ke, Johannes.** See HEVELIUS.

**Hewes** (hūz), **Joseph.** 1730–1779. American Revolutionary leader, b. Kingston, N.J. Member, Continental Congress (1774–77; 1779); signer of Declaration of Independence.

**Hew′ett** (hū′ĕt; -ĭt), **Edgar Lee. 1865–1946.** American archaeologist; engaged in research study in Italy, Greece, Palestine, Egypt, and Mexico (1903–08), and in extensive archaeological exploration and excavation in Colorado, Utah, Arizona, New Mexico, and California, as well as in Central America, Peru and Bolivia; directed excavation of ancient Mayan city of Quiriguá.

**Hew′ish** (hū′ĭsh), **Antony.** 1924– . British astronomer. At Cambridge U. (1952– ); awarded (with Sir Martin Ryle) Nobel prize for physics (1974).

**Hew′it** (hū′ĭt), **Augustine Francis,** *orig.* **Nathaniel Augustus.** 1820–1897. American clergyman; converted to Roman Catholicism (1846); ordained priest (1847), taking name Augustine Francis; joined Redemptorists (1849); assisted Isaac Hecker (*q.v.*) in organizing (1858) the Congregation of the Missionary Priests of St. Paul the Apostle (Paulist Fathers) and succeeded him (1888) as its superior.

**Hew′itt** (hū′ĭt), **Abram Stevens.** 1822–1903. American industrialist and political leader; adm. to bar (1845). With Edward Cooper (*q.v.*) opened iron-manufacturing business, Cooper and Hewitt; introduced first American open-hearth furnace (1862) and made first American-made steel (1870). Active in establishment and management of Cooper Union; aided in overthrowing Tweed Ring. Member, U.S. House of Representatives (1875–79; 1881–86). Mayor of New York (1887–88). His son **Peter Cooper** (1861–1921) was an electrical engineer; invented a mercury-vapor electric lamp and a mercury-vapor rectifier; discovered fundamental principle of vacuum-tube amplifier (used in radio); experimented with hydro-airplanes and helicopters.

**Hewitt, Henry Kent.** 1887–1972. American naval officer, b. Hackensack, N.J.; educ. U.S.N.A., Annapolis (1903–06), entered navy (1908); commander, cruiser division, U.S. fleet; in command of American naval forces supporting North African operations (1942).

**Hewitt, James.** 1770–1827. Violinist and composer, b. Dartmoor, England; to U.S. (1792). His son **John Hill** (1801–1890) was author and composer of many popular ballads, including *The Minstrel's Return from the War*, *Rock Me to Sleep, Mother*, and *Carry Me Back to the Sweet Sunny South.*

**Hewlett, Maurice Henry.** 1861–1923. English essayist, novelist, and poet. Among his many books are *Songs and Meditations* (1897), *The Forest Lovers* (1898), *Little Novels of Italy* (1899), *Richard Yea-and-Nay* (1900), *New Canterbury Tales* (1901), *The Queen's Quair* (1904), *The Fool Errant* (1905), *Rest Harrow* (1910), *Mrs. Lancelot* (1912), *A Lovers' Tale* (1915), *The Song of the Plow* (1916), *Wiltshire Essays* (1922).

**Hext, Harrington.** Pseudonym of Eden PHILLPOTTS.

**Hey′de·brand und der La′sa** (hī′dĕ·bränt ŏŏnt dĕr lä′zä), **Ernst von.** 1851–1924. German jurist and politician; leader of Conservative party.

**Hey′den** (hī′dĕn), **Friedrich von.** 1789–1851. German writer; author of plays, narrative poetry, novels, etc. His son **August** (1827–1897) was a historical painter. August's son **Hubert** (1860–1911) was a painter and designer, identified with the ultramodern school.

**Hey′den** (hī′dĕn), **Jan van der.** 1637–1712. Dutch painter, esp. of streets, city squares, and buildings in Amsterdam.

**Hey′drich** (hī′drĭĸ), **Reinhard.** *Known as* **der Hen′ker** (dĕr hĕng′kĕr), *i.e.* the hangman. 1904–1942. Deputy chief of the Gestapo; Reich "protector" in Czechoslovakia (from Sept., 1941); in reprisal for his assassination, the Nazis demolished the village of Lidice, Czechoslovakia, and executed the male population, only one man reported to have escaped.

**Hey′duk** (hĕ′ĭ·dŏŏk), **Adolf.** 1835–1923. Czech author of lyric, narrative, and allegorical verse.

**Hey′e** (hī′ĕ), **Wilhelm.** 1869–1946. German general. On general staff during World War I; succeeded von Seeckt as commander of Reichswehr (1926–30); a Stahlhelm leader, and advocate of German rearmament.

**Hey′er** (hā′ĕr; hâr), **Georgette.** 1902–1974. English novelist; m. George Ronald Rougier (1925). Among her novels are *The Black Moth, Devil's Cub, Regency Buck, Royal Escape, No Wind of Blame.*

**Hey′lyn** *or* **Hey′lin** (hā′lĭn; hī′-), **Peter.** 1600–1662. English clergyman and church historian; Royalist during Civil War. Chief work, *Ecclesia Restaurata: the History of the Reformation of the Church of England* (1661).

**Hey′mann** (hī′män). See Henrik HERTZ.

**Hey′mann** (hī′män), **Ernst.** 1870–1946. German jurist.

**Hey′mans** (hī′mäns), **Corneille.** 1892–1968. Belgian physiologist; professor of pharmacodynamics, U. of Ghent; awarded 1938 Nobel prize in physiology and medicine for detection of importance of the sinus aorta mechanism in breathing.

**Heymans, Gerardus.** 1857–1930. Dutch philosopher and psychologist.

**Heymans, Jozef.** 1839–1921. Belgian painter.

**Heyn** *or* **Heijn** (hīn), **Piet,** *in full* **Pieter Pieterszoon.** 1578–1629. Dutch admiral; captured Spanish treasure fleet (1628).

**Hey′ne** (hī′nĕ), **Christian Gottlob.** 1729–1812. German classical philologist.

**Heyne, Moriz.** 1837–1906. German scholar; published editions and translations of Anglo-Saxon classics (*Beowulf*, etc.); collaborated on Grimm's *Deutsches Wörterbuch* and compiled a *Deutsches Wörterbuch* himself (3 vols., 1890–95).

**Heyn′lin** (hīn′lĭn), **Johann.** *Also known as* **Jean de la Pierre** (dē lȧ pyâr). *Lat.* **Joannes a Lap′i·de** (ā lăp′ĭ·dē) *or* **Lap′i·da′nus** (lăp′ĭ·dā′nŭs). d. 1496. Theologian and humanist, b. perhaps in Switzerland; to Paris (c. 1460); established (with Fichet) first printing press in France (in Paris, c. 1470); professor of theology, Tübingen (1478). See Ulrich GERING.

**Hey′rov′sky** (hā′rôf·skĭ), **Jaroslav.** 1890–1967. Czechoslovakian physical chemist. Awarded Nobel prize in chemistry (1959) for his discovery and development of polarographic analysis.

**Hey′se** (hī′zĕ), **Johann Christian August.** 1764–1829. German philologist and educator. His son **Carl Wilhelm Ludwig** (1797–1855) was a philologist. Carl's son **Paul von Heyse** (1830–1914; ennobled 1910) was a novelist, playwright, and poet; author of *Gesammelte Novellen in Versen* (1864), *Dramatische Dichtungen* (38 vols., 1864–1905), *Meraner Novellen* (1867), *Deutscher Novellenschatz* (24 vols., 1870–76), *Novellen vom Gardasee* (1902), etc.; awarded Nobel prize for literature (1910).

**Hey′ward** (hā′wĕrd), **DuBose′** (dŭ·bōz′). 1885–1940. American author, b. Charleston, S.C. As a boy, gained firsthand knowledge of Charleston water-front life, later used in his books; devoted himself to writing (from c. 1919). Author of *Skylines and Horizons* (verse; 1924), the novels *Porgy* (1925), *Angel* (1926), *Mamba's Daughters* (1929), *Peter Ashley* (1932), *Lost Morning* (1936), the play *Brass Ankle* (prod. 1931), etc. *Porgy* later became the basis for the operatic work *Porgy and Bess* by George Gershwin. His wife (m. 1923), **Dorothy Hartzell,** *nee* **Kuhns** [kōōnz] (1890–1961), wrote the play *Nancy Ann* (1924) and the novels *Three-a-Day* (1930) and *The Pulitzer Prize Murders* (1932).

**Heyward, Thomas.** 1746–1809. American political leader, b. in St. Luke's Parish, S.C. Member, Council of Safety (1775, 1776) and Continental Congress (1776–78); signer of Declaration of Independence. Served in Revolutionary War. Judge, circuit court (1779–89).

**Hey′wood** (hā′wŏŏd), **John.** 1497?–?1580. English epigrammatist. A favorite with Queen Mary; retired to

Malines at accession of Elizabeth (1558); nothing known of his subsequent career. Wrote interludes, including *The Four P's*, *The Play of the Wether*, *The Play of Love*, which in the personal representation of characters were the predecessors of English comedy. Wrote also *Dialogue on Wit and Folly*, proverbs, epigrams, ballads, etc. His son **Jasper** (1535–1598) entered the Jesuit order (1562); superior of English Jesuit mission (1581–85); deported to France (1585); died in Naples.

**Heywood, Thomas.** 1574?–1641. English playwright and miscellaneous writer, b. in Lincolnshire. Actor on London stage; member of Queen's company (1619). His plays include *The Four Prentices of London* (c. 1600), *Edward IV* (2 parts; 1600, 1605), *A Woman Killed with Kindness* (1603), *The Rape of Lucrece* (1608), *The Royal King and the Loyal Subject* (1637), *The Wise Woman of Hogsdon* (1638). Also wrote *An Apology for Actors* (1612), and verse, including *Hierarchy of the Blessed Angels* (1635).

**Hez'e·ki'ah** (hĕz'ē·kī'ȧ). *In Douay Bible* **Ez'e·chi'as** (ĕz'ē·kī'ăs). *In A. V. of New Testament* **Ez'e·ki'as** (-kī'ăs). 740?–?692 B.C. King of Judah (720?–?692 B.C.). Son and successor of Ahaz. Waged successful war against Philistines (*2 Kings* xviii. 8), prob. in early part of reign; defied Sennacherib, King of Assyria, who invaded Palestine and defeated him and his allies (c. 700 B.C.); thereafter paid tribute to Sennacherib; his reign marked by prophecy of Isaiah; succeeded by his son Manasseh. See *2 Kings* xviii–xx; *Isaiah* xxxvi–xxxix.

**H. H.** Pen name of Helen Hunt JACKSON.

**Hib'bard** (hĭb'ẽrd), **Aldro Thompson.** 1886– . American landscape painter; founder and instructor, Rockport (Mass.) Summer School of Drawing and Painting.

**Hib'ben** (hĭb'ĕn), **John Grier.** 1861–1933. American educator, b. Peoria, Ill. A.B. (1882), Ph.D. (1893), Princeton. Ordained in Presbyterian ministry; pastor at Chambersburg, Pa. (1887–91). Teacher of logic and psychology (1891–1912), professor (1907–12), president (1912–32), Princeton. Author of *Inductive Logic* (1896), *The Problems of Philosophy* (1898), *Deductive Logic* (1905), *A Defense of Prejudice and Other Essays* (1911).

**Hibben, Paxton Pattison.** 1880–1928. American diplomat and journalist, b. Indianapolis, Ind. In U.S. diplomatic service (1905–12). Journalist in Germany (1914–15), Greece (1915–16). Joined U.S. army (1917); served in France (1918–19). In Armenia (1919) and Russia, on relief work (1921–25); because of sympathy with Russian revolutionaries, was twice investigated by U.S. military tribunal, but exonerated and his army commission renewed. Devoted himself to writing (from 1925).

**Hib'bert** (hĭb'ẽrt), **Robert.** 1770–1849. British merchant and philanthropist, b. in Jamaica; merchant and slaveowner in Jamaica (1791–1836); to England (c. 1836). Created Hibbert trust (1847), originally designed for the elevation of the Unitarian ministry, but widened to include other purposes, and now used to defray costs of Hibbert lectures, the *Hibbert Journal*, etc.

**Hich'ens** (hĭch'ĕnz), **Robert Smythe.** 1864–1950. English novelist; author of *The Green Carnation* (1894), *The Garden of Allah* (1905), *Bella Donna* (1909), *Mrs. Marden* (1919), *Doctor Artz* (1929), *The Paradine Case* (1933), *The Journey Up* (1938), *The Million* (1940), *A New Way of Life* (1942). Collaborated in a number of plays, including *The Medicine Man*, *The Garden of Allah*, etc.

**Hickes** (hĭks), **George.** 1642–1715. English nonjuring clergyman and scholar; dean of Worcester (1683); deprived of his living for refusing to take oath of allegiance to William and Mary (1690); remained in hiding (1690–99); consecrated suffragan bishop (1694).

**Hick'ok** (hĭk'ŏk), **James Butler.** *Known as* **Wild Bill Hickok.** 1837–1876. American scout and U.S. marshal, b. Troy Grove, Ill. Stage driver, first on Santa Fe Trail, later on Oregon Trail; fought McCanles gang, Rock Creek Station, Nebr., killing McCanles and two of his gang (July 12, 1861). Scout in Union army, in Civil War. Deputy U.S. marshal, Fort Riley, Kans. (1866–67); U.S. marshal, Hays City, Kans. (1869–71), and Abilene, Kans. (1871). On tour with Buffalo Bill (1872–73). Murdered in Deadwood, Dakota Territory.

**Hickok, Laurens Perseus.** 1798–1888. American philosopher, b. Bethel, Conn. Congregational clergyman (1823–36); professor of philosophy (1852–66), president (1866–68), Union Coll.

**Hicks** (hĭks), **Elias.** 1748–1830. American Quaker minister, b. Hempstead, Long Island, N.Y. Carpenter by trade; Quaker preacher (from c. 1775); identified with liberal thought; responsible for separations in Quaker communities, conservatives known as "Orthodox" and liberals as "Hicksite" (1828).

**Hicks, Frederick Charles.** 1863–1953. American economist, b. Capac, Mich. President, U. of Cincinnati (1920–29).

**Hicks, John Richard.** 1904– . Economist, b. near Stratford, Eng. Educ. Oxford; taught at London, Cambridge, Manchester, and Oxford universities. Author of *Value and Capital* (1939), etc. Shared 1972 Nobel prize in economics with Kenneth J. Arrow for work on general economic equilibrium theory.

**Hicks,** Sir **Seymour,** *in full* **Edward Seymour.** 1871–1949. English actor, playwright, and manager; comedian in Gaiety company (1893–98). Interested in the Globe, Queen's, and Aldwych theaters in London.

**Hicks, Thomas Holliday.** 1798–1865. American politician; governor of Maryland (1858–62). Delayed calling legislature in session (1860–61), thus preventing radical group from allying State with Confederacy. U.S. senator (1862–65).

**Hicks, William.** *Known as* **Hicks Pa'sha** (pȧ'shä). 1830–1883. British general in Egyptian army, commanding troops sent against the Mahdi (1883); ambuscaded, and killed in action (Nov. 4, 1883).

**Hicks Beach** (hĭks' bēch'), Sir **Michael Edward.** 1st Earl **St. Ald'wyn** (ôld'wĭn). 1837–1916. Educ. Oxford. Conservative M.P. (1864–1906). Colonial secretary (1878–80); chancellor of exchequer and house leader (1885–86); opposed Irish home rule and advocated free trade.

**Hi·dal'go y Cos·til'la** (ē·thäl'gō ē kōs·tē'yä), **Miguel.** 1753–1811. Mexican priest and revolutionist; in attempt to improve condition of natives, proclaimed revolt (Sept. 16, 1810) against Spanish government; seized Guanajuato and Guadalajara, and was joined by Allende and Aldama (*qq.v.*). With army of 80,000 marched on Mexico City (Oct., 1810); won first battle but forced to fall back when defeated by Spanish force under Félix Calleja (Nov. 6, 1810); completely defeated by Calleja (Jan., 1811) near Guadalajara. Fled north; was captured and shot. His campaign the beginning of War for Mexican Independence.

**Hi·da·ri Jin·go·ro** (hē·dä·rē jēn·gō·rō), *i.e.* "Left-handed Jingoro." 1584?–1634. Japanese woodcarver and sculptor. Worked in beginning of Tokugawa shogunate; his exquisite temple carvings still to be seen at Kyoto and Nikko.

**Hi·de·ta·da** (hē·dĕ·tä·dä). 1579–1632. Japanese shogun of the Tokugawas (1616–23). Son of Iyeyasu. Accompanied his father on military campaigns (1600–05); shogun with his father (1605–16), alone (1616–23). Tried to carry out Iyeyasu's policies; continued bitter persecutions of Christians (esp. 1622–23); abdicated in favor of his son Iyemitsu (1622).

**Hi·de·yo·ri** (hē·dĕ·yō·rē). 1592–1615. Japanese child ruler; son of Hideyoshi; nominal ruler (from 1598) under four regents, one of whom was Iyeyasu; perished in Toyotomi Castle at Osaka when it was burned by army of Iyeyasu.

**Hi·de·yo·shi** (hē·dĕ·yō·shē), **Toyotomi**. 1536–1598. Japanese general and statesman; son of poor woodcutter. Became follower of Nobunaga; by his military talents rose in the ranks; created lord of Chikuzen (1575); acknowledged leader on death of Nobunaga (1582). With other generals controlled affairs for Nobunaga's infant grandson (1582–86); made peace with Iyeyasu (1583); completed (1585) great Toyotomi Castle at Osaka. Created by the emperor (1585) regent (*Kwampaku*) or military dictator of Japan; issued edict (1587) against Jesuits, not put into effect for ten years; united all Japan under one rule (1590); nominally retired (1591) from regency taking title of Taiko and selecting his nephew, Hidetsugu, as his heir; still actual ruler until his death; chose Iyeyasu as his successor.

**Hiel** (hēl), **Emanuel**. 1834–1899. Flemish poet; a leader in the revival of Flemish language and literature; best known for cantatas and oratorios.

**Hi·emp'sal** (hī·ĕmp'săl). Name of two kings of Numidia: **Hiempsal I** (d. 117? B.C.), grandson of Masinissa; murdered by Jugurtha. **Hiempsal II**, great-grandson of Masinissa; expelled from his kingdom by Domitius Ahenobarbus; restored by Pompey (81 B.C.).

**Hi'er·a'cas** (hī'ĕr·ā'kăs) *or* **Hi'er·ax** (hī'ĕr·ăks). Egyptian ascetic of 4th century A.D.; denied resurrection of the material body. His followers were called Hieracites.

**Hierax, Antiochus**. See ANTIOCHUS HIERAX.

**Hi'er·o** (hī'ĕr·ō) *or* **Hi'er·on** (hī'ĕr·ŏn). Name of two tyrants (kings) of Syracuse:

**Hiero I.** d. 466 B.C. Tyrant (478–466 B.C.). Brother of Gelon. Distinguished himself at battle of Himera (480); succeeded Gelon; founded city of Aetna (475); won naval victory over Etruscans at Cumae (474); by defeat (472) of Thrasydaeus of Aeragas (modern Agrigento), gained supreme control of Sicily; noted for his patronage of poets and philosophers (Pindar, Aeschylus, Simonides, Bacchylides).

**Hiero II.** 308?–215 B.C. Tyrant (270 or 265?–215). Natural son of Hierocles, a Syracusan noble. Fought under Pyrrhus in Sicilian campaigns (278–275); successful against Mamertines at Messina (270); chosen king (270); aided Carthaginians against Mamertines but defeated by Romans (264); concluded treaty with Romans (263); furnished support to Rome in both First and Second Punic wars. A kinsman of Archimedes (*q.v.*).

**Hi·er'o·cles** (hī·ĕr'ō·klēz). Greek Neoplatonic philosopher of Alexandria in 5th century A.D.

**Hi'er·on'y·mus** (hī'ĕr·ŏn'ĭ·mŭs), Saint **Eusebius**. See Saint JEROME.

**Hieronymus of Car'di·a** (kär'dĭ·ȧ). Greek general and historian. Served under Alexander the Great, Eumenes, Antigonus, and Antigonus Gonatas, successively. Author of a history of the Diadochi down to 272 B.C.

**Hieronymus of Prague.** = JEROME OF PRAGUE.

**Hig'den** *or* **Hig'don** (hĭg'dŭn), **Ranulf**. d. 1364. English Benedictine monk and chronicler; author of *Polychronicon*, a general history (in Latin; trans. into English by John de Trevisa, *q.v.*).

**Hig'gins** (hĭg'ĭnz), **Edward John**. 1864–1947. English Salvation Army leader; chief of staff, in England (1919–29); general, succeeding **W. Bramwell Booth** (1929–34).

**Higgins, Eugene.** 1874–1958. American painter and etcher, b. Kansas City, Mo.

**Higgins, Frederick Robert.** 1896–1941. Irish poet and theater director; joint editor with W. B. Yeats of *Broadsides* (1935); managing director of Abbey Theatre in Dublin (from 1935). His volumes of verse include *Salt Air* (1924), *Island Blood* (1925), *The Dark Breed* (1927), *Arable Holdings* (1933), and *The Gap of Brightness*.

**Higgins, Victor.** 1884–1949. American landscape and figure painter, b. Shelbyville, Ind.

**Hig'gin·son** (hĭg'ĭn·s'n), **Francis**. 1587?–1630. Clergyman, b. in Leicestershire, England. Ordained in Anglican church (1614). Became nonconformist; emigrated to America (1629) and settled at Salem, Mass. Drew up confession of faith and covenant for the church there. His son **John** (1616–1708) was also pastor at Salem (from 1660). John's son **Nathaniel** (1652–1708) was a colonial administrator in India (from 1684), governor of Fort Saint George (1692); lieutenant general of India (1694); replaced as governor (1698) and returned to England (1700). Among the descendants of Francis are Thomas Wentworth and Henry Lee Higginson (see the separate articles).

**Higginson, Henry Lee.** 1834–1919. American banker; with Lee, Higginson & Co., Boston banking firm (from 1868). Founded (1881) and financed (1881–1918) Boston Symphony Orchestra. Benefactor of Harvard, Radcliffe, and other educational institutions.

**Higginson, Thomas Wentworth Storrow.** 1823–1911. American clergyman, army officer, and writer, b. Cambridge, Mass. In Unitarian ministry (1847–61); active in antislavery movement. Served in Civil War; colonel of first Negro regiment in Union army (1862–64). After Civil War, devoted himself to writing; author of a number of biographies, including *Francis Higginson* (1891), *Henry Wadsworth Longfellow* (1902), *John Greenleaf Whittier* (1902).

**Hi·lar'i·on** (hĭ·lâr'ĭ·ŏn), Saint. 290?–371 A.D. Palestinian hermit; educated, and coverted to Christian faith, in Alexandria; lived as hermit in desert near Egyptian border; introduced monasticism into Palestine.

**Hi·lar'i·us** (hĭ·lâr'ĭ·ŭs) *or* **Hil'a·rus** (hĭl'ȧ·rŭs) *or* **Hil'a·ry** (hĭl'ȧ·rĭ), Saint. d. 468. Pope (461–468). Continued vigorous policy of Leo I, esp. in Gaul and Spain.

**Hil'a·ry** (hĭl'ȧ·rĭ), Saint. *Latin* **Hi·lar'i·us** (hĭ·lâr'ĭ·ŭs). d. 367? Christian prelate; one of the Doctors of the Church; bishop of Poitiers (c. 353); vigorously opposed Arianism.

**Hilary**, Saint. *Latin* **Hilarius.** Christian ecclesiastic; bishop of Arles (429–449). Endeavored to establish primacy over church in southern Gaul; deposed bishop of Besançon for claiming metropolitan dignity for his see; Pope Leo I deprived Hilary of his rights as metropolitan (444).

**Hil'bert** (hĭl'bĕrt), **David**. 1862–1943. German mathematician; professor, Göttingen (from 1895); worked on the theory of invariants, on the theory of numbers, and on integral equations; reduced geometry to a system of axioms; worked on the axiomatization of arithmetic. Author of *Grundlagen der Geometrie* (1899), *Methoden der Mathematischen Physik* (with R. Courant; 1924).

**Hil'da** (hĭl'dȧ), *more properly* **Hild** (hĭld), Saint. 614–680. English abbess; abbess of Hartlepool (649); founded monastery of Whitby (657), and ruled it (657–680); known as Abbess of Whitby.

**Hil'de·bert** (hĭl'dĕ·bĕrt; *Fr.* ēl'dĕ·bâr'). 1055–1133. French prelate; bishop of Mans (1096) and archbishop of Tours (1125); engaged in struggle with Louis the Fat, King of France, ended by intervention of a papal legate.

**Hil'de·brand** (hĭl'dĕ·brănd). See Pope GREGORY VII.

**Hil'de·brand** (hĭl'dĕ·bränt). See Nikolaas Beets.

**Hil'de·brand** (hĭl'dĕ·bränt), **Bruno.** 1812–1878. German economist; chief work, *Die Nationalökonomie der Gegenwart und Zukunft* (1848). His son **Adolf von Hildebrand** (1847–1921) was a sculptor; studio in Florence (1874–92); carved portrait busts of Clara Schumann, Ludwig of Bavaria; among his other sculptures are *Adam, Father Rhine,* a monument of Brahms, a portrait relief of Kaiser William II.

**Hildebrand, Theodor.** 1804–1874. German historical painter.

**Hil'de·brandt** (hĭl'dĕ·bränt), **Eduard.** 1818–1868. German landscape painter.

**Hil'de·gard** (hĭl'dĕ·gärd; *Ger.* -gärt), Saint. 1098?–1179. German nun; founder and abbess of convent of Rupertsberg; famed for visions and prophecies.

**Hil'ditch** (hĭl'dĭch), **Jacob.** 1864–1930. Norwegian writer, esp. of sea tales and humorous sketches of folk life.

**Hil'dreth** (hĭl'drĕth; -drĭth), **Richard.** 1807–1865. American historian; best known for his *History of the United States* (6 vols., 1849–52).

**Hil'fer·ding** (hĭl'fĕr·dĭng), **Rudolf.** 1877–1941. German statesman, b. Vienna; naturalized German (c. 1920). Leader of independent social democrats; negotiated their union (1922) with Social Democratic party. Finance minister under Stresemann (1923) and Müller (1928); forced to retire (1929) because of failure to control growing deficit.

**Hill** (hĭl), **Aaron.** 1685–1750. English poet and playwright; wrote words for Handel's *Rinaldo;* author of stage productions *Athelwold, Zara, Merope, Alzira* (the last three being translations of plays by Voltaire); conducted the *Plaindealer* (1724).

**Hill, Adams Sherman.** 1833–1910. American grammarian and educator; author of textbooks in rhetoric.

**Hill, Ambrose Powell.** 1825–1865. American army officer; grad. U.S.M.A., West Point (1847). Entered Confederate service (1861); brigadier general (Feb. 26, 1862); major general (May 26, 1862); lieutenant general (1863); initiated attack that began battle of Gettysburg. Killed in action before Petersburg (Apr. 2, 1865).

**Hill, Archibald Vivian.** 1886– . English physiologist. Educ. Cambridge; professor, Manchester (1920–23), University Coll., London (1923–25), Royal Society (1926–51); secretary of Royal Society (1935–1945). Investigated the liberation of energy in muscles. Shared with Otto Meyerhof the 1922 Nobel prize for physiology and medicine (1923).

**Hill, Benjamin Harvey.** 1823–1882. American political leader, b. in Jasper County, Ga. Signer of secession ordinance (1861); aided in organizing government of Confederacy; senator, Confederate Provisional Congress (1861–65). Member, U.S. House of Representatives (1875–77) and U.S. Senate (1877–82).

**Hill, Daniel Harvey.** 1821–1889. American army officer and educator, b. in York District, S.C.; grad. U.S.M.A., West Point (1842). Entered Confederate service; brigadier general (1861); major general (1862); lieutenant general (1863). President, U. of Arkansas (1877–84) and Georgia Military College (1885–89).

**Hill, David Bennett.** 1843–1910. American politician, b. Havana, N.Y. Adm. to bar (1864); practiced, Elmira, N.Y. Joined Tilden in exposing Tweed Ring (1871). Governor of New York (1885–91); U.S. senator (1892–97).

**Hill, David Jayne.** 1850–1932. American historian and diplomat, b. Plainfield, N.J. President, Bucknell (1879–88), U. of Rochester (1888–96). Professor of European diplomacy in School of Comparative Jurisprudence and Diplomacy, Washington, D.C. (1899–1903), and assistant secretary of state (1898–1903). U.S. minister to Switzerland (1903–05), the Netherlands (1905–08), and Germany (1908–11). Author of biographies, and books on political science and diplomacy.

**Hill, David Octavius.** 1802–1870. Scottish painter and photographer; first to apply photography to portraiture, using the calotype process.

**Hill, Edward Burlingame.** 1872–1960. American musician and composer. Professor of music, Harvard (from 1928). Author of choral music, symphonies, sonatas, concertos, etc.

**Hill, Frank Ernest.** 1888–1969. American editor and writer; author of *Stone Dust* (verse, 1928), *What Is American?* (1933), *The Westward Star* (1934), *Listen and Learn* (1937); collaborator with Joseph Auslander in compiling *The Winged Horse* (a poetry anthology, 1927).

**Hill, Frank Pierce.** 1855–1941. American librarian; librarian of Brooklyn (N.Y.) public library (1901–30).

**Hill, Frederick Trevor.** 1866–1930. American lawyer; practiced, New York City (from 1890). Wrote several novels and three books on Lincoln: *Lincoln, the Lawyer* (1906), *Lincoln's Legacy of Inspiration* (1909), *Lincoln, the Emancipator* (1928).

**Hill, George Birkbeck Norman.** 1835–1903. English educator. Nephew of Sir Rowland Hill (1795–1879). Schoolmaster (1858–75); known chiefly as authority on life and works of Dr. Johnson. Edited Boswell's *Life of Johnson* (6 vols., 1887), *Johnson's Letters* (2 vols., 1892), *Johnsonian Miscellanies* (2 vols., 1897), *Johnson's Lives of the English Poets* (3 vols., 1905), etc. See Sir Leonard Erskine Hill.

**Hill, George William.** 1838–1914. American astronomer; known chiefly for his work in celestial mechanics and mathematics.

**Hill, James Jerome.** 1838–1916. American railway promoter, b. near Rockwood, Ontario, Canada; to U.S. (c. 1856); settled in St. Paul, Minn. In mercantile business (1856–65). With associates, bought St. Paul and Pacific Railroad (1878); reorganized and extended line; created Great Northern Railway Co., to merge all properties into one unit (1890); president of road (1882–1907); chairman of board (1907–12). Engaged in stock market battle, J. P. Morgan and Hill against Harriman and Schiff, to control Northern Pacific Railroad, causing panic of 1901. Attempted to insure stability of control by organization of Northern Securities Co., a holding company for all his properties; defeated by U.S. Supreme Court decision (1904). Interests widened to include Canadian railroads, steamship lines to Orient, mines, and banks; became known as "Empire Builder."

**Hill, Joseph Adna.** 1860–1938. American statistician; on staff of U.S. Census Bureau (from 1898); chief statistician (1909); assistant director of 14th and 15th censuses (1921, 1929); chief statistician for historical research (1933).

**Hill,** Sir **Leonard Erskine.** 1866–1952. Son of George Birkbeck Norman Hill. English physiologist. Author of *The Physiology and Pathology of the Cerebral Circulation* (1896), *Caisson Disease* (1912), *Sunshine and Open Air, Common Colds* (1929, with Mark Clement), etc.

**Hill, Louis Clarence.** 1865–1938. American engineer; supervising engineer, U.S. Reclamation Service in Arizona, Southern California, etc. (1905–14); consultant, Boulder Canyon Dam, All American Canal, Bonneville Dam, and other projects.

**Hill, Octavia.** 1838–1912. English reformer; prominent in promoting improvements in housing conditions in poorer districts of London.

**Hill, Rowland.** 1st Viscount **Hill.** 1772–1842. British soldier. Distinguished himself in Peninsular campaign and at Waterloo. Commander in chief in England (1825–39).

**Hill,** Sir **Rowland.** 1795–1879. English postal authority, b. Kidderminster; originator of "penny postage." Schoolmaster for many years. Began advocacy of postal reform with pamphlet submitted to Lord Melbourne, *Post Office Reform; its Importance and Practicability* (1837); appeared before commission and described his invention of the adhesive stamp for use in postage; secured adoption of penny postage in the budget (1839); on post office staff (1840–42); secretary to postmaster general (1846); secretary to the post office (1854–64).

**Hill, Thomas.** 1818–1891. American Unitarian clergyman and educator, b. New Brunswick, N.J. President, Antioch Coll. (1859–62) and Harvard (1862–68).

**Hill, Wills.** 1st Marquis of **Down'shire** (doun'shĭr; -shẽr). 1st Earl *and* 2d Viscount of **Hills'bor·ough** (hĭlz'bŭ·rŭ; -brŭ). 1718–1793. English statesman. Secretary of state for colonies (1768–72) and for northern department (1779–82); opposed concessions to American colonies; favored union of England and Ireland.

**Hil'la·ry** (hĭl'ȧ·rĭ), Sir **Edmund Percival.** 1919– . New Zealand mountaineer, explorer, and author. With Tenzing Norgay, first to reach the summit of Mt. Everest and return (1953); with Antarctic expeditions (1955–58, 1967); reached South Pole Jan. 4, 1958. Wrote *High Adventure* (1955), etc.

**Hil'le·brand** (hĭl'ĕ·bränt), **Joseph.** 1788–1871. German philosopher and historian of literature; orig. a Roman Catholic priest, but adopted Protestant faith. Chief philosophical work, *Philosophie des Geistes* (2 parts, 1835); chief work in literature, *Die Deutsche Nationalliteratur seit dem Anfang des 18. Jahrhunderts* (3 vols., 1845). His son **Karl** (1829–1884) was a journalist and historian; chief historical work, *Geschichte Frankreichs von der Thronbesteigung Ludwig Philipps bis zum Fall Napoleons III.*

**Hil'le·brand** (hĭl'ĕ·brănd), **William Francis.** 1853–1925. American chemist; chemist, U.S. Geological Survey (1880–1908); chief chemist, Bureau of Standards (1908–25).

**Hil'le·brandt** (hĭl'ĕ·bränt), **Alfred.** 1853–1927. German Sanskrit scholar.

**Hil'le·gas** (hĭl'ĕ·găs), **Michael.** 1729–1804. American merchant, b. Philadelphia. Made fortune in sugar refining and iron manufacturing. First treasurer of the U.S. (1777–89).

**Hil'lel** (hĭl'ĕl). fl. 30 B.C.–9 A.D. Jewish teacher who entered Palestine from Babylonia and gained recognition as an authority on interpretation of Biblical law; first teacher to formulate definite hermeneutic principles.

**Hillel II.** Jewish patriarch of middle 4th century A.D.; resident in Tiberias; established rules for calculating Jewish calendar, still the basis of Jewish reckoning.

**Hil'ler** (hĭl'ẽr), **Ferdinand.** 1811–1885. German pianist and composer; concert director, and director of the Conservatory of Music, Cologne (1850–84). Composer of operas, symphonies, oratorios, cantatas, etc.

**Hiller, Johann Adam.** 1728–1804. German composer; identified with musical life of Leipzig (from 1758); founder and director (1781–85) of the Gewandhaus concerts, Leipzig. Composer of operettas, a symphony, orchestral music, choral works, and songs. Influential in establishing the German *Lied* as opposed to the Italian operatic aria.

**Hiller, Kurt.** 1885– . German writer; editor of the yearbook *Das Ziel* (1916–24).

**Hil'lern** (hĭl'ẽrn), **Wilhelmine von.** 1836–1916. Daughter of Charlotte Birch-Pfeiffer. German novelist. Author of *Doppelleben* (2 vols., 1865), *Ein Arzt der Seele* (4 vols., 1869), *Ein Sklave der Freiheit* (1903), etc.

**Hil'ler von Gaer'tring·en** (hĭl'ẽr fôn gẽr'trĭng·ĕn), Baron **Friedrich von.** 1864–1947. German archaeologist; in charge of excavations in Thera (1896–1902); chief work, *Thera* (4 vols., 1899–1909).

**Hil'liard** (hĭl'yẽrd), **Nicholas.** 1537–1619. First English miniature painter; goldsmith, carver, and limner to Queen Elizabeth.

**Hil'lis** (hĭl'ĭs), **Newell Dwight.** 1858–1929. American Congregational clergyman; pastor, Plymouth Congregational Church, Brooklyn, N.Y. (1899–1924).

**Hill'man** (hĭl'măn), **Sidney.** 1887–1946. American labor leader, b. Lithuania; to U.S. at age of 20. Organizer among textile workers; president, Amalgamated Clothing Workers of America (from 1915); vice-president of CIO; chairman of executive council, Textile Workers' Union of America (from 1939); codirector (with William S. Knudsen), Office of Production Management (1941); head of labor division, War Production Board (1942).

**Hill'quit** (hĭl'kwĭt), **Morris.** 1869–1933. Lawyer and Socialist leader, b. at Riga, in Latvia; to U.S. (1886). Practiced law in New York (from 1893). Joined Socialist party (1888); Socialist candidate for mayor of New York (1917). Author of *History of Socialism in the United States* (1903), *Socialism Summed Up* (1912), etc.

**Hills** (hĭlz), **Laura Coombs.** 1859–1952. American miniature and flower painter and pastel artist, b. Newburyport, Mass.; studio in Boston.

**Hillsborough,** Earl and viscount of. See Wills HILL.

**Hill'yer** (hĭl'yẽr), **Robert Silliman.** 1895–1961. American poet, b. East Orange, N.J. Teacher of English at Harvard (1919–26; 1928 ff.; professor from 1937). Among his volumes of verse are *Sonnets and Other Lyrics* (1917), *The Halt in the Garden* (1925), *The Seventh Hill* (1928), *The Gates of the Compass* (1930), and *Collected Verse* (1933; awarded Pulitzer prize for poetry, 1934). Author also of the novels *Riverhead* (1932), *My Heart for Hostage* (1942).

**Hil·mi' Pa·sha'** (hĭl·mĭ' pä·shä'), **Hussein.** 1859?–1923. Turkish public official; minister of interior (1908), of justice (1912); minister to Austria (1912); grand vizier twice (1909, 1914); opposed German influence in Turkey.

**Hil'precht** (hĭl'prĕKt), **Hermann Volrath.** 1859–1925. Assyriologist, b. Hohenerxleben, Germany; to U.S. (1886). Professor, U. of Pennsylvania (1886–1911). Member and (1895) director, university expeditions to excavate at Nippur. Reorganized Imperial Ottoman Museum at Constantinople (1893–1909). Retired (1911) and settled in Germany; after World War, returned to U.S. and became naturalized.

**Hil'ton** (hĭl't'n; -tŭn), **James.** 1900–1954. English novelist; author of *Lost Horizon* (1933; awarded Hawthornden prize, 1934), *Goodbye, Mr. Chips* (1934; dramatized 1938), *We Are Not Alone* (1937), *To You, Mr. Chips* (1938), *Random Harvest* (1941).

**Hilton, John.** 1804–1878. English surgeon and anatomist; author of *On Rest and Pain* (1863).

**Hilton, William.** 1786–1839. English historical painter.

**Hil'ty** (hĭl'tē), **Carl.** 1833–1909. Swiss jurist and philosopher; member of National Council (from 1890).

**Hi·me'ri·us** (hĭ·mẹr'ĭ·ŭs; hī-). Greek Sophist and rhetorician; called to Antioch (362 A.D.) to be secretary to Emperor Julian. Established school of rhetoric in Athens (363).

**Hi·mil'co** (hĭ·mĭl'kō). fl. about 500 B.C. Carthaginian navigator who explored coast of Europe north from Gades (Cádiz) and is believed by some to have sailed as far as the Sargasso Sea.

**Himilco.** Carthaginian general; son of Hanno. Commanded expedition against Sicily (406 B.C.) and, after initial successes, was forced to capitulate by Dionysius; humiliated by the disgrace, committed suicide.

**Himilco.** Carthaginian general of 2d century B.C.; distinguished himself during first part of Third Punic War and then joined Roman army and aided in destruction of Carthage.

**Him'mel** (hĭm'ĕl), **Friedrich Heinrich.** 1765–1814. German composer of operas, oratorios, cantatas, chamber music, and songs.

**Himm'ler** (hĭm'lẽr), **Heinrich.** 1900–1945. German official; joined Nazi party (1925); Reich director of propaganda (1926–30); leader of Schutzstaffel (1929–45); chief of the Gestapo (1936–45); chief of home front and of Wehrmacht inside Germany (1944–45); attempted to negotiate surrender of Germany (Apr., 1945); captured by British; committed suicide (May 23).

**Hinck'ley** (hĭngk'lĭ), **Allen Carter.** 1877–1954. American operatic basso, b. Boston. On staff of Metropolitan Opera Company in New York (3 years) and Chicago Opera Company (2 years). Repertory includes leading oratorios, 75 grand operas, and many songs.

**Hincks** (hĭngks), **Edward.** 1792–1866. Irish Orientalist; rector of Killyleagh (1825–66). Credited with discovering true method of deciphering Egyptian hieroglyphics, and (simultaneously with Rawlinson) discovering the Persian cuneiform vowel system. His brother Sir **Francis** (1807–1885) went to Canada (1831); newspaper editor in Toronto and Montreal; prime minister of Canada (1851–54); governor of Barbados and Windward Islands (1855–62), and of British Guiana (1862–69); finance minister of Canada (1869–73).

**Hinc'mar** (hĭngk'mär). 806?–882. Archbishop of Reims (845); prominent in political and religious issues of his period; opposed Gottschalk's predestinarian doctrines. Author of treatises inspired by religious controversies and of a continuation (from 861) of *Annales Bertiniani.*

**Hind** (hīnd), **John Russell.** 1823–1895. English astronomer; director (1844–95) of observatory founded (1836) by astronomer George Bishop in Regent's Park, London. Author of *The Solar System* (1846), etc.

**Hin'de·mith** (hĭn'dĕ·mĭt), **Paul.** 1895–1963. German violist and composer; concertmeister, Frankfurt (1915–23); professor, Berlin (1927–33). To U.S. (1933); professor, Yale and Berkshire Music Center, Mass. Identified with ultramodern school of composition. Composer of string quartets and other chamber music, sonatas, operas, etc.

**Hin'den·burg** (hĭn'dĕn·bo͝ork; *Angl.* hĭn'dĕn·bûrg), **Karl Friedrich.** 1741–1808. German mathematician; credited with being originator of combinatorial analysis.

**Hindenburg, Paul von.** *Full name* **Paul Ludwig Hans Anton von Be'neck·en·dorff** (bā'nĕ·kĕn·dôrf) **und von Hindenburg.** 1847–1934. German general and president, b. Posen; fought at Königgrätz in Seven Weeks' War (1866); in Franco-Prussian War, was in battles of St.-Privat, Sedan, and siege of Paris (1870–71); won Iron Cross. Completed military course (1872–75); became member of general staff (1877); head of infantry bureau in war department (1889); major general (1896); lieutenant general (1900); commanding general of 4th army corps (1903); retired (1911). Because of intimate knowledge of Masurian Lakes region, summoned at beginning of World War (1914) to command army in East Prussian campaign; won complete victory over Russians at Tannenberg (1914); made field marshal and awarded the order Pour le Mérite (1914). In command in successful campaign against Russia in Poland (1915); promoted to chief of staff (1916) to succeed von Falkenhayn; with Ludendorff, directed all German strategy for remainder of war (1917–18); retired (1919). Wrote autobiography, *Aus meinem Leben* (1920); took no part in politics of the Reich (1919–25). Elected second president (1925–32) on fusion ticket; sought unity of German nation; approved Treaty of Locarno and Germany's admission to League of Nations; re-elected president (1932–34), defeating Adolf Hitler at the polls; compelled to yield to Nazi power by appointing Hitler as chancellor (1933). Buried in the Marshal's Tower of the National War Memorial at Tannenberg. His brother **Bernhard** (1859–1932), author and playwright, wrote biography *Feldmarschall von Hindenburg* (1918).

**Hin'der·sin** (hĭn'dẽr·zĭn), **Gustav Eduard von.** 1804–1872. German soldier; lieutenant general in Prussian army, commanding artillery attack on Düppel in Danish-Prussian War (1864); chief of artillery on the king's staff in Austro-Prussian War (1866) and Franco-Prussian War (1870–71); substituted rifled artillery for the smooth-bore type, and organized the artillery school.

**Hind'man** (hīnd'măn), **Thomas Carmichael.** 1828–1868. American Confederate commander in Civil War.

**Hinds** (hīndz), **Asher Crosby.** 1863–1919. American parliamentarian; author of *Hinds' Precedents of the House of Representatives of the United States* (5 vols., 1907–08).

**Hin'dus** (hĭn'dŭs), **Maurice Gerschon.** 1891–1969. Writer, b. in Russia; to U.S. (1905). Author of *Russian Peasant and Revolution* (1920), *Humanity Uprooted* (1929), *The Great Offensive* (1933), *Moscow Skies* (1936), *We Shall Live Again* (1939), *Mother Russia* (1943), etc.

**Hines** (hīnz), **Frank Thomas.** 1879–1960. American army officer and government administrator, b. Salt Lake City. Brigadier general (Jan. 7, 1920). Chief of embarkation service (1918–19), and responsible for building organization transporting over 2,000,000 soldiers to Europe and bringing them home again. Director, U.S. Veterans Bureau (1923–30); administrator of veterans' affairs (1930–45); ambassador to Panama (1945–48).

**Hines, John Leonard.** 1868–1968. American army officer; brigadier general (Nov. 30, 1918); major general (Mar. 5, 1921). Served in Philippines (1900–01; 1903–05; 1911–12; 1930–32) and in France (1917–21). Chief of staff, U.S. army (1924). Commander of Philippine department (1930). Retired (1932).

**Hines, Walker Downer.** 1870–1934. American lawyer and railroad administrator; U.S. director-general of railroads (1919–20). Practiced law in New York (from 1921). Author of *War History of American Railroads.*

**Hin'kle** (hĭng'k'l), **Beatrice M.**, *nee* **Van Gei'sen** (văn gē'z'n). 1874–1953. American psychiatrist; m. Walter Scott Hinkle (1892; d. 1899). M.D., Stanford (1899). To New York (1905); opened first psychotherapeutic clinic in America, at Cornell Medical College, New York City (1908).

**Hinkmar.** Variant of HINCMAR.

**Hinkson,** Mrs. **Katharine Tynan.** See TYNAN.

**Hino, Ashihei.** Pseudonym of Katsunori TAMAI.

**Hi'no·jo'sa** (ē'nō·hō'sä), **Pedro de.** 1489–1553. Spanish conquistador; with Pizarro in conquest of Peru; fought against the Almagros (1538, 1542); sided with Gonzalo Pizarro rebellion (1545), as captain of fleet; took Panama and Nombre de Diós; deserted to royal side with whole fleet (1546); given army command and governorship of Charcas; murdered by conspirators.

**Hin'richs** (hĭn'rĭks), **Hermann Friedrich Wilhelm.** 1794–1861. German Hegelian philosopher.

**Hin'schi·us** (hĭn'shē·o͝os), **Paul.** 1835–1898. German jurist; professor of ecclesiastical law, Berlin (1872).

**Hin'shaw** (hĭn'shô), **William Wade.** 1867–1947. American operatic baritone, b. Union, Iowa. Member of Metropolitan Opera Company of New York (1910–13). Director of opera productions with his own company (1920–26), presenting especially Mozart operas in English.

**Hin'shel·wood** (hĭn'shĕl·wo͝od), Sir **Cyril Norman.** 1897–1967. British chemist. At Oxford (1937–64); awarded Nobel prize in chemistry (1956) with N. Semenoy for research on mechanism of chemical reaction.

**Hins'ley** (hĭnz'lĭ), **Arthur.** 1865–1943. English Roman Catholic prelate; rector of the English College at Rome (1917–28); archbishop of Westminster (from 1935); created cardinal (1937).

**Hin'ton** (hĭn't'n; -tŭn), **James.** 1822–1875. English aural surgeon (in London) and author of philosophical works, as *Mystery of Pain* (1866), *Philosophy and Religion* (pub. 1881).

**Hint'ze** (hĭn'tsĕ), **Paul von.** 1864–1941. German naval officer and diplomat; ambassador to Mexico (1911–14), Peking (1914–15), Oslo (1915–18); foreign secretary (1918), until fall of the empire.

**Hiouen Tsang.** = HSÜAN TSANG.

**Hip·par'chus** (hĭ·pär'kŭs). Tyrant of Athens (527–514 B.C.); son of Pisistratus and brother of Hippias; assassinated by Harmodius and Aristogiton (*q.v.*). Cf. HIPPIAS.

**Hipparchus.** Greek astronomer; discovered (130 B.C.) precession of the equinoxes; catalogued over 1000 stars; developed trigonometry; devised method of locating geographical positions on the earth by giving their latitude and longitude.

**Hip'pel** (hĭp'ĕl), **Theodor Gottlieb von.** 1741–1796. German humorous writer.

**Hip'per** (hĭp'ĕr), **Franz von.** 1863–1932. German naval officer; rear admiral (1912); commanded reconnaissance forces of German High Seas Fleet (1914) and was engaged at battle of Jutland; commanded force of battle cruisers raiding English coastal areas in World War I; commander in chief of the High Seas Fleet (1918).

**Hip'pi·as** (hĭp'ĭ·ăs). Tyrant of Athens; son of Pisistratus and brother of Hipparchus (*q.v.*), with whom he shared the administration (527–514 B.C.); ruled with great severity after assassination of Hipparchus (514); forced into exile (511 or 510).

**Hippias of E'lis** (ē'lĭs). Greek Sophist of 5th century B.C.; lectured in Athens on mathematics, music, astronomy, and politics. Possibly the Hippias who is reputed to have invented a curve (later termed "quadratrix of Dinostratus") used in connection with the problem of subdivision of an angle.

**Hippius.** Pseudonym of Zinaida Nikolaevna MEREZHKOVSKI.

**Hip·poc'ra·tes** (hĭ·pŏk'rȧ·tēz). 460?–?377 B.C. Greek physician, b. on island of Cos; known as "Father of Medicine." Little is known of his life; reputed to have been a man of high character and noble ideals; said to have devised a code of medical ethics which he imposed on his disciples, the same code being now administered as an oath (Hippocratic oath) to men about to enter medical practice. Eighty-seven treatises, constituting the "Hippocratic collection," are attributed to him.

**Hip·pod'a·mus** (hĭ·pŏd'ȧ·mŭs). Greek architect of 5th century B.C., in Miletus; commissioned by Pericles to lay out the Piraeus; later, planned colonial town of Thurii and laid out city of Rhodes.

**Hip·pol'y·tus** (hĭ·pŏl'ĭ·tŭs), Saint. Perhaps of 3d century. The ecclesiastic, said to be "chief of the bishops of Rome," to whom is attributed the compilation known as *Canons of Hippolytus*, a collection of instructions on election and ordination of Christian priests, rules for baptism, the Eucharist, fasts, etc.

**Hippolytus.** Ecclesiastical writer; according to tradition, martyred in Sardinia (c. 235 A.D.). Chief work, *Philosophumena*, a refutation of heresies.

**Hippolytus a Lapide.** See Bogislaw von CHEMNITZ.

**Hip·po'nax** (hĭ·pō'năks). Greek poet of Ephesus in 6th century B.C., famous for scurrilous and vituperative verse; reputed inventor of the choliamb.

**Hi'ram** (hī'răm) *or* **Hu'ram** (hū'-). 989?–936 B.C. King of Tyre (970–936 B.C.). Improved port of Tyre; friend of Solomon and David; furnished cedar timber and skilled workmen for building of Solomon's temple (*1 Kings* v; *2 Chron.* ii) and David's palace (*2 Sam.* v).

**Hi·ra·nu·ma** (hē·rä·no͞o·mä), Baron **Kiichiro.** 1867–1952. Japanese statesman; minister of justice (1911–12); president of supreme court (1921–38); premier (1939); minister of home affairs (1940); adviser to emperor.

**Hi·ra·ta A·tsu·ta·ne** (hē·rä·tä ä·tso͞o·tä·nĕ). *An adopted name.* 1776–1843. Japanese scholar; specialist in Japanese history and literature. His works contributed to strengthening of Shintoism and of national sentiment and prepared way for abolition of shogunate.

**Hirn** (ērn), **Gustave Adolphe.** 1815–1890. French physicist; known for researches in thermodynamics, esp. on the mechanical equivalent of heat, and for researches in mathematical physics.

**Hi·ro·hi·to** (hē·rô·hē·tô; *Angl.* hē'rô·hē'tō, hĭr'ô-). *Reign name* **Sho·wa** (shō·wä). 1901– . Emperor of Japan (1926– ), 124th in direct lineage. Son of Yoshihito; traveled in Europe; regent (1921–26) during illness of father; m. (1924) Princess Nagako Kuni (b. 1903); heir to throne, Prince Tsugu, born (1933). Reign noted for increase of influence of army and navy, Mukden incident (1931) leading to establishment of Manchukuo, Chino-Japanese War (beginning 1937), tripartite pact (1940) with Germany and Italy, war against United States (beginning Dec. 7, 1941).

**Hi·ro·shi·ge** (hē·rô·shē·gĕ), **Ando.** 1797–1858. Japanese landscape painter; noted for his use of color and treatment of perspective; influenced Whistler in his moonlight interpretations. His name adopted by two of his pupils: **Hiroshige II** (d. after 1863) and **Hiroshige III** (d. 1896).

**Hi·ro·ta** (hē·rô·tä), **Koki.** 1878–1948. Japanese diplomat and politician. In diplomatic service (1906–27); minister to Netherlands (1927–30); ambassador to Russia (1930–32); minister for foreign affairs (1932–36; 1937) and prime minister (1936–37).

**Hirsau** *or* **Hirschau.** See WILHELM VON HIRSAU.

**Hirsch** (hûrsh), **Al'can** (ăl'kăn). 1885–1938. American chemical engineer; established laboratory in New York (1911); a founder of Molybdenum Corp. of America (1920). Inaugurated pyrophoric alloy industry in U.S. (1915).

**Hirsch** (hĭrsh), **Emanuel.** 1888– . German Protestant theologian; a leader (since 1933) of the German "Christens."

**Hirsch** (hûrsh), **Emil Gustav.** 1851–1923. Rabbi, b. in Luxembourg; to U.S. (1866). Rabbi in Chicago (from 1880); liberal in policy; first to have only a Sunday service in the synagogue. Editor, *Reform Advocate* (1891–1923). Professor of rabbinic literature and philosophy, U. of Chicago (from 1892).

**Hirsch** (hĭrsh), **Julius.** 1882–1961. German economist; member of German reparations delegations, at Berlin, Paris, Cannes, Genoa.

**Hirsch, Max.** 1832–1905. German economist; interested himself in trade-union organization in Germany; member of Reichstag (1869–93).

**Hirsch** (hĭrsh), Baron **Moritz**. *Known also by French form of name* **Maurice de Hirsch** (dē ērsh'). 1831–1896. German businessman and philanthropist; amassed fortune in Turkish government railway contracts. Interested himself in improving conditions of Jews, esp. those of Russia; founded and financed Jewish Colonization Assoc. "to assist and promote the emigration of Jews from any part of Europe or Asia...to any part of the world"; initiated the Baron de Hirsch Fund (incorporated in New York, 1891) to assist Jewish immigrants in U.S. to find employment and homes, learn mechanical trades, etc. His wife, **Clara**, *nee* **Bi'schoffs·heim** [bĭsh'ŏfs·hīm] (1833–1899), collaborated in his extensive charities.

**Hirsch, Samson Raphael.** 1808–1888. Jewish theologian; founder of so-called "New Orthodoxy."

**Hirsch'berg** (hĭrsh'bĕrk), **Julius.** 1843–1925. German ophthalmologist.

**Hirsch'feld** (hĭrsh'fĕlt), **Georg.** 1873–1942. German novelist and playwright.

**Hirschfeld, Magnus.** 1868–1935. German psychiatrist.

**Hirschfeld, Otto.** 1843–1922. German historian and epigraphist.

**Hirsh'feld** (hûrsh'fĕld), **Clarence Floyd.** 1881–1939. American electrical engineer; authority on power-plant and power-distribution engineering.

**Hirst** (hûrst), **Francis W.** 1873–1953. English economist. Author of *Adam Smith* (1904), *Political Economy of War* (1915), *Liberty and Tyranny* (1935), *Armaments* (1937), etc.

**Hirt** (hĭrt), **Hermann.** 1865–1936. German philologist; specialized in study of Indo-European language.

**Hirth** (hĭrt), **Friedrich.** 1845–1927. German Chinese scholar; on staff of Chinese maritime customs service (1870–97). Professor of Chinese and head of Chinese department, Columbia U., New York City (1902–17). His brother **Rudolf Hirth du Frênes** [dü frân'] (1846–1916) was a painter, with works represented in galleries in Munich, Frankfurt, Hanover, Nuremberg, etc.

**Hir'ti·us** (hûr'shĭ·ŭs), **Aulus.** 90?–43 B.C. Roman historian and politician; friend of Julius Caesar and Cicero. Consul (43 B.C.); supported senatorial party after Caesar's assassination and was killed in action at Mutina (April, 43). Reputed author of parts of the continuations of Caesar's *Commentaries*, notably the 8th book of the Gallic War and the history of the Alexandrian War.

**His** (hĭs), **Wilhelm.** 1831–1904. German anatomist; known for researches on the embryological development of the nervous system, etc. His son **Wilhelm** (1863–1934), physician, was director of the first medical clinic and professor of internal medicine, U. of Berlin (1907–26); investigated the nervous system of the vertebrate heart. His's bundle, composed of nerve fibers connecting the auricles with the ventricles, is named after him.

**Hi·sham'** (hĭ·shăm') *or* **Hi·shem'** (hĭ·shĕm'). *Arab.* **Hishām.** Name of several Mohammedan rulers.

**Hisham** (d. 743), 10th Ommiad caliph of Damascus (724–743), 4th son of Caliph Abd-al-Malik. Last real ruler of Ommiads in East, marking close of golden age of dynasty; during his reign occurred Kharijite (738) and Shiite (740) revolts in Iraq.

*Three Ommiad rulers of Córdoba:* **Hisham I** (757–796), emir (788–796); son of Abd-er-Rahman I; ruled with firmness; made some successful expeditions against Franks; popular because of his personal interest in his people; completed great Mosque of Córdoba. **Hisham II** (d. 1013?), caliph (976–1009, 1010–13); son of Hakam II; came to throne at age of 12; lived in seclusion most of reign, a puppet under control of the military, esp. of al-Mansur; reign marked decline of Ommiads in Spain. **Hisham III** (d. 1031), caliph (1027–31; deposed), last of Spanish dynasty.

**Hi'sing·er** (hē'sĭng·ĕr), **Wilhelm.** 1766–1852. Swedish geologist and mineralogist.

**His'ti·ae'us** (hĭs'tĭ·ē'ŭs). d. 494 B.C. Tyrant of Miletus, under the Persian king Darius I. Recalled to Susa by Darius in alarm at his power in Ionia; allowed to leave Susa on mission to suppress a rebellion in Ionia. Established himself, perhaps as a pirate, at Byzantium; captured by Harpagus and crucified at Sardis by Artaphernes (494 B.C.).

**Hita, Ginés Pérez de.** See Ginés PÉREZ DE HITA.

**Hitch'cock** (hĭch'kŏk), **Albert Spear.** 1865–1935. American agrostologist, b. Owosso, Mich. B.S., Iowa State (1884). Professor of botany, Kansas State (1892–1901). On staff of U.S. Department of Agriculture (from 1901), and systematic agrostologist (from 1905). Special editor for grasses, *Webster's New International Dictionary, Second Edition.*

**Hitchcock, Edward.** 1793–1864. American geologist, b. Deerfield, Mass. Professor of chemistry and natural history, Amherst (1825–45); president (1845–54); again professor (1854–64). Conducted geological survey of Massachusetts (1830–33, 1837–41); investigated dinosaur tracks in Connecticut Valley sandstone; state geologist of Vermont (1856–61). His son **Edward** (1828–1911) was professor of hygiene and physical education at Amherst (1861–1911), the first such professor in an American college. Another son, **Charles Henry** (1836–1919), was a geologist; state geologist, Maine (1861) and New Hampshire (1868–78); professor, Dartmouth (1868–1908).

**Hitchcock, Ethan Allen.** 1835–1909. American political leader, b. Mobile, Ala. U.S. minister to Russia (1897–98); first U.S. ambassador to Russia (1898). U.S. secretary of the interior (1898–1907); uncovered frauds in administration of public lands; removed incompetent or corrupt officials and prosecuted many; co-operated with Roosevelt in orders (1906–07) enlarging forest reserves and withdrawing mineral lands from exploitation.

**Hitchcock, Frank Harris.** 1869–1935. American lawyer and politician; U.S. postmaster general (1909–13); established postal savings banks and parcel post, and started first air-mail service.

**Hitchcock, Gilbert Mo·nell'** (mô·nĕl'). 1859–1934. American lawyer, newspaper publisher, and politician; practiced law in Omaha, Nebr. (1881–85). Founded Omaha *Evening World* (1885) and consolidated Omaha *Morning Herald* with it (1889) as the Omaha *World-Herald.* Member, U.S. House of Representatives (1903–05; 1907–11) and U.S. Senate (1911–23); chief presidential representative in U.S. Senate during Wilson's administration.

**Hitchcock, Lambert.** 1795–1852. American cabinetmaker and chair manufacturer, b. Cheshire, Conn. Established furniture factory in Barkhamsted (1818); best known for his design and manufacture of Hitchcock chairs; maker also of rocking chairs.

**Hitchcock, Raymond.** 1865–1929. American actor, esp. in comic roles in musical comedies; b. Auburn, N.Y.

**Hitchcock, Roswell Dwight.** 1817–1887. American Congregational clergyman and educator; professor of church history, Union Theol. Sem. (from 1855); president of the faculty (from 1880).

**Hit'ler** (hĭt'lĕr), **Adolf.** 1889–1945. German chancellor and Führer (leader), b. Braunau, Upper Austria, of an Austrian father, whose original name is said to have been **Schick'l·gru'ber** (shĭk''l·grōō'bĕr), and Bavarian mother. Architect's draftsman; moved to Munich

(1912); served in World War in Bavarian regiment and received Iron Cross. Became reactionary leader in Bavaria; with six others, founded (1919–20) National Socialist German Workers' party, known as the Nazi party. Editor of *Der Völkische Beobachter* (c. 1922); won aid of Ludendorff; with him and others, organized unsuccessful revolt in Munich (Nov. 8–9, 1923) known as "Beer Hall Putsch"; sentenced to five years' imprisonment but paroled after nine months (1924). In prison, dictated to his secretary, Rudolf Hess, *Mein Kampf* ("My Battle"; Eng. trans. 1933). Increased strength of Nazi party (1928–32); opposed Hindenburg (1932) as candidate in presidential election, but was defeated. Swept into power (1933) on rising tide of German nationalism and economic discontent; named chancellor by Hindenburg (Jan., 1933); gained control of Reichstag; granted by it (Mar., 1933) dictatorial powers for four years by constitutional amendments; on death of Hindenburg (Aug., 1934), united presidential office and chancellorship, assuming title "Der Führer." Inaugurated violent anti-Semitic policy; established new economic program; broke conditions of Versailles Treaty; reoccupied Rhineland zone (Mar., 1936); annexed Austria (Mar., 1938), the Sudetenland (Oct., 1938), all of Czechoslovakia (Mar., 1939); made nonaggression pact with Russia (Aug., 1939); by invading Poland (Sept. 1, 1939) brought on general war; conquered Denmark, Norway, the Netherlands, Belgium, France (1940), Greece (1941); invaded Russia (June, 1941); committed suicide (Apr., 1945); Germany surrendered to Allies (May 1945).

**Hitomaro.** *In full* **Ka·ki·no·mo·to no Hi·to·ma·ro** (kä·kē·nô·mô·tô nô hē·tô·mä·rô). d. about 729. Japanese poet of the golden age.

**Hi·to·tsu·ba·shi** (hē·tô·tsōō·bä·shē). *Also known as* **Yo·shi·no·bu** (yô·shē·nô·bōō) *and by Chinese form* **Kei·ki** (kā·kē). 1837–1902. Last of the Japanese shoguns; by some called "Last of the Tycoons." Son of daimio of Mito; member of Tokugawa (*q.v.*) family; adopted at age of eleven into feudal house of Hitotsubashi. Proposed for shogunate (1858) by party opposed to foreigners; became (1863) leader of shogun party; sought to avoid factional troubles and bloodshed; on death (1866) of Shogun Iyemochi, chosen (1867) as his successor, but resigned a few months later, after Mutsuhito (*q.v.*) had been chosen emperor; yielded to emperor, thus ending 700 years of the shogunate; lived in retirement (1868–1902), chiefly at Shizuoka.

**Hit'ti** (hĭt'ĭ), **Philip Khuri.** 1886–1978. American Orientalist, b. in Lebanon; B.A., Am. U. of Beirut (1908), Ph.D., Columbia (1915); to U.S. (1913), naturalized (1919); taught at Columbia (1915–20), Beirut (1920–26), Princeton (1926–54; prof. of Semitic lit. from 1936). Author of *The Origins of the Islamic State* (1916), *Syria and the Syrians* (1926), *History of the Arabs* (1937), etc.

**Hit'torf** (hĭt'ôrf), **Johann Wilhelm.** 1824–1914. German physicist. Pioneer in electrochemical research; investigated the migration of ions during electrolysis and worked out the transference number; studied electrical phenomena in rarefied gases, the Hittorf tube being named for him; determined a number of properties of cathode rays, including the deflection of the rays by a magnet, thereby anticipating Crookes, who published a report of researches on cathode rays in 1878.

**Hit'torff'** (ē'tôrf'), **Jacques Ignace.** 1792–1867. French architect. Government architect in Paris (from 1830); built church of Saint Vincent de Paul (1832), and various public and private buildings; designed embellishments for the Place de la Concorde, Champs-Élysées, and Avenue de l'Étoile.

**Hit'zig** (hĭt'sĭκ), **Julius Eduard.** 1780–1849. German jurist.

**Hjär'ne** (yâr'nĕ), **Harald Gabriel.** 1848–1922. Swedish historian.

**Hla'dik** (hlȧ'dyĭk), **Václav.** 1868–1913. Czech writer of tales and plays depicting life in Prague.

**Hlin'ka** (hlĭng'kȧ), **Andrej.** 1864–1938. Slovak Roman Catholic priest and patriot; founder and leader of the Slovakian People's party (also known as the Hlinka party), and founder of its journal *Slovák;* opposed policy of unification with Bohemia, and presented a memorandum to the Peace Conference (1919) demanding a plebiscite in Slovakia. Arrested and jailed, but released when elected to the legislature (1920). Desisted (1926) from continued opposition to unification, but pressed for autonomy in the new Czechoslovak state.

**Hlinka, Vojtěch.** *Pseudonym* **František Prav'da** (prȧv'dȧ). 1817–1904. Czech writer, esp. of realistic tales of Czech village life.

**Hoar** (hōr), **Leonard.** 1630?–1675. American clergyman and educator, b. Gloucester, England; to America as a boy. President, Harvard College (1672–75).

**Hoar, Samuel.** 1778–1856. American lawyer and legislator, b. Lincoln, Mass.; practiced, Concord, Mass. Member, U.S. House of Representatives (1835–37). Sent by Massachusetts to South Carolina to test constitutionality of certain South Carolina laws prohibiting free Negroes (as seamen on Massachusetts vessels) from entering state (1844); forcibly expelled from South Carolina in accordance with vote of South Carolina legislature. His son **Ebenezer Rockwood** (1816–1895) a jurist; U.S. attorney general (1869–70); member, U.S. House of Representatives (1873–75). Another son, **George Frisbie** (1826–1904), served in U.S. House of Representatives (1869–77), U.S. Senate (1877–1904); wrote *Autobiography of Seventy Years* (2 vols., 1903).

**Hoare** (hōr), Sir **Samuel John Gurney.** 1880–1959. English statesman; educ. Oxford. M.P. (from 1910). Secretary of state for air (1922–24, 1924–29, 1940), for India (1931–35), for foreign affairs (1935); first lord of the admiralty (1936–37); secretary of state for home affairs (1937–39); lord privy seal (1939–40); amb. to Spain (1940–44); cr. Viscount **Templewood** (1944).

**Ho'ban** (hō'băn), **James.** 1762?–1831. Architect, b. in County Kilkenny, Ireland; to America (c. 1785). Designed and supervised construction of the White House, Washington, D.C. (1792–1800; destroyed by the British 1814), and the new White House (1815–29) replacing it.

**Ho'bart** (hō'bärt), **Alice Tisdale.** *Nee* **Alice Nourse** (nôrs). 1882–1967. American novelist, b. Lockport, N.Y.; m. Earle Tisdale Hobart (1914); author of *Pidgin Cargo* (1929; republished as *River Supreme,* 1934), *Oil for the Lamps of China* (1933). *Their Own Country* (1940), *Yang and Yin* (1936), etc.

**Ho'bart** (hō'bĕrt; -bärt), **Garret Augustus.** 1844–1899. American lawyer and politician, b. Long Branch, N.J. Vice-president of the U.S. (1897–99).

**Hobart, George Vere.** 1867–1926. Writer, b. in Nova Scotia, Can. Humorous writer on Baltimore *American;* originator and writer (for 16 years) of "Dinkelspiel" papers. Author of *The John Henry Books* (15 volumes of comic stories), *Li'l Verses for Li'l Fellers* (poems for children). Author or adapter of, or collaborator in, many plays, including *Wildfire, Our Mrs. McChesney, Sonny,* and the morality play *Experience.*

**Hobart, John.** 1st Earl of **Buck'ing·ham·shire** (bŭk'ĭng·ăm·shĭr; -shĕr). 1694?–1756. English political leader. Lord lieutenant of Norfolk (1745). His son **John** (1723–1793), 2d earl, was comptroller of the royal household (1755), ambassador to Russia (1762–65), lord lieutenant of Ireland (1777–80). **Robert** (1760–1816), 4th earl, grandson of 1st earl, was chief secretary to lord lieutenant of Ireland (1789–93); governor of Madras (1794–98), recalled on account of differences with Sir John Shore, governor general of India; secretary for war and the colonies (1801–04); chancellor of duchy of Lancaster (1805, 1812); president of board of control for Indian affairs (1812–16). **George Robert** (1789–1849), 5th earl, nephew of 4th earl, added to his surname the name Hampden. **Augustus Charles Hobart-Hamp'den** [-hăm(p)'dĕn] (1822–1886), younger son of 6th earl, known as **Hobart Pa·sha'** (pä·shä'), was British naval officer (1835–63); blockade runner off North Carolina during American Civil War; commanded Turkish Black Sea fleet in Russian War (1877–78). **Vere Henry Hobart** (1818–1875), elder son of 6th earl, was director-general of Ottoman Bank, Constantinople, and governor of Madras (1872–75).

**Hobart, John Henry.** 1775–1830. American Protestant Episcopal bishop, b. Philadelphia. Rector, Trinity Church, New York (from 1816). Bishop of the diocese, from 1816.

**Hob'be·ma** (hŏb'ĕ·mȧ), **Meindert.** 1638–1709. Dutch landscape painter; studied under Jakob van Ruisdael. Among his notable pictures are *The Hermitage, St. Petersburg* (in New York Historical Society collection), *Avenue of Middelharnis, Ruins of Brederode Castle, Entrance to a Village, Water Mill.*

**Hobbes** (hŏbz), **John Oliver.** Pseudonym of Pearl Mary Teresa CRAIGIE.

**Hobbes, Thomas.** 1588–1679. English philosopher. B.A., Oxon. (1608). An exile in France because of his political convictions (1641–52). Returned to England (1652); associated with Earl of Devonshire, and a member of his household (1660 ff.). In his travels on Continent, met Galileo, Gassendi, Mersenne; in England was friendly with Harvey, Ben Jonson, Cowley, Sidney Godolphin, Selden. Received pension from Charles II. Chief works, *De Cive* (1642), *Human Nature* (1650), *Leviathan, or the Matter, Form, and Power of a Commonwealth, Ecclesiastical and Civil* (1651, containing his famous social contract theory), *De Homine* (1658).

**Hobbs** (hŏbz), **William Herbert.** 1864–1953. American geologist, b. Worcester, Mass.; professor of geology and director of geological laboratory, U. of Michigan (from 1906). Director of aerological investigations carried on by U. of Michigan in Greenland (1926–30). Author of *Characteristics of Existing Glaciers* (1911), *Earth Features and Their Meaning* (1912), *Cruises Along By-Ways of the Pacific* (1923), *Peary* (1936), etc.

**Hob'by** (hŏb'ĭ), **Oveta,** *nee* **Culp** (kŭlp). 1905– . Director, U.S. Women's (Auxiliary) Army Corps (1942–45); b. Killeen, Texas; m. William P. Hobby. Sec'y of the dept. of health, education and welfare (1953–55).

**Hobertus, Jakob.** See OBRECHT.

**Hob'house** (hŏb'hous), **John Cam.** Baron **Brough'ton de Gyf'ford** (brô't'n dĕ gĭf'ērd). 1786–1869. British administrator and liberal pamphleteer. M.A., Cantab. (1811). Secretary at war (1832–33); chief secretary for Ireland (1833); president, Board of Control (1835–41, 1846–52). Friend and traveling companion of Lord Byron in Spain, Portugal, Greece, and Turkey; visited Byron in Switzerland and Italy; as Byron's executor, advised destruction of his *Memoirs* (1824). From personal observation, wrote Bonapartist account of the Hundred Days (1816); author also of volume of reminiscences, *Recollections of a Long Life* (1865).

**Hobhouse, Leonard Trelawney.** 1864–1929. English journalist and philosopher. First professor of sociology, London U. (1907–1929). Author of *The Labour Movement* (1893), *The Theory of Knowledge* (1896), *Mind in Evolution* (1901), *Morals in Evolution* (1906), *The Rational Good* (1921), *The Elements of Social Justice* (1922).

**Ho'bohm** (hō'bōm), **Martin.** 1883– . German historian.

**Hobrecht, Jakob.** See OBRECHT.

**Hob'son** (hŏb's'n), **John Atkinson.** 1858–1940. English economist. Author of *Problems of Poverty* (1891), *The Evolution of Modern Capitalism* (1894), *The Problem of the Unemployed* (1896), *The Economics of Distribution* (1900), *Imperialism* (1902), *The Industrial System* (1909), *Work and Wealth...*(1914), *Problems of a New World* (1921), *Wealth and Life...*(1929), *God and Mammon* (1931), *Democracy* (1934), *Confessions of an Economic Heretic* (1938), etc.

**Hobson, Richmond Pearson.** 1870–1937. American naval officer and author, b. Greensboro, Ala.; grad., U.S.N.A., Annapolis (1889). Known esp. for exploit in sinking collier *Merrimac* in Santiago harbor in effort to bottle up Spanish fleet (1898). Resigned from navy (1903). Member of U.S. House of Representatives (1907–15). Awarded Medal of Honor by Congress (1933).

**Hobson, Thomas.** 1544?–1631. English liveryman at Cambridge, whose practice of requiring every customer to take the horse which stood nearest the door gave rise to the expression "Hobson's choice."

**Hoc'cleve** (hŏk'lēv) *or* **Oc'cleve** (ŏk'-), **Thomas.** 1370?–?1450. English poet; clerk in the privy seal office. His longest work is *De Regimine Principum* ("The Regiment of Princes"; a verse homily on virtues and vices).

**Hoch'berg vom Für'sten·stein** (hōᴋ'bĕrᴋ [hôᴋ'-] fôm für'stĕn·shtīn), Count **Volko von.** *Pseudonym* **J. H. Franz** (fränts). 1843–1926. German theater manager and composer; general manager, Court Theater, Berlin (1886–1903). Composer of symphonies, string quartets, choral pieces, songs, and the opera *Die Falkensteiner*, later rewritten and produced under the title *Der Wärwolf* (1881).

**Hoche** (ôsh), **Louis Lazare.** 1768–1797. French Revolutionary soldier; promoted from corporal (1789) to general of brigade and general of division, commanding the army of the Moselle (1792); served with distinction in Alsace (1793), in suppressing the Vendean insurrection (1795–96), and in fighting the Austrians at Neuwied and Altenkirchen (1797).

**Ho Chi Minh** (hō' chē' mĭn'). *originally* **Nguyen That Thanh** 1890–1969. Vietnamese political leader; president of No. Vietnam (1946–69).

**Hoch'stet'ter** (hōᴋ'shtĕt'ēr; hôᴋ'-), **Ferdinand von.** 1829–1884. Austrian geologist. Explored New Zealand on voyage of scientific exploration around the world made by the *Novara* (1857–59).

**Hochstetter, Gustav.** 1873– . German journalist and writer of plays, verse, and fiction.

**Hock'ing** (hŏk'ĭng), **Silas Kitto.** 1850–1935. English clergyman (ordained 1870) and novelist; his novels include *Alec Green* (1878), *Sea Waif* (1882), *Cricket* (1885), *God's Outcast* (1898), *Pioneers* (1905), *Nancy* (1919), *The Mystery Man* (1930), *Gerry Storm* (1934). His brother **Joseph** (1855?–1937), nonconformist clergyman (1884–1910) and novelist; novels include *Jabez Easterbrook* (1891), *Ishmaël Pengelly* (1894), *The Scarlet Woman* (1899), *Follow the Gleam* (1903), *The Trampled Cross* (1907), *The Jesuit* (1911), *Prodigal Daughters* (1922), *Prodigal Parents* (1923), *The Man Who Found Out* (1933).

**Hocking, William Ernest.** 1873–1966. American philosopher; professor, Harvard (from 1914). Author of *The Meaning of God in Human Experience* (1912), *Man and the State* (1926), *Types of Philosophy* (1929),

*Thoughts on Death and Life* (1937), *What Man Can Make of Man* (1942), etc.

**Hodge** (hŏj), **Frederick Webb.** 1864–1956. American ethnologist, b. in Plymouth, England; to U.S. at age of seven. With Bureau of American Ethnology (1889–1901, 1905–18), in charge (1910–18); with Museum of the American Indian, New York City (1918–31); director, Southwest Museum, Los Angeles (from 1932). Conducted archaeological and ethnological expeditions in the Southwest (1917–21, 1923).

**Hodge, Hugh Lenox.** 1796–1873. American obstetrician, b. Philadelphia. Professor, U. of Pennsylvania (1835–63). His brother **Charles** (1797–1878) was a Presbyterian clergyman; professor, Princeton Theol. Sem. (1822–78); exerted conservative influence in Presbyterian Theological teachings.

**Hodge, John.** 1855–1937. British trade-unionist and politician, b. in Ayrshire, Scotland. M.P. (1906–23); minister of labor (1916–17) and of pensions (1917–19).

**Hodg'es** (hŏj'ĕz; -ĭz), **Courtney Hicks.** 1887–1966. American army officer, b. Perry, Ga.; enlisted as private (1906); chief of infantry (1941–43); in command of 3d army (1943), 1st army (1945).

**Hodges, George.** 1856–1919. American Protestant Episcopal clergyman; dean, Episcopal Theol. School, Cambridge, Mass. (from 1894).

**Hodges, John Sebastian Bach.** 1830–1915. American Protestant Episcopal clergyman, b. Bristol, Eng.; to U.S. (1845). Known as an organist, and composer of many anthems and hymns.

**Hodg'kin** (hŏj'kĭn), **Alan Lloyd.** 1914– . British physiologist. Awarded Nobel prize in physiology and medicine (1963) with J. Eccles and A. Huxley for their researches on nerve impulses.

**Hodgkin, Dorothy Crowfoot.** 1910– . British chemist, b. Egypt. Awarded Nobel prize in chemistry (1964) for work on biochemical structures.

**Hodgkin, Thomas.** 1798–1866. English physician, first to describe the glandular disease named after him.

**Hodgkin, Thomas.** 1831–1913. English banker and historian; author of *Italy and her Invaders* (1879–99), *History of England from the Earliest Times to the Norman Conquest* (1906).

**Hodg'son** (hŏj's'n), **Brian Houghton.** 1800–1894. British Orientalist; civil servant in India. Author of *Illustrations of Literature and Religion of the Buddhists* (1841), *Essays on Language, Literature, and Religion of Nepal and Tibet* (1874).

**Hodgson, John Evan.** 1831–1895. English painter; known for genre, historical, and Moorish paintings.

**Hodgson, Ralph.** 1871–1962. English poet; wrote *Eve, The Gipsy Girl, The Bull, The Bride, Last Blackbird.*

**Hodgson, Shadworth Hollway.** 1832–1912. English philosopher; chief works, *Time and Space* (1865), *Metaphysic of Experience* (1898).

**Ho'dler** (hō'dlẽr), **Ferdinand.** 1853–1918. Swiss painter and illustrator; painter of landscapes and portraits; also a lithographer; a leader in the expressionist school.

**Hod'son** (hŏd's'n), **Henrietta.** 1841–1910. English actress; married as 2d husband (1868) Henry du Pré Labouchère (*q.v.*).

**Hodson, William Stephen Raikes.** 1821–1858. British cavalry officer; commissioned during Sepoy Mutiny (1857–58) to raise a troop of cavalry, known as Hodson's Horse. After capture of Delhi (Sept. 20, 1857), seized the king of Delhi, and shot the princes of Delhi when their rescue was attempted.

**Ho'dža** (hô'jà), **Milan.** 1878–1944. Czechoslovak statesman; leader of Agrarian party; prime minister (1935–38).

**Hoe** (hō), **Robert.** 1784–1833. American industrialist, b. in Leicestershire, England; to U.S. (1803). Manufacturer of printing presses (from c. 1805); firm organized as R. Hoe & Co. (from 1823). His son **Richard March** (1812–1886) succeeded him in management of R. Hoe & Co. (1830); invented rotary press (1847), web press (c. 1847), and improvements that made possible the modern newspaper press. Richard's nephew **Robert** (1839–1909) succeeded him as head of R. Hoe & Co. (1886); devised improvements increasing speed of newspaper press; perfected rotary art press (1890); developed color presses.

**Hoeck'e** (ho͞o'kĕ), **Jan van den** (1611–1651) and his half brother **Robrecht van den** (1622–after 1695). Flemish painters of the Flemish school; Jan known for portraits and historical pictures; Robrecht for genre, landscape, and battle scenes.

**Hoe'fer** (hû'fẽr), **Edmund.** 1819–1882. German novelist; collaborator with Hackländer in editing magazine *Hausblätter* in Stuttgart (1854–68).

**Hoef'na'gel** (ho͝of'nä'gĕl), **Joris.** *Ger.* **Georg Huf'na'gel** (*Ger.* ho͞of'nä'gĕl). 1542–1600. Dutch miniature painter and illustrator; his masterpiece is the *Missale Romanum*, preserved in the National Library at Vienna.

**Höegh–Guldberg.** See GULDBERG.

**Hoene** *or* **Hoene–Wroński.** See WROŃSKI.

**Hoens'broech** (ho͞ons'bro͞ok; hōns'brōk), Count **Paul von.** 1852–1923. German writer; entered Jesuit order as a young man, but withdrew (1893) and joined Protestant church (1895); edited *Tägliche Rundschau* (1898) and the monthly *Deutschland* (1902–07).

**Hoepp'ner** (hûp'nẽr), **Ernst von.** 1860–1922. German general; appointed (1916) first commanding general of the German war in the air.

**Hoerbst** (hûrpst), **Hans.** b. 1859. Swiss sculptor; in U.S. (1887–94); executed a number of portrait busts.

**Hoer'nes** (hûr'nĕs), **Moritz.** 1815–1868. Austrian paleontologist; investigated the Tertiary mollusca of the Vienna basin. His son **Rudolf** (1850–1912), geologist and paleontologist, wrote on paleozoology, earthquakes, and the geology of Austria. Another son, **Moritz** (1852–1917), archaeologist and ethnographer, conducted archaeological investigations in Bosnia and Herzegovina, and wrote on the early history of man, the plastic arts in Europe.

**Hoern'le** (hûrn'lē; -lĕ), **Rudolf.** 1841–1918. English Orientalist of German descent, b. in India; authority on Indian antiquities and languages.

**Hoess'lin** (hûs'lĭn), **Franz von.** 1885–1946. German conductor; at Bayreuth (1927, 1928).

**Hoetzsch** (hûch), **Otto.** 1876–1946. German historian; specialized in history of eastern Europe.

**Hoe'ven** (ho͞o'vĕn), **Jan van der.** 1801–1868. Dutch naturalist.

**Ho'fer** (hō'fẽr), **Andreas.** 1767–1810. Tyrolese patriot; led rebellion (1809) against Bavarian government of the Tyrol, and defeated Bavarian army, but was defeated later by combined French and Bavarian army. Forced into hiding, but was betrayed and shot (Feb. 20, 1810).

**Hofer, Karl.** 1878–1955. German painter; identified with ultramodern schools of painting, as abstractionism and expressionism.

**Hoff, Jacobus Hendricus van't.** See VAN'T HOFF.

**Höff'ding** (hûf'dĭng), **Harald.** 1843–1931. Danish philosopher, of positivistic school.

**Hof'fen·stein** (hŏf'ĕn·stīn), **Samuel Goodman.** 1890–1947. Humorous poet and writer, b. in Lithuania; to U.S. in his youth; motion-picture scenario writer (from 1927); author of *Life Sings a Song* (1916), *Poems in Praise of Practically Nothing* (1928), etc.

**Hoffman.** See also HOFFMANN and HOFMANN.

**Hoff'man** (hŏf'măn), **Charles Fenno.** 1806–1884.

American writer, b. New York City. Editor, *American Monthly Magazine* (1835–37). Associated with Horace Greeley in editing the *New Yorker* (1840). Clerk, office of surveyor of customs, New York (1841–43); deputy surveyor (1843–44). Editor, *Literary World* (1847–48). In institution for insane (1849–84). Author of *A Winter in the West* (1835), *Wild Scenes in the Forest and Prairie* (1839), *Greyslaer, a Romance of the Mohawk* (1839), *The Vigil of Faith and Other Poems* (1842), *The Echo* (verse, 1844), *Love's Calendar, Lays of the Hudson* (1847).

**Hoff'man'** (ôf'mån'), **François Benoît.** 1760–1828. French writer; author of verse, dramas, and comic opera librettos, collaborating with Grétry, Kreutzer, Cherubini, and others.

**Hoff'man** (hŏf'măn), **John Thompson.** 1828–1888. American politician, b. Sing Sing (Ossining). Joined Tammany Society (1859). Elected mayor of New York City (1865, 1867); governor of New York (1868, 1870); during administration, activities of Tweed Ring at their height; political future ruined by conviction of Tweed.

**Hoffman, Mal·vi'na** (măl·vē'nȧ). 1887–1966. American sculptor, b. New York City; m. Samuel Bonarios Grimson (1924). Executed bronzes of 101 racial types for Field Museum in Chicago. Awarded 1st prize in Paris (1911) for her *Russian Dancers*. Author of *Heads and Tales* (1930), *Sculpture Inside and Out* (1939).

**Hoffman, Richard.** *Orig. surname* **Andrews.** 1831–1909. Concert pianist and composer, b. Manchester, England; to U.S. (1847); accompanist with Jenny Lind, under Barnum's management (1850). Composed part songs, ballads, anthems, and piano music.

**Hoff'mann** (hôf'män), **August Heinrich.** *Known as* **Hoffmann von Fal'lers·le'ben** (fäl'ērs·lā'bĕn). 1798–1874. German poet, philologist, and historian of literature; librarian (1823) and professor of German (1830–42), Breslau U. Author of lyric verse, as *Lieder und Romanzen* (1821), *Kinderlieder* (1843–47), *Liebeslieder* (1851), *Soldatenlieder* (1851–52), *Vaterlandslieder* (1871), best known poem, *Deutschland, Deutschland über Alles* (1841), used as a national hymn (from 1922). Other works include *Fundgruben für Geschichte Deutscher Sprache und Literatur* (2 vols., 1830–37), *Geschichte des Deutschen Kirchenliedes bis auf Luther* (1832), *Die Deutsche Philologie im Grundriss* (1836).

**Hoffmann, Ernst Theodor Wilhelm.** *As composer, known as* **Ernst Theodor Amadeus Hoffmann,** *in honor of Mozart.* 1776–1822. German composer, music critic, fiction writer, and illustrator, b. Königsberg. His opera, *Undine* (1816, libretto by La Motte-Fouqué), was the inspiration for Offenbach's *Les Contes d'Hoffmann.* His stories and novels are among the finest of the German romantic movement, and include *Die Elixiere des Teufels* (1816), *Nachtstücke* (2 vols., 1817), *Die Serapionsbrüder* (stories, 4 vols., 1819–21).

**Hoffmann, Friedrich.** 1660–1742. German physician; experimented with various remedies, Hoffmann's anodyne and Hoffmann's drops being named after him; brought mineral waters into more general use; adherent of the iatrophysical school of medicine.

**Hoffmann, Hans.** 1848–1909. German novelist; author of *Iwan der Schreckliche und sein Hund* (1889), *Bozener Märchen* (1896), *Ostseemärchen* (1897), etc.

**Hoffmann** *or* **Hoff'mann-Don'ner** (-dôn'ēr), **Heinrich.** 1809–1894. German physician and poet; widely known for his children's books, illustrated by himself, including *Struwwelpeter* (1847), *König Nussknacker, Im Himmel und auf Erden, Prinz Grünewald,* etc.

**Hoffmann, Max.** 1869–1927. German general in the World War; served esp. on the eastern front, succeeding Ludendorff as chief of the general staff under Prince Leopold of Bavaria (1916); negotiated armistice of Brest Litovsk with the Soviets (1917–18); opposed annexation of Poland by Germany.

**Hof'hai'mer** (hōf'hī'mēr), **Paulus von.** 1459–1537. German organist, composer of choral works and songs.

**Hofmann.** See also HOFFMAN and HOFFMANN.

**Hof'mann** (hōf'män; hôf'-), **August Wilhelm von.** 1818–1892. German chemist; founder of the German Chemical Society (1868). Known for researches in organic chemistry, esp. on coal-tar products; discovered methods for preparation of coloring substances from aniline; introduced violet dyes (Hofmann's violets) made from rosaniline; discovered a method for converting an amide into an amine having one less carbon atom, also a method for determining molecular weights of liquids by means of vapor densities.

**Hofmann, Heinrich.** 1824–1902. German historical painter; best known for a series of paintings (many reproduced in engravings) of scenes from the life of Christ.

**Hofmann, Johann Christian Conrad von.** 1810–1877. German Protestant theologian; head of the Erlangen school of theologians.

**Hof'mann** (hŏf'măn; *Pol.* hôf'män), **Jo'sef** (jō'zĕf; -zĭf) **Cas'i·mir** (kăz'ĭ·mĭr). 1876–1957. Polish piano virtuoso, b. in Cracow. Director, dean, and teacher, Curtis Institute of Music, Philadelphia (1926–38). Has toured Europe and U.S. as concert performer. Composer, under pseudonym **Dvor'sky** (dvôr'skĭ), of concertos, a symphony, an orchestral suite, and piano pieces.

**Hof'mann** (hōf'män; hôf'-), **Ludwig von.** 1861–1945. German painter, known esp. for his historical and allegorical canvases and for his murals.

**Hof'manns·thal** (hōf'mäns·täl; hôf'-), **Hugo von.** 1874–1929. Austrian poet and playwright, b. Vienna. Author of *Gestern* (dramatic poem, 1892), *Der Tod des Tizian* (short drama, 1901), *Elektra* (1903), *Ödipus und die Sphinx* (1905), *Ariadne auf Naxos* (1912), also lyric verse, and the libretto for *Der Rosenkavalier* (music by Richard Strauss).

**Hof'mei'ster** (hōf'mī'stēr), **Franz.** 1850–1922. Austro-German physiological chemist; known for work on proteins, metabolism, and colloidal chemistry.

**Hofmeister, Wilhelm.** 1824–1877. German botanist; one of the first to describe the ovule and the development of the embryo from the fertilized ovum; credited with discovery of alternation of generations in mosses and ferns and their relationship to gymnosperms and angiosperms.

**Hof'meyr** (hŏf'mār), **Jan Hendrik.** 1845–1909. South African politician, b. Cape Town. Editor, *Ons Land* (from 1871). Member of Cape Parliament (1879–95); negotiated for Great Britain with President Kruger and arranged Swaziland convention (1890); supported Cecil Rhodes until Jameson Raid (1895). Initiated Bloemfontein conference between Milner and Kruger (1899). Advocated conciliation after the Boer War (1903); favored federation in South Africa.

**Hof'stadt'er** (hōf'stăt·ēr), **Robert.** 1915– . Amer. physicist, b. New York City. At Stanford U. (1950– ); awarded Nobel prize in physics (1961) with R. L. Mossbauer for research on atomic structure.

**Hof'ste'de de Groot** (hŏf'stā'dĕ dĕ grōt'), **Cornelis.** 1863–1930. Dutch art scholar; compiled catalogue of 17th-century Dutch painters (with art historian Wilhelm Valentiner; 8 vols., 1908–27); wrote esp. on Rembrandt and his works.

**Ho'garth** (hō'gärth), **David George.** 1862–1927. English archaeologist; assisted in excavations at Paphos in Cyprus (1888), in Egypt with Egypt Exploration Fund (1894–96), at Naucratis (1899, 1903), Knossos (1900),

Ephesus (1904–05); keeper of Ashmolean Museum, Oxford (1908–27).

**Hogarth, William.** 1697–1764. English painter and engraver, b. London. Originally apprenticed to a silversmith; concentrated on engraving (from c. 1718). Produced first notable work, plates for Butler's *Hudibras* (1726); followed this with *The Harlot's Progress* (1732) and *The Rake's Progress* (1735). Secured legislation (Hogarth's Act, 1735) protecting designers from piracy. Painted historical pictures at St. Bartholomew's Hospital (1736), and published the prints *The Distrest Poet*, *Company of Undertakers*, and *Sleeping Congregation*. Others of his engravings are *Strolling Actresses dressing in a Barn* (1738), *Marriage à la Mode* (1745), *Industry and Idleness* and *Stage Coach* (1747), *Election* (4 prints, 1755–58), *Cockpit* (1759), *Five Orders of Periwigs* (1761), *The Bathos* (1764). Others of his paintings are portraits of Captain Coram and Martin Folkes, a portrait of himself and his dog, *The March to Finchley*, *Moses and Pharaoh's Daughter*, *Paul before Felix*. Regarded as a supreme pictorial satirist.

**Hog′ben** (hŏg′bĕn), **Lancelot.** 1895–1975. English scientist, educator, and writer; professor of social biology, London (1930–37); regius professor of natural history, Aberdeen (from 1937); to U.S. (1940); visiting professor, Wisconsin. Author of *Nature and Nurture* (1933), *Mathematics for the Million* (1936), *Science for the Citizen* (1938), *Dangerous Thoughts* (1940). His wife (m. 1918), **Enid,** *nee* **Charles** (1894– ), sociologist and geneticist, author of technical papers on genetics, vital statistics, etc., and of *The Practice of Birth Control* (1932) and *The Twilight of Parenthood* (1935).

**Hogg** (hŏg), **Douglas McGarel.** See Viscount HAILSHAM.

**Hogg, James.** *Known as* **the Ett′rick Shepherd** (ĕt′rĭk). 1770–1835. Scottish poet, b. in Ettrick, Selkirk. Friend of Scott, Byron, John Wilson, Wordsworth, Southey. Settled in Edinburgh (1810) and at Eltrive Lake in Yarrow (1816). Among his works are *Donald M'Donald* (1800), *Scottish Pastorals* (1801), *The Mountain Bard* (1807), *Forest Minstrel* (1810), *The Queen's Wake* (1813), *Pilgrims of the Sun* (1815), *The Poetic Mirror* (1816), *Queen Hynde* (1826).

**Hogg, Thomas Jefferson.** 1792–1862. English lawyer, close friend of Shelley. Contributed reminiscences of Shelley at Oxford to Bulwer-Lytton's *New Monthly Magazine* (1832), and published two volumes of a biography of Shelley (1858).

**Hogue** (hōg), **Alexandre.** 1898– . American artist, b. Memphis, Missouri; resident of Texas (from 1904). Known for his paintings of Texas drought landscapes, as in *Drouth Survivors* and *Drouth-Stricken Area.*

**Ho′hen·berg** (hō′ĕn·bĕrk), Duchess of. Countess **Sophie Cho′tek** (kô′tĕk). 1868–1914. Morganatic wife (1900) of Francis Ferdinand (*q.v.*), Archduke of Austria; assassinated with him at Sarajevo, Bosnia (June 28, 1914).

**Ho′hen·lo′he** (hō′ĕn·lō′ĕ). A district in Franconia and a German princely family named from it, originating as a countship in early part of 12th century with Henry I (d. 1183) count of Hohenlohe, whose grandsons, supporters of Frederick II, founded (1230) two lines, which soon through marriages and inheritances (such as Langenburg, Ohringen, Neuenstein, Waldenburg, etc.) became divided and subdivided many times, most branches being now extinct; independence of principality lost (1806); lands now parts of Bavaria and Württemberg. Many members of family have held important military or political posts during 19th and 20th centuries. Among prominent members have been:

HOHENLOHE-ING′EL·FING′EN (-ĭng′ĕl·fĭng′ĕn):

**Friedrich Ludwig.** Prince of **Hohenlohe–Ingelfingen.** 1746–1818. Prussian general, b. at Ingelfingen (in north Württemberg). Served with distinction at Weissenburg (1793) and Kaiserslautern (1794); held part of command at German defeat of Jena (1806); capitulated at Prenzlau (1806); retired (1808).

**Kraft Karl August Eduard Friedrich.** Prince of **Hohenlohe–Ingelfingen.** 1827–1892. Prussian general of artillery, b. in Upper Silesia. Served in Crimean War, at Sadowa in Seven Weeks' War, and in Franco-Prussian War, esp. at the siege of Paris (1870–71); rose in rank (1873–89) to full general; wrote several works on military science.

HOHENLOHE-LANG′EN·BURG (-läng′ĕn·bŏŏrk):

**Hermann.** Prince of **Hohenlohe–Langenburg.** 1832–1913. German soldier. Served in armies of Württemberg, Austria (1854–60), Baden (1862–71), and Prussia; member of Imperial Reichstag (1871–80); governor of Alsace-Lorraine (1894–1907); founder and president (1887–94) of Deutsche Kolonialgesellschaft.

**Ernst.** Prince of **Hohenlohe–Langenburg.** 1863– . Son of Hermann; officer in Prussian army (1889–1900); regent of Saxe-Coburg-Gotha (1900–05) for Duke Charles Edward; member of German Reichstag (1907–11).

HOHENLOHE-WAL′DEN·BURG (-väl′dĕn·bŏŏrk):

**Ludwig Aloysius.** Prince of **Hohenlohe–Waldenburg–Bar′ten·stein** (-bär′tĕn·shtīn). 1765–1829. Marshal and peer of France. Entered service of the Palatinate (1784–92); commanded regiment (1792) for emigrant princes of France; fought under Condé (1792–93), and later for Holland; refused reconciliation with Napoleon; entered French service (1814); marshal (1827).

**Alexander Leopold.** Prince of **Hohenlohe–Waldenburg–Schil′lings·fürst** (-shĭl′ĭngs·fürst). 1794–1849. German Roman Catholic priest, b. at Kupferzell, near Waldenburg, Württemberg. Ordained (1815); member of the society of "Fathers of the Sacred Heart"; gained reputation as miracle-worker at Munich and Bamberg; came into conflict with civil authorities; canon of Oradea (1824) and titular bishop of Sardica (1844).

HOHENLOHE-SCHILLINGSFÜRST:

**Chlodwig Karl Viktor.** Prince of **Hohenlohe–Schillingsfürst** (1845) and Prince of **Ra′ti·bor und Cor′vey** [rä′tē·bôr (-bōr) ŏŏnt kôr′vī] (1840). 1819–1901. Chancellor of the German Empire (1894–1900), b. at Rotenburg an der Fulda; active in Bavarian politics (1846–70; minister of foreign affairs 1866–70); labored for a united Germany; German ambassador at Paris (1874–78); a representative of Germany at the Congress of Berlin (1878); German secretary of foreign affairs (1880–85); governor of Alsace-Lorraine (1885–94); became chancellor (1894); strong supporter of Bismarck; wrote memoirs, *Denkwürdigkeiten* (publ. 1906).

**Gustav Adolf.** Prince of **Hohenlohe–Schillingsfürst.** 1823–1896. Brother of Chlodwig; took holy orders (1849); bishop of Edessa in partibus (1857); cardinal (1866); lived at Rome (1876–79); bishop of Albano (1879–84).

**Ho′hen·stau′fen** (hō′ĕn·shtou′fĕn). A German princely family which furnished sovereigns of Germany (1138–1208, 1215–54) and of Sicily (1194–1268). It derived its name from the ancestral castle at Staufen in Swabia (southern Germany) and originated with Conrad III, King of Germany, who was the son of Agnes, daughter of Emperor Henry IV, and Frederick of Hohenstaufen, Duke of Swabia. It included the Holy Roman emperors Frederick I, Henry VI, Otto IV, and Frederick II, the kings of Germany Philip of Swabia and Conrad IV, and the kings of Sicily Henry VI, Frederick II, Conrad IV,

Manfred, and Conradin. During the 12th and 13th centuries, its rivals were the Welfs (*q.v.*). See *Table* (*in Appendix*) for HOLY ROMAN EMPIRE.

**Ho'hen·zol'lern** (hō'ĕn·tsŏl'ērn). A German royal family, deriving its name from the ancestral castle Zollern, later Hohenzollern, in Swabia, with counts dating from the 11th or 12th century. Two branches, Swabian and Franconian, established (1227): (1) *Swabian* branch existed in two petty principalities, **Hohenzollern-Hech'ing·en** [-hĕk'ĭng·ĕn] (became extinct 1869) and **Hohenzollern-Sig'ma·ring'en** [-zēk'mä·rĭng'ĕn] (until 1849). See CAROL I and II, FERDINAND I, and MICHAEL, kings of Rumania, and CHARLES ANTHONY and LEOPOLD, princes of Hohenzollern-Sigmaringen. (2) *Franconian* branch gave support (12th to 15th centuries) to Hohenstaufens and Hapsburgs. From Conrad III (d. 1261) to Frederick VI (1417–40), territory and influence increased. Frederick VI became first elector and margrave of Brandenburg (*q.v.*) as Frederick I and was followed by eleven electors of Brandenburg (1440–1701); the last, Frederick III (1688–1713), became first king of Prussia (*q.v.*) as Frederick I (1701–13), being succeeded by the Hohenzollern kings of Prussia (1713–1871): Frederick William I, Frederick II the Great, his nephew Frederick William II, then Frederick William III and IV, and William I (1861–88). Last kings of Prussia (1871–1918) were also German emperors: William I, Frederick III, and William II. See *Tables* (*in Appendix*) for GERMANY, PRUSSIA, and RUMANIA, and see also individual biographies of rulers mentioned above.

**Ho·jo** (hō·jō). Family of Japanese nobility of Taira origin that succeeded the Minamotos as rulers of Japan (1219–1333). Its first leader, Tokimasa, councilor and father-in-law of Yoritomo, secured power (c. 1204); family came into full control with death of last Minamoto shogun (1219). As regents over a line of weakling Fujiwara shoguns and puppet emperors, Tokimasa's successors were actual rulers during last century of Kamakura shogunate; put down revolts of emperors and (1281) defeated armada sent against Japan by Kublai Khan; overthrown by Ashikaga shogun Takauji (1333).

**Ho·ku·sai.** *Also* **Ka·tsu·shi·ka Ho·ku·sai** (kä·tso͞o·shē·kä hō·ko͞o·sī). 1760–1849. Japanese artist, b. Yedo. Wood engraver; devoted himself to illustration of books and to industrial art; teacher of drawing, with many pupils. His drawings and color prints were of high technical excellence and had considerable influence on art in foreign countries. His many works include the *Mangwa*, or *Ten Thousand Sketches* (in 15 vols.; last publ. in 1836), the *Hundred Views of Mount Fuji* (1835).

**Hol** (hŏl), **Richard.** 1825–1904. Dutch pianist, conductor, and composer of Masses, symphonies, choral works, chamber music, and songs.

**Hol'a·bird** (hŏl'ȧ·bûrd), **John Augur.** 1886–1945. American architect; practiced architecture in Chicago as member of firm of Holabird & Root, which designed Palmolive, Chicago *Daily News*, and Board of Trade buildings, Chicago, and Chrysler building at Chicago's Century of Progress Exposition (1933).

**Holabird, William.** 1854–1923. American architect; office in Chicago; pioneer in designing skeleton steel skyscrapers.

**Holagu.** Var. of HULAGU.

**Hol'bach'** (ôl'bȧk'; *Ger.* hôl'bäk), Baron **Paul Henri Die'trich'** (dē'trēk'; *Ger.* dē'trĭk) **d'.** 1723–1789. French materialistic philosopher, hostile to religious doctrines; a contributor of many articles to the *Encyclopédie*.

**Hol'bein** (hôl'bīn; *Angl.* hōl'-), **Hans,** the Elder. 1465?–1524. German historical painter, b. Augsburg, Bavaria; among many altarpieces executed by him, his masterpiece is the Altar of St. Sebastian, preserved in the Old Pinakothek, in Munich. His son **Hans** the Younger (1497?–1543) was a portrait and historical painter, and a wood engraver; court painter to Henry VIII of England (c. 1536); among his works are portraits of Erasmus, Sir Thomas More, Anne of Cleves, Henry VIII, a famous series of woodcuts entitled *The Dance of Death*, and a number of religious paintings.

**Hol'berg** (hŏl'bărg), **Ludvig.** 1684–1754. Danish man of letters; regarded as founder of Danish literature. Among his many works are the comic heroic poem *Peder Paars* (1719), a number of comedies for the newly opened Danish theater, historical works, and a novel.

**Hol'brook** (hōl'bro͝ok), **John Edwards.** 1794–1871. American naturalist; M.D., Pennsylvania (1818). Aided in founding (1824) Med. Coll. of South Carolina, Charleston; professor of anatomy there (from 1824). Author of *North American Herpetology* (5 vols., 1842), etc.

**Hol'brooke** (hōl'bro͝ok), **Josef.** 1878–1958. English pianist, conductor, and composer. Among his orchestral works are *The Raven*, *Ulalume*, *The Bells*, and *Queen Mab.* Composer also of chamber music, operas, ballets, and various choral works.

**Hol'comb** (hōl'kŭm), **Thomas.** 1879–1965. American marine officer, b. New Castle, Del.; served in World War (1914–18); promoted through the grades to brigadier general (1935); general (1943); commandant of U.S. marine corps (1936–43); U.S. minister to Union of So. Africa 1944–48).

**Hol'croft** (hōl'krŏft), **Thomas.** 1745–1809. English playwright and miscellaneous writer. Successively, stableboy, shoemaker, and tutor in family of Granville Sharp; later, had experience as an actor. Among his plays are *Duplicity* (1781), *The Road To Ruin* (1792); published also comic operas, novels, and translations.

**Hol'de·man** (hōl'dĕ·măn), **John.** 1830–1900. American Mennonite; founder (1859) of a group now known as the Church of God in Christ, Mennonite.

**Hol'den** (hōl'dĕn), Sir **Edward Hopkinson.** 1848–1919. English financier; authority on foreign exchange and international banking.

**Holden, Edward Singleton.** 1846–1914. American astronomer; grad. U.S.M.A., West Point (1870). At Naval Observatory, Washington, D.C. (1873–79); director, Washburn Observatory, U. of Wisconsin (1881). President, U. of California (1885–88) and director of Lick Observatory (1888–97). Librarian, U.S.M.A., West Point (from 1901).

**Holden,** Sir **Isaac.** 1807–1897. British inventor. Obtained patent (1847, jointly with Samuel Cunliffe Lister) for new method of carding, combing, and preparing genappe yarns; established factory near Paris (1848), later moved to Bradford, England (1864). M.P. (1865–68; 1882–95).

**Holden, Perry Greeley.** 1865–1959. American agronomist; director, agricultural extension department, International Harvester Co. (1912–32). Studied potato, corn, and sugar-beet culture. Originated a plan for improving the teaching of agriculture in rural schools.

**Hol'der** (hōl'dēr), Sir **Frederick William.** 1850–1909. Australian statesman; first speaker of Commonwealth house of representatives (1901–09).

**Holder, Joseph Bassett.** 1824–1888. American physician and naturalist, b. Lynn, Mass. On staff, American Museum of Natural History, New York (from 1871); known for his studies of coral formations along Florida reefs, and for his *History of the American Fauna* (1877). His son **Charles Frederick** (1851–1915) was also on staff of American Museum of Natural History (1871–75), and wrote many popular articles and books on natural history and deep-sea fishing.

**Höl'der·lin** (hûl'dĕr·lēn), **Friedrich,** *in full* **Johann Christian Friedrich.** 1770–1843. German poet; insane (from c. 1802), and confined in an asylum (from 1807). Author of *Hyperion* (a romance in the form of letters, 2 vols., 1797, 1799), *Der Tod des Empedokles* (an unfinished tragedy), and poems including *Der Blinde Sänger, An die Hoffnung, Dichtermut.*

**Holderness,** Earls of. See Sir John RAMSAY and his nephew Prince RUPERT.

**Hold'heim** (hôlt'hīm), **Samuel.** 1806–1860. Jewish theologian; preacher of the Jewish reform movement in Berlin (from 1847); at first orthodox; later, leader of extreme reform party.

**Hol'dich** (hōl'dĭch), Sir **Thomas Hungerford.** 1843–1929. English surveyor and explorer in India. Detailed on survey duty on India's northwest border (1865–66, 1878 ff.); served as member of Russo-Afghan boundary commission (1884); superintendent of frontier surveys (1892–98).

**Hol'ding** (hōl'dĭng), **Elisabeth,** *nee* **Sanx'ay** (săngk'sā). 1889–1955. American novelist, b. Brooklyn, N.Y.; m. George E. Holding; author of *The Unlit Lamp* (1922), *The Silk Purse* (1928), *The Death-Wish* (1934), etc.

**Ho'le·ček** (hô'lĕ·chĕk), **Josef.** 1853–1929. Czech writer; author of chronicle romance *Naši*, depicting life in southern Bohemia (11 vols., 1898–1913).

**Hol'i·day** (hŏl'ĭ·dā), **Henry.** 1839–1927. English painter and stained-glass designer and artist; succeeded (1862) Sir Edward Burne-Jones as designer of cartoons for stained glass at James Powell & Sons' glassworks at Whitefriars in London. Among windows designed by him are some in Salisbury Cathedral, Church of the Epiphany in Washington, D.C., and St. Luke's Hospital in New York.

**Hol'ins·hed** (hŏl'ĭnz·hĕd; *often* -ĭn·shĕd) *or* **Hol'lings·head** (hŏl'ĭngz·hĕd), **Raphael.** d. about 1580. English chronicler; employed by Reginald Wolfe, printer, to do translating, and to continue a chronicle of universal history which Wolfe had begun. His work (pub. 1578) included *Chronicles* of England (to 1575), Scotland (to 1571) and Ireland (to 1547); from Holinshed's *Chronicles* Shakespeare took much of his data for his historical plays, and for parts of *Macbeth, King Lear,* and *Cymbeline.*

**Ho'lit·scher** (hō'lĭ·chĕr), **Arthur.** 1869–?1939. Austrian author of essays, books of travel, literary criticism, and fiction.

**Hol'kar** (hōl'kĕr). Name of the Maratha dynasty of the rulers of Indore, one of the native states of Central India. Its founder, **Malhar Rao Holkar** (1693–1766), gained favor of the peshwa, obtained western half of Malwa, with Indore as his capital; joined (1761) league of Hindu princes to oppose Ahmad Shah, the Afghan king; was at Panipat (1761) but fled before the battle and great defeat of Hindus began; suspected of treason. His widow appointed successor (1766), with **Tukaji Rao I Holkar,** a tribesman but not related, as commander of the army, the latter becoming sole ruler (1795–97). His natural son **Jaswant Rao Holkar** seized throne (1797–1811); driven out, but decisively defeated Marathas at Poona (1802); died insane. Descendants of family ruled at Indore (1811–43); new family, appointed by East India Company, succeeded (1843– ), retaining title of Holkar; recent member, **Tukaji Rao III Holkar** (1911–26), dethroned by British.

**Holl** (hōl). Name of a family of English portrait artists, including: **William** (1771–1838), stipple engraver; his son **Francis** (1815–1884), engraver; Francis's son **Francis Montague,** *known as* **Frank** (1845–1888), portrait painter.

**Holl** (hôl), **Elias.** 1573–1646. German architect; designed Augsburg city hall (1615–20), with its famous "Goldner Saal."

**Hol'land** (hŏl'ănd), Barons. See Henry FOX.

**Holland,** Earl of. See Sir Henry RICH.

**Holland, Clifford Milburn.** 1883–1924. American civil engineer, b. Somerset, Mass. Tunnel engineer, Public Service Commission of New York, in charge of the double subway tunnels under the East River (1914–19); chief engineer, New York State and New Jersey Interstate Bridge and Tunnel commissions, building vehicular tunnel ("Holland Tunnel") under Hudson River (1919–24).

**Holland, George.** 1791–1870. Actor, b. London, England; successful on American stage in comedy roles (from 1827). Two sons, **Edmund Milton** (1848–1913) and **Joseph Jefferson** (1860–1926), became noted actors on the American stage.

**Holland, John.** Duke of **Ex'e·ter** (ĕk'sĕ·tĕr) *and* Earl of **Hun'ting·don** (hŭn'tĭng·dŭn). 1352?–1400. 3d son of Sir Thomas Holland, 1st Earl of Kent and half brother to Richard II. Distinguished himself under John of Gaunt in Spain (1386); chamberlain of England (1389); aided Richard II against Gloucester and Arundel (1397) and rewarded with dukedom; executed for conspiracy against Henry IV. His second son, **John** (1395–1447), Duke of Exeter (restored 1443) and Earl of Huntingdon (restored 1416), distinguished himself at Agincourt (1415), commanded fleet off Harfleur (1417), won victory of Fresney (1420), and commanded expedition for relief of Guînes (1438).

**Holland, John Philip.** 1840–1914. Inventor, b. in County Clare, Ireland. Taught school, Ireland (1858–72); became interested in possibilities of submarine boat. To U.S. (1873); settled in Paterson, N.J., as teacher. Offered submarine design to U.S. Navy Department (1875); navy rejected it as impracticable. Fenian Society financed further experiments; successful submarine, *Fenian Ram,* launched in Hudson River (1881); defects in power system rendered it useless for extended operation. Continued experiments, with aid of naval officers; at Elizabeth, N.J. (1898), launched the *Holland* which had internal-combustion engines for surface power and electric motor for submerged cruising, being the first submarine thus equipped; U.S. government purchased *Holland* (1900) and ordered additional submarines. Last years clouded by litigation with financiers who had supported his companies.

**Holland, Josiah Gilbert.** 1819–1881. American editor and writer; associate editor, Springfield (Mass.) *Republican* (1850–66); editor, *Scribner's Monthly* and its successor *Century Magazine* (from 1870). Author of *Titcomb's Letters to Young People, Single and Married* (under pseudonym, **Timothy Tit'comb** [tĭt'kŭm], 1858), *Lessons in Life* (1861), *Life of Abraham Lincoln* (1866), *The Marble Prophecy and Other Poems* (1872), *Sevenoaks* (1875), *Nicholas Minturn* (1877), *The Puritan's Guest and Other Poems* (1881).

**Holland,** Sir **Nathaniel Dance-.** See George DANCE.

**Holland, Philemon.** 1552–1637. English classical scholar; known as "Translator General." Chief translations, *Livy* (1600), Pliny's *Natural History* (1601), Plutarch's *Moralia* (1603), *Suetonius* (1606), Camden's *Britannia* (1610).

**Holland,** Sir **Thomas Erskine.** 1835–1926. English jurist; professor of international law and diplomacy, Oxford (1874–1910).

**Holland,** Sir **Thomas Henry.** 1868–1947. British geologist; director, geological survey of India (1903–09). Principal and vice-chancellor, U. of Edinburgh (1929–44).

**Holland, William Jacob.** 1848–1932. Moravian pastor (1874–91), zoologist, and paleontologist, b. Jamaica. Director of Carnegie Institute, Pittsburgh (1898–1922). Also an authority on museum administration.

**Hol'lan·der** (hŏl'ăn·dẽr), **Bernard.** 1864–1934. Physician, b. Vienna, Austria; in England (from 1883). Known for studies of mind and character and their deviations from the normal; investigated cerebral localization.

**Hollander, Jacob Harry.** 1871–1940. American economist, b. Baltimore. Professor, Johns Hopkins (from 1904). Treasurer of Puerto Rico (1900–01); introduced revenue system in the island. U.S. special commissioner adjusting public debt of Santo Domingo and the Dominican Republic (1905–10). Umpire in Maryland coal-field disputes (1918–20); chairman of tax-survey commission of Maryland (1931–32). Author of *A Study in Municipal Activity* (1894), *The Abolition of Poverty* (1914), *Economic Liberalism* (1925), *Want and Plenty* (1932), etc.

**Hol'lar** (*Ger.* hôl'är; *Angl.* hŏl'är, -ẽr), **Wenceslaus** *or* **Wenzel.** *Czech* **Václav Ho'lar** (hô'lär). 1607–1677. Bohemian engraver; to England (1635). Engraved *Ornatus Muliebris Anglicanus* (1640), *Charles I and his Queen* (after Vandyke, 1641); illustrated Dugdale's *History of St. Paul's Cathedral*, Ogilby's *Vergil*. Executed map of London after the great fire (1666).

**Hol'les** (hŏl'ĭs). Family name of dukes of NEWCASTLE.

**Holles, Denzil.** 1st Baron **Holles** of I'field (ī'vĕl). 1599–1680. Brother-in-law of Strafford. English statesman. M.P. (1624 ff.); one of two members who held speaker in his chair when he tried to adjourn House of Commons at king's order (Mar. 2, 1629); imprisoned and heavily fined, but compensated by Long Parliament. Impeached as one of Five Members (Jan. 3, 1642). Fought in Parliamentary army at Edge Hill and Brentford; later advocated peace with king; impeached by Parliamentary army (1647); fled to France. After Restoration, created baron (1661); ambassador to France (1663–66).

**Hol'ley** (hŏl'ĭ), **Alexander Lyman.** 1832–1882. American metallurgist and mechanical engineer; bought American rights to Bessemer process for making steel (1863); built plant, and began steel production, first in U.S. by Bessemer process, Troy, N.Y. (1865); obtained patents for improvements in Bessemer process.

**Holley, Horace.** 1887–1960. American writer, b. Torrington, Conn. Secretary, National Spiritual Assembly of Bahais of United States and Canada (1924–30; 1932–40); editor of *World Unity Magazine* (1927–35), *The Bahai World* (1926–38). Author of *The Inner Garden* (verse, 1912), *Divinations and Creation* (verse, 1917), *Bahaism, The Modern Social Religion* (1914), *Bahai—The Spirit of the Age* (1921), etc.

**Holley, Marietta.** *Pseudonym* **Josiah Allen's Wife.** 1836–1926. American humorist, b. in Jefferson County, N.Y. Author of *Samantha at the Centennial* (1877), *Samantha at Saratoga* (1887), *Samantha on the Woman Question* (1913), *Josiah Allen on the Woman Question* (1914).

**Holley, Robert William.** 1922– . Amer. biochemist, b. Urbana, Ill. Awarded Nobel prize in physiology and medicine (1968) with H. Khorana and M. Nirenberg for work on genetic code and its function in protein synthesis.

**Hol'lick** (hŏl'ĭk), **Charles Arthur.** 1857–1933. American geologist and botanist; curator of the department of fossil botany (1900–13), honorary curator (1914–21), paleobotanist (from 1921), New York Botanical Garden.

**Hol'lings·head** (hŏl'ĭngz·hĕd), **John.** 1827–1904. English journalist and theater manager. First manager of Gaiety Theatre (1866–88), where he produced burlesque, operas, and serious drama, and introduced Ibsen to England by presenting *The Pillars of Society* (1880).

**Hollingshead, Raphael.** See HOLINSHED.

**Hol'ling·worth** (hŏl'ĭng·wûrth), **Harry Levi.** 1880–1956. American psychologist; at Columbia U. (1907–46).

**Hol'lins** (hŏl'ĭnz), **George Nichols.** 1799–1878. American naval officer; bombarded Grey Town, Nicaragua, in reprisal for outrages on American citizens (1854). Entered Confederate service (1861); in command of naval forces in upper Mississippi (1862).

**Hol'lis** (hŏl'ĭs), **Ira Nelson.** 1856–1930. American engineer and educator; grad. U.S.N.A., Annapolis (1878). Professor of engineering, Harvard (1893–1913). President, Worcester (Mass.) Polytechnic Institute (1913–25).

**Hol'lo·way** (hŏl'ō·wā), **Emory.** 1885–1977. American educator, b. Marshall, Mo.; professor of English, Adelphi, Garden City, N.Y. (1919–37); author of *Whitman—An Interpretation in Narrative* (1926, awarded Pulitzer prize); editor of Whitman's *Leaves of Grass*, etc.

**Hol'low Horn' Bear'.** 1850–1913. American Sioux Indian chief, b. in Sheridan County, Nebr.; his portrait appears on the 14-cent stamp of the 1922 series of United States postage stamps.

**Holls** (hŏlz), **George Frederick William.** 1857–1903. American lawyer; practiced, New York City. Influential in securing U.S. participation in Peace Conference at The Hague, and served as secretary to American delegation (1899).

**Hol'ly** (hŏl'ĭ), **James Theodore.** 1829–1911. American Negro, Protestant Episcopal bishop, b. Washington, D.C. Ordained deacon (1855); priest (1856); encouraged emigration of American Negroes to Haiti; consecrated bishop of Haiti (1874); resident of Haiti (from 1874).

**Holm** (hŏlm), **Gustav Frederik.** 1849–1940. Danish naval officer and explorer of Greenland; on expeditions to south Greenland (1876, 1880–81); explored east coast of Greenland to Angmagssalik (1883–85); discovered Eskimo communities and five ice fiords.

**Holm, Peter Edward.** 1833–1915. Danish historian of Norway and Denmark.

**Hol'man** (hōl'măn), **William Steele.** 1822–1897. American legislator; member, U.S. House of Representatives (1859–65; 1867–77; 1881–95; 1897); earned reputation as "the Watch Dog of the Treasury" by his attitude on appropriation bills and governmental expenditures.

**Holman–Hunt, William.** = Holman HUNT.

**Holme** (hōm), **Ernest Rudolph.** 1871–1952. Australian educator; educ. Sydney, Paris, and Berlin. Professor of English language, Sydney (from 1921). Special editor for Australian terms, *Webster's New International Dictionary, 2d Edition.*

**Holmes** (hōmz), **A·bi'el** (ȧ·bī'ĕl). 1763–1837. American Congregational clergyman and historian, b. Woodstock, Conn. Pastor, First Church, Cambridge, Mass. (1792–1829). Author of *American Annals, or a Chronological History of America* (2 vols. 1805). See Oliver Wendell HOLMES.

**Holmes, Arthur.** 1890–1965. English geologist; author of *The Age of the Earth* (1913), etc.

**Holmes** (hōmz), **Augusta Mary Anne.** *Fr. form of surname* **Hol'mès'** (ôl'mĕs'). 1847–1903. Composer, b. Paris, of Irish parents; naturalized French citizen (1879). Studied under César Franck. Chief works, *In Exitu Israel* (1874), *Irlande* (symphonic poem, 1882), *Ode Triomphale* (1889), *La Montagne Noire* (opera).

**Holmes, Burton,** *in full* **Elias Burton.** 1870–1958.

American traveler, b. Chicago, Ill. Author of *The Burton Holmes Travelogues* (15 vols.), *The Traveler's Russia* (1934), etc.

**Holmes,** Sir **Charles John.** 1868–1936. English landscape painter and art critic; professor of fine art, Oxford (1904–10); director, keeper, and secretary, National Portrait Gallery (1909–16); director of the National Gallery (1916–28). Author of *Leonardo da Vinci* (1919), *Constable, Gainsborough, and Lucas* (1922), *Raphael* (1933), etc.

**Holmes, Harry Nicholls.** 1879–1958. American chemist; professor, Oberlin (from 1914); known for work in colloidal chemistry. Author of *Out of the Test Tube* (1934), *Have You Had Your Vitamins?* (1938), etc.

**Holmes, John Haynes.** 1879–1964. American clergyman, b. Philadelphia. Ordained in Unitarian ministry (1904); pastor (from 1907), Church of the Messiah, later called the Community Church of New York; relinquished Unitarianism to become independent (1919). Associated with Unitarian Fellowship for Social Justice, American Civil Liberties Union, War Resisters League. Author of *New Wars for Old* (1916), *Religion for Today* (1917), *Is Violence the Way Out?* (1920), *Patriotism Is Not Enough* (1925), etc.

**Holmes, Joseph Austin.** 1859–1915. American geologist. In charge, testing laboratories of U.S. Geological Survey (1904–07); chief, technological branch, U.S. Geological Survey (1907); worked for its reorganization into U.S. Bureau of Mines, of which he became first director (1910). A pioneer in accident-prevention practice in coal mines; popularized slogan "safety first."

**Holmes, Mary Jane,** *nee* **Hawes** (hôz). 1825–1907. American novelist, b. Brookfield, Mass.; m. Daniel Holmes (1849). Wrote many novels, popular in latter half of 19th century, including *Tempest and Sunshine* (1854), *Lena Rivers* (1856), *Gretchen* (1887), *Dr. Hathern's Daughters* (1895), *The Abandoned Farm* (1905).

**Holmes, Nathaniel.** 1815–1901. American jurist; practiced, St. Louis, Mo. (to 1865; and 1872–83); justice, Missouri supreme court (1865–68). Best-known work *The Authorship of Shakespeare* (1866), upholding the Baconian theory.

**Holmes, Oliver Wendell.** 1809–1894. Son of Abiel Holmes. American man of letters, b. Cambridge, Mass. Grad. Harvard (1829); M.D., Harvard (1836); practiced, Boston. Professor of anatomy, Dartmouth (1838–40) and Harvard Med. School (1847–82). Wrote *The Contagiousness of Puerperal Fever* (1842). Sprang into literary fame with contributions, *The Autocrat of the Breakfast-Table,* a series of light, witty talks, in the first numbers of the *Atlantic Monthly* (1857, pub. in book form, 1858); followed by series, *The Professor at the Breakfast-Table* (in book form, 1860) and *The Poet at the Breakfast-Table* (book, 1872). Other works: poetry, *Songs in Many Keys* (1862), *Songs of Many Seasons* (1875), *The Iron Gate and Other Poems* (1880), *Before the Curfew and Other Poems* (1887); novels, *Elsie Venner* (1861), *The Guardian Angel* (1867), *A Mortal Antipathy* (1885); essays, *Soundings from the Atlantic* (1864), *Pages from an Old Volume of Life* (1883), *Our Hundred Days in Europe* (1887); biography, *John Lothrop Motley* (1879), *Ralph Waldo Emerson* (1885). Among his best-known poems are *Old Ironsides, The Chambered Nautilus, The Last Leaf, Dorothy Q, The Deacon's Masterpiece, or, The Wonderful One-Hoss Shay,* and the hymn *Lord of all being! throned afar.* Elected to American Hall of Fame (1910). See Oliver Wendell HOLMES (1841–1935).

**Holmes, Oliver Wendell.** 1841–1935. Son of Oliver Wendell Holmes (1809–1894). American jurist, b. Boston. A.B. (1861), LL.B. (1866), Harvard. Served in Union army in Civil War, at Ball's Bluff, Antietam, Fredericksburg. Adm. to bar (1867); practiced in Boston; professor of law, Harvard Law School (1882). Associate justice (1882–99) and chief justice (1899–1902), supreme court of Massachusetts. Associate justice, U.S. Supreme Court (1902–32). Author of *The Common Law* (1881). Some of his opinions were published as *The Dissenting Opinions of Mr. Justice Holmes* (1929). Elected to American Hall of Fame (1965).

**Holmes, Samuel Jackson.** 1868–1964. American zoologist, b. Henry, Ill. Associate professor (1912–17), professor (from 1917), U. of California. Author of *The Evolution of Animal Intelligence* (1911), *Studies in Animal Behavior* (1916), *Studies in Evolution and Eugenics* (1923), *The Negro's Struggle for Survival* (1937), etc.

**Holmes, Thomas Rice Edward.** 1855–1933. British schoolmaster and writer; assistant master of St. Paul's School (1886–1909); author of *A History of the Indian Mutiny* (1883), *Caesar's Conquest of Gaul* (1899), *Sir Charles Napier* (1925), etc.

**Holmes, William Henry.** 1846–1933. American anthropologist and archaeologist. Archaeologist, Bureau of American Ethnology (1889–98); chief, Bureau of American Ethnology (1902–09); head curator of anthropology, U.S. National Museum (1910–20), also curator (1910–20) and director (from 1920), National Gallery of Art. Author of *Pottery of the Ancient Pueblos* (1886), *Handbook of Aboriginal American Antiquities* (1919), etc.

**Holm'gren'** (hôlm'grān'), **Alarik Frithiof.** 1831–1897. Swedish physiologist; known for work in ophthalmology, esp. on color blindness; advocate of Swedish gymnastics (exercises done without apparatus).

**Holofernes.** See JUDITH.

**Hol'royd** (hŏl'roid), Sir **Charles.** 1861–1917. English painter and etcher; first keeper of Tate Gallery, London (1897–1906); director of National Gallery, London (1906–16). Etcher of figure subjects, landscapes, and portraits.

**Holst** (hŏlst), *orig.* **von Holst** (fôn hôlst'), **Gustav.** 1874–1934. English musician, composer, and teacher. Composer of symphonies, operas, orchestral suites, and esp. hymns, psalms, and other choral works.

**Holst** (hŏlst), **Hans Peter.** 1811–1893. Danish writer; dramaturgist at Royal Theater, Copenhagen (1874); established reputation by a short poem on the death of Frederick VI (1839); author of the novel cycle *Der Kleine Hornblaser* (1849), and other novels and plays.

**Holst** (hōlst), **Hermann Eduard von.** 1841–1904. Historian, b. Fellin, Russia (now in Estonia); to U.S. (1867). Called to Germany as professor of history, Strassburg (1872–74) and Freiburg (1874–92). Head, department of history, U. of Chicago (1892–1900). Author of *The Constitutional and Political History of the United States* (8 vols., 1877–92; trans. from German work, 5 vols., 1873–91), *John C. Calhoun* (1882), *The Constitutional Law of the United States* (1887; from German work, 1885), *The French Revolution Tested by Mirabeau's Career* (2 vols., 1894).

**Hol'stein** (hŏl'shtīn), **Franz von.** 1826–1878. German composer of the operas *Der Haideschacht* (1868), *Der Erbe von Morley* (1872), *Die Hochländer* (1876); composer also of overtures, choral works, chamber music, and songs.

**Holstein, Friedrich von.** 1837–1909. German diplomat and statesman. After dismissal of Bismarck (1890), Holstein wielded powerful influence in shaping German foreign policy.

**Holstein–Gottorp.** See OLDENBURG, 3.

**Holstein–Sönderborg.** See OLDENBURG, 4.

**Hol'sti** (hŏl'stĭ), **Eino Rudolf Woldemar.** 1881–1945.

Finnish diplomat; M.A. (1908), Ph.D. (1913), U. of Helsinki; minister to Great Britain (1918–19), to Estonia and Latvia (1923–27); secured recognition of independence of Finland (Paris Peace Conference, 1919); foreign minister (1919–22, 1936–38); delegate to League of Nations (1927–40); professor, Stanford U. (from 1941).

**Holt** (hōlt), **Edwin Bissell.** 1873–1946. American psychologist; author of *The Concept of Consciousness* (1914), *The Freudian Wish* (1915), *Animal Drive and the Learning Process* (vol. 1, 1931).

**Holt, Hamilton.** 1872–1951. American educator; managing editor (1897–1913), editor and owner (1913–21), *The Independent*, New York City. President, Rollins College (1925–49).

**Holt, Harold Edward.** 1908–1967. Australian politician; prime minister of Australia (1966–67).

**Holt, Henry.** 1840–1926. American publisher and author, b. Baltimore, Md. In publishing business (from 1866); organized firm of Henry Holt & Co. (1873). Author of the novels *Calmire, Man and Nature* (1892) and *Sturmsee, Man and Man* (1905), and of *Talks on Civics* (1901), *On the Cosmic Relations* (1914), *Garrulities of an Octogenarian Editor* (1923).

**Holt,** Sir **Herbert Samuel.** 1856–1941. Canadian financier, b. County Kildare, Ireland; to Canada at age of 19. Successively railroad laborer, contractor; organized Montreal Light, Heat & Power Co. (c. 1901). Chairman of the board, Montreal Light, Heat & Power Co. and Royal Bank of Canada; president, Montreal Trust Co.

**Holt,** Sir **John.** 1642–1710. English jurist. Educ. Oxford. Lord chief justice of King's Bench (1689–1710). Known for discouraging prosecutions for witchcraft, for liberal construction of statute compelling church attendance, and for strict views of treason and seditious libel.

**Holt, Joseph.** 1807–1894. American political leader, b. in Breckinridge County, Ky. Adm. to bar; practiced, Elizabethtown, Ky. (to 1832) and Louisville (from 1832). U.S. commissioner of patents (1857); U.S. postmaster general (1859–61); U.S. secretary of war (1861); judge advocate general, U.S. army (1862–75). As judge advocate general, prosecuted those charged with having conspired with John Wilkes Booth in assassination of Lincoln; accused of suppressing evidence and keeping from President Johnson the military commission's recommendation of clemency for Mrs. Surratt.

**Holt, Luther Emmett.** 1855–1924. American physician, b. Webster, N.Y. Specialist in treatment and diseases of children. Author of *The Care and Feeding of Children* (1894), *Diseases of Infancy and Childhood* (1896).

**Holt, Winifred.** d. 1945. American philanthropist, b. New York City; m. (1922) Rufus Graves Mather (1874–1952). Sculptor esp. of portrait busts and bas-reliefs. Founder, New York Association for the Blind, with headquarters, known as "The Lighthouse," in New York City; extended work to France during World War, and then to Poland, Italy, and other countries.

**Holt'by** (hōlt'bĭ), **Winifred.** 1898–1935. English novelist; author of *Anderby Wold, The Crowded Street, Mandoa, Mandoa, Take What You Want* (U.S. title, *South Riding*), etc.

**Hol'tei** (hôl'tī), **Karl von** 1798–1880. German poet, novelist, and playwright.

**Holt'hau'sen** (hôlt'hou'zĕn), **Ferdinand.** 1860–1956. German philologist; authority on Anglo-Saxon and Germanics; editor of Old and Middle English texts.

**Höl'ty** (hûl'tē), **Ludwig Christoph Heinrich.** 1748–1776. German poet; author of the patriotic idyl *Das Feuer im Walde*, and numerous odes, elegies, and songs.

**Holtz** (hôlts), **Wilhelm.** 1836–1913. German physicist; invented an electrostatic induction machine (1865); author of works on the theory of electricity and on lighting protection.

**Holt'zen·dorff** (hôl'tsĕn·dôrf), **Franz von.** 1829–1889. German jurist; authority on criminal law and international law.

**Holtz'mann** (hôlts'män), **Adolf.** 1810–1870. German philologist. His nephew **Heinrich** (1832–1910) was a Protestant theologian.

**Ho'lub** (hô'lo͝op), **Emil.** 1847–1902. Bohemian explorer and naturalist in Africa. Surgeon in diamond fields of South Africa (1872–73); made three exploring trips in southern Africa, reaching the Zambezi and the Victoria Falls (1873–75); on third trip, accompanied by his wife, intended to traverse Africa from Cape Town to Egypt, but was prevented by hostile tribesmen from going more than a third of the distance (1883–87).

**Ho Lung** (hō' lo͝ong'). 1886?– . Chinese Communist leader, b. in Hunan, of a peasant family; early enlisted with revolutionary forces; joined Communist forces (1927); with Chu Teh was defeated in several campaigns; took part in the "Long March" (1934–36) of the Eighth Route Army; one of the leading Communists in the war against Japan (1937 ff.).

**Ho'ly·oake** (hō'lĭ·ōk), **George Jacob.** 1817–1906. English social reformer. A Chartist (1832); an Owenite (1838) and minister to Owenites at Worcester (1840); turned rationalist, and edited *Oracle of Reason* (1841). To London (1843); edited *Reasoner* (1846) and *Leader* (1850). Author of *A History of Co-operation* (1875–77), *Sixty Years of an Agitator's Life* (2 vols., 1892), *Bygones Worth Remembering* (1905).

**Holywood, John of.** See Johannes de SACROBOSCO.

**Holz** (hôlts), **Arno.** 1863–1929. German man of letters; author of lyric poetry, fiction, plays, and esp. literary criticism; regarded as one of the founders of naturalism in German literature.

**Holz'mei'ster** (hôlts'mī'stẽr), **Clemens.** 1886– . Austrian architect; designed the Salzburg Festival Theater, government buildings in Ankara, Turkey, the Dollfuss Memorial in Vienna.

**Holz'schu'her** (hôlts'sho͞o'ẽr), **Hieronymus.** 1469–1529. Councilor of Nuremberg; friend of Dürer.

**Hom'berg** (hôm'bĕrK), **Willem.** 1652–1715. Dutch naturalist and chemist, b. in Batavia, Java. Grad. in medicine at Wittenberg; practiced at Paris (1682–85, and after 1691) and Rome (1685–90); discovered boracic acid (1702); observed the green color produced in flames by copper, the crystallization of salt, etc.

**Home** (hūm). see also HUME.

**Home,** Sir **Alec Douglas-.** 1903– . British politician; educ. Oxford; M.P. (1931–45; 1950–51); minister of state, Scottish office (1951–55); secretary of state for Commonwealth Relations (1955–60); secretary of state for foreign affairs (1960–63); prime minister (1963–64).

**Home, Daniel Dun·glas'** (dŭn·glȧs'). 1833–1886. Scottish spiritualist medium, b. near Edinburgh. To U.S. (c. 1842); adopted by an aunt, but turned out of her home because of mysterious rappings. His séances being attended by prominent persons, including William Cullen Bryant. To England (1855); his séances here also attended by prominent persons, including the Brownings; subject of Robert Browning's poem *Sludge the Medium* (1864). Held séances before French, Prussian, and Dutch sovereigns (1857–58); expelled from Rome as sorcerer (1864); convinced scientist Sir William Crookes by submitting to tests in full light (1871).

**Home,** Sir **Everard.** 1756–1832. Scottish surgeon; first president, Royal Coll. of Surgeons (1821).

**Home, Henry.** Lord **Kames** (kămz). 1696–1782. Scottish jurist and philosopher. Lord of justiciary (1763–82). Author of *Essays on the Principles of Morality and Natural Religion* (1751), *Elements of Criticism* (1762), etc.

**Home, John.** 1722–1808. Scottish clergyman and playwright; educ. Edinburgh U.; took part in rebellion of 1745; minister at Athelstaneford (1747–57); private secretary to Bute, and tutor to prince of Wales; pensioned by George III. His plays include *Douglas* (1756), *Agis* (1758), *Alonzo* (1773).

**Ho'mer** (hō'mẽr). Traditional ancient Greek poet, to whom are ascribed the *Iliad* and the *Odyssey*, epics on the Trojan War and the wanderings of Odysseus (Ulysses). A school of modern criticism maintains that the *Iliad* and *Odyssey* are not the work of any one poet but composite products of many poets who contributed over many generations of history to the growth of these epics to their final form. The so-called "Homeric Hymns," once attributed to Homer, are probably the work of rhapsodists. Various dates have been assigned to the traditional Homer, from the 850 B.C. of Herodotus to a date as early as 1200 B.C.

**Homer** the Younger. Greek tragic poet of 3d century B.C.; ranked as a member of the Pleiad of Alexandria.

**Homer, Sidney.** 1864–1953. American composer, esp. of music for songs, including Tennyson's *Sweet and Low*, Holmes's *Last Leaf*, Stevenson's *Requiem*, and songs for children from Christina Rossetti's *Sing-Song*. He married (1895) **Louise Dilworth Beat'ty** [bē'tĭ] (1871–1947), operatic contralto, b. Pittsburgh, Pa.; with Metropolitan Opera Company, N.Y. (1900–19); with Chicago Civic Opera (from 1920); also sang in recitals throughout U.S.; leading roles, Amneris in *Aïda*, Laura in *La Gioconda*, Delilah in *Samson and Delilah*, Brangäne in *Tristan und Isolde*.

**Homer, Winslow.** 1836–1910. American painter, b. Boston. Apprenticed to lithographer (1855–57). Opened studio, Boston (1857) and New York (1859). Contributed drawings to *Harper's Weekly* (1859–67). Resided Scarboro, Me. (from 1884); there painted notable marines. Examples of his work: *The Gulf Stream; Northeaster; Cannon Rock; Maine Coast;* and twelve fine water colors, now in Metropolitan Museum of Art, New York; *All's Well*, in Museum of Fine Arts, Boston; *A Light on the Sea*, Corcoran Art Gallery, Washington, D.C.; *High Cliff*, in National Gallery of Art, Washington, D.C.; *Early Evening*, in Freer Gallery, Washington, D.C.; *A Summer Night*, in Luxembourg Museum, Paris.

**Hom'mel** (hôm'ĕl), **Fritz.** 1854–1936. German Semitic scholar; authority on southern Semitic philology and Assyriology.

**Ho'molle'** (ô'môl'), **Théophile.** 1848–1925. French archaeologist; director (1890), French school at Athens and its excavations at Delphi (1892–1903); director, national museums in France (1904); director, French National Library (1913–24).

**Hon'de·coe'ter** (hôn'dĕ·kōō'tẽr), **Melchior d'.** 1636–1695. Dutch painter; son of the painter **Gijsbert d'Hondecoeter** [dôn'-] (1604–1653). Melchior was noted as a painter of animals, esp. birds.

**Hon'di·us** (hŏn'dĭ·ŭs), **Jodocus.** *Real name* **Joos de Hondt** (dĕ hônt'). 1563–1611. Flemish engraver in England; illustrated voyages of Drake and Cavendish; engraved portraits; made large globes.

**Hondt, Pieter De.** See Saint Peter CANISIUS.

**Hone** (hōn), **Philip.** 1780–1851. American businessman and diarist; auctioneer, New York (1796–1821). Mayor of New York (1825). His *Diary*, kept from 1828 to 1851, gives valuable impressions of life in New York and of the beginnings of the Whig party.

**Hone, William.** 1780–1842. English satirist and bookdealer. Wrote political satires illustrated by Cruikshank (1817 ff.); established bookshop in London and published *Political House that Jack Built* (1819), *Man in the Moon* (1820), *Political Showman* (1821), etc.

**Ho'neg'ger** (hō'nĕg'ẽr; *Fr.* ô'nĕ'gâr'), **Arthur.** 1892–1955. French composer, of Swiss descent; identified with ultramodern school of music in Paris; leader of a group known as "The Six" (Honegger, Auric, Durey, Milhaud, Poulenc, Taillefere). Among his notable compositions are the oratorios *King David* and *Nicolas de Flue*, biblical drama *Judith*, various stage pieces, symphonic orchestral works (*Pacific 231*, *Song of Joy*, *Rugby*, etc.), chamber music, and songs.

**Ho·no'ri·a** (hō·nō'rĭ·ȧ), **Justa Grata.** fl. 1st half of 5th century A.D. Roman princess; daughter of Emperor Constantius III; brought up in the court of Theodosius II at Constantinople. Reputed to have sought marriage with Attila, the Hun, who through her claimed (c. 450) a portion of the Roman Empire and, his demands being rejected, invaded Gaul.

**Ho·no'ri·us** (hō·nō'rĭ·ŭs). Name of four popes (see *Table of Popes*, Nos. 70, 163, 177, 190) and one antipope:

**Honorius I.** d. 638. Pope (625–638), b. in the Campagna, Italy. Took great interest in affairs of the church in England; worked in accord with Emperor Heraclius; wrote letters (c. 634) to Sergius, Patriarch of Constantinople, favoring the Monothelete doctrine; condemned for this by Council of Constantinople (680).

**Honorius II.** *Real name* **Lamberto Scan'na·bec'chi** (skăn'nä·bāk'kē). d. 1130. Pope (1124–30), b. near Imola, Italy. While cardinal bishop, concluded Concordat of Worms (1122) with Henry V, settling the question of investiture; supported by the Frangipani, esp. in his opposition to antipope Celestine III; recognized Lothair III of Saxony as emperor; confirmed order of Knights Templars.

**Honorius II.** *Real name* **Pietro Cad'a·lo'us** (kăd'ȧ·lō'ŭs). d. 1072. Antipope (1061–64); chosen by Lombard bishops in opposition to Alexander; deposed by Council of Milan.

**Honorius III.** *Real name* **Cencio Sa·vel'li** (sä·vĕl'lē). Pope (1216–27), b. Rome. Urged crusades against the Albigenses and to the Holy Land; active in urging peace in several European countries; confirmed orders of Dominicans (1216) and of Franciscans (1223); author of many ecclesiastical works and letters.

**Honorius IV.** *Real name* **Giacomo Savelli.** 1210?–1287. Pope (1285–87).

**Honorius, Flavius.** 384–423. Roman emperor of the West (395–423). Second son of Theodosius the Great, b. Constantinople. On death of his father received western half of empire under guardianship of Stilicho; resided at Milan and later, for most of his reign, at Ravenna; m. daughter of Stilicho; caused death of Stilicho (408); lived in ease at Ravenna while Alaric ravaged Italy and sacked Rome (410); several provinces lost to empire, Roman power greatly declined; made Constantius III coemperor of the West (421).

**Hont'heim** (hōnt'hīm), **Johann Nikolaus von.** 1701–1790. German Roman Catholic prelate; opponent of ultramontanism. Best known for his *De Statu Ecclesiae et Legitima Potestate Romani Pontificis* (1763), published under pseudonym **Justinus Fe·bro'ni·us** (fā·brō'nē·ōōs), origin of the Febronian doctrine.

**Hont'horst** (hônt'hôrst), **Gerard van.** 1590–1656. Dutch painter; best known as a portrait and figure painter, often of night scenes.

**Hooch** *or* **Hoogh** (hōκ), **Pieter de.** 1629–after 1677. Dutch painter of genre scenes, esp. interiors.

**Hood** (hŏŏd). Name of an English family several members of which were high-ranking British naval officers, including: **Samuel** (1724–1816), 1st Viscount **Hood** (cr. 1796), British admiral; entered navy (1741), in command of the *Vestal* captured French frigate *Bellona* (1759); commander in chief on North American station (1767–70); rear admiral (1780); fought de Grasse (1781) and outmaneuvered him off St. Kitts (1782); commanded rear under Rodney in defeat of De Grasse off Dominica (1782); took possession of Toulon (1793) and Corsica (1794); admiral (1794). His younger brother **Alexander** (1727–1814), 1st Viscount **Brid′port** (brĭd′pōrt); entered navy (1741), commanded the *Robust* at Ushant (1778); rear admiral (1780) and one of Howe's flag officers at relief of Gibraltar (1782); had full share in operations culminating in action of "the Glorious First of June" off Ushant (1794); captured three French ships (1795); as commander in chief of Channel fleet directed blockade of Brest (1797–1800); vice-admiral of England (1796). Two sons of **Samuel**, of Kingsland, Dorset, a purser in the navy and first cousin of Viscount Hood and Viscount Bridport, were also naval officers: Sir **Alexander** (1758–1798), entered navy (1767), accompanied Capt. Cook in the *Resolution* on second circumnavigation (1772); commanded one of Rodney's frigates in victory off Dominica (1782); in command of the *Mars* mortally wounded in victory over French *Hercule* (1798); and his brother Sir **Samuel** (1762–1814), entered navy (1776), served in actions in West Indies leading to Rodney's victory off Dominica (1782); resourcefully extricated his frigate from Toulon (1793); participated in Nelson's attack on Santa Cruz de Tenerife (1797) and in battle of the Nile (1798); commodore at Leeward station (1803–04); lost an arm blockading Rochefort (1805); vice-admiral (1811); commander in chief in East Indies (1811–14). **Arthur William Acland** (1824–1901), 1st Baron **Hood of Av′a·lon** (ăv′ȧ·lŏn); grandson of Sir Alexander Hood (1758–98); entered navy (1836), served before Sevastopol; participated in capture of Canton, China (1857); director of naval ordnance (1869–74); rear admiral (1876); vice-admiral (1880); commanded Channel fleet (1880–82); first sea lord of admiralty (1885–89) and admiral (1885); known for his antagonism to innovation. Sir **Horace Lambert Alexander** (1870–1916), son of 4th Viscount Hood; entered navy (1883), served on the Nile (1897–98) and Somaliland expedition (1903–04); commander of naval college at Osborne (1910–14); rear admiral (1913); commanded 3d battle cruiser squadron at Jutland (1916) and went down with his flagship *Invincible.*

**Hood, Edwin Paxton.** 1820–1885. English Congregationalist clergyman; author of popular biographies of Milton, Marvell, Swedenborg, Wordsworth, Carlyle, Cromwell.

**Hood, John Bell.** 1831–1879. American army officer, b. Owingsville, Ky.; grad. U.S.M.A., West Point (1853). entered Confederate army (1861); brigadier general (Mar. 2, 1862) in command of "Texas Brigade" which won reputation at Gaines's Mill, Second Manassas, and Antietam; major general (Oct. 11, 1862) under Longstreet at Gettysburg; lost right leg at Chickamauga; lieutenant general (1864); transferred to J. E. Johnston's army; replaced Johnston and conducted defense of Atlanta against Sherman; after unsuccessful engagements against Thomas and Schofield, relieved at own request (Jan. 23, 1865). After Civil War, commission merchant in New Orleans.

**Hood, Raymond Mathewson.** 1881–1934. American architect, b. Pawtucket, R.I.; practiced in New York City. Collaborated with John Mead Howells in submitting successful designs in competition for *Tribune* Tower in Chicago (1922) and in design of *Daily News* building in New York; associated with Harvey Corbett in submitting designs for Radio City, in New York City.

**Hood, Thomas.** 1799–1845. English poet and humorist, b. London. Son of **Thomas Hood** (d. 1811), Scottish bookseller. Learned engraving; subeditor, *London Magazine* (1821–23); wrote, with his brother-in-law J. H. Reynolds, *Odes and Addresses to Great People* (1825); won reputation on series of *Comic Annual* (1830–42), treating current events with caricature; showed poetical powers as editor (1829) of the *Gem*, an annual in which appeared *Eugene Aram's Dream* (1829); other serious verse included *The Plea of the Midsummer Fairies* (1827), *The Bridge of Sighs* (1844); began *Hood's Magazine* (1844); his *Song of the Shirt* appeared in *Punch* (1843); other works, *Whims and Oddities* (1826, 1827), *Tylney Hall*, a novel (1834), *Miss Kilmansegg*, comic poem, and *Whimsicalities* (1844). His son **Thomas**, *known as* **Tom** (1835–1874), humorist and journalist, served in the war office five years; became editor of *Fun* (1865), and began series of *Tom Hood's Comic Annuals* (1867).

**Hooft** (hōft), **Pieter Corneliszoon.** 1581–1647. Dutch historian, poet, and playwright; center of a group of artists, poets, and men of letters identified with the Dutch renaissance.

**Hoogh.** See HOOCH.

**Hoog′strae′ten** (hōĸ′strä′tĕn), **Jakob van.** 1460?–1527. Belgian Dominican monk; papal inquisitor for Cologne, Mainz, and Treves; involved in controversy with Reuchlin (*q.v.*); ridiculed in *Epistolae Obscurorum Virorum.*

**Hoogstraeten, Samuel van.** 1627–1678. Dutch painter; studied under his father **Dirck van Hoogstraeten** (1596–1640) and under Rembrandt. Painter of genre pictures, portraits, and still life.

**Hook** (hŏŏk), **James.** 1746–1827. English organist (at Vauxhall Gardens, 1774–1820) and composer of more than 2000 songs. A son, **James** (1772?–1828), was dean of Worcester (1825–28). Another son, **Theodore Edward** (1788–1841), humorist and novelist, edited *John Bull* (1820) and *New Monthly Magazine* (1836–41); author (writing under several pseudonyms, as **Richard Jones,** Mrs. **Rams′bot′tom** [rămz′bŏt′ŭm], **Vi·ces′i·mus Blen′kin·sop** [vī·sĕs′ĭ·mŭs blĕng′kĭn·sŏp]) of *Exchange no Robbery* (farce), *Tentamen* (satire on Queen Caroline), and the novels *Maxwell* (1830), *Gilbert Gurney* (1836), *Jack Brag* (1836), *Births, Marriages, and Deaths* (1839); the original of Mr. Wagg in Thackeray's *Vanity Fair.* A son of James (1772?–1828), **Walter Farquhar** (1798–1875), educ. Oxford, vicar of Leeds (1837–59), dean of Chichester (1859–75), compiled *Church Dictionary* (1842) and *Dictionary of Ecclesiastical Biography* (1845–52), and wrote *Lives of the Archbishops of Canterbury* (12 vols., 1860–76).

**Hook, James Clarke.** 1819–1907. English painter of genre subjects, landscapes, and portraits, including *The Samphire Gatherer, The Stream.*

**Hook, William.** 1600–1677. English Puritan clergyman; to New England (1640); pastor in Massachusetts and Connecticut. Returned to England (1656) and became one of Cromwell's chaplains. Published a sermon, *New England's Teares for Old England's Feares* (1640), and *A Catechisme...for the...Church...at New Haven* (1659, with John Davenport).

**Hooke** (hŏŏk), **Robert.** 1635–1703. English experimental philosopher, b. on Isle of Wight; educ. Oxford. Assistant to Thomas Willis in chemistry researches and to Robert Boyle with his air pump. Gresham professor of geometry, Oxford (1665); surveyor of London and designer of Montague House, Bethlehem Hospital, and Coll. of Physicians. Author of *Micrographia* (1665), in which he explained true nature of combustion. Proved experimentally that center of gravity of earth and moon is the point describing an ellipse around sun; discovered fifth star in Orion; inferred rotation of Jupiter; one of first to use balance spring in watches; expounded correct theory of elasticity and kinetic hypothesis of gases (1678); anticipated Newton in formulation of law of inverse squares; constructed first Gregorian telescope; invented a marine barometer.

**Hook'er** (ho͝ok'ẽr), **Brian,** *in full* **William Brian.** 1880–1946. American writer, b. New York City. Teacher of English at Yale (1905–09), Columbia (1915–18). Author of *The Right Man* (1908) and of several operas, including *Mona* (1911; awarded prize in Metropolitan Opera Company competition), *Fairyland* (1915; awarded prize in American Opera Association competition), *Morven and the Grail* (1915), and a commemorative poem *A.D. 1919*, all with music by Horatio Parker. Translator of *Cyrano de Bergerac* (1923). Collaborator in *June Love* (1920), *The Vagabond King* (1925), etc.

**Hooker, Joseph.** 1814–1879. American army officer, b. Hadley, Mass.; grad. U.S.M.A., West Point (1837). At outbreak of Civil War, appointed brigadier general of volunteers (May 17, 1861); distinguished himself at Williamsburg (May 5, 1862), winning sobriquet of "Fighting Joe"; wounded at Antietam; brigadier general, U.S. army (Sept. 20, 1862). Succeeded Burnside in command of Army of the Potomac (Jan. 26, 1863); failed to defeat Lee at Chancellorsville (May 2–4, 1863); at own request, relieved of command and succeeded by Meade (June 28, 1863); served under Thomas and Sherman. Retired, as major general (1868).

**Hooker, Richard.** 1554?-1600. English theologian; educ. Oxford; held livings in Wiltshire and Kent. Chief work *The Laws of Ecclesiastical Polity* (4 books, 1594; 5th book, 1597; 3 more added after his death).

**Hooker, Thomas.** 1586?–1647. Congregational clergyman, b. in Leicestershire, England. Pastorates in England (1620–30). Puritan sympathies caused him to be cited to appear before Court of High Commission (1630); fled to Holland (1630), and to America, with John Cotton and Samuel Stone (1633). Pastor, Newtown, Mass. (1633–36). Migrated with his congregation to Connecticut and settled Hartford (1636). Active in framing and securing adoption of the "Fundamental Orders" which served as constitution for Connecticut (1639). Favored (from 1639) defensive confederation of New England settlements, accomplished (1643) by organization of "United Colonies of New England."

**Hooker,** Sir **William Jackson.** 1785–1865. English botanist; director of Kew Gardens, where he co-operated with John Stevens Henslow in founding a museum of economic botany (1847). His son Sir **Joseph Dalton** (1817–1911), also a botanist; member of Ross's antarctic expedition (1839–43), publishing botanical results in six volumes (1844–60); collaborated with Darwin in researches on origin of species; explored eastern Nepal (1848–49), and eastern Bengal (1850–51); assistant director of Kew Gardens (1855) and director (1865); extended travels in North Africa and in Rocky Mountains in U.S. in search of botanical specimens; member of Order of Merit (1907).

**Hooker, Worthington.** 1806–1867. American physician; author of *Physician and Patient* (1849); *Human Physiology* (1854), *Rational Therapeutics* (1857), *Natural History* (1860), *First Book in Chemistry* (1862), etc.

**Hoole** (ho͞ol), **John.** 1727–1803. English translator and playwright; author of three tragedies presented at Covent Garden; translator of Tasso's *Jerusalem Delivered* (1763) and Ariosto's *Orlando Furioso* (1783).

**Hoo'per** (ho͞o'pẽr; ho͝op'ẽr), **Ellen,** *nee* **Stur'gis** (stûr'jĭs). 1816?–?1848. American poet; m. Robert W. Hooper. Author of hymns and lyrical verse, including the poem *Beauty and Duty* (beginning "I slept, and dreamed that life was beauty").

**Hooper, Franklin Henry.** 1862–1940. American editor; on staff of Century Co., New York (1883–96), and an editor of *Century Dictionary;* on staff of *Encyclopaedia Britannica* (from 1899), and editor in chief (1932–38).

**Hooper, John.** d. 1555. English prelate and martyr; turned Protestant; fled from England (1539) to escape persecution. Returned to England (1549); bishop of Gloucester (1550), Worcester (1552). Deprived of his see by Queen Mary; condemned for heresy; burned at the stake, at Gloucester (Feb. 9, 1555).

**Hooper, Johnson Jones.** 1815–1862. American humorist, b. Wilmington, N.C.; author of *Some Adventures of Captain Simon Suggs, Late of the Tallapoosa Volunteers* (1846) and *The Widow Rugby's Husband* (1851).

**Hooper, William.** 1742–1790. American Revolutionary leader, b. Boston. Active in pre-Revolutionary agitation. Member, Continental Congress (1774–77); signer of Declaration of Independence.

**Hoorn,** Count of. See HORN.

**Hoo'ton** (ho͞o't'n), **Earnest Albert.** 1887–1954. American anthropologist, b. Clemansville, Wis. Rhodes scholar at Oxford (1910–13). On Harvard faculty (from 1913), professor (from 1930); curator of Peabody Museum, Harvard (from 1914). Author of *Up from the Ape* (1931), *Apes, Men and Morons* (1937), *Crime and the Man* (1939), *Twilight of Man* (1939), *Why Men Behave Like Apes, and Vice Versa* (1940), *Man's Poor Relations* (1942), etc.

**Hoo'ver** (ho͞o'vẽr), **Charles Ruglas.** 1885–1942. American chemist; worked on the determination of atomic weights, the analysis of gases, laboratory construction and equipment, etc.; invented a gas absorbent and a gas detector during World War (1917–18).

**Hoover, Herbert Clark.** 1874–1964. Thirty-first president of the United States, b. West Branch, Iowa. A.B. in mining engineering, Stanford (1895). Mining engineer in many parts of world (1895–1913), with headquarters in London (from 1902). Chairman of American Relief Commission in London (1914–15) and of Commission for Relief in Belgium (1915–19); also, U.S. food administrator (1917–19). Directed various economic measures in Europe during armistice; in charge of relief in countries of eastern Europe (1921). U.S. secretary of commerce (1921–28). President of the U.S. (1929–33).

**Hoover, John Edgar.** 1895–1972. American lawyer and criminologist, b. Washington, D.C. LL.B., George Washington U. (1916). On staff of Department of Justice (1917); director, Federal Bureau of Investigation, Department of Justice (1942–1972).

**Hoover, John Howard.** 1887– . American naval officer; rear admiral (1941); head of Western Caribbean command (Jan., 1942).

**Hoover, W. H.** 1849–1932. American industrialist; started manufacture of vacuum cleaner (invented by J. Murray Spangler, 1907). President of the Hoover Suction Sweeper Co. (to 1922), and chairman of the board of its successor, The Hoover Co. (1922–32).

**Hope** (hōp), **Anthony.** Pseudonym of Sir Anthony Hope HAWKINS.

**Hope,** Sir **George Price Webley.** 1869–1959. British naval officer; engaged in attempt to force the Dardanelles (Feb.–May, 1915); promoted rear admiral (1917), vice-admiral (1920), admiral (1925). Admiralty representative at Peace Conference at Paris (1919). Commanded Mediterranean squadron (1919–21).

**Hope, John.** 1868–1936. American Negro educator; president, Morehouse College, Atlanta, Ga. (1906–31), and Atlanta (Ga.) University (1929–36).

**Hope, John Adrian Louis.** 7th Earl of **Hope′toun** (hōp′tŭn; -toun) *and* 1st Marquis of **Lin·lith′gow** (lĭn·lĭth′gō). 1860–1908. British statesman; governor of Victoria, Australia (1889); paymaster general (1895–98); lord chamberlain (1898). First governor general, Commonwealth of Australia (1901–02). Secretary of state for Scotland (1905). His son **Victor Alexander John** (1887–1951), 8th earl and 2d marquis, soldier and administrator, served in World War (1914–18); chairman of joint select committee on Indian constitutional reform, which prepared the so-called Linlithgow Report (1933); viceroy and governor general of India (1936–43).

**Hope, Thomas.** 1770?–1831. English antiquarian and writer; collector of marbles and sculptures; patron of Canova, Thorvaldsen, and Flaxman.

**Hopewell–Ash, Edwin Lancelot.** See ASH.

**Hop′fen** (hôp′fĕn), **Hans von.** 1835–1904. German poet, playwright, and novelist.

**Hoph′ni** (hŏf′nī). *In Douay Bible* **Oph′ni** (ŏf′nī). In Bible, a degenerate son of Eli (*1 Sam.* ii. 12–iv. 22).

**Hophra.** See APRIES.

**Hop′kins** (hŏp′kĭnz), **Arthur Melancthon.** 1878–1950. American play producer, b. Cleveland, Ohio. Settled in New York City (1912). Among plays produced by him are *Hedda Gabler, The Doll's House, Macbeth, Anna Christie, The Hairy Ape, The Second Mrs. Tanqueray, The Petrified Forest, The Glory Road.*

**Hopkins, Edward.** 1600–1657. Colonial administrator, b. Shrewsbury, England; emigrated to America (1637); settled at Hartford, Conn. Governor of Connecticut (1640, 1644, 1646, 1650, 1652, 1654).

**Hopkins, Edward John.** 1818–1901. English organist and author of *The Organ, its History and Construction* (1855).

**Hopkins, Edward Washburn.** 1857–1932. American philologist; professor of Sanskrit language and literature and comparative philology, Yale (1895–1926).

**Hopkins, Ernest Martin.** 1877–1964. American educator; president of Dartmouth (1916–45).

**Hopkins, Esek.** 1718–1802. American naval officer, b. in what is now Scituate, R.I. New England sea captain; appointed commander in chief of the Continental navy (Dec. 22, 1775). Met insuperable difficulties in equipping and manning the few American ships; censured by Congress for failure (June, 1776); suspended from command (Mar. 26, 1777); dismissed (Jan. 2, 1778).

**Hopkins,** Sir **Frederick Gowland.** 1861–1947. English biochemist; originated a method of quantitative estimation of uric acid; with S. W. Cole, isolated tryptophan; codiscoverer of the connection between lactic acid and muscular contraction; isolated glutathione from living tissue; demonstrated the existence of essential amino acids and of accessory food factors later called vitamins. Shared (with Christiaan Eijkman) the 1929 Nobel prize for physiology and medicine; member Order of Merit (1935).

**Hopkins, Gerard Manley.** 1844–1889. English Jesuit and poet. His poems, published posthumously, include *The Wreck of the Deutschland, The Windhover,* and *Vision of the Mermaids,* and are notable for many technical innovations, such as sprung rhythm and outrides.

**Hopkins, Harry Lloyd.** 1890–1946. American administrator and politician; in social-welfare work in New Orleans and New York (to 1933); appointed federal administrator of emergency relief (1933) and works progress administrator (1935–38); secretary of commerce (1938–40); head of Lend-Lease Administration (1941); President Roosevelt's personal envoy to Russia and Britain (1941); member of War Production Board (1942); member of Pacific War Council (1942); special assistant to President Roosevelt (1942–45).

**Hopkins, James R.** 1877– . American portrait and figure painter.

**Hopkins, John.** See Thomas STERNHOLD.

**Hopkins, John Henry.** 1792–1868. Protestant Episcopal clergyman, b. Dublin, Ireland; to U.S. (1800); first bishop of Vermont (1832).

**Hopkins, Johns.** 1795–1873. American financier, b. in Anne Arundel County, Md. Left fortune to found hospital and university, now located in Baltimore, Md., and named in his honor The Johns Hopkins Hospital and The Johns Hopkins University.

**Hopkins, Lemuel.** 1750–1801. American physician and writer, b. in what is now Naugatuck, Conn. Practiced medicine, Litchfield, Conn. (from 1776) and Hartford (from about 1784). Became associated with group known as "Hartford wits"; wrote satirical political verse, and contributed to the *American Mercury* (from 1791).

**Hopkins, Mark.** 1802–1887. American educator, b. Stockbridge, Mass. Professor of moral philosophy and rhetoric, Williams (1830–87); president (1836–72); known as inspired teacher and lecturer. Author of many books on moral and religious subjects. Elected to American Hall of Fame (1915).

**Hopkins, Samuel.** 1721–1803. American Congregational theologian, b. Waterbury, Conn. Intimate friend of Jonathan Edwards; introduced systematic theological doctrine (*Hopkinsianism*) in his book *System of Doctrines Contained in Divine Revelation, Explained and Defended* (2 vols., 1793).

**Hopkins, Stephen.** 1707–1785. Colonial administrator in America, b. Providence, R.I. Governor of Rhode Island (1755, 1756, 1758–61, 1763, 1764, 1767). Member, Continental Congress (1774–80); signer of Declaration of Independence.

**Hopkins, William John.** 1863–1926. American writer; author of *The Sandman Series* (juveniles, 4 vols., 1902–08), *The Clammer* (1906), *Old Harbor* (1909), *Burbury Stoke* (1914), *She Blows! and Sparm at That* (1922), etc.

**Hop′kin·son** (hŏp′kĭn·s'n), **Charles Sydney.** 1869–1962. American portrait painter and aquarellist.

**Hopkinson, Francis.** 1737–1791. American political leader and writer, b. Philadelphia. Adm. to bar (1761); practiced, Philadelphia, and Bordentown, N.J. (from 1774). Active in pre-Revolutionary agitation; began publishing political satires (1774). Member, Continental Congress (1776); signer of Declaration of Independence; had important part in designing American flag (1777). U.S. district judge, eastern district of Pennsylvania (1789–91). Among his satires, *The Battle of the Kegs* (verse, 1778); *Date Obolum Bellesario* (allegory, 1778); *Modern Learning Exemplified* (1784); *A Letter from a Gentleman in America on White-washing* (1785).

**Hopkinson, John.** 1849–1898. English electrical engineer; patented three-wire system of distributing electricity (1882); with his brother **Edward,** published paper on dynamos which led to improved dynamos.

**Hopkinson, Joseph.** 1770–1842. Son of Francis Hopkinson. American jurist; practiced, Philadelphia. Member, U.S. House of Representatives (1815–19). Judge, U.S. district court, eastern district of Pennsylvania (1828–42). Author of the patriotic song *Hail Columbia* (1798), first sung by Gilbert Fox in Philadelphia.

**Hop′pe** (hŏp′ē), **William F.** 1887–1959. American expert billiard player; world's champion at the 18.1 balk-line game (1906, 1907, 1909–11, 1914), the 18.2 balk-line game (1907, 1910–20, 1923–24), and the three-cushion game (1936, 1940, 1941). Special editor for terms in billiards, *Webster's New International Dictionary, Second Edition.*

**Hop′per** (hŏp′ẽr), **DeWolf,** *in full* **William DeWolf.** 1858–1935. American actor; long associated with Weber and Fields; later starred at head of his own company; excelled in comedy roles, as in *Wang, Pinafore, The Mikado, The Pirates of Penzance,* etc.

**Hopper, Edward.** 1882–1967. American painter, b. Nyack, N.Y. His *Light House at Two Lights* and *House by the Railroad* have often been on exhibition.

**Hop′pe–Sey′ler** (hŏp′ĕ·zī′lẽr), **Felix,** *in full* **Ernst Felix Immanuel.** 1825–1895. German physiologist and chemist; studied properties of hemoglobin and protein, activation of oxygen, fermentation, etc.

**Hop′pin** (hŏp′ĭn), **Augustus.** 1828–1896. American illustrator; excelled in humorous and satirical illustration, as in sketches for Shillaber's *Life and Sayings of Mrs. Partington,* Holmes's *Autocrat of the Breakfast-Table,* and Irving's *Sketch Book.* His nephew **Joseph Clark Hoppin** (1870–1925) was an archaeologist; author of *Euthymides and His Fellows* (1917), *A Handbook of Attic Red-Figured Vases* (2 vols., 1919), *A Handbook of Greek Black-Figured Vases* (1924).

**Hoppin, James Mason.** 1820–1906. American clergyman and educator; Congregational clergyman, Salem, Mass. (1850–59); professor, Yale Divinity School (1861–79); professor of history of art, Yale School of Fine Arts (1879–99).

**Hopp′ner** (hŏp′nẽr), **John.** 1758–1810. English portrait painter, of German descent.

**Hop′ton** (hŏp′tŭn), **Ralph.** 1st Baron **Hopton.** 1598–1652. English Royalist commander. Educ. Oxford; M.P.; as Royalist sympathizer, expelled from House of Commons (1642). After several victories, was defeated at Cheriton (1644); forced to surrender at Truro (1646); left England with Prince Charles (1648).

**Hop′wood** (hŏp′wo͝od), **Avery,** *in full* **James Avery.** 1882–1928. American playwright, b. Cleveland, Ohio. First play, *Clothes,* written with Channing Pollock (produced 1906). Best known for mystery melodramas as *The Bat* (with Mary Roberts Rinehart, 1920), and for ultramodern, clever, often somewhat risqué, farce comedies, as *The Gold Diggers* (1919), *The Demi-Virgin* (1921), *Why Men Leave Home* (1922).

**Hopwood, Ronald Arthur.** 1868–1949. British admiral and writer; specialist in naval gunnery; author of *The Secret of the Ships, The New Navy,* and the poems *The Laws of the Navy* and *Secret Orders.*

**Ho′ra** (hŏ′rä) *or* **Ho′rea** (hŏ′ryä) *or* **Ho′ria** (hŏ′ryä), **Nicolae.** 1730–1785. Rumanian patriot; headed peasant rebellion (Nov.–Dec., 1784); captured and executed (Feb. 28, 1785).

**Hor′ace** (hŏr′ĭs). *In full* **Quintus Ho·ra′tius Flac′cus** (hō·rā′shŭs [-shĭ·ŭs] flăk′ŭs). 65–8 B.C. Roman lyric poet and satirist, b. Venosa, Lucania, the son of a freedman. Educated in Rome and Athens; commanded legion in republican army at Philippi (42). On return to Rome, enjoyed patronage of Maecenas and received from him gift of a villa in the Sabine Hills; also enjoyed favor of Emperor Augustus. Among his works are two books of satires, one book of epodes, four books of odes, two books of epistles, and *Ars Poetica.*

**Hor′a·pol′lon** (hōr′ȧ·pŏl′ŏn; hŏr′-) *or* **Hor′a·pol′lo** (-ō). Greek grammarian of 4th century A.D., in Phaenebythis, Egypt; reputed author of treatises on hieroglyphics.

**Ho·ra′tius** (hō·rā′shŭs; -shĭ·ŭs). *In full* **Marcus Horatius Bar·ba′tus** (bär·bā′tŭs). Roman consul (449 B.C.); published, with Lucius Valerius Potitus, the other consul for that year, two tables of Roman laws to be added to the ten tables previously prepared, thus making the famous Twelve Tables of Roman history.

**Horatius Coc′les** (kŏk′lēz; kō′klēz). Legendary Roman hero of the 6th cent. B.C., a soldier who with two companions held head of Sublician bridge over the Tiber against Etruscan army of Lars Porsena of Clusium, while other Romans were destroying bridge behind him. The story is subject of one of Macaulay's *Lays of Ancient Rome.*

**Horea, Nicolae.** See HORA.

**Hore′–Be·li′sha** (hōr′bĕ·lē′shȧ), **Leslie.** 1893–1957. English political leader, barrister, and journalist. Financial secretary to treasury (1932–34); minister of transport (1934–37) and originator of Belisha beacons, for regulating traffic; secretary for war (1937–40).

**Horemhab** *or* **Horemheb.** Variants of HARMHAB.

**Horen, Theob. van.** Pseudonym of Jacobus van LOOY.

**Hore–Ruthven.** See RUTHVEN family.

**Hor′gan** (hôr′găn), **Paul.** 1903– . American novelist; author of *The Fault of Angels* (1933; winner of Harper prize novel competition), *No Quarter Given* (1935), *Far from Cibola* (1938), *The Habit of Empire* (1941), *The Common Heart* (1942), etc.

**Horgan, Stephen Henry.** 1854–1941. American inventor of a half-tone engraving process that made possible the reproduction of photographs (in N.Y. *Daily Graphic* 1880).

**Horia, Nicolae.** See HORA.

**Ho·ri·no·u·chi** (hō·rē·nō·o͞o·chē), **Kensuke.** 1886– . Japanese diplomat; ambassador to U.S. (1938–40).

**Hor′ler** (hôr′lẽr), **Sydney.** 1888–1954. English author of more than seventy thrillers, including *Hidden Hand, Lord of Terror, Traitor, The Man Who Died Twice.*

**Hor′lick** (hôr′lĭk), Sir **James.** 1844–1921. English manufacturer; founder and subsequently chairman of Horlick's Malted Milk Co.; actively interested in agriculture in Gloucestershire.

**Horlick, William.** 1846–1936. Industrialist, b. in Gloucestershire, Eng.; to U.S. (1869), naturalized (c. 1887); settled in Racine, Wis. (1876). Originated malted milk, dry extract of malt, etc.; president and general manager, Horlick's Malted Milk Corp., with his son **William** (1875–1940), b. Chicago, Ill., as vice-president, later board chairman.

**Hor′mayr** (hôr′mīr), Baron **Joseph von.** 1782–1848. Austrian historian; director of archives, Vienna (1803); imperial historiographer (1816). To Munich (1828) and became Bavarian minister to Hanover (1832) and Bremen (1839); director, Munich royal archives (1846).

**Hor·mis′das** (hôr·mĭz′dăs), Saint. d. 523. Pope (514–523), b. in Campania; effected union of Eastern and Western churches (519).

**Hormizd** *or* **Hormizdas.** See ORMIZD.

**Horn** (hôrn) *or* **Hoorn** (hōrn) *or* **Hornes** (hôrn), Count of. **Philip de Mont′mo·ren′cy** (mŏnt′mō·rĕn′sĭ; *Fr.* môɴ′mō′räɴ′sē′). 1518–1568. Flemish statesman and soldier. Fought at St. Quentin and Gravelines; as admiral of Flanders commanded fleet that carried Philip from Netherlands to Spain (1559); at Spanish court (1559–63); on return joined with William, Prince of Orange, and Egmont in opposing Spanish policies, esp. the Inquisition; after refusing to flee when duke of Alva took control, arrested (1567) with Egmont (*q.v.*); beheaded as a traitor at Brussels.

**Horn** (hôrn), **Alfred Aloysius.** *Known as* "Trader Horn." See under (Mrs.) Ethelreda LEWIS.

**Horn** (ho͝orn), Count **Arvid Bernhard.** 1664–1742. Swedish statesman; general in army of Charles XII (1700); active in deposition of Augustus II of Poland

(1704); counselor to the king (1705) and prime minister (1710); favored summoning the estates (1710, 1713); on death of Charles XII (1718), persuaded Ulrika Eleonora to be elected queen; aided in election of Frederick of Hesse as king (1720); influential over affairs of kingdom, increasing its prosperity (1720–38).

**Horn** (hôrn), **Charles Edward.** 1786–1849. English singer and composer; composer of operas and oratorios, glees and piano pieces, and many popular airs, including *Cherry Ripe* and *I Know a Bank.*

**Horn, George Henry.** 1840–1897. American entomologist; specialist in study of Coleoptera; coauthor with John L. LeConte of *Classification of the Coleoptera of North America* (1883).

**Horn** (ho͞orn), **Gustaf.** Count **till Björ′ne·borg′** (tĭl byûr′nĕ·bôr′y′). 1592–1657. Swedish soldier; field marshal (1615); served in Thirty Years' War under Gustavus Adolphus and with Baner and Bernhard of Saxe-Weimar.

**Horn** (hôrn), **W. O. von.** Pseudonym of Philip Friedrich Wilhelm Örtel.

**Hor′na·day** (hôr′nȧ·dā), **William Temple.** 1854–1937. American zoologist; chief taxidermist, U.S. National Museum (1882–90); director, New York Zoological Park (1896–1926; retired). Promoted game preserves and laws for the protection of wild life.

**Horn′blow** (hôrn′blō), **Arthur.** 1865–1942. Editor and playwright, b. Manchester, Eng.; to U.S. (1889). On staff of various newspapers (1889–1901), and *The Theatre Magazine* (1901–26). Collaborator with Charles Klein in writing *The Third Degree, John Marsh's Millions, The Gamblers, The Money Makers;* and with George Broadhurst in writing *Bought and Paid For, The Price;* and with Eugene Walter in writing *The Easiest Way.*

**Horn′blow′er** (hôrn′blō′ẽr), **Jonathan** (1717–1780) and his son **Jonathan Carter** (1753–1815). English engineers; employees of James Watt; designed a steam engine (patented 1781) on the expansion principle which was judged by the courts (1799) an infringement on Watt's patent. The principle was rediscovered by Arthur Woolf (*q.v.*) and incorporated in the Woolf engine, first practical compound engine (1804).

**Horn′by** (hôrn′bĭ), Sir **Geoffrey Thomas Phipps.** 1825–1895. British naval officer; took fleet through Dardanelles to Constantinople in Russo-Turkish war (1878); admiral (1879); admiral of the fleet (1888). His father, Sir **Phipps** (1785–1867), was also a British admiral (from 1858); and his brother **James John** (1826–1909) was headmaster (1868–84) and provost (1884–1909) of Eton.

**Hornby, Lester George.** 1882– . American painter, illustrator, and etcher.

**Horne** (hôrn), **Henry Sinclair.** 1st Baron **Horne of Stir′koke** (stĭr′ko͝ok). 1861–1929. English soldier; in World War (1914–18), successively artillery commander of 1st corps in France, commander (1915) of 2d division, commander (1916) of 15th corps, general and commander (1916) of 1st army. Commander in chief in the East (1919–23).

**Horne, Richard Henry** *or* **Richard Hengist.** 1803–1884. English writer; commissioner for crown lands, and magistrate, in Australia (1852–69). Author of the epic poem *Orion* (1843), *Ballad Romances* (1846), *Australian Facts and Prospects* (1859), etc.

**Horne, Thomas Hartwell.** 1780–1862. English clergyman and biblical scholar.

**Hor′ner** (hôr′nẽr), **Francis.** 1778–1817. British politician; M.P. (1806 ff.). As chairman of the bullion committee, recommended in his report (Bullion Report) resumption of specie payments (1810), establishing reputation as a sound economist.

**Horner, William Edmonds.** 1793–1853. American physician; M.D., Pennsylvania (1814); practiced in Philadelphia (from 1815). Discovered (1824) tensor tarsi, now known as Horner's muscle. Author of *Treatise on Pathological Anatomy,* first book of its kind in America (1829).

**Hörnes.** Variant of Hoernes.

**Hornes,** Count of. See Horn.

**Horne Tooke.** See Tooke.

**Hor′ney** (hôr′nī), **Karen,** *nee* **Danielsen.** 1885-1952. Psychiatrist, b. Hamburg, of Norwegian father and Dutch mother; m. Oscar Horney (1909). Teacher of technique of psychoanalysis at Berlin Psychoanalytic Institute (1920–32). To U.S. (1932); teacher at New York Psychoanalytic Institute (1934–41); professor, New York Medical Coll. (from 1942).

**Hor′ni·man** (hôr′nĭ·măn), **Annie Elizabeth Fredericka.** 1860–1937. English theater manager; built and managed Abbey Theatre in Dublin for the Irish National Theatre Society (1904); bought and managed Gaiety Theatre in Manchester (1908–21).

**Hor′nung** (hôr′nŭng), **Ernest William.** 1866–1921. English writer of adventure fiction; creator of Raffles, gentleman burglar. Among his many novels are *The Amateur Cracksman* (1899), *Stingaree* (1905), *Mr. Justice Raffles* (1909) and *The Crime Doctor* (1914).

**Ho′ro·witz** (hô′rô·vĭts), **Vladimir.** 1904– . American (Russian-born) pianist; m. Wanda, daughter of Arturo Toscanini; U.S. debut with N.Y. Philharmonic orchestra (1928); concert tours in U.S. (from 1928).

**Hor′ra·bin** (hŏr′ȧ·bĭn), **James Francis.** 1884–1962. English journalist and illustrator; on staff of London *News Chronicle and Star* (from 1911). Author and illustrator of *Adventures of the Noah Family, An Atlas of Current Affairs* (1934), *Atlas of Empire* (1937), and a series (1939 ff.), *Horrabin's Atlas-History of the Second Great War* (simple maps and diagrams with brief explanatory comments).

**Hor′rocks** (hŏr′ŭks), **Jeremiah.** 1617?–1641. English astronomer; made first observation of a transit of Venus (1639), and wrote an account of it in *Venus in Sole Visa.* Assigned to the moon an elliptical orbit with the earth at one of the foci, a discovery accepted by Newton; probably identified solar attraction with terrestrial gravity.

**Horsa.** See Hengist.

**Hors′ford** (hôrs′fẽrd), **Eben Norton.** 1818–1893. American industrial chemist; esp. interested in chemistry of foods (from 1863); developed processes for making condensed milk and baking powder.

**Hors′ley** (hôrz′lĭ; hôrs′-), **Samuel.** 1733–1806. English prelate; bishop of St. Davids (1788), of Rochester (1793), of St. Asaph (1802). Carried on long controversy with Joseph Priestley on the Incarnation (1783–90); edited Newton's works (1779–85).

**Horsley, William.** 1774–1858. English organist and composer; published five collections of glees (between 1801 and 1837), and *The Musical Treasury* (1853). His son **John Callcott** (1817–1903) was a painter, esp. of genre scenes and portraits. Another son, **Charles Edward** (1822–1876), was an organist and composer, notably of oratorios and music for Milton's *Comus.* J. C. Horsley's son Sir **Victor Alexander Haden** (1857–1916), physiologist and surgeon, made special study of the functions of the thyroid gland, protective treatment against rabies, and localization of function in the brain.

**Hort** (hôrt), **Fenton John Anthony.** 1828–1892. English theologian and Biblical scholar. One of revisers of New Testament (1870–80); contributor to Smith's *Dictionary of Christian Biography.*

**Hortense de Beauharnais.** See BEAUHARNAIS.

**Hor·ten′si·us** (hôr·tĕn′sĭ·ŭs; -shĭ·ŭs; -shŭs), **Quintus.** Roman statesman; dictator of Rome (286 B.C.); decreed (*Lex Hortensia*) that resolutions adopted by the mass (plebiscita) of Roman citizens should be binding on all citizens without necessity of senate approval.

**Hortensius, Quintus.** 114–50 B.C. Roman lawyer and orator; a leader of the aristocratic party; quaestor (81); aedile (75); praetor (72); consul (69).

**Hor′thy** (hôr′tĭ), **Miklós von Nagy′bá′nya** (fôn nŏd′y′-bä′nyŏ). 1868–1957. Hungarian admiral and statesman. At outbreak (1914) of World War, commanded Austro-Hungarian cruiser *Novara,* operating in Adriatic; distinguished himself in action at Otranto (May 14, 1917); appointed commander in chief of Austro-Hungarian fleet (1918). After World War, returned to Hungary to combat Bolshevism; became commander in chief of national army in Hungary (1919). Regent of Hungary (1920–1944).

**Hor′ton** (hôr′t'n), **Douglas.** 1891–1968. American clergyman; dean of Harvard Divinity School (1955–59).

**Hor′ton** (hôr′t'n), **George.** 1859–1942. American consular official and writer; U.S. consul at stations in the Near East (from 1893). Author of *Songs of the Lowly* (1891), *In Unknown Seas* (1895), *Aphroessa* (1897), *Modern Athens* (1901), *The Blight of Asia* (1926), *Poems of an Exile* (1931), etc.

**Horton, Samuel Dana.** 1844–1895. American publicist; notable for his works on currency, *Silver and Gold in Their Relation to the Problem of Resumption* (1876), *Silver in Europe* (1892), etc.

**Horush.** See BARBAROSSA I.

**Hor′váth** (hôr′vät), **Mihály.** 1809–1878. Hungarian Roman Catholic clergyman and statesman; involved in revolution, becoming Hungarian minister of public education and worship (1849); after crushing of revolution, lived abroad (1849–66); returned to Hungary (1866); entered lower house of Diet (1876). Author of *History of the War of Independence in Hungary* (3 vols., 1865), and other works on Hungarian history.

**Horváth, Ödön von.** 1901–1938. German-Hungarian novelist; fled to Paris to escape Nazi regime in Germany; author of *A Child of Our Time* (Eng. trans., 1938), *The Age of the Fish* (Eng. trans., 1939).

**Hos′ack** (hŭs′ăk; hŭz′ăk), **David.** 1769–1835. American physician; practiced medicine, Alexandria, Va. (1791). Professor of botany (1795–1811) and of materia medica, Columbia (1797–1811); professor of theory and practice of physic, Coll. of Phys. and Surg., N.Y. (from 1811). His son **Alexander Eddy** (1805–1871) was a surgeon, one of the first to use ether as an anesthetic, and a pioneer in urology.

**Ho·sä′us** (hô·zâ′o͝os), **Hermann.** 1875– . German sculptor; carved Mozart memorial in Dresden, Vasco di Gama statue in Hamburg, statue of Justice in Essen law courts building.

**Ho·se′a** (hô·zē′ȧ; -zā′ȧ). *In Douay Bible* **O′see** (ō′zē). One of the minor Hebrew prophets (fl. during and after reign of Jeroboam II, 8th century B.C.), whose reproof and prophecy for apostate Israel, symbolized by marriage to a faithless wife, the Old Testament book of *Hosea* records.

**Hosein.** Variant of HUSAIN (see HASAN).

**Hosemann, Andreas.** See Andreas OSIANDER.

**Ho·she′a** (hô·shē′ȧ). *In Douay Bible* **O′see** (ō′zē; ō′sē). d. 722? B.C. Last king of Israel (c. 732–722 B.C.). Son of Elah. Murdered Pekah and with aid of Tiglath-pileser III ascended throne (*2 Kings* xv. 30); withheld tribute from Shalmaneser V, King of Assyria; his kingdom invaded; taken captive; Samaria besieged (724–722) and captured by Sargon, who took leading inhabitants away as captives to Media (*2 Kings* xvii).

**Ho′sie** (hō′zĭ), Sir **Alexander.** 1853–1925. British diplomat in China (1876–1912), rising to post of consul general at Tientsin (1908–12; retired). His 2d wife (m. 1913), **Dorothea,** *nee* **Soot′hill** [?so͝ot′hĭl] (1885–1959), b. Ningpo, China; daughter of William Edward Soothill; lecturer and writer on Chinese subjects; author of *Portrait of a Chinese Lady* (1929), and *Brave New China* (1938); editor of her father's translation of the *Analects* of Confucius (1937); collaborator with her husband in editing Philips' *Commercial Map of China.*

**Ho′si·us** (hō′zhĭ·ŭs) *or* **O′si·us** (ō′zhĭ·ŭs). d. about 358 A.D. Spanish prelate. Bishop of Cordova (c. 300); one of presiding bishops at Council of Nicaea (325); said by some to have prepared the Nicene Creed, adopted there. For refusing to condemn Athanasius (355), was banished by Emperor Constantius II; at Council of Sirmium (357); signed under pressure a document favoring Arianism, but still refused to condemn Athanasius; restored to his see.

**Ho′si·us** (hō′zhĭ·ŭs), **Stan′is·laus** (stăn′ĭs·lôs). *Pol,* **Stanisław Ho′zjusz** (hô′zyo͞osh). 1504–1579. Polish Roman Catholic prelate. Bishop of Kulm, or Chełmno (1549), of Ermeland (1551); cardinal (1561). Actively opposed Protestant Reformation; wrote *Confessio Fidei Christianae Catholicae,* adopted by Synod of Piotrków (1557).

**Hos′mer** (hŏz′mẽr), **Harriet Goodhue.** 1830–1908. American sculptor, b. Watertown, Mass. Examples of her work: *Beatrice Cenci,* now in St. Louis Mercantile Library; *Thomas H. Benton,* in Lafayette Park, St. Louis; *Oenone,* in St. Louis Museum of Art.

**Hosmer, James Kendall.** 1834–1927. American author, b. Northfield, Mass.; Unitarian minister (1860). In Union army in Civil War. Professor at Washington U., St. Louis (1874–92). Author of *Short History of German Literature* (1878), *Samuel Adams* (1885), *Short History of Anglo-Saxon Freedom* (1890), *History of the Louisiana Purchase* (1902), *The Appeal to Arms 1861–63* (1907).

**Hos′trup** (hŏs′tro͝op), **Jens.** 1818–1892. Danish poet, playwright, and theologian; author of lyric verse, and a number of plays.

**Hotch′kiss** (hŏch′kĭs), **Benjamin Berkeley.** 1826–1885. American inventor, b. Watertown, Conn. Invented Hotchkiss machine gun and Hotchkiss magazine rifle.

**Ho′tho** (hō′tō), **Heinrich Gustav.** 1802–1873. German art historian.

**Hot′man′** (ôt′mäɴ′), **François.** Sieur **de Vil′liers′ Saint′-Paul′** (dĕ vē′lyā′ săɴ′pôl′). *Latinized surname* **Hot·man′nus** (hŏt·măn′ŭs). 1524–1590. French jurist; a Protestant; fled to Switzerland after the Massacre of Saint Bartholomew. Among his many works are *De Statu Primitivae Ecclesiae* (1553), *Jurisconsultus* (1559), *L'Antitribonien* (1567).

**Hot′son** (hŏt′s'n), **Leslie,** *in full* **John Leslie.** 1897– . Educator and writer, b. in Ontario, Canada. Professor of English, Haverford (1931–41). Author of *The Death of Christopher Marlowe* (1925), *Shelley's Lost Letters to Harriet* (1930), *Shakespeare versus Shallow* (1931), *I, William Shakespeare* (1937).

**Hotspur.** See Sir *Henry Percy* (1364–1403) under PERCY family.

**Hot′ting·er** (hŏt′ĭng·ẽr), **Johann Jakob.** 1783–1860. Swiss historian.

**Hötzendorf, Franz Conrad von.** See CONRAD VON HÖTZENDORF.

**Hou′ben** (ho͞o′bĕn), **Heinrich Hubert.** 1875–1935. German historian of literature; literary director, Brockhaus publishing firm (1907–19).

**Hou'bra'ken** (hou'brä'kĕn), **Arnold.** 1660–1719. Dutch painter of scenes from Dutch history; author of a biography of Dutch painters. His son **Jakob** (1698–1780) was a painter and engraver known for portraits.

**Hou'chard'** (o͞o'shȧr'), **Jean Nicolas.** 1738–1793. French Revolutionary soldier; defeated the British at Hondschoote (1793), but failed to follow up his advantage; was defeated at Courtrai (1793).

**Houdar de La Motte, Antoine.** See LAMOTTE-HOUDAR.

**Hou'de·tot'** (o͞o'dē·tō'), Comtesse **d'.** *Nee* **Élisabeth Françoise Sophie de la Live' de Belle'garde'** (dē lȧ lēv' dē bĕl'gȧrd'). 1730–1813. French beauty; m. Comte d'Houdetot (1748); formed liaison with Saint-Lambert which lasted until his death; especially remembered because of Jean Jacques Rousseau's love for her, which he describes in a chapter of his *Confessions.* Her son Comte **César Louis Marie François Ange d'Houdetot** (1749–1825) was a soldier; governor of Martinique (1803–09).

**Hou'din'** (o͞o'dăN'), **Jean Eugène Robert.** 1805–1871. French magician; took pride in exposing "fakes," esp. those appealing to religious emotions; at the same time, contrived mechanisms to produce more remarkable illusions, always explaining their natural causes; successfully undertook government mission to Algeria (1852) to persuade the Arabs by his magical tricks that the French sorcery was superior to the native. Author of several books on magic, and an autobiography.

**Hou·di'ni** (ho͞o·dē'nĭ; -dĭn'ĭ), **Harry.** *Real name* **Ehrich Weiss** (wīs). 1874–1926. American magician, b. Appleton, Wis., of Hungarian-Jewish parentage. Took name Harry Houdini after French magician Houdin. Known for his ability to extricate himself from handcuffs and locked and sealed containers of all kinds.

**Hou'don'** (o͞o'dôN'; *Angl.* ho͞o'dŏn), **Jean Antoine.** 1741–1828. French sculptor. Among his early figures were *Saint Bruno, Morphée, Vestale, Minerve, Écorché.* Carved bust of Washington. His bust *Voltaire Assis* is considered one of finest works of its kind in modern art. Other busts are of *Catherine II, Turgot, Molière, J. J. Rousseau, Buffon, d'Alembert, Franklin, La Fayette, Louis* XVI, *Mirabeau, Diane Nue.*

**Hou'dry** (ho͞o'drē; -drĭ; *Fr.* o͞o'drē'), **Eugene J.** 1892–1962. American engineer, b. Domont, France; naturalized (Dec., 1941); developed processes to produce motor fuels from coal, lignite, etc., by catalytic methods; invited to U.S. by Vacuum Oil Co. to apply processes to commercial production of gasoline, becoming president of Houdry Process Corporation (1931); began (1936) commercial production of gasoline by catalytic cracking of heavy oil; later developed process for producing aviation gasoline from naphtha, and began research on catalytic methods of producing synthetic rubber.

**Hough** (hŭf), **Emerson.** 1857–1923. American writer, b. Newton, Iowa; known as advocate of the preservation of wild life and national parks. Author of *Story of the Cowboy* (1897), *The Mississippi Bubble* (1902), *The Passing of the Frontier,* in *Chronicles of America* (1918), *The Covered Wagon* (1922).

**Hough, George Washington.** 1836–1909. American astronomer; director, Dearborn Observatory, Chicago, and later Evanston, Ill. (1879–1909). Best known for measurements of double stars, systematic observation and study (1879–1909) of planet Jupiter, invention of many ingenious astronomical instruments.

**Hough** (hŏf), **Lynn Harold.** 1877–1971. American clergyman and educator; president, Northwestern U. (1919–20); at Drew U. (1930–47).

**Hough** (hŭf), **Romeyn Beck.** 1857–1924. American dendrologist; author of *American Woods* (15 vols.), etc.

**Hough, Theodore.** 1865–1924. American physiologist; professor at Simmons Coll. (1903–07), and at U. of Virginia (from 1907). Investigated esp. cardiac inhibition, alcohol and fatigue, physiology of muscular fatigue, effect of temperature on cutaneous circulation.

**Hough, Walter.** 1859–1935. American anthropologist; with division of ethnology (from 1886), curator (from 1910) and head curator of anthropology (from 1922), U.S. National Museum. Studied aboriginal fire making and armor, the Pueblo region of Arizona, Hopi foodstuffs, Malayan ethnography, etc.

**Houghton,** Baron. See Richard Monckton MILNES.

**Hough'ton** (hō't'n), **Alanson Bigelow.** 1863–1941. American industrialist and diplomat, b. Cambridge, Mass.; son of **Amory Houghton** (1837–1909), the founder of the Corning Glass Works at Corning, N.Y. Entered Corning Glass Works (1889); president of the company (1910–18) and chairman of the board (from 1918). Member, U.S. House of Representatives (1919–22). U.S. ambassador to Germany (1922–25), to Great Britain (1925–29).

**Houghton, George Hendric.** 1820–1897. American Protestant Episcopal clergyman; founder and pastor (1849–97) of the Church of the Transfiguration, New York City (better known as The Little Church Around the Corner).

**Houghton, Henry Oscar.** 1823–1895. American publisher, b. Sutton, Vt. Apprenticed to printer, Burlington, Vt. (1836). Opened printing office, Cambridge, Mass.; incorporated as H. O. Houghton & Co. (1852), known as The Riverside Press. Joined partnership in publishing business (1864) which eventually developed into Houghton Mifflin Co. (after 1880). Mayor of Cambridge (1872).

**Hough'ton** (hô't'n), **Stanley,** *in full* **William Stanley.** 1881–1913. English playwright; author of *The Dear Departed* (1908), *The Younger Generation* (1910), *Hindle Wakes* (1912), etc.

**Hour'ticq'** (o͞or'tēk'), **Louis Edmond Joseph.** 1875–1944. French art historian; compiler of *Encyclopédie des Beaux-Arts* (1925); author of *De Poussin à Watteau* (1921), etc.

**House** (hous), **Edward Howard.** 1836–1901. American journalist; war correspondent with New York *Tribune* through Civil War. Professor of English in Japanese Coll. at Tokyo (1871); editor of Japanese-subsidized weekly paper in English, the Tokyo *Times* (1875–77). Author of *The Kagoshima Affair* (1874), *Japanese Expedition to Formosa* (1875), *Yone Santo, a Child of Japan* (1889), *Midnight Warning and Other Stories* (1892).

**House, Edward Man'dell** (măn'd'l). 1858–1938. American diplomat, b. Houston, Tex. *Known as* "Colonel House" because he was a colonel on the staff of Governor Culberson of Texas. Friend and confidant of President Wilson; personal representative of the president to European nations (1914, 1915, 1916). Commissioned special representative of U.S. at interallied conference to effect co-ordination of military and naval action (1917). Designated by the president to act for U.S. in negotiating armistice with Central Powers (1918). Member of American commission to negotiate peace (1918–19); and member of commission to frame the covenant of the League of Nations. Author of *What Really Happened at Paris* (with Charles Seymour).

**House, Henry Alonzo.** 1840–1930. American inventor of a buttonhole machine (patented Nov. 11, 1862) and other attachments to improve sewing machines, and a horseless carriage propelled by a twelve-horsepower steam engine (1866).

**House, Homer Doliver.** 1878–1949. American botanist.

**House, Royal Earl.** 1814–1895. American inventor of a

printing telegraph (patented Apr. 18, 1846). Cf. David Edward Hughes.

**Hous'man** (hous'măn), **Alfred Edward**. 1859–1936. English classical scholar and poet; educ. Oxford. Professor of Latin, University Coll., London (1892–1911), and Cambridge (1911–36). Edited works of Manilius, Juvenal, and Lucan. Published volumes of verse *A Shropshire Lad* (1896) and *Last Poems* (1922). Another volume, *More Poems*, was pub. posthumously (1936), as was the definitive *Collected Poems of A. E. Housman* (1940). His brother **Laurence** (1865–1959), writer and illustrator; author of *The Writings of William Blake* (1893), *The House of Joy* (1895), *Gods and their Makers* (1897), *Rue* (1899), *Bethlehem, a Nativity Play* (1902), *Mendicant Rhymes* (1906), *The Chinese Lantern* (1908), *The Sheepfold* (1918), *Angels and Ministers* (1921), *Little Plays of St. Francis* (1922; 2d series, 1931), *Trimblerigg* (1924), *Nunc Dimittis* (1933), *Victoria Regina* (play; 1934), *A. E. H.* (a memoir of his brother; 1937), etc.

**Hous'saye'** (ōō'sā'), **Arsène**. *Orig.* **Arsène Hous'set'** (ōō'sĕ'). 1815–1896. French writer; manager of the Comédie Française (1849–56). Author of many novels, volumes of verse, books of literary criticism, histories, etc. His son **Henri** (1848–1911) was a historian and literary critic; on staff of *Revue des Deux Mondes* and *Journal des Débats;* made study of Napoleonic period.

**Hous·say'** (ōō·sī'), **Bernardo Alberto**. 1887–1971. Argentine physiologist. Awarded Nobel prize in physiology and medicine (1947) with C. and G. Cori.

**Hous'ton** (hūs'tŭn), **David Franklin**. 1866–1940. American educator and public official; president, Texas A. and M. (1902–05), U. of Texas (1905–08); chancellor, Washington U. (1908–16). U.S. secretary of agriculture (1913–20); U.S. secretary of the treasury (1920–21), and chairman of the Federal Reserve Board and Farm Loan Board. Wrote *Eight Years with Wilson's Cabinet.*

**Houston, Edwin James**. 1847–1914. American electrical engineer; with Elihu Thomson, invented system of arc lighting (patent issued 1881); consulting electrical engineer, Philadelphia (1894–1914).

**Houston, Margaret Bell**. d.1966. American novelist and poet; granddaughter of Sam Houston.

**Houston, Samuel,** *known as* **Sam**. 1793–1863. American soldier and political leader, b. in Rockbridge County, Va. Entered army (1813); lieutenant (1814); resigned (1818). Studied law; adm. to bar; practiced, Lebanon, Tenn. Member, U.S. House of Representatives (1823–27). Governor of Tennessee (1827–29). Moved to the Indian country of Cherokee Nation, now Oklahoma (1829), and on into Texas (1833). As trouble developed with Mexico, Houston was chosen commander in chief of the forces of Texan provisional government; met and defeated Mexican troops under Santa Anna at battle of San Jacinto (Apr. 21, 1836). First president of Republic of Texas (1836–38) and again president (1841–44). On admission of Texas to Union, Houston became U.S. senator (1846–59); strong believer in maintenance of the Union. Governor of Texas (1859–61); deposed for refusal to take oath of allegiance to Confederacy.

**Hout'man** (hout'män), **Cornelis de**. c. 1540–1599. Dutch navigator and one of earliest traders with the East Indies (1595–96); on second expedition (1598–99), visited Madagascar, Cochin China, and Sumatra; murdered by order of the sultan of Achin. His brother **Frederik** (1570–1627), who also went on this expedition, was arrested by the sultan of Achin but released; became governor of Amboina (1605); published first dictionary of the language of the Malays (1603).

**Hou'zeau' de Le·haye'** (ōō'zō' dĕ lĕ·ā'), **Jean Charles**. 1820–1888. Belgian astronomer.

**Hoveden** *or* **Howden, Roger of.** See Roger of Hoveden.

**Ho've·lacque'** (ôv'làk'), **Alexandre Abel**. 1843–1896. French linguist and anthropologist. Author of *Grammaire de la Langue Zende* (1869), *Les Nègres de l'Afrique Sus-équatoriale* (1889), etc.

**Hoven, J.** Pseudonym of Vesque von Püttlingen.

**Ho'ven·den** (hō'vĕn·dĕn), **Thomas**. 1840–1895. Painter, b. in County Cork, Ireland; to U.S. (1863). Studio, New York and Philadelphia. Examples of his work: *The Last Moments of John Brown* and *Jerusalem the Golden*, now in Metropolitan Museum of Art, New York.

**Hov'ey** (hŭv'ĭ), **Alvin Peterson**. 1821–1891. American army officer and political leader; served in Union army through Civil War; brigadier general (1862); credited by Grant with winning key battle of Vicksburg campaign; brevetted major general (1864). U.S. minister to Peru (1865–70). Member, U.S. House of Representatives (1887–89). Governor of Indiana (1889–91).

**Hovey, Charles Mason**. 1810–1887. American horticulturist and editor; introduced the Hovey strawberry, early large-fruited variety (1834); founder and editor, *The American Gardener's Magazine and Register*, later *The Magazine of Horticulture, Botany, and... Rural Affairs* (1835–68).

**Hovey, Richard**. 1864–1900. American poet, b. Normal, Ill. Author of a poetic drama series, *Launcelot and Guenevere* (first part pub. 1891), *Seaward* (elegy, 1893), *Songs from Vagabondia* (with Bliss Carman; 1894, 1896, 1900), *Along the Trail* (1898), *To the End of the Trail* (1908).

**Hov'gaard** (hōv'gärd; *Dan.* hou'gôr), **William**. 1857–1950. Naval architect, b. in Denmark; to U.S. (1901), naturalized (1919). Professor of naval design and construction, M.I.T. (1901–33); also, consulting naval architect for U.S. navy department (1919–26; 1935–38). Author of *Structural Design of Warships* (1915), etc.

**How'ard** (hou'ẽrd). Name of an old English house standing at head of English Catholic nobility, founded by Sir **William Howard** *or* **Haw'ard** [hô'ẽrd] (d. 1308), of Norfolk, a justice of common pleas (1297), whose grandson Sir **John Howard** was admiral of the king's navy in the north. Sir **Robert Howard** (d. before 1436), great-grandson of Sir John, married Margaret, dau. of 1st duke of Norfolk and coheiress of house of Mowbray.

Dukes of Norfolk: Their son Sir **John Howard** (1430?–1485), known as **Jack of Norfolk;** 1st Duke of Norfolk (of Howard line; 1483); fought with Edward IV in France (1475); created by Richard III (1483) earl marshal of England, a distinction borne by his male heirs; served against Lancastrians and in Brittany; envoy to France and Flanders; lord admiral of England, Ireland, and Aquitaine (1483); led archer vanguard at Bosworth Field; slain there in battle.

His son **Thomas I** (1443–1524), 2d Duke of Norfolk, Earl of Surrey (created 1483); wounded and captured at Bosworth Field (1485); imprisoned three years in Tower by Henry VII, then obtained reversal of his own and his father's attainder; as lieutenant general of the north, defeated Scots at Flodden Field (1513); quelled rioting apprentices (1517); common ancestor of all living Howards of main stock.

**Thomas II** (1473–1554), 3d Duke of Norfolk, Earl of Surrey; son of 2d duke; m. (1495) Edward IV's daughter Anne (1475–1512), thus becoming brother-in-law of Henry VII; m. (1513) Elizabeth (d. 1558), daughter of Edward Stafford, Duke of Buckingham; lord high admiral (1513); led vanguard of English at Flodden; lord lieutenant of Ireland (1520–21); raided Boulogne (1522) and south of Scotland; Roman Catholic; headed party hostile to Wolsey; president of privy council (1529); as lord steward presided at trial of Anne Boleyn, his niece; punished rebels of Pilgrimage of Grace (1536); arrested Thomas Cromwell (1540); led English army in Scotland (1542–44); lost court influence upon execution of Catherine Howard (*q.v.*), the second niece of his to be wife of Henry VIII; imprisoned throughout reign of Edward VI under condemnation as accessory to treason of his son Henry, Earl of Surrey (see Henry HOWARD); released and restored on accession of Queen Mary (1553).

Thomas II's brother **William** (1510?–1573); convicted of misprision of treason in concealing offenses of his niece Queen Catherine, but pardoned; lord high admiral (1554–73); made peer for his defense of London against Sir Thomas Wyatt; lord chamberlain (1558); lord privy seal (1572). His son **Charles** (1536–1624), 2d Baron Howard of Effingham, 1st Earl of Nottingham (in Howard line), was ambassador to France (1559); lord chamberlain (1574–85); as lord high admiral (1585–1618), held chief command against Armada (1588); colleague of Essex in Cádiz expedition (1596); commissioner for trial of Mary, Queen of Scots (1586), of Essex (1601), for union with Scotland (1604) and for trial of Gunpowder Plotters (1606).

**Thomas III** (1536–1572), 4th Duke of Norfolk; son of Henry Howard (*q.v.*), Earl of Surrey; tutored by John Foxe, martyrologist; succeeded his grandfather as duke and earl marshal (1554), and in absence of princes of the blood became first subject of England under Elizabeth; lieutenant of north country (1559); one of commissioners to inquire into Scottish affairs (1568); imprisoned (1569–70) for project to marry Mary, Queen of Scots; communicated with Philip of Spain regarding planned Spanish invasion of England to free Mary, Queen of Scots; beheaded on failure of plot. His 3d son, Lord **William** (1563–1640), was a scholar; known to contemporaries as "Belted Will" or "Bauld (bôld) Willie"; m. (1577) Elizabeth Dacre, one of three coheirs of Thomas, Lord Dacre of Gilsland; became Roman Catholic (1584); imprisoned on suspicion of treason (1583, 1585, 1589); attainted (1572).

**Henry** (1628–1684), 6th Duke of Norfolk; 3d son of Henry Frederick Howard, 3d Earl of Arundel (see below); succeeded his brother Thomas, duke by reversal (1660) of attainder of 1572; presented Arundel marbles to Oxford (1667); envoy to Morocco (1669).

Succeeding dukes were lords lieutenant of northern counties, members of Parliament representing Arundel, mostly Roman Catholics, but some supporting and some opposing Reform Bill and Ecclesiastical Titles Bill.

**Henry Fitz·al′an Howard** [fĭts·ăl′ăn] (1847–1917), 15th duke, was special envoy to pope (1887); postmaster general (1895–1900); served in Boer War (1900); worked in cause of his coreligionists; in close connection with Vatican; improved Catholic education and built Gothic churches; one of founders of Sheffield U. His brother **Edmund Bernard Fitzalan-Howard** (1855–1947), 1st Viscount **Fitzalan of Der′went** (dûr′wĕnt), youngest son of 14th duke and uncle of 16th duke of Norfolk; assumed name of **Tal′bot** [tôl′bŭt] (1876–1921); M.P. (1894–1921); deputy asst. adjutant general in Boer War; D.S.O. (1900); a lord of treasury (1905); chief Unionist whip (1913–21); viceroy of Ireland (1921–22).

Members of Howard family in one or another of its branches have enjoyed or still enjoy earldoms, including Carlisle (1661), Suffolk (1603), Berkshire (1626), Surrey (1483), Northampton (1604), Arundel (1580), Nottingham (1596), Effingham (1837), among them the following:

EARLS OF CARLISLE: **Charles Howard** (1629–1685), 1st Earl of Carlisle (in Howard line); great-grandson of Lord William Howard (1563–1640); became Protestant (1645); supported Commonwealth; distinguished himself at battle of Worcester (1651); member of council of state (1653) and of Cromwell's House of Lords (1657); lord lieutenant of Cumberland and Westmorland (1660); created Baron **Da′cre of Gils′land** (dā′kẽr, gĭlz′lănd), Viscount **Howard of Mor′peth** (môr′pĕth; -pĕth), Earl of Carlisle (1661); ambassador to Russia, Sweden, and Denmark (1663–64); governor of Jamaica (1677–81); lieutenant general (1667).

His grandson **Charles** (1674–1738), 3d Earl of Carlisle, Viscount Morpeth; lord lieutenant of Cumberland and Westmorland (1694–1712); first lord of treasury (1701–02, 1715); a lord justice (1714–15).

**Frederick** (1748–1825), 5th earl; headed commission sent by Lord North to attempt reconciliation with American colonies (1778); viceroy of Ireland (1780–82); on regency question took part on side of prince of Wales in opposition to Pitt (1789); grandson of 4th Lord Byron; appointed (1798) guardian of Lord Byron, the poet, who attacked him in *English Bards and Scottish Reviewers* because he refused to introduce his ward to House of Lords; author of two tragedies, *The Father's Revenge* (1783) and *The Stepmother* (1800), and some poems.

Frederick's son **George** (1773–1848); 6th earl; M.A., Oxon. (1792); commissioner for affairs of India in All-the-Talents Administration (1806–07); held positions in cabinets of Canning and Grey.

**George William Frederick** (1802–1864); 7th earl; eldest son of 6th earl; M.A., Oxon. (1827); M.P. (1826) as Viscount Morpeth; as Irish secretary under Lord Melbourne (1835–41), carried Irish reform bills; carried Public Health Bill (1848); chancellor of duchy of Lancaster (1850–52); viceroy of Ireland (1855–58, 1859–64); established on his estate a reformatory for juvenile criminals; author of poems and travel books.

**George James** (1843–1911); 9th earl; nephew of 7th earl; amateur artist; educ. Cambridge; M.P. (from 1879); succeeded his uncle in peerage (1889); trustee for 30 years of National Gallery, to which he transferred his Mabuse's *Adoration of the Kings;* connoisseur of art and skilled painter of landscapes; lifelong temperance advocate. His wife (m. 1864), **Rosalind Frances** (1845–1921), Countess of Carlisle, daughter of Edward John, 2d Baron Stanley of Alderley; promoter of a democratic franchise for women; promoter also of temperance movement; business manager of her husband's northern estates.

Their son **Charles James Stanley** (1867–1912); 10th earl; unionist M.P. (1904–11) and parliamentary whip; succeeded by his son **George Josslyn L'Estrange** (1895– ), 11th earl.

EARLS OF SUFFOLK AND BERKSHIRE: Lord **Thomas Howard** (1561–1626), 1st Earl of **Suffolk** and 1st Baron **Howard de Wal′den** (dĕ wôl′dĕn); second son of 4th duke of Norfolk; distinguished himself against Armada (1588); vice-admiral of fleet sent to capture Spanish ships in Cádiz harbor (1596); lord chamberlain (1603–14); lord high treasurer (1614–18); with his wife, imprisoned for embezzlement (1619) but released after ten days and finally restored to favor; later urged investigation of Lord Bacon's offenses. His 2d son, **Thomas**, was created (1626) earl of Berkshire, a title merged (1645) with that of earl of Suffolk. **Theophilus** (1584–1640), 2d earl of Suffolk and 2d baron Howard de Walden; eldest son of 1st earl; M.A., Oxon. (1605); governor of Jersey (1610); lord lieutenant of Cambridgeshire, Suffolk, and Dorset (1626); warden of Cinque Ports (1628).

**Charles Henry George** (1906–1941), 20th Earl of Suffolk and Berkshire; scientist; went round world in sailing ship; rancher in Australia; collector of paintings. See also Henrietta HOWARD.

EARLS OF SURREY: see Thomas (I) Howard (2d Duke of Norfolk), above, and descendants; Thomas Howard (2d Earl of Arundel), below; Henry HOWARD (1517?–1547).

EARL OF NORTHAMPTON: **Henry Howard** (1540–1614), 1st Earl of **Northampton** (cr. 1604; only one in Howard line); 2d son of Henry Howard (*q.v.*), Earl of Surrey; younger brother of 4th duke of Norfolk; tutored, with his brother and sisters, by John Foxe; M.A., Cantab. (1564); long under suspicion of Elizabeth for mysterious relations with Mary, Queen of Scots; imprisoned for a time after publishing (1583) an attack on judicial astrology suspected of treasonable designs; on accession of James I, created earl of Northampton (1604); lord privy seal (1604); commissioner at trials of Raleigh (1603), Guy Fawkes (1605), Garnet (1606); a commissioner of treasury (1612). Roman Catholic; founder of hospitals; framer of James I's edict against duelling; author of three apothegms in Bacon's collection; builder of Northumberland House.

EARLS OF ARUNDEL: **Philip Howard** (1557–1595), 13th Earl of Arundel (1st in Howard line); eldest son of 4th duke of Norfolk and Lady Mary, daughter and heiress of Henry Fitzalan, 12th Earl of Arundel (see ARUNDEL); suspected of being involved in conspiracy headed by Francis Throckmorton (1583); became Roman Catholic through influence of his wife (1584); imprisoned for attempt to escape from England; died in prison.

His son **Thomas** (1585?–1646), 14th earl (2d in Howard line), Earl of Surrey and of Norfolk; patron of arts and learning; educ. Cambridge; became Protestant (1615); president of committee of peers on Bacon's case (1621); general of army against Scots (1639); as lord high steward presided at trial of Strafford (1641); escorted Queen Henrietta Maria to Continent (1642) and took residence at Padua. One of first large-scale collectors of art in England; collected statues, pictures, guns, coins, manuscripts, books, and the marbles, known as Arundel marbles, presented by his grandson, 6th duke of Norfolk, to Oxford (1667). Thomas's 5th son, **William** (1614–1680), 1st Viscount **Stafford** (cr. 1640), married sister and heiress of last (English) Baron Stafford; was accused by Titus Oates, condemned, beheaded for treason.

**Henry Frederick** (1608–1652); 3d earl (in Howard line); son of 2d earl; Irish privy councilor (1634); fought as Royalist in Civil War; his son **Thomas** succeeded (1660), by reversal of the attainder of 1572, to dukedom of Norfolk (see above) in which the earldom merged.

EARL OF NOTTINGHAM. See *Charles Howard* (1536–1624) under *Dukes of Norfolk*, above.

EARL OF EFFINGHAM: **Kenneth Alexander Howard** (1767–1845), 1st Earl of Effingham (2d creation); soldier; served in Flanders (1793–95), Ireland, and Holland (1799); commander in Peninsular War (from 1811); headed first division of army of occupation after Waterloo; general (1837).

**Howard, Ada Lydia.** 1829–1907. American educator; first president, Wellesley Coll. (1875–81).

**Howard, Benjamin Chew.** See under John Eager HOWARD.

**Howard, Blanche Willis.** 1847–1898. American novelist; m. Julius von Teuffel (1890; d. 1896). Author of *One Summer* (1875), *Aunt Serena* (1881), *Guenn* (1883), *The Open Door* (1889), etc.

**Howard, Bronson Crocker.** 1842–1908. American playwright; in newspaper work until he gained success with play *Saratoga* (produced in New York, 1870). Other notable plays: *Young Mrs. Winthrop* (1882), *One of Our Girls* (1885), *The Henrietta* (1887), *Shenandoah* (1888), *Aristocracy* (1892).

**Howard, Catherine.** 1520?–1542. Fifth queen of Henry VIII of England. Niece of Thomas (II) Howard, 3d Duke of Norfolk (see HOWARD family); a dependent in her grandmother's house; entertained lovers, including her music master Henry Mannock or Manox, her cousin Thomas Culpepper, and Francis Dereham, a retainer of duchess of Norfolk; m. (1540) to King Henry after his divorce from Anne of Cleves; clandestinely met Dereham and Culpepper, who were executed upon Catherine's confession of prenuptial unchastity; attainted by Parliament and beheaded on conviction of adultery.

**Howard,** Sir **Ebenezer.** 1850–1928. English shorthand reporter and social reformer; reporter in London law courts; best remembered as originator of the garden-city movement and founder of Letchworth and Welwyn Garden City.

**Howard, Edward.** See under Sir Robert HOWARD.

**Howard, Esme William.** 1st Baron **Howard of Pen'rith** (pĕn'rĭth). 1863–1939. British diplomat; served in army during Boer War (1900). Consul general in Hungary (1908–11); minister to Switzerland (1911–13) and Sweden (1913–19); ambassador to Spain (1919–24) and U.S. (1924–30).

**Howard, George Bronson.** 1884–1922. American journalist and writer, b. in Howard County, Md.; cousin of Bronson Howard. At various times served on staffs of London *Daily Chronicle*, Baltimore *American*, New York *Herald*, San Francisco *Chronicle*. Author of *Norroy, Diplomatic Agent* (1907), *An Enemy to Society* (1911), *God's Man* (1915), *Birds of Prey* (1918), a number of plays, including *The Only Law* (1909), *Snobs* (1911), *The Passing Show of 1912*, *The Red Light of Mars* (1918), and some motion-picture scenarios.

**Howard, George Elliott.** 1849–1928. American educator; professor of history, U. of Nebraska (1879–91); Stanford (1891–1901); U. of Nebraska (1904–24). Author of *History of Matrimonial Institutions* (3 vols., 1904), *General Sociology* (1907), etc.

**Howard, H. L.** Pseudonym of Charles J. WELLS.

**Howard, Henrietta.** Countess of **Suffolk.** 1681–1767. Mistress of George II. Married Charles Howard (later 9th earl of Suffolk); bedchamber woman to princess of Wales; resided at Marble Hill, Twickenham; on accession of George II, installed in St. James's Palace; cultivated by writers and wits; m. (1735) Hon. George Berkeley.

**Howard, Henry.** Earl of **Surrey** (by courtesy). 1517?–1547. English soldier and poet; son of 3d duke of Norfolk (see HOWARD family); received classical education; m. (1532) Frances de Vere, dau. of John de Vere, 15th Earl of Oxford; wounded when marshal before Montreuil (1544); superseded by rival Lord Hertford; through efforts of Hertford faction, condemned, along with father, on flimsy charges of treasonable ambition; author of amatory verses and elegies, including 40 poems in Tottel's *Miscellany* (1557); as translator of *The Aeneid* (books II and III), introduced into English blank verse in five iambic feet; imitator of Italian, esp. Petrarchan, verse models; with Sir Thomas Wyatt, introduced sonnet (three quatrains and couplet) from Italy to England.

**Howard, Jacob Merritt.** 1805–1871. American legislator; member, U.S. House of Representatives (1841–43). One of organizers of Republican party, Jackson, Mich. (1854). U.S. senator (1862–71); strong supporter of congressional reconstruction policy after Civil War.

**Howard, James.** See under Sir Robert HOWARD.

**Howard, John.** 1726?–1790. English prison reformer.

**Howard, John Eager.** 1752–1827. American Revolutionary leader; major (1777); lieutenant colonel (1778); member, Continental Congress (1784–88); governor of Maryland (1789–91); U.S. senator (1796–1803). His son **Benjamin Chew** (1791–1872) practiced law in Baltimore; member of U.S. House of Representatives (1829–33, 1835–39); reporter, U.S. Supreme Court (1843–62); Maryland delegate to peace conference at Washington, D.C. (Feb., 1861).

**Howard, John Galen.** 1864–1931. American architect; offices in New York City and later in San Francisco; professor of architecture (from 1901) and director of the school of architecture (1913–27), U. of California. Designed many of the buildings of the U. of California.

**Howard, Keble.** Pseudonym of John Keble BELL.

**Howard, Leland Os'si·an** (ŏz'ĭ·ăn). 1857–1950. American entomologist; assistant entomologist (1878–94), chief of Bureau of Entomology (1894–1927), principal entomologist (1927–31), U.S. Dept. of Agriculture. Author of *Mosquitoes*...(1901), *The House-Fly—Disease Carrier* (1911), *Fighting the Insects—the Story of an Entomologist* (1933), etc.

**Howard, Leslie.** 1893–1943. English actor, b. London. Stage debut as Jerry in *Peg o' My Heart* (1917); on tour as Charley in *Charley's Aunt* (1917). On New York stage (1920–25, 1927–28, 1929–33), in *Our Mr. Hepplewhite, Mr. Pim Passes By, Her Cardboard Lover, Berkeley Square, The Petrified Forest*, etc.; in motion pictures (from 1930).

**Howard, Luke.** 1772–1864. English pioneer in meteorology; published *Climate of London* (1818–20; enlarged 1830).

**Howard, Oliver Otis.** 1830–1909. American army officer, b. Leeds, Me.; grad. U.S.M.A., West Point (1854). Served through Civil War; brigadier general (1861) and major general (1862); engaged at Chancellorsville and Gettysburg; commander of right wing of Sherman's army in march to the sea. Commissioner, Bureau of Refugees, Freedmen, and Abandoned Lands (1865–74). Founder and president, Howard U. (1869–74).

**Howard,** Sir **Robert.** 1626–1698. English dramatist; 6th son of Thomas Howard, 1st Earl of Berkshire (see under HOWARD family). Distinguished himself on Royalist side at second battle of Newbury (1644); imprisoned during Commonwealth; at Restoration, made auditor of exchequer; privy councilor (1689). Author of a comedy, *The Committee, or the Faithful Irishman* (1663), featuring the servant Teague. Patron of Dryden, who married his sister Lady Elizabeth Howard, and who assisted him in the *Indian Queen*, a tragedy in heroic verse. Opposed Dryden's contention that rhyme was more suitable to heroic tragedy than blank verse; ridiculed in Shadwell's *Sullen Lovers* (1668). His brother **Edward** (fl. 1669) wrote tragedies, including *The Usurper* (1668), and comedies, including *The Women's Conquest* (1671); ridiculed by George Villiers in *The Rehearsal*. Another brother, **James**, wrote the comedies *All Mistaken, or the Mad Couple* (1667) and *The English Mounsieur* (1666), the latter a success through the acting of Nell Gwyn.

**Howard, Roy Wilson.** 1883–1964. American journalist b. Gano, Ohio. On staff of Indianapolis *News* (1902); New York manager of United Press Association (1907), its president and general manager (1912) and chairman of the board (1921). Also, business director of Scripps-McRae, later Scripps-Howard, newspapers (1921), and editorial director of these papers, with Robert P. Scripps (from 1925). Editor (1931–60) and president (1931–62) of New York *World-Telegram and The Sun*.

**Howard, Sidney Coe.** 1891–1939. American playwright, b. Oakland, Calif. Served in World War (captain, aviation service). Author of *Swords* (1921), *They Knew What They Wanted* (1925; awarded Pulitzer prize), *Salvation* (with Charles MacArthur; 1927), *Yellowjack* (1928), *The Late Christopher Bean* (1933), *Dodsworth* (with Sinclair Lewis; 1934), *Paths of Glory* (with Humphrey Cobb; 1935). Also, adapter of plays from the French, Spanish, and Hungarian for presentation on American stage, and adapter of plays and novels for motion pictures, including *Arrowsmith, Dodsworth, Gone With the Wind.*

**Howe** (hou), **Ed,** *in full* **Edgar Watson.** 1853–1937. American journalist and author, b. Treaty, Ind. Trained in printing office, age of twelve (1865). Editor and proprietor, Atchison (Kans.) *Daily Globe* (1877–1911), *E. W. Howe's Monthly* (1911–37). Author of *The Story of a Country Town, Lay Sermons, Preaching of a Poor Pagan, Ventures in Common Sense, Plain People*, etc.

**Howe, Elias.** 1819–1867. American inventor, b. Spencer, Mass. Apprentice in textile machinery works (1835–37), in watchmaking shop (1837). Worked on design for a sewing machine (from 1843); patent issued (Sept. 10, 1846). First machine marketed in England. Established his rights by patent-infringement suits (1849–54). A perfected sewing machine of Howe's design won gold medal, Paris Exhibition (1867). Elected to American Hall of Fame (1915). Cf. Charles F. WEISENTHAL, Thomas SAINT, Barthélemy THIMONNIER, Walter HUNT.

**Howe, Frederic Clemson.** 1867–1940. American lawyer and political scientist; adm. to bar (1894) and practiced in Cleveland, Ohio (1894–1909). Director, People's Institute, New York City (1911–14). Commissioner of immigration, Port of New York (1914–19). Special adviser in office of the U.S. secretary of agriculture (from 1935). Author of *The City the Hope of Democracy, European Cities at Work, Why War?, Denmark—The Cooperative Way*, etc.

**Howe, George.** 1886–1955. American architect; practiced in Philadelphia. Among buildings designed by his firm are: Goodhart Hall at Bryn Mawr, Coast Guard World War Memorial in Arlington Cemetery, Philadelphia Saving Fund Society building.

**Howe, Harrison Es'tell** (ĕs'tĕl). 1881–1942. American industrial chemist; editor, *Industrial and Engineering Chemistry* (from 1921), *Chemistry in Industry* (vol. I, 1924, vol. II, 1925); author of *The New Stone Age* (1921), *Profitable Science in Industry* (1924), etc.

**Howe, Henry Marion.** See under Samuel Gridley HOWE.

**Howe, John.** 1630–1705. English Puritan clergyman; domestic chaplain to Oliver Cromwell and his son Richard Cromwell. Chief work *The Living Temple of God* (1675).

**Howe, Joseph.** 1804–1873. Nova Scotian editor and politician; edited the *Nova Scotian* (from 1828); governor of Nova Scotia (1873).

**Howe, Julia Ward.** See under Samuel Gridley HOWE.

**Howe, Lu'cien** (lū'shĕn). 1848–1928. American ophthalmologist, b. Standish, Me. Founder of Buffalo (N.Y.) Eye and Ear Infirmary (1876); professor, U. of Buffalo (from 1879); author of the Howe law, N.Y. legislature, requiring application of prophylactic drops to eyes of newly born babies (1890); founder of research laboratory, Harvard, for ophthalmological work (1926).

**Howe, Mark Antony DeWolfe.** 1808–1895. American Protestant Episcopal bishop, b. Bristol, R.I.; bishop of Central Pennsylvania (1871). His son **Mark Antony DeWolfe** (1864–1960) was associate editor of *Youth's Companion* (1888–93, 1899–1913); vice-president of Atlantic Monthly Co. (1911–29); director, Boston Athenaeum (from 1933); author of *Shadows* (1897), *Boston, the Place and the People* (1903), *Harmonies, a Book of*

*Verse* (1909), *Barrett Wendell and His Letters* (awarded Pulitzer prize for biography, 1924), *Yankee Ballads* (1930), etc. His grandson **Mark DeWolfe** (1906–1967), lawyer; A.B. (1928), LL.B. (1933), Harvard; professor of law (1937), dean (1941–43), School of Law, U. of Buffalo; U.S. Army (1943–45); professor of law (1945–67), Harvard.

**Howe, Marshall Avery.** 1867–1936. American botanist; curator, New York Botanical Garden (1906–23), asst. director (1923–35), director (1935–36).

**Howe, Richard.** Earl **Howe.** 1726–1799. English naval officer; rear admiral (1770) and vice-admiral (1775); engaged in the American Revolution (1776–78); admiral (1782); commanded Channel fleet in great victory over the French (June 1, 1794); named admiral of the fleet, and general of marines (1796).

His brother Sir **William** (1729–1814), 5th Viscount **Howe,** an army officer, commanded regiment at capture of Louisburg and defense of Quebec (1759–60); major general (1772); lieutenant general (1775); commanded British at battle of Bunker Hill (1775) and succeeded Gage as commander in chief in America; defeated Americans on Long Island (1776); captured New York City and defeated Americans at White Plains and Brandywine (1776); resigned command (1778); appointed general (1793).

**Howe, Samuel Gridley.** 1801–1876. American humanitarian, b. Boston. Served as soldier and surgeon in Greek war for independence from Turkey (1824–30). Head of Perkins Institution for the Blind (1832–76); also interested himself in care of the feeble-minded, prison reform, abolishment of imprisonment for debt and antislavery movement; edited *The Commonwealth;* chairman, Mass. Board of State Charities (1865–74). His wife (m. 1843), **Julia,** *nee* **Ward** [wôrd] (1819–1910), b. New York City, helped him edit *The Commonwealth;* composed and published *The Battle Hymn of the Republic* (1862); became leader in woman-suffrage movement (from 1868) and participant in move to promote international peace (from 1870); lectured widely in these causes; her books include *Samuel Gridley Howe* (1876), *Modern Society* (1881), *Margaret Fuller* (1883), *Is Polite Society Polite?* (1895), *Reminiscences* (1899), *At Sunset* (1910). Their son **Henry Marion** (1848–1922) was a metallurgist; professor at Columbia (1897–1913); author of *Metallurgy of Steel and Cast Iron* (1916), etc. See Laura E. RICHARDS.

**Howe, Timothy Otis.** 1816–1883. American political leader; U.S. senator from Wisconsin (1861–79). U.S. postmaster general (1881–83).

**Howe, William F.** 1828–1902. American criminal lawyer; partner (from 1869) of Abraham Henry Hummel in firm of Howe & Hummel, New York.

**Howe, William Henry.** 1846–1929. American painter; excelled in landscape and cattle pictures. His *Monarch of the Farm* is now in National Gallery of Art, Washington, D.C.; his *Norman Bull,* in St. Louis Museum of Fine Arts.

**Höwel[c]ke, Johannes.** See HEVELIUS.

**How'ell** (hou'ĕl), **Clark.** 1863–1936. American journalist; on staff of Atlanta *Constitution* (from 1884); managing editor (1889) and editor in chief (from 1897). Director of Associated Press from date of its organization (1900).

**Howell, James.** 1594?–1666. English author. Royalist sympathizer in Civil War; imprisoned (1643–51). At Restoration, named historiographer royal (1661). Chief work *Epistolae Ho-Elianae: Familiar Letters,* mostly written while in prison and chiefly to imaginary correspondents; revised Cotgrave's *French and English Dictionary* (1650), and compiled an English-French-Italian-Spanish dictionary (1659–60).

**Howell, John Adams.** 1840–1918. American naval officer and inventor; grad. U.S.N.A., Annapolis (1858). Served through Civil War; rear admiral (1898); retired (1902). Invented a gyroscopic steering torpedo, disappearing gun carriage and certain high-explosive shells. Published *The Mathematical Theory of the Deviations of the Compass* (1879), first scientific American work on this subject.

**Howell, Thomas Jefferson.** 1842–1912. American botanist; published *Flora of Northwest America* (1897–1903), etc.

**Howell, William Henry.** 1860–1945. American physiologist; professor, Johns Hopkins (1893–1931); author of *Text-book of Physiology* (1905).

**How'ells** (hou'ĕlz), **Herbert Norman.** 1892– . English composer of concertos, sonatas, a song cycle, orchestral and choral works.

**Howells, John Mead.** 1868–1959. American architect; offices in New York City. Designed Title Guarantee and Trust building in New York City; collaborated with Raymond M. Hood in design of *Daily News* building in New York and *Tribune* Tower in Chicago.

**Howells, William Dean.** 1837–1920. American man of letters, b. Martin's Ferry, Ohio. Compositor in printing office (to 1856); on staff, *Ohio State Journal,* Columbus, Ohio (1856–61); contributor of poems to *Atlantic Monthly.* Published (1860) a campaign *Life of Lincoln;* U.S. consul, Venice, Italy (1861–65). Assistant editor, *Atlantic Monthly* (1866–71); editor (1871–81). On editorial staff, *Harper's Magazine* (1886–91) and *Cosmopolitan Magazine* (1891–92). Author of *Venetian Life* (1866), *Their Wedding Journey* (1872), *A Chance Acquaintance* (1873), *A Foregone Conclusion* (1875), *The Lady of the Aroostook* (1879), *A Fearful Responsibility* (1881), *A Modern Instance* (1882), *A Woman's Reason* (1883), *The Rise of Silas Lapham* (1885), *Indian Summer* (1886), *The Minister's Charge* (1887), *April Hopes* (1888), *A Hazard of New Fortunes* (1890), *The Quality of Mercy* (1892), *The World of Chance* (1893), *The Landlord at Lion's Head* (1897), *Story of a Play* (1898), *Their Silver Wedding Journey* (1899), *The Kentons* (1902), *The Son of Royal Langbrith* (1904), *The Leatherwood God* (1916). In addition to this body of fiction, he wrote dramas, farce comedies, travel sketches, literary criticism, reminiscences, and poetry.

**How'i·son** (hou'ĭ·s'n), **George Holmes.** 1834–1916. American philosopher; professor, U. of California (1884–1909). With B. P. Bowne, exponent of the doctrine of personalism. Chief work, *The Limits of Evolution* (1901).

**How'itt** (hou'ĭt), **Alfred William.** 1830–1908. English explorer and anthropologist in Australia. To Australia (1852); explored Central Australia (1859) and made a study of Australian aborigines. Police magistrate of Gippsland (1862–89); chief work, *The Native Tribes of South-East Australia* (1904). His father, **William** (1792–1879), wrote *Book of the Seasons* (1831), *Rural Life of England* (1838), *History of the Supernatural...*(1863), etc. His mother **Mary,** *nee* **Both'am** [bŏth'ăm] (1799–1888), collaborated with her husband in *Literature and Romance of Northern Europe* (1852), *Ruined Abbeys and Castles of Great Britain* (1862, 1864), etc.

**Howze** (houz), **Robert Lee.** 1864–1926. American army officer; grad. U.S.M.A., West Point (1888). Served in battle of Santiago (1898), in Philippines (1899–1900), in Puerto Rico (1901–04, 1909–12), in Mexico (1916). Brigadier general (1917); major general, commanding 38th division, in France and in the army of occupation in Germany (1918–19).

**Hox'ie** (hŏk'sĭ), **Vinnie**, *née* **Ream** (rēm). 1847–1914. American sculptor; m. Richard Leveridge Hoxie (1878). Her full-length marble statue of Lincoln (unveiled 1871) is in the rotunda of the Capitol, Washington, D.C.; her *Gov. Samuel Kirkwood* and *Sequoyah* stand in Statuary Hall; a copy of her *Sappho* is over her grave in the National Cemetery, Arlington, Va.

**Ho Ying-chin** (hŭ' yĭng'jĭn'). 1889– . Chinese military leader and politician; follower of Chiang Kai-shek; chief of staff of generalissimo's headquarters (1927); director-general of military training (1929); chief of staff and minister of military affairs (from 1930); negotiated Ho-Umedzu agreement with Japan (July, 1935), whereby China withdrew troops from Hopei.

**Hoyle** (hoil), **Edmond.** 1672–1769. English writer on card games, esp. whist; his laws of whist were in effect over a hundred years (1760–1864).

**Hoyt** (hoit), **Charles Hale.** 1860–1900. American playwright, b. Concord, N.H. In newspaper work (from 1878). Made success in writing farces, including *A Bunch of Keys* (1882), *A Texas Steer* (1890), *A Trip to Chinatown* (1891), *A Milk White Flag* (1893), *A Stranger in New York* (1897), *A Day and a Night in New York* (1898).

**Ho'zier', d'** (dō'zyā'). Family of French genealogists, including: **Pierre** (1592–1660); his son **Charles René** (1640–1732); Charles's nephew **Louis Pierre** (1685–1767); Louis's son **Antoine Marie d'Hozier de Sé'ri'gny'** [dē sā'rē'nyē'] (1721–?1810); Antoine's nephew **Ambroise Louis Marie** (1764–1830).

**Hrabanus Maurus.** See RABANUS MAURUS.

**Hr'dlič·ka** (hûr'dlĭch·kȧ), **A'leš** (ä'lĕsh). 1869–1943. Anthropologist, b. in Bohemia; to U.S. as a young man. With expeditions under sponsorship of American Museum of Natural History (1899–1903). On staff of U.S. National Museum, Washington, D.C. (from 1903), curator (from 1910). Founder and editor (from 1918), *American Journal of Physical Anthropology.* Supporter of theory that American Indians are of Asiatic origin. Known also for anthropologic survey of Alaska and for work on anthropometry and on the evolution of man.

**Hrolf.** See ROLLO.

**Hrotsvitha** *or* **Hrotswitha.** See ROSWITHA.

**Hroz'ný** (hrôz'nē), **Friedrich**, *Czech* **Bedřich.** 1879–1952. Czech archaeologist and Orientalist, b. Leszno, Poland; professor, Prague (1919). Renowned as decipherer of the Hittite language from a study of records written in Babylonian cuneiform and recovered from excavations at Boghazkeui, 90 miles east of Angora.

**Hru·shev'sky** (hrŏŏ·shăf'skû·ĭ; *Angl.* -skĭ), **Mikhail Sergeevich.** 1866–1934. Ukrainian historian; lived outside Russia (1919–24); professor, Kiev (1924–34); author of works on history and literature of Ukraine; wrote also tales and dramatic sketches.

**Hsia** (shē·ä'). First historical dynasty (c. 2205–1766 B.C.) of Chinese emperors, founded by Yü (d. 2197 B.C.) and according to tradition having seventeen rulers; succeeded by the Shang dynasty.

**Hsieh Ho** (shē·ĕ' hŭ'). fl. end of 5th century A.D. Chinese painter and critic; formulated six canons of painting, the basis for art criticism in the Far East for centuries.

**Hsien Fêng** (shē·ĕn' fŭng'). *Personal name* **I Chu** (ē' jōō'). 1831–1861. Chinese emperor (1851–61), seventh of the Ch'ing, or Manchu, dynasty. Fourth son of Emperor Tao Kuang. Took as a concubine Yehonala (later the Empress Dowager Tzu Hsi, *q.v.*); made her son T'ung Chih his successor. During his reign occurred the Taiping rebellion (1850–64), Treaty of Tientsin (1858) opening eleven ports, and war with England (1859–60); fled to Jehol (1860).

**Hsin.** See WANG MANG.

**Hsüan Tsang** (shü·än' dzäng') *or* **Hüan Chwang** *or* **Hiouen Tsang.** *Also* **Yüan Chwang** *or* **Yüan Tsang.** 600?–664 A.D. Chinese Buddhist traveler in India, b. in Honan. Ordained as Buddhist monk (620); made long pilgrimage (629–631) from Ch'ang-an (modern Sian) to India via Tien Shan and Hindu Kush mountains to Peshawar, thence (633) to Kanauj on the Ganges; visited Kanchi, capital of the Pallavas, and famous Buddhist sites; mastered Sanskrit and the Buddhist philosophy, and returned (645) in time of T'ang dynasty via the Pamirs and Kashgar with 657 sacred Buddhist books and 150 relics of Buddha. Wrote (or, according to some, two of his pupils wrote) a vivid and trustworthy account of his travels, translated into French (1853–58) by Stanislas Julien.

**Hsüan Tsung** (shü·än' dzŏŏng'). 685–762 A.D. Chinese emperor (713–756 A.D.) of the T'ang dynasty; founded Hanlin Academy of Letters (725); presided over a court famous for its poets and artists; in latter part of reign lost territory in Tibet, Turkestan, and the south; faced with serious revolts, abdicated.

**Hsüan T'ung** (shü·än' tŏŏng'). *Personal name* **P'u-i** *or* **P'u-yi** (pōō'ē'). 1906–1967. Last emperor (1908–12) of the Ch'ing, or Manchu, dynasty of China. Son of Prince Ch'un and nephew of Emperor Kuang Hsü. Elected emperor (1908) with his father as regent; abdicated (1912) on establishment of the Republic; lived at Peking (1912–24), studying Chinese classics and modern subjects; restored as "nominal ruler" for a few days (1917) by a coup d'état. Tutored by Sir Reginald Johnston, an English scholar, who suggested that he choose an English name; chose *Henry*, after Henry VIII; henceforth best known by the name **Henry P'u-yi;** m. (1922) Elizabeth Yuang, a Manchu girl. Driven out of Peking (1924) by Feng Yu-hsiang; lived under Japanese protection at Tientsin (1924–31); removed by Japanese to Dairen (1931) and made chief executive of the new state Manchukuo (1932); crowned as emperor (1934) under the name **K'ang Tê** *or* **Kang Teh** (käng' dŭ'), *i.e.* "exalted virtue."

**Hsü Hai-tung** (shü' hī'dŏŏng'). 1900– . Chinese Communist leader, b. near Hankow, of peasant origin. In early years a potter; joined Kuomintang forces as soldier (c. 1923); became a Communist (1927); persecuted by the Kuomintang, with a price of $100,000 on his head; an organizer of Red army; commander of the fifteenth Red army corps (1933); Red military leader in war against Japan (1937 ff.).

**Hsün Tzŭ** (shün' dzŭ') *or* **Hsün K'uang** (kwäng') c. 298–c. 230 B.C. Chinese philosopher. Wrote a treatise in 32 books, setting forth the doctrine that man was bad by nature, but could be improved through proper ethical standards and corrective measures of the state; affirmed the artificial nature of society; lived to an extreme old age (according to legend, 120 years); retired (237 B.C.) to the kingdom of Ch'u, gathering a group of disciples that included Han Fei and Li Ssŭ.

**Hsü Shih-ch'ang** (shü' shĭr'chäng'). 1858–1939. Chinese general and politician, b. in Honan province; grand councilor (1905–06); viceroy of Manchuria (1907–09); held various other offices under the empire (1906–11); at time of Revolution (1911) made grand guardian of the emperor; supported Yüan Shih-k'ai; retired from politics (1917–18). Elected president of China (1918–22); a conservative, friendly to both imperial and republican parties; during his term China refused to sign Treaty of Versailles because of the Shantung clauses; retired to Tientsin.

**Huai-nan Tzu.** See LIU AN.

**Hüan Chwang.** Variant of Hsüan Tsang.

**Huang Hsing** (hwäng' shĭng'). 1873–1916. Chinese general, b. near Changsha, Hunan. Educ. at Tokyo U.; active in revolutionary plots against Manchus; forced to flee to Japan; just before the Revolution (1911), was Sun Yat-sen's representative in China; led forces at Hankow; appointed (1912) commander of southern army; a member and founder of the Kuomintang; clashed with President Yüan Shih-k'ai; visited U.S. (1914).

**Huard** (wär; *Fr.* ü·àr'), **Frances,** *nee* **Wil'son** (wĭl's'n). Baroness **Huard.** 1885– . Writer, b. New York City; m. Charles Huard (1905). Author of *My Home in the Field of Honor* (1916), *My Home in the Field of Mercy* (1917), etc. and translations from the French.

**Huart** (ü·àr'), **Clément Imbault-.** 1854–1926. French Orientalist; in consular service in Oriental countries for twenty-three years; among his books are *Grammaire Élémentaire de la Langue Persane* (1899), *Littérature Arabe* (1902).

**Huás'car** (wäs'kär). 1495?–1533. Inca prince, son of Huayna Capac. Defeated (1532) and put to death by his half brother Atahualpa (*q.v.*).

**Huay'na Ca'pac** *or* **Huai'na Ca'pac** (wī'nä kä'päk). 1450?–1525. Eleventh and greatest Inca ruler of Peru (1487–1525), ruling an empire about 3000 miles long and 400 miles wide, capital Cuzco. Divided it between his sons Atahualpa and Huáscar (see Atahualpa).

**Hubald.** See Hucbald.

**Hu'bay** (hōō'boi), **Jenő.** *Known as* **Hubay von Sza'lat·na** (fôn sŏ'lŏt·nŏ). 1858–1937. Hungarian violin virtuoso and composer; with David Popper (1843–1913), cellist, organized Hubay-Popper string quartet. Among his operas are *Der Geigenmacher von Cremona* (1894), *Anna Karenina* (1924); composed also symphonic works, violin concertos, choral pieces, and songs.

**Hub'bard** (hŭb'ẽrd), **Elbert Green.** 1856–1915. American writer, editor, and printer, b. Bloomington, Ill. Free-lance newspaper writer, Chicago (1872–76). Founded (1895), at East Aurora, N.Y., Roycroft Shop, so called from 17th-century English printer Roycroft, to revive the old handicrafts, esp. artistic printing; founded, edited, and wrote the material in *The Philistine,* a monthly magazine used to express his homely, common-sense philosophy and his opinions on all manner of issues (1895–1915); founded and edited *The Fra* (1908–17). Published *Little Journeys,* monthly sketches, chiefly biographical, ultimately filling fourteen volumes. Other works, *A Message to Garcia* (1899; see Calixto García Íñiguez), *Loyalty in Business* (1921). Went down with the *Lusitania* (May 7, 1915).

**Hubbard, Frank McKinney,** *known as* **Kin** (kĭn). 1868–1930. American caricaturist and humorist, b. Bellefontaine, Ohio; on staff of Indianapolis (Ind.) *News;* creator of rustic character *Abe Martin.*

**Hubbard, Gar'di·ner** (gär'd'n·ẽr) **Greene.** 1822–1897. American lawyer, b. Boston; practiced, Boston; moved to Washington, D.C. (1879). A founder of *Science* (1883); founder and first president, National Geographic Society (1888–97). Hubbard Memorial Hall, Washington, home of this society, is named in his honor.

**Hubbard, Henry Vincent.** 1875–1947. American landscape architect; teacher of landscape architecture, Harvard (1906–29), and professor (1921–29); professor of regional planning, Harvard (from 1929). A founder and editor, *Landscape Architecture* (from 1910), *City Planning Quarterly* (1925–34); consulting editor, *The Planners' Journal* (from 1935).

**Hubbard, Richard William.** 1816–1888. American landscape painter, b. Middletown, Conn., his *Sunrise on the Mountains* is in Metropolitan Museum of Art, N.Y.

**Hubbard, William.** 1621?–1704. Congregational clergyman and historian, b. in England; to America as a boy. Pastorate, Ipswich, Mass. (1658–1702). Author of *Narrative of the Troubles with the Indians in New England* (1677), *A General History of New England...*(1815).

**Hub'bell** (hŭb''l), **Henry Salem.** 1870–1949. American painter, b. Paolo, Kans. Head of school of painting and decoration, Carnegie Tech., Pittsburgh (1918–21).

**Hub'ble** (hŭb''l), **Edwin Powell.** 1889-1953. American astronomer; Rhodes scholar at Oxford (1910–13); B.A. in jurisprudence, Oxford (1912). Astronomer, Mt. Wilson Observatory, Pasadena, Calif. (from 1919); investigator of nebulae.

**Hu'ber** (hōō'bẽr), **Eugen.** 1849–1923. Swiss jurist; life member, Hague Tribunal.

**Hu'ber'** (ü'bâr'), **François.** 1750–1831. Swiss naturalist; at fifteen began to lose sight, and later became wholly blind. With aid of his wife and son and a servant, investigated life and habits of honeybees; credited with discovery of aerial impregnation of the queen bee, killing of males by workers, use of antennae, origin of propolis, ventilation of hives, etc.

**Hu'ber** (hū'bẽr), **Gott'helf** (gŏt'hĕlf) **Carl.** 1865–1934. American anatomist, b. Hubli, India. Professor of histology and embryology (1903–14), of anatomy (from 1914), dean of graduate school (from 1927), U. of Michigan.

**Hu'ber** (hōō'bẽr), **Hans.** 1852–1921. Swiss composer of operas, oratorios, symphonies, piano concertos, overtures, chamber music, choral works, piano pieces, and songs.

**Huber, Johannes.** 1830–1879. German Roman Catholic theologian and philosopher.

**Huber, Ludwig Ferdinand.** 1764–1804. German writer; editor, *Allgemeine Zeitung,* Stuttgart (1798–1803). Author of a number of plays and stories. His wife (m. 1794), **Therese,** *nee* **Hey'ne** [hī'nĕ] (1764–1829), was a novelist. Their son **Victor Ai'mé'** [ĕ'mā'] (1800–1869) was a historian of literature; specialized in study of Spanish language and literature; wrote *Spanisches Lesebuch* (1832), *Die Geschichte des Cid* (1829), *Skizzen aus Spanien* (4 vols., 1828–33), etc.

**Huber, Max,** *in full* **Hans Max.** 1874–1960. Swiss jurist; judge of the Permanent Court of International Justice (from 1921); president of the court (1925–27).

**Hu'ber·mann** (hōō'bẽr·män), **Bronisław.** 1882–1947. Polish violin virtuoso.

**Hu'bert** (hū'bẽrt; *Fr.* ü'bâr'), Saint. d. about 727. Bishop of Maestricht and Liége; according to legend, was converted while hunting by the sight of a stag bearing a luminous cross on his head; hence, patron saint of hunters.

**Hu'ber'ti'** (ü'bẽr'tē'), **Gustave Léon.** 1843–1911. Belgian composer of oratorios, instrumental works, and songs.

**Hubert Walter.** See Hubert Walter.

**Hüb'ner** (hüb'nẽr), **Julius.** 1806–1882. German historical painter. His son **Emil** (1834–1901) was a philologist. Julius's two grandsons, **Heinrich** (1869– ) and **Ulrich** (1872–1932), were both painters.

**Hübner, Karl.** 1814–1879. German genre painter.

**Huc** (hük), **Évariste Régis.** 1813–1860. French Roman Catholic priest and missionary in China, Mongolia, and Tibet.

**Huc'bald** (hŭk'bôld) *or* **Hug·bal'dus** (hŭg·băl'dŭs) *or* **Hu'bald** (hū'bôld) *or* **U·bal'dus** (ū·băl'dŭs) *or* **U'gu·bal'dus** (ū'gū·băl'dŭs). 840?–930 (or 932). Benedictine monk and writer on music; author of *De Harmonica Institutione,* one of the earliest treatises on polyphonic music.

**Huch** (ho͞ok), **Ricarda.** 1864–1947. German authoress; writer of verse, plays, novels, and literary criticism.

**Huch′ten·berg** (hûk′tĕn·bĕrk) *or* **Huch′ten·burgh** (-bûrk), **Johan van.** 1647–1733. Dutch painter and etcher.

**Huck′el** (hŭk′'l), **Oliver.** 1864–1940. American Congregational clergyman, lecturer, and writer; pastorates, Baltimore (1897–1916), Greenwich, Conn. (1917–35). Published religious books, and a series of works on Wagner's operas.

**Hud′dle·ston** (hŭd″'l·stŭn), **Sisley.** 1883–1952. English journalist and writer; Paris correspondent of London *Times;* later, European editorial correspondent of *Christian Science Monitor.* Author of *Peace-making in Paris* (1919), *France and the French* (1925), *Europe in Zigzags* (1929), and *The Book of St. Pierre* (1940).

**Hud′son** (hŭd′s'n), **Henry** [*not* **Hendrick,** *though this name occurs often in references to him*]. d. 1611. English navigator. Conducted expedition (in the *Hopewell*) for English Muscovy Company, to discover northeast passage to Far East (1607); reached Greenland and Spitzbergen; second voyage (in the *Hopewell*) for same company, turned back at Novaya Zemlya (1608). Third voyage (in the *Halve Maen* or *Half Moon*), for Dutch East India Company, discovered Hudson River and sailed up it as far as Albany (1609). Fourth voyage (in the *Discovery*), for group of English enterprisers, reached Hudson Bay (1610–11); mutineers seized Hudson and eight others and set them adrift in a small boat (June 23, 1611); no record of their fate.

**Hudson, Henry Norman.** 1814–1886. American Shakespearean scholar, b. Cornwall, Vt. Grad. Middlebury College (1840). Ordained priest, Protestant Episcopal Church (1849). Editor, *Churchman* (1852–55) and *American Church Monthly* (1857–58). Chaplain, Union army, in Civil War. Author of *Lectures on Shakespeare* (2 vols., 1848), *Shakespeare, his Life, Art, and Characters* (2 vols., 1872); editor of Harvard edition of Shakespeare's works (20 vols., 1880–81).

**Hudson, Jeffery.** 1619–1682. English dwarf; 18 inches tall at age of 30; later grew to about 3 ft. 6 in. Concealed in a pie at a dinner in honor of Charles I; page to Queen Henrietta Maria. Captured by Flemish pirates (1630); captain of horse in Royalist army at beginning of Civil War; captured (c. 1649) by Barbary pirates, but escaped; imprisoned for a time (1679) for supposed connection with Popish plot. His portrait painted by Vandyke. Introduced by Scott in *Peveril of the Peak.*

**Hudson, Manley Ottmer.** 1886–1960. American jurist; professor of international law, Harvard (from 1923) and director of research in international law, Harvard Law School (1927–38). Member of American commission at Paris Peace Conference (1919); member of legal section, Secretariat of the League of Nations (1919–23). Judge, Permanent Court of International Justice (1936–46). Author of *The Permanent Court of International Justice and the Question of American Participation* (1925), *By Pacific Means* (1935), etc.

**Hudson, Stephen.** d. 1944. *Pseud. of* **Sydney Schiff.** English novelist; author of *Richard Kurt* (1919), *Tony* (1924), *Myrtle* (1925), *Richard, Myrtle and I* (1926), *Celeste and Other Sketches* (1930), *The Other Side* (1937).

**Hudson, William.** 1730?–1793. English botanist; an original member of Linnaean Society (1791); published *Flora Anglica* (1762). The genus *Hudsonia* is named after him.

**Hudson, William Henry.** 1841–1922. Naturalist and author, b. in Argentina, of American parentage; spent youth in Argentina; to England (1874), naturalized (1900). Author of *The Purple Land that England Lost* (1885), *The Naturalist in La Plata* (1892), *British Birds* (1895), *Green Mansions* (a romance; 1904), *Adventures among Birds* (1913), *Far Away and Long Ago* (1918), *The Book of a Naturalist* (1919), *A Little Boy Lost* (1920), *A Hind in Richmond Park* (1922).

**Hudson, William Henry.** 1862–1918. English literary critic, b. London. Professor of English literature, Stanford U., Calif. (1892–1901). Among his works are *Studies in Interpretation* (1896), *The Study of English Literature* (1898), *The Story of the Renaissance* (1912), and studies on Scott, Gray, Lowell, Milton, etc.

**Hüe** (ü), **Georges Adolphe.** 1858–1948. French composer, especially of symphonic works and lyric dramas.

**Hueb′ner** (hēb′nẽr), **Solomon Stephen.** 1882–1964. American educator; professor of insurance and commerce, U. of Pennsylvania (from 1908). Author of *The Stock Exchange* (1918), *Property Insurance* (1922), *Life Insurance* (1923), etc. Special editor for terms in insurance, *Webster's New International Dictionary, Second Edition.* His brother **Grover Gerhardt** (1884–1964), professor of transportation, Wharton School, U. of Penn.; author of *Railroad Traffic and Rates* (1911), *Principles of Ocean Transportation* (1918), *Foreign Trade* (1930), etc.; special editor for land transportation terms, *Webster's New International Dictionary, Second Edition.*

**Huef′fer** (hŭf′ẽr), **Ford Madox.** See Ford Madox FORD.

**Huef′fer** (hŭf′ẽr), **Francis.** *Orig. name* **Franz Hüf′fer** (hüf′ẽr). 1845–1889. Son-in-law of Ford Madox Brown, and father of Ford Madox Ford (*qq.v.*). Music critic, b. in Germany; to London (1869); naturalized (1882). Music critic on *The Times* (1879); edited *Musical World* (1886). Author of *Richard Wagner and the Music of the Future* (1874), *The Troubadours* (1878).

**Huep′pe** (hüp′ĕ), **Ferdinand.** 1852–1938. German hygienist and bacteriologist. Professor, German U. in Prague (from 1889). Proved that certain bacteria formerly regarded as specific pathogens were only forms of polymorphic bacteria; investigated protection against infection with pathogenic bacteria by inoculation with related but benign bacteria; led to a simplification of disinfection by his work on the control of infectious diseases; wrote on bacteriology, hygiene, physical training, alcoholism, vegetarianism, etc.

**Huer′ta** (wĕr′tä), **Adolfo de la.** d. 1955. Mexican political leader; joined Obregón and Calles in revolution (1920) against government. After death of Carranza, made provisional president (May–Nov., 1920); minister of finance under Obregón (1920–23); took prominent part in oil question discussions (1921); revolted against Obregón and Calles (1923–24); defeated (1924) and lived in exile in U.S. (1924–33).

**Huerta, Victoriano.** 1854–1916. Mexican soldier and politician, b. Colotlán, Jalisco. Took part in revolution that raised Díaz to power; brigadier general (1902). Served Madero (1911–13) but (Feb., 1913) turned against him, deposed and arrested him, and was supposed to be responsible for Madero's death. Provisional president of Mexico (1913–14); failed of recognition by U.S.; involved in difficulties with U.S. in Tampico and Veracruz; resigned (July 15, 1914). In exile in Europe and U.S. (1914–16); arrested twice in U.S. on Mexican border for conspiracy to incite revolution; died in custody of U.S. government.

**Huerta y Muñoz, Vicente Antonio García de la.** See GARCÍA DE LA HUERTA Y MUÑOZ.

**Huet, Conrad Busken.** See Conrad BUSKEN HUET.

**Huet** (ü·ĕ′), **Paul.** 1804–1869. French painter of landscapes, as *Le Château d'Arques, Le Calme du Bois.*

**Huet, Pierre Daniel.** 1630–1721. French prelate and scholar; renowned as mathematician, Hellenist, and

Hebraist; bishop of Avranches (1691). Editor of Origen's *Commentaria in Sacram Scripturam;* author of a critique on the philosophy of Descartes (*Censura Philosophiae Cartesianae*), etc.

**Hu'fe·land** (hōō'fĕ·länt), **Christoph Wilhelm.** 1762–1836. German physician; professor of pathology and therapeutics, Berlin U.; wrote on Wieland, Herder, Goethe, and Schiller as well as on scientific subjects.

**Hufeland, Gottlieb.** 1760–1817. German jurist and economist; wrote *Neue Grundlegung der Staatswirtschaftskunst* (2 vols., 1807–13).

**Hüf'fer** (hüf'ĕr), **Hermann.** 1830–1905. German historian and legal scholar.

**Hufnagel.** See HOEFNAGEL.

**Hugbaldus.** See HUCBALD.

**Hü'gel** (hü'gĕl), Baron **Friedrich von.** 1852–1925. Roman Catholic theologian and baron of the Holy Roman Empire, b. Florence, Italy; son of Baron Karl von Hügel; to England (1873). Founder of London Society for the Study of Religion; became center of modernist group. Wrote *Mystical Element of Religion* (1908), *Eternal Life* (1912), *The Reality of God* (1931), etc.

**Hügel,** Baron **Karl von.** 1795–1870. Austrian explorer, horticulturist, and diplomat. Served as a soldier; then took up the study of horticulture and natural history; traveled in the East Indies (1830–36) and to New Zealand; ambassador in Florence and Brussels (1850–69). See Friedrich von HÜGEL.

**Hu'gen·berg** (hōō'gĕn·bĕrk), **Alfred.** 1865–1951. German newspaper proprietor, motion-picture magnate, and politician. Member of Reichstag (from 1920); chairman, German National People's party (1928–33). Minister of national economy, food, and agriculture in Hitler cabinet (1933); retired, and his party ("Green Shirts") dissolved (1933), but remained member of new Reichstag.

**Hugensz, Lucas.** See LUCAS VAN LEYDEN.

**Hu·ger'** (ū·jē'), **Isaac.** 1743–1797. American Revolutionary officer, b. in South Carolina; colonel (1776); brigadier general (1779).

**Hug'gen·ber'ger** (hōōg'ĕn·bĕr'gĕr), **Alfred.** 1867–1960. Swiss poet and novelist.

**Hug'gins** (hŭg'ĭnz), **Charles Brenton.** 1901– . Am. surgeon, b. Halifax, Canada. At U. of Chicago (1927– ); awarded Nobel prize in physiology and medicine (1966) with P. Rous for cancer research.

**Huggins, Miller James.** 1879–1929. American professional baseball player, b. Cincinnati, Ohio; played second base, with Cincinnati (1904–08) and St. Louis (1909–17) of the National League; manager, New York, American League (1918–29).

**Huggins,** Sir **William.** 1824–1910. English astronomer, b. London. With William Allen Miller, invented stellar spectroscope; presented to Royal Society results of his first investigations with it, in a paper *Lines of the Spectra of Some of the Fixed Stars* (1863), showing that in structure the stars are like the sun. Made observations of several comets; by use of a refracting telescope determined (1870–75) velocity of stars; photographed spectrum of Vega, of the larger stars, the moon, and the planets; conducted researches into the presence of calcium in the sun (1897). Published *An Atlas of Representative Stellar Spectra* (1900).

**Hugh** (hū). *Fr.* **Hugues** (üg). Name of five dukes of Burgundy: **Hugh I** (1040?–1093); duke (1075–78); abdicated in favor of his brother, Eudes I. His nephew **Hugh II,** *called* **Bo'rel'** (bô'rĕl'); duke (1102–42). His grandson **Hugh III** (1150?–1193); took part in Third Crusade; died in Syria. His grandson **Hugh IV** (1212–1272); duke (1218–72); went on unsuccessful expedition to Palestine (1239–41); taken prisoner with Saint Louis in Egypt on Sixth Crusade (1248–54); granted title of hereditary king of Salonika by Baldwin II (1265); greatly increased strength of duchy. His grandson **Hugh V;** duke (1305–15).

**Hugh' Ca'pet** (hū' kā'pĕt, -pĭt; kăp'ĕt, -ĭt). *Fr.* **Hugues Ca'pet'** (üg' kȧ'pĕ'). 940?–996. Son of Hugh the Great. Duke of France (956–996) and king of France (987–996), first of the Capetians (*q.v.*). Carried on policies of his father. Inherited part of Burgundy (965). Elected king by nobles (987), defeating Charles, Duke of Lorraine. Had difficulty in maintaining his authority because of the many powerful feudal lords of Normandy, Burgundy, Aquitaine, Flanders, etc.

**Hugh of Avranches.** See Earl of CHESTER.

**Hugh of Cyveiliog** *or* **Kevelioc.** See Earl of CHESTER.

**Hugh of Lin'coln** (lĭng'kŭn) *or* **Hugh of Av'a·lon** (ăv'ȧ·lŏn), Saint. 1135?–1200. English prelate, b. Avalon, France; Carthusian monk in La Grande Chartreuse (from 1160); called to England by Henry II (c. 1175) and became his adviser; bishop of Lincoln (1186–1200); excommunicated John (1194); took lead (1198) in first refusal of a money grant. Canonized (1220).

**Hugh of Lincoln.** 1246?–1255. English boy martyr; according to legend, crucified by a Jew at Lincoln; subject of Chaucer's *Prioress's Tale* in *Canterbury Tales;* legend also used in Marlowe's *Jew of Malta.*

**Hugh of Pro'vence'** (prô'väɴs'). *Fr.* **Hugues** (üg). *Ger.* **Hu'go** (hōō'gō). d. 947. Count of Arles (898–947) and duke of Provence (911–945); king of Italy (926–947) jointly with his son, Lothair II (931–947); defeated Rudolf II of Burgundy; compelled to yield control of Italy to Berengar II (945).

**Hugh of St. Cher** (hū' ŭv săɴ' shâr'). *Also known as* Cardinal **Hu'go** (hū'gō). 1200?–1263. French ecclesiastic; entered Dominican order (1225); cardinal (1244); regarded as first compiler of a concordance to the Bible; reputed first to divide Old Testament and New Testament into chapters.

**Hugh** (*or* **Hugo**) **of St. Vic'tor** (hū [hū'gō] ŭv sānt vĭk'tĕr). *Fr.* **Hugues de Saint'-Vic'tor'** (üg' dĕ săɴ'vēk'tôr'). 1096?–1141. Scholastic theologian and mystic philosopher, b. in Flanders or perhaps Saxony; spent most of his adult life in abbey of St. Victor, Paris. Author of *De Unione Corporis et Spiritus, De Arca Noë Mystica, De Vanitate Mundi,* etc.

**Hugh** (*or* **Hugo**) **the Great,** Saint. *Also known as* **Hugh** (*or* **Hugo**) **of Clu'ny'** (klü'nē'). 1024–1109. French Benedictine monk; abbot of Cluny (1049–1109); supported popes Leo IX, Stephen IX, and Gregory VII in their efforts at ecclesiastical reforms.

**Hugh the Great.** *Called also* **the White** (hwīt). d. 956. Son of Robert, Count of Paris. Ruler of large estates in northern France (923–956). At times in conflict with later Carolingian kings; had power to take their thrones from them, but generally supported them. Father of Hugh Capet (*q.v.*).

**Hughes** (hūz), **Charles Evans.** 1862–1948. American jurist, b. Glens Falls, N.Y. A.B., Brown (1881); LL.B., Columbia (1884). Adm. to bar (1884) and practiced in New York City. Counsel for New York State legislative commission ("Armstrong commission") investigating financial methods of life-insurance companies (1905–06). Governor of New York (1907–10). Associate justice, U.S. Supreme Court (1910–16). Unsuccessful candidate for president of United States, defeated by Wilson (1916). U.S. secretary of state (1921–25). Member of Hague Tribunal (1926–30) and judge on Permanent Court of International Justice (1928–30). Appointed chief justice, U.S. Supreme Court (1930; retired, 1941).

**Hughes, Charles Frederick.** 1866–1934. American naval

officer; grad. U.S.N.A., Annapolis (1884). Chief of staff of Atlantic fleet (1913–14); served with British grand fleet, in North Sea (1917–18). Commandant in chief, U.S. battle fleet, and chief of naval operations; retired (Nov. 1, 1930).

**Hughes, David Edward.** 1831–1900. Inventor, b. London, England; to U.S. as a boy. Began experiments with printing telegraph (about 1852); devised improvement over Royal Earl House machine; patent issued (1856); succeeded in having machine adopted for use in foreign countries. Also credited with invention of microphone (1878; his being the first instrument called by this name), induction balance, and Hughes electromagnet. Resident of London (from 1877).

**Hughes, Edwin.** 1884–1965. American piano virtuoso; composer of many songs.

**Hughes, Edwin Holt.** 1866–1950. American Methodist Episcopal clergyman, b. Moundsville, W.Va.; bishop (1908); senior bishop of Methodist Episcopal Church (from 1932).

**Hughes, Hatcher.** 1881–1945. American playwright, b. Polkville, N.C. On English teaching staff, Columbia (from 1912). Author of *A Marriage Made in Heaven* (1918), *Hell-Bent for Heaven* (1922; awarded Pulitzer prize, 1924); coauthor of *Wake Up, Jonathan* (1921), *The Lord Blesses the Bishop* (1932).

**Hughes, Hugh Price.** 1847–1902. English Methodist clergyman; founded *Methodist Times* (1885); opened West London Mission (1886); renowned as pulpit orator.

**Hughes, John.** 1677–1720. English writer; author of plays *Siege of Damascus* (1720) and *Calypso and Telemachus* (1712), and of *Poems on Several Occasions* (publ. 1735); edited Spenser (1715); contributed to *Tatler, Spectator,* and *Guardian.*

**Hughes, John Cei′riog** (kû′ĭ·ryôg). *Pen name* **Ceiriog.** 1832–1887. Welsh poet; author of hundreds of songs and the Welsh pastoral poem *Owain Wyn* (1856).

**Hughes, John Joseph.** 1797–1864. Roman Catholic prelate, b. in County Tyrone, Ireland; to U.S. (1817). Militant defender of Roman Catholicism. Designated coadjutor bishop of New York (1838); consecrated bishop of New York (1842); first archbishop of New York (1850); laid cornerstone of St. Patrick's Cathedral, N.Y. City (1858).

**Hughes, Langston,** *in full* **James Langston.** 1902-1967. American Negro writer, b. Joplin, Mo. Grad., Lincoln U., in Pennsylvania (1929). Variously employed, as seaman, waiter, laundry sorter, garden worker, bus boy, etc. Author of *Weary Blues* (1926), *Not Without Laughter* (1930), *The Dream Keeper* (verse; 1932), *The Ways of White Folks* (1934), *The Big Sea* (autobiographical; 1940), *Shakespeare in Harlem* (1942). Many of his poems have been set to music.

**Hughes, Richard Arthur Warren.** 1900– . English writer; educ. Oxford. Author of *Gipsy-Night and Other Poems* (1922), *The Sisters' Tragedy and Other Plays* (1924), *A Moment of Time* (short stories, 1926), *Confessio Juvenis* (verse, 1926), *A High Wind in Jamaica* (American title *The Innocent Voyage,* 1929), *The Spider's Palace* (children's stories, 1931), *In Hazard* (1938).

**Hughes, Robert Ball.** 1806–1868. Sculptor, b. London, England; to U.S. (c. 1828); studio, Dorchester, Mass. Examples of his work: *Bishop John H. Hobart,* in Trinity Church, New York; *Nathaniel Bowditch,* in Boston Athenaeum; *Chief Justice John Marshall,* in Pennsylvania Academy of Fine Arts; *John Trumbull,* in Yale Art Gallery, New Haven, Conn.

**Hughes, Rupert.** 1872–1956. American author, b. Lancaster, Mo. In editorial work, chiefly with Encyclopaedia Britannica Company (1901–05). Author of biography (*George Washington*), books on music (*American Composers, Music Lovers' Cyclopedia*), plays (*Alexander the Great, All for a Girl, Excuse Me*), and more than twenty-five novels (including *What Will People Say?,* 1914; *Cup of Fury,* 1919; *Souls for Sale,* 1922; *The Patent Leather Kid,* 1927; *No One Man,* 1931; *The Man Without a Home,* 1935).

**Hughes,** Sir **Sam.** 1853–1921. Canadian soldier and statesman, b. in Ontario. Member of Dominion parliament (1892–1921); entered Canadian militia and served in Boer War (1899–1902); major general (1914); minister of militia and defense (1911–16), and organizer of Canadian expeditionary forces in World War; lieutenant general (1916).

**Hughes, Thomas.** 1822–1896. English jurist, reformer, and writer; associated with Frederick Denison Maurice (*q.v.*) in work of Christian Socialism; active in founding Working Men's College; its principal (1872–83); founded model community in Tennessee, U.S.A. (1879), which failed. Served as county-court judge (1882–96). Best known as author of *Tom Brown's School Days* (publ. anon.; 1857) and *Tom Brown at Oxford* (1861); also wrote biographies of Daniel Macmillan, Livingstone, and Alfred the Great.

**Hughes, Thomas Patrick.** 1838–1911. American clergyman and Orientalist, b. in England; compiler and editor of *Dictionary of Islam* (1895).

**Hughes, William Morris.** 1864–1952. Australian statesman, b. in Wales; to Australia (1884). Labor party representative in federal legislature; minister for external affairs (1904); attorney general (1908–09, 1910–13, 1914–21); prime minister of Australia (1915–23); again minister for external affairs (1921–23). Member of imperial cabinet and delegate to Paris Peace Conference (1919). Australian representative at League of Nations Assembly (1932). Vice-president of executive council, Australia (1934–35, 1937–38); minister for health and repatriation (1934–37); minister in charge of territories (1937–38); again minister for external affairs (1937–39); attorney general (1939–41), and minister for industry (1939–40), for the navy (1940–41).

**Hugo′** (hū′gō; *Ger.* hōō′-). See HUGH.

**Hugo,** Cardinal. See HUGH OF ST. CHER.

**Hugo.** One of Four Doctors of Bologna. See BULGARUS.

**Hu′go** (hōō′gō), **Gustav.** 1764–1844. German jurist; professor, Göttingen (1788); privy councilor (1819). Chief work *Lehrbuch eines Civilistischen Cursus* (1792 ff.).

**Hu′go′** (ü′gō′), Comte **Joseph Léopold Sigisbert.** 1773–1828. French general and writer on military subjects; served in the Revolutionary and Napoleonic armies; well known for his defense of Thionville (1813–14). His sons: (1) **Abel** (1798–1855), author of literary and historical works, including *L'Heure de la Mort* (1819), *Histoire de l'Empereur Napoléon* (1833), *France Militaire* (1834); (2) **Eugène** (1800–1837), poet; (3) **Victor Marie** (*q.v.*).

**Hu′go** (hū′gō; *Fr.* ü′gō′), **Victor Marie.** 1802–1885. Son of Comte Joseph Léopold Sigisberg Hugo (*q.v.*). French man of letters, b. Besançon. At age of seventeen, won three prizes in Toulouse at a poetic competition (*Jeux Floraux,* 1819). Published *Odes et Poésies Diverses* (1822), and was granted a pension by Louis XVIII. Then followed the romantic novel *Han d'Islande* (1823), *Nouvelles Odes et Ballades* (1826), the drama *Cromwell* with its famous *Préface* (1827), and *Les Orientales* (verse, 1828), establishing his position as leader of the romantic movement in French literature. The presentation of his *Hernani* (1830) at the Théâtre Français was marked by clashes between the classicists and romanticists for nearly 100 nights. Other works of this period were *Le Dernier Jour d'un Condamné* (1829), *Notre Dame de*

*Paris* (novel, 1831), *Marion Delorme* (play, 1831), *Le Roi s'Amuse* (1832), *Lucrèce Borgia* (1833), *Marie Tudor* (1833), *Ruy Blas* (1838), *Les Burgraves* (1843), and four collections of poems, *Feuilles d'Automne* (1831), *Chants du Crépuscule* (1835), *Voix Intérieures* (1837), *Les Rayons et les Ombres* (1840). Created a peer of France (1845) and elected member of Constituent Assembly (1848); banished from France by Napoleon III and resided on island of Guernsey (to 1870); during this period wrote *Les Châtiments* (1853), *Les Contemplations* (1856), *La Légende des Siècles* (vol. 1, 1859), *Les Misérables* (novel, 10 vols., 1862), *Chansons des Rues et des Bois* (1865), *Les Travailleurs de la Mer* (1866), *L'Homme qui Rit* (1869). Returned to France (1870) and was member of the National Assembly at Bordeaux (1871); resigned after the Commune and fled to Brussels and Luxemburg; wrote *L'Année Terrible* (1872), *Quatre-Vingt-Treize* (1874), *L'Art d'Être Grandpère* (1877), and published (1877) his *Histoire d'un Crime* (written 1852), an account from his Republican point of view of Louis Napoleon's coup d'état of 1851. Thereafter he added other parts to his *La Légende des Siècles*, wrote a few philosophical poems, and published the drama *Torquemada* (1882) at the age of 80. He died in Paris (May 22, 1885). His two sons, **Charles Victor** (1826–1871) and **François Victor** (1828–1873), were journalists and editors.

**Hu'go the Great** *or* **Hu'go of Cluny** (hū'gō). = HUGH THE GREAT.

**Hugues** (üg). See HUGH.

**Hugues, Clovis.** 1851–1907. French poet and politician; involved in communist movement in Marseilles (1871) and imprisoned (1871–75); member of Chamber of Deputies (from 1881). Among his books of verse are *Les Soirs de Bataille* (1882), *Les Évocations* (1885), *La Chanson de Jeanne d'Arc* (1900). His wife, **Jeanne,** *nee* **Roy'an'nez'** [rwȧ'yȧ'nā'] (1855– ), was a sculptor.

**Hugues de Pa'yens'** (dẽ pȧ'yäɴs'). 1070?–1136. Burgundian knight; with Geoffroi de Saint-Omer, founded (1119) at Jerusalem the religious and military order whose members were known as Knights Templars.

**Hu Han-min** (hōō' hän'mĭn'). 1879–1936. Chinese politician, b. in Kwangtung province; aided Sun Yat-sen in organizing revolutionary party; military governor of Canton (1911–13); chief adviser, generalissimo's headquarters (1917–21); acted as chief during Dr. Sun's absence (1924–25); visited Moscow (1925); chairman of Nationalist government at Nanking (1927–28); state councilor (1928–31); member of the Kuomintang (from 1924); with Chiang Kai-shek and Wang Ching-wei formed a triumvirate (1932–35); represented extreme right and reactionary forces.

**Hui Tsung** (hwā' dzŏŏng'). 1082–1135. Chinese emperor (1101–25), next to the last of the Northern Sung dynasty; painter and collector of paintings; founded imperial academy of painting, and was a patron of artists.

**Hui'zing·a** (hoi'zĭng·ȧ), **Johan.** 1872–1945. Dutch historian; author of *The Waning of the Middle Ages* (Eng. trans. 1924), *Erasmus* (1924), etc.

**Hu·la'gu** (hōō·lä'gōō; hōō'lä·gōō') *or* **Ho·la'gu** (hō·lä'gōō; hō'lä·gōō'). 1217–1265. Mongol ruler. Son of Tului and grandson of Genghis Khan, and brother of Mangu Khan and Kublai Khan. Sent (1252) by Mangu Khan to quell uprising in Persia; destroyed sect of the Assassins (1256); founded an astronomical observatory; laid siege to Baghdad; seized and sacked the city (1258), overthrowing Abbasside caliphate; broke Seljuk power in Persia. Invaded Syria (1260), and captured Aleppo and Damascus; on hearing of Mangu Khan's death assumed title of Il-khan (*q.v.*) as ruler of conquered provinces; his armies defeated at Ain Jalut (1260) by Mameluke sultan of Egypt; became a Moslem. Considered by some as the destroyer of Persian medieval culture. His descendants, Il-khans of Persia, were the ruling dynasty for about a century.

**Hul'bert** (hŭl'bẽrt), **Archer Butler.** 1873–1933. American historian and educator; author of many books on American history. His *Forty Niners* received *Atlantic Monthly* prize award (1931).

**Hulbert, James Root.** 1884– . American educator; A.B., Chicago (1907). Teacher of English (from 1907) and professor (from 1926), U. of Chicago. Author of *Chaucer's Official Life* (1912); coauthor of *Effective English* (1929); coeditor of *Dictionary of American English.*

**Hul'burt** (hŭl'bẽrt), **Lorrain Sherman.** 1858–1943. American educator; professor of mathematics, Johns Hopkins (1897–1926). Author of *Differential and Integral Calculus* (1912).

**Hu'lin'** (ü'lăɴ'), Comte **Pierre Augustin.** 1758–1841. French general of the Revolutionary and Napoleonic period; took part in the capture of the Bastille (July 14, 1789). Served in Italian campaign; aided in defense of Genoa, under Masséna (1800); presided at court-martial which tried and condemned the Duc d'Enghien (1804). Distinguished himself at Jena (1806); general of division (1807); comte (1808); governor of Paris; suppressed Malet's conspiracy to overthrow Empire (1812).

**Hull** (hŭl), **Albert Wallace.** 1880–1966. American physicist; known for work on X rays, thermionic vacuum relays, etc.

**Hull, Cordell.** 1871–1955. American statesman, b. in Tennessee. B.L., Cumberland (1891). Adm. to bar (1891); judge, 5th judicial circuit of Tennessee (1903–07). Member, U.S. House of Representatives (1907–21; 1923–31), U.S. Senate (1931–33); author of federal income tax law of 1913, and its revision in 1916, also of the federal inheritance act of 1916. U.S. secretary of state (1933–44; resigned); negotiated reciprocal trade agreements, esp. with Latin-American countries; awarded Nobel Peace Prize for 1945.

**Hull,** Mrs. **Edith Maude.** English novelist; author of *The Sheik* (1921), *Desert Healer* (1925), *Sons of the Sheik* (1926), *Lion-tamer* (1928), *Captive of the Sahara* (1931), *Forest of Terrible Things* (1939), etc.

**Hull, Helen Rose.** 1888–1971. American educator and novelist; teacher (of English), Columbia U. (1916–56); author of *Quest* (1922), *Heat Lightning* (1932), *Frost Flower* (1939), *A Circle in the Water* (1943), etc.

**Hull, Isaac.** 1773–1843. American naval officer, b. Shelton, Conn. Served in war with Tripoli (1803–04). In command of the *Constitution* (popularly called "Old Ironsides") in its defeat of British frigate *Guerrière* (Aug. 19, 1812). Commodore (1823); in command of Pacific squadron (1824–27). In command, Washington Navy Yard (1829–35); in Mediterranean (1839–41).

**Hull, William.** 1753–1825. American Revolutionary officer, b. Derby, Conn. Governor, Michigan Territory (1805–12). Appointed brigadier general (1812); led American attack from Detroit into Canada (July, 1812); outmaneuvered and defeated by British; surrendered (Aug. 16, 1812). Court-martialed; convicted of cowardice and neglect of duty, and sentenced to be shot (1814); sentence approved, but execution not carried out because of Hull's Revolutionary service.

**Hul'lah** (hŭl'ȧ), **John Pyke.** 1812–1884. English organist, composer, and singing teacher; introduced singing classes on the tonic sol-fa method (1840 ff.); composed an opera, *Village Coquettes* (1836; words by Charles Dickens), motets, duets, and songs.

**Hulme** (hūm), **Thomas Ernest.** 1883–1917. English

philosopher and poet; killed in action (1917); author of *Lecture on Modern Poetry*, and *Speculations* (pub. 1924); translator of works by Bergson and Sorel.

**Hulse** (hŭls), **John.** 1708–1790. English clergyman; educ. Cambridge; bequeathed property to Cambridge U. for advancement of religious learning; his bequest endowed the Hulsean professorship of divinity, Hulsean lectures (on divinity and evidences of Christianity), and certain Hulsean prizes.

**Hül'sen** (hül'zĕn), **Christian.** 1858–1935. German historian and classical archaeologist.

**Hul'ton** (hŭl't'n; -tŭn), Sir **Edward.** 1870–1925. English newspaper proprietor and sportsman. Entered (1898) business of his father, **Edward Hulton,** owner of London *Evening Chronicle, Sunday Chronicle, Daily Dispatch, Daily Sketch, Sporting Chronicle,* at whose death (1904), he succeeded to proprietorship of the papers; acquired *Illustrated Sunday Herald* and London *Evening Standard;* served with distinction in World War; purchased string of race horses and won the "War Derby" (1916); sold newspaper properties (1923) to lords Rothermere and Beaverbrook.

**Hu'mann** (hōō'män), **Karl.** 1839–1896. German railway construction engineer and archaeologist; made topographical surveys and built roads in Palestine, Anatolia, and the Balkans; engaged in archaeological excavations in Pergamum (1878–86), northern Syria, Manisa (1891–94), etc.

**Hu·ma'yun** (hŏŏ·mä'yōōn). 1508–1556. Second emperor of Hindustan of the Mogul dynasty (1530–1556). Son of Babor. Ceded Kabul and western Punjab to his brother; failed to conquer Gujarat; defeated (1539, 1540) by Sher Khan (see SHER SHAH) of Bengal. Driven from India, found shelter in court of Persia (1542–1555); recovered Kandahar and Kabul (1545–47); spent next nine years (1547–55) in Afghan kingdom in disturbed conditions; returned to India (1555) and seized Delhi from Afghan ruler; died six months later.

**Hum'bert I** (hŭm'bĕrt). *Ital.* **Um·ber'to** (ōōm·bĕr'tō). 1844–1900. Son of Victor Emmanuel II. Prince of Piedmont of the Savoy-Carignan line, b. Turin. 2d king of Italy (1878–1900). As prince, took part in wars for unification of Italy (1858–70); reign generally tranquil; approved formation (1882) of Triple Alliance (Dreibund) between Italy, Germany, and Austria-Hungary; assassinated at Monza by an anarchist.

**Humbert II.** 1904– . King of Italy (May–June, 1946), formerly prince of Piedmont; son of Victor Emmanuel III; m. (1930) Princess Marie José of Belgium; in exile, as count of **Sar're** (sär'rā).

**Hum'bert'** (ŭɴ'bâr'), **Georges Louis.** 1862–1921. French soldier; general of brigade (1912) and of division (1914). Commanded Moroccan division sent to France at beginning of the World War (1914), and commanded the 3d army (July 22, 1915); engaged on the Marne, the Yser, and in the Argonne; sent to Picardy (1917) and was engaged along the Oise (1918). Governor of Strasbourg (1919); member of supreme war council (1920).

**Hum'boldt** (hŏŏm'bōlt; *Angl.* hŭm'bōlt), Baron **Alexander von,** *in full* **Friedrich Heinrich Alexander von.** 1769–1859. Brother of Baron Wilhelm von Humboldt. German naturalist, traveler, and statesman, b. Berlin. Educ. U. of Frankfort on the Oder, Berlin, and Göttingen, and the mining school in Freiberg. Accompanied Georg Forster on journey through Belgium, Holland, England, and France (1790); superintendent of mines in Frankish principalities (1792). Accompanied French botanist Aimé Bonpland on a scientific journey to South America, Cuba, and Mexico (1799–1804); settled in Paris (1808), worked on the description of his American travels. Resided in Berlin (after 1827); on scientific expedition to Russian Asia (1829); on several diplomatic missions for Prussian government. By writings, fostered introduction and use in Europe of Peruvian guano; provided means, by his delineation of isothermal lines, for comparing climatic conditions of various countries; studied rate of decrease in mean temperature with increase of elevation, also the origin of tropical storms; wrote on plant distribution; discovered decrease in intensity of the earth's magnetic force from the poles to the equator; studied volcanoes, demonstrated igneous origin of certain rocks. Chief among his works is *Kosmos* (pub. 1845–62), a description of the physical universe.

**Humboldt,** Baron **Wilhelm von.** 1767–1835. Brother of Baron Alexander von Humboldt. German philologist and diplomat; Prussian resident minister in Rome (1801–08), Vienna (1810), London (1817), Berlin (1819). His great work was *Über die Kawisprache auf der Insel Jawa,* published posthumously (3 vols., 1836–40); the introduction to this book has been published separately (transl., *On the Difference in the Construction of Language, and its Influence upon the Intellectual Development of the Human Race*). Influential in developing the science of comparative philology.

**Hume** (hūm), **Cyril.** 1900–1966. American writer; author of *Wife of the Centaur* (1923), *Cruel Fellowship* (1925), *The Golden Dancer* (1926), *A Dish for the Gods* (1929), *My Sister My Bride* (1933), etc.

**Hume, David.** 1711–1776. Scottish philosopher and historian, b. Edinburgh. Studied law; judge advocate to General James Sinclair (1747); keeper of Advocates' Library, Edinburgh (1752); on staff of British embassy in Paris (1765); under secretary of state (1767–68). As a philosopher, known esp. for his philosophical skepticism (Humism), restricting human knowledge to experience of ideas and impressions and denying the possibility of obtaining any ultimate verification of their truth; deeply influenced subsequent metaphysical thought. Author of *A Treatise of Human Nature* (1739), *Essays Moral and Political* (1741–42), *An Enquiry Concerning Human Understanding* (orig. title *Philosophical Essays Concerning Human Understanding;* 1748), *Political Discourses* (1752), *Four Dissertations* (1757), *History of England during Reigns of James I and Charles I* (1754 ff.), *Dialogues on Natural Religion* (1779).

**Hume, Fergus.** 1859–1932. British writer of detective stories; adm. to bar in New Zealand; to England (1888). Books include *Mystery of a Hansom Cab* (1887), *The Bishop's Secret* (1900), *Jonah's Luck* (1906), *The Other Person* (1920), and *The Caravan Mystery* (1926).

**Hume, Joseph.** 1777–1855. English physician and radical politician; known as "Adversity Hume." In medical service in India (1797–1807). M.P. (1812; 1818–41; 1842–55), identified with radical group; known for his repeated predictions of national disaster; instrumental in obtaining repeal of corn laws (1834) and laws prohibiting emigration and export of machinery.

**Hume** *or* **Home** (hūm), Sir **Patrick.** 1st Earl of **March'mont** (märch'mŭnt) *and* Baron **Pol'warth** (pōl'wẽrth). 1641–1724. Scottish statesman; member of Argylle's expedition (1684); involved in Rye House Plot, and outlawed (1685); escaped to Utrecht. Became adviser to William of Orange; accompanied him to England (1688); sheriff of Berwickshire (1692–1710) and lord chancellor of Scotland (1696–1702). Passed act for security of Presbyterianism; supported union with England. Father of Lady Grizel Baillie (*q.v.*).

**Hume, Robert Allen.** 1847–1929. American Congregational clergyman and missionary, b. Bombay, India. Missionary in India (1874–1926).

**Humfrey.** See HUMPHREY.

**Hum'mel** (hŭm'ĕl), **Abraham Henry.** 1850–1926. American criminal lawyer, b. Boston, Mass. Partner with William F. Howe in firm of Howe & Hummel, New York City; convicted (1905) on conspiracy charge and imprisoned (1907–08); last years lived in England and France.

**Hummel, Arthur William.** 1884– . American librarian and Oriental scholar; on teaching staff, Commercial U., Kobe, Japan (1912–14), in Shansi, China (1915–24), in Peiping, China (1924–27); chief of division of Orientalia, Library of Congress, Washington, D.C. (1927–54). Consultant in etymology (Chinese) for *Webster's New International Dictionary, Second Edition.*

**Hum'mel** (hŏŏm'ĕl), **Johann Nepomuk.** 1778–1837. German piano virtuoso and composer of sonatas, concertos, chamber music, Masses, and nine operas.

**Hum'per·dinck** (hŏŏm'pĕr·dĭngk), **Engelbert.** 1854–1921. German composer; studied at Cologne and Munich; traveled in Italy; friend of Richard Wagner (1881). Best known as composer of the fairy operas *Hänsel und Gretel* (1893) and *Die Königskinder* (1910); composed also incidental music for Shakespeare's *Merchant of Venice, The Tempest, As You Like It, Winter's Tale,* and Maeterlinck's *Blue Bird.*

**Hum'phrey** (hŭm'frĭ). Duke of **Gloucester** *and* Earl of **Pembroke** (cr. 1414). 1391–1447. Youngest son of Henry IV. Called "the Good Duke Humphrey" because of patronage to men of letters, including Lydgate and Capgrave. Commander of division; wounded at Agincourt (1415); took Cherbourg (1418). Regent of England (1420–21); named protector during Henry VI's minority, by Henry V's will, functioned (1422–29) merely as deputy to his brother John, Duke of Bedford. m. (1422; annulled 1428) Jacoba of Holland, but allowed her realm to be overwhelmed by Burgundy; m. (c. 1430) his mistress, Eleanor Cobham, who was condemned for witchcraft (1441). Made vain attempt to deprive his uncle Henry Beaufort as cardinal of his English see (1432); denounced Beaufort's peace policy in French relations and led short campaign in Flanders (1436); as popular leader of war party, advocated violation of truce with France (1445); suspected of designs on king's life, died in custody. Collector of books; gave first books for library at Oxford; his first library later formed part of Bodleian.

**Humphrey, Doris.** 1895–1958. Amer. dancer, choreographer; with Charles E. Weidman (*q.v.*), formed dance group and opened studio (1928).

**Humphrey, Hubert Horatio.** 1911–1978. American politician; U.S. senator from Minnesota (1949–64, 1970–78); U.S. vice-president (1965–69); Democratic candidate for president of the U.S. (1968).

**Hum'phrey** *or* **Hum'frey** (hŭm'frĭ), **Laurence.** 1527?–1590. English clergyman; educ. Oxford; president, Magdalen Coll., Oxford (1561–90), and vice-chancellor, Oxford (1571–76). Dean of Gloucester (1571) and of Winchester (1580–90).

**Hum'phreys** (hŭm'frĭz), **Albert.** d. ?1925. American sculptor, b. near Cincinnati, Ohio. Made specialty of small animal groups. Carved bust of Mark Twain in the American Hall of Fame.

**Humphreys, Andrew Atkinson.** 1810–1883. American army officer; grad. U.S.M.A., West Point (1831). In charge, survey of Mississippi River delta (1850–51, 1857–61). Served through Civil War; brigadier general (1862); major general (1863). Chief of Engineers, U.S. army (1866–79).

**Humphreys, David.** 1752–1818. American Revolutionary officer and diplomat; lieutenant colonel and aide-de-camp to Washington (1780); U.S. commissioner in Algeria (1793); U.S. minister to Spain (1796–1801). Imported first Merino sheep in United States (1801); interested in woolen manufacturing (from 1801). Associated with Hartford wits; had a share in writing *The Anarchiad* (political satirical poem, 1786–87); also wrote *A Poem on the Happiness of America* (1786).

**Humphreys, Joshua.** 1751–1838. American naval constructor; commissioned to outfit Continental ships under Esek Hopkins (1776). Appointed first U.S. naval constructor (1794–1801); designed and supervised building of frigates *Constitution, President, United States, Chesapeake, Constellation, Congress,* which formed nucleus of U.S. navy for War of 1812.

**Humphreys, William Jackson.** 1862–1949. American physicist; professor of meteorological physics, U.S. Weather Bureau (1905–35); and also, professor at George Washington U. (1911–34). Author of *Physics of the Air* (1920), *Fogs and Clouds* (1926), *Weather Rambles* (1937), etc. Special editor of meteorology, *Webster's New International Dictionary, Second Edition.*

**Hun'e·ker** (hŭn'ĕ·kẽr; -ĭ·kẽr), **James Gibbons.** 1860–1921. American musician and critic, b. Philadelphia; settled in New York (1886); taught in National Conservatory of Music. Edited weekly column of musical comment, *Musical Courier* (1887–1902); dramatic and literary critic, New York *Sun* (1902–17); music critic, New York *World* (1919–21). Author of *Mezzotints in Modern Music* (1899), *Melomaniacs* (1902), *Overtones* (1904), *Iconoclasts* (1905), *Egoists* (1909), *Franz Liszt* (1911), *Ivory Apes and Peacocks* (1915), *Unicorns* (1917), *Steeplejack* (1920), etc.

**Huneric.** See HUNNERIC.

**Hun'fal·vy** (hŏŏn'fŏl·vĭ), **Pál.** 1810–1891. Hungarian philologist and ethnographer; author of treatises on the dialects of the Voguls and the Ostyaks, a Magyar ethnography, a study of the Rumanian language, etc. His brother **János** (1820–1888), geographer and historian, was author of a universal history, a universal geography, an account of the travels of László Magyar, etc.

**Hun'ger·ford** (hŭng'gẽr·fẽrd), **Margaret Wolfe,** *nee* **Hamilton.** *Pseudonym* **The Duchess.** 1855?–1897. Irish novelist; m. Thomas H. Hungerford; author of more than 30 novels, including *Molly Bawn* (1878).

**Hung Hsiu–ch'üan** (hŏŏng' shē·ōō' chü·än'). 1812–1864. Hakka schoolmaster, instigator of the Taiping rebellion (1850–64), b. near Canton. Learned something of Christianity (c. 1833–40); in a long illness had strange religious visions; became leader in a mystic society in Kwangsi; taught and made converts in his district (c. 1840–48), using certain forms from Protestant doctrine. His teachings aroused his disciples to some violence (1848–50) and (1850) into open rebellion, actually a revolt against the Manchus; styled himself **T'ien–wang** (tyĕn'wäng'), *i.e.* "Heavenly Prince," and his dynasty **T'ai P'ing** (tī' pĭng'), *i.e.* "Great Peace"; made Nanking headquarters (1853), where he issued edicts and directed his generals; at first everywhere successful, later his armies became lawless and destructive; defeated (1860–62) by Frederick Ward and his Ever-Victorious Army and completely overcome (1862–64) by forces of General Gordon and Li Hung-chang; seeing collapse of rebellion, poisoned himself.

**Hung Wu.** See CHU YÜAN-CHANG.

**Hun'ne·ric** (hŭn'ĕ·rĭk) *or* **Hu'ne·ric** (hū'nĕ·rĭk). d. 484. King of Vandals in Africa (477–484). Son of Genseric. Sent to Italy as hostage (435); on return to Carthage married daughter of Theodoric I, king of Visigoths. An Arian; persecuted orthodox Christians in his kingdom.

**Hu'nold** (hōō'nōlt), **Christian Friedrich.** *Pseudonym*

**Me·nan'tes** (mȧ·nän'tĕs). 1680–1721. German writer; author of *Die Verliebte und Galante Welt* (2 vols., 1700), *Der Europäischen Höfe Liebes- und Heldengeschichte* (1704), *Satirischer Roman* (1705), and textbooks in rhetoric.

**Hun'sa'ker** (hŭn'sā'kẽr), **Jerome Clarke.** 1886– . American aeronautical engineer; grad. U.S.N.A., Annapolis (1908); chief of aircraft design, Navy Department, Washington, D.C. (1916–23). Designed airship *Shenandoah* and flying boat *NC4*, said to be first aircraft to fly across Atlantic. Head of departments of mechanical and aeronautical engineering, M.I.T.; chairman, National Advisory Committee for Aeronautics (1941).

**Hunsdon,** Baron. See Henry CAREY (1524?–1596).

**Hunt** (hŭnt), **Arthur Surridge.** 1871–1934. English paleographer; engaged in research in Egypt (1895–1907); professor of papyrology at Oxford (1913–34); served in World War (1915–19); collaborated with Bernard Pyne Grenfell (*q.v.*).

**Hunt, Clara Whitehill.** 1871–1958. American librarian; superintendent of children's department, Brooklyn (N.Y.) Public Library (from 1903). Author of juveniles, including *The Little House in the Woods* (1918), *Peggy's Playhouses* (1924).

**Hunt, Edward Eyre.** 1885–1953. American journalist and sociologist; war correspondent in Europe (1914); on relief commission in Belgium (1914–16), and in Red Cross economic rehabilitation work in France (1917–18). Author of *War Bread...Belgium* (1916), *Tales from a Famished Land* (1918), *An Audit of America* (1930), *Greathouse* (1937), etc.

**Hunt, Frazier.** 1885–1967. American journalist; war correspondent of Chicago *Tribune*, in France (1918) and later in northern Russia.

**Hunt, Gail·lard'** (gĭl·yärd'). 1862–1924. American writer, b. New Orleans. In government service (1882–1924). Author of *James Madison* (1902), *John C. Calhoun* (1908), *Life in America One Hundred Years Ago* (1914), etc. Edited *The Writings of James Madison* (9 vols., 1900–10) and vols. 16–25 of *Journals of the Continental Congress* (1910–22).

**Hunt, Henry.** 1773–1835. English radical politician; presided at a reform meeting in Manchester (Aug. 16, 1819) which was broken up forcibly by the yeomanry in what became known as the Peterloo Massacre; sentenced to two years' imprisonment. M.P. (1830–33).

**Hunt, Henry Jackson.** 1819–1889. American army officer; grad. U.S.M.A., West Point (1839). Brigadier general (1862); in charge of artillery that broke Pickett's charge at Gettysburg; brevetted major general (1865).

**Hunt, Holman,** *in full* **William Holman.** 1827–1910. English painter, b. London. Studied at Royal Academy Schools (1844), where he met Millais and D. G. Rossetti; with them founded (1848) Pre-Raphaelite Brotherhood, joined later by Woolner, W. M. Rossetti, James Collinson, and F. G. Stephens; adhered to brotherhood's principles in his work. Member of Order of Merit (1905). His notable paintings include *Rienzi, The Hireling Shepherd, Claudio and Isabella, The Light of the World, The Scapegoat, Isabella and the Pot of Basil, The Shadow of Death, Nazareth, The Triumph of the Innocents.* Author of *Pre-Raphaelitism and the Pre-Raphaelite Brotherhood* (2 vols., 1905).

**Hunt, Leigh,** *in full* **James Henry Leigh.** 1784–1859. English essayist and poet. Editor of *The Examiner* (1808 ff.) and *The Reflector* (1810); sentenced to two years' imprisonment (1813) for articles reflecting on the Prince Regent. Founded and edited *The Indicator* (1819); associated with Byron in editing *The Liberal* (1822–23). His many works include *The Story of Rimini* (poem; 1816), *Foliage* (verse; 1818), *Hero and Leander* (1819), *Lord Byron and Some of his Contemporaries* (1828), *Captain Sword and Captain Pen* (1835), *A Legend of Florence* (play; 1840), *Imagination and Fancy* (1844), *Men, Women, and Books* (1847), *Autobiography* (1850).

**Hunt, Reid.** 1870–1948. American pharmacologist; professor, U.S. Public Health Service (1904–13), Harvard Med. School (1913–36). Joint author of *Studies in Experimental Alcoholism* (1907), *Effects of Derivatives of Choline and Analogous Compounds* (1911), etc.

**Hunt, Richard Howland.** 1862–1931. American architect, b. in France; designed Quintard and Hoffman Halls at U. of the South, Kissam Hall at Vanderbilt U., etc.

**Hunt, Richard Morris.** 1827–1895. Bro. of William Morris Hunt. American architect; offices in New York (from c. 1857). Examples of his work: Administration Building, Chicago World's Fair (1893); main section of Metropolitan Museum of Art, New York; Lenox Library, New York; National Observatory, Washington, D.C.; Fogg Museum, Harvard.

**Hunt, Robert Woolston.** 1838–1923. American metallurgist; with Cambria Iron Co., Johnstown, Pa.; rolled first commercial order for steel rails (1867); assumed charge of company's new Bessemer steel plant (1871). Founded firm of Robert W. Hunt & Co., consulting engineers, with offices in Chicago (1888).

**Hunt, Thomas Sterry.** 1826–1892. American scientist; chemist and mineralogist, geological survey of Canada (1847–72). Noted for researches in general and economic geology and in pure and applied chemistry.

**Hunt, Walter.** 1796–1859. American inventor of eye-pointed needle and double lock stitch for sewing machines (c. 1832; never patented; cf. Elias HOWE), safety pin (pat. 1849), paper collar (1854), etc.

**Hunt, Ward.** 1810–1886. American jurist; associate justice, U.S. Supreme Court (1873–82).

**Hunt, William.** 1842–1931. Church of England clergyman and historian; author of *The English Church in the Middle Ages* (1888) and *The English Church, 597–1066* (1899, being vol. 1 of a history under his editorship); contributor to *Dictionary of National Biography.*

**Hunt, William Henry.** 1790–1864. English water-color artist, known esp. for humorous and still-life sketches.

**Hunt, William Henry.** 1823–1884. American jurist; practiced, New Orleans. Union sympathizer during Civil War. Associate judge, U.S. court of claims (1878–81). U.S. secretary of the navy (1881–82); U.S. minister to Russia (1882–84).

**Hunt, William Morris.** 1824–1879. Bro. of Richard Morris Hunt. American painter; studio, Boston (from 1864). Examples of his work: *Girl Reading, Peasant Girl at Barbizon, Hurdy-Gurdy Boy* (now in Boston Museum of Fine Arts), *Landscape, Girl at a Fountain, The Bathers* (in Metropolitan Museum of Art, N.Y.).

**Hun'ter** (hŭn'tẽr), **David.** 1802–1886. American army officer; grad. U.S.M.A., West Point (1822). Served through Civil War; brigadier general (1861); commanded Department of the South (1862) and issued order (May 9, 1862, annulled by Lincoln, May 19, 1862) freeing the slaves in his department; brevetted major general (1865). President, military commission that tried conspirators for assassination of Lincoln.

**Hunter, George Leland.** 1867–1927. American authority on tapestries; author of *Tapestries, Their Origin, History and Renaissance* (1912), *Practical Book of Tapestries* (1925), etc.

**Hunter, John.** 1728–1793. British anatomist and surgeon, b. in Scotland. Staff surgeon with English army in Portugal (1762). Practiced in London (1763); took house pupils, among whom was Edward Jenner (*q.v.*);

began to lecture on surgery (1773); surgeon extraordinary to George III (1776); surgeon general to army (1793). His investigations include work relating to the descent of the testes in the fetus, course of the olfactory nerves, formation of pus, placental circulation, function of lymphatics, coagulation of blood, digestion in hibernating snakes and lizards, recovery of people apparently drowned, the structure of whales, bees, growth of deer's antlers; discovered that smaller arteries increase in size to compensate when circulation is arrested in larger ones; first to ligate artery for aneurysm (1785). His brother **William** (1718–1783) was a physiologist and anatomist; surgeon-accoucheur, Middlesex Hospital (1748), British Lying-in Hospital (1749); physician-extraordinary to Queen Charlotte Sophia (1764); first professor of anatomy, Royal Academy (1768); claimed some of his brother's discoveries.

**Hunter, Robert.** d. 1734. British administrator in America, b. in Ayrshire, Scotland; captain general, and governor of New York and New Jersey (1710–19); governor of Jamaica (1727–34).

**Hunter, Robert,** *in full* **Wiles Robert.** 1874–1942. American sociologist; secretary, Chicago bureau of charities (1896–1902); head worker in University Settlement, New York City (1902–03); member of Socialist party (1905–14). Lecturer, U. of California (1918–22). Author of *Tenement Conditions in Chicago* (1901), *Poverty* (1904), *Socialists at Work* (1908), *Violence and the Labor Movement* (1914), *Inflation and Revolution* (1934), etc.

**Hunter, Robert Mercer Tal'ia·ferro** (tŏl'ĭ·vẽr). 1809–1887. American political leader; member, U.S. House of Representatives (1837–43, 1845–47); U.S. Senate (1847–61). Secretary of state of the Confederacy (1861–62); member, Confederate senate (1862–65); one of Confederate negotiators at Hampton Roads conference (1865). Treasurer of Virginia (1874–80).

**Hunter, Thomas.** 1831–1915. Educator, b. Ardglass, Ireland; to U.S. (1850). Teacher in New York public schools; organized first evening high school (1866). Organized (1870) and headed (1870–1906) Normal College of the City of New York, whose name was changed (1914) to Hunter College.

**Hunter, Walter Samuel.** 1889–1954. American psychologist, b. Decatur, Ill. Professor, Kansas (1916–25), Clark (1925–36), Brown (from 1936). Author of *General Psychology* (1919), *Human Behavior* (1928).

**Hunter, William.** 1861–1937. English physician; in charge of British mission to Serbia to study epidemics of typhus and relapsing fever (1915). Author of *Jaundice and Liver Diseases* (1898), *Treatment of Anaemia* (1907), etc.

**Hunter,** Sir **William Wilson.** 1840–1900. British civil servant, b. Glasgow; organized and directed statistical survey of Indian Empire (1869–81), whose reports filled 128 volumes, later condensed in *The Imperial Gazetteer of India* (9 vols., 1881); member of governor-general's council (1881–87).

**Hun'ter–Wes'ton** (-wĕs'tŭn), Sir **Aylmer.** 1864–1940. British soldier; brigadier general (1914), major general (1914), lieutenant general (1919). In World War, commanded first in France and Flanders, then at the Dardanelles, and, later, again in France.

**Hun'ting·don,** Earl of (hŭn'tĭng·dŭn). Title of one of three oldest English earldoms still existent, held from just before the Conquest by Scottish kings beginning with David I; by William Herbert (see HERBERT family); by John HOLLAND (1352?–1400) and his son; from 1529 by HASTINGS family.

**Huntingdon,** Countess of. = *Selina Hastings* (1707–1791), under HASTINGS family.

**Hun'ting·ton** (hŭn'tĭng·tŭn), **Archer Milton.** 1870–1955. Son of Collis P. Huntington. American writer and Hispanic scholar, b. New York City. Founded Hispanic Society of America (1904) and gave it a building, an endowment, and a valuable collection. Author of *A Note Book in Northern Spain* (1898), *Lace Maker of Segovia* (verse, 1928), *The Ladies of Vallbona* (verse, 1931), *The Silver Gardens, Alfonso the Eighth Rides By* (verse, 1934), *Vela Venenosa, Rimas* (verse, 1936). His wife, **Anna,** *nee* **Hy'att** [hī'ăt] (1876–1973), sculptor, b. Cambridge, Mass., represented by bronzes of animals in Metropolitan Museum of Art in New York, carved lions in New York City, statues of Joan of Arc in Cathedral of St. John The Divine in New York City and in Blois, France, statues of El Cid in New York City, Seville, Spain, Buenos Aires, Argentina, a memorial monument to Collis P. Huntington at Newport News, Va., and the bust of Louis Agassiz in American Hall of Fame.

**Huntington, Collis Potter.** 1821–1900. Pioneer American railroad builder, b. Harwinton, Conn. Itinerant peddler (1836–42); storekeeper, Oneonta, N.Y. (1842–49). To California (1849). Interested in building of transcontinental railroad (from 1861), completed when Central Pacific Railroad joined Union Pacific (1869). Southern Pacific Railroad organized (1884); president of this road (from 1890). Served as active lobbyist in Washington for favorable railroad legislation (1870–80). Also interested in Chesapeake and Ohio Railroad (from 1869), Pacific Mail Steamship Co., United States and Brazil Steamship Co., Old Dominion Steamship Co. See Henry Edwards HUNTINGTON.

**Huntington, Daniel.** 1816–1906. American painter; studio in New York. Examples of his work: *Atlantic Cable Projectors,* now in Chamber of Commerce, New York City; *Venice,* in J. P. Morgan collection; *The Sibyl,* in New York Historical Society; *President Lincoln,* in Union League Club, New York; *Mercy's Dream* and *Cyrus W. Field,* in Metropolitan Museum of Art, New York.

**Huntington, Edward Vermilye.** 1874–1952. American mathematician; known for work on systems of postulates forming the bases of elementary mathematical theories.

**Huntington, Ellsworth.** 1876–1947. American geographer and explorer, b. Galesburg, Ill. On teaching staff, Euphrates College, Turkey (1897–1901); explored canyons of Euphrates River (1901). On Pumpelly expedition to Russian Turkestan (1903–04) and R. L. Barrett expedition to Chinese Turkestan (1905–06). Teacher of geography (1907–15) and research associate (from 1917), Yale. Served in World War. Author of *The Pulse of Asia* (1907), *Civilization and Climate* (1915), *World Power and Evolution* (1919), *Earth and Sun* (1923), *The Character of Races* (1924), *The Pulse of Progress* (1926), *The Human Habitat* (1927), *Tomorrow's Children—the Goal of Eugenics* (1935), *Season of Birth* (1938), etc.

**Huntington, Frederic Dan.** 1819–1904. American Protestant Episcopal bishop, b. Hadley, Mass. Served in Unitarian ministry (1842–60). Ordained priest, Protestant Episcopal Church (1861); consecrated bishop of Central New York (1869).

**Huntington, George.** 1851–1916. American neurologist; first described the nervous disorder named for him Huntington's chorea.

**Huntington, Henry Edwards.** 1850–1927. Nephew of Collis Potter Huntington. American railway executive, b. Oneonta, N.Y. Installed by uncle in executive positions on Huntington railroads (1881–1900); inherited from uncle large railroad interests; sold control of Southern Pacific Railroad to E. H. Harriman. From about 1903, collected book and art treasures for his library at

San Marino, near Pasadena, which he left to trustees to be maintained for public benefit.

**Huntington, Jedediah.** 1743–1818. American Revolutionary officer; colonel (1775); brigadier general (1777). Member, court of inquiry investigating case of Major John André (1780). Brevetted major general (1783).

**Huntington, Samuel.** 1731–1796. American Revolutionary political leader; member, Continental Congress (1776–84) and its president (1779–81, 1783); signer of Declaration of Independence. Governor of Connecticut (1786–96).

**Huntington, William Reed.** 1838–1909. American Protestant Episcopal clergyman, b. Lowell, Mass. Rectorates, Worcester, Mass. (1862–83), New York City (1883–1909); active in the founding and building of Cathedral of St. John the Divine, New York City.

**Hunt'ly** (hŭnt'lĭ), Earls and marquises of. See GORDON family.

**Hun'tzi'ger'** (ûn'tsē'zhâr'), **Charles Léon Clément.** 1880–1941. French army officer; distinguished himself in World War (1914–18); major (1916); colonel (1924); brigadier general (1928); major general (1934). During German invasion (1940), commanded 2d army; headed delegation that signed peace terms with Germany at Compiègne Forest (July 22, 1940). In Pétain regime, named generalissimo and commander in chief of land forces (Sept., 1940); transferred to Algiers when Darlan became war minister.

**Hu'nya·di** *or* **Hu'nya·dy** (hŏŏ'nyŏ·dĭ). *English* **Hu·ni'a·des** (hū·nī'ȧ·dēz). Name of Hungarian family derived from small family estate of Hunyad in Transylvania. The family includes:

**János,** *Eng.* **John** (c. 1387–1456), national hero of Hungary, leader against Turks; saw first military service under King Sigismund (1410–38); successful against Turks (1437–38); after death of King Albert (1439), successfully supported Ladislas III (*q.v.*) of Poland for throne of Hungary; voivode of Transylvania (1440); won several victories over Turks (1441–43) and secured treaty advantageous to Hungary; in new war, joined forces with Ladislas; with him, suffered overwhelming defeat at Varna (1444); regent (1446–52) for young king, Ladislas V; fought two years (1446–48) against Frederick III and again against Turks, but defeated at Kosovo (1448); his greatest achievement was defense (1456) of Belgrade against Turkish army of Mohammed II; died of plague shortly after siege was raised.

His older son, **László** *or* **Ladislas** (1433–1457), statesman; fought in campaigns with father; after Kosovo, left as hostage (1448) with George Branković, Despot of Serbia; ban of Croatia-Dalmatia (1453); after father's death, accused falsely by enemies of Hunyadi family, condemned without trial, and beheaded.

János's younger son (see MATTHIAS CORVINUS) became king of Hungary.

**Huram.** Variant of HIRAM, King of Tyre.

**Hur'ban** (hŏŏr'bȧn), **Josef Miloslav.** 1817–1888. Slovak patriot and writer. His son **Svetozar Hur'ban-Va'jan·ský** [-vȧ'yȧn·skē] (1847–1916), author of fiction and patriotic verse and founder (1881) of *Národní Noviny.* Svetozar's son **Vladimír S. Hurban** (1883–1949), journalist in Czechoslovakia (1904–14); served in World War (1914–18); military attaché to the Czechoslovak legation, Washington, D.C. (1919–24); chargé d'affaires at Cairo, Egypt (1924–30); minister to Sweden, Norway, and Lithuania (1930–36); minister to U.S. and Cuba (1936–43); ambassador to U.S. (1943–46).

**Hurd** (hûrd), **Henry Mills.** 1843–1927. American psychiatrist; professor, Johns Hopkins (1889–1906), and superintendent of Johns Hopkins Hospital (1889–1911).

**Hurd,** Sir **Percy Angier.** 1864–1950. English publicist. A founder (1898) and editor (1898–1904) of *The Outlook;* London editor of Montreal *Star;* editor of *Canadian Gazette* and, later, of *Canada's Weekly.* M.P. (from 1918). Author of *The Empire, a Family Affair, The New Empire Partnership,* and *Canada, Past, Present and Future.* His brother Sir **Archibald** (1869–1959, publicist, authority on naval matters; on staff of London *Daily Telegraph* (1899–1928); author of official *History of the Merchant Navy in the War* and of *Naval Efficiency..., German Seapower..., The British Fleet in the Great War, The Merchant Navy* (3 vols., 1921, 1924, 1929), *The Eclipse of British Sea Power; An Increasing Peril* (1933).

**Hurd, Peter.** 1904– . American painter, b. Roswell, N.Mex.; studio on his ranch at San Patricio, N.Mex. Painted murals for New Mexico Military Institute and post offices at Big Springs and Dallas, Tex. Represented in Chicago Art Institute and Metropolitan Museum of Art in New York City.

**Hurd, Richard.** 1720–1808. English prelate; bishop of Lichfield and Coventry (1774–81), of Worcester (1781–1808). Author of *Moral and Political Dialogues* (1759), *Letters on Chivalry and Romance* (1762), etc.

**Hurl'but** (hûrl'bŭt), **William.** 1883– . American playwright; author of *The Fighting Hope* (1908), *Little Miss Fix-it* (1911), *Lilies of the Field* (1921), *Hidden* (1927), *Recessional* (1931), etc.

**Hur'ley** (hûr'lĭ), **Edward Nash.** 1864–1933. American industrialist and public official, b. Galesburg, Ill. Originated and developed pneumatic tool industry. U.S. trade commissioner to Latin-American republics (1913); vice-chairman, and later chairman, Federal Trade Commission (to 1917); chairman, U.S. Shipping Board, and president of Emergency Fleet Corp. (1917–19). Author of *The Awakening of Business* (1916), *The New Merchant Marine* (1920), *The Bridge to France* (1927).

**Hurley, Patrick Jay.** 1883–1963. American lawyer, b. in Oklahoma; practiced in Tulsa (from 1908); officer in World War, U.S. secretary of war (1929–33); U.S. minister to New Zealand (Feb., 1942–Mar., 1943); appointed by President Roosevelt his personal representative in Near and Middle East (Mar., 1943) and on missions to Afghanistan and China (1944); temporary major general (Feb., 1944); U.S. ambassador to China (1944–45).

**Hurry,** Sir **John.** See Sir John URRY.

**Hurst** (hûrst), Sir **Cecil James Barrington.** 1870–1963. English jurist; legal adviser to British foreign office (1918–29); British member of Hague Tribunal (from 1929); judge of the Permanent Court of International Justice at The Hague (from 1929), and president of the court (1934–36).

**Hurst, Fannie.** 1889–1968. American fiction writer, b. Hamilton, Ohio; m. Jacques S. Danielson (1915). Author of many novels, including *Stardust* (1919), *Lummox* (1923), *Appassionata* (1925), *A President is Born* (1927), *Five and Ten* (1929), *Imitation of Life* (1932), *Anitra's Dance* (1934), and of plays and motion-picture scenarios.

**Hurst, John Fletcher.** 1834–1903. American Methodist Episcopal bishop and educator; professor (1871–72) and president (1873–80), Drew Theol. Sem. Elected bishop (1880). Chancellor, American U., Washington, D.C. (1891; chartered, 1893; opened, 1917). Author of *History of Rationalism* (1865), *History of Methodism* (7 vols., 1902–04), etc.

**Hurs'ton** (hûrs'tŭn), **Zora Neale.** 1901–1960. American Negro writer, b. Eatonville, Fla. Educ. Howard U., Washington, D.C., and Barnard Coll. in New York City, where she studied anthropology under Franz Boas. Private secretary to Fannie Hurst. Awarded Guggenheim Fellowship (1936). Author of *Jonah's Gourd Vine,*

*Mules and Men, Their Eyes Were Watching God* (1937), *Tell My Horse* (1938), *Moses, Man of the Mountain* (1939), *Dust Tracks on a Road* (autobiography, 1942).

**Hur·ta'd·o de To·le'do** (o͞or·tä'tho̅ thȧ tô·lā'tho̅), **Luis.** 1530?–?1591. Spanish poet, b. Toledo; curate of San Vicente of Toledo; formerly considered author of chivalric novel *Palmerín de Inglaterra* (1547); among his works are pastorals and comedies.

**Hur'ter** (ho͝or'tẽr), **Friedrich von.** 1787–1865. Swiss ecclesiastic and historian; orig. a Protestant clergyman, adopted Roman Catholic faith (1844); historiographer in Vienna (1846).

**Husain.** Son of Ali. See HASAN AND HUSAIN.

**Hu·sain'** (ho͝o·sän'), **Za'kir** (zä'kĭr). 1897–1969. Indian educator; president of India (1967–69).

**Husayn Ali.** See BAHAULLAH.

**Hus'bands** (hŭz'bǎndz), **Hermon.** 1724–1795. American agitator and revolutionist, b. prob. in Cecil County, Md.; leader of malcontents in back country of North Carolina, and identified with "Regulators" (1768–71); also, leader of "Whisky Insurrection" in western Pennsylvania (1794); tried, condemned to death, but pardoned.

**Huse** (hūs), **Harry Pinckney.** 1858–1942. American naval officer; grad. U.S.N.A., Annapolis (1878); rear admiral (1916) in World War (1917–19). Commander of U.S. naval forces in European waters, with rank of vice-admiral (1920); retired (1922).

**Hu·sein'** (ho͝o·sā'ĭn). 1675?–1729. Shah of Persia (1694–1722) of the Safawid dynasty; overwhelmed by Ghilzais and forced to surrender throne; succeeded by his son Tahmasp II.

**Hu·sein' ibn–A·li'** (ho͝o·sīn' ĭb''n·ä·lē'). *Arab.* **Ḥusayn ibn–'Ali.** 1856–1931. First king of the Hejaz (1916–24) and founder of modern Arab Hashimite dynasty. Grand sherif of Mecca (1908–16) as result of Young Turk movement. In World War first sided with Turks; later, on advice of his son Faisal (*q.v.*) and of Col. T. E. Lawrence, joined Allied cause; rendered valuable service in Arabia; on proclamation of Arabian independence chosen (1916) first king of the Hejaz; refused to sign Versailles Treaty (1919) and treaty with Great Britain (1924) because not satisfied with settlement of Arab problems in Near East. Proclaimed himself head of new caliphate (1924) provoking opposition of Wahabis, whose king ibn-Saud invaded the Hejaz; forced to abdicate in favor of his eldest son, Ali ibn-Husein (*q.v.*); in exile in Cyprus (1924–30); died at Amman, capital of his second son, Abdullah ibn-Husein (*q.v.*), amir of Trans-Jordan.

**Hu Shih** (ho͞o' shĭr'). 1891–1962. Chinese philosopher, b. in Shanghai. Educ. in U.S.; B.A., Cornell (1914), and Ph.D., Columbia (1917). Professor of philosophy, later dean (1917–26) at Peking National U.; invented pai-hua, modern simplified Chinese language, and wrote poems in it; professor of philosophy (1927–31) at Kuang Hua U., Shanghai. Editor of a weekly political newspaper; research fellow, China Foundation (1931–37); chairman, Shanghai Conference, Institute of Pacific (1931–37). Ambassador to the United States (1938–42). Author of *Outline of Chinese Philosophy* (1919), *Ancient History of China, Chinese Renaissance* (1934).

**Hus'kis·son** (hŭs'kĭ·s'n), **William.** 1770–1830. English financier and statesman. M.P. (1796–1802; 1804–30); secretary to treasury (1804–05; 1807–09); treasurer of navy and president of Board of Trade (1823–27); colonial secretary, and leader of House of Commons (1827–28).

**Huss** (hŭs), **Henry Holden.** 1862–1953. American pianist and composer of orchestral and choral pieces, piano works, and many songs.

**Huss** *or* **Hus** (hŭs; *Ger. & Czech,* ho͝os), **John.** *Known in German as* **Johannes Hus von Hu'si·netz** (fôn ho͞o'zē·nĕts). *Czech* **Jan Hus.** 1369?–1415. Bohemian religious reformer, b. Husinetz (*Czech* Husinec), near Budweis, of Czech parents. Educ. Prague; became lecturer there (1398) and finally rector (1402–03). Ordained priest (1401). Read, and was influenced by, writings of Wycliffe; became a popular preacher. Excommunicated (1410) for teaching and lecturing on Wycliffe's doctrines. Papal interdict against him (1412). Attended Council of Constance (1414) under protection of King Wenceslaus and Emperor Sigismund. Tried by council for heresy (1415); condemned and burned at the stake (July 6, 1415); act aroused great indignation and led to Hussite War (1419–34). Author of religious works, esp. *De Ecclesia* (*On the Church*).

**Hus'sa·rek** (ho͝os'ä·rĕk), Baron **Max von.** 1865–1935. Austrian statesman; minister of justice (1911–17); Austro-Hungarian chancellor during last days of the monarchy (Feb.–Oct., 1918).

**Hussein.** Variant of HUSEIN.

**Hus·sein' Ibn Ta·lal'** (ho͞o·sān' ĭb''n tȧ·läl'). 1935– Jordanian monarch. King of Jordan (1952– ).

**Hus·sein' Av·ni' Pa·sha'** (hü·sān' äv·nē' pä·shä'). 1819–1876. Turkish general and statesman, b. near Isparta; served in war in Montenegro (1859–60) and in Crete (1867–69). Minister of war (1869–71 and 1875); grand vizier (1874); governor of Smyrna (1875); leader in plot that deposed (1876) Abdul-Aziz and placed Murad V on throne; assassinated.

**Hus·sein' Ka'mil** (ho͞o·sīn' kä'mĭl) *or* **Kem'al** (kĕm'ǎl). 1850?–1917. Sultan of Egypt (1914–17). Son of Ismail Pasha (*q.v.*); educ. Egypt and Paris; held important posts in Egyptian government; as eldest living prince of family of Mohammed Ali, made sultan by British when Khedive Abbas (II) Hilmi was deposed (Dec., 1914). Succeeded by his brother Fuad.

**Hus·sein' Pa'sha** (ho͞o·sīn' pȧ'shä). 1773?–1838. Last dey of Algeria (1818–30), b. Smyrna. During his rule occurred conflict with France; forced to capitulate.

**Hus'serl** (ho͝os'ẽrl), **Edmund.** 1859–1938. German philosopher.

**Hus'sey** (hŭs'ĭ), **Obed.** 1792–1860. American inventor, b. in Maine; invented a reaper (patented 1833; improved model, 1847), which he manufactured (1834–58) in competition with the McCormick reaper.

**Hussey, William Joseph.** 1862–1926. American astronomer; professor, Stanford; on staff of Lick Observatory (1896). Known for his micrometrical measurements of comets, satellites, and double stars, and his discoveries of hundreds of double stars. Director (from 1905) of observatory at Ann Arbor, Mich., and (1911–17) at La Plata, Argentina.

**Hüssgen, Johannes.** See OECOLAMPADIUS.

**Husson, Jules Fleury–.** See CHAMPFLEURY.

**Hus'ton** (hūs'tǔn), **Walter.** 1884–1950. Actor, b. Toronto, Can. On legitimate stage and in vaudeville in U.S. (1908–29). Engaged chiefly with motion pictures from 1929; starred in *Dodsworth, Cecil Rhodes, Benefits Forgot.*

**Hu'szár** (ho͝o'sär), **Károly.** 1882–1941. Hungarian journalist and politician. Head of Christian Social party, and editor of its journals *Népujsag* and *Alkotmány;* imprisoned for Catholic activity during Communist dictatorship in Hungary (1919); prime minister of coalition cabinet (1919–20) which made Admiral Horthy regent of Hungary; member of Upper House of Diet (from 1929).

**Hutch'ens** (hŭch'ĕnz), **Frank Townsend.** 1869–1937. American portrait painter, b. Canandaigua, N.Y. Painted series of 24 portraits of past presidents of Florida's senate, hung in State Capitol at Tallahassee.

**Hutch'e·son** (hŭch'ĕ·s'n), **Ernest.** 1871–1951. Pianist and composer, b. Melbourne, Australia. President and director of Juilliard School of Music, New York City. Composer of piano concertos, a symphony, a violin concerto, and many piano pieces.

**Hutcheson, Francis.** 1694–1746. Scottish philosopher; professor, Glasgow (1729–46); author of *System of Moral Philosophy* (pub. 1755).

**Hutch'ins** (hŭch'ĭnz), **Harry Burns.** 1847–1930. American educator; practiced law (1876–84); professor of law, U. of Michigan (1884–87). Dean of law school, Cornell (1887–95) and U. of Michigan (1895–1910). President, U. of Michigan (1910–20; retired).

**Hutchins, Thomas.** 1730–1789. American cartographer, b. in Monmouth County, N.J. Appointed by Congress "geographer to the United States" (1781); in charge of survey of lands in the Northwest Territory as provided by the Ordinance of 1785.

**Hutchins, William James.** 1871–1958. American educator; ordained in Presbyterian ministry (1896); pastor in Brooklyn, N.Y. (1896–1907); professor of homiletics, Oberlin (1907–20); president of Berea College (1920–39). His son **Robert Maynard** (1899–1977), b. Brooklyn, N.Y., A.B. (1921), LL.B. (1925), Yale, was secretary of Yale (1923–27); dean of Yale Law School (1928–29); president of U. of Chicago (1929–45), chancellor (1945–51); author of *The Higher Learning in America* (1936), and articles on educational problems.

**Hutch'in·son** (hŭch'ĭn·s'n), **Anne,** *nee* **Mar'bur·y** (mär'bẽr·ĭ). 1591–1643. Religious liberal, b. Alford, England; m. William Hutchinson (1612, d. 1642); to America (1634); settled in Boston. Preached salvation by individual intuition of God's grace and love without regard for obedience to the specific laws of church and state; tried for "traducing the ministers and their ministry"; convicted (1637) and banished from Massachusetts Bay Colony. Emigrated (1638) to Aquidneck (Rhode Island); moved (1642) to home near what is now Pelham Bay, N.Y. She and her family were massacred by Indians (1643).

**Hutchinson, Arthur Stuart-Men·teth'** (mĕn·tēth'). 1879–1971. English novelist, b. in India. On staff of London *Daily Graphic* (1907), its editor (1912–16). Novels include *The Happy Warrior* (1912), *If Winter Comes* (1921), *This Freedom* (1922), *One Increasing Purpose* (1925), *Big Business* (1932), *As Once You Were* (1938), *It Happened Like This* (1942).

**Hutchinson, Benjamin Peters.** *Known as* **Old Hutch** (hŭch). 1829–1899. American commodity speculator, b. Middleton, Mass.; engineered corner in September wheat (1888). His son **Charles Lawrence** (1854–1924), b. Lynn, Mass., was one of the organizers and first president (for 42 years) of Chicago Art Institute.

**Hutchinson, John.** 1615–1664. English Puritan soldier and regicide. Governor of Nottingham, and M.P. (1646 ff.); signed death warrant of Charles I; imprisoned after the Restoration. His wife, **Lucy,** *nee* **Aps'ley** [ăps'lĭ] (1620–?1680), wrote his biography, *Life of Colonel Hutchinson* (pub. 1806).

**Hutchinson, John.** 1674–1737. British philosopher of Yorkshire; author of *Moses's Principia* (1724) and works of religious symbolism; taught that Hebrew scriptures contain a complete system of natural science and theology, and gained many followers (known as Hutchinsonians, not to be confused with similarly named followers of Anne Hutchinson).

**Hutchinson,** Sir **Jonathan.** 1828–1913. English surgeon. Hunterian professor at London Hospital (1879–83); specialist in ophthalmology, dermatology, and syphilis.

**Hutchinson, Ray Coryton.** 1907– . English novelist; author of *Thou Hast a Devil* (1930), *The Answering Glory* (1932), *The Unforgotten Prisoner* (1933), *One Light Burning* (1935), *Shining Scabbard* (1936), *Testament* (1938), *Last Train South* (play; 1938), *The Fire and the Wood* (1940).

**Hutchinson, Thomas.** 1711–1780. American colonial administrator, b. Boston. Merchant, Boston (from 1727). In Massachusetts legislature (1737–49); member, governor's council (1749–66); accepted legality of Stamp Act and hence had his house destroyed by mob (1765). Royal governor of Massachusetts (1771–74); upheld British authority and by his policies brought nearer the Revolution. To England (1774); in exile there until his death.

**Hutchinson, Woods.** 1862–1930. Physician and author, b. Selby, England; to U.S. as a child. Practiced medicine, Des Moines, Iowa (1884–96). Professor of comparative pathology, U. of Buffalo (1896–99). From 1905, devoted himself to interpreting medical information for laymen, as in *Instinct and Health* (1908), *Exercise and Health* (1911), *Community Hygiene* (1916), *The Doctor in War* (1918).

**Huth** (hōōth), **Henry.** 1815–1878. English banker and bibliophile, of German descent; collected early English, Spanish, and German books; published *Ancient Ballads and Broadsides* (1867), *Inedited Poetical Miscellanies 1584–1700* (1870), *Fugitive Tracts 1493–1700* (1875), etc.

**Hu'tier'** (ü'tyā'), **Oskar von.** 1857–1934. German soldier; commanded 8th army, and captured Riga (1917); commanded 18th army on the western front (1918) and delivered powerful attacks against Allied lines in the Noyon-Montdidier sector; attacks repulsed and his army fell back in disorder (Aug., 1918).

**Hut'ten** (hŏŏt'ĕn), **Philipp von.** 1511?–1546. German adventurer. One of a contingent sent to conquer Venezuela in behalf of Augsburg family of Welser, to whom province had been granted by Emperor Charles V; in Venezuela (1535–46; captain general from 1540); after years of exploration in interior, returned to coast to find in power a Spanish governor who had him seized and executed.

**Hutten, Ulrich von.** 1488–1523. German nobleman and humanist; friend and supporter of Luther. Educ. at the Benedictine monastery at Fulda (1498–1505); fled from the monastery and studied at various universities in Germany and Italy. Joined imperial army (1513); under patronage of elector of Mainz (1514; 1518). The murder of his uncle by the duke of Württemberg caused him to join the Swabian League against the duke (1519); joined Franz von Sickingen in the struggle of the nobility of the Upper Rhine against the spiritual principalities (1522). Engaged vigorously in defense of Luther, and by his writings appealed to the sympathies and patriotism of the nobility, thus supplementing Luther's appeal to the common folk. Had dispute with Erasmus (1522–23), marked by exchange of bitter communications. Known in literature chiefly as a bitter satirist, and as author of a large share of the second part of *Epistolae Obscurorum Virorum.*

**Hutten zum Stol'zen·berg** (tsŏŏm shtŏl'tsĕn·bĕrк), Baroness **von.** *Nee* **Bettina Rid'dle** (rĭd''l). 1874–1957. Writer, b. Erie, Pa.; m. Baron von Hutten zum Stolzenberg (1897; divorced 1909). Author of *Our Lady of the Beeches* (1902), *Pam* (1905), *Pam at Fifty,* etc., and of *One Way Out* (1906), *Kingsmead* (1909), *Notorious Mrs. Gatacre and Other Stories* (1933), *Lives of a Woman* (1935), *Die She Must* (1936), etc.

**Hut'ter** (hŏŏt'ẽr) *or* **Hüt'ter** (hüt'ẽr), **Leonhard.** 1563–1616. German Lutheran theologian; a champion of Lutheran orthodoxy.

**Hut'ton** (hŭt''n), **Charles.** 1737–1823. English mathematician; computed mean density of the earth (1778); wrote *Principles of Bridges* (1772), *Mathematical Tables* (1785), etc.; compiled *Mathematical and Philosophical Dictionary* (1795).

**Hutton, Frederick Remsen.** 1853–1918. American engineer; on editorial staff, *Johnson's Universal Cyclopaedia* (1893), *Century Dictionary* (1904), *New International Encyclopaedia* (1913).

**Hutton, James.** 1726–1797. Scottish geologist; author of *Investigations of Principles of Knowledge* (1794), *Theory of the Earth* (1795), etc. Credited with originating modern theory of formation of earth's crust.

**Hutton, Laurence.** 1843–1904. American essayist and critic; literary editor, *Harper's Magazine* (1886–98). Author of *Plays and Players* (1875), *Actors and Actresses of Great Britain and the United States* (with James Brander Matthews, 1886), *Edwin Booth* (1893), *A Boy I Knew* (1898), and literary guidebooks to London, Edinburgh, Jerusalem, Venice, Rome, Florence, Oxford, etc.

**Hutton, Maurice.** 1856–1940. Canadian educator and classical scholar, b. in England. Professor of classics (1880–87), of Greek (1887–1928), and principal (1901–28), University Coll., Toronto. Translator for Loeb Classical Library.

**Hutton, Richard Holt.** 1826–1897. English editor, theologian, and man of letters; joint editor and part proprietor of the *Spectator* (1861–97). Author of *Essays on some Modern Guides of English Thought* (1887), *Criticisms on Contemporary Thought and Thinkers* (1894), etc.

**Hutton, Thomas Jacomb.** 1890– . British army officer; in Palestine (1936–39); chief of staff, India (1941); commander of Br. forces in Burma (1942).

**Hutton, William Holden.** 1860–1930. Anglican prelate and historian; fellow of St. John's Coll., Oxford (1884–1923), and tutor in history (1889–1909). Dean of Winchester (1919–30). Author of *The English Church... 1625–1714* (1903), *The Church and the Barbarians* (1906), and biographies of Sir Thomas More and William Laud.

**Hux'ley** (hŭk'slĭ), **Andrew Fielding.** 1917– . British physiologist. Awarded Nobel prize in physiology and medicine (1963) with A. Hodgkin and J. Eccles for research on nerve impulses.

**Huxley, Thomas Henry.** 1825–1895. English biologist; entered Royal Navy medical service (1846); asst. surgeon, H.M.S. *Rattlesnake* (1846–50). Lecturer, Royal School of Mines (1854); Hunterian professor, Royal College of Surgeons (1863–69), and Fullerian professor, Royal Institution (1863–67); president, Royal Society (1883–85). Foremost advocate in England of Darwin's theory of evolution. Author of *Zoological Evidences as to Man's Place in Nature* (1863), *On the Causes of the Phenomena of Organic Nature* (1863), *Lay Sermons* (1870), *Manual of the Comparative Anatomy of Vertebrated Animals* (1871) and *...of Invertebrated Animals* (1877), *The Crayfish* (1880), *Science and Culture* (1881), *Evolution and Ethics* (1893).

His son **Leonard** (1860–1933), editor and author, taught in Charterhouse (1884–1901); editor of *Cornhill Magazine;* wrote *Life of Huxley* (1900), *Anniversaries and other Poems* (1920); edited *Jane Welsh Carlyle, Letters to Her Family* (1924) and *Letters to Her Sister, from Elizabeth Barrett Browning* (1929).

Sir **Julian Sorell** (1887–1975), biologist, son of Leonard Huxley; educ. Oxford; asst. professor, Rice Institute, Texas (1913–16); senior demonstrator in zoology, Oxford (1919–25); professor (1925–27) and honorary lecturer (1927–35), King's College, London; Fullerian professor, Royal Institution (1926–29); author of *The Individual in the Animal Kingdom* (1911), *Essays of a Biologist* (1923), *The Stream of Life* (1926), *The Science of Life* (with H. G. and G. P. Wells; 1929), *Ants* (1929), *What Dare I Think?* (1930), *The Captive Shrew and other Poems* (1932), *If I Were Dictator* (1934), *At the Zoo* (1936), *Evolution Restated* (1940), *Evolution: The Modern Synthesis* (1942), etc.

His brother **Aldous Leonard** (1894–1963), novelist and critic; educ. Oxford; author of *The Burning Wheel* (1916), *The Defeat of Youth* (1918), *Limbo* (1920), *Mortal Coils* (1922), *Antic Hay* (1923), *Those Barren Leaves* (1925), *Jesting Pilate* (1926), *Point Counter Point* (1928), *Brief Candles* (1930), *Brave New World* (1932), *Eyeless in Gaza* (1936), *The Olive Tree and other Essays* (1926), *After Many a Summer Dies the Swan* (1939), etc.

**Huy'de·co'per** (hoi'dĕ·kō'pẽr), **Balthazar.** 1695–1778. Dutch philologist and poet; translator of Horace's *Satires* and *Epistles;* author of *Achilles* (play; 1719); interested himself in critical research into the Germanic language of the Middle Ages and the 17th century.

**Huy'gens,** *or* **Huy'ghens** (hoi'gĕns; *Angl.* hī'gĕnz), **Christian.** 1629–1695. Son of Constantijn Huygens. Dutch mathematician, physicist, and astronomer, b. at The Hague. Studied law and mathematics at Leiden. With his brother, discovered improved method of grinding and polishing lenses (1655); discovered a satellite of Saturn and ring of Saturn (1655); constructed powerful telescopes; devised negative eyepiece for telescopes; described micrometer for use in telescopes; first to use pendulum to regulate movement of clocks (1656), and to determine acceleration due to gravity; enunciated laws governing the impact of elastic bodies (1669); developed wave theory of light (first stated by him in 1678); enunciated principle (Huygen's principle) according to which the surface constituting a wave front is determined; investigated polarization of light. Elected fellow of the Royal Society of England (1663); worked in Paris at invitation of Louis XIV (1666–81). Author of *Horologium Oscillatorium* (1673), *Traité de la Lumière* (1678, pub. 1690), etc.

**Huygens, Constantijn.** 1596–1687. Father of Christian Huygens (*q.v.*). Dutch diplomat and poet; his collected poems (written between 1658 and 1672) appeared under the title *Korenbloemen* (*Eng.* "Cornflowers") in 27 volumes.

**Huysman** *or* **Huysmann, Roelof.** Real name of Rodolphus AGRICOLA.

**Huys'mans** (hois'mäns), **Cornelis.** 1648–1727. Dutch painter; best known for his landscapes and a few large religious pictures.

**Huys'mans** (*Du.* hois'mäns; *Fr.* ü·ēs'mäɴs'), **Joris Karl,** *really* **Charles Marie Georges.** 1848–1907. French novelist, descended from a family of Dutch artists. Author of a series of realistic novels, including *Marthe, Histoire d'une Fille* (1878), *Les Sœurs Vatard* (1879), *En Ménage* (1881), *À Vau-l'Eau* (1882), *En Rade* (1887), followed by novels showing a reaction from materialism, as *Là Bas* (1891), *En Route!* (1895), *La Cathédrale* (1898).

**Huy'sum, van** (vän hoi'sûm). Name of a family of Dutch painters, including **Justus** (1659–1716) and his sons: **Jan** (1682–1749), noted for paintings of flowers and fruit, in oils and water colors; **Justus** (1685–1707), painter esp. of battle scenes; and **Jacobus** (b. 1686), who imitated or copied Jan's paintings.

**Hu'zard'** (ü'zär'), **Antoinette,** *nee* **de Ber'ge·vin'** (dẽ bĕr'zhẽ·văɴ'). *Pseudonym* **Colette Y'ver'** (ē'vâr'). 1874–1953. French novelist; author esp. of works dealing with social problems and the lot of women, including *Les Cervelines* (1903), *Un Cour du Voile* (1912), *Femmes d'Aujourd'hui* (1929), *Cher Cœur Humain* (1932).

**Hviezdoslav.** Pseudonym of Pavol ORSZÁGH.

**Hy'a·cinth** (hī'ȧ·sĭnth), Saint. 1185?–1257. Roman Catholic priest, b. in Silesia; known as "Apostle of the North"; preached and founded priories in Poland, Bohemia, Prussia, Pomerania, Lithuania, and the Scandinavian countries; canonized (1594).

**Hyacinthe,** Père. See Charles LOYSON.

**Hy'am·son** (hī'ăm·s'n), **Albert Montefiore.** 1875–1954. English editor, b. at London. In British civil service (from 1895); transferred to government of Palestine (1921); retired (1934). Compiler of *A Dictionary of Universal Biography* (1915) and *A Dictionary of English Phrases* (1922). Author of *Jewish Surnames* (1903), *A History of the Jews in England* (1908), *The Buccaneers of the Spanish Main* (1912), *Judas Maccabaeus* (1935), *David Solomons* (1939), several books on Palestine, etc.

**Hy'att** (hī'ăt), **Alpheus.** 1838–1902. American naturalist, b. Washington, D.C. Custodian, Boston Society of Natural History (1870–81) and curator (1881–1902). A founder and editor (1867–71) of *American Naturalist;* established marine laboratory at Annisquam, Mass. (1879), later moved to Woods Hole, Mass. Taught zoology and paleontology, M.I.T. (1870–88) and Boston U. (1887–1902). Founded new school of invertebrate paleontology; discovered law of acceleration in evolution of Cephalopoda. Author of *Genesis of the Arietidae* (1889), *Phylogeny of an Acquired Characteristic* (1894).

**Hyatt, John Wesley.** 1837–1920. American inventor, b. Starkey, N.Y. Printer by trade. Invented composition billiard ball; discovered fundamental principle utilized in making celluloid (patent issued 1870); invented water filter and purifier, a type of roller bearing, a lock-stitch sewing machine with fifty needles, and a process of solidifying hard woods.

**Hyde** (hīd), **Arthur M.** 1877–1947. American lawyer and politician; practiced law at Princeton, Mo. (1900–15) and Trenton, Mo. (from 1915). Governor of Missouri (1921–25); U.S. secretary of agriculture (1929–33).

**Hyde, Catherine.** See under *dukes of Queensberry,* under DOUGLAS family.

**Hyde, Douglas.** *Known in Ireland as* **An Craoi'bhín Aoi'bhinn** (ăn krē'vēn ē'vĭn), *i.e.* the Fair Branch. 1860–1949. Irish writer and statesman, b. in County Roscommon. Identified with Irish nationalist movement from its inception; first president of Gaelic League (1893–1915); professor of modern Irish, National University of Ireland (1909–32). President of Ireland (1938–45). Among his many works, including verse, plays, histories, essays, are *Love Songs of Connacht* (1894), *Story of Early Irish Literature* (1897), *Ubhla den Chraoibh* (verse, 1900), *Casadh an Tsugâin* (play in Irish, 1901), *Raftery's Poems* (1904), collection of Irish plays (1905), *Maistin an Bheurla* (play, 1913), *Legends of Saints and Sinners from the Irish* (1915), *An Leath-rann* (1922), *Mise Agus an Connradh* (1938).

**Hyde, Edward.** 1st Earl of **Clar'en·don** (klăr'ĕn·dŭn). 1609–1674. English statesman and historian; slighted study of law for literature and the company of Lord Falkland, Ben Jonson, Edmund Waller and others. Member of Short and Long Parliaments (1640), favoring popular party (till 1641); influential in suppressing earl marshal's court; supported Strafford's impeachment; supporter of Church of England and old constitution; opposed Grand Remonstrance and wrote king's reply; openly joined Royalist cause (1642); composed king's manifestoes and, by his legalistic justification, won half the nation to Charles. Expelled from House of Commons; followed king, as privy councilor and chancellor of exchequer (1643); followed Prince Charles (1646) to Scilly and Jersey, where he began his *History;* engaged in fruitless embassy to Spain for aid in money and for recovery of Ireland (1649–50). Chief adviser to Charles, later Charles II (1651), who appointed him lord chancellor (1658); opposed concessions to Romanists and Presbyterians, encouraged alliance with Levellers, and succeeded in making Restoration a national, not a factional, restoration of king and monarchy. Confirmed as lord chancellor (1660), became virtual head of government in control of all departments of state; adopted religious policy of comprehension but not of toleration; vigorously enforced Act of Uniformity and other repressive measures; endeavored to restore episcopacy in Scotland; supported Ormonde's enlightened Irish administration; one of lord proprietors of colony of Carolina (1663), but supported navigation laws; pursuing feeble foreign policy, initiated disgraceful system of pensions from Louis XIV and dependence on France; became unpopular because of sale of Dunkirk and of Dutch War. Fell victim to court cabal, and to king's resentment at opposition to obtaining Frances Stewart for the royal seraglio, and enmity of Barbara Villiers; dismissed (1667). Fled to France under impeachment by House of Lords; banished, lived in exile six years, compiling his *History* and writing autobiography; died at Rouen, buried Westminster Abbey. Author of *History of the Rebellion* (printed 1702–04 from transcript, 1826 from original ms.), *History of Civil War in Ireland* (1721), *Life of Edward, Earl of Clarendon* (3 vols., 1759), and *Contemplations on the Psalms.* Grandfather of Queen Mary, wife of William III, and Queen Anne, through secret marriage (1660) of his daughter **Anne** (1637–1671) to James II when duke of York.

**Henry** (1638–1709), 2d earl; Royalist adherent; eldest son of 1st earl; M.P. as Viscount **Corn'bur·y** [kôrn'bẽr·ĭ] (1661); privy councilor through influence of duke of York (1680); lord privy seal (1685); viceroy of Ireland (1685–87); opposed settlement of crown on William and Mary; imprisoned (1690, 1691); succeeded in title by his son **Edward** (1661–1723), 3d earl, governor of New York as Viscount Cornbury (1702–08).

Sir **Nicholas** (d. 1631), judge; uncle of 1st earl; M.P. (1601); deserted popular party to defend duke of Buckingham on impeachment charge by House of Commons (1626); chief justice of King's Bench (1627–31); one of judges who condemned the parliamentarians Sir John Eliot, Baron Holles, and Benjamin Valentine for conspiracy (1629).

**Lawrence** (1641–1711), 1st Earl of **Rochester** (cr. 1681); Tory statesman; 2d son by 2d wife of Edward, 1st Earl of Clarendon; M.P. (1660–79); with his elder brother Henry, warmly defended his father on impeachment charge in parliament (1667); first lord of treasury (1679–85); forced to take part in negotiation of Charles II's infamous subsidy treaty with Louis XIV (1681); lord president of the Council (1684; 1710–11); lord high treasurer to James II (1685–87), dismissed because of resistance to Roman Catholicism. Accepted regime of William III; viceroy of Ireland (1700–03). Patron of Dryden; represented as Hushai in Dryden's *Absalom and Achitophel.* His only son, **Henry** (1672–1753), 2d earl, inherited (1724) earldom of Clarendon as well; with his death both titles became extinct; one of his granddaughters, **Charlotte,** daughter of 3d earl of Essex, assumed name Hyde, m. (1752) Thomas Villiers, who was created (1756) Baron Hyde and 1st earl of Clarendon in Villiers family (see under George William Frederick VILLIERS.

**Hyde, Harford Montgomery.** 1907– . British historian, b. Belfast. Author of *The Rise of Castlereagh* (1933), *Princess Lieven* (1938), *Development of the Privy Council in Ireland* (1939), etc.

**Hyde, Helen.** 1868–1919. American etcher and engraver, b. Lima, N.Y. Resident in Japan for fifteen years; known esp. for etchings of Japanese subjects and of Chinese children and scenes in San Francisco. Pioneer in making woodcuts in the Japanese mode.

**Hyde, Henry Baldwin.** 1834–1899. American insurance magnate; founder of Equitable Life Assurance Society of the United States (1859); president (from 1874).

**Hyde, Thomas.** 1636–1703. English Orientalist; librarian of the Bodleian library (1665–1701); Laudian professor of Arabic, Oxford (1691); regius professor of Hebrew (1697); court interpreter of Oriental languages. Chief work, *Historia Religionis Veterum Persarum* (1700).

**Hyde, William DeWitt.** 1858–1917. American educator; ordained in Congregational ministry (1883). President, Bowdoin (from 1885). Author of *Practical Ethics* (1892), *Practical Idealism* (1897), *From Epicurus to Christ* (1904), *Self-Measurement* (1908).

**Hyder Ali.** = HAIDAR ALI.

**Hy·gi′nus** (hī·jī′nŭs), Saint. Pope (bishop of Rome; 136?–?140).

**Hyginus, Gaius Julius.** Latin author of 1st century B.C.; appointed by Augustus superintendent of the Palatine library. Author of biographical and topographical works, literary commentaries, a collection of mythological legends, an elementary work on astronomy, etc.

**Hyk′sos** (hĭk′sōs; -sŏs). Egyptian kings, often called the "Shepherd Kings," of XVth and XVIth dynasties, reigning about 1650–1580 B.C. Very little known about them; probably a barbaric people from the east.

**Hylacomylus.** See Martin WALDSEEMÜLLER.

**Hy′lan** (hī′lăn), **John F.** 1868–1936. American lawyer and politician, b. in Greene County, N.Y. Practiced law in Brooklyn, N.Y. (from 1897); mayor of New York (1918–25); justice, Children's Court, City of New York (1925–36).

**Hy′mans** (hī′mäns), **Paul.** 1865–1941. Belgian statesman; member of Chamber of Deputies (from 1900) and a leader of the Liberal party; Belgian ambassador to Great Britain (1915–17); represented Belgium at the Paris Peace Conference (1919) and at the League of Nations, where he was the first presiding officer (Jan., 1920). His father, **Henri Simon Hymans** (1836–1912), was an art historian; curator of the Bibliothèque Royale (from 1904).

**Hymans, Salomon Louis.** 1829–1884. Belgian historian and novelist; among his novels is *Un Brillant Mariage* (with P. J. Stahl); among his histories, *Histoire Populaire de la Belgique.*

**Hynd′man** (hīnd′măn), **Henry May′ers** (mā′ẽrz). 1842–1921. English Socialist, b. London. Founded (Social) Democratic Federation (1881); opposed Boer War (1899–1902); left British Socialist party and organized National Socialist party (1916); carried on agitation for social improvement. Author of *Economics of Socialism* (1896), etc.

**Hyne** (hīn), **Charles John Cutcliffe Wright.** 1865–1944. English traveler and fiction writer; best known as creator of fictional character Captain Kettle, as in *Adventures of Captain Kettle* (1898), *Captain Kettle on the Warpath* (1916), etc.

**Hy·pa′ti·a** (hī·pā′shĭ·ȧ; -shȧ). Neoplatonic philosopher, renowned for her beauty; taught at Alexandria; murdered (415 A.D.) by a mob incited by Cyril, then archbishop of Alexandria. Heroine of Kingsley's romance *Hypatia.*

**Hy·per′bo·lus** (hī·pûr′bō·lŭs). Athenian politician; succeeded Cleon (d. 422 B.C.) as head of democratic party; assassinated in Samos by the oligarchy (411).

**Hy′pe·ri′des** *or* **Hy′pe·rei′des** (hī′pē·rī′dēz). Athenian statesman and orator; supported anti-Macedonian policy advocated by Demosthenes; promoted Lamian War and, after Athenian defeat at Cranon, was condemned to death (322 B.C.); fled to Aegina, but was captured and executed.

**Hypselantes** *or* **Hypsilantis.** See YPSILANTI.

**Hyrcanus, John.** *Also* **Hyrcanus II.** See MACCABEES.

**Hyrtl** (hĭr′t'l), **Joseph.** 1810–1894. Austrian anatomist; professor at Vienna; known for work on the anatomy of the ear, also work in angiology and in comparative anatomy, esp. of fishes.

**Hys′lop** (hĭs′lŭp), **James Hervey.** 1854–1920. American philosopher, b. Xenia, Ohio. Founder (1906) of American Society for Psychical Research; author of *Elements of Psychology* (1895), *Problems of Philosophy* (1905), *Borderland of Psychical Research* (1906), *Psychical Research and Survival* (1913), *Life After Death* (1918).

**Hys·tas′pes** (hĭs·tăs′pēz). fl. 521 B.C. Persian noble; one of the Achaemenidae of the younger line, kinsman of Cyrus the Great and father of Darius I Hystaspis and Artaphernes. Satrap of Parthia and Hyrcania.

# I

**I·am′bli·chus** (ī·ăm′blĭ·kŭs). 2d-century Syrian-Greek romancer; author of *Babyloniaca*, a story of the adventures of two lovers, Rhodanes and Sinonis.

**Iamblichus.** d. about 333 A.D. Greek philosopher, b. at Chalkis in Syria; a leading representative of Syrian Neoplatonism.

**Iaroslav.** Variant of YAROSLAV.

**I·bá′ñez** *in full* **I·bá′ñez del Cam′po** (ē·bä′nyās thĕl käm′pō), **Carlos.** 1877–1960. Chilean soldier and politician; president of Chile (1927–31; forced to resign); in exile (1931–37); unsuccessful candidate for president (1938; again, 1942); president of Chile (1952–58).

**I·bá′ñez** (ē·bä′nyāth), **Vicente Blasco–.** See BLASCO-IBÁÑEZ.

**I·bá′ñez é I·bá′ñez de I·be′ro** (ē·bä′nyāth ā ē·bä′nyāth thā ē·bā′rō), **Carlos.** 1825–1891. Spanish military engineer and geodesist.

**I′bas** (ī′băs). 380?–?457. Nestorian bishop of Edessa; writer of a letter to the Persian Mari, forming one of the Three Chapters condemned by edict of Emperor Justinian (543).

**I′bert′** (ē′bâr′), **Jacques.** 1890–1962. French composer of piano pieces, orchestral works, symphonic poems, and opéra bouffe, etc.

**I′ber′ville′** (ē′bĕr′vēl′; *Angl.* ē′bẽr·vĭl *or* ī′-), Sieur **d'. Pierre Le·moyne′** (lē·mwȧn′). 1661–1706. Son of Charles Lemoyne (*q.v.*). French-Canadian explorer and commander, b. Montreal. Served in French navy for ten years. Raided British Hudson Bay fur-trading stations in effort to expel British and win Canada for France (1686–97). Founded French colony in Louisiana, first at what is now Biloxi (Miss.), later at Mobile (1698).

**ibn–** (ĭb′'n-). Arabic prefix meaning "son," used frequently as the first element of common form of name in

English; as *ibn-Saud, ibn-Batuta, ibn-Khaldun.* Cf. BEN.

**ibn-abi-Amir.** See al-MANSUR.

**ibn-a·bi'-U·say'bi·ah'** (ĭb'n·ă·bē'ōō·sĭ'bĭ·ă'). *Arab.* **Muwaffaq-al-Dīn abu-al-'Abbās Aḥmad ibn-abi-Uṣaybi'ah.** 1203–1270. Arab physician, b. Damascus. His great work was *'Uyūn al-Anbā'*, a collection of some 400 biographies of Arab and Greek physicians and scientists.

**ibn-A'jur·rum'** (ĭb''n ä'jōōr·rōōm'). *Arab.* **ibn-Ājurrūm.** d. 1323? Arab scholar; author of an elementary Arabic grammar (*Ajrumiya*) long the basis of all grammatical study in the East.

**ibn-al-A·thir'** (ĭb'nōōl·ă·thēr') *or* **ibn-A·thir'** (ĭb''n-ă·thēr'). *Arab.* **'Izz-al-Dīn ibn-al-A·thīr'** (ĭz'zōōd-dēn' ĭb'nĭl·ă·thēr'). 1160–1234. Arab historian; chief work *al-Kāmil,* a general history down to 1231, in part an abridgment of al-Tabari's work. His brother **Majd-al-Din** (măj'dōōd·dēn'), *full Arab. name* **Majd-al-Dīn ibn-al-Athīr** (1149–1210), theologian, wrote encyclopedia giving traditions of the prophets, a book of biographies, and a dictionary of family names. Another brother, **Di·ya'-al-Din'** (dĭ·yä'ōōd·dēn'), *full Arab. name* **Diyā-al-Dīn ibn-al-Athīr** (1163–1239), soldier and man of letters, served under Saladin and his son al-Malik (after 1191) in various campaigns; wrote aesthetic and critical literary studies.

**ibn-al-Bay·tar'** (ĭb'nōōl·bĭ·tär'). *Arab.* **'Abdullāh ibn-Aḥmad ibn-al-Bayṭār.** d. 1248. Arab botanist and pharmacist in Spain; author of a work on materia medica and of a work on simples, the foremost medieval treatise of its kind.

**ibn-al-Fa'ra·di'** (ĭb'nōōl·fă'ră·dē'). *Arab.* **abu-al-Walīd 'Abdullāh ibn-al-Faraḍi.** 962–1013. Arab historian in Andalusia; wrote a collection of biographies of Arab scholars in Spain.

**ibn-al-Fa'rid** (ĭb'nōōl·fă'rĭd) *or* **ibn-Fa'rid** (ĭb''n·fă'rĭd). *Arab.* **'Umar ibn-al-Fāriḍ.** 1181–1235. Arab mystic poet, b. Cairo. Greatest of Sufi poets; his poems (*divan*) considered models of style.

**ibn-al-Haytham.** See ALHAZEN.

**ibn-al-Kha·tib'** (ĭb'nōōl·kă·tēb'). *Arab.* **Lisān-al-Dīn ibn-al-Khaṭīb.** 1313–1374. Arab poet, historian, and general writer; most important work, a history of Granada.

**ibn-al-Mu·qaf'fa** (ĭb'nōōl·mŏ·kăf'fă). *Arab.* **Abu 'Amr** (*later* **Abu Muḥammad**) **ibn-al-Muqaffa'.** d. 757? Persian writer; Zoroastrian converted to Islam; translated into Arabic the Indian fables of Bidpai (*q.v.*).

**ibn-A'ra·bi'** (ĭb''n·ă'ră·bē'). *Arab.* **ibn-'Arabi.** 1165–1240. Arab mystic poet and prose writer; in his poems carried symbolism to extremes; chief work *The Meccan Revelations,* a 12-volume encyclopedia of Sufistic beliefs and doctrines.

**ibn-A'rab·shah'** (ĭb''n·ă'răb·shă'). *Arab.* **ibn-'Arab-Shāh.** 1392?–1450. Arab historian, b. Damascus; taken captive and removed by Tamerlane to Samarkand (1400); secretary to Ottoman sultan at Adrianople; chief work, a biography of Tamerlane, entitled *The Marvels of Destiny.*

**ibn-Bajjah.** See AVEMPACE.

**ibn-Ba·tu'ta** (ĭb''n·bă·tōō'tä). *Arab.* **Muḥammad ibn-'Abdullāh ibn-Baṭṭūṭah.** 1304–1377. Mohammedan traveler, b. Tangier; greatest Arabian traveler of Middle Ages; spent about 25 years (1325–49) in overland traverse of regions of Africa, Asia, and Europe; made four pilgrimages to Mecca.

**ibn-Daud.** See ABRAHAM IBN DAUD.

**ibn-Du·raid'** (ĭb''n·dōō·rĭd'). *Arab.* **abu-Bakr Muḥammad ibn-al-Ḥasan ibn-Durayd.** 837–933. Arab poet and scholar, b. Basra; to Persia (883); won favor of ruler by his panegyric ode *al-Maqṣūra;* compiled large dictionary in Persian; at Baghdad (after 920) wrote genealogical dictionary of Arab tribes (*Kitāb al-Ishtiqāq*).

**Ibn Ez'ra** (ĭb''n ĕz'rä). *More correctly and in full* **Abraham ben Meïr ibn Ezra.** 1092–1167. Jewish scholar, b. Toledo, Spain; a foremost scholar of medieval Spain; master of Hebrew, Arabic, and Aramaic languages; wrote many books on various sciences (mathematics, astronomy, philosophy, and medicine) and poems of high rank; best known for commentaries on Bible; inspiration of Robert Browning's *Rabbi Ben Ezra.*

**ibn-Fad·lan'** (ĭb''n·făd·län'). *Arab.* **Aḥmad ibn-Faḍlān ibn-Ḥammād.** fl. 921–922. Arab traveler; wrote earliest reliable account of Russia.

**ibn-Ga·bi'rol** (ĭb''n·gȧ·bē'rôl) *or* **ben-Ga·bi'rol** (bĕn'-), **Solomon ben Judah.** *Known in Spanish as* **A'vi·ce·brón'** (ä'vē·thȧ·brôn'; -sȧ·brôn'). 1021?–?1058. Jewish poet and philosopher, b. Málaga; wrote many poems in Hebrew, using Arabic meters; contributed lyrical poems of high rank to Jewish liturgy; first teacher of Neoplatonism in Europe; set forth his doctrine of matter and form in his chief philosophical work, *Yanbū 'al-Ḥayāh* (The Well of Life), which had great influence on the Schoolmen although received unfavorably by Jewish scholars, and which was translated (1150) into Latin.

**ibn-Han'bal** (ĭb''n·hăn'băl). *Arab.* **abu-'Abdullāh Aḥmad ibn-Ḥanbal.** 780–855. Arab founder of fourth Sunnite sect (Hanbalites), b. Baghdad. Punished and imprisoned (842) by caliphs for his conservatism; set free (846) by Caliph al-Mutawakkil; compiled the *Musnad,* collection of about 28,000 traditions; revered as a saint by his followers.

**ibn-Haw'qal** *or* **ibn-Hau'kul.** (ĭb''n·hou'kăl). *Arab.* **ibn-Ḥawqal.** fl. 943–977 A.D. Arab geographer and traveler.

**ibn-Hazm** (ĭb''n·hăz''m). *Arab.* **'Ali ibn-Aḥmad ibn-Ḥazm.** 994–1064. Arab theologian of Persian descent, b. Córdoba; at first a Shafiite, gradually became exponent of Zahirite or literalist school of theology; applied these principles to jurisprudence; compiled anthology of love poems; his chief work a book on sects, one of earliest works on comparative religion.

**ibn-Hi·sham'** (ĭb''n·hĭ·shăm'). *Arab.* **ibn-Hishām.** d. 833? Arab historian. Revised ibn-Ishaq's biography (not extant) of the Prophet Mohammed, which became standard authority.

**ibn-Is·haq'** (ĭb''n·ĭs·häk'). *Arab.* **Muḥammad ibn-Isḥāq.** d. 767? Arab historian; lived in Medina, later at Al Kufa and Baghdad; wrote biography of Mohammed, now known only in a later recension.

**ibn-Janah, Abul Walid Merwan.** See Rabbi JONAH.

**ibn-Ju·bayr'** (ĭb''n·jōō·bĭr') *or* **ibn-Jubair.** *Arab.* **abu-al-Ḥusayn Muḥammad ibn-Aḥmad ibn-Jubayr.** 1145–1217. Arab geographer.

**ibn-Kasim** *or* **ibn-Qasim.** See MOHAMMED IBN-KASIM.

**ibn-Khal·dun'** (ĭb''n·kăl·dōōn'). *Arab.* **'Abd-al-Raḥmān ibn-Khaldūn.** 1332–1406. Arab historian, b. Tunis. Wrote comprehensive history, consisting of three parts: (1) Muqaddamah ("Preface"), masterly treatise on philosophy of history, (2) history of Arabs and neighboring peoples, (3) history of Berbers and of Moslem dynasties of North Africa; made pilgrimage to Mecca (1382); remained three years in Cairo, part of time as its grand cadi; held various government positions in Egypt (1385–99); wrote his autobiography (1394). Considered founder of modern science of sociology, and greatest Arabian historian.

**ibn-Khal'li·kan'** (ĭb''n·kăl'lĭ·kän'). *Arab.* **Shams-al-Dīn Aḥmad ibn-Muḥammad ibn-Khallikān.** 1211–1282. Arab biographer; descendant of Barmecides. Wrote first dictionary of national biography in Arabic.

**ibn-Ma'sa·wayh'** (ĭb''n·mä'să·wī'). *Arab.* **Yūḥanna ibn-Māsawayh.** 777–857. Arab Christian physician; in service of caliph of Baghdad; wrote first systematic treatise on ophthalmology extant in Arabic.

**ibn-Qu·tai'ba** *or* **ibn-Ku·tai'ba** (ĭb''n·kōō·tī'bă). *Arab.* **abu-Muḥammad ibn-Muslim ibn-Qutaybah.** 828–?889. Arab philologist and historian; author of several works on history, poetry, and grammar, esp. *Adab al-Kātib,* compendium of Arabic style, and *'Uyūn al-Akhbār,* treatise on a variety of subjects.

**ibn-Rushd.** See AVERROËS.

**ibn-Sab·in'** (ĭb''n·săb·ēn'). *Arab.* **abu-Muḥammad 'Abd-al-Ḥaqq ibn-Sab'īn.** 1217?–1269. Arab philosopher in Spain, b. in Murcia. A Sufi theologian, founder of a mystic sect; wrote work on mysteries of illuministic philosophy.

**ibn-Sa·ud', Abd·ul'-A·ziz'** (ȧb·dōōl'ă·zēz' ĭb''n sōō-ōōd'). *Arab.* **'Abd-al-'Azīz ibn-'Abd-al-Raḥmān al-Faisal ibn-Su 'ūd.** 1880–1953. King of Saudi Arabia (1932–53), b. Riyadh. Son of Abd-al-Rahman, Wahabi sultan of Nejd. In childhood, driven by civil war into exile (1891) at Bahrein and Kuwait; succeeded (1901) father on throne of Nejd; organized force that seized (1901) Riyadh and established (1906) dominance of Wahabis in Nejd; through able administration (1906–14), built up strength of Nejd, replacing Arab patriarchal system by nationalism. In World War, sided with British against Turks; added outlying regions of Arabia to Nejd (1919–22); invaded and conquered (1924–25) the Hejaz, forcing abdication of King Husein and his son Ali; proclaimed himself king of Hejaz (1926). Signed (1927) treaty with Great Britain by which independence of his country recognized; changed (1927) his title from sultan of Nejd to king of the Hejaz and Nejd; by decree (1932), proclaimed official name of Hejaz and Nejd as Kingdom of Saudi Arabia; introduced order in tribal relations and made pilgrimages to Mecca safe for all Mohammedans; after discovery of oil (1938), granted extensive concessions to Standard Oil Co. of California; on outbreak of war (1939) remained neutral, but friendly to British; dismissed Italian legation (Mar., 1942).

**ibn-Shaprut.** See HASDAI IBN-SHAPRUT.

**ibn-Sina.** See AVICENNA.

**ibn-Tash·fin'** (ĭb''n·täsh·fēn'), **Yusuf.** *Arab.* **Yūsuf ibn-Tāshfīn.** d. 1106. Berber chieftain, one of founders of Almoravid empire of northwestern Africa and Spain. King of the Almoravides (1061–1106); founded (1062) Marrakech (Morocco), which became their capital; invaded Spain (1086), defeating Alfonso VI of León and Castile and again (1090), subjugating all Mohammedan Spain as far as Toledo.

**ibn-Tib'bon** (ĭb''n·tĭb'bōn). fl. 12th–13th cent. Jewish family in Provence whose members translated into Hebrew chief Arabic writings of Jews in Middle Ages.

**ibn-Tu·fail'** *or* **ibn-To·fail'** (ĭb''n·tōō·fīl'). *Arab.* **abu-Bakr Muḥammad ibn-'Abd-al-Malik ibn-Ṭufayl.** *Latinized* **Ab'u·ba'cer** (ăb'ū·bā'sẽr). d. 1185. Arab philosopher and physician, b. near Granada, Spain. Friend of Averroës; practiced medicine at Granada, where he was secretary to the governor; later, vizier to caliph of Morocco. His chief work, thought by some to have been original of *Robinson Crusoe,* was an original philosophic romance, *Ḥayy ibn-Yaqẓān* ("the living one, son of the vigilant"), translated by Edward Pococke into Latin (1671) as *Philosophus Autodidactus* and by others into most European languages.

**ibn-Tu'mart** (ĭb''n·tōō'märt). *Arab.* **abu-'Abdullāh Muḥammad ibn-Tūmart.** 1078?–1130. Arab reformer in North Africa, founder of sect of Almohades; preached doctrine of unity of divine being; proclaimed himself Mahdi (1121); protested against many current practices of Islam; gathered following of Berber mountaineers. Succeeded by Abd-al-Mumin (*q.v.*), who founded Almohade dynasty.

**ibn-Yasin, Abdallah.** See ABDALLAH.

**ibn-Zay·dun'** (ĭb''n·zī·dōōn'). *Arab.* **abu-al-Walīd Aḥmad ibn-Zaydūn.** 1003–1071. Arab poet in Spain, b. Córdoba. His love for al-Walladah, poet and daughter of Caliph al-Mustakfi, caused him to be exiled; wrote famous epistle to his rival for hand of al-Walladah; his poems regarded by some as the finest by any Arab of Moslem Spain.

**ibn-Zuhr** *or* **ibn-Zohr.** See AVENZOAR.

**Ib·ra'him'** (ĭb·rä'hēm'). d. 632. Son of Mohammed (*q.v.*).

**Ib·ra'him'** (ĭb·rä'hēm'). *Arab.* **Ibrāhīm.** Name of two Aghlabite (*q.v.*) sultans of North Africa. **Ibrahim I,** *full name* **Ibrāhīm ibn-al-Aghlab** (756–812), founder of Aghlabite dynasty; sultan (800–812); seized Kairouan and Tunis; given government of African province by Harun al-Rashid; received embassy from Charlemagne. **Ibrahim II** (848–902), sultan (875–902).

**Ib·ra·him'** *or* **Ib·ra·him' Pa·sha'** (ĭb·rä·hĭm' pä·shä'). 1493?–1536. Turkish grand vizier. Bought as a slave by Sultan Suleiman I; made vizier (1523); commanded Turkish army in invasion of Hungary (1526); given sultan's sister in marriage and became his close friend and adviser; took command (1533–34) in war with Persia; strangled by sultan's order.

**Ibrahim.** 1615–1648. Ottoman sultan (1640–48). Third son of Ahmed I; by feigning insanity, escaped death from his brother Murad IV; at war with Venice (1645–48); failed in attack on Crete; deposed and strangled by Janizaries.

**Ib·ra·him' Bey** (ĭb·rä·hĭm' bā'). 1735?–1817. Mameluke emir of Egypt (1791–98) jointly with Murad Bey; defeated by Napoleon (1798); escaped massacre of Mamelukes by Mehemet Ali (1811).

**Ib·ra·him' Lo'di** (ĭb·rä·hēm' lō'dē). d. 1526. Afghan king (1517–26) of Delhi of the Lodi dynasty. Defeated and slain (1526) by the Mogul invader, Baber.

**Ib·ra'him' Pa'sha** (ĭb·rä'hēm' pȧ'shä). 1789–1848. Egyptian general and viceroy, b. Kavalla, Rumelia. Son, or adopted son, of Mehemet Ali. Subdued Wahabis (1816–18); in command against Greece (1824–27); led Egyptian army into Syria (1831); took Acre (1832); defeated Turks in several battles (1832); governor of Syria (after 1833); in second war with Turks, won great victory (1839) at Nezib in north Syria; compelled by Great Powers to abandon Syria (1841); appointed viceroy for senile father (1848). See SAID PASHA and ISMAIL PASHA.

**Ib'sen** (ĭb's'n; *Norw.* ĭp'sĕn), **Henrik.** 1828–1906. Norwegian poet and dramatist, b. Skien. Studied medicine and was chemist's assistant at Grimstad (1844–50); helped edit weekly journal *Andhrimner* (1851). Stage director and dramatist at Ole Bull's National Theater, Bergen (1851–57); director of Norwegian Theater, Oslo (1857–62); received traveling scholarship (1863) and government pension (1866). Disapproved Norway's stand in politics, and left Norway (1863) to live chiefly in Italy and Germany (until 1891); returned to Oslo (1891). His works include the unsuccessful tragedy *Catilina* (1850; under the pseudonym **Brynjolf Bjar'me** [byär'mĕ]), the historical dramas *The Banquet at Solhaug* (1856), *The Warriors at Helgoland* (first national Norwegian realistic drama; 1858), *The Pretenders* (1864), and *Emperor and*

*Galilean* (1873), the dramatic poems *Brand* (1866) and *Peer Gynt* (1867), the satirical political prose comedy *League of Youth* (1869), and the satirical social play *Love's Comedy* (1862), precursor of his social and psychological plays *The Pillars of Society* (1877), *A Doll's House* (1879), *Ghosts* (1881), *An Enemy of the People* (1882), *The Wild Duck* (1884), *Rosmersholm* (1886), *The Lady from the Sea* (1888), *Hedda Gabler* (1890), *The Master Builder* (1892), *Little Eyolf* (1894), *John Gabriel Borkman* (1896), and *When We Dead Awaken* (1899).

**Ibsen, Sigurd.** 1859–1930. Son of Henrik Ibsen and son-in-law of B. Björnson. Norwegian politician and writer, b. Oslo. In Swedish-Norwegian foreign office and diplomatic service (1885–89) at Stockholm, Washington, and Vienna; engaged in journalism (1892–95; 1898–99); member of Norwegian State Council, Stockholm (1902–05); favored Swedish-Norwegian union; member of Hague Tribunal (1906, 1912). Author of *Men and Powers* (1894), *Human Quintessence* (1911), the dramas *Robert Frank* (1914) and *The Temple of Reminiscence* (1917), etc.

**Ib'y·cus** (ĭb'ĭ·kŭs). Greek lyric poet of 6th century B.C., in Rhegium (Reggio Calabria), Italy. Fragments extant.

**Ich'a·bod** (ĭk'ă·bŏd). In Bible, posthumous son of Phinehas, son of Eli (*1 Samuel* iv. 19–22).

**Icilius, Quintus.** See GUICHARD.

**Ick'es** (ĭk'ĕs), **Harold LeClair.** 1874–1952. Am. lawyer and politician, b. in Frankstown Township, Pa.; adm. to bar and practiced in Chicago (from 1907); prominent in Republican politics (to c. 1926); worked in interest of Roosevelt-Garner ticket (1932); U.S. secretary of the interior (1933–46), also administrator of public works (1933–39) and petroleum administrator, under various titles (1933 ff.).

**Ic·ti'nus** (ĭk·tī'nŭs). Greek architect of 5th century B.C.; chief designer of Parthenon at Athens, temple to Demeter and Persephone at Eleusis, etc.

**I'da** (ī'dȧ; *A.-S.* ē'dä). d. 559. Chieftain of the Angles; first king (547 ff.) of Bernicia (northern Northumbria).

**Iddesleigh,** Earl of. See Sir Stafford Henry NORTHCOTE.

**Id'dings** (ĭd'ĭngz), **Joseph Paxson.** 1857–1920. American geologist; professor, U. of Chicago (1895–1908). Coauthor, with Cross, Pirsson, and Washington, of *Quantitative Classification of Igneous Rocks* (1903); author of *Rock Minerals* (1906), *Igneous Rocks* (2 vols., 1909–13), *The Problem of Volcanism* (1914).

**Ide** (īd), **Henry Clay.** 1844–1921. American public official; chief justice of Samoa (1893–97). Member, Philippine Commission (1900–04); governor general of the Philippines (1906). U.S. minister to Spain (1909–13).

**I'de·ler** (ē'dĕ·lẽr), **Christian Ludwig.** 1766–1846. German astronomer and chronologist.

**I'del·sohn** (ē'd'l·zōn), **Abraham Ze·bi'** (tsvē). 1882–1938. Jewish music scholar, b. in Kurland; in Jerusalem, founded (1919) a Jewish music school. To U.S. (1922); professor, Hebrew Union College, Cincinnati (1924–34; retired). Writer on Hebrew, Jewish, and oriental music.

**I·dri'si, al-** (ȧl·ĭ·drē'sĭ). *Also* **E·dri'si** (ĕ-). *Arab.* **abu-'Abdullāh Muḥammad ibn-Muḥammad al-Idrīsi.** 1100–1166. Arab geographer and cartographer, b. Ceuta of Hispano-Arab parents; lived in Sicily under patronage of King Roger II; prepared a geography, containing 71 maps, of value as revealing extent of Arab knowledge of geography in 12th century.

**Id'ri·sid** (ĭd'rĭ·sĭd) *or* **Id'ri·site** (-sīt) dynasty. Arab Shiite dynasty of northwestern Africa (788–974) with principal capital at Fez in Morocco; its main line, the Alids (*q.v.*), founded by Idris ibn-Abdullah; overthrown by Berbers.

**Iemitsu.** See IYEMITSU.

**Ieyasu.** See IYEYASU.

**Iff'land** (ĭf'länt), **August Wilhelm.** 1759–1814. German character actor, director, and dramatist.

**I·gle'sias** (ē·glā'syäs), **José María.** 1823–1891. Mexican jurist and statesman; president of supreme court of Mexico (1873); when Lerdo de Tejada was overthrown (1876), assumed presidency of Mexico until Díaz took power.

**Iglesias, Miguel.** 1822–1901. Peruvian general and politician; when Peruvian government refused to meet Chilean terms at end of War of the Pacific (1879–83), was elected president of Peru under Chilean influence (1883–86); negotiated treaty of Ancón (1883). Forced to resign by revolution led by Cáceres (1886).

**Iglesias, Pablo.** 1850–1925. Spanish Socialist leader; editor of *El Socialista*, official Socialist organ (1885 ff.); first Socialist deputy in the Cortes (1910 ff.); president, Unión General de Trabajadores.

**Iglesias de la Ca'sa** (thā lä kä'sä), **José.** 1748–1791. Spanish poet, b. Salamanca; known esp. for satirical epigrams and letrillas (letters in verse) aimed at the moral decay of contemporary society.

**Ig·na'tiev** (ĭg·nȧ'tyĕf), **Nikolai Pavlovich.** 1832–1908. Russian general and diplomat; as attaché at Peking (1858), secured Amur region by Treaty of Aigun; minister plenipotentiary to China (1860–63). Ambassador at Constantinople (1864–77); took leading part in diplomatic proceedings before outbreak of Russo-Turkish War (1877–78); at conclusion of war was mainly responsible for Treaty of San Stefano (1878).

**Ig·na'ti·us** (ĭg·nā'shĭ·ŭs; -shŭs), Saint. *Surnamed* **The·oph'o·rus** (thē·ŏf'ō·rŭs). Christian prelate of late 1st and early 2d century; bishop of Antioch and one of the fathers of the church; martyred under Trajan. Certain of his *Epistles* are extant, written during his journey from Antioch to his martyrdom in Rome.

**Ignatius** of Constantinople, Saint. *Called* **Ni·ce'tas** (nī·sē'tȧs; nĭ-). 799?–878. Son of Emperor Michael I. Patriarch of Constantinople (846–858 and 867–878). Excommunicated Bardas, regent for Michael III; for this was deposed and exiled (858). Replaced by Photius (*q.v.*). Restored by Basil I (867); innocence confirmed by Council of Constantinople (869).

**Ignatius of Loyola,** Saint. See LOYOLA.

**Ihering, Rudolf von.** See JHERING.

**Ih'ne** (ē'nĕ), **Wilhelm.** 1821–1902. German historian.

**Ih're'** (ē'rĕ'), **Johan.** 1707–1780. Swedish philologist.

**I·i Na·o·su·ke** (ē·ē nä·ō·sōō·kĕ), Baron. *Also known by honorific title* **I·i Ka·mon no ka·mi** (ē·ē kä·mōn nō kä·mē). 1815–1860. Japanese statesman. Hated foreigners, but, after Commodore Perry's visit (1853), sought in best interests of Japan to treat them in friendly manner; premier of Shogun Iyesada (1858); opposed Hitotsubashi for shogunate; secured election of 12-year-old Iyemochi as shogun (1858). Without emperor's approval, signed treaties of friendship with U.S., England, Russia, etc., arousing great hostility, esp. among the daimio; assassinated.

**I·ke·da** (ē·kĕ·dä), **Seihin.** 1867–1950. Japanese industrialist. Entered Mitsui banking house (1895); its managing director (1909–36); chairman, Tokyo clearinghouse (1923–33); governor of Bank of Japan (1937); minister of finance and commerce (1938); counselor to government (from 1939).

**I·ke·no** (ē·kĕ·nō), **Seiitiro.** 1866–1943. Japanese botanist.

**Ikh·na'ton** (ĭk·nä't'n) *or* **A'khe·na'ten** *or* **A'khe·na'·ton** (ä'kĕ·nä't'n) *or* **Akh·na'ton** (äk·nä't'n). *Also known as* **A'men·ho'tep IV** (ä'mĕn·hō'tĕp). King of ancient Egypt of the XVIIIth (Diospolite) dynasty (reigned c. 1375–1358 B.C.); called "the Religious Revolutionary." Son of Amenhotep III and Tiy. Established new cult in worship of Aten, the sun god or "solar disk," opposing priests of Amen—hence, his change of name to *Ikhnaton* (meaning "Aten is satisfied"); established new capital at Akhetaton (modern Tell el-Amarna); died young. Reign called the "Amarna Age" in reference to the extant correspondence (Tell el-Amarna letters), written on tablets, between Amenhotep III and IV and Egyptian viceroys in Palestine, kings of Babylon, and a king of the Mitanni. See NEFERTITI; TUTANKHAMEN.

**Ilacomilus.** See Martin WALDSEEMÜLLER.

**Il'de·fon'so** (ēl'dā·fōn'sō), Saint. 607–667. Spanish ecclesiastic; archbishop of Toledo (657).

**Il·de·rîm'** (yĭl·dĭ·rĭm'). = BAJAZET I.

**Ilf** (ēl'y'f), **Ilya Arnoldovich.** 1897–1937. Russian writer, b. Odessa; known esp. for his humorous writings with Evgeni Petrov (*q.v.*).

**Ilg** (ĭlk), **Alfred.** 1852–1916. Swiss engineer; in Ethiopia (from 1878), adviser to King Menelik; obtained concession to build railway connecting Ethiopia with Djibouti (1896); prime minister and imperial councilor of state, in charge of foreign affairs (1897).

**Ilg, Paul.** 1875–1957. Swiss author, poet, and dramatist.

**I'lić** (ē'lĕt·y'; *Angl.* -lĭch). Family of Serbian poets, including **Jovan** (1823–1901), author of poems in the style of Serbian folk songs; and his two sons, **Dragutin** (1858– ), author of novels, plays, and works of criticism as well as verse, and **Vojislav** (1862–1894), author chiefly of elegiac verse.

**I'li·e'scu** (ē'lē·yĕ'skōō), **Dmitri.** 1865– . Rumanian soldier; commanded the Rumanian army, World War I.

**Il-khan'** (ēl·kän'), *i.e.* "provincial, or dependent, khan." Mongol dynasty (1260–1353) in Persia, founded by Hulagu (*q.v.*); its real power terminated (1335); divided between five petty dynasties (1335–53).

**Il'ling·ton** (ĭl'ĭng·tŭn), **Margaret.** 1881–1934. American actress; m. Daniel Frohman (1903), Edward J. Bowes (1909). Played lead in *The Two Orphans, Mrs. Leffingwell's Boots, His House in Order;* starred in *Kindling, Within the Law, Our Little Wife, The Gay Lord Quex* (with John Drew).

**Iltutmish.** See ALTAMSH.

**I·mad'-al-Din'** (ĭ·mä'dōōd·dēn'). *Arab.* **'Imād-al-Dīn al-Kātib al-Iṣfahāni.** 1125–?1201. Arab historian; entered service (1174) of Saladin, accompanied him on campaigns, and wrote his biography.

**I·ma·mu·ra** (ē·mä·mōō·rä), **Akitsune.** 1870–1948. Japanese seismologist.

**Im'ber** (ĭm'bĕr), **Naf·ta'li** [*or* **Naph·ta'li**] (näf·tô'lē) **Herz** (hĕrts). 1856–1909. Itinerant Hebrew scholar and poet, b. Złoczów, Poland; associated with Israel Zangwill in London (1889–92); in U.S. (from 1892); his hymn, *Hatikvah* (The Hope), has become the hymn of the Zionist party all over the world.

**Im'bert'** (ăN'bâr'), **Barthélemy.** 1747–1790. French writer; author of the poem *Le Jugement de Pâris* (1772) and a volume of *Fables* (1773).

**Im'bo'den** (ĭm'bō'd'n), **John Daniel.** 1823–1895. American Confederate officer. Colonel under "Stonewall" Jackson (1862); led raid in West Virginia (Apr.–May, 1863); covered Confederate retreat from Gettysburg.

**Im·ho'tep** (ĭm·hō'tĕp). *Gr.* **I·mou'thes** (ĭ·mōō'thēz). fl. c. 2980–2950 B.C. Physician and sage of ancient Egypt, counselor of King Zoser of IIId (first Memphite) Dynasty. Architect and probable builder of Zoser's pyramid (see ZOSER); skilled in medicine and priestly magic. Later (in Ptolemaic times) regarded by Egyptians as a deity; identified by Greeks with Asclepius (Asklepios).

**Im'mel·mann** (ĭm'ĕl·män; *Angl.* -măn), **Max.** 1890–1916. German aviator in the World War; regarded, with Boelcke, as founder of the German technique of air combat; the maneuver known as the "Immelmann turn" was developed by him; killed in action (July 18, 1916).

**Im'mer·mann** (ĭm'ĕr·män), **Karl Leberecht.** 1796–1840. German poet, dramatist, and novelist. Author of lyric poems, the dramatic poem *Trauerspiel in Tirol* (1827), the poetic satire *Tulifäntchen* (1830), the novels *Die Epigonen* (3 vols., 1836) and *Münchhausen* (4 vols., 1838–39; containing the village idyl *Der Oberhof*), etc.

**Im'misch** (ĭm'ĭsh), **Otto.** 1862–1936. German classical philologist and scholar.

**Imola, Innocenzo da.** See FRANCUCCI.

**Imouthes.** See IMHOTEP.

**Im'pey** (ĭm'pĭ), Sir **Elijah.** 1732–1809. English jurist. Educ. Cambridge. Chief justice of Bengal, India (1774–89); co-operated with Warren Hastings. Impeached (1783) by House of Commons for his conduct in India; successfully defended himself; acquitted (1788). M.P. (1790–96).

**Im·ru'-al-Qays** (ĭm·rōō'ōōl·kīs'). *Also* **Am·ru-'l-Kais** (ăm·rōōl'kīs'). *Arab.* **Imru'-al-Qays.** d. 540? A.D. One of earliest and greatest of Arab poets; native of southern Arabia.

**Ina.** See INE.

**Inca, El.** See GARCILASO DE LA VEGA (1539?–1616).

**Ince** (ĭns), **William.** 18th-century English furniture designer.

**Inch** (ĭnch), **James Robert.** 1835–1912. Canadian educator.

**Inch'bald** (ĭnch'bôld), **Elizabeth,** *nee* **Simp'son** (sĭm(p)'s'n). 1753–1821. English actress and author; m. Joseph Inchbald (1772); wrote comedies and farces, chiefly adaptations from French; best known for two tales, *A Simple Story* (1791) and *Nature and Art* (1796).

**Inch'cape** (ĭnch'kāp), 1st Earl. **James Lyle Mackay.** 1852–1932. British industrialist, financier, and statesman, b. in Forfarshire, Scotland. To India (1874) in shipping business; rose to senior partnership in shipping firm Mackinnon, Mackenzie & Co. Member of legislation council of viceroy of India (1891–93) and of Council of India (1897–1911). During World War (1914–18), served on imperial defense committee and food production committee; after World War, served as chairman of committee to control bank amalgamation (1918–23).

**Inchiquin,** Barons and earls of. Titles borne by O'Brien family (*q.v.*).

**Inclán, Ramón del Valle.** See VALLE INCLÁN.

**In'cle·don** (ĭng'k'l·dŭn), **Charles.** 1763–1826. English tenor; sang in operas (including Gay's *Beggar's Opera*) at Covent Garden (1790–1815); appeared in first performance of Haydn's *Creation*, Covent Garden (1800).

**In'dy'** (ăN'dē'), **Vincent d'.** 1851–1931. French composer; studied under César Franck; a leader of radical modern French school. Founder and director of the Schola Cantorum, in Paris; author of *Cours de Composition Musicale* (1902–09). Composer of operas, chamber music, sonatas, symphonic works, etc.

**I'ne** (*A.-S.* ĭ'nĕ) *or* **I'ni** (*A.-S.* ĭ'nĭ) *or* **I'na** (*Lat.* ī'nȧ). d. 726. West Saxon king (688–726); established power over England south of the Thames; promulgated laws (690–693), earliest extant West Saxon legislation; abdicated (726) and died on pilgrimage to Rome.

**Inés de Castro.** See CASTRO.

**In·fan'te** (ēn·fän'tā), **Manuel.** 1883–1958. Spanish composer, esp. of piano works.

**Infarinato.** See Leonardo SALVIATI.

**In'feld** (ĭn'fĕlt), **Le'o·pold** (lā'ô·pôlt). 1898–1968. Physicist, b. Cracow, Poland; on fellowship at Princeton

U. renewed work with Einstein; professor of applied mathematics, U. of Toronto (from 1939). Known for work on relativity and the quantum theory.

**In'galls** (ĭng'gălz), **James Monroe**. 1837–1927. American army officer; ballistic authority; founded (1882) department of ballistics at U.S. army artillery school, Ft. Monroe, Va.

**Ingalls, John James**. 1833–1900. American politician, orator, and writer, b. Middleton, Mass.; grad. Williams (1855); adm. to bar (1857) and practiced in Atchison, Kans. (from 1860); U.S. senator from Kansas (1873–91).

**Ingalls, Melville Ezra**. 1842–1914. American railroad executive, b. Harrison, Me.; grad. Harvard Law School (1863) and practiced in Boston. Organized Cincinnati, Indianapolis, St. Louis & Chicago Railway (1880); president of this company (1880–89) and also of later consolidated company, Cleveland, Cincinnati, Chicago & St. Louis Railway, known as the Big Four (1889–1905); also, president of Chesapeake & Ohio Railway (1888–1900).

**Inge** (ĭng), **William Ralph**. 1860–1954. Anglican prelate, scholar, and writer, b. Crayke, Yorkshire. Educ. Cambridge. Fellow and tutor, Hertford Coll., Oxford (1889–1904); professor of divinity, Cambridge (1907–11). Dean of St. Paul's, London (1911–34); sometimes referred to as "the gloomy Dean." Among his many books are *Christian Mysticism* (1899), *Faith and Knowledge* (1904), *Outspoken Essays* (two series, 1919, 1922), *Lay Thoughts of a Dean* (1926), *Christian Ethics and Modern Problems* (1930), *Things New and Old* (1933), *Vale* (1934), *Our Present Discontents* (1938).

**Ing'e·borg** (ĕng'ĕ·bŏrg). *French* **In'ge·burge'** (ăN'zhĕ·bürzh') *or* **In'gel'burge'** (ăN'zhĕl'bürzh'). 1176?–?1237. Queen of France, b. in Denmark. Sister of King Canute VI; m. (1193) Philip Augustus. Immediately became object of Philip's dislike; her marriage repudiated but Philip's attempt to secure separation opposed by Popes Celestine III and Innocent III; kept in prison, but finally (1213) regained her rights.

**In'ge·gne'ri** (ĕn'jâ·nyâ'rē), **Marco Antonio**. 1545?–1592. Veronese composer; among his works are *Responsoria Hebdomadae Sanctae* (long attributed to Palestrina), Masses, and madrigals.

**In'ge·low** (ĭn'jĕ·lō), **Jean**. 1820–1897. English poet and writer of fiction. Her verse includes three series of *Poems* (1871, 1876, 1885); her novels include *Off the Skelligs* (1872), and *John Jerome* (1886).

**Ing'e·mann** (ĕng'ĕ·mȧn), **Bernhard Severin**. 1789–1862. Danish poet and novelist; helped spread Late German romanticism in Denmark; author of the romantic tragedy *Blanca* (1815), the historical novels *Valdemar the Victorious* (1827), *Erik Menved's Childhood* (1828), and *King Erik* (1833), the epic *Valdemar the Great and his Men* (1824), the lyrics *Holger Danske* (1837) and *Morning and Evening Hymns* (1839), etc.

**Ing'en·housz** (ĭng'ĕn·hous), **Jan**. 1730–1799. Dutch physician and plant physiologist. Practiced as physician in England (c. 1765, 1779 ff.) and Austria (1768–79). Author of *Experiments on Vegetables* (1779), etc.

**In'ge·nie'ros** (ĕng'hâ·nyā'rōs), **José**. 1877–1925. Argentine psychologist, psychiatrist, and sociologist.

**Ing'e·nohl** (ĭng'ĕ·nōl), **Friedrich von**. 1857–1933. German admiral; head of High Seas Fleet (1913). Admiral in World War, and suffered reverses at Helgoland (1914) and elsewhere; removed from command (1915).

**In'ger·soll** (ĭng'gĕr·sŏl; -s'l), **Ernest**. 1852–1946. American naturalist; on editorial staff of *Standard Dictionary* (1892–95, 1910–12) and *New International Encyclopaedia* (1902–03); conducted department of natural history, Montreal *Star* (from 1899).

**Ingersoll, Jared**. 1722–1781. American lawyer, b. Milford, Conn. London agent for Connecticut colony (1758–61, 1764). Appointed by British government to collect stamp tax in Connecticut (1765); mobbed and forced to resign his post (1765). His son **Jared** (1749–1822) was a jurist; member of Continental Congress (1780, 1781); delegate to Constitutional Convention (1787); attorney general of Pennsylvania (1790–99, 1811–17); Federalist candidate for vice-president of the United States (1812). Jared's son **Charles Jared** (1782–1862) was a member of U.S. House of Representatives (1813–15, 1841–49); U.S. district attorney for Pennsylvania (1815–29).

**Ingersoll, Leonard Rose**. 1880–1958. American physicist; worked on subjects related to the electromagnetic theory of light; invented the "glarimeter," a device for measuring gloss of paper.

**Ingersoll, Robert Green**. 1833–1899. American lawyer and agnostic; served in Union army during Civil War; colonel (1861). Attorney general of Illinois (1867–69). Became noted agnostic lecturer, attacking popular Christian beliefs. Author of *The Gods, and Other Lectures* (1876), *Some Mistakes of Moses* (1879), *Why I am an Agnostic* (1896), *Superstition* (1898).

**Ingersoll, Robert Hawley**. 1859–1928. American industrialist; developed mail-order business and chain-store system; introduced (1892) Ingersoll one-dollar watch, "the watch that made the dollar famous." Insolvent (1921); sold assets to Waterbury Clock Co. (1922).

**Ingersoll, Royal Eason**. 1883–1976. American naval officer, b. Washington, D.C.; grad. U.S.N.A., Annapolis (1905); commanded U.S. Atlantic fleet (1942); admiral commanding western sea frontier (1944).

**Ing'ham** (ĭng'ăm), **Charles Cromwell**. 1796–1863. Painter, b. Dublin, Ireland; to U.S. (1816); studio in New York; excelled in portrait painting.

**Ingham, Samuel Delucenna**. 1779–1860. American politician; U.S. secretary of the treasury (1829–31). Developed anthracite coal fields of Pennsylvania (from 1831).

**In'ghel'brecht'** (ăN'gĕl'brĕsht'), **D. E.** 1880–1965. French music director and composer; impressionistic in his compositions, as in *Le Diable dans le Beffroi*, the *Rapsodie de Printemps*, and piano pieces and songs.

**Inghen, Marsilius von**. See MARSILIUS VON INGHEN.

**In'ghi·ra'mi** (ĕng'gē·rä'mē). Italian noble family, including: **Tommaso** (1470–1516), known as **Fe'dra** (fâ'drä) because of his success in interpreting role of Phaedra in Seneca's *Hippolytus;* author of a number of Latin orations. **Francesco** (1772–1846), an archaeologist, specialist in Etruscan archaeology. **Giovanni** (1779–1851), astronomer and mathematician.

**In'gle·by** (ĭng'g'l·bĭ), **Clement Mansfield**. 1823–1886. English philosopher and Shakespearean critic. Among his works are *Introduction to Metaphysic* (1864, 1869), *Shakespeare Hermeneutics* (1875), and *Shakespeare: the Man and the Book* (1877, 1881).

**In'gle·field** (ĭng'g'l·fēld), Sir **Edward Augustus**. 1820–1894. British naval officer and Arctic explorer; visited Arctic in search for Sir John Franklin (1852, 1853, 1854).

**In'glin** (ĭng'glĭn), **Meinrad**. 1893– . Swiss novelist and short-story writer.

**In'glis** (ĭng'g'lz; -glĭs), Sir **John Eardley Wilmot**. 1814–1862. British soldier, b. in Nova Scotia. Served in Canada (1837) and in the Punjab (1848–49); famed for his gallant defense of Lucknow (1857) during Sepoy Mutiny; major general (1857).

**Ingoldsby, Thomas**. Pseudonym of R. H. BARHAM.

**In'gra·ham** (ĭng'grȧ·hăm; -hăm; ĭng'grăm), **Duncan Nathaniel**. 1802–1891. American naval officer; in command of U.S. ship *St. Louis* at Smyrna and by show of force obtained release of a Hungarian-American from Austrian imprisonment (1853). Resigned from U.S. navy (1861); entered Confederate service; commanded rams which tried to break Union blockade off Charleston (1863).

**Ingraham, Joseph Holt.** 1809–1860. American clergyman and novelist; wrote sensational fiction as a young man: *Lafitte* (2 vols., 1836), *Burton, or, The Sieges* (2 vols., 1838), *The Quadroone* (2 vols., 1841). Ordained priest in Protestant Episcopal Church (1852); wrote religious romances: *The Prince of the House of David* (1855), *The Pillar of Fire* (1859), *The Throne of David* (1860). His son **Prentiss** (1843–1904) was a soldier of fortune and writer of dime novels.

**In′gram** (ĭng′grăm), **Arthur Foley Winnington.** 1858–1946. Anglican prelate and writer; canon of St. Paul's Cathedral and bishop of Stepney (1897–1901); bishop of London (1901–39; retired). Leader in Oxford settlement movement and founder (1888) of Oxford House in London's East End.

**Ingram, Frances.** 1888– . Operatic contralto, b. Liverpool, Eng.; to U.S. (1897); joined Metropolitan Opera Company (1919), singing leads in *Carmen, Il Trovatore, Madame Butterfly, Aïda.*

**Ingram, John Kells.** 1823–1907. British man of letters. Professor of oratory (1852–66) and Greek (1866–77), librarian (1879–87), and vice-provost (1898–99), Trinity Coll., Dublin. Author of *History of Political Economy* (1888), *Outlines of the History of Religion* (1900), *Sonnets and other Poems* (1900), etc.

**In·gras′sia** (ĕng·gräs′syä) *or* **In·gras′sias** (ĕng·gräs′syäs), **Giovanni Filippo.** 1510–1580. Sicilian anatomist and physician.

**In′gres** (ăɴ′gr′), **Jean Auguste Dominique.** 1780–1867. French painter, b. Montauban. Studied under David and in Italy; studio in Paris (1824–34); director of Académie de France in Rome (1834); again in Paris (after 1841); recognized as a leader among the classicists. Best known as an historical painter.

**Ingunthis.** See under LEOVIGILD.

**Ini.** See INE.

**In′jal′bert′** (ăɴ′zhăl′bâr′), **Jean Antoine.** 1845–1933. French sculptor; among his works are *Christ en Croix, Monument de Molière, Le Maréchal Joffre* (a bust), *Titan.*

**In′man** (ĭn′măn), **Henry.** 1801–1846. American painter, b. Utica, N.Y. Apprenticed to John Wesley Jarvis, portrait painter, New York City (1816–23). Studio in New York (1823). Examples of his work: *Martin Van Buren, William C. Macready as William Tell* (now in Metropolitan Museum of Art, New York City), *Fitz-Green Halleck* (in New York Historical Society), *Mumble-the-Peg* (in Pennsylvania Academy of Art).

**Inman, Samuel Guy.** 1877–1965. American educator and writer, b. Trinity, Tex. B.A. (1904), M.A. (1923), Columbia. Teacher of international law, Columbia (1919–34); professor of international relations, U. of Hawaii (1936), U. of Pennsylvania (1937).

**In′nes** (ĭn′ĕs; -ĭs), **Arthur Donald.** 1863–1938. English historian.

**Innes, Cosmo.** 1798–1874. Scottish antiquary; professor of constitutional law, Edinburgh (1846–74). Published *Scotland in the Middle Ages* (1860), *Facsimiles of National Manuscripts of Scotland* (1867), etc.

**Innes, Robert Thorburn Axton.** 1861–1933. British astronomer in South Africa.

**In′ness** (ĭn′ĕs; -ĭs), **George.** 1825–1894. American landscape painter, b. near Newburgh, N.Y.; studios, New York City (c. 1845), Medfield, Mass. (1859–64), New York (1876–78) and Montclair, N.J. (from 1878); known as one of the last and most talented members of the Hudson River school. Examples of his work: *Mill-pond, Florida Pines, Threatening, Rainbow after a Storm* (now in Chicago Art Institute), *Peace and Plenty, Delaware Valley, Autumn Oaks, Spring Blossoms* (in Metropolitan Museum of Art, New York City), *September Afternoon, Georgia Pines, Niagara* (in National Gallery of Art, Washington, D.C.). His son **George** (1854–1926), b. in Paris, France, was also an artist; studied with his father (1870–74); his *Shepherd and Sheep* and *First Snow at Cragsmoor* are in Metropolitan Museum, N.Y.

**In′nit·zer** (ĭn′ĭt·sẽr), **Theodor.** 1875–1955. Roman Catholic prelate, b. in Bohemia; archbishop of Vienna (1932); cardinal (1933). At first publicly endorsed affirmative Roman Catholic vote in Austria prior to Anschluss plebiscite of 1938, but was compelled by the pope to issue partial retraction which was refused publication; later preached and wrote pastoral letters against Nazi regime and provoked demonstrations.

**In′no·cent** (ĭn′ō·sĕnt; -s′nt). Name of thirteen popes (see *Table of Popes,* Nos. 40, 164, 176, 180, 185, 199, 204, 215, 232, 238, 242, 244, 246) and one antipope, including:

**Innocent I,** Saint. d. 417. Pope (bishop of Rome; 402–417), b. Albano, Italy. During his pontificate, Rome was sacked (410) by Alaric.

**Innocent II.** *Real name* **Gregorio Pa′pa·re′schi** (pä′pä·rās′kē). d. 1143. Pope (1130–43), b. Rome. Irregularly elected by a minority; fled to France when Anacletus II was elected as antipope (1130); installed at Rome by Emperor Lothair (1133) but again forced to leave; fully recognized after death of Anacletus (1138).

**Innocent III.** *Real name* **Giovanni Lotario de′ Con′ti** (dā kōn′tē). 1161–1216. Pope (1198–1216), b. Anagni, Italy; son of Count Trasimund, a Roman noble; educ. Paris, Rome, and Bologna. Tried to continue policy of Gregory VII to make papacy supreme over the state; brought papal power to its highest point; urged Fourth Crusade (1202–04), which resulted in capture of Constantinople and establishment of the Latin Empire; promoted a crusade against the Albigenses (1208); supported Philip of Swabia against Otto IV in Germany (1207) and after Otto's election as emperor, excommunicated him (1210); asserted papal rights against King John of England in controversy over Stephen Langton (1206), placed England under an interdict (1208), deposed John (1212), and compelled his submission (1213); deposed Otto IV and crowned Frederick II of Sicily as emperor (1215); presided at fourth Lateran Council (1215).

**Innocent IV.** *Real name* **Sinibaldo de′ Fie′schi** (dā fyĕs′kē). d. 1254. Pope (1243–54), b. Genoa. Carried on continued struggle with Emperor Frederick II and, after his death (1250), with his sons Conrad IV and Manfred; just before his death, suffered severe defeat (1254) by Manfred at Foggia.

**Innocent VI.** *Real name* **Étienne Au′bert′** (ō′bâr′). d. 1362. Pope (1352–62), b. near Pompadour, Limoges. Resided at Avignon.

**Innocent VII.** *Real name* **Cosimo de′ Mi′glio·ra′ti** (dā mē′lyō·rä′tē). 1336?–1406. Pope (1404–06), b. Sulmona, Italy. Pope of the Western Schism; resided at Rome while Antipope Benedict XIII held court at Avignon.

**Innocent VIII.** *Real name* **Giovanni Battista Ci′bo** (chē′bō). 1432–1492. Pope (1484–92), b. Genoa. Declared Henry VII to be lawful king of England (1486); appointed (1487) Torquemada as grand inquisitor of Spain; made treaty (1489) with Sultan Bajazet II; deposed (1489) Ferdinand of Naples but later (1492) restored him; during his pontificate, Moors driven from Spain (1492).

**Innocent X.** *Real name* **Giovanni Battista Pam·fi'li** (päm·fē'lē). 1574–1655. Pope (1644–55), b. Rome. changed papal sympathies from France to Hapsburgs; aided in putting down insurrection in Naples and helped Venice against Turks; protested against Treaty of Westphalia (1648); condemned Jansenism (1653).

**Innocent XI.** *Real name* **Benedetto O'de·scal'chi** (ō'dā·skäl'kē). 1611–1689. Pope (1676–89), b. Como. Engaged in long struggle with Louis XIV; joined Holy League (1684) against Turks; approved League of Augsburg (1686).

**Innocent XII.** *Real name* **Antonio Pi'gna·tel'li** (pē'nyä·těl'lē). 1615–1700. Pope (1691–1700), b. Naples. Active in various church reforms; improved relations with France; his advice to Charles II of Spain as to Charles's successor brought on the War of the Spanish Succession.

**Innocent XIII.** *Real name* **Michelangelo Con'ti** (kōn'tē). 1655–1724. Pope (1721–24), b. Rome. Granted Naples (1722) to Emperor Charles VI; supported "James III" in Scotland as pretender.

*Antipope:* **Innocent III.** *Real name* **Lando de'i Fran'gi·pa'ni** (dā'ē frän'jē·pä'nē). Antipope (1179–80) in opposition to Alexander III.

**Innocenzo da Imola.** See FRANCUCCI.

**İ·nö·nü'** (ĭ·nû·nü'), **İsmet.** *In early life known as* **İsmet Pa·şa'** (pä·shä'). 1884–1973. Turkish statesman, president of Turkey (1938–50); b. Smyrna; received military education; in World War fought in Palestine and against Russians in eastern Turkey; Kemal Atatürk's chief of staff in war against Greeks (1919–22); defeated Greeks twice at village of İnönü, which he adopted as his last name. First prime minister of new republic (1923–37); signed Treaty of Lausanne (1923); in large measure responsible for transformation of Turkey into modern state, introducing many reforms; on Atatürk's death (1938) unanimously elected president (1938); made several important treaties with object of keeping Turkey strongly neutral; visited by Winston Churchill (Jan., 1943); premier (1961–65).

**I·no·u·ye** (ē·nō·ōō·yě), **Junnosuke.** 1869–1932. Japanese banker and statesman; b. in Oita prefecture. Entered service of Bank of Japan (1885); its agent in London (1908–11); its governor (1924, 1927–28). Three times minister of finance (1924, 1929–30, 1931); stabilized Japan's currency and restored gold standard; murdered by hired assassin of reactionary militarist clique.

**I·no·u·ye** *or* **I·no·u·e** (ē·nō·ōō·yě), Marquis **Kaoru** *or* **Kaaru.** 1835–1915. Japanese statesman; a samurai of the Choshu fief. During disturbed period escaped to England (1863) with his friend Hirobumi Ito; sought unsuccessfully (1864) to prevent clash between Choshu clan and foreign war vessels; severely wounded by reactionary samurai. After Restoration (1868) made vice-minister of finance in new government (1870–73); held other important cabinet offices (1878–98), esp. minister for foreign affairs (1881–88); created count (1885), marquis (1907). Special commissioner to Korea (1895); one of five elder statesman of Meiji period; adviser to emperor during Russo-Japanese War (1904–05).

Marquis **Katsunosuke Inouye** (1861–1929), his nephew and adopted son and heir; financier and diplomat; educ. in Europe by Japanese government (seven years in England); envoy to Berlin (1906–08), to Chile (1910–13); ambassador to England (1913–16); succeeded to title (1915); director of South Manchurian Railway and advocate of open door in Manchuria.

**Inouye,** Viscount **Ryokei.** 1845–1929. Japanese admiral; educ. U.S.N.A., Annapolis (grad. 1881), one of earliest Japanese students there. Wounded in bombardment of Kagoshima by British squadron (1863); fought in Chinese-Japanese War (1894–95). Admiral of the fleet (1911–29); baron (1887); viscount (1907).

**Inskip,** Sir **Thomas.** See Viscount CALDECOTE.

**In'sull** (ĭn's'l), **Samuel.** 1859–1938. Public-utility magnate, b. London, Eng.; to U.S. (1881). Private secretary to Thomas A. Edison; on consolidation of Edison interests, became 2d vice-president of Edison General Electric Co. (1889) and, after the merger (1892), of General Electric Co. President, Chicago Edison Co. (1892), Commonwealth Electric Co. of Chicago (1898), Peoples' Gas Light, and Coke Co., Chicago, and various other companies. Overexpansion caused financial difficulties and three of his largest companies went into receivership (1932); he was indicted (1932), arrested (1934), tried (1934, 1935), and acquitted.

**Intrépide, l'.** See Joseph Marie DESSAIX.

**I·nu·kai** (ē·nōō·kī), **Ki Tsuyoshi.** 1855–1932. Japanese journalist and statesman; war correspondent for *Hochi-Shimbun* during Satsuma rebellion (1877) and later its editor (until 1890). Member (1890–1932) of first House of Representatives in Imperial Diet; prime minister (1931–32). Friend of Sun Yat-sen and advocate of peaceful policy toward China.

**I'on** (ī'ŏn). Greek poet of Chios in 5th century B.C.; settled in Athens at early age. Only fragments of his lyrics and tragedies are extant.

**Io·nes'co** (yô·něs'kō), **Eugene.** 1912– . French dramatist, b. Rumania. To Paris (1938); some of his plays are *The Bald Soprano, The Chairs,* etc.; also wrote short stories, essays and ballets.

**Io·ne'scu, Take.** 1858–1922. Rumanian statesman; founded Conservative-Democratic party (1908). Represented Rumania at the peace conference in Bucharest (1913). In World War I, favored Rumanian intervention on Allied side; after the war, represented Rumanian interests in Paris. Minister of foreign affairs in Averescu cabinet (1920); participated in formation of Little Entente; prime minister of Rumania (1921–22).

**Ionescu, Toma.** 1861–1926. Rumanian surgeon; known esp. for attempts to cure angina pectoris, and other diseases, by division of a sympathetic nerve.

**I'o·phon** (ī'ô·fŏn). Greek tragic author of 5th and early 4th centuries B.C.; son of Sophocles; only scattered fragments of his works are extant. According to tradition, he accused his father of insanity in order that he might gain control of his fortune; Sophocles proved his sanity by reciting to the judges the chorus from his *Oedipus at Colonus.*

**Ior'ga** (yŏr'gä), **Nicolae.** 1871–1940. Rumanian historian and politician; founder of Institute for the Study of Southeastern Europe (1914). Founder of National Democratic party (1910) and president, Chamber of Deputies (1919).

**Io'ris** *or* **Jo'ris** (yô'rēs), **Pio.** 1843–1921. Italian painter; known particularly for genre paintings and landscapes.

**I·pa'tieff** *or* **I·pa'tiev** (ĭ·pȧ'tyěf), **Vladimir Nikolaevich.** 1867–1952. Chemist, b. Moscow, Russia; to U.S. (1931); professor, Northwestern U. (1931–35). Authority on high-pressure catalytic reactions, many of which are important for industrial processes, esp. in the refining of petroleum and the synthesis of hydrocarbons; in charge of chemical work for Russian government during World War (1914–18); developed a polymerization process of making high-octane gasoline and a method of making olefins from alcohols; discovered new catalytic agents important in manufacture of fuels and dyes; first to point out action of chemical promoters.

**I·phic'ra·tes** (ī·fĭk'rȧ·tēz). d. 351? B.C. Athenian general; improved armor and discipline of Athenian troops.

Commanded peltasts in defeating Spartans near Corinth (392 or 390 B.C.) and in Thrace (389), and in relieving Corcyra (Corfu) when besieged by Sparta (373). Commanded fleet off Macedonian coast (369) and aided in keeping family of Amyntas on Macedonian throne.

**Ip·po·li′tov–I·va′nov** (ĭp·pŭ·lyē′tôf·ĭ·vȧ′nôf), **Mikhail Mikhailovich.** 1859–1935. Russian composer; made special study of Georgian folk songs. Composer of operas, a concert overture, a symphonic scherzo, choral works, cantatas, and songs. Known esp. for his orchestral suite, *Sketches from the Caucasus* (opus 12).

**Ip′sen** (ĭp′s'n), **Ernest Lud′vig** (lo͝oth′vĕg). 1869–1951. American portrait painter; among his portraits are those of Elihu Root, Dr. Henry van Dyke, Chief Justice William Howard Taft, Cass Gilbert, Gen. Robert E. Lee as superintendent of U.S.M.A., West Point.

**Iq·bal′** (ĭk·bäl′), **Ma·hom′ed** (mo͝o·hăm′mĕd). 1873–1938. Moslem poet and philosopher of India.

**I·ra′la** (ē·rä′lä), **Domingo Martínez de.** 1487–1557. Spanish conquistador; governor of the Spanish colonies on the Plata and Paraguay rivers (1537–42; 1544–57). First to open communications between Paraguay and Peru.

**Ire′dell** (īr′dĕl), **James.** 1751–1799. Jurist, b. Lewes, England; to America as comptroller of customs, Edenton, N.C. (1768); collector of the port (1774–76). Attorney general of North Carolina (1779–81). Member, Council of State (1787). In constitutional ratification convention, supported adoption of Constitution (1788). Associate justice, U.S. Supreme Court (1790–99). His son **James** (1788–1853), b. Edenton, N.C., was a jurist and politician; governor of North Carolina (1827–28); U.S. senator (1828–31).

**Ire′land** (īr′lănd), **John.** 1827–1896. American political leader; served in Confederate army through Civil War. Governor of Texas (1883–87).

**Ireland, John.** 1838–1918. Roman Catholic prelate, b. Burnchurch, County Kilkenny, Ireland; to U.S. (1849). Chaplain in Union army (1862–63). Rector of the cathedral, St. Paul (1867); bishop of St. Paul (1884); archbishop (1888). Influential in founding Catholic U., Washington, D.C. (1889).

**Ireland, John.** 1879–1962. English composer of orchestral works, piano music, and chorals, esp. songs; composer of about 70 songs to poems by Hardy, Symons, Masefield, Housman, and others.

**Ireland, Michael.** Pseudonym of Darrell FIGGIS.

**Ireland, William Henry.** 1777–1835. English forger of Shakespearean manuscripts, including a transcript of *King Lear* and extracts from *Hamlet*, and the pseudo-Shakespearean plays *Vortigern and Rowena* and *Henry II;* confessed the forgeries after their authenticity was challenged by Malone. Author also of original romances, ballads, and narrative verse.

**I′re·nae′us** (ī′rē·nē′ŭs), Saint. Christian prelate, a Father of the Greek Church. Apostle of the Gauls; bishop of Lyon (177); reputed to have been martyred under Emperor Septimius Severus.

**I·re′ne** (ī·rē′nē). Name of three empresses of the Eastern Roman Empire:

**Irene.** 752–803. Athenian by birth; married Leo IV (769); on his death (780) became regent during minority of their son Constantine VI; re-established image worship; summoned Second Nicene Council (787) which defined veneration due to images; abdicated (790) as Constantine took power; title of empress confirmed (792); plotted continuously for return to power (792–797); arrested and imprisoned Constantine (797); became sole ruler (797–802); finally turned against by patricians; dethroned (802) and exiled to Lesbos.

**Irene Du′cas** (dū′kăs). 1066?–?1120. Wife of Alexius I Comnenus; with her daughter Anna Comnena (*q.v.*), plotted against her son John II Comnenus; retired to a nunnery.

**Irene.** d. 1161. First wife (m. 1146) of Emperor Manuel I Comnenus, and sister-in-law of King Conrad III of Germany.

**I·rene′** (ī·rēn′), Sister. *Orig.* **Catherine Fitz·gib′bon** (fĭts·gĭb′ŭn). 1823–1896. Roman Catholic religious, b. London, Eng.; to U.S. as a child; joined community of Sisters of Charity (1850), taking name of (Mary) Irene; founder and director of the first foundling asylum in New York City (1869), later known as the Foundling Hospital.

**Ire′ton** (īr′t'n), **Henry.** 1611–1651. English Parliamentary commander and regicide; son-in-law of Oliver Cromwell. Commanded left-wing cavalry at Naseby, was wounded and captured, but escaped (1645). M.P. (1645 ff.); signed warrant for execution of Charles I. Second in command under Cromwell in Irish campaign (1649); captured Carlow, Waterford, and Duncannon (1650), and Limerick (1651).

**I·riar′te** (ē·ryär′tā), **Ignacio.** 1620–1685. Spanish landscape painter.

**I·riar′te** (*or* **Y·riar′te**) **y O′ro·pe′sa** (ē·ryär′tā ē ō′rō·pā′sä), **Tomás de.** 1750–1791. Spanish poet, b. in Canary Islands; educ. Madrid. Known esp. for *Fábulas Literarias* (1782); author also of didactic poem *La Música* (1779), comedies and numerous translations, as of Horace's *Ars Poetica.* His uncle **Juan de Iriarte** (1702–1771) was a scholar; educ. Paris; fellow-pupil of Voltaire; head librarian, Royal Library, Madrid (1732 ff.); known esp. for his catalog of Greek manuscripts of the Royal Library (vol. 1, 1769); works also include poems in Spanish and Latin, and a Greek paleography.

**I′ri·go′yen** (ē′rē·gō′yān), **Hipólito.** 1850–1933. Argentine lawyer, b. Buenos Aires, of Basque ancestry. Took part in revolution of 1890; leader of Radicals thereafter. President of Argentina (1916–22, 1928–30); forced out by Conservatives (1930).

**Ir·ne′ri·us** (ĭr·nēr′ĭ·ŭs) *or* **War·ne′ri·us** (wär·nēr′ĭ·ŭs) *or* **Guar·ne′ri·us** (gwär-). 1050?–?1130. Italian jurist, b. Bologna; reviver of Roman law in Middle Ages; authority on Justinian Code; author of *Summa Codicis,* first systematic treatise on Roman law, and prob. of *Authentica,* an epitome of Justinian's *Novellae.*

**Iron, Ralph.** Pseudonym of Olive SCHREINER.

**Ironquill.** Pseudonym of Eugene Fitch WARE.

**I′ron·side′** (ī′ērn·sīd′), **William Edmund.** 1st baron of **Archangel and Ironside.** 1880–1959. Brit. army officer, b. Aberdeen. Served in Boer War (1899–1900) and World War (1914–18); commanded Allied forces at Archangel (1918). Commanded mixed contingent at Constantinople (1919) and extricated it from attack; commanded Allied contingent in north Persia (1920) and managed withdrawal before Bolshevik attack. Commanded British army in India (1926), and Middle Eastern forces (1936); governor general of Gibraltar (1938). Chief of imperial general staff (1939–40); commander of Home Defense forces (1940); field marshal (1940).

**Ir′ving** (ûr′vĭng), **Edward.** 1792–1834. Scottish clergyman; to London (1822) as minister at Hatton Garden Chapel; built new church in Regent Square; acquired fame as preacher. Compelled to retire from Regent Square church because of his acceptance of pentecostal phenomena (1832); condemned by presbytery of Annan on charge of heresy (1833). His followers, known as Irvingites, assumed title of Holy Catholic Apostolic Church.

**Irving,** Sir **Henry.** *Orig. name* **John Henry Brod′ribb**

(brŏd′rĭb). 1838–1905. English actor, b. near Glastonbury. On stage in Edinburgh (1857–59) and Manchester (1860–65). Scored first notable success as Digby Grant in Albery's *Two Roses* on London stage (1870), followed by successes as Hamlet (1874), Macbeth (1875), Othello (1876). Lessee and manager of Lyceum Theater, London (1878); professionally associated with Ellen Terry 22 years (1878–1902); acted with her in *Hamlet, Merchant of Venice, Romeo and Juliet, Much Ado About Nothing, Twelfth Night, King Lear,* etc.; triumphed in Tennyson's *Becket* (1893). Made eight American tours (first, 1883–84; last, 1903–04). Knighted (1895), first actor to be so honored; buried in Westminster Abbey. His son **Lawrence Irving,** *orig.* **Sydney Brodribb** (1872–1914), was also an actor and theater manager.

**Irving, Isabel.** 1871–1944. American actress, b. Bridgeport, Conn.; m. William H. Thompson (1899). Member of Augustin Daly's company (1888–94); later, leading woman in company with John Drew, and star with James K. Hackett. Played comedy role in *Smith* with John Drew, and title role in *The Mollusc* with Kyrle Bellew. Costarred with Tom Wise and Constance Collier in *The Merry Wives of Windsor.*

**Irving, Pierre Munro.** See under Washington IRVING.

**Irving, Roland Duer.** 1847–1888. Nephew of Washington Irving. American geologist, b. New York City. Professor, U. of Wisconsin (from 1870). For U.S. Geological Survey, investigated geology of Lake Superior region (from 1880). His son **John Duer** (1874–1918), b. Madison, Wis., was also a geologist; on staff, U.S. Geological Survey (1899–1907); professor, Yale (from 1907).

**Irving, Washington.** *Pseudonyms* **Geoffrey Cray′on** (krā′ŏn), **Jonathan Old′style′** (ōld′stīl′), **Launcelot Wag′staffe** (wăg′stȧf), Friar **Antonio A′ga·pi′da** (ä′gä·pē′thä). 1783–1859. American author, b. New York City. Studied law; adm. to bar. In Europe on trip for health (1804–06). Leading figure in group that published *Salmagundi* (1807–08), a series of whimsical essays somewhat in style of Addison's *Spectator,* in which the name Gotham was first applied to New York City. Established reputation with humorous and genially satirical *History of New York...by Diedrich Knickerbocker* (1809). To Liverpool, representing his brothers' firm of P. and E. Irving (1815); when firm failed (1818), turned seriously to writing to bring in money. Remained in England; under pseudonym Geoffrey Crayon wrote the essays that appeared in *The Sketch Book* (1820); published *Bracebridge Hall* (1822). Traveled in Germany and France (1822–25). On staff of U.S. embassy, Madrid (1826–29); published *History of...Christopher Columbus* (1828) and *A Chronicle of the Conquest of Granada* (1829). Secretary of U.S. legation, London (1829–32); to U.S. (1832). Published *Alhambra* (1832). U.S. minister to Spain (1842–46). To U.S. (1846); resided at "Sunnyside," country home near Tarrytown, N.Y. Published *Oliver Goldsmith* (1849); *Mahomet and His Successors* (2 vols., 1849–50); *Life of Washington* (5 vols., 1855–59). Among his best-known short stories are *The Legend of Sleepy Hollow* introducing Ichabod Crane, and *Rip Van Winkle.* Elected to American Hall of Fame (1900). His brother **William** (1766–1821) was a merchant and politician; member, U.S. House of Representatives (1814–19); contributor of light satirical verse to *Salmagundi* (1807–08). William's son **Pierre Munro** (1803–1876) was author of *Life and Letters of Washington Irving* (4 vols., 1862–64), and collaborator in Washington Irving's *Astoria* (1836).

**Ir′win** (ûr′wĭn), Baron. See Earl of HALIFAX.

**Irwin, George Le Roy.** 1868–1931. American army officer; served in Philippines (1899–1901), in Cuba (1906–09), in Mexico (1914). Brigadier general, National army (1917); served in France (1918–19). Major general (1928).

**Irwin, May.** *Real name* **Ada Campbell.** 1862–1938. Actress, b. at Whitby, Ontario, Can.; m. Frederick W. Keller (1878; d. 1886), Kurt Eisfeldt (1907). Member of Tony Pastor's company (1877–83) and Augustin Daly's company (1883–87). Excelled in farce comedy.

**Irwin, Wallace.** 1875–1959. American journalist and humorist, b. Oneida, N.Y.; educ. Stanford (1896–99). On staff of San Francisco *Examiner* (1900), *Overland Monthly Magazine* (1902), New York *Globe* (1904–05), *Collier's Weekly* (1906–07). Author of *The Love Sonnets of a Hoodlum* (1902), *The Rubaiyat of Omar Khayyam, Jr.* (1902), *Chinatown Ballads* (1905), *Letters of a Japanese Schoolboy* (1909), *Mr. Togo, Maid of All Work* (1913), *Suffering Husbands* (1920), *Lew Tyler and the Ladies* (1928), *Young Wife* (1936), etc.

**Irwin, Will,** *in full* **William Henry.** 1873–1948. American journalist and writer, b. Oneida, N.Y. A.B., Stanford (1899). On staff of San Francisco *Wave* (1899–1900), San Francisco *Chronicle* (1901–04), New York *Sun* (1904–06), *McClure's Magazine* (1906–07), *Collier's Weekly* (1907–08); war correspondent for *Saturday Evening Post* (1916–18). Author of *The Hamadryads* (verse; 1904), *The City That Was* (1907), *The Confessions of a Con Man* (1909), *The House of Mystery* (1910), *Men, Women, and War* (1915), *The Thirteenth Chair* (a play, with Bayard Veiller, 1916), *Christ or Mars* (1923), *Highlights of Manhattan* (1927), *Propaganda and the News* (1936), etc. His wife (m. 1916), **Inez,** *nee* **Haynes** [hānz] (1873–1970), b. Rio de Janeiro, m. 1st Rufus Hamilton Gillmore (1897); writer of fiction, including *June Jeopardy* (1908), *Angel Island* (1914), *The Native Sons* (1919), *Confessions of a Business Man's Wife* (1931), *Strange Harvest* (1934), *Good Manners for Girls* (1937); awarded O. Henry memorial prize for best short story (1924).

**I′saac** (ī′zȧk; ī′zĭk). In Bible, son of Abraham by his wife Sarah in her old age (*Genesis* xxi. 1–5); father of Jacob and Esau (*Genesis* xxv. 20 ff.).

**Isaac.** Name of two rulers of the Eastern Roman Empire: **Isaac I Com·ne′nus** [kŏm·nē′nŭs] (d. 1061); son of Manuel Comnenus (see COMNENUS); emperor (1057–59), first of the Comneni; deposed Michael VI; found empire in bad condition; instituted reforms; repelled Hungarians (1059); abdicated because of severe illness; author of several works on Homer. **Isaac II An′ge·lus** [ăn′jĕ·lŭs] (d. 1204); emperor (1185–95 and 1203–04), first of the Angeli; raised to throne by a revolution; suffered military disasters (1190); dethroned and blinded by his brother Alexius III (1195); restored by crusaders who took Constantinople (1203) but again deposed by Alexius V Ducas.

**Isaac Na·than ben Ka·lon′y·mus** (nā′thăn [-th'n] bĕn kă·lŏn′ĭ·mŭs). French rabbi and philosopher; compiler (1437–47) of the first Bible concordance in Hebrew, the *Meïr Netib* (first pub. at Venice, 1523, under name of Mordecai Nathan).

**Isaac of An′ti·och** (ăn′tĭ·ŏk). 5th-century theologian and poet; identified with the Syrian church, and abbot of a convent near Antioch; best known as reputed author of the poem of 2137 verses on a parrot said to have uttered the Trisagion in the streets of Antioch.

**I′saacs** (ī′zȧks; -zĭks), Sir **Isaac Alfred.** 1855–1948. Australian jurist and statesman, b. Melbourne. Attorney general of Australia (1905–06). Justice of high court of Australia (1906–30); chief justice of Australia (1930–31). Governor general of Australia (1931–36).

**I·saacs′** (ē·säks′; ē·sä′äks), **Jorge.** 1837–1895. Colombian writer, son of an English Jew; author of *Poesías* (1864) and the widely read novel *María* (1867).

**I'saacs** (ī'zȧks; ī'zĭks), **Rufus Daniel.** See Marquis of READING.

**Isaacs, Samuel My'er** (mī'ẽr). 1804–1878. Rabbi and journalist, b. Leeuwarden, the Netherlands; to U.S. (1839). Rabbi of New York congregation (from 1839); founder and editor, *Jewish Messenger* (1857–78); one of founders of Mt. Sinai Hospital, Hebrew Free School Association, United Hebrew Charities; leader among orthodox rabbis in America. His son **Abram Samuel** (1851–1920), b. New York City, was a Hebrew scholar; proprietor and editor, *Jewish Messenger* (1878–1903); professor of Hebrew, N.Y.U. (1886–94), and of German (1887–95); in graduate school, professor of German literature (1895–1906) and of Semitics (from 1906); wrote *A Modern Hebrew Poet...Moses Chaim Luzzatto* (1878) and *What is Judaism?* (1912).

**I'sa·ak** (ē'zä·äk; ē'zäk), **Hein'rich** (hīn'rĭk). *Also* **Isaac, Isac, Izac, Yzac, Yzaac.** 1450?–1517. Composer of the contrapuntal school, b. prob. in Flanders; pioneer in use of melody in the soprano. Lived in Florence (1480?–92) as music teacher in service of Lorenzo de' Medici, also in Rome, Innsbruck, Ferrara, in Vienna as court composer to Maximilian I (1497), and again in Florence (1514–17). Composed Masses, motets, part songs, melodies, etc.

**I'sa'beau'** (ē'zȧ'bō') *or* **Isabella** *or* **Elizabeth** of Bavaria. 1370–1435. Daughter of Stephen II, Duke of Bavaria; m. (1385) Charles VI, King of France; crowned (1389); after king became insane (1392), consorted with duke of Orléans until his death (1407). Sided sometimes with Armagnacs, sometimes with Burgundians. Later (1419–20) went over to the English; instigated the Treaty of Troyes (1420). Her daughter Catherine married Henry V of England (1420).

**Is'a·bel** (ĭz'ȧ·bĕl; *Span.* ē'sä·bĕl'). Spanish form of ISABELLA and ELIZABETH.

**Isabel** *or* **Elizabeth,** Saint. *Also known as* **Elizabeth** (*or* **Isabel**) **of Ar'a·gon** (ăr'ȧ·gŏn). 1271–1336. Queen of Portugal; daughter of Pedro III of Aragon; m. (1283) Diniz, King of Portugal. Lived apart from dissolute court life; on death of king (1325) took habit of Order of St. Francis; died in convent at Coimbra which she had founded; beatified (1516) by Pope Leo X; canonized (1625) by Urban VIII. Called "the Peacemaker."

**Is'a·bel'la** (ĭz'ȧ·bĕl'ȧ; *Ger.* ē'zä·bĕl'ä). 1214–1241. German empress; wife of Frederick II (m. 1235); second daughter of King John of England. Her daughter Margaret (1237–70) married Albert of Thuringia and was thus ancestress of house of Saxe-Coburg-Gotha.

**Is'a·bel'la** (ĭz'ȧ·bĕl'ȧ). *Fr.* **I'sa'belle'** (*or* **I'sa'beau'**) **de Lor'raine'** (ē'zȧ'bĕl' [ē'zȧ'bō'] dẽ lô'rân'). 1410?–1453. Daughter of Charles (II) the Bold, of Lorraine; m. (1420) René of Anjou; queen of Two Sicilies (1439–42) and duchess of Anjou and Lorraine. Her daughter Margaret married Henry VI of England.

**Isabella I.** *Span.* **Isabel.** *Called* **la Ca·tó'li·ca** (lä kä·tō'lē·kä), *i.e.* the Catholic. 1451–1504. Daughter of John II. Queen of Castile (1474–1504); m. Ferdinand II of Aragon (1469); joint sovereign with him as Ferdinand V of Castile and Aragon (1479–1504); gave much aid to Columbus. See FERDINAND V of Castile.

**Isabella II.** *Span.* **Isabel.** *In full* **Ma·ri'a Isabella Lou·i'sa** (mȧ·rē'ȧ, lōō·ē'zȧ). 1830–1904. Daughter of Ferdinand VII and Maria Christina, b. in Madrid. Queen of Spain (1833–68). Became heiress apparent by decree of the Cortes (1830) setting aside Salic law; became queen (1833) on death of her father, with her mother as queen regent; civil war waged by Don Carlos, her uncle (1833–39), resulted in court triumph, followed by reactionary policy against religious orders and the church; queen regent resigned (1840) in favor of Gen. Espartero, who was overthrown (1843) by an insurrection; declared of age by the Cortes (1843); last 25 years of reign (1843–68) a period of continuous strife, political intrigues, attempted insurrections, frequent changes in ministries (Espartero, O'Donnell, Narváez, etc.); m. (1846) her cousin Don Francisco de Asís; overthrown by revolution (1868) headed by Serrano, Prim y Prats, and Topete y Carballo; fled to Paris; abdicated in favor of her son Alfonso XII (1870). See AMADEUS.

**Isabella of An'gou'lême'** (äN'gōō'lâm'). d. 1246. Queen of England, wife of John (m. 1200); daughter of Aymer, Count of Angoulême; mother of Henry III (b. 1207). Imprisoned by John in Gloucester (1214–16); returned to France (1217); m. Hugh (1220), Count of La Marche.

**Isabella of Austria.** 1566–1633. See under ALBERT, Archduke of Austria.

**Isabella of Brazil.** *Port.* **I·sa·bel'** (ē·zȧ·bĕl'). 1846–1921. Brazilian princess, eldest daughter of Emperor Dom Pedro II; b. Rio de Janeiro; m. (1864) Louis Gaston d'Orléans, Comte d'Eu; heir apparent during long period of father's reign; served as regent three times during her father's absence from Brazil (1871–72, 1876–77, 1886–89); during last regency decreed emancipation of slaves without compensation, which contributed to revolution (1889); driven into exile.

**Isabella of France.** Name of two queens of England.
(1) 1292–1358. Daughter of Philip IV of France; m. (1308) Edward II, who treated her with great unkindess; driven to France; raised army with Roger de Mortimer, Earl of March, and formed plot to invade England; landed with army at Harwich (1326) and terminated successful invasion by deposition of Edward (1327); ruled with Mortimer (1327–30) as coregent for her son Edward III; arrested with Mortimer (1330) by Edward III and Henry of Lancaster; lived thereafter in semiretirement.
(2) 1389–1409. Second queen of Richard II (m. 1396); second daughter of Charles VI of France; after Richard's death returned to France (1401); m. the poet Charles d'Orléans, Count of Angoulême.

**Isabella of Hai'naut'** (ĕ'nō'). 1170–1190. First queen of France; wife of Philip Augustus (m. 1180); daughter of Baldwin V, Count of Hainaut; brought to king as dowry the province of Artois; mother of Louis VIII.

**Isabella of Portugal.** 1397–1471. Daughter of John I; m. Philip the Good of Burgundy; Order of the Golden Fleece founded (1429) in honor of the wedding; mother of Charles the Bold; noted for her beauty.

**Isabella of Portugal.** 1503–1539. Wife (m. 1525) and cousin of Holy Roman Emperor Charles V; b. Lisbon; daughter of Emanuel, King of Portugal; mother of Philip II of Spain.

**I'sa'bey'** (ē'zȧ'bā'), **Jean Baptiste.** 1767–1855. French painter of miniatures. His son **Eugène Louis Gabriel** (1804–1886) was also a painter; best known for his marines.

**I·sae'us** (ī·sē'ŭs; -zē'-). Athenian orator and rhetorician of 4th century B.C.; composer esp. of speeches which his clients memorized and delivered in law courts; at one time had Demosthenes as a client. Eleven of his orations have been preserved.

**I·sag'o·ras** (ī·săg'ō·rȧs). Athenian politician; first archon (508 B.C.); on resistance of Cleisthenes and mass of people to his administration, asked help from Spartans, who occupied city; banished 700 families and tried to replace democratic Five Hundred by aristocratic

Three Hundred; fled into exile when Athenians successfully revolted.

**Isai.** See JESSE.

**I·sa'iah** (ī·zā'yȧ; -zī'ȧ). *In Douay Bible* **I·sa'ias** (ī·zā'yȧs; -zī'ȧs). *In A. V. of New Testament* **E·sa'ias** (ē-). One of the major Hebrew prophets; ministered in kingdom of Judah (c. 740–701 B.C.), attacking corrupt national life. The Old Testament book of *Isaiah* contains discourses on the state of Judah and Israel, oracles, a historical passage on the reign of Hezekiah, and (chapters xl ff.) later prophecies. Some authorities regard these last (chapters xl–lxvi or xl–lv) as postexilic writings, the work of another author referred to as *Deutero-Isaiah*, or *Second Isaiah.*

**I·sau'ri·an** (ī·sô'rĭ·ăn). Name given to a dynasty (717–802) of rulers of the Eastern Roman Empire, derived from Isauria, the region in southern Asia Minor whence its founder, Leo III (reigned 717–741), came. Other members were: Constantine V, Leo IV, Constantine VI, and Irene. Zeno (reigned 474–491) was also a native of Isauria.

**Iscanus, Josephus.** See JOSEPH OF EXETER.

**Iscariot.** See JUDAS (ISCARIOT).

**Isdigird.** See YAZDEGERD.

**I'se·lin'** (ēz'lăN'), **Henri Frédéric.** 1826–1905. French sculptor; best known for his portrait busts.

**I'se·lin** (ē'zĕ·lĭn), **Isaak.** 1728–1782. Swiss philosophical writer in Basel; champion of reform in morals, education, and legislation.

**Iselin, Jakob Christoph.** 1681–1737. Swiss theologian and philologist.

**I'sham** (ī'shăm), **Samuel.** 1855–1914. American painter and writer.

**Ish'er·wood** (ĭsh'ẽr·wo͝od), **Benjamin Franklin.** 1822–1915. American naval engineer; responsible for design and building of engines for expansion of U.S. navy during Civil War. Isherwood Hall, at U.S. Naval Academy, Annapolis, is named in his honor.

**Isherwood, Christopher William Brad'shaw-** (brăd'-shô-). 1904– . English playwright and fiction writer; collaborator with W. H. Auden in the plays *The Dog Beneath the Skin* (1935), *Ascent of F. 6* (1936), *On the Frontier* (1938), and in the travel book *Journey to a War* (1939); wrote independently the stories *All the Conspirators* (1928), *Mr. Norris Changes Trains* (1935), *Goodbye to Berlin* (1939), etc.

**Isherwood,** Sir **Joseph William.** 1870–1937. British shipwright.

**I·shi·ha·ra** (ē·shē·hä·rä), **Kanji.** 1889–1949. Japanese general; urged extension of Japanese military strength northward, esp. into Inner Mongolia.

**I·shi·i** (ē·shē·ē), Viscount **Kikujiro.** 1866-1945. Japanese diplomat; educ. for law, Tokyo U. Attaché at legation in Paris (1890–96); consul in Korea (1896–1900); secretary of legation at Peking (1900) during Boxer Rebellion; director of commerce bureau (1904–07); investigated anti-Japanese riots in California and British Columbia (1907). Ambassador to France (1912–15); minister of foreign affairs (1915–16); created viscount (1916). As special envoy to U.S., signed "Gentlemen's Agreement," also known as Lansing-Ishii Agreement, with reference to Japanese immigration into U.S. (1917); again ambassador to France (1920–27); president of council and assembly of League of Nations (1923, 1926); retired (1927).

**Ish'ma·el** (ĭsh'mā·ĕl). *In Douay Version* **Is'ma·el** (ĭs'mā·ĕl). In Bible, Abraham's son by his concubine Hagar (*q.v.*). From him Mohammed claimed descent.

**Is'i·dore of Cha'rax** (ĭz'ĭ·dōr kā'răks). 1st-century Greek geographer; author of *Parthian Stations.*

**Isidore of Se·ville'** (sĕ·vĭl'; sĕv''l, -ĭl), Saint. *Lat.* **Is'i·do'rus His'pa·len'sis** (ĭz'ĭ·dō'rŭs hĭs'pȧ·lĕn'sĭs). 560?–636. Spanish prelate and scholar; archbishop of Seville (600); considered most learned man of his time; a father of the Western Church; known particularly for his vast medieval encyclopedia *Originum seu Etymologiarum Libri XX* (known in Eng. as *Etymologies*).

**Is'i·do'rus** (ĭz'ĭ·dō'rŭs). 370?–?440. Abbot of the monastery at Pelusium; best known for his *Letters* expounding and interpreting the Scriptures.

**Isidorus of Mi·le'tus** (mī·lē'tŭs; mĭ-). Byzantine architect of 6th century A.D.; collaborated with Anthemius of Tralles (Aydin) in designing Church of Saint Sophia in Constantinople.

**I'sin** (ē'sĕn). Fourth dynasty of Babylonian kings, of Semitic race (towards end of 3d millenium B.C.), comprising eleven kings, including Nebuchadnezzar I; its rule centered about the city of Nippur.

**Is·kan·der'** (ĭs·kän·dẽr'). Turkish form of ALEXANDER; esp. = ALEXANDER THE GREAT.

**Iskander.** See Aleksandr HERZEN.

**Iskender Bey.** See SCANDERBEG.

**Is'la** (ēs'lä), **José Francisco de.** 1703–1781. Spanish Jesuit and satirist; known esp. for his satire on bombastic pulpit oratory *Historia del Famoso Predicador Fray Gerundio de Campazas alias Zotes* (1758; banned by Inquisition, 1760).

**Islebius,** Magister. See Johannes AGRICOLA.

**Is'lip** (ĭz'lĭp), **Simon.** d. 1366. English prelate; archbishop of Canterbury (1349–66). His nephew **William Whit'tle·sey** ([h]wĭt''l·sĭ) *or* **Wit'tle·sey** (d. 1374) was also archbishop of Canterbury (1368–74).

**Ismael.** See ISHMAEL.

**Is·ma'il'** (ĭs·mä'ēl'). *Arab.* **Ismā'īl.** d. 760. Son of sixth imam, Jafar al-Sadiq. Designated as successor by his father; died five years before Jafar, but his followers proclaimed him the hidden Mahdi and formed Shiite sect of Ismailians, who claimed imamate and who by developing an effective religio-political doctrine threatened the caliphate and gave rise to other powerful sects, as the Karmathians and Fatimids.

**Is'ma·il'** (ĭs'mȧ·ēl'). Name of two kings (shahs) of Persia of the Safawid dynasty:

**Ismail I.** 1486–1524. Founder of the dynasty; king (1500–24). Regarded by subjects as both saint and shah; enlarged Persian dominions by conquests (1501–09); defeated Uzbegs (1510); overwhelmed in battle (1514) of Chaldiran, near Tabriz, by Sultan Selim I; lost Azerbaijan and Kurdistan. Father of Tahmasp I.

**Ismail II.** 1551–1577. King (1576–77). Son of Tahmasp I.

**Is·ma'il' Pa'sha** (ĭs·mä'ēl' pȧ'shä) *or* **Ismail I.** 1830–1895. Khedive of Egypt (1863–79), b. Cairo. Son of Ibrahim Pasha and father of Tewfik Pasha, Hussein Kamil, and Fuad I (*qq.v.*). Proclaimed viceroy (1863) on death of uncle Said Pasha. Received title of khedive (1867) from sultan of Turkey and established succession in his line; rebuilt Cairo and improved Alexandria; encouraged Suez Canal project as advantageous to Egypt; annexed Darfur (1874); becoming involved financially, sold his canal shares to Great Britain (1875); forced by Great Powers to abdicate (1879) in favor of son Tewfik Pasha.

**Is'ma·il'Pa·sha'** (ĭs'mä·ĭl' pä·shä'). See György KMETY.

**İsmet Paşa.** See İsmet İNÖNÜ.

**Is'nard'** (ēs'når'), **Maximin.** 1755–1825. French Girondist member of the Legislative Assembly (1791), the National Convention (1792), the Council of Five Hundred (1795); loyally supported Napoleon and, later, Louis XVIII.

**I·soc'ra·tes** (ī·sŏk'rȧ·tēz). 436–338 B.C. Athenian orator and rhetorician; founder (392 B.C.) and head of school in Athens; pupils included Ephorus, Theopompus of Chios, Isaeus, Lycurgus, and Hyperides (*qq.v.*).

**I'souard'** (ē'zwȧr'), **Nicolas.** *Known professionally as* **Nic'co·lò'** (nēk'kô·lô'). 1775–1818. Franco-Italian pianist and composer of masses, cantatas, motets, vocal pieces, and 33 operas.

**Is'ra·el** (ĭz'rā·ĕl; -rĭ·ĕl). In Bible = JACOB; so called after he wrestled with the angel (*Genesis* xxxii. 24 ff.).

**Israel ben Eliezer.** See BAAL SHEM-TOB.

**Is'ra·els** (ĭz'rȧ·ĕls), **Jozef.** 1824–1911. Dutch genre painter, b. in Groningen of Jewish parentage. His paintings are chiefly scenes from humble life, esp. of fisherfolk; also produced portraits, water colors, historical pictures, and etchings.

**Is'sa·char** (ĭs'ȧ·kär). In Bible, Jacob's ninth son (*Genesis* xxx. 14–18), ancestor of one of the twelve tribes of Israel.

**Is·takh'ri, al–** (ăl'ĭs·tăk'rĭ). fl. 950. Arab geographer.

**Is'tel** (ĭs'tĕl), **Edgar.** 1880–1948. Ger. composer and writer; in Madrid (1920–36), and U.S. (from 1938).

**I·stra'ti** (ē·strä'tē), **Panait.** 1884–1935. Rumanian novelist writing in French.

**Istria, Dora d'.** See DORA D'ISTRIA.

**Is·tú'riz** (ēs·tōō'rēth), **Francisco Javier de.** 1790–1871. Spanish statesman, b. Cádiz; a leader in revolution of 1820. President of the Cortes (1823); exiled to London (to 1834); premier and minister of foreign affairs (1836); exiled to Portugal (1836–37); president of the Cortes (1838 ff.); premier (1846); ambassador to London (1850–54), St. Petersburg (1856), and Paris (1863–64).

**István.** Hungarian form of STEPHEN.

**I·syl'lus** (ī·sĭl'ŭs). Greek poet of 4th century B.C. (or later).

**I·ta·ga·ki** (ē·tä·gä·kē), **Seishiro.** 1885–1948. Japanese general; minister of war (1938–39); hanged as war criminal.

**Itagaki,** Count **Taisuke.** 1837–1919. Japanese statesman of samurai class. Aided in overthrow of feudalism, supporting emperor against shogun; active in civil war of 1868. As a liberal, favored representative government; privy councilor of the empire (1871–73); organized (1881) first political party (Liberals) and was its leader (to 1900); retired (1900).

**Italicus, Tiberius Catius Silius.** See SILIUS ITALICUS.

**Ito** (ē·tō), Marquis **Hirobumi.** 1841–1909. Japanese statesman, b. in Choshu province. Made early visit to Europe as student; strong supporter of Western ideas; visited U.S. (1871) and reported a system of coinage for Japan; minister of interior (1878–82); four times premier (1886–1901); active in effecting economic reforms; with Saionji prepared new constitution (1888–89). Created marquis (1895) after successful conduct of Chinese-Japanese War (1894–95); special adviser to emperor during Russo-Japanese War (1904–05); sent to Korea (1904) and to Manchuria (1909); assassinated by a Korean at Harbin.

**Ito, Yuko** *or* **Sukenori.** 1843–1914. Japanese admiral; rear admiral (1886); vice-admiral (1892). As commander in chief in Chinese-Japanese War, won battle of the Yalu (1894); chief of naval general staff (1895–1905) through Russo-Japanese War; created count (1907).

**It'ten** (ĭt'ĕn), **Johannes.** 1888–1967. Swiss painter and sculptor; identified with ultramodern school of art.

**I·tur'bi** (ē·tōōr'bē), **José.** 1895– . Spanish pianist and conductor, b. in Valencia; to U.S. (1929) on concert tour; took up residence in U.S.; musical director, Rochester Philharmonic Orchestra.

**I'tur·bi'de** (ē'tōōr·bē'thā), **Agustín de.** 1783–1824. Mexican soldier and emperor, b. Morelia. Commanded Spanish army against Guerrero (1820); later joined Guerrero in setting up Plan of Iguala (1821); forced Spanish government to capitulate (Treaty of Córdoba, 1821), assuring Mexican independence. Head of provisional government; emperor, as Agustín I (1822–23); his harsh measures of repression led to revolution (by Santa Anna, Guerrero, etc.), abdicated (Mar. 19, 1823); exile in Europe. Returned, and was captured and shot (July 19, 1824).

**Itz·co'atl** (ĭsh·kō'ä·t'l) *or* **Iz·co'huatl** (ĭsh·kō'wä·t'l). 1360?–?1440. First emperor of the Aztecs (1427–?40); made Tenochtitlan (Mexico City) independent and the dominant power of the lake valley.

**Iu'ba** (yōō'bȧ), **Iu·gur'tha** (yŭ·gûr'thȧ), **Iul'ius** (yōōl'yŭs), etc. Variants of the Latin names JUBA, JUGURTHA, JULIUS, etc.

**Iu·va'ra** (yōō·vä'rä) *or* **I·va'ra** (ē·vä'rä), **Filippo.** 1676?–1736. Italian architect, b. Messina; chief architect to king (at Turin).

**I·van'** (ĭ·vän'). Name of several grand dukes and czars of Russia.

**Ivan I.** *Called* **Ivan Ka·li·ta'** (kŭ·lyĭ·tä'), *i.e.* "Moneybag." d. 1341. Prince of Vladimir; grand prince or duke of Moscow (1328–41). Vassal of Tatars; made collector of taxes by Tatar Khan; extended boundaries of domain and increased importance of Moscow, laying foundation of Muscovite kingdom; caused metropolitan see to be transferred to Moscow.

**Ivan II.** *Called* **Ivan Kras'ny** (kräs'nû·ĭ), *i.e.* "the Red." 1326–1359. Grand prince or duke (1353–59). Son of Ivan I; father of Demetrius Donskoi.

**Ivan III Vasilievich.** *Called* **Ivan the Great.** 1440–1505. Grand duke (1462–1505); son of Basil II. Continued policy of former rulers to strengthen leadership of Moscow; conquered Novgorod (1471–78) and annexed it; threw off yoke of Tatars (1480); gained further territory by conquest or by voluntary allegiance of princes; m. (1472) Sophia (Zoë), niece of last Byzantine emperor; this marriage important in establishing claim of Russian rulers as protectors of Orthodox Christianity; added two-headed eagle of Byzantine empire to arms of Muscovy; through his wife received new ideas and customs in imperial court; twice invaded (1492, 1501) Lithuania and acquired part of it by treaty (1503).

**Ivan IV Vasilievich.** *Called* **Ivan the Terrible.** 1530–1584. Ruler (1533–84). Son of Basil III and grandson of Ivan III. Ruled under regency of mother (1533–38) and then of powerful boyars (1538–44); assumed control (1544) and (1547) had himself crowned czar, first Russian ruler to use the title formally; m. (1547) Anastasia Romanovna (see ROMANOV); formed advisory Council of Boyars (1547); convoked (1550) first national assembly (*Zemski Sobor*); conquered Kazan and Astrakhan (1552–56); began long war (1557–82) over Livonia, at first successful but later defeated by Poland and Sweden; driven partially mad by death of wife and son (Dmitri) and other causes; ravaged Novgorod (1570); defeated by Swedes (1578) and lost Polotsk (1579); beaten in Livonia by Stephen Báthory (1581); acquired Siberia (1581) through conquest by Cossacks under Ermak Timofeev; in a fit of anger killed his son Ivan (1580).

**Ivan V.** 1666–1696. Romanov czar (1682–89). Son of Czar Alexis I. Physically and mentally weak; affairs administered by his half sister Sophia; associated in rule by Peter, son of Alexis' second wife; deposed (1689) when Sophia was overthrown. Father of Anna Ivanovna (empress 1730–40).

**Ivan VI.** 1740–1764. Czar or emperor (1740–41). Son of Anna Leopoldovna (*q.v.*) and Anthony Ulrich and great-grandson of Ivan V; although only eight weeks old on death of Anna Ivanovna, proclaimed emperor under regency of Biron (*q.v.*); forced to abdicate soon after Biron's overthrow; succeeded by Elizabeth; kept in prison for rest of life (1742–64).

**I·va′nov** (ĭ·vȧ′nôf), **Aleksandr Andreevich.** 1806–1858. Russian painter.

**Ivanov, Nikolai Yudovich.** 1851–1918. Russian general; fought in Russo-Japanese War (1905); commander of 3d army (1914) and on southwest front (1915–16); led army against revolutionists (1918).

**Ivanov, Vyacheslav Ivanovich.** 1866–1949. Russian poet, b. Moscow. Published first volume of poems, *Guiding Stars* (1903); also wrote critical essays and tragedies, and as philologist had considerable influence in molding modern Russian language.

**Ivara, Filippo.** See Filippo IUVARA.

**Iveagh,** Earls of. See under GUINNESS family.

**Ives** (īvz), **Charles Edward.** 1874–1954. American composer, b. Danbury, Conn.; in insurance business in New York (1898 ff.); composer of orchestral, choral, and chamber music, and many songs; known for his use of polytonal harmonies and unusual rhythms.

**Ives, Chauncey Bradley.** 1810–1894. American sculptor, b. Hamden, Conn.; resident in Italy (from 1844).

**Ives, Frederick Eugene.** 1856–1937. American inventor, b. Litchfield, Conn.; credited with invention of the half-tone photoengraving process now universally used (1886); pioneered in color photography, making the first trichromatic half-tone process printing plates (1881) and developing a process for motion pictures in natural colors (1914); invented half-tone photogravure process (anticipating rotogravure), the short-tube single-objective binocular microscope, and the photochromoscope. His son **Herbert Eugene** (1882–1953), physicist; with Bell Telephone Laboratories (from 1919); authority on illuminating engineering; instrumental in the development of television and transmission of pictures by wire.

**Ives, James Merritt.** 1824–1895. American lithographer, b. New York City; partner (from 1857) in firm of Currier & Ives. See Nathaniel CURRIER.

**Ives of Chartres** (ēv, shȧr′tr′; *Angl.* īvz, shär′tr′). = YVES DE CHARTRES.

**I′vo·gün** (ē′vô·gün), **Maria.** *Orig. name* **Irene von Gün′ther** (fôn gün′tẽr). 1891– . Operatic and concert coloratura soprano, b. Budapest; m. 1st (1921) the Munich tenor Karl Erb, 2d (1933) the pianist Michael Raucheisen.

**I′vo·ry** (ī′vô·rĭ), Sir **James.** 1765–1842. Scottish mathematician; author of *Theory of Astronomical Refractions* (1839), etc.

**I′vy** (ī′vĭ), **Andrew Conway.** 1893– . American physiologist; professor and head of department, Northwestern U. Medical School (from 1925); known esp. for work on the functions of the brain.

**I·wa·ku·ra** (ē·wä·kōō·rä), Prince **Tomomi.** 1835–1883. Japanese statesman, b. Kyoto, of one of the great Minamoto families; at first opposed opening of ports to foreigners during revolutionary period (1867–68); finally sided with imperial progressive party and was instrumental in carrying out palace revolution (Jan., 1868); head of unsuccessful mission sent (1871–73) to Western countries to seek revision of treaties; opposed war with Korea (1873); chief councilor of emperor (1873–83).

**I·wa·sa** *or* **I·wa·sa Ma·ta·bei** (ē·wä·sä mä·tä·bā). 1577?–1650. Japanese painter. Originator of the Ukiyoye school, which departed from traditional methods and produced landscape and genre paintings and color prints of everyday life.

**I·wa·sa·ki** (ē·wä·sä·kē). Japanese family influential in modern industry, including: **Yataro Iwasaki** (1834–1885), founder of family; interested in exploring and trading; developed shipping line (1868); expanded business, founding Mitsubishi, a finance and trading company, specializing in banking, shipping, and insurance. **Yanosuke** (d. 1909), younger brother of Yataro; educ. in U.S.; succeeded as head of Mitsubishi; owned most of business district of Tokyo; created baron (1896). Baron **Hisaya** (1866–1955), eldest son of Yataro; educ. U. of Pennsylvania (grad. 1883); became head of Mitsubishi (1883). Baron **Koyata** (1879–1945), son of Yanosuke; educ. Tokyo and Cambridge, England; became president of banking department of Mitsubishi; philanthropist; established in Tokyo the Oriental Library.

**Ix′tlil·xo′chitl II** (ĭsh′tlĭl·shō′chĭt·'l). 1500?–1550. Mexican chief, king of Texcoco; enemy of Montezuma; at war with his brother (1516) for kingdom of Texcoco; aided by Cortes (c. 1520); after becoming king, was faithful ally of Spaniards.

**Ixtlilxochitl, Fernando de Alva Cortés.** 1568?–?1648. Mexican historian, descendant of the kings of Texcoco; commissioned by the Spanish viceroy of Mexico to write histories of the ancient Mexican peoples.

**I·ye·mi·tsu** (ē·yĕ·mē·tsōō) *or* **I·e·mi·tsu** (ē·yĕ-). 1604–1651. Japanese shogun of the Tokugawas (1623–51), son of Hidetada. Endeavored to carry out Iyeyasu's policies; a bitter enemy of the Christians. Closed Japan to all foreign trade; ordered massacre of Christians at Shimabara Castle (1638); put Macao ambassadors to death (1640); confined Dutch and their trading (1641) to island of Deshima in Nagasaki harbor, which became Japan's "window to the West," its only link with western world for more than 200 years; strong supporter of Buddhism and Confucianism; brought Tokugawa shogunate to zenith of its power.

**I·ye·mo·chi** (ē·yĕ·mô·chē) *or* **I·e·mo·chi** (ē·yĕ-). 1846–1866. Japanese shogun of the Tokugawas (1858–66). As boy of 12, chosen heir to shogunate by Iyesada through influence of Ii Naosuke, who remained in control of affairs (to 1860); antiforeign sentiment still very strong; all new treaties with western countries came into force (1858–59); went to Kyoto (1863) in response to summons of emperor; attacks on foreigners brought allied expedition (1864); succeeded (1867) by Hitotsubashi Yoshinobu.

**I·ye·na·ri** (ē·yĕ·nä·rē) *or* **I·e·na·ri** (ē·yĕ-). 1773–1841. Japanese shogun of the Tokugawas (1793–1837); son of Hitotsubashi Harunari; his reign marked by disturbances; resigned shogunate to son Iyeyoshi.

**I·ye·sa·da** (ē·yĕ·sä·dä) *or* **I·e·sa·da** (ē·yĕ-). 1824–1858. Japanese shogun of the Tokugawas (1853–58); brother of Iyeyoshi. After Commodore Perry's demand (see IYEYOSHI) had brought on civil war (see II NAOSUKE), signed with Perry treaty of Kanagawa (Mar. 31, 1854), opening two ports to trade; forced to grant similar privileges to other countries (1854–56); faced with growing prestige of emperor and strength of Ii Naosuke's party (1858); being without heir, appointed Iyemochi as successor.

**I·ye·ya·su** (ē·yĕ·yä·sōō) *or* **I·e·ya·su** (ē·yĕ-). 1542–1616. Japanese general and statesman; founder (1603) of Tokugawa shogunate; descendant of Minamoto clan. Served under both Nobunaga and Hideyoshi; on death of latter (1598) became one of four regents for Hideyori, minor son of Hideyoshi; engaged in conflict with fellow regents, totally defeating them in great battle of Sekigahara (1600); assumed complete control of government, securing commission (1603) from emperor as shogun (thus founding shogunate that lasted until 1867); established his capital at Yedo (modern Tokyo); his many sons put in possession of great fiefs. Abdicated in favor of his son, Hidetada (1605), but actually remained in complete control of affairs. Retired to Shizuoka. Endeavored to establish commercial relations with outside world, esp. the Portuguese and Spanish, but not successful; later (1609–13), through Will Adams (*q.v.*) developed better trade relations with the English and Dutch, but this venture also failed; forbade by decree (1614) all Christian missionaries; besieged and destroyed the Toyotomi Castle at Osaka (1614–15), at which time Hideyori and others perished. Cf. IYEMITSU.

**I·ye·yo·shi** (ē·yĕ·yō·shē) *or* **I·e·yo·shi** (ē·yĕ-). 1792–1853. Japanese shogun of the Tokugawas (1837–53); son of Iyenari. His reign marked by steadily increasing pressure of Occidental ideas and demands for opening of Japan to foreign trade, and by increased sentiment for restoration of emperor; refused (1846) trade to American Commodore James Biddle, visiting Yedo Bay; received communication from Commodore Perry (July, 1853) addressed to emperor and demanding answer to request for open ports and trade; succeeded by his brother Iyesada.

**Izac, Heinrich.** See ISAAK.

**Iz'ard** (ĭz'ẽrd), **Ralph.** 1742–1804. American Revolutionary leader, b. near Charleston, S.C.; to Paris at outbreak of Revolution (1776); appointed American commissioner to Tuscany, but not received there; engaged in dispute with Benjamin Franklin, of American mission in Paris; recalled (1779); member, Continental Congress (1782, 1783); U.S. Senate (1789–95). His son **George** (1776–1828) was major general (1814); served on Canadian front, at Niagara River, and was criticized for failing to push his advantage over the British; resigned (1815); governor of Arkansas Territory (1825–28).

**Izcohuatl.** See ITZCOATL.

**Iz·vol'ski** (ĭz·vôl'y'·skû·ĭ; *Angl.* ĭz·vŏl'skĭ), **Aleksandr Petrovich.** 1856–1919. Russian statesman and diplomat; envoy at Belgrade (1896), Munich (1897–1900), Tokyo (1900–03); at latter post attempted unsuccessfully to warn home government of war with Japan; envoy to Denmark (1903–06); minister of foreign affairs (1906–10); ambassador to France (1910–17); resigned post after Russian Revolution (1917); died in Paris.

**İz·zet' Pa·şa'** (ĭz·zĕt' pä·shä'), **Ahmet.** 1870– . Turkish general and statesman, of Albanian descent; chief of general staff (1908), and commander in chief (1913) during Balkan War; during World War I, led army of the Caucasus.

# J

**Jabir.** See GEBER.

**Ja'bloch·kov** (yȧ'blŭch·kôf), **Paul.** 1847–1894. Russian electrical engineer.

**Ja'bło·now'ski** (yä'blô·nôf'skē), Prince **Jo'seph** (yō'zĕf) **A'le·xan'der** (ä'lĕ·ksän'dẽr) **Pruss** (pro͞os). 1712–1777. Polish patron of arts and letters; moved to Leipzig (1768) and established (1774) Jabłonowski Scientific Foundation, which has published studies on Polish history, economics, mathematics, physics, etc.

**Ja·blon'ski** (yä·blôn'skē), **Daniel Ernst.** 1660–1741. German Reformed theologian; consecrated bishop of Moravian church (1699) and worked with Leibnitz for union between Lutherans and Reformed Protestants.

**Ja·bo·tin'sky** (yĭ·bŭ·tyĕn'skû·ĭ; *Angl.* yăb'ō·tĭn'skĭ), **Vladimir Evgenevich.** 1880–1940. British Zionist leader. Founder of Jewish Legion in Palestine during World War; founder and president (from 1923) of World Union of Zionist-Revisionists; also, president of New Zionist Organization (from 1935).

**Jac·chi'no** (yäk·kē'nô), **Arturo.** Italian admiral; appointed by Mussolini (1940) commander of the fleet at sea.

**Jach'mann** (yäк'män), **Eduard Karl Emanuel von.** 1822–1887. German admiral; commanded Prussians against Danes in naval victory near Jasmund (1864); commander in chief in North Sea (1870–74).

**Jachmann-Wagner, Johanna.** See under Richard WAGNER.

**Jäckh** (yĕk), **Ernst.** 1875–1959. German-born political scientist in England; member of German diplomatic service with general headquarters during World War (1914–18). Member of German delegation at Versailles, Genoa, Locarno, and Geneva conferences; founded League of Nations Union (1918). To London (1933) and became director of the *New Commonwealth* (1933–39). Author of *From Kaiser unto Hitler* (1939), etc.

**Jacks** (jăks), **Lawrence Pearsall.** 1860–1955. English clergyman, philosopher, and writer; Unitarian minister (from 1887). Professor of philosophy (1903–31) and principal (1915–31), Manchester Coll., Oxford. Editor of *Hibbert Journal* (from its foundation, 1902). Author of *Mad Shepherds, and other Human Studies, All Men are Ghosts, The Legends of Smokeover, The Challenge of Life, My Neighbour the Universe* (1928), *Education through Recreation* (1932), *The Revolt against Mechanism* (1934), and *The Last Legend of Smokeover* (1939).

**Jack'son** (jăk's'n), **Abraham Reeves.** 1827–1892. American gynecologist.

**Jackson, Abraham Valentine Williams.** 1862–1937. American educator; professor of Indo-Iranian languages, Columbia (1895–1935).

**Jackson, Andrew.** 1767–1845. Seventh president of the United States, b. Waxhaw, S.C. Adm. to bar, Salisbury, N.C. (1787). Migrated westward (1788); opened law office in Nashville, Tenn. Member, U.S. House of Representatives (1796–97) and U.S. Senate (1797–98). Judge, Tennessee Supreme Court (1798–1804). Major general of Tennessee militia (1802); defeated Creek Indians, battle of Horseshoe Bend (1814). Commissioned major general, U.S. army, and assigned to defend New Orleans (1814); succeeded and became national hero (Jan., 1815); added to fame by operations against Seminole Indians (1818); involved federal government by pursuing Indians into Spanish territory and hanging two English troublemakers. Governor of Florida territory (1821). U.S. senator (1823–25). Unsuccessful Democratic candidate for president (1824); elected (1828) and re-elected (1832). Outstanding features of his administration: introduction of spoils system; social scandal caused by Peggy O'Neale (see under John Henry EATON) incident, which broke up Jackson's cabinet; overthrow of United States Bank by vetoing its charter; the South Carolina nullification issue; the complete paying off of the national debt. Elected to American Hall of Fame (1910).

**Jackson, Benjamin Daydon.** 1846–1927. English botanist; author of *Index Kewensis* (nearly 14 years in preparation; pub. 1893–95; supplement, with T. Durand, 1901–06).

**Jackson, Charles Thomas.** 1805–1880. American scientist; practiced medicine, Boston (1832–36); abandoned medicine for work in chemistry and mineralogy (1836). Claimed to have pointed out to S. F. B. Morse the basic principles of the electric telegraph; also claimed priority in discovery of guncotton; suggested to W. T. G. Morton (*q.v.*) the use of ether as anesthetic for extracting a tooth and thereafter proclaimed himself as discoverer of surgical anesthesia.

**Jackson, Che·va'lier'** (shĕ·và'lyā'). 1865–1958. American laryngologist.

**Jackson, Dugald Caleb.** 1865–1951. American electrical engineer.

**Jackson, Frederick George.** 1860–1938. British explorer; educ. Edinburgh. Served in Boer War (1899–1902) and World War (1914–18). Made exploratory trips in various parts of the world, including the Australian deserts, Lapland and the Arctic tundra, and Africa; commanded polar expedition sent out by Alfred Harmsworth to Franz Josef Land (1894–97).

**Jackson, Frederick John Foakes.** = F. J. FOAKES-JACKSON.

**Jackson, Helen Maria Hunt,** *nee* **Fiske.** 1830–1885. American writer, b. Amherst, Mass.; m. Edward Bissell Hunt (1852; d. 1863), William Sharpless Jackson (1875). Began contributing to magazines (1865) over signature **H. H.** Author of *Verses* (1870), *Sonnets and Lyrics* (1886), the novels *Mercy Philbrick's Choice* (1876), *Hetty's Strange History* (1877), and *Ramona* (1884); also of *A Century of Dishonor* (1881), a document recording government wrongs in dealing with Indians, which resulted in her appointment (1882) as special commissioner to investigate conditions among the Mission Indians of California.

**Jackson, Henry.** 1839–1921. English philosopher and educator; prelector in ancient philosophy (1875–1906), Cambridge; professor of Greek, Cambridge (1906–21). Member of Order of Merit (1908).

**Jackson,** Sir **Henry Bradwardine.** 1855–1929. British naval officer; admiral of the fleet (1919); retired (1924). Known esp. as pioneer in wireless telegraphy (from 1890); responsible for equipment of many vessels in the navy with wireless installations (1900). Chief of war staff of the Admiralty (1913) and remained at the Admiralty (1914–16); president, Royal Naval Coll. at Greenwich (1916–19).

**Jackson, Holbrook.** 1874–1948. English writer, b. Liverpool. Editor, *The Beau* (1910), *T. P.'s Magazine* (1911–12), *T. P.'s Weekly* (1911–16), *To-day* (1917–23). Author of *The Eternal Now* (verse, 1900), *Bernard Shaw* (1907), *Platitudes in the Making* (1911), *All Manner of Folk* (1912), *The Anatomy of Bibliomania* (2 vols., 1930–31), *William Caxton* (1933), *The Printing of Books* (1937).

**Jackson, Howell Edmunds.** 1832–1895. American jurist, b. Paris, Tenn. U.S. senator (1881–86). Associate justice, U.S. Supreme Court (1893–95).

**Jackson, James.** 1777–1867. American physician, b. Newburyport, Mass. One of first to introduce vaccination against smallpox (1800); in article in *New England Journal of Medicine* (1822), gave first description of peripheral alcoholic neuritis. His brother **Patrick Tracy** (1780–1847) was leader of group that established first cotton-textile factories on Merrimac River at site of what is now Lowell, Mass. (1820).

**Jackson, John.** 1778–1831. English portrait painter.

**Jackson, John Adams.** 1825–1879. American sculptor.

**Jackson, John Hughlings.** 1835–1911. English neurologist. Studied speech defects in brain disease, associating them with disease in left cerebral hemisphere, and motor spasms due to local brain irritation and now known as Jacksonian epilepsy.

**Jackson, Laura Riding.** See Laura RIDING.

**Jackson, Robert Hough'wout** (hou'ŭt). 1892–1954. American jurist, b. Spring Creek, Pa. Practiced law in Jamestown, N.Y. General counsel for U.S. Bureau of Internal Revenue (1934). Solicitor general of the U.S. (1938–39); attorney general of the U.S. (1940–41); associate justice, U.S. Supreme Court (1941–54); chief war crimes prosecutor for U.S. (appointed May, 1945).

**Jackson, Samuel Macauley.** 1851–1912. American Presbyterian clergyman. Editor in chief, *New Schaff-Herzog Encyclopedia of Religious Knowledge* (12 vols.).

**Jackson, Thomas.** 1783–1873. English Wesleyan clergyman. Wrote a life of Charles Wesley, and edited John Wesley's works and journals, and Charles Wesley's journals.

**Jackson,** Sir **Thomas Graham.** 1835–1924. English architect; studied under Sir George Gilbert Scott (1858–61). Among buildings of his design are new Examination Schools at Oxford; restoration of Bodleian Library; new law library and law school at Cambridge; churches at Annesley, Wimbledon, and Aldershot; new buildings for Eton, Rugby, Harrow; new buildings for the Inner Temple at London. Author of *Modern Gothic Architecture* (1873), *Reason in Architecture* (1906), etc.

**Jackson, Thomas Jonathan.** *Known as* **Stone'wall'** (stōn'wôl') **Jackson.** 1824–1863. American Confederate general, b. Clarksburg, Va., now W.Va. Grad. U.S.M.A., West Point (1846). Served in Mexican War. Resigned from army (1852). Entered Confederate service at outbreak of Civil War; brigadier general (June 17, 1861); gained sobriquet "Stonewall" by his stand at Bull Run; major general (Oct. 7, 1861). Led Confederates in brilliant Shenandoah Valley campaign (1862). Severely wounded accidentally by fire from his own troops just after routing the federal right wing at Chancellorsville (1863). Elected to American Hall of Fame (1955).

**Jackson, William.** *Known as* **Jackson of Ex'e·ter** (ĕk'sĕ·tēr). 1730–1803. English composer; organist and lay vicar, Exeter Cathedral (1777–1803). Composed the operas *The Lord of the Manor* (1780) and *Metamorphosis* (1783), musical settings for Milton's *Lycidas*, Warton's *Ode to Fancy*, and Pope's *Dying Christian to his Soul*, and church music and songs.

**Jackson, William.** 1815–1866. English organist; composer of two oratorios, a cantata (*The Year*, 1859), glees, songs, etc.

**Jack the Rip'per** (jăk' thē rĭp'ēr). Sobriquet of an unknown criminal, to whom is attributed a series of gruesome murders in the East end of London (1888–89).

**Ja'cob** (jā'kŭb) *or* [*Gen.* xxxii. 28] **Is'ra·el** (ĭz'rā·ĕl; -rĭ·ĕl). In Bible, grandson of Abraham and son of Isaac and Rebekah (*Gen.* xxv. 20 ff.), who, after depriving his twin brother Esau of his birthright and his father's blessing (*Gen.* xxvii), lived many years with his uncle Laban, whose daughters Leah and Rachel he took as wives (*Gen.* xxix). His twelve sons, by his wives and by their handmaidens Zilpah and Bilhah were the ancestors of the twelve tribes of Israel (*Gen.* xxix. 31–xxx. 24; xxxv. 16–19): Reuben, Simeon, Levi, Judah (sons of Leah), Dan, Naphtali (sons of Bilhah), Gad, Asher (sons of Zilpah), Issachar, Zebulun (sons of Leah), Joseph and Benjamin (sons of Rachel).

**Ja'cob'** (zhà'kôb'). Family of French furniture makers including: **Georges** (1739–1814); his son **François Honoré**

Georges, *known as* **Ja'cob'-Des'mal'ter'** [dā'mȧl'tā'] (1770–1841); and François's son **Georges Alphonse,** *also known as* **Jacob–Desmalter** (1799–1870).

**Ja'cob'** (zhȧ'kôb'), **François.** 1920– . French geneticist. At Pasteur Inst. (1950– ); awarded Nobel prize in physiology and medicine (1965) with A. Lwoff and J. Monod for research on genetic control of enzyme and virus synthesis.

**Ja'cob** (jā'kŭb), **John.** 1812–1858. English soldier in India; pacified Upper Sind Frontier district (1841–47); town of Jacobabad named in his honor (1851).

**Ja'cob'** (zhȧ'kôb'), **Max.** 1876–1944. French writer; a precursor of the Dadaist movement in literature; author of a mystical novel (*Saint Matorel*), a symbolic drama (*Siège de Jérusalem*), prose poems, etc.

**Ja'cob** (jā'kŭb), **Naomi Ellington.** *Pseudonym* **Ellington Gray.** 1889–1964. English novelist.

**Jacob, Violet,** *nee* **Ken'ne·dy–Er'skine** (kĕn'ĕ·dĭ·ûr'·skĭn). 1863–1946. Scottish novelist and poet.

**Ja'cob ben Ash'er** (jā'kŭb bĕn ăsh'ēr). d. about 1340. Jewish scholar and Biblical commentator in Spain; greatest work, *Arba Turim* ("Four Turim"), a compilation of religious laws.

**Jacob Bibliophile, P. L.** Pseudonym of Paul LACROIX.

**Ja'cob of E·des'sa** (jā'kŭb, ē·dĕs'ȧ). 640?–708 A.D. Syrian theologian; bishop of Edessa (about 686–700; 708). Best known for his work on the Syriac version of the Old Testament.

**Jacob of Vitry.** = JACQUES DE VITRY.

**Ja·co'bi** (jȧ·kō'bĭ), **Abraham.** 1830–1919. Physician, b. in Westphalia. To U.S. (1853); specialized in diseases of infants and children. At Coll. of Phys. & Surg., N.Y. (1870–1902). His wife (m. 1873), **Mary Corinna Put·nam** [pŭt'nȧm] (1842–1906), dau. of George Palmer Putnam (*q.v.*), was also a physician; at Woman's Med. Coll., N.Y. (1871–81); wrote on women's diseases.

**Jacobi, Frederick.** 1891–1952. American composer.

**Ja·co'bi** (yä·kō'bē), **Friedrich Heinrich.** 1743–1819. German philosopher and writer; champion of philosophy of faith and of feeling (Gefühlsphilosophie). His brother **Johann Georg** (1740–1814), lyric poet, was professor at Halle (1766) and Freiburg (1784), and coeditor of *Iris* (1774–77), to which Gleim, Goethe, and others contributed. F. H. Jacobi's son **Karl Wigand Maximilian** (1775–1858), psychiatrist, was a founder of the somatic school of psychiatry.

**Jacobi, Hermann Georg.** 1850–1937. German philologist. His publications include editions of Sanskrit literature, translations in vols. 22 and 45 of *Sacred Books of the East*, and works on Indian chronology, comparative philology, Prakrit grammar, literature, astronomy, poetry, philosophy, and Jainism.

**Ja·co'bi** (yä·kō'bē), **Karl Gustav Jakob.** 1804–1851. German mathematician; developed (independently of Abel) the theory of elliptical functions (1829); also known for work in differential equations and the calculus of variations. His brother **Moritz Hermann** (1801–1874), physicist and engineer, went to St. Petersburg (1837); claimed discovery of galvanoplasty (1837); worked on the application of electricity for the movement of machinery and boats, also on the arc lamp.

**Ja'co·bi'ni** (yä'kō·bē'nē), **Lodovico.** 1832–1887. Italian prelate; cardinal (1879); papal secretary of state (1880–87); instrumental in securing repeal of May laws, thus ending Bismarck's Kulturkampf.

**Ja'cobs** (yȧ'kŏps), **Aletta.** 1849–1929. Dutch suffragist leader; first woman physician to practice in Holland; opened first birth-control clinic in the world, in Amsterdam (1878).

**Ja'cobs** (yä'kôps), **Christian Friedrich Wilhelm.** 1764–1847. German classical philologist and scholar.

**Ja'cobs** (jā'kŭbz), **Helen Hull.** 1908– . American tennis player, b. Globe, Ariz.; U.S. women's singles champion (1932, 1933, 1934, 1935); Wimbledon singles champion (1936).

**Jacobs, Joseph.** 1854–1916. Jewish scholar and writer, b. Sydney, Australia. Devoted himself to writing and editorial work, in England and in U.S. (from 1900). Author of *Earliest English Version of the Fables of Bidpai* (1888), *The Jews of Angevin England* (1893), *Studies in Biblical Archaeology* (1894), and a series of volumes of fairy tales. Revising editor, *Jewish Encyclopedia,* in New York (from 1900).

**Ja'cobs'** (zhȧ'kôbz'), **Victor.** 1838–1891. Belgian statesman; minister of public works, of finance (1870), of the interior and public instruction (1884); introduced and sponsored the so-called denominational education bill, a law which returned elementary teaching in Belgium to the control of the religious orders.

**Ja'cobs** (jā'kŭbz), **William Plum'er** (plo͝om'ēr). 1842–1917. American Presbyterian clergyman, b. in York County, S.C.; pastorate, Clinton, S.C. (1864–1911). His son **Thornwell** (1877–1956) founded Oglethorpe U., Atlanta, Ga., and became its president (1915).

**Jacobs, William Wymark.** 1863–1943. English writer; author esp. of sea stories, as *Many Cargoes* (1896), *A Master of Craft* (1900), *Captains All* (1905), *Beauty and the Barge* (play, with Louis N. Parker, 1913), *Night Watches* (1914), *Deep Waters* (1919).

**Ja'cob·sen** (yȧ'kŏp·s'n), **Jens Peter.** 1847–1885. Danish novelist and poet.

**Ja'cob·sohn** (yä'kôp·zōn), **Siegfried.** 1881–1926. German dramatic critic and editor.

**Ja'cob·son** (jā'kŭb·s'n), *Dan.* **Ja'kob·son** (yȧ'kŏp·s'n), **Ludvig Le·vin'** (lĭ·vēn'). 1783–1843. Danish surgeon and anatomist.

**Jacobsz, Lucas.** See LUCAS VAN LEYDEN.

**Ja·co'bus** (jȧ·kō'bŭs). See BULGARUS.

**Jacobus Baradaeus.** See BARADAI.

**Jacobus de Benedictis.** See JACOPONE DA TODI

**Jacobus de Va·rag'i·ne** (dē vȧ·răj'ĭ·nē) *or* **Vo·rag'·i·ne** (vŏ-). 1230?–?1298. Italian Dominican and writer; archbishop of Genoa (1292 ff.); author of a chronicle of Genoa to 1296 and of the celebrated *Golden Legend.*

**Ja·co'by** (jȧ·kō'bĭ), **Harold.** 1865–1932. American astronomer, b. New York City; at Columbia U. (1904–30). Author of *Astronomy, a Popular Handbook* (1913); *Navigation* (1917).

**Jacoby, Henry Sylvester.** 1857–1955. American bridge engineer.

**Ja·co'by** (yä·kō'bē), **Johann.** 1805–1877. Prussian physician, radical politician, and publicist. Reform member of Frankfurt Vorparlament (1848–49), Prussian National Assembly, and lower chamber (1849); took part in Rump Parliament at Stuttgart as champion of radical democrats. In Prussian Chamber of Deputies (1862–70), opposed Bismarck and the government; imprisoned (1870) for condemning annexation of Alsace-Lorraine; joined Social Democrats (1872).

**Ja'co·po'ne da To'di** (yä'kô·pō'nā dä tô'dē) *or* **Ja'co·po de'i Be'ne·det'ti** (yä'kô·pō dā'ē bā'nā·dāt'tē). *Lat.* **Ja·co'bus de Ben'e·dic'tis** (jȧ·kō'bŭs dē bĕn'ē·dĭk'tĭs). 1230?–1306. Italian Franciscan monk and writer; reputed author of *Stabat Mater.*

**Jac'quard'** (zhȧ'kȧr'; *Angl.* jă·kärd'), **Joseph Marie.** 1752–1834. French inventor of the Jacquard apparatus used in the Jacquard loom for figured weaving; inventor also of a machine for weaving nets.

**Jacque** (zhăk), **Charles Émile.** 1813–1894. French

painter and engraver; one of chief members of the Barbizon school; well-known for his paintings of sheep, and for his etchings of scenes from rural life.

**Jac'que·mart'** (zhȧk'mȧr'), **Albert Jules.** 1808–1875. French authority on ceramics. His son **Jules Ferdinand** (1837–1880) was an etcher; prepared plates for his father's books.

**Jacquemart, Henri Alfred.** 1824–1895. French sculptor.

**Jacquemart, Nélie.** 1840–1912. French painter; m. Édouard André (1876); excelled in genre paintings; established by bequest in her will the Musée Jacquemart-André in Paris for art works.

**Jac'que·mi'not'** (zhȧk'mē'nō'; *Angl.* jăk'mĭ·nō), Vicomte **Jean François.** 1787–1865. French soldier; served in Napoleonic armies at Austerlitz, Essling, Wagram, and the Russian campaign, and at Waterloo. Member of Chamber of Deputies (1827); strongly supported the July Monarchy (1830). Promoted brigadier general and chief of the general staff of the Paris National Guard; lieutenant general (1838); commander of the National Guard of the Seine (1842); his indecision at a critical moment (1848) made the revolution of 1848 possible. A variety of rose is named in his honor.

**Jac'que·mont'** (zhȧk'môɴ'), **Victor.** 1801–1832. French botanist and traveler; in India (1828–32), collecting specimens of plants new to Europe; remembered for his *Correspondance* (pub. 1834) and his *Voyage dans l'Inde* (edited by Guizot and pub. 1836–44).

**Jacques** (zhȧk), **Jules Marie Alphonse.** Baron **de Dix'mude'** (dē dēks'müd'). 1858–1928. Belgian commander of 12th brigade in its defense of Dixmude (1914) and of 3d division, called the Iron Division, which repulsed the German assault at Merckem (1918).

**Jacques de Vi'try'** (dē vē'trē'). 1180?–1240. French prelate and historian; preached in support of the crusade against the Albigensians; bishop of Acre (1216), and prominent in the Fifth Crusade; cardinal bishop of Tusculum (1227); Latin patriarch of Jerusalem (1239); author of sermons, letters, and *Historia Orientalis*, valuable source book of 13th-century history and customs.

**Jac'quet'** (zhȧ'kĕ'), **Jules** (1841–1913) and his brother **Achille** (1846–1908). French engravers.

**Jac'quin'** (zhȧ'kăɴ'), Baron **Nikolaus Joseph von.** 1727–1817. Austrian botanist.

**Jacquot, Charles Jean Baptiste.** See Eugène de MIRECOURT.

**Ja'das·sohn** (yä'däs·zōn), **Salomon.** 1831–1902. German music theorist and composer of over 125 works for orchestra, chorus, piano, also chamber music and songs.

**Ja'din'** (zhȧ'dăɴ'), **Louis Emmanuel.** 1768–1853. French composer of operas, orchestral works, etc.

**Jad·wi'ga** (yäd·vē'gä). *Ger.* **Hed'wig** (hāt'vĭк). 1370–1399. Queen of Poland (1384–99). Daughter of Louis the Great of Hungary and Poland; married (1386) Jagello, Duke of Lithuania. See JAGELLON dynasty.

**Jad'win** (jăd'wĭn), **Edgar.** 1865–1931. American army officer; assistant to General Goethals in building Panama Canal (1907–11). Served overseas in World War (1917–19); major general and chief of engineers, U.S. army (1926). Retired as lieutenant general (1929).

**Jae'ger** (yā'gẽr), **Werner Wilhelm.** 1888–1961. German classical scholar.

**Jae'gers** (yā'gẽrz), **Albert.** 1868–1925. Sculptor, b. at Elberfeld, Ger.; to U.S. as a youth. Executed statuary for the Buffalo and St. Louis expositions, and for the new Custom House in New York City; received U.S. government commission to erect the Baron von Steuben statue in Washington.

**Ja'el** (jā'ĕl). *In Douay Version* **Ja'hel** (jā'ĕl; -hĕl). In Bible, wife of Heber (*in D. V.* Haber) the Kenite who killed Canaanite general Sisera when he sought refuge with her after fleeing from defeat by Barak (*Judges* iv. 17–22).

**Jaensch** (yĕnsh), **Erich.** 1883–1940. German psychologist and philosopher; carried on experiments and researches in sight and space perception, analyzed eidetics, and sought to establish a closer relation between philosophy and psychology.

**Ja'far.** See BARMECIDES.

**Jafar Ali Khan.** = MIR JAFAR.

**Ja'far al–Sa'diq** (jă'făr ăs·sä'dĭk). *Arab.* **Ja'far al-Ṣādiq.** 699–765. Sixth Shiite imam in direct descent from Ali; father of Ismail (*q.v.*) and of Musa, seventh imam.

**Jaf'fe** (jăf'ē), **Ber'nard** (bûr'närd). 1896– . American writer; chemistry teacher in New York high schools. Author of *Chemical Calculations, Crucibles, Outposts of Science* (1935), *New World of Chemistry* (1935).

**Jaf'fé** (yä'fā), **Philipp.** 1819–1870. German historian.

**Jag'a·tai'** (jăg'ȧ·tī') *or* **Chag'a·tai'** (chăg'-). d. 1242. Mongol ruler. Second son of Genghis Khan. On division of father's empire (1227), received approximately what is now Turkestan as far south as Bokhara; relinquished (1229), to his younger brother Ogadai, office of khan; adviser to Ogadai and keeper of the Mongol law. Founder of House of Jagatai, which (14th century) separated into two dynasties: western with capital at Samarkand, and eastern at Kashgar (later at Yarkand and Agsu). Tamerlane (*q.v.*), or Timur, became leader of Western Jagatai; after his death (1405) a third kingdom, Fergana, founded; all three dynasties swept away by Uzbek Mongols (c. 1500).

**Ja·gel'lon** (yä·gĕl'ŭn). Name of second Polish dynasty (1386–1572), succeeding the Piast; so called from Jagello (*Pol.* Jagiełło, *from Lith.* Jagela), Duke of Lithuania (see LADISLAS II of Poland), who married (1386) Jadwiga, daughter of Louis I of Hungary and granddaughter of Casimir III of Poland. The rulers were: Ladislas II *or* V (1386–1434), Ladislas III *or* VI (1434–44), Casimir IV (1447–92), John Albert (1492–1501), Alexander (1501–06), Sigismund I (1506–48), and Sigismund II (1548–72), last of direct Jagellon line. Catharine Jagello, daughter of Sigismund I and sister of Sigismund II, m. John III, King of Sweden (see VASA); their son was Sigismund III, King of Poland (1587) and of Sweden (1594–1604); his two sons, Ladislas IV *or* VII, and John Casimir, were kings of Poland.

**Ja'ge·mann** (yä'gĕ·män), **Christian Joseph.** 1735–1804. German scholar; wrote on Italian art and literature, translated Dante's *Inferno*, and compiled an Italian-German dictionary (4 vols., 1805). His daughter **Karoline** (1777–1848), tragic actress and singer in Weimar (1797–1828); mistress of Grand Duke Charles Augustus, who called her Frau **von Hey'gen·dorf** [fôn hī'gĕn·dôrf] (from 1809); was cause of Goethe's withdrawal from the theater (1817). His son **Ferdinand** (1780–1820) painted portraits of Schiller, Goethe, and Karl August (all now in Weimar), and other celebrities.

**Jä'ger** (yâ'gẽr), **Gustav.** 1832–1917. German naturalist and hygienist; most widely known for his emphasis upon the use of nothing but woolen clothing.

**Jäger, Oskar.** 1830–1910. German historian and educator.

**Jag'gar** (jăg'ẽr), **Thomas Augustus.** 1871–1953. American geologist; director, Hawaiian Volcano Observatory (1912–19); volcanologist, U.S. Weather Bureau (1919–24); chief, section of volcanology, U.S. Geological Survey (1926–35); volcanologist, National Park Service (from 1935).

**Jag'ger** (jăg'ẽr), **Charles Sargeant.** 1885–1934. English sculptor; among his notable works are *British Memorial to Belgium*, Brussels; *Royal Artillery Memorial* at Hyde Park Corner, London; *G. W. R. Memorial* at Paddington Station, London; statue of King George V, New Delhi, India.

**Ja'gić** (yä'gĕt·y'; *Angl.* -gĭch), **Vatroslav.** 1838–1923. Croatian philologist; author of treatises on Slavic languages and literature, esp. of early times.

**Ja'gow** (yä'gō), **Gottlieb von.** 1863–1935. German statesman; ambassador in Rome (1909–13). Assisted in renewal of Triple Alliance (1912). State secretary of foreign affairs (1913–16) and Prussian secretary of state (1914).

**Jahan,** Shah. See SHAH JAHAN.

**Ja·han'gir** (jȧ·hän'gēr) *or* **Je·han'gir,** *i.e.* "Conqueror of the World." 1569–1627. Emperor of Hindustan (1605–27), fourth of the Mogul dynasty; son of Akbar the Great; known in youth as Prince Selim. Rebelled against his father; after accession carried on long wars in Deccan; added little territory to empire; much influenced, at first for his good, by his empress (m. 1611; d. 1645) **Nur Ja·han'** (no͝or' jȧ·hän'), *i.e.* "Light of the World," *or* **Nur Ma·hal'** (mȧ·häl'), *i.e.* "Light of the Palace"; faced with frequent rebellions (1622–26) by his son Shah Jahan; held captive (1626); visited by first English envoys, Capt. William Hawkins (1609–11) and Sir Thomas Roe as ambassador (1615–18).

**Jahel.** See JAEL.

**Jahn** (yän), **Friedrich Ludwig.** 1778–1852. Prussian gymnastic director and patriot; known as "Father of Gymnastics." Opened in Berlin (1811) a Turnplatz, or athletic field, first of many throughout Germany; used his system of training to inspire patriotism in Prussian youth and a spirit of resistance to Napoleonic domination.

**Jahn, Johann.** 1750–1816. German Roman Catholic Orientalist and Biblical critic; author of *Biblische Archäologie* (5 vols., 1797–1805), *Enchiridion Hermeneuticae* (1812; appendix, 1813–15), an edition of the Hebrew Bible (4 vols., 1806), also grammars, lexicons, etc.

**Jahn, Otto.** 1813–1869. German classical philologist, archaeologist, and music and art critic; pioneer in introducing the scientific philological method into classical archaeology and opponent of the symbolical school of interpretation.

**Jähns** (yâns), **Friedrich Wilhelm.** 1809–1888. German composer, esp. of songs; biographer and bibliographer of Weber.

**Jai'me** (hī'mā). Spanish form of JAMES.

**Jai'me** (hī'mā). *In full* **Jaime Juan Carlos Alfonso Felipe de Bor·bón' An'jou'** (thā bôr·bôn' äN'zho͞o'). Duque **de Ma·drid'** (mä·thrē[th]'). 1870–1931. Spanish nobleman, son of Don Carlos (1848–1909); after Don Carlos's death (1909), the Carlist claimant to the Spanish throne.

**Ja'kob** (yä'kôp), **Ludwig Heinrich von.** 1759–1827. German Kantian philosopher and economist.

**Jakobson, Ludvig L.** See JACOBSON.

**Ja·ku·chu** (jä·ko͞o·cho͞o), **Ito.** Japanese painter of the 18th century.

**Ja·lal'–ad–Din'** *or* **Je·lal' ad–Din'** (jă·lä'lo͝od·dēn'). d. 1231. Shah of Khwarazm. Opposed armies of Genghis Khan; was completely defeated on banks of Indus (c. 1220) and his lands overrun; fled to India; re-established khanate in part but was again overcome by Mongols under Ogadai; assassinated.

**Jalal–al–Din.** See MALIK SHAH.

**Jalal–ud–din.** See FIRUZ SHAH II.

**Jalal–ud–Din Muhammad.** See AKBAR.

**Ja·lal'–ud–din' Ru'mi** (jă·lä'lo͝od·dēn' ro͞o'mē). 1207–1273. Persian poet, b. Balkh; greatest of Oriental mystics. Lived in Asia Minor at Iconium, modern Konya (*Arab.* Rum—hence his name); founded order of dervishes (Maulawiyah), a Sufistic sect. Wrote many exquisite lyrics. His great work was *Mesnevi*, or *Mathnawī*, a large collection of double-rhymed verses containing ethical and moral precepts.

**Ja'loux'** (zhȧ'lo͞o'), **Edmond.** 1878–1949. French novelist and critic.

**Ja·mal'–ud–Din' al'–Af·gha'ni** (jă·mä'lo͝od·dēn' ăl'ăf·gä'nē). Also **Jemaleddin Afghani.** 1838–1897. Moslem teacher and politician, and founder of modern Islamic nationalist movement, b. near Kabul. Leading agitator of Pan-Islamism, his teachings inspiring nationalist movement in Egypt (1881–82) and, later, in Persia and Turkey.

**James** (jāmz). In the New Testament: (1) *Often known as* **St. James the Greater.** One of the twelve apostles, son of Zebedee and brother of John (*Matt.* iv. 21 and x. 2; *Mark* i. 19 and iii. 17; *Luke* vi. 14; *Acts.* i. 13). According to a tradition, after preaching Christianity in Spain, he returned to Judea where he was put to death at Herod's order, his body being miraculously translated to Spain, eventually to Compostela (Santiago de Compostela), which became a famous center of pilgrimage; hence, sometimes known as **St. James of Com'pos·te'la** (kôm'pôs·tā'lä).

(2) Another of the twelve apostles, son of Alphaeus (*Matt.* x. 3; *Mark* iii. 18; *Luke* vi. 15; *Acts* i. 13), often identified with James the Less (*Mark* xv. 40).

(3) A brother of Jesus (*Matt.* xiii. 55; *Mark* vi. 3; *Gal.* i. 19); head of church at Jerusalem in apostolic age; regarded by some as author of New Testament Epistle of James. Identified by Roman Catholics with (2), above. See JUDAS, 3.

**James.** Name of two kings of Great Britain, of house of Stuart:

**James I.** 1566–1625. King of Scotland as James VI (1567–1625) and of Great Britain as James I (1603–25). Son of Mary, Queen of Scots, and Henry Lord Darnley; great-great-grandson of Henry VII of England through Henry's daughter Margaret, queen of James IV of Scotland. Educ. by George Buchanan. After succession of regents (Moray, Lennox, Mar, Morton), ruled Scotland (from 1581) with aid of two favorites, James Stewart, Earl of Arran, and duke of Lennox; seized by Protestant nobles in Raid of Ruthven (1582) and forced to give up his favorites; escaped (1583) but compelled by Protestant nobles to make treaty of Berwick with England (1586). m. Anne, daughter of king of Denmark (1589). Succeeded (1594) in curbing powers of great Roman Catholic nobles of Scotland and centralizing power in monarchy; introduced episcopacy into Scotland; fought Presbyterians more bitterly after killing of leader of extreme Protestant party in alleged Gowrie conspiracy to kidnap the king (1600); connived with Rome. Succeeded to English throne at death of Queen Elizabeth (1603); sought to assert divine right of kings; in foreign relations, favored policy of peace at any price and aroused suspicions of people by truckling to Spain; alienated nonconformist sentiment by severity and rudeness to Puritan divines at Hampton Court conference (1604); his severity toward Roman Catholics engendered Gunpowder Plot (1605). Aspired to literary fame; published works in verse and prose, including famous *Counterblaste to Tobacco* (1604). During reign, a group of scholars prepared new version of Bible (Authorized Version) called in his honor King James Bible (1611).

**James II.** 1633–1701. King of England, Scotland, and

Ireland (1685–88). Son of Charles I and Henrietta Maria; created duke of York. At Restoration, became lord high admiral of England (1660) till forced by Test Act to resign (1673); received grant of New Netherland (1664); won victory over de Ruyter (1672); accepted Roman Catholic faith (prob. before 1672); retired to Continent during national furor over Popish Plot; object of attempt by House of Commons to exclude him from succession to throne (1678–81); as high commissioner in Scotland inflicted cruelties upon Covenanters (1679–80); resumed direction of naval affairs (1684). Succeeded to throne on death of his brother Charles II (1685); began almost at once to show special favor to Roman Catholics; by appointments, gave evidence of intention to restore powers to this church; published declaration of liberty of conscience for all denominations (1687); aroused public fear of Roman Catholic tyranny, resulting in English nobles offering throne to his son-in-law William of Orange; escaped to France (Dec. 23, 1688) after William had landed in England (Nov. 5); landed in Ireland (1689), but was decisively defeated by William at battle of the Boyne (July 1, 1690).

**James.** Name of six kings of Scotland, of the Stewart or Stuart family (*q.v.*):

**James I.** 1394–1437. King (1406–37). Son of Robert III. Sent by father to France for safety (c. 1406), captured on way by English seamen and held prisoner by Henry IV; lodged at Windsor and well treated, after accession of Henry V to English throne (1413); accompanied Henry on French campaign (1420–22). Released (1423) after negotiations by Scottish leaders; crowned king of Scotland at Scone (May 21, 1424); attempt to suppress great feudal lords of Scotland led to plots against his life; murdered at Perth (Feb. 20) by Sir Robert Graham at instigation of a son of Robert II, Walter Stewart, Earl of Atholl. Gained reputation as poet by *The Kingis Quair*, allegorical poem of courtly love.

**James II.** 1430–1460. King (1437–60). Son of James I. Minority marked by bitter conflicts between great Scottish families; assumed control of government (1449); executed his guardian Sir Alexander Livingstone (1450) for having expelled queen mother from joint guardianship; continued father's policy of suppressing great feudal lords; stabbed to death earl of Douglas, who conspired against him (1452), and attainted James, new earl of Douglas, and confiscated his properties; killed by accidental bursting of a cannon during siege of Roxburgh Castle (Aug. 3).

**James III.** 1451–1488. King (1460–88). Son of James II. During minority, government in hands of the unscrupulous Lord Boyd of Kilmarnock, high justiciar (d. 1469?); assumed control (c. 1479); continued policy designed to break power of great nobles; arrested his brothers Alexander, Duke of Albany, and John, Earl of Mar (c. 1479); held in custody by Scottish nobles at outbreak of war following Alexander's escape to England and recognition (1482) by Edward IV as king of Scotland; after Alexander, with aid of English troops, had captured Berwick and marched to Edinburgh, favored peace with English; in resultant rebellion among his nobles, defeated in battle near Bannockburn and murdered shortly afterward (June 11).

**James IV.** 1473–1513. King (1488–1513). Son of James III; m. Margaret, daughter of Henry VII of England, a union which led ultimately to succession of member of Stuart house to English throne (see JAMES I of England). After disputes with Henry VIII, gathered army and invaded England; defeated and killed at Flodden Hill (Sept. 9).

**James V.** 1512–1542. King (1513–42). Son of James IV and Margaret. During minority, regency exercised by mother and, later, by duke of Albany; proclaimed by queen mother competent to rule (1524) on retirement of Albany; held prisoner by Archibald Douglas, Earl of Angus, in turn with other nobles (1525–28); assumed control (1528); introduced reforms designed to protect people from oppression by nobles; waged war on England; defeated at Solway Moss (Nov. 24, 1542) and died soon thereafter (Dec. 14). Succeeded by Mary, Queen of Scots (*q.v.*), his week-old daughter by second wife (m. 1538), Mary of Guise.

**James VI.** = JAMES I of Great Britain.

**James.** *Span.* **Jai′me** (hī′mā). Name of two kings of Aragon:

**James I.** *Called* **El Con′quis·ta·dor′** (ĕl kông′kēs-tä·thôr′), *i.e.* the Conqueror. 1208–1276. Son of Pedro II, b. in Montpellier. King (1213–76). At first under care of Simon de Montfort in England, but returned to Spain after his father's death (1213); m. (1221) Leonor of Castile, but divorced her and married Yolande, daughter of Andrew, King of Hungary; conquered the Balearic Islands (1229–35); took Valencia by siege (1238); signed Treaty of Corbeil with France (1258); spent last 20 years of reign (1256–76) in wars against Moors in Murcia; promulgated new legal code (1247); one of the great organizers among Spanish rulers.

**James II.** *Called* **the Just.** 1260?–1327. Grandson of James I and son of Pedro III. King of Sicily (1285–91). King of Aragon (1291–1327); relinquished Sicily but in recompense made king of Corsica and Sardinia by the pope; m. Blanche (1295), daughter of Charles of Anjou; founded U. of Lérida (1300).

**James, Arthur Lloyd.** See LLOYD JAMES.

**James, Edmund Janes.** 1855–1925. American educator; president, Northwestern U. (1902–04) and U. of Illinois (1904–20). Founded (1890) American Academy of Political and Social Science and was its first president (1890–1901).

**James, Frank Cyril.** 1903–1973. British economist and educator in Canada; principal and vice-chancellor, McGill U., Montreal, Canada (1939–62). Author of *The Economics of Money, Credit, and Banking;* special editor for terms in finance, *Webster's New International Dictionary, Second Edition.*

**James, George Payne Rainsford.** 1799–1860. Grandson of Robert James. English novelist and historical writer; prolific author of historical romances including *Richelieu* (1829; his earliest) and *Philip Augustus* (1831).

**James, George Wharton.** 1858–1923. Explorer and interpreter of the southwestern United States, b. Gainsborough, England; to U.S. (1881). Author of *In and Around the Grand Canyon* (1900), *Indian Basketry* (1900), *The Indians of the Painted Desert Region* (1903), *Prehistoric Cliff Dwellings of the Southwest* (1913), *Indian Blankets* (1914), etc.

**James,** Sir **Henry.** 1803–1877. English military engineer.

**James, Henry.** 1811–1882. American philosopher and author; influenced by Swedenborgianism and Fourierism. Author of *Christianity the Logic of Creation* (1857), *Relation to Life* (1863), *The Secret of Swedenborg, being an Elucidation of his Doctrine of the Divine Natural Humanity* (1869), etc. See Henry JAMES (1843–1916) and William JAMES.

**James, Henry.** 1st Baron **James of Her′e·ford** (hĕr′ĕ·fẽrd). 1828–1911. English jurist. M.P. (1869–85, 1886–95; raised to peerage, 1895); attorney general (1873; 1880–85); chancellor of duchy of Lancaster (1895).

**James, Henry.** 1843–1916. Son of Henry James (1811–

1882); bro. of William James. American novelist, b. New York City. Attended Harvard Law School (1862). Devoted himself to writing, from about 1865; contributor to *Nation, Atlantic, Galaxy* (1865–69). Resident of London, England (from 1876); naturalized British citizen (1915); awarded Order of Merit (1916). Author of *Roderick Hudson* (1876), *The American* (1877), *The Europeans* (1878), *Daisy Miller* (1879), *An International Episode* (1879), *The Portrait of a Lady* (1881), *Washington Square* (1881), *The Bostonians* (1886), *The Princess Casamassima* (1886), *The Tragic Muse* (1890), *The Spoils of Poynton* (1897), *What Maisie Knew* (1897), *In the Cage* (1898), *The Awkward Age* (1899), *The Sacred Fount* (1901), *The Wings of the Dove* (1902), *The Ambassadors* (1903), *The Golden Bowl* (1904), *The American Scene* (1907), *The Ivory Tower* (a fragment, 1917); shorter fiction, *The Madonna of the Future and Other Tales* (1879), *The Author of Beltrafio* (1885), *The Real Thing and Other Tales* (1893), *The Private Life* (1893), *The Wheel of Time* (1893), *Embarrassments* (1896), *The Two Magics* (containing *The Turn of the Screw*, 1898), *The Better Sort* (1903), *The Finer Grain* (1910); essays and criticism, as *French Poets and Novelists* (1878), *Portraits of Places* (1883); biography, as *Life of Hawthorne* (1880), *William Wetmore Story and His Friends* (1903); and autobiographical works, *A Small Boy and Others* (1913), *Notes of a Son and Brother* (1914).

**James, Henry.** 1879–1947. Son of William James (1842–1910). American lawyer and biographer; practiced law in Boston (1904–12); manager, Rockefeller Institute for Medical Research, New York (1912–17). Author of *Richard Olney* (1923), *Charles W. Eliot* (awarded Pulitzer prize, 1931).

**James, James.** Pseudonym of Arthur Henry ADAMS.

**James, Jesse Woodson.** 1847–1882. American desperado, b. in Clay County, Mo. Leader of band of brigands robbing banks and trains (from 1866); treacherously murdered by one of his band at St. Joseph, Mo. (Apr. 3, 1882).

**James, Marquis.** 1891–1955. American journalist and author, b. Springfield, Mo. Served in World War, in France (1917–19); on staff of *American Legion Monthly* (1923–32). Author of *A History of the American Legion* (1923), *The Raven, a Biography of Sam Houston* (1929; awarded Pulitzer prize), *Andrew Jackson* (1937; Pulitzer prize), *Biography of a Business, 1792–1942* (1943), etc.

**James, Montague Rhodes.** 1862–1936. British scholar; provost of King's Coll., Cambridge (1905–18); provost of Eton (from 1918). Among his many works are commentaries on Biblical texts, catalogues of manuscripts in several libraries, printed lectures on antiquarian subjects, and *Ghost Stories of an Antiquary* (1905), *More Ghost Stories* (1911), etc. Member of Order of Merit (1930).

**James, Philip.** 1890– . American conductor and composer of a symphony, three suites, four overtures, various choral works and many songs. Awarded 1st prize ($5000) by National Broadcasting Company for suite for orchestra.

**James, Robert.** 1705–1776. English physician; compiled a *Medical Dictionary* (1743), to which his friend Samuel Johnson contributed.

**James, Thomas Lemuel.** 1831–1916. American politician, b. Utica, N.Y. U.S. postmaster general (1881–82); co-operated with attorney general to stop Star Route frauds.

**James, Thomas Potts.** 1803–1882. American botanist, b. Radnor, Pa. Specialist in study of mosses and liverworts.

**James, Will,** *in full* **William Roderick.** 1892–1942. American writer and illustrator, b. near Great Falls, Mont. Ranch hand on western U.S. and Canadian ranges. Illustrated his own books. Author of *Cowboys, North and South* (1924), *Smoky* (1926; awarded Newbery medal), etc.

**James, William.** d. 1827. British naval historian; published a standard *Naval History of Great Britain from the Declaration of War by France in 1793 to the Accession of George IV* (1822–24).

**James, William.** 1842–1910. Son of Henry James (1811–1882); bro. of Henry James (1843–1916). American psychologist and philosopher, b. New York City. Grad. Harvard Med. School (1869). Taught anatomy, physiology, and hygiene, Harvard (from 1872); professor of philosophy (from 1881). Known esp. as one of the founders of pragmatism. Author of *The Principles of Psychology* (1890), *The Will to Believe and Other Essays* (1897), *The Varieties of Religious Experience* (1902), *Pragmatism* (1907), *The Meaning of Truth* (1909), *A Pluralistic Universe* (1909), *Essays in Radical Empiricism* (1912). See C. G. LANGE.

**James Edward.** = James Francis Edward STUART.

**Jame'son** (jām'sʼn), **Anna Brownell,** *nee* **Mur'phy** (mûr'fĭ). 1794–1860. Irish writer; m. Robert Jameson (1825). Published *Diary of an Ennuyée* (1826), *Characteristics of Women* (1832), and works on art by which she is chiefly known.

**Jameson, John Franklin.** 1859–1937. American historian; director, department of historical research, Carnegie Institution, Washington, D.C. (1905–28); chief, division of manuscripts, Library of Congress (1928–37). Author of *Dictionary of United States History* (1894), *The American Revolution considered as a Social Movement* (1926), etc.

**Jameson,** Sir **Leander Starr.** *Known as* **Doctor Jameson.** 1853–1917. Scottish physician and statesman in South Africa; b. in Edinburgh. M.D., London (1877). To Kimberley, South Africa (1878) and practiced medicine; became friend of Cecil Rhodes, and was used by Rhodes in various negotiations with natives, notably with the Matabele chief Lobengula. During troubles at Johannesburg between Uitlanders and Boer government (1895), led the famous Jameson Raid, an attempt to cross the Transvaal and take help to the Uitlanders in Johannesburg; forced to surrender to General Cronjé (Jan., 1896); handed over by President Kruger to British authorities for trial; sent to England and imprisoned for a short time. Returned to South Africa and entered Cape legislature (1900); became prime minister of Cape Colony (1904–08).

**Jameson, Robert.** 1774–1854. Scottish mineralogist.

**Jameson, Storm,** *in full* **Margaret Storm.** 1897– . English novelist; m. Guy Patterson Chapman. Author of *Happy Highways* (1920), *Farewell to Youth* (1928), *A Richer Dust* (1931), *Here Comes a Candle* (1938), *Farewell Night, Welcome Day* (1939; American title *The Captain's Wife*), *The Fort* (1941).

**Jame'sone** (jām'sʼn), **George.** 1588?–1644. Scottish portrait painter.

**Ja'met'** (zhȧ'mĕ'), **Marie.** *Known as* **Marie Augustine de la Com'pas'sion'** (dē lȧ kôɴ'pä'syôɴ'). 1820–1893. A founder of the French religious order Little Sisters of the Poor, and superior of the order (from 1843).

**Ja'mi** (jä'mĭ). *Pers.* **Nur ud-din 'Abd-ur-raḥman ibn Aḥmad.** 1414–1492. Persian poet and mystic, b. at Jam in Khurasan. Devoted himself to study of Sufi philosophy, which he accepted with all its mysticism. Author of lyric and romantic verse; considered the last great classic poet of Persia.

**Ja'mie·son** (jā'mĭ·sʼn; jăm'ĭ-; jĭm'ĭ-), **John.** 1759–1838.

Scottish clergyman, antiquary, and lexicographer; compiled *Etymological Dictionary of the Scottish Language* (1808).

**Jamieson, Robert.** 1780?–1844. Scottish anthologist and antiquary; compiled *Popular Ballads and Songs* (1806); collaborated with Sir Walter Scott in *Illustrations of Northern Antiquities* (1814).

**Ja'min'** (zhà'măN'), **Jules Célestin.** 1818–1886. French physicist. Devised an electric candle and a powerful electromagnet made up of many laminae; known also for work on capillarity, the interference and velocity of light, and the reflection of light from metallic surfaces.

**Jam'i·son** (jăm'ĭ·s'n), **Cecilia Viets,** *nee* **Da'kin** (dā'kĭn). 1837–1909. Painter and author, b. Yarmouth, Nova Scotia; to Boston as a young girl; m. 1st George Hamilton, 2d Samuel Jamison (1878; d. 1902). In writing, successful in books for children, as *Lady Jane* (1891), *Thistledown* (1903), *The Penhallow Family* (1905), etc.

**Jammes** (zhàm), **Francis.** 1868–1938. French poet and novelist. Among his books of verse are *De l'Angélus de l'Aube à l'Angélus du Soir* (1888–97), *Le Triomphe de la Vie* (1900–01), *Quatre Livres de Quatrains* (1923–25); prose works include *Clara d'Ellébeuse* (1899), *Pomme d'Amis* (1904), *Ma Fille Bernadette* (1910), *Cloches pour Deux Mariages* (1925), *Divine Douleur* (1928).

**Jam'nit·zer** (yäm'nĭt·sẽr) *or* **Ja'mit·zer** (yä'mĭt·sẽr). Name of a family of German Renaissance goldsmiths and ornamental designers and engravers in Nuremberg, including: **Wenzel** (1508–1585), who conducted a workshop with his brother **Albrecht** (until 1550) and later with his sons and sons-in-law; court goldsmith to Charles V, Ferdinand I, Maximilian II (from 1564), and Rudolf II. His grandson **Christoph** (1563–1618) designed ornamental works and published a *Groteskenbuch* (1610) containing 63 fantastic engravings.

**Jan** (yän). Dutch form of JOHN.

**Jan** (yän), **Karl von.** 1836–1899. German scholar in field of ancient Greek music.

**Ja'ná·ček** (yà'nä·chĕk), **Leoš.** 1854–1928. Czech composer of operas, a song cycle, a symphonic poem, and orchestral and vocal works.

**Ja'nau·schek** (yä'nou·shĕk), **Fan'ny** (fän'ē), *in full* **Fran·zi'ska Mag'da·le'na Ro·man'ce** (frän·tsĭs'kä mäk'dä·lā'nä rō·män'tsĕ). 1830–1904. Bohemian tragedienne; learned English in order to interpret Shakespearean roles, and toured U.S. (1863); played in London (1876).

**Jane** (jān), **Frederick T.** 1870–1916. British naval officer; founder and first editor of the annuals *Jane's Fighting Ships* (1898 ff.), an authoritative description of the world's navies, and *All the World's Aircraft* (1910 ff.).

**Jane Seymour.** 1509?–1537. 3d queen of Henry VIII of England. See under SEYMOUR family.

**Ja'ne·quin'** (zhàn'kăN'). 16th-century composer, probably French; published a collection of sacred songs for four voices, a collection *Chansons de la Guerre et de la Chasse;* wrote also much church music.

**Ja'net'** (zhà'nĕ'), **Paul.** 1823–1899. French philosopher.

**Janet, Pierre Marie Félix.** 1859–1947. French psychologist and neurologist. Known esp. for researches on hysteria and neuroses.

**Jane'way** (jān'wā), **Edward Gamaliel.** 1841–1911. American physician, b. New Brunswick, N.J.; practiced New York City. His son **Theodore Caldwell** (1872–1917), physician, practiced with his father in New York; taught at Bellevue Hospital Med. Coll. (1898–1907), Coll. of Phys. & Surg., N.Y. (1907–14), Johns Hopkins Hospital and School of Medicine (1914–17); in U.S. army medical corps during the World War.

**Ja'nin'** (zhà'năN'), **Jules Gabriel.** 1804–1874. French journalist, novelist and critic.

**Jan'is** (jăn'ĭs), **Elsie.** *Real surname* **Bier'bow'er** (bēr'bou'ẽr). 1889–1956. American actress; appeared in vaudeville (1898–1903); starred in *The Belle of New York* (1904), *The Fortune Teller, The Vanderbilt Cup* (1906–08), *The Hoyden, Elsie Janis and Her Gang* (written by herself), etc.; entertainer to A.E.F. (1917–18).

**Ja'ni·tschek** (yä'nē·chĕk), **Hubert.** 1846–1893. Austrian art historian, b. Troppau; m. **Maria Tölk** [tûlk] (1859–1927), poet (*Gesammelte Gedichte*, 1892), and author of tales and novels.

**Jank** (yängk), **Angelo.** 1868–1940. German painter and illustrator.

**Jan'kó** (yŏn'kō), **Paul** (poul) **von** (fôn). 1856–1919. Hungarian pianist; inventor (1882) of the Jankó keyboard, a pianoforte keyboard of six rows of keys.

**Jan'ney** (jăn'ĭ), **Eli Hamilton.** 1831–1912. American inventor of automatic railway car coupler (1st patent, 1868), made standard railroad equipment in 1888.

**Jan'nings** (yän'ĭngs; *Angl.* jăn'ĭngz), **Emil.** 1887–1950. Stage and screen actor, b. in Switzerland of German-American parentage. Appeared with Max Reinhardt's company in Berlin; made screen debut in Ernst Lubitsch films (1916), and worked in American films (1926–29); returned to stage (1932).

**Jan of Leiden** (yän). = JOHN OF LEIDEN.

**János Hollós.** See under MATTHIAS CORVINUS.

**Ja·now'ski** (yä·nôf'skē), **David.** 1868–1927. Polish chess expert; made headquarters in Paris and for twenty years was a leader in international tournaments.

**Jan'sen** (jăn's'n; *Du.* yän'sĕn), **Cornelis.** *Lat.* **Cornelius Jan·se'ni·us** (jăn·sē'nĭ·ŭs; -sĕn'yŭs). 1585–1638. Dutch Roman Catholic theologian, b. Acquoi, near Leerdam; founder of the Jansenists. Head of Dutch theological college of St. Pulcheria, Louvain (1617); professor at Louvain (1630); bishop of Ypres (1636). Author of *Mars Gallicus* (an anti-French, anti-Richelieu attack, 1635), and of *Augustinus* (pub. posthumously, 1640; condemned by Urban VIII, 1642), in which he maintained that the teaching of St. Augustine on grace, free will, and predestination was opposed to the teaching of the Jesuit schools. In the religious controversies that it provoked, his view was championed by Pascal, Arnauld, Nicole, and the Port-royalists. See also Jean DU VERGIER DE HAURANNE.

**Jan'son** (yän'sôn), **Anton.** fl. 1660–1687. Dutch type founder.

**Jan'son** (yän'sŏn), **Kristofer Nagel.** 1841–1917. Novelist, b. Bergen, Norway; to America (1879); Unitarian missionary in Minnesota and Wisconsin region (1881–93); resident of Norway (from 1893). Works, all written in Norwegian, include *Our Grandparents* (1881), *Sara* (1891), *The Outlaw* (1893), *Aspasia* (1914), etc.

**Jan'son'** (zhäN'sôN'; *Angl.* jăn's'n), **Nicolas.** = Nicolas JENSON.

**Jans'sen** (yän'sĕn), **Geraert** *or* **Gerard.** fl. 1616. Tombstone carver in England; known for his portrait bust of Shakespeare at Stratford upon Avon.

**Jans'sen** (yän'sĕn), **Johannes.** 1829–1891. German Roman Catholic priest and historian; champion of ultramontanism.

**Janssen, Peter.** 1844–1908. German historical and portrait painter.

**Jans'sen'** (zhäN'sĕn'), **Pierre Jules César.** 1824–1907. French astronomer, b. Paris. On various scientific missions, as to Peru to determine the magnetic equator (1857–58), to Italy to study the telluric rays in the solar spectrum (1861–62; 1864), to the Azores for magnetic and topographic studies (1867); also on expeditions to observe solar eclipses, etc. Established and directed observatory on Mont Blanc (1893).

**Jans'sen** (yän'sĕn), **Zacharias.** Dutch spectacles maker credited with the invention of the compound microscope (c. 1590).

**Jans'sens** (yän'sĕns), **Abraham.** *Called* **Janssens van Nuys'sen** (vän noi'sĕn). 1575?–1632. Flemish historical painter and colorist. Became master in St. Luke's Guild at Antwerp (1601). He painted chiefly religious, mythological, and allegorical pictures, and portraits.

**Jans'sen van Ceu'len** (yän'sĕn vän kû'lĕn), **Cornelius.** 1593–?1664. Portrait painter in England.

**Jan'u·ar'i·us** (jăn'ū·âr'ĭ·ŭs), Saint. *Ital.* San **Gen-na'ro** (sän jān·nä'rō). 272?–?305. Christian prelate; bishop of Beneventum; martyred, according to legend. Patron saint of Naples, where two phials believed to contain his blood are preserved and exhibited twice a year, in May and September, the substance in the phials miraculously liquefying on these occasions.

**Ja'nus** (yä'nōōs). Pseudonym of J. J. I. von DÖLLINGER.

**Jan'vier** (jăn'vēr), **Thomas Allibone.** 1849–1913. American writer, b. Philadelphia; resident of New York (from 1884). Author of *Color Studies* (1885), *The Aztec Treasure House* (1890), *Stories of Old New Spain* (1891), *In Old New York* (1894), *The Dutch Founding of New York* (1903), *Henry Hudson* (1909), *Legends of the City of Mexico* (1910), *From the South of France* (1912). His wife, **Catharine Ann,** *nee* **Drink'er** [drĭngk'ĕr] (1841–1922), was a painter and author. His sister **Margaret Thomson Janvier** (1844–1913), over pen name **Margaret Van'de·grift** (văn'dĕ·grĭft), wrote a number of books for children.

**Ja'pik·se** (yä'pĭk·sĕ), **Nicolas.** 1872–1944. Dutch historian.

**Jaques'-Dal'croze'** (zhäk'dȧl'krōz'), **Émile.** 1865–1950. Swiss composer and teacher of eurythmics; founder and director (from 1915) of Institut Jaques-Dalcroze, Geneva, where he pursued the teaching of eurythmics.

**Jar'dine** (jär'dēn), **Sir William.** 1800–1874. Scottish naturalist; edited *Naturalists' Library* (1833–45).

**Jar'dine** (jär'dīn), **William M.** 1879–1955. American educator; president, Kansas State (1918–25). U.S. secretary of agriculture (1925–29). U.S. minister to Egypt (1930–33); pres., Wichita Municipal U. (1934–49).

**Ja·rir'** (jä·rēr'). *Arab.* **Jarīr.** d. 729? Arab poet and satirist; lived in Iraq; one of three leading poets (see al-AKHTAL and al-FARAZDAQ) of early Ommiad period; court poet of al-Hajjaj.

**Jar'nac'** (zhȧr'nȧk'), Comte **Guy Chabot de.** French soldier; known for his duel (July 10, 1547) with La Châteigneraie before King Henri II and his court, when Jarnac by a sudden and unexpected blow (whence the expression "coup de Jarnac") won the decision.

**Jar·nach'** (jär·näk'), **Philip.** 1892– . German composer, of Spanish descent. Studied under Busoni, and completed Busoni's opera *Dr. Faust* after Busoni's death. Composer esp. of string quartets.

**Jär'ne·felt** (yăr'nĕ·fĕlt), **Armas.** 1869–1958. Finnish composer and conductor, cofounder of Finnish national music. Composed overtures, the symphonic poem *Korsholm* (1894), the symphonic fantasy *Heimatklang* (1895), a serenade, suites for orchestra, choral works, piano pieces, songs, etc.

**Jar'no·wick** (yär'nō·vĭk). *Real name* **Giovanni Ma'ne** (mä'nā) **Gior'no·vi'chi** (jōr'nō·vē'kē). 1745?–1804. Italian violinist and composer. His grandson **Pierre Louis Hus'-Des'forges'** (üs'dā'fôrzh'), *also known as* **Jarnowick** (1773–1838), was a violoncellist and composer.

**Jar'ves** (jär'vĕs), **Deming.** 1790–1869. Pioneer glass manufacturer in U.S. The pressed glass known as Sandwich glass was manufactured (from 1827) in his factory at Sandwich, Mass. His son **James Jackson** (1818–1888) founded and edited *Polynesian,* in Honolulu, first newspaper published in Hawaiian Islands (1840); settled in Florence, Italy (after 1851) and collected works of art, later (1871) sold to Yale Art School and known as the Jarves Collection; presented collection of Venetian glass to Metropolitan Museum of Art, New York City (1881).

**Jar'vis** (jär'vĭs), **Claude Scu'da·more** (skū'dȧ·mōr). 1879–1953. British soldier and writer. Served in Boer War (1899–1902) and World War (1914–18). Governor of Sinai Peninsula (1923–36); awarded Lawrence Memorial Medal by Royal Central Asian Society (1938).

**Jas'min'** (zhȧs'măN'), **Jacques.** *Pen name of* **Jacques Bo'é'** (bô'ā'). *Known as* **Jasmin d'A'gen'** (dȧ'zhăN') *and* **the Barber Poet.** 1798–1864. Gascon poet; wigmaker by profession; tramped through the Midi reciting his poems, and gaining reputation of being the last of the troubadours. His works include popular songs, patriotic odes, and lyrics, all written in a dialect of the langue d'oc.

**Ja'son of Cy·re'ne** (jā's'n, sī·rē'nē). fl. about 100 B.C. A Hellenistic Jew; author of a history in Greek of the Maccabean revolt from 175–161 B.C. (5 books), the basis of the present *2 Maccabees* (of the Biblical Apocrypha).

**Jas'par'** (zhȧs'pȧr'), **Henri.** 1870–1939. Belgian statesman and lawyer; foreign minister (1920–24), advocate of close co-operation with France and membership in League of Nations; formed ministry of public safety (1926) and acted as minister of interior; formed new government following resignation of Socialists (1927) and a third cabinet (1929–31); finance minister in Broqueville's cabinet (1932–34).

**Jas'pers** (yäs'pērs), **Karl.** 1883–1969. German psychiatrist and philosopher.

**Jas'trow** (yäs'trō), **Ignaz.** 1856–1937. German economist and historian; assistant to Ranke in historical work; economic adviser in Berlin (1903–17), and rector of the Berlin Commercial Hochschule (1906–09).

**Jas'trow** (jăs'trō; yäs'trō), **Marcus,** *known also as* **Morris.** 1829–1903. Rabbi, b. in Prussian Poland. Rabbi of synagogue in Warsaw (1858). Pastorate in Philadelphia (1866–92). Compiler of *Dictionary of the Targumim, the Talmud Babli and Yerushalmi and the Midrashic Literature* (1886–1903). His son **Morris** (1861–1921), b. Warsaw, Poland, was a Semitic scholar; professor, U. of Pennsylvania (from 1892) and librarian (from 1898); special editor, *Webster's New International Dictionary* (1910); author of *The Study of Religion* (1901), *The Book of Job* (1920), *The Song of Songs* (1921). Another son, **Joseph** (1863–1944), psychologist, was professor, U. of Wisconsin (1888–1927); author of *Time Relations of Mental Phenomena* (1890), *The Subconscious* (1906), *Piloting your Life* (1930), *Effective Thinking* (1931), *The House that Freud Built* (1932), *The Life of the Mind* (1938), etc.

**Jaswant Rao Holkar.** See HOLKAR.

**Ja'tho** (yä'tō), **Karl.** 1873–1933. German airplane builder; said to be first to construct a biplane propelled by a gasoline motor (1899); claimed first successful flight in mechanical airplane (August 5, 1903), four months before flight by Wright brothers at Kitty Hawk, N.C. Established airplane works at Hanover (1913); founded one of first aviation schools in Germany.

**Jau'bert'** (zhō'bâr'), **Pierre Amédée Émilien Probe.** 1779–1847. French Orientalist.

**Jau'court'** (zhō'kōōr'), Marquis **Arnail François de.** 1757–1852. French politician; member of Legislative Assembly; émigré (1791). Returned to France after Reign of Terror; member of the Tribunate (1799) and its president (1802); elected to Senate (1803); minister of marine (1815). Member of the privy council and supported July Monarchy (1830); in upper house, voted in favor of Louis Napoleon (1848) and approved the coup d'état (Dec. 2, 1851).

**Jaucourt,** Chevalier **Louis de.** 1704–1779. French scholar; edited articles in the *Encyclopédie* on physiology, chemistry, botany, pathology, and political history.

**Jauregg, Julius Wagner von.** See WAGNER VON JAUREGG.

**Jau'ré'gui'ber'ry'** (zhō'rā'gē'bĕ'rē'), **Jean Bernard.** 1815–1887. French naval officer.

**Jáu're·gui y A'gui·lar'** (hou'rā·gē ē ä'gē·lär'), **Juan Martínez de.** 1583–1641. Spanish poet and painter; supposed painter of Cervantes's portrait now in Real Academia Española, Madrid. Known esp. for verse translation of Tasso's *Aminta* (1607).

**Jau'rès'** (zhō'râs'), **Jean Léon.** 1859–1914. French socialist and politician, b. Castres; deputy from Tarn (1885–89); retired to teaching and writing essays on philosophy (1889). Became interested in socialism; again deputy (1893–98, 1902–14); leader of Socialists in the Chamber of Deputies; founder (with Briand, 1904) and editor of *L'Humanité* (1904–14). Fought militaristic legislation on eve of outbreak of World War I.

**Javier, Francisco.** See Saint Francis XAVIER.

**Jay** (jā), **John.** 1745–1829. American jurist and statesman, b. New York City. Grad. Columbia (1764). Active in pre-Revolutionary agitation. Member, Continental Congress (1774–77, 1778, 1779; president, 1778–79). American minister to Spain (1779); called to Paris by Franklin to join commission for negotiating peace with Great Britain (1782; peace signed, 1783); returned to New York (1784). U.S. secretary of foreign affairs (1784–89). Joined with Hamilton and Madison in writing the *Federalist,* explaining new constitution (1787–88). Chief justice, U.S. Supreme Court (1789–95); negotiated treaty (Jay's treaty) with Great Britain settling outstanding disputes (1794–95). Governor of New York (1795–1801). His son **Peter Augustus** (1776–1843), lawyer, was recorder of New York (1820–21). Another son, **William** (1789–1858), was also a lawyer; prominent abolitionist and advocate of emancipation of slaves. A son of William, **John** (1817–1894), was a lawyer and diplomat; prominent abolitionist; an organizer of Republican Party; U.S. minister to Austria-Hungary (1869–74).

**Ja'ya·de'va** (jŭ'yȧ·dā'vȧ). fl. about 1200 A.D. Hindu poet, probably native of Bengal. Author of a lyric drama in Sanskrit in varied meters, *Gītagōvinda* ("Song of the Cowherd") recounting the love of Krishna for the milkmaid Radha, translated into English (1875) by Sir Edwin Arnold as *The Indian Song of Songs.*

**Jeaf'fre·son** (jĕf'ẽr·s'n), **John Cordy.** 1831–1901. English writer of novels, and biographical sketches, as *The Real Lord Byron* (1883), *The Real Shelley* (1885), *Lady Hamilton and Lord Nelson* (1888). Also published *Book About Doctors* (1860), *Book About Lawyers* (1866), *Book About the Clergy* (1870).

**Jean** (zhäN). French form of JOHN.

**Jean.** 1921– . Grand duke of Luxembourg; son of Grand Duchess Charlotte (*q.v.*); m. Princess Josephine-Charlotte of Belgium (1953); Grand duke (1964– ).

**Jean Bap'tiste' de la Salle'** (zhäN bȧ'tēst' dē lȧ sȧl'), Saint. 1651–1719. Christian saint and educational reformer; priest (1678) at Reims, where he founded (1680–84) the Institute of the Brothers of the Christian Schools (Christian Brothers); canonized (1900).

**Jean de Ma'tha'** (zhäN' dē mȧ'tȧ'), Saint. 1160–1213. French priest; consecrated himself to redemption of Christian captives in the hands of the Turks; founded order of Trinitarians (rule approved, 1198). Canonized (1679). See Saint FÉLIX OF VALOIS.

**Jean de Meung** (zhäN' dē mûn') *or* **Meun.** *Real name* **Jean** *or* **Jehan Clo'pi'nel'** (klô'pē'nĕl') *or* **Cho'pi'nel'** (shô'-). 13th-century French writer; author of second part of the allegorical metrical romance *Roman de la Rose* (cf. GUILLAUME DE LORRIS) and translator of Boethius's *Consolation of Philosophy.*

**Jean'-Au'bry'** (zhäN'ō'brē'), **Georges.** 1882–1950. French writer on music and biographer of Joseph Conrad (*Life and Letters of Joseph Conrad,* 1927).

**Jeanne d'Albret.** See ALBRET.

**Jeanne d'Arc.** See JOAN OF ARC.

**Jeanne de Bour'gogne'** (zhän' dē bo͝or'gôn'y'). Name of two queens of France. (1) d. 1325. Daughter of Count Otto IV of Burgundy; m. (1306) Philip of France, later (1316–22) King Philip V. (2) 1293–1348. Daughter of Duke Robert II of Burgundy; m. (1313) Philip of Valois who, as Philip VI (1328–50), became first king of France of house of Valois. See ORLÉANS and BURGUNDY.

**Jeanneret, Charles Édouard** and **Pierre.** See LE CORBUSIER.

**Jean'nin'** (zhȧ'năN'), **Pierre.** 1540–1623. French lawyer and diplomat; counselor to Parliament of Dijon (1579) and president of the parliament (1581). Intendant of finance under Henry IV (1602). French ambassador to Holland (1607–09).

**Jean'ron'** (zhäN'rôN'), **Philippe Auguste.** 1810–1877. French genre and landscape painter; founded Musée du Luxembourg.

**Jean'roy'** (zhäN'rwȧ'), **Marie Henri Gustave Alfred.** 1859–1953. French Romance language scholar.

**Jeans** (jēnz), Sir **James Hopwood.** 1877–1946. English physicist, astronomer, and author, b. London; educ. Cambridge. Professor of applied mathematics, Princeton (1905–09); lecturer in applied mathematics, Cambridge (1910–12); secretary, Royal Society (1919–29); professor of astronomy, Royal Institution. Worked esp. on kinetic theory of gases and on radiations. Author of *The Dynamical Theory of Gases* (1904), *Theoretical Mechanics* (1906), *The Mathematical Theory of Electricity and Magnetism* (1908), *Radiation and the Quantum-Theory* (1914), *Problems of Cosmogony and Stellar Dynamics* (1919), etc., and of books popularizing science, including *The Universe Around Us* (1929), *The Stars in their Courses* (1931), *Through Space and Time* (1934), *Science and Music* (1937).

**Jeau'rat'** (zhō'rȧ'), **Étienne.** 1699–1789. French painter of genre scenes.

**Je'ba·vý** (yĕ'bȧ·vē), **Václav.** *Pseudonym* **Otakar Bře'zi·na** (bẽr·zhĕ'zĭ·nȧ). 1868–1929. Czech lyric and mystic poet.

**Jebb** (jĕb), Sir **Richard Clav'er·house** (klăv'ẽr·hous). 1841–1905. Scottish Greek scholar, b. in Dundee; educ. Cambridge. Professor, Glasgow (1875–89), Cambridge (1889–1905). M.P. for Cambridge U. (1891–1905). Author of *Attic Orators* (2 vols., 1876), *The Growth and Influence of Greek Poetry* (1893), etc. Edited *Sophocles.* O.M. (1905).

**Jech'o·ni'ah** (jĕk'ō·nī'ȧ) *or* **Jech'o·ni'as** (-ăs). = JEHOIACHIN.

**Jee'jee·bhoy'** (jē'jē·bä'ē), Sir **Jam·set'jee** (jŭm·sāt'jē). 1783–1859. Indian Parsi merchant and philanthropist; founded hospital at Bombay; endowed schools; built public works. Knighted (1842) and created a baronet (1857), first native Indian to be thus honored.

**Jef'fer·ies** (jĕf'rĭz), **Richard.** 1848–1887. English naturalist and writer; best known for the descriptions of nature in his stories *The Gamekeeper at Home* (1877), *Wood Magic* (1881), *Bevis* (1882), *Red-Deer* (1884), etc.

**Jef'fers** (jĕf'ẽrz), **Robinson,** *in full* **John Robinson.** 1887–1962. American poet, b. Pittsburgh, Pa. Author of *Californians* (1916), *Tamar* (1924), *Cawdor* (1928), *Dear Judas* (1929), *Thurso's Landing* (1932), *Solstice* (1935), *Such Counsels You Gave to Me* (1937), etc.

**Jeffers, William Martin.** 1876–1953. American railway official, b. North Platte, Nebr.; rose from office boy (1890) to president (1937–46) of Union Pacific R.R.; U.S. rubber administrator (1942–43).

**Jef'fer·son** (jĕf'ẽr·s'n), **Charles Edward.** 1860–1937. American Congregational clergyman; pastor of Broadway Tabernacle, New York City (1898–1937).

**Jefferson, Joseph.** 1829–1905. American actor, b. Philadelphia; made success in Laura Keene's company, New York, as Asa Trenchard in *Our American Cousin* (1858), and Caleb Plummer in *The Cricket on the Hearth* (1859). Most famous role, Rip Van Winkle in Dion Boucicault's play of that name (from 1865). Also made success of Bob Acres in *The Rivals* (from 1880). His grandfather **Joseph Jefferson** (1774–1832), b. Plymouth, Eng., came to U.S. (1795) and appeared chiefly in comedy roles. See also Eleanor FARJEON.

**Jefferson, Thomas.** 1743–1826. Third president of the United States, b. in Goochland, now Albemarle County, Va. Grad. William and Mary (1762). Adm. to bar (1767). Member, Virginia House of Burgesses (1769–74); with R. H. Lee and Patrick Henry initiated intercolonial committee of correspondence (1773). Member, Continental Congress (1775, 1776); chairman of committee that prepared Declaration of Independence; wrote and presented first draft of declaration to Congress (July 2, 1776); signed Declaration of Independence. Governor of Virginia (1779–81). Again member, Continental Congress (1783–85). U.S. minister to France (1785–89). U.S. secretary of state (1790–93); differing policies caused bitter antagonism with Alexander Hamilton, secretary of treasury. Vice-president of the U.S. (1797–1801); president of the U.S. (1801–09), elected by House of Representatives after tie in popular vote (with Aaron Burr, *q.v.*). Features of administration: purchase of Louisiana, war against Algerian pirates, westward expansion, diplomatic trouble with Great Britain over impressment of American seamen (Embargo Act of 1807), prohibition of the importation of slaves. On retirement from presidency, lived on plantation at "Monticello," near Charlottesville, Va. Instrumental in founding U. of Virginia (1819). Elected to American Hall of Fame (1900).

**Jef'frey** (jĕf'rĭ), **Francis.** Lord **Jeffrey.** 1773–1850. Scottish critic and jurist, b. in Edinburgh. One of founders of *Edinburgh Review* (1802), and its editor (1803–29). Judge of Court of Session (1834–50). Author of the famous devastating criticism of Wordsworth's *Excursion* beginning "This will never do."

**Jef'freys** (jĕf'rĭz), **George.** 1st Baron **Jeffreys of Wem** (wĕm). 1644–1689. English jurist. Solicitor general to duke of York (1677). Lord chief justice (1682) and privy councilor (1683); lord chancellor (1685). On overthrow of James II, attempted to flee from England but was captured and imprisoned in Tower of London (1688), where he died (April 18, 1689). As chief justice and chancellor, made himself notorious by injustice and brutality. The assizes conducted by him (1685) at which those involved in Monmouth's rebellion against James II were tried became known as the Bloody Assizes because of the number of executions decreed.

**Jef'fries** (jĕf'rĭz), **James J.** 1875–1953. American prizefighter; world heavyweight champion from 1899 (winning title from Bob Fitzsimmons) until he retired in 1905; returned to ring for match with Jack Johnson (1910), in which he was defeated.

**Jeffries, John.** 1744–1819. Physician and balloonist, b. Boston; practiced medicine in Boston. Loyalist during American Revolution; resident in England after the war. Interested himself in use of balloons for scientific observations and experiments; with François Blanchard, French aeronaut, crossed English Channel from Dover to forest of Guînes, France, in balloon (Jan. 7, 1785), first crossing of English Channel by air.

**Jehan.** See SHAH JAHAN.

**Jehangir.** See JAHANGIR.

**Je·ho'a·haz** (jē·hō'ȧ·hăz). See AHAZ.

**Jehoahaz.** *In Douay Bible* **Jo'a·chaz** (jō'ȧ·kăz). (1) King of Israel (d. 800? B.C.); son and successor of Jehu; reigned (c. 816–800 B.C.); his kingdom at mercy of Damascus (*2 Kings* xiii). (2) *Called* **Shal'lum** (shăl'ŭm) in *Jeremiah* xxii. 11. King of Judah; son of Josiah; reigned few months only (608 or 607 B.C.); deposed by Necho (II); carried as prisoner to Egypt, where he died (*2 Kings* xxiii. 30–33).

**Jehoash.** See JOASH.

**Je·hoi'a·chin** (jē·hoi'ȧ·kĭn). *In Douay Bible* **Jo'a·chin** (jō'ȧ·kĭn). 615?–?560 B.C. King of Judah (598 or 597 B.C.); son of Jehoiakim; reigned few months only; with Judean leaders, carried away as prisoner to Babylon by Nebuchadnezzar; held captive 37 years; released by Evil-Merodach (*2 Kings* xxiv. 6–16).

**Je·hoi'a·kim** (jē·hoi'ȧ·kĭm). *In Douay Bible* **Jo'a·kim** (jō'ȧ·kĭm). d. 598? B.C. King of Judah (c. 608–598 B.C.). Son of Josiah. Placed on throne by Necho (II), who had deposed Jehoahaz (*2 Kings* xxiii. 34–xxiv. 7); revolted against Babylon after hegemony over Palestine passed (605) from Necho to Nebuchadnezzar at battle of Carchemish; died at siege of Jerusalem just before city was taken; succeeded by Jehoiachin (*q.v.*).

**Je·ho'ram** (jē·hō'răm). *In Douay Bible* **Jo'ram** (jō'răm). (1) King of Israel (d. 843? B.C.); son of Ahab; succeeded older brother Ahaziah as king (c. 852–843 B.C.); with Jehoshaphat of Judah, put down revolt in Moab (*2 Kings* iii); revolt against him by Elisha and his party; slain by Jehu, who seized throne (*2 Kings* ix). (2) King of Judah (d. 844? B.C.); son and successor of Jehoshaphat; reigned (c. 851–844 B.C.); m. Athaliah (*q.v.*), daughter of Ahab and Jezebel; during his reign Edom rebelled; succeeded by son Ahaziah (*2 Kings* viii. 16–29; *2 Chron.* xxi).

**Je·hosh'a·phat** (jē·hŏsh'ȧ·făt). *In Douay Bible* **Jos'a·phat** (jŏs'ȧ·făt). d. 851? B.C. Son and successor of Asa. King of Judah (c. 875–851 B.C.). Ruled righteously and introduced reforms; made alliance with Israel and joined Ahab in battle at Ramoth Gilead against Syrians; practically vassal of Israel; succeeded by son Jehoram (*1 Kings* xxii. 41–50; *2 Kings* iii; *2 Chron.* xvii–xxi).

**Je·hosh'e·ba** (jē·hŏsh'ē·bȧ). *In Douay Bible* **Jos'a·ba** (jŏs'ȧ·bȧ). fl. 9th century B.C. Daughter of King Jehoram of Judah and aunt of Joash. With her husband, high priest Jehoiada, saved life of Joash when royal family was massacred by Athaliah (*2 Kings* xi. 2–3).

**Je'hu** (jē'hū). d. 816? B.C. King of Israel (c. 843–816 B.C.). Founder of new dynasty; soldier under King Ahab; led revolt against him; anointed king by Elisha; killed kings Jehoram and Ahaziah, driving his chariot furiously (*2 Kings* ix. 20) to the attack; seized throne of Israel and controlled Judah by destroying royal family; paid tribute to Shalmaneser III; at war with Hazael of Damascus; succeeded by son Jehoahaz (*2 Kings* ix–x).

**Jehudah** *or* **Jehuda.** Var. of JUDAH.

**Je'la·čić od Bu'ži·ma** (yĕ'lä·chēt'y' [*Angl.* -chĭch] ōd bōō'zhē·mä), Count **Josip.** 1801–1859. Croatian general and governor; lieutenant field marshal and ban of

Croatia (1848). Incited by Austria, led army against Magyar domination in revolutionary Hungary in attempt to separate Croatia from Hungary (1848–49), but was finally defeated (1849). Returned to Zagreb as ban and governor of Croatia and Slavonia; created count (1855).

**Jelal ad-Din.** See JALAL-AD-DIN.

**Je'lí·nek** (yĕ'lē·nĕk), **Hanuš.** 1878– . Czech poet and literary critic.

**Jellachich, Joseph.** = Josip JELAČIĆ OD BUŽIMA.

**Jel'li·coe** (jĕl'ĭ·kō), **John Rush'worth** (rŭsh'wûrth; -wĕrth). 1st Earl **Jellicoe.** 1859–1935. British naval commander; rear admiral (1907); admiral of the fleet (1919). During World War, commander of the grand fleet (1914–16) and chief of the naval staff (1917); commanded the grand fleet in battle of Jutland (May 31, 1916). Governor general of New Zealand (1920–24). Member of Order of Merit (1916).

**Jel'liffe** (jĕl'ĭf), **Smith E'ly** (ē'lĭ). 1866–1945. American neurologist.

**Jel'li·nek** (yĕl'ē·nĕk), **Adolf.** 1821–1893. Austrian theologian, scholar, and orator; rabbi and preacher, Leipzig (1845–56) and Vienna. A son, **Georg** (1851–1911), b. Leipzig, was a jurist. Another son, **Max Hermann** (1868–1938), b. Vienna, was a philologist; professor, Vienna (from 1900); author of *Geschichte der Gotischen Sprache* (1926), etc.

**Jem** (jĕm) *or* **Djem** (jĕm). *Also* **Zi·zim'** (zĭ·zĭm'). 1459–1495. Turkish prince, younger son of Sultan Mohammed II and brother of Bajazet II. Contested throne with Bajazet (1481); proclaimed sultan at Bursa and proposed division of empire; after year of fighting, was defeated and sought refuge with Knights of Rhodes (Hospitalers); betrayed by Aubusson, grand master of the knights; kept in captivity thirteen years. Died under suspicious circumstances, possibly poisoned.

**Jemaleddin Afghani.** See JAMAL-UD-DIN AL-AFGHANI.

**Je'natsch** (yā'näch), **Georg** *or* **Jürg** (yürk). 1596–1639. Swiss soldier and political leader during the Thirty Years' War.

**Jenghiz Khan.** Variant of GENGHIS KHAN.

**Jen'kin** (jĕng'kĭn), **Fleeming,** *in full* **Henry Charles Fleeming.** 1833–1885. British electrician, of Welsh family; collaborator with Lord Kelvin (*q.v.*) in work on insulation and resistance of submarine telegraphy cables; inventor of telpherage (1882).

**Jen'kins** (jĕng'kĭnz), **Charles Francis.** 1867–1934. American inventor of a motion-picture projector having an intermittent movement (patented, 1895), a braking device for airplanes, an altimeter, the conical paper drinking cup, one of the first automobile self-starters, and devices in radiophotography, television, and radiomovies.

**Jenkins, Herbert.** 1876–1923. English publisher and writer; founded publishing house bearing his name; created fictional cockney character Bindle in a series of books, including *Bindle* (1916), *Adventures of Bindle* (1918), etc.

**Jenkins,** Sir **Lawrence Hugh.** 1858–1928. British jurist in India. Chief justice of high court of judicature, Bombay (1899–1908); member of Council of India (1908–09); chief justice of high court, Bengal (1909–15).

**Jenkins, Robert.** fl. 1731–1738. English mariner whose ear was cut off by the Spanish captain Fandino at Havana (1731). The incident was the immediate cause of the war between England and Spain that became known as "the War of Jenkins's Ear" (1739).

**Jenkinson.** Family name of first three earls of LIVERPOOL.

**Jenks** (jĕngks), **Albert Ernest.** 1869–1953. American anthropologist; professor, Minnesota (1907–38); conducted investigations in African desert, southern and eastern Europe, New Mexico, Minnesota, and the Dakotas.

**Jenks, Edward.** 1861–1939. English lawyer, educator, and writer on law; principal and director of legal studies, Law Society (1903–24); professor, London.

**Jenks, George Charles.** *Pseudonym* **W. B. Law'son** (lô's'n). 1850–1929. Printer, journalist, and writer of fiction; b. London, England; to U.S. (1872); author (from 1886) of dime novels, including some of *Nick Carter* series, *Diamond Dick,* and *Jesse James.*

**Jenks, Jeremiah Whipple.** 1856–1929. American educator, b. St. Clair, Mich. Professor of political economy, Cornell (1891–1912); professor of government, N.Y.U. (from 1912). Adviser, U.S. Industrial Commission in its investigation of "trusts" (1899). Sent by U.S. government to the Orient to study currencies, taxation, and police systems (1902). Employed by Mexico on currency reform (1903). Member, U.S. Commission on International Exchange (1904); U.S. Immigration Commission (1907). Assisted Nicaragua in revision of banking laws (1925) and Germany in plans for currency stabilization. Author of *The Trust Problem* (1900), *Principles of Politics* (1909), *The Immigration Problem* (1911).

**Jen'ner** (jĕn'ĕr), **Edward.** 1749–1823. English physician, discoverer of vaccination, b. at Berkeley, Gloucestershire. Apprenticed to surgeon near Bristol; pupil of John Hunter (*q.v.*) in London (1770–72); studied at St. George's Hospital. Began practice in Berkeley (1773). Observed that dairymaids who had had cowpox did not get smallpox; vaccinated James Phipps, a boy of eight, with matter from cowpox vesicles on hands of a milkmaid (1796); several weeks later the boy was inoculated with smallpox but did not contract the disease; published *Inquiry into the Cause and Effects of the Variolae Vaccinae* in which he announced his discovery of vaccination (1798).

**Jenner,** Sir **William.** 1815–1898. English physician and pathological anatomist. Established separate identities of typhus and typhoid fevers.

**Jen'ne·val'** (zhĕn'vȧl'). *Pseudonym of* **Hippolyte Louis Alexandre De·chet'** (dē·shĕ'). 1801–1830. French comedian and poet; on stage in Paris, Lille, Brussels, and finally (1830) at Comédie Française. Fought with Belgian patriots (1830); wrote the words of *La Brabançonne,* adopted as the Belgian national anthem.

**Jen'ney** (jĕn'ĭ), **William Le Baron.** 1832–1907. American architect; designed Home Insurance Co. building, in Chicago, with type of skeleton construction making it the father of modern skyscrapers (1884).

**Jen'nings** (jĕn'ĭngz), **Herbert Spencer.** 1868–1947. American naturalist; professor, Johns Hopkins (from 1906); conducted research work in physiology of microorganisms, animal behavior, and genetics.

**Jennings, Sarah.** See under John CHURCHILL.

**Jen'sen** (yĕn'zĕn), **Adolf.** 1837–1879. German composer, esp. of songs and piano pieces, including the songs in the *Spanisches Liederbuch,* the song cycle *Dolorosa,* and *Gaudeamus* (12 songs for bass). His brother **Gustav** (1843–1895), composer and violinist, wrote chamber music, choruses, piano pieces, and songs.

**Jensen, Hans.** *In Full* **Johannes Hans Daniels Jensen.** 1907–1973. German physicist. Awarded Nobel prize in Physics (1963) with M. G. Mayer and E. P. Wigner for research on nuclear shell structure.

**Jen'sen** (yĕn's'n), **Jens Arnold Diederich.** *Called* (*since 1911*) **J. A. D. J. Bild'söe** (bēl'sû). 1849–1936. Danish naval officer; explored Greenland.

**Jensen, Johannes Vilhelm.** 1873–1950. Danish lyric poet and novelist; opponent of Georg Brandes. Awarded 1944 Nobel prize for literature.

**Jen′sen** (yĕn′zĕn), **Peter Christian Albrecht.** 1861– . German Assyriologist.

**Jensen, Wilhelm.** 1837–1911. German novelist and newspaper editor; author of historical and modern novels and stories, novelettes, and lyric and epic poems and tragedies.

**Jen′son′** (zhäN′sôN′; *Angl.* jĕn′s′n), **Nicolas.** d. about 1480. French engraver and printer; sent by Charles VII to Mainz to learn art of printing; worked three years under Gutenberg; set up printing establishment in Venice (c. 1470) and perfected roman type.

**Jen′yns** (jĕn′ĭnz), **Soame.** 1704–1787. English politician and writer; educ. Cambridge; M.P. (1742–80). Author of *Poems* (1752), *Free Enquiry into the Nature and Origin of Evil* (1757), etc.

**Jeph′thah** (jĕf′thȧ). *In Douay Version* **Jeph′te** (jĕf′tē). In Bible (*Judges* xi), a judge of Israel who sacrificed to Jehovah his only daughter in fulfillment of a vow that if he returned victorious over the Ammonites he would sacrifice whatever came to meet him.

**Jep′son** (jĕp′s′n), **Edgar.** 1863–1938. English novelist.

**Jepson, Helen.** 1907– . American operatic singer; m. George Roscoe Possell (1931). Operatic debut with Philadelphia Grand Opera Company; member of Metropolitan Opera Company in New York City. Also widely known as concert singer.

**Jepson, Willis Linn.** 1867–1946. American botanist; author of works on the flora of California.

**Je′řá·bek** (yĕr′zhä·bĕk), **František.** 1836–1893. Czech playwright.

**Jer′e·mi′ah** (jĕr′ē·mī′ȧ). *In Douay Bible* **Jer′e·mi′as** (-ăs). 650?–?585 B.C. A major Hebrew prophet, whose preaching (of denunciation and judgment) is recorded in Old Testament books of *Jeremiah* and *Lamentations.*

**Jé′rez** (hā′rāth). Modern spelling of XÉREZ.

**Je′ric·hau** (yĭ′rĕk·kou), **Jens Adolf.** 1816–1883. Danish sculptor; pupil of Thorvaldsen. He married **E·li′sa·beth** (ā·lē′zä·bĕt) **Bau′mann** [bou′män] (1819–1881), genre painter, b. in Warsaw of German parents.

**Je′ri·tza** (yĕ′rē·tsä), **Maria.** *Real name* **Marie Je′dlitz·ka** (yĕ′dlĭts·kä). 1887– . Operatic soprano, b. at Brünn, Austria; m. Baron Leopold Popper de Podharagn (div.), (1935) Winfield Sheehan (d. 1945). With Imperial and Royal Opera, Vienna (1913), and Metropolitan Opera Company, New York City (1921). Also widely known as concert singer.

**Jer′myn** (jûr′mĭn), **Henry.** 1st Earl of **St. Al′bans** (sånt ôl′bănz). d. 1684. English courtier and statesman; vice-chamberlain to Queen Henrietta Maria (1628) and her master of the horse (1639). Fought in Royalist army; accompanied queen to France (1644). After execution of Charles I (1649), remained in France with Charles II; after Restoration was created earl (1660) and lord chamberlain (1674).

**Jer′o·bo′am** (jĕr′ō·bō′ăm). Name of two kings of Israel: **Jeroboam I.** d. 912? B.C. An Ephraimite, first king of northern kingdom of Israel (933?–?912 B.C.); leader in plot against Solomon; fled to Egypt on failure of plot, but returned on accession of Rehoboam; chosen king of ten northern tribes; made Shechem his capital; according to Bible account, favored idolatry; succeeded by son Nadab (*1 Kings* xii–xiv).

**Jeroboam II.** d. 744? B.C. King (c. 785–744 B.C.); son and successor of Joash; reconquered lost provinces, seizing Damascus; ruled Israel at height of its power; during his reign, Amos and Hosea prophesied doom of Israel; succeeded by son Zechariah (*2 Kings* xiv. 23–29).

**Je·rome′** (jĕ·rōm′; *Brit. usu.* jĕr′ŭm), Saint. Lat. **Eusebius Hieronymus.** 340?–420. One of the four Doctors of the Church recognized as such during the Middle Ages, b. in Pannonia. Secretary to Pope Damasus (382). Went to Bethlehem in Palestine (386) and in a monastery there devoted himself to study and writing. Published a Latin version of the Bible, known as the Vulgate; wrote also a large number of works of ecclesiastical history and Biblical exegesis.

**Je·rome′** (jĕ·rōm′), **Je·rome′** (jĕ·rōm′) **Klapka.** 1859–1927. English humorist, novelist, and playwright, b. Walsall. Variously, railroad clerk, schoolmaster, actor, journalist. Among his works are *The Idle Thoughts of an Idle Fellow* (1889), *Three Men in a Boat* (1889), *Three Men on the Bummel* (1900), and the plays *Barbara* (1886), *Miss Hobbs* (1899), *Fanny and the Servant Problem* (1908), *The Passing of the Third Floor Back* (1908), *The Great Gamble* (1914).

**Je·rome′** (jĕ·rōm′), **William Travers.** 1859–1934. American lawyer; district attorney, New York County (1901–09); known as vigorous opponent of New York's Tammany Hall organization, and as prosecutor of Harry K. Thaw for the murder of Stanford White.

**Jérôme Bonaparte.** See BONAPARTE.

**Je·rome′ E′mi·lia′ni** (jĕ·rōm′ [jĕr′ŭm] ā′mē·lyä′nē), Saint. 1481?–1537. Venetian soldier; during pestilence in Venice (1518), sold all his property and gave proceeds to the poor, founded orphanages, etc.; founded Somaschian religious order (1532) to engage in charitable works; canonized (1767).

**Jerome of Prague** (präg; prāg). 1360?–1416. Bohemian religious reformer; studied at Oxford and became a convert to the teachings of Wycliffe; preached these doctrines at Prague (1407). An associate and defender of Huss; condemned as heretic by the Council of Constance and burned at the stake (May 30, 1416).

**Jer′ram** (jĕr′ăm), Sir **Martyn,** *in full* **Thomas Henry Martyn.** 1858–1933. British naval officer; rear admiral (1908); admiral (1917); commanded 2d battle squadron at battle of Jutland (May 31, 1916).

**Jer′rold** (jĕr′ŭld), **Douglas William.** 1803–1857. English playwright and humorist; started magazine (1845) and newspaper (1846) bearing his name; editor of *Lloyd's Weekly Newspaper* (from 1852). His most successful plays were *Black-eyed Susan* (1829), *Bride of Ludgate* (1831), *Time Works Wonders* (1845). Among his contributions to *Punch*, the best-known were *Mrs. Caudle's Curtain Lectures.* His son **William Blanchard** (1826–1884) wrote the play *Cool as a Cucumber* (1851); also, *Life of Napoleon III* (1874–82), and a number of novels.

**Jersey,** Earls of. See Edward VILLIERS.

**Jer′vis** (jär′vĭs; jûr′-), **John.** Earl of **St. Vin′cent** (sånt vĭn′s′nt). 1735–1823. English naval commander; commanded the *Foudroyant* in battle of Ushant (1778); captured French *Pégase* (1782); vice-admiral (1793); with Sir Charles Grey captured Martinique and Guadeloupe (1794); commanded Mediterranean fleet (1795); with 15 sail, defeated Spanish fleet of 27 sail off Cape St. Vincent (1797), for which he was created earl. Through foresight and severe discipline, averted mutiny (1798) and subdued spirit of sedition in Channel fleet (1799–1801); first lord of admiralty (1801–04), reformed corruptions of dockyards and brought about impeachment of Melville and reform of naval administration; declined public service till Pitt's death, then resumed command in Channel (1806–07).

**Jer′vis** (jûr′vĭs), **John Bloomfield.** 1795–1885. American engineer; inventor of the railroad truck.

**Jes′per·sen** (yĕs′pĕr·s′n), **Otto,** *in full* **Jens Otto Harry.** 1860–1943. Danish philologist, b. at Randers; educ.

Copenhagen. Professor of English language and literature, Copenhagen (from 1893); rector of the university (1920–21). Proposed an international language, *Novial* (1928), for which he prepared a grammar and lexicon. Among his notable works are *Fonetik* (1897–99; later translated into German as two separate books, *Lehrbuch der Phonetik* and *Phonetische Grundfragen*), *Growth and Structure of the English Language* (1905), *A Modern English Grammar on Historical Principles* (4 parts, 1909–31), *Language, its Nature, Development, and Origin* (1922), *Philosophy of Grammar* (1924), *Analytic Syntax* (1937).

**Jes'se** (jĕs'ē). *In Douay Version* **I'sai** (ī'sī; ī'sā·ī). In Bible, father of David (*1 Samuel* xvi–xvii; *Matthew* i. 5–6), descended from Ruth the Moabitess (*Ruth* iv. 18–22).

**Jesse, Fryniwyd Tennyson.** (d. 1958). Eng. novelist, playwright. Grandniece of Alfred, Lord Tennyson; m. (1918) Harold Marsh Harwood (*q.v.*). Author of *The Milky Way, Beggars on Horseback, Tom Fool, Moonraker, Act of God,* and the plays *The Mask, Billeted, The Pelican, How to be Healthy though Married* (all with her husband), *Quarantine,* and *Anyhouse.*

**Jesse, John Heneage.** 1815–1874. English memoir writer.

**Jes'sel** (jĕs''l), Sir **George.** 1824–1883. English equity judge.

**Jes'sup** (jĕs'ŭp), **Philip Caryl.** 1897– . Amer. authority on international law; prof., Columbia (from 1935); member International Court of Justice (from 1961).

**Jessup, Walter Albert.** 1877–1944. American educator; president, State U. of Iowa (1916–34); president of Carnegie Foundation for the Advancement of Teaching (from 1934) and of Carnegie Corporation of N.Y. (from 1941).

**Jes'up** (jĕs'ŭp), **Mŏrris Ketchum.** 1830–1908. American merchant and banker; benefactor of American Museum of Natural History, several expeditions to the Arctic, Audubon Society.

**Je'sus** (jē'zŭs) [*Greek form of Hebrew name* Joshua, *meaning "Jehovah is salvation"*] *or* **Jesus Christ** (krīst) *or* **Christ Jesus** [*from Greek* Christos, *translation of Hebrew* Messiah, "Anointed," *used as title of Hebrew kings and hence of the promised future king*]. *Called also* **Jesus of Naz'a·reth** [năz'ȧ·rĕth] (*Mark* i. 24). Born between B.C. 8 and B.C. 4 (near end of reign of Herod the Great); crucified about 29 A.D. Legally son of Joseph, carpenter of Nazareth, but believed by his followers to have been miraculously conceived by his mother, the Virgin Mary (*Matt.* i; *Luke* i–ii). Born at Bethlehem (*Matt.* ii. 1–12; *Luke* ii. 1–21); genealogy traced back to David, Abraham, and Adam (*Matt.* i. 1–16; *Luke* iii. 23–38). Lived as child at Nazareth; as young man followed carpenter's trade (*Mark* vi. 3). Lifetime a period of distress in Palestine under rule of three sons of Herod (see HEROD ARCHELAUS, HEROD ANTIPAS, and PHILIP THE TETRARCH) and oppressive Roman procurators. Baptized by John the Baptist (*q.v.*); gathered twelve disciples; preached in Galilee; received with enthusiasm by common people because of extraordinary healing powers, effective teaching by parables, and impression of authority (*Mark* i. 22); strongly opposed by Pharisees and privileged classes because of attacks on hypocrisy and interest in the poor. Regarded by some as long-expected Messiah, hence rulers suspected revolutionary aims. After brief ministry in Galilee went with disciples to Jerusalem to observe Passover; taught in Temple and drove out money changers (*Mark* xi. 15–17), arousing hostility of priestly class. After Last Supper with disciples, betrayed by one of them, Judas Iscariot (*Mark* xiv); seized by Roman soldiers; examined by high priest and Sanhedrin and condemned as blasphemer deserving death; sent to Roman procurator, Pontius Pilate, and by him to Herod Antipas, ruler of Galilee, who sent him back to Pilate; turned over by him to the Jewish authorities. Crucified between two thieves on Golgotha and buried in tomb of Joseph of Arimathea; believed by his followers to have risen from the dead and ascended to heaven (*Matt.* xxvi–xxviii; *Mark* xiv–xvi; *Luke* xxii–xxiv).

Taught redeeming love of God for even the lowest and worst of mankind, necessity of repentance as preparation for the coming Kingdom of God, duty of unselfish devotion to God and man, inward spirituality instead of ritualism and institutionalism. Teachings, personal example, and sacrificial death are the foundation of Christianity; Christian Church grew out of his disciples' proclamation of him as Messiah and Saviour. Supposed date of his birth taken as the beginning of the Christian Era; events of his life are commemorated on such festival days as Christmas, Epiphany, Easter. Sources for his life and teachings are the four Gospels of the New Testament; incidental references in Josephus and Tacitus.

**Jesus, Son of Si'rach** (sī'răk). fl. 200 B.C. Author of the wisdom book (in Protestant O. T. Apocrypha; canonical in Roman Catholic Bible) commonly called *Ecclesiasticus.*

**Jet'té'** (zhĕ'tā'), Sir **Louis Amable.** 1836–1920. Canadian jurist and statesman; puisne judge, Superior Court, Quebec (1878–98); lieutenant governor of Quebec (1898–1908); chief justice, Court of King's Bench (1909–11).

**Jev'ons** (jĕv'ŭnz), **Frank Byron.** 1858–1936. English scholar. Classical tutor (1882–1910) and professor of philosophy (from 1910), Durham; also, master of Hatfield Coll. (1896–1923). Author of *The Development of the Athenian Democracy, An Introduction to the History of Religion* (1896), *Evolution* (1900), *Idea of God in Early Religions* (1910), *Philosophy: What is It?* (1914), etc.

**Jevons, William Stanley.** 1835–1882. English economist and logician. Educ. University Coll., London. Assayer at the mint, Sydney, Australia (1854–59). Professor of logic, political economy, and philosophy, Owens Coll., Manchester (1866–79). Also, professor of political economy, University Coll., London (1876–80). Author of *Pure Logic* (1864), *Elementary Lessons in Logic* (1870), *Studies in Deductive Logic* (1880), *Theory of Political Economy* (1871), *The State in Relation to Labour* (1882), *Methods of Social Reform,* etc. His son **Herbert Stanley** (1875–1955), also an economist; educ. Cambridge; was professor of economics and political science, University Coll. of South Wales and Monmouthshire (1905–11); professor of economics, U. of Allahabad, India (1914–23), and Rangoon (1923–30); author of *Essays on Economics* (1905), *Money, Banking, and Exchange in India* (1922), etc.

**Jew'el** (jōō'ĕl), **John.** 1522–1571. English prelate; bishop of Salisbury (1560–71). Author of *Apologia pro Ecclesia Anglicana* (1562), first methodical statement of the Anglican Church's position against the Roman Catholic Church.

**Jew'ell** (jōō'ĕl), **Marshall.** 1825–1883. American industrialist and politician; leather-belting manufacturer (from 1850); governor of Connecticut (1869, 1871, 1872); U.S. minister to Russia (1873). U.S. postmaster general (1874–76).

**Jew'ett** (jōō'ĕt; -ĭt), **Charles Coffin.** 1816–1868. American librarian; superintendent, Boston Public Library (from 1858). His brother **John Punchard** (1814–1884), a publisher, brought out Harriet **Beecher** Stowe's *Uncle Tom's Cabin* (1852).

**Jewett, Frank Baldwin.** 1879–1949. American electrical

engineer; president, Bell Telephone Laboratories, Inc. (1925–44), National Academy of Sciences (from 1939).

**Jewett, Milo Parker.** 1808–1882. American educator; founded Judson Female Institute, Marion, Ala. (1838–55). Induced Matthew Vassar to endow a women's college, chartered (1861) as Vassar College, with Jewett as first president (1862–64).

**Jewett, Sarah Orne.** 1849–1909. American writer, b. South Berwick, Me.; excelled in stories and sketches of New England life. Author of *Deephaven* (1877), *A Country Doctor* (1884), *Tales of New England* (1890), *The Country of the Pointed Firs* (1896), etc.

**Jewett, William.** 1792–1874. American portrait painter.

**Jews'bur·y** (jo͞oz'bĕr·ĭ; -brĭ), **Maria Jane.** 1800–1833. English writer; m. William K. Fletcher (1832); wrote *Phantasmagoria* (1824), *The Three Histories* (1830). Her sister **Geraldine Endsor** (1812–1880) wrote *Zoe* (1845), *Marian Withers* (1851), *Right or Wrong* (1859).

**Jex'-Blake'** (jĕks'blāk'), **Thomas William.** 1832–1915. English clergyman and educator; headmaster of Rugby (1874–87); dean of Wells (1891–1910). His sister **Sophia Louisa** (1840–1912) was a physician; founded London School of Medicine for Women (1874); gained legal right to practice in Great Britain (1877); practiced in Edinburgh (1878–99), where she also founded (1886) a school of medicine for women.

**Jeż, Teodor Tomasz.** *Pseudonym of* Zygmunt MIŁKOWSKI.

**Jez'e·bel** (jĕz'ĕ·bĕl; -b'l). *In Douay Bible* **Jez'a·bel** (jĕz'ȧ-). fl. 9th century B.C. Phoenician princess; daughter of Ethbaal, King of Tyre and Sidon, and wife of Ahab, King of Israel (*1 Kings* xvi. 31). Mother of Ahaziah, Jehoram, and Athaliah. Introduced worship of Baal and persecuted prophets of Jehovah.

**Jhe'ring** *or* **Ihe'ring** (yā'rĭng), **Rudolf von.** 1818–1892. German legal scholar and writer, a founder of the modern philosophico-historical school of law.

**Ji·mé'nez** (hē·mā'nāth), **Juan Ramón.** 1881–1958. Spanish lyric poet. His works include *Platero y Yo* (1914; trans. *Silver and I*, 1957), etc. Awarded Nobel prize in literature (1956).

**Ji·mé'nez de Cis·ne'ros** (hē·mā'nāth thā thēs·nā'rōs), **Francisco.** 1437–1517. Spanish prelate and statesman. Confessor to Queen Isabella (1492); provincial of Franciscan order in Castile (1494); primate of Spain (1495). Cardinal (1507), and inquisitor general of Castile and León; in expedition to Africa, captured Oran (1509). Regent of Castile for Charles I (1516).

**Ji·mé'nez de Que·sa'da** (hē·mā'nāth [-nās] thā kā·sä'thä), **Gonzalo.** 1500?–?1579. Spanish conquistador; conquered New Granada, and founded Bogotá (1538).

**Ji·mé'nez de Ra'da** (hē·mā'nāth thā rä'thä), **Rodrigo.** 1170?–1247. Spanish prelate and historian; author of *Historia Gothica*, commonly called *Chronica Rerum Gestarum in Hispania.*

**Ji·mé'nez O're·a·mu'no** (hē·mā'nās ō'rā·ä·mo͞o'nō), **Ricardo.** 1859–1945. Costa Rican politician; president of Costa Rica (1910–14, 1924–28, 1932–36).

**Jim·mu** *or* **Jim·mu Ten·no** (jēm·mo͝o tĕn·nō). 711–585 B.C. First emperor (*Jap.* tenno) of Japan in legendary period; regarded by Japanese as founder of present dynasty and believed to be direct descendant of Sun Goddess. Reigned (660–585 B.C.). Japanese Era dated from beginning of his reign (Feb. 11, 660 B.C.).

**Jinghis Khan.** Variant of GENGHIS KHAN.

**Jin'nah** (jĭn'nä), **Mohammed Ali.** *Arab.* **Muḥammad 'Ali Jinnah.** 1876–1948. Moslem lawyer in India; president of All-India Moslem League.

**Ji'rá·sek** (yĭ'rä·sĕk), **Alois.** 1851–1930. Czech historical novelist and playwright.

**Ji're·ček** (yĭ'rĕ·chĕk), **Josef.** 1825–1888. Czech literary historian and scholar. His brother **Hermenegild** (1827–1909), jurist, wrote works on Slavic law, history, and literature. Josef's son **Konstantin Josef** (1854–1918), b. Vienna, was an archaeologist and historian; author of works on south Slavic history and literature.

**Jo'ab** (jō'ăb). In Bible, son of Zeruiah, David's half sister. Made commander of David's army; defeated and killed Abner (*2 Sam.* ii–iii); victorious in wars against Ammonites (*2 Sam.* xi–xii); put down conspiracy of Absalom (*2 Sam.* xviii); deposed by David for killing Absalom; killed his rival Amasa (*2 Sam.* xx) but was executed by Solomon after David's death (*1 Kings* ii. 28–34).

**Joachaz.** See JEHOAHAZ.

**Jo'a·chim** (yō'ä·kĭm; yō·ä'kĭm). Name of three electors of Brandenburg. **Joachim I Ne'stor** [nĕs'tôr] (1484–1535); elector (1499–1535); founded (1506) U. of Frankfurt an der Oder; opponent of Luther. His son **Joachim II Hek'tor** [hĕk'tôr] (1505–1571), elector (1535–71); adopted Protestant religion (1539). His grandson **Joachim Friedrich** (1546–1608), son of John George; elector (1598–1608); bishop of Brandenburg and Havelberg (1553) and administrator of Magdeburg (1566); founded (1607) Joachimsthal Gym.

**Joachim, Georg.** See RHÄTICUS.

**Joachim, Joseph.** 1831–1907. Hungarian violinist and composer, b. Kittsee, near Pressburg, of Jewish parents; concert conductor and violinist to the king at Hanover (1854–66); director of the musical Hochschule at Berlin (from 1868), where he founded (1869) and directed the Joachim Quartet. Composed violin concertos, including *Hungarian Concerto in D minor*, variations, overtures, etc. M. (1863; separated 1884) **Amalie Weiss** (vīs), *real name* **Schnee'weiss** [shnā'vīs] (1839–1898), contralto operatic and concert singer, notably of lieder.

**Jo'a·chim of Flo'ris** (jō'ȧ·kĭm ŭv flō'rĭs). 1145?–?1202. Italian mystic, b. in Calabria. Became Cistercian monk and (1177) abbot of Corazzo; founded monastery of San Giovanni in Fiore and a new order (Ordo Florensis, absorbed by Cistercians, 1505). He divided all time into three ages, of the Father, the Son (from 1–1260 A.D.), and the Holy Spirit.

**Jo'a·chim'sen** (yō'ä·kĭm'zĕn) *or* **Jo'a·chim'sohn** (-zōn), **Paul.** 1867–1930. German authority on history of the Reformation and German humanism.

**Joachin.** See JEHOIACHIN.

**Joad** (jōd), **Cyril Edwin Mitch'in·son** (mĭch'ĭn·s'n). 1891–1953. British philosopher; U. of London (1930–53). Works include *Common Sense Ethics* (1921), *Common Sense Theology* (1922), *The Present and Future of Religion* (1930), *Guide to Philosophy* (1936), *The Testament of Joad* (1937), and *Good and Evil* (1943).

**Joakim.** See JEHOIAKIM.

**Joan** (jōn; jō'ăn; jō·ăn'). *Known as* **the Fair Maid of Kent.** 1328–1385. English noblewoman, probably daughter of Edmund of Woodstock, Earl of Kent, Edward I's youngest son. Taken in charge (1330) by Queen Philippa; noted throughout England for beauty and charm; m. 1st (before 1347) Sir Thomas Holland, 2d (1361) Edward, Prince of Wales (the Black Prince); with her husband in Aquitaine (1362–71); mother of Richard (later Richard II); interposed (1378) for Wycliffe at Lambeth synod; succeeded (1385) in healing breach between her son Richard and John of Gaunt.

**Joan.** *Called* **Joan of the Tower.** 1321–1362. Queen of Scotland. Youngest child of Edward II of England and Isabella, b. in Tower of London; m. (1328) Robert Bruce's son and heir, David, who became king (1329). Shared husband's exile in France (1334–41). After

David's defeat and capture in England (1346), made repeated efforts to obtain his release from prison (1346–57).

**Joan** *or* **Jo·an'na** (jō·ăn'ȧ). 1165–1199. Queen of Sicily (1177–89). Third daughter of Henry II of England, b. Angers; m. (1177) William II of Sicily. After William's death (1189), accompanied (1191) her brother Richard I and his queen, Berengaria, to Holy Land; returned to Europe (1192); m. (1196) Count Raymond VI of Toulouse.

**Jo·an' Mau'ritz** (yō·än' mou'rĭts). Count of **Nassau-Siegen.** See NASSAU-SIEGEN.

**Joan of Arc** (ŭv ärk), Saint. *Fr.* **Jeanne d'Arc** (zhän dȧrk). *Called* **the Maid of Or'le·ans** (ôr'lē·ănz); *Fr.* **La Pu'celle' d'Or'lé'ans'** (lȧ pü'sĕl' dôr'lā'äN') *or, simply,* **La Pucelle.** 1412–1431. French national heroine, b. Domremy-la-Pucelle, of a well-to-do and devout peasant family. At age of thirteen, believed she heard voices from angels or from God, at first giving her advice to help her lead a holy life and, later, directions to aid the dauphin in the then troubled times of France (see CHARLES VII). Visited military commandant at Vaucouleurs (1428) and finally persuaded him to guide her to the dauphin, holding court at Bourges; counseled by the voices to raise the siege of Orléans (1428) by the English; obtained consent of Charles; clad in armor, with small army forced English to withdraw (May 4–8, 1429) and brought relief to Dunois and the besieged, arousing enthusiasm throughout France and changing trend of war. Persuaded dauphin to be conducted to Reims and crowned (July 17, 1429); took part in many conflicts (1429–30), some successful. Captured by Burgundians at Compiègne (May 23, 1430); sold six months later to the English; charged with witchcraft and heresy; subject to long, disgraceful, and unfair trial at Rouen, by tribunal of French ecclesiastics; condemned and burned at the stake (May 30, 1431). Revision of her trial obtained and her innocence proclaimed (1455); beatified by Pope Pius X (Apr. 11, 1909); canonized by Pope Benedict XV (1920). Subject of Schiller's drama *Die Jungfrau von Orleans,* of G. B. Shaw's *Saint Joan,* and of notable biographies by Anatole France, Mark Twain, and Andrew Lang.

**Joan** (*or* **Jo·an'na** [jō·ăn'ȧ]) **of Na·varre'** (nȧ·vär'; *Fr.* nȧ'vȧr'). 1370?–1437. Queen of England (1403–13). Daughter of Charles d'Albret of Navarre; m. 1st (1386) John V, Duke of Brittany, by whom she had eight children; after his death (1399), regent of Brittany for her son John; m. 2d (1403) Henry IV of England; on friendly relations with her stepson King Henry V (1413–22); accused and imprisoned (1419–22) on vague charges of witchcraft.

**Joanes, Juan de.** See Vicente Juan MACIP.

**Jo·an'na** (jō·ăn'ȧ). See JUANA.

**Joanna.** *Ital.* **Gio·van'na** (jō·vän'nä). Name of two queens of Naples:

**Joanna I.** 1326?–1382. Queen (1343–82). Caused first husband, Prince Andrew of Hungary, to be murdered (1345); driven out by Andrew's brother Louis I of Hungary but restored (1352); deposed (1380) by Pope Urban VI; captured and put to death by Charles III (1381–82).

**Joanna II.** 1371–1435. Queen (1414–35). Her reign one of continuous unrest; married three times; second husband driven out, third murdered; long dominated by Muzio A. Sforza; several wars with Angevins, Aragon, and the pope.

**Jo·an'nes** (jō·ăn'ēz; -ĕs). Latin form of name of several rulers of the Eastern Roman Empire. See JOHN.

**Joannitsa.** Variant of *Yoannitsa.* See KALOYAN.

**Jo·ão'** (zhwouN). Portuguese form of JOHN.

**Jo'ash** (jō'ăsh) *or* **Je·ho'ash** (jē·hō'ăsh). *In Douay Bible* **Jo'as** (jō'ăs). (1) c. 844–798 B.C. King of Judah (c. 837–798 B.C.); son of Ahaziah; as infant, saved from death by his aunt Jehosheba (*q.v.*); placed on throne at age of seven by palace revolution; at first, affairs administered by guardians; turned from worship of Jehovah; paid tribute to Hazael of Damascus; assassinated (*2 Kings* xi–xii). (2) d. 785? B.C. King of Israel (c. 800–785 B.C.); son of Jehoahaz; partly successful in war with Damascus; defeated Amaziah of Judah and broke down part of wall of Jerusalem (*2 Kings* xiii–xiv).

**Joatham.** See JOTHAM.

**Job** (jōb). An Old Testament patriarch, the story of whose afflictions, borne with fortitude and faith, is told in the Book of Job, a poem representing chiefly colloquies between Job and his friends.

**Joce'lin de Brake'lond** (jŏs'lĭn dĕ brăk'lŏnd). fl. 1200. English monk and chronicler of abbey of Bury St. Edmunds under Samson of Tottington (*q.v.*).

**Jochanan ben Zakkai.** See JOHANAN BEN ZAKKAI.

**Joch'mus** (yôK'mo͞os), **August Giacomo.** Baron **von Co'ti·gno'la** (kō'tē·nyō'lä). 1808–1881. German general and soldier of fortune; general in British foreign legion during Spanish Civil War (1835–38); general chief of staff of combined Turkish, British, and Austrian forces in Syrian campaign (1840–41); in Turkish war ministry (1848). Returned to Germany (1848) and served as minister of foreign affairs and of the navy (1849); named lieutenant field marshal (1859).

**Jo·cho** (jō·chō). d. 1057. Japanese sculptor.

**Jo'chums·son** (yŏk'kûms·sŏn), **Matthías.** 1835–1920. Icelandic poet who restored old classical meters; drew on Iceland's history for subjects, as in *Grettisljóð* (Grettir Lays), verse series dealing with exploits of Grettir, famous outlaw; also wrote lyrical dramas, hymns and funeral poems; translated plays of Shakespeare and other foreign classics.

**Jo'delle'** (zhô'dĕl'), **Étienne.** Sieur **de Ly'mo'din'** (dē lē'mô'dăN'). 1532–1573. French dramatic poet; member of the Pléiade; regarded as founder of French tragedy.

**Jodl** (yō'd'l), **Alfred.** 1892?–1946. German army officer; chief of staff; signed act of military surrender (May 7, 1945); hanged as war criminal (Oct. 1946).

**Jodl, Friedrich.** 1849–1914. German philosopher.

**Jo'el** (jō'ĕl; -ĕl). A minor Hebrew prophet of uncertain date (assigned by some to about 830 B.C., by others to a postexilic period) whose predictions of judgment on Judah, with exhortation to repentance and promise of final blessing, the Old Testament book of *Joel* records.

**Joest van Cal'car** *or* **Kal'kar** (yōst' vän käl'kär), **Jan.** d. 1519. Dutch painter.

**Jof'fe,** *Russ.* **Iof'fe** (yô'fyĕ), **Adolf Abrahamovich.** 1883–1927. Diplomat of Soviet Russia; minister in Peking (1922–23), Vienna (1924–25), Tokyo (1925–26).

**Jof'fre** (zhô'fr'), **Joseph Jacques Césaire.** 1852–1931. French soldier; general of brigade (1902) and of division (1905). At outbreak of World War (1914), became commander in chief of the French armies, and later of the allied armies in France; hero of the victory in the battle of the Marne (Sept., 1914), which stopped the German advance upon Paris; created field marshal; adviser to the general staff and marshal of France (1917).

**Jogues** (zhôg), Saint **Isaac.** 1607–1646. French Jesuit missionary in America; stationed among Indians south of Lake Huron (1636–39); accompanied Indians to strait which he named Sault de Ste. Marie (1641). Captured by Iroquois, tortured, hands mutilated (1642); rescued by the Dutch and taken (1643) to New Amsterdam (New York). Again on mission to Iroquois (1646). Undertook mission to Mohawks; tomahawked on site of what is now Auriesville, N.Y. (Oct. 18, 1646). Canonized, June 29, 1930.

**Johan.** Swedish form of JOHN.

**Jo·han'an** (*or* **Jo·chan'an**) **ben Zak'ka·i** (jō·hăn'ăn [jō·kăn'ăn] bĕn zăk'ā·ī). d. ab. 80 A.D. Jewish teacher, disciple of Hillel. Taught in Jerusalem; escaped into Roman camp during siege of Jerusalem; founded (with Vespasian's permission) and became first head of the school at Jabneel (Jabneh, Jamnia), where the Sanhedrin was established; headed the Jewish community after destruction of Jerusalem and the Second Temple by the Romans, and helped restore and regenerate Jewish national life.

**Johann** and **Johannes.** German forms of JOHN.

**Jo·hann' von Neu'markt** (yō·hän' [yō'hän] fōn noi'märkt). 1310?–1380. German ecclesiastic and humanist.

**Johannes Corvinus.** See MATTHIAS CORVINUS.

**Jo·han'nes His'pa·len'sis** (jō·hăn'ēz (-ĕs) hĭs'pȧ·lĕn'sĭs) *or* **John of Se·ville'** (sĕ·vĭl'; sĕv''l, -ĭl). fl. middle of 12th century. Jewish scholar (his Jewish name unknown); native of Toledo, Spain. Translated Arabic works on mathematics and philosophy into Spanish or Latin.

**Jo·han'nes Leo** (jō·hăn'ēz; -ĕs). See LEO AFRICANUS.

**Johannes of An'ti·och** (ăn'tĭ·ŏk). = JOHANNES SCHOLASTICUS.

**Johannes Scho·las'ti·cus** (skō·lăs'tĭ·kŭs). d. 577. Patriarch of Constantinople (565–577); prepared collection of ecclesiastical laws, or canons, now known as *Nomocanon in 50 titles* or *Nomocanon of Johannes Scholasticus.*

**Johannes Scotus.** See Johannes Scotus ERIGENA.

**Johannes Secundus.** See SECUNDUS.

**Jo·han'nes von Goch** (yō·hän'ĕs fōn gōĸ'). *Real name* Johann **Pup'per** (pŏŏp'ĕr). 1400?–1475. German Augustinian monk and theologian; attacked Pelagianism and urged return to Bible text as source of religious truth; regarded as a forerunner of Reformation.

**Jo·han'ne·sen** (yō·hän'ĕ·sĕn), **Edvard Holm.** 1844–1901. Norwegian arctic explorer.

**Johannitsa.** Variant of *Yoannitsa.* See KALOYAN.

**Jo'han'not'** (zhō'á'nō'), **Charles** (1783–1825) and his brothers **Alfred** (1800–1837) and **Tony** (1803–1852). French engravers and illustrators.

**Jo·hann'sen** (yō·hän's'n), **Albert.** 1871- 1962. American geologist; author of *A Descriptive Petrography of the Igneous Rocks* (4 vols., 1931–38), etc.; special editor for petrography and petrology, *Webster's New International Dictionary, Second Edition.* His brother **Os'kar** (ŏs'kĕr) **Augustus** (1870-1961), entomologist; professor, Cornell (1912–38; retired).

**Jo·hann'sen** (yō·hán's'n), **Wilhelm Ludwig.** 1857–1927. Danish botanist and geneticist. Pioneer in modern experimental genetics; known for experiments with beans leading to his development of the pure-line theory.

**Jo·han'sen** (yō·hän'sĕn), **Frederic Hjalmar.** 1867–1923. Norwegian polar explorer; accompanied Nansen toward North Pole (1895), and Amundsen to South Pole.

**Jo·han'sen** (yō·hän's'n), **John Christen.** 1876-1964. Portrait painter, b. Copenhagen, Denmark; to U.S. in infancy. Instructor at Art Students' League in New York (from 1912). His wife, **M. Jean Mac·Lane'** [măk·lān'] (1878-1964), also a portrait painter.

**John** (jŏn). In the New Testament:

(1) **John the Bap'tist** (băp'tĭst). Son of Zacharias and Elisabeth and cousin of Jesus (*Luke* i. 36). The forerunner of Jesus (*Luke* i, iii; *Matt.* iii; *Mark* i; *John* i). Baptized Jesus; condemned Jewish aristocracy and publicly rebuked Herod Antipas for his marriage with Herodias; imprisoned and executed at Herodias's instigation (see SALOME).

(2) *Called* **the Evangelist** *and* **the Divine.** One of the twelve apostles, son of Zebedee and brother of James (*Matt.* iv. 21, x. 2; *Mark* i. 19, iii. 17; *Luke* vi. 14; *Acts* i. 13), whose name is attached to the Fourth Gospel, the three epistles of John, and the Book of Revelation (*in Douay Bible* the Apocalypse).

**John.** Name of twenty-one popes (see *Note* at John XV, below, and *Table of Popes,* Nos. 53, 56, 61, 72, 82, 85, 86, 107, 116, 123, 126, 131, 134, 137, 139, 142, 143, 146, 187, 196, 262) and one antipope, especially:

**John I,** Saint. 470?–526. Pope (523–526); b. in Tuscany. Sent (525) by Theodoric, King of the Ostrogoths, as head of an embassy to Constantinople to urge Byzantine emperor to show toleration to Arians; mission only partly successful; hence, on return, was imprisoned at Ravenna, where he died.

**John VIII.** 820?–882. Pope (872–882). Strove to keep Saracens out of Italy but was forced to pay tribute; protected by Emperor Louis II; crowned Charles the Bald (875) and Charles the Fat (881); journeyed to France (878–879).

**John X.** 860?–928. Pope (914–928). Made pope through influence of Empress Theodora; crowned Berengar emperor (915); defeated Saracens (916) on the banks of the Garigliano.

**John XI.** 906–936. Pope (931–936). Son of Marozia and reputed son of Pope Sergius III. Made pope through influence of mother; deposed and died in prison.

**John XII.** 938?–964. Pope (955–964); sometimes called "the Boy Pope." Grandson of Marozia. Called Otto I of Germany to his aid against King Berengar II of Italy (961); crowned Otto emperor (962); conspired against Otto and deposed (963); opposed by Leo VIII who was not recognized.

**John XIII.** d. 972. Pope (965–972); b. Rome. Subservient to Emperor Otto I; driven out by Roman nobles but restored (966); crowned Otto II as joint emperor (967).

**John XV** *or* **XVI.** d. 996. Pope (985–996).

☞ Some papal catalogues list a Pope John XV as immediately following Antipope Boniface VII (974); this has confused the numbering of popes named John—XV to XXI. This book follows the more common system and omits the spurious John XV. There was no Pope John XX, the number being given to either John XIX or John XXI.

**John XXI.** *Real name* **Petrus His·pa'nus** (hĭs·pā'nŭs). d. 1277. Pope (1276–77); b. Lisbon. Tried to improve conditions in Portugal; sent legates to the great khan of Tatary; wrote a popular treatise on logic (*Summulae logicales*) and several books on medicine.

**John XXII.** *Real name* **Jacques d'Euse** (dûz). 1249–1334. Pope (1316–34). Resided at Avignon, under French influence; had long conflict with the emperor, Louis of Bavaria; opposed by Antipope Nicholas V, installed (1328) by Louis; engaged in controversy with Franciscan Spirituals.

**John XXIII.** *Real name* **Angelo Giuseppe Ron·cal'li** (rōng·käl'lē). 1881–1963. Pope (1958–1963). b. Sotto il Monte near Bergamo. Grad. as D.T. in Rome. Ordained priest (1904). Mil. chaplain World War I. Made an aide at Vatican's Sacred Congregation for Propagation of the Faith (1921). Apostolic diplomatic posts: titular Arch. of Bulgaria (from 1925), Nuncio to Turkey and Greece (1935–44) and France (1944–53). Cardinal (1953–58).

*Antipope:* **John XVI.** *Real name* **Phi·lag'a·thus** (fĭ·lăg'ȧ·thŭs). d. 1013? Antipope (997–998).

**John.** *Full German name* **Johann Baptist Joseph**

**Fabian Sebastian.** 1782–1859. Archduke of Austria, b. Florence; younger son of Emperor Leopold II. General; commanded Austrian army in Bavaria (1800); defeated by Moreau at Hohenlinden (1800). Commanded Austrian army in Italy (1809); defeated at Raab (1809). After campaign on the Rhine (1815), retired to private life; chosen regent of the empire (1848–49) by German National Assembly.

**John.** 1296–1346. Count of Luxemburg (1309–46) and king of Bohemia (1310–46). Son of Emperor Henry VII. Aided Louis of Bavaria both before and after he became emperor (Louis IV), esp. in the battle of Mühldorf (1322). Aided Charles IV of France; was unsuccessful in retaining control of southern Italy (1333). Became blind (1339 or 1340). Helped Philip VI of France against the English, but was killed at Crécy (1346). His son became Emperor Charles IV (1347).

**John I,** *Dan.* **Hans.** 1455–1513. Son of Christian I and bro. of Frederick I. King of Denmark (1481–1513) and of Sweden, as John II (1497–1501). Never established himself firmly in Sweden, where Sten Sture was regent (1470–1503).

**John.** Name of eight rulers of the Eastern Roman Empire:

**John I Zi·mis'ces** (zĭ·mĭs'ēz). 925–976. Successful general; guardian for Basil II; assassinated Nicephorus Phocas (969); by intrigue with Empress Theophano, became emperor (969–976); drove Russians out of Bulgaria (970–973); recovered Syria (974–976).

**John II Com·ne'nus** (kŏm·nē'nŭs) *or* **Kal'o·jo·an'·nes** (kăl'ō·jō·ăn'ēz; -ĕs). 1088–1143. Son of Alexius I Comnenus; emperor (1118–43); defeated Hungarians and Turks but did not rid government of corruption.

**John III Du'cas** (dū'kăs) *or* **Va·tat'zes** (vȧ·tăt'sēz). 1193–1254. Son-in-law of Theodore I Lascaris; emperor (1222–54) at Nicaea; soldier and able administrator; made truce with Turks; recovered other regions of Asia Minor (1241); unsuccessful in siege of Constantinople (1235).

**John IV Las'ca·ris** (lăs'kȧ·rĭs). 1250?–?1300. Son of Theodore II Ducas; emperor (1258) under Michael VIII, at Nicaea; dethroned (1259), blinded, and imprisoned by Michael Palaeologus (1261).

**John V** (*or* **VI**) **Pa'lae·ol'o·gus** (pā'lē·ŏl'ō·gŭs; păl'ē-). 1332–1391. Son of Andronicus III; emperor (1341–91) but for two periods virtually superseded by John VI Cantacuzene (1347–55) and by Andronicus IV (1376–79); reign marked by gradual weakening of imperial power and by encroachments of Ottoman Turks.

**John VI** (*or* **V**) **Can'ta·cu·zene'** (kăn'tȧ·kū·zēn'). 1292?–1383. Emperor (1347–55); made guardian for John V (1341); set himself up as emperor in Thrace (1341); civil war with John's supporters followed (1341–47); ruler in Constantinople, nominally jointly with John V (1347–55); period of successful attacks on empire by outsiders (Serbians, Turks, Genoese); driven out, retired to monastery; wrote a history (4 books) of years 1320–56.

**John VII Palaeologus.** 1360–1412. Grandson of John V; seized power for short time (1390); coregent with uncle, Emperor Manuel II (1398–1412); defended Constantinople against Bajazet.

**John VIII Palaeologus.** 1391–1448. Son of Manuel II; emperor (1425–48); ruled with caution; offered no military opposition to Turks, who now encircled the capital; sought aid from western Europe; appeared (1438–39) at councils of Ferrara and Florence; during reign: union of Western and Eastern churches partially effected (1439), but came too late; Turks (Murad II) defeated by János Hunyadi and Ladislas III of Hungary and Poland at Nish (1443), but won victory over Christians at Varna (1444).

**John.** *Often called* **John Lack'land'** (lăk'lănd'). 1167?–1216. King of England (1199–1216), of house of Anjou or Plantagenet (*q.v.*). Son of Henry II. Succeeded to throne on death of his brother Richard I (1199); inherited also French duchies of Normandy, Anjou, Maine, and Touraine, but lost them (by 1205). Refused to recognize Stephen Langton as archbishop of Canterbury (after Pope Innocent III, to whom dispute had been referred, ordered his election, 1206), provoking papal interdict against England (1208) and papal bull (1212) deposing him and charging Philip II of France with task of deposition; made peace by accepting his kingdom in fief from pope (1213) and by paying annual tribute. Invaded France, but was defeated (1214). On return to England, met barons at Runnymede, where he was forced to sign (June 15, 1215) Magna Charta, laying foundation for security of English political and personal liberty; immediately appealed to pope and obtained from him bull annulling charter; thereupon, imported foreign mercenaries to fight against barons; died (Oct. 19) before war was decided.

**John.** *Fr.* **Jean** (zhäɴ). Name of two kings of France:

**John I.** Of Capetian line (*q.v.*); posthumous son of Louis X, born (1316) five and one half months after his father's death, during which period Louis's brother Philip (afterwards Philip V) was regent; lived five days only.

**John II.** *Called* **the Good.** *Fr.* **le Bon** (lẽ bôɴ'). 1319–1364. Of house of Valois (*q.v.*); son of Philip VI; b. near Mans; king (1350–64); rule of first years unwise and tyrannical; defeated by Edward, the Black Prince, at Poitiers (1356) and taken prisoner; detained in England (1356–60) while his son Charles V (*q.v.*) acted as regent; Treaty of Brétigny (1360); secured duchy of Burgundy (1363) for his son Philip (*q.v.*); failing to secure all of his own ransom, returned to England (1364), where he died.

**John.** Name of several dukes of Brittany, including:

**John III.** *Called* **the Good.** *Fr.* **le Bon** (lẽ bôɴ'). 1286–1341. Duke (1312–41).

**John de Montfort.** *By some called* **John IV** of Brittany. d. 1345. Brother of John III; duke (1341–45); waged war against Charles de Blois (see Blois) who claimed the duchy; aided by Edward III of England (1342); died at siege of Hennobont.

**John IV** (*or* **V**). *Called* **the Valiant.** *Fr.* **le Vail'·lant'** (lẽ vȧ'yäɴ'). 1338–1399. Son of John de Montfort; duke (1345–99); during minority affairs of duchy administered by his mother, Jeanne of Flanders; war against Charles de Blois continued (1345–65), terminated by victory of Brittany at Auray (1364) and the Peace of Guérande (1365); remained vassal of France but friendly to English. Married (1386) Joan of Navarre.

**John V** (*or* **VI**). *Called* **le Sage** (lẽ sȧzh'). 1389–1442. Duke (1399–1442); during conflict between Burgundians and Armagnacs tried to remain friendly to both Charles VII of France and Henry VI of England.

**John.** *Called* **John the Fearless.** *Fr.* **Jean sans Peur** (zhäɴ' säɴ' pûr'). 1371–1419. Duke of Burgundy (1404–19). Son of Duke Philip the Bold; b. Dijon. Caused assassination of Louis, Duc d' Orléans (1407); followed by civil war (1411–12) and attainment of great power in France (1412); aided by English (two alliances: 1414, 1416); attempted reconciliation with the dauphin (later Charles VII) but was murdered at his instigation.

**John.** *Called* **Hans of Cüstrin.** 1513–1571. Margrave of **Bran'den·burg–Cü·strin'** [brän'dĕn·bŏŏrk·küs-trĕn′] (1535–71); son of Elector Joachim I of Brandenburg; introduced Reformation (1537).

**John.** *Full Ger. name* **Johann Nepomuk Maria Joseph.** 1801–1873. King of Saxony (1854–73), b. Dresden. Active in Council of State before succeeding his brother Frederick Augustus II as king (1854); supported Austria in Seven Weeks' War; forced by Prussia to enter North German Confederation; active in Franco-Prussian War (1870–71) and assisted in founding German Empire. Student of Italian literature and of Dante; author under pseudonym **Phil′a·le′thes** (fĭl′*ȧ*·lē′thēz; *Ger.* fē′lä·lā′tĕs), *i.e.* "lover of truth"; published metrical translation of *Divina Commedia* (1839–49).

**John.** Kings of Poland. See JOHN II CASIMIR (page 786) and JOHN III SOBIESKI (page 787).

**John.** *Port.* **João.** Name of six kings of Portugal, the first three of the House of Aviz (*q.v.*), the others of the House of Braganza (*q.v.*):

**John I.** *Called sometimes* **the Bastard** *and* **the Great.** 1357–1433. King (1385–1433); natural son of Pedro I. Grand master of Aviz (1364); on death of half brother Ferdinand, became regent and defender of the kingdom (1383–85); throne claimed by John of Castile, resulting in war and siege of Lisbon; defeated Spaniards; chosen king (1385) and with aid of English won victory of Aljubarrota over Castilians (1385); made treaty of friendship and alliance with England (1386); married (1387) Philippa of Lancaster, daughter of John of Gaunt; took Ceuta from Moors (1415); introduced many reforms and encouraged voyages of exploration; a long and prosperous reign; his six sons included Edward, his successor, and Prince Henry the Navigator.

**John II.** *Called* **the Perfect.** *Port.* **O prin′ci·pe per·fec′to** (ōō prēɴ′sē·pĕ pĕr·fâ′tōō). 1455–1495. King (1481–95); son of Alfonso V and great-grandson of John I; b. Lisbon. Acted ably as regent during absences of father; fought against and, with help of Cortes and common people, overcame feudal nobility; had leaders put to death; refrained from conflict with Spain; encouraged explorations, sending out Diogo Cam and Bartholomeu Dias, who discovered mouth of the Congo (1484) and Cape of Good Hope (1488) respectively; concluded Treaty of Tordesillas (1494) with Spain, by which possessions in New World were delimited.

**John III.** 1502–1557. King (1521–57); son of Emanuel, b. Lisbon; m. Catherine, sister of Emperor Charles V; introduced Inquisition (1531); placed U. of Coimbra under Jesuits (1540); during his reign power of Portugal began to decline, although colonial expansion continued, especially in East Indies; title to Brazil confirmed by Congress of Badajoz (1524).

**John IV.** *Called* **the Fortunate.** 1605–1656. Founder of Braganza dynasty; king (1640–56); b. Villaviciosa; son of Theodosio, Duke of Braganza (d. 1630); m. (1633) Luisa de Guzmán, daughter of the duke of Medina-Sidonia; by a conspiracy and bloodless revolution, expelled Spanish usurpers (1640); proclaimed himself king (1640); choice confirmed by Cortes (1641); Spaniards defeated at Montijo (1644); Dutch driven out of Brazil (1654); Portugal restored to respected position among European nations.

**John V.** 1689–1750. King (1706–50); son of Pedro II and grandson of John IV. Came to throne in midst of War of Spanish Succession (1701–14); involved as ally of England; Portuguese several times defeated; by Treaty of Utrecht (1713) Portugal confirmed in possession of Amazon region. John was outwardly religious, devoted much attention to ecclesiastical matters, but his court was profligate and extravagant; church strengthened, but army and navy neglected; granted title (1741) of "Most Faithful King" by Pope Benedict XIV; suffered stroke of paralysis (1744).

**John VI.** 1769 or 1767?–1826. King (1816–26); son of Pedro III and Maria I and grandson of John V; b. Lisbon; m. (1790) Carlota, dau. of Charles IV of Spain; took over government (1792) because of his mother's insanity; formally declared regent (1799); driven out of Portugal by French army under Junot (1807); sailed to Brazil with court (1807–08), remaining there till 1821; was declared king of Portugal on death of his mother (1816); returned to Portugal (1821) and declared for the new constitution, Brazil becoming independent (1822) with his son Dom Pedro I its first ruler; last years troubled with reactionary disturbances and attempted rebellion of Queen Carlota and younger son, Dom Miguel.

**John.** *Span.* **Juan.** Name of two kings of Aragon:

**John I.** 1350–1395. Son of Pedro IV; king (1387–95); lover of music and hunting.

**John II.** 1397–1479. Son of Ferdinand I; king (1458–79); m. Blanche, heiress of Navarre (1420), and Juana Henríquez (1447); caused death of his son and heir, Charles of Viana (1461); mortgaged Roussillon to Louis XI of France (1462); arranged marriage of son Ferdinand with Isabella (1469).

**John.** *Span.* **Juan.** Name of two kings of Castile:

**John I.** 1358–1390. Son of Henry II; king (1379–90); led expedition against England (1380) to punish John of Gaunt for his claims to throne of Castile; defeated at Aljubarrota by John of Portugal (1385); won victory over John of Gaunt in his expedition to Spain (1386–87); settled difficulties by treaty (1387) and married his son and heir, Henry, to a daughter of John of Gaunt.

**John II.** 1405–1454. Son of Henry III; king (1406–54); ruled under regents (1406–19); long reign of intrigue and civil war (1419–54); patron of literature and arts.

**John.** *Swed.* **Johan.** Name of three kings of Sweden:

**John I.** 1201?–1222. King (1216–22).

**John II.** Same as John I, King of Denmark. Nominal ruler only (1483–97) during regency of Sten Sture; king (1497–1501).

**John III.** 1537–1592. King (1568–92); second son of Gustavus Vasa. Duke of Finland (1556). Was seized and imprisoned (1563–67) by his brother King Eric XIV; with brother Charles (later Charles IX) conspired against and deposed Eric (1569). Theological student; held synods (1574–75); finally rejected Protestantism and became Roman Catholic (1578); failed in attempt to Romanize Sweden (1578–84); concluded alliance with Poland in war against Russia (1578–83); m. (1561) Catherine Jagello, sister of king of Poland; had Sigismund, their son, crowned king of Poland (1587).

**John,** Don. = JOHN OF AUSTRIA.

**John, Augustus Edwin.** 1878–1961. British painter and etcher, b. in Wales; identified with impressionist school. Among his canvases are *Spanish Flower Girl, Mother and Child,* and *Seraphita;* among his etchings, *Coster Girl, Maggie and Lucy, Quarry Folk,* and *The Valley of Time;* among his portraits are those of Lloyd George, George Bernard Shaw, Lord Fisher, and Princess Bibesco.

**John** (yōn), **Eugenie.** *Pseudonym* **E. Mar′litt** (mär′lĭt). 1825–1887. German novelist.

**John** (jŏn), **Evan.** Pseudonym of Evan John SIMPSON.

**John,** Sir **William Goscombe.** 1860–1952. British sculptor, b. Cardiff, Wales. Among his works are statues of King Edward VII, at Cape Town, King George V and Queen Mary, at Liverpool, David Lloyd George, at Carnarvon. Designed King George V Silver Jubilee Medal (1935).

**John Albert** *or* **John I.** 1459–1501. King of Poland (1492–1501). Son of Casimir IV. His reign (1496) saw gentry strengthened by privileges at expense of burghers and peasants; unsuccessful in campaign against Moldavia (1497–98).

**John Asen I** and **II.** See Asen.

**John Cas'i·mir** (kăz'ĭ·mĭr). 1543–1592. Count Palatine of the Rhine. Son of Elector Palatine Frederick III; b. Simmern. Joined Calvinist Church; led troops to help French Huguenots and Dutch (1575–78), but with small success; as regent of the Palatinate (1583–92), compelled return of Protestants to Calvinism.

**John II Casimir.** *Sometimes known as* **Casimir V.** 1609–1672. King of Poland (1648–68); son of Sigismund III. A Jesuit and cardinal (1640); absolved by pope on becoming king (1648); during his reign occurred invasion by Tatars and Cossacks (1649) and disastrous 13-year war with Russia (1654–67) ended by Treaty of Andrusovo; at war with Sweden (1655–60); took refuge in Silesia; resigned (1668) and retired to France as abbé de Saint-Germain.

**John Chrysostom,** Saint. See Chrysostom.

**John Frederick.** *Called* **the Magnanimous.** *Ger.* **der Gross'mü'ti·ge** (dĕr grōs'mü'tĭ·gĕ). 1503–1554. Elector of Saxony (1532–47) of the Ernestine line (*q.v.*), b. Torgau, Prussia. Son of John the Constant. Attacked Catholics (1542); a leader of League of Schmalkalden; at war (1546–47) with his cousin Maurice, of the Albertine line (*q.v.*); defeated and made prisoner by Charles V (1547) at Mühlberg; forced to renounce his electorate; set free by Maurice (1552), but unsuccessful in attempt to regain title. His son **John Frederick II** (1529–1595) was duke of Saxony, ruling (1547–65) small part granted him by emperor after division (1547) of his father's lands; received Gotha (1565); deposed (1566) and imprisoned.

**John George.** *Ger.* **Johann Georg.** Name of four electors of Saxony of the Albertine line (*q.v.*):

**John George I.** 1585–1656. Elector (1611–56). Son of Elector Christian I. As ruler of Saxony during Thirty Years' War, held position of great importance; policy during entire reign changeable and treacherous, supporting one side and then the other; at first, fought against Protestants; later (1631), made alliance with Gustavus Adolphus; his troops fought at Breitenfeld (1631) but were routed by Imperialists; after Lützen (1632), negotiated for peace; concluded Treaty of Prague (1635) with Emperor Ferdinand II and received Lusatia; declared war on Sweden (1636) but was beaten at Wittstock; forced to make peace with Swedes (1645); confirmed in possessions by Treaty of Westphalia (1648).

**John George II.** 1613–1680. Elector (1656–80); son of John George I. Friendly to France, under influence and subsidy of Louis XIV; much interested in music and art; spent enormous sums in beautifying Dresden and making it musical center of Germany.

**John George III.** 1647–1691. Elector (1680–91); son of John George II. Joined alliance against France (1683); aided Emperor Leopold I against Turks (1682–85); took part (1688) in war of League of Augsburg against France and made commander in chief of Imperial army.

**John George IV.** 1668–1694. Elector (1691–94); son of John George III. Quarreled with emperor; m. Eleonore of Brandenburg-Anspach; celebrated for romantic attachment for Magdalene Sibylle von Neitschütz (created countess of Rochlitz, 1693).

**John Hyrcanus.** See Maccabees.

**John Maurice.** = *Joan Mauritz,* Count of Nassau-Siegen.

**John Ne'po·muk Sal·va'tor** (jŏn nā'pō·mo͝ok zäl·vä'tôr). 1852–1891. Archduke of Austria and prince of Tuscany, b. Florence. Son of Grand Duke Leopold II of Tuscany. Took part in Austrian campaign in Bosnia (1878–79); brought into disfavor by his writings and by his activity in Bulgarian affairs (1886); relinquished title (1889), assuming name of **Johann Orth** (ôrt); started (1890) alone in sailboat from Hamburg on journey round world; never heard from; officially declared dead (1911). ☞ *Do not confuse with* John of Nepomuk.

**John of An'ti·och** (ăn'tĭ·ŏk). = Johannes Scholasticus.

**John of Austria.** *Span.* **Juan de Aus'tri·a** (hwän' dā ous'trē·ä). *Commonly known as* Don **John** (dŏn jŏn). *Span.* Don **Juan** (dôn hwän). 1547–1578. Spanish general, b. in Ratisbon; natural son of Emperor Charles V and Barbara Blomberg. Taken to Spain (1550); brought up under name Gerónimo by Don Luis de Quijada and wife, near Valladolid; recognized as his son by Charles in his will (1558); granted rank of prince by Philip II; educated together with the Infante Don Carlos and Alessandro Farnese. Given command (1568) of squadron against Barbary pirates; suppressed Morisco rebellion in Andalusia (1569–70); held supreme command of fleet of Holy League that defeated Turks at Lepanto (1571); took Tunis from Turks (1573). Appointed governor general of the Netherlands (1576); Pacification of Ghent (1576) united Dutch provinces against Spain; compelled by it to issue "Perpetual Edict" (1577); entered Brussels (1577) but forced to promise to remove Spanish soldiers from Netherlands; deposed by the Estates-General; defeated Dutch in battle of Gembloux (1578) but failed in campaign because of lack of support from Philip; died suddenly in camp at Namur.

**John of Austria,** the younger. *Called* Don **John.** 1629–1679. Spanish general. Natural son of Philip IV of Spain and María Calderón, an actress; recognized by king as his son, educated, and granted princely rank. Sent to Naples to help in suppressing revolt of Masaniello (1647); made viceroy of Sicily (1647–51); terminated revolt in Catalonia (1651–53); given command in Flanders (1656); defeated by Turenne at the Dunes (1658); led campaign against Portugal (1661–63); defeated at Estremoz (1663); removed from power by queen regent (1665–69); led successful revolution (1677); prime minister (1677–79).

**John of Bri'enne'** (brē'ĕn'). 1148–1237. King of Jerusalem (1210–25); m. (1210) Marie de Montferrat, Queen of Jerusalem; on her death (1212) became regent. Led part of Fifth Crusade (1218–21) against Egypt. Left Jerusalem, living in various parts of western Europe (1223–29). Lost throne to Emperor Frederick II (1225). Elected emperor of Constantinople (1228–37) until Baldwin II came of age. Repelled attacks (1235) by Greeks and Bulgars.

**John of Ca'pi·stra'no** (kä'pē·strä'nō), Saint. *Ital.* San **Giovanni da Capistrano.** *Lat.* **Johannes Cap'is·tra'nus** (kăp'ĭs·trā'nŭs). 1386–1456. Italian ecclesiastic. Entered Franciscan order (1416); ordained priest (1426); papal inquisitor against the Fraticelli; papal delegate to Germany to preach against Hussites (1450); led band of crusaders against Turks besieging Belgrade (1456). Author of *Speculum Conscientiae.* Canonized by Benedict XIII (1724).

**John of Da·mas'cus** (dȧ·măs'kŭs) *or* **Jo·han'nes Dam'a·sce'nus** (jō·hăn'ēz [-ĕs] dăm'ȧ·sē'nŭs) *or* **John Dam'a·scene** (dăm'ȧ·sēn), Saint. *Called* **Chry·sor'rho·as** (krĭ·sŏr'ō·ăs), *i.e.* "stream of gold," *on account of his eloquence.* 700?–?754. Theologian, scholar, and writer, b. Damascus; a doctor of the Eastern Church, and upholder of the doctrine of enhypostasia. Served as financial officer under caliph of Damascus; became monk in convent near Jerusalem, where he was ordained priest; author of the standard textbook of dogmatic theology in the Greek church, *Fount of Knowledge* (3 parts, including *An Exact Exposition of the Orthodox Faith*), also three *Operations*, or discourses on image worship, and, reputedly, the tale *Barlaam and Ioasaph;* organized liturgical song; credited with reform of notation. Canonized by Latin and Greek churches.

**John of Fordun.** See FORDUN.

**John of Gaunt** (gônt; gänt). Duke of **Lan'cas·ter** (lăng'kȧs·tẽr). 1340–1399. 4th son of Edward III and brother of Black Prince; b. Ghent, hence his name; m. (1359) his cousin Blanche, daughter of Henry of Lancaster, 1st Duke of Lancaster. Leading first division of Black Prince's army in Spain, fought in van at Nájara (1367); with Black Prince at sack of Limoges (1370) and his lieutenant in Aquitaine (1371). Assumed by marriage with Constance of Castile kingship of Castile and León (1372); led futile expedition from Calais to Bordeaux (1373). Forced into domestic leadership by Black Prince's illness; reversed proceedings of Good Parliament of 1376; supported John Wycliffe, despite disbelief in his religious opinions, as means of resisting opposition of prelates and incurred anger of Londoners, who rioted; on accession of Richard II, his nephew, retired from government; after disastrous failure in attack on St.-Malo (1378), accepted command of Scottish border; unfortunately unsuccessful in Scottish campaign (1384) and accompanied Richard's expedition (1385); subject of several court intrigues designed to trap him into seeming conspiracy against his nephew (1381–85). In attempt to win his Spanish throne, conquered Galicia and formed alliance with Portugal, but failing in invasion of Castile, surrendered his Castilian claims to his daughter Catherine on her marriage with the son of John of Castile (1387); lieutenant of Aquitaine (1388–89); duke of Aquitaine (1390); exerted influence in support of Richard II (1390–94) and effected truce with France (1394); failed to establish rule over his duchy of Aquitaine; m. (1396) Catherine Swynford, his mistress, and obtained from Richard legitimation of her sons (from eldest of whom descended Henry VII); presided at trial of Arundel (1397); broken in spirit by exile of his son Henry.

**John of God** (gŏd; gôd), Saint. San **Juan de Dios** (sän' hwän' dā thyōs'). *Real name* **Juan Ciu·dad'** (thyōō·thäth'). 1495–1550. Spanish religious, b. in Portugal; shepherd in Castile; fought under Charles V against Turks. Founded Grand Hospital at Granada (1540) and Ignorantine order (Brothers Hospitalers of St. John of God). Canonized (1690) by Alexander VIII.

**John of Kron·shtadt'** *or* **Cron·stadt'** (krŭn·shtȧt'), Father. *Real name* **Ioann Ser'gi·ev** (syăr'gyĭ·yĕf). 1821–1908. Orthodox Russian priest and popular idol, b. in Archangel government; alleged performer of miracles. Carried on charitable work at Kronshtadt and ministered to the poor, sick, and needy.

**John of Lan'cas·ter** (lăng'kȧs·tẽr). Duke of **Bed'ford** (bĕd'fẽrd). 1389–1435. 3d son of Henry IV of England. Warden of Scottish marches till Henry IV's death; lieutenant of England during Henry V's French campaigns; assumed regency; prosecuted war with Charles, Dauphin of France, gaining victory at Verneuil (1424) and other successes up to siege of Orléans (1429); allowed Joan of Arc, bought from Burgundians, to be burnt as a witch (1431); secured Henry VI's coronation as king of France (1431); his cause in France ruined by separate peace made by Philip of Burgundy with Charles VII (1435).

**John of Lei'den** (lī'dĕn; -d'n). *Real name* **Jan Beuc'kels·zoon** (bûk'ĕl·sŭn; -sŏn; -sōn) *or* **Boc'kel·son** (bŏk'ĕl·sŭn; -sŏn) *or* **Beuc'kels** (bûk'ĕls). *Ger.* **Johann Buck'holdt** (bŏŏk'hôlt). 1509–1536. Dutch Anabaptist fanatic, b. near Leiden. Worked at first as journeyman tailor, merchant, and innkeeper; became leader of Anabaptists in Münster (1534); established there a theocracy, or kingdom of Zion, of which he was proclaimed king; introduced polygamy and community of goods; ruled with pomp and severity; imprisoned by bishop of Münster (1535) and cruelly put to death (1536). Subject of Hamerling's *Der König von Sion* (1869) and of Meyerbeer's *Le Prophète* (1849).

**John of Lux'em·burg** (lŭk'sĕm·bûrg; *Ger.* lŏŏk'sĕm·bŏŏrk). King of Bohemia (1310–46). See JOHN (1296–1346), Count of Luxemburg.

**John of Matha.** = JEAN DE MATHA.

**John VI of Nassau.** See NASSAU, 2b.

**John of Ne'po·muk** (nĕ'pô·mŏŏk) *or* **Po'muk** (pô'mŏŏk), Saint. 1340?–?1393. Ecclesiastic and patron saint of Bohemia, b. at Pomuk. Pastor (1380) and student, Prague, where he later became cathedral canon and vicar-general to the archbishop; confessor to the queen of Wenceslaus IV, by whom he was tortured and drowned in the Moldau (in 1383, according to legend) for defending ecclesiastical rights and for refusing to reveal the queen's confession; canonized (1729). According to some historians, there is some confusion between two persons of the same name, who suffered similar fates at the hands of Wenceslaus.

☞ *Do not confuse with* JOHN NEPOMUK SALVATOR.

**John of Oxford.** See John of OXFORD.

**John of Salis'bur·y** (sôlz'bẽr·ĭ; -brĭ). d. 1180. English ecclesiastical leader and classical scholar. Studied at Paris under Abelard (1136–38); attended Pope Eugenius III. Secretary to Archbishop Theobald at Canterbury (1150?–1164), by whom he was sent on missions; in disfavor with Henry II after denouncing exactions on church for Toulouse expedition (1159) and supporting Becket's cause; retired to Reims (1164) and wrote *Historia Pontificalis;* returned to England, and was present at murder of Becket at Canterbury (1170). Bishop of Chartres (1176–80); present at peace made between England and France at Ivry (1177). Author of the *Policraticus* (on court vanities and diplomacy; completed 1159), *Metalogicus* (on logic; 1159), *Entheticus* (an elegiac poem), and biographies of Becket and Anselm.

**John of Seville.** See JOHANNES HISPALENSIS.

**John of the Cross,** Saint. *Span.* San **Juan de la Cruz** (sän' hwän' dā lä krōōth'). *Real name* **Juan de Ye'pis y Ál'va·rez** (yā'pēs ē äl'vä·rāth). 1542–1591. Spanish mystic, b. Fontiveros, Ávila; with St. Theresa, founder of discalced Carmelites; author of *The Ascent of Mount Carmel;* canonized (1726) by Benedict XIII.

**John of We'sel** (vā'zĕl). *Real name* **Johannes Ruch'rath** *or* **Ruch'rad** (rōōk'rät). d. about 1481. German pre-Reformation religious reformer. Wrote against the indulgences (*Disputatio adversus Indulgentias,* printed 1757), and came into conflict with the Inquisition; recanted, and was sentenced to spend rest of life in a monastery (1479).

**John Paul.** Name of two popes (see *Table of Popes,* Nos. 264, 265):

**John Paul I.** *Real name* **Albino Luciani.** 1912–1978. Pope (1978), b. Forno di Canale, Veneto. Ordained priest (1935); archbishop of Venice (1969); cardinal (1973); reigned 34 days.

**John Paul II.** *Real name* **Karol Wojtyla.** 1920– . Pope (1978– ), b. Wadowice, Poland. Ordained priest (1946); archbishop of Krakow (1964); cardinal (1967); first non-Italian pope in 455 years.

**John Paul.** See Charles Henry WEBB.

**John Sig'is·mund** (sĭj'ĭs·mŭnd; sĭg'-; *Ger.* zē'gĭs-mŏŏnt). 1572–1619. Elector of Brandenburg (1608–19) and first duke of Prussia (1618–19); joined Reformation (1613).

**John Sigismund Zápolya.** See ZÁPOLYA.

**John III So·bies'ki** (sô·byĕs'kē; *Pol.* sô-). 1624–1696. King of Poland (1674–96), b. Olesko, near Lemberg, Galicia. Entered military service (1648); fought against Tatars and Cossacks (1651–52), but aided Swedes (1654–55). Made commander in chief of Polish army (1665). Engaged in plotting and intrigue against Poland (1669–72), but retrieved himself by defeating Turks at Hotin (1673). Elected king (1674); with 20,000 Polish troops, relieved Turkish siege of Vienna (1683); combined with Imperial army, drove back Turks to the Raab; climax of career; acclaimed as hero of Christendom; because of wretched political conditions in Poland, later years of reign a failure; patron of science and literature.

**John the Par'ri·cide** (păr'ĭ·sīd). 1290–1313. German prince; nephew of the German king Albert I (of Austria). When Albert refused his demand for his hereditary domains, organized a conspiracy against Albert and murdered him (May 1, 1308); fled after murder; arrested in Pisa (1312).

**John Zápolya.** See ZÁPOLYA.

**Joh'ne** (yō'nĕ), **Heinrich Albert.** 1839–1910. German veterinarian; one of first to describe the enteritis of cattle known as Johne's disease, or paratuberculosis; instrumental in introducing meat inspection.

**Johns, Foster.** Pseudonym of Gilbert Vivian SELDES.

**John'son** (jŏn's'n), **Allen.** 1870–1931. American teacher, writer, and editor; author of *Stephen A. Douglas* (1908); editor of *The Chronicles of America* (50 vols., 1918–21) and (from 1926) of *Dictionary of American Biography.*

**Johnson, Alvin Saunders.** 1874–1971. American economist; editor, *The New Republic,* New York (1917–23); director, New School for Social Research, New York (1922–46).

**Johnson, Amy.** 1903–1941. British aviatrix; m. (1932) James Allan Mollison (*q.v.;* divorced 1938). Licensed as pilot in Australia (1930). First woman to make solo flight from London to Australia (1930); made record solo flight from England to India in six days; established records on flight to Japan and back (1931), and to Cape Town and back (1932); with husband made flight from England to U.S.A. (39 hours; 1933), from England to India (22 hours; 1934); made solo flight from London to Cape Town via west coast and return via east coast (1936). Drowned after bailing out over Thames estuary.

**Johnson, Andrew.** 1808–1875. Seventeenth president of the United States, b. Raleigh, N.C. Apprenticed to a tailor. Moved to Tennessee; settled at Greeneville (1826); engaged in tailoring business. Wholly self-educated. Member, U.S. House of Representatives (1843–53). Governor of Tennessee (1853–57). U.S. senator (1857–62). Loyal to Union during Civil War; military governor of Tennessee, rank of brigadier general (1862). Vice-president of the U.S. (Mar. 4–Apr. 15, 1865); succeeded to presidency on death of Lincoln and served 1865–69. Differences between Congress and the president with regard to reconstruction policies led to impeachment proceedings (1868); acquitted. Again U.S. senator (1875). See E. M. STANTON.

**Johnson, Ban.** See Byron Bancroft JOHNSON.

**Johnson, Bush'rod** (bŏŏsh'rŏd) **Rust** (rŭst). 1817–1880. American Confederate commander.

**Johnson, Byron Bancroft.** *Known as* **Ban** (băn) **Johnson.** 1864–1931. American baseball organizer, b. Norwalk, Ohio; organized American League (1900) and was its president (to 1927). Proposed and inaugurated "World's Series" at the close of each baseball season between the pennant-winning clubs of the two major leagues (National and American).

**Johnson, Cave.** 1793–1866. American political leader; U.S. postmaster general (1845–49).

**Johnson, Charles.** 1679–1748. English playwright; satirized by Pope in his *Dunciad.*

**Johnson, Cornelius.** = Cornelius JANSSEN VAN CEULEN.

**Johnson, Dorothy.** English novelist and short-story writer, b. York.

**Johnson, Douglas Wilson.** 1878–1944. American geologist.

**Johnson, Duncan Starr.** 1867–1937. Amer. botanist.

**Johnson, Eastman,** *in full* **Jonathan Eastman.** 1824–1906. American genre and portrait painter.

**Johnson, Edward.** 1598–1672. American colonist, b. England; to America (1630); a founder of Woburn, Mass. (1640); author of a history of New England.

**Johnson, Edward.** 1881–1959. Operatic tenor, b. at Guelph, Ontario, Canada. To U.S. (1920; naturalized 1922) and joined Chicago Opera Company; with Metropolitan Opera Company, New York City (1922–35); general manager, Metropolitan Opera Assoc. (1935–50).

**Johnson, Emory Richard.** 1864–1950. American educator; professor of transportation and commerce, U. of Pennsylvania (from 1896) and dean of the Wharton School of Finance and Commerce (1919–33). Author of books on transportation and commerce, including *Inland Waterways...* (1893), *American Railway Transportation* (1903), *History of Domestic and Foreign Commerce of the United States* (2 vols., 1915), *Principles of Ocean Transportation* (1918), etc.

**Johnson, Esther.** 1681–1728. Fellow member with Jonathan Swift of Sir William Temple's household, to whom Swift addressed the *Journal to Stella.*

**John'son** (yōōn'sôn), **Eyvind.** 1900–1976. Swedish writer. Wrote *Grupp Krilon* (1941), *Sju liv* (1944), *Drömmar om Rosor och eld* (1949), *Hans nades tid* (1961), etc.; awarded (with Harry Martinson) Nobel prize for literature (1974).

**John'son** (jŏn's'n), **Frank Tenney.** 1874–1939. American painter of western U.S. life and scenes.

**Johnson, Guy.** 1740?–1788. British colonial official, b. in Ireland (perhaps nephew of Sir William Johnson, 1715–1774, *q.v.*); to America as a boy. Superintendent of Indian affairs (1774–82); at outbreak of American Revolution, tried to organize Indians against the American colonials (1775); headquarters at Niagara, directing Indian raids against colonials (1779–81); resident of England (from 1783).

**Johnson, Hall.** 1888–1970. American choral conductor, b. Athens, Ga.; organized and directed Hall Johnson Negro choir, N.Y. City (1925–35); in motion-picture choral work (from 1935); organized Festival Negro Chorus of Los Angeles (1941).

**Johnson, Hiram Warren.** 1866–1945. American politician, b. Sacramento, Calif. Adm. to bar (1888) and practiced in Sacramento (1888–1902) and San Francisco (from 1902); succeeded the attorney, Francis Heney, in prosecuting and securing conviction of political boss Abe Ruef on charges of corruption (1908). Governor of California (1911–17). U.S. senator (1917–45).

**Johnson, Hugh Samuel.** 1882–1942. American lawyer and army officer, b. Ft. Scott, Kans. Grad. U.S.M.A., West Point (1903). Served in World War I; originated (1917) plan for selective draft, formulated rules and policies for it, and supervised its execution (1917–

18); brigadier general (1918). National Recovery Administration administrator (1933–34). Works Progress Administration administrator in New York City (1935). Lecturer, radio publicist, and editorial commentator for Scripps-Howard newspapers (from 1934).

**Johnson, James Weldon.** 1871–1938. American author, b. Jacksonville, Fla. A.B., Atlanta U. (1894). Adm. to Florida bar (1897) and practiced in Jacksonville (1897–1901). U.S. consul, Puerto Cabello, Venezuela (1906) and Corinto, Nicaragua (1909–12). Secretary, National Association for Advancement of Colored People (1916–30). Awarded Spingarn medal (1925). Professor of creative literature, Fisk U. (from 1930). Author of *The Autobiography of an Ex-Colored Man* (1912), *Fifty Years and Other Poems* (1917), *The Book of American Negro Poetry* (1921), *The Book of American Negro Spirituals* (1925), *Black Manhattan* (1930), *Negro Americans, What Now* (1934), etc.

**Johnson, Sir John.** 1742–1830. See under Sir William JOHNSON (1715–1774).

**Johnson, John A.,** *known as* **Jack.** 1878–1946. American Negro heavyweight pugilist; won championship (1908); lost title to Jess Willard (1915).

**Johnson, Josephine Winslow.** 1910– . American novelist; author of *Now in November* (1934; awarded Pulitzer prize), *Winter Orchard* (1935), *Year's End* (1937), etc. Received O. Henry memorial award (1935).

**Johnson, Lionel Pigot.** 1867–1902. British author.

**Johnson, Lyndon Baines** (bānz). 1908–1973. Thirty-sixth president of the United States, b. near Stonewall, Texas; B.S., Southwest Texas State Teachers College (1930); member, U.S. House of Representatives (1937–49); Senate (1949–61); U.S. vice-president (1961–63); president (1963–69).

**Johnson, Manuel John.** 1805–1859. Eng. astronomer.

**Johnson, Martin Elmer.** 1884–1937. Amer. motion-picture photographer of wild life, esp. in Africa; made extensive film of vanishing wild life in Africa for American Museum of Natural History (1924–29). His wife (m. 1910), **Osa Helen,** *nee* **Leighty** (1894–1953), collaborated with him in his work and continued it after his death; m. (1941) Clark H. Getts; author of *Lion* (1929), *I Married Adventure* (1940), etc.

**Johnson, Melvin Maynard.** 1909–1965. American inventor of a semiautomatic rifle (1936), a light machine gun (1937), and an autocarbine (1941), named after him. Captain, U.S. marines (1938).

**Johnson, Mordecai Wyatt.** 1890– . American Negro educator; president of Howard U. (from 1926).

**Johnson, Nelson Trusler.** 1887–1954. American diplomat; U.S. ambassador to China (1929–41), minister to Australia (1941–46).

**Johnson, Oliver.** 1809–1889. American humanitarian; associated with William Lloyd Garrison in antislavery agitation (from 1833).

**Johnson, Owen McMahon.** See under Robert Underwood JOHNSON.

**Johnson, Pauline,** *in full* **Emily Pauline.** 1862–1913. Canadian poet, daughter of George Henry M. Johnson, Mohawk Indian chief. Among her volumes of verse are *The White Wampum* (1894), *Canadian Born* (1903), and *Flint and Feathers* (1912).

**Johnson, Rev'er·dy** (rĕv'ẽr·dĭ). 1796–1876. American jurist and diplomat; represented defense in Dred Scott case. U.S. senator (1845–49). U.S. attorney general (1849–50). Aided in keeping Maryland in Union (1861). Again U.S. senator (1863–68). U.S. minister to Great Britain (1868–69).

**Johnson, Richard Mentor.** 1780–1850. Vice-president of the United States, b. near Louisville, Ky. Adm. to bar (1802). Member, U.S. House of Representatives (1807–19; 1829–37), U.S. Senate (1819–29). In electoral vote for vice-president (1837), no candidate gained majority in electoral college; election thereupon thrown into U.S. Senate; only vice-president ever thus elected; served 1837–41.

**Johnson, Robert Underwood.** 1853–1937. American man of letters; on staff of *Century Magazine* (1873–1913); U.S. ambassador to Italy (1920–21). Author of *The Winter Hour and Other Poems* (1891), *Songs of Liberty...* (1897), *Poems of War and Peace* (1916), *Aftermath* (1933), etc. His son **Owen McMahon** (1878–1952), writer of novels and short stories, including *Arrows of the Almighty* (1901), *The Varmint* (1910), *Stover at Yale* (1911), *The Salamander* (1913), *Children of Divorce* (1927), *Coming of the Amazons* (1931), etc.

**Johnson, Rossiter.** 1840–1931. American author, and editor of *Annual Cyclopedia* (1883–1902), *Cyclopedia of American Biography* (1886–89), and a number of many-volumed anthologies. Author of *A History of the War of Secession* (1888), *Three Decades* (verse; 1895), *Morning Lights and Evening Shadows* (verse; 1902), *The Story of the Constitution of the United States* (1906), etc.

**Johnson, Samuel.** 1696–1772. American clergyman and educator; entered Congregational ministry; converted to Church of England (1722); leader of Church of England movement in New England. First president (1754–63) of King's College, now Columbia U., New York. His son **William Samuel** (1727–1819) was a jurist and educator; judge of Connecticut supreme court (1772–74); member of Continental Congress (1784–87); U.S. senator (1789–91); president of Columbia College (1787–1800).

**Johnson, Samuel.** *Known as* **Dr. Johnson.** *Called* **the Great Cham** (kăm) **of Literature.** 1709–1784. English lexicographer, critic, and conversationalist, b. in Lichfield, son of a bookdealer. Educ. Oxford (1728–29). Married a widow, Mrs. Porter, of Birmingham (1735; d. 1752), and opened a school at Edial, near Lichfield, in which David Garrick was one of his first pupils. To London (1737), accompanied by Garrick; became a contributor to *Gentleman's Magazine.* Published a poem, *London* (1738), in imitation of a satire of Juvenal, and a prose *Life of Savage* (1744). Issued a prospectus of his English dictionary (1747) and worked on it until its publication (1755). Also published *The Vanity of Human Wishes* (1749), produced *Irene* at Drury Lane Theatre (1749), edited the *Rambler* (1750–52), and in a famous letter repulsed Lord Chesterfield's tardy offer of patronage for his dictionary (1755). Publication of the dictionary (1755) brought fame and a degree from Oxford. Contributed book reviews to *Literary Magazine* (1756–58); wrote the *Idler* papers for Newbery's *Universal Chronicle* (1758–60), and the prose romance *Rasselas, Prince of Abyssinia* (1759). Aided in exposing the Cock Lane ghost (1762). Received pension of £300 from Lord Bute, and degrees of LL.D. from Dublin and Oxford. Made acquaintance of James Boswell (May, 1763), and soon after founded his Literary Club, including Reynolds, Garrick, Goldsmith, Boswell, Burke, and others. Published critical edition of Shakespeare (1765); wrote *Lives of the Poets* (vols. I–IV, 1779; V–X, 1781). Traveled in Scotland with Boswell (1773), and wrote *Journey to the Western Isles of Scotland* (1775). Frequently enjoyed hospitality of the Thrales (from 1764), and was Mr. Thrale's executor (1781); quarreled with Mrs. Thrale on learning of her marriage to Piozzi. Organized Essex Head Club (1783). Died Dec. 13, 1784; buried in Westminster Abbey. See James BOSWELL.

**Johnson, Thomas.** 1732–1819. American Revolutionary leader; member, Continental Congress (1774–77); nominated George Washington for commander in chief, Continental army (1775). Raised troops in Maryland for Continental army (1777). First governor of Maryland (1777–79). Associate justice, U.S. Supreme Court (1791–93).

**Johnson, Tom Loftin.** 1854–1911. American politician, b. near Georgetown, Ky. Acquired street-railway interests in Indianapolis, Ind., and then in Cleveland, Ohio. Member, U.S. House of Representatives (1891–95). Mayor of Cleveland (1901–1909); administration noted for efficiency and municipal reforms; marked by long bitter fight with street-railway interests.

**Johnson, Walter Perry.** 1887–1946. American professional baseball player, b. Humboldt, Kans.; pitcher, American League team, Washington (1907–27).

**Johnson,** Sir **William.** 1715–1774. British official in American colonies, b. in Ireland. To America and settled in Mohawk Valley (c. 1738); successful in dealing with Indians, esp. those of the Six Nations; superintendent of Indian affairs (1755–74); created baronet (1755). His son **Sir John** (1742–1830) organized Tories and Indians and inspired raids against colonials in the Mohawk and Schoharie valleys (1777–81); superintendent of Indian affairs (from 1782); granted estate in Canada after the Revolution. See also Guy JOHNSON.

**Johnson, William.** 1771–1834. American jurist, b. Charleston, S.C.; associate justice, U.S. Supreme Court (1804–34).

**Johnson, William Eugene.** 1862–1945. American reformer, b. Coventry, N.Y. Journalist (1884–1905). Chief special officer in U.S. Indian service (1908–11); became known as **Puss'y·foot'** (po͝os'ĭ·fo͝ot') **Johnson** because of his methods in pursuing lawbreakers in Indian Territory. Managing editor, publications of Anti-Saloon League (1912–16); publicity director of the league (1916–18); temperance lecturer.

**Johnson, William Samuel.** 1727–1819. See under Samuel JOHNSON (1696–1772).

**John'ston** (jŏn'stŭn; -s'n), **Albert Sidney.** 1803–1862. American army officer, b. Washington, Ky. Grad. U.S.M.A., West Point (1826). Resigned from army (1834). Brigadier general in Texan army (1837); secretary of war, Texas (1838); resigned (1840). Re-entered U.S. army (1849); resigned to enter Confederate service, as general (1861). In battle at Shiloh Church, surprised and defeated Federal army under Grant, but was killed in action (Apr. 6, 1862). See William Preston JOHNSTON; cf. Joseph E. JOHNSTON.

**Johnston, Alexander.** 1849–1889. American historian, b. Brooklyn, N.Y. Author of books on political and constitutional history.

**Johnston, Alexander Keith.** 1804–1871. Scottish geographer; organized, with his brother Sir **William** (1802–1888), map-publishing firm of W. & A. K. Johnston, at Edinburgh (1826); chief works, the first English atlas of physical geography (1848; prepared at Humboldt's suggestion), and a *Dictionary of Geography* (1850). His son **Alexander Keith** (1844–1879) was also a geographer; published maps of Africa (1866) and East Africa (1870).

**Johnston, Annie,** *nee* **Fel'lows** (fĕl'ōz). 1863–1931. American writer of books for children; m. William L. Johnston (1888, d. 1892). Author of *The Little Colonel* (1895) and *Mary Ware* (1908).

**Johnston, Archibald.** Lord **Warriston.** See WARRISTON.

**Johnston, Denis William.** 1901– . British playwright; director, Dublin Gate Theatre (1931–36); actor and producer for Abbey Theatre, Dublin Gate Theatre, and Earl of Longford's company, at intervals (from 1927). Among his plays are *The Moon in the Yellow River* (1931), *A Bride for the Unicorn* (1933), *Blind Man's Buff* (adapted from Toller's *Die Blinde Gottin;* 1936), *The Golden Cuckoo* (1939).

**Johnston,** Sir **Harry Hamilton.** 1858–1927. British explorer and writer; explored Portugese West Africa and Congo River (1882–83); led Royal Society expedition to Mt. Kilimanjaro (1884); led expedition (1889) which founded British Central Africa Protectorate; consul general for Uganda Protectorate (1899–1901). Author of books on Africa, and the novels *The Gay Dombeys* (1919), *Mrs. Warren's Daughter* (1920), and *The Veneerings* (1922).

**Johnston, John Black.** 1868–1939. American neurologist; professor, Minnesota (from 1909).

**Johnston, Joseph Eggleston.** 1807–1891. American army officer; grad. U.S.M.A., West Point (1829). On frontier duty; served through Mexican War. Resigned (1861) to enter Confederate service; brigadier general (May, 1861); general (July, 1861). In command on Mississippi (1863); lost Vicksburg to Grant. With Army of the Tennessee (1864); outmaneuvered by Sherman; relieved of command (July 17, 1864). Assigned again to Army of the Tennessee (Feb., 1865); surrendered to Sherman (Apr. 26, 1865). Member, U.S. House of Representatives (1879–81). U.S. commissioner of railroads (1887–91).

**Johnston, Mary.** 1870–1936. American author, esp. of historical romances; b. Buchanan, Va. Works include *To Have and to Hold* (1900), *Cease Firing* (1912), *The Great Valley* (1926), *Miss Delicia Allen* (1932), etc.

**Johnston,** Sir **Reginald Fleming.** 1874–1938. British Orientalist and civil-service official in China; to China as private secretary to governor of Hong Kong (1900–02); official at Weihaiwei (1904–30) and tutor (1919–25) to Henry Pu-yi; professor of Chinese, U. of London, and head of department of languages and cultures of the Far East in School of Oriental Studies (1931–37).

**Johnston, Richard Malcolm.** 1822–1898. American writer; author of stories of Georgia life.

**Johnston, Robert Matteson.** 1867–1920. American historian, esp. of Napoleonic period.

**Johnston, William.** 1802–1888. See under Alexander Keith JOHNSTON.

**Johnston, William Andrew.** 1871–1929. American journalist and writer, b. Pittsburgh, Pa.; author of detective stories and humorous books, and of the popular story of a lame boy *Limpy* (1917).

**Johnston, William Hartshorne.** 1861–1933. American army officer in World War; engaged in Toul sector (Aug., 1918), St. Mihiel offensive (Sept., 1918) and Meuse-Argonne offensive (Sept.–Oct., 1918); chief of staff of American forces in Germany (Aug., 1920–May, 1921); brigadier general, U.S. army (Apr., 1921) and major general (Nov., 1924).

**Johnston, William Preston.** 1831–1899. Son of Albert Sidney Johnston. American educator; president, Louisiana State U. (1880–84) and Tulane U. (1884–99).

**Johst** (yōst), **Hanns.** 1890– . German novelist and playwright.

**Join'ville'** (zhwăN'vēl'), Prince **de. François Ferdinand d'Or'lé'ans'** (dôr'lā'äN'). 1818–1900. French naval officer and writer, b. Neuilly; 3d son of King Louis Philippe; m. (1843) Francesca, sister of Pedro II, Emperor of Brazil. Made rear admiral (1843). Commanded French squadron in war with Morocco (1844). To England after Revolution of 1848. With son and two nephews served on staff of Gen. McClellan in U.S. Civil War (1861–62). Forced to leave France (1870) but served as a deputy in the National Assembly (1871–75). Author of several works on naval matters, an account of the American Civil War (1872), and *Vieux Souvenirs* (1894).

**Joinville, Jean de.** 1224?–1317. French chronicler; accompanied Saint Louis (Louis IX) to Egypt on the Sixth Crusade (1248–54); wrote *Histoire de Saint Louis.*

**Jó'kai** (yō'koi), **Mau'rus** (mou'rōōs) *or* **Mór** (mōr). 1825–1904. Hungarian novelist and dramatist. His novels and tales, chiefly political and social, include *A Hungarian Nabob* (1854), *The New Landlord* (German trans., 1862), *Black Diamonds* (1873), *The Romance of the Next Century* (1874); his plays include *The Jew Boy* (1842) and *Milton* (1878).

**Jolas, Eugene.** 1894–1952. American poet; a leader in ultramodern school of verse; editor of *transition.*

**Jo·lin'** (yōō·lēn'), **Johan Kristofer.** 1818–1884. Swedish actor and dramatist.

**Jo'liot'–Cu'rie'** (zhô'lyō'kü'rē'), orig. **Joliot, Frédéric.** 1900–1958. French physicist, b. Paris; professor, Radium Inst., Paris; shared 1935 Nobel prize with wife **Irène** (see under Pierre CURIE); high commissioner for atomic energy (1946–50).

**Jol'li·et'** (jŏl'ĭ·ĕt'; *Fr.* zhô'lyĕ') *or* **Jo'li·et'** (jō'lĭ·ĕt'; *Fr.* zhô'lyĕ'), **Louis.** 1645–1700. Explorer in Mississippi Valley, b. prob. in Beaupré, Canada. Sent west (1669) with supplies for expedition looking for copper in Lake Superior region; met Marquette at Sault Ste. Marie. Chosen (1672) by Canadian authorities to lead expedition to discover the great river reported by Indians; sighted Mississippi (June 17, 1673) and floated down as far as what is now Arkansas; reported discovery in Quebec (1674). Given island of Anticosti. Further explorations in Gulf of St. Lawrence and Hudson Bay region. Canadian royal hydrographer (1697).

**Jol'ly** (yôl'ē; *Angl.* jŏl'ĭ), **Philipp von.** 1809–1884. German physicist; invented an air thermometer and a spring balance (Jolly balance) for determining specific gravity; determined the mass and density of the earth and the coefficient of expansion of air and other gases; studied osmosis. Father of **Friedrich** (1844–1904), psychiatrist, and of **Julius** (1849–1932), philologist and Sanskrit scholar, authority on Hindu jurisprudence.

**Jol'son** (jōl'sŭn), **Al.** *Orig. name* **Asa Yoel'son**(yûl'sŭn). 1886–1950. American entertainer, b. Russia. Appeared in vaudeville shows and films, most notably *The Jazz Singer* and *Singing Fool.*

**Jol'y** (jŏl'ĭ), **John.** 1857–1933. Irish physicist; devised a photometer, meldometer, and a method of color photography; invented a steam calorimeter; perfected (with Walter Stevenson) a method in radium therapeutics for securing uniform radiation; conducted researches on the crust formation of the earth.

**Jo'mard'** (zhô'màr'), **Edme François.** 1777–1862. French geographer and Egyptologist.

**Jo'mi'ni'** (zhô'mē'nē'), Baron **Henri.** 1779–1869. Soldier and writer on military affairs, b. in Switzerland; entered French army as aide-de-camp to Marshal Ney; left French service (1813) and became aide-de-camp to Czar Alexander of Russia, and (1837) military instructor of the cesarevitch, afterward Czar Alexander II. Author of *Histoire...des Campagnes de la Révolution* (1819–24), *Précis de l'Art de la Guerre* (1838), etc.

**Jom·mel'li** (yôm·mĕl'lē) *or* **Jo·mel'li** (yô·mĕl'lē), **Niccolò.** 1714–1774. Italian composer of operas, including *Merope* (1741), *L'Ifigenia in Aulide* (1751), and *Armida* (1770), and oratorios, cantatas, psalms, a Requiem, a Miserere, and other church music.

**Jo'nah** (jō'nȧ). *In Douay Bible* **Jo'nas** (jō'năs). According to the Old Testament book of *Jonah*, a Hebrew prophet who, disobeying God's command to go to Nineveh, took ship for Tarshish, encountered a storm, and had sailors throw him into the sea, where he was swallowed by a large fish (called "whale" in *Matt.* xii. 40) in whose belly he remained for three days.

**Jo'nah** (jō'nȧ), Rabbi. *Arab.* **A·bul' Wa·lid' Mer·wan' ibn–Ja·nah'** (ȧ·bōōl' wă·lēd' măr·wän' ĭb''n jă·nä'). *Called also* **R.** (= Rabbi or Rab) **Ma·ri'nus** (mȧ·rī'nŭs). 990?–?1050. Hebrew grammarian, philologist, and physician, b. Córdoba, Spain; left Córdoba (1012) and subsequently settled in Saragossa; author of a study in Arabic of the Bible and its language.

**Jo'nas'** (zhō'näs'), **Hector Lucien.** 1880–    . French painter and lithographer.

**Jo'nas** (yō'näs), **Justus.** 1493–1555. German Protestant reformer, friend and co-worker of Luther; professor of theology, Wittenberg (1521–41).

**Jó'nas·son** (yō'näs·sŏn), **Hermann.** 1896–    . Premier of Iceland (1934–42; 1956–58).

**Jon'a·than** (jŏn'ȧ·thăn). Son of Mattathias. See MACCABEES.

**Jonathan.** In Bible, eldest son of King Saul; aided father in freeing Israel from Philistines (*1 Sam.* xiii–xiv); became firm friend of David; tried to reconcile Saul and David (*1 Sam.* xx).

**Jonathan ben Uz·zi'el** (bĕn ŭ·zī'ĕl; ŭz'ĭ·ĕl). Jewish scholar, disciple of Hillel; traditional author of the Targum.

**Jonck'bloet** (yôngk'blōōt), **Willem Jozef Andreas.** 1817–1885. Dutch critic and literary historian.

**Jones** (jōnz), **Adrian.** 1845–1938. British soldier and sculptor; served 23 years in the British army, rising to rank of captain. Among statues of his design are *Royal Marines Monument*, London; *Soldiers' National Memorial*, Australia; *Duke of Cambridge*, London.

**Jones, Anson.** 1798–1858. President of Republic of Texas, b. Great Barrington, Mass. M.D., Jefferson Coll., Canonsburg, Pa.; practiced in Philadelphia and in Brazoria, Texas (from 1833). Served in Sam Houston's army. Texas minister to U.S. (1835). Texas secretary of state (1841). President of Texas (1844–46); turned over government to J. P. Henderson, first governor under constitution of the United States.

**Jones, Catesby ap** (ăp) **Roger.** 1821–1877. American naval officer in Confederate service; executive officer of the *Merrimac* (1862); in command during battle with *Monitor* (March 9, 1862).

**Jones, Daniel.** 1881–1967. English phonetician. B.A., Cantab. (1903). Teacher of phonetics, University Coll., London (from 1907; professor from 1921). Asst. secretary (1907–27) and secretary (from 1928), International Phonetic Assoc., and asst. editor of its organ, *Le Maître Phonétique* (from 1907). Among his works are *Outline of English Phonetics* (1916) and *English Pronouncing Dictionary*, based on Southern British speech (1917).

**Jones, David Michael.** 1895–1974. British artist and writer; known as water-color painter. Author of *In Parenthesis* (1937; awarded Hawthornden prize, 1938), *The Anathemata* (1952).

**Jones, Ebenezer.** 1820–1860. English poet; remembered esp. for three poems, *Winter Hymn to the Snow, When the World is Burning, To Death*, written near the close of his life.

**Jones, Edward D.** See under Charles H. Dow.

**Jones, Eli Stanley.** 1884–1973. American missionary and author; evangelist to the high castes of India (from 1907). Author of *The Christ of the Indian Road* (1925).

**Jones, Ernest Charles.** 1819–1869. English Chartist reformer and poet; author of *The Battle Day and Other Poems* (1855), novels, and miscellaneous verse.

**Jones, Francis Coates.** 1857–1932. American painter; best known for his figure paintings.

**Jones, George.** 1811–1891. American newspaper publisher and editor, b. Poultney, Vt.; a founder of New York *Times* (1851); directed fight against Tweed Ring (1871). See H. J. RAYMOND.

**Jones, George William.** 1860–1942. English printer; designer of various type faces, including Linotype Granjon, Linotype Estienne, Linotype Georgian; lecturer in Great Britain, Canada, and U.S. on history and craft of printing.

**Jones, Harold Spencer.** 1890–1960. English astronomer at Cape of Good Hope (1923–33); astronomer royal (1933–55).

**Jones, Henry.** 1831–1899. English physician and writer on whist and other games; known by pseudonym **Cav'en·dish** (kăv'ĕn·dĭsh)—hence the *Cavendish* hand in whist.

**Jones,** Sir **Henry.** 1852–1922. British philosopher, b. in North Wales. Author of *Browning as a Religious and Philosophical Teacher, Idealism as a Practical Creed,* and *Social Powers.*

**Jones, Henry Arthur.** 1851–1929. English playwright, son of a farmer; forced to take employment at age of thirteen; became commercial traveler. First stage success, *The Silver King* (with Henry Herman, 1882). Other plays include *Saints and Sinners* (1884), *The Tempter* (1893), *The Masqueraders* (1894), *Michael and his Lost Angel* (1896), *Mrs. Dane's Defence* (1900), *The Hypocrites* (1906), *Mary Goes First* (1913), *Cock o' the Walk* (1915), and *The Pacifists* (1917).

**Jones,** Sir **Henry Stuart–.** See STUART-JONES.

**Jones, Hilary Pollard.** 1863–1938. American naval officer, b. in Virginia. Grad. U.S.N.A., Annapolis (1884); commanded Newport News division, cruiser and transport force (Apr., 1918–Jan., 1919); vice-admiral commanding 2d battleship squadron of the Atlantic fleet (1919–21); commander in chief, Atlantic fleet (1922–23); American delegate at conference on limitation of naval armaments, at Geneva (1927); retired (1927); commissioned admiral on retired list (1930).

**Jones,** Sir **Horace.** 1819–1887. English architect.

**Jones, Howard Mumford.** 1892– . American educator and writer; author of *Gargoyles* (verse, 1918), *A Bibliography of... Byron* (1924), *The Case of Professor Banoring* (play, 1924), *America and French Culture, 1750–1848* (1927), *The Harp that Once* (1937), etc.

**Jones, Hugh Bolton.** 1848–1927. American landscape painter, b. Baltimore, Md. Studio in New York.

**Jones, Inigo.** 1573–1652. English architect, b. London. Designed stage sets, etc., for court masques written by Ben Jonson, Heywood, Davenant, and others. Appointed surveyor general of works (1615); designed the queen's house at Greenwich, Lincoln's Inn Chapel, banqueting hall at Whitehall (1619–22), reconstruction of St. Paul's Cathedral, Covent Garden piazza, Ashburnham House in Westminster.

**Jones, Jacob.** 1768–1850. American naval officer, b. near Smyrna, Del. Commanded sloop *Wasp* when it fought and captured British brig *Frolic* (Oct. 18, 1812); commanded captured frigate *Macedonian* in Decatur's squadron operating against Algiers (1815).

**Jones, Jesse Holman.** 1874–1956. American businessman, banker, and public official, b. in Robertson County, Tenn. In lumber business, Dallas and Houston, Tex. (1895–1905). Organized Texas Trust Co., Houston (1909, now Bankers Mortgage Co.); chairman of the board, National Bank of Commerce, Houston, Tex.; owner and publisher, Houston *Chronicle.* Chairman, Reconstruction Finance Corporation (1933–39); administrator, Federal Loan Agency (1939–45); U.S. secretary of commerce (1940–45).

**Jones, John.** 1729–1791. American surgeon, b. Jamaica, Long Island, N.Y. Published (1775) first surgical textbook in American colonies (*Plain... Remarks on the Treatment of Wounds and Fractures*); personal physician of Benjamin Franklin; attended George Washington.

**Jones,** Sir **John Morris–.** See MORRIS-JONES.

**Jones, John Paul.** *Orig. full name* **John Paul.** 1747–1792. Naval officer, b. in Scotland. In British mercantile marine (from c. 1759). Settled in Fredericksburg, Va. (c. 1773), and added *Jones* to his name. Entered American navy at outbreak of Revolution; commissioned lieutenant (Dec. 7, 1775); promoted captain (1776); successful cruise as commander of *Ranger* in waters around British Isles (1778). With aid of France, organized fleet to attack British; commanded flagship *Bonhomme Richard* (1779); defeated British ship *Serapis* (Sept. 23, 1779) but *Bonhomme Richard* sank two days later. Served in Russian navy on Black Sea (1788–90); in Paris (1790–92). Remains brought to U.S. (1905). Elected to American Hall of Fame (1925).

**Jones, Le Roi.** See Imamu Amiri BARAKA.

**Jones, Lewis Ralph.** 1864–1945. American botanist; professor, Vermont (1889–1910), Wisconsin (from 1910). Editor of bacteriological terms for *Webster's New International Dictionary,* first edition (1909).

**Jones, Mary,** *nee* **Harris.** 1830–1930. American labor leader, b. in Cork, Ireland; to U.S. as a child. Interested herself in labor movement after death of husband (1867). Became agitator, prominent speaker, and organizer in labor circles; known as "Mother Jones."

**Jones, Owen.** 1741–1814. Welsh antiquary; published *The Myvyrian Archaeology of Wales* (1801–07). His son **Owen** (1809–1874), architect, was superintendent of the London Exhibition (1851); joint director of decoration of Crystal Palace; designed St. James's Hall, London.

**Jones,** Sir **Robert.** 1858–1933. British orthopedic surgeon.

**Jones, Robert Edmond.** 1887–1954. American scene designer, b. Milton, N.H.; A.B., Harvard (1910). Designed sets for many plays, including *The Man Who Married a Dumb Wife, The Jest, Richard III, Macbeth, Green Pastures,* and for color films *La Cucaracha, Becky Sharp,* etc.

**Jones, Robert Tyre,** *known as* **Bobby.** 1902–1971. American golf player, b. Atlanta, Ga. B.S., Georgia Tech. (1922) and Harvard (1924). Adm. to bar (1928) and practiced at Atlanta, Ga. Won U.S. national amateur championship (1924, 1925, 1927, 1928, 1930), U.S. national open championship (1923, 1926, 1929, 1930), British open championship (1926, 1927, 1930); first player to be official champion in national open championships of Great Britain and U.S. in the same year (1930).

**Jones, Samuel Milton.** 1846–1904. American industrialist, politician, and reformer, b. in Wales. To U.S. (1849); worker in the oil fields; later, established manufacturing plant at Toledo, Ohio; advocated Golden Rule policy in all his dealings. Mayor of Toledo (1897–1904); led crusade to wipe out dishonesty and political corruption. Known as "Golden Rule Jones."

**Jones, Samuel Porter,** *known as* **Sam.** 1847–1906. American evangelist and revivalist, b. in Chambers County, Ala.

**Jones, Sidney.** 1869–1946. English composer of light operas.

**Jones, Thomas.** 1731–1792. American lawyer, b. Fort Neck, Long Island, N.Y. Practiced in New York City. Loyalist during American Revolution; resident in England (from 1781). Author of *History of New York during the Revolutionary War*... the only history of the period from the Loyalist standpoint.

**Jones, Thomas Hudson.** 1892–1969. American sculptor; among his works are the Tomb of the Unknown Soldier in Arlington National Cemetery, the bust of Ulysses S. Grant in the Hall of Fame.

**Jones, Thomas Rymer.** 1810–1880. English anatomist and physiologist; first professor of comparative anatomy at King's Coll., London (1836–74); chief work, *General Outline of the Animal Kingdom* (1838–41).

**Jones, Thomas Samuel.** 1882–1932. American poet; author of *The Path o' Dreams* (1904), *Sonnets of the Cross* (1922), *Sonnets of the Saints* (1925), etc.

**Jones, Wesley Livsey.** 1863–1932. American lawyer and politician; member, U.S. House of Representatives (1899–1909), U.S. Senate (1909–32). Author of the Jones Act (1929), providing severe penalties for persons convicted of violation of the Volstead Act.

**Jones** of Nay′land (nā′lănd), **William.** 1726–1800. English ecclesiastic and writer on theology; known as "Trinity Jones" because of his treatises in defense of the doctrine of the Trinity. Curate of Nayland, in Suffolk (1777).

**Jones,** Sir **William.** 1746–1794. English Orientalist and jurist; educ. Oxford. Judge of the high court at Calcutta (1783–94). Founded Bengal Asiatic Society (1784). His notable works include a version of the Arabic *Mu'allaqāt* (1783), a *Dissertation on the Orthography of Asiatick Words in Roman Letters,* and translations of *Hitopadesa* and *Sakuntala,* etc.

**Jonescu.** Variant of IONESCU.

**Jong′en** (yông′ĕn), **Joseph.** 1873–1953. Belgian composer of string quartets, sonatas, and other pieces for violin and violoncello, piano trios and quartets, cantatas, orchestral works, the symphonic poem *Lalla Roukh* (1903), the opera *Jélyane* (1916), choruses, and songs.

**Jong′kind** (yông′kĭnt), **Johan Barthold.** 1819–1891. Dutch luminist landscape painter and etcher of the Fontainebleau school; served as link between naturalism and contemporary impressionism; resident chiefly in France (from 1846); became insane (1860).

**Jon′nart′** (zhô′nár′), **Célestin Auguste Charles.** 1857–1927. French politician; member of Chamber of Deputies (1889–1914) and of the Senate (after 1914); minister of public works (1893–94); governor of Algeria (1909–11, 1918). During World War, served as French high commissioner in Greece; was instrumental in forcing King Constantine's abdication and in securing Greece's participation in the war on the side of the Allies. Ambassador to the Vatican (1921) to renew diplomatic relations between France and the Holy See; recalled (1924).

**Jon·ne′sco** (yŏ·nĕ′skō). Variant of IONESCU.

**Jon′son** (jŏn′s'n), **Ben,** *in full* **Benjamin.** 1573?–1637. English playwright and poet, b. in Westminster. Studied in Westminster school, and perhaps in Cambridge. Served briefly with English army in Flanders; returned to London (c. 1592), and became associated with the stage, as both actor and playwright. His plays include *Every Man in his Humour* (1598), *Every Man out of his Humour* (1599), *Cynthia's Revels* (1600), *The Poetaster* (1601), *Sejanus* (1603), *Volpone* (1605), *Epicoene, The Alchemist, Catiline, Bartholomew Fair, The Devil is an Ass* (5 plays between 1605 and 1616), *The Staple of News* (1625), and a number of court masques. Among his poems (pub. 1616) were epigrams, epistles, and songs, including the famous *Drink to me only with thine eyes.* Generally regarded as first poet laureate, although William Davenant (*q.v.*) was first to receive official title.

**Jóns′son** (yōns′sŏn), **Einar.** 1874–1954. Icelandic sculptor and painter.

**Jónsson, Finnur.** 1704–1789. Icelandic bishop and historian; author of *Historia Ecclesiastica Islandiae* (4 vols., 1772–78), used as a source of Icelandic history and literature.

**Jónsson, Finnur.** 1858–1934. Icelandic philologist and literary historian. Professor of northern literature, Copenhagen (1898–1928). Author of a standard *History of Old Norse and Old Icelandic Literature* (3 vols., 1894–1902); edited many Old Norse texts, and the collection *Norse-Icelandic Scaldic Poetry* (4 vols., 1908–15).

**Joram.** See JEHORAM.

**Jor′daens** (yôr′dàns), **Jacob.** 1593–1678. Flemish painter of scenes of Flemish life, historical, religious, and mythological subjects, murals, portraits, designs for tapestries, etc.

**Jor′dan′** (zhôr′däN′), **Camille.** 1771–1821. French politician; royalist in sympathy during French Revolution; took part in the rebellion at Lyons, and had to flee from France (1793). Became member of Council of Five Hundred (1797) and advocated religious liberty. Opposed dictatorship of Napoleon (1800). Member of Chamber of Deputies (1816).

**Jordan, Camille,** *in full* **Marie Ennemond Camille.** 1838–1922. French mathematician; known for work on Abelian functions, the symmetry of polyhedrons, *n*-dimensional geometry, etc.

**Jor′dan** (jôr′d'n), **David Starr.** 1851–1931. American biologist and educator, b. Gainesville, N.Y. M.S., Cornell (1872), M.D., Indiana Medical College (1875). Professor of natural history, Lombard U. (1872–73), of biology, Butler U. (1875–79), of zoology, Indiana U. (1879–85); president, Indiana U. (1885–91); president (1891–1913), chancellor (1913–16), Stanford U. Author of *Manual of Vertebrate Animals of Northern United States* (1876–1929), *The Fishes of North and Middle America* (with B. W. Evermann; 4 vols., 1896–1900), *Footnotes to Evolution* (1898), *American Food and Game Fishes* (with Evermann; 1902), *Fishes* (1907), *The Genera of Fishes* (4 parts, 1918–20), *Fossil Fishes of Southern California* (9 parts, 1919–26), *Check List of the Fishes... of North and Middle America* (with Evermann and H. Walton Clark; 1928), of books on world peace, war, and related topics, such as *War and Waste* (1914), *Democracy and World Relations* (1918), also of books for children, and miscellaneous writings.

**Jordan,** Mrs. **Dorothea** *or* **Dorothy.** *Stage name of* **Dorothea Bland** (blănd). 1762–1816. Irish actress. Made debut at Drury Lane as Peggy in *The Country Girl* (1785); last part that of Lady Teazle at Covent Garden (1814). Leading comedy actress of her day; praised by Hazlitt, Lamb, Leigh Hunt; mistress of duke of Clarence, later William IV (from c. 1790).

**Jordan, Edwin Oakes.** 1866–1936. American bacteriologist; teacher (from 1893), professor (from 1907), Chicago. Conducted researches on influenza, typhoid fever, food poisoning, and bacterial dissociation.

**Jor·dan′** (jôr·dăn′), **Elizabeth.** 1867–1947. American writer; on editorial staff, *Harper's Bazaar* (1900–13) and of Harper & Bros., publishers (1913–18). Author of *Tales of the City Room* (1898), *May Iverson, Her Book* (1904), *The Lady from Oklahoma* (4-act comedy, produced 1911), *Miss Blake's Husband* (1925), *The Life of the Party* (1935), *Three Rousing Cheers* (autobiography, 1938), etc.

**Jor′dan** (jôr′d'n), **John.** 1746–1809. English antiquarian, b. near Stratford-on-Avon. Collected Shakespeareana; bequeathed his collections to Edmund Malone, the Shakespearean scholar, who found many errors in the material and discovered obvious inventions in a number of stories about Shakespeare.

**Jor′dan** (yōr′dän), **Rudolf.** 1810–1887. German genre

painter, illustrator, and etcher; his works include chiefly scenes from the lives of fisherfolk and sailors.

**Jor'dan** (jôr'd'n; jûr'-), **Thomas.** 1819–1895. American army officer; resigned from U.S. army to enter Confederate service (1861); brigadier general, Beauregard's chief of staff (from 1861). Commander of Cuban insurgents in Cuba (1869–70). Founder and editor, *Financial and Mining Record*, New York City (1870–92).

**Jor'dan** (yôr'dän), **Wilhelm.** 1819–1904. German poet, novelist, and aesthetician. Journalist in Leipzig (1844); championed liberalism and "Young Hegelian" philosophy in his writings and poems *Irdische Phantasien* (1842) and *Schaum* (1846); banished from Saxony for alleged atheism (1846). Author of the metaphysical dramatic epic *Demiurgos* (3 vols., 1852–54) and the epic *Die Nibelunge*, the tragedy *Die Witwe des Agis* (1858), comedies in verse, novels and short stories, translations of Shakespeare, Sophocles, Homer, and the Edda, etc.

**Jor·da'nes** (jôr·dā'nēz) *or* **Jor·da'nis** (jôr·dā'nĭs). *Also, prob. erroneously,* **Jor·nan'des** (jôr·năn'dēz). Sixth-century ecclesiastic and historian; wrote (551) a history of the Goths, condensed from the work of Cassiodorus and others, and a universal history.

**Jor·da'nus Nem'o·rar'i·us** (jôr·dā'nŭs něm'ō·râr'ĭ·ŭs). d. 1237? Mathematician, b. in Germany. Credited with earliest statement of the theory of stereographic projections.

**Jörg** (yûrk), **Joseph Edmund.** 1819–1901. Bavarian politician and historian; headed the "Patriots" (1869) in opposition to Bismarck, and Hohenlohe; member of Center party in Reichstag (1874–78). Author of *Deutschland in der Revolutionsperiode von 1522–26* (1851), etc.

**Jör'gen·sen** (yûr'gĕn·sĕn), **E.** See O. Krag.

**Jörgensen, Johannes.** 1866–1956. Danish poet, journalist, and novelist. Favored realism, and, later, French symbolism; embraced Roman Catholicism (1896); resident in Italy (from 1913).

**Jörgensen, Jör'gen** (yûr'gĕn). 1779–?1845. Danish adventurer; established himself briefly (June–August, 1809) as ruler of Iceland. Driven out by captain of a British sloop of war and carried to England; subsequently found guilty of robbery (1820), and sent to Botany Bay.

**Jo'ris** (yô'rēs). See Ioris.

**Jo'ris** (yō'rĭs), **David.** *Also* **Jan Jo'risz** (yō'rĭs) *or* **Jo'ris·zoon** (yō'rĭ·sŭn; -sōn; -sōn). 1501?–1556. Dutch Anabaptist leader; joined Anabaptists (1533). Founded new sect, known as Davidists or Jorists (1536); assumed role of new Messiah; retired incognito to Basel as **Jan van Brug'ge** [vän brûg'ĕ] (1544–56); identified after death, denounced for heresy; remains exhumed and burned (1559).

**Jornandes.** See Jordanes.

**Jor'tin** (jôr'tĭn), **John.** 1698–1770. English ecclesiastic and historian; author of *Life of Erasmus* (1758), etc.

**Josaba.** See Jehosheba.

**Josaphat.** See Jehoshaphat.

**Jos'a·phat Kun·ce'wicz** (jŏs'ȧ·făt [*Pol.* yô·sä'fät] kōōn·tsĕ'vēch), Saint. *Real name* **Jan Kuncewicz.** 1580–1623. Polish martyr; ordained priest (1609), and labored esp. for the union of churches; archbishop of Polotsk (1617). Murdered by opponents of unification (Nov., 1623).

**Jo'sef·fy** (yō'shĕf·fĭ; *Angl.* jō·zĕf'ĭ), **Ra'fa·el** (rŏ'fŏ·ĕl; *Angl.* răf'ā·ĕl, rā'fâ-). 1852–1915. Pianist, b. Hunfalu, Hungary; debut in Berlin (1872); concert tours in Europe (1872–79) and in U.S. (from 1879); professor, National Conservatory of Music, New York (1888–1906). Author of *School of Advanced Piano Playing* (1902), etc.

**José Manuel.** King of Portugal. See Joseph Emanuel.

**Jo'seph** (jō'zĕf; -zĭf). Husband of Mary, mother of Jesus (*Matt.* i. 16; *Luke* ii. 4).

**Joseph.** In Bible, Jacob's eleventh son, first by his favorite wife, Rachel (*Gen.* xxx. 22–24), eponym of one of the twelve tribes of Israel, which divided into the two tribes of his sons Manasseh and Ephraim (*Gen.* xli. 50–52, *Joshua* xvi). According to account in *Genesis* (xxxvii–l), Joseph was sold by his older brothers because of jealousy of father's favoritism toward him, became a slave in Egypt (xxxvii. 3–36), won favor of the pharaoh, who made him his chief official (xli), and was instrumental in bringing Israelites to settle in Egypt (xlv–xlvi).

**Joseph.** Name of two Holy Roman emperors:

**Joseph I.** 1678–1711. King of Hungary (1687–1711), king of Germany (1690–1711), and Holy Roman emperor (1705–11). Son of Leopold I. War of the Spanish Succession continued throughout his reign. Imperial armies campaigned in Italy, Germany, and Flanders under Prince Eugene. Attempted to settle questions of Austrian inheritance. Hostile to Jesuits.

**Joseph II.** 1741–1790. King of Germany (1764–90) and Holy Roman emperor (1765–90). Son of Francis I and Maria Theresa. Coregent with his mother in Austria (1765–80); acquired territory at first partition of Poland (1772). In full control of Austria on mother's death (1780); prohibited publication of any new papal bulls, suppressed convents, and reduced clergy; published Edict of Toleration (1781). As emperor, had many schemes for territorial aggrandizement, but most of them failed. One of the best examples of Europe's "benevolent despots."

**Joseph** *or* **Jo'seph Au'gust** (*Ger.* yō'zĕf ou'gŏŏst). 1872– . Austrian archduke (1905–18) and field marshal, b. in Hungary; son of Archduke Joseph Charles Louis (1833–1905). In Austro-Hungarian army fought in World War in Serbia, in the Carpathians, on the Isonzo, and in Poland against Russia; regent of Hungary (Aug.–Sept., 1919), but forced to resign by entente powers.

**Jo'seph** (jō'zĕf; -zĭf; *Fr.* zhō'zĕf'), Father. *Real name* **François Le Clerc du Trem'blay'** (lē klâr' dü träN'-blā'). 1577–1638. French Capuchin monk and diplomat; provincial of the Capuchin order in Touraine (1613); became confidant and adviser to Cardinal Richelieu, gaining sobriquet **É'mi'nence' Grise** (ā'mē'näNs' grēz'), *i.e.* "gray eminence" (from the color of his habit), in contrast to Richelieu's sobriquet "Éminence Rouge"; was entrusted with important diplomatic missions by Richelieu.

**Jo'seph** (jō'zĕf; -zĭf). *Indian name* **Hinmaton-Yalaktit.** 1840?–1904. American Indian chief of the Nez Percé tribe; defeated and captured by Gen. Nelson A. Miles (Oct. 5, 1877). Resided in Colville Reservation, in Washington, until his death.

**Joseph Bonaparte.** See Bonaparte.

**Joseph Cal'a·sanc'ti·us** (kăl'ȧ·săngk'shĭ·ŭs) *or* **Joseph of Calasanza,** Saint. = San José Calasanzio.

**Joseph E·man'u·el** (ē·măn'ū·ĕl). *Port.* **José Manuel.** 1715–1777. King of Portugal (1750–77). Son of John V. Made Carvalho e Mello prime minister (1756); government measures against Jesuits begun (1757); created Carvalho marquis de Pombal (1769); Carvalho in control until end of reign (1777).

**Jo'seph Fer'di·nand** (*Ger.* yō'zĕf fĕr'dē·nänt). 1872–1942. Austrian archduke and general, b. Salzburg. Son of Ferdinand IV, Duke of Tuscany. Commander of Austrian armies on Eastern front (1914–16); badly defeated (1916) at Lutsk (Łuck) and resigned.

**Joseph of Ar'i·ma·the'a** (jō'zĕf [-zĭf], ăr'ĭ·mȧ·thē'ȧ). In Bible, a rich Jew of Arimathea who took the body of Jesus and placed it in his own tomb (*Matt.* xxvii. 57 ff.;

*Luke* xxiii. 50 ff.; *John* xix. 38). Believed by some to have introduced Christianity into Britain and to have founded a monastery at Glastonbury. In late medieval legend and modern Arthurian poetry, he is the one who brought the Holy Grail to Britain.

**Joseph of Ex'e·ter** (ĕk'sĕ·tẽr). *Lat.* **Jo·se'phus Is·ca'nus** (jō̇·sē'fŭs ĭs·kā'nŭs). fl. 1190. English ecclesiastic and Latin poet; chief works, *De Bello Trojano* (6 books), *Antiocheis*, and *Panegyricus ad Henricum*.

**Joséphine de Beauharnais.** *Sometimes called* Empress **Josephine.** See BEAUHARNAIS.

**Jo'seph·son** (jō'zĕf·s'n; -zĭf-), **Brian David.** 1940– . British physicist. At Cambridge U. (1967– ); awarded (with Leo Esaki and Ivar Giaever) Nobel prize for physics (1973).

**Jo'seph·son'** (yōō'sĕf·sôn'), **Ernst.** 1852–1906. Swedish painter and poet; championed revival of Swedish art.

**Jo·se'phus** (jō̇·sē'fŭs), **Flavius.** *Orig. name* **Jo'seph ben Mat·thi'as** (jō'zĕf [-zĭf] bĕn mă·thī'ăs). 37–?100. Called "the Greek Livy." Jewish historian and general of priestly and royal descent, b. Jerusalem. Studied Hebrew and Greek literature, and spent 3 years in desert with a hermit; returned to Jerusalem and joined Pharisee sect; served as delegate to Nero, and won favor with Poppaea. Chosen governor of Galilee by Sanhedrin in Jerusalem, and took part in Jewish revolt against Romans (66 ff.); resisted siege of Jotapata for 47 days (67); surrendered finally to Vespasian, and predicted he would become emperor; won his favor and accompanied him to Alexandria. Subsequently freed, and adopted name of Flavius; remained under patronage of Vespasian and his successors Titus (whom he accompanied to Rome after fall of Jerusalem, 70) and Domitian; received tracts of land in Judea and a pension. His works include a *History of the Jewish War* (in Aramaic, later in Greek, 7 books), *Antiquities of the Jews* (a history of the Jews from the Creation to 66 A.D., 20 books), an *Autobiography*, and *Against Apion* (an apology of the Jews).

**Jo·se·tsu** (jō̇·sĕ·tsōō). fl. 1400. Japanese painter; founded school based on Sung and Yuan principles.

**Josh'u·a** (jŏsh'ū̇·ȧ). *In Douay Version* **Jos'u·e** (jŏs'ū̇·ē). In Bible, son of Nun and successor of Moses, who, as recounted in Old Testament Book of Joshua (*Douay* Josue), led Israelites in invasion and settlement of Canaan. Rated in Middle Ages among the "Nine Worthies."

**Jo·si'ah** (jō̇·sī'ȧ). *In Douay Bible* **Jo·si'as** (-ăs). d. 608? B.C. King of Judah (638?–?608 B.C.). Son and successor of Amon. During his reign, book of the law (Deuteronomy?) found in temple; began reform movement; beginning of Jeremiah's prophesying; opposed Necho II (Pharaoh-Nechoh) of Egypt and killed in battle at Megiddo (*2 Kings* xxii–xxiii; *Jer.* xxv. 1–3).

**Josiah Allen's Wife.** Pseudonym of Marietta HOLLEY.

**Jo·si'as** (yō̇·zē'äs), **Friedrich.** Prince of **Saxe'–Co'burg** (săks'kō'bûrg). 1737–1815. Austrian general in Seven Years' War (1756–63) and against Turks (1788–91); given command of army (1793); defeated Dumouriez at Neerwinden (1793); beaten at Fleurus (1794).

**Jó'si·ka** (yō'shĭ·kŏ), Baron **Miklós von.** 1796–1865. Hungarian novelist; introduced the romantic-historical novel into Hungary.

**Jos'lin** (jŏs'lĭn), **Elliott Proctor.** 1869–1962. American physician; authority on diabetes.

**Josquin Deprès.** See DEPRÈS.

**Jost** (yōst), **Isaak Markus.** 1793–1860. German-Jewish historian. Author of *Geschichte der Israeliten* (9 parts, 1820–29), a translation into German of the *Mishnah*, with commentary (6 vols., 1832–34), etc.

**Josue.** See JOSHUA.

**Jo'tham** (jō'thăm). *In Douay Bible* **Jo'a·tham** (jō'ȧ·thăm; -thăm). d. 735? B.C. King of Judah (c. 740–735 B.C.). Son of Uzziah. Regent during father's illness (*2 Kings* xv. 5); during his reign, Isaiah, Hosea, and Micah prophesied; succeeded by his son Ahaz (*2 Kings* xv. 32–38).

**Jou'bert'** (zhōō'bâr'), **Barthélemy Catherine.** 1769–1799. French soldier; served with distinction in Italy (1795–99); chief of the army in Italy (1798–99).

**Joubert, Joseph.** 1754–1824. French moralist; associate of Chateaubriand, and Bonald; selections from his *Pensées* were edited by Chateaubriand (1838).

**Joubert, Jules François.** 1834–1910. French physicist; collaborated with Pasteur in work on spontaneous generation.

**Jou'bert'** (zhōō'bâr'), **Petrus Jacobus,** *known as* **Piet.** 1834–1900. Boer soldier and statesman, b. in Cape Colony. Migrated to the Transvaal and made living as a farmer; studied law. Elected to Volksraad; attorney general of South African Republic (1870) and acting president (1875). Opposed British annexation of the Transvaal and was commandant general of Boer forces in the war (1880–81); won victories at Laing's Nek, Ingogo, and Majuba Hill. Remained prominent in political life, opposing Kruger in presidential elections (1883, 1893, 1898). Held nominal command at outbreak of Boer War (1899) but retired because of ill health.

**Jou'ett** (jōō'ĕt; -ĭt), **Matthew Harris.** 1787–1827. American portrait painter. His son **James Edward** (1826–1902), naval officer, served under Farragut in battle of Mobile Bay (1864); commanded North Atlantic squadron (1884).

**Jouf'froy'** (zhōō'frwȧ'), **François.** 1806–1882. French sculptor.

**Jouffroy, Théodore.** 1796–1842. French philosopher; author of *Mélanges Philosophiques* (1833), *Cours d'Esthétique* (1843), etc.

**Jouffroy d'Ab'bans'** (dȧ'bäɴs'), Marquis **Claude François Dorothée de.** 1751–1832. French engineer; pioneer in steam navigation. Made successful attempt to propel a boat by a steam engine on the Saône (1783).

**Jou'haux'** (zhōō'ō'), **Léon.** 1879–1954. French labor leader and politician; secretary-general of Confédération Générale du Travail (1909–40;1945–47); member of the administrative council, International Labor Office, and French delegate to the League of Nations on economic and disarmament questions (1925–28). President, Economic Council of France (1947–54). Awarded Nobel prize for peace (1951).

**Joukovsky.** French form of ZHUKOVSKI.

**Joule** (joul), **James Prescott.** 1818–1889. English physicist; studied under John Dalton. Published papers (1840) which describe attempt to measure electric current by means of a unit of his own definition; discovered magnetostriction of an iron bar. In paper *On the Production of Heat by Voltaic Electricity* announced the law (Joule's law) that the rate at which heat is produced in any part of an electric circuit is measured by the product of the square of the current into the resistance of that part of the circuit (1840); published paper *On the Heat Evolved during the Electrolysis of Water* (1843); determined the mechanical equivalence of heat in several ways. The joule, a unit of work or energy, is named after him.

**Jour'dan'** (zhōōr'däɴ'), Comte **Jean Baptiste.** 1762–1833. French soldier; commanded army of the North, and defeated Austrians at Wattignies (Oct. 16, 1793) and at Fleurus (June 26, 1794), but was defeated at Höchst (Oct. 11, 1795). Commanded army of the Sambre and

Meuse, and was defeated at Amberg (Aug. 24, 1796) and at Würzburg (Sept. 3, 1796). Commanded army of the Danube and was defeated at Ostrach (Mar. 21, 1799) and Stockach (Mar. 25, 1799). Governor of Piedmont (1800). Created marshal of France (1804). Attended Joseph Bonaparte in Naples and Spain.

**Jou've·nel'** (zhōōv'nĕl'), **Henry de.** 1876–1935. French journalist; editor in chief of *Le Matin;* elected senator (1921); French delegate to the League of Nations (1922 and 1924); French high commissioner in Syria (1925–26). See COLETTE.

**Jou've·net'** (zhōōv'nĕ'), **Jean.** 1644?–1717. French painter of religious subjects.

**Jouy** (zhwē), *called* **de Jouy, Victor Joseph Étienne.** 1764–1846. French writer of tragedies, the opera librettos *La Vestale* (1807), *Fernand Cortez* (1809), *Les Amazones* (1812), *Guillaume Tell* (1829), novels, and several sketches of contemporary life and customs.

**Jo·va'no·vić** (yô·vä'nô·vēt'y'; *Angl.* -vĭch), **Jovan.** *Pseudonym* **Zmaj** (zmī). 1833–1904. Serbian journalist and author esp. of lyrics and humorous verse.

**Jo've·lla'nos** *or* **Jo've–Lla'nos** (hō'vā·lyä'nōs), **Gaspar Melchor de.** 1744–1811. Spanish statesman and writer; chief justice of king's court, Madrid (1778); minister of justice (1797). As enemy of Godoy, exiled to Gijón (1797–1801); imprisoned (1801–08). Member of Central Junta; aided in reorganization of the Cortes. Among his works are the tragedy *El Pelayo,* comedy *El Delincuente Honrado,* poems, and prose works.

**Jo'vel·lar' y So·ler'** (hō'vā·(l)yär' ē sô·lĕr'), **Joaquín.** 1819–1892. Spanish general. Captain in Cuba (1842–51). Lieutenant general under King Amadeus (1872); after revolution of 1868, named military director-general. Governor of Cuba (1873–74, 1876–78); in Spain (1874–76), commanded army against Carlists and assumed ministry of war in new government under Alfonso XII; second administration in Cuba saw end of 10-year war for independence (Convention of Zanjón, Feb. 10, 1878). Under Alfonso XII, held various positions, including governor general of Philippines.

**Jo'vi·an** (jō'vĭ·ăn). *Lat.* **Flavius Claudius Jo'vi·a'nus** (jō'vĭ·ā'nŭs). 331?–364. Roman emperor (363–364). Son of Veronianus of Moesia. General in army of Emperor Julian; on Julian's death in Persia, was chosen his successor by soldiers. To save the army, made peace with Persians by giving up all Roman provinces beyond the Tigris; promulgated edict restoring privileges to Christians; supported Nicene Creed against Arians.

**Jo·vin'i·an** (jô·vĭn'ĭ·ăn). Italian heretic of 4th century; condemned by councils of Rome and Milan (1390) and banished. Jovinianists were suppressed by Pope Honorius.

**Jovius.** Surname of Roman emperor DIOCLETIAN.

**Jovius, Paulus.** See Paolo GIOVIO.

**Jow'ett** (jou'ĕt; -ĭt), **Benjamin.** 1817–1893. English Greek scholar. Professor, Oxford (1855); master of Balliol (1870–93); vice-chancellor of Oxford (1882–86). Best known for his translations of *Plato* (4 vols., 1871), *Thucydides* (2 vols., 1881), and Aristotle's *Politics* (1885). Charged with heresy because of his liberal religious views; acquitted (1860) by chancellor's court of Oxford.

**Jowett, Frederick William.** 1864–1944. English Labor party politician; first commissioner of works in first British Labor cabinet (1924).

**Jowett, John Henry.** 1864–1923. English clergyman, b. Halifax, Eng. Educ. Edinburgh and Oxford. Entered Congregational ministry; pastorates, Newcastle upon Tyne (1889–95), Birmingham (1895–1911), New York City (1911–18); minister of Westminster Chapel, London (1918–23). Author of many religious works.

**Jow'itt** (jou'ĭt), **William Allen.** 1st viscount. 1885–1957. British lawyer; educ. Oxford; attorney general (1929–32); minister without portfolio (1943–44), of national insurance (1944–45); lord chancellor (1945–51).

**Joyce** (jois), **James.** 1882–1941. Irish writer, b. in Dublin. Educ. Belvedere Coll. and Royal U. at Dublin. Author of *Chamber Music* (verse), *Dubliners* (short stories), *A Portrait of the Artist as a Young Man* (fiction), *Exiles* (drama), *Ulysses* (fiction), *Pomes Penyeach* (verse), and *Finnegans Wake* (fiction).

**Joyce, Robert Dwyer.** 1836–1883. Irish physician and poet; practiced medicine in Dublin. To U.S. (1866); published epic *Deirdrê* (1876); other poems appeared in *Ballads of Irish Chivalry* (1872), *Blanid* (1879), etc.

**Joyn'son–Hicks'** (join's'n·hĭks'), Sir **William.** 1st Viscount **Brent'ford of New'ick** (brĕnt'fẽrd, nū'ĭk). *Nicknamed* **Jix** (jĭks). 1865–1932. English politician; M.P. (1908–10, 1911–29). Postmaster general and paymaster general (1923); minister of health (1923–24); home secretary (1924–29).

**Juan** (hwän). Spanish form of JOHN.

**Juan.** 1822–1887. Second son of Don Carlos 1st. Carlist claimant to Spanish throne (1861–68); renounced claims in favor of his son Carlos (VII). See CARLOS.

**Juan de la Cruz.** See JOHN OF THE CROSS.

**Juan Ma·nuel'** (mä·nwĕl'), Don. 1282–?1349. Spanish soldier, politician, and writer; grandson of King Ferdinand III of León and Castile and nephew of Alfonso X. In youth fought against Moors in Granada; regent for his cousin Alfonso XI (1320–25); engaged in long civil war with king (1325–38); secured aid of Portugal and alliance with Granada (1328); in exile (1336–38); made peace with Alfonso and later again fought against Moors. Wrote many works of a didactic, religious, or historical nature, the most important being *El Conde Lucanor* ("The Count Lucanor"; 1328–35), a collection of 49 romantic tales of an Oriental character, with moral lessons, and a model or source for Boccaccio, Chaucer, Lope de Vega, Calderón, and possibly Shakespeare's *Taming of the Shrew.*

**Juan y San'ta·cil'la** (ē sän'tä·thē'lyä), **Jorge.** *Usually called* Don **Jorge Juan.** 1712–1773. Spanish explorer and writer; author of *Relación Histórica del Viaje a la América Meridional* (1748), a treatise on applied mechanics, etc.

**Jua'na** (hwä'nä) *or* **Jo·an'na** (jô·ăn'ȧ). *Called* **la Lo'ca** (lä lō'kä), *i.e.* the mad. 1479–1555. Daughter of Ferdinand II of Aragon and Isabella of Castile; mother of Emperor Charles V; b. in Toledo; m. (1496) Philip, Archduke of Austria (see PHILIP I of Spain); neglected and deserted by Philip (1501–03); inherited crown of Castile on death of Isabella and ruled jointly with Philip (1504–06); driven mad by Philip's death (1506), her father, Ferdinand, assuming power as regent (1506–16).

**Jua'na of Portugal** (*Span.* hwä'nä; *Port.* zhwă'nȧ). 1439–1475. Queen of Castile (1455–74). Daughter of Edward I of Portugal; m. (1455) King Henry IV as 2d wife; unpopular because of her relations with court favorite, Beltrán de la Cueva; though Madrid Cortes judged her daughter Juana heir to throne, on Henry's death (1474) Isabella was chosen to succeed him. Her daughter **Juana** (1462–1530), called **la Bel'tra·ne'ja** (lä bĕl'trä·nĕ'hä), probably natural daughter of Beltrán de la Cueva, contested throne of Castile with Isabella; had support of Spanish nobles and of her husband and uncle, Alfonso V of Portugal, who was decisively beaten at Toro (1476), Isabella being recognized as queen (1479); retired to convent of Santa Clara de Coimbra.

**Juanes** *or* **Joanes, Juan de.** See Vicente Juan MACIP.

**Juá'rez** (hwä'rās), **Benito Pablo.** 1806–1872. Mexican

statesman of Indian parentage, b. Guelatao, Oaxaca. Lawyer in his native state, Oaxaca (1834–46), and elected its governor (1847). Exiled by Santa Anna (1853), returned (1855) and joined Álvarez in revolution against Santa Anna; as minister of justice (1855) under Álvarez wrote "Ley Juárez," law abolishing special courts and reducing power of army and church; minister of interior under Comonfort (1857). Provisional president of Mexico (1857–61); three years of civil war (War of the Reform) successfully terminated; established in Mexico City (1861); elected president (term 1861–65); self-proclaimed president (1865–67; elections impossible because of French invasion, undertaken because of bankruptcy of Mexican government); continued warfare against Maximilian (proclaimed emperor of Mexico, 1864) and French; Maximilian captured and shot (June 19, 1867). Elected president (two terms; 1867–72); administration marked by many reforms, but last years troubled with attempted revolutions; died in office (July 18).

**Ju'ba** (jo͞o'bȧ) *or* **Iu'ba** (yo͞o'bȧ). Name of two kings of Numidia. **Juba I** (d. 46 B.C.), son and successor of Hiempsal; in civil war, sided with Pompey; defeated (49 B.C.) G. Scribonius Curio, Caesar's general; joined Pompey's force which was defeated at Thapsus (46); committed suicide. His son **Juba II** (d. 19? A.D.); carried as a child to Rome by Caesar; reinstated (30 B.C.) by Augustus; m. (29) Cleopatra Selene, daughter of Antony and Cleopatra; transferred (25) from Numidia to Mauretania.

**Jubainville, Marie Henri d'Arbois de.** See ARBOIS DE JUBAINVILLE.

**Juch** (yo͝oK), **Emma Antonia Joanna.** 1865–1939. Operatic soprano, b. in Vienna; to U.S. (1867); m. Francis Lewis Wellman (1894; divorced 1911). Organized and sang in Emma Juch English Grand Opera Company.

**Jud** (yo͞ot), **Leo.** *Known as* **Mei'ster Leu'** (mī'stẽr loi'). 1482–1542. Swiss Protestant clergyman; colleague of Zwingli at Zurich; aided in translating the Zurich Bible and made a Latin translation of the Old Testament.

**Ju'dah** (jo͞o'dȧ). *In Douay Version* **Ju'da** (-dȧ). In Bible, Jacob's fourth son (*Gen.* xxix. 35), ancestor of one of the twelve tribes of Israel, which later became one of main elements of kingdom of Judah (933–586 B.C.).

**Ju'dah** (jo͞o'dȧ) *or* **Je·hu'dah** (jē·hū'dȧ). *Called* **ha'–Na·si'** (hȧ'nä·sē'), *i.e.* the Prince, *or* **ha'–Ḳa·dosh'** (hȧ'kä·dōsh'), *i.e.* the Holy. *Called also* **Judah I** *and often simply* **Rab'bi** (răb'ī). 135?–?220. Jewish scholar long resident in Sepphoris, Palestine. Succeeded his father, Simon ben Gamaliel II, as patriarch; generally believed to have been compiler and redactor of the official collection of laws known as the Mishnah.

**Judah ben Sam'u·el** (bĕn săm'ū·ĕl). d. 1217. German Jewish moralist and mystic; founded in Regensburg a school which attracted many famous pupils.

**Judah ha–Le'vi** (hȧ·lē'vī). *Also* **Judah ben Samuel Ha·le'vi.** *Arab. name* **Abu'l Ḥasan.** 1085?–?1140. Spanish Jewish rabbi, physician, and poet, b. Toledo. Wrote songs, national, secular, and religious; expounded and defended Judaism in his chief philosophic work, *Sefer ha-Kuzari;* set forth revealed religion as superior to philosophic and rational belief.

**Ju'das** (jo͞o'dăs). In the New Testament: (1) **Judas Is·car'i·ot** (ĭs·kăr'ĭ·ŏt). One of the twelve apostles (*Matt.* x. 4; *Mark* iii. 19; *Luke* vi. 16); betrayed Jesus (*Matt.* xxvi. 47 ff.) and afterwards committed suicide (*Matt.* xxvii. 3 ff.; *Acts* i. 18).
(2) Another of the twelve apostles, distinguished from Iscariot (*Luke* vi. 16; *John* xiv. 22; *Acts* i. 13; in Douay Version written **Jude** (jo͞od) in *Luke* and *Acts*, **Judas** in *John*), generally identified with Thaddeus (*Matt.* x. 3; *Mark* iii. 18).
(3) **Jude** *or* **Judas.** Author of the *Epistle of Jude*, which (i. 1) describes him as a "brother of James." (See JAMES, 3.) Identified by Roman Catholics with (2) above.

**Judas Maccabaeus.** See MACCABEES.

**Judas of Gal'i·lee** (găl'ĭ·lē). Jewish leader, b. at Gamala in Gaulanitis; reputed founder of the Zealots, and coleader of a Jewish uprising (6–7 A.D.) against Roman rule and census-taking in Palestine (cf. *Acts* v. 37).

**Judd** (jŭd), **Charles Hubbard.** 1873–1946. Psychologist and educator, b. at Bareilly, British India; to U.S. (1879). Professor and head of department of education, U. of Chicago (1909–38). Author of treatises on psychology and education including *Genetic Psychology for Teachers* (1903), *Psychology: General Introduction* (1907), *Psychology of High School Subjects* (1915), *Psychology of Secondary Education* (1927), *Problems of Education in the United States* (1933), *Education and Social Progress* (1934), etc. Special editor for terms in education, *Webster's New International Dictionary, Second Edition.*

**Judd, Gerrit Parmele.** 1803–1873. Hawaiian statesman; went to Sandwich Islands as missionary physician (1827); resigned from mission to serve king of Hawaii (1842). Hawaiian secretary for foreign affairs (1843–45), minister of the interior (1845–46), minister of finance (1846–53).

**Judd, Norman Buel.** 1815–1878. American political leader; Lincoln's campaign manager (1860); U.S. minister to Prussia (1861–65); member, U.S. House of Representatives (1867–71); U.S. collector of customs, Chicago (1872–76).

**Judd, Orange.** 1822–1892. Agricultural editor; owner, editor, and publisher, *American Agriculturist*, New York (1856–83); responsible for establishment, at Wesleyan U., of first State Agricultural Experiment Station. Moved to Chicago; edited *Prairie Farmer* (1884–88), *Orange Judd Farmer* (1888–92).

**Judd, Sylvester.** 1813–1853. American Unitarian clergyman and author; expressed his religious and social views in novels *Margaret* (1845) and *Richard Edney and the Governor's Family* (1850), and the didactic poem *Philo, an Evangeliad* (1850).

**Jude.** See JUDAS, 2 and 3.

**Judge** (jŭj), **Jack.** 1878–1938. British vaudeville performer; composer of song *It's a Long, Long Way to Tipperary* (1912).

**Judge, William Quan.** 1851–1896. Theosophist, b. Dublin, Ireland; to U.S. as a boy. Became follower of Mme. Blavatsky and charter member of Theosophical Society (1875); established branches in large cities (from 1885); edited and published *The Path* (1886–96); devoted all his time to theosophy (from 1893); after schism, became president of American section of Theosophical Society (1894).

**Ju'dith** (jo͞o'dĭth). See ZAUDITU.

**Judith.** Heroine of the book of *Judith* (in the Protestant O. T. Apocrypha, but a canonical book in the Roman Catholic Bible), who delivered her people by killing **Hol'o·fer'nes** (hŏl'ō·fûr'nēz), general of Nebuchadnezzar.

**Jud'son** (jŭd's'n), **Adoniram.** 1788–1850. American Baptist missionary in Burma (1814–50); compiler of *Dictionary, English and Burmese* (1849). His son **Edward** (1844–1914), b. Moulmein, Burma, was also a Baptist clergyman; a pioneer in developing the institutional church, designed to aid in adjusting people of urban communities to their social, economic, and spiritual environment; pastor of Judson Memorial Church, New York City (1890–1914).

**Judson, Edward Zane Carroll.** *Pseudonym* **Ned Bunt'line** (bŭnt'lĭn; -līn). 1823–1886. American adventurer; b. Stamford, N.Y.; pioneer writer of dime novels and adventure fiction.

**Judson, Egbert Putnam.** 1812–1893. American inventor of blasting explosives; patented a "giant powder" (1873), and "railroad powder," first explosive suitable for use in railroad construction work (1876).

**Judson, Harry Pratt.** 1849–1927. American educator; grad. Williams (1870); president, U. of Chicago (1907–27).

**Juel** (yōōl), **Jens.** 1745–1802. Danish portrait painter.

**Juel, Niels.** 1629–1697. Danish admiral; distinguished himself in war with Sweden (1675–77), notably as commander at Jasmund, off Rügen (1676) and at naval victory in Kjöge Bay (1677).

**Ju·gur'tha** (jōō·gûr'thȧ) *or* **Iu·gur'tha** (yōō-). d. 104 B.C. King of Numidia (113–104 B.C.). Natural son of Mastanabal and grandson of Masinissa. Sent by his uncle Micipsa to Spain (134) to aid Romans; on death of Micipsa (118), shared rule with cousins Adherbal and Hiempsal; murdered both and usurped rule of western Numidia (117?) and eastern Numidia (112). At war (111–106) with Rome (Jugurthine War); defeated by Quintus Metellus; captured by Sulla and exhibited in his triumph at Rome (104); died in prison. Subject of a history by Sallust.

**Juil'li·ard** (jōōl'ĭ·ärd; jōōl'yärd), **Augustus D.** 1836–1919. American merchant and patron of music, b. at sea of French parents. Bequeathed bulk of fortune to a foundation (Juilliard Foundation) for providing musical education for promising students.

**Ju'ji** (jōō'jē) *or* **Ju'chi** (jōō'chē). Eldest son of Genghis Khan (*q.v.*).

**Jukes** (jōōks), **Joseph Beete** (?bēt). 1811–1869. English geologist; director of Irish survey (1850–69).

**Ju·kov'sky** (zhōō·kôf'skû·ĭ; -skĭ). Variant of ZHUKOVSKI.

**Jülg** (yülk), **Bernhard.** 1825–1886. German philologist; specialist in comparative philology and Mongolian folklore.

**Jul'ia** (jōōl'yȧ). 83?–54 B.C. Daughter of Julius Caesar and wife of Pompey.

**Julia.** 39 B.C.–14 A.D. Daughter and only child of Augustus Caesar and Scribonia; m. Marcellus (25; d. 23 B.C.), Marcus Vipsanius Agrippa (23; d. 12 B.C.), Tiberius (11 B.C.). Mother of Gaius and Lucius Caesar, Agrippa Postumus, Julia, and Agrippina. Notorious for vice, she was banished by her father. Her daughter **Julia** (d. 28 A.D.) married Lucius Aemilius Paulus and was mother of Aemilia (1st wife of Emperor Claudius); notorious for profligacy; banished (9 A.D.) by her grandfather Emperor Augustus.

**Julia Dom'na** (dŏm'nȧ). 167?–217 A.D. Roman empress, b. Emesa, Syria; m. Septimius Severus (187 A.D.). Mother of Caracalla and Geta; had intellectual power and literary taste; exerted much influence over husband; committed suicide soon after Caracalla was put to death.

**Jul'ian** (jōōl'yăn). *Lat.* **Flavius Claudius Ju'li·a'nus** (jōō'lĭ·ā'nŭs). 331–363. Roman emperor (361–363). Youngest son of Julius Constantius, who was half brother to Constantine the Great. Escaped general massacre of Flavian family (337); well-educated, studied in philosophical schools at Athens; m. Helena, sister of Constantius II. Created caesar (355) with government of Gaul, Spain, and Britain; defeated Alamanni (357) in great battle near Strasbourg; won popularity with army; proclaimed emperor by his troops (361) and became master of empire on death of Constantius; made expedition against Persians; slain in battle in desert beyond Ctesiphon. Persistent enemy of Christianity; publicly announced his conversion to paganism (361), and hence known as "Julian the Apostate."

**Julian,** Cardinal. See Giuliano CESARINI.

**Ju'li·an'a** (jōō'lĭ·ăn'ȧ; -ä'nȧ; *Du.* yü'lē·ä'nȧ). *In full* **Juliana Lou·i'se** (*Du.* lōō·ē'sĕ) **Em'ma** (*Du.* ĕm'ȧ) **Ma·rie'** (*Du.* mȧ'rē') **Wil'hel·mi'na** (*Du.* vĭl'hĕl-mē'nȧ). 1909– . Queen of the Netherlands (1948– ). Daughter of Queen Wilhelmina; m. (1937) Prince Bernhard of Lippe-Biesterfeld.

**Julianus.** (1) See JULIAN. (2) See DIDIUS JULIANUS.

**Ju'lien'** (zhü'lyăN'), **Noël,** *called* **Stanislas.** 1799–1873. French Orientalist.

**Julien, Pierre.** 1731–1804. French sculptor.

**Jul'ius** (jōōl'yŭs). Name of three popes (see *Table of Popes,* Nos. 35, 218, 223):

**Julius I,** Saint. d. 352. Pope (bishop of Rome; 337–352). Firmly supported Athanasius after his deposition by the Arians.

**Julius II.** *Real name* **Giuliano del'la Ro've·re** (dāl'lä rō'vā·rā). 1443–1513. Pope (1503–13); b. Albissola, near Savona, Italy. Sought to extend papal territory and enlarge temporal power; formed League of Cambrai (1508) against Venice; formed Holy League (1511) against France; convened 5th Lateran Council (1512); commenced to rebuild St. Peter's; patronized arts and aided Raphael, Michelangelo, Bramante, and others.

**Julius III.** *Real name* **Giammaria Cioc'chi del Mon'te** (chôk'kē dāl mōn'tā). 1487–1555. Pope (1550–55); b. Rome.

**Julius.** See Gaius Julius HYGINUS.

**Julius Africanus, Sextus.** See AFRICANUS.

**Julius Agrippa I** and **II.** = *Herod Agrippa I* and *II,* under HEROD.

**Julius Caesar.** See Gaius Julius CAESAR.

**Julleville, Petit de.** See PETIT DE JULLEVILLE.

**Jul'lian'** (zhü'lyäN'), **Camille.** 1859–1933. French historian.

**Jul'lien'** (zhü'lyăN'), **Jean.** 1854–1919. French writer. In his book *Le Théâtre Vivant,* stated his theory that every play should be a "tranche de la vie," a cross section of life; author of *La Sérénade* (1888), *Le Maître* (1890), *La Mer, L'Oasis* (1903), etc.

**Jullien, Louis Antoine.** 1812–1860. French composer and musical director.

**June, Jennie.** Pseudonym of Jane CROLY.

**Ju'neau'** (zhü'nō'; *Angl.* jōō'nō, jōō·nō'), **So'lo'mon'** (sô'lô'môN') **Lau'rent'** (lô'räN'). 1793–1856. Fur trader; b. near Montreal, Canada; first permanent settler in what is now Milwaukee, Wis. (1818); naturalized American citizen (1831); first mayor of Milwaukee (1846).

**Jung** (yōōng), **Carl Gustav.** 1875–1961. Swiss psychologist and psychiatrist, b. Basel. Lecturer, U. of Zurich (1905–13). Conducted experiments in mental association which led him to develop the theory of complexes and brought him into association with Freud with whose earlier views his were in harmony; founded analytic psychology. Differed from Freud in regarding the libido (energy or driving force) as a will to live rather than a manifestation of the sex instinct and holding that a neurosis is to be understood more by analysis of the patient's present problem and inadequate adjustment than by unearthing childhood fixations and conflicts; divided all men into two classes—introverts and extroverts. English translations of his works include *Psychology of Dementia Praecox* (1909), *The Theory of Psychoanalysis* (1912), *Psychology of the Unconscious* (1916), *Studies in Word Association* (1918), *Contribu-*

*tions to Analytical Psychology* (1928), *Modern Man in Search of a Soul* (1933).

**Jung, Heinrich.** See JUNG-STILLING.

**Jung Ba·ha′dur** (jŭng′ bȧ·hä′do͝or), Sir. 1816–1877. Prime minister of Nepal, who sent troops to aid of British during Sepoy Mutiny (1857–58).

**Jung′hans** (yo͝ong′häns), **Sophie.** 1845–1907. German novelist and poet; author of novels and tales chiefly of family life.

**Jung′huhn** (yo͝ong′ho͞on), **Franz Wilhelm.** 1812?–1864. German naturalist and physician; medical staff officer in Dutch East Indies (from 1835); explored Java and Sumatra (1839–48; 1855–64).

**Jung′i·us** (yo͝ong′ē·o͝os) *or* **Jung** (yo͝ong), **Joachim.** 1587–1657. German philosopher and botanist; author of *Logica Hamburgensis* (1638); opponent of scholastic philosophy; emphasized value of study of mathematics in philosophy; set forth a classification of plants in his *Isagoge Phytoscopica* (1678) reputed to have served as a basis for Linnaeus's classification.

**Jung′mann** (yo͝ong′män), **Jo′sef** (yō′zĕf) **Ja′kob** (yä′kôp). 1773–1847. Czech writer and philologist; champion of a revival of Czech national sentiment.

**Jung′-Stil′ling** (yo͝ong′shtĭl′ĭng), **Johann Heinrich.** *Known also by his original name* **Heinrich Jung** *and by his pseudonym* **Heinrich Stilling.** 1740–1817. German mystic and writer. Brought up as Pietist; studied medicine at Strasbourg, where he met Goethe; practicing physician and specialist in cataract operations, Elberfeld (until 1778). Professor of economics, Kaiserlautern (1778) and Marburg (1787–1803); retired to Heidelberg (1803) and Karlsruhe (from 1806) as writer and privy councilor to Charles Frederick of Baden. Author of a 5-volume autobiography (1777–1804, including *Heinrich Stillings Jugend*, edited by Goethe), and of novels and mystical works, textbooks on finance, etc.

**Junípero,** Father. See Junípero SERRA.

**Jun′ius** (jo͞on′yŭs; jo͞o′nĭ·ŭs). Pseudonym of the author of a series of letters (Nov. 21, 1768–Jan. 21, 1772) attacking the British ministry, often attributed to Sir Philip Francis (*q.v.*).

**Jun′ius** (jo͞on′yŭs; jo͞o′nĭ·ŭs; *Ger.* yo͞o′nē·o͝os), **Franciscus.** 1589–1677. German-born philologist and antiquary; librarian and tutor in family of Thomas Howard, 2d Earl of Arundel (1621–51). Presented Anglo-Saxon manuscripts and philological collections to Bodleian Library. Published editions of Caedmon, and of *Codex Argenteus* of the Moeso-Gothic version of Ulfilas; compiled *Etymologicum Anglicanum*, largely used by Dr. Johnson.

**Jun′ker** (yo͝ong′kẽr), **Wilhelm.** 1840–1892. African explorer, b. in Moscow of German parents; explored Nile region (1876–78), reaching Emin Pasha at Lado on the upper White Nile (1883); isolated there by Mahdi revolt but finally reached Zanzibar (1886). Author of *Reisen in Afrika 1875–86* (3 vols., 1889–91).

**Jun′kers** (yo͝ong′kẽrs), **Hugo.** 1859–1935. German airplane engineer and builder. Established at Dessau an airplane factory (1919), a motor works (1924). Credited with designing first all-metal airplane to fly successfully; instrumental in establishing one of first regular mail and passenger air lines, operating in several European countries.

**Ju′not′** (zhü′nō′), **Andoche.** Duc **d′A′bran′tès′** (*Fr.* dȧ′bräN′tĕs′; *Port.* dȧ·brăNn′tĕsh). 1771–1813. French soldier; served under Napoleon in Italian and Egyptian campaigns; general of division (1800). Governor of Paris (1806). Commanded army invading Portugal and capturing Lisbon (1807); created duke. Defeated by Wellesley (afterward duke of Wellington) at Vimeiro (1808) and forced to evacuate Portugal. His wife, **Laure,** *nee* **Per′mon′** [pĕr′môN′] (1784–1838), wrote *Souvenirs Historiques sur Napoléon, la Révolution, le Directoire, le Consulat, l'Empire et la Restauration* (1831–35).

**Jun·quei′ro** (zho͞oNng·kā′ē·ro͞o), **Abílio Manuel Guerra.** 1850–1923. Portuguese poet, b. Freixo. Elected deputy (1872); as ardent Republican, opposed Braganzas; tried for high treason (1907); a founder of Portuguese republic. Known esp. for his lyric poetry and satires.

**Junta** *or* **Junte** *or* **Junti.** See GIUNTA.

**Ju·on′** (zho͞o·ôn′), **Paul.** 1872–1940. Russian composer, b. Moscow; taught at Berlin (1897–1934); resident in Switzerland (from 1934).

**Ju′rien′ de la Gra′vière′** (zhü′ryăN′ dẽ lȧ grȧ′vyâr′), **Jean Pierre Edmond.** 1812–1892. French naval officer; commanded French forces sent to Mexico (1861); vice-admiral (1862) and aide-de-camp to the emperor (1864); protected flight of the empress (1870).

**Ju′rieu′** (zhü′ryû′), **Pierre.** 1637–1713. French Protestant theologian; engaged in religious controversies with Maimbourg, Arnauld, Bayle, Basnage, and others.

**Ju′rin** (jo͞or′ĭn), **James.** 1684–1750. English physician and scientist; supporter of Isaac Newton and his theories. Formulated Jurin's law.

**Jus′se·rand′** (zhüs′räN′), **Jean Jules,** *in full* **Jean Adrien Antoine Jules.** 1855–1932. French writer and diplomat, b. Lyons. French minister at Copenhagen (1890) and Washington, D.C. (1902–25). Student of English literature and history. Among his books are *Le Théâtre en Angleterre depuis la Conquête jusqu'aux Prédécesseurs Immédiats de Shakespeare* (1887), *Le Roman au Temps de Shakespeare* (1887), *Les Anglais au Moyen Âge*...(1884; translated 1889 by Lucy T. Smith under title *English Wayfaring Life in the Middle Ages*), *Histoire Littéraire du Peuple Anglais* (3 vols., 1895–1909), and *The School for Ambassadors, and other Essays* (1924).

**Jus′sieu′, de** (dẽ zhü′syû′). Family of French botanists including: **Antoine** (1686–1758), physician; professor, Jardin des Plantes, Paris; editor of Tournefort's *Institutiones Rei Herbariae* (1719). His brother **Bernard** (1699?–1777), demonstrator at the Jardin des Plantes (1722); established a botanical garden at Trianon at request of Louis XV; laid foundation for a natural system of plant classification. Another brother, **Joseph** (1704–1779), collected plants in South America (1735–71); introduced various ornamental plants into Europe. Their nephew **Antoine Laurent de Jussieu** (1748–1836) studied under his uncle Bernard; professor, Jardin des Plantes; elaborated in his *Genera Plantarum* (1778–89) the system of classification founded by Bernard (see above), which served as basis of modern natural classification. Antoine Laurent's son **Adrien** (1797–1853), professor of botany; author of a textbook of elementary botany, monographs, etc.

**Just** (jŭst), **Ernest Everett.** 1883–1941. American Negro biologist; professor, Howard U. (1912–41); known esp. for researches on marine eggs.

**Juste** (zhüst), **Théodore.** 1818–1888. Belgian historian. Author of *Les Fondateurs de la Monarchie Belge* (27 vols., 1865–82), etc.

**Ju′sti** (yo͝os′tē), **Carl.** 1832–1912. German art historian; professor, Bonn (1872–1901).

**Justi, Ferdinand.** 1837–1907. German philologist; specialist in Iranian. His son **Ludwig** (1876–1957), art historian; director of the National Gallery (1909–33), then custodian of the Public Art Library, in Berlin.

**Justi, Johann Heinrich Gottlob von.** 1705?–1771. German economist; champion of cameralism.

**Jus'tin** (jŭs'tĭn), Saint. 100?–?165. Known as "Justin (the) Martyr" and "Justin the Philosopher." One of the Fathers of the Church; student of philosophy and a teacher of Platonic doctrines; opened first Christian school at Rome; said to have been scourged and martyred at Rome (c. 165).

**Justin.** *Lat.* **Jus·ti'nus** (jŭs·tī'nŭs). Name of two rulers of the Eastern Roman Empire:

**Justin I.** *Called* **the Elder.** 452–527. An uneducated soldier, of Gothic parentage; commander of guards under Anastasius I; emperor (518–527); entrusted administration to Proclus and to his nephew Justinian; issued decrees against Arians.

**Justin II.** *Called* **the Younger.** d. 578. Nephew of Justinian I; emperor (565–578); married Sophia, niece of Empress Theodora; dismissal of Narses as exarch of Ravenna allowed barbarian armies to overrun northern and central Italy (568–574); subject to fits of insanity; turned over administration to Tiberius, one of his generals (574).

**Justin.** *Full Latin name* **Marcus Junianus Justinus.** Roman historian of 3d century A.D. (or later); author of *Historiarum Philippicarum Libri XLIV*, an epitome of a lost history by Trogus.

**Jus·tin'i·an** (jŭs·tĭn'ĭ·ăn). Name of two rulers of the Eastern Roman Empire:

**Justinian I.** *In full* **Flavius Petrus Sabbatius Jus·tin'i·a'nus** (jŭs·tĭn'ĭ·ā'nŭs) *or, according to some,* **Flavius Anicius Justinianus.** *Called* **Justinian the Great.** 483–565. Nephew of Justin I. Probably of Slavonic parentage, b. in Illyricum. Emperor (527–565); m. (523) Theodora (*q.v.*). Reign most brilliant of Eastern Empire. Had no military capacity, but chose able generals, as Belisarius and Narses. Military events of reign: Nika riot (532) of Greens and Blues (circus factions) in the Hippodrome, Belisarius and others with barbarian mercenaries killing 30,000 people; Vandal kingdom of North Africa conquered by Belisarius and reannexed to empire (533–534); imperial authority in Rome restored; Rome occupied (536) but besieged by Goths for a year (537–538); northern Italy, including Ravenna, reconquered (538–540), but after recall of Belisarius, Goths again victorious and nearly all Italy overcome (541–548); southern Spain conquered by imperial armies (554); practically all of Western Empire again in hands of barbarians (550–552) but after 20 years of warfare Goths and Franks finally defeated (552–555); two wars fought with Persia (530–532; 540–545), both somewhat advantageous to Persians; Huns, Bulgars, and Slavs repeatedly invaded Balkan region. A great builder, causing erection throughout the empire of many forts, public buildings, monasteries, and churches, esp. Sant' Apollinare in Classe and San Vitale, both in Ravenna, and Santa Sophia (532–562) in Constantinople. Issued edict (543) against Nestorians and in support of Monophysites. Preserved Roman law for future generations; appointed commissions, with Tribonian in charge, which collected all imperial statutes (*Codex Constitutionum*, 528–529), and issued a digest of all writings of Roman jurists (*Digests* or *Pandects*, 533), a revised *Code* (534), and a textbook for students (*Institutes*, 533), all of which with the new laws (*Novellae*, 534–565), form the *Corpus Juris Civilis*, the foundation of actual law in most of continental Europe today.

**Justinian II.** *Called* **Rhi'no·tme'tus** (rī'nô·t'mē'tŭs), *i.e.* "with the nose cut off." 669–711. Son of Constantine IV. Emperor (685–695; 705–711). Beset by Bulgarians (689) and by Arabs in Armenia (692). Caused dissensions in the Church and persecuted Manichaeans. Overcome by his general, Leontius (695), who cut off his nose (whence his nickname); banished to Cherson in the Crimea (695). Escaped and at head of Bulgarian army captured Constantinople (705); vengeance and atrocities stirred up revolt; killed Leontius (705); seized by Philippicus and put to death (711).

**Jus'to** (hōōs'tō), **Agustín** *or* **Agustín P.** 1876–1943. Argentine general; president of Argentina (1932–38).

**Juvara.** Variant of IUVARA.

**Ju've·nal** (jōō'vĕ·n'l). *Full Latin name* **Decimus Junius Ju've·na'lis** (jōō'vĕ·nā'lĭs). 60?–?140 A.D. Roman lawyer and satirist; satirized with brutal frankness vices of Rome under the empire. Little of his life history is known. Five books of his satires, containing sixteen satires, are extant.

**Jux'on** (jŭk's'n), **William.** 1582–1663. English prelate and statesman; educ. Oxford; president of St. John's Coll., Oxford (1621–33). Bishop of London (1633–49), and lord high treasurer (1636–41). Attended Charles I during his trial and on the scaffold. Archbishop of Canterbury (1660–63).

# K

**Kaa'lund** (kô'lōōn), **Hans Vilhelm.** 1818–1885. Danish lyric poet.

**Ka'b ibn-Zu·hair'** (kăb' ĭb''n·zōō·hīr'). fl. 7th century A.D. Arab poet; contemporary of Mohammed, whom at first he ridiculed; on decree of death wrote a eulogy which became famous.

**Ka·bir'** (kȧ·bēr'). 1450?–1518. Hindu mystic poet in the time of the Lodi kings. A weaver of Benares, disciple of Ramanand; preached and wrote in Hindi, appealing alike to Hindus and Mohammedans; admitted all castes, denounced idol worship; his followers known as Kabirpanthi; Sikh religion based on his teachings.

**Kacz·kow'ski** (kăch·kôf'skē), **Zygmunt.** 1825–1896. Polish novelist.

**Ka'del·burg** (kä'dĕl·bōōrk), **Gustav.** 1851–1925. Austrian actor (1871–94; chiefly in Berlin) and author or coauthor of many comedies and farces.

**Ka'den–Ban·drow'ski** (kä'dĕn·bän·drôf'skē), **Juliusz,** 1885–1944. Polish author of realistic and satirical stories dealing esp. with Polish everyday life.

**Kaempf'fert** (kĕmp'fĕrt), **Wal'de·mar** (väl'dĕ·mär) **Bern'hard** (bĕrn'härt). 1877–1956. American editor and author. Managing editor, *Scientific American* (1911–15); editor, *Popular Science Monthly* (1915–20); science editor, New York *Times* (1927–28 and from 1931). Author of *History of Astronomy* (1910), *Science Today and Tomorrow* (1939); editor of *A Popular History of American Invention* (1924).

**Kaf'ka** (käf'kä), **Franz.** 1883–1924. Austrian poet and writer of psychological and philosophical fiction, b. in Prague of Jewish parentage. His works include the posthumously published novels *The Trial* (1925), *The Castle* (1926), and *America* (1927).

**Kaf'tan** (käf'tän), **Theodor** (1847–1932) and his brother

Julius (1848–1926). German Protestant theologians.

**Ka·ga·no′vich** (kŭ·gŭ·nô′vyĭch), **Lazar Moiseevich.** 1893– . Russian politician. Joined Communist party (1911); member of committee on Red army organization (1917); active in Communist party, esp. in Ukraine; member of Union Central Executive Committee (since 1924); commissar of railways (since 1935); member of Presidium of Supreme Council (since 1938); deputy premier and commissar for heavy industries (1938–39); vice-pres., council of ministers (from 1946).

**Ka·ga·wa** (kä·gä·wä), **Toyohiko.** 1888-1960. Japanese social reformer and evangelist; visited U.S., studying at Princeton; returned to Japan to do missionary work; active in relief work after earthquake (1923); became powerful influence in Japanese social life, esp. in labor matters; organized Japanese co-operatives; less influential after beginning of war with China (1937). Author of verse, essays, religious works, and stories.

**Kahl** (käl), **Wilhelm.** 1849–1932. German jurist; specialized in church and public law.

**Kahn** (kän), **Albert.** 1869–1942. American architect, b. in Westphalia, Germany; to U.S. (1881); established practice in Detroit (1904); became authority on concrete construction and pioneer in modern factory design; architect of many office and factory buildings (esp. in automobile and aircraft industries) in Detroit, New York, and other U.S. cities, and in many parts of the world including Soviet Russia.

**Kahn** (kȧn), **Gustave.** 1859–1936. French poet and novelist. Identified with symbolist school, and a founder of journal *Le Symboliste* (1886); regarded by some as originator of vers libre. Among his books are *Chansons d'Amant* (1891), *Le Roi Fou* (novel, 1895), *Le Livre d'Images* (verse, 1897), *Symbolistes et Décadents* (literary criticism, 1902), *Boucher* (biography, 1905), *Ch. Baudelaire* (1928).

**Kahn** (kän), **Julius.** 1861–1924. American legislator, b. Kuppenheim, Ger.; to U.S. as a child; settled in San Francisco. Member, U.S. House of Representatives (1899–1903; 1905–24).

**Kahn, Otto Hermann.** 1867–1934. Banker and opera patron, b. Mannheim, Ger., of naturalized American parentage; to U.S. (1893). Partner in banking firm of Kuhn, Loeb & Co., New York (from 1897). President and chairman of the board, Metropolitan Opera Company, New York (to 1931).

**Kahn, Reuben Leon.** 1887– . American bacteriologist, b. Lithuania; to U.S. (1899). Immunologist, Michigan Department of Health, Lansing (1920–28); assistant professor of bacteriology, Michigan (1928). Devised a blood serum test (Kahn test) for diagnosis of syphilis (1923–28).

**Kahr** (kär), **Gustav von.** 1862–1934. Bavarian statesman; appointed general commissioner of state (1923); split with Reich government over questions of authority; resigned (1924) after Hitler's "beer-cellar" Putsch at Munich, in which he had at first participated (allegedly because of force) but which he later suppressed. President, administrative court of justice (1924–30).

**Kai′du** (kī′do͞o). d. 1301. Mongol leader; grandson of Ogadai; khan for short period (1248) after his uncle Kuyuk's death; held vast domain in western Asia; long at enmity with descendants of Tului, esp. Kublai Khan.

**Kaim** (kīm), **Franz.** 1856–1935. German music lover; organizer of the Kaim Orchestra and builder of the Kaim Concert Hall in Munich.

**Kai′ser** (kī′zẽr), **Georg.** 1878–1945. German playwright. Author of chiefly farcical, and social and ethical problem plays (suppressed and burned during Hitler's regime) including *Die Jüdische Witwe* (1911), *Die Bürger von Calais* (1914), *Gas* (2 parts, 1918–20), *Kolportage* (1924), *Zweimal Oliver* (1926), the revue *Zwei Krawatten* (1929), etc.

**Kai′ser** (kī′zẽr), **Henry J.** 1882–1967. American industrialist, b. Canajoharie, N.Y.; worked as photographer; went to west coast and engaged in highway construction in British Columbia, Washington, California (1914–29), and Cuba (1930); chairman (1933) of executive committee of companies constructing Boulder and Parker dams; president of companies contracting for piers for Oakland-San Francisco Bay Bridge (1933), Bonneville Dam (1934), Grand Coulee Dam (1939); formed company to produce cheaply cement required for Shasta Dam (1939); became interested in shipbuilding (1940), acquiring (by March, 1942) yards of his own in California and Oregon, and developed methods of prefabrication and assembly that resulted in enormous reductions of time required in ship construction; designed with Howard Hughes plans for giant cargo planes and was awarded (1942) contract to construct three; officer, Brewster Aircraft Corp. (1943–44); chairman, Kaiser-Frazer Corp. (automobiles) and Kaiser Community Homes Corp.

**Kaiser, I′sa·bel′le** (ē′zä·bĕl′ĕ). 1866–1925. Swiss author (in French and German) of idealistic novels and romances, and short stories and poems.

**Ka·ja′nus** (kȧ·yä′no͝os), **Robert.** 1856–1933. Finnish composer and conductor; champion of a national Finnish music. Founded in Helsingfors (1882) and conducted first Finnish symphonic orchestral association. Director of music (1897–1926) and professor, U. of Helsingfors. Composer of symphonies, symphonic poems, Finnish rhapsodies based on Finnish folk melodies, orchestral suites, cantatas, choruses, and songs.

**Ka·jar′** (kä·jär′). A dynasty of seven rulers (1794–1925) of modern Persia (Iran) founded by Agha Mohammed Khan (1794–97); last ruler, Ahmed Shah (*q.v.*). See *Table* (*in Appendix*) for IRAN (Persia).

**Ka·kow′ski** (kä·kôf′skē), **Aleksander.** 1862–1938. Polish Roman Catholic cardinal. Archbishop of Warsaw (1913); one of three regents at head of Polish provisional government in Warsaw (1917–18).

**Ka·la′ka′u·a** (kä·lä′kä′o͞o·ä), **David.** 1836–1891. Hawaiian chief, king of Hawaiian Islands (1874–91). Unsuccessful against Lunalilo (1873); elected king by Assembly (1874) after Lunalilo's death; visited U.S. (1874–75); took trip around world (1881); by his ideas of reform aroused political opposition culminating in revolution (1887); his powers restricted by new constitution (1887); died in San Francisco.

**Kalb** (kälp), **Charlotte von,** *nee* **Mar′schalk von Ost′heim** (mär′shälk fôn ôst′hīm). 1761–1843. German writer; m. Heinrich von Kalb (1783); known for her romantic affair with Schiller (c. 1784 ff.), and later with Jean Paul; portrayed as Linda in Jean Paul's *Titan*.

**Kalb** (kälp; *Angl.* kălb), **Johann.** *Known as* Baron **de Kalb** (dĕ kălb′). 1721–1780. Army officer, b. Hüttendorf, Germany. In French army (1743–?64). On confidential mission to America (1768); commissioned major general in Continental army (1777); served in American Revolution (1777–80); mortally wounded in action (Aug. 16, 1780).

**Kal′beck** (käl′bĕk), **Max.** 1850–1921. German poet, librettist, and music and dramatic critic, resident in Vienna (from 1888).

**Kalck′reuth** (kälk′roit), **Count von.** Title held by members of an old German family of nobles, orig. in Lower Silesia, including: **Friedrich Adolf** (1737–1818), Prussian field marshal; adjutant to Prince Henry in Seven Years' War; distinguished himself at siege of Mainz (1793); commander in chief of Pomerania (1795);

served with distinction in unsuccessful defense of Danzig, and was made field marshal (1807); negotiated truce of Tilsit (1807); governor of Königsberg, Berlin (1809, 1814), Breslau (1812). His grandnephew **Stanislaus** (1820–1894), landscape painter; established (1858) and directed (1860–76) the Weimar Art School; resident in Munich (from 1883); painted chiefly mountain scenery of Switzerland, the Pyrenees, and Italy. Stanislaus's son and pupil **Leopold** (1855–1928), portrait, genre, and landscape painter, a founder of the secessionist movement, strongly influenced by impressionism; his works depict esp. the life of German peasants and fisherfolk.

**Ka·le'din** (kŭ·lyā'dyĭn), **Aleksei Maksimovich.** 1861–1918. Russian general; in World War led cavalry division in successful campaign in Galicia; commanded (1915–16) 12th corps, then 8th army, carrying out Łuck offensive; resigned after Revolution; led Don Cossacks against Bolshevists (1917–18); on failure of campaign shot himself.

**Ka·ler'ges** *or* **Ka·ler'gis** (kä·lâr'yēs), **Demetrios.** 1803–1867. Greek general and politician, b. in Crete. Served in Greek War of Liberation (1821); took part in insurrection that forced Otto to get rid of Bavarian advisers (1843); forced into exile (1845). Recalled at outbreak of Crimean War (1854) and became Greek minister of war (1854–55). Greek minister in Paris (1861), where, after fall of Bavarian dynasty in Greece, he negotiated for accession of Prince George of Denmark to Greek throne.

**Ka'li·da'sa** (kä'lĭ·dä'sȧ). *Better* **Kālidāsa.** fl. 5th century A.D. Hindu dramatist and lyric poet; sometimes called "the Shakespeare of India." Very little known of his life; one of the "Nine Gems," who lived and wrote during reigns of Chandragupta II and Kumaragupta I of the Gupta dynasty; generally recognized as pre-eminent poet of the Orient; his greatest drama (in Sanskrit) was *Sakuntala;* also wrote two other dramas of great merit, two epic poems, and a number of lyrical poems, all translated into modern languages.

**Kaliman I** and **II.** See ASEN (dynasty).

**Ka·li'nin** (kŭ·lyē'nyĭn), **Mikhail Ivanovich.** 1875–1946. Russian statesman, president of Union of Soviet Socialist Republics (1923–46), b. Tver province, of peasant parents. Factory worker (1893); joined Social Democratic party (1898); active in revolutionary planning; once (1904) exiled to Siberia; took prominent part in Revolution (1917); chairman of Central Executive Committee of Russian Socialist Federated Soviet Republic (1919); peasant deputy from Leningrad and president of Union of Soviet Socialist Republics (from 1923) as chairman of the Presidium of the Supreme Council.

**Ka·lin'ni·kov** (kŭ·lyēn'nĭ·kôf), **Vasili Sergeevich.** 1866–1901. Russian composer of two symphonies, two symphonic poems, two intermezzi, an orchestra suite.

**Ka·lir'** (kȧ·lēr'), **Eleazar be-Rab'bi** (bē·răb'ī). Early Hebrew liturgical poet; fl. probably in Palestine in 7th century; author of "piyyutim," or synagogal poetry, festival prayers, and hymns.

**Ka'lisch** (kä'lĭsh), **David.** 1820–1872. German Jewish humorist and journalist; helped found political comic journal *Kladderadatsch* in Berlin (1848); author of numerous farces and many humorous couplets. His son **Paul** (1855–1946), operatic tenor; m. (1888) the soprano Lilli Lehmann (*q.v.*).

**Ka'lisch** (kā'lĭsh; *orig.* kä'-), **Isidor.** 1816–1886. Rabbi, b. Krotoschin, Prussia; to U.S. (1849). Leader of reform party.

**Kalkar** *or* **Kalcker, Jan Stephan van.** See CALCAR.

**Kalk'bren'ner** (kälk'brĕn'ēr), **Christian.** 1755–1806. German pianist and composer; settled in Paris and became choral director at the Opéra; author of several operas in French, and suites for piano and violin. His son **Friedrich Wilhelm** (1784–1849), resident in London (from 1814), composed chamber music and piano pieces.

**Kal'las** (kȧl'lȧs), **Aino Julia Maria,** *nee* **Krohn** (krōōn). 1878–1956. Finnish author. Her works include *The White Ship* (1924), *Eros the Slayer* (1927), *The Wolf's Bride* (1930), and a number of plays.

**Kál'lay** (käl'loi), **Benjamin von.** 1839–1903. Austro-Hungarian statesman; acting minister of foreign affairs (1881); Reichsminister of finance and administrator of Bosnia and Herzegovina (from 1882). Author of a *History of the Serbs* (1877), *Russia's Policy in the East* (1878), etc.

**Kal'len** (kăl'ĕn), **Horace Meyer.** 1882–1974. Educator, b. in Silesia, Ger.; to U.S. as a child (1887). Professor of philosophy, The New School for Social Research, New York (1919–52). Author of *William James and Henri Bergson* (1914), *Why Religion* (1927), *Judaism at Bay* (1932), *A Free Society* (1934), etc.

**Kal'lio** (kȧl'lyō), **Kyösti.** 1873–1940. Finnish statesman; leader of Agrarian party; prime minister (1922–24); president of Finland (1937–40); resisted Russian demands (1939) but his government compelled to yield (1940) as result of war; resigned (Nov., 1940) because of ill health; died a few days later.

**Kal'li·wo'da** (*Ger.* kä'lē·vō'dä; *Czech* kȧ'lĭ·vô'dȧ), **Jo·han'nes** (yō·hän'ĕs; -ĕs) **Wen'zes·laus** (vĕn'tsĕs·lous). 1801–1866. Czech composer and violinist; composed 10 Masses, a Requiem, and other church music, 7 symphonies, overtures, violin concertos and solos, chamber music, piano pieces, male choruses and songs.

**Kallwitz, Seth.** See Sethus CALVISIUS.

**Kalm** (kȧlm), **Peter.** 1715–1779. Swedish botanist; friend of Linnaeus. Traveled in North America on natural-history survey (1748–51), writing an account of his travels, etc., in three volumes (1753–61).

**Kál'mán** (käl'män). See KOLOMAN.

**Kálmán, Em'me·rich** (ĕm'ĕ·rĭk). 1882–1953. Hungarian composer, esp. of operettas.

**Kál'no·ky** (käl'nô·kĭ), Count **Gustav Siegmund.** Baron **von Kö'rös–Pa'tak** (fôn kû'rûsh·pŏ'tŏk). 1832–1898. Austro-Hungarian statesman and diplomat, b. in Moravia. Succeeded Haymerle as minister of foreign affairs of Austria-Hungary (1881); sought to strengthen friendly relations with Russia, brought Italy into Triple Alliance with Germany and Austria (1882), and negotiated secret agreement with Rumania (1883); resigned post (1895).

**Kalojoannes.** = *John II Comnenus* (page 784).

**Ka'lo·yan** (kȧ'lô·yȧn) *or* **Yo'an·ni'tsa** (yō'ȧn·nē'tsȧ). d. 1207. Czar of Bulgaria, third ruler (1197–1207) of Asen dynasty (*q.v.*); brother of John I and Peter Asen. Completed conquest of North Bulgaria (1201); opened negotiations with Pope Innocent III and carried on correspondence with him; quarreled with crusaders, completely defeated their emperor, Baldwin, at Adrianople (1205), and captured and probably murdered him; ravaged Thrace.

**Kal'ten·born** (kôl't'n·bôrn; kăl'-), **H. V.** *In full* **Hans** (häns) **von Kaltenborn.** 1878–1965. American editor and radio commentator.

**Kal·ya'ni** (kȧl·yä'nē). A second (restored) Chalukya dynasty established (973–c. 1190) in western Hyderabad. See CHALUKYA.

**Ka·ma·ku·ra** (kä·mä·kōō·rä). A shogunate of Japan (1192–1333), founded by the Minamoto leader Yoritomo after defeat of Taira clan (1185); its capital the village of Kamakura.

**Ka·mal'–ud–din' Is'ma'il' Is'fa·ha·ni'** (kă·mäl'-

o͝od·dēn′ ĭs′mȧ·ēl′ ĭs′fă·hä·nē′). d. 1237. Persian lyric poet; author of gazels, quatrains, and eulogies.

**Ka·ma·ta·ri** (kä·mä·tä·rē). 614–669 A.D. Head of the Japanese Nakatomi family and founder of Fu·ji·wa·ra (fo͞o·jē·wä·rä) clan; as statesman, responsible for many reforms; as a reward for his services, granted by Emperor Tenchi (669) the surname Fujiwara.

**Kam′ban** (käm′bän), **Gudmundur.** 1888–1945. Icelandic novelist and playwright; his novels include *Ragnar Finnsson, The Virgin of Skálholt,* and *I See a Wondrous Land.*

**Ka·me′ha·me′ha** (kä·mā′hä·mā′hä). Name of five native rulers of Hawaiian Islands (Sandwich Islands):

**Kamehameha I.** *Surnamed* **Nu′i** (no͞o′ē), *i.e.* the Great. 1758?–1819. King (1795–1819); b. Kohala, Hawaii; visited Captain Cook's ships (1778); gained control of northern Hawaii (1782); conquered other islands (1785–1810); organized government; allowed foreign traders to settle.

**Kamehameha II** *or* **Li′ho·li′ho** (lē′hō·lē′hō). 1797–1824. King (1819–24); son of Kamehameha I; overthrew taboo system and ancient religion of Hawaiians; received first American missionaries (1820); with his queen visited England (1823–24), both dying suddenly in England.

**Kamehameha III** *or* **Kau′i·ke·ao′u·li** (kou′ē·kä·ou′o͞o·lē). 1813–1854. Brother of Kamehameha II; king (1825–54); two constitutions adopted (1840, 1852) during his reign; had difficulties with foreign governments; finally secured, from U.S. (1842) and from Great Britain and France (1843), recognition of independence of Hawaii; extended organization of government and established courts; sought closer relations with U.S.

**Kamehameha IV** *or* **Alexander Liholiho.** 1834–1863. Nephew of Kamehameha III; king (1854–63); failed to secure treaty of reciprocity with U.S. (1855, 1863); introduced use of English language in Hawaiian schools.

**Kamehameha V** *or* **Lot** (lŏt) **Kamehameha.** 1830–1872. Brother of Kamehameha IV; king (1863–72); promulgated his own constitution (1864) to supersede that of 1852; in his reign Molokai Leper Settlement established (1864); last of direct line.

**Ka·mel′** *or* **Ca·mel′** (kä·mĕl′) *or* **Ca·mel′lus** (kȧ·mĕl′ŭs), **George Joseph.** 1661–1706. Jesuit missionary, b. in Moravia; sent to Philippine Islands, where he made special study of minerals, animals, and plants. The genus *Camellia* was named by Linnaeus in his honor.

**Ka′me·nev** (kȧ′myĭ·nyĕf), **Lev Borisovich.** *Orig. surname* **Ro′sen·feld** (rô′zyĭn·fyĕly′t). 1883–1936. Russian Communist leader, b. Moscow, of Jewish descent. Joined Social Democratic party (1901); arrested and banished to Siberia (1915–17) for antiwar propaganda; after Revolution took part in establishing Bolshevik government; a vice-president of U.S.S.R. (1923); with Stalin and Zinoviev, member of triumvirate ruling Russia after Lenin's death (1924); held high positions in Soviet government (1924–32) but because of his opportunism read out of Communist party several times; m. Trotsky's sister and at times accused of Trotskyite sympathies; sentenced to imprisonment (1934) during purge of party after murder of Kirov; executed with Zinoviev.

**Kamenev, Sergei Sergeevich.** 1881–1936. Russian general, b. Kiev. Joined czar's army (1900); after Revolution (1917) became commander in Red army; Bolshevik leader in Civil War (1919–20); chief of staff of Red army (1920–34); chief of Soviet air defenses (1934–36).

**Ka′mer·lingh On′nes** (kȧ′mẽr·lĭng ôn′ĕs), **Heike.** 1853–1926. Dutch physicist, b. Groningen; educ. U. of Groningen. Professor, U. of Leiden (from 1882); liquefied helium (1908); attained low temperature, within one degree of absolute zero, in his work on helium; discovered that the electrical resistance of certain metals practically disappears at temperatures close to absolute zero. Awarded 1913 Nobel prize in physics.

**Kames,** Lord. See Henry HOME.

**Ka·mień′ski** (kä·myĕn′y′·skē), **Lucian.** *Pen name* **Do·le′ga–Ka·mień′ski** (dô·lĕ′gä-). 1885– . Composer and writer on music, b. Gniezno, Poland. Composer of many songs in German and Polish, also chamber music, choral and orchestral works, operas, an operetta, etc.

**Kamieński, Mat·thi′as** (mä·tē′äs). 1734–1821. Polish composer, b. in Hungary; wrote Polish and German operas, including *Fortune in Misfortune* (first Polish opera, 1778), and *Village Love* (1779), church music, a cantata, etc.

**Ka·mi·mu·ra** (kä·mē·mo͞o·rä), Baron **Hikonojo.** 1850–1916. Japanese admiral; commanded second Japanese squadron in Russo-Japanese War (1904); gained victory over Russian squadron off Vladivostok; fought in battle of Tsushima; admiral (1910).

**Ka·min′ski** (kä·mĭn′skē), **Heinrich.** 1886–1946. German composer; influenced esp. by Bach; advocate of revival of polyphonic music in modern spirit; composer of a concerto grosso for double orchestra and piano, religious music, motets, choruses, chamber music, etc.

**Kämp′fer** (kĕmp′fẽr), **Engelbert.** 1651–1716. German physician and traveler. Author of *History of Japan and Siam* (publ. first in English translation from manuscripts left by him, London, 1728).

**Kamptz** (kämpts), **Karl Albert Christoph Heinrich von.** 1769–1849. Prussian statesman and jurist; minister of justice (1832–38; 1842); unpopular because of demagogic activities. Author of a *Code of Police Law* (1815; burned by students at Wartburg Festival, 1817), works on Prussian law, etc.

**Ka·na′res** *or* **Ka·na′ris** (kä·nä′rēs), **Konstantinos.** 1790–1877. Greek naval commander and statesman. Renowned for daring exploits against Turkish naval units (1822 ff.); took part in revolution that overthrew Bavarian dynasty in Greece (1862) and seated Prince George of Denmark on Greek throne; prime minister of Greece (1864–65, 1877).

**Ka·na′vel** (kȧ·nā′vĕl), **Allen Buckner.** 1874–1938. American surgeon; authority on infections of the hand.

**Kan·din′ski** (kŭn·dyēn′skû·ĭ; *Angl.* kăn·dĭn′skĭ), **Vasili.** 1866–1944. Russian postimpressionist painter and designer; with Paul Klee founded (1911) new abstract school in Munich; instructor (1922–33) in Bauhaus group at Weimar; aimed at pure aesthetic expression, explaining his viewpoint in *The Art of Spiritual Harmony* (1914).

**Kane** (kān), **Elisha Kent.** 1820–1857. American Arctic explorer, b. Philadelphia. Assistant surgeon, U.S. navy (1842); on duty with U.S. Coast Survey (1850). Senior medical officer with De Haven expedition, known as First Grinnell Expedition, searching Arctic for Sir John Franklin (1850–51). Headed Second Grinnell Expedition into Arctic (1853–55); reached territory not previously discovered. Works include *The U.S. Grinnell Expedition in Search of Sir John Franklin* (1853), *Arctic Explorations, The Second Grinnell Expedition* (2 vols., 1856).

**Kane, Paul.** 1810–1871. Canadian painter. A collection of his paintings of Indians is in the Parliament Building at Ottawa.

**Ka·ne·ko** (kä·nĕ·kō), Viscount **Kentaro.** 1853–1942. Japanese statesman and diplomat; grad. Harvard (1878); representative in U.S. during Russo-Japanese War (1904–05).

**K'ang-hsi** (käng'shē'). *Dynastic name* **Shêng-tsu** (shŭng'dzōō'). 1654–1722. Chinese emperor (1662–1722), second of the Ch'ing dynasty. Third son of Shun Chih. His reign was largely one of internal peace, esp. during latter part (1681–1722). Founded Coll. of Inscriptions (1677); ordered compilation of many books of the Chinese classics; patron of scholars; promoted production of the remarkable Kingtehchen porcelain; traveled over the empire. Added three provinces on north (1662, 1664, 1705); conquered Yünnan (1681) and Formosa (1683); concluded Treaty of Nerchinsk (1689) with Russia on boundaries; reorganized the Khalkha states of Mongolia (1691); secured control of Tibet (1705–21). For many years friendly to the Jesuits and other Christian missionaries but by an anti-Christian decree (1717) refused to allow any of them actively to propagate their faiths; gave Ferdinand Verbiest, Jesuit missionary, and others, responsible scientific posts at the imperial court.

**K'ang Tê** *or* **Kang Teh.** Emperor of Manchukuo. See HSÜAN T'UNG.

**K'ang Yu-wei** (käng' yō'wā'). 1858–1927. Chinese scholar and reformer, b. in Canton. Called "the Rousseau of China" and "the Modern Sage." Studied Western history and philosophy and became leader of a reform party; adviser of Emperor Kuang Hsü; suggested famous reform decrees (1898); proscribed by Empress Dowager Tzu Hsi but escaped; in exile in Hong Kong, Singapore, Europe, etc. (1898–1914); worked for reform and active in Revolution (1911–12), although living outside China; an ardent monarchist, took part in attempted restoration (1917) of Hsüan T'ung; retired and spent last years (1917–27) in lecturing, writing, and collecting.

**Ka·nish'ka** (kȧ·nĭsh'kȧ). d. ?162 A.D. King of India (120?–?162; dates very uncertain; some give reign as c. 78–c. 110) of the Kushan (*q.v.*) dynasty in northern India; ruled from Kashmir, with realm extending to Madura in southern India, to Kabul, and to Bokhara in the north. Adopted Buddhism; his reign of great importance in its effect on Buddhism and because of ideas introduced from the west.

**Ka·no** (kä·nō). Name of a family or school of Japanese painters, from village of Kano, Shizuoka prefecture, birthplace of founder, including among its members: **Masanobu** (c. 1453–c. 1540 or, according to some, 1490), founder of family; descendant of the Fujiwara; page at court of shogun Yoshimasa; studied under Josetsu and Shubun; painted landscapes, birds, and figure compositions, chiefly in ink. His son **Motonobu** (c. 1476–c. 1559), one of foremost artists of Japan; most famous painter of the school and its actual founder; gave school its distinctive characteristic of subordinating color to design; painted landscapes, screens, murals, blending native canons and Chinese style; master of technique; employed exquisite color harmonies. **Eitoku** (1543–1590), grandson of Motonobu; official painter of court and shogunate; departed somewhat from earlier classicism of school; painted screens and landscapes and decorated interiors of royal palaces; displayed energy and inventiveness, introducing gold and brilliant colors. **Tanyu,** *real name* **Morinobu** (1602–1674), grandson of Eitoku; last of the great Kano masters; original and versatile, practically founding new school of his own; painted great variety of works; appointed official painter to shogun Iyeyasu; probably his best works still to be seen at Nikko.

**Kant** (känt; *Angl.* kănt), **Immanuel.** 1724–1804. German metaphysician and transcendental philosopher, b. Königsberg, where he spent most of his life; founder of critical philosophy. Educated as a Pietist (until 1740); studied sciences, mathematics, and philosophy at U. of Königsberg (1740–46), and under private tutor (1747–54); professor of logic and metaphysics, Königsberg (from 1770). Came into conflict with Prussian government as consequence of liberal religious views (1792–94); championed freedom, and sympathized with American colonies and French people in struggles for liberty. Began as Leibnitz-Wolffian disciple; later influenced by David Hume and English empiricists; gradually developed his own critical philosophy in which he sought to determine laws and limits of man's knowledge and to avoid dogmatism and overestimation, and skepticism and underestimation. His many works include the treatise *General History of Nature and Theory of the Heavens,* on the cosmic theory later known as the Kant-Laplacian theory (1755), *Observations on the Sense of the Beautiful and the Sublime* (1764), the inaugural dissertation on critical philosophy *On the Form and Principles of the Sensible and Intelligible World* (1770), *Critique of Pure Reason* (*Kritik der Reinen Vernunft*), containing a scheme of a transcendental philosophy (1781; revised 1787), the essay *What is Enlightenment?* (1784), *Principles of the Metaphysics of Ethics* (1785), *Critique of Practical Reason* (*Kritik der Praktischen Vernunft;* 1788), *Critique of Judgment* (*Kritik der Urteilskraft;* 1790), *Religion Within the Limits of Mere Reason* (1793), *Metaphysics of Morals* (2 parts, 1797), a review of Herder's *Philosophy of History,* etc.

**Kantemir.** = CANTEMIR.

**Kan'tor** (kăn'tẽr), **MacKinlay.** 1904–1977. American writer; in newspaper work (1921–31); scenario writer in motion pictures (1934); author of *Long Remember* (1934), *The Voice of Bugle Ann* (1935), *Arouse and Beware* (1936), *Gentle Annie* (1942), *Happy Land* (1943), etc.

**Kan'to·ro'vich** (kän'tō̆·rôv'ĭch), **Leonid Vitalevich.** 1912– . Russian economist. At Leningrad U. (1932–34), Mathematical Institute, Academy of Sciences (1932–41, 1945–71), Institute of National Economy Control (1971–76); awarded (with Tjalling C. Koopmans) Nobel prize for economics (1975).

**Kan'to·ro'wicz** (kän'tō̆·rō'vĭch), **Hermann.** 1877–1940. German jurist; professor, Freiburg (1913–27); expert of Reichstag committee on origin of the war (1923–29); professor, Kiel (1929–33; dismissed). Lecturer, All Souls College, Oxford (1936–40); assistant director of research in law, Cambridge U. (1937–40). His works include *Der Kampf um die Rechtswissenschaft* (1906; under pseud. **Gnä'us Fla'vi·us** [g'nâ'ŏŏs flä'vē·ŏŏs]), *Dictatorships* (1935), *Studies in the Glossators of the Roman Law* (1938), etc.

**Kao Tsu.** See CHAO K'UANG-YIN and LI YÜAN.

**Kao Tsung** (gä'ō̆ dzŏŏng'). See CH'IEN LUNG.

**Kao Tsung** (gä'ō̆ dzŏŏng'). 628–683 A.D. Emperor of China (650–683), of the T'ang dynasty. Son of T'ai Tsung. Completed conquest of Korea and defeated Western Turks. After his death, throne usurped by his widow, Empress Wu Hou (683–704).

**Ka'pi·la** (kŭ'pĭ·lȧ). fl. before middle of 6th century B.C. Ancient Hindu philosopher; reputed founder of the Sankhya system of Hindu philosophy. His teaching entirely dualistic; the *Sankhya Sutras,* sometimes attributed to him, are much later.

**Ka'pi·tza** (kȧ'pyĭ·tsŭ), **Peter L.** *Russ. name* **Pëtr Leonidovich Ka'pi·tsa.** 1894– . Russian physicist; known for work on magnetism and low temperatures.

**Kap'lan** (kăp'lăn), **Mordecai Men'a·hem** (mĕn'ȧ·hĕm). 1881– . Rabbi and educator, b. in Lithuania; to U.S. (1889). Rabbi of the Jewish Center in New York (1918–22), and a leader of the Society for the Advancement of Judaism (1922–44).

**Kap·nist'** (kŭp·nyĕst'), **Vasili Yakovlevich.** 1757–?1824. Russian dramatist and poet; friend of Derzhavin; produced sensation with his comedy (1798) *Yabeda* (*i.e.* Pettifoggery), dealing with bribery and corruption in Russian judicial circles, which was barred from presentation for several years but much of which has been perpetuated in everyday proverbs.

**Ka'po·di'stri·as** (kä'pô·thē'strē·äs), Count **Ioannes Antonios. Johannes Antonius Cap'o·dis'tri·as** (kăp'ō·dĭs'trĭ·ăs). *Orig.* (*Italian*) *form of surname* **Ca'po d'I'stri·a** (kä'pô dēs'trē·ä). 1776–1831. Greek patriot. Entered Russian service (1809); represented Russia at Congresses of Vienna (1814–15) and Troppau (1820); resigned from Russian service (1822). Devoted himself to cause of Greek independence; elected by Greek national assembly president of Greece (1827); assassinated (Oct. 9, 1831). His brother **Avgoustinos** *or* **Augustinus** (1778–1857) was provisional president of Greece (1831–32).

**Kapp** (käp), **Friedrich.** 1824–1884. German politician and historian; took part in German revolution (1849). To U.S. (1850); lawyer and editor in New York (1850–70); influential among German-Americans. Lived in Berlin (from 1870); National Liberal deputy in Reichstag (1871–78 and 1881–84). Author of several historical works, including lives of Baron von Steuben (1858; pub. 1884) and Johann Kalb (1862), and an important work on the U.S., *Aus und Über Amerika* (2 vols., 1876).

His son **Wolfgang** (1858–1922), German revolutionist, b. New York; underofficer in Prussian government service (1886–1906); in agricultural ministry of East Prussia (1906–16, 1917–20); opposed Bethmann-Hollweg's policy; with von Tirpitz founded German Fatherland party (1917); member of Reichstag (1918); led monarchist revolt (Kapp Putsch) against republican government (Mar., 1920); seized Berlin and declared himself imperial chancellor; failed in revolt because of general strike; fled to Sweden (1920); returned to Germany (1922) but died while awaiting trial.

**Kapp** (kăp; *Ger.* käp), **Gis'bert** (gĭz'bĕrt; *Ger.* gĭs'bĕrt). 1852–1922. Electrical engineer, b. near Vienna, of German father and Scottish mother. With engineering firm at Chelmsford, England (1875–84); professor of electrical engineering, Birmingham (from 1904). Developed a dynamo; designed transformers and power stations; devised methods of electrical testing; applied mathematics in electrical engineering. The Kapp line, a unit of magnetic force, is named after him.

**Kapp** (käp), **Julius.** 1883–1962. German writer on music. Author of *Das Opernbuch* (1922), and of biographical works on Liszt (1909), Wagner (1910), Berlioz (1914), Meyerbeer (1920), Weber (1922), etc.

**Kap'pel** (kăp'ĕl), **Philip.** 1901– . American painter and etcher, b. Hartford, Conn.

**Kap·teyn'** (käp·tīn'), **Jacobus Cornelis.** 1851–1922. Dutch astronomer. Professor, Groningen (from 1878), where he established an observatory. With help of assistants, measured and computed the positions of the stars on David Gill's photographic plates of the southern sky; investigated the structure of fixed-star systems; discovered two streams of stars moving in opposite directions, in the plane of the Milky Way.

**Ka·ra'džić** (kä·rä'jĕt·y'; *Angl.* -jĭch), **Vuk Stefanović.** 1787–1864. Serb scholar; simplified Cyrillic alphabet as used in Serbia. Published anthology of Serbian folk songs, Serbian grammar, and Serbian-German-Latin lexicon.

**Kar'a·george'** (kăr'ȧ·jôrj') *or* **Ka·ra'djor'dje** (kä·rä'·dyôr'dyĕ). *Also* **Czer'ny Djor'dje** (chĕr'nĭ dyôr'dyĕ) *or, Serbian,* **Cr'ni Djor'dje** (tsûr'nē), *i.e.* Black George. *Orig. name* **George Pe'tro·vić** (pĕ'trô·vēt'y'; *Angl.* -vĭch). 1766?–1817. Serbian leader in struggle for independence from Turkish sovereignty; founder of Serbian dynasty of Karageorgevich. Son of peasant; served as sergeant in Austrian army against Turkey (1788–91); deserted Austrian army and settled in Topola (1791); engaged in irregular fighting against Turks (between 1791 and 1804). Elected supreme leader at outbreak of Serb rebellion against Turks (1804); conducted operations with great success until (after treaty of Bucharest, 1812) Turkey was free to throw whole strength against Serbs; decisively defeated (1813) and took refuge in Hungary. Suddenly reappeared in Serbia (1817), prepared to head new rebellion, but was murdered in his sleep, apparently on orders from head of rival Obrenovich house.

**Kar'a·geor'ge·vich** (kăr'ȧ·jôr'jĕ·vĭch). *Serbian* **Ka-ra'djor'dje·vić** (kä·rä'dyôr'dyĕ·vēt'y'). Name of a Serbian dynasty founded (1808) by Karageorge (George Petrović). Its ruling members: Alexander (prince 1842–58), Peter I Karageorgevich (king 1903–21), Alexander (regent 1914–21, king of Yugoslavia 1921–34), and Peter II (king 1934–41) (*qq.v.*). Cf. OBRENOVICH.

**Ka·ra·ï·ska'kes** *or* **Ka'ra·ï·ska'kis** (kä'rä·ē·skä'kyēs), **Georgios.** 1782–1827. Greek leader in war for independence (1821 ff.); killed in action (May 4, 1827).

**Ka'ra·jan** (kä'rä·yän), **Herbert von.** 1908– . Austrian symphony and opera conductor.

**Karajan, Theodor Georg von.** 1810–1873. Austrian philologist; specialist in late medieval language.

**Ka·ra·khan'** (kŭ·rŭ·kän'), **Lev Mikhailovich.** 1889–1937. Russian Communist public official, of Armenian descent. Joined Bolshevists (1917); Soviet ambassador to Poland (1921); head of Soviet embassy to China (1924–27); vice-commissar of foreign affairs (1928–34); ambassador to Turkey (1934–37); disagreed with government on policy toward China; executed with seven other officials on charge of terroristic activities and espionage.

**Ka·ra' Mus·ta·fa'** *or* **Ka·ra' Mus·ta·pha'** (kä·rä' mōōs·tä·fä'). d. 1683. Turkish grand vizier (1676–83); brother-in-law of Ahmed Kuprili, whom he succeeded as vizier; sent by sultan to take Vienna; delayed attack and finally (1683) met complete defeat at hands of John Sobieski and Charles of Lorraine; beheaded by sultan.

**Ka·ram·zin'** (kŭ·rŭm·zyēn'), **Nikolai Mikhailovich.** 1766–1826. Russian historian and novelist, b. Mikhailovka, Orenburg, of noble Tatar family. Described travels (1789–90) in western Europe in *Letters of a Russian Traveler* (in Moscow *Journal*, 1790–92); wrote several novels, esp. *Poor Lisa* (1792) and *Natalia, the Boyar's Daughter* (1792); published two collections of literary masterpieces (one of foreign authors; one of Russian); appointed historiographer (1803); composed *History of Russia* (12 vols., 1819–26; 12th vol. unfinished) down to accession of Romanovs (1613). Reformed the literary language, introducing many Gallicisms to supplant Slavonic words and idioms; had great influence on development of Russian language and literature.

**Ka·ra·the·o·do·ri' Pa·sha'** (kä·rä·tĕ·ŏ·dŏ·rĭ' pä·shä'), **Alexander.** 1833–1906. Turkish statesman; took part in negotiations for Treaty of San Stefano and in Congress of Berlin (1878); Turkish minister of foreign affairs (1878–79); Prince of Samos (1885–95); governor general of Crete (1895–96); forced to resign by uprising (1896).

**Ka·ra·ve'lov** (kȧ·rȧ·vĕ'lôf), **Petko.** 1840–1903. Bulgarian statesman; regarded as founder of liberal party in Bulgaria; minister of finance (1880); premier of Bulgaria (1884–86, 1901–02).

**Karg'–E'lert** (kärk'ā'lĕrt), *orig.* **Karg, Sigfrid.** 1877–1933. German composer of works for organ, many piano pieces, chamber music, chorals, etc.

**Ka·rim' Khan** *or* **Ke·rim' Khan** (kȧ·rēm' kän'). 1699?–1779. Persian sovereign (1750–79), most important of Zand dynasty. Became regent (never took title of shah); made Shiraz his capital (1760); overthrown by Kajars, under Agha Mohammed Khan, after period of civil war.

**Karl** (kärl). German and Swedish form of CHARLES.

**Karl I** and **II.** Dukes of **Brunswick.** See BRUNSWICK.

**Karl Albrecht.** = CHARLES VII, Holy Roman Emperor.

**Karl Alexander, Karl Anton, Karl August, Karl Eduard, Karl Friedrich, Karl Leopold, Karl Ludwig.** See CHARLES ALEXANDER, CHARLES ANTHONY, CHARLES AUGUSTUS, CHARLES EDWARD, CHARLES FREDERICK, CHARLES LEOPOLD, CHARLES LUDWIG.

**Karl Eugen.** = CHARLES II, Duke of Württemberg.

**Karl Franz Josef.** = CHARLES I, Emperor of Austria.

**Karl Friedrich Alexander.** = CHARLES I, King of Württemberg.

**Karl Johan.** = CHARLES XIV of Sweden.

**Karl Knutsson.** = CHARLES VIII of Sweden.

**Karl Wilhelm Ferdinand.** Duke of **Brunswick.** See BRUNSWICK.

**Karl'feldt** (kärl'fĕlt), **Erik Axel.** 1864–1931. Swedish lyric poet; awarded Nobel prize in literature (posthumously, 1931). Author of volumes of poems dealing chiefly with nature and with peasant life of Dalecarlia (Dalarna).

**Karl'gren** (kärl'grān), **Bernhard.** 1889– . Swedish Sinologue. Author of *Analytic Dictionary of Chinese and Sino-Japanese* (1923), *Sound and Symbol in Chinese* (1923), etc.

**Kar'lings** (kär'lĭngz). *Ger.* **Ka'ro·ling'er** (kä'rō·lĭng'ẽr). The Carolingian (*q.v.*) rulers.

**Karlmann.** See CARLOMAN.

**Kar·ło'wicz** (kär·lô'vēch), **Mieczysław.** 1876–1909. Polish composer, b. in Lithuania.

**Karl'stadt** *or* **Carl'stadt** (kärl'shtät) *or* **Ka'rol·stadt** (kä'rōl·shtät). *Real name* **Andreas Rudolf Bo'den·stein** (bō'dĕn·shtīn). 1480?–1541. German Protestant reformer; joined Luther's cause at Wittenberg (1517); championed Augustinian doctrine in Leipzig disputation with Eck (1519); denied Mosaic authorship of Pentateuch (1520); assumed Protestant leadership in Wittenberg during Luther's absence at the Wartburg (1521–22); attacked celibacy of the clergy and monasticism. Opposed Luther's policy of compromise, and championed radical reforms and beliefs. Banished from Saxony as result of reform movements (1524); proclaimed disbelief in Real Presence and Eucharist; accused of participation in Peasants' War during exile; granted refuge in Wittenberg (1525–29) through Luther's intercession following retraction of statements about Lord's Supper. Refused to take part in controversy against Zwingli; became involved in further differences over Lord's Supper, and fled to Holstein, Friesland, and Zurich; received at Zurich by Zwingli and defended against Luther's attacks; preacher and professor at Basel, Switzerland (from 1534).

**Kár'mán** (kär'män), **József.** 1769–1795. Hungarian novelist; author of *Fanni Hagyományai* (*Eng.* "Fanny's Testament").

**Kármán, The'o·dor** (tā'ō·dōr) **von** (fōn). 1881–1963. Physicist and aeronautical engineer, b. Budapest, Hungary. To U.S. (1930); professor of aeronautics and director of Guggenheim Aeronautics Laboratory, Calif. Inst. of Tech. (1930).

**Kar'ne·beek** (kär'nĕ·bāk), **Hermann Adriaan van.** 1874–1942. Dutch statesman, b. The Hague. Secretary of first (1899) and delegate to second (1907) Hague Peace Conference; burgomaster of Hague (1911–18); foreign minister (1918–27); chairman of League of Nations Assembly (1921).

**Karo, Joseph ben Ephraim.** See CARO.

**Ká'ro·lyi** (kä'rō·lyĭ). Noble Hungarian family, including notably: **Mihály Károlyi,** made a baron (1609); his grandson **Sándor** (1668–1743), raised to rank of count (1712), aided Rákóczy in his fight against the Hapsburgs but later made peace with the king and was appointed field marshal in the Austrian army; Count **Aloys** (1823–1889), diplomat; Austrian minister (1860–66), ambassador (1871–78), in Berlin; ambassador in London (1878–88); **Árpád** (1853– ), director of the historical institute in Vienna (from 1920) and author of treatises on 16th- and 17th-century Hungary; **Gyula** (1871–1947), member of the Hungarian House of Magnates (1905 ff.); set up a national government (May–June, 1919) to oppose the Communists; member of the new Upper House (1927 ff.); minister of foreign affairs (1930), and premier (1931–32); **Count Mihály** (1875–1955), politician; after the World War became prime minister of Hungary, and then president of the newly organized Hungarian People's Republic (Nov. 16, 1918–Mar. 12, 1919); was overthrown by Communists (Mar. 12, 1919), and forced to take refuge abroad.

**Kar'pe·les** (kär'pȧ·lĕs), **Gustav.** 1848–1909. Austrian Jewish literary historian and journalist; author of a *History of Jewish Literature* (2 vols., 1885), and of critical works, notably on Heinrich Heine.

**Kar·piń'ski** (kär·pēn'y'·skē), **Franciszek.** 1741?–1825. Polish poet; composed esp. elegies, idyls, and songs.

**Karr** (kȧr), **Alphonse,** *in full* **Jean Baptiste Alphonse.** 1808–1890. French journalist and novelist; editor of *Figaro* (1839) and founder of the satirical review *Les Guêpes.* Author of *Sous les Tilleuls* (1832), *Voyage autour de mon Jardin* (1845), *Histoire d'un Pion* (1854), *Le Credo du Jardinier* (1875), etc.

**Kar'rer** (kär'ẽr), **Paul.** 1889–1971. Swiss chemist; professor, Zurich (1918–59). Awarded (jointly with Walter N. Haworth) the 1937 Nobel prize for chemistry for work on carotenoids, flavins, and vitamins A and B.

**Kar·sa'vi·na** (kŭr·sȧ'vyĭ·nŭ), **Tamara.** 1885–1978. Russian dancer; m. 1st, M. Mochin; 2d, H. J. Bruce. Succeeded Anna Pavlova as première danseuse at Imperial Opera House, St. Petersburg (1910). Appeared in London, under name "La Tamara," in *The Firebird* (1909), and with Imperial Russian Ballet at Covent Garden (1911).

**Karsch** (kärsh) *or* **Kar'schin** (kär'shĭn), **Anna Luise,** *nee* **Dür'bach** (dür'bäk). 1722–1791. German poet; called "the German Sappho." A collection of her selected poems was published (1764). Her daughter **Karoline Luise von Klenck'e** [fōn klĕng'kĕ] (1754–1812), also a poet, was the mother of Helmine de Chézy (*q.v.*).

**Kar'sten** (kär'stĕn), **Hermann.** 1817–1908. German botanist.

**Karsten, Karl Johann Bernhard.** 1782–1853. German mineralogist, mining expert, and metallurgist.

**Kasa.** See THEODORE of Abyssinia.

**Kash'pe·rov** (kȧsh'pyĕ·rôf), **Vladimir Nikitich.** 1827–1894. Russian composer and teacher; among his compositions are the operas *Marie Tudor* (1859), *Rienzi* (1863), and *The Storm* (an attempt at a national Russian opera; 1867).

**Kasimir.** See CASIMIR.

**Kas'ner** (kăs'nẽr), **Edward.** 1878–1955. American mathematician; taught at Columbia U. (from 1900); known for work in conformal geometry, geometry of divergent series, etc.

**Kas·pro'wicz** (käs·prô'vēch), **Jan.** 1860–1926. Polish

lyric poet and translator of works of Aeschylus, Euripides, Shakespeare, Browning, Keats, Rostand, Byron, Tennyson, and others.

**Kassa.** See THEODORE of Abyssinia.

**Ka·stal'ski** (kŭ·stâl'y'·skû·ĭ; *Angl.* kȧ·stăl'skĭ), **Aleksandr Dmitrievich.** 1856–1926. Russian composer; authority on church music, and a leading representative of modern nationalistic tendencies in such music.

**Ka'stl** (käs't'l), **Ludwig.** 1878– . German lawyer and economist; member of reparations section, ministry of finance (1920–25); member of Young committee of experts (1925–33); attorney of the high court, Berlin (1933–36), and Munich (1939 ff.).

**Kast'ler'** (kȧst'lâr'), **Alfred.** 1902– . French physicist. Awarded Nobel prize in physics (1966) for his work on the development of the laser.

**Käst'ner** (kĕst'nēr), **Abraham Gotthelf.** 1719–1800. German mathematician and epigrammatist.

**Kast'ner** (käst'nēr), **Johann Georg.** 1810–1867. German composer, teacher, and writer on music; to Paris (1835). Wrote textbooks on music theory and treatises on instrumentation and vocalization; composer of operas, choral and instrumental works, symphonic tone poems, etc. His son **Georg Friedrich Eugen** (1852–1882), physicist, invented the pyrophone; wrote on the theory of vibration and oscillation, and on the pyrophone.

**Ka'te** (kä'tĕ), **Jan Jacob Lodewijk ten.** 1819–1889. Dutch clergyman and poet; pastorate in Amsterdam (1860); author of *De Schepping* (1866), *De Planecten* (1869), *Palmbladen en Dichtbloemen* (1884), etc.

**Kate, Lambert ten.** 1674–1731. Dutch philologist; forerunner of Jacob Grimm; author of a study on the connection between Gothic and Dutch languages (1710) and an *Introduction* containing a comparative grammar of Germanic languages and an etymological Dutch dictionary (2 vols., 1723).

**Ka'ter** (kā'tēr), **Henry.** 1777–1835. English scientist; army officer (1794–1814). Invented a seconds pendulum (Kater's pendulum) operating by application of Huygens's principle of reciprocity of centers of suspension and oscillation; also invented floating collimator.

**Katharine** *or* **Katharina.** See CATHERINE.

**Kat·kov'** (kŭt·kôf'), **Mikhail Nikiforovich.** 1818–1887. Russian journalist; editor of Moscow *News* (1861–87); a leader of Slavophile movement but a reactionary; personal adviser of Alexander III.

**Ka·to** (kä·tō), Baron **Takaakira.** 1859–1926. Japanese statesman; opposed modernistic reforms; instrumental in forming Conservative party (1913; later known as Kenseikai party); premier of coalition cabinet (1924–26).

**Kato,** Baron **Tomosaburo.** 1859–1923. Japanese admiral and statesman; during Russo-Japanese War in command of Kamimura's squadron; vice-admiral (1908); commanded Japanese fleet at taking of Tsingtao (1914); chief of Japanese delegation at Washington Conference (1921–22); premier (1922–23).

**Ka·tsu·ra** (kä·tsŏŏ·rä), Prince **Taro.** 1847–1913. Japanese statesman and soldier; premier (1901–06, 1908–11, 1912–13).

**Katz** (kăts), Sir **Bernard.** 1911– . British (German-born) physiologist. To London (1935); at Univ. Coll., London (1950– ); awarded Nobel prize in physiology and medicine (1970) with J. Axelrod and U. von Euler for research on nerve and muscle functions.

**Katz'en·bach** (kăt's'n·băk), **Nicholas de·Belle'ville** (dĕ·bĕl'vĭl). 1922– . American lawyer; Rhodes scholar (1947–49); U.S. attorney general (1965–66); U.S. under secretary of state (1966–69).

**Kauff'man** (kouf'măn), **Reginald Wright.** 1877–1959. American writer; war correspondent in Europe during World War I. Author of *Jarvis of Harvard* (1901), *The Things That Are Caesar's* (1902), *What Is Socialism?* (1910), *The House of Bondage* (1910), *The Spider's Web* (1913), *The Mark of the Beast* (1916), *The Ancient Quest* (verse; 1917), *Money to Burn* (1924), *The Overland Trail* (1927), *Front Porch* (1933), etc. His wife (m. 1909), **Ruth,** *nee* **Ham'mitt** (hăm'ĭt), *known as* **Ruth Wright Kauffman** (1883–1952), served as nurse and war correspondent in World War I; novelist: *High Stakes* (1914), *Stars for Sale* (1930), *Dancing Dollars* (1931), *Tourist Third* (1933), *Two Red Roses* (1938), etc.

**Kauff'mann** (*Ger.* kouf'män), **An·ge'li·ca** (*Ger.* äng·gā'lē·kä). 1741–1807. Swiss-born historical and portrait painter; m. 1st Count de Horn (1767; soon separated), 2d Antonio Zucchi (1781). In England (1766–81); one of original academicians (1769).

**Kauf'man** (kôf'măn), **George S.** 1889–1961. American playwright, b. Pittsburgh, Pa. Author of *The Butter and Egg Man* (1925); coauthor of *Dulcy* (1921), of dramatization of *Merton of the Movies* (1922), and *Beggar on Horseback* (1924), with Marc Connelly; of *Minick* (1924), *The Royal Family* (1927), and *Dinner at Eight* (1932), with Edna Ferber; of *June Moon* (1929), with Ring Lardner; coauthor also of *The Dark Tower* (1933), *You Can't Take it With You* (1936), and of the musical comedies *Animal Crackers* (1928), *The Band Wagon* (1931), *Of Thee I Sing* (1932), *I'd Rather Be Right* (1937), etc.

**Kauf'mann** (kouf'män), **Alexander.** 1817–1893. German lyric poet; m. (1857) **Mathilde Bin'der** [bĭn'dēr] (1835–1901), pseudonym **A·ma'ra Ge·or'ge** (ä·mä'rä gā·ôr'gĕ), author of lyric poems, as *Blüten der Nacht* (1856), of *Mythoterpe* (1858; with her husband and G. F. Daumer), and of novels and short tales.

**Kaufmann, Georg Heinrich.** 1842–1929. German historian.

**Kauf'mann** (kouf'mŭn), **Konstantin Petrovich.** 1818–1882. Russian general; took Samarkand (1868); subjugated khanates of Bokhara, Khiva, and Kokand, bringing Russian domain to Afghan border (1868–75).

**Kauf'mann** (kouf'män), **Nicolaus.** Real name of Nicolaus MERCATOR.

**Kauikeaouli.** See KAMEHAMEHA III.

**Kaul'bach** (koul'bäk). Family of German painters, including: **Wilhelm von Kaulbach** (1805–1874), historical painter and illustrator; settled in Berlin (1847–65), where he and his pupils decorated the grand staircase of the Neues Museum with 6 historic murals illustrating the evolution of civilization; director of Munich Academy (1849). His works include many ceiling and mural paintings. His son **Hermann** (1846–1909) was illustrator and painter chiefly of historical genre scenes. **Friedrich Kaulbach** (1822–1903), nephew and pupil of Wilhelm, was historical and portrait painter; court painter in Hanover. **Friedrich August von Kaulbach** (1850–1920), son of Friedrich, was genre and portrait painter; director, Munich Art Academy (1886–91).

**Kaul'bars** (koul'bŭrs), Baron **Nikolai Vasilievich.** 1842–1905. Russian general and cartographer; chief of divisional staff in Turkish war (1877–78); made first Russian maps of South America, Australia, and Africa. His brother Baron **Aleksandr Vasilievich** (1844–1929), explored Tien Shan Mountains and Amu Darya in Central Asia (1869–73; pub. accounts 1874–88); served in Russo-Turkish war (1877–78); a commanding officer in Russo-Japanese War (1904–05).

**Kaun** (koun), **Hugo.** 1863–1932. German composer of operas *Sappho* (1917), *Der Fremde* (1920), and *Menandra* (1925), and of symphonies, overtures, piano pieces, a Requiem, male choruses, chamber music, songs, etc.

**Kau'nitz** (kou'nĭts), Count **Wenzel Anton von.** Prince

**von Kaunitz-Riet'berg** [-rēt'bĕrk] (from 1764). 1711–1794. Austrian statesman; negotiator in interests of Maria Theresa at Peace Congress in Aachen (1748); ambassador at Paris (1750–53). State chancellor and director of foreign policy (1753–92); effected Austro-French coalition against Frederick the Great (1755); represented Austria's interests in first partition of Poland (1772). Acquired Bucovina from Turks (1775); influenced domestic policies of Maria Theresa, Joseph II, and Leopold II.

**Kau'pert** (kou'pĕrt), **Gustav.** 1819–1897. German sculptor, b. Kassel. Executed, after Thomas Crawford's designs, reliefs and figures for a monument in Richmond, Va., and the colossal bronze statue on dome of Capitol in Washington; original works include *Sleeping Lion* on Hessian memorial at Kassel (1874) and *Christ and the Evangelists* at Trier (c. 1880–87).

**Kaut'sky** (kout'skē), **Karl Johann.** 1854–1938. German Socialist writer, champion of Marxism, b. in Prague. Joined Social Democratic party in Vienna (1875); private secretary to Friedrich Engels in London (1881); founded in Stuttgart (1883) and edited in London and Stuttgart (until 1917) Socialist review *Die Neue Zeit.* Chief creator of the Erfurt program (1891); opposed Bernstein's reform Marxist policy ("revisionism"); favored pacifism during World War I. Co-organizer (with Haase) and member of Independent Socialist Democratic party (1917–22); political adviser to Ebert-Haase cabinet; opposed Bolshevism and Russian Revolution, supported Menshevists in Georgia, and refused to join United German Communist party. Settled in Vienna following Bolshevist victory and rejoined Socialist Democratic party; became naturalized citizen of Czechoslovakia (1934); to the Netherlands (1938). Chief editor of *How the World War Originated* (1919).

**Kautzsch** (kouch), **Emil Friedrich.** 1841–1910. German Protestant theologian and Hebrew scholar.

**Ka·vadh'** (kă·väd'). *Arab.* **Ḳo·bādh'** *or* **Qo·bādh'** (kŏ·bäd'). Name of two Sassanid kings of Persia:

**Kavadh I.** King (485–531). Father of Khosrau I. At first favored Mazdakites; deposed (498) by his brother; lived with Ephthalites, who restored him (501) to throne; made war against Romans (503–505, 524–531); withdrew support of Mazdakites and ordered great massacre (523) of them; invaded Syria and defeated Belisarius (531).

**Kavadh II.** King (628). Son of Khosrau II, whom he deposed and slew.

**Kav'a·nagh** (kăv'ȧ·nȧ; -nä), **Julia.** 1824–1877. Irish novelist; author of *Madeleine* (1848), *Daisy Burns* (1853), *Queen Mab* (1863), *John Dorrien* (1875), etc.

**Ka·ve'lin** (kŭ·vyā'lyĭn), **Konstantin Dmitrievich.** 1818–1885. Russian historian and jurist.

**Ka·wa·ba·ta** (kä·wä·bä·tä), **Yasunari.** 1899–1972. Japanese writer. Author of *Izu Dancer* (1924), *Snow Country* (1947), *The Thousand Cranes*, etc. Awarded Nobel prize in literature (1968).

**Ka·wa·ka·mi** (kä·wä·kä·mē), **Kiyoshi Kari.** 1875–1949. Japanese journalist and writer in U.S.A. Author of many works on Japan and Far Eastern questions.

**Ka·wa·mu·ra** (kä·wä·mōō·rä), Viscount **Kageaki.** 1859–1926. Japanese general in command at Mukden (1905).

**Kay** (kā), **John.** fl. 1733–1764. English inventor of flying (or fly) shuttle (patented 1733) used in weaving.

**Kay, John.** 1742–1826. Scottish miniaturist and caricaturist; worked as barber (till 1785); etched plates of eminent contemporary Scotsmen.

**Kaye** (kā), Sir **John William.** 1814–1876. English military historian; succeeded John Stuart Mill as secretary of India Office (1858–74). Author of *History of the Sepoy War* (3 vols., 1864–76), etc.

**Kayenbergh, Marie Émile Albert.** See Albert GIRAUD.

**Kaye'-Smith'** (kā'smĭth'), **Sheila.** 1887–1956. English novelist; m. T. Penrose Fry (1924). Known esp. for tales laid in Sussex; among her novels are *The Tramping Methodist* (1908), *Three Against the World* (1914), *Joanna Godden* (1921), *The End of the House of Alard* (1923), *The Village Doctor* (1929), *Superstition Corner* (1934), *Rose Deeprose* (1936), *The Valiant Woman* (1938), *Ember Lane* (1940).

**Kazimierz.** Polish form of CASIMIR.

**Ka'zin·czy** (kŏ'zĭn·tsĭ), **Ferenc.** 1759–1831. Hungarian writer and linguistic reformer. Sought to promote contemporary Hungarian literary activity; as leader of the neologists, championed a modern Hungarian language. Author of translations into Magyar from German, French, English, and the classical languages, and of plays, poems, and prose works.

**Kea'ble** (kē'b'l), **Robert.** 1887–1927. English clergyman and novelist; missionary in Africa (1912–20); resigned his orders (1920) and devoted himself to writing. Among his works are *Songs of the Narrow Way* (1914), *Simon Called Peter* (1921), *The Mother of All Living* (1922), *Peradventure* (1923), etc.

**Kean** (kēn), **Edmund.** 1787–1833. English actor, b. London. Made striking success at Drury Lane as Shylock (Jan. 26, 1814), and followed this with Hamlet, Othello, Iago, Macbeth, Lear, and Richard III; last stage appearance (Mar. 12, 1833). Unrivaled in his day as a tragedian. His son **Charles John** (1811–1868) acted in his company (1827–33) and independently; visited U.S. (1830, 1839, 1845–47); leased Princess's Theatre (1850) and directed series of revivals of great plays; toured in Australia, America, and Jamaica (1863–66); last professional appearance, Liverpool (1867). m. (1842) **Ellen Tree** (1805–1880), actress at Drury Lane (1826–28), Covent Garden (1829–36), and in America (1836–39 and 1845–47), who played opposite him (1842–67).

**Keane** (kēn), **Augustus Henry.** 1833–1912. British ethnologist and geographer, b. in Cork, Ireland. Professor of Hindustani, University Coll., London. Author of *Ethnology* (1896), *Man, Past and Present* (1899), etc.

**Kear'ney** (kär'nĭ), **Denis.** 1847–1907. Labor leader, b. Oakmount, Ireland; resident in San Francisco (from c. 1868); naturalized (1876). Leader of a workingmen's protest movement (the sand-lot party) against unemployment, dishonest banking, unjust taxes, and esp. Chinese labor.

**Kear'ny** (kär'nĭ), **Lawrence.** 1789–1868. American naval officer; had share in bringing about first commercial treaty between China and U.S. (1844), beginning of open-door policy.

**Kearny, Stephen Watts.** 1794–1848. Cousin of Lawrence Kearny. American army officer; brigadier general in Mexican War; conquered New Mexico; moved westward to California; defeated by Mexicans at San Pascual (Dec. 6, 1846); aided by Robert F. Stockton (see under Richard STOCKTON), occupied Los Angeles (Jan. 10, 1847); after later conflict of authority with Stockton, arrested Lieut. J. C. Frémont (*q.v.;* Stockton's appointee as civil governor) for refusing to carry out his orders; ordered into Mexico; brevetted major general. His nephew **Philip Kearny** (1814–1862) was also an army officer and served through Mexican War; served with French army in Italy (1859); engaged at Magenta and Solferino; awarded cross of the French Legion of Honor; brigadier general of volunteers, Union army (1861), major general (1862); killed on reconnoitering expedition (Sept. 1, 1862).

**Keate** (kēt), **John.** 1773–1852. English schoolmaster; asst. master (1797–1809) and headmaster (1809–34),

Eton, where he enforced discipline in classes with frequent and severe flogging; rector in Hampshire (1824–52). Cf. ORBILIUS PUPILLUS.

**Keats** (kēts), **John**. 1795–1821. English poet, son of London hostler. Studied medicine but never practiced. First-published verse was sonnet printed in Leigh Hunt's *Examiner* (May 5, 1816), followed by sonnet *On First Looking into Chapman's Homer* (Dec., 1816), and other sonnets (1817); with aid of Shelley, published *Poems by John Keats* (March, 1817). Wrote *Endymion* (Apr.–Dec., 1817); finished *The Eve of St. Agnes* (1819) and *La Belle Dame sans Merci* (1819). Fell in love with Fanny Brawne. Published *Lamia and other Poems* (July, 1820). Health failing, went to Italy; died in Rome (Feb. 23, 1821). His *Hyperion* (begun 1818) remained unfinished at death.

**Ke'ble** (kē'b'l), **John**. 1792–1866. English clergyman and poet; educ. Oxford. Professor of poetry, Oxford (1831–41), vicar of Hursley, Hampshire (1836–66). By his sermon on national apostasy (1833), initiated Oxford movement. Published collection of his hymns in *Christian Year* (1827); wrote number of *Tracts for the Times* in support of Oxford movement.

**Keck** (kĕk), **Charles**. 1875–1951. American sculptor, b. New York City. Among his works are: equestrian monuments of Stonewall Jackson at Charlottesville, Va., and Andrew Jackson at Kansas City, Mo.; monuments of Booker T. Washington at Tuskegee, Ala., and James B. Duke at Durham, N.C.; and portrait busts of James Madison, Patrick Henry, and Elias Howe for the American Hall of Fame, New York.

**Keefe** (kēf), **Daniel Joseph**. 1852–1929. American labor leader; U.S. commissioner general of immigration (1908–13).

**Kee'ler** (kē'lẽr), **Charles Augustus**. 1871–1937. American poet and ornithologist; author of *Bird Notes Afield* (1899), and many volumes of verse.

**Keeler, James Edward**. 1857–1900. American astronomer; director, Allegheny Observatory (1891–98) and Lick Observatory (1898–1900). Specialist in spectroscopy; determined wave length of the fundamental green ray of the nebular spectrum; demonstrated truth of Maxwell's theory regarding meteoric constitution of rings of Saturn.

**Keeler, William H.**, *known as* **Wee Willie**. 1872–1923. American professional baseball player, b. Brooklyn, N.Y.; member of New York National League team, the "Giants" (1892–1910); batting champion (1897, 1898).

**Kee'ley** (kē'lĭ), **Leslie E.** 1832–1900. American physician, b. St. Lawrence Co., N.Y.; originator of Keeley cure for alcoholics and drug addicts.

**Keen** (kēn), **William Williams**. 1837–1932. American surgeon, b. Philadelphia. A.M., Brown (1859), M.D., Jefferson Med. Coll. (1862). Surgeon, U.S. army, in Civil War; practiced at Philadelphia (from 1866).

**Keene** (kēn), **Charles Samuel**. 1823–1891. English humorous artist; on staff of *Punch* (from 1851); illustrated Douglas Jerrold's *Caudle Lectures*, etc.

**Keene, Laura**. 1826?–1873. Stage name of an English actress, whose original name is unknown; wife of (1) John Taylor, and (2) John Lutz; on American stage (from 1852). Excelled in light comedy; was acting in *Our American Cousin* at Ford's Theatre, Washington, D.C., the night when President Lincoln was assassinated there.

**Kei'fer** (kī'fẽr), **Joseph Warren**. 1836–1932. American lawyer, soldier, and politician; practiced law, Springfield, Ohio (from 1858). Served through Civil War; brigadier general (1864), and major general (1865). Member, U.S. House of Representatives (1877–85; 1905–11; speaker 1881–83).

**Keight'ley** (kēt'lĭ; kīt'lĭ), **Thomas**. 1789–1872. Irish scholar and writer; published editions of Latin classics and of Milton and Shakespeare.

**Keiki.** See HITOTSUBASHI.

**Keill** (kēl), **John**. 1671–1721. Scottish mathematician and astronomer; defended, against Leibnitz, Newton's claim to be inventor of differential calculus.

**Keir Hardie, James**. See HARDIE.

**Kei'ser** (kī'zẽr), **Reinhard**. 1674–1739. German composer, esp. of operas, oratorios, cantatas, motets, psalms, etc.

**Kei'tel** (kī'tĕl), **Wilhelm**. 1882–1946. German field marshal; entered army (1901); captain in World War (1914–18); colonel (1931), major general (1934), and chief of administration department in ministry of war (1935–38). On army reorganization (Feb., 1938), Hitler himself assumed personal and direct command of Germany's armed forces, exercising his authority through a "supreme command of the armed forces headed by General Wilhelm Keitel"; in reorganized war cabinet (from Aug., 1939); read terms of armistice to French representatives (June, 1940); in command on Russian front (1941); signed act of military surrender (May 9, 1945); hanged as war criminal.

**Keith** (kēth). Name of a Scottish family in which the office of Great Marischal of Scotland was hereditary from grant in 12th century and members of which bore titles of Lord **Keith** and Earl **Mar'i·schal** [mär'shăl] (until 1716) and, after Restoration, Earl of **Kin·tore'** (kĭn·tōr'). Members include the following:

**George Keith** (1553?–1623), 5th Earl Marischal; educ. Aberdeen and Geneva; a firm Protestant, commissioner for executing laws against Catholics; special ambassador to Denmark to arrange marriage of James VI with Princess Anne (1589); founded and endowed Marischal College, Aberdeen (1593); member of commissions, as one for trial of Catholic lords, and one for union with England.

His grandson **William** (1617?–1661), 7th Earl Marischal; a leader of Covenanters in northeast Scotland and chief opponent of marquis of Huntly; co-operated with Montrose (1639); joined duke of Hamilton in invasion of England (1648); entertained Charles II at Dunnottar; committed to Tower; after Restoration, privy councilor and keeper of privy seal of Scotland.

William's brother Sir **John** (d. 1714), 1st Earl of Kintore, held Dunnottar Castle against Cromwell and preserved the regalia of Scotland.

**George** (1693?–1778), 10th Earl Marischal; Jacobite; took part in rising of 1715 and entertained the Pretender (1715); led Spanish Jacobite expedition (1719), fleeing to Spain after its defeat; became favorite of Frederick the Great, who named him Prussian ambassador in Paris (1751), governor of Neuchâtel (1752), ambassador in Madrid (1758); friend of Voltaire and Rousseau.

His brother **James Francis Edward** (1696–1758), *known as* Marshal **Keith**; Jacobite soldier, though Episcopalian; engaged in Alberoni's futile Jacobite expedition (1719); served in Spanish, then in Russian, army (1728 ff.); Russian general in Russo-Turkish war (1737) and Russo-Swedish war (1741–43); created field marshal by Frederick the Great of Prussia (1747) and made governor of Berlin (1749); in Seven Years' War conducted masterly retreat from Olmütz; mortally wounded at battle of Hochkirch (1758).

Through the female line was descended George Keith Elphinstone, Viscount Keith (see ELPHINSTONE family).

**Keith,** Sir **Arthur**. 1866–1955. British anthropologist, b. in Aberdeen, Scot. Author of *Introduction to Study of Anthropoid Apes* (1896), *Human Embryology and*

*Morphology* (1901), *Ancient Types of Man* (1911), *The Human Body* (1912), *Concerning Man's Origin* (1927), *Darwinism and its Critics* (1935), etc.

**Keith, Arthur Berriedale.** 1879–1944. British political scientist and Sanskrit scholar, b. in Dunbar, Scotland; lecturer on the constitution of the British Empire (from 1927). Among his many books are *British Colonial Policy 1763–1917* (2 vols., 1918), *Constitution, Administration, and Laws of the Empire* (1924), *Constitutional History of the First British Empire* (1930), *The British Cabinet System* (1938), etc. In the Sanskrit field, he wrote *The Samkhya System* (1918), *Buddhist Philosophy* (1923), *Sanskrit Drama* (1924), *History of Sanskrit Literature* (1928), etc.

**Keith, Benjamin Franklin.** 1846–1914. American theatrical manager; associated with E. F. Albee (*q.v.*) in operating chain of vaudeville theaters; an organizer of Keith and Proctor Amusement Co., controlling vaudeville theaters (1906).

**Keith, George.** 1638?–1716. Missionary in America, b. in Aberdeenshire, Scotland. Became a Quaker (1664) and was persecuted. To America, and headed separate faction in church, known as Christian Quakers (1692). Entered Anglican Church, and was ordained (1700); Anglican missionary in Pennsylvania, converting many Quakers, esp. Christian Quakers.

**Ke'ku·le von Stra'do·nitz** (kā'ko͞o·lā fôn shträ'dô·nĭts), **Friedrich August.** 1829–1896. German chemist; known esp. for work on constitution of organic compounds; set forth doctrine of the linking of carbon atoms; regarded carbon as tetravalent; originated the ring, or closed-chain, theory of the constitution of the benzene molecule.

**Kekule von Stradonitz, Reinhard.** 1839–1911. German archaeologist; author of works chiefly on Greek and Italian sculpture and archaeology.

**Ké'ler** (kā'lĕr), **Béla.** *Pseudonym of* **Adalbert von Kel'ler** (fôn kĕl'ẽr). 1820–1882. Hungarian conductor and composer of orchestral works, violin solos, marches, and dance music.

**Kel'land** (kĕl'ănd), **Clarence Budington.** 1881–1964. American fiction writer; author of *Mark Tidd* (1913), *Scattergood Baines* (1921), *Dynasty* (1929), *Speak Easily* (1932), *Catspaw* (1934), *Star Rising* (1938), etc., and many short stories including *Opera Hat*, scenarized as *Mr. Deeds Goes to Town* (1936).

**Kel'lar** (kĕl'ẽr), **Harry.** 1849–1922. American magician.

**Kel'ler** (kĕl'ẽr), **Adalbert von.** See Béla KÉLER.

**Keller, Adelbert von.** 1812–1883. German philologist; translator of Cervantes and Shakespeare; compiler of *Altfranzösische Sagen* (2 vols., 1839–40), *Italienischer Novellenschatz* (6 parts, 1851–52), etc. His son **Otto** (1838–1927), classical philologist, was author of a critical edition of Horace (with Alfred Holder; 2 vols., 1864–70), etc.

**Keller, Albert von.** 1844?–1920. Nephew of Friedrich Ludwig Keller (vom Steinbock). Painter, b. in Switzerland; painted in Italy, France (1882–83), England, and the Netherlands; president of Munich Secession Society; ennobled (1898). His paintings are chiefly of Biblical and historical subjects, scenes from antique life with architectural surroundings, and groups and female figures in modern dress.

**Kel'ler** (kĕl'ẽr), **Albert Galloway.** 1874–1956. American educator; professor of science of society, Yale (from 1907). Author of *Homeric Society* (1902), *Societal Evolution* (1915), *Science of Society* (4 vols., 1927, with aid of material left by W. G. Sumner), etc. His son **Deane** (1901– ), painter, assistant professor (1930–36), associate professor (from 1936), Yale school of fine arts; work includes portraits of George P. Baker, Chauncey B. Tinker, James R. Angell, and murals, as *Valley Forge* for the city of New Haven, Conn.

**Keller, Arthur Ignatius.** 1867–1924. American illustrator and painter; studio in New York (from c. 1890); work as illustrator appears in editions of Bret Harte, Longfellow, Irving, S. Weir Mitchell, and F. Hopkinson Smith.

**Keller, Ferdinand.** 1800–1881. Swiss archaeologist and antiquary. Discovered lake dwellings of Obermeilen on Lake Zurich (1853); organized researches on Swiss lake dwellings.

**Keller, Ferdinand.** 1842–1922. German historical, genre, landscape, and portrait painter.

**Keller, Friedrich Gottlob.** 1816–1895. German weaver credited with conceiving the idea of producing pulp for the manufacture of paper by grinding wood on a grindstone with the addition of water.

**Keller,** *or* **Keller vom Stein'bock** (fôm shtīn'bôk), **Friedrich Ludwig.** 1799–1860. Jurist and politician, b. in Zurich. Member (1830) and president (1832, 1834) of grand council, and president of Swiss superior court (1831); fled from Switzerland for political reasons (1839). Professor, Berlin (1847); conservative member in Prussian lower chamber, Erfurt Parliament, and House of Lords.

**Keller, Gottfried.** 1819–1890. Swiss German-language lyric and epic poet and novelist, b. Zurich. Author of collections of verse, novels *Der Grüne Heinrich* (autobiographical; 4 vols., 1854–55) and *Martin Salander* (1886), short stories of Swiss provincial life.

**Keller, Helen Adams.** 1880–1968. American author and lecturer, b. Tuscumbia, Ala. Lost both sight and hearing by illness at age of 19 months. Educ. by **Anne Mansfield** (*nee* **Sullivan**) **Ma'cy** [mā'sĭ] (1887–1936). Lecturer in U.S. and abroad on behalf of the blind. Author of *The Story of My Life* (1902), *Optimism, an Essay* (1903), *The World I Live In* (1908), *Out of the Dark* (1913), *My Religion* (1927), *Helen Keller's Journal* (1938), *Let Us Have Faith* (1940), etc.

**Kel'ler'** (kĕ'lâr'), **Jean Jacques** (1635–1700) and his brother **Jean Balthasar** (1638–1702). Swiss-born French founders of artillery, statues, etc.; cast most of the bronze statues in the gardens at Versailles.

**Kel'ler** (kĕl'ẽr), **Otto.** See under Adelbert von KELLER.

**Keller, Walter.** 1873–1940. American organist and composer of orchestral and choral works, and pieces for organ and piano.

**Kel'ler·mann** (kĕl'ẽr·män), **Bernhard.** 1879–1951. German novelist; author of *Ingeborg* (1906), *Der Tor* (1909; Eng. trans. *The Fool*), *Das Meer* (1910; Eng. trans. *The Sea*), *Der Tunnel* (1913), *Der Neunte November* (1920; Eng. trans. *The Ninth November*), and *Die Brüder Schellenberg* (1925); also of the drama *Die Wiedertäufer von Münster* (1925), and works on his travels in Japan and the East.

**Kel'ler'mann'** (kĕ'lĕr'mån'), **François Christophe.** Duc **de Val'my'** (dē vål'mē'). 1735–1820. French soldier, of German descent; commanded Army of the Moselle (1792) and co-operated with Dumouriez in defeating the duke of Brunswick at Valmy (Sept. 20, 1792). Napoleon appointed him senator (1804), and created him marshal of France and duc de Valmy; Louis XVIII created him a peer (1814). His son **François Étienne** (1770–1835) was one of Napoleon's generals; brigadier general (1797); led decisive charge at Marengo (1800) and was promoted general of division; distinguished himself at Austerlitz and Waterloo.

**Kel'ley** (kĕl'ĭ), **Edgar Stillman.** 1857–1944. American musician, b. Sparta, Wis. Teacher, Cincinnati Conservatory of Music (1910 ff.). Among his compositions are: orchestral suite *Alice in Wonderland;* symphonic poem *The Pit and the Pendulum*, and many choral works and piano pieces. His wife **Jessie Stillman**, *nee* **Gregg** (grĕg), taught piano in San Francisco (1887–94), New York (1894–1902), Berlin (1902–10); lecturer, Cincinnati Conservatory (from 1911); d. 1949.

**Kelley, Edward.** 1555–1595. English alchemist. Pilloried at Lancaster (1580) for fraud or coining; accompanied John Dee (*q.v.*) as scryer in Poland and in Bohemia practicing crystallomancy at court of Emperor Rudolph II (1583–89).

**Kelley, Florence.** 1859–1932. American social-settlement worker, b. Philadelphia; resident at Hull House, Chicago (1891–99), and Henry Street Settlement, New York (1899–1924).

**Kelley, Oliver Hudson.** 1826–1913. American agricultural organizer; one of original organizers of National Grange of the Patrons of Husbandry (1867).

**Kell'gren** (chĕl'grān), **Johan Henrik.** 1751–1795. Swedish lyric poet and critic; cofounder and critic (1778), then owner and editor (from 1788), of the journal *Stockholmsposten;* championed rationalism in controversy with Thorild (1782–84). Librarian (1780), private secretary (from 1785), and literary adviser to Gustavus III. Author of satirical verse influenced chiefly by French aestheticism, lyrical poetry, patriotic verse influenced by the French Revolution, and versification for Gustavus's operas.

**Kel'logg** (kĕl'ŏg; -ŭg), **Clara Louise.** 1842–1916. American dramatic soprano. Organized own company (1873); m. Carl Strakosch (1887). A pioneer in presenting grand opera in English. Important roles: Linda in Donizetti's *Linda di Chamounix*, Gilda in Verdi's *Rigoletto*, Marguerite in Gounod's *Faust.*

**Kellogg, Frank Billings.** 1856–1937. American statesman, b. Potsdam, N.Y.; to Minnesota (1865). Studied law; adm. to bar (1877) and practiced in Rochester, Minn. Served as special counsel for government against the paper trust and Standard Oil trust; also, special counsel for Interstate Commerce Commission in investigating Harriman railroads. U.S. senator (1917–23); U.S. ambassador to Great Britain (1924–25); U.S. secretary of state (1925–29). With Briand negotiated antiwar pact (the Kellogg Pact), a multilateral treaty to outlaw war, signed at Paris (Aug. 27, 1928) by fifteen nations. Awarded Nobel peace prize for 1929. Judge, Permanent Court of International Justice (from 1930).

**Kellogg, John Harvey.** 1852–1943. American surgeon; superintendent and surgeon, Battle Creek (Mich.) Sanitarium (from 1876); founder and president (1923–26), Battle Creek College; founder and medical director, Miami-Battle Creek Sanitarium, Miami Springs, Florida. Inventor of medical instruments and apparatus. Other fields of activity include work on nutrition, light therapy, public health, and race betterment.

**Kellogg, Vernon Lyman.** 1867–1937. American zoologist, b. Emporia, Kans.; professor, Stanford U. (1894–1920). Served in relief work in Belgium, Poland, and Russia (1915–21). Author of *American Insects* (1904), *Darwinism Today* (1907), *The Animals and Man* (1911), *Nuova, the New Bee* (1921), *Mind and Heredity* (1923), *Evolution* (1924), *Biology* (1925), etc.

**Kel'ly** (kĕl'ĭ), **Co'lin** (kŏ'lĭn) **P.** 1915–1941. American army captain; pilot of bomber that destroyed Japanese battleship (Dec. 9, 1941) following attack on Pearl Harbor; when his airplane was damaged by enemy fire, ordered crew to bail out; died in crash. Posthumously awarded Distinguished Service Cross.

**Kelly, Eleanor,** *nee* **Mer'cein'** (mâr'sĕn'; *orig.* -săɴ'). 1880– . American writer, b. Milwaukee, Wis.; m. Robert Morrow Kelly, Jr. (1901; d. 1926). Author under maiden name of *Toya the Unlike* (1913), *The Mansion House* (1923), *Spanish Holiday* (1930), *Arabesque* (1933), *Mixed Company* (1936), etc.

**Kelly, Eric Philbrook.** 1884–1960. American writer; best known for his books for children, as *The Trumpeter of Krakow* (1928, awarded John Newbery medal), *The Blacksmith of Vilno* (1930), *The Christmas Nightingale* (1932), *In Clean Hay* (1937), etc.

**Kelly, George.** 1887–1974. American actor and playwright; author of *The Torch-Bearers, The Show-Off, Craig's Wife* (awarded Pulitzer prize in 1925), *Behold the Bridegroom* (1927), *Maggie the Magnificent* (1929), *Philip Goes Forth* (1931), *Reflected Glory* (1936).

**Kelly, Howard Atwood.** 1858–1943. American surgeon; professor of gynecology, Johns Hopkins (1889–1919), and gynecological surgeon, Johns Hopkins Hospital (1899–1919). Author of *Operative Gynecology* (2 vols., 1898, 1906), *A Scientific Man and the Bible* (1925), etc.

**Kelly, Hugh.** 1739–1777. Irish playwright and miscellaneous writer; author of *Memoirs of a Magdalen* (1767) and plays, including *False Delicacy* (1768) and *A Word to the Wise* (1770).

**Kelly, James Edward.** 1855–1933. American sculptor, b. New York City; became known as "the sculptor of American history." Notable works: *Sheridan's Ride;* bronze busts of Grant, Sherman, Sheridan, Hancock, and other Civil War commanders; *Paul Revere;* equestrian statue of Colonel Roosevelt at San Juan Hill; busts of Admiral Dewey, Admiral Sampson, and other Spanish-American war commanders; bust of Thomas A. Edison.

**Kelly, James Fitzmaurice-.** See FITZMAURICE-KELLY.

**Kelly, John.** 1822–1886. American politician, b. New York City; member of Tammany Hall (from 1853); member, U.S. House of Representatives (1855–58); sheriff, city and county of New York (1859–62, 1865–67). As grand sachem of Tammany Hall, reorganized the Society after it had been discredited by the Tweed Ring exposures. Comptroller of New York (1876–79).

**Kelly, Michael J.** 1857–1894. American professional baseball player, b. Troy, N.Y.; with Cincinnati (1879), Chicago (1880–87), Boston (1887–90; 1892), New York (1893); hero of the popular song *Slide, Kelly, Slide.*

**Kelly, Myra.** 1875–1910. Author, b. Dublin, Ireland; to U.S. as a child. Teacher on New York's East Side (from 1899); m. Allan Macnaughton (1905). Her stories, based on her knowledge of the east side, include *Little Citizens* (1904), *The Isle of Dreams* (1907), *Little Aliens* (1910), etc.

**Kelly, William.** 1811–1888. American inventor, b. Pittsburgh, Pa. Invented converter (later known as Bessemer converter, from an Englishman who invented similar process) for the making of steel, utilizing an air blast on molten iron and the natural carbon content of molten cast iron to obtain greater heat for the process; patent issued (1857).

**Kel'sen** (kĕl'zĕn), **Hans.** 1881– . German jurist; professor, Cologne (1930–33), Geneva Graduate Institute of International Studies (1933–40), Prague German U. (1936–38), in U.S. (1941 ff.). Among his many treatises are *Das Problem der Souveränität und die Theorie des Völkerrechts* (1920), *Sozialismus und Staat* (1925), *Legal Technique in International Law* (1939), etc.

**Kel'sey** (kĕl'sĭ), **Francis Willey.** 1858–1927. American scholar; taught classics, U. of Michigan (1889–1927). An organizer of U. of Michigan expeditions to Near East, which excavated at Antioch, Carthage, and Karanis (in Egypt).

**Kel'tie** (kĕl'tĭ), Sir **John Scott.** 1840–1927. British editor, b. in Dundee, Scot.; editor of *Statesman's Year-Book* (1884–1927). Librarian (1885–92) and secretary (1892–1915), Royal Geographical Society. Author of *The Partition of Africa* (1894), etc.

**Kel'vin** (kĕl'vĭn), 1st Baron. **William Thom'son** (tŏm's'n). 1824–1907. British mathematician and physicist, b. Belfast, Ireland. Educ. Glasgow and Cambridge. Professor, Glasgow (1846–99). While undergraduate wrote paper on *The Uniform Motion of Heat in Homogeneous Solid Bodies, and Its Connection with the Mathematical Theory of Electricity.* Developed Joule's doctrine of convertibility of heat and work; advocated absolute system of measurements; proposed the absolute, or Kelvin, scale of temperature; propounded doctrine of dissipation of energy; by mathematical analysis laid foundation of theory of electric oscillations; investigated electric currents in cables; employed in laying Atlantic telegraph cables (1857–58, 1865–66); invented mirror galvanometer used in receiving telegraph signals, the siphon recorder, and (with Fleeming Jenkin) the curb transmitter; investigated electrodynamic properties of metals and the mathematical theory of magnetism; contributed to theory of elasticity in paper *On Vortex Atoms;* improved mariner's compass (1873–78); devised apparatus for taking soundings (1872); invented tide predictor, a harmonic analyzer, and numerous other devices; estimated age of the earth as not over 100 million years. One of original members of Order of Merit (1902).

**Ke·mal' A·ta·türk'** (kĕ·mäl' ä·tä·türk'). *Formerly* **Mus·ta·fa'** *or* **Mus·ta·pha'** (mo͝os·tä·fä'), **Kemal.** *Later* **Kemal Pa·sha'** (pä·shä'). 1881–1938. Turkish general and statesman; president of Turkish Republic (1923–38); b. Salonika. Ran away from school at Monastir and entered military college in Constantinople; given name Kemal, *i.e.* "perfection," for his excellence in mathematics; because his views too radical, not closely identified with Young Turk movement (1908); served in Turkish-Italian War (1911); military attaché at Sofia (1913–14). In World War had command of army division at Gallipoli (1915), in Caucasus (1916–17), and in Palestine (1918); received title of pasha for efficient service; strongly opposed harsh terms of peace treaty; organized Turkish Nationalist party (1919). Elected president of provisional government by National Assembly (1920); organized forces to oppose occupation of Turkey by Greek army (1920); inspired Turkish nationalist resistance; defeated Greeks at Sakarya River (1921) and took Smyrna (1922); officially named **Gha·zi'** (gä·zē'), *i.e.* "victorious"; secured Treaty of Lausanne (1923) favorable to Turkish cause. After deposition of sultan (1922) unanimously elected first president of Turkish Republic (1923); re-elected (1927, 1931, 1935); inaugurated many major reforms; abolished caliphate (1924), monasteries, ancient modes of dress (1925–26), polygamy; substituted Roman alphabet for Arabic (1928); introduced Gregorian calendar, new civil and penal codes; held a census (1927), and ordered all Turks to register family names (1934); received by act of National Assembly family name of **Atatürk,** *i.e.* "chief Turk"; inaugurated industrial plans; by convention with great powers (1936) secured right to fortify straits of Bosporus and Dardanelles; made friendly alliances with Balkan countries and Russia.

**Ke·mal' Bey** (kĕ·mäl' bā'). *Orig.* **Meh·med' Na·mik'** (mĕ·mĕt' nä·mĭk'). 1840–1888. Turkish poet, writer, and patriot; champion of the Young Turks. Author of much verse in Arabic, Persian, and Turkish, and of translations from Bacon, Rousseau, and others, the dramas *Fatherland* (1872) and *Ākif Bey*, a *History of Turkey,* historical novels, biographies, etc.

**Kem'ble** (kĕm'b'l). Name of English family of actors, including the following:
**Roger Kemble** (1721–1802); m. **Sarah Ward** (1753); formed traveling company in which their children acted; acted Falstaff at the Haymarket, London (1788).
Their children: (1) **Sarah.** = Sarah SIDDONS. (2) **John Philip** (1757–1823), m. (1787) **Priscilla Hopkins** (1756–1845); with Drury Lane company (1783–1802; its manager from 1788); played many Shakespearean roles; regarded as chief founder of declamatory school of acting. (3) **Stephen,** *in full* **George Stephen** (1758–1822), Shakespearean actor; m. (1783) **Elizabeth Satch'ell** [săch'ĕl] (1763?–1841), Shakespearean actress; managed Edinburgh Theatre (1792–1800); played Falstaff at Covent Garden (1806) and Drury Lane (1816). (4) **Elizabeth** (1761–1836), m. (1785) Charles Edward Whitlock; accompanied him to America and acted there. (5) **Charles** (1775–1854), actor at Drury Lane and Covent Garden; manager of Covent Garden (1822 ff.); excelled in comic roles; m. (1806) **Maria Theresa De Camp** [dĕ kămp'; dê] (1774–1838), who played in Gay's *Beggar's Opera* and in her own plays *The Day After the Wedding* and *Smiles and Tears,* as well as Shakespearean roles.
Members of later generations include: Stephen's son **Henry Stephen** (1789–1836). Charles's daughter **Adelaide** (1814?–1879), opera singer, who married (1843) **Edward John Sartoris.** Her older sister, **Frances Anne,** *commonly called* **Fanny** (1809–1893), who appeared first in her father's company at Covent Garden; toured U.S. (1832–34); m. (1834) Pierce Butler of Philadelphia (divorced 1848); gave dramatic readings in England and U.S.; resided in U.S. (1849–68, 1873–78). Charles's grandson **Henry** (1848–1907), who made stage debut at Dublin (1867); excelled in comic roles, as Oliver Surface in *School for Scandal.*
Charles's son **John Mitchell Kemble** (1807–1857) was a philologist; educ. Cambridge; studied under Grimm in Germany; edited *Beowulf* (1833); lectured on Anglo-Saxon at Cambridge; edited *British and Foreign Review* (1835–44); author of *The Saxons in England* (1844); editor of *State Papers* of the period 1688–1714.

**Kemble, Edward Windsor.** 1861–1933. American illustrator and cartoonist; best known for his portrayals of Negro characters. Illustrated *Uncle Tom's Cabin, Huckleberry Finn, Pudd'nhead Wilson;* author of *Kemble's Coons, Comical Coons, Kemble's Sketch Book,* etc.

**Ke'mény** (kĕ'mān·y'), Baron **Zsigmond.** 1814–1875. Hungarian novelist and political writer.

**Kem'eys** (kĕm'ēz), **Edward.** 1843–1907. American sculptor; self-taught; specialized in sculpture of wild animals.

**Kem'mer·er** (kĕm'ẽr·ẽr), **Edwin Walter.** 1875–1945. American economist; professor, Princeton (from 1912). Financial adviser to various governments, including: Mexico (1917), Guatemala (1919), Colombia (1923), Chile (1925), Poland (1926), Ecuador (1926–27), Bolivia (1927), China (1929), Peru (1931).

**Kemnitz, Martin.** See CHEMNITZ.

**Kemp** (kĕmp), **Harry Hibbard.** 1883–1960. American writer; gained experience by working his way around the world, and living as a tramp in U.S. Author of novels: *Tramping on Life* (1922), *More Miles* (1927); verse: *The Cry of Youth* (1914), *Chanteys and Ballads* (1920), *The Sea and the Dunes* (1926); also of a few plays, including *Judas* (1910).

**Kemp, James Furman.** 1859–1926. American geologist; teaching, Columbia (1891–1926). Author of *Ore Deposits of the United States* (1893), *Handbook of Rocks* (1896).

**Kemp** *or* **Kempe** (kĕmp), **John.** 1380?–1454. English prelate; archbishop of York (1426–52) and chancellor of England (1426–32, 1450); archbishop of Canterbury (1452). Created cardinal priest by Pope Eugenius IV (1439) and cardinal bishop by Pope Nicholas (1452).

**Kemp, William.** fl. 1600. English comedian and dancer who had roles in plays by Shakespeare and Ben Jonson.

**Kempe** (kĕmp), **Harry Robert.** 1852–1935. English electrical engineer; associated with Sir Samuel Canning, Sir Charles Wheatstone, and Robert Sabine, British pioneers in telegraphy; author of *The Electrical Engineer's Pocket-Book*, and *The Engineer's Year Book* (36 issues).

**Kem'pe·len** (kĕm'pĕ·lĕn), **Wolfgang von.** 1734–1804. Austrian inventor of an allegedly automatic chess-playing machine (actually operated by a man concealed within) and a machine producing speech sounds.

**Kem'pe·ner** (kĕm'pĕ·nẽr) *or* **Kem'pe·neer** (-nār), **Peter de.** *Called in Spain* **Pedro de Cam·pa'ña** (thā käm·pä'nyä). 1503–1580. Religious painter and tapestry designer, b. Brussels. Lived mostly in Seville (1537–62); again in Brussels (1562); chief engineer to duke of Alba, and director of tapestry works.

**Kem'pen·felt** (kĕm'pĕn·fĕlt), **Richard.** 1718–1782. British naval commander, of Swedish descent. Rear admiral (1780); commanded *Royal George* (sank, 1782).

**Kem'per** (kĕm'pẽr), **Reuben.** d. 1827. American adventurer, b. in Virginia; attempted to overthrow Spanish government in west Florida; led unsuccessful expeditions to capture Baton Rouge (1804), Mobile and Pensacola (1810).

**Kempf** (kĕmpf), **Paul.** 1856–1920. German astronomer; at Potsdam astrophysical observatory (from 1878). Worked on determination of the mass of Jupiter, the period of the sun's rotation, the wave lengths of 300 lines in the solar spectrum, and the brightness of stars; also on the absorption of sunlight by the earth's atmosphere and a photographic survey of the northern skies.

**Kempis, Thomas a.** See THOMAS A KEMPIS.

**Kempner, Alfred.** See Alfred KERR.

**Kemp'–Welch'** (kĕmp'wĕlch'; -wĕlsh'), **Lucy Elizabeth.** 1869–1958. English painter of animals, esp. horses.

**Ken** *or* **Kenn** (kĕn), **Thomas.** 1637–1711. English prelate and hymn writer; bishop of Bath and Wells (1684–91); attended Charles II's deathbed, and Monmouth at his execution (1685). One of the "seven bishops" (see William SANCROFT) who petitioned against James II's Declaration of Indulgence (1688) but were acquitted of a charge of seditious libel; refused to take oath of allegiance to William and Mary (1689). Author of hymns, including *Praise God, from whom all blessings flow* and *Awake, my soul, and with the sun.*

**Ken'dal** (kĕn'd'l), Dame **Madge.** *Nee* **Margaret Brunton Rob'ert·son** (rŏb'ẽrt·s'n). 1849–1935. English actress; sister of T. W. Robertson, the playwright; m. (1869) **William Hunter Grim'ston** [grĭm'stŭn] (1843–1917), *professional name* **Kendal.** Acted with her husband in Shakespearean revivals and old English comedies; excelled in comedy. Dame of the British Empire (1926).

**Ken'dall** (kĕn'd'l), **Amos.** 1789–1869. American politician, b. Dunstable, Mass. U.S. postmaster general (1835–40).

**Kendall, Arthur Isaac.** 1877–1967. American bacteriologist; author of *Bacteriology—General, Pathological and Intestinal* and *Civilization and the Microbe.*

**Kendall, Edward Calvin.** 1886–1972. Amer. biochemist, b. S. Norwalk, Conn. With Mayo Clinic (1921–51); awarded Nobel prize in physiology and medicine (1950) with P. Hench and T. Reichstein for hormone research.

**Kendall, George Wilkins.** 1809–1867. American journalist; founder and editor, the New Orleans *Picayune* (1837); war correspondent during Mexican War.

**Kendall, Henry Clarence.** 1841–1882. Australian poet.

**Kendall, Sergeant,** *in full* **William Sergeant.** 1869–1938. American painter and sculptor, b. Spuyten Duyvil, New York. Dean of the School of Fine Arts, Yale (1913–22). Among his paintings are: *Beatrice*, Pennsylvania Academy of Art, Philadelphia; *An Interlude*, National Gallery, Washington, D.C.; *Narcissa*, Corcoran Gallery, Washington, D.C.; *The Seer* and *Psyche*, Metropolitan Museum of Art, New York City.

**Kendall, William Mitchell.** 1856–1941. American architect; member of firm of McKim, Mead & White, New York, and had a part in designing New York Post Office, New York Municipal Office Building, Arlington Memorial Bridge, etc.

**Ken'drew** (kĕn'drü), **John Cowdery.** 1917– . British molecular biologist. At Cambridge (1945– ). Awarded Nobel prize in chemistry (1962) with M. F. Perutz for studies of the structures of globular proteins.

**Kenmure,** Viscounts of. See GORDON family.

**Ken'nan** (kĕn'ăn), **George.** 1845–1924. American journalist; assistant manager, Associated Press, Washington, D.C. (1877–85). In Russia and Siberia for Century Co. (1885–86). Correspondent in Cuba for the *Outlook* (1898) and in Japan during Russo-Japanese War. Visited Martinique and climbed Mt. Pelée after its eruption in 1902. Author of *Siberia and the Exile System* (2 vols., 1891), *Campaigning in Cuba* (1899), etc.

**Kennan, George Frost.** 1904– . American diplomat and historian, b. Milwaukee, Wis. U.S. ambassador to U.S.S.R. (1952–53), Yugoslavia (1961–63); wrote *Russia Leaves the War* (1956), *Memoirs 1925–1950* (1967).

**Ken'ne·dy** (kĕn'ĕ·dĭ), **Arthur Garfield.** 1880–1954. American philologist; professor, Stanford U. (1914–45). Compiler (with J. S. P. Tatlock, 1927) of *Concordance to Complete Works of Chaucer.*

**Kennedy, David Matthew.** 1905– . American banker; U.S. secretary of treasury (1969–71).

**Kennedy, Edmund B.** d. 1848. Australian explorer; second in command in Sir Thomas Livingstone Mitchell's expedition to trace course of Victoria River (1847).

**Kennedy, John Fitzgerald.** 1917–1963. Thirty-fifth president of the U.S. (1961–63); b. Brookline, Mass.; son of Joseph Patrick Kennedy; B.S., Harvard (1940); member U.S. House of Representatives (1947–53), Senate (1953–60); assassinated at Dallas, Texas, Nov. 22, 1963. His brother **Robert Francis** (1925–1968), lawyer, b. Brookline, Mass.; A.B. Harvard (1948), LL.B., U. of Va. (1951); U.S. attorney general (1961–64); to U.S. Senate (1965–68); assassinated at Los Angeles, California.

**Kennedy, John Pendleton.** *Pseudonym* **Mark Lit'tle·ton** (lĭt''l·tŭn). 1795–1870. American novelist and politician; member, U.S. House of Representatives (1838–39; 1841–45); U.S. secretary of the navy (1852–53). Author of *Horse-Shoe Robinson* (1835), *Quodlibet* (1840).

**Kennedy, Joseph Patrick.** 1888–1969. Amer. businessman and diplomat.

**Kennedy, Margaret.** 1896–1967. English novelist; m. Sir David Davies (1925). Author of *The Constant Nymph* (1924; dramatized 1926), *Red Sky at Morning* (1927), *Together and Apart* (1936), *The Midas Touch* (1938).

**Kennedy, Rann.** 1772–1851. English clergyman and poet; author of *The Reign of Youth* (1840) and other poems. His son **Benjamin Hall** (1804–1889) was headmaster of Shrewsbury (1836–66), professor of Greek at Cambridge (1867–89), author of *Between Whiles* (1877). **Charles Rann Kennedy** (1871–1950), playwright; great-grandson of Rann Kennedy; actor, press agent, theatrical business manager in England (to 1905); to U.S., settled in New York City, devoted himself to writing plays, including *The Servant in the House* (1908), *The Terrible Meek* (1911), *The Idol-Breaker* (1914), *The Army with Banners* (1917), *The Salutation* (1925), *Flaming Ministers* (1932), *Beggar's Gift* (1935). m. (1898) **Edith Wynne Mat'thi·son** (măth'ĭ·s'n), (1875–1955), b. Birmingham, England, actress.

**Kennedy, Walter.** 1460?–?1508. Scottish poet; educ. Glasgow. Considered poetic rival of William Dunbar with whom he carried on a fliting; author of *The Praise of Age, The Passion of Christ*, etc.

**Kennedy, William Sloane.** 1850–1929. American biographer of Longfellow (1882), Whittier (1882), Holmes (1883), etc.

**Ken'nel·ly** (kĕn'l·ĭ), **Arthur Edwin.** 1861–1939. American electrical engineer, b. Bombay, India. To U.S., and became electrical assistant to Thomas A. Edison (1887–94); professor, Harvard (1902–30), M.I.T. (1913–24). Authority on magnetics in engineering and alternating electric currents. Announced in the same year (1902) as Oliver Heaviside the probable existence of the region of ionized air favorable to radio-wave propagation, now known as the Heaviside, or Kennelly-Heaviside, layer or region.

**Ken'net** (kĕn'ĕt; -ĭt), Lady **Kathleen,** *nee* **Bruce** (bro͞os). 1881?–1947. Eng. sculptor; m. (1908) Capt. Robert Falcon Scott, antarctic explorer (d. 1912), and (1922) Sir Edward Hilton Young (1879–1960), 1st Baron Kennet, politician and writer on finance. Among works designed by her are a monument of Captain Smith of the *Titanic*, at Lichfield; of Captain Scott, in Waterloo Place, London; of Adam Lindsay Gordon in Westminster Abbey; and many portrait busts.

**Ken'neth** (kĕn'ĕth; -ĭth). Name of two kings of Scotland. **Kenneth I,** *called* **Mac·Al'pine** [măk·ăl'pĭn; -ôl'pĭn; -ăl'pīn] (d. ?858 A.D.), traditional founder of Scottish kingdom; subdued the Picts (841–846); united them with Gaelic Scots in kingdom first called Scotland; established his capital at Scone. **Kenneth II** (d. 995 A.D.), son of Malcolm I; king (971–995); consolidated his lands; at war almost continually with English.

**Ken'nett** (kĕn'ĕt; -ĭt), **Robert Hatch.** 1864–1932. Anglican clergyman and Orientalist, b. in Ramsgate; regius professor of Hebrew, Cambridge.

**Kennett, White.** 1660–1728. English clergyman and historian; author of *Compleat History of England* (1706).

**Ken'ney** (kĕn'ĭ), **George Churchill.** 1889– . American army officer; educ. M.I.T. (1907–11); railroad engineer (1911–17); officer in U.S. army air service (1917–51); appointed commander of allied air forces in Southwest Pacific (1942).

**Ken'ney** (kĕn'ĭ), **James.** 1780–1849. Irish-born playwright in England; author of farces and comedies, including *Raising the Wind* (1803), *Turn Him Out* (1812), *Sweethearts and Wives* (1823).

**Ken'ni·cott** (kĕn'ĭ·kŭt), **Benjamin.** 1718–1783. English biblical scholar.

**Ken'ning·ton** (kĕn'ĭng·tŭn), **Eric Henri.** 1888-1960. British painter and sculptor.

**Ken'ny** (kĕn'ĭ), **Elizabeth.** 1886–1952. Australian nurse; while working as nurse in back-country districts of Queensland, developed method for treating victims of infantile paralysis, consisting essentially of the stimulating and re-educating of the affected muscles; set up clinic in Townsville (1933); her method reported unfavorably by a royal commission of inquiry (1935) but later (1939) accepted for use in Australian hospitals; to U.S. (1940); under medical sponsorship in Minneapolis established Kenny Institute to train practitioners in her methods; resigned (1945).

**Ken'rick** (kĕn'rĭk), **Francis Patrick.** 1796–1863. American Roman Catholic prelate, b. Dublin; to U.S. (1821); bishop (1830); archbishop of Baltimore (1851).

**Ken'sett** (kĕn'sĕt; -sĭt), **John Frederick.** 1816–1872. American landscape painter; studio in New York (from 1847); known as a painter of the Hudson River school.

**Kent** (kĕnt), Dukes of. (1) **Edward Augustus.** Duke of **Kent and Stra·thern'** (strȧ·thĕrn'; strȧ-). 1767–1820. 4th son of George III of England, and father of Queen Victoria. English soldier; major general (1793), lieutenant general (1796), and general (1799); commander in chief of forces in British North America (1799–1800); governor of Gibraltar (1802–03). Created field marshal (1805). m. (1818) **Victoria Mary Louisa** (1786–1861), daughter of Duke Francis, hereditary prince of Saxe-Saalfeld-Coburg, sister of Leopold I of Belgium, and widow of Emich Charles, hereditary prince of Leiningen-Dachsburg-Hardenburg; their only child became Queen Victoria.

(2) Prince **George Edward Alexander Edmund.** 1902–1942. Brother of King George VI of England; m. (1934) Princess Marina (1906– ), daughter of Prince Nicholas of Greece.

**Kent,** Earls of. Title held by Bishop Odo (d. 1097), Hubert de Burgh, members of Holland family (1360–1408), *Grey de Ruthin* branch of Grey family (1465–1740).

**Kent, Frank Richardson.** 1877–1958. American journalist, b. Baltimore. On staff of Baltimore *Sun* (from 1898), managing editor (1911–21), vice-president (from 1921).

**Kent, James.** 1763–1847. American jurist, b. Fredericksburgh, Putnam County, N.Y.; grad. Yale (1781). Adm. to bar (1785); practiced, Poughkeepsie, N.Y. (1785–93); New York City (from 1793); professor of law, Columbia (1793–98; 1823–26). Judge, New York supreme court (1798–1823) and chief judge (1804–23); chancellor, New York court of chancery (1814–23). His decisions did much to create American system of equity jurisdiction based on principles established in English chancery practice. Author of *Commentaries on American Law* (4 vols.; 1826–30). Elected to American Hall of Fame (1900).

**Kent, Rockwell.** 1882–1971. American artist, b. Tarrytown Heights, N.Y.; known for landscape and figure painting, and for wood engraving and lithography. Wrote *Of Men and Mountains* (1959).

**Kent, William.** 1684–1748. English artist and architect; worked under patronage of earl of Burlington; was criticized and often ridiculed by Hogarth, Chesterfield, and others. Designed Devonshire House in Piccadilly; carved statue of Shakespeare in Westminster Abbey.

**Ken'ti·gern** (kĕn'tĭ·gûrn) *or* **Mun'go** (mŭng'gō), Saint. 518?–603. Apostle of Strathclyde Britons in Scotland; patron saint of Glasgow. Chosen bishop at Cathures (now Glasgow); driven by persecution to take refuge in Wales (c. 553), where he founded monastery at Llanelwy (now St. Asaph's); returned (c. 573) to reclaim Picts of Galloway from idolatry.

**Ken'ton** (kĕn't'n; -tŭn), **Simon.** 1755–1836. American pioneer and Indian fighter, b. in Virginia; associate of Daniel Boone (1775–78).

**Ken'wor'thy** (kĕn'wûr'thĭ), **Joseph Montague.** 10th Baron **Stra·bol'gi** [strȧ·bō'gĭ] (cr. 1318). 1886-1953. British naval commander. Son of **Cuthbert Matthias Kenworthy** (1853–1934), 9th baron. Commander of the *Bullfinch* and the *Commonwealth* in World War I; asst. chief of staff, Gibraltar (1918–20); M.P., Liberal (1919–26) and Laborite (1926–31); chief Labor whip, House of Lords. Author of *Will Civilization Crash?* (1927), *New Wars, New Weapons* (1930), *Sailors, Statesmen—and Others* (1933), *Narvik and After* (1940), *The Campaign in the Low Countries* (1940).

**Ken′yon** (kĕn′yŭn), Sir **Frederic George.** 1863–1952. English classical scholar; director and principal librarian, British Museum (1909–30). Edited classical texts, prepared catalogues of manuscripts in various collections, edited poetical works of the Brownings, etc.

**Kenyon, John.** 1784–1856. English poet and philanthropist, b. in Jamaica; patron and friend of chief literary men of the time, including Coleridge, Wordsworth, Lamb, Browning (whom he first introduced to Elizabeth Barrett), Landor, and George Ticknor the American historian. At his death, bequeathed large fortune to be divided among charitable institutions and friends, leaving specific legacy of £10,000 to Browning.

**Kenyon, John Samuel.** 1874–1959. American phonetician and educator, b. Medina, Ohio. A.B., Hiram College, Ohio (1898), Ph.D., Harvard (1908). Professor of English, Hiram Coll. (from 1916). Author of *American Pronunciation—a Textbook of Phonetics* (1st ed., 1924); coauthor (with Thomas A. Knott, *q.v.*) of *A Pronouncing Dictionary of American English* (1944). Editor of phonetic terms, consulting editor on pronunciation, and reviser of "A Guide to Pronunciation," *Webster's New International Dictionary, Second Edition.*

**Kenyon, William Squire.** 1869–1933. American jurist and legislator; U.S. senator from Iowa (1911–22); cosponsor, with representative Edwin Y. Webb, of the Webb-Kenyon Act (1913) prohibiting shipment in interstate commerce of intoxicating liquors. U.S. circuit court judge, 8th district (1922–33).

**Kenzan Ogata.** See OGATA.

**Ke′o·kuk** (kē′ō·kŭk). fl. 1790–1848. American Indian chief of the Sac tribe; b. near present city of Rock Island, Ill.; aided Americans at time of Black Hawk War (1832); in Washington, arranged peace between Sacs and Sioux (1837). Keokuk, Iowa, is named in his honor.

**Keown** (?kūn), **Anna Gordon.** 1897–1957. English poet and novelist; m. W. H. Seymour (1921; marriage dissolved, 1928). Author of *The Bright of Eye* and *The Winds* (verse), and the novels *The Cat Who Saw God, Mr. Theobald's Devil*, etc.

**Kep′ler** (kĕp′lẽr), **Johannes.** 1571–1630. German astronomer, b. at Weil, Württemberg. Educ. Tübingen, where he was influenced by Copernican principles. Professor, Graz (1594); assistant to Tycho Brahe (*q.v.*) at observatory near Prague (1600); succeeded Brahe at observatory and as imperial mathematician and court astronomer (1601). Mathematician to the states of Upper Austria at Linz (1612); moved to Ulm (1626), and completed and published Brahe's *Rudolphine Tables;* moved to Sagan in Silesia (1628). Discovered the three important laws (Kepler's laws) of planetary motion, announcing the first two in his *Astronomia Nova de Motibus Stellae Martis ex Observationibus Tychonis Brahe* (1609) and the third in *Harmonice Mundi* (1619). Also wrote on optics; approximated the law of refraction. Did pioneer work that led to invention of the calculus.

**Kep′pel** (kĕp′ĕl), **Arnold Joost van.** 1st Earl of **Al′be·marle** (ăl′bē·märl). 1669–1718. Dutch soldier; devoted follower of William III in England, after whose death he returned to Holland; fought at Ramillies and Oudenarde. His son **William Anne Keppel** (1702–1754), 2d earl, British soldier, was governor of Virginia (1737); general on staff at Dettingen (1743); wounded at Fontenoy (1745); fought at Culloden Moor (1746); commander in chief in North Britain (1748); privy councilor (1750). His son **George Keppel** (1724–1772), 3d earl, British soldier, was aide to duke of Cumberland at Fontenoy and Culloden Moor; M.P. (1746–54); general (1759); governor of Jersey (1761); commanded land forces in capture of Havana (1762–63). **Augustus Keppel** (1725–1786), 1st Viscount Keppel, British naval officer, 2d son of 2d earl, was sent to treat with dey of Algiers (1748–51); served under Hawks (1757); captured French settlement of Gorée (1758); commanded leading ship in battle of Quiberon Bay (1759); second in command at capture of Havana (1762); vice-admiral (1770); commander in chief of grand fleet (1778); met French in indecisive action off Ushant and, through disagreement with second in command, allowed French to escape (1778); acquitted by court-martial; first lord of admiralty (1782). **George Thomas Keppel** (1799–1891), 6th Earl of Albemarle, grandson of 3d earl, fought at Waterloo (1815); served at Cape of Good Hope and in India; Whig M.P. (1832); general (1874); wrote *Fifty Years of My Life.* His son **William Coutts Keppel** (1832–1894), 7th Earl of Albemarle and Viscount **Bur′y** (bĕr′ĭ), was superintendent of Indian affairs in Canada (1854–57); M.P. (1857); treasurer of household (1859–66); undersecretary for war (1878–80, 1885–86). Sir **Henry Keppel** (1809–1904), British naval officer, son of 4th earl of Albemarle, served in Opium War (1841–42), in campaign against Borneo pirates (1843–44), in Baltic campaign (1854); commanded naval brigade ashore at Sevastopol (1855); took part in destruction of Chinese fleet (1857); admiral (1869); author of *A Sailor's Life under Four Sovereigns* (3 vols., 1899); member, Order of Merit (1902). His son Sir **Colin Richard Keppel** (1862–1947), naval officer, served in Egyptian War (1882), in Sudan (1884–85), on Nile (1897–98), in battle of Omdurman (1898); commanded Atlantic fleet as rear admiral (1909–10); admiral, retired (1917).

**Keppel, Frederick.** 1845–1912. Art connoisseur and dealer, b. Tullow, Ireland; to Canada (1862) and U.S. (1864); authority on prints and etchings; offices in New York (from 1868).

**Keppel, Frederick Paul.** 1875–1943. American educator; A.B. (1898), dean of college (1910–18), Columbia U.; president of Carnegie Corporation (1923–41).

**Kepp′ler** (kĕp′lẽr), **Joseph.** 1838–1894. Cartoonist, b. Vienna, Austria; to U.S. (1867); founded and edited *Puck*, humorous weekly (from 1876, first in German; English edition inaugurated 1877).

**Ker** (kär; kâr; kûr). (1) Variant of CARR; (2) see KERR family.

**Ker** (kâr), **William Paton.** 1855–1923. British scholar, b. in Glasgow; author of *Epic and Romance* (1897), *The Dark Ages* (1904), *Essays on Medieval Literature* (1905).

**Kerala.** Hindu dynasty. See CHERA.

**Ké′ra′try′** (kā′rȧ′trē′), **Auguste Hilarion de.** 1769–1859. French politician and man of letters; active in July Revolution (1830); councilor of state (1830) and member of the Chamber of Peers (1837); entered private life after the coup d'état (Dec. 2, 1851). His son Comte **Émile de Kératry** (1832–1905) was a soldier and politician; served in the Crimea and in Mexico, and resigned from the army (1865); editor of *Revue Moderne;* member of Chamber of Deputies (1869); prefect of police in Paris (1870); as official under Thiers, suppressed uprisings in the country (1871–72).

**Keraunos.** See PTOLEMY KERAUNOS.

**Ke·ren′ski** (kyĭ·ryān′skû·ĭ; *Angl.* kĕ·rĕn′skĭ), **Aleksandr Feodorovich.** 1881–1970. Russian revolutionary leader, b. Simbirsk (Ulyanovsk). Joined Labor party although in reality a Social Revolutionary; after first Revolution (Feb., 1917) made minister of justice in provisional government; minister of war (May–July, 1917); succeeded Prince Lvov (July–Nov., 1917) as prime minister; overthrown by Bolshevik Revolution (Nov., 1917) because of moderate policies and indecision; fled from Petrograd to Paris; editor of Social Revolutionary paper *Dni* in Paris.

**Ker'gué'len'-Tré'ma'rec'** (kĕr'gā'lĕn'trā'mȧ'rĕk'), **Yves Joseph de.** 1734?–1797. French navigator, b. Quimper. Discovered the subantarctic Kerguelen, or Desolation, Island while searching for new southern continent in southern Indian Ocean (1772).

**Kerhouel, Gaëtan.** Pseudonym of Paul VIGNÉ.

**Kerim Khan.** See KARIM KHAN.

**Ker'le** (kĕr'lĕ), **Jacobus de.** 1531?–1591. Flemish composer and music scholar; composed hymns, vesper psalms, Masses, motets, etc.

**Kerll** (kĕrl), **Johann Kaspar von.** *Surname also* **Kerl** *or* **Kherl** *or* **Cher'le** (kĕr'lȧ). 1627–1693. German organist and composer.

**Kern** (kĕrn), **Hermann.** 1823–1891. German educator of the Herbartian school.

**Kern** (kĕrn), **Jan Hendrik.** 1833–1917. Dutch Indologist and philologist, b. in Java. Professor of Sanskrit, Leiden (1865–1903); edited and translated Indian texts, and wrote a *History of Buddhism in India* (2 vols., 1881–83).

**Kern** (kûrn), **Jerome David.** 1885–1945. American composer, b. New York City. Best known for his scores in light operas, as *Very Good Eddie, Have a Heart, Oh Boy, Rock-a-Bye Baby, Sally, Stepping Stones, Sunny, Show Boat, Blue Eyes, Sweet Adeline, The Cat and the Fiddle, Roberta, Swing Time, When You're in Love,* etc.

**Kern** (kĕrn), **Johann Konrad.** 1808–1888. Swiss statesman. Member of Swiss Diet (1833–48); led Swiss opposition to French demand for expulsion of Prince Louis Napoleon (1838); helped overthrow the Sonderbund (1847), and took part in drawing up new federal constitution (1848). President of federal court (1850); Swiss minister to France (1857–83).

**Kern, Otto.** 1863– . German classical philologist and Hellenist; author of works on history of Greek religion, Greek epigraphy, history of classical philology.

**Ker'na·han** (kûr'nȧ·hăn), **Coulson.** 1858–1943. English writer; author of *A Dead Man's Diary, A World Without a Child, Begging the Moon's Pardon* (1930), *A Dog and his Master* (1932), *A World Without the Christ* (1934). His wife, **Mary Jean Hickling,** *nee* **Gwynne** [gwĭn] (1857–1941), was author of *House of Rimmon, An Unwise Virgin, An Artist's Model, Ashes of Passion, The Temptation of Gideon Holt, The Wireless Call.*

**Ker'ner** (kĕr'nẽr), **Andreas Justinus.** 1786–1862. German lyric poet and physician; formed Swabian School of poetry with his friends Uhland, Gustav Schwab, and others; district physician at Weinsberg (1819–51), where his home became a literary mecca. Besides his verse (including the folk song *Wanderlied*), he wrote a satirical humorous novel of his own experiences, works on occultism, and medical treatises.

**Kerner, Anton.** Ritter **von Ma'ri·laun** (fōn mä'rē·loun). 1831–1898. Austrian botanist; known chiefly for work in systematic botany, ecology, and plant geography.

**Ké'roualle'** (kā'rwȧl'), **Louise Renée de.** Duchess of **Ports'mouth and Au'bi'gny'** (pōrts'mŭth, ō'bē'-nyē'). 1649–1734. A strong-willed subtle Breton, mistress (from 1671) of King Charles II of England. Made duchess of Portsmouth (1673); supported in her intrigue with Charles by French envoy, and rewarded by Louis XIV with fief of Aubigny (1674), for her service in keeping Charles dependent upon France; mother of Charles Lennox (1672–1723), Duke of Richmond.

**Kerr** *or* **Ker** (kär; kâr; kûr). Name of an Anglo-Norman family of Scottish border (from end of 12th century) having two chief branches, the **Cess'ford** (sĕs'fẽrd) and the **Fer'nie·hirst** [fûr'nĭ·hûrst] (in Roxburghshire), to latter of which belonged Robert Carr (*q.v.*), Earl of Somerset.

EARLS AND MARQUISES OF LO'THI·AN (lō'thĭ·ăn; -thyăn):

**Mark Kerr** *or* **Ker** (d. 1609), 1st Earl of Lothian; grandson of Sir **Andrew Ker** of Cessford (fought at Flodden Field, 1513; killed in defeating Scott of Buccleuch, 1526); master of requests (1577–1606); extraordinary lord of session under King James VI; made baron, Lord Newbattle (1587); interim chancellor (1604).

**William Kerr** *or* **Ker** (1605?–1675), descendant of **Andrew Ker** (border chieftain of Ferniehirst branch of family); m. (1631) **Anne,** Countess of Lothian, granddaughter of 1st earl; created 3d earl of Lothian (1631); signed National Covenant (1638); governor of Newcastle (1641); sent by privy council on mission to court of France (1642); joined Argyll in expedition against Montrose (1644); secretary of state (1648–52); member of several commissions sent to treat with Charles II, at Breda and after king's arrival in Scotland (1660); refused to take abjuration oath (1662). His son **Robert Kerr** (1636–1703), 4th Earl and 1st Marquis of Lothian; privy councilor to William III; justice general (1688); united his grandfather Robert's title of earl of **An'crum** (ăng'krŭm) to his own (1690).

**Schom'berg** (shŏm'bûrg) **Henry** (1833–1900), 9th Marquis of Lothian and 4th Baron **Ker of Kers'heugh** (kärz'hū(ᴋ); kârz'-); diplomat; educ. Oxford; held posts in Europe and Middle East; privy seal of Scotland (1874–1900); secretary of state for Scotland in Salisbury's administration (1886–92). His brother Lord **Walter Talbot** (1839–1927), naval commander; served in Baltic expeditions (1854–55) and through Sepoy Mutiny (1857–58); rear admiral (1889); vice-admiral commanding Channel squadron (1895); first sea lord (1899–1904); admiral (1900); promoted reform of system of naval education, proposed by John Arbuthnot Fisher, which resulted in opening of Osborne and Dartmouth (Devon) colleges; admiral of fleet (1904).

**Philip Henry** (1882–1940), 11th Marquis of Lothian; diplomat; educ. Oxford; asst. secretary of intercolonial council of Transvaal and Orange River Colony (1905–08); editor of *The State,* South Africa (1908–09), and *The Round Table* (1910–16); secretary to prime minister Lloyd George (1916–21); secretary of Rhodes trust (1925–39); parliamentary undersecretary, India office (1931–32); British ambassador to U.S., charged with obtaining U.S. supplies and support of Britain's war effort (1939–40; died in office).

EARLS AND DUKES OF ROX'BURGH *or* ROXBURGHE (rŏks'brŭ):

**Robert Ker** (1570?–1650), 1st Earl of Roxburgh; great-grandson of Sir Andrew Ker of Cessford; supported James VI against Bothwell (1594–99); created Baron Roxburgh (1600); accompanied James to London (1603); created earl of Roxburgh (1616); lord privy seal of Scotland (1637–49); Royalist in Civil War. **John Ker** (d. 1741), 5th Earl and 1st Duke of Roxburgh; secretary of state for Scotland (1704); promoted union of Scotland with England and Protestant succession, rewarded with dukedom (1707); keeper of privy seal of Scotland (1714); accompanied rebels under duke of Argyll and distinguished himself at Sheriffmuir (1715); one of lords justices during George I's absence from England (1716, 1720, 1723, 1725). His grandson **John Ker** (1740–1804), 3d duke; bibliophile, b. London; lord of the bedchamber (1767), groom of the stole, and privy councilor (1796); amassed private library containing remarkable collection of books from Caxton's press, dispersed for £23,341 in 45-day sale during which bibliophiles gathered at St. Alban's Tavern and inaugurated the Roxburghe Club, first of the book clubs (1812).

**Kerr** (kĕr), *orig.* **Kemp′ner** (kĕmp′nẽr), **Alfred.** 1867–1948. German writer and dramatic critic, b. in Breslau, of Jewish descent; exile in France. Author of *Die Welt im Drama* (5 vols., 1917), of travel books and sketches, as *Die Welt im Licht* (2 vols., 1920), *New York und London* (1923), *O Spanien!* (1924), of poems, chiefly satirical and in Berlin dialect, as *Die Harfe* (1918) and *Caprichos* (1925), and of *Krämerspiegel* (1922; a group of twelve poems set to music by Richard Strauss).

**Kerr** (kär; kûr), **John.** 1824–1907. Scottish physicist; discovered the Kerr effect. Author of *An Elementary Treatise on Rational Mechanics* (1867).

**Kerr** (kûr), **Orpheus C.** See Robert Henry NEWELL.

**Kerr** (kûr), **Sophie.** 1880–1965. American writer; m. John D. Underwood (1904; divorced 1908). Managing editor of *Woman's Home Companion.* Author of *Love at Large* (1916), *Confetti* (1927), *Tigers Is Only Cats* (1929), *In for a Penny* (1931), *Fine to Look At* (1937), etc., and the play *Big-Hearted Herbert.*

**Ker′saint′** (kĕr′săN′), Comte **de. Armand Gui Simon de Coet′nem′pren′** (kwĕt′nĕm′prĕn′). 1742–1793. French naval officer and politician; Girondist member of Constituent Assembly and Legislative Assembly; promoted vice-admiral (1793), but resigned after execution of Louis XVI; guillotined in Paris (1793). For his daughter Claire, see under DURFORT family.

**Ker′vyn de Let′ten·ho′ve** (kĕr′vĭn dĕ lĕt′ĕn·hō′vĕ), Baron **Joseph Marie Constantin Bruno.** 1817–1891. Belgian scholar; editor of Froissart's *Chronicles;* author of *Histoire de Flandre* (1847–50).

**Ke′shub Chun′der Sen** *or* **Ke′shab Chun′der Sen** (kā′shôb chŏn′drô sān′). 1838–1884. Hindu reformer, b. Calcutta. Educ. Calcutta; clerk in Bank of Bengal; resigned (1861) to devote himself to literature and philosophy; joined Brahmo Samaj (1857); became active leader in samaj (1859); started the *Indian Mirror* (1861); wrote *The Brahma Samaj Vindicated* (1863); caused division in the society (1865), founding (1866) branch known as "Brahma Samaj of India"; visited England (1870); in later years became somewhat of a mystic and exercised less influence over the society. Cf. RAM MOHAN ROY.

**Kes′sel** (kĕs′ĕl), **Jan van.** 1641?–1680. Dutch landscape painter; studied under J. van Ruisdael.

**Kessel, Jeroom.** 1578–?1636. Flemish portrait painter, son-in-law of Jan (Velvet) Brueghel; studio in Antwerp (from c. 1622). His son **Jan van Kessel** (1626–1679), pupil of Jan Brueghel, was a flower and animal painter.

**Kes′sel·ring** (kĕs′ĕl·rĭng), **Albert.** 1887–1960. German field marshal; served in World War I; chief of air staff (1936); air commander, invasion of Poland (1939) and France (1940), attacks on England (1940) and Russia (1941), on Mediterranean and Italian fronts (1942–43), and in western Europe (1945); death sentence as war criminal commuted to life imprisonment (1947).

**Kes′sels** (kĕs′ĕls), **Matthieu.** 1784–1836. Belgian sculptor; his best-known work is the *Discus Thrower* (marble original in England, original model in Brussels museum).

**Kes′ter** (kĕs′tẽr), **Vaughan.** 1869–1911. American novelist, b. New Brunswick, N.J. Author of *John o' Jamestown* (1907), *The Prodigal Judge* (1911). His younger brother **Paul** (1870–1933) was author of *His Own Country, Diana Dauntless,* and a number of plays, including *Zamar, Eugene Abram, When Knighthood Was in Flower* and *Dorothy Vernon* (both from novels of Charles Major), *The Lady in the Case, Lady Dedlock.*

**Kest′ner** (kĕst′nẽr), **Charlotte.** See Charlotte BUFF.

**Ketch** (kĕch), **John,** *known as* **Jack.** d. 1686. English executioner; executed Monmouth (1685); notorious for barbarity; his name a synonym for hangman.

**Ketch′um** (kĕch′ŭm), **Milo Smith.** 1872–1934. American civil engineer; specialized in bridge and structural engineering. Dean of college of engineering, U. of Illinois (1922–34). Author of technical treatises on engineering; special editor for terms in civil engineering, *Webster's New International Dictionary, Second Edition.*

**Ke′tel** (kā′tĕl), **Cornelis.** 1548–1616. Dutch portrait painter; studio in London (1573–81).

**Ket′te·ler** (kĕt′ĕ·lẽr), Baron **Wilhelm Emmanuel von.** 1811–1877. German Roman Catholic ecclesiastic and ultramontane leader, b. Münster. Member, Frankfurt National Assembly (1848–49); was consecrated bishop of Mainz (1850) and became Catholic leader in Germany. At first opposed dogma of papal infallibility at Vatican Council (1870), but subsequently submitted to decrees and supported recognition of new dogmas; represented Center party in Reichstag (1871–73) and became ultramontane leader and strong opponent of Bismarck in Prussian Kulturkampf; championed Christian socialism and social and economic reforms. His nephew Baron **Klemens von Ketteler** (1853–1900) was minister to Mexico (1896–99) and Peking (1899); assassinated by a Chinese during Boxer Rebellion (1900).

**Ket′ter·ing** (kĕt′ẽr·ĭng), **Charles Franklin.** 1876–1958. American electrical engineer and manufacturer; president and general manager, General Motors Research Corporation (1917); vice-president, General Motors Corporation. Inventor of starting, lighting, and ignition system (later known as "Delco") for automobiles and other "Delco" lighting and power equipment.

**Keulen, Ludolph van.** See CEULEN.

**Keuss′ler** (kois′lẽr), **Gerhard von.** 1874–1949. German composer and conductor, b. in Livonia. Composer of music dramas with original texts, oratorios, symphonies, songs and melodies with original words (4 vols., 1925), etc.

**Keut′gen** (koit′gĕn), **Friedrich Wilhelm Eduard.** 1861–1936. German historian.

**Key** (kē), Sir **Astley Cooper.** 1821–1888. British naval commander; first naval lord of the Admiralty (1879). Organized Royal Naval Coll. at Greenwich (1872) and became its president (1873).

**Key, David McKendree.** 1824–1900. American politician, b. in Greene County, Tenn. Served in Confederate army in Civil War. U.S. senator (1875–77); U.S. postmaster general (1877–80). U.S. judge, eastern and middle district of Tennessee (1880–94).

**Key** (kĕ′ĭ), **Ellen Karoline Sofia.** 1849–1926. Swedish feminist and writer, b. in Småland; called "the Pallas of Sweden." Teacher in Stockholm (1880–99) and lecturer at the People's (workingmen's) Institute (1884–1903) and elsewhere; lived abroad (chiefly 1899–1910). Author of works on sociological, literary, and historical subjects, esp. on the feminist movement and child welfare, and on questions of sex, love and marriage, and moral conduct.

**Key, Ernst Axel Henrik.** 1832–1901. Swedish anatomist. Professor of pathological anatomy in the Caroline Institute of Stockholm (1862–97).

**Key** (kē), **Francis Scott.** 1779–1843. American lawyer, writer of *The Star-Spangled Banner,* b. in Frederick County (now Carroll County), Md. Studied law; practiced, Frederick, Md. (1801), Georgetown, D.C. (1802). On mission to obtain exchange of an American held by British fleet, was detained while British bombarded Fort McHenry, key to Baltimore defenses (night of Sept. 13–14, 1814); at sight of U.S. flag still flying over Fort McHenry (morning of Sept. 14), wrote poem *The Star-Spangled Banner,* first scribbled on back of an envelope; song printed on handbills and distributed through Baltimore; published in Baltimore *American* (Sept. 21, 1814). Devoted himself to law practice, Washington, D.C. (from 1830). Wrote no other noteworthy verse. Cf. John Stafford SMITH.

**Key, Pierre van Rensselaer.** 1872–1945. American music critic and editor; editor and publisher of *Pierre Key's Music Year Book* (publ. annually) and *Pierre Key's Musical Who's Who* (publ. quadrennially).

**Keyes** (kīz), **Frances Parkinson,** *nee* **Whee'ler** (hwē'lẽr). 1885-1970. American novelist, b. Charlottesville, Va.; m. Henry Wilder Keyes (1904; d. 1938). Among her novels are *The Old Gray Homestead* (1919), *The Career of David Noble* (1921), *Queen Anne's Lace* (1930), *Senator Marlowe's Daughter* (1933), *Written in Heaven* (1937), *The Great Tradition* (1939), *Fielding's Folly* (1940), *All That Glitters* (1941), *Crescent Carnival* (1942).

**Keyes** (kēz), Sir **Roger John Brownlow.** 1872–1945. British naval officer (from 1885); captain (1905); in charge of submarine service (1910–14); chief of staff, Eastern Mediterranean squadron (1915); grand-fleet captain (1916–17); rear admiral (1917); director of plans at the Admiralty (1917); commander of Dover patrol (1918); commanded operations against Zeebrugge and Ostend (Apr. 23, 1918); vice-admiral (1921), admiral (1926); commander in chief, Mediterranean station (1925–28), Portsmouth station (1929–31); admiral of the fleet (1930); retired (1935); recalled (1940); responsible for organization of commando units (1940–41; see Lord Louis MOUNTBATTEN).

**Keynes** (kānz), **John Maynard,** 1st Baron. 1883–1946. English economist, b. in Cambridge; son of John Neville Keynes. On staff of the Treasury (1915–19), and its principal representative at the Paris Peace Conference (1919). Editor, *Economic Journal* (from 1912). Author of *The Economic Consequences of the Peace* (1919), *A Revision of the Treaty* (1922), *A Tract on Monetary Reform* (1923), *The End of Laissez-Faire* (1926), *A Treatise on Money* (2 vols., 1930), *The General Theory of Employment, Interest and Money* (1936), etc.

**Keynes, John Neville.** 1852–1949. English educator, b. at Salisbury; father of John Maynard Keynes. University lecturer in moral science, Cambridge (1884–1911); registrary, Cambridge (1910–25).

**Key'ser** (kī'zẽr), **Cassius Jackson.** 1862–1947. American mathematician; author of *Science and Religion* (1914), *Mathematical Philosophy* (1922), *Mole Philosophy, and Other Essays* (1927), *Mathematics and the Dance of Life* (1937), etc.

**Key'ser** (kī'sẽr), **Hendrik de.** 1565–1621. Dutch architect and sculptor. Settled in Amsterdam (1591); city architect and sculptor (1594); designed, mostly in Dutch Renaissance style, the Westerkerk (begun 1620), the court of the East India House (1606), and the exchange (1608–17), all in Amsterdam, the town hall at Delft (1620), the monument of William I of Orange at Delft (1614), and the bronze statue of Erasmus at Rotterdam (1621). His son **Thomas** (1596?–1667) was a portrait painter; painted *The Anatomy of Dr. Vrij* (1619; now in Amsterdam), *A Merchant and his Clerk* (1627; in London).

**Key'ser'** (kā'ē'zâr'), **Nicaise de.** 1813–1887. Belgian historical painter.

**Key'ser·ling** (kī'sẽr·lĭng; *Angl.* kī'zẽr-), Count **Alexander.** 1815–1891. German geologist and naturalist, b. in Kurland; friend of Bismarck. His nephew Count **Eduard von Keyserling** (1855–1918) was a writer, long resident in Italy; became blind (1907); author of novels and short stories chiefly about Kurland nobility, and of dramas, as *Benignens Erlebnis* (1906). Alexander's grandson Count **Hermann Alexander Keyserling** (1880–1946), German social philosopher and writer, lived in Paris and England (1903–05), Berlin (1906–07), and on estate in Estonia (1908–46). Acquired admiration for Oriental philosophy; deprived of fortune and estates by Russian Revolution; settled in Darmstadt and founded the "School of Wisdom" (1920); traveled and lectured in many countries, including U.S. (1928). Author of *Reisetagebuch eines Philosophen* (1919), etc.

**Kha'cha·tu'ri·an** (kăch'ȧ·tōōr'ĭ·ăn; kach'-), **Aram Ilich.** 1903– . Soviet composer. Composed symphonies, concertos and ballets (including *Gayne*).

**Khadija.** See MOHAMMED (the Prophet).

**Khaf're** (kăf'rā) *or* **Khaf'ra** (-rä). *Gr.* **Kheph'ren** *or* **Cheph'ren** (kĕf'rĕn). Third king of IVth (Memphite) dynasty of Egypt (reigned c. 2850 B.C.); builder of second pyramid at Giza; possibly also builder of the Sphinx, which is supposed to be his image and a symbol of the god Harmachis. Several statues of him were found in so-called "Temple of the Sphinx".

**Khair ed-Din** *or* **Khaireddin.** See BARBAROSSA II.

**Kha'lid** *or* **Kha'led** (kä'lĭd). *Arab.* **Khālid ibn-al-Walīd.** d. 642 A.D. Arab general and conqueror of Syria; called "Sword of Allah." At first opposed Mohammed; converted to new faith (629); given command of expedition against Syria (633) by abu-Bakr, Mohammed's successor; defeated Byzantine armies of Heraclius south of Damascus (634–635), took Damascus (635), and won final great battle of the Yarmuk (636); replaced in command by Caliph Omar's new general abu-Ubayda.

**Kha·li'fa** (kä·lē'fä), **The,** *i.e.* "the adviser." *Real name* **Abdullah et Taaisha.** 1846?–1899. Arab leader of dervishes in Sudan; first to proclaim Mohammed Ahmed as the Mahdi; succeeded him (1885), extending greatly his dominions (1885–98); defeated at Omdurman by Kitchener (1898).

**Kha·lil'** (kä·lēl'). *Arab.* **al-Khalīl ibn-Aḥmad.** 718?–791 A.D. Arab philologist; first to compile an Arabic dictionary; reputed first to have classified meters of Arabic prosody and determined its rules.

**Khalji.** See KHILJI.

**Kha'ma** (kä'mă). 1835–1923. A Christianized native African chief of a tribe in northern Bechuanaland; aided British South Africa Co. (founded by Rhodes for the colonization and development of South Africa), in defeating the Matabeles (1893); made successful appeal to British government to have his tribal territory set aside as a native reservation (c. 1895).

**Khammurabi.** Variant of HAMMURABI.

**Khan·sa', al-** (ăl'kăn·sä'). *Arab.* **al-Khansā'.** d. ?645 A.D. Arab poet; contemporary of Mohammed; wrote elegies on her father and brothers killed in battle.

**Khayyám, Omar.** See OMAR KHAYYÁM.

**Khemnitser, Ivan Ivanovich.** See CHEMNITZER.

**Khephren.** See KHAFRE.

**Khe·ra'skov** (kyĕ·rä'skôf), **Mikhail Matveevich.** 1733–1807. Russian poet; sometimes called "dean of Russian literature." Composed tragedies, novels, and miscellaneous poems, but esp. the two epic poems *Rossiada* (in 12 books) describing invasion of Kazan by Ivan the Terrible, and *Vladimir* (in 18 books) portraying a struggle between Pagan instincts and Christian faith.

**Khe'ven·hül'ler** (kā'vĕn·hül'ẽr). Family of Austrian nobles, including: Count **Franz Christoph von Khevenhüller-Fran'ken·burg** [-fräng'kĕn·bōōrk] (1588–1650), statesman and diplomat; imperial courtier and minister of Emperor Ferdinand II; author of *Annales Ferdinandei*, on contemporary history. His grandson Count **Ludwig Andreas** (1683–1744) served under Prince Eugene in War of Spanish Succession; fought in War of Polish Succession (1734); field marshal (1737); participated in Turkish War; commanded with distinction against France and Bavaria in Austrian War of Succession (1742).

**Khil·ji′** (kĭl·jē′) *or* **Khal·ji′** (kăl·jē′). A Mohammedan dynasty ruling in India (1290–1320) with Delhi as capital. Founded by Firoz Shah II (known as Jalal-ud-din); its most famous member, Ala-ud-din (sultan 1295–1315).

**Khlesl** (klā′s'l) *or* **Kle′sel** *or* **Klesl, Melchior.** 1553–1630. Austrian cardinal and statesman. Bishop of Vienna (1598); chancellor to Archduke (later Emperor) Matthias (from 1599) and virtual head of imperial politics after latter's succession (1612); cardinal (1615). Came into conflict with Ferdinand II (then archduke) for attempts to negotiate with Protestant princes before considering question of imperial succession; imprisoned at Castle Ambras in Tirol for advising against war with revolting Bohemians (1618); brought to trial before Curia in Rome (1622) and acquitted (1623).

**Khmelnitski, Bogdan.** See CHMIELNICKI.

**Khmel·nits′ki** (kmyăl·y′·nyēts′kû·ĭ; *Angl.* kmĕl-nĭts′kĭ), **Nikolai Ivanovich.** 1789–1846. Russian playwright; governor of Smolensk (1829) and Archangel (1837); author of verse comedies *Castles in Spain, The Russian Faust, The Prattler, The Word of the Czar,* and the historical play *Bogdan Chmielnicki.*

**Kho·mya·kov′** (kô·myŭ·kôf′), **Aleksei Stepanovich.** 1804–1860. Russian poet, b. Moscow; works include *Ermak* (1832) and *Pseudo-Demetrius* (1833).

**Kho·ra′na** (kō·rä′nȧ), **Har Gobind.** 1922– . Amer. chemist, b. India. Awarded Nobel prize in physiology and medicine (1968) with R. W. Holly and M. Nirenberg for studies on the genetic code.

**Kho·srau′** (kŏ·srou′) *or* **Khu·srau′** (kōō·srou′) *or* **Khosru.** *Gr.* **Chos′ro·es** (kŏz′rō·ēz; kŏs′-). Name of two kings of the Sassanidae of Persia:

**Khosrau I.** *Called* **Khosrau A·nu′shir·van′** (ă·nōō′-shēr·vän′), *i.e.* "having an immortal soul." d. 579. King (531–579); son of Kavadh I. At war (531–532; 540–545) with Justinian, Byzantine emperor; sacked Antioch (540); extended power to Black Sea and Caucasus; failed to take Edessa (544); granted a truce (545), forcing Justinian to pay tribute; after nine years of peace (562–571), engaged again in war against Justin II; took fortress of Dara (573); defeated (576). One of the greatest Persian kings; reformed imperial taxation, restored Zoroastrianism in full; ruled Sassanid Empire at its greatest extent; golden age of Pahlavi literature.

**Khosrau II.** *Called* **Khosrau Par·vez′** (păr·vāz′), *i.e.* "the victorious." d. 628. King (590–628). Son of Ormizd IV; grandson of Khosrau I. Aided by Mauricius (*q.v.*), in securing his throne; after murder of Mauricius (602), made war on Eastern Roman Empire; occupied Egypt (616) and reached (617) Chalcedon opposite Constantinople; defeated by Heraclius (623–628).

**Khru·shchev′** (krōōsh·chôf′), **Nikita Sergeevich.** 1894–1971. Soviet leader; first secretary of Communist Party (1953–64); premier of Soviet Union (1958–64).

**Khubilai Khan.** Variant of KUBLAI KHAN.

**Khu′en–Hé′der·vá′ry** (kōō′ĕn·hā′dĕr·vä′rĭ), **Count Karl.** 1849–1918. Hungarian statesman; as ban of Croatia and Slavonia (1883–1903), founded pro-Hungarian Croatian Nationalist party and effected administrative reforms; twice minister president of Hungary (1903); minister in Tisza's cabinet (1904–05); again Hungarian minister president (1910–12); founder and head of National Workers' party (1913).

**Khu′fu** (kōō′fōō). *Gr.* **Che′ops** (kē′ŏps). First king of IVth (Memphite) dynasty of Egypt (reigned c. 2900–2877 B.C.); erected largest of pyramids of Giza. Cf. MENKURE.

**Khusrau.** See KHOSRAU.

**Khwa′riz·mi′, al–** (ăl·kwä′rĭz·mē′). *Also* **al–Khu·wa′-riz·mi′** *or* **al–Kho·wa′riz·mi′** (ăl′kōō·wä′rĭz·mē′). *Arab.* **Muḥammad ibn–Mūsa al–Khwārizmi.** 780–?850 A.D. Arab mathematician; native of Khwarazm (now Khiva); lived at Baghdad; one of the greatest scientific minds of Islam, markedly influencing mathematical thought. Compiled an early work on arithmetic (known only in translation) and the oldest astronomical tables; wrote a treatise on algebra (based on a Hindu work of Brahmagupta), introducing the name (al-jabr) and greatly advancing knowledge of the science; in its Latin translation (by Gerard of Cremona) this treatise was source of much of mathematical knowledge of medieval Europe; wrote also a work on algorism (a term deriving from his name), which introduced Arabic numerals and the art of calculating by decimal notation.

**Kia K′ing.** = CHIA CH'ING.

**Kia·mil′ Pa·sha′** (kyä·mĭl′ pä·shä′). 1832?–1913. Turkish statesman, b. in Cyprus. Served under Egyptian government, and (1861) Ottoman government. Appointed grand vizier (1885–87; 1896); governor of Smyrna (1896–1908); removed by Sultan Abdul-Hamid. Again grand vizier (1908–09), opposed to reform movements. Again grand vizier during Balkan Wars (1912–13); overthrown by coup d'état of Talaat Pasha and Enver Pasha; retired to Cyprus.

**Kid, Thomas.** See KYD.

**Kidd** (kĭd), **Benjamin.** 1858–1916. English sociologist; author of *Social Evolution,* attacking Socialism (1894), *Principles of Western Civilization* (1902), etc.

**Kidd, William.** 1645?–1701. Pirate, b. Greenock, Scotland. Known as "Captain Kidd." Shipowner and sea captain, New York City (1690); in British colonial service against French (1690–95). Commissioned head of expedition against pirates in Indian Ocean; sailed from England (Apr., 1696) for N.Y.; took no prizes before reaching Madagascar almost a year later; during small mutiny, struck and fatally injured one of crew; began to sanction attacks on merchantmen; captured (Jan., 1698) *Quedagh Merchant,* richly laden Armenian vessel, took her for his own ship and captured other prizes; sailed to West Indies, learned he had been proclaimed a pirate, returned to New England and surrendered on promise of a pardon (1699). Sent, with his crew, as prisoner to London (1700); tried and convicted for murder and piracy; hanged (1701). After his death, rumors spread that he had buried his plunder in places along the American coast near New York.

**Kid′de** (kĕth′ĕ), **Harald.** 1878–1918. Danish novelist, author of social and psychological novels of Jutland, Anholt, and Värmland; m. (1907) **Astrid Eh′ren·cron** [ę′rĕn·krōn] (1871-1960), author of mystery novels and stories laid chiefly in parsonages and small Swedish towns.

**Kid′der** (kĭd′ēr), **Kathryn.** 1868?–1939. American actress; m. Louis Kaufman Anspacher (1905). Created roles of Countess Wanda in *Nordeck,* Rachel McCreery in *Held by the Enemy,* Dearest in *Little Lord Fauntleroy,* Elinor in *The Glass House,* Ruth Prescott in *All the King's Horses.* Starred in *Mme. Sans Gêne, School for Scandal,* and Shakespearean roles.

**Ki′der·len–Waech′ter** (kē′dēr·lĕn·vĕk′tēr), **Alfred von.** 1852–1912. German statesman and diplomat. Prussian minister at Hamburg (1894); German minister at Copenhagen (1895), Bucharest (1900), and Constantinople (at various times); deputy for foreign secretary von Schoen (1908), whom he succeeded (under Bethmann-Hollweg; 1910). Negotiated with French ambassador Jules Cambon on Moroccan affairs, and helped bring about Agadir incident (1911), but ultimately signed agreement with France on Moroccan-Congo question (1911).

**Kiel** (kēl), **Friedrich.** 1821–1885. German composer and contrapuntist.

**Kiel'horn** (kēl'hôrn), **Franz.** 1840–1908. German Sanskrit scholar.

**Kiel'land** (kĕl'län), **Alexander Lange.** 1849–1906. Norwegian novelist and playwright, b. Stavanger. Author of *Novelettes* (1879), *Garman and Worse* (1880), *Poison* (1883) and its sequel *Fortune* (1884), *Snow* (1886), and *Jacob* (1891), of satirical comedies, as *Three Couples* (1886) and *Betty's Guardian* (1887), etc.

**Kiel'mey'er** (kēl'mī'ẽr), **Karl Friedrich.** 1765–1844. German naturalist; believed in metamorphosis of species, from simple to complex, through external causes and inherent capacity, with new varieties developing through hybridization and gradually becoming species; recognized facts later formulated by Haeckel (1866) as the "fundamental biogenetic law" (recapitulation theory).

**Kien Lung.** = CH'IEN LUNG.

**Kien'zl** (kēn'ts'l), **Wilhelm.** 1857–1941. Austrian dramatic composer and writer on music. Author of a biography of Wagner (1904), the autobiography *Meine Lebenswanderung* (1926), etc. Composer of the operas *Urvasi* (1886), *Heilmar, der Narr* (1892), *Der Kuhreigen* (1911; Eng. trans. *The Dance of Death*), and *Hassan, der Schwärmer* (1925), and the musical tragicomedy *Don Quixote* (1898); also, of piano pieces, chamber music, orchestral works, songs, etc.

**Kie'pert** (kē'pẽrt), **Heinrich.** 1818–1899. German geographer, cartographer, and philologist; authority on Asia Minor; professor, U. of Berlin (from 1859). Author of *Travels in Asia Minor* (1842 ff.), a *Textbook of Ancient Geography* (1878), *Manual of Ancient Geography* (1879). His cartographic works include *Atlas of Hellas* (1840–46), *Atlas of the Ancient World* (1848), *New Hand Atlas of the Earth* (1857–61), *Atlas Antiquus* (1859 ff.).

**Kier'an** (kḗr'ăn), **John Francis.** 1892– . American journalist, b. New York City. B.S., Fordham (1912). Sports writer, New York *Times* (1915–43); columnist, New York *Sun* (1943 ff.). One of regular members of "Information Please" radio program.

**Kier'ke·gaard** (kĭr'kĕ·gôr), **Sören Aabye.** 1813–1855. Danish philosopher and writer on theology; opposed Hegel's objective philosophy and based his own philosophy on faith and knowledge, and on thought and reality; held that religion is an individual matter and that the relation of the individual to God involves suffering.

**Kie'se·wet'ter** (kē'zĕ·vĕt'ẽr), **Raphael George.** Edler **von Wie'sen·brunn** (fôn vē'zĕn·bro͝on). 1773–1850. Austrian historian of music, b. in Moravia.

**Kie'sing·er** (kē'zĭng·ẽr), **Kurt Georg.** 1904– . German lawyer; chancellor of West Germany (1966–69).

**Kies'ler** (kēs'lẽr), **Frederick John.** 1896–1965. American architect and designer, b. Vienna; identified with ultramodern school of design, esp. with de Stijl group. Designed stage set for play *R.U.R.* in Berlin (1923), and for *Emperor Jones* (1923); architect for Austrian section at International Exposition of Decorative Arts, Paris (1925). To New York (1926); director of laboratory of design correlation, at Columbia U.

**Kil·dare'** (kĭl·dâr'), Earls of. See FITZGERALD family.

**Kil'ham** (kĭl'ăm), **Alexander.** 1762–1798. English Methodist clergyman; expelled from Methodist Connexion (1796); organized Methodist New Connexion (1797); followers are known as Kilhamites.

**Kil'i·an** (kĭl'ĭ·ăn), Saint. See CILIAN.

**Ki'li·an** (kē'lē·än). Family of German copper engravers of Augsburg, including: **Lukas** (1579–1637); his brother **Wolfgang** (1581–1662), portraitist and engraver, esp. after the Venetian masters; Wolfgang's sons **Philipp** (1628–1693) and **Bartholomäus** (1630–1696); and Philipp's great-grandsons **Georg Christoph** (1709–1781) and **Philipp Andreas** (1714–1759).

**Ki·lij' Ars·lan'** (kĭ·lĭj' [*Turk.* kû·lûj'] ärs·län'). Name of two Seljuk sultans: **Kilij Arslan I,** *or* **Su·lei·man'** [sü·lā·män'] (d. 1108), sultan in Holy Land at time of early crusades; defeated by Godfrey of Bouillon at Nicaea and Dorylaeum (1097). **Kilij Arslan II** *or* **IV** (d. 1192), sultan (1155–92); at war with Byzantines under Emperor Manuel Comnenus.

**Kil'li·an** (kĭl'ĭ·ăn), Saint. = Saint CILIAN.

**Kil'li·an** (kĭl'ē·än), **Gustav.** 1860–1921. German laryngologist; known for his methods of removal of foreign bodies in bronchial tubes by bronchoscopic control.

**Kil'li·grew** (kĭl'ĭ·gro͞o), **Thomas.** 1612–1683. English playwright and courtier of Charles II; imprisoned for Royalist sympathies (1642–44); formed company of players, the King's Servants; built original Theatre Royal in Drury Lane (1663); best-known works, a coarse comedy, *The Parson's Wedding* and tragicomedies including *The Prisoners* and *Claracilla.* His niece **Anne Killigrew** (1660–1685) was a poet and painter; subject of one of Dryden's odes.

**Kil'ling·er** (kĭl'ĭng·ẽr), Baron **Manfred von.** 1886– . German Nazi politician and administrator; appointed (1940) ambassador to Rumania.

**Kil'mer** (kĭl'mẽr), **Alfred Joyce.** 1886–1918. American poet, b. New Brunswick, N.J.; on staff of *Standard Dictionary* (1909–12); contributed verse to various periodicals. Volunteered for service at entrance of United States into World War; killed in action (July 30, 1918). Author of *Summer of Love* (1911), *Trees and Other Poems* (1914), *Main Street* (1917); m. (1908) **Aline Murray** (1888–1941), b. Norfolk, Va., author of *Candles That Burn* (1919), *Vigils* (1921), *A Buttonwood Summer* (1929), and other verse.

**Kil·pat'rick** (kĭl·păt'rĭk), **Hugh Judson.** 1836–1881. American army officer; commanded Sherman's cavalry in the march to the sea (1864); brevetted major general (1865).

**Kilpatrick, William Heard.** 1871–1965. American educator; professor, philosophy of education, Teachers College, Columbia (1918–38).

**Kil'vert** (kĭl'vẽrt), **Margaret,** *nee* **Cam'er·on** (kăm'ẽr·ŭn). 1867–1947. American writer, b. Ottawa, Ill.; m. Harrison Cass Lewis (1903; d. 1926), Maxwell Alexander Kilvert (1929). Author of *The Bachelor and the Baby* (1908), *The Golden Rule Dollivers* (1913), *A Sporting Chance* (1926), etc., and of several one-act comedies (*The Kleptomaniac, The Burglar,* etc.).

**Kilwardby, Robert.** d. 1279. English prelate. Entered Dominican order; provincial of order in England (1261). Archbishop of Canterbury (1272–78); crowned Edward I. Cardinal bishop of Porto and Santo Rufina (1278). On going to Rome (1278), took with him registers and judicial records of Canterbury, which have never been recovered.

**Kim'ball** (kĭm'b'l), **Everett.** 1873–1948. American educator; professor of history (1914–19) and of government (from 1919), Smith Coll. Author of *The National Government of the United States* (1919); special editor for terms in history and government, *Webster's New International Dictionary, Second Edition,* and an editor of its "Reference History of the World."

**Kimball, Fiske.** 1888–1955. American architect; engaged in restoration of historical houses, as the home of Jefferson (Monticello), of Robert E. Lee at Stratford, Va. Member of advisory board planning restoration of Williamsburg, Va., and construction of Rockefeller

Center, New York City. Editor of architectural terms for *Webster's New International Dictionary, Second Edition.*

**Kimball, Heber Chase.** 1801–1868. American Mormon leader, known as "Brother Heber." Ordained one of twelve apostles of Mormon Church (1835). Mormon missionary in New England (1836); in England (1837–38, 1839–41); in U.S. (1841–44). Settled in Salt Lake valley (1848). Became one of Brigham Young's chief advisers; chief justice of "State of Deseret"; lieutenant governor (1849–68).

**Kimball, Sumner Increase.** 1834–1923. Organizer of U.S. Lifesaving Service (1871–1916); b. Lebanon, Me.

**Kimball, William Wirt.** 1848–1930. American naval officer; commanded first torpedo boat flotilla, during Spanish-American War. Stanch believer in John P. Holland and in practicability of his submarines.

**Kim'ber·ley** (kĭm'bẽr·lĭ), 1st Earl of. **John Wode'-house** (wŏŏd'hous). 1826–1902. English statesman; as lord lieutenant of Ireland (1864–66), took firm measures against Fenians. Lord privy seal under Gladstone (1868–70) and colonial secretary (1870–74, 1880–82); defended policy of giving Boers self-government (1881); formed Rupert's Land into Province of Manitoba (1870) and brought British Columbia into Dominion of Canada (1872); secretary for India (1882–85, 1892–94). Foreign secretary under Rosebery (1894–95). Leader of Liberal party in House of Lords (1897–1902); supported military operations in Boer War (1899). Kimberley, S. Africa, was named for him. See Shuzo Aoki.

**Ḳim'chi** *or* **Ḳim'ḥi** (kĭm'kē). Medieval Jewish family of Hebrew grammarians and Biblical scholars in Narbonne, Provence, including: **Jo'seph ben I'saac** (jō'zĕf [-zĭf] bĕn ī'zȧk [ī'zĭk]) **Ḳimchi** (1105?–?1170), first to indicate 8 verb classes and to divide Hebrew vowels into 5 short and 5 long vowels. His son **Mo'ses** [mō'zĕz; -zĭz] (d. about 1190), first to introduce the verb "pakad" as a model for conjugation and to introduce the sequence now usual in enumerating stem forms, wrote first methodical manual of Hebrew grammar. Moses' brother and pupil **Da'vid** [dā'vĭd] (1160–1235), *called* **Re·DaK'** [rĕ·dȧk'] (from initials of his name Rabbi David Ḳimchi), author in Hebrew of *Sefer ha-Shorashim* (*Book of Roots;* a dictionary, much used by Christian Hebraists), *Et Sofer* (*The Pen of the Scribe;* a guide to punctuation of Biblical manuscripts), and Biblical commentaries.

**Kim·mei** (kēm·mā). 508?–571 A.D. Emperor of Japan (539?–571); at war with Korea; during his reign (c. 552) Buddhism was introduced in Japan.

**Kim'mel** (kĭm'ĕl), **Hus'band** (hŭz'bănd) **Edward.** 1882–1968. American naval officer, b. Henderson, Ky.; grad. U.S.N.A. (1904); admiral (1941); commander of U.S. Pacific fleet (1941), commander in chief of combined U.S. fleet; relieved of command (Dec., 1941) after Japanese attack on Pearl Harbor.

**Kimp'ton** (kĭm(p)'tŭn), **Lawrence Alpheus.** 1910– American educator; chancellor of Univ. of Chicago (1951–60).

**Kinau, Johann.** See Gorch Fock.

**Kinck** (kĭngk), **Hans Ernst.** 1865–1926. Norwegian novelist and dramatist.

**Kind** (kĭnt), **Johann Friedrich.** 1768–1843. German novelist and dramatist; author of librettos for Weber's *Freischütz* and K. Kreutzer's *Nachtlager von Granada.*

**Kin'di, al-** (ăl·kĭn'dē). *Arab.* **abu-Yūsuf Ya'qūb ibn-Isḥāq al-Kindi.** fl. 9th century A.D. Arab philosopher, b. Al Kufa; called "the Philosopher of the Arabs." One of first Arab students of Greek philosophers; tried to formulate system combining views of Plato and Aristotle; translated Greek works into Arabic and wrote about 265 treatises on scientific subjects.

**Kin'dler** (kĭn'dlẽr), **Hans** (häns). 1893–1949. American violoncellist and conductor; b. Rotterdam; to U.S. (1914), naturalized (1921); founder (1931) and conductor, National Symphony Orchestra of Washington.

**Ki·nea'ly** (kĭ·nē'lĭ), **John Henry.** 1864–1928. American mechanical engineer; patent expert, St. Louis, Mo. (from 1904). Inventor of an air-purifying apparatus, a damper regulator, a thermal valve, etc.

**King** (kĭng), **Basil,** *in full* **William Benjamin Basil.** 1859–1928. Novelist, b. Charlottetown, Prince Edward Island, Canada; rector, Christ Church, Cambridge, Mass. (1892–1900). Author of *The Inner Shrine* (1909), *The Street Called Straight* (1912), *The Side of the Angels* (1916), *The Happy Isles* (1923).

**King, Charles** (1789–1867) and **Charles** (1844–1933). See under Rufus King.

**King, Charles Glen.** 1896– . American chemist; known for isolation (1932) and synthesis (1933) of vitamin C, and for work on enzymes, synthetic fats, nutrition, bacteriology, and dairy sanitation. Cf. Szent-Györgyi von Nagyrapolt.

**King, Clarence.** 1842–1901. American geologist; first head of U.S. Geological Survey (1878–80). Mining engineer (from 1881).

**King, Edward.** 1612–1637. Friend of John Milton; educ. Cambridge. Subject of Milton's elegy *Lycidas.*

**King, Ernest Joseph.** 1878–1956. American naval officer, b. Lorain, Ohio; grad. U.S.N.A., Annapolis (1901); admiral (1941); commander in chief, U.S. Atlantic fleet (1940), combined fleet (Dec., 1941); chief of naval operations (Mar., 1942–Nov., 1945; retired); admiral of the fleet (1944).

**King, Henry.** 1592–1669. English prelate and man of letters; friend of Ben Jonson, Izaak Walton, John Donne; bishop of Chichester (1642–69).

**King, Henry Churchill.** 1858–1934. American educator; professor of philosophy (1891–97) and of theology (1897–1925), Oberlin; president of the college (1902–27).

**King, John.** 1813–1893. American physician; a founder of eclectic school of medicine. Introduced into general use podophyllin, hydrastis and sanguinaria.

**King, John Alsop.** See under Rufus King.

**King, Martin Luther, Jr.** 1929–1968. Amer. clergyman; b. Atlanta, Georgia; founder and president of Southern Christian Leadership Conference; advocate of nonviolence and racial brotherhood; awarded Nobel Peace Prize 1964; assassinated at Memphis, Tenn., April 4, 1968.

**King, Peter.** 1st Baron **King of Ock'ham** (ŏk'ăm). 1669–1734. English jurist; lord chancellor of England (1725–33); author of *History of the Apostles' Creed* (1702).

**King, Rufus.** 1755–1827. American political leader; member, Continental Congress (1784–87); federal Constitutional Convention (1787); Massachusetts ratification convention (1788). To New York City (1788); U.S. senator (1789–96; 1813–25); U.S. minister to Great Britain (1796–1803). Unsuccessful candidate for vice-president of the U.S. (1804 and 1808), and for president (1816). U.S. minister to Great Britain (1825–26). His son **John Alsop** (1788–1867) was member of U.S. House of Representatives (1849–51) and governor of New York (1857, 1858). Another son, **Charles** (1789–1867), was president of Columbia College, New York City (1849–64). A son of Charles, **Rufus** (1814–1876), grad. U.S.M.A., West Point (1833), resigned from army (1836) and engaged in newspaper work (1839–61); brigadier general in Union army (1861–63); U.S. minister to the Papal States (1863–67). Rufus's son **Charles** (1844–1933), grad. U.S.M.A., West Point (1866), was brigadier general of volunteers in Spanish-American War; served under Gen. Lawton in Philippines (1899); author of *Famous and Decisive Battles of the World* (1885), *Rock of Chickamauga* (1907), and a number of novels.

**King, Stanley.** 1883–1951. American lawyer and educator; president of Amherst Coll. (1932–46).

**King, Stoddard.** 1889–1933. American humorist; author of *What the Queen Said* (verse; 1926), *Listen to the Mocking Bird* (1928), and the words of the song *There's a Long, Long Trail.*

**King, Thomas Starr.** 1824–1864. American Unitarian clergyman; pastor in Boston (1848–60), and San Francisco (1860–64); aided in saving California for the Union at outbreak of Civil War.

**King, William.** 1685–1763. English educator and poet; author of mock-heroic poem *The Toast*, and a number of satires praised by Swift.

**King, William Lyon Mackenzie. 1874–1950.** Canadian statesman, b. Ontario; member of Dominion parliament (1908–11; 1919–21; 1921–25; 1926 ff.); minister of labor (1909–11); prime minister of Canada (1921–26; 1926–30; 1935–48).

**King, William Rufus De·Vane′** (dĕ·vān′; dē-). 1786–1853. American politician; settled at Cahaba, Ala. (1818); U.S. senator (1819–44; 1848–53). U.S. minister to France (1844–46). Vice-president of the U.S. (1853).

**King′lake** (kĭng′lāk), **Alexander William.** 1809–1891. English historian; traveled in the East (1835) and wrote *Eothen, or Traces of Travel Brought Home from the East* (1844). Followed British army to Crimea (1854) and, at Lady Raglan's invitation, wrote *Invasion of the Crimea* (8 vols., 1863–87).

**King′o** (kĕng′ō), **Thomas Hansen.** 1634–1703. Danish religious poet and bishop, of Scottish descent; bishop of Fyn (1677); author of collections of hymns (1673, 1681) and of religious and secular poems and pastoral allegories.

**Kingsburgh,** Lord. See Sir John Hay Athole MACDONALD.

**Kings′ford** (kĭngz′fĕrd), **Anna,** *nee* **Bo′nus** (bō′nŭs). 1846–1888. English vegetarian and antivivisectionist. See *Edward Maitland*, under Peregrine MAITLAND.

**Kingsford, Charles Lethbridge.** 1862–1926. English historian and antiquarian; special student and historian of fifteenth-century English literature; published Stow's *Survay of London...*(1908), *First English Life of Henry V* (1911).

**Kingsford, William.** 1819–1898. English soldier, engineer, and historian in Canada; settled in Montreal as civil engineer; author of *History of Canada* (1887–98).

**Kings′ford-Smith′** (-smĭth′), Sir **Charles Edward.** 1897–1935. Australian aviator, b. in Brisbane; served in Royal Flying Corps during World War I (1914–18); in commercial aviation in Australia (from 1919). Made record flight around Australia, 7539 miles in 10 days (with Charles T. P. Ulm; 1927); made transpacific flight from Oakland, Calif., to Brisbane, Australia (with Ulm and others; May 31–June 9, 1928: actual flying time 3 days, 11 hours, 19 min.). Set world's record for flight from Derby, Australia, to London, England (with Ulm and others; June–July, 1929) and for flight from England to Australia, 12,000 miles in 9 days, 23 hours (1930); made record-breaking solo flight, England to Australia, in 7 days, 4 hours, 43 min. (1933); lost en route to Singapore in attempted flight from England to Australia (Nov., 1935).

**Kings′ley** (kĭngz′lĭ), **Charles.** 1819–1875. English clergyman and novelist, b. in Devonshire; educ. King's Coll., London, and Cambridge. Identified with Christian Socialism, and in his early novels *Alton Locke* (1849) and *Yeast* (1849) showed sympathy with the Chartists. Rector at Eversley, in Hampshire; chaplain to Queen Victoria (1859); professor of modern history, Cambridge (1860–69); canon of Westminster (1873). Among his notable works are *Hypatia* (1853), *Westward Ho!* (1855), *Hereward the Wake* (1866), and the children's books *The Heroes*, Greek fairy tales (1856) and *Water Babies* (1863). His younger daughter, **Mary St. Leger Kingsley** (1852–1931), novelist; m. Rev. W. Harrison (1876); under pseudonym **Lucas Mal′et** (măl′ĕt; -ĭt) wrote powerful novels, including *Mrs. Lorimer* (1882), *Colonel Enderly's Wife* (1885), *The Wages of Sin* (1891).

**Henry Kingsley** (1830–1876), novelist; brother of Charles; educ. King's College, London, and Oxford; left Oxford for unsuccessful undertaking in Australian gold fields (1853–58); war correspondent in Franco-Prussian War, and editor, Edinburgh *Daily Review* (1869–70); wrote *Recollections of Geoffrey Hamlyn* (a picture of Australian life; 1859), *Ravenshoe* (1861), *Austin Elliott* (1863), *The Hillyars and the Burtons* (1865).

Another brother, **George Henry Kingsley** (1827–1892), physician; M.D., Edinburgh (1846) and grad. Paris; practiced during outbreak of cholera (portrayed by his brother Henry as Tom Thurnall in *Two Years Ago*); traveled in most countries of the world; wrote books of sport and travel, including *South Sea Bubbles* (with G. R. C. Herbert, 1872). His daughter **Mary Henrietta Kingsley** (1862–1900), traveler and ethnologist, traveled extensively in West Africa, keeping careful record of her experiences and observations; died of typhoid fever while nursing wounded soldiers in South Africa during Boer War; author of *Travels in West Africa* (1897), *West African Studies* (1899), *The Story of West Africa* (1899).

**Kings′ley, Sidney.** 1906– . American playwright; author of *Men in White* (1933), *Dead End* (1935), *Ten Million Ghosts* (1936), and *The Patriots* (1942).

**Kings′mill** (kĭngz′mĭl), **Hugh.** 1889–1949. British novelist and biographer; author of *The Return of William Shakespeare* (1929), *Samuel Johnson* (1933), *D. H. Lawrence* (1938), etc.

**King′ston** (kĭng′stŭn), *in full* **Kingston-upon-Hull** (hŭl), Earls and dukes of. See PIERREPONT family.

**Kingston, William Henry Giles.** 1814–1880. English writer, esp. of books for boys; also, translator of works by Jules Verne.

**Kin·kaid′** (kĭn·kād′), **Moses Pierce.** 1854–1922. American legislator; practiced law in Holt County, Nebr. (from 1881). Member, U.S. House of Representatives (1903–21); author of the Kinkaid Act (1904), allowing 640 acres to each bona fide settler (hence called kinkaider) on certain lands in Nebraska, upon payment of filing fee of **$14.**

**Kinkaid, Thomas Cas′sin** (kăs′ĭn). 1888–1972. American naval officer, b. Hanover, N.H.; grad. U.S.N.A. (1908); rear admiral (1942); task force commander in battles of Coral Sea, Midway, Solomon Islands (1942); commander in chief in North Pacific, carrying out Aleutians campaign (1943); as commander of 7th Fleet (1943–45), supported MacArthur's invasions; admiral (1945); commander, eastern sea frontier (1946).

**Kin′kel** (kĭng′kĕl), **Gottfried.** 1815–1882. German poet and art historian.

**Kin′ley** (kĭn′lĭ), **David.** 1861–1944. Educator, b. in Dundee, Scotland; to U.S. (1872); president, U. of Illinois (1920–30).

**Kin·naird′** (kĭ·nârd′), **Mary Jane,** *nee* **Hoare** (hōr). Lady **Kinnaird.** 1816–1888. English philanthropist; wife of 10th Baron Kinnaird; a founder of the Y.W.C.A.

**Kin′ney** (kĭn′ĭ), **Belle.** 1887–1959. Am. sculpt.; m. (1921)

Leopold Scholz (1874–1946), Vienna-born sculpt. Works include monument to women of the Confederacy, and a bust of Andrew Jackson in the American Hall of Fame.

**Kinney, Troy.** 1871–1938. American painter, b. Kansas City, Mo.; collaborated with his wife, **Margaret,** *nee* **West** [wĕst] (1872–1952), in many illustrations, designs, and murals.

**Ki'no** (kē'nō) *or* **Chi'ni** (kē'nē), **Eusebio Francisco.** 1645?–1711. Jesuit missionary in America, b. Segno, Italy. To Mexico (1681) and Lower California (1682); missionary to Indians in what is now northern Mexico and southern Arizona (1687–1711); discovered and described Casa Grande ruins; prepared and published map of Lower California.

**Kin Ta'tar** (jĭn' tä'tẽr). A Chinese dynasty (1127–1234) of Kin Tatars in the provinces north of the Yangtze, coexistent with most of the Southern Sung dynasty. These Tungus tribes began to get control in the north (1114–27) when called upon by the Sung emperors to drive out the Khitans; conquered by Genghis Khan (1213) but dynasty continued to rule until overcome (1234); finally driven out of China by Kublai Khan (*q.v.*).

**Kint'ner** (kĭnt'nẽr), **Samuel Montgomery.** 1871–1936. American electrical engineer; engaged in radio research for Westinghouse Company (from 1920); vice-president of the company (1931–36).

**Kintore,** Earls of. See KEITH family.

**Kin'zie** (kĭn'zĭ), **John.** 1763–1828. Pioneer fur trader in Chicago region; b. Quebec.

**Kip'ling** (kĭp'lĭng), **Rudyard.** 1865–1936. English writer, b. Bombay, India. Son of **John Lockwood Kipling** (1837–1911), artist and former head of Lahore School of Industrial Art, and curator (1875–93) of Lahore Museum. Educ. United Services Coll., North Devon. To India (1880); on editorial staff of *Civil & Military Gazette and Pioneer*, Lahore (1882–89); began writing verse and tales while in India, and continued in England (from c. 1889). Married (1892) Caroline, sister of Charles Wolcott Balestier (*q.v.*). Awarded Nobel prize for literature (1907). Among his works are *Departmental Ditties* (1886), *Plain Tales from the Hills* (1887), *Soldiers Three, In Black and White, The Story of the Gadsbys, Under the Deodars, Phantom 'Rickshaw, Wee Willie Winkie* (1888–89), *Life's Handicap* (1890), *The Light that Failed* (1891), *Barrack-Room Ballads* (1892), *Many Inventions* (1893), *The Jungle Book* (1894), *Second Jungle Book* (1895), *The Seven Seas* (1896), *Captains Courageous* (1897), *The Day's Work* (1898), *Stalky and Co.* (1899), *Kim* (1901), *Just So Stories for Little Children* (1902), *Traffics and Discoveries* (1904), *Puck of Pook's Hill* (1906), *Actions and Reactions* (1909), *Rewards and Fairies* (1910), *The Harbour Watch* (play; 1913), *A Diversity of Creatures* (1917), *The Years Between* (1918), *Inclusive Verse* (1919), *Debits and Credits* (1926), *A Book of Words* (1928), *Limits and Renewals* (1932), and *Something of Myself* (autobiography, publ. 1937).

**Kip·nis'** (kyĭp·nyĕs'), **Alexander.** 1891– . Operatic basso, b. in Russia; member of Metropolitan Opera Company (from 1939); roles include Wotan in *Die Walküre*, Hagen in *Götterdämmerung*, Sarastro in *The Magic Flute*, Escamillo in *Carmen.*

**Kir'by** (kûr'bĭ), **Rollin.** 1875–1952. American cartoonist; awarded Pulitzer prizes for cartoons *On the Road to Moscow* (1921), *News from the Outside World* (1924), and *Tammany* (1928).

**Kir'by-Smith'** (-smĭth'), **Edmund.** 1824–1893. American army officer; grad. U.S.M.A., West Point (1845); entered Confederate service (1861); major general (Oct., 1861), lieutenant general (Oct., 1862), general (Feb., 1864). In command of Trans-Mississippi Department (from 1863); last Confederate commander to surrender (May 26, 1865). President, U. of Nashville (1870–75); professor of mathematics, U. of the South (from 1875).

**Kirch'bach** (kĭrk'bäk), Count **Hugo Ewald von.** 1809–1887. German general in Franco-Prussian War (1870–71); distinguished himself at Weissenburg, Wörth, Sedan, and siege of Paris.

**Kirchbach, Wolfgang.** 1857–1906. German poet, novelist, playwright, and critic.

**Kirch'ei'sen** (kĭrk'ī'zĕn), **Friedrich Max.** 1877–1933. German historian, esp. of the Napoleonic era.

**Kir'cher** (kĭr'kẽr), **Athanasius.** 1601–1680. German Jesuit and scholar. Taught mathematics and Hebrew at the College of Rome; gave up teaching to study hieroglyphics and archaeology (1643). Credited with invention of the magic lantern.

**Kirch'hoff** (kĭrk'hôf), **Gustav Robert.** 1824–1887. German physicist; credited with discovery, jointly with R. W. Bunsen, of the method of spectrum analysis (1859), which led to their discovery of the elements cesium and rubidium (1860); enunciated the law (Kirchhoff's law) concerning (a) the electric currents and electromotive forces in a network and (b) in optics the emissive power of any body at a definite temperature; investigated thermal conductivity, the solar spectrum, etc.

**Kirchhoff, Johann Wilhelm Adolf.** 1826–1908. German classical philologist and epigraphist. Author of *Die Homerische Odyssee und ihre Entstehung* (1856), and of works on epigraphy; edited *Euripides* (2 vols., 1855), *Plotinus* (2 vols., 1856), etc.

**Kirch'mann** (kĭrk'män), **Julius Hermann von.** 1802–1884. German jurist and writer on law and philosophy; member of Progressive party in Reichstag (1871–76). Author of *Über die Unsterblichkeit* (1865), *Strafgesetzbuch* (1871), *Über das Prinzip des Realismus* (1875), etc.; founded and edited (from 1868) *Philosophische Bibliothek*, a collection of philosophical works of all times, to which he contributed an edition of Kant, translations of Aristotle, Bacon, Grotius, etc.

**Kirch'ner** (kĭrk'nẽr), **Ernst Ludwig.** 1880–1938. German painter and designer; cofounder in Dresden (with Erich Heckel and Karl Schmidt-Rottluff) of "die Brücke" (the Bridge), a group of artists seeking an expressionistic, later a semiabstract, German form of painting rather than academic impressionism (1903; disbanded 1913).

**Kirchner, Theodor.** 1823–1903. German composer; disciple of Schumann. Organist, Winterthur, Switzerland (1843–62); conductor and teacher, Zurich (1862–72); teacher, Leipzig (1875–83) and Dresden Conservatory (1883–90); composed mostly short pieces for piano, songs, and chamber music.

**Kirch'wey** (kûrch'wā), **George Washington.** 1855–1942. American lawyer and criminologist; professor of law, Columbia (1891–1916) and dean of the school of law (1901–10). Warden of Sing Sing prison, Ossining, N.Y. (1915–16). Head of department of criminology, New York School of Social Work (1917–32).

**Kir'dorf** (kĭr'dôrf), **Emil.** 1847–1938. German industrialist. With H. Stinnes, F. Thyssen, A. Vogler (*qq.v.*) formed (1920) the Rhine-Elbe Union, later merged (1926) with important German mining enterprises (incl. Thyssen groups) into the gigantic Vereinigte Stahlwerke (United Steel Works). Opposed the kaiser in government regimentation of business and criticized the democratic system under Weimar Republic; championed a nationalistic policy and was an early supporter of Hitler.

**Kirill Vladimirovich.** Russian name of CYRIL, grand duke of Russia.

**Kirk** (kûrk), **Grayson Louis.** 1903– . American political scientist and educator; president of Columbia Univ. (1953–68).

**Kirk,** Sir **John.** 1832–1922. Scottish administrator in Africa; physician and naturalist with Dr. Livingstone's expedition in Africa (1853–64). Vice-consul of Zanzibar (1867–73), and consul general (1873–87).

**Kirk, John Foster.** 1824–1904. Historian, b. Fredericton, New Brunswick; to U.S. (c. 1842). Editor, *Lippincott's Magazine* (1870–86). Author of *History of Charles the Bold* (1864–68); m. (1879) **Ellen Warner Ol'ney** [ŏl'nĭ] (1842–1928), *pseud.* **Henry Hayes,** novelist.

**Kirk·cal'dy** *or* **Kir·kal'dy** (kûr·kôl'dĭ), Sir **William.** d. 1573. Scottish soldier and politician; involved in murder of Cardinal Beaton (1546); opposed marriage of Mary, Queen of Scots, to Darnley (1565); had knowledge of plot against Rizzio (1566); held Edinburgh for Mary (1568–73), but forced to surrender it; executed.

**Kirke** (kûrk), **Edmund.** See James Roberts GILMORE.

**Kirke, Edward.** 1553–1613. English friend of Edmund Spenser; under initials "E.K.," wrote preface, arguments, and commentary to Spenser's *Shepheardes Calender* (1579).

**Kirke, Percy.** 1646?–1691. English soldier; engaged at Sedgemoor and became notorious for cruelty to rebels (1685).

**Kirk'land** (kûrk'lănd), **Caroline Matilda,** *nee* **Stans'bur'y** (stănz'bĕr'ĭ; -bẽr·ĭ). *Pseudonym* Mrs. **Mary Clav'ers** (?klăv'ẽrz). 1801–1864. American author, b. New York City; m. (1827 or 1828) William Kirkland (d. 1846). Author of *A New Home—Who'll Follow* (1839), *Forest Life* (1842), *Western Clearings* (1845). Her son **Joseph** (1830–1894), lawyer and journalist in Chicago; author of *Zury* (1885), *The McVeys* (1888), *The Captain of Company K* (1891), *The Story of Chicago* (2 vols., 1892–94).

**Kirkland, John.** 1902–1969. American playwright and producer, b. St. Louis, Mo. Adapter of *Frankie and Johnnie* (1928), *Tobacco Road* (1933), *Tortilla Flat* (1938). Author of scenarios for motion pictures.

**Kirkland, Samuel.** 1741–1808. b. Norwich, Conn. American missionary to the Iroquois Indians (from 1764); influential in securing declaration of neutrality from the Six Nations at outbreak of American Revolution (1775); founded Hamilton Oneida Academy (1793), later (1812) chartered as Hamilton College. His son **John Thornton** (1770–1840) was president of Harvard (1810–28), the period of his administration becoming known as the Augustan Age of Harvard history.

**Kirk'man** (kûrk'măn), **Frederick Ber'nulf** (bûr'nŭlf) **Beever.** 1869–1945. British educator and ornithologist, b. in Natal, South Africa; educ. Oxford and Paris. Editor and part author of *British Bird Book* (4 vols., 1911–13), *British Birds* (with F. C. R. Jourdain; 1930), *Bird Behaviour* (1937), *The Highway History* (4 vols., 1936–38).

**Kirk·pat'rick** (kûrk·păt'rĭk), **Alexander Francis.** 1849–1940. Anglican prelate; regius professor of Hebrew, Cambridge, and canon of Ely (1882–1903); dean of Ely (1906–36).

**Kirkpatrick, Frederick Alexander.** 1861–1953. British educator and author of *A History of Argentina, The Spanish Conquistadores, Latin-America,* etc.

**Kirkpatrick, William.** See under ANVARI.

**Kir'kup** (kûr'kŭp), **Thomas.** 1844–1912. British economist; author of treatises on socialism.

**Kirk'wood** (kûrk'wŏŏd), **Samuel Jordan.** 1813–1894. American politician; governor of Iowa (1860–64; 1876–77); U.S. senator (1866–67; 1877–81). U.S. secretary of the interior (1881–82).

**Kirn'ber'ger** (kĭrn'bĕr'gẽr), **Johann Philipp.** 1721–1783. German musical theorist and composer of orchestral, choral, and piano works.

**Ki'rov** (kyē'rôf), **Sergei Mironovich.** 1888–1934. Soviet leader; engaged in revolutionary activities (from 1905). After Revolution (1917), took part in wars against counterrevolutionists (1917–20); member of delegation negotiating Riga peace treaty (1920). Secretary of Communist party in Azerbaijan (1923–26) and in Leningrad area (1926–34); elected to Politburo (1930); one of Stalin's chief aides; member of presidium (1930–34). Assassinated at Leningrad (Dec. 1); his death followed by execution of his murderer and 116 others convicted of widespread conspiracy to overthrow Stalin.

**Kir·shon'** (kyĭr·shôn'), **Vladimir Mikhailovich.** 1902–1937. Russian playwright; author of *Red Rust* (with A. V. Uspenski; produced in New York, 1929), *The City of Winds, Bread, The Wonderful Alloy* (1936), etc.

**Kirt'land** (kûrt'lănd), **Jared Potter.** 1793–1877. American physician and zoologist; discovered parthenogenesis in the silkworm moth, and the bisexual nature of freshwater bivalve mollusks.

**Kir'wan** (kûr'wăn), **Richard.** 1733–1812. Irish chemist and natural philosopher; author of *Elements of Mineralogy* (1784), first English systematic treatise on this subject. Known as "the Nestor of English chemistry."

**Kis'fa·lu·dy** (kĭsh'fŏ·lŏŏ·dĭ), **Sándor.** 1772–1844. Hungarian lyric and epic poet, playwright, and fiction writer. His brother **Károly** (1788–1830) was a poet and dramatist of the romantic school, founder of modern national drama of Hungary; cofounder, with Sándor, and editor (from 1822) of *Aurora,* organ of the romanticists; author of historical dramas of Hungary and of comedies and tragedies of contemporary Hungarian life.

**Kiss** (kĭs), **August.** 1802–1865. German sculptor; his works include *Mounted Amazon Attacked by a Tiger,* an equestrian statue of Frederick the Great, statues of Frederick William III, and *St. George and the Dragon.*

**Kis'sin·ger** (kĭs'ĭn·jẽr), **Henry Alfred.** 1923– . American political scientist and public official, b. Germany. To U.S. (1938); at Harvard U. (1951–69); special assistant to Pres. Nixon for national security affairs (1969–73), U.S. secretary of state (1973-77); awarded Nobel prize for peace (1973).

**Kiss'ling** (kĭs'lĭng), **Richard.** 1848–1919. Swiss sculptor.

**Kis'te·mae'kers** (kĭs'tĕ·mä'kẽrs), **Henry Hubert Alexandre.** 1872–1938. Belgian-born novelist and playwright; naturalized French citizen (1903).

**Ki·ta·za·to** (kē·tä·zä·tō), **Shibasaburo.** 1852–1931. Japanese bacteriologist, b. Kumamoto; studied under Koch in Berlin; isolated bacilli of tetanus and of symptomatic anthrax (1889) and of dysentery (1898). Prepared a diphtheria antitoxin (1890). Discovered etiological agent of bubonic plague, *Bacillus pestis* (1894).

**Kitch'e·ner** (kĭch'ĕ·nẽr), **Horatio Herbert.** 1st Earl **Kitchener of Khar·toum'** (kär·tōōm') **and of Broome** (brōōm). 1850–1916. British soldier, b. Ballylongford, Ireland; educ. Royal Military Acad., Woolwich; commissioned in Royal Engineers (1871). Served in Wolseley's expedition for relief of General Gordon (1884–85). Governor general of Eastern Sudan (1886). Sirdar of Egyptian army (1892); invaded Sudan, annihilated the Khalifa's army at Omdurman, and reoccupied Khartoum (1898); governor general of Sudan (1899). Chief of staff to Lord Roberts in South Africa (1899); organized forces to combat guerrilla warfare of Boers (1900–02). Commander in chief in India (1902–09). Secretary of state for war (1914); engaged in organizing British forces for war (1914–16).

**Ki Tse** *or* **Chi-tsě** *or, better,* **Chi-tzŭ** (jē'dzŭ'). fl. 12th century B.C. Reputed founder of kingdom of Korea. A Chinese feudal lord under Chou Hsin, last ruler of Shang dynasty; on its overthrow left China with 5000 followers; settled (1122 B.C.) probably at Pingyang in Korea, naming the new country Chosen ("Land of the Morning Calm"); introduced Chinese culture and established kingdom, his descendants ruling for more than 900 years. Supposed author of part of the *Shu Ching*, one of the Five Classics.

**Kit'son** (kĭt's'n), **Henry Hudson.** 1865–1947. Sculptor, b. at Huddersfield, Eng.; resident in U.S. for many years. Among his works are: *The Minute Man* in Lexington, Mass.; statues of Gen. N. P. Banks in Boston, Gen. Robert E. Lee in Vicksburg, Miss.; *Pilgrim Maiden* in Plymouth, Mass.; statue of Christ, Drexel Memorial in Philadelphia; statue of James Viscount Bryce in National Museum of Art, Washington, D.C. His first wife, **Theo Alice,** *nee* **Rug'gles** [rŭg''lz] (1871–1932), was sculptor of the statue of General Kosciusko in the public garden, Boston, an equestrian statue of Victory in Hingham, Mass., etc.

**Kit'tel** (kĭt'ĕl), **Rudolf.** 1853–1929. German Protestant theologian and Old Testament scholar.

**Kit'to** (kĭt'ō), **John.** 1804–1854. English Bible scholar; missionary to Malta (1827–29) and Persia (1829–33).

**Kit'tredge** (kĭt'rĭj), **George Lyman.** 1860–1941. American educator, b. Boston. A.B., Harvard (1882). Teacher of English, Harvard (1888–1936); professor (from 1894). Author of *The Language of Chaucer's Troilus* (1894), *Words and Their Ways in English Speech* (with J. B. Greenough, 1901), *English Witchcraft and James I* (1912), *Advanced English Grammar* (with F. E. Farley, 1913), *Chaucer and His Poetry* (1915), *Gawain and the Green Knight* (1916), *Shakespeare* (1916), *Sir Thomas Malory* (1925), *Witchcraft in Old and New England* (1929), etc. Edited, *Albion Series of Anglo-Saxon and Middle English Poetry* (with J. W. Bright, 5 vols., 1900–07), *Complete Works of Shakespeare* (1936). Advisory consultant for synonymy (see John L. LOWES) and reviser of introductory section on history of the English language, *Webster's New International Dictionary.*

**Kiuprili.** See KUPRILI.

**Ki'vi** (kĭ'vĭ), **Alexis.** *Real surname* **Sten'vall** (stān'vȧl). 1834–1872. Finnish dramatist and novelist; author of *Kullervo* (1864; a dramatization of an episode from the *Kalevala*), the comedy *The Shoemakers of the Heath* (1864), and the novel of peasant life *The Seven Brothers* (1870).

**Kiyomasu, Kiyomitsu, Kiyonaga, Kiyonobu.** Japanese painters. See TORII.

**Ki·yo·mo·ri** (kē·yō·mō·rē). 1118–1181. Japanese warrior and statesman; a leader of the Taira clan. Took part in civil war (1156–60) of the Taira, Minamoto and Fujiwara; by overcoming (1160) Yoshitomo and Nobuyori, Fujiwara leader, placed Taira clan in control of affairs; had himself appointed prime minister by the emperor (1167); weakened power of the Buddhists; influence gradually decreased as strength of Minamotos grew (1179–81); Taira clan annihilated four years after his death.

**Kjel'dahl** (kĕl'dȧl), **J.** 1849–1900. Danish chemist; known esp. for skill in devising analytical methods of investigation.

**Kje'rulf** (KĕʹrōōIf), **Halfdan.** 1815–1868. Norwegian composer; representative of national Norwegian music. Composed lyric piano pieces, choruses, and songs made popular by Sontag, Jenny Lind, and Christine Nilsson.

**Kjerulf, Theodor.** 1825–1888. Norwegian geologist; known for studies in southern Norway.

**Kla·bund'** (klä·bōōnt'). *Pseudonym of* **Alfred Hensch'ke** (hĕnsh'kĕ). 1891–1928. German author of lyric verse, including the volumes *Morgenrot* (1913), *Der Himmlische Vagant* (1918), *Dreiklang* (1920), and *Das Heisse Herz* (1923); novels, chiefly historical, as *Moreau* (1915), *Mohammed* (1917), *Pjotr* (1923), and *Rasputin* (1929); plays, as *Der Kreidekreis* (after the Chinese; 1924) and *Cromwell* (1926); a *History of German Literature* (1919) and a *History of Universal Literature* (1921); translations and imitations of Chinese literature, etc.

**Klaf'sky** (kläf'skē), **Ka'tha·ri'na** (kä'tä·rē'nä). 1855–1896. Hungarian operatic soprano; principal star of Hamburg Opera (from 1886); sang with Damrosch Opera Co. in U.S. (1895–96).

**Klaj** (klī). See also CLAJUS.

**Klaj, Johann.** *Lat. surname* **Cla'jus** (klä'yōōs). 1616–1656. German poet; in Nuremberg, founded, with Harsdörfer, literary group known as the Pegnitzorden (1644); author esp. of mystery plays in verse.

**Klap'ka** (klŏp'kŏ), **György.** 1820–1892. Hungarian revolutionary general; led Northern Hungarian army (1849); served in battle of Kápolna and with distinction under Görgey at Komárno and elsewhere; defended Komárno, capitulating on honorable terms (1849). In exile (1849–67); organized Hungarian legion with Kossuth in Italy (1859) and with Bismarck in Upper Silesia (1866). Returned to Hungary following amnesty (1867), and supported Deák party as member of Hungarian parliament.

**Klap'roth** (kläp'rōt), **Martin Heinrich.** 1743–1817. German chemist; known for accurate analyses of minerals and discovery of the elements uranium, titanium, and zirconium. His son **Heinrich Julius** (1783–1835), Orientalist and Asiatic traveler, was author of *Asia Polyglotta* (Paris, 1823; with a language atlas), etc.

**Klau'ber** (klô'bẽr), **Adolph.** 1879–1933. American theatrical producer; m. (1908) Jane Cowl (*q.v.*). Produced Eugene O'Neill's *Emperor Jones*, and, with his wife, *Lilac Time, Smilin' Through, Romeo and Juliet, Pelleas and Melisande, Antony and Cleopatra.*

**Klaus,** Bruder [*or* Brother]. See NICHOLAS OF FLÜE.

**Klaus'ner** (klous'nẽr), **Jo'seph** (yō'zĕf). 1874–1958. Jewish scholar, b. in Russia; champion of modernization of Hebrew language and literature.

**Klau'well** (klou'vĕl), **Otto.** 1851–1917. German composer and writer on music.

**Klaw** (klô), **Marc.** 1858–1936. American theatrical manager (from 1881); partner in firm of Klaw & Erlanger. See Abraham Lincoln ERLANGER.

**Klé'ber'** (klā'bâr'), **Jean Baptiste.** 1753–1800. French soldier of the Revolutionary period; general of brigade (1793); engaged at Charleroi and Fleurus (1794) and in siege of Mainz; commanded army of the Rhine and Moselle (1795); commanded a division in Napoleon's army in Egypt and Syria (1798–1800) and was left as commander in chief when Napoleon returned (1799) to France; assassinated by an Egyptian fanatic (June 14, 1800).

**Klebs** (klāps), **Edwin.** 1834–1913. German pathologist; assistant to Virchow at Berlin (1861). To U.S.; director of a bacteriological laboratory in Asheville, N.C. (1895); professor, Rush Medical College, Chicago (1896); later returned to Germany. Described (1883) the bacillus causing diphtheria, later isolated by Friedrich A. J. Löffler, and known as the Klebs-Löffler bacillus; also, investigated the bacteriology of malaria, anthrax, tuberculosis, etc.

**Klee** (klā), **Paul.** 1879–1940. Swiss modernist painter and pictorial artist, b. Bern; representative of the modern German school. Cofounder in Munich (with Kandinski and Marc) of the German abstract school *Blaue Reiter* (1911), and associate of Kubin, Macke, Feininger, and others; cofounder of the Blue Four movement (1926); developed (from about 1902) an individual style of expressing the subconscious mind and phantasy in art; author of *Pädagogisches Skizzenbuch* (1925).

**Klef'fens** (klĕf'ĕns), **Eelco Nicolaas van.** 1894– . Dutch statesman; minister of foreign affairs (1939–46); delegate to UN (from 1946); author of *The Rape of the Netherlands* (American title, *Juggernaut over Holland*, 1940).

**Klei'ber** (klī'bēr), **Erich.** 1890-1956. Austrian conductor, b. Vienna.

**Klein** (klīn), **Bernhard.** 1793–1832. German composer of oratorios *Job* (1820), *David* (1830), and *Jephthah* (1828), the operas *Dido* (1823) and *Ariadne* (1825), church music, songs, etc.

**Klein, Bruno Os'car** (ŏs'kēr). 1858–1911. Composer, b. Osnabrück, Hanover, Germany; to U.S. (1878); resident of New York City (from 1884); composed numerous pieces for the piano, and the orchestra, and an opera, *Kenilworth*.

**Klein, Charles.** 1867–1915. Dramatist, b. London, England; to U.S. (1883). Examples of his work: *The District Attorney* (with Harrison Grey Fiske, 1895), *The Auctioneer* (with Lee Arthur, 1901), *The Music Master* (1904), *The Lion and the Mouse* (1905), *Maggie Pepper* (1911), *The Third Degree* (1909), *The Gamblers* (1910), *The Moneymakers* (1914), the last three in collaboration with Arthur Hornblow.

**Klein, Felix.** 1849–1925. German mathematician; known esp. for work on geometry and the theory of functions; also interested in the application of mathematics to physics.

**Klein, Julius Leopold.** 1810–1876. German dramatist, literary historian, and art and dramatic critic, b. in Hungary.

**Klein'schmidt** (klīn'shmĭt), **Otto.** 1870–1954. German ornithologist and Protestant theologian; champion of a modern biological group or association theory (Formenkreislehre). Author of *Die Formenkreislehre und das Weltwerden des Lebens* (1926), etc.

**Klein'Smid** (klīn'smĭd), **Rufus Bern'hard** (bûr'närd) **von** (vŏn). 1875-1964. American educator; president, U. of Arizona (1914–21), U. of Southern California (1921–46).

**Kleist** (klīst), **E. G. von.** Dean of the Cathedral of Kamin, Pomerania. Discovered the principle of the Leyden jar (called also Kleistian jar) at about same time (1745) as P. van Musschenbroek of U. of Leiden.

**Kleist, Ewald Christian von.** 1715–1759. German poet and soldier; officer in Danish army (1736) and in Prussian army (from 1740); mortally wounded at battle of Kunersdorf (1759). Author of the descriptive nature poem *Der Frühling* (1749), the *Ode an die Preussische Armee* (1757), the short epic poem *Cissides und Paches* (1759), and other lyrics, odes, idyls, hymns, etc. Said to have been model for Tellheim in Lessing's *Minna von Barnhelm*.

**Kleist, Heinrich von.** 1777–1811. German dramatist, poet, and novelist. Founded in Dresden (with Adam Müller) the journal *Phöbus* (1808); pamphleteer and journalist on Austro-French war front (1809) and in Prague against Napoleon; returned to Berlin (1810) after defeat at Wagram. Edited and contributed to the *Berliner Abendblätter* (suppressed, 1811, for attacks on Hardenberg); became poverty-stricken and despondent, and killed his friend Frau Henriette Vogel and himself by mutual agreement (1811). Author of the tragedies *Die Familie Schroffenstein* (1803) and *Penthesilea* (1808), the romantic chivalric drama *Das Käthchen von Heilbronn* (1810), the patriotic drama *Die Hermannschlacht* (pub. 1821), the comedy *Der Zerbrochene Krug* (1812; Eng. *The Broken Jug*), lyric poetry, etc.

**Kleist, Paul Ludwig Ewald von.** 1881–1954. German colonel general; in command against France (1940), in Yugoslavia (1941), and on southern Russian front (Aug., 1941); advanced through Ukraine and Don region into Caucasus (1941–42) until defeats and withdrawals forced by Russian winter offensive (1942–43).

**Kleist'-Ret'zow** (-rĕt'sō), **Hans Hugo von.** 1814–1892. Prussian politician; champion of extreme conservative government and recognition of church. Led so-called Junker Parliament (1848) and helped found *Kreuzzeitung;* member, Prussian House of Lords (from 1858).

**Kleist von Nol'len·dorf** (fôn nôl'ĕn·dôrf), Count **Friedrich Heinrich Ferdinand Emil.** 1762–1823. Prussian general; corps commander in war with Russia (1812) and in campaign of 1813; fought at Dresden; helped victory of Kulm by defeating French at Nollendorf (1813); was defeated at Etoges in war with France, but distinguished himself at Laon (1814).

**Klemm** (klĕm), **Hanns.** 1885–1961. German airplane designer and constructor.

**Klem'pe·rer** (klĕm'pĕ·rēr), **Otto.** 1885–1973. Orchestra and opera conductor, b. Breslau (Wroclaw). Conductor German Theater (Prague), Hamburg, Bremen, etc., Kroll Opera and State Opera, Berlin; in exile 1933. Led Los Angeles Philharmonic, etc. Known especially for readings of German Romantic composers.

**Kle'nau** (klā'nou), **Paul August von.** 1883–1946. Danish composer and conductor.

**Klencke, Karoline Luise.** See under Anna Luise KARSCH.

**Kleng'el** (klĕng'ĕl), **August Alexander.** 1783–1852. German composer; court organist, Dresden (from 1816).

**Klengel, Paul.** 1854–1935. German violinist, pianist, and composer; teacher at Leipzig Conservatory (1907–31); composed songs, piano pieces, etc. His brother **Julius** (1859–1933), violoncello virtuoso and composer in Leipzig, was teacher at Leipzig Conservatory (from 1881); composed violoncello concertos, suites, sonatas, concert pieces and studies, chamber music, and a *Hymnus* for 12 violoncellos.

**Klen'ze** (klĕn'tsĕ), **Franz Karl Leo von.** 1784–1864. German architect and landscape painter. Author of works chiefly on Greek architecture. He designed, mainly in Italian Renaissance and neo-Greek styles, the Glyptothek (1816), the war department building (1824–30), the palace of Duke Maximilian (1826–30), the Old Pinakothek (1826–36), the king's residence (1826–32) and banquet building (1831–42), and the Propylaea (1846–62), all in Munich.

**Klesel** *or* **Klesl, Melchior.** See KHLESL.

**Klet'ten·berg** (klĕt'ĕn·bĕrk), **Susanne Katharine von.** 1723–1774. German Pietist; original of the "schöne Seele" in Goethe's *Wilhelm Meister*. Friend of Goethe's mother; influenced young Goethe's religious attitude and interest in alchemy during his illness (1768–70).

**Klie'foth** (klē'fōt), **Theodor.** 1810–1895. German Protestant theologian and Lutheran leader.

**Klie'gl** (klē'g'l), **John H.** (1869–1959) and his brother **Anton T.** (1872–1927). Pioneers in development of lighting equipment (including klieg light) and scenic effects for the stage and for motion pictures; b. in Bad Kissingen, Ger. John emigrated to U.S. in 1888, Anton in 1892; formed partnership of Kliegl Bros. (1897).

**Klimsch** (klĭmsh), **Fritz.** 1870–1960. German sculptor; his works include the Virchow monument (1906–10), bronze statues of the virtues for the Reichstag (1914–17), an *Aglaia* (1924), and busts of prominent contemporaries.

**Klinck** (klĭngk), **Leonard Silvanus.** 1877–1969. Canadian agriculturist and educator; president, U. of British Columbia (1919–44).

**Klind′worth** (klĭnt′vôrt), **Karl.** 1830–1916. German pianist, teacher, and composer. In London (1854–68); professor, Moscow Conservatory (1868–84); settled in Berlin, conducted the philharmonic concerts (until 1892, with Joachim and Wüllner), and established a school of piano (combined with Scharwenka Conservatory, 1893); to Potsdam (1893).

**Kling′er** (klĭng′ẽr), **Friedrich Maximilian von.** 1752–1831. German dramatist and novelist; representative of Sturm und Drang period. Childhood friend of Goethe; joined Austrian army (1778), and became officer in Russian army at St. Petersburg (1780) and lieutenant general (1811); ennobled (1780). Curator of Dorpat U. (1803–17). Author of dramatic works, including *Sturm und Drang* (1776), which gave its name to the Sturm und Drang period of German literature, *Simsone Grisaldo* (1776), and *Die Neue Arria* (1776), philosophical and realistic novels, as *Fausts Leben, Taten, und Höllenfahrt* (1791), *Geschichte eines Teutschen der Neuesten Zeit* (1798), and *Der Weltmann und der Dichter* (1798), etc.

**Klinger, Max.** 1857–1920. German etcher, painter, and sculptor. His works include: (1) series of pen-and-ink drawings and cycles of etchings, as *Fantasies upon the Finding of a Glove, Eve and the Future, A Love, Of Death*, the *Brahms Fantasy*, also etched self-portraits and bookplates; (2) paintings, as the *Judgment of Paris, Crucifixion*, a *Pietà, Christ on Olympus*, and frescoes for Leipzig U.; (3) sculptured half-length polychromatic marble figures of Salome and of Cassandra, and the polychromatic statue of Beethoven seated on a decorated chair, busts of Nietzsche, Liszt, and others, a colossal bronze *Athlete*, etc.

**Kling′sor′** (klăɴg′sôr′), **Tristan.** *Pseudonym of* **Léon Le·clère′** (lẽ·klâr′). 1874–1966. French writer, painter, and musician. Among his volumes of verse are *Schéhérazade* (1903), *Poèmes de Bohême* (1913), *Humoresques* (1921); author of critical studies of Chardin, Cézanne, da Vinci; composer of *Chansons de Ma Mère l'Oie* (1905) and *Petite Suite pour deux Violons.* His painting *Environs d'Angers* hangs in the Luxembourg.

**Klo·no′wic** (klô·nô′vēts), **Sebastian.** *Lat. surname* **A·cer′nus** (*ȧ*·sûr′nŭs). 1545?–1602. Polish satirical poet; author of works in Latin and Polish including *Roxolania* (1584; satire on Russia), *Victoria Deorum* (1595; on the oppression of the poor), and *Judas's Knapsack* (1600; on corruption and exploitation of the time).

**Klopp** (klôp), **Onno.** 1822–1903. German historian; wrote *Der Fall des Hauses Stuart* (14 vols., 1875–88), etc.; edited 11 vols. of the works of Leibniz (1864–84).

**Klop′stock** (klôp′shtôk), **Friedrich Gottlieb.** 1724–1803. German poet; studied theology at Jena (1745) and drafted in prose the beginning of the religious epic *Messias* (*The Messiah*); recast it into hexameters at Leipzig (1746), and published the first 3 cantos anonymously in the journal *Bremer Beitrage* (1748). Private tutor at Langensalza (1748), where he fell in love with his cousin, the "Fanny" of his odes; invited to Copenhagen by King of Denmark (on Bernstorff's recommendation) to complete the *Messias* on pensions (1751–70); m. 1st (1754) Margareta [Meta] Moller, the "Cidli" of his odes (d. 1758); in Hamburg (1770–74; 1776 ff.), where he completed (1773) the *Messias* (4 vols., 1751–73). m. 2d (1791) Elisabeth von Winthem, niece of his first wife. Other works include *Oden* (1771), *Geistliche Lieder* (2 vols., 1757, 1769), critical and theoretical writings, including the prose work *Die Deutsche Gelehrtenrepublik* (1774) on his own scheme of poetry and literature, religious dramas, as *Der Tod Adams* (1757) and *David* (1772), and *Hermanns Schlacht* (1769), *Hermann und die Fürsten* (1784), and *Hermanns Tod* (1787), a trilogy of historical prose dramas with bardic choruses (called "Bardiete").

**Klo′ster·man** (klō′stẽr·män), **Karel.** 1848–1923. German-born writer in Bohemia; author of realistic tales of life in southwestern Bohemia.

**Klostermann, Johann.** See John CLOSTERMAN.

**Klotz** *or* **Kloz** (klôts). Family of Bavarian violinmakers in Mittenwald including **Mathias** (1653–1743), prob. pupil of Nicolò Amati in Cremona; active in Padua and (from 1683) in Mittenwald; and his sons **Georg** (b. 1687), **Sebastian** (b. 1696), and **Johann Karl** (b. 1709).

**Klotz, Christian Adolf.** 1738–1771. German classical philologist and scholar; author of Latin poems, satirical writings (as *Genius Saeculi*, 1760, and *Antiburmanus*, 1762), and philological and archaeological works including *Über den Nutzen und Gebrauch der Alten Geschnittenen Steine* (1768), which contains a criticism of Lessing's *Laokoon* answered by Lessing in his *Briefe Antiquarischen Inhalts* (1768–69).

**Klotz** (klŏts), **Otto Julius.** 1852–1923. Canadian civil engineer and astronomer; made survey of the northwest; with Alaskan boundary survey (1893–94); director of the Dominion Observatory, Ottawa. His son **Oskar** (1878–1936), pathologist, was an authority on diseases of the heart and arteries.

**Klü′ber** (klü′bẽr), **Johann Ludwig.** 1762–1837. German publicist; attended Congress of Vienna (1814–15), and collected the *Akten des Wiener Kongresses in den Jahren 1814 und 1815* (8 vols., 1815–18).

**Kluck** (klo͝ok), **Alexander von.** 1846–1934. German soldier. Commanded right-wing army of three main armies invading France (1914), directed upon Paris; by deflecting his attack to southeast as allied troops were forced back on Paris, gave opportunity for flank attack by new and hastily organized French army under Maunoury, his repulse marking beginning of French success in first battle of the Marne (1914); wounded (1915) and forced to give up command.

**Klu′ge** (klo͞o′gĕ), **Friedrich.** 1856–1926. German Germanic scholar and Anglicist; author of works on Gothic, English, and German languages, including *Etymologisches Wörterbuch der Deutschen Sprache* (1883).

**Klu′ge, Gunther von.** 1882–1944. German field marshal; served in World War (1914–18); occupied Polish Corridor (1939); served in France (1940), northwestern Russia (1941); commander on central Russian front (1942) and in western Europe (commander in chief, July, 1944).

**Klug′hardt** (klo͞oᴋ′härt), **August Friedrich Martin.** 1847–1902. German composer of operas, as *Iwein* (1879) and *Gudrun* (1882), oratorios, as *Zerstörung Jerusalems* (1899), symphonies, suites, overtures, chamber music, and songs.

**Kmety** (k'mĕt'y'), **György.** 1810–1865. Hungarian and Turkish general, b. in Hungary. Distinguished himself in Hungarian War of Independence (1848–49); fled to Turkey following Görgey's surrender at Világos, embraced Moslem faith, and, as **Is′ma·il′ Pa·sha′** (ĭs′mä·ēl′ pä·shä′), became general in Turkish army; defended Armenian fortress at Kars against Russians in Crimean War (1854–55).

**Kna′be** (k'nä′bĕ), **Val′en·tine** (văl′ĕn·tīn) **Wil′helm** (vĭl′hĕlm) **Lud′wig** (lo͞ot′vĭᴋ). 1803–1864. Manufacturer, b. Kreuzburg, Prussia; to U.S. (1833); naturalized

(1840); established in Baltimore piano-manufacturing business continued by his sons **Ernst** (1837–1894) and **William** (1841–1889) and grandsons **Ernst J.** (1869–1894) and **William** (1872–1939).

**Knack′fuss** (k'näk′fōōs), **Hermann.** 1848–1915. German painter and writer on art. His works include mural decorations in the courthouse (1892) at Kassel, the altar painting *Holy Family* (1893; in Fulda Cathedral), the historical composition *Entry of Emperor William II into Jerusalem* (1903); also, portraits, and designs for woodcuts.

**Knapp** (k'näp), **Albert.** 1798–1864. German theologian, poet, and hymnologist.

**Knapp, Georg Friedrich.** 1842–1926. German political economist; professor of national economy and statistics, Strassburg (1874–1918).

**Knapp** (năp), **Martin Augustine.** 1843–1923. American specialist in railroad transportation and commerce, b. in Onondaga County, N.Y. Member, U.S. Interstate Commerce Commission (1897–1916).

**Knapp, Seaman Asahel.** 1833–1911. American agriculturist, b. Schroon Lake, N.Y.; conducted colonization experiment at Lake Charles, La., inducing farmers to settle in Louisiana and practice scientific methods of farming; developed rice industry.

**Knatch′bull–Hu′ges·sen** (năch′bŏŏl·hū′jĕ·s'n), **Edward Hugessen.** 1st Baron **Bra′bourne** (brā′bērn). 1829–1893. English political leader; undersecretary for home affairs (1860, 1866), for colonies (1871–74); privy councilor (1873); writer of stories for children. Son of Sir **Edward Knatchbull** (1781–1849).

**Knatchbull–Hugessen,** Sir **Hughe** (hū) **Montgomery.** 1886–1971. British diplomat; ambassador to China (1936–38), Turkey (1939–44), Belgium (1944–47).

**Knaus** (k'nous), **Ludwig.** 1829–1910. German genre and portrait painter. His works include *The Promenade, The Golden Wedding, The Children's Festival, The Holy Family, The Road to Ruin, Old Woman and Cats, The Quarrel,* portraits of Helmholtz and of Mommsen, etc.

**Kne′bel** (k'nā′bĕl), **Karl Ludwig von.** 1744–1834. German poet and translator; associated with Goethe, Schiller, and their literary circle at Weimar. Author of sonnets and translations into German of the *Elegiae* of Propertius (1798), the *De Rerum Natura* of Lucretius (1821), and Alfieri's tragedy *Saul* (1829).

**Kneipp** (k'nīp), **Sebastian.** 1821–1897. German priest; originated and developed (from 1848) "Kneippism" or "Kneipp's cure," a system of treatment of disease by forms of hydrotherapy. Author of *My Water Cure* (1886), etc.

**Knei′sel** (nī′z'l; *Ger.* k'nī′zĕl), **Franz** (fränts). 1865–1926. Violinist, b. Bucharest, Rumania; in U.S. (from 1885); solo violinist, Boston Symphony Orchestra (1885–1903). Organized Kneisel Quartet (debut in Boston, Dec., 1885); devoted himself to leadership of quartet (1903–17). Head of violin department, Institute of Musical Art, New York City (from 1905); disbanded quartet to give all his time to Institute (1917).

**Knel′ler** (nĕl′ēr; *Ger.* k'nĕl′ēr), Sir **Godfrey.** *Orig. name* **Gottfried Knil′ler** (k'nĭl′ēr). 1646–1723. Portrait painter, b. Lübeck, Germany. To England (1675); painted portraits of duke of Monmouth, Charles II, and (for Charles) Louis XIV; principal painter to William III, of whom he did an equestrian portrait; retained favor under Anne and George I; painted ten reigning monarchs in all, including Peter the Great (during Peter's visit to England), and many English celebrities of his day, including members of the Kit-cat Club.

**Kne′se·beck** (k'nā′zĕ·bĕk), Baron **Karl Friedrich von dem.** 1768–1848. Prussian general. Succeeded Gneisenau as commander of army of observation on Polish frontier (1831). Became field marshal general on retirement (1847).

**Kniaź′nin** (k'nyäz′y'·nēn), **Franciszek Dyonizy.** 1750–1807. Polish poet and playwright.

**Knibbs** (nĭbz), **Harry** (or **Henry**) **Herbert.** 1874–1945. Canadian writer, b. Clifton, Ont.; author of *Songs of the Outlands* (1914), *Sundown Slim* (1915), *Riders of the Stars* (1916), *Saddle Songs* (1922), *The Tonto Kid* (1936), etc.

**Knick′er·bock′er** (nĭk′ēr·bŏk′ēr), **Die′drich** (dē′drĭk). Pretended author of Washington Irving's *History of New York* (1809).

**Knickerbocker, Harmen Jansen.** 1650?–?1716. Dutch colonist in New Amsterdam (New York); founder of Knickerbocker family in America; to New Amsterdam (1674) and settled on land near Albany (1682); moved to near Red Hook in Dutchess County (1704).

**Knies** (k'nēs), **Karl.** 1821–1898. German economist; cofounder with Roscher and Hildebrand of the historical school of German economics.

**Knig′ge** (k'nĭg′ĕ), Baron **Adolf von.** 1752–1796. German author of novels and stories, a translation of Mozart's *Figaro* (1791), dramatic poems, etc.

**Knight** (nīt), **Austin Melvin.** 1854–1927. American naval officer; admiral (1917); commanded Asiatic fleet, operating near Vladivostok; retired (1918). Author of *Modern Seamanship* (1901).

**Knight, Charles.** 1791–1873. English publisher of *Penny Magazine* (1832–45), *Penny Cyclopaedia* (1833–44), *Pictorial History of England* (1837–44), *Pictorial Shakespeare* (1838–41), etc.

**Knight, Charles Robert.** 1874–1953. American painter, illustrator, and muralist, b. Brooklyn, N.Y.; specialist in paintings of animals and birds, as for American Museum of Natural History in New York, Field Museum in Chicago, etc.

**Knight, Daniel Ridgway.** 1840–1924. American painter; resident of Paris (from 1872). His *Hailing the Ferry* is in Pennsylvania Academy of Fine Arts; *The Shearer,* in Boston Museum of Art.

**Knight, Edward Henry.** 1824–1883. Patent attorney and mechanical authority; b. London, England; to U.S. (1845). Author of *Knight's American Mechanical Dictionary* (3 vols., 1874–76), and its supplement, *Knight's New Mechanical Dictionary* (1882–84).

**Knight, Eric Mowbray.** 1897–1943. Novelist, b. Menston, Yorkshire, Eng.; to U.S. (1912), naturalized (1942); private in Canadian army in World War I (1914–18); World War II major in U.S. army (1942); killed in airplane crash while on official mission. Author of *Song on Your Bugles* (1936), *The Flying Yorkshireman* (1937), *The Happy Land* (1940), *This Above All* (1941), etc.

**Knight, George Wilson.** 1897– . Canadian educator and literary scholar, b. Sutton, Surrey, Eng.; educ. Oxford. Chancellor's professor of English, Trinity Coll., Toronto; known esp. for Shakespearean studies.

**Knight, Harold.** 1874–1961. English portrait painter. His wife (m. 1903) **Laura** *nee* **Johnson** (1877-1970) painter esp. of circus and theater subjects; created Dame of the British Empire (1929).

**Knight, Howard Lawton.** 1881– . American agriculturist, b. Gardner, Mass. Assistant editor, Experiment Station Record, for U.S. Department of Agriculture (1906–18), associate editor (1918–23), and editor (from 1923). Special editor for agriculture, *Webster's New International Dictionary, Second Edition.*

**Knight, John Prescott.** 1803–1881. English portrait and genre painter. Among his canvases are *The Whist Party, Smugglers Alarmed, Heroes of Waterloo* or *The*

*Waterloo Banquet*, and portraits of duke of Wellington, duke of Cambridge, Sir Charles Lock Eastlake, et al.

**Knight, Jonathan.** 1789–1864. American physician; one of founders of American Medical Association.

**Knight, Joseph Philip.** 1812–1887. English song writer; took holy orders (after 1841); best-known song, *Rocked in the Cradle of the Deep* (1839).

**Knight, William Angus.** 1836–1916. British author; professor of moral philosophy, U. of St. Andrews (1876–1902); known esp. for his editions of works of William and Dorothy Wordsworth.

**Knip′per·dol′ling** (nĭp′ẽr·dŏl′ĭng; *Ger.* k′nĭp′ẽr·dôl′ĭng) *or* **Knip′per·dol′link** (k′nĭp′ẽr·dôl′ĭngk), **Bernhard** *or* **Bernt.** d. 1536. German Anabaptist leader and fanatic in Münster; took active part in Reformation, and joined Anabaptists; supported acts of John of Leiden, under whom he became vice-regent and executioner; tortured and executed (1536).

**Knit′tel** (nĭt′'l; *Ger.* k′nĭt′ĕl), **John.** 1891–1971. Swiss writer, b. in Dahrwar, India, son of a Swiss clergyman. Has lived chiefly in England and Egypt. Among his works are *Aaron West, Into the Abyss, Nile Gold, Via Mala, Dr. Ibrahim.*

**Kno′bels·dorff** (k′nō′bĕls·dôrf), **Georg Wenzeslaus von.** 1699–1753. German architect and painter. Designed Berlin Opera House (1741–43; rebuilt in 1926), new wing of Charlottenburg Castle (1740–43), parts of Castle of Sans Souci at Potsdam (1745–47); helped plan gardens at Rheinsberg, Potsdam, and Sans Souci.

**Knob′lock** (nŏb′lŏk), **Edward.** 1874–1945. British playwright, scenarist, and novelist, b. N.Y. City; A.B., Harvard (1896). His plays include *The Faun* (1911), *Kismet* (1911), *Milestones* (1912; with Arnold Bennett), *My Lady's Dress* (1914), *Marie—Odile* (1915), *Tiger, Tiger* (1918), *The Lullaby* (1923), *London Life* (1924; with Bennett), *The Mulberry Bush* (1930), *The Good Companions* (1931; with J. B. Priestley), *Grand Hotel* (1931; from novel by Vicki Baum), *Evensong* (1932; with Beverley Nichols), *Rolling Stone* (1936), *The Henry Irving Centenary Matinee* (1938). His novels include *The Ant Heap* (1929), *The Man with Two Mirrors* (1931), *The Love Lady* (1933), *Inexperience* (1941).

**Knolles** (nōlz), **Richard.** 1550?–1610. English historian; author of *Generall Historie of the Turkes* (1604).

**Knollys** (nōlz). Name of English family including:

Sir **Francis** (1514?–1596); courtier; educ. Oxford; M.P. (1542 ff.); privy councilor under Elizabeth (1558) and vice-chamberlain of royal household; m. niece of Anne Boleyn; placed in charge of fugitive Mary, Queen of Scots (1568–69), and commissioner at her trial; treasurer of royal household (1572–96).

Sir **William** (1547–1632), Earl of **Ban′bur·y** (băn′bẽr·ĭ; băm′-); 2d son of Sir Francis; soldier and courtier; M.P. (1572 ff.); served in Low Countries under Leicester (1586) and against Spanish Armada (1588); privy councilor (1596); treasurer of royal household (1602); created earl of Banbury (1626) by Charles I.

**Charles** (1662–1740), titular 4th earl, on establishing his right to title of earl of Banbury, was set free after killing his brother-in-law in duel; reputed father of Sir Charles Knowles (*q.v.*), British admiral.

Sir **William Thomas** (1797–1883); soldier; son of 8th earl of Banbury (titular earl up to adverse decision of 1813); served in Peninsular War; organizer of new military camp at Aldershot (1855–60); president of council of military education (1861); treasurer and comptroller of household of prince of Wales (1862–77); gentleman usher of the Black Rod (1877–83). His son **Francis** (1837–1924), 1st Viscount Knollys, was private secretary to King Edward VII (from 1870); excelled as letter writer.

**Knollys** *or* **Knolles** (nōlz), Sir **Robert.** d. 1407. English soldier of a Cheshire family; served under Henry of Lancaster (1357); took prisoner Bertrand Du Guesclin (1359); accompanied the Black Prince on his Spanish expedition (1367); served under Thomas of Woodstock, Earl of Buckingham (1380); active in suppressing Wat Tyler's insurrection.

**Knopf** (k′nŭpf), **Alfred A.** 1892– . American publisher, b. New York City; president, Alfred A. Knopf, Inc., publishers. His father, **Samuel** (1862–1932), was treasurer of the company.

**Knopf** (k′nôpf), **Otto.** 1856– . German astronomer; director, Jena observatory (1900–27).

**Knopf** (k′nŭpf), **S. Adolphus.** 1857–1940. American physician and specialist in tuberculosis, b. Halle-on-the-Saale, Germany. Professor of medicine, Columbia (1908–20). Founder of New York City and National Tuberculosis associations. Author of *Pulmonary Tuberculosis—Its Modern Prophylaxy, and the Treatment . . .* (1899), *Tuberculosis as a Disease of the Masses and How to Combat It* (1900; later published in 30 languages), *Various Aspects of Birth Control* (1928), *The Three Greatest Things on Earth* (1938), etc.

**Knorr** (k′nôr), **Georg.** 1859–1911. German engineer. Developed and manufactured the Knorr air brake, supplanting Westinghouse brake on most German railways.

**Knorr, I·van′,** *Ger.* **I·wan′** (ē·vän′). 1853–1916. German composer and theorist. Wrote three operas, orchestral and chamber music, and Ukrainian love songs; author of works on theory and harmony.

**Knorr, Ludwig.** 1859–1921. German chemist; synthesized pyrazole, quinoline, antipyrine (which he discovered in 1883), etc.; also worked on tautomerism, the morphine alkaloids, etc.

**Knott** (nŏt), **Thomas Albert.** 1880–1945. American educator and editor, b. Chicago. Professor of English, State U. of Iowa (1920–26). General editor (1926–34), *Webster's New International Dictionary, Second Edition.* Professor of English, and editor of Middle English Dictionary, U. of Michigan (1935 ff.). Coauthor of *Elements of Old English* (with Samuel Moore; 1919), *A Pronouncing Dictionary of American English* (with John S. Kenyon, *q.v.*; 1944).

**Know′er** (nō′ẽr), **Henry McElderry.** 1868–1940. American anatomist; conducted researches on termites, muscles of the human heart, etc.

**Knowles** (nōlz), Sir **Charles.** d. 1777. British naval commander; reputed son of titular 4th earl of Banbury (see *Charles*, under KNOLLYS family); governor of Louisburg (1746) and Jamaica (1752–56); vice-admiral (1755), superseded because of miscarriage of expedition against Rochefort; admiral (1760). His son Sir **Charles Henry** (1754–1831) was also an admiral (from 1810).

**Knowles, Dewey Deforest.** 1899– . American electrical engineer; inventor of grid-glow electron tube and other electronic devices.

**Knowles, Farquhar McGillivray Strachan Stewart.** 1860–1932. Painter, b. of English parentage in Syracuse, N.Y. Studio in Toronto, Can. Best known for his landscapes, painted in classical style. His wife, **Elizabeth Annie,** *nee* **Beach** [bēch] (1866–1928), b. Ottawa, Can., was also a painter; best known for her nature studies.

**Knowles, Frederic Lawrence.** 1869–1905. American poet and anthologist; author of *Love Triumphant, On Life's Stairway*, etc.; compiler of anthologies *Golden Treasury of American Songs and Lyrics* (1897), *Poems of American Patriotism* (1926), etc.

**Knowles, James Sheridan.** 1784–1862. Cousin of Richard Brinsley Sheridan. British playwright, b. in Cork, Ireland; served in army, studied medicine, acted, taught school; turned definitely to theater, devoting himself to both acting (till 1843) and writing. Plays include *Caius Gracchus* (1815), *Virginius* (1820), *The Hunchback* (1832), and *The Love Chase* (1837). Published also novels, poems, and miscellaneous works. His father, **James Knowles** (1759–1840), compiled *A Pronouncing and Explanatory Dictionary of the English Language* (1835).

**Knowles,** Sir **James Thomas**. 1831–1908. English architect and editor; practiced as architect in London for thirty years; founded Metaphysical Society (1869); edited *Contemporary Review* (1870–77); founded (1877) and edited (1877–1908) *Nineteenth Century*.

**Knowles, Lucius James.** 1819–1884. American inventor; invented steam pump and improved loom; engaged in manufacturing these (from 1863). The Knowles Pump Co., sold (1879) to Blake Mfg. Co. of Boston, became largest of its kind in U.S.

**Knowl′ton** (nōl′t'n; -tŭn), **Charles.** 1800–1850. American physician and advocate of birth control; author of *Fruits of Philosophy* (1832); prosecuted and imprisoned for three months at Cambridge, Mass. (1832); book made subject of a test case in England (1877).

**Knowlton, Frank Hall.** 1860–1926. American botanist and paleontologist; paleontologist (1900–07) and geologist, U.S. Geological Survey (from 1907); author of *Birds of the World* (1909), *Plants of the Past* (1927).

**Knox** (nŏks), **Edmund George Valpy.** *Pseudonym* **E′voe′** (ē′vē′). 1881–1971. English humorist; editor of *Punch* (1932–49). Author of *The Brazen Lyre, Fiction as she is wrote, Quaint Specimens, Folly Calling,* etc.

**Knox, Frank,** *in full* **William Franklin. 1874–1944.** American newspaper publisher and politician, b. Boston; publisher, Chicago *Daily News* (from 1931). Served in Spanish-American War and World War I. Republican nominee for vice-president of the U.S. (1936); though still a Republican, appointed by President Roosevelt U.S. secretary of the navy (1940–44).

**Knox, Henry.** 1750–1806. American Revolutionary officer; close friend and adviser of Washington; served through war and took part in all notable engagements; brigadier general (Dec. 17, 1776). Took initial steps toward creation of U.S. Military Academy (1779). On court-martial trying Major André (1780). Major general (Nov. 15, 1781). In command at West Point (1782). Founded Society of the Cincinnati (1783). U.S. secretary of war (1785–94).

**Knox, Jean,** Lady **Swaythling.** 1908– . Director of British Auxiliary Territorial Service, b. near London; m. 1st (1925) George Knox; 2d (1945) 3d Baron Swaythling; joined A.T.S. (1939); appointed its commander (July, 1941), with the rank marks of a major general, first British woman accorded such honor.

**Knox, John.** 1505–1572. Scottish reformer, writer, and statesman, b. Haddington. Educ. Glasgow; notary (1540–43). Called to ministry and preached for reformed religion (1547). Captured at St. Andrews and sent to French prison (1548–49); to England, where he was appointed (1551) a royal chaplain. At Mary Tudor's accession (1553), fled to the Continent; at Geneva (1554, 1556–58), where he met Calvin; returned to Scotland (1559). Published six tracts dealing with religious issues in Scotland, including *Blast of the Trumpet against the Monstrous Regiment of Women* (which deeply offended Queen Elizabeth) and *Treatise on Predestination* (1560); issued prayer book *Book of Common Order* (1564). Preached widely throughout Scotland against Roman Catholic priesthood, against image worship and mass, and against Mary, Queen of Scots (whom he called Jezebel); labored to establish Protestantism in Scotland and to organize Presbyterian Church there. Shortly before death, received appointment as minister in Edinburgh. Author of *History of the Reformation of Religioun within the Realme of Scotland* (pub. 1584).

**Knox, Philander Chase.** 1853–1921. American political leader; practiced law, Pittsburgh (from 1875). U.S. attorney general (1901–04); filed suit and won decision against Northern Securities Co. (1901–04); drew up legislation creating U.S. Department of Commerce and Labor (1903). U.S. senator (1904–09). U.S. secretary of state (1909–13); initiated what is known as "dollar diplomacy." U.S. senator (1917–21); prominent in opposition to U.S. entry into League of Nations.

**Knox, Ronald Arbuthnott. 1888–1957.** English Roman Catholic prelate and writer; educ. Oxford. Entered Roman Catholic Church (1917); Roman Catholic chaplain, Oxford U. (1926–39); domestic prelate to pope (1936). Among his books are *Some Loose Stones* (1913), *The Viaduct Murder* (1925), *The Belief of Catholics* (1927), *Caliban in Grub Street* (1930), *The Body in the Silo* (1933), *Let Dons Delight* (1939).

**Knu′bel** (nōō′bĕl), **Frederick Hermann. 1870–1945.** American Lutheran clergyman; vigorous advocate of church unity; president, United Lutheran Church in America (from 1918).

**Knud′sen** (k′nōōt′sĕn), **Gunnar.** 1848–1928. Norwegian statesman, shipowner, and industrialist; minister president (1908–10, 1913–20); championed a neutrality policy during World War, and remained leader of Leftists (until 1922).

**Knud′sen** (nōōd′s'n; *orig. Dan. pron.* k′nōō′s'n), **William S.,** *orig.* **Signius Wilhelm Paul.** 1879–1948. American industrialist, b. Copenhagen, Denmark; to U.S. at age of 20; rose from bicycle mechanic to vice-president (1922), later president, Chevrolet Motor Co.; vice-president (1933–37), president (1937), General Motors Corp. Member of National Defense Commission (1940); codirector (with Sidney Hillman), Office of Production Management (1941); named director of production for War Department, with rank of lieutenant general (Jan., 1942); resigned (1945).

**Knut.** See CANUTE.

**Knut′zen** (k′nōōt′sĕn), **Martin. 1713–1751.** German Wolffian philosopher and Pietist; professor at Königsberg (from 1734) where he taught Kant.

**Knyp′hau′sen** (k′nĭp′hou′zĕn), Baron **Wilhelm von.** 1716–1800. Prussian soldier under Frederick the Great; to America as commander of Hessian troops (1776); commanded at New York City in absence of Sir Henry Clinton (1779–80) and raided Hackensack. Returned to Germany and became military governor of Kassel.

**Kobad.** Variant of KAVADH.

**Kobbé, Gustav.** 1857–1918. American music critic; known as an authority on Wagner.

**Ko′bell** (kō′bĕl). Family of German painters, etchers, and engravers, including: **Ferdinand** (1740–1799), landscape painter and etcher. His brother **Franz** (1749–1822), landscape and architectural painter, etcher, and pen-and-ink draftsman; court painter at Munich. Ferdinand's son and pupil **Wilhelm von Kobell** (1766–1853), landscape and battle painter and etcher.

**Kobell, Franz von.** 1803–1882. Son of Wilhelm (see family entry, above). German mineralogist and poet; invented the stauroscope and a method of galvanography. Author of works on mineralogy and galvanography, and of humorous and fanciful popular poetry chiefly in Upper Bavarian, High German, and Palatine dialects.

**Ko′ber·stein** (kō′bĕr·shtīn), **Karl August. 1797–1870.** German literary historian.

**Kobo Daishi.** See KUKAI.

**Koch** (kôK). See Helius Eobanus HESSUS.

**Koch, Erich.** See KOCH-WESER.

**Koch** (kŏk), **Johan Peter.** 1870– . Danish explorer of Greenland.

**Koch** (kôK), **Johannes.** See COCCEIUS.

**Koch, Joseph Anton.** 1768–1839. Landscape painter and etcher, b. in Tirol; a leader of German artists in Rome; resident chiefly in Rome (after 1795). His etchings include illustrations for Ossian and for Dante's *Divina Commedia;* his landscape paintings include *Historical Landscape, Schmadribachfall, Noah's Sacrifice,* and *San Francesco di Civitella;* painted also four frescoes in the Villa Massimi, Rome (1824–29).

**Koch, Karl.** 1809–1879. German botanist and traveler in Russia and Asia Minor.

**Koch** (kŏk), **Lauge.** 1892–1964. Danish geologist and explorer of Greenland.

**Koch** (kôK), **Max.** 1855–1931. German literary historian; author of a short *History of German Literature* (1893), a biography of Wagner (3 vols., 1907–18), and editions of Shakespeare (12 vols., 1882–84), Platen (4 vols., 1910; with Erich Petzet), etc.

**Koch, Robert.** 1843–1910. German physician and pioneer bacteriologist, b. Klausthal, Hanover. Studied medicine at Göttingen; began bacteriological researches while practicing at Wollstein (1872–80). On mission to Egypt and India to study cholera (1883); professor at U. of Berlin and director of the Institute of Hygiene (1885); director of the Institute for Infectious Diseases, Berlin (1891). First to isolate and obtain a pure culture of the anthrax bacillus (1876), publishing a method of preventive inoculation against this disease (1883). Isolated tubercle bacillus (1882); identified the comma bacillus as the cause of Asiatic cholera (1883); produced tuberculin, of value in diagnosing tuberculosis (1890). Studied rinderpest in South Africa and developed a means of vaccination against it (1896); also investigated bubonic plague in Bombay (1897) and malaria and sleeping sickness in Africa. Awarded 1905 Nobel prize for physiology and medicine.

**Koch** (kōk), **Theodore Wesley.** 1871–1941. American librarian, at Northwestern U. (from 1919). Author of *Dante in America* (1896), *Library Assistant's Manual* (1913), *Tales for Bibliophiles* (1929), etc.

**Ko'cha·now'ski** (kô'Kä·nôf'skē), **Jan.** 1530–1584. Polish lyric poet. Author, in Latin and Polish, of the tragedy *Dismissal of the Greek Envoys* (1578), translations of the Psalms into Polish verse (1579), elegies, songs, etc.

**Ko·chań'ska, Praxede Marcelline.** See Marcella SEMBRICH.

**Ko'cher** (kô'Kẽr), **Emil Theodor.** 1841–1917. Swiss surgeon; professor, Bern (from 1872). Known esp. for work on the physiology, pathology, and surgery of the thyroid gland; also for work on dislocations of the shoulder, on hernia, and on osteomyelitis. Awarded 1909 Nobel prize for physiology and medicine.

**Koch'-Grün'berg** (kôK'grün'bĕrK), **Theodor.** 1872–1924. German ethnologist and explorer; authority on the Indians of Brazil.

**Köch'ly** (kûK'lĭ), **Hermann.** 1815–1876. German classical scholar, philologist, and educational reformer.

**Koch'-We'ser** (kôK'vā'zẽr), **Erich.** *Orig. surname* **Koch.** 1875–1944. German statesman and political reformer; member of Reichstag (1920–30), where he was leader of Democrats (1923–28) and party chairman (1927). Minister of justice (1928–29); founded short-lived German State party (1930).

**Kock** (kôk), **Paul de.** 1794–1871. French novelist and playwright; best known for his depiction of bourgeois life. Among his many novels are *L'Enfant de ma Femme* (1813), *Gustave le Mauvais Sujet* (1821), *La Laitière de Montfermeil* (1827), *La Pucelle de Belleville* (1834), *Un Homme à Marier* (1843), *La Fille aux Trois Jupons* (1861). Author also of a number of melodramas, light operas, vaudeville sketches, pantomimes, etc. His son **Henri** (1819–1892) was a novelist and playwright; author of *Ni Fille, ni Femme, ni Veuve* (1867), *Mademoiselle ma Femme* (1868), *Les Douze Travaux d'Ursule* (1885).

**Ko'dály** (kô'dī), **Zoltán.** 1882–1967. Hungarian composer; exponent of ultramodernism in music. Collector of and writer on Hungarian folk music.

**Ko·da·ma** (kô·dä·mä), Viscount **Gentaro.** 1852–1906. Japanese general; chief of staff of Japanese army in Manchuria in Russo-Japanese War (1904–05); chiefly responsible for successful strategy of the war.

**Kœch'lin'** (kĕsh'lăN'). Family of French textile manufacturers, at Mulhouse, including: **Samuel,** who founded (1746) the business; his son **Jean** (1746–1836); three sons of Jean, **Jacques** (1776–1834), **Nicolas** (1781–1852), and **Daniel** (1785–1871); and **Joseph Kœchlin-Schlum'ber'ger'** [-shlûN'bĕr'zhā'] (1796–1863), a geologist, prepared geological maps of the Rhine region.

**Kœchlin, Charles.** 1867–1950. French composer of melodies, choral works, chamber music, symphonic poems, and ballets.

**Koek'koek** (ko͝ok'ko͝ok), **Barend Cornelis.** 1803–1862. Dutch landscape painter and lithographer.

**Koelreuter, Josef Gottlieb.** See KÖLREUTER.

**Kœ'nig'** (kû'nēg'), **Rodolphe.** *Ger.* **Karl Rudolf Kö'nig** (kû'nĭK). 1832–1901. Physicist, b. in Germany; established a manufactory of acoustic instruments, Paris (1858); conducted researches in acoustics; invented an apparatus (manometric capsule) for studying sound waves, a siren, etc.; produced fine tuning forks.

**Kœ'nigs'** (kû'nēgz'), **Paul Xavier Gabriel.** 1858–1931. French mathematician; known for work in infinitesimal geometry, mechanics, and, esp., general kinematics.

**Koer'ber** (kûr'bẽr), **Er·nest'** (ĕr·nĕst') **von.** 1850–1919. Austrian statesman; minister president and minister of interior (1900) and justice (1902). Tried to solve nationalist question and to carry through a German-Czech agreement in Bohemia; effected a compromise with Hungary (1902) which he later abandoned because of opposition; resigned (1904). Again Austrian minister president (1916).

**Koes'ter** (kĕs'tẽr), **Frank.** *Orig.* **Franz** (fränts) **Kö'ster** (kû'stẽr). 1876–1927. Electrical engineer and expert in city planning and street lighting, b. in Germany; to U.S. (1902). In consulting practice, N.Y. (1911); inventor of devices in power-plant engineering, etc.

**Koest'ler** (kĕst'lẽr), **Arthur.** 1905– . Hungarian-born author, in England. Author of *Darkness at Noon* (1941), *Arrival and Departure* (1943), etc.

**Ko·e·tsu** (kō·yĕ·tso͞o), **Hon-Ami.** 1557?–1637. Japanese painter and lacquerer; skilled in painting on porcelain and in gold lacquering.

**Koff'ka** (kôf'kȧ; kôf'kä), **Kurt** (ko͝ort). 1886–1941. Psychologist, b. Berlin, Germany; to U.S., and became research professor of experimental psychology (1927–32), and professor (from 1932), Smith College.

**Ko'foid** (kō'foid), **Charles Atwood.** 1865–1947. American zoologist, b. Granville, Ill.

**Ko'găl·ni·cea'nu** (kŏ'gȧl·nē·chä'no͞o), **Mihail.** 1817–1891. Rumanian statesman and historian. President of the cabinet (1863–65); minister of interior (1868–70; 1879–80), of foreign affairs (1877–78). Author of *Histoire de la Valachie et de la Moldavie* (1837), etc.

**Köhl** (kûl), **Hermann.** 1888–1938. German military aviator in World War I; with Capt. James Fitzmaurice

(1898–1965) flew *Bremen* on first successful east-to-west transatlantic flight, from Dublin, Ireland, to Greenly Island off the Labrador coast (April, 1928).

**Kohl** (kōl), **Johann Georg.** 1808–1878. German geographer and writer on travel.

**Koh'ler** (kō'lẽr), **Josef.** 1849–1919. German jurist, writer, and poet. Author of works on jurisprudence, and on German patent and copyright law; author also of poetry, as *Lyrische Gedichte und Balladen* (1892), the novel *Eine Faustnatur* (1907), essays on art history, imitations of Dante and Petrarch, etc.

**Koh'ler, Kauf'mann** (kouf'măn). 1843–1926. Rabbi and educator, b. Fürth, Bavaria, Germany; to U.S. (1869). Rabbi of congregation in New York (1879–1903). President, Hebrew Union Coll. (1903–21). Leader of Reformed Judaism in America.

**Köh'ler** (kû'lẽr), **Louis,** *in full* **Christian Louis Heinrich.** 1820–1886. German piano teacher and composer, esp. of piano studies; also wrote instructive musical works.

**Köhler, Reinhold.** 1830–1892. German literary critic and comparative folklorist.

**Köhler, Wolfgang.** 1887–1967. German psychologist, b. in Estonia. One of chief proponents of Gestalt psychology; known esp. for investigations in animal psychology conducted on apes and chimpanzees.

**Kohl'mann** (kōl'măn), **Anthony.** 1771–1836. Jesuit priest, b. in Alsace; to U.S. as missionary (1806). Administrator, diocese of New York (1808–14); won decision in suit brought to compel him to divulge source of information received at confessional; decision responsible for later State legislation (1828) protecting confessional.

**Kohl'rausch** (kōl'roush), **Eduard.** 1874–1948. German jurist; author of *Kommentar zum Strafgesetzbuch*, etc.

**Kohlrausch, Friedrich Wilhelm Georg.** 1840–1910. German physicist; devised improvements in measuring methods in many branches of physics, esp. magnetism and electricity; investigated elasticity, electrolytic conductivity, the reflection of light, etc. Furthered experimental work in physics by instituting a practicum at Göttingen, for which he wrote (1870) *Leitfaden der Praktischen Physik*, a work on physical laboratory methods and measurements which ran into many editions. His father, **Rudolf Hermann Arndt Kohlrausch** (1809–1858), is known for his association with Wilhelm Weber in making the first measurements of an electric current using absolute units.

**Koht** (kōt), **Halvdan.** 1873–1965. Norwegian historian and statesman.

**Ko'hut** (kō'hōōt), **Alexander.** 1842–1894. Rabbi, b. Hungary; to U.S. (1885); congregation in New York; led conservative Judaism. His wife, **Rebekah Kohut** (1864–1951; m. 1887), b. Hungary, social worker and a founder of the National Council of Jewish Women.

**Ko·i·so** (kô·ĕ·sô), **Kuniaki.** 1880–1950. Japanese general; chief of staff of Kwantung army (1932); commander in chief in Korea (1935–38); prime minister (1944–45); sentenced as war criminal to life imprisonment (1948).

**Koizumi, Setsuko** and **Yakumo.** See Lafcadio HEARN.

**Ko'kosch·ka** (kô'kôsh·kä), **Oskar.** 1886– . Austrian expressionist painter, designer, and dramatist; contributed portraits and other drawings to organ of "Sturm" circle in Berlin; professor, Dresden Academy (1918–24). Author of the self-illustrated poem *Die Träumenden Knaben* (1908) and of the expressionistic plays *Mörder, Hoffnung der Frauen* (1907; music by Hindemith, 1921), *Der Brennende Dornbusch* (1911), *Hiob* (1917), and *Orpheus und Eurydike* (1923; music by Křenek). His artistic works include esp. portraits and landscapes.

**Ko'lar** (kō'lär), **Vic'tor** (vĭk'tẽr). 1888–1957. Orchestra conductor, b. in Hungary; with New York Symphony Orchestra (1906–19); conductor at Century of Progress Exposition, Chicago (1934).

**Kol'be** (kôl'bĕ), **Georg.** 1877–1947. German sculptor. His works include the bronze figures *Japanese Girl, Somali Negro, Adam,* and *Girl Seated,* also *The Dancer* and the Rathenau Fountain, both in Berlin; and the group *Man and Wife* for the Heine Memorial (in Frankfurt).

**Kolbe, Hermann,** *in full* **Adolf Wilhelm Hermann.** 1818–1884. German organic chemist; expounded a theory of radicals; indicated the possibility of the existence of secondary and tertiary alcohols before their discovery; credited with first synthesis of acetic and salicylic acids; also, worked on the electrolysis of organic acids.

**Kol'ben·hey'er** (kôl'bĕn·hī'ẽr), **Erwin Guido.** 1878–1962. German poet and author of philosophical and biological studies, novels, philosophical poems, and plays.

**Kol'berg** (kôl'bĕrk), **Os'car** (ôs'kär). 1814–1890. Polish ethnographer and composer of Polish national dances; author of ethnological works on Poland and of an edition of Polish folk songs (1857).

**Kol·chak'** (kôl·chák'), **Aleksandr Vasilievich.** 1874–1920. Russian admiral and counterrevolutionist. Rear admiral in World War (1916) in command of Baltic fleet; promoted to vice-admiral in command of Black Sea fleet. After Revolution (1917) organized a White army in Siberia; at first successful but began to lose control when Omsk was captured by Bolsheviks (1919); retreated to Irkutsk; forced to resign; captured and shot.

**Köl'csey** (kûl'chĕ·ĭ), **Ferencz.** 1790–1838. Hungarian poet, critic, and orator. Cofounder and coeditor (from 1826) of the journal *Life and Literature;* author of the Hungarian national hymn (1823) and of other lyric poetry.

**Kol'de·wey** (kôl'dĕ·vī), **Karl Christian.** 1837–1908. German arctic explorer. In command of first German polar expedition to Spitsbergen (1868), and of second expedition to eastern Greenland (1869) on which he discovered Franz Joseph's Fjord; published accounts of expeditions. On staff of the Imperial Naval Observatory (from 1875).

**Koldewey, Robert.** 1855–1925. German archaeologist; leader in excavation of the ruins of Babylon (1898–1917).

**Kol'lár** (kôl'lär), **Jan.** 1793–1852. Slovak poet and scholar, b. in Hungary; advocate of nonpolitical romantic Pan-Slavism. Author of an edition of Slovakian folk songs (2 vols., 1823–27), the sonnet cycle *Daughter of Slava* (1824), a work in German on Slavic roots and dialects (1837), etc.

**Kol'ler** (kŏl'ẽr), **Carl.** 1857–1944. Ophthalmologist, b. Austria; practiced ophthalmic surgery in New York. His introduction of cocaine as a local anesthetic in eye operations (1884) inaugurated the use of local anesthesia in other types of surgery.

**Köl'li·ker** (kûl'ĭ·kẽr), **Rudolf Albert von.** 1817–1905. Anatomist, histologist, and zoologist, b. in Zurich. Professor, Würzburg (from 1847); known esp. for researches in histology and embryology.

**Kol·lon·tai'** (kŭl·lŭn·tī'), **Aleksandra Mikhailovna.** 1872–1952. Russian Soviet commissar and diplomat; joined Bolsheviks (1917); first Soviet commissar of social welfare (1917); ambassador to Mexico (1927), Sweden (1930); first woman ambassador in the world.

**Koł·łon'taj** *or* **Koł·łą'taj** (kôl·lôɴn'tī), **Hugo.** 1750–1812. Polish priest and politician; vice-chancellor of Poland (1791–92); active in Kosciusko's rebellion (1794) and imprisoned in Austria (1795–1802).

**Koll'witz** (kôl'vĭts), **Käthe,** *nee* **Schmidt.** 1867–1945. German painter, lithographer, and etcher; m. Karl Kollwitz (1891) and settled in Berlin. Her works, often representing life among the poor and the proletariat, include etchings, woodcuts, lithographs, illustrations for *Simplicissimus* (from 1910), and two sculptured figures for a German soldiers' cemetery in Belgium.

**Ko'lo·ko·tro'nes** *or* **Ko'lo·ko·tro'nis** (kô'lô·kô·trô'-nyĕs), **Theodoros.** 1770–1843. Greek leader in war for independence (1821 ff.); commander in chief of Peloponnesus (1823). Conspired against regency governing for King Otto I and was condemned to death for treason (1834); sentence commuted to imprisonment; pardoned at Otto's accession to power (1835) and restored to rank of general.

**Ko'lo·man** *or* **Co'lo·man** (*Ger.* kō'lō·män). *Hungarian* **Kál'mán** (käl'män). 1070–1114. King of Hungary (1095–1114) of Árpád dynasty. Natural son of Geza I. Seized throne on death of his uncle Ladislas I; suppressed rebellion in Croatia; conquered Dalmatia (1097–1102); blinded his brother and his nephew (later King Béla II).

**Ko'lo·wrat–Lieb'stein·sky** (kô'lô·vrät·lēb'stĕ·ĭn·skĭ), Count **Franz Anton.** 1778–1861. Bohemian statesman; promoted revival of Czech language and history; secretary of state to Emperors Franz I and Ferdinand I in Vienna (1826–48).

**Köl'reu'ter** *or* **Koel'reu'ter** (kûl'roi'tẽr), **Josef Gottlieb.** 1733–1806. German botanist; pioneer in hybridization experiments with plants; recognized the importance of insects in pollinating flowers.

**Kol·tsov'** (kŭl·y'·tsôf'), **Aleksei Vasilievich.** 1808–1842. Russian lyric poet; wrote of the Russian peasant; called by Belinski the greatest Russian poet.

**Ko·mei** (kō·mā). 1821–1867. Emperor of Japan (1846–67), last ruler before the Restoration (see MUTSUHITO); under control of shoguns. After Commodore Perry's visits (1853, 1854) his influence gradually increased, opening way for his son's great reforms.

**Komenský, Jan Amos.** See COMENIUS.

**Kom'pert** (kôm'pĕrt), **Leopold.** 1822–1886. Austrian writer of stories of Austrian and Hungarian Jewry.

**Kom'roff** (kŏm'rŏf), **Manuel.** 1890–1974. American writer, b. New York City. To Petrograd at outbreak of Russian Revolution; on staff of *Russian Daily News* (1917); at accession of Bolshevists, fled across Siberia and returned to U.S. (1919). Author of *The Grace of Lambs* (1925), *Coronet* (1929), *Two Thieves* (1931), *A New York Tempest* (1932), *I, the Tiger* (1933), *Waterloo* (1936); editor of Nietzsche's *Zarathustra*, etc.

**Komunduros.** = KOUMOUNDOUROS.

**Ko·mu·ra** (kô·mōō·rä), Marquis **Jutaro.** 1855–1911. Japanese statesman; minister to U.S. (1898–1900) and to Russia (1900); foreign minister twice (1901–06 and 1908–11). Ambassador to Great Britain (1906–08). Created count (1907) and marquis (1911).

**Kon·do** (kôn·dō), **Nobutake.** 1886–1953. Japanese vice-admiral (from 1939); commander of 4th fleet, which attacked Pearl Harbor (Dec. 7, 1941).

**Kon'dou·rio'tes** *or* **Kon'dou·rio'tis** (kôn'dōō·ryô'-tēs). Erroneous variants of KOUNDOURIOTES, KOUNDOURIOTIS.

**Kon'dra·to'wicz** (kôn'drä·tô'vēch), **Ludwik Władysław.** *Pseudonym* **Władysław Sy'ro·kom'la** (sĭ'rô-kôm'lä). 1823–1862. Polish writer, b. in Lithuania. Among his works are *Bavardages* (1853), *Tales in Verse* (1860), *Last Poems* (1862). *Margier* is regarded as his best single poem.

**Kon·dy'les** *or* **Kon·dy'lis** (kôn·thē'lyēs), **Georgios.** 1879–1936. Greek general and statesman; served through Balkan Wars and World War I. Entered Parliament (1923); minister of war, then (1924–25) of interior; engineered coup d'état and became prime minister (Aug. 22, 1926), retired; returned to Greece (1930); minister of war (1932–33, 1933–35) in coalition cabinet of Tsaldares; by coup d'état (Oct. 10, 1935) aided in restoration of monarchy and return of George II to throne (Nov. 25, 1935); acted as premier and temporary dictator.

**Ko'nev** (kô'nyĕf), **Ivan Stepanovich.** 1897–1973. Soviet general. In World War II; became marshal of Soviet Union (1944); commander in chief of Soviet army (1946–60); inspector, ministry of defense (1962–1973).

**Kö'nig** (kû'nĭκ), **Friedrich.** 1774–1833. German printer; inventor of the steam printing press. Cofounder near Würzburg (1817) of König & Bauer, manufacturers of steam printing presses.

**Kö'nig** (kû'nĭκ), **Heinrich Josef.** 1790–1869. German novelist and politician. Excommunicated by Roman Catholic bishop for his writings, notably *Der Christbaum des Lebens* (1831); joined Protestant church. Member, Diet of Hesse (1832). Wrote historical novels and tales, autobiographical sketches, dramas, theological works.

**König, Karl Rudolf.** See Rodolphe KŒNIG.

**König, Paul Leberecht.** 1867–1933. German World War I naval officer; commander of the submarine *Deutschland;* wrote *Die Fahrt der Deutschland* (1916).

**Kö'nigs·ber'ger** (kû'nĭκs·bĕr'gẽr), **Leo.** 1837–1921. German mathematician; worked chiefly in the theory of functions, differential equations, and mechanics.

**Kö'nigs·egg–Ro'then·fels** (kû'nĭκs·ĕk·rō'tĕn·fĕls), Count **Lothar Joseph Georg von.** 1673–1751. Austrian field marshal; in the War of the Austrian Succession, led armies of Bohemia (1742) and the Low Countries (1745); defeated at Chotusitz and Fontenoy.

**Kö'nigs·mark** (kû'nĭκs·märk). Swedish family of German origin, including notably: Count **Hans Christoph Königsmark** (1600–1663); entered Swedish army (1630); commanded Swedish forces in Westphalia (1636 ff.), Swedish left wing at battle of Breitenfeld (1642), and Swedish forces in battle of Prague, the last battle of Thirty Years' War (1648); created field marshal in Swedish army. His grandson Count **Philipp Christoph Königsmark** (1662–?1694); entered army of elector of Hanover; became lover of Sophia Dorothea, wife of the crown prince, and was presumably murdered on discovery of the liaison. Philipp's sister Countess **Maria Aurora Königsmark** (1668?–1728), a beauty and a wit, mistress of Elector Augustus II of Saxony and mother of Maurice of Saxony; regarded by Voltaire as "the most famous woman of two centuries."

**Ko'ninck** (kō'nĭngk) *or* **Ko'ning** (kō'nĭng) *or* **Co'-ningh** (kō'nĭng). Name of several Dutch and Flemish painters including: **Salomon Koninck** (1609–1656), historical, genre, and portrait painter and etcher; imitator of Rembrandt. **Philips de Koninck** (1619–1688), panoramic landscape and portrait painter and colorist; pupil of Rembrandt. **David de Koninck** (1636–?1699), painter of still life and animals, esp. rabbits.

**Ko'nop·nic'ka** (kô'nôp·nēts'kä), **Marja,** *nee* **Wa'si-łow'ska** (vä'sē·lôf'skä). 1842?–1910. Polish novelist and poet; her chief poem, *Mr. Balcer in Brazil,* is a popular epic based on the theme of Polish emigration to the Americas. Another poem, *Rota,* became a national song.

**Ko·now'** (kō·nôv'), **Sten.** 1867–1948. Norwegian Indologist and philologist. Edited Indian texts in the Harvard Oriental series (1901) and elsewhere. Author of a *Bashgali Dictionary* (1913), *India's Religions* (1924), translations, etc.

**Ko·no·ye** (kō·nô·yĕ), Prince **Fumimaro.** 1891–1945. Japanese premier, b. Tokyo; son of Prince Atsumaro Konoye, of an old family of the Fujiwara nobility. Attended Paris Peace Conference (1919) as companion of Prince Saionji; entered House of Peers; elected its president (1933). Premier (1937–39; 1940–41); foreign minister (1938); responsible for much of Japan's policy in the Chino-Japanese War (1937 ff.); committed suicide.

**Kon'rad** (kŏn'rät). See CONRAD.

**Konrad der Pfaf'fe** (dĕr pfäf'ĕ), *i.e.* the Priest. fl. middle of 12th century. Early Middle High German epic poet and priest. Author of the *Rolandslied* (1131?), free German version in verse of the Old French epic *Chanson de Roland*, and probably compiler of the *Kaiserchronik* (c. 1150).

**Konrad von Hoch'sta'den** (fôn hōĸ'shtä'dĕn). d. 1261. German ecclesiastic; archbishop of Cologne (1238–61). Sided with papacy against Frederick II; crowned William of Holland as emperor (1248). Papal legate in Germany (1249–50); effected selection of Richard of Cornwall following William's death (1256) and crowned him at Aix-la-Chapelle (1257).

**Konrad von Mar'burg** (mär'bŏŏrĸ). d. 1233. German priest and papal inquisitor. Confessor (from 1226) to wife of landgrave of Thuringia, later St. Elizabeth of Hungary; papal inquisitor under Gregory IX (1227); zealously combated and punished heretical movements; murdered near Marburg (1233).

**Konrad von Me'gen·berg** (mā'gĕn·bĕrĸ). 1309?–1374. German writer on politics and natural science; author of *Planctus Ecclesiae in Germaniam* (1338), *Deutsche Sphära* (first German handbook of astronomy and physics), and *Das Buch der Natur* (1349–50).

**Konrad von Würz'burg** (vürts'bŏŏrĸ). d. 1287. Middle High German epic poet; author of short epics, narrative poems, and legends and romances in verse often based on Latin and French sources and including *Der Schwanritter* (used by Wagner in *Lohengrin*), the allegorical *Klage der Kunst*, and *Die Goldene Schmiede* (in praise of the Virgin Mary).

**Konstantin.** See CONSTANTINE.

**Kon'ti** (kŏn'tĭ), **Is'i·dore** (ĭz'ĭ·dōr). 1862–1938. Sculptor, b. in Vienna, Austria; to U.S. (1890). Executed works for World's Fair, Chicago (1893); other sculptures include Bishop Horatio Potter memorial in Cathedral of St. John the Divine, New York City, McKinley memorial in Philadelphia, figure *Genius of Immortality* in Metropolitan Museum of Art in New York City.

**Koo** (gōō; *Angl.* kōō), **Vi Kyuin** (wā' jün') **Wel'ling·ton** (wĕl'ĭng·tŭn). *Orig. name* **Ku Wei–chün** (gōō' wā'jün'). 1887– . Chinese statesman and diplomat; educ. at St. John's U., Shanghai, and at Columbia, U.S.A. (B.A. 1908, Ph.D. 1912). Minister (1915–22) to Mexico, United States (1915), and Great Britain. Plenipotentiary for China at Paris Peace Conference (1919) and at Washington conference (1921–22); minister for foreign affairs and acting prime minister (1922–24); minister of finance (1926–27); not in favor with Nationalist government (1928–30) but pardoned and again minister for foreign affairs (1931). Chinese representative on the Council of the League of Nations (1932–34); ambassador to France (1936–41), England (1941–46), U.S. (1946–56).

**Koop·mans** (kōōp'măns), **Tjalling Charles.** 1910– . American economist, b. Netherlands. At U. of Chicago (1944–55), Harvard U. (1960–61); director of Cowles Foundation (1961–67); at Yale U. (1967– ); awarded (with Leonid V. Kantorovich) Nobel prize for economics (1975).

**Kopernik, Mikołaj.** See COPERNICUS.

**Köpfel, Wolfgang Fabricius.** See CAPITO.

**Ko'pisch** (kō'pĭsh), **August.** 1799–1853. German painter and poet; resident in Potsdam (from 1847), where he wrote *Die Schlösser und Gärten zu Potsdam* on royal commission (1854); author of an ode to Frederick William IV (1840), a translation of Dante's *Divina Commedia* (1837), the humorous verse collection *Gedichte* (1836), etc.

**Ko·pi'tar** (kō·pē'tär), **Bartholomäus,** *Slovene* **Jernej Bartel.** 1780–1844. Slovenian Slavic scholar and philologist; author of *Grammatik der Slawischen Sprache in Krain, Kärnthen, und Steiermark* (the first scientific Slavic grammar, 1808), etc.

**Kop'lik** (kŏp'lĭk), **Henry.** 1858–1927. American pediatrician; described spots (Koplik's spots) on mucous membrane of lips and cheeks, used in diagnosis of measles; established first milk depot in U.S., for distribution of milk to infants of the poor.

**Kopp** (kôp), **Georg von.** 1837–1914. German cardinal; served under Bismarck as mediator between state and church, and helped bring about peace measures (1886, 1887) which ended the Kulturkampf. Confidant to government under William II; brought about social reform, built churches and institutions; cardinal (1893).

**Kopp, Hermann Franz Moritz.** 1817–1892. German physical chemist; investigated connection between physical properties and chemical composition of substances; set forth the conception of specific volume.

**Kopp, Joseph Eutych.** 1793–1866. Swiss historian; founder of scientific investigation of Swiss history; showed story of William Tell to be legendary.

**Köp'pen** (*Ger.* kûp'ĕn), **Peter Iwanowitsch von,** *Russ.* **Pëtr Ivanovich.** 1793–1864. Russian archaeologist and ethnologist; published an ethnographical map of European Russia. His son **Friedrich Theodor** (1834–1907), entomologist and dendrologist, was librarian at the Imperial public library, St. Petersburg. Another son, **Wla·di'mir** [vlä·dē'mĭr] (1846–1940), authority on climatology, was meteorologist at the German Naval Observatory, Hamburg (1875–1918).

**Koppernigk, Niklas.** See COPERNICUS.

**Köp'ping** (kûp'ĭng), **Karl.** 1848–1914. German etcher and engraver, esp. of paintings of Rembrandt, etc.

**Köprülü.** See KUPRILI.

**Koraës** *or* **Koraïs.** See CORAY.

**Kor'da** (*Angl.* kôr'dȧ; *Hung.* kôr'dŏ), Sir **Alexander.** 1893–1956. British motion-picture producer, b. Hungary; produced films in Budapest, Vienna, Berlin, Hollywood, and Paris. Founded London Film Productions, Ltd. (1932), and Alexander Korda Film Productions (1939); director, United Artists' Corp. of Am.

**Korff** (kôrf), **Hermann August.** 1882–1963. German literary critic and historian.

**Korin Ogata.** See OGATA.

**Ko'řist·ka** (kôr'zhĭst·kȧ), **Karl von.** 1825–1906. Austrian geodesist and geographer, b. in Moravia; known esp. for determinations of heights and levels in several mountainous regions of Europe.

**Ko'ri·zes'** *or* **Ko'ri·zis'** (kô'rē·zēs'), **Alexandros.** 1885–1941. Greek financier and statesman; premier of Greece (1941); committed suicide after unsuccessful efforts to save his country from Italian and German invasion.

**Kör'men·di** (kûr'mĕn·dĭ), **Ferenc.** 1900–1972. Hungarian writer; author of *Escape to Life* (winner of international novel competition, 1932), etc.

**Korn** (kôrn), **Arthur.** 1870–1945. German physicist; pioneer in telephotography. Credited with first transmission of a photograph by telegraphy over a circuit, from Munich to Nuremberg and return (1904); transmitted pictures by wireless telegraphy from Rome, Italy, to Bar Harbor, Maine (1923).

**Korn'berg** (kôrn'bûrg), **Arthur.** 1918– . Amer. biochemist, b. Brooklyn, N.Y. Awarded Nobel prize in physiology and medicine (1959) with S. Ochoa for work on biological synthesis of nucleic acids.

**Kör'ner** (kûr'nẽr), **Karl Theodor.** 1791–1813. German lyric poet, dramatist, and patriot. Joined Lützow Volunteer Corps at Breslau in war against Napoleon; killed in battle at Gadebusch (1813). Author of librettos, comedies, tragedies, and the collection of patriotic lyrics *Leyer und Schwert* (pub. 1814) containing *Das Schwertlied*, composed on the battlefield. His father, **Christian Gottfried Körner** (1756–1831), jurist and literary critic, was friend of Schiller and correspondent of Goethe; prepared 1st collected edition of Schiller's works (12 vols., 1812–15).

**Korn'gold** (kôrn'gôlt), **Erich Wolfgang.** 1897–1957. Austrian composer, conductor, and pianist; composer of *Sinfonietta* (1912), incidental music for Shakespeare's *Much Ado* (1919), chamber music, sonatas, songs, one-act operas, and the operas *Die Tote Stadt* (1920) and *Das Wunder der Heliane* (1927).

**Kor·ni'lov** (kŭr·nyē'lôf), **Lavr Georgievich.** 1870–1918. Russian general, of Cossack descent. In World War commanded division in Galicia (1914); assumed command (1916) of 20th army corps; in command of troops in Petrograd after Revolution (1917). Checked by Bolsheviks in attempt to make himself dictator; escaped to Caucasus; organized Cossack force; killed in action.

**Ko·ro·len'ko** (kŭ·rŭ·lyān'kô), **Vladimir Galaktionovich.** 1853–1921. Russian novelist; exiled to Siberia (1879–85) for advanced social ideas. Settled in Nizhni Novgorod; editor of a review (from 1895). Representative of older literary traditions; master of style. Author of novels including *Makar's Dream* (his first; 1885), *The Murmuring Forest* (1886), *The Blind Musician* (1886), *Bad Company* (1886), short stories, and an autobiography.

**Kő'rö·si Cso'ma** (kû'rû·shĭ chô'mŏ), **Sándor.** *Known also as* **Cso'ma de Kő'rös** (chô'mŏ dẽ kû'rûsh). 1798?–1842. Hungarian traveler and philologist; to Tibet, where he studied (1827–30) in a Buddhist monastery; published *Tibetan-English Dictionary* (1834), *Grammar of the Tibetan Language* (1834), etc.

**Korsakov, Nikolai A. Rimski-.** See RIMSKI-KORSAKOV.

**Kör'ting** (kûr'tĭng), **Gustav.** 1845–1913. German philologist; specialist in Romance languages and English. Author of *Enzyklopädie und Methodologie der Romanischen Philologie* (3 vols., 1884–86), *Grundriss der Geschichte der Englischen Literatur* (1887), *Handbuch der Romanischen Philologie* (1896), etc.

**Kor'tum** (kôr'tōōm), **Karl Arnold.** 1745–1824. German physician, and author of a burlesque epic *Die Jobsiade* (1784).

**Ko'rze·niow'ski** (kô'zhĕ·nyôf'skē), **Józef.** 1797–1863. Polish playwright, novelist, and teacher; author of dramatized folklore, social plays, including the comedies *The Jews* (1843) and *Married Woman and Widow* (1844), and stories and novels of manners.

**Korzeniowski, Teodor Józef Konrad.** See Joseph CONRAD.

**Kor·zyb'ski** (kôr·zĭp'skē), **Alfred Habdank Skarbek.** 1879–1950. American scientist and writer, b. in Warsaw, Poland; to U.S. (1916) and naturalized (1940). President and director, Institute of General Semantics, Chicago (from 1938). Author of *Manhood of Humanity* (1921), *Science and Sanity, An Introduction to Non-aristotelian Systems and General Semantics* (1933).

**Kó'sa** (kō'shŏ), **György.** 1897– . Hungarian composer and pianist.

**Kosch'witz** (kôsh'vĭts), **Eduard.** 1851–1904. German Romance scholar and philologist; author of *Les Plus Anciens Monuments de la Langue Française* (1879; one of the earliest phonetic anthologies), etc.

**Kos'ci·us'ko** (kŏs'ĭ·ŭs'kō), **Thaddeus.** *Pol.* **Tadeusz Andrzej Bonawentura Koś·ciusz'ko** (kôsh·chōōsh'kô). 1746–1817. Polish patriot, b. in Grand Duchy of Lithuania. Grad. Royal Coll., Warsaw (1769); studied engineering and artillery in France. Went to America to offer services in American Revolutionary army (1776); appointed colonel of engineers in Continental army (Oct. 18, 1776); in charge of construction of fortifications at West Point (1778–80); in charge of transportation during Greene's retreat (1781); engaged before Charleston, S.C. (1782); one of founders of Society of the Cincinnati (1783); brigadier general (Oct. 13, 1783). Returned to Poland (1784); major general in Polish army (1789); led rebellion (1794); became dictator of Poland, but was captured and imprisoned by Russia (1794–96). In America again (1797–98). Resident of France (from 1798); continued efforts to gain freedom for Poland until his death in Switzerland (Oct. 15, 1817).

**Ko'se·gar'ten** (kō'zĕ·gär'tĕn), **Ludwig The'o·bul'** (tā'ô·bōōl'). 1758–1818. German poet and novelist. His son **Johann Gottfried Ludwig** (1792–1860) was an Orientalist and historian.

**Ko·se no Ka·na·o·ka** (kô·sĕ nô kä·nä·ô·kä). fl. 850–880. One of earliest Japanese landscape and figure painters; founded Kose school, following the school of the T'ang dynasty of China; few of his works extant.

**Ko'ser** (kō'zẽr), **Reinhold.** 1852–1914. German historian; authority on Frederick the Great.

**Kos'ken·nie'mi** (kŏs'kĕn·nyĕ'mĭ), **Veikko Antero.** 1885–1962. Finnish scholar and writer. Among his works are *Symphonia Europaea A.D. 1931*, *Nuori Goethe* (1932), *Miekka ja Taltta* (1937).

**Kosloff.** Variant of KOZLOV.

**Kos'sak–Szczuc'ka** (kôs'säk·shchōōts'kä), **Zofia.** 1890–1968. Polish writer; m. (1st) Stefan Szczucki, and (2d) Zygmunt Szatkowski. Her experiences of the Russian Revolution (1917) are contained in her memoirs under the title (translated) *Conflagration*.

**Kos'sel** (kôs'ĕl), **Albrecht.** 1853–1927. German physiological chemist; investigated the chemistry of cells, also of proteins. Awarded the 1910 Nobel prize for physiology and medicine. His son **Walter** (1888–1956), professor of physics, Kiel (from 1921), is known for his theory of the physical nature of chemical valence and researches on the spectra of X rays and gamma rays.

**Kos'sin·na** (kô'sĭ·nä), **Gustaf.** 1858–1931. German prehistorian and archaeologist; author of *Altgermanische Kulturhöhe* (1927), etc.

**Kos'suth** (kô'shōōt; *Angl.* kŏs'ōōth), **Lajos.** 1802–1894. Hungarian patriot and statesman, b. in Monok. Imprisoned on political charges by Austrian government (1837–40). Editor of *Pest Journal*, reform organ (1840–44). Member of the Hungarian Diet (1847–49). Headed Hungarian insurrection (1848–49); persuaded Hungarian national assembly to declare independence of Hungary; was appointed governor of Hungary with dictatorial powers (1848). As insurrection was crushed, Kossuth resigned his powers (Aug. 11, 1849) and fled into exile in Turkey (imprisoned there, 1849–51), U.S. (1851–52), and England. During Austro-Sardinian war (1859), organized a Hungarian legion in Italy; resided thereafter in Turin. His son **Ferenc** (1841–1914), after sharing his father's exile, returned to Hungary (1894) and became a leader of the independence party in the Hungarian parliament; served as minister of commerce in the Wekerle cabinet (1906).

**Kost** (kôst), **Frederick W.** 1861–1923. American landscape painter.

**Koster.** Variant of COSTER.

**Köst'lin** (kûst'lēn), **Christian Reinhold.** *Pseudonym* **C. Rein'hold** (rīn'hôlt). 1813–1856. German jurist, poet, and writer; m. (1842) **Josephine Lang** [läng] (1815–1880), composer of songs. Their son **Heinrich Adolf** (1846–1907) was a theologian and writer on music. Christian's brother **Karl Reinhold** (1819–1894) was a Protestant theologian and philosopher.

**Köstlin, Julius.** 1826–1902. German Protestant theologian.

**Ko·sto·ma'rov** (kŭ·stŭ·ma'rôf), **Nikolai Ivanovich.** 1817–1885. Russian historian and novelist.

**Ko·sy'gin** (kŭ·sē'gĭn), **Aleksei N.** 1904– . Russian politician; premier of Soviet Union (from 1964).

**Kot'ze·bue** (kôt'sĕ·bōō), **August Friedrich Ferdinand von.** 1761–1819. German writer and dramatist, b. Weimar. In Russian civil service (1781–90), living in Paris and Mainz; retired to estate near Reval as writer (1795); dramatist and librettist to court theater, Vienna (1798–1800). Arrested as political suspect on return to Russia and taken to Siberia (1800); won favor of Paul I; released (1801); became director of German theater in St. Petersburg. Won unpopularity in Weimar through continued quarrels with Goethe and open attacks on romantic school; helped edit antiromantic journal *Der Freimütige* in Berlin (1803–05). To Königsberg; attacked Napoleon and France in journals *Die Biene* (1808–10) and *Die Grille* (1811–12); Russian consul general in Königsberg and political observer for Russia in Germany (1817); founded antiliberal weekly journal *Literarisches Wochenblatt* in Mannheim (1818); continued in Weimar. Stabbed to death by university student K. L. Sand for ridiculing Burschenschaft movement (1819). Author of over 200 dramatic works including tragedies, historical verse dramas, as *Die Hussiten vor Naumburg* (1803), and, esp., comedies and farces; also historical and biographical works, and miscellaneous sketches and stories.

His sons include: **Otto** (1787–1846), navigator and explorer; accompanied Krusenstern on voyage around world (1803–06); commanded vessel *Rurik* (accompanied by Chamisso, Eschscholtz, and others) in attempt (1815–18) to find passage across Arctic Ocean and explore Oceania; discovered 399 islands in South Sea, and Kotzebue Sound near Bering Strait (1816); visited California and Hawaii, and discovered Romanzov Island of Marshall group (1817); commanded third round-the-world voyage (1823–26) accompanied by Eschscholtz. **Wilhelm** (1813–1887), diplomat in Russian service; author, under pseudonym **W. Au'gust·sohn** (ou'gŏŏst·zōn), of plays, sketches, novels, and a German translation of V. Alecsandri's collection of Rumanian folk poems.

**Kou'moun·dou'ros** (kōō'mōōn·thōō'rôs), **Alexandros.** 1817–1883. Greek statesman; prime minister of Greece at various periods (between 1865 and 1882); policies characterized by hostility toward Turkey.

**Koun'dou·rio'tes** (kōōn'dōō·ryô'tēs) *or* **Koun'dou·rio'tis** (-tēs) *or* **Koun'tou·rio'tes** (kōōn'dōō-) *or* **Koun'tou·rio'tis, Pavlos.** 1855–1935. Greek admiral and statesman; commanded Greek fleet in Balkan War (1912–13) and twice defeated Turkish fleet in Dardanelles; minister of marine (1915); aided in organizing provisional government at Salonika favorable to Allies. Regent of Greece after death of King Alexander (1920) and again after King George II left country (1923). Elected first provisional president of Greece by Constituent Assembly (1924) and served (with short interruptions) until his resignation (1929).

**Kous'se·vitz'ky** (*Angl.* kōō'sĕ·vĭts'kĭ; *Russ.* kōō·syĭ·vyĕts'kû·ĭ), **Serge** (sûrj; sĕrzh), *or, Russ.,* **Sergei Alexandrovitch.** 1874–1951. Orchestra conductor, b. in Russia; director of Russian State Orchestra (1918–20); conductor in western Europe and England (1920–24), founding in Paris (1921) the Concerts Koussevitzky. Became conductor of Boston Symphony Orchestra (1924); organized Berkshire Music Center for symphonic festivals (held each summer from 1934), receiving gift of "Tanglewood" estate at Lenox, Mass., for its permanent home; also organized Berkshire Music School (1940).

**Kouyoumdjian, Dikran.** Orig. name of Michael ARLEN.

**Ko·va·lev'ski** (kŭ·vŭ·lyāf'skû·ĭ; *Angl.* kŏv'ȧ·lĕf'skĭ), **Aleksandr Onufrievich.** 1840–1901. Russian zoologist; brother-in-law of Sonya Kovalevski; best known for his studies in embryology and structure of ascidians and of Amphioxus, and in embryology and postembryological development of insects.

**Kovalevski, Sonya.** *Russ. name* **Sofya Vasilievna Ko·va·lev'ska·ya** (kŭ·vŭ·lyāf'skŭ·yŭ), *nee* **Korvina-Krukovskaya.** 1850–1891. Russian mathematician, b. Moscow; m. (1868) Vladimir Onufrievich Kovalevski, brother of Aleksandr O. Kovalevski; received Ph.D. degree at Göttingen (1874) for dissertation on theory of partial differential equations. Professor, U. of Stockholm (1884). Besides scientific papers, wrote *The Privatdocent* (a sketch of life in a small German university town, 1877), and an autobiographical sketch, *Recollections of Childhood* (1890); intimate friend of Anne Edgren (*q.v.*).

**Ko'va·řo'vic** (kô'vär·zhô'vĭts), **Karel.** 1862–1920. Czech conductor and composer; conductor and head of opera, Bohemian National Theater, Prague (1899–1920); composed operas, 7 ballets (3 under pseudonym **Charles For'ge·ron'** [shärl' fôr'zhĕ·rôN']), melodramas, the symphonic poem, *Persephone* (1884), string quartets, sonatas for violin and piano, a piano concerto, and songs and choruses, including the *Slovak Song.*

**Kö'vess von Kö'vess·há'za** (kû'vĕsh fôn kû'vĕsh·hä'zŏ), Baron **Her'mann** (hĕr'män). 1854–1924. Austro-Hungarian field marshal in World War; given chief command of Austrian troops by Emperor Charles (1918).

**Kox·in'ga** (kŏk·sĭng'(g)ȧ). *Chin.* **Cheng Ch'eng-kung** (jŭng' chŭng'gŏŏng'). 1623–1663. Chinese general and pirate; called "the pirate-patriot." Fought against the Manchus as they overthrew Ming dynasty (1644); refused to yield and with fleet of 3000 junks ravaged coasts; seized Amoy (1653); made Ch'ung-ming island at mouth of Yangtze his headquarters (1656); defeated Manchus at Amoy (1660); besieged Dutch (1661–62) in Formosa, forcing them to surrender; established Chinese government there.

**Koz·lov'** (kŭs·lôf'), **Pëtr Kuzmich.** 1863–1935. Russian scientist. Made expeditions into Chinese Turkestan (1889), and into Mongolian desert (1899), discovering Karakorum, capital of empire of Genghis Khan; explored Gobi desert (1907–09).

**Krae'pe·lin'** (krâ'pĕ·lēn'), **Emil.** 1856–1926. German pioneer in modern psychiatry; divided mental diseases into dementia-praecox and manic-depressive groups; investigated fatigue and influence of alcohol on mental processes.

**Krafft** (kräft), **Johann Peter.** 1780–1856. German historical and genre painter in Austria; painted many large pictures of battles and public events.

**Krafft'-E'bing** (kräft'ā'bĭng), Baron **Richard von.** 1840–1902. German neurologist; known for work on forensic psychiatry and *Psychopathia Sexualis* (1886; 17th edition, 1924).

**Kraft** *or* **Krafft** (kräft), **Adam.** 1460?–?1508. German stone sculptor in Nuremberg. His works include the following (all in Nuremberg): tomb of Sebald Schreyer, the elaborate late-Gothic tabernacle in the Church of St. Lawrence, *The Seven Stations* (reliefs of scenes from the life of Christ), and many reliefs for public and private buildings.

**Krag** (kräg), **O.** Norwegian inventor who, with **E. Jör'gen·sen** (yûr'gĕn·sĕn), developed Krag-Jörgensen rifle, standard arm of U.S. army (1892–98).

**Krag, Thomas Peter.** 1868–1913. Norwegian poet and novelist; author of *Jon Graeff* (1891), *The Copper Snake* (1895), *Ada Wilde* (1896), and *Master Magius* (1909), the drama *Kong Aagon* (1894), etc. His brother **Vilhelm Andreas Wexels** (1871–1933), lyric poet, dramatist, and novelist, was author of *Fandango* (1891), *Songs from the West* (1898), *Songs of My Island* (1918), and other lyric poetry, dramas, fairy plays, comedies, novels, and humorous sketches of Norwegian life.

**Kraljević** *or* **Kralievich.** See MARKO KRALJEVIĆ.

**Kra'mář** (krȧ'märsh), **Karel.** 1860–1937. Czech statesman; first prime minister of Czechoslovakia (1918–19).

**Kranach, Lucas.** See CRANACH.

**Kra'nich** (krä'nĭĸ), **Friedrich.** 1857–1924. German technical director of the Bayreuth Festival Theater (1882–1924). His son **Friedrich** (1880– ), technical director of Schwerin theater (1906–25); stage director in Hanover and (from 1906) at Bayreuth Festival Theater.

**Krantz** (kränts), **Albert.** 1448–1517. German statesman and historian. Ambassador to France (1497) and England (1499); author of works on ecclesiastical and political history of northern Europe.

**Krapf** (kräpf), **Johann Ludwig.** 1810–1881. German missionary, traveler, and philologist; missionary in Abyssinia (1837–42); traveled with Erhardt and Rebmann through East Africa and discovered Mts. Kilimanjaro (1848) and Kenya (1849); joined English expedition to Abyssinia as interpreter (1867); introduced many Abyssinian manuscripts into Germany and England.

**Krapotkin.** Variant of KROPOTKIN.

**Krapp** (krăp), **George Philip.** 1872–1934. American educator; professor of English, Columbia (from 1910). Author of *The Elements of English Grammar* (1908), *Pronunciation of Standard English in America* (1919), *Comprehensive Guide to Good English* (1927), *Anglo-Saxon Reader* (1929), etc.

**Kra·sic'ki** (krä·sēts'kē), **Ignacy.** 1735–1801. Polish poet and man of letters; enjoyed favor of Frederick the Great. Wrote fables and satires, esp. the mock-heroic *Mousiad* (Pol. *Myszeis*) and *Monachomachia*, a satire on cloistered life of monks (both 1778).

**Kra·siń'ski** (krä·sēn'y'·skē), Count **Zygmunt.** 1812–1859. Polish poet; among his works are *Undivine Comedy* (1834), *Irydion* (1836), *Dawn* (1843).

**Kras'sin** (krȧ'syĭn), **Leonid Borisovich.** 1870–1926. Russian politician; engineer by profession. During civil war following Revolution (1917), organized munition supply for Red army; president of Soviet delegation to conclude trade treaty with England (1920); Russian diplomatic representative in Paris and (1925–26) in London.

**Kra·szew'ski** (krä·shĕf'skē), **Józef Ignacy.** 1812–1887. Polish novelist, b. Warsaw; author of *Jermola*, *Ulana* (1843), *Kordecki* (1852); culture romances *Morituri* (1874–75) and *Resurrecturi* (1876); several political novels under pseudonym **Bo'le·sła·wi'ta** (bô'lĕ·slä·vē'tä). Author also of plays, verse (including epic on history of Lithuania, *Anafielas*, 1840–43), criticism, and historical works.

**Kraus** (krous), **Carl von.** 1868–1952. German philologist; published *Deutsche Gedichte des 12. Jahrhunderts* (1894), *Minnesangs Frühling*, *Untersuchungen* (1939).

**Kraus** (krous), **Charles Au'gust** (ô'gŭst). 1875–1967. American chemist; worked on vacuum-tight seals, chemical processes, electrical conducting systems, etc.

**Kraus, Edward Henry.** 1875–1972. American educator and mineralogist; author of *Descriptive Mineralogy* (1911), *Gems and Gem Materials* (with E. F. Holden, 1925), etc.

**Kraus, Franz Xaver.** 1840–1901. German Roman Catholic theologian; writer on church and art history and archaeology.

**Kraus, Herbert.** 1884–1965. German jurist; author of *Germany in Transition* (1924), *The Crisis of German Democracy* (1932), etc.

**Kraus, John.** 1815–1896. Educator; b. Nassau, Germany; to U.S. (1851). With his wife, **Maria Kraus'-Boel'té** [krous'bûl'tĕ; *Angl.* -bōl'tē] (1836–1918), active in spreading educational doctrines of Pestalozzi and Froebel.

**Kraus, Karl.** 1874–1936. Austrian satirist, critic, and poet, b. in Czechoslovakia. Founder and editor of the polemical review *Die Fackel* (from 1899), attacking middle-class circles and the liberal press; author of essays, verse, dramatic works, etc.

**Krau'se** (krou'zĕ), **Ernst Ludwig.** See CARUS STERNE.

**Krause, Fritz.** 1881–1963. German ethnologist and folklorist.

**Krause, Karl Christian Friedrich.** 1781–1832. German philosopher and writer. Advocated a union (Bund) of mankind to work toward a goal of universal development; created the "all-in-God" philosophical system of panentheism, the doctrine that God includes the world as a part, though not the whole, of His being; sought to purify the German language, etc.

**Krause, Wilhelm.** 1833–1910. German anatomist; credited with first description of nerve end organs in the skin.

**Kraus'kopf** (krous'kŏpf), **Joseph.** 1858–1923. Rabbi, b. Ostrowo, Prussia; to U.S. (1872); congregation in Philadelphia (from 1887); leader in Reformed Judaism in America; prominent in humanitarian work.

**Krauss** (krous), **Clemens.** 1893–1954. Austrian conductor.

**Krauss, Marie Gabriele.** 1842–1906. Austrian soprano.

**Krauth** (krôth), **Charles Philip.** 1797–1867. American Lutheran clergyman; first president, Pennsylvania (now Gettysburg) College (1834–50). His son **Charles Porterfield** (1823–1883) was also a Lutheran clergyman.

**Kravchinski, Sergei Mikhailovich.** See Sergei M. STEPNYAK.

**Kray von Kra'jo·wa** (krī fôn krä'yô·vä), Baron **Paul.** 1735–1804. Austrian general. Commanded in Netherlands against French, and defeated Pichegru at Catrou (1794) and Kléber near Wetzlar (1796); suffered reverses (1797), but won victories at Verona, Legnago, Magnano, and Mantua in Italian campaign (1799); succeeded Archduke Charles Louis as commander of army in Germany (1800); failed in German campaign and was removed from command.

**Krebs** (krĕbz), Sir **Hans Adolf.** 1900– . British (German-born) biochemist. Awarded Nobel prize in physiology and medicine (1953) with F. A. Lipmann for discovery of the citric acid cycle.

**Kreh'biel** (krā'bēl), **Henry Edward.** 1854–1923. American music critic; with New York *Tribune* (from 1880). Served as American editor of Grove's *Dictionary of Music*, 2d edition (1904–10). Author of *Studies in the Wagnerian Drama* (1891), *Afro-American Folk-Songs* (1914), etc.

**Kreis'ler** (krīs'lĕr), **Fritz.** 1875–1962. American violinist, b. Vienna; in Austrian army, World War I; to U.S. (naturalized 1943); composer of arrangements of classical music for violin, many original violin pieces, a string quartet, and the operetta *Apple Blossoms* (1919).

**Kre′ling** (krā′lĭng), **August von.** 1819–1876. German painter and sculptor; works include frescoes and historical paintings, illustrations for *Faust*, etc.

**Krell, Nikolaus.** See CRELL.

**Krem′nitz** (krĕm′nĭts), **Mite** *or* **Marie.** *Nee* **Marie von Bar′de·le′ben** (fôn bär′dĕ·lā′bĕn). *Pseudonym* **George Al′lan** (jôrj ăl′ăn). 1852–1916. German writer; m. Dr. Kremnitz and settled in Bucharest (1875); moved to Berlin (1897). Coauthor, with Queen Elizabeth of Rumania (Carmen Sylva), of the translations *Rumänische Dichtungen* (1881) and, under joint pseudonym **Di′to und I′dem** (dē′tō ŏŏnt ē′dĕm), of the drama *Anna Boleyn* (1886) and novels and stories. Author also of the comedy *Die Kammerwahl* (1917; with Kienzl) and of *Rumänische Skizzen* (1877, 1881), *Rumänische Märchen* (1882), biographies, and novels and collections of stories.

**Kře·nek** (kĕr·zhĕ′nĕk), **Ernst.** 1900– . American (Austrian-born) composer of the modernist school, and writer on music, b. Vienna. Composer of the operas *Orpheus und Eurydike* (1923; text by O. Kokoschka), *Jonny Spielt Auf* (farcical jazz opera; 1927), and of musical plays, ballets, symphonic music, concerti grossi for orchestra, a violin concerto, chamber music, piano pieces, cantatas, etc.

**Kress** (krĕs), **Samuel Henry** (1863–1955) and his brother **Claude Washington** (1876–1940). American merchants; founders of S. H. Kress & Co., operating a chain of five, ten, and twenty-five cent stores in U.S. and Hawaii.

**Kretsch′mer** (krăch′mĕr; krĕch′-), **Edmund.** 1830–1908. German composer and organist; court organist (1863–1901) in Dresden.

**Kretschmer, Ernst.** 1888–1964. German psychiatrist.

**Kret′zer** (krĕt′sĕr), **Max.** 1854–1941. German novelist; disciple of Zola and founder of naturalistic school in Germany. Author chiefly of realistic and social novels and tales, also of plays and verse.

**Kretz′schmar** (krĕts′shmär), **August Ferdinand Hermann.** 1848–1924. German music scholar, critic, and historian. Composed organ works and sacred and secular part songs; author of *Geschichte der Oper* (1919), etc.

**Kreu′ger** (krü′gĕr), **Ivar.** 1880–1932. Swedish industrialist, financier, and swindler; to U.S. (c. 1893) and became successful building-construction engineer. In Sweden, organized with Paul Toll firm of Kreuger & Toll (1908), expanding into the match industry; organized holding company, Swedish Match Co. (1917), and developed an international match monopoly; engaged in vast financing operations, including advances to various governments in return for industrial concessions. Financial stress beginning in 1929 forced collapse of his enterprises, and he committed suicide in Paris (Mar. 12, 1932); subsequent investigation revealed vast irregularities in the finances of his various enterprises.

**Kreut′zer** *or* **Kreu′zer** (kroi′tsĕr), **Konradin.** 1780–1849. German composer and concert pianist. Composed about 30 operas and other dramatic works including *Konradin von Schwaben* (1812) and *Das Nachtlager von Granada* (1834; libretto by J. F. Kind), the oratorio *Die Sendung Mosis* (1814), songs and male choruses, church music, chamber music, etc.

**Kreut′zer** (kroi′tsĕr; *Fr.* krûd′zâr′), **Rodolphe.** 1766–1831. German-French violinist and composer; composed 40 études and caprices (violin studies), 19 violin concertos, about 40 operas and dramatic works, and much chamber music; Beethoven's *Kreutzer Sonata* was dedicated to him.

**Krey** (krā), **Laura Lettie,** *nee* **Smith.** 1890– . American novelist; m. August Charles Krey (1913). Author of *And Tell of Time* (1938), *On the Long Tide* (1940).

**Kreym′borg** (krām′bôrg), **Alfred.** 1883–1966. American poet, b. New York City. Collaborator with Paul Rosenfeld, Lewis Mumford, and Van Wyck Brooks in publication of *American Caravan* (1927, 1928, 1929, 1931), a miscellany of new American literature. Author of *Mushrooms* (verse; 1916), *Plays for Merry Andrews* (1920), *Less Lonely* (verse; 1923), *Lima Beans* (plays; 1925), *Funnybone Alley* (verse; 1927), *Manhattan Men* (1929), *Our Singing Strength* (1929).

**Kriloff.** Variant of KRYLOV.

**Kro′ba·tin** (krō′bä·tĭn), Baron **Alexander von.** 1849–1933. Austro-Hungarian field marshal in World War I.

**Krock** (krŏk), **Arthur.** 1886–1974. American journalist, b. Glasgow, Ky.; A.M., Princeton; editor in chief, Louisville (Ky.) *Times* (1919–23); with N.Y. *World* (1923–27), N.Y. *Times* (from 1927; Washington correspondent, 1932–53), commentator (1953–67). Author of *Memoirs: Sixty Years on the Firing Line* (1970), *Myself When Young: Growing Up in the 1890's* (1973).

**Kroe′ber** (krō′bĕr), **Alfred Louis.** 1876–1960. American anthropologist; known for work on languages, culture, religion, etc., of North American Indians.

**Krogh** (krôg), **August,** *in full* **Schack August Steenberg.** 1874–1949. Danish physiologist; professor, Copenhagen (1916). Discovered the regulation of the motor mechanism of capillaries. Awarded the 1920 Nobel prize for physiology and medicine.

**Kroh** (krō), **Oswald.** 1887–1955. German psychologist.

**Krohg** (krôg), **Christian.** 1852–1925. Norwegian painter and writer; pioneer in open-air painting in Norway. His artistic works include *Port the Helm, Leif Ericson Discovers America, Norwegian Pilot, The Seamstress.*

**Krol** (krōl), **John Joseph.** 1910– . American Roman Catholic clergyman; consecrated bishop (1953); archbishop of Philadelphia (1961); cardinal (1967).

**Kroll** (krōl), **Leon.** 1884–1974. American portrait, landscape, genre, still-life, and mural artist. Painted murals for U.S. Dept. of Justice building, Washington, D.C.

**Kroll** (krôl), **Wilhelm.** 1869–1939. German classical philologist and scholar; published critical editions of Greek and Latin authors, and edited Pauly-Wissowa's *Real-Encyclopädie* (from 1908).

**Kro′may′er** (krō′mī′ĕr), **Johannes.** 1859–1934. German historian, esp. of ancient warfare and battlefields.

**Kronach, Lucas.** See CRANACH.

**Kron′berg** (krŏn′bûrg), **Louis.** 1872–1965. American portrait painter, b. Boston.

**Kro′neck′er** (krō′nĕk′ĕr), **Leopold.** 1823–1891. German mathematician; known chiefly for work in algebra and the theory of numbers.

**Kro′ner** (krō′nĕr), **Richard.** 1884– . German philosopher. Wrote *Von Kant bis Hegel* (1921–24), etc.

**Kro′nes** (krō′nĕs), **Therese.** 1801–1830. Austrian actress and playwright; subject of works of fiction.

**Kro·pot′kin** (krŭ·pŏt′kyĭn), Prince **Pëtr Alekseevich.** 1842–1921. Russian geographer, revolutionist, and social philosopher, b. Moscow. Made valuable contributions (1871–73) to geography by explorations in Siberia, Finland, and Manchuria. Joined (1872) extreme branch of International Workingmen's Association; arrested (1874) but escaped (1876) to England. Condemned in Lyons (1883) and sentenced to five years' imprisonment for anarchistic activities and publications; released (1886) and lived in England (1886–1914) and in Russia (1917–21); visited U.S. (1900). Author (in French) of works on social subjects, esp. *Paroles d'un Révolté* (1885; Eng. trans. *Memoirs of a Revolutionist,* 1899), *The Conquest of Bread* (1888; Eng. trans. 1906, 1916), *Modern Science and Anarchism* (1903), *Terror in Russia* (1909).

**Kröy′er** (krû′ĭ·ĕr), **Peter Severin.** 1851–1909. Painter,

b. Stavanger, Norway. Settled in Denmark as teacher and leader of naturalistic school. His works include pictures of life in Skagen, portraits of his wife, Drachmann, and others, group portraits, genre scenes with figures.

**Krü'de·ner** (krü'dĕ·nẽr), Baroness **Bar'ba·ra** (bär'bä·rä) **Ju'li·a'ne** (yōō'lē·ä'nĕ) **von,** *nee* **von Vie'ting·hoff** (fôn fē'tĭng·hôf). 1764–1824. Russian Pietist and novelist, b. at Riga; m. (1782; separated 1785) Baron von Krüdener, Russian ambassador to Venice and Denmark (d. 1802). Led gay life in Germany, France, Russia, and Switzerland; intimate of Madame de Staël at Coppet (1801) and Paris. Returned to Riga (1804), was converted to teachings of Moravians, and influenced by chiliasts and Pietists and by association with Jung-Stilling in Germany (1808) and ideas of Swedenborg. Devoted herself to preaching and prophesying in Europe; brought Queen Louise of Prussia and Alexander I of Russia under her influence; and played important part in furthering formation of Holy Alliance.

**Krue'ger** (krü'gẽr), **Felix.** 1874–1948. German philosopher and psychologist.

**Krue'ger** (krōō'gẽr), **Walter.** 1881–1967. American army officer, b. Flatow, Germany; joined U.S. army as private (1898); commissioned (1901), served in Spanish-American War, Philippine insurrection (1899–1903), Mexican border (1916), World War I; commander of 3d army (1941), 6th army (1943); general (1945).

**Krue'si** (krōō'zĭ), **John.** 1843–1899. Mechanical engineer, b. Speicher, Switzerland; to U.S. (1870); associated with Thomas A. Edison (from 1871); chief engineer of General Electric Co. (from 1895).

**Krug** (krōōg), **Julius Albert.** 1907–1970. American power engineer, b. Madison, Wis.; public utilities expert, with Wis. (1932–35), Federal Communications Comm. (1935–37), Tenn. Valley Authority (1938–40); War Production Board (1942–45); secretary of the interior (1946–49).

**Krug** (krōōᴋ), **Wilhelm Traugott.** 1770–1842. German philosopher.

**Krü'ger** (krü'gẽr), **Franz.** *Called* **Pfer'de–Krü'ger** (pfĕr'dĕ·krü'gẽr), *i.e.*, "Horse-Krüger." 1797–1857. German portrait and horse painter, at Prussian court (1825) and to Nicholas I of Russia. His works include portraits of the Prussian royal family and court society, Russian nobility, and well-known Berlin personalities.

**Krüger, Paul.** 1840–1926. German jurist and historian.

**Kru'ger** (krü'(g)ẽr; *Angl.* krōō'gẽr), **Stephanus Johannes Paulus.** *Known as* **Oom Paul** (ōōm pō'ōōl). 1825–1904. South African statesman, b. Colesberg, Cape Colony (Cape of Good Hope). Migrated from Cape Colony to north of Orange River (the Great Trek, 1836–40) and became a founder of Transvaal state, whose independence was acknowledged by Great Britain in Sand River Convention (1852). Elected commandant general of Transvaal forces (1864). Transvaal annexed by British (1877) and Kruger dismissed from service (1878) on account of opposition to British domination. A leader of Boer rebellion (1880) and associate of General Petrus Jacobus Joubert and Marthinus Pretorius in negotiating peace (1881). President of Transvaal (1883–1900). Too old to take part in Boer War (1899–1902), went to Europe in vain attempt to get European powers to intervene. Died in Switzerland.

**Kruif, Paul de.** See DE KRUIF.

**Kru'ko·wiec'ki** (krōō'kô·vyĕts'kē), Count **Jan.** 1770?–1850. Polish soldier; president of insurrectionary government in Poland (1830–31); surrendered Warsaw to General Paskevich (Sept. 7, 1831).

**Krum** (krŭm) *or* **Crum'mus** (krŭm'ŭs) *or* **Crumn** (krŭm). d. 814. Bulgarian king or khan (802–814). Gained power by victories over Avars; waged war for five years (808–813) with Byzantine Empire; defeated and killed Emperor Nicephorus (811); besieged Constantinople (813–814); defeated by Leo the Armenian at Mesembria (813).

**Krum'ba'cher** (krŏŏm'bä'ᴋẽr), **Karl.** 1856–1909. German Byzantine scholar; founder of *Byzantinische Zeitschrift* (1892); author of *Geschichte der Byzantinischen Literatur* (1891), etc.

**Krum'ma·cher** (krŏŏm'ä·ᴋẽr). Family of German Protestant clergymen, including: **Friedrich Adolf** (1767–1845), pastor in Bremen (1824–43); author of the classic *Parabeln* (1805), religious poems for children, etc. His son **Friedrich Wilhelm** (1796–1868), court preacher, Potsdam (from 1853); author of *Salomo und Sulamith* (1827), *Elias der Thisbiter* (1828), etc.

**Krüm'mel** (krüm'ĕl), **Otto.** 1854–1912. German geographer and oceanographer.

**Krupp** (krŏŏp; *Angl.* krŭp), **Friedrich.** 1787–1826. German ironmaster; founder (c. 1810) of the Krupp Works, at Essen. His son **Alfred** (1812–1887) succeeded him; developed process of making cast steel, begun by his father; began manufacture of ordnance (c. 1847); his type of breech-loading rifle was adopted by Prussian army (1861). Alfred's son **Friedrich Alfred** (1854–1902) succeeded his father in management of the works; also manufactured machinery. At his death, control passed to his daughter **Bertha** (1886–1957), whose husband (m. 1906), with consent of German government, prefixed *Krupp* to his name and became **Gustav Krupp von Boh'len und Hal'bach** [fôn bō'lĕn ŏŏnt häl'bäᴋ] (1870–1950).

**Krup'ska·ya** (krōōp'skŭ·yŭ), **Nadezhda Konstantinovna.** 1869–1939. Russian social worker; m. (1898) Nikolai Lenin (*q.v.*); active in aiding Lenin in revolutionary program in St. Petersburg (1891–98); exiled to Siberia (1898). Joined Lenin in years of exile in Europe; secretary of Bolshevik section of Social Democratic party (1900–17); returned to Russia (1917). After Lenin's death exerted great influence, esp. in education of Soviet youth; wrote *Memories of Lenin* (transl. 1930).

**Kru'se** (krōō'zĕ), **Heinrich.** 1815–1902. German poet, dramatist, and publicist.

**Kru'sen·stern** (krōō'zĕn·shtĕrn), **Adam Johann von.** 1770–1846. Russian navigator, b. in Estonia. Commissioned by Emperor Alexander I (1803) to explore north Pacific; made valuable geographical discoveries and was first Russian to circumnavigate the globe (1803–06).

**Krutch** (krōōch), **Joseph Wood.** 1893–1970. American critic and essayist; editor, *The Nation* (1924–52); professor, Columbia (1937–1952). Author of *Comedy and Conscience After the Restoration* (1924), *Edgar Allan Poe—A Study in Genius* (1926), *The Modern Temper* (1929), *Was Europe a Success?* (1934), etc.

**Kry·len'ko** (krĭ·lyân'kô; *Angl.* krĭ·lĕng'kō), **Nikolai Vasilievich.** 1885–?1938. Russian revolutionary officer. Joined revolutionary movement (1904), using pseudonym **A·bram'** (ŭ·brâm'); after Revolution, commander of Bolshevist forces (1917–18); later private secretary to Lenin; people's commissar for justice (1922–38).

**Kry·lov'** (krĭ·lôf'), **Aleksei Nikolaevich.** 1863–1945. Russian mathematician and naval architect; director of naval construction (1908–10); professor, naval academy (1910). Investigated the oscillation of ships; devised optical instruments.

**Krylov, Ivan Andreevich.** 1768–1844. Russian fabulist, b. Moscow. Translated La Fontaine's fables; published collections of his own fables (1809, 1811, 1816); chief librarian in Imperial Public Library (1816–41).

**Krylov, Viktor Aleksandrovich.** 1838–1906. Russian dramatist; wrote more than 100 plays including many adapted from the French and several original plays dealing with social problems.

**Kuang Hsü** *or* **Kwang Hsu** (gwäng′ shü′). *Personal name* **Tsai T'ien** (dzī′ tê·ĕn′), *i.e.* "Glorious Succession." 1871–1908. Chinese emperor (1875–1908) of the Ch'ing, or Manchu, dynasty; b. at Peking; son of Prince Ch'un and nephew and adopted heir of Emperor Hsien Fêng. During minority (1875–84) under regency of Prince Kung and of his aunt Tzu Hsi, who continued in control (1884–89) until his marriage. Inclined to adopt reform measures, but on issuing edicts (1898) to bring about reforms, was again compelled to accept regency of his aunt, Dowager Empress Tzu Hsi; for rest of reign (1898–1908) a mere puppet.

**Kuang Wu-ti** (gwäng′ wo͞o′dē′). 6 B.C.–57 A.D. Chinese emperor (25–56); founder of the Later Han dynasty.

**Ku·ba′la** (ko͞o·bä′lä), **Ludwik.** 1838–1918. Polish historian, esp. of the 17th century.

**Ku′be·lik** (ko͝o′bĕ·lĭk), **Jan.** 1880–1940. Czech violinist and composer of violin concertos; Hungarian citizen.

**Ku′bin** (ko͝o′bĭn), **Alfred.** 1877–1959. Painter and illustrator, esp. of phantastic subjects; b. in Bohemia.

**Ku′bi·tschek** (ko͞o′bĭ·chĕk), **Jus′ce·li′no** (zho͞o′sĕ·lē′no͞o). 1901– . Brazilian physician and politician; president of Brazil (1956–61).

**Ku′blai Khan** (kū′blī kän′) *or* **Khu′bi·lai Khan** (ko͞o′bĭ·lī) *or* **Ku′bla Khan′** (ko͞o′blȧ). 1216–1294. Mongol khan and founder of Mongol dynasty in China; son of Tului and grandson of Genghis Khan, and brother of Mangu Khan and Hulagu. With his brother Mangu, then Mongol khan, undertook conquest of southern China (1252–59); advanced into Tonkin and to borders of Tibet; treated conquered peoples humanely. After death of Mangu (1259), was elected khan; completed subjugation of China by expelling Kin Tatars in the north and putting down various rebellions (1260–79); founded (1264–67) Khanbalik ("City of the Khan"), Tai-tu, or Cambaluc (now identified with Peiping), as his capital. Relinquished parts of Mongol empire to other descendants of Genghis Khan, but retained China; completed organization of China and founded Yüan dynasty (1280), succeeding the Southern Sung dynasty. In foreign wars, subdued Korea and Burma, but expeditions to Japan (1274–81) and Java (1293) failed. Visited by Marco Polo (*q.v.*) with father and uncle (1275–92). Ardent Buddhist, but tolerant of other faiths; patron of literature and arts.

**Ku′char·zew′ski** (ko͞o′kär·zĕf′skē), **Jan.** 1876–1952. Polish historian and politician; appointed by regency council prime minister of Polish government (Nov., 1917), but resigned (Feb., 1918) in protest against terms of Brest-Litovsk treaty.

**Kü′chen·mei′ster** (kü′kĕn·mī′stēr), **Friedrich.** 1821–1890. German parasitologist; author of *Die Parasiten des Menschen* (1855), etc.

**Küch′ler** (kük′lēr), **Walther.** 1877–1953. German Romance scholar and writer.

**Ku Chu-tung** (ko͞o′jo͞o′to͝ong′). 1893– . Chinese army off.; com. in chief, 16th route army of antirebel forces; chairman, Kiangsu provincial government (1931–33); member, central executive committee of Kuomintang (from 1931); commander in chief of northern route, communist suppression forces (1933–34); held various commands in Chino-Japanese War (1937 ff.).

**Kück′en** (kük′ĕn), **Friedrich Wilhelm.** 1810–1882. German composer; composed many songs and duets including the Thuringian folk song *Ach, Wie Ist's Möglich Dann* (1827), the operas *Die Flucht nach der Schweiz* (1839) and *Der Prätendent* (1849), sonatas for piano and violin, piano and violoncello, etc.

**Kuehl** (kül), **Gotthardt.** 1850–1915. German painter; painted chiefly views of cities and interiors, often with brilliant lighting effects.

**Kue′nen** (kü′nĕn), **Abraham.** 1828–1891. Dutch Protestant theologian; leader of the modern critical school in Holland.

**Kü′gel·gen, von** (fôn kü′gĕl·gĕn). Family of German painters including: **Gerhard** (1772–1820), who painted chiefly mythological and religious pictures, also portraits of Goethe, Schiller, Herder, and Wieland, etc. His twin brother, **Karl** (1772–1832), who produced chiefly sketches of Crimean landscapes. Gerhard's son and pupil **Wilhelm** (1802–1867), who painted portraits of Goethe and Wieland.

**Ku′gler** (ko͞o′glēr), **Franz.** 1808–1858. German historian, esp. of art, and poet; championed revival of Prussian art.

**Kuh** (ko͞o), **Emil.** 1828–1876. Austrian literary critic and poet, b. of Jewish parents. Embraced Roman Catholicism (1857); author of first biography of Hebbel (2 vols., 1877; completed by R. Valdek), and of literary criticisms, essays, stories, and lyric poetry.

**Kuhhorn, Martin.** See Martin BUCER.

**Kuh′lau** (ko͞o′lou), **Friedrich.** 1786–1832. German composer of operas, as *The Robbers' Castle* (1814), music to Boye's *Shakespeare* (1826) and Johan Ludvig Heiberg's Danish national play *Elverhöj* (*Fairy Hillock*, 1828), chamber music, songs, and male quartets.

**Kuhl′mann′** (ko͞ol′mȧn′), **Charles Frédéric.** 1803–1881. French chemist and industrialist; established near Lille (1825) sulphuric-acid manufactory, from which present Kuhlmann Chemical and Dye Company of Paris developed.

**Kuhl′mann** (ko͞ol′män), **Richard von.** 1873–1948. German statesman; foreign secretary (1917–18); represented Germany in peace negotiations with Russia at Brest-Litovsk and with Rumania at Bucharest (1918). Publicly championed peace by agreement rather than decision by arms alone, and was forced to withdraw from office (1918).

**Kuhn** (ko͞on), **Adalbert,** *in full* **Franz Felix Adalbert.** 1812–1881. German Indo-Germanic philologist and mythologist; a founder of the science of comparative mythology. Cofounder and editor (from 1851) of Kuhn's *Zeitschrift für Vergleichende Sprachforschung*, and editor of a series of Brandenburg, North German, and Westphalian myths, customs, and legends (1843, 1848, 1859). Author of work on Indo-Germanic archaeology and linguistic paleontology, and essays on mythology. His son **Ernst** (1846–1920), Indologist, was coeditor of his father's *Zeitschrift*, and of *Grundriss der Iranischen Philologie* (1895–1904), and author of studies on Pali (1875) and Singhalese (1879).

**Kuhn, Franz.** Baron **Kuhn von Küh′nen·feld** (fôn kü′nĕn·fĕlt). 1817–1896. Austrian master of the ordnance. Chief of general staff under Gyulai in Italian war of 1859. War minister (1868–74); master of ordnance (1873); commanded forces in Styria, Carinthia, and Carniola (1874–88).

**Kuhn, Richard.** 1900–1967. Austrian chemist; professor at Kaiser Wilhelm Institute, Berlin; known for researches on vitamins and carotinoids; declined 1938 Nobel prize for chemistry in accordance with instructions of German government.

**Kuh′nau** (ko͞o′nou), **Johann.** 1660–1722. German composer, organist, and scholar; predecessor of Bach as cantor at St. Thomas's, Leipzig (1701); invented the separate movements of the clavier sonata. Composed *Neue Klavierübung* (2 parts, 1689–92), and *Musikalische Vorstellung Einiger Biblischen Historien in 6 Sonaten*, an example of early program music (1700), also cantatas and other church music, etc.

**Küh'ne** (kü'nĕ), **August.** *Pseudonym* **Jo·han'nes van De·wall'** (yō·hän'ĕs vän dĕ·väl'). 1829–1883. German novelist; army officer (1848–75); author of the humorous tales *Kadettengeschichten* (1878), and novels of army officers and upper-class life.

**Kühne, Ferdinand Gustav.** 1806–1888. German novelist and critic; a leader of Young Germany. Edited the weekly *Europa* (1846–59); resident in Dresden (from 1856). Author of historical novels, critical essays, poems, and dramas.

**Kühne, Wilhelm.** 1837–1900. German physiologist; professor, Heidelberg (from 1871); known esp. for studies on the physiology of muscles and nerves and on the chemistry of digestion.

**Küh'ne·mann** (kü'nĕ·män), **Eugen.** 1868–1946. German philosopher and historian of literature. Professor, Harvard (1909), Wisconsin (1912–13); worked for German cause in U.S. (1914–17). Author of *Herders Leben* (1895), *Schiller* (1905), *Deutschland und Amerika* (1917), *Kant* (2 vols., 1923–24), *Goethe* (2 vols., 1930), etc.

**Kui'by·shev** (kōō'ĭ·bĭ·shĕf), **Valerian Vladimirovich.** 1888–1935. Russian Bolshevik leader, b. Omsk; joined Communist party (1904); with Frunze, led military operations against Kolchak during Civil War. Served as chairman of the Supreme Council of National Economy and as chairman of the Central Committee; head of the Gosplan for nearly 5 years; member of the Politburo (from 1927). The city of Samara was renamed Kuibyshev in his honor.

**Ku·kai** (kōō·kī). *Posthumous name* **Ko·bo Dai·shi** (kō·bō dī·shē). 774–835 A.D. Japanese Buddhist priest. Studied in China (804–806); preached Shingon doctrine, founding (806) Buddhist sect Shingon-shu; established (816) in Kii province Mt. Koya monastery (Koya-san); invented the hiragana syllabary; also noted as a sculptor and calligrapher.

**Ku K'ai-chih** (gōō' kī'jĭr'). 344?–?406 A.D. Chinese painter, who lived under the Eastern Chin dynasty; one of the most famous of Chinese masters, esp. in figure painting; two rolls attributed to him are extant.

**Ku·ku'lje·vić–Sak·cin'ski** (kōō·kōō'lyĕ·vēt'y' [*Angl.* -vĭch]·säk·tsēn'skē), **Ivan.** 1816–1889. Croatian writer; author of verse, drama, fiction, and historical studies; wrote the first Croatian play, *Juran i Sofija* (1839).

**Ku·lik'** (kōō·lyĕk'), **Grigori Ivanovich.** 1890– . Russian military leader and artillery expert; inspector general of artillery (1937); with Timoshenko and Shaposhnikov, directed successful attack on Mannerheim line (Finland, 1940), and with them was awarded rank of marshal; deputy to Supreme Soviet of U.S.S.R.; following Nazi invasion of Russia (1941), member of general staff in charge of all artillery units of Red army.

**Kul'lak** (kōōl'äk). Family of German musicians including: **Theodor** (1818–1882), pianist; cofounder (1850; with Julius Stern and Adolf B. Marx) of the Berlin (later Stern) Conservatory and founder (1855) of the Neue Akademie der Tonkunst; royal professor (1861). His son and pupil **Franz** (1844–1913), pianist, was royal professor (1883). Theodor's brother **Adolf** (1823–1862) was a pianist and music critic.

**Kulm'bach** (kōōlm'bäk), **Hans von.** *Real name* **Hans Süss** (züs). 1476?–1522. German painter; worked under Dürer; court painter at Cracow (1514–18). His works include 8 scenes from the lives of St. Peter and St. Paul (now in Florence), *Adoration of the Magi* (in Berlin), the Tucher altar representing a *Coronation of the Virgin*, etc., in Nuremberg; also designs for stained glass, etc.

**Kül'pe** (kül'pĕ), **Oswald.** 1862–1915. German philosopher and experimental psychologist; disciple of Wundt and exponent of the Würzburg school of psychology; carried on researches in psychology of feeling and thought and sought to find a critical realism.

**Ku·ma'ra·gup'ta I** (kōō·mä'rȧ·gōōp'tȧ). d. A.D. 455. Fourth king of the Gupta dynasty (413–455) of India. Son of Chandragupta II. Ruler during India's golden age of literature.

**Ku·ma'ri·la** *or* **Ku·ma'ri·la Bhat'ta** (kōō·mä'rĭ·lȧ bŭt'tȧ). fl. 700–750 A.D. Hindu philosopher, native of Bihar. Wrote a famous commentary on Mimamsa system of philosophy; a bitter opponent of Buddhism.

**Küm'mel** (küm'ĕl), **Otto.** 1874–1952. German Orientalist.

**Kum'mer** (kōōm'ĕr), **Ernst Eduard.** 1810–1893. German mathematician; contributed to development of differential geometry and the theory of numbers; originated the theory of ideal numbers.

**Kum'mer** (kōōm'ĕr), **Frederic Arnold.** 1873–1943. American writer; author of fiction including *The Green God* (1911), *The Webb* (1919), *Plaster Saints* (1921), *Design for Murder* (1936), of plays including *The Brute* (1912), *The Magic Melody* (1919; musical comedy, music by Sigmund Romberg), *My Golden Girl* (1919; music by Victor Herbert), *The Bonehead* (1920), and of scenarios as *The Slave Market*, *The Ivory Snuff Box*. m. (1895) **Clare Rodman Bee'cher** (bē'chĕr), author of the comedies *Be Calm Camilla*, *Good Gracious Annabelle*, *Successful Calamity*, etc.

**Kum'mer** (kōōm'ĕr), **Friedrich August.** 1797–1879. German violoncellist, composer, and teacher.

**Kumunduros.** = KOUMOUNDOUROS.

**Kun** (kōōn), **Béla.** 1885–1937. Hungarian Jewish Communist, b. in Transylvania. Journalist in Cluj; fought in Austrian army in World War; captured by Russians (1915); became Bolshevist; sent to Hungary (1918) by Communist leaders; edited *Red News* (1918–19); organized Communist revolution in Budapest (1919); succeeded Károlyi as premier (Mar. 22–July 31, 1919); introduced radical changes in government; failed to control Slovakian peasants. In counterrevolution, was defeated with aid of Rumanians (1919); fled to Vienna and later (1920) to Russia; reappeared in Vienna (Apr., 1928), briefly imprisoned, and deported to Russia.

**Kuncewicz, Jan.** See Saint JOSAPHAT KUNCEWICZ.

**Kunck'el** *or* **Kun'kel** (kōōng'kĕl), **Johann.** 1630?–?1702. German alchemist. Discovered processes for making artificial ruby glass and preparing phosphorus.

**Kundt** (kōōnt), **August.** 1839–1894. German physicist; discovered a method of determining the velocity of sound in gases; conducted researches on the conduction of heat and the friction of gases, and on the optical properties of metals.

**Kundt, Hans.** 1869–1939. German army officer; served on von Mackensen's staff in the World War. In Bolivia (1920–26; 1928–30; 1932–33), had a part in directing Bolivian campaign in the Chaco war against Paraguay.

**Kung** (gōōng), Prince. *Personal name* **I Hsin** *or* **Yi Hsin** (ē' shĭn'). 1833–1898. Manchu statesman; sixth son of the emperor Tao Kuang and brother of the emperor Hsien Fêng. In war with British and French (1859–60) left in charge when emperor fled; made best terms possible under Treaty of Peking (1860); first president of the Tsung-li Yamen (1861). Coregent (1862–73) with the empress dowager Tzu Hsi for T'ung Chih during his minority and for his successor Kuang Hsü (1875–84); also prime minister during this period; granted hereditary title **Kung Ch'in-wang** (gōōng' chĭn'wäng') by the empress dowager; his advocacy of reforms and his friendliness to Western ideas led to retirement (1884–94); recalled to presidency of Tsung-li Yamen (1894) and to the state council.

**Kung** (kŏŏng), **H. H.** *Orig.* **K'ung Hsiang-hsi** (kŏŏng' shē·äng'shē'). 1881–1967. Chinese statesman, b. in Shansi province; lineal descendant of Confucius (*Chin.* K'ung Fu-tzŭ) in 75th generation; educ. in U.S. at Oberlin (1906) and Yale (M.A., 1907); founder and principal of Oberlin Coll., T'aiku (or Ta-ku), Shansi. Active in revolutionary years (1911–17); acting minister of finance, Canton government, and in charge of Russian negotiations (1924–27); minister of industry (1928–31); member of the Kuomintang executive committee (1926–28); minister of finance of Nationalist government (1933–38); president, Executive Yuan (1938), vice-president (1939–44; resigned). On outbreak of war with Japan (1937) visited countries of Europe to establish credits; a man of great wealth; gave valuable aid to his brother-in-law Chiang Kai-shek and the Chinese cause. He married **Ai-ling Soong** (ī'lĭng' sŏŏng'), *Chin.* **Sung Ai-ling** [sŏŏng'] (1888–1973), *usually known as* Madame **Kung,** eldest daughter of C. J. Soong (see SOONG family); educ. at Wesleyan Coll., Macon, Ga. (M.A., 1910); on return to China joined revolutionary movement; shrewd in business; of great influence over her husband, esp. in all financial undertakings. Of their four children the eldest, **David Kung,** educ. at St. John's U., Shanghai, became managing director of Central Trust Company, China.

**K'ung Ch'iu.** See CONFUCIUS.

**K'ung Fu-tzŭ** *or* **Kung Fu-tse.** See CONFUCIUS.

**Ku'ni·gun'de** (kōō'nē·gŏŏn'dĕ), Saint. d. about 1039. Wife of Emperor Henry II of Germany; according to legend, when her reputation had been unjustly impugned she vindicated herself by walking barefoot over hot irons. After Henry II's death (1024), retired to a convent which she had founded, and devoted herself to pious works. Canonized (1200).

**Ku'ni·yo'shi** (kōō'nĭ·yō'shĭ), **Ya·su'o** (yä·sōō'ō). 1893–1953. Painter, b. Okayama, Japan; to U.S. as a boy (1906). Awarded Guggenheim Fellowship (1935). His work is represented in Metropolitan Museum of Art in New York, Chicago Art Institute, and other collections.

**Kunkel.** Variant of KUNCKEL.

**Kunth** (kŏŏnt), **Karl Sigismund.** 1788–1850. German botanist; known esp. for classification and description of plants collected by Humboldt and Bonpland in America published in his *Synopsis* (4 vols., 1822–25).

**Kunt'ze** (kŏŏn'tsĕ), **Otto.** 1843–1907. German traveler and botanist. Known for large herbarium and collection of plant pictures, and for publications, esp. the *Revisio Generum Plantarum* (3 vols., 1891–98), dealing with Latin nomenclature.

**Kun'wald** (kōōn'vält), **Ernst.** 1868–1939. Austrian orchestra conductor and pianist. Conductor of Berlin Philharmonic Orchestra (1907–12) and Cincinnati Symphony Orchestra (1912–17). Director of symphony concerts in Königsberg (1920–27) and Berlin (1928–32).

**Kunz** (kŏŏnts), **George Frederick.** 1856–1932. American mineralogist and gem expert, b. New York City; on staff of Tiffany & Co., jewelers (from 1879); special agent, U.S. Geological Survey (1883–1909). Author of *Gems and Precious Stones of North America, The Book of the Pearl* (with Charles H. Stevenson, 1908), *The Ring* (1917), etc. Special editor of gem and jewelry terms, *Webster's New International Dictionary, Second Edition.*

**Kup'ka** (kŏŏp'kȧ), **František** *or* **Frank** (frăngk). 1871–1957. Czech painter, satirist, and illustrator; pioneer in abstract movement called Orphism; settled in Paris (1894).

**Ku'pri·li'** (kōō'prē·lē') *or* **Kiu'pri·li'** (kü'-). *Correct mod. Turk.* **Kö'prü·lü'** (kû'prü·lü'). Name of an Albanian family, prominent in Turkish history in 17th and 18th centuries.

**Mohammed Kuprili** (1586?–1661) was made grand vizier (1656) by Mohammed IV; repressed revolts, reorganized army, and defeated Venetian fleet (1657), regaining Tenedos and Lemnos. His son **Ahmed,** *in full* **Fazil Ahmed** (1635–1676), grand vizier (1661–76), waged war with Austria (1663–64); badly defeated at St. Gotthard (1664) by Count Montecuccoli; concluded at Vasvár peace advantageous to Turkey; successfully terminated war with Venice (1669), obtaining Crete; began war against Poles (1672); twice beaten by John Sobieski; secured peace (Treaty of Zurawno, 1676). Ahmed's brother **Mustafa,** *in full* **Zade Mustafa** (1637–1691), grand vizier (1689–91), reorganized internal affairs and the army and navy, reformed finances and taxation system, and improved state of Christians; killed in battle of Slankamen. Mohammed's nephew **Hussein** (d. 1702), grand vizier (1697–1702), negotiated Treaty of Karlowitz (1699) by which Turkey lost much territory; driven from office.

**Kup·rin'** (kōōp·ryēn'; kōōp'ryĭn), **Aleksandr Ivanovich.** 1870–1938. Russian realistic novelist and short-story writer; wrote stories of army life, including *The Duel,* his most famous novel (1905), also *Gambrinus, Sulamith,* and *Yama* (all translated into English); opposed to Bolshevism; lived in Paris after Revolution (1917).

**Ku·ra'kin** (kŏŏ·rä'kyĭn), Prince **Boris Ivanovich.** 1676–1727. Russian diplomat; brother-in-law of Peter the Great; sometimes called "father of Russian diplomacy." Represented Peter at Rome (1707), London, Hanover, and The Hague (1708–12); Russian emissary at Peace Congress at Utrecht (1713); ambassador at Paris (1716–22); instrumental in preventing Great Britain from siding with Sweden in war against Russia; his autobiography (1709) is an important historical document.

**Kurb'ski** (kŏŏrp'skû·ĭ; *Angl.* -skĭ), Prince **Andrei Mikhailovich.** 1528?–1583. Russian general and writer. Commander under Ivan IV; defeated in Lithuania, fled to Poland; his correspondence with Ivan, criticizing the czar, is of special historical interest.

**Kü'ren·berg, der von** (dār fôn kü'rĕn·bĕrk) *or* **der Kü'ren·ber'ger** (dĕr kü'rĕn·bĕr'gẽr). fl. c. 1160. Earliest-known (by name) German High Alamannic minnesinger, of an Austrian knightly family; author of *Das Falkenlied* and of love songs, etc.; sometimes erroneously credited with authorship of original *Nibelungenlied.*

**Ku·ri·no** (kōō·rē·nō), Viscount **Shinichiro.** 1852–1937. Japanese diplomat; minister to U.S.A. (1894–96), securing treaty whereby U.S. (1894) gave up principle of extraterritoriality as applied to Japan. Minister at Rome (1896), at Paris (1897–1901), and at St. Petersburg (1901–04) just before outbreak of Russo-Japanese War; ambassador to France (1906–12).

**Ku·ro·ki** (kŏŏ·rō·kē), Count **Tamemoto Tamesada.** 1844–1923. Japanese general; commander of first army in Manchuria in Russo-Japanese War (1904–05); won battle of the Yalu and took part in other battles.

**Ku·ro·pat'kin** (kŏŏ·rŭ·pȧt'kyĭn), **Aleksei Nikolaevich.** 1848–1921. Russian general; distinguished himself in Russo-Turkish War (1877–78); lieutenant general and governor of Transcaspian territories (1890–98); minister of war (1898–1904). Given supreme command of Russian forces in Far East and fought in Manchuria (1904) but was opposed to war with Japan because of Russia's unpreparedness; defeated at Mukden (1905) and relieved of chief command; wrote account of the war, *The Russian Army and the Japanese War* (1909).

**Kürschner.** See Konrad PELLICANUS.

**Kurth** (kürt), **Godefroid.** 1847–1916. Belgian historian.

**Ku·ru·su** (kōō·rōō·sōō), **Saburo.** 1888–1954. Japanese diplomat; in diplomatic service (1910–45); as ambassador to Germany (1939–40), signed pact that brought Japan into Axis (Sept., 1940); special envoy to U.S. (Nov.–Dec., 1941).

**Kurz** (kŏŏrts), **Hermann.** 1813–1873. German novelist, poet, and translator. Author of novels, as *Schillers Heimatjahre* (1843) and *Der Sonnenwirt* (1854), verse essays, translations of Ariosto, Cervantes, Shakespeare, etc. His daughter **Isolde** (1853–1944), poet and writer of fiction, author of stories of Italy and the Renaissance.

**Kusch** (kŏŏsh), **Polykarp.** 1911– . American physicist, b. Germany. At Columbia U. (1937–41; 1942–44; 1946– ). Awarded Nobel prize in physics (1955) with W. E. Lamb.

**Ku·shan′** (kŏŏ·shän′) *or* **Ku·sha′na** (kŏŏ·shä′nȧ). Name of a nomadic clan of the Yuechi Tatars in northern India forming a dynasty of kings (c. 78 A.D.–?220); esp. important was Kanishka (*q.v.*). Dynasty disappeared, probably a result of the rise of the Sassanidae.

**Kus′ma·nek von Burg′neu′städ′ten** (kŏŏs′mä·nĕk fôn bŏŏrK′noi′shtĕt′ĕn), Baron **Hermann.** 1860–1934. Austro-Hungarian colonel general; commanded fortress at Przemyśl against Russians (1914–15), defeated.

**Kus′ser** (kŏŏs′ĕr) *or* **Cous′ser′** (*Fr.* kōō′sâr′), **Johann Siegmund.** 1660–1727. Hungarian composer; lived in Paris (1674–82); orchestra conductor at Hamburg, where he presented his operas *Erindo* (1693), *Porus* (1694), *Pyramus and Thisbe* (1694), *Scipio Africanus* (1695), and *Jason* (1697); Kapellmeister, Christ Church Cathedral, Dublin (from 1710), and royal music master for Ireland (from 1716).

**Küssner–Coudert, Amalia.** See COUDERT.

**Kü′ster** (küs′tĕr), **Ernst.** 1874– . German botanist.

**Kutb–ud–din** *or* **Ku′tab–ud–din, Ai′bak** (ī′băk kŏŏt′bŏŏd·dēn′). d. 1210. Founder of the Slave dynasty of the Mohammedan kings (sultans) of Delhi. Born a Turki slave; left (1192) by Mohammed of Ghor as his viceroy in India; conquered Gujarat; on death of Mohammed became (1206) first independent Mohammedan sovereign of northern India. A successful general; consolidated dominion during short reign; his name preserved in the beautiful minaret at Delhi, the Kutb Minar, built by Altamsh.

**Ku·tu′zov** (kōō·tōō′zôf), **Mikhail Ilarionovich.** Prince of **Smo·lensk′** (smŭ·lyănsk′). 1745–1813. Russian field marshal, b. St. Petersburg. Served in Poland (1764–69) and against Turks (1770; 1771–72; 1811–12); ambassador at Constantinople, governor of Finland, and governor of St. Petersburg (1801). Army commander in wars against Napoleon (1805–12); defeated at Austerlitz (1805); military governor of Kiev (1806–11); commander in chief against Turks (1811–12) and against French (1812); defeated at Borodino but won victory over Davout and Ney at Smolensk (Nov., 1812) during French retreat; died at Bunzlau.

**Küt′zing** (küt′sĭng), **Friedrich Traugott.** 1807–1893. German botanist who, in his book *Grundzüge der Philosophischen Botanik* (1851–52), advanced theories of origin of species resembling those later enunciated by Darwin.

**Kuyp.** Variant of CUYP.

**Kuy′per** (koi′pĕr), **Abraham.** 1837–1920. Dutch Protestant theologian and statesman. Represented antirevolutionary party in lower chamber (1874–77). Broke with national church and formed Free Reformed Church (1886). Again member of lower house (1894); effected Conservative and Clerical alliance between Calvinist and Catholic parties; formed a Christian Conservative ministry (1901), and was minister of interior (until 1905); championed social reforms; minister of state (1907).

**Ku′yuk** (kōō′yŏŏk). d. 1248. Mongol khan (1246–48); oldest son of Ogadai. One of Mongol generals in invasion of Europe (1237–41); quarreled with Batu; his court visited by Nestorian Christians.

**Kuyumjian.** Variant of KOUYOUMDJIAN (see Michael ARLEN).

**Kuz′nets** (kŭz′nĕts), **Simon.** 1901– . Am. economist, b. Russia. To U.S. (1907). Member, National Bureau of Economics (1927– ); at U. of Pa. (1930–54), Johns Hopkins U. (1954–60), Harvard U. (1960– ). Awarded Nobel prize in economic science (1971) for studies of gross national product as measure of a nation's economic growth. Author of *National Income and Its Composition, 1919–1938* (1941), etc.

**Kuz·ne·tsov′** (kŏŏs·nyĭ·tsôf′), **Nikolai Gerasimovich.** 1902–1974. Soviet admiral; served in civil war (1919–20); grad., Frunze Naval Academy (1926); attended Voroshilov Naval Academy (1929–32); cruiser commander (1934); commander of Pacific fleet (1937–38); appointed People's commissar of the navy (1939).

**Kva′pil** (kvȧ′pĭl), **František.** 1855–1925. Czech lyric poet; compiler of a Czech anthology of Polish verse.

**Kvapil, Jaroslav.** 1868–1950. Czech poet and dramatist; author of collections of lyric verse, dramas, the libretto to Dvořák's *Water Fairy*, etc.

**Kvie′sis** (kvyĕ′sĭs), **Alberts.** 1882–1944. Latvian statesman; president of Latvia (1930–36).

**Kvit′ka** (kvyēt′kŭ), **Grigori Petrovich.** *Pseudonym* **Os·no·vya′nen·ko** (ŭs·nŭ·vyȧ′nyĕn·kô). 1778–1843. Ukrainian writer; his works, written in Ukrainian, include *Marusya* (1832) and *Pan Khalyavski* (1839).

**Kvitka, Laryssa Petrovna.** See UKRAINKA.

**Kwam·mu** (kwäm·mōō). *Called also* **Kwam·mu Ten·no** (tĕn·nō), *i.e.* Emperor Kwammu. 738?–805 A.D. Fiftieth emperor of Japan (782–805) of the Nara period. Moved capital from Nara to Nagaoka (784) in attempt to free government of Buddhist domination, and again (794) from Nagaoka to Kyoto, the latter change inaugurating the Heian period (794–1185), from the name bestowed by him on the new capital (Heian-kyo).

**Kwang Hsu.** Variant of KUANG HSÜ.

**Kworin Ogata.** See OGATA.

**Kyd** *or* **Kid** (kĭd), **Thomas.** 1557?–?1595. English playwright; chief work, *The Spanish Tragedy* (pub. 1594). Plays of doubtful authorship sometimes attributed to him include *The Tragedy of Solyman and Perseda* (printed 1599), *The First Part of Ieronimo* (pub. 1605), and a lost pre-Shakespearean Hamlet play.

**Kyne** (kīn), **Peter Bernard.** 1880–1957. American fiction writer. Author of *Cappy Ricks* (1916), *The Valley of the Giants* (1918), *The Green Pea Pirates* (1919), *The Go-Getter* (1922), *Never the Twain Shall Meet* (1923), *Jim the Conqueror* (1929), *Comrades of the Storm* (1933), *Cappy Ricks Special* (1935), *Dude Woman* (1940), etc.

**Kynewulf.** See CYNEWULF.

**Kyokutei Bakin.** See BAKIN.

**Kyo·sai** (gyō·sī), **Sho·fu** (?shō·fōō). 1831–1889. Japanese painter, b. Koga, near Tokyo. During Restoration period (1867–68) became Japan's first political cartoonist; influenced by Hokusai; several times arrested; produced sketches and paintings esp. of native folklore.

**Kyrle** (kûrl), **John.** 1637–1724. English philanthropist; known as "the Man of Ross," from his estates at Ross in Hertfordshire; eulogized by Pope (in *Moral Essays*) for his character and charities. The Kyrle Society was founded (1877) as a memorial to him.

**Kyui, Tsezar Antonovich.** See César CUI.

# L

**Laar** *or* **Laer** (lär), **Pieter van.** *Called* **Il Bam·boc′cio** (ēl bäm·bôt′chō). 1592?–1642. Dutch genre and landscape painter and etcher; works include representations of fairs, pastoral scenes, and other much-imitated grotesque scenes from common or rustic life (bambocciades), as *The Quack* (now in Kassel) and *The Game of Ninepins* (Dresden).

**La Argentina.** See ARGENTINA.

**Laas** (läs), **Ernst.** 1837–1885. German positivist philosopher and educator; author of *Idealismus und Positivismus* (3 vols., 1879–84), etc.

**La′ba′die′** (lȧ′bȧ′dē′), **Jean de.** 1610–1674. French religious reformer; originally member of Jesuit order; converted to Calvinism (c. 1650); zealously preached return to primitive Christianity and gained many followers in the Netherlands; because of his doctrines, deposed by Protestant Synod of Netherlands (1668).

**La′ban** (lā′băn). In the Bible, the brother of Rebekah (*Gen.* xxiv. 29 ff.) and father of Leah and Rachel, who became the wives of his nephew Jacob (*Gen.* xxvii–xxix).

**La′band** (lä′bänt), **Paul.** 1838–1918. German jurist; authority on constitutional law.

**La′bar′raque′** (lȧ′bȧ′rȧk′), **Antoine Germain.** 1777–1850. French apothecary; credited with discovery of disinfecting property of Javelle water (also, esp. formerly, called *Labarraque's solution*).

**La′bat′** (lȧ′bȧ′), **Jean Baptiste.** 1663–1738. French Dominican missionary; served in French West Indies (1694–1705); author of *Nouveau Voyage aux Îles de l'Amérique* (1722), etc.

**La′bé′** (lȧ′bā′), **Louise.** *Known as* **la Belle′ Cor′dière′** (lȧ bĕl′ kôr′dyâr′), *i.e.* the Beautiful Ropemaker. 1526–1566. French poet; wife of Ennemond Perrin (d. 1565), a ropemaker; author of many love lyrics, elegies, sonnets, etc.

**La Bé′do′yère′** (lȧ bā′dwȧ′yâr′), Comte **de. Charles Angélique François Hu′chet′** (ü′shĕ′). 1786–1815. French soldier; aide-de-camp to Marshal Lannes (1807–09); rallied to Napoleon during Hundred Days; turned over garrison at Grenoble to emperor; general of division and aide-de-camp to Napoleon; arrested for treason after Waterloo.

**Lab′e·o** (lăb′ē·ō), **Marcus Antistius.** 50 B.C.?–18 A.D. Roman jurist; said to have been founder of the Proculian school of law, named from his disciple Sempronius Proculus.

**Labeo Notker.** See NOTKER.

**La·be′ri·us** (lȧ·bēr′ĭ·ŭs), **Decimus.** 105?–43 B.C. Roman knight and writer; author of mimes (farces), verse satires, an epic on the Gallic War, etc.

**La′ber′thon′nière′** (lȧ′bĕr′tô′nyâr′), **Lucien.** 1860–1932. French theologian and philosopher; developed a doctrine of immanence in his *Essais de Philosophie Religieuse* (1903), a book later placed on the Index.

**La′biche′** (lȧ′bēsh′), **Eugène Marin.** 1815–1888. French playwright; author of many vaudeville sketches, farces, and comedies.

**La·bid′** (lă·bēd′). *Arab.* **Labīd ibn-Rābī'ah.** 560?–?661. Arab poet.

**Lab′i·e′nus** (lăb′ĭ·ē′nŭs), **Titus.** d. 45 B.C. Roman politician; tribune of the plebs (63 B.C.); legate of Caesar in Gaul (to 52); at outbreak of Civil War, joined Pompey; fled to Africa after battle of Pharsalus (48); killed in action at Munda in Spain (45). His son **Quintus** commanded a Roman army which invaded Syria and Asia Minor (40–39 B.C.).

**La Bil′lar′dière′** *or* **La′bil′lar′dière′** (lȧ′bē′yȧr′-dyâr′), **Jacques Julien Hou′tou′ de** (ōō′tōō′ dē). 1755–1834. French naturalist; on expedition in search of La Pérouse (1791).

**La·bitz′ky** (lä·bĭts′kē), **Josef.** 1802–1881. Bohemian-German dance composer.

**La′blache′** (lȧ′blȧsh′), **Luigi.** 1794–1858. Bass singer, b. Naples, son of a Marseilles merchant and Irish mother; sang solos in Mozart's *Requiem*, on death of Haydn (1809); sang at La Scala, Milan (1817); taught singing to Queen Victoria; one of torchbearers round coffin of Beethoven (1827).

**La Bo′é′tie′** (lȧ bô′ā′sē′), **Étienne de.** 1530–1563. French writer; intimate friend of Montaigne; author of sonnets, some Latin verses, and translations.

**La′bor** (lä′bôr), **Josef.** 1842–1924. Bohemian blind pianist, organist, and composer.

**La′borde′** (lȧ′bôrd′), Comte **Henri François de.** 1764–1833. French soldier in siege of Toulon (1793), with Army of the Rhine (1799), in Portugal, and in Russia; rallied to Napoleon during Hundred Days and went into exile after Waterloo (to 1819).

**Laborde,** Marquis **Jean Joseph de.** 1724–1794. French financier; loaned large amounts to French government during Seven Years' War; banker of Louis XV; guillotined (1794). His son Comte **Alexandre Louis Joseph** (1774–1842), archaeologist and politician, wrote *Voyage Pittoresque et Historique de l'Espagne* (1806–26), *Les Monuments de la France Classés Chronologiquement* (1816–26), etc. Alexandre's son Marquis **Léon Emmanuel Simon Joseph** (1807–1869), archaeologist, did research work in Asia Minor, Syria, Egypt, and Arabia.

**La′bo′ri′** (lȧ′bô′rē′), **Fernand Gustave Gaston.** 1860–1917). French lawyer; defense counsel in trial of Dreyfus at Rennes (1899), in the Caillaux affair, etc.

**La′bou′chère′** (lȧ′bōō′shâr′; *Angl.* lăb′ōō·shâr′), **Henry.** Baron **Taun′ton** (tôn′t'n; tän′-; -tŭn). 1798–1869. British statesman; president of Board of Trade in Lord Melbourne's cabinet (1839–41), and under Lord John Russell (1847–52); colonial secretary under Lord Palmerston (1855–58). His nephew **Henry du Pré Labouchère** (1831–1912), journalist and Liberal political leader, was in diplomatic service (1854–64); gained reputation as journalist on *The Daily News* during Franco-Prussian War, and with Edmund Yates on *The World;* founded (1877) and edited *Truth*, remarkable for exposures of sham and corruption; M.P. (1865–66; 1867–68; 1880–1905); advocate of Irish home rule; instrumental in exposing the Irish journalist Pigott; embarrassed Cecil Rhodes party by inquiries into Jameson Raid; advocated abolition of House of Lords; married (1868) the actress Henrietta Hodson.

**La′bou′laye′** (lȧ′bōō′lā′), **Édouard René Le·feb′vre de** (lē·fâ′vr′ dē). 1811–1883. French journalist and politician; founder of *Revue Historique de Droit* (1855); elected member of Chamber of Deputies (1871) and senator for life (1880). Administrator of Collège de France (from 1873). Author of *Questions Constitutionnelles* (1872), *La Liberté Religieuse* (1875), etc.

**La Bour′don′nais′** (lȧ bōōr′dô′nĕ′), Comte **de. Bertrand François Ma′hé′** (mȧ′ā′). 1699–1753. French naval officer; captured Madras from the English (1746); engaged in long dispute with Dupleix, French governor in India, and was imprisoned for two years in the Bastille before being vindicated.

**La′brouste′** (lȧ′brōōst′), **François Marie Théodore**

(1799–1885) and his brother **Pierre François Henri** (1801–1875). French architects.

**Labrunie, Gérard.** See Gérard de NERVAL.

**La Bru'yère'** (lȧ brü'yâr'), **Jean de.** 1645–1696. French moralist, b. Paris; tutor in history to Louis de Bourbon, grandson of the Great Condé (1684); author of *Les "Caractères" de Théophraste, Traduits du Grec, avec les Caractères et les Mœurs de ce Siècle* (1688), which in later editions was largely expanded by additional "caractères" and commentaries.

**La'caille'** (lȧ'kä'y'), **Nicolas Louis de.** 1713–1762. French astronomer; made observations of approximately 10,000 southern stars; determined lunar and solar parallax (with Mars as intermediary); first to measure a South African arc of the meridian.

**La Cal'pre·nède'** (lȧ kȧl'prē·nĕd'), **Gautier de Costes** (kôst) **de.** 1614–1663. French novelist and playwright; author of the tragedies *Le Comte d'Essex* (1638), *Édouard Roi d'Angleterre* (1639), etc., and the novels *Cassandre* (1642–60), *Cléopâtre* (1647–58), etc.

**La'caze'–Du'thiers'** (lȧ'kȧz'dü'tyā'), **Félix Henri de.** 1821–1901. French naturalist; authority on anatomy of mollusks.

**La'cé'pède'** (lȧ'sā'pĕd'), Comte **de. Bernard Germain Étienne De·la'ville'** (dē·lȧ'vēl'). 1756–1825. French naturalist and writer; author of *Poétique de la Musique* (1781–85), *Essai sur l'Électricité* (pub. 1781), *Physique Générale et Particulière* (1782–84); continued Buffon's *Histoire Naturelle.*

**La Cer'da** (lä thĕr'thä). Distinguished princely family of Castile, descended from Ferdinand, eldest son of Alfonso X, King of León and Castile, and prominent in Spanish and French history (1270–1425).

**La Chaise** *or* **La Chaize** (lȧ shâz'), **François d'Aix de** (dĕks' dē). 1624–1709. French Jesuit priest; confessor of Louis XIV (from 1674); approved secret marriage of Louis XIV and Mme. de Maintenon. He often retired to a Jesuit retreat on Mont Louis, northeast of Paris, where a cemetery was later opened (1806) and called after him "Cimetière du Père Lachaise."

**La'chaise'** (lȧ'shâz'), **Gaston.** 1882–1935. Sculptor, b. Paris, France; to U.S. (1906); naturalized (1916). Executed decorative sculpture in Rockefeller Center in New York, in Century of Progress Exhibition in Chicago, etc.

**La Cha'lo'tais'** (lȧ shȧ'lô'tĕ'), **Louis René de Ca'ra'-deuc'** (kȧ'rȧ'dûk') **de.** 1701–1785. French magistrate; procureur général to parliament of Brittany; published *Comptes Rendus des Constitutions des Jésuites* (1761–62), an attack on the Jesuits which was instrumental in causing order to be suppressed in France; wrote also *L'Éducation Nationale* (1763), highly praised by Voltaire.

**La Chaus'sée'** (lȧ shō'sā'), **Pierre Claude Ni'velle'** (nē'vĕl') **de.** 1692–1754. French playwright; creator of the sentimental comedy (*comédie larmoyante*), as in *La Fausse Antipathie* (1733), *Le Préjugé à la Mode* (1735), *Mélanide* (1741), *L'Homme de Fortune* (1751), etc.

**La'che·lier'** (lȧ'shē·lyā'), **Jules.** 1832–1918. French philosopher.

**La'ches** (lā'kēz). Athenian general in Peloponnesian War; commanded Athenian army at Mantinea (418 B.C.), where he was killed in action.

**Lach'mann** (läḵ'män), **Karl Konrad Friedrich Wilhelm.** 1793–1851. German classical philologist and Germanic scholar; a founder of modern philological criticism.

**Lach'ner** (läḵ'nĕr). A family of German musicians, of Rain, Upper Bavaria: **Franz** (1803–1890) was an intimate friend of Schubert; court Kapellmeister (1836–65) and general music director (1852) in Munich; composed operas, oratorios, symphonies, orchestral suites in the tradition of Bach, church music, choruses, chamber music, and songs. His brother **Ignaz** (1807–1895) composed operas, many songs, chamber music, masses, symphonies, etc. Another brother, **Vincenz** (1811–1893), composed overtures, chamber music, songs, etc.

**Lack'land'** (lăk'lănd'). See JOHN, King of England.

**La·clède'** (lȧ·klĕd'; lȧ·klĕd'; *Fr.* lȧ'klĕd'), **Pierre.** *Real name* **Pierre Laclède Li'guest'** (lē'gĕ'). 1724?–1778. Fur trader and pioneer in America, b. Bedous, France; to America (1755); founder of St. Louis, Mo., establishing trading post on site of present city (1764). See CHOUTEAU.

**La Cloche** (lȧ klôsh'), **James de.** 1644?–1669. English adventurer, pretended natural son of Charles II; called himself Prince James Stuart; brought up in France and Holland; became Jesuit (1667); disowned by Charles II in reply to viceroy of Naples.

**La'clos'** (lȧ'klō'), **Pierre Ambroise François Cho'der'-los'** (shô'dĕr'lō') **de.** 1741–1803. French soldier and writer; served with the Army on the Rhine (1792); under the Directory, commanded artillery of the Army on the Rhine (1795); under the Empire, became inspector general of the Army of Southern Italy. His chief written work is a novel, *Liaisons Dangereuses* (1782). See LA ROCHE DU MAINE.

**La'combe'** (lȧ'kôɴb'), **Louis Trouil'lon'** (trōō'yôɴ'). 1818–1884. French pianist and composer of the opera *Winkelried* (1892), the comic operas *La Madone* (1860) and *Le Tonnelier de Nuremberg* (1897), dramatic symphonies, chamber music, piano pieces, songs, a cappella choruses, etc.

**La Con'da'mine'** (lȧ kôɴ'dȧ'mēn'), **Charles Marie de.** 1701–1774. French traveler and mathematical geographer; on expedition to Peru to measure a meridional arc at the equator (1735); explored the Amazon; worked on establishment of a universal unit of length.

**La'cor'daire'** (lȧ'kôr'dâr'), **Jean Théodore.** 1801–1870. French entomologist; in South America (1825–32); author of *Histoire Naturelle des Insectes* (1854–68), etc. His brother **Jean Baptiste Henri** (1802–1861) was a Dominican monk; renowned for his sermons at Notre Dame, and for his funeral orations.

**La'coste'** (lȧ'kôst'), Sir **Alexandre.** 1842–1923. Canadian jurist; chief justice of Quebec (1891–1907; retired).

**Lacoste, René.** French lawn-tennis player; member of Davis Cup team (1925–33) that won the cup (1927) and successfully defended it (1928–32); U.S. singles turf champion (1926, 1927).

**La'cre·telle'** (lȧ'krē·tĕl'), **Jacques de.** 1888– . French novelist; best known for his analytical or psychological studies.

**Lacretelle, Pierre Louis de.** 1751–1824. French journalist and magistrate. Active in French Revolution; member of Commune of Paris and elected to States-General and Legislative Assembly; defended publicly constitution of 1791. Under the Empire, took little part in politics; under Restoration, became coeditor with Benjamin Constant de Rebecque of *Minerve Française.* His brother **Jean Charles Dominique** (1766–1855) was a journalist and historian; on editorial staff of *Journal des Débats* (1790); author of many books on French history, esp. of the period of and after the French Revolution.

**La'croix'** (lȧ'krwä'), **François Antoine Alfred.** 1863–1948. French mineralogist; investigated volcano of Mount Pelée after eruption of 1902 and Vesuvius after eruption of 1906; author of works on volcanoes, eruptive rocks, etc.

**Lacroix, Paul.** *Pseudonyms* **Pierre Du'four'** (dü'fōōr'), **Bi'bli'o'phile' Ja'cob'** (*Fr.* bē'blē'ô'fēl' zhä'kôb'), *and*

**P. L. Jacob, Bibliophile.** 1806–1884. French scholar; author of historical novels, histories, and miscellaneous works, including *La Danse Macabre* (1832), *L'Homme au Masque de Fer* (1836), *Le Moyen Âge et la Renaissance* (1847 ff.), *Vie Militaire et Vie Religieuse au Moyen Âge* (1872), *Mœurs et Usages* (1883). His brother **Jules** (1809–1887) wrote verse, novels, and plays.

**Lacroix, Sylvestre François.** 1765–1843. French mathematician; chief work, *Traité du Calcul Différentiel et du Calcul Intégral* (3 vols., 1799).

**Lac·tan′ti·us Fir′mi·a′nus** (lăk·tăn′shĭ·ŭs fûr′mĭ·ā′nŭs) *or* **Firmianus Lactantius, Lucius Caelius** *or* **Caecilius.** Christian writer; went to Gaul (c. 306) on invitation of Constantine the Great to tutor Constantine's son Crispus. Author of *Divinarum Institutionum Libri Septem.* The treatise *De Mortibus Persecutorum* has been ascribed to him.

**La′cy** (lā′sĭ), **Henry de.** 3d Earl of **Lin′coln** (lĭng′kŭn). 1249?–1311. English soldier and counselor of Edward I and Edward II. Accompanied Edward I to Gascony (1286–89); commanded army in France (1296–98); guardian of kingdom in Edward II's absence (1310). Cf. Earl of LINCOLN.

**Lacy, Hugh de.** 5th Baron **Lacy** and 1st Lord of **Meath** (mēth; mēth). d. 1186. English soldier, conqueror of Ireland. Accompanied Henry II to Ireland (1171); governor of Ireland (1177–81, 1185–86); received submission of Roderic O'Connor, King of Connaught; secured good order; accused of ambition to be king of Ireland; murdered by a native. His second son, **Hugh** (d. 1242?), 1st Earl of **Ul′ster** (ŭl′stẽr), earliest Anglo-Saxon peer of Ireland (cr. 1205), was leader in partisan wars in Ireland.

**La′cy** (lä′sē; *Eng.* lā′sĭ), **Peter.** Count **Lacy.** *Known also as* **Pierre La′scy** (läs′ē). 1678–1751. Irish soldier, field marshal in Russian army; b. Limerick. Served with Irish Jacobite troops in France and Italy and on Rhine (1692 till peace of Ryswick); trained troops of Peter the Great (from 1697) and led them against Danes, Swedes, Turks (1705–21); commanded brigade of right wing at Poltava (1709); field marshal (1736). His son **Francis Maurice Lacy,** *known also as* **Franz Moritz Lascy** (1725–1801), Irish soldier in Austrian service in War of Austrian Succession and Seven Years' War; field marshal (1765); head of military advisory board (1766–73) with full confidence of Maria Theresa and Joseph II; with Laudon, joint Austrian commander in War of Bavarian Succession; suffered ill success in Turkish War (1788–90).

**Ladd** (lăd), **Anna Coleman,** *nee* **Watts** (wŏts). 1878–1939. American sculptor, b. Philadelphia; m. Maynard Ladd (1905). Executed bronzes now in Boston Museum of Fine Arts, Palazzo Borghese in Rome, Cathedral of St. John the Divine in New York; also, carved portrait busts of Eleonora Duse and Pavlova. Author of novels *Hyeronymus Rides* (1912), *The Candid Adventure* (1912).

**Ladd, George Trumbull.** 1842–1921. American psychologist and philosopher; professor, Yale (from 1881). Author of *Philosophy of Mind* (1895), *Philosophy of Religion* (2 vols., 1905), *The Secret of Personality* (1918), etc.

**Ladd, William.** 1778–1841. American advocate of international peace, b. Exeter, N.H.; founder (1828), American Peace Society; author of *An Essay on a Congress of Nations* (1840), proposing a congress of nations and an international court for settling differences by judicial decision or by arbitration, a plan later realized in the League of Nations and the World Court.

**Ladd′-Frank′lin** (lăd′frăngk′lĭn), **Christine.** 1847–1930. American psychologist and logician, b. Windsor, Conn.; m. Fabian Franklin (1882). In field of logic, published original method for reducing all syllogisms to a single formula; in field of psychology, advanced original theory accounting for development of man's color sense.

**La′de·gast** (lä′dĕ·gäst), **Friedrich.** 1818–1905. German organ builder.

**La′den·burg** (lä′dĕn·bo͝ork), **Albert.** 1842–1911. German chemist; known for researches on organic silicon compounds and on piperidine derivatives.

**Lad′is·las** (lăd′ĭs·lăs; -läs). Name of two kings of Bohemia:

**Ladislas I.** = LADISLAS V (*or* VI) of Hungary.

**Ladislas II.** 1456–1516. Son of Casimir IV of Poland; king of Bohemia (1471–1516) and of Hungary (1490–1516); weak and vacillating ruler, dominated by nobles; lost territory to Hapsburgs.

**Lad′is·las** (lăd′ĭs·lăs; -läs) *or* **Lad′is·laus** (-lôs). *Hung.* **Lász′ló** (läs′lō). Name of several kings of Hungary, esp.:

**Ladislas I.** *Called* **the Saint.** 1040?–1095. Son of Béla I; king (1077–95); conquered Croatia and Bosnia (1091); extended domain into Transylvania; supported Pope Gregory VII against Emperor Henry IV; established order and suppressed paganism; introduced a legal code; canonized (1192).

**Ladislas III.** 1199–1205. Son of Emeric I; king (1204–05); driven from throne by Andrew (II).

**Ladislas IV.** *Called* **the Cu·man′** (ko͞o·män′). 1262–1290. Son of Stephen V; king (1272–90); allied with Rudolf of Hapsburg, defeated Ottokar of Bohemia (1278); attacked the Cumans (a Turkish race of southeastern Europe); overcome by them and Tatars; m. Cuman princess and adopted Cuman customs; assassinated by a Cuman.

**Ladislas V.** Designation used by some for LADISLAS III of Poland, who ruled Hungary 1440–44.

**Ladislas V** (*or* **VI**). *Called* **Ladislas Post′hu·mus** (pŏs′tū·mŭs; pŏst′hū·mŭs). 1440–1457. Posthumous son of Emperor Albert II; brought up at court of Emperor Frederick III; king of Hungary (1446–52) under János Hunyadi as regent; king of Bohemia (1452–57), crowned (1453) but control in hands of George of Poděbrad; caused murder of László Hunyadi (1457); fled to Prague; died of plague; succeeded in Hungary by Matthias Corvinus.

**Ladislas VI** (*or* **VII**). = LADISLAS II of Bohemia.

**Ladislas** *or* **Ladislaus.** 1379?–1414. King of Naples (1386–1414). Son of Charles III of Durazzo, of the house of Anjou (*q.v.*). At war with rival, Louis II of Anjou (1391–99); gained support of Pope Boniface IX; planned conquests in central Italy (1400–14). Twice seized Rome (1408–09, 1413); defeated at Roccasecca (1411).

**Ladislas.** *Pol.* **Wła·dy′sław** (vlä·dĭ′släf). *Also Anglicized as* **Lad′is·laus** *or* **Wlad′is·laus** (lăd′ĭs·lôs) *or* **Wlad′is·law** (lăd′ĭs·lô) *or* **Vlad′is·lav** (lăd′ĭs·lăv). Name of several kings of Poland:

**Ladislas I** (*or* **IV**) **Lo·kie′tek** (lô·kyĕ′tĕk). 1260–1333. Duke of Poland (1296) as Ladislas IV; supported by pope; united Great and Little Poland (1305–12); king (1320–33); as ally of Teutonic Order saved Danzig from Brandenburg, but later engaged in six-year war with the order (1327–33), defeating it at Plowce (1332).

**Ladislas II** (*or* **V**) **Ja·gel′lo** (yä·gĕl′ō). *Pol.* **Ja·gieł′ło** (yä·gyĕl′lô). *Lith.* **Jagela.** 1350–1434. Son of Olgierd (*q.v.*); as Jagello, grand duke of Lithuania (1377–86); engaged in first war with Teutonic Order (1377–82); m. (1386) Jadwiga, Queen of Poland; elected king of Poland (1386–1434); adopted Catholic faith; with Lithuanians, defeated the Teutonic Order at Tannenberg (1410); m. as 4th wife Russian princess Sophia; during reign Poland became a great power.

**Ladislas III** (*or* **VI**). 1424–1444. Son of Ladislas II Jagello and Sophia; king of Poland (1434–44) and of Hungary as Ladislas V (1440–44); faced with internal troubles in both Poland and Hungary; led crusade against Turks (1443), terminated by peace of Szeged (1444); broke treaty immediately; killed at Varna while invading Balkans. See János Hunyadi at HUNYADI family.

**Ladislas IV** (*or* **VII**). 1595–1648. Son of Sigismund III; served as youth in Muscovite campaigns (1610–12 and 1617–18); succeeded father as king (1632–48); on accession fought war with Russia, winning victorious peace (1634); made favorable settlement with Turks (1634) and with Sweden (1635); involved in serious internal troubles, esp. from acts of the Sejm; renewed attempt in last years of reign to establish order, but died unsuccessful; lost part of Ukraine to Russia following revolt of Cossacks (1648) under Bogdan Chmielnicki (*q.v.*). See JAGELLON.

**Lad'mi'rault'** (làd'mē'rō'), **Louis René Paul de.** 1808–1898. French general at battle of Solferino (1859); commanded 4th corps at outbreak of Franco-Prussian War, and was engaged at Rezonville; commanded 1st corps suppressing Commune of Paris (1871); military governor of Paris (1871–78).

**La'dré'** (là'drā'). Late 18th-century French street singer, reputed author of the words of *Ça Ira*, the Revolutionary war song.

**Lae'li·us** (lē'lĭ·ŭs), **Gaius.** Roman general and statesman; served with Scipio Africanus in Spain and in Africa, and commanded the cavalry in battle of Zama (202 B.C.). Plebeian aedile (197); praetor of Sicily (196); consul (190); ambassador to Transalpine Gaul (170). His son **Gaius Laelius**, *surnamed* **Sa'pi·ens** (sā'pĭ·ĕnz; săp'ĭ·ĕnz); friend of Panaetius and the younger Scipio and named as one of the speakers in Cicero's essays *De Senectute*, *De Amicitia*, and *De Republica;* tribune (151 B.C.); served against the Carthaginians in Africa (147) and Spain (145); consul (140); helped introduce Greek culture in Rome.

**Laemm'le** (lĕm'lē), **Carl.** 1867–1939. German-born American motion-picture producer; to U.S. (1884); organized and headed Universal Pictures Corp. (to 1936, when he sold his holdings). Produced first full-length photoplay, *Traffic in Souls* (1912), and first million-dollar picture, *Foolish Wives* (1922).

**Laën'nec'** (lā'nĕk'), **René Théophile Hyacinthe.** 1781–1826. French physician; introduced practice of auscultation with the stethoscope, which he invented (c. 1819).

**Laer, Pieter van.** See Pieter van LAAR.

**Laer'mans** (làr'mäns), **Eugène.** 1864–1940. Belgian painter and etcher; works include expressionistic paintings of poor, simple people at work, at prayer, and in sorrow.

**Laess'le** (lĕs'lē), **Albert.** 1877–1954. American sculptor; studio in Philadelphia. His bronzes *Billy* and *The Bronze Penguins* are in Fairmount Park, Philadelphia.

**La Farge** (là färzh'), **Christopher.** 1897–1956. American poet; author of *Hoxsie Sells his Acres* (novel in verse, 1934), *Each to the Other* (novel in verse, 1939), *Poems and Portraits* (1940).

**La Farge, John.** 1835–1910. American artist, b. New York City. Painted chiefly landscapes (1860–76). Commissioned for mural decoration of Trinity Church, Boston (1876–77), his success leading to other work of similar nature, including panels in St. Thomas's Church, New York City, *The Ascension* in the Church of the Ascension, New York City, and lunettes in the supreme court room of the Minnesota State Capitol at St. Paul. Interested himself in production of stained glass; developed opalescent glass; wrote pamphlet, *The American Art of Glass* (1893). Examples of his painting: *Christ and Nicodemus*, in Trinity Church, Boston; *The Three Kings*, in Boston Art Museum; *The Muse of Painting*, in Metropolitan Museum of Art, New York City; *The Arrival of the Magi*, in Church of the Incarnation, New York City. Examples of his work in stained glass are in Second Presbyterian Church, Chicago; Memorial Hall, Harvard U.; Columbia U. Chapel, New York City. Father of:

(1) **Christopher Grant** (1862–1938), architect, b. Newport, R.I.; practiced, New York City (1886–1910); designed Protestant Episcopal cathedral of Saint John the Divine, in New York City; Fourth Presbyterian church and parsonage, New York City; Roman Catholic cathedral, Seattle, Wash.; Packard Memorial Library, Salt Lake City; Morgan Memorial Building, Hartford, Conn.; etc.

(2) **Oliver Hazard Perry** (1869–1936), businessman and amateur artist.

(3) **John** (1880–1963), Roman Catholic priest; editor (1942–48) of Jesuit weekly *America;* author of *The Jesuits in Modern Times* (1928), *Interracial Justice* (1937).

**Oliver Hazard Perry** (1901–1963), *sometimes known as* **Oliver II**; son of Christopher Grant La Farge; author, b. New York City; member of archaeological expeditions to Mexico, Guatemala, and Arizona; president, American Association on Indian Affairs (1933–42; 1948–63); wrote *Tribes and Temples* (with Frans Blom, 1927), *Laughing Boy* (awarded Pulitzer prize for 1929), *Sparks Fly Upward* (1931), *Long Pennant* (1933), *All the Young Men* (1935), *The Enemy Gods* (1937).

**La'farge'** (là'fàrzh'), **Marie Fortunée,** *nee* **Cap'pelle'** (kà'pĕl'). 1816–1853. Frenchwoman convicted of poisoning her husband (1840) and condemned to life imprisonment at hard labor; persisted in asserting her innocence; pardoned (1852); regarded by many as victim of circumstantial evidence and judicial prejudice.

**La'fargue'** (là'fàrg'), **Paul.** 1842–1911. French Socialist politician and writer; son-in-law of Karl Marx. Associated with Jules Guesde (*q.v.*) in organizing Marxian Socialist movement in France.

**La Fa·ri'na** (lä fä·rē'nä), **Giuseppe.** 1815–1863. Italian statesman and historian; exiled from Sicily (1837–48) for participation in revolution; took part in Tuscan movement (1848); elected deputy and minister on return to Sicily (1848–49); again fled Sicily after Revolution of 1848. Associated with Cavour (from 1855) in National Italian Society, its president (1859); aided in deposition of Bourbons in Sicily (1860); sent to Sicily by Cavour as representative of Victor Emmanuel (1860); deputy from Messina in Italian parliament (1861–63). Author of *Storia della Rivoluzione Italiana 1821–48* (1849), *Storia d'Italia 1815–50* (6 vols., 1851), etc.

**La'fa·yette'** (lä'fĭ·ĕt'; lăf'ĭ-; *Fr.* là'fà'yĕt'), Marquis **de. Marie Joseph Paul Yves Roch Gilbert du Mo'tier'** (dü mô'tyā'). 1757–1834. French statesman and officer; entered French military service (1771); withdrew (1776) to enter American service in Revolutionary War (1777); commissioned by Congress major general in Continental army (July 31, 1777). Became intimate associate of George Washington. Spent furlough in France, advancing American cause (1778–80). Served in Virginia (1781). Returned to France (Dec., 1781). Visited U.S. (1784; 1824–25). Member of French National Assembly (1789); showed liberal sympathies; aided in organizing National Guard; instrumental in bringing about adoption of tricolor flag; a founder of the Club of the Feuillants, conservative liberals who sought to establish a constitutional monarchy (1790). In command of force that fired on the mob in the Champ de Mars (1791). Commanded an army in war with Austria. Opposed further advance of Jacobin party; was declared a traitor by National Assembly; fled to Flanders and was imprisoned by Austrians (1792–97). Returned to France (1799); took no part in politics, being opposed to Napoleonic policies. Member, Chamber of Deputies (1815, 1818–24); leader of opposition (1825–30). Commander of the National Guard, Revolution of 1830.

**La Fa·yette'** (lä'fī·ĕt'; lăf'ĭ-; *Fr.* lȧ'fȧ'yĕt'), Comtesse **de.** *Nee* **Marie Madeleine Pioche de La Vergne** (pyôsh' dẽ lȧ vĕr'ny'). 1634–1693. French novelist; m. François Motier, Comte de La Fayette (1655; d. 1683). Friend of La Rochefoucauld. Among her novels are *La Princesse de Montpensier* (1662), *Zayde* (1670), and *La Princesse de Clèves* (1678).

**La Fayette, Gilbert Mo'tier' de** (mô'tyā' dẽ). 1380?–1463. French soldier; served under Marshal Boucicaut and later under John I, Duc de Bourbon; created marshal of France (1420).

**La'fe·nes'tre** (lȧ'fẽ·nâ'tr'), **Georges.** 1837–1919. French writer; author of collections of verse (*Idylles et Chansons,* 1874, etc.) and art criticism.

**La'fer'rière'** (lȧ'fĕ'ryâr'), **Louis Firmin Ju'lien'-** (zhü'lyăN'-). 1798–1861. French jurist. His son **Édouard** (1841–1901) was also a jurist.

**Laf'fan** (lăf'ăn), **William Mack'ay** (măk'ĭ). 1848–1909. Journalist and art connoisseur, b. Dublin, Ireland; to U.S. (1868). Publisher, New York *Sun* (from 1884); founded *Evening Sun* (1887). Trustee, Metropolitan Museum of Art (from 1905). Author of *Oriental Ceramic Art* (1897), etc.

**Laf·fite'** *or* **La·fitte'** (lȧ·fēt'; *Fr.* lȧ'-), **Jean.** c. 1780–c. 1826. Pirate, b. prob. Bayonne, France. In New Orleans, La. (c. 1809). Head of band of privateers and smugglers (1810); when British sought his aid in attack on New Orleans (1814) he revealed their plans to American authorities, many of his band serving on American side in battle of New Orleans. Returned to piracy after War of 1812, with headquarters at Galveston, Texas; captured and scuttled American merchant ship (1820); his headquarters raided and destroyed by American warship; continued piracy on Spanish main; disappeared from view about 1825.

**Laf'fitte'** (lȧ'fēt'), **Jacques.** 1767–1844. French financier and statesman; regent (1809), and governor (1814–19), of the Bank of France; member of Chamber of Deputies (from 1816). Partisan of Louis Philippe; premier and finance minister (1830–31); failed to reconcile parties with his policies.

**Laffitte, Pierre.** 1823–1903. French philosopher; disciple of Auguste Comte.

**La'fi'tau'** (lȧ'fē'tō'), **Joseph François.** 1670–1740. French Jesuit; missionary among the Iroquois in Canada (1712–17).

**La·fleur'** (lȧ·flûr'; *Fr.* lȧ'-), **Eugène.** 1856–1930. Canadian lawyer; professor of international law, McGill (1880–1908).

**La Fol'lette** (lȧ fŏl'ĕt; -ĭt), **Robert Marion.** 1855–1925. American political leader, b. Primrose, Wis. Adm. to bar (1880); practiced, Madison, Wis. Member, U.S. House of Representatives (1885–91). Interested himself in reform of Wisconsin State politics; elected governor of Wisconsin (1900); re-elected (1902, 1904); became known as leader among progressives. U.S. senator (from 1906); leader of progressives and radicals. Opposed U.S. entrance into World War; critical of Wilson's policies during World War; opposed ratification of Covenant of the League of Nations and admission of U.S. to World Court; sponsored resolution authorizing senatorial investigation into Teapot Dome and other naval oil leases. Candidate of League for Progressive Political Action, for U.S. presidency (1924); defeated. Founded *La Follette's Weekly Magazine* (1909); an organizer of National Progressive Republican League (1911). His son **Robert Marion, Jr.** (1895–1953), American legislator; private secretary to his father (1919–25). U.S. senator from Wisconsin, succeeding his father (1925–47). Another son, **Philip Fox** (1897–1965), a lawyer and politician, practiced law in Madison, Wis. (from 1922); governor of Wisconsin (1931–33; 1935–39).

**La'fon'taine'** (lȧ'fôN'tĕn'), **August Heinrich Julius.** 1758–1831. German clergyman and novelist; canon of Magdeburg Cathedral. Author (often under pseudonyms, as **Gustav Frei'er** [frī'ẽr], **Mil'ten·berg** [mĭl'-tĕn·bĕrK], **Sel'chow** [zĕl'Kō]) of about 200 volumes of novels and sketches chiefly of middle-class domestic life.

**La'fon'taine'** (lȧ'fôN'tĕn'), **Henri.** 1854–1943. Belgian lawyer and politician; senator (1895); strong advocate of international arbitration, and of the Permanent Court of International Justice; awarded Nobel prize for peace (1913).

**La Fon'taine'** (lȧ fôN'tĕn'), **Jean de.** 1621–1695. French fabulist, b. Château-Thierry. Friend of Racine, Boileau, and Molière. The first six books of his *Fables* (pub. 1668) were dedicated to the dauphin; the next five books (pub. 1678–79) were prefaced with a eulogy of Mme. de Montespan; the twelfth book (pub. 1694) was dedicated to the duke of Burgundy. Author also of *Contes* (1664–74), poems, and with Champmeslé of opera librettos and plays.

**Lafontaine,** Sir **Louis Hypolite.** 1807–1864. Canadian statesman; supported Papineau in opposition to administration of governor in chief, but disapproved Papineau's extreme measures; leader of French Canadians; refused solicitor generalship but on death of Sydenham formed a first administration with Robert Baldwin (1842–43), and a second, acting as premier and attorney general for Lower Canada (1848–51); passed amnesty bill, which provoked riots in Montreal; chief justice of Lower Canada (1853–64); settled question of land tenure in Canada.

**La Forge** (lȧ fôrzh'), **Frank.** 1879–1953. American pianist and composer of many songs, including *Before the Crucifix, Song of the Open, Retreat.*

**La'forgue'** (lȧ'fôrg'), **Jules.** 1860–1887. French writer; identified with the symbolists.

**La'fosse'** (lȧ'fôs'), **Charles de.** 1636–1716. French historical painter. His nephew **Antoine de Lafosse,** Sieur **d'Au'bi'gny'** [dō'bē'nyē'] (1653–1708), was a poet.

**La'fren'sen** (lȧ'frĕn'sĕn), **Nils.** *Called by the French* **Nicolas La'vreince'** (lȧ'vrăNs'). 1737–1807. Swedish painter. He painted, in gouache and rococo style, social gatherings, ballet scenes, scenes from everyday life, portraits, etc.

**La·fuen'te** *or* **La Fuen'te** (lä fwān'tā), **Modesto.** 1806–1866. Spanish historian and satirist; chief work, *Historia General de España* (30 vols., 1850–66); satires published under pseudonyms of **Fray Ge·run'di·o** (frä'ē hā·rōōn'dyō) and **Ti'ra·be'que** [tē'rä·bā'kā] (1844–50).

**La·gae'** (lȧ·gȧ'), **Jules.** 1862–1931. Belgian sculptor.

**La Gan'da'ra'** (lȧ găN'dȧ'rȧ'), **Antonio de.** 1862–1917. French painter of English-Mexican descent; renowned for his portraits.

**La·garde'** (lä·gärd'), **Paul Anton de.** *Father's surname* **Böt'ti·cher** (bût'ĭ·Kẽr). 1827–1891. German Orientalist. Called (from 1854) after his adoptive mother's surname de Lagarde. Edited Italian works of Giordano Bruno (2 vols., 1888–89); worked on books of the Bible and church fathers; edited and translated Greek, Chaldean, Arabic, Syriac, and Coptic texts.

**La'ger·kvist** (lä'gẽr·kvist), **Pär Fabian.** 1891–1974. Swedish author, playwright, and poet. Works include the novels *Barabbas* (1951), *Pilgrim at Sea* (1964); and the play *Let Man Live* (1949). Awarded Nobel prize in literature (1951).

**La'ger·löf'** (lä'gẽr·lûv'), **Selma Ottiliana Lovisa.** 1858–1940. Swedish novelist and poet. Taught at Landskrona (1885–95); honorary degree at Uppsala U. (1907), Nobel prize for literature (1909), diploma of French Legion of Honor (1930); first woman member of Swedish Acad. (1914). Author of novels including *Gösta Berling* (1891), *The Miracles of Antichrist* (1897), *Jerusalem* (2 vols., 1901–02), *Liljecrona's Home* (1911), *The Emperor of Protugallia* (1914), *The Outcast* (1918), and the trilogy *The Ring of the Löwenskölds* (1931: *The General's Ring,* 1925; *Charlotte Löwensköld,* 1925; *Anna Svärd,* 1928); collections of stories, including *Invisible Links* (1894), *From a Swedish Homestead* (1899), *Christ Legends* (1904), the children's classic *The Wonderful Adventures of Nils* (2 vols., 1906–07), *The Girl from the Marsh Croft* (1908), *Trolls and Men* (2 vols., 1915–21); autobiographical works, as *Mårbacka* (1922) and *The Diary of Selma Lagerlöf* (1937), etc.

**La Gorce** (lȧ gôrs'), **Pierre de.** 1846–1934. French historian; among his works are *Histoire de la Seconde République Française* (2 vols., 1887), *Histoire du Second Empire* (7 vols., 1898–1906).

**La Grange** (lȧ gräɴzh'), Sieur **de. Charles Var'let'** (vår'lĕ'). 1639?–1692. French comedian in Molière's company; collaborated with Vinot in preparing first important edition of Molière's works.

**La'grange'** (lȧ'gräɴzh'), **Joseph Louis.** 1736–1813. French geometer and astronomer, b. Turin, Italy. Educ. Turin Coll. At age of nineteen, became professor of mathematics at artillery school, Turin; communicated to Euler method of solving the isoperimetrical problem from which grew the calculus of variations; with students, founded society which became Turin Acad. of Sciences; awarded prize by French Acad. of Sciences for essay on libration of the moon (1764) and a theory of the satellites of Jupiter (1766). Appointed by Frederick the Great to succeed Euler as director of Berlin Acad. of Sciences, a position he held for twenty years. To Paris (1787) at invitation of Louis XVI; headed commission for reform of weights and measures (1793); professor, École Normale, Paris (1795), and École Polytechnique (1797); under Napoleon I, made senator and count. Publications include *Mécanique Analytique* (1787), *Théorie des Fonctions Analytiques* (1797), and *Leçons sur le Calcul des Fonctions* (1806).

**La'grange'–Chan'cel'** (-shäɴ'sĕl'), **Joseph de.** *Real surname* **Chancel.** 1677–1758. French playwright.

**La Guar'di·a** (lȧ gwär'dĭ·ȧ; lȧ gär'dĭ·ȧ), **Fi'o·rel'lo** (fē'ô·rĕl'ō) **Henry.** 1882–1947. American lawyer, politician, b. New York City. Practiced law in New York (from 1910). Member, U.S. House of Representatives (1917–21; 1923–33). Served in U.S. air service in World War I. Mayor of New York (1934–45); chief, U.S. Office of Civilian Defense (1941–42).

**la Guar'dia** (lä gwär'thyä), **Ricardo Adolfo de.** See GUARDIA.

**La'guerre'** (lȧ'gâr'), **Edmond.** 1834–1886. French mathematician; known for work on linear systems and theory of equations.

**La Halle, Adam de.** See ADAM DE LA HALLE.

**La Harpe** (lȧ årp'), **Frédéric César de.** 1754–1838. Swiss politician; to France (1796) and played important part in establishing the Helvetic Republic (1798), of which he became a director. Fugitive in France (1800–14). Member of the Grand Council of the Canton of Vaud (1816–28).

**La'harpe'** (lȧ'årp'), **Jean François de.** *Orig. known as* **Jean François De·lharpe'** (dē·lȧrp') *or* **De·la'harpe'** (dē·lȧ'ärp'). 1739–1803. French poet and literary critic.

**La'hey** (lā'hĭ), **Richard Francis.** 1893– . American painter, b. Jersey City, N.J. Among his notable paintings are *Head of Joan, My Wife, Maine Inlet, Pont Neuf.*

**La Hire** *or* **La Hyre** (lȧ ēr'), **Laurent de.** 1606–1656. French painter; commissioned by Richelieu to execute paintings which decorated Salle des Gardes of Palais-Royal. Chief work, *La Descente de Croix,* painted for Capuchins of Rouen. His son **Philippe** (1640–1718), astronomer and mathematician, wrote on experimental astronomy, physics, natural history, and geometry.

**Lahm** (läm), **Frank Purdy.** 1877–1963. American aeronaut; first airship and balloon pilot in U.S. army; b. Mansfield, Ohio. Grad. U.S.M.A., West Point (1901). Won Bennett cup in international balloon race in Paris (1906); organized aviation service in Philippine Islands (1912); in charge of air service of 2d Army of A.E.F. in France (1918–19); 9th Corps Area air officer (1924–26); appointed brigadier general for period of four years, and assistant to chief of air corps to organize and command air corps training center (1926–30).

**La'hon'tan'** (lȧ'ôɴ'täɴ'), Baron **de. Louis Armand de Lom d'Arce** (dē lôɴ' dȧrs'). 1666–1715. French officer and traveler; served in Canada (1683). Deserted the army (1693); traveled widely through Europe. Author of *Nouveaux Voyages de M. le Baron de Lahontan dans l'Amérique Septentrionale* (1703).

**Lahor, Jean.** Pseudonym of Henry CAZALIS.

**La Huerta, Adolfo de.** See HUERTA.

**la Huerta y Muñoz, Vicente Antonio García de.** See GARCÍA DE LA HUERTA Y MUÑOZ.

**Laid'law** (lād'lô), **William.** 1780–1845. Scottish friend, steward, and amanuensis of Sir Walter Scott; with James Hogg supplied material for *Minstrelsy of the Scottish Border;* wrote lyrics, including *Lucy's Flittin'.*

**Laid'ler** (lād'lẽr), **Harry Wellington.** 1884–1970. American Socialist leader, b. Brooklyn, N.Y. A founder (1905) and secretary (1910–21), Intercollegiate Socialist Society. Director, National Bureau of Economic Research (from 1920), and its president (1930–32). Socialist candidate for governor of New York (1936). Author of many books on Socialism and on social and economic problems.

**Lai'do·ner** (lī'dô·nĕr), **Johan.** 1884– . Estonian soldier; served in Russian army (1914–17); commanded Estonian army in war for independence (1918). Estonian delegate to League of Nations. Presiding officer, League of Nations commission investigating Mosul frontier dispute between Great Britain and Turkey (1925).

**Lai'né'** (lĕ'nā'), Vicomte **Joseph Louis Joachim.** 1767–1835. French politician; because of his love of liberty, incurred disfavor of Napoleon; at the Restoration, became president of the Chamber of Deputies (1815), minister of the interior (1816), minister of state (1820), and a peer of France (1822).

**Lainez.** See LAYNEZ.

**Laing** (lăng; lāng), **Alexander Gordon.** 1793–1826. Scottish explorer in Africa. Sent by governor of Sierra Leone to Mandingo country to open up commerce and prepare for abolition of slave trade (1822); seeking source of Niger, stopped by natives; frequently defeated Ashantis (1823); sent to explore Niger basin via Tripoli and Timbuktu; murdered by Arabs on reaching Timbuktu.

**Laing, David.** 1793–1878. Scottish antiquary; librarian to Signet Library (1837–78). Edited Scottish ballads and metrical romances and publications of Bannatyne

Club; issued first collected edition of poems of William Dunbar (1834); edited *Letters and Journals of Robert Baillie 1637–62* (1841–42), works of John Knox (1846–64) and Sir David Lindsay.

**Laing, Malcolm.** 1762–1818. Scottish historian; called to Scottish bar (1785); British M.P. (1807–12). Wrote in liberal tone last volume of Robert Henry's *History of England* (1793); published his own *History of Scotland* (1802), and in a second edition (1804) sought to prove Mary, Queen of Scots, the writer of the Casket Letters. His brother **Samuel** (1780–1868) served in Peninsular War (1808–09); wrote on economic and social conditions of Scandinavia; translated *Heimskringla or Chronicle of Kings of Norway* (1844). Samuel's son **Samuel** (1812–1897) was financial secretary to the treasury (1859–60); financial minister in India (1860); author of *Modern Science and Modern Thought* (1885) and *Human Origins* (1892).

**Laird** (lârd), **Donald Anderson.** 1897-1969. American psychologist; director, psychological laboratory, Colgate (1925–39), Ayer Foundation for Consumer Analysis, Philadelphia (1939–40). Founder of periodical *Industrial Psychology;* technical adviser to numerous commercial organizations. Author of *Psychology of Selecting Men* (1923), *Increasing Personal Efficiency* (1925), *Why We Don't Like People* (1931), *How to Use Psychology in Business* (1936), *How to Improve Your Brain Power* (1939), etc.

**Laird, John.** 1887–1946. British philosopher; regius professor of moral philosophy, Aberdeen. Author of *Problems of the Self* (1917), *Modern Problems in Philosophy* (1928), *An Enquiry into Moral Notions* (1935), etc.

**Laird, Macgregor.** 1808–1861. Scottish merchant and South African explorer. Organized company for trade along lower Niger; on first expedition (1832–34), led by Richard Lander (*q.v.*), was first white man to ascend Benue River from confluence with Niger; promoted navigation company for running steamships between England and New York (1837), of which the *Sirius* was first to cross Atlantic from Europe entirely under steam. His father, **William**, shipbuilder, was founder of the Birkenhead house of William Laird & Son.

**Laird, Melvin Robert.** 1922– . American politician; U.S. secretary of defense (from 1969).

**Lai'resse'** (lĕ'rĕs'), **Gerard de.** 1641–1711. Dutch painter, etcher, and writer on art.

**La'is** (lā'ĭs). Name of two Greek hetaerae: the first, probably of Corinth, lived during the Peloponnesian War, was noted for her beauty, her avarice, and her caprices; the second, a contemporary and rival of Phryne (*q.v.*), was stoned to death in the temple of Aphrodite by Thessalian women jealous of her beauty.

**Laj'oi·e** (lăsh'ō·wā), **Napoleon,** *known as* **Larry.** 1875–1959. American professional baseball player, b. Woonsocket, R.I.; known as batsman; second baseman in National League, with Philadelphia (1896–1900), and in American League, with Philadelphia (1901; 1915–16) and Cleveland (1902–14).

**Lajos.** Hungarian form of LOUIS.

**La'ka'nal'** (lȧ'kȧ'nȧl'), **Joseph.** 1762–1845. Name orig. **La'ca'nal'** (lȧ'kȧ'nȧl'), changed to distinguish him from his Royalist brothers. French educator and politician; member of National Convention (1792) and voted for execution of the king; member (1793) and, later, chairman of Committee of Public Instruction. Member of Council of Five Hundred. Under Napoleon, occupied educational posts. In exile in U.S. (1816–33), and president of Louisiana State U. (1817–25).

**Lake** (lāk), **Gerard.** 1st Viscount **Lake.** 1744–1808. British military commander. Descendant of Sir Thomas Lake (1567?–1630), secretary of state (1616). Nephew of the elder George Colman (*q.v.*). Served in Germany (1760–62), America (1781), Low Countries (1793–94); routed Irish rebels at Vinegar Hill (1798), received surrender of French at Cloone; commander in chief in India (1800–03); in Maratha war in northwest India took Delhi and Agra, won battles of Laswari and Farrukhabad; pursued Holkar into Punjab and forced surrender (1805); created baron (1804), viscount (1807).

**Lake, John.** 1624–1689. English royalist and prelate. Bishop of Chichester (1685); one of the Seven Bishops (see William SANCROFT) who petitioned against James II's Declaration of Indulgence (1688), but were acquitted of a charge of seditious libel; refused to take oath of allegiance to William and Mary (1688).

**Lake, Kirsopp.** 1872–1946. Theologian, b. Southampton, Eng.; to U.S. to become professor of early Christian literature (1914–19), of ecclesiastical history (1919–32), and of history (1932–38), at Harvard. Conducted research work on ancient Greek manuscripts, in Greece. Author of *The Historical Evidence for the Resurrection of Jesus Christ* (1905), *The Beginnings of Christianity* (5 vols., 1920–33), *Religion Yesterday and Tomorrow* (1925), etc.

**Lake,** Sir **Percy Henry Noel.** 1855–1940. British soldier; chief of general staff in India (1912–15); commanded Mesopotamian force (1916).

**Lake, Simon.** 1866–1945. American mechanical engineer and naval architect, b. Pleasantville, N.J. Educ. Franklin Institute, Philadelphia. Inventor of even-keel type of submarine; built *Argonaut* (1897), first submarine to operate successfully in the open sea. Also invented submarine apparatus for locating and recovering sunken vessels and their cargoes, and a heavy-oil internal combustion engine for marine use.

**La'laing'** (lȧ'lăN'), Comte **Jacques de.** 1858–1917. Belgian sculptor and painter; his statue of La Salle stands in Chicago.

**La'lande'** (lȧ'läNd'), Saint **John.** d. 1646. French Jesuit missionary in America; martyred by Mohawk Indians at what is now Auriesville, N.Y.; canonized (June 29, 1930).

**Lalande, Joseph Jérôme Le Fran'çais' de** (lẽ fräN'sĕ' dẽ). 1732–1807. French astronomer; sent to Berlin by French Acad. to determine moon's parallax (1751); director of Paris observatory (from 1768). Worked on planetary theory; improved planetary tables of Halley and others; author of *Traité d'Astronomie* (1764), *Histoire Céleste Française* (1801; containing catalog of nearly 50,000 stars), treatises on navigation, etc.

**La Lan'delle'** (lȧ läN'dĕl'), **Guillaume Joseph Gabriel de.** 1812–1886. French writer; best known for his novels of the sea.

**La'lanne'** (lȧ'lȧn'), **Maxime François Antoine.** 1827–1886. French etcher, illustrator, and engraver.

**La'le·mant'** (lȧl'mäN'), Saint **Gabriel.** 1610–1649. French Jesuit missionary in America; to Canada (1646) and a station among the Hurons; martyred by Iroquois Indians; canonized (June 29, 1930).

**La'lique'** (lȧ'lēk'), **René.** 1860–1945. French jeweler and glassmaker; known esp. for manufacture of numerous fine but inexpensive glass objects.

**Lal'le·mand'** (lȧl'mäN'), Baron **Frédéric Antoine.** 1774–1839. French soldier of the Revolutionary and Napoleonic era; after battle of Waterloo, fled to Texas with some companions and tried to establish a colony, but failed because of Spanish opposition.

**Lallemant** *or* **Lallement, Robert Christian Berthold Avé–.** See AVÉ-LALLEMANT.

**Lal'ly'** (lȧ'lē'), Comte **Thomas Arthur de.** Baron **de Tol'len'dal'** (tô'läN'dȧl'). 1702–1766. French soldier, of Irish descent; commander in chief of French East Indies (1756); waged offensive war against the English (1758); was defeated and forced to capitulate to Sir E. Coote (1761); beheaded by order of the Parlement de Paris on charge of treason and cowardice (May 9, 1766). His son Marquis **Trophime Gérard de Lally-Tollendal** (1751–1830) spent years in vindicating his father's good name, and succeeded with Voltaire's aid in having the sentence annulled (1778); an émigré in Switzerland (1790) and later in England; at the Restoration (1815), created a peer of France and a minister of state.

**La'lo'** (lȧ'lō'), **Édouard Victor Antoine.** 1823–1892. French composer of impressionistic school; his compositions include the operas *Fiesque* (1867) and *Le Roi d'Ys* (1888), the ballet *Namouna* (1882), the violin concerto *Symphonie Espagnole*, a violoncello concerto, orchestral works, church and chamber music, piano pieces, and songs.

**Lam'a·chus** (lăm'ȧ·kŭs). d. 414 B.C. Athenian general; distinguished himself as an associate of Alcibiades and Nicias in the Sicilian expedition (415 B.C.); killed in action fighting the Syracusans (414).

**La·mar'** (lȧ·mär'), **Joseph Rucker.** 1857–1916. American jurist, b. in Elbert County, Ga. Associate justice, U.S. Supreme Court (from 1911).

**Lamar, Mir'a·beau** (mĭr'ȧ·bō) **Buonaparte.** 1798–1859. Second president of Republic of Texas, b. in Warren County, Ga. In Texas (from 1836); served in Sam Houston's force at battle of San Jacinto. Vice-president of Texas (1836) and president (1838–41); after 1844, advocated annexation to United States. His nephew **Lucius Quintus Cincinnatus Lamar** (1825–1893) was a lawyer; settled in Mississippi (1855); member of U.S. House of Representatives (1857–60); served in Confederate army in Civil War; supported Jefferson Davis's administration and acted as Confederate commissioner in Europe (1862–63); again member of U.S. House of Representatives (1873–77); U.S. senator (1877–85); U.S. secretary of the interior (1885–88); associate justice, U.S. Supreme Court (1888–93).

**La Marche** (lȧ mȧrsh'), **Olivier de.** 1425?–1502. French chronicler and writer of allegorical poems, as *Le Chevalier Délibéré;* remembered esp. for his *Mémoires*, covering period 1435 to 1488.

**La Marck** (lȧ mȧrk'). A family originating in Westphalia to which later belonged, among others, the families of Bouillon and Turenne (*q.v.*); the seigneury became a county (13th century). **Guillaume de La Marck** (1446?–1485), called "the Wild Boar of Ardennes," a Belgian soldier of Louis XI, killed the bishop of Liége (1482); later was captured and beheaded. **Robert II** (1465?–1536), seigneur de Sedan, accompanied Charles VIII in expedition against Naples (1495); fought at Novara (1513) and Pavia (1524); a friend of Francis I. **Robert III** (see under BOUILLON). His son **Robert IV** (1520?–1556), soldier, was marshal of France (1547). **Évrard** (1475–1538), brother of Robert II, was bishop of Liége. See ARENBERG.

**La'marck'** (lȧ'mȧrk'), Chevalier **de. Jean Baptiste Pierre Antoine de Mo'net'** (dē mô'nĕ'). 1744–1829. French naturalist, b. Bazantin, Picardy. In French army during Seven Years' War. Studied medicine and then botany in Paris; published (1778) *Flore Française;* as royal botanist visited Holland, Germany, and Hungary (1781–82); published *Dictionnaire de Botanique* and *Illustrations de Genres;* custodian of herbarium of Jardin du Roi (c. 1778), the name of which he was later responsible for changing to Jardin des Plantes; professor of zoology, Jardin des Plantes (1793–1818). Forerunner of Darwin in evolutionary theory; proposed theory that changes in environment cause changes in structure of animals and plants, esp. by inducing new or increased use of certain organs or parts, resulting in adaptive modification or greater development, and inducing also disuse and final atrophy of other organs, and that such acquired characters are transmitted to offspring; responsible for classification of animals into vertebrates and invertebrates; among invertebrates, first proposed the classes Infusoria, Annelida, Crustacea, Arachnida, and Tunicata. Author of *Système des Animaux sans Vertèbres* (1801), *Recherches sur L'Organisation des Corps Vivants* (1802), *Philosophie Zoologique* (1809), *Histoire Naturelle des Animaux sans Vertèbres* (1815–22).

**La Mar'mo·ra** (lä mär'mô·rä), Marchese **di. Alfonso Fer·re'ro** (fâr·râ'rō). 1804–1878. Italian soldier and statesman; served in the war of independence (1848–49). As minister of war (1848–59, with a few interruptions), reorganized the Sardinian army; served in Crimean War (1855), and commanded the army in the war of 1859. Prime minister of Sardinia (1859–60; 1864–66). Chief of staff (1866). His older brothers **Alberto Ferrero,** Conte **di La Marmora** (1789–1863), and **Alessandro Ferrero,** Cavaliere **di La Marmora** (1799–1855), were also army officers; Alberto was lieutenant general (1848) in the army of Charles Albert of Sardinia; Alessandro was general of brigade, and is credited with organizing the *Bersaglieri*, a corps d'élite of the Italian army.

**La'marque'** (lȧ'mȧrk'), Comte **Maximilien.** 1770–1832. French general; campaigned in Italy, and captured Gaeta (1806); engaged under Napoleon at Wagram. Member of Chamber of Deputies (1828–32); outspoken in his opposition to the government. His funeral (June 5–6, 1832) was occasion seized by Republicans for an insurrection in Paris.

**La'mar'tine'** (lȧ'mȧr'tēn'), **Alphonse Marie Louis de Prat** (prȧ) **de.** 1790–1869. French poet; best known for his *Méditations Poétiques* (1820), which was immensely popular and strongly influenced history of romantic movement in French literature. Among other of his poetic works are *Nouvelles Méditations Poétiques* (1823), *Harmonies Poétiques et Religieuses* (1830), *Jocelyn* (1836), and *La Chute d'un Ange* (1838). Author also of prose works, as *Histoire des Girondins* (1846), *Graziella* (1852). Known also as an orator; minister of foreign affairs in provisional government (1848).

**Lamas, Carlos Saavedra.** See SAAVEDRA LAMAS.

**Lamb** (lăm), **Arthur Becket.** 1880–1952. American chemist; professor (1920–48), director of chemical laboratory (1912–47), Harvard; dean, Graduate School of Arts and Sciences, Harvard (1940–43). Editor, *Journal of the American Chemical Society* (1917–49).

**Lamb,** Lady **Caroline.** 1785–1828. English novelist. Daughter of Frederick Ponsonby, 3d Earl of Bessborough; m. (1805) William Lamb (later 2d Viscount Melbourne); infatuated with Lord Byron, became notorious for her nine-months devotion to him (1812–13); author of three novels: *Glenarron* (1816, containing a caricature portrait of Byron), *Graham Hamilton* (1822), *Ada Reis* (1823). Mentally deranged after happening to meet Byron's funeral procession.

**Lamb, Charles.** 1775–1834. English essayist and critic. Educ. at Christ's Hospital (1782–89), where he formed friendship with Coleridge; clerk in South Sea House, in India House (1792–1825); lived in straitened circumstances with parents and sister **Mary Ann** (1764–1847), who in fit of insanity killed her invalid mother (1796); gave up projected marriage and devoted himself to guardianship of his sister; himself mentally unhinged and confined in asylum (1795–96). Contributed four sonnets to Coleridge's first volume (1796); wrote *Old Familiar Faces* for volume *Blank Verse*, published with Charles Lloyd (1798); published his little prose romance, *A Tale of Rosamund Gray* (1797). With sister Mary contributed to W. Godwin's Juvenile Library *Tales from Shakespeare*, Charles doing the tragedies and Mary the comedies (1807); wrote with his sister a child's *Ulysses* (1808), and poetry for children. Contributed articles on Hogarth and Shakespeare to Leigh Hunt's *Reflector;* published his collected prose and verse (1818); invited to staff of the new *London Magazine*, to which he contributed (1820–25) the 25 *Essays of Elia* (reprinted; 1st series, 1823; 2d, 1833). Adopted Emma Isola, an orphan; moved to Edmonton; deprived of companionship by increasing frequency of sister's periods of mental alienation and by marriage (1833) of Emma Isola to Edward Moxon.

**Lamb,** Sir **Horace.** 1849–1934. English mathematician and physicist; author of *Hydrodynamics* (1895), *Statics* (1912), *Dynamics* (1914), *Higher Mechanics* (1920), etc.

**Lamb, William.** 2d Viscount **Mel'bourne** (mĕl'bẽrn; -bôrn). 1779–1848. English statesman; m. (1805) daughter of 3d earl of Bessborough (see Lady Caroline LAMB); Whig M.P. (1806); lost seat because of support of Catholic emancipation (1812); Irish secretary (1827, 1828); home secretary under Grey (1830–34), employed in Ireland coercive measures disapproved by governor general; summoned to form ministry, prime minister for few months (1834); again prime minister (1835–41), eminently tactful political adviser of young Queen Victoria. His brother **Frederick James** (1782–1853), 3d Viscount Melbourne and Baron **Beau'vale** (bū'vāl); diplomat; minister at court of Bavaria (1815–20), Spain (1825–27); ambassador at Vienna (1831–41).

**Lamb, Willis Eugene.** 1913– . American physicist, b. Los Angeles, Calif. At Columbia U. (1938–52), Stanford (1951–56), Oxford (1956–62), Yale (1962– ). Awarded Nobel prize in physics (1955) with P. Kusch for work on the hydrogen spectrum.

**Lam'balle'** (läɴ'bȧl'), Princesse **de.** *Nee* **Marie Thérèse Louise de Sa'voie'–Ca'ri'gnan'** (dẽ sȧ'vwȧ'kȧ'rē'nyäɴ'). 1749–1792. Personal friend of Marie Antoinette; m. prince de Lamballe (1766; d. 1767); imprisoned (1792), she refused to subscribe to the oath against the monarchy (Sept. 3), and was torn to pieces by mob.

**Lambart, Frederic Rudolph.** See Earl of CAVAN.

**Lam'beaux'** (läɴ'bō'), **Jef** *or* **Joseph Marie Thomas.** 1852–1908. Belgian sculptor; settled in Brussels (1881). His works include *The Wild Song* and *Human Passions* (Brussels), Brabo Fountain (Antwerp), busts, etc.

**Lamber, Juliette.** See Juliette ADAM.

**Lam'bert** (*Angl.* lăm'bẽrt; *Ger.* läm'bĕrt; *Fr.* läɴ'bâr'), **Franz.** *Known as* **Lambert of A'vi'gnon'** (ȧ'vē'nyôɴ'). 1486?–1530. Protestant theologian; originally a Franciscan friar, he was converted to Protestantism (1522) and joined Luther at Wittenberg (1523); first professor of theology at Marburg.

**Lam'bert** (lăm'bẽrt), **George Washington.** 1873–1930. Portrait and mural painter, b. St. Petersburg, of American father and English mother. Studied in Sydney, Australia; official artist to Australian imperial forces in Egypt and Palestine.

**Lam'bert** (läm'bĕrt; *Angl.* lăm'bẽrt), **Johann Heinrich.** 1728–1777. German physicist, mathematician, astronomer, and philosopher. Conducted researches on heat, light, and color; discovered method of measuring the intensity of light and the absorption of light, the lambert (a unit of brightness) being named after him; constructed a color pyramid; measured the coefficient of expansion of air; formulated a theorem relating to the motion of the planets; demonstrated the irrationality of $\pi$; responsible for conception of hyperbolic functions in trigonometry.

**Lam'bert** (lăm'bẽrt), **John.** 1619–1683. English Parliamentary general in the Civil War. Led cavalry at Marston Moor; commander of army in north (1647) and spokesman of the army; aided Cromwell in destroying Scottish army at Preston (1648); led van at Dunbar (1650); won victory of Inverkeithing; commanded troops on east bank of Severn at battle of Worcester (1651). Leader of council of officers that installed Cromwell as lord protector (1653); at first supported Richard Cromwell; later, headed cabal that retired Cromwell into obscurity; regarded as leader of Fifth Monarchy Men, or extreme republican party; suppressed Royalist insurrection in Cheshire (1659); virtual ruler of country until frustrated by Monck's advance to London; kept prisoner in Guernsey and Drake's Island until his death.

**Lambert, Louis.** Pseudonym of Patrick S. GILMORE.

**Lam'bert von Hers'feld** (läm'bĕrt fôn hĕrs'fĕlt). d. about 1088. Medieval German historian; opponent of Henry IV. Author of *Annales*, a history of the world to 1077, containing a comprehensive treatment of contemporaneous events from the accession of Henry IV, *Vita Lulli*, a biography of Archbishop Lullus of Mainz who founded the monastery at Hersfeld, and the epic *Carmen de Bello Saxonico.*

**Lam'bin'** (läɴ'băɴ'), **Denis.** *Lat.* **Dionysius Lambi'nus** (lăm·bī'nŭs). 1516–1572. French philologist; royal professor of Greek (1561).

**Lam'bros** *or* **Lam'pros** (läm'brôs), **Spyridon.** 1851–1919. Greek historian; author of a history of Athens, a history of Greece; translator of German works on Greek history.

**Lam'bru·schi'ni** (läm'brōō·skē'nē), **Luigi.** 1776–1854. Italian ecclesiastic and statesman; cardinal (1831); papal secretary of state (1836). Active in securing victory of bishop of Cologne over Prussia as author of famous allocutions. Forced to flee Rome during revolution (1848); with Pius IX at Gaeta (to 1850).

**Lamb'ton** (lăm(p)'tŭn), Sir **Hedworth.** See MEUX.

**Lambton, John George.** 1st Earl of **Dur'ham** (dûr'ăm). 1792–1840. English statesman; grandson of **John Lambton** (1710–1794), general. Liberal M.P. (1813); proposed scheme of parliamentary reform rejected as too advanced; privy councilor and lord privy seal in administration of his father-in-law, Lord Grey (1830–33); one of four who drew up the first reform bill; created Viscount Lambton and Earl of Durham (1833); ambassador to St. Petersburg (1835–37); excluded from Melbourne administration. Governor general and lord high commissioner in Canada (1838); took statesmanlike action to placate rebellious Lower Canada; resigned (1838); attempted public justification by means of his *Report on the Affairs of British North America* (1839), outlining principles and schemes of British colonial policy adopted by his successors.

**Lam'burn** (lăm'bẽrn), **Richmal Cromp'ton** (krŭmp'tŭn). *Pen name* **Richmal Crompton.** 1890–1969. English fiction writer; senior classical mistress at S. Elphin's (1915–17) and Bromley High School for Girls (1917–24). Author of *The Innermost Room, The Hidden Light, Ladies First, Chedsy Place,* etc.

**La'mé'** (lȧ'mā'), **Gabriel.** 1795–1870. French mathematician and engineer; engaged in building railroads from Paris to Saint-Germain and from Paris to Versailles; engineer in chief of mining (1836); professor of the calculus of probabilities, U. of Paris (1851).

**La'men'nais',** *orig.* **La Men'nais'** (lȧ'mĕ'nĕ'), **Félicité Robert de.** 1782–1854. French priest and philosopher;

founder of journals *L'Avenir* (with Montalembert; 1830) and *Le Peuple Constituant* (1848), and director of *La Réforme;* his advocacy of policy of freedom in religious matters was not approved by clergy and brought upon him censure and condemnation. His great philosophical work is *Essai sur l'Indifférence en Matière de Religion* (vol. I, 1817; II, 1820; III & IV, 1822–23).

**La'meth'** (lȧ'mĕt'), Comte **Charles Malo François de.** 1757–1832. French politician; member of States-General (1789); an émigré (1792). Returned to France (1801) and was appointed by Napoleon governor of Würzburg, and later of Santoña, Spain. His brother Comte **Alexandre Théodore Victor** (1760–1829) served under Rochambeau in American Revolution; served under La Fayette in war with Austria (1792); prisoner of war with the Austrians (1792–95); returned to France (1799) and was in Napoleon's service.

**La Met'trie'** (lȧ mĕ'trē'), **Julien Of'froy'** (ô'frȧ') **de.** 1709–1751. French physician and materialistic philosopher; forced to flee from France and then from Leiden because of materialistic teachings in his *Histoire Naturelle de l'Âme* (1745); found asylum with Frederick the Great in Berlin. Held that psychical phenomena are due to organic changes in brain and nervous system, that the only pleasures are those of the senses, that life should be spent in enjoyment of pleasures, that the soul ceases to exist with the death of the body.

**La'mi'** (lȧ'mē'), **Louis Eugène.** 1800–1890. French historical painter; known also for his illustrations, as those for works of Alfred de Musset, for Merimée's *Charles IX*, etc.

**Lam'masch** (läm'äsh), **Heinrich.** 1853–1920. Austrian jurist and statesman; authority on criminal and international law. Four times member (from 1900) and president of International Court of Arbitration, The Hague; helped settle Newfoundland fisheries dispute between Great Britain and U.S. (1910). Opposed union with German Reich and later Anschluss movement; favored peace by agreement in World War and a league of nations; last minister president of old Austria (Oct.–Nov., 1918).

**Lam'me** (lăm'ē), **Benjamin Garver.** 1864–1924. American engineer and inventor; devoted himself to designing electrical machinery, as the rotary converter, alternating-current generator, induction motor, twenty-five cycle commutator motor.

**Lam'mers** (läm'ērs), **Hans Heinrich.** 1879–1962. German government official; secretary of state, and head of the Reich chancellery (1933–37); minister and head of the chancellery (1937 ff.).

**La'moi'gnon'** (lȧ'mwȧ'nyôN'). Prominent French family, including: **Guillaume de Lamoignon** (1617–1677), lawyer and first president of the Parliament of Paris (1658); his two sons **François Chrétien** (1644–1709), a lawyer and man of letters, and **Nicolas de Lamoignon de Bâ'ville'** [dē bä'vēl'] (1648–1724), lawyer, intendant at Poitiers and Montpellier (1685–1718); Nicolas's son **Urbain Guillaume de Lamoignon,** *known as* **Cour'son'** [kōōr'sôN'] (1674–1742), intendant at Rouen (1704), Bordeaux (1707), councilor of state (1730); Nicolas's nephew **Guillaume de Lamoignon,** Seigneur **de Blanc'mes'nil'** (bläN'mā'nēl') *and* **de Males'herbes'** [mäl'zĕrb'] (1683–1772), chancellor of France (1750), father of Malesherbes (*q.v.*); and **Chrétien François de Lamoignon** (1735–1789) of the same family, guardian of the seals (1787).

**Lam'on** (lăm'ŭn), **Ward Hill.** 1828–1893. American lawyer and associate of Abraham Lincoln, b. in Frederick County, Va. Law partner of Lincoln in Danville, Ill. (1852). Accompanied Lincoln to Washington (1861); marshal of District of Columbia (1861–65); trusted guard of Lincoln during these years; was on a mission to Richmond night Lincoln was shot. Author of *Life of Abraham Lincoln from His Birth to His Inauguration as President* (1872).

**Lam'ond** (lăm'ŭnd), **Frederic.** 1868–1948. British pianist and composer, b. in Glasgow. Composer of a symphony, overtures, trios, sonatas, etc.

**La·mont'** (lȧ·mŏnt'), **Daniel Scott.** 1851–1905. American political leader, b. in Cortland County, N.Y. Private secretary to President Cleveland (1885–89); U.S. secretary of war (1893–97). Vice-president, Northern Pacific Railway (from 1898).

**La'mont** (lä'mônt), **Johann von.** 1805–1879. Scottish-German astronomer and physicist; professor of astronomy, U. of Munich (1852–79). Executed magnetic surveys of Bavaria, France, Spain, North Germany, Denmark (1849–58); announced discovery of earth currents (1862).

**La·mont'** (lȧ·mŏnt'), **Robert Patterson.** 1867–1948. American engineer and public official, b. Detroit. U.S. secretary of commerce (1929–32). Established astronomical observatory, for U. of Michigan, in South Africa.

**Lamont, Thomas William.** 1870–1948. American banker, b. Claverack, N.Y. Vice-president, Bankers Trust Co., New York (1905–09), First National Bank, New York (1909–11); member of firm, J. P. Morgan & Co. (from 1911), board chairman (Mar., 1943). Overseer of Harvard (1912–25). Trustee, Metropolitan Museum of Art, New York City. His son **Thomas Stilwell (1899–1967),** banker, on staff of J. P. Morgan & Co. (from 1922); member of firm (from 1928).

**La'mo'ri'cière'** (lȧ'mô'rē'syâr'), **Louis Christophe Léon Ju'chault' de** (zhü'shō' dē). 1806–1865. French general; distinguished himself in campaign against Abd-el-Kader, in Algeria (1847). Member of Legislative Assembly (1849–51) and opposed intrigues of Louis Napoleon so vigorously that he was banished from France (1852). Entered military service of the Papacy, and was defeated at Castelfidardo (1860).

**La Mothe Le Va'yer'** (lȧ môt' lē vȧ'yā'), **François de.** 1588–1672. French philosopher; a leader among 17th-century French skeptics; tutor of the duc d'Orléans (1649) and of King Louis XIV (1652); appointed historiographer of France and councilor of state.

**La Motte** (lȧ môt'), Comte **Marc Antoine Nicolas de** (1754–1831) and his wife **Jeanne,** *nee* **de Saint'-Ré'my' de Va'lois'** [dē săN'rā'mē' dē vȧ'lwȧ'] (1756–1791). French adventurers involved in affair of the diamond necklace. The comtesse became mistress of Cardinal de Rohan, pretended to be an intimate of Queen Marie Antoinette. The cardinal purchased a diamond necklace under the impression (given him by the comtesse) that he was authorized to do so by the queen; when the jewelers complained to the queen, the cardinal was arrested, tried, and acquitted (1786); the comtesse was condemned to be whipped, branded, and imprisoned, but escaped from prison; the comte was believed to have fled with the necklace to London.

**La Motte'-Fou·qué'** (lä môt'fōō·kā'), Baron **Heinrich August de.** 1698–1774. German soldier, of Norman-French descent, whose family fled from France after the revocation of the Edict of Nantes. Distinguished himself under Frederick the Great. His grandson Baron **Friedrich Heinrich Karl** (1777–1843), German writer; a romanticist, author of the novel *Undine* (1811) and of libretto for Hoffmann's opera *Undine,* of many lyrics, including the patriotic song *Frisch auf zum Fröhlichen Jagen*, and a number of dramas.

**La'motte'-Hou'dar'** (lȧ'môt'ōō'dȧr'). *Real name* **Antoine Houdar de La Motte.** 1672–1731. French poet and literary critic; translated the *Iliad* into modern French verse, with an introductory *Discours sur Homère* (1714), reopening the long controversy between the ancients and the moderns; wrote also prose tragedies, prose odes, fables, and opera librettos.

**La'mou'reux'** (lȧ'mo͞o'rû'), **Charles.** 1834–1899. French violinist and conductor; established Nouveaux Concerts (later called *Concerts Lamoureux*) at Paris (1881) and popularized music of Wagner and others in France.

**Lam·pa'di·us** (läm·pä'dē·o͝os), **Wilhelm August.** 1772–1842. German chemist; known for contributions to the science of metallurgy.

**Lam·per'ti** (läm·pĕr'tē), **Francesco.** 1813–1892. Italian singing teacher; taught Cruvelli, Sembrich, Artôt, and others; author of a treatise on the art of singing.

**Lamp'man** (lămp'măn), **Archibald.** 1861–1899. Canadian poet; author of *Among the Millet, and Other Poems* (1888), *Lyrics of Earth* (1895).

**Lam'precht** (läm'prĕкt), **Karl.** 1856–1915. German historian, upheld theory that science of history is social-psychological rather than exclusively political. Author of *Deutsche Geschichte* (19 vols., 1891–1909), *Die Kulturhistorische Methode* (1900), etc.

**Lamprecht the Priest.** fl. 1120–1130. Frankish epic poet and divine; author of the Middle Frankish *Alexanderlied* (c. 1130), an epic on the life and deeds of Alexander the Great based on a French original by Albéric de Besançon and on a Latin prose version.

**Lam·prid'i·us** (lăm·prĭd'ĭ·ŭs), **Aelius.** Latin historian of early 4th century A.D.; one of the collaborators in writing *Scriptores Historiae Augustae.*

**Lampros, Spyridon.** See LAMBROS.

**Lamp'son** (lăm(p)'s'n). See also LOCKER-LAMPSON.

**Lampson,** Sir **Curtis Miranda.** 1806–1885. Merchant, b. New Haven, Vt.; moved to England (1830); naturalized British subject (1849); associated with Cyrus W. Field in laying of Atlantic cable (from 1856); created baronet (1866).

**Lampson, Miles Wedderburn.** 1st Baron **Kil·learn'** (kĭl·lûrn'). 1880–1964. British diplomat; minister to China (1926–33); British high commissioner for Egypt and the Sudan (1933–36), and ambassador to Egypt (1936–46). Appointed privy councilor (1941).

**Lams'dorf** (läms'dôrf), Count **Vladimir Nikolaevich.** 1845–1907. Russian statesman; succeeded Muraviëv as minister of foreign affairs (1900); tried unsuccessfully to negotiate peaceful settlement of outstanding issues with Japan (1903–04); resigned (1906).

**Lam'son–Scrib'ner** (lăm's'n·skrĭb'nẽr), **Frank.** *Orig. surname* **Lamson.** *Adopted by family named* **Scribner.** 1851–1938. American botanist, authority on grasses; professor of botany, Tennessee (1888–94); chief, division of agrostology, U.S. Dept. of Agriculture (1894–1901); chief, Insular Bureau of Agriculture, P.I. (1901–04); special agent and expert on exhibits, U.S. Dept. of Agriculture, for fairs and expositions (1904–22). Author of *Grasses of Tennessee* (1894), *American Grasses* (3 vols.; 1897–1900), etc.

**La'my'** (lȧ'mē'), **Bernard.** 1640–1715. French ecclesiastic and scholar; member of the Congregation of the Oratory; suffered ecclesiastical discipline for teaching Cartesian doctrines. Among his works are *Nouvelles Réflexions sur l'Art Poétique* (1668), *Traité de la Grandeur en Général* (1680), *Harmonie Évangélique* (1689).

**Lamy, Étienne Marie Victor.** 1845–1919. French politician; member of National Assembly and Chamber of Deputies (1871–81), where his support of the church caused a break with leftist groups. Among his books are *L'Armée et la Démocratie* (1885), *Études sur le Second Empire* (1895), *Témoins des Jours Passés* (1913).

**Lamy, John Baptist.** *Orig.* **Jean Baptiste l'Amy.** 1814–1888. Roman Catholic prelate, b. Lempdes, France. In U.S. (from 1839); missionary bishop in the Southwest (from 1850); created bishop of Santa Fe (1853); archbishop (1875). Willa Cather's novel *Death Comes for the Archbishop* is based on his career in the Southwest.

**Lan'cas·ter** (lăng'kăs·tẽr), House of. English royal house derived from the fourth son of Edward III, John of Gaunt, created (1362) duke of Lancaster after marriage (1359) with daughter and heiress of Henry, 1st duke of Lancaster; branch of Plantagenet family, rival (after 1399) of house of York. Title traces from creation by Henry III of his second son, Edmund Crouchback, earl of Lancaster (1267). Symbol of house in War of the Roses was the red rose. Reigning Lancastrian kings: Henry IV, Henry V, Henry VI. See *Table (in Appendix)* for ENGLAND.

**Lancaster,** Earls and dukes of.

(1) **Edmund.** *Called* **Crouch'back'** (krouch'băk'). Earl of Lancaster. 1245–1296. 2d son of Henry III, King of England, and Eleanor of Provence; brother of Edward I. Styled king of Sicily by pope (1255; title annulled 1263); crusader (1271); took part in Welsh War (1277–82).

(2) **Thomas.** Earl of Lancaster, Leicester, Derby, Lincoln and Salisbury. 1277?–1322. Eldest son of Edmund, Earl of Lancaster. Leader of barons, because of wealth and position, at accession of Edward II; brought about banishment of Piers Gaveston (1308); obliged Edward to surrender power to 21 "ordainers"; drove Edward and Gaveston from Newcastle and brought about execution of Gaveston (1312); took advantage of English defeat at Bannockburn to wrest control from Edward, but himself equally feeble in administration because of quarrels with barons and private war against Earl Warenne; temporarily reconciled with Edward after Berwick (1318); accused of taking bribes from Scots; withheld himself from government until the Despensers were banished (1321); taken by royal forces in north and beheaded.

(3) **Henry of Lancaster.** 1st Duke of Lancaster. 1299?–1361. English warrior and trusted counselor of Edward III. Son of **Henry of Lancaster** (1281?–1345), Earl of Lancaster, who was brother of Thomas, Earl of Lancaster. Distinguished himself off Sluis (1340) and off Winchelsea (1350); served against Moors at Algeciras (1343); led successful expeditions into Scotland, Gascony, Normandy, and Brittany (1341–57); lieutenant of Aquitaine (1345–47); admiral of western fleet (1351); led forces into Prussia and Poland (1351–52). Frequently employed on diplomatic business; negotiated with French and Flemish (1348–49); negotiated with Pope Innocent VI (1354) upon peace between England and France; assisted in arranging Treaty of Bretigny (1360). Steward of England and one of original knights of the garter. His daughter Blanche married John of Gaunt.

(4) See also JOHN OF GAUNT and HENRY IV of England.

**Lancaster, Bruce.** 1896–1963. American novelist; author of *Guns of Burgoyne* (1939), *Bride of a Thousand Cedars* (with L. Brentano, 1939), *For Us the Living* (1940), *Bright to the Wanderer* (1941).

**Lancaster, G. B.** Pseudonym of Edith J. LYTTLETON.

**Lancaster,** Sir **James.** 1550?–1618. English navigator and pioneer of East Indian trade. Served under Drake against Armada (1588); sailed with earliest English oversea expedition to establish East Indian trade (1591); commanded first fleet of East India Company; promoted search for Northwest Passage.

**Lancaster, John of.** Duke of **Bedford** (1389–1435). See JOHN OF LANCASTER.

**Lancaster, Joseph.** 1778–1838. English educationist. Joined Society of Friends; taught free school of a thousand boys; organized corps of elder boys as monitors to oversee and instruct; the Lancasterian system of education adopted widely by nonconformists in competition with Andrew Bell's system supported by Church of England; emigrated to America (1818).

**Lance** (làns), **George.** 1802–1864. English painter, esp. of flowers, fruit, and dead game.

**Lan'ce·lot'** (läɴs'lō'), Dom **Claude.** 1615?–1695. French priest and educator; a Jansenist.

**Lan'ce·reaux'** (läɴs'rō'), **Étienne.** 1829–1910. French physician; studied alcoholism; credited with discovery of a form of diabetes often associated with pancreatic disease (1877); research on syphilis, malaria, etc.

**Lan'ches·ter** (lăn'chĕs·tĕr; -chĭs-), **Elsa.** See under Charles LAUGHTON.

**Lanchester, Henry Vaughan.** 1863–1953. English architect; designed Cardiff City Hall and Law Courts, St. Bartholomew's Hospital, Birmingham Hospital Centre; interested in town planning, worked in India.

**Lan·cia'ni** (län·chä'nē), **Rodolfo Amadeo.** 1846?–1929. Italian archaeologist; assisted in excavations at Ostia; director of Roman excavations (1875–95); authority on topography of ancient Rome.

**Lan'cret'** (läɴ'krĕ'), **Nicolas.** 1690–1743. French painter in the style of Watteau.

**Land** (lănd), **Edwin Herbert.** 1909– . American inventor and physicist, b. Bridgeport, Conn. Founder (1937) of Polaroid Corp.; developed Polaroid lenses and one-step photographic process (1947).

**Land, Emory Scott.** 1879–1971. American naval officer; grad. U.S.N.A., Annapolis (1902); M.S., M.I.T. (1907); chief of bureau of construction and repair, U.S. Navy Department (1932–37); member of U.S. Maritime Commission (1937–46, chairman from 1938).

**Lan·dau'** (län·dou'), **Lev Davidovich.** 1908–1968. Soviet physicist. Awarded Nobel prize in physics (1962) for theories on condensed matter, esp. liquid helium.

**Lan'dau** (lăn'dô), **Rom** (rŏm). 1899– . British sculptor and writer; advocate of a more spiritual nonsectarian Christianity; member of executive committee of World Congress of Faiths, in London. Author of *Minos the Incorruptible* (1925), *God is My Adventure* (1935), *Thy Kingdom Come* (1937), *Love for a Country* (1939), *Of No Importance* (1940), *We Have Seen Evil* (1941), *Hitler's Paradise* (1941), *Fool's Progress* (1942), etc.

**Landau-Aldanov, Mark Aleksandrovich.** See ALDANOV.

**Land'berg** (lånd'băr·y'), Count **Carlo.** 1848–1924. Swedish Arabic scholar.

**Lan'dé** (län'dĕ), **Alfred.** 1888– . Physicist, b. Germany; known for researches in atomic structure, quantum theory, and related subjects.

**Lan'delle'** (läɴ'dĕl'), **Charles.** 1821–1908. French painter of religious pictures and Algerian, Egyptian, and Moroccan scenes and types.

**Lan'dells** (?lăn'd'lz), **Ebenezer.** 1808–1860. English wood-engraver; conceived idea of *Punch*, projected magazine (first issue July 17th, 1841); contributed to early numbers of *Illustrated London News*. His eldest son, **Robert Thomas** (1833–1877), was war artist for *Illustrated London News* during Crimean War (1856), German invasion of Denmark (1863), Austro-Prussian War (1866), and Franco-Prussian War (1870).

**Lan'den** (lăn'dĕn), **John.** 1719–1790. English mathematician; made researches on elliptic functions; produced Landen's theorem for expressing the arc of a hyperbola in terms of two elliptic arcs (1775).

**Lan'der** (lăn'dĕr), **Richard Lemon** (1804–1834) and his brother **John** (1807–1839). English explorers of the Niger River; reported first expedition (1830–31) in combined journal (3 vols., 1832); discovered confluence of the Niger and Benue. Richard was companion of Hugh Clapperton (*q.v.*) expedition to western Africa and published Clapperton's journal and records (1830); later led expedition up the Niger organized by Macgregor Laird (*q.v.*); settled course and outlet of Niger.

**Landesmann, Heinrich.** See Hieronymus LORM.

**Lan·di'no** (län·dē'nō), **Francesco.** *Sometimes called* **Francesco Cie'co** (chā'kō) *or* **Francesco de'gli Or'ga·ni** (dā'lyē ōr'gä·nē). c. 1325–1397. Florentine musician and composer; blind from childhood; a leading representative of *ars nova* of 14th century.

**Lan'dis** (lăn'dĭs), **James McCauley.** 1899–1964. American lawyer and educator, b. Tokyo, Japan; A.B., Princeton (1921); LL.B. (1924), S.J.D. (1925), Harvard. Professor, Harvard (1928–34); member, Federal Trade Commission (1933–34), Securities and Exchange Commission (1934–37; chairman 1935–37); dean of Harvard Law School (1937–46); director, Office of Civilian Defense (1942–43); U.S. minister to Middle East (1943–44).

**Landis, Ken'e·saw Moun'tain** (kĕn'ĕ·sô moun'tĭn; -tĕn). 1866–1944. American jurist, b. Millville, Ohio. Practiced law in Chicago (1891–1905). U.S. district judge, Northern District of Illinois (1905–22); presided at trial (1907) of Standard Oil of Indiana rebate cases, found defendants guilty, imposed fine of $29,240,000, later reversed by P. S. Grosscup. Baseball commissioner for American and National Leagues of Professional Base Ball Clubs, and National Association of Professional Base Ball Leagues (1920–44).

**Lan'do** (län'dō) *or* **Lan'dus** (lăn'dŭs). d. 914. Pope (913–914).

**Lan'dolt** (län'dōlt), **Hans.** 1831–1910. Physical chemist, b. in Switzerland; professor in Berlin; investigated optical refractivity of organic compounds; devised improvements for polarization apparatus; joint publisher of physical-chemical tables.

**Lan'don** (lăn'dŭn), **Alfred Mossman.** 1887– . American businessman and politician, b. W. Middlesex, Pa. Independent oil producer in Kansas (from 1912). Governor of Kansas (1933–37). Republican nominee for president of the U.S. (1936).

**Landon, Letitia Elizabeth.** 1802–1838. English poet and novelist, using initials **L. E. L.** as pen name; m. George Maclean, governor of Cape Coast, Africa (1838). Published volumes of verse, as *The Fate of Adelaide* (1821), *The Venetian Bracelet* (1829); wrote several novels, including *Ethel Churchill* (1837), and a tragedy *Castruccio Castracani* (1837).

**Lan'dor** (lăn'dôr; -dĕr), **Walter Savage.** 1775–1864. English poet and prose writer, b. Warwick; removed from Rugby for insubordination and intractable temper; rusticated from Oxford (1794); quarreled with family; retired to South Wales on allowance. Gained friendship with Southey through poem *Gebir* (1798); went through fortune; fought as volunteer in Spain (1808). Bought Llanthony Abbey, Monmouthshire, but quarreled with neighbors and tenants; m. Julia Thuillier (1811); lived successively in France, at Como, and at Florence; quarreled with wife and returned to England (1835). Returned to Florence (1858) because of libel action; assisted by Robert Browning; visited by Swinburne. Author of a tragedy *Don Julian* (1812), *Imaginary Conversations* (5 vols., 1824, 1828, 1829), *The Examination of William Shakespeare...Touching Deer-stealing* (1834), *Pericles and Aspasia* (1836), *Pentameron* (1837), *Hellenics* (1847), *Poemata et Inscriptiones* (1847), and *Dry*

*Sticks, Fagoted* (1858). Caricatured as Lawrence Boythorn in Dickens's *Bleak House*. His grandson **Arnold Henry Savage Landor** (1865–1924), artist and traveler, b. in Florence, studied art in Paris; traveled in eastern Asia, America, Azores, Australia, Africa; reached both sources of Brahmaputra River, Asia (1897), explored central Mindanao, where he discovered the "white tribe" Mansakas; went overland from Russia to Calcutta (1902); crossed Africa at its widest part in 364 days (1906); crossed South America (1910–12); long held altitude record in mountain climbing, Mount Lumpa, Nepal (23,490 ft.); dispatch rider for Belgian government in World War; illustrated his own travel books.

**Lan'dou'zy'** (län'dōō'zē'), **Louis.** 1845–1917. French physician; author of works on nervous diseases, serotherapy, syphilis; known esp. for work on tuberculosis.

**Lan·dow'ska** (län·dôf'skä), **Wanda.** 1877–1959. Polish pianist and harpsichordist; interpreter of early keyboard music. Settled in Paris (1919) and founded a school of early-music interpretation. Composer of songs, piano pieces, and orchestral works.

**Lan'dow'ski'** (läN'dôf'skē'), **Paul Maximilien.** 1875–1961. French sculptor; his works include *Monument to the Unknown Artists* (le Panthéon), *Monument to the Reformation* (Geneva), equestrian statues of Edward VII (Place Édouard VII, Paris) and Marshal Haig, numerous busts, etc.

**Land'seer** (lăn(d)'sēr; -syēr), Sir **Edwin Henry.** 1802–1873. English animal painter, b. London; attracted attention with *Fighting Dogs Getting Wind* (1818), *Alpine Mastiffs Reanimating a Distressed Traveller* (1820), *The Cat's Paw* (1824). Visited Sir Walter Scott at Abbotsford and drew the poet and his dogs (1824); saw deer in native haunts. After about 1823 made animal pictures serve to convey a sentiment or idea without sacrificing correctness of draftsmanship; after *High Life* and *Low Life* (1829) chose higher grades of animal society, portraying in civilized settings his dogs, and even wild animals, as in *Jack in Office* (1833), *The Old Shepherd's Chief Mourner, The Swannery Invaded by Eagles.* Painted his most famous pictures between 1838 and 1850, including *A Distinguished Member of the Humane Society* (1838), *Dignity and Impudence* (1839), *Stag at Bay* (1846), *A Random Shot* (1848), *Monarch of the Glen* (1851), *Titania and Bottom* (1851), largely known through engravings by his brother Thomas (see below). Frequently (1839–66) painted Queen Victoria and Prince Albert, whom he taught the art of etching. Completed lions at base of Nelson monument in Trafalgar Square (1866).

His father, **John Landseer** (1769–1852), engraver, painter, and writer on art, illustrated a number of works; engraver to William IV. Sir Edwin's eldest brother, **Thomas** (1795–1880), engraver, pupil of Benjamin Haydon, executed many etchings and engravings of Sir Edwin's animal pictures. Another brother, **Charles** (1799–1879), was a historical painter.

**Land'stei'ner** (lănd'stī'nēr; *Ger.* länt'shtī'nēr), **Karl.** 1868–1943. Pathologist, b. Vienna. M.D., U. of Vienna (1891), where he taught pathology (1909–19); in U.S., member of Rockefeller Institute for Medical Research (1922–39; emeritus). Discovered that there are four main types of human blood; awarded 1930 Nobel prize for physiology and medicine; author of papers on immunology, bacteriology, and pathology.

**Lane** (lān), **Edward William.** 1801–1876. English Orientalist; eminent Arabic scholar. Author of *Manners and Customs of the Modern Egyptians* (1836; a classic), of first accurate version of *A Thousand and One Nights* (1838–40), and *Selections from the Kur-ān* (1843); compiled as life work Arabic thesaurus (5 parts, 1863–74; completed in 3 parts by grandnephew Stanley Lane-Poole, 1877–92). His sister **Sophia** (1804–1891) married (1829) Edward Richard Poole, bibliophile; lived in Egypt (1842–49), wrote *The Englishwoman in Egypt* (1844–46). Sophia's younger son, **Reginald Stuart Poole** [pōōl] (1832–1895), archaeologist, numismatist, and Orientalist, was assistant in antiquities, British Museum (1852); keeper of coins and medals (1870–93).

**Reginald Lane Poole** (1857–1939), grandson of Sophia Poole and nephew of Reginald Stuart Poole, was lecturer on history, Oxford (1886–1910), on diplomatics (from 1896); curator of Bodleian Library (1914–26); author of *The Huguenots of the Dispersion* (1880), *Benedict IX and Gregory VI* (1917), *Studies in Chronology and History* (1934); edited *Historical Atlas of Modern Europe* (1897–1902).

**Stanley Lane'-Poole'** [lān'pōōl'] (1854–1931), brother of Reginald Lane Poole, was a historian and archaeologist; keeper of coin department, British Museum (1874–92); completed Arabic thesaurus of his granduncle E. W. Lane; compiled 14-volume catalogue of Oriental and Indian coins (1875–92); conducted archaeological expeditions to Egypt (1883) and Russia (1886); author of *Histories of the Moors in Spain* (1887), historical works upon Turkey, Barbary corsairs, medieval Egypt, medieval India, biographies, including *Edward William Lane* (1877), *Aurangzib* (1892), *Saladin* (1898).

**Lane, Franklin Knight.** 1864–1921. American political leader, b. near Charlottetown, P.E.I., Canada; to California as a child. Practiced law, San Francisco (from 1894). Member, U.S. Interstate Commerce Commission (1906–13). U.S. secretary of the interior (1913–20).

**Lane, George Martin.** 1823–1897. American classical scholar; author of *Latin Grammar* (1898), the humorous *Lay of the Lone Fishball*, etc.

**Lane, Henry Smith.** 1811–1881. American politician; active in organization of Republican party and a leader of this party in Indiana; governor of Indiana (1861); U.S. senator (1861–67).

**Lane, James Henry.** 1814–1866. American army officer and politician; moved to Kansas (1855); identified himself with the Free State movement in Kansas; elected senator, but not seated by U.S. Senate (1856). Headed an "army of the north" raiding Kansas proslavery districts (1856). U.S. senator (1861–66). Vigorously supported Lincoln; advocated emancipation and arming of the Negroes.

**Lane, John.** American blacksmith and inventor who (c. 1833) made a plow with moldboard and share formed of strips of steel, thus obtaining credit for inventing the first steel plow. Cf. John DEERE. His son **John** (1824–1897), manufacturer of plows in Chicago, invented improvements in steel plows.

**Lane, John.** 1854–1925. English publisher, b. in Devon. Cofounder with Elkin Mathews of Bodley Head Publishing Co. (1887); continued as sole proprietor after partnership dissolved (1894). Also, founder of the *Yellow Book* (1894).

**Lane, Jonathan Homer.** 1819–1880. American physicist, b. Geneseo, N.Y. Invented an optical telegraph and a mercury horizon; first formulated law (Lane's law) that gaseous bodies may from generation of heat by contraction grow hotter as they cool.

**Lane, Joseph.** 1801–1881. American pioneer, soldier, and legislator; governor of Oregon Territory (1849–50); delegate from Oregon Territory to U.S. House of Representatives (1851–59); U.S. senator (1859–61). Candidate for vice-president on Breckinridge ticket (1860); defeated.

**Lane, Margaret.** 1907– . English journalist, novelist, and biographer; m. (1934) Bryan Wallace, son of Edgar Wallace. Author of *Faith, Hope, no Charity* (1935), *Edgar Wallace, the Biography of a Phenomenon* (1938), etc.

**Lane,** Sir **Ralph.** 1530?–1603. English pioneer in America, b. in Northamptonshire. In Queen Elizabeth's service (from 1563); served in Ireland (1583–85). Went to Virginia (1585); in command of colony at Roanoke Island (1585); with colonists, returned to England (1586). Author of an account of the Virginia settlement published in Hakluyt's *Voyages* (1589).

**Lane, Ralph Norman Angell.** Original name of Sir Norman ANGELL.

**Lane, Rose,** *nee* **Wil'der** (wĭl'dẽr). 1887–1968. American writer, b. in De Smet, S.Dak.; m. Gillette Lane (1909; divorced 1918). Author of *Diverging Roads* (1919), *He Was a Man* (1925), *Hill-Billy* (1926), *Cindy* 1928), *Give Me Liberty* (1936), *Free Land* (1938), *The Discovery of Freedom* (1943); coauthor, with Frederick O'Brien, of *White Shadows in the South Seas* (1919).

**Lane,** Sir **William Arbuthnot.** 1856–1943. British surgeon; known for operations for fractures, cleft palates, and intestinal obstruction.

**Lane, William Coolidge.** 1859–1931. American librarian, b. Newton, Mass. A.B., Harvard (1881). Librarian, Harvard (1898–1928).

**Lane Poole** *or* **Lane–Poole.** See under Edward William LANE.

**Lan'franc** (lăn'frăngk). 1005?–1089. Foreign prelate and scholar in England, b. Pavia, Italy; became a Benedictine at Bec (1042), prior (1045); opened school in monastery, to which European scholars flocked; contended against Bérenger in controversy over transubstantiation (1050), and again at council of Tours (1055). Opposed marriage of William the Conqueror with his cousin Matilda but later became reconciled and sought papal dispensation; counseled William in policy of invasion of England; called to England as archbishop of Canterbury (1070–89), continued as chief counselor of William; rebuilt cathedral destroyed by fire in 1067; crowned William II (1087).

**Lan·fran'co** (län·främg'kō), **Giovanni.** 1580–1647. Italian painter of the Eclectic school; master of baroque decorative painting.

**Lan'frey'** (läN'frā'), **Pierre.** 1828–1877. French historian; French ambassador to Switzerland (1871–73); senator for life (1876); author of *Histoire de Napoléon I^er^* (1867–74), in which he tried to destroy the Napoleonic legend.

**Lang** (läng). Name of a family of German potters and wood carvers of Oberammergau, Bavaria, some of whom are known as actors in the famous Oberammergau Passion Plays, as **Andreas Lang** (1862–1933), who played roles of Peter, Simon, King David, and Pilate, and his cousin **Anton** (1875–1938), who enacted role of Christus (1900, 1910, 1922).

**Lang** (lăng), **Andrew.** 1844–1912. Scottish scholar, poet, and man of letters. Keenly interested in history of Stuarts; author of *Pickle the Spy* (1897), a *History of Scotland* (4 vols., 1900–07), *The Mystery of Mary Stuart* (1901), *John Knox and the Reformation* (1905). Took lead in controversy with Max Müller over interpretation of mythology and folk tales; proved folklore the foundation of literary mythology; author of *Custom and Myth* (1884), *The Making of Religion* (1898); a founder of Psychical Research Society. Author of volumes of graceful verse, including *Ballads and Lyrics of Old France* (1872), *xxii Ballads in Blue China* (1880), *Helen of Troy* (1882), *Grass of Parnassus* (1888); author also of *The Monk of Fife* (novel; 1895), *Life and Letters of J. G. Lockhart* (biography; 1896), a series of fairy books, and volumes on Homer, Joan of Arc, and the Baconian claims; translator of Theocritus and Homer (*Odyssey*, with S. H. Butcher, 1879; *Iliad*, with E. Myers and Walter Leaf, 1882).

**Lang, Benjamin Johnson.** 1837–1909. American pianist, conductor, and composer of symphonies, overtures, church music; b. Salem, Mass. His daughter **Margaret Ruthven** (1867– ), b. Boston, composer of songs, and of piano and orchestral works.

**Lang, Cosmo Gordon.** 1864–1945. Anglican prelate, b. Aberdeenshire; bishop of Stepney (1901–08) and canon of St. Paul's; archbishop of York (1908–28); influential member of House of Lords, member of royal commission on divorce, supporter of revised Prayer Book in parliament (1928). Archbishop of Canterbury (1928; resigned 1942); active in social work in industrial centers; lord high almoner to king (from 1933); created baron (1942).

**Lang'dell** (lăng'd'l), **Christopher Columbus.** 1826–1906. American lawyer and educator, b. New Boston, N.H. Grad. Harvard Law School (1853); adm. to bar; practiced, New York City (1854). Professor of law, Harvard Law School (1870–1900) and dean (1870–95); introduced (1870) the "case system" of teaching law, now the system generally used in the U.S. Author of *Cases on the Law of Contracts* (1871), *Cases on Sales of Personal Property* (1872), *Cases on Equity Pleading* (1875).

**Lang'don** (lăng'dŭn), **John.** 1741–1819. American Revolutionary leader, b. Portsmouth, N.H. Active in pre-Revolutionary agitation. Member, Continental Congress (1775, 1776). Naval agent for colonies (1776). Organized and financed Stark's force to oppose Burgoyne, and served in the expedition. Member, Continental Congress (1783). President of New Hampshire (1785); governor of New Hampshire (1788, 1805–09, 1810–11); U.S. senator (1789–1801); 1st pro tempore president of the U.S. Senate (1789).

**Langdon, Samuel.** 1723–1797. American Congregational clergyman; president of Harvard (1774–80).

**Langdon, Stephen Herbert.** 1876–1937. American Assyriologist; professor, Oxford U., England (from 1908). Director of Oxford and Field Museum expedition in Mesopotamia (1923–32). Editor of various Assyrian and Babylonian texts, inscriptions, etc.

**Lang'don–Da'vies** (-dā'vĭs; -dā'vēz), **John.** 1897– . British journalist; author of *Man and his Universe, Inside the Atom, Behind the Spanish Barricades, Invasion in the Snow* (1941), etc.

**Lang'e** (lăng'ē; lăng'ē), **Alexis Frederick.** 1862–1924. American educator; director, school of education, U. of California (1913–22) and dean (1922–24). A leader in junior-high-school movement; originator (with David Starr Jordan) of junior-college movement.

**Lan'ge** (län'gĕ), **Antoni.** 1861–1929. Polish poet and literary critic; to Paris for political reasons (1886). Author of lyric and philosophical poems, historical dramas, of *Studies in French Literature* (1897), and of translations from Baudelaire and other French writers.

**Lang'e** (läng'ĕ), **Carl Georg.** 1834–1900. Danish physician and psychologist; with William James set forth the James-Lange theory of emotion; author of a history of materialism.

**Lang'e** (läng'ĕ), **Christian Louis.** 1869–1938. Norwegian pacifist and historian. Taught history at Norwegian Nobel Institute, Oslo (1890–1909); secretary to Nobel Commission of Norwegian Parliament (1900–09) and member of Nobel Prize Committee; Norwegian representative at International Peace Conference, The Hague (1907); secretary-general of International Parliamentary

Union (1909–33); European correspondent for Carnegie Peace Endowment (1917–30); Norwegian delegate to League of Nations (1920–38); won Nobel peace prize (1921; with Karl Hjalmar Branting); lectured on international problems in Europe and America (1926). Author of *The European Civil War* (1915), *History of Internationalism* (1919), *International Politics* (1924), *Imperialism and Peace* (1938), etc.

**Lang′e** (läng′ĕ), **Ernst Philipp Karl.** *Pseudonym* **Philipp Ga′len** (gä′lĕn). 1813–1899. German novelist; author chiefly of character novels and novels of manners.

**Lange, Friedrich Albert.** 1828–1875. German Neo-Kantian philosopher, sociologist, and economist; introduced Darwinistic sociology and philosophy of history into Germany and paved way for revisionism.

**Lange, Helene.** 1848–1930. German educator and feminist, a leader in movement for women's education in Germany. Edited the monthly journal *Die Frau* (from 1893); author of *Die Frauenbewegung in ihren Modernen Problemen* (1909), etc.

**Lange, Johann Peter.** 1802–1884. German Protestant theologian.

**Lang′e** (lång′ĕ), **Julius Henrik.** 1838–1896. Danish art historian and critic; discovered law of frontality in art representation.

**Lang′e** (läng′ĕ), **Ludwig.** 1825–1885. German classical scholar; author of *Handbuch der Römischen Altertümer* (3 vols., 1856–71), etc.

**Lange, Samuel Gotthold.** 1711–1781. German poet, b. Halle. With his friend Immanuel Jakob Pyra, attacked Gottsched and opposed use of rhyme in poetry; with Pyra, wrote *Thyrsis' und Damons Freundschaftliche Lieder* (1745).

**Lang′e** (lång′ĕ), **Sven.** 1868–1930. Danish writer and critic; dramatic critic of *Politiken*, Copenhagen (from 1900). Author of dramas, novels, and stories.

**Lang′en** (läng′ĕn), **Eugen.** 1833–1895. German engineer; inventor of an early form of internal-combustion engine (with Otto; 1867).

**Lang′en·beck** (lăng′ĕn·bĕk), **Karl.** 1861–1938. American ceramic engineer, b. Cincinnati, Ohio. Originated "Rookwood" faïence and aventurine pottery glazes; consulting ceramic engineer, U.S. Bureau of Standards.

**Lang′en·ho′ven** (läng′ĕn·hōō′fĕn), **C. J.** d. **1932.** South African poet and politician; senator in South African parliament; author of *Die Stem van Suid-Afrika* (*The Voice of South Africa*), put to music by M. L. de Villiers, accepted as a national anthem.

**Lang′er** (lång′ĕr), **František.** 1888–1965. Czech writer; among his novels are *The Golden Venus* (1911), *The Iron Wolf* (1920); among his plays, *Saint Wenceslas* (1911), *The Periphery* (1925), *The Conversion of Ferdyš Pištora* (1929), *The Camel Goes Through the Needle's Eye* (1930).

**Lang′er** (läng′ĕr), **Johann Peter von.** 1756–1824. German portrait and religious painter; conducted school for tapestry painting (until 1801); director of Munich Acad. (1806). His son and pupil, **Robert** (1783–1846), was a painter; works include frescoes in churches in Munich, and sketches illustrating Dante's *Divina Commedia.*

**Langer, Susanne Knauth.** 1895– . American philosopher, b. New York City. At Radcliffe Coll. (1927–42), Columbia U. (1945–50), Conn. Coll. (1954–62); author of *Philosophy in a New Key* (1942), *Feeling and Form* (1953), *Philosophical Sketches* (1962), etc.

**Lang′er·hans** (läng′ĕr·häns), **Paul.** 1847–1888. German physician; authority on pathological anatomy.

**Lan′ge·ron′** (läNzh′rôN′), Count **Andrault de.** 1763–1831. French general in Russian service; general of division at Austerlitz (1805); distinguished himself at Leipzig (1813); stormed Montmartre and entered Paris with Allies (1814); governor general of New Russia (southern Russia, 1822 ff.).

**Lan′ge·vin′** (läNzh′văN′), Sir **Hector Louis.** 1826–1906. Canadian political leader; mayor of Quebec (1858–60); solicitor general (1864–66); postmaster general (1866–67); active in furtherance of confederation; one of commissioners sent to London (1866). Member, Dominion House of Commons (1867–96); secretary of state (1867–69); minister of public works (1869–73, 1879–91).

**Langevin, Paul.** 1872–1946. French physicist; known for work on secondary X rays, the properties of ions in gases, the kinetic theory of gases, Brownian movement, the theory of magnetism, the theory of relativity.

**Lang′feld** (lăng′fĕld), **Herbert Sidney.** 1879–1958. American psychologist, b. Philadelphia, Pa. Professor and director of Psychological Laboratory, Princeton (1924–47). Author of *The Aesthetic Attitude* (1920), etc.; joint author and editor of *Introduction to Psychology* (1939); editor of *Psychological Review.*

**Lang′ham** (lăng′ăm), **Simon.** 1310–1376. English prelate. Monk, prior, abbot of abbey of St. Peter at Westminster; treasurer of England (1360); bishop of Ely (1361); chancellor of England (1363); first to deliver speeches in parliament in English; archbishop of Canterbury (1366); expelled Wycliffe and secular clergy from Oxfordshire Hall; cardinal (1368); forced to resign archbishopric (1368); died at Avignon.

**Lang′hans** (läng′häns), **Carl Gotthard.** 1732–1808. German architect; director of royal buildings, Berlin (1788); designed the Hatzfeld Palace at Breslau (1766–74), the Brandenburg Gate (1788–91) and Bellevue Castle at Berlin, theaters at Charlottenburg, Potsdam, and Berlin, various Protestant churches in Silesia, etc.

**Lang′horne** (lăng′hôrn), **John.** 1735–1779. English poet. Curate in London; rector of Blagdon, Somerset; prebendary of Wells; known for translation, with his brother **William** (1721–1772), of Plutarch's *Lives* (1770).

**Lan·gie′wicz** (län·gyĕ′vēch), **Marjan.** 1827–1887. Polish patriot; leader of Polish insurgents in the district of Sandomierz (1863) and designated by his army dictator of Poland; defeated by Russians, fled to Austria, and was imprisoned. Later, took refuge in Switzerland and France (under name **Lan′glé′** [läN′glā′]); finally, entered Turkish army, and died in Constantinople.

**Lang–Köstlin, Josephine.** See under Christian Reinhold Köstlin.

**Lang′land** (lăng′lănd) *or* **Lang′ley** (-lĭ), **William.** 1332?–?1400. Supposed name of English poet, native of western Midlands; author of the allegorical poem *The Vision of William concerning Piers the Plowman* (usually called *The Vision of Piers Plowman*). Probably educated at monastery of Great Malvern, and engaged on the poem (1362–92). The poem was produced in three versions, held by Skeat and Jusserand to be work of a single author, held by Manly to be work of five different authors. Once thought to be author also of *Richard the Redeless*, poem in remonstrance with Richard II.

**Lan′gle de Ca′ry′** (läN′gl′ dē kȧ′rē′), **Fernand Louis Armand Marie de.** 1849–1927. French soldier; commanded 4th army in the Ardennes, battle of the Meuse, and first battle of the Marne; promoted (Dec., 1915) to command of a group of armies in the center; on mission in Algeria and Tunisia (Mar. 25, 1916–Dec. 1, 1917).

**Lan′glès′** (läN′glĕs′), **Louis Mathieu.** 1763–1824. French Orientalist; instrumental in establishing École des Langues Orientales, in Paris, and its first administrator (1795).

**Lang′ley** (lăng′lĭ), **Edmund of.** 1st Duke of **York.** See York.

**Langley, John Newport.** 1852–1925. English physiologist; proprietor and editor, *Journal of Physiology* (1894–1925). Conducted researches into the sympathetic nervous system (1890–1906).

**Langley, Samuel Pierpont.** 1834–1906. American astronomer and airplane pioneer, b. Roxbury, Mass. Received only high-school education. Interested in astronomy from boyhood. Professor of physics and astronomy, and director of Allegheny Observatory, in Western U. of Pennsylvania, now U. of Pittsburgh (1867–87); conducted observations of solar eclipses in 1869, 1870, 1878. Invented bolometer for measuring distribution of heat in spectrum of sun; by use of bolometer, determined transparency of atmosphere to different solar rays, and measure of increase of their intensity at high altitudes. Organized expedition to top of Mount Whitney, California, for his experiments (1881). Secretary, Smithsonian Institution, Washington, D.C. (from 1887); there continued studies of solar radiation; observed solar eclipse of 1900. Began study of possibilities of flight in heavier-than-air machines; built models of planes; his model no. 5 achieved a flight of 3000 ft. on Potomac River (May 6, 1896), model no. 6 a flight of 4200 ft. (November, 1896), first flights of mechanically propelled heavier-than-air machines in the world. Full-sized machine, designed to carry an operator, failed in two trials (Oct. 8 and Dec. 8, 1903), and funds were lacking at the time for further experiments. Langley now recognized as pioneer in theory and construction of heavier-than-air machines; his machine is on exhibition in the National Museum, Washington, D.C.; the flying field near Norfolk, Va., is named in his honor. See Alexander Graham BELL.

**Lan′glois′** (läN′glwȧ′), **Charles Victor.** 1863–1929. French author of treatises on medieval French history.

**Langlois, Jean Charles.** 1789–1870. French soldier and battle painter; best known for his painting of military panoramas, as *Bataille de la Moskova*, *Incendie de Moscou*, *Prise de Malakof*.

**Langlois, Victor.** 1829–1869. French Orientalist; made study of French-Armenian documents and relations of period of crusades.

**Lang′muir** (lăng′mūr), **Irving.** 1881–1957. American chemist, b. Brooklyn, N.Y. Met.E., Columbia (1903); Ph.D., Göttingen (1906). Research chemist (from 1909), associate director (from 1932), Research Laboratory, General Electric Co., Schenectady, N.Y. Developed gas-filled tungsten electric lamp, electron-discharge apparatus, a high-vacuum pump, a process of welding using atomic hydrogen; with Gilbert N. Lewis, originated the Lewis-Langmuir atomic theory; awarded the 1932 Nobel prize for chemistry for his work in surface chemistry.

**Lang′ston** (lăng′stŭn), **John Mercer.** 1829–1897. American Negro lawyer and educator; professor of law and dean, Howard U. (1869–76); U.S. minister to Haiti and chargé d'affaires to Santo Domingo (1877–85). President, Virginia Normal and Collegiate Institute, Petersburg, Va. (from 1885).

**Lang′stroth** (lăng′strŏth), **Lorenzo Lorraine.** 1810–1895. American apiarist; interested himself in beekeeping; invented a movable-frame beehive which revolutionized the bee industry; also, developed methods of scientific management for large-scale honey production.

**Lang′toft** (lăng′tŏft), **Peter.** d. 1307? English author of a chronicle in French verse dealing with history of England up to death of Edward I. The latter part of the chronicle was translated into English by Robert Mannyng (*q.v.*).

**Lang′ton** (lăng′tŭn), **Stephen.** d. 1228. English theologian, historian, and poet. Doctor in arts and theology, Paris, where he lived 25 years; composed Biblical commentaries, divided Old Testament books of Vulgate into chapters; author of *Questiones* on limits of episcopal power and on papal dispensation. Made cardinal priest (1206); elected and consecrated archbishop of Canterbury (1207) but kept out of see by King John (until 1213); sided with barons against John, and first of subscribing witnesses to Magna Charta; suspended for failing to publish pope's excommunication of barons (1214, reinstated 1218); in synod at Osney (1222) promulgated set of constitutions still recognized as binding in English ecclesiastical courts. Said to have made transition from feudal church of Lanfranc to national church.

**Lang′try** (lăng′trĭ), **Lillie.** *Maiden name* **Emilie Charlotte Le Bret′on** (lĕ brĕt′′n). 1853–1929. Known as "the Jersey Lily." Famed British beauty and actress, b. Island of Jersey; m. Edward Langtry (1874; d. 1897), and Hugo Gerald de Bathe (1899). First appeared professionally on stage in London (1881); acted under own management in London and U.S.

**Lan′guet′** (läN′gĕ′), **Hubert.** 1518–1581. French publicist; known for his *Vindiciae contra Tyrannos sive De Principis in Populum, Populique in Principem Legitima Potestate* (1579), a treatise upholding daring theories on liberty of conscience and of thought, and rights of peoples against their rulers.

**La·nier′** (lȧ·nēr′), **Sidney.** 1842–1881. American poet, b. Macon, Ga. Served in Confederate army in Civil War. After a tragic period of ill health and financial difficulty (1865–73), devoted himself to music and literature. Played in Peabody Symphony Orchestra, Baltimore (1874). Lecturer on English literature, Johns Hopkins U. (1879). Died of tuberculosis. Author of *Tiger-Lilies* (1867), *Poems* (1877), *The Science of English Verse* (1880), *The English Novel* (1883). Among his best-known poems are *Corn*, *The Song of the Chattahoochee*, *The Marshes of Glynn*, *Sunrise*, *The Revenge of Hamish*. Elected to American Hall of Fame (1945).

**Lan′i·gan** (lăn′ĭ·găn), **George Thomas.** 1846–1886. Journalist, b. St. Charles, Canada; to U.S. (c. 1867). Author of humorous and satirical verse fables and ballads, including *Threnody for the Ahkoond of Swat* and *The Amateur Orlando*.

**Lan′jui′nais′** (läN′zhü·ē′nĕ′), Comte **Jean Denis.** 1753–1827. French politician; member of States-General (1789) and National Assembly; Girondist member of the Convention (1792); member of the Council of the Ancients; elected senator (1800); opposed the Consulate (1802) and the establishment of the Empire (1804); voted for abdication of Napoleon (1814).

**Lan′kes·ter** (lăng′kĕs·tẽr; -kĭs-), **Edwin.** 1814–1874. English physician and scientist; published works on physiology and sanitary science. His son Sir **Edwin Ray** (1847–1929) attained distinction as a morphologist; pioneered in researches on embryology of Mollusca; conducted important studies on protozoan parasites; founder, Marine Biological Association (1884); author of *Degeneration* (1880), *Extinct Animals* (1905), *Science from an Easy Chair* (1910; 1912), *Great and Small Things* (1923), etc.

**Lan′man** (lăn′măn), **Charles Rockwell.** 1850–1941. American Oriental scholar; professor of Sanskrit, Harvard (from 1880). Author of *Sanskrit Reader*, *Vocabulary*, *Notes* (8 issues, 1884–1927), *Beginnings of Hindu Pantheism* (1890), etc.

**Lan′ner** (län′ẽr), **Josef.** 1801–1843. Austrian dance composer; creator of the modern Viennese waltz, music director of masquerade balls (1828) and of court balls in Vienna. Composed waltzes, galops, cotillions, quadrilles, polkas, and marches.

**Lannes** (lȧn), **Jean.** Duc **de Mon′te·bel′lo** (dē mōn′-tȧ·bĕl′lō). Prince **de Sié′vers′** (syā′vâr′). 1769–1809. French soldier in the Revolutionary and Napoleonic armies; distinguished himself under Napoleon in the Italian campaign (1796); accompanied Napoleon on Egyptian expedition (1798–99). Won victory of Montebello (1800); engaged at Marengo (1800), Austerlitz (1805), Jena (1806), Friedland (1807), and in Spanish campaign (1808–09). Created marshal of France (1804). Mortally wounded at Essling (May, 1809). His son **Napoléon Auguste Lannes,** Duc **de Montebello** (1801–1874), was a diplomat; minister of foreign affairs (1839) and of marine and colonies (1847); ambassador at St. Petersburg (1858–64). Another son, **Gustave Olivier Lannes,** Comte **de Montebello** (1804–1875), was a soldier; aide-de-camp to Napoleon III; commanded French corps in the occupation of Rome (1862–64), and a cavalry division in the Imperial Guard (1865–69). A son of Napoléon Auguste, **Gustave Louis Lannes,** Marquis **de Montebello** (1838–1907), was a diplomat; ambassador at Constantinople (1886) and at St. Petersburg (1891–1902), where he played important part in negotiating the Franco-Russian alliance.

**La Noue** (lȧ nōō′), **François de.** 1531–1591. French Huguenot soldier; lost an arm at Fontenay-le-Comte (1570), had iron artificial arm made; hence his nickname **Bras de Fer** (brȧ dē fâr). Commanded forces at La Rochelle (1572–73) and in Flanders (1578–80); mortally wounded at the siege of Lamballe (1591).

**Lan′re·zac′** (läɴr′zȧk′), **Charles Louis Marie.** 1852–1925. French general in World War; commanded 5th army at outbreak of war and was driven back by German assaults; was relieved of his command (Sept. 3, 1914).

**Lans′bur·y** (lănz′bĕr·ĭ; -brĭ; *in U.S., also* -bĕr′ĭ), **George.** 1859–1940. British Labor party leader and politician; joined Socialist party (1890); member of parliament (1910–12; 1922 ff.). First commissioner of works (1929–31); leader of Labor party (1931–35); mayor of Poplar (1919–20, 1936–37). Author of *Your Part in Poverty, My Quest for Peace* (1938), etc.

**Lans′downe** (lănz′doun), Baron. See *George Grenville* or *Granville*, under Sir Richard GRENVILLE (1541?–1591).

**Lansdowne,** Marquises of:

Sir **William Pet′ty** (pĕt′ĭ). 2d Earl of **Shel′burne** (shĕl′bĕrn). 1st Marquis of **Lansdowne.** 1737–1805. English statesman; great-grandson of Sir William Petty (*q.v.*). President of Board of Trade (1763); opposed government in regard to Wilkes (1763) and Stamp Act (1764); as secretary of state under Pitt, thwarted in effort toward conciliation of American colonies (1766–68); opposed government, chiefly on American policy (1768–82); home secretary under Rockingham (1782); 1st lord of treasury and prime minister (1782–83); conceded American independence, made peace with France and Spain; overthrown by Fox and North (1783).

His son Sir **Henry Pet′ty–Fitz·mau′rice** (-fĭts·mô′-rĭs). 3d marquis. 1780–1863. Moderate Whig leader; as chancellor of exchequer under Grenville, raised property tax from 6½ to 10 per cent (1806); advocated abolition of slavery (1809–29); president of council (1830–41, 1846–52); member of cabinet without office (1852–63). Father of Sir **Henry Thomas Petty–Fitzmaurice** (1816–1866), 4th marquis, undersecretary of state for foreign affairs under Palmerston (1856–58).

**Henry Charles Keith Petty–Fitzmaurice.** 5th marquis. 1845–1927. Son of 4th marquis. Held minor posts (1868–83) in two Gladstonian administrations; was object of No Rent campaign in Ireland. As governor general of Canada (1883–88), saw completion of Canadian Pacific Railway, Newfoundland fisheries settlement with U.S., and second Riel rebellion. As viceroy of India (1888–93), stabilized rupee by closing Indian mints to free coinage. As secretary for war (1895–1900), received blame for early mistakes of Boer War. As foreign secretary (1900–05), accomplished alliance with Japan (1902) and Anglo-French Entente (1904), handled affairs of Venezuela blockade (1903) and Alaskan boundary (1903) with U.S. Member of coalition administration without portfolio (1915–16); repudiated by the government and by his party for famous letter to *Daily Telegraph* (Nov., 1917), outlining possible peace terms.

**Lansfeld,** Countess of. See Lola MONTEZ.

**Lan′sing** (lăn′sĭng; *Brit.* län′-), **Robert.** 1864–1928. American lawyer and statesman, b. Watertown, N.Y. U.S. associate counsel, Bering Sea arbitration (1892); U.S. counsel, Bering Sea claims commission (1896–97). U.S. solicitor, Alaskan Boundary Tribunal (1903); counsel, North Atlantic Fisheries, at The Hague (1909–10); agent for United States, American and British Claims Arbitration (1912–14). Counselor, U.S. Department of State (1914–15); U.S. secretary of state (1915–20). Resigned at request of President Wilson (Feb. 12, 1920). Practiced law, Washington, D.C. (from 1920). Author of *The Peace Negotiations* (1921), etc. See Kikujiro ISHII.

**Lan′son′** (läɴ′sôɴ′), **Gustave.** 1857–1934. French critic; author of *Histoire de la Littérature Française* (1894), *L'Idéal Français dans la Littérature, de la Renaissance à la Révolution* (1928), etc.

**Lan′ston** (lăn′stŭn), **Tol′bert** (tŏl′bērt). 1844–1913. American inventor, b. Troy, Ohio. Began (1883) working on typesetting machine; received (1887) patent for a "type forming and composing machine," and (1897) introduced commercially his perfected Monotype. Cf. Ottmar MERGENTHALER.

**Lan′syer′** (läɴ′syā′), **Maurice Emmanuel.** 1835–1893. French painter, esp. of marines and landscapes of Brittany.

**Lan′za** (län′tsä), **Giovanni.** 1810?–1882. Italian statesman; prime minister of Italy (1869–73).

**Lan′zi** (län′tsē), **Luigi.** 1732–1810. Italian archaeologist and antiquary; advanced theory of Greek influence on Etruscan civilization. His works include *Saggio di Lingua Etrusca* (1789), *Storia Pittorica dell' Italia* (1792).

**La·od′i·ce** (lā·ŏd′ĭ·sē). Wife of Antiochus II of Syria and mother of Seleucus II and Antiochus Hierax (*qq.v.*).

**Lao–tzu** *or* **Lao–tse** *or* **Lao–tsze** (lou′dzŭ′). *Orig.* **Li Erh.** c. 604–531 B.C. One of the great philosophers of China; lived under the Chou dynasty; b. in Honan province. Founder of Taoism, a liberal religion, setting forth conformity to the *Tao*, right conduct or eternal spirit of righteousness, and believing that forms and ceremonies are entirely useless; differed greatly from Confucianism. Traditionally, author of *Tao Tê Ching* ("teaching of Tao"). His teachings elaborated by Chuang-tzu (4th century B.C.); later Taoism degenerated into a system of magic (see CHANG TAO-LING).

**La′par′ra′** (lȧ′pȧ′rȧ′), **Raoul.** 1876–1943. French composer of the operas *La Habañera* (1908) and *La Jota* (1911), the orchestral suite *Un Dimanche Basque*, a string quartet, violin sonatas, piano pieces, etc.

**La Pé′rouse′** (lȧ pā′rōōz′), Comte **de. Jean François de Ga′laup′** (dē gȧ′lō′). 1741–1788. French sailor and explorer; served against the English in the Seven Years' War (1756–63); promoted captain (1780). Commanded exploring expedition in Asiatic waters (1785–88); discovered La Pérouse Strait (between Sakhalin and Hokkaido); turned back to Australian and Tasmanian coasts; was lost with entire expedition by shipwreck in the New Hebrides (1788).

**Lapide, a.** *Or* **Lapidanus.** See Johann HEYNLIN.

**La'pi·doth–Swarth'** (lȧ'pē·dŏt·swärt'), **Hé'lène'** (ā'lĕn'), *nee* **Swarth.** 1859–1941. Dutch lyric poet; m. F. Lapidoth (1892). Author of poems in French and esp. in Dutch, including the collections *Poetry* (1892) and *Verse* (1893), *Deep Waters* (1897), *Late Roses* (1920), *Evening Dew* (1930); also wrote dramatic poems, as *Dolorosa* (1911), prose stories, and sketches.

**La'place'** (lȧ'plȧs'), **Ernest.** 1861–1924. American surgeon, b. New Orleans; studied abroad under Pasteur, Lister, and Koch. Devised forceps for intestinal anastomosis; wrote on antisepsis and intestinal surgery; worked in brain surgery.

**La Place** (lȧ plȧs'), **Pierre Antoine de.** 1707–1793. French playwright and literary historian; first French writer to attempt (in his *Théâtre Anglais*, 1745–48) translation of Shakespeare's principal plays.

**La'place'** (lȧ'plȧs'), Marquis **Pierre Simon de.** 1749–1827. French astronomer and mathematician, b. in Normandy, son of a farmer. To Paris (1767); demonstrated his gift for mathematics to d'Alembert and through his influence obtained professorship in mathematics at École Militaire; appointed by Bonaparte (1799) minister of interior, but replaced because of incompetence; entered Senate (1799); its vice-president (1803). In celestial mechanics, announced (1773) discovery of the invariability of the planetary mean motions (a discovery of importance in establishing the stability of the solar system); discovered dependence of the moon's acceleration on the secular changes in the eccentricity of the earth's orbit; worked out laws of motion of the first three moons of Jupiter; set forth his nebular hypothesis in a note in *Exposition du Système du Monde* (1796); investigated tides, specific heats, capillary action, electricity, equilibrium of a rotating fluid mass; worked on theory of probability. Chief works: *Théorie du Mouvement et de la Figure Elliptique des Planètes* (1784), *Théorie des Attractions des Sphéroïdes et de la Figure des Planètes* (1785), *Traité de Mécanique Céleste* (5 vols.; 1799–1825), *Théorie Analytique des Probabilités* (1812–20), *Essai Philosophique sur les Probabilités* (1814). See also Immanuel KANT.

**La'pointe'** (lȧ'pwăɴt'), **Ernest.** 1876–1941. Canadian lawyer, politician, and diplomat. Member, Canadian House of Commons (from 1904); minister of marine and fisheries (1921); minister of justice (1924–30, 1935 ff.); also, attorney general (1935 ff.). Canadian delegate at League of Nations (1922); negotiator of treaty with France (1922), and of treaty with U.S. concerning Pacific fisheries; accompanied Mackenzie King to London as representative of Canada to Imperial Conference (1926); head of Canadian delegation to Imperial Conference (1929); member of the delegation at Third Imperial Conference (1937).

**La'pouge'** (lȧ'po͞ozh'), Comte **Georges Va'cher' de** (vȧ'shā' dẽ). 1854–1936. French anthropologist; supported theory of racial significance in cultural development; chief work, *L'Aryen, son Rôle Social* (1899).

**Lap'pa'rent'** (lȧ'pȧ'räɴ'), **Albert Auguste Co'chon' de** (kô'shôɴ' dẽ). 1839–1908. French geologist and mining engineer; author of *Traité de Géologie* (1882), *Leçons de Géographie Physique* (1896), etc.

**Lap'pen·berg** (lăp'ĕn·bĕrĸ), **Johann Martin.** 1794–1865. German historian, b. Hamburg; archivist to Hamburg Senate (1823–63) and collaborator on *Monumenta Germaniae Historica.* Completed Sartorius's history of the Hanseatic League (1830); author of a *Geschichte von England* (2 vols., 1834–37; continued by Pauli and translated, 1845, into English by Benjamin Thorpe), and of works largely on the history of Hamburg.

**La'prade'** (lȧ'prȧd'), **Pierre Marin Victor Ri'chard' de** (rē'shȧr' dẽ). 1812–1883. French poet; his verse includes *Les Parfums de la Madeleine* (1839), *La Colère de Jésus* (1840), *Psyché* (1842), *Odes et Poèmes* (1844), *Symphonies* (1855), *Idylles Héroïques* (1858), and a number of patriotic poems during the Franco-Prussian War (1870–71). Author also of critical essays.

**La Ramée, Pierre.** See Petrus RAMUS.

**Lar'a·mie** (lăr'ȧ·mĭ), **Jacques.** d. 1821. Fur trapper, in Colorado and southeastern Wyoming; b. prob. in Canada. Reputed first white man to reach upper course of Laramie River. Various places and natural features in this region have been named in his honor, as, the Laramie Mountains, Fort Laramie, Laramie County, and the city of Laramie, Wyo.

**Lar'baud'** (lȧr'bō'), **Valéry.** 1881–1957. French journalist and novelist; author of *A. O. Barnabooth, Poésies et Journal Intime* (1908–13), *Fermina Marquez* (1911), *Jaune, Bleu, Blanc* (1927), etc.

**Lar'cher'** (lȧr'shā'), **Pierre Henri.** 1726–1812. French Hellenist; translator of Herodotus.

**Lar'com** (lär'kŭm), **Lucy.** 1824–1893. American author and educator, b. Beverly, Mass. Millworker, Lowell, Mass. (1835–46); schoolteacher in Illinois (1846–52), and at Wheaton College, Norton, Mass. (1854–62). Author of *Similitudes from Ocean and Prairie* (1854), *Poems* (1869), *A New England Girlhood* (1889), *The Unseen Friend* (1892). Collaborated with Whittier in editing anthologies.

**Lard'ner** (lärd'nẽr), **Dionysius.** 1793–1859. Irish writer on science. M.A., Dublin (1819); wrote scientific treatises, as on algebraic geometry, differential and integral calculus, and the steam engine; known esp. for his *Cabinet Cyclopaedia*, for which he wrote articles on hydrostatics, pneumatics, mathematics (1829–44).

**Lardner, Nathaniel.** 1684–1768. English Biblical and patristic scholar; founder of modern school of critical research in early Christian literature.

**Lardner, Ring** (rĭng), *in full* **Ring'gold** (rĭng'gōld) **Wilmer.** 1885–1933. American humorist and short-story writer; author of *Bib Ballads* (1915), *You Know Me, Al* (1915), *Gullible's Travels* (1917), *Treat 'Em Rough* (1918), *The Real Dope* (1918), *The Big Town* (1921), *What of It?* (1925), *Round Up* (collected stories; 1929), etc.; author with George S. Kaufman of play *June Moon* (1929).

**Lar'dy'** (lȧr'dē'), **Charles.** 1847–1923. Swiss diplomat and jurist; first Swiss representative at Hague Tribunal (1899).

**La·re'do Brú** (lä·rā'tho͞ bro͞o'), **Federico.** 1875–1946. Cuban soldier and politician; fought in war of independence (1898–99); led revolutionary movement against Pres. Zayas y Alfonso (1920–24); founder of Union Nationalist party; president of Cuba (1936–40); under influence of Col. Fulgencio Batista (*q.v.*).

**La're·vel'lière'–Lé'peaux'** (lȧr'vĕ'lyȧr'lā'pō'), **Louis Marie.** 1753–1824. French politician; member of States-General (1789), National Convention (1792), Council of Ancients (1795); president of the Directory (1795–99).

**La Rey, Jacobus Hercules De.** See DE LA REY.

**Lar'gil'lière'** *or* **Lar'gi'llierre'** (lȧr'zhē'lyȧr'), **Nicolas de.** 1656–1746. French painter; called to London by James II (1684) and painted portraits of king, queen, prince of Wales, and important persons at court.

**Lar'go Ca'bal·le'ro** (lär'gō kä'bä·lyā'rō), **Francisco.** 1869–1946. Spanish labor leader and statesman. Imprisoned for political activities (1917). Minister of labor in various governments (1931–33); again imprisoned (1934) for complicity in revolt in Asturias; acquitted (1935); resigned as Socialist leader (1935); prime minister

(1936–37); imprisoned by Nazis (1942–45); minister of interior of Republicans in exile (1946).

**La·ri·o′nov** (lŭ·ryĭ·ô′nôf), **Mikhail Fëdorovich.** 1881–1964. Russian painter and decorator.

**La Rive** (lȧ rēv′), **Auguste Arthur de.** 1801–1873. Swiss physicist. Investigated specific heat of gases and temperature of the earth's crust; made discoveries in connection with magnetism, electrodynamics, the properties of the voltaic arc, and the passage of electricity through rarefied media; discovered a process for electrogilding. Author of *Traité d'Électricité Théorique et Appliquée* (1854–58), etc. His father, **Charles Gaspard de La Rive** (1770–1834), physicist and chemist, was inventor of a galvanometer; one of founders of museum of natural history and the botanic garden at Geneva.

**La′ri′vey′** (lȧ′rē′vā′), **Pierre de.** *Orig. surname* **Giun′ta** (jōōn′tä). 1540?–?1612. French playwright and translator, of Italian descent; author of comedies adapted from Italian originals and written in prose, an innovation for the French stage at the time: regarded as one of creators of French comedy.

**Lar′mi′nat′** (lȧr′mē′nȧ′), **Edgard de.** 1895– . French army officer; grad. St. Cyr; served in World War (1915–18), in various colonies (1920–31), in Levant (1936–40); high commissioner of Free French Africa (1940–41); deputy commander in Syria (1941); commander in Libya, Italy, France (1942–45).

**Lar′mi·nie** (lär′mĭ·nĭ), **William.** 1849–1900. Irish poet, associated with Irish literary revival; author of *Glanlua and Other Poems* (1889), *Fand and Other Poems* (1892), *West Irish Folk Tales and Romances* (1893).

**Lar′mor** (lär′môr), Sir **Joseph.** 1857–1942. British mathematician, b. Ireland. Worked on mathematical problems in electrodynamics and thermodynamics; studied atomic structure.

**Lar′ned** (lär′nĕd; -nĭd), **Josephus Nelson.** 1836–1913. Librarian, b. Chatham, Ontario, Canada, of American parentage. Librarian, Buffalo, N.Y. (1877–97). Compiler of Larned's *History for Ready Reference* (5 vols., 1894–95; supplements, 1901 and 1910), and author of volumes of general history.

**Larned, William Augustus.** 1872–1926. American lawn-tennis player, b. Summit, N.J. Seven times national singles champion and six times member of United States Davis Cup team.

**La Roche** (lä rôsh′), **Karl von.** 1796?–1884. German actor; met Goethe in Weimar, and created role of Mephistopheles in Goethe's *Faust* (1829); engaged for life at Burgtheater, Vienna (1833).

**La Roche** (lä rôsh′), **Sophie,** *nee* **Gu′ter·mann** (gōō′tẽr·män). 1731–1807. German novelist. Had love affair with young Wieland; m. (1753) Georg Michael Frank von Lichtenfeld, called La Roche. Grandmother of Clemens Brentano (*q.v.*) and Elisabeth von Arnim (see under Ludwig von ARNIM). Author of novels and stories modeled chiefly after Richardson.

**La Roche du Maine** (lȧ rôsh′ dü mĕn′), Marquis **de. Jean Pierre Louis de Lu′chet′** (dẽ lü′shĕ′). 1740–1792. French writer; collaborated with Rivarol, Laclos, and Mirabeau in writing (1789) *Galerie des États Généraux,* depicting leading political figures of the time.

**La Roche′fou′cauld′** (lȧ rôsh′fōō′kō′), Duc **François de.** 1613–1680. French writer; intrigued against Richelieu; joined the Fronde and was wounded at the siege of Paris; enjoyed the friendship of Mme. de Longueville, Mme. de Sévigné, and especially Comtesse de La Fayette. His literary fame rests upon his *Réflexions ou Sentences et Maximes Morales* (first pub. anonymously, 1665) and *Les Mémoires sur la Régence d'Anne d'Autriche* (1662).

**La Roche′fou′cauld′-Lian′court′** (-lyäɴ′kōōr′), Duc **François Alexandre Frédéric de.** 1747–1827. French philanthropist; founded at Liancourt a school for the education of children of poor soldiers, later called École des Enfants de la Patrie. Member of the States-General (1789); an émigré from France until the Consulate. Created a peer of France at the Restoration (1814).

**La Roche′jac′que·lein′** *or* **La Roche′ja′que·lein′** (lȧ rôsh′zhȧ′klăɴ′). French royalist family, including **Henri Du Ver′gier′** (dü vĕr′zhyā′), Comte **de La Rochejacquelein** (1772–1794), a Vendean leader, generalissimo (Oct., 1793), defeated at Le Mans (1793), killed in action at Nouaillé (Mar. 4, 1794); his brother **Louis Du Vergier,** Marquis **de La Rochejacquelein** (1777–1815), also a Vendean leader, killed in action near Saint-Gilles (June 4, 1815); the wife of Louis, **Marie Louise Victoire,** *nee* **de Do′nis′san′** [dē dô′nē′säɴ′] (1772–1857), intensely royalist in sympathy and publisher of *Mémoires* (1815); another brother, **Auguste Du Vergier,** Comte **de La Rochejacquelein** (1784–1868), involved in the Vendean uprising (1815), field marshal under the Restoration (1818) and took part in Spanish campaign (1823) and the Turkish war (1828); and a nephew of Auguste, **Henri Auguste Georges Du Vergier,** Marquis **de La Rochejacquelein** (1805–1867), leader of Legitimist party in the Chamber of Deputies (1842–48) but later accepted the republic and the Second Empire, becoming senator (1852).

**La′ro′mi′guière′** (lȧ′rô′mē′gyâr′), **Pierre.** 1756–1837. French philosopher; author of *Leçons de Philosophie* (1815–18), etc.

**La Rouërie,** Marquis **de.** See Charles ARMAND.

**La′rousse′** (lȧ′rōōs′; *Angl.* lȧ-), **Pierre Athanase.** 1817–1875. French grammarian, lexicographer, and encyclopedist; prepared series of improved textbooks for elementary instruction; founded a journal for teachers, *L'École Normale* (1859). Best known today for his *Grand Dictionnaire Universel du XIXᵉ Siècle* (1866–76), in preparation of which he spent last years of his life.

**Lar′ra** (lär′rä), **Mariano José de.** *Pseudonym* **Fí′ga·ro** (fē′gä·rō). 1809–1837. Spanish satirist, playwright, and miscellaneous writer; author of a historical play, *Macías* (1834), a comedy, and a novel, but best known for bitter satires published over his pseudonym.

**Lar′rey′** (lȧ′rā′), Baron **Dominique Jean.** 1766–1842. French military surgeon; with Napoleon in Egypt and Russia; surgeon in chief, Hôpital du Gros-Caillou, and Hôtel des Invalides. Credited with introducing the *ambulance volante* (moving hospital).

**L'Ar′ronge′** (lȧ′rôɴzh′), **Adolf.** 1838–1908. German conductor, theater manager, and playwright.

**Lar′sen** (lär′s'n), **Hanna As′trup** (äs′trōōp). 1873–1945. American editor, b. Decorah, Iowa; literary editor (1913–21) and editor (from 1921), *American-Scandinavian Review,* New York City; author of *Knut Hamsun* (1922), *Selma Lagerlöf* (1935); translator of modern Danish books, and editor of anthologies.

**Larsen, Johannes Anker.** See ANKER LARSEN.

**Lar′sen** (lär′s'n), **Karl Halfdan Eduard.** 1860–1931. Danish author of plays, novels, including *Dr. Ix* (1896) and *A Woman's Confession* (1901), and studies of the life and language of Copenhagen's lower classes.

**Lars′son** (lärs′sôn), **Carl.** 1853–1919. Swedish painter and etcher; joined plein-airists at Paris (1877, 1880–85); produced oils and water colors chiefly of his home and family life, including water-color series in book form (*The House,* 1899; *The Larssons,* 1902; *With Us in the Country,* 1907), mural paintings, portraits, witty drawings and caricatures, illustrations, etc.

**Lar′tet′** (lȧr′tĕ′), **Édouard Armand Isidore Hippolyte.**

1801–1871. French archaeologist; one of founders of modern paleontology. Discovered fossils near Auch (1834); investigated anthropological remains in French caves; discovered evidence in cave of Aurignac that man existed contemporaneously with extinct mammals.

**La Rue** (lȧ rü′), **Pierre** *or* **Pier′chon′** (pyĕr′shôN′) **de.** *Latinized* **Petrus Pla·ten′sis** (plȧ·tĕn′sĭs). d. 1518. Composer and contrapuntist, of the Franco-Flemish school; composer of masses, motets, and other church music, French chansons, etc.

**La Salle** (lȧ săl′; *Fr.* lȧ sȧl′), Sieur **de. Robert Ca′ve·lier′** (kȧ′vĕ·lyā′). 1643–1687. French explorer in America. Pioneer settler and trader, near Montreal (1666). On expedition to Lake Ontario region (1669); later claimed to have discovered Ohio River at this time. Backed by Frontenac, governor of Quebec, obtained from Louis XIV grants (1673 and 1678) of lands and trading privileges in west. Descended Mississippi River to Gulf of Mexico (arrived Apr. 9, 1682), claiming whole valley for Louis XIV and naming the region Louisiana. Returned to France; named viceroy of North America. Organized expedition for colonizing; sailed from France (1684); landed by error at what is now Matagorda Bay, Texas. On way to mouth of Mississippi, was murdered by his men (March 19, 1687).

**La Salle** *or* **La Sale** (lȧ sȧl′), **Antoine de.** 1388?–?1462. French courtier and writer; author of a romance, *Jehan de Saintré*, and reputed author of *Les Cent Nouvelles Nouvelles* and *Les Quinze Joyes de Mariage.*

**La′salle′** (lȧ′sȧl′), Comte **Antoine Charles Louis de.** 1775–1809. French soldier in Revolutionary and Napoleonic armies; killed in a charge at battle of Wagram (1809).

**la Salle,** Saint **Jean Baptiste de.** See JEAN BAPTISTE DE LA SALLE.

**La·saulx′** (lä·sō′), **Ernst von.** 1805–1861. German archaeologist and philosopher; author of works on the decadence of Hellenism, the theological basis of all systems of philosophy, the philosophy of fine arts, etc.

**Lasca, Il.** See Antonio Francesco GRAZZINI.

**Las′ca·ris** (lăs′kȧ·rĭs). A Byzantine noble family that first became prominent through **Theodore I Lascaris,** first Nicaean emperor (1206–22) of the Eastern Roman Empire, son-in-law of the Emperor Alexius III. He was succeeded as emperor at Nicaea by his eldest daughter's second husband, John III Ducas, whose son **Theodore II** took the name Lascaris to show his direct descent from the founder.

**Lascaris, Constantine.** *Greek* **La′ska·ris** (*Mod. Gr.* lä′skä·rēs). 1434?–1501. Greek grammarian. Settled in Milan after fall of Constantinople (1453); taken under patronage of Duke Francesco Sforza; published *Greek Grammar*, first book printed in Greek (1476); taught Greek in Rome, Naples, and Messina. His younger brother **Andreas Johannes,** *or* **Janus, Lascaris** (1445?–1535), *called* **Rhyn′da·ce′nus** (rĭn′dȧ·sē′nŭs), was a Greek scholar and teacher; lived at Florence at court of Lorenzo de' Medici; after his patron's death, went to Paris (1495); gave public instruction in Greek; at head of Greek college in Rome (1515) on invitation of Pope Leo X.

**Las Ca′sas** (läs kä′säs), **Bartolomé de.** 1474–1566. Spanish Dominican missionary and historian, b. Seville; called "Apostle of the Indies." To Hispaniola as a planter (1502); ordained priest (1510), first to be ordained in New World. Began (1514) to labor for Indians, preaching against slavery system; devoted life to this cause; to Spain (1515) to intercede with Ferdinand; unsuccessful in his model Indian colony at Cumaná, Venezuela (1520–21); became Dominican at Santo Domingo (1522); secured passage of laws to protect Indians (1542); bishop of Chiapas (1544–47); returned to Spain. Wrote several works on America, esp. *Brief Relation of the Destruction of the Indies* (1552) and *Historia General de las Indias*, important historical source (first printed 1875).

**Las Cases** (lȧs kȧz′), Comte **Emmanuel Augustin Dieudonné de.** 1766–1842. French historian; served in Condé's royalist army (1792); émigré in England (1792–99). To France (1799); prepared an *Atlas Historique* (published under name Lesage, 1803–04); honored by Napoleon. Accompanied Napoleon to St. Helena and wrote from Napoleon's dictation part of his memoirs. Sent away from St. Helena (Nov., 1816) for trying to smuggle a letter to Lucien Bonaparte. Published *Mémoires de E. A. D. Comte de las Cases* (1818), *Mémorial de Sainte Hélène* (1823).

**Las′celles** (lăs′′lz). Name of English family bearing title earl of **Hare′wood** (här′wo͝od; hâr′-), including: **Henry Lascelles** (1767–1841), 2d Earl of Harewood, 2d son of Edward, 1st earl (cr. 1812); M.P. (1796); became Viscount Lascelles on death of elder brother (1814). His grandson Sir **Frank Cavendish Lascelles** (1841–1920), diplomat; consul general in Egypt (1878–79) and Bulgaria (1879–86); minister to Rumania (1887) and Persia (1891); ambassador to Russia (1894) and Berlin (1896–1908); active promoter of Anglo-German amity (till 1914). **Henry George Charles** (1882–1947), 6th earl, soldier; son of Henry Ulick Lascelles (1846–1929), 5th earl; educ. Eton and Sandhurst; member of diplomatic corps; aide-de-camp to governor general of Canada (1907–11); served in World War; D.S.O. and Croix de guerre; as Viscount Lascelles, m. (1922) Princess Mary, only daughter of King George V.

**Lasco, John.** See Jan ŁASKI.

**Lascy, Franz** and **Pierre.** See Peter LACY.

**La Ser′na y Hi′no·jo′sa** (lä sĕr′nä ē ē′nô·hō′sä), **José de.** 1770–1832. Spanish general; major general, commanding Upper Peru (1816); viceroy (1821–24); captured by Sucre, with whole Spanish army, at battle of Ayacucho (Dec. 9, 1824).

**Las′ker** (läs′kẽr), **Eduard.** 1829–1884. German politician, b. in Posen, of Jewish parentage. Took part in Revolution of 1848 at Vienna; entered government service of Prussia (1856); member, Prussian Chamber of Deputies (1865–79), German Reichstag (from 1867); active in Progressive party (until 1866), then as cofounder and a leader of National Liberal party; took part in civil consolidation of German empire and in many legislative and administrative enactments; withdrew from National Liberal party (1880), following differences with Bismarck over financial and economic policies, and joined secessionists (1881).

**Lasker, Emanuel.** 1868–1941. German chess master; won world championship from Steinitz (1894) and held title until defeated by Capablanca at Havana (1921). Author of works on chess, mathematics, and philosophy.

**Las′ker–Schü′ler** (-shü′lẽr), **Else.** 1876–1945. German author of volumes of lyric verse, novels, and the play *Die Wupper* (1908).

**Las′ki** (lăs′kĭ), **Harold Joseph.** 1893–1950. English political scientist; professor, U. of London (from 1926). Author of *The Problem of Sovereignty* (1917), *Authority in the Modern State* (1919), *Communism* (1927), *Liberty in the Modern State* (1930), *Democracy in Crisis* (1933), *Parliamentary Government in England* (1938), *The American Presidency* (1940), etc.

**Łas′ki** (läs′kē), **Jan.** *Angl.* **John Las′ki** (lăs′kĭ) *or* **Las′co** (lăs′kō). *Lat.* **Johannes a Las′co** (ā lăs′kō). 1499–1560. Polish-born religious reformer; friend and associate of Erasmus in Basel (1524–25). Became austere Calvinist; superintendent of London church of foreign Protestants (1550) and influential figure in Edward VI's court. To Poland (1556–60); aided in establishing and spreading principles of Reformation.

**Las'ky** (lăs'kĭ), **Jesse L.** 1880–1958. American motion-picture producer, b. San Francisco. Organizer and head of Jesse L. Lasky Feature Play Co. (from 1914), and assoc. producer of RKO Radio Pictures, Inc.

**La'so de la Ve'ga** (lä'sō thā lä vā'gä), **García** *or* **Gar·cí'as** (gär·sē'äs) *or* **Gar·cí'** (gär·sē'). = GARCILASO DE LA VEGA.

**Las·salle'** (lä·säl'), **Ferdinand.** 1825–1864. German Socialist, b. Breslau; disciple of Karl Marx (from 1848) and Socialist propagandist; imprisoned for six months (1848). Champion of the working classes (from c. 1862); formulated so-called iron law of wages; proposed organization of co-operative associations for production with use of public credit for necessary capital; founded Der Allgemeine Deutsche Arbeiterverein (1863) to promote use of political power by workers; regarded as founder of German Social Democratic party. Killed in a duel. See *Helene von Dönniges*, under Wilhelm von DÖNNIGES.

**Las'salle'** (là'sàl'), **Jean Louis.** 1847–1909. French operatic baritone.

**Las·sell'** (lă·sĕl'), **William.** 1799–1880. English astronomer; built observatory near Liverpool and devised improvements in construction of reflecting telescopes. By means of one of his telescopes verified discovery of Neptune (1847); became first to ascertain clearly the composition of the Uranian system. Catalogued many new nebulae; discovered (Oct. 10, 1846) satellite of Neptune, and (Sept. 19, 1848) the 8th satellite of Saturn, and (Oct. 24, 1851) the two inner satellites of Uranus.

**Las'sen** (läs'ĕn), **Christian.** 1800–1876. Indologist, b. Bergen, Norway; professor, Bonn (1830); introduced study of Indian archaeology into Germany. His works include *Die Altpersischen Keilinschriften von Persepolis* (1836), in which he deciphered Old Persian cuneiform inscriptions, editions of various Sanskrit texts, etc.

**Las'sen** (làs''n), **Eduard.** 1830–1904. Composer, b. Copenhagen; taken to Brussels at age of two. Succeeded Liszt as conductor of the court theater in Weimar. Among his operas are *Frauenlob* and *Le Captif;* also wrote symphonies, songs, and music for Sophocles's *Oedipus*, Goethe's *Faust* and *Pandora.*

**Las'so, Or·lan'do di** (ŏr·län'dō dē läs'sō). *Also* **Or·lan'dus** *or* **Ro'land de Las'sus** (ŏr·län'dŭs [rō'länt] dĕ läs'ŭs). *Orig. name* **Ro'land' De·lat'tre** *or* **de Lat'tre** (rô'läN' dē·làt'r'). 1532?–1594. Composer, b. Mons, Belgium; called to Munich by Duke Albert V of Bavaria (1556); director of court chamber music (1560); ennobled by Maximilian II and made knight of golden spur by the pope. Regarded as leading composer (next to Palestrina) of 16th century; composed over 2000 works, including music for the seven penitential psalms, motets, masses, Magnificats, Italian madrigals and villanelle, French chansons, seven books of sacred and secular German songs, etc.

**Las'son** (läs'ōn), **Adolf.** 1832–1917. German Hegelian philosopher. Translated Aristotle's *Metaphysics* (1907), *Nicomachean Ethics* (1909), etc.; wrote *Das Kulturideal und der Krieg* (1868), *System der Rechtsphilosophie* (1882), *Der Leib* (1898), etc.

**Lass'witz** (läs'vĭts), **Kurd.** 1848–1910. German philosopher; author also of poetic and Utopian novels, including *Auf Zwei Planeten* (1897) and *Nie und Immer* (1902), etc.

**Las'tey'rie' du Sail'lant'** (làs'tĕ'rē' dü sà'yäN'). Name of a French family including: Comte **Charles Philibert de Lasteyrie du Saillant** (1759–1849), journalist who founded (1814) first lithographic establishment in Paris. His son Comte **Ferdinand Charles Léon** (1810–1879), archaeologist; as member of Chamber of Deputies (1842 ff.), protested Louis Napoleon's coup d'état (Dec. 2, 1851) and retired from political life.

**Last'man** (läst'män), **Pieter.** 1583–1633. Dutch painter and engraver; taught Rembrandt in Amsterdam (1623); works include mainly Biblical and mythological subjects, and portraits.

**La'sus of Her·mi'o·ne** (lā'sŭs, hûr·mī'ō·nē). Greek lyric poet of late 6th century B.C.; rival of Simonides and teacher of Pindar.

**Lász'ló** (läs'lō). Hungarian form of LADISLAS.

**László de Lom'bos** (dē lôm'bōsh), **Philip Alexius,** *Hung.* **Fülöp Elek.** 1869–1937. Painter, b. Budapest; to England (1907), naturalized (1914). Best known for his portraits.

**La Taille** (là tä'y'), **Jean de.** 1540?–1608. French writer; author of *Saül* (tragedy; 1572), *Le Négromant* (comedy; 1573), *Discours Notable des Duels* (1607), etc.

**Lat'a·né** (lăt''n·ā), **John Holladay.** 1869–1932. American historian, b. Staunton, Va.; professor, Johns Hopkins (from 1913). Author of *America as a World Power* (1907), *The United States and Latin America* (1920), *History of American Foreign Policy* (1927), etc.

**La'tham** (lā'thăm; -thăm), **John.** 1740–1837. English ornithologist; one of founders of Linnaean Society (1788); author of *A General History of Birds* (11 vols., 1821–28), for which he designed, etched, and colored the illustrations himself.

**Latham, Robert Gordon.** 1812–1888. English philologist and ethnologist; author of textbooks on English language, philology, grammar, etymology; completely revised Johnson's dictionary (1870); author of works on ethnology of British Isles and colonies and Europe. Advanced in *Elements of Comparative Philology* (1862) the view that Aryan race originated not in central Asia but in Europe.

**Lath'bur'y** (lăth'bĕr'ĭ; -bēr·ĭ), **Mary Artemisia.** 1841–1913. American author, b. Manchester, N.Y. Wrote esp. books for children, and hymns, including *Day is Dying in the West*, *Arise and Shine*, and *Break Thou the Bread of Life.*

**La'throp** (lā'thrŭp), **Francis Augustus.** 1849–1909. American mural painter; assisted La Farge in murals of Trinity Church, Boston (1877); painted reredos of St. Bartholomew's Church, New York, and proscenium of Metropolitan Opera House; also executed stained-glass memorial window in Princeton chapel. His brother **George Parsons** (1851–1898) was a journalist and miscellaneous writer; author of *Rose and Roof-tree* (a volume of poems; 1875), *A Study of Hawthorne* (1876), etc. George's wife **Rose** was daughter of Nathaniel Hawthorne (see Mother ALPHONSA).

**Lathrop, Julia Clifford.** 1858–1932. American social-service worker, b. Rockford, Ill. Chief, Children's Bureau, U.S. Department of Labor (1912). Assessor-member of advisory committee on child welfare, League of Nations (1925–32). Resident often of Hull House, in Chicago, and friend of and co-worker with Jane Addams, who wrote her biography (*My Friend, Julia Lathrop;* 1936).

**Lathrop, William Langson.** 1859–1938. American landscape painter, b. Warren, Ill.

**Lathyrus.** See PTOLEMY VIII.

**Lat'i·mer** (lăt'ĭ·mẽr), **Hugh.** 1485?–1555. English champion of Reformation and Protestant martyr; zealous preacher of reformed doctrines; preached two sermons on "the card" showing allegorically how to win salvation by playing trumps (1529); on question of lawfulness of Henry VIII's marriage to Catherine of Aragon, took king's side; on charge of heresy made complete submission (1532); after Henry VIII's repudiation of papal authority, co-operated with Cranmer and Thomas Cromwell in advising king (1534); bishop of Worcester (1535), resigned (1539) because he opposed Act of the Six Articles; by his preaching, established principles of Reformation in popular mind; for refusal to accept the Six Articles sent to Tower (1546); in Edward VI's reign resumed preaching after eight years' silence with sermon against "unpreaching prelates," but refused to resume his see; on Mary's accession committed to Tower; found guilty, with Cranmer and Ridley, of heresy, and burned at stake, with Ridley.

**La·ti'ni** (lä·tē'nē), **Brunetto.** 1212?–?1294. Florentine writer and statesman; member of Guelph party; exile in France (1260–69); chancellor of Florence (1273); friend and counselor of Dante (*Inferno* xv); chief work, the prose encyclopedia *Li Livres dou Trésor* written in dialects of northern France.

**La'touche'** (là'to͞osh'), **Gaston.** 1854–1913. French painter; studied under Manet.

**La Tour** *or* **La'tour'** (là'to͞or'), **Abbé de.** See Isabelle de CHARRIÈRE.

**La Tour, Charles Cagniard de.** See CAGNIARD DE LA TOUR.

**La Tour, Maurice Quen'tin' de** (käN'tăN' dẽ). 1704–1788. French painter, best known for pastel portraits, as of Diderot, Voltaire, d'Alembert, Louis XV, and Jean Jacques Rousseau.

**La Tour d'Au'vergne'** (dô'vĕrn'y'). Name of French family, originally from village of Latour in Auvergne, dating from 10th century; it divided into several branches, including counts of Auvergne, dukes of Bouillon and **Al'bret'** (ȧl'brĕ'), and viscounts of Turenne; see BOUILLON and TURENNE. **Madeleine de La Tour d'Auvergne** (d. 1519) married Lorenzo de' Medici, Duke of Urbino; mother of Catherine de Médicis (*q.v.*). One of best-known members of family was **Théophile Malo Cor'ret'** [kô'rĕ'] (1743–1800); French soldier; added (1771) surname de La Tour d'Auvergne to his own, being descended from an illegitimate half brother of Turenne. Served in army (1767–91); refused to emigrate (1792); fought in early campaigns of Revolution (1792–95). Held prisoner by the English (1795–97); studied Celtic philology; returned as captain to army, serving in Germany and Switzerland (1797–1800); killed in action at Oberhausen. His courage a legend in French army; named by Carnot (1800) "First Grenadier of France"; his name kept on pay roll of his company until 1814, and when called at all parades the answer given was "Mort au champ d'honneur!" (Dead on the field of honor).

**La'tou·rette'** (lä'to͞o·rĕt'), **Kenneth Scott.** 1884–1968. American Baptist clergyman and Oriental scholar, b. Oregon City, Ore. B.A. (1906), Ph.D. (1909), Yale. On teaching staff, College of Yale in China (1910–12); professor of missions, Yale (1921–27). Editor of Chinese terms for *Webster's New International Dictionary, Second Edition.* Author of *Development of China* (1917), *Development of Japan* (1918), *The Chinese, Their History and Culture* (1934), *A History of the Expansion of Christianity* (7 vols., 1937–45), etc.

**La'treille'** (là'trâ'y'), **Pierre André.** 1762–1833. French entomologist; associated with Haüy, Fabricius, and Lamarck in Paris; known esp. for his classification of insects and crustaceans.

**La Tré'moille'** (là trā'mo͞o'y'). Noble French family, the most distinguished member being **Louis de La Trémoille,** Vicomte **de Thou·ars'** (twȧr), Prince **de Tal'mont'** [tȧl'môN'] (1460–1525), soldier, known as **Che·va'lier' sans Re·proche'** (shẽ·vȧ'lyā' säN' rẽ·prôsh'); commanded the army of Italy and conquered the Milanese (1500); governor of Burgundy; admiral of Guienne (1502) and of Brittany (1514); defended Picardy (1521–23); was killed in action at Pavia (Feb. 24, 1525).

**La'tro** (lā'trō), **Marcus Porcius.** 55 B.C.?–3 (or 4) A.D. Spanish-born rhetorician in Rome; friend of the elder Seneca; Ovid was among his disciples.

**La·trobe'** (lȧ·trōb'), **Benjamin Henry.** 1764–1820. Architect and engineer, b. Fulneck, Yorkshire, Eng.; to U.S. (1796). Designed Bank of Pennsylvania building, at Philadelphia (1798); proposed, designed, and built Philadelphia city water-supply system, first in America (1799). Appointed by Jefferson a surveyor of public buildings, Washington, D.C. (1803), he designed south wing of the Capitol, made alterations in the White House, remodeled the Patent Office, and drew plans for the Marine Hospital. Went into partnership with Robert Fulton, Robert R. Livingston, and Nicholas J. Roosevelt to build steamboats for navigation of upper Ohio River; lost his fortune on failure of scheme. After destruction of the Capitol by British in 1814, Latrobe was engaged to rebuild it (1815–17).

**Latrobe, Christian Ignatius.** 1758–1836. English musical composer; took orders in the Unitas Fratrum; composed anthems, chorales, and instrumental works; edited first English edition of *Moravian Hymn Tune Book;* known for his *Selection of Sacred Music from Works of the Most Eminent Composers of Germany and Italy* (6 vols., 1806–25).

**Lat'ti·more** (lăt'ĭ·mōr), **Owen.** 1900– . American Orientalist and writer; educ. Cumberland, Eng., and Harvard; expert on the Far East, esp. central Asia; editor in chief of *Pacific Affairs;* professor, Johns Hopkins; named by Pres. Roosevelt political adviser to Chiang Kai-shek (1941–42); director, Pacific bureau of Office of War Information (1942–45).

**La'tude'** (là'tüd'), **Jean Henry.** *Also variously known as* **Jean Dan'ry'** (däN'rē'), **Dan'ger'** (däN'zhā'), **Je·dor'** (zhẽ·dôr'), **Ma'sers' d'Au'bres'py'** (mȧ'sâr' dō'brā'pē'), **Masers de Latude.** 1725–1805. French army officer who attempted to make himself a hero by sending an imitation infernal machine to Mme. de Pompadour and then warning her not to handle it because he had discovered a plot against her. His scheme was found out; imprisoned without trial for 35 years (1749–84); his fate was cited at outbreak of French Revolution (1789) as one of great injustices of ancien régime; voted pension by Legislative Assembly.

**Latur.** See LAUTARO.

**Latz'ko** (läts'kō), **Andreas.** 1876– . Writer, b. Budapest; resident in Salzburg. Author of plays, including *Ten Years* (1900), *Hans in Luck* (1904), the comedy *Apostle* (1911); novels and stories, as *The Wild Man* (1911), the pacifistic *Men in War* (1917), *Seven Days* (1931); a biography of Lafayette, etc.

**Lau'be** (lou'bẽ), **Heinrich.** 1806–1884. German playwright, novelist, and theater director; active in Young Germany movement and editor of its organ (1833–34; 1843–44). Expelled from Saxony (1834); imprisoned (in Berlin, 1834–35; Muskau, 1837) for participation in liberal movement. To Leipzig as journalist and dramatic critic (1839); director of Hofburgtheater, Vienna (1849–67), Leipzig Stadttheater (1869–70), and Vienna Stadttheater (1872–74, 1875–80). Author of critical works, including *Das Neue Jahrhundert* (essays; 2 vols., 1833); works on the theater; travel sketches and stories, as *Französische Lustschlösser* (3 vols., 1840); plays, including the tragedies *Monaldeschi* (1841) and *Graf Essex* (1856), and the comedies *Rococo* (1846) and *Gottsched und Gellert* (1847), and the Schiller play *Die Karlsschüler* (1847); novels and stories, including the trilogy *Das Junge Europa* (1833–37).

**Laud** (lôd), **William.** 1573–1645. English prelate, b. Reading. Openly expressed antagonism to dominant Calvinism and Puritanism; dean of Gloucester (1616); bishop of St. David's (1621–26). Intimate with Buckingham, gained free scope, from accession of Charles I, for his activities against Calvinists; supported king's prerogative in conflict with parliament; assisted in Buckingham's defense; privy councilor (1626); bishop of London (1628); chancellor of Oxford U. (1630). Archbishop of Canterbury (1633); virtual first minister, with Strafford and Charles I forming triumvirate dedicated to absolutism in church and state; sought to root out Presbyterianism in Scotland, as also Calvinism in England; forbade Englishmen abroad to attend Calvinistic services; sought to supplant, through judgments of Court of High Commission and the Star Chamber, justification by faith, and Sabbatarianism, with ritualism, doctrine of real presence, celibacy, and confession; provoked riot in St. Giles, Edinburgh, which led to Bishops' Wars and the Long Parliament, which impeached him of high treason; committed to Tower (1641); condemned and beheaded (1645) under an ordinance of attainder.

**Lau'der** (lô'dẽr), Sir **Harry.** *Real surname* **Mac-Len'nan** (măk·lĕn'ăn). 1870–1950. Scottish singer; gained great popularity for rendition of Scottish songs and ballads, many of his own composition, including *Roamin' in the Gloamin'*, *Wee Hoose amang the Heather.*

**Lauder, Robert Scott.** 1803–1869. Scottish painter; known for *The Bride of Lammermoor* (1831) and *The Trial of Effie Deans* (1840).

**Lauder, William.** d. 1771. Scottish Latin scholar and literary impostor, who sought to prove (1747), by means of forged, garbled, and interpolated quotations, *Paradise Lost* plagiarized from 17th-century Latin poets. See John DOUGLAS.

**Lauderdale,** Earls and Duke of. See MAITLAND family.

**Lau'don** *or* **Lou'don** (*Ger.* lou'dōn; *Eng.* lou'd'n), Baron **Gideon Ernst von.** 1717–1790. Austrian field marshal, general in Seven Years' War, distinguished himself at Prague and Kolín (1757), and at Hochkirch (1758); victorious at Kunersdorf (1759); defeated La Motte-Fouqué at Landeshut, stormed Glatz, but was defeated at Liegnitz (1760); captured Schweidnitz (1761); commanded army in Bohemia as field marshal in War of Bavarian Succession (1778); commanded in Turkish war at capture of Belgrade (1789); generalissimo of anti-Prussian army in Moravia (1790).

**Lau'don'nière'** (lō'dô'nyâr'), **René Gou'laine'** (gōō'-lĕn') **de.** fl. 1562–1582. French Huguenot, sent by Coligny to establish colony in America (1562 and 1564); escaped to France when his settlement on St. Johns River, Florida, was devastated by Spaniards (Sept. 20, 1565); author of *L'Histoire Notable de la Floride* (publ. Paris, 1586). Cf. Jean RIBAUT.

**Lau'e** (lou'ĕ), **Max von.** 1879–1960. German physicist; discovered (1912) the interference of X rays in crystals and as a result was able to measure the wave lengths of X rays and to study the structure of crystals; contributed to development of the theories of relativity, electromagnetism, and diffraction of light. Awarded the 1914 Nobel prize for physics. Author of *Das Relativitätsprinzip* (1911), *Die Interferenz der Röntgenstrahlen* (1923), etc.

**Lauenburg line.** See ERNESTINE LINE.

**Lau'fer** (lou'fẽr), **Berthold.** 1874–1934. Anthropologist and Orientalist, b. Cologne, Germany; to U.S. (1898); on expeditions to Eastern Siberia (1898–99), to China (1901–04), to Tibet and China (1908–10), to China (1923). On staff of Field Museum of Natural History, Chicago (from 1908; curator of anthropology, from 1915).

**Lauff** (louf), **Joseph von.** 1855–1933. German writer of peasant epics, plays, novels, esp. of the lower Rhine.

**Laugh'lin** (lăf'lĭn), **James Laurence.** 1850–1933. American political economist; professor, Cornell (1890–92), Chicago (1892–1916). Editor of *Journal of Political Economy* (1892–1933). Author of *Study of Political Economy* (1885), *Facts about Money* (1885), *Gold and Prices since 1873* (1887), *Reciprocity* (1903), *Money, Credit, and Prices* (2 vols., 1931), etc.

**Laugh'ton** (lô't'n), **Charles.** 1899–1962. English actor on stage and (from 1932) in motion pictures, chiefly in Hollywood, including *The Private Life of Henry VIII*, *The Barretts of Wimpole Street*, *Ruggles of Red Gap*, *Mutiny on the Bounty.* Married (1929) **Elsa Lan'ches-ter** (lăn'chĕs·tẽr; -chĭs-), English actress, who has appeared in many plays with him.

**Lau'mont'** (lō'môɴ'), **François Pierre Nicolas Gil'let'** (zhē'lĕ') **de.** 1747–1834. French mineralogist; discovered the mineral laumontite, which is named for him.

**Lau'nay'** (lō'nā'). See Baronne de STAAL DE LAUNAY.

**Launay, Bernard René Jor'dan'** (zhôr'däɴ') **de.** 1740–1789. French soldier; last commander of the Bastille, in Paris; murdered by the mob at the taking of the Bastille (July 14, 1789).

**Launay,** Vicomte **Charles de.** Pseudonym of Delphine de GIRARDIN.

**Lau'ra** (lô'rȧ). 1308?–1348. French lady whose praises are sung by Petrarch in his sonnets and canzoni; identified traditionally with **Laure de Noves** (lôr' dẽ nôv'), wife of Hugues de Sade, of Avignon.

**Lau·ra'na** (lou·rä'nä), **Francesco da.** ab. 1420–1503. Italian sculptor and medalist.

**Laurana, Luciano da.** fl. 1468–1482. Italian architect; known esp. for ducal palaces of Urbino and Gubbio executed for Federigo da Montefeltro, Duke of Urbino.

**Lau'rence** (lô'rĕns; lŏr'ĕns). Variant of LAWRENCE.

**Laurence, French.** 1757–1809. English lawyer; aided Burke in preparation of case against Warren Hastings; friend and literary executor of Burke.

**Laurence, Samuel.** 1812–1884. English portrait painter.

**Lau'ren'cin'** (lō'räɴ'săɴ'), **Marie.** 1885–1956. French painter; identified with the modernists. Also known for her designs of decorations and costumes for the Comédie Française and for the Ballets Russes of Diaghilev.

**Lau'rens'** (lō'räɴs'), **Henri.** 1885–1954. French artist, b. in Paris; associated with ultramodern art movement.

**Lau'rens** (lô'rĕns; lŏr'ĕns), **Henry.** 1724–1792. American Revolutionary statesman, b. Charleston, S.C. Export merchant in Charleston (1748?–64); planter (from 1764). President, first provincial congress in South Carolina and of South Carolina Council of Safety (1775). Member, Continental Congress (1777–79); president (Nov. 1, 1777–Dec. 9, 1778). Captured by British (1780) on way to negotiate treaty with Dutch; confined in Tower of London; exchanged for Lord Cornwallis (1782). On mission in France and England (1782–84). His son **John** (1754–1782) was an officer on Washington's staff (from 1777); envoy extraordinary to France (1780); stormed British redoubt at Yorktown; negotiated terms of Cornwallis's surrender. Engaged in irregular warfare in South Carolina; killed in action (1782).

**Lau'rens'** (lō'räɴs'), **Jean Paul.** 1838–1921. French historical painter.

**Lau'rent'** (lō'räɴ'), **Auguste.** 1807–1853. French chemist; studied naphthalene and phenol and their derivatives; propounded the nucleus theory of organic radicals; with C. F. Gerhardt, worked on classification of organic compounds. Laurent's acid is named after him.

**Laurent, François.** 1810–1887. Belgian historian and jurist; championed liberalism and progressive ideas; helped introduce savings banks into Belgium. Author of *Principes de Droit Civil* (33 vols., 1869–78), *Droit Civil International* (8 vols., 1880–81), etc.

**Lau·rent'** (lô·rĕnt'), **Ro·bert'** (rô·bâr'). 1890–1970. Sculptor, b. Concarneau, France; to U.S. (1902). Best known for his wood carving and his direct cutting in stone and marble.

**Lau'ren'tie'** (lô'räN'tē'), **Pierre Sébastien.** 1793–1876. French publicist; founder of *Courrier de l'Europe* (1831); editor of *La Quotidienne* and editor in chief of its successor, *Union.* Vigorous upholder of legitimist cause.

**Lau·ren'ti·us** (lô·rĕn'shĭ·ŭs; -shŭs). See Saint LAWRENCE.

**Laurentius.** Antipope (498–505). Elected in opposition to Pope Symmachus; banished by Theodoric, King of the Goths.

**Laurentius Andreae.** See Lars ANDERSON.

**Laurentius Justinianus.** See LAWRENCE JUSTINIAN.

**Lau'ri·a** (lou'ryä) *or* **Lu'ri·a** (lōō'ryä) *or* **Lo'ri·a** (lô'ryä), **Ruggiero di.** 1250?–1305. Italian naval commander; admiral of fleet defeating French off Malta (1283), Angevin fleet in Bay of Naples (1284), French fleet again off coast of Catalonia (1285); regarded as chief figure in naval war caused by the Sicilian Vespers (1282).

**Lau'ri·er** (lô'rĭ·ā; *Fr.* lô'ryā'), Sir **Wilfrid.** 1841–1919. Canadian statesman, b. St. Lin, Quebec, of French Roman Catholic parents. Practiced law in Montreal and Arthabaska. Member of Quebec legislature (1871) and of Dominion House of Commons (1874); spoke in defense of Riel and for union between French and English races in Canada and for a policy of moderate protection; held post in Liberal cabinet briefly (1877). Liberal leader in succession to Edward Blake (1888); with policy of unrestricted reciprocity with U.S., prime minister of Canada (1896–1911); put into effect fiscal preference of $33\frac{1}{3}\%$ in favor of goods from Great Britain; dispatched Canadian troops to help of Great Britain in Boer War; aided construction of second transcontinental railroad, the Grand Trunk; assumed imperial fortresses of Halifax and Esquimalt; promoted development of western territories, made tariff arrangement with U.S. (1900); defeated (1911) over reciprocity agreement with U.S. and naval question; supported Conservative government's war policy (1914–18) but refused to form coalition (1917).

**Lau'ris'ton'** (*Fr.* lô'rēs'tôN'; *Eng.* lô'rĭs·tŭn), Marquis **de. Jacques Alexandre Bernard Law** (*Fr.* lō, *formerly* läs; *Eng.* lô). 1768–1828. Grandnephew of John Law (*q.v.*). French soldier; aide-de-camp to Napoleon (1800); served in Austerlitz campaign, captured Ragusa (1807), and distinguished himself at Wagram (1809). Rallied to the Bourbon cause at the Restoration; peer of France (1815); created marquis (1817), and marshal of France (1823).

**Lau'rit·sen** (lou'rĭt·s'n), **Charles Christian.** 1892–1968. Physicist, b. in Denmark; assistant professor (1930), professor (from 1935), Calif. Inst. Tech. Known for work on X rays, electron emission, and nuclear physics.

**Laus'se·dat'** (lōs'dà'), **Aimé.** 1819–1907. French army officer and geodesist. Used camera lucida in drawing plans; credited with invention of photogrammetry; invented several astronomical instruments.

**Laut** (lôt), **Agnes C.** 1871–1936. Canadian journalist and writer, b. in Ontario. On staff of Manitoba *Free Press,* at Winnipeg; later, settled in New York City. Author of *Lords of the North* (1900), *Heralds of Empire* (1902), *Pathfinders of the West* (1904), *Pioneers of the Pacific Coast* (1915), *Pilgrims of the Santa Fe* (1931), etc.

**Lau·ta'ro** (lou·tä'rō) *or* **La·tur'** (lä·tōōr'). 1535?–1557. Araucanian Indian chieftain, of Chile; led Indians against Spaniards (1553–57); killed in action at battle of Mataquito. His exploits are celebrated in the *Araucana* of the Spanish poet Ercilla y Zúñiga.

**Lau'tré'a'mont'** (lō'trā'à'môN'), **le Comte de.** *Real name* **Isidore Lucien Du'casse'** (dü'kàs'). 1846–1870. Poet, identified as a precursor of surrealism, b. Montevideo, Uruguay, but settled in Paris (from c. 1860); author of *Chants de Maldoror* (1868–70).

**Lautrec.** See TOULOUSE-LAUTREC.

**Lau'zun'** (lō'zûN'), Duc **de.** See Duc de BIRON.

**Lauzun,** Duc **de. Antonin Nom'par' de Cau'mont'** (nôN'pàr' dē kō'môN'). 1633–1723. French soldier; won favor of Louis XIV and received important military commands. Led French force to Ireland and fought for James II at battle of the Boyne (1690).

**La·val',** **Carl Gustaf Patrik de** (dĕ lȧ·vȧl'; *Angl.* dē' lȧ·văl'). 1845–1913. Swedish engineer; inventor of a steam turbine and of a centrifugal cream separator.

**La'val'** (là'vȧl'; *Angl.* lȧ·văl'), **Pierre.** 1883–1945. French lawyer and politician; member of Chamber of Deputies (from 1914); premier and minister of foreign affairs (1931–32); minister of labor (1932), of colonies (1934), of foreign affairs (1934–35); again premier and minister of foreign affairs (1935–36); vice-premier in Vichy government (July–Dec., 1940); as premier (from Apr., 1942) pursued policy of collaboration with Germany; executed for treason.

**La Va'lette'** (là và'lĕt'), Comte **de. Antoine Marie Cha'mans'** (shà'mäN'). 1769–1830. French politician; accepted (1789) principles of the Revolution and joined Army of the Alps, becoming aide-de-camp to Bonaparte. Under the Empire, served as French minister to Saxony, postmaster general of France, and councilor of state. Condemned to death by Louis XVIII, he escaped by aid of his devoted wife, **Émilie Louise,** *nee* **de Beau'har'nais'** [bō'àr'nĕ'] (1780–1855).

**La Valette, Jean Pa'ri'sot'** (pà'rē'zō') **de.** 1494–1568. French-born grand master (from 1557) of the Knights of Malta (Hospitalers); defended Malta brilliantly against Turkish assaults and siege (1565); built a new city and capital, named Valletta in his honor.

**La Val'lière'** (là và'lyâr'), Duchesse **de. Françoise Louise de la Baume Le Blanc** (dē là bōm' lē bläN'). 1644–1710. A mistress of Louis XIV (1661–c. 1674), and mother by him of four children; superseded by Marquise de Montespan; retired to a convent (1674). Reputed author of *Réflexions sur la Miséricorde de Dieu* (1685).

**La Vallière,** Duc **de. Louis César de la Baume le Blanc.** 1708–1780. French bibliophile, grandson of Duchesse de La Vallière (*q.v.*). Collected large library, later acquired by Comte d'Artois, forming part of the library of the Arsenal.

**La'val'-Mont'mo'ren'cy'** (là'vàl' môN'mô'räN'sē'), **François Xavier de.** 1623–1708. French prelate in Canada; to Quebec (1659) as vicar apostolic; first bishop of Quebec (1674–88). Laval U. is named for him.

**Lav'a·rack** (lăv'ȧ·răk), **John Dudley.** 1885–1957. Australian army officer; major general (1935); chief of general staff (1935–39); commanded southern command, Australian military forces (1939–40), 1st army (1942–44); head of military mission to U.S. (1944–46); governor of Queensland (from 1946).

**La'va·ter** (lä'vä·tēr; lä·vä'tēr), **Johann Kaspar.** 1741–1801. Swiss poet, mystic, and writer on philosophy and theology; founder of so-called science of physiognomy. Author of lyric poems, dramas, epics, etc.

**La've·dan'** (låv'däN'), **Henri Léon Émile.** 1859–1940. French playwright and novelist. Among his novels are *Mam'zelle Vertu* (1885), *Nocturnes* (1891), *Le Bon Temps* (1906), *Le Chemin du Salut* (7 vols., 1920–25); among his plays, *Le Prince d'Aurec* (1894), *Le Nouveau Jeu* (1898), *Les Médicis* (1901), *Le Duel* (1905), *Sire* (1909).

**La've·leye'** (lȧ'vlā'), Baron **Émile Louis Victor de.** 1822–1892. Belgian economist; author of *Le Socialisme Contemporain* (1881), *Éléments d'Économie Politique* (1882), etc.

**La·velle'** (lȧ·vĕl'), **Michael Joseph.** 1856–1939. American Roman Catholic clergyman, b. New York City. Appointed vicar-general of New York diocese (1902), domestic prelate to Pope Pius X (1903), and prothonotary apostolic by Pope Pius XII (1929).

**La'ver** (lā'vẽr), **James.** 1899– . English writer, b. Liverpool. Among his many works are *Cervantes* (Newdigate prize poem; 1921), *The Young Man Dances* (1925), *Whistler* (1930), *Nymph Errant* (musical comedy; 1932), *Winter Wedding* (1934), *Laburnum Tree* (short stories; 1935), *The House that Went to Sea* (children's play; 1936), *The Heart was not Burned* (play; 1938), *Swiss Family Robinson* (children's play; 1938; with Sir Barry Jackson), *Poems of Baudelaire* (1939).

**La've·ran'** (lȧ'vrăN'), **Charles Louis Alphonse.** 1845–1922. French army physician and bacteriologist; while in Algeria to study malarial fever (1878–83) discovered the blood parasite that causes it (1880); army physician (1891–97); chef de service honoraire, Pasteur Institute, Paris. Awarded 1907 Nobel prize for physiology and medicine. Author of *Nature Parasitaire des Accidents de l'Impaludisme* (1881), *Traité des Fièvres Palustres* (1884), etc.

**La Vé'ren'drye'** (lȧ vā'răN'drē'), Sieur **de. Pierre Gaul'tier' de Va'rennes'** (gō'tyā' dē vȧ'rĕn'). 1685–1749. Explorer in America, b. Three Rivers, Canada. Officer in French army, in France (1707–11), in Canada (from 1712). Started western explorations in 1731; erected forts on Lake of the Woods (1732), Lake Winnipeg (1734), Assiniboine River (1738); pushed westward to upper Missouri, the Black Hills region (1742), thus being discoverer of Manitoba, the Dakotas, western Minnesota, perhaps part of Montana, and western Canada.

**La'ver·y** (lā'vẽr·ĭ; lăv'ẽr·ĭ), Sir **John.** 1856–1941. British portrait and figure painter, b. Belfast; studied in Paris, under Bouguereau and Robert-Fleury. Among his best-known canvases are *Polymnia* (now in National Gallery at Rome), *A Lady in Black* (in National Gallery at Berlin), *Spring* (in the Luxembourg), *Game of Tennis* (New Pinakothek, Munich).

**La'vi'ge·rie'** (lȧ'vēzh'rē'), **Charles Martial Al'le·mand'-** (ȧl'mäN'-). 1825–1892. French Roman Catholic prelate; bishop of Nancy (1863), archbishop of Algiers (1867), cardinal (1882). Founded (1874) order of White Fathers (Pères Blancs); opposed slave trade in Africa and founded (1888) Anti-Slavery Society.

**La'vi'gnac'** (lȧ'vē'nyȧk'), **Albert.** 1846–1916. French writer on music; coeditor of *Encyclopédie de la Musique et Dictionnaire du Conservatoire* (1902 ff.); author of *La Musique et les Musiciens* (1895), etc.

**La Ville'mar'qué'** (lȧ vēl'mȧr'kā'), Vicomte **de. Théodore Claude Henri Her'sart'** (ĕr'sȧr'). 1815–1895. French scholar; authority on language and literature of Brittany.

**La'visse'** (lȧ'vēs'), **Ernest.** 1842–1922. French historian; specialized in study of Prussian history, and wrote *Études sur l'Histoire de Prusse* (1879), *Le Grand Frédéric avant l'Avènement* (1893), etc.

**La'voi'sier'** (lȧ'vwȧ'zyā'), **Antoine Laurent.** 1743–1794. French chemist, founder of modern chemistry, b. Paris. Studied astronomy with N. L. de Lacaille, chemistry with G. F. Rouelle, and botany with Bernard de Jussieu. Director of state gunpowder works (1776); farmer-general (1779); member of commission to establish uniform system of weights and measures (1790); commissary of treasury (1791); arrested by order of the Convention and guillotined. Conducted quantitative experiments; disproved the phlogiston theory; explained combustion as the union of the burning substance with the part of the air that he later came to call oxygen; propounded a theory of formation of chemical compounds; conducted experiments to determine composition of water and various organic compounds; with C. L. Berthollet, L. B. Guyton de Morveau, and A. F. Fourcroy, devised system of chemical nomenclature that serves as basis of present system.

**Lavreince, Nicolas.** See Nils LAFRENSEN.

**Lav·rov'** (lŭv·rôf'), **Pëtr Lavrovich.** 1823–1900. Russian revolutionist and scholar; associated with revolutionary activities (1862); arrested (1866); exiled (1868); escaped and took refuge in Paris. Edited Socialist review *Forward* (1873–77). Author of *The Hegelian Philosophy* (1858–59), *An Attempt at a History of Modern Thought* (2 vols., 1859), etc.

**Law** (lô), **Bonar,** *in full* **Andrew Bonar.** 1858–1923. British statesman, b. in New Brunswick, Canada; to Scotland as a boy. M.P. (from 1900); leader of opposition in House of Commons (1911–15); secretary of state for the colonies (1915–16); chancellor of the exchequer (1916–18); lord privy seal (1919–21); prime minister of Great Britain (1922–23).

**Law, Edward.** 1st Baron **El'len·bor'ough** (ĕl'ĕn·bûr'ō; *esp. Brit.*, -bŭ·rŭ, -brŭ). 1750–1818. English judge. Son of **Edmund Law** (1703–1787), metaphysician at Cambridge and bishop of Carlisle (1768–87). Chosen as leading counsel for Warren Hastings (1788) and opened defense (1792); attorney general (1801); chief justice of King's Bench and privy councilor (1802); accepted seat in cabinet of All-the-Talents Administration, retaining chief-justiceship; an authority on mercantile law.

His eldest son, **Edward** (1790–1871), Earl of Ellenborough, became M.P. (1813); lord privy seal (1828); president of Board of Control (1828–30). Succeeded Lord Auckland as governor general of India (1841); entrusted war with the amirs of Sind to Sir Charles Napier, who neglected just and merciful instructions and seized Sind for annexation (1842); invaded Gwalior and pacified the Marathas at Maharajpur (1843); recalled by directors (1844). First lord of admiralty (1846); president of Board of Control for fourth time (1858). Author of home constitution of government of India carried into effect by his successor.

**Thomas** (1759–1834), 7th son of Edmund Law, was in service of East India Co. (1773–91); emigrated to America (1793); m. Anne Custis, daughter of Martha Washington; sought to establish a national currency in U.S.; died at Washington, D.C.

**Law** (*Fr.* lō, *formerly* läs; *Eng.* lô), **Jacques Alexandre Bernard.** See Marquis de LAURISTON.

**Law** (lô; *Fr.* lō, formerly läs) of **Lau'ris·ton** (lô'rĭs·tŭn; *Fr.* lô'rēs'tôN'), **John.** 1671–1729. Scottish financier and speculator, originator of the Mississippi Scheme. Forced to flee to Continent, having killed in a duel (1694) Edward, or Beau, Wilson, a young gentleman who from a mysterious source, never yet uncovered, derived funds for notoriously expensive living. Founded Banque Générale, first bank of any kind in France (1716), which issued paper currency and prospered; gained control of Louisiana for colonization and trade; incorporated

(1717) for development of Louisiana an enterprise called "the Mississippi Scheme," or "the System," which soon absorbed the East India and China companies and the African company, and the mint; became supreme in French colonial and internal finance; director-general of finance (1720); fled on collapse of the scheme, due to overissue of paper currency and hostile government action (1720); died in Venice, poor and forgotten.

**Law** (lô), **Sallie Chapman,** *nee* **Gordon.** 1805–1894. Known as "Mother of the Confederacy," b. in Wilkes County, N.C.; m. Dr. John S. Law (1825). Active in organization and management of hospitals in the South during the Civil War.

**Law, William.** 1686–1761. English devotional writer. Spiritual director of Gibbon family and other persons, including John and Charles Wesley and John Byrom; became ardent admirer of the German mystic Jakob Böhme (1737); author of controversial works, including an attack on Mandeville's *Fable of the Bees* (1723), and the *Case of Reason* (1732), an answer to Tindal the Deist; works on practical divinity, including the *Serious Call to a Devout and Holy Life* (1728), his best-known work, which deeply influenced the Evangelical Revival; mystical works, including *The Way to Divine Knowledge* (1752).

**Lawes** (lôz), **Henry.** 1596–1662. English musical composer; suggested to Milton composition of *Comus* and wrote music for it (performed 1634); composed music for the George Sandys version of *Psalms* and for *Choice Psalmes put into Musick* (the latter with his brother William, 1648); published three books of airs (*Ayres and Dialogues for One, Two, and Three Voices;* first book, 1653; second, 1655; third 1658); composed *Zadok the Priest* for coronation (1660). Commemorated by Milton in sonnet "Harry, whose tuneful and well-measured song." His brother **William** (d. 1645) composed music for Shirley's masque *The Triumph of Peace* (performed 1634) and Davenant's masque *The Triumph of the Prince d'Amour* (1635); killed fighting for Royalist cause.

**Lawes,** Sir **John Bennet.** 1814–1900. English agriculturist; carried out series of agricultural experiments on estate at Rothamsted (from 1843); patented (1842) a mineral superphosphate for manure.

**Lawes, Lewis E.** 1883–1947. American penologist; warden of Sing Sing Prison, N.Y. (1920–41); author of works on prisons and penology, including *20,000 Years in Sing Sing* (1932).

**Law'less** (lô'lĕs; -lĭs), **Emily.** 1845–1913. Irish novelist and miscellaneous writer; among her books are *Hurrish* (novel; 1886), *Grania* (novel; 1892), *With the Wild Geese* (verse; 1902).

**Law'rence** (lô'rĕns; lŏr'ĕns), **Saint.** *Lat.* **Lau·ren'tius** (lô·rĕn'shĭ·ŭs; -shŭs). 3d-century Christian martyr; deacon of Pope Sixtus II. According to tradition he was burned alive on a gridiron; his festival is August 10th.

**Lawrence, Abbott.** See under William LAWRENCE.

**Lawrence,** Sir **Alfred Tristram.** 1st Baron **Tre·veth'in** (trĕ·vĕth'ĭn). 1843–1936. English jurist; lord chief justice of England (1921–22).

**Lawrence, Amos** and **Amos Adams.** See under William LAWRENCE.

**Lawrence, Charles Edward.** 1870–1940. English writer; joint editor of *The Quarterly Review.* Among his writings are *Pilgrimage* (1907), *The Wisdom of the Apocrypha* (1910), *The Gentle Art of Authorship* (1924), *Week-End at Forthries* (1935), *The Gods were Sleeping* (1937), and several plays, including *The Year* (1927), and *The Reckoning* (1934).

**Lawrence, David.** 1888–1973. American journalist, b. Philadelphia. Veteran Washington correspondent. Published *United States Daily* (1926–33); founded *U.S. News* (1933), became *U.S. News & World Report* (1947). Author of widely syndicated political news column and *True Story of Woodrow Wilson* (1924), *Beyond the New Deal* (1934), *Nine Honest Men* (1936), *Diary of a Washington Correspondent* (1942), etc.

**Lawrence, David Herbert.** 1885–1930. English novelist, b. in Nottingham; m. (1914) Frieda von Richthofen, cousin of Baron Manfred von Richthofen, the German military aviator, and divorced wife of Ernest Weekley. Among his novels are *The White Peacock, Sons and Lovers, Kangaroo* (1923), *The Plumed Serpent* (1926), *Lady Chatterley's Lover* (1928). Author also of plays, as *The Widowing of Mrs. Holroyd, David* (1926), etc.; verse, as *Amores, Birds, Beasts, and Flowers* (1925); and essays *Psychoanalysis of the Unconscious, Fantasia of the Unconscious,* etc.

**Lawrence, Ernest Orlando.** 1901–1958. American physicist. Invented the cyclotron (1931), by means of which he made researches into the structure of the atom, effected transmutation of certain elements, and produced artificial radioactivity; applied radiations in the study of problems in biology and medicine. Awarded 1939 Nobel prize for physics and 1957 Fermi Award.

**Lawrence, George Alfred.** 1827–1876. English novelist; author of *Guy Livingstone, or Thorough* (1857) and *Sword and Gown* (1859).

**Lawrence,** Sir **George St. Patrick.** 1804–1884. British soldier, b. in Ceylon, son of Indian army officer. Took part in Afghan War (1838–39); secretary to Macnaghten (killed 1841); political agent at Peshawar (1848), in Mewar, Rajputana (1850–57); commanded forces in Rajputana during Sepoy Mutiny; author of *Forty-three Years in India* (1874). His brother Sir **Henry Montgomery** (1806–1857), soldier and Indian administrator, took part in first Afghan War (1838), Kabul expedition (1842), Sikh Wars (1846, 1848); governor general's agent for foreign relations and affairs of Punjab (1846); president of board of administration of Punjab (1849–53); warned government against imminence of revolt (1856); chief commissioner of Lucknow in charge of Oudh (1856); at outbreak of Sepoy Mutiny put in charge of troops in Oudh (1857); killed while holding Lucknow against mutineers. Another brother, **John Laird Mair** (1811–1879), 1st Baron Lawrence, Indian administrator, became magistrate and land-revenue officer, Delhi; commissioner and then lieutenant governor of Punjab (1853–57); curbed oppression by chiefs and devised land-tenure system; able to disarm mutineers in Punjab and to send loyal Sikh troops to relief of Delhi; viceroy of India (1863–69), developed sanitation, irrigation, railway extension, and opposed intriguing in Afghanistan that led to Afghan war of 1878–79.

**Lawrence, Gertrude.** *Orig.* **Gertrud Alexandra Dagmar Lawrence Kla'sen** (klä's'n). 1901–1952. English actress, b. London, of Danish-Irish parentage; m. 1st Francis Gordon-Hawley (marriage later dissolved), 2d (1940) Richard S. Aldrich, theatrical producer. On stage from 1908, chiefly in musical comedy and revue; to U.S. (1924); first straight dramatic part in *Candlelight* (1929), later playing opposite Noel Coward in his *Private Lives* (1930) and *To Night at Eight-Thirty* (1936–37) and leading roles in *Susan and God* (1935), *Skylark* (1939), *Lady in the Dark* (1940), *The King and I* (1951).

**Lawrence,** Sir **Herbert Alexander.** 1861–1943. English soldier; served in South Africa (1899–1902), at the Dardanelles (1915), in Egypt (1916), in France (1917–19); major general (1915), lieutenant general (1918), general (1919).

**Lawrence, James.** 1781–1813. American naval officer,

b. Burlington, N.J. In command of the *Hornet* (1812–13); raided British shipping; defeated British brig *Peacock* (Feb. 24, 1813). Transferred to the *Chesapeake;* was defeated and mortally wounded in engagement with British frigate *Shannon* (June 1, 1813), crying "Don't give up the ship" as he was carried below; these words became popular slogan of the navy.

**Lawrence, Josephine.** American writer, b. Newark, N.J. Author of *Head of the Family* (1932), *If I Have Four Apples* (1935), *A Good Home With Nice People* (1939), and many juveniles.

**Lawrence, Margery.** 1880?-1969. English journalist and fiction writer, b. in Shropshire; m. Arthur E. Towle. Author of *Miss Brandt, Adventuress; Nights of the Round Table* (short stories); *The Terraces of Night* (short stories); *Overture to Life; The Bridge of Wonder.*

**Lawrence, Marjorie.** 1908– . Australian operatic soprano; known esp. as an interpreter of Wagnerian opera.

**Lawrence, Stringer.** 1697–1775. English soldier in India; known as "Father of the Indian army," for service of organization; served at Gibraltar (1727) and in Flanders; also fought at Culloden Moor (1746); commanded all troops of East India Company (1748); with Clive as junior officer relieved Trichinopoly (1752, and again 1753); defended Fort St. George during siege by French (1758–59); major general (1759).

**Lawrence,** Sir **Thomas.** 1769–1830. English painter, son of innkeeper; limner to king (1791); painted countess of Derby (1790), George III (1792). Principal painter to king in succession to Reynolds; went to Aix-la-Chapelle to paint sovereigns and diplomats (1818). Known for portraits of courtliness and social elegance, including those of Mrs. Siddons, Princess de Lieven, J. P. Kemble as Hamlet.

**Lawrence, Thomas Edward.** *Known as* **Lawrence of Arabia.** 1888–1935. Changed his surname to **Shaw** by deed poll (1927). British archaeologist, soldier, and writer, b. in Portmadoc, Caernarvonshire, Wales; educ. Oxford. On staff of British Museum expedition excavating Carchemish on the Euphrates River (1910–14). Served in World War (1914–18), major (1917), lieutenant colonel (1918); attached to General Wingate's staff in the Hejaz expeditionary force (1917), to General Allenby's staff (1918); leader of the Arab revolt against the Turks (1917–18), which he described in *The Seven Pillars of Wisdom* (1926), and its abbreviated version *Revolt in the Desert* (1927). Invited to Paris Peace Conference (1919); adviser on Arab affairs at the Middle East division of the Colonial Office (1921–22). Withdrew from this position (1922), joined the Royal Air Force as an aircraftsman, under the name of Ross, apparently with the desire to remove himself wholly from public attention. Published a prose translation of the *Odyssey* (1932). Killed in a motorcycle accident (May 19, 1935).

**Lawrence, William.** 1783–1848. American merchant, b. Groton, Mass. An organizer of first incorporated company to manufacture woolen goods, with plant at Lowell, Mass. (c. 1825); participated in establishment of Suffolk Bank System; contributed to endowment of academy in Groton, named Lawrence Academy in his honor (1846). His brother **Amos** (1786–1852) was also a Boston merchant, well known for his benefactions. Another brother, **Abbott** (1792–1855), was in partnership with Amos; founded and developed textile-manufacturing city of Lawrence, Mass. (from 1845); represented his district in Congress (1834–36, 1838–40); U.S. minister to Great Britain (1849–52); contributed to Harvard College, where the Lawrence Scientific School was named in his honor. A son of Amos, **Amos Adams** (1814–1886), was commission merchant and textile manufacturer; contributed to various causes, establishing Lawrence Coll., Appleton, Wis., and a college at Lawrence, Kans., which became nucleus of U. of Kansas; identified himself with antislavery agitation, gave money to John Brown and aided in employing counsel to defend him after the Harpers Ferry raid.

**Lawrence, William.** 1850–1941. American Protestant Episcopal clergyman, b. Boston. Consecrated bishop of Massachusetts (1893); resigned (1926). Author of *The American Cathedral* (1921), *Memories of a Happy Life* (1926), *Life of Phillips Brooks* (1930). His son **William Appleton** (1889-1968), also a Protestant Episcopal clergyman; educ. Harvard and Episcopal Theol. School; pastorate in Lawrence and Lynn, Mass., and Providence, R.I.; consecrated bishop of western Massachusetts (1937).

**Lawrence, William Beach.** 1800–1881. American jurist, b. New York City. Lieutenant governor of Rhode Island (1851); acting governor (1852). Author of many books on law, esp. international law.

**Lawrence, William John.** 1862–1940. British literary historian, b. in Belfast, Ireland. In liquor business for years; abandoned business to devote himself to study and writing. Became authority on history of the Irish stage, and on the history and literature of the drama. Author of *The Elizabethan Playhouse* (1912–13), *Pre-Restoration Stage Studies* (1927), *Shakespeare's Workshop* (1928), etc.

**Lawrence, William Witherle.** 1876–1958. American educator and scholar, b. Bangor, Me. Author of *Medieval Story* (1911), *Beowulf and Epic Tradition* (1928), *Shakespeare's Problem Comedies* (1931).

**Lawrence Jus·tin′i·an** (jŭs·tĭn′ĭ·ăn), Saint. *Lat.* **Lau·ren′ti·us Jus·tin′i·a′nus** (lô·rĕn′shĭ·ŭs [-shŭs] jŭs·tĭn′ĭ·ā′nŭs). 1381–1456. Italian Augustinian monk; became general of his order, and drew up its constitution. First patriarch of Venice (1451).

**Law′rie** (lô′rĭ; lŏr′ĭ), **Lee.** 1877–1963. Sculptor, b. Rixdorf, Ger.; to U.S. in infancy. Consultant in sculpture for Chicago's Century of Progress Exposition (1933) and New York's World's Fair (1939). Best known for architectural decorative sculpture, as for the U.S.M.A. at West Point, the National Academy of Sciences in Washington, the Los Angeles Public Library, etc. Also carved reliefs and statues for Harkness tower and archway at Yale, the Bok "Singing Tower" in Florida, entrance to R.C.A. building in Radio City in New York.

**Law′son** (lô′s'n), **Alexander.** 1773–1846. Engraver, b. in Lanarkshire, Scotland; to U.S. in 1794. Known esp. for his plates in Alexander Wilson's *American Ornithology* (9 vols., 1808–14) and in Charles Lucien Bonaparte's *American Ornithology* (4 vols., 1825–33).

**Lawson, Andrew Cowper.** 1861–1952. American geologist, b. Anstruther, Scotland. Professor of mineralogy and geology (1890–1928; retired), U. of California. Worked in Archean geology, petrography, economic geology, geomorphology, seismology, etc.

**Lawson, Cecil Gordon.** 1851–1882. English landscape painter.

**Lawson, Edward Levy–** and **Harry Lawson Webster.** See Baron BURNHAM

**Lawson, Ernest.** 1873–1939. American landscape painter, b. San Francisco.

**Lawson,** Sir **Harry Sutherland Wightman.** 1875–1952. Australian lawyer and statesman; premier of Victoria (1918–24); senator for Victoria (1928–35); minister in charge of external territories (1934).

**Lawson, Henry Hertzberg.** *Orig. surname* **Lar′sen** (lär′s'n). 1867–1922. Australian writer, b. in New

South Wales. Author of *Short Stories in Prose and Verse* (1895), *Verses, Popular and Humorous* (1900), *Children of the Bush* (1902), *When I Was King, and Other Verses* (1905), etc.

**Lawson,** Sir **John.** d. 1665. English naval commander. Commander in North Sea and the Channel in Parliamentary navy (1642–45, 1651–53, 1654–56); dismissed; Anabaptist and republican, enemy to Oliver Cromwell. On fall of Richard Cromwell, became commander in chief of fleet (1659); escorted Charles to England; fought Algerian pirates; mortally wounded at Lowestoft in Dutch war.

**Lawson, John.** d. 1711. English traveler in America (1700–c. 1708). Surveyor general of North Carolina (1708). With one Christopher de Graffenried, organized a migration of Swiss and German Palatines to settle in North Carolina; a founder of New Bern, N.C. Murdered by Indians (1711). Author of *A New Voyage to Carolina*...(1709).

**Lawson, John Howard.** 1895– . American playwright, b. New York City. Author of *Roger Bloomer* (1923), *Processional* (1925), *The International* (1928), *Gentlewoman* (1934), *Marching Song* (1937), etc.

**Lawson, Robert.** 1892–1957. American illustrator, b. New York City. Illustrated a number of juveniles, including *Four and Twenty Blackbirds*, Arthur Mason's *Wee Men of Ballywooden*, Ella Young's *Unicorn with Silver Shoes*, Munro Leaf's *Story of Ferdinand*, Mark Twain's *The Prince and the Pauper*, Bunyan's *Pilgrim's Progress*.

**Lawson, Thomas William.** 1857–1925. American stock-market speculator and author, b. Charlestown, Mass. Associated with promotion of Amalgamated Copper Co. (1897). Author of *Frenzied Finance* (an account of stock-market operations in Amalgamated Copper; 1902), *Friday, the Thirteenth* (1907), *The Remedy* (1912), etc. See J. E. O. Addicks.

**Lawson, Victor Freemont.** 1850–1925. American journalist, b. Chicago. Proprietor of Chicago *Daily News* (from 1876), first penny newspaper in the West; took over Chicago *Evening Post* (1878); published morning paper, Chicago *Record* (1881), later merged with *Times-Herald* to become Chicago *Record-Herald* (ceased publication, 1914). Director (1893–1925) and president (1894–1900), Associated Press. Pioneer in development of foreign news service.

**Lawson, W. B.** Pseudonym of George Charles Jenks.

**Lawson,** Sir **Wilfrid.** 1829–1906. English radical and temperance advocate. M.P. (1859); first introduced his permissive, or local veto, bill (1864); advocated Sunday closing in Ireland (1875–76); supported disestablishment, abolition of House of Lords, disarmament; denounced Boer War; defended free trade. Writer of light verse; a famous wit.

**Law'ton** (lô't'n), **Henry Ware.** 1843–1899. American soldier, b. near Toledo, Ohio. Served in Union army through Civil War; awarded medal of honor for heroism at Atlanta. Entered regular army (1867); served in Indian frontier fighting; pursued and captured Geronimo (1886). Major general of volunteers, serving in Cuba in Spanish-American War (1898), and in Philippines suppressing rebellion (1899).

**Lax'ness** (läks'nĕs), **Halldór Kiljan.** 1902– . Icelandic novelist; wrote *The Great Weaver of Cashmere* (Eng. trans. 1927), *Salka Valka* (1934), *Independent People* (1939), *Islands Klukkan* (1943), *Gerpla* (1952), etc. Awarded Nobel prize in literature (1955).

**Lay'a·mon** (lā'ȧ·mŭn; -mŏn; lä'yȧ-; lī'ȧ-). fl. 1200. Early English poet. Priest of Ernley (doubtless Areley Regis in Worcestershire); paraphrased Robert Wace's *Roman de Brut* in English unrhymed, alliterative verse, earliest considerable English poem, extant in two manuscripts in British Museum.

**Lay'ard** (lârd; lā'ẽrd), Sir **Austen Henry.** 1817–1894. English archaeologist and diplomat; began excavations near site of ancient Nineveh (1845); found remains of four palaces and sent to British Museum slabs with bas reliefs and cuneiform inscriptions from what was later identified as Assyrian city of Calah. Liberal M.P. (1852); minister at Madrid (1869–77) and Constantinople (1877–80). Author of *Nineveh and its Remains* (1848–49), *Nineveh and Babylon* (1853). See also Hormuzd Rassam and Sir H. C. Rawlinson.

**Lay·nez'** *or* **Lai·nez'** (lī·nāth'), **Diego.** 1512–1565. Spanish Jesuit; ardent disciple of Loyola. General of the Jesuit order (1558); represented the order in the Council of Trent; emphasized importance of education designed to influence the young for the good of the church.

**Lay'ton** (lā't'n), Sir **Geoffrey.** 1884–1964. British naval officer; rear admiral (1935); vice-admiral commanding 1st battle squadron (1939–40); commander in chief of British fleet in China (1940–42), Ceylon (1942–45); admiral (1942).

**Layton, Walter Thomas.** 1st Baron **Layton.** 1884–1966. English economist and publicist; editor of the *Economist* (1922–38); chairman of the News Chronicle, Ltd. (from 1930), and the Star Newspaper Co., Ltd. (from 1937). British member of organization committee of Bank for International Settlements (1929). Author of *Relations of Capital and Labour*, etc.

**La'zar** (lä'zär). Name of princes of Serbia, including: **Lazar I** (d. 1389), prince (1371–89); led allied army of Serbs, Bosnians, Albanians, etc., against Turks under Murad I; totally defeated and slain at battle of Kosovo. **Lazar III** (d. 1458), son of George Branković; prince (1456–58).

**La·za're·vić** (lä·zä'rĕ·vēt'y'; *Angl.* -vĭch), **Laza.** 1851–1890. Serbian novelist, physician by profession; author of several psychological novels.

**Laz'a·rus** (lăz'ȧ·rŭs; lăz'rŭs). In Bible, brother of Mary and Martha, whom (according to *John* xi) Jesus raised from the dead.

**Lazarus, Emma.** 1849–1887. American poet, essayist, and philanthropist, b. New York City. Published *Admetus and Other Poems* (1871), *Alide: an Episode of Goethe's Life* (1874), *The Spagnoletto* (poetic drama; 1876). Championed oppressed Jews during persecution in Russia (1879–83); organized relief work; wrote *Songs of a Semite* (volume of poetry and verse drama; 1882), etc.

**La'za·rus** (lä'tsä·rōōs), **Moritz.** 1824–1903. German philosopher; with H. Steinthal, credited with establishing science of ethnopsychology. Chief work, *Das Leben der Seele* (1855–57).

**La·zear'** (lȧ·zēr'), **Jesse William.** 1866–1900. American physician; entered U.S. army medical corps (1900). Member, with Walter Reed, James Carroll, and Aristides Agramonte, of the Yellow Fever Commission (1900); while in Cuba studying the disease, died from bite of infected mosquito.

**La·zhech'ni·kov** (lŭ·zhăch'nyĭ·kôf), **Ivan Ivanovich.** 1792–1869. Russian novelist and playwright; among his many historical novels are *The Last Novik* (1833), *The House of Ice* (1835), *Basurman* (1838); his drama *The Oprichnik* (1842) used as text of opera by Tschaikowsky.

**Laz'za·ri** (läd'dzä·rē), **Bramante.** See Bramante.

**Laz'za·ri** (läd'dzä·rē), **Silvio.** 1860–1944. Composer, b. in Austrian Tirol; naturalized French citizen (1896); championed cause of Wagner in musical journals. Composer of the pantomime *Lulu* (1887); the operas *L'En-*

*sorcelé* (1903), *La Lépreuse* (1912), *Le Sauteriot* (1920), *La Tour de Feu* (1925); the orchestral suite *Impressions;* symphonic poems, a symphony, a concertstück for piano and orchestra, a festival march, a Spanish rhapsody, chamber music, piano pieces, choruses, songs, etc.

**Lea** (lē), **Fanny Heaslip.** 1884–1955. American writer, b. New Orleans; m. Hamilton Pope A'gee [ā'jē] (1911; divorced 1926). Author of *Quicksands* (1911), *Sicily Ann* (1914), *The Dream-Maker Man* (1925), *Wild Goose Chase* (1929), *Lolly* (a play; 1930), *Half Angel* (1932), *Once to Every Man* (1937), etc.

**Lea, Homer.** 1876–1912. American soldier and author, b. Denver, Colo.; aided in relief of Peking during Boxer rebellion. General in Chinese army (1909); adviser to Sun Yat Sen (1911–12). Author of *The Valor of Ignorance* (1909), *The Day of the Saxon* (1912), etc.

**Lea, Isaac.** 1792–1886. American publisher and naturalist; authority on fresh-water mollusks. His son **Henry Charles** (1825–1909) was a publisher (with M. Carey & Sons, 1843–80) and historian; author of *Superstition and Force* (1866), *A History of the Inquisition . . .* (3 vols., 1888), etc.

**Leach** (lēch), **William Elford.** 1790–1836. English naturalist; expert malacologist; developed system of arrangement in conchology and entomology (1813).

**Lea'cock** (lē'kŏk), **Stephen Butler.** 1869–1944. Canadian economist and humorist, b. in Hampshire, England; professor, McGill U., Montreal (1901–36), and head of economics department (1908–36). Author of *Elements of Political Science* (1906), *Economic Prosperity in the British Empire* (1930), studies of Mark Twain (1932) and Charles Dickens (1933), *Humour: its Theory and Technique* (1935), *Montreal: Seaport and City* (1942), *How to Write* (1943), and many humorous publications, beginning with *Literary Lapses* (1910) and including *Nonsense Novels* (1911), *Arcadian Adventures with the Idle Rich* (1914), *Moonbeams from the Larger Lunacy* (1915), *Frenzied Fiction* (1917), *My Discovery of England* (1922; after a lecture tour in England), *Afternoons in Utopia* (1932), *Funny Pieces* (1936), *Laugh Parade* (1940), *My Remarkable Uncle* (1942).

**Lead** *or* **Leade** (lĕd), **Jane,** *nee* **Ward** (wôrd). 1623–1704. English mystic; impressed by revelations of Jakob Böhme, recorded prophetic visions in *A Fountain of Gardens* (from 1670); founded the Philadelphians, a Boehmenist sect (1697).

**Lea'der** (lē'dẽr), **Benjamin Williams.** *Family name orig.* **Wil'liams** (wĭl'yămz). 1831–1923. English landscape painter, esp. of scenes in Worcestershire and Wales.

**Leaf** (lēf), **Munro.** 1905– . American humorist and illustrator; author of *Grammar Can Be Fun* (1934), *Manners Can Be Fun* (1936), *Noodle* (illust. by Ludwig Bemelmans; 1937), *The Story of Ferdinand* (1936) and *Wee Gillis* (1938), both illust. by Robert Lawson (*q.v.*), *Fair Play* (1939), *Watchbirds—a Picture Book of Behavior* (illust. by the author; 1939).

**Leaf, Walter.** 1852–1927. English banker and Greek scholar, b. in Norwood. Chairman, Westminster Bank. Collaborator with Andrew Lang and E. Myers in prose translation of Homer's *Iliad* (1882); editor of *The Iliad,* with English notes and introduction (1886–88). Author of *Companion to the Iliad* (1892), *Homer and History* (1915), etc.

**Le'ah** (lē'ȧ). *In Douay Version* **Li'a** (lī'ȧ). In Bible, daughter of Laban and wife of her cousin Jacob (*q.v.*).

**Lea'hy** (lā'hĭ), **William Daniel.** 1875–1959. American naval officer; grad. U.S.N.A., Annapolis (1897). Rear admiral (1930); admiral; chief of naval operations (1937–39); retired (1939). Governor of Puerto Rico (1939–40); ambassador to France (1941). Named chief of staff to President Roosevelt (1942). Admiral of the fleet (1944).

**Leake** (lēk), Sir **John.** 1656–1720. English naval commander. As governor of Newfoundland (1702), destroyed French settlements; distinguished himself in relief of Gibraltar (1704); relieved Barcelona (1706).

**Leake, William Martin.** 1777–1860. English antiquarian and classical topographer, b. London. Great-grandson of Stephen Martin, naval captain under Admiral Sir John Leake, whose son became Admiral Leake's heir and assumed his name. Resided in Greece (1808–10); collected coins and inscriptions; presented his marbles to British Museum (1839). Known for topographical researches recorded in *Athens* (1821), *Morea* (1830), *Northern Greece* (1835).

**Lea'key** (lē'kĭ), **Louis Seymour Bazett.** 1903–1972. British anthropologist, b. Kenya. Discovered fossil remains of early humanoids in Africa (1959). Wrote *White African, Adam's Ancestors, The Progress and Evolution of Man in Africa,* etc.

**Le·an'der** (lē·ăn'dẽr), **Saint.** 550?–?601. Spanish monk; friend of Gregory the Great; archbishop of Seville (c. 584); converted the Visigoths from Arianism.

**Leander, Richard.** See Richard von VOLKMANN.

**Lé'an'dre** (lā'äN'dr'), **Charles Lucien.** 1862–1934. French artist, illustrator, and caricaturist; best known for his caricatures, as for *Le Rire.*

**Lear** (lēr), **Ben.** 1879–1966. American army officer, b. Hamilton, Ont.; to U.S. (1881). Enlisted in U.S. army (1898); commander of U.S. 2d army (1940–43).

**Lear, Edward.** 1812–1888. English landscape painter and nonsense poet. Employed by 13th earl of Derby to draw Knowsley menagerie; composed for Edward, the 15th earl, his first *Book of Nonsense* (pub. 1846); left Knowsley (1836) and set up studio as topographical landscape painter in Rome; recounted travels through Mediterranean countries in series of *Illustrated Journals of a Landscape Painter,* with delicately penned sketches; intimate with the Tennysons. Author also of *Nonsense Songs, Stories, and Botany* (1870), *More Nonsense Rhymes* (1871), *Laughable Lyrics* (1876).

**Lear, Tobias.** 1762–1816. American diplomat, b. Portsmouth, N.H. Private secretary (1785–92) and military secretary (1798–99) to George Washington. U.S. consul at Algiers (1803–12); negotiated treaty (1805) with pasha of Tripoli, agreeing to ransom American prisoners. Dismissed by Dey of Algiers at outbreak of War of 1812.

**Learmont, Thomas.** = Thomas of ERCELDOUNE.

**Lear'ned** (lûr'nĕd; -nĭd), **Marion Dexter.** 1857–1917. American Germanic philologist and historian.

**Lea'ry** (lēr'ĭ), **Herbert Fairfax.** 1885–1957. American naval officer, b. Washington, D.C.; grad. U.S.N.A., Annapolis (1905); advanced through the grades to rear admiral (1938); vice-admiral commanding Allied naval forces in Australia-New Zealand area (Feb., 1942); commander of U.S. Pacific Fleet task force (Oct., 1942).

**Leathes** (lēthz), **Stanley.** 1830–1900. English Biblical scholar; member of Old Testament revision committee (1870–85). His son Sir **Stanley Mordaunt** (1861–1938) was joint editor with Sir Adolphus Ward and Sir George Prothero of the *Cambridge Modern History* (1902–12); author also of *Rhythm in English Poetry* (1935).

**Le Bar'gy'** (lē bȧr'zhē'), **Charles Gustave Auguste.** 1858–1936. French actor; among plays in which he appeared were *Hernani, Les Effrontés, Les Romanesques, L'Énigme, Le Dédale, Cyrano de Bergerac.*

**Le Bas** (lē bä'), **Philippe.** 1794–1860. French archaeologist and philologist; on archaeological expedition in Greece and Asia Minor (1842); author of *Antiquités Grecques et Romaines* (1836).

**Le·bau'dy'** (lē·bō'dē'), **Paul.** 1858–1937. French industrialist; with his brother, **Pierre**, built a number of semirigid dirigibles, among which were the first military dirigible (1902) and the first English dirigible, which made the trip across the English Channel and return (1910).

**Le'be·dev** (lyā'byĕ·dyĕf), **Pëtr Nikolaevich.** 1866–1911. Russian physicist; proved existence of, and succeeded in measuring, extremely small pressure exercised on bodies by light; also investigated the earth's magnetism.

**Le Bel** (lē bĕl'), **Jean.** d. 1370. Belgian chronicler, author of *Les Vrayes Chroniques* (1326–61) from which Froissart borrowed material.

**Le Bel, Joseph Achille.** 1847–1930. French chemist; investigated optical activity and fermentation; propounded theory of asymmetric carbon atom independently of van't Hoff (1874); sought to determine existence of optically active compounds of nitrogen (1891).

**Le·bel'** (lē·bĕl'), **Nicolas.** 1838–1891. French army officer and inventor of a gun of small calibre named after him.

**Le·besgue'** (lē·bâg'), **Henri Léon.** 1875–1941. French mathematician; known for contributions to the theory of functions of real variables.

**Lebesgue, Philéas.** 1869–1958. French poet and literary critic.

**Le·blanc'** (lē·bläN'), **Maurice.** 1857–1923. French electrical engineer and inventor. His inventions include a phase advancer, a damper winding, an induction machine, and an exciter.

**Leblanc, Maurice.** 1864–1941. French novelist, known esp. for his detective fiction including a series with Arsène Lupin as the central character.

**Leblanc, Nicolas.** 1742–1806. French chemist. Surgeon to the household of the duke of Orleans (Philippe-Égalité); invented a process for the manufacture of soda from common salt.

**Le Blant** (lē bläN'), **Edmond Frédéric.** 1818–1897. French archaeologist.

**Le Blon** *or* **Le Blond** (lē blôN'), **Jacques Christophe.** 1670–1741. French painter and engraver, noted for his miniatures; went from Amsterdam to London, where he set up process of printing engravings in color to imitate paintings (1720), described in *Il Coloretto* (1730); inventor of modern system of chromolithography.

**Le·blond'** (lē·blôN'), **Marius** and **Ary**, pseudonym of French writers **Georges A'the'nas'** (à'tā'nàs'), 1877–1955, and **Aimé Mer'lo'** (mĕr'lō'), 1880–1958; authors of *Vies Parallèles* (1902), *Les Sortilèges* (1905), *L'Oued* (1907), *En France* (Goncourt prize, 1909), *Les Martyrs de la République* (1927–28), *Histoire d'Afrique* (1937), *Le Paradis Perdu* (1939).

**Le·bœuf'** (lē·bûf'), **Edmond.** 1809–1888. French soldier; distinguished himself in Italian campaign (1859), esp. in use he made of new rifled artillery; aide-de-camp to Napoleon III. Minister of war (1869–70); marshal of France (1870). When war with Prussia was imminent, he assured Emperor Napoleon III that the army was ready, even down to the buttons on the gaiters; appointed major general of the army on the Rhine (July 19, 1870), but was promptly relieved of his command when the unpreparedness of the army became evident. Prisoner of war in Germany (1870–71); lived in retirement in France thereafter.

**Le Bon** (lē bôN'), **Gustave.** 1841–1931. French physician and sociologist; author of *L'Homme et les Sociétés...* (1881), *La Civilisation des Arabes* (1884), *Les Lois Psychologiques de l'Évolution des Peuples* (1894), *La Psychologie des Foules* (1895), *L'Évolution Actuelle du Monde* (1927), etc.

**Le Bon, Joseph.** 1765–1795. French politician; originally a priest; member of the National Convention (1793); commissary of the National Convention at Pas-de-Calais (1794); arrested, tried, convicted, and executed at Amiens (1795).

**Le·bon'** (lē·bôN'), **Philippe.** 1769–1804. French chemist and government civil engineer; pioneer in use of gas for illumination; patented an engine using coal gas.

**Le Bos'su'** (lē bô'sü'), **René.** 1631–1689. French priest and writer; subprior of abbey of Saint Jean de Chartres; author of *Traité du Poème Épique* (1675), praised by Boileau but criticized by Voltaire.

**Le Bou'len'gé'** (lē bōō'läN'zhā'), **Paul Émil.** 1832–1901. Belgian artillery soldier; known for his discoveries in science of ballistics, and for his invention of Le Boulengé chronograph.

**Le·bourg'** (lē·bōōr'), **Albert.** 1849–1928. French landscape painter.

**Le Braz** (lē brà'), **Anatole.** 1859–1926. French writer; most of his stories and essays deal with life and literature of Brittany.

**Lebrija, Elio Antonio de.** See Elio Antonio de NEBRIJA.

**Le·brun'** (lē·brûN'), **Albert.** 1871–1950. French politician, 14th president of the Republic. Mining engineer by profession; author of scientific works. Deputy from Meurthe-et-Moselle (1900–20); senator (1920–32); president of the Senate (1931–32). President of France (1932–40); resigned (July, 1940) when the government headed by Pétain and Pierre Laval assumed power.

**Le Brun** *or* **Le·brun'** (lē·brûN'), **Charles.** 1619–1690. French historical painter; director of the Gobelins; commissioned by Louis XIV to paint at Fontainebleau series of subjects drawn from life of Alexander the Great, and later to decorate small gallery of Louvre; appointed first painter to the king; worked eighteen years on decoration of palace of Versailles; a leader in what is known as the French school; a dominating influence in French art for twenty years (1662–82).

**Lebrun, Charles François.** Duc **de Plai'sance'** (plĕ'zäNs'). *Eng.* Duke of **Pia·cen'za** (pyä·chĕn'tsä). 1739–1824. French writer and politician; translator of Tasso's *Gerusalemme Liberata* and of Homer's *Iliad.* Member of the States-General, National Assembly, Council of Five Hundred; Third Consul (1799), archtreasurer of the Empire (1804), duke of Piacenza (c. 1806). His son **Anne Charles** (1775–1859), aide-de-camp to Napoleon; organized defense of Antwerp (1809).

**Lebrun, Jean Baptiste Pierre.** 1748–1813. French painter and art critic; m. (1776) Marie Anne Élisabeth Vigée (see VIGÉE-LEBRUN).

**Lebrun, Pierre Antoine.** 1785–1873. French poet and playwright.

**Lebrun, Pigault-.** See PIGAULT-LEBRUN.

**Lebrun, Ponce Denis Écouchard.** *Known as* **Le·brun'-Pin'dare'** (-păN'dàr'). 1729–1807. French lyric poet, best known for his epigrams.

**Lebrun, Mme. Vigée-.** See VIGÉE-LEBRUN.

**Le Car'don'nel'** (lē kàr'dô'nĕl'), **Louis.** 1862–1936. French abbé and poet; his volumes of verse include *Carmina Sacra* (1912), *Du Rhône à l'Arno* (1920).

**le Caron,** Major **Henry.** See Thomas Miller BEACH.

**Le Ca'ron'** (lē kà'rôN'), **Joseph.** 1586–1632. French Roman Catholic missionary in Canada; did pioneer work among Huron Indians, and compiled first Huron dictionary; sent back to France (1629) by the English after they captured Quebec.

**Le Cha'pe·lier'** (lē shà'pē·lyā'), **Isaac René Guy.** 1754–1794. French Revolutionary politician; member of States-General (1789); president of Constituent Assembly (1789); became moderate in doctrines (1791) and opposed Robespierre; guillotined (1794).

**Le Châ'te·lier'** (lẽ shä'tẽ·lyā'), **Henry Louis.** 1850–1936. French chemist; conducted researches on chemical equilibrium, the combustion of gaseous mixtures, on metals, alloys, etc.; enunciated Le Châtelier's law dealing with the equilibrium of a system when displaced by a stress; expounded the laws of energy; developed an optical pyrometer.

**Le Che·va'lier'** (lẽ shẽ·vȧ'lyā'), **Jean Baptiste.** 1752–1836. French traveler and archaeologist; collaborated in exploration of Troy (1784–1786). Librarian, Library of Sainte Geneviève (from 1808).

**Le·chits'ki** (lyĕ·chēts'kû·ĭ; *Angl.* lĕ·chĭts'kĭ), **Platon Alekseevich.** 1856– . Russian general; in World War I commanded armies in Galicia (1916–17); conducted successful campaign along Dniester and in Rumania; an organizer of Red army (1918).

**Lech'ler** (lĕk'lẽr), **Gotthard Victor.** 1811–1888. German Protestant theologian; a disciple of J. A. W. Neander.

**Leck'y** (lĕk'ĭ), **William Edward Hartpole.** 1838–1903. Irish historian and essayist; published *Leaders of Public Opinion in Ireland*, essays on Swift, Flood, Grattan, and O'Connell (1862); won success with abstruse and discursive *History of Rationalism in Europe* (1865) and companion work *History of European Morals from Augustus to Charlemagne* (1869); occupied himself 19 years with his magnum opus, *The History of England in the Eighteenth Century* (8 vols., 1878–90). Liberal Unionist M.P. (1895), supported extension of educational facilities for Roman Catholics and Plunkett's agricultural policy, but opposed home rule; one of first members of British Academy; O.M. (1902). Also wrote *Democracy and Liberty* (1896), *The Map of Life* (1899).

**Le·clair'** (lẽ·klâr'), **Jean Marie.** 1697–1764. French violin virtuoso and composer of the opera *Scylla et Glaucus* (1746), violin sonatas, trios, and concertos, etc.

**Le·clan'ché'** (lẽ·kläN'shā'), **Georges.** 1839–1882. French chemist; devised a galvanic cell (Leclanché's cell) that has an electromotive force of about 1½ volts.

**Léclavelé, Roland.** See Roland DORGELÈS.

**Le Clear** (lĕ klẹr'), **Thomas.** 1818–1882. American portrait and genre painter.

**Le·clerc'** (lẽ·klâr'), **Charles Victor Emmanuel.** 1772–1802. French soldier; m. Maria Paulina Buonaparte, sister of Napoleon (1797); served under Napoleon in Egypt; sent by Napoleon (1801) to conquer Santo Domingo; defeated Toussaint L'Ouverture (1802) and sent him a prisoner to France; died of yellow fever.

**Leclerc, Jacques Philippe.** 1902–1947. French army officer; educ. St. Cyr; governor of Cameroons (1940); military commander of Chad Territory (1941–42); led Free French force in 1500-mile march to join British 8th army in Libya (1943); in Normandy invasion (1944).

**Le Clerc** *or* **Le·clerc'** (lẽ·klâr'), **Jean.** *Lat.* **Johannes Cler'i·cus** (klĕr'ĭ·kŭs). 1657–1736. Swiss Protestant theologian and scholar; champion of Arminianism.

**Le Clerc du Tremblay, François.** See Father JOSEPH.

**Le·clercq'** (lẽ·klâr'), **Michel Théodore.** 1777–1851. French playwright.

**Lé'cluse'** *or* **Les'cluse'** (lā'klüz'), **Charles de.** *Latinized* **Carolus Clu'si·us** (kloo͞'zhĭ·ŭs). 1526–1609. French physician and botanist; credited with introducing the potato into Europe.

**Le·cocq'** (lẽ·kôk'), **Alexandre Charles.** 1832–1918. French composer, esp. of operettas, including *Fleur de Thé* (1868), *La Fille de Madame Angot* (1873), *Giroflé-Girofla* (1874), and *Le Petit Duc* (1878).

**Le·comte'** (lẽ·kôNt'), **Georges.** 1867–1958. French writer; known for his gently satirical novels.

**Le Conte** (lĕ kŏnt'), **John.** 1818–1891. American physicist, b. in Liberty County, Ga.; professor, U. of California (1869–91). His brother **Joseph** (1823–1901) was professor of geology, U. of California (1869–96). Their cousin **John Lawrence Le Conte** (1825–1883) became leading entomologist in U.S.; coauthor with G. H. Horn of *Classification of the Coleoptera of North America* (1883).

**Le·conte'** (lẽ·kôNt'), **Sébastien Charles.** 1865–1934. French jurist and poet, identified with the Parnassians.

**Leconte de Lisle** (dẽ lēl'), **Charles Marie.** *Orig. surname* **Leconte.** 1818–1894. French poet, b. in the island of Réunion. Settled in Paris; identified with modern Parnassian school; considered a poet of disillusionment and skepticism; found source of inspiration in the works of the ancients. Author of *Poèmes Antiques* (1852), *Poèmes Barbares* (1862), *Poèmes Tragiques* (1884), etc.

**Le Coq** (lẽ kôk'), **Albert August von.** 1860–1930. German ethnologist and archaeologist.

**Le·coq' de Bois'bau'dran'** (lẽ·kôk' dẽ bwä'bō'dräN'), **Paul Émile,** *called* **François.** 1838?–?1912. French chemist; engaged in spectroscopic researches on the rare earths; credited with discovery of elements gallium (1875), samarium (1879), and dysprosium (1886).

**Le Cor'bu'sier'** (lẽ kôr'bü'zyā'). *Pseudonym of* **Charles Édouard Jean'ne·ret'** (zhän'rĕ'). 1887–1965. French (Swiss-born) architect, painter, and writer; worked with Peter Behrens in Berlin (1911–12); a pioneer in ferroconcrete frameworks and collaborator with his cousin **Pierre Jeanneret** (1896–1967), engineer, in creating modern functional architecture; cofounder, with Ozenfant, of purism in art. His works include a design for the Palace of the League of Nations at Geneva (1927), etc. Author of *Après le Cubisme* (1918) and *La Peinture Moderne* (1924), both with Ozenfant, and of *Vers une Architecture* (1923), etc.

**Le·cou'vreur'** (lẽ·koo͞'vrûr'), **Adrienne.** 1692–1730. French actress both in tragedy and comedy; mistress of Maurice of Saxony and reputedly poisoned by her rival, the duchesse de Bouillon; subject of a play *Adrienne Lecouvreur* by Scribe and Legouvé.

**Leczinski.** French spelling of LESZCZYŃSKI.

**Le Dan'tec'** (lẽ däN'tĕk'), **Félix Alexandre.** 1869–1917. French biologist; connected with Pasteur Institute and sent by Pasteur to Brazil to establish a laboratory for study of yellow fever. Author of *Théorie Nouvelle de la Vie* (1896), *La Crise du Transformisme* (1910), etc., also philosophical works, including *L'Athéisme* (1906) and *L'Egoïsme, Base de Toute Société* (1911).

**Le'de·bour** (lā'dĕ·boo͝r), **Georg.** 1850–1947. German Socialist; Social Democrat member of Reichstag (1900–18); with left wing of his party, opposed war credits in World War I (1914); joined Independent Social Democrats (1916); participated in revolution of 1918; took part in Communist revolt, Berlin (1919); joined new Socialist Labor party (1931).

**Ledebour, Karl Friedrich von.** 1785–1851. German botanist; author of *Flora Rossica* (4 vols., 1841–53), etc.

**Ledebour,** Baron **Leopold Karl Wilhelm August von.** 1799–1877. German historian; author of *Adelslexikon der Preussischen Monarchie* (3 vols., 1854–57), etc.

**Led'er·berg** (lĕd'ẽr·bûrg), **Joshua.** 1925– . American geneticist, b. Montclair, N.J. Awarded Nobel prize in physiology and medicine (1958) with G. W. Beadle and E. L. Tatum.

**Le'de·rer** (lā'dĕ·rẽr), **Emil.** 1882–1939. German economist and sociologist; author of *Grundzüge der Ökonomischen Theorie*, etc.

**Led'er·er** (lĕd'ẽr·ẽr), **George W.** 1861–1938. American theatrical producer, b. Wilkes-Barre, Pa. Pioneer in presentation of better-class vaudeville shows, and in producing musical comedies, fantasies, revues, as *The Belle of New York*, *Madame Sherry*, *The Passing Show*.

**Le·des'ma Bui·tra'go** (lȧ·thās'mä bwē·trä'gō), **Alonso de.** 1562–1633. Spanish poet, whose *Conceptos Espirituales* (1600) and *Juegos de Nochebuena* (1611) established the school of literary mysticism known as *conceptism.*

**le Despenser.** See DESPENSER.

**Le'dó·chow'ski** (lĕ'dōō·kôf'skē), Count **Mieczysław.** 1822–1902. Polish Roman Catholic prelate; archbishop of Posen and Gnesen (1866–86); imprisoned (1873–75) for his opposition to the May laws during the Kulturkampf. Consecrated cardinal (1875); resigned his see (1886); prefect of propaganda, Rome (1892–1902).

**Le·doux'** (lē·dōō'), **Lou'is** (lōō'ĭ) **Vernon.** 1880–1948. American poet and critic, b. New York City. In business as president of Ledoux & Co., chemists and assayers. Author of *Songs from the Silent Land* (1905), *The Soul's Progress and Other Poems* (1907), *Yzdra* (1909), etc. Authority on Japanese art, and author of *The Art of Japan* (1927), *Japanese Prints* (1936), etc.

**Le·dru'–Rol'lin'** (lē·drü' rô'lăN'), **Alexandre Auguste.** 1807–1874. French lawyer and politician; member of Chamber of Deputies (from 1841) and identified with radical groups. Associated with Lamartine and Louis Blanc in seeking reforms; a leader in the revolution (1848) and minister of the interior in the provisional government. Became candidate for president of France, but was defeated (1848). Elected to Legislative Assembly (1849), but was forced to flee to England for safety; not allowed to return to France until 1870. Continued issuing Republican manifestoes; advocated universal suffrage and was largely instrumental in causing its adoption in France. Was again a member of the legislature at the time of his death (Dec. 31, 1874).

**Le' Duc' Tho'** (lā'dŭk'tō'), 1912– . Vietnamese official. Awarded (with Henry Kissinger) but declined Nobel prize for peace (1973).

**Led'widge** (lĕd'wĭj), **Francis.** 1891–1917. Irish poet, b. in County Meath. Worked in fields and as domestic servant, copper miner, overseer of roads. Introduced by Lord Dunsany; enlisted in Kitchener's first army, served through Gallipoli campaign (1915); killed in Belgium. Author of *Songs of the Field* (1915), *Songs of Peace* (1916), *Last Songs* (1918).

**Led'yard** (lĕd'yẽrd), **William.** 1738–1781. American Revolutionary soldier, b. Groton, Conn. With his garrison, was captured and massacred by the British at Fort Griswold, Groton (Sept. 6, 1781). His nephew **John Ledyard** (1751–1789) as corporal of marines accompanied Cook on his last voyage (1776–79); wrote *A Journal of Captain Cook's Last Voyage to the Pacific Ocean* (1783).

**Lee** (lē), **Ann.** 1736–1784. Religious mystic, b. Manchester, Eng.; founder of Shaker society in U.S. Joined Shaking Quakers, or Shakers (1758); m. Abraham Standerin, Stanley, or Standley (1762), a blacksmith. Became acknowledged leader of Shakers, known as "Ann the Word," or "Mother Ann" (1770). To U.S. in 1774; settled with followers at what is now Watervliet, N.Y. (1776), forming first Shaker colony in U.S. Arrested for treason (1780) but soon released. Made two-year tour (1781–83) among Shaker colonies in New England. Died at Watervliet.

**Lee, Arthur.** 1740–1792. American diplomat, b. at "Stratford," Va. (see Richard LEE). Studied law and was admitted to English bar (1775). Appointed (1776) by Continental Congress one of three commissioners to negotiate treaty with France; became suspicious of his associates, Benjamin Franklin and Silas Deane, and circulated charges against them. Treaty was negotiated and signed (1778) but Deane was recalled and charged in turn that Lee did not have the confidence of the French foreign minister. Lee-Deane controversy led Congress to decide that the "suspicions and animosities" aroused were "highly prejudicial to the honor and interests of these United States," and Lee was recalled (1779). Member, Continental Congress (1781–85); member, treasury board (1784–89). Opposed adoption of the Constitution.

**Lee, Arthur Hamilton.** 1st Viscount **Lee of Fare'ham** (fâr'ăm). 1868–1947. English political leader. Conservative M.P. (1900); carried act for suppression of white-slave traffic (1912). Military secretary to Lloyd George, secretary for war (1915–16); director-general of food supplies (1917–18); minister of agriculture (1919), first lord of admiralty (Feb., 1921–Nov., 1922) in Lloyd George's administration; delegate to Washington Conference (1921–22). Chairman, royal commission on public services of India (1923–24). Gave estate of Chequers to nation as residence for prime minister.

**Lee, Charles.** 1731–1782. Soldier, b. Dernhall, Eng. To America (1773); took up land in Berkeley County, Va. At outbreak of Revolution, appointed second ranking major general of Continental army; joined Washington late in 1776. Slow in carrying out Washington's orders; severely criticized Washington, notably in letter to Gen. Gates. Captured by British (Dec. 13, 1776); while prisoner, submitted secret plan to Gen. Howe for defeating Americans; hence now regarded as traitor. Exchanged (1778); put in command of planned attack at Monmouth; instead of attacking began a retreat, which was halted only by arrival of Washington, Greene, Steuben, and their forces. Court-martialed, found guilty of disobedience, of misbehavior before the enemy, and of disrespect to the commander in chief; suspended from command. Continued to abuse Washington; dismissed from the army (1780).

**Lee, Charles.** 1758–1815. American jurist, b. at "Leesylvania," Va. (see Richard LEE). Attorney general of the U.S. (1795–1801).

**Lee, Fitzhugh.** 1835–1905. Grandson of Henry (Light-Horse Harry) Lee. American army officer, b. in Fairfax County, Va.; grad. U.S.M.A., West Point (1856). Resigned from U.S. army and entered Confederate service (1861). Cavalry commander, served notably in Peninsular operations (1861–62), in Chancellorsville campaign (1863), and at Spotsylvania Court House (1864). Governor of Virginia (1886–90). Consul general, Havana (1896–98); major general of volunteers in Spanish-American War; military governor of Havana (1899). Author of *General Lee* (1894), a biography of his uncle Robert E. Lee.

**Lee, Francis Lightfoot.** 1734–1797. American Revolutionary statesman, b. at "Stratford," Va. (see Richard LEE). Member, Virginia House of Burgesses (1758–68, 1769–76); supported revolutionary measures. Delegate to Continental Congress (1775–79); a signer of the Declaration of Independence.

**Lee, George Washington Custis.** 1832–1913. Son of Robert E. Lee. American army officer, b. Fortress Monroe, Va.; grad. U.S.M.A., West Point (1854). Resigned from U.S. army and entered Confederate service (1861); brigadier general (1863); major general (1864). Professor, Virginia Military Institute (1865–71). Succeeded his father as president, Washington and Lee U. (1871–97).

**Lee, Gerald Stanley.** 1862–1944. American Congregational clergyman and writer, b. Brockton, Mass.; lecturer on literature and the arts (from 1898). Author of *The Lost Art of Reading* (1902), *Crowds . . .* (1913), *Seven Studies in Self Command* (1921), *Recreating Oneself . . .*

(1933), etc. He married (1896) **Jennette Barbour Perry** (1860–1951), also a writer, professor of English, Smith (1904–13); director, with her husband, of Training School for Balance and Coördination, New York (from 1926); author of *Kate Wetherill* (1900), *Simeon Tetlow's Shadow* (1909), *Aunt Jane* (1915), *Dead Right* (1925), etc.

**Lee, Hannah Farnham,** *nee* **Saw′yer** (sô′yẽr). 1780–1865. American author, b. Newburyport, Mass.; m. George Gardner Lee (1807). Author of *Three Experiments of Living* (1837), and a number of biographical works.

**Lee, Harriet.** 1757–1851. English novelist and dramatist. Published novels *Errors of Innocence* (1786) and *Clara Lennox* (1797); her comedy *The New Peerage* performed (1787); author of *The Canterbury Tales* (5 vols., 1797–1805), one of which (*Kruitzner*) was dramatized by Byron under title *Werner* (1822) and previously by herself as *The Three Strangers* (performed 1825). Her sister **Sophia** (1750–1824), novelist and dramatist, conducted girls' school at Bath (1781–1803); author of *The Chapter of Accidents* (a five-act comedy; 1780), *The Recess* (a historical romance; 1785), *Almeyda, Queen of Grenada* (a tragedy in blank verse; 1796).

**Lee, Henry.** *Known as* **Light′-Horse′** (līt′hôrs′) **Harry Lee.** 1756–1818. American soldier and statesman, b. at "Leesylvania," Va. (see Richard LEE). Brilliant cavalry commander in Revolutionary War, esp. known for operations covering Greene's retreat across North Carolina to Virginia (1781). Member, Continental Congress (1785–88). Governor of Virginia (1792–95); commanded troops that suppressed Whisky Rebellion in Pennsylvania (1794). Member, U.S. House of Representatives (1799–1801). In his eulogy of Washington (1799) occur the famous words, "First in war, first in peace, and first in the hearts of his countrymen." Last years marred by debt and ill-health. His son **Henry** (1787–1837) was also a soldier, b. at "Stratford," in Westmoreland County, Va.; served in War of 1812; joined Jacksonian party (1826) and aided in preparing Jackson's inaugural address (1829); author of a life of Napoleon Bonaparte and books defending his father's record. Another son was Robert Edward Lee (*q.v.*); Fitzhugh Lee (*q.v.*) was a grandson.

**Lee, Ivy Ledbetter.** 1877–1934. American public-relations counsel; developed profession as public-relations counsel for various large interests (from 1914), notably John D. Rockefeller, Bethlehem Steel Co., Pennsylvania Railroad.

**Lee, James Paris.** 1831–1904. Scottish-born American inventor of the Lee-Enfield rifle, adopted (1904) by Great Britain for both infantry and cavalry. See also W. E. METFORD.

**Lee, Jason.** 1803–1845. Methodist Episcopal missionary in Oregon country (from 1834); b. Stanstead, Quebec. Co-operated in drawing up petition for territorial government (1836–37); presided (1841) at preliminary meeting for territorial organization; influential in establishing provisional government (1843). A founder of Oregon Institute, later Willamette U.

**Lee, Jennette Barbour Perry.** See Gerald Stanley LEE.

**Lee, Jesse.** 1758–1816. American Methodist Episcopal clergyman, b. in Virginia. Assistant to Bishop Asbury (1797–1800). Presiding elder, South District of Virginia (1801–15). Author of first history of the Methodists in the U.S. (1810).

**Lee, John Clifford Hodges.** 1887–1958. American army officer, b. Junction City, Kans.; grad. U.S.M.A., West Point (1909); chief of services of supply for U.S. forces in Europe (1942–44); lieut. general (1944).

**Lee, Manfred B.** 1905– . See Ellery QUEEN.

**Lee, Nathaniel.** 1653?–1692. English dramatist; produced *Nero* (1675), *Gloriana* and *Sophonisba* (two rhyming plays, 1676); made reputation with blank-verse tragedy *The Rival Queens, or the Death of Alexander the Great,* in which both Roxana and Statira (*q.v.*) are wives of Alexander (1677); terminated series of plays from classical history with *Constantine the Great* (1684); collaborated with Dryden in *Oedipus* (1679) and *The Duke of Guise* (1682).

**Lee, Richard.** d. 1664. English settler in Virginia, probably from Shropshire, Eng. Emigrated about 1641; settled in York County; moved to Northumberland County (1651); acquired land, raised tobacco, and traded with England. Many of his descendants were prominent in American history, including his great-grandsons of the branch of the Lees associated with "Stratford" in Westmoreland Co., Va., Richard Henry, Francis Lightfoot, William, and Arthur, and their cousins of the branch associated with "Leesylvania" in Prince William Co., Va., Henry (Light-Horse Harry) and Charles (1758–1815). See the individual biographies.

**Lee, Richard Henry.** 1732–1794. American Revolutionary statesman, b. at "Stratford," Va. (see Richard LEE). Educated in England. Member, Virginia House of Burgesses (1758); prominent in defending colonial rights (from 1764); with Patrick Henry and Thomas Jefferson, initiated intercolonial committees of correspondence (1773). Virginia delegate to Continental Congress (1774–79); on June 7, 1776, moved resolution (adopted July 2) that "these united colonies are, and of right ought to be, free and independent states; that they are absolved from all allegiance to the British crown, and that all political connection between them and the State of Great Britain is, and ought to be, totally dissolved"; a signer of Declaration of Independence and of Articles of Confederation. Again member of Congress (1784–89); its president (1784–85); opposed new constitution. Member, U.S. Senate (1789–92).

**Lee, Robert Edward.** 1807–1870. Son of Henry (Light-Horse Harry) Lee (*q.v.*). American soldier, commander in chief of the Confederate armies, b. at "Stratford," Va. (see Richard LEE). Grad. U.S.M.A., West Point (1829). On engineering duties, U.S. army (1829–46). Served in Mexican War, notably at Vera Cruz, Churubusco, and Chapultepec (1847). Superintendent, West Point (1852). Transferred from corps of engineers to cavalry (1855). On frontier duty in Texas (1856–57; 1860–61). Commanded detachment which suppressed the uprising at Harpers Ferry at time of John Brown's raid (1859). At outbreak of Civil War, resigned from U.S. army and accepted command of Virginia forces. Military adviser to Jefferson Davis (1861–62). Assigned (June 1, 1862) to command troops around Richmond, Va.; designated his troops as the army of northern Virginia; repulsed Federal forces (June 25–July 1, 1862). Started campaign into Maryland; checked at Antietam (Sept. 17, 1862). Turned back Federal move at Fredericksburg (Dec. 13, 1862), and again at Chancellorsville (May 1, 1863). Advanced into Pennsylvania, but was decisively defeated at Gettysburg (July 1–4, 1863). With inferior forces, conducted brilliant defensive operations against Grant (May, 1864–April, 1865); appointed general in chief of all Confederate armies (Feb. 6, 1865); surrendered to Grant at Appomattox Court House (April 9, 1865). President, Washington College (1865–70), now Washington and Lee University. Elected to American Hall of Fame (1900). See George Washington Custis LEE and William Henry Fitzhugh LEE, his sons.

**Lee, Samuel.** 1783–1852. English Orientalist; professor of Arabic at Cambridge (1819–31), of Hebrew (1831–48);

author of Hebrew grammar (1830) and *Hebrew, Chaldaic, and English Lexicon* (1840).

**Lee, Samuel Phillips.** 1812–1897. Grandson of Richard Henry Lee (*q.v.*). American naval officer, b. in Fairfax County, Va. Served in Union navy through Civil War; commanded *Oneida* in attack on New Orleans (1862) and at Vicksburg under Farragut; commanded North Atlantic blockading squadron (1862–64) and Mississippi squadron (1864–65). Retired in 1873.

**Lee,** Sir **Sidney.** 1859–1926. English editor and scholar. Assistant editor (1883–90), coeditor with Sir Leslie Stephen (1890–91), and editor in chief (1891–1917), *Dictionary of National Biography.* Commissioned by King George V to prepare a biography of King Edward VII from original papers. Among his other works are *A Life of William Shakespeare* (1898), *A Life of Queen Victoria* (1902), *Shakespeare and the Modern Stage* (1906), *Shakespeare and the Italian Renaissance* (1915).

**Lee, Tsung Dao.** 1926– . American (Chinese-born) physicist. At Columbia U. (1953–60; 1963– ); awarded Nobel prize in physics (1957) with C. N. Yang for work concerning the parity laws of physics.

**Lee, Vernon.** Pseudonym of Violet PAGET.

**Lee, William.** d. 1610. English clergyman and inventor of the stocking frame (1589). Patent refused by Queen Elizabeth and James I, so set up frames at Rouen, Fr.

**Lee, William.** 1739–1795. American merchant and diplomat, b. at "Stratford," Va. (see Richard LEE). In business in London, Eng. (from 1768); elected sheriff of London (1773) and alderman (1775), the only American ever to hold this office. Appointed (1777) by Continental Congress to act with Thomas Morris as commercial agent at Nantes, France; became involved in the Arthur Lee-Deane controversy (see Arthur LEE). Chosen by Congress to be commissioner to Berlin and Vienna (1777); failed to obtain from these courts recognition of United States; negotiated commercial treaty (never ratified) with Holland (1778), this treaty becoming cause of war declared by England against Holland (1780); recalled by Congress (1779).

**Lee, William Henry Fitzhugh.** 1837–1891. Son of Robert E. Lee. Known as **Rooney Lee** to distinguish him from his cousin Fitzhugh Lee. American Confederate officer, b. Arlington, Va.; cavalry commander in Civil War; with Jeb Stuart (1862–64); in action at Chancellorsville, Fredericksburg, Gettysburg, and around Richmond; major general (1864); member, U.S. House of Representatives (1887–91).

**Lee, William Little.** 1821–1857. American jurist in Hawaii, b. Sandy Hill, N.Y. On trip around Cape Horn to Oregon, stopped at Honolulu (1846); accepted invitation to remain and aid in establishing judiciary; chief justice, supreme court (1852). Hawaiian minister to United States (1855–57). Regarded as one of most influential creators of Hawaiian constitutional monarchy.

**Lee, Willis Augustus.** 1888–1945. American naval officer; entered navy (1904); appointed commander of task force in Southwest Pacific (1942).

**Leeb** (lāp), **Wilhelm Joseph Franz von.** 1876–1956. German field marshal. Commanded on southern flank in invasion of France (1940); in command on Leningrad front in Russian campaign (1941).

**Leech** (lēch), **John.** 1817–1864. English caricaturist; published *Etchings and Sketchings by A. Pen, Esq.* (1835); made hit with caricature of Mulready's design for postal envelope (1840); member of staff of *Punch* (1841–64).

**Leeds,** Dukes of. See Thomas and Francis OSBORNE.

**Lee'–Ham'il·ton** (-hăm'ĭl·tŭn; -t'n), **Eugene Jacob.** 1845–1907. English poet and novelist; disabled by nervous disease, retired to Florence with his half sister Violet Paget (*q.v.*). Author of *Imaginary Sonnets* (1888), *Sonnets of the Wingless Hours* (1894); translated Dante's *Inferno* (1898).

**Lee'–Han'key** (-hăng'kĭ), **William.** 1869–1952. English painter and etcher.

**Lees** (lēz), **Charles Herbert.** 1864–1952. English physicist; author of textbooks of practical physics, papers on the conduction of heat and electricity, etc.

**Lee'ser** (lē'sẽr), **Isaac.** 1806–1868. Rabbi, and pioneer in development of Jewish life in America; b. in Westphalia, Prussia; to U.S. (1824). Rabbi of congregations in Philadelphia (1829–50; 1857–68); founded (1843) and edited (1843–68) *The Occident and American Jewish Advocate;* established Maimonides Coll. (1868).

**Leete** (lēt), **William.** 1613?–1683. English colonist in America, b. in Huntingdonshire, Eng. Became Puritan and sailed to America (1639). One of group founding Guilford, Conn.; town clerk (1639–62). Deputy governor, New Haven Colony (1658–61); governor (1661–64). Deputy governor, Connecticut Colony (1669–76); governor (1676–83).

**Leeu'wen·hoek** *or* **Leu'wen·hoek** (lā'vĕn·ho͝ok), **Anton van.** 1632–1723. Dutch naturalist, b. at Delft. Made simple microscopes through which he observed microorganisms; first to give accurate description of the red blood corpuscles; demonstrated the blood capillaries; described spermatozoa, striated muscle fibers, the crystalline lens of the eye, etc.; observed hydra, rotifers, bacteria, and yeast plants; disproved instances of supposed spontaneous generation; described monocotyledonous and dicotyledonous stems.

**Le Fa·nu** (lĕf'ȧ·nū), **Joseph Sheridan.** 1814–1873. Irish novelist, b. Dublin, of old Huguenot family; editor and proprietor (1839–58), *The Evening Mail,* Dublin. His novels include *The House by the Churchyard* (1863) and *Uncle Silas* (1864).

**Le·fé'bure'–Wé'ly'** (lē·fā'bür'vā'lē'), **Louis James Alfred.** *Orig. surname* **Le·feb'vre** (lē·fâ'vr'). 1817–1870. French organist and composer of religious music and the light opera *Les Recruteurs* (1861).

**Le·feb'vre** (lē·fâ'vr'), **Charles Édouard.** 1843–1917. French composer of the comic opera *Le Trésor* (1883), the operas *Zaïre* (1887) and *Djelma* (1894), the legend *Melka* (1883), the choral works *Judith* (1879) and *Éloa* (1889), the symphonic work *Dalila,* sonatas, psalms, instrumental music, etc.

**Lefebvre, François Joseph.** Duc **de Dant'zig'** (däɴt'sēk'). 1755–1820. French soldier; general of brigade (1793) and of division (1794). Engaged at Fleurus (1794), the crossing of the Rhine (1795), Altenkirchen (1796), Neuwied (1797), Stockach (1799). Created marshal of the Empire (1807), besieged and captured Danzig. Commander of the Imperial Guard (1812–14); engaged at Montmirail and Champaubert. At the Restoration, appointed peer of France by Louis XVIII. His wife **Catherine,** *nee* **Hub'scher'** (üb'shâr'), whom he married (1783) while a common soldier, had been laundress of his company and retained until her death the simplicity, naïveté, and frankness of a woman of the people; heroine of Sardou's comedy *Madame Sans Gêne.*

**Lefebvre, Jules Joseph.** 1836–1912. French historical and portrait painter.

**Lefebvre, Tannegui.** *Latinized* **Tanaquillus Fa'ber** (fā'bẽr). 1615–1672. French philologist and classical scholar; editor of various Greek and Latin classics.

**Le·feb'vre–Des'nou·ettes'** (-dā'nwĕt'), **Comte Charles.** 1773–1822. French soldier; general of brigade (1807) and of division; engaged in Spanish and Russian campaigns; distinguished himself at Bautzen (1813), and at Brienne,

La Rothière, and Vauxchamps (1814); fought at Waterloo (1815).

**Le·fè′vre** (lĕ·fâ′vr'), **Pierre**. See Pierre FAVRE.

**Lefèvre d'É′ta′ples** (dā′tȧ′pl'), **Jacques**. *Lat.* **Jacobus Fa′ber** (fā′bĕr) *or* **Fa′bri** (fā′brī), *surnamed* **Stap′u·len′sis** (stăp′ū·lĕn′sĭs). 1450?–?1537. French scholar, theologian, and reformer, b. Étaples; leader of Biblical humanism in pre-Reformation France. Settled near Paris (1507–20); condemned for heresy in his religious and critical writings; fled to Strasbourg following charges of Reformation sympathies (1525); recalled; became tutor in royal family and royal librarian at Blois; lived under protection of Queen Margaret of Navarre in Nérac (from 1531), where Calvin is said to have visited him (1533).

**Le Fèvre d'Ormesson.** See ORMESSON.

**Leffler, Anne Charlotte.** See EDGREN.

**Le Flô** (lĕ flō′), **Adolphe Emmanuel Charles.** 1804–1887. French soldier and diplomat; general of brigade (1848) and minister to Russia (1848–49). Opposed Louis Napoleon's intrigues and was banished after the coup d'état (1851); returned to France (1857); minister of war (1870; 1871); ambassador to Russia (1871–79).

**Le·fort′** (lĕ·fôr′), **François.** 1656–1699. Officer in the Russian service, of Swiss birth and Scotch descent; favorite of Peter the Great and one of the czar's chief aides in reorganization of Russia.

**Le Fort** (lĕ·fôr′), **Gertrud von.** 1876–1971. German poet and novelist; among her poetical works are *Hymnen an die Kirche* (1924), *Hymnen an Deutschland* (1932); among her novels, *Das Schweisstuch der Veronika* (1928), *Der Papst aus dem Ghetto* (1930), etc.

**Le·franc′** (lĕ·fräɴ′), **Abel Jules Maurice.** 1863–1952. French scholar; founder and president of Société des Études Rabelaisiennes, and editor of a critical edition of the works of Rabelais; wrote studies on Shakespeare.

**Lefranc de Pompignan.** See POMPIGNAN.

**Le·froy′** (lĕ·froi′), **Harold Maxwell.** 1877–1925. British entomologist; imperial entomologist for India (1903–1912); imperial silk specialist, India (1915–16); devised means of controlling beetles in wheat and the deathwatch beetle in old buildings.

**Le·fu·el′** (lĕ·fü·ĕl′), **Hector Martin.** 1810–1881. French architect; appointed architect of the château of Meudon, later of Fontainebleau; designed parts of restoration of the Louvre, succeeding Visconti (after 1853).

**Le Gal·lienne′** (lĕ găl·yĕn′; găl′yĕn), **Richard.** 1866–1947. English man of letters, b. Liverpool. After seven years' apprenticeship in an accountant's office, abandoned business for literature; settled in London. His works include *My Ladies' Sonnets* (1887), *English Poems* (1892), *The Religion of a Literary Man* (1893), *Prose Fancies* (2 series, 1894, 1896), *If I Were God* (1897), *Painted Shadows* (1907), *Little Dinners with the Sphinx* (1909), *Pieces of Eight* (1918), *The Romantic '90's* (1926), *The Magic Seas* (1930), *From a Paris Garret* (1936). His daughter **Eva** (1899– ), actress; founder (1926) and director of the Civic Repertory Theater in New York, appearing there in *Cradle Song, The Cherry Orchard, Peter Pan, John Gabriel Borkman, Twelfth Night, The Sea Gull, Romeo and Juliet, Camille, Alice in Wonderland, L'Aiglon, Rosmersholm,* etc.

**Le·garé′** (lĕ·grē′), **Hugh Swinton.** 1797?–1843. American lawyer, b. Charleston, S.C. Attorney general of the U.S. (1841–43); ad interim secretary of state (1843).

**Legazpe** *or* **Legaspi, Miguel López de.** See Miguel LÓPEZ DE LEGAZPE.

**Le·gen′dre** (lĕ·zhäɴ′dr'), **Adrien Marie.** 1752–?1833. French mathematician. Member of commission to connect Paris and Greenwich geodetically; collaborated in preparing centesimal trigonometric tables; made important researches in the theory of elliptic functions, the theory of numbers, and attractions of ellipsoids; wrote on the method of least squares.

**Legendre, Louis.** 1752–1797. French revolutionary politician; a leader in the mob that stormed the Bastille (July 14, 1789); member of National Convention (1792) and Council of Ancients (1795).

**Le Gen′til'homme′** (lĕ zhaɴ′tē′yôm′), **Paul Louis.** 1884–1975. Fr. army off.; educ. St. Cyr; in World War I; general (1938); governor of Somaliland (1939–40); named Free French commander in chief in Africa (Aug., 1941); high commissioner of Madagascar (Nov., 1942).

**Lé′ger′** (lā′zhā′), **Alexis Saint-Léger.** *Pseudonym* **Saint-John Perse** (pĕrs). 1887–1975. French poet and diplomat. Secy.-general of French foreign ministry (1932–40). Awarded Nobel prize in literature (1960); wrote *Anabase* (1924), *Exil* (1942), *Chronique* (1960).

**Lé′ger′** (lā′zhā′), **Fernand.** 1881–1955. French painter; identified with ultramodern school, esp. with the cubists.

**Le·ger′** (lĕ·zhā′), **Louis Paul Marie.** 1843–1923. French Slavic scholar; among his many books are *Contes Populaires Slaves* (1882), *Histoire de Russie* (1907), *Les Anciennes Civilisations Slaves* (1921).

**Legge** (lĕg). Name of an English family bearing titles of baron and earl of **Dart′mouth** (därt′mŭth), including: **William Legge** (1609?–1670), Royalist army leader; governor of Oxford (1645); helped Charles escape from Hampton Court (1647); imprisoned (1649–53). His eldest son, **George** (1648–1691), 1st Baron Dartmouth, naval commander; served in Dutch war (1665–67) and in Flanders (1678); lieutenant governor of Portsmouth (1670–83); engaged in Tangier expedition (1683–84); commander in chief of fleet, but took oath of allegiance to William and Mary; died in Tower of London, charged with offer to surrender Portsmouth to France. **William Legge** (1672–1750), 1st Earl of Dartmouth; son of 1st baron; secretary of state for southern department (1710–13); lord keeper of privy seal (1713–14). **William Legge** (1731–1801), 2d earl, grandson of 1st earl; president of Board of Trade and foreign plantations (1765–66); colonial secretary (1772–75); lord privy seal (1775–82); advocated (1776) use of force against American colonies; gave name to Dartmouth Coll. (1769). **Henry Bil′son-Legge′** [bĭl′s'n-] (1708–1764), financier; 4th son of 1st earl; ambassador to king of Prussia (1748); chancellor of exchequer (1754–56, 1756–57, 1757–61).

**Legge, Alexander.** 1866–1933. American businessman; president, International Harvester Co. (1922–29; 1931–33); chairman, Federal Farm Board (1929–31).

**Legge, James.** 1815–1897. Scottish missionary and Sinologist, b. Huntly, Aberdeenshire; missionary at Malacca and Hongkong (1839–73); first professor of Chinese, Oxford (1876); published monumental edition of *Chinese Classics*, with translation, prolegomena, and notes (28 vols., 1861–86).

**Le·gin′ska** (lĕ·gĭn′skȧ), **Ethel.** *Orig. surname* **Lig′gins** (lĭg′ĭnz). 1890–1970. English pianist and conductor, b. at Hull. First woman to conduct leading symphony orchestras, as the Berlin Philharmonic, New York Symphony, Boston Philharmonic, Chicago Woman's Symphony Orchestra. Composer of orchestral works.

**Le Gof′fic′** (lĕ gô′fēk′), **Charles.** 1863–1932. French poet, novelist, and critic; best known for his verse and stories written against the background of his native Brittany, as in *Amour Breton* (verse; 1889), *Le Bois Dormant* (verse; 1900), *Le Crucifié de Kéraliès* (novel; 1889), *L'Abbesse de Guérande* (novel; 1921), *L'Illustre Bobinet* (novel; 1922).

**Le·gou·is′** (lĕ·gwē′), **Émile.** 1861–1937. French writer;

professor of English at the Sorbonne (1904); authority on William Wordsworth, as in his *La Jeunesse de William Wordsworth* (1918), *William Wordsworth et Annette Vallon;* author, with Cazamian, of *Histoire de la Littérature Anglaise* (1924).

**Le·gou'vé'** *or* **Le Gou'vé'** (lē·gōō'vā'), **Gabriel Marie Jean Baptiste.** 1764–1812. French playwright; author of *La Mort d'Abel* (1792), *Épicharis* (1793), *Étéocle et Polynice* (1799), *La Mort de Henri IV* (1806). His son **Gabriel Jean Baptiste Ernest Wilfrid** (1807–1903) was also a playwright and miscellaneous writer; author of the novel *Édith de Falsen* (1840), the plays *Louise de Lignerolles* (1848), *Adrienne Lecouvreur* (with Scribe; 1849), *Bataille de Dames* (1851), *Un Jeune Homme qui ne fait rien* (1861), *Miss Suzanne* (1869), the book *L'Art de la Lecture* (1878), and a volume of memoirs.

**Le·grain'** (lē·grăN'), **Georges.** 1865–1917. French Egyptologist; in charge of reconstruction of temple of Ammon at Karnak (1895), where he discovered 800 statues of stone and 17,000 of bronze (1904).

**Le·grand'** (lē·gräN'), **Émile.** 1841–1903. French Hellenist; author of many books on modern Greek.

**Legrand, Louis.** 1863–1951. French painter and engraver; among his illustrations are those for the tales of Edgar Allan Poe.

**Legrand du Saule** (dü sōl'), **Henri.** 1830–1886. French alienist; a founder of the Society of Legal Medicine.

**Le·gren'zi** (lā·grĕn'tsē), **Giovanni.** 1626?–1690. Italian composer of 18 operas, 6 oratorios, psalms, motets for 2–5 voices, many sonatas for 2–7 instruments, and books of chamber cantatas for 1–3 voices.

**Le·gros'** (lē·grō'), **Alphonse.** 1837–1911. Painter and etcher, b. Dijon; encouraged by Whistler, settled in London (1863) and became naturalized (1881); Slade professor of fine art, University Coll., London (1876–93). Specialized in religious subjects and life of vagabonds in his paintings, pen and pencil drawings, and etchings; contributed to revival of draftsmanship in England.

**Le·gros'** (lē·grō'), **Pierre** (1629–1714) and his son **Pierre** (1666–1718). French sculptors.

**Le·guí'a y Sal·ce'do** (lā·gē'ä ē säl·sā'thō), **Augusto Bernardino.** 1863–1932. Peruvian statesman; banker and insurance manager (1886–1903); minister of finance (1903–08). President of Peru (1908–12); president of the Latin-American Chamber of Commerce in London (1912–19). Returned to Peru and with aid of army seized power and expelled President José Pardo y Barreda; provisional president (1919); action legalized by a Constituent Assembly (Jan., 1920); president (1919–30); overthrown by a military revolt (Aug., 1930).

**Le'hár** (lĕ'här; *Angl.* lā'här), **Franz.** 1870–1948. Hungarian composer of operettas; bandmaster of various Austrian regiments (1890–1902); conductor of the Theater an der Wien (1902). Composer of the opera *Kukuška* (1896), of the operettas *The Merry Widow* (1905), *The Count of Luxemburg* (1909), *Gipsy Love* (1910), *Eva* (1911), *Alone at Last* (1914), *The Yellow Jacket* (1923), *Clo-Clo* (1924), *Paganini* (1925), *Friederike* (1928), etc., and of symphonic poems, sonatas, marches and dances for orchestra, etc.

**Leh'man** (lē'măn), **Herbert H.** 1878–1963. American banker and politician, b. New York City; partner in Lehman Bros., bankers, New York (1908); lieut. governor of New York (1928–32), governor (1932–42); appointed director (1942–46) of foreign relief and rehabilitation operations. His brother **Irving** (1876–1945), jurist; practiced in New York City (from 1898); justice, supreme court of New York (1909–36) and judge of the court of appeals (1924–40), chief judge (1940–45).

**Leh'mann** (lā'män), **Ernst August.** 1886–1937. German aeronautical engineer. Engaged in manufacture and piloting of Zeppelins (from 1913); accompanied Hugo Eckener on first Zeppelin trip to the U.S. in the *ZR3* (1924); commander of *Graf Zeppelin*, which made voyages to South America (1928–36), and of the *Hindenburg Zeppelin*, which he piloted on its first voyage from Germany to Lakehurst, N.J. (1936); died when the *Hindenburg* burned at Lakehurst.

**Leh'mann** (*Ger.* lā'män; *Fr.* lā'män'; *Eng.* lā'măn), **Henri,** *in full* **Charles Ernest Rodolphe Henri.** 1814–1882. Historical and portrait painter, b. Kiel, Schleswig; opened studio in Paris (1847) and became naturalized French citizen; among his works are mural paintings and portraits of Liszt, Ingres, Edmond About. His brother **Rudolf** (1819–1905), painter, exhibited at Royal Academy in London (1851, 1856; from 1866) chiefly subject pictures and portraits; lived in Italy (1856–66); became naturalized British subject; intimate friend of Robert Browning. Rudolf's daughter **Liza** (1862–1918), concert vocalist and composer, met with success in Gt. Britain and Germany; m. (1894) Herbert Bedford (1867–1945), Eng. painter and composer; known for her song cycles *In a Persian Garden* and *Nonsense Songs;* composed two operas, *Sergeant Brue* (1904) and *The Vicar of Wakefield* (1906).

**Rudolph Chambers Lehmann** (1856–1929), British journalist and Liberal politician, nephew of Rudolf, was a member of staff of *Punch* (from 1890), author of *Mr. Punch's Prize Novels* (1893), *Anni Fugaces* (1901), etc.

**Leh'mann** (lā'män), **Lilli.** 1848–1929. German dramatic coloratura soprano; interpreter esp. of Wagner and Mozart and of lieder; studied under Wagner (1875) and sang at premières of "Ring" dramas, Bayreuth (1876); at Metropolitan Opera House, New York (1885–89; 1891–92, and later); m. the tenor Paul Kalisch, in U.S. (1888).

**Lehmann, Lotte.** 1888– . German operatic soprano and concert singer; m. Otto Krause (1926; d. 1939); sang in U.S. at Chicago Civic Opera (1930–31), and with Chicago, Philadelphia, San Francisco, and Metropolitan Opera companies.

**Lehmann, Max.** 1845–1929. German historian; author of the biographies *Scharnhorst* (2 parts, 1886–87), and *Freiherr vom Stein* (3 vols., 1902–05), and of *Preussen und die Katholische Kirche seit 1640* (7 parts, 1878–94), etc.

**Leh'mann** (lę'män), **Orla,** *in full* **Peter Martin Orla.** 1810–1870. Danish statesman and lawyer, of German extraction. Head of National Liberal movement in Copenhagen (1848) and member of "March Ministry"; leader of Schleswig movement, and of "Eider Danes" (who regarded Eider as boundary of Denmark); member of Folketing (1851–53), Landsting (1854–70), and Reichsrat (1856–66); minister of interior (1861–63).

**Leh'mann** (lā'măn), **Rosamond.** 1904?– . English novelist; m. Wogan Philipps (1928); author of *A Dusty Answer* (1927), *Invitation to the Waltz* (1933), *The Weather in the Streets* (1936), *No More Music* (1939), etc.

**Leh'mann-Haupt'** (lā'män·houpt'), **Ferdinand Friedrich Carl.** 1861–1938. German historian and archaeologist; among his books are *Armenien Einst und Jetzt* (3 vols., 1910–31), *Geschichte des Alten Orients.*

**Lehm'bruck** (lām'brŏŏk), **Wilhelm.** 1881–1919. German expressionistic sculptor and etcher. His works feature nudes and elongated and exaggerated figures and include *Torso of a Woman, The Kneeling Woman, Youth Rising, Mother and Child,* several portrait heads.

**Leh'mer** (lā'mēr), **Derrick Norman.** 1867–1938. American mathematician and musician; composer of two operas based on American Indian themes (*The Harvest,*

*Necklace of the Sun*), and a number of Indian songs and choral works.

**Lehrs** (lārs), **Karl.** 1802–1878. German classical philologist and Homeric scholar.

**Leibl** (lī'b'l), **Wilhelm.** 1844–1900. German portrait and genre painter; resident in Paris (1869–70), where he associated with Courbet and other realists, and in Munich (1870–73) as member of the so-called Leibl circle; subsequently lived in Bavaria and the Lower Alps. His works include portraits, as of Frau Gedon; the paintings *The Peasant Women of Dachau, The Village Politicians, Three Women in the Village Church.*

**Leib'nitz,** Baron **Gottfried Wilhelm von.** *More correctly* **Leib'niz** (līp'nĭts). 1646–1716. German philosopher and mathematician, b. Leipzig. Educ. at Leipzig, Jena, and Altdorf (grad. 1666). In service of archbishop elector of Mainz (1667–76); spent four years (1672–76) in Paris and visited London (1673), meeting many scholars; discovered new notations of calculus, published (1684) before Newton's, thus causing long-debated controversy. In service of duke of Brunswick as librarian and privy councilor (1676–1716); wrote (1686; publ. 1819) *Systema Theologicum,* an attempt to find common ground for Catholic and Protestant faiths; began (1687) history of Brunswick ducal house (not publ. until 1843–45); received honors at Berlin from the elector of Brandenburg (1700–16); suggested founding of Acad. of Sciences (1700). Spent last thirty years of his life (1687–1716) in study of mathematics, natural science, philosophy, theology, history, law, politics, and other subjects; composed most of his philosophical works, chiefly as essays, treatises, etc., during latter years; left no complete and finished exposition of his philosophy (Leibnitzianism). His principal work in theology, *Théodicée* (1710), in the main a discussion of the problem of evil and a defense of optimism, was ridiculed by Voltaire in *Candide.*

**Leices'ter** (lĕs'tẽr), Earls of. See (1) Robert de BEAUMONT; (2) Robert DUDLEY; (3) Simon de MONTFORT (1208?–1265); (4) SIDNEY family.

**Leicester of Holkham,** Earl of. See Thomas William COKE.

**Leich'hardt** (līĸ'härt), **Friedrich Wilhelm Ludwig.** 1813–1848. German explorer in Australia, b. in Prussia; went to New South Wales (1841) and began geological investigations; crossed Australian continent from Moreton Bay to Port Essington (1844–45), and described expedition in journal (1847); attempted expedition across continent from east to west but disappeared on Cogoon River, without a trace (Apr. 4, 1848).

**Leich'ten·tritt** (līĸ'tĕn·trĭt), **Hugo.** 1874–1951. German composer and writer on music; composer of dramatic music, orchestral works, chamber music, and songs. Author of *Chopin* (1905), *Händel* (1924), and other biographies, and *Geschichte der Motette* (1908), *Analyse der Chopinschen Klavierwerke* (2 vols., 1920–22), etc.

**Lei'dy** (lī'dĭ), **Joseph.** 1823–1891. American naturalist, b. Philadelphia. Professor of anatomy (1853–91) and director of biology department (1884–91), Pennsylvania. Pioneer in researches in American vertebrate paleontology (*On the Fossil Horse of America,* 1847; *On the Extinct Mammalia of Dakota and Nebraska,* 1869); also wrote on parasitology (*Flora and Fauna within Living Animals,* 1853; *Remarks on Parasites and Scorpions,* 1886).

**Leif Ericson, Ericsson, Eriksen, Erikson,** *or* **Eriksson.** See ERICSON.

**Leifs** (lāfs), **Jón.** 1899– . Icelandic composer.

**Leigh'-Mal'lo·ry** (lē'măl'ō·rĭ), **Trafford Leigh.** 1892–1944. British air officer; LL.B., Cantab.; in World War I; air marshal, R.A.F. fighter command (1942); head of allied air offensive in invasion of Europe (1944); lost in flight.

**Leigh'ton** (lā't'n), **Clare.** 1899– . English artist (woodcuts and wood engravings); author and illustrator of *The Farmer's Year* (1933), *Four Hedges* (1935), *Country Matters* (1937), *Sometime, Never* (1939), *Southern Harvest* (1942), etc.

**Leighton, Frederick.** Baron **Leighton of Stret'ton** (strĕt''n). 1830–1896. English painter; won reputation with *Cimabue's Madonna Carried in Procession through the Streets of Florence* (exhibited 1855; bought at once by Queen Victoria); settled in London (1860). Excelled in draftsmanship, as in his classical paintings *Venus disrobing for the Bath, Hercules wrestling with Death, The Daphnephoria, Phryne, Captive Andromache, The Bath of Psyche, The Garden of the Hesperides, Clytie;* also in a few sacred pictures, including *Rizpah.*

**Leighton, Robert.** 1611–1684. Scottish preacher and prelate; signed Covenant (1643); principal of Edinburgh University (1653) and professor of divinity. Persuaded by Charles II to become bishop of Dunblane (1661); labored to preserve best of Episcopacy and of Presbyterianism as basis for a union; because of persecution of Covenanters sought to resign (1665, 1669); continued his fruitless efforts as archbishop of Glasgow (1670–74). His father, **Alexander Leighton** (1568–1649), was a victim of Laudian persecution; as Presbyterian preacher attacked Romanism in *Speculum Belli Sacri* (1624), attacked episcopacy and the queen in *An Appeal to the Parliament, or Sion's Plea against the Prelacie* (1628); sentenced by Star Chamber to public flogging, loss of ears, pillory, branding, life imprisonment; released by Long Parliament after eleven years' confinement.

**Lein'ber'ger** (līn'bĕr'gẽr), **Hans.** 1470?–after 1530. German sculptor, active in Landshut (after 1510). His works mark a direct transition from Bavarian late Gothic to early baroque.

**Leins'dorf** (līns'dôrf), **Erich.** 1912– . Am. (Austrian-born) conductor; assistant to Bruno Walter and Toscanini (1935); conductor, Metropolitan Opera Co., N.Y. (1939–43; 1957–61); musical director, Boston Symphony Orchestra (1962–68).

**Leinster,** Duke of. See *James Fitzgerald* (1722–1773), at FITZGERALD family.

**Lei'per** (lē'pẽr), **Robert Thomson.** 1881–1969. British parasitologist, b. at Kilmarnock; on Egyptian government survey in Uganda (1907); on research expeditions to the Gold Coast (1905), Nigeria (1912), China (1914), British Guiana (1921). Editor, *Journal of Helminthology* and *Helminthological Abstracts.*

**Lei'se·gang** (lī'zĕ·gäng), **Hans.** 1890–1951. German philosopher; author of *Die Gnosis* (1924), *Luther als Deutscher Christ* (1934), etc.

**Leish'man** (lēsh'măn), **John G. A.** 1857–1924. American diplomat, b. Pittsburgh, Pa. Successful steel manufacturer; U.S. minister to Switzerland (1897–1900), Turkey (1900–06); U.S. ambassador to Turkey (1906–09), Italy (1909–11), and Germany (1911–13).

**Leishman,** Sir **William Boog.** 1865–1926. British medical officer; entered army medical service (1887); director-general, army medical service (1923–26). Member of yellow-fever commission in western Africa (1913–15), and the medical research council (1913–23).

**Leis'ler** (līs'lẽr), **Jacob.** 1640?–1691. Insurrectionary leader in New York, b. Frankfort, Germany; to New Amsterdam (1660). Successful merchant and trader in furs, tobacco, and wine. Incurred hostility of aristocratic elements. Led discontented factions (1689); on flight of Lieutenant Governor Francis Nicholson, proclaimed William and Mary sovereign, assumed authority and administered the government with title of lieutenant governor (1689–91). Surrendered his powers to duly appointed governor, Sloughter, but was tried for treason, condemned, and hanged.

**Leitão, João Baptista da Silva.** See ALMEIDA-GARRETT.

**Leitch** (lēch), **William Leighton.** 1804–1883. Scottish water-color painter.

**Lei'ter** (lī'tẽr), **Levi Zeig'ler** (zĭg'lẽr). 1834–1904. American merchant; associated with Marshall Field in dry-goods business, Chicago (1865–81); active in philanthropic work. His son **Joseph** (1868–1932), b. Chicago, attempted to corner wheat market (1897–98) but failed with losses of about $10,000,000.

**Leith** (lēth), **Charles Kenneth.** 1875–1956. American geologist; professor, Wisconsin (from 1903); writer on pre-Cambrian, structural, and economic geology.

**Leith'-Ross'** (lēth'rŏs'), Sir **Frederick William.** 1887–1968. British economist and financier; private secretary to Prime Minister Asquith (1911–13); British member of finance board, Reparations Commission (1920–25); deputy controller of finance, in Treasury (1925–32); chief economic adviser to the government (1932–42); representative at World Economic Conference (1933), war-debts mission to Washington (1933), financial mission to China (1935–36), international sugar conference in London (1937), British export council (1940); member of economic committee of League of Nations (from 1932), and its chairman (1936, 1937); member of British Board of Trade (from 1942).

**Leit'ner** (līt'nẽr), **Gottlieb Wilhelm.** 1840–1899. Orientalist and traveler, b. Budapest; naturalized British subject; director of Punjab U., Lahore (1864–84); founded many schools, libraries, and newspapers in northwestern India, and contributed to study of Greco-Buddhist art.

**Lei'vick** (lā'vĭk), **Hal'per** (hȧl'pẽr). 1888– . Jewish poet and playwright, b. near Minsk, Russia; to U.S. (1913); author of Yiddish plays, including *Der Golem* (1921), and of volumes of poetry.

**Le·jeune'** (lẽ·zhûn'), **John Archer.** 1867–1942. American marine corps officer; brigadier general (1916) and major general (1918). Served in Spanish-American War (1898), Philippine Islands (1908–09), at capture of Vera Cruz (1914), and in France as commander of 2d division (1918–19); commanding officer, U.S. Marine Corps (1920–29; retired); superintendent, V.M.I. (1929–37); lieutenant general (Apr., 1942).

**Le·jeune'** (lẽ·zhûn'), Baron **Louis François.** 1775–1848. French soldier and painter, esp. of battle scenes; served in Revolutionary and Napoleonic armies. Credited with introducing lithography into France.

**Le·kain'** (lẽ·kăN'), **Henri Louis.** *Orig. surname* **Cain** (kăN). 1728–1778. French tragedian; friend of Voltaire; appeared in *Le Mauvais Riche,* Voltaire's tragedy *Brutus,* etc.

**Le·keu'** (lẽ·kû'), **Guillaume.** 1870–1894. Belgian composer of modern French school; composer of a sonata in G for violin and piano, two symphonic studies, a string quartet (finished by d'Indy), and other chamber music and orchestral works.

**L. E. L.** Initials used as pen name by Letitia Elizabeth LANDON.

**Le'land** (lē'lănd), **Charles Godfrey.** 1824–1903. American journalist and humorist, b. Philadelphia. Resident in London (1869–79) and (after 1884) chiefly in Florence, Italy. Contributed to *Graham's Magazine* his famous *Hans Breitmann's Party* (May, 1857); published other ballads, finally collected in *The Breitmann Ballads* (1871). Also wrote *Meister Karl's Sketch-Book* (1855), *A Dictionary of Slang* (with Albert Barrère, 1889), *The Unpublished Legends of Virgil* (1901), etc.

**Leland, Henry Martyn.** 1843–1932. American pioneer automobile manufacturer; organized Leland & Faulconer Mfg. Co., Detroit (1890), and merged it into Cadillac Motor Car Co. (founded by him, 1904); also, founder of Lincoln Motor Co., later sold to Ford Motor Car Co.

**Le'land** *or* **Ley'land** (lē'lănd), **John.** 1506?–1552. English antiquary; king's antiquary (1533); toured England and Wales to search for records, manuscripts, relics of antiquity.

**Le'land** (lē'lănd), **John.** 1691–1766. English Presbyterian minister and Christian apologist. Replied to Matthew Tindal and to Thomas Morgan's *The Moral Philosopher.* Attacked deists in *View of the Principal Deistical Writers* (1754–56).

**Le·leux'** (lẽ·lû'), **Pierre Adolphe** (1812–1891) and his brother **Hubert Simon Armand** (1818–1885). French painters, esp. of genre scenes of rural life.

**Le·le'wel** (lĕ·lĕ'vĕl), **Joachim.** 1786–1861. Polish historian, geographer, and politician, b. Warsaw; of Prussian ancestry; a leader of Polish revolution (1830–31); lived subsequently as exile in Paris and Brussels. His works in Polish include *The History of Poland* (1829) and *The Rebirth of Poland* (1843); his works in French include *Numismatique du Moyen Âge* (3 vols., 1835), *La Pologne au Moyen Âge* (3 vols., 1846–51), *Géographie du Moyen Âge* (4 vols., 1852–57).

**Le·loir'** (lȧ·lwär'), **Luis Federico.** 1906– . Argentine biochemist, b. Paris. Awarded Nobel prize in chemistry (1970) for work in biosynthesis of carbohydrates.

**Le Lor'rain'** *or* **Le·lor'rain'** (lẽ·lô'răN'), **Robert.** 1666–1743. French sculptor.

**Le'ly** (lē'lĭ; *Du.* lā'lē), Sir **Peter.** *Orig.* **Pieter Van der Faes** (văn dẽr fȧs'). 1618–1680. Dutch portrait painter, active chiefly in England; son of military captain known by nickname Lely (from lily on house of his birth). To England (1641); painted at first historical subjects and landscapes, and later, portraits.

**Le Maire** (lẽ mâr'), **Jacques.** fl. 1732. French instrument maker; invented type of reflecting telescope later developed by Herschel (the Herschelian telescope).

**Le Maire** (lẽ mâr'), **Jakob.** 1585–1616. Dutch navigator; with William Cornelis Schouten explored the South Seas and discovered Staten Island (off Tierra del Fuego) and Le Maire Straits (Jan., 1616).

**Le·maire'** (lẽ·mâr'), **Philippe Joseph Henri.** 1798–1880. French sculptor. His *Thémistocle* and his *Laboureur Trouvant des Armes* are in the Tuileries, his statue of Hoche at Versailles, his statue of Napoleon at Lille.

**Lemaire de Belges** (dẽ bĕlzh'), **Jean.** 1470?–?1525. Belgian poet and chronicler.

**Le·maî'tre** (lẽ·mâ'tr'), **Antoine Louis Prosper,** *known as* **Frédérick.** 1800–1876. French actor; made hit as Robert Macaire in the melodrama *L'Auberge des Adrets* (1823); appeared in *Hamlet, Falstaff, Kean, Ruy Blas, Don César de Bazan, Tragaldabas.*

**Lemaître,** Abbé **Georges Édouard.** 1894–1966. Belgian astrophysicist and mathematician; professor of the theory of relativity and of the history of the physical and mathematical sciences, U. of Louvain; known for work relative to the theory of an expanding universe.

**Lemaître, Jules,** *in full* **François Élie Jules.** 1853–1914. French writer; literary critic on staff of *Revue Bleue;* dramatic critic on *Journal des Débats* and *Revue des Deux Mondes;* his critiques appeared in book form, *Contemporains* (7 vols., 1885–99) and *Impressions de Théâtre* (10 vols., 1888–98). Author also of plays, fiction, and verse.

**Le·man'** (lẽ·măN'), **Gérard Mathieu.** 1851–1920. Belgian general (1912); conducted brilliant defense of fortress of Liége against overwhelming German forces (August, 1914).

**Le Mar′chant** (lẽ mär′chănt), **John Gaspard.** 1766–1812. English soldier; drew up plans for schools of instruction for officers, the beginnings of Sandhurst; lieutenant governor of the schools (1801–10); commanded cavalry brigade in Peninsular War (1810–12); fatally wounded at Salamanca.

**Le·may′** (lẽ·mā′), **Leon Pamphile.** 1837–1918. French-Canadian poet and novelist.

**Le·mer′cier′** (lẽ·mĕr′syā′), **Jacques.** 1585?–1654. French architect; appointed architect of the king (1618), and took charge of completion of the Louvre (1624); designed Palais Richelieu, later developed into the Palais Royal; designed the Sorbonne.

**Lemercier, Louis Jean Népomucène.** 1771–1840. French playwright and poet; among his plays are *Agamemnon* (1794), *Ophis* (1798), *Charlemagne*, and a comedy, *Pinto* (1799), reputed to be first French historical comedy.

**Le·merre′** (lẽ·mâr′), **Alphonse.** 1838–1912. French publisher whose establishment became a rendezvous for young literary men of the day, as Leconte de Lisle, François Coppée, Paul Bourget, et al.

**Lé′me·ry′** (lām′rē′; *Angl.* lĕm′ẽr·ĭ), **Nicolas.** 1645–1715. French chemist; established pharmacy in Paris; because of his Calvinistic principles had to flee to England (1683); returned to France, turned Catholic (1686), reopened his pharmacy. Author of *Cours de Chymie* (1675), *Traité de l'Antimoine* (1707), etc.

**Le·mieux′** (lẽ·myû′), **Rodolphe.** 1866–1937. Canadian lawyer and politician; solicitor general of Canada (1904–06); postmaster general (1906–11); minister of marine (1911); speaker of the House of Commons (1922–30); senator (1930 ff.).

**Lem′mens** (lĕm′ĕns), **Nicolas Jacques.** 1823–1881. Belgian organist and composer; won European reputation as teacher. His works include a great *École d'Orgue* and many organ compositions.

**Lem′mon** (lĕm′ŭn), **John Gill.** 1832–1908. American botanist; conducted botanical explorations in California, Nevada, and Arizona; author of *Pines of the Pacific Slope* (1888), *Hand-book of West-American Cone-bearers* (1892), etc.

**Lem′ni·us** (lĕm′nĭ·ŭs; *Ger.* -nē·o͞os), **Simon.** *Real surname* **Lemm′–Mar′ga·dant** (lĕm′mär′gä·dänt). 1511?–1550. German humanist and Latin poet; studied under Melanchthon at Wittenberg, where he antagonized Luther with two books of epigrams (1538) attacking Luther's followers and praising Luther's enemy Archbishop Albert of Mainz; escaped from Wittenberg and sought revenge by writing a 3d book of epigrams (1538) and the bitter satirical poem *Monachopornomachia.* Further works include *Amores* (love poems; 1542), *Raeteïs* (epic of the Swiss war of 1499; pub. 1874), and a Latin translation of the *Odyssey* (1549).

**Le Moine** (lẽ mwån′), Sir **James MacPherson.** 1825–1912. Canadian lawyer, naturalist, and writer, b. Quebec. Author of *L'Ornithologie du Canada* (1860), *Legendary Lore of the Lower Saint Lawrence* (1862), *Quebec, Past and Present* (1876), *Birds of Quebec* (1891), etc.

**Le·moinne′** (lẽ·mwån′), **John Marguerite Émile.** 1815–1892. French journalist; on staff of *Journal des Débats* (1840–92).

**Lem′on** (lĕm′ŭn), **Harvey Brace.** 1885–1965. American physicist; professor, Chicago (from 1928). His researches include work on comet-tail spectra and on the biophysical effects of ultraviolet rays; designed a spectrophotometer; adapted coconut-shell charcoal for gas masks. Author of *From Galileo to Cosmic Rays* (1934) and *Cosmic Rays thus Far* (1936).

**Lemon, Mark.** 1809–1870. English playwright; author of farces, melodramas, operas, novelettes, lyrics, songs, and a few three-volume novels; best known as one of the founders and first editors (later sole editor) of *Punch* (1841–70).

**Le·mon′nier′** (lẽ·mô′nyā′), **Camille,** *in full* **Antoine Louis Camille.** 1844–1913. Belgian author of realistic novels and stories of peasant life, psychological novels, the descriptive novel *Au Cœur Frais de la Forêt* (1900), juveniles, works on art criticism, etc.

**Lemonnier, Pierre Charles.** 1715–1799. French astronomer. At 21 years of age, assisted Maupertuis and Clairaut in measuring a degree of the meridian within the polar circle in Lapland. Investigated the disturbances of the motion of Jupiter caused by Saturn; carried on lunar observations for 50 years; studied terrestrial magnetism and atmospheric electricity; determined positions of numerous fixed stars; observed and recorded Uranus before its discovery as a planet.

**Le·mot′** (lẽ·mō′), Baron **François Frédéric.** 1773–1827. French sculptor; carved statue *Numa Pompilius* for the Council of Five Hundred, *Cicéron* for the Tribunate, *Brutus* and *Lycurgue* for the Corps Législatif, and *Léonidas aux Thermopyles* for the Senate; also, carved the huge bas-relief on the front of the Louvre.

**Le·moyne′** *or* **le Moyne** (lẽ·mwån′), **Charles.** 1626–1685. French colonist in Canada; ennobled by Louis XIV (1668) and presented with seigneury of Longueuil and other seigneuries which descended to his sons, as follows: **Charles** (1656–1729), Baron **de Lon′gueuil′** (lôɴ′gû′y'), commandant general of Canada (1711); governor of Three Rivers (1720); governor of Montreal (1724). **Jacques** (1659–1690), Sieur **de Sainte Hé′lène′** (săɴ′tā′lĕn′), a commander in expedition that sacked Schenectady (1690); mortally wounded in action at Quebec (Oct., 1690). **Pierre** (1661–1706), Sieur **d'Iberville** (see IBERVILLE), naval officer; founded colony of Louisiana. **Paul** (1663–1704), Sieur **de Ma′ri′court′** (må′rē′ko͞or′), army officer; killed (Mar. 21, 1704). **Joseph** (1668–1734), Sieur **de Sé′ri′gny′** (sā′rē′nyē′), naval officer; governor of Rochefort (1723). **Jean Baptiste** (1680–1768), Sieur **de Bienville** (see BIENVILLE), lieutenant of king in Louisiana and, later, governor. **Antoine** (1681–1747), Sieur **de Châ′teau′-guay′** (shä′tō′gā′), governor of Guiana; to Acadia and aided in defense of Louisburg.

**Le·moyne′** (lẽ·mwån′), **François.** 1688–1737. French painter; best-known work, decoration of the vault of the Salon d'Hercule at the Château de Versailles with 142 figures of superhuman proportions.

**Lemoyne, Jean Baptiste.** 1704–1778. French sculptor; carved statues of Louis XV at Rennes and Bordeaux, tombs of Cardinal Fleury and Mignard at Saint-Roch, and many portrait busts.

**Lem·prière′** (lĕm·prẹr′; lĕm′prĭ·ẽr, -âr; läɴ′prē′âr′), **John.** 1765?–1824. English classical scholar; known for his *Bibliotheca Classica* or *Classical Dictionary* (1788), long a reference book in mythology and classical history.

**Le Nain** (lẽ năɴ′). Family of three brothers, French painters: **Antoine** (1588–1648), **Louis** (1593–1648), and **Mathieu** (1607–1677).

**Le′nard** (lā′närt), **Philipp.** 1862–1947. German physicist; head of the radiological institute in Heidelberg (1909). First to observe the peculiar properties of cathode rays penetrating into the outside air from the Crookes tube; these rays are called *Lenard rays* after him. Awarded the 1905 Nobel prize for physics. Author of *Über Kathodenstrahlen* (1906), *Über Äther und Materie*

(1911), *Quantitatives Über Kathodenstrahlen Aller Geschwindigkeiten* (1918), *Probleme Komplexer Moleküle* (1914), *Über das Relativitätsprinzip* (1918), *Grosse Naturforscher* (1929).

**Le'nar·to'wicz** (lĕ'när·tô'vĕch), **Teofil.** 1822–1893. Polish poet; published *Szopka* (1849), *Lirenka* (1851), *Poezje* (1861); translated Dante's *Divina Commedia.*

**Le'nau** (lā'nou), **Nikolaus.** *Pseudonym of* **Nikolaus Niembsch von Streh'le·nau** (nēmpsh' fôn shtrā'lĕ·nou). 1802–1850. Lyric and epic poet, b. in Hungary; in Vienna and Stuttgart (1833–43); became insane (1844). Wrote lyric poems, and the epics *Faust* (1835), *Savonarola* (1837), *Die Albigenser* (1842), etc.

**Len'bach** (lān'bäκ), **Franz von.** 1836–1904. German portrait painter; his works include copies of Rubens, Titian, and others for Schack's gallery in Munich, *The Arch of Titus, The Shepherd Boy,* and portraits.

**Len'clos'** (län'klō'), **Anne.** *Known as* **Ninon de Lenclos.** 1620–1705. French lady of fashion; adopted the epicurean philosophy of her father; her beauty and wit attracted to her a number of the most distinguished men of the day, including Richelieu, St.-Évremond, La Rochefoucauld, D'Estrées, Condé, and Sévigné; in her later years, she enjoyed the friendship of Mme. de Maintenon, Mme. de Lafayette, Queen Christina of Sweden, and her salon was attended by the most select society of the period.

**Le·nep·veu'** (lĕn·vû'), **Jules Eugène.** 1819–1898. French painter; known esp. for his decorative work in many churches and public buildings.

**L'En'fant'** (län'fäN'), **Pierre Charles.** 1754–1825. Engineer and soldier, b. Paris, France. To America (1777) to serve in Continental army; commissioned captain of engineers (1778); served in southern army under John Laurens; honorably retired (1784). Remodeled building in New York City for temporary quarters of new federal government (1789). Invited by George Washington, he laid out plans for the national capital on the Potomac (1791) and began construction; expense entailed by magnitude of his work caused his dismissal (Feb. 27, 1792); excellence of plans recognized by Park Commission (1901) and development of city of Washington carried out in accordance with them.

**Len'glen'** (läN'glĕn'; *Angl.* lĕng'(g)lĕn), **Suzanne.** 1899–1938. French lawn-tennis player; won world's hard-court (women's) singles championship at Paris (1913); won championships in singles, doubles, mixed doubles of France and England (1919–23, 1925–26; not competing in 1924 because of illness); defaulted during tournament in her sole try for American singles title (1921); defeated Helen Wills at Cannes (1926); became professional (1926), touring U.S.; retired (1927).

**Len'gyel** (lĕn'dyĕl), **Emil.** 1895– . Writer, b. Hungary; to U.S. (1921); served in World War I (prisoner in Siberia 20 months); journalist (1919–30); professor of history, Brooklyn Poly. Inst. (1935–42); N.Y.U. (1943); author of *Hitler* (1932), *Millions of Dictators* (1936), *The Danube* (1939), *Turkey* (1941), *Siberia* (1943), etc.

**Le'nin** (lyā'nyĭn), **Nikolai.** *Real name* **Vladimir Ilich Ul·ya'nov** (ōōl·yä'nôf). 1870–1924. Russian Communist leader, b. in Simbirsk (now Ulyanovsk). Began study of works of Karl Marx; influenced by execution (1891) of an older brother for plot against life of czar. Practiced law in Samara (1892); moved to St. Petersburg (1894), where he began Socialist propaganda work; arrested (1895); exiled (1897) to eastern Siberia, where he married (1898) Nadezhda Krupskaya (*q.v.*) and completed his great economic study *The Development of Capitalism in Russia* (1899). To Switzerland (1900); founded *Iskra* (*The Spark*), revolutionary journal intended for circulation in Russia. Collaborated with Plekhanov in working out program of organization and action for Marxian Socialists, accepted by Socialist Congress (1903), which, however, ended in schism, dividing into sections known as Mensheviks (*i.e.* minority party) and Bolsheviks (*i.e.* majority party); became a leader of the Bolsheviks. At time of Russo-Japanese War (1904–05), encouraged revolution in Russia, which was suppressed; continued propaganda and organization work till outbreak of World War I; vigorously denounced the war as imperialistic, and urged Socialists in all countries to rise against their own governments; issued program (Nov. 1, 1914) for creation of a new Socialist International; at congress (Sept., 1915) in Switzerland laid foundations for Communist International. Immediately upon learning of revolutionary disturbances in Russia (Feb., 1917), sought to reach Russia; allowed by Germans to cross Germany by train. In Russia (from April, 1917), assumed leadership of revolutionary movement; overthrew moderate provisional government under Kerenski, and declared that supreme power in Russia was vested in the Soviets; became head of the Soviet of People's Commissars; became premier following dissolution of constituent assembly on his motion (Jan. 7, 1918) and establishment of the dictatorship of the proletariat. Accepted humiliating peace of Brest Litovsk with Germany (1918); defended Russia against counterrevolutionary armies (1918–21); introduced far-reaching socialistic reforms in Russia, later (1921) modified by New Economic Policy. Died at Gorki (Jan. 21, 1924).

**Len·né'** (lĕ·nā'), **Peter Joseph.** 1789–1866. German landscape gardener and architect; known esp. for work on the parks of Berlin and Potsdam and the zoological garden in Berlin.

**Len'nep** (lĕn'ĕp), **Jacob van.** 1802–1868. Dutch novelist, poet, and lawyer. Author of *Legends of the Netherlands* (in verse; 1828–31) and of many romantic and historical novels and stories, of political comedies, works on Dutch history, translations into Dutch from Shakespeare, Byron, Southey, and Tennyson, etc.

**Lenn'gren** (lĕn'grān), **Anna Maria,** *nee* **Malm'stedt** (mälm'stĕt). 1754–1817. Swedish poet; m. Karl Lenngren (1780); wrote satirical poems and epigrams.

**Len'nox** (lĕn'ŭks), Earls and dukes of. See STEWART family.

**Lennox,** Countess of. **Margaret Douglas.** See *earls of Angus,* under DOUGLAS family.

**Lennox.** Name of an English family springing from union of Charles II and Louise Renée de Kéroualle (*q.v.*), Duchess of Portsmouth, and including dukes of **Rich'mond** (rĭch'mŭnd) of fourth creation (peerage of England), of **Lennox** (peerage of Scotland), and of **Au'bi'gny'** [ō'bē'nyē'] (given by Louis XIV). Members include:

**Charles Lennox** (1672–1723), 1st Duke of Richmond, Duke of Lennox (cr. 1675); natural son of Charles II; changing politics and religion, became reconciled to King William; governor of Dumbarton Castle (1681); lord of bedchamber to George I (1714).

The 1st duke's only son, **Charles** (1701–1750), 2d Duke of Richmond and of Lennox, and Duke of Aubigny (in France); lord of bedchamber (1727), privy councilor (1735); a lieutenant general, attended duke of Cumberland in expedition against rebels (1745).

The 2d duke's 3d son, **Charles** (1735–1806), 3d duke; diplomat; grad. Leiden (1753), distinguished himself at Minden (1759); minister at Paris (1765); secretary of state for southern department (1766–67), denounced ministerial policy toward American colonies; pronounced in favor of universal suffrage, with annual elections (1783); master general of ordnance with seat in cabinet (1782–95); turned against all reform (1784).

**Charles Lennox** (1764–1819), 4th duke; nephew of 3d duke; m. (1789) Charlotte Gordon, daughter of 4th duke of Gordon; fought duel with Frederick Augustus, Duke of York (1789); M.P. (1790); lord lieutenant of Ireland (1807–13); general (1814), gave ball at Brussels on eve of Quatre Bras (1815); governor general of British North America (1818).

**Charles Gor′don–Len′nox** [gôr′d'n-] (1791–1860), 5th duke; eldest son of 4th duke; assistant military secretary to Wellington in Portugal (1810–14), postmaster general (1830–34); assumed on death (1836) of his uncle, last duke of Gordon in Gordon line (see under GORDON family), additional surname of Gordon. His brother Lord **William Pitt Lennox** (1799–1881), officer on Wellington's staff, spectator at Waterloo (1815), journalist, author of works of history and fiction, including *The Tuft-Hunter* (1843), also reminiscences.

**Charles Henry Gordon–Lennox** (1818–1903), 6th Duke of Richmond and 1st Duke of **Gordon** in Lennox line; Conservative political leader, aide to Wellington (1842–52), M.P. (1841), president of Board of Trade (1867–69), leader in House of Lords (1868–76); lord president of council (1874–80), secretary for Scotland (1885–86); promoted agricultural legislation, including bill for control of contagious diseases in cattle; chairman of royal commission on agriculture (1879–82).

**Lennox, Charlotte,** *nee* **Ramsay.** 1720–1804. Novelist and poet, b. in New York; to England (1735) where she resided thereafter; m. Alexander Lennox (1747). Friend of Samuel Johnson and Samuel Richardson. Author of *Poems on Several Occasions* (1747); a novel, *The Female Quixote, or the Adventures of Arabella* (1752); *Shakespeare Illustrated* (1753); a play, *The Sister* (1769), and many translations from the French.

**Le·noir′** (lẽ·nwȧr′), **Alexandre,** *in full* **Marie Alexandre.** 1762–1839. French antiquary. Collector of French monuments and works of art saved from convents and churches at the time of the Revolution; worked on the restoration of the tombs of French kings.

**Lenoir, Étienne,** *in full* **Jean Joseph Étienne.** 1822–1900. French inventor of the first practical internal-combustion engine (c. 1859).

**Le·nor′mand′** (lẽ·nôr·mäɴ′), **Henri René.** 1882–1951. French playwright; author of *Les Possédés* (1909), *Le Simoun* (1920), *Une Vie Secrète* (1929), etc.

**Lenormand, Louis Sébastien.** 1757–1839. French chemist and mechanician; credited with first successful parachute descent, made from the tower of the Montpellier observatory, holding an umbrella five feet in diameter in each hand (1783).

**Lenormand, Marie Anne Adélaïde.** *Popularly known as* **La Si′bylle′ du Fau′bourg′ Saint′–Ger′main′** (lȧ sē′bēl′ dü fō′bo͞or′ săɴ′zhĕr′măɴ′). 1772–1843. French fortune teller; gained fame by prophesying marriage of Joséphine de Beauharnais and Napoleon Bonaparte; consulted by such personages as Mme. de Staël, Talma, Alexander I of Russia, the duc de Berry.

**Le·nor′mant′** (lẽ·nôr′mäɴ′), **Charles.** 1802–1859. French archaeologist and numismatist; author of *Introduction à l'Histoire Orientale* (1838) and joint author of *Le Trésor de Numismatique et de Glyptique* (1834–50). His son **François** (1837–1883), Assyriologist and archaeologist, became professor of archaeology, Bibliothèque Nationale (1874); chief work, *Les Origines de l'Histoire d'après la Bible et les Traditions des Peuples Orientaux* (1880–82); recognized existence in cuneiform texts of a non-Semitic language now called the Akkadian.

**Le·nô′tre** (lẽ·nō′tr′), **André.** 1613–1700. French landscape architect; director of royal gardens under Louis XIV; designed, wholly or in part, many famous gardens, as at Versailles, Chantilly, Saint-Cloud, Fontainebleau, Kensington Gardens and St. James's Park (London), the Quirinal and the Vatican (Rome).

**Len′ox** (lĕn′ŭks), **James.** 1800–1880. American bibliophile and philanthropist, b. New York City. Established and gave land and books to the Lenox Library (1870). Published *Washington's Farewell Address...*(1850), *Shakespeare's Plays in Folio* (1861), etc.

**Len·tel′li** (lĕn·tĕl′ĭ; *Ital.* lån·tĕl′lē), **Leo.** 1879–1961. Sculptor, b. Bologna, Italy; to U.S. (1903); naturalized (1912). Best known for his carving of the Saviour and 16 figures for the reredos of the Cathedral of St. John the Divine, New York City.

**Len′thall** (lĕn′tôl; -thôl), **William.** 1591–1662. English parliamentarian; member of Short Parliament (1640); speaker of Long Parliament (1640–53); refused to tell King Charles whether any of the Five Members was in the House of Commons (1642); speaker of parliament of 1654; member of parliament of 1656; speaker of restored Long Parliament (1659); co-operated with Monck in bringing about the Restoration.

**Len′tu·lus** (lĕn′tů·lŭs), **Lucius Cornelius.** *Surnamed* **Crus** (krŭs) *or* **Crus·cel′lo** (krŭ·sĕl′ō). Roman politician, hostile to Caesar; consul (49 B.C.); after battle of Pharsalus (48), fled to Egypt, where he was seized by Ptolemy, and executed.

**Lentulus, Publius Cornelius.** *Surnamed* **Su′ra** (sū′rȧ). d. 63 B.C. Roman praetor (75 B.C.); consul (71). Involved in Catiline's conspiracy; plotted to murder Cicero and burn Rome; executed (Dec. 5, 63).

**Lentulus, Publius Cornelius.** *Surnamed* **Spin′ther** (spĭn′thẽr). Roman politician; curule aedile (63 B.C.), aided Cicero in suppressing conspiracy of Catiline. Praetor (60); governor of Hispania Citerior (59); consul (57); governor of Cilicia (56–53). At outbreak of Civil War (49), joined Pompey; after battle of Pharsalus (48), fled to Rhodes. According to one account, was captured by Caesar, and executed.

**Lenz** (lĕnts), **Heinrich Friedrich Emil.** 1804–1865. German physicist; studied electrical phenomena; enunciated Lenz's law on the direction of the induced current in electromagnetic induction; credited with discovery of the dependence of electrical resistance on temperature.

**Lenz, Jakob Michael Reinhold.** 1751–1792. German lyric poet and dramatist; in Strasbourg (1771), joined Goethe's circle; followed Goethe to Weimar (1776), but forced to leave for bad manners and tactlessness; suffered mental breakdown and led wandering life. Author of lyric poems long attributed to Goethe, including *Die Liebe auf dem Lande* written to Friederike Brion, realistic and social plays, the comedy *Die Freunde Machen den Philosophen* (1776), the satire *Pandaemonium Germanicum* (pub. 1819), and critical works.

**Lenz, Max.** 1850–1932. German historian; disciple of Ranke; author of *Martin Luther* (1883), *Geschichte Bismarcks* (1902), *Napoleon* (1905), the essays *Kleine Historische Schriften* (3 vols., 1910–22), etc.

**Lenz, Oskar,** *in full* **Heinrich Oskar.** 1848–1925. German explorer in West Africa (1874–77); crossed the western Sahara to Timbuktu (1880); made expedition to rescue Junker and Casati, who were isolated because of the Mahdi revolt.

**Lenz, Peter.** *Religious name* Father **De′si·de′ri·us** (dā′zē·dā′rē·o͝os). 1832–1928. German painter, architect, and sculptor; Benedictine monk at Beuron (1876), helped to found Beuron school of art and sought to revive interest in religious art.

**Lenz** (lĕnz), **Sidney S.** 1873–1960. American whist and bridge expert, and writer on bridge.

**Le'o** (lē'ō). Name of thirteen popes (see *Table of Popes*, Nos. 45, 80, 96, 103, 118, 124, 127, 132, 151, 219, 234, 254, 258), especially:

**Leo I,** Saint. 390?–461. Known as "the Great." Pope (440–461); b. probably Rome. Influential as a deacon; sent on a mission to Gaul by Emperor Valentinian III; while there, elected pope (440). Took great interest in affairs in all parts of the realm of the church; had primacy of bishop of Rome recognized by the emperor (445); condemned proceedings of Robber Synod of Ephesus (449); convened Council of Chalcedon (451); persuaded Attila to spare Rome (452) and kept Genseric (455), the Vandal chieftain, from destroying the city; sought to drive out all heresy; active in disciplinary reforms; wrote many sermons and letters of historic interest.

**Leo II,** Saint. d. 683. Pope (682–683); b. in Sicily. Confirmed canons of Council of Constantinople (680); healed schism between sees of Rome and Ravenna.

**Leo III,** Saint. 750?–816. Pope (795–816); b. Rome. Crowned Charlemagne (800) emperor of the West, an act which established the temporal sovereignty of the pope over the Roman city and state.

**Leo IV,** Saint. 800?–855. Pope (847–855); b. Rome. Defended Rome against the Saracens.

**Leo VIII.** d. 965. Pope (963–965). First created pope (963) by the emperor, Otto I, but deposed (964) by synod favoring John XII; after death of John XII and election of Benedict V, again (964) placed in pontifical seat (964–965).

**Leo IX,** Saint. *Real name* **Bru'no** (brōō'nō). 1002–1054. Pope (1049–54); b. in Alsace. Through his father, related to Emperor Conrad II. Elected by influence of Emperor Henry III; enjoined celibacy of the clergy; traveled through Italy, Germany, and France (1050); declared war against Normans in southern Italy (1053); was captured and detained.

**Leo X.** *Real name* **Giovanni de' Medici.** 1475–1521. Second son of Lorenzo the Magnificent (see MEDICI); b. Florence. Pope (1513–21). Destined in childhood for the church; received fine education; created cardinal (1488) at age of 13; taken prisoner in battle of Ravenna (1512); chosen pope at 37; an able administrator, but used his influence to benefit his family; drove French from Italy, but later (1515) defeated by Francis I; made concordat (1516) with France; terminated 5th Lateran Council (1517) and prevented threatened schism; failed to realize importance of rise of Reformation (1519), although he issued (1520) bull excommunicating Luther; a scholar and patron of art in all forms.

**Leo XI.** *Real name* **Alessandro Ottaviano de' Medici** (*q.v.*). 1535–1605. Pope (1605); b. Florence. Archbishop of Florence; cardinal (1574); sent on mission to France (1596) by Pope Clement VIII; reigned less than one month.

**Leo XII.** *Real name* **Annibale Francesco del'la Gen'ga** (dāl'lä jĕng'gä). 1760–1829. Pope (1823–29); b. near Spoleto. Held various high church offices (1793–1823) during Napoleonic era; made cardinal (1816); pontificate marked by energetic efforts for reform.

**Leo XIII.** *Real name* **Gioacchino Vincenzo Pec'ci** (pĕt'chē). 1810–1903. Pope (1878–1903). b. near Anagni, Italy. Received excellent classical education under Jesuits and at the Collegio Romano; sent as nuncio to Brussels (1843); made cardinal (1853). His pontificate one of most notable in recent history of church; wrote many important encyclicals on various matters, such as marriage, freemasonry, study of the Bible, education, modern socialism (*Rerum novarum*, 1891); continued assertion of predecessor as to papal authority, considering himself "prisoner of the Vatican"; won advantage (1887) in struggle with Kulturkampf in Germany; opened Vatican archives (1883) to scholars; constantly strove for promotion of peace; wrote Latin poetry and prose of a high order of excellence; an eminent scholar and statesman.

**Leo.** Name of six rulers of the Eastern Roman Empire:

**Leo I.** *Called* **the Great** *by the orthodox,* **Ma·kel'les** [mȧ·kĕl'ēz] ("the butcher") *by the Arians.* 400?–474. Emperor (457–474); a Thracian, raised to power by Aspar, commander of the guard; his general Anthemius repelled invasions of Huns in Dacia (466, 468); made disastrous expedition against Vandals in Africa (468); caused murder of Aspar (471).

**Leo II.** d. 474. Infant grandson of Leo I; associated as ruler with his grandfather (473–474), but died a few months after him.

**Leo III.** *Called* **the I·sau'ri·an** (ī·sô'rĭ·ăn). 680?–741. Emperor (717–741); first of Isaurian dynasty; in early youth a soldier; overthrew Theodosius III (717); compelled Caliph Suleiman to give up siege of Constantinople; defeated Moslems (726) and especially in great battle at Acroïnum in Phrygia (739); made many administrative reforms in army, finances, and various codes of law; published the *Ecloga Legum* (740); in long strife with church over image worship; an iconoclast, his actions caused insurrections in Greece and Italy (727), and confiscation of papal lands within the empire led to complete rupture with pope (730–732).

**Leo IV.** *Called* **the Kha·zar'** (kä·zär'). 750?–780. Son of Constantine V; emperor (775–780); continued energetic policy against Arabs and Bulgars and upheld a mild iconoclasm; married Irene (later empress).

**Leo V.** *Called* **the Armenian** *because Armenian by birth.* d. 820. Emperor (813–820); a distinguished general under Nicephorus I and Michael I; proclaimed emperor (813), after Michael was driven from throne; conducted long and successful war against Bulgarians (814–817); carried out severe repressions of Paulicians and image worshipers; assassinated by followers of Michael the Amorian.

**Leo VI.** *Called* **the Wise** *and* **the Philosopher.** 866–912. Son of Eudocia and Michael III; emperor (886–912); deposed Photius, Patriarch of Constantinople (886); during his reign Bulgarians established independent church, Moslem pirates captured Thessalonica (904), Moslems conquered Sicily (907); a scholar of some ability, wrote verse and *Orations* (chiefly on theological subjects), and issued *Basilica* (888?), a completion of the digest of the laws of Justinian; m. (1) Theophano (*q.v.*); (2) Zoë (Zaützа); and (3) Zoë (Carbonopsina), whose son Constantine VII succeeded to the throne. See ZOË.

**Le'o** (lā'ō), **Friedrich.** 1851–1914. German classicist; works include critical editions of Seneca's tragedies and of Plautus.

**Le'o** (lā'ō), **Heinrich.** 1799–1878. German historian; conservative and extreme reactionary; author of *Geschichte der Italienischen Staaten* (5 vols., 1829–32), *Lehrbuch der Universalgeschichte* (6 vols., 1835–44), etc., also writings on old Germanic languages, and on religion and politics.

**Le'o** (lâ'ô), **Leonardo.** *Properly* **Lionardo Oronzo Salvatore de Leo.** 1694–1744. Italian composer of the old Neapolitan school; composed over seventy operas, including the serious opera *L'Olimpiade* (1737) and the comic opera *Amor Vuol Sofferenze* (1739), several oratorios, many sacred works, concertos, organ works, piano pieces, etc.

**Le'o Af'ri·ca'nus** (lē'ō ăf'rĭ·kā'nŭs), *i.e.* Leo the African. *Arab.* **al-Ḥasan ibn-Muḥammad al-Wazzan.** fl. 1st half 16th century. Arab traveler and geographer, b. Granada; traveled through northern Africa and western Asia; captured by pirates and sent to Rome (1517); there learned Latin and Italian and became a Christian; took name **Johannes Leo;** wrote *Description of Africa* (first in Arabic; transl. into Italian, 1550), for long time only source of knowledge of geography of Sudan.

**Leo Di·ac'o·nus** (dī·ăk'ō·nŭs). Byzantine historian of 2d half of the 10th century; wrote in ten books a chronicle of events between 959 and 973.

**Leo Hebraeus.** See ABRABANEL.

**Le·och'a·res** (lē·ŏk'ȧ·rēz). Greek sculptor of 4th century B.C.; associated with his master Scopas in decorating the Mausoleum of Halicarnassus.

**Leof'ric** (lā'ôf·rēk). *Latin* **Leu·ri'cus** (lū·rī'kŭs). d. 1057. Earl of Mercia. Succeeded his father as one of three great earls of the realm of England (bet. 1024 and 1032); played part as mediator between Edward the Confessor and Earl Godwin (1051); benefactor of the church, like his wife Godgifu, famed in legend as Lady Godiva (*q.v.*).

**Le·ón'** (lā·ōn'), **Juan Ponce de.** See PONCE DE LEÓN.

**León, Luis Ponce de.** See PONCE DE LEÓN.

**León Hebreo.** See ABRABANEL.

**Le'on of Mo'de·na** (lē'ŏn, mô'dā·nä). 1571–1648. Jewish scholar, rabbi, and poet, b. Venice, of a French family. Author esp. of the much-translated *Historia dei Riti Ebraici* (1637), of *Ari Nohem*, which contains an attack on the cabala (pub. 1840).

**Le·ón' y Gama** (lā·ōn'), **Antonio de.** See GAMA.

**Leon'ard** (lĕn'ẽrd), **Harry Ward.** 1861–1915. American electrical engineer and inventor; associated with Edison (1884) in introducing central station electric system in cities. Patented first electric train lighting system (1889), a system of motor control (1891), electric elevator control (1892), a system of multiple-voltage motor control (1892), a double-arm circuit breaker (1902), etc.

**Leonard, Sterling Andrus.** 1888–1931. American educator; professor of English, Wisconsin (1920–31). Author of *The Doctrine of Correctness in English Usage, 1700–1800* (1928), etc. A report on *Current English Usage* initiated by him was completed by his associates (1932).

**Leonard, William Ellery.** 1876–1944. American educator and poet, b. Plainfield, N.J. On English faculty, U. of Wisconsin (from 1906; professor from 1926). Author of *Sonnets and Poems* (1906), *The Poet of Galilee* (1909), *The Lynching Bee and Other Poems* (1920), *Two Lives* (1925), *A Son of Earth* (collected verse, 1928), and the plays *Glory of the Morning* (1912) and *Red Bird* (1923).

**Le'o·nar'do da Pi'sa** (lā'ō·när'dō dä pē'sä). *Real name* **Leonardo Fi'bo·nac'ci** (fē'bō·nät'chē). *Called also* **Leonardo Pi·sa'no** (pē·sä'nō). *Latin* **Le'o·nar'dus Pi·sa'nus** (lē'ō·när'dŭs pī·sā'nŭs). 1180?–?1250. Italian mathematician; introduced Arabic notation into Europe in his *Liber Abaci* (1202); also published a work on geometry entitled *Practica Geometria* (1220); in the theory of numbers, a certain series of numbers is named after him.

**Leonardo da Vinci.** See Leonardo da VINCI.

**Le'o·nar'do de Argensola** (lā'ō·när'thō), **Bartolomé** and **Lupercio.** See ARGENSOLA.

**Le'o·nar'do Pisano** (lā'ō·när'dō). See Leonardo FIBONACCI.

**Le·on'ca·val'lo** (lā·ōn'kä·väl'lō), **Ruggiero.** 1858–1919. Italian operatic composer and librettist; works include the operas *I Pagliacci* (1892), *Chatterton* (1896), *La Bohème* (1897), *Zaza* (1900), *Der Roland* (1904), and *Edipo Re* (pub. 1920), and their librettos.

**Le'on·hard** (lā'ōn·härt), **Karl Cäsar von.** 1779–1862. German mineralogist and geologist; the mineral leonhardite is named after him.

**Le·o'ni** (lā·ō'nē), **Leone.** *Known as* **il Ca'va·lie're A're·ti'no** (ēl kä'vä·lyâ'rā ä'rā·tē'nō). 1509–1590. Italian medalist, goldsmith, and sculptor; engraver in papal mint, Rome (1537–40), in mint at Milan (1542–45; 1550–90); in service of Charles V of Germany as sculptor and medalist. Works include bronze busts of Charles V and Philip II of Spain, marble statue of Charles V, tomb of marquis of Marignano (in Milan cathedral), medals, as of Michelangelo.

**Le·on'i·das I** (lē·ŏn'ĭ·dăs). fl. early 5th century B.C. King of Sparta (490?–480 B.C.); famous for his defense of the pass of Thermopylae against a vast Persian army; slain with all his force at the pass.

**Leonidas II.** 285?–236 B.C. King of Sparta; dethroned by the ephors (241 B.C.), but regained his power (240 B.C.) and ruled tyrannically until his death (236).

**Leonidas of Ta·ren'tum** (tȧ·rĕn'tŭm). Greek epigrammatic poet of 3d century B.C. Some of his verse is preserved in The Anthology.

**Léonide** *or* **Leonid.** See Léonide BERMAN.

**Le'on·na'tus** (lē'ŏ·nā'tŭs). d. 322 B.C. Macedonian general under Alexander the Great; after Alexander's death (323 B.C.), received the satrapy of Lesser Phrygia; killed in action near Lamia (322).

**Le·o·no'ra Tel'les de Me·ne'ses** (lyō·nō'rȧ tĕ'lyĕzh thĕ mĕ·nā'zĕsh). d. 1386. Mistress, and later queen, of King Ferdinand I of Portugal; regent at his death (1383); driven out by John, Grand Master of Aviz (later John I); imprisoned in convent at Tordesillas.

**Le·o'nov** (lyĭ·ô'nôf), **Leonid Maksimovich.** 1899– Russian novelist, b. Moscow. Author of the prose poem *Tuatamur* (1924); his works translated into English include the novels *The Thief* (1931) and *Soviet River* (1932), and the short stories *By the Bonfire, The Town of Gogulev, Ivan's Misadventure.*

**Le·ont'ief** (lē·ŏnt'yĕf; lyĕ-), **Wassily.** 1906– . American economist, b. Leningrad. At Harvard U. (1932–75), New York U. (1975– ); awarded Nobel prize for economics (1973).

**Le·on'ti·us** (lē·ŏn'shĭ·ŭs). d. 705. Emperor of the Eastern Roman Empire (695–698). An army officer, led revolt against Justinian II, deposed and exiled him; overthrown by Tiberius III Apsimar (698); slain by Justinian.

**Leontius of By·zan'ti·um** (bĭ·zăn'shĭ·ŭm; bī-; -tĭ·ŭm). *Called* **Byz'an·ti'nus** (bĭz'ăn·tī'nŭs) *or* **Scho·las'ti·cus** (skō·lăs'tĭ·kŭs). 485?–?543. A Byzantine monk; writer on theological subjects. Converted from Nestorianism in youth. Lived at various times at Constantinople, where he took part (531) in theological disputes under Justinian, at Rome, and at Jerusalem. Wrote works against the Nestorians, Monophysites, and other heretic sects. Called "the first of the Scholastics."

**Le'o·par'di** (lā'ō·pär'dē), **Alessandro.** d. 1522? Venetian sculptor; known particularly for his completion of Verrocchio's equestrian statue of General Bartolommeo Colleoni; cast the statue in bronze and created its marble pedestal.

**Leopardi,** Conte **Giacomo.** 1798–1837. Italian poet; victim of physical deformities and chronic ailments from early childhood; distinguished as classical scholar and student of modern languages. First known through patriotic poem *All'Italia* (1818); leading Italian lyric poet of pessimism; friend and correspondent of Pietro Giordani; in later years befriended also by Antonio Ranieri. Among his works are *Canzoni* (1824), *Versi* (1826), *Canti* (1836), the poetic satire *I Paralipomeni* *della Batracomiomachia* (1842), and several philological works.

**Le'o·pold** (lē'ô·pōld; *Ger.* lā'ô·pôlt). *Old High Ger.* **Lu'it·pold** (lōō'ĭt·pôlt). Name of several rulers of Austria: (1) Of the Babenberg (*q.v.*) family (10th to 13th century), four margraves (Leopold I to IV) and two dukes (Leopold V and VI), especially:

**Leopold VI.** *Called* **der Glor'rei'che** (dĕr glōr'rī'kĕ), *i.e.* the Glorious. 1176–1230. Duke (1198–1230). Went on crusade (1212) in Spain against the Moors and (1217–19) to Palestine and Egypt; active supporter of Emperor Frederick II.

(2) Of the Hapsburg family (from 1282), dukes and archdukes of Austria, especially:

**Leopold I.** 1290?–1326. Son of King Albert I of Hapsburg and brother of Frederick, rival emperor of Louis IV (of Bavaria); made duke of Austria and Styria; completely defeated by Swiss (1315) at Morgarten; after Frederick's capture at Mühldorf (1322) continued war against Louis.

**Leopold III.** 1351–1386. Nephew of King Albert; duke, jointly with his brother Albert (1365–79); on division of lands (1379) received Styria, Carinthia, Tirol, etc.; a warlike ruler, fought with Bavarians, Venetians, and Swiss; defeated and killed by Swiss at Sempach.

**Leopold V.** 1586–1633. Son of Charles of Styria and brother of Emperor Ferdinand II; archduke (1619–33); bishop of Passau (1605) and of Strassburg (1607); unsuccessful in administration of Jülich and Cleve (1609); received bishopric (1625) from the pope.

**Leopold William.** 1614–1662. Second son of Ferdinand II and nephew of Leopold V; bishop of Passau and other German cities (1625–54); active in command (1639–42) of imperial forces in Thirty Years' War; resigned after defeat at Breitenfeld (1642); took part in campaigns against Swedes and French (1645–47); fought in the Netherlands (1647–55) against the French.

**Le'o·pold** (lē'ô·pōld). Name of three kings of Belgium:

**Leopold I.** *Orig. name* **Georges Chrétien Frédéric.** 1790–1865. First king of independent Belgium (1831–65). Fourth son of Francis Frederick, Duke of Saxe-Coburg-Saalfield (1750–1806); b. at Coburg. Uncle of Queen Victoria of England. Served in Russian army under Alexander I (1805–14); fought at Lützen, Bautzen, and Leipzig (1813); m. (1816) Princess Charlotte of England (d. 1817); lived in England (1817–30); m. (1829) morganatically Karoline Bauer; refused throne of Greece (1830); chosen king of Belgium (1831) on its separation from Holland; m. (1832) Louise d'Orléans, daughter of Louis Philippe. During his reign, treaty signed with Netherlands (1839); friendly relations with France until 1851; after that (1851–65) relations difficult because of policies of Napoleon III; state developed peacefully.

**Leopold II.** *Orig. name* **Louis Philippe Marie Victor.** 1835–1909. King (1865–1909). Son of Leopold I; b. Brussels; m. (1853) Maria Henrietta of Austria. Enforced neutrality of Belgium during Franco-Prussian War (1870–71); organized African International Assoc. (1876); financed expedition of Stanley to the Congo (1879–84); granted sovereignty over Congo by Berlin Conference (1884–85); assumed title of sovereign of Congo Free State (1885); widely criticized (1903–05) for treatment of natives in Congo region; Congo Free State annexed to Belgium (1908). See George GRENFELL.

**Leopold III.** 1901– . King (1934–51). Son of Albert I and grandnephew of Leopold II; m. (1926) Princess Astrid of Sweden who was killed in an automobile accident (Aug. 29, 1935); at invasion of Belgium became Nazi prisoner of war (1940–45); abdicated.

**Leopold.** Name of two Holy Roman emperors:

**Leopold I.** 1640–1705. Second son of Ferdinand III. King of Hungary (1655–1705), Holy Roman emperor (1658–1705). Succeeded (1657) to hereditary Hapsburg dominions (Austria and Bohemia); waged war with the Turks (1661–64), ended by victory of Montecuccoli at St. Gotthard; second war (1682–97), in which Turks were assisted by Hungarian magnates; during this war, Vienna besieged by Turks (July–Sept., 1683); siege raised by John (III) Sobieski, King of Poland, and Charles, Duke of Lorraine; Turks defeated at Senta (1697) by Prince Eugene; signed Treaty of Karlowitz (1699) that ended Turk control of Hungary; urged war against France (1672–79), terminated by Treaty of Nijmegen; joined League of Augsburg (1686) against France and the Grand Alliance (1689); war ended by Treaty of Ryswick (1697); involved in War of the Spanish Succession (1701–14) through Hapsburg family claim to throne of Spain; Prince Eugene given command of imperial armies. Married (1) his niece Margaret Theresa, daughter of Philip IV of Spain; (2) Claudia Felicitas of Tirol; (3) Eleanora of Neuberg—their sons succeeding as Emperor Joseph I (1705–11) and Emperor Charles VI (1711–40).

**Leopold II.** 1747–1792. Holy Roman emperor (1790–92). Third son of Francis I and Maria Theresa, and brother of Joseph II. Grand duke of Tuscany (1765–90) as Leopold I. Formed alliance with Prussia (1792) against revolutionary France. Died just before war was declared.

**Leopold I.** Prince of **An'halt-Des'sau** (än'hält-dĕs'ou). *Called* **der Al'te Des'sau'er** (dĕr äl'tĕ dĕs'ou'ẽr), *i.e.* the Old Dessauer. 1676–1747. Prussian field marshal, b. at Dessau. Son of Prince John George II. Prince (1693–1747); m. (1698) Anna Luise (1677–1745), an apothecary's daughter raised to nobility (1701). Active in War of Spanish Succession; fought at Höchstädt (1703, 1704), Blenheim (1704), Cassano (1705), Turin (1706), and Malplaquet (1709); field marshal (1712); defeated Charles XII of Sweden (1715) at Rügen and Stralsund; a strict disciplinarian, spent years of peace training Prussian army (1715–40); intervened to aid Crown Prince Frederick (later Frederick the Great) when condemned for desertion; aided (1740–45) Frederick in Silesian wars, but not actively; after victory over Austrians at Kesselsdorf (1745) retired to Dessau. His son **Leopold II Maximilian** (1700–1751), prince of Anhalt-Dessau (1747–51), was one of the best of Frederick's generals; captured Glogau (1741) and performed distinguished service in other campaigns (1741–45); made field marshal after battle of Chotusitz (1742).

**Leopold.** *Full name* **Leopold Charles Frederick.** 1790–1852. Grand duke of **Ba'den** [bä'dĕn] (1830–52), b. Karlsruhe. Half brother of Grand Duke Louis. A ruler of liberal tendencies, but reactionary influences, esp. in revolutions of 1830 and 1848, too strong for his policies; driven out (1849) but reinstated (1849) by Prussian troops after several battles.

**Leopold.** *In full* **Maximilian Joseph Maria Arnulf Leopold.** 1846–1930. Prince of Bavaria and field marshal, b. Munich. Second son of Regent Prince Luitpold. Entered Bavarian army (1861); served in Seven Weeks' War and Franco-Prussian War; first lieutenant (1871–91); inspector general (1891–1913); made field marshal (1905); commanded 9th army on eastern front in World War; captured Warsaw (1915).

**Leopold.** 1835–1905. Prince of **Ho'hen·zol'lern-Sig'ma·ring'en** [hō'ĕn·tsôl'ẽrn·zēk'mä·rĭng'ĕn] (1885–1905). Son of Charles Anthony and brother of King Carol I of Rumania. Candidate for throne of Spain (1870) after Revolution of 1868; at first refused, then accepted, then finally withdrew. This became the immediate cause of Franco-Prussian War (1870–71) when King William of Prussia refused to accede to demand of France that Hohenzollern candidacy should never be renewed. See FERDINAND I, King of Rumania.

**Leopold II.** 1797–1870. Grand Duke of Tuscany (1824–59). Son of Grand Duke Ferdinand III. Father of Ferdinand IV, Louis Salvator, and John Nepomuk Salvator (*qq.v.*). His rule mild and progressive; granted (1848) new constitution (abolished 1852) during revolutionary period; refused to join in war on Austria; exiled a few months (1849) but restored by Austrian troops; driven out (1859) on refusing to make alliance with Sardinia; died in Bohemia.

**Le′o·pold** (lā′ô·pōld), **Carl Gustaf af.** 1756–1829. Swedish poet and critic, a champion of French classicism in Sweden. Secretary, court poet, and dramatic collaborator of Gustavus III (1788); author of narrative verse, moral and didactic poems, panegyric odes, lyrics, tragedies, works on philosophy and aesthetics, etc.

**Le′o·tych′i·des** (lē′ō·tĭk′ĭ·dēz). d. about 469 B.C. King of Sparta (491–469 B.C.); commanded Greek fleet, and shared in the glory of the victory over the Persians at Mycale (479). Later, convicted of accepting bribes from the enemy, and banished.

**Le·o′vi·gild** (lē·ō′vĭ·gĭld). King of the Visigoths in Spain (c. 569–586 A.D.); did much to merge Visigoths and Romans in Spain into united people; steadfast Arian. His son **Her·men′e·gild** (hûr·mĕn′ĕ·gĭld; hûr′mĕ·nĕ-) *or* **Er·men′e·gild** (ûr·mĕn′ĕ·gĭld; ûr′mĕ·nĕ-), who had married **In·gun′this** (ĭng·gŭn′thĭs), a Catholic princess, and been converted from his father's Arian faith, revolted against him but was defeated, imprisoned, and killed (585 A.D.).

**Le·pau′tre** (lĕ·pō′tr′). French family of engravers, sculptors, and architects, including: **Jean** (1617?–1682), engraver. His brother **Antoine** (1621–1691), architect. Antoine's son **Pierre** (1660–1744), sculptor.

**Le·pe′le·tier′ de Saint′-Far′geau′** (lĕ·pĕl′tyā′ dĕ săN′fȧr′zhō′), **Louis Michel.** 1760–1793. French politician; member of States-General (1789) and president of the National Assembly (1790); member of the National Convention (1792); assassinated by the Paris garde du corps on eve of execution (Jan. 21, 1793) of Louis XVI, for which he had voted.

**Le·père′** (lĕ·pâr′), **Louis Auguste.** 1849–1918. French engraver and illustrator.

**Lep′i·dus** (lĕp′ĭ·dŭs), **Marcus Aemilius.** Roman general and politician; consul (187 B.C.); pontifex maximus (180 ff.); censor (179); consul again (175). In war, distinguished himself against Antiochus III in Syria, and against the Ligurians. Built the Via Aemilia from Ariminum (Rimini) to Placentia (Piacenza); settled colonies in Mutina (Modena) and Parma.

**Lepidus, Marcus Aemilius.** d. about 77 B.C. Roman politician; praetor of Sicily (81 B.C.); consul (78). After Sulla's death, tried to abrogate the constitution which Sulla had passed. Incurred the enmity of the senate, which ordered him to his province; left Rome, gathered an army, and returned to attack the city (77); defeated by Pompey and Catulus, fled to join Sertorius in Spain; died soon thereafter. His son **Marcus Aemilius** (d. 13 B.C.) joined Caesar's party at outbreak of Civil War (49); consul (46); at time of Caesar's assassination (44), commanded an army near Rome, and sided with Mark Antony; with Antony and Octavius formed Second Triumvirate (43) to administer the Roman government; piqued at being forced by them into a subordinate role, tried to incite a revolt against Octavius in Sicily (36); betrayed by his army, and was retired into private life.

**L'É′pine′** (lā′pēn′), **Ernest.** 1826–1893. French writer who collaborated with Alphonse Daudet in *La Dernière Idole* (1862), *L'Œillet Blanc* (1865), *Le Frère Aîné* (1867).

**Lépine, Raphael.** 1840–1919. French physician; authority on nervous diseases, also kidney diseases and diabetes.

**Lépine, Stanislas Victor Édouard.** 1836–1892. French painter, esp. of landscapes along the Seine River.

**Le Play** (lĕ plā′), **Pierre Guillaume Frédéric.** 1806–1882. French engineer and economist; regarded as founder of modern study of social economy in France.

**Le Prince** (lĕ prăNs′), **Jean Baptiste.** 1733–1781. French painter and engraver, esp. of scenes in Russia and Siberia.

**Lep′si·us** (lĕp′sē·ŏŏs), **Karl Richard.** 1810–1884. German Egyptologist and philologist; headed Frederick William IV's expedition to Egypt (1842–45) and explored Nile valley into the Sudan; author of *Totenbuch der Ägypter* (1842), *Chronologie der Ägypter* (1849), *Denkmäler aus Ägypten und Äthiopien* (1849–59), etc. A son, **Johannes** (1858–1926), Protestant theologian and publicist, devoted himself to helping the Armenians and became director of German Eastern Mission at Potsdam (1897); author of *Armenien und Europa* (1896), *Das Leben Jesu* (2 vols., 1917–18), *Deutschland und Armenien 1914–18* (1919), etc.

**Le Queux** (lĕ kū′), **William Tufnell.** 1864–1927. English novelist, b. London. Author of *Guilty Bonds* (1890), *Secrets of Monte Carlo* (1899), *An Observer in the Near East* (1907), *Where The Desert Ends* (1923), and many detective and mystery stories.

**Ler′che** (lĕr′kĕ), **Vincent Stol′ten·berg** (stŏl′tĕn·băr). 1837–1892. Norwegian genre and architectural painter; works include church and convent interiors, and scenes from monastic life (chiefly humorous), caricatures, wood engravings, etc.

**Ler′chen·feld** (lĕr′kĕn·fĕlt). Bavarian noble family, including: Baron **Maximilian von Lerchenfeld** (1778–1843), Bavarian statesman. Baron **Gustav von Lerchenfeld** (1806–1866), statesman. Count **Hugo von und zu Lerchenfeld-Kö′fe·ring** [-kû′fĕ·rĭng] (1843–1925), diplomat, minister in Berlin (1880–1919). Count **Hugo von und zu Lerchenfeld-Köfering** (1871–1944), statesman and diplomat, German minister in Vienna (1926) and Brussels (1931).

**Ler′do de Te·ja′da** (lĕr′thō thā tĕ·hä′thä), **Miguel.** 1814?–1861. Mexican statesman; secretary of the treasury (1855–57; 1859–60); judge of the Mexican supreme court (1860–61). Noted for his liberalism; sponsor of Lerdo law (1856), which restricted right of civil and ecclesiastical corporations to hold land beyond their operating needs; also aided in passing legislation placing religious orders under government supervision and regulation.

**Lerdo de Tejada, Sebastián.** 1825–1889. Mexican lawyer and politician; judge of supreme court (1855–57); held various cabinet positions (1857–67); strong supporter of Juárez through period of French invasion; chief justice of supreme court (1867–72); president of Mexico (1872–76); overthrown by Porfirio Díaz (Nov., 1876); exiled; died in New York.

**Ler′ma** (lĕr′mä), Duque **de. Francisco Gómez de San′do·val′ y Ro′jas** (thā sän′dō·väl′ ē rō′häs). 1552–1625. Spanish prime minister (1598–1618); practically ruled Spain, having complete ascendancy over Philip III; failed in foreign policy; compelled to make peace with England (1604) and a truce with the Low Countries (1609); drove Moriscos out of Spain (1609–10), a blow from which Spain never recovered; greatly weakened finances of kingdom; driven out by his son, duke of

Uceda (1618); persuaded Pope Paul V to grant him a cardinalate (1618).

**Ler′mi′na′** (lĕr′mē′nȧ′), **Jules Hippolyte.** 1839–1915. French novelist and historian; author of *Les Loups de Paris* (novel; 1876), *Histoire de Cent Ans, Fondation de la République Française* (1884), etc.

**Lermoliev, Ivan.** See Giovanni MORELLI.

**Ler′mon·tov** (lyăr′mŭn·tôf), **Mikhail Yurievich.** 1814–1841. Russian poet and novelist; grad. from military school (1834); became a guards officer; at Pushkin's death (1837), addressed impassioned ode to czar; court-martialed, expelled from guards, and assigned to a line regiment in Caucasus. His best-known poems include *The Demon, Ismail Bey, Hadji-Abrek, Valerik, The Novice, The Song of the Czar Ivan Vasilievich;* and the novel *A Hero of Our Times* (1839).

**Ler′ner** (lûr′nẽr), **Alan Jay.** 1918– . American dramatist, b. New York City. Works include plays, *My Fair Lady* (1956), *Camelot* (1960); and films, *Gigi* (1958), *Paint Your Wagon* (1969).

**Ler′ner, Max.** 1902– . American writer and educator, b. near Minsk, Russia; to U.S. (1907), naturalized (1919). A.B., Yale (1923). Assistant editor (1927), later managing editor, *Encyclopedia of the Social Sciences;* editor of *The Nation*(1936–38); professor, Williams Coll. (1938–43). Author of *It Is Later Than You Think* (1938), *Ideas Are Weapons* (1939), *Ideas for the Ice Age* (1941), *The Age of Overkill* (1962).

**Ler′net-Ho·le′ni·a** (lĕr′nĕt·hō·lā′nē·ä), **Alexander.** 1897– . Austrian novelist and playwright; wrote *Ollapotrida* (1926), *Die Goldene Horde* (1935), *Strahlenheim* (1938), etc.

**Le Ros′si′gnol′** (lẽ rô′sē′nyôl′; *Angl.* lẽ rŏs′ĭg·nŏl), **James Edward.** 1866–1959. Economist and educator, b. Quebec, Canada; at U. of Nebraska (1911). Author of *Monopolies, Past and Present* (1901), *Orthodox Socialism* (1907), *What Is Socialism?* (1921), *Economics for Everyman* (1923), *From Marx to Stalin* (1940).

**Le·roux′** (lẽ·ro͞o′), **Gaston.** 1868–1927. French journalist and author of detective and mystery stories.

**Le Roux** (lẽ ro͞o′), **Henri,** *known as* **Hugues.** 1860–1925. French journalist; on staff of *Le Temps, Le Matin, Le Journal, Figaro;* author of many stories of adventure, romantic novels, and miscellaneous works.

**Leroux, Pierre.** 1797–1871. French philosopher, journalist, and politician; with George Sand founded *Revue Indépendante* (1841); member of Constituent Assembly (1848) and Legislative Assembly (1849); opposed Louis Napoleon's coup d'état; an exile from France until amnesty (1851–59). Wrote *De l'Humanité, de son Principe et de son Avenir* (1840), *De l'Égalité* (1848).

**Leroux, Xavier Henri Napoléon.** 1863–1919. French composer; works include the operas *Evangéline* (1895), *Astarté* (1901), *Le Chemineau* (1907), *Le Carillonneur* (1913), *La Plus Forte* (prod. 1924), the dramatic overture *Harald,* a mass with orchestra, church music, piano pieces, motets, songs, etc.

**Le Roy** (lẽ rwȧ′), **Édouard.** 1870–1954. French philosopher and mathematician; among his books are *Les Origines Humaines et l'Évolution de l'Intelligence* (1928), *Le Problème de Dieu* (1929).

**Le·roy′** (lẽ·rwȧ′), **Julien.** 1686–1759. French horologer. Developed the compensator for clocks; invented horizontal clocks and a repeater for watches. His son **Pierre** (1717–1785) is credited with discovery of the isochronism of spiral springs; originated the detached escapement.

**Le·roy′-Beau′lieu′** (-bō′lyû′), **Anatole,** *in full* **Henri Jean Baptiste Anatole.** 1842–1912. French writer; director of École des Sciences Politiques; among his many books are *La France, La Russie et l'Europe* (1888), *L'Antisémitisme* (1897), *Les États-Unis d'Europe* (1901), *Christianisme et Socialisme* (1905). His brother **Pierre Paul** (1843–1916) was an economist; opposed protective tariffs and Socialism; among his books are *Nouveau Traité...d'Économie Politique* (1895), *Science des Finances* (1899), *L'État Moderne et ses Fonctions* (1900), *Le Collectivisme* (1903), *La Question de la Population* (1913).

**Lers′ner** (lĕrs′nẽr), Baron **Kurt von.** 1883– . German diplomat; head of German delegation to the Peace Conference at Versailles (1919); resigned (Feb., 1920) rather than transmit to German government Allied demand for extradition of certain German leaders.

**Le·sage′** (lẽ·sȧzh′), **Alain René.** 1668–1747. French novelist and playwright; author of the picaresque masterpiece *L'Histoire de Gil Blas de Santillane* (4 vols., 1715–35); among his lesser works are *Le Diable Boiteux* (1707), *Crispin Rival de son Maître* (play; 1707).

**Les′bi·a** (lĕz′bĭ·ȧ). See Gaius Valerius CATULLUS.

**Les·bo′nax** (lĕz·bō′năks). Greek Sophist and rhetorician of 1st century A.D. (or earlier), in Mytilene. Only fragments of his works are extant.

**Les·caze′** (lĕs·käz′), **William.** 1896–1969. Swiss-born architect in America.

**Les′ches** (lĕs′kēz) *or* **Les′cheus** (-kūs). Greek poet of 7th century B.C.; ranked among the cyclic poets; reputed author of *Little Iliad,* continuation of Homer's *Iliad.*

**Le′sche·tiz′ky** (*Ger.* lā′shĕ·tĭts′kē), **The′o·dor** (*Ger.* tā′ō·dōr). *Pol.* **Teodor Le′sze·tyc′ki** (lĕ′shĕ·tĭts′kē). 1830–1915. Teacher of the piano and composer, of Polish parentage; settled in St. Petersburg (1852), and in Vienna as piano teacher (1878). His pupils included Paderewski, Gabrilówitsch, Ethel Leginska. Composer of opera *Die Erste Falte* (1867) and of works for piano.

**Les′cot′** (lĕs′kō′), **Élie.** 1883–1974. Haitian lawyer; minister to U.S. (1937–41); president of Haiti (1941–46).

**Lescot, Pierre.** 1510?–1578. French architect; called the founder of the classic school in France; engaged on the Louvre (from 1546). See Jean GOUJON.

**Les′cure′** (lĕs′kür′), Marquis **de. Louis Marie de Salgues** (dẽ sȧlg′). 1766–1793. French Vendean military leader; died of wounds received in action.

**Les′di′guières′** (lĕs′dē′gyâr′), Duc **de. François de Bonne** (dẽ bôn′). 1543–1626. French soldier; a leader of the Protestant party in the Dauphinate; appointed lieutenant general in Provence and in the Dauphinate by Henri IV; created marshal of France (1608), duke and peer of France (1611), general of all the armies of the king (1621); converted to Roman Catholic faith (1622) and was appointed constable of France.

**Les·kien′** (lĕs·kēn′), **August.** 1840–1916. German Slavic philologist; author of a handbook (1871) and a grammar (1909) of Old Bulgarian.

**Le·skov′** (lyĕ·skôf′), **Nikolai Semënovich.** 1831–1895. Russian novelist; author of *The Blind Alley, The Islanders, Cathedral Folk.*

**Les′ley** (lĕs′lĭ; *Brit. usu.* lĕz′-), **Peter.** *Later signed himself* **J. P. Lesley.** 1819–1903. American geologist, b. Philadelphia. Assisted Rogers in first geological survey of Pennsylvania (1838–41); state geologist, in charge of survey of Pennsylvania (1874–87). Author of *A Manual of Coal and Its Topography* (1856), etc.

**Les′lie** *or* **Les′ly** *or* **Les′ley** (lĕs′lĭ; *Brit. usu.* lĕz′-). Name of a Scottish family originating in pastoral parish of Lesslyn or Leslie in Aberdeenshire; ennobled when George Leslie of Rothes was made earl of **Roth′es** (rŏth′ĭz) and Lord Leslie (1457); held earldom of **Le′ven** (lē′vĕn) and baronies of **Bal·go′nie** (băl·gō′nĭ), **Lin·dores′** (lĭn·dōrz′), and **New′ark** (nū′ẽrk). Members include the following:

ROTHES BRANCH. **Norman Leslie** (d. 1554), Master of Rothes; son of 4th earl of Rothes; led conspirators, including his uncle **John**, against Cardinal Beaton without taking personal part in assassination (1546).

**John Leslie** (1600–1641), 6th Earl of Rothes; grandson of 5th earl; one of ablest leaders among Covenanters, chief organizer of movement against episcopacy (1638); remained (after 1640) at court of Charles I in England.

**David Leslie** (1601–1682), 1st Lord Newark; soldier; son of 1st Lord Lindores, who was a son of 5th earl of Rothes; served in army of Gustavus Adolphus; returned (1643) to Scotland as major general under Alexander Leslie, Earl of Leven (see below); brought Scottish horse to support of Cromwell at Marston Moor; besieged and took Carlisle; routed Montrose at Philiphaugh (1645); held chief command of Scottish armies levied on behalf of Charles II; fought stubborn defensive campaign against Cromwell until battle of Worcester (1651); created Baron Newark (1661).

**John Leslie** (1630–1681), 7th Earl and 1st Duke of Rothes; eldest son of 6th earl; lord of session (1661); lord high treasurer (1663); privy councilor of England (1663); keeper of privy seal (1664); lord chancellor of Scotland (1667); through his two daughters, countesses of Rothes, the earldom passed to their sons in Hamilton family (see earls of HADDINGTON) and Melville family (*q.v.*).

BAL·QUHAIN′ (băl·kwān′; -kwĭn′) BRANCH. **John Leslie** (1527–1596), Roman Catholic prelate and historian; great-grandson of Andrew Leslie of Balquhain; M.A., Aberdeen; studied at Poitiers, Toulouse, and Paris; took orders; at Reformation championed Catholicism, disputed with Knox; one of commissioners sent to bring Mary, Queen of Scots to Scotland (1561) and one of her stanchest partisans, her adviser in her ecclesiastical policy and ambassador at court of Elizabeth; bishop of Ross (1566); for his part in Ridolfi plot to bring about marriage between Mary and duke of Norfolk, imprisoned in Tower of London (1571), banished (1573); while representing Mary's interests in Paris and Rome, published his Latin history of Scotland *De Origine, Moribus, et Rebus Gestis Scotorum* (Rome, 1578), for which he had collected materials during imprisonment; suffragan and vicar general of archbishopric of Rouen (1579).

**Alexander Leslie** (1580?–1661), 1st Earl of Leven; soldier; served thirty years in Swedish army of Gustavus Adolphus; defended Stralsund against Wallenstein (1628); fought at Lützen (1632); took Brandenburg (1634); field marshal (1636); recalled (1639) to command Scottish Covenanting army in war with England; defeated king's troops at Newburn (1640); made earl of Leven and Lord Balgonie (1641); lord general of Scottish forces in Ireland (1642); commanded forces invading England in support of English parliament (1644), took part in battle of Marston Moor, stormed Newcastle; took charge of Charles I (1645–47); after execution of Charles acted with Royalists; prisoner of English parliament (1651–54); entrusted command to David Leslie (see above). See *David Melville*, under MELVILLE family.

**Charles Leslie** (1650–1722), Anglican nonjuror and controversialist; son of John Leslie (1571–1671), "fighting bishop" of Raphoe and Clogher in Ireland; connected with Balquhain branch of family; M.A., Dublin (1673); deprived of chancellorship of cathedral of Connor because of refusal to take oath of allegiance; returning to England (1689), engaged in polemical writing against Quakers, Jews, Papists, Deists, Socinians, and in support of nonjuring (Jacobite) interests, as in pamphlet *The Good Old Cause or Lying in Truth;* joined the Old Pretender (1711), whom he accompanied after failure of 1715 to Italy; known for his *Short and Easy Method with the Deists* (1694).

**Walter Leslie** (1606–1667), Count Leslie, soldier of fortune, a cadet of the Balquhain line, distinguished himself in the Austrian army; created count in reward for bringing about assassination of Wallenstein (1634); ambassador extraordinary to Ottoman Porte (1665).

**Leslie, Charles Robert.** 1794–1859. Painter and author, b. London, Eng., of American parentage. Studio in London. Excelled in genre paintings. Author of *Memoirs of the Life of John Constable, Esq., R.A.* (1843), *A Handbook for Young Painters* (1855), *Life and Times of Sir Joshua Reynolds* (completed by Tom Taylor, 1865).

**Leslie, Frank.** *Orig. name* **Henry Carter.** 1821–1880. Illustrator, journalist, and publisher, b. Ipswich, Eng.; to U.S. (1848). On staff of *Gleason's Pictorial* and *Illustrated News* (1852–53); had his name legally changed to Frank Leslie (1857). Started *Frank Leslie's Ladies' Gazette of Paris, London, and New York Fashions* (1854); made great success with *Frank Leslie's Illustrated Newspaper* (begun 1855); expanded activities to include papers and magazines for all classes and ages; through extravagance and financial depression became bankrupt at close of his life.

His wife (m. 1874) **Miriam Florence**, *nee* **Fol′lin** (fŏl′ĭn) *or* **Fol·line′** [?fŏ·lēn′] (1836?–1914), at his death took over management of his bankrupt enterprises; had her name legally changed (1882) to Frank Leslie, and made remarkable success; author of *Beautiful Women of Twelve Epochs* (1890), *Are Men Gay Deceivers* (1893), *A Social Mirage* (1899).

**Leslie, Henry David.** 1822–1896. English choral conductor and composer of operas, oratorios, cantatas, a festival anthem, symphonies, an overture, songs, etc.

**Leslie,** Sir **John.** 1766–1832. Scottish mathematician and physicist; among his works are *Experimental Inquiry into the Nature and Properties of Heat* (1804), *Philosophy of Arithmetic* (1817), *Elements of Natural Philosophy* (1823).

**Leslie,** Sir **Shane**, 3d baronet, *in full* **John Randolph Shane.** 1885–1971. Irish journalist and writer; editor of Dublin *Review* (1916). Author of *Songs of Oriel*, *Verses in Peace and War*, *The Oppidan* (1922), *Doomsland* (1923), *The Epic of Jutland* (1930), *American Wonderland* (1936), *The Film of Memory* (1938), *The Life of Mrs. Fitzherbert* (1939), etc.

**Leslie, Thomas Edward Cliffe.** 1827?–1882. British economist, b. in County Wexford, Ire.; descendant of Charles Leslie (1650–1722; see LESLIE family). One of founders of English historical school of political economy.

**Les′pi′nasse′** (lĕs′pē′nȧs′), **Julie Jeanne Éléonore de.** 1732–1776. Frenchwoman; natural daughter of the comtesse d'Albon; companion for ten years (1754–64) to Mme. du Deffand; remembered for her relations with d'Alembert, her liaisons with the marquis de Mora and the comte de Guibert, to the latter of whom were written the *Lettres de Mlle. de Lespinasse*, first published in 1809 and valuable for accounts of contemporary life and customs.

**Les′que′reux′** (lā′kā′rû′), **Le′o** (lē′ō). 1806–1889. Paleobotanist, b. in Switzerland; to U.S. (1848). Associate of William S. Sullivant (*q.v.*) in bryological work; recognized authority on Appalachian coal field.

**Les′seps′** (lĕ′sĕps′; *Angl.* lĕs′ĕps), Vicomte **Ferdinand Marie de.** 1805–1894. French diplomat and promoter of the Suez Canal, b. Versailles. In consular service at Lisbon (1825 ff.); minister of France at Madrid (1848–49). First thought of constructing canal across Suez in 1832; received concession for its construction from Said

Pasha, Viceroy of Egypt (1854); one of those who formed company (raising half its funds by popular subscription in France) which carried out construction (1859–69). President of French company that worked on construction of Panama Canal (1881–88) but gave up project because of financial and political difficulties; with son Comte **Charles Aimée Marie** (1849–1923) sentenced to fine and imprisonment by French government for misappropriation of funds, but sentence not carried out.

**Les'sing** (lĕs'ĭng), **Gotthold Ephraim.** 1729–1781. German dramatist and critic; associate of E. von Kleist and Gleim in Leipzig (1755–57); in Berlin (1758); founded, with Nicolai and Moses Mendelssohn, the critical journal *Briefe, die Neueste Literatur Betreffend* (24 vols., c. 1759–67) and contributed letters on Wieland and Klopstock, against Gottsched, and in praise of Shakespeare. While serving as secretary to General Tauentzien, Breslau (1760–65), wrote *Minna von Barnhelm;* dramaturgist to German National Theater, Hamburg (1767); librarian of ducal library, Wolfenbüttel (from 1770). His works include the comedies *Der Junge Gelehrte* (1748), *Der Freigeist* (1749), *Die Juden* (1749), and the classic German drama *Minna von Barnhelm* (1763; pub. 1767); the tragedies *Miss Sara Sampson,* 1st German tragedy of middle-class life (1755), and *Philotas* (1759) and *Emilia Galotti* (1772), both in prose; the dramatic poem on toleration *Nathan der Weise* (1779); the collection of epigrams and Anacreontic poems *Kleinigkeiten* (1751); *Fabeln* (3 vols., 1759); the analysis of the limitations of poetry and the plastic arts *Laokoon* (1766); theatrical criticisms; the archaeological treatise *Wie die Alten den Tod Gebildet* (1769); theological criticisms actually written by Reimarus, *Fragmente eines Ungenannten* (1774–78), from the Wolfenbüttel Library, which involved him in a controversy with Pastor Goeze of Hamburg. See also Christian A. KLOTZ.

**Lessing, Karl Friedrich.** 1808–1880. German historical and landscape painter; grandnephew of Gotthold E. Lessing. Director of Karlsruhe Art Gallery (1858–80). His son **Otto** (1846–1912) was a sculptor and painter.

**Les'si·us** (lĕs'ē·ŭs), **Leonard.** 1554–1623. Flemish Jesuit theologian; author of *Theses Theologicae* (1586; provoked controversy over his doctrine of grace and Biblical inspiration), *De Justitia et Jure* (1605; in defense of absolute monarchy), *De Gratia Efficaci* (1610), etc.

**Les·tocq'** (lĕs·tôk'), Count **Johann Hermann von.** 1692–1767. Favorite of Empress Elizabeth Petrovna of Russia, b. in Prussia of French parents. Entered service of Peter the Great as a surgeon (1713); became surgeon to Princess Elizabeth (1725), whom he helped to the throne by his leadership of the revolution; arrested by the high chancellor (1748) and banished to the province of Archangel (1753); recalled by Peter III (1761).

**L'Es·trange'** (lĕs·trānj'; lĕs-), Sir **Roger.** 1616–1704. English journalist and Royalist pamphleteer; employed by Hyde in service of Charles II abroad; pardoned by Cromwell (1653). At Restoration, surveyor of printing presses and licenser of the press (1663–88); issued *Public Intelligence* and *The News* (1663–66); attacked Whigs, Titus Oates, and dissenters in the *Observator* (1681–87); translator of Quevedo y Villegas (*The Visions of Quevedo;* 1667), Seneca (*Seneca's Morals by Way of Abstract;* 1678), Cicero (*Offices;* 1680), Aesop (*Fables;* 1692), and Josephus (*Works;* 1702).

**Le·su·eur'** (lē·sü·ûr'), **Charles Alexandre.** 1778–1846. French artist and naturalist; explored coasts of Australia (1800–04); with the naturalist François Péron (1775–1810), collected over 100,000 zoological specimens, including about 2500 new species; explored and collected specimens in U.S. (1816–17). Joined Robert Owen's community at New Harmony, Ind.; taught drawing there (1826–37). Author of monographs on reptiles, crustaceans, and esp. American fishes.

**Lesueur, Daniel.** *Pseudonym of* **Jeanne La'pauze'** (lȧ'pōz'), *nee* **Loi'seau'** (lwȧ'zō'). 1860–1921. French writer, b. Paris; m. Henry Lapauze (1904). Among her writings are *Fleurs d'Avril* (verse; 1882), *Le Mariage de Gabrielle* (novel; 1882), *Sursum Corda* (verse; 1885), *Fiancée* (play; 1901), *L'Évolution Féminine* (1905), etc.

**Le Sueur** (lē sü·ûr'), **Eustache.** 1616–1655. French painter; his best-known work, *Vie de Saint Bruno,* is in the Louvre.

**Le Sueur** *or* **Lesueur, Jean François.** 1760–1837. French composer; succeeded Paisiello as court Kapellmeister to Napoleon (1804); superintendent and composer of chapel of Louis XVIII; teacher of Hector Berlioz, Ambroise Thomas, Gounod, etc. He composed eight operas, several oratorios, many masses, and other sacred vocal music.

**Leszczyńska.** See MARIA LESZCZYŃSKA.

**Lesz·czyń'ski** (lĕsh·chĭn'y'·skē). *Fr.* **Lec'zin'ski'** (lĕk'zăN'skē'). Noble Polish family, prominent in 16th to 18th century; esp. Rafael Leszczyński, Polish general, father of Stanislas I, king of Poland. See STANISLAS I LESZCZYŃSKI and MARIA LESZCZYŃSKA.

**Le Tel'lier'** (lē tĕ'lyā'), **Michel.** 1603–1685. Chancellor of France, b. Paris. Minister of war (1643–66) at recommendation of Mazarin; a hard worker and skillful political leader; turned over office of minister (1666) to his son marquis de Louvois (*q.v.*); made chancellor by Louis XIV (1677); an enemy of the Huguenots, signed revocation of Edict of Nantes (1685).

**Lethington,** Lord. See MAITLAND family.

**Let'ter·man** (lĕt'ẽr·măn), **Jonathan.** 1824–1872. American army surgeon, b. Canonsburg, Pa. Medical director, Army of the Potomac (1862–64); reorganized field medical service and introduced ambulance service to recover battlefield casualties. Letterman General Hospital in the presidio of San Francisco is named in his honor.

**Let'tow–Vor'beck** (lĕt'ō·fōr'bĕk), **Paul von.** 1870–1964. German soldier; commanded colonial forces in German East Africa (1914–18); author of *Meine Erinnerungen aus Deutsch-Ostafrika* (1919).

**Letts** (lĕts), **Winifred M.** 1882–1972. Irish writer; m. W. H. Foster Verschoyle (1926). Author of *Songs from Leinster, Hallowe'en and Poems of the War, Diana Dethroned, Christina's Son,* a number of children's books, and two plays performed at the Abbey Theatre, Dublin (*Eyes of the Blind* and *The Challenge*).

**Leuch'ten·berg** (loiK'tĕn·bĕrK). Name of a landgraviate in Bavaria, and its ruling German family of French origin, founded by General Eugène de Beauharnais (see BEAUHARNAIS) when he acquired, by purchase (1817) from Maximilian I Joseph of Bavaria, title and lands, together with principality of **Eich'stätt** (ĭK'shtĕt), and became duke (1817–24). His two sons and four daughters formed connections with several royal families. Eldest son, **Auguste,** *Ger.* **August** (1810–1835), b. Milan; duke (1824–35); m. (1835) Queen Maria of Portugal; died two months later. Second son, **Maximilien,** *Ger.* **Maximilian** (1817–1852), b. Munich; duke (1835–52); m. (1839) Maria Nikolaevna (1819–1876), eldest daughter of Czar Nicholas I of Russia; his descendants granted title of Prince Romanovski. Eldest daughter, **Joséphine** (1807–1876), m. (1823) Oscar I, King of Sweden. Second daughter, **Eugénie Hortense** (1808–1847), m. Frederick William, a prince of Hohenzollern-Hechingen. Third daughter, **Amélie** (1812–1873), m. (1829) Dom Pedro I, Emperor of Brazil. Fourth daughter, **Théodelinde** (1814–1857), m. Count William of Württemberg.

**Leu·cip′pus** (lū̇·sĭp′ŭs). Greek philosopher of 5th century B.C.; proponent of the atomistic theory, and thus founder of the school of philosophy based thereon. Cf. DEMOCRITUS.

**Leuck′art** (loik′ärt), **Rudolf,** *in full* **Karl Georg Friedrich.** 1822–1898. German zoologist, pioneer in the sciences of modern parasitology and animal ecology. Correctly described the structure of sponges and classified them as coelenterates; studied jellyfish; recognized parthenogenesis in numerous insects; first to study the life histories of many parasitic worms.

**Leu′mann** (loi′män), **Ernst.** 1859–1931. Swiss-born Sanskrit scholar; compiler of *Sanskrit-English Dictionary* (with Monier-Williams and Cappeler); author of *Etymologisches Wörterbuch der Sanskrit-Sprache,* etc.

**Leusch′ner** (loish′nẽr), **Ar′min** (är′mĭn) **Otto.** 1868–1953. American astronomer; professor (1907–1938), dean of the graduate school (1913–18 and 1920–23), U. of California. Known for work in theoretical astronomy, on the perturbations of the Watson asteroids, on methods of determining preliminary orbits of comets and planets, etc.

**Leut′hold** (loit′hôlt), **Heinrich.** 1827–1879. Swiss poet; joined Munich group of poets (1857); author of lyric, satirical, and epic poems, and of the translations *Fünf Bücher Französischer Lyrik* (1862; with Geibel).

**Leut′ze** (loi′tsĕ), **E·man′u·el** (ė·măn′ū·ĕl). 1816–1868. Historical painter, b. Gmünd, Württemberg; to U.S. as a child. Studio in Germany (1841–59) and in New York and Washington, D.C. (from 1859). Among his best-known works are *Washington Crossing the Delaware,* now in Metropolitan Museum of Art, New York; *Westward the Course of Empire Takes its Way,* in the Capitol, Washington, D.C.; *Cromwell and Milton,* in Corcoran Art Gallery, Washington, D.C.

**Le′va·di′ti** (lĕ′vä·dē′tē), **Constantin.** 1874–1953. French physician, b. in Rumania; head of the laboratory at Pasteur Institute in Paris. Known for work relating to certain spirochetal diseases, serological diagnostics, neurotropic viruses, and the treatment of syphilis with bismuth.

**Le·vail′lant′** (lē·vȧ′yäɴ′), **François.** 1753–1824. French traveler and ornithologist, b. in Dutch Guiana. Traveled in South Africa, studying the natives and collecting birds (1780–85). Author of *Voyages de Levaillant dans l'Intérieur de l'Afrique* (1790–96) and *Histoire Naturelle des Oiseaux d'Afrique* (1796–1812).

**Le·vant′** (lĕ·vănt′; lē-), **Oscar.** 1906–1972. American pianist and composer, b. Pittsburgh, Pa. On stage in *Burlesque* (1928); later, associated with Twentieth Century-Fox, in Hollywood. Composed music and conducted orchestra for *The American Way* (1939). Known for his range of musical knowledge, esp. on the radio program "Information Please." Composer of two string quartets, a piano concerto, a nocturne, and a number of songs. Author of *A Smattering of Ignorance* (1940).

**Le·vas′seur′** (lē·vȧ′sûr′), **Pierre Émile.** 1828–1911. French economist; student esp. of social and economic history; author of *La Question de l'Or* (1858), *Histoire des Classes Ouvrières en France depuis la Conquête de Jules César jusqu'à la Révolution* (2 vols., 1859) and its sequel, *Histoire...depuis la Révolution jusqu'à nos Jours* (1867), *La Population Française* (1889–92), *Questions Ouvrières et Industrielles sous la Troisième République* (1907), etc.

**Le·vas′sor′** (lē·vȧ′sôr′), Émile. d. 1897. French pioneer in the construction and racing of automobiles. See René PANHARD.

**Le Vau** (lē vō′), **Louis.** 1612–1670. French architect; designed parts of the Louvre and of the Tuileries.

**Leven,** Earls of. See LESLIE and MELVILLE families.

**Le·vene′** (lĕ·vēn′), **Phoebus Aaron Theodore.** 1869–1940. American chemist, b. in Russia; to U.S. (1892); member, Rockefeller Institute (1907–39). Known for work on proteins, nucleins, carbohydrates, lipoids, hexosamines, nucleic acids, etc.

**Le′ver** (lē′vẽr), **Charles James.** 1806–1872. British novelist, b. in Dublin, of English parents. Traveled as student from Göttingen to Weimar; wrote songs, among them "The pope he loved a merry life"; practiced as dispensary doctor in County Clare, Ireland, and in Brussels (1840). Contributed to *Dublin University Magazine* his first novel, *Harry Lorrequer,* which found immediate acceptance (1837), and his most popular book, *Charles O'Malley* (1841), reflecting his own college life in Dublin; edited *Dublin University Magazine* (1842–45), and gathered round him Irish wits. Set off on tour of Central Europe in coach, renting ducal castles; settled at Florence (1850); British consul at Spetsai (1857) and Trieste (1867); wrote essays for *Blackwood's Magazine* under name **Cornelius O'Dowd′** (ō·doud′). Author of many lighthearted, rollicking stories, mostly of Irish life and characters, including *Tom Burke of Ours* (1844), *Arthur O'Leary* (1844), *Roland Cashel* (1850), *The Daltons* (1852); also of two historical romances, *The O'Donoghue* (1845) and *The Knight of Gwynne* (1847); and among his last novels, *Cornelius O'Dowd* (1864), *Luttrell of Arran* (1865), *Lord Kilgobbin* (1872).

**Lever, William Hesketh.** See Viscount LEVERHULME.

**Lev′er·ett** (lĕv′ẽr·ĕt, -ĭt; lĕv′rĕt, -rĭt), **Frank.** 1859–1943. American geologist, b. Denmark, Iowa. With U.S. Geological Survey (from 1886), geologist (1890–1929). Authority on the water resources of Illinois, Indiana, Ohio, and Michigan, on the glacial deposits in the upper Mississippi, Great Lakes regions, and Ohio Valley.

**Leverett, John.** 1616–1679. American colonial governor, b. Boston, Eng.; to America (1633). Massachusetts colonial agent in England (c. 1655–62); member, Massachusetts General Court (1663–65), and of the council (1665–70). Lieutenant governor (1671–73); governor (1673–79). His grandson **John Leverett** (1662–1724), grad. Harvard (1680), was president of Harvard (1707–24).

**Le′ver·hulme** (lē′vẽr·hūm), **1st Viscount. William Hesketh Le′ver** (lē′vẽr). 1851–1925. English soap manufacturer, b. in Bolton, Lancashire. Chairman of Lever Brothers, Ltd., and founder of Port Sunlight, a model industrial town; originator also of a profit-sharing plan for the benefit of his employees. M.P. (1906–10); high sheriff of Lancashire (1917). Created viscount (1922).

**Lev′er·idge** (lĕv′ẽr·ĭj), **Richard.** 1670?–1758. English bass singer in London theaters and writer of songs, including "All in the Downs" and "The Roast Beef of Old England."

**Lev′er·more** (lĕv′ẽr·mōr), **Charles Herbert.** 1856–1927. American educator and world-peace advocate, b. Mansfield, Conn. Founded Adelphi College, Brooklyn, N.Y. (1896); its president (1896–1912). Devoted himself to propaganda for world peace (from 1912).

**Le·ver′rier′** (lē·vĕ′ryā′), **Urbain Jean Joseph.** 1811–1877. French astronomer; produced improved tables of mercury; upon the suggestion of Arago, investigated the disturbance in the motion of Uranus, making calculations indicating the presence of an unknown planet which was later discovered (1846) and named Neptune. Director of the Paris Observatory (1854). See Johann GALLE.

**Le′ver·tin** (lā′vẽr·tēn), **Oscar Ivar.** 1862–1906. Swedish lyric poet, novelist, and critic; began as realist, but became a leader of romanticists (c. 1890). Author of the realistic novel *Conflicts* (1885); the psychological novel

*Enemies of Life* (1891); the romantic novels *Rococo Stories* (1899) and *The Masters of Österås* (1900); verse, as in *Legends and Songs* (1891), *New Poems* (1894), and the cycle *King Solomon and Morolf* (1905); works on literature and art.

**Leve'son–Gower'** (lo͞o's'n·gōr'; lū'-; -gôr'). Name of English family tracing descent from **Lawrence Gower,** who had part in execution of Piers Gaveston (1312), and including among its members:

**John Leveson–Gower** (d. 1754), 1st Earl **Gower;** a lord justice of the kingdom (1740, 1743, 1745, 1748, 1750, 1752); lord privy seal (1742–43, 1744); created Viscount Trentham and Earl Gower (1746) for service against Jacobite rebels.

His son **Granville** (1721–1803), 2d earl, 1st Marquis of **Staf'ford** [stăf'ērd] (cr. 1786); educ. Oxford; M.P. (1744); lord privy seal (1755–57, 1785–94); president of the council (1767–79, 1783–84).

The 1st marquis's eldest son, **George Granville** (1758–1833), 2d marquis, 1st Duke of **Suth'er·land** [sŭth'ēr-lănd] (cr. 1833); inherited Bridgewater estates from his maternal uncle, the 3d duke of Bridgewater (see under EGERTON family); M.P. (1778–84, 1787–98); ambassador in Paris (1790–92); m. (1785) Elizabeth, Countess of Sutherland; constructed roads and bridges in Sutherlandshire, Scotland, of large part of which his wife was proprietress; reduced rents and brought land under cultivation. See his son *Francis* (1800–1857) under EGERTON family.

The 1st marquis's youngest son, **Granville** (1773–1846), 1st Earl **Gran'ville** (grăn'vĭl); ambassador extraordinary at St. Petersburg (1804–05), minister at Brussels (1816), ambassador at Paris (1824–41).

The 1st earl's eldest son, **Granville George** (1815–1891), 2d earl, statesman; educ. Oxford; Whig M.P. (1836); undersecretary for foreign affairs; a free trader in House of Lords (from 1846); one of promoters of great exhibition of 1851; minister for foreign affairs (1851–52) under Lord John Russell; lord president of the council (1852–54); leader of Liberals in House of Lords (from 1855); failed to form ministry (1859); colonial secretary in Gladstone's first ministry (1868–70), again (1886); known chiefly as foreign secretary (1870–74, 1880–85), under Gladstone, and as a supple negotiator but lacking strength to cope with European statesmen, unable to take effective measures in troubles in Egypt and Sudan, against Alabama claims of U.S., or for maintenance of intermediate zone between Russia and Afghanistan; supported Gladstone's home-rule policy; forced to yield to Bismarck over Angra Pequeña in southwest Africa (1883–84).

Lady **Georgiana Charlotte Ful'ler·ton** [fo͝ol'ēr·t'n; -tŭn] (1812–1885), novelist and philanthropist; youngest daughter of 1st earl Granville; m. (1833) Alexander Fullerton, military officer; founder of Poor Servants of the Mother of God Incarnate; author of *Ellen Middleton* (1844), *Too Strange not to be True* (1864), *A Will and a Way* (1881), also lives of saints and two volumes of verse.

**Le'vi** (lē'vī). In Bible: (1) Jacob's third son (*Genesis* xxix. 34), ancestor of one of the twelve tribes of Israel, the Levites, which furnished the priests of the Jews and the men charged with the care of the sanctuary. (2) = MATTHEW (the apostle).

**Le'vi** (lā'vē), **Hermann.** 1839–1900. German musical conductor; conducted 1st performance of *Parsifal* at Bayreuth (1882) and won fame as conductor of Wagner and Mozart.

**Lé'vi'** (lā'vē'), **Israel.** 1856–1939. French rabbi and scholar, b. Paris. Rabbi, Paris (1882); chief rabbi of France (1919). Author of *L'Ecclésiastique* (an edition of the Hebrew Sirach with translation and commentary; 2 vols., 1898–1901).

**Le'vi** (lē'vī; *Ital.* lā'vē), **Le·o'ne** (lā·ō'nā). 1821–1888. Jewish jurist and statistician in England, b. Ancona, Italy; settled in Liverpool as merchant (1844), naturalized as British subject; author of a history of British commerce (1872), works on taxation and international law, and a periodical summary of parliamentary papers (18 vols., 1856–68).

**Lé'vi'** (lā'vē'), **Sylvain.** 1863–1935. French East Indian scholar; author of *Le Théâtre Indien* (1890), *Buddhacarita* (1892), etc.; compiler of *Hôbôgirin, Dictionnaire du Bouddhisme d'après les Sources Chinoises et Japonaises* (1928 ff.).

**Le'vi ben Ger'shon** *or* **Ger'son** (lē'vī bĕn gûr'shŏn, gûr'sŏn). *Called* **Ger·son'i·des** (gûr·sŏn'ĭ·dēz). 1288?–?1344. French Jewish mathematician and religious philosopher. Wrote philosophical work, *Milhamot Adonai* (*Wars of God;* pub. 1560); commentaries on the Bible and the Talmud; treatise on trigonometry (1321).

**Le'vi–Ci'vi·ta** (lā'vē·chē'vē·tä), **Tullio.** 1873–1942. Italian mathematician; professor of mechanics, Padua (1898), Rome (1918–38); author of *Lezioni di Meccanica Razionale* (3 vols., 1923–27), *Lezioni di Calcolo Differenziale Assoluto* (1925), etc.

**Levien, Ilse.** See Ilse FRAPAN-AKUNIAN.

**Le·vine'** (lĕ·vēn'), **Jack.** 1915– . American painter, b. Boston; one of best-known paintings is *String Quartette;* first American soldier artist to be selected (1943) to paint battle scenes.

**Lev'in·thal** (lĕv'ĭn·thôl), **Ber·nard'** (bẽr·närd'; bûr-) **Louis.** 1865–1952. Rabbi, b. in Vilna, Russia; to U.S. (1891). Minister of congregation in Philadelphia (from 1891); founder and president of Orthodox Rabbinical Association of America. His son **Israel Herbert** (1888– ), also a rabbi; minister of congregations in Brooklyn, N.Y. (from 1910); founder and director of Institute for Jewish Studies for Adults; associated with Zionist movement.

**Lé'vis'** (lā'vēs'), Duc **François Gaston de.** 1720–1787. French soldier; distinguished himself in the War of the Austrian Succession; served in Canada (1756), succeeded to command at Montcalm's death, and defended the French colony there; created marshal of France (1783) and duc de Lévis (1784). His son **Gaston Pierre Marc** (1764?–1830) was a writer; an émigré (1792) and served in the Royalist army; returned to France at the Restoration and was appointed peer (1816); author of *Maximes et Réflexions* (1808), *Voyages de Kang-hi, ou Nouvelles Lettres Chinoises* (1812), *L'Angleterre au Commencement du XIXe Siècle* (1814).

**Le·vi'ta** (lē·vī'tȧ; lĕ·vē'tȧ), **E·li'jah** (ē·lī'jȧ) *or* **E·li'as** (ē·lī'ăs). **Elijah ben Ash'er ha–Le'vi** (bĕn ăsh'ēr hȧ·lē'vī). *Known also as* **Elijah Ash'ke·na'zi** (ăsh'kē·nä'zĭ) *or* **Ba·chur'** *or* **Ba·ḥur'** (bȧ·ko͞or'; bô'ko͞or) *or* **Tish'bi** (tĭsh'bē). 1469–1549. Jewish scholar, b. Neustadt, Bavaria; taught at Rome, Padua, Venice. Author of *Sefer ha-Baḥur* (pub. 1518) and other works on Hebrew grammar; the commentary *Massoret ha-Massoret* (1538), and lexical works, including *Tishbi* (1541).

**Le·vi'tov** (lyĕ·vyē'tôf), **Aleksandr Ivanovich.** 1835–1878. Russian writer of folk stories, as *Sketches of the Steppe* (1865), *Moscow Dens and Slums* (1868), *The Sorrows of Country, Highway, and Town* (1874).

**Le·vits'ki** (lyĕ·vyēts'kû·ĭ; *Angl.* lĕ·vĭts'kĭ), **Dmitri Grigorievich.** 1735?–1822. Russian portrait painter.

**Le·vitz'ki** (lyĕ·vyēts'kû·ĭ; *Angl.* lĕ·vĭts'kĭ), **Mischa.** 1898–1941. Russian piano virtuoso.

**Le'vy** (lē'vĭ), **Amy.** 1861–1889. English poet and novelist, of Jewish descent; works include several volumes of poems, as *Xantippe* (1881), and a novel *Reuben Sachs* (1889).

**Le′vy** (lē′vĭ), **Benn Wolfe.** 1900– . English playwright; author of *This Woman Business, Mud and Treacle, Mrs. Moonlight, Art and Mrs. Bottle, The Devil, Topaze* (from the French of Marcel Pagnol), *Springtime for Henry, The Jealous God,* etc.

**Lé′vy′** (lā′vē′), **Émile.** 1826–1890. French portrait and genre painter.

**Le′vy** (lē′vĭ), **Louis Edward.** 1846–1919. American photoengraver and inventor, b. in Bohemia; to U.S. (1855). His inventions include a photochemical engraving process (with David Bachrach, Jr.; pat. 1875), an etched glass grating or screen for making half-tone engravings (with his brother Max Levy; pat. 1893), which made possible the development of photoengraving, and other processes used in photoengraving. His brother **Max** (1857–1926), b. Detroit, Mich., was associated with him in photoengraving industry; devoted himself after 1893 to manufacture of half-tone screens; invented (1917) the hemocytometer.

**Lé′vy′** (lā′vē′), **Maurice.** 1838–1910. French mathematician and engineer. Author of works relating to hydrodynamics, elasticity, statics, etc.

**Lévy, Raphaël Georges.** 1853–1933. French economist; made special study of financial problems; among his many books are *Qualités Monétaires des Voleurs Mobilières* (1899), *Le Triomphe de l'Unité Monétaire* (1901), *Monnaie Saine et Saines Finances* (1919).

**Le′vy** (?lē′vĭ; lĕv′ĭ), **Uriah Phillips.** 1792–1862. American naval officer, b. Philadelphia. Flag officer of Mediterranean Squadron (1860). Purchased Jefferson's home, "Monticello," and willed it to the United States, but successful contest of the will prevented fulfillment of the bequest.

**Lé′vy′–Bruhl′** (lā′vē′brül′), **Lucien.** 1857–1939. French philosopher; author of *L'Idée de Responsabilité* (1884), *La Philosophie d'Auguste Comte* (1900), *La Mentalité Primitive* (1922), etc.

**Levy–Lawson, Edward.** See 1st Baron BURNHAM.

**Le·wal′** (lē·vȧl′), **Jules Louis.** 1823–1908. French general; member of Bazaine's general staff (1870); aided in training the new army (after 1871); commanded École Supérieure de la Guerre at its foundation (1878).

**Le′wald** (lā′vält), **August.** 1792–1871. German writer; author of novels, short stories, travel books, and dramatic works. His cousin **Fanny Lewald** (1811–1889) was a novelist and writer of travel books; m. Adolf Stahr (1855); among her novels are *Clementine* (1843), *Stella* (1883), *Die Familie Darner* (3 vols., 1887).

**Le′wen·haupt** (lā′vĕn·houpt), **Adam Ludvig.** 1659–1719. Swedish general who commanded Swedish army in its defeat by the Russians at Poltava (1709).

**Lew′es** (lū′ĭs), **George Henry.** 1817–1878. English philosopher and literary critic; contributed articles to reviews (1840–49) including many on drama later published as *Actors and Acting* (1875); wrote two unsuccessful novels. Became acquainted (1851) with Marian Evans (George Eliot, *q.v.*), with whom he went to Germany as husband (1854); founded and edited (1865–66) *Fortnightly Review;* published his *Life of Goethe,* a biographical classic (1855); as popularizer of philosophy, recast an earlier work as *The History of Philosophy from Thales to Comte;* as popularizer of science, esp. physiology and psychology, made brilliant suggestions in *Physiology of Common Life* (1859), *Studies in Animal Life* (1862), and *The Problems of Life and Mind* (1874–79), claiming against Comte a place for introspection in psychology, and initiating study of mental phenomena in their relation to social and historical conditions.

**Lew′in** (lū′ĭn), **Thomas.** 1805–1877. English lawyer and Biblical scholar; author of a standard treatise on *The Law of Trusts and Trustees* (1837), an authoritative textbook *The Life and Epistles of St. Paul* (1851).

**Lew′is** (lū′ĭs; lo͞o′-). See also LOUIS.

**Lewis, Agnes,** *nee* **Smith.** 1843–1926. British Orientalist, b. in Irvine, Ayr; m. Samuel Savage Lewis (1887; d. 1891). Studied Greek, Arabic, and Syriac; traveled in the Middle and Near East; discovered (with her sister Mrs. Margaret Dunlop Gibson) in the library of the Convent of St. Catherine on Mount Sinai a text (*Sinai Palimpsest*) of the four Gospels in Syriac, the oldest version then (1892) known.

**Lewis, Alfred Henry.** 1858?–1914. American journalist and author, esp. of stories of the fictitious Arizona town of Wolfville, *Wolfville Days* (1902), *Wolfville Nights* (1902), *Wolfville Folks* (1908), etc.

**Lewis, Andrew.** 1720–1781. American soldier and patriot, b. in Ireland; to America (c. 1732); settled near Staunton, Va. Commanded British contingent that defeated Indians at Point Pleasant (1774), resulting in peace with Indians during early years of Revolution and in the opening up of the way for George Rogers Clark campaign of 1778–79. Brigadier general in Continental army (1776–77).

**Lewis, Cecil Day.** *Orig.* **Cecil Day–Lewis.** 1904–1972. English poet; educ. Oxford; author of verse, as in *Transitional Poem* (1929), *From Feathers to Iron* (1931), *The Magnetic Mountain* (1933), *Time to Dance* (1935), *Overtures to Death* (1938), *Poems in Wartime;* also of *A Hope for Poetry* (1934), *Noah and the Waters* (modern morality play), translation of Vergil's *Georgics* (1940), *Child of Misfortune* (1939) etc., and detective fiction (under pseudonym **Nicholas Blake**); poet laureate (1968).

**Lewis, Charles Bertrand.** *Pseudonym* **M. Quad** (kwŏd). 1842–1924. American journeyman printer, journalist, and humorist, b. Liverpool, Ohio; author of *Brother Gardner's Lime Kiln Club* (1882), *The Life and Troubles of Mr. Bowser* (1902), etc.

**Lewis, Charlton Thomas.** 1834–1904. American lawyer and scholar; with Charles Short, compiled *Harper's Latin Dictionary* (1879); wrote treatises on the law of insurance. His son **Charlton Miner** (1866–1923) was professor of English at Yale (1899–1923); author of *Foreign Sources of Modern English Versification* (1898), *The Principles of English Verse* (1906), etc.

**Lewis, Clarence Irving.** 1883–1964. American philosopher; professor, Harvard (from 1930); author of *Survey of Symbolic Logic* (1918), *Mind and the World-Order* (1929), etc. Special editor for philosophy and logic, *Webster's New International Dictionary, Second Edition.*

**Lewis, Clive Staples.** *Pseudonym* **Clive Hamilton.** 1898–1963. English writer; author of *Pilgrim's Regress, an allegorical apology for Christianity, reason, and romanticism* (1935), *Allegory of Love, a study in medieval tradition* (1936), *Out of the Silent Planet* (1938), etc.

**Lewis, Dominic Bevan Wyndham.** 1891–1969. British journalist and writer; served in France through World War (1914–18); columnist on London *Daily Express* (1919–23) and *Daily Mail* (from 1923). Author of *On Straw and Other Conceits* (1927), *François Villon* (1928), *King Spider: Louis XI of France* (1930), *Emperor of the West, Charles V* (1932), *The Nonsensibus* (1936). ☞ Do not confuse with (Percy) Wyndham LEWIS (*q.v.*).

**Lewis, Mrs. Ethelreda.** d. 1946. English writer; known as editor of the life narrative of Alfred Aloysius Horn, really Smith, under the title *Trader Horn*...(1927).

**Lewis, Francis.** 1713–1803. Merchant, b. Llandaff, Wales; to U.S. (1738). N.Y. delegate to Continental Congress (1774–79); signer of Declaration of Independence. His son **Morgan** (1754–1844), b. New York, was chief of staff for General Gates at Ticonderoga and Saratoga; chief justice of New York Supreme Court (1801–04); governor of New York (1804–07); major general in War of 1812.

**Lewis, Frederick Christian.** 1779–1856. English engraver and landscape painter; engraved works of Raphael, Michelangelo, Claude, Poussin, Flaxman, and Sir Thomas Lawrence's crayon portraits; painted landscapes, esp. of Devonshire, in oils and water colors. His brother **George Robert** (1782–1871), painter of landscapes and portraits, illustrated Thomas F. Dibdin's account of tour through France and Germany. Another brother **Charles** (1786–1836) was an eminent bookbinder. **John Frederick** (1805–1876), painter, son of Frederick Christian, shifted from animal paintings to aquarelles after journey through Germany and Italy, to Spanish genre painting after visit to Spain (1832–34), to Oriental subjects after travel in East (1839–51). Another son, **Charles George** (1808–1880), engraver, is best known for his engravings of Landseer's works.

**Lewis,** Sir **George Cornewall.** 1806–1863. English statesman and man of letters. M.P. (1847); undersecretary for home office (1848); financial secretary to treasury (1850–52); editor of *Edinburgh Review* (1852–55); chancellor of exchequer (1855–58); home secretary under Lord Palmerston (1859–61); secretary for war (1861–63). In his *Enquiry into the Credibility of the Early Roman History* (1855), combated the historical methods of Niebuhr. Author also of a *Dialogue on the Best Form of Government* (1863).

**Lewis,** Sir **George Henry.** 1833–1911. English lawyer; engaged in many famous cases, including the Bravo poisoning case, the Hatton Garden diamond robbery, and several banking prosecutions; solicitor for Parnell and incriminated nationalists (1888–89); discovered Piggott's forgeries.

**Lewis, Gilbert Newton.** 1875–1946. American chemist; work includes studies on thermodynamic theory and its application to chemistry and development of atomic theories, a theory of valence, a theory of photons, concentration of heavy hydrogen, etc. See Irving LANGMUIR.

**Lewis, H. H.** American farm hand and poet; awarded Harriet Monroe lyric prize for his poem *Farmhands' Refrain* (pub. in *Poetry* magazine, June, 1938). Author of *Red Renaissance* (1930), *Thinking of Russia* (1932), *Salvation* (1934), *Road to Utterly* (1935), etc.

**Lewis, Isaac Newton.** 1858–1931. American army officer and inventor; grad. U.S.M.A., West Point (1884). Invented an artillery position finder (pat. 1891), the Lewis machine gun (1911), a system of signals for artillery fire control, a gas-propelled torpedo, etc. Originated modern artillery corps organization, adopted by U.S. army in 1902.

**Lewis, John Llewellyn.** 1880–1969. American labor leader, b. Lucas, Iowa. Coal miner; joined United Mine Workers' Union (an affiliate of the American Federation of Labor); became its vice-president (1917) and president (from 1920). A.F. of L. organizer (1911–17); influential in securing election of William Green (*q.v.*) as its president after death of Gompers (*q.v.*). In disagreement with A.F. of L. policies, organized (1935) Committee for Industrial Organization, reorganized (1938) as Congress of Industrial Organizations (both known as CIO), around a nucleus of ten unions, and entered aggressively into competition with the A.F. of L.; president of CIO (1935–40). Kept promise to resign from presidency of CIO if Franklin D. Roosevelt were elected for a third term, but retained presidency of strong United Mine Workers' Union.

**Lewis, Matthew Gregory.** *Nicknamed* **Monk** (mŭngk) **Lewis.** 1775–1818. English novelist, dramatist, and poet, b. London. Attaché at The Hague (1794), where, inspired by Mrs. Radcliffe's works, he wrote his famous romance *Ambrosio, or the Monk* (1796), in which the supernatural and horrible predominate; M.P. (1796–1802); produced musical drama *The Castle Spectre* at Drury Lane (1798), and *Rolla*, a translation from Kotzebue (1799); made acquaintance of Walter Scott and procured publication of his translation of *Götz von Berlichingen* (1799); on death of his father succeeded to large fortune and made tours of inquiry into grievances and treatment of slaves on West Indian estates, reported in his *Journal of a West Indian Proprietor* (pub. 1834). Author also of *The Bravo of Venice*, *Tales of Terror* (1799), *Tales of Wonder* (to which Sir Walter Scott contributed; 1801), and skillful ballads including *Alonzo the Brave and the Fair Imogen.*

**Lewis, Meriwether.** 1774–1809. American explorer, b. in Albemarle County, Va. Private secretary to President Jefferson (1801–03). Named by Jefferson to lead expedition to explore the Louisiana Purchase; selected William Clark (*q.v.*) as coleader. Lewis and Clark expedition (1804–06) went up the Missouri River to its source, crossed the Great Divide, and descended Columbia River to the Pacific Ocean; brought back valuable information on natural features of country, its flora, fauna, Indian tribes, etc. Governor of Louisiana Territory (1807–09).

**Lewis, Morgan.** See under Francis LEWIS.

**Lewis, Sin'clair** (sĭn'klâr). 1885–1951. American novelist and playwright, b. Sauk Centre, Minn. A.B., Yale (1907). Journalist and editor (1907–16). Author of *Our Mr. Wrenn* (1914), *The Trail of the Hawk* (1915), *The Job* (1917), *Main Street* (1920), *Babbitt* (1922), *Arrowsmith* (1925), *Mantrap* (1926), *Elmer Gantry* (1927), *The Man Who Knew Coolidge* (1928), *Dodsworth* (1929), *Ann Vickers* (1933), *Work of Art* (1933), *It Can't Happen Here* (1935), *Prodigal Parents* (1938), *Bethel Merriday* (1940), *Gideon Planish* (1943), *Cass Timberlane* (1945), *Kingsblood Royal* (1947), etc. First American to be awarded the Nobel prize in literature (1930). See Dorothy THOMPSON.

**Lewis, Tayler.** 1802–1877. American classical scholar and Orientalist, b. Northumberland, N.Y. Specialist in study of religion. Author of *The Six Days of Creation* (1855), *The Bible and Science, or the World Problem* (1856), *The Divine Human in the Scriptures* (1860).

**Lewis, William Thomas.** *Called* **Gentleman Lewis.** 1748?–1811. English comedian, of Welsh descent; created among others characters Faulkland in *The Rivals*, Doricourt in *The Belle's Stratagem*, Jeremy Diddler in *Raising the Wind*, Egerton in *Man of the World*, Rover in *Wild Oats.*

**Lewis, Winford Lee.** 1878–1943. American chemist, b. Gridley, Calif. Captain in Chemical Warfare Service, U.S. army (1917–18). Developed the poison gas (lewisite) named after him (1918).

**Lewis, Wyndham,** *in full* **Percy Wyndham.** 1884–1957. British painter and writer, b. in America of English ancestry; studio in England (from 1911); hailed as leader of vorticist school of post-impressionism; attracted attention by vorticist murals in Eiffel Tower Restaurant, London. Served in France in World War (1914–18). As vorticist movement in painting subsided, became prominent as a writer. Author of *Tarr* (novel; 1918), *The Art of Being Ruled* (1926), *The Childermass* (1929), *The Apes of God* (1930), *The Diabolical Principle and the Dithyrambic Spectator* (1931), *Filibusters in Barbary* (1932), *Doom of Youth* (1932), *Men Without Art*

(1934), *Left Wings Over Europe* (1936), *Blasting and Bombardiering* (1937), *The Mysterious Mr. Bull* (1938), *Wyndham Lewis the Artist* (1939), etc.

☞ Not to be confused with Dominic Bevan Wyndham LEWIS (*q.v.*).

**Lew'i·sohn** (lū'ĭ·zŭn), **Adolph.** 1849–1938. Philanthropist, b. Hamburg, Ger.; to U.S. (c. 1867); donor of Lewisohn Stadium to C.C.N.Y., and benefactor of Columbia, Harvard, Yale, Princeton, and Dartmouth.

**Lewisohn, Ludwig.** 1883–1955. Novelist and critic, b. Berlin, Ger.; to U.S. (1890). On editorial board, *The Nation* (1919–24); traveled in Europe and Near East (1924–25) studying Jewish problem; resident in France from 1927. Author of novels, including *The Broken Snare* (1908), *Don Juan* (1923), *The Case of Mr. Crump* (1927), *The Island Within* (1928), *Stephen Escott* (1930), *The Last Days of Shylock* (1931); critical writings, including *The Modern Drama* (1915), *The Spirit of Modern German Literature* (1916), *The Poets of Modern France* (1918), *Israel* (1925), *Cities and Men* (1927), *Expression in America* (1932; later retitled *Story of American Literature*); the autobiographical *Upstream* (1922) and *Mid-channel* (1929); and many translations from the German.

**Lex'ow** (lĕk'sō), **Clarence.** 1852–1910. American lawyer, b. Brooklyn, N.Y. New York State senator (1893–98); chairman, legislative investigating committee which exposed municipal corruption in New York City government.

**Ley** (lē), **James.** 1st Earl of **Marl'bor·ough** (môl'bŭ·rŭ; -brŭ; märl'-). 1550–1629. English judge; lord chief justice of King's Bench, in Ireland (1604), in England (1622–24); lord high treasurer (1624); succeeded Bacon as speaker of House of Lords (1621) and pronounced judgment of peers upon Bacon.

**Ley** (lī), **Robert.** 1890–1945. German Nazi leader; served in World War; prisoner in France (1917–20). Entered Nazi party (1924); noted for anti-Semitism; appointed head of the party district in the Rhineland (1924). Nazi deputy (1928); leader of the Nazi organization in Munich (1931), in all Germany (1932); as head of Labor Front (from 1933) ruthlessly enforced obedience in labor ranks; committed suicide, awaiting trial as war criminal.

**Ley'bourn** (lē'bērn; -bûrn), **William.** 1626–?1700. English mathematician; coauthor of *Urania Practica* (1648; first book on astronomy written in English); author of *The Compleat Surveyor* (1653), *Cursus Mathematicus* (1690), and *Panarithmologia* (1693; earliest English ready reckoner), etc.

**Ley'den** (lī'dĕn), **Ernst Viktor von.** 1832–1910. German physician. Investigated diseases of the spinal cord, heart, and kidneys; contributed to the development of institutions for the treatment of tuberculosis and to improvement in nursing.

**Ley'den** (lā'd'n), **John.** 1775–1811. Scottish poet and Orientalist. Contributed poems and translations to *Edinburgh Magazine;* contributed to Matthew Gregory Lewis's *Tales of Wonder* (1801); assisted Scott in gathering materials for his *Minstrelsy of the Scottish Border;* published poem *Scenes of Infancy* (1803). Sailed for India as surgeon and naturalist (1802); forced by ill health to visit Malay Peninsula and East Indian islands, where he collected linguistic and ethnographical information among Indo-Chinese tribes, foundation for his essay on the Indo-Persian, Indo-Chinese, and Deccan languages (1807). Translated Gospels into five languages; accompanied Lord Minto to Java as interpreter (1811); died of fever there. Author of important *Dissertation on the Languages and Literatures of the Indo-Chinese Nations.*

**Ley'den** (lī'dĕn), **Lucas van.** See LUCAS VAN LEYDEN.

**Ley'dig** (lī'dĭk), **Franz.** 1821–1908. German zoologist; author of *Lehrbuch der Histologie des Menschen und der Tiere* (1857), *Zelle und Gewebe* (1885), etc.

**Ley'en** (lī'ĕn), **Friedrich von der.** 1873–1966. German scholar; author of *Die Deutschen Heldensagen* (1912), *Deutsche Dichtung in Neuer Zeit* (1922), etc.

**Leygues** (lāg), **Jean Claude Georges.** 1857–1933. French politician; minister of marine under Clemenceau (1917–18), rendering important service in co-ordinating activities of Allied fleets. Premier of France (1920). Again minister of marine (1925–30; 1932–33).

**Leyland, John** (1506?–1552). See LELAND.

**Ley'poldt** (lī'pōlt), **Frederick.** 1835–1884. Publisher and bibliographer, b. Stuttgart, Ger.; to U.S. (1854); naturalized. With Henry Holt established book firm Leypoldt & Holt (1866). Editor and publisher (from 1868) of the *Literary Bulletin*, which became (1873) *The Publishers' Weekly;* and (from 1870) of annual catalogues of books published, which have developed into *The Publishers' Trade List Annual.* A founder of the *Library Journal* (1876), and its publisher.

**Leys** (līs), Baron **Hendrik.** 1815–1869. Belgian painter and etcher; best known as historical and genre painter.

**L'Her'mite'** (lĕr'mēt'), **François,** *known as* **Tristan.** 1601–1655. French poet, playwright, and miscellaneous writer; member of the retinue of the duc d'Orléans. Author of *Plaintes d'Acante* (1633), *Les Amours de Tristan* (1638), *Le Page Disgracié* (autobiographical matter; 1642), *Mariamne* (tragedy; 1636), *La Mort de Sénèque* and *La Mort de Crispe* (tragedies; 1645), *La Parasite* (comedy; 1653), etc.

**L'Hermite** *or* **L'Ermite, Tristan.** See Louis TRISTAN L'HERMITE.

**Lher'mitte'** (lĕr'mēt'), **Léon Augustin.** 1844–1925. French painter, esp. of landscapes.

**Lhé·vinne'** (lâ·vēn'), **Jo'sef** (jō'zĕf; -zĭf). 1874–1944. Russian pianist; American debut, with Russian Symphony Orchestra, New York (1906). Has toured Europe and U.S. frequently; concert tours in U.S. annually (from 1920).

**Lho'pi'tal'** *or* **L'Hô'pi'tal'** (lō'pē'tȧl'), **Guillaume François Antoine de.** Marquis **de Saint-Mesme** (dē săN'mâm'). Comte **d'Au'tre·mont'** (dō'trē·môN'). 1661–1704. French geometer. Studied the differential calculus with Jakob Bernoulli (1692); author of *L'Analyse des Infiniment Petits pour l'Intelligence des Lignes Courbes* (1696) and *Traité Analytique des Sections Coniques* (pub. 1707).

**L'Hos'pi'tal'** (lō'pē'tȧl') *or* **L'Hô'pi'tal'** (lō'-), **Michel de.** 1507–1573. French jurist and statesman; chancellor of France (1560); summoned the States-General (1560) and secured passage of act granting toleration to the Huguenots (1562); policy of tolerance failed and religious wars followed, destroying his influence in government; dismissed from office (1568).

**Lhote** (lōt), **André.** 1885–1962. French painter; identified with ultramodern movements in painting.

**Lia.** See LEAH.

**Lia'dov** *or* **Lya'dov** (lyȧ'dôf), **Anatoli Konstantinovich.** 1855–1914. Russian composer of a symphony, symphonic poems (*Baba Yaga, Kikimora, The Enchanted Lake*, etc.), and piano works.

**Liang** (lē·äng'). A Chinese dynasty (502–557 A.D.), also known as **Southern Liang,** succeeded by the Ch'ên. One of the Five Dynasties (*q.v.*) is known as the **Later Liang** (907–923).

**Liang Ch'i-chao** (chē'chä'ō). 1873–1929. Chinese scholar and revolutionary leader. Started first Chinese daily paper in Peking; fled to Japan (1898); associated with Sun Yat-sen, working for reforms, and also with K'ang Yu-wei; returned (1912) to China after the Revolution; conducted a daily paper in Tientsin; held several government positions for short periods (1912–14); at Paris Peace Conference (1919); spent later years teaching history in various colleges in northern China and in writing books on history, education, literature, etc.; placing Western ideas before the Chinese.

**Liang Shih-yi** (shĭr′ē′). 1869–1933. Chinese statesman; acting director of imperial Chinese postal system (1911–12); held other government offices under Yüan Shih-k'ai (1912–15); aided him in his attempt to overthrow republic (1915–16); retired (1916–18). Speaker of the Senate (1918); sided with Chang Tso-lin (1921) but forced to leave Peking (1922) on Chang's defeat.

**Liap′chev** (lyȧp′chĕf), **Andrei.** 1866–1933. Bulgarian statesman; premier (1926–31); pursued conciliatory foreign policy; avoided war with Yugoslavia.

**Lia·pu·nov′** *or* **Lya·pu·nov′** (lyŭ·pŏŏ·nôf′), **Aleksandr Mikhailovich.** 1857–1918. Russian mathematician; conducted research in field of hydrodynamics.

**Liapunov** *or* **Lyapunov, Sergei Mikhailovich.** 1859–1924. Russian composer of symphonies, symphonic poems, concertos, and piano studies.

**Liard** (lyȧr), **Louis.** 1846–1917. French philosopher; charged (1885–93) with reorganization of the curricula and institutions for higher education; author of *La Science Positive et la Métaphysique* (1879), *Descartes* (1881), etc.

**Li·ba′ni·us** (lĭ·bā′nĭ·ŭs; lī-). Greek Sophist and rhetorician of 4th century A.D., b. at Antioch, Syria. His many works include orations, letters, a life of Demosthenes.

**Li′bau** (lē′bou), **Andreas.** *Latin* **Li·ba′vi·us** (lĭ·bā′vĭ·ŭs). d. 1616. German naturalist, physician, and chemist.

**Lib′by** (lĭb′ĭ), **Willard Frank.** 1908– . Amer. chemist, b. Grand Valley, Colo. Awarded Nobel prize in chemistry (1960) for use of carbon-14 for age determination in archaeology, geology, etc.

**Lib′bey** (lĭb′ĭ), **Laura Jean.** 1862–1924. American fiction writer; b. New York City; m. Van Mater Stilwell. Author of many popular sentimental novels, including *Lovers Once but Strangers Now*, *Miss Middleton's Lover*, *When His Love Grew Cold*.

**Li′belt** (lē′bĕlt), **Karol.** 1807–1875. Polish philosopher and politician; member of Polish revolutionary committee (1845) and the Polish provisional government at Cracow (1846). Arrested and sentenced to twenty years' imprisonment (1847), but released after the March revolution (1848). Member of the Frankfort parliament (1848), and the Prussian Abgeordnetenhaus (1873). In his philosophical works, a disciple of Hegel.

**Li′be·ra′le da Ve·ro′na** (lē′bā·rä′lā dä vā·rō′nä), **Antonio.** 1445?–?1529. Veronese painter; works include miniatures (as illuminations of missals in cathedrals of Chiusi and Siena, and in the Pinacoteca, Verona), frescoes, and religious paintings on wood.

**Li′be·ri** (lē′bā·rē), **Pietro.** *Sometimes called* **il Li′ber·ti′no** (ēl lē′bār·tē′nō). 1605–1687. Venetian painter; known chiefly for his *Battle of the Dardanelles*.

**Li·be′ri·us** (lī·bēr′ĭ·ŭs), **Saint.** d. 366. Pope (bishop of Rome; 352–366). Involved in controversy between Arians and Athanasius; exiled to Thrace (355) because of his support of Athanasius; replaced by Antipope Felix II, but reinstated (358).

**Li′bri–Car·ruc′ci del′la Som·ma′ia** (lē′brē·kär·rōōt′chē dāl′lä sōm·mä′yä), Count **Guillaume Brutus Icilius Timoléon.** 1803–1869. Mathematician, b. Florence; to Paris (1830). Author of *Memoires de Mathématiques et de Physique* (1827), etc.

**Lich·now′sky** (lĭk·nôf′skē), Prince **Karl Max.** 1860–1928. German diplomat; ambassador to Great Britain (1912–14), where he labored futilely to maintain peace between Great Britain and Germany. His wife **Mechtilde** (1879–1958), poet, playwright, and novelist; author of *Gott Betet* (verse; 1916), *Ein Spiel vom Tod* (play; 1913), *Geburt* (novel; 1921).

**Lich′ten·au** (lĭk′tĕ·nou), Countess **von.** *Nee* **Wilhelmine En′ke** (ĕng′kĕ). 1753–1820. Mistress of the Prussian king Frederick William II, to whom she bore five children.

**Lich′ten·berg** (lĭk′tĕn·bĕrk), **Georg Christoph.** 1742–1799. German physicist and satirist; conducted investigations in experimental physics, esp. electricity; ridiculed Lavater's science of physiognomy; wrote satirical work on Greek pronunciation; attacked Sturm und Drang writers; explained Hogarth's etchings.

**Lich′ten′ber′ger′** (lēsh′tăn′bĕr′zhā′), **Frédéric Auguste.** 1832–1899. French Protestant theologian; author of *Encyclopédie des Sciences Religieuses* (1876–82), etc. His nephew **Henri Lichtenberger** (1864–1941) was professor of German literature at U. of Paris and author of works on German literature. Henri's brother **André** (1870–1940), sociologist and writer of fiction; author of *Le Socialisme au XVIII*[e] *Siècle* (1895), *Le Socialisme Utopique* (1898), *La Mort de Corinthe* (novel, 1900), *La Folle Aventure* (1908), *Scènes en Famille* (1921), etc.

**Lich′ten·stein** (lĭk′tĕn·shtīn), **Martin Heinrich.** 1780–1857. German zoologist and traveler in Dutch South Africa; founder of Berlin zoo (opened 1844).

**Licht′wark** (lĭkt′värk), **Alfred.** 1852–1914. German art teacher and critic.

**Licht′wer** (lĭkt′vēr), **Magnus Gottfried.** 1719–1783. German writer of fables.

**Li·ci′ni·o** (lē·chē′nyō), **Bernardino.** fl. 1520–1544. Venetian painter; pupil and relative of Pordenone (*q.v.*); known for his family portrait groups, individual portraits, and religious paintings.

**Licinio, Giovanni Antonio.** See Giovanni Antonio da PORDENONE.

**Li·cin′i·us** (lī·sĭn′ĭ·ŭs). *In full* **Valerius Li·cin′i·a′nus** (lī·sĭn′ĭ·ā′nŭs) **Licinius.** 270?–325 A.D. Roman emperor (308–324), b. in Dacia. Made Augustus in the East by Emperor Galerius (308); became sole emperor in the East (311); m. (313) Constantia, half sister of Constantine the Great; with Constantine issued Edict of Milan (313) recognizing Christianity; defeated Maximinus (314) and in turn was beaten at Cibalae in Pannonia by Constantine (314); made peace but later resumed the war and was defeated at Adrianople (324) by Constantine; surrendered and was executed.

**Licinius Cal′vus Sto′lo** (kăl′vŭs stō′lō), **Gaius.** Roman statesman of 1st half of 4th century B.C.; tribune of the people (377 B.C.); consul (361). Collaborated with Lucius Sextius in introducing measures in favor of the rights of the plebeians.

**Licinius Ma′cer** (mā′sēr), **Gaius.** 110?–66 B.C. Roman politician and historian; head of the democratic party; author of *Annales*. His son **Gaius Licinius Macer Cal′vus** [kăl′vŭs] (82–47 B.C.) was an orator and poet.

**Lick** (lĭk), **James.** 1796–1876. American financier and philanthropist, b. Fredericksburg, Pa. In South America (1820–37), California (from 1847). From his bequest of $700,000 for "a powerful telescope, superior to and more powerful than any telescope ever yet made," Lick Observatory on Mount Hamilton, Calif., was built, and turned over to U. of California (1888).

**Lid′dell** (lĭd′'l), **Henry George.** 1811–1898. English classical scholar; dean of Christ Church (1855–91); headmaster of Westminster School (1846–55). Joint author with Robert Scott of standard *Greek-English Lexicon* (based on Passow, 1843). See Charles L. DODGSON.

**Lid'dell Hart** (lĭd''l härt'), Sir **Basil Henry.** 1895–1970. English military authority and writer. Served through World War (1914–18); twice wounded; retired (1927). Devoted himself to study of military science; military correspondent of London *Daily Telegraph* (1925–35) and London *Times* (1935–39); also, military editor of *Encyclopaedia Britannica.* Among his notable works are a number of military biographies, studies of the life of his friend T. E. Lawrence, and *The Decisive Wars of History* (1929), *The Future of Infantry* (1933), *A History of The World War* (1934), *Europe in Arms* (1937), *The Defence of Britain* (1939; a book reputed to have had influence in determining British strategy at outbreak of war against Germany in 1939), *Dynamic Defence* (1940), *The Current of War* (1941), *The Strategy of Indirect Approach* (1941), *This Expanding War* (1942).

**Lid'don** (lĭd''n), **Henry Parry.** 1829–1890. English pulpit orator; joined Pusey and Keble in Oxford movement; Ireland professor of exegesis, Oxford (1870–82); canon of St. Paul's Cathedral (1870), chancellor (1886); defended Athanasian Creed.

**Lid'ner** (lēd'nẽr), **Bengt.** 1757–1793. Swedish poet; author of *The Death of the Countess Spastara* (1783), the opera *Medea* (1784), the tragedy *Erik XIV* (pub. 1800).

**Lie** (lē), **Jonas.** 1833–1909. Uncle of Jonas Lie (1880–1940). Norwegian writer; among his novels are *The Foreseer* (1870), *The Bark Future, or Life up North* (1872), *The Pilot and his Wife* (1874), *Thomas Ross* (1878), *Adam Schroder* (1879), *Rutland* (1881); among his plays, *Faustina Strozzi* (lyrical drama; 1875), and *Grabows Kat* (comedy).

**Lie** (lē), **Jo'nas** (jō'nȧs; *Norw.* yō'näs). 1880–1940. Painter, b. in Norway; to U.S. (1893). Studied at National Academy of Design and Art Students' League, New York. President, National Academy of Design (from 1934). Among his well-known works are *Wind Swept, The Mill Race, Brooklyn Bridge, A New York Cañon, Fishing Boats at Sunrise.*

**Lie, Sophus,** *in full* **Marius Sophus.** 1842–1899. Norwegian mathematician; worked on transformation groups, differential geometry, and differential equations.

**Lie, Tryg've** (trüg'vĕ) **Halvdan.** 1896–1968. Norwegian lawyer, b. Oslo; legal adviser to Norwegian Labor Party (1922–40); minister of justice (1935–39), of shipping and supply (1939–41), of foreign affairs (1941–46); secretary-general, UN (1946–53).

**Lieb** (lēb), **John William.** 1860–1929. American mechanical and electrical engineer, b. Newark, N.J.

**Lieb** (lēp), **Michael.** See Mihály von MUNKÁCSY.

**Lie'ber** (lē'bẽr), **Francis.** 1800–1872. Publicist and educator, b. Berlin, Ger. Imprisoned as a radical (1819; 1824); fled to England (1826) and to U.S. (1827). Planned and edited *Encyclopaedia Americana* (13 vols., 1829–33). Professor of history and political economy, South Carolina Coll. (1835–56), Columbia (1857–65), Columbia Law School (1865–72). Author of *Manual of Political Ethics* (2 vols., 1838–39), *Legal and Political Hermeneutics* (1839), *On Civil Liberty and Self-government* (2 vols., 1853), *A Code for the Government of Armies* (1863), which in a revised form was issued by U.S. War Department as *Instructions for the Government of Armies in the Field, General Orders No. 100.*

**Lie'ber·kühn** (lē'bẽr·kün), **Johann Nathanael.** 1711–1756. German anatomist; worked on microscopic technique; the crypts of Lieberkühn (glands in the intestines) were named after him.

**Lie'ber·man** (lē'bẽr·mȧn), **Elias.** 1883–1969. Educator and poet, b. St. Petersburg, Russia; to U.S. (1891). Teacher of English in New York City schools (from 1903); author of *Paved Streets* (1918), *Hand Organ Man* (1930), *Man in the Shadows* (1940), *To My Brothers Everywhere* (1954); coauthor of a play *The Awakening of Narradin* (1916).

**Lie'ber·mann** (lē'bẽr·män), **Karl.** 1842–1914. German chemist. Professor, Charlottenburg (from 1873). With Graebe, produced first synthetic alizarin (1869). A reaction for detection of phenol is named after him.

**Liebermann, Max.** 1847–1935. German painter and etcher; among his canvases are notably portraits and genre scenes, as *Woman Plucking Geese, Country Tavern in Bavaria, Going to School in Edam, The Hog Market.* His brother **Felix** (1851–1925), legal historian; author of *Die Gesetze der Angelsachsen* (3 vols., 1898–1916), etc.

**Lie'bert** (lē'bẽrt), **Arthur.** 1878–1946. German philosopher.

**Liebhard, Joachim.** See Joachim CAMERARIUS.

**Lie'big** (lē'bĭk), Baron **Justus von.** 1803–1873. German chemist. Among his numerous contributions to chemical science are the establishment at Giessen of the first practical chemical teaching laboratory, introduction of methods of organic analysis, discovery of chloroform and aldehyde, a method for manufacture of potassium cyanide, and work in collaboration with Wöhler on constitution of bitter oil of almonds and on uric acid; in biochemistry, investigated constitution of body fluids; proved that body heat is the result of combustion of foods in the body; is considered founder of agricultural chemistry; held that transformation of inorganic into organic substance takes place exclusively in plants, and that plants receive carbon and nitrogen from carbon dioxide and ammonia in the atmosphere while they receive mineral elements from soil; experimented with artificial soil fertilizers.

**Lieb'knecht** (lēp'k'nĕкt), **Wilhelm.** 1826–1900. German journalist and politician; in exile (1849–62) in Switzerland and England. Aided by Karl Marx in founding Social Democratic Labor party (1869). Member of Reichstag (1867–70; 1874 ff.). Editor, *Demokratisches Wochenblatt* (merged into *Volksstaat,* 1869), and *Vorwärts.* See also August BEBEL. His son **Karl** (1871–1919) was a lawyer and Communist leader; member, German Reichstag (1912); violently opposed Germany's policy (1913–14) leading to the World War; after war broke out, organized antiwar demonstrations (1915, 1916); arrested, and condemned to two years' penal servitude (1916–18); on release from prison (1918), took leadership with Rosa Luxemburg (*q.v.*) of Spartacus party and was involved in the Spartacist insurrection (Jan., 1919); arrested, and murdered (with Rosa Luxemburg) while being transferred from military headquarters in west Berlin to prison (Jan. 15, 1919).

**Lieb'mann** (lēp'män), **Otto.** 1840–1912. German philosopher.

**Liech'ten·stein** (lĭк'tĕn·shtīn). Principality between Austria and Switzerland and its ruling family originating in the 12th century, which acquired county of Schellenberg (1699) and of Vaduz (1712) and title (1719) to possession of the two as Principality of Liechtenstein, granted by Emperor Charles VI; inheritance has been held by two lines: elder, from Francis Joseph (c. 1781) and younger (extinct 1908) from his brother Charles Borromeus (d. 1789). Chief members of family, holding the title Prince **von und zu Liechtenstein,** are: **Joseph Wenzel** (1696–1772), Austrian general; took prominent part in several wars of Austria, esp. that of the succession (1740–48); minister to France (1737–41); reigning prince (1748–72). His great-nephew **John I Joseph** (1760–1836), Austrian field marshal; fought in

Turkish war (1788–91) and in Napoleonic wars (1799–1814); covered retreat at Austerlitz (1805); ruled principality after death of brother (1805–36). **John II** (1840–1929), nephew of John I; prince (1858–1929), the longest known period of personal rule in European history. His nephew **Alfred** (1842–1907), Austrian politician; member of Austrian parliament (from 1879); founded Catholic political party. **Francis I** (1853–1938), brother of John II; prince (1929–38).

**Lieh-Tzŭ** (lē·ĕ′ dzŭ′). fl. 5th or 4th century B.C. Chinese Taoist philosopher, regarded by some as imaginary and created by the philosopher Chuang-tzu. Eight books of writings, reputed to be his but probably the work of his disciples, still exist.

**Lien′hard** (lēn′härt), **Friedrich.** 1865–1929. German author of *Lieder eines Elsässers* (1895), the plays *Till Eulenspiegel* (1896), *Odilia* (1898), *König Arthur* (1900), *Wieland der Schmied* (1905), and *Odysseus* (1911); the novels *Oberlin* (1910) and *Westmark* (1919); and essays.

**Lietz′mann** (lēts′män), **Hans.** 1875–1942. German Protestant theologian.

**Lie′ven** (lē′vĕn), **Princess de. Dariya Khristoforovna,** *nee* **von Ben′ken·dorff** (fôn bĕng′kĕn·dôrf). 1784–1857. Latvian lady; m. (1800) Russ. gen. Khristofor Andreevich de Lieven (d. 1839) and accompanied him when he was ambassador at Berlin (1809), London (1812–34). Established salon at Paris (after 1839) to which were drawn some of the leading diplomats of Europe; the extent of her diplomatic connections and her oracular utterances gained for her the name "Sibyl of Europe."

**Lie′vens** *or* **Lie′vensz** *or* **Li′vens** (lē′vĕns), **Jan.** 1607–1674. Dutch painter; studio in Leiden (1621–31), England (1631–34), Antwerp (1635–44), Amsterdam (1644–74). Painter of Biblical and allegorical scenes, and portraits.

**Li·far′** (lyĭ·får′y′), **Serge** (sĕrzh). 1905– . Russian choreographer and ballet master in Paris; close friend of and student under Diaghilev; author of *Serge Diaghilev: His Life, His Work, His Legend* (1940).

**Li·gar′i·us** (lĭ·gâr′ĭ·ŭs), **Quintus.** Roman senator; a follower of Pompey and a prisoner of Caesar after battle of Thapsus (46 B.C.); pardoned by Caesar after a brilliant defense conducted by Cicero; later involved in conspiracy of Brutus, and died while under proscription of Second Triumvirate.

**Lig′gett** (lĭg′ĕt; -ĭt), **Hunter.** 1857–1935. American army officer, b. Reading, Pa.; grad. U.S.M.A., West Point (1879); major general (1917). With A.E.F. in France (1917–19), commanding 1st army (1918–19) with rank of lieut. general. Commanded army of occupation on the Rhine (1919). Retired as major general (1921); promoted lieut. general on retired list.

**Liggett, Louis Kroh** (krō). 1875–1946. American businessman, b. Detroit. Founder, president, and director, United Drug Co.; chairman of the board, Liggett Drug Co., Inc., operating a chain of drugstores.

**Light′foot** (līt′fo͝ot), **John.** 1602–1675. English Hebraist and rabbinical scholar; vice-chancellor of Cambridge U. (1654); prebendary of Ely (1668); assisted Brian Walton with the *Polyglot Bible.* Author of harmonies of the Gospels and Old Testament and of *Horae Hebraicae et Talmudicae* (5 vols., 1658–74), his life work.

**Lightfoot, Joseph Barber.** 1828–1889. English theologian. Hulsean professor of divinity, Cambridge (1861); chaplain to prince consort, Whitehall preacher, canon of St. Paul's (1871); bishop of Durham (1879–89). Author of commentaries on Epistles, works on Apostolic Fathers defending authenticity of Epistles of Ignatius; influential member of committee for revision of New Testament (1870–80).

**Light-Horse Harry.** See Henry LEE.

**Ligne** (lēn′y′), Prince **Charles** (shärl) **Jo′seph′** (zhō′zĕf′) **von.** 1735–1814. Austrian soldier, b. in Brussels; distinguished himself in the Seven Years' War (1756–63); served in Austrian diplomatic service at various European courts; was created field marshal by Catherine II of Russia. Maintained correspondence with leading figures of his time, including Frederick the Great, Voltaire, Laharpe, Catherine II, Goethe, Wieland. Selections from his writings form *Mélanges Militaires, Littéraires et Sentimentaires* (34 vols., 1795–1811).

**Lig′o·nier′** (lĭg′ō·nēr′; lē′gô′nyā′), **John,** *known also as* **Jean Louis.** 1st Earl **Ligonier.** 1680–1770. British military officer, of Huguenot descent; fought under Marlborough; colonel of the Black Horse, now 7th Dragoons (1720–49); commanded British foot at Fontenoy (1745); commander in chief in Austrian Netherlands (1746–47); field marshal (1766).

**Li·guo′ri** (lē·gwô′rē), Sant'**Alfonso Maria de′.** *Eng.* Saint **Alphonsus Liguori.** 1696–1787. Italian prelate; bishop of Sant'Agata dei Goti (1762–75); founder (1732) of Congregation of the Most Holy Redeemer, commonly known as Redemptorist Order. Canonized (1839).

**Liholiho.** See KAMEHAMEHA II and IV.

**Li Hung-chang** (lē′ ho͝ong′jäng′). 1823–1901. Chinese statesman, called "the Bismarck of Asia." Associated with Gen. Gordon in suppression of Taiping rebellion (1861–64); governor of Kiangsu (1862); viceroy of Nanking (1865) and of Canton (1867); viceroy of Chihli (1870); China's representative with foreign powers (1870–94); founded Chinese navy; negotiated peace with French (1884–85) over Tonkin difficulties; in supreme command of Chinese forces in Korea at time of outbreak of Chinese-Japanese War (1894); badly defeated through no fault of his own, stripped of honors; negotiated treaty of peace with Japan (1895); prime minister (1895–98); visited Europe and United States (1896); governor of Chihli (1900) and commissioner to restore peace after Boxer uprising (1900).

**Lij Yasu.** 1896–1935. Nephew of Menelik II. Emperor of Ethiopia (1911–16). Named heir to throne by uncle (1909); proclaimed emperor (1911); converted to Islam (1916); deposed by Zauditu (1916); exiled but taken prisoner (1921).

**Li Kung-lin.** = LI LUNG-MIEN.

**Lil′burne** (lĭl′bĕrn), **John.** 1614?–1657. English leader of the Levelers. Sentenced by Star Chamber to whipping, pillory, and imprisonment for share in importing and circulating Puritan publications of John Bastwick and Prynne (1637). Fought in Parliamentary army; resigned as lieutenant colonel because of dissatisfaction with Presbyterian dominance and refusal to take the Covenant (1645); expressed distrust of army leaders. Attacked Cromwell's Commonwealth as too aristocratic; advocated release of trade from restrictions of chartered companies and monopolists (1650); repeatedly imprisoned, tried for sedition but acquitted; exiled for joining his uncle George Lilburne in charges against Sir Arthur Hesilrige (1652–53); on return confined in Jersey, Guernsey, Dover Castle (till 1655); joined Quakers. His brother **Robert** (1613–1665), an officer in Parliamentary army, signed Charles I's death warrant (1649).

**Li′li·en·cron′** (lē′lē·ĕn·krōn′), Baron **Detlev von.** 1844–1909. German writer; served in Prussian army in Austro-Prussian War (1866) and Franco-Prussian War (1870–71); in German government service (to 1887). Among his volumes of verse are *Adjutantenritte* (1883), *Poggfred* (1896 ff.), *Nebel und Sonne* (1900), *Bunte Beute* (1903); among his novels, *Breide Hummelsbüttel* (1886),

*Der Mäcen* (1890); among his dramas, *Der Trifels und Palermo* (1886), *Pokahuntas* (1905).

**Liliencron,** Baron **Rochus von.** 1820–1912. German scholar; chief works are in the field of musical research.

**Lil′ien·thal** (lĭl′yĕn·thôl), **David Eli.** 1899– . American administrator and lawyer, b. Morton, Ill. Chairman, Tenn. Valley Authority (1941–46), Atomic Energy Comm. (1946–50); wrote *TVA: Democracy on the March* (1944), an autobiography, etc.

**Li′li·en·thal′** (lē′lē·ĕn·täl′), **Otto.** 1848–1896. German aeronautical engineer; studied flight of birds and built gliders in which he demonstrated advantages of curved surfaces over flat ones for wings.

**Li·li′u·o·ka·la′ni** (lē·lē′ōō·ō·kä·lä′nē), **Lyd′i·a** (lĭd′ĭ·ȧ) **Ka′me·ke′ha** (kä′mā·kā′hä). 1838–1917. Queen of the Hawaiian Islands, sister of King Kalakaua; m. John O. Dominis (d. 1891). Succeeded her brother on the throne (1891); deposed (Jan. 30, 1893). See J. H. Blount.

**Lil′je·fors** (lĭl′yĕ·fôrs; -fôsh), **Bruno Anders.** 1860–1939. Swedish animal painter.

**Lille, Gautier de.** See Gautier de Lille.

**Lil′lie** (lĭl′ĭ), **Beatrice,** Lady **Peel.** 1898– . Actress and comedienne; b. Toronto, Can.; m. Sir Robert Peel (1920). Debut in London (1914), New York (1924).

**Lillie, Frank Rattray.** 1870–1947. Zoologist, b. Toronto, Can. Professor, Chicago (from 1907). Director, Marine Biological Laboratory, Woods Hole, Mass. (1908–26); president (1925–42).

**Lil′lo** (lĭl′ō), **George.** 1693?–1739. English dramatist, b. London, of mixed Dutch and English parentage. Author of *Silvia, or the Country Burial* (ballad opera; 1730), *The Merchant*, renamed *The London Merchant, or the History of George Barnwell* (domestic tragedy produced by Theophilus Cibber; 1731), *The Christian Hero* (1735), *Fatal Curiosity* (1736). One of first to introduce middle-class characters on English stage.

**Lil′ly** (lĭl′ĭ), **William.** 1602–1681. English astrologer. Published his first almanac *Merlinus Anglicus Junior* (1644) and issued annual pamphlets of prophecy; viewed seriously by members of Long Parliament; author of *Christian Astrology* (1647); ridiculed in character of Sidrophel in Butler's *Hudibras*.

**Li Lung-mien** (lē′ lŏŏng′mē·ĕn′) *or* **Li Kung-lin** (lē′ gŏŏng′lĭn′). c. 1040–1106. Chinese painter, of the early Sung period, held to be one of the greatest of a purely Chinese culture; painted horses, and later chiefly Buddhist subjects; rarely used color, esp. skillful in contrasts of light and shade and in delicate lines.

**Lil′y** *or* **Lil′ye** (lĭl′ĭ), **William.** 1468?–1522. English grammarian; settled in London as private teacher of grammar, said to be first in city to teach Greek; first high master of St. Paul's school (1512–22); known for share in authorship of the old Eton Latin grammar *Brevissima Institutio*, a revision of Colet's *Aeditio*.

**Li′ma e Sil′va** (lē′mȧ ē sĭl′vȧ), **Francisco de.** 1785–1853. Brazilian general and statesman; member of the regency after abdication of Pedro I (1831); ruler of Brazil (1831–35). For his son **Luiz Alves**, see Duque de Caxias.

**Li′man von San′ders** (lē′män fôn zän′dĕrs), **Otto.** 1855–1929. German general; on mission of instruction to the Turkish army (1913); given command of 1st Turkish army at outbreak of World War I; commanded Turkish armies in Dardanelles (1915), Asia Minor and Syria (1918); defeated in Palestine (1918).

**Lim′borch** (lĭm′bŏrĸ), **Philip van.** 1633–1712. Dutch Arminian theologian; pastor and professor in Seminary of the Remonstrants, Amsterdam (from 1657). Chief work, *Theologia Christiana ad Praxim Pietatis ac Promotionem Pacis Christianae Unice Directa* (1686).

**Lim′burg** (lĭm′bûrĸ), **Pol** and his brothers **Hermann** and **Jan.** Early 15th-century Belgian miniature painters.

**Limerick,** Earl of. See Thomas Dongan.

**Lim·nan′der de Nieu′wen·ho′ve** (lĭm·năn′dĕr dĕ nē′-vĕn·hō′vĕ), Baron **Ar′mand′ Ma′rie′ Guis′lain′** (år′mäɴ′ må′rē′ gēs′lăɴ′). 1814–1892. Belgian composer of comic operas, a symphony, sonata, cantatas, *Requiem Mass, Stabat Mater*, and choral works.

**Li·món′** (lē·môn′), **José Arcadio. 1908–1972.** American dancer and choreographer, b. Mexico. Works include *The Moor's Pavane* (1949), *The Traitor* (1954), etc.

**Li′mo′sin′** (lē′mō′zăɴ′). Family of French enamelers, of Limoges, of whom the most famous was **Léonard Limosin** (1505?–?1577), appointed by King Francis I to be head of the royal manufactory at Limoges.

**Li′mou′sin′** (lē′mōō′zăɴ′). = Limosin.

**Lin′a·cre** (lĭn′ȧ·kĕr), **Thomas.** 1460?–1524. English humanist and physician; one of first propagators of the New Learning in England. Lectured on medical subjects at Oxford; formed circle of scholars with John Colet and William Grocyn; had Erasmus and Sir Thomas More as students; tutor to Prince Arthur and physician to Henry VIII; chiefly instrumental in founding College of Physicians (1518); composed Latin grammar *Rudimenta Grammatices* for Princess Mary (1523).

**Li·na′res** (lē·nä′rās), **José María.** 1810–1861. President of Bolivia (1857–61), assuming dictatorial powers; ousted by revolution.

**Linck′e** (lĭng′kĕ), **Paul.** 1866–1946. German composer; among his operatic works are *Lysistrata, Venus auf Erden;* composer of the motion-picture operetta *Der Glückswalzer.*

**Lin′coln** (lĭng′kŭn), Earl of. English title held (1232–1311) by members of Lacy family, including Henry de Lacy (see Lacy), 3d earl; merged with crown on accession of Henry IV (1399); held (1467–87) by John de la Pole (see de la Pole family) and (since 1572) by members of Clinton family, being (since 1768) courtesy title of eldest son of duke of Newcastle.

**Lincoln, Abraham.** 1809–1865. 16th president of the United States, b. in a log cabin in Hardin (now Larue) County, Ky.; son of **Thomas Lincoln** (1778–1851), an illiterate wandering laborer, and **Nancy,** *nee* **Hanks** [hăngks] (d. 1818). Moved to Indiana (1816), to Macon County, Ill. (1830). Had little formal schooling. Settled in New Salem, Ill., clerking in store, managing a mill, splitting rails, and studying law in leisure hours (1831–37); courtship of Ann Rutledge terminated by her death (1835). Elected to Illinois legislature (1834–41). Moved to Springfield (1837); practiced law in partnership with J. T. Stuart (1837–41) and with Stephen T. Logan and William H. Herndon (from 1844); m. Mary Todd, Nov. 4, 1842. Member, U.S. House of Representatives (1847–49). Rose to be prominent Illinois circuit-riding lawyer (from 1849). Entered political life again (1854); became identified with newly formed Republican party (1856); received 110 votes for vice-presidential nomination on Frémont ticket (1856). Nominated for U.S. Senate (1858) after speech before convention in which he said: "A house divided against itself cannot stand; I believe this government cannot endure permanently, half slave and half free." During campaign for senatorship, stumped Illinois in series of debates with his Democratic opponent, Stephen A. Douglas; took stand against slavery; though defeated for senatorship, campaign made him leading candidate for next Republican presidential nomination. Nominated at Chicago (1860); carried election, electoral vote being Lincoln 180, Breckinridge 72, John Bell 39, Douglas 12; inaugurated Mar. 4, 1861. Slave states began seceding; Gen. Beauregard fired upon Fort Sumter in harbor of Charleston, S.C., forcing surrender (Apr. 13, 1861); Lincoln issued call for 75,000 volunteers (Apr. 15, 1861); proclaimed blockade of southern ports (Apr. 19, 1861). During Civil War, Lincoln supported loyally his generals in the field, choosing successively to command the army of the Potomac McClellan, Burnside, Hooker, Meade, and Grant. Issued Emancipation Proclamation (Jan. 1, 1863; preliminary proclamation Sept. 22, 1862), declaring freedom of the slaves of all states in rebellion. After Lee's army was decisively defeated at Gettysburg (July 1–3, 1863), Lincoln made his immortal Gettysburg address dedicating the national cemetery there (Nov. 19, 1863). Renominated and re-elected (1864); electoral vote, Lincoln 212, McClellan 21. Five days after Lee's surrender at Appomattox Court House had ended Civil War, Lincoln was shot in Ford's Theater, Washington, D.C., by John Wilkes Booth, a little-known actor, and died next day (Apr. 15, 1865). Elected to American Hall of Fame (1900). See also Mary Todd LINCOLN, Robert Todd LINCOLN.

**Lincoln, Benjamin.** 1733–1810. American Revolutionary officer, b. Hingham, Mass. Major general in Continental army (Feb. 19, 1777), in command of militia in Vermont; in command of American army in southern department (Sept. 25, 1778). Captured with his army in Charleston, S.C. (May, 1779). Exchanged; served in Yorktown campaign (1781); elected secretary of war by Congress (1781–83). Commanded force that suppressed Shays' Rebellion (1787). Lieutenant governor of Massachusetts (1788).

**Lincoln, Joseph Crosby.** 1870–1944. American novelist, b. Brewster, Mass.; known especially for his Cape Cod stories. Author of *Cape Cod Ballads* (1902), *Cap'n Eri* (1904), *Mr. Pratt* (1906), *Mr. Pratt's Patients* (1913), *Shavings* (1918), *The Portygee* (1919), *Galusha the Magnificent* (1921), *Rugged Water* (1924), *Queer Judson* (1925), *The Big Mogul* (1926), *Storm Signals* (1935), etc.

**Lincoln, Levi.** 1749–1820. American lawyer, b. Hingham, Mass. Attorney general of the U.S. (1801–04). Lieutenant governor of Massachusetts (1807, 1808); acting governor (1808). His son **Levi** (1782–1868) was lieutenant governor of Massachusetts (1823); governor (1825–34); member, U.S. House of Representatives (1834–41). Another son, **Enoch** (1788–1829), was a lawyer and politician; member, U.S. House of Representatives (1818–26); governor of Maine (1826, 1827, 1828).

**Lincoln, Mary Johnson,** *nee* **Bai'ley** (bā'lĭ). 1844–1921. American educator and author, b. South Attleboro, Mass.; m. David A. Lincoln (1865). Director, Boston Cooking School (1879–85). Author of *Mrs. Lincoln's Boston Cook Book* (1884), *Peerless Cookbook* (1885), etc.

**Lincoln, Mary,** *nee* **Todd** (tŏd). 1818–1882. Wife of Abraham Lincoln (m. Nov. 4, 1842). Resided Springfield, Ill. (1842–61); in the White House (1861–65). Adjudged insane (1875); later declared competent to handle her affairs. Pensioned by Congress (from 1870).

**Lincoln, Natalie Sumner.** 1872–1935. American editor and writer, b. Washington, D.C. Author esp. of detective fiction, including *The Trevor Case* (1912), *The Red Seal* (1920).

**Lincoln, Robert Todd.** 1843–1926. Son of Abraham Lincoln. American lawyer, b. Springfield, Ill. Served on Grant's staff last few months of Civil War. U.S. secretary of war (1881–85); U.S. minister to Great Britain (1889–93). President, the Pullman Co. (1897–1911).

**Lind** (lĭnd), **James.** 1716–1794. Scottish physician; experimented with remedies for scurvy, and was instrumental in issue of British admiralty order to supply navy with lemon juice (1795); improved naval hygiene.

**Lind** (lĭnd), **Jen'ny** (jĕn'ĭ), *really* **Johanna Maria.** *Known latterly as* Madame **Jenny Lind–Gold'schmidt** (-gôlt'-shmĭt; *Angl.* -gōld'-). 1820–1887. Swedish soprano singer, unrivaled master of coloratura; called "the Swedish Nightingale." Appeared first at theater in *Der Freischütz* (1838); court singer (1840). Studied in Paris under García (1841); toured German cities; gained popularity in London (1847–48); retired from operatic stage (1849) and devoted herself to concert singing and oratorio. Engaged in America by P. T. Barnum (1850–52); m. (1852) Otto Goldschmidt (*q.v.*); spent last years in England; became naturalized British subject (1859).

**Lind, Samuel Colville.** 1879–1965. American chemist, b. McMinnville, Tenn. Director, school of chemistry (1926–35), and dean, institute of technology (from 1935), U. of Minnesota. Inventor of electroscope for radium measurements; originator of ionization theory of chemical effects of radium rays.

**Lin'dau** (lĭn'dou), **Rudolf.** 1829–1910. German diplomat and writer; to France, and became associate editor of *Revue des Deux Mondes* and *Journal des Débats*. Lived (1859–69) in eastern Asia and California; returned to Germany (1869) and was war correspondent during Franco-Prussian War (1870–71); on German embassy staff in Paris (1872–78). Author of travel books, short stories, and historical sketches. His brother **Paul** (1839–1919) was a playwright, novelist, and essayist; founded *Das Neue Blatt* in Leipzig (1869), *Die Gegenwart* in Berlin (1872), and *Nord und Sud* in Berlin (1878), which he edited (1878–1904).

**Lind'bergh** (lĭn(d)'bûrg), **Charles Augustus.** 1902–1974. American aviator and aviation consultant, b. Detroit, Mich. Air-mail pilot, Chicago to St. Louis (1926). Made first solo nonstop transatlantic flight, from Roosevelt Field, New York, to Le Bourget Air Field, Paris (May 20–21, 1927) in his monoplane *The Spirit of St. Louis*. Toured U.S. cities under auspices of Daniel Guggenheim Foundation for the Promotion of Aeronautics. Worked with Dr. Alexis Carrel (*q.v.*) on physiological experiments. Awarded Congressional Medal of Honor. Appointed brigadier general in U.S. Air Force Reserve (1954). Author of *We* (1936), *The Spirit of St. Louis* (autobiography, 1953; received 1954 Pulitzer prize for biography), *Wartime Journals* (1970). His father, **Charles Augustus Lindbergh** (1859–1924), b. Stockholm, Sweden, to U.S. (1859), grad. Michigan Law School (1883), was a member, U.S. House of Representatives from Minnesota (1907–17). His wife, **Anne Spencer,** *nee* **Mor'row** [mŏr'ō] (1906– ), dau. of Dwight Whitney Morrow (*q.v.*), grad. Smith College (1927), accompanied him as copilot and radio operator in flight of 40,000 miles over five continents; author of *North to the Orient* (1935), *Listen, the Wind* (1938), *The Wave of the Future* (1940), *The Steep Ascent* (1944), *Gift from the Sea* (1955), *The Unicorn and Other Poems* (1956), *Bring Me a Unicorn: Diaries and Letters* (1972), etc.

**Lind'blad** (lĭnd'bläd), **Adolf Fredrik.** 1801–1878. Swedish composer, esp. of songs which, as sung by Jenny Lind (*q.v.*), became widely known.

**Lin'de** (lĭn'dĕ), **Otto zur.** 1873–1938. German writer; with Pannwitz, founded (1904) the poetry society Charon, and edited its monthly magazine *Charon*. Author of *Gedichte, Märchen, Skizzen* (1901), *Die Kugel, eine Philosophie in Versen* (1909), etc.

**Lin'de** (lĕn'dĕ), **Samuel Bogumił.** 1771–1847. Polish lexicographer; compiler of a dictionary of Polish (6 vols., 1807–14).

**Lin'de·man** (lĭn'dĕ·män), **Ludvig Mathias.** 1812–1887. Norwegian organist and music scholar.

**Lin'de·mann** (lĭn'dĕ·män), **Ferdinand.** 1852–1939. German mathematician. Professor, Königsberg (1883) and Munich (1893–1923). Proved that the ratio $\pi$ is a transcendental number (1882), and hence that it is impossible to "square the circle" by ruler-and-compass construction; originated a method of solving equations of any degree by means of transcendental functions (1892).

**Lin'de·mann** (lĭn'dĕ·măn), **Frederick Alexander.** 1886–1957. 1st Viscount **Cher'well** (chär'wĕl). English physicist; served in World War (1914–18). Director of physical laboratory of Royal Air Force, Farnborough. Author of *The Physical Significance of the Quantum Theory* (1932).

**Lin'den'** (lăN'däN'), **Jean Jules.** 1817–1898. Belgian botanist and horticulturist.

**Lin'de·nau** (lĭn'dĕ·nou), Baron **Bernhard August von.** 1779–1854. German astronomer and politician; works include *Tabulae Veneris* (1810), *Tabulae Martis* (1811).

**Lin'den·schmit** (lĭn'dĕn·shmĭt), **Wilhelm.** 1806–1848. German historical painter and muralist. His brother **Ludwig** (1809–1893) was an archaeologist. Wilhelm's son **Wilhelm von Lindenschmit** (1829–1895) was also a historical painter and muralist.

**Lin'den·thal** (lĭn'dĕn·thôl), **Gustav.** 1850–1935. American civil engineer, b. Brünn, Austria; to America (1874). Consulting engineer in bridge and railway construction, Pittsburgh (1877–90); commissioner of bridges, New York City (1902–03); consulting engineer for Pennsylvania R.R. tunnels under Hudson and East rivers, New York; consulting engineer and designer, Hellgate steel-arch bridge over East River, New York.

**Lin'det'** (lăN'dĕ'), **Jean Baptiste Robert.** 1746–1825. French lawyer; member of Legislative Assembly and National Convention; prepared "report on the crimes imputed to Louis Capet," which was basis for act of accusation against Louis XVI; minister of finance (1799).

**Lind'ley** (lĭn(d)'lĭ), **John.** 1799–1865. English botanist and horticulturist. While writing descriptive portions of Loudon's *Encyclopaedia of Plants*, developed preference for classification system of A. L. de Jussieu over that of Linnaeus and later published *A Synopsis of British Flora, arranged according to the Natural Order* (1829) and *An Introduction to the Natural System of Botany* (1830); author of *The Vegetable Kingdom* (1846). His son **Nathaniel** (1828–1921), Baron Lindley, jurist, was lord justice of appeal (1881–97); master of the rolls (1897); lord of appeal in ordinary (1900–05); author of *Introduction to the Study of Jurisprudence* (1855), etc.

**Lind'man** (lĭnd'măn), **Salomon Arvid Achates.** 1862–1936. Swedish admiral and statesman; served in navy (1882–91); member of the Diet (1905); minister of the navy (1905) and prime minister of Sweden (1906–11); minister of foreign affairs (1917) and again prime minister (1928–30).

**Lind'ner** (lĭnd'nẽr), **Theodor.** 1843–1919. German historian; chief work, *Weltgeschichte seit der Völkerwanderung* (9 vols., 1901–16), which he introduced with a philosophy of history.

**Lin'do** (lĭn'dō), **Mark Prager.** *Pseudonym* **De Ou'de Heer Smits** (dĕ ou'dĕ hār' smĭts'), *i.e.* Old Mr. Smits. 1819–1879. Dutch writer, b. London, Eng.; settled in the Netherlands; translator of novels of Scott, Fielding, Thackeray, Dickens, and others. Under pseudonym wrote humorous sketches, later collected and published (1877–79) as *Kompleete Werken van den Ouden Heer Smits.* His serious works include *The Rise and Development of the British People* (2 vols., 1868–74).

**Lind'paint'ner** (lĭnt'pīnt'nẽr), **Peter Joseph von.** 1791–1856. German conductor and composer of operas, ballets, oratorios, cantatas, masses, symphonies, chamber music, and songs.

**Lind'say** (lĭn'zĭ). Name of Scottish family including the earls of **Craw'ford** (krô'fẽrd) and earls of **Bal·car'res** (băl·kăr'ĭs; -ĭz). Among its more important members are the following: Sir **David** (1365?–1407), 1st Earl of Crawford, 10th Baron Crawford; famed for his tournament with Lord Welles at London Bridge (1390), as narrated in Wyntoun's chronicle; having Lord Welles at his mercy, helped him to rise and presented him to queen. **David** (1440?–1495), 5th Earl of Crawford, 1st Duke of **Mont·rose'** (mŏnt·rōz'; mŏn·trōz'); son of 4th earl; lord high admiral (1476); lord chamberlain (1483); ambassador to England. **Alexander** (d. 1607), 1st Baron **Spy'nie** (?spī'nĭ); son of 10th earl of Crawford and brother of 11th earl; vice-chamberlain to James VI; accused of harboring earl of Bothwell (1592); slain while trying to placate quarreling kinsmen, as narrated in an old ballad. **Patrick** (d. 1589), 6th Baron Lindsay of the Byres (bīrz); supported plot for murder of Rizzio (1566); was guardian of Mary, Queen of Scots (1567); aided in defeat of her adherents at Langside (1568); one of first of Scottish nobles to support cause of Reformers. **Alexander** (1618–1659), 1st Earl of Balcarres; Scottish leader of moderate party of Covenanters; a commissioner of the exchequer (1650); hereditary governor of Edinburgh castle (1651). His 2d son, **Colin** (1654?–1722), 3d earl, distinguished himself at Southwold Bay (1672); privy councilor (1680, 1705); joined Prince Charles Edward (1715); published memoirs of 1688–90. Colin's grandson **Alexander** (1752–1825), 6th earl; soldier; forced to surrender at Ticonderoga (1777); governor of Jamaica (1794–1801); general (1803); representative Scottish peer (1784–1825). House of Lords adjudged (1848) earldom of Crawford (which had been dormant since 1808) to 6th earl's son **James**, 7th Earl of Balcarres. James's son **Alexander William Crawford** (1812–1880), 25th Earl of Crawford and 8th Earl of Balcarres; M.A., Cantab. (1833); bibliophile; author of *Lives of the Lindsays* (3 vols., 1849). His son **James Ludovic** (1847–1913), 26th Earl of Crawford and 9th Earl of Balcarres; astronomer and Orientalist. The latter's son **David Alexander Edward** (1871–1940), 27th Earl of Crawford and 10th Earl of Balcarres; lord privy seal in Lloyd George's coalition cabinet (1916–18); author of *Evolution of Italian Sculpture* (1910).

**Lindsay,** Lady **Anne.** See BARNARD.

**Lind'say** *or* **Lynd'say** (lĭn'zĭ), Sir **David.** *Known also as* **Lindsay of the Mount.** 1490–1555. Scottish poet. Satirized vices of clergy and abuses in state; influential in turning common people toward the Reformation. Author of *The Dreme* (1528), *The Monarchy* (1554), the *Satyre of the Thrie Estaitis* (1540).

**Lindsay, David.** 1856–1922. Australian explorer. Traversed Australia from north to south (1888); on 550-mile journey across Victoria Desert, discovered auriferous area which led to discovery of gold fields of West Australia; explored Northern Territory (1916–20).

**Lind'say, Howard.** 1889–1968. American playwright, producer, and actor, b. Waterford, N.Y.; co-author with Bertrand Robinson of *Tommy* (1927), *Your Uncle Dudley* (1929), *Oh Promise Me* (1930), with Russel Crouse (*q.v.*) of musical comedies *Anything Goes* (1934), *Red, Hot, and Blue* (1936), *Hooray for What?* (1937), *Strip for Action* (1942), and a dramatization of Clarence Day's *Life with Father*; also *State of the Union* (1946).

**Lindsay, Norman Alfred William.** 1879–1969. Australian cartoonist, black-and-white artist, and novelist. Artist on staff of Sydney *Bulletin* (from 1901); illustrator of many classics, including works by Theocritus, Boccaccio, Petronius, and modern works. Author of *A Curate in Bohemia* (1913), *The Magic Pudding* (1919),

*Pam in the Parlour* (1934), *Age of Consent* (1938), etc. His son **Philip** (1906–1958), journalist, author of works on history as *Morgan in Jamaica* (1930), *King Richard III* (1933), *King Henry V* (1934), *Kings of Merry England* (1936), *Mirror for Ruffians* (1938), historical novels as *Panama is Burning* (1932), *London Bridge is Falling* (1934), *Gentleman Harry Retires* (1937), *Bride for a Buccaneer* (1938), and scenarios.

**Lindsay, Robert James.** See Baron WANTAGE.

**Lindsay,** Sir **Ronald Charles.** 1877–1945. British diplomat; minister at Paris (1920–21); undersecretary at British Foreign Office (1921–24); ambassador to Germany (1926–28), and United States (1930–39).

**Lindsay, Samuel McCune.** 1869–1959. American educator, b. Pittsburgh, Pa. Commissioner of education, Puerto Rico (1902–04). Professor of social legislation, Columbia (from 1907). Author of *Railway Labor in the United States* (1902), *Financial Administration of Great Britain* (with W. W. and W. F. Willoughby, 1917), etc.

**Lindsay, Va'chel** (vā'chĕl), *in full* **Nicholas Vachel.** 1879–1931. American poet, b. Springfield, Ill. Educ. Hiram College (1897–1900). Studied painting, Chicago Art Institute (1900–03) and New York School of Art (1904–05). Tramped like a troubadour through the south (1906), exchanging his poem *The Tree of Laughing Bells* for bed and board, and through the west (1912). First volume of poems, *General William Booth Enters into Heaven and Other Poems* (1913), was followed by the successful *The Congo and Other Poems* (1914). Lectured and chanted his own verses through U.S. and by invitation (1920) at Oxford U., Eng. Later volumes, *The Chinese Nightingale* (1917), *The Golden Whales of California* (1920), *Going-to-the Sun* (1923), etc.

**Lindsay, Wallace Martin.** 1858–1937. Scottish classical scholar; editor of many Latin texts; author of *The Latin Language* (1894), *Syntax of Plautus* (1907), *Julian of Toledo* (1922), etc.

**Lindsay, William Bethune.** 1880–1933. Canadian soldier; organized 1st Canadian Divisional Engineers (Aug., 1914). Brigadier general and chief engineer, Canadian Army Corps (1916–18); major general, commanding Canadian Engineers (1918); retired (1920).

**Lind'sell** (?lĭn's'l), Sir **Wilfrid Gordon.** 1884– . British army officer (from 1903); served in World War; major general (1938); quartermaster general of B.E.F. (1939–40); lieutenant general (1941); in charge of service of supply, Middle East theater.

**Lind'sey** (lĭn'zĭ), **Benjamin Barr,** *known as* **Ben.** 1869–1943. American jurist, b. Jackson, Tenn. Judge, juvenile court, Denver, Colo. (1900–27). Authority on juvenile court laws and juvenile delinquency. Judge, Superior Court of California (from 1934). Author of *Problems of the Children* (1903), *The Beast* (with Harvey O'Higgins; 1910), *The Revolt of Modern Youth* (in collab. with Wainwright Evans; 1925), *The Companionate Marriage* (with Wainwright Evans; 1927).

**Li·ne'vich** (lyĭ·nyā'vyĭch), **Nikolai Petrovich.** 1838–1908. Russian general; commanded Russian campaign in China (1900) and the Manchurian army (to 1904); commanded Russian left wing in battle of Mukden; succeeded Kuropatkin (Mar., 1905) as commander in chief of Russian forces in Far East.

**Ling** (lĭng), **Pehr Henrik.** 1776–1839. Swedish gymnastic teacher; founded (1813) and headed (1813–39) Gymnastic Central Inst., Stockholm; also known as a poet and playwright.

**Lin'gard** (lĭng'gärd), **John.** 1771–1851. English historian. Author of *The Antiquities of the Anglo-Saxon Church* (1806), a prelude to the labor of his life, a *History of England to 1688* (8 vols., 1819–30), which he defended against attacks in *Edinburgh Review* with erudition and candor.

**Ling'el·bach** (lĭng'ĕl·bäк), **Jan.** 1622–1674. Dutch painter; known esp. for genre scenes and landscapes.

**Lingg** (lĭngk), **Hermann von.** 1820–1905. German physician and writer of verse, as in *Vaterländische Balladen und Gesange* (1869), plays, and fiction.

**Lin'guet'** (lăɴ'gĕ'), **Simon Nicolas Henri.** 1736–1794. French lawyer and journalist; editor of *Annales Politiques* (1777–92); confined in the Bastille (1780–82) and published *Mémoires sur la Bastille* (1783); fled to Brussels to escape the Revolution, but returned to France too soon (1791); guillotined (1794).

**Li'niers'** (*Fr.* lē'nyā'; *Span.* lē·nyĕrs'), **Santiago Antonio María de.** 1756–1810. French-born royalist officer in the Spanish naval service. Seized Buenos Aires from British (1806); installed by act of the people as viceroy; dismissed by Spanish Central Junta (1809); joined revolutionary movement attempting to re-establish royal authority (May, 1810); captured and shot near Buenos Aires (Aug. 26, 1810).

**Link** (lĭngk), **Heinrich Friedrich.** 1767–1850. German botanist; studied esp. plant anatomy and physiology.

**Link'la'ter** (lĭngk'lā'tẽr), **Eric.** 1899–1974. British writer, b. in Orkney Islands; commonwealth fellow in U.S. (1928–30). Author of *White-maa's Saga* (1929), *Poet's Pub* (1929), *Juan in America* (1931), *Ben Jonson and King James* (1931), *The Men of Ness* (1932), *Mary Queen of Scots* (1933), *Robert the Bruce* (1934), *The Devil's in the News* (1934), *The Lion and the Unicorn* (1935), *God Likes Them Plain* (1935), *Juan in China* (1937), *The Impregnable Women* (1938), *The Wind on the Moon* (1944), *Private Angelo* (1946), etc.

**Lin'ley** (lĭn'lĭ), **George.** 1798–1865. English verse writer and composer of fashionable and popular ballads; author of farces and satirical poems, an operetta *The Toymakers* (1861), and a comedietta *Law Versus Love* (1862).

**Linley, Thomas.** 1732–1795. English musical composer; with his son **Thomas** (1756–1778), violinist and composer, composed or compiled music for his son-in-law R. B. Sheridan's comic opera *The Duenna* (1775); musical director at Drury Lane and composer of songs and operas (1776–81). Of the elder Thomas's daughters, **Elizabeth Ann** (1754–1792), prima donna of concerts given by her father, married (1773) Richard Brinsley Sheridan (*q.v.*), **Mary** (1756?–1787), singer, married Richard Tickell, pamphleteer and dramatist, grandson of Thomas Tickell (*q.v.*), and **Maria** (d. 1784) was a concert and oratorio singer.

**Linlithgow,** Marquises of. See John Adrian Louis HOPE.

**Lin·nae'us** (lĭ·nē'ŭs), **Carolus.** *Latinized form of Swed.* **Carl von Lin·né'** (fôn lĭn·nā'). 1707–1778. Swedish botanist, a father of modern systematic botany; b. Råshult, in Småland, Sweden, son of Lutheran pastor. Educ. Lund (1727) and Uppsala, where he became assistant to Dr. Olaf Celsius in compilation of *Hierobotanicon*, treatise on plants of the Bible; wrote essay on sex in plants; assistant to professor of botany, Uppsala (1730). Explored Lapland for Acad. of Sciences (1732), publishing scientific results in *Flora Lapponica* (1737); traveled through Dalecarlia, Sweden; took M.D. at Harderwijk, Holland (1735). Published *Systema Naturae* (1737); wrote *Hortus Cliffortianus* as result of study of plants in garden near Haarlem of his patron George Clifford, a Dutch merchant; while still in Holland, wrote also *Fundamenta Botanica* (1736), *Bibliotheca Botanica* (1736), *Critica Botanica* (1737), *Genera Plantarum* (1737), and *Classes Plantarum* (1738). Traveled to England and France; returned to Sweden and established himself as physican at Stockholm (1738); professor of medicine (1741) and botany (from 1742), Uppsala. Toured Öland and Gotland (1742), publishing results of trip in *Olandska och Gothländska Resa* (1745), in which botanical specific names were first used. Other important publications include *Flora Suecica* and *Fauna Suecica* (1745), *Hortus Upsaliensis* (1748), *Philosophia Botanica* (1750), and *Species Plantarum*, which gives a full account of specific names and is considered foundation for modern system of botanical nomenclature. Issued patent of nobility by Gustavus III of Sweden (1761).

**Lin'nan·kos'ki** (lĭn'nȧn·kŏs'kĭ), **Johannes.** *Real name* **Vihtori Pel'to·nen** (pĕl'tŏ·nĕn). 1869–1913. Finnish writer; among his plays are *Eternal Strife* (1903), *Samson and Delilah* (1911), *Jepthah's Daughter* (1911); among his verse, *The Fugitive* (1908), *The Fiery Red Blossom* (1921).

**Lin·nell'** (?lĭ·nĕl'), **John.** 1792–1882. English portrait and landscape painter; intimate friend of William Blake.

**Lin Piao** (lĭn bê·ä'ô). 1908–?1971. Chinese soldier and Communist leader; served under Chiang Kai-shek (c. 1924–27); joined the Red army (1927); noted as a tactician; a leader of the Long March (1934–35); commanded Communist forces against Japan and against Chiang in post-world war II civil war; Defense Minister, Communist government (1959).

**Lin'scho'ten** (lĭn'skō'tĕn), **Jan Huyghen van.** 1563–1611. Dutch traveler. In Goa, gathered information on Indonesia (1583–89); promoted Dutch attempts to find northeast passage to East Indies; took part in Barents's second voyage into Kara Sea (1594–95); author of *Itinerario, Voyage ofte Schipvaert naer Oost ofte Portugaels Indien* (1596).

**Lin Sên** (lĭn' sĕn') *or* **Lin Shen** (lĭn' shĕn'). 1867?–1943. Chinese politician; lived in California many years; joined Sun Yat-sen's revolutionary movement (1911); member, Kuomintang Central Executive Committee (1924); president, National Government (1932–43).

**Lin'sing·en** (lĭn'zĭng·ĕn), **Alexander von.** 1850–1935. German general in World War I; commanded (1915) southeastern group of armies and checked Russian advances; led forces into Ukraine (1918); chief in command in province of Brandenburg (1918), where his troops joined the revolution (Nov. 9, 1918).

**Lin'thi·cum** (lĭn'thĭ·kŭm), **John Charles.** 1867–1932. American lawyer and legislator, b. in Anne Arundel County, Md. Member, U.S. House of Representatives (1911–31); secured legal recognition of *The Star-Spangled Banner* as the national anthem.

**Lin'ton** (lĭn't'n; -tŭn), **William.** 1791–1876. English classic landscape painter.

**Linton, William James.** 1812–1897. Wood engraver, reformer, and miscellaneous writer, b. London, Eng.; to U.S. (1866). Active in Chartist agitation (1841–42); wrote *Life of Paine* (1839), *To the Future* (1848), *The Plaint of Freedom* (1852), *Claribel and Other Poems* (1865). In U.S., taught wood engraving at Cooper Union, New York (1868–70); made engravings for *Frank Leslie's Illustrated News*, Whittier's *Snow-Bound*, Longfellow's *Building of the Ship*, Bryant's *Thanatopsis* and *The Flood of Years*. His wife (m. 1858) **Eliza,** *nee* **Lynn** [lĭn] (1822–98), novelist, set up as woman of letters in London (1845); newspaper correspondent in Paris (1851–54); published, with her husband, *Lake Country* (1864); later gained success as novelist with *Joshua Davidson* (1872), *Autobiography of Christopher Kirkland* (1885) and with *Girl of the Period* articles in *Saturday Review*.

**Lin'tot** (lĭn'tŏt), **Barnaby Bernard.** 1675–1736. English publisher of Pope's translations of *Iliad* and *Odyssey* and other works of Pope, as well as of poems and plays for Gay, Farquhar, Vanbrugh, Steele, Rowe.

**Lin Tsê–hsü** (lĭn' dzĕ'shü'). 1785–1850. Known as "Commissioner Lin." Chinese official; as governor general of Hunan and Hupeh, suppressed opium traffic (1837); sent by Emperor Tao Kuang to handle opium situation at Canton (1838); ordered (1839) destruction of $6,000,000 worth of opium owned by foreign merchants, which led to Opium War (1839–42); opposed to opening China to foreigners; recalled by emperor (1841) because of difficulties due to his policies; banished to Kulja (1843); recalled (1845) and served as governor of different provinces (1846–50).

**Li'nus** (lī'nŭs), Saint. Pope (bishop of Rome; 67?–?79). Generally considered as the successor to St. Peter.

**Lin Yutang** (lĭn' yü'täng'). *Orig.* **Lin Yu–t'ang.** 1895–1976. Chinese author and philologist, b. at Changchow, Amoy. Educ. at St. John's U., Shanghai, and at Harvard and Leipzig (Ph.D., 1923). Research fellow in philology and English editor, *Academia Sinica* (1929–33); inventor of Chinese indexing system and collaborator in official romanization plan. Author of essays and of *My Country and My People* (1936), *The Importance of Living* (1937), *Moment in Peking* (1939), *With Love and Irony* (1940), *A Leaf in the Storm* (1941), *The Wisdom of China and India*, anthology (editor; 1942), etc.

**Lionel of Antwerp.** 1st Duke of Clarence. 1338–1368. See House of YORK.

**Lionne** (lyôn), **Hugues de.** 1611–1671. French diplomat; associate of Mazarin in negotiating Treaty of Westphalia and Peace of the Pyrenees; councilor of state (1643). French ambassador at Rome (1654), Madrid (1656), Frankfort (1657), Turin (1658). Secretary of state for foreign affairs (1663); adviser to Louis XIV.

**Lio'tard'** (lyô'tȧr'), **Jean Étienne.** 1702–1789. Swiss painter; produced notable pastel sketches, portraits, and genre scenes.

**Liou'ville'** (lyōō'vēl'), **Joseph.** 1809–1882. French mathematician, esp. geometer.

**Li·piń'ski** (lê·pēn'y'·skê), **Karl.** 1790–1861. Polish violinist, and composer of violin concertos, an opera, etc.

**Lip'mann** (lĭp'măn), **Fritz Albert.** 1899– . Amer. biochemist, b. Germany. At Harvard U. (1941–57); awarded Nobel prize in physiology and medicine (1953) with H. Krebs for discovery of coenzyme A.

**Li Po** (lē' bô') *or* **Li T'ai–po** *or* **Li Tai–peh** (lē'tī' bô'). d. 762 A.D. Chinese poet, probably the greatest China has produced, b. in Szechwan. Lived a dissipated life, part of the time at the court of the T'ang emperor and part wandering about in disgrace; was one of a hard-drinking band known as "the Eight Immortals of the Wine Cup"; said to have drowned from a boat in an effort while tipsy to embrace the reflected moon; famous for the exquisite imagery, richness of language, allusions, and cadence of his lyrics.

**Lip'pe** (lĭp'ĕ). A former German principality and its ruling family, which had its origin in the 12th century (1123). Founded by Bernhard I (1113–1144); became a county (1529) under Simon V (1511–1536); divided on death of Simon VI (1555–1613) into two lines: **Lippe–Det'mold** [-dĕt'mōlt] (with two main branch lines, **Lippe–Bie'ster·feld** [-bē'stĕr·fĕlt] and **Lippe–Weis'sen·feld** [-vī'sĕn·fĕlt], and further subdivisions) and the **Lippe–Al'ver·dis'sen** (-äl'vĕr·dĭs'ĕn) line, which later (1643) became the Schaumburg-Lippe county (*q.v.*); became a principality (1720; confirmed 1789). On death (1895) of Prince Woldemar (1875–1895) dispute arose among various branches as to succession; Prince Charles Alexander acted as regent (1895–1905) until dispute settled by courts, Count Leopold (IV) of Lippe-Biesterfeld (1871– ) becoming prince of Lippe (1905–abdicated 1918). Other princes of Lippe-Biesterfeld: Leopold II (ruled 1820–51); Leopold III (1851–75); Bernhard (b. 1911), nephew of Leopold IV, m. (1937) Princess Juliana of the Netherlands.

**Lip′pers·hey** (lĭp′ẽrs·hī), **Hans**. d. about 1619. Dutch spectaclemaker; credited with devising one of first telescopes (1608).

**Lip′pi** (lēp′pē), Fra **Filippo** *or* **Lippo**. *Sometimes called* Fra **Fi·lip′po del Car′mi·ne** (fē·lēp′pō dâl kär′mē·nā). 1406?–1469. Florentine painter. Carmelite monk (1421 ff.); released from monastic vows by Pius II (c. 1461). Protégé of Cosimo de'Medici. His works include the frescoes *Life of St. John the Baptist* and *Life of St. Stephen* (in Prato cathedral) and *Life of the Virgin* (in cathedral at Spoleto), and canvases, as *Coronation of the Virgin, Madonna with Saints, Vision of St. Bernard, Annunciation, St. Lawrence.* His son **Filippo**, *more commonly* **Filippino** *or* **Lippino** (1457?–1504), also a painter, completed frescoes of Masaccio in the Brancacci chapel, as *Sts. Peter and Paul Raising the Dead Youth;* other works include frescoes in church of Santa Maria sopra Minerva at Rome, and in the Strozzi Chapel at Florence, and altarpiece in church of San Michele at Lucca, *Virgin Enthroned, Madonna with Saints, Crucifixion, Adoration of the Kings, The Virgin and Child, with St. Joseph and an Angel.*

**Lippi, Lorenzo**. *Anagrammatic pseud.* **Per·lo′ne Zi′po·li** (pâr·lō′nā tsē′pō·lē). 1606–1664. Florentine poet and painter; known particularly for his comic epic *Il Malmantile Racquistato* (pub. 1676).

**Lip′pin·cott** (lĭp′ĭn·kŭt; *popularly*, -kŏt), **Joshua Ballinger**. 1813–1886. American publisher, b. Juliustown, N.J. Began J. B. Lippincott & Co., Philadelphia (1836); notable publications, a *Pronouncing Gazetteer* (1855), a *Dictionary of Biography and Mythology* (1870). Founded *Lippincott's Magazine* (1868). His son **Joshua Bertram** (1857–1940) was vice-president of the J. B. Lippincott Co. (1886–1911), president (1911–26), chairman of the board (from 1926).

**Lipp′mann′** (lēp′mȧn′), **Gabriel**. 1845–1921. French physicist; educ. École Normale and in Germany. Professor at Sorbonne (from 1882). Enunciated principle of conservation of electricity; invented capillary electrometer; devised process of photography in natural colors in which light is reflected back on itself; awarded 1908 Nobel prize for physics. Author of *Cours de Thermodynamique* (1886) and *Cours d'Acoustique et d'Optique* (1888).

**Lipp′mann** (lĭp′măn), **Walter**. 1889–1974. American editor, journalist, and author, b. New York City. Associate editor, *New Republic;* on editorial staff, New York *World* (until 1931); special writer, New York *Herald Tribune* (1931–67). Assistant to the secretary of war (1917); secretary of E. M. House organization to prepare data for Paris Peace Conference (1918–19). Author of *A Preface to Politics* (1913), *Drift and Mastery* (1914), *The Stakes of Diplomacy* (1915), *Liberty and the News* (1920), *Public Opinion* (1922), *A Preface to Morals* (1929), *The Method of Freedom* (1934), *The New Imperative* (1935), *The Good Society* (1937), *Essays in the Public Philosophy* (1955). Awarded Pulitzer prizes (1958, 1962).

**Lipps** (lĭps), **Theodor**. 1851–1914. German philosopher; chief works, *Die Ethischen Grundfragen* (1899), *Ästhetik* (2 vols., 1903–06), *Psychologische Untersuchungen* (2 vols., 1907–12).

**Lips** (lĭps), **Johann Heinrich**. 1758–1817. Swiss painter and engraver; best known for his engravings after the old masters; also engraved portraits of many of his contemporaries, including Goethe and Wieland.

**Lips′comb** (lĭp′skŏm), **William Nunn, Jr.** 1919– American chemist. At U. of Minnesota (1946–59), Harvard U. (1959– ); awarded Nobel prize for chemistry (1976).

**Lip′si·us** (lĭp′sĭ·ŭs), **Justus**. *Latinized form of* **Joest Lips** (lĭps). 1547–1606. Flemish scholar; published editions of Tacitus (1574), Valerius Maximus (1585), the tragedies of Seneca (1589), Vellejus Paterculus (1591), philosophical works of Seneca (1605).

**Lip′si·us** (lĭp′sē·ōōs), **Richard Adelbert**. 1830–1892. German Protestant clergyman; cofounder of the Evangelical Union. Chief work, *Lehrbuch der Evangelisch-Protestantischen Dogmatik* (1876). His brother **Justus Hermann** (1834–1920) was a classical scholar; author of *Das Attische Recht und Rechtsverfahren* (3 vols., 1905–15). A sister, **Marie** (1837–1927), was a writer, under the pseudonym **La Ma′ra** [lä mä′rä] (1837–1927), on music and musicians.

**Lip′sky** (lĭp′skĭ), **Louis**. 1876–1963. American editor, b. Rochester, N.Y. Editor, *Maccabean Monthly*, official organ of Federation of American Zionists; editor, *The New Palestine.* A leader in the Zionist movement; chairman (1922–24) and president (1924–30), Zionist Organization of America.

**Lip′ton** (lĭp′tŭn), Sir **Thomas Johnstone**. 1850–1931. British merchant and yachtsman, b. in Glasgow of Irish parentage. As a boy and young man, worked for about ten years in U.S.; opened grocery store in Glasgow (1876) which expanded into a large chain of stores throughout Great Britain, dealing in tea, coffee, cocoa, and various groceries and meat products; acquired tea, coffee, and cocoa plantations in Ceylon, packing houses and factories in England and Chicago; organized his business in a limited-liability company (1898). Competed for the America's Cup, symbol of international yachting championship, with five yachts, each named *Shamrock* (1899, 1901, 1903, 1920, 1930).

**Li′sa** (lē′sȧ; -sä), **Man′u·el** (măn′ū·ĕl; mä·nwĕl′). 1772–1820. American fur trader, b. New Orleans; headquarters at St. Louis (from 1790); explored upper Missouri River region, establishing trading posts, in successive expeditions (from 1807).

**Lis′cow** (lĭs′kō), **Christian Ludwig**. 1701–1760. German satirist.

**Li′sen·ko** (lyē′syĕn·kô), **Nikolai Vitalievich**. 1842–1912. Ukrainian composer; regarded as creator of the Ukrainian national opera, with his *Christmas, Nocturne, Winter and Spring;* composed also cantatas, choral works, and songs.

**Lis′franc′ de Saint′-Mar′tin′** (lēs′fräɴ′ dē săɴ′mår′tăɴ′), **Jacques**. 1790–1847. French physician and surgeon; introduced into France from England the surgical method (named after him) of division at the joint between the tarsus and metatarsus in partial amputation of the foot.

**Lisgar**, Baron. See Sir John YOUNG.

**Lisle** (līl; lēl), Viscounts. See (1) John DUDLEY; (2) SIDNEY family.

**Lisle** *or* **l'Isle, de** (dē lēl′). See (1) Sir Beauvoir DE LISLE, (2) Guillaume DELISLE, (3) LECONTE DE LISLE, (4) ROMÉ DE LISLE, (5) ROUGET DE LISLE, (6) VILLIERS DE L'ISLE-ADAM.

**Lisle** (līl; lēl), **Alice**. *Known as* Lady **Alice Lisle.** 1614?–1685. Englishwoman; m. (1630) **John Lisle** (1610?–1664), member of Cromwell's House of Lords and a regicide. Tried by Judge Jeffreys at Bloody Assizes for sheltering two of Monmouth's supporters at her house overnight; beheaded at Winchester.

**Li′so·la** (lē′zō·lä), Baron **Franz von.** 1613–1674. Austrian diplomat; negotiated alliance with Poland while minister there (1655–60); later, ambassador in London and The Hague, where he tried to form a great alliance against Louis XIV of France. Largely instrumental in forming the Austrian-Spanish-Dutch alliance (1673).

**Lis'sa'jous'** (lē'sȧ'zhōō'), **Jules Antoine.** 1822–1880. French physicist; known for researches in acoustics, esp. on vibratory movements, and in optics; invented system of optical telegraphy used during siege of Paris in 1871.

**Lis'sau'er** (lĭs'ou'ẽr), **Ernst.** 1882–1937. German poet and playwright; among his volumes of verse are *Der Acker* (1907), *Der Strom* (1912), *Flammen und Winde* (1922); among his plays, *Eckermann* (1921), *York* (1921), *Luther und Thomas Münzer* (1929). During World War I, gained prominence as author of the *Hymn of Hate*, with its refrain "Gott Strafe England."

**Lissauer, Heinrich.** 1861–1891. German neurologist.

**Lis·sitz'ky** (lyĭ·syĕts'kû·ĭ; *Angl.* lĭ·sĭts'kĭ), **Eliezer.** 1890–1941. Russian painter, b. in Smolensk; identified with ultramodern school.

**Li Ssŭ** (lē' sŏŏ'). d. 208 B.C. Chinese minister of state. Disciple of Hsün Tzŭ; minister of Shih Huang Ti (*q.v.*); said to have advised the emperor to burn the classics, in order to break off absolutely all connection with the past; invented a form of writing; killed as result of a court intrigue.

**List** (lĭst), **Georg Friedrich.** 1789–1846. Political economist, b. Reutlingen, Württemberg. Imprisoned, charged with sedition (1824); to U.S. (1825); naturalized. A leader in advocacy of protective tariff; U.S. consul at Baden (1831–34), Leipzig (1834–37), Stuttgart (1843–45). Author of *Outlines of American Political Economy* (1827), etc.

**List, Siegmund Wilhelm Walther.** 1880–1971. German field marshal; served in World War I; commander of Austrian army (1938), of armies of occupation in Czechoslovakia (1939); governor of Moravia (1939); commander on Slovak sector during invasion of Poland (1939) and of army which broke French defenses at Sedan (1940); field marshal; commander in Balkans (1941), on Moscow front (Dec., 1941), on Stalingrad front (Sept., 1942).

**Lis'ta y A'ra·gón'** (lēs'tä ē ä'rä·gôn'), **Alberto.** 1775–1848. Spanish mathematician, poet, critic, and educator; ordained priest (1803). Founded and directed college of San Mateo (1820–23); in exile (1823–33). Editor, *Gaceta de Madrid* (1833 ff.); aided in founding *Ateneo Científico, Literario, y Artístico.*

**Lis'te·mann** (lĭs'tĕ·män), **Bernhard.** 1841–1917. Violinist, conductor, and teacher, b. in Thuringia, Ger.; to U.S. (1867). Founded Boston Philharmonic Club (1875), out of which developed the Boston Philharmonic Orchestra; concertmaster of Boston Symphony Orchestra (1881–85); taught in Chicago (1893–1907).

**Lis'ter** (lĭs'tẽr), **Joseph Jackson.** 1786–1869. English optician, b. London. Wine merchant by trade. Investigated principles of construction of the object glasses of microscopes and discovered fundamental principle (law of the aplanatic foci) of the modern instrument (1830); first to ascertain true form of red corpuscle of mammalian blood (1834). His son **Joseph,** 1st Baron **Lister of Lyme Re'gis** [lĭm rē'jĭs] (1827–1912), was a surgeon; made special study of inflammation and suppuration following injuries and wounds; deeply influenced by discoveries of Pasteur; used carbolic acid to prevent septic infection; founder of antiseptic surgery. See Sir R. J. GODLEE.

**Lister, Martin.** 1638?–1712. English zoologist; practiced medicine at York (until 1683); proposed to Royal Society a new sort of maps, suggesting idea of a geological survey (1683); contributed to *Philosophical Transactions* articles on spiders, mollusks, minerals, etc.

**Lister, Samuel Cunliffe.** 1st Baron **Mas'ham** (măs'ăm; măsh'ăm). 1815–1906. English inventor. Set up by his father in worsted-milling business; took out 150 patents for inventions, chiefly in clothmaking; advocate of tariff reform; art collector; sportsman; philanthropist.

**Lis'ton** (lĭs'tŭn), **Robert.** 1794–1847. Scottish surgeon; renowned for surgical skill and for invention of a splint (the Liston splint) used in cases of thigh dislocation.

**Liszt** (lĭst), **Franz.** 1811–1886. Hungarian piano virtuoso and composer; studied in Vienna (1821–23) under Czerny and Salieri, and in Paris (1823 ff.) under Paer and Reicha. Withdrew from the concert stage (1833–48), and lived (1835–39) in partial retirement in Geneva with the Comtesse d'Agoult, by whom he had three children (one of whom married, first, Count von Bülow, and second, Richard Wagner). Settled at Weimar with the Princess Sayn-Wittgenstein (1848–61), and devoted himself to composition, writing, and work as conductor at court concerts. To Rome (1861) and became member of the Franciscan order (1865); known as "Abbé Liszt"; passed remainder of his life between Rome and Weimar, with intervals of teaching in the Hungarian Conservatory of Music in Budapest. Among his many notable compositions are his symphonies, symphonic poems, oratorios, Hungarian rhapsodies, and piano pieces.

**Liszt, Franz von.** 1851–1919. Cousin of Franz von Liszt, the composer. German jurist; prominent as a reformer of the theory and practice of criminal law.

**Li Tai-peh** *or* **Li T'ai-po.** See LI PO.

**Lith'gow** (lĭth'gō), **William.** 1582?–?1645. Scottish traveler, mostly on foot, in British Isles, Europe, Asia, Africa; recounted adventures in *The Totall Discourse of the Rare Adventures* (1614).

**Li'tolff** (lē'tŏlf), **Henry Charles.** 1818–1891. Pianist and composer, b. London, of a French father and English mother. Composer of operas, overtures, oratorios, lyric dramas, etc.

**Li Tsung-jên** (lē' dzŏŏng'rĕn'). 1890–1969. Chinese general, b. in Kwangsi. Joined revolutionary forces (1925); member of Kuomintang (1928–29); dismissed from all posts (1929) for opposing policies of Chiang Kai-shek; reinstated (1931); always strongly anti-Japanese. He and the other Kwangsi general, Pai Chung-hsi, are together known as **Li-Pai** (lē'bī').

**Lit·tau'er** (lĭ·tou'ẽr), **Lucius Nathan.** 1859–1944. American industrialist, b. Gloversville, N.Y. Associated (from 1878) with glove-manufacturing business established by his father. Member, U.S. House of Representatives (1897–1907). Donor of $1,100,000 to fund (Lucius N. Littauer Foundation) to be administered so as to promote better understanding among all mankind (1930). Donor of over $2,000,000 to Harvard for establishment of a graduate school of public administration.

**Lit·tell'** (lĭ·tĕl'), **Eliakim.** 1797–1870. American editor and publisher, b. Burlington, N.J. Founded *Littell's Living Age* (1844), containing mainly reprints from British sources.

**Littell, Frank Bowers.** 1869–1951. American astronomer, b. Scranton, Pa. Professor of mathematics, U.S. navy (1901–33); astronomer, U.S. Naval Observatory. With W. S. Eichelberger, made catalogue of 23,521 stars. Special editor on astronomy for *Webster's New International Dictionary, Second Edition.*

**Lit'tle** (lĭt''l), **Arthur De·hon'** (dĕ·hŏn'). 1863–1935. American chemical engineer, b. Boston. Chemist and superintendent of first mill in U.S. making sulphite wood pulp (1884–85). Invented processes of chrome tanning, and of electrolytic manufacture of chlorates, artificial silk, gas, and petroleum.

**Little, Charles Coffin.** 1799–1869. American publisher,

b. Kennebunk, Me. With James Brown as his chief associate (from 1837), established firm of Little, Brown & Co. (1847) in high position among publishers of legal and general works.

**Little,** Sir **Charles James Colebrooke.** 1882– . British naval officer; in World War I, commanded grand fleet submarine flotilla (1916–18), Baltic fleet (1919). Chief of navy personnel (1938–41); member of combined World War II U.S.-British chiefs of staff (1942).

**Little, Clarence Cook.** 1888–1971. American biologist and educator, b. Brookline, Mass. President, U. of Maine (1922–25), Michigan (1925–29); head, Roscoe B. Jackson Memorial Laboratory (1929–56); managing director, American Society for Control of Cancer (1929–56). Conducted researches on inheritance of susceptibility to cancer and on modification of germ plasm.

**Little, Frances.** See Fannie Caldwell MACAULAY.

**Little, Malcolm.** See MALCOLM X.

**Lit′tle·ton** (lĭt′'l·tŭn), Sir **Edward.** 1st Baron **Littleton.** 1589–1645. English judge; chief justice of North Wales; M.P. (1625); chairman of committee of grievances from whose report the Petition of Right was framed (1628); solicitor general (1634); argued against Hampden in ship-money case (1635); chief justice of common pleas (1640); lord keeper of great seal (1641); escaped with great seal to Charles I (1642) but required by parliament to restore it.

**Littleton, Mark.** Pseudonym of John Pendleton KENNEDY.

**Littleton,** Sir **Thomas.** 1407?–1481. English jurist and legal author. According to Paston letters a well-known counsel (1445); sergeant-at-law (1453); a justice of assize in northern circuit (1455); judge of common pleas (1466); knight of the Bath (1475). Gained fame through his treatise *Tenures* (in legal French), a complete view of English land law, one of earliest books printed in London and the earliest treatise on English law ever printed (1481 or 1482). His text was a part of legal education for more than three centuries and was the basis of Sir Edward Coke's (*q.v.*) commentary *Institutes of the Lawes of England* (1628), known as *Coke upon Littleton.*

**Litt′mann** (lĭt′män), **Enno.** 1875–1956. German Semitic scholar; member of American archaeological expeditions in Syria (1899–1900; 1904–05), and head of such an expedition in Abyssinia (1905–06).

**Lit′tre** (lē′tr'), **Alexis.** 1658–?1725. French physician and anatomist; first described type of hernia and urethral mucous glands named after him.

**Lit′tré′** (lē′trā′), **Maximilien Paul Émile.** 1801–1881. French scholar and lexicographer; admired Comte (*q.v.*) and his positivist philosophy; recognized as head of the positivist school after death of Comte (1857). Chief work, *Dictionnaire de la Langue Française* (1863–72).

**Lit′trow** (lĭt′rō), **Joseph Johann von.** 1781–1840. Austrian astronomer; director of Vienna observatory (from 1819). Author of *Die Wunder des Himmels* (1834–36) and *Atlas des Gestirnten Himmels* (1838). His son **Karl Ludwig** (1811–1877) succeeded him as director of Vienna observatory (1842).

**Lit·vi′nov** (lyĭt·vyē′nôf; *Angl.* lĭt·vē′-), **Maksim Maksimovich.** 1876–1951. Russian Communist leader and diplomat. Joined Social Democratic party (1898); in Socialist schism (1903), joined Lenin and the Bolsheviks. After Russian Revolution (1917), represented Russian government in London; headed Russian delegations at disarmament commissions (1927, 1928, 1929), signing Kellogg Pact (1928); people's commissar for foreign affairs (1930–39); succeeded by Molotov (1939). Soviet ambassador to U.S. (1941–43); deputy commissar for foreign affairs (1943–46).

**Litz′mann** (lĭts′män), **Karl.** 1850–1936. German army officer; commanded division under Hindenburg in campaign against Russia in World War I.

**Li Tzŭ–ch′êng** (lē′ dzŭ′chŭng′). 1605?–1645. Chinese rebel leader, b. in Shensi. During disturbances of last years of Ming dynasty, became bandit chieftain (1629–45); overran parts of Hupeh and Honan (1640); captured Kaifeng (1642) and conquered all of Shensi (1642–44); proclaimed himself emperor (1644) and seized Peking; defeated by Gen. Wu San-kuei; driven into Hupeh.

**Liu An** (lê·ōō′ än′). Prince of **Huai–nan.** *Literary name* **Huai–nan Tzŭ** (hwī′nän′ dzŭ′). d. 122 B.C. Chinese ruler and scholar. Grandson of Liu Pang, founder of the Western Han dynasty. Student of Taoism; author of a treatise that became a standard work of the Taoists; became deeply involved in occult studies, such as the search for an elixir of immortality; accused of conspiracy, committed suicide.

**Liu Chi** (lê·ōō′ jē′). 1311–1375. Chinese painter of the Ming dynasty; known esp. for bird and flower pieces.

**Liudprand.** See LIUTPRAND.

**Liu Pang** (lê·ōō′ bäng′). 247–195 B.C. Chinese emperor, founder of the Western Han dynasty (206 or 202 B.C.). Cf. LIU AN.

**Liu Pei** (lê·ōō′ bā′). 162–223. Chinese emperor (221–223), founder, Shu, or Minor Han, dynasty (see HAN).

**Liu Shao–chi** (lē·ōō′ shou′chē′). 1898–1974. Chinese leader. Secy.-general of communist party (1943–54); Chairman, People's Republic of China (1959–69).

**Liu Sung** (lê·ōō′ sŏŏng′). A Chinese dynasty (see SUNG, 1).

**Li′ut·prand** (lē′ŏŏt·pränt) *or* **Lu′it·prand** (lōō′ĭt-). 690?–744 A.D. King of the Lombards (712–744). Seized Ravenna (728); made alliance with Charles Martel (739); defeated dukes of Spoleto and Beneventum and besieged Rome; brought Lombardy to zenith of her power; promulgated *Edicta Liutprandi.*

**Li′ut·prand** *or* **Li′ud·prand** (lē′ŏŏt-). *Known also as* **Liutprand of Cre·mo′na** (krē·mō′nȧ). 922?–?972. Italian prelate and historian; bishop of Cremona (961–972). Among his works are *Antapodosis* (containing events in Italian history 886–c. 952), *De Rebus Gestis Ottonis Magni Imperatoris* (covering period 960–964).

**Livens.** See LIEVENS.

**Live′right** (lĭv′rīt), **Horace Brisbin.** 1886–1933. American publisher and theatrical producer; with Albert Boni founded firm of Boni and Liveright (1918), and was its president (1918–30). Entered theatrical producing field (1924) and produced *Hamlet in Modern Dress, An American Tragedy, Dracula,* etc.

**Liv′er·more** (lĭv′ẽr·mōr), **Mary Ashton,** *nee* **Rice.** 1820?–1905. American suffragette and reformer, b. Boston; m. Rev. Daniel Parker Livermore (1845). With husband, edited church periodical, the *New Covenant,* Chicago (1857–69). Active in woman-suffrage movement; founded (1869) and edited (1869–72) *The Agitator* and the *Woman's Journal* into which it was merged. Also interested in temperance cause.

**Liv′er·pool** (lĭv′ẽr·pōōl), Earls of. Title in English peerage held by members of **Jen′kin·son** (jĕng′kĭn·s'n) and **Fol′jambe** (fŏŏl′jăm) families.

**Charles Jenkinson** (1727–1808), 1st Earl of **Liverpool** and 1st Baron **Hawkes′bur·y** (hôks′bẽr·ĭ; -brĭ); statesman; descendant of Anthony Jenkinson (sea captain, first to penetrate into Central Asia); M.A., Oxon. (1752); M.P. (1761); became leader of king's friends on retirement of Bute; joint secretary to treasury (1763–65); secretary at war in North's ministry (1778–82); president of board of trade and chancellor of duchy of Lancaster (1768–1801), popularly supposed to be confidant of king;

created earl (1796); author of *Coins of the Realm* (1805). **Robert Banks Jenkinson** (1770–1828), 2d earl, statesman; son of 1st earl; educ. Oxford; M.P. (1790); member of India board (1794–1801); master of mint (1799); as Addington's foreign secretary (1801–03), negotiated abortive Treaty of Amiens with Napoleon, and responsible for failure of British to evacuate Malta according to treaty; home secretary and leader in upper house (1804–06); declined premiership on death of Pitt; again home secretary (1807–09); secretary for war and colonies (1809–12); prime minister (1812–27) in Tory ministry; supported Wellington's Peninsular campaign; carried on war with U.S.; prime mover in sending Napoleon to St. Helena; introduced bill of pains and penalties against Queen Caroline; originated severe measures of repression at home (1819–20); increased duty on grain; blamed for apparent British connivance in quelling revolution in Naples; though opposed to Catholic emancipation, advocated minor concessions; recognized (1826) necessity of changing corn laws; stricken with apoplexy.

**Charles Cecil Cope Jenkinson** (1784–1851), 3d earl; half brother of 2d earl; volunteer in Austrian army (1805); undersecretary for home department (1807–09), for war (1809); lord steward (1841–46).

**Cecil George Savile Foljambe** (1846–1907), son of 2d daughter of 3d earl; earl of Liverpool by revival of title (1905) and lord steward of King Edward VII's household (1905–07); succeeded by his son **Arthur William de Brito Savile Foljambe** (1870–1941), lord lieutenant of Ireland (1906–08); governor (1912–17), then governor general (1917–20), of New Zealand.

**Liv'i·a Dru·sil'la** (lĭv'ĭ·ȧ drōō·sĭl'ȧ). 56 B.C.?–29 A.D. Daughter of Livius Drusus Claudianus; wife of Tiberius Claudius Nero, and by him mother of Tiberius and Drusus Senior; divorced husband to marry Octavianus (Augustus), thus becoming the first Roman empress. Secured succession of her son Tiberius; in the early part of his reign she was very influential in public affairs. See DRUSUS.

**Liv'ing·ston** (lĭv'ĭng·stŭn). Surname of an American family prominent in colonial and postcolonial periods. The founder, **Robert Livingston** (1654–1728), b. Ancrum, Roxburghshire, Scotland, emigrated to America (1673); settled at Albany, N.Y.; established manor and lordship of Livingston with estate of 160,000 acres; became lord of the manor; secretary of Indian affairs (from 1695); member, N.Y. provincial assembly (1709–11; 1716–25); speaker (1718); retired (1725). His successor as lord of the manor of Livingston was his son **Philip** (1686–1749). Other important members are the following:

Three sons of Philip; (1) **Peter Van Brugh** [văn brŭk'] (1710–1792), grad. Yale (1731), wealthy N.Y. City merchant; upheld colonial cause in the Revolution. (2) **Philip** (1716–1778), grad. Yale (1737), also successful N.Y. City merchant; one of first to advocate founding of King's College, now Columbia; established a professorship of divinity at Yale; member of Continental Congress (1774–78); signer of Declaration of Independence. (3) **William** (1723–1790), grad. Yale (1741), lawyer; engaged in long political feud with De Lancey family; moved to Elizabethtown, N.J. (1772); member of Continental Congress (1774–76); governor of New Jersey (1776–90); delegate to Constitutional Convention (1787); signer of the Constitution. William's son **Henry Brock'holst** [brŏk'hōlst] (1757–1823), b. New York City, grad. Princeton (1774), served in American Revolution, practiced law in New York (from 1783), was associate justice, U.S. Supreme Court (1806–23).

**Robert R.** (1718–1775), a grandson of the founder through a son, Robert, New York jurist; judge of the admiralty court (1759–63); puisne judge of the supreme court (from 1763); chairman of New York committee of correspondence. His son **Robert R.** (1746–1813), b. New York City, grad. Columbia (1765), lawyer; member of Continental Congress (1775–77; 1779–81); one of committee of five who drew up Declaration of Independence; first U.S. secretary of foreign affairs (1781–83); chancellor of New York State (1777–1801); administered oath of office to Washington (Apr. 30, 1789); U.S. minister to France (1801–04); aided Robert Fulton in building his steamboat and obtained a monopoly (later broken) of steam navigation. His brother **Edward** (1764–1836), b. in Columbia County, N.Y., grad. Princeton (1781), lawyer in New York; member, U.S. House of Representatives (1795–1801); mayor of New York (1801–03); moved to New Orleans (1804), on Jackson's staff at battle of New Orleans (1815); drew up legal code for Louisiana; member, U.S. House of Representatives (1823–29), then U.S. senator, from Louisiana (1829–31); U.S. secretary of state (1831–33); U.S. minister to France (1833–35).

**Livingston, Burton Edward.** 1875–1948. American plant physiologist; professor, Johns Hopkins (1909–40); author of *Rôle of Diffusion and Osmotic Pressure in Plants* (1903).

**Liv'ing·stone** (lĭv'ĭng·stŭn), **David.** 1813–1873. Scottish missionary and explorer in Africa, b. in Lanarkshire. Operative in cotton mill from ten till twenty-four years of age; studied medical and Greek courses in Glasgow, medicine and science in London. Embarked as missionary, reached Bechuanaland in Africa (July, 1841); repulsed by Boers in missionary efforts; m. (1844) Mary Moffat (d. 1862), daughter of the missionary Robert Moffat (*q.v.*); organized exploration expeditions into interior; discovered Lake Ngami (1849), Zambesi River (1851); on great expedition northward from Cape Town through west Central Africa to Loanda and back to Quelimane (1852–56) collected vast amount of information and discovered Victoria Falls of the Zambesi (1855); welcomed back in England and Scotland with enthusiasm; published his *Missionary Travels* (1857); severed connection with missionary society. Returned as consul of Quelimane (1858–64); commanded expeditions exploring Zambesi, Shire, and Ruvuma rivers, discovered lakes Shirwa (Chilwa) and Nyasa (1859); recalled (1863) and on second visit to England published *The Zambesi and its Tributaries* (1865), with intent to expose Portuguese slave traders and get missionary and commercial settlement established near head of the Ruvuma. On proposal of Royal Geographical Society led expedition to explore watershed of Central Africa and sources of Nile (1866); discovered lakes Mweru and Bangweulu (1867–68), explored cannibal country, returned almost dying to Ujiji, where he was rescued (1871) by Henry M. Stanley (*q.v.*); on further exploration to discover source of Nile, died at village of Old Chitambo in Zambia; his remains buried in Westminster Abbey.

**Liv'i·us An'dro·ni'cus** (lĭv'ĭ·ŭs ăn'drō·nī'kŭs; *popularly, often* ăn·drŏn'ĭ·kŭs), **Lucius.** fl. 3d century B.C. Latin epic poet and playwright, of Greek origin; translated and imitated Greek originals.

**Livius Sal'i·na'tor** (lĭv'ĭ·ŭs săl'ĭ·nā'tôr; -tẽr), **Marcus.** Roman general and politician; consul (219 and 207 B.C.); co-operated with Claudius Nero, his associate in the consulship, in defeating the Carthaginians under Hasdrubal in battle of Metaurus (207).

**Liv'y** (lĭv'ĭ). *Latin* **Titus Liv'i·us** (lĭv'ĭ·ŭs). 59 B.C.–17 A.D. Roman historian, b. in Padua. Under patronage of Emperor Augustus, wrote *The Annals of the Roman*

*People* (142 books), a history of Rome from its foundation to the death (9 B.C.) of Drusus, younger brother of Emperor Tiberius. Books I to X, and XXI to XLV, are extant, together with fragments or epitomes of all but two of the other books.

**Li Yüan** (lē′ yü·än′). *As emperor* **Kao Tsu** (gä′ō dzōō′). 565–635 A.D. A general of the Sui dynasty with capital at Ch'ang-an (now Sian); founder of the T'ang dynasty (618); reigned 618–627.

**Li Yüan-hung** (lē′ yü·än′hŏŏng′). 1864–1928. Chinese statesman, b. in Hupeh province. Trained as naval officer; served in Chinese-Japanese War (1894–95); transferred to army; at first opposed to Revolution (1911) of Sun Yat-sen, but later joined it; after Manchus were deposed, elected vice-president of new Chinese Republic (1912–16); on Yüan Shih-k'ai's death became president (1916–17); restored parliament; forced out of presidency, retired (1917–22); again president (1922–23) but again forced out by militarists under Gen. Ts'ao K'un; lived in Tientsin and Shanghai (1923–28); worked for reunification of China by negotiation.

**Lizardi, José Joaquín Fernández de.** See FERNÁNDEZ DE LIZARDI.

**Ljung′gren** (yŭng′grān), **Gustaf.** 1823–1905. Swedish literary critic and historian.

**Llano, Gonzalo Queipo de.** See QUEIPO DE LLANO.

**Llew·el′lyn** (lōō·ĕl′ĭn), **Richard.** *Pen name of* **Richard David Vivian Llewellyn Lloyd** (loid). British novelist, of Welsh descent. Served in British regular army for 5 years (to 1931); employed in motion-picture production (after 1931); rejoined British army (captain in the Welsh guards, 1940). Author of *Poison Pen* (psychological mystery play, 1938), *How Green Was My Valley* (1940), *None But the Lonely Heart* (1943), etc.

**Llewellyn,** Sir **William.** 1863–1941. British portrait painter; painted the State portrait of Queen Mary.

**Llew·el′yn** *or* **Llyw·el′yn** (*Angl.* lōō·ĕl′ĭn; *Welsh* lĕ′ōō-ĕ′lĭn). Name of two Welsh princes:

**Llewelyn ab Ior′werth** (ȧb yôr′wûrth). *Called* **Llewelyn the Great.** d. 1240. Prince of North Wales, afterwards called Prince of Wales. Returned from exile and drove his uncle David I from his territory (1194); m. (1201) Joan (d. 1237), illegitimate daughter of King John; allied with John, extended power to South Wales (1207); deprived of possessions by John (1208–11), won back most of losses with encouragement of the pope, France, and barons; prince of all Wales not ruled by Normans (1216); secured in his rights by clauses in Magna Charta; never desisted from wars against Marchers of South Wales.

**Llewelyn ab Gruf′fydd** (grĭf′ĭth). d. 1282. Grandson of Llewelyn the Great; prince of North Wales; nephew of David II, whom he succeeded (1246); did homage to Henry III and gave up lands east of the Conway (1247); resisted encroachment of officers of Prince Edward; allied himself with forces of Simon de Montfort and in the Barons' War made himself master of south and north Wales; recognized as overlord of Wales by treaty of Shrewsbury (1265); attacked by Edward I for refusal to do homage, forced to submit and hold principality subject to crown of England (1277); revolting again, slain in skirmish with the Mortimers; last champion of Welsh liberty.

**Llo·ren′te** (lyō·rān′tā), **Juan Antonio.** 1756–1823. Spanish priest and historian; general secretary of the Inquisition (1789–1801). Commissioned (1809) by Joseph Bonaparte to examine the archives of the Inquisition and write its history. Withdrew from Spain with the French, and published his history of the Inquisition in Paris (1817–18).

**Lloyd** (loid), **David.** 1656?–1731. Lawyer, b. in Wales; attorney general of Pennsylvania (1686–1700); leader of democratic, or antiproprietary, party in Pennsylvania assembly (from 1703); chief justice of Pennsylvania (1717–31); regarded as leader in securing democratic institutions in Pennsylvania.

**Lloyd, Edward.** fl. 1688–1713. English keeper of coffeehouse first in Tower St., afterwards in Lombard St., London, resort of insurers against sea risk, after whom *Lloyd's List*, devoted to shipping news (from 1726), and the commercial corporation Lloyd's took their names.

**Lloyd, Edward.** 1845–1927. English tenor; first became widely known for his singing in Bach's *St. Matthew* passion music at the Gloucester Music Festival (1871). Excelled in interpretation of music of Handel and Wagner.

**Lloyd, George Ambrose.** 1st Baron **Lloyd of Do·lob′ran** (dō·lŏb′răn). 1879–1941. British colonial administrator, b. in Wales. Served in World War in Egypt, Gallipoli, Russia, Mesopotamia (1914–18). Governor of Bombay (1918–23); high commissioner for Egypt and the Sudan (1925–29); colonial secretary (1940–41). Author of *Egypt since Cromer* (2 vols., 1933, 1934), etc.

**Lloyd, Henry Demarest.** 1847–1903. American writer, b. New York City. On staff of Chicago *Tribune* (1872–85). Wrote for *Atlantic Monthly* magazine sensational *Story of a Great Monopoly* (1881), an exposure of the methods of the Standard Oil Company and the railroads; became known as first of the muckrakers. Joined Socialist party (1903).

**Lloyd, Humphrey.** 1800–1881. British scientist, b. Dublin; best known for researches in optics and magnetism.

**Lloyd, John Selwyn Brooke.** 1904– . British lawyer; secretary of state for foreign affairs (1955–60).

**Lloyd, Llewelyn Southworth.** 1876–1956. English acoustician. Author of *Music and Sound, The Musical Ear, Decibels and Phons* (1938), etc.

**Lloyd, Ma′rie** (mä′rĭ). *Real name* **Matilda Alice Victoria Wood.** 1870–1922. English music-hall comedienne. Known especially for sympathetic character impersonations, esp. of Cockneys, low-comedy roles, and as a popularizer of many comic songs.

**Lloyd, Morton Gith′ens** (gĭth′ĕnz). 1874–1941. American electrical engineer, b. Beverly, N.J.

**Lloyd, Robert.** 1733–1764. English poet; author of *The Actor* (1760) and other poems, and of a comic opera *The Capricious Lovers* (1764).

**Lloyd, William.** 1627–1717. English prelate. Bishop of St. Asaph (1680); one of the Seven Bishops (see William SANCROFT) who petitioned against James II's Declaration of Indulgence (1688) but were acquitted of charge of seditious libel; bishop of Lichfield and Coventry (1692), of Worcester (1700).

**Lloyd, William Watkiss.** 1813–1893. English classical and Shakespearean scholar. Author of *Xanthian Marbles* (1845), *Age of Pericles* (1875), etc. Contended in his edition of *Much Ado About Nothing* that Shakespeare's prose was disguised blank verse.

**Lloyd George** (loid′ jôrj′), **David.** 1st Earl of **Dwy·for** (dōō′ē·vôr). 1863–1945. British statesman, b. Manchester, of Welsh parentage. Solicitor (1884). M.P. (from 1890), won recognition by brilliancy in debate; president of Board of Trade (1905–08); chancellor of the exchequer (1908–15); minister of munitions (1915–16); secretary of state for war (1916). Replaced Asquith as prime minister (1916–22) and, as virtual dictator, directed Britain's policies to victory in war and in settlement of terms of peace; also arranged conference (1921) with Irish leaders and instituted negotiations which resulted in founding of Irish Free State. Author of *War Memoirs* (6 vols., 1933–

36), and *The Truth about the Peace Treaty* (2 vols., 1938). Member of Order of Merit (1919).

**Lloyd-Greame, Philip.** See 1st Viscount SWINTON.

**Lloyd James** (loid′jāmz′), **Arthur.** 1884–1943. British phonetician, b. in South Wales; lecturer in phonetics, University Coll., London (1920–27); engaged in radio broadcasting (from 1924). Author of *Literary Phonetic Reader, English Speech, A Basic Phonetic Reader*, etc.

**Llywelyn.** See LLEWELYN (princes of Wales).

**Lo·ba·chev′ski** (lŭ·bŭ·chăf′skû·ĭ; *Angl.* lō′bȧ·chĕf′skĭ), **Nikolai Ivanovich.** 1793–1856. Russian mathematician; pioneer in non-Euclidean geometry. Author of *Principles of Geometry* (1829–30), *Imaginary Geometry* (1835), *New Principles of Geometry, with a Complete Theory of Parallels* (1835–38), etc.

**Lo·ba′nov-Ro·stov′ski** (lŭ·bȧ′nôf·rŭ·stôf′skû·ĭ; *Angl.* -skĭ), Prince **Aleksei Borisovich.** 1824–1896. Russian statesman; ambassador at Constantinople (1878–79), London (1879–82), Vienna (1882 ff.). Foreign minister of Russia (1895–96).

**Lo′bau′** (lō′bō′), Comte **de.** **Georges Mou′ton′** (mōō′tôN′). 1770–1838. French soldier; aide-de-camp to Joubert (1799), and to Napoleon (1805); general of division (1807), with a command in Spain (1808); engaged at Landshut and Aspern (1809), at Ligny and Waterloo (1815). Commander in chief of National Guard (1830); created marshal of France and peer (1831).

**Lo′be** (lō′bĕ), **Johann Christian.** 1797–1881. German composer of operas, orchestral works, and chamber music.

**Lo′beck** (lō′bĕk), **Christian August.** 1781–1860. German classical scholar; specialized in the study of Greek language, legend, and literature.

**Lo·bei′ra** (lōō·bā′ē·rȧ), **Vasco de.** 1360?–1403. Portuguese knight; reputed author of the romance *Amadis of Gaul.*

**Lo′bel** (lō′bĕl), **Matthias de.** *Latin* **Lo·be′li·us** (lō·bē′lĭ·ŭs; -bĕl′yŭs). 1538–1616. Flemish botanist and physician to James I of England. The plant genus *Lobelia* is named after him.

**Lo′ben·gu′la** (lō′bĕng·gū′lȧ; lō·bĕng′gū·lȧ). 1833–1894. King of the Matabele; yielded concession to British South African Company to develop gold resources in Mashonaland, but attacked the British as they established themselves there (1893); in the decisive battle (Oct. 23, 1893), the Matabele were slaughtered by machine-gun fire and Lobengula forced to yield his capital Bulawayo and flee. Cf. Cecil RHODES.

**Lob′ko·witz** (lôp′kō·vĭts). Noble family of Bohemia, known since 9th century. Prominent members include: **Johann Georg Christian** (1686–1755), Austrian general. **Georg Christian** (1835–1908), Czech politician in Austria; member of Bohemian parliament (from 1865); its president (1871).

**Lo′bo** (lō′bōō), **Francisco Rodrigues.** 1575?–?1627. Portuguese writer; author of an epic (*El Condestable de Portugal,* 1610), a volume of ballads (1596), and most notably a novel in three parts, *A Primevera* (1601), *O Pastor Peregrino* (1608), *O Desenganado* (1614).

**Lobo, Jerônimo.** 1593–1678. Portuguese Jesuit missionary in India and Abyssinia. His manuscript account of his travels was translated into French (*Voyage Historique d' Abissinie,* 1728).

**Lo′bo·dow′ski** (lō′bō·dôf′skē), **Józef.** 1909– . Polish poet; among his works are *Conversation with the Fatherland* (1935), *The Return of Allain Gerbault, Demons of Night* (1936).

**Lo′ca·tel′li** (lō′kä·tĕl′lē), **Pietro.** 1693–1764. Italian violinist and composer, esp. of concerti grossi, sonatas, and caprices.

**Loch** (lŏK; lŏk), **Henry Brougham** (brōōm). 1st Baron **Loch of Dry′law** (drī′lō). 1827–1900. British colonial administrator; in China, negotiated surrender of Taku forts; imprisoned and tortured by Chinese officials; governor of Isle of Man (1863–82), of Victoria (1884–89), of Cape Colony and high commissioner of South Africa (1889–95); assisted in the annexation of Mashonaland and Matabeleland.

**Lochiel.** See CAMERON OF LOCHIEL.

**Loch′ner** (lôK′nēr), **Stephan.** d. 1451. German painter; leading master of the Cologne school. His masterpiece is a three-paneled altarpiece in the cathedral at Cologne.

**Locke** (lŏk), **Al′ain** (ăl′ĭn) **LeRoy.** 1886–1954. American Negro educator, b. Philadelphia. Rhodes scholar at Oxford U. (1907–10). Professor of philosophy, Howard U. (from 1917). Author of *The New Negro* (1925), *The Negro in America* (1933), *The Negro and His Music* (1936), *Negro Art...* (1937), etc.

**Locke, David Ross.** *Pseudonym* **Pe·tro′le·um V. Nas′by** (pē·trō′lē·ŭm, năz′bĭ). 1833–1888. American journalist, b. Vestal, N.Y. In Ohio (from 1852); editor, *The Jeffersonian,* Findlay, Ohio, when he wrote the first of the Petroleum V. Nasby letters (Mar. 21, 1861). Editor, Toledo (Ohio) *Blade* (1865–71); the Nasby letters, political satires marked by humor, caricatures, and aggressiveness, continued in Toledo *Blade* through 1887.

**Locke, John.** 1632–1704. English philosopher, b. in Somersetshire; lecturer in Greek, rhetoric, and philosophy; turned away from subtleties of Aristotle and Schoolmen toward experimental science and philosophy of Descartes and Bacon; expressed views on religion in *An Essay concerning Toleration* (1667). Went to live in house of Anthony Ashley Cooper (later Earl of Shaftesbury), as confidential adviser (from 1667) and tutor; employed by Cooper to draw up constitution of Carolina; made secretary of presentations under Shaftesbury as lord chancellor (1672). During discussion with friends upon morality and religion promised to make attempt at settling what questions the human understanding was or was not fitted to deal with; devoted his best energies for seventeen years to resolving this issue in *An Essay concerning Human Understanding* (1690). Studied medicine in France (1675–79); suspected of complicity in Shaftesbury plots (1684), fled to Holland; returned during Revolution to become commissioner of appeal (1689–1704) and adviser to government on coinage; lived mostly (from 1691) with Sir Francis and Lady Masham in Essex. Author of four letters on *Toleration* (the fourth unfinished at death), *Some Thoughts concerning Education* (1693), *The Reasonableness of Christianity* (1695). Known as the father of English empiricism. See also Edward STILLINGFLEET and John TOLAND.

**Locke, John.** 1792–1856. American scientist and inventor; did geological survey work; investigated terrestrial magnetism and electricity; invented a surveyor's compass, level, and orrery, and an electromagnetic chronograph which revolutionized method of determining longitudes.

**Locke, Matthew.** 1620?–1677. English musical composer; perhaps the earliest English writer of music for stage; joint composer with Christopher Gibbons of music for Shirley's masque *Cupid and Death* (1653) and composer of some music for Davenant's *Siege of Rhodes* (1656), and other contemporary plays.

**Locke, Richard Adams.** 1800–1871. Journalist, b. in Somersetshire, Eng.; to U.S. (1832). Best known as author of the "Moon Hoax" (in the N.Y. *Sun,* 1835), a story purporting to reveal discovery by Sir John Herschel of men and animal life on the moon.

**Locke, William John.** 1863–1930. British novelist, b. in

Barbados. Studied architecture; secretary, Royal Institute of British Architects (1897–1907). Among his many novels are *The Morals of Marcus Ordeyne* (1905), *The Beloved Vagabond* (1906), *Septimus* (1909), *Simon the Jester* (1910), *The Joyous Adventures of Aristide Pujol* (1912), *Stella Maris* (1913), *The Fortunate Youth* (1914), *Jaffery* (1915), *The Golden Adventure of Mr. Paradyne* (1924), *The Great Pandolfo* (1925).

**Lock'er–Lamp'son** (lŏk'ẽr·lăm(p)'s'n), **Frederick.** *Orig. surname* **Locker.** 1821–1895. English poet; took his second wife's maiden name, Lampson (1885). Author of *London Lyrics* (graceful society verse; 1857), *Patchwork* (1879); editor of *Lyra Elegantiarum* (anthology of light verse; 1867).

**Godfrey Lampson Tennyson Locker–Lampson** (1875–1946), his eldest son, held undersecretaryships in home and foreign offices (1917–29); privy councilor (1928); author of works on coins and parliamentary financial procedure, but chiefly of verses and essays, including *A Soldier's Book of Love Poems* and *The Country Gentleman.*

**Oliver Stillingfleet Locker–Lampson** (1881–1954), another son; journalist, soldier, and political leader; naval officer (acting commander, 1915); saw service with armored cars on western front, in Russia, Austria, and Middle East; conducted Victory Loan (1919); lord privy seal (1921).

**Lock'hart** (lŏk'ẽrt; -härt), **John Gibson.** 1794–1854. Scottish editor and novelist and biographer of Scott and Burns. Called to Scottish bar (1816); one of chief contributors to *Blackwood's Magazine* (1817); sketched Edinburgh society in *Peter's Letters to his Kinsfolk* (1819) under pseudonym of **Peter Morris;** married (1820) Sir Walter Scott's eldest daughter, Charlotte Sophia; author of four novels, *Valerius* (1821), *Adam Blair* (1822), *Reginald Dalton* (1823), and *Matthew Wald* (1824); translator of *Ancient Spanish Ballads* (1823); editor of *Quarterly Review* (1825–53); edited Peter Motteux's edition of *Don Quixote* (1822); produced charming biography of Burns (1828), and a *History of Napoleon* (1829); published his magnum opus, his *Life of Sir Walter Scott* (7 vols., 1837–38); by some taxed with ungenerous exposure of his subject, but usually rated by critics next to Boswell's *Johnson* among the great biographies in English.

Sir **William Stephen Alexander Lockhart** (1841–1900), his nephew; British military officer in Sepoy Mutiny, the Bhutan campaign (1864–66), Abyssinian expedition (1867–68), the Hazara Black Mountain expedition (1868–69); served in Afghan War (1878–80), Third Burmese War (1886–87); commander of Punjab frontier force (1890–95); full general (1896); commander in chief in India (1898).

**Lockhart,** Sir **Robert Hamilton Bruce.** 1887–1970. British journalist and writer, b. in Scotland. Acting consul general in Moscow (1915–17); head of special mission to Soviet government (1918), and imprisoned in the Kremlin (Sept.–Oct., 1918). On staff of Anglo-Austrian Bank (1922–28). On staff of London *Evening Standard* (1928 ff.). Author of *Memoirs of a British Agent* (1932), *Retreat from Glory* (1934), *Return to Malaya* (1936), *Guns or Butter?* (1938), etc.

**Lockhart** of Lee (lē), Sir **William.** 1621–1675. British soldier and diplomat. Son of Sir James Lockhart, Lord Lee (d. 1674), Scottish judge. Attached himself to Cromwell; m. Cromwell's niece; became commissioner for administration of justice in Scotland (1652); ambassador in Paris (1656–58, 1673–76). His nephew **George Lockhart** of Carn·wath' (kärn·wŏth') in Lanarkshire (1673–1731), Jacobite leader, was member of Scottish parliament, a commissioner for the union (1705); implicated in rising of 1715, imprisoned but liberated without trial; secret agent to Prince James Edward in Scotland (1718–27), discovered, but permitted to return to Scotland, probably through influence of duke of Argyll; killed in duel; his *Memoirs* form part of *Lockhart Papers,* valued authority on Jacobites.

**Lock'man** (lŏk'măn), **DeWitt McClellan.** 1870–1957. American portrait painter, b. Brooklyn, N.Y.

**Lock'roy'** (lô'krwȧ'), **Joseph Philippe.** *Real surname* **Si'mon'** (sē'môɴ'). 1803–1891. French comedian and playwright; author or coauthor, often with Scribe and Cogniard, of many plays, including *Catherine II* (1831), *Passé Minuit* (1839), *Les Trois Épiciers* (1840), *Deux Compagnons du Tour de France* (1845), etc. His son **Étienne Auguste Édouard** (1840–1913) was a politician; member of Chamber of Deputies (from 1871); minister of commerce and industry (1886–87), of public instruction (1888–89), of marine (1895–96; 1898–99).

**Lock'wood** (lŏk'wo͝od), **Belva Ann,** *nee* **Bennett.** 1830–1917. American lawyer, b. Royalton, N.Y.; m. (1) Uriah H. McNall (1848); (2) Dr. Ezekiel Lockwood (1868). Adm. to bar (1873); practiced, Washington, D.C.; first woman admitted to practice before the U.S. Supreme Court (1879). Leader in women's rights movement. Nominated by National Equal Rights party for president of the United States (1884; 1888).

**Lockwood, James Booth.** 1852–1884. American arctic explorer, b. Annapolis, Md. Commissioned 2d lieutenant, U.S. army (1873). Volunteered for Greely's expedition to arctic (1881). With small detachment, pushed forward (1882) to explore northeastern coast of Greenland; reached 83° 24′ N., 40° 46′ W. (May 13, 1882), then the farthest north reached by explorers. Crossed Grant Land to the western ocean (1883). Died at Cape Sabine two months before Greely party survivors were rescued.

**Lockwood, Ward,** *in full* **John Ward.** 1894–1963. American painter, b. Atchison, Kans. Studio at Taos, N.Mex. (from 1926). Among his notable paintings are *The Plaza in Snow; Rain Across the Valley; Street Scene; Corner Grocery, Taos.* Painted murals for U.S. Post Office Department building in Washington, D.C., Court House at Lexington, Ky., etc.

**Lockwood, Wilton,** *in full* **Robert Wilton.** 1861–1914. American portrait and flower painter, b. Wilton, Conn. Examples of his work: *John La Farge,* now in Boston Museum of Fine Arts; *Grover Cleveland,* at Princeton; *Justice Oliver Wendell Holmes,* in Massachusetts Bar Association; and flower pictures in Metropolitan Museum of Art, N.Y., and Corcoran Gallery, Washington.

**Lock'yer** (lŏk'yẽr), Sir **Joseph Norman.** 1836–1920. English astronomer; clerk in war office, London (1857); devoted leisure time to astronomical studies. Director, Solar Physics Observatory, and professor of astronomical physics, Royal Coll. of Science (1890–1913). Author of *Contributions to Solar Physics* (1873), *The Sun's Place in Nature* (1897), *Inorganic Evolution* (1900), etc. First to observe helium in spectrum of sun's atmosphere (1868).

**Lo·cus'ta** (lō·kŭs'tȧ) *or more correctly* **Lu·cus'ta** (lū-). Roman professional poisoner of 1st century A.D.; she was employed by Agrippina to poison Claudius, and by Nero to poison Britannicus; executed during reign of Emperor Galba.

**Lo'der** (lō'dẽr), **Bernard Cornelius Johannes.** 1849–1935. Dutch jurist; judge, High Court of Justice, the Netherlands (1908–21); first president, Permanent Court of International Justice, The Hague (1922–25).

**Lodge** (lŏj), **Edmund.** 1756–1839. English biographer and writer on heraldry. Blue Mantle pursuivant of arms at College of Arms (1782); Norroy king-of-arms (1822); Clarenceux king-of-arms (1838).

**Lodge, Henry Cabot.** 1850–1924. Great-grandson of George Cabot. American legislator and author, b. Boston. Member, U.S. House of Representatives (1887–93), U.S. Senate (1893–1924). As chairman of foreign affairs committee, led opposition to the Peace Treaty and the Covenant of the League of Nations (1919). Author of *Life and Letters of George Cabot* (1877), *The Story of the Revolution* (2 vols., 1898), *The Senate and the League of Nations* (1925), and biographies of Hamilton, Webster, and Washington. His son **George Cabot** (1873–1909), b. Boston, was a poet; author of *The Song of the Wave* (1898), *Cain, a Drama* (1904), *The Soul's Inheritance* (1909). The latter's son **Henry Cabot, II** (1902– ) on staff of N.Y. *Herald-Tribune* (1924–36); U.S. senator from Massachusetts (1937–44; 1947–52); U.S. representative to the U.N. and Security Council (1953–60); ambassador to South Vietnam (1963–64; 1965–67); ambassador to West Germany (1968–69).

**Lodge,** Sir **Oliver Joseph.** 1851–1940. English physicist and author, b. Penkhull, Staffordshire. Professor, University Coll., Liverpool (1881–1900); principal, U. of Birmingham (1900–19). Investigated lightning, electromagnetic waves, wireless telegraphy; named the coherer used in wireless telegraphy; conducted experiment to determine whether moving matter exerts a drag on the ether, obtaining a negative result; pursued psychical researches; published belief in possibility of communication between living and dead; attempted to reconcile science and religion. Writings include *Elementary Mechanics* (1877), *Modern Views of Electricity* (1889), *Life and Matter* (1905), *The Substance of Faith* (1907), *Man and the Universe* (1908), *The Ether of Space* (1909), *The Survival of Man* (1909), *Raymond, or Life and Death* (containing an account of his supposed communication with dead son Raymond; 1916), *Christopher, a Study in Human Personality* (1919), *Making of Man* (1924), *Atoms and Rays* (1924), *Relativity* (1925), *Evolution and Creation* (1927), *Why I Believe in Personal Immortality* (1928), *Beyond Physics* (1930), *Advancing Science* (1931), *Past Years* (autobiography; 1931) etc.

**Lodge, Oliver William Foster.** 1878–1955. Son of Sir Oliver Lodge. English writer; author of *The Labyrinth* (one-act tragedy; 1911), *Spurgeon Arrives* (one-act comedy), *Poems* (1915), *Love in the Mist* (verse; 1921), *What Art Is* (1927), *The Candle* (1938), etc.

**Lodge, Thomas.** 1558–1625. English poet and dramatist, son of a lord mayor of London. Abandoned law for literature; replied to Stephen Gosson's *Schoole of Abuse* in *A Defence of Plays* (1580). Took part in two sea expeditions, to Terceira and the Canaries (1588) and to South America (1591). Studied medicine; M.D., Oxon. (1602); having turned Catholic, had large practice among his coreligionists; issued *A Treatise of the Plague* (1603), and translations of Seneca and Josephus. One of founders of English drama; author of a second-rate play, *The Wounds of Civile War* (1594) and, with Robert Greene, *A Looking Glasse for London and England* (1594). Author of lyric poems, including the volume *Scillaes Metamorphosis* (1589) and *Phillis* (sonnets; 1593), *A Fig for Momus* (eclogues with satiric cast; 1595); of romances, including the euphuistic romances *Euphues Shadow, the Battaile of the Sences* (1592) and *Rosalynde, Euphues Golden Legacie* (1590), written to beguile the time of the Canaries voyage and supplying the story of Shakespeare's *As You Like It*, of two historical romances, *The Divel Conjured, The Life and Death of William Longbeard,* and of *Wit's Miserie and World's Madnesse* (1596).

**Lo'di** (lō'dē). Name of a weak dynasty of Afghan kings of Delhi (1450–1526), overcome by Baber, founder of the Mogul dynasty. Cf. IBRAHIM LODI.

**Loeb** (lûb), **Jacques** (jäk). 1859–1924. Biophysiologist, b. Mayen, Ger.; to U.S. (1891). Professor, Chicago (1892–1902), California (1902–10); member, Rockefeller Institute for Medical Research (1910–24). Published, before the age of thirty, his tropism theory to account for certain instincts and phenomena of behavior. Conducted researches in comparative physiology and psychology; did pioneer work on artificial parthenogenesis and in analysis of the process of egg fertilization. Author of *Der Heliotropismus der Tiere und seine Übereinstimmung mit dem Heliotropismus der Pflanzen* (1890), *The Dynamics of Living Matter* (1906), *The Mechanistic Conception of Life* (1912), *The Organism as a Whole* (1916), *Regeneration* (1924), etc.

**Loeb** (lōb), **James.** 1867–1933. American banker, b. New York City. A.B., Harvard (1888). Member of banking firm, Kuhn, Loeb & Co. (1888–1901; retired). Projected and subsidized (1912) publication of Loeb Classical Library, a library of about 300 volumes from Greek and Latin authors, with Greek or Latin text on the verso and English translation on the recto of each pair of facing pages. Gave his collection of Arretine pottery to Fogg Museum, Harvard. Founded and endowed in New York City the Institute of Musical Art (1905), incorporated into Juilliard Musical Foundation (c. 1925). Also, established and maintained a clinic in Munich for study of mental disorders and their treatment.

**Loeb, Louis.** 1866–1909. American painter and illustrator; studio in New York (from 1896). Known for illustrations of Mark Twain's *Pudd'nhead Wilson*, F. Marion Crawford's *Via Crucis*, etc. His *Temple of the Winds* is in Metropolitan Museum, New York; *The Siren*, in National Gallery of Art, Washington, D.C.

**Loeb, Morris.** 1863–1912. American chemist, b. Cincinnati. Author of articles on organic and physical chemistry.

**Loeb, Sophie Irene,** *nee* **Si'mon** (sī'mŭn). 1876–1929. Journalist and social worker, b. Rovno, Russia; to U.S. (1882); m. Anselm Loeb (1896; divorced). On staff of New York *Evening World* (1911–20). Campaigned for legislation to aid widowed mothers with dependent children, for model tenements, public baths, play streets, etc. First president, Child Welfare Committee of America. Author of *Epigrams of Eve* (1913), *Everyman's Child* (1920), *Palestine Awake* (1926).

**Loeb, William.** 1866–1937. American businessman; private secretary to Theodore Roosevelt while Roosevelt was governor of New York, vice-president of the U.S., and president of the U.S.

**Loeff'ler** (lûf'lẽr). = LÖFFLER.

**Loef'fler** (lĕf'lẽr), **Charles Martin Tor'nov** (?tôr'nŏf). 1861–1935. Violinist and composer, b. Mulhouse, Alsace; to U.S. (1881). Played with Boston Symphony Orchestra (1883–1903). Composer of symphonic poems (*The Death of Tintagiles, La Bonne Chanson, La Villanelle du Diable, A Pagan Poem*), a suite for violin and orchestra, chamber music, and songs.

**Loe'land** (lû'län), **Rasmus.** 1861–1907. Norwegian writer; his novels portray realistically the life of the Norwegian people, esp. children.

**Loe'ning** (lō'nĭng), **Grover Cleveland.** 1888– . American aircraft manufacturer, b. Bremen, Ger., where his father was U.S. consul. Chief aeronautical engineer, U.S. army air corps (1914–15). President, Loening Aeronautical Engineering Corp., New York (1917–28), and Grover Loening Aircraft Co. (1928–38). Invented strut-braced monoplane and an amphibian airplane; took out numerous airplane patents. Won Wright trophy (1921) and Collier trophy (1922); received distinguished service award from U.S. war department for production of two-seater fighting plane.

**Loer'ke** (lûr'kĕ), **Oskar.** 1884–1941. German novelist, essayist, and poet.

**Loesch'cke** (lûsh'kĕ), **Georg.** 1852–1915. German archaeologist; investigated Mycenaean earthenware vessels and vases and Roman limites.

**Loew** (lō), **Marcus.** 1870–1927. American theater owner and motion-picture producer, b. New York City. His son **Arthur M.** (1897– ) succeeded him as vice-president of Loew's, Inc., and of Metro-Goldwyn-Mayer studios.

**Loe'we** (lû'vĕ), **Johann Karl Gottfried.** 1796–1869. German composer; municipal music director in Stettin (1820–66). Regarded as creator of German ballad as a distinct art form; works include ballads *Edward, Erlkönig, Prinz Eugen, Archibald Douglas,* as well as 5 operas, 16 oratorios, a number of cantatas, piano sonatas, and chamber music. See also J. R. ZUMSTEEG.

**Loewe, Wilhelm.** *Known as* **Loe'we–Kal'be** (-käl'bĕ). 1814–1886. German liberal politician; member of the Frankfort National Assembly (1848), and president of the Rump Parliament in Stuttgart (1849); liberal leader in the Prussian Abgeordnetenhaus (from 1863), and in the Reichstag (1867–81).

**Loe'wen·thal** *or* **Lö'wen·thal** (lû'vĕn·täl), **Johann Jakob.** 1810–1876. Hungarian-English chess player, b. Budapest; settled in London (1851); naturalized; edited *Chess Player's Magazine* (1863–67); manager of British Chess Association (1865–69).

**Loe'wi** (lû'vē), **Otto.** 1873–1961. Amer. (Ger.-born) pharmacologist. Educ. Strassburg and Munich. Professor of pharmacology, Graz (1909–38). With Sir Henry Hallett Dale, investigated chemical transmission of nerve impulses; shared with Dale 1936 Nobel prize for physiology and medicine. To U.S. (1940); research professor of pharmacology, N.Y. Univ. Coll. of Med. (1940 ff.).

**Loe·win·son'–Les'sing** (lyĕ·vyĭn·sôn'lyās'sĭnk), **Franz Yulievich.** 1861–1939. Russian geologist; founder of the Petrographical Institute of the Academy of Arts and Sciences, U.S.S.R.; authority on petrology and volcanism. Author of a standard textbook of petrology.

**Loe'wy'** (lû'vē'), **Maurice.** 1833–1907. French astronomer, b. Vienna. Assistant (1864) and director (1896), Paris observatory. Studied falling stars, influence of planets on sun's photosphere, etc.; invented equatorial coudé, a type of equatorial telescope.

**Löff'ler** (lûf'lĕr), **Friedrich August Johannes.** 1852–1915. German bacteriologist; on staff of Friedrich Wilhelm Inst. in Berlin (1884). Discovered bacillus of glanders and that of swine erysipelas (1882); isolated and made culture of Klebs-Löffler bacillus, the organism causing diphtheria (1884), after it had been first described by Klebs (*q.v.*); developed successful protective serum against foot-and-mouth disease.

**Löfftz** (lûfts), **Ludwig von.** 1845–1910. German painter after the manner of the 16th and 17th century Dutch and German masters.

**Lof'ting** (lŏf'tĭng), **Hugh.** 1886–1947. Writer and illustrator, b. at Maidenhead, Berkshire, Eng.; settled in U.S. (1912). Civil engineer by profession; practiced (to 1912). Served in British army in World War; wounded (June, 1917). Successful in writing and illustrating children's books, including the "Dr. Dolittle" series (*The Voyages of Dr. Dolittle,* 1922, awarded Newbery Medal; *Doctor Dolittle's Caravan,* 1926; *Doctor Dolittle's Return,* 1933), *Porridge Poetry* (1924), *Gub Gub's Book* (1932), etc.

**Lof'tus** (lŏf'tŭs), Lord **Augustus William Frederick Spencer.** 1817–1904. English diplomat. Son of 2d marquis of Ely (Irish peerage). Ambassador at Berlin (1866), at St. Petersburg (1871–79); suggested Anglo-Russian understanding implemented in London; governor of New South Wales (1879–85).

**Loftus, Cissie.** *Stage name of* **Marie Cecilia M'Car'thy** (mȧ·kär'thĭ). 1876–1943. Actress, b. Glasgow, Scotland; m. Justin Huntly M'Carthy (1894; marriage dissolved in U.S., 1899), and 2d (1909) Dr. E. H. Waterman of Chicago. Played Marguerite in *Faust,* supporting Sir Henry Irving, Ophelia in *Hamlet,* supporting E. H. Sothern; starred in Zangwill's *Governess,* and in *Twelfth Night,* produced for her by Mme. Modjeska; later, in motion pictures. Known also for her impersonations of stage and film stars. Author of a number of poems and songs.

**Lo'gan** (lō'găn), **George.** 1753–1821. American physician and politician, b. near Germantown, Pa. Undertook on own initiative and at own expense to visit France in effort to improve relations between France and U.S. (1798–99); efforts disapproved by U.S. government; Congress passed Logan Act (Jan. 30, 1799), forbidding a private citizen to undertake diplomatic negotiations without official authority. U.S. senator from Pennsylvania (1801–07).

**Logan, James.** 1674–1751. Statesman in America, b. of Scottish parentage in County Armagh, Ireland; to America (1699) as secretary to William Penn. Member of the provincial council (1703–47); mayor of Philadelphia (1722); acting executive of the province (1736–38). Chief justice, Pennsylvania supreme court (1731–39). Bequeathed his library to Philadelphia, where as the Loganian Library it is part of the city collection. Interested in botany; friend of John Bartram; the family Loganiaceae and the genus *Logania* were so named by Linnaeus in his honor.

**Logan, James** *or* **John.** *Indian name* **Tah–gah–jute.** 1725?–1780. American Indian leader among the Mingo bands on the Ohio and Scioto rivers. Friendly with the whites until members of his family were massacred (April, 1774); took savage vengeance thereafter, allying himself with the British to whom he turned over scalps and prisoners at Detroit.

**Logan, James Harvey.** 1841–1928. American lawyer and horticulturist, b. near Rockville, Ind. Judge, superior court, Santa Cruz County, Calif. (1880–92). Produced in his garden a new variety of berry, the loganberry, variously regarded as a variety of the western dewberry or as a hybrid between this and the red raspberry.

**Logan, John.** 1748–1788. Scottish clergyman and poet; edited volume of poems by friend Michael Bruce (1770) and published volume of his own (1781); disputed with Michael Bruce authorship of *Ode to the Cuckoo* beginning "Hail, beauteous stranger of the grove," but is acknowledged author of *The Braes of Yarrow.*

**Logan, John Alexander.** 1826–1886. American soldier and legislator, b. in Jackson County, Ill. Member, U.S. House of Representatives (1859–62). Raised Illinois regiment and served in Civil War; brigadier general and major general (1862). Member, U.S. House of Representatives (1867–71), U.S. Senate (1871–77; 1879–86). Candidate for vice-president of the U.S. on Blaine ticket (1884).

**Logan, Stephen Trigg.** 1800–1880. American jurist, b. in Franklin County, Ky. Law partner of Abraham Lincoln in Springfield, Ill. (1841–44). Member of convention that nominated Lincoln (1860).

**Logan,** Sir **William Edmond.** 1798–1875. Canadian

geologist, b. Montreal, of Scottish parents; as manager of copper-smelting company at Swansea made map of coal basin, refuting drift theory of origin of coal by showing character of beds of "stigmaria clay" underneath coal seams of South Wales; head of geological survey of Canada (1842–70).

**Lo'gau** (lō'gou), Baron **Friedrich von.** *Pseudonym* **Salomon von Go'law** (gō'läf). 1604–1655. German poet and epigrammatist. Published *Zweyhundert Teutscher Reimsprüche* (1638), *Deutscher Sinngedichte Dreitausend* (1654).

**Log'hem** (lŏk'ĕm), **Martinus Gesinus Lambert van.** *Pseudonym* **Fio're del'la Ne've** (fyō'rā dāl'lä nā'vā). 1849–1934. Dutch poet and fiction writer; author of *Love in the South* (verse narrative; 1881), *Liana* (lyric cycle; 1882), *Victor* (novel; 1888), and short-story collections.

**Lo'gro·sci'no** *or* **Lo Gro·sci'no** (lō'grō·shē'nō), **Nicola.** 1700?–?1763. Italian composer, esp. of comic operas; in his own day, known as **il Di'o del·l'O'pe·ra Buf'fa** (ēl dē'ō dāl·lō'pā·rä bōōf'fä).

**Logue** (lōg), **Michael.** 1840–1924. Irish Roman Catholic prelate; archbishop of Armagh (from 1888) and primate of all Ireland; cardinal (1893).

**Lo'hen·stein** (lō'ĕn·shtīn), **Daniel Casper von.** 1635–1683. German writer; author of tragedies, a book of lyrics, and a novel.

**Loi'se·leur'–Des'long'champs'** (lwȧz'lûr'dā'lôN'shäN'), **Jean Louis Auguste.** 1774–1849. French botanist; authority on indigenous medicinal plants suitable as substitutes for exotic plants and on classification of indigenous plants; genus *Loiseleuria* is named after him.

**Loi'sy'** (lwȧ'zē'), **Alfred Firmin.** 1857–1940. French Roman Catholic priest, Orientalist, and exegete; condemned as a modernist because of his books *L'Évangile et l'Église* (1902) and *Autour d'un Petit Livre* (1903), he left the church and taught in the Collège de France (1911–27).

**Lok·man'** (lōōk·män'). *Arabic* **Luqmān.** A legendary Arabic writer and wise man of the pre-Islam period, mentioned in the Koran (Sura xxxi); variously identified with ancient Hebrew or Arabic personages. Reputed author of a collection of fables and proverbs. The fables are similar to those of Aesop, many of them being of Greek origin and some going back to Indian stories.

**Lola Montez.** Countess of **Lansfeld.** See Lola MONTEZ.

**Lö'land** (lû'län). = LOELAND.

**Lo'max** (lō'măks), **John Avery.** 1867–1948. American folklorist; edited *Cowboy Songs and Other Frontier Ballads* (1910), *Plantation Songs of the Negro* (1916), and, with his son **Alan** (1915– ), *American Ballads and Folk Songs, Negro Folk Songs as Sung by Lead Belly,* etc.

**Lomb** (lŏm), **Henry.** 1828–1908. American optician, b. in Germany; to U.S. (1849); cofounder (1853; with J. J. Bausch) of Bausch & Lomb Optical Co., Rochester, N. Y.

**Lom'bard** (lôm'bärt), **Johann Wilhelm.** 1767–1812. Prussian statesman, of French Huguenot descent; adviser to Frederick William III (from 1800) in his policy of friendly neutrality toward France and Napoleon; disgraced after the Prussian defeat at Jena, but later restored to favor.

**Lom'bard** (lôm'bärt), **Lambert.** 1505?–1566. Dutch painter and architect.

**Lom'bard** (lŏm'bẽrd; -bärd; lŭm'-), **Peter.** *Lat.* **Petrus Lom·bar'dus** (lŏm·bär'dŭs). 1100?–1160 or 1164. Italian theologian; bishop of Paris (1159). Chief work, *Sententiarum Libri Quatuor,* popularly referred to as *Sententiae,* a collection of opinions of the fathers of the church. This book was widely used as a textbook in medieval theological schools, and was an important influence in crystallizing the doctrine concerning the sacraments of the church.

**Lom·bar'di** (lôm·bär'dē), **Alfonso.** *Real name* **Alfonso Cit'ta·del'la** (chēt'tä·dĕl'lä). 1487–1537. Italian sculptor.

**Lom·bar'do** (lôm·bär'dō) *or* **Lom·bar'di** (-dē). *Real name* **So·la'ro** (sō·lä'rō). Italian family of architects and sculptors, including: **Pietro** (1435–1515), among whose works are Dante's tomb at Ravenna, tombs of Malipiero, Marcello, and Mocenigo at Venice, and tomb of Zanetti in Treviso Cathedral. His son **Antonio** (c. 1458–?1516), who collaborated with his father and brother (see below), among whose works are marble statues *Peter Martyr* and *Thomas Aquinas* in Venice. Another son, **Tullio** (c. 1455–1532), among whose works are the choir chapel in Treviso Cathedral, Vendramini tomb in Venice, and four marble angels in Venice.

**Lom·bro'so** (lôm·brō'sō), **Cesare.** 1836–1909. Italian physician and criminologist; professor of psychiatry at Pavia (1862); later, professor of criminal anthropology at Turin. Held that a criminal represents a distinct anthropological type with definite physical and mental stigmata and that a criminal is the product of heredity, atavism, and degeneracy.

**Lo'mé'nie'** (lô'mā'nē'), **Louis Léonard de.** 1815–1878. French man of letters; author of *Galeries des Contemporains...* (1840–47), *Beaumarchais et son Temps* (1855), *Esquisses Historiques et Littéraires* (1879), etc.

**Loménie de Bri'enne'** (dē brē'ĕn'), **Étienne Charles.** 1727–1794. French cardinal and statesman under Louis XVI. Cardinal (1788); controller general of finance succeeding Calonne (1787); premier of France (1788); convoked meeting of States-General for May 1, 1789; forced out of office by public opposition (Aug. 24, 1788).

**Lo·mo·no'sov** (lŭ·mŭ·nô'sôf), **Mikhail Vasilievich.** 1711–1765. Russian scientist and man of letters; author of odes, epigrams, and plays, an essay on Russian versification, etc.

**Lon'don** (lŭn'dŭn), **Jack.** 1876–1916. American writer, b. San Francisco. Lived life of sailor, waterfront loafer, and hobo (1891–94). Became Socialist; made soap-box speeches; arrested. Spent year in high school and a few months (1896–97) in U. of California. To Klondike and back (1897–98). Acceptance of stories by the *Overland Monthly* (Dec., 1898), *Atlantic Monthly* (July, 1899) and of a book of collected stories by Houghton, Mifflin & Co. (1900) encouraged him in his writing. Wrote 43 books, including *The Son of the Wolf* (1900), *The God of his Fathers* (1901), *A Daughter of the Snows* (1902), *The Call of the Wild* (1903), *The People of the Abyss* (1903), *The Sea Wolf* (1904), *The Game* (1905), *The Road* (1907), *Martin Eden* (1909), *The Cruise of the Snark* (1911), *John Barleycorn* (1913), *The Abysmal Brute* (1913), *The Strength of the Strong* (1914). See Martin E. JOHNSON.

**London, Meyer.** 1871–1926. Socialist and labor leader, b. in Poland; to U.S. (1891). A founder of the Socialist party of America (1899–1901). Member, U.S. House of Representatives (1915–19; 1921–23).

**Londonderry,** Marquises of. See Robert STEWART.

**Long** (lŏng), **Armistead Lindsay.** 1825–1891. American army officer, b. in Campbell County, Va.; military secretary to General Robert E. Lee (1861–63); wrote *Memoirs of Robert E. Lee, His Military and Personal History* (1886).

**Long** (lŏng), **Breckinridge.** 1881–1958. American lawyer and diplomat, b. St. Louis; practiced law in St. Louis (1907 ff.); ambassador to Italy (1933–36); ambassador on special mission to Argentina, Brazil, Uruguay (1938).

**Long, Crawford Williamson.** 1815–1878. American surgeon, b. Danielsville, Ga. Reputedly first to use ether as an anesthetic (8 operations between 1842 and 1846); published account of his experience (Dec., 1849). Previous to this publication, Dr. W. T. G. Morton (*q.v.*), of Boston, at suggestion of Dr. C. T. Jackson, made a public demonstration of the use of ether (1846), and claimed priority in the discovery.

**Long, Earl.** See under Huey P. LONG.

**Long, Esmond Ray.** See under John Harper LONG.

**Long, Ga′bri′elle′** (gȧ′brē′ĕl′) **Margaret Vere,** *nee* **Campbell.** *Pseudonyms* **Marjorie Bow′en** (bō′ĕn) *and* **George Run′nell** (rŭn′′l) **Pree′dy** (prē′dĭ). 1888–1952. English novelist and playwright; m. 1st (1912) Don Zeffirino Emilio Costanzo (d. 1916); 2d (1917) Arthur L. Long. Won Eve's prize (1923) with *Windfalls.* Author also of biographical accounts of Mary, Queen of Scots, Emma, Lady Hamilton, Mary Wollstonecraft Godwin, William Hogarth, William Cobbett, John Wesley, John Paul Jones.

**Long, George.** 1800–1879. English classical scholar; edited *Penny Cyclopaedia* (1833–46); surpassed his contemporaries in knowledge of Roman law; edited *Bibliotheca Classica* (1851–58).

**Long, Huey Pierce.** 1893–1935. American lawyer and politician, b. Winnfield, La. Adm. to bar (1915) and practiced in Winnfield (1915–18) and Shreveport (from 1918). Governor of Louisiana (1928–31). U.S. senator (1931–35); assassinated (1935). Noted for demagoguery and for his dictatorial control over Louisiana through his political machine. His brother **Earl Kemp** (1895–1960), lieutenant governor of Louisiana (1936–38), became governor on resignation of Governor Richard W. Leche (1939); defeated in election for governor (1940).

**Long, James.** 1793?–1822. American adventurer; led expedition to Texas (1819); formed republic with himself as president; declared independence (June 23, 1819). Captured and taken to Mexico City (1822); shot and killed by a sentry.

**Long, John Davis.** 1838–1915. American lawyer and legislator; governor of Massachusetts (1880, 1881, 1882). Member, U.S. House of Representatives (1883–89). U.S. secretary of the navy (1897–1902). Author of *The New American Navy* (2 vols., 1903).

**Long, John Harper.** 1856–1918. American chemist; author of several chemistry textbooks. His son **Esmond Ray** (1890– ), pathologist, b. Chicago; professor, U. of Chicago (1921–32), U. of Pa. (from 1932); government consultant on tuberculosis; army colonel (1943); director, National Tuberculosis Association (from 1947). Special editor of medical terms for *Webster's New International Dictionary, Second Edition.*

**Long, John Luther.** 1861–1927. American novelist and playwright; his short story, *Madame Butterfly* (in *Century Magazine,* Jan., 1898), was adapted for the stage by David Belasco, and used as a basis for the libretto of Puccini's opera. Also wrote, with Belasco, *The Darling of the Gods* (1902) and *Andrea* (1904). His fiction includes *The Fox-Woman* (1900), *The Way of the Gods* (1906), *Baby Grand* (1912).

**Long, Stephen Harriman.** 1784–1864. American army officer and explorer; sent west to explore upper Mississippi (1817). Commanded exploring expedition to Rocky Mountain region (1820); discovered Longs Peak, in Colorado. Explored northern U.S. boundary (1823).

**Long, Walter Hume.** 1st Viscount **Long of Wrax′all** (răk′sôl). 1854–1924. English statesman; M.P. (1880–1921); raised to the peerage (1921). President, Board of Agriculture (1895–1900); president, Local Government Board (1900–05; 1915–16); chief secretary to Ireland (1905–06); secretary of state for the colonies (1916–18); first lord of the admiralty (1919–21).

**Long, William Joseph.** 1866–1952. American Congregational clergyman and writer on nature and animal life (*Ways of Wood Folk,* 1899; *Brier Patch Philosophy,* 1906; *Wood Folk Comedies,* 1920; etc.).

**Long′a′cre** (lŏng′ā′kẽr), **James Barton.** 1794–1869. American engraver, b. Delaware County, Pa. Known especially for his work in *The National Portrait Gallery of Distinguished Americans* (4 vols., 1834–39); chief engraver, U.S. mint (1844–69).

**Long′champ′** (lôɴ′shäɴ′), **William.** d. 1197. English prelate; left service of Geoffrey, Henry II's son, for that of Richard, who on accession as Richard I of England made him chancellor of the duchy of Aquitaine, and bishop of Ely (1189), and on departure from England made him joint chief justiciar with bishop of Durham; ousted bishop of Durham (1190); papal legate (1190). Balanced in power by Walter of Coutances, archbishop of Rouen; forced, by general uprising against his arrogance, to withdraw to Normandy; a loyal servant to Richard, who employed him in diplomatic missions to Germany and France (1194–95).

**Longespée, William de.** See William LONGSWORD.

**Long′fel′low** (lŏng′fĕl′ō), **Henry Wadsworth.** 1807–1882. Son of Stephen Longfellow (*q.v.*). American poet, b. Portland, Me.; grad. Bowdoin (1825). Professor of modern languages, Bowdoin (1829–35), Harvard (1835–54). Devoted himself wholly to his writing from 1854. Among his poetical works: *Voices of the Night* (including the *Psalm of Life;* 1839); *Ballads and Other Poems* (including *The Wreck of the Hesperus, The Skeleton in Armor, The Village Blacksmith;* 1841); *Evangeline: A Tale of Acadie* (1847); *The Seaside and the Fireside* (including *The Building of the Ship;* 1850); *The Golden Legend* (1851); *The Song of Hiawatha* (1855); *The Courtship of Miles Standish* (1858); *Tales of a Wayside Inn* (1863); *The Divine Comedy of Dante Alighieri* (3 vols., 1865–67); *Three Books of Song* (1872); *The Hanging of the Crane* (1874); *Ultima Thule* (1880). Elected to American Hall of Fame (1900).

**Longfellow, Stephen.** 1776–1849. American lawyer, b. Gorham, Me.; practiced, Portland, Me.; father of Henry Wadsworth Longfellow (*q.v.*). Another son, **Samuel** (1819–1892), was a Unitarian clergyman and poet; author of a *Life of Henry Wadsworth Longfellow* (2 vols., 1886), *Thalatta* (poems, 1853), and numerous hymns.

**Long′ford** (lŏng′fẽrd), **Joseph Henry.** 1849–1925. British Orientalist; in British consular service in Japan (1869–1902). Author of *Japan of the Japanese* (1911).

**Lon·ghe′na** (lông·gâ′nä), **Baldassare.** 1604–1682. Venetian architect; known esp. for the domical church, Santa Maria della Salute, Venice.

**Lon′ghi** (lông′gē), **Pietro.** *Orig.* **Pietro Fal′ca** (fäl′kä). 1702–1785. Venetian painter, esp. of contemporary domestic and social Venetian life. His son **Alessandro** (1733–1813), painter and engraver, is known esp. for his portraits and etchings.

**Longimanus.** See ARTAXERXES I.

**Lon·gi′nus** (lŏn·jī′nŭs), **Dionysius Cassius.** Greek Platonic philosopher and rhetorician of 3d century A.D.; studied in Alexandria and taught in Athens. Summoned by Zenobia (*q.v.*) to tutor her children, he became her political adviser; beheaded (273 A.D.) by order of Emperor Aurelian, after Zenobia's fall. Renowned as a scholar and critic; author of *Philological Discourses, On First Principles, On the Chief End.* A famous essay *On the Sublime* has been ascribed to him, but its authorship is disputed.

**Longinus, Johannes.** See Jan DŁUGOSZ.

**Long′man** (lŏng′măn). Name of an English family of

book publishers founded by **Thomas Longman** (1699–1755); shared in publishing Boyle's *Works*, Ainsworth's *Latin Dictionary*, Ephraim Chambers's *Cyclopaedia*, and Johnson's *Dictionary;* took into partnership (1754) his nephew **Thomas Longman** (1730–1797), who brought out a new edition of Chambers's *Cyclopaedia*, and whose son **Thomas Norton** (1771–1842) took into firm (1794) Owen Rees (1770–1837) and published works of Wordsworth, Coleridge, Moore, Southey, and Scott; gained for firm sole proprietorship of *Edinburgh Review* (1826). **Thomas** (1804–1879) and **William** (1813–1877), sons of Thomas Norton Longman, first published Macaulay's *Lays of Ancient Rome* (1842) and his *History of England* (1st two vols., 1848); Thomas issued an illustrated New Testament and William was author of the *History of the Life and Times of Edward III* (1869) and a *History of the Three Cathedrals dedicated to St. Paul* (1873). **Thomas Norton** (1849–1930), son of Thomas (1804–1879), continued control of the firm, now Longmans, Green & Co. Sir **Hubert Harry Longman** (1856–1940) was partner in Longmans, Green & Co. (1880–1933). See RIVINGTON.

**Longman, Mary Evelyn Beatrice.** 1874?–1954. American sculptor; m. Nathaniel Horton Batchelder (1920). Executed bronze doors for the chapel at U.S. Naval Academy, Annapolis, Spanish War Memorial in Hartford, Conn., and a number of portrait busts, as that of Alice Freeman Palmer for American Hall of Fame.

**Lon'gnon'** (lôɴ'nyôɴ'), **Auguste Honoré.** 1844–1911. French scholar; made special study of the historical geography of France.

**Lon'go·mon·ta'nus** (lŏng'gō·mŏn·tā'nŭs) [*Latinized form of Longberg,* Jutland, his birthplace]. *Real name* **Christian Se've·rin'** (sĕ'vĕ·rēn'). 1562–1647. Danish astronomer; assistant to Tycho Brahe (1589–1600); founder of observatory in Copenhagen.

**Long'street'** (lŏng'strēt'), **Augustus Baldwin.** 1790–1870. American Methodist Episcopal clergyman, author, and educator, b. Augusta, Ga. Began (1827) humorous sketches of Georgia life, *Georgia Scenes*, published in book form (1835 and 1840). President, U. of Mississippi (1849–56), U. of South Carolina (1857–65).

**Longstreet, James.** 1821–1904. American army officer, b. in Edgefield District, S.C.; grad. U.S.M.A., West Point (1842). Resigned from U.S. army to enter Confederate service (1861). Commissioned brigadier general, then major general (1861); lieutenant general (1862). Commanded a corps at second battle of Bull Run (1862), the right wing of Lee's army at Antietam (Sept., 1862), a corps at Gettysburg (July, 1863) where his delay in carrying out Lee's orders to attack has been held responsible for the Confederate defeat, the left wing of the Confederate army at Chickamauga; surrendered with Lee at Appomattox Court House (Apr. 9, 1865). U.S. minister to Turkey (1880–81); U.S. marshal (1881–84); U.S. railroad commissioner (1898–1904). Author of a military autobiography, *From Manassas to Appomattox* (1896).

**Long'sword'** (lŏng'sōrd'), **William.** *Also* **William de Long'es'pée'** (dē lôɴ'gā'pā'). 3d Earl of **Salis'bur·y** (sôlz'bĕr·ĭ; -brĭ). d. 1226. Illegitimate son of Henry II of England. Granted by Richard I both hand of heiress of William, Earl of Salisbury, and the title (1198); warden of Cinque Ports (1204–06), of Welsh marches (1208); hopeless of King John's cause, joined Dauphin Louis (1216–17); faithfully supported his own nephew King Henry III. His son **William de Longespée** (1212?–1250), often called Earl of **Salisbury,** joined crusades (1240, 1247); killed at battle near El Mansura.

**Longueuil, de.** See Charles LEMOYNE (1626–83 and 1656–1729).

**Longue'ville'** (lôɴg'vēl'), Duchesse **de. Anne Geneviève,** *nee* **de Bour'bon'–Con'dé'** (dē bōōr'bôɴ'-kôɴ'dā'). 1619–1679. Sister of the Great Condé and of the prince de Conti; m. duc de Longueville (1642; d. 1663); had liaison with La Rochefoucauld (1646); an influential leader in the Fronde; retired to a Carmelite convent.

**Lon'gus** (lŏng'gŭs). fl. 2d or 3d century A.D. Greek writer, to whom is attributed the pastoral romance *Daphnis and Chloë.*

**Longus, Tiberius Sempronius.** See SEMPRONIUS LONGUS.

**Long'worth** (lŏng'wûrth; -wērth), **Nicholas.** 1782–1863. American horticulturist, b. Newark, N.J. Studied law; practiced, Cincinnati, Ohio (from 1803). Experimented with wine grapes (Catawba and Isabella wines), strawberry culture, and black raspberries. Retired (1828) to devote himself to grape cultivation and wine making; known as "father of American grape culture." His great-grandson **Nicholas** (1869–1931), b. Cincinnati, was a lawyer and legislator; member of U.S. House of Representatives (1903–13; 1915–31); m. Alice, daughter of President Theodore Roosevelt, at the White House (1906); speaker of the House of Representatives (1925–31).

**Lo'nit·zer** (lō'nĭt·sēr) *or* **Lo'ni·cer** (lō'nĭ·tsēr), **Adam.** d. 1586. German botanist after whom the genus *Lonicera* was named.

**Lönn'rot** (lûn'rŏt), **Elias.** 1802–1884. Finnish scholar; regarded as one of the founders of modern Finnish literature. Chief work, the collection and editing of Finnish epic songs, which he organized and systematized into a great national epic, *Kalevala.*

**Löns** (lûns), **Hermann.** 1866–1914. German journalist and writer; among his books are nature stories, animal and hunting tales, novels, and verse.

**Lons'dale** (lŏnz'dāl), Earls of and 1st viscount. See LOWTHER family.

**Lonsdale, Frederick.** 1881–1954. British playwright and scenario writer; among his plays are *The King of Cadonia, The Best People, The Last of Mrs. Cheyney;* among his scenarios, *The Devil to Pay, Lovers Courageous.*

**Ló'nyay** (lō'nyoi), Count **Melchior.** 1822–1884. Hungarian statesman; premier (1871–72).

**Loo'mis** (lōō'mĭs), **Alfred Lee.** 1887– . American physicist; practiced law in New York. Director, Loomis Laboratories, Tuxedo Park, N.Y. (from 1926). Major, U.S.A., in charge of experimental and developmental work, Aberdeen (Maryland) Proving Grounds (1917–19). His work includes investigation of the physical and biological effects of high-frequency sound waves and electrical potentials of the brain.

**Loomis, Charles Bat·tell'** (bă·tĕl'). 1861–1911. American humorist, b. Brooklyn, N.Y. Among his best-known books are *Just Rhymes* (1899), *Cheerful Americans* (1903), *Cheer Up* (1906), *A Bath in an English Tub* (1907), *A Holiday Touch* (1908), *Just Irish* (1909).

**Loomis, Chester.** 1852–1924. American portrait, landscape, and figure painter.

**Loomis, Elias.** 1811–1889. American mathematician and astronomer; professor, Western Reserve College (1837–44), U. of the City of New York (1844–47; 1849–60), Yale (1860–89).

**Loomis, Francis Butler.** 1861–1948. American diplomat; U.S. minister to Venezuela (1897–1901), Portugal (1901–02); asst. secretary of state (1902) and secretary of state ad interim (1905). Conducted final negotiations leading to acquisition of Panama Canal Zone by U.S.

**Loomis, Harvey Worthington.** 1865–1930. American pianist and composer of four comic operas, a grand opera, chamber music, cantatas, piano pieces, and songs. Also published *Lyrics of the Red Man*, etc.

**Loomis, Mahlon.** 1826–1886. American dentist and inventor, b. Oppenheim, N.Y.; practiced in Philadelphia; invented a kaolin process for making artificial teeth (patented 1854). Pioneer (from 1860) in experiments with aerial telegraphy (wireless telegraphy); incorporated Loomis Aerial Telegraph Company (1873) but lacked funds to pursue experiments further.

**Loos** (lōōs), **Anita.** 1893– . American humorous writer; b. Sisson, Calif.; m. John Emerson (1919). Collaborated with husband in writing motion-picture scenarios; author of *Gentlemen Prefer Blondes* (1925), *But Gentlemen Marry Brunettes* (1928).

**Looy** (lō′ĭ), **Jacobus van.** 1855–1930. Dutch painter and novelist; as a painter, regarded as a leader of the Amsterdam school; among his novels is the trilogy *Jaapje* (1917), *Jaap* (1923), and *Jakob* (1930).

**Lo′pe de Ve′ga** (lō′pā thā vā′gä). See Vega.

**Lo′pes** (lô′pĕsh), **Fernão.** *Also* **Fernam Lo′pez** (lô′pĕsh). 1380?–?1460. Portuguese historian; commissioned by the Portuguese king to chronicle the history of the kings of Portugal.

**Lopes de Castanheda, Fernão.** See Castanheda.

**Ló′pez** (lō′pās), **Alfonso.** 1886–1959. President of Colombia (1934–38; 1942–45).

**López, Carlos Antonio.** 1790–1862. Paraguayan dictator; nephew of José G. R. Francia. One of the consuls (1841–44); president (dictator) of Paraguay (1844–62; re-elected 1854, 1857, in nominal elections). His son **Francisco Solano** (1827–1870) succeeded as president (1862–70) with dictatorial powers; ambition to dominate South America led to difficulties with Brazil and Argentina (1864–65); declared war against them and Uruguay and invaded Argentina; at first successful but in 5-year war (1865–70) gradually driven back and Paraguay devastated; finally killed by Brazilian troops.

**López, José Hilario.** 1800?–1869. Colombian (New Granadan) general and politician; president of New Granada (1849–53).

**Ló′pez, Narciso.** 1798?–1851. Venezuelan-born filibuster in Cuba; to Cuba (1841) and identified himself with revolutionists; fled to U.S. (1849) and thereafter organized three filibustering expeditions to Cuba; captured and shot, at Havana.

**López, Vicente Fidel.** 1815?–1903. Argentine historian and politician; opposed dictator Rosas; in exile in Chile (1840–52). Back in Argentina, supported Urquiza (1853–61); again expatriated. Author of novels, political tracts, essays, and esp. *Historia de la República Argentina* (10 vols., 1883–93). His father, **Vicente López y Pla′nes** [ē plä′nās] (1784–1856), was author of Argentine national hymn.

**López Con·tre′ras** (kôn·trā′räs), **Eleázar.** 1883–1973. Venezuelan soldier and politician; provisional president of Venezuela (1935) on death of Gómez; elected president (1936–41).

**Ló′pez de A·ya′la** (lō′pāth thā ä·yä′lä), **Pedro.** 1332–1407. Spanish statesman, soldier, historian, and writer; ambassador to France (1379–80; 1395–96); chancellor of Castile (1398–1407); author of the historical work *Crónicas de los Reyes de Castilla Don Pedro, Don Enrique II, Don Juan I, Don Enrique III* (2 vols.; 1779–80); the satiric poem *Rimado del Palacio*, and translations of Titus Livius, Saint Gregory, Boccaccio, etc. See Marqués de Santillana.

**López de Ayala y Herrera.** See Ayala y Herrera.

**López de Gómara, Francisco.** See Gómara.

**Ló′pez de Le·gaz′pe** *or* **Le·gas′pi** (lō′pās thā lā·gäs′pā, lā·gäs′pē), **Miguel.** 1510?–1572. Spanish soldier; conqueror of the Philippine Islands (1564 ff.); founded Manila (1571).

**Ló′pez de Mendoza** (lō′pāth), **Íñigo.** See Marqués de Santillana.

**Ló′pez Do·mín′guez** (lō′pāth thō·mēng′gāth), **José.** 1829–1911. Spanish general and statesman; under the republic, captain general of Burgos (1873); captured Cartagena; lieutenant general; minister of war (1893); president of senate (1905); premier of Spain (1906).

**López y Por·ta′ña** (ē pôr·tä′nyä), **Vicente.** 1772–1850. Spanish painter, esp. of historical scenes and portraits (*Ferdinand VII, Goya, Marshal Suchet*).

**Lor′ca** (lôr′kä), **Federico García.** 1899–1936. Spanish man of letters.

**Lord, Jeremy.** Pseudonym of Ben Ray Redman.

**Lord, Nathan.** 1792–1870. American Congregational clergyman and educator; president, Dartmouth (1828–63). A nephew, **John Lord** (1810–1894), wrote *Beacon Lights of History* (8 vols., 1884–96), etc.

**Lord, Royal Bertram.** 1899–1963. American army officer; B.S., Brown (1919), U.S.M.A., West Point (1923); inventor of portable steel emplacement and portable cableway used by U.S. army; chief of operations (Sept., 1941), asst. director (Apr., 1942), Board of Economic Warfare.

**Loreburn,** Earl of. See Robert Threshie Reid.

**Lo′ree** (lō′rē), **Leonor Fres·nel′** (frā·nĕl′). 1858–1940. American railroad executive; president, Baltimore & Ohio Railroad Co. (1901–04), Delaware & Hudson Co. (1907–38).

**Lo′ren′cez′** (lô′räN′sā′), Comte **de. Charles Ferdinand La′trille′** (là′trē′y′). 1814–1892. Grandson of Marshal Oudinot. French soldier; distinguished himself in Crimean War (1854–55); commanded French expeditionary force in Mexico (1862), was repulsed before Puebla, and replaced. Commanded 3d division of 4th corps (1870), and was interned in Germany after the fall of Metz.

**Lo′rentz** (lō′rĕnts), **Hendrik Antoon.** 1853–1928. Dutch physicist; educ. at Leiden where he became (1878) professor of mathematical physics. Made important contributions to the electromagnetic theory of light and to the electron theory of matter; with Pieter Zeeman (*q.v.*) discovered phenomena known as the *Zeeman effect;* shared with Zeeman the 1902 Nobel prize for physics; did work on phenomena of moving bodies that led to promulgation of the theory of relativity. See George Fitzgerald.

**Lo·rentz′** (lō·rĕnts′), **Pare** (pâr). 1905– . American scenario writer and motion-picture director.

**Lo′renz** (lō′rĕnts), **Adolf.** 1854–1946. Austrian orthopedic surgeon; devised method of reducing congenital dislocation of the hip joint by manipulation, and a method for straightening clubfoot.

**Lorenz, Ottokar.** 1832–1904. Austrian historian.

**Lorenz, Konrad.** 1903– . German ethologist, b. Vienna. At U. of Vienna (1928–40); director of Max-Planck-Institute für Verhaltenphysiologie (1961–73); awarded (with Karl von Frisch and Nikolaas Tinbergen) Nobel prize for physiology or medicine (1973).

**Lo′ren·za′na y Bu·trón′** (lō′rān·thä′nä ē bōō·trōn′), **Francisco Antonio.** 1722–1804. Spanish prelate; archbishop of Mexico (1766–72); archbishop of Toledo, and primate of Spain (1772–1800); cardinal (1789). Chief work, *Historia de Nueva-España* (1770).

**Lo′ren·zet′ti** (lō′rān·tsāt′tē). Name of two Italian painters of the Sienese school: **Ambrogio** (c. 1300–?1348), sometimes called **Ambrogio di Lo·ren′zo** (dē lō·rĕn′tsō), known particularly for his series of frescoes *Good and Bad Government* in Palazzo Pubblico at Siena. His older brother and teacher **Pietro** (c. 1280–?1348), also called **Pietro Lau·ra′ti** (lou·rä′tē) *or* **Laurati da**

**Sie'na** (dä syâ'nä), painter of polyptych in Arezzo cathedral, frescoes at Assisi, etc.

**Lo'ren·zi'ni** (lō'rân·tsē'nē), **Carlo.** 1826–1890. *Pseudonym* **Carlo Col·lo'di** (kôl·lô'dē). Italian writer of books for children; chief work, a series of adventure tales finally brought out in book form as *Le Avventure di Pinocchio* (1882).

**Lo·ren'zo** (lō·rĕn'tsō), **Fiorenzo di.** 1445?–?1525. Umbrian painter; master of Perugino and Pinturicchio.

**Lorenzo, Piero di.** See PIERO DI COSIMO.

**Lorenzo Mo'na·co** (mô'nä·kō). *Also called* Don **Lorenzo** (dōn). c. 1370–1425. Italian Camaldolite monk and painter of the Sienese school; teacher of Fra Filippo Lippi; influenced Giovanni da Fiesole.

**Lorenzo the Magnificent.** See MEDICI family.

**Lorges,** Comte **de.** See *Guy Aldonce de Durfort de Duras*, at DURFORT family.

**Lo'ri·a** (lô'ryä), **Achille.** 1857–1943. Italian economist and sociologist; believer in economic determinism.

**Loria, Ruggiero di.** See LAURIA.

**Lor'i·mer** (lŏr'ĭ·mẽr), **George Claude.** 1838–1904. Baptist clergyman, b. Edinburgh, Scotland; to U.S. (1855). Author of *Isms Old and New* (1881), *Christianity in the Nineteenth Century* (1900), etc. His son **George Horace** (1868–1937), b. Louisville, Ky., was editor in chief of the *Saturday Evening Post* (1899–1936).

**Lorimer, James.** 1818–1890. Scottish jurist; authority on international law.

**Lorimer, John Henry.** 1856–1936. Scottish portrait, figure, and flower painter. His brother Sir **Robert Stodart** (1864–1929), architect, designed the Scottish National War Memorial at Edinburgh Castle.

**Loris, Heinrich.** See Henricus GLAREANUS.

**Lo'ris–Me'li·kov** (lô'ryĭs·myā'lyĭ·kôf), Count **Mikhail Tarielovich.** 1825?–1888. Russian general and statesman, of Armenian descent. Commanded regiment in Crimean War (1854–56); major general (1856); lieutenant general (1863); commanded army invading Turkey from Armenia (1877–78); captured Kars. Chairman of Imperial Administrative Commission (1880), charged with combating Nihilism; minister of interior (1880–81).

**Lorm** (lôrm), **Hieronymus.** *Pseudonym of* **Heinrich Lan'des·mann** (län'dĕs·män). 1821–1902. German writer; among his books of verse are *Abdul* (epic; 1852), *Gedichte* (1870), *Nachsommer;* among his works of fiction, *Wanderers Ruhebank* (1881), *Das Kopftuch der Madonna* (1887); among his essays, *Der Grundlose Optimismus* (1894; 1897); among his philosophical treatises, *Der Naturgenuss. Eine Philosophie der Jahreszeiten* (1876).

**l'Orme** *or* **Lorme, de.** See DELORME.

**Lorne** (lôrn), Marquis of. Title borne by heir (when a son) of duke of ARGYLL.

**Lor·rain',** **Claude** (klōd lô·rān'; lō-; *Fr.* klōd lô'răN'). *Professional name of* **Claude Gel'lée'** (zhĕ'lā') *or* **Ge·lée'** (zhē-). 1600–1682. French landscape painter and engraver, b. in Chamagne, Lorraine; studio in Rome (1627 ff.). His paintings include notably *Le Campo Vaccino, La Vue d'un Port au Soleil Levant, Acis et Galatée,* and *Jacob et les Filles de Laban.*

**Lorrain, Jean.** Pseudonym of Paul DUVAL.

**Lorrain, Robert Le.** See LE LORRAIN.

**Lor·raine'** (lô·rān'; lō-; *Fr.* lô'rân'). Name of ducal family of France, ruling in Lorraine continuously from 11th century (**Gé'rard' d'Al'sace'** [zhā'rȧr' dȧl'zȧs'], 1048–1070) to its union with Hapsburgs (1740), although in the later years under domination of France. Branch houses of Vaudémont and Aumale originated in 15th century with nephew of Charles II the Bold (duke, 1391–1431). Charles's daughter Isabella married René I of Anjou, who became (1434) duke of Lorraine (see RENÉ I). René's second daughter, Margaret, married Henry VI of England. René's grandson René II of Lorraine was in direct line which extended through eight generations to Francis Stephen (1708–65), later Emperor Francis I, who married (1736) Maria Theresa of Austria (see HAPSBURG-LORRAINE). Duchy lost to France (1624–90); see CHARLES IV and V, Dukes of Lorraine, who kept title; see also CHARLES, Prince of Lorraine. Claude, Duc d'Aumale, son of René II, was made count, then duke (1528) of Guise, first of lesser branch of Lorraine (see GUISE), which included dukes François (1519–63) and Henri (1550–88), cardinals Charles (1524–74) and Louis (1555–88), and Mary, who married James V of Scotland. This male line became extinct (1765) with Francis Stephen; duchy had been granted (1737) by Francis to Stanislas I Leszczyński, and on his death (1766) title passed to France. See AUMALE, and individual names.

**Lorraine–Hapsburg.** See HAPSBURG-LORRAINE.

**Lorris, Guillaume de.** See GUILLAUME DE LORRIS.

**Lo'serth** (lō'zĕrt), **Johann.** 1846–?1920. Austrian historian; among his works are *Hus und Wiclif* (1884), *Geschichte des Späteren Mittelalters* (1903).

**Los'sing** (lŏs'ĭng), **Benson John.** 1813–1891. American engraver, journalist, and historian; wood engraver in New York (from 1838). Published *Pictorial Field Book of the Revolution* (2 vols., 1850–52), *Pictorial History of the Civil War* (3 vols., 1866–68), *Our Country* (2 vols., 1876–78), and several popular biographies and histories.

**Lot** (lŏt). In Bible, a nephew of Abraham (*Gen.* xi. 31; xii. 5), who escaped the destruction of Sodom but whose wife is said to have been turned into "a pillar of salt" because she looked back when fleeing from the city (*Gen.* xix).

**Lot Kamehameha.** See KAMEHAMEHA V.

**Lo·thair' II** (lō·thâr'; -târ'). 826?–869 A.D. King of Lorraine (855–869). Second son of Emperor Lothair I. On death of father (855) received part of Austrasia, which was renamed Lotharingia (Lat. *Lotharii regnum*, "kingdom of Lothair"), in modern French Lorraine; had controversy with Pope Nicholas I over divorce of first wife.

**Lo·thair'** (lō·thâr'; -târ'). *Fr.* **Lo'thaire'** (lô'târ'). 941–986. King of France (954–986); son of Louis IV; b. Laon. Next to the last of the Carolingians (*q.v.*). After death of Hugh the Great (956), began aggressive policy; fought with Emperor Otto II (978–980); quarreled with Hugh Capet (980–985). Succeeded by his son Louis V.

**Lo·thair'.** *Fr.* **Lo'thaire'.** *Ger.* **Lo'thar** (lō'tär; lō·tär'). Name of two Holy Roman emperors:

**Lothair I.** 795?–855. King of Germany (840–843) and Holy Roman emperor (840–855). Son of Louis I. In early years associated in the Empire with his father, but revolted against him (829–833). On death of Louis I (840), attempted to seize all authority. Defeated by brothers at Fontenoy (841); by Treaty of Verdun (843), granted title of emperor and sovereignty over northern Italy and Lorraine; divided his kingdom among his three sons (855); troubled with invasions of the Northmen (843–845).

**Lothair II** (*or* **III**). 1070?–1137. Called "the Saxon." King of Germany and Holy Roman emperor (1125–37; crowned 1133). Appointed duke of Saxony (1106). War with the Hohenstaufens (1128–35). Secured allegiance of Frederick of Swabia (1134). Invaded Italy (1136–37).

**Lothair II.** d. 950 A.D. King of Italy, jointly with his father, Hugh, Count of Arles (931–947), alone (947–950); in conflict with Berengar II (945–950) finally overcome; his widow, Adelaide, married Emperor Otto I.

**Lothar** *or* **Lothaire.** See CLOTAIRE and LOTHAIR.

**Lothian,** Earls and marquises of. See KERR family.

**Lo'throp** (lō'thrŭp), **Amy.** Pseudonym of Anna Bartlett Warner (see under Susan Bogert WARNER).

**Lothrop, Daniel.** 1831–1892. American publisher, b. Rochester, N.H. Founder of D. Lothrop & Co., publishers of works of Edward Everett Hale and Thomas Nelson Page, and of several juvenile periodicals. His second wife, **Hariett Mulford,** *nee* **Stone** (1844–1924), pseudonym **Margaret Sidney,** was a writer of juveniles, including *Five Little Peppers and How They Grew* (1881), *A Little Maid of Concord Town* (1898), etc.

**Lo'ti'** (lô'tē'), **Pierre.** *Pseudonym of* **Louis Marie Julien Viaud** (vyō). 1850–1923. French naval officer and novelist, b. Rochefort. Served in French navy, seeing service esp. in waters near Japan, Senegal, and Tonkin; placed on retired list (1910) but recalled to service in World War (1914–18). Among his many books are *Aziyadé* (1879), *Rarahu* (1880; later called *Le Mariage de Loti*, 1882), *Pêcheur d'Islande* (1886), *Madame Chrysanthème* (1887), *Japoneries d'Automne* (1889), *Fantôme d'Orient* (1892), *Matelot* (1893), *Les Derniers Jours de Pékin* (1902), *Vers Ispahan* (1904), *Les Désenchantées* (1906), *Un Pèlerin d'Angkor* (1912), *La Hyène Enragée* (1916), *Le Roman d'un Enfant* (1919). See Judith GAUTIER.

**Lo·tich'i·us** (lō·tĭk'ĭ·ŭs; *Ger.* lō·tē'kē·ōōs). *In full* **Pe'trus** (pē'trŭs; pā'trōōs) **Lotichius Se·cun'dus** (sē·kŭn'dŭs; zā·kōōn'dōōs). 1528–1560. German humanist; professor of medicine, Heidelberg. Author of songs, elegies, and eclogues written in Latin.

**Lot'ti** (lôt'tē), **Antonio.** 1667–1740. Italian composer of 20 operas, 3 oratorios, and many church choral works.

**Lot'to** (lôt'tō), **Lorenzo.** c. 1480–c. 1556. Venetian painter of religious subjects, altarpieces, and frescoes.

**Lotz** (lōts), **Karl.** 1833–1904. Hungarian painter, known esp. for his large murals representing scenes from Hungarian legend and history.

**Lot'ze** (lōt'sē), **Rudolf Hermann.** 1817–1881. German philosopher; opposed the theory of a "vital force"; aided in founding science of physiological psychology; as a philosopher, elaborated a system of teleological idealism.

**Lou'bet'** (lōō'bĕ'), **Émile.** 1838–1929. French statesman, and 7th president of the Republic; studied law at Paris; established himself at Montélimar; its mayor (1870–99). Member, Chamber of Deputies (1876–84); senator (1885–87); minister of public works (1887–88); prime minister (1892); re-elected to Senate (1894); its president (1896–99). On death of Faure elected president of France (1899–1906); administration marked by Dreyfus crises (1899, 1904) and separation of church and state (1905); retired from public life (1906).

**Lou'cheur'** (lōō'shûr'), **Louis.** 1872–1931. French industrialist and politician; in business as contracting engineer (to 1914). Artillery officer at outbreak of World War; called by Briand to be undersecretary in charge of war industries (1916); later, served in various cabinet posts, as minister of munitions (1917–19), minister of industrial reconstruction in the liberated regions (1919–20; 1921–22), minister of labor (1928–30) and of commerce (1930–31).

**Lou'der·back** (lou'dẽr·băk), **George Davis.** 1874–1957. American geologist; discovered benitoite and other minerals. Investigated west coast stratigraphy, basin range structure, physical history of the Pacific Coast, China, and the Philippine Islands.

**Loudon,** Baron **Gideon Ernst von.** See LAUDON.

**Lou'don** (lou'd'n), **John Claudius.** 1783–1843. Scottish horticultural writer; edited *Gardener's Magazine* (1826–43); established and edited *Architectural Magazine* (1834); compiler of several encyclopedic works.

**Loudon, Samuel.** 1727?–1813. Printer, b. prob. in Ireland; to America before 1753. Founded (1776) weekly newspaper *The New York Packet and the American Advertiser*, renamed (1792) *Diary or Loudon's Register.*

**Lou'doun** *or* **Lou'don** (lou'd'n), Earls of. See John CAMPBELL (1598–1663).

**Loughborough,** Baron. See Alexander WEDDERBURN.

**Lou'is** (lōō'ĭs; lōō'ĭ; *Fr.* lwē), Saint. 1274–1297. Son of Charles II of Anjou (see ANJOU); held prisoner (1288–94) in Barcelona in place of his father; became there a Friar Minor; made bishop of Toulouse (1295).

**Louis,** Saint. = LOUIS IX of France.

**Louis.** Name of three Flemish counts:

**Louis of Flanders.** Count of **Ne·vers'** (nĕ·vâr'). 1271?–1322. Fought with Philip IV of France for possession of county; defeated and imprisoned (1312) but escaped; see NEVERS.

**Louis I de Nevers.** Count of **Flanders.** 1304?–1346. Son of Louis of Flanders; became count of Nevers (1322) but extravagance led to revolt; later (1328) a more serious revolt, led by Jacob van Artevelde, broke out in Flanders; forced to flee (1337) to Paris; killed at Crécy (1346).

**Louis II de Male** (mȧl). Count of **Flanders.** 1330–1383. Son of Louis I de Nevers; wounded at Crécy; his rule a long struggle with communes, led by Ghent; caused three districts, previously seized by Philip the Fair, to be restored (1369) to Flanders; extravagances and harsh taxation led to revolt, partly suppressed by defeat of Artevelde at Roosebeke (1382). His daughter Margaret married (1369) Philip the Bold of Burgundy; on his death, Flanders passed to Burgundy.

**Louis.** Name of eighteen kings of France:

CAROLINGIAN (*q.v.*):

**Louis I.** *Called* **le Dé'bon'naire'** (lẽ dā'bô'nâr'). 778–840. King (814–840); see LOUIS I, Holy Roman Emperor.

**Louis II.** *Called* **the Stammerer.** *Fr.* **le Bègue** (lẽ bĕg'). 846–879. Son of Charles the Bald; king (877–879).

**Louis III.** 863?–882. Son of Louis II; king (879–882), jointly with his brother Carloman; ruled north of France; defeated Northmen (881).

**Louis IV.** *Called* **d'Ou'tre·mer'** (dōō'trẽ·mâr'), *i.e.* from beyond the sea. 921?–954. Son of Charles the Simple; king (936–954); carried to England on death of his father (929); accession (936) supported by Hugh the Great, Count of Paris (see CAPETIAN); controlled by Hugh during most of his reign.

**Louis V.** *Called* **the Sluggard.** *Fr.* **le Fai'né'ant'** (fā'nā'äN'). 966?–987. Son of Lothair; king (986–987), last of Carolingians in France; succeeded by Hugh Capet.

CAPETIAN (*q.v.*):

**Louis VI.** *Called* **the Fat.** *Fr.* **le Gros** (lẽ grō'). 1081–1137. Son of Philip I. King (1108–37). By continuous warfare for 24 years subdued robber barons around Paris; engaged in war against Emperor Henry V and Henry I of England (1116–20). Encouraged communal movement among his vassals; granted privileges to towns and aided the church.

**Louis VII.** 1121?–1180. *Called* **the Young.** *Fr.* **le Jeune** (lẽ zhûn'). Son of Louis VI. King (1137–80). Married Eleanor of Aquitaine (1137). Conquered Champagne (1142–44). Joined Second Crusade (1147–49). Divorced Eleanor (1152), who married (1152) Henry of Anjou (see ANJOU), later Henry II of England. Gave up Aquitaine (1154). Long struggle (1157–80) with Henry II; not much actual fighting, but many parts of France held by English king.

**Louis VIII.** *Called* **le Lion** (lē lyôN′) *or* **Cœur′ de Lion′** (kûr′ dē lyôN′; *Angl.* lē′ŏn). 1187–1226. Son of Philip Augustus. King (1223–26); m. (1200) Blanche of Castile. A warrior prince, active in several campaigns (1213–15). Offered English crown by barons in opposition to John; led French expedition to England (1216–17); defeated; returned to France after death of John. Aided in war against Albigenses (1215–19); directed massacre at Marmande. As king, tried to destroy power of Plantagenets and to conquer the south of France. Overpowered Avignon and received submission of the Albigenses of Languedoc (1226).

**Louis IX.** *Known as* Saint **Louis.** 1214–1270. Son of Louis VIII; b. Poissy. King (1226–70). His mother, Blanche of Castile, regent during minority (1226–36). Married (1234) Margaret of Provence. Long and comparatively peaceful reign. Rising of nobles (1242–43). Took crusader's vow (1244); went on Sixth Crusade (1248–54); his mother again regent until her death (1252); defeated and captured (1250) at El Mansûra, Egypt; remained in Syria four years. Signed Treaty of Corbeil (1258); gave up claims of France to Roussillon and Barcelona. Treaty of Paris (1259) with England; claims of Henry III adjusted; Normandy, Anjou, Touraine, Maine, and Poitou became French, while domains in the south went to Henry. Sanctioned conquest (1265) of Naples by his brother Charles of Anjou. Planned another crusade (1266–70); died at Tunis soon after leaving France. Canonized (1297).

**Louis X.** *Called* **the Quarreler.** *Fr.* **le Hu′tin′** (lē ü′tăN′). 1289–1316. Son of Philip IV; b. Paris. King of Navarre (1305–16). King of France (1314–16; period of feudal reaction); granted charters to nobility.

VALOIS (*q.v.*):

**Louis XI.** 1423–1483. Son of Charles VII; b. Bourges; m. (1436) Margaret of Scotland (*q.v.*). Made unsuccessful attempts against his father's throne (1446, 1456); fled to Flanders (1456). King (1461–83). Destroyed power of great feudatories: struggled esp. with Charles the Bold, Duke of Burgundy, who led a conspiracy of nobles (League of Public Weal; 1464–65); nobles detached by diplomacy and bribery, Charles defeated in war (1467–77); after Charles's death (1477), war continued with his daughter Mary of Burgundy. By Treaty of Arras (1482) Burgundian territories lapsed to king of France; also Anjou, Maine, Provence, and other regions united with the crown (1480–81): foundation of absolute monarchy of France, secured by arbitrary and perfidious measures.

**Louis XII.** *Called* **Père du Peu′ple** (pâr′ dü pû′pl′), *i.e.* Father of the People. 1462–1515. Son of Charles, Duc d'Orléans; b. Blois; m. (1) Jeanne (1476), daughter of Louis XI; (2) Anne de Bretagne (1499), widow of Charles VIII; (3) Mary Tudor (1514), sister of Henry VIII of England. Duc d'Orléans (1465–98); opposed Charles VIII; imprisoned (1487–90); took part in French invasion of northern Italy (1494–95). King (1498–1515). A popular ruler; inaugurated widespread reforms in finance and justice. Aided by Cardinal d'Amboise. Led army into northern Italy, overthrew Ludovico Sforza (1499); with Ferdinand of Aragon conquered Naples (1500–01), but quarreled; French driven out (1503). Joined with Pope Julius II, Ferdinand of Aragon, and the emperor Maximilian in the League of Cambrai (1508) against Venice; won battle of Agnadello (1509), in which Venice was overwhelmed. Through jealousy of allies and England, Holy League formed (1511) against France. Gaston de Foix killed at Ravenna (1512) and French driven out of Lombardy. Defeated by Henry VIII in Battle of the Spurs (1513). Peace concluded (1514). See also ORLÉANS and Valentina VISCONTI.

BOURBON (*q.v.*):

**Louis XIII.** 1601–1643. Son of Henry IV and Marie de Médicis; b. Fontainebleau; m. Anne of Austria (1615). King (1610–43). His mother (see MARIE DE MÉDICIS) regent during his minority (1610–17); after murder of marquis d'Ancre (1617), threatened civil war with queen mother and her adherents. For most of reign completely under influence of Richelieu, who had entered council of ministers (1624) and soon became chief adviser; for uprising of Huguenots (1622–28) in south of France, foreign policy toward Hapsburgs, and participation of France in Thirty Years' War (1618–48), see RICHELIEU. Other events: his brother Gaston d'Orléans (see under ORLÉANS) attempted (1632) overthrow of Richelieu by expedition from Spain; conspiracy of Cinq-Mars unsuccessful (1641–42). His eldest son succeeded him as Louis XIV; his second son, Philippe I, Duc d'Orléans, was founder of present house of Orléans (*q.v.*).

**Louis XIV.** *Called* **the Great.** *Also* **le Grand Mo′narque′** (lē grăN′ mô′nȧrk′) *and* **le Roi So′leil′** (lē rwä′ sô′lâ′y′), *i.e.* the Sun King. 1638–1715. Son of Louis XIII and Anne of Austria; b. Saint-Germain-en-Laye. King (1643–1715), acceding at age of five. Regency held by his mother, but power actually with Cardinal Mazarin (1643–61): Peace of Westphalia, concluding Thirty Years' War (1648); civil wars of the Fronde (1648–53); war with Spain terminated by Peace of the Pyrenees (1659); France received Roussillon and part of Spanish Netherlands. Married Marie Thérèse of Spain (1660). On death of Mazarin (1661), assumed control; aided by able ministers, especially Colbert (finance) and Louvois (war). Engaged in long struggle with Spain and the Empire over Franche-Comté, parts of Netherlands, and Luxemburg; first stage, the Queen's War (1667–68), terminated by the Treaty of Aix-la-Chapelle; second, the Dutch War (1672–78), generally successful, esp. with the armies of Turenne up to his death (1675), and closed by the Treaty of Nijmegen; third (1683–97), marked by French invasion of Spanish Netherlands, devastation of the Palatinate, formation of first Grand Alliance against France, under leadership of William III of England (1689), and French naval defeat off La Hogue (1692), and concluded by Treaty of Ryswick, by which France lost certain territories; and fourth, the War of the Spanish Succession (1701–14), the greatest conflict of all, marked by struggle with second Grand Alliance and by several severe defeats of the French by the duke of Marlborough and Prince Eugene in the great battles of Blenheim, Oudenarde, Malplaquet, and concluded by treaties of Utrecht (1713) and Rastatt (1714), by which, although Philip of Anjou, his grandson, retained Spanish throne, French territories were given up, French prestige diminished, and the country burdened with debt. During reign, Huguenots gradually deprived of rights; Edict of Nantes revoked (1685) and thousands fled from France; power of church generally brought under control; morality of society lowered. Much under the influence of his mistresses Louise de La Vallière, Mme. de Montespan, and Mme. de Maintenon, whom he married after death of Marie Thérèse (1683). Inordinately ambitious, his monarchical authority greatly increased and despotically used; condition of poor classes made worse. His idea of government summed up in words attributed to him: "L'état c'est moi" (I am the state). His reign (73 years) longest in European history: France at its zenith, his court the most magnificent in Europe, French letters and arts in their golden age. See CHARLES II of England.

**Louis XV.** *Called* **the Well-Beloved.** *Fr.* **le Bien′-Ai′mé′** (lẽ byăɴ′-nĕ′mā′). 1710–1774. Grandson of Louis the Dauphin (1661–1711) and great-grandson of Louis XIV; b. in Versailles. King (1715–74). During minority (1715–23), under regency of Philippe II, Duc d'Orléans; actual administration by Dubois. Education entrusted to Cardinal Fleury. Disastrous financial schemes of John Law (1717–20). Duc de Bourbon prime minister (1723–26). Married (1725) Maria Leszczyńska (*q.v.*). Bourbon replaced by Fleury as minister (1726–43), whose policy for recovery partly successful while France kept out of war, but who involved France in War of Polish Succession (1733–35; closed by Treaty of Vienna, 1735, which added Lorraine to France), and brought France into Austrian Succession War (1740–48) as ally of Frederick of Prussia, and was blamed for results of Peace of Aix-la-Chapelle which brought no gains to France. After Fleury's death (1743), managed affairs personally but disordered finances were never relieved, administration generally became worse, and discontent and hatred of king by the masses grew steadily more bitter. Had several mistresses, especially Mme. de Pompadour, whose influence (1745–64) was long-continued and most harmful. Engaged in Seven Years' War (1756–63) which by Treaty of Versailles brought disaster in loss of Canada and India. Jesuits suppressed (1764). Parliament of Paris abolished (1771). Mme. du Barry in ascendancy (1768–74). Duc de Choiseul influential cabinet minister (1758–70), and duc d'Aiguillon (1770–74).

**Louis XVI.** 1754–1793. Third son of Dauphin Louis (only son of Louis XV); b. in Versailles. Became dauphin (1765). Married (1770) Marie Antoinette (*q.v.*). King (1774–92). At time of accession, France much disturbed by misery and discontent. At first aided by able ministers—Turgot, Malesherbes, Vergennes, etc.; objectionable taxes remitted, evil laws abolished, and conditions somewhat improved, but soon overruled by extravagant queen and court. Necker made finance minister (1776), succeeding Turgot. America aided in War of Independence (1778–81). Necker (dismissed by Louis in 1781) was succeeded by Calonne (1783), whose unpopular borrowing methods caused opposition to new taxes and criticism of extravagance of court; Necker recalled (1788). States-General met (May, 1789). Next four years (1789–92) coincident with French Revolution. Wavering policy caused king loss of confidence of both Royalists and Revolutionists. Dismissed Necker but compelled to recall him (1789). With family, brought forcibly by Parisian mob (Oct. 5, 1789) from Versailles to live in Tuileries. Endangered by death of Mirabeau, leader of conservatives, sought to escape from France (June 20–21, 1791) but arrested at Varennes and brought back. Took oath as constitutional king (Sept., 1791). Tuileries invaded by organized mob (June 20, 1792); again stormed and Swiss Guard massacred (Aug. 10, 1792). Deposed by National Convention and Republic declared (Sept. 21, 1792); tried for treason (Dec., 1792); found guilty and condemned to death; guillotined (Jan. 21, 1793). Left two children, the dauphin Louis XVII and Marie Thérèse, Duchesse d'Angoulême (*q.v.*).

**Louis XVII.** *Known as* **Louis Charles de France** (dẽ fräɴs′). 1785–1795. Second son of Louis XVI and Marie Antoinette. Became dauphin after death (1789) of his brother Louis Joseph Xavier (b. 1781). Imprisoned in the Temple with royal family (1792). Titular king of France (1793–95). Many accounts (partly legendary) of ill-treatment by guardians, Antoine Simon, the cobbler, and J. J. C. Laurent; according to official reports, died in prison (June 8, 1795). Later, many claimants as real Louis XVII arose; see Karl W. NAUNDORFF and Eleazar WILLIAMS.

**Louis XVIII.** *Full name* **Louis Xavier Stanislas.** *Sometimes called* **Louis le Dé′si′ré′** (lẽ dā′zē′rā′). 1755–1824. Grandson of Louis XV and brother of Louis XVI and Charles X; b. in Versailles. King (1814–15, 1815–24). Comte de Provence. Married Louise Marie Joséphine of Savoy (1771). Interested in politics and literature; remained in Paris after outbreak of revolution (1789–91); fled to Belgium at same time that Louis XVI tried to escape; lived with émigrés in Germany; proclaimed himself regent after death of Louis XVI (1793); took title of Louis XVIII after death of Louis XVII (1795); during Napoleonic regime (1796–1814) led life of constant wandering, living in Germany, Russia, Poland, and England, always engaged in royalist conspiracies; on Napoleon's downfall and restoration of Bourbons through Talleyrand-Périgord's efforts (Mar.–Apr., 1814), issued Declaration of Saint-Ouen, promising a constitution to France; entered Paris (May 2); fled to Ghent during Hundred Days (1815); again entered Paris (July 8, 1815); influenced by Élie Decazes, minister of police (1816–20); general policy prudent and sensible; during last years government controlled by Villèle and ultraroyalists. For "Louis XIX," see his nephew Louis, Duc d'ANGOULÊME. See also LOUIS PHILIPPE.

**Louis.** Name of three dauphins of France:

**Louis de France** (dẽ fräɴs′). *Called* **le Grand Dau′phin′** (lẽ gräɴ′ dō′făɴ′) *and* **Mon′sei′gneur′** (môɴ′sĕ′nyûr′). 1661–1711. Son of Louis XIV of France and Marie Thérèse. Retired to Château of Meudon; spent time in hunting; m. (1679) Marie Christine of Bavaria; given command by king of armies in Rhine campaign (1688) and in Flanders (1693); aided Villars in War of Spanish Succession (1709–10). Had three children: Louis, Duc de Bourgogne; Philip, Duke of Anjou, later Philip V of Spain; Charles, Duc de Berry.

**Louis.** Duc **de Bour′gogne′** (bo͝or′gôn′y′). 1682–1712. Son of Louis le Grand Dauphin, and father of Louis XV; b. in Versailles; educated by Fénelon, who composed for him *Télémaque* and *Fables;* became under his training a prince of exemplary character; m. (1697) Marie Adélaïde of Savoy; dauphin (1711–12); after death of his father (1711) took part in councils of king.

**Louis.** 1729–1765. Son of Louis XV and Maria Leszczyńska. Present at battle of Fontenoy (1745); m. as second wife (1747) Marie Josèphe of Saxony; pious, opposed to new ideas, friendly to Jesuits; had three sons, all of whom became kings of France: Louis XVI, Louis XVIII, and Charles X.

**Louis.** Name of three dukes of Anjou, claimants to throne of Naples:

**Louis I.** 1339–1384. Son of John II of France; count of Provence (1339–84) and titular king of Naples (1382–84). Fought at Poitiers (1356) and took part in war with England; supported by Antipope Clement VII, named as heir to throne of Naples (1380); regent of France (1380–82) for his nephew Charles VI; defeated by his rival Charles III of Durazzo (1384), king of Naples.

**Louis II.** 1377–1417. Son of Louis I; continued struggle for kingdom of Naples after death of father; unsuccessful and forced to retire to France; crowned as king by Clement VII (1389).

**Louis III.** 1403–1434. Son of Louis II and brother of René the Good; attempted to conquer Naples (1420).

**Louis.** Duc **d'Orléans.** 1372–1407. See ORLÉANS, 2; VALOIS, 2 and 3.

**Louis.** *Ger.* **Ludwig.** Name of kings of Germany:

**Louis I.** *Called* **the Pious.** = LOUIS I, Holy Roman Emperor.

**Louis II.** *Called* **the German.** *Ger.* **der Deut′sche** (dĕr doi′chĕ). 804?–876. Son of Louis I. King of Germany (843–876). On death of his father (840), joined with his brother Charles the Bald against Lothair and defeated him at Fontenoy (841). By Treaty of Verdun (843), became king of all Germany east of the Rhine; commonly regarded as the founder of the German kingdom. Fought successful war against Moravia (846–847). War with Charles the Bald (855–858) during attacks of Northmen. Divided kingdom among three sons (865).

**Louis III.** *Called* **the Child.** 893–911. Son of Arnulf. King of Germany (899–911); never crowned as emperor. His government administered by Archbishop Hatto of Mainz; country overrun by the Hungarians (900–910); last of the Carolingians in Germany. See CAROLINGIAN.

**Louis.** *Ger.* **Ludwig.** Name of Holy Roman emperors:

**Louis I.** *Called* **le Dé′bon′naire** (lē dā′bô′nâr′) *and* **le Pieux** (lē pyû′), *i.e.* the Pious. 778–840. King of France and of Germany (814–840) and emperor of the West (814–840; crowned 816). Third son of Charlemagne. Divided the Empire among his three sons (817) to take effect after his death; m. (819) as 2d wife Judith of Bavaria; son (born 823) became Charles the Bald. Reign marked by quarrels with sons and various changes in plans for succession. Civil War (838–840).

**Louis II.** 822?–875. King of Lorraine (872–875) and Holy Roman emperor (855–875). Became king of Italy (844). Son of Lothair I. Crowned by the pope as joint emperor (850) and succeeded his father as sole emperor (855). A weak ruler; the Empire declined rapidly.

**Louis III.** See LOUIS III, King of Germany.

**Louis IV** of Bavaria. 1287?–1347. King of Germany and Holy Roman emperor (1314–47; crowned 1328). Duke of Bavaria (1294–1347) of the Wittelsbach line. Opposed at election of king by Frederick, Duke of Austria; waged war with Frederick (1314–22) and made him prisoner at battle of Mühldorf (1322); in conflict with papacy; invaded Italy (1327–30), seized Rome, and set up antipope Nicholas V; at Diet of Rense (1338), electoral princes declared that emperor did not need papal confirmation.

**Louis.** 1763–1830. Grand duke of Baden (1818–30); son of Charles Frederick; half brother of Grand Duke Leopold; general in Prussian army; as ruler, inclined to absolutism.

**Louis.** Name of nine dukes of Bavaria, especially:

**Louis II.** *Called* **the Strict.** 1228–1294. Duke (1253–94); engaged in many wars; especially powerful in southern Germany; supported Rudolf of Hapsburg in his election to the imperial throne (1273); m. as third wife Rudolf's daughter Mathilde.

**Louis V.** 1315–1361. Duke (1347–61); also, margrave of Brandenburg (1323–51).

**Louis.** Name of three kings of modern Bavaria, of the Wittelsbach family (*q.v.*):

**Louis I.** 1786–1868. King (1825–48). Son of Elector (later king) Maximilian I Joseph; b. in Strasbourg. Patron of art and literature; erected many fine buildings; removed U. of Landshut to Munich; at time of revolution (1848) abdicated in favor of his son Maximilian II; caused scandal by his affair with Lola Montez (*q.v.*).

**Louis II.** 1845–1886. King (1864–86). Son of Maximilian II; b. in Nymphenburg. Supported Austria against Prussia (1866) and joined Prussia in Franco-Prussian War; brought Bavaria into German Empire (1871); patron of art and music, esp. of Richard Wagner; lavish in expenditures for new public buildings, creating great public debt; declared insane by his ministers; committed suicide by drowning three days later.

**Louis III.** 1845–1921. King (1913–18). Son of Prince Regent Luitpold; b. in Munich. Active in Bavarian military matters; m. (1868) Archduchess Maria Theresa of Austria-Este; made regent on death of his father (1912) and king on deposition of his cousin Otto (1913); abdicated (1918); last reigning king of house of Wittelsbach.

**Louis.** Name of six landgraves of Hesse-Darmstadt (*q.v.*), Louis V to Louis X. Louis X became grand duke (1806) as Louis I (*q.v.*).

**Louis.** *Ger.* **Ludwig.** Name of five grand dukes of **Hesse′–Darm′stadt** (hĕs′därm′stăt; -shtät):

**Louis I.** 1753–1830. Landgrave, as Louis X (1790–1806); received title of grand duke (1806); entered Confederation of the Rhine (1806); joined coalition against France (1813).

**Louis II.** 1777–1848. Son of Louis I; grand duke (1830–48). His son Prince Alexander (1823–1888) married (1851) morganatically Julia Teresa, Countess von Haucke, and received revived title of Battenberg (*q.v.*); his daughter Marie married (1841) the cesarevitch (later Czar Alexander II) and took the name Maria Alexandrovna.

**Louis III.** 1806–1877. Son of Louis II; grand duke (1848–77); sided with Austria against Prussia (1866).

**Louis IV.** 1837–1892. Nephew of Louis III; grand duke (1877–92); m. (1862) Alice Maud, 2d daughter of Victoria of England.

**Louis Ernest.** *Ger.* **Ludwig Ernst.** 1868–1937. Son of Louis IV; grand duke (1892–1918); lost throne when Hesse became a republic (1918); five of the six members of his family killed (Nov. 16, 1937) in airplane crash in Belgium a month after his death.

**Louis.** Name of four margraves of Thuringia of the 11th to 13th centuries.

**Louis.** *Hung.* **Lajos.** Name of two kings of Hungary:

**Louis I.** *Called* **the Great.** 1326–1382. King of Hungary (1342–82) and of Poland (1370–82); son of Charles I (*q.v.*); entered into long struggle with Venice (3 wars: 1342–46, 1357–58, 1378–81) for control of Adriatic coast; finally successful (treaty 1381); maintained friendly relations with Holy Roman emperor; appointed successor to Polish crown by Casimir III (1370), but union of two countries not a success. See JADWIGA and MARY of Anjou.

**Louis II.** 1506–1526. King of Hungary (1516–26); lost Belgrade to Turks (1521); killed at battle of Mohács. See MARY OF HUNGARY.

**Louis II.** Prince of Monaco. See MONACO.

**Louis.** *Port.* **Luis** *or* **Luiz.** 1838–1889. King of Portugal (1861–89). Son of Ferdinand II and Maria II da Gloria. Duke of Saxony and duke of Oporto during brother Pedro V's reign (1853–61); m. (1862) Maria Pia of Savoy, daughter of Victor Emmanuel of Italy; as king, attempted various reforms; freed slaves in Portuguese colonies (1868); reign progressive, but disturbed by political strife and many ministerial changes. See BRAGANZA.

**Lou′is** (lo͞o′ĭs), **Joe.** *Real name* **Joseph Louis Bar′row** (băr′ō). 1914– . American Negro pugilist, b. near Lafayette, Ala. Won world's heavyweight championship by defeating James J. Braddock (June, 1937).

**Louis Am′a·de′us** (lo͞o′ĭs [-ĭ] ăm′ȧ·dē′ŭs). = Duke of the ABRUZZI.

**Louis Bonaparte.** See BONAPARTE.

**Louis de Blois.** See BLOIS (the countship).

**Louis I** and **II de Bourbon.** See CONDÉ.

**Louis Frederick Christian.** *Usually called* **Louis Ferdinand.** 1772–1806. Prince of Prussia, son of Prince Augustus Ferdinand and nephew of Frederick the Great. German soldier; distinguished himself in campaigns (1792–95) against French; bitter opponent of

Napoleon; killed at Saalfeld. Devoted to music; a friend of Beethoven; himself a pianist and composer.

**Louis Henri Joseph de Bourbon.** See CONDÉ.

**Louis Joseph de Bourbon.** See CONDÉ.

**Louis Napoleon.** See NAPOLEON III.

**Louis of Anjou.** Name of three titular kings of Naples. See ANJOU, *Third house*, 4.

**Louis of Nas′sau** (*Angl.* năs′ô; *Ger.* näs′ou). 1538–1574. Count of Nassau-Dietz (-dēts); brother of William, Prince of Orange; a leader in revolt against Spain; defeated and killed by duke of Alva at Mookerheide.

**Louis Phi′lippe′** (lwē′ fē′lēp′; *Angl.* lōō′ĭ fĭ·lēp′). *Known as* **Citizen King.** *Fr.* **Roi ci′toy′en′** (rwä′ sē′twȧ′yăN′). 1773–1850. Eldest son of Louis Philippe Joseph (Philippe-Égalité), Duc d'Orléans; b. Paris. King of the French (1830–48); only sovereign of the Bourbon-Orléans line (see ORLÉANS). Duc de Valois (1773–85); duc de Chartres (1785–93); like his father, joined with revolutionists (1789); member of Jacobin Club (1790); colonel in revolutionary army, fought at Valmy and Jemappes (1792); under Dumouriez in Holland (1793); on death of father (1793), became duc d'Orléans. During Napoleonic regime (1796–1814) travelled in Scandinavia, lived in Philadelphia (1796–1800), and later in England and Sicily; m. (1809) Princess Maria Amelia, daughter of King Ferdinand IV of Naples. Returned to France (1814); after two years' exile (1815–17) at Twickenham, England, lived in France (1817–30), administering estates and great wealth. On July revolution (1830) against Charles X, proclaimed "citizen king" by Thiers and elected by deputies (Aug. 7); at first democratic and bourgeois, but fundamentally Bourbon; power weakened by gradual attempts to restore monarchy (see NAPOLEON III) and rise of Radical Socialist party; foreign policy unwise, especially in Spain; deserted by Liberals; overthrown by revolution (Feb., 1848); abdicated; escaped with wife to England; died at Claremont, London. Had eight children: (1) Ferdinand Philippe, Duc d'Orléans (1810–1842); see ORLÉANS; (2) Louise d'Orléans (1812–1850), wife of Leopold I of Belgium; see LEOPOLD I; (3) Marie (1813–1839), wife of Prince Frederick William Alexander of Württemberg; an artist, best known for her statue of Joan of Arc; (4) Louis Charles (1814–1896), Duke of Nemours; see NEMOURS; (5) Clémentine (1817–1907), wife of Prince Augustus of Saxe-Coburg; see ORLÉANS; (6) François Ferdinand (1818–1900), Prince de Joinville; see JOINVILLE; (7) Henri Eugène (1822–1897), Duc d'Aumale; see AUMALE; (8) Antoine Philippe (1824–1890), Duc de Montpensier; see MONTPENSIER.

**Louis Sal·va′tor** (săl·vā′tēr; -tôr; *Ger.* zäl·vä′tôr). 1847–1915. Archduke of Austria of Hapsburg-Lorraine line, b. at Florence. Son of Grand Duke Leopold II of Tuscany. Traveled extensively in Mediterranean regions and visited Asia, Africa, and America; wrote and illustrated (between 1885 and 1913) many descriptive works, esp. about Mediterranean islands and ports.

**Louis the Blind.** 880–?928 A.D. King of Provence (887–905). Grandson of Emperor Louis II and son of King Boso of Provence; by some listed as Louis III, Holy Roman emperor (901–905) in time of Louis the Child; contended with Berengar of Italy for imperial crown; defeated by him (905), captured, and blinded.

**Louis William I.** Margrave of **Ba′den-Ba′den** (bä′dĕn·bä′dĕn). 1655–1707. German soldier and military engineer, b. Paris. Fought against French (c. 1673–78), against the Turks with great distinction (1683–91); captured Heidelberg (1693); served under Marlborough in War of Spanish Succession; marshal (1704).

**Lou·i′sa Hen′ri·et′ta** (lōō·ē′zȧ hĕn′rĭ·ĕt′ȧ). *Ger.* **Luise Henriette.** 1627–1667. Electress of Brandenburg. Daughter of Frederick Henry, Prince of Orange; m. (1646) Elector Frederick William; their son Elector Frederick III later became king of Prussia as Frederick I. See house of PRUSSIA.

**Lou·i′sa Ul·ri′ca** (lōō·ē′zä ŏŏl·rē′kä). 1720–1782. Queen of Sweden (1751–71). Daughter of Frederick William I of Prussia and sister of Frederick the Great, b. Berlin; m. (1744) Adolphus Frederick, heir to Swedish throne; intelligent but domineering; exerted harmful influence over king; patron of literature and science; friend of Linnaeus.

**Lou·ise′ d'Or′lé′ans′** (lwēz′ dôr′lā′äN′). 1812–1850. Queen of Belgium. See LEOPOLD I of Belgium.

**Louise Marie Thérèse d'Artois.** Duchess of Parma (see BERRY family).

**Lou·ise′ of Meck′len·burg–Stre′litz** (lōō·ēz′ ŭv mĕk′lĕn·bŏŏrk·shtrā′lĭts; mā′klĕn-). *Full Ger. name* **Auguste Wilhelmine Amalie Luise.** 1776–1810. Queen of Prussia. Daughter of Duke Charles of Mecklenburg-Strelitz, b. Hanover; m. (1793) crown prince, later King Frederick William III. During Napoleonic Wars, became very popular because of her beauty, dignity, and beneficent acts, and esp. for her courage during years of national calamity; urged the king to resist and, after Prussian defeats at Jena and Eylau, made personal appeal to Napoleon, but without success. Order of Luise (Luisenorden) instituted by king in 1814.

**Lou·ise′ of Sa·voy′** (lōō·ēz′, sȧ·voi′). *Fr.* **Lou·ise′ de Sa′voie′** (lwēz′ dē sȧ′vwȧ′). 1476–1531. Regent of France; m. (1488) Charles, Count of Angoulême (d. 1496). Mother of Francis I of France and of Margaret of Navarre. Regent while Francis was on expeditions to Italy (1515 and 1524–26). With Margaret of Austria signed the treaty of Cambrai (1529), the Ladies' Peace (Paix des Dames).

**Loukaris, Kyrillos.** See Cyril LUCARIS.

**Louns′bur′y** (lounz′bĕr′ĭ; -bēr·ĭ), **Thomas Raynesford.** 1838–1915. American scholar and educator; professor of English, Yale (1871–1906). Author of a *History of the English Language* (1879), *Studies in Chaucer* (3 vols., 1892), *Shakespearean Wars* (3 vols., 1901–06), *The Standard of Pronunciation in English* (1904), *The Standard of Usage in English* (1908), *English Spelling and Spelling Reform* (1909), etc.

**Louth, Robert.** See LOWTH.

**Lou′ther′bourg′** (lōō′tĕr′bōōr′), **Philippe Jacques de.** 1740–1812. French landscape, marine, and battle painter in England. Settled in England (1771) on Garrick's invitation to superintend scene painting at Drury Lane; naturalized British subject. Known for battle scenes, including *Lord Howe's Victory off Ushant* (1794) and *Destruction of the Armada.*

**L'Ouverture, Toussaint.** See TOUSSAINT L'OUVERTURE.

**Lou′vet′ de Cou′vrai′** (lōō′vĕ′ dē kōō′vrā′), **Jean Baptiste.** 1760–1797. French revolutionary politician; member of the National Convention (1792); joined Girondists and attacked Robespierre (Oct. 29, 1792); fled Paris to escape the guillotine; returned (1795) and became member of the Council of Five Hundred. Author of *Aventures du Chevalier de Faublas* (1787–89).

**Lou′vois′** (lōō′vwȧ′), Marquis **de. François Michel Le Tel′lier′** (lē tĕ′lyā′). 1641–1691. French minister of war; succeeded his father, Michel Le Tellier (*q.v.*), as war minister (1666) under Louis XIV; organized French army (1668–72); after death of Colbert (1683) became chief adviser of king, but later lost his influence.

**Louÿs** (lwē), **Pierre.** 1870–1925. French man of letters; author of *Astarté* (collection of verse; 1891), *Les Chansons de Bilitis* (prose poems; 1894), *Aphrodite* (novel;

1896), *La Femme et le Pantin* (novel; 1898), *Sanguines* (stories; 1903), etc.

**Lovat,** Baron. See Simon FRASER (1667?–1747).

**Love'joy** (lŭv'joi), **Elijah Parish.** 1802–1837. American abolitionist; shot and killed by a mob (Nov. 7, 1837) in attempt to save his property; hence known as "the Martyr Abolitionist." His brother **Owen** (1811–1864) was Congregational clergyman; one of first to urge Abraham Lincoln to lead new party; member, U.S. Congress (1856–64) and supporter of Lincoln.

**Love'lace** (lŭv'lās), **Francis.** 1618?–1675. British royalist and colonial governor of New York and New Jersey (1668–73); allowed religious freedom, promoted trade; autocratic in refusal of representative government.

**Lovelace, Richard.** 1618–1658. English Cavalier lyric poet; devoted his fortune to royalist cause; imprisoned in Gatehouse at Westminster for presenting Kentish petition in king's favor (1642), wrote *To Althea from Prison;* prepared for press his *Lucasta: Epodes, Odes, Sonnets, Songs, etc.* (1649).

**Lov'ell** (lŭv'ĕl), Sir **Alfred Charles Bernard.** 1913– . British astronomer. At U. of Manchester (1945– ); specialist in radio astronomy.

**Lo·vén'** (lo͝o·vān'), **Sven Ludwig.** 1809–1895. Swedish zoologist; wrote on sea fauna, esp. polyps, worms, crustaceans, and on distribution of birds in the north.

**Lov'er** (lŭv'ẽr), **Samuel.** 1797–1868. Irish novelist, b. Dublin. Portrait painter, esp. a miniaturist, one of his best-known portraits being of Paganini; produced Irish songs, including *Rory O'More* (1826), *The Angel's Whisper, The Low-backed Car, Molly Bawn, Four-leaved Shamrock;* associated with Dickens in founding *Bentley's Miscellany.* Author of popular novels, including *Rory O'More, a National Romance* (1837; dramatized with **Tyrone** Power [1797–1841] in leading role), *Handy Andy* (1842).

**Lov'ett** (lŭv'ĕt; -ĭt), **Robert Abercrombie.** 1895– . American banker, b. Huntsville, Tex.; B.A., Yale (1918); banker (1921–40); secy. of defense (1951–53).

**Lovett, Robert Morss.** 1870–1956. American educator and author; at U. of Chicago (1893–1936). Author of *A History of English Literature* (1902) and *A First View of English Literature* (1905), both with W. V. Moody (*q.v.*); the novels *Gresham* (1904) and *A Winged Victory* (1907); *Cowards* (a play, 1914); *Preface to Fiction* (1930); and several anthologies.

**Lovett, Robert Scott.** 1860–1932. American lawyer and railroad executive; president, Union Pacific and Southern Pacific systems (1909–13); chairman of executive committee, Union Pacific system (1913–18). On staff of U.S. railway administrator (1918). President, Union Pacific system (1919–20), board chairman (1920–32).

**Low** (lō), **Benjamin Robbins Curtis.** 1880–1941. American lawyer and poet; author of *The Sailor Who Has Sailed* (1911), *Broken Music* (1920), *Winged Victory* (1927), *Off Soundings* (1932), *Turn of the Road* (1933).

**Low,** Sir **David Alexander Cecil.** 1891–1963. British cartoonist and caricaturist, b. New Zealand. On staff of *The Bulletin,* of Sydney, Australia (1911), the London *Star* (1919), and *Evening Standard* (1927). Famous for his political cartoons; created character Colonel Blimp. Cartoons collected in *Caricatures* (1915), *Lloyd George and Co.* (1922), *Low and I* (1923), *Low Again* (1938), *A Cartoon History of Our Times* (1939), *Europe Since Versailles* (1939), *Europe at War* (1940), *A Cartoon History of the War* (1941), etc.

**Low, Juliette,** *nee* **Gordon.** 1860–1927. Founder of Girl Scouts in America; organized first troop of Girl Guides at Savannah, Ga. (Mar. 9, 1912; name changed 1913, to Girl Scouts, and headquarters moved to New York City).

**Low, Mary,** *nee* **Fair'child** (fâr'chīld). 1858–1946. American figure, landscape, and portrait painter; m. (1888) Frederick MacMonnies and (1909) Will Hicok Low (*qq.v.*).

**Low, Maurice,** *in full* **Alfred Maurice.** 1860–1929. British journalist; author of *The American People, a Study in National Psychology* (1909), *Woodrow Wilson, an Interpretation* (1918), etc.

**Low, Seth.** 1850–1916. American merchant, politician, and educator, b. Brooklyn, N.Y. With his father's mercantile house (1870–87). Mayor of Brooklyn (1882–86). President, Columbia U. (1890–1901). Mayor of New York (1901–03). See H. C. POTTER.

**Low,** Sir **Sidney.** 1857–1932. English journalist and writer; editor of *St. James's Gazette* (1888–97). Among his books are *A Vision of India* (1906), *The Call of the East* (1921), *The British Constitution* (1928).

**Low, Will Hicok.** 1853–1932. American illustrator and painter, b. Albany, N.Y. Works include murals, stained-glass windows, and figure paintings. See Mary LOW.

**Low'den** (lou'd'n), **Frank Orren.** 1861–1943. American lawyer and politician; practiced law in Chicago (1887–1906). Member, U.S. House of Representatives (1906–11). Governor of Illinois (1917–21).

**Löwe.** Variant of LOEWE.

**Lowe** (lō), Sir **Hudson.** 1769–1844. British soldier and custodian of Napoleon; continuously active through Napoleonic wars; attached to Prussian army of Blücher, served with distinction. Governor of St. Helena, held strict vigilance against intrigues of Napoleon (1815–21), for which he was attacked by Barry Edward O'Meara, physician to Napoleon; military commander in Ceylon (1825–31).

**Lowe, Robert.** Viscount **Sher'brooke** (shûr'bro͝ok). 1811–1892. British political leader. Practiced law, Sydney, Australia (1842); member of legislative council, New South Wales (1843–50). Liberal M.P. (1852); vice-president of education board (1859–64); an Adullamite, helped to defeat Whig reform bill (1866). Gladstone's chancellor of exchequer (1868–73); home secretary (1873–74).

**Lowe, Thaddeus So'bi·es'ki** (sō'bĭ·ĕs'kĭ) **Constantine.** 1832–1913. American aeronaut and inventor; interested in ballooning (from 1856); chief of aeronautic section, U.S. army (from 1861). Reputed first to manufacture artificial ice in U.S. (1866). Invented and built apparatus for production of water gas (1873–75).

**Low'ell** (lō'ĕl), **Abbott Lawrence.** 1856–1943. (See John LOWELL, 1743–1802.) American political scientist and educator, b. Boston. Grad. Harvard (1877). Practiced law, Boston (1880–97). Professor of science of government, Harvard (1900–09). President of Harvard (1909–33). Author of *Governments and Parties in Continental Europe* (1896), *The Government of England* (1908), *Conflicts of Principle* (1932), etc.

**Lowell, Amy.** 1874–1925. (See John LOWELL, 1743–1802.) American poet and critic; interested herself in the Imagist school then developing in France and issued three yearly numbers (1915, 1916, 1917) of an anthology, *Some Imagist Poets;* wrote much in vers libre, which she preferred to call "unrhymed cadence"; experimented with polyphonic prose. Her volumes of verse include *A Dome of Many-Coloured Glass* (1912), *Sword Blades and Poppy Seed* (1914), *Men, Women, and Ghosts* (1916), *Can Grande's Castle* (1918), *Pictures of the Floating World* (1919), and, posthumously, *What's O'Clock* (1925), *East Wind* (1926), *Ballads for Sale* (1927). Her critical work includes *Six French Poets: Studies in Contemporary Literature* (1915), *Tendencies in Modern American Poetry* (1917), and the biography *John Keats* (2 vols., 1925).

Also published, with Mrs. Florence Ayscough, *Fir-Flower Tablets: Poems Translated from the Chinese* (1921).

**Lowell, Edward Jackson.** 1845–1894. (See John LOWELL, 1743–1802.) American historian, b. Boston. Author of *The Hessians...in the Revolutionary War* (1884), *The Eve of the French Revolution* (1892). His son **Guy** (1870–1927) was an architect; works include buildings at Harvard, Phillips Academy at Andover, Museum of Fine Arts in Boston.

**Lowell, Francis Cabot.** 1775–1817. (See John LOWELL, 1743–1802.) American industrialist, b. Newburyport, Mass. In mercantile business, Boston (1793–1810). With aid of Paul Moody, built at Waltham, Mass. (1812–14), first complete cotton spinning and weaving mill in U.S. Lowell, Mass., is named in his honor. His son **John** (1799–1836) inherited the business; bequeathed funds for establishment of Lowell Institute, providing free or low-cost lectures in various branches of human knowledge.

**Lowell, James Russell.** 1819–1891. (See John LOWELL, 1743–1802.) American poet, essayist, and diplomat, b. Cambridge, Mass. Grad. Harvard (1838), Harvard Law School (1840). Began career with *Poems* (1844), followed (1848) by *Poems, Second Series, A Fable for Critics, The Biglow Papers* and *The Vision of Sir Launfal.* Succeeded to Longfellow's chair at Harvard (1855–86). Editor, *Atlantic Monthly* (1857–61); associate of Charles Eliot Norton in editing *North American Review* (1864 ff.). U.S. minister to Spain (1877–80), Great Britain (1880–85). Elected to American Hall of Fame (1905). His works, in addition to those cited above, include: poetry, as *Commemoration Ode* (1865), *Under the Willows* (1869), *Three Memorial Poems* (1877), *Heartsease and Rue* (1888), and prose, as *Conversations on Some of the Old Poets* (1845), *Fireside Travels* (1864), *Among my Books* (1870; second series, 1876), *My Study Windows* (1871), *Democracy and Other Addresses* (1887), and *Political Essays* (1888), and *Letters of James Russell Lowell* (2 vols., 1893; edited by Charles Eliot Norton).

**Lowell, John.** 1743–1802. American jurist and legislator, b. Newburyport, Mass.; resident of Boston (from 1777). Member, Continental Congress (1782, 1783). U.S. judge, district of Massachusetts (1789–1801); chief judge, first circuit (1801). The following Lowells among his descendants are separately entered: his sons **John** (1769–1840) and **Francis Cabot**; his grandsons **John** (1799–1836; son of Francis) and **Robert Traill Spence** and **James Russell**; his great-grandsons **John** (1824–1897; grandson of John, 1769–1840) and **Edward Jackson** (grandson of Francis); and his great-great-grandchildren, **Percival, Abbott Lawrence** and **Amy** (great-grandchildren of John, 1769–1840) and **Guy** (see under Edward Jackson LOWELL).

**Lowell, John.** 1769–1840. (See John LOWELL, 1743–1802.) American lawyer; active in writing political pamphlets supporting Federalist policies (1806).

**Lowell, John.** 1799–1836. See Francis Cabot LOWELL.

**Lowell, John.** 1824–1897. (See John LOWELL, 1743–1802.) American jurist, b. Boston; expert in insolvency law; circuit judge (1878–84).

**Lowell, Josephine,** *nee* **Shaw.** 1843–1905. American philanthropist; m. Charles Russell Lowell (1863), a nephew of James Russell Lowell. Member, New York State Board of Charities (1876–89); founded *Charity Organization Society.*

**Lowell, Percival.** 1855–1916. (See John LOWELL, 1743–1802.) American astronomer; in business and traveling, chiefly in Japan (1877–93); author of *Chŏson—The Land of the Morning Calm* (1885), *Soul of the Far East* (1888), *Noto* (1891), and *Occult Japan* (1895). Built astronomical observatory on height near Flagstaff, Ariz. (1893–94). Best known for his studies of planet Mars and for mathematical work predicting the discovery of Planet X (discovered by C. W. Tombaugh, Jan., 1930, and named Pluto). Among his astronomical works are *Mars* (1895), *The Solar System* (1903), *Mars and Its Canals* (1906), *Mars as the Abode of Life* (1908), *The Evolution of Worlds* (1909), and *The Genesis of the Planets* (1916).

**Lowell, Robert Traill Spence.** 1816–1891. (See John LOWELL, 1743–1802.) American Protestant Episcopal clergyman; author of *The New Priest in Conception Bay* (1858), *Antony Brade, a Story of a School* (1874), *A Story of Two from an Old Dutch Town* (1878), and of *Poems* (1864), containing the well-known *Relief of Lucknow.*

**Lowell, Robert Traill Spence.** 1917–1977. American poet, b. Boston, Mass. Wrote *Lord Weary's Castle* (1946), *Life Studies* (1959), *Imitations* (1961), etc.

**Lö′wen·dal** (lû′vĕn·däl), Count **Ulrich Friedrich Waldemar von.** *French* Comte **Ulrich Frédéric Valdemar de Lo′wen′dahl′** (dẽ lô′văN′dȧl′). 1700–1755. German-born professional soldier, descended from the Danish royal house. In the Imperial service (1713), Danish (1714), Saxon (1716), Austrian (1717), and Russian (1736). Entered French service (1743); distinguished himself at Fontenoy, Oudenarde, and Nieuport (1746); captured Bergen op Zoom (1747) and was created marshal of France.

**Low′er** (?lō′ẽr), **Richard.** 1631–1691. English physician and physiologist; introduced operation of direct transfusion of blood from one animal into the veins of another.

**Lowes** (lōz), **John Livingston.** 1867–1945. American scholar and educator, b. Decatur, Ind. Grad. W. & J. (1888). Professor of English, Harvard (from 1918). Author of *Convention and Revolt in Poetry* (1919), *The Road to Xanadu* (1927), *The Art of Geoffrey Chaucer* (1931), *Geoffrey Chaucer and the Development of his Genius* (1934), *Essays in Appreciation* (1936), etc.

**Low′ie** (lō′ĭ), **Rob′ert** (rŏb′ẽrt) **Hein′rich** (hīn′rĭK), *known as* **Robert Harry.** 1883–1957. Austrian-born American ethnologist; to U.S. (1893); editor, *American Anthropologist* (1924–33). Authority on the American Indian.

**Low′in** (lō′ĭn), **John.** 1576–1659. English actor; joined king's company (1603); played with Shakespeare, Burbage, John Heming, Condell; acted in chief plays of Shakespeare, Jonson, Beaumont and Fletcher, and Massinger.

**Lowndes** (loundz), **Mrs. Belloc.** See Marie Adelaide BELLOC.

**Lowndes, Rawlins.** 1721–1800. American politician, b. in St. Kitts, British West Indies; to America (1730). Last president of South Carolina (1778–79); zealous opponent of the ratification of the Constitution. His son **William** (1782–1822) was a member of U.S. House of Representatives (1810–22); as chairman of ways and means committee, instrumental in forcing passage of tariff of 1816 recognizing the protective principle; nominated by South Carolina legislature for presidency of the U.S. (1821).

**Lowndes, William Thomas.** 1798–1843. English bookseller and bibliographer. Spent fourteen years compiling *The Bibliographer's Manual of English Literature* (4 vols., 1834), first systematic work of kind in England; left unfinished *The British Librarian* (1839–42).

**Lowth** *or* **Louth** (louth), **Robert.** 1710–1787. English bishop and scholar; professor of poetry at Oxford (1741–50); published his lectures *De Sacra Poesi Hebraeorum* (1753), pointing out parallelism as characteristic of Hebrew poetry, the beginning of modern literary study of Hebrew poetry, that is, of sacred poetry as poetry. Bishop of Oxford (1766–77), of London (1777); dean of Chapel Royal (1777). Author of a life of William of Wykeham (1758), an introduction to English grammar (1762), and a new translation of Isaiah (1778).

**Low'ther** (lou'thẽr). Name of an English family holding earldom of **Lons'dale** (lŏnz'dāl) and tracing descent from Hugh Lowther of Westmorland, attorney general of Edward I (1292), whose descendant Sir **Richard Lowther** (1529–1607) protected Mary, Queen of Scots, at Carlisle Castle (1568). From Sir Richard's eldest son were descended: Sir **Gerard Lowther** (1589–1660), chief justice of common pleas in Ireland (1634), who shifted from king's side to join parliament and became commissioner of great seal in Ireland (1654). Sir **John Lowther** (1655–1700), 1st Viscount Lonsdale (cr. 1696), barrister; M.P. (1676); first lord of treasury (1690–92); lord privy seal (1699–1700). Sir John's great-grandson **James Lowther** (1736–1802), 1st Earl of Lonsdale (cr. 1784) and Viscount Lowther (cr. 1797); exercised great influence in parliamentary elections in north of England (1757–84), usually controlling nine seats in House of Commons. His third cousin **William Lowther** (1757–1844), 2d Earl of Lonsdale (United Kingdom) of second creation (1807); patron of Wordsworth. **William Lowther** (1787–1872), 3d earl, eldest son of 1st earl; M.A., Cantab. (1808); M.P. (1808–41); first commissioner of woods and forests (1828); president of Board of Trade (1834–35); postmaster general (1841); president of council (1852). **James Lowther** (1840–1904), grandnephew of 2d earl; M.A., Cantab. (1866); Conservative M.P. (from 1865); secretary to poor law board (1867–68); undersecretary for colonies (1874–78); chief secretary to lord lieutenant of Ireland (1878–80); breeder of race horses (from 1873). **James William Lowther** (1855–1949), 1st Viscount **Ulls'wa'ter** [ŭlz'wô'tẽr; -wŏt'ẽr] (cr. 1921); educ. King's Coll., London, and Cambridge; represented Penrith in House of Commons (1886–1921); undersecretary for foreign affairs (1891); deputy speaker (1895–1905), speaker of House of Commons (1905–21); chairman of Speakers' Electoral Reform Conference (1916–17), which paved way for extension of franchise and granting of vote to women; chairman of devolution conference (1919), and of commission on London government (1921–22); chairman of Lords and Commons committee on electoral reform (1929–30). **Hugh Cecil Lowther** (1857–1944), 5th earl, Cumberland landowner and sportsman, son of 3d earl; m. daughter of 10th marquis of Huntly; mayor of Whitehaven (1894–96); lord lieutenant of Cumberland and custos rotulorum (1917); founded the Lonsdale championship belt for boxing.

**Loyd, Samuel Jones.** See Baron OVERSTONE.

**Loyd–Lindsay, Robert James.** See Baron WANTAGE.

**Loy·o'la** (*Angl.* loi·ō'lȧ), Saint **Ignatius of.** *Real name* **Íñigo de O·ñez' y Lo·yo'la** (thā ō·nyāth' ē lō·yō'lä). *The name* **Íñigo Ló'pez de Re·cal'de** (lō'pāth thā rā·käl'dā) *is probably a copyist's error.* 1491–1556. Spanish soldier and ecclesiastic, b. in castle of Loyola, Guipúzcoa; founder of the Society of Jesus, known as the Jesuit order. Page at court of Ferdinand V; in military service of duke of Najera (1517–21); wounded (1521) at siege of Pampeluna (now Pamplona); during convalescence, read religious books and resolved to devote himself to the Church. Renounced military career (1522); lived as ascetic; made pilgrimage barefoot to Jerusalem (1523–24). Began education in grammar school (1524); studied at universities of Alcalá and Salamanca (1526–27) and Paris (1528 ff.). While in Paris, planned (1534) a new religious order, to be known as the Society (or Company) of Jesus, devoted to conversion of infidels and to counteraction against the Protestant Reformation; obtained approbation of proposed order in papal bull (Sept. 27, 1540), and became its first superior, or general (1541–56). Author of *Constitutions of the Order* and *Spiritual Exercises*. Canonized by Gregory XV (1622). See Saint Francis XAVIER.

**Loy'son'** (lwȧ'zôɴ'), **Charles.** *Known as* Père **Hya'cinthe'** (pâr yȧ'sănt'). 1827–1912. French priest; ordained in Roman Catholic Church (1851); excommunicated for heterodoxy (1869). Married (1872); although excommunicated, continued to profess his Catholic faith; after being pastor of a liberal Catholic church in Geneva (1873–74), became rector of Gallican Catholic Church in Paris (1879). Author of *La Famille* (1867), *Mon Testament, ma Protestation* (1893), *Christianisme et Islamisme* (1895).

**Lub'be** (lûb'ĕ), **Marinus van der.** 1910–1934. Dutch brick mason and ex-Communist; convicted of high treason for alleged implication in the burning of the German Reichstag building (Feb. 27, 1933); guillotined at Leipzig (Jan. 10, 1934).

**Lub'bock** (lŭb'ŭk), Sir **John William.** 1803–1865. English astronomer and mathematician. Grad. Cambridge (1825). Partner in father's bank. Contributed papers to Royal Astronomical Society; found ways to simplify methods of physical astronomy; gave uniform method for calculation of cometary and planetary orbits (1829); supplementing Laplace, demonstrated stability of solar system; claimed to have reduced tabular errors of moon below those of observation; aided establishment of British Almanac (1827). Author of *An Elementary Treatise on Computation of Eclipses and Occultations* (1835), *On the Theory of the Moon and the Perturbations of the Planets* (1833–61), and *Elementary Treatise on the Tides* (1839).

His son Sir **John Lubbock** (1834–1913), 1st Baron **Ave'bur·y** (āv'bẽr·ĭ; ā'bẽr·ĭ), b. London. From Eton, entered father's banking house at fourteen; partner (1856). Liberal M.P. (1870); instrumental in carrying several banking reforms through Parliament, also measures dealing with shop hours regulation, public libraries, and ancient monuments. Vice-chancellor for London U. (1872–80); president, London Chamber of Commerce (1890–92), and chairman, London County Council. Known best as writer of popular science books, esp. in archaeology and entomology, including *Prehistoric Times*, long used as textbook on archaeology (1865), *The Origin of Civilization and the Primitive Condition of Man* (1870), *Origin and Metamorphoses of Insects* (1874), *British Wild-flowers Considered in Relation to Insects* (1875), *Ants, Bees, and Wasps* (1882), *Senses, Instincts, and Intelligence of Animals* (1888); author also of ethical works, as *Pleasures of Life* (1887–89), *Use of Life* (1894), *Marriage, Totemism, and Religion* (1911).

**Basil Lubbock** (1876–1944), a grandson of Sir J. W. Lubbock; writer of books on ships, as *The China Clippers* (1914), *Western Ocean Packets* (1925), *The Nitrate Clippers* (1932), *The Arctic Whalers* (1937).

**Percy Lubbock** (1879–1965), another grandson of Sir J. W. Lubbock; critic and essayist; author of *The Craft of Fiction*, study of the technique of the novel (1921), *Earlham* (1922), *Shades of Eton* (1929); m. (1926) younger daughter of 5th earl of Desart, Lady **Sybil Marjorie Cuffe** [kŭf] (1879–1943), novelist, editor of her father's memoirs (1936), and author of *A Book of the Sea* (1918), *Four Tales by Zélide* (1925), *Child in the Crystal* (1939).

**Lu'bin** (lōō'bĭn), **David.** 1849–1919. Agriculturist, b. Klodowa, Russian Poland; to U.S. (1855). Successful in dry-goods business, Sacramento, Calif. (1874–84). Engaged in fruitgrowing (1884); interested himself in national agricultural problems; organized fruitgrowers; advocated equalization of protection between industry and agriculture; advocated and finally obtained an international institute of agriculture (1910), planned to make available to agriculturists in all countries information which would enable them to adopt intelligent and progressive policies.

**Lu'bin** (lū'bĭn), **Isador.** 1896–1978. American economist, b. Worcester, Mass.; special expert to War Industries Board (1918–19); U. S. commissioner of labor statistics (1933–46); deputy director, labor division, Office of Production Management (1940–41); statistical asst. to the president (1941–45).

**Lu'bitsch** (lōō'bĭch), **Ernst** (ĕrnst; *Angl.* ûrnst). 1892–1947. Motion-picture director, b. Berlin, Ger.; to U.S. (1922) to direct Mary Pickford. Associated successively with Warner Bros., Metro-Goldwyn-Mayer, and Famous-Players-Lasky Corp. Directed *Passion, Lady Windermere's Fan, Old Heidelberg, Design for Living, Merry Widow, Bluebeard's Eighth Wife, Ninotchka.*

**Lüb'ke** (lüp'kĕ), **Wilhelm.** 1826–1893. German art scholar; chief work, *Grundriss der Kunstgeschichte* (1860), *Geschichte der Renaissance in Deutschland* (1873), etc.

**Lübke, Wilhelm Meyer–.** See MEYER-LÜBKE.

**Lu·bli'ner** (lōō·blē'nēr), **Hugo.** *Pseudonym* **Hugo Bür'ger** (bür'gēr). 1846–1911. German writer.

**Lu'bo·mir'ski** (lōō'bô·mēr'skē). Polish princely family from the early 17th century, including: **Stanisław Szre·nia'wa** [shrĕ·nyä'vä] (1583–1641); defeated the Turks at Choczin (1621). **Jerzy Sebastyan** (1616–1667); won the battle of Cudnow (1660) and later headed a rebellion against King John Casimir. **Stanisław III** (1704–1793), one of the leaders of the patriot party during the partitions of Poland. Prince **Kazimierz Lubomirski** (1863?–1930), first minister from Poland to U.S. (1919), was a member of this same family.

**Lu·bow'ski** (lōō·bôf'skē), **Edward.** 1839–1923. Polish writer, esp. of social comedies and novels.

**Luca, Giuseppe De.** See Giuseppe DE LUCA.

**Luca d'Olanda.** See LUCAS VAN LEYDEN.

**Lucan,** Earl of. See George Charles BINGHAM.

**Lucan,** Titular earl of. See Patrick SARSFIELD.

**Lu'can** (lū'kăn). *Full Latin name* **Marcus Annaeus Lu·ca'nus** (lū·kā'nŭs). 39–65 A.D. Roman poet, b. at Cordova in Spain; educ. in Rome. For a time enjoyed Nero's favor, losing it as his literary reputation grew, until the jealous Nero forbade his public recitals; joined conspiracy of Piso (*q.v.*) against Nero, was betrayed. His sole extant work is an epic, *Pharsalia* (10 books), about the civil war between Caesar and Pompey.

**Lu'ca·ris** *or* **Lu'ka·ris** (lōō'kȧ·rĭs), **Cyril.** *Greek* **Kyrillos Lou'ka·ris** (lōō'kä·rēs). 1572?–1638. Prelate of Greek Church; patriarch of Constantinople (1621). Sent to England (1628) the Codex Alexandrinus, 5th-century manuscript containing third oldest Bible extant. Suspected of Protestantism by his enemies.

**Lu'cas** (lū'kăs), **Albert Pike.** 1861?–1945. American landscape, portrait, and figure painter, and sculptor.

**Lucas, Edward Verrall.** 1868–1938. English publisher and writer. On staff of London *Globe* (1893–1900), *Academy* (1896–1901), and *Punch;* chairman of Methuen & Co., publishers. Author of *The Open Road* (1899), *Highways and Byways in Sussex* (1904), *Character and Comedy* (1907), *Over Bemerton's* (novel; 1908), *Mr. Ingleside* (novel; 1910), *Old Lamps for New* (1911), *London Lavender* (1912), *The King's Visit* (play; 1912), *Landmarks* (1914), *Genevra's Money* (1922), *The Same Star* (1924), *The More I See of Men* (1927), *Pleasure Trove* (1935). Editor of *Letters of Charles and Mary Lamb* (1935).

**Lucas, Frank Laurence.** 1894–1967. English educator and man of letters; author of *The River Flows* (novel), *Cécile* (novel), *The Wild Tulip* (novel), *Poems* (1935), *The Bear Dances* (play; 1932), *Land's End* (play; 1938), *A Journal under the Terror* (1938), etc.

**Lucas, Frederic Augustus.** 1852–1929. American naturalist; osteologist, U.S. National Museum (1882–1904); director, American Museum of Natural History (1911–29). Author of *Animals of the Past* (1901), *Animals before Man in America* (1902), etc.

**Lucas, John Seymour.** 1849–1923. English painter; best known for historical paintings.

**Lucas, St. John Welles.** 1879–1934. English man of letters; author of *Poems* (1904), *Quicksilver and Flame* (1906), *Saints, Sinners, and the Usual People* (1912), *April Folly* (1916), *Certain Persons* (1922).

**Lu'cas van Ley'den** (lü'käs vän lī'dĕn). *Real name* **Lucas Hu'gensz** (hü'gĕns). *Ital. name* **Luca d'O·lan'da** (dô·län'dä). *Also known as* **Lucas Ja'cobsz** (yä'kŏps). 1494–1533. Dutch painter and engraver. Precocious artist; said to have painted *The History of St. Hubert* in water colors at age of 12; known to have engraved large plate *Mahomet* at age of 14, and the plate *Ecce Homo* at age of 16. Among his notable canvases are *Healing of the Blind Man, Virgin with Saints, The Last Judgment;* among his plates, *Conversion of St. Paul, Crucifixion, Abraham Dismissing Hagar.*

**Luc'ca** (lŏŏk'ä; lōōk'kä), **Pauline.** 1841–1908. Austrian operatic soprano, of Italian descent; m. Baron Rahden (1865; divorced) and Emil von Wallhofen (d. 1899). Sang on tour in U.S. (1872–74).

**Luc'che·si'ni** (lōōk'kā·sē'nē), Marchese **Girolamo.** 1751–1825. Italian-born diplomat in the Prussian service; ambassador in Vienna (1793–97), Paris (1802); dismissed after the battle of Jena (1806). Chief chamberlain at the court of Elisa Buonaparte. Grand Duchess of Tuscany (from 1806).

**Luce** (lūs), **Henry Robinson.** 1898–1967. American editor and publisher, b. in Shantung Province, China, of American parentage. A founder (1923), editor, and publisher of weekly magazine *Time;* also, of monthly magazine *Fortune* (1930). Established *Life,* a weekly picture magazine (1936). See Clare BOOTHE.

**Luce, John.** 1870–1932. British naval officer; admiral, commanding H.M.S. *Glasgow* in actions during World War off Coronel (Nov. 1, 1914), Falkland Islands (Dec. 8, 1914), and Juan Fernández (Mar. 14, 1915). On retired list (from 1925).

**Luce** (lüs), **Siméon Auguste.** 1833–1892. French scholar; student esp. of French history of the 14th and 15th centuries.

**Luce** (lūs), **Stephen Bleecker.** 1827–1917. American naval officer; author of textbook *Seamanship* (1863). Advocated and obtained (1884) establishment of Naval War College for postgraduate training of naval officers; became its first president. Rear admiral (1886); retired (1889).

**Lucera,** Duke of. See Matthias GALLAS.

**Lu'chaire'** (lü'shâr'), **Achille.** 1846–1908. French historian; specialized in study of 13th-century France and of the Capetians.

**Luchana,** Count. See Baldomero ESPARTERO.

**Lu'cian** (lū'shăn). Greek satirist and wit of 2d century A.D., b. at Samosata in Syria; regarded as most brilliant writer of the revived Greek literature under the Roman Empire. Among the most notable of his many works are *Dialogues of the Gods, Dialogues of the Dead, Banquet of Philosophers, Demonax, Auction of Philosophers.*

**Lucian.** *Known as* **Lucian of Antioch** *and* **Lucian the Martyr.** 240?–312. Christian martyr, b. at Samosata in Syria; presbyter of Antioch; renowned as a theologian; martyred at Nicomedia in Bithynia.

**Luciani, Sebastiano.** See SEBASTIANO DEL PIOMBO.

**Lucien Bonaparte.** See BONAPARTE.

**Lu'ci·fer** (lū'sĭ·fẽr). d. 371? Sardinian prelate; bishop of Cagliari; known esp. for his vehement opposition to Arianism; defended Athanasius at council of Milan; exiled by Emperor Constantius II (355); formed schismatic sect called Luciferians (363) to combat return of Arian bishops to former rank in orthodox church.

**Lu·cil'i·us** (lů·sĭl'ĭ·ŭs), **Gaius.** Latin satirical poet of 2d century B.C.; regarded as originator of the form of satirical composition later perfected by Horace, Persius, and Juvenal. Only fragments of his works are extant.

**Lu·cio'ni** (lōō·chō'nē), **Luigi.** 1900– . Painter, b. Malnate, Italy; to U.S. (1911) and settled in Jersey City; naturalized (1922). Studio in New York City and in Vermont; known for his New England landscapes.

**Lu'ci·us** (lū'shĭ·ŭs; -shŭs). Name of three popes. See *Table of Popes*, Nos. 22, 166, 171.

**Luck'ner** (lŏŏk'nẽr), Count **Felix von.** 1881–1966. German sailor; served in German navy in World War; engaged in battle of Jutland. Made a world tour (1937–39) in his yacht, *The Sea Devil.* Author of *Der See-Teufel* and *Der See-Teufel Erobert Amerika.*

**Luck'ner'** (lük'nâr'), **Nicolas.** 1722–1794. French soldier, b. in the Palatinate; lieutenant general (1763); marshal of France (1791). Commanded army of the north, invading Belgium (1792); failed to follow up early successes; arrested and guillotined.

**Lu·cre'ti·a** (lů·krē'shĭ·ȧ; -shȧ). *Eng.* **Lu·crece'** (lů·krēs'; lū'krēs). Virtuous wife of Lucius Tarquinius Collatinus; raped by Tarquinius Sextus; killed herself; legend told in Shakespeare's *Rape of Lucrece.*

**Lu·cre'ti·us** (lů·krē'shĭ·ŭs; -shŭs). *In full* **Titus Lucretius Car'us** (kâr'ŭs; kā'rŭs). 96?–55 B.C. Roman philosophical poet; a disciple of Epicurus; committed suicide, according to tradition, in a fit of madness caused by a love philter given to him by his wife. His great work is the *De Rerum Natura* (6 books), a didactic and philosophical poem treating of physics, psychology, and ethics according to the Epicurean doctrine.

**Lu·cul'lus** (lů·kŭl'ŭs), **Lucius Licinius.** Roman general, patron of learning, and epicure. Curule aedile (79 B.C.); consul (74). Campaigned in Asia Minor and defeated Mithridates (74–71) and Tigranes (69). In Rome (from 66), lived in great luxury and established reputation by the splendor of his banquets and the magnificence of his surroundings; enjoyed the company of the leading poets, artists, and philosophers of his time.

**Lucusta.** = LOCUSTA.

**Lu'cy** (lū'sĭ), Sir **Henry.** 1845–1924. British journalist, on staff of Shrewsbury *Chronicle* (1864), London *Pall Mall Gazette* (1870), London *Daily News* (1873); editor of the *Daily News* (1886–87). Began writing for *Punch* (1881), under the pseudonym **To'by, M.P.** (tō'bĭ), presenting humorous and satirical articles on contemporary politics; continued with *Punch* (1881–1916). Published *Men and Manners in Parliament* (1875), *Gideon Fleyce* (novel; 1882), *Peeps at Parliament* (1903), *Memories of Eight Parliaments* (1908), *The Diary of a Journalist* (3 vols., 1920, 1922, 1923), etc.

**Lucy,** Sir **Thomas.** 1532–1600. English Warwickshire squire; justice of peace; according to story told by Nicholas Rowe (1710), prosecuted Shakespeare for stealing deer from Charlecote Park (1585); reputedly caricatured by Shakespeare as Justice Shallow.

**Lud** *or* **Ludd** (lŭd), **Ned.** fl. 1779. A half-witted Leicestershire workman who, about 1779, broke up stocking frames; riots that occurred some years later (1811–16) when workmen broke up labor-saving machinery were called "Luddite riots," and men who took part in them were known as "Luddites."

**Lu'den** (lōō'dĕn), **Heinrich.** 1780–1847. German historian; chief work, *Die Geschichte des Deutschen Volkes* (to 1237; 12 vols., 1825–37).

**Lu'den·dorff** (lōō'dĕn·dôrf), **Erich Friedrich Wilhelm.** 1865–1937. German general and politician. At outbreak of World War (1914), was appointed a quartermaster general; worked with Hindenburg; responsible with him for defeat of Russia, and alone the cause of collapse of Serbians and Rumanians and defeat of Italy at Caporetto (1917); his plan of campaign (1918) on the Western Front almost successful in crushing Allies; after German defeat, fled to Sweden fearing accusations. Returned to live at Munich (1919); took part in reactionary conspiracies, such as the Kapp Putsch (1920) and the Hitler Beer Hall Putsch (1923); in last years almost fanatical in his ideas and actions: accused Hindenburg, led crusades against Jews, Catholics, Masons, and Protestants, supported Hitler and then deserted him; later became a pacifist. Author of several works on World War.

**Lü'ders** (lü'dyẽrs), Count **Aleksandr Nikolaevich.** 1790–1874. Russian general; commanded army in the Crimea (1856); governor of Poland (1861–62).

**Lud'low** (lŭd'lō), **Edmund.** 1617?–1692. English Parliamentary leader and regicide. M.P. (1646); one of chief promoters of Pride's Purge (1648); one of king's judges, signed death warrant. Member of Council of State (1649, 1650). Practically completed subjugation of Ireland; arrested on refusal to acknowledge Cromwell as Protector, but allowed to retire to Essex; on recall of Long Parliament (1659) member of committee of safety and of council of state and commander in chief in Ireland; impeached by restored parliament, escaped to Vevey, Switzerland, where he wrote *Memoirs* (1698–99).

**Ludlow, John Malcolm Forbes.** 1821–1911. English social reformer; one of founders of Christian Socialist movement; founder and editor of *Christian Socialist* (1850).

**Ludlow, Roger.** 1590–?1664. English pioneer in America, b. in Wiltshire, Eng.; to America (1630) as an assistant of Massachusetts Bay Company. A founder of Dorchester, Mass.; deputy governor of Massachusetts (1634). Moved to Windsor, Conn., and presided (1636) over first court held in Connecticut. Reputed to have drafted Fundamental Orders, which remained basis of Connecticut government till 1818. Collected and codified Connecticut laws in *The Code of 1650*, known as *Ludlow's Code.* First settler, Fairfield, Conn. (1639); magistrate of Connecticut colony (1639–54). Returned to England (1654).

**Lud·mil'la** (lōōt·mĭl'ä) *or* **Lud·mi'la** (-mē'lä), Saint. d. 921. Patron saint of Bohemia; first Christian duchess of the country.

**Lu'dolf** (lōō'dôlf), **Hiob.** 1624–1704. German Oriental scholar; regarded as founder of Abyssinian philology.

**Lud'wich** (lōōt'vĭκ; lōōd'-), **Artur.** 1840–1920. German classical scholar, esp. in field of Homeric literature.

**Lud'wig** (lōōt'vĭκ; lōōd'-). German form of LOUIS.

**Ludwig, Alfred.** 1832–1912. Austrian Sanskrit scholar.

**Ludwig, Carl Friedrich Wilhelm.** 1816–1895. German physiologist; one of the founders of nonvitalistic physiology in Germany. Developed graphic methods, using the kymograph to study blood pressure and the circulation of blood; demonstrated the influence of nerves on the distribution of blood and on the secretion of glands; determined the composition of blood.

**Ludwig, Emil.** *Orig. surname* **Cohn** (kōn). 1881–1948. German writer, esp. known as a biographer. Name legally changed to Ludwig (1883). Among his earlier works are a number of plays (*Napoleon*, 1906; *Friedrich von Preussen*, 1914; a trilogy entitled *Bismarck*, 1923), novels (*Manfred und Helene*, 1911; *Diana*, 1918), and essays. Among his notable biographies are *Goethe* (1920), *Napoleon* (1924), *Wilhelm II* (1925), *Der Menschensohn* (1928), *Lincoln*, *Roosevelt*, *Three Titans* (*Michelangelo*, *Rembrandt*, and *Beethoven*), *Bolivar*, *Beethoven* (1943). Also wrote *The Nile* (1939), *The Germans* (1941), *The Mediterranean* (1942), etc.

**Ludwig, Otto.** 1813–1865. German writer; author of an opera *Die Köhlerin*, the tragedies *Der Erbförster* (1850), *Die Makkabäer* (1854), the novel *Zwischen Himmel und Erde* (1856).

**Luf′ber·y** (lŭf′bẽr·ĭ; -bĕr′ĭ), **Ra′oul′** (rȧ′o͞ol′) **Ger′vais′** (zhĕr′vĕ′) **Vic′tor** (vĭk′tẽr; *Fr.* vēk′tôr′). 1885–1918. Aviator in World War; b. Clermont, France, of American father and French mother. Member of Escadrille Lafayette (1916–18); credited with seventeen victories in air combat; commissioned major in U.S. air service (Jan. 10, 1918); killed in combat (May 19, 1918).

**Lufft** (lo͝oft), **Hans.** 1495–1584. Early German printer; known as "the Bible Printer," because at Wittenberg he printed the first complete edition of Luther's Bible.

**Lu·gard′** (lo͞o·gärd′), **Frederick Dealtry.** 1st Baron **Lugard.** 1858–1945. British soldier and colonial administrator; served in Afghan War (1879–80), Sudan campaign (1885), Burma campaign (1886–87); commanded West African frontier force, with rank of brigadier general (1897–99). High commissioner and commander in chief of Northern Nigeria (1900–06); governor of Hong Kong (1907–12); governor of Northern and Southern Nigeria (1912–13); governor general of Nigeria (1914–19).

**Lu′han** (lo͞o′hän), **Mabel,** *nee* **Gan′son** (găn′s′n). *Known as* **Mabel Dodge Luhan.** 1879–1962. American writer, b. Buffalo, N.Y.; m. Carl Evans (1900), Edwin Dodge (1903), Maurice Sterne (1916), Antonio Luhan (1923). Author of *Lorenzo in Taos* (1932), and an autobiographical series under general title *Intimate Memories.*

**Lu·i′ni** (lo͞o·ē′nē) *or* **Lu·vi′ni** (lo͞o·vē′nē), **Bernardino.** c. 1475–c. 1532. Italian painter of Lombard school; excelled in religious frescoes; among his other works are *Beheading of John the Baptist* (in the Uffizi), *Jesus among the Doctors* (in National Gallery, London), *Herodias* (in the Louvre), *Birth of Christ* (in Berlin).

**Luis.** Portuguese form of LOUIS.

**Luis de Granada.** See GRANADA.

**Lui′sa de Guz·mán′** (*Port.* lwē′zȧ thĕ go͞ozh·mäN′; *Span.* lwē′sä thä go͞oth·män′). 1613–1666. Queen of Portugal (1640–56). Daughter of 8th duke of Medina-Sidonia; m. (1633) John, Duke of Braganza, later John IV, King of Portugal; acted as regent for her son Alfonso VI but forced to resign (1662); retired to convent.

**Luise.** See also LOUISA and LOUISE.

**Lu′it·pold** (lo͞o′ĭt·pôlt). Old High German for LEOPOLD.

**Luitpold I.** Margrave of Austria. See BABENBERG.

**Luitpold** *or* **Leopold.** *In full* **Charles Joseph William Louis Leopold.** 1821–1912. Prince regent of Bavaria (1886–1912), b. Würzburg. Second son of Louis I and uncle of Louis II and Otto; m. (1844) Princess Augusta of Tuscany. Officer in Bavarian army (1866–86); chosen (1886) regent of Bavaria for Otto during his entire reign, because of Otto's insanity; succeeded by his son Louis III.

**Luitprand.** See LIUTPRAND.

**Luiz.** Portuguese form of LOUIS.

**Luiz** (lwēs), **Washington.** *Full name* **Washington Luiz Pe·rei′ra de Sou′za** (pĕ·rā′rȧ thĕ sō′zȧ). 1869–1957. Brazilian statesman; prefect of São Paulo (1914–19); governor of São Paulo state (1920–24); senator in National Congress from São Paulo (1924–26). President of Brazil (1926–30); tried with little success to improve finances; faced with difficulties in valorizing coffee during world depression; deposed by revolution led by Vargas in Rio Grande do Sul; to Europe as exile.

**Lukaris.** See LUCARIS.

**Lu′kas** (*Angl.* lo͞o′kȧs), **Paul.** 1895–1971. Hungarian-born actor in U.S., both on the legitimate stage and in motion pictures, including *Watch on the Rhine* (1943).

**Luke** (lūk), Saint. The Evangelist; a physician (*Col.* iv. 14), and companion of St. Paul (*Philemon* 24; *2 Tim.* iv. 11), traditionally regarded as author of the third Gospel and the *Acts of the Apostles* in the New Testament.

**Luke′man** (lūk′măn), **Augustus,** *in full* **Henry Augustus.** 1871–1935. American sculptor; among his many notable works are: statues of William McKinley (Dayton, Ohio), Francis Asbury (Washington, D.C.), and Jefferson Davis (for Statuary Hall, Washington, D.C.), and monument to women of the Confederacy (Raleigh, N.C.).

**Lu′kin** (lū′kĭn), **Lionel.** 1742–1834. English coachbuilder and inventor of an "unsubmergible" boat, according to the patent (Nov., 1785) fitted beneath the gunwale with airtight and watertight projections of cork or hollow chambers.

**Luks** (?lŭks), **George Benjamin.** 1867–1933. American painter; staff artist on Philadelphia *Press* and Philadelphia *Bulletin.* Originator of comic strip *The Yellow Kid*, in New York *World.* Among his many notable canvases are: *The Wrestlers*, *Little Madonna*, *Woman and Black Cat*, *Ducks*, *Morris Canal*, *The Breaker Boys*, *Tango Artist.*

**Lull** (lŭl), **Richard Swann.** 1867–1957. American paleontologist; professor, Yale (from 1911) and director of Peabody Museum (1922–36). Author of *Organic Evolution*, *The Ways of Life*, etc.

**Lul′ly′** (lü′lē′), **Jean Baptiste.** *Ital.* **Giovanni Battista Lul′li** (lo͞ol′lē). 1632–1687. French composer, b. in Florence, Italy; called founder of national French opera. Member of corps of 24 violins attached to service of Louis XIV, whose favor he won; court composer (1653) and superintendent of court music; wrote masques and ballets in which he and Louis XIV himself took part; head of Académie Royale de Musique, now the Grand Opéra (1672–87); became naturalized French citizen and one of king's secretaries (1681). Developed French form of the overture; introduced lively ballets, varied rhythms, simplicity and directness of expression in his operas. Composed operas, with Quinault as librettist, including *Alceste* (1674), *Thésée* (1675), *Atys* (1676), *Proserpine* (1680), *Persée* (1682), and *Armide et Renaud* (1686); also several pastorali, many ballets and masques, church music, the song *Au Clair de la Lune*, etc.

**Lul′ly** (lŭl′ĭ), **Raymond.** *Angl. form of Catalan* **Ramón Lull** (lo͞ol). *Span.* **Raimundo Lu′lio** (lo͞o′lyō). *Lat.* **Raimundus Lul′lus** (lŭl′ŭs). *Fr.* **Raimond Lulle** (lül). *Known as* **Doc′tor Il·lu′mi·na′tus** (dŏk′tẽr [-tôr] ĭ·lū′mĭ·nā′tŭs). 1235?–1315. Catalan ecclesiastic and scholastic philosopher, b. in the Balearic Islands. Converted to the religious life (c. 1266), he resolved to devote himself to missionary work, to the refutation of infidel errors, and to the teaching of foreign languages. Studied Arabic (1266–75) and taught it in the Franciscan monastery at Miramar (1275–85). Planned a spiritual crusade for the conversion of Mohammedans, and preached this crusade stubbornly for the rest of his life. Went as missionary to Mohammedans of north African regions, and was finally stoned to death outside the walls of Bougie. Among his writings are *Blanquerna* (a novel describing a new Utopia), *Libre de Maravelles, Lo Cant de Ramon.*

**Lum'holtz** (lo͝om'hŏlts), **Carl Sofus.** 1851–1922. Norwegian explorer and ethnologist.

**Lu'mière'** (lü'myâr'), **Louis Jean.** 1864–1948. French chemist and industrialist, b. in Besançon. With his brother **Auguste Marie Louis Nicolas** (1862–1954), also a chemist, founded in Lyons a factory for producing photographic plates, paper, and chemicals. They invented the Lumière process of color photography and an early motion-picture camera (1893); also, originated a theory attributing to the properties of colloidal substances the principal part in the various phenomena of life.

**Lum'mer** (lo͝om'ẽr), **Otto.** 1860–1925. German physicist; known for investigations in the fields of optics and radiations; discovered interference in a plane-parallel glass plate, which developed into the Lummer-Gehrcke plate (a type of interferometer); with Brodhun devised an improved photometer which uses a combination of prisms in place of greased paper. See also Ernst PRINGSHEIM.

**Lum'mis** (lŭm'ĭs), **Charles Fletcher.** 1859–1928. American author and editor, b. Lynn, Mass. Lived among Pueblo Indians in New Mexico (1888–91). On ethnological expedition to Peru and Bolivia (1892–94). Interested himself in preserving Spanish missions and other historical relics in California. Author of *Birch Bark Poems* (1879), *A New Mexico David* (1891), *A Tramp Across the Continent* (1892), *The Land of Poco Tiempo* (1893), *The Spanish Pioneers* (1893), *The Awakening of a Nation: Mexico of Today* (1898), *Mesa, Cañon and Pueblo* (1925), *A Bronco Pegasus* (1928), and volumes of Pueblo folk tales and old California Spanish songs.

**Lu'na** (lo͞o'nä), **Álvaro de.** 1388?–1453. Spanish statesman; minister of John II of Castile; appointed constable of Castile (1423). Grand master of the Military Order of Santiago (1445) and commander in chief of the army. Created duke of Trujillo, count of Gormaz, of San Esteban, and of Ledesma, and lord of many cities and castles; raised his brother to archbishop of Toledo and primate of Spain; married his daughter into the royal family.

**Luna, Pedro de.** 1328?–?1423. Antipope as Benedict XIII, at Avignon (1394–1423); b. in Aragon, Spain. A cardinal deacon, joined French cardinals in election (1378) of Antipope Clement VII; legate of Avignon in various countries; deposed at Council of Pisa (1409) but refused to accept decision; again deposed (1417) at Council of Constance; died unsubmissive.

**Lu·na·char'ski** (lo͞o·nŭ·chär'skû·ĭ; *Angl.* -skĭ), **Anatoli Vasilievich.** 1875–1933. Russian Communist leader and writer; joined Social Democratic party (1898); arrested and deported (1899). Escaped to Paris; at schism in Socialist party (1903), joined Bolsheviks under Lenin. Soon after outbreak of Russian Revolution (1917), joined Lenin and Trotsky in Russia and aided in Bolshevik coup d'état (Nov., 1917). Commissar for education (1917–29); introduced widespread reforms in public education in Russia. Author of *Religion and Socialism* (2 vols., 1911), *Culture and the Working Class* (1919).

**Lu'na·li'lo** (lo͞o'nä·lē'lō), **William C.** 1832–1874. King of Hawaiian Islands (1873–74). Elected king to succeed Kamehameha V, last of the direct Kamehameha line; had liberal ideas; worked for improvements in constitution; favored reciprocity treaty with U.S.

**Lu'na y A'rel·la'no** (lo͞o'nä ē ä'rā·lyä'nō), **Tristán de.** fl. 1530–1561. Spanish explorer in America; served under Coronado in New Mexico expedition. Named governor and captain general of Florida; sailed for Florida (1559); landed at Pensacola Bay.

**Lund, Troels Frederik.** *Known as* **Troels'-Lund'** (trōls'lo͝on'). 1840–1921. Danish writer and educator; chief work, a history of Danish and Norwegian culture in the 16th century. Appointed historiographer-royal to the king of Denmark.

**Lun'de·gård** (lŭn'dĕ·gōrd), **Axel.** 1861–1930. Swedish novelist; author of *At Daybreak* (1885), *Titania. A Love Saga* (1892), *Struensee* (1898–1900), *Queen Margaret* (1905–06), etc.

**Lun·dell'** (lŭn·dĕl'), **Johan August.** 1851–1940. Swedish philologist; known for study of Swedish dialects.

**Lund'gren** (lŭnd'grān), **Egron Sellif.** 1815–1875. Swedish water-color painter.

**Lun'dy** (lŭn'dĭ), **Benjamin.** 1789–1839. American abolitionist; organized The Union Humane Society, in St. Clairsville, Ohio (1815), one of the first antislavery societies. Traveled, wrote, and spoke in various states against slavery. Assaulted by Baltimore slave dealer (1827); property destroyed by Philadelphia mob (1838).

**Lü'ne·burg** (lü'nĕ·bo͝ork), Dukes of. See HANOVER.

**Lung'e** (lo͝ong'ĕ), **Georg.** 1839–1923. German chemist; contributed to development of processes for commercial production of soda and inorganic acids.

**Lunt** (lŭnt), **Alfred.** 1893–1977. American actor, b. Milwaukee, Wis.; m. Lynn Fontanne (*q.v.*). Appeared in *Sweet Nell of Old Drury, The Guardsman, Elizabeth the Queen, Design for Living, Taming of the Shrew.*

**Lu·pe'scu** (lo͞o·pĕ'sko͞o), **Magda.** *Orig. name said to be* **Wolff.** 1904?–1977. Rumanian adventuress, b. in Iasi, of a Jewish father and Viennese Catholic mother. Educ. in a convent; m. an army officer; met Prince Carol (1921?); divorced her husband; left Rumania (1925) to live with Carol in Paris; lived in Neuilly (1925–30); returned to Rumania (1930) soon after Carol seized throne; during Carol's reign (1930–40) exerted great influence over political events of kingdom; forced to flee with Carol to Spain (1940), Cuba (1941), Brazil (1944).

**Lu·pi'no** (lo͞o·pē'nō). Name of a family of actors including: **George** (1853–1932), English comedian of Italian descent; his son **Stanley** (1895–1942), b. in London, actor, playwright, and producer of stage and screen plays; Stanley's daughter **Ida** (1916– ), b. in London, actress on English stage and in motion pictures in Holly wood.

**Lu'pot'** (lü'pō'), **Nicolas.** 1758–1824. French violinmaker, b. Stuttgart; especially skillful in imitating the instruments made by Stradivarius.

**Lup'ton** (lŭp'tŭn), **Thomas Goff.** 1791–1873. English mezzotint engraver; one of first to employ steel in his art. Did best work in seascapes and landscapes, esp. in reproductions of J. M. W. Turner's work.

**Luqmān.** See LOKMAN.

**Lu'ria** (lo͞o'ryä), **Isaac ben Solomon Ash'ke·na'zi** (ăsh'kĕ·nä'zĭ). 1534–1572. Hebrew mystic and cabalist, b. in Jerusalem of German descent; founder of a school of mystics. His disciple Hayyim Vital collected notes of his lectures and produced numerous works expounding his doctrines, notably *'Eẓ Ḥayyim* (6 vols., pub. 1772).

**Luria, Ruggiero di.** See LAURIA.

**Luria, Salvador Edward.** 1912– . American biologist, b. Italy. To U.S. (1940); at Mass. Institute of Tech. (1959– ); awarded Nobel prize in physiology and medicine (1969) with M. Delbruck and A. Hershey for work on the genetic structure of viruses.

**Lur'ton** (lûr't'n), **Horace Harmon.** 1844–1914. American jurist; served in Confederate army in Civil War. Associate justice, U.S. Supreme Court (1910–14).

**Lu'schan** (lo͝osh'än), **Felix von.** 1854–1924. Austrian anthropologist and ethnologist. Publications on Bushmen, Hamites, and social anthropology.

**Lusignan** *or* **Lu'si'gnan' d'Ou'tre–mer'** (lü'zē'nyäN' do͞o'trē·mâr'). Name of French family, descended from Hugues VIII of Lusignan, which ruled the island of Cyprus from 1192 to 1474. See esp. GUY OF LUSIGNAN.

**Lusk** (lŭsk), **Graham.** 1866–1932. American physiologist; at Cornell (1909); authority on nutrition.

**Lusk, William Thompson.** 1838–1897. American obstetrician; wrote *Science and Art of Midwifery* (1882).

**Luska, Sidney.** See Henry HARLAND.

**Lust** (lo͝ost), **Ben'e·dict** (bĕn'ē·dĭkt). 1872–1945. American physician and editor, b. in Germany; to U.S. (1892). Founded N.Y. Naturopathic College and Hospital, health resorts, health food store, and publishing business.

**Lutero, di.** See Dosso DOSSI.

**Lu'ther** (lo͝ot'ẽr; *Angl.* lū'thẽr), **Hans.** 1879–1962. German economist and statesman; minister of finance in Stresemann's second ministry and in Marx's ministry; negotiated the Dawes loan for Germany (1924). Chancellor of Germany (Jan., 1925–May, 1926); represented Germany at the conference of Locarno (1924). German ambassador in Washington (1933–37).

**Luther, Martin.** 1483–1546. German religious reformer, b. in Eisleben; father of the Reformation in Germany. M.A., Erfurt (1505). Became an Augustinian friar; ordained priest (1507); lectured in Wittenberg on dialectics, physics, and the Scriptures (1508). On mission to Rome (1510–11), where he was unfavorably impressed by conditions. Professor of Biblical exegesis, Wittenberg (1511–46). Began to preach the doctrine of salvation by faith rather than by works; attacked the church's sale of indulgences; nailed to the church door at Wittenberg (Oct. 31, 1517) his 95 theses questioning the value of the indulgences and condemning the means used by the agents in selling them. Publicly defended his position in appearances before a chapter of his own Augustinian order (May, 1518) and before Cardinal Legate Cajetan (Oct., 1518); appealed from the pope to a general council of the church. Publicly debated the issue in Leipzig with the theologian Johann Eck (July, 1519), and went further than the mere indulgence issue by denying the supremacy of the pope, by asserting that the act of the church council in condemning John Huss had been wrong. Publicized his arguments by pamphlets, *An Address to the Christian Nobility of the German Nation, The Babylonian Captivity of the Church, The Liberty of a Christian Man.* Excommunicated by Pope Leo X (bull issued June 15, 1520); publicly burned the bull. Appeared before Diet of Worms (Apr. 17 and 18, 1521); Diet passed the Edict of Worms, putting Luther under the ban of the empire. Luther's friend Frederick of Saxony concealed him for safety in a castle at Wartburg (1521–22); there he wrote his pamphlet *On Monastic Vows* and translated the New Testament from Greek into German. Returned to Wittenberg (1522) and devoted himself to organization of the church he had inaugurated. Married Katharina von Bora (1525), a former nun. Translated the Old Testament, and wrote many commentaries, catechisms, etc.

**Lu·thu'li** (lŭ·to͞o'lē), **Albert John.** 1898–1967. South African reformer. Former Zulu chief; president, African National Congress (1952–60); awarded Nobel peace prize (1960); wrote *Let My People Go* (1962).

**Lüt'ke** (lüt'kĕ), Count **Fëdor Petrovich.** 1797–1882. Russian naval officer and navigator; explored coasts of Kamchatka and Novaya Zemlya (1821–25); commanded (1826–28) Russian voyage around world, exploring coasts of Siberia and Alaska; admiral (1855).

**Lu'to·sław'ski** (lo͞o'tô·släf'skē), **Wincenty.** 1863–1954. Polish philosopher.

**Lut'yens** (lŭch'ĕnz; lŭt'yĕnz), Sir **Edwin Landseer.** 1869–1944. English architect and artist; R.A. (1920); O.M. (1942); president of the Royal Academy (from 1938). Works include Whitehall Cenotaph, new British embassy (Washington, D.C.), South African War Memorial (Johannesburg).

**Lutz** (lo͞ots), **Frank Eugene.** 1879–1943. American biologist; with American Museum of Natural History (from 1909); curator of entomology (from 1921).

**Lux'em'bourg'** (lük'säN'bo͞or'), Duc **de. François Henri de Mont'mo'ren'cy'–Bou'te·ville'** (dē môN'-mô'räN'sē'bo͞ot'vēl'). 1628–1695. French soldier; aide-de-camp and associate of the Great Condé (*q.v.*). Served in wars against Spain and Holland; won victories at Fleurus (1690), Leuze (1691), Steenkerke (1692), Neerwinden (1693). Created duke and peer (1662) and marshal of France (1675). His son **Chrétien Louis** (1675–1746), best known as **Maréchal de Montmorency,** was also a soldier; served in Flanders and distinguished himself at Oudenarde, Malplaquet, and Denain; created marshal of France (1734).

**Lux'em·burg** (lo͝ok'sĕm·bo͝orK; *Angl.* lŭk'sĕm·bûrg), House of. (1) Founded in 11th century by Count Conrad (d. 1086); held seigniory of Luxemburg; male line became extinct (1136). (2) Founded in 13th century by Henry II, Count of Luxemburg of a collateral line. His great-grandson Count Henry IV elected emperor (1308) as Henry VII, establishing house on throne of Holy Roman Empire. Chief members were: Henry VII, emperor (1308–13); his son John, king of Bohemia, killed at Crécy (1346); Charles IV, son of John, emperor (1346–78); two sons of Charles: Wenceslaus, emperor (1378–1400), and Sigismund, emperor (1411–37). House succeeded (1438) by Albert II of Hapsburg. See *Table (in Appendix)* for HOLY ROMAN EMPIRE.

**Luxemburg, Rosa.** 1870–1919. Known as "Red Rosa." German Socialist agitator; associated with Karl Liebknecht (*q.v.*) as leader of the Spartacus party; involved with him in the Spartacist insurrection; arrested, and killed while being taken to prison (Jan. 15, 1919).

**Luynes** (lü·ēn'), Duc **de.** Title borne by members of French family **d'Al'bert'** (dȧl'bâr'), of Provençal origin, including: **Charles d'Albert** (1578–1621); favorite of King Louis XIII of France; constable of France (1621); died on campaign to suppress Huguenots; **Honoré Théodoric Paul Joseph** (1802–1867); archaeologist; author of *Études Numismatiques,* etc.

**Lu·zán' Cla'ra·munt' de Suel'ves y Gur·re'a** (lo͞o-thän' klä'rä·mo͞ont' dā swĕl'vās ē go͞or·rā'ä), **Ignacio de.** 1702–1754. Spanish writer; chief work, *Poética, ó Reglas de la Poesía en General y de sus Principales Especies* (1737), a critical work advocating observance of strict classic rules in Spanish literary composition.

**Luz·zat'ti** (lo͞ot·tsät'tē), **Luigi.** 1841–1927. Italian economist and statesman, b. Venice. Minister of finance (1891–92; 1896–98; 1903–05; 1906; 1920); minister of agriculture (1909–10); prime minister (1910–11); senator (1921 ff.).

**Lvov** (lyvôf), **Aleksei Fëdorovich.** 1799–1870. Russian composer; conductor of Imperial Court Choir (1836–55); commissioned by czar to compose music for Russian national anthem (words by Vasili Zhukovski). Composer of operas, including *Undine* (1846), church music, songs, and many violin pieces.

**Lvov,** Prince **Georgi Evgenievich.** 1861–1925. Russian statesman; member of 1st Duma (1905); joined right wing of Constitutional Democratic party; after outbreak of Russian Revolution and abdication of czar, became premier in provisional government (Mar. 14, 1917); after formation of first Kerenski government (July 7, 1917), settled in Paris.

**Lwoff** (lŭ·wôf′), **André Michel.** 1902– . French microbiologist. At Pasteur Inst. (1921– ); awarded Nobel prize in physiology and medicine (1965) with F. Jacob and J. Monod for research on genetic control of enzyme and virus synthesis.

**Ly′all** (lī′ăl), Sir **Alfred Comyn.** 1835–1911. British administrator in India and writer. As governor general's agent in Rajputana (1874) drew up statistical gazetteer of Berar and Rajputana, first of its kind; foreign secretary to government of India (1878–81); as lieutenant governor of Northwest Provinces and Oudh (1882–87), administered local self-government and effected legislative reforms; member of India council in London (1887–1902). Author of *Asiatic Studies*, dealing with Hindu religion (1882, 1889), biographies of Hastings, Tennyson, Lord Dufferin, also *Verses Written in India* (1889), including *Theology in Extremis*, soliloquy of an Englishman upon saving his life at price of becoming a Mohammedan.

**Lyall,** Sir **Charles James.** 1845–1920. English Orientalist; served in Bengal civil service (1867–89); chief commissioner of Central Provinces (1895–98); secretary of judicial and public department, India Office (1898–1910); translated and edited early Arabic literature.

**Lyall, David.** Pseudonym of Helen Buckingham (*nee* Mathers) REEVES.

**Lyall, Edna.** Pseudonym of Ada Ellen BAYLY.

**Lyau′tey′** (lyō′tā′), **Louis Hubert Gonzalve.** 1854–1934. French soldier; saved Morocco from German control in World War I; marshal of France (1921).

**Ly′con** (lī′kŏn). Greek philosopher; head of the Peripatetic school (270–226 B.C.).

**Ly′co·phron** (lī′kō·frŏn). Greek poet of Alexandria of 3d century B.C.; one of the Pleiad of Alexandria. His only extant poem is *Alexandra*, or *Cassandra*, in which Cassandra prophesies the fall of Troy and the later adventures of the Greek and Trojan heroes.

**Ly·cur′gus** (lī·kûr′gŭs). According to tradition, a Spartan lawgiver of the 9th century B.C., who by decree imposed upon Sparta its characteristic institutions designed to produce tough and able warriors.

**Lycurgus.** 396?–?323 B.C. Athenian orator and financier; favored anti-Macedonian policy of Demosthenes; renowned for his wise administration of Athenian finances after the battle of Chaeronea (338–323).

**Ly·dek′ker** (lī·dĕk′ẽr), **Richard.** 1849–1915. English naturalist and geologist; in India (1874–82); catalogued fossil mammals, amphibians, reptiles, and birds for the British Museum. Author of *A Manual of Palaeontology* (with H. A. Nicholson; 1889); with W. H. Flower wrote *An Introduction to the Study of Mammals* (1891) and *The Royal Natural History* (1893–96).

**Lyd′gate** (lĭd′gāt; -gĭt), **John.** 1370?–?1451. English poet; disciple and imitator of Chaucer; b. at Lydgate, Suffolk. Benedictine monk; prior of Hatfield Broadoak (1423), retired (1434); court poet at courts of Henry IV, V, and VI. Wrote *Troy Book*, at request of Prince of Wales and containing reverent tributes to his "master" and friend Chaucer (written 1412–20, printed 1513), *Falls of Princes* (written 1430–38, printed 1494), *The Story of Thebes* (written c. 1420, printed c. 1500), *London Lickpenny*, describing contemporary London manners, and two allegorical poems, *Complaint of the Black Knight* and *Temple of Glass*, also devotional, hagiological, philosophical, scientific, historical, and satirical poems.

**Ly′ell** (lī′ĕl), Sir **Charles.** 1797–1875. Son of Charles Lyell. British geologist, b. Scotland. Geological expeditions to various regions of Europe; opposed catastrophic theory advanced to account for great geologic changes; published *Principles of Geology* (3 vols., 1830–33) to refute this theory; regarded as father of modern geology. Also *Travels in North America, with Geological Observations* (1845), *The Antiquity of Man* (1863).

**Lyl′y** (lĭl′ĭ), **John.** 1554?–1606. English author, b. in Kent. M.A., Oxon. (1575); studied at Cambridge; M.P. (1589); supported the bishops in Martin Marprelate controversy. Known chiefly for his didactic romance, in two parts, *Euphues, the Anatomy of Wit* (1579) and *Euphues and his England* (1580), aiming at reform of education and manners, and its affected style (called Euphuism), marked by antithesis, alliteration, similes, and a pervading effort after elegance; ridiculed by Shakespeare and others but admired and imitated by large number of contemporaries, including Lodge and Greene. As a dramatist introduced English high comedy and made prose its vehicle; author of several dramas beginning with *The Woman in the Moone* (produced 1583?), but most are on classical and mythological subjects, as *Alexander and Campaspe* (1584), *Sapho and Phao* (1584), *Endymion* (1591), *Midas* (1592), *Galathea* (1592), *Mother Bombie* (1594), which contain attractive lyrics.

**Ly′man** (lī′măn), **Theodore.** 1874–1954. American physicist; known for work on the properties of light of extremely short wave lengths.

**Lynch, Charles.** 1736–1796. American planter and justice of the peace, b. near Lynchburg, Va. Commanded Virginia volunteer regiment with General Greene at battle of Guilford Court House. During disorganized conditions accompanying American Revolution, presided over extralegal court to punish lawlessness, in which convictions were frequent and followed by summary punishment, usually flogging; hence the term *lynch law* or, formerly, *Lynch's law*.

**Lynch, Robert Clyde.** 1880–1931. American laryngologist, b. Carson City, Nev. Developed frontal sinus operation, known as "Lynch operation."

**Lynch, Thomas.** 1749–1779. American planter; member of 2d Continental Congress (1776–77); a signer of the Declaration of Independence; lost at sea (1779).

**Lynd** (lĭnd), **Robert.** 1879–1949. Irish journalist and man of letters; literary editor, London *News Chronicle.* Author of *Home Life in Ireland* (1909), *Old and New Masters* (1919), *Solomon in All His Glory* (1922), *Dr. Johnson & Company* (1928), *It's a Fine World* (1930), *Searchlights and Nightingales* (1939). His wife (m. 1909), **Sylvia,** *nee* **Dry′hurst** [drī′hûrst] (1888–1952), author of *The Chorus* (novel; 1916), *The Goldfinches* (verse; 1920), *The Mulberry Bush* (short stories; 1925), *The Children's Omnibus* (anthology; 1932).

**Lynd, Robert Staughton.** 1892–1970. American sociologist; professor, Columbia (1931–60). With collaboration of his wife (m. 1921), **Helen,** *nee* **Mer′rell** (mĕr′ĕl), made sociological study of a Middle Western city (Muncie, Ind.) and published *Middletown—a Study in Contemporary American Culture* (1929), *Middletown in Transition* (1937), *Knowledge for What?* (1939); she wrote (1945) *England in the 1880's.*

**Lyndhurst,** Baron. See John Singleton COPLEY (1772–1863).

**Lyndsay,** Sir **David** (1490?–1555). See LINDSAY.

**Lynedoch,** Baron. See Thomas GRAHAM (1748–1843).

**Ly′nen** (lü′nĕn), **Feodor.** 1911–1979. German biochemist. At U. of Munich (1942–79); awarded Nobel prize in physiology and medicine (1964) with K. Bloch.

**Ly′on** (lī′ŭn), **Mary.** 1797–1849. American educator, b. Buckland, Mass.; pioneer in providing advanced education for women. Taught at Ashfield, Mass., Londonderry, N.H., and Ipswich, Mass. (1821–34). Opened

Mount Holyoke Seminary, South Hadley, Mass. (1837), a school of collegiate grade for girls, which later became Mount Holyoke College; remained president (1837–49). Elected to American Hall of Fame (1905).

**Lyon, Nathaniel.** 1818–1861. American army officer; b. Ashford, Conn.; grad. U.S.M.A., West Point (1841). Served through Mexican War and on western frontier duty. Brigadier general in command of Union forces at St. Louis, Mo. (May, 1861); captured Jefferson City (June 15, 1861) and Boonville (June 17).

**Lyon'net'** (lyô'nĕ'), **Pierre.** 1707–1789. Dutch entomologist; published treatise on caterpillars.

**Ly'ons** (lī'ŭnz), **Edmund.** 1st Baron **Lyons.** 1790–1858. English naval commander; commanded frigate at blockade of Navarino (1826); employed on diplomatic service (1840–53) in Greece, Switzerland, Sweden; second in command of British fleet in Black Sea in Crimean War; vice-admiral (1855). His son **Richard Bickerton Pemell** (1817–1887), 1st Earl **Lyons,** was British minister at Washington (1858–65), and conducted negotiations concerning Trent affair; ambassador at Paris (1867–87), accompanied provisional government to Tours (1870); created viscount (1881), earl (1887).

**Lyons, Joseph Aloysius.** 1879–1939. Australian statesman. Educ. U. of Tasmania. Premier of Tasmania and treasurer (1923–28); member of Federal House of Representatives (from 1929) and leader of United Australia party in legislature (from 1931). Prime minister and treasurer of Australia (1932–39).

**Lyot** (lyō), **Bernard Ferdinand.** 1897–1952. French astronomer.

**Ly·san'der** (lī·săn'dẽr). d. 395 B.C. Spartan naval and military commander; son of Aristocritus. Commanded fleet which defeated the Athenians off Notium (407 B.C.); replaced (406) by Callicratidas but chosen commander again and victorious at Aegospotami (405); captured Athens (404), and thus brought the Peloponnesian War to a triumphal end. Ambitious to establish himself as supreme in Sparta, he was relieved of his command by the Spartan ephors and ordered home to answer a charge of insubordination. Escaped punishment, and commanded army against the Boeotians (395).

**Ly·sen'ko** (lĭ·sĕng'kō), **Trofim Denisovich.** 1898–1976. Soviet biologist and agronomist. President, Acad. of Agric. Sciences (1938–56; 1958–62); wrote *Agrobiology* (1952).

**Lys'i·as** (lĭs'ĭ·ăs). 450?–?380 B.C. Athenian orator; settled in Athens (c. 412 B.C.). Fled from city when it fell under control of the Thirty Tyrants (404); when democracy was restored, returned to impeach Eratosthenes, one of the tyrants, in a speech (403) which is still extant. Of most of his orations, only fragments are extant.

**Lysias.** d. 162 B.C. Syrian general and regent under kings Antiochus Epiphanes and Antiochus Eupator. Appointed viceroy (165 B.C.); attempted to quell Jewish insurrection under Maccabees; his great army defeated (165?) by Judas Maccabaeus (*1 Macc.* iii. 38–40; iv. 1–22, 28–35); seized Syrian throne on death of Antiochus Epiphanes; defeated Judas and besieged Jerusalem; compelled to make peace by insurrection in Antioch.

**Ly·sim'a·chus** (lī·sĭm'ȧ·kŭs). 361?–281 B.C. Macedonian general; served under Alexander the Great. At Alexander's death (323 B.C.), received Thrace; assumed title of king (306). Shared in victory at Ipsus (301), and gained large section of Asia Minor; gained Macedonia (287–286). Defeated by Seleucus Nicator (281). See ARSINOË.

**Ly·sip'pus** (lī·sĭp'ŭs). Greek sculptor of Sicyon in 4th century B.C.; brother of Lysistratus (*q.v.*). Credited with developing new system of bodily proportions, making the head smaller, the legs longer, and adjusting details to these changes. A copy of his *Apoxyomenos* is preserved in the Vatican. Made a number of portrait busts of Alexander the Great.

**Ly·sis'tra·tus** (lī·sĭs'trȧ·tŭs). Greek sculptor of 4th century B.C.; brother of Lysippus of Sicyon (*q.v.*).

**Lyte** (līt), **Henry Francis.** 1793–1847. Anglican clergyman and hymn writer; b. Scotland, of Somersetshire family. Remembered for his hymns, including *Abide with me; Pleasant are thy courts; Jesus, I my cross have taken; Praise, my soul, the King of Heaven.*

**Lyt'tel·ton** (lĭt''l·tŭn), **George.** 1st Baron **Lyttelton of Frank'ley** (frăngk'lĭ). 1709–1773. English public official and man of letters. Often called "the Good Lord Lyttelton." Direct descendant of Sir Thomas Littleton, jurist (*q.v.*); first cousin to Earl Temple and to George Grenville and connected by marriage with William Pitt. M.P. (1735–56); a lord of the treasury (1744–54); chancellor of exchequer briefly (1755–56); opposed repeal of Stamp Act (1766). Patron of poet Thomson and other literary men. Author of a treatise on the conversion of St. Paul (1747), *Dialogues of the Dead* (1760), *The History of the Life of Henry the Second* (1767–71); in poetry remembered chiefly for the *Monody* on death of his wife and as having place in Johnson's *Lives of the Poets.* His son **Thomas** (1744–1779), 2d baron, libertine; known as "the Wicked Lord Lyttelton"; prominent in debates in House of Lords on American affairs (1774–78).

**William Henry Lyttelton** (1724–1808), 1st baron of second creation; brother of George; barrister and M.P. (1748); as governor of South Carolina (1755–62), detained as hostages Cherokee chiefs sent to conference, precipitating renewal of Indian war and frontier ravages; governor of Jamaica (1762–66); ambassador to Portugal (1766–71); author of *An Historical Account of the Constitution of Jamaica* (1792). His grandson **George William Lyttelton** (1817–1876), 4th baron; lord lieutenant of Worcestershire (1839); principal of Queen's College, Birmingham (1845); one of founders and first president of Saltley Training College; chief commissioner of endowed schools (1869); student of colonial, esp. Australasian, affairs; undersecretary of state for colonies (1846); chairman of Canterbury Association, which sent Church of England colonists to New Zealand. The 4th baron's 3d son, Sir **Neville Gerald** (1845–1931), distinguished himself at Tel-el-Kebir and Khartoum; major general (1898); commanded brigade in Boer War; chief of general staff (1904–08). The 4th baron's 5th son, **Arthur Temple** (1852–1903), first master of Selwyn College, Cambridge (1882–93), suffragan bishop of Southampton (1878–1903), was author of *Modern Poets of Faith, Doubt, and Unbelief* (1904).

The 4th baron's 8th son, **Alfred** (1857–1913), successful lawyer (1881–1903); M.P. (1895); as colonial secretary in Balfour cabinet (1903–05), introduced Chinese coolies into the Rand, in face of denunciation; laid groundwork for Imperial Conference by dispatch of April, 1905. Alfred's wife (m. 1892), Dame **Edith,** ***nee*** **Balfour** (1865–1948), woman of affairs and playwright, served as member of committees on intellectual co-operation, Stratford Memorial theatre, war refugees, women's employment, waste reclamation (1916–25); president of Society for Psychical Research (1933–34); substitute delegate to League of Nations Assembly (1923, 1926, 1927, 1928, 1931); author of plays *Warp and Woof, The Thumbscrew, Peter's Chance,* biographies of her husband and others, and *Our Superconscious Mind* (1931), *Some Cases of Prediction* (1937). Their only son, **Oliver** (1893–1972), soldier, distinguished himself in Grenadier Guards (1915–18; D.S.O., 1916); controller of nonferrous metals (1930–40); privy councilor and president of Board of Trade (1940); political officer to General Auchinleck, commander in Middle East (1941). Minister of production (1942) and cohead (with Donald Nelson) of combined U.S.-British production and resources board.

**Lyt'tle·ton** (lĭt''l·tŭn), **Edith J.** 1873–1945. *Pseud.* **G. B. Lancaster.** New Zealand writer, b. in Tasmania; taken to New Zealand in childhood. Author of *Pageant* (1933), *Promenade* (1938), and other novels, and many short stories.

**Lyt'ton** (lĭt''n), **Edward George Earle Lytton Bul'wer-** (bo͝ol'wẽr-). 1st Baron **Lytton of Kneb'worth** (nĕb'wûrth; -wẽrth). 1803–1873. English novelist and dramatist. Brother of Sir Henry Bulwer. Educ. Cambridge; m. Rosina Wheeler (1827); separated from her (1836). First novel *Falkland* (1827); second novel *Pelham* (1828). Editor, *New Monthly Magazine* (1831–32). M.P. (1831, 1832–41). Produced three plays, *The Lady of Lyons* (1838), *Richelieu* (1839), and *Money* (1840). Returned to politics; M.P. (1852–66); colonial secretary (1858–59); created baron (1866). Author of poems, including *The New Timon* (1846), of short stories introducing the occult, of historical and romantic novels including *Eugene Aram* (1832), *The Last Days of Pompeii* (1834), *Rienzi* (1835; on which Wagner's opera *Rienzi* is based), *The Last of the Barons* (1843), *Harold* (1848), *The Caxtons* (1849), and of a prophetical romance *The Coming Race* (1871). His son **Edward Robert Bulwer Lytton** (1831–1891), 1st Earl of **Lytton,** statesman and poet (pseudonym **Owen Meredith**), had a career in diplomatic service; as viceroy of India (1876–80), effected internal reforms but failed to avert Afghan War (1879); ambassador at Paris (1887–91); author of several volumes of verse, including long romances *Lucile* (1860) and *Glenaveril* (1885) and the fantastic epic *King Poppy* (1892).

**Lytton,** Sir **Henry Alfred.** 1865–1936. English actor, b. London; appeared first, with his wife, in *Princess Ida* in D'Oyly Carte Opera Company in Glasgow (1884); New York debut (1890); tried management (1899–1907); created sensation as Reggie Drummond in *The Talk of the Town* (1905); appeared on variety stage; rejoined D'Oyly Carte Company and played leading parts in Gilbert and Sullivan operas.

# M

☞ **M'–, Mc–.** Abbreviated forms of MAC-. Names beginning with this prefix are all alphabetized as if spelled MAC-. M' is sometimes written M', esp. in British references.

**Ma.** Chinese general. = MA CHAN-SHAN.

**Maarri, al–.** See ABU-AL-ALA AL-MAARRI.

**Maar'tens** (mär'tĕns), **Maarten.** *Pen name of* **Joost Marius Willem van der Poor'ten–Schwartz'** (vän dẽr pōr'tĕn·shvärts'). 1858–1915. Dutch novelist; studied law in Utrecht; wrote in English realistic and moral novels and stories, chiefly of Holland, including *The Sin of Joost Avelingh* (2 vols., 1889), *An Old Maid's Love* (3 vols., 1891), *A Question of Taste* (1891), *God's Fool* (3 vols., 1892), *The Greater Glory* (3 vols., 1894), *My Lady Nobody* (1895), *Some Women I Have Known* (1901), *The New Religion* (1907), and *Eve* (1912), the one-act play *The Jail-Bird* (1904), the collection *A Sheaf of Sonnets* (1888), etc.

**Maas, Nicolaes.** See Nicolaes MAES.

**Ma'bie** (mā'bĭ), **Hamilton Wright.** 1845?–1916. American editor and critic, b. Cold Spring, N.Y.; practiced law (1869–77). On editorial staff (1879–1916), under Lyman Abbott, of the *Christian Union* (renamed in 1893 the *Outlook*); associate editor from 1884. Author of *Norse Stories Retold from the Eddas* (1882), *My Study Fire* (1890), *Essays in Literary Interpretation* (1892), *Nature and Culture* (1896), *Books and Culture* (1896), *William Shakespeare* (1900), *American Ideals, Character and Life* (1913), *Japan Today and Tomorrow* (1914), etc.

**Ma'bil'lon'** (ma'bē'yôN'), **Jean.** 1632–1707. French Benedictine monk and scholar; lived at abbey of Saint-Germain-des-Prés, Paris (from 1664); among his works are *Acta Sanctorum Ordinis S. Benedicti* (9 vols., 1668–1702), *De Re Diplomatica* (1681), etc.

**Ma'bly'** (ma'blē'), **Gabriel Bonnet de.** 1709–1785. French philosopher and historian; author of *Parallèles des Romains et des Français* (1740), *Droit Public de l'Europe* (1748), *Observations sur l'Histoire de France* (1765), etc.

**Ma·bu·chi** (mä·bo͞o·chē). 1697?–1769. Japanese scholar who tried to restore Shinto, native religion of Japan, to its original purity; advocated return to primitive social simplicity; made Japan's ancient poetry accessible to modern readers.

**Ma'buse'** (ma'büz') *or* **Mal·bo'di·us** (*Flem.* mäl·bō'dē·ûs; *Angl.* măl·bō'dĭ·ŭs), **Jan.** *Real name* **Jan Gos'saert** (gŏs'ärt) *or* **Jenni Gos'sart** (-ärt). 1478?–?1533. Flemish historical and portrait painter, b. in Maubeuge, from which he adopted his name. Entered service of Philip of Burgundy, illegitimate son of Philip the Good; accompanied him to Rome (1508), where he copied old paintings; lived subsequently in Utrecht and Middelburg, Zealand. His works include *Adoration of the Kings* (now in National Gallery, London), Madonnas in Munich, Vienna, Paris, Berlin, and Madrid, *Neptune and Amphitrite* and *The Agony in the Garden* (both in Berlin), portraits, etc.

**Mc·Ad'am** (măk·ăd'ăm), **John Loudon.** 1756–1836. British engineer, b. Ayr, Scotland. Surveyor general of roads, Bristol, Eng. (1815); general surveyor of roads (1827); introduced improved roads, built of crushed stone, known as "macadamized" roads.

**Mc'A·doo** (măk'ȧ·do͞o), **William Gibbs.** 1863–1941. American lawyer, b. near Marietta, Ga.; practiced, Chattanooga, Tenn. (1885–92), New York (from 1892). President, Hudson & Manhattan R.R. Co., which completed (Mar. 8, 1904) first tunnel under Hudson River. U.S. secretary of the treasury (1913–18); U.S. director-general of railways (1917–19). Married Eleanor Wilson, daughter of President Wilson (1914). Prominent candidate for Democratic nomination for president (1920 and 1924). U.S. senator from California (1933–39).

**Mc'A·fee** (măk'ȧ·fē), **Mildred Helen.** 1900– . American educator; B.A., Vassar (1920); dean of women and professor of sociology, Centre College, Danville, Ky. (1927–32); dean of women, Oberlin (1934–36); president of Wellesley College (from 1936); lieut. commander (1942) and head of women's naval reserve ("WAVES"); captain (1943); m. (1945) Douglas Horton (1891–1968), clergyman.

**Mc·Al′ex·an′der** (măk·ăl′ĕg·zăn′dẽr; -ĭg-; *Brit. also* -zän′-), **Ulysses Grant.** 1864–1936. American army officer; in France (1917–19), and engaged in 2d battle of the Marne, Aisne-Marne, St. Mihiel, and Meuse-Argonne offensives. Retired (1924).

**Mac·al′is·ter** (măk·ăl′ĭs·tẽr), Sir **Donald.** 1854–1934. Scottish physician and anatomist; principal and vice-chancellor (1907–29), chancellor (from 1929), Glasgow U. Author of *Nature of Fever* (1887), *Antipyretics* (1888), *Romani Versions* (1928).

**Macalister, Robert Alexander Stewart.** 1870–1950. Irish archaeologist; author of *Studies in Irish Epigraphy* (3 vols., 1897–1907), *Excavations in Palestine* (with Dr. F. J. Bliss; 1902), *Two Irish Arthurian Romances* (1908), *A History of Civilization in Palestine* (1912), *The Excavations of Gezer* (3 vols., 1912), *A Textbook of European Archaeology* (1921), *The Book of the Taking of Ireland* (vol. i, 1938; ii, 1939), etc.

**Mc·Al′lis·ter** (măk·ăl′ĭs·tẽr), **Addams Stratton.** 1875–1946. American electrical engineer. Associate editor (1905–12) and editor (1912–15), *Electrical World.* With U.S. Bureau of Standards (from 1923). Inventor of various alternating-current machinery; formulated law of conservation as applied to illuminating-engineering calculations.

**McAllister, Alister.** 1877–1943. Irish author, under pseudonym of **Anthony Wharton,** of plays and novels, and under pseudonym of **Lynn Brock,** of short stories and detective stories featuring Colonel Gore.

**McAllister, Samuel Ward,** *known as* **Ward.** 1827–1895. American lawyer and social leader, b. Savannah, Ga. Practiced San Francisco (1850–52). Resident, New York City and Newport, R.I. (from 1852). Became arbiter of New York's social world; originated the Patriarchs, a group of heads of old New York families; responsible for phrase "the Four Hundred," referring to the number of people who belonged in New York Society. Author of *Society as I Have Found It* (1890).

**Mc·Al′pine** (măk·ăl′pīn), **William Jarvis.** 1812–1890. American civil engineer, b. New York City; chief engineer or consulting engineer for various bridges, including Eads Bridge at St. Louis and Washington Bridge in New York; built Riverside Drive, New York City.

**Mc′A·nen′y** (măk′ȧ·nĕn′ĭ), **George.** 1869–1953. American municipal official, b. Greenville, N.J. Newspaper reporter in New York (1885–92). President of Borough of Manhattan (1910–13); president of board of aldermen, and acting mayor of New York (1914–16). Executive manager, New York *Times* (1916–21). Chairman, New York Transit Commission (1921). Interested in city planning, development of transit lines, civil-service reform, Negro education, etc.

**Mac·Ar′thur** (măk·är′thẽr), **Arthur.** 1845–1912. American army officer, b. Springfield, Mass. Served through Civil War; awarded (1890) Congressional Medal of Honor for heroism at battle of Missionary Ridge (1863). Major general of volunteers in Spanish-American War, on duty in Havana (1898–99). Military governor of the Philippines (1900–01). Lieutenant general and assistant chief of staff (1906); retired (1909). His son **Douglas** (1880–1964), army officer, b. Little Rock, Ark.; grad. U.S.M.A., West Point (1903); commanded 42d (Rainbow) division in France during World War (1918–19); brigadier general (1920); superintendent, U.S.M.A. (1919–22); major general (1925); in command of Philippine Department (1928); general, and chief of staff, U.S. army (1930–35); director of organization of national defense for the Philippine government (1935–37; retired). Recalled to active service (July, 1941) as lieutenant-general and commander of U.S. forces in the Far East; allied supreme commander in S.W. Pacific (1942) and of occupational forces in Japan (1945–51); general of the army (1944); supreme commander of UN forces, Korea (1950–51). Awarded Congressional Medal of Honor.

**MacArthur, Charles.** 1895–1956. American playwright, b. Scranton, Pa.; m. (1928) Helen Hayes (*q.v.*). Newspaper reporter in Chicago and New York (1914–23); served in Rainbow Division, A.E.F. (1917–19); on staff of *Hearst's International Magazine* (1924). Turned to writing plays (from 1924) and to writing and producing motion pictures and plays (from 1929); partner in Hecht-MacArthur, Inc. Collaborated with E. Sheldon in play *Lulu Belle* (1926), with Sidney Howard in *Salvation* (1927), and with Ben Hecht in *The Front Page* (1928), *Twentieth Century* (1933), and *Ladies and Gentlemen* (1939). With Ben Hecht, adapted *Wuthering Heights* for motion-picture presentation.

**Mc·Ar′thur** (măk·är′thẽr), **Duncan.** 1772–1839. American legislator, b. Dutchess County, N.Y.; settled near Chillicothe, Ohio (1796). Served under Hull at Detroit (1812); brigadier general, U.S. army (1813) in command at Sackets Harbor; commanded army in the Northwest (1814). Member, U.S. House of Representatives (1823–25). Governor of Ohio (1830–32).

**Macarthur, Mary Reid.** See Mary Reid ANDERSON.

**Ma·cart′ney** (mȧ·kärt′nĭ), **George.** 1st Earl **Macartney.** 1737–1806. British diplomat, b. County Antrim, Ireland. British envoy at St. Petersburg (1764–67); chief secretary for Ireland (1769–72); governor of the Caribbean Islands (1775–79). Governor of Fort St. George (Madras, 1780–86). First British diplomatic representative to Peking (1792–94); governor of Cape of Good Hope (1796–98).

**Ma·cau′lay** (mȧ·kô′lĭ), **Catharine,** *nee* **Saw′bridge** (sô′brĭj). 1731–1791. English historian; m. 1st George Macaulay (1760; d. 1766), 2d William Graham (1778). Visited U.S. (1784–85); guest of George Washington for ten days. Author of *The History of England from the Accession of James I to that of the Brunswick Line* (8 vols., 1763–83).

**Macaulay, Fannie,** *nee* **Cald′well** (kôld′wĕl; -wĕl; kōld′-). *Pseudonym* **Frances Lit′tle** (lĭt′'l). 1863–1941. American writer, b. Shelbyville, Ky.; m. James Macaulay of Liverpool, Eng. Kindergarten teacher in Japan (1902–07). Author of *The Lady of the Decoration* (1906), *Little Sister Snow* (1909), *The Lady and Sada San* (1912), *The House of the Misty Star* (1914), etc.

**Macaulay,** Dame **Rose.** 1881–1958. Eng. novelist; author of *Potterism* (1920), *Dangerous Ages* (1921), *Told by an Idiot* (1923), *A Casual Commentary* (essays; 1925), *Keeping up Appearances* (1928), *Staying with Relations* (1930), *Some Religious Elements in English Literature* (1931), *John Milton* (1933), *Personal Pleasures* (1935), *I Would be Private* (1937), *And No Man's Wit* (1940), etc.

**Macaulay, Thomas Babington.** 1st Baron **Macaulay.** 1800–1859. Son of Zachary Macaulay (*q.v.*). English writer and statesman, b. Rothley Temple, Leicestershire. Educ. Cambridge. Called to bar (1826). M.P. (1830–34, 1839–47, 1852–56); raised to peerage (1857). Member, Supreme Council of India (1834–38); secretary of war (1839–41); paymaster of the forces (1846–47). Contributor to *Edinburgh Review* (from 1825). Author of *History of England,* covering reigns of James II and William III (vols. I and II, 1848; III and IV, 1855; V, 1861). Author also of *Lays of Ancient Rome* (1842) and numerous essays (including one on Milton in *Edinburgh Review,* 1825), biographical sketches, speeches, etc. Complete works in 8 volumes, edited by his sister Lady Trevelyan (Hannah More Macaulay), appeared in 1866, a two-volume biography, by his nephew G. O. Trevelyan, in 1876.

**Macaulay, Zachary.** 1768–1838. Father of Thomas Babington Macaulay (*q.v.*). English philanthropist; active in antislavery agitation. Governor of Sierra Leone (1793–99); secretary to Sierra Leone Co. (1799–1808). Editor of abolitionist journal, the *Christian Observer* (1802–16); secretary, African Inst. (1807–12); aided in organizing Anti-Slavery Society (1823).

**Mc·Au'ley** (măk·ô'lĭ), **Catharine.** 1787–1841. Irish religious; founder of the House of our Blessed Lady of Mercy, in Dublin (1827), which became the Order of the Sisters of Mercy.

**McAuley, Jeremiah.** 1839?–1884. Social-service worker, b. in Ireland; to U.S. (1852). Became river thief on New York waterfront; in Sing Sing penitentiary (1858–64). Converted, opened mission in New York slums (1872); incorporated (1876); founded Cremorne mission further uptown (1882). Dictated an autobiography, *Transformed, or the History of a River Thief* (1876).

**McAuley, Thomas.** 1778–1862. Presbyterian clergyman, b. in Ireland. A founder (1835), and first president (1836–40), of Union Theological Seminary.

**Mc·Bain'** (măk·bān'), **Howard Lee.** 1880–1936. Political scientist, b. Toronto, Can.; professor, Columbia U. (1917–36). Author of *The Law and the Practice of Municipal Home Rule* (1916), *American City Progress and the Law* (1917), *The Living Constitution* (1927), etc.

**Mac·beth'** (măk·bĕth'). d. 1057. King of Scotland; slew Duncan and seized kingdom (1040); defeated and slain by Malcolm III (1057); hero of Shakespeare's tragedy *Macbeth.*

**Macbeth, Robert Walker.** 1848–1910. Scottish painter and etcher.

**Mc·Bey'** (măk·bā'), **James.** 1883–1959. Scot.-born Amer. painter and etcher; official artist with Egyptian expeditionary force (1917); made drawings and paintings for British Museum and Imperial War Museum.

**Mac·Bride'** (măk·brīd'), **Ernest William.** 1866–1940. British zoologist, b. Belfast, Ireland. Author of *Textbook of Invertebrate Embryology* (1914), *Introduction to the Study of Heredity* (1924), *Evolution* (1927), *Embryology* (1929), *Huxley* (1934), etc.

**MacBride, Maud Gonne.** See Maud GONNE.

**Mac·Bride'** (măk·brīd'), **Seán.** 1904– . Irish United Nations official, b. Paris. Lawyer, member of Irish legislative Dail (1947–58), minister for external affairs (1948-51); assistant secretary general of UN (1973–77); a founder (1961) of Amnesty International; awarded (with Eisaku Sato) Nobel prize for peace (1974).

**Mc·Bur'ney** (măk·bûr'nĭ), **Charles.** 1845–1913. American surgeon, b. Roxbury, Mass. Grad. Harvard (1866). Professor, Coll. Phys. & Surg., N.Y. (1889–1907). Pioneer in antiseptic surgery. Authority on appendectomy; discoverer of McBurney's point, a tender pressure point important in diagnosis, and of McBurney's incision, a method of operating in appendectomy.

**Mc·Cabe'** (mȧ·kāb'), **Joseph.** 1867–1955. British rationalist philosopher; entered Franciscan order (1883); ordained priest (1890); withdrew from church (1896), devoting himself to lecturing and writing. Author of *Twelve Years in a Monastery* (1897), *Modern Rationalism* (1897), *The Decay of the Church of Rome* (1909), *The Evolution of Mind* (1910), *The Story of Evolution* (1912), *The Bankruptcy of Religion* (1918), *Ice Ages* (1922), *The Twilight of the Gods* (1923), *The Hundred Men who Moved the World* (1931), *The Riddle of the Universe Today* (1934), *A History of the Popes* (1939), etc.

**Mac'ca·bees** (măk'ȧ·bēz). Family of Jewish patriots of 2d and 1st centuries B.C., more correctly called the Hasmonaeans (*q.v.*). See *1–4 Maccabees* in the Apocrypha. The chief members of the family were:

**Mat'ta·thi'as** (măt'ȧ·thī'ăs) *or* **Mat'ta·thi'ah** (-ȧ). d. 166? B.C. Founder of family; priest of Modin, village near Lydda; defied decree of Antiochus IV Epiphanes of Syria to Hellenize the Jews; rose in revolt (167) and fled with five sons to the mountains.

**Ju'das** (jōō'dăs). *Orig.* **Ju'dah** (-dȧ). His third son; became leader (166–160 B.C.); received surname **Mac'ca·bae'us** [măk'ȧ·bē'ŭs] (perhaps meaning "the Hammerer"), later applied to all members of Hasmonaean family; able military leader; defeated several Syrian armies; purified the Temple of Jerusalem, and restored Jewish worship (165 or 164 B.C.; now commemorated by the Jewish Feast of Dedication, or Hanukkah); secured recognition of Jewish religious liberty, and worked for political independence; won victory over Syrian forces of Nicanor (160), but fell in battle of Elasa during second Syrian invasion (160), just before concluding alliance with Romans. Hero of Handel's oratorio *Judas Maccabaeus* (1746). Two other sons, **John** and **El'e·a'zar** (ĕl'ē·ā'zẽr), were killed (before 160) in the revolt.

**Jon'a·than** (jŏn'ȧ·thăn). Youngest son of Mattathias; succeeded his brother Judas as leader (160–143 B.C.); successful as military leader of Hasmonaean bands; allowed by Seleucidae to reside (157–152) at Michmash (town just north of Jerusalem); profited by intrigues at Syrian court; gradually changed Judea into independent principality under a Hasmonaean high priest (from 157); became high priest (152); supported Alexander Balas against Demetrius I (152–150); after Alexander's death (145) supported Antiochus VI; trapped at Bethshean and killed by Tryphon, Syrian usurper.

**Si'mon** (sī'mŭn). Second son of Mattathias; succeeded Jonathan as leader (143–134 B.C.); won independence (142) of Jewish nation (Judea); drove all Syrians from citadel in Jerusalem; achieved peace (*1 Macc.* xiv. 12); chosen civil governor and high priest (141); sent embassy to Rome; began coinage of money; treacherously murdered by his son-in-law.

**John Hyr·ca'nus** (hûr·kā'nŭs). Son of Simon; succeeded father as leader (134–104 B.C.); extended kingdom to include Samaria, Idumaea, and lands east of Jordan; opposed Pharisaic party; for the most part his rule brought prosperity but departed somewhat from earlier ideals of Israel.

**A·ris'to·bu'lus I** (ȧ·rĭs'tō·bū'lŭs; ăr'ĭs·tō-). *Called* **Judah.** 140?–103 B.C. Son and successor of John Hyrcanus; high priest and king of Judea (104–103 B.C.); assumed title of "Philhellene"; supported cause of Sadducees; displayed hatred toward members of his family; completed conquest of Galilee.

**Alexander Jan·nae'us** (jă·nē'ŭs) *or* **Jan'nai** (jăn'ī; -ā·ī). Brother and successor of Aristobulus I; ruled 103–76 B.C.; first Jewish ruler to assume title of priest-king; selfish and savage ruler, one of worst of Jewish kings; his reign marked by continual intrigues and fighting, and by conflicts between Pharisees and Sadducees; at war with Egypt; extended boundaries of kingdom.

**Sa·lo'me Alexandra** (sȧ·lō'mē). *Or simply* **Alexandra.** d. 67 B.C. Wife and successor of Alexander Jannaeus; ruled 76–67 B.C.; reversed husband's policy and supported Pharisees; bitter strife continued between two sects; kingdom threatened by foreign powers.

**Hyrcanus II.** d. 30 B.C. Son of Salome Alexandra; chosen by her as high priest (76–67 B.C.); succeeded her, but only as nominal ruler; engaged in civil war (67–63 B.C.) with his brother **Aristobulus II** (d. 48 B.C.), who was supported by Pompey; lost throne (63), Hasmonaean power being ended by Pompey's seizure of Jerusalem; retained by Pompey as high priest (63–40 B.C.), but lacked real power, Jewish politics being marked by increasing influence (47) of Antipater (*q.v.*) the Idumaean, father of Herod the Great; carried off to Babylon (40) by Parthians; held prisoner (40–36).

**An·tig′o·nus** (ăn·tĭg′ō·nŭs). d. 37 B.C. Son of Aristobulus II; ruled (40–37 B.C.); put on throne of Judea by Parthians to oppose Roman influence; last of the Hasmonaeans. His niece **Mar′i·am′ne** (măr′ĭ·ăm′nē) the Hasmonaean was second wife of Herod the Great (*q.v.*).

**Mc·Cain′** (mȧ·kān′), **John Sidney**. 1884–1945. American naval officer, b. in Carroll Co., Miss.; grad. (1906) U.S.N.A.; chief, Bureau of Aeronautics (1942–43); vice-admiral and deputy chief of naval operations (1943).

**Mc·Cal′lum** (mȧ·kăl′ŭm), **Daniel Craig**. 1815–1878. Civil and railroad engineer, b. Johnston, Scotland; to U.S. as a boy. Invented an arched-truss bridge (1851). Military director and superintendent of railroads with emergency war powers (1862–65).

**Mac·Cam′er·on** (mȧ·kăm′ẽr·ŭn), **Robert**. 1866–1912. American figure and portrait painter; his *Groupe d'Amis*, popularly called *The Absinthe Drinkers*, hangs in Corcoran Art Gallery, Washington, D.C.; *The Daughter's Return* and portrait of *Auguste Rodin*, in Metropolitan Museum of Art, New York.

**Mc·Cann′** (mȧ·kăn′), **Alfred Watterson**. 1879–1931. American pure-food reformer; conducted campaign (from 1912) against use of injurious preservatives in food products.

**Mc·Car′tan** (mȧ·kär′t'n), **Edward**. 1879–1947. American sculptor; works include bust of Washington Irving.

**Mac·Car′thy** (mȧ·kär′thĭ), **Denis Florence**. 1817–1882. Irish poet, b. Dublin. Author of *Ballads, Poems, and Lyrics* (1850), *The Bell-founder* (1857), and *Underglimpses* (1857); translator of the plays of Calderón (1848–73).

**MacCarthy,** Sir **Desmond**. 1878–1952. British writer and critic; author of *The Court Theatre*, *Portraits*, *Experience*, and *Leslie Stephen;* edited *Letters of the Earl of Oxford and Asquith to a Friend* (1933).

**MacCarthy, Hamilton Thomas**. 1847–1939. Canadian sculptor; designed Boer War memorials for Halifax, Ottawa, Quebec, Charlottetown, Brantford, a statue of Sir John A. Macdonald for Toronto, and a monument to Champlain at St. John in New Brunswick.

**Mc·Car′thy** (mȧ·kär′thĭ), **Joseph Raymond**. 1908–1957. U.S. Senator from Wisconsin (1947–57), b. Grand Chute, Wis. Accused many individuals of subversive (Communist) activities (McCarthyism, 1950–54); censured by the Senate (1954).

**M'Car′thy** (mȧ·kär′thĭ), **Justin**. 1830–1912. Irish writer and politician; on staff of *Northern Daily Times* (1853–59), *Morning Star* (1860–68), and *Daily News* (1870 ff.). M.P. and advocate of home rule for Ireland (1879–1900); chairman of the Irish Parliamentary party, the Anti-Parnellites (1890–96). Author of a number of novels, biographies, *History of Our Own Times* (5 vols., I–IV, 1879–80; V, 1897), and two volumes of *Reminiscences* (1899). His son **Justin Huntly** (1861–1936) was a playwright, novelist, and historian; M.P. (1884–92); among his plays are *The Candidate, The Highwayman, If I Were King, Caesar Borgia,* and *Stand and Deliver;* among his stories, *Dolly, A London Legend, The Illustrious O'Hagan, The God of Love, In Spacious Times, Truth and the Other Thing;* among his historical works, *Outline of Irish History, England under Gladstone, Ireland since the Union, The French Revolution, 1789–91, Short History of the United States.* See Cissie LOFTUS.

**Mc·Car′thy** (mȧ·kär′thĭ), **Leighton Goldie**. 1869–1952. Canadian lawyer and businessman, b. Walkerton, Ont.; chairman of board, Canada Life Assurance Co.; Canadian minister to U.S. (1941–43), amb. (1943–44).

**McCarthy, Lillah**. 1875–1960. English actress and manager; m. 1st Harley Granville-Barker (1906; divorced 1918), 2d Sir F.W. Keeble (1920). Assumed management of Little Theatre (1911), the Kingsway (1912 and 1919), the Savoy (1912). Roles include Nora in *John Bull's Other Island*, Ann Whitfield in *Man and Superman*, Gloria in *You Never Can Tell*, Jennifer in *The Doctor's Dilemma*, Margaret Knox in *Fanny's First Play*, Hilda Wangel in *The Master Builder*, Jocasta in *Œdipus Rex*, and Viola in *Twelfth Night*.

**Mac Cathmhaoil, Seosamh**. See Joseph CAMPBELL.

**Mc·Cau′ley** (mȧ·kô′lĭ), **Catharine**. = Catharine MC-AULEY.

**McCauley, Mary,** *nee* **Lud′wig** (?lŭd′wĭg). *Known as* **Molly Pitch′er** (pĭch′ẽr). 1754?–1832. American Revolutionary heroine, b. near Trenton, N.J.; m. 1st John Caspar Hays (1769, d. 1789); 2d George McCauley. At battle of Monmouth (June 28, 1778), carried water to the weary and wounded soldiers (hence the sobriquet "Molly Pitcher"), and when her husband was overcome by the heat, manned his cannon through rest of battle. Awarded annuity (Feb. 21, 1822, "Act for the relief of Molly M'Kolly") by Pennsylvania assembly for her services.

**Macchiavelli.** Variant of MACHIAVELLI.

**Mc·Clel′lan** (mȧ·klĕl′ăn), **George Brinton**. 1826–1885. American army officer, b. Philadelphia; grad. U.S.M.A., West Point (1846). Served through Mexican War. On engineering duty (till 1855); studied military operations abroad (1855–56); recommended new type of cavalry saddle (McClellan saddle) used in U.S. army. At outbreak of Civil War, commissioned major general, U.S. army (May 3, 1861), commanding department of the Ohio; influential in keeping Kentucky in the Union. Commanded division of the Potomac (July, 1861); commissioned general in chief (Nov., 1861). Directed the Peninsula campaign (Mar.–Aug., 1862); commanded at Antietam (Sept. 17, 1862); replaced by Gen. Burnside (1862); Democratic candidate for president (1864); defeated by Lincoln. Governor of New Jersey (1878–81). His son **George Brinton** (1865–1940), b. Dresden, Saxony, was a member of U.S. House of Representatives (1895–1903); mayor of New York (1903–09); professor of economic history, Princeton (1912–31); served overseas in World War I; wrote *The Oligarchy of Venice* (1904), *The Heel of War* (1915), *Venice and Bonaparte* (1931), *Modern Italy* (1933), etc.

**McClellan, Henry Brainerd**. 1840–1904. A cousin of Gen. George B. McClellan. American Confederate officer; chief of staff to J. E. B. Stuart (1863–64) and to Wade Hampton (1864–65). Author of *The Life and Campaigns of Major-General J. E. B. Stuart* (1885).

**Mc·Clel′land** (mȧ·klĕl′ănd), **Robert**. 1807–1880. American lawyer; member, U.S. House of Representatives (1843–49). Governor of Michigan (1851–53). U.S. secretary of the interior (1853–57).

**Mc·Cler′nand** (mȧ·klûr′nănd), **John Alexander**. 1812–1900. American lawyer and soldier; practiced in Illinois. Member, U.S. House of Representatives (1843–51; 1859–61). Served in Civil War; brigadier general (1861); major general (1862). Circuit judge, Sangamon district, Ill. (1870–73).

**Macclesfield,** Earls of. See Charles GERARD; Sir Thomas PARKER.

**Mc·Clin′tic** (mȧ·klĭn′tĭk), **Guthrie**. 1893–1961. American theatrical producer and director, esp. of plays starring his wife Katharine Cornell (*q.v.*).

**Mc·Clin′tock** (mȧ·klĭn′tŭk), Sir **Francis Leopold**. 1819–1907. British naval officer and explorer, b. Dundalk, Ireland. Vice-admiral (1877) and admiral (1884). Served in Arctic expeditions in search of Sir John Franklin under Sir James Clark Ross (1848), Sir Erasmus Ommanney (1850), and Sir Edward Belcher (1852); commanded an expedition in search of Franklin (1857–59) and published story (1859) of fate of the Franklin expedition.

**M'Clin'tock** (mȧ·klĭn'tŭk), **John.** 1814–1870. American Methodist Episcopal clergyman and educator, b. Philadelphia. Pastor, St. Paul's Church, New York (1857–60), American Chapel, Paris, France (1860–64). First president, Drew Theol. Sem. (1867–70). See James STRONG.

**Mc·Clos'key** (mȧ·klŏs'kĭ), **John.** 1810–1885. American Roman Catholic cardinal, b. Brooklyn, N.Y. Archbishop of New York (1864). Created first American cardinal (1875).

**Mc·Clung'** (mȧ·klŭng'), **Clarence Erwin.** 1870–1946. American zoologist; author of *Microscopical Technique* and *Chromosome Theory of Heredity.*

**Mc·Clure'** (mȧ·kloor'), **James Gore King.** 1848–1932. American theologian; president of Lake Forest U. (1897–1901), and Presbyterian Theol. Sem., Chicago (1905–28). Author of *Possibilities* (1896), *Living for the Best* (1903), etc.

**McClure, John.** 1893–1956. American lyric poet, b. Ardmore, Okla.

**McClure,** Sir **Robert John Le Mesurier.** 1807–1873. British naval officer, b. Wexford, Ireland. Commanded an expedition in search for Sir John Franklin (1850–54), and in course of the search discovered the Northwest Passage.

**McClure, Samuel Sidney.** 1857–1949. Editor and publisher, b. in County Antrim, Ireland; to U.S. in his youth. Established McClure Syndicate, first newspaper syndicate in U.S. (1884), purchasing manuscripts from authors and selling them to newspapers for simultaneous publication. Founder (1893) and editor, *McClure's Magazine.*

**Mc·Clurg'** (mȧ·klûrg'), **Alexander Caldwell.** 1832–1901. American bookdealer and publisher; served through Civil War; bought interest in bookseller's business, Chicago (1866); chief owner of business (1886), later reorganized as A. C. McClurg & Co.

**Mc·Col'lum** (mȧ·kŏl'ŭm), **Elmer Verner.** 1879–1967. American physiological chemist; professor, U. of Wisconsin (1913–17), Johns Hopkins (from 1917). Author of *The Newer Knowledge of Nutrition* (1918), *Foods, Nutrition and Health* (1933), etc.

**Mc·Comb'** (mȧ·kōōm'), **Samuel.** 1864–1938. Clergyman, b. in Londonderry, Ireland. Joined Episcopal Church and became associated with Elwood Worcester (*q.v.*) in the Emmanuel movement ("a movement for moral treatment of nervous disorders") at Boston, Mass. (1906–16). Canon, Cathedral of the Incarnation, Baltimore (1916–22). Professor of pastoral theology, Episcopal Theol. School (from 1922). Author of *Religion and Medicine* (1907), *Prayer*...(1913), *Faith* (1915), *The Power of Prayer* (1921), etc.

**Mc·Con'nell** (mȧ·kŏn''l), **Francis John.** 1871–1953. American Methodist Episcopal clergyman; president of DePauw U. (1909–12). Elected bishop (1912). Author of *The Diviner Immanence* (1906), *The Christlike God* (1927), *Christianity and Coercion* (1933), etc.

**Mc·Cook'** (mȧ·kook'), **Alexander McDowell.** 1831–1903. American army officer; grad. U.S.M.A., West Point (1852). Served through Civil War; major general (1862). On frontier duty after Civil War; brigadier general, U.S. army (1890); major general (1894).

**McCook, Edward Moody.** 1833–1909. American army officer; cavalry commander in Civil War; brigadier general (1864). U.S. minister to Hawaii (1866–69); governor of territory of Colorado (1869–75). A brother, **Anson George** (1835–1917), was also an army officer and served with Ohio volunteers through Civil War; brevetted brigadier general (1865); member of U.S. House of Representatives (1877–83); secretary, U.S. Senate (1883–93); chamberlain, New York City (1895–98). A second brother, **Henry Christopher** (1837–1911), was a Presbyterian clergyman and naturalist; chaplain in Civil War (1861–62); pastor in Philadelphia (1870–1902); interested himself in study of spiders and ants; author of *American Spiders and Their Spinning Work* (3 vols., 1889, 1890, 1893). A third brother, **John James** (1843–1927), was a Protestant Episcopal clergyman and educator; served through Civil War; pastor in East Hartford, Conn. (1868–1927); professor of modern languages, Trinity Coll. (from 1886).

**Mac Cool, Finn.** See FINN MAC COOL.

**Mc·Cor'mack** (mȧ·kôr'măk), **John.** 1884–1945. Operatic and concert tenor, b. in Athlone, Ireland; naturalized American citizen (1919). Operatic debut, in *Cavalleria Rusticana,* London (1907). Joined Manhattan Opera Company (1909), and later Chicago Grand Opera Company, Metropolitan Opera Company, Monte Carlo Opera Company. Among his notable roles are Rodolpho in *La Bohème,* Faust, Pinkerton in *Madame Butterfly,* Don Ottavio in *Don Giovanni.* Well known as concert singer, esp. of Irish songs.

**Mc·Cor'mick** (mȧ·kôr'mĭk), **Anne;** *nee* **O'Hare'** (ō·hâr'). 1881–1954. American journalist, b. Yorkshire, Eng.; m. Francis J. McCormick. Free-lance foreign correspondent of New York *Times* (from 1921); awarded Pulitzer prize for European correspondence (1937), first woman to receive a major Pulitzer prize in journalism. Author of *Hammer and the Scythe: Communist Russia Enters the Second Decade* (1928).

**Mac·Cor'mick** (mȧ·kôr'mĭk), **Austin Harbutt.** 1893– . Penologist, b. Georgetown, Ont., Canada; to U.S. in infancy. Associate of Thomas Mott Osborne in study of prison conditions and prison management; with Paul W. Garrett, investigated prisons of U.S., and wrote *The Handbook of American Prisons and Reformatories* (1929). Commissioner of correction, City of New York (1934–40); instituted important reforms in penitentiary on Welfare Island (1934–37) and superintended construction of new modern institution on Ricker's Island.

**McCormick, Robert.** 1780–1846. American inventor, b. in Rockbridge County, Va. Invented a gristmill and hydraulic machine (1830–31) and experimented unsuccessfully with threshing and reaping machines. His son **Cyrus Hall** (1809–1884) invented a successful reaping machine (patented 1834); began its manufacture on a large scale (1847); introduced it into Europe at International Exhibition (London, 1851); in partnership (from 1859) with his brother **Leander James** (1819–1900); formed McCormick Harvesting Machine Co., with himself as president (1879–84) and brother as vice-president (1879–81); succeeded as president (1884–1902) by his son **Cyrus Hall** (1859–1936), who became first president (1902–19; board chairman 1919–35) of International Harvester Co.

**McCormick, Robert Sanderson.** 1849–1919. Grandson of Robert McCormick (*q.v.*). American diplomat, b. in Rockbridge County, Va. U.S. minister to Austria (1901–02) and first U.S. ambassador to Austria-Hungary (1902); U.S. ambassador to Russia (1902–05); U.S. ambassador to France (1905–07); m. Katherine Van Et'ta (văn ĕt'ȧ) Me·dill' (mĕ·dĭl'), dau. of Joseph Medill (*q.v.*), proprietor and editor of the Chicago *Tribune.* Their son **Joseph Medill** (1877–1925), b. Chicago, Ill., was a journalist and politician; on staff of Chicago *Daily Tribune;* proprietor of the *Tribune;* also financially interested in Cleveland *Leader* and Cleveland *News;* member of U.S. House of Representatives (1917–19), U.S. Senate (1919–25). Another son, **Robert Rutherford** (1880–1955), b. Chicago, studied law and took over editorship of Chicago *Tribune;* president, Sanitary District of Chicago (1905–10); practiced law in Chicago (1908–20); with A.E.F. in France (1917–18); editor and publisher, Chicago *Tribune* (from 1920). See Joseph Medill PATTERSON. The wife of Joseph Medill McCormick, **Ruth,** *nee* **Han′na** [hăn′*ȧ*] (1880–1944), dau. of Mark Hanna, m. Joseph Medill McCormick (1903; d. 1925) and Albert G. Simms (1932); interested herself in political, civic, and industrial issues; became Republican national committeewoman from Illinois (1924–28); member, U.S. House of Representatives (1929–31) and Republican candidate for U.S. senator (1930).

**McCormick, Samuel Black.** 1858–1928. American Presbyterian clergyman and educator, b. in Westmoreland County, Pa. President, Coe College (1897–1904), Western U. of Pennsylvania (1904–20), which he transferred to Pittsburgh, renamed U. of Pittsburgh, and organized into a modern institution of learning.

**McCormick, Stephen.** 1784–1875. Son of John McCormick. American inventor, b. Auburn, Va. Invented cast-iron plow with replaceable parts and adjustable wrought-iron point (patented 1819, 1826, 1837).

**McCormick, Vance Cris′well** (krĭs′wĕl; -w*ĕ*l). 1872–1946. American newspaper publisher, b. Harrisburg, Pa. Publisher of Harrisburg *Patriot* and Harrisburg *Evening News.* Chairman, Democratic national campaign committee (1916). Chairman, War Trade Board (1917–19). Adviser to the president, on American commission to negotiate peace, in Paris (1919).

**Mc·Cosh′** (m*ȧ*·kŏsh′), **James.** 1811–1894. Philosopher and educator, b. in Ayrshire, Scotland; grad. Edinburgh U. (1833); professor of logic and metaphysics, Queen's College, Belfast (1852–68). President, Princeton (1868–88). Author of *The Method of the Divine Government...* (1850), *The Intuitions of the Mind Inductively Investigated* (1860), *The Supernatural in Relation to the Natural* (1862), *An Examination of Mr. J. S. Mill's Philosophy ...*(1866), *The Laws of Discursive Thought* (1870), *Christianity and Positivism* (1871), *Psychology* (2 vols., 1886–87), etc.

**Mc·Coy′** (m*ȧ*·koi′), **Frank Ross.** 1874–1954. American army officer; grad. U.S.M.A., West Point (1897). Served in Cuba (1898), the Philippines, in Mexico (1915–16), with A.E.F. in France (1917–19). Assistant to governor general of the Philippines (1921–25); election supervisor in Nicaragua (1928); head of commission on conciliation between Bolivia and Paraguay (1929); retired (1938); head, commission on Japan (1945–46).

**McCoy, Samuel Duff.** 1882–1964. American journalist; investigated and wrote on peonage conditions in Florida (1923–24), and earned for New York *World* the Pulitzer award (1924) for "most disinterested and meritorious public service rendered by any American newspaper during the year." Author of *Tippecanoe* (a novel; 1916), *Merchants of the Morning* (verse; 1919), *This Man Adams* (1929).

**Mac·Crack′en** (m*ȧ*·krăk′*ĕ*n), **Henry Mitchell.** 1840–1918. American Presbyterian clergyman and educator, b. Oxford, Ohio. Professor of philosophy, N.Y.U. (1884–85), vice-chancellor (1885–91), chancellor (1891–1910). His son **John Henry** (1875–1948) was president of Westminster Coll., Missouri (1899–1903), of Lafayette, Easton, Pa. (1915–26). Another son, **Henry Noble** (1880–1970), president of Vassar (1915–46); author of a number of textbooks in English; editor of works of Lydgate, Chaucer, and Shakespeare.

**Mc·Crae′** (m*ȧ*·krā′), **John.** 1872–1918. Canadian physician and poet, b. Guelph, Ontario. Surgeon at Alexandra Hospital in Montreal and lecturer in pathology and medicine, McGill medical school. Lieutenant in Boer War (1899–1902) and surgeon (lieut. colonel) to first brigade of Canadian artillery in World War; killed in action. As poet, remembered chiefly for lyric *In Flanders Fields.*

**Mc·Crie′** (m*ȧ*·krē′), **Thomas.** 1772–1835. Scottish Presbyterian clergyman; ejected from his pastorate for nonconformity (1809). Published *Life of John Knox* (1812), a history of the Reformation in Italy (1827) and in Spain (1829), and other biographical and historical treatises.

**Mc·Cul′lers** (m*ȧ*·kŭl′ẽrz), **Carson,** *nee* **Smith.** 1917–1967. American novelist, b. Columbus, Ga.; m. Reeves McCullers (1937); among her novels are *The Heart is a Lonely Hunter* (1940), *Reflections in a Golden Eye* (1941).

**Mc·Cul′loch** (m*ȧ*·kŭl′*ŭ*k; -*ŭ*ᴋ), **Hugh.** 1808–1895. American lawyer and banker, b. Kennebunk, Me. Practiced law, Fort Wayne, Ind. (1833); bank official, Fort Wayne (1835–63). U.S. comptroller of the currency (1863–65); U.S. secretary of the treasury (1865–69; again, 1884–85).

**Mac·cul′loch** (m*ȧ*·kŭl′*ŭ*ᴋ; -*ŭ*k), **John.** 1773–1835. Scottish geologist; commissioned (1826) to prepare a geological map of Scotland. Among his books are *A Description of the Western Isles of Scotland, including the Isle of Man* (1819), *A Geological Classification of Rocks* (1821), and *Highlands and Western Isles of Scotland* (1824).

**Mc·Cul′loch** (m*ȧ*·kŭl′*ŭ*ᴋ; -*ŭ*k), **John Ramsay.** 1789–1864. Scottish economist; comptroller of the stationery office (1838–64). Author of *Principles of Political Economy* (1825); propounded a wages' fund theory in *Essay on the Circumstances which determine the Rate of Wages and the Condition of the Labouring Classes* (1826); compiled a *Dictionary...of Commerce and Commercial Navigation* (1832).

**Mc·Cum′ber** (m*ȧ*·kŭm′bẽr), **Porter James.** 1858–1933. American lawyer and legislator; U.S. senator (1899–1923); chairman of Senate finance committee (1922–23) and cosponsor of Fordney-McCumber Tariff Act (1922).

**Mac·Cunn′** (?m*ȧ*·kŭn′), **Hamish.** 1868–1916. Scottish composer, esp. of orchestral and choral works.

**Mac·Cur′dy** (m*ȧ*·kûr′dĭ), **George Grant.** 1863–1947. American anthropologist; author of *The Eolithic Problem* (1905), *Some Phases of Prehistoric Archaeology* (1907), *Antiquity of Man in Europe* (1910), *Human Origins—A Manual of Prehistory* (2 vols., 1924), *The Coming of Man* (1932), etc.

**Mc·Cutch′an** (m*ȧ*·kŭch′*ă*n), **Robert Guy.** 1877–1958. American musician and educator; dean of school of music, DePauw U. (1911–37). Author of treatises on church music.

**Mc·Cutch′eon** (m*ȧ*·kŭch′*ŭ*n), **George Barr.** 1866–1928. American novelist, b. near Lafayette, Ind. City editor, Lafayette (Ind.) *Daily Courier* (1893–1901). Author of *Graustark* (1901), *Brewster's Millions* (1902), *Beverly of Graustark* (1904), *Mary Midthorne* (1911), *A Fool and his Money* (1913), *The Prince of Graustark* (1914), *The Merivales* (1929), etc. His brother **John Tinney** (1870–1949), cartoonist on staff of Chicago *Record* (1889–1901), Chicago *Record-Herald* (1901–03), Chicago *Tribune* (from 1903); known esp. for political cartoons, and awarded Pulitzer prize for cartoons (1931).

**Mac·Diar′mid** (m*ȧ*k·dẽr′mĭd), **Hugh.** *Pseudonym of* **Christopher Murray Grieve** (grēv). 1892–1978. Scottish poet; among his books of verse are *Sangschaw, Penny Wheep, A Drunk Man Looks at the Thistle, Stony*

*Limits, First Hymn to Lenin, Cornish Heroic Song for Valda Trevlyn;* wrote also, in prose, *Annals of the Five Senses, Albyn, or the Future of Scotland, Scottish Scene, The Scottish Islands,* etc.

**Mac·Don′agh** (măk·dŭn′ȧ), **Thomas.** 1878–1916. Irish poet; involved in Easter Rebellion in Ireland (1916) and executed. Author of *John-John, Of a Poet-Patriot,* and *Wishes for my Son.*

**Mac·Don′ald** (măk·dŏn′′ld), **Arthur.** 1856–1936. American anthropologist; studied medicine and psychophysics in Europe (1885–89). Specialist with U.S. Bureau of Education (1892–1904). Author of *Abnormal Man* (1893), *Criminology* (1894), *Juvenile Crime and Reformation* (1908), *Mentality of Nations and Social Pathology* (1912), etc.

**Macdonald,** Sir **Claude Maxwell.** 1852–1915. British soldier and diplomat. Served in Egyptian campaign (1882), on the Suakin expedition in eastern Sudan (1884–85); commanded defense of the legations in Peking during the Boxer rebellion (1900). Minister (1900–05) and ambassador (1905–12), Tokyo; endeavored to promote Anglo-Japanese friendship.

**Macdonald, Duncan Black.** 1863–1943. Theologian, b. Glasgow, Scotland; to U.S. (1892). Professor of Semitic languages, Hartford (Conn.) Theol. Sem. (1892-1931). Author of *Religious Attitude and Life in Islam* (1911), *Hebrew Literary Genius...* (1933), *Hebrew Philosophical Genius...* (1935), etc.

**Macdonald, Flora.** 1722–1790. Scottish Jacobite heroine; aided Prince Charles Edward in his escape after the battle of Culloden Moor (1746); m. Allan Macdonald (1750); resident in North Carolina (1774–79), returned to Scotland.

**Macdonald, George.** 1824–1905. Scottish novelist and poet; author of volumes of verse; books for children, including *At the Back of the North Wind* and *The Princess and the Goblin;* a number of "Unspoken Sermons" (1866–89); novels, including *David Elginbrod* (1863), *Alec Forbes* (1865), *Robert Falconer* (1868), *The Elect Lady* (1888), etc.

**Macdonald,** Sir **George.** 1862–1940. Scottish scholar; interested esp. in study of numismatics and archaeology; prepared catalogue of Greek coins in the Hunterian Collection (1899–1905). Author of *Coin Types...* (1905), *The Roman Forts on the Bar Hill* (1907), *The Evolution of Coinage* (1916), *Roman Britain* (1914–28; 1931), and *Agricola in Britain* (1932).

**Macdonald,** Sir **Hector Archibald.** 1853–1903. British soldier; served with distinction in Egypt, in Sudan campaign (1888–91), in expedition to Dongola (1896), at Omdurman (1898); served in the Punjab (1899–1900) and in South Africa (1900–01), where he captured Koodoesberg (Feb., 1900) and opened way to relief of Kimberley, and engaged in actions leading (Feb.–May, 1900) to surrender of Boer generals Cronjé and Prinsloo.

**Mac′do′nald′** (măk′dô′năl′), **Jacques Étienne Joseph Alexandre.** Duc **de Ta′rente′** (dē tȧ′räNt′). 1765–1840. French soldier, of Scottish descent. Served in French Revolutionary and Napoleonic armies; general of brigade (1795) and of division (1796). Distinguished himself at Wagram (1809) and was created marshal of France and duc de Tarente. Commanded a corps in the Russian campaign, and in the campaign for the defense of France (1813–14); negotiated with allies for abdication of Napoleon (1814).

**Mac·Don′ald** (măk·dŏn′′ld), **James Ramsay.** 1866–1937. British statesman, b. Lossiemouth, Scotland. Joined Labor party (1894), its secretary (1900–12), treasurer (1912–24). M.P. (1906–18) and leader of Labor party (1911–14). Pacifist by conviction, opposed England's participation in World War and criticized policies of Asquith and Sir Edward Grey; lost leadership of Labor party (1914) and seat in House of Commons (1918), but regained both (1922). Prime minister and secretary for foreign affairs (Jan., 1924), organizing first Labor ministry in history of Britain; defeated in elections (Oct. 20, 1924). Again prime minister, head of the second Labor ministry (1929–31); remained prime minister as head of coalition cabinet (1931–35); served as lord president of the council in cabinet of Stanley Baldwin; resigned on account of ill health (May 28, 1937). Author of *Socialism and Society, Socialism and Government,* and *The Social Unrest.*

**MacDonald, James Wilson Alexander.** 1824–1908. American sculptor, esp. of portrait busts and bronze statues.

**Macdonald, John.** 1779–1849. Known as "the Apostle of the North." Scottish Presbyterian clergyman; joined Secession Church (1843); influential in advancing evangelical religion in the north of Scotland.

**Macdonald,** Sir **John Alexander.** 1815–1891. Canadian statesman, b. Glasgow, Scotland; settled in Kingston, Canada (1820). Member of House of Assembly (1844–54; 1856–91); premier Upper Canada (1857). Leader of federation movement and influential in securing passage of British North America Act (1867). First prime minister of Dominion of Canada (1867–73); again prime minister (1878–91). Regarded as organizer of Dominion of Canada.

**Macdonald,** Sir **John Hay Athole.** Lord **Kings′burgh** (kĭngz′bŭ·rŭ; -brŭ). 1836–1919. Scottish lawyer, inventor, and military writer. Solicitor general for Scotland (1876–80); lord advocate (1885–86, 1886–88); presided over second division of Court of Session (1888–1915), conducting series of criminal trials. Promoter and officer of volunteer movement; authority on military training and tactics.

**Macdonald, John Sandfield.** 1812–1872. Canadian lawyer and politician; prime minister of Canada (1862–64). First premier, Province of Ontario (1867–71).

**Macdonald, Lawrence.** 1799–1878. Scottish sculptor; noted for his portrait busts.

**Macdonald, Lucy Maud,** *nee* **Montgomery.** 1874–1942. Canadian novelist, b. Prince Edward Island; m. Rev. Ewan Macdonald (1911). Among her books are *Anne of Green Gables* (1909), *Anne of Avonlea, Anne of Ingleside.*

**MacDonald, Malcolm.** 1901– . Son of James Ramsay MacDonald (*q.v.*). British statesman, b. Lossiemouth, Scotland. M.P. (1929 ff.). Secretary of state for colonies (1935), for dominion affairs (1935–38, 1938–39), again for colonies (1938–41). High commissioner for the United Kingdom in Canada (1941–46).

**MacDonald, Ramsay.** See James Ramsay MacDonald.

**MacDonald, William.** 1863–1938. American historian and journalist; on editorial staff, *The Nation* (1918–31). Author of *Jacksonian Democracy* (1905), *Three Centuries of American Democracy* (1923), etc.

**MacDonald, Wilson.** 1880– . Canadian poet; author of *Caw-caw Ballads, Confederation Ode, Flagon of Beauty, Out of the Wilderness, Paul Marchand, Quintrains of Callander, Song of the Undertow,* etc.

**Mac′do·nell′** (măk′dô·nĕl′), **Alastair Ruadh.** *Known as* **Pick′le the Spy** (pĭk′′l). 1725?–1761. Scottish Jacobite; to France (1738) and joined Royal Scots Guards (1743). Entrusted by Highland chiefs with secret mission to Prince Charles Edward (1745); captured by English and confined in Tower of London (1745–47). Under pseudonym "Pickle," acted as spy on Charles (1749–54). Became chief of clan Glengarry (1754).

**Macdonell, Archibald Gordon.** 1895–1941. English journalist and writer; served in World War I. Wrote *Napoleon and His Marshals, Lords and Masters, Autobiography of a Cad,* and *The Spanish Pistol.*

**Mac·don′ell** (măk·dŏn′'l), **Arthur Anthony.** 1854–1930. British Sanskrit scholar, b. in India; professor, Oxford (1899–1926). Author of *Vedic Mythology* (1897), *History of Sanskrit Literature* (1900), *Vedic Grammar* (1910), *India's Past...* (1927), etc.

**Mac·Don′nell** (măk·dŏn′'l), **Antony Patrick.** Baron **MacDonnell of Swin′ford** (swĭn′fẽrd). 1844–1925. British government administrator in India; chief commissioner of the central provinces (1890), lieutenant governor of United Provinces of Agra and Oudh (1895–1901). Member of Council of India (1903).

**Mac′Don·nell′** (*Scot. usu.* măk′dŏ·nĕl′; *Ir. usu.* măk-dŏn′'l), **Sorley Boy.** 1505?–1590. Scoto-Irish chief. Treated with Queen Elizabeth for guarantee of security of settlement of Hebridean Scots on Antrim coast (1560); defeated and held captive by rival Shane O'Neill (1564–67); defeated by earl of Essex (1575); escaped to Scotland (1585); submitted to English government on receipt of grant of all country between Bann and Bush rivers (1586).

**Mac·don′ough** (măk·dŏn′ŭ), **Thomas.** 1783–1825. American naval officer; commanded American fleet on Lake Champlain (1812–14); defeated and captured British squadron in battle of Plattsburg (Sept. 11, 1814).

**Mc·Dou′gall** (măk·do͞o′găl), **Alexander.** 1731?–1786. Revolutionary general in America, b. on island of Islay, Scotland; to America (1738). Commanded British privateers (1756–63). Pamphleteer against British government in New York (1769); imprisoned (1770–71). Served in Revolution; brigadier general (1776); major general (1777); took command of West Point after Arnold's treason. Member, Continental Congress (1781–82; 1784–85).

**Mac·dou′gall** (măk·do͞o′găl), Sir **Patrick Leonard.** 1819–1894. British soldier; served in Canada (1844–54); adjutant general of Canadian militia (1865–69); returned to England (1869) and served as head of intelligence branch at the War Office (1873–78); commander in North America (1877–83).

**McDougall, William.** 1871–1938. Psychologist, b. in Lancashire, Eng. Professor, Harvard (1920–27), Duke (1927–38). Author of *Physiological Psychology* (1905), *Social Psychology* (1908), *Body and Mind* (1912), *Ethics and some Modern World Problems* (1924), *Outline of Abnormal Psychology* (1926), *Janus* (1927), *World Chaos* (1931), *Energies of Men* (1933), etc.

**Mac·Dow′ell** (măk·dou′ĕl), **Edward Alexander.** 1861–1908. American composer, b. New York City. Under patronage of Liszt, produced his *First Modern Suite* at Zürich (1882). Settled in Wiesbaden (1885–88), Boston (1888–96). Professor of music, Columbia (1896–1904). Composer of symphonic poems (*Hamlet, Ophelia, Lancelot and Elaine, Lamia, The Saracens,* etc.), piano sonatas (*Tragica, Eroica, Norse, Keltic*), orchestral suites, concertos for piano and orchestra, and songs and shorter pieces, as in the popular *Woodland Sketches* and *Sea Pieces,* including *To a Wild Rose* and *Thy Beaming Eyes.* Elected to American Hall of Fame (1960).

**Mc·Dow′ell** (măk·dou′ĕl), **Ephraim.** 1771–1830. American surgeon; practiced in Danville, Ky. Pioneer in abdominal surgery; performed (1809) first recorded operation in ovarian surgery in United States.

**McDowell, Franklin Davey.** 1888–1965. Canadian novelist; author of romance *The Champlain Road* (1940), which received first Governor-General's Annual Literary Award (established 1936 by Lord Tweedsmuir).

**McDowell, Irvin.** 1818–1885. American army officer; grad. U.S.M.A., West Point (1838). Served through Mexican War. Promoted brigadier general (May 14, 1861) and put in command of Department of Northeastern Virginia; lost battle of Bull Run (July 21, 1861); superseded by McClellan. Major general and corps commander in second battle of Bull Run (Aug. 29–30, 1862); criticized and relieved of command for his conduct in that battle, but exonerated by court of inquiry. No further field command in Civil War. Major general, U.S. army (from 1872); retired (1882).

**MacDowell, Katherine Sherwood,** *nee* **Bon′ner** (bŏn′ẽr). *Pen name* **Sherwood Bonner.** 1849–1883. American fiction writer, b. Holly Springs, Miss.; m. Edward MacDowell (1871). Writer of stories of southern life and character.

**Macdowell, Patrick.** 1799–1870. Irish sculptor; executed marble statues of William Pitt and the earl of Chatham; designed group typifying Europe for the Albert Memorial in London.

**Mc·Duf′fie** (măk·dŭf′ĭ), **George.** 1790?–1851. American legislator, b. in Georgia. Member, U.S. House of Representatives (1821–34). Governor of South Carolina (1834–36). Member, U.S. Senate (1842–46). Noted orator; prominent in support of doctrine of nullification.

**Ma′cé′** (ma′sā′), **Jean.** 1815–1894. French journalist, educator, and politician; elected senator for life (1883). Among his works are *Théâtre du Petit-Château* (1862), *Morale en Action* (1865), *La France avant les Francs* (1881), and *Philosophie de Poche* (1893).

**Ma·ce′do** (mȧ·sā′tho͞o), **José Agostinho de.** 1761–1831. Portuguese writer; entered Augustinian order (1778) but was expelled because of irregularity of his life. Court chaplain (1802); censor of books (1824–29); court chronicler (1830). Among his verse, *A Meditação* (1813), *O Oriente, Os Burros* (1812–14); among his critical works, *Motim Literário* (1811), *As Pateadas* (1812).

**Macedonian** dynasty. (1) A dynasty (867–1056) of Byzantine emperors; founded by Basil I. (2) See Ptolemy.

**Macedonicus.** See Lucius Aemilius Paulus.

**Mac′e·do′ni·us** (măs′ē·dō′nĭ·ŭs). Patriarch of the Eastern Church; elected bishop of Constantinople by Arian bishops (341 A.D.). Compelled by Emperor Constans to resign his see (348), but reinstalled two years later. Expelled by Council of Constantinople (360) and became leader of a sect (Macedonians).

**Mc′El·roy** (măk′ĕl·roi), **Robert.** 1872–1959. American historian, b. Perryville, Ky. On history faculty at Princeton (1898–1925); professor of American history, Oxford U., England (1925–38). Author of *The Winning of the Far West* (1914), *Grover Cleveland . . .* (2 vols., 1923), *The Pathway of Peace* (1927), etc.

**Mc′En·tee** (măk′ĕn·tē), **Jervis.** 1828–1891. American landscape painter, esp. of winter and autumn scenes.

**Ma·ce′o** (mä·sā′ō), **Antonio** (1848–1896) and his brother **José** (1846–1896). Cuban patriots; fought together in the Ten Years' War (1868–78); joined the rebellion together (1895) and defeated the Spaniards at Jobito and at Sao del Indio (1895).

**Mc′E·voy** (măk′ĕ·voi), **Arthur Ambrose.** 1878–1927. English portrait painter.

**McEvoy, Joseph Patrick.** 1895–1958. American writer, b. New York City. Author of *Slams of Life* (verse; 1919), *The Potters* (comedy; 1924), *Allez Ooop* (revue; 1927), *Show Girl* (novel; 1928), *Denny and the Dumb Cluck* (1930), *New Americana* (revue; 1932), etc.

**Mc·Ew′en** (măk·ū′ĕn), Sir **John B.** 1868–1948. British musician, b. in Scotland. Composer of symphonies, sonatas, orchestral suites, songs, etc.

**Mac·Ew′en** (măk·ū′ĕn), **Walter.** 1860–1943. American painter, esp. of portraits, landscapes, and genre subjects.

**Mac·ew′en** (măk·ū′ĕn), Sir **William.** 1848–1924. Scottish surgeon; known as a pioneer in field of bone surgery.

**Mac·fad′yen** (măk·făj′ĕn), **Allan.** 1860–1907. British bacteriologist; planned and organized Lister Inst., with which the Coll. of State Medicine was merged. Author of *The Cell as the Unit of Life* (1908).

**M'Fall, Frances Elizabeth.** See Sarah GRAND.

**Mac·far′ren** (măk·făr′ĕn), Sir **George Alexander.** 1813–1887. English composer, b. London. Studied at Royal Acad. of Music (1829–36), professor there (1837–46, 1851–75); principal of Royal Acad. of Music, and professor of music at Cambridge (1875–87). Among his operas are *The Devil's Opera* (1838), *Don Quixote* (1846), and *Robin Hood* (1860); oratorios, *St. John the Baptist* (1873), *The Resurrection* (1876), *Joseph* (1877).

**Mc·Fee′** (măk·fē′), **William.** 1881–1966. English writer; son of English father and Canadian mother; b. at sea; to U.S. (1911). Marine engineer by profession; at sea (1905–22). Settled at Westport, Conn. (1922). Author of *An Ocean Tramp* (1908), *Aliens* (1914), *Casuals of the Sea* (1916), *Capt. Macedoine's Daughter* (1920), *Harbours of Memory* (1921), *Swallowing the Anchor* (1925), *Sailors of Fortune* (1929), *The Harbourmaster* (1932), *The Beachcomber* (1935), *Derelicts* (1938), *Watch Below* (1940), *Spenlove in Arcady* (1941), *Ship to Shore* (1943), etc.

**Mac·Gahan′** (má·găn′), **Januarius Aloysius.** 1844–1878. American war correspondent, b. in Perry County, Ohio. Reported the Franco-Prussian War (1870–71), Paris Commune (1871), Russian campaign against Khiva (1873), the *Pandora* expedition to the Arctic (1875), bashi-bazouk massacres in Bulgaria (1876).

**Mc·Gar′rah** (má·găr′á), **Gates W.** 1863–1940. American banker, b. Monroe, N.Y.; chairman of executive committee of Chase National Bank, New York City (1926–27); president, Bank for International Settlements, Basel, Switzerland (1930–33).

**Mc·Gee′** (má·gē′), **Thomas D'Arcy.** 1825–1868. Journalist, politician, and writer, b. in County Louth, Ireland. On staff of *Freeman's Journal* in London, and the *Nation.* A leader in the Young Ireland party (1846); fled to U.S. (1848) and founded *New York Nation* and *American Celt.* To Canada (1857); member of parliament (from 1858); president of the council (1862–63); minister of agriculture (1864–68). Supported policy of federation and was elected member of the first Dominion parliament (1867–68). Assassinated at Ottawa (Apr. 7, 1868), probably because of his statements against the Fenian invasion. Among his books are *A History of the Irish Settlers in North America* (1851), *A Popular History of Ireland* (3 vols., 1862–69), etc.

**McGee, William John.** 1853–1912. American geologist and anthropologist, b. near Farley, Iowa. With U.S. Geological Survey (1883–93), Bureau of American Ethnology (1893–1903).

**Mc·Gif′fert** (má·gĭf′ẽrt), **Arthur Cushman.** 1861–1933. American theologian, b. Sauquoit, N.Y. Ordained in Presbyterian ministry (1888); shifted to Congregationalist (1899). Professor of church history (1893–1927) and president (1917–26), Union Theol. Sem.

**Mc·Gif′fin** (má·gĭf′ĭn), **Philo Norton.** 1860–1897. American soldier of fortune; grad. U.S.N.A., Annapolis (1882). Honorably discharged from U.S. navy (1884); commissioned in Chinese navy (1885); professor at naval college in Tientsin (1885–94). Executive officer of battleship *Chen Yuen* in battle with Japanese off the Yalu River (Sept. 17, 1894).

**Mc·Gill′** (má·gĭl′), **James.** 1744–1813. Scottish-born Canadian businessman and philanthropist, of Montreal; bequeathed £10,000 and land for founding of a college to bear his name. The college became McGill University by royal charter (1821).

**Mac·Gill′** (má·gĭl′), **Patrick.** 1890– . Irish poet and novelist; served in World War I (1914–18). Wrote *Gleanings from a Navvy's Scrap Book, Songs of a Navvy, Songs of the Dead End, Children of the Dead End, The Rat-Pit, The Great Push, Soldier Songs, Songs of Donegal.*

**McGillicuddy, Cornelius.** See Connie MACK.

**Mc·Gil′li·vray** (má·gĭl′ĭ·vrā), **Alexander.** 1759?–1793. American Creek Indian chief; educated in Charleston and Savannah; loyalist during American Revolution, and associated with British trading firm as its agent with the Creeks. Sought to organize confederation of southern Indians to force back the whites (1783 ff.). Incited attacks on American settlements (1785–87). Clever in diplomacy, playing off Spanish against Americans in trying to advance Creek interests. Negotiated treaty with U.S. in New York (1790); later repudiated it (1792) when he obtained better terms from the Spanish.

**Mac·Gil′li·vray** (má·gĭl′ĭ·vrā), **William.** 1796–1852. Scottish naturalist; author of *A History of British Birds* (1837–52).

**Mc·Giv′ney** (má·gĭv′nĭ), **Michael Joseph.** 1852–1890. American Roman Catholic priest, b. Waterbury, Conn. Leader of a group which founded at New Haven, Conn. (1882), the Knights of Columbus.

**Mc·Glach′lin** (má·gläк′lĭn), **Edward Fenton.** 1868–1946. American army officer; grad. U.S.M.A., West Point (1889). Served in Spanish-American War, the Philippines, and with A.E.F. in France, as chief of artillery of the first army (May–Nov., 1918) and commander of the 1st division (1918–19) and the 7th division (1919–21). Retired (1923).

**Mc·Glynn′** (má·glĭn′), **Edward.** 1837–1900. American Roman Catholic clergyman, b. New York City. Pastor of St. Stephen's parish, New York (1866–87). His public advocacy of Henry George's single-tax doctrine and platform appearances (1886) on behalf of George's candidacy for mayor of New York brought condemnation from his superiors; removed from his pastorate (1887) and ordered to Rome; excommunicated (July 4, 1887) on his refusal to obey. Reinstated in Roman Catholic ministry (1892); pastor at Newburgh, N.Y. (1894–1900).

**Mc·Gov′ern** (ma·gŭv′ẽrn), **George Stanley.** 1922– . American politician, b. Avon, S. Dak. U.S. senator from S. Dak. (1963– ); Democratic candidate for U.S. president (1972).

**Mac·gow′an** (má·gou′ăn), **Kenneth.** 1888–1963. American writer and theatrical producer, b. Winthrop, Mass. Dramatic critic (1910–25); independent producer (1927–29); with RKO-Radio Pictures (1933–35); brought out *Little Women, Anne of Green Gables, La Cucaracha, Becky Sharp.* Later, with Twentieth Century-Fox Film Corp. (1935–41).

**Mac·Grath′** (má·gräth′), **Harold.** 1871–1932. American fiction writer, b. Syracuse, N.Y. Author of tales of adventure and romance, including: *Arms and the Woman* (1899), *Hearts and Masks* (1905), *The Carpet from Bagdad* (1911), *Deuces Wild* (1913), *Yellow Typhoon* (1919), *The Green Stone* (1924), etc.

**Mc·Graw′** (má·grô′), **John Joseph.** 1875–1934. American professional baseball player, b. Truxton, N.Y.; third baseman, Baltimore Orioles (1891–99); manager, New York Giants (1902–32).

**Mc·Grea′dy** (?má·grā′dĭ), **James.** 1758?–1817. American Presbyterian revivalist; inspirer of revival movements in Logan County, Ky. (1797, 1798, 1799), forerunners of the great revival which started in his churches in Logan County and swept the West and South in 1800.

**Mac·greg'or** (mȧ·grĕg'ẽr), **John.** 1825–1892. English traveler and writer, under pseudonym **Rob Roy** (rŏb roi). Designed (1865) a short, light, flat-decked canoe (called a Rob Roy) for river cruising, and made long cruises in it (from 1865). Author of *A Thousand Miles in the Rob Roy Canoe* (1866), etc.

**Macgregor** *or* **Campbell, Robert.** *Known as* **Rob Roy** (rŏb roi). 1671–1734. Freebooter of the Scottish highlands, chief of the clan Macgregor; engaged in rustling cattle and exacting tribute for protection against thieves. Arrested and sentenced to be transported, but pardoned (1727). Sir Walter Scott's introduction to his novel *Rob Roy* gives particulars of the freebooter's life history.

**Mc·Grig'or** (mȧ·grĭg'ẽr), Sir **James.** 1771–1858. British army surgeon; chief of medical staff of Wellington's army in the Peninsular War (1811); director-general of army medical department (1815–51).

**Mc·Gro'ar·ty** (mȧ·grō'ẽr·tĭ), **John Steven.** 1862–1944. American lawyer and writer; settled and practiced in Los Angeles (from 1901). Elected poet laureate of California by state legislature (1933). Author of *Just California* (1903), *Wander Songs* (1908), *The King's Highway* (1909), the dramas *La Golondrina, Osceola, Babylon,* and books about California.

**Mc·Guf'fey** (mȧ·gŭf'ĭ), **William Holmes.** 1800–1873. American educator, b. in Washington County, Pa. Professor, U. of Virginia (1845–73). Best known for his series of *Eclectic Readers* (first and second readers, 1836; third and fourth readers, 1837). More than 120,000,000 copies of McGuffey's *Readers* in original and revised editions have been sold.

**Mc·Guire'** (mȧ·gwīr'), **William Anthony.** 1887–1940. American playwright and scenarist, b. Chicago; author of *Six Cylinder Love, Twelve Miles Out,* etc.

**Mach** (mäĸ), **Edmund Robert Otto von.** 1870–1929. German-American art historian; to U.S. (1891); openly championed German cause in World War until U.S. entered conflict; gave up academic career for law (1923). American editor of *Allgemeines Lexikon der Bildenden Künstler;* author of *Greek Sculpture* (1903), *A Handbook of Greek and Roman Sculpture* (1904), *Outline of a History of Painting* (1905), *The Art of Painting in the 19th Century* (1907), etc.

**Mach, Ernst.** 1838–1916. Austrian physicist and philosopher. Investigated in his researches in physics the physiology and psychology of the senses, esp. in relation to the theory of knowledge; one of the founders of *Empiriokritizismus,* a realistic philosophy based on the analysis of sensations.

**Má'cha** (mä'kȧ), **Karel Hynek.** 1810–1836. Czech lyric poet and novelist; representative of Czech romanticism.

**Mach'a·bees** (măk'ȧ·bēz). Var. of MACCABEES.

**Ma·cha'do** (mȧ·shä'thōō), **Augusto d'O'li·vei'ra** (thō'-lē·vā'ē·rȧ). 1845–1924. Portuguese composer, esp. of operettas and comic operas.

**Machado, Bernardino Luiz.** 1851–1944. Portuguese statesman, b. Rio de Janeiro. Entered Parliament (1882); supported republicanism (1897–1921); minister of foreign affairs in provisional government (1910); premier (1914); president of Portugal (1915–17); banished by insurgents (1917); premier of a coalition ministry (1921); again president (1925–26); forced to leave Portugal on charge of insurrection (1927).

**Ma·cha'do** (mä·chä'thō), **Manuel.** 1874–1947. Spanish librarian and writer; director, Madrid Municipal Library and Museum (1918 ff.). Among his poems are *Alma, Caprichos, El Amor y la Muerte;* among his plays, written in collaboration with his brother Antonio (see MACHADO RUIZ), are *Iulianillo Valcarcel, Las Adelfas, Juan de Mañana, La Duquera de Benameji.*

**Ma·cha'do de As·siz'** (mȧ·shä'thōō thē ȧ·sēs'), **Joaquim Maria.** 1839–1908. Brazilian writer; among his poetical works are *Crisálidas* (1864), *Falenas* (1869); among his prose works, *Memórias Póstumas de Braz Cubas* (1881), *Esau e Jacob* (1904).

**Ma·cha'do Ru·iz'** (mä·chä'thō rōō·ēth'), **Antonio.** 1875–1939. Spanish poet, playwright, and scholar, b. Seville. Best known for lyrics; collaborated often with his brother Manuel Machado (*q.v.*).

**Ma·cha'do y Mo·ra'les** (mä·chä'thō ē mō·rä'lās), **Gerardo.** 1871–1939. Cuban politician, b. Santa Clara. Took part in revolution against Spain (1895–98); Liberal party leader, supported by Zayas y Alfonso; president of Cuba (1925–33); deposed by popular revolt (1933); fled to U.S.

**Ma Chan-shan** (mä' jän'shän'). 1887–1950. Chinese general, a Moslem, b. in Fengtien province. Enlisted (1907); garrison commander (1929) in border region of Heiho, north Manchuria; member of Heilungkiang provincial government (1931); opposed Japanese advance in north Manchuria, putting up stubborn defense at Nonni River; bribed by Japanese to join Manchukuoan puppet regime but soon (1931) deserted them with money and official secrets; again led opposition, escaped to Siberia; later (1937) leader of campaigns in Suiyuan against Japanese.

**Ma'char** (mȧ'ĸȧr), **Josef Svatopluk.** 1864–1942. Czech poet. Bank official in Vienna (1891–1918); inspector general of Czech army (1919–24). Author of the lyric trilogy *Confiteor* (1887), sarcastic sonnets (4 vols., 1891–93), political poems, as *Tristium Vindobonae* (1893), the novel in verse *Magdalena* (1893), the satirical epic *Warriors of God* (1897), the religious poem *Golgotha* (1901), the books of verse *In the Glow of the Hellenic Sun* (1905) and *Poison from Judea* (1906).

**Ma'chault' d'Ar'nou'ville'** (mȧ'shō' dȧr'nōō'vēl'), **Jean Baptiste.** 1701–1794. French statesman; comptroller general of finances (1745–54); secretary for the navy (1754–57); opposed alliance with Austria and thus gained ill will of Mme. de Pompadour, who caused his dismissal from office in disgrace (1757); arrested as a suspect and died in prison (1794).

**Machaut** *or* **Machault, Guillaume de.** See GUILLAUME DE MACHAUT.

**Mach'en** (măk'ĕn), **Arthur.** 1863–1947. English novelist and essayist; author of *Eleusinia, The Anatomy of Tobacco, The Chronicle of Clemendy, The Great God Pan, The Hill of Dreams, Dr. Stiggins, The Secret Glory, The Shining Pyramid, Dog and Duck, Ornaments in Jade, Dreads and Drolls, The Children of the Pool,* etc.

**Ma'chen** (mā'chĕn), **John Gres'ham** (grĕs'ăm). 1881–1937. American theologian; a leader of the fundamentalists in the Presbyterian Church; general assembly of the church refused to ratify him for a professorship at Princeton Theol. Sem. (1926) because of his intolerance; investigation of Princeton Theol. Sem. followed and a new board of control was organized. Machen withdrew (1929) to found, head, and teach New Testament at Westminster Theol. Sem., Philadelphia. Assailed liberalism of Presbyterian board of foreign missions (1931) and set up (1933) his own independent board. Tried on disciplinary charges by Presbyterian special court, found guilty, and suspended from ministry (1935). Seceded and, with followers, founded (1936) the Presbyterian Church of America.

**Mc·Hen'ry** (măk·hĕn'rĭ), **James.** 1753–1816. Patriot in American Revolution, b. in County Antrim, Ireland; to America (1771). On medical staff in Continental army (1775–78). Private secretary to General Washington (1778–80), to Lafayette (1780–81). Member, Continental Congress (1783–86). Maryland delegate to Constitutional Convention (1787). U.S. secretary of war (1796–1800).

**Ma′chia·vel′li** (mä′kyä·vĕl′lē; *Angl.* măk′ĭ·ȧ·vĕl′ĭ), **Niccolò.** 1469–1527. Italian statesman and political philosopher, b. in Florence. Secretary to the Dieci di Libertà e Pace, Florence (1498–1512); carried out several diplomatic missions in the Italian states, France, and Germany. Deprived of office by the Medici when they regained power in Florence (1512), and imprisoned for a time. Retired to his estate near San Casciano in Val di Pesa and devoted himself to study and writing. Most famous work, *Il Principe* ("the prince"), containing his theory of government and a number of maxims of practical statecraft; also wrote *Discorsi*, *Istorie Fiorentine*, *Arte della Guerra*, etc.

**Ma·cí′a y Llu′sa** (mä·thē′ä ē lōō′sä), **Francisco.** 1859–1933. Spanish statesman; leader of extremist Catalan party (1917); exiled from Spain. Attempted (1926) to raise rebellion in northern Spain and was imprisoned for a short time; expelled from U.S. and several South American countries for his attempts to raise funds to finance revolutionary activities. After amnesty (1931), returned to Barcelona; organized followers and after collapse of the monarchy (Apr. 14, 1931) proclaimed Catalonia a republic; chosen provisional president; negotiated compromise with Madrid government (1932) whereby Catalonia was recognized as an autonomous region.

**Mc′Il·wain** (măk′ĭl·wān), **Charles Howard.** 1871– . American political scientist; professor, Harvard (1916–46). Author of *The American Revolution* (1923; awarded Pulitzer prize for history), *The Growth of Political Thought in the West, from the Greeks to the End of the Middle Ages* (1932), *Constitutionalism and the Changing World* (1939), *Constitutionalism, Ancient and Modern* (1940), etc.; an editor of the "Reference History of the World," *Webster's New International Dictionary, Second Edition.*

**Mc′Il·wraith** (măk′ĭl·rāth), **Jean Newton.** 1859–1938. Canadian writer, b. Hamilton, Ont.; her works include *The Making of Mary* (1895), *A Book about Shakespeare* (1898), *The Curious Career of Roderick Campbell* (1901), *A Diana of Quebec* (1912), *The Little Admiral* (1924), and *Kinsmen at War* (1927).

**Mc′In·tire** (măk′ĭn·tīr), **Samuel.** 1757–1811. American architect and wood carver, b. Salem, Mass. Designed many of the colonial houses, churches, and public buildings of old Salem.

**Mac′in·tosh** (măk′ĭn·tŏsh), **Charles.** 1766–1843. Scottish chemist and inventor; best known as inventor of waterproof fabric (patented 1823) known as *mackintosh.*

**Macintosh, Douglas Clyde.** 1877–1948. Theologian, b. in Ontario, Canada; Ph.D., U. of Chicago (1909). Ordained in Baptist ministry (1907). Professor of theology, Yale (from 1916). Author of *The Reaction against Metaphysics in Theology* (1911), *The Problem of Knowledge* (1915), *God in a World at War* (1918), *Theology as an Empirical Science* (1919), *Social Religion* (1939), etc. Special editor for Protestant Church terms, *Webster's New International Dictionary, Second Edition.*

**Mc′In·tosh** (măk′ĭn·tŏsh), **Lachlan.** 1725–1806. Officer in American Revolution, b. in Scotland; to U.S. (1736). Brigadier general (Sept. 16, 1776); killed Button Gwinnett in duel (1777); wintered with Washington at Valley Forge (1777–78); failed to carry out plans against Detroit (1778); captured by British at Charleston, S.C. (1780); brevetted major general (1783).

**McIntosh, William.** 1775?–1825. American Creek Indian chief, b. in Carroll County, Ga. Commissioned brigadier general, U.S. army, and served with Andrew Jackson against Seminoles (1817–18). Negotiated treaty ceding lands to the whites (1825); murdered by Indians.

**Mc′In·tyre** (măk′ĭn·tīr), **James Francis Aloysius.** 1886–1979. American Roman Catholic churchman, b. New York City. Ordained (1921); archbishop, Los Angeles (1948–79); cardinal (1953).

**McIntyre, Oscar Odd** (ŏd). 1884–1938. American journalist, b. Plattsburg, Mo. Started journalistic career at Gallipolis, Ohio; conducted syndicated column *New York Day by Day*, appearing in over 300 newspapers (from 1912). Author of *White Light Nights* (1924), *The Big Town* (1935), etc.

**Ma·cip′** (mä·sēp′), **Vicente Juan.** *Known as* **Juan de Jua′nes** *or* **Joa′nes** (hwä′näs). 1500?–1579. Spanish painter, called the "Spanish Raphael"; painted five scenes from the St. Stephen legend for the Church of St. Stephen in Valencia, a Madonna for the Church of St. Andrew in Valencia. His father, **Vicente Macip** (1475?–?1550), was also a painter.

**Mačiulis, Jonas.** See MAIRONIS.

**Mack** (măk), **Con′nie** (kŏn′ĭ). *Real name* **Cornelius Mc·Gil′li·cud′dy** (mȧ·gĭl′ĭ·kŭd′ĭ). 1862–1956. American professional baseball player, b. East Brookfield, Mass.; manager, Philadelphia Athletics (1901–50).

**Mack** (mäk), **Karl.** See Baron MACK VON LEIBERICH.

**Mac·kail′** (mȧ·kāl′), **John William.** 1859–1945. British classical scholar; professor of poetry, Oxford (1906–11). Author of *Latin Literature* (1895), *The Springs of Helicon* (1909), *Lectures on Poetry* (1911), *Classical Studies* (1925), *The Approach to Shakespeare* (1930), *The Odyssey in English Verse* (1932), *Studies in Humanism* (1938), *The Sayings of Christ* (1938); member of Order of Merit (1935). His son **Denis George** (1892–1971), writer of fiction; author of *What Next?* (1920), *Bill the Bachelor* (1922), *The "Majestic" Mystery* (1924), *The Fortunes of Hugo* (1926), *Tales from Greenery Street* (1928), *How Amusing!* (1929), *Having Fun* (1933), *The Wedding* (1935), *London Lovers* (1938), etc.

**Mac·Kay′** (mȧ·kī′), **Alexander Howard.** 1848–1929. Canadian scientist and educator; superintendent of education, Nova Scotia (1890–1926). Author of *The Flora of Nova Scotia*, *Freshwater Sponges*, *Phenology of Canada.*

**Mac·kay′** (mȧ·kī′), **Alexander Murdoch.** 1849–1890. Scottish missionary in Africa. Joined mission of Church Missionary Society to Uganda (1876); gained influence over Mtesa, king of a Uganda tribe, and his people.

**Mac·Kay′** (mȧ·kī′), **Angus.** 1841–1931. Canadian agriculturist; discovered (1885–86) and introduced system of summer fallow for conserving moisture, still used in wheat areas of western Canada; first superintendent of dominion experimental farm, Indian Head (1887–1907), where he carried out for William Saunders (*q.v.*) experiments that aided in development of marquis wheat.

**Mac·kay′** (mȧ·kī′), **Charles.** 1814–1889. British journalist and poet, b. Perth, Scotland. Editor, Glasgow *Argus* (1844–47) and *Illustrated London News* (1852–59); author of many lyrics, collected in *The Salamandrine, or Love and Immortality* (1842), *Voices from the Crowd* (1846), *Voices from the Mountain* (1847), *Gossamer and Snowdrift* (1890), etc.

**Mc·Kay′** (mȧ·kā′), **Claude.** 1890–1948. Negro writer, b. in Jamaica, West Indies; to U.S. (1912). Employed as waiter and porter (1915–18); on staff of *Liberator* magazine (1919–22). Author of *Songs of Jamaica* (1911), *Constab Ballads* (1912), *Harlem Shadows* (poems; 1922), *Home to Harlem* (novel; 1927), *Banjo* (1929), *Banana Bottom* (1933), *Harlem: Negro Metropolis* (1940), etc.

**Mc·Kay′** (mȧ·kā′), **Donald.** 1810–1880. Shipbuilder, b. in Shelburne County, Nova Scotia; to U.S. (1827). Known for designing and building, in his East Boston yards, the finest and fastest packet and clipper ships of the period (1845–55).

**Mac·kay′** (mȧ·kī′), **Eric.** 1851–1899. Son of Charles Mackay. English poet; author of *Love-Letters of a Violinist* (1886), *Gladys the Singer* (1887), *A Lover's Litanies* (1888), *My Lady of Dreams* (1895), *The Lover's Missal* (1898), etc.

**Mc·Kay′** (mȧ·kā′), **Gordon.** 1821–1903. American inventor and industrialist, b. Pittsfield, Mass. Purchased (1859) Lyman R. Blake's patent for a machine to sew the soles of shoes to the uppers; perfected machine (patented 1862); engaged in making shoes and the machines, which he leased to manufacturers. Associated with Charles Goodyear (c. 1880–85); sold his interests to Goodyear Co. (1895), and retired. Benefactor of Harvard.

**Mac·kay′** (mȧ·kī′), **Isabel Ec′cle·stone** (ĕk′′l·stŭn), *nee* **Mac·pher′son** (măk·fûr′s'n). 1875–1928. Canadian poet and novelist; m. Peter John Mackay; resident in British Columbia (from 1909).

**Mac·kay′** (?mȧ·kī′), Sir **Iven Giffard.** 1882–1966. Australian army officer; brigadier general commanding 1st Australian infantry brigade (1918); commander, 2d division, commonwealth military forces (1937–40); commander, 6th division, Australian imperial forces (1940–41), which took part in successful British campaign in Libya (Dec., 1940); commander in chief, Australian home forces (1941–42). In army reorganization (Mar., 1942), appointed to one of two commands embracing entire continent of Australia.

**Mac·kay′** (*prob.* mȧ·kī′), **James.** 1759?–1822. Explorer in America, b. in Scotland; to Canada (1776). Explored region of the upper lakes, for the British. Explored upper Missouri River Valley and region to the westward, for the Spanish (1795–97); his maps of the region were used later by Lewis and Clark (1804–06).

**Mac·kay′** (mȧ·kī′), **John Henry.** 1864–1933. Scottish writer and poet in Germany, b. Greenock, Scotland; champion of an individualistic anarchism.

**Mack′ay** (măk′ĭ), **John William.** 1831–1902. Miner and financier, b. Dublin, Ireland; to U.S. (1840). Moved to California (1851); worked as miner; obtained interest in bonanza mines of the Comstock lode; struck rich ore (1873) and accumulated fortune. Moved to New York (1876). With James Gordon Bennett, founded Commercial Cable Co. (1883) and laid two submarine cables to Europe (1884) to break Gould monopoly. Organized Postal Telegraph Cable Co. (1886) to lay land lines and break the Western Union monopoly. His son **Clarence Hungerford** (1874–1938), b. San Francisco, succeeded him in his interests.

**Mack′ay** (măk′ā), **William Andrew.** 1876–1939. American painter; best known as muralist.

**Mac·Kaye′** (mȧ·kī′), **James Morrison Steele,** *known as* **Steele.** 1842–1894. American actor, dramatist, and producer, b. Buffalo, N.Y. Manager of Madison Square Theater, New York (1879), designed by him, first of so-called "intimate" theaters. Built Lyceum Theater; established there first dramatic school in America. Author of more than twenty plays, including *Rose Michel* (1875), an adaptation from the French, and *Hazel Kirke* (1880). His son **Percy** (1875–1956), b. New York City, grad. Harvard (1897), known as poet and dramatist; author of *The Canterbury Pilgrims* (a comedy, 1903), *Fenris the Wolf* (1905), *Jeanne d'Arc* (1906), *Sappho and Phaon* (1907), tragedies, *The Scarecrow* (a play, 1908); *The Playhouse and the Play* (essays, 1909), *Poems* (1909); *Anti-Matrimony* (a comedy, 1910), *St. Louis* (a masque, 1914), *Caliban* (a masque, 1916), *The Roll Call* (a masque, 1918), *Rip Van Winkle* (a folk opera, 1920), *Winged Victory* (poem, 1927), *The Sphinx* (comedy, 1929), *The Far Familiar* (poems, 1937), etc.

**Mack′e** (mäk′ĕ), **August.** 1887–1914. German painter; member of "Der Blaue Reiter" group, pioneers of impressionism; killed in World War I, France (1914).

**Mc·Kean′** (mȧ·kēn′), **Thomas.** 1734–1817. American statesman, b. in Chester County, Pa. Member (1774–83), president (1781), Continental Congress; signer of Declaration of Independence; chief justice of Pennsylvania (1777–99); governor (1799–1808).

**Mac·kel′lar** (mȧ·kĕl′ẽr), **Patrick.** 1717–1778. British military engineer, b. in Scotland. Accompanied Gen. Braddock to America (1754); chief engineer of frontier forts (1756). Engineer at capture of Louisburg (1758), under Wolfe at capture of Quebec (1759), under Monckton at capture of Martinique (1762), and under Albemarle at siege of Havana (1762–63).

**Mc·Kel′way** (mȧ·kĕl′wā), **St. Clair.** 1845–1915. American journalist; editor, Albany *Argus* (1878–84), Brooklyn *Daily Eagle* (1884–1915). Regent, U. of the State of New York (1883–1915), chancellor (1913–15).

**Mc·Ken′dree** (mȧ·kĕn′drē), **William.** 1757–1835. American Methodist Episcopal bishop (1808), first American-born bishop of his church; associate of Bishop Asbury (1808–16). McKendree Coll. is named in his honor.

**Mackenna, Benjamín Vicuña–.** See VICUÑA-MACKENNA.

**Mc·Ken′na** (mȧ·kĕn′ȧ), **Joseph.** 1843–1926. American jurist, b. Philadelphia. Practiced law in California. Member, U.S. Congress (1885–92). U.S. circuit judge (1892–97). U.S. attorney general (1897–98). Associate justice, U.S. Supreme Court (1898–1925).

**McKenna, Reginald.** 1863–1943. English lawyer, financier, and politician; M.P. (1895–1918); financial secretary of the treasury (1905); president of board of education (1907–08); first lord of the admiralty (1908–11); home secretary (1911–15); chancellor of exchequer (1915–16); chairman, Midland Bank, Ltd. (1919–43).

**McKenna, Siobhan.** 1923– . Irish actress. Appeared in plays and films.

**McKenna, Stephen.** 1888–1967. English novelist; author of *The Reluctant Lover* (1912), *Sonia* (1917), *The Education of Eric Lane* (1921), *Tales of Intrigue and Revenge* (1924), *Due Reckoning* (1927), *Happy Ending* (1929), *Magic Quest* (1933), *A Life for a Life* (1939).

**Mac·ken′nal** (mȧ·kĕn′′l), Sir **Bertram.** 1863–1931. British sculptor, b. in Melbourne, Australia. Among his notable works are: equestrian statue of Edward VII in Trafalgar Square, London; statues of Queen Victoria for India and Australia; war memorial at Islington.

**Mc·Ken′nan** (mȧ·kĕn′ăn), **Thomas McKean Thompson.** 1794–1852. American lawyer; practiced in Pennsylvania. Member, U.S. House of Representatives (1831–39; 1842–43). U.S. secretary of the interior (1850).

**Mc·Ken′ney** (mȧ·kĕn′ĭ), **Ruth.** 1911–1972. American writer, b. Mishawaka, Ind.; newspaper reporter in Ohio and New York; m. Richard Bransten (1939); author of *My Sister Eileen* (1938; later dramatized and scenarized), *Industrial Valley* (1939), *The McKenneys Carry On* (1940).

**Mack′en·sen** (mäk′ĕn·zĕn), **August von.** 1849–1945. German soldier; general field marshal (1915); commanded forces invading Poland (1914–15) and Rumania (1916); retired (1920).

**Mac·ken′zie** (mȧ·kĕn′zĭ), Sir **Alexander.** 1764–1820. Scottish explorer in North America; entered service of Northwest Fur Co. (1779). Explored in the northwest and discovered the Mackenzie River (1789); made overland journey from Fort Chippewyan to the Pacific coast

(1793), first white man to cover this ground. Wrote an account of his explorations (1801).

**Mackenzie, Alexander.** 1822–1892. Canadian statesman, b. in Perthshire, Scotland; to Canada (1842); first liberal prime minister of the Dominion of Canada (1873–78).

**Mackenzie,** Sir **Alexander Campbell.** 1847–1935. British composer, conductor, and teacher, b. in Edinburgh. Concert violinist and teacher; played in Birmingham Festival orchestras (1864–1867, 1870, 1873); director of Novello's oratorio concerts in London (1885–86); principal of Royal Acad. of Music (1888–1924), also conductor of London Philharmonic Society (1892–99). Knighted (1895). His compositions include the cantatas *The Bride* (1881), *Jason* (1882), and *The Story of Sayid* (1882), the choral work *The Cotter's Saturday Night*, oratorios, operas, comic operas, orchestral works, the orchestral ballad *La Belle Dame Sans Merci* (1883), and the *Scottish Rhapsodies*, *Burns* (1881) and *Tam o' Shanter* (1911), the *Pibroch* suite for violin (1889), piano pieces, songs, etc.

**Mackenzie, Alexander Sli′dell** (slī′d'l; *popularly* slī·dĕl′). *Orig.* **Alexander Slidell.** 1803–1848. Brother of John Slidell; name Mackenzie added in 1838. American naval officer, b. New York City. In quashing a planned mutiny (1842), hanged three men from the yardarm of his brig, the *Somers;* court of inquiry and court-martial wholly exonerated him. Author of *A Year in Spain* (2 vols., 1829), *Popular Essays on Naval Subjects* (1833), *Spain Revisited* (2 vols., 1836), and biographies of John Paul Jones, Perry, and Decatur.

**Mackenzie,** Sir **Compton.** 1883–1972. English writer. b. West Hartlepool. In World War I; with Dardanelles expedition (1915); director of intelligence service in Syria (1917). Literary critic, *Daily Mail* (1931–35). Rector, Glasgow U. (1931–34). Author of *Poems* (1907); plays, including *The Gentleman in Grey* (1906), *Carnival* (1912), *Columbine* (1920), *The Lost Cause* (1931); novels, including *The Passionate Elopement* (1911), *Carnival* (1912), *Sylvia Scarlet* (1918), *The Parson's Progress* (1923), *Vestal Fire* (1927) *The Four Winds of Love* (4 vols, 1937–40), *A Musical Chair* (1939), *The Monarch of the Glen* (1941), *Whiskey Galore* (1947); and a ten-volume memoir, *My Life and Times.*

**Mackenzie** of Rose′haugh (rōz′hô; rō·zôκ′), Sir **George.** 1636–1691. Scottish lawyer; as king's advocate (1677), became instrument of Charles II in his policy of inhumanity and relentless persecution of Covenanters, thereby gaining nickname "Bloody Mackenzie." On failure of hopes of his party (1689), retired to Oxford to do literary work; founder of Advocates' Library, Edinburgh. Author of graceful moral essays and legal, political, and antiquarian works.

**Mackenzie, George Henry.** 1837–1891. Chess champion, b. in Scotland; to U.S. (1863); recognized as American chess champion (1880), world champion (1887).

**Mackenzie, Henry.** 1745–1831. Scottish novelist, known as "the Man of Feeling," and sometimes as "the Addison of the North"; attorney for the crown in management of exchequer business; comptroller of taxes (1804–31); chairman of committee investigating Macpherson's *Ossian.* Author of three novels: *The Man of Feeling*, loosely connected series of sketches about a weak sentimental hero which gained instant success (anonymously, 1771), *The Man of the World*, tale of a villain and seducer (1773), *Julia de Roubigné*, novel in manner of Richardson (1777).

**Mackenzie, John Stuart.** 1860–1935. British philosopher; author of *Outlines of Metaphysics* (1902), *Fundamental Problems of Life* (1928), *Cosmic Problems* (1931).

**Mackenzie,** Sir **Morell.** 1837–1892. Engish laryngologist; helped found Hospital for Diseases of the Throat, London (1863). Author of *Diseases of the Throat* (2 vols., 1880–84).

**Mc·Ken′zie** (mȧ·kĕn′zĭ), **Robert Tait.** 1867–1938. Physician and sculptor, b. in Ontario, Canada. Director of physical training, McGill (1896–1904); director of physical education, U. of Pennsylvania (1904–30). Best-known sculptures are war memorials, as the Scottish American War Memorial in Edinburgh, and war memorials in the parliament building at Ottawa, Canada.

**Mackenzie, Stuart–Wortley–.** See *earls of Bute*, under STEWART family.

**Mackenzie,** Sir **William.** 1849–1923. Canadian financier and railroad builder, b. Kirkfield, Ontario. Built sections of the Canadian National and Canadian Pacific railways. With Sir Donald Mann (from 1886), organized and built Canadian Northern R.R., later taken over by the government (1917–18) and finally merged into the Canadian National Railway system.

**Mackenzie, William Douglas.** 1859–1936. Theologian, b. in Orange River Colony, South Africa. Ordained in Congregational ministry (1882). President, Hartford (Conn.) Seminary Foundation (1904–30).

**Mackenzie, William Lyon.** 1795–1861. Canadian insurgent leader, b. near Dundee, Scotland; to Canada (1820). Published *Colonial Advocate* (1824–34), in which he assailed the government; led 800 insurrectionists in Toronto uprising with intention of setting up provisional government (Dec., 1837); on failure, fled to U.S., organized supporters in Buffalo, N.Y., and fortified Navy Island in Niagara River; caused international incident of the *Caroline*, American steamer fitted out to support the insurrectionists which was destroyed by Canadians in Niagara River; imprisoned in U.S. for violation of neutrality laws (till 1840); agitation succeeded in drawing attention of home government to colonial abuses.

**Mc·Ker′row** (mȧ·kĕr′ō), **Ronald Brunlees.** 1872–1940. English scholar and publisher; managing director (from 1917), Sidgwick & Jackson, Ltd., publishers; editor of various English classics, including *Works of T. Nashe* (5 vols., 1904–10), and of a new edition of Shakespeare, for which he wrote *Prolegomena for the Oxford Shakespeare* (1939); noted for his work in bibliography; founder (1925) and first editor of *Review of English Studies.*

**Mc·Kim′** (mȧ·kĭm′), **Charles Follen.** 1847–1909. American architect, b. in Chester County, Pa. Partnership of McKim, Mead, and White formed (1879). Among the works of this firm in which he took a chief part are: Boston Public Library; a group of Columbia University buildings on Morningside Heights; University Club, N.Y.; restoration of the White House, Washington, D.C.

**Mac·kin′der** (mȧ·kĭn′dẽr), Sir **Halford John.** 1861–1947. British geographer. At U. of London (1900–25); pres., British Assoc., geog. section (1895–1931). Wrote *Elementary Studies in Geography* (18th ed.; 1930), etc.

**Mc·Kin′ley** (mȧ·kĭn′lĭ), **John.** 1780–1852. American jurist and legislator, b. in Culpeper County, Va. U.S. senator from Alabama (1826–31). Member, U.S. House of Representatives (1833–35). Associate justice, U.S. Supreme Court (1837–52).

**McKinley, William.** 1843–1901. Twenty-fifth president of the United States, b. Niles, Ohio. Served through Civil War. Practiced law, Canton, Ohio. Member, U.S. House of Representatives (1877–83; 1885–91); as chairman (1889–91) of the committee on ways and means, had major part in framing and passing the protective tariff act (McKinley Tariff) of 1890. With organization directed by Marcus Alonzo Hanna, Republican politician of Cleveland, elected governor of Ohio (1892–96), and president of the U.S. (1896 and 1900). Shot by Leon Czolgosz, an anarchist, at Buffalo, Sept. 6, 1901, and died Sept. 14.

**Mack'in·tosh** (măk'ĭn·tŏsh), **Charles Rennie.** 1868–1928. Scottish architect; designed Glasgow School of Art buildings and Queen's Cross Church in Glasgow; credited with exercising influence on continental European decorative design. After withdrawal from architectural work (1913), devoted himself to landscape painting, esp. in water colors.

**Mackintosh,** Sir **James.** 1765–1832. Scottish philosopher and historian; called to bar (1795); delivered brilliant lectures at Lincoln's Inn on *The Law of Nature and Nations* (1799). Recorder of Bombay (1804–06) and judge in admiralty court, Bombay (1806–11). M.P. (1813); professor of law, Haileybury Coll. (1818–24); commissioner of Board of Control for India in Grey ministry (1830). Author of *Dissertation on the Progress of Ethical Philosophy* (1830; in *Encyclopaedia Britannica,* 7th ed.), history of England from earliest times (1830; in Lardner's *Cabinet Cyclopaedia*), and *History of the Revolution in England in 1688* (incomplete).

**Mack'lin** (măk'lĭn), **Charles.** 1697?–1797. Irish actor and playwright. Son of William McLaughlin of North Ireland. Celebrated for acting of Shylock; author of farce *Love à la Mode* (produced 1759) and comedy *The Man of the World* (produced 1781), creating burlesque character Sir Pertinax Macsycophant.

**Mc·Knight'** (măk·nīt'), **George Harley.** 1871– . American educator; professor of English, Ohio State U. (from 1907). Author of *English Words and Their Background* (1923), *Modern English in the Making* (1928), etc.

**Mac·kub'in** (mȧ·kŭb'ĭn), **Florence.** 1861–1918. Portrait and miniature painter, b. Florence, Italy, of American parentage. Studio in Baltimore.

**Mack von Lei'be·rich** (mäk' fôn lī'bĕ·rĭĸ), Baron **Karl.** 1752–1828. Austrian general, b. in Franconia. Commanded army against the French (1798) and occupied Rome, but was forced to withdraw because of revolt in Naples. Commanded Austrian army in southern Germany (1805); forced to capitulate with 20,000 men at Ulm (1805).

**Mc·Lane'** (măk·lān'), **Allan.** 1746–1829. American Revolutionary officer, b. Philadelphia. Captain of light reconnaissance troops in Philadelphia area (1777–78); with Henry Lee before Stony Point (1779); with Steuben's command in Virginia (1781). His son **Louis** (1786–1857) was a lawyer; member of U.S. House of Representatives (1817–27) and of U.S. Senate (1827–29); U.S. minister to England (1829–31); U.S. secretary of the treasury (1831–33); U.S. secretary of state (1833–34); U.S. minister to England again (1845–46). Louis's son **Robert Milligan** (1815–1898) practiced law, Baltimore, Md. (from 1843); member of U.S. House of Representatives (1847–51); U.S. commissioner to China and Japan (1853–54); U.S. minister to Mexico (1859–60); member of U.S. House of Representatives (1879–83); governor of Maryland (1883–85); U.S. minister to France (1885–89).

**MacLane, M. Jean.** See under John Christen JOHANSEN.

**Maclaren, Ian.** Pseudonym of John WATSON.

**Mc·Laugh'lin** (măk·läf'lĭn), **Andrew Cunningham.** 1861–1947. American historian; professor, Michigan (1891–1906), Chicago (1906–29). Author of *A History of the American Nation* (1899), *The Courts, the Constitution and Parties* (1912), *Foundations of American Constitutionalism* (1933), *A Constitutional History of the United States* (1935), etc.

**Mac·lau'rin** (măk·lô'rĭn), **Colin.** 1698–1746. Scottish mathematician; author of *Geometrica Organica, sive Descriptio Linearum Curvarum Universalis* (1720), *A Treatise of Fluxions* (1742) containing his essay on tides, statement of the conception of level surfaces, and theory for distinguishing between maxima and minima, *A Treatise of Algebra* (pub. 1748), *An Account of Sir Isaac Newton's Philosophy* (pub. 1748).

**Maclaurin, Richard Cock'burn** (kō'bẽrn). 1870–1920. Physicist and educator, b. Lindean, Scotland; to New Zealand (1875). Professor of mathematics, U. of New Zealand, Wellington (1898–1905); professor of mathematical physics, Columbia (1908–09). President, M.I.T. (1909–20). Author of *Lectures on Light* (1909), etc.

**Mc·Laws'** (măk·lôz'), **Lafayette.** 1821–1897. American army officer, b. Augusta, Ga. Grad. U.S.M.A., West Point (1842). Entered Confederate service (1861); at Antietam, Fredericksburg, Chancellorsville, Gettysburg, and Chickamauga. Relieved and court-martialed after failure to capture Knoxville; exonerated by President Davis. In command at Savannah (1864–65).

**Mac·lay'** (măk·lā'), **William.** 1734–1804. American lawyer, b. in Chester County, Pa. U.S. senator (1789–91). His journal (pub. 1880) of senate debates during his term is the only continuous report of the proceedings.

**Mac·Lean'** (măk·lān'), **James Alexander.** 1868–1945. Canadian educator, b. Ontario. President, U. of Idaho (1900–13), U. of Manitoba (1913–34).

**Mc·Lean'** (măk·lān'), **John.** 1785–1861. American lawyer and legislator, b. in Morris County, N.J. Member, U.S. Congress (1813–16). U.S. postmaster general (1823–29). Associate justice, U.S. Supreme Court (1829–61). Unsuccessful candidate for Republican nomination for the presidency (1856, 1860).

**McLean, Sarah Pratt.** See Sarah P. McLean GREENE.

**Mc·Lean'** (măk·lēn'), **William Lip'pard** (lĭp'ärd). 1852–1931. American newspaper proprietor, b. Mount Pleasant, Pa.; publisher of Philadelphia *Evening Bulletin* (1895–1931); director of Associated Press (1896–1924). His son **Robert** (1891– ), b. Philadelphia, succeeded him in his newspaper interests.

**Mac'le·hose** *or* **M'Le·hose** (măk'lĕ·hōz), **Agnes,** *nee* **Craig** (krāg). 1759–1841. Scottish correspondent of Robert Burns, under name of **Cla·rin'da** (klȧ·rĭn'dȧ). Grandniece of Colin Maclaurin. Met Burns (1787); corresponded with him and sent him verses (till 1794). Burns's *Ae fond kiss, and then we sever* commemorates their last meeting (1791).

**Mac·Leish'** (măk·lēsh'), **Archibald.** 1892– . American poet and librarian, b. Glencoe, Ill. Served in World War. Librarian of Congress (1939–44); assistant secretary of state (1944–45). Author of volumes of verse *The Happy Marriage* (1924), *The Pot of Earth* (1925), *Streets in the Moon* (1926), *Conquistador* (1932; awarded Pulitzer prize), *Public Speech* (1936), *America War Promises* (1939), verse plays *Nobodaddy* (1925), *Panic* (1935), *The Fall of the City* (1937), prose essays, etc.

**Mac·Len'nan** (măk·lĕn'ăn), **Hugh.** 1907– . Canadian author, b. Nova Scotia. At McGill U. (1951– ); wrote *Barometer Rising* (1941), *The Precipice* (1948), *The Watch That Ends the Night* (1959), etc.

**McLennan, John Cunningham.** 1867–1935. Canadian physicist; professor, Toronto (1907–31). Known chiefly for work relating to electricity; investigated the superconductivity of metals; liquefied helium (1932).

**McLennan, John Ferguson.** 1827–1881. Scottish sociologist. Author of papers on totemism and of *Primitive Marriage* (1865), setting up exogamy as primitive form of marriage and stimulating research in this field.

**Mac·leod'** (măk·loud'), **Fiona.** Pseudonym of William SHARP (1856?–1905).

**Macleod, Henry Dunning.** 1821–1902. Scottish economist; called to English bar (1849); employed on poor-law reform in Scotland and on codification of law of bills of exchange (1868–70). Author of *The Theory and Practice of Banking* (1856), *Elements of Political Economy*, in which he first applied term "Gresham's law" (1858), and *The Theory of Credit* (2 vols., 1889–91).

**Mc·Leod′** (mă̆k·loud′), **Irene Rutherford**. 1891– . English poet; m. Aubrey De Sélincourt (1919); author of *Songs to Save a Soul* (1915), *Before Dawn* (1918), etc.

**Macleod, John James Rickard**. 1876–1935. Scottish physiologist. Professor, Western Reserve U., Cleveland, Ohio (1903–18), U. of Toronto, Canada (1918–28), U. of Aberdeen, Scotland (from 1928). For share in discovery of insulin, awarded jointly with F.G. Banting (*q.v.*) the 1923 Nobel prize for physiology and medicine. Author of *Practical Physiology* (1903), *Diabetes, Its Physiological Pathology* (1913), *Fundamentals in Physiology* (1916), *Physiology and Biochemistry in Modern Medicine* (7th ed., 1934), etc.

**Macleod, Norman**. 1812–1872. Scottish clergyman and author. Studied divinity under Dr. Thomas Chalmers. A founder of Evangelical Alliance (1847); minister of Barony Church, Glasgow (1851–72). Edited *Good Words* (1860–72), to which he contributed *Wee Davie* and *The Starling;* author of *The Earnest Student* (1854), *Parish Papers* (1862), *Reminiscences of a Highland Parish* (1867), and *Peeps at the Far East* (1871).

**Mac·lise′** (mă̆k·lēs′), **Daniel**. 1806–1870. Irish historical painter; contributed character portraits of men and women of the time to *Fraser's Magazine* under pseudonym **Alfred Cro′quis′** [krô′kē′] (1830–38); made reputation with *All-Hallow Eve* (1833); designed book illustrations for Tennyson and some of Dickens's Christmas books.

**Mc·Lough′lin** (mă̆k·lŏf′lĭn), **Maurice Evans**. 1890–1957. American lawn-tennis player, b. Carson City, Nev. Member of U.S. Davis Cup team (1909, 1911, 1913, 1914). Winner of U.S. championship (1912, 1913).

**Mc·Lu′han** (mă̆k·lo͞o′ă̆n), **Marshall**. *In Full* **Herbert Marshall McLuhan.** 1911– . Canadian educator and author, b. Edmonton, Alberta. Expert on mass communications; wrote *Understanding Media* (1964), *The Medium is the Message* (1967), etc.

**Mac·lure′** (mă̆k·lo͝or′), **William**. 1763–1840. Geologist, b. Ayr, Scotland; visited U.S. (1782, 1796); became naturalized citizen of U.S. (before 1803). Member, U.S. commission to settle spoliation claims between U.S. and France (1803–07). Made geological chart of U.S. (1809; revised and enlarged 1817).

**Mc·Ma′hon** (mă̆k·mä′ŭ̆n), Sir **Arthur Henry**. 1862–1949. British administrator. Revenue and judicial commissioner in Baluchistan (1901); foreign secretary to government of India (1911–14); first high commissioner for Egypt (1914–16); British commissioner of Middle East at Paris Peace Conference (1919).

**Mac′Ma′hon′** (màk′mà′ôɴ′), Comte **Marie Edme Patrice Maurice de.** 1808–1893. Marshal of France and second president of the Third Republic; b. in Sully. In the Crimea, led the assault on Malakoff (1855); led successful campaign against the Kabyles in Algeria (1857–58); in war with Austria (1859) turned defeat into victory at Magenta and helped French win at Solferino; made marshal and duke of Magenta (1859). Governor general of Algeria (1864–70). In Franco-Prussian War (1870); defeated at Weissenburg, Wörth, and Sedan. Aided Thiers in suppressing Commune (1871). Elected president of France (1873–79; retired).

**Mac·Ma′hon** (mă̆k·mä′ŭ̆n), **Percy Alexander**. 1854–1929. English mathematician, b. Malta; professor of physics, Ordnance Coll. (1890–97); deputy warden of standards (1904–20). Specialist in algebraic forms; author of *Combinatory Analysis* (1915).

**Mc·Man′us** (mă̆k·mă̆n′ŭ̆s), **George**. 1884–1954. American cartoonist; on staff of New York *World* (1905), New York *American* (1912). Creator of the comic strip serials *Let George Do It*, *The Newly Weds and Their Baby*, *Bringing up Father*.

**Mac·Man′us** (mă̆k·mă̆n′ŭ̆s), **Seumas**. 1869–1960. Irish writer of verse, fiction, and plays, b. Donegal. Author of *Shuilers* (verse; 1893), *'Twas in Dhroll Donegal* (1897), *Through the Turf Smoke* (1899), *Donegal Fairy Stories* (1900), *The Red Poocher* (1903), *Ballads of a Country Boy* (1905), *Top o' the Mornin'* (1920), *Bold Blades of Donegal* (1935), *Dark Patrick* (1939), and the plays *The Woman of Seven Sorrows*, *Orange and Green*, *Mrs. Connolly's Cashmere*, *Father Peter's Miracle*, etc.

**Mc·Mas′ter** (mă̆k·màs′tẽr), **John Bach**. 1852–1932. American historian, b. Brooklyn, N.Y. Taught engineering, Princeton (1877–83); history, Pennsylvania (1883–1920). Wrote *The History of the People of the United States* (8 vols., 1883–1913), *Benjamin Franklin as a Man of Letters* (1887), *Daniel Webster* (1902), *The United States in the World War* (2 vols., 1918–20).

**Mac·Mech′an** (mă̆k·mĕ̆k′ă̆n), **Archibald M'Kellar**. 1862–1933. Canadian scholar and essayist; author of *Sagas of the Sea* (1923), *The Book of Ultima Thule* (1927), *Red Snow on Grand Pré* (1931), etc.

**Mac·mil′lan** (mă̆k·mĭl′ă̆n), **Daniel**. 1813–1857. Scottish bookseller and publisher; bookseller at Irvine, Glasgow, Cambridge (1833–37), London (1837–43); opened shop with his brother in Cambridge (1843); added publishing (1844), assuming firm name Macmillan & Co.; won first successes with Kingsley's *Westward Ho!* (1855) and *Tom Brown's School Days* (1857). Succeeded (1857) by his brother **Alexander** (1815–1896), who transferred business to London (1863) and opened branch in New York; published *Macmillan's Magazine* (1859–1907) and works of Tennyson, Lightfoot, J. R. Green, Lewis Carroll, among others. Daniel's son Sir **Frederick Orridge** (1851–1936) became president of organization as a limited-liability company (1893); director of American Macmillan Co.

**Mac·Mil′lan** (mă̆k·mĭl′ă̆n), **Donald Baxter**. 1874–1970. American arctic explorer, b. Provincetown, Mass. With Peary on north-polar expedition (1908–09). Led expeditions to arctic lands (1913–37). Author of *Four Years in the White North* (1918), *Etah and Beyond* (1927), *Kahda* (1929), *How Peary Reached the Pole* (1932).

**Mc·Mil′lan** (mă̆k·mĭl′ă̆n), **Edwin Mattison**. 1907– American physical chemist, b. Redondo Beach, Calif. Taught physics, U. of Calif. (1935– ); awarded Nobel prize in chemistry (1951) with G. T. Seaborg for discovery of transuranium elements.

**Mac·mil′lan, Harold**. 1894– . British publisher, economist, and politician. M.P. (1924–29, 1931–45); chancellor of exchequer (1955–57); prime minister (1957–63). Wrote *Reconstruction* (1933), *The Middle Way* (1938), *Economic Aspects of Defense* (1939), etc.

**MacMillan, Harvey Reginald**. 1885– . Canadian lumberman and government administrator, b. in Newmarket, Ontario. Chief forester for British Columbia (1912–15); timber trade commissioner, department of trade and commerce, Ottawa (1915–16); head of wartime requirements board (1940), and of the merchant shipbuilding and shipping program (1941).

**Macmillan, John**. 1670–1753. Scottish minister; founder (1743) of the Reformed Presbyterian Church, composed mostly of Cameronians.

**Mac·mil′len** (mă̆k·mĭl′ĕ̆n), **Francis**. 1885– . American violinist, b. Marietta, Ohio.

**Mac·Mon′nies** (măk·mŏn′ĭz), **Frederick William.** 1863–1937. American sculptor, b. Brooklyn. Studied under Augustus Saint-Gaudens, Falguière, and others. Studio in Paris (1887) and later in New York. Among his notable works are: bronze angels in St. Paul's Church, New York; *Nathan Hale*, in City Hall Park, New York; *Faun with Heron; Sir Henry Vane*, in Boston Public Library; *Bacchante with Infant Faun*, in Metropolitan Museum of Art in New York; *Venus and Adonis; Cupid;* equestrian statues of Gen. Slocum, Theodore Roosevelt, Gen. George B. McClellan; monument on the Marne battlefield, in France; portrait busts of Whistler, Brisbane, Hastings, Motley, and others. See Mary Low.

**Mac·Munn′** (măk·mŭn′), Sir **George Fletcher.** 1869–1952. English soldier; British commander in chief in Mesopotamia (1919–20); quartermaster general in India (1920–24). Author of books on India.

**Mac·Mur′ray** (măk·mûr′ĭ), **John Van Ant′werp** (văn ănt′wûrp). 1881–1960. American diplomat; U.S. minister to China (1925–29), to Estonia, Latvia, and Lithuania (1933–36), to Turkey (1936–42).

**Mc·Mur′rich** (măk·mûr′ĭk), **James Playfair.** 1859–1939. Canadian scientist; professor of anatomy, Michigan (1894–1907) and Toronto (1907–30).

**Mac·Mur′rough** (măk·mûr′ō), **Dermot.** *Irish name* **Diar′maid Mac·mur′cha·da** (dĭr′mĭd mȧk·mûr′κȧ·gȧ). 1110?–1171. Irish ruler; king of Leinster (from 1126); banished by Irish chieftains (1166); introduced the English into Ireland when he invoked (1166) aid of the English in regaining his kingdom against a coalition of Irish kings and nobles; compiled the *Book of Leinster*, a collection of early Gaelic traditions.

**Mc·Mur′ry** (măk·mûr′ĭ), **Frank Morton.** 1862–1936. American educator; professor of elementary education, Teachers College in Columbia U. (1898–1926).

**Mac·nagh′ten** (măk·nô′t′n), Sir **William Hay.** 1793–1841. Anglo-Indian diplomat; secretary to Lord William Bentinck (1830–33); adviser to Lord Auckland, governor general of India (1837); envoy and minister to Afghan court at Kabul (1838); on renewal of rebellion after reduction of subsidies to Afghan chiefs, made error of accepting terms offered by Akbar Khan, which proved trap in which he was murdered at Kabul and retreating British army massacred in Khyber Pass (1841).

**Mc·Nair′** (măk·nâr′), **Lesley James.** 1883–1944. American army officer; grad. U.S.M.A. (1904); assigned to artillery; major general (1939), lieutenant general (1941); named commander of ground forces, U.S. army (Mar., 1942); killed in Normandy (July, 1944).

**Mac·Nal′ly** (măk·năl′ĭ), **Leonard.** 1752–1820. Irish playwright and political informer. Joined United Irishmen but secretly betrayed revolutionists to the government (1794–1820); betrayed political clients whom he defended in court, including Robert Emmet.

**Mc′Na·mar′a** (măk′nȧ·măr′ȧ; măk′nȧ·măr′ȧ), **Robert Strange** (strānj). 1916– . American businessman; U.S. Secretary of Defense (1961–68).

**Mc·Nar′ney** (măk·när′nĭ), **Joseph Taggart.** 1893–1972. American army officer, b. Emporium, Pa.; grad. U.S.M.A. (1915); deputy chief of staff, U.S. Army (1942); general (1945); commander of U.S. forces in Europe (1945–47); retired (1952).

**Mc·Nar′y** (măk·nâr′ĭ), **Charles Lin′za** (lĭn′zȧ). 1874–1944. American lawyer and legislator, b. near Salem, Ore. Adm. to bar (1898), and practiced in Salem (1898–1913). Justice, supreme court of Oregon (1913–15). U.S. senator (1917–44); chairman of senate committee on agriculture and forestry, and cosponsor of the McNary-Haugen bill for farm relief; Republican candidate for vice-president of the United States (1940).

**Mc·Naugh′ton** (măk·nô′t′n), **Andrew George Latta.** 1887–1966. Canadian army officer; B.S., McGill (1910). Artillery officer in World War I (1914–18); chief of general staff (1929–35); World War II commander of Canadian army in Great Britain (Apr., 1942–Sept., 1944); retired, with rank of general; minister of national defense (Nov., 1944–Aug., 1945); chairman, U.S.-Canadian Permanent Joint Defense Board (1945).

**Mac·Neice′** (măk·nēs′), **Louis.** 1907-1963. British poet and classical scholar, b. Belfast. Author of *Blind Fireworks* (1929), *Poems* (1935), *The Agamemnon of Aeschylus* (1936), *The Earth Compels* (1938), *Zoo* (prose; 1938), *Autumn Journal* (1939), *Modern Poetry* (1939), *Plant and Phantom* (1941), *Christopher Columbus* (1944), etc.

**Mac·Neil′** (măk·nēl′), **Hermon Atkins.** 1866–1947. American sculptor; best known for his American Indian subjects, as in *Coming of the White Man*, at Portland, Ore., *Primitive Chant* in Metropolitan Museum of Art, New York City, *The Moqui Prayer for Rain*, in Chicago Art Institute. Other works include several busts in the Hall of Fame. He married (1895) **Carol Brooks** (1871–1944), sculptor, esp. of child life.

**Mc·Neile′** (măk·nēl′), **Cyril.** *Pseudonym* **Sap′per** (săp′ẽr). 1888–1937. British army officer and writer; author of *Sergeant Michael Cassidy; Bull-Dog Drummond* (1920), *Jim Maitland* (1923), *The Final Count* (1926), *Tiny Carteret* (1930), etc.

**Mac·neill′** (măk·nēl′), **Hector.** 1746–1818. Scottish poet; known esp. for his songs, including *I lo'ed ne'er a laddie but one* and *Come under my plaidie.*

**Mc·Neill′** (măk·nēl′), **James.** 1869–1938. Irish statesman, b. in County Antrim; member of committee to draft constitution for Irish Free State (1922); high commissioner for Irish Free State (1923–28) and governor general (1928–32).

**M'Neill′** (măk·nēl′), **John.** 1854–1933. Scottish Presbyterian evangelist; associated with Dwight L. Moody in revival meetings (1892 ff.).

**MacNeill, John Gordon Swift.** 1849–1926. Irish jurist, politician, and historian; called to Irish bar (1875); professor at King's Inn, Dublin, and later (from 1909) in the National U. of Ireland. M.P. (1887–1918). Author of *Constitutional and Parliamentary History of Ireland* (1917), etc.

**McNeill, Ronald John.** See Cushendun.

**Mc·Nutt′** (măk·nŭt′), **Paul Vo′ries** (vō′rēz). 1891–1955. American lawyer and politician, b. Franklin, Ind.; A.B., Indiana (1913), LL.B., Harvard (1916); served in World War I (major); professor of law. Indiana U. (1919–33; dean 1925–33); national commander of American Legion (1928–29); governor of Indiana (1933–37); U.S. high commissioner to the Philippines (1937–39; 1945–46); administrator of Federal Security Agency (1939–45); director of Defense, Health, and Welfare Services (1941–43); chairman of War Man-power Commission (1942–45).

**Ma·comb′** (mȧ·kōm′), **Alexander.** 1782–1841. American army officer, b. Detroit; in War of 1812, defended Plattsburg against British (Sept., 1814); commanding general, U.S. army (1828–41).

**Ma′con** (mā′kŭn), **Nathaniel.** 1758–1837. American legislator, b. in Edgecombe (now Warren) County, N.C. Served in American Revolution. Member, U.S. House of Representatives (1791–1815; speaker 1801–07), U.S. Senate (1815–28).

**Mac Or′lan′** (màk′ ôr′läɴ′), **Pierre.** *Orig.* **Du′mar′chey′** (dü′mȧr′shā′). 1882–1970. French writer; best known for his adventure tales.

**Mac·Phail′** (măk·fāl′), **Agnes Campbell.** 1890–1954. Canadian politician; a leader of Co-operative Commonwealth Federation of Canada; member of Canadian House of Commons (1921, 1925, 1926, 1930, 1935), first woman elected to Canadian legislature. Represented Canada as delegate to Assembly of League of Nations.

**Mac·Phail′** (măk·fāl′), Sir **Andrew**. 1864–1938. Canadian physician and writer; professor of history of medicine, McGill (1906–37). Served in World War I (1914–18). Author of *Essays in Puritanism* (1905), *The Vine of Sibmah* (1906), *Essays in Politics* (1909), *Essays in Fallacy* (1910), *The Book of Sorrow* (1916), *Three Persons* (1929), *The Bible in Scotland* (1931), etc.

**Mac·pher′son** (măk·fûr′s′n), **James**. 1736–1796. Scottish translator (self-alleged) of *The Poems of Ossian*. Schoolmaster in native Ruthven, Inverness; published *The Highlander* (1758) and *Fragments of Ancient Poetry collected in the Highlands of Scotland* (1760); sent by Faculty of Advocates, on subscriptions gathered by Dr. Hugh Blair, to collect more Gaelic poems, obtained mss. which a Captain Morrison and Rev. A. Gallic helped him to translate; announced discovery of a Gaelic epic on Fingal; published *Fingal, an Ancient Epic Poem in Six Books* (1762) and *Temora* (1763), alleged translations from Gaelic of 3d-century poet Ossian, in poetry or rhythmic prose admired (by Goethe among others) for romantic rhythm and occasional passages of striking beauty; asserted by Dr. Johnson to have woven romance himself from fragments of poems and stories (1775); never produced his originals or rebutted charge of forgery. M.P. (1780–96); London agent to Mohammed Ali, nabob of Arcot (1781). Author also of *The History of Great Britain from the Restoration to the Accession of the House of Hanover* (2 vols., 1775).

**McPherson, James Birdseye**. 1828–1864. American army officer, b. near Clyde, Ohio; grad. U.S.M.A., West Point (1853). Chief engineer on Grant's staff (1862); major general (Oct. 8, 1862), serving through Vicksburg campaign (1862–63). Commanded army of the Tennessee (1864) co-operating with Sherman in Georgia; killed by skirmishers near Atlanta, Ga. (July 22, 1864).

**Mac′quer′** (mȧ′kâr′), **Pierre Joseph**. 1718–1784. French chemist; author of a dictionary of chemistry (5 vols., 1789).

**Mc·Rae′** (măk·rā′), **James Henry**. 1863–1940. American army officer; grad. U.S.M.A., West Point (1886). In World War I commanded 78th division in France (major general, N.A., 1918–19); commanded Philippine department (1924–26), 2d corps area (1926–27).

**McRae, Milton Alexander**. 1858–1930. American newspaper publisher, b. Detroit. In partnership (from 1889) with Edward W. Scripps (*q.v.*), developed the Scripps-McRae Press Association which became later the United Press Associations. Author of *Forty Years in Newspaperdom* (1924).

**Mac·rea′dy** (măk·rē′dĭ), **William Charles**. 1793–1873. English tragedian; first London appearance (1816); gained leading place by his Richard III (1819); transferred from Covent Garden to Drury Lane (1823); played successfully in America (1826) and in Paris (1828); during his management of Covent Garden (1837–39), produced Shakespeare, Browning's *Strafford*, and Bulwer-Lytton's *Lady of Lyons* and *Richelieu*, himself playing principal characters; manager of Drury Lane (1841–43); in America, was confronted by mob and riot resulting from bitter jealousy of actor Edwin Forrest (1849); took farewell of stage, at Drury Lane, as Macbeth (1851). Numbered among chief roles Macbeth, Cassius, King Lear, Henry IV, Iago, and title roles in Sheridan Knowles's *Virginius* and *William Tell*.

**Mc·Reyn′olds** (măk·rĕn′′ldz), **James Clark**. 1862–1946. American jurist, b. Elkton, Ky.; practiced, Nashville, Tenn. U.S. attorney general (1913–14); associate justice, U.S. Supreme Court (1914–41).

**Ma·cri′nus** (mȧ·krī′nŭs). *In full* **Marcus Opelius Macrinus.** 164–218. Roman emperor (217–218), b. in Caesarea, Mauretania, of humble parentage. Prefect of the praetorians under Caracalla; plotted and brought about murder of Caracalla (217); succeeded him as emperor; defeated by Parthians; became unpopular with army for his severe discipline; defeated near Antioch and succeeded by Heliogabalus.

**Ma·cro′bi·us** (mȧ·krō′bĭ·ŭs), **Ambrosius Theodosius**. Latin grammarian of late 4th and early 5th century A.D. Extant works, *Commentarius ex Cicerone in Somnium Scipionis* and *Conviviorum Saturnaliorum Libri Septem* (usually called the *Saturnalia*).

**Mac·Swi′ney** (măk·swē′nĭ), **Terence**. 1879–1920. Irish Nationalist politician and agitator; identified with Sinn Fein from its beginning; a leader in Easter Rebellion (1916); elected lord mayor of Cork. Arrested by English government on charges preferred under Defence of the Realm Act and sentenced (Aug. 17, 1920) to two years' imprisonment; went on hunger strike and died of starvation in Brixton jail, London (Oct. 25, 1920).

**M'Tag′gart** (măk·tăg′ẽrt), **John M'Taggart Ellis**. 1866–1925. English philosopher; author of *Some Dogmas of Religion* (1906), *Commentary on Hegel's Logic* (1910), and *The Nature of Existence* (2 vols., 1921, 1927).

**Mc·Tyeire′** (măk·tẹr′), **Holland Nimmons**. 1824–1889. American bishop (1866 ff.) of Methodist Episcopal Church, South. Influential in founding Vanderbilt U., obtaining aid from Cornelius Vanderbilt.

**Mac·Veagh′** (măk·vā′), **Isaac Wayne**, *known as* **Wayne**. 1833–1917. American jurist, b. near Phoenixville, Pa.; vigorous opponent of machine politics and corruption in Pennsylvania (from 1871); U.S. attorney general (1881); ambassador to Italy (1893–97); chief counsel for U.S. in Venezuela arbitration (1903). His brother **Franklin** (1837–1934), lawyer (1864–66); U.S. secretary of the treasury (1909–13). Wayne's son **Charles** (1860–1931), lawyer in N.Y. City (from 1883); U.S. ambassador to Japan (1925–29). Charles's son **Lincoln (1890–1972)**, publisher and diplomat; the Dial Press founded (1924); U.S. minister (1933–41) and ambassador (1943–47) to Greece, Portugal (1948), Spain (1952).

**Mac·Whir′ter** (măk·hwûr′tẽr), **John**. 1839–1911. Scottish painter, esp. of landscapes and studies of trees.

**Ma′cy** (mā′sĭ), **Jesse**. 1842–1919. American political scientist; professor, Grinnell (1884–1912). Author of *Our Government* (1886), *Political Parties in the United States, 1846–61* (1900), *Party Organization and Machinery* (1904), etc.

**Macy, John Albert**. 1877–1932. American author and critic, b. Detroit, Mich.; became socialist (1909). Literary editor, Boston *Herald* (1913–14), *The Nation* (1922–23). Author of *The Spirit of American Literature* (1913), *Socialism in America* (1916), *The Story of the World's Literature* (1925), *The Romance of America as Told in Our Literature* (1930), *About Women* (1930). Edited Helen Keller's *Story of My Life* (1903).

**Ma′dách** (mŏ′däch), **Imre**. 1823–1864. Hungarian poet and dramatist. Author notably of a dramatic poem dealing with the life and fall of the human race, *The Tragedy of Man* (1861).

**Mad′an** (măd′′n; mā′d′n), **Martin**. 1726–1790. English barrister and Methodist divine; chaplain of Lock Hospital, London (1750–80); stirred storm of protest with his *Thelyphthora* ("ruination of women"), advocating polygamy as remedy for evils of prostitution (1780).

**Ma′da·ria′ga y Ro′jo** (mä′thä·ryä′gä ē rô′hō), **Salvador de.** 1886–1978. Spanish writer and diplomat; ambassador in Washington (1931); League of Nations council (1931–36); ambassador to France (1932–34); chief, Spanish delegation to the League of Nations (1934–35). Among his works are *Shelley and Calderón*, *The Genius of Spain*, *The Price of Peace*, *Anarchy or Hierarchy* (1937), *The World's Design* (1938).

**Mad'den** (măd''n), Sir **Charles Edward.** 1862–1935. British naval officer; rear admiral in the home fleet (1911–14); vice-admiral (1916); engaged at battle of Jutland (1916); second in command of grand fleet (1917–19). Commander in chief of Atlantic fleet (1919–22); first naval aide-de-camp to king (1922–24); admiral of the fleet (1924); first sea lord of the admiralty and chief of naval staff (1927–30); retired (1930). Member of Order of Merit (1931).

**Madden,** Sir **Frederic.** 1801–1873. English paleographer, of Irish extraction. Keeper of mss. in British Museum (1828–66). Edited *Havelok the Dane* (1828), *William and the Werwolf* (1832), early English versions of *Gesta Romanorum* (1838), Layamon's *Brut* (1847), and Wycliffe's *Bible* (1850).

**Madden, Richard Robert.** 1798–1886. Irish surgeon, traveler, and author. Special magistrate for administering abolition of slavery in Jamaican plantations (1833–41); special commissioner on African west coast (1841–43); colonial secretary of Western Australia (1847–50). Author of *The United Irishmen* (7 vols., 1843–46), etc.

**Madden, Samuel.** 1686–1765. Irish philanthropist and writer of tragedy, history, poetry; author of the oft-quoted panegyric poem *Boulter's Monument* (1745).

**Mad'dox** (măd'ŭks), **Ernest Edmund.** 1860–1933. British ophthalmologist; developed method of treating squint in children; authority on heterophoria.

**Ma'dec'** (mȧ'dĕk'), **René Marie.** *Known as* **Me·doc'** (?mĕ·dŏk') *in Anglo-Indian references.* 1736?–1784. French adventurer in India; served under Dupleix and Lally; captured by British and enlisted in Bengal army; deserted and entered service of some of native princes, notably Emperor Shah Alam (1772); rejoined French (1778) and took part in defense of Pondichéry; returned to France after fall of this city.

**Ma'de·lin'** (mȧ'dlăN'), **Louis,** *in full* **Émile Louis Marie.** 1871–1956. French historian; author of *Fouché* (1901), *Rome de Napoléon* (1904), *La Révolution* (1910), *Danton* (1912), *Histoire de la Nation Française*, and *Consulat de Bonaparte* (1929), etc.

**Ma'de·lung** (mä'dĕ·lo͝ong), **Georg.** 1889– . German aeronautical engineer.

**Ma·der'na** (mä·dĕr'nä) *or* **Ma·der'no** (-nō) *or* **Ma·der'ni** (-nē), **Carlo.** 1556–1629. Italian architect; exponent of Roman baroque style; nephew and pupil of Domenico Fontana; protégé of Clement VIII and Paul V; succeeded Fontana as architect of St. Peter's (1603); altered Michelangelo's Greek cross plan to that of present Latin cross. Among his other works are Palazzo Mattei di Giove, church of Santa Maria della Vittoria, continuation of Palazzo Quirinale and Palazzo Barberini.

**Ma·de'ro** (mä·thā'rō), **Francisco Indalecio.** 1873–1913. Mexican revolutionist and politician; a liberal and idealist; opposed re-election of Díaz to presidency (1910), but failed of election; demanded effective suffrage and no re-election, and plotted against Díaz; fled to U.S. (Nov., 1910); led military campaign ending in capture of Ciudad Juárez, where capital was established (May 11, 1911); forced resignation of Díaz and became president (1911–13); after revolts and street fighting in Mexico City (Feb., 1913), overthrown by Huerta, arrested, and shot while allegedly attempting escape.

**Ma'de·to'ja** (mȧ'dĕ·tŏ'yȧ), **Leevi Antti.** 1887–1947. Finnish composer; professor, Helsinki (from 1916), and musical critic for the *Helsingin Sanomat* (1916–32). Composer of operas, symphonies, cantatas, chamber music, and a Finnish national anthem. His wife, **Onerva** (1882– ), writer, under the pseudonym **L. O'ner·va** (ŏ'nĕr·vȧ), of poetical works including *The Crushed Gods*, *Evening Bells*, *The Struggle of Souls;* novels including *Mirdja* and *The Lonely People;* and plays including *The Prosecutors* and *Legends.*

**Ma'dha·va** *or* **Ma'dha·va·char'ya** (mä'dȧ·vä·chär'yȧ). fl. about 1380 A.D. Hindu scholar and royal counselor. Elder brother of Sayana. Lived at court in Vijayanagar as minister to the king; wrote on philosophical and religious subjects and collaborated with his brother on commentaries on the Vedas. Founder of the Madhvas, a Vaishnava sect.

**Ma'dhu Ra'o** (mä'do͞o rä'o͞o). Name of two peshwas of the Marathas: **Madhu Rao I** (1754–1772); fourth peshwa (1761–72); son of Balaji Baji Rao; succeeded to throne after great defeat of Marathas at Panipat (1761); nominal head of the first great Maratha houses; withstood attack of Mohammedan prince of Hyderabad; defeated Haidar Ali of Mysore (1770–71). **Madhu Rao II** (1774–1795); sixth peshwa (1774–95); posthumous son of the fifth peshwa, **Na·ra'yan Rao** [nä·rä'yȧn] (1772–73); during entire life, power held by Maratha minister, Nana Farnavis; First Maratha War (1775–82) against British occurred in his reign.

**Mad'i·son** (măd'ĭ·s'n), **Dolley,** *nee* **Payne.** *Often spelled* **Dolly.** 1768–1849. American hostess, b. in Guilford Co., N.C.; m. John Todd, Jr. (1790; d. 1793), James Madison (1794). Famous Washington hostess while her husband was secretary of state (1801–09) and president (1809–17).

**Madison, James.** 1749–1812. American Episcopal clergyman and educator, b. near Staunton, Va. Grad. William and Mary (1771); president of the college (1777–1812). Elected first bishop of Virginia (1790).

**Madison, James.** 1751–1836. Fourth president of the United States, b. Port Conway, Va. Grad. Princeton (1771). Member, Continental Congress (1780–83), Constitutional Convention (1787). Co-operated with Hamilton and Jay in writing a series of papers (pub. 1787–88 under title of *The Federalist*) explaining the new constitution and advocating its adoption. Member, U.S. House of Representatives (1789–97); leader of Democratic-Republican party in opposition to Hamilton's financial measures. With Jefferson, drafted the Virginia Resolutions (1798) inspired by resentment at the Federalist alien and sedition laws. U.S. secretary of state (1801–09). President of the U.S. (1809–17). Rector, U. of Virginia (1826–36). Elected to American Hall of Fame (1905).

**Mäd'ler** (mâd'lĕr), **Johann Heinrich von.** 1794–1874. German astronomer.

**Mad'oc** (măd'ŭk). = MADOG AB OWAIN GWYNEDD.

**Ma'dog ab O'wain Gwy'nedd** (mȧ'dŏg ȧb ō'wân go͞o'ĭ·nâth). 1150–?1180. Legendary Welsh prince; said (in 15th-century Welsh poem) to have sailed away in ten ships and long supposed by his countrymen to have discovered America (c. 1170); subject of Southey's poem *Madoc.*

**Madonella.** See Mary ASTELL.

**Ma'dou'** (mȧ'do͞o'), **Jean Baptiste.** 1796–1877. Belgian genre painter and lithographer.

**Ma·doz'** (mä·thôth'), **Pascual.** 1806–1870. Spanish politician and writer; governor of Barcelona (1854); Spanish minister of finance (1855); had important part in furthering secularization of church lands. Published

*Diccionario Geográfico, Estadístico é Histórico de España* (1848–50).

**Ma·dra′zo** (mä·thrä′thō). Family of Spanish painters, including: **José de Madrazo** (1781–1859), historical and portrait painter. His son **Federico** (1815–1894), also historical and portrait painter, appointed court painter and curator of the Madrid Gallery of Art. Federico's son **Raimundo** (1841–1920), portrait and genre painter with studio in Paris.

**Mad′vig** (màth′vēg), **Johan Nicolai.** 1804–1882. Danish classical scholar; professor, Copenhagen (1829–79); worked esp. for improvement of classical schools. President of the council (1856–63) and leader of the National Liberal party.

**Mae·ce′nas** (mē·sē′năs), **Gaius.** 70?–8 B.C. Roman statesman and patron of literature; close friend of Horace and Vergil, and of Octavianus (who became emperor under title Augustus). Entrusted by Octavianus with administration of Rome while Octavianus fought with Pompey the Younger (38–36); after battle of Actium (31), urged Octavianus to establish an empire. Retired to private life (16). Presented Horace with the Sabine farm which Horace celebrated in his verse; requested Vergil to write his *Georgics.* Only fragments of his own writings are extant.

**Ma′ël′** (mà′ĕl′), **Pierre.** Joint pseudonym of two French novelists, **Charles Causse** [kōs] (1862–1905) and **Charles Vin′cent′** [văN′säN′] (1851–1920), collaborators in writing many romances, including *L'Alcyone* (1888), *Mer Bleue* (1890), *Mer Bénie* (1894), *Fleur de France* (1896), *Le Cœur et l'Honneur* (1898), *Bonheur Conquis* (1901), *Au Pays du Mystère* (1904). After Causse's death, Vincent used same pseudonym for a number of his own novels.

**Mael′zel** *or* **Mäl′zel** (mĕl′tsĕl), **Johann Nepomuk.** 1772–1838. German musician and inventor of musical mechanisms; settled in Vienna as music teacher (1792) and won fame for mechanical inventions including a kind of orchestrion called the panharmonicon (or panharmonion), an automatic trumpeter (1808), and ear trumpets used by Beethoven among others; named court mechanician (1808). Constructed the Maelzel metronome (1816) from the idea advanced by Winkel of Amsterdam; aided his friend Beethoven in writing *The Battle of Vittoria* (1813) for panharmonicon (later also for organ). Settled in Paris (1817), in U.S. (from 1826). His brother **Leonhard** (d. 1855) became court musical mechanician (1827).

**Maer′lant** (màr′länt), **Jacob van.** 1235?–?1300. Flemish poet, b. near Bruges; founder of the didactic school in the Netherlands. Author esp. of rhymed versions of Latin and French originals, of didactic works, of the rhymed Biblical history *Rhyme Bible* (1271; after Petrus Comestor's *Biblia Scolastica*), and the rhymed world chronicle *The Mirror of History* (begun 1282; chiefly after Vincent of Beauvais's *Speculum Historiale*), etc.

**Maes** *or* **Maas** (màs), **Nicolaes.** 1632–1693. Dutch genre and portrait painter; studied under Rembrandt. His works include *The Idle Maid, The Card Players, The Listener, Old Woman at the Spinning Wheel, The Inquisitive Servant, Old Woman Peeling an Apple, Saying Grace, Hagar's Farewell.*

**Mae′ter·linck** (*Flem.* mà′tẽr·lĭngk; *Fr.* mĕ′tĕr′lăNk′; *Angl.* mā′tẽr·lĭngk, mĕt′ẽr-, mä′tẽr-), Count **Maurice.** 1862–1949. Belgian poet, dramatist, and essayist, b. in Ghent of Flemish origin. Settled in Paris (1896), where he came under influence of French symbolists; won Nobel prize for literature (1911); did relief work in France and Belgium during World War (1914–18) and wrote against German rule in Belgium; visited U.S. for lecture tour (1921); created count (1932); to U.S. (1940). Author of the volume of melancholy poems *Hothouses* (1889) and of the lyrics *Twelve Chansons* (1896); of chiefly mystic and symbolistic plays including *The Princess Maleine* (1889), *The Intruder* (1890), *The Blind* (1890), *The Seven Princesses* (1891), *Pelléas et Mélisande* (1892), adapted for opera (1902) by his friend Debussy; of marionette plays *The Death of Tintagiles* (1894), *Aglavaine and Sélysette* (1896), *Arione* and *Sister Beatrice* (1899), *Monna Vanna* (1902), *Joyzelle* (1903), *The Miracle of St. Anthony* (1905), *The Blue Bird* (1909) and its successor *The Betrothal* (1918), *Mary Magdalene* (1910), *The Burgomaster of Stilemonde* (1918), etc.; of essays and studies chiefly on philosophy and nature including *The Treasure of the Humble* (1896), *Wisdom and Destiny* (1898), *The Life of the Bee* (1901), *The Buried Temple* (1902), *The Double Garden* (1904), *Life and Flowers* (1907), *Death* (1912), *The Great Secret* (1921), *The Life of Space* (1927), *The Life of the Ant* (1930), *The Magic of the Stars* (1930), and *Before God* (1937); and of an essay on *King Lear* and a French translation of *Macbeth* (1910). Most of his works have been translated into English.

**Maf·fe′i** (mäf·fâ′ē), Marchese **Francesco Scipione di.** 1675–1755. Italian author and scholar; cofounder of *Giornale dei Letterati d'Italia* (1710). Known particularly for his contributions to Italian drama; author of *Merope* (1713), first notable Italian tragedy, used later as basis for Voltaire's *Mérope* (1743); also wrote *Trattato de' Teatri Antichi e Moderni.* Among his other works are *Storia Diplomatica* (1727), *Galliae Antiquitates* (1733), *Storia Teologica...*(1742), *Dell'Impiego del Denaro* (1746).

**Ma·ga·lhaens′** (mă·gȧ·lyăĕNsh′), **Gabriel de.** 1609–1677. Portuguese Jesuit missionary to China.

**Ma·ga·lhães′** (mă·gȧ·lyāēs′), **Domingo José Gonçalves de.** Viscount of **A·ra·gua′ya** (ă·rȧ·gwī′yȧ). 1811–1882. Brazilian poet, philosopher, and statesman; leader of the romantic school in Brazilian literature. Brazilian ambassador successively in Naples, Turin, Vienna and Washington. Among his poetical works are *A Confederação dos Tamóios* (epic; 1857), *Mistérios* (1858), *Urânia* (1862). Author also of a literary history of Brazil (1834).

**Magdalene** *or* **Magdalen.** See MARY MAGDALENE.

**Ma·gee′** (mȧ·gē′), **William.** 1766–1831. Irish prelate, of Scottish family origin; archbishop of Dublin (1822–31). Author of *Discourses on the Scriptural Doctrines of Atonement and Sacrifice,* a polemic against Unitarianism (1801). His grandson **William Connor Magee** (1821–1891), orator and prelate of Church of England, made strong defense of Irish Church at time of disestablishment proposals (1868); bishop of Peterborough (1868–91); archbishop of York (1891); condemned disestablishment bill in celebrated speech in House of Lords (1869); opposed excess in ritual.

**Magee, William Kirkpatrick.** *Pseudonym* **John Eg′lin·ton** (ĕg′lĭn·tŭn). 1868– . Irish essayist and poet, b. Dublin. Asst. librarian, National Library, Dublin. Author of *Two Essays on the Remnant* (1896), *Pebbles from the Brook* (1902), *Bards and Saints* (1906), *Irish Literary Portraits,* etc.

**Ma·gel′lan** (mȧ·jĕl′ăn; *Brit.* -gĕl′ăn), **Ferdinand.** *Port.* **Fernando de Ma·ga·lhães′** (thĕ mă·gȧ·lyăĕNsh′). 1480?–1521. Portuguese navigator. In service of Emanuel (1495); in India and the East (from 1505); explored Spice Islands [Moluccas] (1511–12); dropped from Emanuel's service (1514). Offered services to Spain (1517); acquired approval of Charles V for voyage to Spice Islands by western route. Left Spain (Sept. 20, 1519) with five vessels; sighted South America near

Pernambuco (Nov. 29); explored La Plata estuary; wintered at Port St. Julian (Mar. 31, 1519–Aug. 24, 1520); crushed mutiny; sailed through strait now known as Strait of Magellan (Oct. 21–Nov. 28, 1520); reached Ladrone Islands (Mar. 6, 1521); discovered Philippines (Mar. 16), arriving Cebu (Apr. 7); made alliance with treacherous native sovereign; killed on expedition on his behalf to island of Mactan (Apr. 27, 1521); survivors of party escaped to Moluccas (Nov. 6); one vessel completed circumnavigation of globe (1522). See J. S. del CANO.

**Ma'gen'die'** (mȧ'zhăɴ'dē'), **François.** 1783–1855. French physiologist; pioneer in experimental physiology in France; demonstrated the functions of the spinal nerves; investigated the mechanisms of blood flow, deglutition, and vomiting; credited with introduction of strychnine and morphine, and compounds of iodine and bromine, into medical practice.

**Mag·gi'ni** (mäd·jē'nē), **Giovanni Paolo.** 1580–?1632. Italian violinmaker.

**Ma·ginn'** (mȧ·gĭn'), **William.** 1793–1842. Irish periodical writer and poet; first success as parodist and writer of humorous Latin verse in *Blackwood's Magazine* (1819); in association with Hugh Fraser, writer and Bohemian, initiated *Fraser's Magazine* (1830), contributing *Gallery of Literary Characters* and *Homeric Ballads* (from 1838); adapted Lucian's *Dialogues of the Dead* into blank-verse comedies; his best story, *Bob Burke's Duel with Ensign Brady* (1834). Portrayed as Captain Shandon in Thackeray's *Pendennis.*

**Ma'gi'not'** (mȧ'zhē'nō'; *Angl.* măzh'ĭ·nō), **André.** 1877–1932. French politician; member of Chamber of Deputies (from 1910); served in World War. Minister of colonies (1917), of pensions (1921), of war (1922–24; 1926–29; 1929–30; 1931). Vigorous advocate of military preparedness; the Maginot line was named in his honor.

**Ma'glia·be'chi** (mä'lyä·bā'kē) *or* **Ma'glia·bec'chi** (-bāk'kē), **Antonio.** 1633–1714. Florentine bibliophile and scholar; librarian to Cosimo III, Grand Duke of Tuscany (1673–1714); bequeathed personal library (Magliabechiana) of 30,000 volumes to grand duke, now part of Biblioteca Nazionale of Florence.

**Ma'gnan'** (mȧ'nyäɴ'), **Bernard Pierre.** 1791–1865. French soldier; served at Waterloo (1815), in Spain (1823) and Algeria (1830); general of brigade (1839) and of division (1845); suppressed uprising in Lyons (1849); took active part in ensuring success of coup d'etat (Dec. 2, 1851) and was created marshal of France; senator (1852); commander of army of Paris (1859).

**Ma·gna'sco** (mä·nyäs'kō), **Alessandro.** *Called* **Lis'-san·dri'no** (lēs'sän·drē'nō). 1667?–1749. Italian painter, esp. of genre scenes.

**Mag·nen'ti·us** (măg·nĕn'shĭ·ŭs; -shŭs), **Flavius Popilius.** d. 353 A.D. Roman emperor of the West (350–353), of barbarian birth; in command of troops on the Rhine; plotted against and caused death of Constans (350); defeated by Constantius II at Mursa (351); fled to Gaul; committed suicide.

**Mag'nes** (măg'nēz). Athenian writer of comedies in early 5th century B.C.; reputed first of the comedy writers to win dramatic prize. None of his work is extant beyond titles of a few plays.

**Mag'nes** (măg'nĕs), **Judah Leon.** 1877–1948. American rabbi, b. San Francisco. Rabbi, Temple Emanu-El, New York (1906–10), B'nai Jeshurun, New York (1911–12). Leader, Society for Advancement of Judaism (1912–20). Chancellor (1925–35) and president (1935 ff.), Hebrew U., Jerusalem.

**Ma'gnin'** (mȧ'nyăɴ'), **Charles.** 1793–1862. French scholar; author of *Origines du Théâtre en Europe* (1838), *Histoire des Marionnettes en Europe...*(1852), etc.

**Ma'gnol'** (mȧ'nyôl'), **Pierre.** 1638–1715. French physician and botanist; originated classification of plants by families. Linnaeus named the genus of trees *Magnolia* after him.

**Mag'nus** (*Dan.* måg'nōōs; *Angl.* măg'nŭs). King of Denmark. = MAGNUS I of Norway.

**Mag'nus** (*Norw.* mäng'nōōs; *Angl.* măg'nŭs). Name of seven kings of Norway:

**Magnus I.** *Called* **the Good.** d. 1047. Son of St. Olaf. King of Norway (1035–47) and of Denmark (1042–47).

**Magnus II Ha'ralds·son** (hä'räld·sŏn). 1035–1069. King (1066–69). Son of Harold Haardraade. Divided kingdom with brother Olaf III; took north and west portion.

**Magnus III.** *Called* **Barefoot.** 1073–1103. Son of Olaf III. King (1093–1103). At first ruled only southern third (1093–95); after death (1095) of Haakon Magnusson, ruled all Norway; harried Orkneys and Hebrides (1098–99); waged war with Sweden (1099–1100); led another expedition south; landed on Orkneys and Isle of Man; killed on coast of Ireland.

**Magnus IV.** *Called* **the Blind.** 1115?–1139. Son of Sigurd and grandson of Magnus III. King (1130–35). Engaged in civil war with Harold Gille (1134–35); defeated, had his eyes put out, and imprisoned; later, killed in naval battle with sons of Harold.

**Magnus V Er'lings·son** (âr'lĭng·sŏn). 1156–1184. Son of Erling Skakke. King (1162–84), under regency (1162–64); crowned at Bergen (1164); fought long civil war with Sverre Sigurdsson; finally defeated (1179) and fled to Denmark; slain in naval battle in attempt to recover kingdom.

**Magnus VI.** *Called* **La'ga·bö'ter** (lä'gä·bû'tẽr), *i.e.* the law mender. 1238–1280. Son of Haakon IV. King (1263–80).

**Magnus VII E'riks·son** (ā'rĭk·sŏn). See MAGNUS II, King of Sweden.

**Mag'nus** (*Swed.* mång'nŭs; *Angl.* măg'nŭs). Name of two kings of Sweden:

**Magnus I.** *Called* **Magnus La'du·lås'** (lä'dōō·lōs'), *i.e.* barn lock. 1240–1290. Second son of Birger of Bjälbo. King (1275–90). Deposed his brother Waldemar; opposed nobles and protected peasantry by wise legislation.

**Magnus II.** *Also known as* **Magnus E'riks·son** (ā'rĭk·sôn). *Called* **Smek** (smāk). 1316–1374. Son of Duke Eric and grandson of Haakon V of Norway. King of Norway as Magnus VII (1319–43) and as regent (1343–55) for his son Haakon VI; king of Sweden (1319–65). Ruled under a regent (1319–32); lived almost all the time in Sweden; tried to control nobility; gave Norway to three-year-old son Haakon (1343); deposed (1356–59) by his son Eric XII; lost southern districts of Sweden to Waldemar IV of Denmark (1360); deposed by Royal Council of Swedes (1363); succeeded by Duke Albert of Mecklenburg; retired to Norway; drowned.

**Mag'nus** (mäg'nōōs), **Heinrich Gustav.** 1802–1870. German chemist and physicist; work includes studies of tellurium and selenium, and the gases in the blood, and contributions to mineralogical chemistry. His investigation of the deviation of projectiles led him to discover the "Magnus effect," the sideways thrust on a rotating cylinder when placed in a current of air. This phenomenon was later utilized in the rotor ship for propulsion.

**Mag'nus** (*Swed.* mång'nŭs; *Angl.* măg'nŭs), **Olaus.** 1490–1558. Swedish Roman Catholic ecclesiastic and historian; to Rome (1527) where he lived chiefly in the monastery of Saint Brigitta. Author of *Historia de*

*Gentibus Septentrionalibus* (1555), long accepted in Europe as authoritative on Swedish history. His brother **Johannes** (1488–1544) was archbishop of Uppsala.

**Mag′nus·sen** (mäg′nōō·sĕn), **Har′ro** (här′ō). 1861–1908. German sculptor; executed portrait busts of Haeckel, Frederick the Great, and Bismarck, and memorial monuments to Bismarck in Kiel, Bismarck, Moltke, to Roon in the Hall of Fame in Görlitz, and to William I in Bonn.

**Mag′nús·son** (mäg′nōōs·sŏn), **Árni.** 1663–1730. Icelandic antiquary and philologist; founder of the Arna-Magnæan Collection of Old Norse manuscripts at U. of Copenhagen.

**Mag′nús·son** (mäg′nōōs·sŏn) *or* **Mag′nú·sen** (-nōō-sĕn) *or* **Mag′nús·sen** (-nōōs·sĕn), **Finnur.** 1781–1847. Icelandic archaeologist; author of treatises on the elder Edda, and on Norse mythology and antiquities.

**Ma′go** (mā′gō). Name of several prominent Carthaginians of the same family, including: (1) A general of 6th century B.C., reputed organizer of Carthaginian military system. (2) A naval commander; engaged against Syracusans (396–392 B.C.); suffete of Carthage. (3) An army commander in Sicily (343 B.C.); guilty of cowardice, committed suicide. (4) A younger brother of Hannibal; accompanied Hannibal to Italy (218 B.C.); supported Hasdrubal in Spain (215); defeated by Scipio Africanus at Silpia (206). (5) The reputed author, of unknown date, of a book on agriculture which by order of the Roman senate was taken to Rome after destruction of Carthage and translated into Latin.

**Ma·gon′i·gle** (mȧ·gŏn′ĭ·g'l), **Harold Van Buren.** 1867–1935. American architect; designed the McKinley National Memorial, at Canton, Ohio, National Maine monument, in New York.

**Ma·goon′** (mȧ·gōōn′), **Charles Edward.** 1861–1920. American lawyer and administrator; practiced in Nebraska. Governor of Canal Zone (1905–06); provisional governor of Cuba (1906–09).

**Ma·gru′der** (mȧ·grōō′dẽr), **John Bankhead.** 1810–1871. American army officer, b. Winchester, Va.; grad. U.S.M.A., West Point (1830). Resigned from U.S. army (1861) to enter Confederate service, commanding district of Texas (1862–65). Major general under Emperor Maximilian of Mexico (1866–67). His niece **Julia Magruder** (1854–1907) was a novelist, her works including *Princess Sonia* (1895), *A Manifest Destiny* (1900).

**Ma′gyar** (mŏ′dyŏr), **László.** 1817–1864. Hungarian traveler in Africa; author of *Reisen in Südafrika, 1849–57* (1st vol., 1859).

**Ma·haf′fy** (mȧ·hăf′ĭ), Sir **John Pentland.** 1839–1919. Irish classical scholar, b. in Switzerland. First professor of ancient history at Dublin (1869–1901), provost of Trinity (from 1914); directed defense of college in Easter Rebellion (1916). Known for works on life, literature, and history of ancient Greeks, including *History of Classical Greek Literature* (1880) and *The Silver Age of the Greek World* (1906).

**Ma·han′** (mȧ·hăn′), **Alfred Thayer.** 1840–1914. American naval officer and historian, b. West Point, N.Y.; grad. U.S.N.A., Annapolis (1859). President, Naval War College, Newport, R.I. (1886–89; 1892–93); published his lectures as *The Influence of Sea Power Upon History, 1660–1783* (1890) and *The Influence of Sea Power upon the French Revolution and Empire, 1793–1812* (2 vols., 1892). Retired (1896). U.S. delegate to first Hague Peace Conference (1899). Other works include: *Types of Naval Officers* (1901), *Sea Power in Its Relations to the War of 1812* (2 vols., 1905), *Naval Strategy* (1911), and biographies of Farragut and Nelson. His father **Dennis Hart Mahan** (1802–1871), grad. U.S.M.A., West Point (1824), was professor of engineering at West Point (1832–71) and author of textbooks on military engineering and descriptive geometry.

**Ma·hā′vī′ra, Var·dha·mā′na Jñā′ti·pu′tra** (mȧ-hä′vē′rȧ vȧr·dȧ·mä′nȧ j'nyä′tĭ·pōō′trȧ). fl. 6th century B.C. Historical founder of Jainism in India. Contemporary with Buddha; practiced asceticism for 12 years, then devoted himself to preaching and teaching; in Jain legendary accounts held to be the 24th or last jina, or saint. The name *Mahavira*, in Sanskrit, means "great hero."

**Mah′di, al-** (ăl·mă′dē). d. 785. Third Abbasside caliph (775–785). Son of al-Mansur and father of Harun al-Rashid. Waged successful war against Byzantines; his reign beginning of Abbasside ascendancy.

**Mahdi, the.** See MOHAMMED AHMED.

**Mahendra-varman.** See PALLAVA.

**Ma′hieu′** (mȧ′yû′), **Thomas.** 16th-century French bibliophile famed for the excellent and distinctive bindings of volumes in his collection. Secretary to Catherine de Médicis; treasurer of France (1572). Because of the device on the bindings of his books, he was long erroneously believed to be **Tommaso Ma·io′li** (mä·yô′lē), and the name *Maioli* was given in his honor to a style of binding contemporary with Jean Grolier de Servières.

**Mah′ler** (mä′lẽr), **Gustav.** 1860–1911. Bohemian composer and conductor; director, Imperial Opera in Vienna (1897–1907); conducted in U.S. (1907–10). Among his compositions are ten symphonies (the last unfinished), *Das Klagende Lied* (a cantata), many songs, a set of *Humoresken* for orchestra, and *Das Lied von der Erde* (1908). Also edited and completed Weber's unfinished opera *Die Drei Pintos* (1887).

**Mahl′mann** (mäl′män), **Siegfried August.** 1771–1826. German poet; many of his folk songs have been set to music.

**Mäh′ly** (mâ′lē), **Jakob.** 1828–1902. Swiss philologist and poet; among his works are *Mathilde* (1854), *Paix* (1862), *Byrsopolias* (1875), *Histoire de la Littérature Antique* (1880).

**Mah·mud′** (mä·mōōd′). Name of two sultans of Turkey: **Mahmud I** (1696–1754) succeeded his uncle Ahmed III on throne (1730); forced Austria to cede Belgrade (1739). **Mahmud II** (1785–1839) succeeded his brother Mustafa IV on throne (1808); waged unsuccessful war against Russia (1809–12); attempted to suppress Greeks in their struggle for freedom (1821–29) and was forced by Greek allies, France, England, and Russia, to sign Treaty of Adrianople securing Greek independence (1829); started war with Mehemet Ali, Viceroy of Egypt (1839).

**Mahmud Ne·dim′ Pa·sha′** (nĕ·dēm′ pä·shä′). 1810–1884. Turkish statesman; grand vizier (1871–75, with some interruptions); minister of interior (1879–83).

**Mah·mud′ of Ghaz′ni** (mȧ·mōōd′, gŭz′nē). 971?–1030. Moslem sultan (997–1030) of Ghazni (see GHAZNEVID); called "the Idol Smasher." Son of Subuktigin. Extended small Afghan kingdom from the Tigris to the Ganges and northward to the Oxus (Amu Darya); invaded India seventeen times (1001–30), the most important being called the *Twelve Expeditions;* overwhelmed Hindu ruler of Lahore; sacked Somnath (1024) in Gujarat; carried away much booty; made the Punjab an outlying province of Afghan kingdom. Many legends told of him by Mohammedan chroniclers. Cf. FIRDAUSI.

**Mah·mud′ Shah** (mȧ·mōōd′ shä′). Amir of Afghanistan (1799–1803; 1810–1818).

**Mah·mud′ Shev·ket′ Pa·sha′** (mä·mōōd′ shĕf·kĕt′ pä·shä′). 1855 (or 1858)–1913. Turkish general, b.

Baghdad. Leader of Young Turk cause (1908–09); marched against Constantinople and caused deposition of Sultan Abdul-Hamid (1909). Minister of war (1912); grand vizier (1913); assassinated (June 11, 1913).

**Mahomet** *or* **Mahomed.** See MOHAMMED.

**Ma'hon'** (mȧ'ôɴ'), Ducs **de.** See CRILLON family.

**Ma·hon'** (mȧ·hōōn'; -hōn'), Viscount. Courtesy title of eldest living son of earls STANHOPE.

**Ma·hon'** (mȧ·hōōn'; -hōn'), Sir **Bryan Thomas.** 1862–1930. British soldier. In Boer War (1899–1902), distinguished himself at relief of Mafeking, and in World War I. Commander in chief in Ireland (1916–18).

**Mahon, Charles James Patrick.** *Known as* **the O'Gor'man** (ō·gôr'măn) **Mahon.** 1800–1891. Irish adventurer and political leader. Quarreled with O'Connell (1831); M.P. (1847–52); served in Russian, Turkish, and Austrian armies; fought on government side in Uruguayan civil war; commanded Chilean fleet against Spain; colonel in Brazilian army; fought in Union army in American Civil War; M.P. (1879–91).

**Ma·hone'** (mȧ·hōn'), **William.** 1826–1895. American Confederate officer; with army of northern Virginia (from 1862); served at Malvern Hill, Second Manassas, the Wilderness. Leader of Readjuster party in Virginia (1879); U.S. senator (1881–87).

**Mah'o·ny** (mä'ō·nĭ; mä'nĭ), **Francis Sylvester.** *Pseudonym* **Father Prout** (prout). 1804–1866. Irish humorist. Master of rhetoric at a Jesuit college; expelled from the Jesuit order (1830), abandoned priesthood for literary pursuits. Contributed to *Fraser's Magazine* and *Bentley's Miscellany* translations from Horace and French writers interspersed with Greek, Latin, and French translations of Thomas Moore's poems and songs which he presented as originals; foreign correspondent to newspapers (1846–66). Author of *The Bells of Shandon.*

**Mai** (mä'ē), **Angelo.** 1782–1854. Italian prelate, classical philologist, and antiquary; Jesuit (from 1797); Vatican librarian (1819–25); created cardinal (1838). Known chiefly for his discovery and publication of old manuscripts and palimpsests, as Cicero's *De Re Republica* (1820), Plautus's *Vidularia,* Fronto's letters, Eusebius of Caesarea's *Chronicon,* and Dionysius' *Roman Antiquities.*

**Ma·ia'no** (mä·yä'nō), **Benedetto da.** 1442–1497. Florentine sculptor and architect; his sculptural works include pulpit of Santa Croce, tomb of Filippo Strozzi in church of Santa Maria Novella, Florence, and portrait busts; his chief architectural work is Palazzo Strozzi, Florence. His brother and teacher **Giuliano** (1432–1490) was also an architect and sculptor.

**Maid of Norway.** See MARGARET, Queen of Scots.

**Maier** (mâr), **Guy.** 1892–1956. American pianist; long associated with Lee Pattison (*q.v.*) in concerts for two pianos, frequently appearing with symphony orchestras.

**Mai'gnan'** (mĕ'nyäɴ'), **Albert Pierre René.** 1844–1908. French painter; best known for historical paintings.

**Maigrot, Émile.** See Émile HENRIOT.

**Mai'kov** (mī'kôf), **Apolloni Nikolaevich.** 1821–1897. Russian poet; published two lyrical dramas, epics, and a volume of shorter poems (1842).

**Mai'láth** (moi'lät), Count **János.** 1786–1855. Hungarian historian and poet.

**Mai'ler** (mā'lẽr), **Norman Kingsley.** 1923– . Amer. author, b. Long Branch, N.J. Wrote *The Naked and the Dead* (1948), *An American Dream* (1965), *The Armies of the Night* (1968), etc.

**Mail'lart'** (mȧ'yȧr'), **Louis,** *known as* **Aimé.** 1817–1871. French composer; among his works are the operas *La Croix de Marie* (1852), *Les Dragons de Villars* (1856), *Lara* (1864).

**Mail'let'** (mȧ'yĕ'), **Jacques Léonard.** 1823–1894. French sculptor.

**Mail'lol'** (mȧ'yôl'), **Aristide.** 1861–1944. French sculptor; was painter before attempting sculpture; carved monuments to Blanqui and Cézanne and a number of large graceful statues executed in the Greek tradition of 5th century B.C.

**Maim'bourg'** (măɴ'bōōr'), **Louis.** 1620?–1686. French ecclesiastical historian; entered Jesuit order (1636); dismissed from order because of his *Traité Historique de l'Établissement et des Prérogatives de l'Église de Rome* (1685), which defended Gallicanism; wrote also *Histoire du Luthéranisme* (1680), *Histoire du Calvinisme* (1682), etc.

**Mai'mon** (mī'mōn), **Salomon.** 1754–1800. German philosopher, b. in Polish Lithuania of Jewish descent.

**Mai·mon'i·des** (mī·mŏn'ĭ·dēz). *Or* Rabbi **Moses ben Mai·mon'**(bĕn mī·mōn'). *Also known as* **RaM·BaM'** (răm·bȧm') *from initials of his names.* 1135–1204. Jewish philosopher, b. in Córdoba, Spain. Studied under Arabic scholars. After Moslem capture of Córdoba (1148), emigrated to Cairo, Egypt; became physician to Saladin, Sultan of Egypt, and (1177) rabbi of Cairo. His philosophical system attempted to reconcile Rabbinic Judaism with Aristotelian philosophy as modified by Arabic interpretation; believed in freedom of the will; condemned asceticism; taught care of body as well as of soul. Among his notable works are Arabic commentary on the Mishnah, entitled *Siray* (*Illumination*), Arabic *Book of Precepts,* Hebrew work *Mishneh Torah* (*Second Law*), Arabic *Guide of the Perplexed,* and various works on logic, mathematics, medicine, law, and theology.

**Mai·nar'di** (mī·när'dē), **Sebastiano.** 1460?–1513. Italian painter; pupil of, and assistant to, Ghirlandajo.

**Maine** (mān), Sir **Henry James Sumner.** 1822–1888. English jurist; regius professor of civil law, Cambridge (1847–54); published lectures as *Ancient Law* (1861), which made his reputation. Legal member of council in India (1863–69), shaped plans for codification of Indian law; member of secretary of state's council for India (1871–88); appointed to new chair of comparative jurisprudence at Oxford (1869–78); master of Trinity (1877–88), professor of international law (1887–88), Cambridge. Author of works on philosophy of law, history, and politics, including *Early History of Institutions* (1875), *Early Law and Custom* (1883).

**Maine de Bi'ran'** (mân' dē bē'räɴ'). *Real name* **Marie François Pierre Gon'thier'** (gôɴ'tyā') **de Biran.** 1766–1824. French philosopher; member of Council of Five Hundred (1797) and councilor of state (1816). Author of *Influence de l'Habitude* (1802), *L'Aperception Immédiate* (1807), *Examen des Leçons de Philosophie de Laromiguière* (1817), etc.

**Main'te·non'** (măɴt'nôɴ'), Marquise **de. Françoise d'Au'bi'gné'** (dō'bē'nyā'). 1635–1719. Mistress and second wife of Louis XIV; spent childhood in Martinique, until father's death (1645); educ. in a convent (1645–49); converted to Roman Catholic faith; m. poet Scarron (1652); left in poverty at his death (1660). Favored by Mme. de Montespan; entrusted with education of her children (1669). Became favorite of Louis XIV; purchased estate of Maintenon (1674), which was later (1678) made a marquisate. After death of Queen Marie Thérèse (1683) m. Louis privately (1685); exerted strong religious influence over king, and had considerable control over his foreign policy and over domestic affairs, esp. those of the church; favored revocation of Edict of Nantes; on Louis's death (1715), retired to convent of St.-Cyr, which she had previously founded. Noted esp. for her beauty and intellectual gifts. Much of her correspondence preserved, published at Paris (1854–66; 1888).

**Maioli, Tommaso.** See Thomas MAHIEU.

**Mair, John.** See MAJOR.

**Mai'ret'** (mĕ'rĕ'), **Jean.** 1604–1686. French dramatist; wrote *Sylvie* (1621), *Virginie* (1628), *Cléopâtre* (1630), *L'Illustre Corsaire* (1637), etc.

**Mai·ro'nis** (mī·rô'nĭs). *Real name* **Jonas Ma·čiu'lis** (mä·chŏŏ'lĭs). 1862–1932. Lithuanian poet; among his poems are *Young Lithuania, Our Sufferings, Magdalen of Raseiniai;* among his dramas are *Where is Salvation?, The Death of Kestutis.* His songs are widely sung in Lithuania.

**Mais** (māz), **Stuart Petre Brodie.** 1885– . English journalist, lecturer, broadcaster, and miscellaneous writer; literary critic, London *Evening News* (1918) and *Daily Express* (1921–23); literary editor, *Daily Graphic* (1923–26); on staff of *Daily Telegraph* (1926–31). Works include textbooks, treatises on education, essays, and local English guidebooks, as *See England First* (1927), *Highways and Byways in the Welsh Marches* (1939).

**Maisières, Philippe de.** See MÉZIÈRES.

**Mai'sky** (mī'skû·ĭ; *Angl.* -skĭ), **Ivan Mikhailovich.** 1884– . Ambassador of the U.S.S.R. in Great Britain (1932–43).

**Mai'son'** (mā'zôN'), **Nicolas Joseph.** 1771–1840. French soldier in Revolutionary army (1792) and under Napoleon; general of division (1812); remained loyal to Louis XVIII during the Hundred Days; created marquis (1817); commanded expedition (1828) to Peloponnesos (Morea) and was created marshal of France; minister of foreign affairs (1830); ambassador at Vienna (1831) and St. Petersburg (1833); minister of war (1835–36).

**Mai'son'neuve'** (mā'zô'nûv'), Sieur **de.** **Paul de Cho'me·dey'** (shôm'dā'). 1612–1676. French colonial administrator; founder and governor of Montreal (1642–64).

**Maisonneuve, Jules Germain François.** 1810–1894. French surgeon; one of the first in surgery to apply the theory of regeneration of bone by the periosteum.

**Mais'tre** (mĕs'tr'), Comte **Joseph Marie de.** 1753–1821. French philosopher, statesman, and man of letters; emigrated to Switzerland and Italy during French Revolution (1792); ambassador of Victor Emmanuel I at St. Petersburg (1802–16); remained opponent of French Revolution and its results. Among his works are *Considérations sur la France* (an attack on the Revolution; 1796), *Les Soirées de Saint Pétersbourg* (1821), and *Examen de la Philosophie de Bacon* (pub. 1836). His brother Comte **Xavier** (1763–1852) was also a writer and Royalist sympathizer; served in Austrian and Russian armies (1799); lived for most of his life in Russia.

**Maistre, Paul André Marie.** 1858–1922. French general in the World War; commander of a group of armies of the center in final months of the war.

**Mait'land** (māt'lănd). Name of a Scottish family possessing the ancestral keep of **Thirle'stane** (thîrl'stān), the lands of **Leth'ing·ton** (lĕth'ĭng·tŭn), and the earldom and dukedom of **Lau'der·dale** (lô'dẽr·dāl), which descended from an Anglo-Norman family that settled in Berwick in reign of William the Lyon (1165–1214). The family includes:

Sir **Richard Maitland,** Lord **Lethington** (1496–1586), lawyer, poet, and collector of Scottish verse; educ. St. Andrews and Paris; lost his sight (1561); an ordinary lord of session and privy councilor (1561); keeper of great seal (1562–67); author of poems of social and political satire and a history of family of Seton; his collection of Scottish poetry is in Pepysian collection at Cambridge.

His eldest son, **William Maitland** of Lethington (1528?–1573), known as "Secretary Lethington"; educ. at St. Andrews; secretary of state to queen regent of Scotland (1558), but joined lords of the congregation against her (1559); secretary of state (1561–66), entrusted with foreign policy of Mary, Queen of Scots, whom he supported in opposition to extreme proposals of Knox; conciliatory toward England, worked for union between two crowns; shared in murder of Darnley; driven by enmity with Bothwell to side of insurgents against Mary at Langside, but after her flight tried to exculpate her and formed a party of her adherents; with Kirkcaldy held Edinburgh castle against the regent Morton (till 1573); died in prison.

Sir Richard's second son, Sir **John** (1545?–1595), 1st Baron **Maitland of Thirlestane;** lord privy seal of Scotland (1567), supported cause of Mary, Queen of Scots, against Presbyterians; secretary of state (1584); vice-chancellor (1586); influenced King James VI to consent to act establishing the Kirk on a strictly Presbyterian basis. His son **John** (d. 1645), 2d baron, was created 1st earl of **Lauderdale** (1624).

The 1st earl's eldest son, **John Maitland** (1616–1682), 2d Earl and first Duke of **Lauderdale.** Scottish statesman and English Cabal minister. Began career as zealous adherent of Presbyterian cause, the hope of the ultra-Covenanters' party; commissioner for Solemn League and Covenant (1643–46) sent to Westminster Assembly; one of commissioners sent to confer with Charles I at Carisbrooke, who gained from him the Engagement (1647); shifted to Royalist side (1647); joined Prince Charles in Holland and accompanied him to battle of Worcester, where he was captured (1651); lay prisoner (1651–60), liberated by Monck. As secretary of state for Scottish affairs (1660–80), spent seven years eliminating rivals, then became virtual ruler of Scotland; made his object the bringing to the crown of absolute power of church and state in Scotland; persecuted Covenanters; goaded peasants of west country into rebellion (1666); called in Highland host to suppress Scottish conventicles (1677–78); drilled Episcopal Church into submission; held seat in the Cabal ministry; aroused hatred of the other ministers and both countries by arrogance and debauched life; through favor of Charles II and corrupt practices in English parliament foiled repeated petitions of parliament for his removal; by triumph over William Douglas, 3d Duke of Hamilton, in Convention of Estates retained power two more years, until by voting for condemnation of Roman Catholic Lord Stafford he alienated Charles II and was stripped of offices (1682).

**Charles Maitland** (d. 1691), 3d Earl of **Lauderdale,** brother of 2d earl, assisted him in management of Scottish affairs (1674–81) and succeeded him (1682). His son **Richard** (1653–1695), 4th earl; joint general of the mint with his father; lord justice general (1681–84); died in exile because of refusal to agree to revolution settlement.

Sir **Frederick Lewis Maitland** (1777–1839), naval commander, grandson of 6th earl of Lauderdale; as commander of the *Bellerophon* after Waterloo (1815) refused Napoleon permission to sail to U.S., and carried him to England; rear admiral (1830); commander in chief in East Indies and China (1837–39).

**James Maitland** (1759–1839), 8th Earl of **Lauderdale,** political leader and author; educ. at Edinburgh, Oxford, and Glasgow; advocate (1780); M.P. (1780–89); Scottish representative peer (1790); opposed Pitt's policy toward France; created Baron **Lauderdale of**

**Thirlestane** (peerage of Great Britain and Ireland, 1806); lord high keeper of great seal of Scotland (1806); shifted to Tory principles (1821) and voted (by proxy) against Reform Act (1832); author of *Inquiry into the Nature and Origin of Public Wealth* (1804; revised 1819) and *The Depreciation of the Paper-currency of Great Britain Proved* (1812).

**Maitland, John Alexander Fuller–.** See FULLER-MAITLAND.

**Maitland,** Sir **Peregrine.** 1777–1854. English soldier and colonial administrator; lieutenant governor of Upper Canada (1818–28); governor and commander in chief at Cape of Good Hope (1844–47); general (1846). His nephew **Edward Maitland** (1824–1897), mystical writer, went to California as a forty-niner; settled in London as writer (1857); published autobiographical *The Pilgrim and the Shrine* (1867); collaborated with Mrs. Anna Kingsford, vegetarian and antivivisectionist, in *Keys of the Creeds* (1875) and *The Perfect Way; or the Finding of Christ* (1882); with her, founded Hermetic Society (1884).

**Maitland, Samuel Roffey.** 1792–1866. English historian, of Scottish descent; published monograph on Albigenses and Waldenses (1832); edited (1839–49) *British Magazine*, to which he contributed papers later published as *The Dark Ages* (1844) and *The Reformation in England* (1849). His grandson **Frederic William Maitland** (1850–1906), jurist and historian, was founder of Selden Society for study of history of English law and edited several volumes for it (1887); with Sir Frederick Pollock, wrote *History of English Law before the time of Edward I* (2 vols., 1895), standard authority on the subject; author also of *Domesday Book and Beyond* (1897), *Roman Canon Law in the Church of England* (1898), etc.

**Ma·ja′no** (mä·yä′nō). = MAIANO.

**Majd–al–Din.** See under IBN-AL-ATHIR.

**Ma′jor** (mā′jẽr), **Charles.** *Pseudonym* Sir **Edwin Cas·ko′den** (kăs·kō′d'n). 1856–1913. American novelist, b. Indianapolis, Ind.; practiced law (from 1877); author of *When Knighthood was in Flower* (1898), *Dorothy Vernon of Haddon Hall* (1902), *A Gentle Knight of Old Brandenburg* (1909), etc.

**Major, Clare,** *nee* **Tree** (trē). d. 1954. Grandniece of Ellen Tree, English actress. Theatrical director; to U.S. (1914) and joined Washington Square Theatre Company, New York; later, director of the Princess Theatre, N.Y. Established Clare Tree Major Children's Theatre, sending out on tour a number of companies each summer.

**Ma′jor** (mä′yôr), **Georg.** 1502–1574. German Lutheran theologian, who expounded at Wittenberg the doctrine (Majorism) that good works are necessary to salvation as evidence of vital faith.

**Ma′jor** (mā′jẽr) *or* **Ma′ir** (mā′ẽr; mâr), **John.** 1469–1550. Scottish scholastic writer; professor of philosophy and divinity, Glasgow (1518); taught philosophy and logic, St. Andrews (1522), having Patrick Hamilton and George Buchanan, and perhaps John Knox, as students; provost of St. Salvator's Coll., St. Andrews (1533–50). Maintained doctrinal position of Rome and the Scotist position that civil authority was derived from popular will; approved Gallicanism and reform of ecclesiastical abuses; one of last eminent scholastic teachers, contestant of the Renaissance and Reformation.

**Majorano, Gaetano.** See CAFFARELLI.

**Ma·jo′ri·an** (mȧ·jō′rĭ·ăn). *Lat.* **Julius Valerius Ma·jo′ri·a′nus** (mȧ·jō′rĭ·ā′nŭs). d. 461 A.D. Roman emperor in the West (457–461); made emperor by Ricimer; won battle (458) over Vandals on coast of Campania; lost fleet off Spain (460); promulgated a number of laws for the reform of the empire; forced to abdicate.

**Ma·ka′rov** (mŭ·kȧ′rôf), **Stepan Osipovich.** 1848–1904. Russian admiral; distinguished himself in Russo-Turkish War (1877–78); vice-admiral and commander of Baltic fleet (1897); commanded Russian naval forces in Far East (1904); lost on flagship *Petropavlovsk* when it was blown up by a mine (Apr. 13, 1904).

**Ma′kart** (mä′kärt), **Hans.** 1840–1884. Austrian historical and figure painter.

**Make′ham** (māk′ăm), **William.** d. 1892. British mathematician who formulated (c. 1860) the law of human mortality known as *Makeham's law*, still widely used in computing joint life contingencies. Work not officially recognized by the Institute of Actuaries until 1887.

**Ma·kem′ie** (mȧ·kĕm′ĭ; -kā′mĭ), **Francis.** 1658?–1708. Presbyterian clergyman, b. in Donegal, Ireland; to America (1683). Evangelist (1683–98); settled in eastern Virginia (1699); organized first American presbytery (1706). Regarded as founder of Presbyterianism in America.

**Ma·ki·no** (mä·kē·nō), **Count Nobuaki.** 1861–1949. Japanese statesman, son of Marquis Okubo; member of Japanese cabinet, successively as minister of education, agriculture, commerce, and foreign affairs. Represented Japan at Paris Peace Conference (1919) and was one of the so-called Big Five.

**Makkari.** Variant of MAQQARI.

**Makrisi** *or* **Makrizi.** Variant of MAQRIZI.

**Ma′ku·szyń′ski** (mä′ko͞o·shĭn′y'·skē), **Kornel.** 1884–1953. Polish poet and essayist; among his works are *Hunting the Stars, The Milky Way, Sinless Summertime, Song of the Fatherland.*

**Ma·la·ba′ri** (mȧ·lȧ·bä′rē), **Behramji Maharbanji** *or* **Merwanji.** 1854–1912. Hindu poet and social reformer, Parsi by birth. Proprietor and editor of the *Indian Spectator* (1880–1900); editor of *East and West* (1901–12); advocated improving the status of women in India. Published *The Indian Muse in English Garb* (1877), *Gujarat and the Gujaratis* (1884), and *The Indian Eye on English Life* (an account of his visits to England; 1893).

**Mal′a·chi** (măl′ȧ·kī). *In Douay Bible* **Mal′a·chi′as** (-kī′ăs). Minor Hebrew prophet, reputed author of Old Testament book of *Malachi* (ascribed to Persian period, c. 464–424 B.C.), which contains reproof of the priests for laxity in service and of the people for foreign intermarriage.

**Mal′a·chy** (măl′ȧ·kĭ), Saint. 1094?–1148. Irish prelate and reformer. Abbot of Bangor, County Down (1121); bishop of Connor (1124); after sacking of seat of his bishopric, built monastery of Ibrach in south of Ireland; archbishop of Armagh (1132–36); bishop of Down (1136); journeyed to Rome (1140); died at Clairvaux in arms of St. Bernard, his future biographer. Canonized (1199).

**Ma·la′las** (mȧ·lā′lăs), **Ioannes.** 491?–578 A.D. Byzantine historian; author of a chronicle (18 books) of world history notable esp. because written in vulgar language for instruction of monks and common people.

**Mal′an** (măl′ăn; *Fr.* mȧ′läɴ′), **Solomon Caesar,** *orig.* **César Jean Salomon.** 1812–1894. British Orientalist and Biblical scholar, b. in Geneva.

**Ma′la·te′sta** (mä′lä·tĕs′tä). Italian family of Rimini, prominent from the 13th to the 16th century, and including: **Malatesta da Ve·ruc′chio** [dä vā·ro͞ok′kyō] (1212–1312), determined foe of the Ghibellines and placed in Hell (*Inferno*) by Dante; **Giovanni Malatesta,** husband and murderer of Francesca da Rimini, whose love for Giovanni's brother **Paolo** is told by Dante; **Carlo** (1364?–1429), man of letters and patron of the arts; **Sigismondo Pandolfo** (d. 1468), patron of art and letters and accomplished soldier, made war against the pope and was excommunicated (1460); **Pandolfo** (1475–1534), last of the line to hold Rimini.

**Malatesta, Errico.** 1850–1932. Italian anarchist; founder and editor of *Le Révolté*, in Paris, and of *La Question Sociale*, in U.S.

**Malbodius, Jan.** See Jan MABUSE.

**Mal'bone** (môl'bōn), **Edward Greene.** 1777–1807. American miniature painter; studio in Providence, R.I. (1794–96), Boston (1796), Charleston, S.C. (1801–04), Boston (1804–05).

**Mal'colm** (măl'kŭm). Name of four kings of Scotland:

**Malcolm I Mac·Don'ald** (măk·dŏn''ld). d. 954. Succeeded to throne (943); received Cumbria from West Saxon king, Edmund I (945); lost Northumbria (954).

**Malcolm II Mac·ken'neth** (mȧ·kĕn'ĕth; -ĭth). d. 1034. Succeeded (1005); grandson of Malcolm I; annexed Lothian and Cumbria north of the Solway to Scotland; pledged allegiance to Canute (1031).

**Malcolm III Mac·Dun'can** (măk·dŭng'kăn). *Surnamed* **Can'more** (kăn'mōr). d. 1093. Son of Duncan I; with help of Siward defeated (1054) and killed Macbeth (1057); king (1059–93); m. (c. 1067) Margaret, sister of the Saxon Edgar the Ætheling, provoking retaliation by William the Conqueror (1072); carried on war with England (1077–80); by marriage with Margaret, who brought the Black Rood to Scotland, started transition from Celtic culture and Columban religious rites to feudal system and Roman ritual.

**Malcolm IV.** *Surnamed* **the Maiden.** 1141–1165. Succeeded (1153) his grandfather David I (*q.v.*), who was youngest son of Malcolm III; forced to surrender to Henry II of England, Northumberland and Cumberland with all fiefs his grandfather David had received from Matilda in return for his support against Stephen.

**Malcolm,** Sir **John.** 1769–1833. British colonial administrator, b. Dumfriesshire, Scotland. Sent by Lord Wellesley as envoy to Persian court to form alliance against Bonaparte (1799–1801). After Second Maratha War, reduced conquered states to order (1804–05); thrice ambassador to Persia (1800, 1807, 1810). Distinguished himself in wars (1817–18) against the Pindaris and Holkar (*q.v.*). Governor of Bombay (1827–30); M.P. (1831). Author of *A History of Persia* (2 vols., 1815), *A Political History of India, from 1784* (1811), and a life of Clive.

**Malcolm X.** *Originally* **Malcolm Little.** 1925–1965. Amer. religious and political leader, b. Omaha, Nebr. Leader, Black Muslims (1963–64); formed Organization of Afro-American Unity (1964).

**Mal·czew'ski** (mäl·chĕf'skē) *or* **Mal·cze'ski** (-chĕ'skē), **Antoni.** 1792?–1826. Polish poet; friend of Byron; chief work, a narrative poem *Marja* (1825).

**Malczewski, Juliusz.** 1872–1927. Polish general; served on Austrian general staff (1914–18); prepared defense of Warsaw against Russian attack (1920); minister of war (1926) and ousted after two days by Pilsudski's coup d'état (May 12, 1926); imprisoned at Wilno (1926).

**Mal'do·na'do** (mäl'dō·nä'thō), **Juan.** *Lat.* **Johannes Mal'do·na'tus** (măl'dô·nā'tŭs). 1533–1583. Spanish Jesuit theologian; commissioned by Pope Gregory XIII to make a new edition of the *Septuagint*.

**Mâle** (mäl), **Émile.** 1862–1954. French art historian.

**Male'branche'** (mål'bränsh'), **Nicolas de.** 1638–1715. French metaphysician, b. Paris. His philosophical system, known as Malebranchism, embodies the doctrine that the mind cannot have knowledge of anything external to itself except through its relation to God. His chief work is *Recherche de la Vérité* (4 vols., 1674 ff.). Engaged in long controversy with Bossuet and Arnauld occasioned by his *Traité de la Nature et de la Grâce*, and terminated by *Traité de l'Amour de Dieu*.

**Ma'len·kov'** (mäl'yĕn·kôf'), **Georgi Maximilianovich.** 1902– . Soviet premier, b. Orenburg, Russia. WW II head of aircraft and tank production; deputy premier of U.S.S.R. (1946–53); premier (1953–55).

**Males'herbes'** (mål'zĕrb'), **Chrétien Guillaume de La'moi'gnon' de** (dē là'mwà'nyôN' dē). 1721–1794. French statesman and writer on political and legal subjects. Largely instrumental in securing publication of the *Encyclopédie* (1751–72). Banished by Louis XV; recalled by Louis XVI (1774); minister of the interior (1775–76); minister of state (1787–88). Took no part in early stages of Revolution; later (1792) received permission to defend Louis XVI, but was arrested (Dec., 1793), tried for treason, and executed (Apr., 1794).

**Ma'let'** (mà'lĕ'), **Claude François de.** 1754–1812. French general in Revolutionary and Napoleonic armies; conspired against Napoleon and was shot (1812).

**Mal'et** (măl'ĕt; -ĭt), Sir **Edward Baldwin.** 1837–1908. English diplomat; negotiated meeting between Jules Favre and Bismarck (1870); in charge of Paris embassy (Mar.–June, 1871); as agent and consul general in Egypt (1879–83), aided in restoring financial stability and native confidence; ambassador to Berlin (1884–95); British member of Hague Tribunal (1899).

**Malet, Lucas.** Pseudonym of Mary St. Leger Kingsley (see under Charles KINGSLEY).

**Ma·le'vich** (mŭ·lyā'vyĭch), **Kazimir Severinovich.** 1878–1935. Russian painter; identified with ultramodern school; founded school of abstract art known as "suprematism."

**Mal·fat'ti** (mäl·fät'tē), **Giovanni Francesco Giuseppe.** 1731–1807. Italian mathematician; known for proposing (1803) and solving the problem (Malfatti's problem) which in its simplest form is: to inscribe in a given triangle three circles each tangent to the other two and to two sides of the triangle.

**Mal'fi'lâ'tre** (mål'fē'lä'tr'), **Jacques Charles Louis de Clin'champ' de** (dē klăN'shäN' dē). 1732–1767. French poet; author of ode *Le Soleil Fixe au Milieu des Planètes* (1759), *Églogues*, and mythological poem *Narcisse dans l'Île de Vénus*, revealing an appreciation of Greek literature.

**Mal'gaigne'** (mål'gĕn'y'), **Joseph François.** 1806–1865. French surgeon; inventor of surgical instruments.

**Malhar Rao Holkar.** See HOLKAR.

**Mal'herbe'** (mà'lĕrb'), **François de.** 1555–1628. French poet; court poet to Henry IV and Louis XIII; composed odes, sonnets, and other lyrics in style of the period; his emphasis on choice of the exact word to express a desired meaning helped to make Parisian French the standard language of France and to give French thinkers an ideal of logical clarity and precision in expression.

**Malherbe, Henry.** 1886– . French novelist; awarded Goncourt prize (1917) for his *La Flamme au Poing* (transl. by Van Wyck Brooks as *The Flame That Is France*).

**Ma'li'bran'** (mà'lē'bräN'), **María Felicia,** *nee* **Gar·cí'a** (gär·thē'ä). 1808–1836. French opera singer; daughter of the Spanish singer Manuel García; m. Malibran (1826; separated 1827) and De Bériot (1836). Operatic debut in *Il Barbiere di Siviglia* at Rome (1825); sang in New York (1826).

**Ma'li·e·to'a** (mä'lē·ā·tō'ä). *In full* **Malietoa Lau·pe'pa** (lou·pā'pä). d. 1898. King of Samoan Islands (1880–87, 1889–98). United islands (1880), with government seat at Apia; made treaty with U.S.; in conflict with German interests in islands (1886–87); deposed and deported by Germany (1887); restored (1889) after tripartite conference (U.S., Germany, Great Britain); subdued (1894) his rival Mataafa (*q.v.*).

**Ma'lik ibn-A·nas'** (mä'lĭk ĭb''n·ă·năs'). *Arab.* **Mālik ibn-Anas.** 715?–795. Moslem jurist, b. Medina. Opened school of jurisprudence in Medina; wrote *al-Muwaṭṭa'* ("The Leveled Path"), a record of Moslem traditions, conventions, and customs which were to be taken as guides to legal decisions; founder of Malikite school, a sect whose members were known as Malikis.

**Ma·lik' Shah** (mă·lĭk' shä'). *Arab.* **Malikshāh.** *Called* **Ja·lal'–al–Din'** (jă·lä'lo͝od·dēn'), *i.e.* Majesty of Religion. Sultan of Seljuk Turks (1072–92). Son of Alp Arslan. Affairs ably administered by his vizier, Nizam-al-Mulk; ruled an extensive empire, Seljuks reaching zenith of power; during his reign, Ismailian fraternity of Assassins founded (see HASAN IBN-AL-SABBAH); calendar reformed (1079) at his suggestion by group of astronomers including Omar Khayyám and called Jalalaean calendar after him.

**Malines, Gerard (de).** See MALYNES.

**Ma·li'nov** (mȧ·lē'nôf), **Aleksandr.** 1867–1938. Bulgarian statesman; premier of Bulgaria (1908–11; 1918; 1931); signed the armistice (1918) and offered the Bulgarian crown to Boris III.

**Ma'li·now'ski** (mä'lē·nôf'skē), **Bronisław Kasper.** 1884–1942. Anthropologist, b. Cracow, Poland; Ph.D., Polish U. (1908). On expedition to New Guinea (1914–20); reader in social anthropology (1924–27), professor (1927), U. of London. To U.S. (1938); at Yale (from 1939). Author of *Argonauts of the Western Pacific* (1922), *Sex and Repression in Savage Society* (1926), *The Sexual Life of Savages in N.W. Melanesia* (1929), etc.

**Malintzin.** See MARINA.

**Ma'li·pie'ro** (mä'lē·pyâ'rō), **Gian Francesco.** 1882–1973. Italian composer; among his works are the symphonic drama *Pantea*, a trilogy of dramas *L'Orfeide*, a drama *San Francesco d'Assisi*, eight symphonies, five oratorios, several chamber works, many operas, piano pieces, and songs.

**Mal'lar'mé'** (mȧ'lȧr'mā'), **Stéphane.** 1842–1898. French poet; originator (with Paul Verlaine) and a leader of the symbolist group of poets, and prominent among those known as the decadents. Author of *L'Après-Midi d'un Faune* (1876), *Vers et Prose* (1893), etc.; translator of poems of Edgar Allan Poe (1888).

**Mal'le·son** (măl'ĕ·s'n), **George Bruce.** 1825–1898. Anglo-Indian military historian; author of *The History of the Indian Mutiny*, continuation of Kaye's *History of the Sepoy War* (3 vols., 1878–80), *History of the French in India* (1868), and *The Decisive Battles of India* (1883).

**Mal'let'** (mȧ'lĕ'; *Angl.* măl'ĕt, -ĭt), **Anatole.** 1837–1919. Swiss locomotive engineer; designed Mallet locomotive.

**Mal'let'** (mȧ'lĕ'), **Claude François de.** = MALET.

**Mal'let** (măl'ĕt; -ĭt), **David.** *Orig. surname* **Mal'loch** (-ŭk; -ŭk). 1705?–1765. Scottish poet; gained reputation with ballad *William and Margaret* (1723), which made him known to Pope and Young; undersecretary to Frederick, Prince of Wales (1742), at whose request he wrote, with James Thomson, *The Masque of Alfred* (1740; music by Thomas A. Arne), containing patriotic song *Rule Britannia;* to please his patron, Bolingbroke, attacked Pope (1749); for zealous support of Lord Bute and Tories, rewarded with sinecure (1760). Author also of three tragedies, and of poems, including *The Excursion* (1728) and *The Hermit* (1747).

**Mal'let' du Pan** (mȧ'lĕ' dü päɴ'), **Jacques.** 1749–1800. Swiss journalist; openly avowed royalist sympathies at outbreak of French Revolution (1789), sent on confidential mission to Frankfort by Louis XVI (1792). To England (1798), founded *Mercure Brittanique.*

**Mal'linc·krodt** (mäl'ĭngk·krōt), **Hermann von.** 1821–1874. German politician; leader of Catholic party in resistance to May Laws during Kulturkampf.

**Malloch, David.** See MALLET.

**Mal'lock** (măl'ŭk), **William Hurrell.** 1849–1923. English writer, b. in Devonshire. Author of *The New Republic* (1877), *Is Life Worth Living?* (1879), *Poems* (1880), *The Old Order Changes* (novel; 1886), *Aristocracy and Evolution* (1898), *The Reconstruction of Belief* (1905), etc.

**Mal'lo·ry** (măl'ō·rĭ), **Stephen Russell.** 1813?–1873. Political leader in the Confederacy; b. in Trinidad; to U.S. as a child. U.S. senator from Florida (1851–61); secretary of the navy, Confederate States of America (1861–65).

**Malmesbury,** Earls of. See James HARRIS.

**Malmesbury, William of.** See WILLIAM OF MALMESBURY.

**Malm'gren** (mȧlm'grān), **Finn.** 1895–1928. Swedish meteorologist; joined Amundsen on voyage in north-polar basin (1922); on voyage in airship *Norge* across north-polar basin (1926); meteorologist of expedition under Gen. Nobile, which sailed over North Pole in airship *Italia* (May 24, 1928).

**Malm'ström** (mȧlm'strûm), **Bernhard Elis.** 1816–1865. Swedish scholar and writer; professor of aesthetics and history of literature, Uppsala (1856). Among his works are the epic *Ariadne* (1838), the elegiac cycle *Angelica* (1840), the narrative poem *The Fisher Maid of Tunnelsö*, *Studies in Literary History*, and *Elements of the History of Swedish Literature* (5 vols., 1866–68).

**Ma'lon'** (mȧ'lôɴ'), **Benoît.** 1841–1893. French politician.

**Ma·lone'** (mȧ·lōn'), **Dumas.** 1892– . American historian and editor, b. Coldwater, Miss.; Ph.D., Yale (1923); editor in chief (1931–36), *Dictionary of American Biography;* director, Harvard U. Press (1936–43); professor Columbia U. (1945–1959).

**Malone, Edmund** *or* **Edmond.** 1741–1812. Irish Shakespearean scholar and literary critic; son of a judge, Edmund Malone (1704–1774). Called to Irish bar (1767); settled in London, visited Dr. Johnson frequently, aided Boswell in revising and proofreading *The Life of Samuel Johnson, LL.D.;* encouraged by George Steevens (*q.v.*), attempted to ascertain order in which plays of Shakespeare were written; published results (1778), which are still for most part accepted; published his own edition of Shakespeare (11 vols., 1790) and left to James Boswell the younger materials for a new octavo edition (third variorum edition, 21 vols., 1821). Among first to detect Rowley forgeries of Chatterton and Ireland forgeries of Shakespeare mss.; edited works of Dryden (1800). The Malone Society, founded (1907) for making accessible dramatic texts and documents, was named for him.

**Mal'o·ry** (măl'ō·rĭ), Sir **Thomas.** fl. 1470. English translator and compiler of English prose epic *Le Morte d'Arthur* (finished between March, 1469, and March, 1470; printed by Caxton, 1485), abridged compilation of the body of French Arthurian romance in direct, idiomatic, elevated style. Identified by George Lyman Kittredge with Sir Thomas Malory, knight, of Newbold Revell in Warwickshire, who was a retainer of Richard Beauchamp, Earl of Warwick, and who, as a result of quarrels with a neighboring priory, brought himself imprisonment (from 1451 or 1452). If this identification is correct, he apparently finished *Le Morte d'Arthur* in prison.

**Ma'lot'** (mȧ'lō'), **Hector Henri.** 1830–1907. French critic and novelist.

**Ma'lou·et'** (mȧ'lwĕ'), Baron **Pierre Victor.** 1740–1814.

French politician; member of Constituent Assembly; defended royalist cause in the assembly, and fled from France (1792). Returned to France (1803) and was appointed by Napoleon commissary general of marine at Antwerp; became councilor of state (1810). Appointed by Louis XVIII minister of marine (1814).

**Mal·pi'ghi** (mäl·pē'gē), **Marcello.** 1628–1694. Italian anatomist, b. near Bologna. Because of early use of microscope in biological studies, called founder of microscopic anatomy; studied structure of secreting glands; discovered capillary circulation in the lung and bladder of the frog, the deeper portion of the epidermis known as the *Malpighian layer*, loops of capillaries (or Malpighian tufts) in the kidney, and masses of adenoid tissue (or Malpighian corpuscles) in the spleen; described structure of human lung, development of the chick, structure of the brain and spinal cord, and the metamorphosis of the silkworm.

**Mal'raux'** (mål'rō'), **André.** 1901–1976. French novelist; author of *Les Conquérants* (1929), *La Condition Humaine* (1933; awarded Goncourt prize; trans. into English as *Man's Fate*), *L'Espoir* (1938; trans. as *Man's Hope*), etc.

**Mal'te–Brun'** *or* **Mal'te·brun'** (*Fr.* mål'tē·brûN'), **Conrad.** *Orig. name* **Malte Conrad Bruun** (bro͞on). 1775–1826. Geographer, b. Thisted, Denmark; banished from Denmark because of sympathy with French Revolution (1800); settled in Paris; founder of *Annales des Voyages* (1808); author of *Précis de Géographie Universelle* (1810–29).

**Mal'ten** (mäl'tĕn), **Therese.** *Real surname* **Müller.** 1855–1930. German operatic soprano; sang at the Court Theater, in Dresden (1873–1903); noted for interpretation of Wagnerian roles.

**Mal'thus** (măl'thŭs), **Thomas Robert.** 1766–1834. English economist; curate at Albury, Surrey (1798). Aroused controversy by his argument, in *An Essay on the Principle of Population* (1798), that population when unchecked tends to increase in a geometric ratio while means of subsistence tend to increase only in an arithmetic ratio and that preventive checks on increase of population are necessary as an alternative to the exclusive operation of positive checks, such as overcrowding, disease, war, poverty, and vice; in second edition (1803), documented his argument, relinquished question of mathematical ratios, recognized influence of moral restraint as a preventive check, remained pessimistic of possibilities of future progress of mankind. Author also of *An Inquiry into the Nature and Progress of Rent* (1815) and *Principles of Political Economy* (1820).

**Mal'titz** (mäl'tĭts), Baron **Friedrich Franz von.** 1794–1857. German poet; in Russian diplomatic service (1811–54); published collected verse, a tragedy (*Demetrius*, 1817), and translations from French classics, as Racine and Voltaire. His brother Baron **Apollonius** (1795–1870), in the Russian diplomatic service (1811–65) and consul in Weimar (1841–65), wrote poems, a humorous novel, and several plays, including *Virginia* (1858), *Anna Boleyn* (1860), and *Spartacus* (1861).

**Maltz** (môlts), **Albert.** 1908– . American writer, b. Brooklyn, N.Y. Collaborated with George Sklar in writing plays *Merry Go Round* (1932), *Peace on Earth* (1934), *Black Pit* (1935). Scenarist; author of one-act plays, short stories, novels (*The Underground Stream*, 1940; *The Cross and the Arrow*, 1944).

**Mal'tzan** (mäl'tsän). German noble family, including: **Heinrich von Maltzan,** Baron **zu War'ten·berg und Penz·lin'** [tso͞o vär'tĕn·bĕrK o͝ont pĕnts·lēn'] (1826–1874), traveler and scholar, author of *Meine Wallfahrt nach Mekka* (2 vols., 1865), *Reise nach Südarabien* (1873), etc. **Adolf Georg Otto** (*known by the acrostic name* **A'go** [ä'gō]) **von Maltzan,** Baron **zu Wartenberg und Penzlin** (1877–1927), diplomat, ambassador to U.S. (1925).

**Ma'lus'** (må'lüs'), **Étienne Louis.** 1775–1812. French engineer and physicist; made researches in optics; discovered polarization of light by reflection; won prize from the Institute with memoir on the theory of double refraction of light in crystalline substances (1810).

**Mal'vy'** (mål'vē'), **Louis Jean.** 1875–1949. French politician; Radical Socialist member of Chamber of Deputies (1906 ff.); minister of commerce (1913), of the interior (1914); forced to resign after Clemenceau's attacks upon his position with regard to the enforcement of laws against defeatists, etc. (1917). Accused of having communication with the enemy, he was acquitted by the Senate assembled as a high court, but was condemned to banishment for five years for laxity in performance of his duties as minister of the interior (1918). Again member of Chamber of Deputies (1924) and minister of the interior (1926).

**Ma·lynes'** *or* **Ma·lines'** *or* **de Ma·lines'** (dĕ mă·lēn'), **Gerard.** fl. 1586–1641. English merchant and economist; commissioner of trade in Low Countries (1586), of the mint (1609); attempted to develop English lead and silver mines. One of first English writers to apply natural law to economic science; lifelong exponent of foreign exchange.

**Mälzel, Johann Nepomuk** and **Leonhard.** See MAELZEL.

**Ma·mae'a** (mă·mē'ȧ), **Julia.** d. 235 A.D. Roman matron; wife of Gessius Marcianus and mother of Emperor Alexander Severus; slain with Alexander by mutinous soldiers.

**Ma·me'li** (mä·må'lē), Marchese **Goffredo.** 1827–1849. Italian poet and patriot; volunteer under Garibaldi (Lombardy, 1848); chief of general staff, Roman republic (1849); known for his battle hymns *Fratelli d'Italia* (music by Michele Novaro) and *L'Alba.*

**Mam'e·luke** (măm'ĕ·lūk). *Arab.* **Mamlūk.** Name given to Egyptian sultans, divided into two dynasties (see BAHRI and BURJI), founded by Aybak (1250) and extending until Egypt was conquered and became Turkish province (1517).

**Ma·mer'tus** (mȧ·mûr'tŭs), Saint. d. about 475. Bishop of Vienna (462); instituted or introduced into Gaul the ceremonial processions of Rogation days.

**Ma·mia'ni** (mä·myä'nē), **Terenzio.** Conte **del'la Ro'·ve·re** (dāl'lä rō'vå·rā). 1799–1885. Italian statesman and philosopher; minister of interior under Pius IX (1848); professor of philosophy, Turin (1857–60); minister of public instruction under Cavour (1860).

**Mam·mae'a** (mă·mē'ȧ). = MAMAEA.

**Ma·mun'** *or* **Ma·moun', al–** (ăl·mă·mo͞on'). *Arab.* **abu–al–'Abbās 'Abdullāh al–Ma'mūn.** 786–833. Younger son of Harun al-Rashid. Seventh Abbasside caliph of Baghdad (813–833); renowned patron of philosophy and astronomy; reign disturbed because of his preference for Persians; a rationalist and Mutazilite.

**Man** (män), **Hendrik de.** 1885–1953. Belgian Socialist writer and politician; minister of public works and unemployment (1935–36), and of finance (1936–38). Author of *The Remaking of a Mind* (1919), *The Psychology of Socialism* (1927), *Joy in Work* (1928), etc.

**Man** (măn), **Ray.** See Man RAY.

**Ma·nas'seh** (mȧ·năs'ĕ). *In Douay Version and in A. V. in New Testament* **Ma·nas'ses** (-ēz). In Bible, Joseph's elder son (*Gen.* xli. 50–51), ancestor of a tribe of the Israelites (*Joshua* xvi). See JOSEPH.

**Manasseh.** *Gr.* **Manasses.** d. 639? B.C. King of Judah (692?–639? B.C.; longest reign in history of Judah). Son of Hezekiah. Vassal of Assyria; for some time captive in Babylon (*2 Kings* xxi; *2 Chron.* xxxiii). The *Prayer of Manasses* (Old Testament Apocrypha) attributed to Manasseh when in prison (*2 Chron.* xxxiii. 18).

**Manasseh ben Is′ra·el** (bĕn ĭz′râ·ĕl; ĭz′rĭ·ĕl). 1604–1657. Jewish theologian and cabalist. Chief rabbi at synagogue, Amsterdam, at age of eighteen; set up Hebrew printing press at Amsterdam (1626). To England (1655) to petition Long Parliament and Cromwell for abolition of legislation excluding Jews from England. Author of *El Conciliador* (in Spanish, a harmony of the Pentateuch; 1632), and *Spes Israelis* (1650).

**Mana-Zucca.** See ZUCCA.

**Mance** (măns), Sir **Henry Christopher**. 1840–1926. English electrical engineer; invented method of locating faults in submarine cables, method of testing internal resistance of electric batteries, and the heliograph used by Indian government for transmitting messages in frontier warfare.

**Mance** (mäɴs), **Jeanne**. 1606–1673. French philanthropist in Canada; founded (1644) Hôtel Dieu, Montreal.

**Manchester,** Earls and dukes of. See MONTAGU.

**Man′chu′** (măn′chōō′; *attrib. also* măn′chōō). Chinese dynasty (1644–1912), usually called Ch'ing (*q.v.*).

**Man·ci′ni** (män·chē′nē). Roman patrician family. Among prominent members were four sisters, nieces of Cardinal Mazarin, whom the cardinal introduced to the French court: **Laure** (1635–1657), wife of Louis de Vendôme, Duc de Mercœur, and mother of Louis, Duc de Vendôme, who served brilliantly in the armies of Louis XIV; **Olympe** (1639?–1708), wife of Eugène Maurice de Savoie-Carignan, mother of Prince Eugene, mistress of Louis XIV; **Marie** (1640?–1714), wife of Godefroy Maurice de la Tour, Duc de Bouillon, and patroness of men of letters, including La Fontaine, Corneille, and Molière; **Hortense** (1646?–1699), wife of marquis de La Meilleraye, who took the name and arms of Mazarin and treated his brilliant wife with such severity that she took refuge in England, where she had a liaison with King Charles II.

**Mancini, Antonio.** 1852–1930. Italian genre, portrait, and landscape painter.

**Mancini, Pasquale Stanislao.** 1817–1888. Italian statesman and jurist; fled from Naples to Turin (1849) after revolutionary activities; professor of international law, U. of Turin (1849 ff.). Minister of justice (1876–78), of foreign affairs (1881–85); concluded Triple Alliance (1882); accomplished occupation of Eritrea (1884–85).

**Man′co Ca′pac** (mäng′kō kä′päk). Traditional founder of Inca dynasty in Peru; supposed to have consolidated Indians (Quechuas) of highlands of Peru (early 11th century).

**Manco Capac.** *Also known as* **Manco In′ca** (ēng′kä; ĭng′kȧ). 1500?–1544. Brother of Huáscar. Indian sovereign of Peru; recognized by Pizarro after death of Atahualpa and Huáscar (1533), and crowned at Cuzco. Raised army and attacked Spaniards (1536); defeated (1537) and fled to mountains; assassinated by fellow refugees (1544).

**Man′del′** (mäɴ′dĕl′), **Georges**. *Orig. name* **Jé′ro′bo′am′ Roth′schild′** (zhā′rô′bô′àm′ rôt′shēld′). 1885–1943. French politician; chef de cabinet to Clemenceau (1917–20); member, Chamber of Deputies (from 1932); minister of colonies (Apr.–Sept., 1938) in Daladier cabinet; minister of interior in Reynaud cabinet (Mar.–July, 1940); arrested following defeat of France by Germany.

**Man′der** (män′dēr), **Karel van.** 1548–1606. Dutch painter and writer; best-known work, *Schilderboeck* (1604), a collection of biographical studies of painters of various epochs.

**Man′de·ville** (măn′dĕ·vĭl; *Fr.* mäɴd′vēl′), **Bernard.** 1670?–1733. Philosopher and satirist, b. Dordrecht, Holland. Settled in London in medical practice and, on behalf of Dutch distillers, advocated dram drinking. Known as author of *The Fable of the Bees: or, Private Vices, Public Benefits* (1714; first published as *The Grumbling Hive*, 1705), a political satire in octosyllabic verse maintaining that every virtue is at bottom some form of selfishness; involved in controversy in which Berkeley, William Law, John Brown, Warburton, and Hutcheson took exception to his view of the essential vileness of human nature.

**Man′de·ville** (măn′dĕ·vĭl), **Geoffrey de.** 1st Earl of **Es′sex** [ĕs′ĕks; -ĭks] (cr. 1141). d. 1144. English baron. Constable of Tower (c. 1130); gained vast lands and great power by betraying first King Stephen, then Matilda (Empress Maud); raised rebellion; turned bandit in Fens, where fatally wounded. His son **William** (d. 1189), 3d Earl of **Essex** and Earl or Count of **Au′male′** [ō′mȧl′] (by marriage), went to England (1166) from court of Philip of Flanders, with whom he went on crusade (1177–78); attended Henry II faithfully through rebellion and French wars; chief justiciar under Richard I (1189).

**Mandeville,** Sir **John**. Name assumed by unknown compiler (d. 1372), in role of author, of book of travels written in French (pub. between 1357 and 1371) describing journeys in the East, including India and the Holy Land, combining geography with romance, describing such marvels as anthills of gold dust, anthropophagi, and men whose heads grew beneath their shoulders. Borrowed travel accounts largely from works of others, as Friar Oderic of Pordenone, Giovanni de Piano Carpini (probably mostly at second hand through Vincent of Beauvais), which he interpolated with extravagant particulars; may have contributed some details from own experience. Usually identified with a physician of Liége, Jehan de Bourgogne or Burgoyne, otherwise Jehan à la Barbe, who, as chamberlain to John, Baron de Mowbray, participated in Mowbray's unsuccessful contest with the Despensers and fled England (1322).

**Ma·nén′** (mä·nān′), **Juan**. 1883– . Spanish violin virtuoso and composer.

**Ma′nes** (mā′nēz) *or* **Ma′ni** (mä′nē) *or* **Man′i·chae′us** (măn′ĭ·kē′ŭs). 216?–?276 A.D. Persian sage; founder of the sect of Manichaeans. Began new religious movement (c. 246); preached his doctrines, a system compounded of Zoroastrian dualism and Christian soteriology, at court of Persian King Shapur I and on long journeys in Turkestan, India, and China; claimed that he himself received divine revelations and that he was the final prophet of God in the world. The Magians bitterly opposed his preaching and finally caused his condemnation and crucifixion. The Manichaean heresy survived for centuries. His works have been lost.

**Má′nes** (mä′nĕs), **Josef**. 1820–1871. Czech painter; regarded as founder of the modern Czech school of painting.

**Ma′net′** (mȧ′nĕ′), **Édouard**. 1832–1883. French painter, b. Paris. Studied under Couture; became originator and leader of impressionism in painting.

**Man′e·tho** (măn′ĕ·thō). Egyptian priest and historian of 3d century B.C.; author of a history of Egypt, written in Greek, of which only fragments are extant.

**Man′fred** (măn′frĕd; -frĭd). 1232?–1266. King of Naples and Sicily (1258–66); natural son of Emperor Frederick II. Prince of Tarentum (1250–57); regent for Conradin in southern Italy (1254); crowned at Palermo (1258); excommunicated by Pope Alexander IV (1258);

defeated papal forces and seized Tuscany; his dominions bestowed as papal fief on Charles of Anjou by Pope Urban IV; defeated and killed at Benevento.

**Man′gan** (măng′găn), **James Clarence.** 1803–1849. Irish poet; author of *German Anthology* (2 vols., 1845); known esp. for *Dark Rosaleen*, *O'Hussey's Ode to the Maguire*, and the tragic autobiographical ballad *The Nameless One.*

**Man′gin′** (mäN′zhăN′), **Charles Marie Emmanuel.** 1866–1925. French soldier; promoted general of division (1914). Commanded defense of Verdun (1916) and offensive along Chemin des Dames (1917); commanded 10th army in its counterattack at Villers-Cotterets (July 18, 1918) which halted German advance; pushed forward into Lorraine at the time of the armistice (Nov. 11, 1918). Member of Conseil Supérieur de la Guerre (from 1921).

**Man′gu Khan** (mäng′gōō kän′; măng′gōō kăn′). 1207?–1259. Mongol khan. Eldest son of Tului and nephew of Ogadai. As a general of Ogadai conquered the Kipchaks (1237); friendly to Batu; elected khan (1251) as successor to Ogadai; sent his brother Hulagu (*q.v.*) to Persia to quell disturbances; with other brother Kublai conquered (1252–59) nearly all of China; died of dysentery on return from campaign; succeeded by Kublai (see KUBLAI KHAN).

**Mani** *or* **Manichaeus.** See MANES.

**Ma·nil′i·us** (mȧ·nĭl′ĭ·ŭs), **Gaius.** Roman politician; tribune of the people (66 B.C.); sponsor of law (Manilian law) to recall Roman commanders in Asia and extend power of Pompey over all the East. Cicero supported the law in his oration *Pro Lege Manilia* (or *De Imperio Gnaei Pompeii*).

**Manilius, Marcus** *or* **Gaius.** Reputed author of Latin poem on astrology called *Astronomica;* lived probably in late 1st century B.C. or early 1st century A.D.

**Ma·nin′** (mä·nēn′), **Daniele.** 1804–1857. Italian patriot and statesman; active as leader of liberal opinion in Venice (1831 ff.); imprisoned for opposition to Austrian rule (1847–48); led patriotic movement in Venice (1848) as president of restored Republic of St. Mark; led defense of Venice against Austrian siege (Apr.–Aug., 1849); lived in exile (Paris, 1849–57).

**Man′ing** (măn′ĭng), **Frederick Edward.** 1812–1883. New Zealand jurist, b. in County Dublin, Ireland; to New Zealand (1824). Settled among Maoris (1833), was adopted into a native tribe, and married a native. Judge of native land courts (1865–81). Author of *Old New Zealand* (1876), etc.

**Man′ion** (măn′yŭn), **Robert James.** 1881–1943. Canadian physician and politician; served in France in World War (1914–18). Member of Canadian House of Commons (1917–35) and member of the cabinet (1921, 1926, 1930–35); again member of parliament, and leader of Conservative party in Canada (1938–Mar., 1940).

**Ma·niu′** (mä·nyōō′), **Iuliu.** 1873–1951. Romanian statesman; a founder and leader of the National Peasants party. Prime minister of Romania (1928–30; 1932–33). Senator (1939 ff.).

**Man′ley** (măn′lĭ), **Mary de la Ri′vière′** (dē lȧ rē′vyâr′). 1663?–1724. English playwright and political pamphleteer; decoyed into bigamous union with her cousin John Manley; lived with Barbara Villiers, Duchess of Cleveland, fell into disreputable ways. Achieved literary triumph with *Secret Memoirs and Manners of Several Persons of Quality of both Sexes, from the New Atalantis* (sic), usually known as *The New Atalantis* (1709), a scandalous chronicle involving Whig notables; arrested for libel but discharged (1710); author of political pamphlets; succeeded Swift as editor of *Examiner* (1711); author of plays, including *Lucius* (1717), of *Memoirs of Europe* (1710), *The Power of Love, in Seven Novels* (1720), and autobiography *The Adventures of Rivella* (1714).

**Man′li·us** (măn′lĭ·ŭs). Name of Roman patrician gens, including among its members:

**Marcus Manlius Cap′i·to·li′nus** [kăp′ĭ·tō·lī′nŭs] (d. 384 B.C.), consul (392 B.C.); savior of Rome (390) when, according to tradition, awakened by cackling of sacred geese, he discovered surprise night attack by besieging Gauls, quickly raised band of fighters and repelled invaders; later, suspected of catering to people in effort to make himself tyrant of Rome, was arrested, tried, and condemned to be thrown from Tarpeian Rock.

**Titus Manlius Im·pe′ri·o′sus Tor·qua′tus** (ĭm-pēr′ĭ·ō′sŭs tôr·kwā′tŭs), general; military tribune (362 B.C.); served against Gauls (361); dictator (353, 349) and consul (347, 344, 340); executed own son for disobedience of orders (340).

**Titus Manlius Torquatus** (d. 202 B.C.), general; consul (235, 224) and dictator (208); gained important victory over Carthaginians in Sardinia (215).

**Man′ly** (măn′lĭ), **John Matthews.** 1865–1940. American educator; professor of English, Chicago (from 1898). Served through World War. Author of *Some New Light on Chaucer* (1926), *Chaucer and the Rhetoricians* (1926); collaborator in many textbooks in English; editor of *Macbeth* (1896), *Specimens of Pre-Shakespearean Drama* (1897), *Chaucer* (1928). His brother **Charles Matthews** (1876–1927), mechanical engineer, was associated with Samuel P. Langley in experiments with airplanes; designed light 5-cylinder radial gasoline engine for airplane use, regarded as first modern aircraft engine; took out about fifty patents on power generation and transmission systems; awarded posthumously (1930) Langley gold medal for aerodromics.

**Mann** (măn), Sir **Donald D.** 1853–1934. Canadian railroad builder; partner of William Mackenzie (*q.v.*) in contracting firm (1886); had important part (from 1895) in building and organizing Canadian Northern R.R., absorbed (1922) into Canadian National R.R. Co.

**Mann** (män; *Angl.* măn), **Erika.** 1905–1969. Author and actress, b. Munich, Germany; daughter of Thomas Mann (*q.v.*); m. (1935) W. H. Auden (*q.v.*), English poet. Wrote, acted in, and directed *Peppermill;* author of *School for Barbarians*, *Children in Goose-Step*, *Escape to Life* (1939; with her brother Klaus, *q.v.*), *The Other Germany* (1940; with Klaus), *The Lights Go Down* (1940).

**Mann** (män), **Fritz Karl.** 1883– . German political economist.

**Mann** (män; *Angl.* măn), **Heinrich.** 1871–1950. Brother of Thomas Mann (*q.v.*). German writer, b. Lübeck; exile in France (1933–40); interned (1940) but escaped to U.S. Author of novels, short stories, plays, and essays, including the following translated into English: *The Goddess*, *The Poor* (1917), *The Chief* (1925), *Mother Mary*, *The Little Town* (1931), *The Blue Angel* (1932), *Young Henry of Navarre*, and *Henry, King of France.*

**Mann** (măn), Sir **Horace.** 1701–1786. English diplomat. British envoy at Florence, Italy (1740–86), by appointment of Sir Robert Walpole, to watch over doings of the Old Pretender and the Young Pretender. Friend and correspondent of Horace Walpole (1741–85) in thousands of letters avowedly written, on both sides, for publication.

**Mann, Horace.** 1796–1859. American educator, b. Franklin, Mass. Practiced law (1823–37). First secretary, Massachusetts Board of Education (1837–48); revolutionized public school organization and teaching; instrumental in establishing first normal school in U.S.

(1839). Member, U.S. House of Representatives (1848–53). President, Antioch College (1852–59). Elected to American Hall of Fame (1900).

**Mann, James Robert.** 1856–1922. American lawyer and legislator, b. near Bloomington, Ill. Member, U.S. House of Representatives (1897–1922). His name is associated with important laws, including the Mann-Elkins Act for railroad rate regulation, the Mann Act (or White-slave-traffic Act), etc.

**Mann** (män; *Angl.* măn), **Klaus.** 1906–1949. Author; son of Thomas Mann (*q.v.*); left Germany (1937); later to U.S.; author of *The Fifth Child* (1927), *Alexander* (1929), *Journey into Freedom* (1936), *Escape to Life* (1939; with his sister Erika, *q.v.*), *The Other Germany* (1940; with Erika), *The Turning Point* (autobiography; 1942), *André Gide* (1943).

**Mann** (măn), **Louis.** 1865–1931. American actor, b. New York City; excelled in comedies, esp. in German and Jewish dialect roles; costarred in *Friendly Enemies* (1918–20).

**Mann** (män; *Angl.* măn), **Thomas.** 1875–1955. Brother of Heinrich Mann and father of Erika and Klaus Mann (*qq.v.*). Author, b. Lübeck, Germany; recipient of Nobel prize for literature (1929); refugee from Germany (1933); to U.S. (1938), naturalized (1944). Author of novels, plays, essays, including the following translated into English: *Buddenbrooks* (1901), *Fiorenza* (play; 1906), *Death in Venice* (1912), *Tonio Kröger* (1914), *Royal Highness* (1916), *Bashan and I* (1923), *The Magic Mountain* (1924; German title *Der Zauberberg*), *Children and Fools* (1928), *Mario and the Magician* (1929), *Joseph and His Brothers* (1934), *Joseph in Egypt* (1938), *The Beloved Returns* (1940), *The Transposed Heads* (legend of India; 1941).

**Mann** (măn), **Tom.** 1856–1941. English labor leader, b. in Warwickshire. Employed in mines (1867–70) and in engineering work in Birmingham (1870–77); settled in London (1877). Joined trade-union movement (1881) and Socialist party (1885). Author of *A Socialist's View of Religion*, *Tom Mann's Memoirs*, *What I Saw in China* (1927), etc.

**Mann** (män; *Angl.* măn), **William Julius.** 1819–1892. Lutheran clergyman in Philadelphia; b. Stuttgart, Württemberg, Germany; to U.S. (1845); professor, Lutheran Sem. (from its founding, 1864). Author of *Lutheranism in America* (1857), *Life and Times of Henry Melchior Mühlenberg* (1887), etc.

**Man'ner·heim** (män'nĕr·hām), **Baron Carl Gustaf Emil von.** 1867–1951. Finnish soldier and statesman; served in Russian army, distinguished himself in Russo-Japanese War (1904–05), and rose to rank of major general (1914). After Bolshevik Revolution in Russia (1917), withdrew from Russian army to Finland, where he took command of White Guard and suppressed Finnish Workers' Republic. Regent of Finland (1918); appointed president of council of defense (1931) and given rank of field marshal (1933); planned and supervised construction of a line of defense (Mannerheim line) against Russia. Commanded Finnish army against Russia (1939; and in war beginning 1941). Regarded by some as liberator of Finland. President (1944–46).

**Man'ner·ing** (măn'ĕr·ĭng), **Mary.** *Professional name of* **Florence Friend** (frĕnd). 1876–1953. Actress, b. London; stage debut in Manchester and London (1892); to U.S. (1896) and appeared under Daniel Frohman's management; m. 1st James K. Hackett (*q.v.*), 2d Frederick E. Wadsworth. Starred in *Janice Meredith*, *The Truants*, *A Man's World*, and *The Garden of Allah.*

**Man'ners** (măn'ĕrz). Name of north of England family descended from barons **Ros of Ham'lake** (rŏs, hăm'lāk) and possessing earldom and dukedom of **Rut'land** (rŭt'lănd) and marquisate of **Gran'by** (grăn'bĭ), including among its members:

**John Manners** (1638–1711), 9th Earl and 1st Duke of Rutland; lord lieutenant of Leicestershire (1677–87, 1689–1711); aided in raising forces for William of Orange; created marquis of Granby and duke of Rutland (1703).

**John Manners** (1721–1770), Marquis of Granby; soldier; eldest son of John, 3d Duke of Rutland (1696–1779); educ. Cambridge; M.P. (1741); colonel and, later, commander of Leicester "blues" (1745–59); commander in chief of British contingent in Germany during Seven Years' War (from 1759); commander in chief of the forces (1766); subject of Junius's invectives.

His eldest son, **Charles** (1754–1787); succeeded grandfather as 4th duke of Rutland (1779); M.A., Cantab., and M.P. (1774); protested against government policy of taxing American colonies (1775); lord privy seal in Pitt's ministry; lord lieutenant of Ireland (1784), advocated legislative union of Ireland with England.

**John James Robert Manners** (1818–1906), 7th duke; grandson of 4th duke; a Conservative leader in Parliament (1841–88); twice postmaster general (1874–80, 1885–86); held offices in Conservative ministries (between 1852 and 1892); a leader of Young England party (1843–47); advocate of public holidays, factory reform, and general system of allotments; advocate of Irish disestablishment; accepted Disraeli's Reform Act of 1867; opposed extension of franchise without redistribution (1884–85); made Baron **Roos of Bel'voir** [rŏs, bē'vĕr] (1896). Author of *England's Trust and other Poems* (1841), *English Ballads and other Poems* (1850), and notes on Irish and Scottish tours (1848–49). More or less prominent figure in Disraeli's *Coningsby* (1844), *Sybil* (1845), and *Endymion* (1880).

Lady **Diana Manners** (see under Alfred Duff COOPER), daughter of 8th duke of Rutland.

For **Manners-Sutton** branch, see Charles and Thomas MANNERS-SUTTON, sons of Lord George Manners-Sutton, son of John Manners, 3d Duke of Rutland.

**Manners, Charles.** *Professional name of* **Southcote Man'sergh** (măn'sĕr). 1857–1935. English operatic and concert basso.

**Manners,** Lady **Diana.** See under Alfred Duff COOPER.

**Manners, John Hartley.** 1870–1928. Actor and playwright, b. London, Eng.; first appearance in U.S., with Lily Langtry's company (1902). Author of *The Crossways*, *Peg o' My Heart* (1912), *Happiness* (1914), *The National Anthem* (1922). See Laurette TAYLOR.

**Man'ners-Sut'ton** (măn'ĕrz·sŭt''n), **Charles.** 1st Viscount **Can'ter·bur'y** (kăn'tĕr·bĕr'ĭ; -bĕr·ĭ; -brĭ). 1780–1845. English Tory leader; judge advocate general (1809); speaker of House of Commons (1817–35). His father, **Charles** (1755–1828), bishop of Norwich (1792–1805), archbishop of Canterbury (1805–28), and his uncle **Thomas** (1756–1842), 1st Baron Manners, solicitor general (1802), lord chancellor of Ireland (1807–27), were grandsons of 3d duke of Rutland (see MANNERS family). His son **John Henry Thomas** (1814–1877), 3d Viscount Canterbury, was lieutenant governor of New Brunswick (1854–61), governor of Trinidad (1864–66), of Victoria, Australia (1866–73).

**Man'nes** (măn'ĕs), **David.** 1866–1959. American violinist and director, b. New York City. Concertmaster, New York Symphony Orchestra (1902–11). With his wife, **Clara,** *nee* **Damrosch** (1869–1948), dau. of Leopold and sister of Walter Damrosch, gave sonata recitals in New York, Boston, London, and other cities, and directed the David Mannes Music School.

**Mann'hardt** (män'härt), **Wilhelm.** 1831–1880. German mythologist.

**Man'nin** (măn'ĭn), **Ethel.** 1900– . English journalist and novelist, b. London. On staff of theatrical journal *The Pelican* (1918). Author of *Martha* (1923), *Sounding Brass* (1925), *Crescendo* (1929), *Ragged Banners* (1931), *Men are Unwise* (1934), *The Pure Flame* (1936), *Rose and Sylvie* (1938), and *Julie* (1940).

**Man'ni·nen** (män'nĭ·nĕn), **Otto.** 1872–1950. Finnish poet and translator; published *Säkeitä I–II* (1905–10), *Virrantyven* (1925), and translations of works of Homer, Sophocles, Goethe, Ibsen, Molière, and others.

**Man'ning** (măn'ĭng), **Daniel.** 1831–1887. American journalist and financier; U.S. secretary of the treasury (1885–87).

**Manning, Henry Edward.** 1808–1892. English cardinal, b. Totteridge, Hertfordshire; grad. Oxford (1830). In colonial office (1830). Curate in Church of England (1832); archdeacon of Chichester (1840–51). Became Roman Catholic (1851); superior of Congregation of the Oblates of St. Charles, Bayswater, London (1857); appointed at Rome domestic prelate and monsignor (1860); archbishop of Westminster (1865); cardinal (1875). Controversialist in matters ecclesiastical. Author of *The Unity of the Church* (1842), *The Grounds of Faith* (1852), *The Temporal Mission of the Holy Ghost* (1865; 2d vol., 1875), *The Vatican Decrees* (1875), *The Eternal Priesthood* (1883), etc.

**Manning, James.** 1738–1791. American Baptist clergyman and educator; first president, Brown (1765–91).

**Manning, William Thomas.** 1866–1949. American Protestant Episcopal bishop, b. Northampton, Eng.; grad. U. of the South (1893); rector, Trinity Parish, New York City (1908–21); bishop of New York (1921–46).

**Mann'li·cher** (män'lĭ·kĕr), **Ferdinand.** 1848–1904. Austrian engineer; known for inventions in small arms, esp. the development of a breech-loading repeater rifle and a self-loading pistol.

**Man·nuc'ci** (män·no͞ot'chē), **Man·nuz'zi** (-no͞ot'tsē). Italian forms of MANUTIUS.

**Man'ny** (măn'ĭ) *or* **Mau'ny** (mō'nĭ), Sir **Walter de.** Baron **de Manny.** d. 1372. Military commander, b. in Hainaut; distinguished himself in service of King Edward III of England against Scots, Flemings, and French, and as negotiator; accompanied John of Gaunt in invasion of France (1369). Founder of house of Carthusian monks, Charterhouse, in London (1371).

**Man'nyng** (măn'ĭng), **Robert.** *Or* **Robert de Brun'ne** (dĕ bro͝on'nĕ). fl. 1288–1338. English chronicler and poet. Native of Lincolnshire; joined Gilbertine canons at Sempringham (1288). Author of *Handlyng Synne* (c. 1300), a free translation with his own additions of a French text *Manuel des Pechiez* by an English writer of Edward I's time, including metrical homilies and stories on Commandments, Seven Deadly Sins, and Sacraments, and depicting social life of time; author also of chronicle *The Story of Inglande*, translation in verse of Wace's *Brut* and French chronicle of Peter Langtoft; represents in works development of national sentiment under Plantagenets and, linguistically, dropping of inflections, introduction of French words, and furthering of Midland dialect, that is, transition from early to later Middle English.

**Manoel.** See MANUEL.

**Manoel do Nascimento, Francisco.** See NASCIMENTO.

**Ma'nou'vri'er'** (må'no͞o'vrē'ā'), **Léonce Pierre.** 1850–1927. French anthropologist; known esp. for work on the brain and its functions, and on the philosophy of science.

**Man·ri'que** (män·rē'kā), **Gómez.** 1415?–?1490. Spanish soldier, statesman, and poet; prominent in rebellious outbreaks during reigns of John II and Henry IV; author of lyrics and political satires, and most notably of dramatic compositions which were precursors of later dramatic forms. His nephew **Jorge Manrique** (1440?–1479) was author of lyrics, satires, and acrostics, and most notably of an elegy in 40 stanzas on the death of his father.

**Man'sart'** (mäɴ'sȧr'; *Angl.* măn'särt) *or* **Man'sard'** (mäɴ'sȧr'; *Angl.* măn'särd), **François,** *in full* **Nicolas François.** 1598–1666. French architect. His works include the churches of Sainte-Marie de Chaillot and Visitation de Sainte-Marie, the Hôtel de la Vrillière (later the Hôtel de la Banque de France), in Paris, and several châteaux. Usually credited with invention of the mansard roof, which he brought into general use. His grandnephew **Jules Har'douin'–Mansart** (ȧr'dwăɴ'-) *or* **Hardouin–Mansard,** *orig.* **Hardouin** (1646–1708), was building superintendent and architect of Louis XIV; enlarged Château de Saint-Germain; built Château de Clagny (1676–1680); commanded by king to complete the Palace of Versailles begun by Le Vau. His other works include the Grand Trianon, the dome of the Hôtel des Invalides, the Place Vendôme, the Place des Victoires at Paris.

**Mans'bridge** (măns'brĭj), **Albert.** 1876–1952. English educator; pioneer in field of adult education; founded Workers' Educational Assoc., in England (1903) and Australia (1913), and served as its secretary (1903–15); president of World Assoc. for Adult Education.

**Man'sel** (măn's'l), **Henry Longueville.** 1820–1871. English metaphysician, of so-called Scottish school. Maintained duality of consciousness as testifying to existence of self and external world; followed Sir William Hamilton in holding limitation of knowledge to the finite and conditioned.

**Mans'feld** (mäns'fĕlt), Count **Peter Ernst.** 1517–1604. German soldier; served under Emperor Charles V and under Philip II of Spain; governor of Luxemburg and of Netherlands. His natural son Count **Peter Ernst II** (1580–1626), German general, saw military service in Austria and Netherlands (1603–09); in Thirty Years' War, fought on Protestant side, leading attack against Austria (1625); defeated by Wallenstein at Dessau (1626).

**Mans'field** (măns'fēld), Earl of. See William MURRAY (1705–1793).

**Mansfield, Katherine.** *Pseudonym of* **Kathleen,** *nee* **Beau'champ** (bē'chăm), **Mur'ry** (mûr'ĭ). 1888–1923. British writer, b. Wellington, New Zealand; m. 1st George Bowden (1909; divorced 1918), 2d (1918) John Middleton Murry (*q.v.*). Afflicted with tuberculosis; passed most of her life (from 1918) in Italy, Switzerland, and France. Author of short stories collected in *In a German Pension* (1911), *Prelude* (1918), *Je ne parle pas français* (1919), *Bliss* (1920), *The Garden Party* (1922), *The Doves' Nest* (1923), and *Something Childish* (1924). Her *Poems* (1923), *Journal* (1927), and *Letters* (1928) were collected, edited and published after her death.

**Mansfield, Richard.** 1854–1907. Actor, b. Berlin, Ger., of English parentage; to U.S. (1872). On English stage (1877–82); on American stage (from 1882). Appeared in *Dr. Jekyll and Mr. Hyde, Beau Brummell, Merchant of Venice,* Shaw's *Arms and the Man,* Rostand's *Cyrano de Bergerac, Henry V, Peer Gynt,* etc.

**Man'ship** (măn'shĭp), **Paul.** 1885–1966. American sculptor; his bronze statue of Lincoln as a young man stands in Fort Wayne, Ind., his *Centaur and Dryad* in Detroit Museum of Art.

**Man'si** (män'sē), **Giovanni Domenico.** 1692–1769. Italian prelate and historian; archbishop of Lucca (1765 ff.); known esp. for his history of church councils to 1509.

**Man'so de Ve·las'co** (män'sō thā vä·läs'kō), **José Antonio.** Conde **de Su'pe·run'da** (thā sōō'pā·rōōn'dä). 1695?–after 1762. Spanish soldier and colonial administrator; captain general of Chile (1735–45); viceroy of Peru (1745–61).

**Man'son** (măn's'n), **George.** 1850–1876. Scottish water-color painter; depicted humble Scottish life; also known as an etcher.

**Manson,** Sir **Patrick.** 1844–1922. British physician and parasitologist, b. Aberdeen. To Amoy, China, becoming head of a missionary society's hospital and dispensary and engaging in private practice (1871); settled in Hong Kong (1883); instituted school of medicine which developed into university and medical school of Hong Kong. To Scotland (1889), and London (1890); instrumental in foundation of London School of Tropical Medicine (1899). First to enunciate hypothesis, afterwards confirmed by others, that the mosquito was the host of the malarial parasite at one stage of its existence, and thus an active agent in spreading malaria. Called father of tropical medicine.

**Man'stein** (män'shtīn), **Fritz Erich von.** *Orig. surname* **von Le·win'ski** (fôn lā·vĭn'skē). 1887–1973. German army officer; captured Sevastopol after long siege (Oct., 1941–July, 1942); field marshal (July, 1942).

**Man·sur'** *or* **Man·sour', al–** (ăl'măn·sōōr'). *Sometimes Anglicized as* **Al·man'zor** (ăl·măn'zẽr; -zôr) *or* **Al·man'sor** (-sẽr; -sôr). Arabic surname meaning "victorious," assumed by many Moslem princes.

**Mansur, al–.** *Arab.* **abu–Ja'far 'Abdullāh al–Manṣūr.** 712?–775. Second Abbasside caliph (754–775); succeeded his brother abu-al-Abbas. Transferred (762) seat of government to new city of Baghdad; patron of learning; firmly established new dynasty; suppressed revolts; encouraged translation of Greek and Latin classics into Arabic.

**Mansur, al–.** *Arab.* **Muḥammad ibn–abi–'Āmir.** 939–1002. Moslem regent of Córdoba, Spain. Rose from humble professional position to minister of finance under Caliph Hakam II; seized power as regent in reign of Hisham II, Hakam's successor; became royal chamberlain (Hajib; *Arab.* al-Ḥājib) and vizier; victorious in campaigns against Christian kingdoms in north; as result of triumphs assumed (981) honorific title **al–Mansur bi–Allah,** *Arab.* **al–Manṣūr bi–Allāh.** Checked separatist movements in religion; extended and sustained power of Ommiad caliphate just before its decline; patronized learning and literature.

**Mansur, al–.** *Arab.* **abu–Yūsuf Ya'qūb al–Manṣūr.** d. 1199. Almohade caliph in Spain (1184–99); grandson of Abd-al-Mumin; sent aid to Saladin in his war against the Crusaders; his reign important for its architectural monuments in Spain and Morocco, esp. the Giralda.

**Man'te·gaz'za** (män'tā·gät'tsä), **Paolo.** 1831–1910. Italian physiologist and anthropologist; founder of Museum of Anthropology and Ethnology at Florence, the Italian Anthropological Society, and an anthropological and ethnological journal. His publications include works on the physiology of pleasure, pain, and love, spontaneous generation, physiognomy, and political treatises and fiction.

**Man·te'gna** (män·tā'nyä), **Andrea.** 1431–1506. Italian painter and engraver, b. near Padua; chief master of Paduan school; adopted son and pupil of Squarcione. To Mantua (1459) as protégé of Lodovico Gonzaga, Marquis of Mantua; called to Rome (1488–90) by Innocent VIII to decorate Belvedere Chapel. Among his works executed at Padua are murals in church of the Eremitani, *Sts. Bernardinus and Antonius* in church of Sant'Antonio, *St. Euphemia* (now in Naples Museum); among his works executed at Mantua are a series of nine cartoons *Triumph of Caesar* (now in Hampton Court), *Triumph of Virtue over Vice, Parnassus* (both in the Louvre), *Triumph of Scipio* (in National Gallery, London), *St. Sebastian* (in Vienna museum), *St. George* (in Venice Academy), *Adoration of the Magi* (in New York Historical Society collection), and *Infancy of Jesus* (in Metropolitan Museum, N.Y.); among his engravings are *Flagellation of Christ, Christ at the Gates of Hell, Resurrection of Christ,* and *Entombment,* the last particularly notable for its effect on the subsequent art of Raphael, Holbein, and Dürer.

**Man·tell'** (măn·tĕl'), **Gideon Algernon.** 1790–1852. English geologist and paleontologist; studied paleontology of the Secondary rocks, esp. in Sussex; discovered four of the five genera of dinosaurs known in his time. Author of *The Wonders of Geology* (1838), etc.

**Mantell, Robert Bruce.** 1854–1928. Actor, b. Irvine, Ayrshire, Scotland. Identified with American stage (from 1884), playing esp. melodramas, romantic dramas, and in later years Shakespearean roles (Romeo, Othello, Hamlet, Richard III, Macbeth, Iago, King Lear, etc.).

**Man'teuf'fel** (män'toi'fĕl). German noble family, including: Baron **Otto Theodor von Manteuffel** (1805–1882), Prussian conservative statesman, minister of the interior (1848–50) and prime minister and minister of foreign affairs (1850–58); member of the Herrenhaus (from 1864). Baron **Edwin Hans Karl** (1809–1885), Prussian soldier, served in Danish War (1864), Austro-Prussian War (1866), and Franco-Prussian War (1870–71); created field marshal and commander of Prussian army of occupation in France (1871–73); governor of Alsace-Lorraine (1879).

**Man'tle** (măn't'l), **Burns,** *in full* **Robert Burns.** 1873–1948. American journalist, editor, and critic, b. Watertown, N.Y. On staff of New York *Evening Mail* (1911–22), New York *Daily News* (from 1922). Editor of the annuals *Best Plays* and *Year Book of the Drama* (from 1919); author of *American Playwrights of Today* (1929).

**Man'ton** (măn't'n; -tŭn), **Joseph.** 1766?–1835. English gunmaker in London; patented improvements in guns, including a hammer and breeching; instrumental in introduction of percussion system.

**Man'toux'** (mäɴ'tōō'), **Charles.** 1877–1947. French physician; educ. Paris; settled near Cannes; known for work relating to tuberculosis, esp. development of an intracutaneous tuberculin test called the "Mantoux test," production of artificial pneumothorax, and pictures of cavities in the lungs.

**Ma·nuc'ci** (mä·nōōt'chē), **Ma·nuz'zi** (mä·nōōt'tsē). Italian forms of MANUTIUS.

**Man'u·el** (măn'ū·ĕl). Name of two emperors of the Eastern Roman Empire: **Manuel I Com·ne'nus** [kŏm·nē'nŭs] (1120?–1180); son of John II; distinguished as a soldier; emperor (1143–80); m. as first wife (1146) Irene (*q.v.*); granted Crusaders passage through his dominions (Second Crusade, 1147–49); reign marked by many military victories (against Italians, Venetians, Serbs, Turks, etc.), most of them not decisive, and by serious defeats (as by Seljuks in Phrygia, 1176); empire weakened financially. **Manuel II Pa'lae·ol'o·gus** [pā'lē·ŏl'ō·gŭs] (1350–1425); son of John V; emperor (1391–1425); coregent with John VII (1398–1412); made journey (1399–1403) to Western countries to seek aid in establishing union of churches and in defending Constantinople, which was besieged by Turks; failed to take action when defeat (1402) of Bajazet I by Tamerlane at

Angora (Ankara) made Turks vulnerable; attacked by Murad II (1422).

**Ma·nuel'** (*Port.* mȧ·nwĕl'). *Earlier Port.* **Ma·noel'** (mȧ·nwĕl'). Name of two kings of Portugal: **Manuel I;** see EMANUEL. **Manuel II** (1889–1932); king (1908–10). Second son of Carlos I. Duke of Beja; trained for naval career; overthrown by naval revolt (1910); fled to Gibraltar, then to England; lived in exile in England during rest of life, as a country gentleman; m. (1913) Augusta Victoria, daughter of Prince William of Hohenzollern.

**Ma'nu·el'** (mȧ'nü·ĕl'), **Eugène.** 1823–1901. French man of letters; author of *Pages Intimes* (verse; 1865), *Les Ouvriers* (social drama; 1870), *Poèmes Populaires* (1872), *L'Absent* (comedy; 1873), *En Voyage* (verse; 1888), etc.

**Ma·nuel'** (mä·nwĕl'), Don **Juan.** 1282–1349. Spanish prince, general, statesman, and writer; nephew of Alfonso X, the Learned. Coregent for Alfonso XI during his minority (1320–25); general in chief of the Spanish army fighting the Moors. Chief literary work, *El Conde Lucanov*, a collection of tales in the Oriental manner, each with a little moral in verse at the end.

**Ma'nu·el** (mä'nōō·ĕl), **Nikolaus.** *Also known as* **Nikolaus Deutsch** (doich). 1484–1530. Swiss painter and wood engraver; studied in Venice under Titian. Works include 45 frescoes of *Dance of the Dead*, at Berne. Ardent supporter of Reformation; author of satirical comedies and polemical verse.

**Manuela.** See Marie d'UZÈS.

**Ma·nu'ti·us** (mȧ·nū'shĭ·ŭs), **Aldus.** *Latin form of* **Aldo,** *in full* **Teobaldo, Man·nuc'ci** (män·nōōt'chē) *or* **Ma·nu'zi·o** (mä·nōō'tsyō). 1450–1515. Italian printer and classical scholar, founder of the Aldine press. Settled in Venice (1490); gathered Greek scholars and assistants; published fine editions of Greek, Latin, and Italian classics. First to use italic type (in an edition of Vergil, 1501). Founded the New Academy (1500) of Hellenic scholars. His son **Paulus,** *Ital.* **Paolo** (1512–1574), succeeded to management of Aldine press (1533) and devoted himself esp. to publication of Latin classics, notably the works of Cicero, working (from 1561) chiefly under the patronage of the Papacy. Paolo's eldest son, **Aldus** (1547–1597), continued editorial and printing work, and was called to Rome (1588) by Pope Sixtus V to direct the Vatican printing press.

**Man·zo'ni** (män·dzō'nē), **Alessandro Francesco Tommaso Antonio.** 1785–1873. Italian novelist and poet; leader of Italian Romantic school. To Paris (1805–07); influenced by Voltairism of contemporary literary salons; m. 1st (1808; d. 1833) Enrichetta Blondel, 2d (1837) Teresa Borri; father-in-law of Massimo d'Azeglio. Abandoned earlier skepticism in favor of ardent religious orthodoxy; participated in Milanese revolt (1848); appointed senator of the kingdom (1860). Known especially for his novel *I Promessi Sposi* (1825–26), an historical study of 17th-century Italy and a model of modern Italian prose. Among his other works are *Inni Sacri* (1810), *Osservazioni sulla Morale Cattolica* (1819), the tragedies *Il Conte di Carmagnola* (1820) and *Adelchi* (1822), an ode on Napoleon's death *Il Cinque Maggio* (1822), and *Storia della Colonna Infame* (1842).

**Mao Tse-tung** (mou' dzŭ'dōōng'). 1893–1976. Chinese Communist leader; president of first Chinese Peasants Union (1927); took part in "Long March" (1934–36); chairman of new Central People's Government (1949); established people's communes (1958); relinquished his position as head of state (1959) but retained chairmanship of Communist party.

**Map** (măp), **Walter.** *Surname Latinized* **Ma'pes** (mā'pēz). c. 1140–c. 1209. Medieval Welsh ecclesiastic, author, and wit, b. probably in Herefordshire. Clerk of royal household and itinerant justice; sent on missions abroad; canon of St. Paul's Cathedral, Lincoln; archdeacon of Oxford (from 1197). Author of *De Nugis Curialium* (*i.e.* "Courtiers' Triflings"; c. 1182–1192), notebook of court gossip, daily events, theological arguments, accounts of miracles, largely satirical. Reputed author of some of goliardic verses, satires upon vices of monks, including one converted into drinking song "Meum est propositum in taberna mori." Probably the man who linked up Arthur legend proper to cycle of the Holy Grail; credited with lost Latin prose romance of *Lancelot du Lac* and prose romances *Mort Artus* and *Queste*, too long to be work of a busy court official, but more probably he was author in early years of poem on Lancelot, original of the German version.

**Maq'di·si** *or* **Mu'qad·da·si, al** (ăl·măk'dĭ·sē). *Arab.* **Muḥammad ibn-Aḥmad al-Maqdisi.** fl. latter part of 10th century. Moslem geographer, b. Jerusalem; traveled widely in Moslem countries (except India and Spain) gathering material for his *Aḥsan al-Taqāsīm.*

**Maq'qa·ri, al-** (ăl·măk'kă·rē). 1591?–1632. Moorish historian, b. Tlemcen, Algeria. Chief work, *Nafḥ al-Ṭīb* ("Breath of the Perfumes"), part of which has been translated into English by Gayangos y Arce as *History of the Mohammedan Dynasties of Spain.*

**Maq·ri'zi, al-** (ăl'măk·rē'zē). *Arab.* **Tagi-al-Dīn Aḥmad Maqrīzi.** 1364–1442. Moslem historian; teacher in various mosques in Cairo. Wrote topographical history of Egypt, history of Egypt from 1181 to 1440, history of Moslem rule in Abyssinia, and treatise on Arabic weights and measures.

**Ma'quet'** (mȧ'kĕ'), **Auguste.** 1813–1888. French writer; best known as collaborator with Alexandre Dumas père in many novels and plays, doing research to establish historical facts used by Dumas in his plots.

**Mar** (mär), Earls of. See (1) *earls of Douglas and earls of Angus*, under DOUGLAS family; (2) under John ERSKINE (d. 1572); (3) *Alexander Stewart* (1375?–1435) and *James Stewart* (1531?–1570), Earl of Moray, under STEWART family.

**Mara, La.** See *Marie Lipsius* under Richard LIPSIUS.

**Ma·ral'di** (mä·räl'dē), **Giacomo Filippo.** 1665–1729. Nephew of J. D. Cassini. Astronomer, b. near Nice; lived in Paris (from 1687). Discovered that the dark division observed by Cassini (*q.v.*) was the line of demarcation between two of Saturn's rings; recognized the variability of one of the stars in the constellation Hydra (1704); author of a star catalogue.

**Ma'ran'** (mȧ'räN'), **René.** 1887–1960. French Negro novelist; awarded Goncourt prize (1921) for *Batouala.*

**Ma'rat'** (mȧ'rȧ'), **Jean Paul.** 1743–1793. Swiss-born French Revolutionary politician; studied medicine; took active part in prerevolutionary agitation; published paper called *L'Ami du Peuple* (1789) inciting the people to violence. Member of National Convention (1792) and identified with radical Jacobins; attacked by Girondists, arrested, and tried, but acquitted (Apr. 24, 1793). Joined Danton and Robespierre in overthrowing power of the Girondists. Assassinated by Charlotte Corday (*q.v.*) while in his bath (July 13, 1793).

**Ma·rat'ti** (mä·rät'tē) *or* **Ma·rat'ta** (-tä), **Carlo.** 1625–1713. Italian painter of the Roman school; commissioned by Clement XI to restore Raphael's frescoes in Vatican (1702–03). Eclectic; chief master of Roman late baroque style. Among his works are *Annunciation* (now in Turin Gallery), *Holy Night* (in Dresden museum), *Portrait of a Cardinal* (at Munich), *Portrait of Clement IX* (at Leningrad).

**Mar'be** (mär'bĕ), **Karl.** 1869–1953. German philosopher and psychologist.

**Mar'beau'** (mȧr'bō'), **Jean Baptiste Firmin.** 1798–1875. French philanthropist; founded at Chaillot (1844) first foundling hospital (crèche) in France.

**Mar'beck** (mär'bĕk) *or* **Mer'beck** (mär'-), **John.** d. 1585? English organist and theologian. Early adherent of Calvinism; arrested and condemned to burn at stake, but pardoned through Bishop Gardiner of Winchester. Published earliest concordance of whole English Bible (1550) and *The Boke of Common Praier Noted*, an adaptation of plain chant of older rituals to liturgy of Edward VI (1550).

**Mar'ble** (mär'b'l), **Alice.** 1913– . American tennis champion, b. in Plumas County, Calif.; won American national titles in singles and mixed doubles (1936, 1938–40), doubles (1937–40), and Wimbledon titles in mixed doubles (1937–39), doubles (1938–39), singles (1939); turned professional (1940).

**Mar'bo** (mär'bō) *or* **Mar'o·bod'u·us** (măr'bô·bŏd'ū-ŭs). 18 B.C.?–?41 A.D. Germanic chieftain; king of the Marcomanni; negotiated alliance of Germanic tribes against the Romans; secured a treaty with Emperor Tiberius (6 A.D.); driven from the throne by the Gothic Catualda (19 A.D.).

**Marbois,** Marquis **de Barbé-.** See BARBÉ-MARBOIS.

**Mar'bot'** (mȧr'bō'), Baron **Jean Baptiste Antoine Marcelin, de.** 1782–1854. French soldier; aide-de-camp of Augereau at Austerlitz, Jena, Eylau, of Lannes at Saragossa, of Masséna at Wagram; commissioned field marshal (after 1830) and lieutenant general (1836); appointed peer of France (1845).

**Mar'burg** (mär'bo͝orK), **Otto.** 1874–1948. Neuropathologist, b. Moravia; director, neurological institute of U. of Vienna (1919–38); resident in U.S. from 1938.

**Marc** (märk), **Franz.** 1880–1916. German painter; known esp. as an animal painter; killed in action near Verdun (Mar. 4, 1916). See Paul KLEE.

**Mar'ca'** (mȧr'kȧ'), **Pierre de.** 1595–1662. French Roman Catholic prelate; governor of Catalonia (1644–51); archbishop of Toulouse (1652) and minister of state; archbishop of Paris (1662); author of *De la Concorde du Sacerdoce et de l'État* (1641).

**Mar'ca'bru'** (mȧr'kȧ'brü'). 12th-century Gascon troubadour, one of earliest troubadours known.

**Mar'ceau'** (mȧr'sō'), **François Séverin.** *Orig.* **Mar'-ceau'-Des'gra'viers'** (-dā'grȧ'vyā'). 1769–1796. French soldier; took part in assault on the Bastille (1789); served in revolutionary armies in La Vendée (1793), where he was promoted general, at Fleurus (1794), and along the Rhine (1795–96).

**Mar'cel'** (mȧr'sĕl'), **Étienne.** d. 1358. French politician; provost of the merchants of Paris (from 1354). Leader in the States-General (1356); succeeded in inducing the dauphin Charles (later King Charles V of France) with the support of the States-General to issue an edict of reform; King John the Good, then a prisoner of the English, forbade execution of the edict; whereupon, Marcel turned from the dauphin to support the claims of Charles the Bad, King of Navarre. Led the Paris mob into the palace of the dauphin (Feb. 22, 1358) and in the presence of the dauphin murdered the marshals of Champagne and Normandy. Was himself murdered (July 31, 1358) by Jean Maillart, an agent of the dauphin, when on the point of opening the gates of Paris to the troops of the king of Navarre.

**Mar'cel·li'nus** (mär'sĕ·lī'nŭs), Saint. d. 304. Pope (bishop of Rome; 296–304); pontiff during the persecutions under Diocletian.

**Mar·cel'lo** (mär·chĕl'lō), **Benedetto.** 1686–1739. Italian composer; chief work, *Estro Poetico-Armonico* (1724–27), a musical setting for a paraphrase of fifty of the Psalms.

**Mar·cel'lus** (mär·sĕl'ŭs). Name of two popes. See *Table of Popes*, Nos. 30, 224.

**Marcellus.** Name of Roman plebeian family, including: **Marcus Claudius Marcellus** (268?–208 B.C.), general; consul five times (between 222 and 208); defeated Gauls (222), slaying their king, Britomartus, with his own hand; defeated Hannibal at Nola (216); commanded army in Sicily (214), captured Syracuse (212), and subjugated whole island; fought Hannibal (210–208); ambushed and killed on reconnoitering expedition (208).

**Marcus Claudius Marcellus,** orator and politician; consul (51 B.C.); opponent of Caesar; withdrew to Mytilene after Pompey's defeat at Pharsala (48); pardoned by Caesar after request by the Senate (46); Caesar thanked in speech (*Pro Marcello*) by Cicero; murdered on way to Rome by one of his retinue.

**Marcus Claudius Marcellus** (43–23 B.C.), nephew and favorite of Augustus; adopted by Augustus (25) and named as his successor; his untimely death is referred to by Vergil in *The Aeneid* (Book VI, ll. 860–886).

**Mar'cel'lus'** (mȧr'sĕ'lüs'), Comte **de. Marie Louis Jean André Charles du Ty'rac'** (dü tē'rȧk'). 1795–1865. French diplomat who discovered the statue of Venus de Milo (1820) and caused it to be taken to France.

**Marcellus, Nonius.** See NONIUS MARCELLUS.

**March** (märch), Earls of (in the English peerage). See MORTIMER family.

**March,** Earls of (in the Scottish peerage). See *Patrick Dunbar* (1285–1369), under Agnes DUNBAR; *Alexander Stewart* (1454?–1485) under STEWART family; *William Douglas* (1724–1810) under DOUGLAS family; Francis WEMYSS-CHARTERIS-DOUGLAS.

**March** (märk), **Ausías.** 1397?–?1460. Catalan poet; author of poems on love, death, religion, and morals, written in the style of Petrarch.

**March** (märch), **Francis Andrew.** 1825–1911. American philologist, b. Millbury, Mass. Professor, Lafayette Coll. (1857–1906). Best known for researches in English historical grammar. Director (from 1879) of American staff of *Oxford English Dictionary.* Consulting editor of the *Standard Dictionary* (1893–95). Author of *A Comparative Grammar of the Anglo-Saxon Language...* (1870); *Introduction to Anglo-Saxon: An Anglo-Saxon Reader* (1870); etc. His son **Francis Andrew** (1863–1928) was a lexicographer; taught at Lafayette (1882–1928), professor (from 1891); in charge of etymological work for the *Standard Dictionary* (1893–95); coeditor with his father of *A Thesaurus Dictionary of the English Language* (1902). Another son, **Peyton Conway** (1864–1955), army officer; grad. U.S.M.A., West Point (1888); served in World War as artillery commander in the A.E.F. in France (1917) and as general and chief of staff in Washington (1918). Retired (1921).

**March, Fredric.** 1897–1975. *Orig. name* **Frederick McIntyre Bick'el** (bĭk''l). American actor, b. Racine, Wis.; on stage in *Deburau* (1920), *Shavings, The Royal Family, The Skin of Our Teeth* (1942), etc., often with his wife (m. 1927) **Florence El'dridge** [el'drij] (1901– ); also in motion pictures including *The Dummy, Dr. Jekyll and Mr. Hyde, Sign of the Cross, Design for Living, Death Takes a Holiday, The Barretts of Wimpole Street, The Dark Angel, Mary of Scotland, A Star Is Born, Nothing Sacred, The Best Years of Our Lives, Death of a Salesman;* received award of Acad. of Motion Picture Arts and Sciences (1932, 1947).

**March, William.** *Pen name of* **William Edward March Campbell.** 1894–1954. American novelist and short-story writer; withdrew from business (1938) to devote himself to writing. Author of *Company K* (1933), *The Tallons* (1936), *The Looking-Glass* (1943).

**Mar′chand′** (mȧr′shäN′), **Jean Baptiste.** 1863–1934. French soldier and explorer; served in Africa (1889 ff.), traced Niger River to its source, explored region from Ivory Coast to Tengrela; commanded across-continent expedition which reached and occupied Fashoda (July 10, 1898), causing serious crisis in Anglo-French relations, and later (Dec. 11, 1898–May, 1899) marched through Ethiopia to Djibouti. In World War, general of brigade and of division; commanded 10th colonial division in Champagne offensive (1915), on the Somme (1916) and Chemin des Dames (1917), in battle of Verdun (1917), and on the Marne (1918).

**Marchand, Jean Hippolyte.** 1883–1941. French painter; identified with cubist group.

**Mar·che′si** (mär·kā′zē), Cavaliere **Pompeo.** 1789–1858. Italian sculptor; among his works are statues, as of Volta, Goethe, and Francis I of Austria, a large group including the notable *Mater Dolorosa*, and a funeral monument to Duke Emmanuel Philibert of Savoy.

**Marchesi, Salvatore.** Cavaliere **de Ca·stro′ne** (dā käs·trō′nā). Marchese **del′la Ra·ja′ta** (dāl′lä rä·yä′tä). 1822–1908. Italian baritone singer and composer; expelled from Italy (1848), sang in U.S. and various cities of Europe, and finally settled in Paris. Composed a number of songs, and made Italian translations of French and German operas. His wife, **Ma·thil′de** (*Ger.* mä·tĭl′dĕ; *Fr.* mȧ′tēld′), *nee* **Grau′mann** [grou′män] (1826–1913), was a concert singer and singing teacher; established the École Marchesi in Paris (after 1881); author of *L'Art du Chant*, *Marchesi and Music*, etc. Her daughter **Blanche** [bläNsh] (1863–1940) was also a concert and opera singer.

**Mar·chet′ti** (mär·kāt′tē), **Filippo.** 1831–1902. Italian composer, esp. of operas, as *Gentile da Varano* (1856), *Ruy Blas* (1869), *Don Giovanni d'Austria* (1880).

**Marchmont,** Earl of. See Sir Patrick HUME.

**Mar′ci·a′nus** (mär′shĭ·ā′nŭs; mär′sĭ-). *Also* **Mar′cian** (mär′shăn). 392–457. Emperor of the Eastern Roman Empire (450–457). A Thracian of humble birth; on death of Theodosius II chosen consort by Pulcheria; successfully defended empire in Syria and Egypt (452) and on Armenian frontier (456); refused tribute to Attila (450). Council of Chalcedon (451) held in his reign.

**Mar′cin** (?mär′sĭn), **Max.** 1879–1948. Playwright and producer, b. in province of Posen, Ger.; to U.S. as a child. Author of *The House of Glass* (with George M. Cohan, 1915), *See My Lawyer* (1915), *Cheating Cheaters* (1916), *Silence* (1925), *Los Angeles* (with Donald Ogden Stewart, 1927); author and producer of *The Humbug* (1929); producer of *Give and Take* (1923).

**Mar′ci·on** (mär′shĭ·ŏn; -sĭ·ŏn). Christian Gnostic of 2d century; regarded as a heretic by orthodox writers; founded sect (Marcionites) with churches in northern Africa, Gaul, Asia Minor, and Egypt. His doctrine of eternity of matter was developed by Hermogenes, a teacher of 2d century with Gnostic tendencies.

**Mar·co′ni** (mär·kō′nē), Marchese **Guglielmo.** 1874–1937. Italian electrical engineer and inventor, b. of Italian father and Irish mother at Bologna. Carried out successful experiments with wireless telegraphy near Bologna (1895). To England (1896); made successful tests between Penarth and Brean Down, finally sending signals distance of nine miles. To La Spezia at invitation of Italian government, where wireless station was erected (1897); Marconi's Wireless Telegraph Co., Ltd., formed in London (1897); established communication across English Channel between England and France (1898); succeeded in receiving and sending signals across the Atlantic between Poldhu, Cornwall, and St. John's, Newfoundland (1901); patented magnetic detector (1902) and horizontal directional aerial (1905); introduced timed-spark system for generating continuous waves (1912). Shared (with Karl Ferdinand Braun) the 1909 Nobel prize for physics.

**Marco Polo.** See POLO.

**Mar′cos** (mär′kōs), **Ferdinand Edralin.** 1917– . President of the Philippines (1965– ).

**Mar′cos·son** (mär′kŭ·s'n), **Isaac Frederick.** 1877–1961. American journalist, b. Louisville, Ky. On staff of Louisville *Times* (1894–1903), *World's Work* (1903–07), *Saturday Evening Post* (1907–10), *Munsey's Magazine* (1910–13), and again *Saturday Evening Post* (1913–36). Author of *The Business of War* (1917), *Peace and Business* (1919), *An African Adventure* (1921), *Caravans of Commerce* (1927), *Turbulent Years* (1938), etc.

**Mar′cou′** (mȧr′kōō′), **Jules.** 1824–1898. Geologist, b. Salins, France; settled in Cambridge, Mass. (1860–98). Author of *Geology of North America* (1858), *Geological Map of the World* (1862), *De la Science en France* (1869), *Life, Letters and Works of Louis Agassiz* (2 vols., 1895).

**Mar′cous′sis′** (mȧr′kōō′sē′), **Louis Casimir La′dis′las′** (lȧ′dēs′läs′). *Orig. surname* **Mar′kus** (mär′kōōs). 1882?–1941. Polish painter; to Paris under Lefebvre (1903); associated with Picasso; one of the early cubists.

**Mar′coux′** (mȧr′kōō′), **Vanni.** 1879–1962. Operatic baritone, b. Turin, of French parentage; sang at Covent Garden, London (1905–12); member of Chicago Opera Company (from 1912); created roles in Massenet's *Don Quichotte*, Musorgski's *Boris Godunov*.

**Mar′cus Au·re′li·us** (mär′kŭs ô·rē′lĭ·ŭs; ô·rēl′yŭs). *Surnamed* **An′to·ni′nus** (ăn′tô·nī′nŭs). *Original name* **Marcus An′ni·us Ve′rus** (ăn′ĭ·ŭs vẹr′ŭs). 121–180. Roman emperor (161–180), b. Rome. Son of Annius Verus and nephew of Emperor Antoninus Pius, by whom he was adopted (138) and created Caesar (139); m. (c. 145) Faustina, daughter of emperor; became consul (140); held various public offices (140–161). As emperor made Lucius Verus his colleague (161); his generals subdued Parthians (162–166) and revolting tribes in Pannonia (167–168); won victories (170–175) over Marcomanni and Quadi (episode of the Thundering Legion, 174); visited Egypt; returned to Italy (176); again fought barbarians in the north (177–180); died at Sirmium or Vindobona (Vienna). One of the most eminent of Stoic philosophers; a man of gentle character and wide learning, yet an opponent of Christianity, supporting persecutions. Author of *Meditations* (written in Greek), a collection of precepts of practical morality.

**Marcus Aurelius Antoninus.** See CARACALLA.

**Mar′cy** (mär′sĭ), **Randolph Barnes.** 1812–1887. American army officer; chief of staff to Gen. McClellan (1861). Inspector general, U.S. army (1878–81).

**Marcy, William Learned.** 1786–1857. American statesman; b. Sturbridge, Mass.; member of dominant political group known as the "Albany Regency." Comptroller, New York State (1823–29); associate justice, New York supreme court (1829–31); U.S. senator (1831–32). Coined phrase "spoils system" by a speech in which he said he could see "nothing wrong in the rule that to the victor belong the spoils" (1832). Governor of New York (1833–39); U.S. secretary of war (1845–49); U.S. secretary of state (1853–57).

**Mar′cza·li** (mŏr′tsŏ·lĭ), **Henrik.** *Surname orig.* **Mor′gen·stern** (mŏr′gĕn·shtĕrn). 1856–1940. Hungarian historian.

**Mar′den** (mär′d'n), **Charles Carroll.** 1867–1932. American philologist, b. Baltimore; professor of Spanish, Princeton (1916–32). With Frederick C. Tarr, wrote *A First Spanish Grammar* (1926).

**Marden, Orison Swett.** 1850–1924. American journalist; founded and edited (1897–1912; 1918–24) magazine *Success*, New York. Author of *Pushing to the Front* (1894), *Ambition and Success* (1919), *Masterful Personality* (1921), etc.

**Mardochai.** See MORDECAI.

**Mar·do′ni·us** (mär·dō′nĭ·ŭs). d. 479 B.C. Persian general. Son of Gobryas and son-in-law of Darius Hystaspis. Led unsuccessful expedition (492) against Eretria and Athens. After accession of Xerxes, commanded army at time (480) of Persian defeat at Salamis; defeated and probably killed at Plataea (479).

**Ma·rées′** (mä·rā′), **Hans von.** 1837–1887. German painter; chief work, frescoes in library of zoological museum at Naples.

**Ma·ren′co** (mä·rĕng′kō), Count **Carlo.** 1800–1846. Italian dramatist; influenced by the Romantic movement; wrote historical tragedies, as *Buondelmonte, Corso Donati*, and *Arnaldo da Brescia.*

**Ma·ren′zi·o** (mä·rĕn′tsyō), **Luca.** 1560?–1599. Italian composer of madrigals, villanelles and airs, motets, and a mass.

**Ma′ret′** (må′rĕ′), **Hugues Bernard.** Duc **de Bas·sa′no** (dĕ bäs·sä′nō). 1763–1839. French statesman; ambassador to England (1792, 1797) and Naples (1793); imprisoned at Brünn by Austrians (1793–96). Confidential adviser to Napoleon; created duke of Bassano (1809); minister of foreign affairs (1811–13); minister of state during Hundred Days; exiled after Waterloo (1815–20). Created peer of France by Louis Philippe (1831).

**Ma′rets′** (må′rā′), **Nicolas Des.** Seigneur **de Mail′le·bois′** (dĕ mä′y′·bwä′). 1648–1721. Nephew of Colbert (*q.v.*). French intendant of finances (1678–83); director of finances (1703–08), and comptroller general of finances (1708–15).

**Mar′ett** (măr′ĕt), **Robert Ra′nulph** (rā′nŭlf). 1866–1943. English anthropologist; works include *The Threshold of Religion* (1909), *Anthropology* (1912), *Psychology and Folklore* (1920), *Heart and Hands in Human Evolution* (1935), etc.

**Ma′re·tzek** (mä′rā·tsĕk), **Max.** 1821–1897. Conductor and composer, b. Brünn, Moravia; conducted and produced Italian opera in New York (1849–79). Composer esp. of operas and ballet music.

**Ma′reuil′** (må′rû′y′), **Arnaud** *or* **Arnault** *or* **Arnaut de.** Late 12th-century Provençal troubadour.

**Ma′rey′** (må′rā′), **Étienne Jules.** 1830–1904. French physiologist; known for work on the physiology of the heart and circulation, animal heat, electrical phenomena in animals, action of poisons on nerves and muscles, and the flight of birds and insects; invented the sphygmograph (1863).

**Mar′ga·ret** (mär′gȧ·rĕt; -rĭt), Saint. 255?–?275. Christian martyr; beheaded at Antioch (c. 275).

**Margaret,** Saint. d. 1093. See MALCOLM III of Scotland.

**Margaret.** *Dan.* **Margrete.** 1353–1412. Known as "Semiramis of the North." Daughter of Waldemar IV, King of Denmark. Queen of Denmark, Norway, and Sweden; m. (1363) Haakon VI, King of Norway. Regent of Denmark for her son Olaf (1376–87) and, on death of Haakon (1380), became regent of Norway, also for Olaf; on Olaf's death (1387), seized control of both kingdoms; elected as joint sovereign by Denmark (1387) and by Norway (1388); had Eric of Pomerania, her grandnephew, proclaimed her successor (1389); offered throne of Sweden by disaffected citizens; defeated and took prisoner (1389) Swedish king, Albert of Mecklenburg; after complete conquest of Sweden (1389–97), effected Union of Kalmar, a dynastic union that nominally lasted until 1523; kept effective control, although Eric crowned king (1397) of the three nations; no monarchy in Europe equal in extent at the time.

**Margaret.** 1282?–1318. Queen of Edward I of England; daughter of Philip III of France; m. (1299) Edward as his second wife; never crowned queen.

**Margaret.** 1237–1270. Daughter of Isabella, German empress. See ISABELLA.

**Margaret.** 1240–1275. Queen of Scots. Eldest daughter of Henry III of England; m. Alexander III of Scotland (1251); looked upon with suspicion as representing English influence, confined in Edinburgh castle by guardians of king and queen until released through intervention by her father. Her daughter Margaret married Eric Magnusson of Norway. Their daughter **Margaret,** *known as* **the Maid of Norway** (1283–1290), titular queen of Scotland on death of her grandfather (1286), was affianced to Prince Edward, son of Edward I of England (1287); died in Orkneys, en route to England, under mysterious circumstances (1290).

**Margaret.** 1882–1920. Daughter of duke of Connaught; m. (1905) Gustavus Adolphus, crown prince of Sweden.

**Margaret Beaufort.** Countess of **Richmond and Derby.** See Margaret BEAUFORT.

**Margaret of An′jou** (ăn′jōō; *Fr.* äN′zhōō′). 1430–1482. Queen of Henry VI of England. Daughter of René of Anjou; m. to Henry VI by proxy (1445) as result of negotiations by William de la Pole, Duke of Suffolk, to confirm truce with France in defiance of popular will to continue war (the Hundred Years' War); supported Beaufort-Suffolk peace party; later supported Edmund Beaufort, Duke of Somerset, who lost Normandy and Guienne; during Henry VI's insanity, strove against Richard, Duke of York's protectorate; failed to crush York, who again became protector after death of Somerset in defeat at first battle of St. Albans (1455), the inauguration of wars between houses of Lancaster and York. After victory at Wakefield (1460), defeated Richard Neville, Earl of Warwick, at St. Albans (1461) and brutally executed her enemies; defeated at Towton (1461); retired to Scotland with Henry; invaded Northumberland with help from Louis XI, but failed (1462); given refuge in Flanders and Lorraine; her forces defeated at Hexham (1464); arranged with Warwick a temporarily successful invasion of England (1470–71) and placed Henry VI on throne; defeated at Barnet (1471), Henry VI a prisoner; defeated and captured at Tewkesbury (1471), where her son Edward was killed; prisoner for five years; ransomed by Louis XI (1476) on surrender of all rights of succession to French territory.

**Margaret of Austria.** 1480–1530. Daughter of Emperor Maximilian I and Mary of Burgundy; b. Brussels. Duchess of Savoy and regent of the Netherlands (1507–30); m. 1st (1497) Infante Juan of Spain, who died a few months later; 2d (1501) Philibert II (1480–1504), Duke of Savoy. Appointed (1507) by her father regent of the Netherlands and guardian of her nephew Charles (later Emperor Charles V); negotiated treaty of Cambrai (1529) with Louise of Savoy for France.

**Margaret of Austria.** See MARGARET OF PARMA.

**Margaret of Burgundy.** *Fr.* **Mar′gue·rite′ de Bour′gogne′** (mår′gē·rēt′ dē bōōr′gôn′y′). 1290?–1315. Queen of Navarre; daughter of Robert II, Duke of Burgundy; m. Louis le Hutin (1305), King of Navarre (see LOUIS X of France). Convicted of adultery, imprisoned, and smothered to death by order of king.

**Margaret of Ca·rin′thi·a** (kȧ·rĭn′thĭ·ȧ). *Ger.* **Mar′ga·re′te von Kärn′ten** (mär′gä·rā′tĕ fōn kĕrn′tĕn).

*Called* **Maul′tasch** (moul′tăsh). 1318–1369. Daughter of Henry, Duke of Carinthia; m. John Henry, Prince of Bohemia (1330); discarded this husband (1341) and m. Louis, son of the emperor (1342); inherited Carinthia and Tirol (1335), but finally (1363) forced to abdicate in favor of Austrian Hapsburg house.

**Margaret of Flan′ders** (flăn′dẽrz). *Fr.* **Mar′gue·rite′ de Flan′dre** (mȧr′gẽ·rēt′ dẽ flăɴ′dr′). *Also known as* **Margaret of Constantinople.** 1200?–1280. Daughter of Emperor Baldwin I, Count of Flanders and Hainault; m. 1st Bouchard d'Avesnes and 2d (1223) William of Dampierre. Inherited Flanders and Hainault; struggle ensued between children of two marriages; settled by appeal to Louis IX of France as arbiter, who gave Hainault to sons of Bouchard d'Avesnes and Flanders to sons of William of Dampierre (1246).

**Margaret of Flanders.** *Fr.* **Marguerite de Flandre.** 1350–1405. Countess of Flanders and duchess of Burgundy. Daughter of Louis II de Male; m. 1st Philippe de Rouvre (1357), 2d Philip the Bold (1369); mother of Duke John; inherited (1383) Flanders, Artois, etc.

**Margaret of France.** *Fr.* **Marguerite de France** (dẽ frăɴs′). *Also known as* **Margaret of Savoy.** 1532?–1574. Daughter of Francis I of France; m. Emmanuel Philibert, Duke of Savoy (1559); patron of literature; corresponded with Ronsard and du Bellay.

**Mar′ga·ret** (mär′gȧ·rĕt; -rĭt) *or* **Mar′gue·rite′** (mär′gĕ·rēt′) **of Na·varre′** (nȧ·vär′; *Fr.* nȧ′vȧr′). *Also known as* **Margaret of An′gou′lême′** (äɴ′gōō′lâm′) *or* **of Or′lé·ans** (ôr′lê·ănz; *Fr.* ôr′lā′äɴ′) *or* **of Va′lois′** (vȧ′lwȧ′). 1492–1549. Daughter of Charles d'Orléans, Count of Angoulême, who was son of John of Angoulême, and Louise of Savoy; sister of Francis I; b. Angoulême. Queen of Navarre (1544–49); m. 1st (1509) duc d'Alençon (d. 1525), 2d (1527) Henri d'Albret, titular king (as Henry II) of Navarre. Their daughter Jeanne d'Albret was mother of Henry of Navarre (Henry IV of France); see ALBRET, BOURBON. Active in politics and a supporter of Protestantism, but inclined to mysticism; a friend of literature, and a writer of prose and poetry; courts at Nérac and Pau most brilliant intellectually in Europe at that time. Her best-known works: *Les Marguerites de la Marguerite des Princesses*, collection of dramatic and religious poems (1547), *Dernières Poésies* (pub. 1896), *Lettres* (pub. 1841–42), and esp. the *Heptaméron*, a collection of tales, probably a joint work with writers of her court (1559).

**Margaret of Par′ma** (pär′mȧ). *Ital.* **Mar′ghe·ri′ta di Par′ma** (mär′gā·rē′tä dē pär′mä). *Also known as* **Margaret of Austria.** *Ger.* **Mar′ga·re′te von Ös′ter·reich′** (mär′gä·rā′tĕ fōn û′stẽr·rīĸ′). 1522–1586. Natural daughter of Emperor Charles V; m. Alessandro, Duca di Firenze (1536; d. 1537), and Ottavio Farnese, Duca di Parma (1538); regent of Netherlands (1559–67).

**Margaret of Provence.** *Fr.* **Mar′gue·rite′ de Pro′vence′** (mȧr′gẽ·rēt′ dẽ prô′văɴs′). 1221?–1295. Queen of France; daughter of count of Provence; m. King Louis IX (1234).

**Margaret of Savoy.** See MARGARET OF FRANCE.

**Margaret of Savoy.** *Ital.* **Mar′ghe·ri′ta di Sa·vo′ia** (mär′gā·rē′tä dē sä·vô′yä). 1851–1925. Queen of Italy, b. Turin; daughter of duke of Genoa; m. Crown Prince Humbert (1868) and became queen when he succeeded to throne (1878). Queen dowager (from 1900).

**Margaret of Scotland.** 1425?–1445. Scottish poet; daughter of James I of Scotland; m. (1436) Dauphin Louis (afterward Louis XI of France), who mistreated her; author of rondeaus and laments. Cf. Saint MARGARET (d. 1093); MARGARET, Queen of Scots (1240–75).

**Margaret of Va′lois′** (vȧ′lwȧ′) *or* **Margaret of France.** *Known as* **Queen Margot.** *Fr.* **Reine Mar′got′** (rân mȧr′gō′). 1553–1615. Daughter of Henry II of France and Catherine de Médicis. Queen of Navarre, noted for her beauty and learning; also, notorious for her loose living; m. Henry of Navarre (1572) just before St. Bartholomew's Day. After Henry's accession (1589), marriage dissolved by pope (1599). Wrote *Mémoires* (first pub. 1628) and *Lettres*.

**Margaret of York.** Countess of Salisbury. = *Margaret Pole*, under POLE family.

**Margaret Rose.** 1930– . Princess of Great Britain. Dau. of George VI, sister of Elizabeth II; m. Sir Antony Armstrong-Jones, Earl of Snowdon (1960; div. 1978).

**Mar′ga·ret The·re′sa** (mär′gȧ·rĕt [-rĭt] tĕ·rē′sȧ[-zȧ]) of Spain. 1651–1673. Empress of Germany (1666–73), b. at Madrid; younger daughter of Philip IV of Spain; first wife (m. 1666) of her uncle Emperor Leopold I; their daughter Maria Antonia married Maximilian II Emanuel of Bavaria.

**Margaret Tu′dor** (tū′dẽr). 1489–1541. Queen of James IV of Scotland. Daughter of Henry VII of England; m. (1503) James IV (d. 1513 at Flodden); supported English party against French; regent (1513) and guardian of young king, her fourth child, later James V; made peace with England; m. (1514) Archibald Douglas, 6th Earl of Angus; forced to give up regency and young king to John Stewart, Duke of Albany (1515), and flee to England. Returned to Scotland, joined French party, allied herself with Albany, repeatedly shifted from one side to the other; abrogated Albany's regency with aid of James Hamilton, proclaimed her son James V (1524); on divorce from Angus, m. (1528) Henry Stewart, 1st Baron Methven; became chief adviser to James on fall of Angus (1528); interceded with her brother Henry VIII for her daughter Lady Margaret Douglas (1536), whose marriage had displeased him, and made various other complaints to him; prevented from escaping to England (1537). Her great-grandson James VI of Scotland became king of England as James I (1603).

**Marg′graf** (märk′gräf), **Andreas Sigismund.** 1709–1782. German chemist; discovered sugar in the sugar beet; founder of beet-sugar industry (1747).

**Mar′ghi·lo·man′** (mär′gē·lō·män′), **Alexandru.** 1854–1925. Rumanian statesman; during World War I, advocated Rumanian neutrality; prime minister of Rumania (1918).

**Mar·go′lies** (mär·gō′lēz), **Morris S. 1851–1936.** American rabbi; chief rabbi of the orthodox congregation, Boston (1889); rabbi of congregation Kehilath Jeshurun, New York (1906–36).

**Mar·go′li·outh** (*orig.* mär·gō′lĭ·ŭth; *later* mär′gŭl-yōōth), **David Samuel.** 1858–1940. English Arabic scholar. Laudian professor of Arabic, Oxford (1889–1937); specialized in study of Arabic commentaries on Aristotle and history of Mohammedanism; Hibbert lecturer (1913); president of Royal Asiatic Society (1934–37); author of *Eclipse of the Abbasid Caliphate* (with H. F. Amedroz; 7 vols., 1920–21), etc.

**Mar·go′lis** (mär·gō′lĭs), **Max Leopold.** 1866–1932. Semitic philologist, b. Merech, Vilna, Russia; to U.S. (1889); professor of Biblical philology, Dropsie Coll. (1909–32). Editor in chief of a Jewish translation of the Scriptures into English (1917). Author of *The Hebrew Scriptures in the Making* (1922), *A History of the Jewish People* (1927; with Alexander Marx), etc.

**Mar·gre·the II** (mär·grā′tĕ), 1940– . queen of Denmark (1972– ). Eldest daughter of King Frederik IX.

**Mar′gue·ritte′** (mȧr′gẽ·rēt′), **Paul.** 1860–1918. French novelist; author of *Tous Quatre* (1885), *Jours d'Épreuve* (1889), *La Force des Choses* (1891), and *Âme d'Enfant* (1894); collaborator with his brother **Victor** (1866–1942) in period between 1896 and 1908, writing *Pariétaire* (1896), *Le Carnaval de Nice* (1897), *Poum* (1897), *Le Désastre* (1898), *Les Braves Gens* (1901), *La Commune* (1904), and *Le Prisme* (1905). Victor published independently a number of novels, and interested himself in emancipation of women, internationalism, and communism.

**Mar·gu'lies** (mär·gū'lēz), **Joseph.** 1896– . Portrait painter, b. in Austria; to U.S. as a boy.

**Mar·hei'ne·ke** (mär·hī'nĕ·kĕ), **Philipp.** 1780–1846. German Protestant theologian and historian; chief works, *Christliche Symbolik* (1810–14), *Geschichte der Deutschen Reformation* (1816–34).

**Marholm, Laura.** Pseudonym of Laura Mohr HANSSON.

**Maria.** Italian and German form of MARIE.

**Maria,** Princess. See FIAMMETTA.

**Ma·ri'a** (*Port.* mȧ·rē'ȧ). Name of two reigning queens of Portugal:

**Maria I.** *In full* **Maria Fran·cis'ca** (frăN·sēsh'kȧ). 1734–1816. Queen (1777–1816). Eldest daughter of King Joseph Emanuel; m. (1760) her uncle, Pedro, younger brother of Joseph Emanuel; crowned with him as joint sovereign (1777); both feeble and weak-minded; control of affairs seized by her mother, Marianna Victoria, who had Pombal (*q.v.*) dismissed, tried, and banished from court; after Pedro's death (1786) Maria became demented; government taken over by her second son, John (1792), who was declared regent (1799–1816; see JOHN VI); died at Rio de Janeiro.

**Maria II.** *Usually known as* **Maria da Glo'ria** (thȧ glô'ryȧ). 1819–1853. Queen (1826–53); dau. of Dom Pedro I, Emperor of Brazil, and granddaughter of John VI of Portugal, b. Rio de Janeiro. Became queen after her father had renounced his rights (1826); fled to England and Brazil because of Civil War (1828–33) that resulted when her uncle Dom Miguel (*q.v.*), regent, usurped the throne; with her father's help, forced Dom Miguel to yield (1834); was declared of age (1834); m. (1835) Duke Auguste of Leuchtenberg (d. 1835), and (1836) Duke Ferdinand of Saxe-Coburg-Gotha (see FERDINAND II). During her reign: new constitution granted (1838–42); insurrections (1846, 1851). Succeeded by son, Pedro V, with Ferdinand as regent.

**Ma·ri'a** (*Ruman.* mä·rē'ä). 1899–1961. Daughter of Ferdinand I, King of Rumania; m. (1922) Alexander I of Yugoslavia.

**Ma·ri'a A·le·xan'drov·na** (mä·rē'ä [*Ger.*] ŭ·lyĭ·ksȧn'-drôv·nŭ [*Russ.*]). 1824–1880. Daughter of Louis II, Grand Duke of Hesse-Darmstadt; m. (1841) Alexander II of Russia; mother of Alexander III.

**Ma·ri'a An'na** (*Ger.* mä·rē'ä än'ä) of Bavaria-Neu'burg (-noi'bŏŏrk). 1667–1740. Queen of Spain; m. Charles II (1689; d. 1700); heroine of Victor Hugo's *Ruy Blas.*

**Ma·ri'a An'nun·zia'ta** (*Ital.* mä·rē'ä än'nōōn·tsyä'tä). 1843–1871. Princess of Sicily; m. (1862) Charles Louis, Archduke of Austria.

**Ma·ri'a An·to'ni·a** (*Ger.* mä·rē'ä än·tō'nē·ä). 1669–1692. Daughter of Emperor Leopold I and Margaret Theresa; m. (1685) Maximilian II Emanuel of Bavaria.

**Ma·ri'a Ca'ro·li'na** (*Ital.* mä·rē'ä kä'rô·lē'nä). 1752–1814. Queen of Naples and the Two Sicilies; daughter of Francis I and Maria Theresa, b. Vienna; m. (1768) Ferdinand I, King of the Two Sicilies, over whom she exercised bad influence; made her favorite Sir John Acton prime minister; forced by Napoleon to leave Naples (1805).

**Ma·ri'a Chris·ti'na** (*Eng.* mȧ·rī'ȧ [mȧ·rē'ȧ] krĭs-tē'nȧ). *Span.* **María Cristina.** Name of two queens of Spain:

**Ma·rí'a Cris·ti'na de Bor·bón'** (mä·rē'ä krēs·tē'nä thā bôr·bôn'). 1806–1878. Daughter of Francis I, King of the Two Sicilies, b. in Naples. Queen of Spain (1829–33) as fourth wife (m. 1829) of Ferdinand VII (*q.v.*); at his death (1833) became regent for her daughter Isabella; during Carlist war (1833–39) her supporters known as Cristinos; took little interest in affairs; on signing law depriving communes of right to elect councils, forced to resign regency (1840); retired to France; after fall of Espartero (1843) returned to Madrid; because of intrigues, very unpopular; driven from Spain by revolution (1854); died at Havre.

**María Cristina.** 1858–1929. Daughter of Archduke Charles Ferdinand of Austria, b. Gross-Seelowitz, Austria; m. Alfonso XII (1879); queen regent from his death (Nov., 1885) until their son Alfonso XIII (b. May, 1886) was declared of age (1902); showed ability and tact; did not oppose real rulers—the army, church, and party leaders; her reign a period of peace and some progress, except for Spanish-American War (1898); American possessions lost; retired at end of regency (1902).

**Ma·ri'a E'le·o·no'ra** (*Ger.* mä·rē'ä ā'lā·ô·nō'rä) of Brandenburg. 1599–1655. Queen of Sweden; daughter of Elector John Sigismund of Brandenburg; m. Gustavus Adolphus of Sweden (1620).

**Ma·ri'a Fë'do·rov'na** (*Russ.* mŭ·ryē'yŭ fyô'dŭ·rôv'nŭ). *Orig.* **Marie Sophia Frederika Dagmar.** 1847–1928. Empress of Russia; daughter of King Christian IX of Denmark, and wife (from 1866) of Grand Duke Aleksandr Aleksandrovich, who became (1881) czar of Russia as Alexander III. Widely known throughout Russia for her philanthropies. After husband's death (1894), lived in retirement until the World War; returned to Russia (1914) and was allowed by the Bolsheviks to live (1917 ff.) in the Crimea under guard. Returned to Denmark after the Treaty of Versailles (1919) and died at Copenhagen.

**Ma·ri'a Hen'ri·et'ta** (*Eng.* mȧ·rī'ȧ [mȧ·rē'ȧ] hĕn'-rĭ·ĕt'ȧ). *Fr.* **Ma'rie' Hen'ri·ette'** (mȧ'rē' äN'ryĕt'). 1836–1902. Daughter of Archduke Joseph of Austria (1776–1847), palatine of Hungary, 5th son of Emperor Leopold II; m. (1853) Prince Leopold of Belgium, later Leopold II.

**Ma'ria Lesz·czyń'ska** (*Pol.* mä'ryä lĕsh·chĭn'y'·skä). *Fr.* **Ma'rie' Lec'zin'ska'** (mȧ'rē' lĕk'zăN'skȧ'). 1703–1768. Daughter of Stanislas Leszczyński, King of Poland; b. Breslau. Settled in Alsace with her father after his expulsion from Poland (1709); m. Louis XV of France (1725); lived in retirement.

**Ma·ri'a Lou·i'sa** (*Eng.* mȧ·rī'ȧ [mȧ·rē'ȧ] lōō·ē'zȧ). *Span.* **María Luisa.** Name of two queens of Spain:

**Ma·rí'a Lu·i'sa Te·re'sa** (*Span.* mä·rē'ä lōō·ē'sä tā·rā'sä) of Parma (1751–1819); daughter of Philip, Duke of Parma; m. Charles IV (1765); queen of Spain (1788–1808); had influence over weak-minded king and controlled affairs; made Godoy minister and with him ruined Spain's finances, finally (1808) bringing about intervention of Napoleon; spent last part of life in France and Italy. **María Luisa Ga'bri·e'la** (gä'brē·ā'lä) of Savoy (1688–1714); daughter of Victor Amadeus II, Duke of Savoy; m. Philip V (1701); queen of Spain (1701–14), greatly aiding Philip in his administration of affairs; acted as regent during absence of Philip in Naples (1701–03) during War of Spanish Succession; mother of two succeeding kings of Spain: Louis I and Ferdinand VI.

**Ma·rí'a Lu·i'sa** (*Span.* mä·rē'ä lōō·ē'sä). 1782–1824.

Queen of Etruria; daughter of Charles IV of Spain and María Luisa of Parma; b. Madrid; m. (1795) eldest son of Duke Ferdinand III of Parma, Louis de Bourbon, who was granted kingdom of Etruria (Tuscany) by Napoleon (1801); on his death (1803) became regent for her son Charles Louis (1803–07); lost kingdom (1807); lived at Madrid, Parma, Nice; failed in attempt to flee to England (1811); prisoner in cloister in Rome (1811–14); granted Lucca by Congress of Vienna (1814).

**Ma·ri'a Ni·ko·la'ev·na** (*Russ.* mŭ·rē'yŭ nyĭ·kŭ·lȧ'-yĕv·nŭ). 1819–1876. Eldest daughter of Nicholas I of Russia; m. (1839) duke of Leuchtenberg (*q.v.*).

**Ma·ri'a Pi'a** (*Ital.* mä·rē'ä pē'ä; *Port.* mȧ·rē'ȧ pē'ȧ). 1847–1911. Queen of Portugal (1862–89); daughter of Victor Emmanuel II of Italy; b. Turin; m. (1862) King Louis; unpopular because of her extravagances and absolutist ideas; dowager queen during reign of Carlos I (1889–1908); returned to Italy after overthrow of Manuel (1910).

**Ma·ri'a So·phi'a A·ma'li·a** (*Ger.* mä·rē'ä zō·fē'ä ä·mä'lē·ä). 1841–1925. Duchess in Bavaria; last queen of the Two Sicilies; sister of Empress Elizabeth of Austria; m. (1859) crown prince of Naples, Francesco Maria Leopoldo, who succeeded to throne (1859) as Francis II and lost crown (1861) when joint campaign of Garibaldi in Sicily and of Piedmontese against Naples succeeded in uniting Italy under Victor Emmanuel II of Sardinia.

**Ma·ri'a The·re'sa** (*Eng.* mȧ·rī'ȧ [mȧ·rē'ȧ] tĕ·rē'sȧ; -zȧ). *Ger.* **Ma·ri'a The·re'si·a** (mä·rē'ä tā·rā'zē·ä). 1717–1780. Archduchess of Austria; queen of Hungary and Bohemia; daughter of Emperor Charles VI; m. (1736) Francis Stephen, Duke of Lorraine (later Francis I, Holy Roman Emperor). By virtue of the Pragmatic Sanction, succeeded to the Hapsburg dominions (1740). Opposed by France, Prussia, Spain, etc., in War of Austrian Succession (1740–48). Lost Silesia to Frederick II of Prussia and Austrian lands in Italy to Naples (1748). By financial reforms and aids to commerce and agriculture, strengthened Austria's resources. Made alliance with France which brought on Seven Years' War (1756–63). Austria humiliated. After death of Francis (1765), associated her son Joseph II, Holy Roman Emperor (1765–90), with her as ruler of hereditary states (1765–80). Joined Russia and Prussia in partition of Poland (1772). See MARIE ANTOINETTE.

**Maria Theresa.** See MARIE THÉRÈSE.

**Mar'i·am'ne** (măr'ĭ·ăm'nē). Name of two of the wives of Herod the Great (*q.v.*): (1) **Mariamne the Has'-mo·nae'an** [hăz'mō·nē'ăn] (60?–?29 B.C.), granddaughter of Hyrcanus II; m. Herod (37 B.C.); mother of Alexander and Aristobulus and grandmother of Herod of Chalcis and Herod Agrippa I; ordered executed by Herod in fit of jealousy. Subject of various works of literature, as those by Voltaire, Hebbel, Tristan L'Hermite, etc. (2) **Mariamne** (d. about 20 B.C.), daughter (or sister) of High Priest Simon; mother of Herod Philip.

**Ma·ria'na** (mä·ryä'nä), **Juan de.** 1536–1623 or 1624. Spanish Jesuit and historian; taught in Jesuit schools in Rome (1561), Sicily (1565), and Paris (1569). Chief work, a history of Spain, written originally in Latin (1592–1605) and later translated into Spanish.

**Ma·ria'na de Aus'tri·a** (mä·ryä'nä thā ous'trē·ä). 1634–1696. Daughter of Emperor Ferdinand III, b. Vienna. Queen of Spain, as wife of Philip IV (m. 1649); regent (1665–75) during minority of their son Charles II; made German Jesuit, Nithard, inquisitor general and minister (1665–69); recognized independence of Portugal (1668); at war with France (1673–75).

**Maricourt,** Sieur **de. Paul Lemoyne.** See under Charles LEMOYNE.

**Marie.** French form of MARIA and MARY.

**Ma·rie'** (*Eng.* mȧ·rē' *or Brit.* mä'rĭ, măr'ĭ). *In full* **Marie Al'ex·an'dra Vic·to'ri·a** (*Eng.* ăl'ĕg·zăn'drȧ [ăl'ĭg-] vĭk·tō'rĭ·ȧ) of Saxe-Coburg. 1875–1938. Queen of Rumania (1914–27; queen dowager, 1927–38); eldest daughter of Alfred (*q.v.*), Duke of Edinburgh and of Saxe-Coburg-Gotha; b. in London; m. (1893) Ferdinand, who became (1914) king of Rumania; influential in determining government policies; on surrender of Rumania to Germany (1917–18) showed great courage and heroism in working for the Red Cross and her people, winning their affection; crowned with Ferdinand (1922) as rulers of Greater Rumania; greatly disturbed over actions of eldest son (see CAROL II); visited the United States (1926); lived in retirement during rule of her grandson Michael (1927–30). Author of several books (all in English) including *My Country* (1916), *Ilderim* (1925), and *The Mask* (1935), fiction; *The Story of My Life* (1934–35); and Rumanian fairy tales. For children, see FERDINAND.

**Ma'rie'** (mȧ'rē'), **Pierre.** 1853–1940. French neurologist; authority on acromegaly, and on diseases of the medulla.

**Ma'rie' A'dé'la'ïde'** (*Fr.* mȧ'rē' ȧ'dā'lȧ'ēd'). 1685–1712. Duchesse de Bour'gogne' (bōōr'gôn'y'); daughter of Victor Amadeus II of Savoy; m. (1697) the dauphin, Louis; mother of Louis XV.

**Marie Adélaïde.** 1894–1924. Daughter of Grand Duke William IV, of the House of Nassau. Grand duchess of Luxemburg (1912–19); dominions overrun by Germans (1914–18); abdicated (1919) in favor of her sister Charlotte and entered a convent in Italy.

**Ma'rie' A'mé'lie' de Bour'bon'** (mȧ'rē' ȧ'mā'lē' dē bōōr'bôɴ'). *Ital.* **Maria Amelia.** 1782–1866. Queen of France (1830–48); daughter of Ferdinand IV, King of Naples; b. Caserta; m. Louis Philippe (1809); lived at Neuilly (1817–28); exiled (1848), lived at Claremont, England (1848–66).

**Ma·rie' An'toi·nette'** (mȧ·rē' [*Brit. also* mä'rĭ, măr'ĭ] ăn't(w)ŏ·nĕt'; *Fr.* mȧ'rē' äɴ'twȧ'nĕt'). *In full* **Josèphe Jeanne Marie Antoinette.** 1755–1793. Daughter of Emperor Francis I and Maria Theresa; b. Vienna. Queen of France; wife of Louis XVI, whom she married (1770) while he was dauphin. Made enemies at French court; unpopular because of foolish pleasantries and dislike for etiquette; after Louis's accession (1774) particularly disliked because of her love of luxury and extravagance and her indifference to miseries of lower classes. Called in contempt **l'Au'tri'chienne'** (lō'trē'-shyĕn'), *i.e.* the Austrian woman. Affair of diamond necklace increased feeling against her (see Cardinal de ROHAN; and Comte de LA MOTTE). Strongly opposed summoning of States-General (1789). Forced to live in Tuileries (1789); see LOUIS XVI. Influenced Louis to attempt flight from France (1791). Tried to secure aid from Austria; insulted by mobs at Tuileries (June 20 and Aug. 10, 1792). Consigned to Temple as prisoner with king and children (1793); tried by Revolutionary Tribunal, found guilty of treason, and guillotined (Oct. 16, 1793). Charges of treason just, but many accusations and much slander against her false. Her courage and frankness at trial and her tragic fate the subject of much literature, treated from many viewpoints.

**Marie Caroline Ferdinande Louise** of Naples. Duchess de Berry (see Charles Ferdinand de BERRY).

**Ma·rie' Cas'i·mir** (*Eng.* mȧ·rē' [*Brit. also* mä'rĭ, măr'ĭ] kăz'ĭ·mĭr). 1641–1716. Queen of Poland; m. John Sobieski (1665), who became king of Poland (1674); expelled from Poland by Polish Diet after death of Sobieski (1696).

**Ma·rie′ Chris·tine′** (*Eng.* mȧ·rē′ krĭs·tēn′; *Fr.* mȧ′rē′ krēs′tēn′). *In full* **Marie Anne Christine Victoire de Bavière.** 1660–1690. Dauphiness of France. See Louis, Grand Dauphin (1661–1711).

**Marie de Bourgogne.** See Mary of Burgundy.

**Ma′rie′ de France** (mȧ′rē′ dē fräns′). Late 12th-century French poet, resident most of her life in England; author of *Fables* and *Lais* (dedicated to Henry II of England).

**Ma′rie′ de Mé′di′cis′** (mȧ′rē′ dē mā′dē′sēs′). *Ital.* **Ma·ri′a de′ Me′di·ci** (mä·rē′ä dā mâ′dē·chē). 1573–1642. Daughter of Francesco de' Medici, Grand Duke of Tuscany; b. Florence; m. as 2d wife Henry IV of France (1600). After murder of Henry (1610), made regent for her son Louis XIII (1610–17), but capricious rule aroused nobles to revolt (1614). Confided in her favorite, Concini, Marquis d'Ancre. Exiled to Blois by king on assumption of rule (1617). Restored to place in king's council (1621) but finally forced by Richelieu to leave France (1631). Until her death, vainly plotted against Richelieu. See Medici.

**Ma′rie′ Jo′sé′** (mȧ′rē′ zhō′zā′), Princess. 1906– . Daughter of King Albert I of Belgium and sister of King Leopold III; m. (1930) Prince Humbert of Italy.

**Ma′rie′ Jo′sèphe′** (*Fr.* mȧ′rē′ zhō′zĕf′) *or* **Ma·ri′a Jo·se′pha** (*Ger.* mä·rē′ä yō·zā′fä) of Saxony. 1731–1767. Daughter of Augustus III, Elector of Saxony and King of Poland. Dauphiness of France; see Louis, Dauphin (1729–65).

**Ma·rie′ Lou·ise′** (*Eng.* mȧ·rē′ [*Brit. also* mä′rĭ, măr′ĭ] lo͞o·ēz′; *Fr.* mȧ′rē′ lwēz′). *Ger.* **Ma·ri′a Lu·i′sa** (mä·rē′ä lo͞o·ē′zä). 1791–1847. Daughter of Archduke Francis, afterward Emperor Francis I, of Austria. Second wife (1810) of Napoleon I; mother of Napoleon II (b. 1811). On Napoleon's abdication, went with son to Schönbrunn, Vienna (1814–16). Made duchess of Parma, Piacenza, and Guastalla (1816–31); her rule mild but wholly without political sagacity. Contracted morganatic marriage (1821) with Count von Neipperg. Secretly married (1833) Count Bombelles.

**Ma′rie′ Lou·ise′ d'Or′lé′ans′** (*Fr.* mȧ′rē′ lwēz′ dôr′-lā′äN′). 1662–1689. Queen of Spain; daughter of Philippe, Duc d'Orléans, brother of Louis XIV of France; m. Charles II of Spain (1679). Promoted French interests at Spanish court; died suddenly, perhaps poisoned by friends of Austria.

**Ma·rie′ of Bra·bant′** (mȧ·rē′ [*Brit. also* mä′rĭ, măr′ĭ] ŭv brȧ·bănt′). *Fr.* **Ma′rie′ de Bra′bant′** (mȧ′rē′ dē brȧ′bäN′). 1260?–1321. Queen of France; m. Philip III of France (1274); patron of the trouvères.

**Ma·rie′ of Würt′tem·berg** (mȧ·rē′ [*Brit. also* mä′rĭ, măr′ĭ] ŭv vür′tĕm·bĕrK; *Ger.* mä·rē′ĕ, mä·rē′). 1813–1839. Wife of Prince Frederick William Alexander. See Louis Philippe.

**Ma′rie′ Thé′rèse′** (*Fr.* mȧ′rē′ tā′râz′). *Called also* **Ma·ri′a The·re′sa** (mȧ·rī′ȧ [mȧ·rē′ȧ] tĕ·rē′sȧ [-zȧ]) of Austria. 1638–1683. Daughter of Philip IV of Spain; b. at the Escorial. Queen consort of Louis XIV of France (m. 1660); by Treaty of the Pyrenees (1659) renounced any claim to Spanish succession; neglected by king for his mistresses. Only one of six children survived her, Dauphin Louis (d. 1711).

**Ma′rié′ton′** (mȧ′ryā′tôN′), **Paul.** 1862–1911. French writer, a leader among the Félibrige; founder of *Revue Félibréenne* (1885); author of several books of verse, literary studies, *La Terre Provençale* (1890), and *La Provence Nouvelle* (a history of Félibrige, 1901).

**Ma′ri·ette′** (mȧ′ryĕt′), **Auguste Édouard.** 1821–1881. French Egyptologist; excavated the Serapeum near modern Saqqara and tombs of Apis bulls (1851); director of governmental excavations in Egypt; cleared historic spots, including ancient temples, great Sphinx, and tombs of Saqqara; suggested the story used in the libretto of Verdi's opera *Aïda.*

**Ma′ri′gnac′** (mȧ′rē′nyȧk′), **Jean Charles Galissard de.** 1817–1894. Swiss chemist; known for determinations of atomic weights and researches in crystallography and on certain rare-earth elements.

**Ma′ri·gnol′li** (mä′rē·nyōl′lē), **Giovanni de′.** fl. 1290–1357. Italian traveler. Sent on mission to khan of Cathay by Pope Benedict XII (1338), reaching Peking (1342), where he remained three or four years; at Columbum (Quilon) in Malabar, discovered church of Latin communion; returned to Europe, delivering letter from khan to Pope Innocent VI.

**Ma′ri′gny′** (mȧ′rē′nyē′), **Enguerrand de.** 1260–1315. French statesman; favorite of Philip the Fair, and grand chamberlain and chief minister of the king (1304 ff.). After death of the king (1314), the feudal lords seized Marigny, had him condemned on a charge of sorcery, and hanged.

**Ma′ril′lac′** (mȧ′rē′yȧk′). Name of a family of Auvergne, including: **Guillaume de Marillac** (d. 1573), master of royal accounts (1555) and comptroller general of France (1569). **Charles** (1501?–1560), ecclesiastic and diplomat, ambassador to Constantinople (to 1538) and to London (to 1543); in Switzerland (1547) and Brussels (1548–49); archbishop of Vienna (1557) and an opponent of the Guises. **Michel** (1563–1632), councilor of state, guardian of the seals (1626). **Louis** (1573–1632), soldier, marshal of France (1629); involved in intrigues against Richelieu; executed.

**Ma′rin′** (mȧ′răN′), **Louis.** 1871–1960. French politician; member of Chamber of Deputies (from 1905); head of political group known as L'Union Républicaine Démocratique (from 1925).

**Ma·ri′na** (mä·rē′nä) *or* **Ma·lin′tzin** (mä·lĭn′tsĭn). 1501?–?1550. Aztec slave, mistress of Hernando Cortes (*q.v.*); acted as Maya and Nahua interpreter and otherwise aided Cortes in Spanish conquest of Mexico.

**Ma′ri·net′ti** (mä′rē·nāt′tē), **Emilio Filippo Tommaso.** 1876–1944. Italian poet and writer; founded futurist movement in literature (1911). War correspondent, Libya and the Balkans (1911–14); officer in World War (1914–18); joined Fascist party (1919). Among his works are *La Conquête des Étoiles* (1902), *Mafarka le Futuriste* (1910), *Le Futurisme* (1911), *Otto Anime in una Bomba* (1919), *Il Tamburo di Fuoco* (1922), *Futurismo e Fascismo* (1924), and *Novelle colle Labbra Tinte* (1928).

**Ma·ri′ni** (mä·rē′nē) *or* **Ma·ri′no** (-nō), **Giambattista.** *Known as* **il Ca′va·lier′ Ma·ri′no** (ēl kä′vä·lyĕr′). 1569–1625. Italian poet; protégé of Cardinal Pietro Aldobrandini (Rome); accompanied patron to Ravenna (1605) and Turin (1608); won favor of Charles Emmanuel I (Turin). To Paris (1615); protégé of Marie de Médicis (Paris, 1615–23). Notable as leading exponent of concettism in Italian 17th-century literature; works include *Adone* (1623), a leading example of concettism, and subject of a long and bitter literary polemic.

**Ma·rin′ko·vić** (mä·rēn′kō·vēt′y′; *Angl.* -vĭch), **Vojislav.** 1876–1935. Yugoslav statesman; member of the Serbian legislature (1908 ff.); member of the coalition cabinet (1914–17) during the World War. Aided in drafting declaration (1917) for formation of a kingdom of Serbs, Croats, and Slovenes, each with their own constitution. Active in organization of the Democratic Union party (1919). Member of various cabinets (from 1918), and premier of Yugoslavia for a few months (April–June, 1932).

**Ma′ri′no′ni′** (mȧ′rē′nô′nē′), **Hippolyte.** 1823–1904.

French inventor of a rotary press capable of printing 40,000 impressions per hour, and another capable of printing 20,000 six-color polychromes per hour; editor of *Petit Journal* (from 1883).

**Ma·ri'nus** (mȧ·rī'nŭs). Name of two popes (see *Table of Popes*, Nos. 108, 129): **Marinus I,** *also known as* **Martin II;** pope (882–884). **Marinus II,** *also known as* **Martin III;** pope (942–946).

**Marinus of Tyre** (tīr). Greek geographer of the early 2d century A.D.; regarded as founder of mathematical geography; predecessor of Ptolemy.

**Ma'ri·o** (mä'ryō), **Giuseppe.** Marchese **di Can'di·a** (dē kän'dyä). 1810–1883. Italian operatic tenor; among his chief roles were Otello in Rossini's *Otello*, Almaviva in *Il Barbiere di Siviglia*, Manrico in *Il Trovatore;* m. the soprano singer Giulia Grisi (*q.v.*).

**Mar'i·on** (măr'ĭ·ŭn; mâr'-), **Francis.** 1732?–1795. Known as "the Swamp Fox." American Revolutionary commander, b. prob. in Berkeley County, S.C. Served through Revolutionary War; commanded militia troops in South Carolina, harassing British forces by raids, and escaping into the swamps and forests when hard pressed. Took part in battle of Eutaw Springs.

**Ma'ri·otte'** (mȧ'ryôt'), **Edme.** 1620?–1684. French physicist; made many discoveries in hydrodynamics. The name *Mariotte's law* is sometimes given to Boyle's law since Mariotte discovered independently the principle previously formulated by Boyle.

**Mariotti, Luigi.** See A. C. N. GALLENGA.

**Ma'ris** (mä'rĭs). Name of three brothers, Dutch painters, closely associated in their work: **Jacob** (1837–1899), best known as a landscape painter, esp. of Dutch scenes. **Matthijs** (1839–1917); to London (1885) to design stained-glass windows. **Willem** (1844–1910); resided chiefly in London; excelled in pastoral scenes.

**Marischal,** Earls. See KEITH family.

**Ma·ris'co** (mȧ·rĭs'kō) *or* **Marsh** (märsh), **Richard de.** d. 1226. English ecclesiastic; one of King John's worst advisers. Advised persecution of Cistercians (1210); justiciar (1213–14), chancellor (1214), bishop of Durham (1217–26). His nephew **Adam de Marisco** *or* **de Marsh** (d. ?1257) was a Franciscan scholar and theologian; student and friend of Bishop Robert Grosseteste; spiritual adviser of Simon de Montfort.

**Ma'ri'tain'** (mȧ'rē'tăN'), **Jacques.** 1882–1973. French philosopher; Ph.D., Sorbonne; brought up Protestant; became Roman Catholic (1906); known as liberal Catholic apologist; prof. at Institut Catholique, Paris (1913–40), Columbia (1940–44), Princeton (1948–53); amb. to Holy See (1945–48). Of his many works those translated into English include *Prayer and Intelligence* (with his wife **Raïssa** 1883–1960), *Art and Scholasticism, An Introduction to Philosophy, The Angelic Doctor, The Degrees of Knowledge, True Humanism, Religion in the Modern World.*

**Mar'i·us** (mâr'ĭ·ŭs), **Gaius.** 155?–86 B.C. Roman general and political leader; tribune of plebs (119); praetor (115); consul (107, 104, 103, 102, 101, 100, 86). Fought against Jugurtha (107–106) and against the Cimbri and Teutones (104–101), winning decisive victories over Teutones at Aix (102) and over Cimbri near Vercellae (101). Rivalry with Sulla led to civil war (88); at first driven from Rome, but returned and, with aid of Cinna, captured city and revenged himself by proscribing leaders of aristocratic party. His adopted son, **Gaius** (109–82? B.C.), consul (82), continued resistance against Sulla; defeated and committed suicide.

**Ma'ri·us** (mä'rē·o͝os), **Simon.** *Properly* **Mayr** (mīr). 1570–1624. German astronomer; credited with independent discovery of four moons of Jupiter (1610).

**Mar'i·us Victorinus** (mâr'ĭ·ŭs). See VICTORINUS.

**Ma'ri'vaux'** (mȧ'rē'vō'), **Pierre Car'let' de Cham'-blain' de** (kȧr'lĕ' ·dē shäN'blăN' dē). 1688–1763. French playwright and novelist; after studying law, turned to the theater and wrote *L'Amour et la Vérité* (comedy; 1720), *Annibal* (tragedy), *Arlequin Poli par l'Amour, La Surprise de l'Amour* (1722), *Le Jeu de l'Amour et du Hasard* (1730), *L'Heureux Stratagème* (1733), *Le Legs* (1736), and *L'Épreuve* (1740); his outstanding novels are *La Vie de Marianne* (1731–41) and *Le Paysan Parvenue* (1735).

**Mar'jo·ri·banks** (märch'băngks), **Edward.** 2d Baron **Tweed'mouth** (twēd'mŭth; -mouth). 1849–1909. English cabinet minister. Liberal M.P. (1880–94) and chief Liberal whip under Gladstone (1892); lord privy seal and chancellor of Duchy of Lancaster (1894–95); first lord of admiralty (1905–08), speeded naval construction to meet German rivalry; resigned because of furor over his alleged premature disclosure of naval estimates to German emperor.

**Mark** (märk), Saint. *In full* **John Mark.** The Evangelist; fellow worker with Paul and Barnabas (*Acts* xii. 25, xv. 37 ff.; *Col.* iv. 10; *Philemon* 24); traditionally regarded as author of the second Gospel.

**Mark,** Saint. Pope (bishop of Rome; 336).

**Mark Antony** *or* **Anthony.** See Marcus ANTONIUS (83?–30 B.C.).

**Mark'ham** (mär'kăm), Sir **Clements Robert.** 1830–1916. English geographer and historical writer. Served in navy (1844–52); member, Board of Control (1854), East India Co., and in charge of geographical work (1867–77); introduced Cinchona culture from South America into India. Author of works on Peru, Tibet, Persia, lives of Fairfax, the fighting de Veres, John Davys the navigator, and *The Lands of Silence*, a history of Arctic and Antarctic explorations (completed posthumously). His cousin and biographer Sir **Albert Hastings Markham** (1841–1918), Arctic explorer, entered navy (1856), brought back survivors of *Polaris* American Arctic expedition (1873); commanded the *Alert* in British Arctic expedition of Sir George Nares (1875–76), reaching without dogs northern point not exceeded till 1895; rear admiral (1891).

**Markham, Edwin,** *in full* **Charles Edwin.** 1852–1940. American poet, b. Oregon City, Ore.; taken to California as a child of five; educ. San Jose Normal School. Teacher, school principal, and school superintendent in California. Moved to New York (1899) and engaged in lecturing and writing. Achieved sensational success with *The Man With the Hoe* (1899). Other works: *Lincoln, and Other Poems* (1901), *The Shoes of Happiness, and Other Poems* (1915), *California the Wonderful* (1915), *Gates of Paradise* (1920), *The Ballad of the Gallows Bird* (1926), *Eighty Songs at Eighty* (1932), *The Star of Araby* (1937).

**Markham, Gervase** *or* **Jervis.** 1568?–1637. English soldier in Low Countries and Ireland; translator, compiler, and original writer on forestry, agriculture, veterinary art; author of *A Discource of Horsemanshippe* (1593), *The Most Honorable Tragedie of Sir Richard Grinvile, Knight* (1595; poem on the last fight of the *Revenge*), *The English Arcadia* (1607; poem in continuation of Sidney's *Arcadia*), *Country Contentments* (1611), and other poems and plays.

**Markham, William.** 1635?–1704. English colonial governor in America; commissioned deputy governor of Pennsylvania (1681); provincial secretary (1685–91); deputy governor of the lower counties (1691–93); lieutenant governor or governor of province (1693–99).

**Mar·kie'vicz** (mär·kyĕ'vēch), Countess **de. Constance Georgine,** *nee* **Gore'-Booth'** (gōr'bo͞oth'). 1876–1927.

Irish politician; m. Polish Count Casimir Dunin de Markievicz (1900). Joined Sinn Fein movement and became noted orator and leader; sentenced to death for being involved in the Easter Rebellion (1916), but released after the amnesty (1917). Vigorous supporter of Eamon de Valera, and minister of labor in his cabinet; elected member of Dail Eireann (1922, 1923, 1927).

**Mar'ko Kra'lje·vić** (mär'kô krä'lyĕ·vēt'y'; *Angl.* -vĭch), *i.e.* "Marko, son of the king." 1335?–1394. Serbian hero, son of King Vukašin; according to tradition, lived 300 years and used his great physical strength against oppressors, esp. the Turks. Hero of Serbian, Rumanian, and Bulgarian folk literature.

**Mar'ko·va** (mär'kô·vȧ), Dame **Alicia**. *Originally* **Lilian Alicia Marks.** 1910– . British ballerina. Vice president, Royal Acad. of Dancing (1958); director, Metropolitan Opera Ballet (1963– ).

**Marks** (märks), **Percy.** 1891–1956. American teacher and writer; author of *The Plastic Age* (1924), *Martha* (1925), *Which Way Parnassus?* (1926), *The Unwilling God* (1929), *Craft of Writing* (1932), *And Points Beyond* (1937), *Full Flood* (1942), etc.

**Markus.** See MARCOUSSIS.

**Marlborough,** Duke and Duchess of: see John CHURCHILL; Duke of: see SPENCER family.

**Marlborough,** Earl of. See James LEY.

**Marle'berge** (märl'bûrg), **Thomas de.** *Also* **Thomas of Marl'bor·ough** (môl'bŭ·rŭ; -brŭ; märl'-). d. 1236. English ecclesiastic and scholar of canon and civil law.

**Marlinski, Cossack.** Pseudonym of A. A. BESTUZHEV.

**Marlitt, E.** Pseudonym of Eugenie JOHN.

**Mar'lowe** (mär'lō), **Christopher.** 1564–1593. English dramatist, b. Canterbury, son of shoemaker. M.A., Cantab. (1587); attached himself early as dramatist to the Admiral's Men, the earl of Nottingham's theatrical company which produced most of his plays; in *Tamburlaine the Great* (acted 1587 or 1588; pub. 1590), first dramatist to discover vigor and variety of blank verse; wrote *The Tragedy of Dr. Faustus* (entered at Stationers' Hall, 1601); produced *The Jew of Malta* (after 1588; pub. 1633) and *Edward II* (1593; pub. 1594), and inferior plays, as *The Massacre at Paris* and *Tragedy of Dido* (finished by Nash). Credited on internal evidence with part authorship of *Titus Andronicus;* credited with second and third parts of *Henry VI*, completed and revised by Shakespeare; translated Ovid's *Amores* and Lucan's *Pharsalia;* paraphrased part of Musaeus's *Hero and Leander* in heroic couplets (1598); author of short poems, including *Come live with me and be my love* (to which Raleigh wrote a reply, *If all the world and love were young*). Denounced for holding and propagating atheistical opinions and for revolt against conventional morality.

**Marlowe, Julia.** *Stage name of* **Sarah Frances Frost** (frôst). 1866–1950. Actress, b. in Cumberlandshire, Eng.; to U.S. (1871); m. 1st Robert Taber (divorced 1899), 2d (1911) Edward Hugh Sothern (*q.v.*). Starred (1888–1924) in Shakespearean and other dramatic roles.

**Mar'mier'** (mȧr'myā'), **Xavier.** 1809–1892. French man of letters; curator (1846) and administrator (1884) of Bibliothèque Sainte-Geneviève in Paris; author of number of travel books, histories of German, Danish, and Swedish literatures, and translations.

**Mar'mi·on** (mär'mĭ·ŭn), **Shackerley** *or* **Shakerley.** 1603–1639. English dramatist; imitated Ben Jonson. Author of epic *Cupid and Psyche* (1637) and three comedies, *Holland's Leaguer* (1632), *A Fine Companion* (1633), and *The Antiquary* (pub. 1641).

**Már'mol** (mär'môl), **José.** 1818?–1871. Argentine writer; banished by the dictator Rosas (*q.v.*); author of plays, poetry, and the historical novel *La Amalia* (1855).

**Mar'mont'** (mȧr'môɴ'), **Auguste Frédéric Louis Viesse de** (vyĕs' dē). Duc **de Ra'guse'** (dē rȧ'güz'). 1774–1852. French soldier; served in Napoleonic campaigns, notably at Marengo (1800), Ulm (1805), Znojmo (1809) and in Germany (1813–14); created duc de Raguse (1808) and marshal of France (1809). Honored by Louis XVIII at Restoration; created peer of France (1814) and commissioned major general; tried unsuccessfully to suppress Revolution of 1830. Retired thereafter to Vienna.

**Mar'mon'tel'** (mȧr'môɴ'tĕl'), **Jean François.** 1723–1799. French writer; author of tragedies *Denys le Tyran* (1748), *Aristomène* (1749), *Cléopâtre* (1750), *Les Héraclides* (1752), and *Funérailles de Sésostris* (1753); contributed to the *Encyclopédie*, and published collections of his articles; wrote also *Contes Moraux* (1761), *Bélisaire* (philosophical novel, 1767), *Les Incas* (historical novel), and librettos for several light operas.

**Mar'nix** (mär'nĭks), **Philip van.** Baron **Sint Al'de·gon'de** (sĭnt äl'dĕ·gôn'dĕ). 1538–1598. Flemish diplomat and writer; dispatched on a number of missions by William of Orange, and finally taken prisoner by the Spaniards. Translated the *Psalms* of David into Flemish, and wrote the national song *Wilhelmuslied.*

**Maro, Publius Vergilius.** See VERGIL.

**Maroboduus.** See MARBO.

**Ma'ro·chet'ti** (mä'rô·kāt'tē), **Carlo.** 1805–1867. Sculptor, b. Turin, Italy, under French Empire; French citizen through father's naturalization (1814). Executed sculptures in Paris, including relief of *Assumption* in the Madeleine; at Revolution of 1848, moved to London where he produced equestrian statue of Richard Cœur de Lion for Great Exhibition (1851) and statues of Queen Victoria, duke of Wellington, and others, and obelisk in Waterloo Place.

**Ma'ró·czy** (mŏ'rō·tsĭ), **Géza.** 1870– . Hungarian chess master; won first prize at Monte Carlo (1902; 1904) and Ostend (1905), and tied with Alekhine and Bogoljubow for first prize at Karlsbad (1923).

**Ma'rot'** (mȧ'rō'), **Clément.** 1495?–1544. French poet; long resident in court of Francis I; among his works are *Le Temple de Cupido* (allegorical poem, 1515), *L'Enfer* (1532), various *Épîtres, Rondeaux, Épigrammes, Ballades,* etc.; also, translations of fifty-two *Psalmes* and of selections from Vergil, Ovid, and Petrarch. His father, **Jean Marot,** *orig.* **Des'ma'retz'** [dā'mȧ'rā'] (d. 1524), was also a poet in court of Francis I.

**Marot, Jean.** 1619?–1679. French architect. His son **Daniel** (1660?–?1712), also an architect, accompanied William of Orange to England, returning to Holland in 1702; designed great audience chamber in palace at The Hague.

**Ma·ro'zi·a** (mȧ·rō'zhĭ·ȧ; *Ital.* mä·rô'tsyä). d. before 945. Daughter of Theodora and Theophylact; wife (1st) of Alberic, (2d) of Guido of Tuscany, and (3d) of Hugh, King of Italy; exercised great influence at the papal court, and succeeded in elevating her son to the papal throne as John XI; finally imprisoned by her son Alberic II (932).

**Mar·quand'** (mär·kwŏnd'), **Henry Gurdon.** 1819–1902. American financier, b. New York City. One of organizers and benefactors of Metropolitan Museum of Art, New York City; president of the museum (1889–1902). His son **Allan** (1853–1924) was an educator; professor of history of art, Princeton (1883–1924); on editorial staff of *American Journal of Archaeology* (1885–1924); founded and financed *Princeton Monographs in Art and Archaeology* and contributed several studies on the della Robbias; author of *Greek Architecture* (1909); coauthor, with A. L. Frothingham, of *A Textbook of the History of Sculpture* (1896).

**Marquand, John Phillips.** 1893–1960. American writer, b. Wilmington, Del. Lieutenant of field artillery in World War; engaged in Marne-Aisne, St. Mihiel, and Meuse-Argonne offensives. Author of *The Unspeakable Gentleman* (1922), *The Black Cargo* (1925), *Haven's End* (1933), several detective novels around the character Mr. Moto, *The Late George Apley* (1937; Pulitzer prize), *Wickford Point* (1939), *H. M. Pulham, Esq.* (1941), *So Little Time* (1943), *Repent in Haste* (1945).

**Mar′quardt** (mär′kvärt), **Joachim.** 1812–1882. German antiquarian; made special study of Roman antiquities. Continued to completion W. A. Becker's *Handbuch der Römischen Alterthümer*, and later collaborated with Theodor Mommsen and other scholars in preparing a revision of the entire work.

**Mar′quet′** (mȧr′kĕ′), **Albert.** 1875–1947. French painter; admirer of Cézanne; best known for landscapes of Paris, Le Havre, Honfleur, Rouen, Rotterdam, etc.

**Mar′quette′** (mȧr′kĕt′; *Angl.* mär·kĕt′), **Jacques.** *Known as* **Père Marquette** (pâr; *Angl.* pẹ̄r). 1637–1675. Jesuit missionary and explorer in America, b. Laon, France. To New France (1666); on mission among Ottawa Indians (1668); founded mission of St. Ignace on north shore of Straits of Mackinac (1671). Accompanied Jolliet on voyage down Wisconsin and Mississippi rivers, to the mouth of the Arkansas River, and back to Lake Michigan via the Illinois River (1673). His journal of the voyage was first published in 1681.

**Mar′quis** (mär′kwĭs), **Don,** *in full* **Donald Robert Perry.** 1878–1937. American journalist and humorist, b. Walnut, Ill. Associated with Joel Chandler Harris in editing *The Uncle Remus Magazine* (1907–09). On staff, New York *Sun* (1912–22), conducted column "The Sun Dial," in which he introduced mehitabel the cat, archy the cockroach, the Old Soak, etc. On staff, New York *Tribune* (1922–25). Much of the material in his column was collected and printed in book form, as *The Old Soak* (1921), *archy and mehitabel* (1927), *Off the Arm* (1930), *archy does his part* (1935), etc. His play *The Old Soak* was successfully produced (1922).

**Marquis au court nez.** See GUILLAUME D'ORANGE.

**Marr** (mär), **Carl von.** 1858–1936. American-born painter in Germany, b. Milwaukee, Wis.; professor (1893–1925) and director (1919–25), Munich Academy of Fine Arts.

**Mar·ra′di** (mär·rä′dē), **Giovanni.** *Pseudonym* **G. La·bro′nio** (lä·brô′nyō). 1852–1922. Italian poet, b. Leghorn; teacher at Leghorn; known chiefly as nature poet. Among his works are *Canzoni Moderne* (1879), *Fantasie Marine* (1880), *Ballate Moderne* (1894), *Rapsodia Garibaldiana* (1899), *Poesia della Riscossa* (1918), and prose criticisms.

**Mar′ri·ott** (măr′ĭ·ŭt), **Charles.** 1869–1957. English novelist and art critic; apothecary dispenser (1890–1901); art critic on London *Times* (from 1924). Author of *The Column* (1901), *The Kiss of Helen* (1908), *The Catfish* (1913), *Modern Art* (1917), *A Key to Modern Painting* (1938), etc.

**Marriott,** Sir **John Arthur Ransome.** 1859–1945. English historian; M.P. (1917–29). Author of *Makers of Modern Italy* (1889), *George Canning and his Times* (1903), *England since Waterloo* (1913), *The Eastern Question*...(1917), *Syndicalism*...(1921), *England under the Tudors* (1922), *The Mechanism of the Modern State* (2 vols., 1927), *A History of Europe from 1815 to 1923* (1931), *Evolution of Modern Europe, 1453–1923* (1932), *The Evolution of the British Empire and Commonwealth* (1939), etc.

**Mar′ro·quín′** (mär′rō·kēn′), **José Manuel.** 1827–1908. Colombian politician and philologist. President of Colombia (1900–04); lost Panama by revolution (1903). Author of books on Castilian grammar and spelling.

**Mar′ry·at** (măr′ĭ·ăt), **Frederick.** *Known as* Captain **Marryat.** 1792–1848. English naval commander and novelist of sea life, b. London; grandson of **Thomas Marryat** (1730–1792), physician and wit of Bristol. In Burmese War, commanded successful expedition up Bassein River (1825); retired (1830). Visited Canada during Papineau's revolt (1837) and toured U.S., where he wrote *The Phantom Ship* (1839); settled on farm, Langham, Norfolk (1843). Author of novels of sea life largely based on his own experiences, including *Frank Mildmay* (1829), *Peter Simple* (1834), *Jacob Faithful* (1834), *Mr. Midshipman Easy* (1836); also of *Japhet in Search of a Father* (autobiography of a foundling, 1836), *Snarleyyow, or the Dog Fiend* (historical novel, 1837), and *Poor Jack* (1840); in his last days, of books expressly for boys, including *Masterman Ready* (1841), *The Settlers in Canada* (1844), *The Children of the New Forest* (1847). His daughter **Florence** (1838–1899), successively Mrs. Church and Mrs. Lean, novelist, lecturer, operatic singer, and comedienne, wrote his biography (1872), also many novels, a few plays, and works on spiritualism.

**Mars** (mȧrs), Mlle. *Stage name of* **Anne Françoise Hippolyte Bou′tet′** (bo͞o′tĕ′). 1779–1847. French actress; renowned as comedienne; member of Théâtre Français company, and a favorite with Napoleon I; excelled in interpretations of plays of Molière and Marivaux; retired from stage (1841). See MONVEL.

**Marsal, Frédéric François.** See FRANÇOIS-MARSAL.

**Mar′schall von Bie′ber·stein** (mär′shäl fôn bē′bẽr·shtīn). German noble family, including: Baron **Karl Wilhelm** (1763–1817), Baden diplomat and representative at the Congress of Vienna (1814). His brother Baron **Friedrich August** (1768–1827), traveler and botanist. Karl Wilhelm's grandson Baron **Adolf Hermann** (1842–1912), German statesman and diplomat, member of the Baden upper chamber (1875–83) and of the imperial diet (1878–81), Prussian minister of state (1894–97), and German ambassador in Constantinople (1897–1912) and London (1912); regarded as important factor in influencing Turkey in favor of German policies.

**Marsch′ner** (märsh′nẽr), **Heinrich.** 1795–1861. German composer; director, Dresden court opera (1823), at Leipzig (1827–31), and at Hanover (from 1831). Among his compositions are the operas *Vampyr* (1828), *Hans Heiling* (1833).

**Marsh** (märsh), **Adam de** and **Richard de.** See MARISCO.

**Marsh,** Sir **Edward Howard.** 1872–1953. English writer and wit; B.A., Cambridge (1895). Private secretary to Winston Churchill (1917–22, 1924–29), J. H. Thomas (1929–36), and others. Author of *Memoir of Rupert Brooke* (1918), *A Number of People* (1939), etc.

**Marsh, George Perkins.** 1801–1882. American lawyer, diplomat, and philologist; member of U.S. House of Representatives (1843–49); U.S. minister to Turkey (1849–53), to Italy (1861–82); American collaborator on *Oxford English Dictionary;* author of *The Origin and History of the English Language* (1862), *Man and Nature* ...(1864), etc.

**Marsh, James.** 1794–1846. British chemist; engaged by Woolwich arsenal; assistant to Faraday at Royal Military Academy; invented test (Marsh test) for arsenic.

**Marsh,** Dame **Ngai′o** (nī′ō). 1899– . New Zealand writer; known esp. for her detective fiction.

**Marsh, Othniel Charles.** 1831–1899. American paleontologist, b. Lockport, N.Y. Professor, Yale (1866–99). Led expeditions to the West in search for fossils (from

1870). Made large fossil collection, now at Yale. Author of *Introduction and Succession of Vertebrate Life in America* (1877) and monographs including *Extinct Order of Gigantic Mammals*, etc.

**Marsh, Reginald.** 1898–1954. American painter, b. in Paris, France, of American parentage. Illustrator for New York journals; known esp. for his paintings of New York City scenes. His *Sorting Mail* and *Transfer of Mail from Liner to Tugboat* are among the murals in the U.S. Post Office Department building in Washington, D.C.

**Marsh, Sylvester.** 1803–1884. American inventor and promoter; projected and built inclined railway up Mount Washington, N.H. (1866–69), inventing special designs of engines for ascending grades, a cog rail (patented 1867), and an atmospheric brake (patented 1870).

**Mar'shal** (mär'shăl). Name of an English family of hereditary marshals including among its members earls of Pembroke:

**William Marshal** (d. 1219), 1st Earl of **Pem'broke** (pĕm'bro͝ok) and **Strig'ul** (?strĭg'ŭl) through marriage, on accession of Richard I, with daughter of Richard de Clare, 2d Earl of Pembroke and Strigul (see CLARE family); performed exploits as crusader in Holy Land (c. 1185–87); one of regents during Richard's absence (1190); declared for King John (1199); supported royal side in Barons' War; one of John's executors and regent of kingdom (1216); led young King Henry III's army against Prince Louis and rebels at battle of Lincoln (1217) and effected settlement by Treaty of Lambeth (1217). Succeeded by his five sons successively in the earldom.

**William** (d. 1231), 2d earl; eldest son of 1st earl; one of 25 executors of Magna Carta (1215); fought alongside his father at Lincoln (1217); as justiciar in Ireland, forced submission of Hugh de Lacy (1224); m. Henry III's sister Eleanor (1224); fought with Henry III in Brittany and conducted raids in Normandy and Anjou.

**Richard** (d. 1234), 3d earl; 2d son of 1st earl; led baronial party in appeal to Henry III to dismiss foreigners (1233); made terms with Llewelyn ab Iorwerth, defeated royal forces, and ejected Peter des Roches and king's other advisers that had come from Poitou (1234); treacherously betrayed (1234).

**John Marshal** (1170?–1235), 1st Baron **Marshal of Hing'ham** (hĭng'ăm); nephew of 1st earl; received grants of land for service in Flanders with his uncle and in Ireland, where he was marshal (1207); supported King John against barons; fought against French at Lincoln (1217); justice and diplomatic agent (after 1225).

**Mar'shall** (mär'shăl), **Alfred.** 1842–1924. English economist; professor, Cambridge (1885–1908). Author of *Principles of Economics* (1890), *Industry and Trade* (1919), and *Money, Credit and Commerce* (1923).

**Marshall, Archibald.** 1866–1934. English novelist; founder (1905) and head (1905–07) of publishing house of Alston Rivers. Novels include *The House of Merrilees* (1905), *The Graftons* (1919), *The Education of Anthony Dare* (1924), *Simple People* (1928), *The Claimants* (1933), and a series about the fictional Clinton family, including *The Squire's Daughter* (1909), *The Honour of the Clintons* (1913), etc.

**Marshall, Bruce.** 1899– . Scottish novelist; author of *Father Malachy's Miracle* (1931), *The Uncertain Glory* (1935), *Luckypenny* (1937), etc.

**Marshall, Christopher.** 1709–1797. Revolutionary leader in America, b. prob. in Dublin, Ireland; to America (1727). Best known for his *Remembrancer*, a diary he kept during the Revolution (first pub. at length, 1877).

**Marshall, Edison.** 1894–1967. American writer of stories dealing with western U.S.; awarded O. Henry memorial prize for short story *The Heart of Little Shikara* (1921).

**Marshall, Francis Hugh.** 1878–1949. English physiologist; author of *The Physiology of Reproduction* (1910), *Introduction to Sexual Physiology* (1925), etc.

**Marshall, Frank James.** 1877–1944. American chess master, b. New York City. Winner in international competitions, Cambridge Springs, Pa. (1904), Nuremberg, Ger. (1906), Budapest, Hung. (1912). Won chess championship of U.S. from J. W. Showalter (1909) and held it continuously until his resignation (1936).

**Marshall, George Catlett.** 1880–1959. American army officer, b. Uniontown, Pa.; educ. V.M.I. (1897–1901). Served with A.E.F. in France in World War I (1917–19); engaged at battle of Cantigny, and in the Aisne-Marne, St. Mihiel, and Meuse-Argonne offensives. Aide-de-camp to Gen. Pershing (1919–24). Served in China (1924–27). Chief of staff, U.S. army (1939–45; retired); general of the army (1944). U.S. ambassador to China (1945–47); secretary of state (1947–49); of defense (1950–51). President, Amer. Red Cross (1949–50); originator of Marshall Plan; awarded Nobel peace prize (1953).

**Marshall, Henry Rutgers.** 1852–1927. American psychologist, b. New York City. Practiced architecture (from 1878). Interested himself in psychology (from 1888), and wrote *Pain, Pleasure, and Aesthetics* (1894), *The Relation of Aesthetics to Psychology* (1905), *Mind and Conduct* (1919), *The Beautiful* (1924), etc.

**Marshall, Humphry.** 1722–1801. Cousin of John Bartram (*q.v.*). American botanist, b. in Chester County, Pa. Author of *Arbustrum Americanum, the American Grove* (1785), a catalogue on the Linnaean plan of American forest trees and shrubs.

**Marshall, James Wilson.** 1810–1885. American pioneer in California, b. in Hunterdon County, N.J.; to California (1844–45). Discovery of gold (Jan. 24, 1848) during excavation for a sawmill that he was building in partnership with John A. Sutter (*q.v.*) started famous gold rush of 1849.

**Marshall, John.** 1755–1835. Son of Thomas Marshall. American jurist, b. near Germantown, Fauquier County, Va. Served in Continental army with his father through American Revolution; at Brandywine, Germantown, Monmouth, Valley Forge. Admitted to bar in Fauquier County (1780); practiced, Richmond, Va. (from 1783). Member of Virginia executive council (1782–95), of House of Burgesses (1782–88). Became recognized Federalist leader in Virginia. Served as one of American commissioners to France (1797, 1798) to obtain redress for French hostile actions. Member, U.S. House of Representatives (1799–1800). U.S. secretary of state (1800–01). Chief justice of U.S. Supreme Court (1801–35). Fundamental principles for constitutional interpretation were established by his important decisions, as in Marbury vs. Madison, McCulloch vs. Maryland, Dartmouth College vs. Woodward, Cohens vs. Virginia, Gibbons vs. Ogden. Elected to American Hall of Fame (1900).

**Marshall, Louis.** 1856–1929. American Jewish lawyer and leader, b. Syracuse, N.Y. Member of New York State constitutional conventions (1890, 1894, 1915). Mediator in effecting settlement of New York cloakmakers' strike (1910); arbitrator in clothingworkers' strike (1919). A founder of Jewish Welfare Board; chairman, American Jewish Relief Committee, organized to raise funds during World War I. Championed minority protective clauses in Versailles peace treaties (1919). Labored in Zionist cause (from 1917).

**Marshall, Stephen.** 1594?–1655. English Presbyterian preacher and leader, one of five clergymen who wrote (1641) as Smectymnuus (*q.v.*). Powerful preacher; influenced elections for Short Parliament (1640); swayed House of Commons by sermons on episcopal and liturgical reform; member of Westminster Assembly (1643); participated in preparation of Shorter Catechism (1647).

**Marshall, Thomas.** 1730–1802. American Revolutionary leader, b. in Westmoreland County, Va. Member, Virginia House of Burgesses (1761–67; 1769–73; 1775). Served in Continental army through American Revolution; at battle of Trenton and battle of Brandywine. Opened surveyor's office in Kentucky and moved his family there (1783); served as surveyor of revenue for the District of Ohio (to 1797). His oldest son (see John MARSHALL) was chief justice of the United States.

**Marshall, Thomas Riley.** 1854–1925. Vice-president of the United States, b. North Manchester, Ind.; practiced law, Columbia City, Ind. (1875–1908). Governor of Indiana (1909–13); vice-president of the United States (1913–21).

**Marshall, Thurgood.** 1908– . American lawyer, b. Baltimore, Md.; associate justice, U.S. Supreme Court (from 1967).

**Marshall, William Calder.** 1813–1894. Scottish sculptor; designed symbolic group *Agriculture* on Albert Memorial, Hyde Park.

**Marshall, William Louis.** 1846–1920. American army engineer, b. Washington, Ky.; grad. U.S.M.A., West Point (1868). On river and harbor work (1876–99); headquarters at New York City (1899–1908), where he completed Ambrose Channel. Chief of engineers, U.S. army (1908–10).

**Marshall,** Sir **William Raine.** 1865–1939. British lieutenant general; during World War, served in France (1914–15), at Gallipoli and Salonika (1916), in Mesopotamia (1916–19); held southern command in India (1919–23).

**Mar′shall–Corn′wall** (-kôrn′wăl; -wôl), Sir **James Handyside.** 1887– . British army commander; served in World War (1914–18); chief of military mission to Egyptian army (1937–38); director of air and coast defense, War Office (1939–40); lieutenant general, commanding British troops in Egypt (June, 1941); head of western command, in Great Britain (Nov., 1941).

**Marsh′man** (märsh′măn), **Joshua.** 1768–1837. English missionary and Orientalist; Baptist missionary at Serampore (1799), where he took leading part in translating Bible into various dialects; aided by his son **John Clark Marshman** (1794–1877), established newspapers and Serampore Coll.; published first complete Chinese Bible; translated Confucius (1809).

**Mar·si′gli** (mär·sē′lyē), Count **Luigi Ferdinando.** 1658–1730. Italian naturalist, geographer, and soldier; founded Institute of Science and Arts (Bologna, 1714); pioneer in field of oceanography. Among his works are *Breve Ristretto del Saggio Fisico intorno alla Storia del Mare* (1711) and *Lo Stato Militare dell'Impero Ottomano* (1732).

**Mar·sil′i·us of Pad′u·a** (mär·sĭl′ĭ·ŭs, păd′ū·ȧ). *Ital.* **Mar·si′glio de′i Mai′nar·di′ni** (mär·sē′lyō dā′ē mī′när·dē′nē). 1290?–?1343. Italian scholar; professor of philosophy, Paris (1311 ff.); rector, U. of Paris (1313 ff.); participated in Ghibelline struggles in northern Italy. With John of Jandun, wrote *Defensor Pacis* (1324, publ. 1522), a juridical treatise against temporal power of pope; forced to flee Paris (1326); condemned and excommunicated by Pope John XXII (1327); protégé of Louis IV of Bavaria; aided in patron's conquest of Rome (1328); appointed ecclesiastical vicar of Rome.

**Mar·si′li·us von Ing′hen** (mär·zē′lē·ōōs fôn ĭng′ĕn). 1330?–1396. German scholastic; appointed rector of newly founded U. of Heidelberg by Rupert. Author of textbooks in philosophy; exponent of Thomas Aquinas's theology, Ockham's logic, and Buridan's physics.

**Mar′ston** (mär′stŭn), **John.** 1575?–1634. English dramatist, b. Coventry. B.A., Oxon. (1594). Published, under pseudonym **W. Kin·say′der** (?kĭn·sā′dẽr), erotic poem *The Metamorphosis of Pigmalion's Image* (1598) and *The Scourge of Villanie,* eleven coarse and vigorous satires (1598, 1599) burned by order of archbishop of Canterbury; published all his plays (except possibly *The Insatiate Countesse,* of uncertain authorship, 1613) between 1602 and 1607; took orders (?1609); incumbent of Christ Church, Hampshire (1616–31). Pilloried by Ben Jonson as Crispinus in *Poetaster* (1601) for his melodramatic and exaggerated writing in *The History of Antonio and Mellida* and its sequel, *Antonio's Revenge* (entered at Stationers' Hall, 1601); retaliated by collaborating with Dekker in *Satiromastix,* attacking Jonson (1602). Known chiefly for gay and entertaining comedies and a few bombastic and rather coarse tragedies: *The Malcontent* (comedy with additions by Webster and dedicated to Jonson, 1604); *Eastward Hoe* (comedy written in collaboration with Jonson and Chapman, 1605, and including reflections on Scots for which the authors were confined in prison); *The Dutch Courtezan* (comedy, 1605); *Parisitaster, or the Fawne* (comedy, 1606); *The Wonder of Women, or the Tragedy of Sophonisba* (1606); *What You Will* (comedy, 1607).

**Marston, John Westland.** 1819–1890. English dramatic poet, b. in Lincolnshire. Solicitor's clerk; belonged to mystical society resembling New England transcendentalists; edited mystical periodical *Psyche;* author of dozen metrical dramas with well-constructed plots and fine diction, including *The Patrician's Daughter* (1841), *Strathmore* (1849), *Marc de Méranie* (1850), *A Life's Ransom* (1857), *A Hard Struggle* (1858), *Donna Diana* (1864), and a comedy, *The Favourite of Fortune* (1866). His son **Philip Bourke** (1850–1887), poet, lost his sight at early age; author of idylls of flower life, *The Rose and the Wind,* and three collections of poems, *Song-tide* (1871), *All in All* (1875), *Wind Voices* (1883); subject of elegy by Swinburne and of Mrs. Dinah Maria Craik's *Philip, my King.*

**Mar′strand** (mär′strän), **Vilhelm.** 1810–1873. Danish painter, esp. of genre scenes and historical subjects.

**Mar′sus** (mär′sŭs), **Domitius.** Roman poet, 1st cent. B.C.

**Martel, Charles.** See CHARLES MARTEL.

**Mar·tel′** (mär·tĕl′), Sir **Giffard Le Quesne** (lẽ kān′). 1889–1958. British army officer; in World War I aided in developing use of first tanks; constructed first one-man tank (1925); assistant director of mechanization at War Office (1936–38); deputy director (1938–39); commander of Royal Armored Corps (1940); lieut. general (1942); military head of Moscow mission (1943).

**Mar′tel′** (mȧr′tĕl′), **Louis Joseph.** 1813–1892. French politician; member of Legislative Assembly (1849), Corps Législatif (1863–70), and National Assembly (1871); elected senator for life (1875); minister of justice (1876–77); president of Senate (1879–80).

**Mar′tel′ de Jan′ville′** (mȧr′tĕl′ dẽ zhäɴ′vēl′), Comtesse **de. Sibylle Gabrielle Marie Antoinette,** *nee* **de Ri′quet′ti′ de Mi′ra′beau′** (dẽ rē′kĕ′tē′ dẽ mē′rȧ′bō′). *Pseudonym* **Gyp** (zhēp). 1850–1932. French novelist; author of *Petit Bob* (introducing the type of the "enfant terrible," 1882), *Autour du Mariage* (1883), *Autour du Divorce* (1886), *Un Ménage Dernier Cri* (1903), *L'Affaire Débrouillard-Delatamize* (1911), *Les Profitards* (1918), etc. See Comtesse de MIRABEAU.

**Mar·tel′li** (mär·tĕl′lē) *or* **Mar·tel′lo** (-lō), **Pier Jacopo.** 1665–1727. Italian poet and scholar; attempted to create an Italian counterpart to classical French tragedy; invented verse of two seven-syllable hemistichs (now called *verso Martelliano*) as substitute for French Alexandrines; author of several tragedies in imitation of the French.

**Mar′ten** (mär′tĭn; -t'n), **Henry.** 1602–1680. English regicide. M.P. (1640); supported attainder against Strafford and supremacy of Parliament; expelled from Parliament (1643–46) for advocating extirpation of royal family. Leader of extreme party, sided with army against Parliament; raised troop of horse to prevent restoration of Charles I (1648); a leading judge in trial of Charles I and signer of death warrant (1649). At Restoration, conducted own defense; imprisoned for life.

**Mar′tens** (mär′tĕns), **Frédéric Fromm′hold** (frŏm′hōlt) **de.** *Russ.* **Fëdor Fëdorovich Martens.** 1845–1909. Russian jurist, b. in Livonia. On staff of Russian ministry of foreign affairs (1868); professor, Imperial School of Law and Imperial Alexander Lyceum (1872); diplomatic representative of Russia in various international arbitration proceedings. Established reputation as authority on international law; author of *International Law of Civilized Nations;* editor of *Recueil des Traités et Conventions Conclus par la Russie avec les Puissances Étrangères* (13 vols., 1874–1902). Awarded Nobel prize for peace (1902).

**Mar′tens** (mär′tĕns), **Georg Friedrich von.** 1756–1821. German journalist and diplomat; professor of law, Göttingen (1783). Published *Recueil des Traités* (7 vols., 1791–1801; 4 supplements, 1802–08), *Nouveau Recueil* (16 vols., 1817 ff.).

**Mar′tha** (mär′thȧ). In New Testament, sister of Mary and Lazarus (*John* xi. 1 ff.). In medieval and later Christian allegory she often symbolizes the active life, as Mary symbolizes the contemplative life (cf. *Luke* x. 38–42).

**Mar·tí′** (mär·tē′), **José Julian.** 1853–1895. Cuban patriot; lawyer by profession; consul in New York for Argentina, Uruguay, and Paraguay. Founded Cuban Revolutionary party (1892); inspired Cuban revolt (1895) and, with a few companions, landed in Cuba to command rebel troops; killed by Spanish in skirmish (May, 1895).

**Mar′tial** (mär′shăl). *Full Latin name* **Marcus Valerius Mar′ti·a′lis** (mär′shĭ·ā′lĭs). Roman epigrammatist of 1st century A.D., b. Bilbilis, Spain; long resident in Rome. Friend of Juvenal; enjoyed patronage of emperors Titus and Domitian. Fourteen books of his epigrams are extant.

**Mar′ti·a′nus Ca·pel′la** (mär′shĭ·ā′nŭs kȧ·pĕl′ȧ). Latin writer of 5th century A.D., from northern Africa; probably practiced law in Carthage. Chief work, an allegory in prose and verse entitled *Satyricon* or *De Nuptiis Philologiae et Mercurii et de Septem Artibus Liberalibus Libri Novem,* containing 2 books of allegory and 7 books of exposition, constituting altogether an encyclopedia of contemporary culture.

**Mar′ti′gnac′** (mȧr′tē′nyȧk′), Vicomte **de. Jean Baptiste Sylvère Gay** (gā). 1778–1832. French politician; royalist in sympathy; appointed procurator-general of Limoges (1815). Accompanied French expedition into Spain (1823); created vicomte (1825); as secretary of the interior (1828–29), superintended final attempt to reconcile monarchy with the people; removed by king (Apr., 1829).

**Mar′ti′gny′** (mȧr′tē′nyē′), **Joseph Alexandre.** 1808–1881. French priest and writer; compiler of *Dictionnaire des Antiquités Chrétiennes* (1865).

**Martin.** See also Martyn.

**Mar′tin** (mär′tĭn; -t'n; *Fr.* mȧr′tăN′), Saint. *Also known as* Saint **Martin of Tours** (to͞or). 315?–?399. French prelate; bishop of Tours (c. 371); founder of the monastery of Marmoutier. Patron saint of France; regarded as patron of publicans and innkeepers. The feast of St. Martin (Martinmas) is Nov. 11.

**Mar′tin** (mär′tĭn; -t'n). Name of five popes (see *Table of Popes,* Nos. 74, 108, 129, 189, 208):

**Martin I,** Saint. d. 655. Pope (649–655). Condemned Monotheletism at Lateran Synod (649); deposed (653) by Emperor Constans II; exiled to the Crimea.

**Martin II** and **III.** = Marinus I and II.

**Martin IV.** *Real name* **Simon de Brie** (dē brē′). 1210?–1285. Pope (1281–85), b. in Touraine, France. Excommunicated (1281) Michael Palaeologus, Emperor of the East, thus weakening union of Eastern and Western churches; labored to save Sicily for France, after Sicilian Vespers (1282).

**Martin V.** *Real name* **Ottone** *or* **Oddone (Otto) Co·lon′na** (kō·lōn′nä). 1368–1431. Pope (1417–31), b. Genazzano, near Rome. Elected at the Council of Constance after the deposition of Benedict XIII, Gregory XII, and John XXIII; made special concordats with several countries; brought peace to the Papacy and the end of the Western Schism.

**Martin, Archer John Porter.** 1910- . British chemist. Awarded Nobel prize in chemistry (1952) with R. Synge for inventing partition chromatography.

**Mar′tin′** (mȧr′tăN′), **Bon Louis Henri.** 1810–1883. French historian; member of National Assembly (1871) and senator (1876). Edited *Histoire de France,* a sequence of selections from important chroniclers and historians (15 vols., 1833–36); wrote *Histoire de France* (19 vols., 1837–54; awarded Gobert prize, 1856).

**Mar′tin** (mär′tĭn; -t'n), **Edward Sandford.** 1856–1939. American editor and writer; a founder of *Harvard Lampoon* (1876); founder and first editor of *Life* magazine (1883), and editorial writer for it (1887–1933). On editorial staff, *Harper's Weekly* (1893–1913), and writer of the "Easy Chair" in *Harper's Magazine* (1920–35). Author of *A Little Brother of the Rich* (verse, 1890), *Lucid Intervals* (1900), *Reflections of a Beginning Husband* (1913), *Abroad With Jane* (1918), *What's Ahead, and Meanwhile* (1927), etc.

**Mar′tin** (mär′tĕn), **Ernst.** 1841–1910. German philologist.

**Mar′tin** (mär′tĭn; -t'n), **Everett Dean.** 1880–1941. American educator; ordained in Congregational ministry (1907); lecturer on social philosophy (from 1916), asst. director (1917–22), and director (from 1922), People's Institute of New York. Author of *The Behavior of Crowds, The Meaning of a Liberal Education, Liberty, Civilizing Ourselves, Farewell to Revolution,* etc.

**Mar′tin** (mär′tĭn; -t'n; *Fr.* mȧr′tăN′), **François Xavier.** 1762–1846. Jurist, b. France; to America in youth. U.S. judge for Mississippi Territory (1809) and for Territory of Orleans (1810). Attorney general of Louisiana (1813). Judge, Louisiana supreme court (1815–46), and chief justice (1836–46). Published *History of Louisiana* (1827), *History of North Carolina* (1829).

**Mar′tin** (mär′tĭn; -t'n), **Franklin Henry.** 1857–1935. American surgeon; gynecologist, Women's Hospital, Chicago; founder and editor (1905), *Surgery, Gynecology and Obstetrics;* founder, Am. College of Surgeons.

**Martin, Glenn L.** 1886–1955. American airplane manufacturer, b. Macksburg, Iowa. Established one of first airplane factories in U.S. (1909); received first government order (1913). Merged with Wright Co. (1917) to form Wright-Martin Aircraft Corp., but withdrew same year to form The Glenn L. Martin Co., Cleveland, Ohio; located at Baltimore (1929). Chief business, manufacture of bombers and transoceanic flying boats; designer and builder of clipper airplanes used in transpacific service. Awarded Collier trophy (1932) for greatest achievement in aeronautics in America.

**Martin, Gregory.** d. 1582. English Biblical translator. M.A., Oxon. (1565); tutor to Philip Howard (later earl of Arundel); stanch Roman Catholic, fled to Douai, Flanders (1570), where he taught Hebrew; sent to help organize new English college at Rome (1577); moved (1578) with Douay Coll. to Reims, where he spent rest of life translating Bible into English from the Latin Vulgate, collated with Greek and Hebrew versions; his translation, after revision by Cardinal Allen, his assistant Richard Bristow (1538–1581), and others, published (New Testament, 1582; Old Testament, 1609–10) as Douay Bible.

**Martin, Helen,** *nee* **Rei'men·sny'der** (rē'mĕn·snī'dẽr). 1868–1939. American novelist; b. Lancaster, Pa.; m. Frederic C. Martin (1899). Author of many novels, including: *Tillie, a Mennonite Maid* (1904; later dramatized), *Sabina, a Story of the Amish* (1905), *Barnabetta* (1914; dramatized as *Erstwhile Susan*), *Wings of Healing* (1929), *Deliverance* (1935), *Emmy Untamed* (1937), etc.

**Mar'tin'** (mȧr'tăN'), **Henri Jean Guillaume.** 1860–1943. French painter; identified with impressionistic school of painting; known esp. for decorative work.

**Mar'tin** (mär'tĕn), **Hipsch** *or* **Hübsch.** See Martin SCHONGAUER.

**Mar'tin** (mär'tĭn; -t'n), **Homer Dodge.** 1836–1897. American landscape painter; studio in New York (from 1865). His *Evening on the Seine* hangs in the National Gallery, Washington, D.C.; *Harp of the Winds, Sand Dunes, Lake Ontario, Mounts Adams and Jefferson,* in Metropolitan Museum of Art, New York City.

**Martin, John.** 1789–1854. English historical and landscape painter; known chiefly for *Belshazzar's Feast* (1821), *The Fall of Nineveh* (1828), *The Deluge* (1826), and *The Eve of the Deluge* (1840), showing wild imaginative power.

**Martin, Joseph William.** 1884–1968. American politician, b. North Attleboro, Mass.; publisher of North Attleboro *Evening Chronicle* (from 1908). Member of U.S. House of Representatives (1925–67), speaker (1947–49; 1953–55). Eastern manager (1936), manager (1940), Republican national campaign.

**Martin, Josiah.** 1737–1786. British colonial governor of North Carolina (1771–75). Served with British forces (1776–81). Returned to England (1781).

**Mar'tin'** (mȧr'tăN'), **Louis.** 1864–1946. French physician and bacteriologist; a pioneer in use of injections of antidiphtheric serum; director of the Pasteur Institute, Paris.

**Mar'tin** (mär'tĭn; -t'n), **Luther.** 1748?–1826. American lawyer and Revolutionary leader, b. near New Brunswick, N.J. Practiced in Maryland (from c. 1772). Member, Continental Congress (1785), and federal Constitutional Convention (1787); opposed plan of strong central government and adoption of Constitution. Defended Chase in impeachment trial before U.S. Senate (1804) and Aaron Burr in treason trial at Richmond, Va. (1807). Chief judge, court of oyer and terminer, Baltimore (1813–16).

**Martin, Martin.** d. 1719. Scottish traveler; M.D., Leiden; author of *Voyage to St. Kilda* (1698) and *A Description of the Western Islands of Scotland* (1703).

**Mar'tin** (mär'tĕn), **Paul.** Pseudonym of Paul Martin RADE.

**Mar'tin'** (mȧr'tăN'), **Pierre Émile.** 1824–1915. French engineer; director of the steel mills of Sireuil; inventor of a process (Martin process) of making steel from pig iron.

**Mar'tin** (mär'tĭn; -t'n), **Ric·car'do** (rĭ·kär'dō). *Real name* **Hugh Whitfield Martin.** 1874–1952. Am. operatic tenor; member, Metropolitan Opera Company (1907–15), Boston Opera Company (1915–17), Chicago Opera Company (1920). Also sang at Covent Garden, London.

**Martin,** Sir **Theodore.** 1816–1909. British poet, translator, and essayist; solicitor in Edinburgh; joined firm of parliamentary agents in London (1846). Collaborated with William Edmonstoune Aytoun in *The Bon Gaultier Ballads* (witty parodies, 1845), and *Poems and Ballads of Goethe* (1858). Fascinated by acting of Helen Faucit (*q.v.*), adapted for her, from Danish of Hertz, *King René's Daughter* (1849); married her (1851). Wrote on dramatic themes in *Fraser's Magazine* (1858–65), *Quarterly Review*, and *Blackwood's Magazine;* translator in verse of Oehlenschläger's *Aladdin* (1854) and *Correggio* (1857), works of Horace (1860) and of Catullus (1861), Dante's *Vita Nuova* (1862), Goethe's *Faust* (1865, 1866), poems and ballads of Heine (1878); won lifelong friendship of Queen Victoria by his *Life of His Royal Highness the Prince Consort* (5 vols., 1875–80).

**Martin, Thomas Commerford.** 1856–1924. Editor, b. London, Eng.; to U.S. (1877). Assistant in Edison Laboratory, Menlo Park, N.J. (1877–79). Editor, *Electrical World* (1883–90), *Electrical Engineer* (1890–1909). Author of *Nikola Tesla* (1894), *Edison, His Life and Inventions* (2 vols., 1910), *The Story of Electricity* (2 vols., 1919–22), etc.

**Martin, Violet Florence.** *Pseudonym* **Martin Ross.** 1862–1915. Irish novelist, b. in Galway. Collaborated with her cousin Edith Oenone Somerville (*q.v.*) on vivid tales of Irish life, including *The Real Charlotte* (1894), *Mount Music* (pub. 1919), *The Enthusiast* (pub. 1921), and a series of sporting stories, beginning with *Some Experiences of an Irish R. M.* (1899).

**Martin, William Alexander Parsons.** 1827–1916. American Presbyterian missionary in China, b. Livonia, Ind. To China (1850); founded mission in Peking (1863). President, and professor of international law, **T'ungwên** Kuan, a Chinese college in Peking (1869–94). President, Imperial U., Peking (1898–1900); assisted in defense of legations during Boxer uprising (1900). Professor of international law, Wuchang U. (1902–05). Author of many books in Chinese, and many in English about China and the Chinese, including *A Cycle of Cathay* (1896), *The Awakening of China* (1907).

**Martin Du Gard, Roger.** See Roger Martin DU GARD.

**Martin of Tours,** Saint. See Saint MARTIN.

**Mar'tin of Trop'pau** (mär'tĭn [*Ger.* mär'tēn], trŏp'ou). *Also* **Martin the Pole** *or* **Mar·ti'nus Po·lo'nus** (mär·tī'nŭs pō·lō'nŭs). d. 1278. Dominican monk and chronicler, b. in Troppau; papal chaplain to Pope Nicholas III and later popes; archbishop of Gnesen (1278). Author of a history of the popes and emperors (to 1277).

**Mar'ti·neau** (mär'tĭ·nō; -t'n·ō), **Harriet.** 1802–1876. English novelist and economist; delicate and deaf from childhood. Gained success and became authority on economics upon publication of *Illustrations of Political Economy* (1832–34), *Poor Laws and Paupers* (1833), and *Illustrations of Taxation* (1834); settled in London, consulted by cabinet ministers. Visited America (1834–36), where she gave offense by abolitionist views and by *Society in America* (1837). Settled at Ambleside in English Lake District (1845). In *Eastern Life, Present and Past* (1848), expounded philosophic atheism; alienated friends by agnostic views in her correspondence published as *Letters on the Laws of Man's Nature and*

*Development* (1851); issued condensed translation of Comte's *Philosophie Positive* (1853). Author also of two novels, *Deerbrook* (1839) and *The Hour and the Man* (1840), of popular tales for children, of *History of England during the Thirty Years' Peace* 1816–46 (1849) and *Autobiographical Memoir* (1877).

Her brother **James** (1805–1900), Unitarian theologian, was preacher in chapel in Liverpool (1832–57); professor of mental and moral philosophy, Manchester New Coll. (1840–69), and principal (1869–85); author of influential philosophical works, including *Rationale of Religious Inquiry* (1836), *Ideal Substitutes for God* (1879), *Study of Spinoza* (1882), *The Study of Religion* (1888), *The Seat of Authority in Religion* (1890).

**Mar'ti'net'** (mȧr'tē'nĕ'; *Angl.* mär'tĭ·nĕt', -t'n·ĕt'). 17th-century French army officer under Louis XIV; devised a new system of military drill given his name.

**Martinet, Achille Louis.** 1806–1877. French engraver; engraved after Raphael, Rembrandt, Murillo, Delaroche, Cogniet, and other masters.

**Mar·tí'nez** (mär·tē'nās), **Maximiliano Hernández.** 1882– . Salvadoran general and politician; vice-president of El Salvador (1931); chosen president by a military directorate (Dec., 1931; confirmed by Congress Feb., 1932) to succeed deposed president Arturo Araújo; president (1931–34) but not recognized by U.S. until 1934; elected president (1935); resigned (1944).

**Martínez, Tomás.** 1812–1873. Nicaraguan general and politician, b. León. Fought against William Walker, American filibuster (1856–57); president of Nicaragua (1857–67); defeated in war with Honduras and El Salvador.

**Mar·tí'nez de Cam'pos** (mär·tē'nāth thā käm'pōs), **Arsenio.** 1834–1900. Spanish soldier and statesman; served in Morocco (1859), Mexico (1861), and Cuba (1869–72). Aided in restoring monarchical government in Spain (1874–75), seated Alfonso XII on the throne, and defeated the Carlists (1876). Suppressed Cuban insurrection (1878). Premier of Spain (1879); minister of war (1881–84); president of the Senate (1886; 1891; 1899). Again commanded in Cuba (1895–96).

**Martínez de la Ro'sa** (lä rô'sä), **Francisco.** 1789–1862. Spanish statesman and writer; supported constitution of 1812, and when it was abolished (1814) was imprisoned (1814–20). Premier of Spain (1820–23; 1834). Lived for long periods in Paris, where he served as Spanish ambassador (1847–51). Author of poetry, plays, historical works, and the historical novel *Doña Isabel de Solís*.

**Martínez de To·le'do** (tô·lā'thō), **Alfonso.** 1398?–?1466. Spanish prelate and writer; archbishop of Talavera; author of a satirical work on the foibles of women, *Reprobación del Amor Mundano* (better known as *El Corbacho*).

**Mar·tí'nez Pas·qua'lis** (mĕr·tē'nĕsh pȧsh·kwä'lēsh). 1715?–1779. Portuguese mystic; founder (1754) of a society of mystics later led by Marquis Louis Claude de Saint-Martin (*q.v.*).

**Mar·tí'nez Ruiz** (mär·tē'nāth), **José.** See Ruiz.

**Martínez Sier'ra** (syĕr'rä), **Gregorio.** 1881–1947. Spanish playwright and novelist; among his novels are *Sol de la Tarde* (1904), *Tú Eres la Paz* (1907); among his plays, *Canción de Cuna* (1911), *Reino de Dios* (1915).

**Mar·tí'nez Zu'vi·rí'a** (mär·tē'nās sōō'vē·rē'ä), **Gustavo.** *Pseudonym* **Hu'go Wast** (ōō'gō väst'). 1883– . Argentine lawyer and writer, b. Córdoba. Member, House of Deputies (1916–20); director, National Library, Buenos Aires (from 1931). Among his works are *Alegre* (1907), *Valle Negro* (*Black Valley*, 1918; awarded Royal Spanish Academy prize), *Desierto de Piedra* (*Stone Desert*, 1925; awarded Argentine national prize), *Sangre en el Umbral* (1927), *Lucía Miranda* (1929), *El Camino de las Llamas* (1930), *Naves-oro-sueños* (1936).

**Mar·ti'ni** (mär·tē'nē), **Ferdinando.** 1841–1928. Italian writer; minister of education (1892–93), and colonial minister (1914–16). Author of *I Nuovi Ricchi* (1863), *La Marchesa* (1876), *La Vipera* (comedy; 1894), and *Peccato e Penitenza* (stories; 1913).

**Mar·ti'ni** (mär·tē'nē), **Frédéric de.** 1832–1897. Inventor, b. in Hungary; mechanical engineer at Frauenfeld, Switzerland; invented rifle adopted by British army (1871), used until 1889, and replaced with the Martini-Henry rifle, the invention of Henry.

**Martini, Giovanni Battista.** *Known as* **Pa'dre Martini** (pä'drā). 1706–1784. Italian Franciscan monk, composer, and music scholar.

**Mar'ti'ni'** (*Fr.* mȧr'tē'nē'; *Ger.* mär·tē'nē), **Jean Paul Égide.** *Real name* **Johann Paul Ägidius Schwar'zen·dorf** (shvär'tsĕn·dôrf). *Also known as* **Mar·ti'ni il Te·de'sco** (*Ital.* mär·tē'nē ēl tā·dās'kō). 1741–1816. French composer of German birth; settled at Nancy, and later in Paris, where he became music director successively for the prince de Condé and the comte d'Artois. Composer of dramatic works, military pieces, and choral music; his best-known composition is the romance *Plaisir d'Amour*.

**Mar·ti'ni** (mär·tē'nē), **Simone.** *Surname sometimes* **di Mar·ti'no** (dē mär·tē'nō) *and, incorrectly,* **Mem'mi** (mĕm'mē). 1283?–1344. Italian painter; one of leading representatives of Sienese school; employed at Siena (to 1333), Assisi (1333–39), and at papal court of Benedict XII at Avignon (1339–44). Among his works are the altarpiece *Annunciation* in collaboration with his brother-in-law **Lippo Memmi**, frescoes illustrating life of St. Martin (in lower church, Assisi), and frescoes illustrating life of St. John (in papal palace and cathedral, Avignon).

**Mar·ti'ni** (*Ital.* mär·tē'nē), **Vicente.** *Real name* **Mar·tín' y So·lar'** (*Span.* mär·tēn' ē sō·lär'). 1754–1810. Spanish composer; director, Italian Opera, in St. Petersburg (1788–1803).

**Mar'tin·son'** (mär'tēn·sôn'), **Harry Edmund.** 1904–1978. Swedish writer and poet. Wrote *Nasslorna blomma* (1935), *Vägen ut* (1936), *Passad* (1945), *Aniara* (1956), etc.; awarded (with Eyvind Johnson) Nobel prize for literature (1974).

**Mar·ti'nus** (mär·tī'nŭs). One of Four Doctors of Bologna. See Bulgarus.

**Martinus Polonus.** See Martin of Troppau.

**Mar'ti·nuz'zi** (mär'tē·nōōt'tsē), **George.** *Croatian name* **Juraj U'tje·še'no·vić** (ōō'tyĕ·shĕ'nō·vēt'y'; *Angl.* -vĭch). *Known as* **Fra'ter Ge·or'gi·us** (frä'tĕr gā·ôr'gē·ōōs). 1482–1551. Hungarian statesman, of Croatian origin; treasurer and chief adviser (from c. 1529) to John Zápolya, King of Hungary. Bishop of Nagyvárad (1534); later, cardinal and archbishop of Esztergom. After death of Zápolya (1540), served as guardian and regent for Zápolya's son John Sigismund. Attacked by alliance headed by Isabella, the queen mother (1550); defeated the alliance and concluded treaty whereby Isabella renounced rights to Transylvania in favor of Ferdinand I, Holy Roman Emperor. Secured unity of Hungary, but was forced to pay tribute to Turkey because Ferdinand was too weak to defend Hungary. Suspected of disloyalty and assassinated by order of Ferdinand (Dec. 17, 1551).

**Mar·ti'ny** (mär·tē'nĭ), **Philip.** 1858–1927. Sculptor, b. Strasbourg, Alsace; to U.S. as a young man. Executed sculptured decorations for the agricultural building at Columbian Exposition, Chicago (1893), for Pan-American Exposition, Buffalo (1901), and for St. Louis

World's Fair (1904). Other works include marble carvings in balustrade of staircase of Library of Congress, Washington, D.C.; *Soldiers' and Sailors' Monument*, Jersey City, N.J.; bronze doors, Saint Bartholomew's Church, New York City.

**Martín y Solar.** See Vicente MARTINI.

**Mar'ti·us** (mär'tsē·ōōs), **Karl Friedrich Philipp von.** 1794–1868. German naturalist and traveler. On expedition to Brazil (1817); professor in Munich (1826–64); author of works on plants of Brazil; with help of others, began *Flora Brasiliensis* (1840).

**Mar·tuc'ci** (mär·tōōt'chē), **Giuseppe.** 1856–1909. Italian pianist and composer.

**Mar'tyn** (mär'tĭn; -t'n), **Edward.** 1859–1923. Irish critic and playwright; associated with Lady Gregory, W. B. Yeats, and George Moore in founding Irish Literary Theatre. President of Sinn Fein (1904–08). Founded Irish Theatre, at Dublin (1914), for presentation of plays in Irish language. Author of the plays *The Heather Field, Maeve, The Placehunters, The Dream Physician, Regina Eyre,* etc.

**Martyn, Henry.** 1781–1812. English missionary to India; chaplain under East India Co. (1805); translated New Testament and Prayer Book into Hindustani, New Testament and Psalms into Persian, and Gospels into Judaeo-Persian.

**Martyn, John.** 1699–1768. English botanist; contributed to Bailey's *Dictionary* (1725); professor of botany, Cambridge (1732–62), and at same time practicing physician. Author of *Historia plantarum rariorum* (1728–37); translator of Vergil's *Georgics* (1741) and *Bucolics* (1749), with agricultural and botanical notes. His son **Thomas** (1735–1825) was professor of botany, Cambridge (1762–1825), and introduced Linnaean system; published translation and continuation of Rousseau's *Letters on the Elements of Botany* (1785), long a standard work.

**Martyn, Wyndham.** 1875– . Writer, b. in England; to U.S. (1904). Author chiefly of detective fiction, including: *Anthony Trent, Master Criminal* (1918), *Anthony Trent, Avenger* (1927), *Murder Walks the Deck* (1938), etc.

**Martyr, Peter.** See PETER MARTYR.

**Ma·ruc'chi** (mä·rōōk'kē), **Orazio.** 1852–1931. Italian archaeologist; authority on Egyptology and on Christian archaeology, esp. of Rome.

**Maruyama Okyo.** See OKYO.

**Marvel, Ik.** Pseudonym of Donald Grant MITCHELL.

**Mar'vell** (mär'vĕl; -v'l), **Andrew.** 1621–1678. English poet and satirist; educ. under his father, Andrew Marvell (1586?–1641), at Hull grammar school. Tutor to daughter of Lord Fairfax (c. 1650); wrote poems on gardens and country life and *Horatian Ode upon Cromwell's Return from Ireland* (1650); tutor of William Dutton, Cromwell's ward (1653); Milton's colleague in Latin secretaryship (1657); M.P. (1660), with republican leanings, but favorite of Charles II. As political writer, vigorously opposed government after Restoration in pamphlets and satires, as *Growth of Popery and Arbitrary Government in England* (1677) and *The Last Instructions to a Painter*, on Dutch War; defended Milton; turned satire on Charles II (c. 1672) and monarchy, endangering his life. Author of a few poems of high poetic quality, as *The Emigrants in the Bermudas, The Nymph Complaining for the Death of her Fawn, Thoughts in a Garden, To his Coy Mistress.*

**Mar'vin** (mär'vĭn), **Charles Frederick.** 1858–1943. American meteorologist; chief, U.S. Weather Bureau (1913–34).

**Mar·wan'** (măr·wän'). Name of two Ommiad caliphs of Baghdad: **Marwan I.** *Arab.* **Marwān ibn-al-Ḥakam.** d. 685. Caliph (683–685); founder of Marwanid branch and father of Abd-al-Malik. **Marwan II.** d. 750. Last of Ommiad caliphs (744–750); overthrown by Abbassides.

**Mar'witz** (mär'vĭts), **Georg von der.** 1856–1929. German general in the World War (1914–18); served on the Russian front (1914–16) and the western front (1916–18).

**Marx** (märks), **Adolf Bernhard.** 1795–1866. German composer and music scholar; composer of an opera, oratorio, symphony, piano sonata, and songs; cofounder with Julius Stern and Theodor Kullak of Berlin (later Stern) Conservatory.

**Marx, Karl.** 1818–1883. German political philosopher, b. Treves, Prussia. Educ. U. of Bonn and U. of Berlin. Editor of *Rheinische Zeitung* at Cologne (1842), which was suppressed by the government (1843). Exile in Paris and Brussels, but returned to Cologne at outbreak of revolutionary activity (1848) and founded *Neue Rheinische Zeitung* (1848); expelled from Prussia (1849). Settled in London and devoted himself to the philosophical development of his theory of socialism and to agitation for social reforms and the spread of socialism; proposed scheme of International Workingmen's Association at public meeting in London (Sept. 28, 1864); aided Liebknecht and his associates in Germany in founding Social Democratic Labor party (1869). His great work, *Das Kapital* (3 vols., 1867, 1885, 1895), was carried to completion by his collaborator, Friedrich Engels (*q.v.*). His other most notable work, also written in collaboration with Engels, was the *Communist Manifesto* (1847), often referred to as the *Workers' Declaration of Independence.* Regarded by some as founder of modern socialism.

**Marx, Wilhelm.** 1863–1946. German statesman; member of the Reichstag (from 1910); chancellor of Germany (1923–24; 1926; 1927–28).

**Mar'y** (mâr'ĭ). In Old Testament (Douay Version): = MIRIAM.

**Mary.** In New Testament: (1) Saint **Mary** *or* (the Blessed) **Virgin Mary.** The mother of Jesus. (2) = MARY MAGDALENE. (3) **Mary of Beth'a·ny** (bĕth'ȧ·nĭ). Sister of Martha and Lazarus, *qq.v.* (*John* xi. 1–xii. 8). In medieval and later Christian allegory she often symbolizes the contemplative life, as Martha symbolizes the active life (cf. *Luke* x. 38–42).

**Mary.** Name of several queens of England or of Great Britain.

(1) *Known as* **Mary I** *or* **Mary Tudor.** *Often called* **Bloody Mary.** 1516–1558. Queen of England and Ireland (1553–58), of house of Tudor; daughter of Henry VIII. Succeeded to throne on death of her half brother Edward VI and after deposition of Lady Jane Grey; m. Philip II of Spain (July 25, 1554); repealed laws establishing Protestantism in England and re-established Roman Catholicism (1555); persecuted Protestants, total number martyred during her reign being about 300; accepted Cardinal Pole as chief adviser; lost Calais (1558), last English foothold on the Continent.

(2) **Mary II.** 1662–1694. Queen of England, Scotland, and Ireland (1689–94), of house of Stuart; eldest child of James II and Anne Hyde; m. (1677) her cousin William, Prince of Orange; with husband, invited by influential English nobles to assume English crown in order to prevent James II from establishing Roman Catholicism in country; landed in England (1688); crowned joint sovereign with William (Apr. 11, 1689). See WILLIAM III, Prince of Orange.

(3) **Mary Beatrice.** *Known as* **Mary of Mo'de·na** (mô'dâ·nä). 1658–1718. Daughter of Alfonso IV, Duke

of Modena; second wife (m. Nov. 21, 1673) of James, Duke of York, who became (1685) James II; after invasion of England by William of Orange and Mary (1688), joined James in his refuge in France.

(4) Queen of George V. See *Victoria Mary*, under TECK.

**Mary.** *In full* **Victoria Alexandra Alice Mary.** 1897–1965. Princess Royal of England; daughter of George V; m. (1922) Henry George Charles Lascelles, 6th Earl of Harewood (see LASCELLES family).

**Mary.** *Also known as* **Mary of An'jou** (ăn'jōō; *Fr.* äN'zhōō'). 1370–1395. Queen of Hungary (1382–85); daughter of Louis the Great; became queen on death of father; m. Sigismund of Luxemburg; deposed (1385) by Charles III of Naples; imprisoned (1386) but freed by Sigismund (1387); queen with Sigismund (1387–95).

**Mary, Queen of Scots.** *Or* **Mary Stu'art** (stū'ẽrt). 1542–1587. Only lawful surviving child of James V of Scotland; b. at Linlithgow; daughter by his second wife, Mary of Guise (*q.v.*); next heir (through her grandmother, Margaret Tudor, James IV's queen) to English throne after Henry VIII's children. Queen of Scotland when six days old on death of James V. Brought up with royal children of France in Roman Catholic faith; m. (1558) Francis (crowned Francis II of France, 1559; d. 1560); on fall from power of her uncles, duke of Guise and cardinal of Lorraine, returned to Scotland (1561) to rule her kingdom, left without government since her mother's death (1560) and largely Protestant through the Reformation. Sent her loyal secretary, William Maitland of Lethington, to England to claim right of succession to Elizabeth (1563), but received no declaration from Elizabeth. Distrusted in Scotland for her religion and regarded as frivolous because of her culture; victim of intrigues among nobles for disposal of her hand; suddenly married (1565) her cousin Henry Stewart, Lord Darnley (see DARNLEY), a Catholic, and gave him title of king; easily quelled consequent insurrection by Moray and the Hamiltons. Set out to make herself absolute monarch and to impose Roman Catholicism, with David Rizzio, musician, as her French secretary and chief minister; refused Darnley's demand that crown be secured to him for life and to his heirs, whereupon he formed compact with Moray, Ruthven, Morton, and other nobles, who murdered Rizzio (1566); temporarily reconciled with her husband, had help of James Hepburn, 4th Earl of Bothwell, in banishing murderers of Rizzio; bore son (1566), later James VI of Scotland; finally estranged from Darnley, whose conduct had alienated all Scotland; considered divorce; conveyed him, sick with smallpox, to Kirk o' Field, outside Edinburgh, where during her temporary absence the house was blown up by gunpowder and Darnley found strangled in the yard (Feb., 1567); probably connived at murder, which was universally ascribed to Bothwell, despite his acquittal in a mock trial; her guilt of complicity in the murder plot revealed in the Casket Letters, the genuineness of which has not been definitely established; abducted (Apr. 24, 1567) by Bothwell, probably at her own instigation; m. Bothwell in a Protestant church (May 15, 1567). Having provoked Scottish nobles to rebellion by this marriage, and deserted by her army at Carberry Hill (June, 1567), was forced to dismiss Bothwell, deliver herself up to confederate lords, and sign an abdication in favor of her son; escaped from imprisonment at Loch Leven, gathered army of six thousand, but was defeated by Moray at Langside (1568). Fled to England; held prisoner there rest of her life by Elizabeth; imperiled by a number of unsuccessful Catholic risings in her behalf, including Ridolfi plot (1570–71); consented to divorce from Bothwell. Implicated in Throckmorton plot for invasion by the Guises, for which help of pope and Philip II of Spain was solicited (1582); charged with being an accomplice in Babington's plot (1586); tried at Fotheringhay and, before Star Chamber, condemned to death largely on evidence of copies of letters, in Walsingham's hands, approving assassination of Elizabeth; beheaded at Fotheringhay (Feb. 8, 1587). Subject of dramas by Swinburne, Schiller, and Alfieri.

**Mary Mag'da·le'ne** (măg'dȧ·lē'nē; măg'dȧ·lēn). *Or in Douay Version* **Mary Mag'da·len** (măg'dȧ·lĕn; -lĭn). *Also* **Mary of Mag'da·la** (măg'dȧ·lȧ). In New Testament, a woman whom Jesus healed of evil spirits and who was present at the crucifixion. Her identification with the sinful woman who anointed Jesus' feet (whence the use of the term *Magdalen* for a reformed prostitute) is based merely on the fact that the first mention of her (*Luke* viii. 2) follows closely after that story (*Luke* vii. 36 ff.).

**Mary of Bur'gun·dy** (bûr'gŭn·dĭ). *Fr.* **Ma'rie' de Bour'gogne'** (mȧ'rē' dẽ bōōr'gôn'y'). 1457–1482. Daughter of Charles the Bold; b. Brussels. On death of her father (1477) became duchess and heiress of Burgundy; her duchy seized by Louis XI, who sought her in marriage for the dauphin, Charles; declined; m. (1477) Maximilian of Austria, later Holy Roman Emperor (1493); signed (1477) the Great Privilege, the Magna Charta of the Netherlands. Mother of Philip I of Spain and of Margaret of Austria (*q.v.*).

**Mary of France.** *Nee* **Mary Tu'dor** (tū'dẽr). 1496–1533. Queen of Louis XII of France; daughter of Henry VII and Elizabeth. Betrothed (1508–14) to Charles, Prince of Castile (later Emperor Charles V); m. (1514) by Henry VIII to Louis XII (d. 1515); secretly m. (1515) Charles Brandon, 1st Duke of Suffolk, with whom she went to Field of the Cloth of Gold (1520); refused to accompany Anne Boleyn to meeting with Francis I (1532). Her daughter Frances was mother of Lady Jane Grey.

**Mary of Guise** (*Fr.* gü·ēz', gēz; *Angl.* gēz, gwēz). *Also known as* **Mary of Lor·raine'** (lŏ·rān'; lô·rān'; *Fr.* lô'rân'). 1515–1560. Queen of Scotland; daughter of Claude, Duke of Guise; m. (Aug. 4, 1534) Louis d'Orléans (d. 1537), and (June, 1538) James V of Scotland; mother of Mary, Queen of Scots; regent of Scotland (1554–59).

**Mary of Hungary.** 1505–1558. Queen of Hungary (1522–26) and regent of the Netherlands (1531–52); daughter of Philip of Burgundy (Philip I of Spain of house of Hapsburg) and sister of Emperor Charles V; m. (1522) Louis II of Hungary. Ably administered affairs of Netherlands for twenty years under direction of Charles.

**Mary of Modena.** See MARY, Queen of England.

**Mary of the Incarnation.** *Real name* **Marie**, *nee* **Guy'ard'** (gü·ē'yȧr'), **Mar'tin'** (mȧr'tăN'). 1599–1672. French Ursuline nun and educator in Canada, b. Tours, France. Entered Ursuline order at Tours; accompanied Mme. de la Peltrie, church benefactress, to Canada; superior of Ursuline convent at Quebec (1639); aided work of French missionaries in Canada.

**Mary Stuart.** See MARY, QUEEN OF SCOTS.

**Mary Tudor.** See (1) MARY I of England; (2) MARY OF FRANCE.

**Maryborough,** 1st Baron. See under WELLESLEY family.

**Ma·sac'cio** (mä·zät'chō). *Real name* **Tommaso Gui'di** (gwē'dē). 1401–1428. Sometimes called "Father of Modern Art." Italian painter of Florentine school; works mark advance from medieval to Renaissance

Florentine painting; pupil of Masolino; aided master in frescoing Church of San Clemente at Rome and Brancacci Chapel in Santa Maria del Carmine at Florence, succeeding him in latter work; influenced future course of Florentine painting by his Brancacci frescoes, studied as exemplary by Michelangelo, Raphael, etc.

**Ma'sa·niel'lo** (mä'zä·nyĕl'lō). *Properly* **Tom·ma'so A·niel'lo** (tôm·mä'zō ä·nyĕl'lō). 1623?–1647. Amalfi fisherman; leader of revolt at Naples (1647) against Spanish viceroy, Duque de Arcos; led people, maddened by new tax on fruit, in uprising, driving viceroy out of city; later agreed to settlement; lost confidence of people; murdered by mob. Subject of opera by Auber, *La Muette de Portici* (1828).

**Masanobu.** See KANO.

**Ma'sa·ryk** (mȧ'sȧ·rĭk), **Tomáš Gar·rigue'** (gă·rēg'). 1850–1937. Czechoslovak statesman and philosopher, b. in Moravia; m. (1878) an American, Charlotte Garrigue (d. 1923). Professor, Prague (1882); founded monthly reviews *The Athenaeum* (1883) and *Our Epoch* (1893). Member of parliament (1891–93; 1907 ff.); vigorous critic of Austrian policy. At outbreak of World War escaped from Austria (Dec., 1914); became president of a central revolutionary committee known as the Czechoslovak National Council, which at the end of the World War gained recognition (1918) as the de facto government of the future state of Czechoslovakia. First president of Czechoslovakia (1918–35). Among his philosophical and political writings are *Suicide and Modern Civilization* (1881), *Essay on Concrete Logic* (1885), *The Philosophical and Sociological Foundation of Marxism* (1898), *Russia and Europe* (1913), *The New Europe* (1918), *The Making of a State...1914–1918* (1927), etc. His son **Jan Garrigue** (1886–1948); grad. U. of Prague; in diplomatic service (from 1919); minister to Britain (1925–38); lectured in U.S. (1939–40); foreign minister (1940–48) and vice-premier (1941–45) of Czechoslovak provisional government in London.

**Ma·sca'gni** (mäs·kä'nyē), **Pietro.** 1863–1945. Italian composer. Kapellmeister, Teatro Constanzi, Rome (from 1909). Composer of the famous one-act opera *Cavalleria Rusticana* (1890) and of less successful operatic works including *Iris* (1898), *Le Maschere* (1901), *Isobel* (1911), and *Si* (1919); also of various symphonic works, chamber and church music, etc.

**Mascarenhas de.** See GARCIA DE MASCARENHAS.

**Mas'ca'ron'** (mȧs'kȧ'rôɴ'), **Jules de.** 1634–1703. French ecclesiastic; famous esp. for funeral orations, as for Anne of Austria, Duc de Beaufort, Turenne.

**Mas'cart'** (mȧs'kȧr'), **Éleuthère Élie Nicolas.** 1837–1908. French physicist; known for work in spectroscopy, on electrical units, atmospheric electricity, and terrestrial magnetism.

**Ma'sche·ro'ni** (mäs'kȧ·rō'nē), **Lorenzo.** 1750–1800. Italian mathematician; his works include *Geometria del Compasso* (1797), a collection of geometrical constructions in which the compass is used exclusively.

**Mas'cov** (mäs'kō), **Johann Jakob.** 1689–1761. German historical and legal writer; professor, Leipzig (from 1719). Author of *Principia Juris Publici Romano-Germanici* (1729), *Commentarii de Rebus Imperii Romano-Germanici* (3 vols., 1741–53), etc.

**Mas·deu'** (mäs·thā'ōō), **Juan Francisco de.** 1744–1817. Spanish Jesuit and historian; author of *Historia Crítica de España y de la Cultura Española* (1783–1805).

**Mase'field** (mās'fēld), **John.** 1878–1967. English poet, playwright, and fiction writer, b. Ledbury. Ran away to sea at age of thirteen (1891); settled in or near London, and devoted himself to writing (from c. 1897). Poet laureate (from 1930); member of Order of Merit (1935). Among his notable works are *Salt Water Ballads* (1902), *A Mainsail Haul* (stories of the sea; 1905), *Captain Margaret* (romance; 1908), *The Tragedy of Nan and Other Plays* (1910), *The Tragedy of Pompey the Great* (1910); the verse narratives *The Everlasting Mercy* (1911), *The Widow in the Bye Street* (1912), and *Dauber* (1913); *The Story of a Roundhouse and Other Poems* (1912), *Philip the King* (drama; 1914), *Gallipoli* (prose sketches; 1916), *Reynard the Fox* (narrative poems; 1919); novels of adventure, as *Sard Harker* (1924), *Odtaa* (1926), *Dead Ned* (1938) and *Live and Kicking Ned* (1939); *Basilissa* (fictional biography of Empress Theodora; 1940); *Generation Risen* (poems; 1942).

**Ma'sères'** (mȧ'zâr'), **Francis.** 1731–1824. English mathematician and lawyer; cursitor baron of exchequer (1773–1824). Author of treatises on the negative sign (1758) and on permutations and combinations (1795).

**Mas'ham** (măs'ăm; măsh'ăm), Baron. See Samuel Cunliffe LISTER.

**Masham,** Lady **Abigail,** *nee* **Hill.** d. 1734. English confidante of Queen Anne. First cousin of Sarah, Duchess of Marlborough, through whose influence she became bedchamber woman to Queen Anne. Superseded duchess of Marlborough in Anne's favor; m. (1707) **Samuel Masham,** 1st Baron **Masham** (1679?–1758; M.P. and brigadier general, 1710; gentleman of bedchamber to Prince George of Denmark). Gained dismissal of duke of Marlborough and a peerage for her husband (1712), also dismissal of Harley; continued to engage in Jacobite plots; retired after death of Anne. Sir **Francis** and Lady **Masham,** parents of Samuel, cared for John Locke in his last years.

**Mashar, abu–.** See ALBUMAZAR.

**Mas'i·nis'sa** *or* **Mas'si·nis'sa** (măs'ĭ·nĭs'ȧ). 238?–149 B.C. King of Numidia; fought as a Carthaginian ally (to 206) and later as a Roman ally; commanded cavalry on the right wing of the Roman army under Scipio Africanus at the battle of Zama (202); under Roman protection, gained mastery over all of Numidia (201). See SOPHONISBA.

**Masip.** Variant of MACIP.

**Mas'ke·lyne** (măs'kĕ·lĭn; -lĭn), **Nevil.** 1732–1811. English astronomer; deputed to observe transit of Venus at St. Helena, experimented en route on determination of longitude by method of lunars, which method he introduced in his *British Mariner's Guide* (1763); astronomer royal (1765), improved methods, obviated effects of parallax; invented prismatic micrometer; published *Nautical Almanac* (1st vol. 1766 to 1811); suggested to Royal Society the Schiehallion experiment for determining earth's density from deviations of the plumb line and carried out the plan (1774).

**Masoch, Leopold von Sacher–.** See SACHER-MASOCH.

**Ma'so·li'no da Pa'ni·ca'le** (mä'zō·lē'nō dä pä'nē·kä'lā). *Identified with* **Tommaso di Cri·sto'fo·ro Fi'ni** (dē krēs·tô'fō·rō fē'nē). 1383?–?1447. Florentine painter; assistant of Lorenzo Ghiberti; master of Masaccio (*q.v.*); to Hungary (1427) as protégé of Filippo Scolari; at Castiglione d'Olona (1428–35).

**Ma'son** (mā's'n), **Alfred Edward Woodley.** 1865–1948. English novelist and playwright; author of *A Romance of Wastdale* (1895), *The Philanderers* (1897), *The Four Feathers* (1902), *Col. Smith* (comedy; 1909), *At the Villa Rose* (detective story; 1910), *The Witness for the Defence* (play; 1911), *Open Windows* (play; 1913), *The Four Corners of the World* (stories; 1917), *The Winding Stair* (1923), *The Three Gentlemen* (1932), *Dilemmas* (1934), *Fire Over England* (1936), *The Drum* (motion picture scenario; 1937), *Königsmark* (1938), *The Life of Francis Drake* (1941).

**Mason, Charles.** 1730–1787. English astronomer. Assistant at Greenwich Observatory (1756–60); with Jeremiah Dixon, employed by proprietors of Maryland and Pennsylvania to survey boundary line between these states (1763–67), the line afterwards being known as Mason and Dixon's line; with Dixon, measured arc of the meridian in America; returned to England (1769).

**Mason, Daniel Gregory.** See Lowell MASON.

**Mason, Edith,** *nee* **Barnes.** 1893–1973. American operatic soprano; m. 1st Giorgio Polacco (1919), 2d Maurice A. Bernstein (1929), 3d Giorgio Polacco again (1931), 4th William Ragland (1938). Member of Metropolitan Opera Company of New York (1915–17), Chicago Opera Association (1921–22), and Chicago Civic Opera Company (1923–30).

**Mason, Francis van Wyck.** 1897–1978. American novelist, b. Boston; served with A.E.F. (1918–19). Author of detective fiction and historical novels.

**Mason, Frank Stuart.** 1883–1929. American musician, b. Weymouth, Mass. On faculty of New England Conservatory of Music (from c. 1909); conductor, People's Symphony Orchestra, Boston; composer of chamber music, songs, piano pieces, and an orchestral suite (*Bergerie*).

**Mason, George.** 1629?–?1686. English colonist in America; took up lands in Westmoreland County, Va. (1655, 1664, 1669). Burgess in Virginia assembly (1676). Well known as Indian fighter. Among his notable descendants were: **George Mason** (1725–1792), planter and Revolutionary statesman, resident of Gunston Hall in Fairfax County; active in opposition to the Stamp Act and the Townshend duties; drew up nonimportation resolutions presented by Washington to the burgesses and passed on to the Continental Congress; member of Virginia constitutional convention (1776) and prepared the Declaration of Rights and most of the constitution for Virginia; outlined (1780) plan, later adopted, by which Virginia ceded her western land claims to the United States; member of federal Constitutional Convention (1787) but did not sign constitution and took active measures to oppose Virginia's ratification; chosen first U.S. senator from Virginia, but refused to serve. George's brother **Thomson** (1733–1785) was also a Revolutionary leader; member of Virginia assembly (1758–61; 1765–74; 1777–78; 1779; 1783–85); a leader in saving the territory gained by George Rogers Clark in his northwest campaign; author of nine letters of a "British American" (1774), upholding colonial position in dispute with Great Britain. Thomson Mason's son **Stevens Thomson** (1760–1803) was U.S. senator from Virginia (1794–1803); and Stevens Thomson Mason's grandson **Stevens Thomson Mason** (1811–1843) was first governor of the State of Michigan (1836–40). A grandson of the younger George Mason, **James Murray Mason** (1798–1871), was a lawyer and Confederate diplomat; practiced Winchester, Va. (from 1820); member, U.S. House of Representatives (1837–39) and U.S. Senate (1847–61); drafted fugitive slave law (1850); member of Confederate Congress (1861); commissioner of the Confederacy to Great Britain and France (1861–65); seized (with John Slidell, *q.v.*) on board British mail steamer *Trent*, the seizure almost bringing war between U.S. and Great Britain (Nov. 8, 1861); released Jan. 2, 1862, and proceeded to London; lived in Virginia (1868–71).

**Mason, George Heming.** 1818–1872. English landscape and figure painter; painted English and Roman subjects in idyllic style.

**Mason, Henry.** See Lowell MASON.

**Mason, Henry Lowell.** See Lowell MASON.

**Mason, James Murray.** See George MASON.

**Mason, Jeremiah.** See John MASON (1600?–1672).

**Mason,** Sir **John.** 1503–1566. English diplomat; sent on missions to the Continent by Henry VIII, Edward VI, Mary, and Elizabeth; chancellor of Oxford (1552–56, 1559–64); under Elizabeth, directed foreign policy.

**Mason, John.** 1586–1635. English settler in America, b. King's Lynn, England. Governor of Newfoundland (1615). Joined Gorges and others in organizing Laconia Company (1629) to found agricultural settlement on Piscataqua River, thus becoming a founder of New Hampshire.

**Mason, John.** 1600?–1672. English colonist in America; to Massachusetts (before 1633); one of first settlers of Windsor, Conn. (1635). Commanded mixed force of colonials and Indians that decisively defeated the Pequots (1637). Magistrate in Connecticut colony (1642–60); deputy governor (1660–69); assistant governor (1669–72). A founder of Norwich, Conn. (1660). Fifth in direct descent from John Mason was **Jeremiah Mason** (1768–1848), lawyer and legislator; attorney general of New Hampshire (1802–05); U.S. senator (1813–17).

**Mason, John.** 1858–1919. See Lowell MASON.

**Mason, John Young.** 1799–1859. American legislator and diplomat, b. in Greensville County, Va. Member, U.S. House of Representatives (1831–37); U.S. district judge for eastern Virginia (1837–44); U.S. secretary of the navy (1844–45 and 1846–49); U.S. attorney general (1845–46); U.S. minister to France (1853–59). See Pierre SOULÉ.

**Mason, Joseph.** 1807–1883. American artist and naturalist, b. Cincinnati, Ohio. Devoted companion of Audubon, accompanying him on many of his expeditions (from c. 1820), and painting with great skill the details of vegetation that illuminate the earlier *Birds of America*.

**Mason, Lowell.** 1792–1872. American musician, b. Medfield, Mass.; organizer of Boston Academy of Music (1833). Devised system of musical instruction for children, based on Pestalozzian methods, and published *Manual of Instruction* (1834). Teacher of music in Boston schools (1838–41). Compiler of several collections of music, esp. church music, and author of tunes for many hymns, including *Nearer, my God, to Thee; From Greenland's icy mountains; My faith looks up to Thee.* A son **William** (1829–1908) was a concert pianist, teaching and giving piano recitals in New York (from 1855); author of books on piano method and technique, and composer of piano pieces. Another son, **Henry** (1831–1890), piano manufacturer, founded, with Emmons Hamlin, the Mason and Hamlin Organ Co., Boston (1854), extended into piano manufacturing (from 1882) and reorganized as Mason and Hamlin Organ and Piano Co.; his son **Henry Lowell** (1864–1957), succeeded him as president of the company (1906–29). Another son of Henry, **Daniel Gregory** (1873–1953), was professor of music, Columbia; composer of two symphonies, string quartet, *Chanticleer Overture*, and piano pieces; author of *From Grieg to Brahms* (1902), *Beethoven and his Forerunners* (1904), *Contemporary Composers* (1919), etc. **John Mason** (1858–1919), a grandson of Lowell Mason, and nephew of Henry Mason, was an actor; member, Boston stock company (1879–90).

**Mason, Mary,** *nee* **Knight** (nīt). 1857–1944. American song composer, b. Easthampton, Mass.; m. Charles Greenleaf Wood (1879; d. 1913), Alfred Bishop Mason (1914; d. 1933). Among her songs are *Ashes of Roses, Songs of Sleep, Song of Joy, Egyptian Love Song, Songs of Tangier.*

**Mason, Max.** 1877–1961. American mathematician, b. Madison, Wis. Professor, U. of Wisconsin (1908–25); president, U. of Chicago (1925–28); president (1929–36), Rockefeller Foundation, N.Y. Inventor of devices for submarine detection.

**Mason, Otis Tufton.** 1838–1908. American ethnologist, b. Eastport, Me. Curator of ethnology in National Museum (1884–1902); head curator of anthropology (1902–08). Author of *Woman's Share in Primitive Culture* (1894), etc.

**Mason, Stevens Thomson.** See George MASON.

**Mason, Thomson.** See George MASON.

**Mason, Walt.** 1862–1939. Humorist and poet, b. Columbus, Ontario, Canada; to U.S. (1880); associated with William Allen White on the Emporia (Kans.) *Gazette* (from 1907). His prose poems were syndicated, appearing daily in more than 200 newspapers. Author of *Uncle Walt* (1910), *Horse Sense* (1915), *Terse Verse* (1917), *Walt Mason, His Book* (1918), etc.

**Mason, William.** 1724–1797. English poet; wrote *Musaeus* (lament for Pope in imitation of *Lycidas;* 1747); denounced supposed Jacobitism of Oxford U. in poem *Isis* (1748). Author of two plays in pseudoclassical style, *Elfrida* (1752) and *Caractacus* (1759); *Heroic Epistle* to Sir William Chambers, satirizing fashions in gardening (1773); *The English Garden*, in blank verse (1772–81). As Gray's executor, wrote *Life and Letters of Gray* (1774).

**Mason, William.** 1829–1908. See Lowell MASON.

**Mas'pe·ro'** (màs'pē·rō'), Sir **Gaston Camille Charles.** 1846–1916. French Egyptologist; discovered royal mummies at Deir el-Bahri (1881). His works include *Histoire Ancienne des Peuples de l'Orient Classique* (3 vols., 1895–97), *L'Archéologie Égyptienne.*

**Mas'sa·soit'** (măs'ȧ·soit'). d. 1661. Chief of Wampanoag Indians, living in Massachusetts between Cape Cod and Narragansett Bay. Negotiated peace (1621) with the Pilgrims, and remained friendly with the whites all his life. His son was King Philip (*q.v.*).

**Mas'sé'** (mà'sā'), **Victor,** *really* **Félix Marie.** 1822–1884. French dramatic composer; chorus master at the Opéra (1860–76). His compositions include the cantata *Le Renégat de Tanger* (1844), operas and operettas as *Galatée* (1852), *Les Saisons* (1856), *Fior d'Aliza* (1866), *Paul et Virginie* (1876), and *Une Nuit de Cléopâtre* (produced 1885), etc.

**Mas'sé'na'** (mà'sā'nà'), **André.** 1758–1817. French marshal under Napoleon; played important part in French victory at Loano (1795); triumphed under Napoleon in Italy (1796–97), esp. in battle of Rivoli Veronese (1797). Commanded French army in Switzerland and won battle at Zurich (Sept. 26, 1799). Defended Genoa (1800); appointed by Napoleon marshal of France (1804). Commanded army in Italy (1805) and defeated Austrians under Archduke Charles Louis at Caldiero (Oct. 30, 1805). Created duc **de Ri'vo·li** [dē rē'vô·lē] (1808). Distinguished himself in battles of Aspern-Essling and Wagram (1809); created prince **d'Ess'ling** (dĕs'lĭng). Commander in chief of French army in Spain (1810–11); defeated by Sir Arthur Wellesley.

**Mas'sen·bach** (mäs'ĕn·bäκ), Baron **Christian von und zu.** 1758–1827. Prussian army officer; fought in Holland (1787) and against France (1792–95); was held responsible for surrender at Jena (1806). Retired and devoted himself to writing. Was charged with high treason for alleged publication of state secrets and sentenced to fourteen years' imprisonment; pardoned by Frederick William III (1826).

**Mas'se·net'** (màs'nĕ'; *Angl.* măs''n·ā'), **Jules Émile Frédéric.** 1842–1912. French composer; professor, Paris Conservatory (1878–94). His compositions include operas, as *Don César de Bazan* (1872), *Hérodiade* (1881), *Manon* (1884), *Le Cid* (1885), *Thaïs* (1894), *Sapho* (1897), *Le Jongleur de Notre-Dame* (1902), *Don Quichotte* (written for Chaliapin, 1910), and *Amadis* (produced 1922), incidental music to Leconte de Lisle's *Les Érinnyes* containing the *Élégie* (1873), oratorios, as *Marie Magdaleine* (1873) and *Ève* (1875), cantatas, Biblical dramas, a requiem mass, overtures, notably to Racine's *Phèdre* (1901), seven orchestral suites including *Scènes Hongroises* (1871) and *Scènes Alsaciennes* (1881), ballets, chamber music, songs, etc.

**Mas'sey** (măs'ĭ). Name of a distinguished Canadian family, including: **Hart Almerin Massey** (1823–1896), manufacturer of agricultural machinery; made first harvesters produced in Canada. His son **Chester D.** (1850–1926), president of the company (1901); benefactor of religious and educational foundations; established and headed Massey Foundation. Chester's son **Vincent** (1887–1967), diplomat; minister without portfolio, dominion cabinet (1925); Canadian minister to U.S. (1926–30); high commissioner for Canada in U.K. (1935–46); governor-general (1952–59). Vincent's brother **Raymond** (1896– ), actor and producer; joint manager, Everyman Theatre (1926 ff.); U.S. citizen (1944); acted in plays, as *The Constant Nymph, Ethan Frome, Idiot's Delight, Abe Lincoln in Illinois,* and motion pictures, as *The Scarlet Pimpernel, The Prisoner of Zenda, The Hurricane, Abe Lincoln in Illinois.*

**Massey,** Sir **Edward.** 1619?–?1674. English soldier; commanded advance guard of Royalists in invasion of England (1651) and was taken prisoner; made governor of Gloucester by Charles II (1660).

**Massey, Gerald.** 1828–1907. English poet; joined Chartists; joined Christian Socialist movement; became known as editor of *Spirit of Freedom;* published *Voices of Freedom and Lyrics of Love* (1850) and *The Ballad of Babe Christabel* (1854), followed by other volumes of verse. Journalist; lectured on spiritualism; in closing years, sought source of psychic and spiritualistic phenomena in ancient Egyptian civilization and produced *A Book of the Beginnings* (1881), *The Natural Genesis* (1883), and *Ancient Egypt: the Light of the World* (1907). Discovered a secret drama in Shakespeare's sonnets. His career suggested to George Eliot the theme of her *Felix Holt.*

**Massey, William Ferguson.** 1856–1925. New Zealand statesman, b. in County Londonderry, Ireland; to New Zealand (1870), and settled as farmer near Auckland. Member of House of Representatives (1894–1925); opposition whip (1895–1903); leader of Conservative opposition (1903–12); prime minister of New Zealand (1912–25); signed Treaty of Versailles (1919) on behalf of New Zealand.

**Mas'sil'lon'** (mà'sē'yôɴ'), **Jean Baptiste.** 1663–1742. French ecclesiastic; bishop of Clermont (1717); pronounced funeral orations for Prince de Conti, the grand dauphin, and Louis XIV.

**Mas·sine'** (mŭ·syēn'), **Léonide.** 1896–1979. Russian-born dancer and choreographer. Studied under Fokine. With Diaghilev ballet company, played leading roles (Paris and London, 1914); succeeded Fokine as choreographer (1915), his first production being *The Midnight Sun* (New York, 1916). Dancer and choreographer with Ballet Russe de Monte Carlo (1932–38); founder (1938) and artistic director (1938–42) of new Ballet Russe de Monte Carlo. Later with American Ballet Theatre and Royal Ballet of England.

**Mas'sin·ger** (măs'ĭn·jẽr), **Philip.** 1583–1640. English dramatist; collaborated with Nathaniel Field, Cyril Tourneur, Dekker, and Fletcher (1613–25) for the king's players; with Dekker, wrote *The Virgin Martyr* (entered at Stationers' Hall, 1621), and with Field, *The Fatal Dowry* (1632), which are attributed in large part to Shakespeare; had many patrons, among them the Herbert family, earl of Carnarvon, Sir Anton Cokayne, Lord Mohun. Supported democratic views of Philip Herbert; introduced thinly veiled reflections on current politics into his plays; denounced Buckingham in *The Bondman* (1624); thought to have been Roman Catholic from evidence in certain plays; rhetorical and picturesque in expression, fluent and flexible in verse, had few rivals in art of plot construction. Sole author of fifteen plays, chiefly romantic dramas, including (in probable order of composition; date of 1st printing given): *The Duke of Milan* (1623), *The Unnatural Combat* (1639), *The Renegado* (1630), *The Parliament of Love* (1805), *The Roman Actor* (1629), *The Maid of Honour* (1632), *The Picture* (1630), *The Great Duke of Florence* (1635), *The Emperor of the East* (1631), *The City Madam* (1658), *The Guardian* (1655), *The Bashful Lover* (1655), and comedy *A New Way to Pay Old Debts* (1632), dealing with discomfiture of the extortionist and cheat, Sir Giles Overreach.

**Mas′sing·ham** (măs′ĭng·ăm), **Henry William.** 1860–1924. English journalist; editor, London *Daily Chronicle* (1895–99), and the *Nation* (1907–23), which he molded into an influential liberal organ. His son **Harold John** (1888–1952), journalist; author of literary criticism, writings on bird and animal life, studies of the English countryside, folklore, mythology, etc., including *Pre-Roman Britain* (1927), *The Heritage of Man* (1929), *The Friend of Shelley* (1930), *Country* (1934), *Genius of England* (1937), *Remembrance* (autobiography; 1942).

**Massinissa.** See MASINISSA.

**Mas′sis′** (mȧ′sēs′), **Henri.** 1886–1970. French writer, one of the seventeen forming the group known as "Jury." Author of *Jeunes Gens d'Aujourd'hui* (1913), *Impressions de Guerre, 1914–1915* (1916), *Le Sacrifice, 1914–1916* (1917), *Défense de l'Occident* (1927), *Avant-Postes* (1929), etc. Awarded grand prize in literature (1928).

**Mass′mann** (mäs′män), **Hans Ferdinand.** 1797–1874. German philologist; professor, Munich (1829); to Berlin (1843) as organizer of a gymnastics curriculum for Prussia, and professor of Old German language and literature, U. of Berlin (1846). Author of works on Germanic philology.

**Mas′son′** (mȧ′sôN′), **Antoine.** 1636–1700. French engraver, esp. of portraits, as *Comte d'Harcourt*, *Olivier d'Ormesson*, *Marie de Lorraine*, *Duchesse de Guise;* his *Pèlerins d'Emmaüs*, after Titian, is also well-known and is often called in English *The Tablecloth* because of the delicacy with which texture of the table linen is rendered.

**Mas′son** (măs′′n), **David.** 1822–1907. Scottish man of letters; edited *Macmillan's Magazine* (1859–68); editor of register of Scottish privy council (1880–99); historiographer royal for Scotland (1896); edited works of Goldsmith (1869), Milton (3 vols., 1874), and De Quincey (14 vols., 1889–90). Author of *Essays, Biographical and Critical* (1856), *British Novelists* (1859), *Drummond of Hawthornden* (1873), *Chatterton* (1873), *De Quincey* (in "English Men of Letters" series, 1878), and his magnum opus, *Life of Milton* (6 vols., 1859–80), the standard authority.

**Mas′son′** (mȧ′sôN′), **Frédéric.** 1847–1923. French historian; friend and secretary to Prince Napoleon, and entrusted with family papers of Napoleon for classification; from these papers he drew material for a number of books on Napoleon I.

**Mas′son** (măs′′n), **Tom,** *in full* **Thomas Lansing.** 1866–1934. American humorist and editor, b. Essex, Conn.; literary and managing editor of *Life* magazine (1893–1922); assoc. editor of *Saturday Evening Post* (1922–30). Author of *A Bachelor's Baby, and Some Grown-Ups* (1907), *In Tune With the Finite* (1928), *Ascensions* (1929), etc.

**Mas′sue′** (mȧ′sü′), **Henri de.** Marquis **de Ru′vi′gny′** (dẽ rü′vē′nyē′). 1605–1689. French soldier; zealous Protestant, deputy general of Huguenots at French court (1653); friend of Turenne; naturalized in England (1680), to which he emigrated (1686) after revocation of Edict of Nantes. His son **Henri** (1648–1720), 2d Marquis de Ruvigny and 1st Earl of **Gal′way** (gôl′wā), soldier, was aide-de-camp to Turenne (1672–75); retired to England (1688); commanded cavalry regiment of French refugees in service of William III (1691); commander in chief in Ireland (1692); one of lords justices of Ireland (1697–1701); commander of English forces in Portugal in War of Spanish Succession, entering Madrid (1706); defeated at Almansa (1707); lord justice in Ireland (1715–16).

**Mas′sys** (mäs′ĭs) *or* **Mat′sys** (mät′sĭs) *or* **Mes′sys** (mĕs′ĭs) *or* **Met′sys** (mĕt′sĭs), **Quentin** *or* **Quinten.** 1466?–1530. Flemish painter; a leading representative of the early Flemish school of Antwerp. Painted Biblical and genre pictures, portraits, and decorations, including *The Money Changer and his Wife*, portraits of Erasmus, *Man with the Eyeglasses.* His son **Jan** (1509–1575), religious and genre painter, painted at first in imitation of his father and then after the Roman masters.

**Mas′ters** (mȧs′tẽrz), **Edgar Lee.** 1869–1950. American writer, b. Garnett, Kans. Studied law; adm. to bar (1891). Author of *A Book of Verses* (1898), *Blood of the Prophets* (1905), *Spoon River Anthology* (1915), *Starved Rock* (verse; 1919), *Mitch Miller* (1920), *The New Spoon River* (1924), *Lincoln—the Man* (1931), *Vachel Lindsay, a biography* (1935), *Whitman* (1937), *The New World* (poem; 1937), *Mark Twain* (1938), *More People* (verse; 1939), *Illinois Poems* (1941).

**Mas′ter·son** (mȧs′tẽr·s′n), **William Barclay,** *known as* **Bat** (băt). 1853–1921. American sports writer, b. in Iroquois County, Ill. Indian fighter, scout, gambler, sheriff, and U.S. marshal, in western frontier towns (to 1900). Sports writer on New York *Morning Telegraph* (1902–21).

**Ma·suc′cio di Salerno** (mä·zōōt′chō dē sä·lĕr′nō). *Real name* **Tommaso de′i Guar·da′ti** (dā′ē gwär·dä′tē). fl. 15th century. Italian writer of novelle; secretary to Roberto Sanseverino, Prince of Salerno; known for his *Novellino* (1476), collection of 50 novelle written in Neapolitan dialect, source book for Shakespeare's *Romeo and Juliet.*

**Mas·u′di, al-** (ăl′măs·ōō′dē). *Arab.* **Abu-al-Ḥasan ʻAli al-Masʻūdi.** d. 956. Arab historian, b. Baghdad. Chief work, *Annals* (a chronological sketch of general history, 30 vols.), and an abridgment of two parts of the *Annals* under title *Meadows of Gold and Mines of Gems.*

**Ma′ta·a′fa** (mä′tä·ä′fä). King of Samoan Islands (1888–89). Chosen king after dethronement of Malietoa (*q.v.*); in conflict with German marines (1888); aspired to throne after Malietoa's restoration but was defeated; friend of Robert Louis Stevenson.

**Ma′ta Ha′ri** (mä′tȧ hä′rē) [perhaps from Malayan *matahari*, "sun"]. *Real name* **Gertrud Margarete Zel′le** (zĕl′ĕ). 1876–1917. Dancer on the French stage; executed as a spy by the French.

**Ma′ta·mo′ros** (mä′tä·mō′rōs), **Mariano.** 1770?–1814. Mexican priest and patriot; served with insurgents under command of Morelos (1811–14); captured in battle of Puruarán (Jan. 5, 1814) and executed at Valladolid (Feb. 3, 1814). The town of Matamoros on the Rio Grande is named in his honor.

**Ma·tej'ko** (mä·tĕ'ē·kô), **Jan.** 1838–1893. Polish historical painter, chiefly of scenes from Polish history.

**Ma·ter'na** (mä·tĕr'nä), **Amalie.** 1845–1918. Austrian dramatic soprano, notably in Wagnerian opera; m. the actor Karl Friedrich.

**Math'er** (măth'ẽr; măth'ẽr), **Cotton.** 1663–1728. Son of Increase Mather (*q.v.*; see also Richard MATHER). American Congregational clergyman, b. Boston; grad. Harvard (1678). Ordained (1685); assisted his father in Second Church pastorate, Boston (1685–1723); succeeded him in the pastorate (1723–28). Active in opposition to royal governor Andros (1689) and in support of Andros's successor. Countenanced witchcraft trials and executions (1692–93) but later supported view that the trials were unfair. Defeated as candidate for presidency of Harvard; aided Yale; invited to be president of Yale (1721), but refused. Continued as leader in his church; active in charitable and educational fields. Author of numerous religious books, including *Wonders of the Invisible World* (1693), *Magnalia Christi Americana* (1702), *Bonifacius* or, later, *Essays to Do Good* (1710), *Ratio Disciplinae* (1726), etc.

**Mather, Frank Jewett.** 1868–1953. American educator, author, and art critic, b. Deep River, Conn. Professor of art and archaeology, Princeton (1910–33). Author of *Homer Martin, Poet in Landscape* (1912), *Estimates in Art* (1916), *Modern Painting* (1927), *Concerning Beauty* (1935), *Venetian Painters* (1936), etc.

**Mather, Increase.** 1639–1723. Son of Richard Mather (*q.v.*). American Congregational clergyman, b. Dorchester, Mass.; grad. Harvard (1656). Preached in England (1658–61); returned to America after the Restoration. Pastor, Second Church, Boston (1664–1723). President of Harvard (1685–1701). In England, representing Massachusetts colonial interests and securing new charter and new governor (1688–92). His *Cases of Conscience Concerning Evil Spirits* (1693) is credited with ending executions for witchcraft. Continued until his death a leader in his church and a spokesman for Congregationalism. Author of a large number of religious treatises, political pamphlets, sermons, and *A Brief History of the Warr with the Indians* (1676).

**Mather, Kirtley Fletcher.** 1888– . American geologist, b. Chicago. Professor (from 1927), director of summer school (from 1934), Harvard; geologist, U.S. Geological Survey (1919–37). Author of *Old Mother Earth* (1928), *Science in Search of God* (1928), *Sons of Earth* (1930), *Adult Education, a Dynamic for Democracy* (with Dorothy Hewitt; 1937), *A Source Book in Geology* (with S. L. Mason; 1939), etc.

**Mather, Richard.** 1596–1669. Congregational clergyman, b. Lowton, Lancashire, Eng. Ordained in Anglican Church (1618); suspended from ministry (1633, 1634) because of his Puritanism. To America (1635); pastorate at Dorchester (1636–69). Leader of Congregationalism in Massachusetts; author of treatises defending and expounding Congregationalism. His son was Increase Mather; his grandson, Cotton Mather; his great-grandson, Samuel Mather (1706–1785). Also among his descendants in America were Samuel Mather (1851–1931), Samuel Livingston Mather, Stephen Tyng Mather. See the separate biographies.

**Mather, Samuel.** 1706–1785. Son of Cotton Mather (*q.v.*; see also Richard MATHER). American Congregational clergyman, b. Boston. Grad. Harvard (1723). Pastor, Second Church, Boston (1732–41); dismissed. Organized and remained pastor of new congregation (1741–85). Author of *A Life of...Cotton Mather* (1729).

**Mather, Samuel Livingston.** 1817–1890. Descendant of Richard Mather (*q.v.*). American financier, b. Middletown, Conn. Exploited iron-ore deposits on borders of Lake Superior; president and treasurer, Cleveland Iron Mining Co. (1869–90). His son **Samuel** (1851–1931) entered employ of Cleveland Iron Mining Co. (1873); organized Pickands, Mather & Co., dealers in iron ore, coal, and pig iron (1883); expanded iron and steel interests inherited from father (from 1890).

**Mather, Stephen Tyng.** 1867–1930. Descendant of Richard Mather (*q.v.*). First director, National Park Service, in U.S. Department of the Interior (1917–29); established co-ordinated system of national parks and principles for their preservation and use.

**Mathers, Helen Buckingham.** See REEVES.

**Math'e·son** (măth'ĕ·s'n), Sir **Charles George.** 1876–1948. English ship captain; commodore of the Orient Line (retired, 1938); served in navy during World War, esp. with the "Q" ships (1914–18); knighted (1937); author of *Fifty Years of Ocean Hazard* (1939).

**Matheson, Samuel Pritchard.** 1852–1942. Canadian prelate of the Anglican Church, b. in Manitoba; chancellor, U. of Manitoba (1900–34); archbishop of Rupert's Land (1905–31); primate of all Canada (1909–31); retired (1931).

**Math'ew** (măth'ū), **Theobald.** 1790–1856. Irish priest and orator. Known as "Apostle of Temperance." Roman Catholic priest in Capuchin order; inaugurated total-abstinence movement (1838) and carried on crusades in Irish, English, and Scottish cities and (1849–51) in America.

**Math'ews** (măth'ūz). See also MATTHEWS.

**Mathews, Albert Prescott.** See William S. B. MATHEWS.

**Mathews, Arthur Frank.** 1860–1945. American painter; best known for his murals, as in California State Capitol, Sacramento, Calif., and in State Supreme Court chamber in San Francisco.

**Mathews, Charles.** 1776–1835. English comedian; played in chief London houses (from 1803); introduced entertainments known as "at homes," including songs, recitations, ventriloquial imitations; joint manager with Frederick Henry Yates of Adelphi (from 1825). His son **Charles James** (1803–1878), actor and playwright, practiced architecture several years; gave up architecture for stage (1835); excelled as light comedian; author of many slight plays of one, two, and three acts, largely adaptations. His wife **Lucia Elizabeth** *or* **Elizabetta** (1797–1856), actress and stage singer; known as **Madame Ves'tris** (vĕs'trĭs); daughter of an engraver, Bartolozzi; married, at sixteen, Armand Vestris, and (1838) Charles James Mathews; appeared first in Italian opera (1815); gained fame in light comedy and burlesque in London theaters; lessee of Olympic (from 1831); aided her husband in management of Covent Garden (1839–42) and Lyceum (1847–54).

**Mathews, Samuel.** 1600?–1660. English colonial governor in Virginia, b. in England; to Virginia (1622). Member of the council (from 1623); a leader in revolt against tyranny of the governor; engaged in measures to secure Maryland for Virginia (1642–57). Last governor of Virginia under the Commonwealth (1658–60); died in office.

**Mathews, Shailer.** 1863–1941. American educator, b. Portland, Me.; assoc. professor (1894–97) and professor (1897–1908) of New Testament history and interpretation, divinity school of U. of Chicago, and dean of the school (1908–33). Author of *The Social Teaching of Jesus* (1897), *The Church and the Changing Order* (1907), *The Spiritual Interpretation of History* (1916), *The Faith* *of Modernism* (1924), *Creative Christianity* (1935), etc. Also wrote *The French Revolution, 1789–1815* (1922), and, with G. B. Smith, compiled *Dictionary of Religion and Ethics* (1921).

**Mathews, William Smith Babcock.** 1837–1912. American teacher of music, b. London, N.H. Organist, Centenary Methodist Episcopal Church, Chicago (1867–93). Author of many popular and educational books on music. His son **Albert Prescott** (1871–1957), physiological chemist, professor of biochemistry, U. of Cincinnati (from 1918); known esp. for research work in parthenogenesis, nerve impulses, and chemical biology.

**Math′ew·son** (măth′ū·s'n), **Christopher,** *known as* **Christy.** 1880–1925. American baseball pitcher, b. Factoryville, Pa.; educ. Bucknell. Pitcher for New York National League baseball team, the "Giants" (1900–16); manager, Cincinnati team (1916–18).

**Ma·thi′as** (mȧ·thī′ăs), **Thomas James.** 1754?–1835. English satirist and Italian scholar; caused sensation with satirical poem *The Pursuits of Literature* (1794); edited Gray (1814); passed latter part of life at Naples; wrote Italian verse, edited works of Italian authors including Tiraboschi.

**Ma·thi′as·sen** (mȧ·tē′ȧ·s'n), **Therkel.** 1892– . Danish archaeologist; leader of several expeditions to Greenland (1929–34); authority on Eskimo archaeology.

**Ma′thieu′** (mȧ′tyû′), **Émile Louis Victor.** 1844–1932. Belgian composer; director, Louvain Music School (1881–98) and Royal Conservatory, Ghent (1898–1924). Composed operas and comic operas, including *Georges Dandin* (1876), *La Bernoise* (1880), and *L'Enfance de Roland* (1895), music to Séjour's *Cromwell* (1874), the ballet *Les Fumeurs de Kiff* (1876), choruses, cantatas, symphonic poems, concertos for piano and for violin, French and Flemish songs, etc.

**Mathieu, François Désiré.** 1839–1908. French Roman Catholic prelate; bishop of Angers (1893), archbishop of Toulouse (1896–99), cardinal (1899). Among his writings are *L'Ancien Régime dans la Province de Lorraine* (1878) and *Le Concordat de 1801* (1904).

**Ma·til′da** (mȧ·tĭl′dȧ), Saint. 890?–968. Queen of Germany; daughter of Saxon Count Theodoric; m. Henry the Fowler (909), who became king of Germany (919). Noted for philanthropies; founded many convents, in one of which she spent her last years.

**Matilda.** Name of three queens of England: (1) **Matilda of Flanders.** d. 1083. Wife (m. about 1053) of William I (the Conqueror); crowned (1068) on her arrival in England after serving ably as regent in Normandy during William's absences. (2) **Matilda** *or* **Maud** (môd). 1080–1118. Daughter of Malcolm III of Scotland; first wife (m. Nov. 11, 1100) of Henry I of England. (3) **Matilda.** 1103?–1152. Daughter of Eustace III, Count of Boulogne; wife (m. before 1125) of Stephen of Blois, who seized English crown (1135).

**Matilda.** 1156–1189. Daughter of Henry II of England; m. (1168) Henry the Lion.

**Matilda** *or* **Maud** (môd), Empress. 1102–1167. Daughter of Henry I of England and Matilda; m. Holy Roman Emperor Henry V at Mainz (1114); returned to England after his death (1125); recognized by barons as Henry I's successor; married (1128) by her father to Geoffrey Plantagenet, son of count of Anjou (see ANJOU family) in order to insure Anjou's noninterference in Normandy. On assumption by Stephen of English throne, invaded England with her half brother, Robert, Earl of Gloucester (1139); captured Stephen (1141); established herself as "Lady of England and Normandy"; after six months, driven from London by citizenry as result of her greed; returned to Normandy (1148); jointly with husband ceded (1150) duchy of Normandy to their son Henry, who became (1154) King Henry II of England.

**Matilda of Tuscany.** 1046–1115. Known as "the Great Countess." Countess of Tuscany and inheritor of power over large part of northern Italy; strong supporter of papacy against the empire.

**Ma′tisse′** (mȧ′tēs′), **Henri.** 1869–1954. French painter; studied under Gustave Moreau; identified with post-impressionism and a leader among the Fauvists; among his canvases are *Desserte, Italienne, Le Jeune Marin, Odalisque, Femme au Turban, La Musique, Fenêtre à Tanger, Les Trois Sœurs,* and *Torse de Jeune Fille.*

**Ma′tos Fra·go′so** (*Span.* mä′tōs frä·gō′sō), **Juan de.** 1608?–1689. Portuguese-born playwright in Madrid; author esp. of comedies, including *El Redentor Cautivo, La Dicha por el Desprecio, El Yerro del Entendido.*

**Ma·tsu·dai·ra** (mä·tsōō·dī·rä), **Tsuneo.** 1872–1949. Japanese diplomat; vice-minister for foreign affairs (1923); ambassador to U.S. (1925–28), and Great Britain (1928–36).

**Ma·tsu·i** (mä·tsōō·ē), Baron **Keishiro.** 1868–1946. Japanese diplomat; ambassador to France (1914–20); minister of foreign affairs (1924); ambassador to Great Britain (1925–28).

**Ma·tsu·ka·ta** (mä·tsōō·kä·tä), Prince **Masayoshi.** 1835–1924. Japanese statesman, b. Kagoshima, son of a samurai of Satsuma clan; minister of home affairs (1880) and finance (1881–91, 1898–1900); premier of Japan (1891–92, 1896–98); keeper of privy seal (1917–22). Created prince (1922)

**Matsuo Basho** *or* **Matsuo Munefusa.** See BASHO.

**Ma·tsu·o·ka** (mä·tsōō·ō·kä), **Yosuke.** 1880–1946. Japanese statesman; to U.S. (1893); grad. law school, U. of Oregon (1900). Secretary to premier of Japan (1919); director of South Manchurian railway (1920–26) and its vice-president (1927). Resigned position with railway (1930); represented Japan in Geneva at League of Nations (1932) in pleading for recognition of Japanese policy in Manchuria (Manchukuo); lost his case, but led Japanese delegation out of league and gained great repute in Japan. President, South Manchurian railway (1935–39). Minister of foreign affairs (1940–41); allied Japan with Axis powers and concluded nonaggression pact with Russia. Died while on trial as war criminal.

**Matsys, Quentin.** See Quentin MASSYS.

**Mattaniah.** See ZEDEKIAH.

**Mattathias.** See ANTIGONUS II of Judea; MACCABEES.

**Mat·te′o da Ba′scio** (mät·tā′ō dä bä′shō) *or* **Bas′si** (bäs′sē). c. 1495–1552. Italian monk, b. Bascio; founder and first vicar-general of Capuchin order (1529).

**Mat′te·ot′ti** (mät′tā·ôt′tē), **Giacomo.** 1885–1924. Italian Socialist politician; member of Italy's legislature, and secretary of the Italian United Socialist party; murdered by Fascisti (June 10, 1924).

**Mat′ter′** (mȧ′târ′), **Jacques.** 1791–1864. French historian and philosopher; author of *Histoire de l'École d'Alexandrie* (1820), *Histoire Critique du Gnosticisme...* (1828), *Schelling...* (1842), *Le Mysticisme en France au Temps de Fénelon* (1864), etc.

**Mat′te·son** (măt′ĕ·s'n), **Tompkins Harrison.** 1813–1884. American historical and genre painter, b. Peterboro, N.Y. Studio in New York City (1841–50); many of his popular historical paintings became widely known from their reproductions, as *Spirit of Seventy-six, Washington Crossing the Delaware, The First Sabbath of the Pilgrims, Washington's Inaugural, Eliot Preaching to the Indians.*

**Mat′te·uc′ci** (mät′tā·ōōt′chē), **Carlo.** 1811–1868. Italian physicist; investigated physiological effects of electricity.

**Mat′the·son** (mät′ĕ·zôn), **Johann.** 1681–1764. German composer and writer on music; tenor opera singer in Hamburg (1697–1705); befriended Handel (1703); musical director (1715–28) and canon at Hamburg Cathedral; contributed to development of church cantata and introduced female singers into his choir. Author of biography of Handel (1761), and translations of English works. Composer of eight operas, 24 oratorios and cantatas, suites for clavier, flute sonatas, a Passion, a mass, etc.

**Mat′thew** (măth′ū), Saint. In the Bible, a collector of customs at Capernaum, who at the summons of Jesus became one of the twelve apostles (*Matt.* ix. 9 and x. 3; *Mark* iii. 18; *Luke* vi. 15; *Acts* i. 13); commonly identified with **Le′vi** (lē′vī), the son of Alphaeus (*Mark* ii. 14; *Luke* v. 27); traditionally regarded as author of the First Gospel.

**Matthew, Thomas.** Pseudonym of John ROGERS, used for version of Bible.

**Matthew, Tobias** *or* **Tobie.** 1546–1628. English prelate; archbishop of York (1606); as political agent in the north, actively forced recusants to conform to Church of England. His son Sir **Tobias** *or* **Tobie** (1577–1655), courtier and diplomat, became Roman Catholic in Florence (1606); sent to Madrid as adviser to Prince Charles and Buckingham (1623); secretary to Strafford in Ireland (1633); suspected by Puritans of being papal spy, driven abroad (1640); died at Ghent; friend of Francis Bacon, whose essays he translated into Italian (1618); Bacon's essay *Of Friendship* written for him.

**Matthew of Westminster.** See WESTMINSTER.

**Matthew Paris.** d. 1259. See Matthew PARIS.

**Mat′thews** (măth′ūz). See also MATHEWS.

**Matthews, Brander,** *in full* **James Brander.** 1852–1929. American educator and author, b. New Orleans. Professor of literature (1892–1900) and of dramatic literature (1900–24), Columbia. Author of plays, as *Margery's Lovers* (with G. H. Jessop), *A Gold Mine*, and *On Probation*, essays, novels, and books on the drama, including *The Development of the Drama* (1903), *Playwrights on Playmaking* (1923), *Rip Van Winkle Goes to the Play* (1926).

**Matthews, Stanley.** 1824–1889. American jurist, b. Cincinnati; practiced law, Cincinnati (from 1844); served in Civil War (colonel, 1861–63); U.S. senator (1877–79); associate justice, U.S. Supreme Court (1881–89).

**Matthews, William.** 1822–1896. Bookbinder, b. Aberdeen, Scotland; to U.S. (1843); opened bindery in New York (1846); head of bindery, D. Appleton & Co. (1854–90). Collaborator with William Loring Andrews in *A Short Historical Sketch of the Art of Bookbinding* (1895).

**Mat·thi′as** (mă·thī′ăs). In the Bible, the apostle chosen by lot to fill the place of Judas Iscariot (*Acts* i. 21–26).

**Mat·thi′as** (mă·thī′ăs; *Ger.* mä·tē′äs). 1557–1619. Holy Roman emperor (1612–19). Younger son of Maximilian II. Appointed governor of Austria (1593) by his brother Emperor Rudolf. After formidable insurrection of Hungarian Protestants (1606), declared head of the Hapsburg house (*q.v.*). Forced from Rudolf by treaty (1608) cession of Austria, Hungary, and Moravia, and (1611) crown of Bohemia. Chosen emperor (1612). Attempted to establish peace between Protestant states and Catholic League but failed. Bohemians revolted (1617); uprising in Prague (1618) was beginning of Thirty Years' War.

**Mat·thi′as Cor·vi′nus** (mă·thī′ăs kôr·vī′nŭs). *Hung.* **Mátyás Hol′lós** (hôl′lōsh). 1440–1490. King of Hungary (1458–90). Second son of János Hunyadi. His election contested (1459) by Emperor Frederick III, who finally (1462) signed treaty relinquishing claims; fought successfully against Turks (c. 1462–68); waged long war against Bohemia (1468–78); proclaimed king of Bohemia (1469); by Treaty of Olomouc (1478), obtained cession of Moravia, Silesia, and Lusatia; in war with Frederick III, seized Vienna (1485); built up most powerful kingdom of Central Europe; improved internal conditions and strengthened army; held annual diets; patron of science and literature; established one of finest libraries (*Bibliotheca Corvina*) in Europe. Chose as heir to throne of Hungary his natural son **Johannes Corvinus,** *Hung.* **János Hollós** (1473–1504), but Ladislas II of Bohemia was elected instead; Johannes became ban of Croatia and Dalmatia.

**Matthison, Edith Wynne.** See under Rann KENNEDY.

**Mat′this·son** (mät′ĭ·sôn), **Friedrich von.** 1761–1831. German lyric poet. In service (1794 ff.) of Princess Louise of Anhalt-Dessau; chief librarian in service of king of Württemberg at Stuttgart (1812). Author of *Gedichte* (1787), poem *Adelaide* (set to music by Beethoven), and *Erinnerungen* (5 vols., 1810–15).

**Mat′ti·o′li** (mät′tē·ô′lē), Conte **Ercole Antonio.** 1640–1703. Italian statesman and diplomat; settled at Mantua and served as secretary of state under Charles III and Charles IV. Regarded by many as the famous secret prisoner known as "the Man in the Iron Mask," incarcerated in the Bastille (1698–1703) for revealing secret negotiations for sale of the Mantuan fortress of Casale to France.

**Matt′son** (măt′s′n), **Henry E′lis** (ē′lĭs). 1887–1971. Painter, b. Gothenburg, Sweden; to U.S. (1906); naturalized (1913). Known for landscapes and marines.

**Mat′u·rin** (măt′ū·rĭn), **Charles Robert.** 1780–1824. Irish novelist and dramatist, of Huguenot ancestry Author of Gothic romances *The Fatal Revenge* (1807), *The Wild Irish Boy* (1808), and *The Milesian Chief* (1812). Attracted notice of Sir Walter Scott, who recommended his tragedy *Bertram, or the Castle of St. Aldobrand* (1816) to Kemble and Byron; wrote two more tragedies, *Manuel* (1817) and *Fredolfo* (1819). Author of novels *Women* (1818), *Melmoth the Wanderer* (1820), and *The Albigenses* (1824).

**Mátyás Hollós.** See MATTHIAS CORVINUS.

**Mat′ze·nau′er** (mät′sĕ·nou′ẽr), **Mar′ga·re′te** (mär′gä·rā′tĕ). 1881–1963. Operatic mezzo-soprano, b. at Temesvár, Hungary; m. Ernst Preuse (1902–11), Edoardo Ferrari-Fontana (1912–17), Floyd Glotzbach (1921). Joined Metropolitan Opera Company, New York (1911); became naturalized U.S. citizen (1918). Roles include Carmen, Brünnhilde, Isolde, Herodias, Donna Elvira, Mignon.

**Mätz′ner** (měts′nẽr), **Eduard Adolf Ferdinand.** 1805–1892. German philologist; author of *Syntax der Neufranzösischen Sprache* (2 vols., 1843–45), *Französische Grammatik* (1856), *Englische Grammatik* (1860–65), and *Altenglische Sprachproben* (begun 1867; not completed), etc.

**Mau** (mou), **August.** 1840–1909. German archaeologist; concerned esp. with excavations at Pompeii.

**Mauch** (mouĸ), **Karl.** 1837–1875. German traveler in Africa; discovered gold fields (1867) and ruined city of Zimbabwe, in Mashonaland (1871).

**Mau′clair′** (mō′klâr′), **Camille.** *Orig. surname* **Faust** (fōst). 1872–1945. French writer; among his many works are *Éleusis* (prose, 1893), *Sonatines d'Automne* (verse, 1894), *Couronne de Clarté* (novel, 1895), *M. Maeterlinck* (literary criticism, 1900), *Auguste Rodin* (art criticism, 1901), *L'Impressionisme* (art criticism, 1904), *Histoire de la Musique Européenne 1850–1915* (1914), *Un Siècle de Peinture Française 1820–1920* (1929), studies of Baudelaire (1927), Heine (1930), Poe (1932), Mallarmé (1937).

**Maud** (môd). = MATILDA (1080–1118), Queen of England.

**Maud,** Empress. = MATILDA (1102–1167).

**Maud Char'lotte Mar'y Vic·to'ri·a** (môd shär'lŏt mâr'ĭ vĭk·tō'rĭ·*ȧ*). 1869–1938. Queen of Norway; youngest child of Edward VII of Great Britain; m. Prince Charles of Denmark (1896), who became King Haakon VII of Norway when Norway seceded from Sweden (1905).

**Maude** (môd), **Aylmer.** 1858–1938. English man of letters; taught in Moscow (1877–80); in business in Moscow (1890–97). Best known as biographer, translator, and interpreter of Tolstoi, of whom he was a personal friend.

**Maude, Cyril.** 1862–1951. English actor; comanager of Haymarket, London (1896–1905); builder and manager of The Playhouse (to 1915). Appeared in *The Second Mrs. Tanqueray, The Little Minister, The Manoeuvres of Jane, Cousin Kate, Grumpy,* etc.

**Maude, Frederic Nat'usch** (năt'o͝osh). 1854–1933. English military writer; entered Royal Engineers (1873); staff college graduate (1891). Author of *Cavalry versus Infantry* (1896), *Leipzig Campaign, 1813* (1908), *Jena Campaign, 1806* (1909), and *Ulm Campaign, 1805* (1912), etc.

**Maude,** Sir **Frederick Stanley.** 1864–1917. British soldier; commander of 13th division at Dardanelles (1915); took division to Mesopotamia and there assumed command of army (1916); drove Turks out of Kut-el-Amara and captured Baghdad (1917); died of cholera.

**Mauds'lay** (môdz'lĭ), **Henry.** 1771–1831. English mechanical engineer; took out patents for printing calico (1805–08); made improvements in lathe and marine engines; invented slide rest. His elder son, **Thomas Henry** (1792–1864), built up father's firm, which constructed engines for ships of British navy for quarter century. His younger son, **Joseph** (1801–1861), patented marine engines, built engines for first screw steamer for admiralty, patented feathering screw propeller and direct-acting annular-cylinder screw engine.

**Mauds'ley** (môdz'lĭ), **Henry.** 1835–1918. English psychologist; author of *Body and Mind* (1870), *Responsibility in Mental Disease* (1874), *Pathology of Mind* (1883), and *Heredity, Variation, and Genius* (1908).

**Maugham** (môm), **William Somerset.** 1874–1965. English novelist and playwright; educ. Heidelberg; grad. in medicine at St. Thomas's Hospital, London, but never practiced. Author of novels, including *Mrs. Craddock* (1902), *Of Human Bondage* (1915), *The Moon and Sixpence* (1919), *On a Chinese Screen* (1922), *Cakes and Ale* (1930), *First Person Singular* (1931), *Theatre* (1937), *The Hour Before Dawn* (1942), *The Razor's Edge* (1944); short stories, including *Rain* (1932); and plays, including *A Man of Honour* (1903), *Lady Frederick* (1907), *Smith* (1909), *Caroline* (1916), *East of Suez* (1922), *The Constant Wife* (1927), *The Sacred Flame* (1929), *The Bread-Winner* (1930), *Sheppey* (1933).

**Mau'nou'ry'** (mō'no͞o'rē'), **Michel Joseph.** 1847–1923. French soldier; in World War, commanded hastily organized 6th army and checked von Kluck's drive on Paris (Aug.–Sept., 1914); severely wounded at Soissons (Mar., 1915); military governor of Paris.

**Mauny,** Sir **Walter de.** See MANNY.

**Mau'pas'sant'** (mō'pȧ'säɴ'), **Guy de,** *in full* **Henri René Albert Guy de.** 1850–1893. French short-story writer and novelist; protégé of Flaubert. First gained attention with short story *Boule de Suif* (1880), followed by collections of short stories establishing him as supreme in this field, *La Maison Tellier* (1881), *Mademoiselle Fifi* (1883), *Contes de la Bécasse* (1883), *Les Sœurs Rondoli* (1884), *Contes et Nouvelles* (1885). Among his novels are *Une Vie* (1883), *Bel-Ami* (1885), *Mont-Oriol* (1887), *Le Horla* (1887), *Pierre et Jean* (1888), *Fort comme la Mort* (1889), *Notre Cœur* (1890), etc.

**Mau'peou'** (mō'po͞o'), **René Nicolas Charles Augustin de.** 1714–1792. French statesman; chancellor of France (1768–74); instrumental in overthrowing Parliament of Paris (1771); joined with duc d'Aiguillon and Abbé Joseph Marie Terray in forming triumvirate to administer government; forced into retirement at accession of Louis XVI (1774).

**Mau'per'tuis'** (mō'pĕr'tü·ē'), **Pierre Louis Moreau** (mô'rō') **de.** 1698–1759. French mathematician and astronomer; head of expedition sent by Louis XV into Lapland to measure a degree of longitude (1736–37); supported Newtonian theory; originated principle of least action; involved in numerous quarrels, a notable one being that with Voltaire, who satirized him.

**Mau'pin'** (mō'păɴ'), Mme. *Nee* **d'Au'bi'gny'** (dō'bē'nyē'). 1673–?1707. French operatic contralto; heroine of T. Gautier's novel *Mademoiselle de Maupin* (1835).

**Mau'ra y Mon'ta·ner'** (mou'rä ē môn'tä·nĕr'), **Antonio.** 1853–1925. Spanish statesman; member of the legislature (1881 ff.); prime minister of Spain (1903–04; 1907–09; 1918; 1919; 1921).

**Mau'rel'** (mô'rĕl'), **Victor.** 1848–1923. French operatic baritone; sang in Paris Opéra (1879–94, with short interruptions). Chosen by Verdi to create role of Iago in his *Otello* (1887) and role of Falstaff (1893) at La Scala, Milan; with Metropolitan Opera Co. (1894–95); returned to Opéra Comique (1896–1904), where he created role of Mathias in Erlanger's *Le Juif Polonais* (1901); settled in New York City as voice teacher (1909).

**Mau'ren·bre'cher** (mou'rĕn·brĕ'κĕr), **Wilhelm.** 1838–1892. German writer on history, specialist on Reformation and Counter Reformation periods.

**Mau're·pas'** (môr'pȧ'), Comte **Jean Frédéric Phélipeaux.** 1701–1781. French minister of state (1738–49). Dismissal caused by Mme. de Pompadour because of a satirical couplet against her. Lived in exile (1749–74). Prime minister at accession of Louis XVI (1774). Alarmed at Turgot's reforms, helped bring about his downfall (1776); also, later, dismissal of Necker (1781).

**Mau'rer** (mou'rĕr), **Georg Ludwig von.** 1790–1872. German statesman and law historian; member of regency during minority of King Otto in Greece (1832–35); Bavarian minister of foreign affairs and justice (briefly, 1847). Author of *Das Griechische Volk Vor und Nach dem Freiheitskampf* (3 vols., 1835–36), and a series (1854–71) of works on early German systems of government. His son **Konrad** (1823–1902) was law historian and specialist in North Germanic law, history, and literature; professor, Munich (1847–93).

**Mau'rer** (mou'rĕr; mour'ĕr), **Louis.** 1832–1932. Artist, b. Germany; to U.S. (c. 1851); member of staff of Currier and Ives (*qq.v.*); painted many water colors of American scenes.

**Mau'riac'** (mô'ryȧk'), **François.** 1885–1970. French writer; on staff of *Revue de Temps Présent;* author of *Les Mains Jointes* (verse; 1909), *Adieu à l'Adolescente* (poem; 1911), and a number of novels, including *Le Baiser au Lépreux* (1922), *Genitrix* (1924), *Le Noeud de Vipères* (1932), *La Pharisienne* (1941), *L'Agneau* (1954), etc. Awarded Nobel prize in literature (1952).

**Mau'rice** (mô'rĭs; mŏr'ĭs). *Ger.* **Moritz.** 1521–1553.

Duke of Saxony (1541–53) and elector in the Albertine line (1547–53), b. Freiberg. Son of Henry the Pious. Supported Reformation and aided Charles V in various wars (1542–44) and esp. against Elector John Frederick (1546–47). In opposition to Charles, granted favorable terms to Magdeburg (1550), concluded treaty with Henry II of France (1552), and refused to recognize Augsburg Interim (1548); finally forced Charles to leave Germany and to conclude the Treaty of Passau (1552); rule ended by struggle with Albert Alcibiades; mortally wounded at Sievershausen.

**Maurice.** *Commonly known as* **Maurice of Nas'sau** (năs'ô; näs'ou). 1567–1625. Stadholder of the Dutch Republic (1587–1625). Son of William the Silent. Prince of Orange (1618) and Count of Nassau. Elected stadholder by northern provinces (1584–91); in command of armed forces; a great military leader; seized Zutphen, Deventer, and Nimeguen (1591), Gertruydenberg (1593), and Province of Groningen (1594); defeated Spaniards at Turnhout (1597) and Nieuport (1600); lost Ostend (1604); agreed to truce with Spain (1609) but renewed struggle (1621); worked with Jan van Olden Barneveldt from 1587 to 1609 but thereafter his enemy; caused his death (1619).

**Maurice,** Sir **Frederick Barton.** 1871–1951. British soldier; served in Boer War (1899–1900) and World War (1914–18); director of military operations, imperial general staff (1915–18). Author of *Russo-Turkish War, 1877-78; Forty Days in 1914; Robert E. Lee, the Soldier* (1925); *British Strategy* (1929); and *Life of Lord Haldane* (2 vols., 1937–38).

**Maurice, Frederick Denison,** *in full* **John Frederick Denison.** 1805–1872. English theologian, of Broad Church party, and chief founder of Christian Socialism. Ordained priest (1834); wrote one novel, *Eustace Conway* (1834); professor of English history and literature, King's Coll., London (1840), and of theology (1846–53), but deprived (1853) for alleged unorthodoxy in *Theological Essays,* dealing with atonement and eternal life. Helped to found Queen's Coll., London (1848), and Working Men's Coll. (1854); professor of moral philosophy, Cambridge (1866). Active supporter of all attempts at co-operation among working men; with Thomas Hughes and Charles Kingsley, founded Christian Socialism movement. Author of *The Religions of the World and their Relations to Christianity* (1847), *Moral and Metaphysical Philosophy* (1848), *The Doctrine of Sacrifice* (1854), and *Social Morality* (1869). His son Sir **John Frederick** (1841–1912), professor of military history at staff college (1885), was author of prize essay that influenced army reform at beginning of twentieth century, and of books on military history.

**Maurice of Nassau.** (1) = Joan Mauritz, Count NASSAU-SIEGEN. (2) = MAURICE (1567–1625).

**Maurice of Saxony.** See Hermann Maurice, Comte de SAXE.

**Mau·ri'ci·us** (mô·rĭsh'ĭ·ŭs; -shŭs). *In full* **Flavius Tiberius Mauricius.** *Also known by English name* **Maurice.** 539?–602. Emperor of the Eastern Roman Empire (582–602). Of Roman descent, b. in Cappadocia; made emperor by Tiberius II; married (582) Tiberius's daughter Constantina; successfully concluded Persian war (591); through his general, Priscus (d. 612), defeated Avars several times (598–601); faced by mutiny of Danube army, forced to abdicate (602); killed by Phocas.

**Mau'ro·cor·da'tos** *or* **Mau'ro·kor·da'tos** (mä'vrô-kôr·thä'tôs). = MAVROKORDATOS.

**Mau'rois'** (mô'rwä'), **André.** *Pseudonym of* **Émile Salomon Wilhelm'** (vē'lĕlm') **Her'zog'** (ĕr'zôg'). 1885–1967. French writer; liaison officer with British forces in World War I (1914–18). Among his many works are *Les Silences du Colonel Bramble* (1918), *Les Discours du Docteur O'Grady* (1921), *Ariel ou la Vie de Shelley* (1923), *Vie de Disraeli* (1927), *Byron* (1930), *Le Peseur d'Âmes* (1931), *Tourguéniev* (1931), *Voltaire* (1932), *Dickens* (1934), *Histoire d'Angleterre* (1937), *Châteaubriand* (1938).

**Mau'ro·mi·cha'lis** (mä'vrô·mē·kä'lyēs). = MAVROMICHALIS.

**Maur'ras'** (mô'rä'), **Charles.** 1868–1952. French writer; on staff of *L'Événement, Revue Bleue, Revue Encyclopédique;* contributor to *Le Soleil, La Gazette de France,* and *Le Figaro,* where he campaigned against democratic ideas; coeditor with Léon Daudet of Royalist journal *L'Action Française.* Among his many works are *Jean Moréas* (1891), *Le Chemin de Paradis* (1895), *Enquête sur la Monarchie* (1900), *Les Amants de Venise, George Sand et Musset* (1902), *Kiel et Tanger* (1910), *Tombeaux* (1921), *L'Allée des Philosophes* (1924), and *La Musique Intérieure* (verse, 1925).

**Mau'rus** (mô'rŭs) *or* **Maur** (*Fr.* môr), Saint. 512?–584. French monk; disciple of Saint Benedict; founder and first abbot of Benedictine monastery Saint-Maur-de-Glanfeuil at Saint-Maur-sur-Loire.

**Maurus, Terentianus.** See TERENTIANUS MAURUS.

**Mau'ry'** (mô'rē'), **Jean Siffrein.** 1746–1817. French Roman Catholic prelate; member of States-General (1789) and Constituent Assembly (1789–91); emigrated from France (1792). Created cardinal (1794). Returned to France under Napoleon; archbishop of Paris (1810–14); fled to Rome at Restoration. Among his writings, best-known is *Essai sur l'Éloquence de la Chaire.*

**Maury, Louis Ferdinand Alfred.** 1817–1892. French scholar and archaeologist; general director of the national archives (1868–1888). Works include *Essai sur les Légendes Pieuses du Moyen Âge* (1843) and *Croyances et Légendes de l'Antiquité* (1863).

**Mau'ry** (mô'rĭ), **Matthew Fon·taine'** (fŏn·tān'). 1806–1873. American naval officer and oceanographer, b. near Fredericksburg, Va. Superintendent, Depot of Charts and Instruments, and of the Naval Observatory (1842–61); conducted researches on ocean winds and currents; made wind and current charts of Atlantic, Pacific, and Indian oceans; published (1855) *The Physical Geography of the Sea,* first textbook of modern oceanography; prepared chart of sea bottom in Atlantic between U.S. and Europe to show practicability of submarine cable. Resigned from U.S. navy to enter Confederate service (1861); agent of Confederacy in England (1862–65). Professor of meteorology, V.M.I. (1868–73). Author of *First Lessons in Geography* (1868), *The World We Live In* (1868), etc. Maury Hall, U.S. Naval Academy, Annapolis, is named in his honor. His birthday, Maury Day (Jan. 14), is a school holiday in Virginia. Elected to American Hall of Fame (1930).

**Maur'ya** (mä'ŏŏr·yȧ). A dynasty (322?–185 B.C.) of Hindu kings of India, founded by Chandragupta (*q.v.*). Its greatest ruler was Asoka (273–232 B.C.), whose kingdom comprised nearly all of India.

**Mau'ser** (mou'zẽr), **Peter Paul** (1838–1914) and his brother **Wilhelm** (1834–1882). German inventors; produced a needle gun (1863); to Liége (1867), where they perfected breech-loading gun which became "Mauser model 1871" after its adoption by Prussian government in 1871; purchased arsenal at Oberndorf am Neckar to manufacture their guns; invented a pistol, a revolver, and repeating rifle. Peter Paul Mauser invented the Mauser magazine rifle (1897).

**Mau·so'lus** (mô·sō'lŭs). d. about 353 B.C. Ruler of

Caria; chiefly known because of magnificent monument (named from him, *Mausoleum*) erected in his memory at Halicarnassus by his sister and widow, Artemisia (*q.v.*).

**Mauth′ner** (mout′nẽr), **Fritz.** 1849–1923. German writer; author of collection of parodies on contemporary poets, of satirical novels, historical novels, and philosophical works, esp. on speech.

**Mau′ve** (mou′vĕ), **Anton.** 1838–1888. Dutch landscape and animal painter, both in oils and water colors.

**Mau′vil′lon′** (mō′vē′yôɴ′), **Jakob.** 1743–1794. German military engineer and political economist; champion of physiocratic doctrine in economics.

**Mav′er·ick** (măv′ẽr·ĭk), **Samuel Augustus.** 1803–1870. American pioneer in Texas (from 1835); engaged in revolutionary agitation and fighting which led to Texan independence; member of convention which established Republic of Texas (1836); mayor of San Antonio (1839); member of Texas congress (1845) and of first legislature of State of Texas. Owned large cattle ranch (385,000 acres). The term *maverick* (for an unbranded animal) arose from his practice of not branding his calves.

**Ma′vor** (mā′vẽr), **James.** 1854–1925. Scottish-born Canadian economist and educator; professor, U. of Toronto (1892–1923). Uncle of James Bridie.

**Mavor, O. H.** Real name of James Bridie.

**Ma′vro·kor·da′tos** (mä′vrô·kôr·thä′tôs), **Alexandros.** 1791–1865. Greek statesman, scholar, and patriot; devoted himself to cause of Greek independence; president of first national assembly (1822); distinguished himself in defense of Missolonghi (1822–23); prime minister of Greece (1833, 1854).

**Ma′vro·mi·cha′lis** (mä′vrô·mē·ĸä′lyēs), **Petros.** *Often called* **Pe·tro′ Bey** (pĕ·trô′ bā). 1775–1848. Greek patriot; bey of Maina (1816); led Greek revolt in the Morea (1821). Opposed Kapodistrias (*q.v.*) and his pro-Russian policy, and was imprisoned. Supported King Otto I (from 1832) and was appointed vice-president of the council of state.

**Ma·war′di, al–** (ăl′mä·wăr′dē). *Arab.* **abu–al–Ḥasan ʻAli ibn–Muḥammad al–Māwardi.** 974?–1058. Arab jurist, b. Basra; chief justice in Baghdad. Chief work, *Principles of Government*, a Utopian treatise.

**Maw′son** (mô′s′n), Sir **Douglas.** 1882–1958. British Antarctic explorer and geologist; on scientific staff of Sir Ernest Shackleton's Antarctic expedition (1907); leader of Australasian Antarctic expedition (1911–14) and British, Australian, and New Zealand Antarctic expedition (1929–31); professor, U. of Adelaide (1920 ff.).

**Max** (màks), **Adolphe.** 1869–1939. Belgian politician and patriot; burgomaster of Brussels (1909–14); stubbornly opposed German abuses of power and requisitions on the people of the occupied city (1914) until the Germans removed him to an internment camp in Germany. Returned after Nov. 11, 1918. Elected to the Chamber of Representatives (1919) and appointed minister of state.

**Max** (mäks), **Gabriel von.** 1840–1915. German historical and genre painter and illustrator; studied under his father, **Joseph Max** (1803–1854), sculptor, and under Piloty at Munich (1863–69); settled in Munich and taught at Munich Acad. (1879–83).

**Max·en′ti·us** (măk·sĕn′shĭ·ŭs; -shŭs), **Marcus Aurelius Valerius.** d. 312. Roman emperor (306–312). Son of Maximian (*q.v.*); passed over in appointment of new Caesars on abdication (305) of his father and Diocletian; led uprising in Rome (306) and was proclaimed Caesar by praetorians; overthrew Severus and drove Galerius out of Italy; quarreled with his father and banished him (308); engaged in war (312) with Constantine and was totally defeated at battle of Milvian Bridge (or Saxa Rubra); drowned in the Tiber.

**Max′im** (măk′sĭm), Sir **Hiram Stevens.** 1840–1916. Inventor, b. Sangerville, Me. In engineering works, Fitchburg, Mass. (c. 1865); chief engineer, United States Electric Lighting Co., first company of its kind in America (1878). To England (1881); became naturalized; organized Maxim Gun Co. (1884), merged with Nordenfeldt Co. (1888), absorbed into Vickers' Sons and Maxim (1896); knighted by Queen Victoria (1901). Best known of his many inventions is the Maxim gun, a recoil-operated machine gun. His brother **Hudson** (1853–1927), originally named **Isaac** after his father, was an inventor and explosives expert; became chief engineer of Columbia Powder Manufacturing Co., Squankum, N.J.; organized Maxim Powder Co. (1893) and took over plant in Squankum; sold out his plant and smokeless powder patents to E. I. Du Pont de Nemours & Co. (1897); consultant for this company (1897–1927); invented high explosive, maximite, a smokeless powder, improvements for torpedo boats, a process for making calcium carbide, etc. Sir Hiram's son **Hiram Percy** (1869–1936) was an American inventor; invented many electrical instruments, automobile improvements, but best known for Maxim silencer for firearms; author of *Life's Place in the Cosmos* (1933).

**Max·im′i·an** (măk·sĭm′ĭ·ăn). *Lat.* **Marcus Aurelius Valerius Max·im′i·a′nus** (măk·sĭm′ĭ·ā′nŭs). *Surnamed* **Her·cu′li·us** (hûr·kū′lĭ·ŭs). *Sometimes known as* **Maximianus I.** d. 310. Roman emperor (286–305, 306–308), b. of humble origin in Pannonia. Made Caesar by Diocletian (285) and Augustus (286); ruled in Italy and Africa (293–305); abdicated simultaneously (305) with Diocletian (*q.v.*); recalled to aid his son Maxentius (306) who had caused himself to be proclaimed emperor at Rome; again emperor (306–308); expelled by Maxentius (308); fled to Gaul, but on discovery of conspiracy against Constantine, committed suicide.

**Maximianus I.** See Maximian.

**Maximianus II.** A title sometimes given to Galerius (*q.v.*).

**Max′i·mil′ian** (măk′sĭ·mĭl′yăn; -mĭl′ĭ·ăn; *Ger.* mäk′sē·mē′lē·än). *In full* **Ferdinand Maximilian Joseph.** 1832–1867. Brother of Francis Joseph, Emperor of Austria. Archduke of Austria and (1864–67) emperor of Mexico. Trained for naval service; in command of Austrian navy (1854). Viceroy of Lombardo-Venetian kingdom (1857–59). After French had partially conquered Mexico, an assembly of Mexican notables in exile met under French auspices, adopted imperial form of government for Mexico (July, 1863), and offered throne to Maximilian. He accepted throne (Apr. 10, 1864); reached Mexico City (June 12, 1864); with aid of French troops, drove Juárez over northern frontier. U.S. government refused to recognize empire and demanded (Feb. 12, 1866) that French withdraw their army; Napoleon III ordered troops withdrawn, breaking his pledge of military support for Maximilian. Juárez returned to attack (1867); besieged Maximilian at Querétaro and forced surrender (May 15, 1867). Maximilian condemned by court-martial and shot, at Querétaro (June 19, 1867). Married (1857) Princess Carlota (*q.v.*), daughter of Leopold I of Belgium.

**Maximilian.** *Known as* Prince **Max of Ba′den** (mäks, bä′dĕn). *Full Ger. name* **Maximilian Alexander Friedrich Wilhelm.** 1867–1929. Heir presumptive to grand ducal throne of Baden; b. Baden-Baden. President of Baden diet (1907–18). During World War, did much to improve conditions of British prisoners in Germany and of German prisoners in Russia; on collapse of German military system (Oct., 1918), appointed imperial chancellor; initiated negotiations for

Armistice and insisted that kaiser abdicate; resigned government to Socialist leader Ebert (Nov., 1918); retired to Salem Castle on Lake of Constance. Wrote *Erinnerungen und Dokumente* (1927) defending his war actions against charges by Ludendorff and monarchists.

**Maximilian.** Name of two kings of Bavaria:

**Maximilian I.** *In full* **Maximilian I Joseph.** 1756–1825. Elector of Bavaria (1799); sided with France against allied powers (1805); gained territory by Treaty of Pressburg (Dec. 26, 1805) and by its terms assumed title of king (1806). Remained loyal to Napoleon until just before battle of Leipzig (1813); negotiated with allies in effort to save his kingdom. Granted his people liberal constitution (1818).

**Maximilian II.** *In full* **Maximilian II Joseph.** 1811–1864. Son of King Louis I of Bavaria; succeeded to throne when his father abdicated (1848). Pursued ultraconservative policy (1848–59), but later instituted moderate constitutional government in kingdom.

**Maximilian.** Name of three electors of Bavaria:

**Maximilian I.** *Called* **the Great.** 1573–1651. Duke of Bavaria (1597–1651); as elector (1623–51). Educated by Jesuits; active opponent of Protestant cause; established Catholic League (1609) and served as its head. In Thirty Years' War (1618–48), allied himself with Emperors Ferdinand II and III; his army under count of Tilly defeated that of Elector Frederick V at White Mountain (1620); effected Wallenstein's dismissal (1630); driven from Munich by Swedish army (1632); fought against Swedes and French (1637–38); made separate peace (Truce of Ulm, 1647).

**Maximilian II Emanuel.** 1662–1726. Elector (1679–1726). Son of Elector Ferdinand Maria; married (1685) Maria Antonia, daughter of Emperor Leopold I and Margaret Theresa. Fought for Austria against Turks (1683–87). Appointed governor of Spanish Netherlands (1692); resigned on death of his son Joseph Ferdinand (1699). Aided France in War of the Spanish Succession (1701–14), but after defeat of Höchstädt (1704), forced to take refuge in Netherlands. Restored (1714).

**Maximilian III Joseph.** 1727–1777. Elector (1745–77). Son of Emperor Charles VII. Forced to renounce candidacy for imperial election; sided with Maria Theresa in Seven Years' War (1756–63).

**Maximilian.** Name of two Holy Roman emperors:

**Maximilian I.** 1459–1519. Called "the Last of the Knights." King of Germany (1486–1519) and Holy Roman emperor (1493–1519). Son of Frederick III; m. Mary of Burgundy (1477). Inaugurated many administrative reforms (1495–1512). Defeated in war with Swiss Confederacy (1499), which meant practical independence of the latter. Became involved in war with France (1494) for sovereignty of Milan and Naples. Joined League of Cambrai (1508) against Venice and (1513) the Holy League against France. As ally of Henry VIII of England, helped win battle of Guinegate (1513) against France. After victory of Francis I of France at Melegnano (1515), forced to cede Milan to the French. Author of several autobiographical works and a work on hunting.

**Maximilian II.** 1527–1576. Archduke of Austria and king of Hungary and Bohemia and Holy Roman emperor (1564–76). Son of Ferdinand I. Concluded disadvantageous truce (1568) with Selim II, Sultan of the Turks. Observed tolerant attitude toward Protestants of Germany.

**Maximilian Franz** (fränts). 1756–1801. Youngest son of Empress Maria Theresa. Archbishop and (1784–1801) elector of Cologne. Raised Bonn academy to university status (1786).

**Maximilian Henry.** 1621–1688. Son of Duke Albert VI of Bavaria. Archbishop and (1650–88) elector of Cologne. Fought in alliance with Louis XIV against States-General of Holland, the emperor, and Spain (1672–74); when enemy besieged Bonn (1673), fled to Cologne and initiated negotiations for peace.

**Maximilian Joseph.** *Pseudonym* **Phan′ta·sus** (*Ger.* făn′tä·zŏŏs). 1808–1888. Bavarian duke and writer; author of plays, novels, and travel book *Wanderung nach dem Orient...*(1839).

**Maximilian of Saxony,** Prince. 1870–1951. Saxon scholar, b. Dresden; son of King George of Saxony. Ordained priest (1896); professor of liturgics, theological seminary, Cologne (1912–16); professor of culture and literature of the ancient East, Freiburg, Switzerland (1921).

**Max′i·mi′nus** (măk′sĭ·mī′nŭs). *Also known as* **Max′i·min** (măk′sĭ·mĭn). Name of two Roman emperors: (1) **Gaius Julius Verus Maximinus.** *Surnamed* **Thrax** (thrăks), *i.e.* the Thracian. 173–238. A Thracian of unusual size and strength; made emperor (235–238) by soldiers on the Rhine after murder of Alexander Severus; cruelty and oppression caused a revolt under Gordianus in Africa; slain by his own soldiers. (2) **Galerius Valerius Maximinus.** *Originally* **Da′za** (dā′zȧ). d. 314. Roman emperor (308–314), b. in Illyria. Nephew of Galerius. Made Caesar (305) and given government of Syria and Egypt; became emperor (308); on death of Galerius (311) given command of Asia; quarreled with Licinius; totally defeated by him near Heraclea Pontica.

**Max′i·mus** (măk′sĭ·mŭs), Saint. *Called* **the Confessor.** 580?–662. Christian theologian of the East, b. Constantinople; served under Emperor Heraclius (610–630); entered monastery at Scutari (c. 630). Vigorous opponent of Monothelite doctrine; banished to Thrace (655); recalled to Constantinople (662) and commanded to accept Monothelite heresy; on refusal to do so, tortured and again banished; died soon afterward.

**Maximus.** Name of four Roman emperors: (1) **Magnus Clemens Maximus.** d. 388. Emperor (383–388), b. Spain. Led insurrection in Britain (383); defeated Gratian in Gaul (383); recognized as Augustus in Gaul, Spain, and Britain by Theodosius and Valentinian II; invaded Italy (387), driving out Valentinian; defeated and killed at Aquileia by Theodosius. (2) **Marcus Clodius Pupienus Maximus.** See PUPIENUS MAXIMUS. (3) **Petronius Maximus.** d. 455. Emperor (455). Friend of Valentinian III; formed conspiracy against Valentinian, because of emperor's treatment of his wife; after death of Valentinian, ruled three months only; slain by Vandals. (4) **Maximus Ty·ran′nus** (tĭ·răn′ŭs; tī-). d. 422. Emperor (409–411). Proclaimed in Spain (409) by rebel Gerontius; defeated and deposed by Constantine the usurper (411); killed in a second insurrection (418–422).

**Max Mül′ler** (mäks′ mül′ĕr; *Angl.* măks′ mŭl′ĕr, mĭl′ĕr), **Friedrich.** 1823–1900. British philologist, b. Dessau, Germany; son of Wilhelm Müller, poet and ducal librarian. Naturalized British subject. Engaged by East India Co. to bring out edition of Sanskrit *Rigveda* (pub. 1849–73); deputy (1850) and full (1854–68) Taylorian professor of modern European languages, Oxford; a curator of Bodleian Library (1856–63, 1881–94). First professor of comparative philology at Oxford (1868); gave up professorial activities (1875) to edit *Sacred Books of the East* (51 vols., from 1875) and devote himself to comparative mythology and comparative study of religions; exerted extraordinary stimulating influence on Oriental linguistic and mythological studies. Author of *History of Ancient Sanskrit Literature* (1859),

*Science of Language* (1861–63), *Science of Religion* (1870), *Origin and Growth of Religion* (Hibbert lectures, 1878), *Natural, Physical, Anthropological, and Psychical Religion* (Gifford lectures, 1889–93), and *Chips from a German Workshop* (collected essays; 4 vols., 1867–75).

**Max of Baden,** Prince. See MAXIMILIAN.

**Max'ton** (măks'tŭn), **James.** 1885–1946. British labor leader; organizer in Scotland for Glasgow Federation of Independent Labor party (1919–22) and chairman of this party (1926–31, 1934–39); M.P. (from 1922). Author of *Lenin* (1932) and *If I were Dictator* (1935).

**Maxtone Graham, Joyce.** See Jan STRUTHER.

**Max'well** (măks'wĕl; -wĕl). Name of Scottish family that migrated from England (c. 1100), holding titles of earl of **Mor'ton** (môr't'n), earl of **Niths'dale** (nĭths'-dāl), Lord **Maxwell,** Lord **Her'ries** (hĕr'ĭs), and including among its members:

**John Maxwell,** 4th Baron **Maxwell;** killed at Flodden (1513). His son **Robert** (d. 1546), 5th baron; member of royal council under James V; extraordinary lord of session (1533); warden of west marches; taken prisoner by English at rout of Solway Moss (1542). Robert's grandson **John** (1553–1593), 7th or 8th baron, earl of Morton; granted earldom of Morton on death of 4th earl (1581) but deprived on reversal of the attainder (1586); helped expel James VI's favorite, James Stewart, Earl of Arran (1585); assembled followers to assist invading Spaniards (1588). John's (1553–1593) son **John** (1586?–1612), 8th or 9th baron; carried on feuds with laird of Johnstone over his father's death, with Douglases over earldom of Morton; shot Johnstone, escaped to the Continent (1608); on return, beheaded for treason. John's (1586?–1612) brother **Robert** (d. 1646); restored to lordship of Maxwell and created earl of Nithsdale (1620); fought under Montrose for Charles I.

**William Maxwell** (1676–1744), 5th Earl of Nithsdale; joined English Jacobites (1715); taken prisoner at Preston (1715); joined Chevalier James Edward at Rome after escaping (1716) by aid of his wife, **Winifred** (m. 1699; d. 1749), Countess of Nithsdale, daughter of William Herbert, 1st Marquis of Powis (see HERBERT family), who wrote an account of her husband's escape.

Sir **John Maxwell** of Ter·reg'les [tĕ·rĕg''lz] (1512?–1583), Master of Maxwell, 4th Baron Herries; 2d son of Robert Maxwell, 5th Baron Maxwell; partisan of Mary, Queen of Scots; warden of west marches (1552–53, 1561); joined Mary with strong force at Dunbar (1566); called to peerage as Baron Herries in right of his wife (1566); commanded Mary's horse at Langside (1568); assisted in depriving Morton of regency (1578); on Morton's return to power, was appointed to succeed his nephew Lord Maxwell as warden of west marches; joined Lennox after raid of Ruthven.

**Maxwell, Anna Caroline.** 1851–1929. Known as "the American Florence Nightingale." American nurse, b. Bristol, N.Y. In France during World War, aiding in organizing nursing service for A.E.F. The nurses' home at Medical Center, New York, was named Anna C. Maxwell Hall in her honor.

**Maxwell, James Clerk** (klärk). 1831–1879. Scottish physicist, b. Edinburgh; educ. U. of Edinburgh and Cambridge. Professor of physics, Marischal Coll., Aberdeen (1856–60); professor of physics and astronomy, King's Coll., London (1860–65); first professor of experimental physics, Cambridge (from 1871), where he supervised building of Cavendish laboratory. At fifteen, wrote paper on a mechanical method of tracing Cartesian ovals and, at eighteen, one *On the Equilibrium of Elastic Solids;* awarded prize for essay *On the Stability of Saturn's Rings* (1859). Investigated color perception and color blindness, and kinetic theory of gases; worked on theory of electromagnetism, publishing his *Treatise on Electricity and Magnetism* (1873); demonstrated that electromagnetic action travels through space in transverse waves similar to those of light and having the same velocity, advancing hypothesis that light and electricity are the same in their ultimate nature.

**Maxwell, Jane.** Duchess of **Gordon.** See GORDON family.

**Maxwell,** Sir **John Grenfell.** 1859–1929. British soldier; served in Egypt under Kitchener (1892–1900), commanding the 2d brigade at the battle of Omdurman; in South Africa (1900–02), where he was military governor of Pretoria; in command of British forces in Egypt (1914–16); commander in chief in Ireland after the Easter Rebellion (1916), and commander in chief of the Northern command, based at York (1916–19).

**Maxwell, Mary Elizabeth.** See under Sir Edward N. C. BRADDON.

**Maxwell, Russell La·monte'** (lȧ·mŏnt'). 1890–1968. American army officer, b. Oakdale, Ill.; grad. U.S.M.A., West Point (1912); promoted through the grades to brigadier general (1941); major general commanding U.S. troops in North Africa (1942).

**Maxwell, William Babington.** 1866–1938. English novelist; served (captain) in World War (1914–18). Author of *Vivien* (1905), *The Rest Cure* (1910), *In Cotton Wool* (1912), *A Remedy Against Sin* (1920), *Gabrielle* (1926), *This is my Man* (1933), *Jacob's Ladder* (1937), etc.

**Maxwell, William Hamilton.** 1792–1850. Irish novelist; descendant of Scottish Maxwells of Nithsdale. First of school of military fiction; author of *O'Hara* (1825), *Stories of Waterloo* (1829), and *Life of the Duke of Wellington* (1839–41).

**Maxwell,** Sir **William Stirling-.** See STIRLING-MAXWELL.

**May** (mā), **Andrew Jackson.** 1875–1959. American politician; member from Kentucky, U.S. House of Representatives; chairman, House military affairs committee (from 1938).

**May** (mā'ĭ), **Lev Aleksandrovich.** = L. A. MEI.

**May** (mā), **Philip William,** *called* **Phil.** 1864–1903. English illustrator and caricaturist. Made reputation with *Phil May's Winter Annual* (from 1892), depiction of low life in *Daily Graphic* and other papers, *Sketch Book* (1895), and *Guttersnipes: Fifty Original Sketches* (1896); took du Maurier's place on staff of *Punch* (from 1896); East London types his specialty, such as habitués of the racecourse, the prize ring, the stage.

**May, Sophie.** Pseudonym of Rebecca Sophia CLARKE.

**May, Thomas.** 1595–1650. English poet and parliamentary historian; published tragedies *Antigone* and *Agrippina* and comedy *The Heir* (1622); translator of Vergil's *Georgics* and of Lucan; produced at command of Charles I poems on King Henry II (7 books) and on Edward III (7 books); secretary to Long Parliament and its historian in *The History of the Parliament of England, which began Nov. 3, 1640* (1647).

**May,** Sir **Thomas Erskine.** 1st Baron **Farn'bor'ough** (färn'bûr'ō; *esp. Brit.*, -bŭ·rŭ, -brŭ). 1815–1886. English constitutional jurist. Clerk of House of Commons (1871–86). Author of *Rules, Orders, and Forms of Procedure of the House of Commons* (1854), *The Constitutional History of England since the Accession of George III* (1861), *Democracy in Europe* (1877), etc.

**Ma·ya·kov'ski** (mŭ·yŭ·kôf'skû·ĭ; *Angl.* -skĭ), **Vladimir Vladimirovich.** 1893–1930. Russian poet; identified with futurist school; member of Bolshevik party from age of 14. His poems include *The Cloud in Trousers*

(1916), *Mystery Bouffe* (1918), *150 Million* (1920).

**May'bach** (mī'bäk), **Wilhelm.** 1847–1929. German pioneer automobile builder. In partnership with G. Daimler at Cannstatt (1882), where they produced one of first gasoline motors; technical director, Daimler Motor Co. (1895). Constructed first Mercedes automobile; credited with invention of spray-nozzle carburetor, honeycomb radiator, and change-speed gear.

**Mayenne,** Duc **de Charles de Lorraine.** 1554–1611. See under GUISE family.

**May'er** (mā'ẽr· mâr), **Brantz** (brănts). 1809–1879. American lawyer and historian, b. Baltimore. Secretary, U.S. legation in Mexico City (1841–44). Served in U.S. army; retired (1875). Wrote books on Mexico. His nephew **Alfred Marshall Mayer** (1836–1897), physicist, did research in acoustics, heat and light, gravity, electricity. Alfred's son **Alfred Goldsborough** (1868–1922), who legally changed surname to **May'or** (mā'ẽr; mâr) in 1918, was a biologist; accompanied Alexander Agassiz on Atlantic and Pacific research trips; director of marine laboratory in the Florida Keys (1904–22); conducted researches into growth of coral and coral reefs.

**May'er** (mī'ẽr), **Johann Simon.** See MAYR.

**Mayer, Johann Tobias.** 1723–1762. German mathematician, physicist, and astronomer; introduced improvements in map making; investigated libration of moon; known esp. for lunar tables.

**Mayer, Julius Robert von.** 1814–1878. German physician and physicist; claimed discovery of first law of thermodynamics, but claim was later contested.

**May'er** (mā'ẽr; mâr), **Louis Burt** (bûrt). 1885–1957. Motion-picture producer, b. in Minsk, Russia; naturalized U.S. citizen (from 1912). Organizer and vice-president, Metro Pictures Corp., and Louis B. Mayer Pictures Corp., merged into the Metro Pictures Corp. (1924) and later merged with Goldwyn Co. to become Metro-Goldwyn-Mayer Corp. First vice-president in charge of production, Metro-Goldwyn-Mayer Corp.

**May'er** (mī'ẽr), **Maria Goeppert.** 1906–1972. American (German-born) physicist. Awarded Nobel prize in physics (1963) with J. H. Jenson and E.P. Wigner for studies on nuclear shell structure.

**May'er** (mī'ẽr), **Otto.** 1846–1924. German jurist; specialist in administrative law.

**May'hew** (mā'hū), **Henry.** 1812–1887. English journalist; with Gilbert à Beckett, started comic weekly *Figaro in London* (1831–39); a founder of *Punch;* made hit with one-act farce *The Wandering Minstrel* (1834); published his chief work *London Labour and the London Poor* (1851–64); with his brother **Augustus Septimus** (1826–1875), wrote clever works of fiction, including *The Greatest Plague of Life* (1847) and *The Good Genius that Turned Everything to Gold* (1847).

**Mayhew, Thomas.** 1593–1682. English colonist in America; settled in Medford, Mass. (c. 1632); bought (1641) Martha's Vineyard, Nantucket, and the Elizabeth Islands; moved to Martha's Vineyard (1646), and acted as magistrate there. Commissioned governor of Martha's Vineyard (1671–82). His son **Thomas** (1621?–1657) was a Congregational clergyman; led colonists in settlement of Martha's Vineyard (1641). The latter's grandson **Ex·pe'ri·ence** (ĕks-pẹ̄r'·ĭ·ĕns; ĭks-) **Mayhew** (1673–1758), also a clergyman and missionary in Martha's Vineyard, wrote an Indian version of the Psalms, a number of theological works, and *Indian Converts* (1727). His son **Jonathan** (1720–1766), pastor, West Church, Boston (1747–66), was known for his liberalism in religious doctrine and his defense of liberal theories of government.

**May'nard** (mā'nẽrd; -närd), **Edward.** 1813–1891. American dentist; practiced, Washington, D.C. (1836–91); invented improvements in firearms, esp. in breech-loading rifles. His son **George Willoughby** (1843–1923) painted murals and portraits.

**May'nard'** (mā'nȧr'), **François.** 1582–1646. French poet; author of sonnets, odes, and epigrams, published in *Les Œuvres de Maynard* (1646).

**May'nard** (mā'nẽrd; -närd), **Horace.** 1814–1882. American politician, b. Westboro, Mass.; practiced law, Knoxville, Tenn. (from 1844). Member, U.S. House of Representatives (1857–63; 1866–75); Unionist during Civil War; attorney general of Tennessee (1863–65); U.S. minister to Turkey (1875–80); U.S. postmaster general (1880–81).

**Mayne** (mān), **Ethel Colburn.** d. 1941. English writer; author of *The Clearer Vision* (stories; 1898), *Jessie Vandeleur* (novel), *Blindman* (stories), *Inner Circle* (1925), biographies including *Byron,* literary criticism, and translations from the German.

**Mayne, Jasper.** 1604–1672. English dramatist and clergyman; author of *The City Match* (comedy; 1639) and *The Amorous War* (tragicomedy; 1648), the latter containing line "Time is a feathered thing." After Restoration, canon of Christ Church, Oxford; archdeacon of Chichester.

**May'nor** (mā'nôr), **Dorothy.** 1910– . American Negro soprano, b. Norfolk, Va.; debut in New York (1939) with encouragement of Koussevitzky.

**May'o** (mā'ō), **Henry Thomas.** 1856–1937. American naval officer; commander in chief, Atlantic fleet (1916–19), through whole period of American participation in World War.

**Mayo, John.** See John MAYOW.

**Mayo, Katherine.** 1867–1940. American writer, b. Ridgeway, Pa. Author of *Isles of Fear* (1925), *Mother India* (1927), *General Washington's Dilemma* (1938), etc.

**Mayo, William Worrall.** 1819–1911. Physician, b. Manchester, Eng.; to U.S. (1845). Provost surgeon for southern Minnesota, headquarters at Rochester, Minn. (from 1863). Hospital erected there by Order of St. Francis (1885) developed into present St. Mary's Hospital in which his sons Charles and William (see below) organized the Mayo Clinic (1889). His son **William James** (1861–1939), surgeon in Rochester, Minn. (from 1883); cofounder (1915, with his brother Charles) of the Mayo Foundation for Medical Education and Research in affiliation with the U. of Minn., to which he and his brother gave $2,800,000. Known esp. for operations for cancer and gallstones. Another son, **Charles Horace** (1865–1939), also a surgeon in Rochester (from 1888); surgeon, Mayo Clinic; cofounder of the Mayo Foundation (see above); known esp. for operations for goiter.

**May'or** (mā'ẽr; mâr), **Alfred Goldsborough.** See under Brantz MAYER.

**Mayor, John Eyton Bickersteth.** 1825–1910. English classical scholar; librarian (1863–67), professor of Latin (1872–1910), master (1902), St. John's Coll. Edited thirteen satires of Juvenal (1853); published *Bibliographical Clue to Latin Literature* (1873). His brother **Joseph Bickersteth** (1828–1916), classical scholar, m. niece of George Grote, historian; Grote's literary executor; editor of Cicero's *De Natura Deorum* (3 vols., 1880–85), *A Guide to the Choice of Classical Books* (1880); author of handbooks on English meter and sermons.

**May'o–Smith'** (mā'ō·smĭth'), **Richmond.** 1854–1901. Brother of Henry Preserved Smith (*q.v.*). American economist; teacher, Columbia (1877–1901), professor (from 1883); author of *Science of Statistics* (2 vols., 1895–99), etc.

**May'ow** *or* **May'ouwe** *or* **May'o** (mā'ō), **John.** 1640–

1679. English physiologist and chemist; known for work relating to respiration, chemistry of combustion, and muscular action.

**Mayr** (mīr), **Georg von.** 1841–1925. German economist and statistician.

**Mayr** (mīr) *or* **May'er** (mī'ẽr), **Johann Simon.** 1763–1845. German operatic composer in Italy; teacher at music school (1805) in Bergamo, where Donizetti was his pupil; said to have been first to introduce crescendo of the orchestra, much used by Rossini. Composed about 70 operas, also oratorios, cantatas, and other church music.

**Mayr, Richard.** 1877–1935. Austrian operatic baritone or basso cantante; member of Vienna opera (from 1902).

**Mayr, Simon.** See Simon MARIUS.

**Ma'zade'** (mȧ'zȧd'), **Charles de,** *in full* **Louis Charles Jean Robert de.** 1821–1893. French journalist; on staff of *Revue de Paris* and *Revue des Deux Mondes.* Author of *L'Espagne Moderne* (1855), *Lamartine...* (1872), *Cavour* (1877), *Thiers* (1884), *Metternich* (1889), etc.

**Ma'za'rin'** (mȧ'zȧ'răɴ'; *Angl.* măz'ȧ·rĭn, măz'ȧ·rēn'), **Jules.** *Ital.* **Giulio Ma'za·ri'ni** (mä'dzä·rē'nē). 1602–1661. French cardinal and statesman, b. of Sicilian parentage at Pescina, Abruzzi e Molise. Educ. by Jesuits at Rome (to 1619); at university of Alcalá, Spain (1619–22). Captain of infantry under Calonna (1625). Executed several diplomatic missions for Pope Urban VIII (1629–34); nuncio to France (1634–36). Entered service of Richelieu and became naturalized Frenchman (1639). Made cardinal (1641); succeeded Richelieu as prime minister (1642); retained by queen regent, Anne of Austria, after Louis XIII's death (1643–61). Foreign policy, based on that of Richelieu, generally successful during final period of Thirty Years' War (1643–48). War of the Fronde (1648–53) for a while upset his domestic policy; twice exiled (1651–52 and 1652–53). Destroyed remaining power of feudal nobles. By alliances and treaties (esp. Treaty of the Pyrenees, 1659) greatly strengthened France as a power in Europe; laid foundation for Louis XIV's later successes. Amassed a great private fortune; pensioned literary leaders and founded (1642) great library, Bibliothèque Mazarine.

**Ma'zas'** (mȧ'zȧ'), **Jacques Féréol.** 1782–1849. French violin virtuoso and composer of violin studies, concertos, the one-act comic opera *Le Kiosque* (1842), etc.

**Maz'dak** (măz'dăk). Persian religious reformer of the 5th century A.D.; originally a Magian priest; founded a new sect; preached community of property (including women), simplicity of life, and abstinence from meat.

**Ma'ze·line'** (mȧz'lēn'), **Guy.** 1900– . French novelist and journalist; author of *Les Loups* (Goncourt prize, 1932), etc.

**Ma·ze'pa** (mŭ·zyā'pŭ; *Angl.* mȧ·zĕp'ȧ), **Ivan Stepanovich.** 1640?–1709. Cossack hetman. Brought up in Polish court; after discovery of his intrigue with a lady of the court he was, by command of the lady's husband, bound naked on the back of a Ukrainian wild horse, which on being freed galloped off to its native haunts, where it was caught and Mazepa rescued; this incident the subject of Byron's poem *Mazeppa.* Remained among Ukrainian cossacks and was elected hetman (1687); given by Peter the Great title of prince of the Ukraine; sought to gain independence of the Ukraine, intriguing with Poles and later with Swedes; fled to Turkey with Charles XII of Sweden after his defeat at Poltava (1709).

**Ma'zo** (mä'thō), **Juan Bautista Martínez del.** 1612?–1667. Spanish painter; pupil and son-in-law of Velázquez; chief court painter of Philip IV (from 1661); painted figures, landscapes, and portraits.

**Ma·žu'ra·nić** (mä·zhōō'rä·nēt'y'; *Angl.* -nĭch), **Ivan.** 1814?–1890. Croatian poet and statesman; first chancellor of Croatia and Slavonia (1861); governor (ban) of Croatia (1873–80). Chief poetical work, an epic *Smrt Ismail Age Čengića.*

**Maz·ze'i** (mät·tsā'ē), **Philip.** 1730–1816. Italian physician and merchant; wine merchant in London (1755–73). In Virginia, trying to introduce viticulture (1773–78). Colonial American agent in Europe (1779–84), sending information to Jefferson. Recipient of a letter from Jefferson (the Mazzei letter, 1796) in which Jefferson bitterly attacked Federalist leaders, publication of which caused a political scandal in U.S.

**Maz·zi'ni** (mät·tsē'nē; mäd·dzē'nē), **Giuseppe.** 1805–1872. Italian patriot, b. in Genoa; practiced law in that city. Associated himself with the democratic movement in Italy; joined the Carbonari (1830); imprisoned for six months and released only after he pledged himself to leave Italy. Made his home in Marseilles; wrote a letter to Charles Albert of Sardinia which caused a decree of perpetual banishment to be announced against him. Organized (1832) secret revolutionary society, *Young Italy,* whose purpose was the unification of Italy under a republican form of government. On outbreak of revolution in Italy (1848) he returned to become a member of the triumvirate, with Aurelio Saffi and Armellini, in the Republic of Rome (1849), but went into exile when papal control of the city was re-established. Instigated rebel manifestations in Mantua (1852), Milan (1853), Genoa (1857); aided in organizing Garibaldi's expeditions (1860; 1862; 1867). Refused to take seat in Italian parliament under a monarchical government. Involved in revolutionary movement at Palermo and was captured (1870), but soon released under an amnesty issued after the fall of Rome. Remained until his death an uncompromising republican.

**Mazzola, Girolamo Francesco Maria.** See Il PARMIGIANINO.

**Maz'zo·li'no** (mät'tsō·lē'nē). *Really* **Lodovico Maz·zo'li** (mät·tsô'lē) *or* **Maz·zuo'li** (mät·tswô'lē). *Sometimes called* **Il Fer'ra·re'se** (ēl fär'rä·rā'sā). 1478?–1528. Italian painter of Ferrara school; known particularly for small canvases; as *Nativity, Adoration of the Magi, Holy Family,* and *Circumcision.*

**Maz·zo'ni** (mät·tsō'nē), **Guido.** *Called* **Il Mo'da·ni'no** (ēl mō'dä·nē'nō). 1450–1518. Italian sculptor; employed at Naples (to 1495); accompanied Charles VIII to France (1495–1515); worked chiefly in terra cotta. Designed tomb of Charles VIII, bronze bust of King Ferdinand, and a group *Adoration.*

**Mazzoni, Guido.** 1859–1943. Italian poet and literary scholar; professor of Italian language and literature, Florence (1894 ff.); senator (1910 ff.); disciple of Carducci. Among his poetic works are *Poesie* (1883), *Liber, Libro, Libertà* (1919), *Fiamelle* (1926); among his critical works, *Poeti Giovani* (1888), *Storia Letteraria d'Italia: L'Ottocento* (2 vols., 1905–13), *Francesco Ferrucci nel Racconto dei Contemporanei* (1930); edited Tasso's *Gerusalemme Liberata* (1883), *Rinaldo* and *Aminta* (1884), works of Giovanni Rucellai (1887), memoirs of Goldoni (2 vols., 1907), works of Parini, and works of Machiavelli (1929).

**Maz'zu·chel'li** (mät'tsōō·kĕl'lē), Conte **Giovanni Maria.** 1707–1765. Italian biographer and literary historian; known esp. for literary encyclopedia *Gli Scrittori d'Italia...* (through letter B, 6 vols., 1753–63). Also wrote biography of Pietro Aretino.

**Mazzuoli, Girolamo Francesco Maria.** See Il PARMIGIANINO.

**Mazzuoli, Lodovico.** See MAZZOLINO.

**Mc-.** Names beginning with this prefix are alphabetized as if spelled MAC-.

**Mdi·va'ni** ('m·dē·vä'nē). Name of a former princely family of Georgia (in the Caucasus).

**Mead** (mēd), **George Herbert.** 1863–1931. American philosopher; author of the posthumously edited and published *Mind, Self, and Society* (1934), *The Philosophy of the Act* (1938), etc.

**Mead, Larkin Goldsmith.** 1835–1910. American sculptor. Examples of his work: *Ethan Allen,* in capitol at Montpelier, Vt.; *Lincoln Monument,* in Springfield, Ill.; *The Father of Waters,* in Minneapolis, Minn. His brother **William Rutherford** (1846–1928) was an architect; associated with C. F. McKim and Stanford White, in New York City (from 1879).

**Mead, Margaret.** 1901–1978. American anthropologist; m. Gregory Bateson (1936; div. 1951). Asst. curator of ethnology, American Museum of Natural History (1926–42); assoc. curator (1942–64); curator (1964–69). At Fordham U. (1968–71). On expedition to New Guinea (1931–33), Bali and New Guinea (1936–39). Author of *Coming of Age in Samoa* (1928), *Growing Up in New Guinea* (1930), *Sex and Temperament in Three Primitive Societies* (1935), *And Keep Your Powder Dry* (1942), etc.

**Mead, Richard.** 1673–1754. English physician; author of account of venomous snakes (1702), treatise on influence of sun and moon on human bodies (1704), paper on parasitic nature of scabies.

**Meade** (mēd), **George Gordon.** 1815–1872. American army commander. Aided in defense of Washington (1861); present at battles of Mechanicsville and Gaines's Mill; wounded at Glendale; served at second Bull Run, Antietam and Chancellorsville. Placed in command of army of the Potomac (June 28, 1863); repulsed Confederate army under Lee at Gettysburg (July 1–4, 1863), but was criticized for lack of aggressiveness in following up repulse to obtain decisive victory.

**Meade, James Edward.** 1907– . British economist. At Oxford U. (1930-37), London School of Economics (1947–57), Cambridge U. (1957–74); awarded (with Bertil Ohlin) Nobel prize for economics (1977).

**Meade, Richard Kidder.** 1746–1805. American Revolutionary officer, b. in Nansemond County, Va. Aide-de-camp to Washington (1777–81). Planter, Frederick County, Va. (from 1781).

**Mea'gher** (mä'ẽr; -hẽr; -KẽR), **Thomas Francis.** 1823–1867. Politician and soldier, b. Waterford, Ireland. Member, Young Ireland party (from 1845); a founder of the Irish Confederation. Banished to Tasmania (1849) for advocating insurrection in Ireland. Escaped to U.S. (1852); became naturalized citizen and leader of Irish-Americans in New York City. Served through Civil War; organized and commanded the Irish Brigade, recruited from New York City; engaged at first Bull Run, in Peninsular Campaign, at second Bull Run, Antietam, Fredericksburg, Chancellorsville; brigadier general (1864). Territorial secretary of Montana (1865) and acting governor (1865–66).

**Mea'ny** (mē'nĭ), **George.** 1894– . American labor leader, b. New York City. President, N.Y. State Federation of Labor (1934–39), Am. Federation of Labor (1952–55), Am. Federation of Labor-Congress of Industrial Organizations (1955– ).

**Mearns** (mûrnz), **Hughes.** 1875–1965. American educator and writer, b. Philadelphia. Professor, Philadelphia School of Pedagogy (1905–20); on staff of Rockefeller Foundation (1920–25); chairman, department of creative education, N.Y.U. (1926–46). Author of *Creative Youth* (1925), *Creative Power* (1929), *Creative Adult* (1940), and a number of light novels (*Richard, Richard,* 1916; *The Vinegar Tree;* etc.).

**Mears** (mērz), **Helen Farnsworth.** 1876–1916. American sculptor, b. Oshkosh, Wis. Among her works are busts of Dr. William T.G. Morton in Smithsonian Institution, Augustus Saint-Gaudens in Peabody Institute, Baltimore, Edward MacDowell in Metropolitan Museum of Art, N.Y., and a marble statue of Frances E. Willard for the Capitol, Washington, D.C.

**Meath,** Earl of. See Reginald BRABAZON.

**Meath,** Lord of. See Hugh de LACY.

**Me·ce'nas** (mē·sē'năs). = MAECENAS.

**Me'che·lin'** (mĕ'kĕ·lēn'), **Leo** *or* **Leopold von.** 1839–1914. Finnish statesman and law scholar. Liberal member of Diet (from 1872); senator in Finnish government (1882); minister of economics (1882–90). Defended Finland's constitutional rights against Russian attacks.

**Mechnikov.** See Élie METCHNIKOFF.

**Meck'el** (mĕk'ĕl), **Johann Friedrich.** 1724–1774. German anatomist; discovered sphenopalatine ganglion (Meckel's ganglion) on fifth cranial nerve. His grandson **Johann Friedrich Meckel** (1781–1833) was professor of anatomy and physiology at Halle.

**Meck'len·burg** (mĕk'lĕn·bo͝orK; mā'klĕn-). A former German duchy and its ruling family (the only one of Western Europe of Slavonic origin), claiming to be the oldest sovereign house in the Western world. Reputedly founded by Niklot (d. 1160), whose successors comprise 26 generations; ruler made prince of the empire (1170) by Emperor Frederick I; made a duchy (1348; see ALBERT II); Duke Albert III (*q.v.*) made king of Sweden (1363); possessions divided (1701) between Mecklenburg-Schwerin and Mecklenburg-Strelitz:

**Mecklenburg-Schwe·rin'** (shvā·rēn'). Made grand duchy (1815). Recent rulers: Frederick (ruled 1756–85), Frederick Francis I (1756–1837; duke 1785–1815; grand duke 1815–37), Paul Frederick (1800–1842; ruled 1837–42), Frederick Francis II (*q.v.*) [1842–83], Frederick Francis III (1851–1897; ruled 1883–97), Frederick Francis IV (1882– ; ruled 1897–1918, abdicated). Alexandrine Augustine, sister of Frederick Francis IV, m. (1898) Christian X of Denmark; Cecile, another sister, m. (1905) Frederick William, German crown prince. Elizabeth (1869– ), sister of Frederick Francis III, m. (1896) Grand Duke Frederick Augustus of Oldenburg; Henry (1876–1934), her brother, m. (1901) Queen Wilhelmina of Netherlands.

**Mecklenburg-Stre'litz** (-shtrā'lĭts). Made grand duchy (1815). Recent rulers: George (1816–60), Frederick William (1819–1904; ruled 1860–1904), Adolf Frederick V (1848–1914; ruled 1904–14), Adolf Frederick VI (1882–1918; ruled 1914–18, abdicated).

**Me·dar'dus** (mē·där'dŭs), Saint. *Fr.* **Mé'dard'** (mā'dȧr'). 456?–?545. Bishop of Noyon and Tournai, b. Salency, France, of Frankish and Gallo-Roman parents; patron of farmers, wine harvests, and good weather. Instituted famous rosary of Salency and is hero of many legends.

**Med'a·war** (mĕd'ȧ·wẽr; -wär), Sir **Peter Brian.** 1915– . British biologist, b. Brazil. At U. of London (1951–62); director, Nat. Inst. of Med. Research (1962–71). Awarded Nobel prize in physiology or medicine (1960) with F. Burnet for study of immunological tolerance.

**Me'di·ci** (mâ'dē·chē; *Angl.* mĕd'ĕ-, mā'dē-). *Fr.* **Mé'di'cis'** (mā'dē'sēs'). Name (meaning, literally, "physicians" or "doctors") of an Italian family powerful in Florence and Tuscany, esp. from 14th to 16th century. Name recorded in Florence as early as 12th century. Real founder of family was **Giovanni de' Medici,** *also* *known as* **Giovanni di Bic′ci de′** (dê bēt′chê dâ) **Medici** (1360–1429), Florentine merchant; amassed very large fortune by skill in trade; strong supporter of smaller guilds and common people; virtual ruler of Florence (1421–29). From his two sons, Cosimo (1389–1464) and Lorenzo (1395–1440), derive the two great branches of the Medici family:

ELDER BRANCH.

**Cosimo** *or* **Cosmo** (1389–1464), known as "Cosimo the Elder," son of Giovanni. Florentine banker, patron of the arts, and ruler of the republic; called "father of his country"; acquired great wealth from his father and ruled through controlling appointments to chief offices; rival of the Albizzi; expelled from Florence (1433) but returned (1434); for 30 years patron of literature and fine arts; welcomed to his palace Greek refugee scholars driven out of Constantinople after its capture (1453).

His son **Piero** (1414–1469), known as "Piero the Gouty," ruler of Florence (1464–69), whose grandson **Giulio** (1478–1534; son of Piero's second son **Giuliano**, 1453–1478) became pope as Clement VII (*q.v.*).

**Lorenzo** (1449–1492), known as "Lorenzo the Magnificent" (*Ital.* il Ma·gni′fi·co [ēl mä·nyē′fê·kō]), eldest son of Piero. Florentine statesman, ruler, and patron of arts and letters; conjointly with his brother Giuliano, succeeded (1469) to great wealth and power of Medici family; engaged in struggle with Pazzi family and Pope Sixtus IV; after assassination of Giuliano (1478), became sole ruler (1478–92); with help of King Ferdinand of Aragon, made peace with pope (1480). Immoral, and tyrannical ruler, but contributed greatly to make Florence prosperous; a polished prose writer and original poet; participated actively in intellectual achievements of Florence; esp. influential in causing the Tuscan dialect to become national speech of Italy.

Lorenzo the Magnificent's sons: **Pietro** (1471–1503), ruled two years only, driven from Florence (1494) by Savonarola and his followers (the Piagnoni); **Giovanni** (1475–1521), pope as Leo X (*q.v.*); **Giuliano** (1479–1516), Duke of **Ne·mours′** (nē·mōōr′), whose natural son **Ippolito** (1511?–1535) became a cardinal.

**Lorenzo** (1492–1519), son of Pietro; created (1516) duke of **Ur·bi′no** (ōōr·bē′nô) by his uncle Pope Leo X; m. Madeleine de La Tour d'Auvergne. His natural son **Alessandro** (1510–1537), last of the direct male line of elder branch of family; first duke of Florence (1531–37), under imperial patent of Charles V; murdered, for his tyrannical rule, by a distant kinsman **Lorenzo,** *known as* **Lorenzino** (1514–1548), a grandson of Lorenzo the Younger (see below). For **Caterina** (1519–1589), daughter of Lorenzo (1492–1519), see CATHERINE DE MÉDICIS.

YOUNGER BRANCH.

**Lorenzo** (1395–1440), known as "Lorenzo the Elder," second son of Giovanni di Bicci; confined himself to family's banking interests. His grandsons: **Lorenzo** the Younger (1463–1507), enemy of Savonarola, and **Giovanni** (1467–1498), who married Caterina Sforza.

**Giovanni** (1498–1526), known as Giovanni del′le Ban′de Ne′re (dāl′lâ bän′dâ nā′râ), *i.e.* John of the Black Bands; son of Giovanni and Caterina; Italian general, killed at battle of Mantua.

**Cosimo I** (1519–1574), known as "Cosimo the Great," son of Giovanni delle Bande Nere; granted title of duke of Florence (1537–74) on extinction of elder branch; capable ruler, but despotic and cruel; conquered Siena (1555); given title of grand duke of Tuscany by the pope (1569), but title generally dated from its bestowal under imperial grant (1575) on his son Francesco (1541–1587).

Children of Cosimo I: **Francesco** (1541–1587), tool of Emperor Maximilian II and of Philip II of Spain; father of **Maria** (= MARIE DE MÉDICIS), wife of Henry IV of France. **Ferdinand I** (1549–1609), Grand Duke of Tuscany (1587–1609); increased strength and prosperity of duchy; from him descended direct line of younger branch of family.

**Cosimo II** (1590–1620), son of Ferdinand I; grand duke (1609–20); gave up all practice of banking and commerce; protected Galileo Galilei; m. Maria Magdalena of Austria, sister of Emperor Ferdinand II, by whom he had seven children, including: **Ferdinand II** (1610–1670), grand duke (1620–70), patron of art and letters, whose rule was subservient to Rome and was disturbed by wars.

**Cosimo III** (1642–1723), son of Ferdinand II; grand duke (1670–1723); weak ruler, under whom Tuscany's power further declined; m. Marguerite Louise d'Orléans (d. 1721), daughter of Gaston, Duc d'Orléans. Their children included **Giovan** (*or* **Gian**) **Gastone** (1671–1737), last grand duke of Tuscany (1723–37), weak and dissolute ruler, who was driven out of Tuscany at its annexation by Austria (1737), and **Anna Maria Ludovica** (1667–1743), known as "the last of the Medici."

**Medici, Alessandro Ottaviano de′.** = Pope LEO XI. (Not a member of the famous Medici family of Florence, but descended from a brother of the grandfather of Giovanni di Bicci, founder of the Florentine family. See MEDICI.)

**Médicis, Catherine de** and **Marie de.** See CATHERINE DE MÉDICIS and MARIE DE MÉDICIS; see also MEDICI family.

**Me·dill′** (mĕ·dĭl′), **Joseph.** 1823–1899. Journalist, b. near St. John, New Brunswick, Canada; to U.S. (1832); adm. to bar (1846) in Ohio. Founded Cleveland *Leader* (1852); participated in conferences (1854) leading up to formation of new antislavery party, the Republican party, to replace the Whigs. Bought interest in Chicago *Tribune* (1855); vigorously supported Lincoln in campaign for presidency and during his administration; gained control of the *Tribune* (1874) and continued as publisher and editor until his death. One daughter, Katherine Van Etta Medill, married Robert Sanderson McCormick and their children, Joseph Medill McCormick and Robert Rutherford McCormick, inherited an interest in the Chicago *Tribune;* another daughter, Elinor Medill, married Robert Wilson Patterson, and their children, Joseph Medill Patterson and Eleanor Medill Patterson, inherited the remaining interest in the *Tribune.* See under Robert Sanderson MCCORMICK, Joseph Medill PATTERSON, and Eleanor Medill PATTERSON.

**Me·di′na An′ga·ri′ta** (mâ·thē′nä äng′gä·rē′tä), **Isaías.** 1897–1953. Venezuelan soldier (chief of staff, 1935; general, 1940) and statesman; minister of war and the navy (1935–40); president of Venezuela (from 1941).

**Me·di′na–Si·do′nia** (-sê·thō′nyä), 7th Duke of. **Alonso Pérez de Guzmán.** 1550–1615. Spanish admiral; a wealthy nobleman with no ability or training, placed (1588) by Philip II in command of "Invincible Armada"; completely defeated by English; in spite of incompetence retained as "admiral of the ocean"; responsible for loss of Cádiz (1596) to the English; also for defeat of Spanish squadron off Gibraltar (1606).

**Medoc.** See MADEC.

**Medolla, Andrea.** See Andrea SCHIAVONE.

**Medt′ner** (mĕt′nēr), **Nikolai** *or* **Nikolaus.** 1879–1951. Pianist and composer of classical-romantic school, b. Moscow, of German descent.

**Med′wall** (mĕd′wôl), **Henry.** fl. 1490. English writer of interludes; chaplain to Morton, Archbishop of Canterbury, for whose entertainment he wrote earliest secular play in English, *Fulgens and Lucres*, from medieval Latin original, with comic underplot.

**Med′win** (mĕd′wĭn), **Thomas.** 1788–1869. Cousin, schoolfellow, and biographer of Shelley; associated with Shelley and Byron in Italy (1821) and from notes of their conversations wrote *Memoir of Shelley* (1833), later expanded into *The Life of Shelley* (2 vols., 1847).

**Mee** (mē), **Arthur.** 1875–1943. English journalist, editor, and writer. Member of editorial staff of Sir George Newnes (1896) and, later, of Alfred Harmsworth (Lord Northcliffe). Editor of *The Children's Encyclopedia* (1908–33), *Harmsworth Self-Educator* (1906), *Harmsworth History of the World* (1907), *Harmsworth Popular Science* (1912), etc. Author of *Joseph Chamberlain* (1900), *Arthur Mee's Golden Year* (1922), *The Children's Shakespeare* (1926), *The Rainbow Books* (1939), *The King's England* (survey of English towns and villages; 1936 ff.).

**Meek** (mēk), **Fielding Bradford.** 1817–1876. American paleontologist; with Smithsonian Institution, Washington, D.C. (1858–76). Collaborated with F. V. Hayden, James Hall, and others in geological survey work. Author, with Hayden, of *Paleontology of the Upper Missouri* (1865), etc.

**Meel, Jan.** See Jan MIEL.

**Meer** (mār), **Jan van der.** *Usually called* **Jan van der Meer** (*or* **Jan Ver·meer′** [vẽr·mār′]) **van Haar′lem** (vän här′lĕm). Name of two Dutch landscape painters, father (1628–1691) and son (1656–1705), b. Haarlem. The former painted the downs and flatlands of Holland in brown-green tones; his son and pupil painted chiefly landscapes with animals.

**Meersch** (mārs), **Maxence van der** (vän dẽr). 1907–1951. French writer, Flemish born; won Goncourt Prize (1936) for novel *L'Empreinte du Dieu* [*Hath Not the Potter*].

**Meer van Delft, Jan van der.** See Jan VERMEER.

**Mees** (mēz), **Charles Edward Kenneth.** 1882–1960. Photographic authority, b. at Wellingborough, Eng.; to U.S. (1912); director of research laboratory, Eastman Kodak Co., Rochester, N.Y. (from 1912). Author of *Photography of Colored Objects* (1909), *The Fundamentals of Photography* (1920), *Photography* (1937), etc. Special editor for terms in photography, *Webster's New International Dictionary, Second Edition.* See F. C. L. WRATTEN.

**Meg′a·cles** (mĕg′ȧ·klēz). Athenian political leader, member of great family of the Alcmaeonidae; aided Pisistratus to gain power in Athens (560–559 B.C.); later opposed Pisistratus and was forced with others of family to flee Athens.

**Me·gas′the·nes** (mē̇·găs′thē̇·nēz). fl. 3d century B.C. Greek historian; sent (302 B.C.) by Seleucus Nicator as ambassador to court of Indian king Chandragupta Maurya; remained at Pataliputra [now Patna] (302–298). Wrote *Indica*, a description of Indian customs, flora, and fauna; only fragments of his work are extant.

**Megerle, Hans Ulrich.** Real name of ABRAHAM A SANCTA CLARA.

**Me·grue′** (mĕ·grōō′), **Roi** (roi) **Cooper.** 1883–1927. American playwright, b. New York City; grad. Columbia (1903). Author of *Under Cover* (1913), *It Pays to Advertise* (with Walter Hackett, 1914), *Under Fire* (1915), *Under Sentence* (with Irvin S. Cobb, 1916), *Tea for Three* (1918).

**Mehemet Aali.** See AALI.

**Me·he·met′ A·li′** (mĕ·mĕt′ ä·lī′) *or* **Mo·ham′med Ali** (mō̇·hăm′ĕd; -ĭd). 1769–1849. Viceroy of Egypt (1805–48), b. Kavalla, Rumelia, of Albanian parentage. Father of Said Pasha and (or adoptive father) of Ibrahim Pasha (*qq.v.*); fought against Napoleon at Abukir (1799); proclaimed loyalty to sultan (1804); made pasha by sheiks of Cairo (1805); strengthened his position (1807–10) and, by massacre of Mamelukes (1811), left without rival in Egypt; carried on war against Wahabis (1811–18), brought to successful conclusion by Ibrahim Pasha; subdued Nubia and Kordofan (1820–22); laid foundations of Khartoum (1823); persuaded by sultan to aid him in Greek revolt (1824–27); lost fleet at Navarino (1827); granted possession of Crete (1830); sent Ibrahim to conquer Syria (1831–33), his conflict with Turkey becoming vital part of Eastern question of the time; his forces completely defeated Turks at Nizib (1839), but deprived by Great Powers of spoils of victory; retired to hereditary viceroyalty of Egypt (1841); during last years weakened in mind, Ibrahim Pasha being appointed viceroy (1848).

**Mehemet Ali Pa·sha′** (pä·shä′). *Real name* **Karl De·troit′** (dĕ·trō̇·ä′). 1827–1878. German-born Turkish general; to Turkey (1843) and became protégé of Aali Pasha; went to Turkish military school, adopted Mohammedan religion, and entered army (1853). Served in Crimean War; promoted brigadier general (1865) and created pasha. Commanded Turkish army in Bulgaria in Russo-Turkish War (1877–78); forced to retreat and replaced by Suleiman Pasha (1878). Mobbed and killed by insurgents in Albania (Sept. 7, 1878).

**Mehmed Namik.** See KEMĀL BEY.

**Meh′ring** (mā′rĭng), **Franz.** 1846–1919. German Socialist historian and pamphleteer; joined opposition at outbreak (1914) of World War and became member of early Spartacus group (c. 1916).

**Meh′ta** (mā′tä), Sir **Phe·ro′ze·shah′** (fē·rō′zĕ·shä′) **Mer·wan′ji** (mār·wän′jē). 1845–1915. Indian lawyer; first Parsi to be called to the English bar (1868); successful practitioner in Bombay; justice of the peace (1869) and member of the new Bombay Corporation (1872–1915); also, member of Bombay legislature for 30 years.

**Meh-tzŭ.** = Mo TI.

**Mé′hul′** (mā′ül′), **Étienne Nicolas.** 1763–1817. French composer of operas, including *Mélidore et Euprosine* (1794), *Le Jeune Henry* (1797), *Adrien* and *Ariodant* (1799), *L'Irato* (1801), *Joseph* (1807) and *La Journée aux Aventures* (1816), and of ballets, cantatas, symphonies, piano sonatas, and many songs, including patriotic hymns.

**Mei** (mā′ĭ), **Lev Aleksandrovich.** 1822–1862. Russian poet; translator of works of Milton, Byron, Schiller, Goethe, Heine, Victor Hugo; author of the dramas *The Bride of the Czar*, *Servilia*, *The Woman of Pskov.*

**Mei′bom** (mī′bōm), **Heinrich.** 1638–1700. German physician; discoverer of the glands (Meibomian glands) that lubricate the eyelids.

**Me·ière′** (mē̇·âr′), **Marie Hildreth.** 1893?–1961. American painter, known esp. for her murals, as in the dome of the National Academy of Sciences building in Washington and in the Nebraska State Capitol.

**Mei′er–Grae′fe** (mī′ẽr·grâ′fĕ), **Julius.** 1867–1935. German writer and art critic, b. in Rumania; specialist in 19th-century French painting and champion of impressionism.

**Mei′er·o′vics** (mā′ĕr·ō′vĭts), **Zigfrids Anna.** 1887–1925. Latvian statesman; became first foreign minister of independent Latvia (1918) and held office almost continuously until death; minister president (1921–23, 1923–24).

**Meigh′en** (mē′ĕn), **Arthur.** 1874–1960. Canadian statesman, b. in Ontario; adm. to bar (1903). Member, Canadian House of Commons (1908–21, 1922–26); solicitor general of Canada (1913), secretary of state (1917), minister of the interior (1917); member of imperial war cabinet (1918); prime minister of Canada

(1920–21, 1926); minister without portfolio (1932–35) and government leader in the senate.

**Meigs** (mĕgz), **Cornelia Lynde.** 1884–1973. American writer, b. Rock Island, Ill. On English staff, Bryn Mawr. Among her many works, a number of them juveniles, are: *Kingdom of the Winding Road* (1915), *The Steadfast Princess* (1916; Drama League prize play), *Helga and the White Peacock* (a play; 1922), *Rain on the Roof* (1925), *Trade Wind* (1927; winner of $2000 prize offered by Little, Brown & Co.), *Invincible Louisa* (1933; awarded Newbery medal, 1934), *Railroad West* (1937).

**Meigs, Re·turn′** (rē·tûrn′) **Jonathan.** 1740–1823. American Revolutionary officer, b. Middletown, Conn.; served through Revolution, taking part in Arnold's expedition against Quebec, raid on Sag Harbor (1777), and storming of Stony Point under Anthony Wayne; pioneer in Tennessee region and commissioner for treating with Indians. His son **Return Jonathan** (1764–1824), lawyer, practiced in Marietta, Ohio (from 1788); first chief justice, State of Ohio (1803–04); U.S. senator (1808–10); governor of Ohio (1810–14); U.S. postmaster general (1814–23).

**Meiji.** See MUTSUHITO.

**Mei′kle** (mĭk′'l), **Andrew.** 1719–1811. Scottish millwright and inventor; patented machine for dressing grain (1768); invented drum threshing machine (1784; patented 1788).

**Mei′kle·john** (mĭk′'l·jŏn), **Alexander.** 1872–1964. Educator, b. Rochdale, England; to U.S. (1880). President, Amherst (1912–24). Director of experimental college in U. of Wisconsin (1926–33). Instructor in School for Social Studies, San Francisco (from 1933).

**Meiklejohn, John Miller Dow.** 1836–1902. Scottish schoolmaster; first professor of education in St. Andrews (1876); author of *English Language* (1886), *The Art of Writing English* (1899), and *English Literature* (pub. 1904).

**Meil′hac′** (mĕ′yȧk′), **Henri.** 1831–1897. French playwright; among his plays are *Le Petit-fils de Mascarille* (1859), *La Vertu de Célimène* (1861), *Les Demoiselles Clochart* (1886), *Décoré* (1888), and *Brevet Supérieur* (1892). Collaborator with a number of other playwrights, including Delavigne, Gille, Massenet, and esp. with Ludovic Halévy, as in many light operas and comedies (*Froufrou*, 1869; *Loulou*, 1876; etc.).

**Mei′li** (mī′lē), **Friedrich.** 1848–1914. Swiss jurist; authority on international law.

**Meil′let′** (mĕ′yĕ′), **Antoine.** 1866–1936. French philologist; author of *Les Dialectes Indo-Européens* (1908), *Linguistique Historique et Linguistique Générale* (1921), *Introduction à l'Étude Comparative des Langues Indo-Européennes*, etc.

**Mei′neck·e** (mī′nĕ·kĕ), **Friedrich.** 1862–1954. German historian.

**Mei′ne·ke** (mī′nĕ·kĕ), **August,** *in full* **Johann Albrecht Friedrich August.** 1790–1870. German classical scholar; author of *Fragmenta Comicorum Graecorum* (5 vols., 1839–57), *Analecta Alexandrina* (1843).

**Meingre, Jean Le.** See BOUCIQUAUT.

**Mein′hof** (mīn′hōf), **Carl.** 1857–1944. German specialist in African languages.

**Mei′nong** (mī′nông), **Alexius.** Ritter **von Hand′schuhs·heim** (fôn hänt′shōōks·hīm). 1853–1920. Austrian philosopher and psychologist; professor, Graz (1882), where he established (1894) first psychological institute in Austria; established a general theory of value (*Werttheorie*) on psychological grounds.

**Mei Shêng** (mā′ shŭng′). d. 140 B.C. Chinese poet; sometimes called "the father of modern Chinese poetry"; credited with introducing five-character line.

**Meis′le** (mīs′lē), **Kathryn.** 1899–1970. American operatic contralto; m. Calvin M. Franklin (1917). Debut in New York as Amneris in *Aïda*, with Metropolitan Opera Association (1935); sang with symphony orchestras in Philadelphia, Boston, Detroit, Chicago, etc.

**Meiss′ner** (mīs′nĕr), **Alexander.** 1883–1958. Austrian radio engineer; credited by some with invention of regenerative coupling and introduction of heterodyne reception.

**Meissner, August Gottlieb.** 1753–1807. German author of several historical novels, plays, and operettas. His grandson **Alfred Meissner** (1822–1885), poet, novelist, and dramatist, wrote volume of revolutionary verse, *Gedichte* (1845), the lyrical epic *Ziska* (1846; banned in Austria), and novels and stories, as *Sansara* (4 vols., 1857), *Schwarzgelb* (8 vols., 1862–64); also, the tragedy *Das Weib des Urias* (1851).

**Meissner, Bruno.** 1868–1947. German Assyriologist.

**Meissner, Georg.** 1829–1905. German physiologist and anatomist; professor in Göttingen; known for work relating to the skin, organs of sight, and respiration. Meissner's corpuscles, small tactile end organs in the skin, are named after him. See Rudolf WAGNER.

**Meis′so′nier′** (mā′sô′nyā′), **Jean Louis Ernest.** 1815–1891. French painter; studied under Cogniet; best known for small genre pictures painted with great delicacy and often representing military subjects. Among his famous canvases are *Hallebardier*, *La Partie d'Échecs*, *Le Grand Fumeur*, *Le Liseur*, *L'Attente*, *La Halte*, *Le Rieur*, *Campagne de France*, *Castiglione*, *Les Cuirassiers*, *Iéna*, *Le Cavalier à sa Fenêtre*, and a Napoleonic cycle of four paintings including *1807*, *1814*, *1815*.

**Meis′son′nier′** (mā′sô′nyā′), **Just Aurèle.** 1695?–1750. French goldsmith and decorator; regarded as a master of rococo; appointed goldsmith and furniture designer to King Louis XV.

**Mei′ster** (mī′stĕr), **Aloys.** 1866–1925. German historian.

**Meit′ner** (mīt′nĕr), **Lise.** 1878–1968. Physicist, b. Vienna; professor in Berlin and member of Kaiser Wilhelm Inst.; to Stockholm (1938); known for her work on disintegration products of radium, thorium, and actinium and on behavior of beta rays; discovered (1918) with Otto Hahn protoactinium and accomplished (1938) with Hahn and Fritz Strassmann the fission of uranium. Fermi Award (1966) with Hahn and Strassmann.

**Meit′zen** (mī′tsĕn), **August.** 1822–1910. German statistician and political economist; author of *Geschichte, Theorie, und Technik der Statistik* (1886), etc.

**Me·jí′a** (mĕ·hē′ä), **Tomás.** 1812?–1867. Mexican general, of native Indian descent; supported Maximilian and was executed with him at Querétaro (June 19, 1867).

**Mejía Colindres, Vicente.** See COLINDRES.

**Me′khi·tar′** *or* **Me′chi·tar′** (mĕ′kē·tär′), **Peter Manoug.** 1676–1749. Armenian religious reformer; founded (1701) at Constantinople a congregation (Roman Catholic) designed to introduce western culture among Armenian people; abbot of monastery which he founded (1702) in the Morea (then ruled by Venice) and transferred (1715) to San Lazzaro, near Venice, and widely known for its work in printing Armenian classics and an Armenian translation of the Bible.

**Mekum, Friedrich.** See Friedrich MYCONIUS.

**Me′la** (mē′lȧ), **Pomponius.** Latin geographer of 1st century A.D.; his *De Situ Orbis* is earliest known description of ancient world written in Latin.

**Me·lanch′thon** (mē·lăngk′thŭn; *Ger.* mā·länk′tôn) *or* **Me·lan′thon** (mē·lăn′thŭn; *Ger.* mā·län′tôn). *Grecized surname of* **Philipp Schwarz′ert′** (shvärts′ārt′). 1497–1560. German scholar and religious reformer; collaborator with Martin Luther in the Protestant Reformation;

b. in Bretten, Baden; educ. Tübingen; professor of Greek at Wittenberg (1518) and of theology (1526). Published *Loci Communes Rerum Theologicarum* (1521), first great Protestant treatise on dogmatic theology. Noted for vast learning, skill in dialectics and exegesis, and a moderation that tempered Luther's vehemence. Drafted the Augsburg Confession (1530), thus making important contribution to the Protestant cause. Sought consistently to reconcile Protestantism with Roman Catholicism and thus attain Christian unity.

**Me·lan′der** (mĕ·lăn′dẽr), **Axel Leonard.** 1878–1962. American zoologist, b. Chicago, Ill.; authority on classification of Diptera. Author of *Key to Families of North American Insects* (with C. T. Brues; 1915), *Classification of Insects* (with C. T. Brues; 1932), etc.

**Melanthon.** See MELANCHTHON.

**Me·lan′thus** (mē·lăn′thŭs) *or* **Me·lan′thi·us** (-thĭ·ŭs). Greek painter of 4th century B.C.; studied under Pamphilus (*q.v.*); representative of Sicyonian school.

**Me′lar·tin** (mĕ′lär·tĭn), **Erkki Gustaf.** 1875–1937. Finnish composer of the opera *Aino* (1907), symphonies, symphonic poems, orchestral suites, a violin concerto, string quartets and other chamber music, piano pieces, and songs.

**Me′las** (mā′läs), Baron **Michael Friedrich Benedikt von.** 1729–1806. Austrian general; commanded Austrian army in Italy; with Suvorov at Cassano d'Adda, the Trebbia River, and Novi (1799), and alone at victory over French at Genola; defeated by Napoleon in battle of Marengo (1800); commanding general in Bohemia (1801–03).

**Mel′ba** (mĕl′bȧ), Mme. **Nellie.** *Stage name of* **Helen Porter Mitchell.** 1861 –1931. Operatic soprano, b. near Melbourne, Australia; m. Charles Nesbitt Frederick Armstrong (1882). Operatic debut, as Gilda in *Rigoletto*, at Brussels (1887), adopting name of Melba from Melbourne, Australia; London debut, as Lucia in *Lucia di Lammermoor* (1888). First appeared in New York (1893) and later toured U.S. Prima donna at the Royal Opera, Covent Garden, London. Created dame of the British Empire (1918).

**Melbourne,** Viscounts. See William LAMB.

**Mel′chers** (mĕl′chẽrz), **Gar′i** (gâr′ĭ), *in full* **Julius Gari.** 1860–1932. American painter, b. Detroit; excelled in genre pictures of Dutch peasant life, religious paintings, and mural decorations. His *The Nurse and the Children* is in the Luxembourg, Paris; *Dutch Skaters*, in Pennsylvania Academy, Philadelphia; *The Madonna*, in Metropolitan Museum of Art, New York; portrait of Colonel Theodore Roosevelt, in National Gallery, Washington; his mural *Peace and War* is in the Congressional Library, Washington, D.C.

**Mel′chers** (mĕl′kẽrs), **Paulus.** 1813–1895. German Roman Catholic prelate; archbishop of Cologne (1866). Imprisoned six months for participation in Kulturkampf (1874) and declared removed from office by tribunal for church affairs (1876); fled to Holland (1875–85), whence he administered his diocese. Resigned as archbishop (1885) and was created cardinal at Rome; joined Jesuits (1892).

**Melchett,** Baron. Sir **Alfred Moritz Mond.** See under Ludwig MOND.

**Melchiades.** See Saint MILTIADES.

**Mel′chi·or** (mĕl′kē·ôr), **Carl Joseph.** 1871–1933. German banker; represented financial interests of Germany at international conferences following World War (Spain, Brussels, London, Genoa, The Hague, Lausanne, etc.); member (1926–30) and chairman (1930) of finance committee of League of Nations; deputy chairman of board of Bank for International Settlements at Basel (1930–33).

**Mel′chior′** (mĕl′kyôr′), **Charles Jean.** See Marquis de VOGÜÉ.

**Mel′chior** (mĕl′kyŏr), **Lauritz Lebrecht Hommel.** 1890–1973. Operatic tenor, b. Copenhagen, Denmark; operatic debut, Copenhagen, as baritone (1913) and as tenor (1918); sang at Covent Garden, London (1925); appeared in chief cities of Europe; member of Metropolitan Opera Company, New York (1926–1950), specialized in Wagnerian roles; naturalized (1947).

**Mel·chiz′e·dek.** *In Douay Version* **Mel·chis′e·dech** (mĕl·kĭz′ĕ·dĕk). In Bible, a pre-Aaronic and pre-Levitical priest-king to whom Abraham paid tithes (*Gen.* xiv. 18 ff.).

**Melch′thal** (mĕlκ′täl), **Arnold von.** *Called also* **Arnold an der Hal′den** (än dẽr häl′dĕn). Legendary Swiss patriot of 14th century; one of three liberators in Swiss struggle for independence against Austria; said to be a founder of the Rütli league (1307). A principal character in Schiller's *Wilhelm Tell.*

**Melcombe,** Baron. See George Bubb DODINGTON.

**Mel′do·la** (?mĕl′dô·lȧ), **Raphael.** 1849–1915. English chemist; engaged in color works in London; made researches on triphenyl methane dyes; produced first oxazine dyestuff, Meldola's blue (1879).

**Meldolla, Andrea.** See Andrea SCHIAVONE.

**Mel′e·a′ger** (mĕl′ē·ā′jẽr). Greek epigrammatist of 1st century B.C.; compiled earliest known anthology, *The Garland*, containing epigrams of many authors and including 130 epigrams of his own composition.

**Me·lén′dez Val·dés′** (mā·lān′dāth väl·dās′), **Juan.** 1754–1817. Spanish poet; associated himself with the Napoleonic government in Spain and became unpopular with the people; forced into exile when French troops were withdrawn from Spain. As a poet, known esp. for his lyrics and pastorals.

**Mélesville.** Pseudonym of Anne Honoré Joseph DUVEYRIER.

**Me·le′ti·us** (mē·lē′shĭ·ŭs). d. 381 A.D. Greek ecclesiastic; bishop of Antioch (360); orthodox in doctrine, he was subject to attack from the Arians, at that period very powerful in Syria. Died while presiding over Council of Constantinople.

**Meletius.** Christian ecclesiastic of 4th century; bishop of Lycopolis; founder of a sect (Meletians).

**Mel′ga·re′jo** (mĕl′gä·rĕ′hō), **Mariano.** 1818–1871. Bolivian general, b. Cochabamba; president of Bolivia (1865–71), deposing José María de Achá; gave up much of Bolivia's claim to nitrate regions of Atacama Desert.

**Me′li** (mā′lē), **Giovanni.** 1740–1815. Sicilian physician and poet; wrote chiefly in dialect; author of *Bucolica*, *Fata Galante*, *Favole Morali*, *Ditirambo*, the mock heroic epic *Don Chisciotte e Sancio Panza*, canzonets, odes, pastorals, and collections of Sicilian proverbs.

**Melikov,** Count **Loris–.** See LORIS-MELIKOV.

**Mé′line′** (mā′lēn′), **Félix Jules.** 1838–1925. French statesman; premier of France (1896–98); elected to senate (1903); minister of agriculture (1915–16).

**Mel′ish** (mĕl′ĭsh), **John.** 1771–1822. Merchant, cartographer, and author, b. Methven, Scotland; merchant in Philadelphia, U.S.A. (from 1811); known esp. as map publisher (from 1816).

**Me·lis′sus** (mē·lĭs′ŭs). Greek Eleatic philosopher of Samos in 5th century B.C.; disciple of Parmenides. Only fragments of his works are extant.

**Mel′i·to** (mĕl′ĭ·tō). Christian prelate of late 2d century; bishop of Sardis and upholder of orthodoxy. Only fragments of his many works are extant.

**Mel·lin′** (mĕ·lēn′), **Gustaf Henrik.** 1803–1876. Swedish author of historical novels and of works on Scandinavian history.

**Mel'lo** (mâ'lo͞o), **Custodio José de.** 1845?–1902. Brazilian admiral who led revolt against Peixoto government (1893–94); was defeated and gave himself up (Apr. 16, 1894).

**Mello, Francisco Manuel de.** = MELO.

**Mello Fran'co** (fräNng'ko͞o), **Afranio de.** 1870–1943. Brazilian jurist and statesman; Brazilian representative in the League of Nations, and former president of the council of the league; judge of the Permanent Court of International Justice, at The Hague (1923–29); Brazilian minister of foreign affairs (1930–33).

**Mel'lon** (mĕl'ŭn), **Andrew William.** 1855–1937. American financier, b. Pittsburgh, Pa.; educ. U. of Pittsburgh. Largely interested in coal, coke, and iron enterprises, aluminum manufacture, and banking; president, Mellon National Bank of Pittsburgh. U.S. secretary of the treasury (1921–32); U.S. ambassador to Great Britain (1932–33).

**Mel·lo'ni** (mâl·lō'nē), **Macedonio.** 1798–1854. Italian physicist; to Naples (1839); director of Vesuvius observatory (until 1848). Known for discoveries in radiant heat; studied power of various substances to transmit infrared rays and changes undergone by heat rays in passing through various substances; showed similarity of heat and light; coined term "diathermancy" to denote property of transmitting infrared radiation.

**Me'lo** (*Span.* mā'lō) *or* **Mel'lo** (*Port.* mâ'lo͞o), **Francisco Manuel de.** 1611–1666. Portuguese historian and poet; served in Spanish army (to 1640), and then under the house of Braganza (after 1640). Accused falsely of attempted assassination of King John IV, he was imprisoned (1644–53) and then banished to Brazil (1653–59); lived thereafter in Lisbon. Wrote principally in Spanish; chief work, *Historia de los Movimientos, Separación, y Guerra de Cataluña* (1645); collected poems first published under title *Las Tres Musas de Melodino* (1649).

**Me·lo'ney** (mĕ·lō'nĭ), **William Brown.** 1878–1925. American journalist and army officer in World War; engaged in Meuse-Argonne offensive. Author of *Graft* (play; 1911), *The Girl of the Golden Gate* (1913), *The Heritage of Tyre* (1916). He married (1904) **Marie Mat'ting·ly** [măt'ĭng·lĭ] (d. 1943), journalist; editor, *Woman's Magazine* (1914–20), *The Delineator* (1920–26), New York *Herald Tribune Sunday Magazine* (from 1926) and its successor *This Week* (from 1934).

**Me·loz'zo da For·lì'** (mâ·lôt'tsō dä fôr·lē'). 1438–?1495. Italian painter of Umbrian school; known for skill in perspective, esp. in foreshortening; pupil of Piero della Francesca.

**Mel'sted** (mĕl'stād), **Henning Finne von.** 1875– . Swedish writer and lawyer; author of brochures on modern legal and social questions, of plays, and of many novels dealing esp. with modern problems.

**Meltzer.** See HALOANDER.

**Melt'zer** (mĕl'tsẽr), **Samuel James.** 1851–1920. Physiologist, b. in Kurland, Russia; to U.S. (1883). Head of department of physiology and pharmacology, Rockefeller Institute for Medical Research (1906–20).

**Mel'ville** (mĕl'vĭl), Viscounts. See DUNDAS of Arniston.

**Melville.** Name of a Scottish family holding barony and earldom of Melville:

**Robert Melville** (1527–1621), 1st Baron Melville; son of Sir John Melville of Raith, Fifeshire; representative of Mary, Queen of Scots, at English court; opposed Darnley marriage; released as noncombatant after Langside (1568); privy councilor (1583); begged Elizabeth for Mary's life; chancellor (1589); extraordinary lord of session (1594); accompanied James VI to England (1603); commissioner for union (1605).

**George Melville** (1634?–1707), 4th Baron and 1st Earl of Melville; joined Monmouth against the Covenanters (1679); implicated in Rye House Plot (1683); returned to England after revolution of 1688; secretary for Scotland (1689); created earl (1690); entrusted by king with propitiation of Presbyterians; lord privy seal (1691); president of Scottish privy council (1696–1702).

His son **David Melville** (1660–1728), 3d Earl of **Le'ven** (lē'vĕn), 2d Earl of Melville, fought for William III at Killiecrankie (1689) and in Irish campaign, in Flanders, and as commander in chief of Scottish forces suppressed Jacobite uprising (1708); became 3d earl of Leven (1681) through his mother, Catherine, Countess Leven, granddaughter of 1st earl of Leven (see LESLIE family).

**Mel'ville** *or* **Mel'vill** (mĕl'vĭl), **Andrew.** 1545–1622. Scottish religious reformer. Principal of Glasgow U. (1574–80), of St. Mary's Coll., St. Andrews (1580–1606); reorganized Scottish universities; promoted study of Aristotle and taste for Greek. Had part in drawing up *The Second Book of Discipline* (sanctioned 1581), shaping Presbyterian Church; preached boldly before General Assembly against absolute spiritual authority of king and hierarchy (1582); escaped to England until after Arran's fall (1585). Headed deputation to remonstrate with James VI (1596) against encroachments of government; dean of faculty of theology (1599). Summoned before English privy council for ridiculing service in Chapel Royal; delivered two long speeches on behalf of freedom of assemblies and against popery and superstition as encouraged by archbishop of Canterbury (1606); sent to Tower for four years; released through Henri de la Tour d'Auvergne, Duc de Bouillon, and made professor of Biblical theology in U. of Sedan (1611). His nephew **James Melville** *or* **Melvill** (1556–1614), religious reformer, devoted himself (from 1586) to church controversy and antagonism toward episcopal schemes of king; attended his uncle to London (1606); detained (1607). Remembered for his *Diary*, giving portrait of Knox.

**Melville, George John Whyte-.** See WHYTE-MELVILLE.

**Melville, George Wallace.** 1841–1912. American naval officer and explorer; chief engineer of the *Jeannette*, George W. De Long's ship in arctic exploration (1879); after wreck of ship, led a detachment to safety through Siberia. Headed relief expedition which discovered dead bodies of De Long and his companions, and rescued ship's records. Chief engineer on the *Thetis* of Greely relief expedition (1884). Chief, bureau of steam engineering, U.S. navy (1887–1903); retired as rear admiral (1903).

**Melville, Herman.** 1819–1891. American novelist, b. New York City; ran away to sea (1837); on whaler *Acushnet* (1841–42); deserted his ship at the Marquesas Islands and found temporary refuge among cannibal natives; escaped on Australian whaler *Lucy Ann* but left her at Papeete; enlisted (Aug. 17, 1843) as seaman on frigate *United States;* discharged at Boston (Oct. 14, 1844). Devoted himself to writing stories based on his experiences: *Typee* (1846), *Omoo* (1847), *Mardi* (1849), *Redburn* (1849), *White-Jacket* (1850), *Moby Dick* (1851; now accepted as a classic), *Pierre: or the Ambiguities* (1852), *Israel Potter* (1855), *The Piazza Tales* (1856). U.S. customs inspector on New York docks (1866–85). In addition to novels, published three volumes of verse.

**Melville** of Hall'hill' (hôl'hĭl'), Sir **James.** 1535–1617. Scottish soldier and British diplomat; offered allegiance to Mary, Queen of Scots (1561); ambassador to Queen Elizabeth, sought to win her approval of Darnley marriage; loyal to Mary Stuart up to her commitment to Loch Leven Castle. Sent on diplomatic missions during

James VI's minority; privy councilor under Queen Anne. Presented historical data in autobiography *Memoirs* (discovered 1660; pub. 1683).

**Mel'zi** (mĕl'tsē), **Francesco.** 1492–?1570. Italian painter; favorite pupil, friend, and heir of Leonardo da Vinci; accompanied Leonardo to Rome (1513) and France (1515).

**Mel'zi** (mĕl'thē), **José de Palafox y.** See PALAFOX Y MELZI.

**Mem'bré'** (mäɴ'brā'), **Ze·no'bi·us** (zē·nō'bĭ·ŭs). 1645–?1687. Roman Catholic missionary in America; member of Recollect order; sent to Canada (1675). Accompanied La Salle in exploration of Mississippi Valley (1681–82) and on expedition which landed in Texas (1684). Murdered by Indians.

**Mem'ling** (mĕm'lĭng) *or* **Mem'linc** (-lĭngk), **Hans.** 1430?–1495. Flemish painter of early Flemish school; studied in Cologne and under Rogier van der Weyden in Brussels; lived in Bruges (from c. 1466). Works include Madonnas, portraits, and religious paintings, as the triptych of *The Marriage of St. Catherine*, etc., the Floreins triptych with *Adoration of the Magi*, and the *St. Christopher* altarpiece, all in Bruges; the large *Last Judgment* altarpiece painted for a Florence church, *Thomas Portinari and Wife*, *Man with an Arrow*, etc.

**Memmi, Simone** and **Lippo.** See Simone MARTINI.

**Mem'min·ger** (mĕm'ĭn·jẽr), **Christopher Gustavus.** 1803–1888. American Confederate financier, b. Nayhingen, Württemberg, Germany; to U.S. as a child; secretary of the treasury, Confederate States of America (1861–64).

**Mem'phite** (mĕm'fīt). Name of several dynasties of Egyptian kings, the IIId to VIIIth (reigning c. 2980–2445 B.C.) of the Old Kingdom; so called from the capital city, Memphis. See *Table* (*in Appendix*) for EGYPT.

**Me'na** (mā'nä), **Juan de.** 1411–1456. Spanish poet; secretary to King John II of Castile; chief work, *El Laberinto de Fortuna* (1496), popularly called *Las Trezientas* (*The Three Hundred*, in allusion to its 300 stanzas).

**Mena, Pedro de.** d. about 1693. Spanish sculptor; carved in high relief figures of 40 saints for the choir stalls in Málaga cathedral, an equestrian statue of St. James in Toledo cathedral, and a Madonna and child with St. Joseph in the church of St. Isidoro, Madrid.

**Me'na·bre'a** (mā'nä·brâ'ä), Count **Luigi Federigo.** 1809–1896. Italian soldier and statesman; chief of staff of engineers in Sardinian army (1859); directed sieges of Ancona, Capua, and Gaeta (1860); minister of marine (1861–62) and public works (1862–64); premier (1867–69); ambassador to London (1876 ff.), Paris (1882–92).

**Mé'nage'** (mā'nȧzh'), **Gilles.** 1613–1692. French scholar; author of *Origines de la Langue Française* (1650), *Origines de la Langue Italienne* (1669), *Menagiana* (pub. 1693), etc.

**Men'a·hem** (mĕn'ȧ·hĕm). King of Israel (744?–738 B.C.).

**Me·nan'der** (mē·năn'dẽr). 343?–?291 B.C. Athenian writer of comedies; student of Theophrastus and friend of Epicurus. Author of more than 100 comedies noted for literary style, ingenuity of plot, and wit. Only fragments of his work survive; several plays of Plautus and Terence, however, are adaptations of his plays.

**Menander.** *Known as* **Mi·lin'da** (mĭ·lĭn'dȧ) *in Buddhist traditions.* fl. 150 B.C. A Greek king of India; one of a powerful Greco-Bactrian dynasty set up at Kabul; invaded India, conquered and apparently held for some time the valley of the Indus, the Punjab, Gujarat, etc.; many coins bearing his name found over an extensive area.

**Me·nant'** (mē·näɴ'), **Joachim.** 1820–1899. French Assyriologist and jurist; judge of court of appeals, Rouen (to 1890); studied cuneiform and became, with Oppert, founder of Assyriology in France.

**Menantes.** See C. F. HUNOLD.

**Mé'nard'** (mā'nȧr'), **Louis Nicolas.** 1822–1901. French scholar, poet, scientist, and artist; discovered collodion; published *Poèmes* (1855) and *Rêveries d'un Païen Mystique* (1876); author of *Du Polythéisme Hellénique* (1863), *Études sur les Origines du Christianisme* (1894), etc. His brother **René Joseph** (1827–1887) was a landscape and animal painter. René's son **Auguste Émile René** (1862–1930) was a landscape and portrait painter.

**Me·nard'** (*Angl.* mĕ·närd'; *Fr.* mā'nȧr'), **Michel Bran'a·mour** (*Angl.* brăn'ȧ·mo͝or; *Fr.* brȧ'nȧ'mo͞or'). 1805–1856. Fur trader in western region, esp. Arkansas and Texas; b. Laprairie, Lower Canada. Located claim (1834) to about six square miles of land on Galveston Island, Texas, and organized company (1838) to settle it, thus founding the city of Galveston. Menard County, Texas, was named after him.

**Menard, Pierre.** 1766–1844. Fur trader and pioneer, b. St. Antoine, Quebec, Canada; to Vincennes, Ind. (c. 1787). An organizer of St. Louis Missouri Fur Co. (1809); first lieutenant governor of State of Illinois (1818).

**Me·nas'seh ben Israel** (mē·năs'ĕ). = MANASSEH BEN ISRAEL.

**Men'ci·us** (mĕn'shĭ·ŭs). *Latinized form of Chinese* **Mêng-tzŭ** *or* **Meng-tse** (mŭng'dzŭ'). 372?–?289 B.C. Chinese philosopher, under the Chou dynasty; b. in Shantung province. A pupil of the grandson of Confucius; teacher by profession, traveling from place to place; fearless expounder of Confucianism; author of the second (by some listed as the fourth) of the Four Books of the Chinese classics, the *Book of Mencius*, a record of his sayings.

**Menck'e** (mĕng'kĕ) *or* **Menck'en** (mĕng'kĕn). Family of German scholars including: **Otto Mencke** (1644–1707), professor of moral philosophy, Leipzig, and cofounder (1682) and editor of *Acta Eruditorum*, first literary and scientific periodical in Germany. His son **Johann Burkhard** (1674–1732), writer and historian, succeeded his father as editor of *Acta Eruditorum* and founded *Neue Zeitungen von Gelehrten Sachen* (1715); patron of Johann Christian Günther; editor of *Scriptores Rerum Germanicarum, Praecipue Saxonicarum* (3 vols., 1728–30); author of poems (4 vols., 1705–10) under pseudonym **Philander von der Lin'de** (fôn dẽr lĭn'dĕ).

**Menck'en** (mĕng'kĕn), **Henry Louis.** 1880–1956. American editor and satirist, b. Baltimore. On staff of Baltimore *Morning Herald* (1899–1905); editor, Baltimore *Evening Herald* (1905–06). On staff of Baltimore *Sun* (1906–10), *Evening Sun* (1910–16, 1918–36), and on both *Sun* and *Evening Sun* (from 1936). Literary critic, *Smart Set* (1908–23), and coeditor (1914–23). Founder, with George Jean Nathan (*q.v.*), coeditor, and editor, *American Mercury* (1924–33). Contributing editor, *The Nation* (1921–32). Author of *Ventures into Verse* (1903), *George Bernard Shaw—His Plays* (1905), *In Defense of Women* (1917), *The American Language* (1918; later editions, revised), *Prejudices* (in 6 series, 1919–27), *Notes on Democracy* (1926), *Treatise on the Gods* (1930), *Treatise on Right and Wrong* (1934), *A New Dictionary of Quotations* (1942), the autobiographical *Happy Days, 1880–1892* (1940), *Newspaper Days, 1899–1906* (1941), and *Heathen Days, 1890–1936* (1943), etc.

**Men·da'ña de Ney'ra** (mān·dä'nyä thā nĕ'ē·rä), **Álvaro de.** 1541–1595. Spanish mariner and explorer; discovered and explored Solomon Islands (c. 1567) and Marquesas Islands (c. 1595).

**Men'del** (mĕn'dĕl), **David.** Orig. name of Johann August Wilhelm NEANDER.

**Mendel, Gregor Johann.** 1822–1884. Austrian botanist; entered order of Augustinians at Brünn (1843); became abbot. Known for breeding experiments with peas in monastery garden; discovered Mendel's law, a law observed in inheritance of many characters in animals and plants. Law was published by natural history society of Brünn (1865) but not widely recognized until brought into prominence by De Vries and others (1900).

**Mendel, Lafayette Benedict.** 1872–1935. American physiological chemist, b. Delhi, N.Y. Known for researches connected with digestion and nutrition, protein metabolism, growth, discovery of vitamin A (1913), and function of vitamin C.

**Men·de·le'ev** (myĕn·dyĭ·lyā'yĕf; *Angl.* mĕn'dĕ·lā'(y)ĕf), **Dmitri Ivanovich.** 1834–1907. Russian chemist, b. Tobolsk, Siberia. Educ. St. Petersburg, where he later (1866) became professor. Director, bureau of weights and measures (from 1893). Known for bringing into prominence periodic system of classification of chemical elements, on basis of which system he was able to make predictions, many of which were afterwards fulfilled; author of *The Principles of Chemistry* (written 1868–70; translated into English, 1905).

**Men'del·sohn** (mĕn'dĕl·zōn; *Angl.* -s'n), **Eric.** 1887–1953. German-born architect in England; naturalized British subject (1938). Designed Einstein Tower at Potsdam, Columbus House in Berlin, Hebrew U. and Medical Center in Jerusalem. Author of *The International Conformity of the New Architecture—or Dynamics and Function* (1923), *Architecture and the Changing Civilisation* (1940), etc.

**Men'dels·sohn** (mĕn'dĕls·zōn; *Angl.* -dĕl-s'n). Family of German bankers, including founders of Berlin banking house Mendelssohn & Co. (1805). **Joseph Mendelssohn** (1770–1848) and his brother **Abraham** (1776–1835; father of Felix Mendelssohn-Bartholdy, *q.v.*), sons of philosopher Moses Mendelssohn (*q.v.*). Their successors include **Ernest von Mendelssohn–Bar·thol'dy** [-bär·tōl'dē] (d. 1906) and **Franz von Mendelssohn** (1865–1935), partner and senior head of firm, president of German Chamber of Industry and Commerce (1921–31) and of International Chamber of Commerce (1931).

**Mendelssohn, Arnold Ludwig.** 1855–1933. Son of a cousin of Felix Mendelssohn-Bartholdy (*q.v.*). German composer of choral and orchestral works, including *Abendkantate* (1881), *Frühlingsfeier* (1891), *Der Paria* (1905), and *Psalm 137* (1913); also of three operas, including *Elsi, die Seltsame Magd* (1896), symphonies, chamber music, and songs.

**Mendelssohn, Dorothea.** See Dorothea SCHLEGEL.

**Mendelssohn, Felix.** *In full* **Jakob Ludwig Felix Mendelssohn–Bar·thol'dy** (bär·tōl'dē). 1809–1847. Son of Abraham Mendelssohn (*q.v.*) and grandson of Moses Mendelssohn (*q.v.*). Added *Bartholdy* to his surname following conversion to Christianity in early childhood. German composer, pianist, and musical conductor, b. Hamburg. Made first public appearance as pianist (1818) and presented original compositions at musical gatherings in father's house. Formed close friendships with Weber and Goethe (1821), and Moscheles. Gave initial impetus to Bach revival and successfully conducted Bach's *Matthew Passion* in Berlin (1829), first time after death of the composer. Appeared successfully as pianist and conductor in London (1829); toured (until 1832) in England, Italy, and on the Continent; again to London in 1833 and repeatedly thereafter. Musical director in Düsseldorf (1833); director of famous Gewandhaus concerts in Leipzig (from 1835), which became center of musical world of Europe; helped found Berlin Acad. of Arts and reorganized Cathedral choir; cofounder (1843) and director of Leipzig Conservatory; first met Jenny Lind 1844, for whom he composed special music. Collapsed from overwork and from nervous prostration following death of his sister **Fanny** (1805–1847), composer and pianist, wife of painter Wilhelm Hensel. Mendelssohn composed five symphonies, including *Symphony in C Minor* (1824), *Italian Symphony* (1833), *Scotch Symphony* (1842), *Reformation Symphony,* and symphony cantata *Lobgesang* (Eng. *Hymn of Praise;* revised 1840); overtures, including *The Hebrides*, or *Fingal's Cave* (1830), Goethe's *A Calm Sea and a Prosperous Voyage, The Lovely Melusine* (1833), *Ruy Blas* and the *Trumpet Overture* (1839); concertos, including a violin concerto (1844) and two piano concertos; works for piano and orchestra, dramatic works, including music to Shakespeare's *A Midsummer Night's Dream* (overture, 1826; completed, 1842), Goethe's *First Walpurgis Night* (1831), Sophocles's *Antigone* (1841) and *Oedipus at Colonus* (1845), Racine's *Athalie* (1843–45), comic opera *The Wedding of Camacho* (prod. 1827), Singspiel *Son and Stranger* (1829), and unfinished fragments of opera *Lorelei;* much chamber music, piano works, including eight books of *Songs Without Words* (1830–45), four sonatas, three books of *Variations*, six preludes and fugues, various fantasias (including one on *The Last Rose of Summer*), organ sonatas, vocal music, including oratorios *St. Paul* (1836) and *Elijah* (1846), and songs, psalms, motets, and other choral works, etc. Father of historian **Karl Mendelssohn–Bartholdy** (1838–1897) and grandfather of **Albrecht Mendelssohn–Bartholdy** (1874–1936), professor of civil and international law at Würzburg (1905) and Hamburg (1920).

**Mendelssohn, Moses.** 1729–1786. Called "the German Socrates." German Jewish philosopher, b. Dessau. Formed close friendship with Lessing (1754), which inspired latter's *Nathan der Weise*, and was befriended by Nicolai, Lavater, and others; corresponded with Kant; helped found and contributed as critic to Nicolai's *Bibliothek* and Lessing's *Briefe, die Neueste Literatur Betreffend.* Author of *Philosophische Gespräche* (1755), the satire *Pope ein Metaphysiker* (1755), the essay *Abhandlung über die Evidenz in den Metaphysischen Wissenschaften* (1764; Berlin Acad. prize), *Phädon* (in support of immortality of the soul, 1767), translations into German of the Psalms and the Pentateuch (1783), which helped advance education and culture of the Jews, *Jerusalem oder über Religiöse Macht und Judentum* (plea for religious tolerance, 1783), *Morgenstunden oder über das Dasein Gottes* (1785), etc. Father of the writer Dorothea Schlegel (*q.v.*) and the bankers Joseph and Abraham Mendelssohn (see MENDELSSOHN family).

**Men'den·hall** (mĕn'dĕn·hôl), **Thomas Corwin.** 1841–1924. American physicist, b. near Hanoverton, Ohio. President, Rose Polytechnic Institute, Terre Haute, Ind. (1886–89), Worcester Tech. (1894–1901). Known for his researches in gravity, seismology, electricity, and atmospheric electricity.

**Men'dès'** (măɴ'dĕs'), **Catulle,** *in full* **Abraham Catulle.** 1841–1909. French man of letters; to Paris and founded (1859) *Revue Fantaisiste;* became founder of Parnassian school of poetry, the origins of which he described in *Légende du Parnasse Contemporain* (1884). Dramatic critic of *Le Journal* (from 1893). Wrote verse, as *Philoméla* (1864), *Hespérus* (1869), *Contes Épiques* (1870), *Odelettes Guerrières* (1871); plays, as *La Femme de Tabarin* (1887), *La Reine Fiammette, Médée, Scarron;* librettos, as *Gwendoline* (1886), *Isoline* (1888), *La Carmélite* (1902), *Ariane* (1906); romances, as *Le Roi*

*Vierge* (1881), *Monstres Parisiens* (1882), *Gog* (1894).

**Men′des** (mĕn′dĕs), **Frederic de So′la** (dĕ sō′lȧ). 1850–1927. Rabbi, b. in Jamaica, B.W.I. Rabbi in New York City (1878–1920); a founder and editor, *American Hebrew* (1879–85); revising editor, *Jewish Encyclopedia;* author of *Outlines of Jewish History* (1886), etc.

**Mendes Pinto, Fernão.** See PINTO.

**Mén′dez** (mān′dās). **Miguel Abadía.** 1867–1947. Colombian lawyer; president of Colombia (1926–30).

**Men′di·bu′ru** (mān′dē·bōō′rōō), **Manuel de.** 1805–1885. Peruvian statesman and scholar; served in Peruvian army in war for independence (1821–30); in government service (1834–70), including service as minister successively to Great Britain, Bolivia, and Chile. Chief work, *Diccionario Histórico-Biográfico del Perú* (1874–85), of which only the first part has been published.

**Men·die′ta** (mān·dyā′tä), **Carlos.** 1873–1960. Cuban political leader; active in revolution against Spain (1896–98). Led attacks against administrations of Menocal and Machado; arrested (1931) and went into exile in New York; after Machado's fall (1933), led opposition to radical government of Grau San Martín. Provisional president of Cuba (1934–35); disturbance led to military dictatorship; resigned (Dec. 12, 1935).

**Men·do′za** (mān·dō′sä), **Antonio de.** 1485?–1552. Spanish colonial governor; first viceroy of New Spain (Mexico; 1535–49) and viceroy of Peru (1551–52). Brought first printing press to New World (1535); sent out expedition under Coronado which explored much of what is now New Mexico and Colorado.

**Men·do′za** (mān·dō′thä), **Diego Hurtado de.** 1503?–1575. Spanish statesman and man of letters; ambassador to Venice (1539); representative at Council of Trent (1545); governor of Siena (1547); imperial representative in Rome (1549). Author of verse and the history *Guerra de Granada;* reputed author of novel *Lazarillo de Tormes.*

**Mendoza, Íñigo López de.** See Marqués de SANTILLANA.

**Mendoza, Juan de Palafox de.** See PALAFOX DE MENDOZA.

**Mendoza, Juan Gonzales de.** 1540?–1617. Spanish prelate; member of Augustinian order. On mission from Philip II to China (1580–83); later, bishop of Lipari Islands, of Chiapas, and of Popayán. Published (1586) an account of China.

**Mendoza, Pedro de.** 1487?–1537. Spanish soldier, colonizer, and explorer; appointed by Charles V military governor of lands between Plata River and Strait of Magellan. Equipped expedition largely at own expense (1534); sailed up Plata River and founded first colony of Buenos Aires (1536).

**Mendoza, Pedro González de.** 1428–1495. Spanish prelate, statesman, and soldier, b. Guadalajara; son of Íñigo López de Mendoza, Marqués de Santillana. Bishop of Calahorra (1452); fought in battle of Olmedo (1467); bishop of Sigüenza (1468); created cardinal (1473); archbishop of Seville and chancellor of Castile; aided Isabella I in securing Spanish throne; archbishop of Toledo (1482). Occupied Granada in name of Ferdinand and Isabella (Jan. 2, 1492).

**Men′e·de′mus** (mĕn′ĕ·dē′mŭs). 350?–?276 B.C. Greek philosopher, of Eretria; reputed student under Phaedo, whose school (Elian school) he is said to have transferred to Eretria, where it became known as Eretrian school. His doctrines are said to have resembled those of Megarian school.

**Men′e·lik II** (*Angl.* mĕn′ĕ·lĭk). *Abyssinian* **Negus Negusti,** *i.e.* King of Kings. 1844–1913. Emperor of Abyssinia, son of king of Shoa. Succeeded to throne of Abyssinia (1889) and signed treaty placing empire under Italian domination. Abrogated treaty (1893); defeated Italians at Aduwa (Mar. 1, 1896); established independence of Abyssinia. Negotiated boundary settlement between Abyssinia and British Sudan (1902) and between Abyssinia and Italian Somaliland (1908). Unable to continue rule because of apoplectic attacks, succeeded by a regency (1910). See LIJ YASU.

**Me·nén′dez** (mā·nān′dās), **Manuel.** 1790?–?1845. Peruvian politician; acting president of Peru (1841–45); twice driven from power during his administration, which was one of civil war and confusion, once (1842) by Juan Crisóstomo Torrico, again (1843) by Manuel Ignacio de Vivanco. Supported by Ramón Castilla.

**Me·nén′dez de A′vi·lés′** (mā·nān′dāth thā ä′vē·lās′), **Pedro.** 1519–1574. Spanish mariner; captain general of the Indies fleet (1554); made three trips to America (between 1555 and 1563). Adelantado of Florida (1565), charged with exploration, colonization, and defense of the province; built fort at St. Augustine and defeated and massacred French Protestant colony on St. John's River (1565); firmly established Spanish power in Florida.

**Menéndez Pi·dal′** (pē·thäl′), **Ramón.** 1869–1968. Spanish philologist; professor of Romanic philology, Madrid (1899 ff.); editor of *Revista de Filología.* Author of *L'Epopée Castillane à travers la Littérature Espagnole* (1910; lectures delivered in 1909 at Johns Hopkins U., Baltimore) and *El Romancero Español* (lectures delivered at Columbia U., New York). Chief work, *Gramática Histórica Española.*

**Menéndez y Pe·la′yo** (ē pā·lä′yō), **Marcelino.** 1856–1912. Spanish literary critic and historian; chief works, *Historia de los Heterodoxes Españoles* (3 vols., 1880–82) and *Historia de las Ideas Estéticas en España* (1883–91).

**Me·ne′ni·us A·grip′pa** (mē·nē′nĭ·ŭs ȧ·grĭp′ȧ). According to legend, Roman patrician who, during plebeian secession to Sacred Mount (c. 494 B.C.), induced plebeians to compromise by telling fable of interdependence of the belly and members of the body.

**Meneptah.** Variant of MERNEPTAH.

**Me′nes** (mē′nēz). *Sometimes* **Me′na** (mē′nȧ). fl. 3400 (3500?) B.C. First king of Ist (Thinite) dynasty of Egypt; formerly held to be legendary; now substantiated as uniting north and south kingdoms under one scepter and as founder of city on site of Memphis.

**Meng′el·berg** (mĕng′ĕl·bĕrk), **Willem,** *in full* **Josef Willem.** 1871–1951. Dutch orchestra conductor, pianist, and composer, b. Utrecht, of a German family; a leading interpreter of Richard Strauss and Gustav Mahler; conductor of London Symphony Orchestra and Royal Philharmonic Society (1911–14); appeared with New York Philharmonic Society (1905) and as conductor of National Symphony Orchestra of New York (1921 ff.), which two merged (1922) on his suggestion; coconductor with Toscanini of newly formed (1928) New York Philharmonic-Symphony Orchestra; professor, Utrecht (1933).

**Meng′er** (mĕng′ĕr), **Karl.** 1840–1921. Austrian economist; a leading theorist of Austrian school of economics; professor, Vienna (1873–1903). Favored theory and speculation and opposed historical method in economics; cofounder of school of marginal utility. His brother **Anton** (1841–1906) was a jurist and social politician; championed politically centralized government with decentralized economic functions.

**Men·ghin′** (mĕn·gēn′), **Oswald.** 1888– . Austrian historian; Austrian minister of education (1938). Author of *Weltgeschichte der Steinzeit* (1931), *Geist und Blut* (1934), etc.

**Mengs** (mĕngs), **Anton Raphael.** 1728–1779. German

historical and portrait painter and art critic; representative of late baroque and classical schools. To Dresden (1744), where he became court painter to Elector Augustus III (1745); in Madrid as first painter to Charles III of Spain (1761–69, 1774 ff.), and in Rome (1769–73; from 1777). Painted *Holy Family, Annunciation,* and *Antony and Cleopatra* (all now in Vienna), *Nativity* (in Madrid), frescoes for the royal palace in Madrid, many oil and pastel portraits, and self-portraits.

**Mêng T'ien** (mŭng' tē·ĕn'). d. 209 B.C. Chinese general; a commander in chief of Emperor Shih Huang Ti; appointed by the emperor to superintend the building of the Great Wall (214–209 B.C.); reputed to have been the inventor of the pen or writing brush.

**Mêng-tzŭ** *or* **Meng-tse.** See MENCIUS.

**Me·nier'** (mē·nyā'), **Émile Justin.** 1826–1881. French chocolate manufacturer and politician; author of works on economics.

**Mé'nière'** (mā'nyâr'), **Prosper.** 1801–1862. French physician; specialist in diseases of the ear; described symptoms of disease known as *Ménière's disease.* His son **Émile Antoine** (1839–1905) was also a physician.

**Me·nip'pus** (mē·nĭp'ŭs). Greek cynic philosopher and satirist of 3d century B.C., b. Gadara, Syria; originally a slave; bitterly satirized, in verse varied with prose, foibles of men, esp. of fellow philosophers.

**Men'ken** (mĕng'kĕn), **Adah Bertha,** *known as* **Adah I'saacs** (ī'zăks; ī'zĭks). 1835?–1868. American actress, b. New Orleans; m. A. I. Menken (1856) and then, under impression that she was divorced, John Carmel Heenan (1859), pugilist; became central figure in divorce scandal. Successful on stage, esp. in *Mazeppa.* Wrote poems later collected and published (1868) under title *Infelicia.*

**Men·ku're** (mĕn·kōō'rā) *or* **Men·kau're** (-kou'-). *Gr.* **Myk'e·ri'nos** (mĭk'ĕ·rī'nŏs). *Lat.* **Myc'e·ri'nus** (mĭs'ĕ·rī'nŭs). King of IVth (Memphite) dynasty of Egypt; reigned about 2800 B.C. Builder of third pyramid of Giza, smallest but most perfect of the pyramids (cf. KHUFU); reign marked beginning of decline of the dynasty.

**Men'ning·er** (mĕn'ĭng·ẽr), **Karl Augustus.** 1893– . American psychiatrist; M.D., Harvard; in practice in Topeka, Kans., in Menninger (neuropsychiatric) Clinic. Author of *The Human Mind* (1930), *Man Against Himself* (1938), *Love Against Hate* (1942), etc.

**Men'no Si'mons** (mĕn'ō sē'mōns). 1496–1561. Religious reformer, b. in Friesland; leader of conservative Anabaptists, from whom Mennonites took their name. Roman Catholic priest in his native Witmarsum (1531–36); came under influence of Lutheran and Anabaptist thought and withdrew from Roman Catholic Church (1536); was rebaptized and ordained elder at Groningen (1537); active as organizer and leader of Anabaptist groups in East Friesland, Holland, and Germany.

**Me'no·cal'** (mā'nō·käl'), **Mario García.** 1866–1941. Cuban engineer and political leader; served in patriot army in revolution (1895–98); Conservative president of Cuba (1913–21); administration businesslike and friendly to U.S., but only partly successful in reform measures. Defeated for presidency by Machado (1924).

**Me·no'her** (mĕ·nôr'; -nō'ẽr), **Charles Thomas.** 1862–1930. American army officer in World War I; served in Lunéville sector, Champagne-Marne offensive, St. Mihiel attack, and Meuse-Argonne offensive.

**Me·not'ti** (mā·nôt'tē), **Ciro.** 1798–1831. Italian patriot; member of the Carbonari; led insurrection (Modena; Feb., 1831).

**Menotti, Gian-Carlo.** 1911– . American (Italian-born) composer. Wrote chamber music, songs, concertos, operas, cantatas, ballets, etc. Founder, Festival of Two Worlds (1958; director, 1958– ).

**Me·nou'** (mē·nōō'), Baron **Jacques François de.** 1750–1810. French soldier in the Revolutionary and Napoleonic armies; commanded French army in Egypt after death of Kléber (1800); was defeated by English at Alexandria (Mar. 21, 1801) and capitulated.

**Men'pes** (mĕm'pĭs), **Mortimer.** 1859–1938. British painter and etcher, b. in Australia; acted as war correspondent in Africa for *Black and White* (1900); superintended reproduction of *The Menpes Series of Great Masters.* Published *War Impressions* (1901), *The Durbar* (1903), *Whistler as I Knew Him* (1904), *India* (1905), *Thames* (1906), etc.

**Mens'dorff-Pouil'ly'** (mĕns'dôrf·pōō'yē'), Count **Alexander von.** 1813–1871. Austrian soldier and statesman; general (1850); minister of foreign affairs (1864–66); failed in efforts to prevent Austro-Prussian war. His son **Count Albert von Mensdorff-Pouilly-Die'trichstein** [-dē'trĭk·shtīn] (1861–1945) was Austro-Hungarian ambassador to London (1904–14).

**Men'shi·kov** (myān'y'·shĭ·kôf), Prince **Aleksandr Danilovich.** 1672–1729. Russian soldier and statesman in service of Peter the Great; commissioned general (1704) and created prince of Holy Roman Empire. At death of Peter the Great (1725), was instrumental in having empress dowager proclaimed empress under title of Catherine I; at Catherine's death (1727), became regent for her grandson Peter II; exiled to Siberia by Peter II (1727). Great-grandfather of Aleksandr Sergeevich MENSHIKOV.

**Menshikov,** Prince **Aleksandr Sergeevich.** 1787–1869. Great-grandson of Aleksandr Danilovich Menshikov (*q.v.*). Russian soldier; served against Napoleon (1812–15) and the Turks (1828–29). Governor general of Finland (1831); Russian minister of marine (1836). Commanded Russian naval and military forces in the Crimea (1854–55); noted for his conduct of operations in defense of Sevastopol.

**Men·teith'** (mĕn·tēth'), Sir **John de.** d. after 1329. Scottish knight who captured Wallace at Glasgow and took him to London (1305).

**Men'tel** (mĕn'tĕl) *or* **Men'te·lin** (mĕn'tĕ·lĭn), **Johann.** 1410?–1478. German printer in Strassburg. Probably associated with Gutenberg at Mainz after latter's quarrel with Faust; citizen of Strassburg (from 1447), where he was first to establish a press; printed the 49-line Bible (1460–61). Invention of printing was attributed by some to him, but the claim has been demonstrated as without ground.

**Men'tu·ho'tep** (mĕn'tōō·hō'tĕp). Name of five kings of ancient Egypt of XIth (Theban) dynasty. Dates of all reigns are uncertain but, according to one authority (Breasted), last five rulers of dynasty, Mentuhotep I to V, were in power c. 2160 to 2000 B.C. **Mentuhotep II,** *also known as* **Nib·ha'pet·re** (nĭb·hä'pĕt·rā) *or* **Neb·ha'pet·re** (nĕb-) **Mentuhotep,** completed conquest of Heracleopolitan dynasty and began establishment of supremacy of Thebes. **Mentuhotep IV** *or* **Nib·he'pet·re Mentuhotep** (nĭb·hĕ'pĕt·rā), greatest ruler of the dynasty, organized and strengthened kingdom; reigned about fifty years. **Mentuhotep V** was displaced by a new and stronger Theban family, led by Amenemhet I, first of XIIth (Theban) dynasty.

**Men'u·hin** (mĕn'ŭ·ĭn), **Ye·hu'di** (yĕ·hōō'dĭ). 1916– . American violinist, b. New York City; child prodigy, appearing at age of 7 as soloist with San Francisco orchestra, and at 8 in recital at Manhattan Opera House, New York. On concert stage from 1937.

**Menu von Minutoli,** Baron **Heinrich.** See MINUTOLI.

**Men'zel** (mĕn'tsĕl), **Adolph Friedrich Erdmann von.**

1815–1905. German historical and genre painter, illustrator, and lithographer; produced six pen-and-ink drawings for lithographs illustrating Goethe's *Künstlers Erdenwallen* (*Artist's Earthly Pilgrimage*), over 400 designs for woodcuts illustrating Kugler's *History of Frederick the Great* (from 1839), which gave new impetus to art of wood engraving in Germany, 200 sketches for woodcuts for an edition de luxe of the works of Frederick the Great on commission of Frederick William IV (1843–48), 600 sketches for lithographs illustrating *Frederick the Great's Army in Uniform* (3 vols., 1842–57), oil paintings, esp. of historical scenes, gouache paintings for *Kinderbuch* (1858–80), fresco portraits in the Marienburg refectory, aquarelles, etc.

**Menzel, Wolfgang.** 1798–1873. German critic and historian; follower of Jean Paul; in literature a romanticist. Helped found Burschenschaft at Jena (1818); resident mostly in Stuttgart (from 1825), where he edited and contributed to literary periodicals. Member of Württemberg parliament (1830–38); actively opposed Young Germany and was bitterly attacked by Börne, Heine, and others. Author of witty poems *Streckverse* (1823), and of *Geschichte der Deutschen* (3 vols., 1824–25), *Die Deutsche Literatur* (an attack on Goethe's views; 2 vols., 1827), *Die Deutsche Dichtung* (3 vols., 1858–59), *Allgemeine Weltgeschichte* (16 vols., 1862–70), the historical novel *Furore* (2 vols., 1851), romances, fairy tales, etc.

**Men'zies** (mĕn'zēz), Sir **Robert Gordon.** 1894–1978. Australian lawyer and politician; called to the bar (1918); king's counsel (1929); attorney general of Australia (1935–39); prime minister (1939–41; 1949–66); member of advisory war council.

**Merbeck, John.** See John MARBECK.

**Mer'ca·dan'te** (mär'kä·dän'tā), **Saverio.** 1795–1870. Italian composer in various Italian cities and in Vienna (1824), Spain (1827–29), Paris (1836), etc.; director of Royal School of Music, Naples (1840–62); totally blind (from 1862). Composed about 60 operas, 20 masses, many psalms, motets, and other church music, cantatas, orchestral pieces, fantasias, funeral symphonies, songs, etc.

**Mer'ca'dier'** (mĕr'kȧ'dyā'), **Ernest Jules Pierre.** 1836–1911. French telegraphic engineer; known for work relating to acoustics, electricity, telegraphy, and telephony, esp. wireless telephony.

**Mer·cal'li** (mâr·käl'lē), **Giuseppe.** 1850–1914. Italian priest and geologist; devised scale for measuring earthquake shocks; studied glacial action in northern Italy and volcanoes at Etna and Vesuvius.

**Mer·ca'tor** (mûr·kā'tēr; *Flem.* mĕr·kȧ'tôr), **Gerhardus.** *Lat. form of* **Gerhard Kre'mer** (krā'mēr). 1512–1594. Flemish geographer; founded geographical establishment at Louvain (1534); published his earliest known map (1537), a map of the Holy Land, now lost; produced map of Flanders (1537–40), map of world showing north and south hemispheres (1538), terrestrial globe (1541), celestial globe (1551), and six-sheet map of Europe (1554). To Duisburg (1552); cosmographer to duke of Jülich and Cleves (1559). Known esp. for use in map of 1568 of the projection which has since borne his name; began great atlas (1585) completed by his son after his death.

**Mer·ca'tor** (mûr·kā'tēr; *Ger.* mĕr·kä'tôr), **Nicolaus.** *Real name* **Kauf'mann** (kouf'män). c. 1620–1687. German mathematician, astronomer, and engineer; to London (1660); later, engineer to construct Versailles fountains; in mathematics, credited with discovery of series for log $(1+x)$.

**Mercein, Eleanor.** See Eleanor Mercein KELLY.

**Mer'cer** (mûr'sēr), **James.** 1736–1793. American Revolutionary leader, b. in Stafford County, Va. Member, Virginia House of Burgesses (1762–76), Continental Congress (1779, 1780). Judge, Virginia general court (1779–89), first Virginia court of appeals (1789–93). His half brother **John Francis Mercer** (1759–1821) served through Revolutionary War; aide-de-camp to Gen. Charles Lee (1778–79); commanded militia grenadiers with rank of lieutenant colonel, at Yorktown (1781); delegate from Virginia to Continental Congress (1782–85); moved to Maryland (1785); member, U.S. House of Representatives (1792–94); governor of Maryland (1801–03).

**Mercer, John.** 1791–1866. English calico printer and chemist; discovered dyes suitable for printing calico orange, yellow, and bronze; partner in printworks (1825); discovered process named *mercerization* after him (1850).

**Mercer, Samuel Alfred Browne.** 1880– . Clergyman and Egyptologist, b. Bristol, Eng.; educ. in Newfoundland, U.S., and Europe (Ph.D., Munich, 1910); ordained priest in Protestant Episcopal Church (1904); professor of Hebrew, Western Theol. Seminary, Chicago (1910–22); professor of Semitic languages and Egyptology, and dean of divinity, Trinity Coll., Toronto (1923–24). Author of *Egyptian Grammar* (1915, 1927), *The Book of Genesis* (1919), *Growth of Religious and Moral Ideas in Egypt* (1919), *Ethiopic Grammar* (1919), *Life and Growth of Israel* (1921), *Assyrian Grammar* (1921), *Tutankhamen and Egyptology* (1923), *The Tell el-Amarna Tablets* (1939), etc. Special editor for Egyptology, *Webster's New International Dictionary, Second Edition.*

**Merchiston,** Laird of. See John NAPIER.

**Mer'cié'** (mĕr'syā'), **Marius Jean Antonin.** 1845–1916. French sculptor; among his carvings are *Thiers* (at Saint-Germain), *Quand Même* (at Belfort), *Guillaume Tell* (at Lausanne), and *Jeanne d'Arc* (at Domremy).

**Mer'cier'** (mĕr'syā'), **Désiré Joseph.** 1851–1926. Belgian cardinal and philosopher; disciple of Thomas Aquinas. Professor of Thomist philosophy, Louvain (1882–1906), where he was founder and editor of *Revue Néo-Scolastique* (1894–1906). Archbishop of Malines and primate of Belgium (1906); created cardinal (1907). Spiritual leader and spokesman of Belgians during German occupation of Belgium in World War (1914–18). Issued series of pastoral letters, including *Patriotism and Endurance* (Jan. 1, 1915), a protest which the German authorities sought to suppress. Visited U.S. (1919) to thank America for assistance to Belgium. Aimed toward unification of Anglican, Protestant Episcopal, and Roman churches.

**Mercier, Louis Sébastien.** 1740–1814. French man of letters; championed romanticism in his *Essai sur l'Art Dramatique* (1773). Author of several plays for the Comédie Italienne, also of miscellaneous works, including *L'Homme Sauvage* (1767), *L'An 2440 ou Rêve s'il en fut jamais* (1770), *Tableau de Paris* (1781–90), *Néologie* (1801).

**Mercier de la Ri'vière'** (dē lȧ rē'vyâr'), **Paul Pierre.** 1720–1794. French economist; associate of Quesnay, Du Pont de Nemours, and others of the physiocrats in spreading propaganda encouraging economic liberalism.

**Merck** (mĕrk), **Johann Heinrich.** 1741–1791. German writer and literary critic. Friend of Goethe, whose *Götz von Berlichingen* he published at his own expense.

**Mer'cœur'** (mĕr'kûr'), Duc **de. Philippe Emmanuel de Lor'raine'** (dē lô'rân'). 1558–1602. French soldier. Governor of Brittany (1582). After assassination of duc de Guise (1588), declared for the Catholic, or Holy, League and allied himself with Philip II of Spain; fought unsuccessful war (1588–98), but succeeded in negotiating advantageous peace with Henry IV (1598); married his daughter to César de Bourbon, Duc de Vendôme (*q.v.*).

For his grandson **Louis de Vendôme,** Duc de Mercœur, see Duc de VENDÔME.

**Mer'cy'** (mĕr'sē'), Baron **Franz von.** d. 1645. Bavarian field marshal; served in the Thirty Years' War; mortally wounded in action at Nördlingen (1645). His grandson Count **Claudius Florimund Mercy** (1666–1734) was an Austrian field marshal; killed in action near Parma (1734). The nephew and adopted son of Count Claudius, Count **Anton Mercy d'Ar'gen'teau'** [dȧr'zhäɴ'tō'] (1691–1767), was an Austrian field marshal. A grandnephew of Count Claudius, Count **Florimund Mercy d'Argenteau** (1727–1794), was in the Austrian diplomatic service.

**Mer'e·dith** (mĕr'ĕ·dĭth), **Edwin Thomas.** 1876–1928. American journalist and political leader; editor and publisher, *Farmers' Tribune,* Des Moines, Iowa (1896–1904); founder and editor, *Successful Farming* (1902–28). U.S. secretary of agriculture (1920–21).

**Meredith, George.** 1828–1909. English novelist and poet, b. Portsmouth. Articled to London solicitor (1845) but turned to journalism; contributed to *Household Words, Chambers's Edinburgh Journal, Fraser's Magazine;* parodied German romance in *Farina* (1857); worked for Ipswich *Journal* (1859–75). Met Swinburne and Pre-Raphaelite group; lodged with Rossetti and Swinburne in Cheyne Walk, Chelsea (1861–62); published *Modern Love and Poems of the English Roadside* (1862), considered his best poetical work. Reader to Chapman & Hall (1862–94). Published novels serially; delivered lecture *The Idea of Comedy and the Uses of the Comic Spirit* (1877); won popular approval for first time with *Diana of the Crossways* (1885), which had Sheridan's granddaughter the Hon. Mrs. Norton as prototype; published characteristic poems of natural realism, including volumes *Poems and Lyrics of the Joy of Earth* (1883), *Ballads and Poems of Tragic Life* (1887), *A Reading of Earth* (1888); disabled (from 1893) by paraplegia; his conversational comedy, *The Sentimentalists,* produced (1910). Criticized for obscurity and affectation, accentuated in *The Egoist* (1879) and later novels; acclaimed for stimulative thought on politics, sociology, and ethics, penetrating character analysis, lively humor, and resilient optimism in his best novels, including *The Shaving of Shagpat* (1856), *The Ordeal of Richard Feverel* (1859), *Evan Harrington* (1861), *Emilia in England* (1864; later called *Sandra Belloni*) and its sequel *Vittoria* (1867), *Rhoda Fleming* (1865), *The Adventures of Harry Richmond* (1871), *Beauchamp's Career* (1876), *The Tragic Comedians* (1880).

**Meredith, Owen.** Pseudonym of E. R. Bulwer LYTTON.

**Meredith, William Morris.** 1799–1873. American lawyer, b. Philadelphia; U.S. secretary of the treasury (1849–50); attorney general of Pennsylvania (1861–67).

**Meres** (mērz), **Francis.** 1565–1647. English clergyman; educ. Cambridge and Oxford; schoolmaster at Wing (1602); author of *Palladis Tamia: Wits Treasury* (1598), reviewing 125 English authors each in comparison with a Latin, Greek, or Italian author, listing Shakespeare's plays, and narrating Marlowe's death.

**Me·rezh·kov'ski** (myĕ·ryĕsh·kôf'skû·ĭ; *Angl.* mĕr'ĕsh·kôf'skĭ), **Dmitri Sergeevich.** 1865–1941. Russian writer, b. St. Petersburg; after revolution (1917), settled in Paris. Author of critical essays, as *The Causes of Decadence in Modern Russian Literature* (1893) and *Tolstoi and Dostoevski* (1901); also of *Christ and Antichrist* (trilogy of historical novels; 1901–05); biographies of Napoleon (1929), Michelangelo (1930), Leonardo da Vinci (1938); plays, including *Paul I* (1908) and *Alexander I* (1913); and, among later works, *Not Peace but a Sword, The Menace of the Mob, The Secret of the West,* and (1933) *Jesus the Unknown.* His wife, **Zinaida Nikolaevna Me·rezh·kov'ska·ya** [-kôf'skŭ·yŭ] (1869–1945), *pseudonym* **Hip'pi·us** (gyēp'pĭ·o͝os; *Angl.* hĭp'ĭ·ŭs), poet, novelist, and critic, b. St. Petersburg; author of fiction, as *The Red Sword* (1906), *Black and White* (1908), and *Devil's Doll* (1910); and (with her husband, during exile in Paris) a picture of Russia under Bolshevik regime entitled *The Reign of the Antichrist.*

**Mer'gen·tha'ler** (mĕr'gĕn·tä'lẽr), **Ottmar.** 1854–1899. Inventor, b. Hachtel, Germany; to U.S. (1872), naturalized (1878). After many experiments, invented first Linotype typesetting machine (patented 1884); produced improved machine (1885) with automatic justification; later patented further improvements.

**Me'ri·an** (mā'rē·än), **Matthäus,** *Eng.* **Matthew.** 1593–1650. Swiss engraver and bookseller; took over business of his father-in-law, Jean Théodore de Bry (c. 1623), in Frankfurt. Produced copperplate engravings for Abelin's *Historische Chronica,* the Bible, *Theatrum Europaeum* (begun 1635), *Basler Totentanz* (1644), and, esp., began series of *Topographia,* with text by the Austrian topographer Martin Zeiller, showing perspective views of various European cities, towns, castles, etc. (16 vols., 30 parts, 1642–88). His son and successor **Matthäus** (1621–1687) was a portrait and religious painter and engraver. Another son, **Kaspar** (1627–1686), etcher and engraver, produced portraits, landscapes, views of cities, and festive scenes. Matthäus the elder's daughter **Maria Sibylla** (1647–1717), painter, engraver, and naturalist, m. (1668) the painter Johann Andreas Graff; traveled in Surinam and made study of native insect and plant life (1699–1701); painted flowers, fruits, and insects; author of works on natural science, often with original copperplate illustrations.

**Merici,** Saint **Angela.** See ANGELA MERICI.

**Méricourt, Théroigne de.** See THÉROIGNE DE MÉRICOURT.

**Mé'ri·da** (mā'rē·thä), **Carlos.** 1893– . Guatemalan painter; executed paintings based on folklore themes. Exhibited in Mexico City (1919) and joined group of Mexican revolutionary painters under leadership of David Alfaro Siqueiros. Turned toward surrealism (c. 1930). Known esp. for his frescoes.

**Me·ri'gi** (mâ·rē'jē). Variant of *Merisi* (see Michelangelo da CARAVAGGIO).

**Me'ri·kan'to** (mĕ'rĭ·kän'tŏ), **Oskar.** 1868–1924. Finnish organist, opera conductor, and composer, b. Helsingfors. Works include operas, several popular Singspiels, concerto for violin, clarinet, horn, and string quartet, works for organ, piano, and violin, choruses, and many Finnish songs.

**Mé'ri'mée'** (mā'rē'mā'), **Prosper.** 1803–1870. French man of letters; appointed inspector general of historical remains in France (1841); elected senator (1853). Among his literary works are *La Jacquerie* (1828), *La Chronique du Temps de Charles IX* (historical novel; 1829), *Colomba* (novel; 1840), *Arsène Guillot* (novel; 1844), *Carmen* (novel; 1845), *L'Abbé Aubain* (novel; 1846), *Histoire de D. Pèdre Ier de Castille* (1848), *Le Faux Démétrius* (1852), *Les Cosaques d'Autrefois* (1865), and many translations from Russian classics, which served to make Russian literature known in France. His *Lettres* and *Correspondance* were published after death.

**Merire.** = PEPI I.

**Merisi** *or* **Merisio, Michelangelo.** See CARAVAGGIO.

**Mer'i·vale** (mĕr'ĭ·vāl), **John Herman.** 1779–1844. English barrister, translator, and minor poet. His second son, **Charles** (1808–1893), historian; dean of Ely (1869–93); author of *A History of the Romans under the Empire* (7 vols., 1850–64), in which he unduly glorified imperialism. An elder son, **Herman** (1806–1874), lawyer and historical writer; undersecretary for colonies, transferred to India office (1859–74). Herman's son **Herman Charles** (1839–1906), playwright and novelist; collaborated in highly successful plays *All for Her* (1875) and *Forget Me Not* (1879); adapted foreign dramas; author of poetic drama *The White Pilgrim* (1883), farces and burlesques, *Faucit of Balliol* (novel, 3 vols., 1882), and a fairy tale *Binko's Blues* (1884).

**Mer′kel** (mĕr′kĕl), **Adolf.** 1836–1896. German jurist and authority on criminal law.

**Merkel, Paul Johannes.** 1819–1861. German jurist and law historian.

**Mer′ker** (mĕr′kẽr), **Paul.** 1881–1945. German philologist and literary historian.

**Merle d'Au′bi′gné′** (mĕrl′ dō′bē′nyā′), **Jean Henri.** 1794–1872. Swiss Protestant theologian, b. near Geneva. Pastor in Hamburg (1819); court preacher, Brussels (1823); professor of church history in Geneva (1831). Wrote *Histoire de la Réformation au XVI^e Siècle* (4 vols., 1835–47) and *Histoire de la Réformation en Europe au Temps de Calvin* (8 vols., 1862–78).

**Mer′lin′, Antoine Christophe.** *Called* **Mer′lin′ de Thi·on′ville′** (mĕr′lăɴ′ dē tyôɴ′vēl′). 1762–1833. French politician; member of Legislative Assembly (1791–92), National Convention (1792–95), and Council of Five Hundred (1795–98); director-general of posts (1798–99).

**Merlin,** Comte **Philippe Antoine.** *Called* **Merlin de Dou·ai′** (dwā). 1754–1838. French jurist and politician; member of States-Général (1789) and president of criminal court of the North (1791). Member of National Convention (1792) and its president for a time after the Reign of Terror (1793). Minister of justice (1795–99); procureur général at the Court of Cassation (1801); councilor of state (1808); created comte by Napoleon (1810). Expelled from France at the Restoration (1815), returning fifteen years later.

**Merlo, Aimé.** See Marius and Ary LEBLOND.

**Mer′mil′lod′** (mĕr′mē′yō′), **Gaspard.** 1824–1892. Swiss Roman Catholic cardinal, orator, and ultramontane leader. Named bishop of Lausanne and Geneva by Pope Leo XIII (1883) with see at Freiburg; lived as cardinal in Rome (from 1890). Founder of *L'Observateur Catholique.*

**Merm′na·dae** (mûrm′nȧ·dē). Name of third dynasty of Lydia, founded by Gyges (685 B.C.) and terminated by overthrow of Croesus by Cyrus the Great (546).

**Mer′ne·ptah′** (mĕr′nĕp·tä′) *or* **Me′ne·ptah′** (mĕ′-nĕp·tä′). King of ancient Egypt of XIXth (Diospolite) dynasty; reigned about 1225–1215 B.C. Son of Ramses II. Generally supposed to be the pharaoh of the Exodus; defeated (c. 1221 B.C.) Libyans who had invaded Egypt.

**Me·ro′dach–bal′a·dan** (mē·rō′dăk·băl′ȧ·dăn; mĕr′ō-). Name of several kings of Babylon, esp.: **Merodach–baladan II.** *Assyrian* **Marduk–apal–iddina.** d. ?700 B.C. King (721–710). As ruler of a part of Chaldea, submitted to Tiglath-pileser III (729–728); made alliance with Elamites (721) against Sargon II of Assyria; defeated and driven out by Sargon (710); in Chaldea (709–705); after Sargon's death (705), renewed alliance against Assyria; sent embassy to Hezekiah (*Isaiah* xxxix. 1 and, as **Be·ro′dach–bal′a·dan** [bē·rō′dăk-; bĕr′ō-], *2 Kings* xx. 12); defeated by Sargon's son Sennacherib (703); fled to Elam.

**Mé′rode′** (mā′rôd′), **Le Maître de.** See FLÉMALLE.

**Mérode,** Comte **Philippe Félix Ghislain de.** 1791–1857. Belgian statesman; minister of state (1831); minister of war ad interim (1832); minister of foreign affairs (1833); minister of finance; Belgian ambassador at Paris (1839). His son **Frédéric Xavier Ghislain** (1820–1874) was a Roman Catholic prelate; appointed by Pope Pius IX minister of war, Papal States (1860–65); titular archbishop of Mytilene and grand almoner of the pope (1866).

**Mé′ro′vée′** (mā′rô′vā′). *Ger.* **Me′ro·wig** (mā′rô·vĭĸ). *Lat.* **Mer′o·vae′us** (mĕr′ô·vē′ŭs). Second Frankish king (448–458), who gave his name to the Merovingian dynasty (*q.v.*).

**Mer′o·vin′gi·an** (mĕr′ô·vĭn′jĭ·ăn). Name of the first Frankish dynasty ruling from Clodion (428–448) to Childeric III (dethroned 751), when it was succeeded by Pepin, first of the Carolingians. The family began with rulers of the Salian Franks only (428) but later, after the death (511) of Clovis, its first ruler of importance, it had often two or more kings at a time (over Neustria, Austrasia, Burgundy, etc.). All possessions were united under Clotaire II (584–628) and Dagobert I (628–639). After 639 the power of the Merovingian rulers, **les Rois Fai′né′ants′** (lā rwä′ fā′nā′äɴ′), declined and they were under the control of the mayors of the palace. See PEPIN, CAROLINGIANS; see also *Table (in Appendix)* for FRANCE.

**Mer′ri·am** (mĕr′ĭ·ăm). Family of printers, bookmakers, and booksellers of Massachusetts. **Dan Merriam** (1771–1823), of West Brookfield; married (1802) Thirza Clapp (b. 1781); with his brothers **Ebenezer** (1777–1858) and **George** (1773–1802), founded (1798) firm of E. Merriam & Co.; published newspaper (1798–1801), later (1799) printed and published books; under several names, published for more than 50 years law books, Bibles, dictionaries (Perry's dictionary, editions of 1801, 1806, 1809), etc. Among Dan's eight children were: **George** (1803–1880), eldest child, b. Worcester; apprentice, later partner (1824–31), in West Brookfield printing business (E. & G. Merriam); moved to Springfield (1831); with brother Charles, established there (1831) firm of Merriam, Little & Co., later (1832) G. & C. Merriam, printers and booksellers. **Charles** (1806–1887), b. West Brookfield, served apprenticeship as printer at Hartford (1820–23) and at West Brookfield; worked few years in printing office of T. R. Marvin of Boston (until 1831). George and Charles Merriam, at first general publishers (1831–43), purchased (1843) rights of publication of Webster's *An American Dictionary of the English Language* from heirs of Noah Webster (*q.v.*) and became dictionary publishers, bringing out (1847) first dictionary of Merriam-Webster series, an enlarged revision by Chauncey A. Goodrich (*q.v.*) of original *American Dictionary* of Webster. **Lewis** (1811–1892), in printing business in Greenfield (1843–69); postmaster of Greenfield (1861–82). **Homer** (1813–1908), b. West Brookfield; in printing business in Greenfield, with brother William, and in Troy, N.Y.; joined G. & C. Merriam firm in Springfield (1856), president (1892–1904).

**Merriam, Augustus Chapman.** 1843–1895. American classical scholar and archaeologist; author of *The Greek and Latin Inscriptions on the Obelisk-Crab in the Metropolitan Museum, N.Y.* (1884), *The Sixth and Seventh Books of Herodotus* (1885), etc.

**Merriam, Clinton Hart.** 1855–1942. Brother of Florence Augusta Bailey (*q.v.*). American naturalist, b. New York City. In medical practice (1879–85); chief, U.S. Biological Survey (1885–1910). Biological investigator financed by special trust fund established by Mrs. E. H. Harriman (from 1910). Author of *The Birds of Connecticut* (1877), *Life Zones and Crop Zones of the United States* (1898), *Indian Population of California* (1905), *Review of the Grizzly and Big Brown Bears of America* (1917), *The Acorn, a Neglected Source of Food* (1918), *The Buffalo in Northern California* (1926), etc.

**Merriam, Florence Augusta.** See Florence A. BAILEY.

**Merriam, John Campbell.** 1869–1945. American paleontologist, b. Hopkinton, Iowa; president, Carnegie Institution (1920–38). Author of *The Occurrence of Human Remains in California Caves* (1909), *The Emergence of Man* (1919), *Spiritual Values and Constructive Life* (1933), *Science and Belief...* (1939), etc.

**Merriam, William Rush.** 1849–1931. American politician; governor of Minnesota (1889–93); director, twelfth U.S. census (1899–1903).

**Mer′rick** (mĕr′ĭk), **Leonard.** *Orig. surname* **Miller** *changed by deed poll.* 1864–1939. English novelist and playwright. After two years' experience on the stage, devoted himself to writing. Author of novels, including *Cynthia, a Daughter of the Philistines* (2 vols., 1896), *The Actor-Manager* (1898), *The Worldlings* (1900), *Conrad in Quest of his Youth* (1903), *While Paris Laughed* (1918), *To Tell You the Truth* (1922); plays, including *When the Lamps are Lighted, My Innocent Boy, The Elixir of Youth.*

**Mer′rill** (mĕr′ĭl), **Elmer Drew.** 1876–1956. American botanist, b. East Auburn, Me.; authority on taxonomy and phytogeography of Philippine, Polynesian, and Indo-Malayan plants.

**Merrill, George Perkins.** 1854–1929. American geologist, b. Auburn, Me.; on staff, U.S. National Museum (1881–1929), curator (from 1887), head curator (from 1897); developed geological and paleontological collection in museum; known esp. for his studies of meteorites.

**Merrill, Paul Willard.** 1887–1961. American astronomer; astronomer, Mt. Wilson Observatory (from 1919); known for work on stellar spectroscopy.

**Merrill, Selah.** 1837–1909. American Congregational clergyman, b. Canton Center, Conn. Archaeologist (1874–77) and leader (1876–77) of Eastern Palestine exploring expedition. American consul at Jerusalem (1882–85, 1891–93, 1898–1907) and at Georgetown, British Guiana (1907–08). Author of *East of the Jordan* (1881), *Ancient Jerusalem* (1908), etc.

**Merrill, Stuart Fitzrandolph.** 1863–1915. Poet, b. Hempstead, Long Island, N.Y.; resident in Paris (from 1889). His chief works, all written in French, are *Les Gammes* (1887), *Les Fastes* (1891), *Petits Poèmes d'Automne* (1895), *Les Quatre Saisons* (1900), *Une Voix dans la Foule* (1909).

**Mer′ri·man** (mĕr′ĭ·măn), **Henry Seton.** Pseudonym of Hugh Stowell SCOTT.

**Merriman, John Xavier.** 1841–1926. South African statesman, b. in Somersetshire; to South Africa as a child. Diamond dealer in Kimberley (1871), wine merchant in Cape Town (1874–75); friend of Cecil Rhodes. Prime minister of Cape of Good Hope (1908–10).

**Merriman, Mansfield.** 1848–1925. American civil engineer, b. Southington, Conn.; author of *Method of Least Squares* (1884), *Treatise on Hydraulics* (1889), *Strength of Materials* (1897), etc.; editor in chief, *American Civil Engineers' Pocket Book* (1911).

**Mer′ritt** (mĕr′ĭt), **Anna,** *nee* **Lea** (lē). 1844–1930. Artist, b. Philadelphia; m. Henry Merritt (1877); resident chiefly in London (from 1871). Her *Love Locked Out* hangs in the Tate Gallery, London; *Piping Shepherd,* in Pennsylvania Academy of Fine Arts, Philadelphia; *James Russell Lowell,* in Harvard U.

**Merritt, Leonidas.** 1844–1926. American mining prospector, b. Chautauqua County, N.Y.; discovered iron ore deposits in Mesabi region of Minnesota (1890).

**Merritt, Wesley.** 1834–1910. American army officer, b. New York City; grad. U.S.M.A., West Point (1860). Served through Civil War; on frontier duty (1866–79); superintendent, U.S.M.A., West Point (1882–87). Commanded first Philippine expedition (1898).

**Mer′ry** (mĕr′ĭ), **Robert.** 1755–1798. English poet of dilettante Della-Cruscan school; made member of Accademia della Crusca in Florence. Under pseudonym **Del′la Crus′ca** (dĕl′ȧ krŭs′kȧ) wrote affected verse in England; carried on sentimental correspondence in verse with Mrs. Hannah Cowley (1787), wrote unsuccessful plays.

**Mer′ry del Val** (mĕr′rē thĕl väl′), **Rafael.** 1865–1930. Roman Catholic prelate, b. London, son of secretary of Spanish legation there. Ordained priest in the diocese of Westminster (1888). Served on various missions, including one to Canada (1897); consecrated titular archbishop of Nicaea (1900). Papal secretary of state (1903–14) under Pope Pius X; created cardinal (1903); secretary of the Holy Office (1914–30).

**Mer′senne′** (mĕr′sĕn′), **Marin.** 1588–1648. French mathematician; fellow pupil of Descartes; settled in Paris (1620); defended Descartes against clerical critics; made researches in mathematics, physics, and astronomy; wrote on theory of music and musical instruments.

**Mer′sey** (mûr′zĭ), 1st Viscount. **John Charles Big′ham** (bĭg′ăm). 1840–1929. English jurist; judge, King's Bench Division, High Court of Justice (1897–1909); president, probate, divorce, and admiralty division (1909–10). Member of board of inquiry investigating *Titanic* (1912) and *Lusitania* (1915) disasters.

**Mer·shon′** (mẽr·shŏn′), **Ralph Davenport.** 1868–1952. American electrical engineer and inventor; inventor of 6-phase rotary converter, compounded rotary converter, system of lightning protection for electrical apparatus, and compensating voltmeter.

**Mer′son′** (mĕr′sôɴ′), **Luc Olivier.** *Also* **Luc Olivier-Merson.** 1846–1920. French painter, best known for historical canvases; also known as illustrator and bank-note designer.

**Mer′ten Pa′sha** (mĕr′tĕn pä′shä), **Hans.** 1857–1926. German naval officer; naval adviser to sultan of Turkey during Allied attack on the Dardanelles (1915).

**Mer′ton** (mûr′t'n), **Thomas.** *Known as* **Father M. Louis.** 1915–1968. American clergyman and writer, b. in France. Ordained priest (1949); wrote *The Seven Storey Mountain* (1948), poems, etc.

**Merton, Walter de.** d. 1277. English prelate and founder (1264–74) of Merton Coll., Oxford, first English college; chancellor of England (1261–63, 1272–74) and justiciar (1271); bishop of Rochester (1274).

**Me′ru·lo** (mā′rōō·lō), **Claudio.** *Real surname* **Mer·lot′ti** (mâr·lôt′tē). *Called also* **Claudio da Cor·reg′gio** (dä kôr·rād′jō). 1533–1604. Italian organist and composer; organist at St. Mark's, Venice (1557–86); later, court organist at Parma. Composed ricercari, canzoni, and toccatas for organ; also, many madrigals, motets, and masses for five to twelve voices.

**Mer′win** (mûr′wĭn), **Samuel.** 1874–1936. American author and editor, b. Evanston, Ill.; associate editor, *Success Magazine* (1905–09), and editor (1909–11). Author of *The Road to Frontenac* (1901), *Drugging a Nation* (1908), *Anthony the Absolute* (1914), *The Passionate Pilgrim* (1919), *In Red and Gold* (1921), *Bad Penny* (1933), etc.

**Merx** (mĕrks), **Adalbert.** 1838–1909. German Protestant theologian and Orientalist; author of a Syrian grammar (1867–70), and other philological works, criticisms of the Old Testament, etc.

**Mé′ry′** (mā′rē′), **Joseph.** 1798–1865. French writer of poetry, novels, plays, and travel books, including *Nain Jaune* (1824), *Les Nuits de Londres* (1840), *Héva* (1843), *Le Fou et le Sage* (1852), *Les Nuits d'Orient* (1854), *L'Essai du Mariage* (1855), *Les Nuits Parisiennes* (1855). Collab. with Barthélemy in satirical verse.

**Mé'ry·on'** (mā'ryôɴ'), **Charles.** 1821–1868. French etcher and engraver.

**Mes'dag** (mĕs'däк), **Hendrik Willem.** 1831–1915. Dutch marine painter; settled in The Hague, and helped promote Dutch art. His paintings are chiefly of the North Sea. Presented to The Hague (1903) the Mesdag Museum together with his collection of impressionistic French and Dutch paintings, bronzes, porcelains, and other objets d'art, and a collection of his own works and those of his wife **Sientje Mesdag–Van Hou'ten** [-vän hou'tĕn] (1834–1904), impressionistic landscape and still-life painter.

**Me'sha** (mē'shȧ). King of Moab (c. 850 B.C.); paid tribute to Ahab (*2 Kings* iii), but after Ahab's death, ceased payments; resisted attack by Jehoram and Jehoshaphat; sacrificed his first-born son to avert defeat. The Moabite stone is a stele (discovered 1868) on which this event is recorded and is oldest known Semitic monument.

**Meshach.** See SHADRACH.

**Mes'mer** (mĕs'mĕr; *Angl.* mĕz'-), **Franz** *or* **Friedrich Anton.** 1734–1815. Austrian physician after whom mesmerism was named, b. Weil, near Lake of Constance. Studied medicine at Vienna. Having made experiments on supposed curative power of the magnet, was led to believe that some kind of occult force resided in himself; developed theory of animal magnetism; to Paris (1778), where he devoted himself to curing diseases; his séances investigated by commission of physicians and scientists appointed by French government; denounced as impostor.

**Me'so·ne'ro y Ro·ma'nos** (mā'sō·nā'rō ē rō·mä'nōs), **Ramón de.** 1803–1882. Spanish journalist and essayist; on staff of *Cartas Españolas;* founder and editor (1836–42) of *Semanario Pintoresco Español.* Among his volumes of essays are *Escenas Matritenses* (2 vols., 1836) and *Memorias de un Setentón* (1880).

**Mes·rob'** (mĕs·rōp'). 350?–439 A.D. Armenian bishop (consecrated 390) and scholar; reputed inventor of Armenian and Georgian alphabets.

**Mes'sa'ger'** (mĕ'sȧ'zhā'), **André Charles Prosper.** 1853–1929. French composer and conductor; director of Opéra Comique, Paris (1898–1908), and artistic director of Covent Garden Theater, London (1901–07); co-director of Grand Opéra, Paris (1908–14); conductor of conservatory concerts (1908–19); toured U.S. (1918–19); again director of Opéra Comique (1919–20); subsequently musical director at Casino, Cannes. Composed comic operas and operettas, including *La Béarnaise* (1885), *Madame Chrysanthème* (1893), *Les P'tites Michu* (1897), *Véronique* (1898), and *Monsieur Beaucaire* (1919), many ballets, piano pieces, songs, etc.

**Mes·sa'la** (*or* **Mes·sal'la**) **Cor·vi'nus** (mĕ·sā'lȧ [-săl'ȧ] kôr·vī'nŭs), **Marcus Valerius.** Roman general, statesman, and patron of letters; held a command in republican army at battle of Philippi (42 B.C.); commanded center of Octavius's fleet in battle of Actium (31); consul (31); as proconsul of Aquitania, subjugated that province.

**Mes'sa·li'na** (mĕs'ȧ·lī'nȧ), **Valeria.** d. 48 A.D. Roman empress, noted for vices and profligacy; daughter of Marcus Valerius Messala Barbatus; 3d wife of Emperor Claudius. Caused death of number of persons who attempted to thwart her desires. Executed by order of the emperor after she had, during his temporary absence from Rome, gone through public marriage ceremony with her favorite, Silius. See NARCISSUS.

**Mes'sel** (mĕs'ĕl), **Alfred.** 1853–1909. German architect, exponent of modernism; taught architecture in Berlin (1886–96); designed National Museum in Darmstadt (1906); made original plans for new Berlin museum (1907–09); designed many business buildings and private residences in Berlin.

**Mes·se'ni·us** (mĕs·sā'nĭ·ŭs), **Johannes.** 1579–1636. Swedish historian, dramatist, and lyric poet.

**Mes'ser** (mĕs'ĕr), **August.** 1867–1937. German philosopher and pedagogue; author of *Empfindung und Denken* (an attempt to unite Husserl's phenomenology and psychology; 1908), *Geschichte der Philosophie* (3 parts, 1912–13), *Pädagogik der Gegenwart* (1926), the novel *Katholische Studenten* (1905; under pseudonym **A. Fried'walt** [frēt'vält]), etc.

**Mes'ser·schmitt** (mĕs'ĕr·shmĭt), **Wilhelm.** 1898–1978. German aircraft designer and manufacturer; designed his first plane (1916) and founded manufacturing firm under own name (1923); also, chief engineer of Bayerische Flugzeugwerke until it was merged (1938) with Messerschmitt company. Awarded Lilienthal prize for research in aviation (1937).

**Mes'ser·smith** (mĕs'ĕr·smĭth), **George S.** 1883–1960. American diplomat, b. Fleetwood, Pa.; entered U.S. consular service (1914); consul general in Belgium (1923–28), Argentina (1928), Berlin (1930–34); U.S. minister to Uruguay (1934), Austria (1934); asst. secretary of state (1937–40); ambassador to Cuba (1940–41), Mexico (1941–46), Argentina (1946–47).

**Mes'sier'** (mĕ'syā'), **Charles.** 1730–1817. French astronomer in Paris; credited with discovery of 21 comets and compilation of catalogue of nebulae.

**Messina, Antonello da.** See ANTONELLO.

**Messys, Quentin.** See Quentin MASSYS.

**Meš'tro·vić** (mĕsh'trō·vēt'y'; *Angl.* -vĭch), **Ivan.** 1883–1962. Yugoslav sculptor, b. in Dalmatia; apprentice to marble carver in Spalato; exhibited at London, Paris (where he became friend of Rodin), Rome, and Venice (1914); resident chiefly in Zagreb (after 1918) and Spalato. Dealt with religious and mythological subjects and Slav folklore, and produced many portraits and portrait busts, medals in relief, vases, etc. Works include seated figure of Bishop Strossmayer, Croatian patriot (1926; Zagreb), memorial chapel to unknown soldier (Belgrade), monument to Brătianu (Bucharest), *The Archangel Gabriel* (Brooklyn museum), portraits and busts of Lady Cunard (1915), Sir Thomas Beecham (1915), President Masaryk, etc. To U.S. (1947); at Syracuse U. (1947–55), Notre Dame U. (1955–62).

**Mé'szá·ros** (mā'sä·rōsh), **Lázár.** 1796–1858. Hungarian general and politician; colonel in Radetzky's army in Italy (1848); minister of war (1848–49); organized revolutionary army (1849), was defeated at Szöreg and Temesvár (Timişoara), and fled to Turkey.

**Metacomet.** Indian name of American chief PHILIP (d. 1676).

**Me·tag'e·nes** (mē·tăj'ē·nēz). See CHERSIPHRON.

**Me'ta·sta'si·o** (mā'tä·stä'zyō). *Orig.* **Pietro Antonio Domenico Bonaventura Tra·pas'si** (trä·päs'sē). 1698–1782. Italian poet and dramatist; protégé of Gravina, a jurist. To Naples (1720); gained patronage of singer Marianna Bulgarelli; called to Vienna (1730) as court poet to Charles VI, Holy Roman Emperor. Known particularly for melodramas, in development of which he succeeded Apostolo Zeno. Works include lyric dramas (set to music by various composers), as *Didone Abbandonata, Catone in Utica, Ezio, Ciro, Temistocle, Demofoonte, Semiramide, La Clemenza di Tito, A Hilio Regolo, Achille in Sciro,* etc., oratorios, poems for cantatas, and operas.

**Me'ta·xas'** (mĕ'tä·ksäs'; *Angl.* mē·tăk'sȧs). Greek family of Cephalonia, including notably: **Andreas** (1786–1860), premier of Greece (1843–44). **Joannes** (1871–1941), chief of general staff (1915); member of cabinet of national union (1926–28); dictator of Greece in position of prime minister, minister of foreign affairs, and acting minister of war, marine, and air (1936–40).

**Met′calf** (mĕt′kăf; -kȧf), **Victor Howard.** 1853–1936. American lawyer and cabinet officer, b. Utica, N.Y.; member, U.S. House of Representatives (1899–1904); U.S. secretary of commerce and labor (1904–06); U.S. secretary of the navy (1906–08).

**Metcalf, Willard Leroy.** 1858–1925. American painter, b, Lowell, Mass.; studio in New York (from c. 1890); excelled in depiction of New England landscapes. His *The Family of Birches* is in National Gallery, Washington, D.C.; *Twin Birches,* in Pennsylvania Academy of Fine Arts, Philadelphia; *Ice Bound,* in Art Institute, Chicago.

**Met′calfe** (mĕt′kăf; -kȧf), Sir **Charles Herbert Theophilus.** 1853–1928. English civil engineer in South Africa (1882–1914), where he served as engineer in construction of important railway lines; closely associated with Cecil Rhodes (1890–1902).

**Metcalfe, Charles Theophilus.** Baron **Metcalfe.** 1785–1846. English colonial administrator, b. Calcutta. As envoy to Sikh states signed (1809) boundary treaty with Ranjit Singh; lieutenant governor of North West Provinces and Oudh (1836–38); governor of Jamaica (1839–42); governor general of Canada (1843–45).

**Metch′ni′koff′** (*Fr.* mĕch′nē′kôf′), **Élie.** *Russian* **Ilya Ilich Mech′ni·kov** (myăch′nyĭ·kôf). 1845–1916. Russian zoologist and bacteriologist, b. Ivanovka, in Kharkov. Professor of zoology and comparative anatomy, Odessa (1870); resigned to devote himself to research (1882). To Paris, where Pasteur gave him a laboratory (1888); succeeded Pasteur as director of Pasteur Inst. in Paris (1895). Investigated intracellular digestion; formulated theory of phagocytosis; made microscopic studies of diseases of the blood. Shared (with Paul Ehrlich) 1908 Nobel prize for physiology and medicine. Author of *The Comparative Pathology of Inflammation* (French, 1892; English translation, 1893), *Immunity in Infectious Diseases* (French, 1901; English translation, 1905), and *The Nature of Man* (French, 1903; English translation, 1904).

**Me·tel′lus** (mē·tĕl′ŭs). Name of prominent Roman family of Caecilian gens, including among members: **Lucius Caecilius Metellus** (d. about 221 B.C.), general who defeated Carthaginians at Panormus (250 B.C.). **Quintus Caecilius Metellus** (d. 115 B.C.), surnamed **Mac′e·don′i·cus** (măs′ē·dŏn′ĭ·kŭs), distinguished for victories in Macedonia and Greece (148–146 B.C.); consul (143), censor (131). **Quintus Caecilius Metellus** (d. 99 B.C.), surnamed **Nu·mid′i·cus** (nū·mĭd′ĭ·kŭs), nephew of Metellus Macedonicus; consul (109 B.C.) and proconsul (108); defeated Jugurtha in Numidia (109–108). **Quintus Caecilius Metellus** (d. about 64 B.C.), surnamed **Pi′us** (pī′ŭs), son of Metellus Numidicus; served with Sulla in civil wars and commanded in Spain against Sertorius; consul (80 B.C.). **Quintus Caecilius Metellus Ce′ler** [sē′lẽr] (d. 59 B.C.), statesman; praetor (63 B.C.); opponent of Catiline and hostile to his conspiracy; consul (60). His brother **Quintus Caecilius Metellus Ne′pos** [nē′pŏs] (d. about 55 B.C.), who sided with Pompey in civil wars; tribune (62 B.C.), consul (57). **Quintus Caecilius Metellus Pius Scip′i·o** [sĭp′ĭ·ō] (committed suicide 46 B.C.), adopted son of Metellus Pius; consul with Pompey (52 B.C.); commanded armies for Pompey in Syria and Egypt. **Quintus Caecilius Metellus** (d. about 56 B.C.), surnamed **Cre′ti·cus** (krē′tĭ·kŭs), consul (69 B.C.); subjugated Crete (68–67).

**Met′ford** (mĕt′fẽrd), **William Ellis.** 1824–1899. English inventor; invented explosive rifle bullet, adopted by government (1863); pioneer of shallow grooving and hardened cylindrical bullet; produced his first match rifle (1865), his first breech-loading rifle (1871); his type of bore combined by an American, James P. Lee, with bolt action and detachable magazine in the Lee-Metford rifle, selected for British use (1888).

**Meth′fes′sel** (mĕt′fĕs′ĕl), **Albert Gottlieb.** 1785–1869. German composer of male choruses and songs, an opera, an oratorio, and piano pieces.

**Methodius,** Saint. See under Saint CYRIL (827–869 A.D.).

**Meth′u·en** (mĕth′ū·ĭn), 3d Baron. **Paul Sanford Methuen.** 1845–1932. British soldier; served in Ashanti War (1874), Egyptian War (1882), Boer War (1899–1902), in the last of which he commanded 1st division of the 1st army corps and was defeated by Cronjé at Magersfontein and later (1902) taken prisoner by De La Rey. Commander in chief in South Africa (1907–09); governor of Natal (1909); governor of Malta (1915–19); governor and constable of the Tower (1920 ff.).

**Methuen,** Sir **Algernon Methuen Marshall.** *Original surname* **Sted′man** (stĕd′măn). 1856–1924. Changed name to Methuen (1899). English publisher; opened small publishing office in London under name Methuen & Co. (1889); made initial publishing success by issuing Kipling's *Barrack-Room Ballads* (1892). Expanded business greatly, being publisher for Belloc, Chesterton, Conrad, "Anthony Hope," W. W. Jacobs, Lankester, Sir Oliver Lodge, Maeterlinck, Masefield, Gilbert Parker, Stevenson, Oscar Wilde, and many others. Compiled two anthologies, *An Anthology of English Verse* (1921) and *Shakespeare to Hardy* (1922).

**Me′ti·us** (mā′tē·ŭs), **Adriaan.** *Also known as* **Adriaan A′dri·aans′zoon** (ä′drē·än′sŭn; -sŏn; -sōn). 1571–1635. Dutch geometer; author of works on astronomy, geometry, arithmetic, trigonometry, etc. His brother **Jacobus** was credited by Descartes and others with invention of the refracting telescope.

**Me′ton** (mē′tŏn). fl. 5th century B.C. Greek astronomer of Athens; instituted cycle of nineteen years, named *Metonic cycle* after him (432 B.C.).

**Met′ro·do′rus** (mĕt′rō·dō′rŭs). Greek philosopher of Chios, of 4th century B.C.; a leading representative of atomistic school.

**Me·tsu′** *or* **Me·tzu′** *or* **Me·tsue′** (mĕ·tsü′), **Gabriel.** 1629?–1667. Dutch genre painter; settled in Amsterdam (after 1650). Works include *The Sportsman* (1661), *Music Lovers, Old Poultry Seller, The Music Lesson, Visit to the Nursery,* and *Artist and his Wife.*

**Metsys, Quentin.** See Quentin MASSYS.

**Met·tau′er** (mĕ·tô′ẽr), **John Peter.** 1787–1875. American surgeon, b. in Prince Edward County, Va.; best known for operations for cataract and for stricture of the urethra; pioneer in genitourinary surgery.

**Met′ter·nich** (mĕt′ẽr·nĭκ), Prince **Klemens Wenzel Nepomuk Lothar von.** *Family name* **Metternich-Win′ne·burg** (-vĭn′ĕ·bŏŏrκ). 1773–1859. Austrian statesman and diplomatist; brought up in courts of Rhine electorates where his father (Prince Georg Karl, 1746–1818) was Austrian ambassador. At Mainz and Brussels (1790–94) where, as a witness of certain acts of French revolutionists, he acquired the basis of lifelong reactionary ideas. Westphalian representative at Congress of Rastadt (1797–99); Austrian envoy to Saxony (1801–03) and ambassador at Berlin (1803–05) and Paris (1806–09); after war declared between France and Austria (1809), returned to Vienna. Austrian minister of foreign affairs (1809–48); influential in securing Marie Louise as 2d wife of Napoleon (1810). By skillful diplomacy and deceit, kept Austria out of war between France and Russia (1812–13) but finally joined alliance with Russia against France (1813); created hereditary prince of Austrian Empire (1813); at Congress of Vienna (1814–15), at height of his power. Largely responsible for policy of stability of European governments and of suppression of liberal ideas or revolutionary movements that marked European history (1815–30), esp. through the Holy Alliance. Weakened somewhat by revolutions of 1830 but did not resign until forced by Vienna mob (1848). Although power lost, never gave up his political beliefs; lived in retirement in England and Belgium (1848–51) and in Vienna (1851–59). His son Prince **Richard** (1829–1895), Austrian diplomat, was ambassador in Paris (1859–70); m. (1856) **Pauline**, *nee* Countess **Sán'dor** [shän'dôr] (1836–1921), with whom he played important role in the political and social life at the court of Napoleon III.

**Mettrie, Julien Offroy de la.** See La Mettrie.

**Metz** (mĕts), **Christian.** 1794–1867. Sectarian leader, b. Neuwied, Prussia. Leader of sect known as Community of True Inspiration (from 1817); established communistic colony on site near Buffalo, N.Y. (1842–54); colony emigrated to Iowa frontier site, christened Amana (1855); community incorporated (1859) as Amana Society, with Metz as its head until his death.

**Metz'ger** (mĕts'gẽr), **Josef.** 1870–1921. Austro-Hungarian general; commanded Austro-Hungarian army in battle against Italians along Isonzo River (Apr., 1917).

**Met'zin'ger'** (mĕt'săN'zhā'), **Jean.** 1883–1956. French painter, b. Nantes; one of the first of the cubist painters; author of *On Cubism* (1910, with Albert Gleizes).

**Metz'ler** (mĕts'lẽr), **William Henry.** 1863–1943. American mathematician, b. Ontario, Can.; professor (1896–1923), dean of college of liberal arts (1921–23), Syracuse U.; dean, New York State Coll. for Teachers (1923–33). Author of *College Algebra* (1906) and *A Treatise on the Theory of Determinants* (1929).

**Metzu, Gabriel.** See Gabriel Metsu.

**Meu'len** (mû'lĕn), **Adam Frans van der.** 1632–1690. Flemish painter; court painter to Louis XIV of France (c. 1666), whom he accompanied on campaigns; painted chiefly battles and sieges engaged in by Louis XIV, and landscapes.

**Meu'mann** (moi'män), **Ernst.** 1862–1915. German psychologist; adherent of Wundt's school of psychology; applied experimental methods in aesthetics, esp. in pedagogy.

**Meung** *or* **Meun, Jean de.** See Jean de Meung.

**Meu'nier'** (mû'nyā'), **Constantin.** 1831–1905. Belgian sculptor and painter, b. near Brussels. Pupil of his brother **Jean Baptiste** (1821–1900). Works deal with historical and religious subjects and, esp., with workers in mines and factories, and include paintings *Burial of a Trappist, Martyrdom of St. Stephen*, and *Tobacco Factory at Seville;* sculptures *The Hammersmith, The Puddler, The Mower, The Prodigal Son, The Mine Girl*, and *The Old Mine Horse.*

**Meu'rice'** (mû'rēs'), **François Paul.** 1820–1905. French dramatist; editor of Victor Hugo's *L'Événement* (1848); imprisoned nine months (1851) for devotion to Hugo's cause; helped found Hugo journal *Le Rappel* (1869); a literary executor of Victor Hugo, whose works he edited (46 vols., 1880–85). Works include *Falstaff* (1842; with T. Gautier and A. Vacquerie; based on Shakespeare), metrical translation of *Hamlet* (1847; with A. Dumas), dramas *Benvenuto Cellini* (1852), *Schamyl* (1854), *Struensée* (1898), dramatic version of *Les Misérables* (1878), romances *La Famille Aubry* (1857) and *Le Songe de l'Amour* (1889), etc.

**Meur'si·us** (mûr'sē·ŭs), **Johannes.** *Lat. form of* **Jan de Meurs** (dĕ mûrs'). 1579–1639. Dutch classical philologist and antiquary; historiographer to States-General; royal historiographer. Author of archaeological works and editions of Greek authors reprinted in Gronovius's *Thesaurus Antiquitatum Graecarum.*

**Meus'nier'** (mû'nyā'), **Jean Baptiste Marie.** 1754–1793. French general and savant; defended fort of Königstein against Prussians (1793); enounced theorem (named after him) relating to center of curvature of any plane section (1777); contributed to knowledge of balloons.

**Meux** (mūks; mūz), Sir **Hedworth.** *Orig. surname* **Lamb'ton** (lăm(p)'tŭn). 1856–1929. English naval commander; brought up naval guns to support garrison of Ladysmith (Oct., 1899); commander in chief, China (1908–10); admiral of the fleet (1915). At outbreak of World War I, successfully safeguarded passage of transports of B.E.F. to France. Changed name to Meux on becoming Lady Meux's heir (1911).

**Mew** (mū), **Charlotte Mary.** 1869–1928. English poet; frequent contributor to *Temple Bar, The Nation, The New Statesman, The Englishwoman*, and *The Chap-book.* Published two volumes of verse, *The Farmer's Bride* (1915) and *The Rambling Sailor* (1929).

**Mey'en·dorff** (mī'ĕn·dôrf), Baron **Alexander.** 1869–1964. Russian jurist, politician, and historian; member of the Duma (1907–17), vice president (1907–09); teacher in King's Coll., London, and in London School of Economics (1922–34). Author of *Background of the Russian Revolution, The Cost of the War to Russia*, etc.

**Mey'er** (mī'ẽr), **Adolf.** 1866–1950. American psychiatrist, b. near Zurich; to U.S. (1892). Docent in psychiatry at Clark U. (1895–1902); protessor of psychiatry, Cornell U. medical college (1904–09); professor, Johns Hopkins, and director, Henry Phipps Psychiatric Clinic, Johns Hopkins Hospital (1910–41).

**Meyer, Albert.** 1870–1953. Swiss journalist and statesman; commercial editor, *Neue Züricher Zeitung;* president of Swiss Confederation (1936–38).

**Meyer, Albert Gregory.** 1903–1965. American Roman Catholic churchman, b. Milwaukee, Wis. Ordained (1926); archbishop, Milwaukee (1953–58), Chicago (1958–65); cardinal (1959).

**Meyer, Annie,** *nee* **Na'than** (nā'thăn). 1867–1951. American educator and writer, b. New York City; m. Alfred Meyer (1887). Known as founder of Barnard College, Columbia U. Author of *Woman's Work in America* (1891), *The Dominant Sex* (1911), *The District Attorney* (play; 1920), *The Advertising of Kate* (play; 1921), *Black Souls* (play; 1932), *Barnard Beginnings* (1935), etc.

**Meyer, Arnold Oskar.** 1877–1944. German historian; specialized in English history of time of Reformation and Counter Reformation; also wrote *Metternich* (1924), *Bismarck* (1925), etc.

**Me'yer'** (mā'yâr'), **Arthur.** 1844–1924. French journalist; with E. Tarbé des Sablons, founded *Le Gaulois* (1865).

**Mey'er** (mī'ẽr), **Bal·tha'sar** (bäl·tä'zär) **Henry.** 1866–1954. American economist, b. Mequon, Wis.; member, U.S. Railroad Securities Commission (1910) and Interstate Commerce Commission (from 1911); author of *History of Transportation in the United States before 1860* (1917), etc.

**Meyer, Conrad Ferdinand.** 1825–1898. Swiss poet and historical novelist, b. Zurich; translated French historical works at Zurich (1853); m. Luise Ziegler (1875) and settled in Kilchberg near Zurich (1877); called himself **Meyer–Zie'gler** [-tsē'glẽr] (from 1879). Author of volumes of poetry, as *Zwanzig Balladen* (1864) and the collection *Gedichte* (1882), the lyric epic poem *Huttens Letzte Tage* (1871), the narrative poem *Engelberg* (1873), and of prose fiction chiefly on Renaissance subjects.

**Meyer, Eduard.** 1855–1930. German historian; attempted to justify Germany's position in World War. Author of *Geschichte des Altertums* (5 vols., 1884–1902), *England* (1915), *Ursprung und Anfänge des Christentums* (3 vols., 1920–23), etc. His brother **Kuno** (1858–1919) was authority on Celtic philology; professor of Celtic, Liverpool (1895–1911) and Berlin (from 1911); cofounder and director, Summer School of Irish Learning, Dublin (1903); contributed to promotion of Celtic scholarship; edited many middle Irish texts with translations, and contributed to *Revue Celtique, Zeitschrift für Celtische Philologie,* founded by him (1896), *Archiv für Celtische Lexikographie* (1898–1907), of which he was cofounder, and journal *Erin.*

**Meyer, Georg Hermann von.** 1815–1892. German anatomist; professor in Zurich; known for work on the mechanics of the human skeleton and on the structure of bone.

**Meyer, George von Leng'er·ke** (vŏn lĕng'ẽr·kĕ). 1858–1918. American politician, b. Boston; U.S. ambassador to Italy (1900–05), to Russia (1905–06); U.S. postmaster general (1907–09); U.S. secretary of the navy (1909–13).

**Meyer, Gustav.** 1850–1900. German philologist; authority on Balkan speech and culture.

**Meyer, Hans Heinrich.** 1760–1832. Swiss painter and writer on art, b. Zurich; close friend of Goethe; professor at Weimar Acad. of Design through Goethe's influence (1792), director (from 1807). Coeditor of Winckelmann's works (8 vols., 1808–20); author of *Neudeutsch Religiös-Patriotische Kunst* in Goethe's *Über Kunst und Altertum* (1817), *Geschichte der Bildenden Künste bei den Griechen und Römern* (3 vols., 1824–36; continued by Riemer), etc.

**Meyer, Heinrich August Wilhelm.** 1800–1873. German Protestant theologian and Biblical commentator.

**Meyer, Johann Georg.** *Called* **Meyer von Bre'men** (fôn brā'mĕn). 1813–1886. German genre painter; painted esp. pictures of children and of peasant life in Hessian, Bavarian, and Swiss mountain districts.

**Meyer, Joseph.** 1796–1856. German publisher, industrialist, and publicist, b. Gotha; founded at Gotha well-known publishing house Bibliographisches Institut (1826), which he removed to Hildburghausen (1828). His son **Hermann Julius** (1826–1909) was at first active in his father's enterprises; to U.S. as political fugitive (1849), where he founded book business in N.Y.; returned to Germany (1854) and took over at Hildburghausen his father's Bibliographisches Institut (1855), which he reorganized and removed to Leipzig (1874); retired (1885). Hermann's son **Hans** (1858–1929) studied science and political economy, and entered the Bibliographisches Institut (1884), of which he was director (1885–1914); traveled in Africa; climbed Kilimanjaro (1889) and reached top of Kibo and found crater; member of German colonial council (1901); studied volcanoes and glaciation of Ecuadorian cordilleras (1903); traveled in German East Africa (1911); professor of colonial geography, Leipzig (1915–28). Hans's brother **Hermann** (1871–1932), traveler and explorer, accompanied anthropologist Karl Ranke to central Brazil and headwater region of the Xingú (1895–97) and discovered the Atelchú, tributary of the Ronuro; visited German colonies in Rio Grande do Sul (1898–1900) and, with Koch-Grünberg and others, navigated upper course of the Ronuro as far as mouth of the Xingú (1899); founded and financed colonies for Germans in Rio Grande do Sul; co-owner (1903–32) and chief director (after 1915) of Bibliographisches Institut in Leipzig.

**Meyer, Julius Lothar.** 1830–1895. German chemist; professor, Tübingen; studied physiology of the blood; known esp. for independent work relating to periodic law (1863).

**Meyer, Jürgen Bona.** 1829–1897. German philosopher; championed psychological philosophy of experience; author of *Kants Psychologie* (1869), *Probleme der Lebensweisheit* (1887), etc.

**Meyer, Karl.** 1885–1950. Swiss historian.

**Meyer, Kuno.** See under Eduard MEYER.

**Me'yer'** (mā'yâr'), **Paul,** *in full* **Marie Paul Hyacinthe.** 1840–1917. French philologist and literary historian, b. Paris; authority on medieval French and Provençal languages and literatures; secretary (1872–76) and director (1882), École des Chartes; professor, Collège de France (1876–1906). Edited many old French texts and published *Les Derniers Troubadours de la Provence* (1872), *La Chanson de la Croisade contre les Albigeois* (2 vols., 1875–79), *Recueil d'Anciens Textes Bas-Latins, Provençaux, et Français* (2 parts, 1874–77), etc.

**Mey'er** (mī'ẽr), **Viktor.** 1848–1897. German chemist; known for researches in organic and physical chemistry, esp. relating to nitric and nitrous compounds, and the discovery of thiophene; developed method for determination of vapor density of steam.

**Mey'er·beer** (mī'ẽr·bār; *sometimes Anglicized to* -bēr), **Gia'co·mo** (jä'kō·mō). *Real name* **Jakob Lieb'mann** (lēp'män) **Beer** (bār). 1791–1864. Brother of Michael and Wilhelm Beer (*qq.v.*). German opera composer, b. Berlin; pianist, Vienna; in Italy (1816), where he composed Italian operas in Rossini's style; settled in Paris (from 1826) and composed in French style; general music director, Berlin Opera (1842). His operas include *Il Crociato in Egitto* (1824), *Robert le Diable* (1831), *Les Huguenots* (1836), *Das Feldlager in Schlesien* (1844), *Le Prophète* (1849), *Dinorah* (1859), *L'Africaine* (first performed 1865); composed also cantatas, overtures, orchestral marches, ceremonial music, etc.

**Mey'er–För'ster** (mī'ẽr·fûr'stẽr), **Wilhelm.** 1862–1934. German writer and playwright; became blind (1904). Works include novels and stories *Eldena* (1896), *Derby* (1897), *Heidenstamm* (1898), *Süderssen* (1902), *Durchlaucht von Gleichenberg* (1923); dramas *Kriemhild* (1891), *Eine Böse Nacht* (1893), *Der Vielgeprüfte* (1898); and the successful romantic drama *Alt-Heidelberg* (1901; dramatization of his story *Karl Heinrich,* 1899), which was translated into other languages (Eng. *Old Heidelberg*) and from which the American operetta *The Student Prince* was adapted. His wife (m. 1890), **Elsbeth** (1868–1902), wrote plays and, esp., novels, as *Das Drama eines Kindes* (1895) and *Also Sprach die Frau* (1900).

**Mey'er·heim** (mī'ẽr·hīm). Name of a family of German painters including: **Eduard,** *in full* **Friedrich Eduard** (1808–1879), genre painter, who painted scenes from German peasant and middle-class life in oils and water colors. His son and pupil **Paul** (1842–1915), who painted chiefly animal pictures, genre scenes, landscapes, and portraits. Eduard's brother **Wilhelm Alexander** (1815–1882), who painted battle scenes, horses, etc.

**Mey'er·hof** (mī'ẽr·hōf), **Otto.** 1884–1951. German physiologist. Professor in Kiel (1918–24); member of Kaiser Wilhelm Inst. for Biology, Berlin-Dahlem (1924); director of department of physiology, Kaiser Wilhelm Inst. for Medical Research, Heidelberg (1929). Investigated conversion of energy and process of spasm in muscle; shared (with A. V. Hill) 1922 Nobel prize for physiology and medicine.

**Mey'er·hold** (mī'ẽr·hōlt), **Vsevolod Emilievich.** 1874–1940. Russian actor and theatrical producer; on staff of Moscow Art Theater; manager, Revolutionary Theater, Moscow; produced a number of political propaganda dramas; carried simplicity to extreme in stage sets, often using no curtain and a bare stage with merely formal scenery. Author of *The Theater* (1913).

**Mey'er–Lüb'ke** (mī'ẽr·lüp'kĕ), **Wilhelm.** 1861–1936. Swiss Romance philologist; author of *Grammatik der Romanischen Sprachen* (4 vols., 1890–1902), *Italienische Grammatik* (1891), *Historische Grammatik der Französischen Sprache* (2 vols., 1908–21), *Romanisches Etymologisches Wörterbuch* (1911), *Das Katalanische* (1925), etc.

**Mey·er'o·witz** (mī·âr'ŏ·wĭts), **William.** 1893– . Painter and etcher, b. in Russia; to U.S. (1905). See Theresa BERNSTEIN.

**Me'yer'son'** (mā'yĕr'sôN'), **Émile.** 1859–1933. French philosopher, b. Lublin, of Polish Jewish ancestry; naturalized French. Author of *Identité et Réalité* (1907), *La Déduction Relativiste* (1925), etc.

**Mey'er·stein** (mī'ẽr·stīn), **Edward Harry William.** 1889–1952. British writer; educ. Oxford; author of verse, as in *The Door* (1911), *Selected Poems* (1935), *The Elegies of Propertius* (transl.; 1935), *Sonnets* (1939), *Eclogues* (1940), *The Visionary* (1942), novels, short stories, and plays.

**Meyer–Ziegler.** See Conrad Ferdinand MEYER.

**Meyn'ell** (mĕn''l), **Wilfrid.** 1852–1948. English journalist and biographical writer; editor of works of Francis Thompson (1913); author of books of verse and biographies of Disraeli (1903) and Johnson (1913). His wife (m. 1877), **Alice Christiana Gertrude,** *nee* **Thomp'son** [tŏm(p)'s'n] (1847–1922), poet and essayist, published her first poems in *Preludes* (1875), praised by Ruskin, Rossetti, and Browning; aided her husband in editing the Catholic periodical *Weekly Register* (1881–98), and *Merry England* (1883–95), through which the Meynells discovered and aided Francis Thompson, the poet; gained literary fame with publication of volume of prose essays, *The Rhythm of Life* (1893); published anthologies and a life of Ruskin (1900), also poems in *A Father of Women* (1917), and essays in *Hearts of Controversy* (1917). Their son **Francis** (1891– ), book designer and writer on typographical subjects; founder of Nonesuch Press (1923). Their daughter **Viola** (1886–1956), nov. and poet, m. John Dallyn (1922); author of *Second Marriage, A Girl Adoring, Alice Meynell, a Memoir* (1929), *The Frozen Ocean* (verse; 1931), *Kissing the Rod* (1937), etc.

**Mey'nert** (mī'nẽrt), **Theodor Hermann.** 1833–1892. Psychiatrist, b. Dresden; professor and director of Psychiatric Clinic, Vienna; known for work on structure and function of various parts of brain.

**Mey'rink** (mī'rĭngk), **Gustav.** 1868–1932. Bavarian writer, b. Vienna; banker in Prague (1889–1902); left Protestant church for Mahayana Buddhism (1927); author of often grotesque and mystic works, including collection of satirical stories *Des Deutschen Spiessers Wunderhorn* (3 vols., 1913), novels *Der Golem* (1915), *Das Grüne Gesicht* (a fantastic novel of the world crisis, 1916), *Walpurgisnacht* (1917), and *Der Engel vom Westlichen Fenster* (1927).

**Mé'ze·ray'** (māz'rā'), **François Eudes de** (ûd' dẽ). 1610–1683. French historian; after campaign in Flanders (1635), wrote some memoirs for Richelieu; appointed historiographer to king; chief work is *Histoire de France* (3 vols., 1643, 1646, 1651).

**Me'zes** (mā'zēz), **Sidney Edward.** 1863–1931. American educator, b. Belmont, Calif.; president, U. of Texas (1908–14), C.C.N.Y. (1914–27). Director of a staff of experts which gathered information used by President Wilson in formulating his Fourteen Points, and his policy at the Versailles Peace Conference.

**Mez'ger** (mĕts'gẽr), **Edmund.** 1883–1962. German jurist; professor; author of *Strafrecht* (1933), *Deutsches Strafrecht* (1936, 1938), etc.

**Mé'zières'** (mā'zyâr'), **Alfred Jean François.** 1826–1915. French literary critic; author of studies on Shakespeare, Dante, Petrarch, and Goethe.

**Mé'zières'** *or* **Mai'sières'** (mā'zyâr'), **Philippe de.** 1327?–1405. French crusader; served under Humbert II, Dauphin de Vienne, against Turks (1345–47); founded Order of the Passion of Jesus Christ to fight the infidels (1347); councilor of Charles V (1373) and tutor of the dauphin; devoted himself to thoughts and plans for crusades to restore Holy Land to Christian power.

**Mez'zo·fan'ti** (mĕd'dzō·fän'tē), **Giuseppe.** 1774–1849. Italian linguist and cardinal; professor of Arabic, Bologna (1803 ff.); chief keeper of Vatican library (1833); cardinal (1838).

**Mi'all** (mī'ăl), **Edward.** 1809–1881. English Congregationalist minister and journalist; lifelong advocate of disestablishment of Church of England; founded and edited weekly *Nonconformist* (1841); sought to amalgamate with Chartists (1842); led in founding of British Anti-State Church Assoc. (1844).

**Mi·an'to·no'mo** (mī·ăn'tō·nō'mō). d. 1643. American Indian sachem of the Narragansetts; friendly with English settlers; deeded Rhode Island to William Coddington and his associates (1638); captured and executed by Uncas, a sachem of the Mahicans.

**Mi·aou'les** *or* **Mi·au'lis** (mē·ou'lyēs), **Andreas Vokos.** 1768?–1835. Greek naval commander; in war for Greek independence, commanded Greek fleet (1821 ff.) and successfully engaged Turkish squadrons (Mar. and Sept., 1822); involved in uprising of 1831; destroyed his fleet to keep it from Russians; one of delegation sent (1832) to offer Greek crown to Prince Otto of Bavaria.

**Mi'cah** *or* **Mi'chah** (mī'kȧ). *In Douay Bible* **Mi·che'as** (mī·kē'ăs). A minor Hebrew prophet, of 8th century B.C., whose prediction of impending judgment on Israel and esp. Judah, with proffer of Messianic hope, the Old Testament book of Micah records.

**Mi'chael** (mī'kĕl; -k'l). Name of nine rulers of Eastern Roman Empire: **Michael I Rhan'ga·be** [răng'gȧ·bē] (reigned 811–813; d. 845). **Michael II,** *called* **the A·mo'ri·an** [ȧ·mō'rĭ·ăn] (reigned 820–829). **Michael III,** *called* **the Drunkard** (reigned 842–867); waged wars with Saracens, Bulgarians, and Russians. **Michael IV,** *called* **the Paph'la·go'ni·an** [păf'lȧ·gō'nĭ·ăn] (reigned 1034–41), a weakling and epileptic, left government to his brother John the Eunuch; m. Zoë, dau. of Constantine VIII; during his reign, Saracens were defeated, Serbs and Bulgarians revolted. **Michael V Cal'a·pha'tes** [kăl'ȧ·fā'tēz] (reigned 1041–42). **Michael VI Strat'i·ot'i·cus** [străt'ĭ·ŏt'ĭ·kŭs] (reigned 1056–57). **Michael VII Du'cas** (dū'kăs), ruled under regency of Romanus IV and Eudocia (1067–71), alone (1071–78); lost Italian possessions (1071); gave territory to Seljuk Turks (1074). **Michael VIII Pa'lae·ol'o·gus** [pā'lē·ŏl'ō·gŭs; păl'ē-] (1234–1282); in youth a soldier; emperor of the East (1259–82); ostensibly regent for John IV Lascaris (1258) but proclaimed himself emperor (1259) and was crowned at Nicaea; conquered Constantinople and drove out Baldwin II (1261); successful against rulers of Greece (1263–64), and in wars with Genoese and Venetians; consented to papal supremacy (1274); opposed by alliance of Charles of Anjou and Pope Martin IV (1281), the failure of which aroused discontent and was a partial cause of the Sicilian Vespers (1282). See PALAEOLOGUS. **Michael IX Palaeologus,** coruler (1295–1320) with his father Andronicus II.

**Michael.** *Romanian* **Mi·hai′** (mē·hī′). 1921– . King of Romania (1927–30, 1940–47), b. Sinaia; son of Carol II and grandson of Ferdinand I. On death of his grandfather (1927), made king under council of regency (his father having renounced throne, 1925); supplanted by Carol (1930), but again made king (1940) when Germany seized control of Romania; abdicated (Dec. 1947).

**Michael I** and **II** of Transylvania. See APAFFY.

**Michael.** *Russ.* **Mikhail Fëdorovich.** 1596–1645. Czar of Russia, first of the Romanov house; son of Patriarch Philaret (see ROMANOV). Elected (1613) to bring unity at time when Russia was being invaded from west and torn by internal anarchy; made peace with Sweden (1617), truce with Poland (1618), and reorganized government of Russia; called in experts from other lands to improve army and country's industrial methods; advanced Russian power in Siberian regions.

**Michael.** *Russ.* **Mikhail.** Name of three grand dukes of Russia: **Mikhail Nikolaevich** (1832–1909), 4th son of Emperor Nicholas I; president (1881) of privy council of state and commander in chief of cavalry. **Mikhail Mikhailovich** (1861–1929) served in Russo-Turkish War (1877); exiled (1891) because of morganatic marriage with Countess Sophie Nikolaevna (b. 1868), lived thereafter in England. **Mikhail Aleksandrovich** (1878–1918), army commander, declined succession to throne of Russia (1917) after emperor's abdication (Mar. 15, 1917) in his favor.

**Michael.** 1825–1868. Prince of Serbia of house of Obrenovich (*q.v.*), second son of Miloš; succeeded his brother Milan (1839) and was driven from throne (1842); again on throne, succeeding his father (1860–68); with help of Great Powers, succeeded in freeing Balkans from Turkish rule; assassinated (1868).

**Michael Asen.** See ASEN.

**Mi′chael At′ta·li·a′tes** (mī′kĕl [-k'l] ăt′ȧ·lĭ·ā′tēz; mē′-kä·ēl′ ä′tä·lyä′tēs). Byzantine jurist; published (1073) by command of Michael Ducas, Emperor of the East, a compendium of law; wrote a history of period 1034–79.

**Mi′chael of Wa·la′chi·a** (mī′kĕl [-k'l], wŏ·lā′kĭ·ȧ). d. 1601. Known as "Michael the Bold." Prince of Walachia (1593–1601); engaged in continual war in effort to gain and maintain independence; assassinated (1601).

**Mi′chael Wiś′nio·wiec′ki** (vēs′y'·nyô·vyĕts′kē). 1638–1673. King of Poland (1669–73); chosen by vote of people; under influence of Hapsburgs; reign marked by revolt of Cossacks; succeeded by John III Sobieski.

**Mi′cha·e′lis** (mī′kä·ā′lĭs), **Adolf.** 1835–1910. German archaeologist; author of a history of ancient art, works on the Parthenon, the ancient marbles in Great Britain, etc.

**Michaelis, Georg.** 1857–1936. German statesman; succeeded Bethmann-Hollweg as imperial chancellor and Prussian minister president (July, 1917), but was replaced by Hertling (Nov., 1917) following difficulties with civil authorities over peace terms; president of Pomerania (1918–19).

**Michaelis, Johann David.** 1717–1791. German Protestant theologian and Orientalist; pioneer in use of historico-critical study in Biblical interpretation; professor, Göttingen (1746–91); author of an introduction to the New Testament (1750), and of *Mosäisches Recht* (1770), a Hebrew grammar (1778), etc.

**Michaelis, Karoline.** See under Joaquim da Fonseca e VASCONCELLOS.

**Mi·cha·e′lis** (mē·kȧ·ę′lēs), **Sophus.** 1865–1932. Danish writer, b. Odense, of German origin; educ. Copenhagen. Author of lyric poetry, including volumes *Poems* (1888), *Sirens* (1898), *Festival of Life* (1900), *Palms* (1904), *Blue Rain* (1913); plays, *Revolutionary Wedding* (1906; set to music by D'Albert) and *The Ship of Heaven* (1921); novels, as the historical novel *Aebelo* (1895), Napoleonic novels *1812* and *Eternal Sleep* (1912), etc. His wife **Karin Michaelis,** *later* **Michaelis–Stang′e·land** (-stăng′-ĕ·lăn), *nee* **Bech–Brön′dum** [bĕk′brûn′do͝om] (1872–1950), Danish-German writer, b. in Denmark; m. 2d (1912) Prof. Charles E. Stangeland; lived in Germany, Austria, U.S., England, and (from 1918) Denmark; worked in interests of the underprivileged and suffering; actively pro-German in World War; author of novels and stories dealing with social questions, women's problems, and the war, including *The Child* (1902), *The Dangerous Age* (1910), *The Girl with the Flowerpot* (1925 ff.), etc.

**Mi′chal** (mī′kăl; -kăl). In the Bible, younger daughter of Saul and wife of David (*1 Samuel* xviii. 20; xix. 12; *2 Samuel* vi. 16).

**Mi′cha·la·ko′pou·los** (mē′kä·lä·kô′po͞o·lôs), **Andreas.** 1875–1938. Greek statesman; leader of Conservative Republican party; premier of Greece (1924); minister of foreign affairs (1926, 1932, 1933).

**Mi′chaud′** (mē′shō′), **Joseph François.** 1767–1839. French journalist and historian; editor of *La Quotidienne,* ultraroyalist journal (1815); author of *Histoire des Croisades* (1811–22); with his brother **Louis Gabriel** (1773–1858), compiled *Biographie Universelle* (1811–28); Louis became director of the royal press (1823) and published several biographies, as of Louis Philippe (1849) and Talleyrand (1853).

**Mi′chaux′** (mē′shō′), **André.** 1746–1802. French botanist and traveler; in Tigris and Euphrates valleys (1782–85), in U.S. (1785–96), and in Madagascar (1801–02). From his collections and field notes were prepared *Histoire des Chênes . . . de l'Amérique Septentrionale* (1801) and *Flora Boreali-Americana . . .* (1803). His son **François André** (1770–1855) accompanied him to U.S. and managed his botanical garden; traveled extensively beyond the Alleghenies and along the Atlantic coast; published *Voyage à l'Ouest des Monts Alléghanys . . .* (1804), *Histoire des Arbres Forestiers de l'Amérique Septentrionale,* translated as *The North American Sylva* (3 vols., 1810–13).

**Micheas.** See MICAH.

**Mi′chel′** (mē′shĕl′), **André.** 1853–1925. French art critic; curator of the Louvre (1896) and professor at Collège de France.

**Michel, Claude.** See CLODION.

**Mich′el** (mĭch′ĕl) of North′gate (nôrth′gāt; -gĭt; -gĕt), **Dan.** fl. 1340. English translator into Kentish dialect of French treatise *La somme des vices et des vertues* by Laurentius Gallus (1279), known as *Ayenbite of Inwyt* (or *Remorse of Conscience*) and valued philologically as dated example of southern dialect.

**Mi′chel′** (mē′shĕl′), **Francisque Xavier.** 1809–1887. French scholar; editor of *Chroniques Anglo-Normandes* (3 vols., 1836–40); author of *Théâtre Français du Moyen Âge* (1839), *Le Pays Basque . . .* (1857), *Les Écossais en France et les Français en Écosse* (1862), etc.

**Michel, François Émile.** 1828–1909. French landscape painter and writer on art, esp. on Dutch masters.

**Michel, Louise,** *in full* **Clémence Louise.** 1830–1905. French anarchist agitator; took part in the Commune of Paris (1871) and was deported to New Caledonia; returned after amnesty (1880) and at once engaged in anarchist plots; sentenced to six years' imprisonment (1883) and refused to accept a pardon (1885); in London (1886–95), and returned to Paris (1895), always continuing to spread anarchist propaganda. Among her books are *Le Livre du Jour de l'An* (1872), *Les Microbes Humains* (1886), *La Commune* (1898).

**Mi'chel·an'ge·lo** (mī'kĕl·ăn'jĕ·lō; mĭk'ĕl-; *Ital.* mā'kăl-ăn'jā·lō) *or* **Mi'chael An'ge·lo** (mī'kĕl ăn'jĕ·lō). *Full Ital. name* **Mi'chel·an'ge·lo Buo'nar·ro'ti** (mā'kăl-ăn'jā·lō bwô'när·rô'tē). 1475–1564. Italian sculptor, painter, architect, and poet of the High Renaissance, b. Caprese. Apprenticed to painter Ghirlandajo (1488); studied esp. ancient paintings in Medici collection; lived in palace of Lorenzo de' Medici (1490–92). Fled shortly before downfall of the Medici to Bologna (1494–95); influenced there by work of Jacopo della Quercia; at Rome (1496–1501); at Florence (1501–05) studied Leonardo's art. Summoned by Pope Julius II to Rome; decorated ceilings of Sistine Chapel (1508–12); worked on Julius memorial (1513–16). Sent (1516) by Pope Leo X to Florence to work on new façade for San Lorenzo (to 1520; not completed) and to procure marbles from quarries of Carrara and Seravezza. Active chiefly in Florence (to 1534); one of nine citizens in charge of defense of city (1529). Again at Rome (from 1534); in service of popes Clement VII and Paul III; succeeded Sangallo as architect of St. Peter's, Rome (1547); vice-president of Florence Acad. (1563). Died (1564) at Rome; buried at Santa Croce, Florence. Friend of painter Sebastiano del Piombo (1516–34), of Roman nobleman Tommaso Cavalieri (from 1532), and of Vittoria Colonna (1538–47); for the last two, wrote religious and love sonnets and made allegorical chalk drawings. Among his sculptures are the bas-reliefs *Battle of the Centaurs* and *Madonna of the Steps* (Casa Buonarroti, Florence); incomplete model *River God* (Florence Acad.); statuettes *Kneeling Angel*, *St. Proculus*, and *St. Petronius* (all at Bologna); *Bacchus* (Florence National Museum); *Pietà* (St. Peter's, Rome); colossal figure of young David carved out of single marble block and incomplete statue of Matthew (both in Florence Acad.); a Madonna for Church of Notre Dame, Bruges; bronze statue of Pope Julius II (Bologna; destroyed 1511); the "tragedy of his life," the Julius tomb for Pope Julius II with the famous statue of Moses (now in San Pietro in Vincoli, Rome); and the figure *Victory* (Florence Acad.); the athletic nude *Christ Risen* for Santa Maria sopra Minerva, Rome; tombs of several Medici in San Lorenzo, Florence; *Youth Crouching* (now in Leningrad); *Cupid Kneeling* (Victoria and Albert Museum, London); *Deposition from the Cross* (Florence Cathedral; later restored) and the Rondanini *Pietà* (Rondanini Palace, Rome), both intended for his own tomb. Among his paintings are the circular painting *Holy Family*, also called *Doni-Madonna* (Uffizi Gallery); cartoon *Battle of Cascina*, executed in rivalry with Leonardo da Vinci and intended for a gigantic fresco of Florentine history for council room of Palazzo Vecchio in Florence; ceiling decorations in Sistine Chapel for Julius II; colossal fresco for Clement VII and Paul III, *The Last Judgment*, on altar wall of Sistine Chapel; for Paul III, frescoes *Conversion of Paul* and *Martyrdom of Peter* (both in Pauline Chapel of Vatican). Among his pen and chalk drawings and sketches are *Phaeton*, *Tityus*, *Ganymede*, and the series *Crucifixion*, *Entombment*, and *Resurrection*. His architectural works include façade for Medici sepulchral chapel, Florence; for Clement VII, plans for Laurentian Library in Florence (built 1530–34); plans for completion of St. Peter's, Rome, begun by Sangallo, and alterations in Bramante's original plans of a Greek cross; plans for Farnese Palace (1546 ff.) and general plans for new Capitoline Place (begun 1546), Rome, with equestrian statue of Marcus Aurelius in center; plans for Porta Pia (building begun 1564), for transformation of Baths of Diocletian into Church of Santa Maria degli Angeli, both at Rome, and for new fortifications of Rome. His poetry includes many lyric poems, mostly sonnets and madrigals, love poems, and religious and philosophical poems.

**Mi'che·let'** (mēsh'lĕ'), **Jules.** 1798–1874. French historian; head of historical section in National Archives (1831); professor, Collège de France (1838–51). Among his notable works are *Tableau Chronologique de l'Histoire Moderne* (1825), *Introduction à l'Histoire Universelle* (1831), *Histoire Romaine* (1831), *Origines du Droit Français* (1837), *Histoire de France* (17 vols., 1833–67), and *Histoire de la Révolution Française* (1847–53). His wife, **Adèle Athénaïs,** *nee* **Mia'la'ret'** [myȧ'lȧ'rĕ'] (1826–1899), writer, collaborated with her husband in *L'Oiseau* (1856), *L'Insecte* (c. 1857), and *La Mer* (1861); also wrote *Les Mémoires d'un Enfant* (1866) and *La Nature* (1872).

**Michelet, Karl Ludwig.** 1801–1893. German philosopher, b. Berlin, of French descent; member of left wing of Hegelian school; assisted in publishing Hegel's works (1832–42). Author of *Geschichte der Letzten Systeme der Philosophie in Deutschland von Kant bis Hegel* (2 vols., 1837–38), *Geschichte der Menschheit* (2 vols., 1859–60), *Das System der Philosophie als Exakter Wissenschaft* (5 vols., 1876–81), etc.

**Mi'che·lin'** (mēsh'lăN'), **André** (1853–1931) and his brother **Édouard** (1859–1940). French industrialists and philanthropists; partners (Michelin & Cie) in the manufacture of rubber tires for use on vehicles; first to apply pneumatic tires to automobiles (1895); instituted scheme of making family allowances among employees based on the size of the family.

**Mi·che'lis** (mē·KA'lĭs), **Friedrich.** 1815–1886. German theologian and philosopher; refused to agree with Vatican council on definition of papal infallibility (1870) and was excommunicated (1871); became leader in Old Catholic movement.

**Mich'ell** (mĭch'ĕl), **John.** 1724–1793. English physicist and astronomer; credited with invention of torsion balance and founding of seismology; described method of magnetization.

**Michell,** Sir **Lewis Loyd.** 1842–1928. Banker and politician in South Africa; general manager in South Africa of the Standard Bank (1895–1902); close friend of Cecil Rhodes (from c. 1885); in accordance with Rhodes's request, resigned from bank to identify himself with Rhodes's interests after Rhodes's death (1902); became chief director of the Rhodes trust and the British South Africa Co. Published a life of Cecil Rhodes (1910).

**Mi'che·loz'zo** (mā'kā·lôt'tsō) *or* **Mi'che·loz'zi** (-tsē). *In full* **Michelozzo di Bar'to·lom·me'o** (dē bär'tō-lôm·mā'ō). 1396–1472. Florentine architect, sculptor, and goldsmith; after Brunelleschi, principal Florentine architect of early Renaissance. Aided Ghiberti on doors of baptistery; associate of Donatello (1425–35); protégé of Cosimo de' Medici; succeeded Brunelleschi as superintendent of Cathedral of Florence (1446). Sculptural works include *St. John the Baptist* (Opera del Duomo, Florence), *St. John the Baptist* (the Bargello, Florence), and an undetermined part of the works of Donatello and Luca della Robbia. Architectural works include the Riccardi Palace for Cosimo de' Medici, Medici chapel in Church of Santa Croce, and Convent of San Marco (all in Florence), San Giorgio Maggiore Library (Venice), Palazzo Rettorale (Ragusa, Dalmatia), Holy Cross tabernacle in Church of San Miniato (Florence), and reconstruction of Medici Bank (Milan) and of Palazzo Vecchio (Florence).

**Mi'chels** (mĭK'ĕls), **Robert.** 1876–1936. German economist and sociologist; author of *Storia del Marxismo in Italia* (1908), *Sexual Ethics* (1914), *Italien von Heute* (1930), etc.

**Mi′chel·sen** (mĭk′kĕl·sĕn), **Christian,** *in full* **Peter Christian Hersleb Kjerschow.** 1857–1925. Norwegian statesman; practiced law (1879–85); minister of finance (1903–05); formed new cabinet following Hagerup's resignation (1905) and received support of Storting in bringing about dissolution of union with Sweden; played a leading part in election of Prince Charles of Denmark as King Haakon VII; first premier of independent Norway (1905–07); retired (1907).

**Mi′chel·son** (mī′kĕl·s'n), **Albert Abraham.** 1852–1931. American physicist, b. in Germany; to U.S. (1854); grad. U.S.N.A., Annapolis (1873); studied in Europe (1880–82); professor and head of the department of physics, U. of Chicago (1892–1929). Determined with a high degree of accuracy the speed at which light travels; invented an interferometer for measuring distances by means of the length of light waves; measured a meter in terms of the wave length of cadmium light for the Paris Bureau International des Poids et Mesures; performed experiment (with E. W. Morley) which showed that the absolute motion of the earth through the ether is not measurable. This demonstration served as the starting point in the development of the theory of relativity. Received 1907 Nobel prize in physics. Elected to American Hall of Fame (1970).

**Miche′ner** (mĭsh′nẽr), **Daniel Roland.** 1900– . Canadian statesman, b. Lacombe, Alberta. Practiced law, Toronto (1923–57); ambassador to India (1964–67); governor-general of Canada (1967– ).

**Mich′e·ner** (mĭch′ĕ·nẽr), **James Albert.** 1907– . American author, b. New York City. Wrote *Tales of the South Pacific* (1947; made into musical play, 1949, and film as *South Pacific*), *Hawaii* (1960), etc.

**Mi·chet′ti** (mē·kāt′tē), **Francesco Paolo.** 1851–1929. Italian painter; representative leader of modern school of realism in painting; known particularly for genre paintings of southern Italian peasant life.

**Mi·chi·na·ga** (mē·chē·nä·gä). 966–1027. Leader of Fujiwara clan who brought it to zenith of its power; enlisted Minamoto soldiers in his service; married five of his daughters to successive emperors; governed country as regent (kwampaku) for 30 years (998–1027); his reign the classical period of Japanese literature.

**Mi′chon′** (mē′shôN′), **Jean Hippolyte.** 1806–1881. French Roman Catholic ecclesiastic and writer; author of *La Révolution et le Clergé* (1858), *Le Concordat* (1862), and irreligious novels, published anonymously.

**Mi·cip′sa** (mĭ·sĭp′sȧ). d. 118 B.C. Eldest son of Masinissa, King of Numidia; succeeded Masinissa (c. 148 B.C.) and pursued policy of friendship with Rome.

**Mic·kie′wicz** (mēts·kyĕ′vēch), **Adam.** 1798–1855. Polish poet; arrested in Vilna as a revolutionary (1824) and sent to St. Petersburg; to Odessa (1825) as teacher in lyceum; in service of governor general at Moscow (1825–28); allowed to travel abroad (1829); first professor of Slavic literatures, Collège de France, Paris (1840–44). Regarded as greatest of Polish poets; wrote *Crimean Sonnets*, *Dziady* (*Ancestors*), *Grażyna* (historical epic), *Books of the Polish Nation and Polish Pilgrimage* (1832), and *Pan Tadeusz* (*Sir Thaddeus*, 1834).

**Mick′le** (mĭk′'l), **William Julius.** 1735–1788. Scottish poet; corrector for Clarendon Press, Oxford (1765–71); published *The Concubine* (or *Syr Martyn*) in manner of Spenser; won success with his translation of *The Lusiad* from the Portuguese of Camoëns (1775); author of ballad *Cumnor Hall* (1784), which suggested to Sir Walter Scott the writing of *Kenilworth;* reputed author of lyric *The Sailor's Wife*, from which comes "There's nae luck aboot the house."

**Mi′con** (mī′kŏn). Athenian painter and sculptor of 5th century B.C.; associate of Polygnotus (*q.v.*) in decoration of the Theseum, or Temple of Theseus, and Temple of the Dioscuri, in Athens.

**Mid′del·schul′te** (mĭd′ĕl·shōōl′tĕ), **Wilhelm.** 1863–1943. Organist and composer, b. in Dortmund, Ger.; to U.S. (1891); with Theodore Thomas orchestra (1894–1917); widely known as interpreter of Bach.

**Mid′dle·sex** (mĭd′'l·sĕks), Earl of. See *Charles Sackville*, under SACKVILLE family.

**Mid′dle·ton** (mĭd′'l·tŭn), **Arthur.** 1681–1737. Acting colonial governor in America, b. Charleston, S.C. In South Carolina House of Commons, led movement overthrowing proprietary control (1719). Acting governor during absence of crown representative (1725–31); administration marked by conflict with House of Commons. His son **Henry** (1717–1784) was a Revolutionary leader; member of Continental Congress (1774–76); and its president (Oct. 22, 1774–May 10, 1775). Henry's son **Arthur** (1742–1787) was a Revolutionary leader; member of Continental Congress (1776–78 and 1781–83) and signer of Declaration of Independence. A son of Arthur, **Henry** (1770–1846), was governor of South Carolina (1810–12); member of U.S. Congress (1815–19); U.S. minister to Russia (1820–30). Another son of Arthur, **John Iz′ard** [ĭz′ärd] (1785–1849), an archaeologist, wrote *Grecian Remains in Italy...* (1812). A son of Henry, **Henry** (1797–1876), an economist, wrote *The Government and the Currency* (1844), *Economical Causes of Slavery in the United States, and Obstacles to Abolition* (1857).

**Middleton, Conyers.** 1683–1750. English clergyman and controversialist; librarian, Cambridge U. (1719); attacked Roman Catholic ritual in *Letter from Rome* (1729); assailed on ground of latitudinarianism in his remonstrance with Daniel Waterland on historical accuracy of the Bible, professed to be answering Tindal but laid himself open to accusation of being freethinker; criticized for latitudinarian treatise on miracles (1748); increased reputation with *Life of Cicero* (1741), largely borrowed from William Bellenden.

**Middleton, George.** 1880–1967. American playwright, b. Paterson, N.J.; author of a large number of one-act plays produced at various little theaters; also wrote the plays *The Cavalier* (with Paul Kester, 1902), *The Sinner* (with L. Westervelt, 1907), *The Prodigal Judge* (1913), *Hit-the-Trail Holliday* (with George M. Cohan and Guy Bolton, 1915), *Polly with a Past* (with Guy Bolton, 1917), *Accused* (with E. H. Sothern, 1925), *The Big Pond* (with A. E. Thomas, 1929), etc.

**Middleton, John.** 1st Earl of **Middleton.** 1619–1674. Scottish soldier, of a Kincardineshire family holding lands at Middleton from 12th century. Served in France; second in command of Parliamentary army at Philiphaugh (1645); suppressed Royalist uprising (1647); distinguished himself at Preston (1648); led highland force dispersed by Monck (1654); commander in chief, governor of Edinburgh Castle, lord high commissioner to Scottish parliament (1660); deprived as result of accusations by earl of Lauderdale (1663). His eldest son, **Charles** (1640?–1719), 2d Earl of Middleton and titular Earl of **Mon′mouth** (mŏn′mŭth; mŭn′-); envoy extraordinary at Vienna (1660); joint secretary for Scotland (1682); secretary of state for England (1684); became chief adviser to James II at St.-Germain (1693) and his secretary of state; became Roman Catholic (1703); responsible for abortive invasion of Scotland (1707). A kinsman, Sir **Charles Middleton,** 1st Baron **Bar′ham** (băr′ăm), was comptroller of navy (1778–90); M.P. (1784); admiral (1795); as first lord of admiralty (1805), at age of 80, devoted his experience and energy to successful organization and execution of campaign culminating at Trafalgar.

**Middleton, Peter.** d. 1781. Physician; b. probably in Scotland; one of first professors (1767) in medical school of King's College, New York City (now Columbia). See John BARD.

**Middleton, Thomas.** 1570?–1627. English dramatist; began (c. 1599) to write for stage with *The Old Law* (later drafts bearing names of William Rowley and Philip Massinger); one of Philip Henslowe's established playwrights (1602); collaborated (1602) with Munday, Drayton, Webster on a lost play, *Caesar's Fall;* collaborated on part I of Dekker's *The Honest Whore* (1604); produced in one year six satirical comedies of contemporary London manners (1607–08); later, with Rowley, turned to romantic comedy; devised pageant for installation of lord mayor (1613, and repeatedly afterwards); wrote entertainment for opening of New River by philanthropic goldsmith Hugh Myddelton (1613); city chronologer, London (1620), his ms. history extant in 18th century; for satirizing policy of court on matter of Spanish marriage in political drama *A Game at Chesse* (1624), censured along with actors. Author of *Michaelmas Terme* (1607), *The Phoenix* (1607), *A Tricke to Catch the Old One* (1608), *The Familie of Love* (1608), *A Mad World, my Masters* (1608), *The Roaring Girl* or *Moll Cut-Purse* (1611; with Dekker), *A Fair Quarrel* (1617; with Rowley), *A Chast Mayd in Cheapeside* (pub. 1630), *More Dissemblers besides Women* (pub. 1657), *No Wit, No Help like a Woman's* (pub. 1657), *Women Beware Women* (pub. 1657), *The Spanish Gipsy* (tragicomedy, pub. 1653), *The Changeling* (performed 1621; pub. 1653; with Rowley), and *Any Thing for a Quiet Life* (pub. 1662; with Rowley).

**Midg'ley** (mĭj'lĭ), **Thomas.** 1889–1944. American chemist; discovered (1922) the antiknock properties of tetraethyl lead; vice-president of Ethyl Gasoline Corp. (from 1923).

**Mid·hat' Pa·sha'** (mĭd·hät' pä·shä'). 1822–1884. Turkish statesman; grand vizier (1872, 1876–77); accused of complicity in assassination of Sultan Abdul-Aziz; exiled to Arabia.

**Midleton,** Earl of. See W. St. J. F. BRODRICK.

**Mie** (mē), **Gustav.** 1868–1957. German physicist; author of *Die Einsteinsche Gravitationstheorie, Naturwissenschaft und Theologie, Die Denkweise der Physik,* etc.

**Miel** (mēl) *or* **Meel** (māl), **Jan.** *Called* **Giovanni del'la Vi'te** (dāl'lä vē'tā). 1599–1663. Flemish genre painter and engraver; in service of Pope Alexander VII at Rome, and at Turin under patronage of Charles Emmanuel of Savoy; painted esp. hunting and pastoral scenes, carnivals, and landscapes.

**Mie'latz** (mē'läts), **Charles Frederick William.** 1860–1919. Etcher, b. Breddin, Germany; to U.S. as a child; studio in New York (from 1903); best known for etchings of views in New York City.

**Mie're·velt** *or* **Mie're·veld** (mē'rĕ·vĕlt), **Michiel Janszoon van.** 1567–1641. Dutch portrait painter; worked chiefly in Delft and The Hague; court painter to house of Orange. Painted portraits of William of Orange and other princes of Orange-Nassau (now in The Hague), of other celebrities, including Dutch poet Jakob Cats (Amsterdam), etc. Sketched *The Anatomy Lesson* (now in Delft Hospital), which was executed by his son and pupil **Pieter** (1596–1623), also a portrait painter.

**Mie'ris** (mē'rĭs). Family of Dutch painters of Leiden including: **Frans van Mieris** (1635–1681), painter of small genre pictures and portraits. His sons and pupils **Jan** (1660–1690), painter of portraits and genre pictures, and **Willem** (1662–1747), painter of portraits and genre and mythological pictures. Willem's son **Frans** (1689–1763), genre and portrait painter, etcher, and historian.

**Mie'ro·sław'ski** (myĕ'rô·slăf'skē), **Ludwik.** 1814–1878. Polish revolutionist; took part in Polish insurrection (1830–31) and in subsequent revolutionary movements in Poland (1846, 1848, 1863). Author of a history of revolution in Poland.

**Mie'ses** (mē'zĕs), **Jacques.** 1865–1954. German chess-master; won 1st prize in international tournaments at Vienna (1907) and Liverpool (1923).

**Miess'ner** (mēs'nẽr), **William Otto.** 1880– . American music educator, b. Huntingburg, Ind.; director of the school of music at Milwaukee State Teachers College (1914–22), and of Miessner Institute of Music, in Chicago (1924–37). Composer of many pieces for children (*Art Song Cycles,* 1910; *The Three Bears,* opera; *Sleeping Beauty,* opera; *Rumpelstiltskin;* etc.), and songs and piano pieces.

**Mies Van Der Rohe** (mēs' văn dẽr rō'[ĕ]), **Ludwig.** 1886–1969. American architect, b. in Germany. Projected designs for steel and glass skyscrapers (1919–21).

**Mieszko.** See BOLESLAV.

**Miff'lin** (mĭf'lĭn), **George Harrison.** 1845–1921. American publisher, b. Boston; on staff of publishing house Hurd & Houghton (1867); admitted to firm (1872) and continued as partner in successor firms; president, Houghton Mifflin Co. (1908–21); also, president of The Riverside Press, Cambridge, Mass.

**Mifflin, Lloyd.** 1846–1921. American poet, b. Columbia, Pa.; studied painting (to 1872); devoted himself to literary work (from 1872); esp. known for his sonnets. Author of *At the Gates of Song* (1897), *The Field of Dawn* (1900), *The Fleeing Nymph* (1905), *My Lady of Dream* (1906), *Flower and Thorn* (1909), *As Twilight Falls* (1916), etc.

**Mifflin, Thomas.** 1744–1800. American Revolutionary leader; active in prerevolutionary agitation. Member, Continental Congress (1774–76, 1782–84), president (1783). Aide-de-camp to Washington (1775); quartermaster general, Continental army (1775–77). Involved in Conway cabal to replace Washington with Gates (1777–78), but upon failure of plan repudiated his connection with it. Member, Constitutional Convention (1787); governor of Pennsylvania (1790–99).

**Mi'gnard'** (mē'nyȧr'), **Pierre.** 1610–1695. French painter; best known as painter of portraits, as of Louis XIV, Mme. de Maintenon, Mme. de Montespan, Mme. de La Vallière, Mme. de La Fayette, Mme. de Sévigné, Bossuet, Turenne, Colbert. His brother **Nicolas** (1606–1668), also a painter, was commissioned by king to decorate certain chambers in the Tuileries; painted also portraits of many members of the court.

**Migne** (mēn'y'), **Jacques Paul.** 1800–1875. French Roman Catholic priest and editor; settled in Paris (1833) and founded and edited *L'Univers Religieux;* established publishing house for religious books; among important publications of this house were the 28 volumes of *Scripturae Sacrae Cursus Completus,* 100 volumes of *Collection . . . des Orateurs Sacrés,* 383 volumes of *Patrologiae Cursus Completus,* and 171 volumes of *Encyclopédie Théologique.*

**Mi'gnet'** (mē'nyĕ'), **François Auguste Marie.** 1796–1884. French historian; friend and associate of Thiers; with Thiers and Carrel founded and edited *Le National,* an anti-Bourbon journal (1830); director of archives in ministry of foreign affairs (1830–48). Among his histories are *Histoire de la Révolution Française* (2 vols., 1824), *Antonio Perez et Philippe II* (1845), *Histoire de Marie Stuart* (1851), *Charles Quint. . .* (1854), *Éloges Historiques* (1863), and *Nouveaux Éloges Historiques* (1877).

**Mi′gnon′** (mē′nyôN′), **Abraham.** 1640–1679. Dutch painter of flowers, fruit, animals, birds, and insects.

**Mi·guel′** (mē·gĕl′). *In full* **Miguel Maria Evaristo de Bra·gan′ça** (thē brȧ·găN′sȧ). *Usually known as* **Dom Miguel** (dōN). 1802–1866. Aspirant to Portuguese throne; third son of John VI of Portugal; brought up in Brazil; returned to Portugal (1821); plotted against father (1821–26); on accession (1826) of young niece, Maria da Gloria, betrothed to her and made regent (1828) by Maria's father, Dom Pedro of Brazil; usurped throne and brought on civil war (1828–33); overthrown by Dom Pedro and followers (1834) and forced by England and France to give up all claims to throne; lived in Italy and Germany in exile.

**Mi′gu·la** (mē′gōō·lä), **Walter.** 1863–1938. German botanist; author of works on a system of bacteriology (2 vols., 1897–1900), cryptogamic flora of Germany, Austria, and Switzerland (13 vols., 1904–31), biology of plants (1909), and mushrooms (1925).

**Mihai.** See MICHAEL, King of Rumania.

**Mi·haj′lo·vić** (mē·hī′lô·vēt′y′; *Angl.* -vĭch), **Draža.** 1893?–1946. Serbian soldier; distinguished for bravery during World War I. Following German conquest of Yugoslavia (1941), organized an army to carry on guerilla warfare against German and Italian armies; minister of war in Yugoslavian government in exile, and head of Free Yugoslavian army (1942).

**Mi·ja′to·vić** (mē·yä′tô·vēt′y′; *Angl.* -vĭch), **Čedomilj.** 1842–?1932. Serbian statesman and writer; minister of finance (1873–75, 1894) and foreign affairs and finance (1880); senator (1875 ff.); minister to Great Britain (1895–1900, 1902–03); wrote on Serbian history.

**Mi·kha·il′** (myĭ·kŭ·ēl′). Russian form of MICHAEL.

**Mikhailovitch, Draja.** Variant of Draža MIHAJLOVIĆ.

**Mik′kel·sen** (mēk′ĕl·s′n), **Ejnar.** 1880–1971. Danish explorer, b. Jutland; on expeditions to east coast of Greenland (with Amdrup, 1900), Franz Joseph's Land (Baldwin-Ziegler expedition, 1901–02), etc.; commanded expeditions to northeastern Greenland (1909–12), Scoresby Sound (1924), west Greenland (1925), and east Greenland (1932). Author of *Conquering the Arctic Ice* (1908), *Lost in the Arctic* (1913), *Frozen Justice* (1920).

**Mi′klas** (mĭk′läs), **Wilhelm.** 1872–1956. Austrian politician; leader in Christian Socialist party (1907–38) and member of Austrian Parliament; president of the Nationalrat (1923–28); president of Austrian republic (1928–38); resigned (Mar. 13, 1938), Austria being proclaimed a part of the Third (German) Reich.

**Mi′klo·šić** (mē′klô·shēt′y′; *Ger.* -shĭch), **Franz von.** 1813–1891. Slavic philologist in Austria; lawyer by profession, practicing in Vienna; devoted himself to philological study (from c. 1844); professor, Vienna (1850–86); regarded as founder of modern Slavic philology. Wrote *Comparative Grammar of Slavic Languages* (1852–74) and *Etymological Dictionary of Slavic Languages*, etc.

**Mi·ko·yan′** (myĭ·kŭ·yȧn′), **A·na·stas′** (ŭ·nŭ·stȧs′) **Ivanovich.** 1895–1978. Soviet leader; Communist party leader in Baku (1917–19); member of Politburo (from 1934); commissar for supplies (1931–34), food industry (1934–38), foreign trade (1938–49); president U.S.S.R. (1964–65).

**Mi′lan** (mē′län). 1819?–1839. Prince of Serbia of house of Obrenovich (*q.v.*), succeeding his father, Miloš, who abdicated (1839); died same year; succeeded by his brother Michael (*q.v.*).

**Milan.** 1854–1901. Prince (1868–82) and king (1882–89) of Serbia, of house of Obrenovich (*q.v.*); m. (1875) Natalie (*q.v.*); initiated wars against Turkey to gain Serbian independence (1876, 1877); with Austrian aid, won recognition of independence at Congress of Berlin (1878); took title of king (1882); engaged in unsuccessful war against Bulgaria (1885); abdicated (1889) in favor of son Alexander; returned to Belgrade (1894); became commander in chief of Serbian army (1897); again withdrew from Serbia after Alexander's marriage (1900).

**Mi′la·ne′si** (mē′lä·nā′sē), **Gaetano.** 1813–1895. Italian art historian; director of Tuscan archives, Florence (1889 ff.). Among his works are *Documenti per la Storia dell'Arte Senese* (3 vols., 1854–56) and the standard edition of Vasari's *Vite de' Più Eccelenti Pittori, Scultori, ed Architetti Italiani* (9 vols., 1878–85).

**Mi′la·nés′ y Fuen′tes** (mē′lä·nās′ ē fwān′tās), **José Jacinto.** 1814–1863. Cuban poet; best known for his lyrics.

**Mi·lá′ y Fon′ta·nals′** (mē·lä′ ē fôn′tä·näls′), **Manuel.** 1818–1884. Spanish literary critic and historian; author of *Elementos de Literatura, Teoría Literaria, Los Trovadores en España* (1861), and *La Poesía Heróico-Popular* (1874).

**Mil′bank** (mĭl′băngk), **Joseph.** 1848–1914. American philanthropist, b. New York City; donor, with his sister Elizabeth Milbank Anderson (*q.v.*), of $3,000,000 to Teachers Coll. and Barnard Coll., Columbia, of $650,000 to establish social welfare bureau, and of $500,000 to Children's Aid Society. Milbank Memorial Chapel at Teachers Coll. and Milbank Hall at Barnard are so named in their honor.

**Milbanke, Anne Isabella.** See under George Gordon BYRON.

**Mil′burn** (mĭl′bērn), **Devereux.** 1881–1942. American polo player; member (1909–27), captain (1921–27), of all U.S. international polo teams.

**Milch** (mĭlK), **Erhard.** 1892–1972. German air-force commander; army pilot in World War I; after war, became civilian aviator (1920); appointed secretary of state in air ministry (1933); lieutenant general (1935), general (1936), colonel general (1938); air field marshal in Tunisia (Dec., 1942).

**Miles** (mīlz), **Eustace.** 1868–1948. English athlete, physical culturist, and dietitian; won championships at lawn tennis and racquets; a master at Rugby. Among his many books are *Better Food for Boys; Racquets, Tennis, and Squash; The Power of Concentration; The Daily Mirror Food Test; The E. M. System of Physical Culture; Self-Health as a Habit.*

**Miles, Nelson Appleton.** 1839–1925. American army commander, b. near Westminster, Mass.; served through Civil War; awarded Congressional Medal of Honor. Colonel, U.S. army (1866); engaged in frontier Indian fighting (1869–80); brigadier general, U.S. army (1880) and major general (1890); led successful campaigns against Apache and Sioux Indian tribes; senior commander, U.S. army (1895); in Cuba and Puerto Rico (1898); lieutenant general, U.S. army (1901); retired (1903).

**Milford Haven,** Marquises of. See under BATTENBERG.

**Mi′lhaud′** (mē′yō′), **Darius.** 1892–1974. French composer of the polytonal school, b. Aix-en-Provence; settled in Paris and became member of "The Six" (see Arthur HONEGGER); visited U.S. as conductor and lecturer (1923); to U.S. (1940); on staff of Mills Coll., Oakland, Calif.; returned to France (1947). Works include operas *La Brebis Égarée* (1923), *Les Malheurs d'Orphée* (1926), *Le Pauvre Matelot* (1926), *Médée* (1939); music for Paul Claudel's *Christophe Colomb* (1928), and *Maximilien* (1930); ballets *Le Boeuf sur le Toit* (1919; after Jean Cocteau's farce), *La Création du Monde* (1923), *Salade* (1924), and *Le Train Bleu* (1924); incidental music to Claudel's translation of the *Orestes* trilogy of Aeschylus; symphonies, chamber music; piano pieces, songs, etc.

**Milhaud, Gaston.** 1858–1918. French philosopher; professor, U. of Montpellier (1894) and the Sorbonne, Paris (1910).

**Mi'líč** (mĭ'lĕch), **Jan.** *Known as* **Milíč of Krem'sier** (krĕm'zẽr). d. 1374. Moravian-born Roman Catholic prelate; in Rome (1367), expounding his criticism of ecclesiastical abuses; imprisoned by Inquisition; released by Pope Urban V (1367), he returned to Prague and continued preaching. Regarded as a predecessor of John Huss and the Reformation.

**Mi·li'će·vić** (mē·lē'tyĕ·vĕt'y'; *Angl.* -chĕ·vĭch), **Milan.** 1831–1908. Serbian educator and writer; librarian of Belgrade National Library (1886 ff.). Among his books are *Serbian Peasant Life* (1867), *Schools in Serbia* (1868).

**Mi'licz** *or* **Mi'litsch** (mĭ'lĕch). Variants of MILÍČ.

**Milinda.** See MENANDER.

**Militchevitch.** Variant of MILIĆEVIĆ.

**Mil·kow'ski** (mēl·kôf'skē), **Zygmunt.** *Pseudonym* **Teodor Tomasz Jeż** (yĕsh). 1824–1915. Polish novelist; involved in Hungarian insurrection (1848) and Polish revolutionary movement (1863); lived thereafter in exile, chiefly in Switzerland. Author of historical romances, and stories of contemporary life portraying esp. manners and customs of the southern Slavs and the Hungarians.

**Mill** (mĭl), **Hugh Robert.** 1861–1950. Scottish geographer and meteorologist; editor of *British Rainfall* and *Symons's Meteorological Magazine* (1901–19). Author of *Realm of Nature* (1892), *The English Lakes* (1895), *The Siege of the South Pole* (1905), *The Life of Sir Ernest Shackelton* (1923), etc.

**Mill, James.** 1773–1836. Scottish philosopher, historian, and economist in England; father of John Stuart Mill. Son of shoemaker; to London (1802) with Sir John Stuart, M.P.; became editor of *St. James's Chronicle* (1805), and wrote for *Edinburgh Review* (1808–13) and other reviews to support his family; spent twelve years on his *History of India* (1818); appointed official in East India Co. (1819), rose to examiner and head of office (1830). Met Jeremy Bentham (1808), adopted his principles, became his companion and chief promulgator of Bentham's utilitarian philosophy in England; contributed utilitarian articles to *Encyclopaedia Britannica* (1816–23) and to *Westminster Review*, Benthamite organ (from 1824). As head of association for setting up "chrestomathic" school for higher education, took leading part in founding London U. (1825). Known as founder of philosophic radicalism, author of *Elements of Political Economy*, intended for education of his eldest son and based on Ricardo (1821), *Analysis of the Mind*, his magnum opus, providing in associationism psychological basis for utilitarianism (1829), and *Fragment on Mackintosh*, supporting doctrine that morality is based on utility (1835).

**Mill, John.** 1645–1707. English Biblical scholar; spent thirty years on critical edition of Greek New Testament for which he collected 30,000 various readings from mss., commentaries, and writings of the fathers (1707).

**Mill, John Stuart.** 1806–1873. English philosopher and economist, b. London; eldest son of James Mill (1773–1836), who subjected him to a systematic education from age of three with a view to his succession as chief exponent of utilitarian philosophy; a precocious student, at ten read Plato and Demosthenes with ease; on visit to France (1820), gained interest in French literature, politics, and social conditions; abandoned intention to enter law and became junior clerk in India House (1823), asst. examiner (1828), in charge of relations with native states (1836–56), chief of office (1856), retired with pension on dissolution of East India. Co. (1858). Formed Utilitarian Society for reading and discussion of essays at Bentham's house (1823–26); chief contributor to *Westminster Review* and recognized as champion of utilitarian school before age of twenty; edited Bentham's *Rationale of Judicial Evidence* (1825), but after period of mental crisis and self-analysis (1826–27), departed from utilitarianism of Bentham by recognizing differences in quality as well as quantity of pleasure and by further humanizing and widening the inherited philosophy by infusing an element of idealism. Contributed to *London Review* (from 1835), organ of philosophical radicalism; created profound impression with his *System of Logic* (1843), treating methods of inductive logic; followed Ricardo's abstract theory in *Principles of Political Economy* (1848) but applied economic doctrines to social conditions. Produced series of his best-known treatises (1859–65), including *On Liberty* (1859), *Thoughts on Parliamentary Reform* (1859), *Representative Government* (1861), *Utilitarianism* (1863), and *Examination of Sir William Hamilton's Philosophy*, presenting defense of association psychology (1865); M.P. (1865–68), voted with advanced Radical party and advocated women's suffrage; returned to literary pursuits with *The Subjection of Women* (1869), *The Irish Land Question* (1870), and *Autobiography* (1873); lived last years of life at Avignon.

**Mil·lais'** (mĭ·lā'), Sir **John Everett.** 1829–1896. English painter, b. Southampton, of old Norman family of Jersey; exhibited at Royal Acad. *Pizarro seizing the Inca of Peru* (1846). Originated, with Holman Hunt and D. G. Rossetti, Pre-Raphaelite movement (1848); his first picture on new principles, banquet scene from Keats's *Isabella* (1849); contributed to what has been called the trilogy of Pre-Raphaelite art his *Christ in the House of His Parents* (1850), which drew upon him a storm of abuse because of its unconventionality. Executed in minute Pre-Raphaelite manner also *The Return of the Dove to the Ark* and *Mariana of the Moated Grange* (1851), *The Huguenot* and *Ophelia* (1852), *The Proscribed Royalist* and *The Order of Release* (1853). Works of transitional period include *Autumn Leaves* and *Peace Concluded* (1856), *Sir Isumbras at the Ford* and *The Escape of a Heretic* (1857), *Apple Blossoms* and *The Vale of Rest* (1859), *The Black Brunswicker* (1860). Illustrated Trollope's works (1860–69) and Tennyson's poems; exhibited *The Eve of St. Agnes* (1863), *Jephthah* (1867), *Rosalind and Celia* (1868); deviated from Pre Raphaelite manner, abandoned imaginative themes, developed greater individuality and breadth and brilliant coloring of his mature phase (from 1870), as in *The Boyhood of Raleigh* (1870), *Chill October* (1871). Turned to portraits, landscapes, and single figures, as in *Cherry Ripe*, with occasional figure pieces, such as *The Northwest Passage* (1874) and *Effie Deans* (1877); painted portraits of Gladstone, Lord Beaconsfield, Wilkie Collins, Carlyle, John Bright, Irving, Tennyson. His 4th son, **John Guille** [gwĭl] (1865–1931), was an animal painter, naturalist, and big-game hunter.

**Mil'lar** (mĭl'ẽr), **Andrew.** 1707–1768. British publisher, b. Scotland; published Johnson's *Dictionary*, Thomson's *Seasons*, Fielding's *Tom Jones* and *Amelia*, and histories of Robertson and Hume.

**Mil'lar'det'** (mē'yȧr'dĕ'), **Alexis.** 1838–1902. French botanist; originated plan of hybridization of French and American grapevines and treatment of them with copper compounds against mildew.

**Mil·lay'** (mĭ·lā'), **Edna St. Vincent.** 1892–1950. American author, b. Rockland, Me.; m. (1923) Eugen Jan Boissevain. Author of volumes of verse, as *Renascence and Other Poems* (1917), *A Few Figs from Thistles* (1920), *Second April* (1921), *The Harp Weaver and Other Poems*

(1923; awarded Pulitzer prize), *The Buck in the Snow* (1928), *Wine from these Grapes* (1934), *Conversation at Midnight* (1937), *Huntsman, What Quarry?* (1939), *There Are No Islands, Any More* (1940); the plays *Aria da Capo* (1921), *The Lamp and the Bell* (1921), *Two Slatterns and a King* (1921); the sonnet sequence *Fatal Interview* (1931); and the libretto for *The King's Henchman*, opera composed by Deems Taylor (produced, 1927).

**Mille** (mēl), **Pierre.** 1864–1941. French journalist and fiction writer; war correspondent of *Le Journal des Débats* in Greco-Turkish War (1897) and of *Le Temps* in World War I (1914–18). Among his books are *De Thessalie en Crète* (1897), *Le Congo Léopoldien* (1903), *L'Ange du Bizarre* (1921), *Christine et Lui* (1926), *Mes Trônes et mes Dominations* (1930).

**Mil'ledge** (mĭl'ĭj), **John.** 1757–1818. American legislator and statesman, b. Savannah, Ga.; served in American Revolution; member, U.S. House of Representatives (1792–93, 1795–99, 1801–02); governor of Georgia (1802–06); U.S. senator (1806–09). Gave (1800) land needed for building the U. of Georgia, and hence credited with being founder of the university. Milledgeville, Georgia's capital (1807–67), was named in his honor.

**Mil'ler** (mĭl'ẽr), **Alice,** *nee* **Duer** (dūr). 1874–1942. American novelist, b. New York City; m. Henry Wise Miller (1899). Author of *The Modern Obstacle* (1903), *Are Women People?* (1915), *The Charm School* (1919), *The Springboard* (a play; 1927), *Forsaking All Others* (1930), *The White Cliffs* (narrative poem; 1940), etc.

**Miller, Arthur.** 1915– . American author and playwright, b. New York City. Wrote *Death of a Salesman* (1949), *The Crucible* (1953), *View from the Bridge* (1955), *Incident at Vichy* (1964), etc.

**Miller, Charles Henry.** 1842–1922. American etcher and landscape painter; his *Bouquet of Oaks* hangs in Metropolitan Museum of Art, New York; *Sunset, East Hampton*, in Brooklyn Museum of Art. Author, under pseudonym **Carl De Mul'dor** (?dĕ mŭl'dôr), of *The Philosophy of Art in America* (1885).

**Miller, Charles Ransom.** 1849–1922. American journalist; with N.Y. *Times* (1875–1922; editor, 1883–1922).

**Miller, Cin'cin·nat'us** (sĭn'sĭ·năt'ŭs) **Hi'ner** (hī'nẽr) *or* **Hei'ne** (hī'nĕ). *Pen name* **Joa·quin'** (wä·kēn') **Miller.** 1839–1913. American poet, b. Liberty, Ind.; ran away from home (1856); led adventurous life in California mining camps, among Digger Indians, with horse thieves (1856–59); studied law; adm. to bar, Portland, Ore. (1861); edited newspaper in Eugene, Ore. (1863), which was suppressed because of his Confederate sympathies. Published two volumes of poetry, *Specimens* (1868) and *Joaquin et al* (1869); visited England (1871) and published *Songs of the Sierras* (1871); attracted attention in literary circles both by his verse and by his western clothes, chaps, and sombrero; published *Songs of the Sunlands* (1873), *Life Among the Modocs* (1873), *The Ship in the Desert* (1875), *The Baroness of New York* (1877), *Songs of Italy* (1878), *Shadows of Shasta* (1881), *The Danites in the Sierras* (1881).

**Miller, David Hunter.** 1875–1961. American lawyer, b. New York City; practiced in New York City. Legal adviser on Colonel House's mission in Paris (1918), and to American commission at Paris Peace Conference (1919); collaborated in drawing up final draft of Covenant of the League of Nations. Author of *My Diary at the Conference of Paris, with Documents* (21 vols., 1924–26), *The Drafting of the Covenant* (2 vols., 1928), *The Peace Pact of Paris* (1928), etc.

**Miller, Dayton Clarence.** 1866–1941. American physicist; professor, Case School of Applied Science (from 1893). Author of *Laboratory Physics* (1903), *Sound Waves, Shape and Speed* (1937), and *Sparks, Lightning, Cosmic Rays* (1939).

**Miller, Edward.** 1760–1812. American physician, b. near Dover, Del.; practiced in New York City (from 1796). A founder of *Medical Repository* (1797), first medical periodical in U.S.; aided in establishing College of Physicians and Surgeons, New York (1807), and was its first professor of the practice of physic (1807–12); interested himself esp. in study of yellow fever. His brother **Samuel** (1769–1850) was a Presbyterian clergyman; pastor, in New York City, of First Presbyterian Church (from 1813); professor of church history and government, Princeton Theological Seminary (from 1813). Samuel's son **John** (1819–1895) was also a clergyman; resided in Princeton, N.J. (from 1871); withdrew from Presbyterian church (1877) and established at Princeton an independent church (1880), of which he remained pastor; received into Cumberland Presbyterian church (1893).

**Miller, Ferdinand von.** 1813–1887. German bronze founder; director of Royal Foundry, Munich (from 1844); among works cast here were the bronze door of the Capitol at Washington. His son and pupil, Baron **Ferdinand** (1842–1929), cast statues of Humboldt, Shakespeare, and Columbus for St. Louis, figures for a fountain at Cincinnati, statues of a soldier for Soldiers' Monument, Charleston, S.C., and of William I at Metz (1892), etc. Another son, **Oskar** (1855–1934), electrical engineer; organized first German electrical exposition, Munich (1882); in U.S. (1883), where he conferred with Edison and Weston; cofounder (with Rathenau) and director of German Edison Co., from which developed Allgemeine Elektrizitäts-Gesellschaft (A.E.G.), or General Electric Co., and Berlin Electrical Works (1883–90); president and technical director of International Electrical Engineering Exhibition at Frankfurt.

**Miller, Frank Ebenezer.** 1859–1932. American physician, b. Hartford, Conn.; began practice in New York (1896); made scientific study of the voice; originated "vocal art-science," a method of voice production.

**Miller, George Abram.** 1863–1951. American mathematician, b. Lynnville, Pa.; professor, Illinois (from 1907). Author of *Determinants* (1892) and *Historical Introduction to Mathematical Literature* (1916).

**Miller, Harriet,** *nee* **Mann** (măn). *Pen name* **Olive Thorne Miller.** 1831–1918. American ornithologist, b. Auburn, N.Y.; m. Watts Todd Miller (1854; d. 1904). Writer esp. of children's books on birds, as *Little Folks in Feathers and Fur, and Others in Neither* (1875), *Bird-Ways* (1885), *The Children's Book of Birds* (1915), etc.

**Miller, Helen Topping.** 1884–1960. American writer, b. Fenton, Mich.; m. Frank Roger Miller (1910). Author of *Sharon* (1931), *The Flaming Gahagans* (1932), *Splendor of Eagles* (1935), *Storm Over Eden* (1937), *Long After Midnight* (1939), etc.

**Miller, Henry John.** 1860–1926. Actor and theater manager, b. London, England; to Toronto, Can., as a boy; leading man, Charles Frohman's Empire Theater stock company (c. 1890–96); opened Princess Theatre, New York, as manager and star in *The Great Divide* (1906), *The Servant in the House* (1908), *The Faith Healer* (1910); manager, director, and star of the Henry Miller Theatre, New York City (1918–26).

**Miller, Henry Valentine.** 1891– . American author, b. New York City. Wrote *Tropic of Cancer* (1934), *Tropic of Capricorn* (1938), both long banned in U.S.

**Miller, Hugh.** 1802–1856. Scottish geologist and man of letters; worked as stonemason (to 1834); published volume of poems (1829); accountant in bank at Cromarty (1834); contributed to Mackay Wilson's *Tales of the*

*Borders;* wrote *Scenes and Legends in the North of Scotland* (1835); editor of *The Witness*, organ of nonintrusionists (1840–56), in which he began geological articles collected as *The Old Red Sandstone* (1841). Pioneer in popularizing of geology by means of chief works *Footprints of the Creator* (1849), *The Testimony of the Rocks* (pub. 1857), *Sketch Book of Popular Geology* (pub. 1859); wrote *First Impressions of England and its People* (1847) and *My Schools and Schoolmasters* (1854).

**Miller, James Russell.** 1840–1912. American Presbyterian clergyman; wrote many devotional books, including *Devotional Hours with the Bible* (8 vols., 1909–13), of which more than 2,000,000 copies were sold.

**Miller, Joaquin.** See Cincinnatus Hiner MILLER.

**Miller, Johann Martin.** 1750–1814. German novelist and lyric poet, b. Ulm; works include *Siegwart, eine Klostergeschichte* (2 vols., 1776), imitation of Goethe's *Werther*, and the volume of lyric poems *Gedichte* (1783), containing *Was Frag ich Viel nach Geld und Gut.*

**Miller, John.** See under Edward MILLER.

**Miller, John Peter.** 1709–1796. Clergyman, b. in Germany; to America (1730); minister of Dutch Reformed Church (1730–35); entered the Ephrata cloister (1735), a monastic community at Ephrata, Pa., of German Seventh-Day Baptists, known as Dunkers; succeeded Johann Conrad Beissel as head of the community (1768–96); engaged by Continental Congress to translate Declaration of Independence into several European languages (1776).

**Miller, Joseph** *or* **Josias,** *commonly* **Joe.** 1684–1738. English comedian. Member of Drury Lane company (from 1709); a favorite as Trinculo in *The Tempest*, First Gravedigger in *Hamlet*, Marplot in *The Busybody.* His name unwarrantably used after his death in title *Joe Miller's Jest-book, or The Wit's Vade Mecum* (by John Mottley; pub. 1739), collection of coarse jests, only three of which are told of Miller.

**Miller, Leonard.** See Leonard MERRICK.

**Miller, Lewis.** 1829–1899. American inventor and philanthropist, b. Greentown, Ohio; invented improvements in agricultural machinery, esp. reapers and binders. With John H. Vincent (*q.v.*), founded the Chautauqua movement (1874).

**Miller, Max.** 1901–1967. American writer, b. Traverse City, Mich.; author of *I Cover the Waterfront* (1932), *The Beginning of a Mortal* (1933), *The Second House From the Corner* (1934), *The Man on the Barge* (1935), *Fog and Men on Bering Sea* (1936), *Mexico Around Me* (1937), *A Stranger Came to Port* (1938), *Reno* (1941), *Land Where Time Stands Still* (1943), etc.

**Miller, Olive Thorne.** Pen name of Harriet MILLER.

**Miller, Oskar von.** See under Ferdinand von MILLER.

**Miller, Patrick.** 1731–1815. Scottish inventor; conducted experiments with steamboat (1788–89); credited by some with invention of steamboat.

**Miller, Perry Gilbert Eddy.** 1905–1963. American literary critic and scholar, b. Chicago, Ill. At Harvard U. (1931–63); wrote *The New England Mind* (1939), *Consciousness in Concord* (1958), etc.

**Miller, Richard E.** 1875–1943. American painter, b. St. Louis, Mo. His painting *The Chinese Statuette* hangs in Metropolitan Museum of Art, New York City; *The Boudoir*, in Corcoran Gallery, Washington, D.C.; *Old Maiden Ladies*, in Luxembourg Gallery, Paris.

**Miller, Samuel.** See under Edward MILLER.

**Miller, Samuel Freeman.** 1816–1890. American jurist, b. Richmond, Ky.; practiced law, Keokuk, Iowa (1850–62); associate justice, U.S. Supreme Court (1862–90).

**Miller, William.** 1782–1849. American sectarian leader, b. Pittsfield, Mass.; farmer, Poultney, Vt. (1803–12), and Hampton, N.Y. (from 1813); experienced conversion (1816); in study of Biblical prophetic books, believed he discovered that Christ was to return to earth about 1843; lectured and preached on the Second Coming of Christ (from 1831); published *Evidence from Scripture and History of the Second Coming of Christ, about the Year 1843* (1836). His followers, known as Millerites, or Adventists, prepared for Christ's coming, both in 1843 and 1844, by neglecting worldly pursuits, donning ascension robes, and gathering at appointed times on hilltops, in cemeteries, etc. Adventist Church was organized (1845), with Miller as its head; existing Adventist bodies are descended from this organization.

**Miller, William.** 1795–1861. British soldier in Peninsular War (1811–14) and in North America (1815); distinguished himself in Chile and in Peru in war for expulsion of Spaniards; intimate with Bolívar; grand marshal under Santa Cruz in Peru; narrates Spanish-American Revolution in *Memoirs.*

**Miller, William.** 1810–1872. Scottish poet; made reputation by contributions of songs in *Whistle Binkie* (1832–53); author of *Wee Willie Winkie* and other nursery lyrics.

**Miller, William Allen.** 1817–1870. English chemist; known for early experiments in spectrum analysis, esp. as applied to stellar chemistry. See Sir William HUGGINS.

**Miller, William Hallowes.** 1801–1880. English mineralogist; developed system of crystallography still in common use, set forth in his *Treatise on Crystallography* (1838).

**Miller, William Henry Harrison.** 1840–1917. American jurist; practiced, Indianapolis, as partner of Benjamin Harrison; attorney general of the U.S. (1889–93).

**Miller, Willoughby Dayton.** 1853–1907. Dentist, b. near Alexandria, Ohio; conducted researches in bacteriology and chemistry as related to dental and oral diseases.

**Mil′le·rand′** (mēl′räN′), **Alexandre.** 1859–1943. French statesman and 11th president of the republic; proprietor and editor of socialist journals (1883–98); elected as Radical Socialist to Chamber of Deputies (1885–1920); worked for reforms in social legislation; held various cabinet offices (1899–1915). After World War, commissioner general of Alsace (1919–20); prime minister (1920); elected president of France (1920–24); forced to resign by parties of the left; senator (1925–40).

**Mil′les** (mĭl′lĕs), **Carl,** *in full* **Vilhelm Carl Emil.** *Orig. surname* **An′der·son** (ån′dĕr·sôn). 1875–1955. Swedish sculptor; settled in Stockholm and became professor at Art Acad. (1920–31). Works include colossal Sten Sture monument near Uppsala, statue of Gustavus Vasa (Nordic Museum, Stockholm), *Playing Bears* groups in granite for Berzelius Park, Stockholm, Europa fountain, Halmstad, Poseidon fountain in front of Göteborg museum, and sculptures at Rockefeller Center, New York.

**Mil′let′** (mē′lĕ′; *Angl.* mĭ·lā′, mĭl′ā), **Aimé.** 1819–1891. French sculptor; studied painting with his father, **Frédéric Millet** (1786–1859), portrait painter, and sculpture with Viollet-le-Duc and David d'Angers; gave up painting (after 1852). Works include statues *Narcissus, Ariadne*, and *Bacchante*, the marble figure *Mercury*, the colossal *Apollo* group in bronze for Paris Opéra façade, *Phidias*, portrait bust of George Sand, portrait statues of Chateaubriand and Edgar Quinet, etc.

**Mil′let** (mĭl′ĕt; -ĭt), **Francis Davis.** 1846–1912. American artist, b. Mattapoisett, Mass.; illustrator for London *Graphic* (1878). With Poultney Bigelow, journeyed 1700 miles down Danube (1891; for *Harper's Magazine*); war correspondent of New York *Sun*, London *Times*, and *Harper's Weekly* in the Philippines (1899); on special U.S. government mission to Tokyo (1908); lost on the

*Titanic* (Apr. 15, 1912). Painted historic murals for the Minnesota and Wisconsin State capitols and the Baltimore customhouse. His *A Cozy Corner* and *An Old-Time Melody* hang in the Metropolitan Museum of Art, New York City; *Between Two Fires* in the National Gallery, known as the Tate Gallery, London. Author, with Poultney Bigelow, of *From the Black Forest to the Black Sea* (1893).

**Mil'let'** (mē'lĕ'; *Angl.* mĭ·lā', mĭl'ā) *or* **Mi'lé'** (mē'lā'; *Angl.* mĭ·lā', mĭl'ā), **Jean François.** *Often called* **Fran'cisque'** (fräN'sēsk'). 1642?–1679. Landscape painter, b. Antwerp, of French parentage; settled in Paris (1660); painted Italian and Arcadian landscapes in imitation of Poussin.

**Millet, Jean François.** 1814–1875. French genre and landscape painter of Barbizon school; lived alternately in Normandy and Paris (1840 ff.) and painted religious, classical, and genre subjects; settled in Barbizon (1849), joined Fontainebleau group of landscape artists, and painted chiefly peasant subjects; intimate friend of Rousseau. Works include *The Sower*, *The Water Carrier*, *The Shepherdess*, *Knitting Lesson*, *The Gleaners*, *The Angelus*, *Spring*, *Harvesters Resting*, *Shepherdess Seated*, *Potato Diggers*, *Breaking the Flax*, *Man with the Hoe*, *Woman Feeding Chickens*, *Death and the Woodcutter*. His brother **Jean Baptiste** (1831–1906), sculptor and painter, produced water colors and landscapes of Fontainebleau and environs of Paris and sculptures at Notre Dame de Paris and Madeleine de Vézelay.

**Mil'li·kan** (mĭl'ĭ·kăn), **Robert Andrews.** 1868–1953. American physicist, b. Morrison, Ill.; taught at U. of Chicago (1896–1921; professor from 1910); director, Norman Bridge Laboratory of Physics, Calif. Inst. Tech. (from 1921). Credited with being first to isolate the electron and measure its charge. His other work includes investigations on the penetrating power of cosmic rays, also on the absorption of X rays, and the Brownian movement in gases, the photoelectric determination of Planck's constant, and the extension of the ultraviolet spectrum. Received 1923 Nobel prize in physics. Author of textbooks and *The Electron* (1917), *Evolution of Science and Religion* (1927), *Science and the New Civilization* (1930), *Time, Matter, and Value* (1932), *Protons, Photons, Neutrons and Cosmic Rays* (1935), etc.

**Mil'lin** (mĭl'ĭn), **Sarah Gertrude,** *nee* **Lieb'son** (lēb's'n). 1889–1968. South African writer; m. Philip Millin. Author of *Rhodes, a Life* (1933), *General Smuts* (1936), and a number of novels, including *The Dark River* (1920), *God's Stepchildren* (1924), *What Hath a Man?* (1938), etc.

**Mil'lis** (mĭl'ĭs), **Harry Alvin.** 1873–1948. American economist and educator; A.B., Indiana U. (1895); Ph.D., U. of Chicago (1899); professor (1916) and head of economics department, U. of Chicago (1928–38); chairman, National Labor Relations Board (1940–45).

**Millis, Walter.** 1899–1968. American journalist, b. Atlanta, Ga.; on staff of New York *Herald Tribune* (from 1924). Author of *Sand Castle* (1929), *Road to War* (1935), *Why Europe Fights* (1940), etc.

**Mil'löck·er** (mĭl'ûk·ẽr), **Karl.** 1842–1899. Austrian composer of operettas, and orchestra conductor; a representative of older Viennese light opera. Compositions include *Der Bettelstudent* (1882), *Der Feldprediger* (1884), *Der Arme Jonathan* (1890), *Der Probekuss* (1894), musical farces, piano works, etc.

**Mills** (mĭlz), **Clark.** 1815–1883. American sculptor and bronze founder, b. in Onondaga County, N.Y. His bronze equestrian statue of Andrew Jackson, the first large bronze statue cast in U.S., stands facing the White House in Washington; his portrait busts of Calhoun and Washington are in Corcoran Art Gallery, Washington.

**Mills, Darius Ogden.** 1825–1910. American financier and philanthropist, b. North Salem, N.Y.; to California (1848–49); merchant and banker, Sacramento; organizer and first president (1864–73) of Bank of California, San Francisco. Moved to New York (1878); established series of hotels for the very poor. Benefactor of Metropolitan Museum of Art and New York Botanical Garden. For his daughter **Elizabeth,** see Whitelaw Reid. His grandson **Ogden Livingston** (1884–1937), lawyer, was U.S. secretary of the treasury (Feb., 1932–Mar., 1933).

**Mills, Enos Abijah.** 1870–1922. American lecturer and writer; b. near Kansas City, Kans.; explorer of the Rocky Mountain region and author of books on the Rockies (*Wild Life in the Rockies*, 1909; *Rocky Mountain Wonderland*, 1915; etc.). Known as "Father of the Rocky Mountain National Park."

**Mills, Lawrence Heyworth.** 1837–1918. Orientalist, b. New York City; professor of Zend philology, Oxford U., England (from 1887); author of books and papers on the Avesta and Zoroastrianism.

**Mills, Robert.** 1781–1855. American architect and engineer, b. Charleston, S.C.; office in Washington, D.C. (from 1830); architect of public buildings, Washington (1836–51); designed the Treasury building, General Post Office, Patent Office building, Washington monument.

**Mills,** Sir **William.** 1856–1932. English inventor; pioneer in researches on alloys; invented Mills hand grenade used by British and Allies during World War (1914–18).

**Mills'paugh** (mĭlz'pô), **Arthur Chester.** 1883–1955. American diplomat and financier, b. Augusta, Mich.; on staff of U.S. State Department (1918–22); administrator general of finances, Persia (1922–27); financial adviser and receiver of customs, Haiti (1927–29); research associate, Brookings Institution (1929–39). Author of *The American Task in Persia* (1925), *Haiti under American Control* (1931), etc.

**Mil'man** (mĭl'măn), **Henry Hart.** 1791–1868. English poet and historian; son of Sir **Francis Milman,** physician to George III. Wrote tragedies (*Fazio*, 1815; acted 1818), epic poems (*Samor*, 1818), hymns, and translations from the classics; professor of poetry, Oxford (1821–31); dean of St. Paul's (1849); known chiefly for historical works, including *History of the Jews* (1830), *History of Christianity under the Empire* (1840), and *History of Latin Christianity* (6 vols., 1854–55).

**Mil'more** (mĭl'mōr), **Martin.** 1844–1883. Sculptor, b. Sligo, Ireland; to U.S. (1851); studio in Boston. Examples of his work: bust of Charles Sumner, in Capitol, Washington, D.C.; *Soldiers' and Sailors' Monument*, on Boston Common; portrait bust of George Ticknor, in Boston Public Library; bronze statue of Sylvanus Thayer, at West Point, N.Y. Over his grave in Forest Hills Cemetery, Roxbury, stands Daniel Chester French's famous work *Death and the Young Sculptor*.

**Miln** (mĭln), **Louise,** *nee* **Jor'dan** (jôr'd'n). 1864–1933. American writer, b. Macomb, Ill.; m. George Crichton Miln (d. 1917); actress (1882 ff.); visited China first time (1888) and interested herself in study of Chinese life; author of a number of novels and short stories about China, including *The Feast of the Lanterns* (1920), *In a Shantung Garden* (1924), *The Soul of China* (short stories; 1925), *It Happened in Peking* (1926), *The Flutes of Shanghai* (1928), *Rice* (1930), *Peng Wee's Harvest* (1933).

**Milne** (mĭln), **Alan Alexander.** 1882–1956. English poet and playwright; asst. editor of *Punch* (1906–14); served in World War (1915–19). Author of *The Day's Play* (1910), *Once on a Time* (1917), *Two People* (1931), *It's Too Late Now* (1939); of plays, including *Make-Believe* (1918), *Mr. Pim Passes By* (1919), *The Romantic Age*

(1920), *The Truth about Blayds* (1921), *The Dover Road* (1922), *Ariadne* (1925), *Michael and Mary* (1930), *Toad of Toad Hall* (1930), *Miss Elizabeth Bennet* (1936), *Gentleman Unknown* (1938); of the series of juveniles (verse and prose) *When We Were Very Young* (1924), *Winnie-the-Pooh* (1926), *Now we are Six* (1927), and *The House at Pooh Corner* (1928).

**Milne, Edward Arthur.** 1896–1950. English astronomer; professor of mathematics, Oxford (from 1928). Author of *Thermodynamics of the Stars, The White Dwarf Stars* (1932), *Relativity, Gravitation, and World-Structure* (1935).

**Milne, George Francis.** 1st Baron **Milne.** 1866–1948. British soldier in South Africa (1899–1902) and World War (1914–18); major general (1915); general (1920); field marshal (1928); commanded British Salonika force and the army of the Black Sea; commander in chief, Eastern Command (1923–26); chief of Imperial general staff (1926–33); governor and constable, Tower of London (1933–38).

**Milne, John.** 1850–1913. English mining engineer and seismologist; first professor of seismology, Imperial U., Tokyo; returned to England (1894); instrumental in establishing seismological stations throughout world.

**Milne, Joshua.** 1776–1851. English actuary whose treatise on valuation of annuities and tables of mortality (1815) revolutionized actuarial science.

**Milne′-E′dwards′** (*Fr.* mēl′nā′dwȧrs′; *Eng.* mĭln′ĕd′-wẽrdz), **Henri.** 1800–1885. French zoologist, b. in Bruges, son of an Englishman; professor at the Sorbonne (1843); director of the Muséum d'Histoire Naturelle. Emphasized physiological division of labor in the economy of organisms; worked esp. on mollusks, crustaceans, and anthozoans; author of work on comparative anatomy and physiology of men and animals. His son **Alphonse** (1835–1900), professor of mammalogy and ornithology (1876), director (1891), Muséum d'Histoire Naturelle; known for work relating to crustaceans and mammals, deep-sea fauna, and the fauna of Madagascar.

**Mil′ner** (mĭl′nẽr), **Alfred.** 1st Viscount **Milner.** 1854–1925. British administrator in South Africa, b. Giessen, Hesse-Darmstadt; on staff of *Pall Mall Gazette* (1881–85); private secretary to the chancellor of the exchequer (1886–89); undersecretary for finance in Egypt (1890–92); governor of Cape of Good Hope (1897–1901); demanded, after conference with Kruger at Bloemfontein (1899), enfranchisement of Johannesburgers; administrator (1900–02) and governor (1902–05) of the Transvaal and Orange River colonies; also, high commissioner for South Africa (1897–1905). Created baron (1901) and viscount (1902). Headed mission to Egypt (1919) that recommended recognition of Egyptian independence.

**Milner, John.** 1752–1826. English vicar apostolic of Roman Catholic Church (1803–26), called "the English Athanasius." Established at Winchester refugee Benedictine nuns from Belgium; obtained substitution of oath not contrary to Roman Catholic doctrine in Pitt's Catholic relief bill (1791); bishop of Castabala (1803); opposed crown's claim of veto power over appointment of Roman Catholic bishops. Author of *Antiquities of Winchester* (1798–1801), *The End of Religious Controversy* (1818), and treatise on English ecclesiastical architecture in Middle Ages (1835).

**Milner, Joseph.** 1744–1797. English ecclesiastical historian; author of *The History of the Church of Christ* (3 vols., 1794–97), written from evangelical point of view. His brother **Isaac** (1750–1820), mathematician, was first professor of natural philosophy, Cambridge (1783–92), and Lucasian professor of mathematics (1798–1820); dean of Carlisle (1791).

**Milner-Gibson, Thomas.** See Gibson.

**Milnes** (mĭlz), **Richard Monckton.** 1st Baron **Hough′-ton** (hou′t′n). 1809–1885. English poet, b. London. At Cambridge, a leader in the Union and member of Apostles Club, with Tennyson, Hallam, and Thackeray. M.P. (1837); interested in copyright legislation; advocated penny banks; left Peel's party on account of corn-law controversy; made peer (1863); championed oppressed nationalities and slaves; m. (1851) the Hon. Annabel Crewe, daughter of 2d Lord Crewe. Remembered as a Maecenas of young writers: secured laureateship for Tennyson; helped to make Emerson known to Britons; eased dying hours of David Gray; one of first to recognize Swinburne's gifts and Keats as of first rank. Author of volumes of graceful verse, including the shorter poems *The Brookside, The Beating of My Own Heart*, and *Strangers Yet*, and *Life of Keats* (1848).

**Mi′lo** (mī′lō) *or* **Mi′lon** (mī′lŏn). Greek athlete of late 6th century B.C., of Crotona, Magna Graecia, Italy; renowned for his strength; victor six times at Olympic games and six times at Pythian games.

**Milo, Titus Annius Papianus.** 95–48 B.C. Roman politician; tribune of the people (57); his bitter rivalry with Clodius culminated in murder of Clodius by Milo's followers; defended by Cicero in trial for death of Clodius but found guilty and condemned to exile; killed in action near Thurii, southern Italy.

**Mi·lo·ra′do·vich** (myĭ·lŭ·rȧ′dŭ·vyĭch), **Mikhail Andreevich.** 1771–1825. Russian general; general of division at Austerlitz (1805); engaged at Borodino (1812) and Lützen (1813); governor of St. Petersburg (1819–25); killed while attempting to crush Decembrist uprising.

**Mi′loš** (mē′lôsh). 1780–1860. Prince of Serbia, of house of Obrenovich (*q.v.*); led Serbian war of liberation (1815) and became ruler of Serbia (1817); proclaimed hereditary prince (1827); recognized by sultan (1830); abdicated (1839); succeeded (1839) by son Milan (who died same year) then by another son, Michael; again prince of Serbia (1858–60); regarded as creator of modern Serbia.

**Mi′lo·va′no·vić** (mē′lô·vä′nô·vēt′y′; *Angl.* -vĭch), **Milovan.** 1863–1912. Serbian jurist and statesman; minister of foreign affairs (1908–11); premier of Serbia (1911–12); initiated negotiations for formation of a Balkan league.

**Mil′stein** (mĭl′stīn), **Na′than** (nā′thăn). 1904– . Russian concert violinist, b. Odessa; pupil of Leopold Auer and of Eugène Ysaye.

**Mil·ti′a·des** (mĭl·tī′ȧ·dēz), Saint. *Also, less correctly,* **Mel·chi′a·des** (mĕl·kī′ȧ·dēz). Pope (bishop of Rome; 310 or 311–314). Persecution of Christians ended during his pontificate; witnessed final triumph of the cross (312) when Constantine the Great defeated Emperor Maxentius; settled controversy with Donatists.

**Miltiades.** 540?–?489 B.C. Athenian general; chosen one of ten Greek generals to resist second invasion of Persians; commanded allied Athenian and Plataean army which decisively defeated Persians at Marathon (490).

**Mil′titz** (mĭl′tĭts), **Karl von.** 1490?–1529. German Roman Catholic ecclesiastic; papal chamberlain and notary (1515); presented golden rose to Prince Frederick the Wise of Saxony (1518); conferred with Luther in Saxony on matter of indulgences (1519–20).

**Mil′ton** (mĭl′t′n; -tŭn), **John.** 1608–1674. English poet, b. London. Son of **John Milton** (1563?–1647), a scrivener and composer of motets, madrigals, and melodies, who was disinherited because of his conversion to Protestantism while at Oxford. Educ. Christ's Coll., Cambridge, where he was nicknamed "the Lady of Christ's"; wrote first poem on death of sister's first child,

*On the death of a Fair Infant* (1626); wrote at university ode *On the Morning of Christ's Nativity* (1629), sonnet to Shakespeare (1630), Latin and English poems. Having given up idea of entering the church, devoted himself to study of classics at father's home at Horton (1632–38), where he wrote *L'Allegro* and *Il Penseroso* (1632), *Arcades* (1633), *Comus* (a masque, 1634; pub. 1637), and the elegy *Lycidas* (1637; pub. 1638); traveled in France and Italy (1638–39). Settled in London as tutor to his nephews Edward and John Phillips; published series of pamphlets against episcopacy, including *Reformation of Church Discipline in England* (1641) and his replies to Bishop Hall, and in defense of Smectymnuus (*q.v.*). Married (1642 or 1643) Mary Powell, daughter of Oxfordshire Cavalier, a girl of seventeen, who returned to her father's house after a month, became reconciled (1645), died (1652). Published pamphlets relating to divorce, including *The Doctrine and Discipline of Divorce* (1643) and *Tetrachordon: The Four Chief Places of Scripture Which Treat of Marriage* (1645), which provoked enmity of Presbyterians and threat of prosecution by parliamentary committee; replied to this threat in his most famous prose work, *Areopagitica* (1644), on liberty of the press; published *Tractate of Education* (1644) and defended execution of Charles in *The Tenure of Kings and Magistrates* (1649); Latin (or foreign) secretary to Council of State (1649); officially replied to Dr. Gauden's *Eikon Basilike* in *Eikonoklastes* (1649) and to Salmasius in *Pro Populo Anglicano Defensio* (1650). Having become blind (1652), was assisted in official duties by Andrew Marvell until Restoration; m. 2d (1656) Catherine Woodcock, who died (1658); in this period of prose writing, composed sonnets on massacre of Vaudois in Piedmont, on his blindness, to Fairfax, to Cromwell, also Greek and Latin poems. At Restoration, lost greater part of fortune but, through intercession of Marvell and perhaps Davenant, was included in amnesty; m. 3d (1663) Elizabeth Minshull, aged 25, who assured his domestic happiness. Bitterly disappointed in republican principles; completed, by dictation to an amanuensis, long-contemplated poem on the fall of man, *Paradise Lost* (completed by 1665, perhaps 1663; pub. 1667 in 10 books; enlarged to 12 books, 1674), of which 1300 copies were sold in 18 months. Cf. Giovanni Battista ANDREINI. Published (1671) *Paradise Regained*, written at suggestion of Thomas Ellwood, and the lyrical drama *Samson Agonistes*, lamenting his own old age and his nation's apostasy. Turned to works upon grammar and logic, of little value, and a Latin *Treatise of Christian Doctrines*, showing him an Arian; execrated as regicide by most of countrymen; succumbed to attacks of gout; buried beside his father, at Cripplegate, London.

**Mi·lyu·kov′** (myĭ·lyŏŏ·kôf′), **Pavel Nikolaevich.** 1859–1943. Russian politician and historian; a founder of Constitutional Democratic party; aided in drafting Viborg Manifesto (1906); member of 3d and 4th dumas and a leader of opposition groups; minister of foreign affairs in Prince Lvov's provisional government (1917); fled after Bolshevik revolution; settled in Paris after the peace (1919) and edited a journal (1921) advocating a patriotic Socialist alliance.

**Mi·lyu′tin** (myĭ·lyōō′tyĭn), **Dmitri Alekseevich.** 1816–1912. Russian general; as minister of war (1862–81), put into effect his program for army reorganization; created field marshal (1888). Author of *A History of the War of 1799...*(1853). His brother **Nikolai Alekseevich** (1818–1872) was a statesman who assisted Emperor Alexander II in introducing important administrative reforms and in effecting emancipation of the serfs; secretary of state for Poland (1866–68).

**Mim·ner′mus** (mĭm·nûr′mŭs). Greek elegiac poet of late 7th century B.C., of Colophon; only fragments of his works are extant.

**Mi′na** (mē′nä), **Francisco Es·poz′ y** (ās·pôth′ē). 1781–1836. Spanish soldier; conducted guerrilla warfare against the French in Spain (1808–14). In exile (1815–20), but returned to fight for liberals of Galicia, León, and Catalonia (1820); later, was involved in insurrection against King Ferdinand (1830); recalled from exile to command Spanish army fighting the Carlists (1835); induced regent, Maria Christina, to grant new constitution (1836). His nephew **Francisco Javier Mina** (1789–1817) fought with him against the French in Spain (1808–09); was prisoner of war (1810–14); took up arms against Ferdinand (1814) and went to U.S.; interested himself in cause of Mexican revolutionists and led force into Mexico; captured and shot.

**Mi·na·mo·to** (mē·nä·mô·tô). *Also known, esp. contemporaneously, by Chinese name* **Gen·ji** (gĕn·jē). A Japanese military feudal clan, or family, whose shoguns were in power, 1185–1219. The clan originated with younger princes of an emperor of 9th century A.D.; as the families became numerous, they were divided into four branches, in one of which Yoritomo (*q.v.*) gained leadership after defeat of Taira clan (1185) and became first Minamoto shogun (1192–99). Descendants of Minamoto Yoritomo ceased to rule (1219) but family remained influential for many years in the Ashikagas and Tokugawas.

**Mincho.** See CHO DENSU.

**Mind** (mĭnt), **Gottfried.** 1768–1814. Called the "Raphael of Cats." Cretinic Swiss painter, sketcher, and lithographer, esp. of cats and other animals, and of groups of children.

**Ming** (mĭng), *i.e.* Illustrious. A Chinese dynasty (1368–1644) founded by Chu Yüan-chang (as emperor, Hung Wu), who overthrew the Yüan or Mongol dynasty (1368). Under its seventeen rulers (chief ones: Yung Lo, Chia Ching, and Wan Li), the Portuguese and Jesuits established themselves in China, the Manchus set up a rival kingdom at Mukden (1625), which later overthrew the Mings. The Mings upheld a high level of culture and art; esp. famous for bronze vases and porcelains; in painting, Tai Chin was important; in philosophy, the teachings of Chu Hsi still predominated although opposed by Wang Yang-ming.

**Ming′er** (mĭng′ẽr), **Rudolf.** 1881–1955. Swiss statesman; member of Federal Council (from 1929); elected its president (1935).

**Min·ghet′ti** (mēng·gāt′tē), **Marco.** 1818–1886. Italian statesman, writer, and scholar; served in Piedmontese army under Charles Albert; minister of exterior (1860–61), interior (1861–62), finance (1862–63), agriculture and commerce (1869); premier (1863–64, 1873–76); ambassador to London (1868) and Vienna (1870–73). Among his works are *Dell'Economia Pubblica* (1859), *Stato e Chiesa* (1878), a biography of Raphael (1885).

**Min·got′ti** (mēng·gôt′tē), **Re·gi′na** (*Ital.* rā·jē′nä; *Ger.* -gē′-), *nee* **Va′len·ti′ni** (vä′lān·tē′nē). 1722?–1808. Italian operatic soprano, b. Naples, of German parentage; m. Pietro Mingotti, impresario of Dresden opera; rival of Faustina Bordoni, wife of the composer Hasse; sang in Naples, Madrid (1752–54), Paris, and London.

**Ming Ti** (mĭng′ dē′). 28–75 A.D. Chinese emperor (58–75), second of the Eastern Han dynasty; according to legend sent envoys to India, as the result of a dream, to inquire about Buddhism, which later was introduced into China.

**Mi′nié′** (mē′nyā′; *Angl.* mĭn′ĭ·ā), **Claude Étienne.** 1814–1879. French army officer; inventor of a rifle and a conical lead bullet which expanded to take the rifling.

**Min·kow′ski** (mĭng·kôf′skē), **Hermann.** 1864–1909. Mathematician, b. in Russia; professor, Königsberg (1895), Zurich (1896), Göttingen (1902). Made studies in field of theory of numbers; credited with laying mathematical foundation for theory of relativity in his *Raum und Zeit* (1907) and *Zwei Abhandlungen über die Grundgleichungen der Elektrodynamik* (1909).

**Minnewit, Peter.** See Peter MINUIT.

**Min′ni·ge·rode** (mĭn′ĭ·gĕ·rōd), **Meade.** 1887–1967. American writer, b. in London, Eng., of American parentage. Author of *Laughing House* (1920), *The Big Year* (1921), *Oh, Susanna* (1922), *The Fabulous Forties* (1924), *Some American Ladies* (1926), *Presidential Years* (1928), *Jefferson, Friend of France* (1928), *The Magnificent Comedy* (1931), *Marie Antoinette's Henchman* (1936), *Black Forest* (1937), etc.

**Mino da Fiesole.** See Mino da FIESOLE.

**Mi′nor** (mē′nôr), **Jakob.** 1855–1912. Austrian literary historian and philologist; professor of Germanic philology, Vienna (from 1885). Author of *Schiller* (2 vols., 1889–90), *Neuhochdeutsche Metrik* (1893), of a commentary on part I of Goethe's *Faust* (2 vols., 1901), and of editions of works of Novalis (4 vols., 1907), Ferdinand von Saar (12 vols., 1909), A. W. and F. Schlegel, Ludwig J. von Arnim, Tieck, Wackenroder, and others.

**Mi′nor** (mī′nēr), **Robert Cran′nell** (krăn′'l). 1839–1904. American landscape painter, b. New York City; known for paintings in the style of the Barbizon school.

**Mi′not** (mī′nŭt), **Charles Sedgwick.** 1852–1914. American biologist and educator; taught in Harvard medical school (1880–1914). Wrote *Human Embryology* (1892), *The Problem of Age, Growth, and Death* (1908), etc.

**Minot, George Richards.** 1885–1950. American physician, b. Boston; grad. Harvard (1908); professor of medicine, Harvard (1928–48). Awarded, jointly with William P. Murphy and George H. Whipple, Nobel prize in medicine (1934) for researches on liver treatment of the anemias.

**Minot, Laurence.** 1300?–?1352. English lyric poet; author of spirited war songs celebrating in various meters battle of Halidon Hill (1333), capture of Berwick, battle of Crécy, siege of Calais, and other triumphs of Edward III.

**Min′sheu** (mĭn′shōō), **John.** fl. 1617. English lexicographer; teacher of languages in London; published Spanish dictionary and grammar and *Guide into Tongues*, a lexicon with equivalents in eleven languages (1617), first English book published by subscription.

**Min′to** (mĭn′tō), Baronets, barons, and earls of. See ELLIOT family.

**Minto, William.** 1845–1893. Scottish man of letters and critic; contributor to *Encyclopaedia Britannica;* author of *English Prose Writers* (1872), *English Poets* (1874), and three novels.

**Min′ton** (mĭn′t'n; -tŭn), **Sherman.** 1890–1965. American jurist, b. Georgetown, Ind. Member, U.S. Senate (1935–41); assoc. justice, U.S. Supreme Court (1949–56).

**Minton, Thomas.** 1765–1836. English pottery manufacturer at Stoke on Trent; maker of majolica and reproductions of works of della Robbia and Palissy. His son **Herbert** (1793–1858), his partner (1817–36), sole proprietor thereafter, produced under direction of Léon Arnoux porcelain rivaling that of Sèvres.

**Min′turn** (mĭn′tērn), **Robert Bowne** (boun). 1805–1866. American merchant and shipowner, b. New York City; proprietor of packet lines to Liverpool and London; instrumental in founding in New York the Association for Improving the Condition of the Poor; aided his wife, **Anna Mary,** *nee* **Wen′dell** (wĕn′d'l), in promoting the project for establishing Central Park.

**Mi·nu′ci·us Fe′lix** (mĭ·nū′shĭ·ŭs [-shŭs] fē′lĭks), **Marcus.** Latin writer of 3d century A.D.; converted to Christianity and wrote a dialogue, *Octavius* (earliest known work of Latin Christian literature), purporting to be a colloquy between a Christian and a pagan in which the Christian refutes all charges brought by people against the new religion.

**Min′u·it** (mĭn′ū·ĭt; mē′nwē′) *or* **Min′ne·wit** (mĭn′ĕ·wĭt), **Pe′ter** (pē′tēr). 1580–1638. Colonial official in America, b. Wesel, Duchy of Cleves; in New Netherland (New York) about 1626; director-general of Dutch colony of New Netherland (1626–31); purchased Manhattan Island from the Indians for trinkets valued at sixty guilders ($24); established forts for colonial defense; recalled (1631). Commissioned by West India Company to establish Swedish colony on Delaware Bay; sailed (1637) and bought (1638) land near what is now Trenton, N.J., from Indians; named country New Sweden and served as its governor. Lost at sea (1638).

**Mi·nu′to·li** (mē·nōō′tō·lē), Baron **Heinrich Me′nu von** (mā′nōō fōn). 1772–1846. Prussian officer and archaeologist, b. Geneva, of Italian extraction. Distinguished himself in Rhenish campaign against France (1793). Head of Prussian archaeological expedition to Egypt (1820–21); made valuable Egyptian collection, bought for Berlin museum by king of Prussia; retired to Lausanne.

**Mio′man′dre** (myô′mäɴ′dr'), **Francis de.** 1880–1959. French writer; author of *Écrit sur de l'Eau* (awarded Goncourt prize; 1908), *Figures d'Hier et d'Aujourd'hui* (1911), *La Cabane d'Amour* (1919), *L'Ombre et l'Amour* (1925), *Baroque* (1930), etc.

**Mion′net′** (myô′nĕ′), **Théodore Edme.** 1770–1842. French numismatist.

**Miot de Me·li′to** (myō′ dē mȧ·lē′tō), Comte **André François.** 1762–1841. French politician; secretary-general of foreign affairs (1793–95); aided Joseph Bonaparte in pacification of Corsica (1796); secretary-general of war department (1798) and a councilor of state; with Joseph Bonaparte in Italy and Spain (1806–13); created comte (1814). Author of translations of Herodotus (3 vols., 1822) and Diodorus (7 vols., 1835–38).

**Mi′quel** (mē′kĕl), **Johannes von.** 1828–1901. German statesman; converted to socialism by writings of Karl Marx; a founder of German Nationalverein. Member of Prussian parliament (1867); entered Reichstag (1887); minister of finance (1890–1900); reformed Prussian system of taxation; attempted to improve condition of poor.

**Mi′ra′beau′** (mē′rȧ′bō′; *Angl.* mĭr′ȧ·bō), Marquis **de. Victor Ri′que·ti′** (rēk′tē′). 1715–1789. French soldier and economist; in economics, disciple of Quesnay and the physiocrats; author of *L'Ami des Hommes ou Traité sur la Population* (1756), *Philosophie Rurale* (1763), *Économiques* (1769), etc. Father of Honoré Gabriel Victor Riqueti, Comte de Mirabeau (see Comte de MIRABEAU), and **André Boniface Louis Riqueti,** Vicomte **de Mirabeau** (1754–1792), soldier and politician; served in American army (1780–85); member of States-General (1789); royalist in sympathy; an émigré (from c. 1790).

**Mirabeau,** Comte **de. Honoré Gabriel Victor Ri′que·ti′** (rēk′tē′). 1749–1791. Son of Victor Riqueti, Marquis de Mirabeau. French orator and revolutionary leader, b. near Nemours; joined cavalry regiment (1767); imprisoned several times for intrigues and wild conduct (1774–80); lived in England (1784); wrote pamphlets attacking Necker (1787–89); made three visits to Germany (1786–88); published *De la Monarchie Prussienne sous Frédéric le Grand* (1788). Sent by the Third Estate as deputy for Aix and Marseilles to States-General (1789);

most important figure in first two years of French Revolution. Influence in the National Assembly exerted by oratory and personality; believed strongly in a limited or constitutional monarchy; ably defended his conservative constitutional measures; often defeated, but his ideas influenced assembly. Broke with Necker and Lafayette. President of Jacobin Club (1790); elected president of National Assembly (1791), but died soon after.

**Mirabeau,** Comtesse **de.** *Nee* **Marie de Gonne′ville′** (dē gôn′vēl′). 1827–1914. French writer; m. Comte Arundel Joseph de Mirabeau (d. 1860). Wrote for *La Mode, Le Figaro, La Vie Parisienne;* author of *Les Jeunes Filles Pauvres* (1863), *Hélène de Gardannes* (1868), *Jane et Germaine* (1875), *Chut!!!* (1880), *Cœur d'Or* (1896). Mother of Comtesse de Martel de Janville (*q.v.*).

**Mi′ra de A·mes′cua** (mē′rä thā ä·mās′kwä), **Antonio.** 1578?–1644. Spanish ecclesiastic and playwright; chaplain to Cardinal Prince Ferdinand of Austria (from 1619). Among his dramas are *El Esclavo del Diablo, El Galan Valiente y Discreto,* and *El Palacio Confuso.*

**Mi′ra·flo′res** (mē′rä·flō′rās), Marqués **de. Manuel de Pan′do** (dā pän′dō). 1792–1872. Spanish statesman; ambassador in London (1834) and Paris (1838–40); premier of Spain (1846, 1863); author of works on contemporary Spanish history.

**Mi′ra′mion′** (mē′rå′myôɴ′), **Marie,** *nee* **Bon′neau′ de Ru′belles′** (bô′nō′ dē rü′bĕl′). 1629–1696. French philanthropist; m. Jean Jacques de Beauharnais, Seigneur de Miramion (1645; d. 1646); devoted herself to charitable undertakings; established community for girls at Sainte-Pélagie which developed into Congrégation des Miramiones, of which she became superior.

**Mi′ra·món′** (mē′rä·môn′), **Miguel.** 1832–1867. Mexican soldier; head of reactionary political faction (1859) and commander of forces fighting against Juárez (1859–60); defeated (Dec. 22, 1860), he fled into exile. Supported Maximilian in Mexico (1866–67); captured and shot with him.

**Mi·ran′da** (mē·rän′dä), **Francisco.** 1750?–1816. Venezuelan revolutionist, b. Caracas; served in Spanish army (1773–82); general of division in French revolutionary armies (1792–93); commanded patriot army in Venezuela (1810); dictator of Venezuela (Apr., 1812); fought vainly against royalists and finally forced to sign treaty (July 25, 1812) yielding country to them; was arrested, sent to Spain, and died in prison.

**Mi·ran′da** (mē·räɴn′då), **Sá de.** See Sá de Miranda.

**Mirandola.** See Pico della Mirandola.

**Mir′beau′** (mēr′bō′), **Octave Henri Marie.** 1850–1917. French journalist; dramatic critic on *L'Ordre;* a founder of weekly satirical paper *Grimaces* (1882); known as a radical, attacking vigorously all forms of social organization. Among his novels are *Le Calvaire* (1886), *La Famille Cannettes* (1888), *Le Jardin des Supplices* (1898), and *Dingo* (1912); among his plays, *Les Mauvais Bergers* (1897), *L'Épidémie* (1898), *Le Portefeuille* (1902), and *Les Affaires sont les Affaires* (1903).

**Mir′bel′** (mēr′bĕl′), **Charles François Bris′seau′ de** (brē′sō′ dē). 1776–1854. French botanist; known for work on the cell and in embryology.

**Mirbel, Lizinka Aimée Zoé,** *nee* **Rue** (rü). 1796–1849. French portrait painter; m. Charles François Brisseau de Mirbel (1823); portrait painter to Louis XVIII and Charles X.

**Mir′cea** (mēr′chä). d. 1418. Known as "Mircea the Great." Prince of Walachia; famed for success in maintaining independence of Walachia in spite of designs of Hungary, Poland, and Turkey (to 1412); forced to acknowledge sovereignty of Turkey (1412).

**Mi′re·court′** (mēr′kōōr′), **Eugène de.** *Pseudonym of* **Charles Jean Baptiste Jac′quot′** (zhå′kō′). 1812–1880. French journalist; author of series of biographical sketches (*Galerie des Contemporains, Les Contemporains*) which resulted in his being forced to leave Paris; also wrote *Les Confessions de Marion Delorme* (1848–52), *Mémoires de Ninon de Lenclos* (1854), *Histoire Contemporaine* (1866–67), etc.

**Mir′i·am** (mĭr′ĭ·ăm). *In Douay Version* **Mary.** In the Bible, sister of Moses and Aaron (*Exodus* xv. 20; cf. ii. 4–8).

**Mi′riam** (mē′ryäm). See Zenon Przesmycki.

**Mir Ja′far** (mēr jä′fēr). 1691–1765. Indian general and ruler; in service of nawab, Siraj-ud-daula, of Bengal; plotted against him in secret agreement with Clive and the British; his treason at Plassey (1757) aided the British; as reward was made nawab but forced to cede much territory; deposed by British (1760); reinstated (1763–65).

**Mir Ka′sim** (mēr kä′sĭm). d. 1777. Nawab of Bengal (1760–63); opposed East India Company and sought independence; quarrels with company led to general uprising against British (1763); caused massacre at Patna of more than 125 British; deposed (1763) and completely defeated in battle of Buxar (1764); fled to Oudh.

**Mir·khond′** (mēr·ĸŏnd′). *Orig. Pers. name* **Mir·khvand′** (mēr·ĸvänd′). *Properly* **Muḥammad ibn-Khavand Shah ibn-Maḥmud.** 1433–1498. Persian historian; author of *Rauẓat-uṣ-Ṣafā* (*Garden of Purity*), containing brief biographies of Persian notables from legendary times to his own day.

**Mi·ró′** (mē·rô′), **Esteban Rodríguez.** 1744–1795. Spanish governor of Louisiana (1785–91), b. Catalonia, Spain; notorious for his intrigue with James Wilkinson (*q.v.*).

**Miró, Joan** (zhwän). 1893–1974. Spanish painter, engraver, and sculptor, b. in Catalonia; associated with surrealist and abstract movements; lived alternately in Spain and France (from 1919).

**Mi′ro·ne′scu** (mē′rŏ·nĕ′skōō), **George.** 1874–1949. Rumanian lawyer and statesman; leader, National Peasant party; minister of foreign affairs (1928–31); prime minister of Rumania (1930, 1930–31); vice-premier (1932–33); minister without portfolio (1938).

**Mir·za′** (mēr·zä′). A title of honor in Persia.

**Misach.** See Shadrach.

**Misch** (mĭsh), **Georg.** 1878–1965. German philosopher; author of *Lebensphilosophie und Phänomenologie,* etc.

**Mi′ses** (mē′zes) **Ludwig Edler von.** 1881–1973. Austrian economist; professor successively at Vienna and Geneva; author of *Theorie des Geldes und der Umlaufsmittel* (1912), *Liberalismus* (1927), *Grundprobleme der Nationalokonomie* (1933), etc.

**Mises, Richard von.** 1883–1953. German mathematician; authority on aerodynamics, hydrodynamics, elasticity, and probability; professor, Dresden (1919), Berlin (1920–33), Istanbul (1933–39), Harvard U. (from 1939).

**Mi′šić** (mē′shēt·y′; *Angl.* -shĭch), **Živojin.** 1855–1921. Serbian general; commanded 1st Serbian army in World War (1914–18); chief of staff (June, 1918).

**Misitheus.** See Timesitheus.

**Mis′tral′** (mēs′trål′), **Frédéric.** 1830–1914. Provençal poet; helped found Félibrige organization of modern Provençal poets (1854) and became active leader in Provençal renaissance and its establishment as literary language; shared Nobel prize for literature with José Echegaray y Eizaguirre (1904). Works include Provençal-French dictionary *Tresor dou Félibrige* (2 vols., 1879–86), and, in Provençal and French, the pastoral poem *Mirèio* (1859), the collection of lyrics and narrative poems *Lis Isclo d'Or* (1875), the historical epic *Nerto* (1884), the dramatic poem *La Rèino Jano* (1890), the epic *Lou Pouèmo dou Rose* (1897), and the collection *Lis Oulivado* (1912).

**Mis·tral'** (mēs·träl'), **Gabriela.** *Real name* **Lucila Go·doy' de Al'ca·ya'ga** (gō·thoi' thā äl'kä·yä'gä). 1889–1957. Chilean poet and educator, b. Vicuña; consul (from 1933) in Madrid, Lisbon, Genoa, etc., and in Los Angeles (from 1946); poems collected in *Gabriela Mistral's Anthology* (1942); awarded 1945 Nobel prize for literature.

**Mitch'el** (mĭch'ĕl), **John.** 1815–1875. Irish patriot, b. in County Londonderry, Ireland; practiced law (from 1840); joined Young Ireland movement (1845); founded and edited *United Irishmen* (1847) to advocate repeal of the Act of Union and armed resistance to England; tried, convicted, and transported (1848); escaped from Van Diemen's Land to America (1853); in newspaper work and lecturing in U.S. (1853–75); elected to English parliament from Tipperary (1875), but declared ineligible. Author of *Jail Journal* (1854); *The Crusade of the Period: and Last Conquest of Ireland: Perhaps* (1873). His grandson **John Pur'roy** (pûr'oi) **Mitchel** (1879–1918), b. Fordham, N.Y., was a lawyer; mayor of New York (1914–18); killed in airplane accident (July 6, 1918) while training for army aviation corps.

**Mitchel, Ormsby MacKnight.** 1809–1862. American astronomer, b. in Union County, Ky.; grad. U.S.M.A., West Point (1829); resigned from U.S. army (1832); professor, Cincinnati Coll. (1836–59); did much to popularize astronomy; director, Dudley Observatory, Albany, N.Y. (1859–61); commissioned brigadier general at outbreak of Civil War; promoted major general (1862); died of yellow fever. Author of *Planetary and Stellar Worlds* (1848), *Popular Astronomy* (1860).

**Mitch'ell** (mĭch'ĕl), **Donald Grant.** *Pseudonym* **Ik** (ĭk) **Mar'vel** (mär'vĕl; -v'l). 1822–1908. Grandson of Stephen Mix Mitchell. American author, b. Norwich, Conn.; U.S. consul at Venice, Italy (1853–54); resident at his estate "Edgewood," near New Haven, Conn. (from 1855). Author of *Reveries of a Bachelor* (1850), *Dream Life* (1851), *My Farm of Edgewood* (1863), *Doctor Johns* (1866), *English Lands, Letters and Kings* (4 vols., 1889–97), *American Lands and Letters* (2 vols., 1897–99).

**Mitchell, Elisha.** 1793–1857. American geologist and botanist, b. Washington, Conn.; professor, U. of North Carolina (1818–57); known for his explorations of North Carolina mountain regions. Mount Mitchell, in Yancey County, is named in his honor.

**Mitchell, Henry.** 1830–1902. American hydrographer, b. Nantucket, Mass.; with U.S. Coast Survey (1849–88); author of *Tides and Tidal Phenomena* (1868), *The Under-Run of the Hudson* (1888), etc. His sister **Maria** (1818–1889) was an astronomer, discoverer of a new comet (Oct., 1847), first professor of astronomy at Vassar College (1865–89). Elected to American Hall of Fame (1905).

**Mitchell, John.** d. 1768. Physician, botanist, and cartographer; appeared in Virginia about 1725; best known for his large-scale *Map of the British and French Dominions in North America...* (1755), a map used in various boundary negotiations in later history.

**Mitchell, John.** 1870–1919. American labor leader, b. Braidwood, Ill.; coal miner (from 1882); member, Knights of Labor (1885–90), United Mine Workers of America (from 1890); president, United Mine Workers of America (1898–1908). Organized and directed anthracite coal miners' strike (1902) in such way as to gain reputation as greatest labor leader of his time. Chairman, New York State Industrial Commission (1915–19). Author of *Organized Labor* (1903), *The Wage Earner and His Problems* (1913).

**Mitchell, John Ames.** 1845–1918. American artist, editor, and novelist, b. New York City; founded and edited *Life* magazine (1883–1918).

**Mitchell, Langdon Elwyn.** *Pseudonym* **John Philip Var'ley** (vär'lĭ). 1862–1935. American playwright, b. Philadelphia; son of S. Weir Mitchell. Author of *Becky Sharp* (a dramatization of Thackeray's *Vanity Fair*), *The New York Idea*, *The Kreutzer Sonata* (adapted from the Yiddish of Jacob Gordin), and volumes of verse.

**Mitchell, Margaret.** 1900–1949. American writer, b. Atlanta, Ga.; m. John R. Marsh (1925); author of the novel *Gone With the Wind* (1936; awarded Pulitzer prize, 1937).

**Mitchell, Margaret Julia,** *known as* **Maggie.** 1837–1918. American actress, b. New York City; excelled in comedy roles, esp. as Fanchon in *Fanchon the Cricket*, a play adapted for her from George Sand's *Le Petite Fadette*.

**Mitchell, Nahum.** 1769–1853. American jurist, b. East Bridgewater, Mass.; collaborator with Bartholomew Brown and others on the "Bridgewater collection" (*The Columbian and European Harmony: or Bridgewater Collection of Sacred Music;* 1802).

**Mitchell,** Sir **Peter Chalmers.** 1864–1945. British zoologist, b. Dunfermline; author of *Outlines of Biology* (1894), *The Nature of Man* (1904), *Materialism and Vitalism in Biology* (1930), *My House in Málaga* (1938).

**Mitchell, Peter Dennis.** 1920– . English biochemist. At Cambridge U. (1943–55), U. of Edinburgh (1955–63); awarded Nobel prize for chemistry (1978).

**Mitchell, Ruth Comfort.** d. 1954. Amer. writer, b. San Francisco; m. Sanborn Young. Author of *The Night Court and Other Verse* (1916), *Play the Game* (1921), *Narratives in Verse* (1923), *The Wishing Carpet* (1926), *Army with Banners* (1928), *The Legend of Susan Dane* (1933), *Strait Gate* (1935), etc.

**Mitchell, Samuel Augustus.** 1792–1868. American geographer, b. Bristol, Conn.; settled in Philadelphia, where he prepared textbooks, maps, and geographic manuals, including *Mitchell's Geographical Reader* (1840), *Map of the United States and Territories* (1861), etc.

**Mitchell, Silas Weir.** 1829–1914. American physician and author, b. Philadelphia; grad. Jefferson Med. Coll. (1850); practiced, Philadelphia; surgeon in Union army in Civil War. Specialized in study and treatment of nervous disorders; author of *Wear and Tear* (1871), *Injuries of Nerves and Their Consequences* (1872), *Fat and Blood* (1877), etc.; also wrote poetry and fiction: poetry, *The Hill of Stones* (1882), *A Psalm of Deaths, and Other Poems* (1890), *Francis Drake—A Tragedy of the Sea* (1893), *The Mother and Other Poems* (1893), *The Comfort of the Hills* (1909); fiction, *In War Time* (1885), *Roland Blake* (1886), *Hugh Wynne, Free Quaker* (1898), *The Adventures of François* (1899), *The Autobiography of a Quack* (1900), *Constance Trescott* (1905), *The Red City* (1907), *John Sherwood, Inn Master* (1911), *Westways* (1913).

**Mitchell, Stephen Mix.** 1743–1835. American jurist and legislator, b. Wethersfield, Conn.; member, Continental Congress (1783–88), U.S. Senate (1793–95); chief justice, Connecticut supreme court (1807–14). See Donald Grant MITCHELL.

**Mitchell,** Sir **Thomas Livingstone.** 1792–1855. Scottish explorer in Australia; deputy surveyor general, New South Wales (1828); known for four expeditions into interior of Australia (1831–45); seeking overland route to Gulf of Carpentaria, found sources of Barcoo River (1845–47).

**Mitchell, Wesley Clair.** 1874–1948. American economist, b. Rushville, Ill.; professor, U. of California (1909–12), Columbia (1914–19; from 1922); director of New School for Social Research (1919–31). Author of *A His-*

*tory of the Greenbacks* (1903), *Gold Prices and Wages Under the Greenback Standard* (1908), *Business Cycles, the Problem and its Setting* (1927), *The Backward Art of Spending Money* (1937), etc.

**Mitchell, William.** 1879–1936. American army officer, b. at Nice, France, of American parentage; entered army as private soldier (1898); promoted through grades to brigadier general (1920); served in Spanish-American War, Philippine Insurrection, on Mexican border, and in France in World War; commander of the air forces, A.E.F. (1917–18). Court-martialed for insubordination because of his criticism of War and Navy Departments for mismanagement of aviation service (1925); convicted, and sentenced to suspension from the service for five years; resigned from U.S. army (1926). Author of *Our Air Force* (1921), *Winged Defense* (1925), *Skyways* (1930).

**Mitchell, William DeWitt.** 1874–1955. American lawyer, army officer, and politician, b. Winona, Minn.; practiced law in St. Paul; served in Spanish-American War and World War I; U.S. solicitor general (1925–29), attorney general (1929–33); chief counsel (1945) for Congressional investigation of Pearl Harbor attack.

**Mitchell–Thomson, William.** See Baron SELSDON.

**Mitch′ill** (mĭch′ĭl), **Samuel Latham.** 1764–1831. American physician and legislator, b. North Hempstead, N.Y.; practiced in New York; professor, Columbia (1792–1801); defended Lavoisier's chemical theories; a founder of the *Medical Repository*, and editor of it (1797–1820). Member, U.S. House of Representatives (1801–04; 1810–13), U.S. Senate (1804–09). Professor, Coll. Phys. & Surg., New York (1807–26); an organizer and vice-president, Rutgers Med. Coll. (1826–30). Author esp. of papers on natural history.

**Mitch′i·son** (mĭch′ĭ·s'n), **Naomi Margaret,** *nee* **Hal′dane** (hôl′dān). 1897– . British writer, b. Edinburgh; m. G. R. Mitchison (1916). Author of *Cloud Cuckoo Land* (1925), *The Laburnum Branch* (verse; 1926), *Barbarian Stories* (1929), *The Delicate Fire* (stories and poems; 1933), *The Fourth Pig* (1936), *The Blood of the Martyrs* (1939).

**Mit′ford** (mĭt′fērd), **John.** 1781–1859. English clergyman; friend of Samuel Rogers and Charles Lamb; editor and contributor to *Gentleman's Magazine* (1834–50); author of *Miscellaneous Poems* (1858); did chief critical work and research for *Works of Thomas Gray* (1814) and eleven memoirs for "Aldine" edition of English poets (1835–43).

**Mitford, Mary Russell.** 1787–1855. English novelist and dramatist; daughter of spendthrift physician; at age of ten, drew £20,000 in a lottery; published poems (1810, 1811, 1812, 1813); reduced to poverty by father's improvidence, wrote for magazines and stage; contributed to *Lady's Magazine* sketches of country life that ultimately became *Our Village* (5 vols., 1824–32), her best-known work. Author also of *Belford Regis* (novel, 1835), *Recollections of a Literary Life* (1852), *Atherton* (novel, 1854), and four tragedies, *Julian* (1823), *The Foscari* (1826), *Rienzi* (1828), and *Charles I* (1834).

**Mitford, William.** 1744–1827. English historian; on advice of Gibbon, his fellow officer in militia, undertook *History of Greece* (5 vols., 1784–1810), which enjoyed long-continued popularity and held highest place among scholars until superseded by histories of Grote and Thirlwall. His brother **John Free′man–Mit′ford** [frē′măn-] (1748–1830), 1st Baron **Redes′dale** (rēdz′dāl); barrister; M.P. (1788); Welsh judge (1789); solicitor general (1793); attorney general (1799); speaker of House of Commons (1801); lord chancellor of Ireland with title Baron Redesdale (1802); unpopular in Ireland because of outspoken opposition to Roman Catholic emancipation; active in House of Lords (after 1806); author, with Samuel Tyler, of *Pleadings and Practice in Equity.* William's great-grandson **Algernon Bertram Freeman–Mitford** (1837–1916), 1st Baron Redesdale of 2d creation, was attaché in Japan (1866–70); secretary to Board of Works (1874–86); assumed additional name and arms of cousin (1886); M.P. (1892); author of *Tales of Old Japan* (1871) and autobiography.

**Mith′ri·da′tes** (mĭth′rĭ·dā′tēz). *More correctly* **Mith′ra·da′tes** (mĭth′rȧ-). Name of five kings of Parthia, of Arsacid dynasty, especially:

**Mithridates I.** *Called also* **Arsaces VI.** King (171–138 B.C.). Brother of Phraates I. Assumed title **Phil′hel·lene** (fĭl′hĕ·lēn; fĭl·hĕl′ēn). Real founder of Parthian Empire; conquered Babylonia and Media, defeating the Seleucids; also, later, added Elam, Persia, etc.

**Mithridates II.** *Called* **the Great.** King (124?–87 B.C.). Defeated Scythians; established trade with China along Silk Route; made treaty with Rome (92 B.C.); conquered Mesopotamia (90?); after his death, Parthia overrun by Tigranes of Armenia.

**Mithridates III.** King (56–55 B.C.). Usurped throne; killed after short reign.

**Mithridates V.** King (129?–147 A.D.).

**Mithridates.** *More correctly* **Mithradates.** Name of six kings (the **Mith′ri·da′tids** [mĭth′rĭ·dā′tĭdz], *Lat.* **Mith′ri·dat′i·dae** [-dăt′ĭ·dē]) of Pontus, especially:

**Mithridates IV Phi·lop′a·tor Phil′a·del′phus** (fĭ·lŏp′ȧ·tôr fĭl′ȧ·dĕl′fŭs). King (170?–?150 B.C.).

**Mithridates V Eu·er′ge·tes** (ū·ûr′jĕ·tēz). King (150?–?121 B.C.); made alliance with Romans; assassinated.

**Mithridates VI Eu′pa·tor** (ū′pȧ·tôr). *Called* **the Great.** c. 132–63 B.C. King (120–63 B.C.); son of Mithridates V; little known of his youth or early part of his reign; gradually became master of Cappadocia, Paphlagonia, Bithynia, and all southern and eastern coast regions of Black Sea; conflict with kings of Bithynia aroused opposition of Romans; waged three wars against Rome: First Mithridatic War (88–84 B.C.); successful at first until his general in Greece was defeated by Sulla at Chaeronea and at Orchomenus (86); forced to sign peace (84) by Sulla and pay heavy damages. Second Mithridatic War (83–81 B.C.); defeated Roman army that invaded Pontus. Third Mithridatic War (74–64 B.C.); occupied Bithynia, which had been bequeathed to Rome; driven out of Pontus (72–71) by L. Licinius Lucullus to court of Tigranes of Armenia; reconquered Pontus (68–67), but defeated by Pompey (66); fled to the Crimea (65); committed suicide. Had great military ability; one of most formidable opponents Rome ever had.

**Mi′tra** (mĭ′trȧ), **Ra·jen′dra·la′la** (rä·jān′drȧ·lä′lȧ). 1824–1891. Indian Orientalist, b. Calcutta; appointed librarian of the Asiatic Society (1846); devoted his life to work of the society as philological secretary, vice-president, and first Indian president (1885); edited about 80 Sanskrit texts. Most important of his works are *The Antiquities of Orissa* (2 vols., 1875, 1880), *Buddha Gaya, the Hermitage of Sakya Muni* (1878), and *Indo-Aryans* (2 vols., 1881).

**Mi′tre** (mē′trā), **Bartolomé.** 1821–1906. Argentine statesman, military leader, and historian, b. Buenos Aires. As fugitive from Rosas regime, lived as journalist in Bolivia, Chile, and Peru. Supported Urquiza (1851); active in affairs of Buenos Aires province (1853–62); defeated Urquiza at Pavon (1861); president of Argentina (1862–68); in alliance with Brazil and Uruguay, conducted successful war against Paraguay (1865–70). Author of *Historia de Belgrano y de la Independencia Argentina* (1858–76) and *Historia de San Martín y de la Emancipación Sud-Americana* (1887).

**Mi·tro′pou·los** (mē·trô′po͞o·lôs), **Di·mi′tri** (thē·mē′-trē). 1896–1960. Greek orchestra conductor and composer; director and conductor, Minneapolis Symphony Orchestra (from 1937); composer of orchestral, piano, and vocal works, music dramas, and chamber music.

**Mi′try′** (mē′trē′), **Marie Antoine Henry de.** 1857–1924. French general in the World War; engaged with distinction on the Marne, the Aisne, and in 2d battle of the Marne.

**Mitsch′er·lich** (mĭch′ēr·lĭk), **Eilhardt.** 1794–1863. German chemist; discovered isomorphism of permanganic acid and selenic acid; decomposed benzoic acid into carbon dioxide and benzene; from benzene, produced nitrobenzene, benzenesulphonic acid, and other derivatives; made researches in chemical geology; produced artificial minerals.

**Mi·tsu·i** (mē·tso͞o·ē). *Orig.* **Ta·ka·hi·sa** (tä·kä·hē·sä). Name of Japanese family, powerful commercially, founded (17th century) by **Takatoshi Mitsui;** after Restoration (1868), accumulated great wealth, expanding to include banking, manufacturing, insurance, shipping, etc. Recent heads of family include barons **Hachiroemon Mitsui** (1857–1948; educ. U.S. and England; created baron, 1900), **Takayasu Mitsui** (1850–1922), and **Takamine Mitsui** (d. 1933).

**Mi·tsu·no·bu** (mē·tso͞o·nō·bo͞o), **Tosa.** 1434–1525. Japanese painter, one of most famous of Tosa school.

**Mitsuyori, Kimura.** See Kano SANRAKU.

**Mit′tel′hau′ser′** (mē′tĕl′ō′zâr′), **Eugène.** 1873–1949. French army commander; served in Algeria and Morocco; general of division (1918); chief of French mission in Czechoslovakia (1919–26).

**Mit′ten** (mĭt′′n), **Thomas Eugene.** 1864–1929. Business executive, b. Brighton, England; to U.S. (1877); street-railway executive (from 1896); official of Philadelphia transit lines (from 1911); known especially for establishment of Mitten Co-operative Plan, giving employees representation on the board of directors and a voice in matters affecting wages and working conditions. Established Mitten Management, Inc., and took over operation of Philadelphia Rapid Transit Co. (1924); failed to live up to contracts; investigation ordered (July, 1929); Mitten drowned, perhaps by suicide (Oct. 1, 1929). Transit Company ordered into receivership (1931) and Mitten management condemned as a "colossal conspiracy against the taxpayers."

**Mit′ter·mai′er** (mĭt′ēr·mī′ēr), **Karl Joseph Anton.** 1787–1867. German jurist and politician, specialist in criminal law. Author of *Grundsätze des Gemeinen Deutschen Privatrechts* (2 vols., 1821), *Das Deutsche Strafverfahren* (2 vols., 1827), and other works on jurisprudence.

**Mi′vart** (mī′värt; -vērt; mĭv′ērt), **St. George Jackson.** 1827–1900. English biologist; professor of biology, Roman Catholic University Coll., Kensington (1874–84); professor of philosophy of natural history, Louvain (1890–93); an evolutionist, insisting upon action of divine power in development of man's mind; critic of Darwin and Huxley as regards natural selection theory; sought to reconcile science and religion; excommunicated for liberalism and repudiation of ecclesiastical authority (1900). Author of *The Genesis of Species* (1871), *American Types of Animal Life* (1894), etc.

**Mjö′en** (myû′ĕn), **Jon Alfred.** 1866– . Norwegian biologist and eugenist; made study of inheritance in man, esp. of mental characteristics.

**Mnemon.** See ARTAXERXES II.

**Mnes′i·cles** (nĕs′ĭ·klēz). Greek architect; designer (c. 437 B.C.) of Propylaea of the Acropolis, Athens.

**Moawiyah** *or* **Mo'awiya.** = MUAWIYAH.

**Mo′berg′** (mo͞o′băr′y′), **Carl Artur Vilhelm.** 1898– Swedish novelist; author of *Väld* (1933), *Sömnlös* (1937), *The Earth is Ours* (1941), etc.

**Mo′ber·ly** (mō′bēr·lĭ), **George.** 1803–1885. English prelate, b. St. Petersburg, Russia; headmaster, Winchester Coll. (1835–66); bishop of Salisbury (1869); urged omission of damnatory clauses in Athanasian Creed (1872); opposed the confessional, esp. in schools (1877). His son **Robert Campbell** (1845–1903) was regius professor of pastoral theology, Oxford, and canon of Christ Church (1892–1903).

**Mö′bi·us** (mû′bē·o͝os), **August Ferdinand.** 1790–1868. German mathematician and astronomer; chief mathematical publication, *Der Baryzentrische Kalkül* (1827), in which he subjects analytical geometry to a new treatment through introduction of homogeneous co-ordinates as well as the principle of duality. His son **Theodor** (1821–1890), professor of Scandinavian language and literature, Kiel (1865–89), edited Norse sagas.

**Möbius, Karl August.** 1825–1908. German zoologist; investigated artificial culture of oysters.

**Möbius, Paul Julius.** 1853–1907. German neurologist; known for work relating to pathological traits of men of genius such as Rousseau, Goethe, Schopenhauer, and Nietzsche.

**Moch·nac′ki** (môk·näts′kē), **Maurycy.** 1803–1835. Polish writer; champion of romanticism in Polish literature.

**Moc′kel′** (mô′kĕl′), **Albert Henri Louis.** 1866–1945. Belgian-French poet and critic; founder and editor (1886–92) of journal *La Wallonie*, organ of Belgian symbolists.

**Moc′quard′** (mô′kȧr′), **Jean François Constant.** 1791–1864. French politician; private secretary of Prince Louis Napoleon (1848) and chief of the cabinet (1848–64).

**Moc′que·reau′** (mô′krō′), Dom **André.** 1849–1930. French Benedictine and music scholar; specialist in Gregorian music; founder and editor of *Paléographie Musicale* (13 vols., 1889–1928), which published photographic reproductions of medieval manuscripts with researches on history of liturgical chants of Roman Catholic Church.

**Moctezuma.** See MONTEZUMA.

**Modanino, Il.** See Guido MAZZONI (1450–1518).

**Mo′der·sohn** (mō′dēr·zōn), **Otto.** 1865–1943. German landscape painter; m. **Paula Beck′er** [bĕk′ēr] (1876–1907), known as **Paula Becker-Modersohn** *and* **Modersohn-Becker,** painter of still lifes, landscapes, and portraits.

**Mod′es·ti′nus** (mŏd′ĕs·tī′nŭs), **Herennius.** fl. about 250 B.C. Roman jurist; studied under Ulpian, and ranked with him, Papinian, Paulus, and Gaius among distinguished Roman jurists.

**Mo′di·glia′ni** (mō′dē·lyä′nē), **Amedeo.** 1884–1920. Italian painter and sculptor; settled in Paris (1906); a leader in modernism in art.

**Mo·djes′ka** (mô·jĕs′kȧ), *orig.* **Mo′drze·jew′ska** (mô′-jĕ·yĕf′skä), **He·le′na** (hĕ·lā′nȧ), *nee* **O′pid** (ô′pēt). 1840–1909. Actress, b. Cracow, Poland; to U.S. (1876); m. Gustav Modrzejewski; Charles Bozenta Chlapowski; on American stage (from 1877); excelled in serious dramatic roles, including Shakespeare's Lady Macbeth, Juliet, Ophelia, Imogen, Ibsen's Nora, Dumas's Camille.

**Mo·djes′ki** (mô·jĕs′kĭ), **Ralph.** *Orig. surname* **Mo′-drze·jew′ski** (mô′jĕ·yĕf′skē). 1861–1940. Engineer, b. Cracow, Poland; son of Helena Modjeska; to U.S.

(1876). Consulting bridge engineer in Chicago (from 1892); chief engineer of McKinley Bridge (St. Louis), Broadway Bridge (Portland, Ore.), Delaware River Bridge (Philadelphia), Huey P. Long Bridge (New Orleans), etc. Member, board of engineers, Quebec Bridge (reconstruction) and Trans-Bay Bridge (San Francisco).

**Moe** (mō), **Jörgen Ingebretsen**. 1813–1882. Norwegian poet, folklorist, and theologian; edited collection of folk songs, ballads, and staves in Norwegian dialects (1840), and *Norwegian Folk and Fairy Tales* (1842–44; with Asbjörnsen); bishop of Kristiansand (1875–81). His son **Moltke** (1859–1913), folklorist and scholar, collaborated with Asbjörnsen and continued collections of tales and folk songs begun by his father and Asbjörnsen.

**Moel′ler** (?mŭl′ẽr), **Philip**. 1880–1958. American playwright, b. New York City; a founder (1914) and director of the Washington Square Players; also, a founder and a director of New York Theatre Guild. Author of *Madame Sand* (1917), *Molière* (1919), *Sophie* (1919), etc.

**Moel′ler van den Bruck** (mûl′ẽr vän [fän] dĕn brŏŏk′), **Arthur**. 1876–1925. German writer on politics, literary history, and sociology; did much to influence new Young Conservative movement and other national groups. Editor, in German, of Poe's works (10 vols., 1901–04) and coeditor of first German edition of Dostoevski's works (22 vols., 1906–15; with Merezhkovski); author of *Das Recht der Jungen Völker* (1919), and *Das Dritte Reich* (1923), title of which became slogan of the Nazis.

**Mof′fat** (mŏf′ăt), **Robert**. 1795–1883. Scottish missionary to South Africa; sent to Namaqualand (1817); moved mission station to Kuruman in Bechuanaland (1825); completed translation of New Testament into Sechuana (1839); visited England (1839–43); established mission among Matabeles; translated Old Testament into Sechuana (1857), also *Pilgrim's Progress* and hymns.

**Mof′fatt** (mŏf′ăt), **James**. 1870–1944. Theologian, b. Glasgow, Scotland; to U.S. (1927) and became professor of church history at Union Theol. Sem., New York (from 1927); author of *Historical New Testament* (1901), *Presbyterianism* (1928), etc.; translator of the New Testament (*The Moffatt New Testament;* 1913), etc.

**Mof′fett** (mŏf′ĕt; -ĭt), **Cleveland Langston**. 1863–1926. American writer of many books of adventure and some successful plays, including *Money Talks* (1906) and *Greater Than the Law* (1912).

**Moffett, William Adger**. 1869–1933. American naval officer; served under Admiral Dewey in battle of Manila Bay (1898); was at Vera Cruz under Admiral Mayo (1914); chief, bureau of aeronautics, with rank of rear admiral (1921–33). Awarded Congressional Medal of Honor for his conduct at the capture of Vera Cruz.

**Mo·gi′la** (mŭ·gyē′lŭ), **Peter**. 1596?–1647. Russian Orthodox Eastern Church prelate, b. in Moldavia, of a noble Wallachian family; metropolitan of Kiev (1632); noteworthy as responsible for *Orthodox Confession*, prepared under his direction by Abbot Kosslowski at Kiev, approved by a provincial synod (1640), and accepted by patriarchs of Constantinople, Jerusalem, Alexandria, and Antioch (1642–43), and by synod of Jerusalem (1672).

**Mogk** (mŏk), **Eugen**. 1854–1939. German philologist; cofounder and editor of *Altnordische Sagabibliothek* (16 vols., 1892–1927); editor of old Norse *Gunnlaugssaga* (1886); author of *Germanische Mythologie* (1890), and contributions on Icelandic literature and Germanic mythology to Paul's *Grundriss der Germanischen Philologie*, etc.

**Mo·gul′** (mô·gŭl′; mō′gŭl). *More correctly* **Mu′ghul** (mōō′gōōl). *Persian* **Mo′ghul** (mō′gōōl). Dynasty of Mongol rulers of India: Baber (1526–30), Humayun (1530–56), Akbar the Great (1556–1605), Jahangir (1605–27), Shah Jahan (1628–58), and Aurangzeb (1658–1707), at whose death it lost its power. Later rulers (1707–1857) were mostly titular emperors only; the last, Bahadur Shah II, was deposed (1857) at the time of the Sepoy Mutiny.

**Mo·ham′med** (mô·hăm′ĕd; -ĭd). Common English form of Arabic *Muḥammad* (from *muḥammad*, "praiseworthy, highly praised"); name of founder of Islam and of other Moslems, and the spelling generally used in this dictionary. **Ma·hom′et** (mȧ·hŏm′ĕt, -ĭt; mā′ô·mĕt, -mĭt) is another Occidental spelling that has been fairly common; other variants are **Mo·ham′ed** (mô·hăm′ĕd; -ĭd) and **Ma·hom′ed** (mȧ·hŏm′ĕd; -ĭd). **Ma·hound′** (mȧ·hound′; -hōōnd′) is an archaic form, influenced by English *hound*. **Mahmud** (Persian and Arabic *Maḥmūd*) is used by some for names of the sultans of Turkey and for Mahmud of Ghazni. **Mehemet** (French *Méhémet*) or **Mehmet** is a modern spelling retained in name of viceroy of Egypt, Mehemet Ali.

**Mohammed.** 570–632 A.D. Son of Abdallah. Arabian prophet and founder of Mohammedan religion, b. Mecca, of tribe of Koreish. Left an orphan and brought up by his uncle abu-Talib; shepherd boy and camel driver, learning habits and languages of the Bedouin; m. (595) Khadija (555?–?620), a rich widow; became merchant; disturbed about low condition of Arabs, their superstition and ignorance; after years of meditation, felt (c. 610) that he had a call as prophet and teacher for his race; for a few years, taught the new religion in secret at Mecca, converting his wife, his cousin and adopted son Ali, his friend abu-Bakr, and a small number of proselytes; first taught openly (c. 613); followers persecuted by Meccan leaders and himself strongly opposed because of his struggle against ancient tribal and religious customs; sought refuge in Taif (c. 620); with loyal followers, fled from Mecca to Yathrib (modern Medina), arriving Sept. 20, 622; Arabic year of the flight (*hegira*) later used to mark beginning of Mohammedan era; enthusiastically received; sought to attain public security at Medina; waged civil war against Meccans, finally successful (620–627); established principles of Islam, embodied in the *Koran;* returned to Mecca as master (629); publicly recognized as chief and prophet (630); extended power to include all Arabia (630–632); died at Medina. After death of Khadija (620), married several wives, chief among them being Aisha, or Ayesha (611–678), daughter of abu-Bakr, "Mother of the Believers," who had great influence over him; **Ibrahim,** his son by the concubine Mary of Egypt, died (632) a few months before his father.

**Mohammed V.** 1913–1961. Sultan of Morocco (1927–57); King of Morocco (1957–61).

**Mohammed.** *Arab.* **Mu·ḥam′mad** (mōō·hăm′măd). Name of several Moorish rulers in southern Spain, esp. **Mohammed I,** Ommiad emir of Córdoba (852–886).

**Mohammed.** Name of eleven Moslem kings of Granada, including: **Mohammed I** (1203–1273), founder of the kingdom, patron of commerce and literature, and builder of palace of the Alhambra. His son and successor **Mohammed II** (1234–1302) increased territory. **Mohammed V** (1334–1391) succeeded to throne (1354) and brought Granada great prosperity. **Mohammed X,** known as "the Brave" (1445?–?1500), warred against Boabdil and against Ferdinand and Isabella; defeated and assassinated. **Mohammed XI** (see BOABDIL).

**Mohammed.** 1029–1072. See ALP ARSLAN.

**Mohammed.** Name of six sultans of Turkey: **Mohammed I** (1387–1421), reigned (1413–1421), consolidated empire. **Mohammed II** (1430–1481), called "the

Conqueror" or "the Great," succeeded father, Murad II (1451); besieged and captured Constantinople (1453), subdued Serbia (1456–58) and conquered Trebizond, Greece, and Crimea, also Albania after death of Scanderbeg (1468); waged first great war with Venice (1463–79), and unsuccessfully besieged Rhodes. **Mohammed III** (1566–1603) succeeded father, Murad III (1595), and waged unsuccessful war against Persia. **Mohammed IV** (1641–1691) succeeded father (1648); surrendered exercise of power to the Kuprili; deposed (1687). **Mohammed V** (1844–1918) succeeded deposed brother, Abdul-Hamid II (1909). **Mohammed VI** (1861–1926) succeeded brother Mohammed V (1918); deposed (1922).

**Mo·ham′med Ah′med** (*Arab.* mŏŏ·hăm′măd ă′măd). *In full* **Mohammed Ahmed ibn-Seyyid Abdullah.** *Called* **the Mah′di** (mä′dē). 1843?–1885. Moslem agitator, b. in province of Dongola, Egyptian Sudan; proclaimed himself mahdi (c. 1880) and overran Egyptian Sudan; besieged and captured Khartoum (1885; see Charles George GORDON). Died at Omdurman (June 22, 1885); succeeded by the Khalifa (*q.v.*).

**Mo·ham′med A·li′** (*Pers.* mô·hàm′măd à·lē′). 1872–1925. Shah of Persia (1907–09) of Kajar dynasty; son of Muzaffar-ed-Din; sought by force to overthrow constitution; deposed; left Persia to live in Europe (1911). Succeeded by his son Ahmed Shah.

**Mo·ham′med A·li′** (mô·hăm′ĕd [-ĭd] ä·lī′). = MEHEMET ALI.

**Mo·ham′med ibn-Abd-al-Wa·hab′** (*Arab.* mŏŏ-hăm′măd ĭb′′n·ăb·dŏŏl′wă·häb′). 1703?–1791. Arab religious reformer; proclaimed himself (1745) reformer of Islam; founded new school of theology; converted to his doctrines the Arab chief Mohammed ibn-Saud, ancestor of ibn-Saud, ruler (1932–53) of Saudi Arabia. Founder of Wahabite sect.

**Mo·ham′med ibn-Ab·dul·lah′** (*Arab.* mŏŏ·hăm′măd ĭb′′n·ăb·dŏŏl·lä′). d. 1920. Called "the Mad Mullah." Somali dervish who, as mullah and religious agitator in eastern Africa, esp. in British Somaliland, engaged in hostilities (1902–20) against the government.

**Mo·ham′med ibn-Ka′sim** *or* **ibn-Qa′sim** (*Arab.* mŏŏ·hăm′măd ĭb′′n kä′sĭm). fl. 1st part of 8th century A.D. Mohammedan general; first Mohammedan conqueror in India; with Arab army, crossed Makran (Baluchistan), invaded Indus valley, and conquered Sind (712–715); established kingdom with Multan as capital.

**Mo·ham′med Na′dir Khan** (*Afghan* mô·hŭm′măd nä′dĕr KÄN′). See NADIR SHAH, of Afghanistan.

**Mo·ham′med of Ghor** (*Pers.* mô·hàm′măd, gōr). *Also known as* **Mu·ham′mad Gho·ri′** (*Pers.* mô·hàm′măd gō·rē′). *Real name* **Mu′izz-ad-din.** d. 1206. Sultan of Ghazni; most important ruler (1173–1206) of Ghuri dynasty of Persia. Established as sultan of conquered city of Ghazni (1173); began invasions of India (1175), carried on for thirty years; subdued Sind (1182); occupied the Punjab (1187); defeated and wounded at Narain (1191) by Hindu army; completely defeated Hindus (1192); made all northern India tributary to Ghor; defeated (1203) in Khwarazm (Khiva); assassinated. Considered founder of Moslem power in India.

**Mo·ham′med Ri·za′ Pah′le·vi** (*Pers.* mô·hàm′măd rĭ·zä′ pă′lă·vē). 1919– . Shah of Iran (Persia); succeeded to throne upon abdication of his father, Riza Shah Pahlavi (1941); deposed (1979).

**Mo·ham′med Shah** (mô·hăm′ĕd [-ĭd] shä′). 1700?–1748. Mogul emperor of India (1719–48); lost Hyderabad and Oudh; reign marked by revolts; defeated in invasion of Nadir Shah from Persia (1739); suffered first Afghan attack (1748) by Ahmad Shah.

**Mo·ham′med Shah** (*Pers.* mô·hàm′măd shä′). 1810–1848. King of Persia (1835–48) of Kajar dynasty; grandson and successor of Fath Ali and son of Abbas Mirza (*q.v.*). Under Russian influence; laid siege to Herat (1837–38) but failed to take it; his death left Persia on verge of bankruptcy and revolution. Succeeded by his son Nasr-ed-Din.

**Mo·ham′med Tugh·lak′** (*Arab.* mŏŏ·hăm′măd tăg-lăk′). d. 1351. Second king (1325–51) of the Tughlak (*q.v.*) dynasty of the kings of Delhi. Son of Ghiyas-ud-din. Inherited a great Mohammedan empire; alienated Hindus by his bigoted zeal for Islam and caused revolt among Mohammedans by his cruel and vicious temper; bought off Mogul hordes in northwestern India; failed disastrously in attempts to invade Persia and China (1337–38); faced by repeated revolts of his provinces (1338–51).

**Mo·ham′med Za′hir Shah** (*Afghan* mô·hŭm′măd zä′hĕr shä′). 1914– . King of Afghanistan; succeeded his father, Mohammed Nadir, on throne (1933); deposed (1973).

**Mohl** (mōl), **Hugo von.** 1805–1872. German botanist; known for anatomical researches important to modern histology and history of development; first used term *protoplasm* to denote substance of cell body as opposed to that of the nucleus (1846); author of works on anatomy and physiology of the plant cell and on use of the microscope. He was brother of: **Julius Mohl** (1800–1876), Orientalist, **Moritz Mohl** (1802–1888), politician and economist, **Robert von Mohl** (1799–1875), statesman, imperial minister of justice (1848), ambassador in Munich (1867), author of works relating to civil law.

**Möh′ler** (mû′lĕr), **Johann Adam.** 1796–1838. German Roman Catholic theologian; works include polemical writing in defense of Catholic doctrine, which stirred up a controversy with his Protestant colleague F. C. Baur.

**Moh′ler** (mō′lĕr), **John Robbins.** 1875–1952. American pathologist; with U.S. Bureau of Animal Industry (from 1897), chief of pathological division (1902–14), chief of bureau (from 1917). Author of articles and reports on pathology, bacteriology, and meat inspection. Special editor for veterinary terms, *Webster's New International Dictionary, Second Edition.*

**Mohn** (mōn), **Henrik.** 1835–1916. Norwegian meteorologist; investigated dynamics of the atmosphere, storms, meteorology of the North Atlantic, and climate of Norway.

**Mo′holy-Nagy′** (mô′hoi·nŏd′y′), **László** *or* **La′dis·laus** (*Ger.* lä′dĭs·lous). 1895–1946. Hungarian painter, designer, and photographer; member of constructivist school; director of short-lived New Bauhaus, or American School of Design, Chicago, with Dr. Walter Gropius (*q.v.*) as adviser (1937–38); opened own school of design in Chicago (1939). Experimented and worked in painting, drawing, photography, stage sets, sculpture, film cartoons, and other arts.

**Mohr** (mōr), **Friedrich,** *in full* **Karl Friedrich.** 1806–1879. German pharmacist; known esp. for work in volumetric analysis.

**Mohr, Joseph.** 1792–1848. Austrian theologian and poet; author of Christmas song *Stille Nacht, Heilige Nacht* (1818).

**Mohs** (mōs), **Friedrich.** 1773–1839. German mineralogist; introduced scale of hardness still commonly used.

**Mohun** (mŏŏn), **Charles.** 4th Baron **Mohun.** 1675?–1712. English duelist; engaged in protracted lawsuit regarding real estate with James Douglas, 4th Duke of Hamilton; forced duke into duel in which both were mortally wounded, an incident figuring in Thackeray's *Henry Esmond.*

**Mohun, Michael.** 1625?–1684. English actor; performed at the Cockpit in Drury Lane, London; served in Royalist army; at Restoration, joined Killigrew's company.

**Moi'gno'** (mwä'nyō'), **François Napoléon Marie.** 1804–1884. French mathematician; author of works on differential and integral calculus, analytical mechanics, molecular physics, saccharimetry, and faith and science.

**Moineaux, Georges.** See Georges COURTELINE.

**Moir** (moir), **David Macbeth.** 1798–1851. Scottish physician; known as Δ (dĕl'tȧ) from his signature to essays and poems contributed to *Blackwood's Magazine.* Author of Scottish novel *The Life of Mansie Wauch* (1828) and *Outlines of Ancient History of Medicine* (1831).

**Moira,** Earl of. See Francis Rawdon-HASTINGS.

**Mois'san'** (mwä'säN'), **Henri.** 1852–1907. French chemist; professor of toxicology and inorganic chemistry, School of Pharmacy, Paris (1889), of inorganic chemistry, Sorbonne (1900). First to isolate fluorine (1886); developed electric arc furnace (1892); produced minute artificial diamonds; awarded **1906** Nobel prize for chemistry.

**Mo'is·si** (mō'ĭ·sē), **Alexander.** 1880–1935. Actor, b. Trieste, Austria (now Italy), of Italian parentage; won fame chiefly in Max Reinhardt productions in Berlin; admitted to Italian citizenship shortly before death. Played many roles, including Hamlet, Romeo, Othello, Mark Antony, Shakespeare's fools, Faust, Orestes, Cyrano de Bergerac, Everyman; appeared in Tolstoi's *Living Corpse* and Ibsen's *Ghosts;* starred in motion picture *The Royal Box.*

**Moj'si·so'vics von Mojs'vár** (mô'ĭ·shĭ·shô'vĭch fôn mô'ĭsh·vär), **Edmund.** 1839–1907. Austrian geologist and paleontologist; chief geologist (1870) and asst. director (1892–1900), Imperial Geological Inst.; coeditor with Melchior Neumayr of *Beiträge zur Paläontologie Österreich-Ungarns und des Orients* (from 1880). His nephew **Roderich Mojsisovics von Mojsvár** (1877–1953), composer and writer on music, conductor of Styrian Musical Society, Graz (from 1912); professor (1925); composed symphonies, piano and violin concertos, chamber music, organ and piano works, songs and choruses, stage music, operas.

**Mo·kan'na, al-** (ăl'mōō·kăn'nă). *Real name* **Hashim ibn-Hakim.** d. about 780. Arab religious charlatan who appeared (c. 774) in Khurasan, pretended to be a god, and wore a veil to hide the (alleged) brightness of his face; committed suicide (c. 780) to escape capture; hero of a tale (*Mokanna, or the Veiled Prophet of Khorassan*) in Moore's *Lalla Rookh.*

**Mo'la** (mō'lä), **Emilio.** 1887–1937. Spanish soldier; joined insurrection led by General Franco; under Franco, held command of northern army in Spain during first year of civil war; killed in airplane accident.

**Mo'la** (mô'lä), **Pierfrancesco.** *Sometimes called* **Mola di Ro'ma** (dē rō'mä). 1612–1666. Italian painter; notable for mythological and religious paintings, esp. for their landscape backgrounds.

**Mo'lay', Jacques de** (dē mô'lā'; *Angl.* dē' mô·lā'). 1243?–1314. Last grand master of the Templars (elected 1297); seized by direction of King Philip IV of France and taken before French Inquisition; burned at the stake in Paris.

**Mol'bech** (mŏl'bĕk), **Christian.** 1783–1857. Danish philologist and historian; author of Danish dictionary (2 vols., 1828–33), Danish dialect lexicon (1833–41), and Danish glossary (1853–66). His son **Christian Knud Frederik** (1821–1888), poet, dramatist, and literary critic; author of lyric verse, dramas, and a translation of Dante's *Divina Commedia* (4 vols., 1851–63), etc.

**Mo'lé'** (mô'lā'), Comte **Louis Mathieu.** 1781–1855. French statesman; member of Council of State under Napoleon I; created peer of France during Restoration; minister of marine (1817–18) and member of privy council; minister for foreign affairs (1830); premier of France (1836–39); one of deputies who opposed the coup d'état (Dec. 2, 1851).

**Molé, Mathieu.** 1584–1656. French jurist and politician; procureur général (1614); upheld authority of Parliament against royal usurpation (1631) and was for a time suspended from office as a result; appointed first president of Parliament (1641–53) and keeper of the seals (1651–56).

**Mo'le·naer** *or* **Mo'le·naar** (mō'lĕ·när), **Jan Miense.** 1605?–1668. Dutch genre and portrait painter; known esp. for humorous Dutch folk scenes.

**Mo'le·schott** (mō'lĕ·sKŏt), **Jacob.** 1822–1893. Physiologist and writer on dietetics, b. in Holland; professor, Rome (1879); Italian senator (1876). His researches were concerned with blood, gall, respiration, innervation of the heart, etc.; advocate of scientific materialism.

**Moles'worth** (mōlz'wûrth; -wĕrth), **Mary Louisa,** *nee* **Stew'art** (stū'ĕrt). *Pseudonym* **Ennis Gra'ham.** 1839–1921. Scottish fiction writer, b. Rotterdam; m. Major R. Molesworth (1861); best known as writer of children's books.

**Molesworth, Robert.** 1st Viscount **Molesworth.** 1656–1725. Irish political leader, b. and educ. Dublin; in Revolution of 1688, supported William of Orange, who sent him on missions to Denmark (1689, 1692); M.P. (1695); member, Irish privy council (1697). His second son, **Richard** (1680–1758), 3d viscount, soldier, saved Marlborough's life at Ramillies (1706); Irish privy councilor (1735); field marshal (1757). **John Edward Nassau Molesworth** (1790–1877), great-grandson of 1st viscount, High-Church vicar of Rochdale (1840), fought losing fight in behalf of church rates for whose abolition John Bright campaigned. John's son **William Nassau** (1816–1890), vicar of Spotland, near Rochdale (1844–89), was author of *History of England 1830–1871* (1871–73) and *History of the Church of England* (1882). Another son, Sir **Guilford Lindsey** (1828–1925), civil engineer and economist, was engineer at Woolwich arsenal during Crimean War; consulting engineer to government of India (1871); author of works on railways, bimetallism, political economy, etc.

**Molesworth,** Sir **William.** 1810–1855. English political leader; ardent champion of measures for colonial self-government; denounced penal transportation; first commissioner of works in Aberdeen's government (1853); colonial secretary in Palmerston's government (1855); editor of Hobbes's works.

**Mo'ley** (mō'lĭ), **Raymond Charles.** 1886–1975. American journalist; assoc. professor of government, Columbia (1923–28), and professor of public law (1928–54); asst. secretary of state (1933) and member of the so-called "brain trust," a group to whom President F.D. Roosevelt is reputed to have turned for advice from time to time. Editor of magazine *Today* (1933–37); contributing editor to *Newsweek* (1937–68); author of *Lessons in American Citizenship* (10 eds., 1917–30), *Parties, Politics, and People* (1921), *Tribunes of the People* (1932), etc.

**Mo'lière'** (mô'lyâr'). *Pseudonym of* **Jean Baptiste Po'que·lin'** (pô'klăN'). 1622–1673. French actor and playwright, b. Paris. Formed own company and performed in Paris and in the provinces (from 1643); gained patronage of the court in Paris (from 1658) and his troupe became known as King's Comedians. As playwright, made first outstanding success with *Les Précieuses Ridicules* (1659), followed by a series of comedies which established his reputation as supreme in this field. Among his most notable comedies are *École des Maris* (1661), *Les Fâcheux* (1661), *École des Femmes* (1662), *Le Mariage Forcé* (1664), *Le Misanthrope* (1666), *Le Médecin Malgré Lui* (1666), *Amphitryon* (1667), *L'Avare* (1668), *Tartufe* (1669), *Le Bourgeois Gentilhomme* (1670), *Les Fourberies de Scapin* (1671), *Les Femmes Savantes* (1672), *Le Malade Imaginaire* (1673).

**Molijn, Pieter de.** See Pieter de MOLYN.

**Mo·li'na** (mô·lē'nä), **Alfonso Qui·ñó'nez** (kē·nyō'nās). 1873–1950. Salvadoran physician and political leader; provisional president of El Salvador (1914–15), vice-president (1915–23), elected president (1923–27).

**Molina, Luis.** 1535–1600. Spanish Jesuit and theologian; propounded doctrine (Molinism) that divine grace is a free gift to all, but that its efficacy depends upon the will that accepts it; caused theological controversy.

**Molina, Tirso de.** See TIRSO DE MOLINA.

**Mo'li·na'ri** (mō'lē·nä'rē), **Bernardino.** 1880–1952. Italian orchestra conductor; appeared with St. Louis Symphony in American debut (1927); coconductor of New York Philharmonic-Symphony Orchestra (1929).

**Mo'li'na'ri'** (mô'lē'nà'rē'), **Gustave de.** 1819–1912. Belgian political economist, in Paris (1843–51; 1857 ff.); became editor of *Journal des Débats* (1867), *Journal des Économistes* (1881); helped establish other economic journals; author of many works on political economy.

**Mo'li'net'** (mô'lē'nĕ') *or* **Mou'li'net'** (mōō'-), **Jean.** d. 1507. French poet and chronicler; historiographer of Charles the Bold; librarian of Mary of Burgundy; continued Chastellain's *Chronique* for years 1474 to 1504; a leader among the "Rhétoriqueurs," a Burgundian school of poetry.

**Mo·li'nos** (mô·lē'nōs), **Miguel de.** 1640–?1697. Spanish priest and mystic; founder of quietism; condemned by the Inquisition (1687).

**Mo·lique'** (mô·lēk'), **Wilhelm Bernhard.** 1802–1869. German violinist and composer; settled in London (1849–66) as successful teacher and concert violinist. Compositions include six violin concertos, a violin concertino, a violoncello concerto, eight string quartets and other chamber music, and the oratorio *Abraham* (1860).

**Mo'lisch** (mō'lĭsh), **Hans.** 1856–1937. German botanist; professor, Vienna (1909–28).

**Mo'li'tor'** (mô'lē'tôr'), Comte **Gabriel Jean Joseph.** 1770–1849. French soldier in Revolutionary and Napoleonic armies; distinguished himself esp. at Essling and Wagram (1809); governor general of Holland (1811); retired (1815), but recalled to service (1818) and commanded corps in French expedition to Spain (1823); created marshal of France and a peer (1824).

**Mo'li·tor** (mō'lē·tôr), **Raphael Fidelis.** 1873– . German Roman Catholic theologian and writer on history of church music; authority on Gregorian Chant; abbot (1906) of St. Joseph monastery, Westphalia.

**Moll** (môl), **Albert.** 1862–1939. Psychiatrist, b. Lissa (Leszno); physician in Berlin; introduced hypnosis and psychotherapy into Germany; strove for scientific investigation of occultism; investigated sexual problems.

**Moll, Bruno.** 1885– . German political economist.

**Möl'len·dorff** (mûl'ĕn·dôrf), **Wichard von.** 1724–1816. Prussian soldier; commanded army in partition of Poland (1793); commanded Prussian army on the Rhine, and won battle of Kaiserslautern (1794), but was defeated by Hoche at Wissembourg; wounded at Auerstedt (1806) and captured.

**Mol'len·hau'er** (mŏl'ĕn·hou'ēr), **E'mil** (ā'mĭl). 1855–1927. American violinist, and conductor of Germania, later called Boston Festival, Orchestra (1888–99), and of the Handel and Haydn Society (1899–1927).

**Mol'ler** (môl'ēr), **Georg.** 1784–1852. German architect; court architect to grand duke of Hesse (from 1810); his works include public buildings in Darmstadt, and the ducal palace at Wiesbaden.

**Möll'hau'sen** (mûl'hou'zĕn), **Heinrich Balduin.** 1825–1905. Traveler and author, b. near Bonn, Germany; to U.S. (1849); on scientific expeditions in western U.S. (1851–52; 1853–54; 1857–58); befriended by Alexander von Humboldt; appointed custodian of royal libraries in and near Potsdam; author of novels of adventure based on experiences in the western U.S.

**Mol'lien'** (mô'lyăN'), Comte **François Nicolas.** 1758–1850. French statesman; councilor of state (1804) and finance minister (1806) under Napoleon; count of the Empire (1808); again finance minister during Hundred Days; created peer of France (1819).

**Mol'li·son** (mŏl'ĭ·s'n), **Amy Johnson.** See JOHNSON.

**Mollison, James Allan.** 1905–1959. British aviator; m. (1932; divorced 1938) Amy Johnson (*q.v.*). Established numerous records for airplane flights, including that from Australia to England (8 days, 19 hours, 28 minutes; 1931), England to Cape Town via west coast (4 days, 17 hours, 5 minutes; 1932), England to India (with wife; 22 hours, 1934); made first solo westward flight across North Atlantic (1932), first flight from England to South America (1933), first flight from England to U.S. (with wife; 1933). Author of *Death Cometh Soon or Late* (autobiography) and *Playboy of the Air* (1937).

**Mol·men'ti** (môl·mĕn'tē), **Pompeo Gherardo.** 1852–1928. Italian historian and politician; deputy (1890 ff.), senator (1909 ff.); known as student of Venetian history and, particularly, for his *Storia di Venezia nella Vita Privata* (3 vols., 1880; 7th ed., 1929).

**Mol'nár** (môl'när), **Ferenc.** 1878–1952. Hungarian playwright, novelist, and short-story writer, b. Budapest; war correspondent on German-Austrian front (1914–18); to U.S. (Jan., 1940). Author of short stories and novels, as *A Derelict Boat* (1901), *The Paul Street Boys* (1907), and *A War Correspondent's Diary*, and esp. plays, chiefly comedies, including *The Devil* (1907), *Liliom* (1909), *The Guardsman* (1910), *Carnival* (1917), *The Swan* (1922), *The Red Mill* (1923), *The Glass Slipper* (1924), *The Play's the Thing* (1925), *Olympia* (1928), *The Good Fairy* (1930), *No Greater Glory* (1934), *Delicate Story* (1940), etc.

**Mo'lo** (mō'lō), **Walter von.** 1880–1958. German novelist and playwright.

**Mo'lo·tov** (mô'lŭ·tôf), **Vyacheslav Mikhailovich.** *Orig. surname* **Skrya'bin** (skryà'byĭn). 1890– . Russian statesman; prominent in revolution of October, 1917; associate of Lenin; member of Politburo, and secretary of central committee of Communist party in Russia (1922 ff.); president (1930–41), vice-chairman (1941 ff.), of Council of People's Commissars; commissar of foreign affairs (1939 ff.); member of state committee of defense (1941 ff.); presided at Anglo-Soviet conference in Moscow (Sept., 1941); visited England and U.S. for conferences (1942); delegate to the UN General Assembly.

**Molt'ke** (môlt'kĕ), Count **Helmuth von.** 1800–1891. Prussian soldier; on mission in Turkey aiding in reorganization of the Turkish army (1835–39); as chief of Prussian general staff (1858–88), reorganized Prussian army (1858–63) with parliamentary support of Bismarck, the chancellor, and von Roon, the minister of war; directed strategy in war against Denmark (1864), against Austria (1866), and against France (1870–71); created field marshal (1871).

**Moltke, Helmuth von.** 1848–1916. Nephew of Field Marshal Helmuth von Moltke. German soldier; chief of general staff (from 1906) and director of German strategy at outbreak of World War (1914); lost the first battle of the Marne (1914); relieved of his command (Nov. 3, 1914) and succeeded by General von Falkenhayn.

**Molt'ke** (mŏlt'kĕ), Count **Joachim Godske von.** 1746–1818. Danish minister of finance (1781–84) and of foreign affairs (1813). His son Count **Adam Wilhelm** (1785–1864) was premier of Denmark (1848–52) and member of the Rigsraad (1854–61).

**Mo'lyn** (mō'lĭn) *or* **Mo'lijn** (mō'lĭn), **Pieter de.** 1595–1661. Dutch landscape and genre painter and etcher.

**Mol'y·neux** (mŏl'ĭ·nōōks; -nŭks; -nū). Name of Irish family descended from Sir **Thomas Molyneux** *or* **Mol'i·nel** [mŏl'ĭ·nĕl] (1531–1597), b. Calais, settled in Ireland (1576), chancellor of Irish exchequer (1590). His great-grandson **William Molyneux** (1656–1698), philosopher and friend of Locke, published his version of Descartes's *Meditations* (1680); M.P. (1692); author of works on optics, including *Dioptrica nova* (1692), and *The Case of Ireland's being bound by Acts of Parliament in England stated* (1698). William's son **Samuel** (1689–1728), astronomer, M.A., Dublin (1710), secretary to prince of Wales, M.P. (1715), made experiments in construction of reflecting telescopes (1724) and was sent by British Royal Society to interview Leeuwenhoek; first lord of admiralty (1727).

**Mol'za** (môl'tsä), **Francesco Maria.** 1489–1544. Italian lyric poet; known esp. for his *Ninfa Tiberina;* also wrote sonnets, romances, elegies, etc.

**Mom'bert** (môm'bĕrt), **Alfred.** 1872–1942. German lyric and symbolistic poet.

**Momm'sen** (môm'zĕn), **Friedrich.** 1818–1892. German jurist.

**Mommsen, Theodor.** 1817–1903. German classical scholar and historian, b. Garding, Schleswig; professor of law, Leipzig (1848); dismissed (1850) for participation in democratic movement; professor of Roman law, Zurich (1852) and Breslau (1854), and of ancient history, Berlin (1858); member of Progressive party (1863–66) and National Liberal party (1873–79) in Prussian House of Representatives, and strong opponent of Bismarck; member of Liberal Union (1881 ff.) and German Liberal party (1884 ff.) in Reichstag; awarded Nobel prize for literature (1902). Editor in chief (from 1854) of *Corpus Inscriptionum Latinarum* (1863 ff.) for Berlin Acad., and editor of *Auctores Antiquissimi* section of *Monumenta Germaniae Historica*, to which he also contributed editions of Cassiodorus (1861), Solinus (1864), etc.; author of famous *Römische Geschichte* (Eng. *History of Rome;* vols. 1–3, 1854–56; vol. 5, Eng. *The Provinces of the Roman Empire*, 1885), *Die Geschichte des Römischen Münzwesens* (Eng. *History of Roman Coinage;* 1860), *Römisches Staatsrecht* (vols. 1–3, 1871–88), *Römisches Strafrecht* (1899), editions of Edict of Diocletian (1851), *Codex Theodosianus* (2 vols., 1905; with P. Meyer), *Digest* (in vol. 1 of *Corpus Juris Civilis*, 1866–70), and other works chiefly on epigraphy, archaeology, and Roman law. His brother **Tycho** (1819–1900) was a classical philologist. Another brother, **August** (1821–1913), was also a classical philologist; author of works chiefly on Greek and Roman chronology and heortology. Theodor's grandson **Wilhelm** (1892–1966), historian.

**Mo'na·ci** (mô'nä·chē), **Ernesto.** 1844–1918. Italian Romance philologist; professor, U. of Rome (1876 ff.); a founder of *Rivista di Filologia* (1872–76). His works include *Crestomazia Italiana dei Primi Secoli* (1889, 1912), *Archivio Paleografico Italiano* (48 brochures, 1884–1915).

**Mon'a·co** (mŏn'ȧ·kō), House of. Modern princely house descended from Goyon-Matignon house (1715–92; see GRIMALDI); dispossessed by Revolution; restored (1814); placed under Sardinia (1815–61). Its recent heads have been: **Florestan I** (1785–1856); prince (1841–56). His son **Charles III** (1818–1889); prince (1856–89); sold rights over towns of Menton and Roquebrune to France (1861). Charles's son **Albert I** (1848–1922); prince (1889–1922); acquired fame as an oceanographer and student of paleontology; equipped four yachts for deep-sea dredging and investigation of ocean currents; put private estate at Monte Carlo at disposal of U.S. government as retreat for convalescent soldiers (1917–19). Albert's son **Louis II** (1870–1949); prince (1922–49).

**Mo·na'gas** (mô·nä'gäs), **José Tadeo.** 1784–1868. Venezuelan general and statesman; fought under Bolívar in War of Independence (1812–21); military leader of Venezuelans when union with Greater Colombia dissolved (1830); was choice of Páez as his successor to presidency (1846), but broke with Páez (1847); president of Venezuela (1846–51, 1855–58); actually a dictator; revised constitution (1857); overthrown by a revolution (1858) and banished. Returned to power (1868), but died soon after. His brother **José Gregorio** (1795–1858) was president of Venezuela (1851–55; placed in office by brother); signed law abolishing slavery (1854). José Tadeo's son **José Ruperto** was president of Venezuela (1868–70); overthrown by Gen. Guzmán Blanco (1870).

**Mo'nal·de'schi** (mō'näl·dās'kē), Marchese **Giovanni.** d. 1657. Italian nobleman and adventurer; favorite of Queen Christina of Sweden, lost favor and was assassinated at her command (Nov. 10, 1657); subject of plays by Dumas père (1830) and Heinrich Laube (1845).

**Mo'na Li'sa** (mō'nȧ lē'zȧ; *Ital.* mô'nä lē'zä). *More correctly* **Mon'na** (mŏn'ȧ; *Ital.* môn'nä) **Li'sa.** *In full* **Lisa di Anton Maria Ghe'rar·di'ni** (gā'rär·dē'nē). *Sometimes called* **La Gio·con'da** (lä jō·kōn'dä). fl. about 1495. Florentine noblewoman; wife of Francesco di Bartolommeo del Giocondo; subject of da Vinci's painting *Mona Lisa.*

**Mo'nash** (mō'năsh), Sir **John.** 1865–1931. Australian soldier, b. Melbourne; served as brigade commander at Gallipoli (1915) and in defense of Suez Canal; commanded 3d Australian division in France (1916–18); promoted lieutenant general (1918) and commanded Australian army corps in France during final months of the war; retired (1930) with rank of general.

**Mon·bod'do** (mŏn·bŏd'ō), Lord. **James Bur'nett** (bûr'nĕt; -nĭt). 1714–1799. Scottish judge and pioneer anthropologist; lord of session (1767); visited at Monboddo by Samuel Johnson (1773). Author of *The Origin and Progress of Language* (1773–92), bringing man into affinity with orangutans and tracing elevation of man to social state as a natural process.

**Mon·ca'da** (mông·kä'thä), **Francisco de.** Conde **de O·su'na** (thā ō·sōō'nä). Marqués **de Ai·to'na** (ī·tō'nä). 1586–1635. Spanish soldier and historian; commander of Spanish army in Netherlands (1633); author of *Expedición de los Catalanes y Aragoneses contra Turcos y Griegos* (1623).

**Moncada, José María.** d. 1945. Nicaraguan politician; president of Nicaragua (1929–32); opponent of Sandino (*q.v.*); faced with intervention of U.S. (1932), declared martial law.

**Mon'cey'** (môN'sā'), **Bon Adrien Jeannot de.** Duc **de Co'ne·glia'no** (kō'nā·lyä'nō). 1754–1842. French soldier in Revolutionary and Napoleonic armies; commander of army which defeated Spaniards and forced peace (1795); created marshal of the Empire (1804) and duc de Conegliano (1808); commanded national guard in Paris (1814) and defended city against allied forces; created peer of France by Louis XVIII; commanded corps in French expedition in Spain (1823).

**Monck** (mŭngk), **Charles Stanley.** 4th Viscount **Monck** (in Irish peerage) and 1st Baron **Monck** (in peerage of U.K.). 1819–1894. British administrator, b. in County Tipperary, Ireland; governor general (1861–68) of British North America (Canada); induced reform leader, George Brown, to enter coalition ministry that governed while federation was being effected.

**Monck** *or* **Monk** (mŭngk), **George.** 1st Duke of **Al′be·marle** (ăl′bĕ·märl). 1608–1670. English soldier; commanded regiment against Irish rebels (1642–43). After imprisonment, took negative oath of covenant; as major general in Ulster and at Dunbar (1650), commended himself to Cromwell; entrusted by Cromwell with subjugation of Scotland (1652); won two sea fights over Tromp (1653) which ended first Dutch-English war. Governor of Scotland (1654); at Coldstream, Berwick, organized regiment known as Coldstream Guards (1659–60); promised support to Parliament, crossed border, and marched to London (1660); general in chief of land forces and joint commander of navy; entered into direct communication with Charles II; freed Rump Parliament from army; caused election of new parliament, which restored monarchy (May 1, 1660); welcomed Charles II at Dover (May 23). Created Baron Monck, earl of **Tor′ring·ton** (tŏr′ĭng·tŭn), and duke of Albemarle; privy councilor, chamberlain, lord lieutenant of Devon and Middlesex; soon withdrew from political affairs. Maintained order and supervised preventive measures through plague in London (1665); took to sea with Rupert; defeated by de Ruyter off Dunkirk (1666); month later won complete victory over de Ruyter off North Foreland. Buried in Westminster Abbey.

**Monck′ton** (mŭngk′tŭn), **Mary.** Countess of **Cork and Or′rer·y** (kôrk, ŏr′ēr·ĭ). 1746–1840. English bluestocking, dau. of 1st Viscount Galway; made her mother's London house a rendezvous of literary celebrities, including Dr. Johnson, Sheridan, Burke, Reynolds; m. (1786) Edmund Boyle, 7th Earl of Cork and Orrery (see BOYLE family); entertained Canning, Castlereagh, Lord John Russell, Byron, Scott. Supposed original of Lady Bellair in Disraeli's *Henrietta Temple* and Mrs. Leo Hunter in *Pickwick.*

**Monckton, Robert.** 1726–1782. British general in America; served in Nova Scotia (1752); captured French Fort Beausejour (1755); lieutenant governor of Nova Scotia (1755); second in command in Wolfe's expedition against Quebec (1759); major general, and governor of New York (1761); commander of expedition conquering Martinique (1761–62). To England (1763); commissioned lieutenant general (1770).

**Mon·crieff′** (mŏn·krēf′; mŭn-). See also SCOTT-MONCRIEFF.

**Moncrieff, Alexander.** 1695–1761. See under Ebenezer ERSKINE.

**Moncrieff,** Sir **Alexander.** 1829–1906. British army engineer; originated (about 1868) Moncrieff system of gun mountings for heavy batteries, utilizing energy of recoil to depress gun below parapet for loading and to return gun to firing position over parapet; replaced counterweights with hydropneumatic device for storing energy of recoil (1869).

**Moncrieff, James.** 1744–1793. British military engineer, b. in Fifeshire; distinguished himself at defense of Savannah (1779) and as chief engineer in capture of Charleston (1780); mortally wounded at siege of Dunkirk.

**Moncrieff, William Thomas.** 1794–1857. English playwright and producer; gained first successes with *The Dandy Family* at Astley's and *The Lear of Private Life* (1820); joined Robert William Elliston at Drury Lane (1820) and produced farce, romantic drama, and melodrama of own composition; with William Oxberry, comedian and printer, published Pierce Egan's *Boxiana* (1818 ff.); dramatized Egan's *Life in London* as *Tom and Jerry* (1821), an instant success; managed Vauxhall Gardens (1827).

**Mond** (mŏnd; *Ger.* mōnt), **Ludwig.** 1839–1909. German chemist and industrialist, b. Kassel; to England (1862); naturalized British subject (1867). Partner in firm at Widnes, where his patented method for recovering sulphur lost in Leblanc alkali process was used; with J. T. Brunner, started alkali works (1872) which became firm of Brunner, Mond, and Co., manufacturers of alkali by ammonia-soda process; developed Mond gas, a producer gas; devised a gas battery; discovered nickel carbonyl and a method of extracting nickel from its ores; formed Mond Nickel Co. with mines in Canada; took out 49 patents; founded Davy-Faraday Research Laboratory at Royal Institution (1896). His son Sir **Alfred Moritz** (1868–1930), 1st Baron **Mel′chett** (mĕl′chĕt; -chĭt), was an industrialist, financier, and politician; educ. Cambridge and Edinburgh; chairman of Mond Nickel Co.; liberal M.P., Chester (1906), Swansea (1910–23), Carmarthen (1924–28); first commissioner of works (1916–21); minister of health (1921–22); Zionist; instituted conferences to discuss problems between employers and employees (1927). Sir **Robert Ludwig** (1868–1938), another son of Ludwig Mond, was an industrialist; educ. Cheltenham Coll., Cambridge, Zurich Polytechnicum, Edinburgh, and Glasgow; made researches in theoretical and applied chemistry, electrochemistry, and color photography; conducted archaeological excavations in Thebes, Palestine, and Brittany.

**Mon′dale′** (mŏn′dāl′), **Walter Frederick.** 1928– . American politician, b. Ceylon, Minnesota. Attorney general of Minnesota (1960–64); U.S. senator (1964–77); U.S. vice-president (1977– ).

**Mon·di′no de′ Luz′zi** (mōn·dē′nō dā lōōt′tsē) *or* **de Luic′ci** (dā lwēt′chē). 1275–1326. Italian anatomist; author of textbook which remained authoritative until appearance of Vesalius's anatomical work.

**Mon′dri·aan** (mŏn′drē·än), **Pieter Cornelis.** 1872–1944. Dutch painter; identified with ultramodern school; studio in Paris. See Georges van TONGERLOO.

**Mo′net′** (mô′nĕ′), **Claude.** 1840–1926. French landscape painter; recognized as one of greatest of the impressionists. Among his many notable canvases are *Embouchure de la Seine à Honfleur, Un Déjeuner sur l'Herbe, Camille ou la Dame en Vert, Le Jardin de l'Infante, La Grenouillère, Gare Saint-Lazare,* a series of landscapes along the Seine, a series on Rouen cathedral, *Bordighera, Palazzo Dario, Venice,* and *Le Meules.*

**Mo·ne′ta** (mô·nâ′tä), **Ernesto Teodoro.** 1833–1918. Italian journalist and pacifist, b. Milan; general staff officer under Garibaldi; in Italian army (1861–67). Director of Milanese newspaper *Il Secolo* (1867–96); became interested in cause of international peace, founding several peace societies; president, international peace congress at Milan (1906); shared Nobel peace prize (1907), given in recognition of his book *Le Guerre, le Insurrezioni, e la Pace nel Secolo XIX* (3 vols., 1903 ff.).

**Monge** (mônzh), **Gaspard.** Comte **de Pé′luse′** (dē pā′lüz′). 1746–1818. French mathematician and physicist; active in establishment of École Polytechnique, where he taught descriptive geometry; considered inventor of descriptive geometry.

**Mon′gol** (mŏng′gŏl; -gŭl). A name sometimes given to the Yüan (*q.v.*) dynasty of China.

**Mon′i·ca** *or* **Mon′ni·ca** (mŏn′ĭ·kȧ), Saint. 332?–387 Mother of Saint Augustine of Hippo.

**Mo'nier'** (mô'nyā'), **Joseph.** 1823–1906. French inventor of reinforced concrete; patented idea of using iron rods in concrete for strengthening.

**Mon'i·er–Wil'liams** (mŭn'ĭ·ēr·wĭl'yămz; mŏn'-), Sir **Monier.** 1819–1899. English Sanskrit scholar, b. Bombay; son of Colonel Monier Williams; assumed additional surname Monier (1887). As professor of Sanskrit at Oxford (1860), conceived and established Indian Inst. (begun 1875, completed 1896). Author of Sanskrit grammars and dictionaries, and works on Indian poetry, philosophy, religious and sacred books.

**Moñino y Redondo, José.** See Conde de FLORIDABLANCA.

**Mo'nis'** (mô'nēs'), **Ernest,** *in full* **Alexandre Emmanuel Ernest.** 1846–1929. French statesman; member of Chamber of Deputies (1885–89) and of the Senate (1891–1920); minister of justice (1899); premier of France (1911); again minister of justice (1913).

**Mo·niusz'ko** (mô·nyŏŏsh'kô), **Stanisław.** 1819?–1872. Polish composer of operas, orchestral works, chamber and church music, and songs.

**Mo·niz'** (mōō·nēsh'), **Antonio Caetano de Abreu Freire Egas.** 1874–1955. Portuguese neurologist and diplomat. Led delegation to Paris Peace Conf. (1919). Nobel prize in physiology and medicine (1949) with W. Hess.

**Monk** (mŭngk). See also MONCK.

**Monk, Maria.** 1817?–1850. Canadian impostor; in two books, *Awful Disclosures by Maria Monk* (1836) and *Further Disclosures* (1836), claimed to reveal revolting practices in a nunnery at Montreal from which she said she had escaped; fraud exposed by William Leete Stone in *Maria Monk and the Nunnery of the Hôtel Dieu* (1836).

**Monk, William Henry.** 1823–1889. English organist and composer; musical editor of Church of England hymnbook *Hymns Ancient and Modern* (1st ed., 1861), for which he composed many original tunes, including *Abide with Me.*

**Monk'house** (mŭngk'hous), **Allan Noble.** 1858–1936. English dramatist and novelist; his plays produced mainly by repertory theaters in England and America. Wrote *A Deliverance* and *Farewell Manchester;* among his plays, *Mary Broome, The Conquering Hero, O Death Where is thy Sting?, Cecilia.*

**Monkhouse, William Cosmo.** 1840–1901. English poet and art critic; author of *A Dream of Idleness,* showing influence of Wordsworth and Tennyson (1865), *Corn and Poppies* (1890), and *The Christ on the Hill* (1898).

**Monks'well** (mŭngks'wĕl; -wĕl), 1st Baron. **Robert Porrett Col'lier** (kŏl'yĕr; -ĭ·ĕr). 1817–1886. English judge. As counsel to admiralty (1859), gave decision that would have prevented *Alabama* from going to sea had it been acted upon. Solicitor general (1863–66); attorney general (1868–71); member, judicial committee of privy council (1871–86).

**Mon'luc'** (môN'lük'). = MONTLUC.

**Mon'mouth** (mŏn'mŭth; mŭn'-), Duke of. **James Scott.** 1649–1685. Claimant to British throne and leader of rebellion; b. in Holland; natural son of Charles II of England by Lucy Walter, Charles II's mistress during his exile. Known as **James Fitz·roy'** (fĭts·roi') and **James Crofts** (krŏfts), and as "the Protestant Duke." Entrusted to William Crofts (1611?–77), Baron Crofts, courtier to Charles II, and diplomat; reared a Protestant; went to England with queen dowager (1662). Acknowledged by Charles II as his son (1663); m. Anne Scott, Countess of Buccleuch; created duke of **Buc·cleuch'** (bŭ·klōō'); took surname of Scott; created duke of Monmouth (1663). Captain general of Charles II's forces (1670), on death of Monck; commanded forces sent to aid French in Dutch war; sent against Scottish Covenanters (1675–79), ending their rebellion by victory at Bothwell Bridge, where his clemency won him popularity. Exiled by Charles II, returned and championed Protestantism; favored by exclusionists; after semiroyal progresses (1680, 1682), became idol of populace; voted for Exclusion Bill in House of Lords; implicated in Rye House Plot, with Whig leaders Russell, Essex, and Sidney; fled to Low Countries (1683). At Charles's death arranged to join Argyll and Ferguson's expedition to England; landed at Lyme Regis, Dorsetshire, with 82 supporters, and claimed "legitimate and legal" right to crown in place of James II (1685); proclaimed king of Taunton; defeated by Feversham and Churchill at Sedgemoor; captured; his supporters were punished by the Bloody Assizes. His mistress **Henrietta Maria Went'worth** [wĕnt'wûrth; -wĕrth] (1657?–1686), Baroness Wentworth, succeeded (1667) her grandfather, 4th baron Wentworth; lived with Monmouth in Bedfordshire (1680); supplied him funds for invasion of England (1685).

**Monmouth,** Earl of. See *Robert Carey,* under Henry CAREY (1524?–1596).

**Monmouth, Geoffrey of.** See GEOFFREY OF MONMOUTH.

**Monna Lisa.** See MONA LISA.

**Monnica.** Variant of MONICA.

**Mon'nier'** (mô'nyā'), **Henri Bonaventure.** 1805–1877. French caricaturist and playwright; creator of famous characters Mme. Gibou and Joseph Prudhomme.

**Monnier, Marc.** 1829–1885. French writer; author of books on Italy, and poetry, fiction, plays, and *Histoire Générale de la Littérature Moderne* (1884).

**Mo'nod'** (mô'nō'), **Frédéric Joël Jean Gérard.** 1794–1863. French Protestant clergyman; founder (1849) of Free Church of France. His brother **Adolphe Théodore** (1802–1856), also a Protestant clergyman, was renowned as preacher. A third member of the family, **Wilfred Monod (1867–1943), was also a Protestant clergyman.**

**Monod, Gabriel.** 1844–1912. French historian; founder and director of *Revue Historique* (1875); works include *Allemands et Français* (1872), *Carolingienne* (1898), and *Renan, Taine, Michelet* (1894).

**Monod, Jacques.** 1910– . French biochemist. At Pasteur Inst. (1946– ); awarded Nobel prize in physiology and medicine (1965) with F. Jacob and A. Lwoff for studies on genetic control of enzyme and virus synthesis.

**Mon'rad** (mŏn'räth), **Ditlev Gothard.** 1811–1887. Danish statesman and theologian; bishop of Lolland-Falster (1849–54); removed from office for opposition in Rigsdag to Örsted ministry; minister president (1863); withdrew from office (1864) following war with Prussia; lived in New Zealand (1865); returned to Denmark (1869); again bishop of Lolland-Falster (1871); member of opposition party in Danish parliament (1882–86).

**Mon'rad** (mŏn'räd), **Marcus Jacob.** 1816–1897. Norwegian philosopher; sought to unite Hegelian point of view with Christian doctrine.

**Mon·ro'** (mŭn·rō'). See also MUNRO.

**Monro** pri'mus (prī'mŭs), **Alexander.** 1697–1767. Scottish anatomist; first professor of anatomy, Edinburgh (1720). His youngest son, **Alexander Monro** se·cun'dus (sē·kŭn'dŭs), of Craiglockhart (1733–1817), anatomist, succeeded to his father's chair (1759–1808); described communication between lateral ventricles of the brain, called after him *foramen of Monro;* described bursea mucosae (1788); author of works on the nervous system (1783), physiology of fishes (1785), the brain, eye, and ear (1797). His son **Alexander Monro** ter'ti·us [tûr'shĭ·ŭs] (1773–1859), joint professor with his father

(1800), wrote on hernia, the stomach, and human anatomy. Alexander tertius's grandson Sir **Charles Carmichael Monro** (1860–1929) served in Boer War; evolved new system of infantry-fire tactics; in France (1914–16); commanded Mediterranean expeditionary force at Gallipoli and effected withdrawal;commander in chief in India (1916–20); governor of Gibraltar (1923–28). **David Binning Monro** (1836–1905), classical scholar, maternal grandson of Alexander tertius, wrote *Grammar of Homeric Dialect* (1882) and *Modes of Ancient Greek Music* (1894); edited *Iliad* and *Odyssey*.

**Monro, Harold Edward.** 1879–1932. English poet and critic; devoted himself to propagation of poetry by founding magazines *Poetry Review* (1911) and *Poetry and Drama* (refounded after war as *The Chapbook*) and *The Poetry Bookshop*, in a slum (1912), which he made a meeting place for poets. Author of volumes of poetry (from 1906), including *Before Dawn* (1911), *Trees* (1916), *Elm Angel* (1930), and critical works.

**Mon·roe′** (mŭn·rō′), **Harriet.** 1861?–1936. American poet and editor, b. Chicago; founded (1912) and edited (1912–36) *Poetry: a Magazine of Verse.* Author of *Valeria and Other Poems* (1892), *The Columbian Ode*, read and sung at ceremonies celebrating the 400th anniversary of the discovery of America (Oct. 21, 1892), *The Passing Show—Modern Plays in Verse* (1903), *You and I* (1914), *The Difference and Other Poems* (1924).

**Monroe, James.** 1758–1831. Fifth president of the United States, b. in Westmoreland County, Va. Served in American Revolution; member, Continental Congress (1783–86); practiced law, Fredericksburg, Va.; U.S. senator (1790–94); U.S. minister to France (1794–96); governor of Virginia (1799–1802); one of negotiators of the Louisiana Purchase (1803); U.S. minister to England (1803–07); again governor of Virginia (1811); U.S. secretary of state (1811–17), also secretary of war (1814–15). President of the U.S. (1817–25); period known as "era of good feeling," because of lack of vigorous factional quarrels; Florida acquired (1819); Missouri Compromise legislation enacted (1820); Monroe Doctrine promulgated (1823). Elected to American Hall of Fame (1930).

**Monroe, Marilyn.** *Originally* **Norma Jean Mortenson.** 1926–1962. American film actress, b. Los Angeles, Calif. In *Some Like It Hot* (1959), *The Misfits* (1961).

**Monroe, Paul.** 1869–1947. American educator; professor of education (from 1902) and director of school of education (1915–23), Teachers College, Columbia; president of Robert College, Istanbul, Turkey; editor in chief, *Cyclopedia of Education* (5 vols., 1910–13).

**Mon·sieur′** (mẽ·syû′). Title of oldest brother of king of France.

**Mon′si′gny′** (mônˈsē′nyē′), **Pierre Alexandre.** 1729–1817. French composer, regarded with Grétry and Philidor as a creator of French comic opera. Composed operas *Les Aveux Indiscrets* (1759), *On ne s'Avise Jamais de Tout* (1761), *Le Déserteur* (1769), *Félix, ou l'Enfant Trouvé* (1777), etc., with librettos mostly by Sedaine (from 1761).

**Mon′son** (mŭn′s'n), Sir **William.** 1569–1643. English naval commander; distinguished himself in Cádiz expedition (1596); vice-admiral of squadron sent to intercept Spanish treasure fleet (1602); admiral of narrow seas (1604); arrested Lady Arabella Stuart (1611); deprived of command on suspicion of complicity in Overbury murder; vice-admiral (1635) in Dutch campaign.

**Mons′tre·let′** (môns′trĕ·lĕ′), **Enguerrand de.** 1390?–1453. French chronicler; in service of John of Luxemburg and present at Compiègne when Joan of Arc was captured by Burgundians; author of *Chronique...* (covering period 1400–44).

**Mon′ta·cute** (mŏn′tȧ·kūt; mŭn′-) *or* **Mon′ta·gu** (-gū), **de** (dĕ). An English family holding the earldom of **Salis′bur·y** [sôlz′bĕr·ĭ; -brĭ] (1337–1428):

**William de Montacute** (1301–1344), 3d Baron Montacute and 1st Earl of Salisbury, grandson of **Simon Montacute,** 1st Baron Montacute (d. 1317; admiral of fleet, 1310); soldier; with Edward III in Scotland (1327) and abroad (1329); rewarded with lands for arresting Mortimer (1330); fought in Scotland, concluding truce (1336); marshal of England (1338).

**William** (1328–1397), 2d earl; son of 1st earl; distinguished himself at Poitiers (1356); served under John of Gaunt in north of France (1369); attended Richard II in meeting Wat Tyler's rebels at Smithfield, during Peasants' Revolt (1381).

**John** (1350?–1400), 3d earl; nephew of 2d earl; a favorite adviser of Richard II; prominent Lollard; deputy marshal of England (1398–1400); joint ambassador to France; raised troops to resist duke of Lancaster (later Henry IV) and conspired against him; beheaded by anti-Lollard mob.

**Thomas** (1388–1428), 4th earl (restored 1421); took part at Agincourt (1415) and in naval engagement before Harfleur (1416); lieutenant general of Normandy (1419) and chief English general in France (to 1428), completing subjugation of Champagne and Maine (1425); undertook siege of Orléans (1428), near which he was mortally wounded. His daughter Alice married Richard Neville (1425) and was mother of Warwick the Kingmaker.

**Mon·ta′gna** (môn·tä′nyä), **Bartolommeo.** 1450?–1523. Italian painter; founder of school of Vicenza. Among works are frescoes illustrating life of St. Blasius (Church of Santi Nazaro e Celso, Verona), *Madonna and Child* (Metropolitan Museum, New York), and *Madonna with Saints* (Philadelphia).

**Mon′ta·gna′na** (mōn′tä·nyä′nä), **Domenico.** 1690?–?1750. Italian maker of violins, esp. of alto violins and violoncellos; active in Cremona and (from 1720) Venice.

**Mon′ta·gu** (mŏn′tȧ·gū; mŭn′-). See also MONTACUTE; MONTAGUE.

**Montagu.** Family name of barons and dukes of Montagu, including:

Sir **Edward Montagu** (d. 1557), English judge; chief justice of King's Bench (1539); transferred to Court of Common Pleas (1545); member of council of regency under Henry VIII's will. His grandson **Edward Montagu** (1562–1644), 1st Baron **Montagu of Bough′ton** (bô′t'n; bou′-); brother of Henry Montagu (*q.v.*), 1st Earl of Manchester; imprisoned as a Royalist; died in Tower of London. Edward's son **Edward** (1616–1684), 2d baron, conducted Charles I to Holmby House and aided him in escape (1647).

**Ralph Montagu** (1638?–1709), 1st Duke of Montagu; diplomat; son of 2d baron; took part in negotiations with Louis XIV (1669) and in arranging neutrality of England in war between France and Holland (1676); intrigued to obtain secretaryship of state; escaped to France but found favor with James II and welcomed William III; married his son **John** (1688?–1749), 2d duke, to daughter of duke of Marlborough (1705); duke of Montagu and marquis of Mon′ther′mer′ [?môn′tĕr′mā′] (1705).

**Montagu.** Family name of earls and dukes of **Man′ches′ter** (măn′chĕs′tẽr; -chĭs·tẽr), including:

Sir **Henry Montagu** (1563?–1642), 1st Earl of Manchester; brother of 1st Baron Montagu of Boughton, uncle of Edward Montagu, 1st Earl of Sandwich, and grandfather of Charles Montagu, 1st Earl of Halifax. English judge and statesman; sergeant-at-law and king's sergeant (1611); opened case against earl and countess of Somerset (1616); as chief justice of King's Bench, condemned Sir Walter Raleigh (1618); lord high treasurer (1620); created Viscount **Man'de·ville** [măn'dĕ·vĭl] (1620); head of Virginia commission (1624); one of guardians of realm during Charles I's absence (1641).

His son **Edward** (1602–71), 2d earl; statesman; M.P. (1623) as Viscount Mandeville (courtesy title); created Baron **Montagu of Kim·bol'ton** [kĭm·bōl't'n; -tŭn] (1626); a leader of Puritans in House of Lords, one of twelve peers to petition king to call Long Parliament (1640); sided with Pym and Hampden; impeached by king for high treason (1642), but cleared; served under Essex; made major general in eastern counties (1643); held nominal command at Marston Moor (1644); charged by Cromwell before House of Commons with neglect and incompetency, and resigned (1645); opposed trial of king and formation of the Commonwealth (1649); actively promoted the Restoration; privy councilor and lord chamberlain (1660).

**Charles Montagu** (1660?–1722), 1st Duke of Manchester; grandson of 2d earl; after succeeding as 4th earl (1683), supported William of Orange in Ireland (1690); sent as ambassador extraordinary to Venice (1697), Paris (1699), Venice (1707); created duke (1719).

**Mon'ta·gu** *or* **Moun'ta·gu** (mŏn'tȧ·gū; mŭn'-). Family name of earls of **Sand'wich** (săn(d)'wĭch; -wĭj), including:

**Edward Montagu** (1625–1672), 1st Earl of Sandwich; English naval commander; nephew of Henry Montagu, 1st Earl of Manchester, and of Edward Montagu, 1st Baron Montagu of Boughton (*qq.v.*). Joined Parliamentary army (1643); raised regiment with which he fought at Marston Moor (1643), Naseby (1645), Bristol (1645). Member of Cromwell's council of state (1653); general at sea (1656), colleague of Robert Blake; at odds with General Monck, as revealed in diary of his secretary, Samuel Pepys; sent with fleet to arrange peace with Sweden and Denmark (1659). Assisted in restoration of Charles II; general at sea (1660), carried fleet to side of Charles and conducted Charles to England from Holland. In command of squadron in battle with Dutch off Lowestoft (1665); ambassador to Madrid (1666–69), concluded treaty with Spain (1666); in renewal of Dutch war, took conspicuous part in action in Southwold Bay, where he was blown up with his flagship; buried in Westminster Abbey. See under Elizabeth MONTAGU and Mary Wortley MONTAGU.

**John Montagu** (1718–1792), 4th earl; diplomat; succeeded his grandfather, 3d earl (1729); educ. Cambridge; a lord commissioner of the admiralty (1744); plenipotentiary to congress at Breda (1746); first lord of admiralty (1748, 1763, 1771–82); a principal secretary of state (1763–65); notorious for part he took in prosecution of Wilkes, for association with Mad Monks of Medmenham Abbey (see Sir Francis DASHWOOD), and for bribery and corruption in management of the admiralty, whence his nickname **Jemmy Twitch'er** (twĭch'ẽr). Sandwich Islands (now Hawaiian Islands) named after him by Captain Cook. Traditionally held to be inventor of the sandwich for eating at the gaming table. See Basil MONTAGU.

**Montagu, Basil.** 1770–1851. English lawyer. Son of 4th earl of Sandwich by his mistress Martha Ray; intimate of Coleridge and Wordsworth at Cambridge; editor of Bacon (1825–37); author of essays.

**Montagu, Charles.** 1st Earl of **Hal'i·fax** (hăl'ĭ·făks). Baron **Halifax.** 1661–1715. English wit, statesman, and patron of literature; grandson of Sir Henry Montagu, 1st Earl of Manchester. M.P. (1689–95); as a lord of treasury (1692), originated English national debt by inducing Parliament to raise a million pounds by life annuities; carried through a bill proposed earlier by William Paterson to raise loan, the subscribers to which were to form a corporation, thus originating the Bank of England (1694); chancellor of exchequer and privy councilor (1694); reformed the currency (1695) with help of Somers, Locke, and Newton; first introduced exchequer bills; carried through scheme for forming consolidated fund to meet interest on government loans (1696); first lord of treasury and prime minister (1697); obliged to resign on account of unpopularity (1699); auditor of exchequer and Baron Halifax (1700); impeached (1701) for obtaining grants from William III in trust for himself and for promoting second Partition Treaty, and (1703) for neglect of duties as auditor, but not prosecuted; supported union with Scotland. On George I's accession, was created earl of Halifax (1714) and became 1st lord of treasury and prime minister. Collaborated with Matthew Prior in *The City Mouse and the Country Mouse* (1687), a parody on Dryden's *Hind and the Panther.* Friend and patron of Addison, Steele, and Congreve.

His nephew **George Montagu** (d. 1739) succeeded him as Baron Halifax; created earl of Halifax (1715); succeeded by his son **George Montagu Dunk** [dŭngk] (1716–1771), 2d earl; took name of Dunk on marriage (1741) with heiress of large fortune of Sir Thomas Dunk; as president of Board of Trade (1748–61), aided founding of colony of Nova Scotia, the chief town of which was named Halifax after him (1749), and zealously extended American commerce; lord lieutenant of Ireland (1761–63); first lord of admiralty (1762); secretary of state (1762); joined triumvirate with Grenville and Egremont; dismissed (1765); lord privy seal in administration of his nephew Lord North (1770).

**Montagu, Elizabeth,** *nee* **Robinson.** 1720–1800. English author, wit and beauty, leader of bluestocking circles; m. (1742) Edward Montagu (d. 1775), grandson of 1st earl of Sandwich and cousin of Edward Wortley Montagu (see under Mary Wortley MONTAGU). Made her salon in Mayfair center of literary and social life; held assemblies for literary discussion, to which epithet *bluestocking* was first applied; among guests were Lord Lyttelton, Burke, Garrick, Sir Joshua Reynolds, Hannah More, Fanny Burney; her conversation praised by Dr. Johnson. Contributed three dialogues to Lord Lyttelton's *Dialogues of the Dead* (1760); author of essay on *Writings and Genius of Shakespear* (1769), defending him against strictures of Voltaire.

**Montagu,** Lady **Mary Wort'ley** (wûrt'lĭ). 1689–1762. English poet and letter writer; daughter of Evelyn Pierrepont, 1st Duke of Kingston (see PIERREPONT family); precocious child, taught herself Latin; clever and witty in presiding at father's table; m. (1712) **Edward Wortley Montagu** (d. 1761), whose father, 2d son of 1st earl of Sandwich, took name Wortley on his marriage (cf. under Elizabeth MONTAGU). Accompanied husband on embassy to Constantinople (1716–18), whence she wrote sparkling *Letters from the East;* on return, introduced into England inoculation for smallpox, which she had observed in Turkey; settled in Twickenham, leader of society and fashion, and renewed friendship with Pope and Swift; quarreled with Pope (1722); bitterly attacked by Pope and Swift; left husband and country to live in Italy (1739–61), whence she wrote letters to her daughter Countess of Bute. Author of *Town Eclogues* (1716). Her son **Edward** (1713–1776), writer and traveler, toured Europe, studying Arabic and European languages; secretary at Congress of Aix-la-Chapelle (1748); author of *Reflections on the Rise and Fall of Antient Republics* (1759).

**Mon′ta·gu** *or* **Moun′ta·gue** (mŏn′tȧ·gū; mŭn′-), **Richard.** 1577–1641. English prelate and controversialist; archdeacon of Hereford and chaplain to James I (1617); defended himself against charges of Arminianism and popery, in *Appello Caesarem* (1625); through influence with Laud, became bishop of Chichester (1628), bishop of Norwich (1638).

**Montagu, Samuel.** Baron **Swayth′ling** (swāth′lĭng). 1832–1911. English financier and philanthropist; b. Liverpool, of Jewish family named Samuel, later Montagu by royal license. Founded with brother and brother-in-law foreign-exchange and banking firm (1853); profited in arbitrage; instrumental in making London clearinghouse of international money market. Liberal M.P. (1885); member of gold and silver commission (1887–90), supported bimetallism. Zealous supporter of Jewish religious, social, and charitable work. His son **Edwin Samuel Montagu** (1879–1924) was parliamentary undersecretary of state for India (1910–14), financial secretary to treasury (1914–16), minister of munitions (1916), secretary of state for India (1917–22); toured provinces of India in preparation for drafting of *Report on Indian Constitutional Reforms* (1918); rallied public opinion to support of his scheme, enacted as Government of India Act (1919), extending self-government through the dyarchy; resigned because of differences over Turkish policy.

**Mon′ta·gue** (mŏn′tȧ·gū; mŭn′-). See also MONTAGU.

**Montague** *or* **Mon′ta·cute** (mŏn′tȧ·kūt; mŭn′-), Baron. See *Henry Pole*, under POLE family.

**Montague, Charles Edward.** 1867–1928. British journalist and man of letters; son of Irish parents. Member of staff of *Manchester Guardian* (1890–1914, 1919–25); enlisted in army as private (1914); cited three times for bravery. Chief editorial writer and dramatic critic on *Guardian;* author of the novels *A Hind Let Loose* (1910), *Disenchantment* (1922), *Rough Justice* (1926), and a collection of essays (1924).

**Mont′ai′glon′** (môɴ′tĕ′glôɴ′), **Anatole de Courde** (ko͝ord) **de.** 1824–1895. French scholar; published editions of Gringore, Rabelais, Molière, La Fontaine.

**Mon′taigne′** (môɴ′tĕn′y′; -tân′y′; *Angl.* mŏn·tān′), **Michel Ey′quem′** (ĕ′kĕm′) **de.** 1533–1592. French essayist; courtier (1561–63) at court of Charles IX and present with king at siege of Rouen (1562). Retired to his estate, Château de Montaigne, and wrote *Essais* (1571–80); mayor of Bordeaux (1581–85); wrote third book of *Essais* (1588). Fame rests on these *Essais*, reflecting spirit of scepticism and inspired by his studies in Latin classics, esp. Plutarch, and by his consideration of lives and ideals of leading figures in his own time; both in style and thought, the *Essais* exercised important influence on French and English literature.

**Mon·ta′le** (mōn·tä′lā), **Eugenio.** 1896– . Italian poet. Wrote *Ossi di seppia* (1925), *La casa dei doganieri* (1932), *Quaterno di traduzione* (1948), *La bufèra e altro* (1956), *Satura* (1962), etc. Elected senator for life (1967); awarded Nobel prize for literature (1975).

**Mont′a′lem′bert′** (môɴ′tȧ′läɴ′bâr′), Marquis **de. Marc Re·né′** (rē·nā′). 1714–1800. French military engineer; specialized in study of fortifications.

**Montalembert,** Comte **de. Charles Forbes** (fôrb). 1810–1870. French journalist and politician; founder, with Lamennais, of journal *L'Avenir* (1830); entered House of Peers (1835); champion of Roman Catholic Church interests; member of Constituent Assembly (1848) and Corps Législatif; opposed Napoleon III's policies from date of the coup d'état (Dec. 2, 1851). Among notable works are *Des Intérêts Catholiques au XIXᵉ Siècle* (1852) and *L'Église Libre dans l'État Libre* (1863).

**Mon′tal·vân′** (môn′täl·vän′), **Juan Pé′rez de** (pā′rāth thā). 1602–1638. Spanish ecclesiastic, playwright, and novelist.

**Mon·tal′vo** (môn·täl′vō), **García Or·dó′ñez de** (ôr-thō′nyāth thā). Spanish writer of late 15th century; published (c. 1500) *Amadís de Gaula* (*Amadis of Gaul*), perhaps translated and arranged in part from Portuguese originals now lost.

**Montalvo, Luis Gálvez de.** See GÁLVEZ DE MONTALVO.

**Mon′ta·nel′li** (mōn′tä·nĕl′lē), **Giuseppe.** 1813–1862. Italian writer and statesman; triumvir of Florentine republic after uprising of 1849; at Paris (1849–59). On return to Italy unsuccessfully advocated formation of central Italian kingdom; member, Italian Parliament (1861–62). His works include *Versi* (1837), a dramatic poem *La Tentazione*, a tragedy *Camma* (1857), and politico-historical works.

**Mon·ta′nus** (mŏn·tā′nŭs). 2d-century Christian schismatic of Phrygia in Asia Minor, who claimed to unite in his own person God the Father, God the Son, and God the Holy Ghost; his followers became known as Montanists. Most distinguished convert to Montanism was Tertullian (*q.v.*). The remnants of the sect were suppressed during the reign of Justinian (527–565).

**Montauban, Charles Cousin-.** See COUSIN-MONTAUBAN.

**Mon′tau′sier′** (môɴ′tō′zyā′), Duc **de. Charles de Sainte′-Maure′** (dē săɴt′môr′). 1610–1690. French lieutenant general (1645); governor of Normandy (1663); created duc de Montausier (1665); guardian of the dauphin (1668–79); patron of Boileau and Racine.

**Mont′ba′zon′** (môɴ′bȧ′zôɴ′). A ducal branch of the Rohan family of France, deriving its name from the ancestral château near Tours. At first a seigneury, later (1547) a county, and then (1588) a duchy with **Louis de Ro′han′** (dē rô′äɴ′), Prince **de Gué′mé′née′** [gā′-mā′nā′] (d. 1594) the first duke. His brother Hercule de Rohan (see under ROHAN), inherited the title. **Louis de Rohan,** Duc **de Montbazon,** son of Hercule, married (1617) Anne de Guéménée, thus uniting the two branches. See GUÉMÉNÉE.

**Mont′calm′ de Saint′-Vé′ran′** (môɴ′kȧlm′ dē săɴ′-vā′räɴ′; *Angl.* mŏnt·käm′), Marquis **Louis Joseph de.** 1712–1759. French field marshal (1756) and commander of French troops in Canada; fought heroically to save Canada from the British, but was defeated and mortally wounded in the battle of Quebec (Sept. 13, 1759).

**Mont′chré′tien′** (môɴ′krā′tyăɴ′), **Antoine de.** 1575?–1621. French playwright and economist; credited with introduction of the term *political economy* into French by publication of his book *Traicté de l'Œconomie Politique* (1615); author of a number of tragedies.

**Montcorbier, François de.** See François VILLON.

**Mont·ea′gle** (mŏnt·ē′g'l), 4th Baron. **William Par′ker** (pär′kẽr). 1575–1622. English adventurer; 11th Baron **Mor′ley** (môr′lĭ) through descent from Robert de Morley, 2d Baron Morley (1296?–1360), admiral, victor at Sluys (1340). Succeeded his mother's father as Baron Monteagle; supported cause of Roman Catholic families; imprisoned and fined for participation in Essex's rebellion (1601); became Protestant; member of House of Lords as Baron Monteagle (1605). Reported to Lord Salisbury letter of warning of Gunpowder Plot, probably written by his brother-in-law Francis Tresham (1605); received £700 a year as reward. Subscriber to, and member of council of, Virginia Company (1709).

**Montebello,** Duc **de.** See Jean LANNES.

**Mon′te·cuc′co·li** (môn′tā·ko͞o′kô·lē) *or* **Mon′te·cuc′-cu·li** (-ko͞o·lē), Count **Raimund.** 1609–1680. Austrian general; defeated Turks (1664) in battle of St. Gotthard (Szentgotthard); commanded imperial army in war of empire and Holland against France (1672–75), opposing Turenne. For his services, given duchy of Melfi by the king of Naples (1679). Wrote memoirs (published 1770) and works on military science.

**Mon'te·fel'tro** (mōn'tā·fāl'trō) *or* **Mon'te·fel'tre** (-trā). Distinguished Italian family of Renaissance period, including: **Federigo da Montefeltro** (1422–1482), created duke of **Ur·bi'no** (ōōr·bē'nō) by Pope Sixtus IV; his son **Guido Ubaldo** *or* **Guidobaldo da Montefeltro** (d. 1508), expelled from Urbino by Cesare Borgia (1502), but regained power there later in same year; bequeathed his coronet (1508) to Francesco Maria della Rovere, Duke of Urbino (*q.v.*).

**Mon'te·fi·o're** (mŏn'tē·fĭ·ō'rē; -ô'rē), **Claude Joseph Gold'smid–** (gōld'smĭd-). 1858–1938. British Jewish leader; grandson of Sir Isaac Lyon Goldsmid (*q.v.*); grad. Oxford (1881); assumed surname Goldsmid by letters patent; Hibbert lecturer (1892); active in educational and philanthropic work; president of Anglo-Jewish Association (1896–1921), of Liberal Jewish synagogue, of University College, Southampton (1915–34). Author of *Truth in Religion, Elements of Liberal Judaism,* etc.

**Montefiore,** Sir **Moses Haim.** 1784–1885. British Jewish philanthropist, b. at Leghorn of Anglo-Italian family of Jewish merchants; brother-in-law of Benjamin Gompertz. Amassed fortune in London Stock Exchange; retired (1824); devoted himself to alleviating hardships of his coreligionists; journeyed seven times to Orient (1827–75) in behalf of his people; founded girls' school and hospital at Jerusalem (1855); obtained from sultan of Morocco edict giving equality to Jews (1864); interceded with Prince Carol of Rumania in behalf of Moldavian Jews (1867).

**Mon'té'gut'** (môɴ'tā'gü'), **Jean Baptiste Joseph Émile.** 1826–1895. French literary critic; on staff of *Revue des Deux Mondes* (1857), *Moniteur Universel* (1862), *Journal de Paris* (1865), and again *Revue des Deux Mondes* (1870); translated Macaulay's *History of England* and Shakespeare's *Complete Works;* introduced Emerson to French readers by essay in *Revue des Deux Mondes.*

**Mon·te'li·us** (môn·tā'lĭ·ŭs), **Oskar.** 1843–1921. Swedish archaeologist; author of *The Civilization of Sweden in Heathen Times* (1888), etc.

**Mon'te·ma·yor'** (*Span.* môn'tā·mä·yôr'), **Jorge de.** 1521?–1561. Portuguese-born romancer and poet, writing in Spanish; joined entourage of the principe (later Philip II) and traveled in Italy and Flanders. Author of the unfinished pastoral romance *Diana Enamorada,* written in prose with passages of verse included and widely popular in Europe; an English translation by Bartholomew Young (1598) was possibly used by Shakespeare in *Two Gentlemen of Verona.*

**Mon'te·mez'zi** (mōn'tā·mĕd'dzē), **Italo.** 1875–1952. Italian composer, b. in Verona province.

**Mon'te·môr'** (mōɴn'tē·môr'). Portuguese form of Spanish MONTEMAYOR.

**Mon'ten** (môn'tĕn), **Dietrich.** 1799–1843. German painter of battle scenes.

**Mon'te·ne'gro** (môn'tā·nā'grō), **Roberto.** 1885– . Mexican artist, b. in Guadalajara; best known for his surrealist murals; first director, Museum of Mexican Popular Art (from 1934).

**Mon'té'pin'** (môɴ'tā'păɴ'), **Xavier de.** 1823–1902. French novelist and playwright; author of many popular novels, including *Les Chevaliers du Lansquenet* (1847), *Les Viveurs de Province* (1860), *La Sorcière Blonde* (1876), *La Porteuse de Pain* (1884), *La Demoiselle de Compagnie* (1899); his plays include *La Policière* (1890), *Le Médecin des Folles* (1891), *La Joyeuse d'Orgue* (1897), *La Marchande de Fleurs* (1901), and dramatizations of many of his novels.

**Mon·te'ro** (môn·tā'rō), **Juan Esteban.** 1878?–1948. Chilean political leader; acting president of Chile (Nov., 1931–June, 1932); forced to resign by a revolution.

**Montero Rí'os** (rē'ōs), **Eugenio.** 1832–1914. Spanish jurist and statesman; president of Spanish commission to negotiate peace after Spanish-American War (1898); premier of Spain (1905).

**Monterrey,** Conde **de.** *Eng.* Count of **Monterey.** See Gaspar de ZÚÑIGA Y AZEVEDO.

**Mon'tes** (môn'tās), **Ismael.** 1861–1933. Bolivian lawyer, statesman, and soldier; president of Bolivia (1904–09, 1913–17); minister to England (1911) and France (1917); lived in exile in France (from 1920); returned to become head of Liberal party (1928).

**Mon'te·si'nos** (môn'tā·sē'nōs), **Fernando.** 1600?–?1655. Spanish historian of Peru; government official in Peru (1629?–?1650); investigated early Indian history. Chief works, *Anales Nuevas del Perú* and *Memorias Antiguas Historiales del Perú,* both first published in French and later translated into Spanish.

**Mon'tes'pan'** (môɴ'tĕs'päɴ'; *Angl.* mŏn'tĕs·păn'), Marquise **de.** *Nee* **Françoise Athénaïs Roche'chou·art'** (rôsh'shwȧr'). 1641–1707. Maid of honor to Queen Marie Thérèse (1661); b. Tonnay-Charente, near Rochefort, France; m. marquis de Montespan (1663). Became mistress of King Louis XIV (1667); education of their older children (legitimatized 1673) entrusted to Mme. Scarron, later Mme. de Maintenon, who gradually (1674–85) replaced her in the favor of the king; left the court (1687) and retired to Convent of St. Joseph (1691).

**Mon'tes'quieu'** (môɴ'tĕs'kyû'; *Angl.* mŏn'tĕs·kū'), Baron **de La Brède** (brĕd) **et de. Charles de Se·con'dat'** (sē·gôɴ'dȧ'). 1689–1755. French lawyer, man of letters, and political philosopher, b. near Bordeaux; counselor of Bordeaux parliament (1714) and its president (1716); withdrew from practice of law to devote himself to study and writing. Best known for *Lettres Persanes* (1721), cleverly criticizing French society of the day by representing it as seen through the eyes of two Persians traveling in Europe, *Considérations sur les Causes de la Grandeur des Romains et de leur Décadence* (1734), and *L'Esprit des Lois* (1748), a book which profoundly influenced political thought in Europe and America.

**Mon'tes'quiou'–Fe·zen'sac'** (môɴ'tĕs'kyōō'fē·zäɴ'-sȧk'), Comte **Robert de.** 1855–1921. French poet and essayist; among his volumes of verse are *Les Chauves-souris* (1891), *Les Perles Rouges* (1899), and *Prières de Tous* (1902); among his prose works are *Les Roscaux Pensants* (1897), *Autels Privilégiés* (1899), *Assemblées de Notables* (1909), etc.

**Mon'tes·so'ri** (mōn'tās·sô'rē; *Angl.* mŏn'tĕ·sō'rē), **Maria.** 1870–1952. Italian physician and educator; originator of Montessori method of education for children; educ. U. of Rome, where she was first woman in Italy to receive medical degree (1894); became interested in education as assistant physician at university psychiatric clinic, and studied psychiatry and pedagogy; founder and principal (1898 ff.) of Orthophrenic School for feeble-minded and defective children; successfully put into practice educational ideas of Édouard Seguin, and determined to apply similar principles and methods to education of normal children; lecturer on pedagogy, U. of Rome (1900–07). Opened first Montessori school for children (casa dei bambini) in slum districts of Rome (1907); featured development of child's initiative and sense and muscle training by means of specially prepared teaching materials and games, and stressed freedom of child with the teacher as supervisor and guide rather than formal instructor. Director of Montessori Institute, Barcelona (1917), and of training courses in London (1919); government inspector of schools in Italy (1922); founder of Montessori Training Center, Laren, the Netherlands (1938). Author of *The Montessori Method* (1912), *Pedagogical Anthropology* (1913), *Advanced Montessori Method* (1917), *The Child in the Church*, etc.

**Mon'tet'** (môɴ'tĕ'), **Pierre.** 1885–1966. French Egyptologist; professor, Strasbourg (from 1919); director of excavations at Abu Roāsh (1913–14), Byblos in Syria, where oldest alphabetical inscriptions discovered up to that time were found (1921–24); engaged in study of ruins of Tanis in Lower Egypt (from 1929), where he discovered (Feb., 1940) tomb of Pharaoh Psousennes.

**Mon'teux'** (môɴ'tû'), **Pierre.** 1875–1964. American (French-born) orchestra conductor; director of Diaghilev's Ballet Russe and conductor of Stravinsky's *Petrouchka* (1911) and *Sacre du Printemps* (1914), etc. In army (1914–16); to U.S. (1916), where he conducted series of concerts with the Civic Orchestra in New York (1917) and French operas at the Metropolitan Opera House (1917–19); conductor, Boston Symphony Orchestra (1919–24), Paris Symphony Orchestra (1930–38), San Francisco Symphony Orchestra (from 1935).

**Mon'te·ver'de** (mōn'tā·vār'dā), **Giulio.** 1837–1917. Italian sculptor; one of leaders of naturalist movement. Among his works are *Mazzini* (at Buenos Aires), equestrian statue of Victor Emmanuel (at Bologna), and *Madonna and Child* (in Campo Santo, Genoa).

**Mon'te·ver'di** (mōn'tā·vār'dē) *or* **Mon'te·ver'de** (-dā), **Claudio.** 1567–1643. Italian composer and music reformer; music director, St. Mark's Church, Venice (from 1613); became priest (1633). His many innovations in musical composition include the development and elaboration of the recitative with enlarged orchestral support, and the use of unprepared discords. Composer of eleven books of madrigals, esp. 5-part madrigals, canzonets (1583–1650), and operas, as *Orfeo* (1607), *Arianna*, containing the *Lamento* (1608), and *L'Incoronazione di Poppea* (1642), also masses, psalms, motets, and other sacred music.

**Mon'tez** (mŏn'tĕz), **Lo'la** (lō'lȧ). *Stage name of* **Marie Dolores Eliza Rosanna Gilbert.** 1818?–1861. British dancer and adventuress, b. Limerick, Ireland; m. 1st Capt. Thomas James (1837; divorced 1842), 2d G. T. Heald (1849; d. 1853), 3d P. P. Hull (1853). Mistress of Louis I of Bavaria (1847–48); created baroness of **Ro'sen·thal** (rō'zĕn·täl) and Countess of **Lans'feld** [läns'fĕlt] (1847); controlled Bavarian government (1847–48); opposed Jesuits; ousted by Austrian and Jesuit influences (1848). On stage in U.S. (1852) and Australia (1855–56); settled in New York; wrote *The Art of Beauty;* devoted herself to helping fallen women.

**Mon'te·zu'ma** (mŏn'tē·zōō'mȧ; *Span.* môn'tā·sōō'mä) *or* **Moc'te·zu'ma** (môk'tā·sōō'mä). *Nahuatl* **Mo'te·cuh·zo'ma** (mō'tā·kwä·sō'mä). Name of two Aztec rulers: **Montezuma I** (1390?–?1464); "emperor" of Mexico (1436?–?64); domain said to have extended from Atlantic to Pacific; enlarged and beautified Mexico City. **Montezuma II** (1480?–1520); Aztec emperor and ruler at time of Spanish conquest (1502–20); waged wars with Tlascalans; tried to persuade Cortes not to come to Mexico City (1519); seized by Cortes and held as hostage; after uprising of Aztecs against Spaniards, wounded as he exposed himself to address them; died a few days later (June, 1520).

**Mont'fau'con'** (môɴ'fō'kôɴ'), **Bernard de.** 1655–1741. French Benedictine monk and scholar; called to Paris (1687) to prepare edition in Latin of works of Greek church fathers; his *Palaeographia Graeca* (1708) won him recognition as founder of science of paleography.

**Mont'fer'rat'** (môɴ'fĕ'rȧ'). *Ital.* **Mon'fer·ra'to** (mōn'fâr·rä'tō). Name of a marquisate in northwest Italy between Maritime Alps, Genoa, and the Po, acquired (967) by a Lombard family, several members of which took part in the crusades (see CONRAD). **Boniface III**, Count of **Montferrat** (d. 1207), joined Fourth Crusade (1201); chosen leader after death of Thibaut III, Count of Champagne; as king of Thessalonica, ruled Greece and Macedonia (1204 ff.). **Marie de Montferrat** (d. 1212), dau. of Conrad; m. (1210) John of Brienne. Marquisate passed (c. 1305) to Palaeologi by marriage of Yolande of Montferrat to Andronicus II; main line extinct (1533); marquisate acquired (1536) by Gonzaga family (*q.v.*) of Mantua by marriage of Margaret of Montferrat to Federigo, Duke of Mantua. Marquisate became duchy (1573); ceded to Savoy (1631, 1703); part of Italy (1797–1815; and again from 1859).

**Mont'fort'** (môɴ'fôr'), **Eugène.** 1877–1936. French novelist; author of *Les Cœurs Malades* (1904), *Les Noces Folles* (1913), *La Soirée Perdue* (1921), *César Casteldor* (1927), etc.

**Mont'fort** (mŏnt'fẽrt; *Fr.* môɴ'fôr'), **Simon de.** Earl of **Leices'ter** (lĕs'tẽr). 1208?–1265. English statesman and soldier, b. in Normandy of a French noble family; through an English grandmother, inherited earldom of Leicester; to England (1229); expelled Jews from Leicester; m. (1238) Eleanor, sister of Henry III; formally invested with earldom of Leicester (1239); became reconciled with Henry III, after quarrel over a debt, by accompanying him on crusade (1240) and in disastrous French expedition (1242); king's deputy in disaffected province of Gascony; put down with severity excesses of seigneurs; acquitted on charges of oppression but yielded to demand of jealous Henry III for his resignation (1252). In parliament led opposition in resisting king's demand for subsidy (1254); in Mad Parliament at Oxford headed opposition, with earl of Gloucester, and was one of fifteen signers of Provisions of Oxford (1258); on Henry's revocation of assent to provisions withdrew to France in despair (1261). On invitation of barons who accused king of falseness to his oath, led rebellion against all violators of the provisions, in the Barons' War (1263–65); injudiciously accepted arbitration of Louis IX of France, who declared the provisions invalid (1264); renewed rebellion, triumphed over royal forces and captured king at battle of Lewes (1264); virtually governor of kingdom, summoned (Jan., 1265) parliament of churchmen, barons, four knights from each shire, and two citizens from each borough, the beginning of the modern parliament. Made alliance with Welsh that aroused resentment of Welsh Marchers, who united with Prince Edward against him; defeated and killed at Evesham (Aug. 4, 1265). Long popularly revered as a martyr and saint, known as "Simon the Righteous."

His father **Simon IV de Mont'fort' l'A'mau'ry'** [dē môɴ'fôr' lȧ'mō'rē'] (1160?–1218), Earl of Leicester and Comte **de Tou'louse'** (tōō'lōōz'), son of Simon III (d. 1181) and of daughter of Robert de Beaumont, 3d Earl of Leicester, went twice to Palestine as crusader and undertook at call of pope crusade against enemies of the church in Languedoc, the Albigenses (1209), and fell at siege of Toulouse.

**Mont'gail'lard'** (môɴ'gȧ'yȧr'), Comte **de.** *Pseudonym of* **Maurice Jacques Roques** (rôk). 1761–1841. French political adventurer; royalist secret agent during French

Revolution; used by Napoleon (1796–1814) and was instrumental in discovering Pichegru's treason; ingratiated himself with Louis XVIII at the Restoration.

**Mont'ge·las'** (môɴzh'lä'), Count **Maximilian Joseph von.** *Original family name* **de Gar'ne·rin'** (dĕ gȧr'-nĕ·răɴ'). 1759–1838. Bavarian statesman; private minister of state (1799); minister of finance (1803–06), of the interior (1806–09), and again of finance (1809–17). His grandson Count **Max von Montgelas** (1860–1938), Bavarian infantry general and politician, commanded 4th Bavarian infantry division (1912–15).

**Mont'gol'fier'** (môɴ'gôl'fyā'; *Angl.* mŏnt·gŏl'fĭ·ẽr), **Joseph Michel** (1740–1810) and his brother **Jacques Étienne** (1745–1799). French inventors; built first practical balloon, inflated with heated air, which made ascent of ten minutes at Annonay on June 5, 1783.

**Mont·gom'er·ie** (mŏn(t)·gŭm'ẽr·ĭ; -gŭm'rĭ; -gŏm'-). Name of a Scottish family descended from Sir **John Montgomerie,** 9th lord of **Ea'gle·sham** (ē'g'l·shăm), who distinguished himself at Otterburn (1388), and whose great-great-grandson **Hugh** (1460?–1545), 3d Baron **Montgomerie,** created earl of **Eg'lin·ton** *or* **Eg'lin·toun** [ĕg'lĭn·tŭn] (1506), was justice general of northern Scotland (1527) and one of council of regency (1536). Other members include: **Hugh** (1531?–1585), 3d earl; great-grandson of 1st earl; supported Roman Catholic policy of Mary, Queen of Scots, fought for her at Langside (1568), and sought to win toleration for Romanists; approved Ruthven raid, which made virtual prisoner of James VI (1582). **Alexander** (1556?–?1610), poet laureate of King James VI; author of *The Cherrie and the Slae* (1597) and *Flyting betwixt Montgomery and Polwart* (1621), and his brother **Robert** (d. 1609), titular archbishop of Glasgow (from 1581). **Alexander** (1588–1661), 6th earl, known as **Grey'steel'** (grā'stēl'); 3d son of **Robert Se'ton** (sē't'n), 6th Lord Seton, and Mary Montgomerie, daughter of 3d earl of Eglinton; took name of Montgomerie when he succeeded his cousin the 5th earl (1612); a prominent Covenanter, distinguished himself at Marston Moor (1644); urged recall of Charles II and policy of Argyll. **Archibald William** (1812–1861), 13th Earl of Eglinton and 1st Earl of **Win'ton** [wĭn't'n; -tŭn] (peerage of U.K.); grandson of 12th earl; lord lieutenant of Ireland (1852, 1858–59); remembered chiefly for his splendid reproduction of a tournament at Eglinton Castle (1839), described by Disraeli in *Endymion.*

**Mont·gom'er·y** (mŏn(t)·gŭm'ẽr·ĭ; -gŭm'rĭ; -gŏm'-). (1) Earls of (cr. 1605). See HERBERT family, 1. (2) Countess of. See *Anne Clifford,* under CLIFFORD family.

**Montgomery,** Sir **Bernard Law.** 1st Viscount **Montgomery of A'la·mein'** (ăl'ȧ·mān'). 1887– . British soldier, b. in Donegal; educ. Sandhurst; captain in World War I; commanded a division in France (1939–40); as commander of 8th army in Egypt (1942) began offensive at El Alamein which drove Rommel's forces from Egypt, Libya, and Tripolitania and forced him to abandon Mareth Line in southern Tunisia (1943); commander, allied armies in northern France (1944); field marshal; commander, British-occupied zone in Germany (1945–46); chief of imperial general staff (from 1946).

**Mont'go'me·ry'** (môɴ'gôm'rē'), Comte **Gabriel de.** 1530?–1574. French army officer; by accident, wounded mortally King Henry II in a joust (1559); fled to England; became Protestant; served under prince de Condé; captured, and executed at Paris.

**Mont·gom'er·y** (mŏn(t)·gŭm'ẽr·ĭ; -gŭm'rĭ; -gŏm'-), **James.** 1771–1854. British poet; editor and proprietor (till 1825) of paper in Sheffield, the *Sheffield Iris.* Author of descriptive poems *The Wanderer of Switzerland* (1806), *Greenland* (1819), *The Pelican Island* (1826), and of hymns, including *Hail to the Lord's Anointed, Prayer is the Soul's Sincere Desire.*

**Montgomery, Leslie Alexander.** See Lynn DOYLE.

**Montgomery, Lucy Maud.** See Lucy Maud Montgomery MACDONALD.

**Montgomery, Richard.** 1736–1775. General in American Revolution, b. Swords, County Dublin, Ireland; in British service (1756–72); to America (1772). At outbreak of Revolution, appointed brigadier general in Continental army; second in command under Schuyler in expedition against Montreal; captured Montreal; killed leading assault on Quebec (Dec. 31, 1775).

**Montgomery, Robert.** 1807–1855. English poet, natural son of one Robert Gomery; B.A., Oxon. (1833); ordained (1835); held various preferments. Touched popular religious sentiment in *Omnipresence of the Deity* (1828) and *Satan* (1830). Immortalized by Macaulay's attempt to demolish his reputation, in *Edinburgh Review.*

**Mont·gom'er·y–Mas'sing·berd** (-măs'ĭng·bûrd), Sir **Archibald Ar'mar** (är'mẽr). 1871–1947. British soldier; orig. name Montgomery; served in Boer War (1899–1902), World War (1914–18); lieutenant general (1926); field marshal (1935); chief of Imperial general staff (1933–36).

**Mon'ther'lant'** (môɴ'tĕr'läɴ'), **Henry Millon de.** 1896–1972. French writer; severely wounded in World War I. Author of *La Relève du Matin* (1920), *Le Songe* (1922), *Chant Funèbre pour les Morts de Verdun* (1924), *Pages de Tendresse* (1928), and a series entitled *Les Jeunes Filles* (1938–39).

**Mon'tho'lon'** (môɴ'tô'lôɴ'), Comte **Charles Tristan de.** 1783–1853. French soldier in Napoleonic armies; general of brigade (1811); aide-de-camp to Napoleon at Waterloo (1815); accompanied Napoleon to St. Helena and was named an executor of his will. Editor of *Mémoires pour Servir à l'Histoire de France sous Napoléon* (with General Gourgaud; pub. 1822–23). Aided Louis Napoleon in attempt to seize throne (1840); imprisoned (1840–47); member of Constituent Assembly (1849).

**Mon'ti** (mōn'tē), **Vincenzo.** 1754–1828. Italian poet; professor of eloquence, U. of Pavia (1802 ff.), Collège de France; historiographer of the kingdom of Italy under Napoleon (to 1814). Among his works are *Saggio di Poesie* (1779), *Bassevilliana* (1793), *Sermone sopra la Mitologia* (1825); plays, as *Aristodemo* (1786), *Caio Gracco* (1802); translations, esp. of the *Iliad;* and prose works, as *Lezioni di Eloquenza, Dialoghi.*

**Mon'ti'cel'li'** (môɴ'tē'sĕ'lē'), **Adolphe Joseph Thomas.** 1824–1886. French landscape, genre, and portrait painter; known esp. as a superb colorist.

**Mont'lo'sier'** (môɴ'lô'zyā'), Comte **de. François Dominique de Rey'naud'** (dĕ rā'nō'). 1755–1838. French journalist; an émigré (1791); commissioned by Napoleon to write articles against the English for *Bulletin de Paris;* published attack on Jesuits; peer of France (1832); supported July Monarchy (1830–38).

**Mont'luc'** (môɴ'lük'), Seigneur **de. Blaise de Las'se·ran'–Mas'sen'come'** (dĕ lȧs'räɴ' mȧ'säɴ'kôm'). 1501?–1577. French soldier; served in armies of Francis I, Henry II, Charles IX, and Henry III; created marshal of France (1574); left *Commentaires* (pub. 1592) on wars between 1521 and 1574.

**Mont'mo'ren'cy'** (môɴ'mô'räɴ'sē'; *Angl.* mŏnt'mō-rĕn'sĭ). Name of distinguished French family, including: Baron **Bouchard IV de Montmorency** (d. after 1124). Baron **Mathieu II** (d. 1230); distinguished himself in wars under Louis VIII and entrusted by him with guardianship of his children. Baron **Mathieu IV** (d. about 1305); grand chamberlain of France. Baron **Charles** (d. 1381); marshal (1343) and chamberlain (1346) of

France, and captain general of the Flemish borders. Baron **Jean II** (1402–1477); chamberlain of France. Duc **François** (1530–1579); soldier; m. Diane de France, natural daughter (legitimized) of Henry II; marshal of France (1559). Duc **Henry I** (1534–1614), soldier; revolted against Henry III and allied himself with Protestants; recognized Henry IV; created constable of France (1595). See also ducs Anne and Henri II de MONTMORENCY and duc de LUXEMBOURG.

**Montmorency,** Duc **Anne de.** 1493–1567. French soldier; marshal (1522); led French against Charles V in Provence (1536); constable of France (1537); Catholic leader against Protestants (1551–67); defeated at St.-Quentin (1557), commanded at Dreux (1562), mortally wounded at St.-Denis. His grandson Duc **Henri II de Montmorency** (1595–1632), marshal of France (1630–32), joined Gaston d'Orléans in revolt against Richelieu; was captured and beheaded (Oct. 20, 1632).

**Mont'pen'sier'** (môɴ'päɴ'syā'). Name of a French ducal family, originating about 1400, a branch of the Bourbons; duchy was held (1626–1789) by the House of Orléans. The family included: **Catherine Marie de Lor'raine'** [dĕ lô'rân'] (1552–1596), Duchesse de Montpensier; daughter of François de Lorraine; m. (1570) Louis II de Bourbon, Duc de Montpensier; active in court politics (1588–96); enemy of Henry III; strongly supported her brother Charles de Lorraine (see GUISE) against Henry IV. **Anne Marie Louise d'Or'lé'ans'** [dôr'lā'äɴ'] (1627–1693), Duchesse de Montpensier; known as **la Grande Ma'de·moi'selle'** (lȧ gräɴd' mȧd'mwȧ'zĕl'; mȧm'zĕl'); daughter of Gaston d'Orléans; opposed by Mazarin; aided Condé in revolt of the Fronde (1651–52); commanded one of the armies; banished from the court (1652–57); had violent love affair with duc de Lauzun, who as a result was imprisoned in the Bastille (1670–80); wrote *Mémoires* (pub. 1729). **Antoine Marie Philippe Louis d'Orléans** (1824–1890), Duc de Montpensier; 5th son of King Louis Philippe; b. Neuilly; fought in African campaigns (1842–45); m. Infanta Luisa de Bourbon, sister of Queen Isabella II of Spain; made his residence in Seville; served in Spanish army (1857–59); offered himself as candidate for Spanish throne (1870) but failed.

**Mon'tré·sor** (mŏn'trĕ·sôr), **James Gabriel.** 1702–1776. British military engineer; served at Gibraltar (1731–54); chief engineer with Gen. Braddock in America (1754); wounded at the Monongahela. His son **John** (1736–1799), also a military engineer, joined Braddock's army in America (1755); present at capture of Louisburg and Wolfe's siege of Quebec; after French and Indian War, continued on duty improving fortifications in New York, Boston, and Philadelphia; chief engineer in America (1775); relieved of command and returned to England (1778).

**Mon'treuil'** (môɴ'trû'y'), **Gerbert de.** 13th-century French poet; author of *Roman de la Violette* and a continuation of the *Perceval* of Chrétien de Troyes.

**Mont·rose'** (mŏnt·rōz'; mŏn·trōz'), Earls, marquises, and dukes of. After extinction of title of duke of Montrose created (1488) for David Lindsay (see LINDSAY family), his niece's husband, **William Graham,** 4th Lord **Graham,** was created earl of Montrose (1505), a title held by his descendants, including the 3d earl, chancellor and viceroy of Scotland, till creation (1644) of 5th earl as marquis of Montrose.

**James Graham** (1612–1650), 1st Marquis and 5th Earl of **Montrose,** often called "the Great Marquis"; son of 4th earl and daughter of William Ruthven, 1st Earl of Gowrie; traveled several years; returned (1636) amid religious service-book tumults; joined party of resistance; signed National Covenant; made military expeditions for coercing Aberdeen into subscription; kidnaped marquis of Huntly (1639); one of covenanting leaders to meet Charles I at Berwick; began his apostasy from Presbyterianism and national cause; invaded England with Covenanters, displayed gallantry at Newburn (1640); imprisoned for intrigue against Argyll and communicating with king. During Civil War, created marquis and lieutenant general, allowed by king to make a diversion in Scotland (1644); met Scoto-Irish auxiliaries and rallied Highland clans; routed Covenanters under earl of Wemyss at Tippermuir, took Aberdeen, crushed Campbells under Argyll at Inverlochy (1645), captured and pillaged Dundee, routed Scottish general William Baillie at Alford and defeated him at Kilsyth, making himself master of Scotland; made lord lieutenant and captain general of Scotland by king; called a parliament; going to help of king after defeat at Naseby, was surprised and routed by David Leslie at Philiphaugh (1645) while his highlanders had slipped off home to secure booty; embarked for Norway, escaped to the Continent, where, as field marshal of Emperor Ferdinand III, he levied troops for Charles I. Burning to revenge death of king, undertook another invasion of Scotland (1650); lost part of army by shipwreck; tried in vain to raise the clans; surprised and routed at Carbiesdale in Ross-shire; betrayed by Neil Macleod of Assynt; sentenced to death by parliament; hanged at Edinburgh, protesting to last that he was a Covenanter. Author of a few loyal poems and other vigorous verses, also of "My one and only love." Introduced as character in Scott's novel *The Legend of Montrose*.

His son **James** (1631?–1669), 2d marquis, called "the Good Marquis"; received back his estates, but joined rising in favor of Charles II, under command of 9th earl of Glencairn (1653); declined to vote at trial of his hereditary enemy, Argyll (1661).

**James** (d. 1742), 4th Marquis and 1st Duke of Montrose; grandson of 2d marquis; lord high admiral of Scotland (1705); lord president of the council (1706); created duke for services in support of union of Scotland with England (1707); one of representative peers and one of regents of kingdom on death of Queen Anne (1714); made keeper of privy seal of Scotland for activity in suppressing Jacobite rising (1715).

**James** (1755–1836), 3d duke, held office in Pitt's administrations (1783, 1804); commissioner for India (1791–1803); lord justice general of Scotland (1795–1836); held office in duke of Portland's administration (1807–30); lord chamberlain (1821–27, 1828–30).

**Monts** (môɴ), Sieur **de. Pierre du Guast** (dü gä'). 1560?–?1630. French explorer and colonizer of Canada; with Samuel Champlain and others sailed to Canada (1603) and founded Port Royal on present site of Annapolis Royal, Nova Scotia; established Tadoussac as fur-trade depot on St. Lawrence River; returned to France; continued to send out expeditions, during one of which Champlain founded Quebec (1608).

**Montt** (mônt), **Jorge.** 1847–1922. Chilean naval officer and political leader, b. Santiago; captain in navy at time of uprising against President Balmaceda (1891); following victory of naval forces and insurgents, became provisional president of Chile (Sept., 1891); elected president (1891–96); liberal and progressive; reorganized army and navy.

**Montt, Manuel.** 1809–1880. Chilean statesman, b. Petorca; president of Chile (1851–61; two 5-yr. terms); administration marked by progress in education, construction of railways and telegraphs, tax reform, etc.; president of supreme court (1861–80). His son **Pedro**

(1848–1910) was president of Chile (1906–10); died in office.

**Mon'tu'cla'** (môN'tü'klȧ'), **Jean Étienne.** 1725–1799. French mathematician; published anonymous treatise on history of the quadrature of the circle (1754) and first part of his history of mathematics, first good book of its kind (1758), completed by J. J. Le F. de Lalande.

**Mon'tyon'** (môN'tyôN'), Baron **de. Jean Baptiste Antoine Au'get'** (ō'zhĕ'). 1733–1820. French lawyer, economist, and philanthropist; councilor of state (1775); chancellor to Monsieur, brother of the king (1780); émigré (1789–1814); used great wealth to aid fellow émigrés and to encourage improvement in French arts and manufactures; instituted by bequest in his will what became known as the Montyon prize for virtue (*Prix de Vertu*), awarded annually to a worthy French man or woman of poor circumstances.

**Mon'vel'** (môN'vĕl'). *Stage name of* **Jacques Marie Bou'tet'** (bōō'tĕ'). 1745–1812. Father of Mlle. Mars. French actor and playwright; excelled as comedian; author of several comic operas and comedies, including *L'Amant Bourru* (1777), *Les Amours de Bayard* (1786).

**Monvel, Louis Maurice Boutet de.** See BOUTET DE MONVEL.

**Mony, Stéphane.** See under Eugène FLACHAT.

**Mon'y·pen'ny** (mŭn'ĭ·pĕn'ĭ), **William Fla·velle'** (flȧ·vĕl'). 1866–1912. British journalist, b. in County Armagh, Ireland; author of authoritative *Life of Benjamin Disraeli, Earl of Beaconsfield* (vol. i, 1910; ii, 1912; completed by George Earle Buckle, *q.v.*).

**Monzaemon, Chikamatsu.** See CHIKAMATSU.

**Monzambano.** See PUFENDORF.

**Mon'zie'** (môN'zē'), **Anatole de.** 1876–1947. French politician and scholar; finance minister (1925); minister of education (1925); minister of justice (1925); minister of public works (1925–26); founder and president, *Encyclopédie Française* (21 vols.).

**Moo'dy** (mōō'dĭ), **Dwight Lyman.** 1837–1899. American evangelist, b. Northfield, Mass.; shoe salesman, Boston and Chicago (to 1860); gave up business to devote himself to missionary work; organized North Market Sabbath School (1858) in Chicago; met Ira D. Sankey (1870); with him made two tours in Great Britain (1873–75 and 1881–83); campaigned in many cities in U.S. Founded Northfield Seminary for girls (1879), Mount Hermon School for boys (1881), Chicago Bible Institute (1889; now called Moody Bible Institute). His son **Paul Dwight** (1879–1947), Presbyterian clergyman; president of Middlebury (Vt.) College (1921–42).

**Moody, Helen Wills.** See Helen WILLS.

**Moody, James.** 1744–1809. American loyalist; spied on troops of Washington, Sullivan, and Gates (1779–80); after Revolution, received pension from British government and settled in Nova Scotia.

**Moody, John.** 1868–1958. American financial analyst, b. Jersey City, N.J.; on staff of Spencer Trask & Co., bankers (1890–1900); founded (1900) *Moody's Manual of Railroads and Corporation Securities;* founded (1905) and edited *Moody's Magazine*, an investor's monthly; founded (1909) *Moody's Analyses of Investments*, an annual publication. Author of *The Truth about Trusts* (1904), *How to Analyze Railroad Reports* (1911), *Profitable Investing* (1925), etc.

**Moody, Paul.** 1779–1831. American inventor, b. Newbury, Mass.; associate of Francis C. Lowell (*q.v.*); devised improvements in cotton spinning and weaving machinery at Waltham and Lowell, Mass.

**Moody, Paul Dwight.** See under Dwight L. MOODY.

**Moody, William Henry.** 1853–1917. American jurist, b. Newbury, Mass.; member, U.S. House of Representatives (1895–1902); U.S. secretary of the navy (1902–04); U.S. attorney general (1904–06); associate justice, U.S. Supreme Court (1906–10).

**Moody, William Vaughn. 1869–1910. American** poet and playwright, b. Spencer, Ind.; grad. Harvard (1893); teacher of English, U. of Chicago (1895–1907). Author of a volume of poems (1901); two dramas in verse, *The Masque of Judgment* (1900) and *The Fire-Bringer* (1904); and two important plays, *The Great Divide* (1906) and *The Faith Healer* (1909). With Robert Morss Lovett, wrote a *History of English Literature* (1902) and a textbook, *A First View of English Literature* (1905).

**Mook** (mōk), **Hubertus Johannes van.** 1895–1965. Dutch East Indian official; b. Java; director of department of economic affairs; appointed to negotiate with Japanese mission (Sept., 1940); by delaying negotiations, gained time to arm Netherlands East Indies; appointed minister of colonies in Netherlands government in exile (Nov., 1941), lieutenant governor general of Netherlands East Indies (Dec., 1941); after escape (Mar., 1942) from N.E.I. joined Dutch government in exile in England.

**Moon** (mōōn), **Parker Thomas.** 1892–1936. American educator, b. New York City; professor of international relations, Columbia (1931–36). Author of *Imperialism and World Politics* (1926), etc.; coauthor of history textbooks.

**Moon, William.** 1818–1894. English inventor (1845) of a system of embossed type (Moon's type) for the blind, easier to learn than Braille but requiring more space; totally blind (1840); issued Bible in his system, which he extended to Irish and Chinese.

**Moo'ney** (mōō'nĭ), **James.** 1861–1921. American ethnologist, b. Richmond, Ind.; on staff, Bureau of American Ethnology (1885–1921), esp. as investigator of Indians of the South and West. Coauthor of *Handbook of American Indians* (2 vols., 1907–10).

**Mooney, Thomas Joseph.** 1882–1942. American labor leader; with **Warren K. Bil'lings** [bĭl'ĭngz] (1893–1972), convicted of responsibility for bomb explosion that killed nine persons and wounded about 40 others in San Francisco during Preparedness Parade (July 22, 1916). Mooney condemned to death and Billings to life imprisonment; Mooney's sentence commuted by governor (Nov. 29, 1918) to life imprisonment. Both Mooney and Billings protested their innocence; case subject of several investigations. Mooney pardoned and released (Jan. 7, 1939); Billings released (Oct. 20, 1939); pardoned (Dec. 21, 1961).

**Moor** (mōr), **Karel de.** 1656–1738. Dutch portrait and genre painter and etcher, b. in Leiden.

**Moore** (mōōr; mōr), **Addison Webster.** 1866–1930. American philosopher; an adherent of pragmatism as expounded by John Dewey.

**Moore, Albert Joseph.** See under Henry MOORE (1831–1896).

**Moore, Alexander Pollock.** 1867–1930. American editor and diplomat, b. Pittsburgh, Pa.; editor in chief of Pittsburgh *Leader* (from 1904); bought New York *Daily Mirror* and Boston *Advertiser* (1928). U.S. ambassador to Spain (1923–25) and to Peru (1928–30). Husband of Lillian Russell (*q.v.*).

**Moore, Alfred.** 1755–1810. See under Maurice MOORE.

**Moore, Benjamin.** 1748–1816. American Protestant Episcopal clergyman, b. Newtown, Long Island, N.Y.; loyal to Great Britain through the Revolution; rector of Trinity Church (1800) and bishop (from 1801); professor at Columbia (1784–86) and president (1801–11). His son **Clement Clarke** (1779–1863) compiled *A Compendious Lexicon of the Hebrew Language* (1809); best known for authorship of the ballad *'Twas the night before Christmas*

(1822). Benjamin Moore's nephew **Nathaniel Fish Moore** (1782–1872), was president of Columbia (1842–49); author of works on the classics.

**Moore, Charles Herbert.** 1840–1930. American painter, b. New York City; specialized in study of medieval architecture; first curator of Fogg Museum (1895–1909). Author of *Character of Renaissance Architecture* (1905), etc.

**Moore, Clement Clarke.** See under Benjamin MOORE.

**Moore, Clifford Herschel.** 1866–1931. American classical scholar; professor, Harvard (from 1898).

**Moore, Daniel McFarlan.** 1869–1926. American electrical engineer; took out over 100 U.S. patents including many early inventions in the fields of radio, X ray, and tube lighting; invented gaseous conduction lamps used in facsimile reception of photographs by radio (1924); developed television and facsimile lamps.

**Moore, Douglas.** 1893–1969. American musician; composed opera *The Devil and Daniel Webster* (produced 1939), choral music, songs, etc.

**Moore, Edward.** 1712–1757. English playwright; author of a domestic tragedy of great vogue, *The Gamester*, produced with Garrick as Beverly the gambler (1753), and of *Fables for the Female Sex* (1744).

**Moore, Edward.** 1835–1916. British Dante scholar; canon of Canterbury (1903); editor of *Tutte le opere di Dante Alighieri* (1894), known as "the Oxford Dante."

**Moore, Edward Caldwell.** 1857–1943. American clergyman; professor of theology (1901–29) and Christian morals (1915–29), Harvard. Author of *History of Christian Thought since Kant* (1912), *The Nature of Religion* (1936), etc. His brother **Frank Gardner** (1865–1955) was professor of classical philology (1910–19) and Latin (1919–37), Columbia U.; author of *The Roman's World* (1936), etc.

**Moore, Eliakim Hastings.** 1862–1932. American mathematician; professor, U. of Chicago (1892–1931).

**Moore, Eva.** 1870–1955. English actress; m. Henry V. Esmond (d. 1922); appeared in *Duke of Killiecrankie*, *Sweet Kitty Bellairs*, *Little Lord Fauntleroy*, *The Dangerous Age*, and *The Holmses of Baker Street;* and in motion pictures, *Chu Chin Chow*, *Jew Süss*, *La Vie Parisienne*, and *Pride and Prejudice* (1936–37).

**Moore, Frank.** See under Jacob Bailey MOORE.

**Moore, Frank Frankfort.** 1855–1931. British poet, novelist, and playwright, b. in Ireland; journalist (1876–92). His verse includes *Flying from a Shadow*, *Dawn*, and *The Discoverer;* his novels, often sensational in character, include *The Silver Sickle* (1890), *They Call it Love* (1895), *The Sale of a Soul* (1895), *The Artful Miss Dill* (1906), *Fanny's First Novel* (1913), and *The Hand and Dagger* (1928); his plays include *A March Hare* (1877), *Moth and Flame* (1878), and *Kitty Clive, Actress* (1895).

**Moore, George.** 1852–1933. Irish novelist. Son of **George Henry Moore** (1811–1870), M.P. for Mayo. Educ. at Roman Catholic school and under a tutor in London; from age of eighteen studied art in Paris, joining group including Manet, Degas, Renoir, Monet; deserted brush for poetry under influence of Gautier, Baudelaire, Mallarmé, Verlaine, and produced *Flowers of Passion* (1878) and *Pagan Poems* (1882); worked hard at journalism in London (from 1882), acquiring English idiom to replace his French. Wrote his first novels, *A Modern Lover* (1883) and *A Mummer's Wife* (1885), showing influence of Flaubert and Zola, with intent of freeing English fiction from Victorian shackles; wrote successful novels in 1890's, returning to realism of Fielding tradition; received his first recognition for *Esther Waters* (1894); followed with *Evelyn Innes* (1898) and its sequel, *Sister Teresa* (1901). Championed impressionist painters in his art criticism, publishing *Impressions and Opinions* (1891), *Modern Painting* (1893). Returned to Ireland (1901), partly because of detestation of Boer War, and assisted Edward Martyn and W. B. Yeats with Irish literary revival, writing two plays, *The Bending of the Bough* (1900) and *The Strike at Arlingford* (1893), wrote also a novel *The Lake* (1905) and short stories *The Untilled Field* (1903) with Irish setting. Back in London, at Ebury Street (1911), renewed his autobiographical writings; visited Palestine in preparation for writing *The Brook Kerith* (the story of Jesus; 1916); believed he attained peak of his artistry in *Héloïse and Abélard* (1921); rewrote his first novel, *A Modern Lover*, as *Lewis Seymour and Some Women* (1917). Turned to drama; published *The Coming of Gabrielle* (1920); won a success with *The Making of an Immortal* (1928); his other late fiction, *Daphnis and Chloe* (1924), and *Ulick and Soracha*, an Irish story of Middle Ages. Author of reminiscences and autobiographical works including *Confessions of a Young Man* (1888), *Memoirs of my Dead Life* (1905), *Hail and Farewell* (*Ave*, 1911; *Salve*, 1912; *Vale*, 1914).

**Moore, George Edward.** 1873–1958. English philosopher; author of *Principia Ethica* (1903), *Philosophical Studies* (1922), etc.

**Moore, George Foot.** 1851–1931. American Orientalist; professor, Andover Theol. Sem. (1883–1902); professor of the history of religion, Harvard (1902–28). Author of *History of Religions* (2 vols., 1913–19), etc.

**Moore, George Henry.** See under Jacob Bailey MOORE.

**Moore, George Thomas.** 1871–1956. American botanist; in charge of botany, Marine Biological Laboratory, Woods Hole, Mass. (1909–19); professor, Washington U. (1909–12). Discovered a method for preventing pollution of water supplies by algae and certain bacteria; perfected method for inoculating soil with bacteria to enable certain plants to utilize atmospheric nitrogen.

**Moore,** Sir **Henry.** 1713–1769. English colonial governor in America, b. in Jamaica; acting governor of Jamaica (1756–62); governor of New York (1765–69).

**Moore, Henry.** 1831–1896. English marine painter; occupied himself with landscapes and animals, until diverted to seascapes (from 1857), including *The Newhaven Packet*, *Catspaws off the Land*, *Mount's Bay;* R.A. (1893). His brother **Albert Joseph** (1841–1893) executed decorative work for theaters and churches, at first following Pre-Raphaelites; developed a style classic in character, using figures of women of Greek mold with gay, diaphanous draperies. Another brother, **John Collingham** (1829–1880), was a painter in water color, known for portraits of children and for Italian landscapes. Their father, **William Moore** (1790–1851), of York, was a successful portrait painter in oils, water color, and pastel.

**Moore, Henry.** 1898– . English sculptor; works represented in Tate Gallery in London, Museum of Modern Art in New York, and Victoria and Albert Museum.

**Moore, Henry Ludwell.** 1869– . American economist; professor, Columbia (1902–29). Author of *Laws of Wages* (1911), *Synthetic Economics* (1929), etc.

**Moore, Hugh Kelsea.** 1872–1939. American chemical engineer; invented unsubmerged diaphragm cell (1897), new method of making calcium arsenate (1925–27), stationary furnace for recovery of soda from black liquor (1913–15), acid-resisting hydraulic cement (1926–27), etc.

**Moore, Jacob Bailey.** 1797–1853. American journalist and historian, b. Andover, N.H.; librarian, New Hampshire Historical Society (1823–30; 1837–39), New York Historical Society (1848–49). Published *Collections of the New Hampshire Historical Society* (1824–32), *Laws of Trade in the United States* (1840), and other historical compilations. A son, **George Henry** (1823–1892), was librarian of the New York Historical Society (1849–76) and of the Lenox Library in New York (1872–92). Another son, **Horatio Franklin,** *known as* **Frank** (1828–1904), was a miscellaneous writer and compiler, esp. of works on the Revolutionary and Civil war periods.

**Moore, James.** 1737–1777. See under Maurice MOORE.

**Moore, James Hobart.** See at William Henry MOORE.

**Moore,** Sir **John.** 1761–1809. British general, b. Glasgow; served in America (1779–83); assisted in reduction of French garrisons in Corsica (1794); served in West Indies, Ireland, and Holland; distinguished himself before Alexandria and Cairo (1801); commander in chief in Portugal (1808); ordered to expel French from Peninsula; approached Madrid only to find that Napoleon with 70,000 men had occupied Madrid and cut off his retreat to Portugal; forced to make disastrous retreat through mountainous country to La Coruña, about 250 miles, in winter; attacked by Soult at beginning of embarkation, defeated French, killing 2000, but fell mortally wounded in moment of victory (Jan. 16, 1809); buried in ramparts of La Coruña, as related in Charles Wolfe's poem *The Burial of Sir John Moore.*

His father, **John Moore** (1729–1802), Scottish physician, surgeon in navy and army; traveled with young duke of Hamilton (1772–78); author of travel books, medical sketches, and an account of French Revolution, but remembered chiefly for novel *Zeluco* (1786), which suggested Byron's *Childe Harold.*

**Moore, John Bassett.** 1860–1947. American jurist and publicist, b. Smyrna, Del.; professor of international law and diplomacy, Columbia (1891–1924); member, Hague Tribunal (1912–28); judge, Permanent Court of International Justice (1921–28). Author of *History and Digest of International Arbitrations* (6 vols., 1898), *A Digest of International Law* (1906).

**Moore, Julia A.** 1847–1920. American poet; known as the "Sweet Singer of Michigan"; published *The Sentimental Song-Book* (1878).

**Moore, Marianne Craig.** 1887–1972. American poet, b. St. Louis, Mo.; A.B., Bryn Mawr (1909). Edited *The Dial* (1925–1929); author of *Poems* (1921), *Complete Poems* (1967); Pulitzer prize in poetry (1952).

**Moore, Maurice.** 1735–1777. American jurist, b. in New Hanover County, N.C.; prominent in pre-Revolutionary activities, upholding colonial cause short of actual separation from Great Britain. His brother **James** (1737–1777) was brigadier general commanding forces in North Carolina; died while planning march northward to join Washington. Maurice's son **Alfred** (1755–1810) served in American Revolution; was attorney general of North Carolina (1782–91); associate justice, U.S. Supreme Court (1799–1804).

**Moore, Nathaniel Fish.** See under Benjamin MOORE.

**Moore, Richard Bishop.** 1871–1931. American chemist; specialized in study of rare gases and radium; with U.S. Bureau of Mines (1912–23); surveyed radium deposits in Colorado and supervised production of first radium salts in U.S.; pioneer in advocating use of helium in balloons and dirigibles; influential in determining policy of conservation of helium gas.

**Moore, Roger.** See Rory O'MORE (3).

**Moore, Stanford.** 1913– . Biochemist, b. Chicago. Ph.D., Wisconsin, 1938. Shared 1972 Nobel prize for chemistry with C. B. Anfinsen and W. H. Stein for enzyme studies.

**Moore, Thomas.** *Pseudonyms* **Thomas Little** *and* **Thomas Brown** the younger. 1779–1852. Irish poet, b. Dublin; son of grocer and wine merchant; educ. Trinity Coll., Dublin (1794), and Middle Temple, London (1799). Admiralty registrar, Bermuda (1803), left post in charge of deputy and traveled through U.S. and Canada. Published translation of *Odes of Anacreon* (1800), *Poetical Works of late Thomas Little* (1801), and *Odes and Epistles* (1806); gained reputation as national lyrist of Ireland by his *Irish Melodies,* with music by Sir John Stevenson (irregularly pub. 1807–34), and *National Airs* (1818–27); m. (1811) Bessie Dyke, actress. Found vent for his wit in pungent satirical verses collected (1813) in *The Twopenny Post Bag,* lampooning prince regent because of failure to support Roman Catholic emancipation. Contracted with Longmans for metrical romance on Eastern subject, and after being forestalled by Byron's *The Giaour* and *The Bride of Abydos,* produced *Lalla Rookh* (1817), which earned him European reputation. Forced to retire to Continent by embezzlement of £6000 by his deputy in Bermuda (1818); traveled in Italy with Lord John Russell; visited Byron, whose memoirs he received in trust and later destroyed; wrote in Paris *The Loves of the Angels,* an Oriental poem (1823); after *The Epicurean,* an imaginative work (1827), confined himself to prose, including lives of Sheridan (1825), Lord Edward Fitzgerald (1831), Byron (1830), and *History of Ireland* (1827); edited Byron's works; received literary pension (1835). Author also of *The Fudge Family in Paris* (1818), *The Fudges in England* (1835), *Fables for the Holy Alliance* (1823), and *Rhymes on the Road.*

**Moore, Thomas Sturge.** 1870–1944. English writer and wood engraver; among his books of verse are *The Vine-dresser and other Poems* (1899), *Absalom* (1903), *The Sicilian Idyll and Judith* (1911), *The Powers of the Air* (1920), and *The Unknown Known...* (1939); among his prose works, studies of Dürer (1904), Correggio (1906), *Art and Life* (1910), *Some Soldier Poets* (1919), and *Armour for Aphrodite* (1929).

**Moore, Veranus Alva.** 1859–1931. American bacteriologist and pathologist; professor, Cornell U. veterinary college (1896–1929); author of *Principles of Microbiology* (1912), *Bovine Tuberculosis and its Control* (1913), etc.

**Moore, William Henry** (1848–1923), b. Utica, N.Y., and his brother **James Hobart** (1852–1916), b. Berkshire, N.Y. American promoters and stock-market operators, active (1898–1904) in merging corporations, esp. in the steel industry and in the railroad field. The resulting steel corporations, such as American Steel Hoop Co. and American Sheet Steel Co., were later absorbed into Morgan's creation The United States Steel Corp. The railroad promotions, beginning with the Chicago, Rock Island & Pacific, and expanding to include the St. Louis & San Francisco, Chicago & Alton, and Lehigh Valley, finally brought disaster, the Rock Island treasury being exhausted and the road forced into receivership.

**Moore, Zephaniah Swift.** 1770–1823. American Congregational clergyman and educator; professor, Dartmouth (1811–15); president, Williams (1815–20); first president, Amherst (1821–23).

**Moore'–Brab'a·zon** (mo͝or'brăb'ȧ·z'n; mōr'-), **John Theodore Cuthbert.** 1st Baron **Brabazon of Tara.** 1884–1964. British aviator and government administrator; educ. Cambridge; M.P. (1918–29); winner of first British Empire Michelin cup; served in flying corps in World War I (1914–18); developed aerial photography.

**Moore'head** (mo͝or'hĕd; mōr'-), **Warren King.** 1866–1939. Archaeologist, b. Siena, Italy, of American parentage; explored mounds and remains in Ohio Valley, Utah, Colorado, and New Mexico, for Chicago Exposition (1893). Author of *The Stone Age in North America,* etc.

**Mor, Anthonis.** See Sir Anthony MORE.

**Mo′ra** (mō′rȧ), **Francis Lu′is** (lo͞o′ĭs). 1874–1940. Painter, b. in Montevideo, Uruguay; to U.S. in childhood; did murals for Red Cross headquarters in Washington, D.C. His portrait of President Warren G. Harding hangs in the White House.

**Mo·raes′** (mo͞o·rĭsh′), **Francisco de.** 1500?–1572. Portuguese romancer; author of famous romance of chivalry *Palmeirim de Inglaterra.*

**Mo·raes′ Bar′ros** (mo͞o·rīs′ bȧr′ro͞os), **Prudente José de.** 1841–1902. Brazilian lawyer and political leader; president of Brazil (1894–98; "first civilian president").

**Mo·raes′ e Sil′va** (mo͞o·rīz′ ē sĭl′vȧ), **Antonio de.** 1757?–1825. Brazilian lexicographer; compiler of *Diccionario da Lingua Portugueza* (2 vols., 1789).

**Mo·ra′is** (mô·rä′ĭs), **Sa·bat′o** (sȧ·băt′ō). 1823–1897. Rabbi, b. Leghorn, Italy; to U.S. (1851); rabbi of congregation in Philadelphia (1851–97); founder and president, Jewish Theological Seminary, N.Y. (1886–97).

**Mo·ra′les** (mô·rä′lās), **Agustín.** 1810–1872. Bolivian general; president of Bolivia (1871–72); assassinated.

**Morales, Luis de.** *Called* **El Di·vi′no** (ĕl dē·vē′nō). 1510?–1586. Spanish religious painter; called (1563) by Philip II to assist in decorating the Escorial. His works include an *Ecce Homo* (New York Historical Society gallery), *Pietà* (in Madrid Academy), *Virgin and Child, Mater Dolorosa* and *Presentation in the Temple* (all in the Prado).

**Mo·ran′** (mô·răn′), **Edward** (1829–1901) and his brothers **Thomas** (1837–1926) and **Peter** (1841–1914). Painters, b. Bolton, England; to U.S. (1844). Edward is known as a marine painter; Thomas was a landscape painter and etcher, best known for his paintings of the Yellowstone region of western U.S. Peter is best known for his paintings and etchings of animal life. Edward's son **Edward Percy** (1862–1935) was also an artist, specializing in subjects drawn from American history. Thomas's son **John Léon** (1863–1941) was known esp. as a figure painter.

**Mo′ran** (mō′răn), **Patrick Francis.** 1830–1911. Roman Catholic cardinal, b. County Carlow, Ireland; private secretary to his uncle Archbishop Cullen (*q.v.*); archbishop of Sydney, Australia (1884); cardinal (1885). Controversialist on religious questions; builder of churches, schools, hospitals.

**Mo′rand′** (mô′räɴ′), **Paul.** 1888– . French diplomat and writer; made reputation with stories and novels of postwar cosmopolitan Europe, as in *Ouvert la Nuit* (1922), *Fermé la Nuit* (1923), *Lewis et Irène* (1924), *L'Europe Galante* (1925), *Magie Noire* (1928).

**Mo·rant′** (mô·rănt′), Sir **Robert Laurie.** 1863–1920. English educator; in Siam as tutor to royal family and educational organizer; reported to Board of Education (from 1895) on education in France, Switzerland, England; instrumental in passage of Education Act (1902); as secretary, remodeled Board of Education (1903–11); chairman of national health insurance commission (1911–19) and first secretary of ministry of health (1919–20).

**Mo′ran·zo′ni** (mō′rän·tsō′nē), **Roberto.** 1882–1959. Italian opera conductor in Bologna, Milan, Turin, and other Italian cities, also in Paris and London; conductor, Boston Opera Co. (1910–16), Metropolitan Opera House, New York (1917–27), and Chicago Civic Opera (1924).

**Mo·ra′ta** (mô·rä′tä), **Olimpia Fulvia.** 1526–1555. Italian classical scholar, b. at Ferrara; in addition to Latin treatises, she wrote poetry, chiefly in Greek.

**Mo′ra·tín′** (mō′rä·tēn′), **Nicolás Fernández de.** 1737–1780. Spanish playwright and poet; introduced principles of French literary classicism in Spanish play construction; among his poetical works are *Diana, Las Naves de Cortés Destruidas*, and verses on a bullfight. His son **Leandro Fernández** (1760–1828) was also playwright and poet; among his plays are *El Viejo y la Niña* (1790), *El Barón* (1803), *La Mojigata* (1804), and *El Si de las Niñas* (1806); wrote also a history of Spanish stage.

**Mo·ra′via** (mô·rä′vyä), **Alberto.** Pseudonym of **Alberto Pincherle.** 1907– . Italian writer of post-World War II realistic school. Novels include *La Romana* (*The Woman of Rome*, 1947). *Il Conformista* (*The Conformist*, 1951), *La Ciociara* (*Two Women*, 1957), *Io e lui* (*Two*, 1972).

**Mor′ay** (mûr′ĭ). See also MURRAY.

**Moray,** Earls of. See (1) Sir Thomas RANDOLPH; (2) STEWART family.

**Mo′ra·zán′** (mō′rä·sän′), **Francisco.** 1799–1842. Central American statesman, b. in Honduras; after Honduras gained independence (1821), aided in organizing new government; led army in victories over reactionaries in El Salvador (1828) and Guatemala (1829); elected president of Central American Confederation (1830–40); failed to keep country united, fled to Peru; organized army and invaded Costa Rica with intention of restoring Confederation (1842); captured and shot.

**Mor′car** (môr′kär) *or* **Mor′ke′re** (môr′kĕ′rĕ). fl. 1066. Earl of the Northumbrians; aided Northumbrians to expel Tostig (1065), and was chosen earl; defeated by Norsemen at Fulford Gate; left Harold to fight alone at Hastings; submitted to William the Conqueror; but later (1068) rebelled; joined insurgents in Isle of Ely.

**Mor′dacq′** (môr′dȧk′), **Jean Jules Henri.** 1868–1943. French general of brigade (1916) and of division (1917); appointed by Clemenceau chief of his military cabinet (1917–20); author of treatises on the last stages of the World War I, the armistice, and the peace of 1919.

**Mor′daunt** (môr′d'nt). Name of an English family holding the earldom of **Pe′ter·bor′ough** [pē′tẽr·bûr′ô; -bŭ·rŭ; -brŭ] (cr. 1628) and barony of Mordaunt, and including: Sir **John Mordaunt** (d. 1504), speaker of House of Commons. His son **John** (1490?–1562), 1st Baron **Mordaunt of Tur′vey** (tûr′vĭ); participated in trial of Anne Boleyn. **John** (1627–1675), 1st Baron **Mordaunt of Rei′gate** (rī′gĭt) *and* Viscount **Mordaunt;** son of **John Mordaunt** (d. 1642), 1st Earl of Peterborough; during Commonwealth, planned insurrections in king's favor; lord lieutenant of Surrey (1660). **Charles** (1658–1735), 3d Earl of Peterborough; son of John (1627–1675); military and naval commander and diplomat; accompanied expeditions to Barbary Coast (between 1674 and 1680); intrigued against James II in Holland; on William III's accession, became privy councilor and first lord of treasury (1689); imprisoned (1697) on suspicion of complicity in Sir John Fenwick's plot; sent to command in Spain in War of Spanish Succession (1705), captured Barcelona, made triumphal entry into Valencia, returned to assume command of fleet and raised siege of Barcelona; recalled (1707); joined Tories; sent on special embassies to southern Europe; commander in chief of naval forces under George I; acknowledged **Anastasia Robinson** (d. 1755), famous operatic singer whom he married secretly (1722?), as countess shortly before death; patron of letters; friend of Swift, Pope, Arbuthnot, Gay. **Henry Mordaunt** (1681?–1710) and Sir **John Mordaunt** (1697–1780), son and nephew of 3d earl, naval and military commanders, respectively, were charged with failures but acquitted by courts-martial.

**Mordaunt, Elinor.** *Maiden name* **Evelyn May Clowes** (?klouz; klo͞oz). 1877–1942. English traveler, novelist, and short-story writer; m. 1st Mordaunt, 2d Robert Rawnsley Bowles (1933); in Mauritius (1897–99), Australia (1902–08); on trip around the world for the *Daily*

*News* (1923). Among her books are *The Garden of Contentment*, *The Ship of Solace*, *Lu of the Ranges*, *Reputation* (1923), *Shoe and Stocking Stories* (1926), *Father and Daughter* (1928), *Full Circle* (1931), *The Family* (1934), *Pity of the World* (1938), *Roses in December* (1939).

**Mor′de·cai** (môr′dē·kī; môr′dē·kā′ī). *In Douay Version* **Mar′do·chai** (mär′dō·kī; mär′dō·kā′ī). In the Bible, cousin of Esther who saved the Jews from destruction planned by Haman. Cf. ESTHER.

**Mord′kin** (môrt′kyĭn), **Mikhail.** 1882?–1944. Russian dancer; ballet master in Moscow, and partner of Anna Pavlova; appeared in U.S. (1924) with own company.

**More** (mōr), Sir **Anthony.** *Known as* **Antonio Mo′ro** (mô′rō). *Properly* **Anthonis Mor** (môr). 1512?–?1576. Flemish portrait painter; invited to Madrid by Emperor Charles V; sent to England, where he painted his masterpiece, portrait of Queen Mary for her bridegroom, Philip of Spain (1553), also portraits of Sir Thomas Gresham and Sir Henry Lee.

**More** (mōr), **Hannah.** 1745–1833. English religious writer, daughter of village schoolmaster at Stapleton, Bristol. Wrote verse early and came before the public with the pastoral drama *The Search after Happiness* (1762) and *The Inflexible Captive* (1774), based on an opera by Metastasio. To London (1774); became clever writer of verse and witty talker in circle of Johnson, Reynolds, and Garrick; taken up by Elizabeth Montagu; had two dramas produced, *Percy* (1777) and *Fatal Falsehood* (1779); after Garrick's death thought playgoing wrong and on publication of *Sacred Dramas* (1782) and *Thoughts on Importance of the Manners of the Great to General Society* (1788) devoted herself to social and religious amelioration; set up Sunday schools in Cheddar neighborhood (1789); shared evangelical views of William Wilberforce and Zachary Macaulay; wrote *An Estimate of the Religion of the Fashionable World* (1790), and to counteract teachings of Tom Paine and the French Revolution, a tract *Village Politics* (1792), the beginning of the series known as "Cheap Repository Tracts," including the *Shepherd of Salisbury Plain.* Author of many other ethical books and tracts including *Hints Towards Forming the Character of a Young Princess* (written at request of queen; 1805), *Coelebs in Search of a Wife* (a novel in name only, her most popular work; 1809), *Practical Piety* (1811), *Moral Sketches* (1819).

**More, Henry.** 1614–1687. English philosopher of Cambridge Platonist school; M.A., Cantab. (1639); fascinated by Neoplatonism; remained in Cambridge all his life; declined mastership of his college and two bishoprics; composed books in verse and prose under spiritual stimulus of one of his pupils, Anne, Viscountess Conway, at her country seat at Ragley, Warwickshire. Author of *Psychozoia Platonica* (verse; 1642), *Philosophicall Poems* (1647), and *Divine Dialogues* (summarizing his view of philosophy and religion; 1668).

**More, Louis Trenchard.** 1870–1944. American physicist, b. St. Louis, Mo.; professor (from 1900), dean (1910–13), dean of graduate school (from 1916), U. of Cincinnati. Author of *The Limitations of Science*, *The Dogma of Evolution*, *Life of Isaac Newton.*

**More, Paul Elmer.** 1864–1937. American essayist and critic, b. St. Louis, Mo.; taught Sanskrit, Harvard (1894–95), Bryn Mawr (1895–97). Literary editor, *The Independent* (1901–03), New York *Evening Post* (1903–09); editor, *The Nation* (1909–14). Lectured on Plato at Princeton U.; associated with Irving Babbitt as champion of humanism. Author of many critical essays published in more than 11 vols. as *Shelburne Essays* (1904 ff.), and of *Life of Benjamin Franklin* (1900), *Platonism* (1917), *The Religion of Plato* (1921), *Hellenistic Philosophies* (1923), *The Demon of the Absolute* (1928), *The Sceptical Approach to Religion* (1934), etc.

**More,** Sir **Thomas.** Also Saint **Thomas More.** 1478–1535. English statesman and author; son of Sir John More, judge. Page in household of Archbishop Morton (1491), who sent him to Oxford; friend of Erasmus, Colet, and Lyly and pupil of Linacre and Grocyn; called to bar, where he was eminently successful; subjected himself to discipline of Carthusian monk (1499–1503); M.P. (1504); successfully opposed Henry VII's demand for aid in money on marriage of Princess Margaret; undersheriff of London (1510). While envoy to Flanders sketched description in Latin of imaginary island of Utopia which he completed and published (1516). Impressed king by arguments in a celebrated Star Chamber case; master of requests (1514); privy councilor (1518); at Field of Cloth of Gold met Guillaume Budé, or Budaeus, Greek scholar (1520); accompanied Wolsey to Calais and Bruges (1521); recommended by Wolsey, elected speaker of House of Commons; chancellor of duchy of Lancaster (1525). Appeared as champion of king against Luther's measures of reform (1523); directed his first English controversial book, *Dialogue*, against Tyndale's writings (1528). On fall of Wolsey succeeded against his will as lord chancellor of England, the first layman to hold the office (1529); despatched cases with unprecedented rapidity but treated heretics without mercy; sought more rational theology and radical reform of clergy but supported historic church; quarreled with Henry VIII over relaxation of heresy laws, refused to take oath renouncing jurisdiction of any but the sovereign over the church; resigned (1532). Charged with high treason, along with Elizabeth Barton, the "holy maid of Kent"; steadfastly refused (1534) along with John Fisher, Bishop of Rochester, to take oath impugning pope's authority or upholding Henry VIII's divorce from Catherine of Aragon; during imprisonment prepared a *Dialogue of Comfort against Tribulation;* sentence to be hanged commuted by king to decapitation; his head fixed upon London Bridge. Beatified by Leo XIII (1886), canonized (1935). Critic and patron of art; known for his *Utopia*, describing communal ownership of land, educations of men and women alike, and religious toleration. Author also of *Life of John Picus, Earl of Mirandula* (1510), showing his humanistic ideals, and *History of Richard III.*

**Mo′ré′as′** (mô′rā′äs′), **Jean.** *Pseudonym of* **Ioannes Pa′pa·dia′man·to′pou·los** (pä′pä·thyä′män·tô′pōō-lôs). 1856–1910. Poet, b. Athens, Greece; settled in Paris (1882); at first identified with symbolists and decadents (as by his *Les Syrtes*, 1884, and *Les Cantilènes*, 1886), he organized with Maurras and others what was called École Romane, and published *Pèlerin Passionné* (1890), *Ériphyle* (1894), *Sylves* (1896), etc.; finally, in conventional verse, wrote six books of short poems, *Stances* (1899–1901).

**Mo′reau′** (mô′rō′), **Émile.** 1852–1922. French writer and playwright; among plays are *Camille Desmoulins* (1879), *Un Divorce* (1884), *Matapan* (1886), *La Peur de l'Être* (1889), *L'Auberge des Mariniers* (1891), *Mme de la Valette* (1899), and *La Reine Élisabeth* (1912); collaborated with Sardou in *Cléopâtre* (1890) and *Mme Sans-Gêne* (1893).

**Moreau, Gustave.** 1826–1898. French painter; regarded as showing reaction from naturalism of Courbet and Manet; bequeathed his home and its furnishings to city of Paris for Musée Gustave Moreau.

**Moreau, Jean Victor.** 1763–1813. French soldier of Revolutionary and Napoleonic armies; commanded army of the Rhine and Moselle (1796) and drove Austrians back to the Danube; commanded army in Italy (1799) and was defeated at Cassano d'Adda; commanded army of the Rhine (1800) and won battle of Hohenlinden (Dec. 3, 1800); headed Republican and Royalist conspiracy against Napoleon and was exiled after being convicted of complicity in the Cadoudal and Pichegru plots; lived near Trenton, N.J. (1805–13); entered Russian service and was mortally wounded at battle of Dresden (Aug. 27, 1813), dying Sept. 2.

**Moreau, Louis Gabriel.** 1740–1806. French painter, a precursor of modern landscape school. His brother **Jean Michel** (1741–1814) was an engraver and illustrator; best known for illustrations of Molière, Voltaire, and Rousseau.

**Moreau, Luc Albert.** 1882–1948. French painter, lithographer, and illustrator.

**Moreau de Saint'-Mé'ry'** (dē săɴ'mā'rē'), **Médéric Louis Élie.** 1750–1819. French lawyer and historian, b. Fort Royal, Martinique; practiced law in Santo Domingo. In Paris, published *Loix et Constitutions des Colonies Françaises de l'Amérique sous le Vent* (6 vols., 1784–90). A founder and president (1787) of the Museum of Paris. Ruled Paris for three days after the fall of the Bastille (1789); fled to America (1794) to escape the guillotine; opened bookselling and publishing house in Philadelphia, which became (1794–98) a meeting place of French émigrés. Returned to Paris (1798); historiographer, ministry of marine; councilor of state (1800); administrator of Parma, Piacenza, and Guastalla (1802–06); recalled by Napoleon (1806).

**Mo·reel'se** (mō·rāl'sĕ), **Paulus.** 1571–1638. Dutch portrait and historical painter and architect.

**More'house** (mōr'hous), **Daniel Walter.** 1876–1941. American astronomer, b. Mankato, Minn.; professor (from 1900), dean of college of liberal arts (1923–30), president (from 1923), Drake U. Discovered comet named after him (1908).

**Morehouse, Ward.** 1899–1966. American journalist and playwright, b. Savannah, Ga.; on staff of New York *Tribune* (to 1926), New York *Sun* (from 1926). Author of *Gentlemen of the Press* (a play); coauthor of *Forsaking All Others.*

**Moreira Penna.** See PENNA.

**Mo'rel'** (mô'rĕl'). Family of French printers and scholars, including: **Fédéric** (1523–1583), royal printer (1571–83); known for his excellent editions of ancient classics. His son **Fédéric** (1552–1630), Hellenic scholar. Two sons of Fédéric the younger, **Fédéric III** (b. 1573?), royal printer (1602–24), and **Claude** (1574–1626), royal printer (1625–26). Claude's two sons **Charles** (b. 1612), royal printer (1635–39) and secretary to the king (1639), and **Gilles** (b. 1616?), who took over the press from his brother Charles (1639), printed *Magna Bibliotheca Patrum* (1643), transferred the business to his partner Simon Piget and became counselor to the Grand Council (1650–75).

**Mo·rell'** (mō·rĕl'), **Thomas.** 1703–1784. English classical scholar; supplied libretti for Handel's oratorios, including *Judas Maccabaeus* (1746) and *Joshua* (1748), in both of which appeared the song "See the conquering hero comes"; editor of Chaucer and Spenser.

**Morella,** Conde **de.** See Ramón CABRERA.

**Mo'rel'-La'deuil'** (mô'rĕl'là'dû'y'), **Léonard.** 1824–1888. French sculptor and goldsmith, regarded as one of the masters of repoussé; engaged in England (from 1859) by Birmingham goldsmith firm Messrs. Elkington.

**Mo'rel'let'** (mô'rĕ'lĕ'), **André.** 1727–1819. French philosopher and man of letters; contributor to Diderot's *Encyclopédie.*

**Mo·rel'li** (mō·rĕl'lē), **Domenico.** 1826–1901. Italian painter; with Filippo Palizzi, leader of the Realist movement in Italy; known especially for his historical and genre paintings, and later, for his Biblical scenes.

**Morelli, Giovanni.** *Pseudonym* **Ivan Ler·mol'iev** (lyĕr·môl'yĕf). 1816–1891. Italian art critic; member, Italian parliament (1860–70); senator (1873 ff.); secured art-conservation law now bearing his name; developed successful principles of art criticism based chiefly on observation that rendition of details (hair, ears, fingers, etc.) is conventional and uniform for each master and hence an accurate means of identification.

**Mo·re'los y Pa·vón'** (mō·rā'lōs ē pä·vôn'), **José María.** 1765–1815. Mexican priest and patriot; joined insurrection led by Hidalgo (1810) and succeeded Hidalgo as leader of rebels; at first successful, issued a declaration of independence from Spain (Nov. 6, 1813); finally defeated by royalists, captured, and shot. Hidalgo (*q.v.*) and Morelos y Pavón are honored as earliest martyrs in struggle for Mexican independence.

**Moreno, Alfredo Baquerizo.** See BAQUERIZO MORENO.

**Mo're'ri'** (mô'rā'rē'), **Louis.** 1643–1680. French Roman Catholic priest and scholar; compiler of *Grand Dictionnaire Historique ou Mélange Curieux de l'Histoire Sacrée et Profane* (1674).

**Mores'by** (mōrz'bĭ), Sir **Fairfax.** 1786–1877. English naval commander; suppressed slave trade at Mauritius (1821–23); admiral (1864); admiral of the fleet (1870). Grandfather of Lily Adams Beck (pseud. **Louis Moresby**). See BECK.

**Mo'ret'** (mô'rĕ'), **Alexandre.** 1868–1938. French Egyptologist.

**Mo·re'to y Ca·va'ña** (mō·rā'tō ē kä·vä'nyä), **Agustín.** 1618?–1669. Spanish playwright; friend of Calderón; among his plays are *El Valiente Justiciero*, *El Lindo Don Diego*, *El Desdén con el Desden*, and *Rico Hombre de Alcalá.*

**Mo·ret'ti** (mō·rāt'tē), **Marino.** 1885– . Italian writer; one of so-called "twilight poets" (poeti crepuscolari).

**Mo·ret'to, Il** (ēl mō·rāt'tō). *Real name* **Alessandro Bon'vi·ci'no** (bōn'vē·chē'nō) *or* **Buon'vi·ci'no** (bwôn'-). 1498–1554. Italian painter, b. Brescia; leading master of Brescian school; known esp. for color harmony. His *Entombment of Christ* and *Christ in the Desert* are in Metropolitan Museum, New York.

**Mo'reux'** (mô'rû'), **Théophile,** *known as* **Abbé Théophile.** 1867–1954. French meteorologist and astronomer; founder and director of observatory at Bourges.

**Mo'rey** (mō'rĭ), **Samuel.** 1762–1843. American inventor, b. Hebron, Conn.; known for his experiments (1790–97) with steamboats and his claim that Fulton profited from his ideas; also, obtained patent (Apr. 1, 1826) for a type of internal-combustion engine.

**Mor'fill** (môr'fĭl), **William Richard.** 1834–1909. English Slavonic scholar; author of grammars of Polish, Serbian, Russian, Czech, Bulgarian.

**Mor'ford** (môr'fērd), **Henry.** 1823–1881. American miscellaneous writer; best known for his guidebooks, including *Morford's Short-Trip Guide to Europe* (1868) and *Morford's Short-Trip Guide to America* (1872).

**Mor·ga'gni** (môr·gä'nyē), **Giovanni Battista.** 1682–1771. Italian physician; founder of pathological anatomy.

**Mor'gan** (môr'găn), **Angela.** d. 1957. American poet, b. Washington, D.C. *The Hour Has Struck* (1914), *Utterance and Other Poems* (1916), *Forward March!* (1918), *Hail, Man!* (1919), *Because of Beauty* (1922), *Crucify Me!* (1933), etc. Her poem *The Unknown Soldier* was read over the bier of the unknown soldier in the rotunda of the Capitol, Washington, D.C.

**Morgan, Arthur Ernest.** 1878– . American civil engineer and educator, b. Cincinnati; president, Antioch Coll. (1920–36); chairman, Tennessee Valley Authority (1933–38); dismissed by President Roosevelt for refusing to submit evidence to support his charges against other members of the commission.

**Morgan, Augustus de.** See De Morgan.

**Morgan, Charles.** 1795–1878. American shipping and railroad magnate; established steamer lines from New Orleans to Texan, Mexican and Central American ports; founder of the Morgan Line from New York to New Orleans; also bought railway lines in Louisiana and Texas to give him monopoly of transportation business in Gulf of Mexico region.

**Morgan, Charles Langbridge.** 1894–1958. English novelist and dramatic critic; served in navy (1907–13, 1914–18); dramatic critic for London *Times* (from 1921). Author of *The Gunroom* (1919), *My Name Is Legion* (1925), *Portrait in a Mirror* (1929), *The Fountain* (1932; awarded Hawthornden prize), *Sparkenbroke* (1936), *The Flashing Stream* (play; 1938), *The Voyage* (1940), *The Empty Room* (1941). Married (1923) **Hilda Vaughan** (vôn) (1892– ), author of *The Battle to the Weak, The Invader, The Soldier and the Gentlewoman, A Thing of Nought, Harvest Home,* etc.

**Morgan, Conway Lloyd.** 1852–1936. English zoologist and psychologist; professor (from 1884), principal (1887–1909), first vice-chancellor, U. of Bristol; sometimes called founder of comparative psychology. Author of *Animal Life and Intelligence* (1890), *Introduction to Comparative Psychology* (1895), *Psychology for Teachers* (1895), *Habit and Instinct* (1896), *Animal Behaviour* (1900), *The Interpretation of Nature* (1905), *Instinct and Experience* (1912), *Emergent Evolution* (1923), *Life, Mind, and Spirit* (1926), *Mind at the Cross-ways* (1929), *The Animal Mind* (1930), *The Emergence of Novelty* (1933).

**Morgan, Daniel.** 1736–1802. American Revolutionary soldier, b. prob. in Hunterdon County, N.J.; served under Arnold in assault on Quebec (Dec. 31, 1775), under Gates in opposing Burgoyne (1777); as brigadier general, commanded troops in western North Carolina, and defeated British at Cowpens (Jan. 17, 1781); commanded Virginia militia in suppressing Whisky Insurrection (1794) in western Pennsylvania.

**Morgan, Edmund Morris, Jr.** 1878–1966. American lawyer and educator; professor, U. of Minnesota (1912–17), Yale (1917–25), Harvard (from 1925). Coauthor of *Cases on Common Law Pleading* (1917) and *Cases on Evidence* (1934).

**Morgan, Edwin Barber.** 1806–1881. American merchant and express executive, b. Aurora, N.Y.; first president, Wells, Fargo & Co. (1852); a founder, U.S. Express Co. (1854); benefactor of Wells College, at Aurora, and Auburn Theological Seminary. His first cousin, **Edwin Denison Morgan** (1811–1883), b. Washington, Mass., moved to New York (1836) and succeeded in business; was governor of New York (1859–63) and U.S. senator (1863–69); benefactor of Williams College, Union Theological Seminary, and New York City hospitals.

**Morgan, George Campbell.** 1863–1945. English clergyman; ordained in Congregational ministry (1889); after pastorates in Birmingham and London, lectured in U.S. on the Bible (1919–29) and served as pastor of Tabernacle Presbyterian Church in Philadelphia (1929–32).

**Morgan, George Washington.** 1820–1893. American army officer; U.S. consul at Marseilles (1856–58); U.S. minister to Lisbon (1858–61); brigadier general (1861); served under Buell (1861–62) and Sherman (1863); resigned (June 8, 1863); member, U.S. House of Representatives (1867–68; 1869–73); practiced law, Mount Vernon, Ohio (from 1873).

**Morgan, Har′court** (här′kōrt) **Alexander,** *in full* **John Harcourt Alexander.** 1867–1950. Entomologist and educator, b. Strathroy, Ontario, Canada; on staff, Louisiana State U. and Agricultural Experiment Station (1889–1905); director, U. of Tennessee Agricultural Experiment Station, and professor of zoology and entomology (1905–19); president, U. of Tennessee (1919–33); member, Tennessee Valley Authority (1933–48), and chairman (1938–41).

**Morgan, Sir Henry.** 1635?–1688. British buccaneer, b. in Wales; said to have been kidnaped and sold as slave at Barbados; sailed with buccaneers, who chose him admiral (1666); commissioned by governor of Jamaica, captured Porto Bello and sacked it, took large sum from governor of Panama, ravaged coast of Cuba, sacked Maracaibo and Gibraltar (1669), recaptured Santa Catalina (1670), and took Panama City (1671); after treaty between Spain and England, called to England to answer for conduct (1672); gained favor of king; appointed lieutenant governor of Jamaica and commander in chief.

**Mor′gan′** (môr′gäɴ′), **Jacques Jean Marie de.** 1857–1924. French archaeologist; to Egypt as director-general of French antiquarian service (1892); made discoveries at Ombos and Karnak; transferred to Persia (1897); explored Pusht-i-Kuh range and Mesopotamia; discovered Hammurabi stele.

**Mor′gan** (môr′găn), **James Appleton,** *known as* **Appleton.** 1845–1928. American lawyer and Shakespearean scholar; founder and president, Shakespeare Society of New York (1885–1925). Author of *The Shakespearean Myth* (1880), *Shakespeare in Fact and Criticism* (1884), *Digesta Shakespeareana* (1887); editor of *The Bankside Shakespeare* (22 vols., 1888–92).

**Morgan, John.** 1735–1789. American physician, b. Philadelphia; founded U. of Pennsylvania Med. Coll. (1765); professor there (from 1765); director-general of hospitals and physician in chief of American army (1775–77); removed by Congress (Jan. 9, 1777); exonerated of neglect or wrongdoing by Washington and by Congress; practiced, Philadelphia (from 1777).

**Morgan, John Hunt.** 1825–1864. American Confederate cavalry commander, b. Huntsville, Ala.; entered Confederate service (1861); famed for cavalry raids (1862–63) in Tennessee and Kentucky; killed in action near Greenville, Tenn. (Sept. 4, 1864).

**Morgan, John Livingston Rutgers.** 1872–1935. American physical chemist; professor, Columbia (from 1905); known esp. for researches on the liquid state.

**Morgan, John Pierpont.** 1837–1913. Son of Junius Spencer Morgan (*q.v.*). American banker and financier, b. Hartford, Conn.; educ. in Switzerland and Germany; apprentice with representatives of his father's firm in London and New York (1856–60); New York agent for this firm (1860–64); member, Dabney, Morgan & Co. (1864–71) and Drexel, Morgan & Co. (1871–93). Formed J. P. Morgan & Co. (1895) closely linked with Drexel & Co. of Philadelphia, with Morgan, Harjes & Co. of Paris, and J. S. Morgan & Co. of London. Best known for his government financing (from 1873), his reorganization of important American railroads, and his industrial consolidations (esp., his formation of United States Steel Corporation, 1901). Renowned as collector of art and rare books; president, Metropolitan Museum of Art, New York City. Benefactor of the Cathedral of St. John the Divine, Metropolitan Museum of Art, New York Public Library, New York hospitals, and many other institutions. See James J. Hill and Jacob H. Schiff.

His son **John Pierpont** (1867–1943), b. Irvington, N.Y., grad. Harvard (1889), succeeded to his father's position as head of J. P. Morgan & Co., acted as agent of Allied governments in floating large loans in U.S. during World War (1914–18).

**Morgan, John Tyler.** 1824–1907. American lawyer and legislator, b. Athens, Tenn.; served in Confederate army through Civil War; brigadier general (1863); U.S. senator from Alabama (1877–1907); vigorous advocate of Nicaraguan interoceanic canal; appointed one of American arbitrators in Bering Sea fisheries dispute (1892), and one of three commissioners to draft legislation for Hawaii (1898).

**Morgan, Junius Spencer.** 1813–1890. Father of John Pierpont Morgan. American banker and financier, b. West Springfield, Mass.; merchant in New York, Hartford, and Boston (to 1854); partner in George Peabody & Co. (1854), international bankers of London, Eng.; on retirement of Peabody (1864), reorganized firm as J. S. Morgan & Co.; president of the company (1864–90). Benefactor of Metropolitan Museum of Art (New York), and other institutions.

**Morgan, Lewis Henry.** 1818–1881. American ethnologist, b. near Aurora, N.Y.; practiced law (from 1844); interested himself in study of the American Indian culture. Author of *League of the Ho-dé-no-sau-nee, or Iroquois* (1851), *Houses and House-Life of the American Aborigines* (1881), etc.

**Morgan, Sydney.** Lady **Morgan.** *Nee* **Sydney Ow'en·son** (ō'ĕn·s'n). 1783?–1859. Irish woman of letters; daughter of an actor and theatrical manager; wrote precocious volume of sentimental poetry (1801); attracted attention with a novel, *St. Clair* (1804); made reputation with *The Wild Irish Girl* (1806), extolling Ireland; m. (1812) surgeon of Abercorn family, Sir **Thomas Charles Morgan** (1783–1843), author of *Sketches of the Philosophy of Life* (1818), *Sketches of the Philosophy of Morals* (1822). Continued to produce novels, verse, travel books, including patriotic novels *O'Donnel* (1814) and *Florence Macarthy* (1818), a life of Salvator Rosa (1823).

**Morgan, Thomas.** d. 1743. English deist of Welsh origin; independent minister, dismissed for heterodoxy (1720); author of controversial works.

**Morgan, Thomas Hunt.** 1866–1945. American zoologist, b. Lexington, Ky.; grad. State College of Kentucky (1886); Ph.D., Johns Hopkins (1890); professor, Columbia (1904–28); director, Kerckhoff Laboratories of Biological Sciences, Calif. Inst. Tech. (from 1928); awarded Nobel prize (1933) for discoveries relating to laws and mechanism of heredity. Author of *Regeneration* (1901), *Evolution and Adaptation* (1903), *Experimental Zoology* (1907), *Heredity and Sex* (1913), *Mechanism of Mendelian Heredity* (1915), *Critique of the Theory of Evolution* (1916), *The Physical Bases of Heredity* (1919), *The Theory of the Gene* (1926), *Embryology and Genetics* (1933), etc.

**Morgan, William.** 1774?–?1826. American Freemason, b. prob. in Culpeper County, Va.; royal arch mason (1825); disappeared (Sept., 1826), after it became known that he was writing a book to expose the secrets of Freemasonry. Charges were made that he was murdered to prevent the publication of the book; charges strongly denied by Freemasons. His disappearance became a political issue. The book, *Illustrations of Masonry*, appeared late in 1826.

**Morgan, William de.** See DE MORGAN.

**Mor'gen·stern** (mŏr'gĕn·shtĕrn), **Christian.** 1805–1867. German landscape painter. His grandson **Christian Morgenstern** (1871–1914) was a lyric poet; author of *Ich und die Welt* (1898), *Einkehr* (1910), *Ich und Du* (1911), and *Epigramme und Sprüche* (1919), of grotesque and ironic poems, and of translations of Ibsen and Björnson, etc.

**Mor'gen·stern** (môr'gĕn·stûrn), **Julian.** 1881– . American rabbi, b. St. Francisville, Ill.; professor of Bible and Semitic languages, Hebrew Union College (from 1907), and president of the college (from 1922).

**Mor'gen·stern** (mŏr'gĕn·shtĕrn), **Lina,** *nee* **Bau'er** (bou'ĕr). 1830–1909. German writer and social reformer; m. Dr. Theodor Morgenstern (1854); worked esp. in field of children's education and protection of young girls. Author of *Universalkochbuch* (1881) and *Der Häusliche Beruf* (1875), and of books for children.

**Mor'gen·thau** (môr'gĕn·tou), **Henry.** 1856–1946. American diplomat, b. Mannheim, Ger.; to U.S. (1865); practiced law, New York City (1879–99); U.S. ambassador to Turkey (1913–16), taking over at outbreak of World War diplomatic interests of various allied countries; U.S. ambassador to Mexico (1920); U.S. technical expert, London monetary and economic conference (1933). Author of *Ambassador Morgenthau's Story* (1918), *All in a Lifetime* (1922), *I Was Sent to Athens* (1929), etc. His son **Henry Morgenthau, Jr.** [-thô] (1891–1967), b. New York City; publisher of *American Agriculturist* (1922–33); governor, Farm Credit Administration (1933); undersecretary of the treasury (1933); U.S. secretary of the treasury (1934–45).

**Mor'ghen** (môr'gān), **Raffaello.** 1758–1833. Italian engraver; among his works are *Aurora* (after Guido Reni), *Transfiguration, Poetry, Theology, Madonna della Sedia* (all after Raphael), *Last Supper* (after Leonardo da Vinci), and portraits.

**Mor'hof** (mŏr'hōf), **Daniel George.** 1639–1691. German literary historian and scholar; author of *Unterricht von der Teutschen Sprache und Poesie* (1682), first historical treatment by a German of German grammar and European literature, of *Polyhistor*, in Latin (1688–92), first history of universal literature by a German writer, etc.

**Mo'rice'** (mô'rēs'), **Charles.** 1861–1919. French poet and critic; associated with symbolism; author of *La Littérature de Tout à l'Heure*, supposed to contain a theory of symbolism (1899), *Rodin* (1900), *Tristan Corbière* (1912), *Poèmes en Prose* (1919), and *Le Rideau de Pourpre* (verse; pub. 1921).

**Mó'ricz** (mō'rĭts), **Zsigmond.** 1879–1942. Hungarian novelist, playwright, and journalist; his novels treat chiefly of Hungarian peasant life.

**Mor'i·er** (mŏr'ĭ·ā), **James Justinian.** 1780?–1849. British diplomat and novelist; son of **Isaac Morier** (1750–1817), British consul at Smyrna. Served at court of Persia as secretary of legation and envoy (1809–15); described journeys in Turkey, Armenia, Asia Minor; known for his *Adventures of Hajji Baba of Ispahan* (1824) and *The Adventures of Hajji Baba of Ispahan in England* (1828), satire on Western civilization. His brother **David Richard** (1784–1877), diplomat, served in Egypt, Dardanelles, Constantinople. The latter's son Sir **Robert Burnett David** (1826–1893), diplomat, b. Paris, acquired intimate acquaintance with German politics and friendship with crown prince during service in German courts (1853–76), arousing hatred of Bismarck; minister at Lisbon (1876–81), at Madrid (1881–84); ambassador at St. Petersburg (1884–93), avoided war with Russia (1885).

**Mo·ri'gi** (mô·rē'jē). Variant of *Merisi* (see Michelangelo da CARAVAGGIO).

**Mö'ri·ke** (mû'rĭ·kĕ), **Eduard.** 1804–1875. German lyric poet and novelist, a leader of the Swabian school. His works include the romantic novel *Maler Nolten* (2 vols.,

1832) and the story *Mozart auf der Reise nach Prag* (1856), the idyll *Der Alte Turmhahn*, the poem *Schön Rotraut*, the collection *Gedichte* (1838), and other lyrics and ballads.

**Mo·ril'lo** (mô·rē'(l)yō), **Pablo.** Conde **de Car'ta·ge'na** (thā kär'tä·hā'nä). 1777–1838. Spanish general in South America; defeated by Bolívar; published (1826) *Memoirs* of his campaigns in South America.

**Mo'rin'** (mô'răN'), **Jean.** *Lat.* **Johannes Mo·ri'nus** (mô·rī'nŭs). 1591–1659. French Roman Catholic theologian and Orientalist; joined the Oratory (1618) and became head of a college at Angers; was summoned to Rome (1640) to discuss union of Greek and Roman churches, but was soon recalled by Richelieu; writer on church history and, esp., on textual criticism.

**Mo·ri'ni** (mô·rē'nē), **Erika.** 1906– . Austrian concert violinist; on tour in U.S. (1921–23) and in Europe and America (after 1927); m. (1938) Felice Siracusano.

**Mo·rí'ni·go** (mô·rē'nē·gō), **Higinio.** 1887– . Paraguayan army officer and politician; minister of war (May–Sept., 1940); president of Paraguay (1940–48).

**Morinobu.** See KANO.

**Mor'i·son** (mŏr'ĭ·s'n). See also MORRISON.

**Morison, James.** 1816–1893. Scottish minister of United Secession church; deposed for preaching universal atonement; with three other ministers deposed for anti-Calvinistic views, founded (1843) the Evangelical Union, whose members are sometimes called Morisonians.

**Morison, James Augustus Cotter.** 1832–1888. English author and positivist; author of lives of St. Bernard (1863), Gibbon (1878), and Macaulay (1882), and of *The Service of Man*, a positivist essay (1887).

**Morison, Robert.** 1620–1683. Scottish botanist; fought on Royalist side; physician to Gaston, Duc d'Orléans (1649); senior physician, king's botanist, superintendent of royal gardens (1660); professor of botany, Oxford (1669); revived study of systematic botany. The genus *Morisonia* was named for him.

**Morison, Samuel Eliot.** 1887–1976. American historian, b. Boston; on teaching staff, Harvard (from 1915); also, Harmsworth professor of American history, at Oxford U. (1922–25); served in World War (1918–19); Author of *Life of Harrison Gray Otis* (1913), *Oxford History of the United States* (1927), *Builders of the Bay Colony* (1930), *Tercentennial History of Harvard University* (5 vols., 1930–36; awarded Jusserand medal and Loubat prize), *The Growth of the American Republic* (with Henry Steele Commager, 1930), *Admiral of the Ocean Sea* (1942; awarded Pulitzer prize), *History of U.S. Naval Operations in World War II* (1947–62), *John Paul Jones* (1959; Pulitzer prize).

**Mo'ri'sot'** (mô'rē'zō'), **Berthe.** 1841–1895. French painter; influenced by her brother-in-law the impressionist painter Édouard Manet.

**Mo'ritz** (mō'rĭts). See MAURICE (of Saxony).

**Moritz.** Prince of **An'halt–Des'sau** (än'hält·dĕs'ou). 1712–1760. Son of Prince Leopold I, b. Dessau; entered Prussian army (1727); fought in Polish war (1734–35), Silesian campaigns, and Seven Years' War; severely wounded at Hochkirch (1758).

**Moritz.** *Known as* **der Ge·lehr'te** (dĕr gĕ·lār'tĕ), *i.e.* "the Scholar." 1572–1632. Landgrave of Hesse-Cassel (from 1592); founded (1599) Collegium Adelphicum Mauritianum at Cassel for sons of nobility; planned union of all Protestant sects; attacked by Catholic army during Thirty Years' War; abdicated (1627).

**Moritz, Karl Philipp.** 1757–1793. German writer of the Sturm und Drang period; editor of the *Vossische Zeitung;* friend of Goethe; professor of archaeology at Academy of Art, Berlin (1789). Author of aesthetic writings, of contributions on psychology, of the mainly autobiographical novels *Anton Reiser* (4 vols., 1785–90) and *Andreas Hartkopf* (1786), and of travel books.

**Morkere.** See MORCAR.

**Mor·lac'chi** (môr·läk'kē), **Francesco.** 1784–1841. Italian composer; rival of Karl von Weber as conductor in Dresden; composed over twenty operas, chiefly comic operas, also several oratorios, ten masses with orchestra, and other church music.

**Mor'land** (môr'lănd), **George.** 1763–1804. English genre, animal, and landscape painter; exhibited at age of ten at Royal Academy; gained reputation at seventeen as copyist of Flemish and Dutch masters; his first original painting, *The Angler's Repast* (1780). Painted 4000 pictures, specializing in inn yards, pastoral scenes, animals, esp. pigs. Known esp. for the Laetitia series of moralities after Hogarth, and for his masterpiece *The Interior of a Stable* (1791).

**Morland,** Sir **Samuel.** 1625–1695. English diplomat and inventor; Cromwellian emissary to Sweden (1653); successful in mission to remonstrate with duke of Savoy on Waldensian massacres (1655). Overheard plot to entice Charles II to Sussex coast in order to assassinate him; thereafter deserted Commonwealth and favored Restoration. Devoted himself to mathematics and mechanics, hydrostatics and hydraulics; invented a speaking trumpet; improved plunger pumps and fire engines; suggested use of steam and published what some regard as a virtual description of a steam engine (1682).

**Morland,** Sir **Thomas Lethbridge Napier.** 1865–1925. British soldier, b. Montreal, Canada; entered service (1884); major general (1913), lieutenant general (1919), and general (1922). During World War, commanded 5th division in first battle of Ypres (Oct., 1914); commanded 10th army corps (1915–17) in the battle of the Somme (July, 1916), the battle of Messines (June, 1917), and the battle of Passchendaele (Sept.–Oct., 1917); commanded 13th army corps (1918–19) in action around Cambrai (Aug., 1918); commanded 10th corps again, in army of occupation at Cologne (1919), and later (1920) became commander in chief of the army of occupation.

**Mor'ley** (môr'lĭ), **Christopher Darlington.** 1890–1957. American writer, b. Haverford, Pa.; A.B., Haverford Coll. (1910); Rhodes scholar, Oxford (1910–13). On editorial staff, Doubleday, Page & Co. (1913–17), *Ladies' Home Journal* (1917–18), Philadelphia *Evening Public Ledger* (1918–20), New York *Evening Post* (1920–24); contributing editor, *Saturday Review of Literature* (1924). Initiated and conducted column, "The Bowling Green," in New York *Evening Post* (1920–24) and in *Saturday Review of Literature.* Among his books are *Parnassus on Wheels* (1917), *Shandygaff* (1918), *The Haunted Book Shop* (1919), *Kathleen* (1920), *Tales from a Rolltop Desk* (1921), *Where the Blue Begins* (1922), *Thunder on the Left* (1925), *Off the Deep End* (1928), *Human Being* (1932), *Mandarin in Manhattan* (1933), *The Trojan Horse* (1937), *Kitty Foyle* (1939), *Thorofare* (1942). Editor of revised edition of *Bartlett's Quotations* (1937). His brother **Felix Muskett** (1894– ), b. Haverford; A.B., Haverford (1915); Rhodes scholar, Oxford (1919–21); on staff of Baltimore *Sun* (1922–29); editor of Washington *Post* (1933–40); president of Haverford College (1940–45).

**Morley, Edward Williams.** 1838–1923. American chemist and physicist, b. Newark, N.J.; professor, Western Reserve (1869–1906). Known for his researches in the variations of atmospheric oxygen content, the ether drift, thermal expansion of gases, conduction of heat through water vapor, vapor tension of mercury, densities of oxygen and hydrogen. See Albert A. MICHELSON.

**Morley, Henry.** 1822–1894. English man of letters, b. London; edited the *Examiner* (1859–65); professor of English literature, University Coll., London (1865–89) and Queen's Coll., London (1878); principal of University Hall, Gordon Square, London (1882–90); edited classics in Morley's Universal Library, Cassell's National Library, and the Carisbrooke Library; wrote monographs on *Palissy the Potter* (1852), *Jerome Cardan* (1854), *Cornelius Agrippa* (1856), *Clément Marot* (1870), and a monumental history of English literature down to death of Shakespeare, *English Writers* (10 vols., 1864–94), his principal work.

**Morley, John.** Viscount **Morley of Black'burn** (blăk'bẽrn; -bûrn). 1838–1923. English statesman and man of letters, b. Blackburn, Lancashire; journalist in London (1860 ff.); on staff of *Saturday Review* (1863); editor of *Fortnightly Review* (1867–82) and *Pall Mall Gazette* (1880–83); M.P. (1883–95, 1896–1908); raised to peerage (1908). Supporter of Gladstone; chief secretary for Ireland (1886, 1892–95); secretary of state for India (1905–10). Among his notable works are *Edmund Burke* (1867), *Voltaire* (1872), *Rousseau* (1876), *Diderot and the Encyclopaedists* (1878), *Richard Cobden* (1881), *Ralph Waldo Emerson* (1884), *Studies in Literature* (1891), *Oliver Cromwell* (1900), *Life of Gladstone* (1903), *Critical Miscellanies* (1908), and *Recollections* (1917).

**Morley, Sylvanus Griswold.** 1883–1948. American archaeologist; connected with Carnegie Institution of Washington (from 1915); in charge of expeditions to Central America; director of Chichen Itza project (1924–40). Author of *Introduction to Study of Maya Hieroglyphs* (1915), *Inscriptions at Copán* (1920), etc.

**Morley, Thomas.** 1557–?1603. English musical composer, excelling in madrigals, canzonets, and ballets.

**Mor'nay'** (môr'nā'), **Philippe de.** Seigneur **du Ples'-sis'-Mar'ly'** (dü plĕ'sē'mår'lē'). *Commonly known as* **Duplessis-Mornay.** 1549–1623. French Huguenot leader; escaped Massacre of St. Bartholomew (1572) and became trusted adviser to king of Navarre (1576); after Prince Condé's death (1588), his power and influence gained him nickname of "Huguenot Pope"; disappointed by Henri IV's abjuration of Protestantism (1593), withdrew from the court and devoted himself to writing.

**Mornington,** Earls of. See WELLESLEY family.

**Mor'ny'** (môr'nē'), Duc **Charles Auguste Louis Joseph de.** 1811–1865. Half brother of Napoleon III. French politician; chief agent in successful coup d'état (Dec. 2, 1851); minister of interior (1851–52); president of Corps Législatif (1854–65); created duc de Morny (1862).

**Moro, Antonio.** See Sir Anthony MORE.

**Mo·ro'ni** (mō·rō'nē) *or* **Mo·ro'ne** (-nā), **Giambattista.** 1525?–1578. Italian portrait painter of the Brescian school; his *Bartolommeo Bonga* is in Metropolitan Museum, New York; his *Old Man and Boy* is in Boston Museum.

**Mo·ro·no·bu** (mō·rō·nō·bōō). *Family name* **Hi·shi·ka·wa** (hē·shē·kä·wä). 1618–1703. Japanese painter, orig. of Tosa school; later, a founder of Ukiyoye school, with scenes from everyday life.

**Mo'ro·si'ni** (mō'rō·sē'nē). Name of patrician family of Venice, including notably: **Domenico** (d. 1156), doge of Venice; **Marino** (d. 1252), doge of Venice (1249–52); **Michele** (d. 1382), doge of Venice (1382); **Antonio** (late 14th and early 15th century), Venetian historian; **Andrea** (1558–1618), historian of Venice and its eastern possessions.

**Morosini, Francesco.** 1618–1694. Venetian general; forced to yield Candia to Turks (1667–69); later, wrested Morea from Turks; doge of Venice (1688).

**Mo'rot'** (mō'rō'), **Aimé Nicolas.** 1850–1913. French painter of portraits, historical works, and murals; his murals are in the Nancy Hôtel de Ville and the Paris Hôtel de Ville; portraits include *Prince d'Arenberg, Édouard Dumont, E. Hébert.*

**Mor'peth** (môr'pĕth; -pĕth), Viscounts. See *earls of Carlisle,* under HOWARD family.

**Mor'phy** (môr'fĭ), **Paul Charles.** 1837–1884. American chess player, b. New Orleans. Matches in U.S., England, and France established him as world's chess master (1857–59); on staff of *Chess Monthly* and New York *Ledger* (1859–60); in later life, was mentally deranged.

**Mor'rill** (mŏr'ĭl), **Justin Smith.** 1810–1898. American legislator, b. Strafford, Vt.; merchant in Strafford (1831–48); member, U.S. House of Representatives (1855–67); author of tariff act (Morrill Tariff Act) of 1861, and Land-Grant College Act, giving lands to states and territories which would provide colleges for teaching agriculture and the mechanic arts, approved by Lincoln in 1862; U.S. senator (1867–98).

**Morrill, Lot Myrick.** 1812–1883. American statesman, b. Belgrade, Me.; governor of Maine (1858–60); U.S. senator (1861–76); U.S. secretary of the treasury (1876–77).

**Mor'ris** (mŏr'ĭs), **Charles.** 1745–1838. English song writer of Welsh origin; served as soldier in America; punchmaker and bard of Beefsteak Society (1785); wrote political songs for party of Fox. Author of *The Town and the Country, A Reason Fair to Fill My Glass, The Triumph of Venus, Ad Poculum,* included with others in *Lyra Urbanica* (1840).

**Morris, Charles.** 1784–1856. American naval officer, b. Woodstock, Conn.; midshipman (1799); served on the *Constitution* in its victory over the *Guerrière* (1812); member, Board of Navy Commissioners (1823–25, 1826–27, 1832–41); commandant, Boston Navy Yard (1827–32). Sometimes called "Statesman of the American Navy" because of his success in administrative work.

**Morris, Clara.** 1848?–1925. Actress, b. Toronto, Canada; to U.S. as a child; m. Frederick C. Harriott (1874). In Augustin Daly's company (1870–73); achieved recognition as great emotional actress. Wrote *Life on the Stage* (1901), *A Pasteboard Crown* (1902), *The Life of a Star* (1906), etc.

**Morris,** Sir **Daniel.** 1844–1933. English agriculturist; imperial commissioner, West Indian agricultural dept. (1898–1908); scientific adviser in tropical agriculture to colonial office (1908–13); introduced successful cultivation of sea-island cotton into West Indies.

**Morris, Edward Patrick.** 1st Baron **Morris.** 1858–1935. Newfoundland jurist and statesman; attorney general and minister of justice (1902–07); premier of Newfoundland (1909–19). Edited *Newfoundland Law Reports, 1800–1900,* commonly referred to as *Morris' Reports.*

**Morris, George Pope.** 1802–1864. American journalist and poet, b. Philadelphia; founded (1823) and edited (1824–42) *New York Mirror and Ladies' Literary Gazette;* with N. P. Willis, edited the *Evening Mirror* (a daily paper begun 1844), and the *Home Journal* (a weekly begun 1846). His collected poems contain the well-known *Woodman, Spare that Tree, Near the Lake, My Mother's Bible, We Were Boys Together, A Long Time Ago.*

**Morris, Gou'ver·neur'** (gŭv'ẽr·nẽr'). 1752–1816. Grandson of Lewis Morris. American statesman and diplomat, b. Morrisania, N.Y.; practiced law, New York City; associated with colonial cause from outbreak of Revolution; member of New York provincial congress (1775–77); signer of the Articles of Confederation (1775);

member of Continental Congress (1777–78); assistant minister of finance (1781–85); member of Constitutional Convention (1787). To Paris on business (1789); U.S. commissioner to England (1790–91); U.S. minister to France (1792–94). Kept diary, edited (1939) by his great-granddaughter Beatrix Cary Davenport as *A Diary of the French Revolution 1789–1893*, a valuable historical source. U.S. senator (1800–03). Chairman, Erie Canal Commission (1810–13). His half brother **Lewis Morris** (1726–1798) also took colonial side in Revolution; member of Continental Congress (1775–77) and a signer of the Declaration of Independence. Another half brother, **Richard Morris** (1730–1810), practiced law in New York (from 1752); was chief justice, New York supreme court (1779–90). A son of Richard, **Lewis Richard** (1760–1825), engaged in business at Springfield, Vt. (from 1786); U.S. marshal (1791–1801); member of U.S. House of Representatives (1797–1803); by withholding his vote on the 36th ballot in the Jefferson-Burr contest for the presidency, turned the election to Jefferson.

**Morris, Gouverneur.** 1876–1953. Great-grandson of Gouverneur Morris (1752–1816). American writer, b. New York City; president, the Monterey (Calif.) Bank (from 1930). Author of *Tom Beauling* (1901), *Aladdin O'Brien* (1902), *The Pagan's Progress* (1904), *Ellen and Mr. Man* (1904), *Putting on the Screws* (1909), *When My Ship Comes In* (1915), *We Three* (1916), *The Wild Goose* (1919), *Tiger Island* (1934), etc.

**Morris, Ira Nelson.** See under Nelson MORRIS.

**Morris, Lewis.** 1671–1746. Grandfather of Lewis, Richard, and Gouverneur Morris. American jurist, b. New York; judge of the court of common right, East Jersey, and member of governor's council (1692); after establishment of New Jersey as royal colony, member of governor's council and member of the assembly (1707); chief justice, New York supreme court (1715); governor of New Jersey (1738). His son **Robert Hunter** (1700?–1764) was a member of the governor's council in New Jersey (1738), chief justice of New Jersey (1738–54), governor of Pennsylvania (1754–56), again chief justice of New Jersey (1756–64). Robert Hunter Morris's natural son **Robert** (1745?–1815) practiced law; chief justice, New Jersey supreme court (1777–79); judge, U.S. district court for New Jersey district (1789–1815).

**Morris, Lewis.** 1726–1798. See under Gouverneur MORRIS (1752–1816).

**Morris,** Sir **Lewis.** 1833–1907. Welsh lawyer and writer of English verse; great-grandson of the Welsh poet, philologist, and antiquary **Lewis Morris** (1700–1765). M.A., Oxon. (1858); winner of chancellor's prize for English essay (1858). Practiced as conveyancer (1861–81); helped to establish U. of Wales (1893). Author of *Songs of Two Worlds* (1872), *The Epic of Hades* (1876–77), *Gwen* (1879), *Songs Unsung* (1883), *Gycia* (1886), *A Vision of Saints* (1890), *The New Rambler* (1906).

**Morris, Lewis Richard.** See under Gouverneur MORRIS.

**Morris, Michael.** Lord **Morris and Kill·an'in** (kĭl-ăn'ĭn). 1826–1901. Irish jurist; solicitor general and attorney general for Ireland (1866); lord chief justice of Ireland (1887–1900); opponent of home rule.

**Morris, Nelson.** 1838–1907. Meat packer, b. Hechingen, Germany; to U.S. as a boy; pioneer in transporting dressed beef from Chicago to eastern seaboard; built up large packing business as head of Morris & Co. His son **Ira Nelson** (1875–1942), b. Chicago, served as U.S. minister to Sweden (1914–23), and wrote *With the Trade Winds* (1897) and *From an American Legation* (1926).

**Morris, Richard.** 1730–1810. See under Gouverneur MORRIS (1752–1816).

**Morris, Richard.** 1833–1894. English philologist; edited publications for Early English Text Society and Chaucer Society; published works on etymology of local names and on English grammar.

**Morris, Robert.** 1734–1806. American financier and statesman, b. near Liverpool, Eng.; to America (c. 1747); in commission shipping business, Philadelphia (from c. 1748). Favored colonial cause at outbreak of Revolution; member, Continental Congress (1776–78) and signer of the Declaration of Independence; performed important service to American cause by arranging for financing the purchases of supplies for Washington's armies (1776–78); served as superintendent of finance (1781–84); founded and organized the Bank of North America (1782); delegate, Constitutional Convention (1787); U.S. senator from Pennsylvania (1789–95); financially ruined by speculation in western lands.

**Morris, Robert.** 1745?–1815. See under Lewis MORRIS.

**Morris, Robert Clark.** 1869–1938. American lawyer, b. Bridgeport, Conn.; appointed to represent United States before United States and Venezuelan Claims Commission (1903); also, agent and general counsel representing United States before Mixed Claims Commission (1922–23). Author of *International Arbitration and Procedure* (1911), *The Pursuit of Happiness* (1930), etc.

**Morris, Robert Hunter.** See under Lewis MORRIS.

**Morris, Robert Tuttle.** 1857–1945. American surgeon, b. Seymour, Conn.; specialist in appendectomy; the Morris point, used in diagnosing chronic appendicitis, was discovered by and named for him.

**Morris, Roland Sle'tor** (slā'tẽr). 1874–1945. American lawyer and diplomat, b. Olympia, Wash.; U.S. ambassador to Japan (1917–21); on special mission to Siberia (1918, 1919).

**Morris, William.** 1834–1896. English poet and artist, b. Walthamstow; B.A., Oxon. (1856); close friend of Burne-Jones; worked at architecture and painting (1857–62); one of originators of *Oxford and Cambridge Magazine*, through which he became friend of Dante Gabriel Rossetti; published his first poetry, *The Defence of Guenevere* (1858); m. (1859) Jane Burden, a model; with Rossetti, Burne-Jones, and others, helped to found decorating firm which effected reform of Victorian taste in color and design. Translated into English verse the *Aeneid* (1875), the *Odyssey* (1887); after travel in Iceland (1871) produced *Three Northern Love Stories* (1875) and the epic *Sigurd the Volsung* (1876). Studied practical arts of dyeing and carpet weaving; founded, with the architect Philip Webb, Society for the Protection of Ancient Buildings (1877). Joined Democratic Federation (1883); advocated doctrine of socialism; led group of seceders (1884) in organizing the Socialist League, and edited its organ *The Commonweal;* relinquished membership and editorship when anarchist faction became dominant; described a socialist commonwealth in England in *News from Nowhere* (1891) and *A Dream of John Ball* (1888). Turned his attention back to art and literature; added typography to his activities and started the Kelmscott Press (1890) at Hammersmith, for which he designed special type and ornamental letters and borders for use in publishing medieval French romances, Shelley, Keats, Rossetti, Herrick, his own works, and finally his magnificent *Kelmscott Chaucer.* Author of other volumes of verse, *The Life and Death of Jason* (1867), *The Earthly Paradise* (1868–70), *Love is Enough* (1873), and *Poems by the Way* (his last volume of original verse; 1891), and of prose romances including *The House of the Wolfings* (1889), *The Roots of the Mountains* (1890), *The Story of the Glittering Plain* (1891), *The Wood Beyond the World*

(1895), *The Well at the World's End* (1896), *The Water of the Wondrous Isles* (1897), *Story of the Sundering Flood* (1898). Member of so-called "fleshly school" of poets; contributor to Gothic revival; producer of illuminated manuscripts, including two of FitzGerald's *Omar Khayyám;* one of leaders of modern romantic school; disciple of beauty for beauty's sake. His daughter **May** (1863?–1938), embroiderer and lecturer on embroidery and jewelry work, edited his works.

**Morris, William Richard.** 1st Viscount **Nuf'field** (nŭf'ēld). 1877–1963. English automobile manufacturer; chairman of Morris Motors, Ltd., Morris Commercial Cars, Ltd., etc. Benefactor of hospitals, charitable institutions, and Oxford U.; established (1943) Nuffield Foundation, for medical, scientific, and social research.

**Mor'ris–Jones'** (mŏr'ĭs·jōnz'), Sir **John.** 1864–1929. Welsh poet and grammarian; one of the leaders in the revival of Welsh literature; author of *A Welsh Grammar* (1913), *Cerdd Dafod* (a study of Welsh metric art), and a number of poems in Welsh.

**Mor'ri·son** (mŏr'ĭ·s'n). See also MORISON.

**Morrison, Arthur.** 1863–1945. English journalist, novelist, and playwright; on staff of *National Observer;* author of *Tales of Mean Streets* (1894), *A Child of the Jago* (1896), *The Green Eye of Goona* (1904), *The Painters of Japan* (1911), *Fiddle o' Dreams* (1933), and a series of detective stories centered about the fictional character Martin Hewitt; coauthor of the plays *That Brute Simmons, The Dumb Cake,* and *A Stroke of Business.*

**Morrison, George Ernest.** 1862–1920. Australian-born British journalist and traveler; correspondent of London *Times* in Peking (1895–1912); political adviser to Li Yüan-hung (*q.v.*), President of China (1916–17); author of *An Australian in China* (1895).

**Morrison,** Baron **Herbert Stanley. Morrison of Lambeth.** 1888–1965. English labor leader and politician; M.P. (1923–24, 1929–31, 1935 ff.); chairman, National Labor party (1928–29); minister of transport (1929–31); alderman and leader, London County Council (from 1934); minister of supply (1940); home secretary and minister of home security (1940–45); member of war cabinet (1942–45); lord president of the council and leader of House of Commons (1945–51).

**Morrison, Richard James.** *Pseudonym* **Zad'ki·el** (zăd'kĭ·ĕl). 1795–1874. English astrologer; served in British navy (1806–29; resigned); recommended to admiralty registration of merchant seamen (1824) and provision of seamen without impressment (1835). Issued *Herald of Astrology* (1831), cont. as *Zadkiel's Almanac.*

**Morrison, Robert.** 1782–1834. Scottish missionary; first Protestant missionary to China; sent by London Missionary Society to Canton (1807); translator to East India Company (1809); translated into Chinese New Testament (1809–14) and, with some help, Old Testament (1819); completed his *Chinese Dictionary* (1823); established Anglo-Chinese College at Malacca (1820).

**Morrison, William Ralls.** 1824?–1909. Am. legislator, b. near Waterloo, Ill.; member, U.S. House of Representatives (1863–65; 1873–87); advocate of tariff reductions; member I.C.C. (1887–97; chairman 1892–97).

**Morrison, William Shepherd.** Viscount **Dun·ros'sil** (dŭn·rŏs''l) 1893–1961. Brit. polit.; M.A. Edinburgh; in World War (1914–1918); M.P. (1929 ff.); minister of agriculture and fisheries (1936–39), of food (1939–40); postmaster general (1940–43); speaker, House of Commons (1951–59); gov. gen. of Australia (1959–61).

**Mor'row** (mŏr'ō), **Dwight Whitney.** 1873–1931. American lawyer, banker, and diplomat, b. Huntington, W.Va.; partner in J. P. Morgan & Co. (1914–27); U.S. ambassador to Mexico (1927–30); U.S. delegate to London Naval Conference (1930); U.S. senator from New Jersey (1930–31). He married (1903) **Elizabeth Cut'ter** [kŭt'ẽr] (1873–1955), B.L., Smith (1896), acting president of Smith (1939–40), author of *The Painted Pig* (1930), *Quatrains for My Daughter* (1931), *Beast, Bird, and Fish* (1933), *Pint of Judgment* (1939). See Anne Spencer Morrow LINDBERGH.

**Morrow, Hon'o·ré'** (ŏn'ō·rā'), *nee* **Mc·Cue'** (mȧ·kū'). *Known as* **Honoré Will'sie** (wĭl'sĭ) **Morrow.** 1880?–1940. American novelist, b. Ottumwa, Iowa; m. Henry Elmer Willsie (c. 1901; divorced, 1922), William Morrow (1923); editor of *The Delineator* (1914–19). Among her many books are *Heart of the Desert* (1913), *We Must March* (1925), *With Malice Toward None* (1928), *Mary Todd Lincoln* (1928), *Argonaut* (1933), *Yonder Sails the Mayflower* (1934), *Let the King Beware* (1935), *Demon Daughter* (1939).

**Morrow, Jay Johnson.** 1870–1937. American army officer; grad. U.S.M.A., West Point (1891); chief engineer, 1st army, A.E.F., in France (1918); engineer of maintenance, Panama Canal (1919–21); governor of Canal Zone (1921–24); chairman, Special Commission on Boundaries, Tacna-Arica Arbitration (1925–29).

**Morrow, Prince Albert.** 1846–1913. American physician; specialized in dermatology and venereal and genitourinary diseases; pioneer in education of public to need for disseminating knowledge of sex hygiene.

**Mors'bach** (môrs'bäκ), **Lorenz.** 1850–1945. German Anglicist; among his works are *Ursprung der Neuenglischen Schriftsprache, Mittelenglische Grammatik, Shakespeares Dramatische Kunst und ihre Voraussetzungen.*

**Morse** (môrs), **Anson Daniel.** 1846–1916. American political scientist; professor, Amherst (1877–1907); specialized in study of American political parties. His brother **Harmon Northrop** (1848–1920) taught chemistry at Johns Hopkins (1876–1916); known esp. for his researches in accumulating accurate data on the osmotic pressure of aqueous solutions.

**Morse, Charles Henry.** 1853–1927. American music educator; first professor and director, College of Music, Wellesley College (1875–84); founder and director, Northwestern Conservatory of Music, Minneapolis (1885–91); organist and choirmaster, Plymouth Church, Brooklyn (1891–99); first director of music (1901–16) and professor (1916–18), Dartmouth College.

**Morse, Charles Wyman.** 1856–1933. American promoter, b. Bath, Me.; in New York (from 1897); organized merger of ice companies and coastwise shipping companies; gained control of chain of banks in New York; indicted, tried, and convicted (1908) of making false entries in books of the Bank of North America and misapplying its funds; served term in prison (1910–12). Re-entered New York financial field (1913) with consolidation of shipping interests; at U.S. entrance into World War, contracted with U.S. Shipping Board to build vessels for government use; indicted (1922) for conspiracy to defraud the government, tried, and acquitted; later civil suit resulted in judgment against him; placed under guardianship as an incompetent (1926).

**Morse, Edward Sylvester.** 1838–1925. American zoologist, b. Portland, Me.; studied under Louis Agassiz at Harvard; director, Peabody Museum, Salem, Mass. (from 1880); curator of Japanese ceramics, Boston Museum of Fine Arts (from 1892). Author of *First Book of Zoology* (1875), *Japanese Homes and Their Surroundings* (1886), *Glimpses of China and Chinese Homes* (1902).

**Morse, Harmon Northrop.** See under Anson Daniel MORSE.

**Morse, Jedidiah.** 1761–1826. Known as "the Father of

American Geography." American Congregational clergyman, b. Woodstock, Conn.; pastor, Charlestown, Mass. (1789–1819); active in maintaining orthodoxy and forcing Unitarian believers out of Congregational Church. Published (1784) *Geography Made Easy*, the first geography appearing in U.S.; also, *The American Geography* (1789), *Elements of Geography* (1795), *Annals of the American Revolution* (1824), *A Compendious History of New England* (with Elijah Parish; 1804). See also biographies of his sons, Samuel Finley Breese MORSE and Sidney Edwards MORSE.

**Morse, John Torrey.** 1840–1937. American lawyer and biographer, b. Boston; practiced law, Boston (1862–80); author of *Law Relating to Banks and Banking* (1870), *Famous Trials* (1874), and biographies of Hamilton, Oliver Wendell Holmes, Henry Lee, Abraham Lincoln, John Quincy Adams, Thomas Jefferson, John Adams, Benjamin Franklin.

**Morse, Richard Cary.** 1841–1926. Grandson of Jedidiah Morse. American Presbyterian clergyman; general secretary, international committee of Y.M.C.A. (1869–1915).

**Morse, Samuel Finley Breese.** 1791–1872. Son of Jedidiah Morse. American artist and inventor, b. Charlestown, Mass.; portrait painter in Boston, Charleston, S.C., and New York (1815–c. 1837); a founder and first president (1826–42) of National Academy of Design; professor, N.Y.U. (from 1832). Interested himself in possibilities of magnetic telegraph (from 1832); conducted experiments with technical aid of Leonard Dunnell Gale (1800–1883) and financial aid of Alfred Vail; invented Morse alphabet or code for use in telegraph instrument; filed a caveat at patent office in Washington (1837) and endeavored in vain to get European patents; made public exhibitions of his apparatus (from 1837). U.S. congress (1843) voted him $30,000 for experimental line between Washington and Baltimore; line built by Ezra Cornell, and Morse sent (May 24, 1844) the first message, "What hath God wrought!" Involved in much litigation over rights to his invention, but courts upheld him and he enjoyed prosperity in his later years. A statue of him stands in Central Park, New York; member of American Hall of Fame (1900).

**Morse, Sidney Edwards.** 1794–1871. Son of Jedidiah Morse; bro. of Samuel F. B. Morse. American journalist and inventor, b. Charlestown, Mass. With his brother Richard Cary Morse (1795–1868), founded the New York *Observer* (1823) and edited it (1823–58). Invented a method (cerography) of making stereotype plates from inscribed sheets of wax, and a bathometer for exploring the depths of the sea. Continued the work of his father in publishing geographies, including *The Cerographic Atlas of the United States* (1842–45), *The Cerographic Bible Atlas* (1844), *The Cerographic Missionary Atlas* (1848), etc.

**Mor·ta′ra** (mŏr·tä′rä), **Edgar.** 1852–1940. Italian Jew, principal in the "Mortara case." Allegedly abducted in early childhood (1858) from his father's house in Bologna by papal guards on ground that he had been secretly baptized into Christianity by a Roman Catholic maid servant; was held despite parents' repeated attempts at recovery, strong indignation in Europe against authorities, and appeals to pope; was discovered during occupation of Rome (1870), but decided to remain Roman Catholic. Became Augustinian monk and preached as missionary in German cities and in New York City.

**Mor′tens·son–Eg′nund** (mŏr′tĕn·sŏn·ĕng′no͞on), **Ivar.** *Orig. surname* **Mortensson** (until 1920). 1857–1934. Norwegian writer, journalist, and theologian; champion of Landsmaal, or New Norwegian, as a national language, and supporter of Kropotkin; collaborated with Moltke Moe in collecting folk songs. Author of works in poetry and prose, including biographies of Arne Garborg (1897, 1924) and Ivar Aasen (1903), the mythological drama *Desecration of the Temple* (1901), and translations of songs from the *Edda* and of the Bible into Landsmaal.

**Mor′tier′** (môr′tyā′), **Alfred.** 1865–1937. French editor and playwright; on staff of *L'Événement* and *Soir;* founder of *L'Idée Libre* (1894) and *Petit Monégasque* (1897). His plays include *La Fille d'Artaban* (1896), the verse tragedies *Marius Vaincu* (1910) and *Sylla* (1913), and *Le Divin Arétin* (comedy of manners; 1930); author also of poetry and literary criticism. His wife, **Marie Antoinette,** *nee* **de Fau′cam′berge′** [fō′käɴ′bĕrzh′] (1882?– ), author, under pseudonym **Au′rel′** (ō′rĕl′), of *Pour en Finir avec l'Amant* (1908), *Voici la Femme* (1909), *La Semaine d'Amour* (1913), *Le Miracle de la Chair* (1928), etc.

**Mortier, Édouard Adolphe Casimir Joseph.** Duc **de Tré′vise′** (dẽ trā′vēz′). 1768–1835. French soldier in Revolutionary and Napoleonic armies; created marshal of France (1804); distinguished himself esp. at Friedland (1807), in Spain (1808–09), in Russian campaign (1812), and in defense of France (1813–14); member of Chamber of Deputies (1816) and, later, of Chamber of Peers; premier of France (1834–35); mortally wounded at side of Louis Philippe by Fieschi's infernal machine.

**Mor′til′let′** (môr′tē′yĕ′), **Gabriel,** *in full* **Louis Laurent Gabriel.** 1821–1898. French anthropologist; investigated Swiss lake dwellings; with Broca (*q.v.*) planned École d'Anthropologie.

**Mor′ti·mer** (môr′tĭ·mẽr). Name of Anglo-Norman family of Welsh marches holding earldoms of **March** (märch) and **Ul′ster** (ŭl′stẽr), including among members: **Roger de Mortimer** (fl. 1054–1074), the founder; son of Hugh, Bishop of Coutances (c. 990); named from his castle, Mortemer-en-Brai. His son **Ralph** (d. 1104?); settled on Welsh marches; enriched by award of forfeited lands of earl of Hertford, including Wigmore, henceforth the family seat (1074), which were entered in Domesday Book. **Ralph,** 5th Baron of **Wig′more** (wĭg′mōr); m. daughter of Llewelyn, Prince of Wales. **Roger** (1231?–1282), 6th Baron of Wigmore; further added to estates by marriage (1247) with Maude de Breuse (Matilda de Braose); sided with barons against Henry III (1258); became royalist (1261), fought against Llewelyn ab Gruffydd; after battle of Lewes, exiled to Ireland but prepared resistance and aided Prince Edward to escape from de Montfort (1265); commanded rear guard at Evesham (1265); became a guardian of realm (1272). **Roger (IV) de Mortimer** (1287–1330), 8th Baron of Wigmore and 1st Earl of March; acquired Irish estates by marriage with Joan de Genville; defeated kinsfolk, the Lacys, in Ireland; lieutenant (1316) and justiciar (1319) of Ireland; helped uncle in fight to maintain independent position of house of Mortimer in Wales against threat of the Despensers (1320), Edward II's favorites; forced to surrender to king at Shrewsbury (1322); escaped after two years' imprisonment to France (1324), where Isabella, Queen of England, became his paramour and joined him in invasion of England (1326) and execution of the Despensers; acquired lands of Despensers and of Arundel; compelled Edward II to abdicate (1327) in favor of his son Edward III; with Isabella, ruled the realm, procured murder of Edward II; responsible for failure of Scots expedition (1327); justiciar of Wales (1327); created earl (1328); by his arrogance, excited jealousy of Henry, Earl of Lancaster, who persuaded young Edward III to assert his independence and seize and imprison his mother's paramour; condemned without trial by his peers for assuming royal power, procuring Edward II's murder and execution of Edmund of Woodstock, Earl of Kent; hanged, drawn, and quartered at Tyburn. His grandson **Roger V** (1327?–1360), 2d Earl of March, was gradually restored by Edward III to family estates and honors.

**Edmund de Mortimer** (1351–1381), 3d earl; son of 2d earl; m. (1368) Philippa, daughter of Lionel of Antwerp, Duke of Clarence, 3d son of Edward III, thereby becoming representative of one of chief Anglo-Norman lordships in Ireland and, on death of his wife's father, next in succession to English crown after the Black Prince and his sickly son; lieutenant of Ireland (1379); handed on to house of York claim to throne, which was contested in Wars of the Roses; his elder daughter, Elizabeth, married Henry Percy (Hotspur).

**Roger (VI) de Mortimer** (1374–1398), 4th Earl of March and Ulster; son of 3d earl; proclaimed heir presumptive to English throne (1385); m. niece of King Richard II (1388); lieutenant of Ireland (1397); killed in battle of Kells in Ireland; his grandson Richard, Duke of York (offspring of his daughter Anne and Richard, Earl of Cambridge, grandson of Edward III), was father of King Edward IV, who acquired Mortimer estates.

**Edmund (IV) de Mortimer** (1391–1425), 5th Earl of March and 3d Earl of Ulster; son of 4th earl of March; recognized as heir presumptive by Richard II (1398); during Lancastrian revolution, held in custody with his brother by Henry IV (1399–1413); restored to estates (1413) by Henry V, whom he accompanied through wars in France (1415–21); member of council of regency; lieutenant of Ireland (1423), died of plague while negotiating with native septs, leaving earldom to become merged with crown on accession of his nephew's son to throne as Edward IV (see preceding ¶).

**Mor′ton** (môr′t'n), **Earls of.** See (1) Douglas family; (2) Maxwell family.

**Morton, Charles.** 1627?–1698. English Puritan clergyman, b. Cornwall; to Boston (1686), expecting to become president of Harvard; minister at Charlestown (1686); Harvard fellow (1692), first vice-president (1697); urged prosecutions for witchcraft at Salem; author of treatises on science and logic used as Harvard textbooks, and of *The Spirit of Man* (1693).

**Morton, David.** 1886–1957. American journalist, teacher, and poet, b. Elkton, Ky.; on staff of Associated Press, Louisville *Courier-Journal*, Louisville *Herald;* teacher of English (from 1915), and professor (from 1924), Amherst College; author of *Ships in Harbour* (1921), *Harvest* (1924), *Nocturnes and Autumnals* (1928), *A Man of Earth* (1930), *Earth's Processional* (1932), *Spell Against Time* (1936), etc.

**Morton, George.** 1585–1624. English colonist in America, b. prob. near Scrooby, Eng.; with the Pilgrims in Leiden (c. 1612–23); agent of Pilgrims in negotiations with London merchants (1619); published account sent to him from the Plymouth colony in 1622 of the new settlement there, ...*The English Plantation setled at Plimoth in New England.* To the New England colony (1623), but died in June, 1624. His son **Nathaniel** (1613–1685), b. Leiden, was taken to Plymouth (1623) and brought up in family of Governor Bradford, his uncle by marriage; secretary of Plymouth Colony (1647–85); author of *New Englands Memoriall* (1669). Among his descendants was Levi Parsons Morton.

**Morton, Guy Mainwaring.** *Pseudonym* **Peter Traill** (trāl). 1896–1968. English novelist and playwright, son of Captain Harry Mainwaring Dunstan, but assumed family name of his stepfather, the dramatist **Michael Morton** (1864–1931), with whom he collaborated in the plays *Fallen Angels* (1924), *After the Theatre* (1924), *By Right of Conquest* (1925), *Salvage* (1926), *The Stranger in the House* (1928), and *Because of Irene* (1929). Among Guy Morton's novels are *Woman to Woman* (1924), *The Divine Spark* (1926), *Great Dust* (1932), *The Angel* (1934), and *Not Proven* (1938).

**Morton, Henry.** 1836–1902. American scientist, b. New York City; first president, Stevens Tech. (1870–1902).

**Morton, Henry Vollam.** 1892– . English journalist and writer, esp. of travel books; author of *The Heart of London* (1925), a series *In Search of England* (1927), *In Search of Scotland* (1929), etc., *In the Steps of the Master* (1934), *Through Lands of the Bible* (1938), *I, James Blunt* (1942), etc.

**Morton, James St. Clair.** See under Samuel Morton.

**Morton, John.** 1420?–1500. English prelate and statesman; present with Lancastrians at battle of Towton (1461); attainted by Yorkists; lived with exiled court of Margaret of Anjou; aided formation of coalition between Richard Neville, Earl of Warwick, and George, Duke of Clarence; landed with Warwick at Dartmouth (1470) but after battle of Tewkesbury (1471), submitted to Edward IV. Master of rolls (1473); a negotiator of Treaty of Picquigny (1475); bishop of Ely (1479); one of executors of Edward IV's will (1483); escaped imprisonment by Richard III and aided earl of Richmond (later Henry VII), whose adviser he became. Archbishop of Canterbury (1486–1500); lord chancellor (1487); cardinal (1493); chancellor of Oxford (1495).

**Morton, John.** 1724?–1777. American patriot, b. Ridley, Pa., of Swedish descent; delegate to Stamp Act Congress (1765); member, Continental Congress (1774–77) and signer of the Declaration of Independence.

**Morton, John Bingham.** 1893– . English journalist and story writer; served in World War. Author of *The Barber of Putney* (1919), *Tally Ho* (1922), *Mr. Thake* (1929), *Who's Who at the Zoo* (1933), *Gallimaufry* (1936), *Pyrenean* (1938), *Saint Just* (1939), etc.

**Morton, John Maddison.** See under Thomas Morton.

**Morton, Joy.** 1855–1934. American salt merchant; founder of Morton Arboretum, at Lisle, Ill.

**Morton, Julius Sterling.** 1832–1902. American agriculturist, b. Adams, N.Y.; settled at Nebraska City, Nebraska (1855); edited Nebraska City *News.* Secretary of Nebraska Territory (1858–61); U.S. secretary of agriculture (1893–97); originator of Arbor Day. His son **Paul** (1857–1911) became a railroad executive on the Santa Fe (1896–1904); U.S. secretary of the navy (1904–05); chairman of board of directors, and later president, Equitable Life Assurance Association (1905–11).

**Morton, Levi Parsons.** 1824–1920. A descendant of George Morton. American banker and politician, b. Shoreham, Vt.; established banking firm in New York (1863); member, U.S. House of Representatives (1879–81); U.S. minister to France (1881–85); vice-president of the U.S. (1889–93); governor of N.Y. (1895–97).

**Morton, Nathaniel.** See under George Morton.

**Morton, Oliver Hazard Perry Throck,** *known as* **Oliver Perry.** 1823–1877. American legislator, b. Salisbury, Ind.; lieutenant governor of Indiana (1860), succeeding to governorship (1861) and being elected governor (1864); known for his able and vigorous war policies in support of Union cause; U.S. senator (1867–77).

**Morton, Samuel George.** 1799–1851. American physician and naturalist, b. Philadelphia, Pa.; specialist in anthropology, esp. craniology. His son **James St. Clair** (1829–1864), grad. U.S.M.A., West Point (1851), served in engineer corps, U.S. army (to 1861); brigadier general

(1862); killed leading attack on Petersburg, Va. (June 17, 1864).

**Morton, Sarah Wentworth,** *nee* **Ap'thorp** (ăp'thôrp). *Pseudonym* **Phi·len'ia** (fĭ·lĕn'yȧ; -lē'nĭ·ȧ; fĭ-). 1759–1846. American poet, b. Boston; m. Perez Morton (1781); contributed lyric and narrative verse to the periodicals of the time.

**Morton, Thomas.** d. 1646 or 1647. English adventurer in America; settled in Quincy, Mass.; built house at Merry Mount, where his licentious life brought him in bad repute with the Pilgrim fathers; arrested and sent to England (1628, and again 1630); arrested and imprisoned at Boston (1644–45). Author of *New English Canaan* (1637), a description of New England.

**Morton, Thomas.** 1764–1838. English playwright; produced number of comedies in which John Emery, Charles and John Kemble, and Macready played, including *A Cure for Heartache* (1797), *Speed the Plough* (with its invisible Mrs. Grundy, 1798), *The Blind Girl* (1801), *The School of Reform* (1805), *Town and Country* (1807), *A Roland for an Oliver* (1819), *School for Grown Children* (1826). His son **John Maddison** (1811–1891), playwright, showed facility in adapting French pieces; scored a hit with farce *Box and Cox* (1847); author of a hundred other farces.

**Morton, Thomas.** 1781–1832. Scottish shipbuilder, inventor of the patent slip (patented 1819) for docking vessels, a submerged carriage on an inclined railway, used as a substitute for a dry dock.

**Morton, Thomas George.** 1835–1903. American surgeon; specialized in orthopedics; first to describe Morton's disease.

**Morton, William Thomas Green.** 1819–1868. American dentist; practiced in Boston (from 1842); associated one year (1842–43) with Horace Wells; also (1844) with Charles T. Jackson, a professor of chemistry, who had experimented with sulphuric ether as an anesthetizing agent. Morton, aware of Jackson's experiments, tested ether on animals and on himself, and finally (Sept. 30, 1846) on a patient; a fortnight later (Oct. 16, 1846), Dr. John C. Warren removed tumor from the neck of a patient anesthetized by Morton's process. Public announcement of the discovery was made Nov. 18, 1846; Morton and Jackson received patent for use of "letheon" (Nov. 12, 1846). Morton's claims and attempts to profit largely by the discovery brought conflicting claims from Jackson, Horace Wells, and Crawford W. Long; last years embittered by controversy, litigation, and poverty. Elected (1920) member of American Hall of Fame. His son **William James** (1845–1920), grad. Harvard Med. School (1872), was a neurologist in New York City (from 1878); editor, *Journal of Nervous and Mental Disease* (1882–85); devoted himself especially to study of electrotherapeutics; one of first physicians in U.S. to use X rays in treatment of skin diseases.

**Morveau, Guyton de.** See GUYTON DE MORVEAU.

**Mor'y·son** (mŏr'ĭ·s'n), **Fynes.** 1566–1630. English traveler on Continent (1591–95), in Holy Land, Constantinople, and Scotland (1598); helped to suppress Tyrone's rebellion; published account of his travels and experiences in Ireland in *An Itinerary* (1617).

**Mo·san'der** (mo͞o·sän'dĕr), **Carl Gustav.** 1797–1858. Swedish chemist; credited with discovery of the elements lanthanum, didymium, erbium, and terbium.

**Mos'by** (mŏz'bĭ), **John Singleton.** 1833–1916. American lawyer and Confederate officer, b. Edgemont, Va.; practiced, Bristol, Va. (from 1855). In Confederate army, on Gen. J. E. B. Stuart's staff in the Peninsula Campaign, at Manassas and at Antietam (1862); commanded independent cavalry unit (Mosby's Rangers), raiding federal pickets and supplies; captured General Stoughton and his staff behind Federal lines at Fairfax Court House (Mar. 9, 1863). After war, resumed practice of law; U.S. consul, Hong Kong (1878–85); assistant attorney, U.S. Department of Justice (1904–10). Author of *Mosby's War Reminiscences, and Stuart's Cavalry Campaigns* (1887), *Stuart's Cavalry in the Gettysburg Campaign* (1908).

**Mo'sca** (mōs'kä), **Gaetano.** 1858–1941. Italian political scientist; senator (1919 ff.). Among his works are *Sulla Teoria dei Governi e sul Governo Parlamentare* (1884), *Elementi di Scienza Politica* (1896, 1923), *Diritto Costituzionale* (1908).

**Mo'sche·les** (mŏsh'ĕ·lĕs), **Ignaz.** 1794–1870. Bohemian piano virtuoso, composer, and teacher, b. in Prague of Jewish parents; gave lessons to Mendelssohn in Berlin (1824) and became his lifelong friend; settled as composer and teacher in London (1826); taught at Leipzig Conservatory (from 1846). Composed 142 opus numbers, including piano concertos, sonatas, three *Allegri di Bravura*, chamber music, variations, and studies for pianoforte. Known as a gifted improvisator and as inventor of the "singing tone," later developed by the Liszt school.

**Mo'sche·rosch** (mŏsh'ĕ·rŏsh), **Johann Michael.** *Properly* **Mo'sen·rosh** (mō'zĕn·rŏsh). *Pen name* **Philander von Sit'te·wald** (fŏn zĭt'ĕ·vält). 1601–1669. Called "the Dreamer." German satirist, b. in Willstätt of an old Spanish family. Author of the satirical "book of visions" *Wunderliche und Wahrhafftige Gesichte Philanders von Sittewald* (1643), and of other satires on the customs and manners of his day.

**Mos'chi·on** (mŏs'kĭ·ŏn). Greek medical writer of the 2d century A.D.; wrote earliest known treatise on obstetrics.

**Mos'chus** (mŏs'kŭs). Greek pastoral poet of 2d century B.C., of Syracuse. His extant works are usually published in editions of Theocritus and Bion.

**Mos̈·cic'ki** (mŏsh·chēts'kē), **Ignacy.** 1867–1946. Polish chemist, b. near Lwów; taught at technical high school, Lwów (1912–26); established Polish Inst. of Chemical Research (1916); president of Poland (1926–39); in exile and Swiss citizen (from 1939).

**Mos·co'so de Al'va·ra'do** (mōs·kō'sō thā äl'vä·rä'thō), **Luis de.** fl. 1530–1543. Second in command under Hernando de Soto in the conquest of Florida; designated by de Soto to succeed to the command of the expedition; built boats (1542–43), descended Mississippi, and crossed the Gulf to Mexico, with 311 survivors of the original army.

**Mo·se'le'ka'tse** *or* **Mo·si'li'ka'tze** (mŭ·zĭ'lē'kȧ'tsĭ). d. 1870. Zulu chieftain who fled from Zululand and set up new kingdom north of Vaal River; defeated by the Boers, withdrew across Limpopo River, where he established the Matabele kingdom.

**Mose'ley** (mōz'lĭ), **Henry Gwyn-Jeffreys.** 1887–1915. English physicist; known for researches on X-ray spectra of elements; killed at Gallipoli in World War. His father **Henry Nottidge Moseley** (1844–1891) acted as naturalist on *Challenger* expedition around the world (1872–76), wrote book on Oregon, was professor of human and comparative anatomy, Oxford (1881); son of **Henry Moseley** (1801–1872), professor of natural and experimental philosophy and astronomy, King's Coll., London (1831–44); author of textbook on mechanics.

**Mo'sel'ly'** (mō'zĕ'lē'), **Émile.** *Pen name of* **Émile Ché'nin'** (shā'năN'). 1870–1918. French writer; author chiefly of novels, including *Terres Lorraines* (1907; awarded Goncourt prize).

**Mo'sen** (mō'zĕn), **Julius.** 1803–1867. German poet,

novelist, and playwright; settled in Dresden as lawyer (1834); dramaturgist of court theater, Oldenburg (1844–48); pensioned because of illness (1850). Author of the epics *Lied Vom Ritter Wahn* (1831) and *Ahasver* (1838), of the collection *Gedichte* (1836) containing the ballads *Andreas Hofer*, *Der Trompeter an der Katzbach*, and *Die Letzten Zehn vom Vierten Regiment*, later popular as folk songs, of the novel *Der Kongress von Verona* (2 vols., 1842), of the tragedies *Cola Rienzi*, *Die Bräute von Florenz*, *Kaiser Otto III*, *Herzog Bernhard* (1855), and *Der Sohn des Fürsten* (1858).

**Mosenrosh, Johann Michael.** See MOSCHEROSCH.

**Mo'sen·thal** (mō'zĕn·täl; -thôl), **Joseph.** 1834–1896. German-American violinist, composer, and conductor, b. in Kassel; to U.S. (1853); played 40 years with first violins in Philharmonic orchestra, and second violin in Mason-Thomas soirees (1855–68). He composed anthems, hymns, and other sacred and secular music.

**Mo'sen·thal** (mō'zĕn·täl), **Salomon Hermann.** 1821–1877. German dramatic poet, b. in Kassel of Jewish ancestry. His works include the folk plays *Deborah* (1850; later eds. known in English as *Leah the Forsaken*), *Der Sonnenwendhof* (1856), and *Der Schulz von Altenbüren* (1868), the literary drama *Die Deutschen Komödianten* (1863), and opera librettos, as for Nicolai's *Merry Wives of Windsor*.

**Mo'ser** (mō'zẽr), **Gustav von.** 1825–1903. German writer of comedies and farces, including *Ultimo* (1874), *Der Bibliothekar* (1878), *Der Registrator* (1879; with L'Arronge), *Krieg im Frieden* (1881; with Franz von Schönthan).

**Moser, Hans Joachim.** 1889–1967. German concert basso and writer on music; author of *Geschichte der Deutschen Musik* (1920), *Musiklexikon* (1933), etc.

**Moser, Johann Jakob.** 1701–1785. German jurist and publicist; first legal scholar to bring out a complete presentation of German constitutional law. Author of *Teutsches Staatsrecht* (50 vols., 2 suppl., and index; 1737–54), *Deutsches Staatsarchiv* (13 vols., 1751–57), etc. His son Baron **Friedrich Karl** (1723–1798), statesman and political writer; privy councilor and minister in Hesse-Darmstadt (1772–80); took part in the struggle against the despotism of the small princes and worked for secularization of the ecclesiastical states of Germany.

**Mö'ser** (mû'zẽr), **Justus.** 1720–1794. German historian, statesman, and publicist; opposed French Revolution, and influenced Goethe and Herder on questions of history and economics.

**Mo'ses** (mō'zĕz; -zĭz). Hebrew prophet and lawgiver who, according to Biblical book of *Exodus*, led Israelites from Egypt through the wilderness to Canaan (c. 1200 B.C. according to some authorities); brother of Aaron (*q.v.*).

**Moses, Bernard.** 1846–1930. American political scientist; authority on history of the colonial era in Spanish America.

**Moses, George Higgins.** 1869–1944. American publicist and legislator; U.S. minister to Greece and Montenegro (1909–12); U.S. senator from New Hampshire (1918–33), and president pro tempore of the senate (1925–33).

**Moses, Robert.** 1888– . American state and municipal official, b. New Haven, Conn.; secretary of state, New York (1927–28); chairman, State Council of Parks (from 1924), Metropolitan Conference on Parks (1926–30), etc. Republican candidate for governor of New York (1934). Appointed New York City park commissioner (1934) with problem of consolidating and administering city park system and co-ordinating it with state and suburban systems.

**Moses of Cho·re'ne** *or* **Kho·re'ne** (kō·rē'nē). Armenian scholar of 5th century A.D.; reputed author of *A History or Genealogical Account of Armenia Major* and a *Geography of Armenia*. Some authorities maintain that these works show evidence of having been written two centuries or more later.

**Mo'ses·sohn** (mō'zĕz·zōn), **Nehemiah.** 1853–1926. Editor, theologian, and lawyer, b. in Crimea, Russia; to U.S. (1888); rabbi in Philadelphia, Dallas, Tex., and Portland, Ore. (to 1902). Founded and edited, with his sons as publishers, *The Jewish Tribune*, in Portland, Ore. (1902–18) and New York City (1918–26). His son **David Nehemiah** (1883–1930) was a lawyer and editor; practiced, Portland, Ore.; moved to New York City (1918); planned and effected reorganization of garment industry in New York, and became executive director of Associated Dress Industries of America (1918); edited *The Jewish Tribune* (1926–30). Another son, **Moses Dayyan** (1884–1940), law partner of his brother David in Portland, Ore. (to 1918), and New York City (from 1918), succeeded his brother as executive chairman of Associated Dress Industries of America (1930–33); published *The Jewish Tribune* (1903–31); author of *Guide to American Citizenship*, etc.

**Mos'heim** (môs'hīm), **Johann Lorenz von.** 1694–1755. German Protestant theologian, ecclesiastical historian, and pulpit orator; helped found U. of Göttingen, where he became professor and chancellor (1747); pioneer in modern preaching and founder of modern pragmatic ecclesiastical historical writing in Germany.

**Mo'sher** (mō'zhẽr), **Thomas Bird.** 1852–1923. American publisher; specialized in publication of little-known masterpieces in fine format at low cost; founded *The Bibelot* (1895).

**Mosilikatze.** See MOSELEKATSE.

**Mos'ko·witz** (mŏs'kō·wĭts), **Belle,** *nee* **Lind'ner** (lĭnd'nẽr). 1877–1933. American social-service worker, b. New York City; m. Charles Henry Israels (1903; d. 1911), Henry Moskowitz (1914); on staff of *The Survey* magazine (1908–10); public relations counselor (from 1917); also, secretary of Mayor's Committee of Women on National Defense (1916–17), secretary of New York State Reconstruction Commission (1919–21), secretary of the governor's labor board (1920–21), and secretary of the Educational Council, Port of New York Authority (from 1921).

**Mos'ler** (mŏz'lẽr), **Henry.** 1841–1920. American genre painter, b. New York City; war artist for *Harper's Weekly* (1862–63); studio in Paris (1877–94), and New York (from 1894). His *Wedding Feast in Brittany* hangs in the Metropolitan Museum of Art, New York; *Saying Grace*, in the Corcoran Art Gallery, Washington.

**Mos'ley** (?mŏz'lĭ; mōz'-), Sir **Oswald Ernald.** 1896– . English politician; served in France in World War (1914–18); M.P., successively as Conservative, Independent, and Labor representative (1918–24, 1926–31); chancellor of the duchy of Lancaster (1929–30). Left Labor party (1931) to found new party; became leader of British Union of Fascists, known as Blackshirts. Taken into custody by the British government (May, 1940).

**Mos·que'ra** (môs·kā'rä), **Tomás Cipriano de.** 1798–1878. Colombian soldier and politician; president of New Granada (1845–49); headed revolt (1859–61); assumed power (1861); called assembly which created United States of Colombia and voted him dictatorial powers; elected president for two-year term (1863, 1866); again assumed dictatorial powers, but was deposed (1867) and banished for three years.

**Moss** (mŏs), **Frank.** 1860–1920. American lawyer, b. Cold Spring, N.Y.; practiced, New York City (from

1881); prominent as counsel for the Society for the Prevention of Crime (from 1887) in prosecution of crime and investigation of municipal corruption. One of counsel for Lexow investigating committee; president, board of police commissioners, New York City (1897).

**Moss, John Calvin.** 1838–1892. American pioneer photoengraver, b. Bentleyville, Pa.; first to establish photoengraving as a commercial enterprise in U.S.

**Möss'bau'er** (mûs'bou'ẽr), **Rudolf Ludwig.** 1929– German physicist. Awarded Nobel prize in physics (1961) with R. Hofstadter for studies on gamma radiation in crystals (known as the Mössbauer effect).

**Mos'so** (môs'sō), **Angelo.** 1846–1910. Italian physiologist; known esp. for work on the circulation of the blood and on muscular fatigue; developed an ergograph and a sphygmomanometer; established a mountain laboratory to study the physiological effects of high altitude.

**Mos'taert** (mŏs'tàrt), **Jan.** 1475?–?1556. Dutch painter, chiefly of Biblical pictures and portraits.

**Mosz·kow'ski** (môsh·kôf'skē), **Alexander.** 1851–1934. Polish writer; settled in Berlin; music critic for *Deutsches Montagsblatt*, coeditor, *Berliner Wespen* (until 1886), and editor, *Lustige Blätter* (from 1886). His brother **Moritz** (1854–1925), concert pianist and composer in Paris; composed the opera *Boabdil* (1892), the ballet *Laurin* (1896), the symphonic poem *Jeanne d'Arc*, overtures, concert suites, a violin concerto, a piano concerto, etc.

**Moth'er·well** (mŭth'ẽr·wĕl; -wĕl), **William.** 1797–1835. Scottish poet, newspaper editor, and antiquary; published collections of ballads, *The Harp of Renfrewshire* (1819) and *Minstrelsy Ancient and Modern* (1827); author of *Poems, Narrative and Lyrical* (1832), including *Jeanie Morrison, My Heid Is Like to Rend, Willie,* and *Wearie's Cauld Well.*

**Mo Ti** (mô' dē') *or* **Mo–tzŭ** (mô'dzŭ') *or* **Meh–tzŭ** (mô'dzŭ'). fl. 5th century and 4th century B.C. Chinese philosopher, lived and taught in the period between Confucius and Mencius. His system (Moism) one of universal love as the foundation of society; taught pacifism and utilitarianism, and believed that all institutions should be judged by their ability to promote human welfare; strongly opposed by Mencius; his doctrines never had a wide appeal among the Chinese.

**Mot'ley** (mŏt'lĭ), **John Lothrop.** 1814–1877. American historian, b. Dorchester, Mass.; grad. Harvard (1831); secretary, U.S. legation at St. Petersburg (1841); interested in Dutch history. Published *The Rise of the Dutch Republic* (1856), *The History of the United Netherlands* (1st 2 vols., 1860–61; 2d 2 vols., 1867–68), *The Life and Death of John of Barneveld* (2 vols., 1874). U.S. minister to Austria (1861–67), to Great Britain (1869–70). Elected to American Hall of Fame (1910).

**Mo'ton** (mō't'n), **Robert Rus'sa** (rŭs'ȧ). 1867–1940. American Negro educator, b. in Amelia County, Va.; grad. Hampton Institute, Va. (1890); head of Hampton Institute (1890–1916); succeeded Booker T. Washington as principal of Tuskegee Normal and Industrial Institute (1915). Author of *Racial Good Will* (1916), an autobiography, *Finding a Way Out* (1920), *What the Negro Thinks* (1929).

**Motonobu.** See KANO.

**Mo·to·o·ri No·ri·na·ga** (mō·tō·ō·rē nō·rē·nä·gä). 1730–1801. Japanese scholar and poet; authority on customs, poetry, and religion of ancient Japan; published *Kojikiden* ("Records of Ancient Matters"), oldest extant Japanese book (1764–96).

**Mott** (mŏt), **Frank Luther.** 1886–1964. American journalist, b. Keokuk Co., Iowa; taught at U. of Iowa (1921–42); dean, School of Journalism, U. of Mo. (1942–51). Author of *Six Prophets out of the Middle West* (1917), *Rewards of Reading* (1926), *A History of American Magazines* (3 vols., 1930), *American Journalism... 1690–1940* (1941). Awarded Pulitzer prize for American history (1939).

**Mott, James.** 1788–1868. American abolitionist, b. North Hempstead, Long Island, N.Y.; commission merchant, Philadelphia (1822–52); active in antislavery agitation (from 1827); with his wife, aided in founding American Anti-Slavery Society, Philadelphia (1833); made his home a refuge for escaped slaves (from 1850); assisted in founding Swarthmore College (1864). His wife (m. 1811), **Lucretia,** *nee* **Cof'fin** [kŏf'ĭn] (1793–1880), b. Nantucket, Mass., became a Quaker minister; co-operated with her husband in his antislavery activities; associated with Elizabeth Cady Stanton in calling and directing the first woman's rights convention, Seneca Falls, N.Y. (July 19–20, 1848).

**Mott, John Ra'leigh** (rô'lĭ). 1865–1955. American Y.M.C.A. leader, b. Livingston Manor, N.Y.; student secretary, International Committee, Y.M.C.A. (1888–1915); general secretary (1915–31). Chairman, World's Committee of Y.M.C.A.'s (from 1926); general secretary, World's Student Christian Federation (1895–1920), and chairman (1920–28); chairman, International Missionary Council (from 1921); honorary chairman (from 1942); shared with Emily G. Balch (*q.v.*) 1946 Nobel prize for peace.

**Mott,** Sir **Nevill Francis.** 1905– English physicist. At U. of Bristol (1933–54), Cambridge U. (1930–33; 1954–71); awarded (with Philip W. Anderson and John H. Van Vleck) Nobel prize for physics (1977).

**Mott, Valentine.** 1785–1865. American surgeon, b. Glen Cove, Long Island, N.Y.; established reputation as bold and skillful surgeon; authority on surgical anesthesia (after 1846). His son **Valentine** (1852–1918) was also a surgeon; studied under Louis Pasteur in France; introduced Pasteur treatment for hydrophobia in U.S.

**Mot'ta** (môt'tä), **Giuseppe.** 1871–1940. Swiss lawyer and statesman; member of the Federal Council (from 1911); president of the Swiss Confederation (1915, 1920, 1927, 1932, 1937); opened first session of the Assembly of the League of Nations (1920) and was president of the Assembly (1924).

**Motte–Fouqué,** Baron **de La.** See LA MOTTE-FOUQUÉ.

**Motte–Guyon, Jeanne Marie de la.** See GUYON.

**Mot'tel·son** (mät'l·sŏn; -sôn'), **Ben Roy.** 1926– . Danish physicist, b. U.S. At Nordic Institute for Theoretical Physics (1957– ); awarded (with Aage N. Bohr and L. James Rainwater) Nobel prize for physics (1975).

**Mot'teux'** (mô'tû'), **Peter Anthony,** *orig.* **Pierre Antoine.** 1660 or 1663–1718. English playwright and translator, b. at Rouen, France; settled in London after revocation of Edict of Nantes; edited *The Gentleman's Journal,* containing verses by himself and wits of the day. Edited book III of Thomas Urquhart's translation of Rabelais, translated books IV and V (1693–1708); wrote comedies, masques, and operas, including *Love's a Jest* (1696); published free translation of *History of the Renowned Don Quixote de la Mancha* (1701).

**Mot'te·ville'** (môt'vēl'), Dame **Lan'glois' de** (läɴ'glwȧ' dē). *Nee* **Françoise Ber'taut'** (bĕr'tō'). 1621?–1689. French lady of the court of Anne of Austria; m. Nicolas Langlois, Seigneur de Motteville (1639; d. 1641); remained as femme de chambre of queen until queen's death (1666). Author of *Mémoires de Mme de Motteville* (first printed 1723).

**Mottistone,** Baron. See John Edward Bernard SEELY.

**Mottl** (mŏt''l), **Felix.** 1856–1911. Austrian composer and conductor, esp. of Wagner's music; appeared often in London (1894 ff.) and at Metropolitan Opera House (1903–04); director of Royal Opera, Munich (1907); edited various works of Berlioz, Bach, Wagner, and other classics, and composed operas, the festival play *Eberstein* (1881), a string quartet (1898), songs, etc.

**Mott′ley** (mŏt′lĭ), **John.** 1692–1750. English clerk in excise office (1708–20), playwright, author of successful comedies and two dull pseudoclassical tragedies, biographer of Peter I of Russia (1739) and Catherine the Great (1744), and author of *Joe Miller's Jest-book, or The Wit's Vade Mecum* (1739). Cf. Joseph MILLER.

**Mot′tram** (mŏt′răm), **Ralph Hale.** 1883–1971. English writer; served in World War I. Among his many books are *The Spanish Farm, The Crime at Vanderlynden's, Poems New and Old* (1930),*The Headless Hound* (1931), *Early Morning* (1935), *Journey to the Western Front* (1936), *Old England* (1937),*Traders' Dream* (1939), *The World Turns Slowly Round* (1942).

**Mo–tzŭ.** See Mo TI.

**Mou′che·ron′** (mo͞osh′rôɴ′), **Frederik de.** 1633–1686. Dutch landscape painter; painted chiefly Italian rivers and mountain landscapes. His son and pupil, **Isaac** (1670–1744), painted landscapes in his father's style and etched views of gardens and landscapes.

**Mou′chez′** (mo͞o′shĕz′), **Amédée Ernest Barthélémy.** 1821–1892. French naval officer and astronomer; director of the Paris Observatory (from 1878); planned international photographic chart of the heavens; founded the Montsouris Observatory, Paris.

**Mou′chot′** (mo͞o′shō′), **Augustin Bernard.** 1825–1911. French physicist.

**Moule** (moul), **Henry.** 1801–1880. English clergyman; indefatigable in relief work during cholera epidemic (1849–54); inventor of dry-earth system of sewage disposal. His sons: **George Evans** (1828–1912), missionary in China (from 1857), first bishop of mid-China (1880–1906); **Arthur Evans** (1836–1918), missionary at Ningpo, China (1861–69, 1871–76), Hangchow (1876–79), in Shanghai (1882–94); retired (1898) but returned to Chehkiang and Kiangsu (1902–10); author of works on Chinese people and missions; and **Handley Carr Glyn** (1841–1920), principal of Ridley Hall, Cambridge (1880–99), Norrisian professor of divinity (1899–1901), bishop of Durham (1901–20). A. E. Moule's son **Walter Stephen** (d. 1949) was vice-prin., prin., and pres. of Trinity College, Ningpo (1888–1925), and author of Biblical commentaries in Chinese. G. E. Moule's son **Arthur Christopher** (1873-1957), architect in China (1898–1903), was professor of Chinese language and history, Cambridge (1933–38).

**Mou′lié′** (mo͞o′lyā′), **Charles.** *Pseudonym* **Thier′ry′ San′dre** (tyĕ′rē′ säɴ′dr′). 1890– . French novelist; awarded Goncourt prize (1924) for his three works, *Le Chevrefeuille* (novel), *Purgatoire* (memoirs of his life as prisoner of war in Germany), and *Athenée* (translation from Greek).

**Moult** (mōlt), **Thomas.** 1895– . English journalist; music critic for Manchester *Guardian;* art and dramatic critic for *The Athenaeum, The English Review,* etc.; sports writer for various English and Australian journals. Among his many books are *Snow over Elden* (novel; 1920), *Down Here the Hawthorn* (verse; 1921), *Barrie* (literary criticism; 1928), *Saturday Night* (novel; 1931), *Bat and Ball, a New Book of Cricket* (1935), and *How We Write Our Poems* (1940); well known as anthologist, esp. for his series of poetry collections *The Best Poems* (pub. annually, 1923–39).

**Moul′ton** (mōl′t′n; -tŭn), **Ellen Louise,** *nee* **Chandler.** 1835–1908. American poet, b. Pomfret, Conn.; m. William U. Moulton (1855). Her collected verse appeared in *The Poems and Sonnets of Louise Chandler Moulton* (1909).

**Moulton, Forest Ray.** 1872–1952. American astronomer, b. Le Roy, Mich.; grad. Albion Coll. (1894); taught at U. of Chicago (1898–1927; professor 1912–27); associate editor, *Transactions of American Mathematical Society* (1907–12). With Thomas C. Chamberlin, propounded the planetesimal hypothesis, also called the spiral-nebula hypothesis. Author of *Celestial Mechanics* (1902), *Descriptive Astronomy* (1911), *Periodic Orbits* (1920), *Astronomy* (1931), *Consider the Heavens* (1935), etc. His brother **Harold Glenn** (1883–1965), grad. U. of Chicago (1907), economist; teacher at U. of Chicago (1909–22); director, Institute of Economics, Washington, D.C. (1922–29); president of Brookings Institution, Washington, D.C. from its founding in 1927; author of *Principles of Money and Banking* (1916), *Financial Organization of Society* (1921), *The American Transportation Problem* (1933), *Income and Economic Progress* (1935), etc.

**Moulton, John Fletcher.** Baron **Moulton.** 1844–1921. English jurist; queen's counsel (1885), specialized in patent actions; M.P. (1885); lord justice of appeal (1906–12); lord of appeal in ordinary and member of juridical committee of privy council (from 1912); director-general of explosive supplies in ministry of munitions (1914). His brother **Richard Green** (1849–1924), educator and critic in America, was professor of literary theory and interpretation, U. of Chicago (1892–1919); re-edited *Modern Reader's Bible,* dividing books into prose narrative, dramatic dialogue, lyric verse, etc. (1907); author of *Shakespeare as a Dramatic Artist* (1885), *The Moral System of Shakespeare* (1903), *The Modern Study of Literature* (1915). Another brother, **William Fiddian** (1835–1898), Wesleyan Methodist clergyman, translated and enlarged Georg B. Winer's *Grammar of New Testament Greek* (1870); one of revisers of New Testament (1870–81); first headmaster of Leys school, Cambridge (1874–98); author of *History of English Bible.* William's son **James Hope** (1863–1917), B.A., Cantab., was professor of Greek and Indo-European philology, Manchester (1908); Iranian scholar and student of Zoroastrianism.

**Moul′trie** (mo͞ol′trĭ), **John.** 1799–1874. English poet; grandnephew of William Moultrie, who fought on side of independence in American Revolution; rector at Rugby, friend of Dr. Arnold (from 1828). Author of *My Brother's Grave, Godiva* (1820), and hymns.

**Moultrie, William.** 1730–1805. American Revolutionary general, b. Charleston, S.C.; repulsed British attack on Sullivan's Island, now Fort Moultrie, in Charleston harbor (June 28, 1776); brigadier general in Continental army (1776); defended Charleston (1779); held prisoner by British (1780–82); exchanged and served (major general, 1782) to end of war; governor of South Carolina (1785–87; 1794–96).

**Mou′net′** (mo͞o′nĕ′), **Jean Sully.** *Called* **Mounet-Sul′ly′** (-sü′lē′). 1841–1916. French tragedian; engaged at Comédie Française (1872); among his notable roles are Orestes, Hamlet, Oedipus, Nero, Achilles, and Hippolytus. His brother **Jean Paul** (1847–1922) was also a tragedian; on stage of the Odéon (1880) and Comédie Française (1889); among his roles are Heracles, Iago, Hamlet, Othello, and Anthony.

**Mou′nier′** (mo͞o′nyā′), **Jean Joseph.** 1758–1806. French lawyer and politician; member and, later, president of Constituent Assembly (1789) and the man who introduced motion not to adjourn before giving the constitution to France; émigré (1790–1801); appointed by Napoleon a councilor of state (1805). His son **Claude**

**Philibert Édouard** (1784–1843) was sec. to Napoleon (1809); rallied to the Bourbons (1814) and became councilor of state (1816) and peer of France (1819).

**Mount** (mount), **William Sidney.** 1807–1868. American portrait and genre painter, b. Setauket, Long Island, N.Y.; painted portraits of Daniel Webster, Robert Schenck, Benjamin F. Thompson.

**Mountagu** *or* **Mountague.** Variants of MONTAGU.

**Moun′tain** (moun′tĭn; -tĕn), **Jacob.** 1749–1825. Founder of Anglican Church in Canada, b. Norfolk, England; first Protestant bishop of Quebec (1793). His son **George Jehoshaphat** (1789–1863), b. Norwich, England, was ordained priest in Canada (1813); suffragan bishop of Montreal (1836); bishop of Quebec (1850).

**Mount·bat′ten** (mount·băt′'n). See BATTENBERG.

**Mountbatten, Louis.** 1st Earl **Mountbatten of Burma.** *Known until 1917 as* Prince **Louis Francis Albert Victor Nicholas of Bat′ten·berg** (băt′'n·bûrg). 1900–1979. Brit. naval and mil. leader; great-grandson of Queen Victoria; son of 1st marquis of Milford Haven (see BATTENBERG). Entered Brit. navy (1913); promoted through the grades to capt. (1937), vice-adm. (1942); chief (1942) of Brit. combined operations (Commandos); strategist for Madagascar invasion (1942); supreme allied com. S.E. Asia (1943–46); viceroy of India (1947), gov. gen. (1947–48); adm. of the fleet (1953–59); chief of defense staff (1959–65).

**Mountbatten, Philip.** Duke of Edinburgh. See Prince PHILIP (1921– ).

**Mount′fort** (mount′fẽrt), **William.** 1664?–1692. English actor and playwright; author of popular comedies *Successful Strangers* (1690), *King Edward the Third* (1691), *Greenwich Park* (1691).

**Mountjoy,** Barons. See Charles and William BLOUNT.

**Mount Stephen,** Baron. See George STEPHEN.

**Mou′rey′** (mōō′rā′), **Gabriel.** 1865–1943. French essayist, art critic, and translator; author of *Miroir* (verse, 1908), *Cœurs en Détresse* (novel, 1898), *D. G. Rossetti et les Préraphaélites Anglais* (1910), *La Peinture Anglaise du XVIII^e Siècle* (1928); translator of works of Edgar Allen Poe, Swinburne, and Ruskin.

**Mousouros, Markos.** See Marcus MUSURUS.

**Moussorgsky.** Variant of MUSORGSKI.

**Mou′ton′** (mōō′tôN′; mōō·tŏn′), **Alexander.** 1804–1885. American lawyer and planter; U.S. senator from Louisiana (1837–42); governor of Louisiana (1843–46); presided at Louisiana secession convention, and voted for secession (1861).

**Mou′ton′** (mōō′tôN′), **Georges.** See Comte de LOBAU.

**Mow′att** (mou′ăt), **Anna Cora,** *nee* **Ogden.** 1819–1870. Writer and actress, b. Bordeaux, France, of American parentage; m. James Mowatt (1834, d. 1851); William Foushee Ritchie (1854). Wrote plays, novels, cookbooks, books on etiquette, etc.; best-known play, *Fashion; or Life in New York* (first produced, 1845; published, 1850). On stage (1845–54), often playing opposite E. L. Davenport. Near close of her life, wrote romantic fiction.

**Mow′bray** (mō′brā; -brĭ). Name of an Anglo-Norman baronial house derived from Montbrai, Normandy, which was founded at the Conquest by Geoffrey (de Montbrai), Bishop of Coutances. His nephew and heir, **Robert de Mowbray** (d. 1125?), became earl of North-um′ber·land [nôr·thŭm′bẽr·lănd] (c. 1080), rebelled against William Rufus (1088); killed Malcolm of Scotland at Alnwick (1093); imprisoned for rebellion in favor of Count Stephen of Aumâle (1095).

Robert's wife Mathilde was allowed by the pope to marry Nigel de Albini (d'Aubigny), another nephew of Bishop Geoffrey of Coutances; Nigel founded the second house of Mowbray, and his son **Roger de Mowbray** (d. 1188?), 2d Baron Mowbray, having changed his name, went on crusades (1147, 1164); joined Scots in rebellion (1174); went on third crusade (1186). Roger's grandson **William de Mowbray** (d. 1222?), 4th baron, was a leader of rising against King John and one of 25 executors of Magna Charta (1215); captured fighting against Henry III at Lincoln (1217). William's great-grandson **John I de Mowbray** (1286–1322) became involved in dispute with Despensers (1320) over the lordship of Gower in South Wales, received through his wife; harried Glamorgan, with other lords marchers; pardoned on temporary fall of Despensers (1321), but on king's taking up arms was captured, with Thomas, Earl of Lancaster, at Boroughbridge and executed. (See Sir John MANDEVILLE.) John's grandson **John III de Mowbray** (1328?–1368) acquired by marriage earldom of Not′ting·ham (nŏt′ĭng·ăm) and marshalship of England.

John III's second son, **Thomas I** (1366?–1399), 12th Baron Mowbray and 1st Duke of Nor′folk (nôr′fŭk), was summoned to parliament as earl of Nottingham (1383); created marshal of England for life (1385); joined his brother-in-law Arundel and the duke of Gloucester in routing royal favorite Robert de Vere, Earl of Oxford (1388); one of five appellants in proscribing king's friends in the Wonderful Parliament (1388); detached from other appellants by Richard II, who appointed him warden of Scottish marches (1389), captain of Calais (1391), and emissary to arrange Richard's marriage with Isabella, daughter of Charles VI of France (1396); helped arrest his former fellow appellants, Gloucester, Arundel, and Warwick, perhaps responsible for murder of Gloucester in prison; received as reward Arundel's lands and was created duke of Norfolk (1397); sought to protect himself by allying with duke of Hereford (later Henry IV), who betrayed him to king; banished, died at Venice; his downfall recounted in act I of Shakespeare's *Richard II.*

Thomas I's son **Thomas II** (1386–1405), Earl Marshal and 3d Earl of Nottingham, in resentment at exclusion from his father's dukedom and marshalship joined Archbishop Scrope in denouncing Henry IV as usurper and in treasonable movement to join Northumberland (1405); seized with Scrope at Shipton's Moor and beheaded. **John V** (1389–1432), 2d Duke of Norfolk, younger brother of Thomas II, on whose death he became earl marshal and 4th earl of Nottingham, was prominent in French wars (1417–30); one of protector's council (1422); restored to dukedom (1425).

John V's son **John VI** (1415–1461), 3d duke, earl marshal, 5th earl of Nottingham, and warden of East March (1437), supported Richard, Duke of York, his uncle by marriage, in effort to control King Henry VI's policy, but overshadowed in influence by the Nevilles; took special oath to Lancastrian succession (1459) but on turning of tables at Northampton (June, 1460) adhered again to Yorkist cause and shared Warwick's defeat at St. Albans (1461); one of Yorkist lords who chose Edward, Duke of York, accompanied him to his enthronement; fought at Towton and rewarded with royal offices (1461). His son **John VII** (1444–1476), 4th duke, last of the line, figured in Paston letters, exchanged Gower and Chepstow estates with William Herbert, 1st Earl of Pembroke for manors in Norfolk and Suffolk. On death (1481) of John VII's daughter Anne, dukedom of Norfolk passed to the Howard family (*q.v.*), descendants of Margaret, daughter of 1st duke of Norfolk; the earldom of Nottingham was revived for Charles Howard (1596) of the eldest of cadet branches of the ducal house.

**Mowbray, George Mordey.** 1814–1891. Industrialist, b. Brighton, Eng.; to U.S. (1854); produced first refined oil, in Titusville (Pa.) field (c. 1859); manufactured nitroglycerin for blasting purposes (from 1866); received many patents for improvements in explosives. His nephew and adopted son, **Henry Siddons Mowbray** (1858–1928), was an artist; studio in New York (1886); excelled in mural painting (the J. P. Morgan library, New York; U.S. courtroom, Federal Building, Cleveland; University Club Library, New York City).

**Mow'er** (mou'ẽr), **Joseph Anthony.** 1827–1870. American soldier; commanded division in Sherman's army in its march to the sea.

**Mo'winck'el** (mō'vĭng'kĕl), **Johan Ludwig.** 1870–1943. Norwegian statesman and shipowner, b. in Bergen; director of Norwegian-American line (1911); Liberal member (1906–09, 1912–18, 1921 ff.), president (1915–18, 1927), and vice-president (1928), Storting; minister of commerce (1921–22); head of Norwegian delegation to Genoa Conference (1922); minister for foreign affairs (1923); prime minister and minister for foreign affairs (1924–26, 1928–31, 1933–35); member (1925) and president (1928–30, 1933–34) of delegation to Assembly of League of Nations; member of committee for Nobel peace prize awards.

**Mow'rer** (mour'ẽr), **Paul Scott.** 1887–1971. American journalist, b. Bloomington, Ill.; on staff of Chicago *Daily News* (from 1905); its Paris correspondent (1910); war correspondent, in Balkans (1912–13) and France (1914–18); at Peace Conference (1918–19) and the limitation-of-armaments conferences (1921–33); editor, Chicago *Daily News* (1935–44); awarded Pulitzer prize for best foreign-correspondence service (1928). Author of *Balkanized Europe...*(1921), *Our Foreign Affairs...*(1924), *The Foreign Relations of the United States* (1927), and two volumes of verse.

**Mox'on** (mŏk's'n), **Edward.** 1801–1858. English publisher and writer of verse; set up as London publisher (1830), his first publication being Lamb's *Album Verses;* published for Bryan Waller Procter, Southey, Wordsworth, Tennyson, Monckton Milnes, Landor, Coventry Patmore, Browning; visited Wordsworth at Rydal Mount (1846); legally compelled to delete passages from Shelley's *Queen Mab* as blasphemous (1841). Author of *The Prospect and Other Poems* (1826) and second volume of sonnets (1837).

**Mo'ya** (mō'yä) *or* **Mo'za** (-thä), **Pedro de.** 1610–1666. Spanish painter; studio at Granada, where he painted many canvases for the cathedral.

**Moyano, Sebastián.** See Sebastián de BELALCÁZAR.

**Moyne,** Baron. See under GUINNESS family.

**Moy'ni·han** (moi'nĭ·hăn), **Berkeley George Andrew.** 1st Baron **Moynihan of Leeds** (lēdz). 1865–1936. English surgeon; author of *Abdominal Operations, Duodenal Ulcer,* etc.

**Mo'zart** (mō'tsärt). Name of a family of Austrian musicians of German origin, including: **Leopold,** *in full* **Johann Georg Leopold** (1719–1787), violinist, composer, and teacher, b. in Augsburg, Bavaria; court composer (1757) and assistant conductor (1762), and teacher at the cathedral choir school (1777); works include a celebrated early violin method *Versuch einer Gründlichen Violinschule* (1756), piano pieces, much church music, oratorios, operas, symphonies, trio sonatas, pieces for violin and for organ, etc. His daughter **Maria Anna,** *nicknamed* **Nan'nerl** [nän'ẽrl] (1751–1829), pianist and teacher, b. in Salzburg; toured leading capitals of Europe (1762–66) as child prodigy with father and brother (see below); taught at Salzburg until marriage (1784) to Baron von Berchthold zu Sonnenberg, and after his death (1801). Leopold's son **Wolfgang Amadeus,** *real name* **Johannes Chrysostomus Wolfgangus Theophilus** (1756–1791), composer, b. in Salzburg; one of chief exponents of the Viennese or classical school; showed unusual musical ability as child, esp. on harpsichord and as composer, and toured as child prodigy with his father and sister; composed his first published violin sonatas and improvisations in Paris and six violin sonatas in London after style of J. C. Bach and Abel; returned to Salzburg (1766) and studied counterpoint under father's direction; again in Vienna (1768), where he received imperial commission to compose and conduct an opera, and honorary appointment as concertmaster to archbishop of Salzburg (1769); to Italy with his father (1769), where he was named chevalier of Golden Spur by the pope; in Milan (1770–71) and Salzburg (1771); broke with Archbishop Hieronymus of Salzburg (1781); settled in Vienna as teacher and composer; m. (1782) **Constanze Weber** (1763–1842), soprano; lived in poverty in spite of position as royal chamber composer to Emperor Joseph II of Austria (1787); traveled (1789) to Berlin, visiting Dresden and Leipzig on the way; at work on his *Requiem* at the time of his death in Vienna; his grave is unknown. He composed over 600 works including operas *La Finta Semplice* (1768), *Mitridate, Rè di Ponto* (1770), *Idomeneo, Rè di Creta* (1781), *Die Entführung aus dem Serail* (1782), *Le Nozze di Figaro* (1786; Eng. *The Marriage of Figaro*), *Don Giovanni* (1787), *Così fan Tutte* (1790), *Die Zauberflöte* (1791; Eng. *The Magic Flute*); operettas, dramatic cantatas, etc., 47 arias, duets, tercets, and quartets with orchestral accompaniment; oratorios and cantatas, church music, including fifteen orchestral masses (1768–80), the unfinished *Requiem* containing the *Lacrimosa* (1791), 39 litanies, vespers, offertoriums, kyries, hymns, and other smaller works; 48 symphonies, 33 cassations, serenades, and divertimenti, 29 orchestral sets, 41 collections of dances, piano works, chamber music. Wolfgang's son **Karl Thomas** (1784–1858) was a gifted pianist. Another son, **Franz Xaver Wolfgang,** *later known as* **Wolfgang Amadeus** (1791–1844), composer, pianist, and music conductor, was active in Lemberg and Vienna.

**Mo'zier** (mō'zhẽr), **Joseph.** 1812–1870. American sculptor, b. Burlington, Vt.; studio in Rome, Italy (from 1845). His *Wept of Wish-ton-Wish* is in New Haven, Conn.; *Il Penseroso,* in National Gallery of Art, Washington, D.C.; *Rebecca,* in New York Public Library.

**Moz'ley** (?mŏz'lĭ; mōz'-), **Thomas.** 1806–1893. English clergyman and journalist; m. John Henry Newman's sister Harriet Elizabeth (1836); took part in Oxford movement. His brother **James Bowling** (1813–1878), theologian, formally allied with Tractarianism, studied theology under Pusey and Newman; attempted reconciliation of Christian tradition about baptism with Calvinistic theology in several treatises, agreeing with Gorham decision of 1850, by judicial committee of privy council, that doubt of conference of spiritual regeneration in sacrament of baptism might be regarded as consistent with subscription to the articles of Church of England; regius professor of divinity at Oxford (1871).

**Mu·a'wi·yah** *or* **Mo·a'wi·yah** (mo͝o·ä'wĭ·yă). *Arab.* **Mu'āwiyah.** Name of two Ommiad caliphs: **Muawiyah I.** *Arab. name in full* **Mu'āwiyah ibn–abi–Sufyān** (d. 680), b. Mecca; first ruler (661–680) of Islam after legitimate caliphs, and founder of Ommiad dynasty; submitted to Islam; secretary to Mohammed; general under abu-Bakr, directing conquest of Syria and Egypt; disputed with Ali (657–661) for caliphate; proclaimed caliph (661) at Jerusalem with capital at

Damascus; strengthened Arab power, unifying Moslem empire; made succession to caliphate hereditary. His grandson **Muawiyah II** (d. 683), caliph (683).

**Much** (mōōk), **Hans.** 1880–1932. German physician and writer; devoted himself esp. to study of tuberculosis. In addition to medical treatises, wrote verse, treatises on art, and studies in Buddhism and mysticism.

**Mu'cha** (mōō'kȧ), **Alphonse Marie.** 1860–1939. Czech decorative painter and illustrator.

**Muck** (mŏŏk), **Karl.** 1859–1940. German orchestra conductor; conductor of Royal Opera (1892–1912) and general music director (1908) in Berlin; guest conductor of opera and concerts in London (1899), Vienna (1903–06; with Mottl), Boston (1906–08), Paris, and other cities; regular conductor of Boston Symphony Orchestra (1912–18) and conductor of concerts at Panama-Pacific International Exposition in San Francisco (1915); conductor of Philharmonic concerts in Hamburg (1922–33).

**Mück'e** (mük'ĕ), **Heinrich.** 1806–1891. German painter, chiefly of historical and religious paintings and portraits.

**Muck'er·mann** (mŏŏk'ēr·män), **Hermann.** 1877–1962. German biologist; director, department of eugenics, Kaiser Wilhelm Inst. (1927–33).

**Mudge** (mŭj), **Isadore Gilbert.** 1875–1957. American librarian and bibliographer; reference librarian, Columbia U. (1911–41). Collaborated with M. E. Sears in compiling *Thackeray Dictionary* (1910) and *George Eliot Dictionary* (1924).

**Mu'die** (mū'dĭ), **Charles Edward.** 1818–1890. English publisher and founder of Mudie's Lending Library, London (1842); became limited company (1864). Published first edition in England of Lowell's *Poems* (1844).

**Mu'dra** (mōō'drä), **Bruno von.** 1851–1931. German infantry general; commanding general of army corps (1913), which he led into France and in battle of the Argonne (1914–16); also commanded army on eastern front (1916).

**Muel'ler-Ott'fried** (mül'ēr·ŏt'frēt), **Paula.** 1865–1946. German social thinker and leader of the Protestant feminist movement.

**Muench** (mĭnch), **Aloisius Joseph.** 1889–1962. Amer. Roman Catholic leader, b. Milwaukee, Wis. Ordained (1913); bishop, Fargo, N.D. (1935–59); cardinal (1959).

**Müff'ling** (müf'lĭng), Baron **Karl von.** 1775–1851. Prussian field marshal; quartermaster general of Blücher's Silesian army (1813–14); Prussian attaché at Wellington's headquarters (1815); chief of general staff of army (1821); devoted himself esp. to advancement and improvement of military cartography; negotiated treaty of peace between Russia and Turkey (1829).

**Müg'ge** (müg'ĕ), **Theodor.** 1806–1861. German novelist; author of *Toussaint* (1840), *Der Voigt von Sylt* (2 vols., 1851), *Afraja* (1854), etc.

**Mug'gle·ton** (mŭg''l·tŭn; -t'n), **Lodowicke.** 1609–1698. English Puritan tailor who presented himself and his cousin John Reeve (1608–1658) as the two witnesses of *Revelation* xi, messengers of a new dispensation (1652); made converts, called Muggletonians, a sect lasting into 18th century; denied Trinity; held that devil became incarnate in Eve; imprisoned for blasphemy (1653); quarreled with Quakers; prepared autobiography and doctrinal letters.

**Mughal.** See MOGUL (dynasty).

**Mu·gno'ne** (mōō·nyō'nā), **Leopoldo.** 1858–1941. Italian conductor; one of founders of interpretive conducting in Italy; known esp. for his work with symphonic scores of modern Italian school; directed première of *Cavalleria Rusticana* (1890), *Falstaff* (1892); associated with Toscanini at La Scala.

**Muhammad Ghori.** See MOHAMMED OF GHOR.

**Mu·ha'si·bi, al-** (ăl'mōō·hä'sĭ·bē; -bĭ). *Arab.* **Ḥārith ibn-Asad al-Muḥāsibi.** d. 857. Sufi teacher in Baghdad.

**Mühlbach, Luise.** Pseudonym of Klara MUNDT.

**Müh'len·berg** (mü'lĕn·bĕrk; *Angl.* mū'lĕn·bûrg), **Henry Melchior.** 1711–1787. Lutheran clergyman, b. Einbeck, Hanover, Germany; to U.S. (1742) to serve as pastor to congregations in Pennsylvania; did constructive pioneer work in organizing Lutheran churches in Pennsylvania; known as virtual founder of Lutheranism in America. Three of his sons, **John Peter Gabriel Muhlenberg** (1746–1807), **Frederick Augustus Conrad Muhlenberg** (1750–1801), and **Gott'hilf** (gŏt'hĭlf; *Ger.* gōt'-) **Henry Ernest Mühlenberg** (1753–1815), became Lutheran clergymen. John Peter served in American Revolution; brigadier general (Feb. 21, 1777); supported Anthony Wayne in assault on Stony Point; second in command under von Steuben (1780); stormed British redoubts at Yorktown (1781); brevetted major general (1783); member, U.S. House of Representatives (1789–91; 1793–95; 1799–1801), and U.S. Senate (1801). Frederick Augustus was a member of Continental Congress (1779–80); member of U.S. House of Representatives (1789–97) and first speaker. Gotthilf Henry served as pastor of Holy Trinity Church, Lancaster, Pa. (1780–1815); was first president of Franklin College (1787); interested himself in botanical studies. Gotthilf Henry's son **Henry Augustus Philip Muhlenberg** (1782–1844) was also a Lutheran clergyman; member of U.S. House of Representatives (1829–38); U.S. minister to Austria (1838–40). Gotthilf Henry's grandson **Frederick Augustus Muhlenberg** (1818–1901) was also a Lutheran clergyman; taught in Franklin Coll. (1840–50), Pennsylvania Coll. (1850–67); first president, Muhlenberg Coll. (1867–76); professor, U. of Pennsylvania (1876–88); president, Thiel Coll. (1891–93). A grandson of Frederick Augustus Conrad, **William Augustus Muhlenberg** (1796–1877), was a Protestant Episcopal clergyman; rector in New York City (1846–58); founder of St. Luke's Hospital, New York, with which he was associated from 1858; author of a number of hymns, including *I would not live alway* (1824).

**Muh·tar' Bey** (mōōk·tär' bā'), **Ahmet.** 1871–1934. Turkish diplomat; ambassador to Russia (1923–25) and U.S. (1927–34).

**Muir** (mūr), **Edwin.** 1887–1959. British writer; author of *The Marionette*, *Poor Tom*, *First Poems*, *Chorus of the Newly Dead* (verse), *Latitudes* (literary criticism), *Structure of the Novel*, *John Knox* (biography), etc.

**Muir, John.** 1810–1882. Scottish Orientalist; civil servant of East India Company in Bengal (1829–53); founded chair of Sanskrit and comparative philology, Edinburgh (1862). His brother Sir **William** (1819–1905), Indian administrator and Arabic scholar, was head of intelligence department at Agra during Sepoy Mutiny (1857); foreign secretary to Indian government (1865); lieutenant governor of North-West provinces (1868–74); member of council of India in London (1876–85); principal of Edinburgh U. (1885–1905); helped found and endow Muir College and University at Allahabad; author of standard *Life of Mahomet* (4 vols., 1858–61), *Mameluke Dynasty of Egypt* (1896), etc.

**Muir, John.** 1838–1914. Naturalist, b. Dunbar, Scotland; to U.S. (1849); educ. U. of Wisconsin (1859–63); toured Wisconsin, Illinois, and Indiana studying botanical specimens; tramped from Indianapolis to California, keeping a diary of his observations and thoughts (1867–68); centered his studies in Yosemite Valley (1868–74), then in Nevada, Utah, and Alaska; settled on fruit farm near Martinez, Calif. (1881–91). With Robert Underwood Johnson, campaigned (from 1889) for establishment of Yosemite National Park, finally provided for by Congress (October, 1890); conducted propaganda to save forest reserves (from 1897); on camping trip with President Theodore Roosevelt (1903), gained his support, and had influence in Roosevelt's acts setting aside 148,000,000 acres of additional forest reserves. Among his books are *The Mountains of California* (1894), *Our National Parks* (1901), *Stickeen* (1909), *My First Summer in the Sierra* (1911), *The Yosemite* (1912), *Travels in Alaska* (1915), etc.

**Muir, Ramsay.** 1872–1941. British historian; author of *Atlas of Modern History* (1911), *The Expansion of Europe* (1917), *History of the British Commonwealth* (2 vols., 1920, 1922), *How Britain Is Governed* (1930), *A Brief History of Our Own Times* (1934), etc.

**Muir,** Sir **Thomas.** 1844–1934. British mathematician, b. in Scotland; educ. Glasgow; superintendent general of education, Cape of Good Hope (1892–1915); author of works relating to determinants.

**Muir′head** (mūr′hĕd), **John Henry.** 1855–1940. British philosopher, b. Glasgow; educ. Glasgow and Oxford; professor, Birmingham. Author of *Elements of Ethics* (1892–1934), *Philosophy and Life* (1902), *The Service of the State* (1908), *The Use of Philosophy* (1928), *Rule and End in Morals* (1932), etc.

**Muirhead, Russell,** *in full* **Litellus Russell.** 1896– . British editor of guidebooks (the *Blue Guides*, from 1930; the *Penguin Guides*, 1938–49).

**Mu′ker·ji′** (mŏŏ′kẽr·jē′), **Dhan Gopal.** 1890–1936. Writer, b. Calcutta, India; to U.S.; best known for his children's books, as *Kari the Elephant* (1923) and *Gay Neck* (1927; awarded Newbery medal). Author also of *Caste and Outcast* (1923), *A Son of Mother India Answers* (1928), *Path of Prayer* (1934), etc.

**Mukh·tar′ Pa·sha′** (mŏŏκ·tär′ pä·shä′), **Ahmed.** 1832–1919. Turkish general; held command in Erzurum during Russo-Turkish War (1877–78); suppressed Cretan insurrection (1878); held command on Greek frontier (1879); Turkish high commissioner in Egypt (1885); grand vizier of Turkey (July–Oct., 1912). His son **Mahmud** (1867–1935) was a soldier and diplomat; trained in Germany; commanded 1st army corps (1908) and 3d army corps in Balkan War (1912); ambassador to Germany (1913–15).

**Mu·kun′da Ram** (mŏŏ·kŏŏn′dŏ räm′). fl. 17th century. Bengali poet; first writer of original poetry in Bengali, and author of two narrative poems based on religious traditions and legends of his country.

**Mul·ca′hy** (mŭl·kă′hĭ), **Richard James.** 1886–1971. Irish politician. Lieutenant in Easter Rebellion (1916); Sinn Fein M.P. (1918–22); member of Dail Eireann (1921–37); Irish Free State minister of defense (1922); commander in chief of Free State army, succeeding Michael Collins (1922–23); minister for local government (1927–32).

**Mul′cas′ter** (mŭl′kăs′tẽr), **Richard.** 1530?–1611. English schoolmaster; first headmaster of Merchant Taylors' school, London (1561–86); high master of St. Paul's school, London (1596–1608). Author of *Positions* (on the training of children; 1581) and *Elementarie* (on the writing of English; 1582).

**Mul′der** (mŭl′dẽr), **Gerardus Johannes.** 1802–1880. Dutch chemist; known for work on proteins and their derivatives; isolated fibrin from blood.

**Muldor, Carl De.** Pseudonym of Charles Henry Miller.

**Mul′ford** (mŭl′fẽrd), **Clarence Edward.** 1883–1956. American author of Western novels, including the "Bar-20" and "Hopalong Cassidy" series.

**Mulgrave,** Barons and earls of. See (1) Phipps family; (2) John and Edmund Sheffield.

**Mul′hall** (mŭl′hôl), **Michael George.** 1836–1900. Irish statistical compiler; emigrated to Buenos Aires (1858), where he founded the *Buenos Ayres Standard* (1861), said to be the first daily newspaper in English to be printed in South America. Wrote a *Handbook of the River Plata*, first English book published in Argentina (1869). Devoted himself to statistics in England (from 1878); published *Dictionary of Statistics* (1883), *History of Prices* (1885).

**Mul′hol′land** (mŭl′hŏl′ănd), **John.** 1898–1970. American magician, b. Chicago, Ill.; author of *Magic in the Making* (1925), *Quicker Than the Eye* (1932), *Story of Magic* (1935). Special editor for terms in magic, *Webster's New International Dictionary, Second Edition.*

**Mu·lier′** (mü·lēr′), **Pieter.** *Called in Italy* **Ca′va·lie′re Tem·pe′sta** (kä′vä·lyâ′rā tām·pĕs′tä). 1637–1701. Dutch painter, chiefly of landscapes and stormy marines.

**Mül′len·hoff** (mül′ĕn·hôf), **Karl.** 1818–1884. German philologist; succeeded J. Grimm at Prussian Acad. of Sciences (1864); author of works chiefly on Germanic philology and antiquities; editor of *Denkmäler Deutscher Poesie und Prosa aus dem 8.–12. Jahrhundert* (1864; with W. Scherer), *Das Deutsche Heldenbuch* (1866–73; with others), including his own edition of *Laurin* (1871), *Deutsche Altertumskunde* (1870 ff.). His glossary to Klaus Groth's *Quickborn* (1856) was the first grammatical and lexicographical treatment of Plattdeutsch.

**Mullens, Priscilla.** *Also* **Mullines** *or* **Mullins.** See Myles Standish.

**Mül′ler** (mül′ẽr), **Adam Heinrich.** *Called* **Müller von Ni′ters·dorf** [fôn nē′tẽrs·dôrf] (from 1827). 1779–1829. German political economist; representative of romantic school of German political economy; friend of Friedrich von Gentz and disciple of Edmund Burke; cofounder, with Heinrich von Kleist, of journal *Phöbus* (1808). As Austrian consul general for Saxony in Leipzig (1816–27), opposed Prussian customs policy; active in Vienna (1827) as journalist and political correspondent of state chancellery. Author of *Elemente der Staatskunst* (3 vols., 1810), *Versuche einer Neuen Theorie des Geldes* (1816).

**Müller, August.** 1848–1892. German Orientalist.

**Müller, Carl Christian.** 1831–1914. Orchestra leader, teacher, and composer, b. in Germany; to U.S. (1854); taught at New York Coll. of Music (1879–95); composer of organ sonatas, a string quartet, choral works, and piano and organ pieces.

**Mul′ler′** (mü′lâr′), **Charles Louis.** *Called* **Muller de Pa′ris′** (dē pȧ′rē′). 1815–1892. French historical painter; director of Gobelin factory in Paris (1850). His *Marie Antoinette* (1857) and *Charlotte Corday in Prison* are in Corcoran Gallery, Washington, D.C.

**Mül′ler** (mül′ẽr), **David Heinrich.** 1846–1912. Austrian Jewish Semitic scholar; a leader of Arabian expedition of Vienna Acad. (1897–98).

**Müller, Eduard.** 1848–1919. Swiss statesman, b. Dresden; president of Swiss Confederation (1899, 1907, 1913); contributed to unification of Swiss civil and penal law and to procedure in military courts.

**Müller,** Baron **Ferdinand von.** 1825–1896. German naturalist; to Australia (1847); government botanist for Victoria (1852); director of Melbourne botanical garden (1857); instrumental in introducing Australian blue-gum tree (*Eucalyptus globulus*) into California, Africa, Europe, and South America.

**Müller, Frederik Paludan–.** See Paludan-Müller.

**Müller, Friedrich.** *Called* **Ma′ler** (mä′lẽr) **Müller.** 1749–1825. German poet, painter, and engraver of the Sturm und Drang period; to Mannheim (1774); electoral court painter (1777). Author of dramas, as *Fausts Leben* (part I, 1778) and *Golo und Genoveva* (begun c. 1775) in imitation of Goethe's *Götz*, of the idylls *Die Schafschur* (1775) and *Das Nusskernen* (1811), and of lyric poems, as *Soldatenabschied.*

**Müller, Friedrich.** 1834–1898. Austrian philologist and ethnologist; professor, Vienna (from 1869); author of linguistic and anthropological parts of account of trip of Austrian frigate *Novara* around world and of work on elements of philology.

**Müller, Fritz.** 1821–1897. German zoologist, b. Erfurt; one of first Darwinians; pioneer in enunciating recapitulation theory which he set forth in *Für Darwin* (1864); studied development of crustaceans, mimicry, olfactory apparatus of butterflies, etc.

**Müller, George.** 1805–1898. German evangelist and philanthropist in England, b. in Prussia; settled as pastor at Teignmouth in England (1829); conducted philanthropic work at Bristol (from 1832), where, without endowment or committee of organization, he established an orphan house; toured world as evangelist. Author of *The Lord's Dealings with George Müller* (1845).

**Müller, George Elias.** 1850–1934. German psychologist; known esp. for work relating to psychophysical method, memory, and color perception.

**Müller, Günther.** 1890–1957. German literary historian; author of *Deutsches Dichten und Denken...* (1934), etc.

**Müller, Hans.** 1882–1950. Austrian playwright; author of *Könige, Flamme, Der Schöpfer, Kleiner Walzer in A Moll,* and musical comedy *Im Weissen Rössl.*

**Müller, Heinrich M.** 1820–1864. German anatomist after whom the fibers of Müller, in the retina, and certain other anatomical structures are named.

**Müller, Hermann.** *Also known as* **Müller–Fran′ken** (-fräng′kĕn). 1876–1931. German politician; a Social Democrat, editor of a socialist journal at Görlitz (1899–1906); member of the executive committee of the Social Democratic party (1906 ff.); member of the Reichstag (1916–18, 1920), and of the National Assembly at Weimar (1919); succeeded Count von Brockdorff-Rantzau as minister of foreign affairs (1919–20), and signed the Treaty of Versailles (1919); chancellor of Germany (Mar.–June, 1920); head of a coalition cabinet (1928–30).

**Mul′ler** (mŭl′ẽr), **Hermann Joseph.** 1890–1967. American geneticist, b. New York City; professor, U. of Texas (1925–36), Amherst Coll. (1942–45), Indiana U. (1945–64); on staff, U.S.S.R. Inst. of Genetics (1933–37), U. of Edinburgh (1937–40); awarded 1946 Nobel prize for medicine, for work on artificial transmutation of the gene by X rays.

**Mül′ler** (mül′ẽr), **Johann.** *Known as* **Re′gi·o·mon·ta′nus** (rē′jĭ·ō·mŏn·tā′nŭs; *Ger.* rā′gē·ō·mōn·tä′nŏŏs) [*Latin for* Königsberg, *his birthplace*]. 1436–1476. German mathematician and astronomer; established at Nuremberg, with the help of the wealthy patrician Bernhard Walther, an observatory, a mechanical workshop, and a printing plant; observed the comet afterwards known as Halley's comet (1472); published, with Walther, *Ephemerides ab Anno 1475–1506* (1473), used by Columbus and other navigators; advanced the study of algebra and trigonometry in Germany; called to Rome by Pope Sixtus IV to assist in reforming the calendar.

**Müller, Johann Gotthard von.** 1747–1830. German copper engraver; founded school of engraving in Stuttgart (1776). Works include engravings of Raphael's *Madonna della Sedia*, Domenichino's *St. Cecilia*, and Trumbull's *Battle of Bunker's Hill*, and portrait engravings of Schiller, Louis XVI, and King Jérôme of Westphalia. His son **Johann Friedrich Wilhelm** (1782–1816) was also a copper engraver; produced engraving of Raphael's *Sistine Madonna*, also portrait engravings.

**Müller, Johannes von.** 1752–1809. Swiss historian, b. Schaffhausen; entered service of Vienna (1792) shortly before French occupation of Mainz and became member of Aulic Council (1793) and custodian of imperial library (1800–04); historiographer at Berlin in Prussian service (1804); introduced to Napoleon (1806), under whom he became secretary of state in new kingdom of Westphalia (1807) and director-general of public education (1808). Author of *Reisen der Päpste* (1782), *Darstellung des Fürstenbundes* (1787), *24 Bücher Allgemeiner Geschichte* (3 vols., 1811 ff.), etc.

**Müller, Johannes Peter.** 1801–1858. German physiologist and comparative anatomist; professor, Berlin (from 1833); introduced concept of specific energy of nerves; gave explanation of color sensations produced by pressure on retina; wrote work on general pathology; investigated blood, lymph, chyle, and mechanism of voice; discovered fetal pronephric ducts (Müllerian ducts) and lymph-hearts in the frog; explained nature of hermaphroditism; studied embryology and metamorphoses of echinoderms. Chief publication, *Handbuch der Physiologie des Menschen* (1833–40).

**Müller, Josef.** 1855– . German philosopher and Roman Catholic theologian; leader of Reform Catholic movement and editor of its monthly organ, *Renaissance* (8 vols., 1900–07).

**Müller, Karl.** 1852–1940. German Protestant theologian.

**Müller, Karl von.** 1873–1923. German naval officer; captain in World War I of German raiding cruiser *Emden;* destroyed by Australian cruiser *Sydney.*

**Müller, Karl Alexander von.** 1882–1964. German historian; author of *Der Altere Pitt* (1923, 1938), *Deutsche Geschichte und Charakter* (1927), *Die Ausbreitung Englands* (1928), etc.

**Müller, Karl Otfried.** 1797–1840. German classical philologist and archaeologist; professor, Göttingen (1819). Author of *Geschichten der Hellenischen Stämme und Städte* (1820, 1824), *Prolegomena zu einer Wissenschaftlichen Mythologie* (1825), *Handbuch der Archäologie der Kunst* (1830), *A History of the Literature of Ancient Greece* (1840), and treatises on ancient Macedonians (1825) and Etruscans (2 vols., 1828). His brother **Julius** (1801–1878) was a Protestant antirationalist theologian; author of *Die Christliche Lehre von der Sünde* (1839), etc.

**Müller, Ludwig.** 1883–1945. German Protestant prelate; navy chaplain (1914–26) and army chaplain (1926–33); member of National Socialist party and a founder of German Christian Movement; consecrated Reichsbishop (Sept., 1934).

**Mül′ler** (mül′ẽr; *Angl.* mŭl′-, mĭl′-), **Max,** *in full* **Friedrich Max.** See MAX MÜLLER.

**Mül′ler** (mül′ẽr), **Otto.** 1816–1894. German novelist and newspaper editor; author of *Charlotte Ackermann* (1854), *Der Stadtschultheiss von Frankfurt* (1856), *Eckhof und seine Schüler* (2 vols., 1863), *Der Professor von Heidelberg* (3 vols., 1870), etc.

**Müller, Paul Hermann.** 1899–1965. Swiss chemist. Awarded Nobel prize in physiology and medicine (1948) for developing DDT (1939; originally by Othmar Zeidler, 1874, but value not then known).

**Müller, Peter Erasmus.** 1776–1834. Danish theologian and antiquary; bishop of Zealand (1830). Works include *Sagabibliothek* or *Library of the Sagas* (3 vols., 1817–20), *Critical Examination of the Traditional History of Denmark and Norway* (2 vols., 1823–30), first critical edition of Saxo Grammaticus's *History of Denmark* (3 vols., pub. 1839–58), etc.

**Müller, Sophus Otto.** 1846–?1921. Danish prehistorian

and archaeologist; director of prehistoric, ethnological, and antique collections (1892–1921) in new National Museum; specialized in study of Bronze and Iron ages and Oriental influence on prehistoric Europe.

**Müller, Wenzel.** 1767–1835. German composer of cantatas, symphonies, masses, and, esp., many fairy operas, operettas, and pantomimes.

**Müller, Wilhelm.** 1794–1827. Father of Friedrich Max Müller (see MAX MÜLLER). German lyric poet, b. Dessau; took part in War of Liberation against Napoleon; teacher (1819) and ducal librarian in Dessau. Author of lyric poems *Müller-Lieder* (1818), including *Die Schöne Müllerin* and *Winterreise* (both set to music by Schubert, 1824), of *Lieder aus dem Meerbusen von Salerno*, of collections *77 Gedichte aus den Hinterlassenen Papieren eines Reisenden Waldhornisten* (1821–27), *Lieder der Griechen*, inspired by Greek struggle for independence (5 parts, 1821–24), and *Neugriechische Volkslieder* (1825), of *Lyrische Reisen* (1827), of stories, works on philology, translations, etc.

**Mül'ler** (mül'ẽr; *Angl.* mĭl'ẽr), **Wilhelm Max.** 1862–1919. Orientalist, b. Gliessenberg, Bavaria; to U.S. (1888). Author of *Asien und Europa nach Altägyptischen Denkmälern* (1893), *Egyptological Researches* (vol. i & ii, 1906–10). Contributor to *Encyclopaedia Biblica*, the *Jewish Encyclopedia*, and technical journals.

**Müller, William John.** 1812–1845. English landscape and figure painter; painted first the scenery of Gloucestershire and Wales, and later oil and water-color paintings of the Orient.

**Mül'ler** (mül'ẽr), **Wolfgang.** *Called* **Müller von Kö'nigs·win'ter** (fŏn kû'nĭks·vĭn'tẽr). 1816–1873. German lyric and epic poet and novelist, b. Königswinter; practiced medicine in Düsseldorf (1842–48); settled in Cologne (1853) and Wiesbaden (1869). Author of *Gedichte* (1847), including *Mein Herz Ist am Rheine*, of the epic of the Rhine in ballad form *Lorelei* (1851), the idyl in verse *Eine Maikönigin* (1852), novels, and dramatic works, including comedy *Sie Hat Ihr Herz Entdeckt.*

**Müller–Erz'bach** (-ärts'bäκ; -ĕrts'bäκ), **Rudolf.** 1874–1959. German jurist.

**Müller–Franken.** See Hermann MÜLLER.

**Müller–Frei'en·fels** (-frī'ĕn·fĕls), **Richard.** 1882–1949. German psychologist; founder of "Lebenspsychologie"; author of psychological works relating to art, poetry, personality, religion, etc.

**Müller–Gut'ten·brunn** (-gŏŏt'ĕn·brōōn), **Adam.** *Pseudonym* **Ig·no'tus** (ĭg·nō'tŭs; *Ger.* -tōōs). 1852–1923. Austrian writer and theater director; critic and literary editor, *Deutsche Zeitung*, Vienna (1873–88); director of Raimund Theater (1892–96) and Kaiser Jubiläum Theater (1898–1903); author of dramas, novels, historical, literary, and theatrical treatises, etc.

**Müller–Ly'er** (-lē'ẽr), **Franz.** 1857–1916. German sociologist and philosopher; founded phaseological method in cultural history. Author of *Phasen der Kultur* (1908), *Die Familie* (1912), *Phasen der Liebe* (1913), etc.

**Mul'ler–U'ry** (mōōl'ẽr·ū'rĭ), **A·dol'fo** (ȧ·dŏl'fō). 1864–1947. Portrait painter, b. in Switzerland; to U.S. (1888); studios in New York and London. Among his subjects have been: Pope Pius X, Cardinal Merry del Val, Pope Benedict XV, Lord and Lady Strathcona, President McKinley, General Grant, Senator Hanna, James J. Hill, Emperor William II of Germany, President Wilson, Mrs. Wilson, Cardinal Mercier.

**Mul'li·gan** (mŭl'ĭ·găn), **Charles J.** 1866–1916. Sculptor, b. Riverdale, Ireland; to U.S. (1883). Among his works are *Lincoln as Railsplitter* and *President McKinley*, in Chicago; *George Rogers Clark*, in Quincy, Ill.; *Soldiers' Monument*, in Decatur, Ill.

**Mul'li·ken** (mŭl'ĭ·kĕn), **Robert Sanderson.** 1896– . American chemist, b. Newburyport, Mass. At U. of Chicago (1921–23; 1928– ); awarded Nobel prize in chemistry (1966) for work on chemical bonds and electronic structure of molecules.

**Mullines** *or* **Mullins.** See MULLENS.

**Müll'ner** (mül'nẽr), **Adolf.** 1774–1829. German writer and playwright; author of fate tragedies, and comedies in verse modeled after the French.

**Mu'lock** (mū'lŏk), **Dinah Maria.** See CRAIK.

**Mulock,** Sir **William.** 1844–1944. Canadian jurist; vice-chancellor, U. of Toronto (1881–1900), and chancellor (from 1924). Postmaster general of Canada (1896–1905), and minister of labor (1900–05); chief justice, exchequer division, Supreme Court of Ontario (1905–23); chief justice of Ontario (1923–36).

**Mul·read'y** (mŭl·rĕd'ĭ; mŭl'rĕd'ĭ), **William.** 1786–1863. Irish genre painter, b. County Clare, Ireland; began painting as illustrator of children's books; exhibited figure subjects and domestic scenes at Royal Acad. Illustrated *Vicar of Wakefield* (c. 1840); furnished design of Rowland Hill's first postal envelope (1840).

**Multatuli.** Pseudonym of Eduard Douwes DEKKER.

**Mum'ford** (mŭm'fẽrd), **Ethel,** *nee* **Watts** (wŏts). 1878?–1940. American writer; m. George Dana Mumford (1894), Peter Geddes Grant (1906). Author of *Dupes* (1901), *Whitewash* (1903), *The Cynic's Calendar* (1905–10), *Out of the Ashes* (1913), the plays *The Young Idea* and *Good Night Nurse*, and several scenarios.

**Mumford, Lewis.** 1895– . American writer, b. Flushing, Long Island, N.Y. Author of *Civilization in the United States, by 30 Americans* (1922), *The Story of Utopias* (1922), *Sticks and Stones* (1924) *The Golden Day* (1926), *Herman Melville* (1929), *American Taste* (1929), *The Brown Decades* (1931), *Technics and Civilization* (1934), *The Culture of Cities* (1938), *Men Must Act* (1939), *Faith for Living* (1940), *The Condition of Man* (1944), etc.

**Mum'mi·us** (mŭm'ĭ·ŭs), **Lucius.** *Surnamed* **A·cha'·i·cus** (ȧ·kā'ĭ·kŭs). Roman general and politician; consul (146 B.C.); commanded Roman army in Achaean war; captured Corinth, thus completing (146) Roman conquest of Greece.

**Mumtaz Mahall.** See under SHAH JAHAN.

**Mun** (mûɴ), Comte **Adrien Albert Marie de.** 1841–1914. French politician; devoted himself to social betterment; founder of Circles of Catholic Workmen (1871); member of Chamber of Deputies (1876). A Boulangist; prominent figure in Dreyfus trial; opponent (1905) of bill for separation of church and state; advocated repeal of three year conscription law (1913); at outbreak of World War I, wrote articles in *L'Écho de Paris* to support morale of French people. Among books are *La Loi des Suspects* (1900), *Contre la Séparation* (1905), *Ma Vocation Sociale* (1908), and *L'Heure Décisive* (1913).

**Mun** (mŭn), **Thomas.** 1571–1641. English writer on economics; early definer of theory of balance of trade; merchant in Italy and the Levant; director of East India Co. (1615); defended East India Co. against charge of bullionists, that such foreign trade as did not yield direct balance of bullion (specie) was harmful, in his *Discourse of Trade from England unto the East Indies* (1621), further developed in *Discourse on England's Treasure by Forraign Trade* (1664).

**Munatius Plancus, Lucius.** See PLANCUS.

**Munch** (mŏŏngk), **Edvard.** 1863–1944. Norwegian painter and designer; studied under Krohg in Oslo, and in Paris (1889–92), Italy, and Germany.

**Munch, Peter Andreas.** 1810–1863. Norwegian historian and philologist; leader of Norwegian historical school and a representative of Norwegian national romanticism; maintained that so-called Icelandic literature was really Old Norse. Author of *History of the Norwegian People* (8 vols., 1852–63), etc. His cousin **Andreas Munch** (1811–1884), lyric poet and dramatist; author of *Ephemera* (1837), *Poems Old and New* (1848), and *Grief and Consolation* (1852), and the dramas *King Sverre's Youth* (1838), *An Evening at Giske* (1855), and *Lord William Russell* (1857).

**Munchausen.** See Baron Karl von MÜNCHHAUSEN.

**Münch–Bellinghausen,** Baron **Eligius von.** See Friedrich HALM.

**Münch'hau'sen** (münk'hou'zĕn), Baron **Börries von.** 1874–1945. German poet; a leading representative of ballad writing; author of *Gedichte* (1897), *Balladen* (1901), etc.

**Münchhausen,** Baron **Karl Friedrich Hieronymus von.** *Eng. corruption* Baron **Mun·chau'sen** (mŭn-chô'z'n). 1720–1797. German huntsman and soldier, b. in Hanover; served with distinction as officer in Russian campaign against Turks. Reputed to have told exaggerated anecdotes of his adventures and exploits; his name is now proverbially associated with absurdly exaggerated stories. Real author of Baron Munchausen tales was Rudolph Erich Raspe (*q.v.*).

**Mun'day** (mŭn'dĭ), **Anthony.** 1560–1633. English poet, playwright, and compiler; went to Rome (1578), a journalist, if not a spy, reporting activities and designs of English Roman Catholics in France and Italy in *The English Romayne Lyfe* (1582). Actor in earl of Oxford's company (1579–84); had hand in eighteen plays (1584–1602), four extant, including two about a Robert, Earl of Huntingdon, identified with Robin Hood, and one on Sir John Oldcastle; ballad writer; compiler of religious works; translator of *Amadis de Gaule* (1589–95), *Palladino of England* (1588), and other French romances; as literary executor, revised Stow's *Survay of London* (1618); wrote most of London city pageants (1592–1623); chief pageant writer (1605–16); rival of Ben Jonson and Middleton.

**Mun'de·lein** (mŭn'dĕ·līn), **George William.** 1872–1939. American Roman Catholic cardinal, b. New York City; archbishop of Chicago (from 1915); elevated to cardinalate (Mar. 24, 1924).

**Mun·del'la** (mŭn·dĕl'ȧ), **Anthony John.** 1825–1897. English cabinet member and philanthropist; formed first British board of conciliation between employers and employed (1866); instrumental in passing of legislation regulating factories and education; privy councilor (1880); secured passage of compulsory-education act (1881); president of board of trade (1886, 1892–94); created labor department (1886).

**Mun'den** (mŭn'dĕn), **Joseph Shepherd.** 1758–1832. English comedian; known now chiefly for Charles Lamb's encomium, in *Essays of Elia*, as king of broad comedy.

**Mundt** (mo͝ont), **Theodor.** 1808–1861. German novelist and critic, b. in Potsdam; a leader of the "Young Germany" school. Among his novels are *Madonna* (1835), *Carmela* (1844), *Mendoza* (2 vols., 1846–47), *Die Matadore* (2 vols., 1850), and *Graf Mirabeau* (4 vols., 1858); also wrote works on history, cultural history, travel, and aesthetics. His wife (m. 1839) **Klara,** *nee* **Müller** (1814–1873), pseudonym **Luise Mühl'bach** (mül'bäk), was author of social novels, as *Aphra Behn* (3 vols., 1849), and, esp., of historical novels of Prussia, Austria, and France, including *Friedrich der Grosse und sein Hof* (1853), etc.

**Mun'dy** (mŭn'dĭ), **Talbot.** 1879–1940. Writer, b. London, Eng.; to U.S. (1911). Among his many books of adventure are *Winds of the World* (1915), *Om* (1923), *Queen Cleopatra* (1929), *Jimgrim* (1931), *East and West* (1937), etc.

**Mun'ford** (mŭn'fẽrd), **William.** 1775–1825. American lawyer and classical scholar, b. in Mecklenburg County, Va.; published a blank-verse translation of Homer's *Iliad* (pub. 1846). His father, **Robert Munford** (d. 1784), served in American Revolution and was author of plays and poems (collected and published, 1798).

**Mungo,** Saint. See Saint KENTIGERN.

**Mu'ni** (mū'nĭ), **Paul** (pôl). *Real surname* **Wei'sen-freund** (wī'z'n·frĕnd). 1895–1967. Actor, b. in Lemberg, Austria; to U.S. (1902), naturalized (1923). Member of stock company in Yiddish Art Theatre, New York (1918–25); alternated between stage and motion pictures (1932–35); under contract to Warner Brothers Pictures (from 1935). Starred in *I am a Fugitive from a Chain Gang, Life of Louis Pasteur* (received the Motion Picture Academy award, 1936), *The Good Earth, Life of Émile Zola,* etc.

**Munk** (mo͝ongk), **Salomon.** 1803?–1867. Orientalist, b. Glogau in Lower Silesia; member of staff in department of manuscripts at Bibliothèque Royale, Paris (1835); professor of Hebrew, Collège de France (1864).

**Mun'ká·csy** (mo͞on'kä·chĭ), **Mihály von.** *Real name* **Mi'cha·el Lieb** (mĭ'kä·ĕl lēp). 1844–1900. Hungarian historical and genre painter; settled near Paris (1872); art inspector, Budapest (1895). His *The Pawnbroker's Shop* (1874), *The Music Room,* and *The Two Families* are in the Metropolitan Museum, New York.

**Mün'nich** (mün'ĭk), Count **Burkhard Christoph von.** 1683–1767. Russian field marshal and statesman; commander in chief of Russian army (1727); field marshal and president of war council (1732). Captured Danzig in War of Polish Succession (1734) and won distinction in Crimean campaigns (1736–39). Overthrew Regent Biron (1740) and became chief minister in regency of Anna Leopoldovna (1740–41); given sentence of death (1741), following accession to throne of Empress Elizabeth Petrovna, which was changed at scaffold to exile in Siberia; recalled by Peter III (1762) and restored to estates. Director-general of Baltic ports under Catherine II.

**Mun'nings** (mŭn'ĭngz), Sir **Alfred James.** 1878–1959. Eng. painter esp. of sporting subjects; painted 45 war pictures under commission from Canadian govt. (1917–18).

**Mu·ñoz'** (mo͞o·nyôth'), **Gil Sánchez.** See CLEMENT VIII, antipope.

**Mun·ro'** (mŭn·rō'). See also MONRO.

**Munro, Charles Kirkpatrick.** *Real name* **Charles Walden Kirkpatrick Mac·Mul'lan** (măk·mŭl'ăn). 1889– . British playwright and essayist; son of Professor S. J. MacMullan, Queen's Coll., Belfast; educ. Cambridge. Author of *Wanderers* (1915), *At Mrs. Beam's* (1922), *Mr. Eno* (1928), *Bluestone Quarry* (1931), *Coronation Time at Mrs. Beam's* (1937).

**Munro, Dana Carleton.** 1866–1933. American historian, b. Bristol, R.I.; professor, Princeton (1915–33); specialist in study of medieval history. Author of *The Middle Ages* (1902); editor of L. J. Paetow's *A Guide to the Study of Medieval History* (1931). His son **Dana Gardner** (1892– ), diplomat and historian; in Latin-American division, U.S. Department of State (1921–25); chief, division of Latin-American affairs, U.S. Department of State (1929–30); U.S. minister to Haiti (1930–32); professor of Latin-American history and affairs, Princeton (from 1932).

**Munro, Hector Hugh.** *Pseudonym* **Sa'ki** (sä'kĭ). 1870–

1916. British writer of humorous short stories and novels, b. Burma; wrote political satires for *Westminster Gazette* under name of Saki; published his only serious book, *The Rise of the Russian Empire* (1900); correspondent in Balkans, Russia, and Paris (1902–08). Began series of short stories with *Reginald* (1904) and *Reginald in Russia* (1910), about an irrepressible young man of the world, followed by *The Chronicles of Clovis* (1911), *Beasts and Super-Beasts* (1914), *The Square Egg* (1924); author of two novels, *The Unbearable Bassington* (1912) and *When William Came* (1913). In World War, served in Royal Fusiliers; killed in France.

**Munro, Hugh Andrew Johnstone.** 1819–1885. British Latinist, b. Elgin, Scotland; collated Vatican and Laurentian manuscripts of Lucretius, inspected manuscripts at Leiden, edited Lucretius and Horace; author of *Criticisms and Elucidations of Catullus* (1878).

**Munro, Neil.** 1864–1930. Scottish novelist and journalist; chief reporter and art, dramatic, and literary critic, Glasgow *Evening News;* editor in chief (1918). Began as novelist with *The Lost Pibroch* (1896) and *John Splendid* (1898); turned from historical and romantic fiction to realistic stories of modern life, beginning with *Bud* (or *The Daft Days*, 1907); author of humorous novels, verse (1931), and essays.

**Mun·ro′** *or* **Mon·ro′** (mŭn·rō′), **Robert.** d. 1680? Scottish soldier; served in Scottish rebellion against Charles I; sent on expedition against Catholic rebels in Ireland (1642); commanded (1644) Parliamentary forces in Ulster; captured Belfast (1644); defeated by O'Neill at Benburb (1646); on making of terms between Parliament and Charles's lieutenant Ormonde, refused to surrender Carrickfergus and Belfast, and was imprisoned and superseded by Monck (1648). His cousin **Robert** (d. 1633), called "the Black Baron," distinguished himself as a colonel under Gustavus Adolphus.

**Munro, William Bennett.** 1875–1957. Political scientist, b. at Almonte, Ontario, Canada; professor, Harvard (1912–29), Calif. Inst. Tech. (from 1929). Author of *The Government of European Cities* (1909), *The Government of the United States* (1919), *Municipal Government and Administration* (2 vols., 1923), *The Governments of Europe* (1925), *American Government Today* (1930), etc.

**Mun·roe′** (mŭn·rō′), **Charles Edward.** 1849–1938. American chemist, b. Cambridge, Mass.; authority on explosives, and inventor of a smokeless powder.

**Munro-Ferguson, Ronald Craufurd.** See Viscount NOVAR.

**Mun·sell′** (mŭn·sĕl′), **Albert Henry.** 1858–1918. American portrait painter, b. Boston, Mass.; inventor of instruments for color measurement and a system of pigment colors. Author of *Atlas of the Color System* (1910), *Color Balance* (1913), etc.

**Mun′sey** (mŭn′sĭ), **Frank Andrew.** 1854–1925. American publisher, b. Mercer, Me.; telegraph operator, Portland and Augusta, Me. (to 1882). To New York and started (1882) publishing magazines; expanded into newspaper field (owning New York *Evening Sun* and *Evening Telegram*), grocery field (Mohican grocery stores). Among his magazine successes were *Munsey's Magazine* and the *Argosy All-Story Weekly.* Bequeathed bulk of fortune to Metropolitan Museum of Art.

**Mun′son** (mŭn′s'n), **Gorham B.** 1896–1969. American editor and critic, b. Amityville, N.Y.; editor, *New Democracy* (from 1933). Author of *Robert Frost* (1927), *American Literature Since 1900* (1928), *Style and Form in American Prose* (1929), *The Dilemma of the Liberated* (1930).

**Munson, Walter David.** 1843–1908. American shipping magnate, b. Cheshire, Conn.; settled in Havana, Cuba (1868); with one schooner, began freight service between New York and Havana (1873), the beginning of the Munson Steamship Line (incorporated, 1899). Resident in New York City (from 1882). Expanded shipping interests to include lines to Mexican, Central American, Haitian, Jamaican, and Colombian ports.

**Mün′ster** (mün′stẽr). Name of Westphalian family including: Count **Ernst Friedrich Herbert zu Münster-Der′ne·burg** (-dĕr′nĕ·bŏŏrк), Baron **von Grot′haus** (grōt′hous). 1766–1839. Hanoverian statesman; ambassador to Russia (1801–04); minister for Hanoverian affairs in London (1805–31); helped bring about entente between Russia and England; framed constitution of new kingdom of Hanover (1819) and introduced two-chamber system. His son Count **Georg Herbert zu Münster–Le′den·burg** (-lā′dĕn·bŏŏrк), Baron von Grothaus and (from 1899) Prince **Münster von Derneburg** (1820–1902); German diplomat and publicist; entered Prussian diplomatic service (1866); member of Prussian house of lords (from 1867); in imperial Reichstag (1871–73); German ambassador at London (1873) and Paris (1885–1900); member of International Peace Conference (1899).

**Münster, Sebastian.** 1489–1552. German theologian and cosmographer; professor of theology and Hebrew at Heidelberg, then of mathematics at Basel; known esp. for *Cosmographia Universa*, first detailed description of the world in German.

**Mün′ster·berg** (mün′stẽr·bĕrк), **Hu′go** (hōō′gō; *Eng.* hū′gō). 1863–1916. Psychologist, b. Danzig; taught at Harvard (1892–95; 1897–1916); superintended construction of laboratory at Harvard especially equipped for experimental psychology; known as pioneer in field of applied psychology. Among his books are *Psychology and the Teacher* (1909), *Psychology and Industrial Efficiency* (1913), *Psychology and Social Sanity* (1914), etc.

**Mun′ta·ner′** (mōōn′tä·nĕr′), **Ramón.** 1265–1336. Spanish soldier, minstrel, and chronicler; wrote *Cronica Catalana*, valuable as source for history of his period.

**Mun′the′** (mŭn′tĕ′), **Axel Martin Fredrik.** 1857–1949. Swedish physician and writer; practiced Paris and Rome; author of anti-German *Red Cross and Iron Cross* (1916), *The Story of San Michele* (1929), etc.

**Mun′the** (mŏŏn′tĕ), **Ludvig.** 1841–1896. Norwegian landscape painter, chiefly of autumn and winter scenes in rainy or foggy weather. His cousin **Gerhard Peter Frants Wilhelm Munthe** (1849–1929), painter and illustrator; works include landscapes, fantastic designs influenced by Norwegian fairy tales and sagas and reproduced in figured tapestries, decorative water colors, woodcuts illustrating Snorri Sturluson's *Heimskringla* (1893–1900), decorations for private residences and public buildings, etc.

**Müntz** (münts), **Eugène.** 1845–1902. French art historian; authority on Renaissance art. His brother **Achille Charles** (1848–1917) was an agronomist.

**Mün′zer** *or* **Mün′tzer** (mün′tsẽr), **Thomas.** 1489?–1525. German religious enthusiast and Anabaptist leader; led peasant insurrection in Thuringia during Peasants' War and inaugurated war against nobility and clergy; defeated at Frankenhausen (1525), captured and beheaded.

**Mun′zing·er** (mŏŏn′tsĭng·ẽr), **Werner.** 1832–1875. Swiss explorer and traveler in Africa; traveled among Bogos (1855–61); member of German expedition to inner Africa (1861) and north and northwest of Abyssinia (1864); British consul at Massaua (1865) and served as guide to British forces in Anglo-Abyssinian War (1868); named governor by khedive of Egypt (1870); pasha and governor general of eastern Sudan (1872); died from wounds suffered at Aussa while on expedition against Abyssinia.

**Muqaddasi, al-.** See MAQDISI.

**Mu·rad′** (mōō·rät′; -räd′) *or* **A′mu·rath′** (ăm′mōō-rät′). Name of five sultans of Turkey: **Murad I** (1319–1389); succeeded to throne (1359); killed by Serbian noble in battle (1389). **Murad II** (1403?–1451); succeeded (1421); extended Turkish conquests in southeastern Europe. **Murad III** (1546–1595); succeeded (1574); conquered parts of Persia. **Murad IV** (1609–1640); succeeded (1623); waged war against Poland and Persia, and established order in internal affairs. **Murad V** (1840–1904); succeeded Abdul-Aziz (1876); suspected of liberalism by conservative group, declared insane, and replaced on throne by Abdul-Hamid II (*q.v.*).

**Mu·rad′ Bey** (mōō·rät′ [-räd′] bā′). d. 1801. Egyptian Mameluke chief; ally of Ibrahim Bey and opponent of Ali Bey; fought the French at Alexandria (1798) but was defeated in battle of the Pyramids and withdrew to Upper Egypt; later (1800), allied himself with French general Desaix de Veygoux against Turks; died of plague (1801).

**Murad Efendi.** Pseudonym of Franz von WERNER.

**Murano.** See under VIVARINI.

**Mu·ra·sa·ki** (mōō·rä·sä·kē), Lady. *Full Jap. name* **Murasaki Shi·ki·bu** (shē·kē·bōō). Japanese writer of 11th century; author of *Genji Monagatari, or The Tale of Genji* (trans. by Arthur Waley, 1925–32).

**Mu′rat′** (mü′rȧ′), **Joachim.** 1767?–1815. French cavalry commander; served in Italy (1796–97) and Egypt (1798–99), rising to rank of general of division; aided Napoleon Bonaparte in coup d'état (1799); m. (1800) Napoleon's sister Maria Annunciata Bonaparte. Appointed governor of Paris; created marshal of France (1804) and prince and high admiral (1805). Commanded cavalry at Austerlitz (1805), Jena (1806), Eylau and Friedland (1807). Became king of Naples under title Joachim I Napoleon (1808); known as the "Dandy King." Joined Napoleon's cause on emperor's return from Elba; defeated by Austrian army at Tolentino (May 2–3, 1815); captured and executed (Oct. 13, 1815). His eldest son, **Napoléon Achille** (1801–1847), emigrated to U.S. (1821); settled on estate near Tallahassee, Fla.; published, in French, commentaries on American system of government. His second son, Prince **Napoléon Lucien Charles** (1803–1878); to U.S. (1825), but made continued efforts to recover for himself father's throne in Naples; settled in France (after 1848), created senator after coup d'état (Dec. 2, 1851), and given formal recognition as prince of imperial family.

**Mu′ra′tore′** (mü′rȧ′tôr′), **Lucien.** 1878–1954. French dramatic tenor; created leading tenor roles in Hahn's *La Carmélite* (1902), Massenet's *Ariane* (1906), *Bacchus* (1909), and *Roma* (1912), and Hüe's *Le Miracle* (1910), and appeared in Strauss's *Salome* (1910), Giordano's *Siberia* (1911), and Saint-Saëns's *Déjanire* (1911), etc. Member of Chicago Opera Company (1913 ff.); to France for war duty (1915); sang at Buenos Aires (1917). His wife (m. 1913), **Lina,** *nee* **Ca′va·lie′ri** [kä′vä·lyâ′rē] (1874–1944), Italian operatic soprano, sang in many leading European cities and in U.S. at Metropolitan Opera House (1906–07), Manhattan Opera House (1908–09), and with Chicago Opera Co. (1915–16).

**Mu′ra·to′ri** (mōō′rä·tō′rē), **Lodovico Antonio.** 1672–1750. Italian antiquary and historian; librarian to duke of Modena (1700 ff.); discovered treatise on Bible canon, now called *Muratorian fragment,* in Ambrosian Library (1740).

**Mu·rav·iëv′** (mōō·rŭf·yôf′). Name of distinguished Russian family, including: **Mikhail Nikitich** (1757–1807), appointed by Catherine II tutor to her grandchildren Alexander and Konstantin; **Nikolai Nikolaevich** (1768–1840), served against Napoleon (1812–14), head of a military school for general staff officers (1797–1823); Nikolai's son **Aleksandr Nikolaevich** (1792–1864), major general, served in Crimean War (1854–56); Alexander's brother **Nikolai Nikolaevich** (1794?–1866), major general, engaged in suppressing Polish rebellion (1830) and served in Crimean War (1854–56); another brother, **Mikhail Nikolaevich** (1796?–1866), also an army officer, suppressed Polish rebellion (1863) with cruel severity; Mikhail's grandson, Count **Mikhail Nikolaevich** (1845–1900), diplomat, minister of foreign affairs (1897–1900). Representatives of another branch of this same family were Count **Nikolai Nikolaevich Muraviëv-A·mur′ski** [ŭ·mōōr′skû·ĭ; *Angl.* -skĭ] (1809?–1881), major general, governor general of eastern Siberia (1848–61), and conqueror of Amur region ceded by China to Russia (1858); his nephew **Nikolai Valerianovich** (1850–1908), jurist and diplomat, minister of justice (1894), chairman of The Hague court which adjudicated Venezuela claims controversy (1903), ambassador to Italy (1905–08).

**Mur′chi·son** (mûr′chĭ·s′n), **Charles.** 1830–1879. Cousin of Sir Roderick I. Murchison. British physician, b. Jamaica; settled in London (1855); authority on tropical fevers.

**Murchison,** Sir **Roderick Impey.** 1792–1871. British geologist, b. Scotland. Investigated lower fossiliferous strata of England and Wales; established Silurian system; with Adam Sedgwick, established Devonian system; collaborated with Édouard P. de Verneuil and Keyserling in geological survey of Russia; studied geology of Scottish Highlands; director-general of geological survey and director of Royal School of Mines (1852).

**Mur′doch** (mûr′dŏk), **Walter.** 1874–1970. Scottish-born educator and anthologist in Australia; author of *The Making of Australia* (history), *Lucid Intervals* (essays); compiler of anthologies, as *The Oxford Book of Australian Verse.*

**Mur′dock** (mûr′dŏk), **William.** 1754–1839. British engineer and inventor, b. Scotland; superintendent of fitting Watt's engines in Cornwall; lighted exterior of factory at Soho with coal gas produced by process he had invented (1802); invented improvements in steam engine; made working model of locomotive steam engine (1784); worked on a steam carriage or road locomotive; invented slide valve (1799) and apparatus for utilizing compressed air; credited with invention of sun-and-planet motion patented by Watt.

**Mure** (mūr), Sir **William.** 1594–1657. Scottish poet; member of Scottish parliament (1643); wounded at Marston Moor (1644). Author of *The True Crucifixe for True Catholickes* (1629), a paraphrase of the Psalms (1639), and *The Cry of Blood and of a Broken Covenant* (1650).

**Murel, John A.** See MURRELL.

**Mu·re′na** (mū·rē′nȧ), **Lucius Licinius.** Roman general who commanded army against Mithridates (83–82 B.C.). His son **Lucius Licinius,** consul (62 B.C.), was accused of bribery by a defeated rival for office; defended by Cicero and acquitted.

**Mu′ret′** (mü′rĕ′), **Eduard.** 1833–1904. German lexicographer; collaborator with Daniel Sanders (*q.v.*) and J. Schmidt in compiling *Enzyklopädisches Wörterbuch der Englischen und Deutschen Sprache* (4 vols., 1891–1901).

**Mu′ret′** (mü′rĕ′), **Jules Henri Maurice.** 1870–1954. Swiss journalist and writer; editor, *Journal des Débats* and *Gazette de Lausanne;* author of *L'Esprit Juif...* (1901), *Le Crépuscule des Nations Blanches* (1926), etc.

**Muret, Marc Antoine.** 1526–1585. French poet and scholar; teacher of the classics; ordained priest (1576); editor of many Latin classics and author of important commentaries.

**Mur'free** (mûr'frē), **Mary No·ailles'** (nō·ī'). *Pseudonym* **Charles Egbert Crad'dock** (krăd'ŭk). 1850–1922. American novelist, b. near Murfreesboro, Tenn.; established reputation as short-story writer by her stories in the *Atlantic Monthly* (from 1878), afterwards published in book *In the Tennessee Mountains* (1884). Other works include the novels *Where the Battle was Fought* (1884), *Down the Ravine* (1885), *The Despot of Broomsedge Cove* (1889), *The Juggler* (1897), *A Spectre of Power* (1903), *The Frontiersman* (1904), *The Storm Centre* (1905), *The Windfall* (1907), *The Ordeal* (1912).

**Mur'ger'** (mür'zhā'), **Henri.** 1822–1861. French writer; best known for sketches of Bohemian life in Paris, as in *Scènes de la Vie de Bohème* (appeared in the journal *Le Corsair*, 1847–49), *Scènes de la Vie de Jeunesse* (1851).

**Mu·ril'lo** (mōō·rē'lyō; *Angl.* mū·rĭl'ō), **Bartolomé Esteban.** 1617–1682. Spanish painter of Andalusian school, b. Seville; succeeded Pacheco as head of Seville school (1654); president of Seville Acad. (1660 ff.); known esp. as colorist, particularly as a master of color contrast. Works include *Founding of Santa Maria Maggiore* (4 pictures in Santa María Blanca, Seville), *Immaculate Conception* (15 examples; in the Louvre, Seville museum, Prado, etc.), *La Purísima* (Seville Cathedral), *St. John of God Attending the Sick* and *Miracle of the Loaves and Fishes* (Church of St. George, Seville), *Adoration of the Shepherds* and *St. Elizabeth of Hungary* (the Prado), *Birth of the Virgin* (the Louvre), *St. John on Patmos* (Metropolitan Museum, New York).

**Mu·ril'lo To'ro** (mōō·rē'yō tō'rō), **Manuel.** 1815–1880. Colombian lawyer, journalist, and statesman; president of Colombia (1864–66, 1872–74).

**Mu'ris, Johannes de** (dē mū'rĭs). *Called* **Nor·ma'nus** (nôr·mā'nŭs). English musical theorist, astronomer, and mathematician of 14th century; master of mathematics at Oxford. Author of treatise *Speculum Musicae* (between 1340–50). Identified by some with **Johannes** (*or* **Julianus**) **de Muris,** *called* **de Fran'ci·a** (dē frăn'shĭ·ȧ), French musical theorist of 14th century; professor (1321) and rector (1350) at the Sorbonne; author of *De Musica Practica* (1321), *De Musica Speculativa* (1323).

**Mur'na·ghan** (mûr'nȧ·hăn), **Francis D.** 1893– . American mathematician, b. in Omagh, Ireland; M.A., National U. of Ireland (1914), Ph.D., Johns Hopkins (1916); to U.S. (1914), naturalized (1928); on teaching staff, Johns Hopkins (from 1918; prof. of applied mathematics from 1928). Author of *Vector Analysis and the Theory of Relativity* (1922), *Theoretical Mechanics* (with Joseph S. Ames; 1929); *Theory of Group Representations* (1938). Special editor for mathematics, *Webster's New International Dictionary, Second Edition.*

**Mur'ner** (mōōr'nẽr), **Thomas.** 1475–1537. German priest and satirist, opponent of Reformation; author of humorous satires *Narrenbeschwörung* (1512), *Schelmenzunft* (1512), and *Geuchmatt* (1519), the biting anti-Lutheran attack *Von dem Grossen Lutherischen Narren* (1522), translation of the *Aeneid* (1515), textbook on logic, metrics, and law, etc.

**Mu'rom·tsev** (mōō'rŭm·tsyĕf), **Sergei Andreevich.** 1850–1910. Russian jurist; elected by Constitutional Democratic party to 1st Russian Duma; chosen its president (1905–06); aided in drafting Viborg Manifesto (1906); arrested and imprisoned by Russian government. Author of legal treatises.

**Mur'phy** (mûr'fĭ), **Arthur.** 1727–1805. Irish actor and playwright; acted roles of Richard III, Othello, Biron (in *Fatal Marriage*), and Osmyn (in *Mourning Bride*). Author of many farces and satires, as *The Apprentice* (1756), *The Upholsterer* (1757), *Know Your Own Mind* (1777); wrote biographies of Fielding and Garrick, an essay on the genius of Samuel Johnson (1792), and translations of Sallust and Tacitus (1793).

**Murphy, Charles Francis.** 1858–1924. American politician; head of Tammany Hall (1902–24).

**Murphy, Edgar Gardner.** 1869–1913. American Protestant Episcopal clergyman, b. Fort Smith, Ark.; labored to improve social conditions in the South.

**Murphy, Frank.** 1890–1949. American lawyer and jurist, b. Harbor Beach, Mich.; LL.B., Michigan (1914). Mayor of Detroit (1930–33), resigning to become governor general of Philippine Islands; U.S. high commissioner to Philippine Islands (1935–36); governor of Michigan (1936–38); attorney general of the U.S. (1939–40); associate justice, U.S. Supreme Court (1940–49).

**Murphy, Franklin.** 1846–1920. American industrialist and governor, b. Jersey City, N.J.; served through Civil War; at Antietam, Chancellorsville, Gettysburg, Missionary Ridge, Lookout Mountain. Organized and headed varnish-manufacturing business (1865–1915). Governor of New Jersey (1902–05); instrumental in securing primary-election law, child-labor law, tenement-house commission law, and workshop-ventilation law.

**Murphy, Hermann Dudley.** 1867–1945. American painter, esp. of landscapes and aquarelles.

**Murphy, John Benjamin.** 1857–1916. American surgeon, b. near Appleton, Wis.; practiced in Chicago; specialist in abdominal surgery; invented (1892) Murphy, or Murphy's, button, a device for rapid and accurate intestinal anastomosis.

**Murphy, John Francis.** 1853–1921. American landscape painter, b. Oswego, N.Y.; self-taught; opened studio in New York (1875). His *October* hangs in the Corcoran Art Gallery, Washington, D.C.; *Indian Summer*, in National Gallery, Washington, D.C.; *The Old Barn*, in Metropolitan Museum of Art, New York.

**Murphy, Lambert.** 1885–1954. American operatic tenor, b. Springfield, Mass.; with Metropolitan Opera Company (1911–15); resigned to devote himself to concert appearances, music festivals, and teaching.

**Murphy, Michael Charles.** 1861–1913. American athletic trainer, b. Westboro, Mass.; trainer of track and football athletes at Yale (1887–89; 1892–96; 1900–05), and at U. of Pennsylvania (1896–1900; 1905–13); coach of American Olympic teams of 1908 and 1912.

**Murphy, Robert Daniel.** 1894–1978. American diplomat, b. Milwaukee; vice-consul, Munich (1921–24); consul (1930–39), counselor of embassy (1939), Paris; chargé d'affaires, Vichy (1940); special representative in North Africa (1940–43); U.S. political advisor for Germany (1944); ambassador to Belgium (1949–52), Japan (1952–53).

**Murphy, Walter Patton.** 1873–1942. American industrialist and philanthropist, b. Pittsburgh, Pa.; in railroad supply business (from 1898); organizer of Walter P. Murphy Foundation; donor (1939) of $6,735,000 to Northwestern U. to establish an institute of technology.

**Murphy, William Parry.** 1892– . American physician, b. Stoughton, Wis.; practiced, Boston (from 1923); research worker on diabetes and diseases of the blood, esp. pernicious anemia; codiscoverer with Dr. George R. Minot of liver treatment for pernicious anemia; joint recipient, with Dr. George Minot and Dr. George H. Whipple, of Nobel prize in medicine (1934).

**Mur'ray** (mûr'ĭ). Family name of earls of DUNMORE.

**Murray.** *Recently* **Stewart–Murray.** Family name of earls, marquises, and dukes of ATHOLL.

**Murray,** Earl of. *English spelling of Scottish title* **Moray.** See (1) Sir Thomas Randolph; (2) Stewart family.

**Murray, Alexander.** 1775–1813. Scottish philologist; grad. Edinburgh and professor of Oriental languages there (1812); author of *History of the European Languages* (1823).

**Murray, Alexander Stuart.** 1841–1904. British archaeologist, b. Arbroath, Scotland; educ. Edinburgh and Berlin; asst. keeper and keeper of Greek and Roman antiquities, British Museum (from 1867); directed excavations in Cyprus (1894–96); author of *A History of Greek Sculpture* (2 vols., 1880–83), *Handbook of Greek Archaeology* (1892), *Sculptures of the Parthenon* (1903).

**Murray, Charles.** 1864–1941. Scottish poet and engineer, b. Aberdeenshire; secretary for public works, Union of South Africa (1910); director of defense, South Africa (1917). Author of *Hamewith* (1900), *A Sough o' War* (1917), and *In Country Places* (1920).

**Murray,** Sir **David.** 1849–1933. Scottish landscape painter, b. Glasgow; took as chief subjects landscapes of Scotland, Picardy, southern England, and Italian lakes.

**Murray, David Christie.** 1847–1907. English novelist and journalist; newspaper and parliamentary reporter; during Russo-Turkish war, special representative of London *Times* (1877–78). Author of novels *A Life's Atonement* (1880), *Joseph's Coat* (1881), *Rainbow Gold* (1885), *Aunt Rachel* (1886), *The Martyred Fool* (1895), *A Race for Millions* (1898).

**Murray,** Lord **George.** 1700?–1760. Scottish Jacobite commander; son of 1st duke of Atholl (*q.v.*); fought in rebellion of 1715 under earl of Mar and in highland expedition of 1719; pardoned; settled (1724–45) at Tullibardine; joined Prince Charles Edward and won victory at Prestonpans (1745); during retreat from Derby, kept Cumberland's dragoons in check; defeated (1746) General Hawley, Scottish commander in chief, at Falkirk; commanded (1746) right wing at Culloden Moor; died in exile.

**Murray,** Sir **Gideon.** See under James Murray.

**Murray, Gilbert,** *in full* **George Gilbert Ai'mé'** (ā'mā'). 1866–1957. British classical scholar, b. Sydney, New South Wales; professor of Greek, Glasgow (1889–99); regius professor of Greek, Oxford (1908–36); professor of poetry, Harvard (1926). Sat in foreign office committee that participated in drafting covenant of League of Nations; member of South African delegation to Assembly of League of Nations (1921, 1922, 1923), of British delegation (1924); interested in protection of minorities by league; promoter of League of Nations Union (from 1918), chairman (1923–38). Author of *History of Ancient Greek Literature* (1897), plays *Carlyon Sahib* (1899) and *Andromache* (1900), and works on Greek drama, including *Rise of Greek Epic* (1907), *Four Stages of Greek Religion* (1913), *Euripides and his Age* (1913), *The Classical Tradition in Poetry* (1927), *Aristophanes* (1933), *Aeschylus, Creator of Tragedy* (1940). Known chiefly for his critical edition of Euripides (3 vols., 1901, 1904, 1910) and Aeschylus (1937) and verse translations of Euripides, acted in England and America. Writer of works on foreign policy and international understanding, including *Faith, War, and Policy* (1918), *The Ordeal of this Generation* (1929), *Liberality and Civilization* (1938).

**Murray, Grenville,** *in full* **Eustace Clare Grenville.** 1824–1881. English journalist; illegitimate son of 2d duke of Buckingham. Founded *Queen's Messenger*, first of English satirical society papers (1869); horsewhipped for libel; driven from England, acted as news correspondent, pioneer journalist of gossip and scandal. Author of novels *The Member for Paris* (1871) and *Young Brown* (1874), but known for *The Roving Englishman* (1854), *Embassies and Foreign Courts* (1855), and *Men of the Second Empire* (1872).

**Murray, James.** 1721–1794. British soldier in America. 5th son of 4th Baron Elibank, descended from Sir **Gideon Murray,** Lord **El'i·bank** (ĕl'ĭ·băngk), of Blackbarony, Peeblesshire (d. 1621). Commander of brigade at Louisburg (1758); one of Wolfe's three brigadiers in expedition against Quebec (1759); commander of left wing in battle for Quebec (1759); left to defend city against French. Governor of Quebec (1760), of Canada (1763–66), of Minorca (1774); obliged to surrender to besieging French and Spaniards under De Crillon (1782); general (1783).

**Murray,** Sir **James Augustus Henry.** 1837–1915. British philologist and lexicographer, b. in Roxburghshire, Scotland. As author of article on English language in *Encyclopaedia Britannica* and *The Dialect of the Southern Counties of Scotland* (1873), gained reputation as philologist. Undertook (1879) chief work of his life, the planning and editing of Philological Society's *New English Dictionary*, often called *Oxford English Dictionary* (based on materials accumulated since 1857 and completed, except supplements, 1928); moved to Oxford (1885); editorially responsible for half the dictionary.

**Murray, John.** 1741–1815. Known as "the Father of American Universalism." Universalist clergyman, b. Alton, England; converted to Universalism by preaching and teaching of James Relly (c. 1759); to America (1770). Began itinerant preaching of universal salvation; chaplain in American Revolution; first settled pastorate in newly organized Independent Church of Christ, Gloucester, Mass. (1779–93); pastor of Universalist society in Boston (1793–1809). His wife, **Judith** (*nee* **Sar'gent** [sär'jĕnt]) **Ste'vens** [stē'vĕnz] (1751–1820), widow of John Stevens (d. 1786 or 1787), is known for her essays, poems, and plays collected and published (1798) as *The Gleaner*.

**Murray, John.** Name of several successive generations of proprietors of a London publishing house. The founder, **John Mac·Mur'ray** [măk·mûr'ĭ] (1745–1793), retired lieutenant of marines, Scotsman of stock of Murrays of Athol, bought bookselling business of William Sandby in Fleet Street; dropped Scottish prefix Mac; started monthly *English Review;* published Mitford's *Greece*, Langhorne's *Plutarch's Lives*, and first part of Isaac D'Israeli's *Curiosities of Literature*. His son **John Murray** (1778–1843), called by Byron "the Anak of publishers," as London agent for A. Constable shared in publication of *Marmion* (1807); launched *Quarterly Review* (1809) in competition with *Edinburgh Review;* moved business to Albermarle Street (1812); broke off business relations with Constable (1813); published works of Byron, his close friend, of Jane Austen, Crabbe, Lyell, Borrow, Moore, Campbell, Irving. His son **John** (1808–1892), M.A., Edinburgh (1827), projected the series of Murray "Handbooks for Travelers"; published works of Hallam, Gladstone, Lyell, Dean Stanley, Darwin, Livingstone, and Campbell's *Lives of the Chancellors*, Smith's dictionaries, and many books of travel. His son Sir **John** (1851–1928) edited Gibbon's autobiography and Byron's correspondence.

**Murray,** Sir **John.** 1841–1914. British marine zoologist and oceanographer, b. in Ontario, Canada; naturalist to *Challenger* expedition (1872–76) and editor of reports of expedition's scientific results (1882–95); carried out bathymetrical survey of fresh-water lochs of Scotland (1897); explored North Atlantic (1910).

**Murray, John Gardner.** 1857–1929. American Protestant Episcopal bishop, b. Lonaconing, Md.; bishop of

Maryland (1911–29); elected presiding bishop of the Protestant Episcopal Church (1925).

**Murray, Lindley.** 1745–1826. Scottish-American grammarian, called "Father of English Grammar"; b. in Pennsylvania, of Scottish immigrants who joined Quakers; to England to regain health (1784), retired to Holdgate, outside York, and devoted himself to gardening and production of schoolbooks, including *Grammar of the English Language* (1795), with corresponding *Exercises* and *Key* (1797), *English Reader* (1799), and *An English Spelling Book* (1804), all widely circulated in England and U.S.; author of religious tracts, as *Power of Religion on the Mind* (1787).

**Murray, Margaret,** *nee* **Pol′son** (pōl′s'n). 1844–1927. Canadian patriot, b. in Paisley, Scotland; m. John Clark Murray (1865); founder of Imperial Order of the Daughters of the Empire (I.O.D.E.).

**Murray, Philip.** 1886–1952. American labor leader, b. Lanarkshire, Scotland; to U.S. (1902). Vice-president, United Mine Workers of America (1920–42); succeeded John L. Lewis as president of CIO (1940).

**Mur′ray** *or* **Mor′ay** (mûr′ĭ), Sir **Robert.** 1600?–1673. Scottish statesman; secret envoy to negotiate treaty between Scotland and France, formed plan for escape of Charles I from Newcastle which Charles failed to take advantage of (1646); joined Charles II in Paris (1654). After Restoration, lord of exchequer for Scotland and deputy secretary (1663); one of triumvirate, with Lauderdale and king, that ruled Scotland (to 1670); a founder of Royal Society (1662).

**Murray, Sinclair.** Pseudonym of Alan SULLIVAN.

**Murray, Walter Charles.** 1866–1945. Canadian philosopher and educator; president, U. of Saskatchewan (1908–37).

**Mur′ray** (mûr′ĭ), **William.** 1st Earl of **Mans′field** (măns′fēld). 1705–1793. British judge and parliamentary debater, b. Scone, Perth, Scotland; son of 5th Viscount Stormont. M.A., Oxon. (1730); solicitor general (1742), attorney general (1754); privy councilor (1756); lord chief justice (1756–88); created Baron Mansfield (1756); found technical flaw allowing substitution for fine and imprisonment for Wilkes's outlawry (1768); on unpopular side in cases of seditious libel, bitterly attacked by Junius; created earl (1776); during Gordon riots (1780), his house was burned. Reduced commercial law and doctrine of quasi contract to coherent body of rules; favored coercion of American colonies; called by Macaulay "father of modern toryism."

**Mur·rell′** *or* **Mur·rel′** *or* **Mu·rel′** (mŭ·rĕl′), **John A.** 1804?–1844. American desperado, b. in central Tennessee; organized criminal bands in several states, and established co-operation in disposing of stolen goods (1826–34); captured (1834) and sentenced to ten years' imprisonment for stealing Negro slaves; testimony introduced during his trial indicating he was planning a Negro uprising in the southwest.

**Mur′ri** (mōōr′rē), **Romolo.** 1870–1944. Italian Roman Catholic clergyman and politician; leader of Christian Democracy in Italy and founder (1905) of the Lega Democratica Nazionale; excommunicated (1909).

**Mur·rie′ta** (mōōr·ryā′tä), **Joaquín.** 1832?–1853. Desperado in California (c. 1849–53).

**Murrone** *or* **Morone, Pietro di.** See Pope CELESTINE V.

**Mur′row** (mûr′ō), **Edward Roscoe.** *Orig. name* **Egbert Roscoe Murrow.** 1908–1965. American news commentator, pioneer in broadcast journalism, b. Greensboro, N.C. With CBS (1935–61); television narrator, *See It Now* (1951–58), *Person to Person* (1953–59). Head of U.S. Information Agency (1961–64).

**Mur′ry** (mûr′ĭ), **John Middleton.** 1889–1957. English writer, b. London; editor, the *Athenaeum* (1919–21) and *Adelphi* (1923–30). Author of *Still Life* (1917), *Poems* (1919), *The Evolution of an Intellectual* (1920), *The Things We Are* (1922), *Pencillings* (1923), *Things to Come* (1928), *God* (1929), *Son of Woman* (1931), *The Necessity of Communism* (1932), *Between Two Worlds* (autobiographical; 1934), *Shakespeare* (1936), *The Necessity of Pacifism* (1937), etc. Collaborator with Ruth E. Mantz in writing a biography (1933) of his wife, Katherine Mansfield (*q.v.*).

**Mu·sae′us** (mū·zē′ŭs). *Surnamed* **Gram·mat′i·cus** (gră·măt′ĭ·kŭs). Greek poet of 5th century A.D. or later; author of *Hero and Leander* (340 verses extant).

**Mu′sa ibn–Nu·sayr′** (mōō′sä ĭb″n nōō·sīr′). *Arab.* **Mūsa ibn–Nuṣayr.** 660?–?714. Moslem governor of North Africa; dispatched his general, Tariq (*q.v.*), into Spain (711), thus initiating Moorish conquest of Spain; campaigned in Spain himself (712–713).

**Mu·sä′us** (mōō·zâ′ōōs), **Johann Karl August.** 1735–1787. German writer; author of satirical novels, including a parody on Richardson's then much-admired *Grandison* called *Grandison der Zweite* (3 vols., 1760–62); also wrote ironical and fanciful tales *Volksmärchen der Deutschen* (5 vols., 1782–86), etc.

**Mu′se·lier′** (mü′zē·lyā′), **Émile Henry.** 1882–1965. French naval officer; commander in chief, Free French navy and air force (1940); led naval forces in occupation of St. Pierre and Miquelon islands (1942).

**Mush′et** (mŭsh′ĕt; -ĭt), **Robert Forester.** 1811–1891. English metallurgist; invented process of adding spiegeleisen during Bessemer process and a special self-hardening steel for engineer's tools.

**Musi, Agostino de′.** See Agostino VENEZIANO.

**Mu′sick** (mū′zĭk), **Edwin C.** 1894–1938. American aviator, b. St. Louis, Mo.; in U.S. army air corps during World War I; commercial aviator after the war; commanded first trial flight of the *China Clipper* (Apr., 1935) and the first regular transpacific commercial air flight, California to Manila (Nov., 1935); received Harmon award for 1935 as world's outstanding aviator.

**Mu′sil** (mōō′sĭl), **A′lois** (ä′lois). 1868–1944. Austrian Orientalist and explorer; undertook expeditions (from 1896) to Biblical countries of Moab, Edom, and Negeb, and to northern Arabia and southern Mesopotamia. Published maps of Arabia and southern Mesopotamia, and wrote *Kuseir 'Amra* (2 vols., 1907), *Arabia Petraea* (3 vols., 1907–08), *The Northern Hejaz* (1926), *Arabia Deserta* (1927), *Palmyrena* (1928), *The Manners and Customs of the Ruwalah Bedouins* (1928), etc.

**Mu′sin′** (mü′zăN′), **Ovide.** 1854–1929. Violinist and composer, b. near Liège, Belgium; to U.S. (1882), playing with New York Symphony Society and New York Philharmonic Society. Established and headed violin school in New York (1908–29). Author of many violin virtuoso compositions.

**Mus′kie** (mŭs′kĭ), **Edmund Sixtus.** 1914– . American politician, b. Rumford, Me. Governor of Maine (1955–59); member, U.S. Senate (1959– ). Democratic candidate for U.S. Vice-President (1968).

**Mu·sorg′ski** *or* **Mous·sorg′sky** (mōō·sôrg′skû·ĭ; *Angl.* mōō·sôrg′skĭ), **Modest Petrovich.** 1835–1881. Russian composer; gained livelihood in a subordinate government position while devoting himself to study of music. Most notable work, opera *Boris Godunov*, based on Pushkin's play of same name. Composer also of orchestral works and songs, and unfinished operas based on Gogol's *Marriage Broker* and Flaubert's *Salammbô*. His incomplete *Khovanshchina* was finished by his friend Rimski-Korsakov.

**Mus′pratt** (mŭs′prăt), **James.** 1793–1886. British chemical manufacturer, b. Dublin; in Liverpool (1822), manufactured prussiate of potash; shifted (1823) to manufacture of soda from salt by Leblanc process; introduced iron pyrites as raw material for sulphuric acid. His eldest son, **James Sheridan** (1821–1871), chemist, founded Liverpool Coll. of Chemistry; edited dictionary of chemistry (1854–60).

**Mus·sa′fi·a** (mōōs·säf′fyä), **Adolf.** 1835–1905. Austrian Romance scholar; regarded as a founder of Romance philology.

**Mus′schen·broek** (mûs′ĕn·brōōk), **Pieter van.** 1692–1761. Dutch mathematician and physicist; discovered principle of Leyden jar (called also Kleistian jar) at about same time (1745) as E. G. von Kleist of Pomerania.

**Mus′sert** (mûs′ĕrt), **Anton.** 1894–1946. Dutch engineer; leader of National Socialist party in Netherlands (from 1931); named by Hitler leader of the Netherlands people (Dec., 1942); executed for treason.

**Mus′set′** (mü′sĕ′), **Alfred de,** *in full* **Louis Charles Alfred de.** 1810–1857. French poet, b. Paris; began publishing verse at an early age, as *Contes d'Espagne et d'Italie* (1830) and *Un Spectacle dans un Fauteuil* (1832). Conceived a grand passion for George Sand and accompanied her to Italy (1833); quarreled with her in Venice and returned to Paris alone (1834); a number of his finest poems revealed his suffering at this period, as *La Nuit de Mai, La Nuit de Décembre, La Nuit d'Août, Stances à la Malibran, L'Espoir en Dieu;* published a novel, *La Confession d'un Enfant du Siècle* (1836). Author also of a number of plays, as *Fantasio* (1833), *Les Caprices de Marianne* (1833), *On ne Badine pas avec l'Amour* (1834), *Barberine* (1835), *Un Caprice* (1837), many stories in prose and verse, and a *Souvenir.* His brother **Paul Edme** (1804–1880) was author of a number of novels and *Biographie d'Alfred de Musset* (1877).

**Mus′so·li′ni** (mōōs′sō·lē′nē), **Benito.** 1883–1945. Italian dictator, b. Dovia, province of Forlì; studied in Lausanne and Geneva; expelled from Switzerland because of Socialist party activities. Engaged in journalism in Italy and continued his political agitation; arrested and imprisoned at various times, and always under police surveillance as a suspected revolutionary; editor of *Avanti* (1912), official organ of Socialist party in Italy. Resigned as editor of *Avanti* (1914); founded (Nov. 15, 1914) own paper, *Il Popolo d'Italia,* in which he appealed for Italian entry into war on side of Allies; after Italy entered war (May 24, 1915), volunteered and served as private until wounded (Feb. 23, 1917); after recovery, returned to editorship of *Popolo d'Italia.* Engaged in political campaign against Communism and Bolshevism; organized first Fascio di Combattimento at Milan (Mar. 23, 1919), the beginning of Fascism in Italy; organized Fascism as political party (1921) with system of strict discipline for party members; supervised spread of Fascist movement throughout Italy. Led Fascists in march on Rome (1922); when Facta cabinet resigned, he was summoned by king to form ministry (1922); undertook reform of government of Italy; took over a number of ministries himself; changed electoral law to assure Fascist control of government; suppressed all opposition parties and newspapers; signed treaty (Feb. 11, 1929) with papacy, ending 59-year-old dispute. Became aggressive in foreign affairs; denounced (1930) provisions of Versailles Treaty, causing strained relations with France; conquered Ethiopia (1935–36) and annexed it to Italy; withdrew from League of Nations (1937) because it approved sanctions against Italy; conquered and annexed Albania (1939); aided Franco in Spanish civil war. In internal affairs, proposed corporative state and established it (1934); caused Chamber of Deputies to vote itself out of existence (1938). Led Italy into war on German side after fall of France (1940); after allied invasion of Italy, deposed (July, 1943) and imprisoned; rescued by Germans (Sept., 1943); assassinated by Italian partisans (April 28).

**Mussolini, Ed′da** (ĕd′dä). See under Galeazzo Ciano.

**Mussorgski.** Variant of Musorgski.

**Mus·ta·fa′** *or* **Mus·ta·pha′** (mōōs·tä·fä′). Name of four sultans of Turkey: **Mustafa I** (1591–1639); reigned during two periods (1617–18; 1622–23); deposed. **Mustafa II** (1664–1704); succeeded to throne (1695); waged unsuccessful war against the Imperialists; decisively defeated by Prince Eugene at Senta (1697); by Peace of Karlowitz (1699) yielded Morea, Ukraine, and a large part of Hungary; deposed (1703). **Mustafa III** (1717–1774); succeeded to throne (1757); involved Turkey in unsuccessful war with Russia (from 1768). **Mustafa IV** (1779–1808); elevated to throne by Janizaries (1807); deposed and assassinated (1808).

**Mus′ta·fa el–Na·has′ Pa′sha** (mōōs′tä·fä ăn′nä·häs′ pá′shä). *Arab.* **Muṣṭfa al–Naḥḥās Pasha.** 1876– . Egyptian statesman; chairman of the Wafd party (from 1927); prime minister of Egypt (1928; 1930; 1936–37; 1942–44; 1950–52).

**Mus·ta·fa′ Fazl Pa·sha′** (mōōs·tä·fä′ fä′z'l pä·shä′). 1830–1875. Egyptian prince, son of Ibrahim Pasha; successively minister of public instruction, minister of finance, and minister without portfolio; head of Young Turk party.

**Mus′ta·fa Ka·mel′** (mōōs′tä·fä kȧ·mâl′). 1874–1908. Egyptian political leader and publicist, b. Cairo; sought to free Egypt from European domination; established (1900) influential paper *Al Liva;* founded Egyptian Nationalist party (1907).

**Mustafa** (*or* **Mustapha**) **Kemal Pasha.** See Kemal Atatürk.

**Mus·ta·sim′** (mōōs·tä·sĭm′). *Arab.* **al–Musta'ṣim.** 1221–1258. Last of Abbasside caliphs; overcome by Hulagu.

**Mus′tel′** (müs′tĕl′), **Charles Victor.** 1815–1890. French manufacturer and inventor of musical instruments; established harmonium factory in Paris (1853) and patented a "double expression" (1854) and made other improvements in the harmonium; invented the typophone, which his son **Auguste** (1842–1919) patented (1868) as the celesta.

**Mu·su′rus** (mṳ·sōō′rŭs), **Marcus.** *Gr.* **Markos Mousou′ros** (mōō·sōō′rôs). 1470?–1517. Greek scholar; associated with Aldus Manutius (from 1493) and others in promoting Greek studies; supervised publication of many of the Aldine classics.

**Mu′sy′** (mü′zē′), **Jean-Marie.** 1876–1952. Swiss jurist and statesman; president of Federal Council, Swiss Confederation (1925, 1930).

**Mu′ta·mid, al–** (äl·mōō′tă·mĭd). *Arab.* **al–Mu'tamid.** 1040–1095. Moslem ruler of Seville; also known as lyric poet.

**Mu·ta·nab′bi, al–** (ăl′mōō·tă·năb′bĭ). *Arab.* **Aḥmad ibn-al-Ḥusayn al–Mutanabbi'.** 915–965. Arabic poet, b. in Syria; lived in Aleppo (948–957), Egypt (957–961), Baghdad, and Shiraz; murdered (965). His *Divan,* collection of verse containing 289 poems, has been translated into German by Hammer-Purgstall as *Motenebbi der Grösste Arabische Dichter* (1824).

**Mu′ta·sim, al–** (ăl·mōō′tă·sĭm). *Arab.* **al–Mu'taṣim.** 794–842. Eighth Abbaside caliph (833–842); son of Caliph Harun al-Rashid; first to establish Turkish bodyguard; removed (836) capital from Baghdad to Samarra; at war with Byzantium (837–842).

**Muth, Conrad.** See Conradus MUTIANUS RUFUS.

**Mu'ti·a'nus Ru'fus** (mū'shĭ·ā'nŭs rōō'fŭs; *Ger.* mōō'-tsē·ä'nōōs rōō'fōōs), **Conradus.** *Real name* **Conrad Muth** (mōōt). *Also called* **Mu'tian** (mū'shăn; *Ger.* mōō'tsē·än'). 1471?–1526. German Humanist; fellow pupil of Erasmus; canonicus in Gotha (from 1503); became center of Mutianischer Bund, which opposed Scholasticism and favored Humanism and which was probably responsible for *Epistolae Obscurorum Virorum;* championed Reuchlin in Reuchlinian controversy.

**Mutio** *or* **Mutius.** See MUZIO.

**Mu'tis** (mōō'tēs), **José Celestino.** 1732–1808. Spanish naturalist; one of first disciples of Linnaeus, in Spain; to New Granada (Colombia) as physician to Spanish viceroy (1760); collected numerous plants, making special study of different species of *Cinchona.*

**Mu·tsu** (mōō·tsōō), Count **Munemitsu.** 1842–1897. Japanese statesman; ambassador to U.S. (1888–90); minister of foreign affairs (1892–96); negotiated treaty (1894) with Great Britain by which Great Britain gave up privilege of extraterritorial jurisdiction in Japan.

**Mu·tsu·hi·to** (mōō·tsōō·hē·tō). *Reign name* **Mei·ji** (mā·jē). 1852–1912. Emperor of Japan (1867–1912), 122d in direct lineage; son of Komei, b. at Kyoto; named crown prince (1860); on accession, found Japan in a seriously disturbed state; promised reforms, many of which were carried out during his reign (called *the Restoration*); crowned at Osaka (1868); m. (1869) Princess Haruko; transferred capital to Tokyo (1869). During his reign: feudal system abolished (1868–69) and fiefs of four great clans surrendered; Western ideas, arts, laws, customs, schools, business methods, etc., introduced; Gregorian calendar adopted (1873); formidable Satsuma rebellion (1877) put down; new constitution promulgated (1889); Chinese-Japanese War (1894–95), Anglo-Japanese alliance (1902), and Russo-Japanese War (1904–05). Succeeded by his son Yoshihito.

**Muy'bridge** (mī'brĭj), **Ead'weard** (?ĕd'wērd). *Orig.* **Edward James Mug'ger·idge** (mŭg'ēr·ĭj). 1830–1904. Motion-picture pioneer, b. Kingston on Thames, Eng.; to U.S. as a boy; in photographic survey work for U.S. Coast and Geodetic Survey; requested (1872) by Leland Stanford to prove by photography that a running horse at one period of his stride has all four feet off the ground, devoted himself to photographing animals in motion; invented the zoopraxiscope, by which he reproduced moving pictures on a screen; continued experiments (from 1884) under auspices of U. of Pennsylvania.

**Mu·zaf'far–ed–Din'** (mōō·zăf'fēr·ĕd·dēn'). 1853–1907. King of Persia (1896–1907), b. Teheran; son of Nasr-ed-Din; unable to withstand pressure of Great Powers for concessions; granted new constitution (1906); succeeded by his son Mohammed Ali.

**Mu·zia'no** (mōō·tsyä'nō), **Girolamo.** *Also* **Girolamo Bres·sa'no** (brās·sä'nō) *or* **Bre'scia·ni'no** (brā'shä-nē'nō). 1528?–1592. Italian painter and mosaicist, b. near Brescia; known for landscapes and for development of mosaic art as imitation of oil painting; one of founders of Acad. of St. Luke in Rome.

**Mu'zio** (mōō'tsyō) *or* **Mu'tio** (mōō'tsyō). *Lat.* **Mu'-ti·us Jus·ti'no·pol'i·ta'nus** (mū'shĭ·ŭs jŭs·tī'nō·pŏl'-ĭ·tā'nŭs). *Real name* **Girolamo Nu'zio** (nōō'tsyō). 1496–1576. Italian writer and diplomat; known esp. for polemics against the theologian Pietro Paolo Vergerio and Bernardino Ochino, important for history of Reformation in Italy.

**Muz'zey** (mŭz'ĭ), **David Sav'ille** (săv'ĭl). 1870–1965. American historian; professor, Columbia (from 1920). Author of *An American History* (1911), *History of the American People* (1927), etc.

**Mycerinus** *or* **Mykerinos.** See MENKURE.

**My·co'ni·us** *or* **My·ko'ni·us** (mü·kō'nē·ōōs), **Friedrich.** *Real surname* **Me'kum** (mā'kōōm). 1491–1546. German Lutheran theologian; friend and co-worker of Luther; entered Franciscan cloister (1510), ordained priest (1516); preached Lutheran doctrine at Gotha (1524) and Leipzig (1539); sent to England to discuss articles of Augsburg Confession. Author of *Historia Reformationis* (1517–42; pub. 1715).

**Myconius** *or* **Mykonius, Oswald.** *Real surname* **Geis'hüs'ler** (gīs'hüs'lēr). 1488–1552. Swiss divine; co-worker of Zwingli; helped draw up 1st and 2d Basel Confessions (1534, 1536); first biographer of Zwingli (1532).

**Myd'del·ton** *or* **Myd'dle·ton** (mĭd''l·tŭn), Sir **Hugh.** 1560?–1631. Welsh goldsmith, banker, and clothmaker in London; M.P. (1603); on authority of Parliament, took over project of supplying London with water from springs in Hertfordshire by means of canal thirty-eight miles long discharging into a reservoir called New River Head (completed 1613).

**My'er** (mī'ēr), **Albert James.** 1829–1880. American army officer; assigned task of organizing and commanding a signal corps for U.S. army (1861); commanded corps through Civil War; proposed establishment of weather bureau under direction of army signal corps; founded and supervised U.S. weather bureau (1870–80). Fort Myer, Va., is named in his honor.

**My'ers** (mī'ērz), **Charles Samuel.** 1873–1946. English psychologist, b. London; editor, *British Journal of Psychology* (1911–24); consulting psychologist with British armies in France (1914–19); director, psychological laboratory, Cambridge U.

**Myers, Frederic William Henry.** 1843–1901. English poet and essayist; school inspector under education department (1872–1900); studied mesmerism and spiritualism (from c. 1870); took lead among founders of Society for Psychical Research (1882); helped to revise society's proceedings, which were published as *Phantasms of the Living* (1886), and made contributions on the subliminal self. Author of poems, including *Saint Paul* (1867), essays, including one on Wordsworth (1881) in *English Men of Letters Series* and one on Shelley (1880) for T. Humphrey Ward's *English Poets,* and of *Human Personality and its Survival of Bodily Death* (2 vols., 1903). His brother **Ernest James** (1844–1921), poet and translator, published four volumes of verse (1877–1904) and prose translations of Pindar's *Odes* (1874), and collaborated in translation of concluding eight books of the *Iliad* (1882).

**Myers, Jerome.** 1867–1940. American painter, b. Petersburg, Va.; studio in New York. Work represented in Metropolitan Museum of Art in New York, Art Institute in Chicago, Corcoran Gallery in Washington, D.C., etc.

**Myers, Philip Van Ness.** 1846–1937. American historian, b. at Tribes Hill, N.Y.; A.B., Williams (1871); professor, U. of Cincinnati (1890–1900), and dean of the faculty (1895–97). Author of history textbooks, as *Ancient History* (1882), *General History* (1889), *The Modern Age* (1903).

**Mykonius.** See MYCONIUS.

**My'li·us–E'rich·sen** (mü'lē·ōōs·ē'rĕk·s'n), **Ludvig.** 1872–1907. Danish explorer in Greenland; led Danish literary expedition (1902–04) to explore unknown shores of Melville Bay and study language, customs, and traditions of Eskimos; led *Danmark* expedition (1906–07) to chart coastline of northeast Greenland; with Lieut. Hagen and an Eskimo, Brönlund, made two attempts to reach Independence Bay, the three perishing of cold, hunger, and exhaustion on 2d attempt. Author of

*Grönland* (1906: with Harald Moltke) and of travel reports, tales, poems, etc

**Mynn** (mĭn), **Alfred.** 1807–1861. English cricketer; member of touring All-England eleven (1846–54); made chief reputation as first fast round-arm bowler of eminence.

**Myn'ster** (mün'stẽr), **Jacob Pier.** 1775–1854. Danish Protestant theologian and pulpit orator; bishop of Zealand (from 1834); opposed Grundtvig and rationalism and was attacked by Kierkegaard.

**Myr'dal'** (mür'däl'; mûr'-; mĭr'-), **Gunnar,** *in full* **Karl Gunnar.** 1898– . Swedish economist. Made study of Negroes in America published as *An American Dilemma* (1944); awarded (with Friedrich von Hayek) Nobel prize for economics (1974).

**My'ron** (mī'rŏn). Greek sculptor of 5th century B.C., b. in Boeotia; studied under Ageladas (*q.v.*); most celebrated work, *Discobolus,* or *Discus Thrower,* replicas of which are in the Vatican and the British Museum.

**My'sl·bek** (mĭ'sʼl·bĕk), **Josef Václav.** 1848–1922. Czech sculptor, b. Prague; his works include statue of Jan Žižka for Tabor (destroyed 1876) and, in Prague, sandstone groups for Palaczký Bridge (1881–97), tomb of Prince Bishop Schwarzenberg in St. Veit Cathedral (1891–95), and statue *Music* in Czech National Theater (1912).

**Mys'li·ve'ček** *or* **Mys'li·we'czek** (mĭs'lĭ·vĕ'chĕk), **Josef.** *Called* **Il Bo·e'mo** (ēl bō·ā'mō) *or* **Ve'na·to·ri'ni** (vā'nä·tō·rē'nē) *by Italians.* 1737–1781. Czech composer; composed about 30 operas, including *Il Bellerofonte* (1764) and *Olimpiade* (1778), oratorios, symphonies, trio sonatas, string quartets, and violin and flute concertos.

**Mzilikatse.** = MOSELEKATSE.

# N

**Na'a·man** (nā'ȧ·măn). In the Bible, a Syrian captain cured of leprosy by Elisha (*2 Kings* v).

**Na·bar'ro** (nä·bär'rō), **David Nu'nes** (nū'nĕz). 1874–1958. English physician; associated with Sir David Bruce and Prof. Aldo Castellani in investigating the cause and mode of transmission of sleeping sickness.

**Nabbes** (năbz), **Thomas.** b. 1605. English dramatist; produced *Covent Garden* (comedy; 1632–33); *Hannibal and Scipio* (tragedy; 1635); noted as writer of masques.

**Na'bi·gha, al-** (ăl·nä'bĭ·gă). *Arab.* **al-Nābighah al-Dhubyāni.** Arab poet of the 6th century A.D.

**Na'bis** (nā'bĭs). Tyrant of Sparta (207–192 B.C.); attacked by Achaeans, and defeated at Scotitas (201); attacked by Romans under Flamininus (195) and forced to surrender control of Argos; murdered.

**Na·bo'kov** (nȧ·bô'kŏf; năb'ŭ·kôf), **Vladimir Vladimirovich.** 1899–1977. Amer. (Russian-born) author. Wrote *Lolita* (1955), *Pale Fire* (1962), *Ada* (1969), etc.

**Nab'o·nas'sar** (năb'ō·năs'ẽr). *Assyrian* **Nabū-nasir.** d. 734 B.C. King of Babylon (747–734 B.C.); a vassal of Tiglath-pileser III, King of Assyria; controlled by Assyrian king and his Aramaean hordes; respected Babylonian gods. His reign supposed to have begun (at noon, Feb. 26, 747) a new Babylonian astronomical era (Era of Nabonassar), later adopted by the Greeks.

**Nab'o·ni'dus** (năb'ō·nī'dŭs). *Assyrian* **Nabū-na'id.** d. 539? B.C. Last king of Babylonia (556–539 B.C.); son of a priestess of Haran, Syria; called the "antiquarian king" because of his great interest in antiquities and many records (cylinders) found bearing his name; showed only partial devotion to gods Marduk and Nebo and thus incurred enmity of priesthood; neglected defenses of kingdom; built temples. Joined Croesus, King of Lydia, against rising power of Cyrus the Great, but was conquered (540–539) and Babylon taken by Cyrus's general Gobryas. Father of Belshazzar (*q.v.*).

**Nab'o·po·las'sar** (năb'ō·pō·lăs'ẽr). King of Babylonia (reigned 625–605 B.C.); founder of Chaldean empire; not of royal birth; viceroy of Chaldea, then part of Assyria; declared Chaldea's independence and began long struggle to throw off control of Assyria; formed alliance with Cyaxares of Media; with allies, captured and destroyed Nineveh (612); at war (610–605) with Necho (II) of Egypt (see NEBUCHADNEZZAR II); founded new Babylonian empire with Chaldea the dominant power. Succeeded by his son Nebuchadnezzar II.

**Nabu-.** See names beginning NABO-.

**Nabuchodonosor** *or* **Nabugodonosor.** = NEBUCHADNEZZAR.

**Nach'baur** (näκ'bour), **Franz.** 1835–1902. German operatic tenor.

**Nach'ti·gal** (näκ'tē·gäl), **Gustav.** 1834–1885. German traveler in Africa; received commission to deliver gifts from Prussian king to sultan of Bornu; traveled to Fezzan and, as the first European, to Tibesti (1869), Kuka (1870), Kanem and Borku (1871), Baguirmi (1872), Wadai (1873), Darfur (1874), and returned over Egypt to Germany (1875). German consul in Tunis (1882); visited W. Africa as imperial commissioner (1884) and annexed Togoland, Kamerun, and Lüderitzland (1884). Author of *Sahara und Sudan* (1879 ff.).

**Na'dab** (nā'dăb). King of Israel (912–911 B.C.); son and successor of Jeroboam I (*1 Kings* xiv). See BAASHA.

**Na'dar'** (nȧ'dȧr'). *Pseudonym of* **Félix Tour'na'chon'** (to͞or'nȧ'shôɴ'). 1820–1910. French caricaturist, writer, and balloonist; founded *Revue Comique* (1849); leader of a company of airmen during the siege of Paris (1870–71). Author of *Les Ballons en 1870* (1871), *Le Monde Où l'On Patauge* (1883), etc.

**Na'daud'** (nȧ'dō'), **Gustave.** 1820–1893. French song writer; composer also of operettas; author of the two-act comedy *Dubois d'Australie* (1874).

**Na'del·man** (nä'dʼl·măn), **E'lie** (ĕ'lĭ). 1882–1946. Sculptor, b. in Warsaw, Poland; to U.S. (1917); naturalized (1927).

**Na'den** (nā'dʼn), **Constance Caroline Woodhill.** 1858–1889. English poet; author of *Songs and Sonnets of Springtime* (1881) and *A Modern Apostle and Other Poems* (1887), including "The Pantheist's Song of Immortality." Formulated, with Robert Lewins, philosophical system Hylo-Idealism.

**Nadir, A. A.** See Achmed ABDULLAH.

**Na'dir Shah** (nä'dẽr shä'). *Orig. name* **Mo·ham'med Nadir Khan** (mō·hŭm'măd, kän'). 1880–1933. King of Afghanistan (1929–33); b. Dehra Dun, India; Afghan minister at Paris (1924–26); returned to East, organized army, overthrew usurper, and became king (1929); effected reforms; granted new constitution (1932); assassinated.

**Na'dir Shah** (nä'dĭr shä'). *Also known as* **Tahm·asp' Ku'li** [*i.e.* Slave of Tahmasp] **Khan** (tă·mäsp' ko͞o'lē κän'). 1688–1747. King of Persia (1736–47); a Turk,

b. in Khurasan; held prisoner by Uzbeks (1705–09); aided Tahmasp II against Afghan usurper (1726–31); granted government of several provinces; deposed Tahmasp (1732) and made Tahmasp's infant son, Abbas III, shah (1732–36); assumed throne; to win support of Afghans, made Sunnite form of Mohammedanism the state religion; renewed war with Turks successfully; to revenge murder of embassy, ravaged Northwest Provinces, took and sacked Delhi (1739); carried off Koh-i-noor diamond and the Peacock Throne; subjugated Bokhara and Khwarazm (Khiva); assassinated.

**Nae′ge·le** (nā′gĕ·lĕ), **Charles Frederick.** 1857–1944. American portrait and figure painter, b. Knoxville, Tenn.

**Nae′vi·us** (nē′vĭ·ŭs), **Gnaeus.** Roman poet and playwright of 3d century B.C.; author of epic on First Punic War, and a number of tragedies and comedies, many of them adapted for Roman stage from the Greek. Only fragments of his works are extant.

**Na·ga·no** (nä·gä·nō), **Osami.** 1888–1947. Japanese admiral; representative at naval conferences and League of Nations; minister of the navy (1936–37); commander in chief, Japanese fleet (1937); chief of naval general staff (1941); fleet marshal (1943); died on trial as war criminal.

**Na·gar′ju·na** (nä·gär′jŏŏ·nȧ) *or* **Na′ga·se′na** (nä′gȧ·sā′nȧ). fl. latter part of 2d century A.D. Buddhist sage and teacher; founder of Mahayana school of northern Buddhism; contemporary of King Kanishka.

**Na′gel** (nä′gĕl), **Charles.** 1849–1940. American lawyer, b. in Colorado County, Tex.; practiced, St. Louis (from 1873); U.S. secretary of commerce and labor (1909–13).

**Nä′ge·li** *or* **Nae′ge·li** (nâ′gĕ·lē), **Karl Wilhelm von.** 1817–1891. Botanist, b. near Zurich, Switzerland; professor, Munich (from 1858); investigated the living matter and nuclei of cells and the mode of growth of cells; credited with discovery of the antheridia and spermatozoids of ferns; originated micellar theory to account for the structure of organized bodies.

**Na′gle** (nā′g'l), **Nano.** 1728–1784. Irish foundress of the Roman Catholic Order of the Presentation of the Blessed Virgin Mary (1777), devoted to visitation of the sick and education of poor children.

**Na′gler** (nä′glẽr), **Georg Kaspar.** 1801–1866. German antiquary and writer on art; author of *Neues Allgemeines Künsterlexikon* (22 vols., 1835–52), etc.

**Naharro, Bartolomé de Torres.** See TORRES NAHARRO.

**Nahas Pasha, Mustafa el–.** See MUSTAFA EL-NAHAS PASHA.

**Nahl** (näl), **Johann August.** 1710–1781. German sculptor and decorator. His son **Samuel** (1748–1813) was a sculptor. Another son, **Johann August** (1752–1825), was a painter of mythological and historical subjects.

**Na′hum** (nā′(h)ŭm; -hŭm). One of the minor Hebrew prophets, who flourished before the fall of Nineveh (c. 606 B.C.) and whose prediction of its fall the Old Testament book of Nahum records.

**Nai′du** (nä′ĭ·dŏŏ) *or* **Nā′ya·du** (nä′yȧ·dŏŏ), **Sarojini.** 1879–1949. Hindu poet and reformer, b. at Hyderabad of Bengali Brahmin stock; m. (1898) Dr. M. G. Naidu, principal medical officer in the service of the Nizam; organized flood-relief work in Hyderabad (1908), for which King Edward VII gave her gold Kaiser-i-Hind medal; lectured widely in India and (1928–29) in U.S.; first Indian woman president (1925) of the Indian National Congress. Author of three books of poetry (translated into many Indian vernaculars): *The Golden Threshold* (1905), *The Bird of Time* (1912), and *The Broken Wing* (1915–16).

**Nain de Tillemont, Sébastien Le.** See Sébastien Le Nain de TILLEMONT.

**Nairne** (nârn), **Carolina,** *nee* **Ol′i·phant** (ŏl′ĭ·fănt). Baroness **Nairne.** 1766–1845. Scottish song writer, daughter of a Jacobite leader. Her poems published as *Lays from Strathearn* (1846); excelled in humorous ballads, including "Land o' the Leal," "Charlie is My Darling," "The Laird o' Cockpen."

**Nai′smith** (nā′smĭth), **James.** 1861–1939. Director of physical education, b. Almonte, Ontario, Can.; on staff of McGill U. (1887–90), of Y.M.C.A. College, Springfield, Mass. (1890–95), of Y.M.C.A., Denver, Colo. (1895–98), and of U. of Kansas (from 1898); originated the game of basketball (1891). See Luther H. GULICK.

**Na·ja′ra** (nȧ·jä′rä), **Is′ra·el ben Mo′ses** (ĭz′râ·ĕl [-rĭ·ĕl] bĕn mō′zĕz [-zĭz]). 1530?–?1599. Hebrew poet, liturgist, preacher, and scholar, b. Damascus; author of secular poems, and of religious hymns, often to Arabic and Turkish tunes, dirges, songs, verse, and prayers for holy days, Sabbaths, etc., many of which have been taken into Jewish rituals and prayerbooks, esp. in Italy and Palestine. *Zemiroth Yisrael* (Songs of Israel), a collection of his poems, was published in 1587.

**Na·ka·to·mi** (nä·kä·tō·mē). A noble Japanese family. See FUJIWARA.

**Na′lèche′** (nȧ′lĕsh′), Comte **Étienne de.** 1865–1947. French journalist; editor, *Journal des Débats* (1897 ff.).

**Nal·kow′ska** (näl·kôf′skä), **Zofja.** 1885–1954. Polish novelist and playwright; among her novels are *The Bad Love* (1928), *The Limit* (1936), *The Impatient* (1938); among her plays, *The Day of his Return* (1931), *Renata* (1935).

**Namatianus.** See Claudius RUTILIUS NAMATIANUS.

**Namby–Pamby.** Nickname of Ambrose PHILIPS.

**Na′nak** (nä′nȧk). *Called* **Gu′ru** (gŏŏ′rŏŏ), *i.e.* teacher. 1469–1538. Founder of Sikhism, a religious faith of India, b. near Lahore. In early years a Hindu in beliefs; lived with Kabir (*q.v.*), who influenced him greatly; made pilgrimages to Mecca and Medina; compiled part of the sacred scriptures of the Sikhs, later (1604) known as the *Granth*, or *Adigranth;* traveled widely, proclaiming new religion; strongly monotheistic, inviting Hindus and Mohammedans alike to become his followers; first of the ten gurus (cf. GOVIND SINGH).

**Na′na Sa′hib** (nä′nä sä′hĭb). *Real name* **Dan′dhu Panth** (dŭn′dŏŏ pŭnt′). 1825?–?1860. A Maratha, one of the leaders of the Sepoy Mutiny; became adopted son of Baji Rao II, last Peshwa of Poona, but not allowed to inherit his pension; hostile to British; when mutiny broke (1857) assumed leadership in Cawnpore; promised English troops safety if they would capitulate, but treacherously murdered the men and later directed that the women and children be killed and cast in a well; often defeated by British and finally (1859) driven into Nepal; probably perished in the jungle.

**Na·ni′ni** (nä·nē′nē) *or* **Na·ni′no** (-nō), **Giovanni Maria.** 1545?–1607. Italian composer; founded public school of musical composition in Rome; associated with Palestrina; maestro di cappella, Santa Maria Maggiore, Rome (1571), and Sistine Chapel (1604–07). Among his works are six-part motet *Hodie Nobis Caelorum Rex*, madrigals, psalms, canzonets, etc.

**Nan·kiv′ell** (năn·kĭv′ĕl), **Frank Arthur.** 1869–1959. Cartoonist and painter, b. Maldon, Australia; to San Francisco (1894); on staff of *Puck*, American humorous weekly (1896); early experimenter in animated motion pictures in full color; portrait painter, illustrator, and etcher in New York.

**Nan′sen** (nän′sĕn), **Fridtjof.** 1861–1930. Norwegian arctic explorer, zoologist, and statesman; curator, Museum of Natural History, Bergen (1882); headed first expedition to cross ice fields of Greenland (1888); headed expedition (1893) aiming to reach across North Pole by drifting; made fast his exploring vessel, *Fram*, to an ice floe, New Siberian Islands; drifted to about 84°N; left the *Fram* and, accompanied by F. H. Johansen (1895), pushed across to 86° 14′N, then the highest latitude reached by man; spent winter of 1895–96 in Franz Josef Land; returned to Vardö, Norway, in a ship of the Harmsworth-Jackson expedition (1896), followed eight days later by O. N. Sverdrup in the *Fram*, which had drifted to 85° 57′N and returned via Spitsbergen. Professor of zoology, Royal Frederick U. (1897); explored North Atlantic Ocean (1900); director, International Commission for Study of the Sea (1901); took active part in separation of Norway and Sweden (1905); first Norwegian minister to Great Britain (1906–08). Professor of oceanography, Royal Frederick U. (1908); made further oceanographic expeditions, chiefly in North Atlantic Ocean (1910–14). Chairman, Norwegian Association for League of Nations (1918); worked for repatriation of World War prisoners (after 1918) and directed famine-relief work for Russia, sponsored by Red Cross (1921–23), and relief work of League of Nations for Russian, Armenian, and Greek refugees; awarded Nobel peace prize (1922); represented Norway on Disarmament Committee, League of Nations (1927). Author of *Across Greenland* (2 vols., 1891), *Eskimo Life* (1891), *Farthest North* (2 vols., 1897), *In Night and Ice* (2 vols., 1897), *The Norwegian North Polar Expedition 1893–96* (with others; 6 vols., 1900–06), *Norway and the Union with Sweden* (1905), *Through Siberia* (1914), *Russia and Peace* (1923), *Armenia and the Near East* (1928), etc.

**Nan′sou′ty′** (näɴ′sōō′tē′), Comte **de. Étienne Marie Antoine Cham′pion′** (shäɴ′pyôɴ′). 1768–1815. French cavalry commander in Napoleonic armies; distinguished himself esp. in campaign for defense of France (1813–14).

**Nan′teuil′** (näɴ′tû′y′), **Robert.** 1623–1678. French engraver; appointed engraver and illustrator to the king (1658); among his engravings are portraits of Louis XIV, Mazarin, Colbert, Le Tellier, Turenne, etc.

**Na′o·mi** (nā′ō·mī, -mĭ; nā·ō′mī, -mĭ). *In Douay Version* **No′e·mi** (nō′ĕ·mī). In the Bible (*Ruth* i–iv), the mother-in-law of Ruth (*q.v.*).

**Nao·ro′ji** (nou·rō′jē), **Dadabhai.** 1825–1917. Indian political leader and first Indian member of British House of Commons; son of a Parsi priest; prime minister to prince of Baroda (1874); president, Indian National Congress (1886, 1893, 1906); Liberal M.P. (1892–95).

**Naosuke.** = II NAOSUKE.

**Naph′ta·li** (năf′tȧ·lī). *In Douay Version* **Neph′ta·li** (nĕf′-). In the Bible, Jacob's sixth son (*Genesis* xxx. 7–8), ancestor of one of the twelve tribes of Israel.

**Na′pi·er** (nā′pĭ·ẽr; nȧ·pḗr′), Sir **Charles James.** 1782–1853. British army officer; eldest son of Col. **George Napier** (1751–1804; a staff officer of Sir Henry Clinton in American Revolution); served in Portugal (1810), against U.S. (1813); as military resident of Cephalonia (1822–33) met Byron and declined offer to become commander of Greek army; undertook (1842) the conquest of Sind; completed it by victory of Hyderabad (1843); subdued hill tribes (1844–45); resigned government of Sind (1847); given command in war against Sikhs but arrived after victory of Gujrat (1849); quelled mutiny of the 66th native regiment; author of books on colonial administration and on the government of India. His next younger brother, Sir **George Thomas** (1784–1855), major general (1837), was governor of Cape of Good Hope (1837–43); general (1854). His second younger brother, Sir **William Francis Patrick** (1785–1860), served in Portugal (1809–11), where he was wounded; retired (1819); lieutenant governor of Guernsey (1842–47); lieutenant general (1851); author of *History of Peninsular War* (1828–40) and *History of Conquest of Scinde* (1844–46), a defense of his brother Sir Charles James's decision to annex the Sind. His third younger brother, **Henry Edward** (1789–1853), naval officer and historian, captain (1830), wrote *Florentine History* (1846–47). Sir **Charles** (1786–1860), first cousin of the half blood of Gen. Charles James Napier, was a naval officer; served in Mediterranean (1811) and on coast of America (1814); commanded Portuguese fleet in service of Dom Pedro I of Brazil against usurper Dom Miguel, won victory off Cape St. Vincent (1833), raised siege of Oporto (1834), and brought civil war to an end, resulting in restoration of Maria II to Portuguese throne; restored to British command (1839), forced evacuation of Beyrouth and concluded a convention with Mehemet Ali (1840); commanded Baltic fleet in Crimean War (1854), but was removed because of failure to storm Kronshtadt; M.P. (1855–60); admiral (1858).

**Napier,** Sir **Francis.** 9th Baron **Napier** *and* Baron **Et′trick** (ĕt′rĭk). 1819–1898. British diplomat, of Scottish family; ambassador at St. Petersburg (1860), at Berlin (1864); as governor of Madras (1866–72), developed public works, esp. irrigation; active in interest of Scottish crofters and cotters (1883 ff.).

**Na′pi·er** (nā′pĭ·ẽr; nȧ·pḗr′) *or* **Ne′per** (nā′pẽr), **John.** Laird of **Mer′chis·ton** (mûr′kĭs·tŭn). 1550–1617. Scottish mathematician, b. at Merchiston Castle, near Edinburgh; published *A Plaine Discovery of the Whole Revelation of St. John* (1593); invented logarithms, which he described in his *Mirifici Logarithmorum Canonis Descriptio* (1614), explaining in his *Constructio* (pub. 1619) their method of construction; pioneer in use of present system of decimal notation; invented mechanical devices for computing, described in his *Rabdologia* (1617).

**Napier,** Sir **Joseph.** 1804–1882. Irish political leader and champion of the Church of Ireland, b. in Belfast; M.P. (1848–58); carried through house *Napier's Ecclesiastical Code* (1849), a boon to Irish protestant church; lord chancellor of Ireland (1858–59); tried to avert disestablishment of Church of Ireland; after disestablishment (1871), actively furthered its reconstruction; member of judicial committee of privy council at Westminster (1868–81).

**Napier, Robert.** 1791–1876. Scottish marine engineer; built engines for first four steamers of Cunard Company (1840); built the *Persia* for Cunard Company (1854), and one of the earliest ironclad warships, *H.M.S. Black Prince* (1860).

**Napier, Robert Cornelis.** 1st Baron **Napier of Mag′da·la** (măg′dȧ·lȧ). 1810–1890. British army officer, b. in Ceylon; engineer, chiefly of public works (1828–45); showed special engineering skill in first (1845) and second (1848) Sikh wars; built roads, canals, and defenses; in the Sepoy Mutiny (1857), instrumental in relieving and in recapturing Lucknow; by cutting road through jungle, effected capture of rebel leader Tantia Topi (1859); commanded 2d division in Chinese expedition (1860); lieutenant general of Bombay army (1867); commanded British punitive expedition against Abyssinia (1868), which within five months stormed native stronghold of Magdala; commander in chief in India (1870); general (1874); field marshal (1883).

**Na·po′le·on I** (nȧ·pō′lē·ŭn; -pōl′yŭn). *Full French name* **Na′po′lé′on′ Bo′na′parte′** (ná′pô′lā′ôɴ′ bô′ná′pårt′). *Ital.* **Na′po·le·o′ne Buo′na·par′te** (nä′pô·lā·ō′nā bwô′-

nä·pär′tȧ) *used by Napoleon until 1796. Called* **le Pe·tit′ Ca′po′ral′** (lẽp·tē′ kȧ′pô′rȧl′), *i.e.* the Little Corporal, *and* **the Corsican.** 1769–1821. For parentage and family relationships, see BONAPARTE. Emperor of the French; b. Ajaccio, Corsica. At military schools of Brienne le Château (1779–84) and Paris (1784–85); second lieutenant in the La Fère regiment of artillery (1785–91); in French revolutionary forces in Paris (1792), in Corsica (1792), at Marseilles, and in command of artillery that decided the conflict at siege of Toulon (1793); made general of brigade; joined Jacobins, held in prison after downfall of Robespierre (1794); took part in defense of Tuileries, driving Parisian mob from the streets with a "whiff of grapeshot" from his artillery (13th Vendémiaire, 1795); became commander of the Army of the Interior (1795).

*Italian and Egyptian Campaigns, and First Consulate* (1796–1804): m. Joséphine de Beauharnais (1796); sent by Directory to conduct Italian campaign (1796); won brilliant victory at Lodi; occupied Milan, defeated Austrians at Arcole (1796), and captured Mantua (1797); conquered northern Italy for France and forced Austrians beyond Alps; displayed genius for military strategy, won enthusiasm of troops; negotiated Treaty of Campoformio (Oct. 17, 1797), contrary to orders of Directory. Returned to France; proposed conquest of Egypt as first step toward India; set sail secretly from Toulon with large force (1798); landed at Alexandria, won battle of the Pyramids; his fleet destroyed by Nelson in battle of the Nile (Aug. 1–2, 1798); invaded Syria (1799), returned to Egypt, won victory at Abukir (July 25, 1799), and thence suddenly returned to France on learning of formation of Second Coalition of powers (1799). Aided by Sieyès and Lucien Bonaparte, carried out coup d'état of 18th Brumaire (Nov. 9, 1799); overthrew Directory, dispersed Council of Five Hundred. With Sieyès and Roger Ducos as consuls, formed provisional government; promulgated Constitution of Year VIII (1799); became first consul (Dec. 24, 1799). Suddenly raised new army to aid Masséna in northern Italy; crossed Alps by Great St. Bernard; occupied Milan (1800); won at Marengo (June 14), greatly aided by Dessaix; Austrians defeated at Hohenlinden by Moreau; signed Treaty of Lunéville (1801), and Treaty of Amiens with England (1802), favorable to France. Thus far had most of central Europe under control, partly by military skill and partly by shrewd diplomacy; extended boundaries of France; reorganized government on grand scale; negotiated Concordat of 1801 with Pius VII, restoring Catholic Church to former position; reconstructed educational system; established Legion of Honor (1802); effected codification of laws of France (*Code Napoléon*, 1804–10). Secured cession of Louisiana from Spain (1800) but failed to conquer Haiti (1802–03); abandoned dream of empire overseas by selling Louisiana to United States (1803). Third Coalition formed (1804), led by Pitt in England. Counterplots against him hastened decision to make France a hereditary empire; condemned for execution of duc d'Enghien (*q.v.*); crowned emperor at Paris (Dec. 2, 1804); assumed title of king of Italy (1805).

*Emperor* (period 1805–09): Planned invasion of England from Boulogne (1805), but finally recognized it as impossible; turned to campaign in Bavaria and Austria; operated from Ulm; won at Austerlitz (Dec. 2, 1805) over Austria (Emperor Francis) and Russia; forced Treaty of Pressburg on Austria, ending Third Coalition; dissolved Holy Roman Empire (Aug. 6, 1806); virtual master of the Continent, but lost supremacy of the seas to England in defeat of Villeneuve by Nelson at Cape Trafalgar (Oct. 21, 1805). Made his brother Joseph Bonaparte king of Naples (1806), and another brother, Louis, king of Holland. Fourth Coalition formed (1806–07): Prussia, Russia, England, and Sweden; hostilities begun by Frederick William III of Prussia (1806). Led army into Germany, defeated Prussians at Jena (Oct. 14) while Davout was defeating Karl Wilhelm Ferdinand, Duke of Brunswick-Lüneburg at Auerstedt; completely dominated Germany; issued Berlin decree (1806) and, later (1807), Milan decree, both against English commerce (*Continental system*); entered Warsaw; victorious in Polish campaign (1807) at Eylau and Friedland; had meeting with Emperor Alexander I of Russia on raft at Tilsit; forced Treaty of Tilsit (1807) that humbled Russia and ended Fourth Coalition. Ordered commerce laws obeyed; when Portugal refused, sent French army under Junot into Portugal; later sent another army into Spain, under Murat; invited Ferdinand of Spain to conference at Bayonne and imprisoned him (1808–14); proclaimed Joseph Bonaparte king of Spain (June, 1808); Peninsular War (1808–14) begun. Fifth Coalition (Austria and England) formed (1809); led army into Austria, driving Archduke Charles Louis back; entered Vienna; fought indecisive battles of Aspern and Essling (May, 1809); defeated (July 6) Charles Louis at Wagram; signed Treaty of Vienna (Schönbrunn). After Swedish revolution (1808), his marshal, Bernadotte, brother-in-law of Joseph Bonaparte, elected heir to throne (see BERNADOTTE). Erected kingdom of Westphalia in Germany for Jérôme Bonaparte; enlarged France by many annexations (Tuscany, Papal States, Holland, etc.); made Murat, who had married his sister, Maria Annunciata, king of Naples (1808). Divorced Josephine (1809).

*Emperor* (period 1810–14): m. (1810) Archduchess Maria Luisa of Austria, daughter of Emperor Francis (see MARIE LOUISE); one child born (1811)—see NAPOLEON II, below. Except for war in Spain, rule peaceful (1810–11), but Austria was preparing under Metternich, Prussia arming under Stein, Scharnhorst, and Hardenberg, and Russia, discontented with alliance, became ally of England. Entered Saxony and Poland (May–June, 1812); led army of 400,000 across Russian frontier; won Borodino against Kutuzov; entered Moscow (Sept. 14); retreated with terrible losses (Oct.–Nov., 1812); lost prestige, found strong nationalist uprisings in Europe; defeated Allies at Bautzen (1813). Faced strong Sixth Coalition of powers; won last great victory at Dresden (Aug. 26–27, 1813); attacked by Allies and defeated in 3-day "Battle of the Nations" at Leipzig; retreated to France; defeated Blücher and Schwarzenberg in brief brilliant defensive campaign (Jan.–Feb., 1814) but was later overwhelmed by numbers of Allies; Congress of Châtillon (Feb.–Mar., 1814); Paris taken by Allies (Mar.); his generals (Ney, Soult, Suchet, Eugène de Beauharnais) defeated; deserted by Murat; abdicated at Fontainebleau (April 11); sent to Elba; Louis XVIII placed on throne by Allies.

*Waterloo and Exile* (1815–21): Congress of Powers in session at Vienna (1814–15). Left Elba; landed at Cannes (Mar. 1, 1815); entered Paris (Mar. 20; beginning of Hundred Days); raised new armies; defeated Blücher at Ligny (June 16) while Ney fought Wellington at Quatre Bras on same day; overthrown at Waterloo (June 18); fled to Paris; abdicated second time (June 22); Allies entered Paris (July 7); surrendered to British (July 15) on board the *Bellerophon;* transferred to *Northumberland* and landed on St. Helena (Oct. 16, 1815); under British governor, Sir Hudson Lowe (1816–21); died (May 5, 1821); remains removed (1840) by direction of Louis Philippe to Hôtel des Invalides, Paris. Subject of biographers, some depicting him as champion of French people and defender of principles of Revolution and democracy, others as an adventurer and despot, exploiting Revolution to his own ends; possessed undoubted military genius and almost equally great organizing and administrative ability.

**Napoleon II.** *Full name* **François Charles Joseph Bonaparte.** *Called* **l'Ai'glon'** (lĕ'glôɴ'), *i.e.* the eaglet. 1811–1832. Titular king of Rome, b. Paris; son of Napoleon I; named as successor on abdication of his father (Apr., 1814), but Allies refused to accept him; lived at court of Vienna (1814–32); created duc **de Reich'stadt** [dē rīk'shtät] (1818); under control of Metternich.

**Napoleon III.** *Known as* **Louis Napoleon.** *Full name* **Charles Louis Napoleon Bonaparte.** *Called* **Car'bo·na'ro** (kär'bō·nä'rō) *and by Victor Hugo* **Na'po'lé'on' le Pe·tit'** (nȧ'pô'lā'ôɴ' lĕp·tē'). 1808–1873. Son of Louis Bonaparte, King of Holland, and Hortense de Beauharnais; nephew of Napoleon I (see BONAPARTE). Emperor of the French, b. Paris; lived in exile with his mother in Germany and Switzerland (1815–30); acquired "liberal" ideas; took part in uprisings in Romagna (1830–31); forced to flee to France. On death of Napoleon II (1832), assumed headship of Bonaparte family; plotted revolt in Strasbourg (1836); discovered, sent to America, but soon returned (1837); formed another conspiracy (Boulogne; 1840); arrested, condemned to life imprisonment at fortress of Ham (1840), but escaped (1846) to England; wrote social and military papers while in prison. Welcomed Revolution of 1848 in Paris; elected to National Assembly (1848) and later president of the Republic (Dec. 10, 1848). Immediately began to acquire absolute authority, to work against republicans, and to put down the press; called for revision of constitution to allow his re-election (1851); by coup d'état (Dec. 2, 1851), made himself dictator; elected president for 10 years (Dec. 21). Proclaimed himself emperor as Napoleon III (Dec. 2, 1852); at first (1852–56) successful in policy of concentration of power in emperor and of subordination of elected assemblies; m. (Jan. 29, 1853) Eugénie de Montijo, a Spanish countess (see EUGÉNIE); caused France to join in Crimean War (1854–56); joined Sardinia against Austria (1859–60), aiding Italy in attaining unity; Savoy and Nice annexed (1860); by sending Archduke Maximilian of Austria to Mexico, dreamed of establishing a Catholic and French empire in America (1863–67), but his plans were frustrated by Juárez, the Mexican people, and the threatening attitude of the U.S. Faced rising opposition in France; confronted by founding of German unity by Bismarck; bitterly attacked by opposition party; successful in a managed plebiscite seeking approval (1870). Several imprudent acts and foolish boasts (1866–70) gave opportunity to Bismarck to involve France in the disastrous Franco-Prussian War (1870–71); joined army, captured at Sedan (Sept. 2, 1870); held as prisoner near Kassel, Germany, until end of war; deposed by National Assembly at Bordeaux (Mar. 1, 1871); retired with wife and son to Chislehurst, England; died (Jan. 9, 1873). His only son, **Eugene Louis Jean Joseph Napoleon** (1856–1879), known as "the Prince Imperial," b. Paris, educ. at Woolwich (1872–75), joined English expedition against Zulus, South Africa (1879), and was killed in an ambush (June 1, 1879).

**Napoleon,** Prince. See Napoléon Joseph Charles Paul BONAPARTE.

**Napper–Tandy, James.** See TANDY.

**Ná'prav·ník** (nä'pråv·nyēk), **Eduard.** 1839–1915. Bohemian pianist, conductor, and composer; chief conductor (from 1869) of Imperial Russian Opera, at St. Petersburg; composer of operas and various orchestral works.

**Na'quet'** (nȧ'kĕ'), **Alfred Joseph.** 1834–1916. French chemist and politician; member of Chamber of Deputies (1871) and of the Senate (1882); among his works are *Principes de Chimie* (1865), *Socialisme Collectiviste et Socialisme Libéral* (1890), *Temps Futurs* (1900), etc.

**Na·ra** (nä·rä). Name given to the period in Japanese history (710–784 A.D.) when Nara was the first permanent capital of the emperors; both the *Kojiki* and the *Nihongi*, early chronicles of Japan, were completed during this period; Buddhism was especially flourishing.

**Na·ram'–Sin'** (nä·räm'sĭn'). fl. about 2550 B.C. King of Babylon, one of great rulers of dynasty of Akkad; supposed to be son of Sargon I. Events of his reign uncertain, but records indicate that he made wide conquests, invading Arabia and Syria; capital at Susa.

**Narasimha–varman.** See PALLAVA.

**Na·ra'yan** (nä·rä'yȧn), **Ja'ya·pra·kash'** (jŭ'yȧ·prȧ·käsh'). 1901?– . Hindu politician; educ. at universities in U.S.; became a Marxist and returned to India; supported Nehru; organized (1933) first session of Congress Socialist party, a left-wing bloc.

**Narayan Rao.** See under MADHU RAO II.

**Nar'brough** (när'brŭ), Sir **John.** 1640–1688. English naval commander; distinguished himself in action against Dutch off The Downs (1666) and at Southwold Bay (1672); suppressed Tripoli corsairs (1674) and Algerian corsairs (1677); admiral (1674).

**Nar·cis'sus** (när·sĭs'ŭs). d. 54 A.D. Freedman of Roman Emperor Claudius; with Empress Messalina (*q.v.*), established ascendancy over Claudius; assisted Messalina in procuring death of a number of persons; after Messalina's public marriage to her favorite, Silius, betrayed her to Claudius and secured from Claudius order for her execution; himself executed at Nero's accession.

**Nar·di'ni** (när·dē'nē), **Pietro.** 1722–1793. Italian violinist; director of music at Tuscan court (1770–93); composer of concertos, sonatas, string quartets, etc.

**Nares** (nârz), **Robert.** 1753–1829. English philologist; assistant librarian, British Museum (1795–1807); cofounder of the *British Critic* (1793); published a glossary of Elizabethan literature (1822). His cousin **Edward Nares** (1762–1841), regius professor of modern history at Oxford (1813–41), wrote theological works, including *The Plurality of Worlds* (1801), and memoirs of Lord Burghley (1828–31). Sir **George Strong Nares** (1831–1915), grandnephew of Edward Nares, was a naval officer; dispatched on exploration in the Antarctic in the *Challenger* (1872–74), first steamship to cross Antarctic Circle, and on Arctic expedition (1875–76); rear admiral (1887); vice-admiral (1892).

**Na·ri·ma'nov** (nŭ·ryĭ·mȧ'nôf), **Nariman.** 1870–1925. Russian Communist leader; representative of Transcaucasian Soviet Socialist Republic on the Union Central Executive Committee, and one of its four chairmen.

**Nar'ses** (när'sēz). Variant of NERSES.

**Nar'ses** (när'sēz) *or* **Nar'sah** (-sȧ). A Sassanid king of Persia (reigned 293–302); son of Shapur I; seized throne from his grandnephew Bahram III; made war on Rome; defeated Galerius (296) but, badly beaten in Armenia (297), concluded a peace with Romans.

**Narses.** 478?–?573. Byzantine general under Justinian I; a eunuch; aided Belisarius in putting down Nika riot (532); sent to Italy (538) to support Belisarius; in command in Italy (548–552) after recall of Belisarius; conquered Totila, leader of the Ostrogoths, and finally the last Gothic army in Italy (553); by subduing Alamanni and Franks (553–555), brought Italy again under Justinian's rule; prefect of Italy (554–567); dismissed by Justin II.

**Na'ru·sze'wicz** (nä'rōō·shĕ'vĕch), **Adam Stanisław.** 1733–1796. Polish ecclesiastic, historian, and poet; bishop of Smolensk, and later, of Lutsk (Łuck); chief historical work, *History of the Polish Nation* (6 vols., 1780–86); his *Idylls* and *Satires* were collected and published (1778) under title *Lyrica.*

**Na'ru·to'wicz** (nä'rōō·tô'vĕch), **Gabrjel.** 1865–1922. Polish civil engineer; elected president of Poland to succeed Piłsudski; assassinated (Dec. 16, 1922) by a madman a few days after he assumed office.

**Nar·vá'ez** (när·vä'äth; -äs), **Pánfilo de.** 1480?–1528. Spanish soldier; to America (c. 1498); aided in conquest of Cuba (1511); sent by Diego Velásquez to Mexico to arrest Cortes and bring him back (1520); surprised near Veracruz by Cortes, captured, and kept prisoner for two years (1520–22); returned to Spain; secured permission to conquer and govern territory of Florida; sailed from Spain (1527); reached Florida (1528) after great hardships and losses; constructed small boats at Apalachee Bay, and set out for Mexico; lost at sea in Gulf of Mexico.

**Nar·vá'ez** (när·vä'äth), **Ramón María.** Duke of **Va·len'ci·a** (vȧ·lĕn'shĭ·ȧ; -shȧ; *Span.* vä·lān'thyä). 1800–1868. Spanish general and statesman; as supporter of Isabella II fought in Catalonia against Carlists (1834–36); opposed Espartero (1840–43); succeeded him in the council (1843); created duke of Valencia (1844); prime minister (1844–46); again in power (1847); thoroughly reactionary in his policy, lost support, and quarreled with former Queen Maria Christina; in power (1856–57, 1864–65, and 1866–68), his chief rival being O'Donnell; overthrown, with Isabella, in revolution (1868).

**Nasby, Petroleum V.** Pseudonym of David Ross LOCKE.

**Nas·ci·men'to** (nȧsh·sē·mäNn'tōō), **Francisco Manoel do** (dōō). *Pseudonym* **Fi·lin'to E·ly'sio** (fē·lēNn'tōō ē·lē'zyōō). 1734–1819. Portuguese poet; ordained priest (1754); ordered arrested by Inquisition on charge of heterodoxy, fled to France (1778); settled in Paris; his poetry collected in 22 vols. (1836–40).

**Nash** (năsh), **Abner.** 1740?–1786. American politician, b. Amelia County, Va.; settled in North Carolina (1762); active in pre-Revolutionary agitation; governor of North Carolina (1780, 1781); member of Continental Congress (1782–86). His brother **Francis** (1742?–1777), also active in pre-Revolutionary agitation, served (from 1775) in Continental army; brigadier general (Feb. 5, 1777); killed in action (Oct., 1777). Nash County, N.C., and Nashville, Tenn., are named in honor of Francis.

**Nash, Charles William.** 1848–1926. Ornithologist and ichthyologist, b. in Sussex, Eng.; to Canada (1869); chief work, *Manual of the Vertebrates of Ontario* (1908).

**Nash, John.** 1752–1835. English architect; known for street improvements in London; laid out Regent's Park and its terraces (1811); designed Regent Street (1813–20); redesigned Buckingham House, which became known (1825) as Buckingham Palace.

**Nash, Joseph.** 1809–1878. English water-color painter and lithographer.

**Nash, Ogden.** 1902–1971. American writer, b. Rye, N.Y.; author esp. of humorous verse, as in *Hard Lines* (1931), *The Primrose Path* (1935), *I'm a Stranger Here Myself* (1938), *Good Intentions* (1942).

**Nash, Paul** (1889–1946) and his brother **John Northcote** (1893– ). English painters, engravers, designers; both served in World War I. John was later commissioned to paint war pictures for Imperial War Museum. Paul, known esp. for landscapes and water colors; official war artist on western front (1917), to air ministry (1940), to ministry of information (1941).

**Nash, Richard.** 1674–1762. English gamester and social arbiter; known as "Beau Nash" and "King of Bath"; master of ceremonies at Bath (1705); virtually abolished dueling; invented new games of chance to evade gaming laws (until stricter legislation of 1745); pensioned by town of Bath.

**Nash** *or* **Nashe** (năsh), **Thomas.** 1567–1601. English satirical pamphleteer and dramatist. Probable first work, *Anatomie of Absurdities* (1589). Impelled by hatred of Puritanism, joined in Martin Marprelate controversy on side of the episcopacy, under pseudonym **Pas'quil** (păs'kwĭl). Waged bitter controversy with Gabriel Harvey, defending both Robert Greene, author of *Menaphon*, and himself, with *Pierce Pennilesse, His Supplication to the Divell* (1592), *Christes Teares* (1593), *Have With You to Saffron Walden* (1596), until controversy was suppressed by archbishop of Canterbury (1599). Pioneered English novel of adventure in his romance *The Unfortunate Traveller, or The Life of Jack Wilton* (1594), in realism approaching Defoe; wrote satirical masque *Summers Last Will* (1592); finished Marlowe's tragedy *Dido* (1596); imprisoned because of pointed satire of abuses in the state in his comedy *The Isle of Dogs;* last work, a burlesque panegyric of red herring of Yarmouth, *Lenten Stuffe* (1599).

**Nash, Walter.** 1882–1968. New Zealand politician, b. Eng.; to N.Z. (1909); Laborite member of N.Z. Parliament (1929–35); minister of finance (1935), of marketing (1936–40), of social security (1940–41); minister to U.S. (1942–44); member of Pacific War Council (1942–44); prime min., New Zealand (1957–60).

**Nasier, Alcofribas.** Anagrammatic pseudonym of François RABELAIS.

**Na'sir, al–** (ăl·nä'sĭr). *Arab.* **al–Malik al–Nāṣir.** 1284–1340. Mameluke sultan of Egypt (1293–94, 1298–1308, 1309–40) of Bahri dynasty. His reign one of longest in Moslem annals; his army defeated (1299) by Mongols, who for a time occupied northern Syria; subjected Druses and Maronites of Lebanon (1300–02).

**Nas'mith** (nāz'mĭth; nā'smĭth; năz'mĭth), **David.** 1799–1839. Scottish originator of city missions.

**Na'smith** (nā'smĭth), Sir **Martin Eric Dun·bar'** (dŭn-bär'). 1883–1965. Eng. naval officer; served in World War (1914–19); given Victoria Cross for courage and daring as commander of submarine *E11* when it destroyed eleven Turkish vessels in the Sea of Marmora; rear admiral (1928), vice-admiral (1932), and commander in chief of East Indies station (1932–34); a lord commissioner of the admiralty and chief of naval personnel (1935–38); admiral (1936).

**Nas'myth** (nāz'mĭth; nā'smĭth; năz'mĭth), **Alexander.** 1758–1840. Scottish portrait and landscape painter; studio in Edinburgh; intimate with Robert Burns and painted his portrait (Scottish National Gallery); became "father of Scottish landscape art"; invented bowstring bridge (1794). His elder son, **Patrick** (1787–1831), was a landscape painter. His younger son, **James** (1808–1890), engineer, began manufacture of machine tools at Manchester (1834), developed Bridgewater Foundry; invented steam hammer (1839), constructed and patented it (1842); devised a planing machine, a nut-shaping machine, a steam pile driver, a hydraulic punching machine; also studied astronomy.

**Naso, Publius Ovidius.** See OVID.

**Na'sr–ed–Din'** (nä'sĕr·ĕd·dēn'). 1831–1896. King of Persia (1848–96); son of Mohammed Shah; began reign with reform measures, assisted by his vizier, Mirza Taki Khan; at war with England (1856–57); made tours of Europe (1873, 1878, 1889); persecuted the Babis; assassinated. Succeeded by his son Muzaffar-ed-Din.

**Nas'sau** (năs'ô; näs'ou). Princely family of Europe, deriving its name from a county on the east bank of the Rhine, north of Mainz; founded by Walram I; divided (c. 1250) into two branches. (1) The elder line (German), founded by Walram II; occupied south part of region continuously till its absorption by Prussia (1866); Adolf of Nassau (*q.v.*), son of Walram II, was king of Germany (1292–98); later, line divided into several branches but by 1816 all extinct except **Nas'sau–Weil'burg** (-vīl'-bo͝ork); erected into a duchy (1806); when Duke Adolf (1817–1905) sided with Austria (1866), Prussia seized duchy; grand duchy of Luxemburg passed to duke of Nassau (1890); see MARIE ADÉLAÏDE and CHARLOTTE, grand duchesses.
(2) The younger or cadet line (Dutch), founded by Otto I (d. about 1292); occupied north part of region; division of territory among Otto's three sons gave rise to several branches: (a) Engelbert (or Engelbrecht) I, of **Nas'sau–Dil'len·burg** (-dĭl'ĕn·bo͝ork) branch, acquired by marriage (1404) lands in the Low Countries; a descendant, Henry III, inherited both German and Dutch possessions; Henry's son René also inherited (1530) from his mother (see ORANGE) the principality of Orange; at René's death (1544) without issue, all lands went to his cousin William I, Count of Nassau (later, William the Silent, stadholder), who founded first line of **Or'ange–Nas'sau** (ŏr'ĭnj-). Stadholders of the Netherlands who, as princes of Orange-Nassau, succeeded William I were: Maurice, Frederick Henry, William II, and William III (who became William III of England). This line became extinct (1702). (b) The four sons of John VI, Count of Nassau, a younger brother of Henry III, who ruled Nassau-Dillenburg (to 1606), founded new branches, two of these being extinct by 1739; the eldest son was Joan Mauritz, Prince of **Nas'sau–Sie'gen** [-zē'gĕn] (see NASSAU-SIEGEN), this branch being extinct by 1743; the third son, Ernest Casimir, founded (1606) line of **Nas'sau–Dietz'** (-dēts'), or second line of Orange-Nassau; a descendant, John William Friso, inherited possessions of Orange in the Netherlands; his son William IV, reunited (1743) all lands of house of Orange and became hereditary stadholder (1747); title lost by William V (1795) when driven out by Napoleon; his son William VI lost Nassau (1806) by refusing to adhere to Confederation of the Rhine, but became king of the Netherlands (1815) as William I; family has continued as house of Orange (sometimes still called Orange-Nassau) on throne of the Netherlands (from 1815); see WILLIAM I, II, and III; WILHELMINA.

**Nas'sau–Sie'gen** (-zē'gĕn), Prince **Charles Henri Nicolas Othon de.** 1745–1808. Military adventurer; in French service accompanied Bougainville on voyage around the world (1766–69); commanded Russ. fleets which defeated Turks (1788) and Swedes (1789; 1790).

**Nassau–Siegen,** Count **Jo·an'** (yô·än') **Mau'ritz** (mou'rĭts) **van.** 1604–1679. Dutch general and administrator, b. Dillenburg; eldest son of John VI, Count of Nassau (see NASSAU); served with distinction at Breda (1625) and Maastricht (1632); governor of Dutch possessions in Brazil (1637–44); defeated Spanish and Portuguese fleet (1640); entered service of Brandenburg (1647) as governor of Cleves; made prince of Nassau-Siegen (1664); made field marshal (1671); active in war against Louis XIV (1672–74).

**Nas'ser, Ga·mal' Abd·el** (gȧ·mäl' ȧb·do͝ol·nä'sẽr). 1918–1970. Egyptian politician and army officer. Pres. of Egypt (1956–58), of United Arab Rep. (1958–70).

**Nast** (năst), **Condé.** 1874–1942. Amer. pub.; pres. of magazine *Vogue* (from 1909), *House and Garden*, etc.

**Nast, Thomas.** 1840–1902. Cartoonist, b. Landau, Ger.; to U.S. (1846); illustrator on staff of *Frank Leslie's Illustrated Newspaper* (1855–59); staff artist of *Harper's Weekly* (1862–86); at height of career, attacked (1869–72) Tweed Ring in New York; his cartoons largely responsible for overthrow of the ring; U.S. consul, Guayaquil, Ecuador (1902).

**Nat'a·lie** (năt'ȧ·lĭ) *or* **Na·tha'lia** (nȧ·thāl'yȧ; -thăl'-; -thäl'-). *Russ. name* **Natalya Kesh·ko'** (kyĕsh·kô'). 1859–1941. Queen of Serbia (1882–89), b. Florence; daughter of a Russian colonel; m. (1875) Milan, Prince (later King) of Serbia; divorced (1888), reconciled (1893); royal rights restored; retired to Biarritz.

**Na'than** (nā'thăn; -th'n). In the Bible, a Hebrew prophet in the reign of David, who (*2 Samuel* xii) reproved David for causing Uriah's death.

**Nathan, George Jean** (jēn). 1882–1958. American editor, author, and dramatic critic, b. Fort Wayne, Ind.; founder, and editor (1924) with H. L. Mencken, of *The American Mercury;* contributing editor (1925–30). A founder and editor, with others, of *The American Spectator* (1932). Author of *The Eternal Mystery* (1913), *Another Book on the Theatre* (1916), *The Critic and the Drama* (1922), *The New American Credo* (1927), *Passing Judgments* (1934), *The Morning After the First Night* (1938), *Encyclopedia of the Theatre* (1940), *The Entertainment of a Nation* (1942), etc.

**Nathan, Robert.** 1894– . American novelist, b. New York City; author of *Peter Kindred* (1919), *Autumn* (1921), *Youth Grows Old* (1922), *The Fiddler in Barly* (1926), *The Bishop's Wife* (1928), *One More Spring* (1933), *Winter in April* (1937), *Journey of Tapiola* (1938), *Portrait of Jennie* (1940), *They Went On Together* (1941), *The Sea-Gull Cry* (1942), etc., also of *Selected Poems* (1935), *Dunkirk* (ballad; 1942), *Journal for Josephine* (personal memoir; 1943), etc.

**Na·than'a·el** (nȧ·thăn'ā·ĕl). In the Bible, a native of Galilee (*John* i. 45 ff.), identified by some with the apostle Bartholomew.

**Na'thans** (nā'thănz; -th'nz), **Daniel.** 1928– American microbiologist. At Johns Hopkins U. (1962– ); awarded (with Werner Arber and Hamilton O. Smith) Nobel prize for physiology or medicine (1978).

**Nat'horst** (nȧt'hôrst), **Alfred Gabriel.** 1850–1921. Swedish geologist, paleobotanist, and Arctic explorer; member of Nordenskjöld's expedition to Greenland (1883); director of a division of the Riks-Museum of Natural History, Stockholm (1885–1918); led an expedition to Bear Island, Spitsbergen, and King Charles Island (1898); visited (1899) Jan Mayen, eastern Greenland, and Franz Josef Fiord, and discovered King Oscar Fiord.

**Na'tion** (nā'shŭn), **Carry Amelia,** *nee* **Moore.** *First name often erroneously spelled* **Carrie.** 1846–1911. American temperance agitator, b. in Garrard County, Ky.; m. 1st Dr. Charles Gloyd (1867), 2d David Nation (1877; divorced, 1901). Resident in Kansas (from 1889), a prohibition state; maintained that, since the saloon was illegal in Kansas, any citizen could destroy liquor, furniture, and fixtures in a place selling intoxicants; armed with a hatchet, went on wrecking expeditions through Kansas cities and towns (1900–10); became country-wide notorious figure, often arrested, imprisoned, fined, and clubbed or shot at.

**Na'torp** (nä'tôrp), **Bernhard Christoph Ludwig.** 1774–1846. German educator and theologian; author of works chiefly on pedagogy, music, and theology; supporter of Pestalozzi. His great-grandson **Paul Gerhard Natorp** (1854–1924), Neo-Kantian philosopher and composer, chiefly of piano pieces and songs; author of

*Platos Ideenlehre* (1903), *Allgemeine Psychologie* (1912), *Sozialidealismus* (1920), etc.

**Nat'ta** (nät'tä), **Giulio.** 1903–1979. Italian chemist. With Inst. of Tech., Milan (1938–74); awarded Nobel prize in chemistry (1963) with K. Ziegler for studies on the chemistry and technology of high polymers.

**Nat'ter** (nät'ẽr), **Heinrich.** 1846–1892. Austrian sculptor, b. in the Tirol; resident in Vienna (from 1875).

**Natter, Johann Lorenz.** 1705–1763. German gem engraver and medalist; in England (c. 1741 and after 1754) and northern Europe (1743); wrote on ancient and modern methods of engraving gems (1754).

**Nat'tier'** (nȧ'tyā'), **Jean Marc.** 1685–1766. French portrait painter; summoned by Peter the Great to paint portraits of leading figures in his entourage (1715); painter to Chevalier d'Orléans (1734).

**Nau** (nō), **John Antoine.** *Orig. name* **André Tor'quet'** (tôr'kĕ'). 1873–1918. French poet and novelist, b. San Francisco, Calif.; awarded first Goncourt prize for novel *La Force Ennemie* (1903).

**Nauck** (nouk), **Johann August.** 1822–1892. German classical scholar and philologist.

**Nau'dé'** (nō'dā'), **Gabriel.** 1600–1653. French bibliographer and historian; librarian to Cardinal Mazarin, and collector of the Mazarin library.

**Nau'en** (nou'ĕn), **Heinrich.** 1880–1940. German expressionistic painter.

**Nau'lin'** (nō'lăɴ'), **Stanislas.** 1870–1932. French general in World War I; commanded army in Morocco against Abd-el-Krim (1925).

**Nau'mann** (nou'män), **Friedrich,** *in full* **Joseph Friedrich.** 1860–1919. German Protestant theologian, publicist, and socialist politician; champion of the Mittel-europa plan; cofounder (with Hellmuth von Gerlach and others; 1896) and first president, National Socialist party; member of the Reichstag (1907–12, 1913–18); cofounder and a leader (1919) of the German Democratic party, German National Assembly, Weimar. Founded and edited *Die Hilfe* (1895) and *Die Zeit* (1896–97; 1901–03). Wrote *Mitteleuropa* (1915; in which he set forth a central-European empire for Germany), etc.

**Naumann, Hans.** 1886–1951. German folklorist and Germanic scholar; wrote *Althochdeutsche Grammatik* (1914), *Höfische Kultur* (with Günther Müller, 1929), etc.

**Naumann, Johann Andreas.** 1747–1826. German ornithologist and agriculturist. His son **Johann Friedrich** (1780–1857), ornithologist, was author of *Naturgeschichte der Vögel Deutschlands* (12 vols., 1820–44), etc.

**Naumann, Johann Gottlieb.** 1741–1801. German composer; composed 23 operas, including *Amphion* (1776), *Cora* (1782), and *Gustav Wasa* (1786), oratorios, masses, psalms, chamber music, cantatas, songs, etc. His son **Karl Friedrich** (1797–1873), mineralogist, was publisher of *Geognostische Spezialkarte,* on Saxony (12 plates, 1834–43; with Cotta), etc. Another son, **Moritz Ernst Adolf** (1798–1871), physician and physiologist, wrote *Handbuch der Medizinischen Klinik* (1829–39). K. F. Naumann's son **Karl Ernst** (1832–1910), organist, director, and professor in Jena (1860–1906), composed chiefly chamber music. M. E. A. Naumann's son **Emil** (1827–1888), composer and writer on music, pupil of Mendelssohn, was court director of sacred music, Berlin (1856); in Dresden (chiefly from 1873); composer of operas (*Judith,* 1858; *Loreley,* prod. 1889), oratorios, etc.

**Naun'dorff** *or* **Naun'dorf** (noun'dôrf), **Karl Wilhelm.** d. 1845. French clockmaker; in Germany (1812–28); claimed to be the Dauphin Louis Charles (son of Louis XVI and Marie Antoinette), whom he greatly resembled in appearance; went to Paris (1833) to push claims; expelled from France (1836). See LOUIS XVII.

**Naun'ton** (nôn't'n; -tŭn), Sir **Robert.** 1563–1635. English political leader; communicated political news from Europe to earl of Essex (c. 1594–c. 1600); secretary of state (1618–23); master of court of wards (1623–35); wrote a valuable account of Elizabeth's courtiers, *Fragmenta Regalia* (pub. 1641).

**Na'var·re'te** (nä'vär·rĕ'tā), **Domingo Fernández.** 1610–?1689. Spanish Dominican monk and missionary; apostolic prefect of Chekiang province, China (1659–73); archbishop of Santo Domingo (1677 ff.).

**Navarrete, Fernández.** See FERNÁNDEZ NAVARRETE.

**Navarrete, Martín Fernández de.** 1765–1844. Spanish navigator and writer; with Spanish navy in attack on Gibraltar (1782); commissioned to collect documents relating to Spanish naval history (1789–92); director, Royal Acad. of History (1824 ff.); created senator and councilor of state.

**Na·var'ro, Mary Anderson de** (thā nä·vär'rô). = Mary Antoinette ANDERSON.

**Na·var'ro** (nä·vär'rô), **Pedro.** Conde **de Al·vet'to** (thā äl·vāt'tô) *or* **O'li·vet'to** (ō'lē-). 1460?–1528. Spanish soldier; known esp. for his developments in use of mines in warfare; in service of Gonzalo de Córdoba against Naples (1500); with Cardinal Cisneros in conquest of Oran (1509).

**Navarro, Tomás.** *In full* **Tomás Navarro To·más'** (tô·mäs'). 1884– . Spanish phonetician; professor, Madrid; professor of Spanish philology, Columbia (1939 ff.); author of textbook of Spanish phonetics *Manual de Pronunciación Española* (1918), of study on phonetics of Basque *Pronunciación Guipuzcoana,* etc.

**Navero, Emiliano González.** See GONZÁLEZ NAVERO.

**Na'vez'** (nȧ'vĕz'), **François Joseph.** 1787–1869. Belgian painter; influenced esp. by David; inaugurated 19th-century renaissance in Belgian painting.

**Na'ville'** (nȧ'vēl'), **Édouard,** *in full* **Henri Édouard.** 1844–1926. Swiss Egyptologist; author of *Das Ägyptische Todtenbuch der 18ten bis 20ten Dynastie* (1886), *Bubastis* (1889), *La Religion des Anciens Égyptiens* (1906), *Archaeology of the Old Testament* (1913), *The Law of Moses* (1920), etc.

**Nawanagar,** Maharaja of. See RANJITSINHJI VIBHAJI.

**Nāyadu, Sarojini.** See Sarojini NAIDU.

**Nay'ler** (nā'lẽr), **James.** 1617?–1660. English Quaker minister; served in Parliamentary army (1642–50); convinced that he was incarnation of Christ, rode into Bristol in imitation of Christ; convicted of blasphemy (1656) and sentenced to pillory, whipping, branding, and imprisonment.

**Na·zi'mo·va** (nŭ·zyē'mŭ·vŭ; *Angl.* nȧ·zĭm'ō·vȧ), **Alla.** 1879–1945. Actress, b. in the Crimea, Russia; m. Charles Bryant; debut in St. Petersburg (1904), in New York (1905); best known for interpretation of Ibsen roles.

**Nea'gle** (nē'g'l), **John.** 1796–1865. American portrait painter, b. Boston; studio in Philadelphia; his *Gilbert Stuart* hangs in Boston Museum of Fine Arts; his *Washington,* in Independence Hall, Philadelphia.

**Neal, Neale** (nēl). See also NEILE, NEILL.

**Neal** (nēl), **Daniel.** 1678–1743. English clergyman and historian of the Puritans; author of *History of the Puritans* (covering period to 1689: 4 vols., 1732–38).

**Neal, David Dal'hoff** (?dăl'hŏf). 1838–1915. American figure and portrait painter, b. Lowell, Mass.; among his portraits are *Mark Hopkins, Whitelaw Reid.*

**Neal, John.** 1793–1876. American miscellaneous writer, b. Portland, Me.; successively, a store clerk, law student, magazine editor, writer of narrative poems, essayist, and novelist. His works include *Keep Cool* (1817), *Seventy-Six* (1823), *The Down-Easters* (1833), *True Womanhood* (1859), etc.

**Neale** (nēl), **Edward Vansittart.** 1810–1892. English co-operator and Christian Socialist; founded first co-operative store in London; director in co-operative newspaper and insurance societies; general secretary of Central Co-operative Board (1875–91); instrumental in passing of co-operative legislation, esp. the Consolidation Act of 1862; author of pamphlets on socialism and co-operation.

**Neale, John Mason.** 1818–1866. English hymnologist; embraced High-Church views; founded Anglican nursing sisterhood of St. Margaret's (1854); translated ancient and medieval hymns, and Bernard of Cluny's *De Contemptu Mundi* including the hymns "For thee, O dear, dear country," "Jerusalem the golden." Author of *An Introduction to the History of the Holy Eastern Church* (2 vols., 1850).

**Ne·an'der** (nā·än'dēr), **Johann August Wilhelm.** *Orig. name* **David Men'del** (mĕn'dĕl). 1789–1850. German Protestant church historian and theologian, of Jewish parentage; pupil of Schleiermacher; embraced Christianity (1806); professor of church history, Berlin (from 1813).

**Ne·ar'chus** (nē·är'kŭs). Macedonian officer under Alexander the Great; commanded fleet in its journey from mouth of the Indus to head of Persian Gulf (325–324 B.C.); after death of Alexander (323), joined Antigonus and was given government of provinces of Lycia and Pamphylia.

**Nea'ring** (nēr'ĭng), **Scott.** 1883– . American sociologist, b. Morris Run, Pa.; lecturer, Rand School of Social Science, New York (1916); socialist candidate for Congress, in New York (1919). Author of *Social Adjustment* (1911), *Poverty and Riches* (1916), *Education in Soviet Russia* (1926), *War* (1931), *Must We Starve?* (1932), etc.

**Nebhapetre Mentuhotep.** = MENTUHOTEP II.

**Ne·bri'ja** (nā·brē'hä) *or* **Le·bri'ja** (lā·brē'hä), **Elio Antonio de.** *Lat.* **Aelius Antonius Neb'ris·sen'sis** (nĕb'rĭ·sĕn'sĭs). *Real name* **Elio Antonio Mar·tí'nez de Ja·ra'va** (mär·tē'näth thā hä·rä'vä). 1444–1532. Spanish humanist, b. Lebrija (Nebrija). Works include *Institutiones Grammaticae* (1481), *Juris Civilis Lexicon* (1486), *Dictionarium Latino Hispanicum et Hispano Latinum* (1492), and *Gramática sobre la Lengua Castellana* (1492).

**Neb'u·chad·nez'zar** (nĕb'ū·kăd·nĕz'ēr). *More correctly* **Neb'u·chad·rez'zar** (-rĕz'ēr). *Bab.* **Nabu-kudurri-uṣur.** *Gr.* **Nab'u·cho·don'o·sor** (năb'ū·kō·dŏn'ō·sôr) *or* **Nab'u·go·don'o·sor** (-gō-). Name of two kings of Babylon: **Nebuchadnezzar I.** King (1146–1123 B.C.), of the Isin dynasty; fought wars against Elam and Assyria.

**Nebuchadnezzar II.** d. 562 B.C. Chaldean king of Babylon (605–562 B.C.); son of Nabopolassar; sent by father on expedition against Necho II of Egypt (610); defeated Necho at Carchemish (605); conquered Palestine, capturing Jerusalem (597); carried Jewish king, Jehoiachin, and many Jews as prisoners to Babylon; appointed Zedekiah king, as his vassal; after Zedekiah's rebellion (588), besieged Jerusalem for 16 months (587–586), destroyed it (cf. APRIES), and for second time carried Jews in exile to Babylon (Babylonian Captivity); took Tyre (573) after siege of 13 years; conducted campaign against Egypt (568); restored Babylon and other cities; rebuilt walls, palaces, temples, etc.; one of greatest of Chaldean kings; according to tradition (*Daniel* iv), suffered strange malady (lycanthropy) for several years during his reign. Succeeded by his son Evil-Merodach (*q.v.*).

**Ne'cho** (nē'kō): (1) *Sometimes known as* **Necho I.** fl. 664–663 B.C. Prince of **Sa'ïs** (sā'ĭs) and **Mem'phis** (mĕm'fĭs) and chief of Egyptian lords of the delta; apparently never recognized as regular king of Egypt; kept in power by Assyrians (see ASHURBANIPAL); father of Psamtik I (*q.v.*), founder of XXVIth (Saite) dynasty. (2) **Necho (II)** *or* **Nech'a·o** (nĕk'ā·ō). *In the Bible* **Phar'aoh–Ne'choh** *or* **Phar'aoh–Ne'coh** (fâr'ō-nē'kō; fā'rō-). *Assyrian* **Ni'ku** (nē'kōō). Son of Psamtik I and father of Psamtik II; second king of XXVIth (Saite) dynasty of Egyptian kings (reigned c. 609–593 B.C.); completely defeated (c. 608 B.C.) Jews under Josiah at Megiddo in Palestine (*2 Chron.* xxxv. 20–24); lost Asiatic possessions when defeated (605) by Nebuchadnezzar at Carchemish (*Jer.* xlvi); maintained fleet at Nile delta and on Red Sea; attempted to dig canal through Goshen from Bubastis to Red Sea; said by Herodotus to have sent an expedition (c. 600) under Phoenician leaders that circumnavigated Africa.

**Neck'am** (nĕk'ăm) *or* **Nech'am** (nĕκ'ăm), **Alexander.** *Punningly nicknamed* **Ne'quam** (nē'kwăm), *Latin* "wicked." 1157–1217. English scholar; abbot of Cirencester (1213). In *De naturis rerum* and *De utensilibus*, recorded for first time outside of China use of a magnetic needle by mariners.

**Neck'el** (nĕk'ĕl), **Gustav.** 1878–1940. German philologist.

**Nec'ker'** (nĕ'kâr'; *Angl.* nĕk'ēr), **Jacques.** 1732–1804. French financier and statesman, b. Geneva; apprentice in Paris banking house (1747–62); set up banking business (1762) and gained fortune during Seven Years' War (1756–63). After removal of Turgot, became minister of finance (1776–81); succeeded in introducing some order into French finances, with reforms, systematized administration, and more just taxation; dismissed by Louis XVI for his Protestantism, and esp. for his insistence on retrenchment. Recalled as director-general of finance (1788); virtually premier of France; recommended calling of States-General (1789); his second dismissal (not effective) immediate cause of storming of Bastille (July 12–14, 1789); resigned (Sept., 1790); retired to his estate near Geneva. Best-known work *Administration des Finances* (pub. 1784). His wife, **Suzanne,** *nee* **Cur'chod'** [kür'shō'] (1739–1794), daughter of a pastor near Lausanne, was a talented author, and hostess to political, financial, and literary leaders of the time. Their daughter was Madame de Staël (*q.v.*). Their niece **Albertine Adrienne Necker de Saus'sure'** [dē sō'sür'] (1766–1841), cousin of Mme. de Staël, daughter of the Swiss naturalist, Horace Bénédict de Saussure, was an author; lived and wrote at Geneva; chief work, *L'Éducation Progressive* (1828).

**Necker, Olivier.** *Known as* **O'li'vier' le Dain** (ô'lē'vyā' lē dăN') *or* **le Daim** (dăN'). *Also* **Olivier le Dia'ble** (dyä'bl'). 1440?–1484. French barber who became favorite and privy councilor of King Louis XI; hanged by order of the Parliament of Paris after Louis's death. A character in Scott's *Quentin Durward.*

**Nec·tan'e·bo** (nĕk·tăn'ē·bō). Name of two kings of Egypt under Persian rule: **Nectanebo I** (reigned c. 382–364 B.C.). **Nectanebo II** (reigned 361–340 B.C.), last native king (XXXth, or Persian, dynasty), who fled to Nubia when Persians under Artaxerxes Ochus conquered Egypt.

**Ned'bal** (nĕd'bäl), **Os'kar** (ôs'kär). 1874–1930. Bohemian violist, conductor, and composer of operettas, ballets, and orchestral, piano, and chamber music.

**Need'ham** (nēd'ăm), **John Turberville.** 1713–1781. English naturalist; ordained Roman Catholic priest (1732); collaborated with Buffon on scientific work; believed in spontaneous generation.

**Neef** (nāf), **Hermann.** 1904– . German political leader; head of civil service of Nazi party.

**Nee'fe** (nā'fĕ), **Christian Gottlob.** 1748–1798. German musician and composer; music director (1782–94) at Bonn, where he taught Beethoven.

**Neefs** *or* **Neeffs** *or* **Nefs** (nāfs). A family of Dutch architectural painters of Antwerp, including: **Pieter** (1578?–?1661), painter esp. of church interiors, often illuminated. His sons and imitators, **Lodewyck** (1617–?) and **Pieter** (1620–after 1675).

**Né'el'** (nā'ĕl'), **Louis Eugène Félix.** 1904– . French physicist. With U. of Strasbourg (1928–45), Grenoble (1945– ); awarded Nobel prize in physics (1970) with H. Alfven for studies in solid state physics.

**Neer** (nār), **Aart** *or* **Aert** *or* **Aernout van der.** 1603?–1677. Dutch landscape painter, active in Amsterdam (from c. 1640). His son and pupil **Eglon Hendrik** (1635?–1703), court painter to the elector palatine at Düsseldorf (from 1690), painted group and genre scenes, landscapes with Biblical or mythological figures, and small portraits.

**Neer'gaard** (nẹ̄r'gôr), **Niels.** 1854–1936. Danish statesman, historian, and journalist; prime minister (1908–09; 1920–24); delegate to Paris Peace Conference (1919).

**Nee·si·ma** (nē·shē·mä), **Joseph Hardy.** 1843–1890. Japanese educator; with Yamamoto Kakuma founded (1874) the Doshisha School (now University) in Kyoto, most important Christian university in Japan; taught at Doshisha (1874–90).

**Nees von E'sen·beck** (nās' fŏn ā'zĕn·bĕk), **Christian Gottfried.** 1776–1858. German botanist and naturalist; author of books on fungi, mosses, natural philosophy, etc. His brother **Theodor Friedrich Ludwig** (1787–1837) was a botanist and pharmacognosist.

**Nef** (nĕf), **John Ulric.** 1862–1915. Swiss chemist; to U.S. (1868); pioneer investigator of bivalent carbon, fulminates, and mechanism of organic reactions.

**Ne'fer·ti'ti** (nĕ'fĕr·tē'tē) *or* **Ne'fer·ti'–it** (-tē'ĭt) *or* **Nof're·te'te** (nŏf'rĕ·tē'tē). fl. 1st half of 14th century B.C. Egyptian queen, wife of Ikhnaton; probably of Asiatic (Hittite) birth; noted for beauty and influence on her husband's religious ideas.

**Neff'tzer'** (nĕf'tsâr'), **Auguste.** 1820–1876. French journalist; founder and editor (1861–71) of *Le Temps.*

**Ne·fi' of Er·zu·rum'** (nĕ·fē', ĕr·zōō·rōōm'). Turkish poet of early 17th cent. Known for eulogies and satires.

**Nef're·ti'ri** (nĕf'rĕ·tē'rē). Variant of NEFERTITI.

**Nefs.** See NEEFS.

**Neghelli,** Marchese **di.** See Rodolfo GRAZIANI.

**Ne'gri** (nā'grē), **Ada.** 1870–1945. Italian poetess, b. Lodi; m. Federigo Garlanda; her works include *Fatalità* (1893), *Maternità* (1904), *Dal Profondo* (1910), *Esilio* (1914), *Le Solitarie* (1916), *Finestre Alte* (1923), *Sorelle* (1929), *Il Dono* (1936).

**Negri, Po'la** (pō'lȧ). *Nee* **Appolonia Cha·lu'pez** (?kä·lōō'pĕs). 1899– . Actress, b. in Poland; m. (1st) Count Dombski and (2d) Prince Serge Mdivani (divorced). To U.S. (1923) and starred in motion pictures, as *Carmen, The Spanish Dancer,* etc.

**Ne·gruz'zi** (nĕ·grōō'tsē), **Constantin.** 1808–1868. Rumanian writer; author of *Alexander Lăpuşneanu* (1857), regarded as a masterpiece of the Rumanian short story; translator of works of Victor Hugo, Pushkin, and others.

**Ne'he·mi'ah** (nē'(h)ĕ·mī'ȧ). *In Douay Bible* **Ne'he·mi'as** (-ăs). A Jewish leader of the 5th century B.C., appointed by Artaxerxes I governor of Judea (445) and authorized to rebuild Jerusalem. The story of the rebuilding of the walls of Jerusalem and of Nehemiah's administration and reforms is told in the Old Testament book of *Nehemiah* (named in Douay Bible *2 Esdras, alias Nehemias*). See also EZRA.

**Ne'her** (nā'ĕr), **Michael.** 1798–1876. German painter, esp. of murals, Gothic churches, etc. His brother **Bernhard** (1806–1886), historical painter and muralist, painted more than 60 murals in the Weimar Castle illustrating works of Goethe and Schiller.

**Neh'ru** (nā'rōō), Pundit **Mo'ti·lal** (mō'tĭ·läl). 1861–1931. Indian Nationalist leader, a Kashmiri Brahman; educ. Muir Coll., Allahabad; practiced law in Allahabad (from 1883); member of United Provinces legislative council; became associated with Gandhi in the Nationalist movement (1919); founded its paper, the *Independent;* president of Indian National Congress (1920); with C. R. Das organized Swaraj party (1922); member of Indian Legislative Assembly (1923–24, 1926); framed Nehru report, formulating plan for dominion status for India (1928); advocated campaign of civil disobedience (1930). His son **Ja·wa'har·lal** [jȧ·wä'hȧr·läl] (1889–1964), b. Allahabad, educ. Harrow and Cambridge, returned to India (1912); joined Gandhi's movement (1919); served seven terms (5½ years) in jail (1921–34) for his Nationalist activities; secretary of National Congress (1929–39); three times president of the Indian National Congress; first prime minister of India (1947–64); author of an autobiography (1936), *The Unity of India* (1941), etc.; the latter's daughter, **In'di·ra** (ĭn'dĭ·rȧ) **Nehru Gan'dhi** [gän'dē; *Angl.* -dĭ] (1917– ), prime minister (1966–77).

**Neid'hart von Reu'en·thal** (nīt'härt fŏn roi'ĕn·täl). Bavarian knight and Middle High German lyric poet of the 13th century; founder of the popular lyric poetry of the courts. His works include chiefly dance songs and, reputedly, poems ridiculing the rude life and manners of the wealthy peasantry, for which he was nicknamed **Neidhart Fuchs** (fŏŏks), *i.e.* Neidhart the Fox.

**Nei'hardt** (nī'härt), **John Gnei'se·nau** (g'nī'zĕ·nou). 1881–1973. American poet, b. Sharpsburg, Ill.; at U. of Nebraska (1923), U. of Mo. (1949-66); literary editor, St. Louis *Post-Dispatch* (1926–38); by act of Nebraska legislature (1921), named poet laureate of Nebraska. His works include *The Divine Enchantment* (1900), *The Lonesome Trail* (1907), *Man-Song* (1909), *The River and I* (1910), *The Song of Three Friends* (1919), *Black Elk Speaks* (1932), *The Song of the Messiah* (1935), etc.

**Neile, Neill** (nēl). See also NEAL, NEALE.

**Neile** (nēl), **Richard.** 1562–1640. English ecclesiastic; archbishop of York (1631–40); sat regularly in courts of Star Chamber.

**Neill** (nēl), **Edward Duffield.** 1823–1893. American clergyman and historian, b. Philadelphia; author of *History of the Virginia Company of London* (1869), *The English Colonization of America during the 17th Century* (1871), etc.

**Neill, James George Smith.** 1810–1857. British army officer, b. in Scotland; organized and reformed Turkish contingent in Crimean War (1854–56); at outbreak of Sepoy Mutiny ruthlessly crushed mutineers at Benares (1857); led famous march from Cawnpore to join in assault upon Lucknow, where he was killed in action.

**Neil'son** (nēl's'n), **George.** 1858–1923. Scottish antiquary and historian; expert paleographer, authority on charters. His *Trial by Combat* (1890) is definitive work on the origin and history of the duel. Also, student of Middle Scots verse; author of *John Barbour, Poet and Translator* (1900), *Huchown of the Awle Ryale, the Alliterative Poet* (1902).

**Neilson, James Beaumont.** 1792–1865. Scottish inventor of the hot blast in the manufacturing of iron, and of improvements in the manufacturing of gas.

**Neilson, John.** 1776–1848. Journalist, b. Kircudbrightshire, Scotland; to Canada (1790); edited Quebec *Gazette* (from 1797), first newspaper to be published in Canada.

**Neilson, Julia.** 1869–1957. English actress; studied music at Wiesbaden, Germany, and Royal Academy, London; first appeared as Cynisca in *Pygmalion and Galatea* (1888); toured U.S. and Canada; as Rosalind in *As You Like It*, played longest run on record in a London theater; theater manager with her husband, Fred Terry (*q.v.*). Their son **Dennis Neil′son–Ter′ry** [-tĕr′ĭ] (1895–1932) was an actor. Their daughter **Phyllis Neilson–Terry** (1892– ), an actress. See under Ellen TERRY.

**Neilson, Lilian Adelaide.** *Stage name of* **Elizabeth Ann Brown.** 1848–1880. English tragic actress; made debut as Juliet (1865); met success (1870–71) as Amy Robsart in *Kenilworth;* her chief characters were Rosalind in *As You Like It*, Beatrice in *Much Ado about Nothing*, Imogen in *Cymbeline*, and Rebecca in *Ivanhoe.*

**Neilson, William Allan.** 1869–1946. Educator, b. Doune, Scotland; M.A., Edinburgh (1891); Ph.D., Harvard (1898). Teacher in Upper Canada Coll., Toronto (1891–95); instructor in English, Bryn Mawr (1898–1900), Harvard (1900–04), Columbia (1904–06); professor of English, Harvard (1906–17); president, Smith Coll. (1917–39). Author of *Essentials of Poetry* (1912), *The Facts About Shakespeare* (with A. H. Thorndike; 1913), *Robert Burns* (1917), *A History of English Literature* (1920); editor of the Cambridge edition of Shakespeare's works (1906; 1942); editor in chief, *Webster's New International Dictionary, Second Edition* (pub. 1934).

**Neilson–Terry, Dennis** and **Phyllis.** See under Julia NEILSON.

**Neip′perg** (nī′pĕrK), Count **Wilhelm Reinhard von.** 1684–1774. German field marshal. His grandson Count **Adam Adalbert von Neipperg** (1775–1829), Austrian general and diplomat, married Marie Louise after the death of Napoleon (1821).

**Neis′ser** (nī′sẽr), **Albert Ludwig Siegmund.** 1855–1916. German physician; specialist in dermatology and venereal diseases; discoverer (1879) of the gonococcus, the bacterium that causes gonorrhea; demonstrated the existence of the bacillus of leprosy.

**Neit′hardt** (nīt′härt), **August Heinrich.** 1793–1861. German composer and choral conductor; royal music director (1839); composed an opera, instrumental and vocal compositions, including the song *Ich Bin Ein Preusse* (1826).

**Neithardt von Gneisenau,** Count. See August GNEISENAU.

**Neit′zel** (nī′tsĕl), **Otto.** 1852–1920. German pianist, composer, conductor, and writer on music; composed operas, a piano concerto and other piano works; author of *Führer durch die Oper der Gegenwart* (3 vols., 1890–93), *Saint-Saëns* (1898), translations of opera texts, etc.

**Ne·kra′sov** (nyĕ·krȧ′sôf), **Nikolai Alekseevich.** 1821–1877. Russian poet; among his individual poems are *Red-Nosed Frost*, *Fatherland*, *Peasants' Children*, *Last Songs*, and the long poem *To Whom Is Life in Russia Worth Living.*

**Né′la′ton′** (nā′lȧ′tôN′), **Auguste.** 1807–1873. French surgeon; devised a probe used in military surgery in searching for bullets; known for operating skill; originated an operation for stones.

**Ne·li′dov** (nyĕ·lyē′dôf), **Aleksandr Ivanovich.** 1838–1910. Russian diplomat; aided in negotiating Treaty of San Stefano after Russo-Turkish War (1877–78), and Treaty of Berlin (1878); Russian ambassador to Turkey (1883–97), Italy (1897–1903), and France (1903–10).

**Nell** (nĕl), **William Cooper.** 1816–1874. American Negro author, b. Boston; agitator for removal of discriminations against colored children in Massachusetts public schools; clerk in Boston post office (1861–74), first Negro to be given a federal position. Author of *Services of Colored Americans in the Wars of 1776 and 1812* (1851), *The Colored Patriots of the American Revolution* (1855), with introduction by Harriet Beecher Stowe.

**Nel′son** (nĕl′s′n), **Donald Marr.** 1888–1959. American merchant and administrator, b. Hannibal, Mo.; B.S., U. of Missouri (1911); with Sears, Roebuck & Co. (1912–42); executive vice-president (1939–42); executive director of supply priorities, Office of Production Management (1941); chairman, War Production Board (1942–44); president, Society of Independent Motion Picture Producers (1945–47).

**Nelson, Edward William.** 1855–1934. American naturalist, b. Manchester, N.H.; on staff of bureau of biological survey, U.S. Department of Agriculture (from 1890), chief of bureau (1916–27), principal biologist (1927–29).

**Nelson, Horatio.** Viscount **Nelson.** 1758–1805. British naval hero; saw first active service in West Indies (1780); commanded H.M.S. *Boreas* in West Indies (1784); m. (1787) Frances Nisbet (1761–1831), a widow. Served under Hood in taking of Bastia and of Calvi (where sight of his right eye was destroyed), completing the reduction of Corsica (1794); served later under Jervis; met (1793) Emma Hamilton, wife of British ambassador at court of Naples; appointed commodore (1796); returned from mission at Elba in time to join Jervis in victory off Cape St. Vincent over French and Spanish fleets (Feb., 1797); rear admiral (1797). Failed in desperate attempt to take Santa Cruz de Tenerife (July, 1797); shot through right elbow, suffered badly performed amputation; returned to fleet in H.M.S. *Vanguard;* pursued French fleet in eastern Mediterranean; discovered them in Abukir Bay, and allowed only two frigates to escape (battle of the Nile; Aug., 1798). Blockaded Malta and Naples, held by French and Neapolitan Jacobins, annulled Cardinal Ruffo's proposed terms to rebels, received absolute surrender; restored Neapolitan royal family to power; returned overland to England with Sir William and Lady Hamilton (1800); separated from his wife (1801). Vice-admiral (1801); although second-in-command to Sir Hyde Parker, attacked Copenhagen (1801); created Viscount Nelson (1801); shared houses with Hamiltons in London and at Merton in Surrey. Appointed on reopening of war to Mediterranean command (1803); blockaded French in Toulon for two years; on their escape pursued to West Indies and back to Cádiz; in battle of Trafalgar (1805) formed fleet in two columns; with his ship, the *Victory*, restrained enemy's van; in breaking through enemy's center ran afoul of the French ship *Redoutable* from whose mizzentop he was struck by a sharpshooter's musket ball that broke his spine; died as victory was completed with annihilation of enemy fleet; buried in St. Paul's Cathedral (1806).

**Nelson, John.** 1654–1734. New England fur trader and statesman; settled in Boston; led in demand for Andros's discharge as governor of Massachusetts (1689); captured by French (1691), imprisoned in France, released after Treaty of Ryswick (1697); addressed memorial to Board of Trade in London and repeatedly argued for English conquest of Canada and expulsion of French; influential factor in the cession of Nova Scotia and Newfoundland to England by the Treaty of Utrecht (1713).

**Nelson, Knute** (k′no͞ot). 1843–1923. Lawyer and legislator, b. Evanger, Norway; to U.S. as a child; settled in Wisconsin (1850–71) and Minnesota (from 1871); member, U.S. House of Representatives (1883–89); governor of Minnesota (1893–95); U.S. senator (1895–1923).

**Nelson, Nelson Ol′sen** (ōl′s'n). 1844–1922. Industrialist, b. in Norway; to U.S. (1847); manufacturer of building and plumbing supplies, St. Louis (from 1877); introduced profit-sharing plan in his business (1886); advocated general adoption of profit-sharing plans to reconcile conflicting interests of capital and labor.

**Nelson, Samuel.** 1792–1873. American jurist, b. Hebron, N.Y.; associate justice, N.Y. supreme court (1831–37), and chief justice (1837–45); associate justice, U.S. Supreme Court (1845–72).

**Nelson, Thomas.** 1780–1861. Scottish publisher; founder of firm of Thomas Nelson & Sons. His elder son, **William** (1816–1887), who entered the business (1835), improved Edinburgh, restoring Old Scottish Parliament House. His younger son, **Thomas** (1822–1892), established a London branch of the firm (1844), invented a rotary press (1850).

**Nelson, William.** 1711–1772. Virginia merchant and planter, b. near Yorktown, Va.; acting governor of Virginia (1770–71). His son **Thomas** (1738–1789) was active in pre-Revolutionary agitation; member of Continental Congress (1775–77) and signer of the Declaration of Independence; governor of Virginia (1781).

**Nelson, William Rockhill.** 1841–1915. American journalist, b. Fort Wayne, Ind.; founder and editor of Kansas City *Evening Star* (1880–1915).

**Ne′ma·nya** (nĕ′mä·nyä). *Serbian* **Ne′ma·nja** (-nyä). Name of a family of Serbian princes: **Stephen Nemanya** founded the Nemanyich dynasty in the latter half of the 12th century; the dynasty reached its height during the reign of **Stephen Dushan Nemanya IX** (1331–1355), and ended with the reign of **Nemanya X** (1355–1371), who was conquered by the Turks.

**Ne·me′si·us** (nē·mē′zhĭ·ŭs; -shĭ·ŭs). Christian philosopher of late 4th century; bishop of Emesa (Homs), Syria; author of treatise *On the Nature of Man.*

**Ne·mours′** (nē·mōōr′). Name of a ducal French family, created as a county by Charles V in latter part of 14th century; first held (c. 1415–1503) by the Armagnacs (branch of the house of Orléans); see ARMAGNAC. Gaston de Foix was created duke of Nemours (1505); see under FOIX. Second ducal house of Nemours held by a branch of the house of Savoy (1528–1659); its chief member was **Philippe de Sa′voie′** [sȧ′vwȧ′] (1490–1533); made count of Geneva (1510); made duke of Nemours (1528) by his nephew Francis I, to win his support. Of later house of Orléans was **Louis Charles Philippe Raphaël d'Or′lé′ans′** [dôr′lā′äN′] (1814–1896), Duke of Nemours; 2d son of King Louis Philippe; b. Paris; served in Algerian campaigns (1836–37, 1841); made general (1837); lived in England (1848–70) and in France (1870–86); expelled from France (1886) but returned later; died at Versailles.

**Ne·na′do·vić** (nĕ·nä′dō·vēt′y'; *Angl.* -vĭch), **Matija.** *Known as* **Pro′ta Ma·ti′ja** (prō′tä mä·tē′yä). 1777–1854. Serbian priest and patriot; one of the leaders of the Serbian insurrection (1804); represented Serbia at Congress of Vienna (1814–15).

**Nen·cio′ni** (nân·chō′nē), **Enrico.** 1837–1896. Italian literary critic and poet; translated works of Browning, Tennyson, Swinburne, etc.; wrote *Medaglioni* (1883), and *Studi di Letterature Straniere* (1897–98).

**Nen′ni·us** (nĕn′ĭ·ŭs). fl. 796 A.D. Welsh compiler of a British history in Latin, *Historia Britonum* (first printed 1691). See GEOFFREY OF MONMOUTH.

**Neper, John.** See John NAPIER.

**Nephtali.** See NAPHTALI.

**Nepomuk,** Saint **John of.** See JOHN OF NEPOMUK.

**Ne′pos** (nē′pŏs; nĕp′ŏs), **Cornelius.** fl. 1st century B.C. Roman historian; friend of Cicero; only extant work is *Vitae Excellentium Imperatorum,* a section of a larger work (*De Viris Illustribus*).

**Nepos, Gaius Duilius.** See DUILIUS.

**Nepos, Julius.** d. 480. Roman emperor in the West (474–475), the last but one; made emperor by Leo I, Byzantine ruler; deposed by Orestes, one of his generals (475), who placed his son Romulus Augustulus on the throne; killed in Dalmatia.

**Nep·veu′** (nē·vû′), **André.** See Luc DURTAIN.

**Nep·veu′** *or* **Ne·veu′** (nē·vû′), **Pierre.** *Known as* **Trin′-queau′** (trăN′kō′). d. about 1542. French architect; designer of several of the finest châteaux in the Loire valley, notably Amboise, Chenonceaux, and Chambord.

**Ne′ri** (nā′rē), San **Filippo de′.** *Angl.* Saint **Philip Neri.** 1515–1595. Italian priest; founder (1564) of the society Fathers of the Oratory, Rome. From musical services held in his oratory in Rome came name *oratorio* for one form of musical composition.

**Néricault, Philippe.** See DESTOUCHES.

**Neri Tanfucio.** See Renato FUCINI.

**Nernst** (nĕrnst), **Walther Hermann.** 1864–1941. German physicist and chemist; invented an electric incandescent lamp (Nernst lamp) using a comparatively weak current; did research on the theories of ions, chemical equilibrium, and solutions, and on the generation of current in the galvanic cell; introduced theorem (Nernst heat theorem) in thermodynamics concerning the energy change in a reaction; awarded 1920 Nobel prize for chemistry (1921).

**Ne′ro** (nē′rō; nēr′ō). *In full* **Nero Claudius Caesar Drusus Ger·man′i·cus** (jẽr·măn′ĭ·kŭs). *Originally* **Lucius Domitius A·he′no·bar′bus** (ȧ·hē′nō·bär′bŭs; ȧ·hĕn′ō-). 37–68 A.D. Roman emperor (54–68); son of Domitius Ahenobarbus, Roman consul, and Agrippina, daughter of Germanicus Caesar; b. at Antium in Latium; educated by Seneca and Burrus; adopted by his stepfather Emperor Claudius (50); m. first Octavia, daughter of Claudius (53). Made emperor by Agrippina, who had poisoned Claudius; caused death of Britannicus (55) and procured assassination of his mother (59); first few years of reign in general marked by wise conduct of public affairs, with Seneca and Burrus as advisers; private life profligate and dissipated; murdered Octavia and her sister Antonia; m. Poppaea Sabina (62) and later caused her death; accused of kindling fire (64) that destroyed a great part of Rome; instituted cruel persecutions of Christians; discovered plot against him (65) and brought about deaths of many Romans, including Seneca; visited Greece (67–68); competed for prizes at festivals; declared a public enemy by the Senate; committed suicide.

**Nero, Gaius Claudius.** Roman general and politician; consul (207 B.C.); joined with his colleague in the consulship, Marcus Livius Salinator (see LIVIUS SALINATOR), in defeating Hasdrubal in decisive battle of Metaurus (207).

**Nero, Tiberius Claudius.** d. 38 B.C.? Roman officer, supporter of Caesar and Antony; m. Livia Drusilla (who in 39 became wife of Octavianus); father of Tiberius (later emperor) and of Drusus Senior.

**Ner′ses** (nûr′sēz). Name borne by many patriarchs of Armenia, including notably: **Nerses the Great** (c. 310–374), patriarch (340–374); fought the Persians and resisted Emperor Valens's efforts to introduce Arianism into Armenia. **Nerses** (480–538); presided at Council of Tvin (537), where the break between the Armenian and Greek churches was consummated. **Nerses the Gracious** (1098–1173); labored for union of the Armenian and Greek churches and against the monophysite heresy.

**Nerses Lampronetsi.** *Angl.* **Nerses of Lam'bron** (lăm'brŏn). Bishop of Tarsus in the 12th century; sat in the Council of Tarsus (1178), where he advocated union of Armenians with Greeks; honored as a saint among Armenians; author of theological treatises, homilies, poems, and translations from Greek, Latin, and Syriac.

**Ne'ru·da** (nĕ'rŏŏ·dȧ). A family of musicians, including: **Jo'sef** (*Czech* yô'sĕf; *Ger.* yō'zĕf) **Neruda** (1807–1875), cathedral organist in Brünn, Moravia. His daughter **Wil'ma** (vĭl'mä) **Ma·ri'a** (mä·rē'ä) **Fran·zis'ka** (frän-tsĭs'kä) **Neruda** *or* **Nor'man–Neruda** [nŏŏr'mȧn-] (1839–1911), violin virtuoso; m. 1st (1864) the Swedish composer **Fredrik Vilhelm Ludvig Norman** (1831–1885), 2d (1888) Sir Charles Hallé (*q.v.*); on concert tours chiefly in Germany, England, Russia, and France; resident in London (1869–1900); teacher, Stern Conservatory, Berlin (from 1900).

**Neruda, Jan.** 1834–1891. Czech lyric poet, novelist, and journalist; author of *Cosmic Songs* (1878), *Ballads and Romances* (1883), novels and sketches, dramas, etc.

**Ne·ru'da** (nâ-rōō'thä), **Pablo.** *Orig. name* **Neftalí Ricardo Re'yes Ba·sual'to** (rā'yās bä·swäl'tō). 1904–1973. Chilean poet and diplomat. Ambassador to Mexico (1940–42), to France (1971–72). Awarded Nobel prize in literature (1971); wrote *Canto General* (1950), *Cantos Ceremoniales* (1962), etc.

**Ner'va** (nûr'vȧ), **Marcus Coc·ce'ius** (kŏk·sē'yŭs). 35 (or 30? or 32?)–98. Roman emperor (96–98), b. in Umbria; held offices of trust under Vespasian and Titus (71–81); consul with Domitian (90) but banished by him to Tarentum (93); as emperor, unable to repress excesses of Praetorian Guard; adopted Trajan as successor. His grandfather, **Nerva Cocceius** (d. 33), consul (22), was a celebrated jurist; friend of Emperor Tiberius.

**Ner'val'** (nĕr'vȧl'), **Gérard de.** *Pen name of* **Gérard La'bru'nie'** (lȧ'brü'nē'). 1808–1855. French writer; an eccentric who became insane near the end of his life; author of *Voyage en Orient* (1848–50), *Les Chimères* (verse), *Les Faux Sauniers* (1851), *Les Illuminés* (1852), *Les Filles de Feu* (containing the romance *Sylvie*, 1854), *La Bohème Galante* (1855); trans. Goethe's *Faust*.

**Ner'vi** (nĕr'vē), **Pier Luigi.** 1891–1979. Italian architect. Pioneer in the use of reinforced concrete.

**Nes'bit** (nĕz'bĭt), **Edith.** 1858–1924. English novelist, poet, and writer of juvenile books; m. (1880) **Hubert Bland** [blănd] (d. 1914), Socialist writer; with him helped found Fabian Society; collaborated with him in a novel *The Prophet's Mantle* (1885). Attained success with stories of the "Bastable Children" as *The Wouldbegoods* (1901), *New Treasure Seekers* (1904), and *The Five Children*. Her best-known novel, *The Red House* (1903); her last, *The Lark* (1922).

**Nesbitt, Louisa Cranstoun.** See NISBETT.

**Nes'field** (nĕs'fēld), **William Eden.** 1835–1888. English architect; author of *Sketches from France and Italy* (1862), which became a textbook of Victorian Gothicists.

**Nesiotes.** See CRITIUS.

**Nes·sel·ro'de** (nyĕs·sĭl·y'·rô'dyĕ; *Angl.* nĕs''l·rōd), Count **Karl Robert.** 1780–1862. Russian statesman; member of the Congress of Vienna (1814–15); Russian minister of foreign affairs (1816); vice-chancellor (1829); chancellor (1844); concluded Treaty of Paris after the Crimean War (1854–56).

**Ness'ler** (nĕs'lẽr), **Julius.** 1827–1905. German agricultural chemist; authority on winegrowing; known for development of analytical methods, the Nessler jar and Nessler reagent being named after him.

**Nessler, Viktor.** 1841–1890. German choral director and composer. Wrote operas *Fleurette* (1864), *Der Wilde Jäger* (1881), *Der Trompeter von Säckingen* (1884), etc.

**Nes'tlé** (*Eng.* nĕs'lē; *Fr.* nĕs'lā'), **Henri.** *Orig. surname* **Nest'le** (*Ger.* nĕst'lĕ). 1814–1890. German-born Swiss chocolate manufacturer, with original factory at Vevey, Switzerland; sold his interest in the business (1875).

**Nes'tor** (nĕs'tôr; -tẽr). 1056–1114. Russian monk and chronicler; in monastery at Kiev (from 1073); reputed author of first Russian chronicle of a national character.

**Nes·to'ri·us** (nĕs·tō'rĭ·ŭs). d. about 451 A.D. Patriarch of Constantinople (428–431); preached the doctrine (Nestorianism) that in Jesus Christ a divine person (the Logos) and a human person were joined in perfect harmony of action but not in the unity of a single individual; deposed for heresy by the Council of Ephesus (431) and banished to the Libyan desert. Nestorians spread widely in Persia, India, Mongolia, and China.

**Ne'swad·ba** (nĕ'svȧd·bȧ), **Joseph.** 1824–1876. Czech conductor and composer of the opera *Bluebeard*, of orchestral works, ballets, and songs.

**Neth'er·sole** (nĕth'ẽr·sōl), **Olga.** 1870–1951. English actress and manager; well known in America in *Camille*, *Carmen*, Clyde Fitch's *Sapho*, and as Paula in Pinero's *Second Mrs. Tanqueray;* created title role in Maeterlinck's *Mary Magdalene*, New York (1910).

**Net'scher** (nĕch'ẽr), **Caspar.** 1639–1684. Painter of small portraits and genre subjects, b. Heidelberg; resident at The Hague (from 1661). His sons **Theodor** (1661–1732) and **Constantijn** (1668–1723) were also portrait and genre painters.

**Net'tle·ship** (nĕt''l·shĭp), **Henry.** 1839–1893. English classical scholar; professor of Latin, Oxford (1878–93); completed and revised Conington's edition of Vergil (1883); published *Contributions to Latin Lexicography* (1889), etc. His brother **John Trivett** (1841–1902) was an animal painter. Another brother, **Richard Lewis** (1846–1892), philosopher, succeeded T. H. Green in teaching philosophy at Oxford; wrote *The Theory of Education in Plato's Republic* (1880).

**Net'tle·ton** (nĕt''l·tŭn), **Walter.** 1861–1936. American painter, b. New Haven, Conn.; esp. known for his Breton and his New England landscapes.

**Netto, Henrique Coelho.** See COELHO NETTO.

**Neu'bau'er** (noi'bou'ẽr), **A'dolf** (ä'dôlf). 1832–1907. English Orientalist, b. Hungary; studied medieval Jewish manuscripts in Bodleian Library, Oxford (1868–99).

**Neu'bur'ger** (noi'bŏŏr'gẽr), **Max.** 1868–1955. Austrian neurologist and historian of medicine; founded first institute for the history of medicine. His works include *Handbuch der Geschichte der Medizin* (with Julius Leopold Pagel; 3 vols., 1901–05) and *Geschichte der Medizin* (2 vols., 1906–10).

**Neu'en·dorff** (noi'ĕn·dôrf), **Adolph Heinrich Anton Magnus.** 1843–1897. Pianist, violinist, conductor, and composer, b. Hamburg, Ger.; to U.S. (1854); conductor, Metropolitan Opera House, New York (1897); composer of symphonies, overtures, cantatas, and comic operas.

**Neufchâteau, François de.** See Nicholas Louis FRANÇOIS.

**Neu'hof** (noi'hōf), Baron **Theodor von.** 1686?–1756. German adventurer; crowned as Theodore I, King of Corsica (1736); driven out by the Genoese (1738).

**Neu'huys** (nû'hois), **Albert.** 1844–1914. Dutch historical, portrait, and genre painter.

**Neu'komm** (noi'kôm), **Sigismund von.** 1778–1858. Austrian composer, organist, pianist, and orchestra leader; pupil (1798 ff.) of Joseph Haydn in Vienna, and virtually his adopted son. To Paris (1809); became friend of Grétry, Cherubini; ennobled and made chevalier of the Legion of Honor (1815) for his requiem in honor of Louis XVI. To Rio de Janeiro (1816); Kapellmeister to Dom Pedro (until 1821). Returned to Europe and rejoined Talleyrand. Author of church music, oratorios, songs, operas, organ pieces, piano music.

**Neu′mann** (noi′män), **Alfred.** 1895–1952. German author of historical novels, as *The Devil* (1926; awarded Kleist prize), *The Rebels* (1928) and its sequel, *Guerra* (1929), *The Hero* (1930), *Mirror of Fools* (1932), of novelettes and short stories, dramas, a biography of Musset (1925), translations of Molière, Musset, and Lamartine, essays, poems, etc.

**Neumann, An′ge·lo** (äng′gȧ·lō). 1838–1910. Austrian theater director and opera singer; tenor with Vienna Royal Opera (1862–76); as codirector of Leipzig Stadttheater (1876), produced Wagner's *Nibelungen* for first time outside Bayreuth; theater director in Prague (1885–1910). His son **Karl Eugen** (1865–1915) translated Buddhist works into German.

**Neumann, Balthasar.** 1687–1753. German architect, master of the German baroque school; designed archbishop's residence at Würzburg with its staircase (1719–44), summer castle at Werneck (1731–37), the abbey church at Neresheim (1745–92), etc.

**Neumann, Carl.** 1860–1934. German author of works on Byzantine history, on history of Italian, German, and Dutch art, and esp. on Rembrandt.

**Neumann, Franz Ernst.** 1798–1895. German physicist and mineralogist; formulated law of electromagnetic induction from results of experiments of Faraday and Henry; worked on reflection, refraction, and double refraction of light, and on conduction of heat. His son **Carl Gottfried** (1832–1925) was also a mathematician; developed the potential theory; reputed founder of logarithmic potentials; his work was continued by his nephew **Ernst Richard** (1875– ).

**Neumann, Isidor von.** 1832–1906. Austrian dermatologist; professor in Vienna.

**Neumann, John von.** 1903–1957. American mathematician, b. in Hungary. With Inst. for Advanced Study, Princeton, N.J. (1933–45). Fermi Award (1956) for work on theory, design, and construction of computers.

**Neumann, Karl Eugen.** See under Angelo NEUMANN.

**Neumann, Karl Friedrich.** 1793–1870. German Orientalist and historian; to China (1830–31), where he collected Chinese books and manuscripts; professor of Armenian and Chinese, Munich (1833–52; removed because of his liberal political views); resident in Berlin (from 1863). Author of histories of the British empire in Asia (1857), of the United States (1863–66), etc.

**Neumann, Karl Johannes.** 1857–1917. German classical scholar and historian.

**Neumann, Robert.** 1897– . Austrian novelist, poet, and playwright; author of *Flood* (1929), *Mammon*, *Zaharoff*, *The Queen's Doctor*, *A Woman Screamed*, *Scene in Passing* (1942), *Mr. Tibbs Passes Through* (1943).

**Neu′mark** (noi′märk), **Georg.** 1621–1681. German poet, librarian, and musician; author of the song *Wer Nur den Lieben Gott Lässt Walten*, etc.

**Neu′may′er** (noi′mī′ẽr), **Georg von.** 1826–1909. German meteorologist and hydrographer; founder (1857) and director (until 1864) of observatory in Melbourne, Australia; director of German Marine Observatory, Hamburg (1876–1903); active in organizing polar expeditions, esp. to the South Pole.

**Neu′mei′ster** (noi′mī′stẽr), **Erdmann.** 1671–1756. German Lutheran theologian and hymn writer; opponent of pietism; author of the hymns *Jesus Nimmt die Sünder an* and *Jesu, Grosser Wunderstern*, the text for several of Bach's cantatas, a literary history of Germany (1695).

**Neu′rath** (noi′rät), Baron **Konstantin von.** 1873–1956. German diplomat; ambassador in Constantinople (1914); minister to Denmark (1919); ambassador to Italy (1922), Britain (1930–32); minister of foreign affairs (1932–38); "protector" for Bohemia and Moravia (1939–41); sentenced to 15 years imprisonment as war criminal.

**Neu′reu′ther** (noi′roi′tẽr), **Eugen Napoleon.** 1806–1882. German painter, etcher, and illustrator; assisted Cornelius in the decorations of the Glyptothek, Munich; art director, Nymphenburg royal porcelain manufactory (1848–56). His works include illustrations, largely marginal drawings, for German legends, ballads, and romances, notably those of Goethe (1829–40), woodcut designs for Herder's *Cid* (1838), oil paintings, etc. His brother **Gottfried von Neureuther** (1811–1887) was an architect in the Italian Renaissance style.

**Neu′ville′** (nû′vēl′), **Alphonse Marie de.** 1836–1885. French battle painter.

**Neu·wied′** (noi·vēt′), Prince **Maximilian Alexander Philipp von.** 1782–1867. German explorer and naturalist in Brazil (1815–17) and western North America (1833).

**Ne·va′da** (nĕ·vä′dȧ), **Emma.** *Stage name of* **Emma Wix′om** (wĭk′sŭm). 1862–1940. American operatic soprano, b. at Austin, Nevada; m. Dr. Raymond Palmer (1885); resident in Paris.

**Ne·vers′** (nē·vâr′). Name of a county, from the town in north central France, originating in the 10th century (see LOUIS, Flemish counts, page 919); made a dukedom (1538) by Francis I and passed by marriage to the family of Gonzaga (*q.v.*), the ducal house of Mantua.

**Neveu, Pierre.** See NEPVEU.

**Ne·veux′** (nē·vû′), **Pol Louis.** 1865–1939. French essayist and critic; author of *Golo*, *Roman de Compagne*, *Guy de Maupassant*, *Reims et la Champagne*, etc.

**Nev′ille** *or* **Nev′ill** (nĕv′'l; -ĭl). Family name of an English noble house descended from Dolfin, receiver of a grant of territory in Durham (1131), which was held by the family four centuries with Raby as its seat and, after union with Bulmer family, with Brancepeth as second seat. **Ralph de Neville** (1291?–1367), 4th Baron Neville, participated in victory of Neville's Cross (1346) and capture of David Bruce; governor of Berwick (1355). His son **John** (d. 1388), 5th baron, fought in French wars of Edward III (1345, 1349, 1360); admiral of fleet (1370); as lieutenant of king in Aquitaine (1378) recovered towns, castles, and forts; warden of Scottish border (after 1381).

*Earls of West′mor·land* (wĕs(t)′mẽr·lănd): Family became closely connected with houses of Lancaster and York by marriages with heiresses. **Ralph Neville** (1364–1425), 6th Baron Neville, son of 5th baron, was created 1st earl of Westmorland (1397); warden of Scottish marches; m. (as 2d wife) a daughter of John of Gaunt; took part against Richard II (1399) and made marshal of England by Henry IV; warden of west marches after battle of Shrewsbury and death of Hotspur (1403); put down a rebellion by Northumberland, Mowbray, and Archbishop Scrope (1405); one of regents for Henry V's son. **Charles Neville** (1543–1601), 6th Earl of Westmorland, joined Northumberland in abortive attempt to release Mary, Queen of Scots (1569); was attainted (1571) and lost estates.

*Earls of Salis′bur·y* (sôlz′bẽr·ĭ; -brĭ): **Richard Neville** (1400–1460), 1st Earl of Salisbury; son of 1st Earl of Westmorland; m. (1425) Alice, dau. of Thomas de Montacute (*q.v.*); warden of both marches (1434); chancellor during protectorate of Richard Plantagenet, 3d Duke of York (1454–55); fled to France with York on their defeat at Ludford; returned (1460) with his son the earl of Warwick (see below); became chamberlain; captured after battle of Wakefield and murdered; succeeded by his son, who became Warwick the Kingmaker.

*Earl of War'wick* (wŏr'ĭk): **Richard Neville** (1428–1471), Earl of Warwick (in right of his wife) and of Salisbury (by succession after his father, 1st earl); known as "the Kingmaker"; aided Yorkists in War of the Roses to win battle of St. Albans (1455); was rewarded with captaincy of Calais (1456); gained in stature as naval commander by capture of three carracks of Spain and Genoa (1459); aided the Yorkists to victory at Northampton (1460) and took Henry VI captive; opposed duke of York's claim to throne till the latter's death in Lancastrian success at Wakefield (1460); defeated by Queen Margaret at 2d battle of St. Albans (1461); joined Edward, duke of York's son, in march on London and victory at Towton (1461) and proclaimed him Edward IV, becoming himself virtual ruler of England during first three years of Edward's reign; displaced during mission to France by Woodville (1467), plotted revenge; married his daughter to George, Duke of Clarence (1469); instigated revolt of Yorkshire rebel known as Robin of Redesdale (1469), forced Edward IV to flee to Flanders; joined Lancastrians, and aided Queen Margaret in invasion of England (1470–71); in meantime placed Henry VI on throne (1470); defeated and slain by Edward IV's forces at Barnet (1471). Subject of Bulwer-Lytton's historical novel *The Last of the Barons* (1843).

*Earl of North·um'ber·land* (nôr·thŭm'bẽr·lănd): **John Neville** (d. 1471), Marquis of Mon'ta·gu (mŏn'tȧ·gū; mŭn'-) and Earl of Northumberland; son of Richard, 1st Earl of Salisbury; took part in Yorkist battles (1453, 1457); imprisoned after 2d battle of St. Albans but liberated by Edward IV after battle of Towton (1461); defeated Lancastrians at Hexham (1464); joined Lancastrians upon restoration (1469) to Percy of earldom of Northumberland, which had been promised to him; killed at Barnet (1471), fighting on Lancastrian side.

The youngest son of Richard, 1st Earl of Salisbury, **George Neville** (1433?–1476), M.A., Oxon. (1452), bishop of Exeter (1458), chancellor of England (1460–67), archbishop of York (1464), chancellor to Henry VI (1470–71); surrendered himself and Henry VI to Edward IV after battle of Barnet (1471); imprisoned in France (till 1475).

**Neville, Wendell Cushing.** 1870–1930. American marine officer, b. Portsmouth, Va.; grad. U.S.N.A., Annapolis (1890); served in the Aisne-Marne offensive, battle of Château-Thierry, battle of Belleau Wood, and the St.-Mihiel and Meuse-Argonne offensives in the World War; major general (1923); commandant, U.S. Marine Corps (1929–30).

**Nev'in** (nĕv'ĭn), **Ethelbert Woodbridge.** 1862–1901. American composer, b. Edgeworth, Pa.; debut as pianist, Pittsburgh (Dec. 10, 1886); excelled in lyrical music, composing seventy songs, published in *Sketch Book* (1888), *Water Scenes* (1891), *In Arcady* (1892), *May in Tuscany* (1896), *A Day in Venice* (1898). Best-known compositions, *Narcissus* and *The Rosary.* His brother **Arthur Finley** (1871–1943), also a composer; author of American Indian opera *Poia* (1910) and *Daughter of the Forest* (1918), and piano and orchestral works.

**Nevin, George Balch** (bôlsh). 1859–1933. American baritone choir singer and composer of songs and church music, b. Shippensburg, Pa.; author of cantatas, anthems, and songs (including *It was a Lover and his Lass* and *O, Little Mother of Mine*).

**Nevin, John Williamson.** 1803–1886. American theologian, b. in Franklin County, Pa.; professor of Biblical literature, Western Theol. Sem., Allegheny, Pa. (1830–40); German Reformed Church Seminary at Mercersburg, Pa. (1840–53); acting president, Marshall Coll. (1841–53); president, Franklin and Marshall Coll. (1866–76). His teachings with regard to sacraments, mystical union, liturgy, etc., became basis of so-called Mercersburg theology. See F. A. RAUCH.

**Nev'ins** (nĕv'ĭnz), **Allan.** 1890–1971. American historian, b. Camp Point, Ill.; on editorial staff, New York *Evening Post* (1913–23), also *The Nation*, New York (1913–18), New York *World* (1925–31); professor of American history, Columbia (1931–58); author of books on American history, and *Grover Cleveland—A Study in Courage* (1932; awarded Pulitzer prize), *Hamilton Fish—The Inner History of the Grant Administration* (1936; Pulitzer prize), *The Gateway to History* (1938), etc.; editor of diaries of Philip Hone (1927), J. Q. Adams (1928), Polk (1929), etc.

**Nev'in·son** (nĕv'ĭn·s'n), **Henry Woodd.** 1856–1941. English newspaper correspondent and essayist; correspondent of London *Daily Chronicle* during Greek and Turkish war (1897) and other wars; exposed Portuguese slave trade in Angola in *A Modern Slavery* (1906); official correspondent at Dardanelles (1915), where he was wounded; writer for *Nation* (1907–23); Manchester *Guardian* correspondent at international conferences; president of London P.E.N. club (1938). Author of *Essays in Freedom* (1909), *Essays in Rebellion* (1913), *Changes and Chances* (an autobiography, 1923), *Between the Wars* (1936), *Films of Time: Twelve Fantasies* (1939).

**Nevski.** See ALEXANDER NEVSKI.

**New** (nū), **Harry Stewart.** 1858–1937. American journalist and politician, b. Indianapolis, Ind.; on staff of Indianapolis *Journal* (1878–1903); U.S. senator from Indiana (1917–23); U.S. postmaster general (1923–29).

**New'all** (nū'ăl), **Cyril Louis Norton.** Baron **Newall of Clifton-upon-Dunsmoor.** 1886–1963. British administrator; served in World War I (1914–18); deputy chief of the air staff (1926–31), chief (1937–40); marshal of Royal Air Force (1940); governor general of New Zealand (1941–46).

**Newark,** Lord. See LESLIE family.

**New'ber'ry** (nū'bĕr'ĭ; -bẽr·ĭ), **John Strong.** 1822–1892. American geologist, b. Windsor, Conn.; professor, School of Mines, Columbia U., New York (1866–92); author of *The Paleozoic Fishes of North America* (1889).

**Newberry, Percy Edward.** 1869–1949. English Egyptologist; in charge, archaeological survey of Egypt (1890); made survey of necropolis at Thebes (1895–1901); collaborated with Flinders Petrie, Howard Carter, and others.

**Newberry, Truman Handy.** 1864–1945. American businessman and politician, b. Detroit, Mich.; in railway business, steel business, and banking, Detroit (1885–1905); assistant secretary, U.S. navy (1905–08); secretary, U.S. navy (1908–09); U.S. senator from Michigan (1919–22); tried and convicted in Michigan courts for corruption in obtaining the nomination, but case dismissed in U.S. Supreme Court; exonerated by U.S. Senate committee on privileges and elections (1922); resigned (Nov., 1922).

**New'ber·y** (nū'bẽr·ĭ), **John.** 1713–1767. English publisher; set up bookshop and publishing house in St. Paul's Churchyard (1744); started newspapers and had among contributors Goldsmith and Dr. Johnson; published children's books, including *Giles Gingerbread, Goody Two Shoes, Tommy Trip;* published *Mother Goose's Nursery Rhymes* (c. 1760). He is portrayed in the *Vicar of Wakefield.* Commemorated by the "Newbery Medal," annually awarded since 1921 for most distinguished contribution to literature for children from the pen of an American writer.

**New'bold** (nū'bōld), **Charles.** American inventor, of Burlington, N.J., who patented (1797) first American cast-iron plow.

**Newbold, William Romaine.** 1865–1926. American philosopher and psychologist, b. Wilmington, Del.; author of *The Cipher of Roger Bacon* (pub. 1928).

**New'bolt** (nū'bōlt), Sir **Henry John.** 1862–1938. English poet and man of letters; practiced law (1887–99); editor of *Monthly Review* (1900–05). His first book, *Taken from the Enemy*, a historical novel (1892); second, *Mordred*, a tragedy in blank verse (1895); won literary reputation with ballads *Admirals All* (1897), followed by *The Island Race* (1898), *The Sailing of the Long-Ships* (1902), *Songs of the Sea* (stirring patriotic verse; 1904); published two novels, *The Old Country* (1906), *The New June* (1909). Professor of poetry, Oxford (1911–21). Controller of wireless and cables during the World War (1917–18). Wrote a *Naval History of the Great War* (1920) and vol. iv (1928) of the cumulative *Naval Operations*, official history of the British navy. Also wrote *Drake's Drum and Other Sea Songs* (1914), *Studies Green and Gray* (essays, 1926), *The Book of the Thin Red Line* (1915).

**Newburgh, William of.** See WILLIAM OF NEWBURGH.

**New'cas'tle** (nū'kȧs''l; *locally, in Northumberland,* nū̇·kăs''l), Duke of. Title in the British peerage (four creations) borne by members of Cavendish, Holles, Pelham, and Clinton families, including:

**William Cavendish** (1592–1676), Duke of Newcastle (cr. 1665), Royalist leader and patron of letters; nephew of 1st earl of Devonshire (see CAVENDISH family); educ. Cambridge; entertained James I (1619) and Charles I (1633) at Welbeck, Nottinghamshire; governor of prince of Wales (1638); maintained troops at own expense in aid of king in Scottish war (1639) and for invasion of Yorkshire (1642); raised siege of Hull (1643); after battle of Marston Moor (1644), engaged against his advice, resided abroad until Restoration; regained part of estates, burdened with debts on account of expenditures of nearly £1,000,000 for royal cause; devoted himself to training horses and wrote and translated works on manège. Author of comedies, including *The Humorous Lovers* and *The Triumphant Widow* (1677); patron of Ben Jonson, Shirley, Davenant, Dryden, and others. His second wife (m. 1645), **Margaret,** *nee* **Lu'cas** [lū'kăs] (1624?–1674), wrote (1653–68) several folio volumes of poems, letters, plays, and an autobiography.

**Thomas Pel'ham–Hol'les** [pĕl'ăm·hŏl'ĭs] (1693–1768), 1st Duke of Newcastle (cr. 1715), statesman; son of Sir Thomas Pelham, 1st Baron Pelham; succeeded to estates of his maternal uncle **John Holles** (1662–1711; duke of Newcastle; lord privy seal 1705–11). Supported Whigs and Walpole, who chose him secretary of state (1724–54); succeeded his brother Henry Pelham (*q.v.*) as prime minister (1754–56); returned as prime minister (1757–62), with William Pitt as leader in House of Commons and director of foreign affairs and the war; as a statesman, credited with holding Whig party together despite George III's opposition.

**Henry Pelham Fiennes** (fīnz) **Pelham Clin'ton** [klĭn'-t'n; -tŭn] (1811–1864), 5th Duke of Newcastle (cr. 1756), statesman; B.A., Oxon. (1832); secretary for war and the colonies (1852–54); secretary for war (1854–55); resigned on account of sufferings of army at Sevastopol; colonial secretary (1859–64); accompanied prince of Wales on visit to Canada (1860).

**New'comb** (nū'kŭm), **Simon.** 1835–1909. Astronomer, b. Wallace, Nova Scotia; ran away from home (1853); taught country school in Maryland; computer, Nautical Almanac Office (1857–77); superintendent, American Ephemeris and Nautical Almanac (1877–97); professor of mathematics, U.S. navy (1861–97), stationed at the Naval Observatory; professor of mathematics and astronomy, Johns Hopkins U. (1884–94; 1898–1900). In addition to many contributions to scientific journals, he wrote *Popular Astronomy* (1878), *The Stars* (1901), *Astronomy for Everybody* (1902), *Reminiscences of an Astronomer* (1903), and some books on economics. Elected to American Hall of Fame (1935).

**New'combe** (nū'kŭm), **Edmund Leslie.** 1859–1931. Canadian jurist, b. at Cornwallis, Nova Scotia; judge, Canadian supreme court (1924); author of a handbook on the British North America acts.

**New'co·men** (nū'kō·mĕn; nū̇·kŭm'ĕn), **Matthew.** 1610?–1669. See SMECTYMNUUS.

**Newcomen, Thomas.** 1663–1729. English blacksmith, inventor of an atmospheric steam engine; in association with John Calley (or Cawley), invented (1705) an engine in which steam admitted to a cylinder was condensed by a jet of cold water and the piston driven by atmospheric pressure; entered partnership with Thomas Savery, whose primitive steam engine for pumping water from mines (patented 1698) he improved and built into a practical working engine in common use in collieries (1725). See also James WATT.

**New'di·gate** (nū'dĭ·gĭt; -gāt), Sir **Roger.** 1719–1806. English antiquary; collected ancient marbles, vases, casts of statues; founded at Oxford the Newdigate prize of 21 guineas for English verse (1805).

**New'ell** (nū'ĕl), **Edward Theodore.** 1886–1941. American numismatist, b. Kenosha, Wis.; author of treatises on numismatics, esp. on ancient coins.

**Newell, Frederick Haynes.** 1862–1932. American civil engineer, b. Bradford, Pa.; hydraulic engineer, U.S. Geological Survey (1888–1902); chief engineer, U.S. Reclamation Service (1902–14); head, civil engineering department, U. of Illinois (1915–20); author of works on water supply and irrigation engineering.

**Newell, Peter Sheaf Hersey.** 1862–1924. American cartoonist and illustrator, b. near Bushnell, Ill.; contributor of comics and illustrations to *Harper's Weekly* and *Harper's Bazaar;* illustrator of John Kendrick Bangs's *A House-Boat on the Styx* (1896), *The Pursuit of the House-Boat* (1897), and Lewis Carroll's *Alice in Wonderland* (1901); creator of illustrated books for children, as *Topsys and Turvys* (1893), *Jungle Jangle* (1909), etc.

**Newell, Robert Henry.** *Pseudonym* **Orpheus C. Kerr** (kûr). 1836–1901. American journalist and humorist, b. New York City; author of *The Orpheus C. Kerr Papers* (3 vols., 1862–65), *The Palace Beautiful and Other Poems* (1865), *There Was Once a Man* (1884).

**New'land** (nū'lănd), **Abraham.** 1730–1807. English banker; chief cashier of Bank of England (from 1782), whose signature on bank notes gave them the nickname of "Abraham Newlands."

**New'lands** (nū'lăndz), **Francis Griffith.** 1848–1917. American legislator, b. Natchez, Miss.; to Nevada (1888); member, U.S. House of Representatives (1893–1903), U.S. Senate (1903–17); associated with the Newlands Act (1913), providing for mediation and conciliation in labor disputes.

**New'man** (nū'măn), **Allen George.** 1875–1940. American sculptor, b. New York City; among his sculptures are the *Henry Hudson Monument* in New York City, *Joel Chandler Harris Monument* in Atlanta, Ga.

**Newman, Ernest.** 1868–1959. English music critic; author of musical studies of Wagner, Elgar, Hugo Wolf, Richard Strauss.

**Newman, Francis William.** 1805–1897. English scholar

and man of letters; bro. of Cardinal Newman; lost sympathy with Anglicanism and became nonconformist; unsectarian missionary to Baghdad for three years; classical tutor and professor (1834–69); took part in religious controversy on the rationalistic side, opposed to his brother; published anonymously *History of the Hebrew Monarchy* (1847), *The Soul* (1849), *Phases of Faith* (1850); joined Unitarian association (1876). Author of educational, social, and political works, including translations of *Odes of Horace* into "unrhymed meter," *Handbook of Modern Arabic* (1866), and of a much-criticized *Early History of Cardinal Newman* (1891).

**Newman,** Sir **George**. 1870–1948. British medical officer; chief medical officer, ministry of health (1919–35); author of *Bacteriology and the Public Health, Outline of the Practice of Preventive Medicine* (1919), *Towards a Healthier Britain* (1939), etc.

**Newman, Horatio Hackett**. 1875–1957. American zoologist, b. near Seale, Ala.; author of *The Biology of Twins* (1917), *Readings in Evolution, Genetics, and Eugenics* (1921), *Evolution Yesterday and Today* (1932), etc.

**Newman,** Cardinal **John Henry**. 1801–1890. English theologian; Anglican leader of the Oxford movement and later Roman Catholic cardinal; B.A., Oxon. (1820); elected fellow (1822) and tutor (1826–32) of Oriel Coll., where he was associated with Edward Pusey and John Keble, and later R. H. Froude; vicar of the university church (1828–43); wrote *Lead, Kindly Light* (1833) on boat from Palermo to Marseilles, and in Rome, other poems making up *Lyra Apostolica* (pub. 1834); acknowledged leader of the Tractarian, or Oxford, movement; published *The Arians of the Fourth Century* (1833) and contributed to *Tracts for the Times* (from 1833), especially the fateful *Tract XC* (1841), opposing religious liberalism, urging Anglican reaffirmation of the doctrine of apostolical succession, maintaining that the Thirty-nine Articles were opposed only to abuses, not to Roman Catholic doctrine; edited *British Critic* (1833–41). After three years of seclusion, retracted all criticisms of Roman Catholicism, wrote the *Essay on Development of Christian Doctrine* (1845), and became a Roman Catholic (1845); ordained priest in Rome (1847); established in Birmingham the Congregation of the Oratory (1847), English branch of the brotherhood of St. Philip Neri; replied to the No-Popery agitation with *Lectures on the Present Position of Roman Catholics* (1851). Rector of Dublin Catholic U. (1851–58); delivered lectures which were revised and published as *The Idea of a University Defined* (1873), maintaining the duty of a university to be the training of the mind, rather than diffusion of useful knowledge; replied to Charles Kingsley's charge of Roman Catholic indifference to truthfulness, in *Apologia pro Vita Sua* (1864), an exposition of his spiritual history, recognized as a literary masterpiece. On election (1877) honorary fellow of Trinity Coll., revisited Oxford after absence of 32 years. On the side of the Inopportunists, opposed pronouncement of pope's personal infallibility as likely to alienate Anglicans; in reply to Gladstone's accusation, affirmed belief in papal infallibility and bitterly opposed ultramontanes. Created, by Pope Leo XIII, cardinal of St. George in Velabro (1879), and allowed to live in England. Author of *The Dream of Gerontius* (a dramatic monologue in verse of a soul's withdrawal from the body; 1866), *Verses on Various Occasions* (1874), *The Grammar of Assent* (on the philosophy of faith; 1870); two religious novels, *Loss and Gain* (1848) and *Callista* (1856); and various volumes of sermons.

**New'march** (nū'märch), **William**. 1820–1882. English banker, economist, and statistician; author of *The New Supplies of Gold* (1853) and, with Thomas Tooke, *A History of Prices* (vols. V and VI, 1857).

**Newnes** (nūnz), Sir **George**. 1851–1910. English magazine publisher; founded *Strand Magazine* (1891), in which first appeared Sherlock Holmes stories; a Gladstonian Liberal M.P., started *Westminster Gazette* as Liberal organ (1893); fitted out a Norwegian south polar expedition (1898).

**New'port** (nū'pōrt), **Christopher**. d. 1617. English mariner; in service of Virginia Company (1606–11), taking over colonists for settlement at Jamestown, and making trips to provision them.

**New'ton** (nū't'n), **Alfred**. 1829–1907. English zoologist; first professor of zoology and comparative anatomy, Cambridge (from 1866); author of *Dictionary of Birds* (1893–96), etc.

**Newton, Alfred Edward**. 1863–1940. American bibliophile, b. Philadelphia; in electrical manufacturing business (1890–1931); author of *The Amenities of Book-Collecting and Kindred Affections* (1918), *Doctor Johnson* (a play, 1923), *The Greatest Book in the World...* (1925), *End Papers* (1933), etc. Known as an authority on Samuel Johnson.

**Newton,** Sir **Charles Thomas**. 1816–1894. English archaeologist; superintended excavations at Bodrum, discovered site of ancient Halicarnassus, and recovered chief remains of the mausoleum (1854–55); keeper of Greek and Roman antiquities, British Museum (1861–85).

**Newton, Gilbert Stuart**. 1794–1835. British portrait and genre painter, b. in Nova Scotia; nephew of Gilbert Stuart.

**Newton, Hubert Anson**. 1830–1896. American mathematician, b. Sherburne, N.Y.; grad. Yale (1850); professor of mathematics, Yale (1853–96); contributor to technical journals; editor of mathematical and astronomical definitions for *Webster's International Dictionary* (1890).

**Newton,** Sir **Isaac**. 1642–1727. English natural philosopher and mathematician, b. Woolsthorpe near Grantham, Lincolnshire; B.A., Cantab. (1665); professor (1669–1701); showed the usefulness of the binomial theorem; credited with invention of differential calculus (1665) and integral calculus (1666); conceived idea of universal gravitation (set forth in his *Principia*, first published by Halley in 1687) after seeing apple fall in his garden (1665), according to Voltaire, who is reputed to have had it from Newton's stepniece; deduced from Kepler's third law that the force between the earth and the moon must be inversely proportional to the square of the distance between them (1665), being able later (c. 1685) to show by calculation that the force which he had deduced corresponded to fact. Studied light and color; read his *New Theory about Light and Colours* to the Royal Society (1672); originated the emission, or corpuscular, theory of light; constructed reflecting telescope (1668); summed up optical researches in *Optics* (1704). Warden of the mint (1696), master (1699); M.P. (1689; 1701–02); president of the Royal Society (1703–27). Cf. G. W. von LEIBNITZ.

**Newton, John**. 1622–1678. English mathematician and astronomer.

**Newton, John**. 1725–1807. English clergyman; impressed on board a man-of-war, made midshipman, deserted; spent four years in African slave trade; tide surveyor at Liverpool (1755–60); curate of Olney; intimate friend of Cowper and joint producer of the *Olney Hymns* (1779), including his "Glorious things of thee are spoken" and "One there is above all others." Author of *Cardiphonia* (1781).

**Newton, John.** 1823–1895. American army officer and engineer; grad. U.S.M.A., West Point (1842); served through Civil War, at Antietam, Fredericksburg, Chancellorsville, Gettysburg, and in the Atlanta campaign; brevetted major general; brigadier general, U.S. army, chief of engineers (1884–86; retired); president, Panama Railroad Co. (1888–95).

**Newton, Joseph Fort.** 1878–1950. American clergyman, b. Decatur, Tex.; ordained in Baptist ministry (1893); pastor, nonsectarian churches in London, Eng. (1916–19), New York City (1919–25), Philadelphia (1925–35); author of *Abraham Lincoln* (1910), *Lincoln and Herndon* (1910).

**Newton, Richard.** 1812–1887. Protestant Episcopal clergyman, b. Liverpool, Eng.; to U.S. (1824); grad. U. of Pennsylvania; rector in Philadelphia (from 1840); especially successful in his sermons for children. His two sons, **Richard Heber** (1840–1914) and **William Wilberforce** (1843–1914), were also Protestant Episcopal clergymen.

**Nex'ö** (nĭk'sû), **Martin An'der·sen** (än'ēr·s'n). 1869–1954. Danish novelist of German descent; champion of working class; author of *Pelle the Conqueror* (autobiographical social novel of Danish labor movement; 4 vols., 1906–10), *Ditte* (novel about a servant girl; 5 vols., 1917–22), *In God's Land* (1929), and novelettes chiefly about proletariat and peasant classes.

**Ney** (nī), **E·li'sa·bet** (å·lē'zä·bĕt). 1833–1907. Sculptor, b. Münster, Westphalia; m. Edmund Duncan Montgomery (1863); to U.S. (1870); settled in Texas. Among her works: busts of Schopenhauer, Garibaldi, Bismarck, Stephen F. Austin, Samuel Houston; the Albert Sidney Johnston Memorial, at Austin, Tex.; and the heroic figure *Prometheus Bound.*

**Ney** (nā), **Michel.** Duc **d'El'ching·en** (dĕl'kĭng·ĕn). Prince **de La Mos'ko'va'** (dē là môs'kô'vá'). 1769–1815. French soldier in the Revolutionary and Napoleonic armies; commanded army on the Rhine (1799); created marshal of France (1804); won victory of Elchingen (Oct. 14, 1805); created duc d'Elchingen; engaged at Jena (1806), Eylau and Friedland (1807), in Spain (1808–11), at Borodino (1812); created prince de La Moskova; commanded rear guard in retreat from Russia (1812); engaged at Lützen, Bautzen, and Leipzig (1813), and the campaign for the defense of France (1814); created peer by Louis XVIII at the Restoration, but rallied to Napoleon during the Hundred Days; commanded the Old Guard at Waterloo (June 18, 1815); tried and condemned for treason by the Chamber of Peers; shot (Dec. 7, 1815). Three of Marshal Ney's sons rose to be officers in the French army, **Napoléon Joseph** (1803–1857), Prince de La Moskova, **Michel Louis Félix** (1804–1854), Duc d'Elchingen, **Napoléon Henri Edgar** (1812–1882), Prince de La Moskova; and two grandsons also served in the army, **Michel Aloys Ney** (1835–1881), Duc d'Elchingen, who served in the campaign in Mexico (1863) and was promoted general (1875), and **Napoléon Joseph Paul Ney** (1849–1900), who served in defense of Paris (1870–71) and in the colonial armies.

**Ngag'–Wang' Lob'sang'** (ngäg'wäng' lôb'säng'). 1617–1682. Fifth dalai lama of Tibet; grand lama of the Yellow Hat order, a religious sect; established at Lhasa by the ruling Mongol prince (1640) as the dalai lama; reputed to have inaugurated the doctrine of the perpetual incarnation of the lama.

**Ngag–Wang Lobsang Thub'den' Gya'–Tsho'** (tŏŏb'dĕn' gyä'chō'). 1876–1933. Thirteenth dalai lama and head of the Tibetan government (1893–1933); chosen in infancy; reared for his high office in a lamasery; spiritual ruler over 10,000,000 Lamaists in central Asia; forced to wander in Mongolia and India (1904–12) when driven out of Lhasa by expedition of Indian government under Sir Francis Younghusband; after the Chinese Revolution (1912), restored to power as Tibetans claimed their independence; drove out all remaining Chinese (1917, 1920); often gave aid to British explorers in their expeditions to Mt. Everest.

**Ng Poon Chew** (*Pekingese pron.* wōō' pän' jou'). 1866–1931. Presbyterian clergyman and editor, b. in South China; to U.S. (1881); in ministry (1892–99); founder and editor of *Chinese Western Daily* (*Chung Sai Yat Po*), first Chinese daily newspaper published in U.S. (1900–31).

**Nguyen.** Name of a dynasty in Annam (1801– ), founded by Nguyen-Anh, better known as Gialong (*q.v.*); through French help, it acquired control over Annam, Tonkin, and Cochin China.

**Niall.** King of Ireland. See O'NEILL family.

**Nibhapetre Mentuhotep** and **Nibhepetre Mentuhotep.** = MENTUHOTEP II and IV.

**Nib'lack** (nĭb'lăk), **Albert Parker.** 1859–1929. American naval officer, b. Vincennes, Ind.; grad. U.S.N.A., Annapolis (1880); commanded section of Atlantic fleet based on Gibraltar (1917–18), and in Eastern Mediterranean (1919); rear admiral (1918–23; retired).

**Nib'lo** (nĭb'lō), **William.** 1789–1878. Proprietor (1829–61) of Niblo's Garden, a combined coffeehouse and theater in New York; b. in Ireland; to U.S. as a boy.

**Ni·can'der** (nī·kăn'dēr; nī-). fl. 2d century B.C. (or earlier). Greek poet, physician, and grammarian; member of the Pleiad of Alexandria; author of *Theriaca* and *Alexipharmaca*, extant poems on venomous animals and antidotes for poisons. Lost works include *Aetolica*, *Heteroeumena*, and *Georgica* and *Melissourgica*, which Vergil is said to have imitated.

**Ni·can'der** (nē·kän'dēr), **Karl August.** 1799–1839. Swedish poet; author of *The Runic Sword* (1820), *The Death of Tasso* (1826), which won him the Swedish Academy award and an opportunity to visit Italy (1827–29), *Reminiscences of the South* (1831–39), lyric poems, *The Hesperides* (1835), *The Lion in the Wilderness* (a eulogy of Napoleon; 1838), translations of Schiller for the royal theater, etc.

**Ni·ca'nor** (nī·kā'nôr; nī-; -nēr). In the Bible, commander of Syrian army defeated by the Maccabees; made governor of Judea by Demetrius I; slain (160 B.C.) in battle against Judas Maccabaeus (*1 Macc.* vii. 27–49; *2 Macc.* xv. 1–36).

**Nicator.** See DEMETRIUS II of Syria; SELEUCUS I of Babylon.

**Nic'co·li'ni** (nēk'kō·lē'nē), **Giovanni Battista.** 1782–1861. Italian playwright and scholar; ardent patriot. Among his plays are *Polyxena* (1811), *Antonio Foscarini* (1827), *Lodovico Sforza* (1834), *Beatrice Cenci* (1838–44), *Arnaldo da Brescia* (1843), and *Filippo Strozzi* (1847).

**Niccolò.** See Nicolas ISOUARD.

**Nic'co·lò' d'A·rez'zo** (nēk'kō·lō' dä·rāt'tsō). *Orig.* **Niccolò di Pie'ro** (*or* **Pie'tro**) **de' Lam·ber'ti** (dē pyâ'rō [pyâ'trō] dā läm·bĕr'tē). 1350?–?1417. Italian sculptor and architect, b. Arezzo; freed Venetian art from Byzantine tradition by introduction of new art of Florence.

**Ni·ceph'o·rus** (nī·sĕf'ō·rŭs). Name of three rulers of Eastern Roman Empire: **Nicephorus I** (d. 811); minister of finance under Irene, whom he overthrew (802); emperor (802–811); defeated (806) by Harun al-Rashid; at first successful in war with Bulgarians (811), but killed by Krum in battle. **Nicephorus II Pho'cas** [fō'kăs; -kås] (913?–969); emperor (963–969); soldier under emperors Constantine VII and Romanus II; led expedition that captured Crete from Saracens (960–961); on death of Romanus made coregent emperor with two young princes, Basil II and Constantine VIII; married their mother, Theophano; conquered northern Syria and Cilicia (964–966); reduced Antioch and Aleppo (969); murdered by his nephew John Zimisces. **Nicephorus III Bo·tan'i·a'tes** [bō·tăn'ĭ·ā'tēz] (d. 1081); emperor (1078–81); a soldier, chosen emperor by Asiatic troops; forced to abdicate by Alexius I Comnenus.

**Nicephorus** *or* **Nicephorus Pa'tri·ar'cha** (pā'trĭ·är'kȧ; păt'rĭ-). 758?–829. Patriarch of Constantinople (806–815) and Byzantine historian; opposed iconoclasts in controversy at Second Nicene Council (787); refused to obey Emperor Leo's edict (814) against worship of images; deposed (815); wrote a history of Constantinople and a chronology.

**Nicephorus Bryennius.** See BRYENNIUS.

**Nicephorus Gregoras.** See GREGORAS.

**Ni·ce'tas Ac'o·mi·na'tus** (nī·sē'tȧs ăk'ō·mĭ·nā'tŭs) *or* **Ni·ce'tas Cho'ni·a'tes** (kō'nĭ·ā'tēz). d. about 1215. Byzantine historian; author of a history of the Greek emperors between 1180 and 1206.

**Ni·ce'ti·us** (nī·sē'shĭ·ŭs; -shŭs), Saint. d. 566. Last Celto-Roman bishop of Treves (c. 527); exiled (555?) for his excommunication of Kings Théodebert I and Clotaire I of the Franks, but restored (561) by Sigebert, Clotaire's son.

**Ni·chi·ren** (nē·chē·rĕn). 1222–1282. Japanese religious teacher; founder of a sect of Buddhists known as Hokkes.

**Nich'ol** (nĭk'ŭl; -'l). See also NICOL; NICOLL.

**Nichol, John Pringle.** 1804–1859. Scottish astronomer; credited with earliest suggestion for study of sunspots by photography; worked on the physical features of the moon and on the nebular hypothesis. His son **John** (1833–1894) was author of *Fragments of Criticism* (1860), *Hannibal* (historical drama; 1873), *Death of Themistocles and other Poems* (1881), *Robert Burns* (1882), *Francis Bacon* (1888–89), etc.

**Nich'o·las** (nĭk'ō·lȧs), Saint. 4th-century Christian prelate; bishop of Myra, in Lycia, Asia Minor; patron saint of Russia; also, considered as patron saint of mariners, thieves, virgins, and children; according to legend, saved three dowerless maidens from being forced into shameful means of earning a livelihood by throwing in at their window on three successive nights purses of gold, thus providing each with a dowry. Hence may come custom of distributing gifts at Christmas and identification of Saint Nicholas with the givers.

**Nicholas.** Name of five popes (see *Table of Popes*, Nos. 105, 155, 188, 191, 210) and one antipope, especially:

**Nicholas I,** Saint. *Sometimes called* **Nicholas the Great.** 800?–867. Pope (858–867); a strong pontiff in the years after the breaking up of Charlemagne's empire; supported Ignatius, Patriarch of Constantinople, and excommunicated Photius (863); conducted long struggle with Lothair, King of Lorraine, forbidding his divorce; upheld right of bishops to appeal to Rome; recognized the pseudo-Isidorian decretals (865).

**Nicholas II.** *Real name* **Gerard of Burgundy.** 980?–1061. Pope (1059–61); under influence of Hildebrand; established regulations for election of popes.

**Nicholas III.** *Real name* **Giovanni Gaetano Or·si'ni** (ôr·sē'nē). 1216?–1280. Pope (1277–80); made new constitution for Rome which freed city of foreign influence.

**Nicholas V.** *Real name* **Tommaso Pa'ren·tu·cel'li** (pä'rân·tōō·chĕl'lē) *or* **Tommaso da Sar·za'na** (dä sär·dzä'nä). 1397?–1455. Pope (1447–55), b. Sarzana; during his pontificate, resignation of Felix V (1449) removed last antipope; a great patron of art and literature.

**Nicholas V.** *Real name* Pietro **Rai'nal·duc'ci** (rī'näl·dōōt'chē). Antipope (1328–30) in opposition to John XXII.

**Nicholas.** *Dan.* **Niels** (nēls). 1063?–1134. King of Denmark (1104–34); son of Sweyn.

**Nicholas.** Name of two rulers of Russia, of the Holstein-Gottorp-Romanov line (see ROMANOV):

**Nicholas I.** *Russ.* **Nikolai Pavlovich.** 1796–1855. Czar of Russia, 3d son of Paul I; succeeded his brother Alexander I (1825); quelled uprising in Poland (1830–31); aided Austria in quelling uprising in Hungary (1849). His designs upon Constantinople provoked war with Turkey (1853) into which other European powers were drawn (Crimean War, 1854–56).

**Nicholas II.** *Russ.* **Nikolai Aleksandrovich.** 1868–1918. Czar of Russia; eldest son of Alexander III; succeeded his father (1894); made peace proposals (1898) which led to International Peace Conference at The Hague (1899) and to the founding of the Hague Tribunal; directed construction of the Trans-Siberian railroad; waged unsuccessful war with Japan (1904–05), forced to grant Constitution of 1905; sought to still popular discontent by liberal reforms under prime minister Stolypin; joined Allies in World War (1914). Dissatisfaction with both his foreign and his domestic policies culminated in Russian Revolution (1917); he abdicated (Mar. 15, 1917) and was executed at Ekaterinburg with his whole family by the Bolsheviks (July, 1918). Last of the Holstein-Gottorp-Romanov line.

**Nicholas.** *Russ.* **Nikolai Nikolaevich.** 1831–1891. Russian grand duke; 3d son of Czar Nicholas I; commanded Russian army of the Danube in Russo-Turkish War (1877–78). His son Grand Duke **Nicholas,** *Russ.* **Nikolai Nikolaevich** (1856–1929), was commander in chief, St. Petersburg military district (1905–14); in the World War, viceroy and commander in chief in the Caucasus; after Russian Revolution (1917), lived in the Crimea (1917–19) and in France (from 1919); chosen leader of Russian monarchists in exile in France (1926).

**Nicholas.** *Russ.* **Nikolai Mikhailovich.** 1859–1919. Russian grand duke; son of Grand Duke Mikhail Nikolaevich; interned by Bolsheviks after Russian Revolution (1917), and executed (Jan. 28, 1919).

**Nicholas I.** 1841–1921. King of Montenegro. Proclaimed prince of Montenegro after the assassination of his uncle Prince Danilo I (1860); obtained from European powers recognition of independence of Montenegro, in the Treaty of Berlin (1878); received title of king of Montenegro by vote of the national legislature (1910); vigorously pursued war of Balkan allies against Turkey (1912); went to aid of Serbia when Serbia was attacked by Austria-Hungary at outbreak of World War (1914).

**Nicholas of Clémanges.** *Fr.* **Ni'co'las' de Clé'manges'** (nē'kô'lä' dē klā'mänzh'). 1360–?1434. French theologian; rector, U. of Paris (1393); secretary to Pope Benedict XIII, at Avignon; author of *Discussion sur le Concile Général*, and a series of letters.

**Nich'o·las of Cu'sa** (nĭk'ō·lȧs, kū'sȧ). *Ger.* **Ni'ko·la'us von Cu'sa** (nē'kō·lä'ŏŏs [nē'kō·lous] fôn kōō'zä). *Lat.* **Nic'o·la'us Cu·sa'nus** (nĭk'ō·lā'ŭs kū·sā'nŭs). 1401–1464. Roman Catholic prelate and philosopher, b. in Cusa (Kues), near Trier, Germany; created cardinal (1448), bishop of Bressanone (1450). Author of *De Concordantia Catholica* (1431–36; written for the Council of Basel), *De Docta Ignorantia*, and philosophical and mathematical treatises. Anticipated Copernicus by his belief in the earth's rotation and revolution around the sun.

**Nicholas of Da·mas′cus** (dȧ·măs′kŭs). *Lat.* **Nic′o·la′us Dam′a·sce′nus** (nĭk′ō·lā′ŭs dăm′ȧ·sē′nŭs). Greek historian of 1st century B.C.; friend of Augustus and Herod the Great. Only fragments of his universal history have been preserved.

**Nicholas of Flü′e** (flü′ĕ). *Ger.* **Nikolaus von der Flüe.** *Orig. name* **Nikolaus Lö′wen·brug′ger** (lû′vĕn-brŏŏg′ẽr). *Often called* **Bru′der Klaus** (brōō′dẽr klous′). 1417–1487. Swiss holy hermit, b. on the Flüeli plateau, near Sachseln, Unterwalden; abandoned family (1467) and lived as hermit in Ranft ravine, near Basel; saved Swiss Confederation by plea for union at Diet of Stans (1481). Canonized (1872).

**Nicholas of Ly′ra** (lī′rȧ). *Lat.* **Nic′o·la′us Ly·ra′nus** (nĭk′ō·lā′ŭs lī·rā′nŭs; lĭ·rā′nŭs). 1270?–?1340. Biblical scholar, b. in Normandy; professor at the Sorbonne; provincial in Burgundy of the Franciscan order.

**Nicholl, Nicholls.** See NICOL; NICOLL; NICOLLS.

**Nich′ols** (nĭk′ŭlz; -'lz), **Anne.** 1891–1966. American playwright; author of *Abie's Irish Rose,* which ran continuously in New York from 1922 to 1927, the longest run on record up to that time; also wrote *The Gilded Cage* (1920), *Love Dreams* (1921), and *Just Married* (with Adelaide Matthews; 1921).

**Nichols, Beverley.** 1899– . English writer; author of *Prelude* (1920), *Self* (1922), *Crazy Pavements* (1927), *The Star Spangled Manner* (1928), *Evensong* (in collaboration with E. Knoblock, 1932), *Cry Havoc* (1933), *Green Grows the City* (1939), etc.

**Nichols, Edward Leam′ing·ton** (lĕm′ĭng·tŭn). 1854–1937. American physicist, b. at Leamington, Eng., of American parentage; professor, Cornell (1887–1919); founder and editor, *Physical Review* (1893–1912); author of *Outlines of Physics* (1897), and collaborator in studies of luminescence and fluorescence.

**Nichols, Ernest Fox.** 1869–1924. American physicist; esp. known for his experiments in measuring planetary heat, determining light pressure, etc., by means of an extremely sensitive radiometer devised by him.

**Nichols, George Ward.** 1831–1885. American music and art promoter; founder and first president (1879–85) of College of Music of Cincinnati; largely responsible for Cincinnati's development as a musical center.

**Nichols, John.** 1745–1826. English printer and author; succeeded (1777) to business of William Bowyer, learned printer; edited the *Gentleman's Magazine* (1778–1826); published *Bibliotheca Topographica* (10 vols., 1780–1800); edited works of Swift (19 vols., 1801) and Hogarth (c. 1808); published *Anecdotes* (9 vols., 1812–15) and *Illustrations* (6 vols., 1817–31), both concerned with 18th-century literary history. His son **John Bowyer** (1779–1863) became proprietor of *Gentleman's Magazine* (1833); added two volumes to his father's *Illustrations* (1848, 1856); published county histories; wrote antiquarian and topographic works. His grandson **John Gough Nichols** (1806–1873), editor of *Gentleman's Magazine* (1851–56), printed many volumes for the Camden Society, of which he was a founder (1838); edited *The Topographer and Genealogist* (1846–58) and *The Herald and Genealogist* (1863–73); wrote antiquarian works.

**Nichols, Robert Malise Bowyer.** 1893–1944. English poet and dramatist; son of the poet **John Bowyer Buchanan Nichols** (1859–1939), of same family as John Nichols (1745–1826). Author of three volumes of poetry, *Invocation* (1915), *Ardours and Endurances* (1917), *Aurelia* (1920); of plays including *Guilty Souls* (1922); of *Fantastica* (1923), including *The Smile of the Sphinx* and other imaginative philosophical tales; etc.

**Nichols, Spencer Baird.** 1875–1950. American muralist, portrait painter, and illustrator. His brother **Henry Hobart, Jr.** (1869–1962), also a painter.

**Nichols, Thomas.** fl. 1554. English merchant; author of a description of Canary Islands and Madeira included in Hakluyt's *Principall Navigations* (1589).

**Nich′ol·son** (nĭk′ŭl·s'n; -'l·s'n). See also NICOLSON.

**Nicholson,** Sir **Francis.** 1655–1728. English administrator in America, b. near Richmond, Yorkshire, Eng.; to America (1686) as captain of foot, under Sir Edmund Andros; lieutenant governor of the Dominion of New England (1688), of Virginia (1690–92); governor of Maryland (1694–98), of Virginia (1698–1705); commanded force capturing Port Royal (1710); governor of Nova Scotia (1713), of South Carolina (1720–25).

**Nicholson, Francis.** 1753–1844. English water-colorist; made advances in water-color art, esp. in production of depth of tone and variety of shade and color; hence called "Father of Water-Color Painting."

**Nicholson, Henry Alleyne.** 1844–1899. English biologist; regius professor of natural history, Aberdeen (1882–99). His son **Reynold Alleyne** (1868–1945), Orientalist; lecturer in Persian (1902–26) and professor of Arabic (1926–33), Cambridge; works include *The Mystics of Islam* (1914), *Studies in Islamic Poetry* (1921), translations, etc.

**Nicholson, James** (1736?–1804) and his brother **Samuel** (1743–1811). Captains in the Continental navy during the American Revolution; b. in Maryland. A grandson of Samuel, **James William Augustus Nicholson** (1821–1887), was also a naval officer; with Perry's squadron to Japan (1853); served through Civil War, at battle of Port Royal, capture of Jacksonville and St. Augustine, and at battle of Mobile Bay; retired as rear admiral (1883).

**Nicholson, John.** 1821–1857. British military officer and administrator, b. in North of Ireland; deputy commissioner (1851–56) in Punjab; became among natives object of hero worship under title of Nik′kul Seyn (nĭk′ŭl sān′); in mutiny of 1857, led first column in assault on Delhi; fell mortally wounded.

**Nicholson, Joseph Shield.** 1850–1927. English economist; authority on currency and banking; author of *Principles of Political Economy* (an attempt to combine historical and mathematical methods; 3 vols., 1893–1901), *Thoth* (1888), *Toxar* (1890), and *Revival of Marxism* (1920), etc.

**Nicholson, Kenyon,** *in full* **John Kenyon.** 1894– . American playwright; author of *The Meal Ticket* (1926), *The American Scene* (with Barrett H. Clark; 1930), *The Barker, Love Is Like That* (with S. N. Behrman), *Eva the Fifth* (with John Golden), *Sailor Beware, June Night,* etc.

**Nicholson, Margaret.** 1750?–1828. English housemaid who attempted (1786) to stab George III with dessert knife; died in Bedlam; subject of burlesque verses by Shelley and Hogg.

**Nicholson, Meredith.** 1866–1947. American novelist and diplomat, b. Crawfordsville, Ind.; U.S. minister to Paraguay (1933–34), Venezuela (1935–38), Nicaragua (from 1938). Author of *Short Flights* (poetry; 1891), *The Main Chance* (1903), *The House of a Thousand Candles* (1905), *The Port of Missing Men* (1907), *The Lords of High Decision* (1909), *A Hoosier Chronicle* (1912), *The Valley of Democracy* (essays; 1918), *Blacksheep! Blacksheep!* (1920), *Broken Barriers* (1922), *The Cavalier of Tennessee* (1928), etc.

**Nicholson, Peter.** 1765–1844. English mathematician and architect; improved mechanical processes of building; invented the centrolinead (c. 1814); devised new method of extracting cube root (pub. 1844).

**Nicholson, William.** 1753–1815. English scientist; waterworks engineer for Portsmouth and Gosport; pioneer in the electrolytic decomposition of water; invented a hydrometer (Nicholson's hydrometer) and a machine for printing on linen (1790); compiler of a *Dictionary of Practical and Theoretical Chemistry* (1808).

**Nicholson, William.** 1781–1844. Scottish painter and etcher of portraits.

**Nicholson, William.** 1816–1865. Australian statesman; "father of the Australian ballot"; b. England; to Melbourne (1841); mayor (1850); premier of Victoria (1859).

**Nicholson,** Sir **William Coldingham Masters.** 1863–1932. British naval officer; served at Jutland (1916); third sea lord (1919–20); vice-admiral, commanding first battle squadron (1921–22); admiral (1925).

**Nicholson,** Sir **William Newzam Prior.** 1872–1949. English painter and wood engraver; designed posters with his brother-in-law James Pryde, under name of Beggarstaff Brothers, which led to a series of original and witty books; published a series of woodcuts including *The Square Book of Animals* (1896), *An Almanac of Twelve Sports* (in collaboration with Rudyard Kipling; 1898), *Twelve Portraits.* Painter of portraits, figure subjects, still-life and open-air studies.

**Nicholson, Wilmot Stuart.** 1872–1947. British naval officer; captain during World War (1914–18); rear admiral (1920); chief of submarine service (1923–25); vice-admiral (1925); admiral, retired (1930).

**Ni′ci·as** (nĭsh′ĭ·ăs). Athenian general and statesman; political opponent of Cleon and Alcibiades; with Alcibiades and Lamachus, placed in command of Sicilian expedition (415 B.C.), although he had opposed project; captured by Syracusans and executed (413).

**Nicias of Ath′ens** (ăth′ĕnz; -ĭnz). Greek painter of 4th century B.C.; contemporary of Praxiteles.

**Nick′alls** (nĭk′ălz; -′lz), **Guy** (d. 1935) and his brother **Vivian** (1871– ). English oarsmen; rowed on many winning crews at Eton and Oxford, and subsequently in numerous Henley regattas.

**Ni′co′dé′** (nē′kô′dā′), **Jean** (zhäN) **Lou·is′** (lwē). 1853–1919. Pianist, conductor, and composer in Germany, b. near Posen; composer of *Marie Stuart* (symphonic poem for orchestra, 1881), *Das Meer* (symphonic ode, 1889), the symphony *Gloria* (1904), orchestral suites, male choruses, chamber music, piano pieces, etc.

**Ni′co·de′mi** (nē′kō·dâ′mē), **Dario.** 1877–1934. Italian dramatist, b. Livorno.

**Nic′o·de′mus** (nĭk′ō·dē′mŭs). In the Bible (*John* iii. 1–21; vii. 50–52; xix. 39), a Pharisee, and ruler of the Jews, who came to talk to Jesus by night.

**Nic′ol** (nĭk′ŭl; -′l), **Erskine.** 1825–1904. Scottish genre painter; depicted Scottish and Irish life.

**Nicol, William.** 1744?–1797. Scottish schoolmaster; host to Robert Burns (1787, 1789), who immortalized him in *Willie Brewed a Peck o'Maut.*

**Nicol, William.** 1768?–1851. British physicist; invented the Nicol prism (1828) for producing and analyzing polarized light.

**Ni′co·la′i** (nē′kō·lä′ē), **Christoph Friedrich.** 1733–1811. German writer, critic, and bookseller; champion of German enlightenment (Aufklärung) and opponent of authority and orthodoxy in religion, so-called extravagance in contemporary literature, and the philosophy of Kant and Fichte; literary associate of Lessing and Moses Mendelssohn, with the latter of whom he founded (1757) in Berlin the critical journal *Bibliothek der Schönen Wissenschaften und Freien Kunste*, and with both of whom he collaborated in the literary review *Briefe, die Neueste Literatur Betreffend;* edited *Allgemeine Deutsche Bibliothek* (268 vols., 1765–1806) and wrote satirical novels, attacks on Goethe, Schiller, and his other literary critics, several biographies, etc.

**Nicolai, Otto,** *in full* **Carl Otto Ehrenfried.** 1810–1849. German composer and conductor; director of cathedral choir and Kapellmeister of royal opera, Berlin (1847); composer of Italian operas, the comic opera *Merry Wives of Windsor* (1849), a mass (1843), a requiem, motets, overtures, chamber music, etc.

**Nicolaie, Louis François.** See CLAIRVILLE.

**Ni′co·lai′er** (nē′kō·lī′ẽr), **Arthur.** 1862– . German physician; professor of internal medicine, U. of Berlin; discovered bacillus of tetanus (1894).

**Nicolas.** See NICHOLAS.

**Nic′o·las** (nĭk′ō·lăs), Sir **Nicholas Harris.** 1799–1848. English antiquary; devoted himself to genealogical and historical studies; author of *History of the Orders of Knighthood of the British Empire* (1841–42), *Synopsis of the Peerage of England* (1825), etc.

**Nicolaus.** See NICHOLAS (OF CUSA, DAMASCUS, LYRA).

**Nic′o·lay′** (nĭk′ō·lā′), **John George.** 1832–1901. Biographer, b. Essingen, Bavaria; to U.S. (1838); private secretary to Abraham Lincoln (1860–65); U.S. consul at Paris (1865–69); marshal of U.S. Supreme Court (1872–87); collaborator with John Hay in a biography of Abraham Lincoln (1890), and in an edition of *Complete Works of Abraham Lincoln.*

**Ni′cole′** (nē′kôl′), **Pierre.** 1625?–1695. French Jansenist; involved in important theological controversies of his time, as against Fénelon and Mme. Guyon, against Quietism, against the Jesuits, etc.

**Ni′co′let′** (nē′kô′lĕ′), **Jean.** 1598–1642. French explorer in America; brought to New France (Canada) by Champlain (1618); lived among Indians on upper Ottawa River; made expedition to Lake Michigan and Wisconsin regions (1634), first white man to reach that region.

**Nic′oll** (nĭk′ŭl; -′l), **Allardyce,** *in full* **John Ramsay Allardyce.** 1894– . British scholar and teacher of English drama; professor, Yale; author of a series of histories of Restoration, 18th-century, and 19th-century drama, studies in Shakespeare, etc.

**Nicoll, Robert.** 1814–1837. Scottish poet; author of two volumes of folk songs and dialect poems (1835, 1844).

**Nicoll,** Sir **William Robertson.** *Pseudonym* **Claudius Clear** (klẹr). 1851–1923. Scottish man of letters; Free Church minister (1874); founded the *Bookman* (1891), a literary monthly; turned nonconformist support to Lloyd George's social legislation and to government during World War; edited *The Expositor's Greek Testament* (1897) and works of Charlotte Brontë (1902).

**Ni′colle′** (nē′kôl′), **Charles Jean Henri.** 1866–1936. French physician and bacteriologist, b. Rouen; director, Pasteur Institute, Tunis (1903); professor, Collège de France (1932); discovered that typhus fever is transmitted by the body louse; awarded 1928 Nobel prize for physiology and medicine.

**Ni′col′let′** (nē′kô′lĕ′), **Jo′seph′** (zhō′zĕf′) **Ni′co′las′** (nē′kô′lä′). 1786–1843. Mathematician and explorer in America, b. in Savoy, France; to America (1832); explored region of upper Mississippi (1836) and upper Missouri (1838, 1839) rivers; prepared map of region northwest of the Mississippi.

**Nic′olls** (nĭk′ŭlz; -′lz), **Mathias.** 1626–?1687. Secretary of New York province (1664–73; 1674–80), b. Plymouth, Eng.; to America (1664); mayor of New York City (1671–72; 1674–75); judge, court of oyer and terminer (1683–87); chief collaborator in preparing the legal code known as "the Duke's Laws," promulgated by Governor Richard Nicolls in 1665.

**Nicolls, Richard.** 1624–1672. First British governor of New York, b. in Bedfordshire; commanded troop of horse in Royalist army (1643); in exile with the Stuarts, on staff of duke of York; governor of New York, taken over from the Dutch (1664–68); made transition from Dutch government to English as gradual as possible; issued "the Duke's Laws," prepared in collaboration with Mathias Nicolls (1665); killed at battle of Southwold Bay (1672).

**Nic'ol·son** (nĭk'ŭl·s'n; -l·s'n). See also NICHOLSON.

**Nicolson,** Sir **Arthur.** 1st Baron **Car'nock** (kär'nŭk). 1849–1928. English diplomat; ambassador to Madrid (1904–06) and St. Petersburg (1906–10); conducted negotiations leading to Algeciras Conference (1906) and entente with France and Russia. His son Sir **Harold** (1886–1968), biographer and critic, b. Teheran, Persia; entered foreign office (1909); m. (1913) Victoria Mary Sackville-West (*q.v.*); served on British delegation to Paris Peace Conference (1919); member of embassy, Berlin (1927–29); literary editor on London newspapers. Author of biographies of Paul Verlaine (1921), Tennyson (1923), Byron (1924), Swinburne (1926), of his father (*Portrait of a Diplomatist*, 1930), of Lord Curzon (1934), Dwight Morrow (1935); also of *Peacemaking* (1919), *Diplomacy* (1939), etc. M.P. (1935 ff.).

**Nicolson, James Brindly.** 1917–1944. Cousin of Harold Nicolson. English aviator; in Royal Air Force (1939); awarded Victoria Cross for exploit in fight with German plane (Aug. 16, 1940).

**Ni·com'a·chus** (nĭ·kŏm'ȧ·kŭs; nī-). Neo-Pythagorean philosopher and mathematician of 2d century A.D., b. Gerasa, Arabia Petraea. Two of his works are extant: *Introductio Arithmetica* and *Enchiridion Harmonices.*

**Nic'o·me'des** (nĭk'ō·mē'dēz). Name of three kings of Bithynia: **Nicomedes I** (reigned 278–250 B.C.); founder (264) of Nicomedia, capital of Bithynia. **Nicomedes II,** *surnamed* **E·piph'a·nes** [ē·pĭf'ȧ·nēz] (reigned 142–91 B.C.), hero of Corneille's *Nicomède.* **Nicomedes III** (reigned 91–74 B.C.), opponent of Mithridates and loyal friend of the Romans, who reduced Bithynia to the status of a Roman province.

**Ni'cot'** (nē'kō'), **Jean.** 1530?–1600. French diplomat and scholar; ambassador in Portugal (1559–61); introduced use of tobacco from Portugal into France. The terms *nicotine* and *Nicotiana* (genus to which the tobacco plant belongs) derive from his name.

**Ni·co'te·ra** (nē·kô'tā·rä), Baron **Giovanni.** 1828–1894. Italian statesman; active in Revolution of 1848; minister of interior (1876–77, 1891–92).

**Nie'buhr** (nē'bo͝or), **Carsten.** 1733–1815. German traveler and explorer, chiefly in Danish service; accompanied Forskål on scientific expedition (1761–67) to explore Arabia, Palestine, Syria, Persia, and Asia Minor; edited and published the results of Forskål's work. His son **Barthold Georg** (1776–1831), historian, statesman, and philologist, was official publicist and defender of Prussian cause during War of Liberation; Prussian ambassador at Rome (1816–23); discovered the *Institutes of Gaius*, an introduction to Roman private law (1816), and fragments of the works of Cicero and Livy (1820), which he helped decipher; created the *Corpus Scriptorum Historiae Byzantinae;* author of *History of Rome* (3 vols., 1811–32), *Griechische Heroengeschichten* (pub. 1842), etc.

**Nie'buhr** (nē'bo͝or), **Rein'hold** (rīn'hōld). 1892–1971. American clergyman; professor of applied Christianity, Union Theol. Sem. (1930–60); author of *Does Civilization Need Religion?* (1927), *Moral Man and Immoral Society* (1932), *Beyond Tragedy* (1937), *The Nature and Destiny of Man* (vol. I, 1941; vol. II, 1943), etc. His brother **Hel'mut** (hĕl'mo͞ot) **Rich'ard** [rĭch'ẽrd] (1894–1962), clergyman; author of *The Kingdom of God in America* (1937), etc.

**Niecks** (nēks), **Frederick.** 1845–1924. British musical authority, b. Düsseldorf; contributed to *Musical Times* (from 1879); compiled *Concise Dictionary of Musical Terms* (1884); professor of music, Edinburgh (1891–1914).

**Nie'der·mey'er** (nē'dẽr·mī'ẽr), **Louis.** 1802–1861. Swiss composer, esp. of sacred music, and of music for poems by Victor Hugo, Deschamps, Lamartine, and others.

**Nie'haus** (nē'hous), **Charles Henry.** 1855–1935. American sculptor, b. Cincinnati, Ohio. His sculptures include: portrait busts of Ingalls, Allen, Garfield, and Morton in rotunda of the Capitol, Washington, D.C.; statues of Garfield in Cincinnati, of Hooker and Davenport in Connecticut State Capitol, Hartford, of Lincoln in Buffalo, N.Y., and Muskegon, Mich., of Gen. Forrest (equestrian) in Memphis, Tenn., of William McKinley for his tomb in Canton, Ohio, of Henry Clay and Ephraim McDowell in Statuary Hall, Washington, D.C., and the *John Paul Jones Monument* in Washington, D.C.

**Nieheim, Dietrich von.** See NIEM.

**Niel** (nyĕl), **Adolphe.** 1802–1869. French soldier; distinguished himself in the Crimean War, esp. at the siege of Sevastopol (1855), and became aide-de-camp to Emperor Napoleon III; engaged at Magenta and Solferino (1859); marshal of France; minister of war (1867–69).

**Niels.** King of Denmark. See NICHOLAS.

**Niel'sen** (nēl's'n), **Alice.** 1876–1943. American soprano, b. Nashville, Tenn.; m. (1st) Benjamin Nentwig, (2d) LeRoy R. Stoddard (1917). Among plays in which she starred were *The Fortune Teller, The Singing Girl.* Sang in grand opera, at Covent Garden, London (1905), with Boston Opera Company (1910–11), and later with Metropolitan Opera Company, New York City.

**Niel'sen** (nḛl's'n), **Carl August.** 1865–1931. Danish composer; conductor of the music society and codirector of the conservatory, Copenhagen (1915–27); composed symphonies, the operas *Saul and David* (1903) and *Maskerade* (1907), orchestral fantasy *Pan and Syrinx* (1926), a violin concerto, violin sonatas, string quartets, piano pieces, stage music, choruses, ballads, songs, etc.

**Ni'em** (nē'ĕm) *or* **Nie'heim** (nē'hīm) *or* **Ny'em** (nē'ĕm), **Dietrich von.** 1340?–1418. German historian, b. Nieheim, Westphalia; officer in papal chancellery, Avignon, and later (1376) in Rome under Boniface IX. Author of *De Schismate Libri III* (a history of the Great Western Schism, completed 1410), *Historia de Vita Johannis XXIII, Nemus Unionis* (a collection of documents of the Council of Pisa), etc.

**Nie'mann** (nē'män), **Albert.** 1831–1917. German Wagnerian and dramatic tenor; appeared in first production of *Tannhäuser* in Paris (1861), in first Bayreuth festival (1876), and at the Metropolitan Opera, New York (1886–88); m. (1859; divorced 1868) the actress Marie Seebach (*q.v.*) and (1871) the actress Hedwig Raabe.

**Niemann–Raabe, Hedwig.** See RAABE.

**Niemann–Seebach, Marie.** See SEEBACH.

**Niembsch von Strehlenau, Nikolaus.** Real name of Nikolaus LENAU.

**Niem·ce'wicz** (nyĕm·tsĕ'vēch), **Julian Ursyn.** 1758–1841. Polish patriot and man of letters; aide and adviser of Kosciusko; to U.S. (1796) and married Mrs. Livingston Kean of New York; returned to Poland (1807); involved in revolution (1830–31), was forced into exile; died in Paris. Among his works are *Historical Ballads* (1816–19), *Meditations at Ursynow* (verse), *The Envoy's Return* (play), *Johann of Tenczyn* (novel), *History of Sigismund III's Reign* (3 vols., 1819).

**Nie'mey'er** (nē'mī'ẽr), **August Hermann.** 1754–1828. Great-grandson of August Hermann Francke. German

Protestant rationalistic theologian and pedagogue; author of *Charakteristik der Bibel* (5 vols., 1775–82), *Grundsätze der Erziehung und des Unterrichts* (1796), *Religiöse Gedichte* (1814), etc. His grandson **Felix von Niemeyer** (1820–1871), physician, wrote *Lehrbuch der Speziellen Pathologie und Therapie* (2 vols., 1858–61).

**Niemeyer Soares Filho, Oscar.** 1907– . Brazilian architect. A designer of U.N. buildings in New York (1947), director of architecture for the new capital of Brasilia (1957– ).

**Niemeyer, Theodor.** 1857–1939. German law scholar; authority on international law.

**Nie'möl'ler** (nē'mûl'ẽr), **Martin.** 1892– . German anti-Nazi Protestant theologian, b. in Westphalia; submarine officer in World War I; ordained (1924); manager, Westphalian Provincial Union for Inner Missions (1924); pastor, Berlin-Dahlem (1931–37); championed nationalism, opposed Communism; at first joined (briefly) the Nazi party, but became leader (1933) of opposition to Nazi and state totalitarian control of Lutheran Church, leader of Pastors' Emergency League (*Pfarrernotbund*), and (1935) member of the board (*Bruderrat*) of the Confessional Church (*Bekenntniskirche*), for which he helped draw up the six principles at the Synod of Barmen (1934); imprisoned in a concentration camp (1937). Wrote *From U-Boat to Pulpit* (1934).

**Niepce** (nyĕps), **Joseph Nicéphore.** 1765–1833. French physicist; produced permanent "heliotypes" by means of glass plates coated with bitumen (1824); associated with Daguerre (from 1829) in experiments resulting in invention of photography. A relative, **Claude Félix Abel Niepce de Saint'-Vic'tor'** [dē săN'vēk'tôr'] (1805–1870), physicist, devoted himself to furthering development of photography as invented by Joseph Niepce and Daguerre, and was first to use albumen, one of first to try fixing images on glass, and one of first to produce steel engravings by photographic means.

**Nie'rem·berg** (nē'rĕm·bĕrg), **Juan Eusebio.** 1595?–1658. Spanish Jesuit naturalist and author, for whom the genus *Nierembergia* is named.

**Nie'se** (nē'zĕ), **Benediktus.** 1849–1910. German classical philologist and historian; editor of Josephus (7 vols., 1885–95). His sister **Charlotte** (b. 1854), writer under pseudonym **Lucian Bürger.**

**Nies'sel'** (nyā'sĕl'), **Henri Albert.** 1866–1955. French general in World War I.

**Nietz'sche** (nē'chĕ), **Friedrich Wilhelm.** 1844–1900. German philosopher and poet; educ. U. of Bonn and U. of Leipzig (1864–67), where he studied Schopenhauer's writings; professor of classical philology, Basel (1869–79), where he was at first the friend and follower and later (about 1874) a strong opponent of Wagner in art and philosophy; opponent of Schopenhauer's philosophy; suffered mental breakdown (1889); spent last years in care of his mother at Naumburg and his sister Elisabeth Förster-Nietzsche (*q.v.*) at Weimar. He denounced all religion and championed the "morals of masters," the doctrine of perfectibility of man through forcible self-assertion and glorification of the superman or overman (*Übermensch*). His theories are regarded as influencing the German attitude in World War I and in the Third Reich (1933). His works, chiefly on philology, music, Greek antiquity, and, esp., philosophy, include *Die Geburt der Tragödie aus dem Geiste der Musik* (1872), *Die Philosophie im Tragischen Zeitalter der Griechen* (1873), *Menschliches-Allzu Menschliches* (2 vols., 1878–80), *Morgenröte* (1881), *Die Fröhliche Wissenschaft* (1882), *Also Sprach Zarathustra* (proclaiming the gospel of the superman; 4 parts, 1883 ff.), which he interpreted in *Jenseits von Gut und Böse* (1886) and *Zur Genealogie der Moral* (1887), *Der Fall Wagner* (1888), *Der Antichrist* (1888), *Der Wille zur Macht* (1888; unfinished), *Götzendämmerung* (1889), the autobiography *Ecce Homo* (1888).

**Nieu'port'** (nyû'pôr'), **Édouard.** 1875–1911. French aviator and airplane builder; constructed biplanes of a type much used in the World War.

**Nieuwenhove.** See LIMNANDER DE NIEUWENHOVE.

**Nieu'wen·huis** (nē'vĕn·hois), **Anton Willem.** 1864– . Dutch explorer and ethnologist; physician of the Dutch expedition to Borneo (1889), and first to cross Borneo from west to east (1896–97); author of *In Central Borneo* (2 vols., 1901); editor of the *Internationale Archiv für Ethnographie* (from 1909).

**Nieuwenhuis, Ferdinand Domela.** 1846–1919. Dutch Socialist; Lutheran pastor (1870–79); became leader of Social Democrats and helped found Socialism in Holland; at Socialist congresses of Brussels (1891) and Zurich (1893) opposed Liebknecht; became anarchist.

**Nieuw'land** (nū'lănd), **Julius Arthur.** 1878–1936. American chemist and botanist, b. Hansbeke, Belgium; ordained Roman Catholic priest (1903); taught at Notre Dame (from 1904); known for synthesis of organic compounds, esp. artificial rubber, from acetylene.

**Nie'vo** (nyā'vō), **Ippolito.** 1831–1861. Italian novelist and poet; known esp. for his historical novel *Confessioni di un Ottuagenario* (1867).

**Ni'fo** (nē'fō), **Agostino.** *Lat.* **Augustinus Ni'phus** (nī'fŭs). 1473?–?1538. Italian philosopher; renounced Averroism in favor of orthodoxy; commissioned by Leo X to answer Pomponazzi's *De Immortalitate Animi.* Among works are *De Infinitate Primi Motoris Quaestio* (1504), *De Immortalitate Animi* (1518).

**Ni'gel** (nē'jĕl; *in mod. Eng.*, nī'jĕl). d. 1169. English prelate and statesman; bishop of Ely (from 1133); in charge of exchequer of Henry I (from 1130); offered resistance to King Stephen (1139) but was reconciled and restored (1142); summoned by Henry II to reorganize exchequer, the work of his life; chief justiciar (1165); probable compiler of the *Black Book of the Exchequer.*

**Nigel.** *Called* **Ni'gel Wi're·ker** (nē'jĕl wī'rĕ·kĕr). fl. 1190. English monk and satirist; author of *Speculum Stultorum,* in Latin elegiac verse, ridiculing vices of both clergy and society, and of *Contra Curiales et Officiales Clericos,* in prose. Quoted by Chaucer in *Nun's Priest's Tale.*

**Night'in·gale** (nīt'ĭn·gāl; nīt''n-; -ĭng·gāl), **Florence.** 1820–1910. English nurse, hospital reformer, and philanthropist; known as "the Lady with the Lamp"; b. at Florence, Italy, of wealthy parents; underwent training as nurse; superintendent of hospital for invalid women, London (1853); took 38 nurses to Scutari (1854) early in Crimean War and organized barrack hospital; introduced sanitation, lessened cases of typhus, cholera, and dysentery; by means of £50,000 testimonial fund, founded institution for training of nurses (1860); first woman to receive Order of Merit (1907).

**Ni'gra** (nē'grä), Conte **Constantino.** 1828–1907. Italian diplomat; secretary to Cavour at Congress of Paris (1856); minister (later ambassador) to France (1861–76); ambassador, St. Petersburg (1876–82), London (1882–85), Vienna (1885–1904); senator (1890); Italian representative at first International Peace Conference (1899).

**Ni·jin'sky** (*Angl.* nĭ·zhĭn'skĭ; *Russ.* nyĭ·zhēn'skû·ĭ), **Was·law'** (vŭts·läf'). 1890–1950. Russian dancer, of Polish descent; debut in Imperial Ballet, St. Petersburg (1907); first appeared in Paris (1909) with Diaghilev's Ballet Russe. Among ballets in which he appeared were *Les Sylphides, Cléopâtre, Pétrouchka, L'Après-Midi d'un Faune, Schéhérazade, Le Spectre de la Rose.* Later, became insane and was confined in an asylum.

**Nik'i·as** (nĭk'ĭ·ăs). Variant of NICIAS.

**Ni'kisch** (nē'kĭsh), **Ar'thur** (är'tŏŏr). 1855–1922. Hungarian violinist, pianist, and orchestral conductor; conductor, Leipzig opera (1879–89), Boston Symphony Orchestra (1889–93), Berlin Philharmonic Orchestra, with which he toured Europe (from 1897); toured U.S. with London Symphony Orchestra (1912); composed a symphony, a string sextet, a cantata, etc.

**Nikita.** See ROMANOV.

**Ni·ki'tin** (nyĭ·kyē'tyĭn), **Ivan Savvich.** 1824–1861. Russian lyric poet; among popular individual poems are *Russia, The Moneylender, The Volga Boatman, The Ploughman: A Winter Night in Village.*

**Nikolai.** Russian form of NICHOLAS.

**Nikolas** *or* **Nikolaus.** See NICHOLAS.

**Ni'kon** (nyē'kôn). 1605–1681. Russian ecclesiastical prelate; metropolitan of Novgorod (1648); patriarch of Moscow (1652–60); convened synod at Moscow (1654) to institute reforms in church ceremonial and in the text of church books; reforms were unpopular and caused schism in the church, and the founding of the Raskolnik sect; deposed by Russian government (1680).

**Niku.** See NECHO (II).

**Niles** (nīlz), **Blair,** *nee* **Rice.** 1887?–1959. Am. explorer and writer, b. Coles Ferry, Va.; m. Robert Niles, Jr.; on exploring expeditions to Mexico, Venezuela, British Guiana, and the Far East; made special study of Devil's Island, and Dutch and French Guiana (1927). Author of *Black Haiti* (1926), *The Biography of an Unknown Convict* (1928), *Condemned to Devil's Island* (1928; presented as a talking motion picture), *Free* (1930), *Peruvian Pageant* (1937), *The James* (1939), *Passengers to Mexico* (1943), etc.

**Niles, Hezekiah.** 1777–1839. American editor, b. in Chester County, Pa.; editor, Baltimore *Evening Post* (1805–11), *Niles' Weekly Register* (1811–36).

**Niles, John Milton.** 1787–1856. American lawyer and editor, b. Windsor, Conn.; practiced, Hartford, Conn. (1817); founded Hartford *Weekly Times* (1817); U.S. senator (1835–39; 1843–49); U.S. postmaster general (1840–41).

**Nil'son** (nĭl'sôn), **Lars Fredrik.** 1840–1899. Swedish physicist; discoverer (1879) of the metallic element scandium.

**Nils'son** (nĭls'sôn), **Christine.** 1843–1921. Swedish concert and operatic soprano, and violinist; m. 1st (1872) the Parisian Auguste Rouzaud (d. 1882), 2d (1887) the Spanish Count di Miranda (d. 1902).

**Nim'itz** (nĭm'ĭts), **Chester William.** 1885–1966. American naval officer, b. Fredericksburg, Texas; grad. U.S.N.A., Annapolis (1905); advanced through the grades to rear admiral (1938); commander of 1st battleship division (1938–39); chief of bureau of navigation, U.S. Navy Department (1939–41); commander in chief of U.S. Pacific fleet (Dec., 1941–Nov., 1945); admiral (Dec., 1941); admiral of the fleet (Dec., 1944); chief of naval operations (Nov., 1945–Nov., 1947).

**Nimrod.** Pseudonym of Charles James APPERLY.

**Nim·zo'witsch** (nĭm·tsō'vĭch), **A'ron** (ä'rôn). 1886–1935. Chess master, b. Riga, Latvia.

**Nin'i·an** (nĭn'ĭ·ăn; nĭn'yăn) *or* **Nin'i·as** (nĭn'ĭ·ăs), Saint. *Lowland Scots form* **Ring'an** (rĭng'ăn). d. 432?. Scottish apostle of Christianity, b. Cumberland (c. 360), son of a British chieftain; made pilgrimage to Rome; after fifteen years' study consecrated bishop; founded church at Whithorn (397); evangelized the southern Picts.

**Ni'ño** (nē'nyō), **Pedro Alonso.** *Called* **el Ne'gro** (ĕl nā'grō). 1468–?1505. Spanish navigator; accompanied Columbus on third voyage (1498); associated with Cristóbal Guerra in first successful commercial voyage to America (1499–1500).

**Ninon de Lenclos.** See Anne LENCLOS.

**Nin y Cas'tel·la'no** (nēn' ē käs'tā·(l)yä'nō), **Joaquín.** 1879–1949. Spanish pianist, composer, and writer, b. Havana, Cuba. Compositions include *Suite de Valses Lyriques, Danza Ibérica,* and *En el Jardín de Lindaraja.*

**Ni'pher** (nī'fẽr), **Francis Eugene.** 1847–1927. American physicist; studied the nature of electrical discharges, variations in the magnetic needle, magnetic storms, gravitational attraction between small masses, etc.

**Niphus, Augustinus.** See Agostino NIFO.

**Nip'kow** (nĭp'kō), **Paul Gottlieb.** 1860–1940. German television pioneer; credited with invention of scanning disk (1884).

**Nip'pold** (nĭp'ôlt), **Friedrich.** 1838–1918. German Protestant theologian and church historian, a founder of the Evangelical Union. His son **Otfried** (1864–1938), jurist and pacifist, authority on international law, worked to promote peace and international understanding, notably during World War I.

**Nir'en·berg** (nĭr'ĕn·bûrg), **Marshall Warren.** 1927– . American biochemist, b. New York City. With Nat. Inst. of Health (1957– ); awarded Nobel prize in physiology and medicine (1968) with R. W. Holley and H. Khorana for studies on the genetic code.

**Ni'sard'** (nē'zȧr'), **Désiré,** *in full* **Jean Marie Napoléon Désiré.** 1806–1888. French journalist and literary critic; on staff of *Journal des Débats* and *Le National;* professor at the Sorbonne; director of École Normale Supérieure; author of *Études sur les Poètes Latins de la Décadence* (1834), *Histoire de la Littérature Française* (1844–61), etc.

**Nis'bet** (nĭz'bĕt; -bĭt), **Robert Hogg.** 1879–**1961.** American landscape painter and etcher, b. Providence, R.I.

**Nis'bett** (nĭz'bĕt; -bĭt) *or* **Nes'bitt** (nĕz'bĭt), **Louisa Cranstoun.** 1812?–1858. English comedy actress; m. (1831) Capt. J. A. Nisbett (killed 1831); won triumph in Sheridan Knowles's *The Love Chase;* the original Lady Gay Spanker in *London Assurance;* returned to stage (1846) to play Lady Teazle.

**Nis'sel** (nĭs'ĕl), **Franz.** 1831–1893. Austrian dramatist; author of *Heinrich der Löwe* (1858), *Dido* (1863), *Agnes von Meran* (1877), *Ein Nachtlager Corvins* (1887), etc.

**Nis'sen** (nĭs'ĕn), **Heinrich.** 1839–1912. German archaeologist and historian; writer on early Roman history.

**Nissl** (nĭs''l), **Franz.** 1860–1919. German neurologist; worked esp. on the anatomy of the brain.

**Nit'hard** (nēt'härt). 795?–?844. Frankish historian; natural son of St. Angilbert and of Bertha, daughter of Charlemagne; sided with Charles the Bald in quarrels between sons of Louis the Pious; fought at Fontenoy (841); wrote history of the times, in Latin.

**Nit'hard** (nēt'härt), **Johannes Eberhard.** 1607–1681. German Jesuit; favorite and minister (1665–69) of Queen Mariana of Spain; made cardinal (1672). See MARIANA DE AUSTRIA.

**Nithsdale,** Earls and countess of. See MAXWELL family.

**Ni·to·be** (nē·tō·bĕ), **Inazo.** 1863–1933. Japanese scholar and statesman; president, Imperial College, Tokyo (1906 ff.); author of *Bushido* (1898; American title, *Bushido, the Soul of Japan,* 1900).

**Nit'ti** (nēt'tē), **Francesco Saverio.** 1868–1953. Italian economist and statesman; minister of commerce and agriculture (1911–17); minister of finance (1917–19); prime minister (1919–20). Wrote *Il Capitale Straniero in Italia* (1915), *Europa Senza Pace* (1921), *The Decadence of Europe* (1922), *Bolshevism, Fascism, and Democracy* (1927), *L'Inquiétude du Monde* (1934).

**Nit′tis** (nē̆t′tēs), **Giuseppe de.** 1846–1884. Italian painter; to Paris (1868); associated with Gérôme and Meissonier; known for scenes of Parisian life.

**Nit′ze** (nĭt′sē), **William Albert.** 1876–1957. American professor of Romance languages, Chicago (from 1909); author of *A History of French Literature* (with E. P. Dargan, 1922), and works on Arthurian romance.

**Nitzsch** (nĭch), **Karl Ludwig.** 1751–1831. German Protestant theologian. His son **Karl Immanuel** (1787–1868), Protestant theologian, was a founder of the mediation theology, and champion of the positive evangelical union. Karl Immanuel's brother **Gregor Wilhelm** (1790–1861) was a classical philologist and Homeric scholar. Gregor's son **Karl Wilhelm** (1818–1880), historian and pupil of Niebuhr, was author of a history of Germany to the peace of Augsburg (3 vols., pub. 1883–85), a history of the Roman Republic (2 vols., pub. 1884–85), etc.

**Ni′velle′** (nē′vĕl′), **Robert Georges.** 1856–1924. French soldier in World War I; general of brigade (1914) and of division (1915); replaced Pétain in command of the 2d army (May, 1916), and succeeded Joffre as commander in chief of the French armies of the North and Northeast (Dec., 1916); relieved of command when his offensive (culminating Apr. 16, 1917) failed; exonerated by committee of inquiry from blame for the failure.

**Nivelle de La Chaussée.** See LA CHAUSSÉE.

**Niv′en** (nĭv′ĕn), **Frederick John.** 1878–1944. Scottish author of songs and poems, books and articles on Canada, and novels.

**Ni′ver′nais′** (nē′vĕr′nĕ′) *or* **Ni′ver′nois′** (-nwȧ′), Duc **de. Louis Jules Man′ci′ni′ Ma′za′ri′ni′** (mäɴ′sē′nē′ mȧ′zȧ′rē′nē′; *Ital.* män·chē′nē mä′dzä·rē′nē). 1716–1798. French soldier and diplomat; ambassador at Rome (1748–52), Berlin (1756), London (1762–63); minister of state in Necker's cabinet (1788).

**Nix′on** (nĭk′s′n), **John.** 1733–1808. American Revolutionary leader, b. Philadelphia; member of Committee of Safety (1775); led Philadelphia guard in defense of Amboy, N.J. and in battle of Princeton (Jan. 3, 1777); an organizer of the Bank of Pennsylvania (1780), formed to aid in supplying Continental army; president, Bank of North America (1792–1808).

**Nixon,** Sir **John Eccles.** 1857–1921. British soldier; commanded southern army of India (1912), and northern army (1915); commanded Mesopotamian expedition in World War I (1915–16); failed in attempt to relieve Gen. Townshend, who had been besieged in Kut-el-Amara.

**Nixon, Lewis.** 1861–1940. American naval architect, b. Leesburg, Va.; grad. U.S.N.A. (1882); designed battleships *Oregon, Indiana, Massachusetts;* engaged in shipbuilding for commercial firms. Leader of Tammany Hall, New York City (1901–02); superintendent of public works, New York State (1919); public service commissioner, New York State (1919–20).

**Nixon, Richard Mil′hous′** (mĭl′hous′). 1913– . Thirty-seventh president of the United States, b. Yorba Linda, Calif. Member, U.S. House of Repr. (1947–51), U.S. Senate (Calif., 1951–53); U.S. vice-president (1953–61); U.S. president (1969–74); resigned (Aug. 9, 1974), after "Watergate" revelations.

**Ni′za** (nē′sä), **Mar′cos** (mär′kōs) **de** (thā). *Also known as* **Fray Marcos** (frä′ē). d. 1558. Franciscan missionary and explorer in America, b. Nice, duchy of Savoy; explored parts of what is now Arizona and western New Mexico (1539); returned with glowing accounts of the wealth in that region; accompanied Coronado (1540) on his expedition of conquest, reaching the upper Rio Grande Valley; lost repute because of Spaniards' failure to find wealth.

**Ni·zam′–al–Mulk′** (nĭ·zä′-mo͝ol·mo͝olk′; nĭ·zäm′ăl-mo͝olk′), **Has·san′ ibn–A·li′** (hă·săn′ ĭb′′n ă·lĭ′). 1018–1092. Persian statesman; vizier of Persia under sultans Alp Arslan (1063–72) and Malik Shah (1072–92).

**Ni·za·mi′** (nĭ·zä·mē′). *In full* **Abu Muhammad Ilyas ibn Yusuf Sheikh Nizam eddin.** 1141–1202. Persian poet; lived as an ascetic. Among his poetical works are *The Storehouse of Mysteries, Khosrau and Shīrīn* (an epic), *Laila and Majnun, The Book of Alexander* (or *The Fortunes of Alexander*), *The Seven Beauties.*

**Ni·zo′li·us** (nĭ·zō′lĭ·ŭs), **Marius.** *Ital.* **Mario Niz′zo·li** (nēt′tsô·lē). 1498–1576. Italian humanist; known esp. as a Cicero scholar.

**Nkru′mah** (ĕn·kro͞o′mȧ), **Kwame.** 1909–1972. Ghanaian statesman. Prime min. (1957–60), president (1960–66) of Ghana. Wrote *Africa Must Unite* (1963), etc.

**No′ah** (nō′ȧ), **Mordecai Manuel.** 1785–1851. American journalist, b. Philadelphia; as consul to Tunis and special agent to Algiers (1813–15), secured release of American prisoners held by Algerian pirates; founder and editor, New York *Enquirer* (1826), New York *Evening Star* (1834), New York *Union, Noah's Times and Weekly Messenger;* surveyor of port of New York (1829–33).

**No′ailles′** (nô′á′y′). Distinguished French family, including: **Antoine de Noailles** (1504–1562), admiral of France, ambassador to England (1553–56). Duc **Anne Jules de Noailles** (1650–1708), marshal of France (from 1693). Anne Jules's brother **Louis Antoine** (1651–1729), archbishop of Paris (1695), cardinal (1700). Anne Jules's son Duc **Adrien Maurice** (1678–1766), marshal of France (from 1734). Adrien Maurice's son Duc **Louis** (1713–1793), marshal of France (from 1766). Louis's brother **Philippe de Noailles** (1715–1794), Duc **de Mou′chy′** (mo͞o′shē′), marshal of France, guillotined (June 27, 1794). Duc **Jean François Paul de Noailles** (1739–1824), son of Louis (1713–1793), émigré in Switzerland and abroad during French Revolutionary and Napoleonic period. Jean François Paul's brother Marquis **Emmanuel Marie Louis** (1743–1822), French diplomat. Philippe's first son, Duc **Philippe Louis Marc Antoine de Noailles** (1752–1819), Prince **de Poix** (pwä), peer of France under Louis XVIII. Philippe's second son, Vicomte **Louis Marie de Noailles** (1756–1804); served under his brother-in-law La Fayette in America, was member of the States-General (1789); initiated measures there whereby the nobles stripped themselves of their rights and privileges (Aug., 1789); emigrated to America and fought under Rochambeau against the British in Santo Domingo. Duc **Paul de Noailles** (1802–1885), peer of France (from 1827) and author of *Histoire de M^me de Maintenon...* (1848–58). Paul's son Duc **Jules Charles Victurnien** (1826–1895), economist and author. Jules's brother Marquis **Emmanuel Henri Victurnien** (1830–1909), diplomat, minister in Washington (1872), Italy (1873), ambassador in Constantinople (to 1886), and in Berlin (1896–1902). Comtesse **Anne Elisabeth Ma′thieu′** (mȧ′tyû′) **de Noailles** (1876–1933), Princesse **Bran′co′van′** (bräɴ′-kô′väɴ′), novelist and poet.

**No·bel′** (nô·bĕl′), **Alfred Bernhard.** 1833–1896. Swedish manufacturer, inventor, and philanthropist, b. Stockholm; educ. in St. Petersburg and the U.S., where he studied mechanical engineering (1850–54); invented dynamite (1866), Ballistite, one of the first smokeless powders (1888), artificial gutta percha, and over 100 other patented items; acquired wealth through the manufacture of dynamite and other explosives in various parts of the world and through his interests in the Baku oil fields in Russia; bequeathed fund of $9,200,000 for establishment of Nobel prizes, first awarded in 1901.

**No′bi·le** (nô′bē·lā), **Umberto.** 1885–1978. Italian aeronautical engineer and Arctic explorer; designed airships *Norge* and *Italia;* flew across North Pole in *Norge* with Amundsen and Ellsworth (May, 1926); commanded polar expedition in dirigible *Italia* (May, 1928); rescued (June 22, 1928) after wreck of *Italia* (May 25, 1928), for which he was later adjudged responsible; resigned commission as general (1929); to U.S.S.R. (1932), U.S. (1936); reinstated in Italian Air Service (1945).

**No′bi·li** (nô′bē·lē), **Leopoldo.** 1784–1835. Italian physicist; inventor (1825) of astatic type of galvanometer, in which the effect of the earth's magnetism is reduced.

**No′ble** (nō′b'l), **Alfred.** 1844–1914. American civil engineer, b. Livonia, Mich.; engineer on improvement of river navigation between lakes Superior and Huron (1870–82); on construction of various bridges, including the Washington bridge, New York (1886–87), and the Memphis bridge over the Mississippi (1888–92). Member, U.S. Nicaragua Canal Commission (1895), Isthmian Canal Commission (1899–1903); chief engineer, East River division Pennsylvania Railroad, superintending tunnel and terminal construction (1902–09).

**Noble,** Sir **Andrew** 1831–1915. Scottish physicist and artillerist; his experiments in ballistics led to changes in composition of gunpowder and in design of guns.

**Noble, Edward.** 1857–1941. English master mariner, novelist, and short-story writer; author of *The Edge of Circumstance, Moving Waters, The Pulse of Darkness.*

**Noble, John Willock.** 1831–1912. American lawyer, b. Lancaster, Ohio; practiced, St. Louis, Mo. (from 1865); U.S. secretary of the interior (1889–93).

**Noble,** Sir **Percy Lockhart Harnam.** 1880–1955. British admiral; served in World War (1914–18); captain (1918), rear admiral (1929), vice-admiral (1935), admiral (1939); commander in chief of China Station (1938–40), of western approaches of Britain (1941); head of British Admiralty delegation in Washington (Nov., 1942).

**No·bre′ga** (nōō·brâ′gȧ), **Manuel de.** 1517–1570. Portuguese Jesuit missionary in Brazil; first provincial of the Jesuits in the New World (1553–59).

**No·bu·na·ga** *or* **O·da No·bu·na·ga** (ō·dä nō·bōō·nä·gä). 1534–1582. Japanese general and statesman of the Taira clan; succeeded to his father's fief (1549); joined by Hideyoshi (1558); secured support of shogun (1561); acting shogun (1568–82), actually head of central government; began subjugation of feudal lords, establishing order in many provinces and making a start toward unification of the empire; by humbling Buddhist priests, destroyed political power of Buddhism in Japan; assassinated by a discontented general.

**No′card′** (nô′kȧr′), **Edmond Isidore Étienne.** 1850–1903. French veterinarian and biologist; credited with discovering the bacteria of bovine farcy, of ulcerative lymphangitis of the horse, etc., and with discovering the identity of the bacillus of avian tuberculosis with that of mammalian tuberculosis; demonstrated transmission of tuberculosis to man through the milk and meat of infected cattle. See Pierre ROUX.

**No′dier′** (nô′dyā′), **Charles.** 1780–1844. French man of letters; identified with romantic movement in French literature, as by his tales *Jean Sbogar* (1818), *Thérèse Aubert* (1819), *Les Vampires* (1820), *Smarra* (1821), *Trilby ou le Lutin d'Argail* (1822), *La Fée aux Miettes* (1832), *La Neuvaine de la Chandeleur* (1839), *Le Chien de Brisquet* (1844).

**No·dzu** (nô·dzōō), Marquis **Michitsura.** 1841–1908. Japanese soldier; served in Chinese-Japanese War (1894–95), commanding a division and capturing Pingyang (Heijo); commanded 4th army in Russo-Japanese War (1904–05).

**No′é′** (nô′ā′), Comte **Amédée de.** *Pseudonym* **Cham** (kȧm). 1819–1879. French caricaturist; best known for his contributions to *Charivari.*

**No′el** (nō′ĕl). See NOWELL.

**Noel, Roden Berkeley Wriothesley.** 1834–1894. English poet and miscellaneous writer.

**Noel, Thomas.** 1799–1861. English poet; author of song *Rocked in the Cradle of the Deep.*

**Noel-Baker, Philip John.** *Orig. name* **Philip John Baker.** 1889– . British statesman and author. Awarded Nobel peace prize (1959). Wrote *The Arms Race: A Programme for World Disarmament* (1958), etc.

**Noel-Buxton, Edward.** See Thomas Fowell BUXTON.

**Noemi.** See NAOMI.

**Noe′ther** (nû′tẽr), **Max.** 1844–1921. German mathematician; specialist in algebra.

**Nofretete.** See NEFERTITI.

**No′ga′ret′** (nô′gȧ′rĕ′), **Guillaume de.** d. 1313. French jurist and statesman; chief adviser to Philip IV in his struggle with the Papacy and the Templars.

**Nogaret de La Valette, Jean Louis de.** See ÉPERNON.

**Nög′ge·rath** (nûg′ĕ·rät), **Johann Jakob.** 1788–1877. German mineralogist and geologist.

**No·gi** (nô·gē), Count **Maresuke.** 1849–1912. Japanese general; in Chinese-Japanese War (1894–95), at battles of Kinchow and Port Arthur; in Russo-Japanese War (1904–05), captured fortress at Port Arthur, in battle of Mukden (1905).

**No·gu·chi** (nô·gōō·chē; *Angl.* nō·gōō′chē), **Hideyo.** 1876–1928. Bacteriologist, b. in northern Japan; to U.S. (1899) and entered laboratory of pathology at U. of Pennsylvania; published *The Action of Snake Venom upon Cold-blooded Animals* (1904); at Rockefeller Institute (from 1904); made important studies in etiology of syphilis and paresis; devised new method (Noguchi test or reaction) for diagnosis of syphilis; succeeded in producing culture medium for development of spirochaetae, thus forwarding study of these organisms; investigated yellow fever, Oroya fever, and trachoma.

**Noguchi, Isamu.** 1904– . American sculptor, b. Los Angeles, Calif. Son of **Yone Noguchi.** Known for his abstract sculptures.

**Noguchi, Yone.** 1875–1947. Japanese poet; resident in U.S. (1893–1902); lectured on Japanese poetry at Oxford U., England (1913–14). Among his books are *Seen and Unseen* (1897), *The Voice of the Valley* (1898), *The Summer Cloud* (1906), *Lafcadio Hearn in Japan* (1911), *The Spirit of Japanese Poetry* (1914), etc.

**No′guès′** (nô′gĕs′), **Auguste.** 1876–1971. French general; artillery captain in World War I; served against Riffs (1924–26); held various posts in France and in North Africa (1927–36); resident general of Morocco (1936) and commander in chief in North Africa (1939); became member of French Imperial Council and deputy high commissioner for North Africa (1942–43).

**Nohl** (nōl), **Ludwig,** *in full* **Karl Friedrich Ludwig.** 1831–1885. German music scholar and biographer.

**Nolasco, Peter.** See Saint PETER NOLASCO.

**Nol′de** (nôl′dĕ), **Emil.** 1867–1956. German expressionist painter and illustrator.

**Nöl′de·ke** (nûl′dĕ·kĕ), **Theodor.** 1836–1930. German Orientalist; author of works chiefly on Semitic languages and the history of Islam.

**No′lhac′** (nô′lȧk′), **Pierre de,** *in full* **Anet Marie Pierre Gi′rauld′ de** (zhē′rō′ dĕ). 1859–1936. French writer; curator of museum at Versailles (1892–1920); director of museum Jacquemart-André, Paris (1920). Among his books are *Le Dernier Amour de Ronsard* (1882), *Érasme en Italie* (1888), *La Reine Marie Antoinette* (1889), *Pétrarque et l'Humanisme* (1892), *Louis XV et Mme de*

*Pompadour* (1904), *Versailles sous Louis XIV* (1911), *Ronsard et l'Humanisme* (1921).

**No'li** (nō'lĭ), **Fan** (fŭn) **Sty'li·an** (stĭ'lĭ·ŭn). 1882–1965. Ecclesiastic; consecrated bishop of the Russian Orthodox Church, in charge of the Albanian community in Boston (1908); grad. Harvard (1912); prime minister of Albania, after coup overthrowing Ahmed Zogu (6 months, 1924); ousted; returned to U.S.

**Nol'le·kens** (nŏl'ĕ·kĕns; *Angl.* -kĕnz), **Joseph Franciscus.** 1706–1748. Flemish painter in the style of Watteau and Panini. His son **Joseph** (1737–1823) was an English sculptor, b. in London; executed portrait busts of Sterne, Garrick, George III, Pitt, Canning, Lord Castlereagh, Lord Liverpool, and the mausoleum of Manners in Westminster Abbey.

**Nol'let'** (nô'lĕ'), **Charles Marie Édouard.** 1865–1941. French general in the World War (1914–18).

**Nollet, Jean Antoine.** 1700–1770. French abbé and physicist; credited with discovery of endosmosis; improved on the Leyden jar; invented an electroscope.

**No·mu·ra** (nō·mōō·rä), **Kichisaburo.** 1877–1964. Japanese naval officer and diplomat; naval attaché, Washington, D.C., during World War (1914–18); admiral (1926); commander in chief of 3d fleet (1932) during Shanghai incident; foreign minister (1939–40); Japanese ambassador to U.S. (Nov., 1940–Dec., 1941); conducted the "peace" negotiations with U.S. interrupted by Japanese attack on Pearl Harbor (Dec. 7, 1941).

**Nonius, Petrus.** See Pedro NUNES.

**No'ni·us Mar·cel'lus** (nō'nĭ·ŭs mär·sĕl'ŭs). Latin grammarian and lexicographer of 4th century A.D.

**Non'nus** (nŏn'ŭs). Greek epic poet of Egypt in late 4th or early 5th century A.D.

**Noon** (nōōn), Ma'lik (mä'lĭk) Sir **Fi'roz·khan'** (fē'rōz-кän'). 1893– . Indian statesman; commissioner for India in United Kingdom (1936–41); member of viceroy's executive council (1941 ff.); author of *Canada and India* (1939), *Wisdom from Fools* (1940), *Scented Dust* (1941), etc.

**Noort** (nōrt), **Adam van.** 1557–1641. Flemish painter; one of the masters of Rubens and Jordaens.

**Nor'bert** (nôr'bērt), Saint. 1085?–1134. Ecclesiastic, b. in duchy of Cleves; founded near Laon religious order of Premonstratensians, or Premonstrants, devoted to penitence and preaching; archbishop of Magdeburg (1126). Canonized (1582).

**Nord A'lex'is'** (nôr' à'lĕk'sē'), **Pierre.** 1820–1910. Haitian general and politician, b. Cap-Haitien; soldier from his youth; minister of war under Sylvain Salnave; exiled by Salnave's successor, President Michel Domingue; took part in revolution (1888) and was appointed governor of the departments of the north and the northwest by General Hippolite (1888–1902); president of Haiti (1902–08); overthrown by a revolt (1908) and took refuge on a French naval vessel.

**Nor'dau** (nôr'dou), **Max Simon.** *Orig. surname* **Süd'feld** (züt'fĕlt). 1849–1923. German physician and author, b. in Hungary of Jewish parentage; practiced medicine in Budapest (1878–80) and Paris; became an active Zionist leader in Europe (from 1895) and supported Herzl in approving acceptance of East Africa as a Jewish settlement. Author of critical and satirical works on moral and social questions including *Conventional Lies of Civilization* (1883), *Paradoxes* (1885), and *Degeneration* (an attempt to relate genius and degeneracy, 2 vols., 1892–93); novels and stories including *The Malady of the Century* (1888), *A Comedy of Sentiment* (1891), *The Drones Must Die* (1898), and *Morganatic* (1904); also *The Interpretation of History* (1909), *Biologie der Ethik* (1921), and essays, plays, travel books, fairy tales, etc.

**Nor'den** (nôr'd'n), **Carl Lukas.** 1880–1965. Dutch inventor of the Norden bombsight; b. Java; to U.S. (1904).

**Nor'den** (nôr'dĕn), **Eduard.** 1868–1937. German classical philologist.

**Nor'den·berg'** (nōōr'dĕn·băr'y'), **Bengt.** 1822–1902. Swedish genre painter, chiefly of Swedish peasant life.

**Nor'den·flycht'** (nōōr'dĕn·flükt'), **Hedvig Charlotta.** 1718–1763. Swedish poetess; champion of the feminist movement and (with Dalin) of French taste in Swedish literature; founder of the first Swedish literary salon, center (from 1753) of the literary "Order of Thought Builders," to which Count Creutz belonged; author of *The Sorrowing Turtledove* (collection of lyrics inspired by the death of her husband; 1743), the collection *A Woman's Play of Thoughts, by a Shepherdess in the North* (4 vols., 1744–50), etc.

**Nor'den·skjöld'** (nōōr'dĕn·shûld'), Baron **Nils Adolf Erik.** 1832–1901. Swedish geologist and arctic explorer, b. Helsingfors, Finland; went on several expeditions to Spitsbergen (first in 1858); led expedition that reached highest northern latitude (81° 42') then attained in the eastern hemisphere (1868); accomplished Northeast Passage in the *Vega* (1878–80); visited Greenland, studying the icecap (1870; 1883). His sons: **Gustaf Erik Adolf** (1868–1895), explorer and scholar, and Baron **Nils Erland Herbert** (1877–1932), ethnologist, who traveled in various South American countries and wrote on South American Indians. Their cousin **Nils Otto Gustaf Nordenskjöld** (1869–1928), geologist and explorer, traveled in Tierra del Fuego (1895–97), Alaska (1898), Greenland (1900; 1909), the Andes (1904–05; 1920–21); led expedition to the Antarctic (1901), being rescued by the Argentine government after his ship, the *Antarctica*, had been crushed by ice (1903).

**Nord'hau'sen** (nôrt'hou'zĕn), **Richard.** *Pseudonym* **Cal'i·ban** (kăl'ĭ·băn; -băn; *Ger.* kä'lē·bän). 1868– . German writer and publicist in Berlin.

**Nord'hoff** (nôrd'hŏf), **Charles.** 1830–1901. Writer, b. in Westphalia; to U.S. as a child; in U.S. navy (1844–47), and merchant marine and fishing vessels (1847–53); author of *Man-of-War Life* (1855), *The Merchant Vessel* (1855), *Whaling and Fishing* (1856), *Politics for Young Americans* (1875), etc.

**Nordhoff, Charles Bernard.** 1887–1947. Writer, b. London, Eng., of American parentage; served in World War, from 1916 to 1919; ambulance driver, Lafayette Flying Corps, U.S. air service. Author of *The Fledgling* (1919), *The Pearl Lagoon* (1924), *Picaro* (1924), *The Derelict* (1928). Collaborator in a number of books with James Norman Hall (*q.v.*). Edited, under title of *In Yankee Windjammers* (1940), journals of his grandfather Charles Nordhoff (*q.v.*).

**Nor'di·ca** (nôr'dĭ·kȧ), **Lillian.** *Pseudonym of* **Lillian Norton.** 1857–1914. American operatic soprano, b. Farmington, Me.; m. (1882) Frederick A. Gower (disappeared, 1886), Zoltan Döme (1896, divorced 1904), George W. Young (1909); devoted herself esp. to Wagnerian roles (from 1894), chiefly with Metropolitan Opera House, New York (1896–1907), Oscar Hammerstein's Manhattan Opera Company (1907–08); on concert tours (after 1908).

**Nor'draak** (nôr'drôk), **Rikard.** 1842–1866. Norwegian composer; studied and collected Norwegian folk songs; met Grieg (1864) and inspired him to develop a Norwegian national school of music; composed the music for the national hymn *Ja, Vi Elsker Dette Landet*, written by his cousin Björnson (*q.v.*), incidental music to Björnson's *Mary Stuart* and *Sigurd Slembe*, piano pieces, etc.

**No·reen'** (nōō·rān'), **Adolf Gotthard.** 1854–1925. Swedish philologist; professor of Scandinavian languages, Uppsala (1887–1919).

**Nor'folk** (nôr'fŭk), Earls and dukes of. Titles in English peerage. Title of earl of Norfolk held first by Ralph de GUADER (fl. 1070); conferred by Stephen (1136) upon Hugh BIGOD and held by members of the Bigod family until it became extinct (1306) with death of Roger Bigod, 5th earl; granted (1312) by Edward II to his half brother THOMAS OF BROTHERTON, from whom it descended to the latter's daughter Margaret (cr. duchess of Norfolk, 1397), then to dukes of Norfolk, becoming extinct with death of Anne, daughter of 4th duke and wife of young Richard, Duke of York, who was murdered in the Tower. Ducal title, created (1397) for Margaret, Countess of Norfolk, and her grandson Thomas (I) Mowbray (1366?–1399), held by members of Mowbray family (*q.v.*) until death (1476) of John, 4th duke; re-created (1483) for Richard (1472–1483), the younger of the princes doomed by Richard III in the Tower, and held (from 1483) by members of Howard family (*q.v.*); still the premier dukedom of England, ranking next after princes of the blood.

**Norman, Fredrik Vilhelm Ludvig.** See NERUDA.

**Nor'man** (nôr'măn), Sir **Henry.** 1858–1939. English journalist, traveler, and radio-engineering expert; asst. editor, *Daily Chronicle* (1895–99); Liberal M.P. (1900–10); founded the (English) magazine *World's Work* (1902); asst. postmaster general (1910); chairman of imperial and international committees on radiotelegraphic research and broadcasting; author of books on Far East, Near East, and the Russias, and a play *Will No Man Understand?* (1934).

**Norman,** Sir **Henry Wylie.** 1826–1904. British military officer and colonial governor; took active part in Sikh war (1848–49), and in Sepoy Mutiny at siege of Delhi, relief of Lucknow, capture of Cawnpore (1857); first secretary to Indian government in military department (1862–70); member of council of India (1878–83); governor of Jamaica (1883–89), of Queensland (1889–95); field marshal (1902).

**Norman, Montagu Collet.** 1871–1950. 1st Baron **Norman of St. Clere** (sânt klâr'; sĭn[g]'klâr). English banker; governor (1920–44), Bank of England; with chancellor of exchequer, Stanley Baldwin, arranged funding of British war debt to U.S. (1922); privy councilor (1923).

**Normanby,** Viscount and marquises of. See PHIPPS family.

**Nor'man·dy** (nôr'măn·dĭ), Dukes of. Rulers of duchy of northern France set up in 912 with Rollo as first duke. See esp. WILLIAM I the Conqueror (duke 1035–87) who conquered England (king 1066–87). See also other rulers of Normandy under RICHARD, ROBERT, WILLIAM.

**Nor'mann** (nôr'män), **Eilert Adelsteen.** 1848–1918. Norwegian landscape painter, esp. of Norwegian fiords.

**Normann-Neruda, Wilma.** See NERUDA.

**Nor'reys** (nŏr'ĭs). See also NORRIS.

**Nor'ris** (nŏr'ĭs), **Frank,** *in full* **Benjamin Franklin.** 1870–1902. American novelist, b. Chicago; war correspondent in South Africa for San Francisco *Chronicle* (1895–96), and in Cuba for *McClure's Magazine* (1898–99); on staff of Doubleday, Page & Co. (from 1899); author of *McTeague* (1899), *A Man's Woman* (1900), *The Octopus* (1901), *The Pit* (1903). His brother **Charles Gilman (1881–1945), assistant editor, *Country Life in America* (1903), *Sunset Magazine* (1905), and art editor, *American Magazine* (1908–13); author of *The Amateur* (1915), *Salt, or the Education of Griffith Adams* (1917), *Brass* (1921), *Bread* (1923), *Pig Iron* (1925), *Seed* (1930), *Zest* (1933), *Hands* (1935),** etc. Charles G. Norris married (1909) Kathleen Thompson, a novelist thereafter known as **Kathleen Norris** (1880–1966); author of *Mother* (1911), *Saturday's Child* (1914), *Sisters* (1919), *The Sea Gull* (1927), *My California* (1933), *Heartbroken Melody* (1938), etc.

**Norris, George William.** 1861–1944. American statesman, b. in Sandusky County, Ohio; member, U.S. House of Representatives (1903–13); U.S. senator from Nebraska (1913–43). Led contest for overthrow of arbitrary rule of Speaker Joseph G. Cannon in the house (1910); opposed U.S. entry into World War I; led long struggle for federal power control in Tennessee Valley and secured passage of act creating Tennessee Valley Authority (1933), the first TVA-built dam, whose gates were closed Mar. 4, 1936, being called Norris Dam in his honor. Also known as "Father of the Twentieth Amendment," popularly known as the "Lame Duck Act" (in effect, 1933), providing for inauguration of a newly elected president on January 20th instead of Mar. 4th and for annual meetings of Congress beginning Jan. 3, thus eliminating the former short session from January to March.

**Norris,** Sir **John.** 1547?–1597. English military commander; won fame under Essex in guerrilla war against Irish (1573), in service in Netherlands (1577–85); ambassador to Dutch States (1588); commanded with Sir Francis Drake fleet that ravaged coasts of Spain and Portugal (1589); returned to Ireland (1597) to aid in reducing Tyrone; failed to pacify Connaught.

**Norris, John.** 1657–1711. English philosopher and clergyman; became sole English advocate of Malebranchist theories; drawn into controversy with Quakers over Malebranchist theory of divine illumination.

**Norris, Kathleen.** See under Frank NORRIS.

**Norris, William Edward.** 1847–1925. English novelist; son of chief justice of Ceylon; encouraged by Leslie Stephen, editor of *Cornhill Magazine,* to try novel; wrote *Heaps of Money* (1877), *Trevalion* (1925), etc.

**Nor'rish** (nŏr'ĭsh), **Ronald George Wreyford.** 1897– . British chemist. At U. of Cambridge (1930–65); awarded Nobel prize in chemistry (1967) with M. Eigen and G. Porter.

**North** (nôrth). Name of an English family, some of whose members bore the title of Baron North; including: Sir **Thomas** (1535?–?1601), 2d son of 1st Baron North (cr. 1554); translator of *The Diall of Princes* (1557; from a French version of Guevara's *Relox de Príncipes*) with mannerisms and antitheses foreshadowing euphuism, of *The Morall Philosophie of Doni* (1570), eastern fables, from the Italian, and of Plutarch's *Lives* from the French of Amyot (1579, with added *Lives* 1595, 1603), the chief source from which Shakespeare drew his knowledge of ancient history.

**Roger** (1585?–?1652), great-grandson of 1st baron; accompanied Raleigh to Guiana (1617), forced to return by disaffection; made successful voyage to the Amazon (1619–21), and obtained letters patent to settle Guiana (1627).

**Francis** (1637–1685), 1st Baron **Guil'ford** (gĭl'fẽrd); son of 4th Baron North; solicitor general (1671), attorney general (1673), chief justice of common pleas (1675–82), lord chancellor (1682); participated in coronation of James II (1685); an accomplished musician.

Sir **Dudley** (1641–1691), economist, brother of Francis North; agent at Smyrna and at Constantinople (1662–80), amassing a fortune; commissioner for customs and for treasury; anticipated Adam Smith in *Discourses Upon Trade* (1691); advocated free trade.

**Roger** (1653–1734), lawyer, brother of Francis and Sir Dudley North; solicitor general to Duke of York (1684); attorney general to James II's queen (1686); quit politics

(1688) and turned to writing. Author of *Memoires of Musick* (ed. 1846) on progress from Greeks to 1728; eulogistic biographies of three of his brothers; and an *Examen* (1740) or criticism of White Kennett's *Compleat History of England.*

**Frederick** (1732–1792), 2d Earl of Guilford, statesman; son of 7th Baron North; known as Lord North (by courtesy until 1790); M.A., Oxon. (1750); entered House of Commons at 22; chancellor of the exchequer (1767); first lord of treasury (1770); as prime minister, made himself pliant agent of George III, who dominated the ministry and, against protests of Fox and Burke, pursued ruinous policy leading to revolt and loss of American colonies; opposed Wilkes, supported American stamp tax and Townshend's tea duty; resigned (1782); united with Fox to overthrow Shelburne ministry (1783).

**Brownlow** (1741–1820), clergyman, half brother of Frederick North; M.A., Oxon. (1766); dean of Canterbury (1770); bishop of Coventry and Lichfield (1771), of Worcester (1774), of Winchester (1781).

**North, Christopher.** Pseudonym of John Wilson (1785–1854).

**North, Elisha.** 1771–1843. American physician, b. Goshen, Conn.; American pioneer in vaccination against smallpox.

**North, Marianne.** 1830–1890. English naturalist and flower painter; traveled in every continent, painting native flora; erected at own expense a gallery for her paintings at Kew Gardens (1882).

**North·amp'ton** (nôr·thămp'tŭn), Earls of. Title held by different English families: first by a Norman noble, **Simon de Sen'lis** (dĕ sĕn'lĭs; *Fr.* säN'lēs'), builder of Northampton Castle, and his son **Simon** (d. 1153), who fought for Stephen at Lincoln (1141); by William de Bohun (d. 1360), captain general in Brittany, who fought at Cressy; by Henry Howard (cr. 1604; see earl of Northampton under Howard family); by members of Compton family, including William Compton (d. 1630), 1st earl, and his son Spencer Compton (*q.v.*), 2d earl.

**Northampton, John de.** fl. 1376–1390. English draper and Wyckliffite; as lord mayor of London (1381–83) obtained revocation of fishmongers' monopoly and reduced price of fish; arrested (1384) by rival and successor, Sir Nicholas Brembre, on charge of sedition; im prisoned (till 1387).

**Northbrook,** Baron and 1st earl of. See Baring family.

**Northcliffe,** Viscount. See Alfred Charles William Harmsworth.

**North'cote** (nôrth'kŭt; -kōt), **James.** 1746–1831. English historical and portrait painter; assistant to Sir Joshua Reynolds; employed by Boydell to paint nine pictures for the Shakespeare Gallery (1786), including *The Murder of the Princes in the Tower;* best known for portraits.

**Northcote,** Sir **Stafford Henry.** 1st Earl of **Iddes'leigh** (ĭdz'lā; -lĭ). 1818–1887. English statesman and financier; M.P. (1855–85), in the confidence of Disraeli; president of Board of Trade (1866); secretary for India (1867); chairman of Hudson's Bay Company (1869–74); chancellor of exchequer (1874–80); leader of House of Commons (1876), of the opposition (1880–85); foreign secretary (1886). His son **Henry Stafford** (1846–1911), colonial administrator, accompanied his father to Washington on settlement of Alabama claims (1871–73); as governor of Bombay (1899–1903), dealt with plague and famine and obtained passage of land revenue reform measures; as governor general of Australia (1904–08), contributed to imperial unity and encouraged immigration.

**Nor'they** (nôr'thĭ), **Edward.** 1868–1953. English military officer in Boer War (1899–1902) and in World War I; governor of Kenya Colony and Zanzibar (1918–22).

**Northington,** 1st Earl of. See Robert Henley.

**Nor'throp** (nôr'thrŭp), **Cyrus.** 1834–1922. American educator, b. near Ridgefield, Conn.; president, U. of Minnesota (1884–1911).

**Northrop, John Howard.** 1891– . American scientist, b. Yonkers, N.Y.; Ph.D., Columbia (1915); with Rockefeller Inst. (from 1916); shared with Wendell M. Stanley and James B. Sumner (*qq.v.*) 1946 Nobel prize for chemistry, for work on enzymes and virus proteins.

**North·um'ber·land** (nôr·thŭm'bẽr·lănd), Earls and dukes of. Titles of British peerage held by John (1502?–1553) and Sir Robert Dudley and the Percy and Neville families.

**Nor'ton** (nôr't'n), **1st Baron.** See Charles Bowyer Adderley.

**Norton, Andrews.** 1786–1853. American Biblical scholar and educator, b. Hingham, Mass.; professor of Sacred Literature, Harvard Divinity School (1819–30); author of *The Evidences of the Genuineness of the Gospels* (3 vols., 1837, 1844). His son **Charles Eliot** (1827–1908), author and educator, was editor, with James Russell Lowell, of *North American Review* (1864 ff.); with E. L. Godkin and others, founded *The Nation* (1865); professor, Harvard (1873–97), beginning first course in the fine arts as associated with social, cultural, and literary development of a people. Author of *Historical Studies of Church-Building in the Middle Ages* (1880); translator into English prose of Dante's *Divine Comedy* (1891–92); editor of *Poems of John Donne* (2 vols., 1895), *Poems of Mrs. Anne Bradstreet* (1897), Thomas Carlyle's *Correspondence*, etc.

**Norton, Caroline Elizabeth Sarah,** *nee* **Sheridan.** 1808–1877. English author; known as "the Hon. Mrs. Norton"; one of the three granddaughters of Richard Brinsley Sheridan; m. 1st (1827) Hon. George Chapple Norton (d. 1875), barrister; contributed to family support by writing for periodicals; led by marital troubles to publish pamphlet and address the queen on divorce laws; George Meredith's model for Diana in *Diana of the Crossways;* m. 2d (1877) Sir William Stirling-Maxwell; remembered chiefly for her poetry.

**Norton, Fletcher.** 1st Baron **Grant'ley** (grănt'lĭ). 1716–1789. English jurist; solicitor general (1762) and attorney general (1763–65); speaker of House of Commons (1770–80); subject of an attack in the 39th letter of Junius (*q.v.*).

**Norton, Grace Fallow.** 1876– . American poet, b. Northfield, Minn.; author of *Little Gray Songs from St. Joseph's* (1912), *The Sister of the Wind* (1914), *Roads* (1916), *The Miller's Youngest Daughter* (1924), etc.

**Norton, Lillian.** See Lillian Nordica.

**Norton, John.** 1606–1663. Puritan clergyman, b. in Hertfordshire, Eng.; to America (1635), and settled at Ipswich; pastor in Ipswich (1638–56) and Boston (1656–63); active in persecution of Quakers in Massachusetts colony; author (1645) of a Latin treatise, *Responsio ad Totam Quaestionum Syllogen*, on New England church government, first Latin book composed in the colonies (pub. in London, 1648).

**Norton, Thomas.** 1532–1584. English lawyer and poet; amanuensis to Protector Somerset; eloquent debater in parliament for anti-Catholic measures; as censor, conducted examinations of Catholics under torture. Translated Calvin's *Institutes* (1559); contributed to Tottel's *Miscellany;* collaborated with Thomas Sackville (*q.v.*) in blank-verse *Tragedy of Gorboduc*, the earliest English tragedy (1561), probably writing first three acts.

**Norton, Thomas Herbert.** 1851–1941. American chemist; as U.S. consul at Chemnitz, Germany (1906–14), studied European chemical industry and issued a report on dyestuffs that formed the foundation of domestic dye industry during the World War (1914–18).

**Norton–Griffiths,** Sir **John.** See GRIFFITHS.

**Norway, Nevil Shute.** See Nevil SHUTE.

**Norwich,** Earl of. See George GORING.

**Norwich, Edward of.** 2d Duke of **York.** See YORK.

**Nos'ke** (nŏs'kĕ), **Gustav.** 1868–1946. German statesman and politician; on staff of various Social Democratic periodicals (from 1897); member of Reichstag (from 1906); to Kiel during November revolution of 1918, where he re-established order; member, Council of National Deputies (1918); commanded troops which suppressed Berlin Spartacan revolts (1919); became first Reichminister of defense (1919), but resigned following the Kapp Putsch (1920); president, Hanover province (1920–33); author of an autobiography (1919), *Von Kiel bis Kapp* (1920), etc.

**Nos·kow'ski** (nôs·kôf'skē), **Zygmunt.** 1846–1909. Polish composer; invented a system of musical notation for use of the blind; conductor of Warsaw Philharmonic Orchestra; composed operas, a ballet, two cantatas, three symphonies, a symphonic poem, etc.

**Nos'tra·da'mus** (nŏs'trȧ·dā'mŭs). *Lat. name of* **Michel de No'tre·dame'** *or* **Nos'tre·dame'** (nô'trē·dȧm'). 1503–1566. French physician and astrologer; published book of rhymed prophecies under the title *Centuries* (1555); prophesied correctly the manner of the death of Henry II of France; gained favor of Catherine de Médicis; became physician to Charles IX.

**Notestein, Ada Comstock.** See Ada Louise COMSTOCK.

**Noth'na'gel** (nōt'nä'gĕl), **Carl Wilhelm Hermann.** 1841–1905. German physician; known for work on the physiology and pathology of the nervous system, on Addison's disease, and on heart and stomach diseases.

**No'thomb'** (nô'tômb'), **Jean Baptiste.** 1805–1881. Belgian statesman; premier of Belgium (1843–45); Belgian minister at Berlin (1845–81).

**Not'ker** (nŏt'kĕr; -kẽr). *Called* **Bal'bu·lus** (băl'bŭ·lŭs), *i.e.* the stammerer. 840?–912. Swiss monk; best known for his sacred music. Beatified (1512).

**Not'ker** (nŏt'kĕr; -kẽr). *Called* **Lab'e·o** (lăb'ē·ō), *i.e.* the thick-lipped. 952?–1022. Swiss-German Benedictine scholar; his translations of Latin classics into German influential in fixing the form of the German language.

**Notredame, Michel de.** See NOSTRADAMUS.

**Nott** (nŏt), **Abraham.** 1768–1830. American jurist, b. Saybrook, Conn.; judge of the circuit court (1810–30), and president of court of appeals (1824–30). His son **Josiah Clark** (1804–1873) was a physician and ethnologist; practiced in Mobile, Ala. (from 1835); served in Confederate army in Civil War; author of papers in technical journals, including papers on yellow fever, hypnotism, and ethnology; coauthor, with George R. Gliddon, of *Types of Mankind* (1854) and *Indigenous Races of the Earth* (1857).

**Nott, Samuel.** 1754–1852. American Congregational clergyman; pastor, Franklin, Conn., for 70 years (1782–1852). His brother **Eliphalet** (1773–1866) was a Presbyterian clergyman; president of Union College for 62 years (1804–66); invented a base-burning stove adapted for use of anthracite coal.

**Not'te·bohm** (nŏt'ĕ·bōm), **Martin Gustav.** 1817–1882. German music scholar; authority on Beethoven; resident in Vienna (from 1845); composed chiefly works for piano.

**Not'ting·ham** (nŏt'ĭng·ăm), Earl of. English title held by MOWBRAY family (1383–1476), HOWARD family (1596–1681), FINCH family (1681–1729), united (since 1729) with earldom of Winchilsea.

**Noue.** See LA NOUE.

**Nou'guès'** (nōō'gĕs'), **Jean.** 1876–1932. French composer, esp. of operas.

**Noureddin.** See NUREDDIN.

**Nourse** (nûrs), **Elizabeth.** 1860?–1938. American painter, b. Cincinnati; studio in Paris; among her paintings are *A Mother and Child, Closed Shutters* (Luxembourg Museum, Paris), *The First Communion, The Family Repast, Mother and Children, Happy Days.*

**Novachovitch, Lippe B.** See Morris WINCHEVSKY.

**No'vák** (nô'väk), **Vítězslav.** 1870–1949. Czech composer of operas, ballets, symphonies, chamber music, songs.

**No·va'ko·vić** (nŏ·vä'kŏ·vēt'y; *Angl.* -vĭch), **Stojan.** 1842–1915. Serbian writer and statesman; premier and minister of foreign affairs (1895–96).

**Novalis.** See Baron Friedrich von HARDENBERG.

**No·var'** (nŏ·vär'), 1st Viscount. **Ronald Craufurd Mun·ro'–Fer'gu·son** (mŭn·rō'fûr'gŭ·s'n). 1860–1934. British administrator, b. in Scotland; M.P. (1884–1914); governor general of Australia (1914–20); secretary for Scotland (1922–24).

**No·va'ti** (nŏ·vä'tē), **Francesco.** 1859–?1915. Italian Romance philologist and literary historian; known for his medieval and Renaissance studies; a founder of *Giornale Storico della Letteratura Italiana* (1883).

**No·va'tian** (nŏ·vā'shăn). *Latin* **No·va'ti·a'nus** (nŏ·vā'shĭ·ā'nŭs). 3d-century Christian sectarian, perhaps native of Phrygia; on a point of ecclesiastical discipline, opposed elevation of Cornelius to bishopric of Rome (pope) and had himself consecrated bishop of Rome (antipope) by his sympathizers (251); he thus became founder of sect known as Novatians.

**No·vel'li** (nŏ·vĕl'lē), **Ermete.** 1851–1919. Italian actor, b. Lucca; known esp. for Shakespearean roles.

**No·vel'lo** (nŏ·vĕl'ō), **Ivor.** *Orig. name* **Ivor Novello Davies.** 1893–1951. Son of Clara Novello Davies (*q.v.*). English actor, composer, and film star; composer of over sixty songs, including *Keep the Home Fires Burning,* and musical plays and reviews, including *Tabs, The House that Jack Built;* actor-manager (1924) with *The Rat,* written in collaboration with Constance Collier, and with his own plays *The Truth Game* (1928), and *Symphony in Two Flats* (1929); to Hollywood for writing and acting (1931); actor-manager with his plays, *Murder in Mayfair* (1934), *Glamorous Night* (1935), *Careless Rapture* (1936), *Crest of the Wave* (1937).

**Novello, Vincent.** 1781–1861. English organist and composer of sacred music; b. London, son of Italian father and English mother; arranged collection of sacred music (1811), which marked founding of publishing house of Novello & Co.; introduced to England unknown compositions of Haydn, Mozart, and Palestrina; original member and frequent conductor of Philharmonic Society. His son **Joseph Alfred** (1810–1896), bass singer and music publisher, inaugurated, with success, many popular concert enterprises, introduced Mendelssohn's works to English public, and devised a system of printing cheap editions of standard musical works. His daughter **Clara Anastasia** (1818–1908), Countess **Gi·gliuc'ci** (jē·lyōōt'chē), oratorio and operatic singer, at age of 14 took soprano part in Beethoven's *Missa Solemnis;* praised by Mendelssohn and Schumann; m. Count Gigliucci (1843).

**Novello–Davies, Clara.** See Clara Novello DAVIES.

**No'verre'** (nô'vâr'), **Jean Georges.** 1727–1810. French dancing master; dance director at the Opéra (1776–80); did much to improve and develop the ballet.

**No'vi·kov** (nô'vyĭ·kôf), **Nikolai Ivanovich.** 1744–1818. Russian journalist and philanthropist; satirized foreign influence in Russia, the institution of serfdom, and other evils of conditions in his country; leased Moscow *Gazette*, with its printing plant (1779–89), and tried to inculcate a love for good literature by publishing many low-priced editions of classics.

**Novikov, Nikolai Vasilievich.** 1903– . Russian diplomat, b. Leningrad; minister to Egypt (1943–44), to U.S. (1944–46); ambassador to U.S. (1946–47).

**Novikov, Olga,** *nee* **Ki·re′ev** (kyĭ·ryā′yĕf). *Pseudonym* **O. K.** (ō′kȧ′; *Eng.* ō′kā′). 1840–1925. Russian journalist, b. in Moscow; m. General Novikov; lived many years in England; friend of Gladstone, Froude, Kinglake, and Carlyle; attempted to promote friendship between Russia and England. Among her books are *Is Russia Wrong?* (1877), *Friends or Foes* (1878), *Russia and England* (1880).

**No′vi·us** (nō′vĭ·ŭs). Latin writer of comedies. Cf. POMPONIUS.

**No′vot·na** (nô′vôt·nȧ), **Jarmila.** 1911– . Czech soprano, b. Prague; m. (1931) George Daubek; with Metropolitan Opera Co., N.Y. (1939–45).

**No′vy** (nō′vĭ), **Frederick George.** 1864–1957. American bacteriologist, b. Chicago; studied in Koch's laboratory, Berlin (1888), and at Pasteur Inst., Paris (1897). Author of *Cocaine and its Derivatives* (1887), *Laboratory Work in Physiological Chemistry* (1899), *Cellular Toxins* (with Victor Clarence Vaughan; 1904), etc.

**Now′ell** *or* **Now′el** *or* **No′el** (nō′ĕl), **Alexander.** 1507?–1602. English clergyman; dean of St. Paul's, London (1560–1602); inclined to Calvinism; author of the *Large Catechism*, the *Middle Catechism*, and the *Small Catechism*, which last is practically that of the *Book of Common Prayer.*

**No′wo·wiej′ski** (nô′vô·vyā′skē), **Feliks.** 1877–1946. Polish composer of operas, oratorios, ballets, symphonies, masses, choral works, and songs.

**Nox, Owen.** Pseudonym of Charles Barney CORY.

**Noyes** (noiz), **Alfred.** 1880–1958. English poet, b. in Staffordshire; m. (1907) Garnett Daniels (d. 1926), dau. of a U.S. army officer; m. 2d (1927) Mary Weld-Blundell; professor of modern English literature, Princeton U. (1914–23); attached to British foreign office (1916); published first volume of poems, *The Loom of Years* (1902); gained popularity with *The Flower of Old Japan* (1903); turned to poetry of the sea in *Forty Singing Seamen* (1907), and *Drake* (a blank-verse epic about Elizabethans, 1908); treated Elizabethan poets in *Tales of Mermaid Tavern* (1912). Author also of poetic plays, including *Sherwood, or Robin Hood and the Three Kings* (1912, produced 1927), *Rada: A Belgian Christmas Eve* (1915); short stories, including *Walking Shadows* (1917); novels, including *The Winepress* (1913), *The Sun Cure* (1929); and an epic trilogy *The Torch Bearers* (1922, 1925, 1930).

**Noyes, Arthur Amos.** 1866–1936. American chemist, b. Newburyport, Mass.; known esp. for work in development of thermodynamic chemistry and of the ionic theory, in qualitative analysis, and in chemical education.

**Noyes, Clara Dutton.** 1870–1936. American Red Cross nurse, b. Port Deposit, Md.; director, department of nursing service, American Red Cross (1918–36); awarded Florence Nightingale medal by International Committee of the Red Cross (1923) and French medal of honor (1929).

**Noyes, Crosby Stuart.** 1825–1908. American journalist, b. Minot, Me.; editor of Washington (D.C.) *Star* (1867–1908). One son, **Theodore Williams** (1858–1946), succeeded him (1908) as editor of the paper. A second son, **Frank Brett** (1863–1948), became president of Washington (D.C.) Evening Star Newspaper Co. (1910) and president of Associated Press (1900–38).

**Noyes, Frances Newbold.** See Frances Noyes HART.

**Noyes, Harry Alfred.** 1890– . American research chemist; specialist in food technology; developed contact freezing processes for foods.

**Noyes, John Humphrey.** 1811–1886. American social reformer, b. Brattleboro, Vt.; studied for ministry; announced (1834) that he had attained sinlessness, or perfection; gathered group at Putney, Vt.; expounded gospel of perfectionism and formed society of Bible communists (1836), attempting to return to the communism of the early Christian church. His views on monogamic marriage and his belief in promiscuity, or free love, practiced in the Putney community, caused his arrest (1846). Fled to central New York State, followed by the Bible communists, and established (1848) Oneida Community in which the group members were free to try their social experiment. Under his organization and leadership, community flourished, abandoned free love, or complex marriage, feature (1879), was capitalized at $600,000 when incorporated (1881), and became known esp. for manufacture of mousetraps and so-called Community silverware. Noyes fled to Canada to escape prosecution for adultery; died Niagara Falls, Ontario. His views were set forth in *The Berean* (1847), *Bible Communism* (1848), *Male Continence* (1848), *Scientific Propagation* (c. 1873), *Home Talks* (1875).

**Noyes, La Verne.** 1849–1919. American inventor, b. Genoa, N.Y.; invented wire dictionary holder and opened factory in Chicago to manufacture it; also invented a tractor wheel (1885), harvester reel (1885), sheaf carrier for self-binding harvesters (1888), cord knotter for grain binders (1889), improved steel windmill (1890), etc.; organized and headed Aërmotor Company, Chicago, to manufacture his windmills.

**Noyes** (nois), **William Albert.** 1857–1941. American chemist; professor and director of chemical laboratory, Illinois (1907–26); known esp. for organic synthesis and atomic weight determinations.

**Nu·bar′ Pa′sha** (nōō·bär′ pȧ′shä). 1825–1899. Egyptian diplomat and statesman; premier of Egypt (1878–79; 1884–88; 1894–95).

**Nuffield,** 1st Viscount. See William Richard MORRIS.

**Nu′gent** (nū′jĕnt), Baron. See GRENVILLE family.

**Nugent,** Sir **George.** 1757–1849. English military officer; served in American Revolution (1777–83), in Flanders under duke of York (1793); lieut. governor of Jamaica (1801–06); commander in chief in India (1811–13); field marshal (1846).

**Nugent, John Charles.** 1878–1947. American actor and playwright, b. Niles, Ohio; acted in vaudeville in sketches of his own composition and by other authors, as *The Dumb-Bell*, *The Rising Son*, *The Trouper*, and *God Loves Us.* His son **Elliott** (1899– ), also an actor and playwright; author of motion-picture scenarios; collaborated with his father in *The Dumb-Bell*, *The Rising Son*, *The Trouper*, etc., and with J. G. Thurber in *The Male Animal* (1940); joined Metro-Goldwyn-Mayer staff (1929) as actor, author, and director; had part in *College Life*, *Not So Dumb*, *The Nervous Wreck*, *Expressing Willie*, etc.

**Nugent, La·val′** (lȧ·văl′). Count **Nugent von West′meath** (fôn wĕst′mēth). 1777–1862. Field marshal in Austrian army, b. in Ireland; general chief of staff (1809); conquered Croatia, Istria, and the Po region (1813); commanded forces in Italy (1815), besieged Rome, and conquered Murat at Ceprano and San Germano; became a prince of the Holy Roman Empire (1816); supported Radetzky against the Piedmontese (1848); field marshal (1849); took part in Italian campaign of 1859.

**Nu·it'ter'** (nü·ē'târ'). *Anagrammatic pseudonym of* **Charles Louis Étienne Tru·i'net'** (trü·ē'nĕ'). 1828–1899. French playwright; author of, or collaborator in, *Une Tasse de Thé* (1860), *J'Ai Perdu Mon Andalouse* (1869), and librettos for *Roméo et Juliette, La Princesse de Trébizonde, Hellé*, etc.

**Nüll** (nül), **Eduard van der.** 1812–1868. Austrian architect; collaborated with August Siccard von Siccardsburg in designing Vienna Opera House (1861 ff.).

**Nu'ma Pom·pil'i·us** (nū'mȧ pŏm·pĭl'ĭ·ŭs). Second legendary king (715–673 B.C.) of early Rome, a Sabine.

**Nu·me'ni·us** (nů·mē'nĭ·ŭs). Greek Neo-Pythagorean philosopher of late 2d century A.D., b. Apamea, Syria; regarded as a forerunner of Neoplatonists. Only fragments of his works are extant.

**Nu·me'ri·a'nus** (nů·mĕr'ĭ·ā'nŭs), **Marcus Aurelius.** d. 284. Roman emperor (283–284) jointly with his brother Carinus (*q.v.*); younger son of Emperor Carus (*q.v.*); accompanied his father on expedition against Persians; after death of Carus, died in camp on returning from the East; succeeded by Diocletian.

**Nun'co·mar** (nŭn'kō·mär). *Also* **Nan'da Ku·mar'** (nŭn'dȧ kōō·mär'). d. 1775. Bengali Brahmin official in India; governor of Hugli (1756); replaced Warren Hastings as collector of Burdwan (1764); accused Hastings of peculation as governor general; indicted for forgery, condemned, executed.

**Nu'nes** (nōō'nĕsh) *or* **Nu'nez** (nōō'nĕsh), **Pedro.** *Lat.* **Petrus No'ni·us** (nō'nĭ·ŭs). 1492–1577. Portuguese mathematician; wrote on navigation and geometry; invented device (the nonius) for graduating instruments, later improved into the vernier. See Pierre VERNIER.

**Nú'ñez** (nōō'nyās), **Rafael.** 1825–1894. President of Colombia (1880–82; 1884–86; 1887–88); succeeded in putting down a revolution (1880); supported new constitution of 1886 which further centralized the government.

**Nú'ñez Cabeza de Vaca** (nōō'nyāth), **Álvar.** See CABEZA DE VACA.

**Nú'ñez de Ar'ce** (nōō'nyāth thā är'thā), **Gaspar.** 1834–1903. Spanish poet, playwright, and statesman; foreign correspondent for *La Iberia* in African campaign (1859–60); deputy to Cortes (1865 ff.); civil governor of Barcelona (1868); minister of colonial affairs (1882). Author of lyrics *Gritos del Combate* (1875), *Idilio* (1879), *Elegía* (1879), *Última Lamentación de Lord Byron* (1879), *Vértigo* (1879), *La Visión de Fray Martín* (1880), and *La Pesca* (1884), and tragedy *El Haz de Leña* (1872).

**Núñez de Balboa, Vasco.** See BALBOA.

**Núñez de Guz·mán'** (thā gōōth·män'), **Hernán.** *Known as* **el Pin·cia'no** (ĕl pēn·thyä'nō) *and* **el Co'men·da·dor' Gri·e'go** (kō'män·dä·thôr' grē·ā'gō). 1478?–1553. Spanish Greek scholar; edited and translated Greek and Latin classics.

**Núñez de Vil'la·vi·cen'cio** (thā vē'lyä·vē·thān'thyō), **Pedro.** 1635–1700. Spanish painter; pupil and associate of Murillo; his works, sometimes confused with those of Murillo, include esp. portraits and historical scenes.

**Nun'ges'ser'** (nûɴ'zhā'sâr'), **Charles.** 1892–1927. French military aviator in the World War, credited with bringing down 45 enemy planes; lost in attempted transatlantic flight (May, 1927).

**Nu·nó'** (nōō·nō'), **Jaime.** 1824–1908. Conductor and composer, b. San Juan de las Abadesas, Spain; a director, National Conservatory of Music, Mexico City (1854–55); in U.S. (from 1855). Composer of music of Mexican national hymn, to a poem by F. G. Bocanegra; Nunó's *Himno Nacional Mejicano* officially adopted (1854).

**Nur'ed·din'** *or* **Nour'ed·din'** (nōō'rĕd·dēn'). *Arab.* **Malik al-'Ādil Nūr-al-Dīn Maḥmūd.** 1118?–1174. Sultan of Syria and Egypt, b. Damascus; succeeded his father Zangi in control of northern Syria (1146) and changed capital from Mosul to Aleppo; defeated the Christian armies of the Second Crusade, before Damascus; extended his dominion over all Syria and Egypt.

**Nu·re'yev** (nōō·rā'yĕf), **Rudolph Hametovich.** 1938– . British (Soviet-born) ballet dancer. With Kirov Ballet (to 1961); with Royal Ballet (1962- ).

**Nur Jahan** *or* **Nur Mahal.** d. 1645. Mogul empress. See JAHANGIR.

**Nur'mi** (nōōr'mĭ), **Paavo.** 1897–1974. Finnish long-distance runner; winner at the Olympic Games, in Antwerp (1920), Paris (1924), Amsterdam (1928).

**Nutt** (nŭt), **Alfred Trüb'ner** (trōōb'nẽr). 1856–1910. English folklorist and Celtic scholar; head (1878) of father's publishing business; published works of W. E. Henley; founded *Folklore Journal;* aided formation of Irish Texts Society (1898); author of *Studies on the Legend of the Holy Grail* (1888).

**Nut'tall** (nŭt'ôl), **George Henry Falkiner.** 1862–1937. Biologist, b. San Francisco; professor, Cambridge U., England (from 1906); founder and chief editor, *Journal of Hygiene* (1901) and *Journal of Parasitology* (1908); discoverer (1892) of *Bacillus aerogenes;* author of *The Bacteriology of Diphtheria* (with others, 1908), and papers in bacteriology, parasitology, and physiology.

**Nuttall, Thomas.** 1786–1859. Botanist and ornithologist, b. Settle, Yorkshire, Eng.; to U.S. (1808); first interested in botany; curator, Botanical Garden, Harvard (1822–32); turned attention to ornithology and published (1832) *A Manual of the Ornithology of the United States and Canada.*

**Nuttall, Zelia.** 1858–1933. American archaeologist, b. San Francisco, Calif.; m. Alphonse L. Pinart (1880; divorced, 1887); authority on ancient and colonial history of Mexico.

**Nut'ting** (nŭt'ĭng), **Charles Cleveland.** 1858–1927. American zoologist; collected birds and antiquities in Nicaragua and Costa Rica for Smithsonian Institution (1881–82); led exploring expeditions into Saskatchewan (1891) and to the Bahamas for study of marine life (1893), and to West Indies (1918), Fiji Islands, and New Zealand (1922).

**Nutting, Wallace.** 1861–1941. American clergyman, painter, and antiquarian, b. Marlboro, Mass.; in Congregational ministry (1888–1905); landscape painter and antique collector (from 1905); author of *Old New England Pictures* (1913), *Furniture Treasury* (3 vols., 1928, 1933), *The Clock Book* (1924), and a series of illustrated descriptive books on the beauties of several states (as *Maine Beautiful, Vermont Beautiful*, etc.).

**Nuyssen, Abraham van** *or* **Janssens van.** = Abraham JANSSENS.

**Nuzio, Girolamo.** See MUZIO.

**Ny'blom'** (nü'blōōm'), **Carl Rupert.** 1832–1907. Swedish lyric poet and critic; translated Moore's *Melodies* (1858) and Shakespeare's *Sonnets* (1871).

**Nye** (nī), Sir **Archibald E.** 1896–1967. British army officer, b. Dublin, Ire.; brigadier general (1939); major general (1940); vice-chief of British general staff (Nov., 1941).

**Nye, Edgar Wilson,** *known as* **Bill.** 1850–1896. American humorist, b. Shirley, Me.; wandered westward to Laramie City, Wyoming Territory (1876); founded and edited *Laramie Boomerang* (1881–84), in which appeared first the humorous pieces later collected in his books; on staff, New York *World* (1887–91); popular as lecturer, with James Whitcomb Riley (1887–90). Author of *Bill Nye and Boomerang* (1881), *Forty Liars and Other Lies* (1882), *Baled Hay* (1884), *Bill Nye's History of the*

*United States* (1894), *Bill Nye's History of England* (1896).

**Nye, Gerald P.** 1892–1971. American legislator, b. Hortonville, Wis.; settled in Cooperstown, N.Dak. (1919); editor and manager, Griggs County *Sentinel-Courier;* U.S. senator from North Dakota (1925–45).

**Nye, James Warren.** 1814–1876. American politician, b. De Ruyter, N.Y.; first and only territorial governor of Nevada (1861–64); one of first two senators from State of Nevada (1864–73).

**Nyem, Dietrich von.** See NIEM.

**Ny'gaards·vold** (nü'gôrs·vôl), **Johan.** 1879–1952. Norwegian statesman; Laborite member of the Storting (from 1916; Labor party leader, 1932); president of the Storting (1934); prime minister and minister of public works (1935–40); following German invasion of Norway, prime minister of the Norwegian government in exile.

**Ny'ren** (nī'rĕn), **John.** 1764–1837. English authority on cricket; author of *The Young Cricketer's Tutor* (edited by Charles Cowden Clarke, 1833).

**Ny'rop** (nü'rŏŏp), **Martin.** 1849–1921. Danish architect; designed the new courthouse (1892–1903) and the Bispebjerg Hospital (1908–13), Copenhagen. His cousin **Kristoffer** (1858–1931), Romance scholar and modern pioneer in Romance philology in Denmark, was professor at Copenhagen (1894–1928) and author of *Grammaire Historique de la Langue Française* (6 vols., 1899–1930), *The Life of Words* (1901), *Manuel Phonétique de Français Parlé* (1902), *Études de Grammaire Française* (5 vols., 1919–23), a work on medieval legends and songs (books 1–6, 1907–09), etc.

**Nys** (*Fr.* nēs; *Flem.* nīs), **Ernest.** 1851–1920. Belgian jurist; member of Hague Tribunal; known for his treatises on international law.

# O

**Oake'ley** (ōk'lĭ), Sir **Charles.** 1751–1826. English colonial administrator; governor of Madras (1790–95). His youngest son, **Frederick** (1802–1880), joined the Tractarian movement; introduced ritualism into Margaret Chapel, London (1839–45); followed Newman into Roman Catholic communion (1845); canon of Westminster diocese (1852–80); translator of Latin hymn *Adeste Fideles* (*O Come All Ye Faithful;* 1841). Sir **Herbert Stanley Oakeley** (1830–1903), organist and composer, nephew of Frederick Oakeley, was composer of songs, anthems, church services, and hymn tunes.

**Oakes, George Washington Ochs.** See under Adolph S. OCHS.

**Oak'ley** (ōk'lĭ), **Annie.** *Real name* **Phoebe Anne Oakley Mozee.** 1860–1926. American markswoman, b. in Darke County, Ohio; m. Frank E. Butler, a vaudeville actor; starred as a markswoman in Buffalo Bill's Wild West Show (1885–1902).

**Oakley, Violet.** 1874–1961. American mural painter, b. New York City; studio in Philadelphia; designed murals for Church of All Angels in New York, governor's reception room in state capitol at Harrisburg, Pa., etc.

**Oast'ler** (ōst'lẽr), **Richard.** 1789–1861. English reformer; led agitation against employment of children in factories and for ten-hour working day; imprisoned (1840–44) for a debt, which was paid by subscription; published *Fleet Papers* from prison.

**Oates** (ōts), **Lawrence Edward Grace.** 1880–1912. English explorer; member of Antarctic expedition led by Captain R. F. Scott, R.N. (1910); member of party that reached South Pole (Jan., 1912); on return trip, when his illness threatened to delay whole party, he deliberately walked to his death in blizzard in unavailing attempt to facilitate companions' return.

**Oates, Titus.** 1649–1705. English impostor and fabricator of the Popish Plot. Son of an Anabaptist preacher; employed by Israel Tonge, English divine, who was obsessed with notion of popish plots; feigned conversion to Catholicism; expelled from two Jesuit seminaries (1677, 1678). "Uncovered" (1678) plot forged by him and Tonge, whereby Roman Catholics were supposed pledged to massacre Protestants, burn London, assassinate the king, and swore to its truth before a magistrate, Sir Edmund Berry Godfrey; gained credence of populace on murder of Godfrey, with result that about thirty-five persons were judicially murdered; implicated Queen Catherine and her physician, on whose acquittal he lost prestige; convicted and fined for calling duke of York a traitor, and imprisoned; found guilty (1685) of perjury and sentenced to be pilloried and flogged and imprisoned for life. Pardoned (1689) on accession of William of Orange, and allowed a pension.

**O'ba·di'ah** (ō'bȧ·dī'ȧ). *In Douay Bible* **Ab·di'as** (ăb·dī'ăs). One of the minor Hebrew prophets, of uncertain date, whose judgment on Edom for siding with Israel's enemy the Old Testament book of *Obadiah* records.

**Obaidallah.** Variant of *Ubaydullah* (see FATIMID dynasty).

**O'ber** (ō'bẽr), **Frederick Albion.** 1849–1913. American ornithologist, b. Beverly, Mass.; explored esp. Florida, the West Indies, and Mexico, collecting specimens. Wrote *Travels in Mexico* (1884), *Guide to the West Indies* (1908), etc.

**Oberge, Eilhart von.** See EILHART VON OBERGE.

**O'ber·holt'zer** (ō'bẽr·hōlt'sẽr), **Ellis Paxson.** 1868–1936. American historian, b. Philadelphia; author of *The Referendum in America* (1893), *Robert Morris, Patriot and Financier* (1903), *Jay Cooke, the Financier of the Civil War* (2 vols., 1907), *Henry Clay* (1909), *A History of the United States Since the Civil War* (1917 ff.), etc.

**Oberholtzer, John H.** 1809–1895. American Mennonite religious leader; ordained as bishop (1847) and founded (1860) General Conference of the Mennonite Church of North America, now the second largest Mennonite branch in America.

**O'ber·kampf** (ō'bẽr·kämpf), **Christophe Philippe.** 1738–1814. Textile manufacturer and colorist, b. at Wiesenbach; naturalized Frenchman (1770). Opened studio at Jouy-en-Josas, France, for coloring cloth (1759), and became sole proprietor of the textile factory there (1785).

**O'ber·län'der** (ō'bẽr·lĕn'dẽr), **Adolf.** 1845–1923. German painter and caricaturist.

**O'ber'lin'** (*Fr.* ō'bĕr'lăɴ'; *Ger.* ō'bẽr·lēn; *Angl.* ō'bẽr·lĭn), **Jérémie Jacques.** 1735–1806. Alsatian philologist. His brother **Jean Fréderic** (1740–1826) was a Protestant clergyman, famed for success in improving agriculture, industry, education, and morals in his pastorate in the Steinthal.

**Obertus, Jakob**. See OBRECHT.

**O·bo·len′ski** (ŭ·bŭ·lyān′skû·ĭ; *Angl.* ŏb′ô·lĕn′skĭ). Princely Russian family, including: Prince **Evgeni** (1795–after 1856); exiled to Siberia for his part in Decembrist plot (1825); wrote *Memories of an Exile in Siberia.* **Mikhail Andreevich** (1805–1873); served in army (to 1831); later devoted himself to publication of a collection of historical annals. **Dmitri Aleksandrovich** (1822–1881); reorganized ministry of marine; member of Council of Empire.

**O'Boyle′** (ô·boil′), **Patrick Aloysius**. 1896– . American Roman Catholic churchman, b. Scranton, Pa. Ordained (1921); archbishop of Washington, D. C. (1948); cardinal (1967).

**O·bra′do·vić** (ô·brä′dô·vēt′y′; *Angl.* -vĭch), **Dimitrije**. *Religious name* **Do·sith′e·us** (dô·sĭth′ē·ŭs). 1742?–1811. Serbian writer; his *Life and Adventures* (1783) was first book published in the Serbian popular language; translated *Aesop's Fables* (1788).

**O′brecht** (ō′brĕKt) *or* **Ho′brecht** (hō′brĕKt) *or* **O·ber′tus** (ô·bûr′tŭs) *or* **Ho·ber′tus** (hô·bûr′tŭs), **Jakob.** 1430?–?1505. Dutch conductor, composer, and contrapuntist, a master of the second Netherlandish school; composed masses, motets, a *Passion*, chansons.

**O′bre·gón′** (ō′brā·gôn′), **Álvaro.** 1880–1928. Mexican soldier and politician, b. near Álamos, Sonora; planter in Sonora (1910–12); entered service of Madero against revolutionists (1912); suppressed Pascual Orozco (1912) and supported Carranza against Victoriano Huerta (1913–14); also aided Carranza against Villa and Emiliano Zapata (1915); defeated Villa at Celaya and León (1915); in command of army during presidency of Carranza (1915–20) and of Huerta (1920). President of Mexico (1920–24); drove Carranza from Mexico City; improved relations with United States; put down revolt of Adolfo de la Huerta (1923–24).

**O·bre′no·vich** (ô·brĕ′nô·vĭch). *Serbian* **O·bre′no·vić** (-vēt′y′). Name of a Serbian dynasty founded (1817) by Prince Miloš. For its ruling members, Miloš (prince 1817–39, 1858–60), Michael (prince 1839–42, 1860–68), Milan (prince 1868–82, king 1882–89), and Alexander I (king 1889–1903), see these names. Rule of dynasty interrupted (1842–58) by Prince Alexander of the Karageorgevich (*q.v.*) rival dynasty.

**O'Bri′en** (ô·brī′ĕn). Name of Irish family of northern Munster descended from Turlough O'Brien (1009–1086) and his line of Irish chieftains, kings of **Tho′mond** (to͞o′mŭnd), including:

**Conor O'Brien** (d. 1539), last independent prince of Thomond; sided with Fitzgeralds in their feud with the Butlers. His brother **Murrough** (d. 1551), 1st Earl of Thomond and Baron **In′chi·quin** (ĭn′chĭ·kwĭn), gave up his kingship to Henry VIII on creation as earl and baron (1543). Conor's grandson **Conor** (1534?–1581), 3d earl; intrigued with Fitzgerald against English, was defeated, and formally surrendered (1571). Conor's (1534?–1581) son **Donough** (d. 1624), Baron of **I·brick′an** (ē·brĭk′ăn) and 4th Earl of Thomond; known as "the Great Earl"; assisted English in suppressing Tyrone's Rebellion (1595); obtained transfer of Clare to jurisdiction of Munster (1602); president of Munster (1605); governor of Clare (1619). With death of **Henry,** 8th earl (d. 1741), earldom of Thomond became extinct.

**Murrough O'Brien** (1614–1674), 1st Earl of Inchiquin and 6th Baron Inchiquin; attended Strafford into Leinster at outbreak of Irish rebellion (1641); governor of Munster (1642); compelled to submit to Parliament (1644) and became president of Munster; gathered force in southern Ireland, fortified southern ports against Parliament, and was joined by Ormonde; driven westward by Cromwell, fled to France (1650); created earl of Inchiquin (1654); served with French in Catalonia (1654); captured by Algerines (1660); high steward of Queen Henrietta Maria's household. **Murrough** (1724?–1808), 5th earl, was created marquis of Thomond. His brother **James** (1769–1855), 3d Marquis of Thomond and 7th Earl of Inchiquin; admiral in British navy (1847); at his death, marquisate became extinct.

**O'Brien, Edward Joseph Harrington.** 1890–1941. American author, editor, and anthologist, b. Boston. Assoc. editor, *The Poetry Journal* (1912–15), and *Poet Lore* (1914–15); founder and editor, *New Stories* (1933–35); author of *White Fountains* (verse; 1917), *The Bloody Fool* (play; 1917), *Son of the Morning* (1932), etc. Originator and editor of *The Best Short Stories* (1915–40) and of *The Best British Short Stories* (1921–40). See *Martha Foley*, under Whit BURNETT. His wife (m. 1923) **Florence Roma Muir**, *nee* **Wilson,** *pen name* **Romer Wilson** (1891–1930), British author; wrote *Martin Schüler* (1918), *The Grand Tour of Alphonse Marichaud* (1923), *Dragon's Blood* (1926), *Greenlow* (1927), *The Social Climbers* (play; 1927), *All Alone* (life of Emily Brontë; 1928), etc.

**O'Brien, Frederick.** 1869–1932. American writer, b. Baltimore; as sailor, casual laborer, and tramp traveled in various parts of the world; spent considerable time on South Sea islands. Writings include *White Shadows in the South Seas* (with Rose Wilder Lane, 1919), *Mystic Isles of the South Seas* (1921), *Atolls of the Sun* (1922).

**O'Brien, James,** *later* **James Bron·terre′** (?brŏn·târ′). 1805–1864. Irish journalist and Chartist; one of best-informed of the Chartists, advocated revolutionary violence; imprisoned for seditious speaking.

**O'Brien, Lawrence Francis.** 1917– . American government official, b. Springfield, Mass. U. S. postmaster general (1965–68).

**O'Brien, Lucius Richard.** 1832–1899. Canadian watercolor landscape painter.

**O'Brien, Smith,** *in full* **William Smith.** 1803–1864. Irish political insurgent; joined with Daniel O'Connell in movement for repeal of legislative union between Great Britain and Ireland (1843); took part in abortive insurrection in south of Ireland (1848); his death sentence commuted to transportation (to Tasmania).

**O'Brien, William.** 1852–1928. Irish journalist and Nationalist leader; appointed by Parnell editor of *United Ireland* (1881); arrested when paper was suppressed (1881); in jail, drew up the "No Rent" manifesto; M.P. (1883–95); started the "No Reduction, No Rent" slogan (1887); imprisoned under Coercion Act of 1887; initiated new agrarian movement, the United Irish League (1898); participated in conference (1902) that led to Land Purchase Act (1903), abolishing Irish landlordism; founded "All for Ireland" party (1910), with motto "Conference, Conciliation, Consent"; in general election (1918), caused his party to retire, thereby securing Sinn Fein victory and extinction of Irish party.

**O′bru·chev** (ô′bro͝o·chĕf), **Vladimir Afanasevich.** 1863–1956. Russian geologist and traveler; traveled in Russian Asia; wrote on geology of this region. His son **Sergei Vladimirovich** (1891–1956) wrote on geology of north Russia and Arctic islands.

**O'Bry′an** (ô·brī′ăn), **William.** 1778–1868. English Wesleyan convert and founder (1816) of the sect of Arminian Bible Christians, or Bryanites.

**O·cam′po** (ô·käm′pō), **Florián de.** 1499–1555. Spanish chronicler, b. at Zamora; canon of Zamora, and historiographer to Charles V.

**O'Car'o·lan** (ō·kăr'ō·lăn) *or* **Car'o·lan** (kăr'ō·lăn), **Tor'logh** (thōōr'lō). 1670–1738. Irish bard; became blind from smallpox (1684); itinerant among houses of gentry, repaying hospitality with songs to harp accompaniment; wrote and composed about two hundred songs in Irish; ten were adapted by Thomas Moore.

**O'Ca'sey** (ō·kā'sĭ), **Sean.** 1880–1964. Irish playwright; wrote for production at Abbey Theatre in Dublin *The Shadow of a Gunman* (1923), working-class plays including *Juno and the Paycock* (1924), *The Plough and the Stars* (1926), *The Silver Tassie* (1928; war play), *Within the Gates* (1933), *Purple Dust* (1940); also wrote *I Knock at the Door* (1939), *Pictures in the Hallway* (1941).

**Occam, William of.** See OCKHAM.

**Occhino, Bernardino.** See OCHINO.

**Occleve, Thomas.** See HOCCLEVE.

**O'chil·tree** (ō'kĭl·trē; ō'kĭl-; ŏ'kĭl-; ŏ'kĭl-), Barons. See under STEWART family.

**O·chi'no** (ō·kē'nō) *or* **Oc·chi'no** (ŏk·kē'nō), **Bernardino.** 1487–1564. Italian theologian and reformer; Franciscan, then Capuchin; elected vicar-general of Capuchins (1538, 1541); confessor of Pope Paul III; influenced toward Protestantism by Juan de Valdés; fled to Geneva (1542); at odds with Calvin; to Augsburg (1545–47), London (1547–53), Zurich (1555), Basel, Nuremberg, etc. Antitrinitarian; upheld polygamy. His works include *Tragedy or Dialogue of the Unjust Usurped Primacy of the Bishop of Rome* (1549), reputed to have influenced Milton's *Paradise Lost.*

**O·cho'a** (ō·chō'ä), **Eugenio de.** 1815–1872. Spanish writer and scholar; edited, with F. Baudry (librarian at Versailles), *Colección de los Mejores Autores Españoles;* published the collection of poems *Ecos del Alma* (1841) and translations, as of Vergil's complete works, Victor Hugo's *Hernani, Notre Dame de Paris,* etc.

**Ochoa, Severo.** 1905– . American biochemist, b. Spain. To U.S. (1940); at N.Y.U. (1942– ); awarded Nobel prize in physiology and medicine (1959) with A. Kornberg for work on the biological synthesis of nucleic acids.

**Ochozias.** See AHAZIAH.

**Ochs** (ŏks), **A'dolph** (ā'dŏlf) **Simon.** 1858–1935. American newspaper publisher, b. Cincinnati; proprietor and publisher, Chattanooga (Tenn.) *Times* (1878–1935); publisher, New York *Times* (1896–1935); proprietor, Philadelphia *Times* (1902–12) and Philadelphia *Public Ledger* (1902–12); originator and founder, Chattanooga-Lookout Mountain Park. By gift of $500,000 made possible publication of *Dictionary of American Biography.* His brother **George Washington Ochs Oakes** (1861–1931) legally added name *Oakes* at entrance of United States into World War (1917); was associated with him in newspaper work. Another brother, **Milton Barlow Ochs** (1864–1955), became managing editor of Chattanooga *Times* (1879–90; 1892–99; 1913–22); proprietor, Nashville *American* (1909–11); general manager, Philadelphia *Public Ledger* (1912–13).

**Ochs** (ōks), **Siegfried.** 1858–1929. German choral conductor and composer.

**Och'ter·lo'ny** (ŏk'tĕr·lō'nĭ; ŏk'-), Sir **David.** 1758–1825. British army officer, b. Boston, Mass., of Scottish descent; defended Delhi against Holkar (1804); brought both Nepal War (1814–15) and Pindari War (1817–18) to successful conclusion.

**Ocht'man** (ŏkt'măn), **Leon'ard** (lĕn'ẽrd). 1854–1934. Painter, b. in the Netherlands; to U.S. (1866); best known for his landscapes of American scenes. His daughter **Dorothy** (1892– ), landscape painter.

**Ochus.** See ARTAXERXES III; DARIUS II.

**Ockeghem.** See OKEGHEM.

**Ockenfuss, Lorenz.** See OKEN.

**Ockenheim, Johannes.** See OKEGHEM.

**Ockham.** Baron **King of Ockham.** See Peter KING.

**Ock'ham** *or* **Oc'cam** (ŏk'ăm), **William of.** *Known as* **Doc'tor In'vin·cib'i·lis** (dŏk'tẽr [-tôr] ĭn'vĭn·sĭb'ĭ·lĭs) *and* **Ven'er·ab'i·lis In·cep'tor** (vĕn'ẽr·ăb'ĭ·lĭs ĭn·sĕp'tôr). 1300?–?1349. English scholastic philosopher, b. Ockham; joined Franciscans; pupil, later rival, of Duns Scotus. In Franciscan controversy defended evangelical poverty against Pope John XXII, in *Opus nonaginta Dierum* (c. 1330); escaped from imprisonment and probably spent rest of life in Munich. With Michael of Cesena, general of the Franciscan order, joined side of Emperor Louis of Bavaria in contesting temporal power of the pope; laid foundations in *Dialogues* (1343) of modern theory of independence of civil rule. Practically closed the scholastic controversy over universals with his nominalistic doctrine that the real is always individual, not universal, that universals have no real existence but are only abstract terms, and the corollary that "entities must not be unnecessarily multiplied" (called *Occam's Razor*), thus preparing the way for Francis Bacon's philosophy.

**Ock'ley** (ŏk'lĭ), **Simon.** 1678–1720. English Orientalist; author of the *History of the Saracens* (3 vols., 1708–57).

**O'Cle'ry** (ō·klẽr'ĭ), **Michael,** *orig.* **Tadhg.** 1575–1643. Irish chronicler; baptized Tadhg, took name Michael on becoming Franciscan friar; with other scholars composed *Royal List* (1630) of Irish kings and *Annals of the Four Masters* (1636), a digest of old Irish annals.

**O'Con'nell** (ō·kŏn''l), **Daniel.** 1775–1847. Irish national leader; known as "the Liberator." United Irish Roman Catholics under leadership of their priests into a league for urging Irish claims; originated the Catholic Association (1823) and perfected its constitutional method of agitation for repeal of civil disabilities by mass meetings. Elected M.P. (1828); took seat only after Wellington and Peel, forced by public opinion, carried through Catholic emancipation (1829); fought Coercion Act (1833); led agitation for abolition of tithes and of established church in Ireland; opposed poor law and movement against rent. Lord mayor of Dublin (1841); revived earlier demand for repeal of union of Great Britain and Ireland; re-created the Catholic Association and held monstrous mass meetings (1842–43); arrested for seditious conspiracy (1843) but released (1844) on writ of error by House of Lords. Found his power broken by dissension, opposition by revolutionaries of Young Ireland (1845), distress from potato famine, and ill health; died at Genoa on way to Rome.

**O'Connell, William Henry.** 1859–1944. American cardinal, b. Lowell, Mass.; rector, American Coll., Rome (1895); bishop of Portland, Me. (1901); archbishop of Constance, and coadjutor with succession of Boston (1906); bishop of Boston (1907); cardinal (1911).

**O'Con'nor** (ō·kŏn'ẽr). Name of an ancient Irish clan that shared with the O'Rourkes the sovereignty of Connaught into the eleventh century, including the following kings: **Cathal O'Connor** (d. 1010), King of Connaught (from 980); bridged the Shannon (1000); retired to a monastery (1003). His grandson **Aedh,** as king, fought continually with rival O'Rourkes; killed near Oranmore (1067). His great-grandson **Roderic,** *Irish* **Ruaidhri** (d. 1118), king from 1076; won victory at Cunghill (1087); was treacherously blinded (1092). Roderic's son **Turlough,** *Irish* **Toirdhealbhach** (1088–1156); assumed kingship of Ireland (1120); deposed (1135); regained kingship (1141–49). His son **Roderic** *or* **Rory** (1116?–1198), King of Connaught (from 1156); regained high kingship of Ireland (1166); forced by Anglo-Norman invasion to submit to Henry II (1175) and pay tribute as vassal of England; last of high kings of Ireland. **Cathal** (1150?–1224); succeeded as king (1201); resisted English expeditions (1220, 1224) under Walter de Lacy, elder son of Hugh de Lacy, 5th Baron Lacy.

**O'Connor, Andrew.** 1874–1941. American sculptor; studio in Paris; among his works are a marble statue of Gen. Lew Wallace in the Capitol at Washington, D.C., a statue of Daniel O'Connell in Dublin, Ire., and a statue *Mourning Woman* in National Gallery, London.

**O'Connor, Feargus Edward.** 1794–1855. Irish Chartist leader; M.P.; unseated as radical through Daniel O'Connell's influence; joined Chartists in England; advocated rise of physical violence in his paper, the *Northern Star;* presented the monster Chartist petition in Parliament (1848). His uncle **Arthur O'Connor** (1763–1852), lawyer, joined United Irishmen; later, went to France (1803) and was appointed general of a division by Napoleon (1804).

**O'Connor,** Sir **Richard Nugent.** 1889– . British army officer; served in World War (1914–18); military governor of Jerusalem (1938–39); under Gen. Wavell in campaign in Libya (1939–41); prisoner of war (1941–44; escaped); commander in Europe and India (1944–46); general (1945).

**O'Connor, Thomas Power.** *Popularly known as* **Tay Pay** (tā′ pā′). 1848–1929. Irish journalist and nationalist leader. While free-lance journalist wrote a scathing *Life of Lord Beaconsfield* (1876); in Parliament, a supporter of Parnell; founded radical newspapers (1887, 1893), a literary paper *T. P.'s Weekly* (1902), and other weeklies; privy councilor (1924). Author of *The Parnell Movement* (1886) and *Memoirs of an Old Parliamentarian* (1929). Called "Father of the House of Commons" because of unbroken period of service (continuously from 1885).

**O'Connor, William Douglas.** 1832–1889. American journalist, b. Boston; close friend and benefactor of Walt Whitman (from 1862); author of *Harrington* (1860), *The Good Gray Poet* (1866), etc.

**O'Con′or** (ō·kŏn′ẽr), **Charles.** 1804–1884. American lawyer; practiced, New York City (from 1824); U.S. district attorney (1853–54); as special deputy attorney general, State of New York, prosecuted Tweed and his associates (1871–75), causing dissolution of Tweed Ring. Nominated by Straight-Out Democrats for president of the United States (1872).

**O'Conor, Nor′reys** (nŏr′ĕz; -ĭs) **Jephson.** 1885–1959. American poet, b. New York City; author of *Celtic Memories* (1914), a poetic drama *The Fairy Bride* (1916), *Songs of the Celtic Past* (1918), *There Was Magic in Those Days* (1929), *A Servant of the Crown* (1938), etc.

**Oc·ta′vi·a** (ŏk·tā′vĭ·ȧ). d. 11 B.C. Roman matron; sister of Octavius (Emperor Augustus) and 2d wife (40 B.C.) of Mark Antony, who divorced her (32) after he had become infatuated with Cleopatra.

**Octavia.** 42?–62 A.D. Roman empress; daughter of Emperor Claudius and Messalina, and wife (53) of Nero; executed by order of Nero (62).

**Octavian** *or* **Octavianus.** See AUGUSTUS (emperor).

**Oc·ta′vi·us** (ŏk·tā′vĭ·ŭs). Family of Roman soldiers and politicians, including: **Gnaeus Octavius** (d. 162 B.C.), general and politician; distinguished himself in campaign against Persians; consul (165 B.C.); assassinated in Syria. **Gnaeus** (d. 87 B.C.), consul (87 B.C.); adherent of Sulla and opponent of his colleague in the consulship, Lucius Cornelius Cinna; murdered by followers of Cinna. **Marcus**, Roman general; belonged to Senate party during Civil War; defeated Dolabella at sea; joined Pompey and fought at Thapsus (46 B.C.) and Actium (31).

**Octavius, Gaius.** d. 59 B.C. Roman general; father of the Emperor Augustus (*q.v.*).

**Octavius, Gaius.** See AUGUSTUS (emperor).

**Octon, Vigné d'.** See Paul VIGNÉ.

**O'Cur′ry** (ō·kûr′ĭ), **Eugene.** 1796–1862. Irish antiquary and Gaelic scholar.

**Od′e·na′thus** *or* **Od′ae·na′thus** (ŏd′ē·nā′thŭs). d. 266 or 267 A.D. Prince of Palmyra; ally of Rome; defeated Persians and restored large part of the East to Roman Empire; acknowledged by Rome as independent ruler; assassinated; succeeded by his wife, Zenobia (*q.v.*).

**Od′e·ric** (ŏd′ẽr·ĭk) *or* **Od′o·ric** (ŏd′ō·rĭk) **of Por′de·no′ne** (pōr′dȧ·nō′nȧ). *Ital.* **O′de·ri′co** (ō′dȧ·rē′kō) *or* **O′do·ri′co** (ō′dō-) **da** (dä) **Pordenone.** 1286–1331. Italian Franciscan missionary and traveler in Asia.

**O′de·ri′gi** (ō′dȧ·rē′jē) *or* **O′de·ri′si** (-zē) **da Gub′bio** (dä gōōb′byō). 1240–1299. Italian miniaturist and manuscript illuminator, noted by Dante in his *Divina Commedia* (*Purgatorio* xi, 79).

**O·dets′** (ō·dĕts′), **Clifford.** 1906–1963. American playwright, b. Philadelphia; on stage in minor roles (1923–30); author of *Waiting for Lefty* (1935), *Awake and Sing!* (1935), *Till the Day I Die* (1935), *Paradise Lost* (1935), *Golden Boy* (1937), *The Silent Partner* (1938), *Rocket to the Moon* (1939), *Night Music* (1940), *Clash by Night* (1942).

**Odle,** Mrs. **Alan.** See Dorothy M. RICHARDSON.

**O′do** (ō′dō). Count of Paris. = EUDES (see CAPETIAN dynasty).

**O′do** (ō′dō) *or* **Eudes** (ûd) **of Ba′yeux′** (bȧ′yû′; *Angl.* bȧ·yōō′). 1036?–1097. Anglo-Norman prelate; half brother of William the Conqueror; bishop of Bayeux (1049); fought at Hastings (1066); was granted Dover Castle and earldom of Kent; as regent during William's absence, ruled tyrannically; left England after rebelling against his nephew William II Rufus (1088); died on way to join First Crusade.

**O′do·a′cer** (ō′dō·ā′sẽr). *Also* **O′do·va′car** *or* **O′do·va′kar** (ō′dō·vā′kẽr). 434?–493. Barbarian ruler of Italy (476–493); joined Roman army; as German tribal leader (a king of the Heruli) in the army, led insurrection (476) and was proclaimed king; caused death of Roman general Orestes, and abdication of his son the puppet emperor Romulus Augustulus, whose title and office were abolished, thus terminating the Western Roman Empire. Shut up in Ravenna (489–493) and several times defeated by Theodoric, King of the Ostrogoths; treacherously slain by the latter.

**O'Don′nell** (ō·dŏn′'l). Name of an ancient Irish family, lords of **Tyr·con′nel** [tĭr·kŏn′'l] (approximately modern Donegal), rivals of the O'Neills in Ulster, and including: **Manus O'Donnell** (d. 1564), deputy governor of Tyrconnel during father's pilgrimage to Rome (1510–11); chief (1537); united with Con O'Neill to overthrow English rule in Ireland but was defeated (1539); harassed (from 1547) by his eldest son, **Calvagh** (d. 1566), who, with aid obtained from Scotland, imprisoned him and usurped authority (1558) and was later surprised, captured, and tortured by Shane O'Neill (1561), being restored by arrival of supporting forces sent in response to appeal to Queen Elizabeth (1566). **Hugh Roe O'Donnell** (1571?–1602), nephew of Calvagh; held as hostage by English lord deputy; escaped (1591) and received chieftainship from his father, Hugh MacManus (1592); secretly worked against the English and appealed to Philip II of Spain for assistance; invaded Connaught (1595, 1597); helped Tyrone to defeat English at Yellow Ford (1598); lost fortresses of Lifford and Donegal by treachery of Niall Garv (1600); failed in attack on English besiegers of newly landed Spanish forces; laid complaint before Philip III of Spain but died in Spain of poison. Sir **Niall Garv O'Donnell** (1569–1626), grandson of Calvagh; in resentment at election of his cousin Hugh Roe, made terms with English government, was promised grant of Tyrconnel, but quarreled with deputy over lordship of Inishowen (1601); his claims of chieftainship (1602) passed over in favor of Rory O'Donnell by English government; charged with complicity in seizure of Culmore Castle and sacking of Derry (1608); died in Tower of London. **Rory O'Donnell** (1575–1608), 1st Earl of Tyrconnel, younger brother of Hugh Roe, assumed chieftainship on brother's flight to Spain (1602); gave allegiance to English lord deputy, but fled with Hugh O'Neill when his designs for tribal independence and seizure of Dublin were known (1607); reached Rome, where his grievances, emphasizing religious disabilities, were heard; died of Roman fever.

**O'Dón'nell** (ō·thō'nĕl), **Leopoldo.** Conde **de Lu·ce'na** (thā lōō·thā'nä; -sā'nä). Duque **de Te·tuán'** (tā-twän'). 1809–1867. Spanish marshal and politician of Irish descent, b. Santa Cruz, Tenerife. Fought for Isabella II against Carlists (1833–39); general in army of Queen Maria Christina and accompanied her into exile (1840); fought against Espartero (1843); governor of Cuba (1843–48); minister of war under Espartero (1854–56); led successful revolution against him (1856); prime minister of Spain (1856; 1858); led successful expedition into Morocco (1859); again prime minister (1863; 1865–66).

**O'Don'nell** (ō·dŏn''l), **Patrick.** 1856–1927. Irish prelate, b. in Donegal; archbishop of Armagh and Roman Catholic primate of all Ireland (1924); cardinal (1925).

**O'Do'no·jú'** (ō·thō'nō·hōō'), **Juan.** 1755?–1821. Spanish soldier; captain general and acting viceroy (1821) of New Spain (Mexico); on arrival at Vera Cruz (July 30, 1821), found the country conquered by Iturbide, with whom he signed a treaty at Córdoba (Aug. 24, 1821) surrendering Mexico; served as one of the five regents governing Mexico until regular constitutional government could be inaugurated.

**O'Don'o·van** (ō·dŏn'ō·văn), **John.** 1809–1861. Irish archaeologist; author of works on Irish history and antiquities and a Gaelic grammar (1845).

**O'Donovan, William Rudolf.** 1844–1920. American sculptor. His bust of Gen. Joseph Wheeler is in National Gallery of Art; his statue of Washington stands at the top of Battle Monument, Trenton, N.J.

**Odoric of Pordenone.** See ODERIC OF PORDENONE.

**O'Dowd, Cornelius.** Pseudonym of Charles James LEVER.

**O'Duf'fy** (ō·dŭf'ĭ), **Owen,** *Irish* **Eoin.** 1892–1944. Irish soldier; member of Irish Republican army (1917), chief of staff (1921–22); in charge of forces of Irish Free State (1924–25); director of Blue Shirt organization; organized and led Irish brigade fighting on side of General Franco in Spain (1936–37); brigadier general in Spanish army.

**O'Dwy'er** (ō·dwī'ẽr), **Joseph.** 1841–1898. American physician; practiced in New York City; pioneer in successful use of intubation to prevent asphyxia in diphtheria, and in use of diphtheria serum as a remedy.

**Oe'chel·häu'ser** (û'kĕl·hoi'zẽr), **Wilhelm von.** 1820–1902. German industrialist and Shakespearean scholar; director, German Continental Gas Co., Dessau (1857–90); helped found (1864) German Shakespeare Society; coeditor of complete stage edition of 27 of Shakespeare's plays (7 vols., 1870–78).

**Oe'co·lam·pa'di·us** (ē'kō·lăm·pā'dĭ·ŭs; ĕk'ō-), **Johannes.** *Real surname* **Heuss'gen** (hois'gĕn) *or* **Hüss'gen** (hüs'gĕn). 1482–1531. German theological leader in Swiss Reformation; cathedral preacher at Basel (1518), where he helped Erasmus edit the New Testament in Greek, and at Augsburg (1518); entered Brigittine convent, Altmünster (1520), but left under Luther's influence to become chaplain to Franz von Sickingen, Ebernburg (1522); returned to Basel (1522) as professor and preacher, and helped introduce the Reformation; sided with Zwingli in his views on the Lord's Supper, and took part in the controversy with Luther and Melanchthon at Marburg (1529).

**Oeh'len·schlä'ger** (û'lĕn·shlâ'gẽr), **Adam Gottlob.** 1779–1850. Danish epic and lyric poet and dramatist, a pioneer of the romantic movement in Europe; professor of aesthetics, Copenhagen (1810); engaged in literary feuds notably with Baggesen (1813–19) and J. L. Heiberg (1827–30); crowned as "king of the Scandinavian singers" by Tegnér at Lund (1829), and publicly acclaimed as national poet (1849). Author of *Guldhornene* (symbolic poem, 1803), *Sanct-Hansaften-Spil* (lyric drama, 1803), *Aladdin* (verse fantasy, 1805), the historical tragedies *Hakon Jarl* (1807), *Baldur hin Gode* (1808), *Palnatoke* (1809), and *Axel og Valborg* (1810), *Correggio* (drama, in German, 1809), *Nordens Guder* (an Eddaic epic cycle, 1819), *Helge* (a cycle of verse romances, 1814), the epic *Regnar Lodbrok* (1848), reminiscences, etc.

**Oe·nop'i·des** (ē·nŏp'ĭ·dēz) *or* **Oi·nop'i·des** (oi-) **of Chi'os** (kī'ŏs). fl. 5th century B.C. Greek astronomer and mathematician; had knowledge of the obliquity of the ecliptic; fixed length of solar year at 365 days and somewhat less than nine hours; credited with discovering 12th and 23rd propositions of the first book of Euclid and the quadrature of the meniscus.

**Oer'sted** *or* **Ör'sted** (ûr'stĭth), **Hans Christian.** 1777–1851. Danish physicist; discovered (1819) that a pivoted magnetic needle turned at right angles to a conductor carrying a current, thus founding the science of electromagnetism. His brother **Anders Sandöe** (1778–1860), jurist, was prime minister (1853).

**Oertel.** See ÖRTEL.

**Oertel, Abraham.** See ORTELIUS.

**Oer'tel** (ûr'tĕl), **Max Joseph.** 1835–1897. German physician; known for his method of treating heart and circulatory diseases, obesity, etc., by regulation of diet, restriction of fluid intake, and exercise.

**Oe'ser** *or* **Ö'ser** (û'zẽr), **Adam Friedrich.** 1717–1799. German painter, sculptor, and etcher; champion of reform in art on antique lines; in Leipzig (from 1759), director of the art academy (1764), where he taught Winckelmann and Goethe. His works include frescoes, allegorical murals, and decorative ceilings, and etchings.

**Oesterley.** See ÖSTERLEY.

**Oe'ting·er** (û'tĭng·ẽr), **Friedrich Christoph.** 1702–1782. German Protestant theologian and theosophist; leader of Pietists and disciple of Böhme and Swedenborg.

**Oexmelin.** See ESQUEMELING.

**O'Fao'láin** (ō·f(w)ā'lōn), **Seán.** 1900– . Irish writer; author of short stories, as in *Midsummer Night Madness* (1932), *A Purse of Coppers* (1937), novels including *A Nest of Simple Folk* (1933), *A Born Genius* (1936), *Come Back to Erin* (1940), biographies of Constance Markievicz (1934), de Valera (1933), Daniel O'Connell (1938), *The Great O'Neill* (1942), etc.

**Of'fa** (ŏf'ȧ). d. 796. King of Mercians in Anglo-Saxon England (757–796); wrested Bensington from Cynewulf of Wessex (779); took territory beyond Severn from Welsh; built Offa's Dyke from mouth of Wye to mouth of Dee, against Welsh; formed bishopric of Lichfield with sanction of Pope Hadrian I (788); caused beheading of Ethelbert (d. 794), King of East Anglia; traded and corresponded with Charlemagne as an equal.

**Offaly,** Barons of. See FITZGERALD family.

**Of'fen·bach** (ŏf'ĕn·bäk; *Fr.* ô'fĕn'bȧk'), **Jacques.** 1819–1880. Musician and composer, b. at Cologne; became naturalized Frenchman; orchestra conductor at Comédie Française (1847); opened his own theater (1855) and played one-act operettas of his own composition, as *Les Deux Aveugles, Les Violoneux, Ba-ta-clan, Croquefer, Le Mariage aux Lanternes.* Contributed successful operettas and opéra bouffe to other theaters in Paris, as *La Belle Hélène, Barbe-Bleue, La Vie Parisienne, La Grande Duchesse de Gérolstein.* Managed the Gaiety Theatre in Paris (1872–76). His famous *Contes d'Hoffmann* (*Tales of Hoffmann*), finished by Ernest Guiraud, was not produced until after his death.

**O'Fla'her·ty** (ō·flă'hēr·tĭ), **Li'am** (lē'ȧm). 1896– . Irish novelist, b. in Aran Islands; first novel, *Thy Neighbor's Wife* (1924); won prize in France with *The Informer* (1925), subsequently made into a motion-picture scenario (received Motion Picture Academy award, 1935).

**Og'a·dai'** (ŏg'ȧ·dī') *or* **Og'dai** (ŏg'dī) *or* **Og'o·tai'** (ŏg'ō·tī'). 1185–1241. Mongol khan (1229–41); third son of Genghis Khan; attempted organization of empire set up by Genghis; built a palace at Karakorum; put down revolts in Korea, China, and Turkestan; aided in his reign by wise counsels of Ye-lü Ch'u-ts'ai; sent great army under Batu Khan (*q.v.*) and Subotai into Russia (1237–41) which plundered Moscow, destroyed Kiev, and overran Poland and Hungary; died in midst of these wars. His death followed by a confused period of ten years, which included short reigns of his son Kuyuk (1246–48) and his grandson Kaidu (1248); his family displaced (1251) by Mangu Khan and Kublai Khan.

**O·ga·ta** (ō·gä·tä). Japanese family of artists of 17th and 18th centuries, especially: **Ogata Ko·rin** (kō·rēn) *or* **Kwo·rin** [kwō·rēn] (1653?–1716); influenced by Koetsu and the Kano and Tosa schools, but displayed originality in designs; created new epoch in Japanese decorative art; excelled in gold lacquer work but designs equally good for woven goods, porcelain, or metal. His brother **Ogata Ken·zan** [kĕn·zän] (1663–1743), noted esp. for high quality of lacquer and porcelain work.

**Og'den** (ŏg'dĕn), **Aaron.** 1756–1839. American lawyer, b. Elizabethtown, N.J.; served with New Jersey troops through American Revolution; practiced law in New Jersey; U.S. senator (1801–03); governor of New Jersey (1812). Operation of steamboat line between Elizabethtown and New York brought litigation with Thomas Gibbons, conducting a rival line under monopoly rights originally granted by the New York legislature to Livingston and Fulton. The Gibbons-Ogden case was carried to U.S. Supreme Court, where Marshall's decision (1824) established the principle of freedom for interstate commerce.

**Ogden, Charles Kay.** 1889–1957. British psychologist and educator; inventor of *basic English,* simplified system of learning English through a selected vocabulary of 850 words; coauthor of *Foundations of Aesthetics* (with I. A. Richards and James Wood; 1921) and *The Meaning of Meaning* (with I. A. Richards; 1923); author of *The Basic Vocabulary* (1930), *Debabelization* (1931), *The System of Basic English* (1934).

**Ogden, George Washington.** 1871–1966. American author of adventure stories against the background of the American old West.

**Ogden, Henry Alexander.** 1856–1936. American painter and illustrator, b. Philadelphia; specialized in historical, uniform, and costume painting.

**Ogden, Peter Skene.** 1794–1854. Fur trader, b. Quebec, Canada; one of first white men to visit Great Salt Lake region; discovered what is now known as Humboldt River in northern Nevada; rescued remnants of Marcus Whitman's expedition from Cayuse Indians (1847). Ogden, Utah, is named in his honor.

**Ogden, Robert Curtis.** 1836–1913. American merchant and philanthropist, b. Philadelphia; associated with John Wanamaker, in the Philadelphia retail store (1879–96); sole manager (1889–93); opened Wanamaker store in New York (1896–1907); president of Southern Education Board, trustee of Hampton Institute, and of Tuskegee Institute; director, Union Theol. Sem.

**Ogden, Rollo.** 1856–1937. American journalist; editor, New York *Evening Post* (1903–20), New York *Times* (1922–37).

**Ogden, William Butler.** 1805–1877. American railroad executive, b. Walton, N.Y.; to Chicago (1835); first mayor of city of Chicago (1837); interested in railroad development out of Chicago; first president, Union Pacific Railroad (1862). Ogden Graduate School of Science in U. of Chicago is named in his honor.

**O'gé'** *or* **O'jé'** (ô'zhā'), **Jacques Vincent.** 1755–1791. Haitian mulatto insurgent; defeated, captured, tortured, and killed. Regarded as a martyr by the natives of Haiti, who rose in rebellion to avenge his death and nearly exterminated the whites on the island.

**Og·gio'no** (ôd·jô'nō) *or* **Og·gio'ne** (-nā) *or* **Ug·gio'ne** (o͞od-), **Marco da.** 1475?–?1530. Italian painter of the Milanese school; pupil and imitator of Leonardo da Vinci; known chiefly for his copies of Leonardo's *Last Supper.*

**O'gil·by** (ō'g'l·bĭ), **John.** 1600–1676. British translator and printer, b. near Edinburgh; published translations in verse of Vergil, Homer, Aesop's *Fables;* satirized by Dryden and Pope.

**O'gil·vie** (ō'g'l·vĭ), **Frederick Wolff.** 1893–1949. British educator and executive; president and vice-chancellor, Queen's U., Belfast (1934–38); director-general of British Broadcasting Corporation (1938–42).

**Ogilvie, John.** 1797–1867. Scottish lexicographer; compiler of *The Imperial Dictionary, English, Technological, and Scientific* (2 vols., 1850), including encyclopedic features.

**Ogilvie, William Henry.** 1869–1964. Scottish journalist and writer of hunting and sporting verse.

**Ogilvie Gor'don** (gôr'd'n), **Maria M.,** *nee* **Ogilvie.** ?–1939. Scottish geologist; specialist in geology of South Tyrol and Dolomites. D.B.E. (1935).

**O·giń'ski** (ô·gēn'y'·skē), **Michał Kazimierz.** 1731–1803. Lithuanian hetman; defeated by the Russians and forced into exile; returned to his estates (1776) and built the Ogiński Canal connecting the Niemen with the Dnieper. His nephew **Michał Kleofas Ogiński** (1765–1831) commanded his own regiment of cuirassiers in the Kosciusko rebellion (1794); refugee (1794–1802); returned to Poland (1802), and served as mediator for his people with Czar Alexander after the Treaty of Tilsit (1807); became Russian senator (1810); withdrew to Italy (1815); composed polonaises and sentimental songs.

**O'gles·by** (ō'g'lz·bĭ), **Richard James.** 1824–1899. American legislator; practiced law in Illinois (from 1845); served in Mexican War and in Union army in Civil War; major general (1863); governor of Illinois (1865–69; 1873); U.S. senator (1873–79); again governor (1885–89), first man to be elected three times governor of Illinois.

**O'gle·thorpe** (ō'g'l·thôrp), **James Edward.** 1696–1785. English philanthropist, founder of Georgia, b. London, Eng.; member of British parliament (1722–54); interested himself in prison reform; planned project for colonizing unemployed men freed from debtor's prison on lands in America; received charter (1732) for a colony of Georgia. Accompanied first band of emigrants; landed in America (Jan., 1733) and administered affairs of colony until return to England (end of 1734); founded Savannah. Again in Georgia (1735–36; 1738–43); fought against Spaniards; repulsed Spanish attack on Georgia (1742). In England (from 1743); lieutenant general (1746); general (1765). Surrendered Georgia charter to British government (1752).

**Ogotai.** Variant of OGADAI.

**O'Gra'dy** (ō·grā'dĭ), **Standish James.** 1846–1928. Irish man of letters, pioneer of Celtic renaissance; author of *History of Ireland: Heroic Period* (2 vols., 1878), Irish historical romances, etc.

**O'Ha'gan** (ō·hā'găn), **Thomas.** 1st Baron **O'Hagan.** 1812–1885. Irish jurist; lord chancellor of Ireland (1868–74, 1880–81), first Roman Catholic in the office since time of James II.

**O'Har'a** (ō·hâr'ȧ), **Geoffrey.** 1882–1967. Composer and song writer, b. Chatham, Ontario, Canada; to U.S. (1904), naturalized (1919). Among his works are the operettas *Peggy and the Pirate* (1927), *Riding Down the Sky* (1928), *Harmony Hall* (1933); the songs *There Is No Death, K-K-K-Katy, Wreck of the Julie Plante, Leetle Bateese, If Christ Came Back.*

**O'Hara, John Henry.** 1905–1970. American journalist and novelist, b. Pottsville, Pa.; author of *Appointment in Samarra* (1934), *Butterfield 8* (1935), *Hope of Heaven* (1938), and many short stories, as in *The Doctor's Son* (1935), *Files on Parade* (1939), *Pal Joey* (1940; which he adapted as musical comedy, 1940).

**O'Hara, Theodore.** 1820–1867. American soldier and poet, b. Danville, Ky.; served (colonel) in Confederate army through Civil War; known esp. for one poem, *The Bivouac of the Dead*, a dirge commemorating the reburial at Frankfort, Ky. (1847) of Kentuckians killed in the battle of Buena Vista.

**O'Hig'gins** (*Eng.* ō·hĭg'ĭnz; *Span.* ō·ē'gēns), Don **Ambrosio.** Marqués **de O·sor'no** (thā ō·sôr'nō). *Orig. name* **Ambrose Hig'gins** (hĭg'ĭnz). 1720?–1801. Irish soldier and administrator in South America, b. in County Meath, Ireland; captain of cavalry in Chilean service; defeated Araucanian Indians and founded fort of San Carlos (1770); built road from Santiago to **Valparaíso**; captain general of Chile (1789–96); prefixed **O'** to his name; rebuilt Osorno (1792) and was created marquis; as viceroy of Peru (1796–1801), improved defenses and lines of communications. His natural son **Bernardo O'Higgins** (1778–1842), Chilean soldier and statesman; known as "Liberator of Chile"; military leader of Chilean patriots (from 1810); made commander of army (from 1813); with Carrera was defeated at Rancagua (1814) but after joining with San Martín, decisively defeated the Spanish at Chacabuco (Feb. 12, 1817); dictator of Chile (1817–23; progressive administration); deposed by revolution, retired to Peru.

**O'Hig'gins** (ō·hĭg'ĭnz), **Harvey Jerrold.** 1876–1929. Journalist and novelist, b. London, Ontario, Canada; author of *The Smoke-Eaters* (1905), *A Grand Army Man* (1908), *Julie Crane* (1924), *Clara Barron* (1926).

**O'Hig'gins** (ō·hĭg'ĭnz), **Kev'in** (kĕv'ĭn) **Christopher.** 1892–1927. Irish lawyer and politician; joined the Sinn Fein movement (c. 1916) and was interned; minister of justice, and vice-president of the executive council in the provisional government of Ireland (1922); also, minister for external affairs (1927); established the Civic Guard and restored order in Ireland; assassinated.

**Ohiyesa.** See Charles Alexander EASTMAN.

**Oh'lin** (ō'lĭn), **Bertil Gotthard.** 1899–1979. Swedish economist and politician. Member of parliament (1938–70); minister of trade (1944–45); leader of Liberal Party (1944–67); awarded (with James E. Meade) Nobel prize for economics (1977).

**Ohm** (ōm), **Georg Simon.** 1787–1854. German physicist; discovered the relationship between the strength or intensity of an unvarying electrical current, the electromotive force, and the resistance of a circuit, now known as Ohm's law. The ohm, the practical unit of electrical resistance, was named in his honor. Known also for work in mathematics and acoustics, and on interference in crystals.

**Oh'net'** (ō'nĕ'), **Georges.** 1848–1918. French novelist; author of series under general title *Batailles de la Vie.* Several of his novels have been dramatized.

**Oinopides.** See OENOPIDES.

**Oisin.** See OSSIAN.

**Ojé.** See OGÉ.

**O·je'da** (ō·hā'thä), **Alonso de.** 1465?–1515. Spanish explorer; to America with Columbus (1493); active in conquest of Hispaniola (1493–95); with Juan de la Cosa and Amerigo Vespucci took part in exploration of northern coast of South America (1499–1500); as governor of Nueva Andalucía (Darien) unsuccessfully attempted settlement near Cartagena (1508–09); later founded colony at Darien.

**O·jet'ti** (ō·yāt'tē), **Ugo.** 1871–1946. Italian writer and art critic; editor in chief *Corriere della Sera* (1926–27). His works include criticisms, a collection of essays *Cose Viste* (1923–26), novels, short stories, and plays.

**O·ka·da** (ō·kä·dä), **Keisuke.** 1868–1952. Japanese naval officer; admiral and supreme war councilor (1924); minister for navy (1927–29, 1932–33); prime minister (1934–36).

**O·ka·ku·ra** (ō·kä·kōō·rä), **Kakuzo.** 1862–1913. Japanese art historian; studied in Europe and U.S. (1884–87); director of new art school in Tokyo (1887–98). Author of *The Ideals of the East* (1904), *The Awakening of Japan* (1904), *The Book of Tea* (1906).

**Ok'ba** *or* **Oq'ba** (ŏŏk'bă). *Arab.* **'Uqbah ibn-Nāfi'.** d. 683 A.D. Arab general in North Africa, nephew of Amr ibn-al-As; sent by Caliph Muawiyah to conquer North Africa; founded (670) Kairouan; continued conquests as far as Tangier; killed at Biskra on return; raised to sainthood by Arabs; great mosque in Kairouan dedicated to him.

**O'Keeffe'** (ō·kēf'), **Georgia.** 1887– . American muralist and landscape painter, b. Sun Prairie, Wis.; m. (1924) Alfred Stieglitz. Known esp. for New Mexican desert scenes and for symbolic abstractions in many of her later paintings.

**O'Keeffe, John.** 1747–1833. Irish actor and playwright; gained reputation as author of *Tony Lumpkin in Town* (produced 1778); author of farces including *Wild Oats*, and of the song "I am a Friar of Orders Grey," in his opera *Merry Sherwood.*

**O'ke·ghem** (ō'kĕ·gĕm) *or* **Ock'e·ghem** (ŏk'ĕ-), **Jean** (zhäN) **d'** *or* **Jan** (yän) **van.** *Also known by numerous other variants, including* **Johannes Ock'en·heim** (ŏk'ĕn·hīm). 1430?–1495. Composer and contrapuntist, b. in East Flanders; a master of the second Netherlandish school; at court of Charles VII in Paris (from 1453) and head of the chapel (1454); served under Louis XI as treasurer of St. Martin's abbey, Tours (1459); again in Paris (from 1461); royal Kapellmeister (from 1465). His compositions include masses (*Missa Cujusvis Toni*), motets, canons, and chansons.

**O'Kel'ly** (ō·kĕl'ĭ), **Seán Thomas.** 1883–1966. Irish journalist and political leader; one of founders of Sinn Fein; speaker of first Dail Eireann (1919–21); Irish envoy to U.S. (1924–26); vice-president of executive council and minister for local government and public health (1932–39), minister of finance (1939–45), president (1945–59), Republic of Ireland.

**O'Kelly, Seumas.** 1881–1918. Irish writer; editor of *Sinn Fein;* author of *The Matchmakers* (1908), *The Shuiler's Child* (1909), *Three Plays* (1912), *The Bribe* (a 3-act play, 1913), *The Golden Barque and The Weaver's Grave* (1919).

**O'ken** (ō'kĕn), **Lorenz.** *Surname properly* **Ock'en·fuss** (ŏk'ĕn·fōōs). 1779–1851. German naturalist and philosopher; sought to unify the natural sciences; in his speculations, foreshadowed theories of the cellular structure of organisms and of the protoplasmic basis of life.

**O·khlop'kov** (ŭ·klôp'kôf), **Nikolai.** 1902?–1967. Russian theater manager and producer; interested in devising means of presenting plays to Russian masses (the so-called Mass Theater Movement).

**O·ku** (ō·kōō), Count **Yasukata.** 1846–1930. Japanese field marshal; served in war with China (1894–95); general (1903); took important part in Russo-Japanese War (1904–05), participating in battles of Liaoyang, Shaho, and Mukden; considered one of Japan's great military strategists; chief of staff (1906–12); count (1907); field marshal (1911).

**O·ku·bo** (ō·kōō·bō), Marquis **Toshimichi.** 1830 or 1832–1878. Japanese statesman and reformer, member of Satsuma clan; one of five leaders in restoration of emperor to power (1867–68); cabinet officer (1870–78); aided government in putting down Satsuma rebellion; murdered by Satsuma clansmen.

**O·ku·ma** (ō·kōō·mä), Marquis **Shigenobu.** 1838–1922. Japanese statesman; one of younger leaders in Restoration period (1867–68); as minister of finance (1869–81) organized fiscal system on sound basis; established (1882) Progressive party; prime minister (1898 and 1914–16, during first part of World War); popular for his liberal views; founder (1882) and president of Waseda U. at Tokyo.

**O·kyo** (ō·kyō). *Also called* **Ma·ru·ya·ma Okyo** (mä-rōō·yä·mä). 1733–1795. Japanese painter; influenced by Chinese masters; founded Maruyama school representative of Japanese 18th-century realism.

**O'laf** (ō'läf; *formerly* ō'läv; *Angl.* ō'lăf). Name of two kings of Denmark:

**Olaf I.** d. 1095. Nicknamed "Hunger" because of famines during reign; son of Sweyn II; king (1086–95).

**Olaf II.** 1370–1387. Son of Haakon VI Magnusson of Norway and Margaret of Denmark; king of Denmark (1376–87) and of Norway, as Olaf V (1380–87), his mother ruling as regent of both countries during his minority (1376–87). See MARGARET.

**O'laf** (ō'läf; *Angl.* ō'lăf) *or* **O'lav** (ō'läv). *Lat.* **O·la'us** (ō·lā'ŭs). Name of five kings of Norway:

**Olaf I.** *Known as* **Olaf Trygg'ves·son** (trüg'vĕ·sŏn). 969–1000. King (995–1000); born while parents were in exile; brought up at court of Vladimir I, Grand Prince of Russia; m. Gyda, a princess of Dublin, and lived in England and Ireland several years (c. 990–993); converted to Christianity in Scilly Islands; led viking expedition, ravaging coasts of France, England, and Ireland (994); sailed to Norway and was accepted as king (995); began to convert country to Christianity; quarreled with King Sweyn of Denmark; in an expedition to Wendish country, waylaid off Svöld, near Rügen, by combined Swedish and Danish fleets; on total defeat of Norwegians, leaped overboard and disappeared. A great warrior and popular sovereign about whose deeds many legends have arisen.

**Olaf II.** *Known as* **Olaf Ha'ralds·son** (här'räl·sŏn). *Called also* **Saint Olaf.** 995?–1030. King (1016–28). Son of Harold Grönske and a descendant of Harold I. Took part in viking expeditions; accepted Christianity; endeavored to complete conversion of Norway; made enemies of petty kings of Norway who sought help of Canute the Great of Denmark; fled to Sweden (1028); tried to reconquer Norway but defeated and killed at Stiklestad; became national hero and patron saint of Norway; canonized (1164).

**Olaf III.** *Known as* **Olaf Haraldsson.** *Also called* **Olaf Kyr're** (*Norw.* kür'rĕ; *Old Norse* kür'rĕ), *i.e.* the Quiet. d. 1093. King (1066–93), son of Harold Haardraade; after death of Harold at Stamford Bridge (1066), brought back fleet to Norway; divided kingdom with brother Magnus (II) Haraldsson; reigned jointly with him (1066–69) and alone (1069–93); entire reign marked by peace and progress and growth of Christianity.

**Olaf IV.** *Known as* **Olaf Mag'nus·son** (*Norw.* mäng'nōō·sŏn; *Old Norse* mäg'nōō·sŏn). 1100?–1115. Son of Magnus III; king (1103–15); proclaimed joint king with his two brothers, Eystein and Sigurd.

**Olaf V.** See OLAF II, King of Denmark.

**O'laf God'frey·son** (ō'lăf gŏth'frĕ·ĭ·sŏn) *or* **O'lafr** (ō'lä'vĕr) **Godfreyson.** d. 941. Danish king of Northumbria and Dublin; kinsman of Olaf Sitricson; leader of Ostmen; king of Dublin (934), of Deira (southern Northumbria, 940).

**O'laf Sit'ric·son** (ō'lăf sĭt'rĭk·s'n) *or* **An'laf Sit'ric·son** (ăn'läf sĭt'rĭk·s'n) *or* **O'lafr Sig'tryggs·son** (ō'lä'-vĕr sĕg'trüg·sŏn). *Known in sagas as* **Olaf the Red.** d. 981. Danish king of Northumbria and Dublin; leader of Ostmen; one of princes defeated by Athelstan at Brunanburh (937); driven from Northumbria by Edmund (944); his dominion in Ireland destroyed by defeat of Danes at Tara (980).

**Olai, Georgius.** See Georg STIERNHIELM.

**Olaus Magnus.** See MAGNUS.

**O·la'ya Her·re'ra** (ō·lä'yä ĕr·rĕ'rä), **Enrique.** 1881–1937. Colombian diplomat and politician; president of Colombia (1930–34); administration notable for financial measures to combat economic depression.

**Ol'bers** (ōl'bĕrs), **Heinrich Wilhelm Matthäus.** 1758–1840. German physician and astronomer; devised method of determining the orbit of a comet; discovered several comets (the one of 1815 with a period of 72 years being named after him), rediscovered the asteroid Ceres, and discovered the asteroids Pallas (1802) and Vesta (1807); advanced hypothesis (Olbers's hypothesis) accounting for origination of asteroids by explosion of a primordial planet.

**Ol'brich** (ōl'brĭk), **Joseph Maria.** 1867–1908. German architect and craftsman; champion of modernism in architecture and handicraft; helped organize the Vienna Secession, a group sympathetic to modernist tendencies in the applied arts (1897). Author of *Ideen* (1899), *Architektur* (3 vols., 450 plates; 1901–14), *Der Frauen-rosenhof* (30 plates; 1907), etc.

**Ol'cott** (ŏl'kŭt), **Chauncey,** *really* **Chancellor John.** 1860–1932. American tenor singer and actor; successful as star in Irish musical dramas (from 1891), some of which he wrote himself; introduced song *Mother Machree* in U.S.; wrote and sang *My Wild Irish Rose.*

**Olcott, Henry Steel.** 1832–1907. American theosophist, b. Orange, N.J.; studied occult science under Madame Blavatsky (1874); cofounder (with Madame Blavatsky, 1875) and first president of the Theosophical Society. With Madame Blavatsky traveled and made "converts" in India and Ceylon (1879–84); after exposure of Madame Blavatsky's frauds (1884), devoted himself to developing Theosophical Society on legitimate basis. Lectured widely in India, Ceylon, Japan; opened free schools in India for pariahs; co-operated with Mrs. Annie Besant in work of Theosophical Society.

**Old'berg** (ōld'bûrg), **Ar'ne** (är'nĕ). 1874–1962. American pianist and composer of chamber music, orchestral numbers (symphonies and a symphonic poem), concertos, and piano pieces.

**Old′cas′tle** (ōld′kàs′'l), Sir **John**. 1377?–1417. English Lollard leader. Titled Baron **Cob′ham** (kŏb′ăm), after his marriage to Joan, Lady Cobham (1409). Won friendship of Henry, Prince of Wales (later Henry V), during Welsh campaigns; commanded army sent to France by Henry (1411). Arrested by Henry's orders and convicted of heresy (1413); escaped; headed a Lollard conspiracy and other plots; captured, hanged as heretic and traitor, and burned while hanging. Portrayed as boon companion of the prince in *The Famous Victories of Henry V*, adapted by Shakespeare in *Henry IV*, in which Falstaff was originally named Oldcastle. Cf. Sir John FASTOLF.

**Ol′den·bar′ne·veldt** (ŏl′dĕn·bär′nĕ·vĕlt), **Jan van.** See Jan van Olden BARNEVELDT.

**Ol′den·berg** (ôl′dĕn·bĕrk), **Hermann.** 1854–1920. German Indologist.

**Ol′den·burg** (ôl′dĕn·bo͝ork). A German family of nobility which became prominent in the 15th century. It is divided into several lines:

(1) Counts of Oldenburg (region in northwestern Germany), extinct (1667).

(2) Dynasties of Denmark: (a) Rulers of Denmark (1448–1863) and Norway (1450–1814), and at times of Sweden; began with Christian (I), Count of Oldenburg (ruled 1448–81), who descended through his mother from Eric (V) Klipping (see CHRISTIAN I), and who was offered crown of Denmark (1448) on death of Christopher III (of Bavaria); succeeded by John (or Hans) [1481–1513] and thereafter by 14 sovereigns alternately named Christian (II–VIII) and Frederick (I–VII), becoming extinct with Frederick VII (1863). (b) **Glücks′burg** (glüks′bo͝ork) line (see CHRISTIAN IX), the present reigning house of Denmark (Christian IX, Frederick VIII, and Christian X). See 4(b) below; see also *Table (in Appendix)* for DENMARK.

(3) **Got′torp** (gôt′ôrp), or **Hol′stein-Got′torp** (hôl′shtīn-), line (named from a castle in Schleswig), a branch of the Danish line; founded (1586) by Duke Adolf, a younger son of King Frederick I of Denmark; line ruled (as counts, 1586–1773) in a part of Schleswig-Holstein under Danish kings; their county became a duchy (1777); held by Napoleon (1806–13); became a grand duchy (1815) but title not adopted until later (1829); last rulers: Nicholas Frederick Peter (1827–1900) and Frederick Augustus (1852–1931; ruled 1900–18; abdicated). Two other royal lines have branched from this: (a) *Russian:* **Holstein-Gottorp-Romanov,** founded by Peter III (czar, 1762), son of Anna (daughter of Empress Catherine I) and Charles Frederick of Holstein-Gottorp. See ROMANOV. (b) *Swedish:* **Holstein-Gottorp** line (see VASA), founded by Adolphus Frederick of Holstein (1751–71), uncle of Peter III and brother of Charles Frederick. See *Table (in Appendix)* for SWEDEN.

(4) **Holstein-Sön′der·borg** (-sûn′ẽr·bôrg) line, originating (1582) with Duke John (Hans) [1545–1622], third son of Christian III of Denmark; divided into two lines: (a) **Sönderborg-Au·gu′sten·burg** (-ou·go͞os′tĕn·bo͝ork), beginning (1770); recent head, Prince Christian (1831–1917), m. Princess Helena of Great Britain; (b) **Schleswig-Holstein-Sönderborg-Glücksburg,** beginning (1825), of which one branch is 2(b) above, another (through George I) the royal line of Greece (1863–1923, 1935 ff.).

**Ol′den·burg** (ôl′dĕn·bo͝ork), **Sergei Fëdorovich.** 1863–1934. Russian Indologist.

**Old′field** (ōld′fēld), **Anne.** 1683–1730. English actress; made reputation as Lady Betty Modish in Cibber's *Careless Husband* (1704); excelled as Lady Townley in the *Provoked Husband;* created many parts in genteel comedy; in tragedy created role of Jane Shore (1714); excelled as Cleopatra and as Calista in Rowe's *Fair Penitent;* created role of Sophonisba (1730).

**Old′ham** (ōl′dăm), **John.** 1600?–1636. English colonist; to America (1623), landing at Plymouth; murdered by Pequot Indians (July, 1636), his murder being one of causes of Pequot War.

**Oldham, John.** 1653–1683. English satirical poet; author of *Satires Upon the Jesuits* (1681) and Pindaric odes.

**Oldham, Thomas.** 1816–1878. Irish geologist; discovered fossil *Oldhamia* at Bray Head (1849).

**Oldham, William Fitzjames.** 1854–1937. American Methodist Episcopal clergyman; missionary bishop for southern Asia (1904–12); bishop (1916).

**Old′mix′on** (ōld′mĭk′s'n), **John.** 1673–1742. English historian; published partisan histories of England, Scotland, Ireland, and America; attacked Clarendon in his *Critical History of England* (1724–26); provoked Pope's retaliation in the *Dunciad.*

**Old Pretender.** See James Francis Edward STUART.

**Olds, Ransom Eli.** 1864–1950, American automobile inventor and manufacturer, b. Geneva, Ohio. President, Reo Motor Car Co. (1904–24), chairman (1924–36); Reo and Oldsmobile named in his honor.

**Oldstyle, Jonathan.** Pseudonym of Washington IRVING.

**Ol′dys** (?ōl′dĭs; ōldz), **William.** 1696–1761. English antiquary; collaborated with Dr. Johnson on *Harleian Miscellany* (1744–46); Norroy king-of-arms (1755–61).

**O·le·vi·a′nus** (ō·lā·vē·ä′no͞os; *Angl.* ō·lē′vĭ·ā′nŭs), **Kaspar.** 1536–1587. German theologian; a founder of the German Reformed Church; introduced Calvinist Reformation in Nassau-Siegen, Solms, and Wied, and founded (1584) the Herborn school.

**Ol′ga** (ŏl′gȧ; *Russ.* ôl′y′·gŭ), Saint. d. 969. Wife of Prince Igor of Kiev; ruled Kiev (945–955) after Igor's death as regent for her minor son; baptized at Constantinople (c. 955).

**Olga Kon·stan·ti′nov·na** (kŭn·stŭn·tyē′nŭv·nŭ). 1851–1926. Queen of Greece; daughter of Grand Duke Constantine of Russia; m. (1867) George I of Greece; mother of Constantine I of Greece.

**Ol′gierd** (*Pol.* ôl′gyĕrt) *or* **Ol′gerd** (*Russ.* ?ôl′y′·gyĕrt). *Lith.* **Al′gir·das** (äl′gĭr·däs). d. 1377. Grand duke of Lithuania (1345–77); son of Gedimin (*q.v.*); extended domain of Lithuania; defeated Teutonic Knights (1360); supported Michael of Tver in Russian civil conflicts; led his armies into southern Russia as far as Black Sea and defeated Tatars (1368); succeeded by his son Jagello (see JAGELLON and LADISLAS II of Poland).

**O·lid′** (ō·lēth′), **Cristóbal de.** 1492?–1524. Spanish captain under Cortes in conquest of Mexico (1519–21).

**O′lier′** (ō′lyā′), **Jean Jacques.** 1608–1657. French Roman Catholic priest; founder (1641) of the Sulpician order for training men for the priesthood, and founder also (1646) of the church and seminary of Saint Sulpice in Paris; sent priests to Canada to est. communities.

**O·lin′sky** (ō·lĭn′skĭ; *Russ.* ŭ·lyēn′skû·ĭ), **I·van′** (ĭ·vän′) **Gre·go′re·witch** (gryĕ·gô′ryĕ·vyĭch). 1878–1962. Painter. b. in southern Russia; to U.S. (1891).

**Ol′i·phant** (ŏl′ĭ·fănt), **Carolina.** See Carolina NAIRNE.

**Oliphant, Laurence.** 1829–1888. English war correspondent, travel writer, and mystic, b. Cape Town. Published *A Journey to Katmandu* (1852), the satirical novel *Piccadilly* (1870). Fell under influence of Thomas Lake Harris, spiritualist prophet in U.S. (1867–81). With his wife wrote *Sympneumata* (1884), expressing strange mystical views; wrote a mystical novel, *Massollam* (1885), and *Scientific Religion* (1888).

**Oliphant, Margaret Oliphant,** *nee* **Wilson.** 1828–1897. Scottish novelist and historical writer. First novel, *Mrs. Margaret Maitland* (1849); m. (1852) her cousin **Francis Wilson Oliphant** (1818–1859), painter and designer of stained glass. Author of *Adam Graeme* (1852), a series of four novels entitled *Chronicles of Carlingford* (1863–76), *The Primrose Path* (1878), *A Widow's Tale* (1898). Author also of *The Makers of Venice* (1887) and a *Literary History of England 1790–1825* (1882).

**O'li·va'res** (ō'lē·vä'rās), Conde **de. Gaspar de Guzmán.** Duque **de San·lú'car** (sän·lo͞o'kär). *Known as* **El Conde–Duque de Olivares.** 1587–1645. Spanish statesman; prime minister for Philip IV (1621–43); introduced great extravagance into Spanish court; renewed war with Holland (1621); caused Spain to enter Thirty Years' War against France (1636); levied taxes that stirred Catalonia and Portugal to revolt (1640–43); dismissed through influence of queen and exiled (1643).

**Ol'i·ver** (ŏl'ĭ·vẽr), **Andrew.** 1706–1774. American colonial political leader, b. Boston; member of Provincial Council (1746–65); secretary of the province (1756–71); appointed stamp officer after passage of the Stamp Act (1765), he was unpopular, hanged in effigy, his house damaged by mob violence; lieutenant governor of Massachusetts (1771–74); again suffered unpopularity when Benjamin Franklin secured and published (1773) certain private letters of his describing unrest in the colonies and suggesting remedies.

**Oliver, George Tener.** 1848–1919. Lawyer and industrialist; practiced law in Pittsburgh (1871–81); engaged in steel manufacturing (1881–1901); U.S. senator (1909–17). His older brother, **Henry William** (1840–1904), was a pioneer in developing Minnesota iron-ore deposits.

**Oliver, Henry Kemble,** *orig.* **Thomas Henry.** 1800–1885. American teacher, musician, and industrialist; teacher at Salem, Mass. (1818–43); superintendent of cotton mills, Lawrence, Mass. (1848–58); first commissioner of labor in Massachusetts (1869–73); composer of church music.

**Oliver, Henry William.** See under George T. OLIVER.

**Ol'i·ver** (ŏl'ĭ·vẽr) *or* **O·liv'i·er** (ō·lĭv'ĭ·ẽr; -ā), **Isaac.** 1556?–1617. English miniature painter of French extraction. His eldest son, **Peter** (1594–1648), was employed by Charles I to make copies in miniature of paintings in his collection.

**Oliver, James.** 1823–1908. Industrialist, b. Scotland; to U.S.(1835); invented process for manufacturing hard-faced plows (patents, 1868, 1869); president of Oliver Chilled Plow Works until his death.

**Oliver, John Rathbone.** 1872–1943. American psychiatrist and novelist, b. Albany, N.Y.; author of the novels *Fear* (1927), *Victim and Victor* (1928), *Rock and Sand* (1930), and *Article Thirty-two* (1931); also of *Psychiatry and Mental Health* (1932), *The Ordinary Difficulties of Everyday People* (1935), etc.

**Oliver, Paul Ambrose.** 1830–1912. American soldier and inventor; credited with inventing dynamite and black powder explosives, contemporaneously with and independently of Nobel and Schultze.

**O'li'vé'tan'** (ō'lē'vā'tän'), **Pierre Robert.** d. 1538. French Protestant scholar; trans. Bible (1535).

**O·liv'i·er** (ō·lĭv'ĭ·ẽr; -ā), **Isaac** and **Peter.** See OLIVER.

**O'li'vier'** (ō'lē'vyā'), **Juste Daniel.** 1807–1876. Swiss writer; author of books on Swiss history, and patriotic poems, hymns, and short stories.

**O·liv'i·er** (ō·lĭv'ĭ·ā), **Laurence Kerr.** Baron **Olivier** of **Brigh'ton** (brī't'n). 1907– . British actor, director, and producer. Knighted (1947); created life peer (1970).

**O·liv'i·er** (ō·lĭv'ĭ·ẽr; -ā), **Sydney.** 1st Baron **Olivier of Rams'den** (rămz'dĕn). 1859–1943. English colonial administrator; one of founders of Fabian Society; colonial secretary of Jamaica (1899–1904) and governor (1907–13); assistant comptroller of exchequer (1917–20); secretary for India in first Labor cabinet (1924).

**O'li'vier' le Dain** (ō'lē'vyā') *or* **le Daim** *or* **le Diable.** See Olivier NECKER.

**Ol'len·dorff** (ôl'ĕn·dôrf), **Heinrich Gottfried.** 1803–1865. German teacher and grammarian in Paris; developed a simplified method of learning modern languages by examples and exercises rather than by rules, and wrote many textbooks employing this method.

**Ol'lier'** (ô'lyā'), **Léopold Louis Xavier Édouard.** 1825–1900. French bone and joint surgeon.

**Ol'li·vant** (ŏl'ĭ·vănt), **Alfred.** 1874–1927. English novelist; achieved success with first book, the dog story *Owd Bob* (1898), American title, *Bob, Son of Battle;* author also of *The Gentleman* (1908; romance of the sea), *The Royal Road* (1912; about Cockney London), etc.

**Ol'li'vier'** (ô'lē'vyā'), **Olivier Émile.** 1825-1913. French politician; headed ministry (Jan. 2, 1870), and was outmaneuvered by Bismarck in the days preceding the Franco-Prussian War; forced to retire (Aug. 9, 1870) after French defeats revealed folly of the ministry in plunging country into war.

**Ol·me'do** (ôl·mā'thō), **José Joaquín.** 1782–1847. Ecuadorian politician and poet; best known for his lyrics, as in *The Victory of Junín, Hymn to Bolívar.*

**Olm'stead** (?ŏm'stĕd; -stĭd), **Dawson.** 1884– . American army officer; grad. U.S.M.A., West Point (1906); promoted through the grades to major general and chief signal officer, U.S. army (Oct., 1941).

**Olm'sted** (ōm'stĕd; -stĭd), **Denison.** 1791–1859. American scientist; professor of mathematics and natural philosophy, Yale (1825–59); responsible for introducing experiments into his lectures, and inaugurating laboratory work at Yale; conducted investigations of meteors, hailstorms, auroras.

**Olm'sted** (ōm'stĕd; -stĭd), **Frederick Law.** 1822–1903. American landscape architect, b. Hartford, Conn.; received appointment as superintendent of Central Park, then under construction in New York City (1857). In association with Calvert Vaux, designed new plans for building this park, and also planned Prospect Park in Brooklyn, South Park in Chicago, a municipal park in Buffalo, the grounds of the national capitol at Washington, and the Boston park system. Instrumental in securing the Yosemite as a national reservation. Uncle and stepfather of **John Charles Olmsted** (1852–1920), who was associated with him (from 1875) and became (1895) senior partner in firm of F. L. and J. C. Olmsted.

**Ol'ney** (ŏl'nĭ), **Richard.** 1835–1917. American statesman, b. Oxford, Mass.; U.S. attorney general (1893–95); U.S. secretary of state (1895–97); directed U.S. policy in settlement of Venezuela boundary dispute with Great Britain (1895).

**O·ló'za·ga** (ō·lō'thä·gä), **Salustiano.** 1803–1873. Spanish lawyer and politician; involved in conspiracy to assassinate King Ferdinand VII (1831); took refuge in Paris. Returned to Spain after Ferdinand's death and became supporter of Queen Maria Christina; ambassador in Paris (1840; 1855–65; 1868 ff.).

**Ol'rik** (ŏl'rēk), **Axel.** 1864–1917. Danish folklorist, specialist in Norse mythology and epic poetry.

**Ol'sen** (ōl'sĕn), **Ole.** 1850–1927. Norwegian composer.

**Ols'hau'sen** (ōls'hou'zĕn), **Hermann.** 1796–1839. German Protestant theologian and exegete. His brother **Theodor** (1802–1869), politician and writer, championed independence of Holstein; resident (1851–65) in New

York and in St. Louis, where he published German newspapers. Their brother **Justus** (1800–1882), Orientalist, wrote esp. on Persian topics, the Old Testament, and Hebraic languages. Justus's son **Robert von Olshausen** (1835–1915), gynecologist, was director of the university clinic for women at Berlin. Robert's brother **Justus von Olshausen** (1844–1924), criminologist, was on supreme court council, Berlin (1887); Reichs counsel (1890); attorney general (1899); president of supreme court senate (1907–10).

**O·lyb'ri·us** (ō·lĭb'rĭ·ŭs), **Anicius**. Roman emperor (472); native of Rome but fled to Constantinople (after 455); m. (c. 464) Placidia, daughter of Valentinian III; sent to Italy by Emperor Leo; made emperor of the West by Ricimer (472); reigned only a few months.

**O·lym'pi·as** (ō·lĭm'pĭ·ăs). d. 316 B.C. Wife of Philip II of Macedon; daughter of Neoptolemus, King of Epirus; mother of Alexander the Great. Married Philip (359 B.C.); retired to Epirus when Philip married (337) Cleopatra; gained much influence during Alexander's reign (337–323); said to have caused death of Cleopatra and her daughter; again withdrew to Epirus (323); joined Polysperchon in alliance against Cassander; besieged in Pydna by Cassander, captured and killed.

**O·lym'pi·o·do'rus** (ō·lĭm'pĭ·ō·dō'rŭs). Greek historian of 5th century A.D., b. Thebes, Egypt; long resident at court of Theodosius; author of a history of the Western Roman Empire from 407 to 425, an abstract of which (by Photius) is extant.

**O'Ma'ho·ny** (ō·mä'hō·nĭ), **John**. 1816–1877. Irish political leader, b. in County Cork, Ireland; suggested (1856) and aided in organizing the Irish Republican Brotherhood under James Stephens (1858); headed American branch known as Fenian Brotherhood, popularly Fenians (1858–66); resigned after dissension following fiasco of Fenian attack on Canada (1866); again Fenian leader (1872–77).

**O'Mal'ley** (ō·măl'ĭ), **Frank Ward**. 1875–1932. American journalist on staff of New York *Sun* (1906–20); established reputation as accurate and brilliant reporter.

**O'man** (ō'măn), Sir **Charles William Chadwick**. 1860–1946. British historian, b. in India; professor of modern history, Oxford (from 1905). Author of histories of Greece (1888), of Europe from 476 to 918 (1893), of the art of war in Middle Ages (1898) and in 16th century (1937), of Peninsular War (7 vols., 1902–30), of England before the Norman Conquest (1910), and of *Warwick the Kingmaker* (1891), *Wellington's Army* (1912), *Napoleonic Studies* (1929), *On the Writing of History* (1939), etc.

**O'mar** (ō'mär; ō'mẽr). Name of two caliphs:

**Omar I.** *Arab.* **'Umar ibn-al-Khaṭṭāb.** 581?–644. Second orthodox caliph (634–644), succeeding abu-Bakr; called "Emperor of Believers." Opposed Mohammed and followers (before 617); then converted to Islam and aided abu-Bakr in conquests of new religion; greatly extended Moslem empire, defeating Persians (637) at Qadisiya (Kadesia) and (641) at Nehavend; conquered Syria and Palestine (635–640); sent (639) his general Amr ibn-al-As to invade Egypt, who conquered it by 642; assassinated at Medina by a Persian slave; organizer of Moslem power; inaugurated system of dating Mohammedan events from the hegira.

**Omar II.** *Arab.* **'Umar ibn-'Abd-al-'Azīz.** d. 720. Ommiad caliph (717–720); attempted unsuccessfully to reorganize finances of empire.

**O'mar Khay·yám'** (ō'mär [ō'mẽr] kī·(y)äm' [kī-]). d. about 1123. Persian poet and astronomer, b. in Nishapur, Khurasan. Member of group of eight scholars appointed by Sultan Malik Shah (Jalal-al-Din) to reform the Moslem calendar (1079); their reform inaugurated the Jalalaean era. Published a series of astronomical tables, known as *Ziji Malikshahi*, and a treatise on algebra. Best known as a poet for his *Rubáiyát*, a collection of quatrains in which the 1st, 2d, and 4th lines rhyme, known to English readers esp. through the translation by Edward FitzGerald (*q.v.*).

**Omar Pasha.** See OMER PASHA.

**Omayyad.** See OMMIAD.

**O'Mea'ra** (ō·mä'rȧ), **Barry Edward**. 1786–1836. Irish surgeon; Napoleon's physician at St. Helena; dismissed by Sir Hudson Lowe for intrigues with Napoleon (1818). Author of *Napoleon in Exile; or a Voice from St. Helena* (2 vols., 1822).

**O'mer Pa·sha'** (ō'mẽr pä·shä'). *Also* **O'mar** (ō'mär; ō'mẽr) **Pasha**. *Real name* **Michael Lattas**. 1806–1871. Turkish general, b. in Croatia; fled to Bosnia (1828) and became Mohammedan; governor of Lebanon (1842); suppressed several revolts; defeated Russians at Oltenița (1853); commanded army in Crimea (1855); governor of Baghdad (1857–59); put down insurrections in Montenegro (1862) and in Crete (1867); created marshal (1864).

**O·mi'chund** (ō·mē'chŭnd). *Real name* **A·mir' Chand** (ȧ·mēr' chŭnd'). d. 1767. Wealthy Sikh banker at Calcutta; intermediary between British and the nawab Siraj-ud-daula; blackmailed British for large amount of treasure involved in their secret treaty with Mir Jafar for deposition of nawab; deceived by Clive who substituted a forged duplicate.

**Om·mi'ad** (ō·mī'ăd) *or* **O·may'yad** (ō·mī'yăd). *Arab.* **U·may'yad** (ŏŏ·mī'yăd). (1) Arab dynasty of caliphs (661–750) with capital at Damascus, deriving its name from **O·may'ya** [ō·mī'yȧ] (*Arab.* **U·may'yah** [ŏŏ·mī'yă]), an ancestor of its founder, Muawiyah, who was proclaimed caliph (661) after death of Ali, fourth and last of the orthodox caliphs. The dynasty had fourteen members, the last, Marwan II, being overthrown by Abbassides. (2) Moorish emirate (756–929) at Córdoba, later a caliphate (929–1031), founded by Abd-er-Rahman I, member of the Ommiad dynasty who escaped the Abbassides. This dynasty had eleven members, reaching height of power in reigns of Abd-er-Rahman III (912–961) and Hakam II (961–976); overthrown by Berbers.

**Omodeo.** See Giovanni Antonio AMADEO.

**O'mont'** (ō'môɴ'), **Henry Auguste**. 1857–1940. French librarian and scholar; on staff of Bibliothèque Nationale (from 1881), and curator of manuscripts there (1899).

**O'More'** (ō·mōr'), **Rory**. *Irish* **Ruaidhri og ua Mordha.** Name of three Irish rebel chieftains of Laoighis (formerly Leix): (1) **Rory** (fl. 1554), captain of Leix. (2) His son **Rory** (*or* **Rury**) **Oge** (d. 1578); fought against forces of both Elizabeth and earl of Ormonde (1572); participated in Kildare plots (1574); pardoned; rebelled again on hope of help from Spain; defeated by Sir Henry Sidney; finally caught and killed by the Fitzpatricks. (3) **Rory** (fl. 1620–1652); called often **Roger Moore**; organized a conspiracy to recover lands of Irish families; failed to seize Dublin Castle (1641), but led Ulster rebellion; won victory at Julianstown (1641); commanded forces in Kings and Queens counties (1643), in Connaught and Leinster; after failure of uprising of 1650, was driven away to island of Bofin (1652).

**Omp'te·da** (ômp'tā·dä), Baron **Georg von.** *Pseudonym* **Georg E'ge·storff** (ā'gĕ·shtôrf). 1863–1931. German writer, esp. of novels and stories, poems, dramas, translations of de Maupassant, etc.

**Om'ri** (ŏm'rī). *In Douay Version* **Om'rai** (ŏm'rī). d. 875? B.C. King of Israel (887?–875? B.C.); proclaimed king by army; gained control of Israel by overcoming

Tibni, claimant to throne, and made Samaria his capital; made Moab subject to him; succeeded by his son Ahab (*1 Kings* xvi. 15–28).

**O·na′tas** (ō·nā′tās). Greek sculptor of 5th century B.C., in Aegina; works highly praised by Pausanias. The Aeginetan marbles, or sculptures, may be in part his work or represent his style.

**O·ña′te** (ō·nyä′tā), **Juan de.** 1549?–?1624. Conqueror and colonizer of New Mexico; led expedition to explore and conquer territory now New Mexico (1598); sent out exploring parties into Kansas (1601) and to Gulf of California (1605).

**Onck′en** (ông′kĕn), **August.** See under Wilhelm ONCKEN.

**Oncken, Hermann.** 1869–1946. German historian; author of political biographies of Ferdinand Lassalle (1904) and Rudolf von Bennigsen (2 vols., 1910), and of *Deutschlands Weltkrieg und die Deutschamerikaner* (1914), *Das Deutsche Reich und die Vorgeschichte des Weltkrieges* (2 vols., 1933), etc.

**Oncken, Wilhelm.** 1838–1905. German historian; author of *Athen und Hellas* (2 parts, 1865–66), *Österreich und Preussen im Befreiungskrieg* (2 vols., 1876–79), etc. His brother **August** (1844–1911), economist, wrote *Adam Smith und Immanuel Kant* (part 1, 1877), *Geschichte der Nationalökonomie* (part 1, 1902), etc.

**O'Neal′, O'Neale′, O'Neil′** (ō·nēl′). See also O'NEILL.

**O'Neale′** *or* **O'Neill′** (ō·nēl′), **Margaret,** *known as* **Peggy.** See under John Henry EATON.

**O·ne′gin** (ŭ·nyā′gyĭn), **Evgeni B.** 1883–1919. Russian composer of operas (*Icarus, Marie Antoinette,* etc.), a comic opera, ballet, choral works, and songs. His wife (m. 1912) **Si′grid** (zē′grĭt; -grēt), *nee* **Hoff′mann** [hŏf′män] (1891–1943), mezzo-soprano dramatic and concert singer.

**O'Neill′** (ō·nēl′). An Irish family descended, through his son Owen (*Irish* Eoghan), from **Niall** [nēl] (d. 405), King of Ireland, who fought against rulers in Ireland, Britain, and Gaul. Of the O'Neills, who were chief rivals in Ulster of the O'Donnells (*q.v.*), the following were important leaders: **Con O'Neill** (1484?–?1559), called "Ba′cach" [bä′kȧk] (the Lame), 1st Earl of **Ty·rone′** (tĭ·rōn′); thrice invaded the Pale, English-controlled district (1520, 1539, 1541); made submission at Greenwich after three invasions of Tyrone (1542) and was created earl of Tyrone by Henry VIII; privy councilor of Ireland (1543). His son **Shane** (1530?–1567), 2d earl; captured Calvagh O'Donnell and harassed English army until Elizabeth recognized him chieftain of Tyrone and granted his terms (1563); attacked Scottish settlements in Antrim, took chiefs of MacDonnells prisoner (1565); invaded the Pale (1566), but was defeated by O'Donnells (aided by English under Sidney) at Letterkenny (1567); took refuge with MacDonnells, by whom he was slain for the reward. Sir **Turlough Luineach** (1530?–1595), Earl of **Clan·con′nell** (klăn·kŏn′'l); cousin of Shane; resisted earl of Essex through alliances with O'Donnells, MacDonnells, and MacQuillans; created earl of Clanconnell (1578), but continued to intrigue against English, resigned (1593) in favor of his cousin Hugh (see next). **Hugh** (1540?–1616), 3d Baron of **Dun·gan′non** (dŭn·găn′ŭn) and 2d Earl of **Tyrone;** on inauguration, united with Hugh Roe O'Donnell in petitions to Spain for help in behalf of religious and political liberty for Irish; destroyed English force at Yellow Ford on Blackwater (1598); received supplies and supporting troops from Spain (1601); failed in attack on Mountjoy (1601–02); made submission and was confirmed in title and estates by James I (1603); fell under suspicion and, with Rory O'Donnell, Earl of Tyrconnel, fled to Spanish Netherlands (1607), thence to Rome, where he died. Sir **Phe′lim** *or* **Fe′lim** (fā′lĭm), *Irish* **Fei′dli·midh ru′adh** [fā′lĭ·mĭ rōō′ȧ] (1604?–1653); participated with Randal MacDonnell, earl of Antrim and nobles of the Pale in insurrection (1641), seized Charlemont Castle (1641); as commander in chief of Northern Irish forces, responsible for failure to capture Drogheda after siege (1641–42); yielded command to Owen Roe O'Neill; went into hiding after surrender of Charlemont (1650); betrayed, captured, executed as a traitor. **Owen Roe** (1590?–1649), nephew of Hugh; served thirty years in Spanish army; became general of Ulsterman (1642); defeated Scottish army under Munro (1646); was co-operating with Ormonde and Catholic confederates at arrival of Cromwell in Ireland (1649). **Daniel** (1612?–1664), nephew of Owen; became a Protestant at court of Charles I; impeached for participation in army plots; escaped from Tower, and served with Prince Rupert at Marston Moor, battles of Newbury (1643, 1644), and Naseby (1645); negotiated between Ormonde and Owen Roe O'Neill in Ireland (1649); commanded Ulster army temporarily; joined Charles II at The Hague, accompanied him to Scotland (1650), and carried on active intrigue for him until Restoration; postmaster general (1663).

**O'Neill, Eliza.** Lady **Be′cher** (?bē′chẽr). 1791–1872. Irish tragic actress; played Juliet in Dublin and (1814) in London; a success in tragic characters including Belvidera, Mrs. Haller, and Mrs. Beverley; m. William Wrixon Becher and retired from stage (1819).

**O'Neill, Eugene Gladstone.** 1888–1953. American playwright, b. New York City; educ. Princeton (1906–07) and Harvard (1914–15); awarded Pulitzer prize for drama (1920, 1922, 1928), and Nobel prize for literature (1936). Author of *The Moon of the Caribbees* (1919), *Beyond the Horizon* (1919), *Emperor Jones* (1921), *Anna Christie* (1922), *The Hairy Ape* (1922), *Desire Under the Elms* (1924), *The Great God Brown* (1925), *Lazarus Laughed* (1926), *Strange Interlude* (1927), *Mourning Becomes Electra* (a trilogy; 1931), *Ah, Wilderness!* (1932), *The Iceman Cometh* (1946), etc.

**O'Neill, John.** 1834–1878. Soldier and Fenian leader, b. in County Monaghan, Ireland; to U.S. (1848); led raid into Canada from Buffalo (1866); raided Canada again (1870), and was arrested and put in jail; made final attempt against Canada (1871) but again failed.

**O'Neill, Moira.** Pseudonym of Agnes Higginson SKRINE.

**O'Neill, Norman.** 1875–1934. English composer of music for Maeterlinck's *Blue Bird* (1909), Barrie's *Mary Rose* (1920), *The Gods of the Mountain,* and other plays, as well as instrumental music and songs.

**O'Neill, Rose Cecil.** 1874–1944. American illustrator and author, b. Wilkes-Barre, Pa.; m. (1902) Harry Leon Wilson (*q.v.*); on staff of *Puck* (1897–1903); originator and designer of kewpies; author of *The Loves of Edwy* (1904), *The Lady in the White Veil* (1909), *Garda* (1929), *The Goblin Woman* (1930), and several "Kewpie" books.

**Onerva, L.** See under Leevi MADETOJA.

**On′e·san′der** (ŏn′ē·săn′dẽr). = ONOSANDER.

**Ongaro, Francesco dall′.** See DALL'ONGARO.

**O·ni′as** (ō·nī′ăs). Name of several Jewish high priests of time of the Second Temple in 3d and 2d centuries B.C. **Onias III** (*or* **IV**), high priest (c. 185–c. 170 B.C.); fled to Egypt during period of religious persecution; supposed to have built Temple of Onias at Leontopolis. **Onias Men′e·la′us** (mĕn′ē·lā′ŭs) *or* **Menelaus** (*2 Maccabees* iv. 23), believed to have been a usurper of the priesthood.

**On′ions** (ŭn′yŭnz), **Charles Talbut.** 1873-1965. English philologist and lexicographer; member of editorial staff of *Oxford English Dictionary* (from 1895); editor of *Shorter Oxford English Dictionary* (1933, 1936); editor of

*Medium Ævum;* revising editor of Sweet's *Anglo-Saxon Reader* (1922).

**Onions, Oliver,** *orig.* **George Oliver.** *Known in private life as* **George Ol'i·ver** (ŏl'ĭ·vẽr). 1873–1961. English novelist; wrote first book, *The Compleat Bachelor* (1901), at urging of Gelett Burgess; his first novel, *The Odd-Job Man* (1903); attacked methods of the Yellow Press in *Little Devil Doubt* (1909); rewrote psychological trilogy (*In Accordance with the Evidence, The Debit Account,* and *The Story of Louie*) as one novel, *Whom God Has Sundered* (1926); author of crime stories, ghost stories, and social novels. His wife, **Berta,** *nee* **Ruck** [rŭk] (1878–1978), wrote *His Official Fiancée* (1914), *Sir or Madam, The Unkissed Bride* (1929), *Change Here for Happiness, Half-past Kissing-time, Mock Honeymoon.*

**Onkel Adam.** Pseudonym of Carl Anton WETTERBERGH.

**On'ke·los** (ŏng'kĕ·lŏs). *Often called* **The Proselyte.** fl. 1st or 2d century A.D. Reputed author of the Aramaic paraphrase of the Pentateuch known as the Targum of Onkelos.

**Onkel Tom.** Pseudonym of Ludwig HEVESI.

**Onnes, Heike Kamerlingh.** See KAMERLINGH ONNES.

**On'o·mac'ri·tus** (ŏn'ō·măk'rĭ·tŭs). 530?–?480 B.C. Athenian priest and seer; said to have influenced development of Orphic mysteries; banished by Hipparchus when he made his own additions to an oracle of Musaeus.

**On'o·san'der** (ŏn'ō·săn'dẽr). Greek writer of 1st century A.D.; author of commentaries on Plato's *Republic,* and a treatise on military art.

**On'sa·ger** (ŏn'sä'gẽr), **Lars.** 1903–1976. American chemist, b. in Norway. To U.S. (1928); at Yale U. (1933–72); awarded Nobel prize in chemistry (1968) for work on thermodynamic activity.

**Ons'low** (ŏnz'lō). Name of an English family descended from **Richard Onslow,** speaker of House of Commons (1566–71), and including: **Arthur** (1691–1768), M.P. (1720–61); as speaker of house (1728–61), supported firmly privileges of house. His son **George** (1731–1814), 1st Earl of **Onslow,** M.P. (1754–76), privy councilor (1767), moved in validation of Wilkes's election (1769); supported parliamentary privilege. **George** (1784–1853), composer, grandson of 1st earl, lived in France; composed three comic operas, symphonies, quintets, sonatas, and trios. **William Hillier Onslow** (1853–1911), 4th earl, great-great-grandson of 1st earl, was governor of New Zealand (1889–92); undersecretary for India (1895–1900), for colonies (1900–03); joined cabinet as president of board of agriculture (1903). His son **Richard William Alan** (1876–1945), 5th earl, member of war mission, Paris (1918–19); chairman of committees in House of Lords (since 1931).

**Oom Paul.** See Stephanus Johannes Paulus KRUGER.

**Oost** (ōst), **Jacob van** (1600–1671) and his son **Jacob van** (1639–1713). Flemish painters.

**Oos'ter·wyck** (ōs'tẽr·vīk), **Maria van.** 1630–1693. Dutch painter of flowers and fruit.

**Ophni.** See HOPHNI.

**O'pie** (ō'pĭ), **Eugene Lindsay.** 1873–1971. American pathologist; author of studies on malarial parasites, anatomy and pathology of the pancreas, diseases of the liver, respiratory diseases, etc.

**Opie, John.** 1761–1807. English portrait and historical painter and illustrator; known as "the Cornish Wonder." Taken (1780) to London by Dr. Wolcot ("Peter Pindar"); did portraits of authors, including Dr. Johnson, Burke, Southey, William and Mary Godwin, and court ladies; illustrated Boydell's *Shakespeare.* His second wife (m. 1798), **Amelia,** *nee* **Al'der·son** [ôl'dẽr·s'n] (1769–1853), novelist and poet, acquaintance of the Kembles and Mrs. Siddons, gained reputation with *Father and Daughter* (1801) and volume of poems (1802); based her *Adeline Mowbray* (1804) upon history of Mary Wollstonecraft; published memoir of her husband (1809), *Valentine's Eve* (1816), *Madeline* (1822).

**O·pim'i·us** (ō·pĭm'ĭ·ŭs), **Lucius.** Roman politician; consul (121 B.C.); opposed reforms of Gaius Gracchus, and led the mob of optimates that killed Gracchus and 3000 of his followers. Wine of the vintage of this year (121), was called in his honor *Opimian wine.*

**O'pitz** (ō'pĭts), **Martin.** *Sometimes called* **Opitz von Bo'ber·feld** (fŏn bō'bẽr·fĕlt). 1597–1639. German poet, critic, and metrical reformer; founder of the so-called first Silesian school of poets; secretary and historiographer to King Ladislas IV of Poland (from c. 1635). Author of *Aristarchus,* which championed purity of German language, verse, style, etc. (in Latin, 1617), *Buch von der Deutschen Poeterey* (on versification and style, 1624), the didactic poems *Zlatna* (1623) and *Vesuvius* (1633), the prose idyl *Hercinia* (1630), *Daphne,* a German version of Rinuccini's Italian text, which became the oldest German opera (1627; music by Heinrich Schütz), hymns, translations, etc.

**Opp, Julie.** See under William FAVERSHAM.

**Op'peln–Bro'ni·kow'ski** (ŏp'ĕln·brō'nē·kôf'skē), **Friedrich von.** 1873–1936. German biographer and historian; in World War I; wrote biographies of Cagliostro, Frederick the Great, Machiavelli, Heine, etc.

**Oppenheim.** See also OPPENHEIMER.

**Op'pen·heim** (ŏp'ĕn·hīm), **Edward Phillips.** 1866–1946. English novelist; published first novel, *Expiation* (1887); author of over 100 novels of adventure and intrigue.

**Oppenheim, James.** 1882–1932. American poet and fiction writer, b. St. Paul, Minn.; wrote: poetry, *Monday Morning and Other Poems* (1909), *War and Laughter* (1916), *Golden Bird* (1923); prose, *Wild Oats* (1910), *The Olympian* (1912), *Idle Wives* (1914), etc.

**Op'pen·heim** (ŏp'ĕn·hīm; *Ger.* ŏp'-), **Las'sa** (lăs'ȧ; *Ger.* läs'ä) **Francis Lawrence.** 1858–1919. Jurist, b. in Germany; naturalized in England (1900); Whewell professor of international law, Cambridge (1908–19).

**Oppenheimer.** See also OPPENHEIM.

**Op'pen·hei'mer** (ŏp'ĕn·hī'mẽr) *or* **Op'pen·heim** (-hīm), **Franz.** 1864–1943. German economist and sociologist; champion of liberal socialism. His brother **Carl** (1874–1941), physiologist and biochemist, specialist in ferments.

**Oppenheimer, Robert.** *In Full* **Julius Robert Oppenheimer.** 1904–1967. American physicist, b. New York City. At U. of Calif. and Calif. Inst. Tech. (1929–47); director, Inst. for Advanced Study, Princeton, N.J. (1947–66). Instrumental in the development of the atomic bomb; received Enrico Fermi Award (1963).

**Op'per** (ŏp'ẽr), **Frederick Burr.** 1857–1937. American illustrator and cartoonist; at various times on staffs of *Frank Leslie's Magazine, Puck,* and New York *Journal;* illustrated books by Bill Nye, Mark Twain, Finley Peter Dunne, etc. Creator of comic-strip characters Happy Hooligan, Alphonse and Gaston, etc.

**Op'pert'** (*Fr.* ō'pâr'; *Ger.* ŏp'ẽrt), **Jules.** 1825–1905. Orientalist, b. Hamburg; settled in France (1847), naturalized (1854). Wrote *Éléments de la Grammaire, Assyrienne* (1860), *Babylone et les Babyloniens* (1869), *Études Sumériennes* (1881), etc.

**Op'pi·us** (ŏp'ĭ·ŭs), **Gaius.** Roman writer of 1st century B.C.; close friend of Julius Caesar, who, during his absences from Rome, entrusted to him the management of his private affairs.

**Op'pol·zer** (ŏp'ŏl·tsẽr), **Johann von.** 1808–1871. Austrian physician. His son **Theodor** (1841–1886), astronomer, author of *Canon der Finsternisse* (1887), giving a table of lunar and solar eclipses from 1207 B.C. to 2163 A.D.

**Optic, Oliver.** Pseudonym of William Taylor ADAMS.

**Op'zoo'mer** (ŏp'sō'mẽr), **Cornelis Willem.** 1821–1892. Dutch philosopher and jurist; leader of the empirical-positivistic school of philosophy and champion of modern theology; wrote on jurisprudence and philosophy; translated Sophocles, Shakespeare, etc.

**Oqba.** See OKBA.

**Or'ange** (ŏr'ĕnj; -ĭnj). Princely family of Europe, deriving its name from a principality (from c. 11th century) forming an enclave in the ancient province of Venaissin, near the Rhone north of Avignon. Its rulers were: 9 princes of the house of Baux (1174–1393); 5 princes of the Burgundian house of Chalon (1393–1530), the last of whom, Philibert (see CHALON), for services to Emperor Charles V was granted (1522) extensive possessions in the Low Countries; and René (son of Philibert's sister Claudia, who had married Henry III of Nassau; see NASSAU), who succeeded Philibert (1530) and on whose death (1544) all possessions passed to William I, Count of Nassau (later stadholder as William the Silent). Principality of Orange seized by Louis XIV (1660) and incorporated in France; by Treaty of Utrecht (1713) title of prince of Orange granted only to John William Friso, his son William IV, and successors; now name of reigning house of the Netherlands (see NASSAU, 2b; *Table* [*in Appendix*] for NETHERLANDS). One sovereign of England, William III, was a prince of Orange; see WILLIAM III, Count of Nassau.

**Orange–Nassau.** See NASSAU, 2a and b.

**Or'bi'gny'** (ôr'bē'nyē'), **Alcide Des'sa'lines'** (dā'sȧ'lēn') **d'.** 1802–1857. French naturalist; on scientific mission to South America (1826–34), resulting in a series of works including *l'Homme Américain* (1840), an ethnological publication; author also of *Paléontologie Française* (begun in 1840 and continued by others after his death).

**Or·bil'i·us Pu·pil'lus** (ôr·bĭl'ĭ·ŭs pū·pĭl'ŭs). Roman schoolmaster of 1st century B.C.; teacher of Horace, who describes him as fond of flogging and by his reference has made him typical of such a teacher. Cf. John KEATE.

**Or·ca'gna** (ôr·kä'nyä). *Corrupted form of* **Ar·ca'gno·lo** (är·kä'nyō·lō). *Real name* **Andrea di Cio'ne** (dē chō'nā). 1308?–?1368. Florentine painter, sculptor, and architect; a leading representative of Gothic style; head architect, Or San Michele, Florence (1355), Orvieto Cathedral (1358–60). Works include marble tabernacle at Or San Michele, murals (as *Paradise*, in Strozzi Chapel, Santa Maria Novella, Florence), and façade of Orvieto Cathedral (now partly in Victoria and Albert Museum, London).

**Orchan.** Variant of ORKHAN.

**Or'chard·son** (ôr'chẽrd·s'n), Sir **William Quiller.** 1832–1910. Scottish painter, in London (1862); took subjects from history and literature; won wide acclaim with *Napoleon on Board the Bellerophon* (1880); also won success as portrait painter.

**Or'czy** (ôr'tsĭ; *Hung.* ôr'-), Baroness **Em'mus·ka** (ĕm'mŏŏsh·kŏ). 1865–1947. English novelist and playwright, b. in Hungary; daughter of Baron Felix Orczy; m. Montagu W. Barstow. Began writing fiction (1900) with a series of detective stories, *The Old Man in the Corner;* won reputation with *The Scarlet Pimpernel* (1905; dramatized in collaboration with husband, 1905), first of a series of adventure stories with background of French Revolution. Author of many other novels, including *A Son of the People* (1906), *Beau Brocade* (1908; dramatized 1910), *Castles in the Air* (1921), *Nicolette* (1923), *The Divine Folly* (1937).

**Or'de·ri'cus Vi·ta'lis** (ôr'dĕ·rĭ'kŭs vĭ·tā'lĭs) *or* **Or'de·ric' Vi'tal'** (*Fr.* ôr'dē·rēk' vē'tȧl'; *Angl.* ôr'dĕ·rĭk). 1075–?1143. Anglo-Norman chronicler, son of French priest and Englishwoman; spent life as monk in Norman abbey of St. Evroult; completed (1141) his *Historia Ecclesiastica*, a history of Normandy and England.

**Or'din–Na·shcho'kin** (ôr'dyĭn·nŭ·shchô'kyĭn), Afanasi Lavrentievich. d. 1680. Russian statesman; minister of foreign affairs and keeper of the great seal (1667); retired to monastery near Kiev (1671). Usually regarded as Russia's first chancellor or prime minister.

**Ordóñez de Montalvo, García.** See MONTALVO.

**Or·do'ño** (ôr·thō'nyō). Name of three kings of Asturias and León: **Ordoño I** (d. 866); son of Ramiro I; king of Asturias (850–866); won territory from the caliphate of Córdoba. **Ordoño II** (d. 923); son of Alfonso III; given Galicia by his father; became king of Galicia (914–923), including León. **Ordoño III** (d. 955); son of Ramiro II; king (950–955); at war with his father-in-law, Fernán González, Count of Castile.

**Or·dzho·ni·kid'ze** (ŭr·jŭ·nyĭ·kyēd'zĕ), **Grigori Konstantinovich.** 1886–1937. Russian politician; joined Communist party (1903); exiled to Siberia, and released under general amnesty at outbreak of Revolution (Feb., 1917). Friend and associate of Stalin; member of Politburo of Central Executive Committee; one of organizers of Five-Year Plan; chairman, Supreme Economic Council; commissar for heavy industries.

**O'Reil'ly** (ō·rī'lĭ), **Alexander.** 1722–1794. Irish soldier in Spanish army; headed Spanish army which punished rebels in Louisiana (1768–69) and drew up regulations for government of the country; intrigued against Floridablanca and was banished to Galicia (1786).

**O'Reilly, John Boyle.** 1844–1890. Poet and editor; joined Fenians and enlisted (1863) in British army unit with intention of exciting a revolt; discovered (1866), tried, sentenced to death, but sentence commuted to twenty years' penal servitude; deported to Australia (1868). Escaped to U.S. (1869); on editorial staff of Boston *Pilot* (from 1870); proprietor and editor (1876–90); became naturalized American citizen. Author of *Songs from Southern Seas* (1873), *Songs, Legends and Ballads* (1878), *The Statues in the Block* (1881), *In Bohemia* (1886), etc.

**O'Reilly, Miles.** Pseudonym of Charles Graham HALPINE.

**O'Rell, Max.** Pseudonym of Paul BLOUET.

**O'rel·la'na** (ō'rā·(l)yä'nä), **Francisco de.** 1500?–1549. Spanish soldier and explorer; lieutenant in Gonzalo Pizarro's expedition to the Napo (1540–41); continued journey down the Napo to the valley of the Amazon, and explored the course of the Amazon from the Andes to the Atlantic Ocean (1541).

**O'rel·la'na** (ō'rā·yä'nä), **José María.** 1872–1926. Guatemalan general and politician; chosen provisional president (1921–22) on deposition of Carlos Herrera; elected president (1922–26).

**O'resme'** (ō'râm'), **Nicole.** 1330?–1382. Roman Catholic prelate; bishop of Lisieux (1377); his translations of various classical works served to popularize science and to fix the form of the French language.

**Orff** (ôrf), **Carl.** 1895– . German composer. Composed *Carmina Burana* (1936), *Der Mond* (1938), *Antigone* (1948), *Oedipus the Tyrant* (1959), etc.

**Or'fi'la'** (ôr'fē'lȧ'), **Matthieu Joseph Bonaventure.** 1787–1853. French chemist; reputed founder of toxicology; founder of a museum (Musée Orfila) of comparative anatomy.

**Or'ford** (ôr'fẽrd), Earls of. See (1) RUSSELL family; (2) Horace and Sir Robert WALPOLE.

**Or·get′o·rix** (ôr·jĕt′ō·rĭks). Helvetic chieftain of 1st century B.C. who led his people in a migration to the southwest to gain safety.

**O·ri·a′ni** (ō·ryä′nē), **Alfredo.** 1852–1909. Italian writer on social problems; outstanding intellectual forerunner of Fascism in Italy; among his works are novels, historicocritical writings, essays, plays, and a volume of poems.

**Oriani, Barnaba.** 1752–1832. Italian priest and astronomer; showed by calculating its orbit that Uranus is a planet, not a comet as at first supposed.

**Or′i·ba′si·us** (ŏr′ĭ·bā′zhĭ·ŭs). c. 325–c. 400 A.D. Greek physician of Pergamum; personal physician of Emperor Julian; compiled a medical encyclopedia. Reputed discoverer of the salivary glands.

**O·ri′be** (ō·rē′bā), **Manuel.** 1796?–1857. Uruguayan general and political leader, b. Montevideo; entered patriot army of Rio de la Plata as a boy; later was one of the "thirty-three immortals" who liberated Uruguay (after 1825); minister of war under Rivera (1833–35); president of Uruguay (1835–38); deposed by Rivera and fled to Buenos Aires; allied with Rosas began long civil war (1842–51), marked esp. by siege of Montevideo; leader of the Blancos; finally defeated by combined Colorados, Brazilians, and Argentine revolutionists under Urquiza.

**Or′i·gen** (ŏr′ĭ·jĕn; -jĕn). *Lat.* **O·rig′e·nes** (ō·rĭj′ĕ·nēz), *surnamed* **Ad′a·man′ti·us** (ăd′ȧ·măn′shĭ·ŭs). 185?–?254 A.D. Christian writer and teacher, of Alexandria; one of the Greek Fathers of the Church; head of the catechetical school in Alexandria (c. 211–232); later, founded a school in Caesarea. His many works include textual studies on Old Testament (*Hexapla* and *Tetrapla*), a treatise on prayer, an exhortation to martyrdom, *Commentaries* and *Homilies*, and a defense of Christianity against attacks by the philosopher Celsus (*Contra Celsum*).

**Orinda.** See Katharine PHILIPS.

**O'Rior′dan** (?ō·rēr′d'n), **Conal Holmes O'Connell.** *Pseudonym* **Norreys Con′nell** (kŏn′'l). 1874–1948. Irish dramatist and novelist; won reputation with *The Fool and his Heart* (1896); had plays produced in Birmingham, London, and Abbey Theater, Dublin; succeeded J. M. Synge as director of Abbey Theater (1909). Author of *The Pity of War* (1905), *The Age of Miracles* (1925), *Soldier's Wife* (1935), *Judith Quinn* (1939); plays, including *Shakespeare's End* (1912), *Captain Falstaff* (1936).

**Orizzonte.** See *Jan Frans van Bloemen*, under Pieter van BLOEMEN.

**Or′kan** (ôr′kän), **Władysław.** *Pseudonym of* **Franciszek Smre·czyń′ski** (smrĕ·chĭn′y'·skē). 1876–1930. Polish writer of verse, plays, and prose works including *Yesterday, The Journalists, The Cattle Plague.*

**Or·khan′** *or* **Or·chan′** (ôr·ḵän′). 1279–1359. Sultan of Turkey; succeeded his father, Osman I (1326); conquered western part of Asia Minor (1329–38); probably originated the military corps of Janizaries; crossed into Europe and settled in Thrace (1354–59).

**Ork′ney** (ôrk′nĭ), Earls of. See Lord George HAMILTON (1666–1737); STEWART and SINCLAIR families.

**Or·lan′do** (ôr·län′dō), **Vittorio Emanuele.** 1860–1952. Italian statesman; prime minister (1917–19); led Italian delegation at Paris Peace Conference (1919–20). Retired from political activity after advent of Fascism.

**Or′lé′ans′** (ôr′lā′äN′; *Angl.* ôr′lē·ănz). Name of cadet branch of Valois and Bourbon houses of France; there have been four distinct houses: (1) **Philippe** (1336–1375); 5th son of Philip VI, Valois king of France, and Jeanne de Bourgogne; made duc d'Orléans (1344); having no heirs, title lapsed. (2) Chief members: **Louis I** (1372–1407); 2d son of King Charles V and brother of Charles VI; comte de Valois (see VALOIS); made duc d'Orléans (1392); m. Valentina Visconti of Milan; purchased countship of Blois (1397); unpopular; engaged in long struggle with Philip the Bold of Burgundy and his son John, the latter of whom caused his assassination, thus bringing about civil war between Burgundians and Armagnacs (supporters of Orléans). Had eight legitimate children (among them, John, Count of Angoulême; see ANGOULÊME) and illegitimate son Dunois (see DUNOIS). See also MARGARET OF NAVARRE. His eldest son, **Charles d'Orléans,** *Eng.* **Charles of Orleans** (1391–1465), poet and nobleman, brought up at court of Blois, succeeded him (1407) as duc d'Orléans and head of the Armagnacs; joint commander at Agincourt (1415); taken prisoner; kept in England for nearly 25 years; ransomed (1440); returned to France; m. (1441) Mary of Cleves as 3d wife; court at Blois resort of poets (Villon, Chastelain, etc.); author of rondels, especially on love and spring; father of Louis XII of France (see LOUIS XII). **Charles d'Orléans** (1522–1545), Duc d'Orléans; 3d son of Francis I and grandson of Louis XII; in command of armies in Low Countries (1542–44). (3) Chief members: **Gaston Jean Baptiste d'Orléans** (1608–1660); 3d son of Henry IV and Marie de Médicis and brother of Louis XIII; b. in Fontainebleau; made duc d'Orléans (1626); m. (1626) Marie de Bourbon, Duchesse de Montpensier; spent most of his life conspiring against Richelieu and Mazarin; after death of Louis XIII, led armies with credit against Spain; joined Condé against court in the Fronde (1648–52). His daughter Anne Marie Louise was duchesse de Montpensier (see MONTPENSIER). (4) BOURBON-ORLÉANS HOUSE (see BOURBON). Chief members: **Philippe I** (1640–1701); son of Louis XIII, King of France, and brother of Louis XIV; made duc d'Orléans (1660); thus became founder of present house of Orléans (Orleanists; see BOURBON); m. (1661) Henrietta Anne (*q.v.*), sister of Charles II of England, and, 2d, Charlotte Elisabeth, daughter of the elector palatine. **Philippe II** (1674–1723); son of Philippe I; b. Saint-Cloud; became duc d'Orléans (1701); distinguished himself in battles (1692–97) of war against England and Grand Alliance and (1701–06) in War of the Spanish Succession; in command in Spain (1707–08); during minority of Louis XV, made regent of France (1715–23); able and popular, but left affairs to his minister Dubois; during last years led a very profligate life. **Louis** (1703–1752); son of Philippe II; b. in Versailles; made duc d'Orléans (1723); governor of Dauphiné (1719–42); student of literature and sciences; retired (1742) from public life. His son **Louis Philippe d'Orléans** (1725–1785); b. in Versailles; served in Austrian wars and Seven Years' War (1742–57); made duc d'Orléans (1752). **Louis Philippe Joseph** (1747–1793); son of the preceding; b. Saint-Cloud; known as **Philippe-É′ga′li′té′** (-ā′gȧ′-lē′tā′); duc de Mont′pen′sier′ [môN′päN′syā′] (1747–52) and duc de Char′tres [shär′tr'] (1752–85); became duc d'Orléans (1785); liberal in views, a reformer and friend of common people; incurred enmity of Louis XVI and the queen; advocated cause of American colonies (1778); in Assembly of Notables (1787), declared against proposals of king's minister; aided French Revolutionists (1789); sent abroad by Louis but returned (1790) to work with Mirabeau and Danton against him (1791–93); renounced title and assumed name of Philippe-Égalité; included in National Convention list of Bourbons whose estates were voted for confiscation by Jacobins (1793); imprisoned at Marseilles; later sentenced to death by Revolutionary Tribunal at Paris and guillotined. His wife (m. 1769), **Louise Marie Adélaïde de Bour'bon'-Pen'thiè'vre** [dē bōōr'bôN'päN'tyâ'vr'] (1753–1821), was noted later in life for her charities. Their son Louis Philippe became king of France (1830–48); see LOUIS PHILIPPE. **Ferdinand Philippe Louis Charles Henri** (1810–1842), Duc de Chartres; son of Louis Philippe; b. Palermo; soldier; active in revolution of 1830 and in Belgium (1831–32); made duc d'Orléans (1830); served in campaigns in Algeria (1835–40); m. (1837) **Hélène Louise Élisabeth** (1814–1858), daughter of Grand Duke Frederick Louis of Mecklenburg-Schwerin. Their two sons were Louis Philippe Albert (see comte de PARIS) and Robert Philippe Louis Eugène Ferdinand (see duc de CHARTRES). **Louise,** *in full* **Marie Thérèse Caroline Isabelle Louise, d'Orléans** (1812–1850); eldest daughter of Louis Philippe; m. (1832) Leopold I of Belgium (*q.v.*). **Clémentine,** *in full* **Marie Clémentine Caroline Léopoldine Clotilde d'Orléans** (1817–1907); 2d daughter of Louis Philippe; m. (1843) Prince August of Saxe-Coburg-Gotha; mother of four children, the youngest being Ferdinand I, King of Bulgaria. **Louis Philippe Robert** (1869–1926); son of comte de Paris; b. Twickenham, England; banished from France by law of 1886, made home in England; offered his services to France (1890) but arrested and imprisoned; traveled in Asia (1890–95); became duc d'Orléans (1894) and pretender to throne of France; supported French army in Dreyfus affair (1897) but won disfavor by action; offered in vain services to France and other Entente countries at outbreak of World War (1914); a scientist of distinction; led expeditions to Arctic regions (1905, 1907, 1919) and to British East Africa (1922–23). His cousin **Henri d'Orléans** (1867–1901); also known as **Prince d'Orléans;** son of duc de Chartres; b. Ham; explorer; made journeys in central Asia, eastern Africa, Ethiopia, and Annam. For other members of house of Orléans see: AUMALE; EU; JOINVILLE; LOUISE; MONTPENSIER; NEMOURS.

**Orléans, the Bastard of.** = Jean DUNOIS.

**Orleans, the Maid of.** See JOAN OF ARC.

**Or'ley** (ôr'lĭ), **Bernaert van.** 1492?–1542. Flemish painter.

**Or'lik** (ôr'lĭk), **E'mil** (ā'mēl). 1870–1932. Painter, etcher, and lithographer, b. in Prague. His works include stage scenery for Reinhardt's productions, portrait etchings of Gustav Mahler, Haeckel, Hodler, Richard Strauss, Bach, Beethoven, and others, genre pictures of Bohemian village life, portfolios of etchings, etc.

**Or·lov'** (ŭr·lôf'). Russian noble family, including: Count **Grigori Grigorievich** (1734–1783), general and statesman; leader in plot (1762) to dethrone and assassinate Peter III and place Catherine on throne; paramour of Czarina Catherine II; advocate of improvement in condition of the serfs. His brother **Aleksei Grigorievich** (1737–1809); also involved in the plot against Peter III; said to have carried Peter away and strangled him; commanded fleet which defeated Turks at Çeşme (July 5, 1770); commanded a militia district in war against Napoleon (1806–07). Another brother, **Fëdor Grigorievich** (1741–1790); also involved in plot against Peter III; distinguished himself as naval commander in first Turkish war (1770); retired (1775). Prince **Aleksei Fëdorovich** (1787–1862), natural son of Fëdor; engaged in wars against Napoleon (1805–07; 1812–14), and in Turkish war (1828–29); ambassador to Turkey (1833); Russian diplomat at conference which negotiated Peace of Paris (1856) after Crimean War. Prince **Nikolai Alekseevich** (1827–1885), son of Prince Aleksei; represented Russia in Belgium (1860–70), France (1870–82), and Germany (1882–85).

**Or·lov'ski** (ŭr·lôf'skû·ĭ; *Angl.* -skĭ), **Boris Ivanovich.** 1796–1837. Russian sculptor.

**Orm** (ôrm) *or* **Or'min** (ôr'mĭn). fl. ?1200. English Augustinian monk; author of the *Ormulum,* metrical paraphrases (c. 10,000 lines) of gospels for the year, followed by metrical homilies in English vernacular.

**Or'man·dy** (ôr'măn·dĭ; *Hung.* ôr'män'dĭ), **Eugene.** 1899– . Orchestra conductor, b. Budapest, Hungary; to U.S. (1921); naturalized (1927); conductor of Minneapolis Symphony Orchestra (1931–36) and Philadelphia Symphony Orchestra (from 1936).

**Orme** (ôrm), **Philibert de l'.** See Philibert DELORME.

**Orme** (ôrm), **Robert.** 1728–1801. Anglo-Indian historian; associated with Lord Clive; historiographer to East India Company (1769).

**Orme'rod** (ôrm'rŏd), **Eleanor Anne.** 1828–1901. English economic entomologist; consulting entomologist to Royal Agricultural Society of England (1882–92); author of *Notes for Observations of Injurious Insects* (1877), *A Text Book of Agricultural Entomology* (1892), *Flies Injurious to Stock* (1900), etc.

**Or'mes'son'** (ôr'mĕ'sôN'). Family of noted French lawyers, including: **Olivier Le Fè'vre d'Or'mes'son'** [lē fâ'vr' dôr'mĕ'sôN'] (1525–1600). His son **André Le Fèvre d'Ormesson** (1577–1665). André's son **Olivier III Le Fèvre d'Ormesson** (1616–1686). Olivier III's son **André II Le Fèvre d'Ormesson** (1644–1684). André II's son **Henri François de Paule Le Fèvre d'Ormesson** (1681–1756). Henri's sons Marquis **Marie François de Paule Le Fèvre d'Ormesson** (1710–1774) and Marquis **Louis François de Paule Le Fèvre d'Ormesson** (1718–1789). Louis's sons **Henri François de Paule Le Fèvre d'Ormesson d'Am'boile'** [däN'bwål'] (1751–1807) and **Anne Louis François de Paule Le Fèvre d'Ormesson de Noy'seau'** [dē nwå'zō'] (1753–1794).

**Or'mizd** (ôr'mĭzd) *or* **Or'mazd** (-măzd). *Also* **Hor'mizd** (hôr'mĭzd) or **Hor·miz'das** (hôr·mĭz'dăs). Name of four kings of the Sassanidae of Persia, esp.: **Ormizd IV,** son of Khosrau I and father of Khosrau II; king (579–590); carried on war against Eastern Roman Empire but was defeated; deposed and assassinated.

**Or'monde** (ôr'mŭnd), Earls, marquises, and dukes of. Titles in Irish peerage (that of duke also in English peerage) held by members of Irish family of **But'ler** (bŭt'lĕr), foes of the Geraldines (*q.v.*), including: **James Butler** (1305?–?1337), created earl chiefly because his wife, Eleanor de Bohun, was granddaughter of Edward I. His son **James** (1331–1382), 2d earl, several times viceroy of Ireland, as was his great-grandson **James** (d. 1452), 4th earl, soldier and scholar. **James** (1420–1461), 5th Earl of Ormonde and Earl of Wilt'shire [wĭlt'shĭr; -shĕr] (English peerage); eldest son of 4th earl; lord high treasurer of England (1455, 1458); captured by Yorkists after battle of Towton (1461) and beheaded; and his brothers **John** and **Thomas,** 6th and 7th earls, English ambassadors to Continental courts. Sir **Piers** (pērz) *or* **Pierce** (1467?–1539), 8th earl (cousin of 7th earl) and 1st earl of **Os'so·ry** (ŏs'ō·rĭ); lord treasurer of Ireland, as was his son **James** (1490?–1546), 9th earl, and his grandson, **Thomas** (1532–1614), 10th earl, a Protestant, who took side of Queen Elizabeth against Irish rebels, probably in order to crush hereditary foe, earl of Desmond; vice-admiral of Ireland (1612). **James** (1610–1688), 12th earl and 1st duke, created marquis (1642) and duke in Irish peerage (1661) and in English peerage (1682); born in London; m. cousin Elizabeth Preston, ending feud with Desmond family, to which his wife belonged; supported Strafford against Irish rebels (from 1640); as lord lieutenant of Ireland (1644) made terms with rebels (1647) and concluded peace (1649); retired to France on Cromwell's conquest of Ireland; again lord lieutenant of Ireland (1661); encouraged Irish manufacturing and learning; dismissed (1669) but recalled (1677–82); resisted some of James II's arbitrary acts (1687). **James** (1665–1745), 2d duke; son of Thomas (see OSSORY) and grandson of 1st duke; joined prince of Orange (1688); commanded regiment at battle of Boyne; served on Continent under William; lord lieutenant of Ireland (1703–05, 1710–11); succeeded Marlborough as captain general (1711–14); impeached for Jacobitism; settled in Spain; buried in Westminster Abbey.

**Orms'by** (ôrmz'bĭ), **John.** 1829–1895. English author, b. in Ireland; author of verse translation of *Poema del Cid* (1879), and translation of *Don Quixote* (1885).

**Orms'by–Gore'** (-gōr'), **William George Arthur.** 4th Baron **Har'lech** (här'lĕk; -lĭ). 1885–1964. English expert in colonial affairs; colonial secretary (1936–38).

**Or'na'no'** (*Fr.* ôr'nȧ'nō'; *Ital.* ōr·nä'nō), **Alphonse d'.** 1548–1610. Soldier of Corsican birth; naturalized Frenchman in Charles IX's service, loyal to royalist cause in struggle against Catholic League; was one of first to recognize Henry IV; created marshal of France (1595). His son **Jean Baptiste** (1581–1626) was also a soldier in French service; followed Henry IV in the war in Savoy (1600–01); kept Guienne and Languedoc loyal to Louis XIII (1610); tutor in administration of Gaston d'Orléans (1619) and created marshal of France. Also of Corsican birth was Comte **Philippe Antoine d'Ornano** (1784–1863), general in the French army; distinguished himself at Austerlitz (1805) and Jena and Lübeck (1806); engaged at Borodino; rallied to Napoleon during the Hundred Days, and was exiled at the second restoration (1815); returned to France (1818) and French service (1828); member of the Corps Législatif (1848) and supporter of cause of Louis Napoleon; created marshal of France (1861).

**Orn'stein** (ôrn'stīn), **Leo.** 1895– . Pianist and composer, b. in Russia; to U.S. (1907); soloist with leading American orchestras; director of Ornstein School of Music, Philadelphia; composer of sonatas, concertos, orchestral suites, songs, etc.

**Orontius Fineus.** See Oronce FINE.

**O·ro'si·us** (ō·rō'zhĭ·ŭs), **Paulus.** Spanish priest of 5th century A.D.; author of *Adversus Paganos Historiarum Libri VII*, a favorite medieval textbook of universal history, translated into old English by Alfred the Great.

**O·roz'co** (ō·rōs'kō), **José Clemente.** 1883–1949. Mexican painter; identified with Mexican modernist school, and an associate of Siqueiros, Rivera, Mérida, and others of that school; painted murals in the National Preparatory School, in Mexico City.

**Orozco Romero, Carlos.** See Carlos Orozco ROMERO.

**Or'pen** (ôr'pĕn), Sir **William Newenham Montague.** 1878–1931. British painter, b. Stillorgan, County Dublin; appointed an official artist by British government during World War. His paintings include portraits of Wilson, Foch, Viscount Bryce, and others.

**Orr** (ôr), **Alexandra Sutherland,** *nee* **Leigh'ton** (lā't'n). 1828–1903. English biographer of Robert Browning; sister of Frederick Leighton (*q.v.*).

**Or·ren'te** (ôr·rān'tā), **Pedro.** 1570?–1644. Called "the Spanish Bassano." Spanish painter; known esp. for his landscapes and animal paintings.

**Orrery,** Earls and countess of. See BOYLE family; Mary MONCKTON.

**Or'say'** (ôr'sā'), Count **Alfred Guillaume Gabriel d'.** 1801–1852. French society leader in Paris and London; wit, painter, sculptor, conversationalist, and arbiter of fashion; friend of Lady Blessington.

**Or·si'ni** (ōr·sē'nē). Roman princely family, including: **Giovanni Gaetano,** who became Pope Nicholas III (1277); **Paolo** (d. 1416), condottiere; **Virginio** (c. 1497), fought for the Papacy; **Flavio,** Duca **di Brac·cia'no** [brät·chä'nō] (d. 1695), and his wife, the duchess of Bracciano, **Anne Marie de la Tré'mouille'** [dē lȧ trā'mōō'y'] (1635–1722), a supporter of French policy at the papal court and a confidential adviser of King Philip V of Spain; **Pietro Francesco** (1649–1730), who was pope as Benedict XIII (1724–30).

**Orsini, Felice.** 1819–1858. Italian revolutionist; member of Young Italy; active in revolution of 1848–49; known esp. for his attempted assassination of Napoleon III (Jan. 14, 1858), the explosion of bombs killing 10 persons and wounding 150; executed with an accomplice, Joseph Pieri, at Paris (Mar. 13, 1858).

**Orsini, Giulio.** See Domenico GNOLI.

**Örsted.** See OERSTED.

**Or'szágh** (ôr'säg), **Pavol.** *Pseudonym* **Hviez'do·slav** (hvyĕz'dô·släf). 1849–1921. Slovak epic and lyric poet; translator of Shakespeare's *Hamlet*, poetry of Goethe, Schiller, etc.

**Ortala,** Count of. See Lennart TORSTENSON.

**Or·te'ga y Gas·set'** (ôr·tā'gä ē gä·sĕt'), **José.** 1883–1955. Spanish philosopher, writer, and statesman; professor, U. of Madrid (1911 ff.); editor, *Revista del Occidente;* member, constituent Cortes (1931). Among his works are *España Invertebrada* (1922), *El Tema de Nuestro Tiempo* (1923), *Espíritu de la Letra* (1927), and *La Rebelión de las Masas* (1930; translated as *The Revolt of the Masses,* 1932).

**Or'teig** (ôr'tĕg), **Raymond.** 1870–1939. French-born American restaurateur; proprietor of the Lafayette and Brevoort hotels, New York. Offered (1919) prize of $25,000 for first nonstop New York to Paris flight; prize won by Charles Lindbergh (1927).

**Ör'tel** *or* **Oer'tel** (ûr'tĕl), **Philipp Friedrich Wilhelm.** *Pseudonym* **W. O. von Horn** (fōn hôrn'). 1798–1867. German writer of popular stories, b. Horn, Prussia.

**Or·te'li·us** (ôr·tē'lĭ·ŭs). *Lat. name of* **Abraham Oer'tel** (ōōr'tĕl) *or* **Or'tell** (ŏr'tĕl). 1527–1598. Flemish geographer; his atlas *Theatrum Orbis Terrarum* (1570) long remained the basis for geographic works.

**Ortell, Abraham.** See ORTELIUS.

**Orth, Johann.** See JOHN NEPOMUK SALVATOR.

**Or·tiz'** (ôr·tēs'), **Roberto M.** 1886–1942. Argentine politician; minister of finance (1935–37); president of Argentina (1938–42; in temporary retirement from 1940).

**Ortiz Ru'bio** (rōō'byō), **Pascual.** 1877–1963. Mexican politician; minister to Germany (1923); ambassador to Brazil (1926); president of Mexico (1930–32), elected (1929) to succeed provisional president Emilio Portes Gil and to fill out the unexpired term of Álvaro Obregón; resigned (Sept., 1932).

**Or'ton** (ôr't'n), **Arthur.** 1834–1898. English butcher and impostor; emigrant to Australia (1852); alias **Thomas Cas'tro** (kăs'trō). Notorious as the Tichborne Claimant (*q.v.*). Returned to England (1866) on invitation of widow of Sir James Francis Doughty Tichborne, 10th baronet; impersonated her eldest son, who had been lost at sea, and convinced Lady Tichborne and many others; brought action (1871–72) for ejectment against the 12th baronet; on collapse of his suit after trial of 102 days, was committed for perjury after trial of 188 days; confessed his imposture (1895).

**Orton, Edward Francis Baxter.** 1829–1899. American geologist and educator; president, Ohio A.&M., later Ohio State U. (1873–81) and professor of geology (1873–99). His son **Edward** (1863–1932) was instrumental in establishing (1894) first school for instruction in technology of clay, glass, and cement industries, at Ohio State U., and was its director (1894–1916).

**Orton, James.** 1830–1877. American naturalist; three expeditions(1867, 1873, 1876) to S. America, collecting specimens in Andes and Amazon River region.

**Or·vie′to** (ôr·vyâ′tô), **Angiolo.** 1869– . Italian poet.

**O Ry′an** (ô·rī′ăn), **John Francis** 1874–1961. Am. lawyer and army commander; practiced law in New York City; commanded National Guard of New York (1912); commanded New York division on Mexican border (1916); commanded division, U.S. army, in France (1917–19); police commissioner, New York City (1934).

**O′sann** (ō′zän), **Emil.** 1787–1842. German physician; professor, Berlin; regarded as founder of balneology.

**Os′born** (ŏz′bẽrn), **Henry Fairfield.** 1857–1935. American paleontologist, b. Fairfield, Conn.; professor, Columbia (from 1890); curator of vertebrate paleontology, American Museum of Natural History (from 1891); also associated with U.S. Geological Survey. Author of *The Age of Mammals* (1910), *Men of the Old Stone Age* (1915), *Origin and Evolution of Life* (1917), *Evolution and Religion in Education* (1926), etc.

**Osborn, Herbert.** 1856–1954. American biologist; engaged in various entomological researches for State and Federal governments; author of *EconomicZoology* (1908), *Agricultural Entomology* (1916), etc.

**Osborn, Sherard.** 1822–1875. English naval officer and explorer, b. in Madras, India; commanded vessels on two expeditions (1850–51, 1852–54) in search of Sir John Franklin; took leading part in Chinese war of 1857–59; helped to lay cable between Great Britain and Australia.

**Os′borne** (ŏz′bẽrn), **Francis.** 1593–1659. English miscellaneous writer; author of *Advice to a Son* (1656, 1658), observations somewhat in the manner of Lord Chesterfield, said to be one of three most popular books of the time.

**Osborne, George Alexander.** 1806–1893. Irish pianist and composer; intimate with Berlioz and Chopin; composed chamber music, duets for violin and piano, and a popular piano solo *La Pluie de Perles*.

**Osborne, John James.** 1929– . British playwright, producer, and actor. His works include *Look Back in Anger* (1956), *The Entertainer* (1957), the filmscript of *Tom Jones* (1963), etc.

**Osborne, Thomas.** 1st Earl of **Dan′by** (dăn′bĭ). Marquis of **Car·mar′then** (kẽr·mär′thĕn). Duke of **Leeds** (lēdz). 1631–1712. English statesman; M.P. (1665); treasurer of navy (1671); lord high treasurer (1673) and earl of Danby (1674); tried in House of Commons to maintain national credit and neutralize predominance of France; pressed for enforcement of laws against Roman Catholics and dissenters; contrived marriage of Mary, daughter of duke of York, to William of Orange (1677); made peace with Holland. Engaged in corrupt politics; betrayed by Ralph Montagu as Charles II's negotiator with Louis XIV for increased bribes, and was impeached (1678) for treasonable negotiations with foreign powers and concealment of Popish Plot; although pardoned by Charles, was imprisoned in Tower of London (till 1684). Reconciled with Whigs, signed invitation to William of Orange; rewarded with marquisate; lord president of council (1689–99) and virtually prime minister; created duke (1694); accused of Jacobite intrigues; again impeached (1695) for accepting bribe from East India Company in connection with grant of a charter, but escaped condemnation when charge was not pressed.

His descendant **Francis Osborne** (1751–1799), 5th Duke of Leeds, known (till 1789) as Marquis of Carmarthen; privy councilor (1777); ambassador extraordinary to Paris (1782); foreign secretary under Pitt (1783–91).

**Osborne, Thomas.** d. 1767. English bookseller; proposed, with Charles Rivington, having their friend Samuel Richardson write a series of letters, the inception of *Pamela* (1740); was satirized by Pope in the *Dunciad* and beaten for impertinence by Dr. Johnson.

**Osborne, Thomas Burr.** 1859–1929. American biochemist; known esp. for investigations of vegetable proteins, and discovery of vitamin in cod-liver oil.

**Osborne, Thomas Mott.** 1859–1926. American penologist, b. Auburn, N.Y.; chairman, New York State Commission for Prison Reform (1913); served secretly a week in Auburn prison to know conditions at firsthand; warden, Sing Sing prison (1914–16); commanding officer, Portsmouth Naval Prison (1917–20); founded and organized Mutual Welfare League, whereby prisoners had a measure of self-government and might acquire a sense of responsibility. Author of *Within Prison Walls* (1914), etc.

**Os′bourne** (ŏz′bẽrn), **Lloyd.** 1868–1947. American writer, b. San Francisco; stepson of Robert Louis Stevenson, and his collaborator in *The Wrong Box* (1889), *The Wrecker* (1892), and *The Ebb Tide* (1894). Author of *Memories of Vailima* (with his sister, Isobel Strong, 1902), *Wild Justice* (1906), *An Intimate Portrait of R.L.S.* (1925), etc.

**Os′car** (ŏs′kẽr). *Swed.* **Oskar.** Name of two kings of Sweden and Norway:

**Oscar I.** 1799–1859. King (1844–59); son of King Charles XIV John, formerly Marshal Bernadotte; b. Paris. Became duke of **Sö′der·man·land′** [sû′dẽr·män·lānd′] (1810); educ. Uppsala; sympathized with Liberals; on accession, introduced reforms, as freedom of the press; improved Sweden's economic position; on account of ill health, relinquished rule to Charles XV, his eldest son (1857–59); m. (1823) Joséphine Beauharnais (Leuchtenberg), granddaughter of Empress Josephine.

**Oscar II.** 1829–1907. King of Sweden (1872–1907) and of Norway (1872–1905); son of Oscar I and brother of Charles XV, b. Stockholm; m. (1857) Princess Sophia Wilhelmina, youngest daughter of Duke William of Nassau. Found problem of preserving union between Sweden and Norway increasingly difficult; insisted on peaceful solution; gave up throne of Norway (1905) to Haakon VII; served as mediator in several international disputes (1889, 1897, 1899); wrote a play, poems, a number of historical works, and translations from the German. See BERNADOTTE.

**Oscar of the Waldorf.** See Oscar TSCHIRKY.

**Os′ce·o′la** (ŏs′ē·ō′lȧ). 1800?–1838. American Indian leader, b. probably in Georgia; leader of Seminoles in Florida during Second Seminole War (1835–37); seized when he appeared for a conference (Oct., 1837) and died in prison at Fort Moultrie, near Charleston, S.C. (Jan. 30, 1838).

**Osee.** See HOSEA.

**Öser.** See OESER.

**Os′good** (ŏz′gŏŏd), **Frances Sargent,** *nee* **Locke** (lŏk). 1811–1850. American poet, b. Boston; m. Samuel Stillman Osgood, a portrait painter (1835); closely associated with Edgar Allan Poe (1845–47); author of *A Wreath of Wild Flowers from New England* (1838), *The Cries of New York* (1846), etc.

**Osgood, Samuel.** 1748–1813. American Revolutionary officer and political leader, b. Andover, Mass.; served at Lexington and Concord; aide to Gen. Artemas Ward; member of Continental Congress (1781–84); first commissioner, U.S. Treasury (1785–89); postmaster general (1789–91); naval officer, port of New York (1803–13).

**Osgood, William Fogg.** 1864–1943. American mathematician, b. Boston; professor, Harvard (1903–33).

**O'Shaugh'nes·sy** (ō·shô'nĕ·sĭ), **Arthur William Edgar.** 1844–1881. English poet. Associated with Rossetti and the pre-Raphaelites; author of *The Epic of Women* (1870), *Lays of France* (1872), adapted from works of Marie de France.

**O'Shaughnessy, Michael Maurice.** 1864–1934. Hydraulic engineer, b. Limerick, Ire.; to U.S. (1885); city engineer of San Francisco (1912–32); builder of Hetch-Hetchy Water and Power Supply for San Francisco and a number of dams, aqueducts, tunnels, etc. O'Shaughnessy Dam in California is so named in his honor.

**O'Shea'** (ō·shā'), **William Henry.** 1840–1905. Irish home-rule advocate; tried to bring about compromise between Parnell and Liberal leaders (1882–84); divorced wife (1890), who married Parnell, the corespondent.

**O·si·an'der** (ō·zē·än'dĕr), **Andreas.** *Orig. surname* **Ho'se·mann** (hō'zĕ·män). 1498–1552. German Lutheran theologian; first Evangelical preacher in Nuremberg (1522–48), where he helped introduce the Reformation; opposed the Augsburg Interim (1548); preacher and professor of theology, Königsberg (from 1549); engaged in theological disputes (carried on after his death, until 1567, by his followers, the Osiandrists) with Martin Chemnitz and Melanchthon; published astronomical work of Copernicus, a *Harmony* of the Gospels (1537), etc., and wrote theological treatises.

**Osland-Hill, George Edward.** See Nora WALN.

**Os'ler** (ōs'lĕr), Sir **William.** 1849–1919. Physician, b. Bondhead, Ontario, Canada; M.D., McGill (1872); professor, McGill Med. School (1875–84) and physician to Montreal General Hospital (1878–84); professor, U. of Pennsylvania (1884–88); physician in chief, Johns Hopkins Hospital, Baltimore (1889–1905) and professor of medicine, Johns Hopkins U.; regius professor of medicine, Oxford U., England (1905–19); created a baronet (1911). His teaching and personality strongly influenced medical progress. A chance allusion in a public address referring to the relative uselessness of men over sixty was interpreted as a suggestion that all men over this age should be chloroformed, and brought him much undesirable notoriety. Author of *Principles and Practice of Medicine* (1891); editor, with Thomas McCrae, of *Modern Medicine* (7 vols., 1907–10). Many of his addresses have been published, such as *Science and Immortality*, *Man's Redemption of Man*, and *The Old Humanities and the New Science.*

**Os·man'** (*Turk.* ŏs·män') *or* **Oth·man'** (*Arab.* ŏŏth·män'). *Surnamed* **al'–Gha·zi'** (ĕl'gä·zē'), *i.e.* the Conqueror. *Also known as* **Osman I.** 1259–1326. Founder of Ottoman Empire, b. Bithynia; succeeded his father Ertogrul (1288) as leader of Seljuk Turks; conquered northwestern Asia Minor; assumed title of emir (c. 1299); father of Orkhan (*q.v.*).

**Osman II.** 1604–1622. Ottoman sultan of Turkey (1618–22); assassinated (1622).

**Osman III.** 1696–1757. Ottoman sultan (1754–57); younger son of Mustafa II and brother of Mahmud I.

**Os·man' Dig'na** (ŏŏs·män' [ŏŏth·män'] dĭg'nă). 1836–1926. Arab soldier; follower of the Mahdi, in the Sudan; commanded an army near Suakin, and defeated Baker Pasha (Feb. 4, 1884); his ability contributed largely to capture of Khartoum and death of General Gordon (*q.v.*); was defeated by Grenfell at Suakin (1888).

**Os·man' Nu·ri' Pa·sha'** (ŏs·män' nōō·rē' pä·shä'). *Surnamed* **al'–Gha·zi'** (ĕl'gä·zē'), *that is*, the Conqueror. 1837?–1900. Turkish general, b. in Asia Minor; educ. Turkish military academy; served in Crimean War (1854–56); aided in suppressing revolt in Crete (1867–69); general of brigade (1874); general of division (1875); marshal (1876). In Russo-Turkish War (1877–78), distinguished himself by his defense of Pleven against Russian attacks; forced to surrender (Dec. 10, 1877). Commander in chief of the Imperial Guard (1878); minister of war (1878–85), and grand marshal of the palace.

**Os·man' Pa'sha** (ŏŏs·män' [ŏŏth·män'] pä'shä). See Duke of RIPPERDA.

**Os·me'ña** (ōs·mā'nyä), **Sergio.** 1878–1961. Philippine lawyer and statesman; educ. Santo Tomás U.; speaker of first Philippine assembly (1907–16), of House of Representatives (1916–22); senator (1922 ff.); vice-president of Commonwealth of Philippines (1935–44) and secretary of public instruction (1936–44); president (1944–46).

**Os'mund** (ŏz'mŭnd) *or* **Os'mer** (ŏz'mĕr), Saint. 1006?–1099. Norman prelate; nephew of William the Conqueror; bishop of Salisbury (1078–99); noted chiefly for formation of the Sarum use.

**O·sor'kon** (ō·sôr'kŏn). (1) Two kings of ancient Egypt of XXIId (Bubastite) Dynasty: **Osorkon I** (reigned c. 924–895 B.C.); son of Sheshonk I and father of Takelot I; inherited kingdom of great wealth and prosperity. **Osorkon II** (reigned c. 874–853 B.C.), under whom, because of family feuds, power of Egypt declined. See also TAKELOT II, SHESHONK II. (2) Two kings of XXIIId (Tanite) Dynasty, **Osorkon III** and **IV,** reigning in 8th century B.C.

**Os'sen·dow'ski** (ôs'sĕn·dôf'skē), **Ferdynand Antoni.** 1876–1945. Polish writer; among his many books are *Beasts, Men and Gods* (1922), *Shadow of the Gloomy East* (1925), *Lenin* (1926), *Wonders of Poland* (6 vols., 1930–37), *The Devils* (1938).

**Os'sian** (ŏsh'ăn; ŏs'ĭ·ăn) *or* **Oi·sin'** (ŭ·shēn'). Legendary Irish warrior and bard; son (or associate) of Finn MacCool, 3d-century hero of Gaelic literature; hero and author of supposed Gaelic poetry from which James Macpherson (*q.v.*) alleged that he translated the Ossianic poems, including *Fingal* (1762) and *Temora* (1763).

**Os'sian·nils'son** (ŏŏ'shän·nĭls'sôn), **Karl Gustav.** *Orig. surname* **Ossian–Nilsson.** 1875– . Swedish lyric poet and novelist.

**Os'si·etz'ky** (ôs'ē·ĕts'kē), **Carl von.** 1889–1938. German pacifist and writer; served in German army through the World War (1914–18); on staff of *Berliner Volks-Zeitung*, and later (1928) editor of *Weltbuehne;* wrote vigorously in defense of pacifism. Imprisoned on charge of revealing military secrets (1931–32) and on charge of being an enemy of the state (1933–36); while in prison, was awarded Nobel peace prize (1935); the Hitler government considered the award a "challenge and an insult," and prohibited Germans thenceforth from accepting such awards.

**Ossoli,** Marchioness. See Margaret FULLER.

**Os'so·liń'ski** (ôs'sô·lēn'y'·skē), Count **Józef Maximilian.** 1748–1826. Polish patriot and scholar; bought an old Carmelite cloister at Lwów (1807), and made it a national institute (opened to public 1833), known as *The Ossolineum*, which later became one of chief centers of Polish intellectual life.

**Os'so·ry** (ŏs'ō·rĭ), Earls of. Members of **Butler** family (see under ORMONDE) beginning with Piers, or Pierce, 1st earl of Ossory. Another member, **Thomas** (1634–1680), eldest son of 1st duke of Ormonde, was called by courtesy earl of Ossory to distinguish him from his father; m. Emilia, a relative of prince of Orange (1659); became lord deputy of Ireland (1664–65, 1668–69); distinguished himself in naval battles in Dutch war; rear admiral (1673); general of British forces in Holland (1678).

**Ossuna.** See OSUNA.

**Os·ta'de** (ŏs·tä'dē), **Adriaen van.** 1610–1685. Dutch genre painter and etcher, chiefly of village life; pupil of Frans Hals; influenced by Brouwer and Rembrandt; his *The Old Fiddler* and *The Smokers* are in the Metropolitan Museum, N.Y. His brother and pupil **Isaac** *or* **Isack** (1621–1649) was also a genre painter and etcher, esp. of Dutch village and tavern scenes, interiors, and winter scenes.

**Öst'berg'** (ûst'băr'y'), **Ragnar.** 1866–1945. Swedish architect; designer of the Stockholm Town Hall (1911–23), the Stockholm Marinmuseum, a restoration of the old Uppsala castle, etc.

**O'sten–Sack'en** (ŏs'tĕn·zäk'ĕn; ō'stĕn-), **Carl Ro'bert Ro·ma'no·vich von der** (kärl rō'bĕrt rô·mä'nô·vĭch fôn dĕr). 1828–1906. Russian entomologist; secretary to Russian legation, Washington, D.C. (1856–62); Russian consul general in New York City (1862–71); conducted research work on the Diptera of North America.

**Osten–Sacken,** Count **Dmitri von der.** 1793?–1881. Russian general; commandant of Sevastopol (1855) in Crimean War.

**Os'ten·so'** (ŏs'tĕn·sō'), **Martha.** 1900–1963. Author, b. Bergen, Norway; to U.S. as a child; resident of Minneapolis, Minn.; author of *A Far Land* (poetry, 1924), *Wild Geese* (prize-winning novel, 1925), *The Mad Carews* (1927), *Waters Under the Earth* (1930), *Prologue to Love* (1931), *White Reef* (1934), *The Stone Field* (1937), etc.

**O'ster·hout** (ō'stẽr·hout), **Winthrop John Van·leu'ven** (văn·lū'vĕn). 1871–1939. American botanist and physiologist, b. Brooklyn, N.Y.; teacher of botany, Harvard (1909–25; professor 1913–25). Author of *Experiments with Plants* (1905), *Nature of Life* (1924), *Some Fundamental Problems of Cellular Physiology* (1927), etc.

**Ö'ster·ley** *or* **Oe'ster·ley** (û'stẽr·lī), **Karl Friedrich Wilhelm.** 1805–1891. German art scholar and historical and portrait painter; court painter, Hanover (1845). His son and pupil **Karl August Heinrich** (1839–1930) was a landscape and genre painter.

**Ö'ster·ling'** (û'stẽr·lĭng'), **Anders.** 1884– . Swedish literary critic and lyric poet.

**O·ster·mann'** (ŭ·styẽr·mȧn'). Russian noble family, including: Count **Andrei Ivanovich** (1686–1747), diplomat in service of Peter the Great, Catherine I, and Anna Ivanovna; vice-chancellor under Catherine I; disgraced by Czarina Elizabeth Petrovna and exiled to Siberia. His great-grandson Count **Aleksandr Ivanovich Ostermann–Tolstoi** (1770–1837), general; distinguished himself in wars against Napoleon, esp. at Eylau, Friedland, Borodino, and Bautzen.

**Ost'hoff** (ôst'hôf), **Hermann.** 1847–1907. German Indo-Germanic scholar and comparative philologist; specialist in phonetics and morphology; a leader of the "New Grammarians" (Junggrammatiker); professor, Heidelberg (from 1877). Coeditor (with Brugmann) of *Morphologische Untersuchungen* (5 vols., 1878–90; vol. 6 pub. 1910).

**O·stro·gor'ski** (ŭ·strŭ·gôr'skû·ĭ; *Angl.* ŏs'trô·gôr'skĭ), **Moisei Yakovlevich.** 1854–1919. Russian political scientist; best known for treatise on English and American political parties, *Democracy and the Organization of Political Parties* (2 vols., 1902).

**O·strog'ski** (ŭ·strôg'skû·ĭ; *Angl.* ŏs·trŏg'skĭ), Prince **Konstantin Vasili.** 1526–1608. Voivode of Kiev (1559–1608); at his home in Ostrog, founded an academy with a printing press on which the Ostrog Bible, first complete Bible printed in Slavonic, was printed (1581).

**O·strov'ski** (ŭ·strôf'skû·ĭ; *Angl.* ŏs·trŏf'skĭ), **Aleksandr Nikolaevich.** 1823–1886. Russian author of plays, chiefly comedies.

**Ost'wald** (ôst'vält), **Hans Otto August.** 1873–1940. German author of tales, sketches, and novels dealing chiefly with common people and the underworld.

**Ostwald, Wilhelm.** 1853–1932. German physical chemist and philosopher; discovered law (Ostwald's dilution law) concerning the dilution of an electrolyte (1888); conducted research on the electrical conductivity of organic acids and the parallel relationship between their electrolytic dissociation and their power of chemical reaction; developed new theory of color; invented a process for the preparation of nitric acid by oxidizing ammonia, important in the production of explosives in Germany during the World War; awarded 1909 Nobel prize for chemistry. President, German Monists' League (1911); exponent of energism.

**O'Sul'li·van** (ô·sŭl'ĭ·văn), **Seumas.** Pseudonym of James Sullivan STARKEY.

**O'Sullivan, Vincent.** 1872–1940. American writer; author of *Poems* (1896), *The Houses of Sin* (verse; 1897), *Human Affairs* (1905), *Sentiment* (1913); the plays *The Hartley Family* and *The Lighthouse*, etc.

**Osuna,** Conde **de.** See Francisco de MONCADA.

**O·su'na** (*Span.* ô·sōō'nä) *or* **Os·su'na** (*Ital.* ôs·sōō'nä), Duke of. **Pedro Tél'lez y Gi·rón'** (tā'lyāth ē hē·rôn'). 1574?–1624. Spanish soldier and statesman, b. Osuna; count of Ureña, marquis of Peñafiel, and grandee of Spain; viceroy of Sicily (1611), Naples (1616); abetted Bedmar's conspiracy against Venetian state; suspected of attempting to usurp Kingdom of the Two Sicilies; recalled to Spain (1620) and imprisoned by Philip IV (1621–24).

**Os'wald** (ŏz'wȧld), Saint. 605?–642. English martyr; nephew of Edwin. King of Northumbrians (634–642). Converted to Christianity during exile in Iona (from 617); aided brothers to drive out Anglian invaders, defeated and killed Caedwalla (634) and succeeded older brother on throne; introduced Christianity with aid of St. Aidan; killed in battle against pagan king Penda of Mercia.

**Oswald,** Saint. d. 992. English prelate; Benedictine monk at Fleury, France; bishop of Worcester (961–992) and archbishop of York (972–992), administering both sees; co-operated with Saints Dunstan and Ethelwold in restoring ecclesiastical discipline in England; founded monasteries.

**Oswald, Richard.** 1705–1784. British diplomat, b. in Scotland; as Shelburne's agent, conducted negotiations with Franklin at Paris concluding American Revolution (1782); chief negotiator of treaty with U.S.

**Os'wald von Wol'ken·stein** (ôs'vält fôn vôl'kĕn·shtīn). 1377?–1445. Late medieval German lyric poet and adventurer; one of the last of the minnesingers.

**Os'wy** (ŏs'wĭ; ŏz'-) *or* **Os'wiu** (ŏs'wĭ'ŏŏ). 612?–670. English king of Northumbrians, brother of Oswald (605?–642); warred constantly with Penda and Britons; after death of Oswin, last king of Deira, ruled all Northumbria (651–670); gave his daughter to king of Middle Angles on condition that he accept Christianity; defeated Penda (655); gained supremacy over all Mercia, the South Angles, East Angles, East Saxons, as well as sections of Britons and Scots; presided at Synod of Whitby (664).

**Otakar.** Variant of OTTOKAR.

**O·te'scu** (ŏ·tĕ'skōō), **Non'na** (nŏ'nä). 1888–1940. Rumanian composer. His compositions include comic operas, ballets, symphonic poems, etc.

**Ot'frid** *or* **Ot'fried** (ôt'frēt). 800?–?880. German monk and religious poet in Lower Alsace; author of *Liber Evangeliorum Domini Gratia Theodisce Conscriptus* (completed c. 868), an Old High German poetical version of the life of Jesus based on the Gospels, the oldest German poem using the end rhyme.

**Othman.** See OSMAN.

**Oth·man′** (ŏŏth·män′). *Arab.* **'Uthmān.** 575?–656 A.D. Third caliph of the Moslems; succeeded Omar (644 A.D.). Made conquests in Persia, northern Africa, Armenia, and Cyprus; assassinated (656) by Mohammed, son of abu-Bakr.

**Otho.** See OTTO.

**O′tho** (ō′thō), **Marcus Salvius.** 32–69. Roman emperor (69); governor of Lusitania under Nero (58–68); at first supported, later overthrew Galba by a conspiracy (69); proclaimed emperor by soldiers; ruled for three months; defeated in battle by generals of Vitellius; committed suicide. See POPPAEA SABINA.

**O′tis** (ō′tĭs), **Bass.** 1784–1861. American portrait painter and engraver, and pioneer in lithography.

**Otis, Elisha Graves.** 1811–1861. American inventor, b. Halifax, Vt.; devised automatic safety appliance for elevators (1852–53); patented a steam elevator (Jan. 15, 1861), the foundation of the Otis elevator business.

**Otis, Elwell Stephen.** 1838–1909. American army officer, b. Frederick, Md.; served through Civil War; major general of volunteers (1898), commander of Department of the Pacific and military governor of the Philippines (1898–1900); suppressed Philippine insurrection (1899–1900).

**Otis, Fessenden Nott.** 1825–1900. American physician; professor of genitourinary and venereal diseases, Coll. of Phys. & Surg., New York (1871–90); known as the first to cure stricture.

**Otis, George Alexander.** 1830–1881. American army surgeon; served in Civil War and thereafter; edited *Medical and Surgical History of the War of the Rebellion* (vol. I, 1870; II, 1876).

**Otis, Harrison Gray.** 1765–1848. Nephew of James Otis. American statesman, b. Boston; practiced law, Boston (from 1786); member, U.S. House of Representatives (1797–1801); delegate to the Hartford Convention (1814–15); U.S. senator (1817–22); mayor of Boston (1829–32).

**Otis, Harrison Gray.** 1837–1917. American army officer and journalist, b. Marietta, Ohio; served through Civil War and in the Philippines in Spanish-American War; brigadier general and (1899) brevet major general. Settled in California (1876); edited Santa Barbara *Press* (1876–79), Los Angeles *Times* (from 1882). As a result of the *Times* opposition to union labor, the Times building was dynamited and twenty-one employees killed (Oct. 1, 1910); the McNamara brothers confessed to the crime (1911).

**Otis, James.** 1725–1783. American Revolutionary statesman, b. West Barnstable, Mass.; practiced law in Boston (from 1750). Was king's advocate general (1760) when royal customs collectors applied for writs of assistance to search for evidence of violation of Sugar Act of 1733; resigned his office and appeared as counsel for Boston merchants to oppose issuance of writs; made brilliant speech basing opposition on principles of natural law, superior to acts of Parliament (1761). In Massachusetts legislature (from 1761); took place among leaders of those upholding colonial cause; published *The Rights of the British Colonies Asserted and Proved* (1764), a closely reasoned argument based on the principles of natural law. With Samuel Adams and Joseph Hawley, directed majority in Massachusetts legislature (1766–69) in opposition to various revenue acts.

**Otrante, Duc d'.** See Joseph FOUCHÉ.

**Ot′ter·bein** (ŏt′ẽr·bīn; *Ger.* ôt′-), **Philip William.** 1726–1813. Clergyman, b. Dillenburg, Ger.; to U.S. (1752); in German Reformed Church pastorates in Pennsylvania and Maryland (1752–1813). In friendly association with Martin Boehm (from 1768); with Boehm and six lay evangelists, formed (1789) a simple organization and adopted a profession of faith, thus originating the sect which became known as the United Brethren in Christ. The first annual conference of United Brethren in Christ was held in 1800. Cf. Martin BOEHM.

**Ot′to** (ŏt′ō; *Ger.* ôt′ō). 1865–1906. Archduke of Austria; son of Archduke Charles Louis, nephew of Emperor Francis Joseph, and father of Charles I; m. (1886) Princess Maria Josepha of Saxony; cavalry general in Austrian army. His grandson archduke **Otto** (1912– ), son of Charles I; pretender to Austro-Hungarian throne; in exile (from 1919).

**Ot′to** (ŏt′ō; *Ger.* ôt′ō) *or* **O′tho** (ō′thō; *Ger.* ō′tō). Name of four Holy Roman emperors:

**Otto I.** 912–973. Called "the Great." Son of Henry I, the Fowler; king of Germany and Holy Roman emperor (936–973; crowned 962). Spent early years of reign in subduing revolts of nobles; aided Adelaide, Queen of Lombardy, against Berengar II (951); m. Adelaide; defeated Hungarians in great battle on the Lechfeld (955); defeated Berengar II (961). Coronation (962) revived the empire of Charlemagne. Deposed Pope John XII (963). His son Otto crowned as joint emperor (967) by Pope John XIII.

**Otto II.** 955–983. Holy Roman emperor (973–983); son of Otto I. Subdued revolt of cousin Henry II of Bavaria (976); drove French out of Lorraine but unsuccessful in siege of Paris (978); claimed provinces in southern Italy but disastrously defeated by Saracens and Greeks (982); m. at Rome (972) **The·oph′a·no** [thē·ŏf′ȧ·nō; *Ger.* tā·ō′fä·nō] (955?–991), daughter of Byzantine emperor, Romanus II, who had great influence at his court, introducing much of the refinement of Constantinople, and who, after his death, ruled (983–991) for her son Otto III as coregent with the boy's grandmother Adelaide.

**Otto III.** 980–1002. Holy Roman emperor (983–1002); son of Otto II. During minority (983–991), under coregency (see Otto II); after his mother's death, under regency (991–996) of the archbishop of Mainz; assumed direction of government (996); lived in Rome (998–1002) and sought to make it the capital of a new Roman empire; established Sylvester II as pope (999).

**Otto IV** of Brunswick. 1174?–1218. Holy Roman emperor (1198–1215; crowned 1209); son of Henry the Lion, Duke of Bavaria and Saxony; educ. in England. Put forward (1198) by Guelphs as rival to Philip, Duke of Swabia, as king and emperor; fought civil war against Philip (1198–1208); crowned emperor after Philip's death; excommunicated (1210) by Pope Innocent III. With John of England, defeated at Bouvines (1214) by Philip II Augustus of France supported by Innocent III; forced to retire (1215) to estates in Brunswick.

**Otto.** 1848–1916. King of Bavaria (1886–1913); became insane (1873); succeeded his brother Louis II as king (1886) under regency of his uncle Prince Luitpold (1886–1912) and of his cousin Louis (1912–13); deposed (1913) and succeeded by cousin as King Louis III.

**Otto.** Name of five margraves of Brandenburg (*q.v.*) of 12th to 14th centuries, especially **Otto III** (d. 1267), who ruled jointly with his brother John I (1220–67) and made important acquisitions to the territory.

**Otto.** Called **the Child,** *Ger.* **das Kind** (däs kĭnt′). 1204–1252. First duke of Brunswick-Lüneburg (see

Brunswick). Grandson of Henry the Lion; inherited Brunswick (1218) and Lüneburg (1227); held captive after defeat by Waldemar of Denmark; joined his lands in a single duchy (1235).

**Otto I.** d. about 1292. Founder of younger Nassau line. See Nassau, 2.

**Ot'to** (ŏt'ō; *Ger.* ôt'ō) **I** *or* **O'tho** (ō'thō; *Ger.* ō'tō). *In full* **Otto Friedrich Ludwig.** 1815–1867. King of Greece (1832–62); second son of Louis I of Bavaria; b. at Salzburg, Austria; chosen "King of the Hellenes" by London conference (1832); ruled under regency of three Bavarian advisers (1832–35); unpopular throughout his reign because of his religion, his taxation, his use of German officials, and interference of his wife (Princess Amalie of Oldenburg); forced by insurrection to grant a constitution (1843); deposed by a revolutionary government (1862).

**Ot'to** (ŏt'ō; *Ger.* ôt'ō), **Bo'do** (bō'dō). 1711–1787. Physician, b. Hanover, Ger.; to America (1755); surgeon in Continental army (1776–82). His grandson **John Conrad Otto** (1774–1844) was also a physician; known for original description of hemophilia (1803); succeeded Benjamin Rush as physician to Pennsylvania Hospital (1813–34). John Conrad's son **William Tod** [tŏd] (1816–1905) was a jurist; arbitrator for U.S. in adjudicating with Spain damages sustained by Americans in Cuba (1871–75); reporter, U.S. Supreme Court (1875–83).

**Otto, Nikolaus August.** 1832–1891. German technician; inventor of an early form of internal-combustion engine (with Langen, 1867), and of the first four-cycle Otto gas engine, or Otto motor (1876).

**Otto, Walter.** 1878–1941. German scholar, specialist in ancient history and papyrology.

**Otto of Bam'berg** (bäm'bĕrk; *Angl.* băm'bûrg), Saint. 1060?–1139. Called "Father of the Monks." Bishop of Bamberg and apostle of the Pomeranians; appointed bishop (1102) by Emperor Henry IV; consecrated at Rome (1106); devoted himself to work of his bishopric, founding more than twenty monasteries; made journeys to Pomerania (1124–28), converting many; canonized (1189).

**Otto of Frei'sing** (frī'zĭng). 1114?–1158. German bishop and historian; grandson of Emperor Henry IV and half brother of Conrad III; studied in Paris; abbot of Cistercian monastery of Morimond in Burgundy (1136); made bishop of Freising (1137), in Bavaria; took part in Conrad's disastrous crusade (1147–49). Wrote (1143–46) one of the most remarkable of the medieval histories, *De Duabus Civitatibus* (Eng. ed. pub. 1928 as *The Two Cities*), a philosophical work in eight books, following in part Augustine and Orosius; began chronicle of reign of Frederick I (*Gesta Friderici Imperatoris*).

**Otto of Nord'heim** (nôrt'hīm). d. 1083. Duke of Bavaria (1061–70, 1074–83); active in plots (1062–70) against Emperor Henry IV in his minority; deprived of his duchy (1070), restored (1074); took part in Saxon uprising (1075) and was in arms against Henry until his death, supporting Rudolf.

**Otto of Wit'tels·bach** (vĭt'ĕls·bäk). Name of three members of Wittelsbach family: **Otto I** (1120?–1183); strong supporter of Emperor Frederick I, accompanied him to Italy; made (1156) count palatine and (1180) first duke of Bavaria; founder of ruling Wittelsbach (*q.v.*) family of that kingdom. His nephew **Otto** (d. 1209), count palatine, murderer of King Philip of Swabia (1208). **Otto II** (d. 1253); called "the Illustrious"; grandson of Otto I; duke (1231–53); increased lands by purchase.

**Ot'to·kar** (ŏt'ō·kär; *Angl.* ŏt'-). *Also* **Ot'to·car** (*Angl.* ŏt'ŏ·kär) *and* **O'ta·kar** (ō'tä·kär). Name of two kings of Bohemia: **Ottokar I** (d. 1230), king (1197–1230); received (1192) duchy of Bohemia from Emperor Henry IV; deposed (1193) but restored (1197); took advantage of many conflicts in Germany to further own interests; weakened by long struggle with clergy (1214–21). **Ottokar II** (1230?–1278), called "the Great"; son of Wenceslaus I; king (1253–78), and possessor of duchy of Austria (1251–76); greatly extended Bohemian dominion (1260–69); on election of Rudolf I (1273) as Holy Roman emperor, ceded Austria, Styria, etc., to him; revolted and was defeated at Marchfeld and slain.

**Ot'way** (ŏt'wā), **Thomas.** 1652–1685. English dramatist; infatuated with Elizabeth Barry, who played with the Bettertons in his first play, *Alcibiades* (1675); scored success with *Don Carlos* (1676); adapted plays by Racine and Molière. His first blank-verse tragedy, *The Orphan*, was produced in 1680; his masterpiece, *Venice Preserved*, in which he caricatured Shaftesbury as Antonio and in which Mrs. Barry played Belvidera, in 1682; his last play, *The Atheist* (a comedy, 1684).

**Oud** (out), **Jacobus Johannes Pieter.** 1890–1963. Dutch architect, a leader of the de Stijl group and champion of modernism in art; city architect, Rotterdam (1918–33).

**Ou'de·mans** (ou'dĕ·mäns), **Jean Abraham Chrétien.** 1827–1906. Dutch astronomer.

**Ou'di'né'** (ōō'dē'nā'), **Eugène André.** 1810–1887. French sculptor and engraver of medals; among his sculptures are *La Vierge et l'Enfant Jésus* at the church of Saint Gervais in Paris, *Hébé* in the palace of the Tuileries; among his medallions are *Prince Napoléon*, *Le Duc d'Orléans*, *Berthollet*, *Deux Décembre 1851*.

**Ou'di'not'** (ōō'dē'nō'), **Nicolas Charles.** Duc **de Reg'gio** (dē rād'jō). 1767–1847. French soldier in the Revolutionary and Napoleonic armies; distinguished himself at Austerlitz (1805), Friedland (1807), Wagram (1809); created marshal of France and duc de Reggio (1809); engaged in the Russian campaign (1812), at Bautzen (1813), and in the defense of France (1813–14); remained loyal to the monarchy during the Hundred Days; appointed to command the National Guard, and created a peer of France. His son **Nicolas Charles Victor** (1791–1863), Duc de Reggio, served in the Napoleonic armies, esp. in the defense of France (1813–14); commanded expedition against Rome and captured the city (1849).

**Ou'dry'** (ōō'drē'), **Jean Baptiste.** 1686–1755. French painter, esp. of animals; superintendent of the Gobelins' factory.

**Ough'tred** (ô'trĕd; -trĭd), **William.** 1575–1660. English mathematician; invented (c. 1600) horizontal instrument for delineating dials on any plane; invented trigonometric abbreviations and introduced signs of multiplication and proportion in his *Clavis Mathematicae* (1631).

**Ouida.** Pseudonym of Marie Louise de la Ramée.

**Oui'met** (wē'mĕt), **Francis.** 1893–1967. American golfer, b. Brookline, Mass.; winner of the United States open championship in 1913, after a sensational play-off with Harry Vardon and Ted Ray, and of the United States amateur championship in 1914.

**Ould** (ōld), **Hermon.** 1886–1951. English dramatist, poet, and critic.

**Ou'less** (ōō'lĕs; -lĭs), **Walter William.** 1848–1933. English portrait painter; did well-known portraits of Darwin and Cardinal Newman.

**Ou·man'sky** (ŏŏ·mån'skû·ĭ; *Angl.* -skĭ), **Constantine Alexandrovich.** 1902–1945. Russian diplomat; ambassador to U.S. (1939–41).

**Ours'ler** (ou(r)z'lĕr), **Charles Fulton.** 1893–1952. American journalist, playwright, and fiction writer, b. Baltimore; author of novels, as *Poor Little Fool* (1928), *The Great Jasper* (1930); detective stories (under pseudonym

**Anthony Abbot**), as *About the Murder of the Choir Singer*, *About the Murder of a Man Afraid of Women;* plays, as *The Spider* (1927), *All the King's Men* (1929); and motion-picture scenarios. Married (1925) **Grace Perkins** (1900–1955), b. Boston, author of *Angel Child* (1927), *Ex-Mistress* (1930), *Boy Crazy* (1931), *The Unbreakable Mrs. Doll* (1938), etc.

**Ouse′ley** (o͞oz′lĭ). Name of an Irish family distinguished in English history, including: Sir **Gore Ouseley** (1770–1844), diplomat and Orientalist; active in collection and translation of Oriental texts. His brother Sir **William** (1767–1842), also an Orientalist; author of *Persian Miscellanies* (1795), *Oriental Collections* (3 vols., 1797–99); translator of a Persian geography and Persian tales. Sir **William Gore** (1797–1866), son of Sir William; British diplomat holding posts in Washington (1825–32), Brazil (1838), Argentina (1844). Sir **Frederick Arthur Gore** (1825–1889), son of Sir Gore; musical theorist and composer of church music, as anthems, oratorios, a cantata, and piano trios and sonatas; author of *Harmony* (1868), *Counterpoint, Canon, and Fugue* (1869).

**Out′cault** (out′kôlt), **Richard Felton.** 1863–1928. American cartoonist; originator of the *Yellow Kid* and *Buster Brown* comic strips.

**Ou′tram** (o͞o′trăm), Sir **James.** 1803–1863. British army commander in India; known as "the Bay′ard (bā′ẽrd) of India." Joined Bombay native infantry (1819); made famous eight-day journey of 355 miles with dispatch to governor of Bombay (1839); defended his residency at Hyderabad against 8000 Sikhs (1843); conducted brilliant war against Persia (1857); in Sepoy Mutiny, a volunteer under his old lieutenant Havelock in first relief of Lucknow; commanded Lucknow garrison through siege until relieved by Sir Colin Campbell; held the city through evacuation until third relief (1857); chief commander of Oudh and lieutenant general (1858). His cousin **George Outram** (1805–1856), Scottish humorous poet, was collaborator with Christopher North in *Dies Boreales*.

**Ou′vrard′** (o͞o′vrȧr′), **Gabriel Julien.** 1770–1846. French speculator and financier; advanced large sums to finance Napoleon's campaigns; later (1807) incurred enmity of Napoleon and was imprisoned (1809–13); during the Hundred Days was appointed supply officer to Napoleon's army; convicted of illegal transactions on the Paris Bourse, was again imprisoned (1823–28).

**Ou·wa′ter** (ou·vȧ′tẽr), **Albert van.** fl. c. 1430–1460. Dutch painter, founder of the Haarlem school.

**Ou′we** (ou′wĕ), **Hart′man** (härt′män) **von.** = HARTMANN VON AUE.

**O·van′do** (ō̇·vän′dō), **Nicolás de.** 1460?–?1518. Spanish colonial administrator; succeeded Francisco de Bobadilla as governor of Spanish possessions in America (1502–09); began first extensive importation of Negro slaves.

**O′vens** (ō′vĕns), **Juriaen.** 1623–1678. Dutch painter, chiefly of group portraits, nocturnal scenes, and historical and allegorical subjects.

**O′ver·beck** (ō′vẽr·bĕk), **Christian Adolf.** 1755–1821. German lyric poet; author of popular lyrics, including *Blühe* and *Liebes Veilchen.* His son **Johann Friedrich** (1789–1869), religious and portrait painter, formed, with Schadow-Godenhaus, Cornelius, Veit, and others, the Nazarenes, or Pre-Raphaelites (1815–30), who established themselves at San Isidoro Convent, Rome, and aimed to restore religion in art; became Roman Catholic convert (1813); his works include oil paintings, frescoes, and religious drawings and cartoons. J. F. Overbeck's nephew **Johannes Adolf Overbeck** (1826–1895) was an archaeologist and art historian.

**O′ver·bur·y** (ō′vẽr·bẽr·ĭ; -bĕr′ĭ), Sir **Thomas.** 1581–1613. English poet; courtier, protégé of Robert Carr, Viscount Rochester (later Earl of Somerset); confidant to intrigue between Rochester and the profligate Frances Howard, Countess of Essex; opposed marriage of Rochester and Lady Essex; imprisoned in Tower (1613) on charge of disrespect to king, and slowly poisoned with blue vitriol by Lady Essex's agents. Known especially for *A Wife* (1614), a didactic poem, and the prose *Characters*, sketches modeled upon Theophrastus and important in development of the English essay.

**Ö′ver·land** (û′vẽr·län), **Arnulf.** 1889–1968. Norwegian lyric poet, novelist, and playwright.

**O′ver·stone** (ō′vẽr·stŭn), Baron. **Samuel Jones Loyd** (loid). 1796–1883. English economist and financier; created Baron **Overstone of Overstone and Foth′er·in·gay′** [fŏth′ẽr·ĭng·gā′] (1860); authority on banking and finance. See Baron WANTAGE.

**O′ver·ton** (ō′vẽr·t'n; -tŭn), **Grant Martin.** 1887–1930. American journalist and fiction writer; author of *When Winter Comes to Main Street* (1922), *The Thousand-and-first Night* (1924), etc.

**O′ver·weg** (ō′vẽr·väk), **Adolf.** 1822–1852. German traveler and explorer in Africa.

**Ov′id** (ŏv′ĭd). *Full Latin name* **Publius O·vid′i·us Na′so** (ō̇·vĭd′ĭ·ŭs nā′sō). 43 B.C.–?17 A.D. Roman poet, b. Sulmona, Italy; educated for the law, but devoted himself to literature; for some unknown cause, banished by Augustus (8 A.D.) from Rome to Tomi (Constanţa), near Black Sea, where he remained until death. Chief work, *Metamorphoses*, a narrative poem recounting legends involving miraculous transformations of form from the creation to time of Julius Caesar. Author also of number of elegies.

**O·vi′dio** (ō̇·vē′dyō̇), **Francesco d'.** 1849–1924. Italian philologist and critic; among his works are *Studies on the Divina Commedia* (1901), and *Benevenuto da Imola e la Legenda Vergiliana* (1916).

**O·vie′do y Val·dés′** (ō̇·vyā′thō ē̇ väl·dās′), **Gonzalo Fer·nán′dez de** (fĕr·nän′dāth [-dās] thā). 1478–1557. Spanish chronicler; to America (1514) as inspector general of trade; governor of Cartagena (1526 ff.), Santo Domingo (1535–45); appointed historiographer of the New World by Charles V; known esp. for his *Historia General y Natural de las Indias Occidentales* (21 vols., 1535).

**O′ving·ton** (ō′vĭng·tŭn), **Earle.** 1879–1936. American aeronautical engineer; first U.S. Air Mail pilot (1911); invented various electrical appliances, including Ovington high-frequency apparatus.

**O′wain Cy·veil′iog** (ō̇′wän kŭ·vŭ′ĭl·yŏg). d. 1197. Welsh poet; prince of Powis (1160–97); joined Owain Gwynedd in repelling Henry II (1165); obtained outside help to expel Rhys ap Gruffydd, prince of South Wales, from Powis (1167–71); founded Cistercian house, where he died a monk. Author of *Hirlas*, a poem in which each of victorious chieftains is toasted in the long drinking horn.

**Owain Gwy′nedd** (go͞o′ĭ·nĕth). d. 1169. King of Gwynedd (North Wales); succeeded father Gruffydd ab Cynan (1137); submitted to Henry II after invasion (1157); aided Owain Cyveiliog in repelling Henry II's invasion of South Wales (1165).

**Ow′en** (ō′ĕn; -ĭn). See also OWAIN.

**Owen,** Sir **Hugh.** 1804–1881. Welsh promoter of education; helped establish teacher-training colleges; founded Aberystwyth University College (opened 1872); reformed and revived the eisteddfod.

**Owen, John.** *Latin* **Au′do·e′nus** (ō̇′dō̇·ē′nŭs) *or* **O·ve′nus** (ō̇·vē′nŭs). 1560?–1622. Welsh epigrammatist; master of Latin idiom and author of shrewd and pointed epigrams.

**Owen, John.** 1616–1683. English Puritan clergyman and theologian; adopted Independent or Congregational principles and preached to parliament day after execution of Charles I (1649); Cromwell's chaplain; vice-chancellor of Oxford (1652–58).

**Owen, John.** 1854–1926. Welsh church leader; bishop of St. David's (from 1897); strenuous opponent of disestablishment of church in Wales.

**Owen,** Sir **Richard.** 1804–1892. English comparative anatomist and zoologist; superintendent of natural history department of British Museum (1856–83); confirmed original observations of Sir James Paget (*q.v.*) on parasite, *Trichina spiralis;* regarded as successor of Cuvier in vertebrate paleontology.

**Owen, Robert.** 1771–1858. Welsh socialist, pioneer of co-operation in industry, and philanthropist; b. Newtown, Wales. Bought New Lanark mills at Manchester from David Dale (1799); with William Allen, Quaker philanthropist, and Jeremy Bentham as partners (1814), initiated program of amelioration in conditions of operatives; stopped employment of children, established sickness and old-age insurance, opened educational and recreational facilities. Contended in *A New View of Society* (1813) that man's character is wholly determined by environment; instrumental in drafting Factory Act of 1819, emasculated in House of Commons. Founded several communities of "Owenites" on the co-operative principle in Great Britain and the United States, including one at New Harmony, Indiana (1825–28), all unsuccessful. Withdrew from New Lanark after disagreements with partners (1829). Spent fortune on social schemes; (after 1834) devoted himself to preaching his educational, moral, secularist, and other ideas; at age of 82 took up spiritualism. Author of *Revolution in Mind and Practice* (1849) and autobiography (1857–58). A son, **Robert Dale** (1801–1877), accompanied his father to U.S. (1825) and to New Harmony, Ind.; taught school and edited New Harmony *Gazette;* to New York (1829) and edited *Free Enquirer;* again in New Harmony (1832); member of U.S. House of Representatives (1843–47); U.S. minister to Italy (1855–58); advocate of emancipation of slaves (1858–63); author of *The Policy of Emancipation* (1863), *The Wrong Slavery* (1864), *Beyond the Breakers* (a novel; 1870), *Threading My Way* (autobiographical; 1874).

**Owen, Robert La'tham** (lā'thăm). 1856–1947. American lawyer and legislator; U.S. senator from Oklahoma (1907–25); aided in drafting Federal Reserve Act, known as the Glass-Owen Currency Act, and Farm Loan Act; advocated initiative, referendum, recall, and cloture in U.S. Senate.

**Owen, Russell.** 1889–1952. American journalist, b. Chicago; on staff of New York *Sun* (1906–20), New York *Times* (from 1920); covered Scopes trial at Dayton, Tenn. (1925); with Amundsen and Byrd expeditions at Spitsbergen (1926); with Byrd's first antarctic expedition (1929–30). Wrote *South of the Sun* (1934).

**Owen, Ruth,** *nee* **Bryan.** See Ruth Bryan ROHDE.

**Owen, Wilfred.** 1893–1918. English poet of World War I; served in France (1916–17); invalided home; company commander on Western front (1918). His poems edited by Siegfried Sassoon (23 titles in 1920 ed.).

**Ow'ens** (ō'ĕnz; ō'ĭnz), **Jesse.** *Orig. name* **James Cleveland Owens.** 1913– . American athlete, b. Alabama. Set three track and field world records and tied one on May 25, 1935; awarded four gold medals in Olympic Games (1936).

**Owens, Michael Joseph.** 1859–1923. American inventor and manufacturer; invented automatic bottle-blowing machine (patented 1895 and 1904); organized Owens Bottle Machine Co. (1903); vice-president (1915–23); also organized Libbey-Owens Sheet Glass Co. (1916); vice-president (1916–23).

**Owens, Robert Bowie.** 1870–1940. American electrical engineer; credited with discovery of alpha rays; invented an electromagnetic system for guiding ships and airplanes, a differentiation machine, and an electric accelerometer.

**Owenson, Sydney.** See Sydney MORGAN, Lady Morgan.

**Ox'en·ford** (ŏk's'n·fẽrd; -fôrd), **John.** 1812–1877. English dramatic critic (on London *Times,* from 1850), playwright, and translator.

**Ox'en·ham** (ŏk's'n·ăm; ŏks'năm), **John.** d. 1575. English mariner; with Drake in Central America (1572); headed a second expedition to the New World; was defeated by the Spaniards, captured, and hanged at Lima, Peru. A fictional account of his expedition is introduced by Charles Kingsley in his *Westward Ho!*

**Oxenham, John.** *Pseudonym of* **William Arthur Dun'ker·ley** (dŭng'kẽr·lĭ). 1861?–1941. English businessman and writer; author of several volumes of verse, as *Bees in Amber* (1913), *The Vision Splendid* (1917), many popular novels, including *God's Prisoner* (his earliest; 1898), *Broken Shackles* (1914), *God's Candle* (1929), *Anno Domini* (1932), *Christ and the Third Wise Man* (1934).

**Ox'en·stier'na** *or* **Ox'en·stjer'na** (o͝ok'sĕn·shâr'nȧ) *or* **Ox'en·stiern** (ŏk's'n·stẽrn), Count **Axel Gustafsson.** 1583–1654. Swedish statesman; appointed chancellor by Gustavus Adolphus (1612); arranged peace treaties with Denmark at Knäred (1613) and with Russia at Stolbova (1617); took part in campaigns against Poland (1621); governor general of Prussia (1626); negotiated a truce with Poland (1629) by which Sweden retained Livonia; held supreme control in Rhine region in Thirty Years' War (from 1631); succeeded Gustavus Adolphus as director of Swedish foreign policy in Germany (after 1632); director of the Evangelical League, Heilbronn (1633); negotiated treaty of Wismar with France (1636); became a guardian of Queen Christina (1636) and remained virtual director of Swedish foreign and domestic policy after her ascension (1644); negotiated peace of Brömsebro with Denmark (1645); ennobled (1645).

**Oxenstierna** *or* **Oxenstjerna,** Baron **Bengt Bengtsson.** 1591–1643. Swedish statesman and traveler; traveled in Palestine (1613) and in Asia Minor, Persia, Egypt, etc. (1616); in diplomatic service of Gustavus Adolphus of Sweden (1620); governor general of Livonia and Ingria (1634). His nephew Count **Bengt Gabrielsson Oxenstierna** (1623–1702) was a statesman and diplomat in the service of Charles X and Charles XI; as governor of Poland led the defense of Thorn (1657); governor general of Livonia (1662–66); delegate to Congress of Nijmegen (1676); chancellor president and director of Swedish foreign policy (1680–97); member of regency council of Charles XII (1697).

**Oxenstierna** *or* **Oxenstjerna,** Count **Johan Gabriel.** 1750–1818. Swedish poet; court poet to Gustavus III and Charles XIII; author of poem cycles, the comic poem *Disa,* lyrics, epigrams, epistles, a translation of Milton's *Paradise Lost,* etc.

**Ox'ford** (ŏks'fẽrd), Earls of. See Robert and Edward HARLEY; VERE family.

**Oxford, John of.** d. 1200. English prelate; bishop of Norwich (1175); charged (1179), with two other bishops, with reconstruction of judicial system.

**Oxford and Asquith,** Earl and Countess of. See ASQUITH.

**O·ya·ma** (ō·yä·mä), Prince **Iwao.** 1842–1916. Japanese general (1891) and field marshal (1898); in Chinese-Japanese War (1894–95), commanded second army and captured Port Arthur and Weihaiwei; in Russo-Japanese War (1904–05), commanded the Manchurian army and defeated the Russians under Kuropatkin in the battles of Liaoyang, the Shaho, and Mukden; created count (1884), marquis (1895), prince (1907).

**O'za'nam'** (ô'zȧ'nȧm'), **Antoine Frédéric.** 1813–1853. French historian; a leader in the Catholic movement; a founder of the Society of Saint Vincent de Paul (1833); cofounder of *Ère Nouvelle*. Author of *Dante et la Philosophie Catholique* (1838), *Études Germaniques* (1847–49), etc.

**O'zen'fant'** (ô'zäN'fäN'), **Amédée.** 1886–1966. French painter; identified with the cubist school; collaborated with Le Corbusier (*q.v.*) in writing *Après le Cubisme* (1918) and *La Peinture Moderne* (1924); to U.S. (1938).

**Ozias.** See UZZIAH.

# P

**Paaltjens, Piet.** Pseudonym of François HAVERSCHMIDT.

**Paa'sche** (pä'shĕ), **Hermann.** 1851–1925. German economist and authority on sugar production.

**Paas'sen** (pȧ'sĕn), **Pierre** (pyâr) **van.** 1895–1968. Dutch-born journalist and author in U.S.; to Canada (1914) and served in Canadian army in World War; joined staff of Toronto *Globe* (1919), Atlanta (Ga.) *Constitution* (1921), New York *Evening World* (1924–31), Toronto *Star* (1932–35); became American citizen; author of *Days of Our Years* (1939), *That Day Alone* (1941), etc.

**Pa'ca** (pā'kȧ; *now usu.* păk'ȧ), **William.** 1740–1799. American Revolutionary leader, b. near Abingdon, Md.; practiced law (from 1764); member of Continental Congress (1774–79) and signer of Declaration of Independence; governor of Maryland (1782–85); U.S. district judge for Maryland (1789–99).

**Pac'ca** (päk'kä), **Bartolommeo.** 1756–1844. Italian prelate and diplomat; cardinal (1801); secretary of state, Papal States (1806 ff.); imprisoned by Napoleon for anti-French policies (1809–13); induced Pius VII to break concordat of Fontainebleau (1813); banished by Napoleon (1814); recalled after fall of the Empire; camerlingo, nuncio to Vienna (1816); governor of Rome (1817); bishop of Ostia and Velletri (1830 ff.). Author of memoirs, important as historical source material.

**Pac'ca·na'ri** (päk'kä·nä'rē), **Niccolo.** Early 19th-century Italian monk; founded order of Regular Clerks of the Faith of Jesus (approved 1797 and absorbed by Society of Jesus, 1814), known generally as Paccanarists.

**Pac·chio'ni** (päk·kyō'nē), **Antonio.** 1665–1726. Italian anatomist; investigated esp. structure of dura mater. The Pacchionian bodies in the brain are named after him.

**Paccioli, Luca.** See PACIOLI.

**Pace** (pās), **Richard.** 1482?–1536. English diplomat; dean of St. Paul's (1519); sent by Wolsey to induce Swiss to attack forces of Francis I (1515), to influence imperial electors in favor of Henry VIII as successor to Emperor Maximilian (1519), and to further Wolsey's papal ambition (1521, 1523). His dispatches are historically important.

**Pacelli, Eugenio.** See Pope PIUS XII.

**Pa·che'co** (pä·chā'kō). See VILLENA.

**Pacheco, Francisco.** 1564?–1654. Spanish portrait and religious painter; teacher and father-in-law of Velázquez; employed at Seville (1625 ff.); author of *Arte de la Pintura* (1649).

**Pacheco, María.** See Juan López de PADILLA.

**Pachitch.** = PAŠIĆ.

**Pach'mann, Vladimir de** (dyĕ päκ'män). 1848–1933. Russian pianist; won renown as an interpreter of Chopin.

**Pa·cho'mi·us** (pȧ·kō'mĭ·ŭs), Saint. Christian monk, of Egypt; founded (c. 318 A.D.) on island in the Nile first monastic institution, in which members agreed to observe rules of life and conduct established by him.

**Pa·cif'i·co** (pȧ·sĭf'ĭ·kō; *Port.* pȧ·sē'fē·kōō), **David.** 1784–1854. Portuguese Jew, b. at Gibraltar; a British subject; Portuguese consul general in Greece (1837–42); made claim against Greek government for burning of his house by a mob; almost precipitated a war when French and British quarreled in their attempt to compel settlement of his claim. See Viscount PALMERSTON.

**Pa·ci'ni** (pä·chē'nē), **Filippo.** 1812–1883. Italian anatomist; rediscovered (1835) nerve terminations (described earlier by Abraham Vater) that came to be called *Pacinian corpuscles*, or *bodies*, after him.

**Pacini, Giovanni.** 1796–1867. Italian composer, esp. of operas, as *Niobe* (1826), *Saffo* (1840), *La Regina di Cipro* (1846).

**Pa'ci·not'ti** (pä'chē·nôt'tē), **Antonio.** 1841–1912. Italian physicist; invented dynamo with ring winding (1860), same type of winding being independently discovered and used in dynamo by Z. T. Gramme (1870).

**Pa·cio'li** (pä·chō'lē) *or* **Pac·cio'li** (pät·chō'lē), **Luca.** *Called also* **Luca di Bor'go** (dē bōr'gō). 1450?–?1520. Italian mathematician and Franciscan friar; author of *Summa de Arithmetica, Geometria, Proporcioni e Proporcionalità* (1494), which contains the first printed description of bookkeeping by double entry, and *De Divina Proportione* with plates engraved by his friend Leonardo da Vinci (1509).

**Pa'ci·us** (pä'sĭ·ŏŏs), **Fredrik.** 1809–1891. Finnish violinist and composer, esp. of operas and patriotic songs, including Finnish national anthem *Maamme*.

**Pack'ard** (păk'ērd), **Alpheus Spring.** 1839–1905. American entomologist; studied under Agassiz at Harvard; a founder and editor in chief of *American Naturalist* (1867–87); professor of zoology and geology, Brown U. (1878–1905); author of *Guide to the Study of Insects* (1869), *Text-Book of Entomology* (1898), *Monograph of the Bombycine Moths* (3 vols., 1895–1914).

**Packard, Frank Lucius.** 1877–1942. Canadian writer, b. Montreal, Que.; author of novels, as *Greater Love Hath No Man* (1913), *The Miracle Man* (1914), *The Beloved Traitor* (1916), *The Night Operator* (1919), and detective fiction, including the Jimmie Dale series.

**Packard, James Ward.** 1863–1928. American engineer and inventor; with brother **William Doud** (1861–1923), founded Packard Electric Co. (1890); designed and built first Packard automobile (1899); president, Packard Motor Car Co. (to 1915).

**Pack′er** (păk′ẽr), **Asa.** 1805–1879. American businessman, b. Groton, Conn.; to Pennsylvania (1822); acquired coal lands and canalboats to carry coal; built, and held controlling interest in, Lehigh Valley Railroad; founded and endowed Lehigh U. (chartered 1866).

**Packington.** = PAKINGTON.

**Pa·cu′vi·us** (pȧ·kū′vĭ·ŭs), **Marcus.** 220?–?132 B.C. Roman playwright, poet, and painter; nephew of Ennius; noted esp. for tragedies. Only fragments of his works are extant.

**Pad′dock** (păd′ŭk), **Benjamin Henry.** 1828–1891. American Protestant Episcopal clergyman; bishop of Massachusetts (1873–91).

**Pa′de·loup′** (pä′dlo͞o′). Family of Paris bookbinders, including: **Antoine,** 17th-century founder of the family, and his three sons, **Nicolas** (b. 1642), **Philippe** (1650–1728), and **Michel** (1654–1725); three sons of Michel, **Sylvestre Antoine** (1676–1720), **Philippe** (1680–1754), and **Antoine Michel** (1685–1758), most famous of the family, known for his mosaics and dentelle borders; a son of Antoine Michel, **Jean** (b. 1716).

**Pa′de·rew′ski** (pä′dĕ·rĕf′skē; *Angl.* păd′ĕ-), **I′gnace′** (*Fr.* ē′nyȧs′), *Pol.* **Ignacy, Jan** (yän). 1860–1941. Polish pianist and statesman, b. in Podolia, then a province of Russian Poland; studied in Warsaw, and in Vienna under Leschetizky; professional debut in Vienna (1887), Paris (1889), London (1890), U.S. (1891); established himself as interpreter of Schumann, Chopin, Liszt, and Rubinstein. Composer of an opera (*Manru*), a symphony in B minor, concertos, and many orchestral and piano pieces, including well-known minuet. During World War I, he devoted himself to the Polish cause; aided in organizing a "general committee of assistance for the victims of the war in Poland" (1914); toured U.S., raising funds by concerts for Polish relief. After war, went to Warsaw and formed coalition ministry, in which he was prime minister and minister of foreign affairs, and which held office for ten months (Jan. 17, 1919–Nov. 27, 1919).

**Pa·dil′la** (pä·thē′yä), **Ezequiel.** 1890–1971. Mexican lawyer and politician; foreign minister of Mexico (1940–45).

**Padilla, Juan de.** 1500?–?1544. Spanish Franciscan missionary; to New Spain (c. 1528); accompanied Coronado into New Mexico (1540–42); established first mission in the Southwest; murdered by Indians.

**Pa·dil′la** (pä·thē′lyä), **Juan López de.** 1490–1521. Spanish revolutionist; led uprising of the communes against absolutism (1520); defeated, captured, and executed. His wife, **María Pa·che′co** [pä·chā′kō] (d. 1531), led rebellion after husband's death and defended Toledo (1521–22); took refuge in Portugal after fall of Toledo.

**Pad′ma·sam′bha·va** (pŭd′mȧ·sŭm′bȧ·vȧ), *i.e.* "born of the lotus." *Real name not known.* fl. 8th century A.D. Buddhist scholar and monk; from Kafiristan carried Buddhist religion into Tibet; founded Lamaism (c. 770); his life and work obscured in legends.

**Padovanino, il.** See under Dario VAROTARI.

**Pae·o′ni·us** (pē·ō′nĭ·ŭs). Greek sculptor of late 5th century B.C., of Mende in Thrace; chiefly known for his Nike (Victory), carved for Messenians and Naupactians and placed at Olympia as a trophy, discovered in 1875.

**Pa′er** (pä′ĕr), **Ferdinando.** 1771–1839. Italian composer, esp. of operas; appointed by Napoleon director of Théâtre Italien; became (1832) music director for Louis Philippe, and a professor at conservatory of music, Paris. Among his notable operas are *Circe* (1791), *Camilla* (1801), *Sargino* (1803), *Eleonora* (1804), *L'Agnese* (1811), and *Un Caprice de Femme* (1834).

**Paes** (pīsh), **Sidônio Bernardino Cardosa da Silva.** 1872–1918. Portuguese statesman; active in republican movement; member of cabinet (1911); minister to Germany (1913–16); a leader in the revolt (1917); president of Portugal (Dec., 1917–Dec., 1918); assassinated.

**Paesiello.** See PAISIELLO.

**Paets** (păts). = PÄTS.

**Paetus, Caecina.** See ARRIA.

**Pá′ez** (pä′ās), **Federico.** Ecuadorian political leader; made provisional president of Ecuador (called "Supreme Head of the State") by the army (Sept. 26, 1935); elected provisional president (Aug. 10, 1937); resigned (Oct. 23) under pressure of armed forces

**Páez, José Antonio.** 1790–1873. Venezuelan soldier and political leader; in War of Independence (1810–22), won victories over Spanish that were chiefly responsible for bringing Venezuela into new republic of Great Colombia; led in revolt against Bolívar (1829) and became first president of new republic of Venezuela (1830); president and dictator (1831–46); led revolt, as leader of conservatives, against President Monagas (1847); was captured and imprisoned (1847–50); went into exile (1850); returned (1858) and was made minister to U.S. (1860). Again proclaimed dictator (1861), but forced to resign (1863) and go into exile.

**Pa′ga·ni′ni** (pä′gä·nē′nē), **Niccolò.** 1782–1840. Italian violinist; toured Europe with great success (1798–1801, 1805 ff.). Among his compositions are 6 violin concertos, 24 caprices, 12 sonatas for violin and guitar, and sets of variations for violin.

**Page** (pāj), **Charles Grafton.** 1812–1868. American physicist, b. Salem, Mass.; developed induction apparatus which in principle is the modern induction coil; made a small reciprocating electromagnetic engine (1846), and an electric locomotive (1850–51).

**Page, Curtis Hidden.** 1870–1946. American educator and writer; professor of English, Dartmouth (from 1911); author of *A History of Japanese Poetry* (1923); translator of many French works, including Molière's *Tartuffe*, Anatole France's *The Man Who Married a Dumb Wife.*

**Page, Frederick Handley.** 1885–1962. English airplane manufacturer; managing director, Handley Page, Inc.

**Page, John.** 1743–1808. American Revolutionary leader and close friend of Thomas Jefferson; lieutenant governor of Virginia (1776–79); colonel in Continental army in Yorktown campaign; member, U.S. House of Representatives (1789–97); governor of Virginia (1802–05). His grandson **Thomas Jefferson Page** (1808–1899) was a naval officer and explorer; commanded *Water Witch* in exploring La Plata River (1853–56); his ship was fired upon (Feb. 1, 1855) by a Paraguayan fort; second formidable expedition, with Page as fleet captain, negotiated treaty with Paraguay, and Page continued explorations up Paraguay River (1859–60); served in Confederate navy through Civil War. See also Thomas Nelson PAGE.

**Page, Leigh.** 1884–1952. American physicist; professor of mathematical physics (1922–52), Yale; developed a theory of electromagnetism.

**Page, Thomas Nelson.** 1853–1922. Great-grandson of John Page (1743–1808). American novelist and diplomat, b. in Hanover County, Va.; practiced law, Richmond, Va. (1874–93); moved to Washington, D.C. (1893), and devoted himself to writing; U.S. ambassador to Italy (1913–19). Among the best known of his books are *In Ole Virginia* (1887), *Two Little Confederates* (1888), *The Old South* (1892), *Social Life in Old Virginia* (1897), *The Old Gentleman of the Black Stock* (1897), *Red Rock* (1898), *The Old Dominion* (1908), *Robert E. Lee, Man and Soldier* (1911), *Italy and the World War* (1920).

**Page, Walter Hines.** 1855–1918. American journalist and diplomat, b. Cary, N.C.; on staff of the *Forum*, New York (1887–95), *Atlantic Monthly* (1895–98), of which he was editor (1898–99); partner in Doubleday, Page & Co., publishers (from 1899); founded and edited *The World's Work* (1900–13); U.S. ambassador to Great Britain (1913–18), during period of World War. Author of *The Rebuilding of Old Commonwealths* (1902); *A Publisher's Confession* (1905); *The Southerner* (1909), a novel published under the pseudonym **Nicholas Worth** (wûrth). His letters appeared in B. J. Hendrick's *The Life and Letters of Walter H. Page* (3 vols., 1922–25).

**Page, William.** 1811–1885. American portrait painter, b. Albany, N.Y. His portraits of John Quincy Adams and William Lloyd Garrison hang in the Boston Art Museum; *Ruth and Naomi*, in New York Historical Society; *The Young Merchants*, in Pennsylvania Academy of Fine Arts, Philadelphia.

**Pag′et** (păj′ĕt; -ĭt), Sir **Henry William.** 1st Marquis of **An′gle·sey** (ăng′g'l·sĭ). 1768–1854. Descendant of William Paget, 1st baron. M.P. (1790–1810). Military commander; served in Flanders (1794), Holland (1799), Peninsula (1808); commanded cavalry and lost leg at Waterloo; lord lieutenant of Ireland (1828–29, 1830–33); favored Catholic emancipation; opposed by O'Connell; field marshal (1846). His son Lord **George Augustus Frederick** (1818–1880) served brilliantly in Crimean War; commanded third line in famous cavalry charge at Balaklava; general (1877); author of *Crimean Journals* (1875). The marquis's nephew Sir **Augustus Berkeley Paget** (1823–1896) was a diplomat; held posts throughout Europe; envoy extraordinary (1867–76), ambassador (1876–83), to King Victor Emmanuel; ambassador at Vienna (1884–93).

**Paget,** Sir **James.** 1814–1899. English surgeon and pathologist. At St. Bartholomew's hospital, London, detected (1835) minute parasite *Trichina spiralis* (a discovery usually credited to Richard Owen); professor of anatomy at Royal Coll. of Surgeons (1847–52) and published the *Lectures on Surgical Pathology* (1853); specialized in pathology of tumors and diseases of bones and joints; first to advocate enucleation of tumors; described (1877) *osteitis deformans*, later called Paget's disease; vice-chancellor of U. of London (1883–95). Successor to John Hunter in surgery and, with Rudolf Virchow, one of founders of modern science of pathology. His brother Sir **George Edward** (1809–1892), physician, was regius professor of medicine, Cambridge (1872–92).
Sons of Sir James Paget were: **Francis** (1851–1911), theologian; regius professor of pastoral theology, Oxford, and canon of Christ Church (1885–92); dean of Christ Church (1892–1901); bishop of Oxford (1901–11); author of an introduction to 5th book of Hooker's *Ecclesiastical Polity* and an essay in *Lux Mundi* (1889) on "Sacraments." **Henry Luke** (1853–1937), prelate; bishop of Chester (1919–32). **Stephen** (1855–1926), surgeon (1885–97); abandoned surgery for propaganda in social struggle against disease; produced *Experiments on Animals* (1900) in justification of vivisection, biographical sketches of surgeons, and a series of essays offering a criticism of life, including *I Wonder* (1911), *Essays for Boys and Girls* (1916), *I Have Reason to Believe* (1921).

**Paget, Violet.** *Pseudonym* **Vernon Lee** (lē). 1856–1935. English essayist and art critic, b. in Normandy; lived in Italy (from 1871). Author of essays, philosophic dialogues, stories, novels, including *Studies of the Eighteenth Century in Italy* (1880), *Limbo* (essays; 1897), *Ariadne in Mantua* (a play; 1903), *Satan the Waster* (1920), *Music and its Lovers* (1932). See E. J. LEE-HAMILTON.

**Paget, William.** 1st Baron **Paget of Beau′de·sert′** (bō′dē·zâr′). 1505–1563. English statesman; sent on diplomatic missions by Henry VIII; privy councilor and secretary of state (1543) and one of Henry's chief advisers; committed to Tower, with Somerset, on charge of conspiring against Warwick's life (1551); degraded from Order of Garter (1552) ostensibly because of discovery of low birth; restored to privy council by Queen Mary (1553); lord privy seal (1556–58).

**Paglia, Antonio della.** *Or* **Antonio degli Pagliaricci.** See PALEARIO.

**Pa′gnol′** (pȧ′nyôl′), **Marcel.** 1895–1974. French playwright and film producer and director; author of *Jazz* (1926), *Topaze* (1928), *Marius* (1929).

**Pahlavi** *or* **Pahlevi.** See RIZA SHAH PAHLAVI; MOHAMMED RIZA PAHLAVI.

**Pai Chung-hsi** (bī′ jŏŏng′shē′). 1893–1966. Chinese general, b. in Kwangsi; commander of various army corps (1926–29); dismissed (1929–31) from all posts because of opposition to Chiang Kai-shek's policies; closely associated with Gen. Li Tsung-jên (*q.v.*) in northern campaigns and later (from 1931) in Nationalist army; vice-chief of staff of Nationalist army (from 1935); assistant to Gen. Joseph W. Stilwell.

**Paige** (pāj), **Leroy Robert.** *Known as* **Satch′el** (săch′ĕl). 1906– . American baseball pitcher, b. Mobile, Ala. Played for Negro teams until he became the first Negro pitcher in the American League (1948).

**Pail′le·ron′** (pä′y'·rôɴ′), **Édouard.** 1834–1899. French writer of verse and plays, including *L'Étincelle* (1879), *Le Monde où l'on s'Ennuie* (1881), *La Souris* (1887); part owner of *Revue des Deux Mondes*, in which many of his poems appeared, including *Le Départ* and *Prière pour la France.*

**Pain** (pān), **Barry Eric Odell.** 1865–1928. English humorist; contributor to *Cornhill Magazine* (1889) and *Punch;* won fame with *Eliza* (1900); author of parodies, including *Another Englishwoman's Love Letters* and *Madge Askinforit*, and ghost stories.

**Pain, James C.** 1837–1923. English fireworks manufacturer; to U.S. (1877); began giving pyrotechnic displays with exhibition at Manhattan Beach, N.Y. (1878). His son **Henry J.** (1858–1935) continued business until its sale (1927) to other interests.

**Paine** (pān). See also PAYNE.

**Paine, Albert Bigelow.** 1861–1937. American author and editor, b. New Bedford, Mass.; on editorial staff of *St. Nicholas Magazine* (1899–1909); author of *The Mystery of Evelin Delorme* (1894), *The Dumpies* (1897), *The Autobiography of a Monkey* (1897), *The Bread Line* (1900), *The Commuters* (1904), *The Tent Dwellers* (1908), *Mark Twain, a Biography* (1912), *Dwellers in Arcady* (1919), *Joan of Arc—Maid of France* (1925), etc.

**Paine, Charles Jackson.** 1833–1916. Great-grandson of Robert Treat Paine (1731–1814). American lawyer and yachtsman, b. Boston; practiced in Boston; served through Civil War. Bore expense of building and sailing two American cup defenders (*Mayflower*, 1886; *Volunteer*, 1887) in the international yacht races, winning both contests against the British challengers.

**Paine, Elijah.** 1757–1842. American jurist, b. Brooklyn, Conn.; migrated to Vermont and developed large stock farm there; justice, state supreme court (1791–93); U.S. senator (1795–1801); judge, U.S. district court for Vermont (1801–42).

**Paine, John Knowles.** 1839–1906. American organist, music teacher, and composer, b. Portland, Me.; teacher of music, Harvard (1862–1906), professor (from 1875), the first professor of music in an American university; composer of oratorios, symphonies, cantatas, songs, and choral music for a performance of Sophocles's *Oedipus Tyrannus*, and organ pieces.

**Paine, Ralph Delahaye.** 1871–1925. American journalist and author; b. Lemont, Ill.; on staff of New York *Herald* (1902) exposing the Beef Trust; author of *The Ships and Sailors of Old Salem* (1909), *The Dragon and the Cross* (1912), *The Call of the Offshore Wind* (1918), *Roads of Adventure* (1922), etc.

**Paine, Robert Treat.** 1731–1814. American jurist, b. Boston; member of Continental Congress (1774–78) and signer of Declaration of Independence; attorney general of Massachusetts (1777–90); judge, Massachusetts supreme court (1790–1804). His son **Robert Treat** (1773–1811) was a poet; grad. Harvard (1792); founded and edited *Federal Orrery* (1794–96), in which his satirical attacks on personages of the day brought social ostracism and physical attacks; best-known poems were *The Invention of Letters* (1795), *The Ruling Passion* (1797), *Adams and Liberty* (1798).

**Paine, Thomas.** 1737–1809. Political philosopher and author, b. Thetford, Eng., son of a Quaker corsetmaker; after various occupations (1757–74), went bankrupt (1774) and emigrated to America; supported himself by contributions to contemporary periodicals; published *Common Sense* (Jan. 10, 1776), a forty-seven page pamphlet urging immediate declaration of independence, which had wide circulation and great influence in concentrating sentiment in favor of immediate independence; served in Continental army (1776); published the *Crisis*, twelve issues during the Revolutionary War, a periodical upholding the colonial cause (1776–83); secretary to congress's committee on foreign affairs (1777–79); clerk of Pennsylvania assembly (1779–81). To Europe (1787); interested in French Revolution (1789); inspired to write *The Rights of Man* (1791–92), defending measures taken in revolutionary France and appealing to the English to overthrow their monarchy and organize a republic; took refuge in France (1792); was tried, convicted of treason, and outlawed from England (1792); became member of French Convention (1792–93); arrested and imprisoned in Paris as an Englishman (Dec., 1793–Nov., 1794); released on request of American minister, James Monroe, who said Paine was an American citizen; remained in Paris, writing and studying (to 1802); published *The Age of Reason* (Part I, 1794; Part II, 1796), a philosophical discussion of his deist belief. Returned to America (1802); found himself involved in political conflict between Jefferson and John Q. Adams; lived last years in ostracism and relative poverty. Elected to American Hall of Fame (1945).

**Paine, Willis Seaver.** 1848–1927. American lawyer and banker; compiled and revised New York State banking laws (enacted 1882); superintendent of banking, State of New York (1885–89); president, The State Trust Co. (1889 ff.). Author of *Paine's New York Banking Laws, Paine's National Banking Laws*, etc.

**Pain'le·vé'** (păɴl'vā'), **Paul.** 1863–1933. French mathematician and statesman; member of Chamber of Deputies (from 1910); minister of public instruction (1915–16), of war (1917), and premier of France (1917); president of Chamber of Deputies (1924) and unsuccessful candidate for presidency of France; again premier of France (1925); minister of war in later cabinets (1925–29) and minister of air (1930–32). Author of books in field of higher mathematics.

**Pain'ter** (pān'tẽr), **William.** 1540?–1594. English translator; published *The Palace of Pleasure* (1566), a collection of tales translated from Boccaccio, Bandello, Cynthius, and other Italian and classical authors, freely used by Elizabethan dramatists.

**Paish** (pāsh), Sir **George.** 1867–1957. English economist and financier; on editorial staff of the *Statist* (1881–1916); adviser to the chancellor of the exchequer (1914–16) and on official mission to U.S. government (Nov., 1914); author of *Railways of Great Britain* (1904), *Railroads of the United States* (1913), *The Road to Prosperity* (1927), *World Economic Suicide* (1929), *The Way Out* (1937).

**Pa'i·siel'lo** (pä'ē·zyĕl'lō) *or* **Pa'e·siel'lo** (pä'ā-), **Giovanni.** 1741–1816. Italian composer, esp. of operas and religious music; called to St. Petersburg by Catherine the Great (1776–84); Kapellmeister to Ferdinand IV in Vienna (1784); called to Paris (1802) by Napoleon to organize chapel music; returned to Naples (1804) under patronage of Joseph Bonaparte and Murat. Among operas are *Il Barbiere di Siviglia* (1780), *Il Re Teodoro* (1784), *Nina Pazza per Amore* (1787), and *La Molinara* (1788); among religious works, masses, oratorios, cantatas, motets, and two Te Deums.

**Paisley,** Baron. See *Claud Hamilton*, under HAMILTON family.

**Pai'va** (pī'vä), **Félix.** 1877– . Paraguayan political leader; provisional president (Aug., 1937–Oct., 1938); elected president (Oct., 1938).

**Paix'hans'** (pĕk'säɴ'), **Henri Joseph.** 1783–1854. French artillery officer; general of division (1848); inventor of the Paixhans gun, one of earliest guns throwing explosive shells.

**Pa'jol'** (pȧ'zhôl'), Comte **Claude Pierre.** 1772–1844. French general in Napoleon's armies; won distinction in battles of Austerlitz, Jena, and Wagram, and in Russian campaign; general of division (1812) and engaged at Lützen, Dresden, and Leipzig; rallied to Napoleon during the Hundred Days; engaged at Waterloo; took active part in Revolution of 1830; appointed peer of France and governor of Paris by Louis Philippe.

**Pa'jon'** (pȧ'zhôɴ'), **Claude.** 1626–1685. French Protestant theologian; founder of theological system known as Pajonism.

**Pa'jou'** (pȧ'zhōō'), **Augustin.** 1730–1809. French sculptor; under commission from Louis XVI, carved decorations for façades of Palais Royal and Palais Bourbon and decorated the opera house at Versailles; executed portrait busts of Descartes, Turenne, Pascal, Bossuet, Buffon, and other notables. His *Psyché* stands in the Louvre.

**Pak'en·ham** (păk'ĕn·ăm), Sir **Edward Michael.** 1778–1815. Irish officer in British army; served with Wellington in the Peninsular War; distinguished himself at Salamanca (1812); major general (1812); defeated by Andrew Jackson and killed in attack upon New Orleans (1815).

**Pak'ing·ton** (păk'ĭng·tŭn). Name of an English Worcestershire family springing from **John Pakington** (d. 1560), lawyer and courtier, to whom Henry VIII gave Worcestershire estates, and represented by barons **Hamp'ton** (hăm(p)'tŭn), including: Sir **John Somerset Pakington** (1799–1880), 1st Baron **Hampton** (orig. surname **Russell;** took name of maternal uncle Sir John Pakington, 8th baronet), secretary for war and colonies under Lord Derby (1852), first lord of admiralty (1858, 1866), secretary for war (1867–68), chief civil-service commissioner (1875–80). **Humphrey Arthur Pakington** (1888– ), son of 3d baron; served in navy (1903–20; retired as lieutenant commander); practiced architecture; rejoined navy (1939); author of books on architecture and of novels including *Four in the Family, The Roving Eye, Family Album, Aunt Auda's Choir* (1942).

**Pa·la'cio Val·dés'** (pä·lä'thyō väl·dās'), **Armando.** 1853–1938. Spanish novelist; member of the Ateneo;

edited *La Revista Europea* (1875–78); known esp. for psychological and naturalistic novels, as *El Señorito Octavio* (1881), *El Idilio de un Enfermo* (1884?), *José* (1885), *El Maestrante* (1893), *Los Majos de Cádiz* (1896), *La Aldea Perdida* (1903), *Tristán o el Pesimismo* (1906), *Los Papeles del Doctor Angélico* (1911).

**Pa′lac·ký** (pȧ′lȧts·kē), **František.** 1798–1876. Czech historian and politician; Bohemian historiographer (1839); member of Slavic congress at Prague (1848) and of first Austrian Reichstag; sought creation of an autonomous Czech nation to include Bohemia, Moravia, and Silesia; member of Austrian Herrenhaus (from 1861); chief work, *History of Bohemia* (5 vols., 1836–67). See Baron Franz von RIEGER.

**Pa·la′de** (pȧ·lä′dē), **George Emil.** 1912– . American biologist, b. Rumania. At U. of Bucharest (1940–45), Rockefeller Institute for Medical Research, later Rockefeller U. (1946–73), Yale U. (1973– ); awarded (with Albert Claude and Christian de Duve) Nobel prize for physiology or medicine (1974).

**Pa′lae·ol′o·gus** (pā′lē·ŏl′ō·gŭs; păl′ē-). *Plural* **Pa′lae·ol′o·gi** (-jī). Name of a (Greek) Byzantine family which furnished the last eight emperors of the Eastern Roman Empire (1259–1453): Michael VIII, Andronicus II and III, John V, VII, and VIII, Manuel II, and Constantine XI (or XIII). See these names, also *John VI Cantacuzene*, page 784. Branch families of the Palaeologi ruled in the Italian marquisate of Montferrat (1305–1533) and in the Morea (1383–1460).

**Pa′la·fox′ de Men·do′za** (pä′lä·fōks′ thā mān·dō′thä), **Juan de.** 1600–1659. Spanish prelate; appointed bishop of Puebla de los Ángeles, Mexico (1639); viceroy (1642); pursued charitable policy toward Indians; laid Jesuits under interdict (1647); transferred to bishopric of Osma, Castile (1653). Author of historical, judicial, and theological works.

**Palafox y Mel′zi** (ē mĕl′thē), **José de.** Duke of **Sar′a·gos′sa** (săr′ȧ·gŏs′ȧ). 1775–1847. Spanish soldier; known particularly for his defense of Saragossa in Peninsular War (1808–09); captain general of Aragon (1841 ff.); ardent defender of absolutism under Ferdinand VII; created duke of Saragossa and grandee of Spain (1836).

**Pal′a·mas** (păl′ȧ·mȧs; pä·lä·mäs′), **Gregorius.** 1296?–1359. Greek mystic and chief apologist for the Hesychasts, also called Palamites; in late life, archbishop of Thessalonica.

**Pa·la·mas′** (pä·lä·mäs′), **Kostes.** 1859–1943. Greek poet; author of *The Songs of My Country* (1886), *Life Immovable* (1904; Eng. trans. 1919), *Royal Blossom* (Eng. trans. 1923), etc.

**Pa·lan′der** (pȧ·lăn′dēr), **Louis.** 1842–1920. Swedish naval officer and arctic explorer; knighted and took name **Palander af Ve′ga′** (äv vā′gȧ′) because he was navigator of ship *Vega* on Nordenskjöld's expedition (1878–80) to discover Northeast Passage; admiral (1910).

**Pa′la′prat′** (pȧ′lȧ′prȧ′), **Jean.** Sieur **de Bi′got′** (dē bē′gō′). 1650–1721. French playwright; coauthor of comedies with David Augustine de Brueys (*q.v.*).

**Pa′le·a′rio** (pä′lā·ä′ryō), **Aonio.** *Also* **Antonio del′la Pa′glia** (dāl′lä pä′lyä) *or* **de′gli Pa′glia·ric′ci** (dā′lyē pä′lyä·rēt′chē). *Lat.* **A·o′ni·us Pal′e·ar′i·us** (ā·ō′nĭ·ŭs păl′ē·âr′ĭ·ŭs; pā′lē-). 1503?–1570. Italian humanist; works branded as heretical; objected chiefly to doctrine of purgatory; after two previous trials for heresy, seized by Inquisition; imprisoned for three years and burned at stake. His works include a didactic poem *De Immortalitate Animarum* (1536) and tracts.

**Pa′lé′o′logue′** (pȧ′lā′ō′lôg′), **Maurice.** 1859–1944. French diplomat; minister to Bulgaria (1907–12); ambassador to Russia (1914–17); director-general of French foreign office (1921–25); author of *La Russie des Tsars pendant la Grande Guerre* (3 vols., 1921) and *Un Grand Réaliste* (biography of Cavour, 1926).

**Pa′le·stri′na** (pä′lā·strē′nä; *Angl.* păl′ĕs·trē′nȧ), **Giovanni.** *In full* **Giovanni Pier·lui′gi da** (pyĕr·lwē′jē dä) **Palestrina.** 1526?–1594. Italian composer of church music, b. Palestrina; protégé of Pope Julius III; maestro di cappella, Cappella Giulia, Rome (1551), St. John Lateran (1555–61), and Santa Maria Maggiore (1561 ff.); composer to Papal chapel (1565); master of music, Cappella Giulia (1571 ff.). Composed exclusively in medieval church modes; works mark apex of attainment in field of older music; compositions include masses, hymns, as *Stabat Mater*, motets, litanies, magnificats, and madrigals.

**Pa′ley** (pā′lĭ), **Frederick Apthorp.** 1815–1888. English classical scholar; private tutor, Cambridge (1860–74); professor of classical literature, Kensington (1874–77); edited *Tragedies of Euripides* (1857), *Epics of Hesiod* (1861), and translations of Aeschylus, Aristophanes, Propertius, Pindar, with English commentary; author of a *Manual of Gothic Mouldings* (1845).

**Paley, William.** 1743–1805. English theologian and utilitarian philosopher; archdeacon of Carlisle (1782); subdean of Lincoln (1795); published lectures, *The Principles of Moral and Political Philosophy* (1785), which became ethical textbook at Cambridge; his most original essay, *Horae Paulinae* (1790), showed improbability of hypothesis that New Testament is a "cunningly devised fable"; author also of a compendium of orthodox arguments in refutation of the deists, *View of the Evidences of Christianity* (1794), and a presentation of the a posteriori argument for existence of God, *Natural Theology* (1802).

**Pal′frey** (pôl′frĭ), **John Gorham.** 1796–1881. American Unitarian clergyman and historian; proprietor and editor, *North American Review* (1835–43); member, U.S. House of Representatives (1847–49); postmaster, Boston (1861–67); author of *History of New England* (4 vols., 1858–75), and volumes of sermons and theological treatises.

**Pal′grave** (păl′grāv; pôl′-), Sir **Francis.** 1788–1861. English historian; son of Meyer Cohen, a Jewish stockbroker in London; changed name by royal permission (1823); deputy keeper of public records (1838–61); author of *History of Normandy and England* (4 vols., 1851–64), carrying down to 1101. His sons were: **Francis Turner** (1824–1897), poet and critic; friend of Tennyson; official of education department (1855–84); professor of poetry, Oxford (1885–95); published volumes of poetry, including *Visions of England* (1880–81) and *Amenophis* (1892), critical essays, including *Landscape in Poetry* (1897); edited well-known anthologies *Golden Treasury of the best Songs and Lyrical Poems in the English Language* (1861; a second series, 1897) and *Treasury of Sacred Song* (1889). **William Gifford** (1826–1888), traveler and diplomat, became a Jesuit missionary in Syria and Arabia, often traveling in disguise as a Syrian doctor; held many posts through the Orient; minister to Uruguay (1884); author of travel narratives. Sir **Robert Harry Inglis** (1827–1919), banker and economist, edited *The Economist* (1877–83), and *Dictionary of Political Economy* (3 vols., 1894–99); author of books on banking and taxation.

**Palikao,** Comte **de.** See COUSIN-MONTAUBAN.

**Pa′lis′sot′ de Mon′te·noy′** (pȧ′lē′sō′ dē môɴt′nwȧ′), **Charles.** 1730–1814. French writer; attacked the Encyclopedists, notably Rousseau and Diderot, as in his comedies *Le Cercle* (1755) and *Les Philosophes* (1760), and his poem *La Dunciade ou la Guerre des Sots* (1764).

**Pa'lis'sy'** (pȧ'lē'sē'), **Bernard.** c. 1510–1589. French potter, known for a superior kind of rustic pottery, esp. his "rustiques figulines," faïence with reliefs of small animals, fish, reptiles, etc. Author of an autobiography, a description of his investigations in ceramics (unsuccessful attempts to discover secret of making white enamel), and of works on agriculture, natural philosophy, and religion.

**Pa'litzsch** (pä'lĭch), **Johann Georg.** 1723–1788. German peasant astronomer; first discovered Halley's comet (1758) and the periodic variability of the star Algol (1782).

**Pa·liz'zi** (pä·lēt'tsē), **Filippo.** 1818–1899. Italian painter, b. Vasto, Chieti; cofounder (with Domenico Morelli) of Neapolitan naturalist school; known esp. for paintings of animals.

**Pal'la·das** (păl'ȧ·dȧs). Greek epigrammatist of Alexandria, of early 5th century A.D.

**Pal'la·di'no** (päl'lä·dē'nō), **Eusapia.** 1854–1918. Italian spiritualistic medium who succeeded for a time in deceiving many noted scientists, including Sir Oliver Lodge; during exhibitions in U.S. (1909–10), she was caught in use of trickery by Professor Hugo Münsterberg of Harvard.

**Pal·la'dio** (päl·lä'dyō), **Andrea.** 1508-1580. Italian architect; adapted principles of Roman architecture to requirements of his time; revolted against ornamentation; responsible for popularity of motif (Palladian motif) of the bay with a round-headed opening flanked by two square-headed openings. Works include, in Venice, San Giorgio Maggiore and Capuchin churches, and palaces on Grand Canal. Inigo Jones imported Palladio's classic style into England and, later, architects of Georgian period founded on it designs which came to be characterized as *Palladian.*

**Pal·la'di·us** (pȧ·lā'dĭ·ŭs). 368?–?431. Greek Christian ecclesiastic and writer; bishop of a see in Asia Minor; author of *Historia Lausiaca*, addressed to Lausus, a chamberlain at imperial court, and containing descriptions of monkish life in Egypt and Palestine.

**Palladius, Rutilius Taurus Aemilianus.** Roman writer of 4th century (or later); author of a calendar of Roman agriculture, *De Re Rustica*, widely read in the Middle Ages.

**Pal'las** (päl'äs), **Peter Simon.** 1741–1811. German naturalist and traveler, esp. in eastern and southeastern Russia and Siberia (1768–74), and southern Russia and the Crimea (1793–94). Known for his collection of natural history specimens, accounts of his travels, and contributions to geography, geology, botany, zoology, archaeology, and ethnology.

**Pal'la·va** (pŭl'lȧ·vȧ). A warrior dynasty of Hindu kings, of uncertain origin, ruling (300?–888 A.D.) in the Tamil country of southern India; used both Prakrit and Sanskrit languages; capital at Kanchi (modern Conjeeveram), near Madras; overcame Cholas and Cheras; height of their power (550–750); disputed control of Deccan with Chalukyas for more than two centuries; made great contributions to art and architecture; two greatest rulers were **Ma·hen'dra–var'man** [mȧ·hān'drȧ·vŭr'mȧ] (600–625) and **Na'ra·sim'ha–var'man** [nŭ'rȧ·sĭɴ'hȧ-] (625–645); defeated (740) and declined; completely overthrown by Chalukyas and Cholas (end of 9th century); especially important for their voyages to and settlements in Malay lands.

**Pal'la·vi·ci'no** (päl'lä·vē·chē'nō) *or* **Pal'la·vi·ci'ni** (-nē), **Pietro Sforza.** 1607–1667. Italian prelate and writer; joined Society of Jesus (1637); created cardinal by Alexander VII (1659); known esp. for *Storia del Concilio di Trento* (2 vols., 1656–57), written to refute the history by Fra Paolo Sarpi which had been placed on the Index.

**Pal'la·vi·ci'no–Tri·vul'zio** (-trē·vōōl'tsyō), Marchese **Giorgio Guido.** 1796–1878. Italian patriot; member of Carbonari; involved in Confalonieri trial; sentenced to 20 years at hard labor; freed and exiled (1835–40); senator (Turin, 1859); prodictator of Naples; prefect of Palermo (1861–62); created senator of the kingdom.

**Pal'len** (păl'ĕn), **Con'dé' Be·noist'** (kôɴ'dā' bĕ·nwȧ'). 1858–1929. American editor, b. St. Louis, Mo.; managing editor, the *Catholic Encyclopedia* (16 vols., 1907–14); author of *The Philosophy of Literature* (1897), *New Rubaiyat* (1898), *Death of Sir Launcelot and Other Poems* (1902), *Ghost House* (1928), etc.

**Pal'les** *or* **Pal'lis** (pä'lyēs), **Alexandros.** 1851–1935. Modern Greek scholar and poet; advocate of use of modern popular Greek as a literary medium; published a modern popular Greek translation of the *Iliad* and of Euripides's *Cyclops*, and of the four Gospels.

**Pal'li·ser** (păl'ĭ·sẽr), **John.** 1807–1887. Canadian geographer and explorer, b. in Ireland; explored (from 1847) western British America; made topographical determination of boundary between U.S. & Canada from Lake Superior to Pacific Coast. His brother Sir **William** (1830–1882), British cavalry officer, invented method of converting smooth bores into rifled guns (1862); invented chilled cast-iron shot (1863).

**Palm** (pälm), **Johann Philipp.** 1766–1806. German bookdealer; published (1806) pamphlet *Deutschland in seiner Tiefen Erniedrigung* (by an unknown author) attacking Napoleon and conduct of French army in Germany; arrested by order of Napoleon, tried by military court, and shot.

**Pal'ma** (päl'mä), **Jacopo.** *Called* **Palma Vec'chio** (vāk'kyō) *or* **Il Vecchio** (ēl), *i.e.* the Elder. 1480?–1528. Italian painter of Venetian school; among his works are *Adam and Eve, The Three Sisters, Holy Family with St. Catharine, Sleeping Venus, Adoration of the Shepherds, Christ and the Adulteress.* His grandnephew **Jacopo** (1544–1628), *called* **Palma Gio'va·ne** (jō'vä·nā) *or* **Il Giovane** [ēl] (*the Younger*), was also a Venetian painter; marks beginning of transition to the decadence; among his works are *Resurrection of Lazarus, The Brazen Serpent*, and 27 engravings.

**Pal'ma** (päl'mä), **Ricardo.** 1833–1919. Peruvian writer; on staff of Peruvian National Library; active in agitation (1886) resulting in expulsion of Jesuit order from Peru; author of *Los Annales de la Inquisición de Lima* (1863), *Poesías* (1887), and *Tradiciones* (collection of Peruvian legends).

**Palma, Tomás Estrada.** 1835–1908. Cuban patriot and statesman; served in Cuban revolution (1868–78); president of provisional government of Cuba; captured (1877) and imprisoned (1877–78); in exile in Honduras and U.S. (to 1902); during Cuban revolution (1898), served as minister plenipotentiary in the U.S. for the Republic of Cuba; elected first president of Cuba (1902–06); re-elected (Mar., 1906); resigned (Sept., 1906).

**Palm'blad'** (pälm'bläd'), **Wilhelm Fredrik.** 1788–1852. Swedish author of philological, historical, and geographical treatises, translations of Aeschylus and Sophocles, and two novels.

**Pal'mei·rim'** (päl'mȧ·ē·rēɴ'), **Luiz Augusto.** 1825–1893. Portuguese poet; known esp. for patriotic and popular poems, and for comedies.

**Palm'er** (päm'ẽr), **Albert Marshman.** 1838–1905. American theater manager, in New York (from 1872); founded Actor's Fund of America (1882).

**Palmer, Alexander Mitchell.** 1872–1936. American lawyer and politician, b. Moosehead, Pa.; member, U.S.

House of Representatives (1909–15); alien property custodian (1917–19); attorney general of the U.S. (1919–21).

**Palmer, Alice Elvira,** *nee* **Free′man** (frē′măn). 1855–1902. American educator, b. Colesville, N.Y.; professor of history, Wellesley Coll. (1879–82); president, Wellesley (1882–87); m. (1887) George Herbert Palmer (*q.v.*); dean of women, U. of Chicago (1892–95); author of a book of verse, *A Marriage Cycle* (pub. 1915). Elected to American Hall of Fame (1920).

**Palmer, Austin Norman.** 1859–1927. American penman and educator; originated method of handwriting (Palmer method) taught widely in American schools.

**Palmer, Charles Skeele.** 1858–1939. American chemist; invented basic process for cracking oils to obtain gasoline (1900); sold rights to Standard Oil Co. (1916).

**Palmer, Daniel David.** 1845–1913. Founder of chiropractic, b. near Toronto, Can.; practiced magnetic healing, Burlington (1883–95) and Davenport, Iowa (1895); developed system of adjusting the joints, esp. of the spine, by manual manipulation for the cure of disease and opened (1898) Palmer School of Chiropractic in Davenport, carried on (after 1903) by his son **Bartlett Joshua** (1881–1961). Author of *Textbook of the Science, Art and Philosophy of Chiropractic* (1910), *The Chiropractor* (1914), etc.

**Palmer, Edward Henry.** 1840–1882. English Orientalist; lord almoner's professor of Arabic, Cambridge (1871–81); during Egyptian rebellion (1882) sent by Gladstone on pacificatory mission among Arabs; interpreter in chief to force in Egypt; ambushed and murdered by Arab robbers. Author of *The Desert of the Exodus* (1871), etc.

**Palmer, Erastus Dow.** 1817–1904. American sculptor, b. Pompey, N.Y.; studio, Albany, N.Y. (1846). Among his works are: *Indian Girl* and *White Captive*, now in Metropolitan Museum of Art, New York City; *Chancellor Robert R. Livingston*, in the Capitol, Washington, D.C.; and portrait busts of Washington Irving, Erastus Corning, Henry Burden, etc. His son **Walter Launt** (1854–1932) was a painter; studio in New York (1877) and Albany (1891); excelled in landscapes, esp. of winter scenes.

**Palmer, Frederick.** 1873–1958. American war correspondent and writer, b. Pleasantville, Pa.; correspondent in Greek War (1897), from Klondike and the Philippines (1897–98), relief of Peking (1900), Russo-Japanese War (1904–05), Balkan War (1912), etc., and with British army and fleet (1914–16); served in A.E.F. in France (1917–19). Among his many books are *Going to War in Greece* (1897), *With Kuroki in Manchuria* (1904), *America in France* (1918), *Newton D. Baker—America at War* (1931), *The Man With a Country* (1935), etc.

**Palmer, George Herbert.** 1842–1933. American scholar and educator, b. Boston; grad. Harvard (1864); teacher, in Harvard, of Greek (1870–72), philosophy (1872–89), natural religion, moral philosophy, and civil polity (1889–1913). Author of *The Odyssey of Homer* (a translation, 1884), *The Antigone of Sophocles* (1899), *The Field of Ethics* (1901), *The Nature of Goodness* (1903), *The Life of Alice Freeman Palmer* (1908), *The Problem of Freedom* (1911), *Formative Types in English Poetry* (1918), *Altruism; Its Nature and Varieties* (1919), etc. See Alice Freeman PALMER.

**Palmer, Horatio Richmond.** 1834–1907. American composer and music director; dean of Summer School of Music at Chautauqua, N.Y. (1877–91); composer of church music, esp. hymns; author of words and music for *Yield not to temptation; Galilee, blue Galilee;* and music for *Just for Today*, etc.

**Palmer, James Crox′all** (?krŏk′sôl). 1811–1883. American naval surgeon; with Wilkes exploring expedition (1838–42), on the steam frigate laying first Atlantic cable (1857), served through Civil War, surgeon general of the navy (1872–73). His brother **John Williamson** (1825–1906) was a journalist; to California in '49 gold rush; settled in New York as writer (c. 1852); in Confederate service during Civil War; again free-lance writer in New York (from 1870); author of poetry, travel books, plays, and essays; best-known poems, *Stonewall Jackson's Way*, *Ned Braddock*, and *The Maryland Battalion.*

**Palmer, James Shedden.** 1810–1867. American naval officer; during Civil War, in command of *Iroquois* under Farragut in passing Vicksburg batteries (June, 1862) and of Farragut's flagship, the *Hartford*, in passing Port Hudson (Mar., 1863); rear admiral (1866).

**Palmer, John Leslie.** 1885–1944. English dramatic critic and novelist; on staff of *Saturday Review* (1910–15); in war-trade division of intelligence dept. (1915–19); delegate to Peace Conference, Paris (1919); member of permanent secretariat of League of Nations (1920). Author of studies on the theater, works on Molière (1930) and Ben Jonson (1934), and *The Happy Fool* (1922), *Jennifer* (1926), *Timothy* (1931), *The Hesperides* (1936). Collaborator with **Hilary Aidan St. George Saunders** under joint pseudonym **Francis Bee′ding** (bē′dĭng), on novels, including *Death Walks in Eastrepps, Five Flamboys, Little White Hag, Pretty Sinister, Three Fishers.*

**Palmer, John McCauley.** 1817–1900. American lawyer and political leader, b. in Scott County, Ky.; served through Civil War; brigadier general (1861); major general (1862); governor of Illinois (1869–73); U.S. senator (1891–97); presidential candidate of Gold Democrats (1896).

**Palmer, Ray.** 1808–1887. American Congregational clergyman and hymn writer, b. Little Compton, R.I.; among his hymns are *My faith looks up to Thee; Away from earth my spirit turns; Take me, O my Father, take me.*

**Palmer, Roger.** Earl of **Cas′tle·maine′** (kȧs′'l·mān′). 1634–1705. English royalist and Roman Catholic pamphleteer; m. (1659) Barbara Villiers (*q.v.*); accused of complicity in Popish Plot; as James II's envoy, offended Pope Innocent XI by insistence on appointments; exempted from Act of Indemnity, escaped to Continent.

**Palmer, Roundell.** 1st Earl of **Sel′borne** (sĕl′bôrn; -bĕrn). 1812–1895. English jurist and hymnologist; solicitor general (1861); attorney general (1863–66); opposed Gladstone's Irish Church policy; as lord chancellor (1872–74, 1880–85) instituted judicature reforms. Edited hymnal; wrote liturgical and ecclesiastical articles. His son **William Waldegrave** (1859–1942), 2d earl, Viscount **Wol′mer** (wo͝ol′mẽr); M.P. (1885); undersecretary for colonies (1895–1900); 1st lord of admiralty (1900–05); as high commissioner for South Africa and governor of Transvaal and Orange River colonies (1905–10), facilitated reconstruction requisite for setting up responsible government in these colonies; uncompromising opponent of Parliament Bill; minister of agriculture (1915), resigned (1916) because of Asquith's policy of compromise with Irish. The 2d earl's son **Roundell Cecil** (1887– ), 3d earl, Viscount **Wolmer,** M.P. (1910–40); director of cement, ministry of works and buildings (1940–42); minister of economic warfare (Feb., 1942).

**Palmer, Samuel.** 1805–1881. English ideal landscape painter and etcher; influenced by mystic genius of William Blake; known for his illustrations of *L'Allegro* and *Il Penseroso.*

**Palmer, Walter Launt.** See under Erastus Dow PALMER.

**Palm'er·ston** (päm'ẽr·stŭn), 3d Viscount (in Irish peerage). **Henry John Temple.** *Nickname* **Pam** (păm). 1784–1865. English statesman; Tory M.P. (1807); secretary for war (1809–28), repeatedly refusing preferment; supported Canning and friends (from 1822) and left ministry (1828); committed himself to parliamentary reform, lent support to Catholic emancipation, associated himself with Whig party (1830); foreign secretary under Lord Grey (1830); effected independence of Belgium (1830–31); saved Portugal and Spain from absolutism by supporting constitutional party and queens Donna Maria and Isabella through his quadruple alliance (1834); rescued Turkey from Russia and maintained her integrity by treaty (1840); effected the closing of Bosporus and Dardanelles (1841); annexed Hong Kong and opened the five ports (1840–41); retired (1841). Foreign secretary under Lord John Russell (1846); supported Swiss against French and Austrian interference, Sicilians against king of Naples, king of Sardinia against Austria; supported David Pacifico's claims on Greek government by sending fleet to Peiraeus and defended his action in House of Commons in a five-hour speech (1850), including the "civis Romanus sum" phrase; on expressing to French ambassador personal approval of Louis Napoleon's coup d'état, dismissed by Lord John Russell (1851); home secretary (1853–55); prime minister (1855–65, except short interval); maintained integrity of Turkey and Turkish territories in Africa; opposed construction of Suez canal; approved advance of Italian independence by French invasion but suspected Napoleon III; supported policy of neutrality in American Civil War; made vain attempt to protect Poles (1863) and Denmark (1864) from Austria and Prussia. Conceded to have held office with more general acceptance than any minister since Chatham.

**Palm'gren'** (pȧlm'grān'), **Selim.** 1878–1951. Finnish pianist and composer of operas (*Daniel Hjort*, 1910, etc.), orchestral works, and many piano pieces, including the well-known *Refrain du Berceau.*

**Pal·mie'ri** (päl·myâ'rē), **Luigi.** 1807–1896. Italian physicist; inventor of a rain gauge, a seismograph, an electrometer, etc.

**Pa'lo·mi'no de Cas'tro y Ve·las'co** (pä'lō·mē'nō thā käs'trō ē vā·läs'kō), **Antonio Aciscio** *or* **Acislo.** 1653–1726. Spanish painter; court painter at Madrid (1688 ff.) Paintings include frescoes in churches of San Juan del Mercado and Nuestra Señora de los Desamparados at Valencia. Known esp. for his treatise on painting *El Museo Pictórico y Escala Óptica* containing a history of painting and a biographical dictionary of Spanish artists.

**Pa·lo'u** (pä·lō'ōō), **Francisco.** 1722?–?1789. Franciscan missionary in America, b. in Majorca; accompanied Junípero Serra to Mexico (1749); with Serra, headed Franciscan group that replaced Jesuits in Lower California (1768); went northward (1773); set boundary stone between Lower and Upper California, used (1848) to fix boundary between U.S. and Mexico; explored San Francisco peninsula and founded (1776) mission still standing in heart of San Francisco. Author of a chronicle of the Franciscans in California.

**Pals'grave** (pălz'grāv; pôlz'-), **John.** 1480?–1554. English grammarian; author of one of earliest French grammars for English use, *Lesclarcissement de la Langue Francoyse* (1530).

**Pal'tock** (?pôl'tŭk), **Robert.** 1697–1767. English attorney and author of original and striking romance, *The Life and Adventures of Peter Wilkins, a Cornish Man* (1751).

**Pa'lu·dan–Mül'ler** (pȧ'lōō·dȧn·mül'ẽr), **Frederik.** 1809–1876. Danish poet; among his works are *The Dancing Girl* (1833), *Amor and Psyche* (lyrical drama, 1834), *Zuleima's Flight* (narrative poem, 1835), *Venus* (1841), *Tithonus* (1844), *Adam Homo* (in ottava rima, 1841–48), and *Kalanus* (lyrical drama, 1857).

**Pam.** Nickname of Viscount PALMERSTON.

**Pam'phi·lus** (păm'fĭ·lŭs). Greek painter of early 4th century B.C.; succeeded Eupompos (*q.v.*) as head of Sicyonian school; teacher of Apelles.

**Pamphilus.** Greek grammarian and lexicographer of 1st century A.D.; prepared in collaboration with **Zo·pyr'i·on** (zō·pĭr'ĭ·ŏn) a Greek lexicon (95 books, all now lost), an epitome of which, by Diogenianus (*q.v.*), is extant.

**Pamphilus of Caes'a·re'a** (sĕs'ȧ·rē'ȧ; sĕz'ȧ-; sē'zȧ-). d. 309. Christian writer and teacher of Caesarea; founded school at Caesarea; imprisoned (307–309) during persecution under Emperor Maximinus, and martyred; collaborated with Eusebius of Caesarea (*q.v.*) in edition of the Septuagint from text in Origen's *Hexapla;* wrote an apology for Origen (5 books, now lost).

**Pa·nae'ti·us** (pȧ·nē'shĭ·ŭs). Greek Stoic philosopher of 2d century B.C., of Rhodes; studied under Diogenes; taught in Athens and Rome; friend of Laelius and the younger Scipio (*qq.v.*).

**Pan Chao** and **Pan Ch'ao.** See under PAN KU.

**Panc'koucke'** (päɴ'kōōk'). Family of French booksellers and writers, including: **André Joseph** (1700–1753), who founded the business in his native city, Lille. His son **Charles Joseph** (1736–1798), who established the business in Paris, bought and directed the *Mercure de France* (with his brother-in-law J. B. A. Suard), founded (1789) *Moniteur.* Charles Joseph's son **Charles Louis Fleury** (1780–1844), who carried on business in Paris. Charles Louis Fleury's son **Ernest** (1808–1886).

**Pan'cras** (păng'krăs), Saint. *Lat.* **Pan·cra'ti·us** (păn·krā'shĭ·ŭs; păng-). c. 290–304. Child Christian martyr at Rome in reign of Diocletian; later regarded as patron saint of children.

**Pan'der** (pän'dẽr), **Christian Heinrich.** 1794–1865. Russian zoologist; regarded as a founder of science of embryology; famed for studies of development of the chick within the egg.

**Pan'do** (pän'dō), **José Manuel.** 1848?–1917. Bolivian soldier and Liberal political leader, b. La Paz; head of revolt (1899); president of Bolivia (1899–1904); settled boundary disputes with Brazil and Chile.

**Pando, Manuel de.** See MIRAFLORES.

**Pan'dulf** (păn'dŭlf). d. 1226. Roman papal envoy to England; excommunicated King John (1211); received King John's submission (1213); elected bishop of Norwich (1216); exercised practically royal authority in England during minority of Henry III (1219–21).

**Panduro, Lorenzo Hervás y.** See HERVÁS Y PANDURO.

**Pan'dya** (pän'dyȧ) *or* **Pan'da·ya** (pän'dȧ·yȧ). An early Hindu (Tamil) dynasty ruling (from c. 4th century B.C.) in extreme south of India (modern Madura and Tinnevelly); by some identified with the Pandavas whose early wars for the conquest of India are described in the great Indian epic *Mahabharata;* carried on trade with Romans at beginning of Christian Era; succeeded by Cholas and Cheras, but retained control of small kingdom until overthrown by Mohammedans (1304 A.D.), thus boasting continuous succession for more than 2000 years.

**P'an Fei** (pän' fā'). d. 501 A.D. Favorite concubine of a Chinese emperor of the Ch'i dynasty; said to have introduced the practice of binding feet of Chinese women.

**Pan'ga·los** (päng'gä·lôs), **Theodoros.** 1878–1952. Greek soldier and statesman; commander in chief of army in Thrace (1922); seized power as dictator (1925–26); proclaimed president of Republic of Greece (1926); overthrown (Aug., 1926) and imprisoned (1926–28).

**Pa′nhard′** (på′når′), **René**. 1841–1908. French automotive engineer; with Levassor, mounted an internal combustion engine on a chassis (1891); founder and director of firm of Panhard and Levassor, an early automobile manufactory.

**Panicale, Masolino da.** See MASOLINO DA PANICALE.

**Pa′nin** (pä′nyĭn). Russian noble family, including: Count **Nikita Ivanovich** (1718–1783), ambassador to Denmark (1747) and Sweden (1749), and minister of foreign affairs under Catherine II. His brother Count **Pëtr Ivanovich** (1721–1789), general, distinguished himself in Seven Years' War. Pëtr's son Count **Nikita Petrovich** (1770–1837), minister to the Netherlands and later to Prussia, vice-chancellor and foreign minister at beginning of Paul I's reign; banished (1804). And the second Nikita's son Count **Viktor Nikitich** (1801–1874), minister of justice (1841–62).

**Pa′ni·ni** (pä′nĭ·nĭ). fl. 350 B.C. Sanskrit grammarian, of whom little is known, b. probably in northern Punjab; wrote the oldest Sanskrit grammar that has been preserved; systematized all preceding works; marked the line between Vedic and classical Sanskrit.

**Pa·niz′zi** (pä·nēt′sē), Sir **Anthony**. 1797–1879. British librarian, b. in Italy; implicated in conspiracy against Modenese government and escaped to England (1823); assistant librarian, British Museum (1831), keeper of printed books (1837), chief librarian (1856–66). Edited Boiardo's *Orlando Innamorato*, Ariosto's *Orlando Furioso*.

**Pankhi.** Variant of PIANKHI.

**Pank′hurst** (păngk′hûrst), **Emmeline**, *nee* **Goul′den** (gōōl′dĕn). 1858–1928. English woman-suffragist; m. (1879) **Richard Marsden Pankhurst** (d. 1898), barrister, a radical and a woman-suffrage advocate, with whom she effected legislation upon married women's property rights and joined Fabian society. Adopted (from 1905) sensational methods of suffragist propaganda, including (from 1909) window smashing, arson, bombing, hunger strikes; lived to see full and equal suffrage given to men and women. Her daughters supported the suffragist movement with ability and energy: **Christabel** (1880–1958), **Estelle Sylvia** (1882–1960), who published biography of her mother (1935); **Adela** (1885– ).

**Pan Ku** (bän′ gōō′). 32–92 A.D. Chinese historian, of the time of the Eastern Han dynasty; developed a system of philosophy, but chiefly famous for his history of the Western Han dynasty; accused of conspiracy; thrown into prison, where he died; his history completed by his sister **Pan Chao** [jou′] (c. 50–112 A.D.), who also wrote *Lessons for Women*, a work on feminine morality still read. Their brother **Pan Ch'ao** [chou′] (c. 31–102 A.D.) was one of the greatest of Chinese generals; after a successful expedition against the Hsiung-Nu, advanced to Kashgar and Bactria and subdued many petty kingdoms in Turkestan.

**Pan′ne·ton′** (pån′tôɴ′), **Philippe**. *Pseudonym* **Rin′-guet′** (răɴ′gĕ′). 1895–1960. Canadian novelist; author of *30 Arpents* (trans. as *Thirty Acres*, 1940).

**Pann′witz** (pän′vĭts), **Rudolf**. 1881–1969. German philosopher; cofounder (1904) with Otto zur Linde of periodical *Charon;* author of *Deutschland und Europa* (1918), *Kosmos Atheos* (2 vols., 1926), etc.

**Pan·tae′nus** (păn·tē′nŭs). Greek Christian philosopher; head of catechetical school in Alexandria (c. 180–200); master of Clement of Alexandria.

**Pan·ta′le·on** (păn·tā′lē·ŏn), Saint. d. 305. Roman physician, originally, it is believed, from Nicomedia (Izmit) in Bithynia; personal physician to Emperor Galerius; martyred because of his Christian faith; patron saint of physicians.

**Pan′ta·le·o′ni** (pän′tä·lā·ō′nē), **Maffeo**. 1857–1924. Italian economist; favored Italian intervention on Allied side from the outbreak of the World War (1914); supported Fascist movement in Italy and was one of first senators appointed. Author of *Principii d'Economia Pura* (1889).

**Pan·to′ja de la Cruz** (pän·tô′hä thā lä krōōth′), **Juan**. 1551–1608. Spanish painter; court painter to Philip II and Philip III. Among his works are *Birth of the Virgin* and *Nativity*, and portraits, as of Philip II, Archduke Albert, and Infanta Ana.

**Pan′y·a′sis** (păn′ĭ·ā′sĭs; pȧ·nī′ȧ·sĭs) *or* **Pan′y·as′sis** (păn′ĭ·ăs′ĭs). Relative of Herodotus. Greek epic poet of 5th century B.C., in Halicarnassus. Chief works, *Heracleias* and *Ionica;* only fragments extant.

**Pan·zac′chi** (pän·tsäk′kē), **Enrico**. 1840–1904. Italian writer; deputy (1882–85, 1897–1904); in ministry of public instruction (1900–01). Work includes verse, as *Lyrica* (1878), *Racconti e Liriche* (1882), and *Cor Sincerum* (1898), critical works, as *Prosatori e Poeti*, a drama *Villa Giulia*, and several novelle.

**Pan′zer** (pän′tsẽr), **Friedrich**. 1870–1956. German scholar; specialized in study of the literature of legends and sagas.

**Pan·zi′ni** (pän·tsē′nē), **Alfredo**. 1863–1939. Italian writer of literary criticisms, novels and novelle, and a biography of Cavour (1931).

**Pa′o·li** (pä′ô·lē), **Betty**. See Barbara Elisabeth GLÜCK.

**Pa′o·li** (pä′ô·lē), **Pasquale di.** 1725–1807. Corsican patriot; son of Hyacinth Paoli, leader in revolt of 1734. Commanded Corsican forces in expulsion of Genoese (1755); continued struggle for independence after cession of Corsica by Genoa to France; defeated (1769), took refuge in England, where he was welcomed as friend by Dr. Johnson and pensioned; first biographized in Boswell's *Account of Corsica* (1768). Recalled to Corsica (1789) as military governor; led revolt against France (1793); with British help expelled the French and turned island over to England; disappointed in hope of being viceroy, retired to England (1796).

**Paolo**, Fra. See Paolo SARPI.

**Paolo Veronese.** See VERONESE.

**Paolotto**, Fra. See Fra Vittore GHISLANDI.

**Pape** (pāp), **Eric**. 1870–1938. American painter, b. San Francisco; known as historical, landscape, and genre painter, and as illustrator.

**Pa′pen** (pä′pĕn), **Franz von.** 1879–1969. German diplomat, soldier, and statesman; military attaché in Mexico (1913–15) and Washington (1915); recalled by request of U.S. State Department because of "improper activities" (1915); attached to general staff of 4th Turkish army in Palestine until end of World War (1918); member of Prussian Landtag (1921–32); chancellor of Germany (May 31–Nov. 17, 1932); premier of Prussia (to Apr. 11, 1933); vice-chancellor of Germany in Hitler's chancellorship (1933–34); special minister to Austria (1934), ambassador to Austria (1936–38), and Turkey (1939–44); acquitted (1946) of major war crimes.

**Paph·nu′ti·us** (păf·nū′shĭ·ŭs), Saint. Bishop of Thebes, in Upper Egypt; renowned for sanctity of his life; participated in first ecumenical council; present at Synod of Tyre (335).

**Pa′pi·as** (pā′pĭ·ăs). 2d-century Christian prelate and writer; an Apostolic Father; bishop of Hierapolis in Phrygia. Chief work, *Exposition of the Lord's Oracles*, only fragments extant.

**Pa'pin'** (pȧ'păN'), **Denis.** 1647–?1712. French physicist. Pupil and assistant of Huygens; lived (after 1675) mostly in England; assistant of Boyle in physical experiments; experimented with hydraulics and pneumatic transmission of power; made improvements in air pump; invented the condensing pump; invented (1679) a "steam digester" (for softening bones), with which he showed how boiling point is raised or lowered as the pressure exceeds or falls below atmospheric pressure; invented the safety valve; discovered principle of the siphon; credited with being the first (1690) to apply steam to raise a piston; constructed (1690) boat equipped with paddle wheels driven by a waterwheel.

**Pa'pi'neau'** (pȧ'pē'nō'), **Louis Joseph.** 1786–1871. French-Canadian insurgent; cousin of Denis Benjamin Viger; elected (1809) to legislative assembly of Lower Canada; speaker (1815–37); successful in mission of protest to England against projected union of Upper and Lower Canada (1823); led French-Canadian demand for financial reform and an elective provincial council; led legislative assembly of Lower Canada in denial of supplies to governor, and arranged for co-operation of William Lyon Mackenzie and revolutionary party of Upper Canada (1835); attended meeting of delegates at St. Charles that decided upon rebellion (1837); charged with high treason, fled to U.S.; declared a rebel; returned by benefit of general amnesty (1847); member of lower house of Canadian parliament (to 1854).

**Pa·pi'ni** (pä·pē'nē), **Giovanni.** 1881–1956. Italian philosopher and writer, b. Florence; founded and managed several periodicals; at first, caustic opponent of Christianity and iconoclast; converted later (1920) to Roman Catholic orthodoxy. Works include *Il Crepuscolo dei Filosofi* (1907), *L'Altra Metà* (1911), *Le Memorie d'Iddio* (1911), his autobiography *Un Uomo Finito* (1912; Eng. trans. *The Failure*, 1924), *Maschilità* (1915), *L'Esperienza Futurista* (1919), *Storia di Cristo* (1921; Eng. trans. *Life of Christ*, 1923), *Pane e Vino* (1926), *Gog* (1929), *Dante Vivo* (1933), and *Storia della Letteratura Italiana* (1937). See Giuseppe PREZZOLINI.

**Pa·pin'i·an** (pȧ·pĭn'ĭ·ăn). *Full Latin name* **Aemilius Pa·pin'i·a'nus** (pȧ·pĭn'ĭ·ā'nŭs). d. 212 A.D. Roman jurist; friend of Emperor Septimius Severus, who appointed him praetorian prefect (203); executed by Emperor Caracalla (212). Chief works, *Quaestiones* (37 books) and *Responsa* (19 books). Regarded as one of the greatest of Roman jurists.

**Pa·pir'i·us** (pȧ·pĭr'ĭ·ŭs), **Lucius.** *Surnamed* **Cur'sor** (kûr'sẽr; -sôr). Roman general and politician; consul (325, 319, 318, 314, 312 B.C.); dictator (323, 308 B.C.); campaigned successfully against Samnites. His son **Lucius Papirius Cursor** was consul (293, 272) and a general in Third Samnite War.

**Pap'pen·heim** (păp'ĕn·hīm), Count **Gottfried Heinrich zu.** 1594–1632. German imperial army cavalry general in Thirty Years' War; suppressed peasant revolt in Upper Austria (1626); took part in storming of Magdeburg (1631) and battle of Breitenfeld (1631); mortally wounded at battle of Lützen.

**Pap'pus** (păp'ŭs). Greek geometer of late 3d and early 4th century, in Alexandria; regarded as last of great Greek mathematicians. Chief work, *Collection* (8 books), is extant only in incomplete form. Centrobaric method of reckoning area and volume of revolutes is also called *theorem of Pappus.*

**Par'a·cel'sus** (păr'ȧ·sĕl'sŭs), **Philippus Aureolus.** *Real name* **Theophrastus Bombastus von Ho'hen·heim** (fôn hō'ĕn·hīm). 1493?–1541. Alchemist and physician, b. Einsiedeln, Switzerland; investigated mechanics of mining, minerals, and diseases of miners, in mines of Tirol; propounded own theories of treating diseases; forced to leave university because of his defiance of tradition; practiced at various places in Germany and Switzerland, finally settling at Salzburg; opposed humoral theory of disease; taught that diseases are specific entities and can be cured by specific remedies; emphasized value of observation and experience; introduced use of therapeutic mineral baths and of opium, mercury, lead, sulphur, iron, arsenic, and copper sulphate as medicinal substances. Author of medical and occult works, including *Die Grosse Wundartznei* (1530).

**Paradol.** See PRÉVOST-PARADOL.

**Pa·ra'mi·no** (pȧ·rä'mĭ·nō), **John Francis.** 1888–1956. American sculptor; studio in Boston. Among his works are a bronze bust of John Adams, in American Hall of Fame; Declaration of Independence Monument, on Boston Common; World War Memorial, at Yarmouth, Mass.

**Par'do** (pär'tħō), **Manuel.** 1834–1878. Peruvian political leader and banker, b. Lima. Father of José Pardo y Barreda. First civilian president of Peru (1872–76); attempted to restore financial stability; made treaty with Bolivia (1873) which led to War of the Pacific. President of the Senate (1876–78); assassinated.

**Pardo Ba·zán'** (bä·thän'), **Emilia.** 1852–1921. Spanish novelist and critic; m. (1868) José Quiroga (d. 1912); settled at Madrid; founded review *Nuevo Teatro Crítico* (1891–93); professor of literature, U. of Madrid (1916 ff.). Her works include realistic novels, as *Un Viaje de Novios* (1881), *La Madre Naturaleza* (1887), *Insolación* (1889), *La Prueba* (1890), *Adán y Eva* (1894), *La Quimera* (1905), *Belcebú* (1912); critical works, as *La Cuestión Palpitante* (1883) and *La Literatura Francesa Moderna* (3 vols., 1910–14); and short stories, as *Novelas Ejemplares* (1906).

**Par'doe** (pär'dō), **Julia.** 1806–1862. English author of travel books and essays on French history.

**Par'do y Bar·re'da** (pär'tħō ē bär·rĕ'tħä), **José.** 1864–1947. Peruvian political leader, b. Madrid, Spain; son of Manuel Pardo; president of Peru (1904–08; 1915–19); deposed (1919) by Augusto B. Leguía y Salcedo; went to France to live.

**Pa'ré'** (pȧ'rā'), **Ambroise.** 1517?–1590. French surgeon; often called father of modern surgery; served as army surgeon, and physician to Henry II, Francis II, Charles IX, Henry III; introduced use of ligature of arteries instead of cauterization in treatment of wounds. Author of works in French on anatomy, surgery, treatment of wounds, plague, generation, obstetrics, and monsters.

**Pa·re'des** (pä·rā'tħās), **Diego García de.** See Diego GARCÍA DE PAREDES.

**Paredes y Ar'ril·la'ga** (ē är'rē·yä'gä), **Mariano.** 1797–1849. Mexican general; leader of extreme conservative group; supported Santa Anna (1841), but later revolted against him and (1845) led attack against Herrera; president of Mexico (Jan. to July, 1846); his actions largely responsible for war with U.S.; went into exile (1847).

**Pa·re'ja** (pä·rĕ'hä), **Juan de.** *Called* **El Es·cla'vo** (ĕl ȧs·klä'vō), *i.e.* "the Slave." 1606?–1670. Spanish painter, b. Seville, of slave parents of West Indian descent; slave of Velázquez, reputedly freed through intervention of Philip IV; later, pupil and servant of Velázquez. Painter of religious pictures and portraits.

**Pa·re'pa–Ro'sa** (pȧ·rā'pȧ·rō'zȧ), **Euphrosyne,** *nee* **Pa·re'pa de Bo·ye'sku** (*Ruman.* pä·rĕ'pä dĕ bŏ·yĕ'skōō). 1836–1874. English operatic soprano; sang chiefly in England (after 1857); m. Carl Rosa in New York (1867).

**Pa·re'to** (pä·râ'tō), **Vilfredo.** 1848–1923. Economist

and sociologist, of Italian descent; professor, Lausanne (from 1894); developed methods of mathematical analysis in study of economic and sociological problems; widely known for his contempt for democracy and democratic methods; the ideology of Italian Fascism is largely based on the theories of Pareto. Among his books are *Cours d'Économie Politique* (2 vols., 1896–97), *Les Systèmes Socialistes* (2 vols., 1902), *Trattato di Soziologia Generale* (2 vols., 1916; trans. as *The Mind and Society*, 1935), *Compendio di Soziologia Generale* (1920), etc.

**Par′faict′** (pȧr′fĕ′), **François.** 1698–1753. French historian; collaborated with his brother **Claude** (1705–1777) in publishing *Histoire Générale du Théâtre Français* (12 vols., 1734–49), *Dictionnaire des Théâtres de Paris* (7 vols., 1749–56), etc.

**Pa·ria′ni** (pä·ryä′nē), **Alberto.** 1876–1955. Italian army officer; commanded 6th inter-Allied army at close of World War (1914–18); on staff at Peace Conference at Paris (1919); military adviser to Albanian army (1928–33); undersecretary of state for war and chief of general staff (1936–39).

**Pa′rieu′** (pȧ′ryû′), **Marie Louis Pierre Félix Es′qui′rou′ de** (ĕs′kē′rōō′ dē). 1815–1893. French lawyer, politician, and economist.

**Pa·ri′ni** (pä·rē′nē), **Giuseppe.** 1729–1799. Italian poet; professor of fine arts at the Brera, Milan (1773 ff.); given place in municipal government by Napoleon (1796–99); known esp. for his satirical epic *Il Giorno*, in which he caustically criticized vicious conditions of the time.

**Pa′ris′** (pȧ′rē′; *Angl.* păr′ĭs), Comte **de. Louis Philippe Albert d'Orléans.** 1838–1894. Eldest son of Ferdinand, Duc d'Orléans (see Orléans, 4). Pretender to crown of France and head of Legitimist party; became heir apparent on death of his father (1842); lived in England and traveled (1848–61); served as captain of volunteers on staff of Gen. McClellan in U.S. Civil War (1861–62); returned to France (1871) and relinquished claim of his family to throne (1873); on death of count of Chambord (1883) became head of Legitimists; exiled from France (1886); wrote books on travel and on labor in England, and esp. *Histoire de la Guerre Civile en Amérique* (1874–89).

**Pa′ris′** (pä′rēs′), **Alexis Paulin.** 1800–1881. French scholar; special student of old French literature; editor and publisher of several chansons de geste; author of *Histoire Littéraire de la France.* His son **Gaston,** *in full* **Bruno Paulin Gaston** (1839–1903), romance philologist and medievalist, was professor at Collège de France, succeeding his father (1872), and director of the school (1895); author of *Histoire Poétique de Charlemagne* (1865), *Chansons du XV<sup>e</sup> Siècle* (1875), *La Poésie du Moyen Âge* (1885), *François Villon* (1901), etc.

**Pâ′ris′** (pä′rēs′), **François de.** *Known as* **Dia′cre** (dyȧ′kr') **Pâris.** 1690–1727. French Jansenist theologian; opposed the bull *Unigenitus* (1713); buried in cemetery of St. Médard, Paris, where his grave became place of pilgrimage.

**Par′is** (păr′ĭs), **Matthew.** 1200?–1259. English historian of Middle Ages; entered monastery of St. Albans (1217); succeeded (1236) Roger of Wendover as chronicler; carried on (from summer 1235 to 1259) and expanded scope of the *Chronica Majora*, adding foreign events (standard ed. by Henry Richards Luard, 7 vols., 1869–83); reorganized and reformed an abbey in Norway on commission from Innocent IV (1248–49); wrote an abridgment of longer chronicles called *Historia Minor* or *Historia Anglorum*, extending from 1067 to 1253 (ed, 3 vols., 1866–69); author also of lives of monks and a book of *Additamenta.*

**Par′ish–Al′vars** (păr′ĭsh·ăl′värz), **Elias.** 1808–1849. English harpist and composer of harp concertos, fantasias, romances; compiler of Greek, Bulgarian, and Turkish melodies.

**Parisot de La Valette, Jean.** See La Valette.

**Park** (pärk), **Edwards Am′a·sa** (ăm′ȧ·sȧ). 1808–1900. American Congregational clergyman, b. Providence, R.I.; one of last champions of old New England theology; editor in chief *Bibliotheca Sacra* (1852–84).

**Park, Maud,** *nee* **Wood.** 1871–1955. Amer. woman-suffragist, b. Boston; m. Charles Edward Park (1898; d. 1904); first president, National League of Women Voters (1920–24).

**Park, Mungo.** 1771–1806. Scottish African explorer; surgeon in mercantile marine (1792); ascended Gambia River, crossed Senegal, followed course of Niger (1795–96); captured by Arab chief and escaped after four months' imprisonment; after nineteen months in interior, reached England (1799) and wrote *Travels in the Interior of Africa* (1799); on second expedition to the Niger (1805), reached Bamako.

**Park, William Hallock.** 1863–1939. American physician and bacteriologist, b. New York City; authority on public-health aspects of diphtheria, pneumonia, tuberculosis, and poliomyelitis.

**Parke** (pärk), **John Grubb.** 1827–1900. American army officer, b. near Coatesville, Pa.; grad. U.S.M.A., West Point (1849); served through Civil War; at Antietam, Fredericksburg, Vicksburg, Petersburg; with Northwest Boundary Commission (1866–69); retired (1889).

**Par′ker** (pär′kẽr), **Alton Brooks.** 1852–1926. American jurist, b. Cortland, N.Y.; judge, New York court of appeals (1889–96), appellate division of supreme court (1896–97); chief justice, court of appeals (1898–1904); Democratic candidate for the presidency (1904).

**Parker, Arthur Caswell.** 1881–1955. American archaeologist; authority on American Indians. Editor of *American Indian Magazine* (1912–15); author of *Myths and Folk Tales of the Seneca* (1923), *Indian How Book* (1927).

**Parker, Cornelia,** *nee* **Strat′ton** (străt′'n). 1885–1972. American writer, b. Oakland, Calif.; m. Carleton Hubbell Parker (1907; d. 1918); investigator of, and writer and lecturer on, labor problems (1919–26); author of *An American Idyll* (1919), *Working with the Working Woman* (1922), *Ports and Happy Places* (1924), *English Summer* (1931), *German Summer* (1932), *Wanderer's Circle* (1934), etc.

**Parker, Dorothy,** *nee* **Roths′child** (?rŏths′chīld). 1893–1967. American writer, b. West End, N.J.; m. Edwin Pond Parker II (1917; divorced 1928), Alan Campbell (1933); author of verse, collected in *Enough Rope* (1926), *Sunset Gun* (1928), *Death and Taxes* (1931), *Not So Deep As a Well* (1936), *Sunset Guns* (1939); and of short stories, as in *Laments for the Living* (1930), *After Such Pleasures* (1933), *Here Lies* (1939).

**Parker, Francis Wayland.** 1837–1902. American educator, b. Bedford, N.H. In Germany (1872–75). Called for a more progressive educational system in the U.S. (from 1875). Founder of Chicago Inst. (1899; became U. of Chicago School of Education, 1901).

**Parker, George Howard.** 1864–1955. American zoologist, b. Philadelphia; teacher at Harvard (1888–91 and from 1893), professor (1906–35). Author of *Biology and Social Problems* (1914), *What Evolution Is* (1925), *Color Changes in Animals in Relation to Nervous Activity* (1936), etc.; coauthor of *The Evolution of Man* (1922), *The Problem of Mental Disorder* (1934), etc.

**Parker,** Sir **Gilbert,** *in full* **Horatio Gilbert.** 1862–1932. Canadian novelist, b. in Ontario; associate editor, *Sydney Herald*, Australia (1885–89); wrote *Round the Compass in Australia* (1892); devoted himself to portrayal of

Canadian woodsmen, Canadian life and character (up to 1900); settled in London; Conservative M.P. (1900), champion of imperialism; in charge of British propaganda in America (1914–17); wrote *The World in the Crucible* (1915). Author of a few plays, *Vendetta* (1889), *No Defence* (1889); a volume of poems, *A Lover's Diary* (1894); short stories, including *Pierre and his People* (1892), *Northern Lights* (1909), *Wild Youth* (1919); novels, including *Mrs. Falchion* (his first, 1893), *When Valmond Came to Pontiac* (1895), *Seats of the Mighty* (1896; dramatized 1897), *Right of Way* (1901), *The Weavers* (1907); the story of La Salle, *The Power and the Glory* (1925); his final book, a Biblical story, *The Promised Land* (1928).

**Parker, Henry Taylor.** 1867–1934. American drama and music critic, b. Boston; on staff of Boston *Transcript* (1905–34).

**Parker, Herschel Clifford.** 1867–1944. American mining engineer, physicist, and mountain climber; teacher of physics at Columbia (1901–11); consulting engineer; made first ascents of various mountains in Canada (1897–1903); made first ascent of highest peak of Mt. McKinley (1912); invented a helioscope and a motor torpedo.

**Parker, Horatio William.** 1863–1919. American composer, b. Auburndale, Mass.; professor of music, Yale (1894–1919), and dean of Yale Music School (1904–19); composer of oratorios (*Hora Novissima*, 1893), operas (*Mona*, 1911; *Fairyland*, 1915; both prize-winning operas, with Brian Hooker writing the librettos), odes (*A.D. 1919*), choral works (*A Star Song*, *The Legend of St. Christopher*), and organ pieces.

**Parker,** Sir **Hyde.** 1714–1782. English naval commander; vice-admiral (1780); fought Dutch on Dogger Bank (1781). His son Sir **Hyde** (1739–1807) commanded fleet sent to Baltic against coalition of Russia, Sweden, and Denmark; showed irresolution, whereupon Nelson engaged, contrary to orders, in battle of Copenhagen.

**Parker, Isaac.** 1768–1830. American jurist, b. Boston; associate justice, Massachusetts supreme court (1806–30), and chief justice (from 1814); professor of law, Harvard (1816–27); instrumental in creation of Harvard Law School.

**Parker, James Cutler Dunn.** 1828–1916. American organist, composer, and teacher of music in Boston; organist of Trinity Church (from 1864); composer of oratorios, cantatas, anthems, and hymns.

**Parker, John.** 1729–1775. American Revolutionary patriot, b. Lexington, Mass.; commanded the force of minutemen in the battle of Lexington (April 19, 1775).

**Parker, Joseph.** 1830–1902. English Congregationalist minister; made five visits to America; fervid pulpit orator; edited *The People's Bible* (25 vols., 1885–95); author of *Ecce Deus* (1867), *A Preacher's Life* (1899), and some fiction.

**Parker, Lawton S.** 1868–1954. American portrait painter.

**Parker, Louis Napoleon.** 1852–1944. English dramatist and musical composer; director of music, Sherborne school, Dorsetshire (1873–92); composer of cantatas including *Silvia*, *The 23d Psalm;* author or translator of plays, including *A Buried Talent* (1890), *Rosemary* (1896), *The Monkey's Paw*, *Beauty and the Barge* (1904), *Pomander Walk* (comedy; 1910), *Disraeli* (1911), *Drake* (1912), *Joseph and His Brethren* (1913), *Lourdes* (1921), *The Abyss* (1930).

**Parker, Martin.** 1600?–?1656. English Royalist ballad writer; author of 18th-century Jacobite song, "When the king enjoys his own again."

**Parker, Matthew.** 1504–1575. English prelate; chaplain to Anne Boleyn (1535); married (1547); dean of Lincoln (1552); deprived of preferments during reign of Mary; appointed second Anglican archbishop of Canterbury by Elizabeth (consecrated 1559). Joining party later called Anglicans, strove to set limits to reformers' doctrines, the beginnings of Puritanism, which he called mutinous individualism; sought to establish ecclesiastical forms midway between Romanism and Puritanism in order to keep the church together; revised Edwardian articles of convocation (1562), reducing the 42 articles to 39 and shaping them into final form (adopted 1571); proposed, supervised (1563–68), and published a revised translation, the *Bishops' Bible* (1572); drew up ecclesiastical enactments, called *Advertisements* (1565), in controversy over regulation of the service; prepared earliest editions of Gildas, Asser, Ælfric, Matthew Paris, and other chroniclers; author of a Latin treatise *De Antiquitate Britannicae Ecclesiae* (1572), said to be first privately printed English book.

**Parker,** Sir **Peter.** 1721–1811. British naval officer; commanded squadron in unsuccessful attack on Fort Moultrie, Charleston (1776); aided Howe in capture of New York; reduced Rhode Island; admiral of fleet (1799); remembered as patron of Nelson.

**Parker, Peter.** 1804–1888. American medical missionary, b. Framingham, Mass.; M.D., Yale (1834); first Protestant medical missionary in China (1834–57).

**Parker, Robert John.** Baron **Parker of Wad′ding·ton** (wŏd′ĭng·tŭn). 1857–1918. English judge; chancery judge (1906); specialized in patent cases; lord of appeal and privy councilor (1913); dealt with prize appeals during World War (1914–18); laid before House of Lords a definite, logically constructed, detailed scheme for a League of Nations (1918).

**Parker, Samuel.** 1640–1688. English philosophical and ecclesiastical writer; regarded as tool of James II; bishop of Oxford (1686); author of *Ecclesiastical Politie* (1670), a popular controversial work (cf. Richard HOOKER).

**Parker, Theodore.** 1810–1860. Grandson of John Parker (1729–1775). American Unitarian clergyman, b. Lexington, Mass. Liberality of his sermons and writings caused severe criticism and resignation of some members of his congregation. Accepted (1845) invitation to be minister of a new "Congregational Society" in Boston; took a leading part in antislavery agitation; was one of the secret committee that aided John Brown's scheme for a raid at Harpers Ferry. *Theodore Parker's Works*, a collected edition, published in 14 vols. (1863–70).

**Parker,** Sir **Thomas.** 1st Earl of **Mac′cles·field′** (măk″lz·fēld′). 1666?–1732. English judge; lord chief justice (1710); favorite of George I on account of vehemence against Jacobites; lord chancellor (1718); impeached and found guilty of defalcation (1725).

**Parker, Thomas Jeffery.** 1850–1898. British zoologist; known for *Text-Book of Zoölogy* (with W. A. Haswell; 1897).

**Parker, Willard.** 1800–1884. American surgeon; professor, Coll. of Phys. & Surg., N.Y. (1839–70); reputedly first in America to operate successfully on abscessed appendix (1867).

**Parker, William.** 1575–1622. Baron Monteagle and Baron Morley. See 4th Baron MONTEAGLE.

**Parker,** Sir **William.** 1781–1866. English naval commander; as vice-admiral, captured Amoy, Ningpo, and other ports, bringing Opium War to end (1842); commander in chief in Mediterranean (1845–52); retired (1852); admiral of fleet (1863).

**Parkes** (pärks), **Alexander.** 1813–1890. English chemist and inventor; took out 66 patents, mostly connected with electrometallurgy; discovered the Parkes process of using zincs for desilverizing lead (1850); invented celluloid (first patented 1855); discovered cold vulcanization process (1841).

**Parkes, Edmund Alexander.** 1819–1876. English physician; superintended civil hospital in Dardanelles in Crimean War; founder of science of modern hygiene; known through Europe for achievement in military hygiene.

**Parkes,** Sir **Harry Smith.** 1828–1885. English diplomat in Orient; employed in negotiating first European treaty with Siam (1855); precipitated with his vigorous protest capture of Canton (1856) and became virtual governor of city (1858–61); consul at Shanghai; minister to Japan (1865–83), where he forwarded cause of the reformers of Liberal party; minister to China (1883–85), concluded treaty opening Korea to British trade.

**Parkes,** Sir **Henry.** 1815–1896. Australian statesman; ivory turner, Birmingham; emigrated to Sydney (1839); led agitation against transportation of convicts; edited (1850–57) liberal newspaper, the *Empire,* demanding responsible government (established 1858); colonial secretary (1866–68); prime minister of New South Wales (1872–75, 1878–82, 1887–89); instituted free-trade policy; reformed civil service; excluded Chinese immigrants; advocated and laid foundations for establishment of the Australian Commonwealth; author of works on Australian political history and poems.

**Park′hurst** (pärk′hûrst), **Charles Henry.** 1842–1933. American Presbyterian clergyman, b. Framingham, Mass.; grad. Amherst (1866); pastor, Madison Square Presbyterian Church, New York City (1880–1918); president, Society for Prevention of Crime (1891); attacked political corruption and organized vice in sermon (Feb. 14, 1892) that aroused New York, caused the Lexow Investigation (1894), Tammany's defeat, and the election of the reform administration of Mayor William L. Strong.

**Par′kin** (pär′kĭn), Sir **George Robert.** 1846–1922. Canadian educator and advocate of Imperial Federation.

**Par′kin·son** (pär′kĭn·s'n), **James.** 1755–1824. English surgeon and paleontologist; writer of first article (1812) on appendicitis and first to recognize perforation as cause of death; described Parkinson's disease (1817); author of *Organic Remains of a Former World* (3 vols., 1804, 1808, 1811) and medical works.

**Parkinson–Fortescue, Chichester Samuel.** See FORTESCUE.

**Park′man** (pärk′măn), **Francis.** 1823–1893. American historian, b. Boston; made trip over the old Oregon trail westward out of St. Louis (1846) and wrote an account of it, *The California and Oregon Trail* (1849). In spite of severe nervous trouble, devoted himself to historical study and writing, publishing *History of the Conspiracy of Pontiac* (2 vols., 1851), *Pioneers of France in the New World* (1865), *The Jesuits in North America* (1867), *The Discovery of the Great West* (1869), *The Old Régime in Canada* (1874), *Count Frontenac and New France under Louis XIV* (1877), *Montcalm and Wolfe* (2 vols., 1884), *A Half-Century of Conflict* (2 vols., 1892). Elected to American Hall of Fame in 1915.

**Parley, Peter.** Pseudonym of Samuel Griswold GOODRICH.

**Par′low** (pär′lō), **Kathleen Mary.** 1890–1963. Canadian violinist; concert debut in London (1905), and called to a command performance before the queen.

**Par′ma** (pär′mȧ; *Ital.* -mä), Dukes of. Rulers of the duchy of Parma and Piacenza, northern Italy, esp. the Farnese (*q.v.*) family (1545–1731); Spanish Bourbons (1731–96; twice temporarily interrupted by Austrian rule); French empress Marie Louise (1814–47); Spanish Bourbons again (1847–60). Duchy became part of Italy (1860). See CHARLES, dukes of Parma.

**Par·men′i·des** (pär·mĕn′ĭ·dēz). Greek philosopher of 5th century B.C., in Elea; head of Eleatic school; author of a didactic poem, *Nature,* which contained essential elements of his doctrines. Only fragments of his work are extant. One of Plato's dialogues was named after him.

**Par·me′ni·o** (pär·mē′nĭ·ō) *or* **Par·me′ni·on** (-ŏn). Macedonian general under Philip of Macedon and Alexander the Great; engaged in battles of Granicus, Issus, and Arbela (Erbil); assassinated (330 B.C.) by order of Alexander, who had reason to doubt his continued loyalty. See PHILOTAS.

**Par′mi·gia·ni′no** (pär′mē·jä·nē′nō) *or* **Par′mi·gia′no** (-jä′nō), **Il** (ēl). *Real name* **Girolamo Francesco Maria Maz·zuo′li** (mät·tswô′lē) *or* **Maz·zo′la** (mät·tsô′lä). 1503–1540. Italian painter, b. Parma; influenced chiefly by Correggio; last representative of north Italian High Renaissance painting; employed chiefly at Parma, also at Rome (1523–27) and Bologna (1527–31). Among his works are *Betrothal of St. Catherine, Vision of St. Jerome, Madonna with a Rose, Cupid Making a Bow,* and portraits.

**Parm′ly** (pärm′lĭ), **Eleazar.** 1797–1874. American dentist, b. Braintree, Vt.; offices in New York (1821–66). A leader in causing recognition of dentistry as an organized profession.

**Parmoor,** Baron. See Charles Alfred CRIPPS.

**Par·nell′** (pär·nĕl′; pär′n'l), **Charles Stewart.** 1846–1891. Irish Nationalist leader; M.P. (1875); initiated calculated policy of obstruction, standing always on opposition side, in order to obtain concessions; united Nationalists, including Fenians of Ireland and America and Land League (organized 1879), in a fight for home rule; imprisoned (1881) on charge of obstructing operation of new land act; gained in power through imprisonment; from prison directed tenants to pay no rent, in retaliation for outlawing of Land League; released from prison upon Kilmainham treaty by which he agreed to declare against all outrage; frustrated in legislative policy by Phoenix Park murders of Lord Cavendish and Thomas Burke by Irish Invincibles (1882); denounced the murders, which were followed by dynamiting outrages in England; brought about defeat of Gladstone government (1885) in protest against fresh coercive legislation; reached apex of career on return of Gladstone to power with definite commitment to adoption of Irish home-rule measure (1886); urged tenants' relief bill (1886); accused by articles in *The Times* of connivance in crime and outrage; denied in House of Commons authenticity of letter purporting to express his extenuation of Phoenix Park murders; was vindicated (1890) by special commission of judges of high court after letter was proved a forgery by Richard Pigott (*q.v.*), who sold it to *The Times.* Ruined (1890) by proof of his adultery with wife of William Henry O'Shea, a former enthusiastic follower, in divorce suit; lost support of English liberals; abandoned by majority of parliamentary colleagues; led a minority in bitter losing fight.

**Parnell, Thomas.** 1679–1718. Anglo-Irish poet, b. Dublin; contributor of allegorical papers to the *Spectator* and *Guardian* (1712–13); member of Scriblerus Club; wrote *Essay on Homer* prefixed to Pope's translations; known for his poems *The Hermit* and *The Fairy Tale.*

**Pa′ro′di′** (pȧ′rô′dē′), **Dominique Alexandre.** 1842–1901. Poet and playwright, b. a Greek, became naturalized Frenchman (1881); author of *Passions et Idées* (1865), *Vaincus et Vainqueurs* (1898), etc., and the plays *Ulm* *le Parricide* (1872), *Rome Vaincue* (1876), *La Reine Juana* (1893), *Le Pape* (1899), etc. His son **Dominique** (1870–1955) known as a philosopher; author of *Traditionalisme et Démocratie* (1909), *Du Positivisme à l'Idéalisme* (1930), etc.

**Parr** (pär), **Catherine.** 1512–1548. Sixth wife of Henry VIII of England; married 1st Lord Burgh, 2d Lord Latimer, 3d (1543) Henry VIII; tried to lessen religious persecution; acted kindly toward Prince Edward and Princesses Elizabeth and Mary; married (1547) Sir Thomas Seymour, Baron Seymour of Sudeley.

**Parr, Samuel.** 1747–1825. English pedagogue and Latin scholar; a political writer of strong Whiggish prejudices (1787); through friendship with Priestley was almost victim of riots (1791); involved in several literary quarrels; published *Characters of Fox* (1809). Known as a vastly learned but dogmatic conversationalist.

**Parr, Thomas.** 1483?–1635. English centenarian; known as "Old Parr"; celebrated by John Taylor, the "water poet"; said to have gone into service (1500) and to have done penance for incontinence at age of 105; exhibited at court by earl of Arundel (1635).

**Par'ran** (păr'ăn), **Thomas, Jr.** 1892–1968. American physician, b. St. Leonard, Md.; on staff of U.S. Public Health Service (1917–30); commissioner, New York State Department of Health (1930–36); surgeon general, U.S. Public Health Service (1936–48); leader in efforts to control and eradicate venereal diseases, especially by open and informative publicity.

**Par·rha'si·us** (pă·rā'zhĭ·ŭs; -shĭ·ŭs). Greek painter of 5th century B.C., b. Ephesus; worked in Athens; recognized as one of greatest painters of antiquity. According to legend, Zeuxis, in a competition with Parrhasius, having painted grapes so perfectly that birds attempted to eat them, asked that Parrhasius draw aside the curtain and exhibit his painting, only to discover that the curtain was itself the painting.

**Par'ring·ton** (păr'ĭng·tŭn), **Vernon Louis.** 1871–1929. American educator; professor of English, U. of Washington (1908–29); author of *Main Currents in American Thought: An Interpretation of American Literature from the Beginning to 1920* (3 vols., 1927–30).

**Par'ris** (păr'ĭs), **Samuel.** 1653–1720. Clergyman, b. London, Eng.; to America (before 1674); pastor in Salem (1689–96). From him and his family originated the accusations of witchcraft that started the famous Salem witchcraft delusions (1692–94) and were responsible for the trials of many persons and the execution of twenty.

**Par'rish** (păr'ĭsh), **Anne.** 1760–1800. American philanthropist, b. Philadelphia; founded in Philadelphia a house of industry for employment of needy women (1795; incorporated 1815), the first charitable organization for women in America.

**Parrish, Anne.** 1888–1957. American writer, b. Colorado Springs, Colo.; m. Charles Albert Cor'liss [kôr'lĭs] (1915). Author of *Pocketful of Poses* (1923), *Semi-Attached* (1924), *The Perennial Bachelor* (awarded Harper prize, 1925), *Tomorrow Morning* (1926), *Floating Island* (1930), *Golden Wedding* (1936), etc.

**Parrish, Maxfield.** 1870–1966. American painter and illustrator, b. Philadelphia; best known as an illustrator, as of *Mother Goose in Prose*, *Knickerbocker's History of New York*, etc.

**Par'ro'cel'** (pá'rô'sĕl'). Family of French painters, including: **Barthélemy** (1600?–?1660), painter of religious subjects; his two sons, **Louis** (1634–1694) and **Joseph** (1646–1704); two sons of Louis, **Ignace Jacques** (1667–1722) and **Pierre** (1670–1739); a son of Joseph, **Charles** (1688–1752); a son of Ignace Jacques, **Étienne** (b. 1696); a son of Pierre, **Joseph François** (1704–1781).

**Par'rott** (păr'ŭt), **Robert Parker.** 1804–1877. American army officer and inventor, b. Lee, N.H.; grad. U.S.M.A., West Point (1824); resigned from army (1836) and entered foundry business (1836–77); invented a method of strengthening cast-iron guns by shrinking wrought-iron hoops on the breech (patented 1861), and an expanding projectile for rifled cannon (patented 1861). Parrott guns were used by Union forces through the Civil War.

**Parrott, Ursula,** *in full* **Katherine Ursula,** *nee* **Towle** (tōl). 1902– . American novelist, b. Boston; m. 1st Lindesay Marc Parrott (1922; divorced), 2d Charles T. Greenwood (1931; divorced). Author of *Ex Wife* (1929), *When Summer Returning* (1936), *Road Leading Somewhere* (1941), *Storm at Dusk* (1943), etc.

**Par'ry** (păr'ĭ), Sir **Charles Hubert Hastings.** 1848–1918. English composer and musical historian; professor of composition and musical history, Royal Coll. of Music (1883); director (1894); professor of music, Oxford (1899–1908). Composer of symphonies and chamber music but better known for choral compositions, including *Ode to St. Cecilia's Day* (1889), *Invocation to Music* (1895), *Te Deum* (1900); oratorios, including *Judith* (1888), *Job* (1892), *King Saul* (1894); incidental music to *The Birds* (1883) and *The Frogs* (1892) of Aristophanes; author of *The Evolution of the Art of Music* (1896), *Johann Sebastian Bach* (1909), and *Style in Musical Art* (1911).

**Parry, Joseph.** 1841–1903. Welsh composer; won prizes at eisteddfods at Danville, Pa. (1860) and in Wales (1863, 1864, 1866); composer of operas *Blodwen* (1878), *Virginia* (1882), *Sylvia* (1889), and oratorios, cantatas, hymn tunes, and anthems.

**Parry,** Sir **William Edward.** 1790–1855. English Arctic explorer, in search of Northwest Passage (1819–20, 1821–23, 1824–25); attempted to reach North Pole by sledge boats from Spitzbergen (1827) and reached latitude 82° 45′, which was not reached again until 1876; rear admiral (1852).

**Par'se·val** (pär'zȧ·väl), **August von.** 1861–1942. German aeronautical engineer; designed medium-sized nonrigid airship, known as a *Parseval*, having single large gasbag from which a car was suspended (1901–03).

**Par'shall** (pär'shăl), **Douglass Ewell.** 1899– . American painter.

**Par'sons** (pär's'nz), **Alfred William.** 1847–1920. English landscape painter and book illustrator.

**Parsons,** Sir **Charles Algernon.** See under William PARSONS.

**Parsons, Elizabeth.** 1749–1807. English child impostor, "the Cock Lane Ghost"; made at age of eleven certain scratchings purporting to proceed as signals from ghost, answering questions (1762); exposed by Dr. Johnson in *Gentleman's Magazine.*

**Par'sons** *or* **Per'sons** (pär's'nz), **Robert.** 1546–1610. English Jesuit missionary and plotter; joined Jesuits (1575); as missionary to England (1580), with Edmund Campion carried on political intrigue toward subjection of England to papal authority; escaped to Continent (1581); urged invasion of England by Philip II of Spain to restore Catholic Church; founded seminaries for English Catholics in France and Spain; rector of English Coll., Rome (1597).

**Parsons, Theophilus.** 1750–1813. American jurist, b. Byfield, Mass.; practiced law (from 1774); active in discussions of new constitution proposed (1778) for Massachusetts; law office in Boston (1800–06); chief justice, Massachusetts supreme court (1806–13). His son **Theophilus** (1797–1882) was also a jurist; practiced in Boston (from 1827); author of many legal treatises, including *Law of Contracts* (2 vols., 1853–55), *Mercantile*

*Law* (1856), *Maritime Law* (2 vols., 1859), *The Constitution* (1861). A Swedenborgian, he wrote also *Outlines of the Religion and Philosophy of Swedenborg* (1875).

**Parsons, Thomas William.** 1819–1892. American poet and translator of Dante, b. Boston. His translation of Dante's *Inferno*, with Doré's illustrations, appeared in 1867; about two thirds of the *Purgatorio* appeared in the *Catholic World* (between 1870 and 1883); of his own verse (*Ghetto di Roma*, 1854; *The Magnolia*, 1866; *The Shadow of the Obelisk*, 1872; etc.), the best-known poems are *On a Bust of Dante* and *Paradisi Gloria*.

**Parsons, Usher.** 1788–1868. American surgeon; with Perry at battle of Lake Erie and distinguished himself by his operations and treatment of the wounded. Author of surgical account of the battle of Lake Erie and a number of medical articles.

**Parsons, William.** 3d Earl of **Rosse** (rŏs). 1800–1867. English astronomer; studied methods of improving construction of speculum of reflecting telescope (from 1827); discovered way to obviate cracking of surface on cooling; mounted giant speculum 6 feet in diameter and 54 feet in focal length at Parsonstown (Birr), Ireland (1845); resolved certain spiral nebulae into groups of stars; discovered binary and triple stars. His eldest son, **Laurence** (1840–1908), 4th earl, astrophysicist, studied radiations of heat from moon (from 1868). His 4th son, Sir **Charles Algernon** (1854–1931), became proprietor of engineering works at Newcastle upon Tyne; invented Parsons compound steam turbine (introduced c. 1884), added a condenser (1891), adapted it to maritime use (1897); invented nonskid automobile chains, a geared turbine (1910).

**Parsons, William Barclay.** 1859–1932. American civil engineer, b. New York City; designed and built first units of New York's subway railway system (1899–1904); member, Isthmian Canal Commission (1904); built East River Tunnel, New York City; chief engineer, Cape Cod Canal (1905–14), chairman, Chicago Transit Commission (1916); served in France as colonel, 11th U.S. engineers (1917–18). Author of *An American Engineer in China* (1900), *The American Engineers in France* (1920), *Robert Fulton and the Submarine* (1922), etc.

**Parsons, William Edward.** 1872–1939. American architect; consulting architect to U.S. government, in the Philippines (1905–14); designed Philippine General Hospital, U. of the Philippines, Manila Hotel; designed various city improvements, as in Chicago, St. Paul, Pasadena, Palm Beach, Washington, D.C.

**Par·the′ni·us** (pär·thē′nĭ·ŭs). Greek grammarian and poet, originally of Bithynia; captured by Romans in war against Mithridates (72 B.C.) and taken to Rome. Only extant work is *Love's Woes*, a collection of 36 love stories.

**Par′ton** (pär′t'n), **Arthur.** 1842–1914. American landscape painter; studio in New York (from 1865). His *Evening, Harlem River* and *A Night in the Catskills* hang in Metropolitan Museum of Art, New York City.

**Parton, James.** 1822–1891. Writer, b. Canterbury, Eng.; to U.S. as a child; wrote esp. biographies, including *Horace Greeley* (1855), *Aaron Burr* (1857), *Andrew Jackson* (1859–60), *Benjamin Franklin* (1864), *John Jacob Astor* (1865), *Thomas Jefferson* (1874). His wife, **Sara Payson,** *nee* **Willis** (1811–1872), sister of N. P. Willis, was also an author, best known under her pseudonym **Fanny Fern** (fûrn); m. 1st Charles H. Eldredge (1837, d. 1846), 2d Samuel P. Farrington (1849, divorced), 3d James Parton (1856); author of several books for children.

**Par′tridge** (pär′trĭj), **Alden.** 1785–1854. American educator, b. Norwich, Vt.; educ. Dartmouth (1802–05) and U.S.M.A., West Point (1805–06); taught at West Point (1806–17); superseded by Maj. Sylvanus Thayer (1817); resigned from army (1818); founded a military academy at Norwich, Vt. (1819), beginning of the present Norwich U. (now located at Northfield, Vt.), and other similar academies in Virginia, Pennsylvania, Delaware, New Hampshire; regarded as founder of elementary and secondary grade military academies.

**Partridge,** Sir **Bernard.** 1861–1945. English caricaturist and illustrator; worked at decorative painting and church ornament (1880–84); at illustration for press and book illustration (from 1884); joined staff of *Punch* (1891) and became chief cartoonist.

**Partridge, Eric Honeywood.** 1894–1979. British literary critic and lexicographer, b. in New Zealand; served in World War (1914–18). Author of *Eighteenth Century English Romantic Poetry*, *The Scene is Changed* (novel), *Slang Today and Yesterday*, *A Dictionary of Slang and Unconventional English*, *The World of Words*, *A Dictionary of Clichês*, *A Guide to Good English*, etc.

**Partridge, John.** 1644–1715. English astrologer and almanac maker; shoemaker by trade; studied Latin, Greek, Hebrew, medicine, astrology; issued an almanac, *Merlinus Liberatus* (from 1680), with patently equivocal predictions, which was parodied by Jonathan Swift under name of Isaac Bickerstaff (1708) in almanac predicting Partridge's death, and in pamphlet and epitaph recording his death; tried in vain to convince public that he was still alive.

**Partridge, William Ordway.** 1861–1930. Sculptor, b. Paris, France, of American parentage; among his works are portrait busts of Chief Justice Fuller, S. Weir Mitchell, Robert Peary, Whittier, and statues of Grant, Nathan Hale, Horace Greeley. Author of *Art for America* (1894), *Technique of Sculpture* (1895), etc.

**Parvez.** See KHOSRAU II.

**Par′vus** (pär′vŭs). = JOHN OF SALISBURY.

**Pa·rys′a·tis** (pȧ·rĭs′ȧ·tĭs). d. 395? B.C. Persian queen; daughter of Artaxerxes I, wife of Darius II Ochus, and mother of Artaxerxes II Mnemon and Cyrus the Younger; exerted evil influence at Persian court through favoritism for Cyrus the Younger.

**Pas′cal′** (päs′kȧl′; *Angl.* păs′kăl′, păs′kăl), **Blaise.** 1623–1662. French scientist and philosopher, b. Clermont; mathematical prodigy as a child; completed original treatise on conic sections at age of sixteen; studied infinitesimal calculus; solved problem of general quadrature of the cycloid; contributed to development of differential calculus; originated, with Fermat, mathematical theory of probability. Various mathematical propositions and demonstrations have been named in his honor, as *Pascal's arithmetical triangle*, *Pascal's law* or *principle*, *Pascal's mystic hexagram*. In field of natural philosophy, carried on experiments on equilibrium of fluids and on differences in barometric pressure at differing altitudes. Significant literary work began with his entrance into Jansenist community at Port Royal (1655) and resulted from his exegesis and defense of Jansenism against Jesuitic attacks; works include *Lettres Écrites par Louis de Montalte à un Provincial de ses Amis*, popularly known as *Provinciales* (1656 ff.), and *Pensées*, published after his death from manuscript notes left by him. The perfection of literary style in the *Provinciales* and the mastership of the weapon of irony have made them classic.

**Pascal, François.** See François GÉRARD.

**Pa′sca·rel′la** (päs′kä·rĕl′lä), **Cesare.** 1858–1940. Italian dialect poet; chief representative of Roman dialect poetry after Giuseppe Gioacchino Belli.

**Pasch** (päsh), **Moritz.** 1843–?1933. German mathematician; professor, Giessen (1873–1911); author of *Vor-*

*lesungen über Neuere Geometrie,* containing system of axioms for descriptive geometry (1882), and works on differential and integral calculus, analysis, and variables and functions. Pasch's axiom is named after him.

**Pas'chal** (păs'kăl). Name of two popes (see *Table of Popes,* Nos. 98, 160) and one antipope:

**Paschal I,** Saint. d. 824. Pope (817–824); b. Rome.

**Paschal II.** *Real name* **Ra·nie'ri** [rä·nyâ'rē] (**Rai·ne'ri·us** [rī·nēr'ĭ·ŭs]). 1050?–1118. Pope (1099–1118), b. near Viterbo, Italy; conducted long struggle with emperors Henry IV and V over investitures, and with Henry I of England; seized and imprisoned (1111) by Henry V; released on promise to restore right of investiture; withdrew promise and excommunicated emperor (1112).

**Paschal III.** *Real name* **Guido of Cre'ma** (krâ'mä). d. 1168. Antipope (1164–68) in opposition to Alexander III.

**Paschitsch.** = PAŠIĆ.

**Pa'sco·li** (päs'kô·lē), **Giovanni.** 1855–1912. Italian poet; succeeded Carducci as professor at Bologna (1904); among his works are three volumes of verse *Myricae* (1892, 1895, 1897), anthologies *Lyra Romana* (1895) and *Epos* (1897), *Odi e Inni* (1906), *Poemi Conviviali* (1907), *Poemi del Risorgimento* (1913), translations from Greek and Latin poets, and critical studies of Dante.

**Pas'de·loup'** (pä'dlōō'), **Jules Étienne.** 1819–1887. French orchestra conductor; founded (1851) Société des Jeunes Artistes du Conservatoir, a symphony orchestra which gave public concerts for some years; conducted popular concerts (1861–84) at Cirque d'Hiver which popularized works of classical composers and introduced many works by young contemporary composers, as Saint-Saëns, Massenet, Bizet, etc.

**Pa'sek** (pä'sĕk), **Jan Chryzostom.** 1630?–1701. Polish soldier; follower of King John II (or Casimir V) of Poland; his memoirs (covering period 1656–88) furnish curious and lively picture of the times.

**Pashić** *or* **Pashich** *or* **Pashitch.** = PAŠIĆ.

**Pa'šić** (pä'shēt·y'; *Angl.* -shĭch), **Nikola.** 1845?–1926. Serbian and Yugoslav statesman; radical in politics; member of legislature (1878 ff.); condemned to death on charge of plotting against King Milan, but escaped into Austria; remained in exile (to 1889); premier of Serbia (1891); ambassador to Russia (1893–94); banished from Serbia (1899) for conspiracy against king; returned to Serbia (1903) and supported Karageorgevich house in its accession to throne; minister of foreign affairs (1904); premier of Serbia and of its successor state, Yugoslavia (1906–26, with few interruptions); guided Serbian policy through World War (1914–18) and creation and organization of Yugoslavia; gained reputation as "Old Fox of the Balkans."

**Pa·si'ni** (pä·zē'nē), **Alberto.** 1826–1899. Italian painter; known chiefly for Oriental paintings and also for Venetian and Spanish works.

**Pasiphilus.** See Hermann von dem BUSCHE.

**Pasitch.** = PAŠIĆ.

**Pa·sit'e·les** (pȧ·sĭt''l·ēz). Greek sculptor of 1st century B.C.; native of Magna Graecia, Italy; wrote extensively on art.

**Pa·ske'vich** (pŭ·skyā'vyĭch), **Ivan Feodorovich.** Count of **E·ri·van'** (â·ryĭ·vȧn'y'). Prince of **Warsaw.** 1782–1856. Russian soldier; field marshal (from 1828); suppressed Polish rebellion (1830–31), captured Warsaw, and became governor of Poland; commanded Russian army sent to aid Austria in suppressing rebellion in Hungary (1849) and received Hungarian surrender at Világos. Commanded army of the Danube (1854); defeated at Silistra (June 9, 1854).

**Pas'ley** (păz'lĭ), Sir **Charles William.** 1780–1861. British army officer and engineer, b. in Scotland; introduced (1811) course of instruction for noncommissioned officers in military engineering, which was established at Chatham with him as director (1812–41); general (1860); author of treatises on military engineering.

**Pasqualis, Martínez.** See MARTÍNEZ PASQUALIS.

**Pas'quier'** (pä'kyā'), **Étienne.** 1529–1615. French jurist; advocate general at Paris Chambre des Comptes (1585); author of *Recherches de la France* (1560 ff.), *Interprétation des Institutes, Plaidoyer pour l'Université,* etc. A descendant, Duc **Étienne Denis de Pasquier** (1767–1862), was named by Napoleon councilor of state and prefect of police (1810); minister of state (1815) and president of Chamber of Representatives (1816) at the Restoration; peer of France (1821) and president of Chamber of Peers under Louis Philippe; chancellor of France (1837); created duc (1844). See AUDIFFRET-PASQUIER.

**Pasquin, Anthony.** Pseudonym of John WILLIAMS (1761–1818).

**Pas·sa'glia** (päs·sä'lyä), **Carlo.** 1812–1887. Italian theologian; joined Society of Jesus (1827); professor of canon law (1844) and dogmatic theology (1845 ff.), Collegium Romanum; advocate of Italian unity; broke with Jesuits (1859) and attacked temporal power of pope; appointed professor of moral philosophy at Turin by Victor Emmanuel II (1861); member of Turin parliament (1863 ff.).

**Pas'sa·vant'** (pä'sä·väɴ'), **Johann David.** 1787–1861. German painter and art scholar; best known as author of *Rafael von Urbino und sein Vater Giovanni Santi* (3 vols., 1839–58) and *Le Peintre-Graveur* (6 vols., 1860–64).

**Passfield,** Baron. See Sidney James WEBB.

**Passos, John Dos.** See DOS PASSOS.

**Pas'sow** (päs'ō), **Franz Ludwig Karl Friedrich.** 1786–1833. German classical philologist; professor, Breslau (1815); founded (1831) *Neue Jahrbücher für Philologie und Pädagogik;* edited dictionary of Greek and wrote *Grundzüge der Griechischen und Römischen Literatur- und Kunstgeschichte.*

**Pas'sy'** (pȧ'sē'), **Frédéric.** 1822–1912. French economist and statesman; member, Chamber of Deputies (1874–89); interested himself in promoting move for establishment of international peace; founded (1868) International League of Peace; aided Sir W. R. Cremer in founding Interparliamentary Union; shared with Jean Henri Dunant first Nobel peace prize (1901). His son **Paul Édouard** (1859–1940), phonetician, asst. director of École des Hautes Études, Paris; founder of International Phonetic Association, chief originator of its phonetic alphabet, and editor of *Le Maître Phonétique* (1889–1940). Wrote *Les Sons du Français* (1887), *Dictionnaire Phonétique de la Langue Française* (with H. Michaelis; 1897), and *International French-English and English-French Dictionary* (with G. Hempl; 1904).

**Pa'sta** (päs'tä), **Giuditta,** *nee* **Ne'gri** (nā'grē). 1798–1865. Italian operatic soprano; sang in many roles expressly written for her by Rossini and Bellini.

**Pa·ster·nak'** (pŭ·styĕr·nȧk'), **Boris Leonidovich.** 1890–1960. Russian poet and author. Wrote *The Twin in the Clouds* (1914), *Above the Barrier* (1917), *Themes and Variations* (1923), *The Year 1905* (1927), *The Second Birth* (1932), *Doctor Zhivago* (1958), trans. of Shakespeare, etc. Awarded Nobel prize in literature (1958). His father, **Leonid Osipovich** (1862–1945), was a painter and draftsman, esp. of genre scenes.

**Pas'teur'** (päs'tûr'), **Louis.** 1822–1895. French chemist, b. Dôle, Jura; educ. Besançon and École Normale, Paris;

professor of physics at Dijon (1848) and Strasbourg (1849); dean and professor of chemistry, Lille (1854–47); director, École Normale Supérieure (1857–63); professor of geology, physics, and chemistry, École des Beaux-Arts (Paris; 1863); professor of chemistry at the Sorbonne (1867–89); director of Institut Pasteur, Paris. Did pioneer work in modern stereochemistry in proving that racemic acid is a mixture of two optically different forms of tartaric acid; investigated diseases of wine and beer; demonstrated that lactic, alcoholic, and other fermentations are caused by minute organisms; proved that these organisms do not arise by spontaneous generation; discovered the bacilli causing two distinct diseases of silkworms and found method of preventing spread of the diseases, thus saving silk industry in France; discovered bacteria to be cause of anthrax; developed method of inoculating with attentuated cultures of germs of anthrax and chicken cholera to protect animals against severe attacks of these diseases; developed curative and preventive treatment for hydrophobia in man and for rabies in dogs.

**Pas'ton** (păs'tŭn). Name of a well-to-do Norfolk family, whose private correspondence from 1422 to 1509, collected and published (first two vols. 1787) along with state papers and other documents, provide historical material upon interfamily violence, domestic conditions, and lawsuits prevalent in reigns of Henry VI, Edward IV, and Richard III. Members of the family include: Sir **William** (1378–1444), "the Good Judge," and his son **John** (1421–1466), letter writer and friend of Sir John Fastolf; Sir **Robert** (1631–1683), 1st Earl of **Yar'mouth** (yär'mŭth), who entertained his friend Charles II at Oxnead (1676); his son Sir **William** (1652–1732), 2d earl, last representative of the family, who married a natural daughter of Charles II, sold some of the family correspondence to an antiquary, Peter Le Neve.

**Pas'tor** (pȧs'tẽr), **An·to'ni·o** (ăn·tō'nĭ·ō; -nyō), *known as* **To'ny** (tō'nĭ). 1837–1908. American actor and theater manager, b. New York City; on stage from childhood; opened Tony Pastor's Opera House, 201 Bowery, New York City (1865); moved to Metropolitan Theater, on Broadway (1875); secured Fourteenth Street Theater, thereafter known as Tony Pastor's (1881); developed legitimate vaudeville in his theaters.

**Pa'stor** (päs'tôr), **Ludwig von.** Baron **von Cam'pers-fel'den** (käm'pĕrs·fĕl'dĕn). 1854–1928. German Roman Catholic historian; author of *Geschichte der Päpste seit dem Ausgang des Mittelalters* (to 1800; 16 vols., pub. 1886–1933).

**Pasture, Elizabeth M. de la.** See Elizabeth DASHWOOD.

**Pasture,** Mrs. **Henry de la.** See Lady CLIFFORD.

**Pat,** Princess. See under CONNAUGHT.

**Pa·tan'ja·li** *or* **Pa·tañ'ja·li** (pȧ·tŭn'jȧ·lĭ). fl. 2d half of 2d century B.C. Indian scholar and grammarian; wrote *Mahābhāshya* ("Great Commentary"); also generally by Hindu scholars identified with the founder of the Yoga system and author of the *Yogasūtras* (a work that first gave literary form to the Yoga doctrines), though some scholars believe that the Yoga philosopher was a different person, living in the 4th century A.D.

**Patch** (păch), **Alexander McCarrell.** 1889–1945. American army officer; grad. U.S.M.A. (1913); commander, army forces in New Caledonia and Guadalcanal (1942), U.S. 7th army in Europe (1944).

**Patch'en** (păch'ĕn), **Kenneth.** 1911–1972. Poet, b. Niles, Ohio. Poems published in *Collected Poems* (1969), *Out of the World of Patchen* (4 vols., 1970), etc. Author of novels *Journal of Albion Moonlight* (1941), *Memoirs of a Shy Pornographer* (1945), and *Sleepers Awake* (1946).

**Pa·tel'** (pȧ·tāl'), **Vith'thal·bha'i** (vĭt'tȧl·bä'ē) **Jah·ver'-bha·i** (jȧ·vär'bä·ē). 1873?–1933. Indian Nationalist leader, b. in Gujarat; studied law and practiced in Bombay; represented Indian National Congress at London Conference (1919) on Government of India Act; joined Gandhi's non-co-operation movement (1920); a leader of Swarajist party; opposed to British rule; died in exile in Switzerland. His younger brother Sardar **Val'labh·bha'i** (vŭl'lȧb·bä'ē) **Jahverbhai Patel** (1877–1950) studied law in India and England; practiced law at Ahmadabad; entered politics (1916), a supporter of Gandhi; active as party organizer and leader of right-wing nationalists.

**Patenier.** See PATINIR.

**Pa'te·nô'tre** (pȧt'nō'tr'), **Jules.** 1845–1925. French diplomat; minister to Sweden (1880–83), China (1883–86), Tangiers (1888–91), U.S. (minister, 1891–93; ambassador, 1893–97); ambassador to Spain (1897–1902); author of *Souvenirs d'un Diplomate* (2 vols., 1913).

**Pa'ter'** (pȧ'târ'), **Jean Baptiste Joseph.** 1695–1736. French painter of genre pictures much after manner of Watteau; his *La Fête Champêtre* hangs in the Louvre.

**Pa'ter** (pā'tẽr), **Walter Horatio.** 1839–1894. English essayist and critic; fellow of Brasenose Coll., Oxford, which was his principal home. Made his life work the interpretation to his age of the humanism of the Renaissance in art and literature; published collection of reviews of da Vinci, Botticelli, Pico della Mirandola, and Michelangelo, as *Studies in the History of the Renaissance* (1873); associated with Pre-Raphaelites; published essays upon aesthetic poetry, style, Shakespeare, Lamb, Sir Thomas Browne in *Appreciations* (1889); published (1885) his masterpiece, *Marius the Epicurean*, a philosophical romance of the time of Marcus Aurelius, presenting his ideal of the aesthetic life.

**Paterculus, Velleius.** See VELLEIUS PATERCULUS.

**Paternò Castelli, Antonino.** See SAN GIULIANO.

**Pat'er·son** (păt'ẽr·s'n). See also PATTERSON.

**Paterson, Andrew Barton.** 1864–1941. Australian journalist and poet; war correspondent (1900–15); officer, Australian remount service (1915–18); author of books of verse including *The Animals Noah Forgot* (1933), *Happy Despatches* (personal recollections of celebrities; 1934), *The Shearer's Colt* (racing story; 1936).

**Paterson, Isabel,** *nee* **Bow'ler** (bō'lẽr). 1886?–1961. Journalist and novelist, b. Manitoulin I., Canada; m. Kenneth Birrell Paterson; book reviewer and columnist (*Turns with a Bookworm*), N.Y. *Herald-Tribune;* author of the novels *The Shadow Riders* (1916), *The Fourth Queen* (1926), *The Golden Vanity* (1934), etc.

**Paterson, John.** 1744–1808. American Revolutionary leader, b. New Britain, Conn.; served through Revolutionary War; at Bunker Hill, on retreat from Crown Point to Ticonderoga, at battles of Trenton and Princeton, at Valley Forge; brigadier general (1777) and brevet major general (1783); settled in Broome County, N.Y. (1791); judge, Broome County (1798 and 1806); member, U.S. House of Representatives (1803–05).

**Paterson, Robert.** 1715–1801. Scottish stonecutter; deserted his family and devoted forty years to repairing and erecting headstones on Covenanters' graves; the original of Scott's character "Old Mortality."

**Paterson, William.** 1658–1719. British financier, originator of Bank of England; b. in Scotland; acquired fortune in trade; made first overtures to government for establishment of Bank of England (1691), adopted by Parliament (1694); resigned from directorate on issue of narrow scope of bank's operations; persuaded Scottish parliament to create company for settlement of Isthmus of Darien (now Isthmus of Panama); accompanied expedition (1698) and returned with survivors a broken man (1699); took prominent part in promoting Scottish union with England and framing articles of the treaty (1701–07); advocated (from 1701) financial measures forming basis of Walpole's sinking fund and the scheme for conversion of national debt (1717); free trader before Adam Smith. Cf. Charles MONTAGU.

**Paterson, William.** 1745–1806. Jurist, b. in County Antrim, Ireland; to America as a child; practiced law (from 1769); attorney general of New Jersey (1776–83); member of Constitutional Convention, Philadelphia (1787); a leader in introducing the New Jersey plan which, though rejected, was effectual in forcing a compromise on methods of representation in U.S. Senate and House of Representatives; U.S. senator (1789–90); governor of New Jersey (1790–93); associate justice, U.S. Supreme Court (1793–1806).

**Pa'thé'** (pȧ'tā'; *Angl.* pă·thā', pä·thā', *attributively* păth'ā, pä'thā), **Charles.** 1863–1957. French motion-picture pioneer; inaugurated newsreel, in France (1909) and U.S. (1910).

**Pa'ti·a'la** (pŭ'tĭ·ä'lȧ), Maharaja of. Sir **Bhu·pin'dar Singh** (bōō·pĭn'dẽr sĭɴ'hȧ). 1891–1938. Native Indian prince; chancellor, Indian Princes Chamber (1926–30; 1933–35; 1937–38); leader of the Indian states delegation to the Indian round-table conference (1930); honorary lieutenant general in the British army; served with Indian expeditionary force in World War (1914–18); head of the Sikh community in India.

**Pa'tig·ian'** (pä'tĭg·yän'), **Haig** (hīg). 1876–1950. Sculptor, b. in Armenia; studied in Paris (1906–07); among his notable works are sculptures on the Machinery Palace at the Panama-Philippines Exposition; statue of Gen. Funston, at City Hall, San Francisco; portrait bust of President Hoover, in the White House, Washington, D.C.; statue of Thomas Starr King, in Statuary Hall, Washington, D.C.

**Pa'ti·nir'** (pȧ'tē·nĭr') *or* **Pa'ti·nier'** (-nēr') *or* **Pa'te·nier'** (pȧ'tĕ·nēr'), **Joachim (de).** 1485?–1524. Dutch painter; among his canvases are *The Temptation of Saint Anthony, The Underworld,* and *The Baptism of Christ.*

**Pa·ti'ño** (pä·tē'nyō), **Simón Ituri.** 1862–1947. Bolivian industrialist and diplomat; owned and operated tin mines in Bolivia; minister plenipotentiary to Spain (1920–26), France (1926–41); reputed to have financed Bolivian war against Paraguay (1932–35; finally settled by peace treaty, 1938); resident in New York (from 1940).

**Pat'kul** (pät'kōōl), **Johann Reinhold von.** 1660–1707. Livonian nobleman and adventurer; entered service of Augustus the Strong, Elector of Saxony and King of Poland, and proposed and negotiated alliance against Sweden (1698 ff.). After peace was finally negotiated at Altranstädt (1706), Patkul was delivered to Charles XII of Sweden and broken alive on the wheel as a traitor to his country.

**Pat'man** (păt'măn), **Wright.** 1893– . American lawyer and legislator, b. near Hughes Springs, Tex.; served in World War (1917–19); member, U.S. House of Representatives (from 1929); sponsor of the Patman Act, or "Bonus bill" (passed over the president's veto, 1936) providing for payment of a bonus to American soldiers who served in World War, and cosponsor of the Robinson-Patman Act. See Joseph T. ROBINSON.

**Pat'more** (păt'mōr), **Coventry Kersey Dighton.** 1823–1896. English poet. Son of **Peter George Patmore** (1786–1855), an author. Assistant librarian, British Museum (1846–65); contributed to Pre-Raphaelite organ, *The Germ;* published poems, *Tamerton Church Tower* (1853); issued his masterpiece, a poetic celebration of married love, *The Angel in the House,* comprising *The Betrothal* (1854), *The Espousals* (1856), *Faithful For Ever* (1860), *The Victories of Love* (1862). After death of first wife became a Roman Catholic (1864). Published *The Unknown Eros,* odes on exalted themes (1877); *Amelia,* an idyll (1878); *Rod, Root, and Flower,* meditations chiefly upon religious subjects (1895).

**Pa'ton** (pā't'n), Sir **Joseph Noël.** 1821–1901. Scottish painter, chiefly of historical, allegorical, fairy, and religious subjects, including companion pictures of *Oberon* and *Titania, Luther at Erfurt* (1861), etc. His son **Diarmid Noël** (1859–1928), regius professor of physiology, Glasgow (1906–28), was a pioneer in study of metabolism and nutrition.

**Pa'tou'** (pȧ'tōō'), **Jean.** 1887–1936. French dressmaker and designer.

**Pa'tri** (pä'trē), **An'ge·lo** (ăn'jȧ·lō). 1877–1965. American educator and writer, b. in Italy; A.B., C.C.N.Y. (1897); teacher (from 1898), principal (from 1908), in New York public schools; author of *Pinocchio in Africa* (1911), *A School Master of the Great City* (1917), *Spirit of America* (1924), *Pinocchio in America* (1928), *The Questioning Child* (1930), *The Parents Counsellor* (1939), *Your Children in Wartime* (1943), etc.

**Patricia,** Princess. See under CONNAUGHT.

**Pat'rick** (păt'rĭk), Saint. *British name* **Suc'at** (sŏŏk'ăt). *Latin* **Pa·tri'ci·us** (pȧ·trĭsh'ĭ·ŭs). 389?–?461. Apostle and patron saint of Ireland, b. near the Severn, Britain, son of Calpurnius, a decurion of Celto-Roman family of high rank. Captured at age of sixteen by Irish marauders, sold as a slave in Antrim, escaped after six years into Gaul; returned to parents in Britain. Heeded call which came to him in a dream to preach to Irish; spent about fourteen years at Auxerre, France, in preparation. Entrusted by Pope Celestine I with conversion of Irish race, and consecrated bishop (432); landed in Wicklow, attacked by druids, proceeded to Lough Strangford; converted brother of King Leoghaire (reigned 428–467) and received protection; according to tradition, plucked shamrock from sward as an illustration in explaining the Trinity (Easter, 433?), and later smote Cromm Cruaich, a chief idol; imprisoned and condemned twelve times by druids. Founded churches and planted the faith through north of Ireland and organized churches and consecrated bishops in the south; introduced Latin as language of church; founded church and monastery at Armagh; died at Saul, Ireland, leaving writings in rude Latin, the *Confession,* an account of his career, and a letter to Coroticus, a British king of Strathclyde who had killed some neophytes in a raid.

**Patrick, Mary Mills.** 1850–1940. American educator, b. Canterbury, N.H.; specialized in study of Near Eastern languages; president, Istanbul Woman's Coll. (1890–1924); author of *Sappho and the Island of Lesbos* (1912), *Under Five Sultans* (1929), *A Bosporous Adventure* (1934), etc.

**Patrick, Mason Mathews.** 1863–1942. American army engineer, b. Lewisburg, W.Va.; grad. U.S.M.A., West Point (1886); promoted through the grades to major general (1921); chief of air service, A.E.F. (May, 1918–July, 1919); again, chief of air service, U.S. army (1921–27); retired (1927).

**Päts** (păts), **Konstantin.** 1874–?1956. Estonian lawyer and statesman; organized first temporary government after the World War (1914–18); head of the government of Estonia (1921–22; 1923–24; 1931–33); dictator (1934–38); elected president (1938–40).

**Pat'ta·ni** (pŭt'tȧ·nē), Sir **Pra'bha·shan'ker** (prŭ'bä·shŭng'kẽr) **Dal'pat'ram** (dŭl'pŭt'rȧm). 1862–1938. Indian political leader; member, Council of India (1917–19); president of state council, Bhaunagar State (1931);

member Indian delegation, League of Nations (1932); elected member, Council of State, India (1936).

**Pat·tee′** (pă·tē′), **Fred Lewis.** 1863–1950. American educator and author of *The Wine of May and Other Lyrics* (1893), *The House of the Black Ring* (1905), *The Breaking Point* (1911), *Tradition and Jazz* (1924), etc.

**Pat′ten** (păt′'n), **Gilbert.** *Pseudonym* **Burt L. Stan′dish** (stăn′dĭsh). 1866–1945. American writer of adventure stories for boys, centering around the fictional hero Frank Merriwell.

**Patten, James A.** 1852–1928. American grain operator; profited largely by grain corners (1908, 1909) and later by a corner in cotton. His cousin **Simon Nelson Patten** (1852–1922) was an economist; professor, U. of Pennsylvania (1888–1917); author of *The Economic Basis of Protection* (1890), *The Theory of Prosperity* (1901), *The New Basis of Civilization* (1907), *The Reconstruction of Economic Theory* (1912), etc.

**Pat′ter·son** (păt′ẽr·s'n). See also PATERSON.

**Patterson, Austin McDowell.** 1876–1956. American chemist, b. Damascus, Syria, of American parents. Ph.D., Johns Hopkins (1900); editor, *Chemical Abstracts* (1909–14); professor, Antioch College (1921–41); vice-president (1930–41). Authority on chemical nomenclature; special editor for chemistry, *Webster's New International Dictionary, Second Edition.* Author of *A German-English Dictionary for Chemists* (1917), *A French-English Dictionary for Chemists* (1921), and *A Guide to the Literature of Chemistry* (with E. J. Crane, 1927).

**Patterson, Elizabeth.** See Elizabeth BONAPARTE.

**Patterson, Frank Allen.** 1878–1944. American educator; on English-teaching staff, Columbia (from 1912), and professor (from 1931); general editor of definitive edition, *Complete Works of John Milton* (18 vols., 1931).

**Patterson, Joseph Medill.** 1879–1946. Grandson of Joseph Medill. American journalist, b. Chicago; B.A., Yale (1901); on staff of Chicago *Tribune* (1901–05); commissioner of public works, Chicago (1905–06); war correspondent in Germany, Belgium, and France (1914–15); served on Mexican border (1916) and in France (1917–18); coeditor of Chicago *Tribune* (with his cousin Robert Rutherford McCormick, to 1925); editor of the New York *Daily News* (from 1925). Author of *A Little Brother of the Rich, Dope, By-Products, Rebellion.* His sister **Eleanor Medill** (1884–1948), also a newspaper editor, married Count Joseph Gizycki (1904) and Elmer Schlesinger (1925); inherited an interest in Chicago *Tribune;* a member of its board of directors; interested with her brother in New York *Daily News;* herself owner and publisher of Washington (D.C.) *Herald* and Washington *Times;* author, under pen name **Eleanor M. Gi·zyc′ka** (gē·zĭts′kä), of *Glass Houses* (1926), *Fall Flight* (1928). See under Joseph MEDILL.

**Patterson, Robert Porter.** 1891–1952. American lawyer, b. Glens Falls, N.Y.; adm. to N.Y. bar (1915) and practiced in New York City; judge, U.S. District Court, southern N.Y. (1930–39); judge, U.S. Circuit Court of Appeals (1939–40); U.S. undersecretary of war (1940–45); secretary of war (1945–47).

**Patterson, Wilfrid Rupert.** 1893–1954. British rear admiral; chief of staff, later head, of British Admiralty delegation in U.S. (1942); a lord commissioner of admiralty and assistant chief of naval staff (Mar., 1943).

**Pat′te·son** (păt′ē·s'n), **John Coleridge.** 1827–1871. English missionary in Melanesia (1855); consecrated bishop (1861); spoke 23 languages; killed by natives in retaliation for kidnaping of laborers by traders.

**Pat′ti** (pät′tē), **Adelina.** 1843–1919. Operatic coloratura soprano, b. Madrid, of Italian parentage; m. Marquis Henri de Caux (1868), the tenor singer Nicolini (1886), and the Swedish baron Cederström (1899). Among her well-known roles were Linda, Norina, Luisa Miller, Lucia, Violetta, and Zerlina. Her sister **Carlotta** (1835?–1889) was also a coloratura singer; had voice of extraordinary compass, extending to G in altissimo.

**Pat′ti·son** (păt′ĭ·s'n), **Andrew Seth Pringle-.** See Andrew SETH.

**Pattison, Lee Marion.** 1890– . American pianist and composer; long associated with Guy Maier (*q.v.*) in concerts for two pianos; composer of piano pieces, songs, etc.

**Pattison, Mark.** 1813–1884. English scholar and author; a Puseyite and follower of Newman, helped in translation of Thomas Aquinas's *Catena Aurea;* gradually separated from high-church party after Newman entered Roman Catholic church; investigated Continental systems of education (1859–60); rector of Lincoln College (1861); continued literary activity, writing for reviews and preparing a history of learning, of which the *Life of Isaac Casaubon* (1875) was a fragment; collected material for a life of Joseph Scaliger. Author of an excellent *Life of John Milton* (1879) and *Memoirs* (to 1860). See Emilia Frances DILKE. His sister **Dorothy Wyndlow** (1832–1878), known as "Sister Dora," philanthropist, joined sisterhood of the Good Samaritan (1864); became a surgical nurse; resigned from sisterhood to become head of municipal hospital at Walsall.

**Pat′ton** (păt′'n), **Francis Landey.** 1843–1932. Presbyterian clergyman and educator, b. in Bermuda; professor, Princeton Theol. Sem. (1881–88) and in Princeton U. (1884–1913); president of Princeton (1888–1902) and of Princeton Theol. Sem. (1902–13).

**Patton, George Smith.** 1885–1945. American army officer, b. San Gabriel, Calif.; grad. (1909) U.S.M.A., West Point; served in cavalry; aide-de-camp to Gen. Pershing in Mexico (1916–17) and in Europe (May–Nov., 1917); first man detailed to tank corps, U.S. army (Nov., 1917); in command of 2d armored division (Nov., 1940); major general (1941); in command, under Gen. Eisenhower, of U.S. forces in Morocco (Nov., 1942); commanded 2d army corps in Tunisia (Mar.–Apr., 1943); commanded U.S. 7th Army in Sicily (1943) and 3d Army in Western Europe (1944–45); general (Apr., 1945).

**Pau** (pō), **Paul Marie Césare Gérald.** 1848–1932. French general; served in Franco-Prussian War; commanded troops in Alsace (1914); on diplomatic duty (1915 ff.).

**Pau′er** (pou′ẽr), **Ernst.** 1826–1905. Austrian pianist and composer.

**Paul** (pôl), Saint. *Orig.* **Saul** (sôl). A Jew of Tarsus whose conversion to Christianity (*Acts* ix. 3 ff.; xxii. 1 ff.; xxvi. 1 ff.) was attended by a vision; became apostle to the Gentiles, making several missionary journeys and founding many churches, to which he sent epistles (the "Pauline epistles," now part of New Testament canon); supposed to have been martyred at Rome (c. 67 A.D.).

**Paul.** Name of six popes (see *Table of Popes,* Nos. 93, 212, 221, 224, 234, 263), especially:

**Paul II.** *Real name* **Pietro Bar′bo** (bär′bō). 1417–1471. Pope (1464–71), b. Venice; attempted interference in the affairs of Venice, France, and Hungary; a patron of scholars, probably introduced printing into Rome; established (1470) ordinary jubilees at 25-year intervals.

**Paul III.** *Real name* **Alessandro Farnese** (see FARNESE family). 1468–1549. Pope (1534–49), b. in Tuscany; received excellent education; excommunicated Henry VIII of England (1538); approved decree (1540) establishing order of Jesuits; aided Emperor Charles V in his wars against the Protestants of Germany; introduced Inquisition into Italy; convened Council of Trent (1545).

**Paul IV.** *Real name* **Giovanni Pietro Ca·raf'fa** (kä-räf'fä). 1476–1559. Pope (1555–59), b. near Benevento, Italy; founded (with Cajetan of Thiene) order of Theatines (1524); as pope, continued reforms of Paul III, reorganizing the Inquisition; opposed Elizabeth's rule in England; unpopular because of nepotism.

**Paul V.** *Real name* **Camillo Borghese** (see BORGHESE family). 1552–1621. Pope (1605–21), b. Rome; aroused France and England to enmity by his extreme ideas of prerogative and his arrogance; weakened papal authority through struggle with Venice (1606–07); began the Villa Borghese and added to the Vatican Library.

**Paul VI.** *Real name* **Giovanni Battista Mon·ti'ni** (mōnt·ē'nē). 1897–1978. Pope (from 1963), b. Concesio near Brescia. Ordained priest (1920); archbishop of Milan (1954); cardinal (1958).

**Paul I.** King of Greece. See under GEORGE **II.**

**Paul I.** *Russ.* **Pavel Petrovich.** 1754–1801. Emperor of Russia; son of Peter III and Catherine the Great; succeeded Catherine (1796); ruled despotically; inaugurated some reforms in treatment of serfs; joined Second Coalition against France (1798) and his army under Suvorov aided in expelling French from northern Italy (1799); later, participated in organization of northern maritime league of Russia, Sweden, and Denmark against Great Britain (1800–01); assassinated. See ROMANOV dynasty.

**Paul.** *Russ.* **Pavel Aleksandrovich.** 1860–1919. Grand Duke of Russia, fifth son of Emperor Alexander II, b. Tsarskoe Selo (Detskoe Selo); m. 1st (1889) Princess Alexandra of Greece and 2d Olga Valerianovna (morganatic marriage); served in World War as commander and inspector general of guards; shot at Petrograd.

**Paul.** 1893–     . Prince of Yugoslavia; cousin of King Alexander I; m. (1923) Princess Olga of Greece; appointed first regent for his nephew King Peter II on death of Alexander (1934); deposed with other members of regency (Mar., 1941), Peter assuming sovereignty.

**Paul, Eden,** *in full* **Maurice Eden.** 1865–1944. English physician and writer; practiced medicine in Japan, China, Perak, Singapore, and England (1895–1912); collaborator with his wife, **Gertrude Mary,** *nee* **Dav'en·port** (dăv'ĕn·pōrt), *known professionally as* **Cedar Paul,** in many translations of important works of French, German, and Russian authors.

**Paul, Elliot Harold.** 1891–1958. American writer, b. Malden, Mass.; author of *Low Run Tide, Lava Rock, Concert Pitch, The Life and Death of a Spanish Town, The Stars and Stripes Forever, The Last Time I Saw Paris,* etc., and a few mystery stories.

**Paul, Herbert Woodfield.** 1853–1935. English biographer and historian; author of *Men and Letters* (1901), *History of Modern England* (5 vols., 1904–06), and biographies of Gladstone, Matthew Arnold, Lord Acton.

**Paul** (poul), **Hermann.** 1846–1921. German philologist; professor, Freiburg (1874) and Munich (1893). Among his works are *Prinzipien der Sprachgeschichte* (1880), *Mittelhochdeutsche Grammatik* (1881), *Grundriss der Germanischen Philologie* (3 vols., 1891–93), and *Deutsche Grammatik* (5 vols., 1916–20).

**Paul** (poul), **Jean** (zhäN). Pen name of Jean Paul Friedrich RICHTER.

**Paul** (pôl), **John.** See Charles Henry WEBB.

**Paul, Kegan,** *in full* **Charles Kegan.** 1828–1902. English publisher and author; B.A., Oxon. (1849); ordained in Church of England (1852); became vegetarian and positivist (1854); joined a Unitarian society; resigned office of vicar (1874); published biography of William Godwin (2 vols., 1876); took over publishing business of H. S. King (1877–99). Published *Last Journals of General Gordon,* works of Tennyson, Hardy, Meredith, Stevenson; was joined (1881) by Alfred Trench and (1889) by Messrs. Trübner & Co. and George Redway, to form a company, Kegan Paul, Trench, Trübner & Co., Ltd., later incorporated in publishing house of Geo. Routledge & Sons, Ltd. Joined Roman Catholic Church (1890) and wrote tracts for Catholic Truth Society. Wrote *Biographical Sketches* (1883), *Maria Drummond* (1891).

**Paul, Louis.** 1901–1970. American novelist and short-story writer, b. Brooklyn; author of *The Pumpkin Coach* (1935), *Emma* (1937), *The Reverend Ben Pool* (1941), etc.

**Paul, Randolph Ev'erng·him** (ĕv'ĕrng·hĭm). 1890–1956. American lawyer, b. Hackensack, N.J.; LL.B., N.Y. Law School (1913); expert on taxation; general counsel, U.S. Treasury Dept. (1942–44).

**Paul, Robert W.** 1869–1943. British engineer who exhibited (1896) a theatrograph (later called an animatograph), an early form of the motion-picture projector, following Edison's kinetoscope (1893). Cf. Thomas A. EDISON.

**Paul,** Saint **Vincent de.** See VINCENT DE PAUL.

**Paul of Ae·gi'na** (ē·jī'nȧ). *Lat.* **Pau'lus Ae'gi·ne'ta** (pô'lŭs ē'jĭ·nē'tȧ). Greek surgeon of late 7th century A.D.; chief work (extant) *De Re Medica Libri Septem.*

**Paul of Sa·mos'a·ta** (sȧ·mŏs'ȧ·tȧ). Christian ecclesiastic; bishop of Antioch (260 A.D.); deposed from his see (272); dynamic monarchian; denied a distinction of persons in God; taught that Christ was a mere man, raised above other men by the indwelling Logos (the impersonal power of God). His followers, regarded as heretics, were called Paulianists. Fragments of his writings are extant.

**Paul of Thebes** (thēbz), Saint. *Called also* Saint **Paul the Hermit.** Christian hermit of 3d and 4th century; said to have lived 113 years; lived as hermit in desert in Upper Egypt; teacher of Saint Anthony; called by Saint Jerome the founder of monasticism.

**Paul of the Cross,** Saint. *Orig. name* **Paolo Francesco Da'ne·i** (dä'nā·ē). 1694–1775. Italian priest; ordained (1727); founder of Passionist order, first community of which was settled on Monte Argentario (c. 1737); canonized by Pope Pius IX (1867).

**Paul the Deacon.** See PAULUS DIACONUS.

**Paul'-Bon'cour'** (pôl'bôN'kōōr'), **Joseph.** 1873–1972. French lawyer and statesman; minister of labor (1911); in World War I; joined Socialist party (1919); entered senate (1931) and resigned from Socialist party; minister of war (1932); premier of France (1932–33); foreign minister (1932–34, 1938). Known for his support of League of Nations; member of League council (1933–34); World War II member of resistance to German occupation. Member, later head, of French delegation to UN conference at San Francisco (1945).

**Paul'ding** (pôl'dĭng), **Hiram.** 1797–1878. American naval officer, b. in Westchester County, N.Y.; acting lieutenant of the *Ticonderoga* at the battle of Lake Champlain (1813); served against Barbary pirates, cruised in the South Seas (1825) in pursuit of mutineers, visited China (1844–47), suppressed Walker's filibustering expedition against Nicaragua (1857).

**Paulding, James Kirke.** 1778–1860. American writer, b. in Putnam County, N.Y.; associated with Washington Irving in publication of humorous periodical, *Salmagundi* (1807–08); published *The United States and England* (1815), a defense against English criticisms; prominent in literary war with English writers, publishing *A Sketch of Old England* (1822) and a burlesque, *John Bull in America* (1825). U.S. navy agent for New York (1824–37); U.S. secretary of the navy (1838–41). Author of *The Dutchman's Fireside* (1831), *Westward Ho!* (1832), *A Life of Washington* (1835), etc.

**Pau'ler** (pou'lĕr), **Gyula von.** 1841–1903. Hungarian historian; author of *History of the Hungarian People under the Árpáds* (1893).

**Pau'let** *or* **Paw'let** *or* **Pou'let** *or* **Pow'lett** (pô'lĕt; -lĭt). An English family named from the parish of Pawlett, Somerset, including Sir **Amias Paulet** (1536?–1588), lieutenant governor of Jersey, commissioner at trial of Mary, Queen of Scots, and famous as her Puritan guardian, who refused to take suggestion to murder her privately; and the following dukes of Bolton and marquises of Winchester, members of a younger branch of family: Sir **William Paulet** *or* **Pawlet** *or* **Poulet** (1485?–1572), 1st Marquis of **Win'ches'ter** (wĭn'chĕs'tĕr; -chĭs·tĕr); honored by Henry VIII; lord president of council and one of council of regency; lord treasurer (1547); joined lords at Baynard Castle who proclaimed Queen Mary in place of Lady Jane Grey; gained favor of Queen Elizabeth and was treasurer (1550–72). His grandson Sir **William Paulet** (1535?–1598), 3d Marquis of Winchester; one of commissioners at trial of Mary, Queen of Scots, and lord steward of her funeral. **John Paulet** (1598–1675), 5th Marquis of Winchester; grandson of the 3d marquis; known as "the great Loyalist" after fortifying and garrisoning Basing House, in Hampshire, against Cromwell's forces (1643–45); suffered long imprisonment and loss of property. **Charles Paulet** *or* **Powlett** (1625?–1699), 1st Duke of **Bol'ton** (bōl't'n; -tŭn) and 6th Marquis of Winchester; son of 5th marquis; deserted Stuart cause, supported Whigs and William of Orange on his landing, and said to have precipitated Marlborough's disgrace by disclosures to king. **Charles Paulet** *or* **Powlett** (1661–1722), 2d Duke of Bolton and 7th Marquis of Winchester; son of the 1st duke; privy councilor (1690); lord chamberlain (1715); lord lieutenant of Ireland (1717–22). Sir **Charles Paulet** *or* **Powlett** (1685–1754), 3d Duke of Bolton and 8th Marquis of Winchester; son of 2d duke; deprived of offices because of opposition to Sir Robert Walpole; married Lavinia Fenton, actress (1751). **Harry Paulet** *or* **Powlett** (1719–1794), 6th Duke of Bolton and 11th Marquis of Winchester; nephew of 3d duke; became admiral (1770).

**Pau'lhan'** (pô'läN'), **Louis.** 1883–1963. French aviator; reached height of 4149 ft. in airplane at Los Angeles, California (1910); won London *Daily Mail* prize of £10,000 for flight from London to Manchester (1910); in French Aviation Corps in World War I.

**Pau'li** (pou'lē), **Reinhold.** 1823–1882. German historian; author esp. of books on English history.

**Pauli, Wolfgang.** 1900–1958. Physicist, b. Vienna; professor, Zurich (1928–40); with Inst. for Advanced Study, Princeton (from 1940); won 1945 Nobel physics prize.

**Pau'ling** (pô'lĭng), **Linus Carl.** 1901– . American chemist, b. Portland, Ore. Applied quantum mechanics to chemistry; worked on the structure of molecules, and on chemical bond; won 1954 Nobel chemistry prize, 1962 peace prize. First to win two full Nobel prizes.

**Pau·li'nus** (pô·lī'nŭs), Saint. *Full Latin name* **Pontius Meropius Anicius Paulinus.** 353–431. Christian prelate, b. Bordeaux; bishop of Nola, Italy; author of 32 songs in various meters and about 50 letters (addressed to Augustine, Jerome, Sulpicius Severus, and others).

**Paulinus,** Saint. d. 644. Roman missionary to England; joined Augustine in Kent (601); consecrated bishop (625); converted Edwin, king of Northumbria, thereupon becoming bishop of York (received archbishop's pallium 634); on death of Edwin (633), fled to Kent and became bishop of Rochester.

**Pau·litsch'ke** (pou·lĭch'kĕ), **Philipp.** 1854–1899. Austrian geographer and explorer, esp. in Africa.

**Paul'lin** (pô'lĭn), **Charles Oscar.** (d. 1944). American naval historian and geographer; author of *Atlas of the Historical Geography of the United States* (1932).

**Paul'sen** (poul'zĕn), **Friedrich.** 1846–1908. German philosopher; author of *System der Ethik* (1889), *Schopenhauer, Hamlet, Mephistopheles* (1900), etc. His son **Rudolf** (1883–1966) was a poet.

**Pau'lus** (pou'lo͝os), **Heinrich Eberhard Gottlob.** 1761–1851. German Protestant theologian; champion of rationalism.

**Pau'lus** (pô'lŭs), **Julius.** Roman jurist of late 2d and early 3d century A.D.; appointed by Emperor Alexander Severus praetorian prefect (*i.e.*, chief judicial officer of Roman Empire). Author of commentaries on Civil law and praetorian (or equity) law. Ranked with Papinian and Ulpian as among the greatest of Roman jurists.

**Paulus, Lucius Ae·mil'i·us** (ē·mĭl'ĭ·ŭs; ē·mĭl'yŭs). (1) Roman consul (219 and 216 B.C.); colleague of Varro in battle of Cannae (216), where he was killed. (2) His son (229?–160 B.C.), surnamed **Mac'e·don'i·cus** (măs'ē·dŏn'ĭ·kŭs), Roman general; praetor in Spain (191–189); consul (168); defeated Perseus in battle of Pydna (168); given triumph in Rome (167); censor (164).

**Paulus Aegineta.** See PAUL OF AEGINA.

**Paulus Di·ac'o·nus** (dī·ăk'ō·nŭs). 720?–?797. *Eng.* **Paul the Deacon.** Italian (Lombard) Benedictine monk and historian; inmate of the Benedictine monastery at Monte Cassino (from before 782 A.D.). Chief works *Historia Gentis Langobardorum* (a history of the Lombards from 568 to 747 in 6 books), *Historia Romana* (a continuation of Eutropius's Roman history).

**Paulus Jovius.** See Paolo GIOVIO.

**Pau'ly** (pou'lē), **August.** 1796–1845. German classical philologist; editor of Pauly's *Real-Encyclopädie der Classischen Altertumswissenschaft* (1839 ff.). A new edition was edited (1893 ff.) by Georg Wissowa (*q.v.*).

**Paunce'fote** (pôns'fo͝ot; -fŭt), **Julian.** 1st Baron **Pauncefote.** 1828–1902. English diplomat; attorney general at Hong Kong (1865–72); chief justice, Leeward Islands (1874); permanent undersecretary of foreign office (1882); delegate to Suez Canal commission, Paris (1885); envoy extraordinary to U.S. (1889), ambassador (1893); negotiated successfully disputes over Canadian seal fishing in Bering Sea (1892), and over boundary between Venezuela and British Guiana (1895–99); negotiated revision of Clayton-Bulwer Treaty, signed Hay-Pauncefote Treaty providing equal passage for all nations through Panama Canal (1901); died in Washington.

**Paur** (pour), **Emil.** 1855–1932. Austrian violinist and orchestra conductor; director, National Conservatory of Music, New York (1899); conductor, Pittsburgh Symphony Orchestra (1904–10) and Royal Opera in Berlin (1912).

**Pau·sa'ni·as** (pô·sā'nĭ·ăs). Spartan general; regent for Pleistarchus (479 B.C.); commanded allied Greek army in decisive victory at Plataea (479); admiral of Greek fleet (478); subjugated most of Cyprus, and captured Byzantium from the Persians; became tyrannical and overbearing, alienating his Greek allies; entered into treasonable correspondence with Persian king; recalled to Sparta, where he plotted a revolt against the government; on discovery of his plot, fled to sanctuary on the Spartan Acropolis, where he was starved to death.

**Pausanias.** Greek traveler and geographer of 2d century A.D.; author of *Periegesis of Greece*, a valuable source of information on topography, local history, religious customs, architecture, and sculpture in Greece.

**Pau'si·as** (pô'sĭ·ăs). Greek painter, of Sicyon, in 4th century B.C.; studied under Pamphilus (*q.v.*); renowned as a decorative artist, esp. in encaustic.

**Pau′wels** (pou′vĕls), **Wil′helm** (vĭl′hĕlm) **Ferdinand.** 1830–1904. Belgian historical painter; among canvases are *The Youth of Luther*, *Reception of the Delegation of the Doge of Genoa by Louis XIV*, and *Banished by Alva.*

**Pa′ve·lić** (pä′vĕ·lēt′y′; *Angl.* -lĭch), **Ante.** 1889–1959. Croat statesman; president of the Senate of Yugoslavia (1932); accused of being involved in assassination of King Alexander in Marseilles (1934), and sentenced in absentia to death; adopted strong pro-Axis policy (1939); appointed by Hitler head of the small Croat state set up under German-Italian protection after the Axis conquest of the Balkans (1941).

**Pa·ví′a y Al′bur·quer′que** (pä·vē′ä ē äl′bōōr·kĕr′kā), **Manuel.** 1828?–1895. Spanish general; on staff of General Prim y Prats (1865) and engaged with him in revolution (1868); used his troops to gain control of political situation in Madrid (1874) and turned over power to Marshal Serrano to organize a coalition government; appointed senator for life (1880) and served as president of supreme council of war.

**Pa′vlov** (pá′vlôf), **Ivan Petrovich.** 1849–1936. Russian physiologist; director, department of physiology, Institute of Experimental Medicine (from 1890) and professor in the Military Medical Acad. (1895–1914), St. Petersburg; director, physiological laboratories, Russian Acad. of Medicine, and Institute of Experimental Medicine. Made researches on the physiology of the heart and on the secretion of the glands, esp. the digestive glands; conducted famous experiment demonstrating conditioned reflex in a dog; awarded 1904 Nobel prize for physiology and medicine.

**Pa′vlo·va** (pá′vlô·vŭ), **Anna.** 1882–1931. Russian dancer; studied at Imperial Ballet School, St. Petersburg; toured Europe and U.S. (from 1911). Famed for dance creations, among best known of which were *The Death of the Swan* (*Le Cygne*, ballet composed especially for her by Michel Fokine), *The Butterflies* (*Papillons*), and *Autumn Bacchanal.* Settled in Paris; m. (1914) Victor d'André (d. 1944); founded school for teaching interpretative dancing. See also Léon BAKST.

**Pa′vo·li′ni** (pä′vô·lē′nē), **Paolo Emilio.** 1864–1942. Italian philologist and Sanskrit scholar.

**Pa′vy** (pā′vĭ), **Frederick William.** 1829–1911. English physician; a pioneer among modern chemical pathologists; made life study of carbohydrate metabolism and founded modern theory of diabetes; known for *Pavy's test* for sugar and use of sugar tests and albumin tests in solid form.

**Pawlet.** Variant of PAULET.

**Pax′son** (păk′s'n), **Frederic Logan. 1877–1948.** American historian; professor, U. of Wisconsin (1910–32), U. of California (from 1932). Author of *The Last American Frontier* (1910), *The Civil War* (1911), *History of the American Frontier* (1924; awarded Pulitzer prize), *American Democracy and the World War...*(1936), etc.

**Pax′ton** (păks′tŭn), Sir **Joseph.** 1801–1865. English architect and horticulturist; designed conservatory in gardens at Chatsworth (1836–40), which served as a model for his design of the Crystal Palace, built of glass and iron for the London Exhibition of 1851 and re-erected into a palace at Sydenham (1853–54).

**Paxton, William McGregor.** 1869–1941. American portrait painter.

**Pay′er** (pī′ĕr), **Julius von.** 1842–1915. Austrian arctic explorer, and painter; with Weyprecht led the Austro-Hungarian North Polar expedition in steamship *Tegetthoff*, which resulted in discovery of Franz Josef Land (1872–74); upon return to Europe, devoted himself to painting pictures relating to his polar experiences.

**Payn** (pān), **James.** 1830–1898. English novelist; editor of *Chambers's Journal* (1859–74), and of *Cornhill Magazine* (1883–96); author of *Lost Sir Massingberd* (published in *Journal;* 1864) and other novels, including *Carlyon's Year* (1868), *The Talk of the Town* (1885), *Another's Burden* (1897).

**Payne** (pān). See also PAINE.

**Payne, John.** 1842–1916. English poet and translator; author of *A Masque of Shadows* (1871), *Lautrec* (narrative poem, 1878), and *New Poems* (1880); translator of Villon's poems (1878), *Arabian Nights* (9 vols., 1882–84), Boccaccio's *Decameron*, poems of Hafiz (3 vols., 1901), and standard French poetry.

**Payne, John Barton.** 1855–1935. American lawyer and public official; practiced at Kingwood, W.Va. (1877–82), Chicago (1883–93; 1898–1918); judge of superior court of Cook County, Ill. (1893–98); general counsel for U.S. Shipping Board Emergency Fleet Corp. (1917–18), and U.S. Railroad Administration (1917–19); chairman, U.S. Shipping Board (1919–20); U.S. secretary of the interior (1920–21) and director general of the railroads; chairman, American Red Cross (from 1921).

**Payne, John Howard.** 1791–1852. American actor and playwright, b. New York City; succeeded in his play *Brutus, or the Fall of Tarquin* (1818); leased Sadler's Wells Theatre, London (1820); failed, and was imprisoned for debt (1820). Immortalized by a single song, *Home, Sweet Home*, in his opera *Clari, or, the Maid of Milan* (1823). Collaborated with Washington Irving (1823–26) in plays. U.S. consul at Tunis (1842–45, 1851–52). Altogether, was author, translator, and adapter of more than sixty plays.

**Payne, Roger.** 1739–1797. English bookbinder.

**Payne, Sereno Elisha.** 1843–1914. American lawyer and politician; practiced in Auburn (from 1866); member of U.S. House of Representatives (1883–87; 1889–1914); associated esp. with tariff legislation (Payne-Aldrich Tariff Act, 1909).

**Payne′ Smith′** (pān′ smĭth′), **Robert.** 1819–1895. English theologian and Orientalist; published first part of his Syriac dictionary, the *Thesaurus Syriacus* (1868), which occupied him the rest of his life; regius professor of divinity, Oxford (1865–70); dean of Canterbury (1870–95); member of Old Testament revision committee (1870–85).

**Payn′ter** (pān′tĕr). = PAINTER.

**Pay′son** (pā′s'n), **William Farquhar.** 1876–1939. American publisher and writer; president, Payson & Clarke, publishers (1924–28), and William Farquhar Payson, Inc. (1928–31). Author of *The Triumph of Life* (1903), *Debonnaire* (1904; later dramatized), *Barry Gordon* (1908; later screened), *Periwinkle* (1910; later screened), *Candles in the Sky* (play; 1931), *Give Me Tomorrow* (novel; 1935), etc.

**Páz′mány** (päz′män·y'), **Péter.** 1570–1637. Hungarian Roman Catholic prelate and writer; cardinal (1629); leader of Counter Reformation in Hungary.

**Pea′bod′y** (pē′bŏd′ĭ; -bŭd·ĭ), **Andrew Preston.** 1811–1893. American Unitarian clergyman and educator; editor and proprietor, *North American Review* (1853–63); professor of Christian morals, Harvard (1860–81); author of books of essays, philosophy, etc.

**Peabody, Elizabeth Palmer.** 1804–1894. American educator; mistress of private schools (1820–23; 1825–34); assistant to Bronson Alcott in Temple School, Boston (1834–36). Opened bookshop in Boston (1839); interested herself in educational theory and methods; published elementary textbooks in grammar and history. Studied Froebel and (1860) opened first American kindergarten, Boston; published the magazine *Kindergarten Messenger* (1873–75). Lectured at Alcott's Concord School of Philosophy (1879–84). Wrote a life of

William Ellery Channing, an account of Bronson Alcott's school methods (*Records of a School*, 1835).

**Peabody, Endicott.** 1857–1944. American educator, b. Salem, Mass.; grad. Cheltenham Coll., Eng. (1876), and Episcopal Theological Seminary at Cambridge, Mass.; ordained priest (1885) of Protestant Episcopal Church. A founder (1884), and the first headmaster (1884–1940), of Groton School, Groton, Mass.

**Peabody, Francis Greenwood.** 1847–1936. American Unitarian theologian, b. Boston; professor, Harvard (1881–1913). Among his many books are *Happiness* (1903), *The Christian Life in the Modern World* (1914), *The Rhythm of Life* (1932).

**Peabody, George.** 1795–1869. American merchant and philanthropist, b. South Danvers, now Peabody, Mass.; partner in Riggs and Peabody, wholesale dry goods house, Baltimore (1815–37); settled in London, Eng. (1837), as banker and broker; admitted Junius Spencer Morgan to partnership (1854). Used his credit to support American credit abroad in years following panic of 1837; fitted out Kane's ship, the *Advance*, to search for John Franklin in the arctic. Founded and endowed Peabody Institute, Baltimore; Peabody Institute, Peabody, Mass.; Peabody Museum, Yale; Peabody Museum, Harvard; Peabody Education Fund to advance education in the South, etc. Elected to American Hall of Fame (1900).

**Peabody, George Foster.** 1852–1938. American banker and philanthropist, b. Columbus, Ga.; government director, Federal Reserve Bank, New York (1914–21). Interested himself in promoting educational work, esp. in southern U.S.; director, General Education Board and treasurer, Southern Education Board (Rockefeller philanthropies); trustee, Hampton Institute and Tuskegee Institute, etc.

**Peabody, Josephine Preston.** 1874–1922. American poet and playwright, b. Brooklyn, N.Y.; m. Lionel Simeon Marks (1906), professor at Harvard. Author of *The Wayfarers* (1898), *Fortune and Men's Eyes* (1900), *Marlowe* (1901), *The Singing Leaves* (1903), *Pan, a Choric Idyl* (1904), *The Book of the Little Past* (1908), *The Piper* (1909; awarded prize in the Stratford-on-Avon play competition), *The Singing Man* (1911), *The Wings* (1912), *The Wolf of Gubbio* (1913), *Harvest Moon* (1916), *Portrait of Mrs. W.* (1922).

**Peabody, Robert Swain.** 1845–1917. American architect; in partnership with John G. Stearns, Peabody and Stearns (1870–1915); designed Chamber of Commerce, Boston; City Hall, Worcester, Mass.; Machinery Hall at World's Columbian Exposition, Chicago (1893); Chamber of Commerce, Cleveland.

**Peabody, Selim Hobart.** 1829–1903. American educator; professor of mechanical engineering and physics, Illinois Industrial U. (1878–80), and regent (1881–85); when its name was changed to U. of Illinois, he became first president (1885–91).

**Peace** (pēs), **Charles.** 1832–1879. English criminal; robber in Manchester; shot would-be captor at Whalley Range; shot one Arthur Dyson in quarrel; lived as gentleman of means, committing burglaries nights, until captured almost by accident (1879), and hanged.

**Pea'cham** (pē'chăm), **Henry.** 1576?–?1643. English author, painter and engraver of portraits and landscapes, musical composer, student of heraldry, mathematician; first book, *Graphice* (1606), treatise on pen and water-color drawings, reissued under title *The Gentleman's Exercise;* made reputation with his epigrams; his magnum opus *The Compleat Gentleman* (1622), from the last edition of which (1661) Dr. Johnson drew the heraldic definitions in his dictionary.

**Pea'cock** (pē'kŏk), **George.** 1791–1858. English mathematician; with Herschel, Babbage, and Woodhouse, translated Lacroix's *Differential and Integral Calculus* (1816) and furthered introduction of Continental mathematical notation into Cambridge; published his *Algebra* (1830); dean of Ely (1839–58); member of commission on weights and measures, advocated system of decimal coinage.

**Peacock, Thomas Love.** 1785–1866. English novelist and poet; self-educated from age of thirteen; published minor poetical and dramatic works; close friend of Shelley (from 1812), and Shelley's executor; clerk and examiner to East India Company (1819–56). His satirical novels, which are of scanty plot, but full of odd characters and interspersed with lyrics, include *Headlong Hall* (1816), *Melincourt* (1817), *Nightmare Abbey* (containing caricatures of Byron, Coleridge, and Shelley; 1818), *Crotchet Castle* (1831), and *Gryll Grange* (1860 or 1861); his more romantic novels include *Maid Marian* (1822), *The Misfortunes of Elphin* (1829). *Rhododaphne* (1818), his best long poetical composition, shows Shelley's influence.

**Peake** (pēk), **Frederick Gerard.** 1886–1970. British army officer, in India (to 1913) and in Egypt (from 1913); recruited and led the Arab Legion (1922 ff.).

**Peale** (pēl). Name of a family of American artists, including: **Charles Willson Peale** (1741–1827), portrait painter; an officer in American Revolution, at battles of Trenton and Princeton; an engraver in Philadelphia (c. 1781–90); best known for paintings of George Washington, who sat for him repeatedly (1772–95). His brother **James** (1749–1831), miniaturist, with studio in Philadelphia; painted miniatures of Martha and of George Washington (1782) and one of George Washington (1788). Charles's three children: **Raphael** (1774–1825), best known for his miniatures and still-life paintings; **Rembrandt** (1778–1860), best known for his portraits and historical scenes; painted portrait of Washington from life (1795), Jefferson (1804), Napoleon Bonaparte (1810); author of *Notes on Italy* (1831), *Portfolio of an Artist* (1839); **Titian Ramsay** (1799–1885), painter and naturalist with Maj. Long's expedition to the Upper Missouri (1819); agent in Florida for Charles Lucien Bonaparte to collect specimens and make drawings for Bonaparte's *American Ornithology* (4 vols., 1825–33); on staff of Wilkes's exploring expedition to the South Seas (1838–42); examiner, U.S. Patent Office (1849–72). James Peale's two children: **Anna Claypoole** (1791–1878), miniaturist; m. William Staughton (1829, d. 1829) and Gen. William Duncan (1841); **Sarah Miriam** (1800–1885), painted portraits of Lafayette, Commodore Bainbridge, Caleb Cushing, Senator Benton.

**Pé'an'** (pā'äN'), **Jules Émile.** 1830–1898. French surgeon; a founder of modern gynecological surgery.

**Pe·a'no** (pā·ä'nō), **Giuseppe.** 1858–1932. Italian mathematician and linguist; one of the originators of the science of symbolic logic. In linguistics, devised an international auxiliary language known as *Latino sine flexione*, or *Interlingua*, whose vocabulary consists of words common to Latin, French, German, and English (1903).

**Pearce** (pērs). See also PEARSE, PEIRCE, PIERCE.

**Pearce, Charles Sprague.** 1851–1914. American painter, b. Boston; studio in France. His *Fantaisie* hangs in Pennsylvania Academy of Art; *Meditation*, in Metropolitan Museum of Art, New York; his murals symbolizing *Family, Religion, Labor, Study, Recreation, Rest* are in the Library of Congress, Washington, D.C.

**Pearl** (pûrl), **Raymond.** 1879–1940. American biologist,

b. Farmington, N.H.; professor of biology (from 1930), school of hygiene and public health, Johns Hopkins; professor of biology, medical school, Johns Hopkins (from 1923). Author of *The Biology of Death* (1922), *The Biology of Population Growth* (1925), *The Ancestry of the Long-lived* (with his daughter Ruth DeWitt Pearl; 1934), *The Natural History of Population* (1939), etc.

**Pearse** (pērs). See also PEARCE, PEIRCE, PIERCE.

**Pearse, Padhraic** *or* **Patrick Henry**. 1879–1916. Irish educationist, author, and Sinn Fein leader; commander in chief of Irish forces in the Easter Rebellion (1916). Author of poems, stories, plays, literary studies.

**Pear'son** (pēr's'n), Sir **Cyril Arthur**. 1866–1921. English newspaper proprietor; after failure of sight (1910–12), devoted fortune to amelioration of conditions of the blind, esp. soldiers and sailors.

**Pearson, Edmund Lester**. 1880–1937. American writer, b. Newburyport, Mass.; wrote esp. stories of real persons and crimes, as *Studies in Murder* (1924), etc.

**Pearson, John**. 1613–1686. English prelate and theologian; Royalist chaplain until collapse of royal cause; defended church against Romanist and Puritan attacks and promoted London Polyglot Bible. At Restoration showered with honors; defended authenticity of the letters of Ignatius; bishop of Chester (1673). Author of *Exposition of the Creed* (1659).

**Pearson, John Loughborough**. 1817–1897. English architect; revived art of vaulting, employed geometrical type of Gothic; best-known work, Truro Cathedral (1880).

**Pearson, Karl**. 1857–1936. English scientist, b. London; at U. of London (1882–1936). Disciple of Galton; applied statistics to biological problems, esp. evolution and heredity. Editor, *Biometrika* (1902–35), *Annals of Eugenics* (1925–33), also of *Tables of the Incomplete Gamma Function* (1923), etc.; his other publications include *The Ethic of Free Thought* (1887), *The Chances of Death, and other Studies in Evolution* (1897), *The Grammar of Science* (1899), *The Life, Letters, and Labours of Francis Galton* (1915), *The Portraiture of Oliver Cromwell* (with Geoffrey M. Morant, 1935), etc.

**Pearson, Lester Bowles**. 1897–1972. Canadian statesman, b. Ontario. At U. of Toronto (1924–28); entered diplomatic service (1928); amb. to U.S. (1945–46); M.P. (1948–68); secy. of state for external affairs (1948–57); pres., U.N. Gen. Assembly (1952–53); prime minister (1963–68). Awarded Nobel peace prize (1957).

**Pearson, Weetman Dickinson**. = Viscount COWDRAY.

**Pea'ry** (pēr'ĭ), **Robert Edwin**. 1856–1920. American arctic explorer, b. Cresson, Pa.; grad. Bowdoin (1877); draftsman, U.S. Coast and Geodetic Survey, Washington, D.C. (1879–81); civil engineer, U.S. navy (from 1881); retired with rank of rear admiral (1911). Started arctic exploration with voyage to interior of Greenland (1886); made voyage to northern Greenland (1891–92); third voyage, intended to reach North Pole, failed in its objective (1893–95). Granted five years' leave of absence from the navy (1897) for further arctic exploration, and presented by Lord Northcliffe with a ship, the *Windward*, which had been used for a British expedition, he left for his fourth voyage (1898–1902), during which he reached 84° 17′ N., furthest north in the American arctic. Granted three years' leave (1903); sailed in the *Roosevelt* (1905–06) in attempt to reach the North Pole; reached 87° 6′ N., only 174 miles from the Pole, before he had to turn back. Final and successful expedition (1908–09); reached the North Pole (Apr. 6, 1909). When announcing success of expedition, learned that Dr. Frederick A. Cook, who had been a surgeon on the 1891 Peary expedition, had claimed five days earlier that he had reached the Pole Apr. 21, 1908, a year before Peary. Scientific investigation later discredited Cook and recognized Peary's attainment. Author of *Northward over the Great Ice* (2 vols., 1898), *Nearest the Pole* (1907), *The North Pole* (1910). His wife (m. 1888), **Josephine**, *nee* **Die'bitsch** [dē'bĭch] (1863–1955), accompanied him on his 1891 and 1893 expeditions; wrote *My Arctic Journal* (1894), *The Snow Baby* (1901). His daughter **Marie Ah'ni·ghi'to** (ä'nē·gē'tō) was born (Sept., 1893) farther north than any other white child.

**Pease** (pēz), **Alfred Humphreys**. 1838–1882. American pianist and song writer (*Hush Thee, My Baby; When Sparrows Build; Blow, Bugle, Blow; Stars of the Summer Night*).

**Pease, Edward**. 1767–1858. English railway promoter; constructed first steam railway line in England, between Stockton and Darlington (opened 1825), planned as tramway but built for steam traction in co-operation with George Stephenson. His grandson **Joseph Albert Pease** (1860–1943), 1st Baron **Gain'ford of Head'lam** (gān'fērd, hĕd'lăm); M.P. (1892); junior Liberal whip (1897–1905); a lord of treasury (1905–08); postmaster general (1916).

**Pease, Francis Gladheim**. 1881–1938. American astronomer; optician and observer, Yerkes Observatory (1901–04); instrument designer (1904–07; 1908–13), astronomer (from 1911), Mt. Wilson Observatory, Pasadena, Calif. Known for direct photographs and spectrograms of nebulae, star clusters, the moon, and planets, measurement of stellar diameters with the interferometer, and measurement of ether drift and of the velocity of light; designed 100-inch telescope and other instruments; developed method for grinding mirror of the 200-inch telescope of the California Inst. of Technology.

**Peas'lee** (pēz'lē), **Edmund Randolph**. 1814–1878. American gynecologist; practiced in New York City (from 1858). Author of *Ovarian Tumors* (1872), etc.

**Peat'tie** (pēt'ĭ), **Donald Culross**. 1898–1964. American botanist and writer; author of *Almanac for Moderns* (1935), *Singing in the Wilderness* (1935), *Green Laurels* (1936), *Flowering Earth* (1939), *The Road of a Naturalist* (1941), *Forward the Nation* (1942), and with his wife *Up Country* (1928), *Down Wind* (1929), *The Happy Kingdom* (1935). His wife, **Louise**, *nee* **Red'field** [rĕd'fēld] (1900–1965), wrote also *Pan's Parish* (1931), *Wife to Caliban* (1934), *American Acres* (1936), *Tomorrow is Ours* (1937), *The Californians* (1940), etc. His brother **Roderick** (1891–1955), professor of geography, Ohio State (1925 ff.), author of *Geography in Human Destiny* (1940), *The Incurable Romantic* (1941), etc.

**Pe·ça'nha** (pĕ·să'nyȧ), **Nilo**. 1867–1924. Brazilian jurist and political leader; vice-president of Brazil (1906–09); succeeded to presidency (1909–10) on death of President Penna; foreign minister (1917–18).

**Pech'stein** (pĕk'shtīn), **Max**. 1881–1955. German painter and designer. See Erich HECKEL.

**Pecht** (pĕkt), **August Friedrich**. 1814–1903. German painter of frescoes of statesmen and soldiers in the Maximilianeum in Munich and scenes from the city's history in the council chamber in Constance.

**Peck** (pĕk), **Annie Smith**. 1850–1935. American mountain climber, b. Providence, R.I.; public lecturer (from 1890) on archaeology, mountain climbing, and South America. Ascended the Matterhorn (1895), Popocatepetl and Orizaba (1897); made first ascent of Mt. Huascarán, Peru, 21,812 ft., highest point in America ever reached by an American (Sept. 2, 1908). Author of *A Search for the Apex of America* (1911), *The South American Tour* (1914), *Flying over South America...* (1932), etc.

**Peck, Charles Horton.** 1833–1917. American mycologist; pioneer in U.S. in investigation of fungi; author of *Mushrooms and Their Use* (1897), etc.

**Peck, George Wilbur.** 1840–1916. American journalist, humorist, and politician; to Milwaukee and published the *Sun* (1878–90), in which appeared Peck's Bad Boy stories; mayor of Milwaukee (1890–94); author of *Peck's Bad Boy and His Pa* (1883), *Peck's Bad Boy with the Cowboys* (1907), etc.

**Peck′ham** (pĕk′ăm), **John.** d. 1292. English prelate; taught in Oxford (from 1270); summoned to Rome as theological lecturer; returned to England as archbishop of Canterbury (1279); insisted on discipline and attempted to magnify ecclesiastical power. Author of treatises on science, scriptural and moral subjects, and of hymns and poems of lyrical tenderness.

**Peckham, Wheeler Hazard.** 1833–1905. American lawyer, b. Albany, N.Y.; practiced in New York City; assisted prosecution in Tweed trial; district attorney, New York City (1884); nominated for justice, U.S. Supreme Court (1894), but not confirmed because of opposition by New York's senators Hill and Murphy. His brother **Rufus W.** (1838–1909) was also a lawyer; justice, New York State supreme court (1883–86) and court of appeals (1886–95); associate justice, U.S. Supreme Court (1896–1909).

**Pe′cock** (pē′kŏk), **Reginald.** 1395?–?1460. British theologian, Welsh by birth; bishop of St. Asaph (1444), of Chichester (1450); privy councilor (1454). Issued (1455?) his chief work, *Repressor of Over-Much Weeting* [blaming] *of the Clergie*, directed against Lollard teachings, and of importance as a model of 15th-century English; wrote *Book of Faith*, also in the vernacular. In the *Provoker* denied authenticity of Apostles' Creed; in general, exalted authority of reason and denied Scriptures to be only standard of right and wrong; found guilty of heresy; expelled from privy council (1457).

**Pe·co′ra** (pē·kō′rȧ), **Ferdinand.** 1882–1971. American jurist, b. in Italy; to U.S. (1887) and naturalized; practiced in New York. On New York County's district attorney's staff (1918–30). Counsel to U.S. Senate committee investigating banking and stock-market practices (1933–34); aided in drafting laws creating Securities and Exchange Commission; one of original members of this commission (1934–35). Justice of New York supreme court (from 1935); designated by governor to preside at trial of indictments for racketeering crimes (1936). Author of *Wall Street under Oath* (1939).

**Pec′quet′** (pĕ′kĕ′), **Jean.** 1622–1674. French physician and anatomist; credited with discovery of course of lacteal vessels, of the cistern chyli (or reservoir of Pecquet), and of the termination of the thoracic duct at the opening into the left subclavian vein.

**Pec′queur′** (pĕ′kûr′), **Constantin.** 1801–1887. French economist; after association with Saint-Simonianism and with Fourierism, adopted a social doctrine of his own, a kind of religious communism.

**Pe′der·sen** (pę′dĕr·s'n), **Christiern.** 1480?–1554. Danish theologian and historian; loyal follower of Christian II, accompanied him in exile; joined Reformation and made first translation of New Testament into Danish. Returned to Denmark (1532) and collaborated in translating Bible into Danish (known as Christian III Bible). By his work, furnished Denmark with beginnings of a national and theological literature in language of the people.

**Pedersen, Holger.** 1867–1953. Danish philologist and Celtic scholar.

**Pe′der·sen** (pā′dĕr·sĕn), **Knut.** See Knut HAMSUN.

**Pedo.** See ALBINOVANUS PEDO.

**Pe·dra′rias** *or* **Pe·dra′rias Dá′vi·la** (pȧ·thrä′ryäs thä′vē·lä). *Uncontracted form* **Pedro A′rias de Á′vi·la** (ä′ryäs thȧ ä′vē·lä). 1440?–1531. Spanish soldier and administrator, b. near Segovia; sent to New World as governor of Darien, or Panama (1514–26); quarreled with Balboa; had him tried and executed (1519); founded Panama City (1519); sent Francisco de Córdoba to Nicaragua (1522); on Córdoba's revolt, surprised and killed him (1526); both aided and hindered Pizarro and Almagro; transferred to Nicaragua (1526).

**Pe·dra′za** (pȧ·thrä′sä), **Manuel Gómez.** 1788?–1851. Mexican general and politician; elected president (1829) but election annulled; took part in revolts (1832); president of Mexico (Dec., 1832–Apr., 1833).

**Pe·drell′** (pȧ·thrĕl′), **Felipe.** 1841–1922. Spanish composer of operas, church music, chamber music, songs, cantatas, and author of critical and historical works on music.

**Pe′dro** (pā′thrōō), Dom. Name of two emperors of Brazil:

**Pedro I,** Dom. *Also* Dom **Pedro IV** of Portugal. *Full name* Dom **Antonio Pedro de Al·cán′ta·ra Bour·bon′** (thē äl·kăNn′tȧ·rȧ bōōr·bōN′). 1798–1834. Second son of John VI, King of Portugal, of house of Braganza (*q.v.*), b. Lisbon. Fled to Brazil (1807) to escape French; made regent of Brazil by King John (1821); took sides with Brazilians against Portuguese reactionary policy; declared independence of Brazil (Sept. 7, 1822); crowned emperor (Oct. 22, 1822); at first popular, his influence weakened by despotic regime; promulgated new constitution (1824); abdicated (1831) and went to Europe; proclaimed king of Portugal (1826); resigned in favor of his daughter Donna Maria da Gloria (see MARIA II of Portugal); waged successful war against the usurper, his brother Dom Miguel (1832–34); m. twice: (1) archduchess Maria Leopoldina of Austria (1818); (2) princess Amélie of Leuchtenberg (1829; see LEUCHTENBERG).

**Pedro II,** Dom. *Full name* Dom **Pedro de Al·cán′·ta·ra** (thē äl·kăNn′tȧ·rȧ). 1825–1891. Son of Dom Pedro I, b. Rio de Janeiro. Became emperor (1831–89) on abdication (Apr. 7, 1831) of his father; crowned 1841; in early years of reign, many revolutionary disturbances; aided Urquiza (1851–52) against Rosas in Argentina and joined Argentina and Uruguay in war (1865–70) against Paraguay; opened Amazon to commerce (1867) and worked for abolition of slavery (1871–88); absent several times in Europe during which periods his daughter Isabella acted as regent. Forced to abdicate (1889) on proclamation of republic (Nov. 15). Sent to Europe; died in Paris. A man of wide culture; his rule marked by great progress of Brazil.

**Pedro.** *Eng.* **Peter.** Name of five kings of Portugal, Pedro I being of house of Burgundy (*q.v.*), the others of house of Braganza (*q.v.*):

**Pedro I.** 1320–1367. King (1357–67); called "the Severe." Son of Alfonso IV, b. Coimbra; m. (1336) Constance Manuel (d. 1345), dau. of Juan Manuel de Villena; as prince, had unfortunate love affair with Inés de Castro (*q.v.*); as king, dispensed strict justice in person; avoided political relations with other kingdoms.

**Pedro II.** 1648–1706. King (1683–1706); called "the Pacific." Third son of John IV, b. Lisbon; dethroned his brother (1667) Alfonso VI, who was paralyzed and mentally weak; chosen regent for rest of Alfonso's reign (1667–83); concluded peace with Spain (1668); improved Portugal's financial condition; negotiated commercial treaty with England (1703); tried to remain neutral in War of Spanish Succession, but in last years definitely sided with Grand Alliance.

**Pedro III.** 1717–1786. Second son of John V and brother of King Joseph Emanuel; m. (1760) his niece Maria (see MARIA I); joint ruler with her (1777–86).

**Pedro IV.** See PEDRO I of Brazil.

**Pedro V.** *In full* **Pedro de Al·cán'ta·ra** (thē äl-kăɴn'tȧ·rȧ). 1837–1861. Son of Maria II (*q.v.*) and Ferdinand II. King (1853–61); under regency of father (1853–55); m. (1857) Princess Stephanie of Hohenzollern; died of cholera in Lisbon.

**Pe'dro** (pā'thrō). *Eng.* **Peter.** Name of four kings of Aragon:

**Pedro I.** 1074?–1104. King of Navarre and Aragon (1094–1104); defeated Moors (1094–96).

**Pedro II.** 1174–1213. King (1196–1213); fought at Navas de Tolosa (1212); killed in battle (1213).

**Pedro III.** 1236–1285. Called "the Great." King (1276–85); claimed Naples and Sicily from Charles of Anjou (1282); conquered Sicily; beginning of strife between Angevins and Aragonese.

**Pedro IV.** 1319–1387. Called "the Ceremonious." Son of Alfonso IV; king of Aragon (1336–87); annexed Balearic Islands (1344); fought with Peter the Cruel of Castile (1357–61); conquered Sicily (1377); ceded it to his son Martín.

**Pedro el Cru·el'** (ĕl krōō·ĕl'). *Eng.* **Peter the Cruel.** 1334–1369. King of Castile and León (1350–69). Son of Alfonso XI, b. in Burgos. Government marked by great cruelties; continually in conflict with his brother Henry of Trastamara; war with Pedro IV of Aragon (1357–61); with help of Edward, the English Black Prince, defeated Henry, Du Guesclin, and other allies at Nájera, or Navarrete (1367); after Edward's retirement, whole kingdom rose in rebellion; defeated at Montiel (1369), captured by Du Guesclin, and slain by Henry.

**Peek** (pēk), **Frank William.** 1881–1933. American electrical engineer; specialized in study of high-voltage phenomena and power transmission.

**Peek, George Nelson.** 1873–1943. American industrialist; president, Moline Plow Co. (1919–23); administrator, Agricultural Adjustment Act (1933); adviser to the president on foreign trade (1934–35), and president of the government export-import banks.

**Peel** (pēl), **John.** 1776–1854. English huntsman; maintained pack of hounds for 55 years at Caldbeck in Cumberland; celebrated in song *D'ye ken John Peel,* written impromptu by John Woodcock Graves.

**Peel,** Sir **Robert.** 1788–1850. English statesman. Son of **Robert Peel** (1750–1830), wealthy calico printer in Lancashire and contributor toward Pitt's war policy. Tory M.P. (1809); undersecretary for war and colonies (1810–12); chief secretary for Ireland (1812–18); combated successfully advocates of Roman Catholic emancipation; instituted Irish constabulary, nicknamed after him *peelers;* abused Daniel O'Connell and challenged him to duel, prevented by police. M.P. (1817); began to build financial reputation upon carrying resolutions embodying recommendations of Huskisson, Ricardo, and other economists for resumption of cash payments (1819). As house secretary (1821–27), defeated upon question of Roman Catholic emancipation, carried bills embodying reformation and humanizing of criminal law. Joined cabinet of duke of Wellington as home secretary and leader of House of Commons (1828–30) and was forced by circumstances to propose Roman Catholic emancipation. First lord of treasury, chancellor of exchequer, and prime minister (1834–35); outvoted in House of Commons, resigned; set about building up the Conservative party with policy of maintaining intact constitution of church and state. As first lord of treasury and prime minister (1841), with majority in both houses, imposed income tax and abated import duties on food and raw materials, with result that national debt and taxes were reduced; reorganized Bank of England; initiated reforms in Ireland; removed penal laws against Roman Catholics and municipal disabilities of Jews; carried measure repealing the corn laws (1846); defeated on Irish coercion bill by protectionists led by Lord Bentinck and Benjamin Disraeli and Whigs (1846). Supported Whigs in free-trade principles, emancipation of Jews; made last speech on Greek question in opposition to Palmerston's policy of interference (1850); mortally injured by fall from his horse.

Sir Robert's son **Arthur Wellesley** (1829–1912), 1st Viscount Peel, M.P. (1865), was speaker of House of Commons (1884–95) in a stormy period, and first invoked closure in combating Irish obstruction. The 1st viscount's son **William Robert Wellesley** (1867–1937), 1st earl, Viscount **Clan'field** (klăn'fēld) of Clanfield, was minister of transport (1921–22); secretary for India (1922–24, 1928–29); first commissioner of works (1924–28); lord privy seal (1931); member of Indian joint committee (1933), Palestine royal commission (1936–37).

**Peele** (pēl), **George.** 1556–1596. English dramatist and poet; doubtless a successful player, as well as versatile playwright. Author of *The Arraignment of Paris* (a pastoral comedy presented to Queen Elizabeth by the chapel children, c. 1581, printed 1584); a chronicle play, *King Edward the First* (1593); *The Battle of Alcazar* (acted 1588–89, printed 1594); *The Old Wives' Tale* (1595), characterized by a play within a play, and thought to have suggested subject of Milton's *Comus; The Love of King David and Fair Bethsabe* (1599); also of *Polyhymnia* (1590) and *The Honours of the Garter* (1593), and other occasional poems, and pageants.

**Pef'fer** (pĕf'ẽr), **Nathaniel.** 1890–1964. American educator, b. N.Y. City; A.B., Chicago (1911); professor of international relations, Columbia; authority on Far Eastern affairs.

**Peg'ler** (pĕg'lẽr), **Westbrook,** *in full* **James Westbrook.** 1894–1969. American journalist, b. Minneapolis, Minn.; on staff of United Press, as war correspondent (1916–18) and sports commentator (1919–25), Chicago *Tribune* (1925–33), New York *World-Telegram,* etc.

**Pé'goud'** (pā'gōō'), **Adolphe.** 1889–1915. French aviator; known for acrobatic flying feats; credited with first "looping the loop" in an aircraft; killed in aerial combat.

**Peguilhan, Aimeric de.** See AIMERIC DE PEGUILHAN.

**Pé'guy'** (pā'gē'), **Charles Pierre.** 1873–1914. French writer, b. Orléans; educ. at École Normale, where he came under influence of Henri Bergson, and at the Sorbonne. Founded (1900) the journal *Cahiers de la Quinzaine,* in which his chief works appeared. Author of studies on Joan of Arc, Victor Hugo, and Henri Bergson, and of religious meditations. Killed at first battle of the Marne.

**Peh Kü-jih.** Variant of Po CHÜ-I.

**Peirce** (pûrs; pērs). See also PEARCE, PEARSE, PIERCE.

**Peirce** (pûrs), **Benjamin.** 1809–1880. American mathematician and astronomer; professor, Harvard (1833–80); consulting astronomer for *American Nautical Almanac* (1849–67); superintendent, U.S. Coast Survey (1867–74). Renowned for accurate computation of the general perturbations of Uranus and Neptune, for his researches on the rings of Saturn, and for his papers in a new mathematical field *Linear Associative Algebra* (1870), first circulated in lithographed form and later (1881) printed in *American Journal of Mathematics.* Author of many mathematical textbooks, and *A System of Analytic Mechanics* (1855). His son **James Mills** (1834–1906) was also a mathematician; taught at Harvard (1861–1906), professor (from 1869); co-operated with President Eliot in introduction of liberal elective system in Harvard. Another son, **Charles Sanders** (1839–1914), was a physicist, mathematician, and logician; on staff of U.S. Coast Survey (1861–91); prepared numerous technical papers on logic (1867–85), laying foundations of the logic of relations, the instrument for logical analysis of mathematics, and contributing to the theory of probability and the logic of scientific methodology; lectured on logic, Johns Hopkins U. (1879–84); founder of pragmatism, first outlined in paper contributed to *Popular Science Monthly* (1878) and developed later by William James, and of pragmaticism, which Peirce differentiated from James's philosophy; now regarded as most original thinker and greatest logician of his time.

**Peirce** (pûrs), **Benjamin Osgood**. 1854–1914. American mathematician and physicist; taught at Harvard (1881–1914), professor (from 1888). Developed courses in pure mathematics and mathematical physics; conducted researches in electricity, magnetism, and hydrodynamics.

**Peirce** (*prob.* pûrs), **Cyrus**. 1790–1860. American educator; principal of first state normal school in Massachusetts, at Lexington (1839–42, 1844–49); pioneer work in this position did much to advance the normal-school system.

**Peirce** (pûrs), **George James**. 1868–1954. American botanist; author of textbooks of plant physiology.

**Peirse** (pērs), Sir **Richard Edmund Charles**. 1892–1970. British air chief marshal; deputy director of operations, air ministry (1930–33); commander in Palestine and Transjordan (1933–36); deputy chief of air staff (1937–40); vice-chief, and head of bomber command (1940–42); commander in India (1942–43); allied air chief in southeast Asia (1943–45).

**Peisander.** Variant of PISANDER.

**Peisistratus.** Variant of PISISTRATUS.

**Pei·xo′to** (pā·ē·shō′tōō), **Floriano**. 1842 (1839?)–1895. Brazilian general; a leader in establishment of Brazilian independence (1889); vice-president (1891); president (1891–94); put down naval revolt of Admiral Mello (1893–94).

**Pei·xot′to** (pā·shō′tō), **Ernest Clifford**. 1869–1940. American painter and illustrator, b. San Francisco; illustrated Theodore Roosevelt's *Life of Cromwell* and Henry Cabot Lodge's *Story of the Revolution;* painted murals for Cleveland Library. Attached to A.E.F. (captain) as official artist; his drawings now in National Museum in Washington, D.C. Author of *By Italian Seas* (1906), *Through Spain and Portugal* (1922), *A Bacchic Pilgrimage* (1932), etc.

**Pé′la′dan′** (pā′lȧ′däɴ′), **Joseph**, *called* **Joséphin**. 1858–1918. French writer; established reputation as mystic and master of the occult; founded order of "Rose-Croix" (1892–98), took to himself title of "Sar" (sȧr), and called attention to himself by his eccentricities. Published series of strange novels under general title *Décadence Latine.*

**Pe·la′gi·us** (pē·lā′jĭ·ŭs). Name of two popes (see *Table of Popes*, Nos. 60, 63): **Pelagius I**; pope (556–561). **Pelagius II**; pope (579–590).

**Pelagius.** 360?–?420. British monk and theologian; led theological disputation in Rome, refuting the Augustinian doctrines of predestination and total depravity, and asserting freedom of the will to do good and to do evil. Joined by Coelestius, a bold preacher, crossed to Africa (after sack of Rome by Goths, 410), and met Augustine; proceeded to Palestine. Accused of heresy (415); acquitted by synod of Jerusalem; called upon by Innocent I to abjure his teachings; through enmity of Emperor Theodosius, condemned by Zosimus and banished from Rome (418). His tenets (Pelagianism) persisted in modified form as semi-Pelagianism. Author of works *On the Trinity, On Free Will, Commentary on Paul's Epistles.*

**Pe·la′yo** (pā·lä′yō). d. 737. First Christian king (718–737) in Asturias after the conquest of Spain by the Arabs. A Gothic chieftain in the mountains, defeated Moslems at Covadonga (718); the beginning of the Christian recovery; deeds partly legendary.

**Pel′ham** (pĕl′ăm). Name of an English family of Hertfordshire dignified by the barony of Pelham, earldoms of **Clare** (klâr), **Chich′es·ter** (chĭch′ĭs·tẽr), and **Yar′bor′ough** (yär′bûr′ō; -bŭ·rŭ; -brŭ), and the dukedom of **New′cas′tle** (nū′kȧs′'l; *locally* nū·kăs′'l), including: Sir **William Pelham** (d. 1587), soldier; served on the Continent; strengthened defenses of kingdom; lord justice of Ireland (1579–80), joined with Ormonde in crushing Munster; became marshal of Leicester's forces in Netherlands, wounded at Doesburg (1586); from Sir William were descended the earls of Yarborough; from his half brother were descended the dukes of Newcastle (see NEWCASTLE). **Henry Pelham** (1695?–1754), statesman; a lord of treasury (1721) on recommendation of Walpole; secretary for war (1724); paymaster of the forces (1730); by union of parties, prime minister and chancellor of exchequer (1743–54); in Parliament reigned supreme, with his brother, Sir Thomas Pelham-Holles, Duke of Newcastle; an able financier, successful in holding together discordant elements chiefly by system of corruption. **Thomas Pelham** (1756–1826), 2d Earl of Chichester; M.A., Cantab. (1775); surveyor general of ordnance (1782); Irish secretary (1795–98); home secretary (1801–03); joint postmaster general (1807–23), postmaster general (1823–26). His brother **George** (1766–1827), bishop successively of Bristol (1803), Exeter (1807), and Lincoln (1820). **Henry Francis Pelham** (1846–1907), scholar and historian, grandson of 2d earl of Chichester; B.A., Oxon. (1869); tutor (1870–89), professor of ancient history (1889), curator of Bodleian (1892), president of Trinity Coll. (1897); author of *Outlines of Roman History* (1893).

**Pelham-Holles, Thomas.** Duke of **Newcastle.** See NEWCASTLE.

**Pé′lis′sier′** (pā′lē′syā′), **Aimable Jean Jacques**. Duc **de Ma′la′koff′** (dē mȧ′lȧ′kôf′). 1794–1864. French soldier; general of brigade (1846); governor general of Oran (1848); general of division (1850). Supported coup d'état (Dec. 2, 1851); commanded 1st army corps in Crimean War (1854–55) and succeeded Marshal Canrobert in supreme command; stormed the Malakoff (Sept. 8, 1855); created marshal of France, duc de Malakoff, and senator. French ambassador at London (1858–59); governor general of Algeria (1860–64).

**Pell** (pĕl), **John**. 1610–1685. English mathematician; professor, Amsterdam (1643–46), Breda (1646–52); diplomat for Cromwell in Switzerland (1654–58). Introduced the sign "÷" into England. The Pellian equation is so named from solutions of indeterminate equation $x^2 - Dy^2 = 1$ in his book.

**Pel′lé′** (pĕ′lā′), **Maurice César Joseph**. 1863–1924. French general in World War.

**Pellegrini, Pellegrino** and **Domenico Tibaldi de′**. See Pellegrino TIBALDI.

**Pel′le·tan′** (pĕl′täɴ′), **Pierre Clément Eugène**. 1813–1884. French journalist and politician; member of Corps Législatif (1864–76) and of Senate (1876–84); author of *Les Droits de l'Homme* (1858), *La Famille, La Mère* (1865), *Nouvelles Heures de Travail* (1870), etc. His son **Charles Camille** (1846–1915) was also a journalist and politician.

**Pel'le·tier'** (pĕl'tyā'), Sir **Charles Alphonse Pantaléon.** 1837–1911. Canadian lawyer and statesman; member of Canadian House of Commons (1869–77) and Senate (1877–1905); minister of agriculture (1877–78); speaker of the Senate (1896–1901); judge, superior court, Province of Quebec (1905–08); lieutenant governor of Quebec (1908).

**Pelletier, Pierre Joseph.** 1788–1842. French chemist; professor, and then assistant director, School of Pharmacy, Paris. With J. B. Caventou discovered strychnine, brucine, quinine, cinchonine, and other alkaloids.

**Pellew,** Sir **Edward.** See Viscount EXMOUTH.

**Pel'li·ca'nus** (pĕl'ē·kä'nōōs; *Angl.* pĕl'ĭ·kā'nŭs), **Konrad.** *Real name* **Kürsch'ner** (kürsh'nĕr). 1478–1556. Swiss scholar; originally a Franciscan monk, joined Reformation movement (c. 1526) and became professor of theology and librarian in Zurich. Chief work, *Commentaria Bibliorum* (7 vols., 1532–39).

**Pel'li·co** (pĕl'lē·kō), **Silvio.** 1789–1854. Italian writer and patriot; undertook management of *Il Conciliatore,* a politico-Romantic periodical; sentenced as a Carbonarist to 15 years at hard labor at Spielberg (1822); released (1830); lived at Turin (from 1834) as librarian to the marchesa di Barolo, reformer of Turin prisons. Known esp. for memoirs of his imprisonment *Le Mie Prigioni* (1832); author also of tragedies, as *Francesca da Rimini* (1815; Eng. transl. by Byron), *Laodamia, Ester d'Engaddi* (Eng. transl. 1836), and *Tommaso Moro* (1833), a translation of Byron's *Manfred,* mystic and religious poetry, and *Cantiche.*

**Pellione di Persano,** Count **Carlo.** See PERSANO.

**Pel'liot'** (pĕ'lyō'), **Paul.** 1878–1945. French traveler and Orientalist; explored central Asia, returning with collection of Chinese, Tibetan, Sanskrit, and Uigur manuscripts of dates earlier than 11th century (1906–08).

**Pel'lis'sier'** (pĕ'lē'syā'), **Georges Jacques Marie.** 1852–1918. French literary critic; author of *Traité...de Versification Française* (1882), *Études de Littérature Contemporaine* (1900–01), *Le Réalisme du Romantisme* (1912), etc.

**Pel·loux'** (pål·lōō'), **Luigi.** 1839–1924. Italian soldier and statesman; served in Africa (1885–89); lieutenant general (1891); elected deputy (1880); senator (1896); minister of war (1891–93, 1896–97); premier (1898–1900); retained army command to 1902.

**Pe·lop'i·das** (pē·lŏp'ĭ·dăs). Theban general; friend of Epaminondas, whom he aided in victory at Leuctra (371 B.C.); won battle of Cynoscephalae (364), but was killed in action.

**Pe·lou'bet** (pĕ·lōō'bĕt), **Francis Nathan.** 1831–1920. American Congregational clergyman; known esp. for his annual publication, *Select Notes on the International Sunday School Lessons* (1875–1920).

**Pe·louze'** (pē·lōōz'), **Théophile Jules.** 1807–1867. French chemist; assistant to Gay-Lussac in Paris; professor, Collège de France; collaborated with Liebig in Germany in work on organic chemistry. Discovered nitrosulphates; introduced use of sodium sulphate in glassmaking; studied effect of sunlight on colored glass; worked on enamels.

**Pel'tier'** (pĕl'tyā'), **Jean Charles Athanase.** 1785–1845. French physicist and meteorologist; discovered the Peltier effect, the production or absorption of heat at the junction of two metals on the passage of an electric current.

**Peltonen, Vihtori.** See Johannes LINNANKOSKI.

**Pelz** (pĕlts), **Paul Johannes.** 1841–1918. Architect, b. at Seitendorf, in Silesia, Germany; to U.S. as a boy. With John L. Smithmeyer, won competition for design of the Library of Congress (1873); also designed Army and Navy Hospital, Hot Springs, Ark., and buildings at Georgetown U. and U. of Virginia.

**Pem'ber·ton** (pĕm'bĕr·t'n; -tŭn), Sir **Francis.** 1625–1697. English judge; lord chief justice (1681); chief justice of common pleas (1683); removed from bench probably for lack of zeal in trial of Lord Russell (see *William Russell,* 1639–1683, under RUSSELL family); defended successfully (1688) the Seven Bishops (see Thomas KEN), precipitating the revolution which placed William of Orange upon British throne.

**Pemberton, John Clifford.** 1814–1881. American army officer, b. Philadelphia; grad. U.S.M.A., West Point (1837). In Florida Indian wars, Mexican War, and western frontier duty (to 1861). Resigned from U.S. army to enter Confederate service (1861); brigadier general (1861), major general (Feb., 1862) and lieutenant general (Oct., 1862). In charge of defense of Vicksburg, besieged by Grant; surrendered Vicksburg (July 4, 1863).

**Pemberton,** Sir **Max.** 1863–1950. English editor and novelist; editor of *Cassell's Magazine* (1896–1906). First novel, *The Diary of a Scoundrel* (1891). Author of many romances, including *The Iron Pirate* (1893), *The Hundred Days* (1905), *The Mad King Dies* (1928); of plays, including *The Finishing School, Lights Out;* of revues, including *Hullo, Ragtime;* of *The Life of Sir Henry Royce* (1934), *Sixty Years Ago and After* (1936).

**Pem'broke** (pĕm'brŏŏk), Countess of. See (1) *Anne Clifford,* under CLIFFORD family; (2) Lady Catherine SEYMOUR.

**Mary Her'bert** (hûr'bĕrt), *nee* **Sid'ney** (sĭd'nĭ). Countess of **Pembroke.** 1561–1621. English author and literary patron; sister and literary executor of Sir Philip Sidney; m. (1577) Henry Herbert, 2d Earl of Pembroke. Suggested Sidney's *Arcadia,* composed for her amusement (1580–81); collaborated with her brother in metrical psalms; translated French works; patron of Samuel Daniel, Nicholas Breton, Ben Jonson. Depicted by Spenser as Urania in *Colin Clouts Come Home Againe* and as Clorinda in *Astrophel.*

**Pembroke,** Earl of. Title first conferred (1138) by King Stephen of England upon Gilbert de Clare and held, by several different creations, by members of de Clare family (see CLARE), Marshal family (*q.v.*), de Valence family (see William de VALENCE), Hastings family (*q.v.*), by Humphrey, Duke of Gloucester (see HUMPHREY), William de la Pole (see de la POLE family), Jasper Tudor (*q.v.*), and thenceforth by members of Herbert family (*q.v.*, ¶1).

**Pe'ña·ran'da** (pā'nyä·rän'dä), **Enrique.** 1892– . President of Bolivia (1940–43).

**Pe'ña y Pe'ña** (pā'nyä ē pā'nyä), **Manuel de la.** 1789–1850. Mexican jurist; judge of supreme court (from 1824) and later its president; cabinet officer (1837, 1845); senator (1843–47); provisional president of Mexico (Sept.–Nov., 1847; Jan.–June, 1848). During latter term, Treaty of Guadalupe Hidalgo signed (Feb. 2), ending war with U.S.

**Penck** (pĕngk), **Albrecht.** 1858–1945. German geographer; professor, Berlin (1906–26) and director of the Institute for Oceanography and of the Geographical Institute. Proposed a uniform map for all countries of the world on a scale of one to 1,000,000 (1891).

**Pencz** *or* **Penz** (pĕnts), **Georg** *or* **Jörg.** 1500?–1550. German painter and engraver; one of group known as "the Little Masters." Painter of portraits and religious and mythological subjects; studio in Nuremberg.

**Pen'da** (pĕn'dȧ). 577?–655. King of Mercia; probably actually became king (633) on defeating and killing Edwin of Northumbria; champion of paganism against Christianity; defeated (634) and slew (642) Oswald of

Northumbria; drove King Cenwalh out of Wessex; routed East Angles and slew their king, Anna (654); on invasion of Northumbria, was defeated and slain by Oswy.

**Pen′de** (pĕn′dā), **Nicola.** 1880– . Italian physician; specialist in endocrinology.

**Pen′der** (pĕn′dẽr), **Harold.** 1879–1959. American electrical engineer; did work at Sorbonne proving existence of magnetic field around a moving electrically charged body (1903). Author of *Principles of Electrical Engineering* (1911), *Direct Current Machinery* (1921), etc.

**Pen′dle·ton** (pĕn′d'l·tŭn), **Edmund.** 1721–1803. American jurist, b. in Caroline County, Va.; leader in pre-Revolutionary activities; member, Committee of Correspondence (1773); member of Continental Congress (1774, 1775); president, Committee of Safety (1775); governor of Virginia (1774–76); presiding judge, Virginia supreme court of appeals (1779–1803). A great-grandnephew, **George Hunt Pendleton** (1825–1889), was a political leader, b. Cincinnati, Ohio; admitted to bar, Cincinnati (1847); member of U.S. House of Representatives (1857–65) and U.S. Senate (1879–85); as chairman of senate committee on civil service, secured passage of bill (1883) providing for civil service commission and for competitive examinations; U.S. minister to Germany (1885–89).

**Pendleton, Ellen Fitz.** 1864–1936. American educator, b. Westerly, R.I.; A.B. (1886), A.M. (1891), Wellesley; teacher of mathematics (1886–1911), president (1911–36), Wellesley.

**Pendragon.** See UTHER PENDRAGON.

**Pen′field** (pĕn′fēld), **Edward.** 1866–1925. American painter and illustrator, b. Brooklyn, N.Y.; art editor, *Harper's Magazine*, *Harper's Weekly*, and *Harper's Bazaar* (1890–1901).

**Penfield, Frederic Courtland.** 1855–1922. American diplomat, b. East Haddam, Conn.; diplomatic agent and consul general, Cairo, Egypt (1893–97); U.S. ambassador to Austria-Hungary (1913–17). Author of *Present Day Egypt* (1899), *East of Suez* (1907).

**Penfield, Wilder Graves.** 1891– . American surgeon; professor of neurology and neurosurgery, McGill U.; surgeon at Royal Victoria and Montreal General hospitals (1928–54), and first director of Montreal Neurological Institute (1934–60).

**Penfield, William Lawrence.** 1846–1909. American jurist; solicitor, U.S. Department of State (1897–1905); represented U.S. before international arbitral tribunals in fifteen cases, including the Pious Fund claim against Mexico.

**P'êng Têh-huai** (pŭng′ dŭ′hwī′). 1899– . Chinese Communist leader; joined Sun Yat-sen's army; joined (1927) Communist party; led insurrection in Hunan (1928); active in Red army campaigns; took part in "Long March" (1934–36); second in command, under Chu Teh, in Eighth Route Army in war against Japan (1937 ff.).

**Pen·hal′low** (pĕn·hăl′ō), **Samuel.** 1665–1726. Merchant and historian in America, b. in Cornwall, England; to America (1686) and settled (1687) at Portsmouth, N.H.; treasurer of the province (1699–1726); chief justice, superior court (1717). Author of *The History of the Wars of New-England with the Eastern Indians...1703–1713 and 1722–1725* (1726), a valuable historical source book.

**Penn** (pĕn), **John.** 1741?–1788. American Revolutionary leader, b. in Caroline County, Va.; practiced law in Virginia (1762–74) and in North Carolina (from 1774); member, Continental Congress (1775–80), and a signer of Declaration of Independence (1776).

**Penn,** Sir **William.** 1621–1670. English Parliamentary naval commander and father of William Penn (1644–1718; *q.v.*). Engaged in pursuit of Prince Rupert (1651–52); as vice-admiral under Robert Blake took part in victory off Portland (1653); commanded fleet sent against Spanish possessions in America; took Jamaica (1655); corresponded secretly with Royalists; at Restoration became Pepys's superior officer; won victory over Dutch near Lowestoft (1665).

**Penn, William.** 1644–1718. Son of Admiral Sir William Penn. Founder of proprietary colony of Pennsylvania, in America, b. London, England. Studied law; in charge of family estates in Ireland (1666). Joined Society of Friends, and preached and wrote as a Friend; imprisoned for nonconformity (1666, 1669, 1670). Engaged in English political campaigns, championing religious tolerance, frequent elections, and uncontrolled parliaments (1675–80). As a trustee to manage West Jersey colony in America, had important part in framing its charter (1677) with its famous Concessions and Agreements. Inherited from his father a large financial claim against Charles II; petitioned the king for a grant of land in the New World as payment of the debt; received grant of Pennsylvania (1681); visited the colony in person (1682) and took to the colonists his frame of government. In Pennsylvania, amended frame of government to meet popular demands; made peace treaties with the Indians; superintended laying out of Philadelphia. In England (1684–99) through accession of James II (1685), and revolution of 1688; ordered foundation of a public grammar school in Philadelphia (1689), which still exists as the William Penn Charter School; presented (1697) to London Board of Trade a plan for union of American colonies. Again in Pennsylvania (1699–1701); renewed peace treaties with Indians; granted a liberal charter (1701) to the colony. Stricken with apoplexy (1712) and his affairs managed by his wife, Hannah, until his death (July 30, 1718). He bequeathed his proprietary interests in Pennsylvania to his widow as executrix for their four sons, John, Thomas, Richard (1706–1771), and Dennis (d. before 1727). Elected to American Hall of Fame (1935). **Thomas** (1702–1775) managed the proprietorship in person in the colony (1732–41), and thereafter resided in England. A son of Richard Penn, **John** (1729–1795), was lieutenant governor of Pennsylvania (1763–71, 1773–76) and was a loyalist during American Revolution. A second son of Richard, **Richard** (1735–1811), served as lieutenant governor of Pennsylvania during John's absence (1771–73); to England (1775).

**Pen′na** (pĕn′ȧ), **Affonso Augusto Mo·rei′ra** (mōō-rā′rȧ). 1847–1909. Brazilian politician; member of commission that drafted Brazilian Civil Code (1888); supported new republic (1889); president of Bank of Brazil (1894–98); senator, then vice-president of Brazil (1902–06); president of Brazil (1906–09).

**Pen′nant** (pĕn′ănt), **Thomas.** 1726–1798. British naturalist, born of old Welsh family. Author of *British Zoology* (1766), *History of Quadrupeds* (1781). Chiefly remembered for *Tours in Scotland* (3 vols., 1771–90), *Tours in Wales* (3 vols., 1778); praised as traveler by Dr. Johnson.

**Pen′nell** (pĕn′'l), **Joseph.** 1857–1926. American etcher, b. Philadelphia; studio in Philadelphia (1880). First drawings, of a marsh in South Philadelphia, appeared in *Scribner's Monthly* (1881) and won him commission to illustrate articles by George W. Cable, published in a book *The Creoles of Louisiana* (1884). The Century Company sent him to Italy to illustrate articles by William Dean Howells on Tuscan cities. He and his wife (m. 1884), **Elizabeth,** *nee* **Rob′ins** [rŏb′ĭnz] (1855–1936), published *A Canterbury Pilgrimage* (1885), a small book with text by Mrs. Pennell and etchings by Pennell; continued this series by trips in various parts of Europe. Studio in London; etchings appeared in *Century*, *Harper's*, and leading English periodicals (from 1885). Interested himself in lithography (from 1895) and produced notable work in this medium. Returned to U.S. (1917) and made vivid drawings depicting industrial war activities.

**Pen'ne·thorne** (pĕn'ē·thôrn), **John.** 1808–1888. English architect; first discovered curved lines in Parthenon and upset belief that Greek architecture was absolutely rectilinear.

**Pen'ni** (pān'nē), **Gianfrancesco.** *Called* **Il Fat·to're** (ēl fät·tō'rā). 1488?–?1528. Italian painter of the Roman school; pupil of Raphael; aided master in many of his frescoes; after Raphael's death, continued, with Giulio Romano, his uncompleted works, as *The Baptism of Constantine by Pope Sylvester* (in the Vatican), and the *Cupid and Psyche* frescoes (in the Villa Farnesina, Rome).

**Pen'ni·man** (pĕn'ĭ·măn), **James Hosmer.** 1860–1931. American educator and historian, b. Alexandria, Va.; collector of Washingtoniana and authority on 18th-century American history. Author of books on education, and *George Washington as Commander-in-Chief* (1917), *George Washington as Man of Letters* (1918), *George Washington at Mount Vernon* (1921), *Philadelphia in the Early Eighteen Hundreds* (1923), etc. His brother **Josiah Harmar** (1868–1941), b. Concord, Mass., A.B. (1890) and Ph.D. (1895), Pennsylvania, was professor of English (from 1896), dean of faculty (1897–1909), vice-provost (1911–20), provost (from 1923), president (1923–30), U. of Pennsylvania.

**Pen'ny·pack'er** (pĕn'ĭ·păk'ēr), **Elijah Funk.** 1804–1888. American abolitionist, b. in Chester County, Pa.; joined Quakers (1841); made his house, near Phoenixville, Pa., a station on the underground railroad for escape of fugitive slaves. His nephew **Galusha Pennypacker** (1844–1916) served through Civil War, brigadier general of volunteers (1865), and was awarded Congressional Medal of Honor for heroism at Fort Fisher (Jan. 15, 1865). A distant relative, **Samuel Whitaker Pennypacker** (1843–1916), was a jurist; judge, court of common pleas, Philadelphia (1889–1902); governor of Pennsylvania (1903–07); president, Pennsylvania Historical Society (1900–16), and collector of large library of Pennsylvania history.

**Pen'rose** (pĕn'rōz), **Boies.** 1860–1921. American politician; U.S. senator from Pennsylvania (1897–1921); identified with high protective tariff legislation and opposed to prohibition, woman's suffrage, and measures regarded popularly as progressive. Republican boss of Pennsylvania after Quay's death (1904).

**Penrose, Francis Cranmer.** 1817–1903. English architect, archaeologist, and astronomer; detected alteration in pitch of pediment of Pantheon at Rome; practiced exact mensuration of Greek classical buildings, supported theories of John Pennethorne (*q.v.*), and expounded entasis; published *Principles of Athenian Architecture* (1851); designed British school at Athens (1882–86). Observed eclipses of sun at Jerez (1870) and at Denver (1878); author of *The Prediction and Reduction of Occultations and Eclipses* (1869).

**Pen'ry** (pĕn'rĭ), **John.** 1559–1593. Welsh Puritan writer of pamphlets; with his Puritan colleagues John Udall, Job Throckmorton, and the printer Robert Waldegrave, published *Martin Marprelate* tracts (1588) satirizing the bishops and defending the Presbyterian system of discipline; hanged on charge of exciting rebellion. See John Bridges (d. 1618).

**Penshurst,** Barons. See under Sir Thomas Smythe (1558?–1625).

**Pen'thiè'vre** (päN'tyâ'vr'), Duc **de. Louis Joseph de Vendôme.** 1654–1712. See under César de Bourbon, Duc de Vendôme.

**Penthièvre,** Duc **de. Louis Jean Marie de Bour'bon'** (dē bōōr'bôN'). 1725–1793. Admiral of France and governor of Brittany; distinguished himself at Fontenoy (1745) and Raucoux [Rocourt] (1746); patron of men of letters.

**Penz.** See Pencz.

**Pen'zi·as** (pĕn'zē·ăs), **Arno Allan.** 1933–     . American astrophysicist, b. Germany. With Bell Laboratories (1961–     ); awarded (with Robert W. Wilson) Nobel prize for physics (1978).

**Pe'pe** (pā'pā), **Guglielmo.** 1783–1855. Neapolitan soldier; as a Carbonarist, led Liberal revolution (1820); defeated by Austrians at Rieti (Mar. 7, 1821); banished under penalty of death; assumed command over Neapolitan troops sent to Lombardy against Austrians (1848); after recall of Neapolitan troops, participated as volunteer in defense of Venice (1849). Author of *Relations des Événements Politiques et Militaires à Naples, 1820–21* (1822), and memoirs. His brother **Florestano** (1780–1851) served in army of Murat in Spain (1809), in Russia (1812), and in Italy (1814, 1815); lieutenant general (1815); commanded Bourbon troops sent to quell Sicilian uprising (1820); retired to private life (1821) as an opponent of the reaction.

**Pe'pi** (pā'pĭ). Name of two kings of ancient Egypt of VIth (Memphite) dynasty: **Pepi I** *or* **Phi'os** (fī'ŏs) *or* **Mer'i·re'** (mĕr'ĭ·rā'). Third and greatest king of the dynasty (reigned c. 2590–2570 B.C.); sent several punitive expeditions against Bedouins of Sinai and into Palestine; left many monuments throughout Egypt, esp. pyramid Men-no-fer near Memphis; founder of Memphis [Greek form of *Men-no-fer*, "White Wall"]. **Pepi II** *or* **Phi'ops** (fī'ŏps). Son of Pepi I; reigned 90 years (c. 2566–2476 B.C.), longest reign known in history; generally uneventful, a period of decline, with king much of time controlled by influential nobles. His pyramid at Saqqara (opened 1881) contained religious texts.

**Pep'in** (pĕp'ĭn). *Fr.* **Pé'pin'** (pā'păN'). Name of two kings of Aquitaine:

**Pepin I.** 803?–838. Son of Louis the Pious; king (817–838); united with his brother Charles (later Charles the Bald) in wars against his father.

**Pepin II.** d. 870?. Son of Pepin I; king (838–864); defeated in war with Charles the Bald and deposed.

**Pepin.** *Fr.* **Pépin.** *Ger.* **Pip·pin'** (pĭ·pēn'). *Also* **Pep'pin** (pĕp'ĭn). Name of three Frankish mayors of the palace, ancestors of the Carolingian kings:

**Pepin the Elder** *or* **Pepin of Lan'den** (län'dĕn). *Ger.* **Pippin von Landen.** d. 640?. Mayor of the palace (628–639) for the Merovingian king Dagobert I; with Arnulf, Bishop of Metz, controlled the policy of the state.

**Pepin of Her'stal** (hĕr'stäl) *or* **Pepin II.** *Fr.* **Pépin d'Hé'ris'tal'** (dā'rēs'tal'). d. 714. Son of Pepin the Elder; became ruler of Austrasia (c. 679); mayor of the palace and ruler over all Franks (687–714).

**Pepin the Short.** *Fr.* **Pépin le Bref** (lē brĕf'). 714?–768. Son of Charles Martel; king of the Franks (751–768); as king of Germany, known as **Pepin III;** mayor of the palace (741–751); m. Bertha, daughter of Caribert, Count of Laon; deposed Childeric III (751), last of the Merovingian kings; founded the Carolingian dynasty (*q.v.*); aided Pope Stephen II against the Lombards (754–755); conquered them and bestowed upon the pope the sovereignty of the exarchate of Ravenna (Donation of Pepin); fought against the Saxons but left completion of their subjugation to his son Charlemagne.

**Pe'po·li** (pä'pō·lē), Marchese **Gioacchino Napoleone.** 1825–1881. Italian statesman; grandson of Murat; participated in defense of Bologna against Austrians (1848); headed provisional government of Bologna (1859); deputy to Italian parliament; minister of agriculture (1862); ambassador to St. Petersburg (1863–64) and Vienna (1868–70); senator (1868 ff.).

**Pep'per** (pĕp'ẽr), **Claude Denson.** 1900– . U.S. senator from Florida (1936–51).

**Pepper, George Seckel.** 1808–1890. American lawyer and philanthropist, b. Philadelphia; on board, Pennsylvania Academy of Fine Arts (1850–90) and president (from 1884); endowed professorship of hygiene, U. of Pennsylvania; bequeathed fund for establishment of free public library. His brother **William** (1810–1864), physician; practiced in Philadelphia. William's son **William** (1843–1898) was also a physician; instrumental in founding University Hospital, attached to medical school of U. of Pennsylvania (1874); provost of U. of Pennsylvania (1880–94) and professor of medicine (1884–98); as provost, had important part in enlarging educational opportunities afforded by university; liberal benefactor to U. of Pennsylvania and the city of Philadelphia.

**Pepper, George Wharton.** 1867–1961. American lawyer, b. Philadelphia; U.S. senator (1922–27). Author of *The Way* (1909), *A Voice from the Crowd* (1915), *Men and Issues* (1924), *In the Senate* (1930), *Family Quarrels* (1931), and legal treatises.

**Pep'per·ell** (pĕp'ẽr·ĕl), Sir **William.** 1696–1759. American general, b. Kittery Point, Me.; member of governor's council (1727–59); chief justice of Massachusetts (1730); commanded American force co-operating with British in capture of French fortress of Louisburg, on Cape Breton (1745); promoted to colonelcy (1745) and created baronet (1746), first native American so honored; raised regiment to serve in French and Indian War; major general (1755) and lieutenant general (1759).

**Pe'pusch** (pā'po͝osh), **John Christopher,** *Ger.* **Johann Christoph.** 1667–1752. Musician and composer, b. in Berlin; to London (1688); arranged tunes and composed overture for Gay's *Beggar's Opera* and *Polly* and other ballad operas.

**Pepys** (pēps; pĕps; pĕp'ĭs), **Samuel.** 1633–1703. English official in navy office and diarist; son of a London tailor; appointed clerk of the king's ships and clerk of the privy seal (1660); surveyor general of victualing office (1665) through naval war with Holland, sticking at his post through plague of 1666; secretary of the admiralty (1673); imprisoned during fanatical period of the Popish Plot, chiefly because of being trusted servant of duke of York (1679–80); visited Tangier and arranged for its evacuation (1683–84); reappointed secretary of admiralty (1684–89). Left to Magdalene College collection of books, manuscripts, prints, including 2000 ballads. Author of *Memoirs of the Royal Navy* (1690) and of a unique diary (Jan. 1, 1660–May 31, 1669), written in Thomas Shelton's system of shorthand, complicated with foreign words and invented ciphers, and offering an honest presentation of conduct of naval administration, ways of court and everyday life, as well as a candid self-portrait. Cf. Arthur BRYANT.

**Per'ce·val** (pûr'sē·văl), Sir **John.** 1st Earl of **Eg'mont** (ĕg'mŏnt; -mŭnt). 1683–1748. British political leader, b. in Ireland; great-grandson of Sir **Philip Perceval** (1605–1647) of Somerset, who settled in Ireland. British M.P. (1727–34); aided James Edward Oglethorpe in founding Georgia colony. His son Sir **John** (1711–1770), 2d earl, 1st Baron **Lov'el and Hol'land** (lŭv'ĕl, hŏl'ănd), was M.P. (1741, mostly to 1761); first lord of admiralty (1763–66). **Spencer Perceval** (1762–1812), statesman, was second son of 2d earl; in parliament supported Pitt's policy of war with France (from 1796); solicitor general (1801); attorney general (1802); opponent of Catholic emancipation; chancellor of exchequer under duke of Portland (1807), whom he succeeded as prime minister (1809); insisted on continuance of war; made bank notes legal tender (1811); assassinated by a bankrupt broker, John Bellingham.

**Per'cier'** (pĕr'syā'), **Charles.** 1764–1838. French architect; collaborator with Pierre Fontaine in remodeling Malmaison; with Fontaine, appointed architect for the Opéra (1794) and the Louvre and Tuileries (1802).

**Per'ci·val** (pûr'sĭ·văl), **James Gates.** 1795–1856. American scholar, b. Kensington, Conn.; gained reputation as poet by volumes of verse (1821, 1822, 1827), but his poetry is now seldom read; learned several foreign languages and assisted Noah Webster in revising and proofreading his dictionary (1827–28). State geologist of Connecticut (1835–38), and of Wisconsin (1855–56).

**Percival, John.** 1779–1862. Known as "Mad Jack" or "Roaring Jack." American naval officer, b. West Barnstable, Mass.; renowned for his exploits in War of 1812 and in later commands against West Indian pirates, in the South Seas, on a cruise around the world (1844–46). Hero in H. A. Wise's *Tales for the Marines* (1855).

**Per'cy** (pûr'sĭ). Name of a North of England noble family, originally Norman, whose founder **William de Percy** (1030?–1096), 1st Baron Percy, accompanied William the Conqueror to England, whose honors included dukedom and earldom of **North·um'ber·land** (nôr·thŭm'bẽr·lănd) and earldom and barony of **Percy,** and whose chief members were:

**Richard de Percy** (1170?–1244), 5th baron; one of the 25 barons entrusted with execution of Magna Charta.

**Henry de Percy** (1272?–1315), 1st Baron **Percy of Aln'wick** [ăn'ĭk] (from 1309 principal seat of family); aided Edward I in subjugation of Scotland. His son **Henry** (1299?–1352), 2d baron; took prisoner David II of Scotland at victory of Neville's Cross (1346).

Sir **Henry Percy** (1342–1408), 1st Earl of Northumberland (created 1377); grandson of the 2d Baron Percy of Alnwick; earl marshal of England (1377); at first supported Richard II in his despotism (1397); joined Henry of Lancaster (1399); was given Isle of Man in fief; revolted with his son (1403), submitted (1404), and restored to offices and lands; conspired with Owen Glendower and Edmund, son of 3d earl of March, to place the latter on the throne (1405); slain on Bramham Moor while invading England. His brother Sir **Thomas** (1344?–1403), Earl of **Worces'ter** (wo͝os'tẽr); served on mission to Flanders with Geoffrey Chaucer (1377); served on French and Spanish expeditions; deserting Richard II for Henry IV (1399), joined his brother's rebellion; captured at Shrewsbury and beheaded.

Sir **Henry Percy** (1364–1403), *called* **Hot'spur'** (hŏt'spûr'); eldest son of 1st earl of Northumberland; associated with his father as warden of the marches (1384) and in placing Henry IV on throne (1399); led English force in battle of Otterburn (1388); with George Dunbar, Earl of March, defeated Scots at Homildon Hill (1402), taking Douglas prisoner; forbidden by Henry IV to ransom his brother-in-law Sir Edmund de Mortimer, revolted (1403) with his father and Owen Glendower; slain at battle of Shrewsbury (1403); introduced as a fiery-tempered soldier in Shakespeare's *Henry IV,* Part I. Sir **Henry** (1394–1455), 2d Earl of Northumberland; son of Hotspur; liberated by Henry V and restored to titles and estates, from which time the family was loyal to house of Lancaster; furnished wardens of eastern and western marches. Sir **Henry** (1446–1489), 4th earl; grandson of 2d earl; temporarily deprived of titles and estates by Edward IV in favor of John Neville, Lord Montagu; restored (1469); murdered by populace on attempting to enforce a subsidy by order of Henry VII. Sir **Thomas Percy** (1528–1572), 7th earl; great-grandson of 4th earl; favored by Mary as a Roman Catholic and restored (1557) to earldom, which had been forfeited after the Pilgrimage of Grace insurrection (1537); beheaded after failure of revolt (1569) against Elizabeth in behalf of Mary, Queen of Scots. His brother Sir **Henry** (1532?–1585), 8th earl, was shot in prison under charge of participating in the Throckmorton conspiracy with Mary, Queen of Scots. **Thomas Percy** (1560–1605), great-grandson of 4th earl; upon nonfulfillment of James I's assurances of toleration for Roman Catholics, took active part in Gunpowder Plot and was mortally wounded in flight. Sir **Henry** (1564–1632), 9th earl; son of 8th earl; father of Lucy Hay (*q.v.*); called the "Wizard Earl" because of his scientific experiments; was imprisoned 15 years on condemnation for implication in the Gunpowder Plot; his brother **George** (1580–1632) was deputy governor of Virginia Colony (1609–10, 1611). Sir **Algernon** (1602–1668), 10th earl; son of 9th earl; lord high admiral (1638); endeavored to negotiate reconciliation with Charles I and opposed, in House of Lords, Charles's trial; with death of his son, the 11th earl, the family became extinct in direct line (1670).

Sir **Hugh Percy,** *orig.* Sir **Hugh Smith′son** [smĭth′s'n] (1715–1786), 1st Duke of **Northumberland** (3d creation); married (1740) granddaughter of 6th duke of Somerset and his wife, Lady Elizabeth Percy (1667–1722), heiress of 11th earl of Northumberland; assumed surname and arms of Percy; succeeded to earldom (1750) and was made duke (1766); lord lieutenant of Ireland (1763–65). His son Sir **Hugh** (1742–1817), 2d duke, fought in American Revolution (1774–77). Sir **Algernon** (1792–1865), 4th duke, 1st Baron **Prud′hoe** (prŭd′ō; -hō); 2d son of 2d duke; first lord of admiralty (1852–53); admiral (1862); sponsored publication (1863) of Edward William Lane's Arabic thesaurus. **Henry Algernon George Percy** (1871–1909), Earl **Percy;** eldest son of 7th duke; won Newdigate Prize at Oxford (1892); undersecretary for India (1902–03), for foreign affairs (1903–05); authority on Ottoman affairs; author of travel books about Turkey. His brother **Alan Ian** (1880–1930), 8th duke; educ. at Oxford (1897–99); served in Boer War, in Egypt (1907–10), in intelligence dept. in World War I; lord lieutenant of Northumberland; chancellor of Durham U. (1929–30).

**Percy, Florence.** Pseudonym of Elizabeth ALLEN.

**Percy, John.** 1817–1889. English metallurgist; discovered process of extracting silver from its ores and improved process of making Bessemer steel.

**Percy, Thomas.** 1729–1811. English antiquary and poet; bishop of Dromore (1782–1811); edited *Reliques of Ancient English Poetry* (1765), usually called *Percy's Reliques;* published a translation from French, *Northern Antiquities* (1770); author of *The Hermit of Warkworth* (1771) and other ballads. His nephew **Thomas Percy** (1768–1808) edited the *Reliques* and defended genuineness against Ritson's criticism.

**Per′di·ca′ris** (?pûr′dĭ·kä′rĭs), **Ion.** d. 1925. American citizen whose abduction (1904) from Tangier by Riff bandit Raisuli (*q.v.*) occasioned message by U.S. secretary of state Hay to sultan of Morocco: "Perdicaris alive or Raisuli dead."

**Per·dic′cas** (pûr·dĭk′ăs). Name of three kings of Macedon: **Perdiccas I** (fl. 700 B.C.), founder of Macedonian dynasty, an Argive who emigrated to Macedonia; **Perdiccas II** (d. about 413 B.C.), king during Peloponnesian War; **Perdiccas III** (d. 359 B.C.), brother of Philip.

**Perdiccas.** d. 321 B.C. Macedonian general under Alexander the Great; on death of Alexander (323 B.C.), appointed regent for Roxana (*q.v.*) and her infant son Alexander IV; held chief military command in Macedonia under Arrhidaeus, who had been elected king by Alexander's soldiers. When Antipater, Antigonus, Craterus, and Ptolemy formed league against him (322), invaded Egypt; killed in mutiny of his soldiers.

**Perdita.** See Mary ROBINSON.

**Pe·re′da** (pā·rā′thä), **Antonio de.** 1599–1669. Spanish painter, b. Valladolid. His *Ecce Homo* hangs in the Prado, Madrid.

**Pereda, José María de.** 1833–1906. Spanish novelist; originally, a military engineer. Among his novels are *El Buey Suelto* (1877), *Pedro Sánchez* (1883), *La Montálvez* (1888), *La Puchera* (1889), *Nubes de Estío* (1891), and *Peñas Arriba* (1895).

**Peregrina, La.** See AVELLANEDA Y ARTEAGA.

**Per′e·gri′nus Pro′teus** (pĕr′ē·grī′nŭs prō′tūs; prō′tē·ŭs). Cynic philosopher of 2d century; traveled to Rome, but was expelled for an insult to Emperor Antoninus Pius; taught in Athens. Realizing his popularity was passing, immolated himself on a funeral pyre at Olympic games (165). Subject of a novel by Wieland.

**Pe·rei′ra** (pĕ·rā′rȧ), **George Edward.** 1865–1923. English soldier and traveler; military attaché with Japanese army (1905), at Peiping (till 1910); commanded brigade in World War. Traveled from Peiping to Lhasa, interviewed Dalai Lama, crossed to Calcutta (1921–23), nearly seven thousand miles, more than half on foot.

**Pe·rei′ra** (pĕ·rā′ē·rȧ), **Nuno Álvares.** 1360–1431. Portuguese soldier and national hero; as constable of Portugal (1385) engaged in the battle of Aljubarrota, and aided in conquest of Ceuta (1415); retired to a Carmelite monastery (1423). Beatified by Pope Benedict XV (1918).

**Pereira de Souza, Washington Luiz.** See Washington LUIZ.

**Pereira Gomes, Wenceslau Braz.** See BRAZ PEREIRA GOMES.

**Pe′reire′** (pā′râr′), **Jacob Rodrigue.** *Orig. surname* **Pe·rei′ra** (pā·rĕ′ē·rä). 1715–1780. Spanish teacher of deaf mutes in France and originator of a sign language for their use. His grandsons **Jacob Émile** (1800–1875) and **Isaac** (1806–1880) were French financiers and brokers in Paris; founded (1852) the Crédit Mobilier.

**Per′el·man** (pûrl′măn), **Sidney Joseph.** 1904– . American writer: *Dawn Ginsbergh's Revenge* (1929), *Strictly from Hunger* (1937), *Look Who's Talking* (1940), *The Dream Department* (1943), etc.

**Pe·rey′** (pē·rā′), **Lucien.** *Pseudonym of* **Clara Adèle Luce Her′pin′** (ĕr′păN′). 1845–1914. French writer of biographies and 18th-century historical studies.

**Pe·rey′ra** (pā·rĕ′ē·rä), **Carlos.** 1871–1942. Mexican historian; chief work, *Historia de la América Española* (8 vols., 1922–26).

**Pé′rez** (pā′rāth), **Antonio.** 1539–1611. Spanish statesman; secretary of state to Philip II (1567); for Philip II, procured assassination of Juan de Escobedo, agent of John of Austria (1578); lost Philip's favor through relationship with Princesa de Éboli, mistress of the king; escaped to Aragon (1589), receiving protection of Aragonese courts. Prosecuted by Inquisition on instigation of Philip (1591); liberated by Aragonese people, whose constitutional privileges were abolished by Philip II in consequence; fled to London and Paris.

**Pé′rez** (pā′rās), **José Joaquín**. 1800–1890. Chilean political leader; president of Chile (1861–71).

**Pérez, Santiago**. 1830–1900. Colombian Liberal political leader; president of Colombia (1874–76).

**Pé′rez de A·ya′la** (pā′rāth thā ä·yä′lä), **Ramón**. 1881–1962. Spanish novelist, poet, critic, and diplomat; ambassador to London (1931–36). Author of lyrics, as *La Paz del Sendero* (1903), *El Sendero Innumerable* (1915), and *El Sendero Andante* (1921), and novels, as *Troteras y Danzaderas* (1913), *Prometeo* (1916), and *Tigre Juan* and sequel *El Curandero de Su Honra* (1926).

**Pérez de Guzmán.** See GUZMÁN.

**Pérez de Hi′ta** (thā ē′tä), **Ginés**. 16th-century Spanish writer and soldier; participated in war against Moriscos in the Alpujarras (1569–70). Author of historical novel *Historia de los Bandos de los Zegríes y Abencérajes*, better known as *Las Guerras Civiles de Granada* (Part I, 1595; Part II, 1604), important as antecedent of similar works in various literatures.

**Pérez de Montalván, Juan**. See MONTALVÁN.

**Pérez Gal·dós′** (gäl·dōs′), **Benito**. 1843–1920. Spanish novelist and playwright. His fiction includes a series of historical romances under the title *Episodios Nacionales* (46 volumes in all), and many novels reflecting contemporary life and its problems, as *Doña Perfecta* (1876), *Ángel Guerra* (1891); his plays include *La Loca de la Casa* (1893), *La de San Quintín* (1894), *Electra* (1900), *Mariucha* (1903).

**Per′fall** (pĕr′fäl), Baron **Karl von.** 1824–1907. German theater manager and composer; director of court music (from 1864) and of court theater (1867–93); composed esp. operas and choral works; author of *Die Entwicklung des Modernen Theaters* (1899). His nephews barons **Karl** (1851–1924) and **Anton** (1853–1912) **von Perfall** were novelists.

**Per′gaud′** (pĕr′gō′), **Louis**. 1882–1915. French writer, esp. of animal stories; his *De Goupil à Margot: Histoires de Bêtes* (1910) won the Goncourt prize.

**Per′go·le′si** (pār′gō·lā′sē) *or* **Per′go·le′se** (-sā), **Giovanni Battista**. 1710–1736. Italian composer; strongly influenced development of operatic and instrumental music. Among his notable works is the operetta *La Serva Padrona* (1733), which determined form of comic opera until time of Rossini. Composed also church music (including unfinished *Stabat Mater*) and chamber music.

**Pe′ri** (pā′rē), **Jacopo**. 1561–1633. Italian composer; music director at court of the Medici in Florence. In effort to reconstruct musical forms used by Greeks in representation of their tragedies, developed new recitative style adapted to stage use and with libretti of poet Rinuccini wrote *Dafne* (1594), now regarded as the first opera; also composed opera *Euridice* (1600).

**Per′i·an′der** (pĕr′ĭ·ăn′dĕr). d. 585 B.C. Greek statesman; son of Cypselus; tyrant of Corinth (625–585 B.C.); promoted Corinthian commerce; conquered Epidaurus; annexed Corcyra (Corfu); patron of men of letters. One of the Seven Wise Men of Greece.

**Per′i·cles** (pĕr′ĭ·klēz). d. 429 B.C. Athenian statesman, son of Xanthippus; leader of Democratic party. Secured ostracism of his political opponents, Cimon and Thucydides, and gained complete ascendancy over city (from c. 460 B.C.). While preparing Athens for inevitable conflict with Sparta, strove also to make city the center of art and literature and most beautiful city architecturally in world; responsible for building Parthenon, Propylaea, Odeon, and other noted buildings; gathered about himself group of noted people, including Anaxagoras and Phidias. His conduct of Peloponnesian War (begun 431) was vigorous and successful as long as he lived; stricken by plague (430) and died the next year (429). See ASPASIA.

**Pericoli, Niccolò**. See Il TRIBOLO.

**Pé′rier′** (pā′ryā′), **Casimir Pierre**. 1777–1832. French statesman; with brother **Antoine Scipion** (1776–1821), engaged in banking business in Paris (1801–17). Chosen deputy from Paris (1817); a leading member of opposition to Charles X (1824–30); after revolution of July, 1830, became prime minister to Louis Philippe (1831–32); restored civic order in France and re-established her prestige in Europe. His son **Auguste Casimir Périer** (1811–1878), politician and minister in Thiers administration (1871–72), who adopted (1873) the surname **Casimir-Périer,** was father of Jean Paul Pierre Casimir-Périer (*q.v.*).

**Pé′ri′gnon′** (pā′rē′nyôN′), **Pierre**. 1638–1715. French Benedictine monk, put in charge of the vineyards at his monastery; reputed discoverer of sparkling wines (champagne, etc.).

**Per′kin** (pûr′kĭn), Sir **William Henry**. 1838–1907. English chemist; produced mauve, the first synthetic dye (1856); with father and brother, established works near Harrow for manufacture of mauve, thus founding aniline dye industry (1857). Developed process for producing alizarin; first to synthesize coumarin; discovered the Perkin reaction for making aromatic unsaturated acids, such as cinnamic acid (1878); studied relation between chemical constitution and rotation of polarized light in a magnetic field.

**Per′kins** (pûr′kĭnz), **Charles Callahan**. 1823–1886. American writer on art; lectured on Greek and Roman art, and on sculpture and painting. Author of *Tuscan Sculptors* (1864), *Raphael and Michaelangelo* (1878), *Historical Handbook of Italian Sculpture* (1883), etc.

**Perkins, Frances**. 1882–1965. American social worker, b. Boston; m. Paul Caldwell Wilson (1913). Executive director, N.Y. Council of Organization for War Service (1917–19); member of N.Y. Industrial Commission (1919–21, 1929–33), of N.Y. Industrial Board (1923–33; chairman 1926–29); secretary of labor (1933–45); member, Civil Service Commission (1946–52).

**Perkins, George Walbridge**. 1862–1920. American financier, b. Chicago; partner in J. P. Morgan & Co. (1901–10). Joined Progressive party in support of Theodore Roosevelt (1912); wrote and spoke on current political and industrial problems.

**Perkins, Grace**. See under Charles Fulton OURSLER.

**Perkins, Jacob**. 1766–1849. American inventor, b. Newburyport, Mass.; invented machine to cut and head nails and tacks in one operation (c. 1790), a steel check plate for printing bank notes (c. 1808), improved high-pressure steam boilers and engines (1823–36). Established factory in England for printing bank notes; received contract (1840) for printing first penny postage stamps.

**Perkins, James Breck**. 1847–1910. American lawyer and author of works on French history, as *France Under Mazarin...* (2 vols., 1886), *France Under Louis XV* (2 vols., 1897), *France in the American Revolution* (1911).

**Perkins, Justin**. 1805–1869. Known as "the Apostle of Persia." American missionary to Nestorian Christians in northwestern Persia (1833). Established mission in Urmia (1835); opened schools, established printing press, reduced modern Syriac to writing, and issued books for the people. Author of *Missionary Life in Persia*, etc.

**Perkins, Milo Randolph**. 1900– . American government official, b. Milwaukee, Wis.; assistant to U.S. secretary of agriculture (1935–37); assistant administrator, Farm Security Administration (1937–39); associate administrator, Agricultural Adjustment Administration, and president of Federal Surplus Commodities Corporation (from 1939); executive director of Economic Defense Board (from 1941), renamed Board of Economic Warfare after Pearl Harbor.

**Perkins, Thomas Han′da·syd** (hăn′dȧ·sĭd). 1764–1854. American merchant, b. Boston; amassed fortune in trading ventures, esp. in Chinese goods; benefactor of Massachusetts General Hospital and Boston Athenaeum; deeded his home to New England Asylum for the Blind (1833), since renamed the Perkins Institute and Massachusetts School for the Blind.

**Perkins, William.** 1558–1602. English Puritan theologian.

**Per′ley** (pûr′lĭ), Sir **George Halsey.** 1857–1938. Canadian businessman and statesman, b. Lebanon, N.H.; naturalized Canadian citizen; in family lumber business in Ottawa; member, Canadian House of Commons (1904, 1908, 1911, 1925 ff.); minister without portfolio (1912–16; 1930–35), and acting premier (1912–13; 1933); secretary of state (1926). With other members of family, established Perley Home for Incurables (1897); presented to Ottawa a tuberculosis hospital (1912).

**Pern′ter** (pĕrn′tẽr), **Joseph Maria.** 1848–1908. Austrian geophysicist and meteorologist; did research on higher layers of the atmosphere and in meteorological optics.

**Pé′ro′chon′** (pā′rô′shôɴ′), **Ernest.** 1885–1942. French poet and novelist; winner of the Goncourt prize (1920) with his *Nène;* author also of *Chansons Alternées* (1908), *Les Ombres* (1922), *Bernard l'Ours* (1928), etc.

**Pe·rón′** (pâ·rôn′), **Juan Domingo.** 1895–1974. Argentine politician; entered army (1913); minister of war and secretary of labor and provision (from 1944); vice-president (1944–45); president of Argentina (1946–55, 1973–74).

**Pe·ro′si** (pâ·rô′zē), **Lorenzo.** 1872–1956. Italian secular priest and composer; music director, St. Mark's, Venice (1894), and Sistine Chapel, the Vatican, Rome (1897–1915). Among his compositions are oratorios *The Transfiguration*, *The Passion of Christ*, and *The Entry of Christ into Jerusalem*, choral works, as *Moses* and *Stabat Mater*, masses, motets, orchestral suites, quartets, etc.

**Per′o·ti′nus** (pĕr′ô·tī′nŭs). *French* **Pé′ro′tin′** (pā′rô′tăɴ′). 12th-century French composer.

**Pérouse, La.** See LA PÉROUSE.

**Pe·rowne′** (pē·rōn′), **John James Stewart.** 1823–1904. English prelate; member of Old Testament revision committee (1870–84); bishop of Worcester (1891–1901).

**Peroz.** See FIRUZ II.

**Per′raud′** (pĕ′rō′), **Jean Joseph.** 1819–1876. French sculptor.

**Per′rault′** (pĕ′rō′). Name of four brothers, prominent in the 17th century: **Pierre** (1608–1680), receiver-general of finances for U. of Paris, and writer. **Nicolas** (1611?–?1661), a Jansenist, and author of *La Morale des Jésuites Extraite Fidèlement de Leurs Livres.* **Claude** (1613–1688), physician and architect; dissected animals to study anatomy; designed façade on the Louvre and Paris Observatory. **Charles** (1628–1703), famous for his *Contes de Ma Mère l'Oye* (*Mother Goose Tales*) for children.

**Per′rers** (pĕr′ẽrz) *or* **de Wind′sor** (dē wĭn′zẽr), **Alice.** d. 1400. Mistress of Edward III of England; as lady of honor of Queen Philippa (from 1366), acquired influence over king; her banishment by Good Parliament (1376) for influencing judge's decisions revoked (1379).

**Per′ret** (pĕr′ĕt), **Frank Alvord.** 1867–1943. American volcanologist, b. Hartford, Conn.; founder and later director, Volcanological Museum, St. Pierre, Martinique.

**Per′rier′** (pĕ′ryā′), **Edmond,** *in full* **Jean Octave Edmond.** 1844–1921. French zoologist; professor (1876) and director (from 1900), Muséum d'Histoire Naturelle. Publications include *Les Colonies Animales et la Formation des Organismes* (1881), *Philosophie Zoologique avant Darwin* (1884), *L'Intelligence des Animaux* (1887), *Le Transformisme* (1888).

**Per′rin′** (pĕ′răɴ′), **Jean Baptiste.** 1870–1942. French physicist and chemist; studied X rays, cathode rays, and electrons; investigated Brownian movement of particles; awarded 1926 Nobel prize for physics for work on the discontinuous structure of matter and for discovery of equilibrium of sedimentation. Publications include *Traité de Chimie Physique* (1903), *Les Atomes* (1913), and *Les Éléments de la Physique* (1930).

**Perrin, Pierre.** 1620–1675. French writer; collaborated with Robert Cambert (*q.v.*) in writing first musical comedies in French.

**Per·rine′** (pĕ·rīn′), **Charles Dillon.** 1867–1951. American astronomer, b. Steubenville, Ohio; astronomer (1895–1909), Lick Observatory; director, Argentine National Observatory, S. America (1909–36). Discovered thirteen comets, motion in nebulosity about the new star in Perseus (1901), and the sixth and seventh satellites of Jupiter; investigated solar eclipse problems.

**Per·ro′ne** (pâr·rō′nâ), **Giovanni.** 1794–1876. Italian Jesuit theologian; active in condemnation of Hermesian heresy and in formulation of doctrine of Immaculate Conception. Known particularly for *Praelectiones Theologicae* (9 vols., 1835–42).

**Per′rot′** (pĕ′rō′), **Georges.** 1832–1914. French archaeologist; on archaeological expedition to Asia Minor (1861) which resulted in his reconstruction of text of *Monumentum Ancyranum.* Coauthor of *Histoire de l'Art dans l'Antiquité* (1882), etc.

**Per′rot** (pĕr′ŭt), Sir **John.** 1527?–1592. English governor in Ireland; reputed son of Henry VIII by Mary Berkley. Forced submission of the Irish rebel James Fitzmaurice Fitzgerald (1573); lord deputy of Ireland (1584–88); guilty of indiscretions of speech about Elizabeth; returned to London in disgrace; died in prison.

**Per′ro′tin′** (pĕ′rô′tăɴ′), **Henri Joseph Anastase.** 1845–1904. French astronomer at Nice (from 1880).

**Per′ry** (pĕr′ĭ), **Bliss.** 1860–1954. American educator and literary critic, b. Williamstown, Mass.; professor of English, Williams (1886–93), Princeton (1893–1900), Harvard (1907–30); editor, *Atlantic Monthly* (1899–1909); general editor, series of Cambridge editions of the poets (1905–09). Author of *The Broughton House* (1890), *The Powers at Play* (1899), *A Study of Prose Fiction* (1902), *Walt Whitman* (1906), *Whittier* (1907), *The American Mind* (1912), *Carlyle* (1915), *The American Spirit in Literature* (1918), *A Study of Poetry* (1920), *The Praise of Folly* (1923), *Pools and Ripples* (1927), *Emerson Today* (1931), *And Gladly Teach* (1935), etc.

**Perry, James De Wolf.** 1871–1947. American Protestant Episcopal clergyman, b. Germantown, Pa.; A.B., Pennsylvania (1891), B.D., Cambridge Theol. School (1895); bishop of Rhode Island (1911 ff.); primate of Protestant Episcopal Church in America (1930–37).

**Perry, Matthew Cal′braith** (kăl′brĕth). 1794–1858. American naval officer, b. Newport, R.I.; brother of Oliver Hazard Perry; pioneer advocate of naval steamships; with rank of captain, commanded the *Fulton*, one of the first naval steamships (1837) and is sometimes called father of the steam navy. Served (1843) on African coast in suppression of the slave trade; in command of squadron that captured (1846) Frontera, Tabasco, Laguna, Túxpam, and co-operated (1847) with Scott in siege of Vera Cruz during Mexican War. Sent (Nov., 1852) in command of squadron to Japan to negotiate a treaty which would open up that country to commerce; delivered his message and papers to representatives of the emperor (July 14, 1853) and sailed to

China to give Japanese time to consider proposals; returned and obtained treaty (signed Mar. 31, 1854) granting U.S. trading rights at ports of Hakodate and Shimoda; from this treaty dates the contact of Japan with western powers.

**Perry, Oliver Hazard.** 1785–1819. American naval officer, b. South Kingston, R.I.; brother of Matthew Calbraith Perry. In War of 1812, ordered to Erie, Pa. (1813), to build, equip, and man a fleet to contest control of Lake Erie with the British; fought battle of Lake Erie (Sept. 10, 1813); the *Lawrence*, his flagship, was so badly injured that he left it during the battle and was rowed to the *Niagara* where he continued the fight and forced the surrender of the British fleet. After the battle, he sent the famous brief dispatch to General Harrison: "We have met the enemy and they are ours." For his victory he received the thanks of Congress and a gold medal. Commander of the *Java*, in the Mediterranean (1816–17). On mission to Venezuela with small fleet (1819); contracted yellow fever on the Orinoco River, and died.

**Perry, Ralph Barton.** 1876–1957. American philosopher and educator; A.B., Princeton (1896), Ph.D., Harvard (1899); professor, Harvard (1913–46); author of *Approach to Philosophy* (1905), *The New Realism* (1912), *The Present Conflict of Ideals* (1918), *Annotated Bibliography of the Writings of William James* (1920), *General Theory of Value* (1926), *The Thought and Character of William James* (1935; Pulitzer prize biography), *Shall Not Perish From the Earth* (1940), *On All Fronts* (1941), *Puritanism and Democracy* (1944), *One World in the Making* (1945).

**Perry, Roland Hinton.** 1870–1941. American painter and sculptor, b. New York City; specialized in portrait painting (from 1917). Among his sculptures are *Fountain of Neptune*, in the Library of Congress; statue of Dr. Benjamin Rush, in Washington, D.C.; statue of Gen. George S. Greene, at Gettysburg, Pa.

**Perry, William James.** d. 1949. Eng. anthropologist; reader in compar. religion, U. of Manchester (1919–23); lecturer in history of religions, Oxford (1924–27); reader in cultural anthropology, U. of London. Author of *The Megalithic Culture of Indonesia* (1918), *The Children of the Sun* (1923), *The Origin of Magic and Religion* (1923), *The Growth of Civilisation* (1924), *Gods and Men* (1927), *The Primordial Ocean* (1935).

**Perry, William Stevens.** 1832–1898. American Protestant Episcopal clergyman and historian; historiographer of Episcopal Church (from 1868); bishop of Iowa (1876–98). Author of *Historical Collections Relating to the American Colonial Church* (5 vols., 1870–78), *The History of the American Episcopal Church, 1587–1883* (1885), etc.

**Per·sa′no** (pår·sä′nō), Count **Carlo Pel·lio′ne di** (pål·lyō′nā dē). 1806–1883. Italian naval officer; assumed command of fleet against Austrians in War of 1866; defeated by Admiral Tegetthof at Vis (July 20, 1866); deprived of rank by senate (1867).

**Perse, St. John.** See Alexis Saint-Leger LEGER.

**Per′seus** (pûr′sūs; -sē·ŭs). Last king of Macedon; succeeded his father, King Philip V, on the throne (179 B.C.); fought against Rome (172); defeated at Pydna (168), dethroned and taken captive to Rome (167).

**Per′shing** (pûr′shĭng), **John Joseph.** 1860–1948. American army commander, b. in Linn County, Mo.; grad. U.S.M.A., West Point (1886). On frontier duty (to 1898); served in Cuba (1898) and the Philippines (1899–1903). U.S. military attaché, Tokyo (1905–06), and with Kuroki's army in Manchuria (1905); brigadier general, U.S. army (1906); in command of Department of Mindanao; suppressed Moro uprising (1913); commanded expeditionary force sent into Mexico in pursuit of Francisco Villa (1916). Promoted major general (1916); commander in chief, American Expeditionary Force (1917–19); promoted general (1917); chief of staff, U.S. army (1921–24); retired from active service. Author of *My Experiences in the World War* (1931; awarded Pulitzer history prize, 1932). See Francis E. WARREN.

**Per′sian** (pûr′zhăn; -shăn). Name of XXVIIth to XXXth dynasties of kings of Egypt (525–332 B.C.) when Egypt was a Persian province. Some of rulers of these dynasties were natives under Persian control.

**Per′si′gny′** (pĕr′sē′nyē′), Duc **de. Jean Gilbert Victor Fia′lin′** (fyȧ′lăN′). 1808–1872. French politician; ardent propagandist for succession of Louis Napoleon to throne in France; involved in Bonapartist attempts at coups d'état in Strasbourg (1836), Boulogne (1840), and the final success at Paris (Dec. 2, 1851); minister of interior (1852–54; 1860–63); ambassador to Great Britain (1855–58; 1859–60).

**Per′sius** (pûr′shŭs; -shĭ·ŭs). *In full* **Aulus Persius Flac′cus** (flăk′ŭs). 34–62 A.D. Roman satirist, b. Volterra in Etruria; educ. Rome (from 46); friend of Stoic philosopher Cornutus and poet Lucan. Author of six satires, composed in hexameters.

**Persons, Robert.** See PARSONS.

**Per′tab Singh** (pŭr′tȧb sĭN′hȧ), Sir. 1845–1922. Indian soldier and statesman; placed at head of Jodhpur government by his brother Maharaja Sir Jaswant Singh; introduced railroads and irrigation; led force from India to China (1900) to relieve embassies in Peking; maharaja of Idar (1901–11); as regent of Jodhpur (1911–16, 1918–22) commanded Jodhpur Lancers in World War.

**Perth,** Earls and dukes of. See DRUMMOND family.

**Per′thes** (pĕr′tĕs). Name of family of German publishers, including: **Johann Georg Justus** (1749–1816), who founded a publishing house in Gotha. His son **Wilhelm** (1793–1853), who specialized in publication of geographical works. Johann's nephew **Friedrich Christoph** (1772–1843), who founded a firm in Hamburg (1796) and the national museum there (1810), and moved to Gotha (1822), where he specialized in publication of historical and theological works. Friedrich's son **Friedrich Andreas** (1813–1890), head of the firm Friedrich Andreas Perthes, Stuttgart. Johann's great-grandson **Joachim** (1899– ), who continued business founded by his great-grandfather.

**Per′ti′nax′** (pĕr′tē′nȧks′; *Angl.* pûr′t′n·ăks). *Pseudonym of* **Charles Gé′rault′** [zhā′rō′] (1878– ) and of **André Gé′raud′** [zhā′rō′] (1882–1974). French journalists. Gérault was prominent during World War (1914–18). Géraud succeeded to the pseudonym as writer on staff of *Écho de Paris* (to 1938), then becoming editor of *L'Europe Nouvelle;* to U.S. as refugee (1940).

**Per′ti·nax** (pûr′t′n·ăks), **Publius Helvius.** 126–193 A.D. Roman emperor (193), b. in Liguria; held consulship twice; chosen emperor against his will to succeed Commodus; reigned three months; killed in a mutiny of the Praetorian Guard.

**Pert′wee** (pûrt′wē), **Roland.** 1886–1963. English writer; author of the plays *Seein' Reason* (1913), *Hell's Loose* (1929), *Heat Wave* (1929), *A Prince of Romance* (1932), *Such an Enmity* (1936), of plays in collaboration with Harold Dearden and J. H. Turner, and of short stories and novels.

**Pertz** (pĕrts), **Georg Heinrich.** 1795–1876. German historian; archivist in Hanover (from 1816); chief librarian in Berlin (from 1842); editor of *Monumenta Germaniae Historica* (1823–73).

**Pe′ru·gi′no, Il** (ēl pā′rōō·jē′nō). *Real name* **Pietro Van·nuc′ci** (vän·nōōt′chē). *Also called* **Pier del′la Pie′ve** (dāl′lä pyâ′vā). 1446–1523. Italian painter;

leading Umbrian master of early Renaissance; master of Raphael; employed at Rome, Florence, and, particularly, Perugia. Among his works are *Crucifixion*, *Pietà*, frescoes, as *Delivery of the Keys to St. Peter*, in the Sistine chapel, Vatican, *Entombment*, in the Pitti Palace; also frescoes, a triptych, and portraits.

**Perugino, Il.** c. 1635–1700. See Pietro Santi BARTOLI.

**Pe·rutz′** (pĕ·ro͞ots′), **Max Ferdinand.** 1914– . British (Austrian-born) biochemist. To England (1936); awarded Nobel prize in chemistry (1962) with C. Kendrew for studies of the structures of globular proteins.

**Pe·ruz′zi** (pâ·ro͞ot′tsē), **Baldassare.** 1481–1536. Italian architect and painter; leading artist of High Renaissance; to Rome (1504); appointed architect of St. Peter's by Leo X (1520); to Siena after sack of Rome (1527); returned to Rome (1532). Among his paintings are frescoes in Church of Sant'Onofrio, on the ceiling of the Stanza d'Eliodoro in the Vatican, and in Church of Santa Maria della Pace (all in Rome); his architectural works include designs for Villa Farnesina and Ossoli Palace at Rome, fortifications of Siena, and (his chief work) Palazzo Massimi alle Colonne at Rome.

**Pesarese, Il.** See Simone CANTARINI.

**Pescara,** Marqués **de.** See Fernando de ÁVALOS.

**Pe′schel** (pĕsh′ĕl), **Oskar.** 1826–1875. German geographer; pioneer in modern geomorphology.

**Pe′sel·li′no, Il** (ēl pā′sâl·lē′nō). *Real name* **Francesco di Ste′fa·no** (dē stā′fä·nō; stâ′fä·nō). c. 1422–1457. Florentine painter; known esp. as painter of predelle and chests; among works are *Scenes from the Argonauts* (in Metropolitan Museum, N.Y.), *Crucifixion* (in Kaiser Friedrich Museum, Berlin), and *Birth of Christ* (in Uffizi Gallery, Florence).

**Pes·sô′a** (pĕ·sō′ȧ), **Epitacio da Sil′va** (thȧ sĭl′vȧ). 1865–1942. Brazilian political leader and jurist; elected (1919) president of Brazil to fill out term (1919–22) of Rodrigues Alves; member of Permanent Court of International Justice at The Hague (1924–30).

**Pes′ta·loz′zi** (pĕs′tä·lôt′sē), **Johann Heinrich.** 1746–1827. Swiss educational reformer, b. Zurich; established school for poor children on his estate at Neuhof and endeavored to put in practice educational theories of Jean Jacques Rousseau (*Émile*); although school failed (1780), derived from his experience a knowledge of certain principles for effective education; explained doctrines in didactic novel *Lienhard und Gertrud, ein Buch für das Volk* (1781–85). Principal of a school at Burgdorf (1799–1804); moved to Münchenbuchsee (1804) and Yverdon (1805–25). His emphasis upon concrete approach in education, with objects used to develop powers of observation and reasoning, has influenced strongly methods of instruction in elementary schools throughout Europe and America.

**Pé′tain′** (pā′tăN′), **Henri Philippe.** 1856–1951. French soldier; promoted general of division (1914); commanded corps that broke German front in battle of Artois (1915); commanded defense of Verdun (from Feb., 1916); commander in chief of the French armies, under Marshal Foch (1918); created marshal of France (1918); vice-president, Higher Council of War (1920–30); commanded French troops in Morocco (1925–26); minister of war (1934); ambassador to Spain (1939). Premier of Unoccupied France (1940–44); fled to Switzerland after Allied invasion; returned (Apr., 1945) for trial; convicted (Aug., 1945) of intelligence with enemy; death sentence commuted by de Gaulle to life imprisonment.

**Pe·tau′** (pē·tō′), **Denys.** *Latinized* **Pe·ta′vi·us** (pē·tā′vĭ·ŭs). 1583–1652. French Roman Catholic theologian and scholar; entered Jesuit order (1605). Wrote *Opus de Doctrina Temporum* (1627), *Tabulae Chronologicae* (1628), *Uranologion* (1630), *Rationarium Temporum* (1633–34), *Theologicorum Dogmatum* (1644–50), etc.

**Pe′ter** (pē′tẽr). See also PEDRO.

**Pe′ter** (pē′tẽr), Saint. *Lat.* **Pe′trus** (pē′trŭs). *Originally called* **Sim′e·on** (sĭm′ē·ŭn) *or* **Si′mon** (sī′mŭn). *Later* **Simon Peter.** *Sometimes* **Ce′phas** (sē′făs). d. 67? Son of Jona. A disciple of Jesus. After the Resurrection, made Jerusalem headquarters for preaching and proselyting in Palestine (c. 33–44 A.D.); imprisoned by Herod Agrippa I, but escaped; established see of Antioch. By well-founded tradition, went to Rome and died a martyr during persecutions of Nero. Roman Catholics accept Christ's words (*Matthew* xvi. 16–19) as appointing him his vicar on earth. Probably wrote two Epistles (included in the New Testament canon).

**Peter.** *In full* **Peter Or·se′o·lo** (pē′tẽr ôr·zâ′ô·lō). 1011–after 1050. King of Hungary (1038–46), second of the Árpád dynasty. Son of sister of St. Stephen and the doge of Venice; declared successor by Stephen; driven out (1041) by Samuel Aba, brother-in-law of Stephen, but restored (1044) with aid of Emperor Henry III.

**Peter I** of Montenegro. 1760?–1830. Prince bishop of Montenegro; succeeded his great-uncle in power (1782); allied himself with Russia and Austria against Turkey; later (1813), allied with Russia against France, and forced French out of Cattaro. Published a code of civil and administrative law for his country. His nephew **Peter II** (1812–1851) succeeded him (1830) as prince bishop, maintained civil order, opened schools, built roads, and made himself known as a poet by writing an epic, a five-act historical play, and a number of lyrics.

**Peter.** Name of three rulers of Russia:

**Peter I.** *Russ.* **Pëtr Alekseevich.** *Known as* **Peter the Great.** 1672–1725. Son of Alexis; reigned jointly with half brother Ivan (1682–89) and alone thereafter. Married (1689) Eudoxia (*q.v.*), sent her to a monastery and later (1712) married Catherine (*q.v.*). Traveled in Germany, Netherlands, England, and Austria (1696–97); returned to Russia and suppressed rebellion of the Strelitzi (1698). Engaged in long northern war (1700–21); defeated by Charles XII of Sweden at Narva (1700) and in turn decisively defeated him at Poltava (1709); concluded peace (1721) with Sweden at Nystadt (Uusikaupunki) and acquired Livonia, Estonia, Ingermanland (Ingria), and part of Karelia. Founded new capital, St. Petersburg (1703); renowned as introducing western European civilization into Russia and raising Russia to recognized place among great European powers.

**Peter II.** *Russ.* **Pëtr Alekseevich.** 1715–1730. Grandson of Peter the Great; succeeded Catherine I (1727; crowned, 1728); fell under influence of Dolgoruki family and was betrothed to one of its members; died a few days before the wedding date.

**Peter III.** *Russ.* **Pëtr Feodorovich.** 1728–1762. Grandson of Peter the Great; succeeded his aunt Elizabeth Petrovna (Jan. 5, 1762); mentally weak; deposed by group of nobles (see ORLOV) with connivance of his wife (July 8); abdicated (July 9); assassinated (July 17); succeeded by his wife, Catherine II (*q.v.*).

**Peter II** of Yugoslavia. 1923–1970. Son of King Alexander and grandson of King Peter I of the Karageorgevich line. King of the Serbs, Croats, and Slovenes (king of Yugoslavia); succeeded to the throne on death of Alexander (1934); government under a regency headed by his uncle Prince Paul (1934–41); assumed sovereignty (Mar., 1941); after German invasion (Apr., 1941), set up government in London; reign ended when Yugoslavia became republic (Nov., 1945).

**Peter, Hugh.** *Surname often* **Pe′ters** (pē′tẽrz). 1598–1660. English clergyman, b. in Cornwall; to America

(1635); pastor, Salem, Mass. (1636); active in establishment of colony at Saybrook, Conn., and in the building of Harvard College. Appointed (1641) to represent Massachusetts Bay Colony in England. Served as chaplain with Parliamentary forces (1642–49), and as a preacher before the Council during the Protectorate; reprimanded for attempts to mediate Dutch War (1652–53). At Restoration, arrested, tried as an accomplice in the execution of Charles I, condemned, and executed at Charing Cross (Oct. 16, 1660).

**Peter Chry·sol′o·gus** (krĭ·sŏl′ō·gŭs), Saint. 406–450. Doctor of the Church; consecrated bishop of Ravenna (433); famed as orator and writer; vigorous opponent of Monophysitism.

**Pe′ter Cla·ver′** (pē′tẽr klä·vĕr′), Saint. *Span.* San **Pe′dro Cla·ver′** (sän pā′thrō klä·vĕr′). 1580–1654. Spanish Jesuit missionary in South America, working esp. among African slaves; known as "Apostle of the Negroes." Canonized (1888).

**Pe′ter des Roches** (pē′tẽr dā rôsh′). d. 1238. English prelate, native of Poitou; knight and clerk under Richard I; bishop of Winchester (from 1205); stood by King John through struggle with barons; justiciar (1213). Led a royal division at battle of Lincoln (1217); left on crusade of Emperor Frederick II (1228); won distinction as soldier and diplomatist between emperor and pope. Returned, lost contest with Richard Marshal, 3d Earl of Pembroke, on denunciation by Edmund Rich, Archbishop of Canterbury. Assisted Gregory IX to defeat Romans (1235) at Viterbo.

**Pe′ter I Kar′a·geor′ge·vich** (pē′tẽr kăr′ȧ·jôr′jĕ·vĭch). *Serbian* **Pe′tar Ka·ra′djor′dje·vić** (pĕ′tär kä·rä′-dyôr′dyĕ·vēt′y′). 1844–1921. King of Serbia (1903–21), oldest son of Prince Alexander of the Karageorgevich line; trained in French military schools, and fought in the French army in the Franco-Prussian War (1870–71); commanded a corps in the rebellion of Bosnia and Herzegovina against Turkey (1875); lived most of time in exile until, after assassination of Alexander I Obrenovich (1903), he was proclaimed king by the army and elected unanimously by parliament; followed policy of alliance with Russia and friendship with France; after World War, received title of king of the Serbs, Croats and Slovenes (1918–21).

**Peter Lombard.** See LOMBARD.

**Pe′ter Mar′tyr** (pē′tẽr mär′tẽr). Name commonly used in English for:

(1) Saint **Peter Martyr.** *Properly* **Peter of Ve·ro′na** (vĕ·rō′nȧ; *Ital.* vå·rō′nä). d. 1252. Dominican in service of Inquisition in Lombardy; killed near Como by members of Catharist sect. Canonized (1253); patron saint of Spanish Inquisition.

(2) **Pietro Mar′ti·re d′An·ghie′ra** (mär′tē·rā däng-gyâ′rä) *or* **d′An·ghe′ra** (däng·gâ′rä). *Lat.* **Pe′trus Mar′tyr An·gle′ri·us** (pē′trŭs mär′tẽr ăng·glẽr′ĭ·ŭs). 1457–1526. Italian historian; royal chronicler, tutor to royal children, diplomatic representative of court of Ferdinand and Isabella of Spain (from 1487); dean of Cathedral of Granada (from 1505). Author of *De Rebus Oceanicis et Novo Orbe* (1516), giving first account of discovery of America; *Opus Epistolarum* (pub. 1530), letters on contemporary events.

(3) **Pietro Martire Ver·mi′gli** (vâr·mē′lyē). 1500–1562. Florentine Augustinian and promoter of Reformation. Read Bucer and Zwingli; accepted Reformed faith; fled from Italy as suspected heretic (1542); divinity professor, Strasbourg (1542–47, 1553–56). Brought to London by Cranmer; divinity professor, Oxford (1547–53); aided Cranmer with second *Book of Common Prayer.* Hebrew professor, Zurich (1556 ff.).

**Pe′ter No·las′co** (pē′tẽr nō·lăs′kō), Saint. d. 1256. French-born knight who distributed his wealth to the poor; in Barcelona (1208 ff.) and helped to ransom Christian captives in hands of the Moors; founded (c. 1218), with aid of James I of Aragon and Raymond of Peñafort, religious Order of Our Lady of Mercy for the Redemption of Captives; members of the order became known as Mercedarians. Cf. RAYMOND OF PEÑAFORT.

**Peter of Al·cán′ta·ra** (äl·kän′tä·rä), Saint. 1499–1562. Spanish ecclesiastic; ordained (1524); provincial of province of Saint Gabriel (1538); founded new branch of Franciscan order, members of which became known as Alcantarines; canonized (1669) by Pope Clement IX.

**Peter of Amiens.** See PETER THE HERMIT.

**Peter of Blois** (blwȧ). *Lat.* **Petrus Ble·sen′sis** (blē-sĕn′sĭs). c. 1135–c. 1208. French writer; tutor to William II of Sicily (1167–70); employed by Henry II of England; chancellor to archbishop of Canterbury (1173?); sent on missions to Rome; secretary to Queen Eleanor (1191–95); his *Epistolae* an important historical source.

**Peter of Bruys.** = Pierre de BRUYS.

**Peter of Courtenay.** *Fr.* **Pierre de Cour′te·nay′** (pyâr′ dē kōōr′tē·nā′). d. 1217. Latin emperor of Constantinople (1216–17); m. Yolande, sister of Emperor Baldwin I. Accompanied Philip Augustus on Third Crusade (1189–91); fought at Bouvines (1214). Chosen emperor (1216) but made prisoner on his journey east by despot of Epirus and died in captivity. Yolande ruled as regent (1217–19). See COURTENAY.

**Peter of Montboissier.** See PETER THE VENERABLE.

**Peter of Sa·voy′** (sȧ·voi′). Earl of **Rich′mond** (rĭch′-mŭnd). 1203?–1268. Savoyard diplomat in English service; son of count of Savoy. Resigned ecclesiastical preferments, married, received in England by Henry III with earldom and estates (1240); associated with Simon de Montfort and barons (from 1252); sent by Henry III on diplomatic missions to pope and Louis IX of France; assumed title of count of Savoy (1263).

**Peter of Verona.** See PETER MARTYR.

**Peter the Cruel.** See PEDRO EL CRUEL.

**Peter the Hermit.** *Known also as* **Peter of A′miens′** (ȧ′myăN′). 1050?–?1115. French hermit and monk; one of the preachers of the First Crusade (1095); led one section of the crusade to Constantinople (1096), where he joined section led by Walter the Penniless and crossed over to Asia Minor. His followers were destroyed by the Turks; he returned to Constantinople, joined the army of the princes (1097), and accompanied them through Asia Minor to Jerusalem. After the conquest of Jerusalem by the crusaders under Godfrey of Bouillon, Peter sailed back westward (late in 1099) and little is known of him thereafter.

**Peter the Lom′bard** (lŏm′bẽrd; -bärd; lŭm′-). *Lat.* **Pe′trus Lom·bar′dus** (pē′trŭs lŏm·bär′dŭs). 1100?–1160. Italian-born scholastic theologian; studied at Bologna, Reims, and Paris (under Abelard); bishop of Paris (1158). Renowned as author of *Sententiarum Libri Quatuor,* important as crystallizing the doctrine concerning the sacraments of the church.

**Peter the Venerable.** *Known also as* **Peter of Mont′bois′sier′** (môN′bwȧ′syā′). 1092?–1156. French-born monk; abbot of Cluny (from c. 1122); present at the Council of Pisa (1134); reputed instrumental in placing Innocent II on the papal throne and in gaining general church recognition of him instead of the antipope Anacletus; befriended Abelard in his last years.

**Peterborough,** Earls and countess of. See MORDAUNT family.

**Pe′ter·kin** (pē′tẽr·kĭn), **Julia**, *nee* **Mood** (mōōd). 1880–1961. American fiction writer, b. in Laurens County, S.C.; m. (1903) William George Peterkin. Author of *Green Thursday* (1924), *Black April* (1927), *Scarlet Sister Mary* (1928; awarded Pulitzer prize and subsequently dramatized), *Bright Skin* (1932), *Roll, Jordan, Roll* (1933), *Plantation Christmas* (1934).

**Pe′ter·mann** (pā′tẽr·män), **August**. 1822–1878. German geographer and cartographer; promoted geographical expeditions to Africa and to polar regions. Chief works include an atlas of physical geography and maps of inner Africa and the Transvaal.

**Pe′ters** (pā′tẽrs), **Carl**. 1856–1918. German explorer; founder of German East Africa colony. Founded German Colonization Society (1884); made treaties with native chiefs in East Africa (1884); returned to Europe and formed German East Africa Co. (1885). Led expedition into Africa for relief of Emin Pasha (1888–90); attempted to extend German sphere of influence in Africa; imperial high commissioner to district of Kilimanjaro (1891). Formed company in London for exploitation of Rhodesia and Portuguese East Africa (1898); discovered deserted gold mines and traces of ancient cities along the Zambezi (1899).

**Pe′ters** (pē′tẽrz), **Charles Rollo**. 1862–1928. American painter, b. San Francisco.

**Pe′ters** (pā′tẽrs), **Christian August Friedrich**. 1806–1880. German astronomer; professor, U. of Kiel (1874); wrote on nutation and on proper motion of Sirius.

**Pe′ters** (pē′tẽrz; *Ger.* pā′tẽrs), **Christian Henry Frederick**. 1813–1890. Astronomer, b. in Schleswig, Germany; to U.S. (1854); on staff of U.S. Coast Survey (1854–58); director, Hamilton College observatory (from 1858). Discovered forty-eight new asteroids and two comets; labored on preparation of charts of the zodiac, locating positions of all stars visible in this belt.

**Pe′ters** (pē′tẽrz), **Curtis Arnoux**. See Peter ARNO.

**Peters, Edward Dyer**. 1849–1917. American mining engineer and metallurgist, b. Dorchester, Mass.; professor of metallurgy, Harvard (from 1904); author of *Modern American Methods of Copper Smelting* (1887), *The Principles of Copper Smelting* (1907), etc. His first cousin **John Pun·nett′** (pŭ·nĕt′) **Peters** (1852–1921) was a Protestant Episcopal clergyman and archaeologist; in charge of excavations on site of ancient Nippur (1888–90) and director of the archaeological work there (to 1895).

**Peters, Hugh**. See PETER.

**Peters, Richard**. 1744–1828. American jurist; secretary of Continental Board of War (1776–81); member of Continental Congress (1782–83); judge, U.S. district court of Pennsylvania (1792–1828).

**Peters, Samuel Andrew**. 1735–1826. American Anglican clergyman, b. Hebron, Conn.; loyalist in sympathy at American Revolution; fled to England (1774) and lived (until 1804) on government pension; returned to America (1805) to press land claims along Mississippi River; claims disallowed by Congress (1826). Author of *A General History of Connecticut* (1781), containing the famous blue laws said to have been enacted in early days of New Haven Colony.

**Pe′ter·sen** (pā′tẽr·zĕn), **Eugen**. 1836–1919. German archaeologist.

**Petersen, Julius**. 1878–1941. German literary critic and historian.

**Petersen, Peter**. 1884–1952. German philosopher and educator.

**Pe′ter·son** (pē′tẽr·s'n), **Frederick**. 1859–1938. American physician and poet, b. Faribault, Minn.; on Columbia teaching staff (from 1897), professor (from 1903). Author of *Poems and Swedish Translations* (1883), *In the Shade of Ygdrasil* (1893), *A Song of the Latter Day* (1904), *Chinese Lyrics* (1916), *The Flutter of the Gold-Leaf* (1922), *Creative Re-education* (1936), and of professional treatises.

**Peterson, Henry**. 1818–1891. American editor, b. Philadelphia; edited *Saturday Evening Post* (1846–74); author of poetry and novels.

**Peterson**, Sir **William**. 1856–1921. British classical scholar and educational administrator, b. Edinburgh; first principal of University Coll., Dundee (1882–95); principal of McGill U., Montreal (1895–1919); editor of works of Quintilian, Tacitus, and Cicero.

**Pe′ters·sen** (pā′tẽr·sĕn), **Eilif**. 1852–1928. Norwegian landscape and genre painter.

**Pet′i·gru** (pĕt′ĭ·grōō), **James Louis**. 1789–1863. American lawyer, b. in Abbeville District, S.C.; member, South Carolina House of Representatives (1830–33) and head of Union party opposed to nullification; opposed secession (1860) but remained loyal to Southern cause after decision was made. His bust stands in Charleston's city hall.

**Pé′tion′** (pā′tyôɴ′), **Alexandre Sabès**. 1770–1818. Haitian general and politician, b. Port-au-Prince; a mulatto, well educated; fought in rebellion under Toussaint L'Ouverture and Rigaud (1791–97); in France (1800–02); served under Dessalines (1802–06); with Christophe assassinated Dessalines (1806); became president of independent republic in southern Haiti (1807); at war with Christophe (1811–18); his rule comparatively moderate and progressive.

**Pé′tion′ de Ville′neuve′** (pā′tyôɴ′ dē vēl′nûv′), **Jérôme**. 1756–1794. French revolutionist; deputy to States-General (1789); member of Jacobin Club and ally of Robespierre; mayor of Paris (1791–92); first president of National Convention (1792); favored Girondists, suspected of being a Royalist; imprisoned (1793) but escaped; committed suicide.

**Pe·tit′** (pē·tē′), **Alexis Thérèse**. 1791–1820. French physicist; with P. L. Dulong, developed methods for determining thermal expansion and specific heat of solid bodies; also with Dulong, enunciated principle (*law of Dulong and Petit*) that the elements in the solid state have nearly the same atomic heat (1819).

**Petit, Jean Louis**. 1674–1750. French surgeon; served as army surgeon and then gave private lectures on anatomy and surgery in Paris; originated numerous methods of operation; chief publication, *L'Art de Guérir les Maladies des Os* (1705).

**Petit de Julle′ville′** (dē zhül′vēl′), **Louis**. 1841–1900. French historian; professor, Faculté des Lettres, Paris; author of *Histoire Grecque* (1875), *Histoire Littéraire* (1884), *Histoire du Théâtre en France* (1880–86), etc.

**Pe·ti′tot′** (pē·tē′tō′), **Jean**. 1607–1691. Swiss painter in enamel; attached to court of Charles I of England; after Charles I's execution, moved to France, and was given lodgings in the Louvre by Louis XIV (1649); being a Protestant, fled to Geneva after revocation of Edict of Nantes (1685).

**Pet·lyu′ra** (pyĕt·lyōō′rŭ), **Simon**. 1879–1926. Ukrainian political and military leader; led Ukrainian army in opposition to Bolsheviks (1918–20); was defeated, and fled to Poland and, later, to Paris; assassinated in Paris.

**Pe′tő·fi** (pĕ′tû·fĭ), **Sándor**. *Surname orig.* **Pe′tro·vics** (pĕ′trô·vĭch). 1823–1849. Hungarian poet; early lyrics (*Verses*, 1844) were sponsored by the poet Vörösmarty, and his later work firmly established his place among the first of Hungary's lyric poets; active in Hungarian revolution (1848–49) and by his patriotic songs gained recognition as Hungary's national poet; believed killed in battle of Segesvár, or Schässburg. Among his collected volumes of verse are *Cypress Leaves on Etelka's Grave, Pearls of Love, Starless Nights,* and *Clouds.*

**Pe'trarch** (pē'trärk). *Ital.* **Francesco Pe·trar'ca** (pȧ-trär'kä), *orig.* **Pe·trac'co** (pȧ-träk'kō). 1304–1374. Italian poet, b. Arezzo; educ. Avignon; studied law at Montpellier (1319 ff.) and Bologna (1323 ff.); devoted himself to study of classics (1326 ff.). Assumed minor ecclesiastical orders (1326); lived at Avignon, where (c. 1327) he met Laura (see LAURA), who inspired his *Rime.* Visited Rome (1337); retired to Vaucluse; crowned poet laureate (Rome, 1341); entrusted with diplomatic mission by Clement VI (1343); settled in Milan (1353); on diplomatic missions for duke of Visconti (1356, 1360). Friend of Boccaccio; protégé of Colonna and Visconti families. Known particularly for *Canzoniere* or *Rime,* a collection of his Italian lyrics, chiefly sonnets and odes written to Laura; other works include, in Italian, allegory *I Trionfi,* and, in Latin, epic poem *Africa, Epistolae Metricae, Bucolica,* the treatises *De Contemptu Mundi, De Vita Solitaria, De Remediis Utriusque Fortunae, De Vera Sapientia, De Otio Religiosorum,* and *De Viris Illustribus,* letters, orations, etc.

**Pe'tre** (pē'tẽr), Sir **Edward.** 1631–1699. English Jesuit confessor of James II and promoter of policies leading to Revolution of 1688.

**Pe'tri** (pā'trē), **Egon.** 1881–1962. Pianist, b. Hanover, Germany; son of Dutch violinist **Henri Petri** (1856–1914), who was first violinist in orchestras at Hanover and (1889–1912) Dresden; studied violin and piano from childhood, as well as other instruments; concentrated on piano from 1900; first concert appearance in Holland (1902); taught in Manchester, England (1905–11), in Berlin (1911–17; 1920–25), Zakopane, Poland (1917–20), Basel (1920); settled in Zakopane (1925), teaching during summers, on tour during winters; U.S. concert debut (1932); fled Poland and settled in U.S. (1940).

**Pe'tri'** (pā'trĭ'), **Olaus.** 1493–1552. Swedish Lutheran clergyman; wrote one of earliest prose histories of Sweden, collaborated with his brother **Laurentius** (1499–1573), first Lutheran archbishop of Uppsala (1531), in translation of the Old Testament into Swedish.

**Pe'trie** (pē'trĭ), Sir **Flinders,** *in full* **William Matthew Flinders.** 1853–1942. English Egyptologist; grandson on mother's side of Capt. Matthew Flinders (*q.v.*); studied ancient British remains at Stonehenge (1875–80); wrote *Inductive Metrology* (1875); investigated pyramids at Giza and other Egyptian antiquities (1880–1914); excavated Tanis, discovered Naucratis (1885) and Daphnae (1886); uncovered funeral portraits and collections of papyri in Faiyum; excavated ancient Hawara, Kahun, Lachish; discovered temple at Medum (1891). Professor of Egyptology, University Coll., London (1892–1933); founded British School of Archaeology in Egypt (1894); discovered remains of a prehistoric race at Nagada (1895); uncovered stele of Merneptah at Thebes (1896), containing unique mention of Israel; investigated tombs of 1st dynasty at Abydos (1899) and site of palaces of Memphis, Tarkhan; excavated in Palestine (1927–38).

**Petrie, George.** 1789–1866. Irish landscape painter, antiquary, and collector of Irish songs and airs.

**Petro Bey.** See Petros MAVROMICHALIS.

**Pe'tro·nil'la** (pā'trō·nē'lyä). Queen of Aragon. See Ramón BERENGUER.

**Pe·tro'ni·us** (pē·trō'nĭ·ŭs), **Gaius.** *Surnamed* **Ar'bi·ter** (är'bĭ·tẽr). Roman exquisite of first century A.D.; proconsul in Bithynia; director of entertainments at Nero's court; called by Tacitus **Arbiter E'le·gan'ti·ae** (ĕl'ē-găn'shĭ·ē) or **E'le·gan'ti·a'rum** (-găn'shĭ·ā'rŭm), *i.e.* "judge of elegance." Generally regarded as author of *Satyricon,* satirical picaresque romance, in prose interspersed with verse, extant only in fragments, the chief episode being the "Cena Trimalchionis" ("Trimalchio's Dinner *or* Banquet"), describing a rich feast given the hero by the vulgar upstart Trimalchio.

**Pe·trov'** (pyĭ·trôf'), **Evgeni.** *Pen name of* **Evgeni Petrovich Ka·ta'ev** (kŭ·tȧ'yĕf). 1903–1942. Russian writer; war correspondent (1941–42); known for humorous writings, including the novels (in collaboration with Ilya Ilf) *Diamonds To Sit On* (trans. 1930), *Little Golden Calf* (1933), *Little Golden America* (1937).

**Pe·trun·ke'vitch** (pyĕ·tro͝on·kyā'vyĭch), **Alexander.** 1875–1964. American zoologist, b. in Russia; professor, Yale (from 1917). Author of *Free Will* (1905), *An Inquiry Into the Natural Classification of Spiders* (1933), etc.; also, *The Russian Revolution* (1917).

**Pe'trus Au·re'o·lus** (pē'trŭs ô·rē'ō·lŭs). d. about 1321. Franciscan monk and scholastic philosopher; archbishop of Aix; attacked realist doctrines of Duns Scotus (*q.v.*); regarded as precursor of William of Ockham (*q.v.*) in revival of nominalism.

**Petrus de Vinea** *or* **Vineis.** See PIETRO DELLA VIGNA.

**Petrus Lombardus.** See PETER THE LOMBARD.

**Petrus Ramus.** See RAMUS.

**Pe'trus Ven'er·ab'i·lis** (pē'trŭs vĕn'ẽr·ăb'ĭ·lĭs). = PETER THE VENERABLE.

**Pet'ten·ko'fen** (pĕt'ĕn·kō'fĕn), **August von.** 1822–1889. Austrian painter and lithographer; best known for military pictures and genre scenes.

**Pet'ten·ko'fer** (pĕt'ĕn·kō'fẽr), **Max von.** 1818–1901. German hygienist; founder of experimental hygiene in Germany; made researches on ventilation of dwellings, on gaseous metabolism in man, and on the function of clothing; as result of his observations on cholera, developed theory emphasizing importance of ground water and contamination of soil in origin of epidemics; in chemistry, originated method for detecting bile acids; also for quantitative determination of carbon dioxide.

**Pet'tie** (pĕt'ĭ), **George.** 1548–1589. English writer of romances; author of *A Petite Pallace of Pettie his Pleasure* (1576), including twelve modernized classical tales, titled by publisher in imitation of Painter's *Palace of Pleasure* (1566).

**Pettie, John.** 1839–1893. Scottish painter; took subjects from Scott's novels; exhibited historical and genre paintings, and portraits.

**Pet'ti·grew** (pĕt'ĭ·gro͞o), **James Bell.** 1834–1908. Scottish anatomist; published *Animal Locomotion* (1873) and *Design in Nature* (1908).

**Pettigrew, James Johnston.** 1828–1863. American Confederate general; served under Johnston through Peninsular campaign; in command, defenses of Petersburg (1862); in command of an advance on left of Pickett in charge at Gettysburg (July 3, 1863).

**Pet'ty** (pĕt'ĭ), Sir **William.** 1623–1687. English political economist and pioneer in science of comparative statistics; physician to army in Ireland (1652); completed in 13 months (1654) fresh survey, the "Down Survey," of Irish lands forfeited in 1641; served as commissioner of distribution of land grants to soldiers; secretary to Henry Cromwell (who became lord deputy of Ireland, 1657); made surveyor general of Ireland by Charles II; set up ironworks, opened mines, quarries, and fisheries. One of authors of first book on vital statistics (1662); one of first to point out errors in mercantilist position that abundance of precious metals sets standard of prosperity; showed unsoundness of prohibition upon exportation of money; his *Treatises of Taxes and Contributions* (1662, 1667, 1685) state doctrine that price depends upon labor necessary for production. His only daughter married

Thomas **Fitz·mau′rice** (fĭts·mô′rĭs; -mŏr′ĭs), 1st Earl of **Ker′ry** (kĕr′ĭ), whose son assumed (1751) name Petty and whose grandson was Sir William Petty, 1st Marquis of Lansdowne (see LANSDOWNE). Later marquises of Lansdowne, strictly named **Petty–Fitzmaurice,** used family name Fitzmaurice.

**Pet′zoldt** (pĕt′sôlt), **Joseph.** 1862–1929. German positivist philosopher; disciple of Ernst Mach.

**Peu′cer** (poi′tsẽr), **Kaspar.** 1525–1602. Son-in-law of Melanchthon. German physician and Protestant theologian; court physician to August, Elector of Saxony. Imprisoned (1574–86) for activity as leader of crypto-Calvinistic movement in Germany.

**Peuerbach, Georg.** See Georg PURBACH.

**Peu′ting·er** (poi′tĭng·ẽr), **Konrad.** 1465–1547. German humanist and antiquary; syndic of Augsburg (1493); known esp. as owner of a parchment map (called *Peutingerian table* after him) showing military roads of ancient Roman empire, which was bequeathed to him by Conradus Celtis (*q.v.*), who discovered it in a Benedictine monastery of Tegernsee, Upper Bavaria.

**Pey′er** (pī′ẽr), **Johann Konrad.** 1653–1712. Swiss physician and anatomist; professor in Schaffhausen; first to describe lymph follicles in walls of small intestine, now known as *Peyer's patches* or *glands* (1677).

**Pey′ré′** (pā′rā′), **Joseph.** 1892–1968. French novelist; author of *L'Escadron Blanc* and *Sang et Lumière* (awarded Goncourt prize, 1935).

**Pey′ro′net′** *or* **Pey′ron′net′** (pā′rô′nĕ′), Comte **Charles Ignace de.** 1778–1854. French politician; ultraconservative in sympathies, became minister of justice (1821–28) and minister of interior (1830); countersigned Ordinances of July 25, which were immediate cause of outbreak of the July revolution (1830). Convicted of treason and sentenced to life imprisonment and loss of civil rights; in prison (1830–34) and pardoned (1834).

**Pey′rou′ton′** (pā′rōō′tôɴ′), **Marcel B.** 1888?– . French politician; held administrative posts in French West Africa, Algeria, and Morocco; ambassador to Argentina (1936–40); resident general in Tunisia (1940); minister of interior in Pétain government at Vichy (1940–41); ambassador to Argentina (1941–42); governor general in Algiers (1943).

**Pezza, Michele.** See FRA DIAVOLO.

**Pfaff** (p′făf), **Johann Friedrich.** 1765–1825. German mathematician; known for work on the theory of series and on the solution of differential equations.

**Pfef′fer** (p′fĕf′ẽr), **Wilhelm.** 1845–1920. German botanist; known for work in plant physiology, esp. on osmotic pressure.

**Pfef′fer·korn** (p′fĕf′ẽr·kôrn), **Johannes.** 1469–1524. German controversialist; engaged in controversy with Reuchlin and other Humanists and instigated preparation and publication by Humanists of great satirical work *Epistolae Obscurorum Virorum.* See Ulrich von HUTTEN.

**Pfeif′fer** (p′fī′fẽr), **Franz.** 1815–1868. German scholar; specialized in study of Middle High German works.

**Pfeiffer, Ida Laura,** *nee* **Rey′er** (rī′ẽr). 1797–1858. Traveler, b. Vienna; m. Dr. Pfeiffer, a lawyer of Lemberg (1820); traveled extensively (after 1842), making two trips around the world; author of *Eine Frauenfahrt um die Welt* (1850), *Meine Zweite Weltreise* (1856), etc.

**Pfeiffer, Richard Friedrich Johann.** 1858–1945. German bacteriologist; army surgeon (1879–89); assistant to Robert Koch (1887); head of research department, Inst. for Infectious Diseases, Berlin (1891); professor of hygiene and director, Inst. of Hygiene, Königsberg (1899); professor in Breslau (1909–1926). Discovered a bacillus (Pfeiffer's bacillus) found in cases of influenza (1892); worked on a specific immune serum against influenza; gave account of reaction (Pfeiffer reaction or phenomenon) serving for determination of cholera (1894). Pfeiffer reaction consists of loss of motility, granular degeneration, and subsequent solution of bacteria following their injection into peritoneal cavity of a guinea pig immunized against them.

**Pfeil** (p′fīl), Count **Joachim.** 1857–1924. German explorer in Africa and the western Pacific area.

**Pfi′ster** (p′fĭs′tẽr), **Albrecht.** d. before 1466. German printer, one of earliest printers in Germany. At one time, supposed to be printer of the *Bible of 36 lines,* sometimes called *Pfister's Bible.*

**Pfis′ter′** (fēs′târ′), **Christian.** 1857–1933. French historian; author of treatises on medieval French history.

**Pfitz′ner** (p′fĭts′nẽr), **Hans.** 1869–1949. German composer; director of Conservatory of Music, municipal concerts, and (from 1909) the opera, Strassburg (1908–18); teacher in composition at Acad. of Art, Berlin (1919–29) and Munich (1929 ff.). Among his operas are *Der Arme Heinrich* (1895), *Palestrina* (1917), and *Das Herz* (1931); among his choral works, *Kolumbus* (1905), *Das Dunkle Reich* (1930); among his instrumental works, *Scherzo in C-minor,* concertos, quartets.

**Pflan′zer–Bal′tin** (p′flän′tsẽr·bäl′tēn), Baron **Karl von.** 1855–1925. Austro-Hungarian general in World War; driven back by Russian army under Brusilov (June, 1916) and relieved of command; commanded on Albanian front (1918).

**Pflei′de·rer** (p′flī′dĕ·rẽr), **Otto.** 1839–1908. German Protestant theologian. His brother **Edmund** (1842–1902) was a philosopher.

**Pflü′ger** (p′flü′gẽr), **Eduard Friedrich Wilhelm.** 1829–1910. German physiologist; known for work on sensory function of the spinal cord, on intestinal nerves, on electrical stimulation of motor nerves, and on digestive and metabolic processes.

**Pflugk′–Hart′tung** (p′flŏŏk′här′tŏŏng), **Julius von.** 1848–1919. German historian; in charge of secret government archives in Berlin (1893). Author of *Geschichte des Mittelalters* (1888), *Napoleon I* (in collaboration; 2 vols., 1900–01), etc.

**Pford′ten** (p′fôr′tĕn), Baron **Ludwig von der.** 1811–1880. Bavarian jurist and statesman; professor, Würzburg (1834); councilor, court of appeal, Aschaffenburg (1841); premier of Bavaria (1849–59, 1864–66).

**Pforr** (p′fôr), **Franz.** 1788–1812. German painter; a leader of the Nazarenes.

**Phae′do** (fē′dō) *or* **Phae′don** (-dŏn). Greek philosopher of early 4th century B.C., of Elis; disciple of Socrates; founder of Elian school of philosophy. Appears as principal speaker in Plato's dialogue *Phaedo,* which treats of immortality of the soul and purports to record Socrates' last conversation. None of his works is extant.

**Phae′drus** (fē′drŭs). Greek philosopher of 5th century B.C.; contemporary of Socrates and Plato; one of Plato's dialogues (attacking prevailing conception of rhetoric) bears his name.

**Phaedrus.** Roman fabulist of early 1st century A.D.; apparently a freedman of Augustus, originally a Macedonian slave; author of *Fabulae Aesopiae* (5 books), chiefly versifications of fables of the Aesop cycle.

**Phaer** (fâr) *or* **Phay′er** (fā′ẽr; fâr), **Thomas.** 1510?–1560. English lawyer, physician, and translator of nine books of Vergil's *Aeneid* into English verse (1555–60).

**Phal′a·ris** (făl′ȧ·rĭs). Greek politician; tyrant of Agrigento in Sicily (570–554 B.C.). According to tradition, he was notoriously cruel, burning human sacrifices inside a brazen bull; finally overthrown and executed by being burned in the same brazen bull.

**Phantasus.** Pseudonym of MAXIMILIAN JOSEPH.

**Pharaoh–Nechoh** *or* **Pharaoh–Necoh.** See NECHO.

**Phar′na·ba′zus** (fär′nȧ·bā′zŭs). Persian commander; negotiated alliance with Sparta against Athens (413 B.C.); later, aided Athenians under Conon in defeating Spartan fleet at Cnidus (394); engaged in expeditions against Egypt (385 and 373), but failed.

**Phar′na·ces** (fär′nȧ·sēz). Name of two kings of Pontus: **Pharnaces I** (reigned c. 183–170 B.C.). **Pharnaces II** (reigned c. 63–47 B.C.), son of Mithridates the Great; sided with Pompey in the Roman Civil War and was defeated by Caesar in battle near Zela (47), after which Caesar sent to the senate at Rome his famous laconic message announcing victory, *Veni, Vidi, Vici.*

**Phei′di·as** (fī′dĭ·ăs). = PHIDIAS.

**Phei·dip′pi·des** *or* **Phi·dip′pi·des** (fī·dĭp′ĭ·dēz) *or* **Phi·lip′pi·des** (fī·lĭp′ĭ·dēz). Athenian long-distance runner, dispatched to Sparta asking for aid just before battle of Marathon. Often confused with unknown Greek runner who reputedly carried news of Greek victory at Marathon (490 B.C.) from field of battle to Athens, the feat after which the modern "marathon race" is named.

**Phelps** (fĕlps), **Edward John.** 1822–1900. American lawyer and diplomat, b. Middlebury, Vt.; practiced in Burlington, Vt. (from 1845); comptroller, U.S. Treasury (1851–53); U.S. minister to Great Britain (1885–89); counsel for U.S. in fur seal arbitration with Great Britain (1893).

**Phelps, Elizabeth Stuart.** See Elizabeth S. WARD.

**Phelps, John Wolcott.** 1813–1885. American soldier, b. Guilford Centre, Vt.; grad. U.S.M.A., West Point (1836); brigadier general of volunteers (May 17, 1861); co-operated with Farragut in clearing lower Mississippi River (Apr., 1862); organized, in New Orleans, first Negro troops for service in federal armies (1862); resigned (Aug. 21, 1862) when federal government disavowed his act and ordered troops disbanded and men be used as common laborers. American Party nominee for president of U.S. (1880).

**Phelps, Oliver.** 1749–1809. American land speculator, b. near Poquonock, Conn.; deputy commissary of Continental army (1777–81). With one Nathaniel Gorman, formed syndicate to buy Massachusetts' land holdings in western New York; contracted for purchase of 6,000,000 acres (1788); failed to interest buyers and turned back to Massachusetts most of the tract.

**Phelps, Samuel.** 1804–1878. English actor-manager; appeared in Haymarket Theatre, London, as Shylock (1837); colessee of Sadler's Wells Theatre (1844–62), where he produced 34 of Shakespeare's plays.

**Phelps, William Lyon.** 1865–1943. American educator and literary critic, b. New Haven, Conn.; on Yale faculty (from 1892), professor (from 1901). Author of *Essays on Modern Novelists* (1910), *Browning* (1915), *The Advance of the English Novel* (1916), *The Advance of English Poetry* (1918), *The Twentieth Century Theatre* (1918), *Reading the Bible* (1919), *As I Like It* (1923), *Happiness* (1926), *What I Like in Poetry* (1934), *What I Like in Prose* (1934), *Autobiography with Letters* (1939).

**Phelps, William Walter.** 1839–1894. American lawyer and diplomat, b. Dundaff, Pa.; member, U.S. House of Representatives, from New Jersey (1873–75, 1883–89); U.S. minister to Austria (1881), Germany (1889–93).

**Phe·rec′ra·tes** (fĕ·rĕk′rȧ·tēz). Greek playwright; winner of prize for comedy (438 B.C.); inventor of a meter called *Pherecratic,* or *Pherecratean,* after him.

**Pher′e·cy′des of Le′ros** (fĕr′ĕ·sī′dēz, lē′rŏs). Greek philosopher of 5th century B.C.; only fragments of his works extant.

**Pherecydes of Sy′ros** (sī′rŏs). Greek philosopher of 6th century B.C., sometimes counted among Seven Wise Men of Greece; reputed originator of doctrine of metempsychosis. Only fragments of works extant.

**Phid′i·as** (fĭd′ĭ·ăs). Greek sculptor of 5th century B.C.; regarded as greatest of ancient Greek sculptors. Studied under Ageladas; commissioned, during ascendancy of Pericles at Athens, to execute greatest of city's monuments and charged with general supervision of all public works under construction; charged, by political enemies of Pericles, with sacrilege because he represented himself and Pericles on shield of goddess Athena; said to have been convicted on this charge and imprisoned and to have died in prison. Among his notable works were sculptures on the Parthenon and the Propylaea, statue of Olympian Zeus at Elis, statue *Athene Parthenos,* and statue of an Amazon at Ephesus.

**Phidippides.** See PHEIDIPPIDES.

**Philadelphus.** See (1) ANTIOCHUS XI of Syria; (2) ATTALUS II; (3) PTOLEMY II.

**Philalethes.** Pseudonym of JOHN, King of Saxony.

**Philander von Sittewald.** Pen name of Johann Michael MOSCHEROSCH.

**Phi·la·ret′** (fyĭ·lŭ·ryât′). *Lay name* **Fëdor Nikitich Ro·ma′nov** (rŭ·mȧ′nôf). 1553?–1633. Patriarch of Moscow; cousin of Czar Fedor I (see ROMANOV), and after his death (1598) an unsuccessful candidate for the throne. Forced by Czar Boris Godunov to take monastic vows under the name of Philaret (c. 1601); metropolitan of Rostov (1605); patriarch of Moscow (1619).

**Philaret.** *Lay name* **Vasili Mikhailovich Droz·dov′** (drŭs·dôf′). 1782–1867. Metropolitan of Moscow (1825 ff.); author of standard catechism adopted (1829) by Holy Synod of Church of Russia.

**Phil′by** (fĭl′bĭ), **Harry St. John Bridger.** 1885–1960. British explorer in Arabia; author of *The Heart of Arabia* (1922), *Sheba's Daughters* (1939), etc.

**Philelphus.** See Francesco FILELFO.

**Phi·le′mon** (fĭ·lē′mŏn; fī-). 361?–?263 B.C. Greek playwright; author of comedies; rival of Menander, defeating him several times in contests; only fragments extant.

**Philemon.** A friend and probable convert of St. Paul, living in Colossae, to whom is addressed the New Testament *Epistle to Philemon.*

**Philenia.** Pseudonym of Sarah Wentworth Apthorp MORTON.

**Phil′e·tae′ros** (fĭl′ĕ·tē′rŏs). Paphlagonian eunuch; governor of Pergamum; won independence of Pergamum, and reigned there (283–278 B.C.); founder of the Attalid dynasty (283–133 B.C.), named after his nephew Attalus, who defeated the Gauls (c. 230 B.C.).

**Phi·le′tas** (fĭ·lē′tăs; fī-). fl. late 4th century B.C. Greek poet, of Cos; tutor in Alexandria to son of Ptolemy I of Egypt and to Theocritus and Zenodotus; author of number of elegies.

**Phil′i·bert** (fĭl′ĭ·bĕrt; *Fr.* fē′lē′bâr′). Name of two dukes of Savoy. For Philibert I, see SAVOY.

**Philibert de Chalon.** See CHALON.

**Phi′li′dor′** (fē′lē′dôr′). Name of a family of French musicians whose proper family name was **Da′ni′can′** (dȧ′nē′käɴ′) but who used the sobriquet "Philidor" (after Filidori, eminent Sienese oboist), said to have been bestowed by Louis XIII on **Michel Danican** (d. 1659?) for skill on the oboe. **André Danican** (1647?–1730), nephew of Michel, player of bassoon, cromorne, oboe, and marine trumpet; composed comic divertissements and an opera ballet, *La Princesse de Crête,* for Louis XIV's court; prepared the *Collection Philidor* (originally 57 vols.) of dance tunes from reign of Henry III, operas of Lully, old airs, bugle calls, marches, hunting fanfares, etc. **Anne** (1681–1728), oboist and composer, son of André, had three pastorales produced at court. **François André** (1726–1795), chess player and composer, youngest son of André; commemorated by "Philidor's defense" and "Philidor's legacy"; composed one-act opera, *Blaise le Savetier* (1759), and many full-length operas, including *Ernelinde* (1767).

**Phil'ip** (fĭl'ĭp). See also PHILLIP.

**Philip.** In the New Testament: (1) One of the twelve apostles (*Matthew* x. 3; *Mark* iii. 18; *Luke* vi. 14; *John* i. 43; *Acts* i. 13). (2) One of the seven deacons of early Christian church at Jerusalem, who later became an evangelist (*Acts* vi. 5 and viii. 4 ff.).

**Philip.** (1) Son of Herod the Great and Mariamne; see HEROD PHILIP. (2) Son of Herod the Great and Cleopatra; see PHILIP THE TETRARCH.

**Philip,** Prince. *In full* **Philip Mountbatten.** Duke of Edinburgh. 1921– . Prince consort of England; m. (1947) Princess Elizabeth Alexandra Mary (Queen Elizabeth II).

**Philip.** *Fr.* **Philippe.** Name of six kings of France, five Capetians, the sixth of the house of Valois:

**Philip I.** 1052–1108. Son of Henry I. King (1060–1108). Reigned (1060–66) under regency of his mother, Anne of Russia, and Baldwin V of Flanders. Kingdom at low ebb of strength because of powerful feudatories, especially Normandy, but royal domain increased in various ways. Excommunicated (1095) for disowning first wife, Bertha of Holland, and for marriage with Bertrada, wife of Count Fulk of Anjou.

**Philip II** *or* **Philip Au·gus'tus** (ô·gŭs'tŭs). 1165–1223. Son of Louis VII. King (1180–1223); engaged in various wars (1181–85), increasing kingdom; persecuted Jews (1182); waged war with England (1187–89). Set out on Third Crusade (1190) with Richard I of England, but they quarreled in Sicily and in Syria; on return to France (1191), conspired with Richard's brother John to seize English lands in France. War lasted six years (1194–99). Attacked John and deprived him of Normandy, Maine, and other English provinces in France (see ANJOU), which were annexed to the kingdom (1202–04). War with Flanders (1213–14) resulted in alliance against France of Otto IV of Brunswick, John of England, and counts of Flanders and in defeat of Allies at Bouvines (1214). Consolidated new possessions (1214–23). One of the greatest of Capetian kings; built many churches and institutions, encouraged trade, and gave first charter to University of Paris (1200). Made France a power in Europe. Married three times: 1st (1180) Isabella of Hainaut, who brought him as dowry the province of Artois, 2d (1193) Ingeborg (*q.v.*) whom he repudiated, and 3d (1196) Agnes (d. 1201), daughter of Bertold IV, Duke of Meran, from whom he was obliged to separate (1201).

**Philip III.** *Called* **the Bold.** *Fr.* **le Har'di'** (lẽ àr'dē'). 1245–1285. Son of Louis IX. King (1270–85); a weak sovereign, pious but uneducated; influenced by favorites, by his wife, Marie of Brabant, by his mother, Margaret of Provence, and by Charles of Anjou; engaged in unsuccessful war for crown of Aragon (1283–85).

**Philip IV.** *Called* **the Fair.** *Fr.* **le Bel** (lẽ bĕl'). 1268–1314. Son of Philip III; b. in Fontainebleau. King (1285–1314); held long controversy with papacy, especially with Pope Boniface VIII (1294–1303). Forbidden to tax clergy, by papal bull *Clericis laicos* (1296). Royal authority challenged by bulls *Ausculta Fili* (1301) and *Unam Sanctam* (1302). First States-General summoned for support (1302). His creature, Clement V, new pope (1305–14), resided at Avignon (beginning Babylonian captivity, 1309–78). Reign one of most momentous of medieval history, marked by new developments of French monarchy and restriction of feudal usages. Increased expenditures brought about confiscations, seizure of Guienne (1294; later restored) and war with England (1294–98), war with Guy de Dampierre, Count of Flanders (1297–1305), in which French were badly defeated at Courtrai (1302), persecutions of Jews (1306), and cruel suppression of Order of Templars in France (1307–13). m. (1284) Jeanne de Navarre, daughter of Henry, King of Navarre, whereby that kingdom annexed to France. Their three sons became kings of France and Navarre.

**Philip V.** *Called* **the Tall.** *Fr.* **le Long** (lẽ lôɴ'). 1294–1322. Son of Philip IV. King (1316–22). Received Poitiers as appanage. Appointed regent on death of Louis X (1316); became king on death of infant John I. Assembly confirmed succession (1317) by adopting Salic law. Ended war with Flanders (1320). Fined Jews heavily; effected some administrative reforms but opposed by States-General in others. Tried especially to unify coinage, weights and measures.

**Philip VI.** 1293–1350. Son of Charles de Valois. First king (1328–50) of the house of Valois (*q.v.*). Before accession held several countships (Valois, Maine, Anjou, etc.); m. 1st (1313) Jeanne de Bourgogne (d. 1348) and 2d (1349) Blanche of Navarre. Appointed regent at death of Charles IV. Won battle of Cassel and reinstated count of Flanders (1328). Disputes over several matters with Edward III of England led to beginning of Hundred Years' War (1337). English naval victory at Sluis (1340). Normandy invaded by Edward and French defeated at Crécy (1346). Calais taken by English (1347). Dauphiné added to France (1349).

**Philip.** Name of two dukes of Burgundy of the cadet line:

**Philip the Bold.** *Fr.* **Phi'lippe' le Har'di'** (fē'lēp' lẽ àr'dē'). 1342–1404. Fourth son of John the Good, King of France (1350–64). Present at Poitiers (1356), where he earned his nickname for bravery in trying to save his father. Granted duchy of Burgundy (1363), after the Capetian line of dukes became extinct (1361); see BURGUNDY. m. (1369) Margaret, daughter of Louis II de Male, Count of Flanders. On death of King Charles V of France (1380), appointed one of four guardians of Charles VI. Put down Flemish revolt (1382). Received Flanders and Artois (1384). Appointed, with his brother Jean de France, Duc de Berry, as regent to govern France when Charles VI became insane (1392).

**Philip the Good.** *Fr.* **Philippe le Bon** (lẽ bôɴ'). 1396–1467. Son of Duke John the Fearless; b. Dijon. Duke of Burgundy (1419–67). Made alliance with Henry V of England (Treaty of Troyes, 1420), in which Henry was recognized as heir to throne of France. Gradually withdrew from this alliance (1429–35) and made peace with Charles VII of France (1435). Retired to his court during latter part of life; a patron of arts. Founded Order of Golden Fleece (1429) in honor of marriage with Isabella of Portugal (*q.v.*). Burgundy most wealthy and prosperous of all Europe at this time.

**Philip** of Swa'bi·a (swā'bĭ·ȧ). *Ger.* **Philipp.** 1180?–1208. Holy Roman emperor and king of Germany (1198–1208), youngest son of Frederick I; educated for the church but resigned his see (1192); made duke of Tuscany (1195) and of Swabia (1196); chosen king and emperor (1198), but never crowned as emperor. Entire reign a struggle with Otto, leader of the Guelphs. Murdered at Bamberg (June, 1208) by Otto of Wittelsbach.

**Philip.** Duke of **Par'ma** (pär'mȧ; *Ital. & Span.* -mä). 1720–1765. Second son of Philip V of Spain and of

Elizabeth Farnese; m. (1738) Louise Elisabeth of France, daughter of Louis XV; aided by French, conquered (1745) Parma, Piacenza, and Milan; recognized as duke (1748); his daughter María Luisa became queen of Spain (1788–1808).

**Philip** of Mac′e·don (măs′ē·dŏn). Name of five kings of Macedon:

**Philip I** (reigned c. 700 B.C.).

**Philip II.** 382–336 B.C. Son of Amyntas II; m. (359) Olympias (*q.v.*). Succeeded to the throne (359); proved himself military genius; carried out aggressive campaigns in Greece, calling forth from Demosthenes the famous orations of warning known as the *Philippics;* crushed combined Athenian and Theban army at Chaeronea (338) and completed conquest of all Greece by overrunning the Peloponnesus; was chosen (337) commander of the Greek forces against Persia; assassinated (336) by Pausanias, a Macedonian youth; succeeded by his son Alexander the Great (*q.v.*).

**Philip III Ar′rhi·dae′us** (ăr′ĭ·dē′ŭs). = ARRHIDAEUS. Natural son of Philip II.

**Philip IV.** Reigned for a few months (c. 297 B.C.).

**Philip V.** 237–179 B.C. Son of Demetrius II; succeeded to the throne (220 B.C.); warred against Rome (214–205; 200–197); was decisively defeated at Cynoscephalae (197) and forced to renounce hegemony in Greece (196).

**Philip.** *Lat.* **Marcus Julius Phi·lip′pus** (fĭ·lĭp′ŭs). *Called* **the Arabian.** d. 249. Roman emperor (244–249). Became praetorian prefect after death of Misitheus; caused death of young emperor, Gordianus III (244); after being proclaimed emperor made disgraceful peace with Persians; founded Philippopolis; celebrated 1000th anniversary of founding of Rome by great exhibition of secular games (248); killed in struggle with Decius.

**Philip.** *Sp.* **Felipe.** Name of five kings of Spain, four of the house of Hapsburg (*q.v.*), the last a Bourbon (*q.v.*):

**Philip I.** *Called* **the Handsome.** *Sp.* **el Her·mo′so** (ĕl ĕr·mō′sō). 1478–1506. Son of Hapsburg Emperor Maximilian I and Mary of Burgundy, b. in Bruges. Archduke of Austria; as duke of Burgundy inherited vast domains of Burgundy on death of his mother (1482); m. (1496) Juana, daughter of Ferdinand V and Isabella, who succeeded to throne of Castile at Isabella's death (1504); joint ruler with Juana (1504–06), although her father, Ferdinand, was actual ruler because of their absence in Flanders; returned with wife to Spain (June, 1506); died three months later (Sept. 25), perhaps poisoned; Juana became insane (see JUANA); founded Hapsburg dynasty in Spain; their sons later became emperors Charles V and Ferdinand I of the Holy Roman Empire.

**Philip II.** 1527–1598. King (1556–98), only son of Emperor Charles V and Isabella of Portugal, b. in Valladolid; educated by clergy; married four times: Maria of Portugal (1543), Mary I of England (1554), Elizabeth of Valois, daughter of Henry II of France (1560), and Anna, daughter of Emperor Maximilian II (1570); given government of Milan (1540), of Naples and Sicily (1554), of Netherlands (1555), and of Spain (1556); inherited also vast possessions in new world; ruled from Netherlands (1556–59); from there waged successful war against France, won battle of St. Quentin (1557); put down revolt of Moriscos and expelled them (1569–70); sent expedition under his half brother, Don John of Austria, who, with the Genoese, defeated the Turks at Lepanto (1571); determined to crush all opposition to Roman Catholicism; developed Inquisition and at great cost failed to put down revolt in Netherlands (1567–79); supported Guises against Henry of Navarre (1562–98); conquered Portugal (1580–81); lost naval supremacy in defeat of Armada (1588) in war with England (1587–89); Treaty of Vervins (1598) ended war with France; bigoted and morose, his policies caused decline in Spain's power, especially in commerce and industry; encouraged art and built Escorial (1563–84). By first wife (Maria) left son Don Carlos, and by fourth wife his successor, Philip III.

**Philip III.** 1578–1621. Son of Philip II, b. Madrid. King (1598–1621). Inherited Spanish possessions and problems of a declining power, but took no interest in government; left all direction of affairs to his favorite, duke of Lerma (1598–1618) and later to duke of Uceda, Lerma's son; spent time in court festivities; had reputation for extreme piety; final expulsion of Moriscos decreed (1609), an event of economic disaster to Spain; independence of Northern Provinces (Netherlands) recognized (1609).

**Philip IV.** 1605–1665. Eldest son of Philip III. King (1621–65); left administration to Olivares (1623–43); during his reign: Spain's industry and commerce continued to decline and country impoverished by disastrous foreign wars, especially with France, Germany, and Holland; independence regained by Portugal (1640); Olivares overthrown (1643), succeeded by Luis de Haro; rebellion of Masaniello in Naples put down (1647) by Don John of Austria; Holland lost by Treaty of Westphalia (1648); Catalonia revolted (1640) and declared allegiance to Louis XIII of France; Roussillon lost permanently; Treaty of the Pyrenees (1659) a victory for France.

**Philip V.** 1683–1746. King (1700–24, 1724–46); founder of Bourbon dynasty in Spain. Grandson of Louis XIV and son of Dauphin Louis and Marie Christine, daughter of Ferdinand Maria, Elector of Bavaria; b. at Versailles, in youth was duke of Anjou; educated by Fénelon. Named heir to throne by Charles II. Accession was beginning of War of Spanish Succession (1701–14); m. (1701) Maria Louisa of Savoy and (1714) Elizabeth Farnese of Parma, both of whom strongly influenced him. Spain invaded by archduke of Austria; lost Gibraltar to England (1704). Recognized as king by Treaty of Utrecht (1713), but Italian possessions and Netherlands given up to Austria. French ideas in control at the court and French institutions introduced; intrigued against House of Orléans; abdicated (Jan., 1724) in favor of his son Louis but, when Louis died (Aug.), again took the throne (1724–46); joined in War of Austrian Succession against Maria Theresa (1741).

**Philip.** *Indian name* **Met′a·com′et** (mĕt′ȧ·kŏm′ĕt; -ĭt). d. 1676. Son of Massasoit. American Indian chief, sachem of the Wampanoags (from 1662). Encroachments by English settlers on Indian lands and execution (1675) of three of his warriors caused him to make war, King Philip's War (1675–76), upon the New England colonists. Killed by raiding party (Aug. 12, 1676).

**Philip, Hoffman.** 1872–1951. American diplomat; minister to Colombia (1917–22), Uruguay (1922–25), Persia (1925–30), Norway (1930–35); ambassador to Chile (1935–38).

**Philip, John Woodward.** 1840–1900. American naval officer, b. Kinderhook, N.Y.; grad. U.S.N.A., Annapolis (1861); commanded the *Texas* in battle off Santiago (July 3, 1898).

**Philip,** Sir **Robert William.** 1857–1939. Scottish physician; best known for his measures for prevention and cure of tuberculosis.

**Philip Augustus.** = PHILIP II (of France).

**Philip Neri,** Saint. See San Filippo de' NERI.

**Philip the Magnanimous.** *Also called* **Philip of**

**Hesse** (hĕs). 1504–1567. Landgrave of Hesse (1509–67); son of William II; declared of age (1518); m. (1523) Christine of Saxony. Won to cause of Reformation (1525) and one of its leaders in Germany; with John, Elector of Saxony, formed (1526) Protestant League of Gotha and Torgau in support of Martin Luther; arranged at Marburg (1529) disputation between Luther and Zwingli; signed the Augsburg Confession, and, with other Protestant leaders, formed (1530–31) League of Schmalkalden against Charles V; m. (1540) Margaret of Saale as second wife, although first wife was still living; this bigamy, although consented to by Luther and Melanchthon, caused great scandal. Made peace with Charles (1541) but later badly defeated by him in Schmalkaldic War (1546–47); taken prisoner at Mühlberg and held in confinement (1547–52); liberated by Maurice. Divided Hesse (*q.v.*) among four sons (1567).

**Philip the Te′trarch** (tē′trärk; tĕt′rärk). *Lat.* **Philippus.** d. 34 A.D. Tetrarch of Batanaea, Trachonitis, etc. (4 B.C.–34 A.D.); son of Herod the Great and Cleopatra of Jerusalem; educ. Rome with his half brothers Archelaus and Antipas; appointed tetrarch by Augustus (4 B.C.); m. Salome, daughter of Herod Philip and Herodias; a just ruler; has been confused with Herod Philip (*q.v.*).

**Philip William.** d. 1618. Eldest son of William the Silent; see WILLIAM I (of Nassau).

**Phi′li′pon′** (fē′lē′pôɴ′), **Charles.** 1800–1862. French journalist and caricaturist.

**Phi·lip′pa of Hai′naut′** (fĭ·lĭp′ȧ, ĕ′nō′). 1314?–1369. Queen of Edward III, King of England; daughter of William the Good, Count of Holland and Hainaut; m. (1328) to her second cousin, Edward III; brought Flemish weavers to England; encouraged coal mining; said to have harangued English troops before battle of Neville's Cross (1346); patron of Froissart, her secretary (1361–1366); mother of Edward, the Black Prince.

**Philippa of Lan′cas·ter** (lăng′kăs·tẽr). 1359–1415. Queen of John I of Portugal; daughter of John of Gaunt; mother of Edward I of Portugal, Don Pedro the traveler and regent, Prince Henry the navigator, and Ferdinand the saint.

**Philippe I.** Count of Savoy. See SAVOY.

**Philippe de Rouvre.** Duke of Burgundy. See BURGUNDY.

**Philippe–Égalité.** See ORLÉANS, 4.

**Philippi.** See SLEIDANUS.

**Phi·lip′pi** (fē·lĭp′ē), **Felix.** 1851–1921. German playwright and novelist.

**Phi·lip′pi·cus** (fĭ·lĭp′ĭ·kŭs). *Orig. name* **Bar·da′nes** (bär·dā′nēz). Emperor of the Eastern Roman Empire (711–713); soldier under Justinian II; a leader in revolt at Cherson; proclaimed emperor (711); drove out Justinian; defeated by Arabs; overthrown by conspiracy of Anastasius.

**Philippides.** See PHEIDIPPIDES.

**Phi′lip′po′teaux′** (fē′lē′pô′tō′), **Henri Emmanuel Félix.** 1815–1884. French painter; specialized in historical and battle scenes.

**Phi·lip′po·vić** (fē·lĭp′ō·vĭch), **Joseph.** Baron **Philippović von Phi′lipps·berg** (fōn fē′lĭps·bĕrĸ). 1818–1889. Austrian soldier, of Bosnian descent; served under Jelačić od Bužima against Hungary (1848–49), in Italian War (1859), and Seven Weeks' War (1866). Commanding general in Prague (1874, 1882–89) and Vienna (1881–82). His brother **Franz Philippović,** Baron **Philippović von Philippsberg** (1820–1903), was also an Austrian soldier; commanding general (1877–81) in Agram (Zagreb). Their nephew **Eugen Philippović,** Baron **Philippović von Philippsberg** (1858–1917), was an Austrian economist; professor, Vienna (1893–1917).

**Phil′ips** (fĭl′ĭps). See also PHILLIPPS, PHILLIPS.

**Philips, Ambrose.** *Nickname* **Nam′by–Pam′by** (năm′bĭ păm′bĭ). 1675?–1749. English poet; M.A., Cantab. (1700); friend of Steele and Addison; involved in long quarrel with Alexander Pope after praise by the *Guardian* of his pastorals over Pope's. Author of *The Distrest Mother*, an adaptation of Racine's *Andromaque* (1712), and other plays.

**Philips, John.** 1676–1709. English poet; author of *The Splendid Shilling* (1701), mock-heroic poem in Miltonic verse; composed *Blenheim* (1705) on commission of Harley and St. John to offset Addison's *Campaign;* imitated Vergil's *Georgics* in *Cyder* (1708), didactic poem.

**Philips, Katherine,** *nee* **Fowler.** *Pseudonym* **O·rin′da** (ō·rĭn′dȧ). 1631–1664. English poet; called "Matchless Orinda"; m. James Philips, Welsh Royalist; instituted a Society of Friendship, a literary salon for discussion of poetry and religion, described in *Letters of Orinda to Poliarchus*. Her translation of Corneille's *La Mort de Pompée* was acted in Dublin.

**Phil′ipse** (fĭl′ĭps), **Frederick.** 1626–1702. Merchant trader in New York Colony, b. in Friesland, Holland; to New Amsterdam (1647); acquired manorial estate in upper Yonkers (between 1672 and 1693), where he established himself in Castle Philipse; member of the council (1675–98). His Manor Hall of Yonkers is preserved by New York State as historical relic.

**Phi·lis′tus** (fĭ·lĭs′tŭs). Greek historian, b. Syracuse, Sicily; banished (386 B.C.) for marrying a niece of Dionysius without the tyrant's consent; recalled by Dionysius the younger and entrusted with command of fleet operating against Dion and Syracusan rebels; defeated and killed (356). Author of history of Sicily.

**Phi·li′tas** (fĭ·lī′tăs; fī-). = PHILETAS.

**Phil′li·more** (fĭl′ĭ·mōr), Sir **Robert Joseph.** 1810–1885. English judge; judge of high court of admiralty (1867); author of *Commentaries on International Law* (1854–61). His son Sir **Walter George Frank** (1845–1929), 1st Baron **Phillimore,** judge, ecclesiastical lawyer, and international jurist, was a lord justice of the court of appeal (1913–16); chairman of naval prize tribunal (1918); a member of committee that drew up statute constituting Permanent Court of International Justice at The Hague (1920). **John Swinnerton Phillimore** (1873–1926), classical scholar and poet, first cousin of 1st Baron Phillimore, pre-eminent as classical scholar at Oxford, succeeded Gilbert Murray in chair of Greek at Glasgow (1899); professor of humanity (from 1906).

**Phil′lip** (fĭl′ĭp). See also PHILIP.

**Phillip, Arthur.** 1738–1814. English naval commander and founder of New South Wales; commanded fleet carrying convicts on eight-month voyage to Sidney Cove, Australia, landing Jan. 26, 1788 (subsequently celebrated as Foundation Day); established and administered penal colony (1788–92); vice-admiral (1810).

**Phillip, John.** 1817–1867. Scottish genre and portrait painter.

**Phil′lipps** (fĭl′ĭps). See also PHILIPS, PHILLIPS.

**Phillipps, James Orchard Halliwell–.** See HALLIWELL.

**Phillipps,** Sir **Thomas.** 1792–1872. English antiquary and collector of rare manuscripts; established a private printing press (c. 1822) on which he printed genealogical and topographical works, chartularies, manuscript catalogues.

**Phil′lips** (fĭl′ĭps). See also PHILIPS, PHILLIPPS.

**Phillips, Albert.** 1875–1940. American actor; widely known in his roles as Ulysses S. Grant in Drinkwater's

*Abraham Lincoln* and Stephen Douglas in Sherwood's *Abe Lincoln in Illinois.*

**Phillips, Bert Greer. 1868–1952.** American painter, b. Hudson, N.Y.; best known for paintings of Indian subjects and for murals. Studio at Taos, N.Mex.; known as founder of the Taos Art Colony.

**Phillips, Charles.** 1880–1933. American poet and educator; author of *Back Home* (1913), *The Divine Friend* (a poetic drama, 1915), *High in Her Tower* (1927), etc.

**Phillips, David Graham.** 1867–1911. American novelist, b. Madison, Ind.; excelled in novels designed to expose current evils in society, business, and government, as *The Cost* (1904), *The Husband's Story* (1910), *The Conflict* (1911), *Susan Lenox: Her Fall and Rise* (1917).

**Phillips, Edward.** 1630–?1696. English compiler and biographer of John Milton; son of Milton's only sister, Ann; educ. by Milton; tutor (1663–72) to son of John Evelyn and to Philip Herbert (later, Earl of Pembroke); hack writer in London. Compiler of *A New World in Words* (a philological dictionary, 1658), and of *Theatrum Poetarum* (a catalogue of poets of all countries, 1675).

**Phillips, George.** 1593–1644. Clergyman in America, b. South Rainham, England; to America (1630); pastor at Watertown (1630–44). Credited by some with being first minister of Massachusetts Bay Colony to introduce the Congregational form of church polity. Among his descendants were Samuel, John, Thomas Wharton, and Wendell Phillips (*qq.v.*).

**Phillips, John.** 1719–1795. Descendant of George Phillips. American merchant and philanthropist, b. Andover, Mass.; settled in Exeter, Mass., where he taught school, conducted a country store, loaned money at interest, and invested in real estate. Contributed liberally to establishment and development of Phillips Academy, Andover; was founder and benefactor of Phillips Exeter Academy, Exeter (incorporated 1781, opened 1783). His nephew **Samuel Phillips** (1752–1802) was an industrialist and political leader; grad. Harvard (1771); manufactured powder for Continental army (from 1775); founder and benefactor of Phillips Academy, Andover (opened 1778), first of the great endowed academies in America; member of board of trustees of the academy (from 1778) and president of the board (from 1796); lieutenant governor of Massachusetts (1802) and died in office. A cousin of Samuel, **William Phillips** (1750–1827), was lieutenant governor of Massachusetts (1812–23); trustee of Phillips Academy, Andover (from 1791) and president of the board of trustees (from 1821).

**Phillips, John.** 1800–1874. English geologist; nephew of geologist William Smith, with whom he made geological studies of various parts of England. Works include *Geological Map of the British Isles* (1842).

**Phillips, Montague Fawcett. 1885–1969.** English organist and composer of two light operas, overtures, ballet music, orchestral suites and melodies, and more than 150 songs.

**Phillips, Philip.** 1834–1895. Known as "the Singing Pilgrim." American gospel singer and music editor; head of Philip Phillips & Co., Cincinnati, a music publishing house (1863–67); author or compiler of many collections of sacred songs, as *New Hymn and Tune Book* (1867), *The Gospel Singer* (1874).

**Phillips, Stephen.** 1868–1915. English poet and playwright; member of Frank R. Benson's theatrical company (1885?–92); published *Eremus* (1894), a long philosophical poem in blank verse; won fame with *Poems* (1897), containing *Christ in Hades* and *Marpessa;* commissioned to write a play, *Paolo and Francesca* (1900); his *Herod* produced by Beerbohm Tree (1900); declined in popularity after *Nero* (1906).

**Phillips, Thomas.** 1770–1845. English historical and portrait painter.

**Phillips, Thomas Wharton.** 1835–1912. Descendant of George Phillips. Oil producer and legislator, b. near Mount Jackson, Pa.; pioneer in developing Pennsylvania oil fields (from 1861); member of U.S. House of Representatives (1893–97); member of U.S. industrial commission (1898–1902), whose report (19 vols., 1900–02) led to creation of bureau of corporations and to constructive research by departments of labor and commerce.

**Phillips, Ulrich Bon·nell'** (bŏ·nĕl'). 1877–1934. American historian, b. La Grange, Ga.; author of *Georgia and State Rights* (awarded Justin Winsor prize by American Historical Assoc., 1901), *Life of Robert Toombs* (1913), *Life and Labor in the Old South* (awarded Little, Brown & Co. prize, 1929), etc.

**Phillips, Walter Alison.** 1864–1950. English historian; chief assistant editor, ***Encyclopaedia Britannica*, 11th** edition (1903–11); Lecky professor of modern history, Dublin (1914–39); contributor to *Cambridge Modern History;* specialist in early 19th-century diplomatic history. Author of histories of Ireland (1909–21), Poland (1915), French Revolution (1929), etc.

**Phillips, Wendell.** 1811–1884. Descendant of George Phillips. American reformer, b. Boston; prominent abolitionist (from 1837), associated with William Lloyd Garrison; president of Anti-Slavery Society (1865–70). In later years, advocated prohibition, penal reforms, woman suffrage, regulation of corporations, and organization of the laboring class.

**Phillips, William.** 1750–1827. See under John PHILLIPS (1719–1795).

**Phillips, William.** 1775–1828. English mineralogist and geologist; wrote textbooks and (with W. D. Conybeare) *Outlines of the Geology of England and Wales* (1822).

**Phillips, William.** 1878–1968. American diplomat, b. Beverly, Mass.; U.S. minister to the Netherlands and Luxemburg (1920–22), U.S. ambassador to Belgium (1924–27), minister to Canada (1927–29), ambassador to Italy (1936–Dec., 1941); head of London division of Office of Strategic Services (1942); personal representative of President Roosevelt in India (1942–45); political adviser to Eisenhower (1943–44).

**Phill'potts** (fĭl'pŏts), **Eden.** *Early pseudonym* **Harrington Hext** (hĕkst). 1862–1960. English novelist and playwright, b. in Rajputana Province, India; studied for the stage; clerk in Sun Fire Insurance office, London (1880–90). In his early novels, *Lying Prophets* (1896) and *Children of the Mist* (1898), described Devonshire with charm and romantic coloring suggestive of Blackmore. Author also of realistic, often tragic, novels of Devonshire, including *Sons of the Morning* (1900), *Widecombe Fair* (1913), *Children of Men* (1923), *The Jury* (1927); wrote also historical novels, including *Evander* (1919), *The Treasures of Typhon* (1924); mystery stories and fairy stories, short stories, and poems, including *The Iscariot* (1912), *Pixies' Plot* (1922), *Sonnets from Nature* (1935), and plays, including *The Farmer's Wife* (1917), *Buy a Broom* (1929), *A Cup of Happiness* (1933), and *Yellow Sands* (1926), this last in collaboration with his daughter **Mary Adelaide Eden** (1896–    ), novelist and playwright.

**Phillpotts, Henry.** 1778–1869. English prelate; bishop of Exeter (1830–69); engaged in polemic in opposition to Catholic emancipation (1825); opposed Reform Bill in House of Lords; attacked Tract 90 and Oxford movement.

**Phi'lo** (fī'lō), **Quintus Publilius.** Roman politician; consul (339 B.C.) and sponsor of three laws (Publilian laws) enlarging power of plebeians.

**Philo Byb'li·us** (bĭb'lĭ·ŭs) *or* **He·ren'ni·us Byblius** (hē·rĕn'ĭ·ŭs). fl. late 1st and early 2d century A.D. Greek scholar and teacher, of Byblus in Phoenicia; only fragments of his works are extant.

**Philo Ju·dae'us** (jōō·dē'ŭs) *or* **Philo of Alexandria.** fl. late 1st century B.C. and early 1st century A.D. Hellenistic Jewish philosopher of Alexandria; known as "the Jewish Plato"; headed embassy of five Jews who went to Rome (c. 40 A.D.) to plead with emperor not to demand divine honors from the Jews. As philosopher, sought to harmonize philosophy of religion as derived from a study of Plato, Aristotle, and other Greek philosophers, with the doctrines of the Pentateuch.

**Phi·loch'o·rus** (fĭ·lŏk'ō·rŭs). Athenian politician and historian; opposed policies of Demetrius Poliorcetes and his son Antigonus Gonatas (*qq.v.*); executed by Antigonus Gonatas (c. 260 B.C.). Author of a history of Athens, extant only in fragments.

**Phil'o·de'mus** (fĭl'ō·dē'mŭs). Epicurean philosopher of 1st century B.C., b. Gadara, Syria; taught in Rome; friend of Calpurnius Piso. Thirty-four of his epigrams are in the Greek anthology; thirty-six treatises attributed to him were discovered in the ruins of Herculaneum.

**Philoff.** Variant of FILOV.

**Phil'o·la'us** (fĭl'ō·lā'ŭs). Greek Pythagorean philosopher of 5th century B.C.; only fragments of his works extant.

**Phil'o·me'tor** (fĭl'ō·mē'tôr). See ANTIOCHUS VIII of Syria, ATTALUS III of Pergamum, DEMETRIUS III of Syria, PTOLEMY VI.

**Phi·lop'a·tor** (fĭ·lŏp'ȧ·tôr). See ANTIOCHUS IX of Syria, SELEUCUS IV, PTOLEMY IV.

**Philopator Neos Dionysos.** See PTOLEMY XI.

**Philopator Philometor Caesar.** See PTOLEMY XIV.

**Phil'o·poe'men** (fĭl'ō·pē'mĕn). 253?–183 B.C. Greek general of Achaean League; known as "last of the Greeks"; distinguished himself at battle of Sellasia (222 or 221); appointed general (208), he improved armor and discipline of league's army; victorious over Spartans at Mantinea (c. 207) and defeated Nabis, Tyrant of Sparta (192). Captured in skirmish before Messina (184) and executed.

**Phi·los'tra·tus** (fĭ·lŏs'trȧ·tŭs). 170?–245 A.D. Greek Sophist philosopher; studied and taught at Athens and later at Rome; author of *Lives of the Sophists* and biography of Apollonius of Tyana.

**Phi·lo'tas** (fĭ·lō'tȧs; fī-). Macedonian general, son of Parmenio (*q.v.*); served under Alexander the Great; on campaign in the East, was charged with conspiracy, tried by army, convicted, and executed (330 B.C.).

**Phi·lox'e·nus** (fĭ·lŏk'sē·nŭs). Christian leader of Eastern Church, b. in Persia; educ. Edessa; vigorous defender of Monophysite doctrine; bishop of Hierapolis (485 A.D.); banished from his see by Justin I (519) and killed in Paphlagonia (523). Revised Syriac version of Bible; produced (with Polycarp) Philoxenian version of Bible, used during 6th century by Monophysites; wrote thirteen homilies on Christian life.

**Phin'e·has** (fĭn'ē·ăs; -hăs). *In Douay Version* **Phin'e·es** (-ĕs; -ēs). In Bible: (1) Son of Eleazar and his successor as high priest of the Jews (*Exodus* vi. 25; *Numbers* xxv; *Judges* xx. 28). (2) One of the degenerate sons of Eli (*1 Samuel* ii. 12–iv. 22).

**Phintias.** See DAMON AND PYTHIAS.

**Phiops.** = PEPI II.

**Phios.** = PEPI I.

**Phipps** (fĭps). Name of an English family bearing titles of earl of **Mul'grave** (mŭl'grāv), viscount and marquis of **Nor'man·by** (nôr'mȧn·bĭ), descendants of Sir **Constantine** (1656–1723), defender of Henry Sacheverell (1710), and lord chancellor of Ireland (1710–14), including: Sir **Henry** (1755–1831), 3d Baron Mulgrave, 1st Viscount Normanby, 1st Earl of Mulgrave; military commander; great-grandson of Sir Constantine; entered army (1775); Pitt's chief military adviser; general (1809); chancellor of duchy of Lancaster (1804); foreign secretary (1805–06); first lord of admiralty (1807–10); master of the ordnance (1810–18) and cabinet member (1810–20); patron of art. His brother **Constantine John** (1744–1792), 2d Baron Mulgrave; naval captain; commanded a polar expedition (1773); distinguished himself off Ushant (1778). Sir **Constantine Henry** (1797–1863), 1st Marquis of Normanby and 2d Earl of Mulgrave; eldest son of 1st earl; M.A., Cantab. (1818); governor of Jamaica (1832–34); lord privy seal under Lord Melbourne (1834); lord lieutenant of Ireland (1835–39); colonial secretary (1839); home secretary (1839–41); ambassador at Paris (1846–52); minister at Florence (1854–58); conflicted with Palmerston and Gladstone on French and Italian policy. Sir **George Augustus Constantine** (1819–1890), 2d Marquis of Normanby; son of 1st marquis; became liberal whip in House of Commons; lieutenant governor of Nova Scotia (1858–63); governor of Queensland (1871–74), of New Zealand (1875–79), of Victoria (1879–84). See also Sir William PHIPS.

**Phipps, Sir Eric Clare Edmund.** 1875–1945. British diplomat; minister at Paris (1922–28), Vienna (1928–33); ambassador at Berlin (1933–37) and at Paris (1937–39).

**Phipps, Henry.** 1839–1930. American industrialist and philanthropist, b. Philadelphia; associate of Andrew Carnegie in development of steel industry (1867–1901); director, U.S. Steel Corp. (from 1901). Founder and benefactor of Henry Phipps Institute for the Study, Treatment, and Prevention of Tuberculosis, Philadelphia (1903), Phipps Tuberculosis Dispensary at Johns Hopkins Hospital, Baltimore (1905), Henry Phipps Psychiatric Clinic, at Johns Hopkins Hospital (1913).

**Phips** (fĭps) *or* **Phipps,** Sir **William.** 1651–1695. Colonial governor in America, b. in Maine; ship's carpenter by trade; cousin of Sir Constantine Phipps (see PHIPPS family). Financed by Charles II and the duke of Albemarle in search for sunken treasure; recovered treasure from a vessel sunk off Haiti (c. 1685); knighted (1687). Associated with Increase Mather in seeking governmental changes in Massachusetts Colony (from 1688). Commanded Massachusetts troops in capture of Port Royal (1690) and in unsuccessful attack on Quebec. Royal governor of Massachusetts (1692–94).

**Phiz.** See Hablot Knight BROWNE.

**Pho'cas** (fō'kȧs). d. 610. Emperor of the Eastern Roman Empire (602–610); a centurion of army fighting Avars on the Danube; raised to emperor (602) by mutinous soldiers; had Emperor Mauricius slain; notorious for cruelty; defeated by Persians under King Khosrau II, who penetrated even to Bosporus; overthrown by plot against him by Heraclius, Exarch of Africa, and his son Heraclius, who became emperor (610); tortured and beheaded.

**Pho'ci·on** (fō'shĭ·ŏn). 402?–317 B.C. Athenian general and statesman; first distinguished himself in naval battle of Naxos (376); opposed anti-Macedonian policy in Athenian assembly; negotiated favorable terms for Athens after her defeat at Chaeronea by Philip of Macedon (338). After Alexander's death (323), became virtual dictator in Athens under Antipater's domination; on restoration of democracy (318), condemned to death by Democratic party in Athens on false charge of treason; executed (317).

**Pho·cyl'i·des** (fō·sĭl'ĭ·dēz). Greek gnomic poet, of

Miletus, in 6th century B.C. Only a few fragments of his maxims are extant.

**Phoenix, John.** Pseudonym of George Horatio DERBY.

**Pho'ti·us** (fō'shĭ·ŭs). 820?–891. Patriarch of Constantinople; made patriarch by Emperor Michael III (858–867), replacing Ignatius. Excommunicated by Pope Nicholas I (863); issued encyclical (867) against pope and the doctrines (especially the filioque doctrine) of Western Church—the immediate cause of the schism (Great Eastern Schism) between the East and West. Formally deposed by Council of Constantinople (869), Ignatius having been reinstated as patriarch after Michael's death (867). Again made patriarch (877); called council (879) that passed upon all theological issues between East and West; again excommunicated (882); banished (886) by Emperor Leo VI to an Armenian cloister. Wrote *Amphilochia*, treating doctrinal and exegetical questions and many other topics, and *Myriobiblion* or *Bibliotheca*, a summary of 280 works of classical authors now mostly lost.

**Phra·a'tes** (frȧ·ā'tēz). Name of five kings of Parthia of Arsacid dynasty, especially: **Phraates I** *or* **Ar'sa·ces** (är'sȧ·sēz) **V.** King (176?–171 B.C.). **Phraates II.** King (138?–128 B.C.); defeated Antiochus VII in Media (129), but overcome while fighting the Tochari. **Phraates III.** King (70–57 B.C.); restored order; sought alliance with Rome (69); deceived by Pompey (64–62); forced to give back territory to Tigranes. **Phraates IV.** King (38?–?2 B.C.); defeated Antony (36), but lost Armenia (34); lost influence as Roman power increased; murdered.

**Phran'tzes** (frăn'tsēz; *Mod. Grk. pron.*, frän·tsēs'), **Georgios.** 1401–?1477. Byzantine historian, author of a chronicle, covering history of Eastern Roman Empire from 1258 to 1476.

**Phra·or'tes** (frȧ·ôr'tēz). *Greek form of* **Fravartish.** d. about 625 B.C. Second king of Media (646?–?625 B.C.); son of Deïoces and father of Cyaxares; began Median conquests, subjugating many Asiatic peoples, but was defeated and killed in war on Assyrians.

**Phry'ne** (frī'nē). Greek hetaera of 4th century B.C., noted for her beauty; reputedly the model for Praxiteles' statue of Aphrodite at Cnidus and for Apelles' painting *Aphrodite Anadyomene.*

**Phryn'i·chus** (frĭn'ĭ·kŭs). Name of two Athenian playwrights: (1) fl. late 6th and early 5th centuries B.C. Author of tragedies, including *Capture of Miletus* and *Phoenissae;* credited with important innovations in dramatic presentation. (2) fl. late 5th century B.C. Writer of comedies, including *Solitary* and *Muses;* accused by Aristophanes, in his *Frogs*, of using vulgar tricks for their comic effect and of plagiarism and poor versification.

**Phryn'i·cus** (frĭn'ĭ·kŭs). *Surnamed* **A·ra'bi·us** (ȧ·rā'bĭ·ŭs). Greek grammarian of Bithynia in 2d century A.D.; only fragments of his work extant.

**Phyfe** (fīf), **Duncan.** 1768–1854. Cabinetmaker, b. in Scotland; to America (c. 1783); apprenticed to cabinetmaker, near Albany (1784); had joiner's shop in New York (from c. 1792); retired from business (1847). Renowned for excellence and artistic beauty of his furniture, esp. mahogany chairs, couches, and tables.

**Phyfe, William Henry Pinkney.** 1855–1915. American orthographer and orthoëpist, b. New York City; author of *5,000 Words Often Misspelled, 12,000 Words Often Mispronounced,* etc.

**Phy·lar'chus** (fī·lär'kŭs; fī-). Greek historian of late 3d century B.C., b. in Egypt, but long resident in Athens. Chief work, history of Greece of period 272–221 B.C., only fragments of which are extant.

**Physcon.** Nickname of PTOLEMY VII.

**Phys'ick** (?fĭz'ĭk), **Philip Syng.** 1768–1837. Known as "Father of American Surgery." American surgeon, b. Philadelphia; one of the first to use animal ligatures in surgery and leave them in the tissues to be absorbed; esp. successful in operating for stone in the bladder; devised a number of new surgical instruments of great service.

**Pia'cen·ti'ni** (pyä'chân·tē'nē), **Marcello.** 1881–1960. Italian architect.

**Pi'a de'i To'lo·me'i** (pē'ä dā'ē tō'lō·mâ'ē). 13th-century Sienese woman, immortalized in Dante's *Divina Commedia* (*Purgatorio* V, 133–136); m. Nello della Pietra de' Pannocchieschi, who, because of jealousy or a desire to remarry, shut her up in his castle in the Tuscan Maremma, where she died.

**Piag'gia** (pyäd'jä), **Carlo.** 1827–1882. Italian explorer in the Sudan and Central Africa.

**Pian'khi** (pyăng'kĭ) *or* **Pan'khi** (păng'-). An Ethiopian king in Egypt (c. 741–721 B.C.) with capital at Napata on the Nile in Nubia; conquered nearly all Nile Valley; captured Memphis and most of delta cities; in control during nominal rule of XXIIId (Tanite) dynasty; erected granite stele, which still exists, covered with inscriptions describing his campaign in Egypt; brother of Shabaka (*q.v.*).

**Piano Carpini, Giovanni de.** See CARPINI.

**Piast** (pyäst). Name of first Polish dynasty; so called from its legendary founder of 9th century (c. 840), a peasant named Piast. Its first historical personage was Mieszko (end of 10th century; see BOLESLAV); it ended with Casimir III (1370), although branches ruled in Mazovia (to 1526) and in Silesia (to 1675).

**Piatakov.** Variant of PYATAKOV.

**Pia·ti·gor'sky** (pyŭ·tyĭ·gôr'skû·ĭ; *Angl.* pyä'tĭ·gôr'skĭ), **Gregor.** 1903– . Russian concert violoncellist.

**Pi'att** (pī'ăt), **Donn.** 1819–1891. American journalist, b. Cincinnati; founder and coeditor of the *Capital* (1871–80), a weekly paper published in Washington, D.C., in which he tried to expose the weaknesses and corruption of the politicians. Indicted (Feb. 21, 1877), on charge of inciting insurrection, but case was dropped after Hayes's inauguration.

**Piatt, John James.** 1835–1917. American journalist and poet, b. Milton, Ind. Author of *Poems of Two Friends* (with William Dean Howells, 1860), *Poems in Sunshine and Firelight* (1866), *Landmarks* (1872), *Idyls and Lyrics of the Ohio Valley* (1881), *Little New-World Idyls* (1893), *Odes in Ohio* (1897), etc. His wife, **Sarah Morgan,** *nee* **Bryan** (1836–1919), was also a poet; author of *Child's World Ballads* (1887), *An Irish Wild-Flower* (1891), *An Enchanted Castle* (1893), etc.

**Piaz·zet'ta** (pyät·tsāt'tä), **Giovanni Battista.** 1682–1754. Italian painter; after Tiepolo, the last important representative of Venetian baroque painting; director of Venetian Acad. (1750).

**Piaz'zi** (pyät'tsē), **Giuseppi.** 1746–1826. Italian Theatine monk and astronomer; professor, Palermo (from 1781), where he was founder and director of the observatory; director of government observatory in Naples (from 1817). Discovered and named Ceres, first known asteroid (1801); published catalogues of fixed stars, the second (1814) listing 7646 stars.

**Pi'ca'bia'** (pē'kȧ'byȧ'), **Francis.** 1879–1953. French painter of the post-impressionistic school, associated with the cubists and their successors; a pioneer in Dadaism; among his canvases are *Paris, Adam et Eve, Cannes, Antibes, Mésange.*

**Pi·can'der** (pē·kän'dẽr). Pseudonym of C. F. HENRICI.

**Pi'card'** (pē'kȧr'). See also PICCARD.

**Picard, Charles Émile.** 1856–1941. French mathematician; known esp. for work on theory of functions and on differential equations. His works include *Traité d'Analyse* (3 vols., 1893), *Théorie des Fonctions Algébriques de Deux Variables Indépendantes* (with Simart; 1897–1906).

**Picard, Edmond.** 1836–1924. Belgian jurist and author of novels, poetry, travel accounts, and plays.

**Picard, Jean.** 1620–1682. French astronomer; first to apply telescope to measurement of angles; known esp. for accurate measurement of a degree of a meridian; determined latitude and longitude of Tycho Brahe's observatory at Uranienburg on island of Hven.

**Picard, Louis Benoît.** 1769–1828. French playwright; manager of Théâtre Louvois, the Odéon and the Opéra at various times. Author of many comedies, including *Les Visitandines* (comic opera, 1792), *Médiocre et Rampant* (verse comedy, 1797), *La Petite Ville* (prose comedy, 1801), etc.

**Picard, Louis Joseph Ernest.** 1821–1877. French lawyer and politician; member of the Corps Législatif (1858) and opponent of imperial policies. After fall of the empire, became member of government of national defense (1870) and minister of interior (1871); senator for life (1875).

**Pi·cas'so** (pē·kä'sō), **Pablo.** *In full* **Pablo Ru·iz' y Picasso** (rōō·ēth' ē). 1881–1973. Spanish painter and sculptor, b. Málaga; studied at Pontevedra, Coruña, and Barcelona; published review *El Renacimiento* at Barcelona; settled in France (1903). Known as one of foremost figures in twentieth century art.

**Pic'card'** (pē'kär'), **Auguste.** 1884–1962. Swiss physicist; investigated radioactivity and atmospheric electricity; with his assistant Kipfer, made balloon ascent of 51,793 feet into the stratosphere in airtight gondola of own invention, Augsburg, Germany (1931); with his assistant Max Cosyns, made ascent of 55,577 feet at Zurich, Switzerland (1932); made observations of cosmic rays and other scientific phenomena. His twin brother **Jean Felix** (1884–1963), chemist and aeronautical engineer; to U.S. (1916); naturalized (1931); professor of aeronautical engineering (from 1937), Minnesota; with his wife, made stratosphere ascent in balloon from Ford Airport, Dearborn, Michigan, reaching altitude of 57,979 feet (1934).

**Pic·ci'ni** (pēt·chē'nē) *or* **Pic·cin'ni** (pēt·chēn'nē), **Niccolò** *or* **Nicola.** 1728–1800. Italian opera composer; made debut as opera composer with the opera buffa *Le Donne Dispettose* in Naples (1754); composed over 60 serious and comic operas (1754–76); called to Paris by Marie Antoinette (1776) and became nonparticipating rival of Gluck in public feud between his followers (Piccinists) and admirers of Gluck (Gluckists); composed French and Italian operas. Returned to Naples at outbreak of French Revolution (1789), and lived on pension from king; kept prisoner 4 years in own house on suspicion of republicanism; returned to Paris (1798), and obtained inspectorship of music at National Conservatory. Among his works are Italian operas, as *La Cecchina Zitella, ossia la Buona Figliuola* (1760), *L'Olimpiade* (1761), and *I Viaggiatori* (1774), and French operas, as *Roland* (1778), *Atys* (1780), also several oratorios, psalms, and other church music.

**Pic'ci·ni'no** (pēt'chē·nē'nō), **Niccolò.** 1375–1444. Italian condottiere, in service of Filippo Maria Visconti, Duke of Milan; captured Bologna (1438) and ruled as overlord (1438–43).

**Pic'ci·ril'li** (pēt'chē·rēl'lē), **Attilio** (1866–1945) and his brother **Furio** (1868–1949). Sculptors, b. at Massa, Italy; to U.S. (1888); joint studio in New York (from 1898). Attilio carved *The Dancing Faun, Thought, Mater Consolatrix*, and portrait busts. Furio is best known for delicately carved reliefs and statues, as *The Young Mother.*

**Pic'co·lo'mi·ni** (pēk'kō·lō'mē·nē). Illustrious Italian family, including: **Enea Sylvio** (1405–1464), who was Pope Pius II (*q.v.*). **Alessandro** (1508–1578), prelate and writer, coadjutor to archbishop of Siena (1574), author of *L'Istituzione di Tutta la Vita dell'Uomo* (1542), *Della Grandezza della Terra e dell'Acqua* (1553), translations of works by Ovid and Vergil, and commentaries on Aristotle. **Francesco** (1520–1604), philosopher, author of *Universa Philosophia de Moribus* (1583), *Libri de Scientiae Natura* (1596), *Comes Politicus* (1601). **Ascanio** (1550?–1597), who succeeded his uncle Alessandro as coadjutor to archbishop of Siena. **Alfonso** (1550?–1591), Duca **di Mon'te·mar·cia'no** (dē mōn'tā·mär·chä'nō), one of the last of the condottieri, in French service (1582–90), defeated at Stagnia (1591) and hanged by order of Grand Duke Ferdinand. **Octavio** (1599–1656), Duca **d'A·mal'fi** (dä·mäl'fē), soldier, a general in the Thirty Years' War in the imperialist service, passing (1643) to the Spanish service, recalled to imperial service and promoted field marshal (1648), operated against the Swedes in Bavaria and Bohemia, represented Austria at the Congress of Nuremberg (1649), and was created prince of the Holy Roman Empire (1654). **Maria** (1836–1899), operatic singer in Italy, Paris, and London, retired (c. 1863) after her marriage with Marchese Gaetani della Forgnia.

**Pi'che·gru'** (pēsh'grü'), **Charles.** 1761–1804. French general; commanded armies of the Rhine and the Moselle (1793–94) and army of the North (1794); conquered the Netherlands and suppressed an insurrection in Paris (1795); member of Council of Five Hundred; plotted overthrow of government (1797); arrested and deported, but escaped and returned to France. Involved in Cadoudal plot against Napoleon (1803); committed suicide, or was murdered, in prison (Apr. 5, 1804).

**Pich'ler** (pĭk'lēr), **Karoline,** *nee* **von Grei'ner** (fōn grī'nēr). 1769–1843. Austrian novelist; among her novels are *Agathokles* (1808), *Die Belagerung Wiens 1683* (3 vols., 1824), *Die Schweden in Prag* (1827), and *Die Wiedereroberung von Ofen* (2 vols., 1829).

**Pi'chon'** (pē'shôɴ'), **Stéphen Jean Marie.** 1857–1933. French journalist, politician, and diplomat; minister of foreign affairs (1906–11, 1917–20); close personal friend and consistent supporter of Clemenceau.

**Pick'ard** (pĭk'ärd), **Greenleaf Whittier.** 1877–1956. American electrical engineer and inventor; patented inventions in radio communication, including crystal detector, radio compass, and static eliminator.

**Pickel, Konrad.** See Conradus CELTIS.

**Pick'ens** (pĭk'ĕnz), **Andrew.** 1739–1817. American Revolutionary commander, b. near Paxtang, Pa.; settled in South Carolina (1763). In the revolution, served with distinction at Cowpens (1781); promoted brigadier general, captured Augusta, Ga. (1781); wounded at Eutaw Springs. Member of U.S. House of Representatives (1793–95). His grandson **Francis Wilkinson Pickens** (1805–1869) was member of U.S. House of Representatives (1834–43); U.S. minister to Russia (1858–60); governor of South Carolina (1860–62).

**Pick'er·ing** (pĭk'ēr·ĭng), **Timothy.** 1745–1829. American statesman, b. Salem, Mass.; adjutant general of Continental army (1777–78); quartermaster general (1780–83); U.S. postmaster general (1791–95); U.S. secretary of war (1795); U.S. secretary of state (1795–1800). U.S. senator (1803–11); member, U.S. House of Representatives (1813–17). His son **John** (1777–1846) was a lawyer and philologist; practiced, Salem (to 1827) and Boston (from 1827); compiler of a lexicon of the Greek language (1826) and the first dictionary of Americanisms. A grandson of Timothy and nephew of John, **Charles Pickering** (1805–1878), was a naturalist; chief zoologist in U.S. exploring expedition under Lieut. Charles Wilkes (1838–42); resident in Boston (from 1842); author of *Races of Men and Their Geographical Distribution* (1848), *The Chronological History of Plants* (1879), etc. A great-grandson of Timothy and nephew of Charles, **Edward Charles Pickering** (1846–1919), was an astronomer; director, Harvard observatory (1877–1919); renowned for his work in stellar photometry, his collection of a photographic library of the stars, his researches in stellar spectroscopy; established observation station at Arequipa, Peru (1891), to study southern stars. Edward's brother **William Henry** (1858–1938) was also an astronomer; led expeditions to observe solar eclipses; discovered Phoebe, 9th satellite of Saturn; predicted existence of, and located, 9th planet, Pluto (1919); co-operated with Edward in establishing observation station at Arequipa, Peru (1891); erected observatory and telescope at Flagstaff, Ariz. (1894).

**Pickering, William.** 1796–1854. English publisher; raised standard of design in printing; began (1825) to bind books in boards covered with cotton cloth; adopted (1830) the dolphin-and-anchor device of Aldine press (see Aldus MANUTIUS) with inscription "Aldi Discipulus Anglus"; issued Aldine edition of English poets (53 vols.).

**Pick′ett** (pĭk′ĕt; -ĭt), **George Edward.** 1825–1875. American army officer, b. Richmond, Va.; grad. U.S.M.A., West Point (1846); resigned from U.S. army to enter Confederate service (1861); brigadier general (Feb., 1862) and major general (Oct., 1862). Held Confederate center at Fredericksburg; his command (4500 men) made famous charge at Gettysburg (July 3, 1863) across half a mile of broken ground against Union positions on Cemetery Ridge, only to be repulsed with loss of three fourths of his division. Fought brilliantly at Five Forks (Apr., 1865).

**Pick′ford** (pĭk′fẽrd), **Mary.** *Orig. surname* **Smith.** 1893–1979. Actress, b. in Toronto, Canada; m. Owen Moore (divorced 1920), Douglas Fairbanks (1920; divorced 1935), Charles (Buddy) Rogers (1937). Especially successful in motion pictures; starred in *Tess of the Storm Country, Stella Maris, Daddy Long Legs, Pollyanna, Rebecca of Sunny Brook Farm, Poor Little Rich Girl, Little Lord Fauntleroy.* Also a producer, head of Mary Pickford Co. and part owner of United Artists.

**Pick′thall** (pĭk′thôl), **Marjorie Lowry Christie.** 1883–1922. Canadian author, b. London, Eng.; to Canada (c. 1889); author of verse and fiction, including *Wood Carver's Wife, and Other Poems.*

**Pickthall, Marmaduke William.** 1875–1936. English novelist; lived in close association with natives in Near East and in Egypt. Author of *Saïd the Fisherman* (1903), *Enid* (1904), *The House of Islam* (1906), *Pot-au-feu* (1911), *Veiled Women* (1913), *Knights of Araby* (1917), *Sir Limpidus* (1919), etc.

**Pi′co del′la Mi·ran′do·la** (pē′kō dāl′lä mē·rän′dō·lä), Count **Giovanni.** 1463–1494. Italian Humanist, a leading scholar of Italian Renaissance; settled at Florence (1484) as protégé of Lorenzo de' Medici and Marsilio Ficino; studied Hebrew, Arabic, and the cabala; posted publicly (Rome, 1486) a list of 900 theses dealing with logic, ethics, theology, mathematics, cabalistic lore, physics, etc., which he proposed to defend publicly against any opponent; accused by Innocent VIII of heresy (cleared later by Alexander VI); reconverted to orthodoxy by Savonarola; poisoned by his secretary. Works include *In Astrologiam Libri XII, De Concordantia Platonis et Aristotelis, De Dignitate Hominis, Heptaplus* (1489).

**Pi·cón′ y Bou′chet′** (pē·kōn′ ē bōō′shĕ′), **Jacinto Octavio.** 1852–1923. Spanish writer of art criticisms, short stories, and novels.

**Pi′cot′** (pē′kō′), **François Édouard.** 1786–1868. French painter; best known for historical paintings.

**Pic′quart′** (pē′kár′), **Georges.** 1854–1914. French general; played important part in defense of Dreyfus, for which he was retired from army (1898) and imprisoned; upon Dreyfus's vindication, Picquart was restored to active service with commission of general of division (1906); minister of war (1906–09).

**Pic′tet′** (pēk′tĕ′), **Raoul.** 1842–1929. Swiss physicist; known for work on production of low temperatures and for liquefaction of oxygen, nitrogen, hydrogen, and carbon dioxide about the same time as it was accomplished by Cailletet (1877); studied properties of substances at low temperatures.

**Pictet de la Rive** (dē là rēv′), **François Jules.** 1809–1872. Swiss zoologist and paleontologist; author of *Traité de Paléontologie* (1845–46), etc.

**Pic′ton** (pĭk′tŭn), Sir **Thomas.** 1758–1815. British army officer, b. in Wales; distinguished himself in capture of St. Lucia (1796); governor of Trinidad; tried in court of King's Bench on charge of cruelty in permitting torture, allowed under Spanish law (1806), with no judgment delivered; served as one of Wellington's principal subordinates in Portugal (from 1810); took prominent part in battle of Fuentes d'Oñoro (1811) and conducted siege of Badajoz (1812); held command in battles of Pyrenees; killed at Waterloo.

**Pier′an·to′ni** (pyĕr′än·tô′nē), **Augusto.** 1840–1911. Italian jurist; participated in Garibaldi's Sicilian expedition (1860); a founder of Institut de Droit International (1873).

**Pierce** (pērs). See also PEARCE, PEARSE, PEIRCE.

**Pierce, Franklin.** 1804–1869. Fourteenth president of the United States, b. Hillsboro, N.H.; grad. Bowdoin (1824); adm. to bar (1827); practiced in Hillsboro; member, U.S. House of Representatives (1833–37), U.S. Senate (1837–42); served in Mexican War; brigadier general (1847); president of the United States (1853–57). His father, **Benjamin Pierce** (1757–1839), was a soldier in American Revolution; governor of New Hampshire (1827 and 1829).

**Pierce, George Washington.** 1872–1956. American physicist; authority on radio communication.

**Pierce, Gilbert Ashville.** 1839–1901. American politician and author, b. East Otto, N.Y.; governor of Territory of Dakota (1884–86); first U.S. senator from North Dakota (1889–91). Author of the play, *One Hundred Wives* (1880), the novels *Zachariah, the Congressman* (1876) and *A Dangerous Woman* (1883), and compiler of *The Dickens Dictionary* (1872).

**Pier′ma·ri′ni** (pyĕr′mä·rē′nē), **Giuseppe.** 1734–1808. Italian architect; official architect and inspector general of architecture at Milan (1770–94); among his works are the La Scala Theater, Porta Orientale, and façade of Belgioioso Palace (all at Milan).

**Pier′né′** (pyĕr′nā′), **Henri Constant Gabriel.** 1863–1937. French conductor and composer; organist, Church of St. Clotilde, Paris (1890–1908); conductor of Concerts Colonne (from 1910). Among his operas are *Salomé* (1895) and *Vendée* (1897); among his comic operas, *Le Docteur Blanc* (1893) and *La Princesse Lointaine* (1895); composer also of orchestral suites, piano concertos, chamber music, oratorios and other choral works, and songs.

**Pie'ro di Co'si·mo** (pyâ'rō dē kô'zē·mō). *Also* **Piero di Lo·ren'zo** (lō·rĕn'tsō). 1462–1521. Florentine painter; among his pupils were Fra Bartolommeo and Andrea del Sarto. Works include *Destruction of Pharaoh's Host,* in Sistine Chapel; *Perseus Delivering Andromeda,* in Uffizi Gallery, and portraits.

**Pié'ro·la** (pyā'rō·lä), **Nicolás de.** 1839–1913. Peruvian general and political leader; stirred up revolts against both Pardo (1874) and Prado (1877–78); took part in War of the Pacific (1879–83) and assumed presidency of Peru when Prado left country (1879–81); finally driven from office by defeats of Peruvian army; overthrew government (1894) when Cáceres was deposed. Again president (1895–99); administration marked by strengthening of army and advances in legislation.

**Pierozzi, Antonio.** See Saint ANTONINUS.

**Pier'pont** (pẽr'pŏnt), **James.** 1660–1714. American Congregational clergyman, b. Roxbury, Mass.; pastor, New Haven, Conn. (1685–1714); one of the founders and original trustees of Yale College (chartered 1701). His great-grandson **John Pierpont** (1785–1866) was a Unitarian clergyman and poet; pastor in Boston (1819–45), Troy (1845–49), West Medford (1849–58); clerk in Treasury Department, Washington, D.C. (1858–66); author of *Airs of Palestine and Other Poems* (1840), *The Anti-Slavery Poems of John Pierpont* (1843). John Pierpont Morgan was his grandson.

**Pierre, Jean de la.** See Johann HEYNLIN.

**Pierre'pont** (pẽr'pŏnt). Name of an English family of Nottinghamshire bearing titles of earl and duke of **King'ston-up·on'-Hull'** [kĭng'stŭn·ŭ·pŏn'hŭl'] (1628–1773), and marquis of **Dor'ches'ter** (dôr'chĕs'tẽr; -chĭs·tẽr), including: **Robert Pierrepont** (1584–1643), 1st Viscount **New'ark** (nū'ẽrk) and 1st Earl of Kingston; declined at beginning of Civil War to lend Charles I money, but joined king (1643); taken prisoner and accidentally killed. His eldest son, **Henry** (1606–1680), 2d Earl of Kingston and 1st Marquis of Dorchester; educ. Cambridge; represented Charles I in negotiations at Uxbridge; paid large fine to Parliament (1647); studied law and medicine; at Restoration, privy councilor (1660–73). **William** (1607?–1678), 2d son of 1st earl; Parliamentarian and leader of peace party at beginning of Civil War; became one of committee of both kingdoms (1644); withdrew from politics at time of Pride's Purge; at Restoration, elected to council of state and sat in Convention Parliament. Sir **Evelyn** (1665?–1726), Marquis of Dorchester and 1st Duke of Kingston; grandson of William Pierrepont; member of Convention Parliament (1689), privy councilor (1714), lord president of council (1719–20); a leader in society. One of his daughters was Lady Mary Wortley Montagu (*q.v.*). His grandson Sir **Evelyn** (1711–1773), 2d duke; raised "Kingston light horse" regiment and opposed Jacobites at Culloden Moor (1746); lieutenant general (1759). His wife, **Elizabeth Chud'leigh** [chŭd'lĭ] (1720–1788), Countess of **Bris'tol** (brĭs't'l), self-styled Duchess of Kingston; maid of honor to Augusta, Princess of Wales (1743); secretly married and had son by Augustus John Hervey (who became in 1775, 3d earl of Bristol); became mistress of 2d duke of Kingston; obtained separation from husband and declared spinster by court; married Kingston (1768) and became his heiress (1773); accused of bigamy by Kingston's nephew; found guilty by House of Lords (1776); lived on Continent.

**Pierrepont, Edwards.** 1817–1892. American lawyer; descendant of James Pierpont; practiced in New York City (from 1846); U.S. attorney general (1875–76); U.S. minister to Great Britain (1876–77).

**Pier'son** (pẽr's'n), **Abraham.** 1609–1678. Congregational clergyman in America, b. in Yorkshire, Eng.; to America, and admitted to church at Boston (1640); first pastor of Southampton, Long Island, N.Y. 1640–47), Branford, Conn. (1647–67), Newark, N.J. (1667–78). His son **Abraham** (1645?–1707) was also a Congregational clergyman; assisted his father at Newark, N.J. (1669–78) and succeeded him (1678–92); pastor, Clinton, Conn. (1694–1707); active in founding Yale College (chartered 1701), and elected its first rector (Nov. 11, 1701).

**Pie'ters** (pē'tẽrz), **Adrian John.** 1866–1940. American agronomist; known esp. for work in connection with introduction into U.S. of new variety of Lespedeza important as forage crop.

**Pieterszoon, Jan.** See Jan Pieters SWEELINCK.

**Pieterszoon, Nicolaes** *or* **Claes.** See TULP.

**Piet Paaltjens.** See François HAVERSCHMIDT.

**Pietro, Giovanni di.** See SPAGNA.

**Pie'tro del'la Vi'gna** (pyâ'trō dāl'lä vē'nyä) *or* **del'le Vi'gne** (dāl'lā vē'nyā). *Lat.* **Pe'trus de Vin'e·a** (pē'trŭs dē vĭn'ē·ȧ) *or* **Vin'e·is** (-ĭs). 1190?–1249. Italian jurist and statesman; prime minister of Emperor Frederick II; aided in drafting Sicilian constitution (1231); suddenly imprisoned on charges of seeking to poison the emperor, committed suicide; his extant letters and speeches are sources for history of the period.

**Pieve, Pier della.** See Il PERUGINO.

**Pi'ga·fet'ta** (pē'gä·fāt'tä), **Antonio.** 1491–?1534. Italian traveler; accompanied Magellan (*q.v.*) on trip around world and completed journey in the *Victoria* (Sept., 1519–Sept., 1522); wrote for Charles V an account of the voyage, which the sovereign published.

**Pi'galle'** (pē'gȧl'), **Jean Baptiste.** 1714–1785. French sculptor; among his works are *Vênus, L'Amour et l'Amitiê* (now in the Louvre), the mausoleum of Marshal Maurice de Saxe in Strasbourg.

**Pi'gault'–Le·brun'** (pē'gō'lē·brûɴ'). *Real name* **Charles Antoine Guillaume Pigault de l'É'pi'ney'** (dē lā'pē'nā'). 1753–1835. French writer of fiction, b. Calais; among his novels are *L'Enfant du Carnaval* (1792), *Mon Oncle Thomas* (1799), and *Monsieur Botte* (1802).

**Pig'gott** (pĭg'ŭt), Sir **Francis Taylor.** 1852–1925. English legal scholar and Orientalist; legal adviser to prime minister of Japan (1887–91); acting chief judge, Mauritius (1895–97), advocate general (1894–1905); chief justice of Supreme Court, Hongkong (1905–12). Author of works on international law, and of books on Japanese gardens and music.

**Pig'ott** (pĭg'ŭt), **Richard.** 1828?–1889. Irish journalist and forger; Dublin newspaper proprietor and violent Nationalist (until 1879); sold (1886) to Loyal and Patriotic Union, an Irish anti home-rule society, papers incriminating Parnell in Phoenix Park tragedy and forming basis of *Times* articles *Parnellism and Crime;* confessed that papers were forged by him; fled to Madrid, shot himself.

**Pi'gres** (pī'grēz). Greek poet of 5th century B.C.; said to have introduced the iambic trimeter and to have written mock-heroic *Batrachomyomachia* (*i.e.* "battle between the frogs and the mice"), a parody on the *Iliad.*

**Pike** (pīk), **Zebulon Montgomery.** 1779–1813. American army officer and explorer, b. Lamberton, N.J.; commissioned first lieutenant, U.S. army (1799); led exploring party to headwaters of Mississippi River (1805–06), and of Arkansas and Red rivers (1806–07); reached site of present Pueblo, Colo., and discovered peak now named Pikes Peak in his honor. Promoted brigadier general (1813); commanded troops against York, now Toronto, Canada; killed in the assault (Apr. 27, 1813).

**Pi′lat** (pĭ′lät), **Ig′naz** (ĭg′näts) **An′ton** (ăn′t′n). 1820–1870. Landscape gardener, b. St. Agatha, Austria; to U.S. (1848); laid out Central Park, New York City, after plans designed by Frederick Law Olmsted and Calvert Vaux.

**Pi′late** (pī′lȧt), **Pontius.** Procurator of Judea under Emperor Tiberius, in 1st half of 1st century A.D.; in this capacity, tried and condemned Jesus Christ.

**Pi′lâ′tre de Ro′zier′** (pē′lä′tr′ dē rō′zyā′), **Jean François.** 1756–1785. French physicist and aeronaut; first human being to ascend in a balloon (1785); killed with companion in attempt to cross English Channel in an apparatus composed of two balloons, one filled with hydrogen and the other with warm air.

**Pile** (pīl), Sir **Frederick Alfred.** 1884– . British army officer; served in World War I; major general (1937); as head, Antiaircraft Command (1939–45), organized defense of London; general (1941); director-general, ministry of works (1945).

**Pil′lers·dorf** (pĭl′ẽrs·dôrf), Baron **Franz.** 1786–1862. Austrian statesman; head of the government for a few weeks (1848); his conciliatory policy was disapproved, and he was retired (July 8, 1848).

**Pil′ling** (pĭl′ĭng), **James Constantine.** 1846–1895. American ethnologist; pioneer in collecting ethnological and bibliographical material about Indian tribes and their languages.

**Pil′low** (pĭl′ō), **Gideon Johnson.** 1806–1878. American army officer, b. in Williamson County, Tenn.; entered Confederate service, brigadier general (1861); second in command under Gen. John B. Floyd at Fort Donelson (1861–62); when Gen. Floyd, in disagreement with decision to surrender, relinquished command, Pillow passed it on to Gen. Simon B. Buckner, and he and Floyd escaped before fort was surrendered (Feb., 1862); suspended from command by Confederate secretary of war, and held guilty of grave errors of judgment.

**Pills′bur′y** (pĭlz′bĕr′ĭ; -bẽr·ĭ), **Harry Nelson.** 1872–1906. American chess expert, b. Somerville, Mass.; U.S. champion (from 1898); excelled in blindfold exhibition games.

**Pillsbury, John Elliott.** 1846–1919. American naval officer, b. Lowell, Mass.; grad. U.S.N.A., Annapolis (1867); on duty with U.S. Coast Survey (1875–91); investigated Gulf Stream; on blockade duty before Santiago in Spanish-American War; rear admiral (1908). Author of *The Gulf Stream* (1891), etc.

**Pillsbury, Parker.** 1809–1898. American abolitionist, b. Hamilton, Mass.; lectured widely on antislavery issue; after Civil War, worked for political reforms, international peace, and esp. for woman suffrage.

**Pillsbury, Walter Bowers.** 1872–1960. American psychologist; author of *Attention* (1908), *Essentials of Psychology* (1911), *An Elementary Psychology of the Abnormal* (1932), etc.

**Pil·nyak′** (pyĭl·y′·nyȧk′). *Pseudonym of* **Boris Andreevich Vo′gau** (vō′gou). 1894–1937. Russian novelist; author notably of tales dealing with transition period from old czarist Russian conditions to new world planned by Soviets. Among his works translated into English are *Tales of the Wilderness* (1925), *The Naked Year* (1928), *The Volga Flows into the Caspian Sea* (1931).

**Pi′lon′** (pē′lôɴ′), **Germain.** 1537?–?1590. French sculptor; among his works are statues of the king and the queen on monument of Henry II in the Church of St. Denis, a bronze statue of Cardinal René de Birague, and *Trois Grâces* in marble (now in the Louvre). Regarded as one of leading sculptors of the Renaissance in France.

**Pi·lo′ty** (pē·lō′tē), **Ferdinand.** 1786–1844. German lithographer. A son, **Karl von Piloty** (1826–1886), was a historical painter; among his canvases are *Columbus Discovers America*, *Death of Alexander the Great in Babylon*, *Galileo in Prison*, *Death of Caesar*, and *The Triumph of Germanicus.* Another son, **Ferdinand Piloty** (1828–1895), was also a historical painter; painted *Queen Elizabeth Reviewing Her Army in Sight of the Armada* and *Sir Thomas More in Prison.*

**Pilpay** *or* **Pilpai.** See BIDPAI.

**Pils** (pēl), **Isidore Alexandre Augustin.** 1813–1875. French painter, esp. of historical and military subjects.

**Pił·sud′ski** (pēl·so͞ot′skē), **Józef.** 1867–1935. Polish general and statesman, b. in province of Wilno; joined organization of Young Poles; sentenced to five years' penal servitude in Siberia on charge of conspiring to assassinate Czar Alexander III (1887). On return to Poland (1892), became a leader of Polish Socialist party; founded radical journal *The Workman* (1894); arrested (1900), but escaped to England. Returned to Poland (1902) and continued political agitation; organized secretly a private Polish army; at outbreak of World War (1914), offered army of 10,000 under his command to Austria, and fought against Russians; resigned command (1916) because of German and Austrian interference in Polish affairs; worked actively for Polish independence; gained recognition by Central Powers (Nov. 16, 1916) of independence of Russian Poland, and accepted position as head of military commission there. Imprisoned by Germans (1917–18) when his troops refused to join Central Powers in war. After collapse of Central Powers, returned to Warsaw; elected chief of state, generalissimo of Polish army, and (1920) first marshal of Poland. Directed war against Lithuanians, Ukrainians, and Bolsheviks (1919–20); absolute dictator of Poland as provisional president until Polish constitution drafted and accepted by Polish parliament (1921). Again intervened in Polish political affairs by moving troops into Warsaw (May 12, 1926), overturning the Witos cabinet, and installing a new cabinet under Kazimierz Bartel, in which he himself accepted position as minister of war; in this position, he was virtual dictator of Poland; became premier of Poland (1926–28, 1930) and continued to keep position as minister of war and commander in chief of army, thereby absolutely controlling Polish policies until his death.

**Pimenta, Diogo Bernardes.** See Diogo BERNARDES PIMENTA.

**Pinch′back′** (pĭnch′băk′), **Pinckney Benton Stewart.** 1837–1921. American politician, son of a white planter and a Negro slave; raised volunteer Negro company for service with Union army in Civil War (1862–63); engaged in post-war Louisiana politics; lieutenant governor (1871); acting governor (1872–73). Elected to U.S. House of Representatives (1872), but not seated, and to U.S. Senate (1873) but again not seated.

**Pinch′beck′** (pĭnch′bĕk′), **Christopher.** 1670?–1732. London watchmaker and toymaker; invented copper and zinc alloy (pinchbeck) resembling gold.

**Pincherle, Alberto.** See Alberto MORAVIA.

**Pin′chot** (pĭn′shō), **Gifford.** 1865–1946. American political leader, b. Simsbury, Conn.; studied forestry in Europe; became first professional American forester; chief of Forest Service, U.S. Department of Agriculture (1898–1910); instituted charges against U.S. secretary of the interior, Richard A. Ballinger, maintaining that the secretary had reversed the Roosevelt conservation policy; President Taft upheld Ballinger and dismissed Pinchot (1910) for insubordination. Professor of forestry, Yale (1903–36); founder, with his brother Amos, of Pinchot School of Forestry at Yale; commissioner of forestry, Pennsylvania (1920–22). Governor of Pennsylvania (1923–27, 1931–35); prominent in initiating measures to settle great coal strike of 1923. Author of *The White Pine* (with H. S. Graves, 1896), *The Adirondack Spruce* (1898), *A Primer of Forestry* (1899–1905), *The Fight for Conservation* (1909), *To the South Seas* (1930), *Just Fishing Talk* (1936), etc.

**Pinck′ney** (pĭngk′nĭ), **Charles.** 1757–1824. American legislator, b. Charleston, S.C.; served in American Revolution; member, Continental Congress (1784–87); submitted to federal convention of 1787 a plan for a constitution, known as the "Pinckney Draught," containing more than thirty provisions later incorporated in the finished constitution. Governor of South Carolina (1789–92, 1796–98, 1806–08); U.S. senator (1798–1801); U.S. minister to Spain (1801–05) during period when Louisiana was relinquished to France and then sold to U.S.; member, U.S. House of Representatives (1819–21).

**Pinckney, Charles Cotesworth.** 1746–1825. American statesman, b. Charleston, S.C.; member, Council of Safety (1776) and one of committee to draft plan for temporary government of South Carolina; served in revolution; at defense of Fort Sullivan, battles of Brandywine and Germantown, captured by British at fall of Charleston, exchanged (1782) and rejoined Continental army, brevetted brigadier general (1783); member of federal convention (1787) and aided in framing the constitution. Sent to France on special mission (1796–97) but his status not recognized by France; forced to leave France; in Amsterdam, was approached by emissary of French government with an offer of terms under which negotiations might be begun; his report, and that of his colleagues, known in history as the XYZ Correspondence, aroused intense feeling both in U.S. and in France, since U.S. commissioners frankly charged that French emissaries attempted bribery to gain their ends; commissioned major general when war with France was expected (1798–1800). Federalist candidate for vice-president (1800) and for president (1804, 1808). His brother **Thomas** (1750–1828) was also educated at Oxford, and admitted to English bar (1774) and American bar (1774); served in Revolution, escaped capture at Charleston and joined Continental army, on Gates's staff, wounded and captured at Camden; governor of South Carolina (1787–89); U.S. minister to Great Britain (1792–94), and special commissioner to Spain (1795–96) where he negotiated treaty settling southern U.S.-Spanish boundary line and navigation rights on Mississippi River; Federalist candidate for vice-president (1796); member of U.S. House of Representatives (1797–1801).

**Pin′dar** (pĭn′dẽr). 522?–443 B.C. Greek lyric poet, b. in Cynoscephalae, near Thebes; little is known of his life history. Among his extant works are 44 complete *Epinicia* (*Odes of Victory*), celebrating victories in great national games. Among fragments of other works are *Hymns* (to Persephone, to Fortune, etc.), *Paeans* (to Apollo and to Zeus), *Choral Dithyrambs* (to Dionysus), *Processional Songs*, *Choral Songs for Maidens*, *Choral Dance Songs*, *Encomia* or *Laudatory Odes*, *Scolia* or *Festive Songs*, and *Dirges*.

**Pindar, Peter.** Pseudonym of John WOLCOT (1738–1819).

**Pin′de·mon′te** (pēn′dȧ·mōn′tȧ), Cavaliere **Ippolito.** 1753–1828. Italian poet; precursor of Romanticism; known particularly for translation into blank verse of Homer's *Odyssey* (1809–22).

**Pine** (pīn), **Robert Edge.** 1730–1788. Painter, b. London, Eng.; successful painter in England (to 1784); to U.S. (1784) and exhibited a series of pictures illustrating scenes from Shakespearean drama. His *Mrs. Reid in the Character of a Sultana* hangs in the Metropolitan Museum of Art, New York; portrait of George Washington, in Independence Hall, Philadelphia; portrait of Martha Washington, in Virginia Historical Society, Richmond, Va.

**Pi·ne′do** (pē·nâ′dō), **Francesco de.** 1890–1933. Italian aviator; flew from Tokyo to Rome in 21 days (1925); killed in airplane accident when taking off from New York City for attempted nonstop flight to Baghdad.

**Pi′nel′** (pē′nĕl′), **Philippe.** 1745–1826. French physician; known for advocacy and practice of more humane treatment for the insane, set forth in his *Traité Médico-Philosophique sur l'Aliénation Mentale*.

**Pi·ne′lo** (pē·nā′lō). *Real name* **Antonio de Le·ón′** (thā lā·ōn′). 1590?–?1660. Spanish jurist and historian; secretary, Council of the Indies; royal historiographer (1637 ff.); known particularly for his codification of colonial laws.

**Pi·ne′ro** (pĭ·nēr′ō), Sir **Arthur Wing.** 1855–1934. English dramatist; actor (1874–81). His first play acted on stage, *£200 A Year* (1877); won financial independence with *The Money Spinner* (1880) and a series of farces, and with *Sweet Lavender* (1888); attempted serious drama in *The Squire* (1881) and returned to it in *The Profligate* (1889); marked off a new era of modern drama with *The Second Mrs. Tanqueray* (1893), first of a series of problem plays with serious intent, including *The Notorious Mrs. Ebbsmith* (1895), *The Benefit of the Doubt* (1895), *Iris* (1901), *The Thunderbolt* (1908), *Mid-Channel* (1909). Author also of plays reflecting contemporary manners and morals, including *The Gay Lord Quex* (1899); satirical comedies, including *The Princess and the Butterfly* (1897); later plays mostly in lighter vein, including *The Enchanted Cottage* (1922), *Child Man* (1930), *Dr. Harmer's Holidays* (1930), *A Cold June* (1932).

**Pin′gré′** (păN′grā′), **Alexandre Gui.** 1711–1796. French astronomer; author of *Cométographie* (1783).

**Pin′ker·ton** (pĭng′kẽr·t'n; -tŭn), **Allan.** 1819–1884. Detective, b. Glasgow, Scotland; emigrated to U.S. (1842); settled in Illinois; established private detective agency, first in U.S., at Chicago (1850); gained national prominence by solving Adams Express robberies; guarded Lincoln on his trip to Washington for the inauguration; during Civil War, organized and conducted secret service activities for General McClellan (1861–62). Prominent in breaking up "Molly Maguires" in coal disorders. Author of *Strikers, Communists, Tramps, and Detectives* (1878), *The Spy of the Rebellion* (1883), *Thirty Years a Detective* (1884), etc.

**Pink′ney** (pĭngk′nĭ), **William.** 1764–1822. American lawyer and legislator, b. Annapolis, Md.; in England as joint commissioner to adjust American claims against British government for maritime losses (1796–1804); U.S. minister to Great Britain (1807–11); U.S. attorney general (1811–14); member, U.S. House of Representatives (1815–16); U.S. minister to Russia (1816–18); U.S. senator from Maryland (1819–22); influential in securing the Missouri Compromise. His son **Edward Coote** (1802–28) was a poet; in U.S. navy (1815–24); practiced law, Baltimore (from 1824); published *Look Out Upon the Stars, My Love...* (1823), *Rodolph, A Fragment* (1823), and a volume of *Poems*, including lyrics *A Health* and *Serenade*.

**Pin′ski** (pĭn′skĭ), **Da′vid** (dā′vĭd). 1872–1959. Dramatist and novelist, b. in Russia; to U.S. (1899); author of six volumes of plays and fourteen volumes of stories, all written in Yiddish. Also published in English *Temptations* (a volume of short stories, 1919), *Ten Plays* (1919),

*The Final Balance* (a play, 1928), *The Generations of Noah Edon* (a novel, 1931), etc.

**Pin'ter** (pĭn'tẽr), **Harold.** 1930– . British playwright and actor. Author of plays, including *The Birthday Party* (1958), *The Homecoming* (1965), also filmscripts, etc.

**Pint'ner** (pĭnt'nẽr), **Rudolf.** 1884–1942. Psychologist, b. in Lytham, Eng.; to U.S. (1912); interested esp. in nature and value of intelligence tests; author of *A Scale of Performance Tests* (1917), *Intelligence Testing* (1923).

**Pin'to** (pēn'tō), **Aníbal.** 1825–1884. Chilean political leader; president of Chile (1876–81); began war with Peru and Bolivia (1879).

**Pin'to** (pēɴn'tōō), **Fernâm Mendes.** 1509?–1583. Known as "the Prince of Liars." Portuguese adventurer and writer; traveled, traded, and fought in Far East; returned to Portugal (1558), settled near Almada, and wrote account of his travels, *Peregrinação* (first published, 1614). Reputation as liar is undeserved; ordinarily, an accurate observer and honest narrator.

**Pinto, Serpa.** See SERPA PINTO.

**Pin'tu·ric'chio** (pēn'tōō·rēk'kyō) *or* **Pin'to·ric'chio** (pēn'tō-). *Real name* **Bernardino Bet'ti** (bāt'tē), *or* **di Bet'to** (dē bāt'tō), **di Bia'gio** (dē byä'jō). 1454–1513. Italian painter of Umbrian school, b. Perugia; collaborated with Perugino in painting frescoes in Sistine Chapel; leading historical painter of Umbrian school. Works include *Holy Family with St. John, Baptism of Christ, Journey of Moses*, frescoes from life of St. Bernardino, decorative works, and portraits.

**Pin·zón'** (pēn·thōn'), **Martín Alonso.** 1440?–1493. Spanish navigator, b. Palos; with brothers helped Columbus prepare expedition; commanded the *Pinta* on first voyage (1492); after landfall at Guanahani separated from Columbus; discovered Haiti; on return voyage separated from Columbus by storm but reached Palos on same day (Mar. 15, 1493). A younger brother, **Vicente Yáñez** (1460?–?1524), b. Palos, commanded the *Niña* on first voyage; made later voyages (1497–1500), discovering coast of Brazil (1500) and sailing north as far as Costa Rica; made voyage with Juan Díaz de Solís (1508–09) along Atlantic coast of South America, perhaps as far south as La Plata. Another brother, **Francisco Martín** (1440?–?1493), was master of the *Pinta* under Martín Alonso.

**Piombo, Sebastiano del.** See SEBASTIANO DEL PIOMBO.

**Pioz'zi** (pyôt'tsē), **Hester Lynch,** *nee* **Salus'bur·y** (sôlz'bẽr·ĭ; -brĭ). *Known mostly as* Mrs. **Thrale** (thrāl). 1741–1821. Writer and friend of Dr. Johnson, b. in northeast Wales; m. (1763) Henry Thrale, Southwark brewer; began (1764) a twenty-year intimacy with Dr. Johnson, who became more or less domesticated in home of the Thrales and accompanied them to Wales (1774) and to France (1775); saved her husband from threatened bankruptcy and disposed of business on his death (1781); m. (1784) Gabriel Piozzi, Italian musician, to the displeasure of Dr. Johnson; traveled in Italy (till 1787), where she associated with the Della-Cruscans and contributed verses; retained her vivacity through last days at Bath. Second only to Boswell in fame among writers on Dr. Johnson.

**Pi'per** (pī'pẽr), Mrs. **Leonora E.** American psychic medium, whose psychic powers were investigated by William James of Harvard, Sir Oliver Lodge in England (1889–90), and other eminent scientists.

**Pippi, Giulio.** See Giulio ROMANO.

**Pip·pin'** (pĭ·pēn'). German form of PEPIN.

**Pi'ran·del'lo** (pē'rän·dĕl'lō), **Luigi.** 1867–1936. Italian novelist and dramatist, b. Agrigento, Sicily; lecturer in literature, Rome (1897–1922); visited U.S. (1923, 1935); member, Italian Acad. (1929 ff.); awarded Nobel prize for literature (1934); a leading exponent of contemporary drama, esp. of the grotesque school. Among his works are poems, as *Mal Giocando*, short stories, as *Amori Senza Amore* (1894), *Quando Ero Matto* (1903), *Bianche e Nere* (1904), *La Vita Nuda* (1910), *La Trappola* (1915), *Il Carnevale dei Morti* (1919), and *Tu Ridi* (1919), novels, as *L'Esclusa* (1901), *Il Fu Mattia Pascal* (1905), *I Vecchi e I Giovani* (1923), and plays, as *Se Non Così* (1917), *Liola* (1917), *Così È Se Vi Pare* (1918), *Sei Personaggi in Cerca d'Autore* (1918; produced in N.Y., 1922), *Tutto per Bene* (1920), *L'Innesto* (1921), *Enrico IV* (1922), *Vestire gli Ignudi* (1923), *La Vita Che Ti Diedi* (1924), *La Nuova Colonia* (1925), *L'Amica della Moglie* (1927), *O di Uno o di Nessuno* (1929), *Come Tu Mi Vuoi* (1930), *Non Si Sa Come* (1935).

**Pi'ra·ne'si** (pē'rä·nā'sē), **Giambattista.** 1720–1778. Italian architect, decorative painter, and engraver; known esp. for copperplate engravings which have become a source book for Louis XIV, Adam, and Empire architectural styles. Among important plates are *Column of Trajan, Fountain of Trevi, Colisseum, Pantheon, Castel Gandolfo*, and *Pæstum*.

**Pirckheimer.** = PIRKHEIMER.

**Pire** (pēr), **Dominique Georges.** 1910–1969. Belgian priest. Founder of charitable organizations, including Aid to Displaced Persons (1949); awarded Nobel peace prize (1958).

**Pi'renne'** (pē'rĕn'), **Henri.** 1862–1935. Belgian historian; during World War I, interned in German prison camp; wrote *Histoire de Belgique, Les Villes du Moyen Âge*, and *La Belgique et la Guerre Mondiale*.

**Pirk'hei'mer** (pĭrk'hī'mẽr), **Willibald.** 1470–1530. German Humanist; at outbreak of Reformation, associated himself with Reuchlin and Dürer. Author of a history of the Swiss War, books on science and politics, and translations of Greek classics into Latin.

**Pi'ron'** (pē'rôɴ'), **Alexis.** 1689–1773. French poet and playwright; author of many epigrams, the dramatic monologue in three acts *Arlequin-Deucalion*, comic opera *Endriaque*, and comedy *La Métromanie*.

**Pir·quet'** (pĭr·kē'), Baron **Clemens von.** 1874–1929. Austrian pediatrist; general commissioner, American Relief Administration for Austria's Children (1919–23).

**Pir'rie** (pĭr'ĭ), **William James.** Viscount **Pirrie.** 1847–1924. British shipbuilder; b. in Quebec of Irish parents; became partner (1874) and later chairman of board of Harland & Wolff, sole builders for White Star line; controller general of merchant shipping (1918).

**Pir'ro'** (pē'rō'), **André.** 1869–1943. French music historian; author of works on Johann Sebastian Bach.

**Pirs'son** (pĭr's'n), **Louis Valentine.** 1860–1919. American geologist; taught at Yale (1893–1919; professor from 1897). Author of *Rocks and Rock Minerals* (1908), *Quantitative Classification of Igneous Rocks* (with Cross, Iddings, and Washington; 1903), which has new system of classification and new terminology.

**Pi·san'der** *or* **Pei·san'der** (pī·săn'dẽr). Greek epic poet of 7th century B.C., of Camirus in Rhodes; author of *Heracleia*, only a few lines of which are extant.

**Pisander** *or* **Peisander.** Athenian politician; a leader of oligarchical party in Peloponnesian War (431 B.C. ff.); a commander of Greek fleet (412); helped establish Council of the Four Hundred at Athens (411); fled to Sparta when oligarchy fell.

**Pi·sa'no** (pē·sä'nō), **Andrea.** *Also called* **Andrea da Pon'te·de'ra** (dä pōn'tā·dâ'rä). 1270?–1348. Italian sculptor of Pisan school, b. probably at Pontedera; succeeded Giotto as chief artist for Cathedral of Florence (1336); chief artist for Cathedral of Orvieto (1347);

known esp. for the bronze doors of the baptistery of the Cathedral of Florence, consisting of twenty reliefs from life of St. John the Baptist and eight representing Christian virtues. His son **Nino** (1315?–?1368) was a sculptor, goldsmith, and architect; leading representative of mature Gothic style; collaborated with his father.

**Pisano, Antonio,** *often called* **Vittore.** *Known as* **Il Pi'sa·nel'lo** (ēl pē'sä·nĕl'lō). 1397?–?1455. Veronese painter and medalist; one of first representatives of early Renaissance in northern Italy; collaborated with Gentile da Fabriano (c. 1409–14) in decoration of Venetian ducal palace; in service of Este family and, later (1448), of King Alfonso of Naples; known chiefly as a medalist; notable also for drawings of animals.

**Pisano, Giovanni.** See under Nicola PISANO.

**Pisano, Giunta.** See GIUNTA PISANO.

**Pisano, Leonardo.** See Leonardo FIBONACCI.

**Pisano** *or* **da Pi'sa** (dä pē'sä), **Nicola** *or* **Niccolò.** 1220–1284. Italian sculptor; works mark apex of Romanesque style; first important precursor of Renaissance; known esp. for his hexagonal marble pulpit of the baptistery at Pisa, particularly the bas-reliefs from the life of Christ, as *Nativity* and *Adoration of the Kings.* Among his other works are an octagonal pulpit in Siena Cathedral, designs for *Arca di San Domenico* in Church of San Domenico, Bologna, and sculptural decorations for fountain at Perugia; reputedly also an architect. His son **Giovanni** (1245–1314) was a sculptor, painter, and architect; chief Italian sculptor of Middle Ages; founder of Italian Gothic sculpture; chief architect, Cathedral of Pisa (1278 ff.) and Cathedral of Siena (1284–99, 1314 ff.); assisted father in execution of pulpit in Siena Cathedral and of fountain of Perugia; among his architectural works are the Campo Santo at Pisa and the façade of Siena Cathedral; sculptural works include holy-water font of San Giovanni Fuorcivita, pulpit of Sant'Andrea Pistoia at Siena, a pulpit in Cathedral of Pisa, statues of Madonna, monument of Urban IV (Perugia).

**Pi'schel** (pĭsh'ĕl), **Richard.** 1849–1908. German Indologist; wrote esp. on classical Sanskrit drama and Prakrit.

**Pi'sem·ski** (pyĕ'syĕm·skû·ĭ; *Angl.* -skĭ), **Aleksei Feofilaktovich.** 1820–1881. Russian writer; educ. Moscow; twenty years in government service. Among his chief novels are *A Muff* (1850), *A Thousand Souls* (1858), and *A Troubled Sea* (1863); among his plays, *A Bitter Fate* (1859).

**Pi Sheng** (bē' shŭng'). Reputed inventor of movable type for printing (in China, c. mid-11th century A.D.).

**Pisida** *or* **Pisides.** See GEORGE THE PISIDIAN.

**Pi·sis'tra·tus** *or* **Pei·sis'tra·tus** (pī·sĭs'trȧ·tŭs). d. 527 B.C. Tyrant of Athens; first distinguished himself in the war with Megara (570–565). In politics, took up cause of working classes, and seized government of the city (560); driven out (560 and 556–554), but established control (554–527). See HIPPIAS and HIPPARCHUS.

**Pi'so** (pī'sō). Roman plebeian family, gens Calpurnius, including notably: **Lucius Calpurnius Piso,** *surnamed* **Fru'gi** (frōō'jī); tribune of the plebs (149 B.C.) and sponsor of first law against extortion; praetor (136), consul (133), censor (120); opposed reforms of the Gracchi; author of a history of Rome, extant only in a few fragments. **Lucius Calpurnius Piso Cae'so·ni'nus** (sē'zō·nī'nŭs); father-in-law of Julius Caesar; consul (58 B.C.); involved in plot with Clodius to get rid of Cicero; governor of Macedonia (57–55); at outbreak of civil war, offered to mediate between Caesar and Pompey; after assassination of Caesar, opposed Mark Antony, but later joined his party. **Gaius Calpurnius Piso;** robbed of his wife (37 A.D.) by Caligula and banished from Rome; conspired to take Nero's life.

**Pis'sar'ro'** (pē'sȧ'rō'), **Camille.** 1830–1903. French landscape painter, identified with impressionist school and, later, with pointillism; among his canvases are *Marchés à Rouen, Vues de Paris,* and *Quais de la Seine.*

**Pistoia, Cino da.** See CINO DA PISTOIA.

**Pis'ton** (pĭs'tŭn), **Walter.** 1894–1976. American composer, b. Rockland, Me. At Harvard U. (1926–60); composer of symphonies, ballets, orchestral works, etc.

**Pi·struc'ci** (pē·strōōt'chē), **Benedetto.** 1784–1855. Italian gem engraver and medalist in England; executed the St. George and the dragon used on the reverse of British gold coins; chief engraver (from 1817); chief medalist (1828).

**Pit'cairn** (pĭt'kârn), **John.** 1722–1775. British officer of the Royal Marines; in command of advance detachment engaged by Americans at Lexington and Concord (1775); mortally wounded at Bunker Hill (June 17, 1775). His son **Robert** (1747?–?1770), midshipman on the *Swallow,* was first to sight (July 2, 1767) the island later to be called Pitcairn Island and to become the refuge of the mutineers of the *Bounty* (1789).

**Pit'cairne** (pĭt'kârn), **Archibald.** 1652–1713. Scottish physician; Jacobite; satirist of Presbyterianism; reputed atheist; author of Latin verses.

**Pitcher, Molly.** See Mary MCCAULEY.

**Pi'thou'** (pē'tōō'), **Pierre.** 1539–1596. French jurist; at first a Protestant, became a convert (1573) to the Roman Catholic faith; renowned as a supporter of Gallicanism and as a humanist; among his works are a number of legal treatises written in Latin, and *Libertés de l'Église Gallicane,* which was used as the basis for the Declaration of the Clergy of France (1682).

**Pit'kin** (pĭt'kĭn), **Walter Boughton.** 1878–1953. American writer, b. Ypsilanti, Mich.; A.B., Michigan (1900); professor of journalism, Columbia U. (from 1912); author of *How to Write Stories* (1922), *The Psychology of Happiness* (1929), *Life Begins at Forty* (1932), *Making Good before Forty* (1939), *On My Own* (1944), etc.

**Pitkin, William.** 1635–1694. Lawyer, b. at Marylebone, London, Eng.; to America (c. 1659) and settled in Hartford, Conn.; became leading lawyer in the colony and one of the champions of colonial liberties. His grandson **William Pitkin** (1694–1769) was a jurist; governor of Connecticut (1766–69). The latter's son **William** (1725–1789) was a jurist and industrialist; manufactured powder for army during Revolution; assistant on governor's council (1766–85); judge of superior court (1769–89), and chief judge (1788–89). His nephew **Timothy Pitkin** (1766–1847) was a lawyer and statesman; member of U.S. House of Representatives (1805–19); member of Connecticut legislature (1819–30); author of *A Political and Civil History of the United States* (2 vols., 1828), covering period 1763–97.

**Pit'man** (pĭt'măn), Sir **Isaac.** 1813–1897. English phonographer; invented an original system of shorthand, based upon phonographic or phonetic, rather than orthographic, principles and published it as *Stenographic Soundhand* (1837); established institution for shorthand instruction at Bath; advocated spelling reform; proposed a phonetic printing alphabet with new letters; author of *Phonography* (1840). His brother **Benjamin,** *known in U.S. as* **Benn** (1822–1910), was a teacher of shorthand; b. Trowbridge, Wiltshire; sent by his brother to U.S. to teach shorthand system (1852); founded Phonographic Institute, Cincinnati (1853), where he taught the Pitman shorthand system; refusal by Benn to adopt certain minor changes by Isaac caused his system to differ somewhat; invented electrochemical process of relief engraving (1855); teacher of wood carving and decorative art, Cincinnati Art School (from 1873).

**Pit'ney** (pĭt'nĭ), **Mah'lon** (mā'lŭn). 1858–1924. American jurist, b. Morristown, N.J.; practiced, Dover, N.J. (1882–89) and Morristown (from 1889); member, U.S. House of Representatives (1895–99); chancellor of New Jersey (1908–12); associate justice, U.S. Supreme Court (1912–22).

**Pi·to'ni** (pē·tō'nē), **Giuseppe Ottavio.** 1657–1743. Italian composer of church music.

**Pi'tra'** (pē'trȧ'), **Jean Baptiste François.** 1812–1889. French Roman Catholic prelate; cardinal (1863) and cardinal bishop of Frascati (1879), of Porto (1884); author of *Analecta Sacra* (1876–81), *Analecta Novissima* (1888), etc.

**Pi·trè'** (pē·trĕ'), **Giuseppe.** 1843–1916. Italian folklorist; physician by profession; founded *Archivio per lo Studio delle Tradizioni Popolari* (1883). Among his works are *Biblioteca delle Tradizioni Popolari Siciliane* (25 vols., 1870–1913), *Curiosità Popolari Tradizionali* (16 vols., 1885–99), etc.

**Pitt** (pĭt), **Thomas.** *Known as* **Diamond Pitt.** 1653–1726. Grandfather of William Pitt, Earl of Chatham. English merchant in East Indian trade; carried on trade as interloper until East India Company, unable to check him in courts, received him into service (1694); governor of Madras (1697–1709); obtained Regent (or Pitt) diamond (1701), sold it (1717) to French regent to be placed with state jewels of France.

**Pitt, William.** Earl of **Chat'ham** [chăt'ăm] (cr. 1766). 1708–1778. Called "the Elder Pitt" and later "the Great Commoner." English statesman. Grandson of Thomas Pitt; entered Parliament (1735) and gained power over commons with his oratory; dismissed from army for supporting prince of Wales in feud with George II and for satire directed against George II; opposed Carteret's Hanoverian policy and system of subsidies to Continental powers; paymaster general and privy councilor (1746); dismissed (1755) for opposition to foreign policy of Newcastle cabinet; called reluctantly (1756) by George II as secretary of state and leader of House of Commons, virtually prime minister; dismissed (1757), but immediately recalled and given full control in foreign and military affairs; by vigorous prosecution of war brought about defeats of French in India, Africa, Canada, and on the seas; compelled to resign by refusal of majority of cabinet to declare war on Spain (1761). Pensioned; continued to oppose attempts to tax American colonists; formed new ministry (1766) with office only as privy seal on account of poor health as result of gout, which caused resignation (1768). Collapsed in House of Lords protesting disruption of empire by peace-at-any-price policy and duke of Richmond's motion for withdrawal of forces from America.

His eldest son, Sir **John Pitt** (1756–1835), 2d Earl of Chatham; lord privy seal (1794–96); president of council (1796–1801); commander of Walcheren Expedition (1809) and charged with its failure; general (1812).

**Pitt, William.** 1759–1806. Called "the Younger Pitt." Second son of 1st earl of Chatham; statesman, probably England's greatest prime minister; M.A., Cantab. (1776). M.P. (1781); assailed Tory ministry of Lord North but declined office until became chancellor of exchequer under Shelburne (1782); declined to form cabinet on fall of Shelburne's ministry (1783); brought forward scheme for parliamentary reform, only to be defeated, as also upon bill for modifying East India Company's charter. On dismissal of Fox-North coalition ministry (Dec., 1783), took office as chancellor of exchequer, 1st lord of treasury, and prime minister, the only member of cabinet in House of Commons; despite hostile votes, refused to dissolve parliament until public feeling on his side; received huge majority in general election (1784). Undertook ordering of finances by funding and reducing national debt, abating customs duties, instituting sinking fund for paying national debt; established new constitution for East India Company (1784); lost his third parliamentary reform bill, providing for purchase of 36 rotten boroughs (1785); first statesman to attempt adoption of teachings of Adam Smith; negotiated favorable commercial treaty with France (1786); failed to carry House of Commons in favor of Wilberforce's proposed abolition of slave trade (1792). Formed (1793) First Coalition with Russia, Sardinia, Spain, Naples, Prussia, Austria, Portugal, granting these allies subsidies, in struggle against Napoleon; suspended Habeas Corpus act, forced to levy income taxes; formed Second Coalition against France (1798), including Portugal, Naples, Russia, the Porte, and Austria, which was facilitated by victory of Nile; compelled by George III to withdraw proposal of Catholic emancipation introduced for quieting Irish rebellion of 1798, temporarily allayed by union with Ireland (1800–01) secured through political corruption. Resigned (1801) during Treaty of Amiens negotiations; assisted ministry of Addington with financial measures until its weakness and declaration of war on France (May, 1803) required him to return to office (May, 1804); assumed vigorous measures and formed Third Coalition with Russia, Austria, and Sweden (Apr., 1805); increased property tax by 25 per cent (1805); raised loan of twenty million pounds; seriously affected in health by charge of misappropriation of public funds against his friend Melville, head of admiralty (1805); broken by news of capitulation at Ulm (Oct., 1805); dealt death blow by defeat of Austria and Russia at Austerlitz (Dec., 1805).

**Pit'ta·cus** (pĭt'ȧ·kŭs). 650?–?570 B.C. Greek ruler of Mytilene, in Lesbos; one of Seven Wise Men of Greece; overthrew Melanchrus, Tyrant of Lesbos (c. 611); became tyrant of Mytilene (589–579); voluntarily resigned power (579).

**Pit'te·ri** (pēt'tȧ·rē), **Riccardo.** 1853–1915. Italian poet.

**Pit'ti** (pēt'tē; *Angl.* pĭt'ĭ). Prominent 15th-century Florentine family, a rival of the Medicis, including notably **Buonaccorso** (1370?–after 1430), ambassador of Florence to Duke Rupert of Bavaria, newly elected king of Germany (1400–10), and **Luca**, who began building (c. 1440) the famous Pitti Palace in Florence.

**Pitt'man** (pĭt'măn), **Key.** 1872–1940. American lawyer and legislator, b. Vicksburg, Miss.; began practice in Seattle, Wash. (1892); settled at Tonopah, Nev. (1901); U.S. senator from Nevada (from 1912); president pro tempore of the Senate (73d Congress); chairman, Senate Committee on Foreign Relations (from 1933).

**Pitt'–Riv'ers** (pĭt'rĭv'ẽrz), **Augustus Henry.** *Orig. surname* **Lane Fox** (lān' fŏks'). 1827–1900. English army officer and archaeologist; served in Crimean War; assumed name Pitt-Rivers upon inheriting estates of great-uncle George Pitt, 2d Baron Rivers. Made collection of weapons and other instruments illustrative of human invention; made excavations on British battle sites.

**Pi'us** (pī'ŭs). Name of twelve popes (see *Table of Popes*, Nos. 10, 212, 217, 226, 227, 252, 253, 255, 257, 259, 261, 262), especially:

**Pius I,** Saint. 90?–?157. Pope (bishop of Rome; 140?–?154).

**Pius II.** *Real name* **Enea Silvio de Pic'co·lo'mi·ni** (dā pēk'kô·lô'mē·nē). *Known in literature as* **Ae·ne'as Sil'vi·us** *or* **Syl'vi·us** (ē·nē'ăs sĭl'vĭ·ŭs). 1405–1464. Pope (1458–64), b. near Siena, Italy; in youth, lived at

Basel (1431–35); engaged in various missions of the church; resided at court of Emperor Frederick III of Germany (1442–47), where he was poet laureate; made bishop of Siena (1449); as pope, took the name Pius as a reminiscence of Vergil's "pius Aeneas"; became a leader of the humanists; issued bull (1460) against belief that councils were superior to popes; quarreled (1461) with Louis XI of France and with George of Poděbrad of Bohemia (1462–64) on questions of doctrine; sought to lead crusade against Turks but died of fever at Ancona. A patron of learning and prolific writer, his works including a novel (*Lucretius et Euryalus*), poems (in Latin), letters and dialogues, a valuable history of his times, and a work on geography that is said to have influenced Columbus.

**Pius IV.** *Real name* **Giovanni Angelo Me'di·ci** (mâ'dē·chē; *Angl.* mĕd'ĕ-, mā'dē-). 1499–1565. Pope (1559–65), b. Milan; adopted policy of conciliation toward emperor and Philip II of France; reconvened the suspended Council of Trent (1562); issued bull (1564) confirming its decisions (*Creed of Pius IV*).

**Pius V,** Saint. *Real name* **Michele Ghis·lie'ri** (gēz-lyâ'rē). 1504–1572. Pope (1566–72), b. near Alessandria, Italy; endeavored to enforce reforming decrees of Council of Trent; a foe of toleration of any kind; attempted to depose Elizabeth of England; aided Catholics in France against the Huguenots and helped Spain in Netherlands; with Spain and Venice, formed the Holy League (1570) against the Turks; revised the breviary (1568) and missal (1570).

**Pius VI.** *Real name* **Giovanni Angelo Bra'schi** (bräs'kē). 1717–1799. Pope (1775–99), b. Cesena, Italy; released American clergy (after 1781) from jurisdiction of vicar apostolic in England; established see of Baltimore (1789); had long controversies with Emperor Joseph II and the king of Naples; deprived of parts of papal dominions by the French (1791, 1796, 1798); carried a prisoner to Valence, France (1798), where he died.

**Pius VII.** *Real name* **Luigi Barnaba Chia'ra·mon'ti** (kyä'rä·mōn'tē). 1742–1823. Pope (1800–23), b. Cesena, Italy; ratified concordat with France (1801); visited Paris and crowned Napoleon (1804); gradually came to oppose Napoleon's aggressions (1805–09); lost several provinces to French (1808); held prisoner by Napoleon at Savona and Fontainebleau (1809–14); re-entered Rome (1814); restored Jesuit order (1814); suppressed Carbonari and restored order (1815–23).

**Pius IX.** *Real name* **Giovanni Maria Ma·stai'-Fer·ret'ti** (mäs·tä'ē·fâr·rāt'tē). 1792–1878. Pope (1846–78), b. Senigallia; archbishop of Spoleto (1827); on becoming pope, proclaimed political amnesty (1846) to meet critical conditions in Papal States; granted a constitution and embarked on policy of wide reforms; after insurrection at Rome (1848), forced to flee to Gaeta; restored by French (1850); henceforth became extremely reactionary; supported ultramontanism; proclaimed dogma of the Immaculate Conception (1854); in Italian War (1859–60), lost greater part of papal dominions; convened Vatican Council (1869–70), which promulgated the dogma of papal infallibility (Pastor aeternus); lost temporal power to Victor Emmanuel (1870); from that, became the first "prisoner of the Vatican"; pontificate longest in history of the church.

**Pius X,** Saint. *Real name* **Giuseppe Melchiorre Sar'to** (sär'tō). 1835–1914. Pope (1903–14), b. Riese, near Venice; became bishop of Mantua (1884), and created cardinal (1893); greatly interested in social questions, esp. improving the condition of the poor; abolished traditional right of veto at papal elections (1903); inaugurated reforms in church music; began revision (1904) of ecclesiastical laws (Codex Juris Canonici); issued encyclical (Pascendi) against Modernism (1907); death hastened by outbreak cf World War.

**Pius XI.** *Real name* **Achille Ambrogio Damiano Rat'ti** (rät'tē). 1857–1939. Pope (1922–39), b. Desio, Italy; taught at Milan (1882–88); director and prefect of Ambrosian Library, Milan (1888–1910); subprefect and prefect of the Vatican Library (1911–18); sent to Poland (1918); nuncio (1919–20); became cardinal and archbishop of Milan (1921); celebrated Holy Year (1925); issued several encyclicals of importance, esp. one on the Roman Catholic Church in Mexico; signed (Feb. 11, 1929) Lateran Treaty with Mussolini by which Vatican City was established and arrangement made for recognition by Italian government of the Roman Catholic religion.

**Pius XII.** *Real name* **Eugenio Pa·cel'li** (pä·chĕl'lē). 1876–1958. Pope (1939–58) b. Rome; nuncio in Bavaria and Germany (1917–20); archbishop of Sardi (1917); made cardinal (1929); sent on various important papal missions (1934–38); secretary of state to Holy See (1930–39); author of several works.

**Pix'é'ré'court'** (pēk'sā'rā'kōōr'), **René Charles Guil'-bert' de** (gēl'bâr' dē). 1773–1844. French playwright; author and coauthor of more than 100 melodramas.

**Pix'ii'** (pēk'sē'), **Hippolyte.** French instrument maker; credited with invention of first magnetoelectric machine (1832).

**Pi·zar'ro** (pĭ·zär'ō; *Span.* pē·thär'rō, -sär'rō). Name of a Spanish family prominent in the early history of South America, including Francisco, the conquistador (see separate entry), and his three half brothers: **Gonzalo** (1506?–1548); went with Francisco to Peru (1531); governor of Quito (1539–46); disputed government with Gasca (1547–48); defeated and executed. **Hernando** (1475?–1578); went with Francisco to Peru (1531); returned to Spain with royal fifth of ransom of Atahualpa (1534); again in Peru; seized at Cuzco by Almagro (1537); released; commanded brother's army, defeated Almagro (1538), and executed him; imprisoned in Spain (1540–60). **Juan** (1500?–1536); killed in fighting at Cuzco.

**Pizarro, Francisco.** 1470?–1541. Spanish conqueror of Peru, b. at Trujillo, Estremadura; sailed to America (1509); made journey with Ojeda in Caribbean (1509); settled in Panama (1519); joined Diego de Almagro (1522) in plan to explore west coast of South America; first expedition (1524–25) a failure; second (1526) after great hardships explored Gulf of Guayaquil. Returned to Spain (1528) and secured from Charles V authority to conquer and govern new territory; enlisted large force, including his three half brothers; arrived in Panama (1530) and started for Peru (1531); overcame Atahualpa (1532), Inca chieftain, and executed him (1533) at Cajamarca for refusal to accept Christian faith; marched to Cuzco (1533), captured it, and secured immense amount of gold; founded new capital, Lima (1535). Waged civil war with Almagro (1537–38), who was defeated and killed; slain by followers of Almagro in revenge (1541).

**Piz·zet'ti** (pēt·tsāt'tē), **Ildebrando.** 1880–1968. Italian composer of operas, stage music, and orchestral works.

**Place** (plās), **Francis.** 1771–1854. English reformer; journeyman leather-breeches maker; led successful campaign to repeal legislation forbidding trade-unionism (1814–24); campaigned against national sinking fund (1816–23); framed placard "To Stop the Duke, go for Gold," producing run on banks, forcing Wellington from office, and assuring passage of Reform bill (1832). Author of pamphlets and articles on social and economic questions; drafted the *National*, or *People's, Charter* in the form of an act of Parliament (published May 8, 1838) setting forth the platform of the Chartists.

**Placidia, Galla.** See GALLA PLACIDIA.

**Plácido.** See Gabriel VALDÉS.

**Plan·ché'** (?plăn·shā'), **James Robinson.** 1796–1880. English playwright and antiquary, of Huguenot descent; his first play a burlesque, *Amoroso, King of Little Britain* (1818); gained reputation for knowledge of costume and heraldry; translated or adapted plays and wrote original plays, at his best bringing out pieces for Madame Vestris (1831–56); made Somerset herald (1866) and sent on Continental missions to invest with Order of Garter. Author of valuable works on British costume.

**Planck** (plängk), **Gottlieb Jakob.** 1751–1833. German Protestant theologian. One grandson, **Julius Wilhelm von Planck** (1817–1900), was a jurist; chief work, *Das Deutsche Gerichtsverfahren im Mittelalter* (2 vols., 1879). See Max Karl Ernst Ludwig PLANCK.

**Planck, Karl Christian.** 1819–1880. German philosopher.

**Planck, Max Karl Ernst Ludwig.** 1858–1947. Son of Julius Wilhelm von Planck. German physicist, b. Kiel; professor, Kiel (1885) and Berlin (from 1889). As result of work on radiation from black bodies, originated and developed quantum theory (from 1901); awarded 1918 Nobel prize for physics; known also for work relating to thermodynamics and mechanics and to electrical and optical problems associated with radiation of heat and with the quantum theory.

**Plan'çon'** (pläɴ'sôɴ'), **Pol.** 1854–1914. French operatic basso profundo; created roles of Norfolk in *Henry VIII*, Don Gormas in *Le Cid*, and François I in *Ascanio*.

**Plan'cus** (plăng'kŭs), **Lucius Munatius.** Roman soldier and politician; served under Caesar in Gaul; after assassination of Caesar (44 B.C.), joined Mark Antony; consul with Lepidus (42 B.C.); in civil war between Octavius and Antony, sided with Octavius; sponsored in Senate motion to confer on Octavius title of Augustus (27). One of Horace's odes is addressed to him.

**Plan'quette'** (pläɴ'kĕt'), **Robert,** *in full* **Jean Robert Julien.** 1848–1903. French composer; best known for light operas, including *Les Cloches de Corneville* (1877; commonly known in English as *The Chimes of Normandy*), *Le Chevalier Gaston* (1879), *Rip* (1884), *Le Talisman* (1893), *Le Paradis de Mahomet* (1906).

**Plan·tag'e·net** (plăn·tăj'ĕ·nĕt; -nĭt). Surname, originally a nickname, historically associated with English royal house called house of **An'jou** (ăn'jōō; *Fr.* äɴ'-zhōō') or the **An'ge·vin** (ăn'jĕ·vĭn) royal house, founded by Geoffrey, Count of Anjou, and his wife Matilda, daughter of Henry I of England, and occupying English throne (1154–1399) in persons of Henry II (ruled 1154–89), Richard I (1189–99), John (1199–1216), Henry III (1216–72), Edward I (1272–1307), Edward II (1307–27), Edward III (1327–77), Richard II (1377–99) in the direct line of descent and thereafter through its descendants in two contending branches, the houses of Lancaster and of York (*qq.v.*), until the death of Richard III (1485). Other members of house, which assumed surname Plantagenet in middle of fifteenth century, after its adoption by Richard, Duke of York, for sake of prestige in his conflict with Lancastrians, include the following (see separate entries as indicated by small-capital type): Edmund (1245–1296), called "Crouchback," Earl of LANCASTER; Edmund of Langley (1341–1402), 1st Duke of YORK; Edward, the Black Prince (1330–1376)—see EDWARD; Edward of Norwich (1373?–1415), 2d Duke of YORK; Edward (1475–1499), Earl of Warwick—see under dukes of CLARENCE; Geoffrey (d. 1212), Archbishop of York—see GEOFFREY; George (1449–1478), Duke of CLARENCE; Henry of Cornwall (1235–1271)—see under RICHARD, Earl of Cornwall; Henry (1281?–1345), Earl of LANCASTER; Henry (1299?–1361), 1st Duke of LANCASTER; Humphrey (1391–1447), Duke of Gloucester —see HUMPHREY; John of Gaunt (1340–1399), Duke of Lancaster—see JOHN OF GAUNT; John of Lancaster (1389–1435), Duke of Bedford—see JOHN OF LANCASTER; Margaret (1473–1541), Countess of Salisbury—see POLE family; Richard (1209–1272), Earl of Cornwall and King of the Romans—see RICHARD; Richard (1411–1460), 3d Duke of YORK; Richard (1472–1483), Duke of YORK; Thomas (1277?–1322), Earl of LANCASTER; Thomas of Woodstock (1355–1397), Duke of Gloucester—see THOMAS OF WOODSTOCK; Thomas (1388?–1421), Duke of CLARENCE. See also *Table (in Appendix)* for ENGLAND.

**Plan'té'** (pläɴ'tā'), **Gaston.** 1834–1889. French physicist; invented first practical storage battery (1860).

**Plan'tin'** (pläɴ'tăɴ'), **Christophe.** 1520?–1589. French bookbinder, printer, and publisher; settled in Antwerp (c. 1550). Books published by him became famous for typographical excellence and beauty.

**Pla·nu'des Max'i·mus** (plȧ·nū'dēz măk'sĭ·mŭs) *or* **Maximus Planudes** 1260?–?1330. Byzantine monk and scholar; by his translations from Greek into Latin, aided in introducing knowledge of Greek literature in western Europe.

**Plas'kett** (plăs'kĕt; -kĭt), **John Stanley.** 1865–1941. Canadian astronomer, b. near Woodstock, Ontario; director, Dominion Astrophysical Observatory, Victoria, B.C. (1917–35); authority on the motion of faint stars, rotation of the Milky Way, and matter in interstellar space. A pair of large stars (Plaskett's Twins) are named after him.

**Pla'teau'** (plȧ'tō'), **Joseph Antoine Ferdinand.** 1801–1883. Belgian physicist; professor, Ghent, until he became blind (c. 1840); investigated physiological optics and molecular forces; originated stroboscopic method of studying vibratory motion.

**Pla'ten** (plä'tĕn), **August.** Count **von Platen Hal'ler·mund** (häl'ĕr·mōōnt) *or* **Hal'ler·mün'de** (häl'-ĕr·mün'dĕ). 1796–1835. German writer; among his poetical works are *Ghaselen* (1821), *Der Gläserne Pantoffel* (dramatic poem, 1824), *Sonette aus Venedig* (1825), and *Die Abbassiden* (epic, 1834); among plays, *Der Schatz des Rhampsinit* (1824) and *Die Liga von Cambrai* (1833).

**Platina.** See Bartolommeo de' SACCHI.

**Plat'ner** (plät'nĕr), **Ernst.** 1744–1818. German philosopher and physician.

**Pla'to** (plā'tō). *Orig. name* **A·ris'to·cles** (ȧ·rĭs'tō·klēz). 427?–347 B.C. Surnamed Plato because of his broad shoulders. Greek philosopher; disciple of Socrates and teacher of Aristotle; studied under and with Socrates until Socrates's trial, conviction, and death (399 B.C.), then left Athens; stayed for a while in Megara; traveled in Egypt, Cyrene, Sicily, and Magna Graecia. Returned to Athens permanently (387) and there founded his school of philosophy known as the Academy. This academy was later endowed and became in form a university, the first university known in history; it flourished until closed by Justinian (529 A.D.). His extant works are in form of dialogues, in each of which his master, Socrates, is represented in a leading role; these dialogues include *Republic* (generally regarded as his greatest work; a search for justice in construction of an ideal state), *Laws* (on same theme; unfinished), *Symposium* (on ideal love), *Phaedrus* (attacking prevailing conception of rhetoric), *Timaeus* (embodying a theory of the universe and containing story of the lost Atlantis),

*Apology* (purporting to give Socrates's speech in own defense at his trial), *Phaedo* (on immortality of the soul; purporting to be a record of Socrates's last conversation before death), also *Charmides, Cratylus, Critias, Crito, Euthydemus, Euthyphro, Georgias, Ion, Laches, Lesser Hippias, Lysis, Menexenus, Meno, Parmenides, Philebus, Politicus, Protagoras, Sophist, Theaetetus.*

**Plato.** Athenian playwright of late 5th and early 4th century B.C.; reputed author of thirty comedies (only fragments extant).

**Pla·ton′** (plŭ·tôn′). *Orig. name* **Peter Lev·shin′** (lyĕf-shēn′). 1737–1812. Russian prelate; became monk, adopting name of Platon; religious instructor to future czar Paul I (1762); bishop of Tver [Kalinin] (1770); archbishop of Moscow (1775); metropolitan of Moscow (1787).

**Pla·to′nov** (plŭ·tô′nôf), **Sergei Feodorovich.** 1860–1933. Russian historian.

**Pla′tov** (plȧ′tôf), Count **Matvei Ivanovich.** 1751–1818. Russian general, of Greek descent; hetman of the Cossacks (1801); distinguished himself in attacks upon French rear guard during French retreat from Russia (1812); defeated French at Laon (1813); captured Nemours (1814), and entered Paris with the allies. Created count by Emperor Alexander I (1812).

**Platt** (plăt), **Charles Adams.** 1861–1933. American artist, b. New York City; early work in landscape painting, largely of New England views; later, devoted himself to landscape architecture and the designing of buildings. With Charles L. Freer, designed Freer Art Gallery, Washington, D.C.; also designed nine buildings for U. of Illinois (1922–30). Planned landscape architecture for Phillips Academy, Andover, Mass., and served as consulting architect (from 1927). Also excelled as an etcher, his subjects often being Dutch scenes.

**Platt, Orville Hitchcock.** 1827–1905. American lawyer and legislator, b. Washington, Conn.; U.S. senator (1879–1905). His name is attached to the Platt Amendment, an amendment to the army appropriation bill (1901) requiring Cuba to enter into no foreign agreements contrary to interests of the U.S., and to grant to U.S. the right to intervene in Cuban affairs, if necessary to keep order.

**Platt, Thomas Collier.** 1833–1910. American politician, b. Owego, N.Y.; political associate of Roscoe Conkling (from 1870); member, U.S. House of Representatives (1873–77); U.S. senator (1881); resigned (May, 1881) along with Conkling in disagreement with President Garfield over a civil-service appointment for collector of the port of New York; tried for re-election and vindication at the polls, but was defeated. Continued influential in Republican party machine in New York.

**Platt, William.** 1885– . British army officer; served in World War I; commandant of Sudan defense force (1938–41); commander in chief in East Africa (1941–45); general (1943).

**Plau′tus** (plô′tŭs), **Titus Maccius.** 254?–184 B.C. Roman playwright, b. Sarsina in Umbria. Little is known of his life; settled in Rome as writer of comedies adapted from Greek originals. Of 21 plays commonly accepted as genuine, following are extant (some of them in incomplete form): *Amphitruo, Asinaria, Aulularia, Bacchides, Captivi, Casina, Cistellaria, Curculio, Epidicus, Menaechmi, Mercator, Miles Gloriosus, Mostellaria, Persa, Poenulus, Pseudolus, Rudens, Stichus, Trinummus, Truculentus.* Only parts of *Vidularia* extant.

**Play′fair′** (plā′fâr′), **John.** 1748–1819. Scottish mathematician and geologist; succeeded Dugald Stewart as professor of mathematics in Edinburgh (1785); transferred to chair of natural philosophy (1805). Author of *Elements of Geometry* (1795); proponent of Huttonian theory of the earth.

**Playfair, Lyon.** 1st Baron **Playfair.** 1818–1898. British chemist; as member of commission on health of towns, helped to lay foundations of modern sanitation; an organizer of Crystal Palace exposition (1851). M.P. (1868–92); postmaster general (1873); reorganized the civil service; discovered a new class of salts, the nitroprussides.

**Playfair,** Sir **Nigel.** 1874–1934. English actor and manager; manager of Lyric Theatre, Hammersmith (from 1919); produced Drinkwater's *Abraham Lincoln* (1919) and revival of Gay's *Beggar's Opera* (1920).

**Pleas′on·ton** (plĕz′′n·tŭn), **Alfred.** 1824–1897. American army officer; grad. U.S.M.A., West Point (1844). In Civil War, served at Antietam, Fredericksburg, Chancellorsville; major general of volunteers (1863); commanded Union cavalry at Gettysburg.

**Pleekschans.** Variant of *Pliekšans* (see Jan RAINIS).

**Pleh′we** (plā′vĕ), **Wenzel von.** *Russ. name* **Vyacheslav Konstantinovich Ple′ve** (plyā′vyĕ). 1846–1904. Russian lawyer and government administrator; director of secret police, ministry of the interior (1881); secretary of state for Finland (1894); minister of the interior (1902), noted for the harsh rigor of his administration; killed by a bomb (July 28, 1904).

**Ple·kha′nov** (plyĕ·kȧ′nôf), **Georgi Valentinovich.** 1857–1918. Russian political philosopher; chief exponent in Russia of philosophic Marxism. Spent about 40 years in exile, chiefly at Geneva; became intellectual leader of Russian Social Democratic movement; influenced thought and philosophy of Lenin. During World War, advocated defense of Russia, contrary to Bolshevik policy of working for defeat of government; thereafter, opposed Bolshevik revolution. Credited with exercising great influence on development of socialist thought and policy in Russia.

**Ple′ner** (plā′nẽr), Baron **Ignaz von.** 1810–1908. Austrian statesman; minister of finance (1860–65) and commerce (1867–70); member of Herrenhaus (1873 ff.). His son Baron **Ernst** (1841–1923) was also a statesman; succeeded to leadership of German liberals, and was selected (1888) as head of United German Left party; minister of finance (1893–95); member of the Herrenhaus (from 1900).

**Ple·shche′ev** (plyĕ·shchā′yĕf), **Aleksei Nikolaevich.** 1825–1893. Russian poet; accused of plotting against emperor and sentenced to be shot (1849), but sentence commuted to banishment; served in army and distinguished himself in Crimean War (1854–56); pardoned (1857). Translated works of Heine, Byron, and Tennyson; published collection of his original verse (1887).

**Pletho, Georgius Gemistus.** *Or* **Georgius Plethon.** See GEMISTUS PLETHO.

**Plet′ten·berg** (plĕt′ĕn·bĕrk), **Walter von.** 1450?–1535. Prince of Livonia, Kurland, and Estonia; defended his country against Russian invasion (1494); defended the Teutonic Knights against the Poles (1515), and received from the head of the order the title of grand master; designated by Emperor Charles V a prince of the empire (1527).

**Pley′el** (plī′ĕl; *Fr.* plĕ′yĕl′), **Ignaz.** 1757–1831. Austrian composer and piano manufacturer.

**Pliekšans, Jan.** See Jan RAINIS.

**Plim′soll** (plĭm′s'l; -sŏl), **Samuel.** 1824–1898. English leader of shipping reform; known as "the Sailors' Friend." Coal merchant in London (1853); M.P. (1868–80); with his book, *Our Seamen* (1872), helped overcome obstruction of shipowners to Merchant Shipping Act (1876), giving powers of inspection to Board of Trade;

gave his name to *Plimsoll*, or *Plimsoll's, mark*, the load line allowed by law.

**Plin'y** (plĭn'ĭ). *Lat. name* **Gaius Plin'i·us Se·cun'dus** (plĭn'ĭ·ŭs sē·kŭn'dŭs). *Known as* "the Elder." 23–79 A.D. Roman scholar, b. Como, Italy; to Rome in youth; served in Africa and Germany; procurator in Spain (c. 70–72); studied and wrote in fields of history, rhetoric, natural science, military tactics. Died while trying to observe closely an eruption of Vesuvius (79). Of his many works, only one is extant, *Historia Naturalis* (37 books), an encyclopedia of natural science esp. as it touches human life. His nephew **Gaius Plinius Cae·cil'i·us** (sē·sĭl'ĭ·ŭs) **Secundus,** *known as* "the Younger" (62–113); consul (100); governor of Bithynia and Pontica (111 or 112); best known for his *Letters*, including one written to Emperor Trajan with regard to treatment of Christians in Bithynia and Pontica, this being one of earliest historical references to Christianity.

**Plis'nier'** (plēs'nyā'), **Charles.** 1897–1952. Belgian writer; author of *Mariages* (1936) and *Faux Passeports* (1937; awarded Goncourt prize, 1937).

**Ploetz** (plûts), **Alfred.** 1860–1940. German physician; author of treatises on racial hygiene and social anthropology.

**Plo'mer** (?plōō'mẽr), **William Charles Franklyn.** 1903– . South African novelist, b. in North Transvaal, descendant of Sir Thomas Plumer (1753–1824; *q.v.*). Farmer in Stormberg Mountains, South Africa; trader in Zululand. Author of novels, including *Turbott Wolfe*, with scenes laid in Africa (1926), of volumes of short stories, including *I Speak of Africa* (1927), biographical works, including *Cecil Rhodes* (1933) and poems including *Visiting the Caves* (1936).

**Plo·ti'nus** (plō·tī'nŭs). 205?–270 A.D. Roman Neoplatonic philosopher, b. in Egypt, of Roman parentage; studied at Alexandria under Ammonius Saccas; lectured in Rome on philosophy (from 244); chief exponent of Neoplatonism.

**Plotz** (plŏts), **Harry.** 1890–1947. American bacteriologist, b. Paterson, N.J.; pathologist, Mt. Sinai Hospital, New York City (1913–14); on staff of surgeon general, U.S. army (1917–19); on typhus fever commission to Serbia (1915); chief of service, Pasteur Inst., Paris (1921–39). Demonstrated identity of Brill's disease with typhus (1914); developed protective vaccine against typhus; investigated cause of measles and worked on development of serum for treatment of measles; studied virus diseases.

**Ploug** (ploug), **Parmo Carl.** *Pseudonym* **Poul Ryt'ter** (rüt'ẽr). 1813–1894. Danish poet and politician; wrote collected poems *Viser og Vers* (1847) and a satirical comedy, *Atellaner;* also *New Songs and Poems* (1869), *New Poems* (1883). Member of constitutional convention (1848–49), Folketing (1854–57), and Landsting (from 1859).

**Plow'den** (plou'd'n), **Edmund.** 1518–1585. English jurist; member of a Shropshire Catholic family. A kinsman, Sir **Edmund Plowden** (1592–1659), received a charter (1634) for colonizing New Albion, the first English grant of the present New Jersey area; sailed with party (1642) to Virginia, where his party mutinied; returned to England (1648), where land suits detained him till his death.

**Plow'man** (plou'măn), **George Taylor.** 1869–1932. American architect and etcher, b. Le Sueur, Minn.; author of *Etching and Other Graphic Arts* (1914), *Manual of Etching* (1924).

**Plück'er** (plük'ẽr), **Julius.** 1801–1868. German mathematician and physicist; professor in Bonn (from 1836); known in mathematics for work in analytical geometry; in physics, developed a theory of diamagnetism and worked on optics of crystals and on theory of the spectrum; investigated effect of a magnetic field on electrical discharges in rarefied gases.

**Plumb** (plŭm), **Glenn Edward.** 1866–1922. American lawyer, b. Clay, Iowa; specialized in railroad law; devised plan (1919), known as the Plumb plan, for government ownership of railroads; plan was endorsed by railroad employer groups, American Federation of Labor, Nonpartisan League, and was debated in Congress, but no action taken.

**Plu'mer** (plōō'mẽr), **Herbert Charles Onslow.** 1st Viscount **Plumer.** 1857–1932. English military commander; served in Matabele campaign (1896) and Boer War; promoted major general (1902); leader of 2d army on western front, World War (1915–17), held Ypres salient and won victory at Messines ridge (1917); commanded Italian expeditionary force (1917–18); resumed leadership of 2d army, in Belgian Flanders; general (1916), field marshal (1919); governor of Malta (1919–25); high commissioner for Palestine (1925–28).

**Plumer,** Sir **Thomas.** 1753–1824. English judicial officer; one of three to defend Warren Hastings (1787); defended Lord Melville on impeachment (1806); assisted in defense of Caroline, Princess of Wales (1806); solicitor general (1807); attorney general (1812); first vice-chancellor of England (1813); master of the rolls (1818). See W. C. F. PLOMER.

**Plum'er** (plŭm'ẽr), **William.** 1759–1850. American politician, b. Newburyport, Mass.; U.S. senator (1802–07); governor of New Hampshire (1812–13, 1816–19). His recommendation to the legislature that the charter of Dartmouth College be altered was the initial step in the famous Dartmouth College case (decision rendered by Chief Justice Marshall, 1819).

**Plum'mer** (plŭm'ẽr), **Alfred.** 1841–1926. Church of England clergyman; author of theological works and books on church history.

**Plump'tre** (plŭm(p)'trē), **Edward Hayes.** 1821–1891. English theological and classical scholar; member of Old Testament Revision Committee (1869–74); dean of Wells (1881). Author of theological works, verse translations of Sophocles and Aeschylus, and biography of Bishop Ken (1888).

**Plun'ket** (plŭng'kĕt; -kĭt), **Oliver.** 1629–1681. Irish Roman Catholic theologian; archbishop of Armagh and primate of Ireland (1669); imprisoned after passing of Test Act and accused of share in Irish branch of Popish Plot; convicted of treason by London jury on inadequate evidence; hanged, drawn, and quartered.

**Plunket, William Conyngham.** 1st Baron **Plunket.** 1764–1854. Irish lawyer and judge; led Whigs in Irish parliament; fiercest of adversaries of Pitt's project of union (1798); solicitor general (1803) and attorney general for Ireland (1805); prosecuted Emmet (1803); succeeded Grattan (1820) as foremost champion of emancipation and recognized as one of best orators in House of Commons; paradoxically opposed agitation by O'Connell and Catholic Association (1825); as Irish attorney general (1822), attempted to put down Orange faction; chief justice of common pleas in Ireland (1827); lord chancellor of Ireland (1830–41).

**Plun'kett** (plŭng'kĕt; -kĭt), **Charles Pesh'all** (pĕsh''l). 1864–1931. American naval officer; grad. U.S.N.A., Annapolis (1884); in the battle of Manila Bay (May 1, 1898); in charge of batteries of 14-inch naval guns on railway mounts in France (1918); promoted rear admiral (1919).

**Plunkett,** Count (*of Rome*) **George Noble.** 1851–1948. Irish poet and writer on art; editor of literary and artistic reviews; minister for foreign affairs and of fine arts, Irish Free State. Author of *Sandro Botticelli* (1900), *Echoes* (1928), and other poems. His eldest son, **Joseph Mary** (1887–1916), editor and lyric poet, died after Easter Rebellion (1916).

**Plunkett,** Sir **Horace Curzon.** 1854–1932. Irish agricultural reformer and political leader; 3d son of 16th Baron Dunsany; cattle raiser (1879–89); founder of modern co-operative movement in Irish agriculture (1894). M.P. (1892–1900); commissioner of congested-districts board in Ireland (1891–1918); endowed trust in his name for development of agriculture (1919); presiding officer of Irish convention (1917–18), strove for understanding with British government; senator of Irish Free State (1922–23). Author of *Ireland in the New Century* (1904), *Some Tendencies of Modern Medicine* (1913), *Home Rule and Conscription* (1918). His nephew Lord Dunsany won fame as poet and dramatist (see DUNSANY). Sir **Reginald Aylmer Ranfurly Plun′-kett–Ern′le–Erle′–Drax′** [-ûrn′'l·ûrl′drăks′] (1880–1967), British naval commander, brother of Lord Dunsany the poet, was aboard *H.M.S. Lion* at Heligoland action, Dogger Bank, and Jutland; rear admiral (1928), vice-admiral (1932), admiral (1936); head of diplomatic delegation to Russia (1939).

**Plu′tarch** (ploo͞′tärk). 46?–?120 A.D. Greek biographer, b. Chaeronea in Boeotia; educ. Athens; traveled widely; taught in Rome. In later life, returned to Chaeronea. Author of *Moralia* (a collection of more than 60 essays on all manner of questions). Best known for his *Parallel Lives*, in which he presented character studies of distinguished Greeks and Romans in pairs, from the age of Theseus and Romulus down to his own time.

**Plym′ley** (plĭm′lĭ), **Peter.** Pseudonym of Sydney SMITH (1771–1845).

**Po·be·do·nos′tsev** (pŭ·byĕ·dŭ·nôs′tsĕf), **Konstantin Petrovich.** 1827–1907. Russian jurist and government administrator; member of council of empire (1872). Believer in absolutism; consistent opponent of liberal reforms; upheld influence of Orthodox Greek Church on Russian policy.

**Po′ca·hon′tas** (pō′kȧ·hŏn′tăs). *Indian name* **Matoaka.** 1595?–1617. American Indian princess, dau. of Powhatan; said by Captain John Smith in his *Generall Historie of Virginia* (1624) to have saved his life (1608) by holding his head in her arms to prevent Powhatan's warriors from clubbing him to death. Taken prisoner by the English (1612); converted to Christianity and baptized Rebecca; married (Apr., 1614) John Rolfe, colonist, whom she accompanied to England (1616); received with royal honors and presented to the king and queen. Died while preparing to return to America.

**Poc·cet′ti** (pôt·chāt′tē), **Bernardino.** *Real name* **Bernardino** *or* **Bernardo Bar′ba·tel′li** (bär′bä·tĕl′lē). 1548?–1612. Italian painter; known esp. for his decorative frescoes, as those depicting scenes from the life of St. Anthony in court of Church of San Marco, and others in Church of Santa Maria Novella and in the Pitti Palace (all in Florence).

**Poc′ci** (pôt′chē), Count **Franz von.** 1807–1876. German artist, musician, and poet; as artist, attained fame with humorous silhouettes and drawings for *Fliegende Blätter;* as musician, composed an opera, a number of songs, and incidental music for popular marionette shows; as playwright, wrote folk plays.

**Po Chü–i** (bô′ jü′ē′). 772–846 A.D. Chinese poet, under the T'ang dynasty, b. in Honan; government official in several capacities; president of the council of justice (841–846); produced more than 70 books; his lyrics are especially fine.

**Po′cocke** (pō′kŏk), **Edward.** 1604–1691. English Orientalist; discovered and edited four missing Syriac versions of New Testament Epistles (1630); first Oxford professor of Arabic (1636); advanced to chair of Hebrew (1648; confirmed at Restoration); his magnum opus an edition of Arabic text with Latin translation of Arabic history of Bar-Hebraeus (1663); compiled a *Lexicon Heptaglotton* (1669).

**Pococke, Richard.** 1704–1765. English traveler; published accounts of travels up the Nile, in Greece and the near East; a pioneer of Alpine travel; bishop of Ossory (1756–65), of Meath (1765).

**Pod′bi·el′ski** (pôt′bē·ĕl′skē), **Theophil von.** 1814–1879. Prussian general; quartermaster general in Franco-Prussian War (1870–71); inspector general of artillery (1872).

**Po′dě·brad** (pô′dyĕ·brȧt), **George of.** *Czech* **Jiří z Po′dě·brad** (spô′dyĕ·brȧt). 1420–1471. King of Bohemia; appointed regent of Bohemia (1451) during minority of King Ladislas; after death of Ladislas (1457), elected king (1459). A leader of the Calistins; excommunicated by Pope Paul II (1466), who inspired a crusade against him. Resisted invasion by Matthias Corvinus, King of Hungary, who had himself crowned king of Bohemia and margrave of Moravia (1469); gained aid of Poland by promising Bohemian succession to Ladislas, son of the Polish king Casimir IV; with this aid forced Matthias to come to terms.

**Pod·gor′ny** (pôd·gôr′nĭ), **Nikolai V.** 1903– . Soviet politician; U.S.S.R. president (1965–77).

**Pod′more** (pŏd′mōr), **Frank.** 1855–1910. English writer on psychical research; associated with Edmund Gurney and F. W. H. Myers in psychical research; argued for psychological causality; supposed to have originated name of Fabian Society, and one of its founders (1884).

**Poe** (pō), **Edgar Allan.** 1809–1849. American poet and story writer, b. Boston; on death of his mother, was taken into family of **John Allan** (1780–1834), a merchant of Scottish descent in Richmond, Va. Studied one term at U. of Virginia (1826); after quarrel with foster father, ran away from home (1827); in Boston, published *Tamerlane and Other Poems* (1827). His resources exhausted, enlisted in U.S. army (May, 1827), from which his foster father procured his discharge (Apr., 1829). Published at Baltimore *Al Aaraaf, Tamerlane, and Minor Poems* (1829). Student at U.S.M.A., West Point (1830–31); dismissed for neglect of duty and disobedience of orders. Published *Poems by Edgar A. Poe* (1831), dedicated to the cadets at the military academy. Resident at the house of Mrs. Clemm and her daughter, Virginia (1831–35); with his story *A MS. Found in a Bottle* won a short-story competition (1833). Aided by John P. Kennedy of Baltimore, taken on staff of *Southern Literary Messenger*, Richmond, Va. (1835–37), and contributed poems, essays, short stories, and critical reviews to that magazine. Married Virginia Clemm (May, 1836). Resident in New York (1837) and Philadelphia (1838), gaining a meager living by his writing. Associate editor, *Burton's Gentleman's Magazine*, Philadelphia (1839–40), to which he contributed reviews, poems, and some of his most famous stories (*The Fall of the House of Usher, Ligeia*, etc.). Published collection of his stories in book *Tales of the Grotesque and Arabesque* (1840). Literary editor, *Graham's Magazine* (1841–42). Precarious health and irregular habits caused loss of this position (1842). Again won short-story prize with *The Gold Bug* (1843); developed his writing of mystery stories, as in *The Murders in the Rue Morgue* and *The Mystery of Marie Rogêt.* To New York (1844) where *The Raven* appeared (Jan. 29, 1845) and brought him fame; published later in book form, *The Raven and Other Poems* (1845). Editor of the *Broadway Journal* (1845–46). Period of abject poverty and despondency followed, climaxed by death of his wife from tuberculosis (Jan. 30, 1847). In abnormal mental condition, aggravated by alcoholic excesses (1847–49); during intermittent periods of sanity wrote *For Annie, Ulalume, Annabel Lee, The Bells, El Dorado.* Died in Baltimore (Oct. 7, 1849). Elected to American Hall of Fame (1910). See also Sarah Helen WHITMAN.

**Poe, Orlando Metcalfe.** 1832–1895. American army officer, b. Navarre, Ohio; grad. U.S.M.A., West Point (1856); brigadier general of volunteers (1862); chief engineer, Army of the Ohio (1863–64); chief engineer on Gen. Sherman's staff in the march to the sea (1864); aide-de-camp to Gen. Sherman (1873–84). As engineer, had charge of improving the St. Mary's and Detroit rivers, the ship canal between Chicago, Duluth, and Buffalo, and the building of locks at Sault Sainte Marie.

**Poel** (pōl), **William.** *Orig. surname* **Pole** (pōl). 1852–1934. English actor and theatrical manager known for reviving old plays; son of William Pole (*q.v.*); revived *Hamlet* with text of first quarto and without scenery (1881); founded Elizabethan Stage Society (1895); revived plays of Shakespeare, Marlowe, Ben Jonson; produced for first time Swinburne's *Locrine* (1900), *Fratricide Punished* (1924); dramatized Howells's *A Foregone Conclusion* (1884). Author of plays, including *Lillies that Fester*, and comediettas.

**Poe'laert** (pōō'lärt), **Joseph.** 1817–1879. Belgian architect; designed Palace of Justice, Brussels, largest building in modern Europe.

**Poe'len·burgh** (pōō'lĕn·bûrk), **Cornelisz van.** 1586–1667. Dutch painter; studied under Bloemaert; painted portraits, landscapes, and religious pictures.

**Poel'zig** (pûl'tsĭk), **Hans.** 1869–1936. German architect; head of advanced studio in architecture at Acad. of Art, Berlin (1920 ff.), and professor at Inst. of Technology, Charlottenburg (1924 ff.). Designed buildings and gardens of Centenary Exhibition (in Berlin) and many notable buildings in Berlin and elsewhere.

**Po·e'rio** (pô·â'ryô), **Alessandro.** 1802–1848. Italian poet and patriot; volunteer under Pepe against Austrians (1821) and exiled after Austria regained control of Naples; mortally wounded serving under Pepe against the Austrians (1848); author of lyrics, esp. of the patriotic poem *Il Risorgimento.* His brother **Carlo** (1803–1867) was a lawyer and patriot; sentenced (1849) to 19 years in irons and served 9 years before being released and exiled; returned to Italy and was elected (1860) member of Turin parliament.

**Po·ey' y A·loy'** (pô·ĕ'ē ē ä·loi'), **Felipe.** 1799–1891. Cuban naturalist; professor, Havana. Chief work, *Catálogo Razonado de los Peces Cubanos*, in ten volumes, with many of his own drawings and accounts of numerous fish previously undescribed.

**Pof'fen·ber'ger** (pŏf'ĕn·bûr'gẽr), **Albert Theodore.** 1885– . American psychologist.

**Po·ga'ny** (pŏ·gä'nĭ; *Hung.* pŏ'gän·y'), **Wil'ly** (wĭl'ĭ; *Hung.* vĭl'lĭ), *in full* **William Andrew.** 1882–1955. Illustrator, mural painter, stage and costume designer, and art director of motion pictures, b. in Szeged, Hungary; studio in Hollywood, Calif.; widely known as illustrator of children's books, as *Home Book of Verse for Children* (Stevenson), *Tales from the Arabian Nights, Bible Stories, Gulliver's Travels.*

**Pog'ge** (pŏg'ĕ), **Paul.** 1839–1884. German explorer in Central Africa and Portuguese West Africa.

**Pog'gen·dorff** (pŏg'ĕn·dôrf), **Johann Christoff.** 1796–1877. German physicist; investigated problems in electricity and magnetism; published biographical work on scientists of all times and works on history of science, esp. physics.

**Pog'gio Brac'cio·li'ni** (pôd'jô brät'chô·lē'nē), **Giovanni Francesco.** 1380–1459. Italian Humanist; papal secretary (1404 ff.); chancellor of Florence (1453 ff.); known chiefly for discoveries, in various monasteries in Germany, Switzerland, and France, of lost Latin classics, including eight orations of Cicero, Lucretius's *De Rerum Natura*, Quintilian's *Institutio Oratoria*, twelve plays of Plautus, Ammianus Marcellinus's history, part of Valerius Flaccus's *Argonautica*, and Tacitus's *Dialogus* and *Germania.*

**Po·go'din** (pŭ·gô'dyĭn), **Mikhail Petrovich.** 1800–1873. Russian historian and archaeologist; amassed notable collection of Russian antiquities, later purchased by government; vigorously advocated policy of Pan-Slavism.

**Pohl** (pōl), **Hugo von.** 1855–1916. German admiral; commanded German battle fleet (Feb., 1915–Jan., 1916).

**Pohl, Richard.** 1826–1896. German writer on music; friend of Liszt, in Weimar (1854–64); author of studies on Wagner, Liszt, and Berlioz; translator of Berlioz's works.

**Poin'ca'ré'** (pwăɴ'kȧ'rā'), **Jules Henri.** 1854–1912. Cousin of Raymond Poincaré. French mathematician; at U. of Paris (from 1881), professor of physical mechanics (1885), of mathematical physics and calculus of probabilities (1886), and, finally, of celestial mechanics. Reconstituted analytical mathematics; developed automorphic functions; introduced Fuchsian functions; applied analysis to rational mechanics, physics, and astronomy; worked on electromagnetic theory of light, electric oscillations, and diffraction of hertzian waves.

**Poincaré, Lucien.** 1862–1920. Brother of Raymond Poincaré. French physicist and educator; author of works on physics and electricity.

**Poincaré, Raymond.** 1860–1934. French statesman and writer, 9th president of the Republic. Elected deputy (1887–1902); a leader of the progressive Republicans, esp. as an economist; held several cabinet offices (1893–1903); senator (1903–12); prime minister (1912–13); vigorously supported entente with Great Britain and alliance with Russia. Elected president (1913–20); influenced legislation much more than previous presidents; strengthened French defenses; served through entire period of World War, sustaining patriotism by his oratory and by fighting defeatism. After termination of presidency returned to Senate (1920); stood for strong nationalist policy; again prime minister (1922–24); disagreed with Great Britain on reparations; sent French army to occupy the Ruhr (1923); was defeated by Radicals and Socialists (1924). Again prime minister and minister of finance (1926–29) to meet financial crisis; caused measures to be passed that stabilized the franc. Member of French Academy (1909).

**Poin'dex'ter** (poin'dĕks'tẽr), **Joseph Boyd.** 1869–1951. American jurist and administrator; governor of the Territory of Hawaii (from 1934).

**Poin'sett** (poin'sĕt; -sĭt), **Joel Roberts.** 1779–1851. American legislator and diplomat, b. Charleston, S.C.; member, U.S. House of Representatives (1821–25); first U.S. minister to Mexico (1825–29); U.S. secretary of war (1837–41). *Poinsettia*, a genus of tropical American woody plants, is named in his honor.

**Poin'sot'** (pwăɴ'sō'), **Louis.** 1777–1859. French mathematician; originated theory of couples, set forth in his *Les Éléments de la Statique* (1803); originated theorem relating to motion of a free solid.

**Poise** (pwȧz), **Ferdinand,** *in full* **Jean Alexandre Ferdinand.** 1828–1892. French composer; known esp. for comic operas, including *Les Charmeurs* (1855), *Joli Gilles* (1884), etc.

**Poi'seuille'** (pwȧ'zû'y'), **Jean Louis Marie.** 1799–1869. French physician, anatomist, and physiologist; known for investigations of circulation of the blood, for his work *Le Mouvement des Liquides dans des Tubes de Petits Diamètres* (1844), and for discovery (1843) of Poiseuille's law (concerning velocity of flow of a liquid through a capillary tube).

**Pois'son'** (pwȧ'sôɴ'), **Siméon Denis.** 1781–1840. French mathematician; known for application of mathematics to physics, esp. to electrostatics and magnetism; author of works on definite integrals, Fourier's series, calculus of variations, probability.

**Poi'te·vin'** (pwȧt'văɴ'), **Prosper.** 1810?–1884. French scholar; author of *Grammaire Générale et Historique de la Langue Française* (1856); compiler of *Nouveau Dictionnaire Universel de la Langue Française* (1854–60).

**Poitiers, Guillaume de.** See GUILLAUME DE POITIERS.

**Po·kor'ny** (pô·kôr'nē), **Julius.** 1887–1970. German philologist and Celtic scholar.

**Po·krov'ski** (pŭ·krôf'skû·ĭ; *Angl.* -skĭ), **Mikhail Nikolaevich.** 1868–1932. Russian historian and politician; joined Bolsheviks (1905); forced to live abroad (1908–17). After Bolshevik revolution (1917), became delegate of Moscow workmen's council and member of peace conference at Brest Litovsk; general director of government archives, Moscow (1921). Among his works are *Russian History* (4 vols., 1924) and *Sketches of the History of the Revolutionary Movement in Russia in the 19th and 20th Centuries* (1924).

**Pol** (pôl), **Wincenty.** 1807–1872. Polish poet; author of *Songs of our Land* (1843), *Mohort* (1855), and *Wit Stwosz* (1857).

**Po·lac'co** (pô·läk'kô), **Giorgio.** 1875–1960. Ital.-born Amer. operatic conductor; interpreter of Wagner; music director and conductor, Chicago Civic Opera Assn. (1920–30). See Edith MASON.

**Po·lá'šek** (pô·lä'shĕk; *orig.* pô'lä·shĕk), **Al'bin** (ăl'bĭn). 1879–1965. Sculptor, b. in Moravia; among his sculptures are *Theodore Thomas Memorial* in Chicago, *Woodrow Wilson Memorial* in Prague, Czechoslovakia, and the portrait bust of Daniel Boone in American Hall of Fame.

**Polastron, Yolande Martine Gabrielle de.** Duchesse **de Polignac.** See POLIGNAC.

**Pol de Mont** (pŏl' dĕ mônt'). *Properly* **Karel Marie Po'ly·door'** (pō'lē·dōr') **De Mont.** 1857–1931. Flemish poet and art critic; author of *Loreley* (1882), *Fladderende Vlinders* ("Fluttering Butterflies," 1885), *Iris* (1895), and *Zomervlammen* ("Flames of Summer," 1922).

**Pole** (pōl). Name of English family descended from Geoffrey Pole, Buckinghamshire squire, whose son Sir Richard (d. 1505) married (?1491) a princess of the royal house, **Margaret Pole** (1473–1541), Countess of **Salis'bur·y** (sôlz'bēr·ĭ; -brĭ), daughter of George Plantagenet (1449–78), Duke of Clarence. She was given family lands of earldom of Salisbury by Henry VIII as some amends for judicial murder of her brother Edward, Earl of Warwick; was discharged as governess to Princess Mary on refusal to give up Princess Mary's jewels after Henry VIII's marriage to Anne Boleyn and was beheaded as consequence of Henry's antagonism toward her son Reginald.

**Reginald Pole** (1500–1558), Roman Catholic prelate. B.A., Oxon. (1515); friend of Sir Thomas More; sent by Henry VIII to Rome to study (1521–27); made dean of Exeter and initiated by Thomas Cromwell into statesmanship (1527); while traveling abroad, criticized Henry VIII in his book *Pro Ecclesiasticae Unitatis Defensione* (1536), giving adverse opinion on question of Henry's divorce and warning of temporal punishment in event of nonsubmission to divine institution of papal supremacy, thus provoking execution of his mother and brother Henry in England; created cardinal by Pope Paul III (1536) and sent as emissary to incite Francis I and Charles V to send expedition to depose Henry VIII (1537, 1539); legate at Viterbo (from 1541) amid scholars interested in discussion of justification by faith; one of presiding legates at Council of Trent, which embodied in its decree Pole's views of original sin and his doctrines of justification by faith; just missed election as pope (1549). Papal legate to Queen Mary on her accession and, on reversal of attainder, returned to England (1554); cardinal priest (1555); absolved kingdom and those ordained under old rite or in schism, instituted reforms; archbishop of Canterbury (1556) on Cranmer's deprivation; attempted to restore ecclesiastical system disrupted by Henry VIII; summoned by his old enemy Caraffa, now Paul IV, to answer charge of heresy; breve containing summons intercepted by Queen Mary; broken by the blow and ill health.

His brother **Sir Henry** (1492?–1538), Baron **Mon'tague** (mŏn'tȧ·gū; mŭn'-) *or* **Mon'ta·cute** (-kūt), distinguished himself in France (1513, 1523); beheaded on charge of treasonable conversations because of Reginald's book and opposition. Another brother, **Sir Geoffrey** (1502?–1558), through Spanish ambassador urged Charles V to invade England; made confessions involving his brother Sir Henry, fled to Rome to join his brother the cardinal; his sons died in prison as plotters against Elizabeth.

**Pole, de la** (dĕl'ȧ·pōl'). Name of a rich English family descended from a Hull merchant, Sir **William de la Pole** *or* **at'te Pool'** [ăt'ĕ pōl'] (d. 1366), who held offices under Edward III in recognition of loans of money, and including earls and dukes of Suffolk:

**Michael de la Pole** (1330?–1389), 1st Earl of **Suf'folk** (sŭf'ŭk); eldest son of Sir William; took part in Black Prince's siege of Limoges (1370); became most trusted personal adviser of Richard II; chancellor of England (1383); impeached (1386) by organized opposition of Thomas of Woodstock (Duke of Gloucester) on a charge of misappropriation of funds and, after brief reinstatement by Richard II, compelled to flee the realm (1387).

**William de la Pole** (1396–1450), 4th Earl and 1st Duke of **Suffolk,** and, by reversion of title, Earl of **Pem'broke** [pĕm'brŏŏk] (1447); grandson of 1st earl; served fourteen years in French wars, first under Henry V, later under duke of Bedford, and in chief command (1428); taken prisoner by Joan of Arc at Jargeau (1429); occupied himself with home politics (from 1431); led peace party in opposition to Humphrey, Duke of Gloucester, and the war party; negotiated successfully match between Henry VI and Margaret of Anjou and two-year truce (1444); left without rival by death of Gloucester while under arrest and five days later, of Cardinal Beaufort; promoted to dukedom (1448); banished Richard of York as lieutenant of Ireland, replacing him with Edmund Beaufort, Duke of Somerset, in French command; became unpopular after ceding to France as part of truce all of Anjou and Maine and after renewal of war, partly in consequence of treacherous attack on Fougères during truce; accused by House of Commons of maladministration and of selling the realm to France; banished by Henry VI; intercepted off Dover and beheaded at sea; his farewell letter to his son included in the Paston letters.

**John de la Pole** (1442–1491), 2d Duke of **Suffolk;** son of 1st duke; joined Yorkists and married Elizabeth, sister of Edward IV and Richard III; became steward of England at coronation of Edward IV (1461) and was trusted by Richard III and Henry VII despite fact that three of his sons were pretenders to throne on death of Richard III, as follows: **John de la Pole** (1464?–1487), Earl of **Lin′coln** (lĭng′kŭn); lord lieutenant of Ireland (1484); promoted Simnel's plot; killed at battle of Stoke. Sir **Edmund de la Pole** (1472?–1513), Earl of **Suffolk;** repaired to Emperor Maximilian in Tyrol on promise of help to throne (1501); was delivered to Henry VII by king of Castile and beheaded on accession of Henry VIII. **Richard de la Pole** (d. 1525); recognized as king of England by Louis XII (1512); fought for French in Spain and Netherlands; prepared for invasion of England with German mercenaries; killed at battle of Pavia.

**Pole** (pōl), **William.** 1814–1900. English engineer, musician, and writer on whist; professor of engineering, Bombay (1844–47), and University Coll., London (1859–67); examiner for musical degrees, U. of London (1878–91). His son, William Poel (*q.v.*), actor, altered the spelling of his name.

**Po′lenz** (pō′lĕnts), **Wilhelm von.** 1861–1903. German writer of plays and novels.

**Po·le·voi′** (pŭ·lyĕ·voi′), **Nikolai Alekseevich.** 1796–1846. Russian writer; author of plays, novels, and *History of the Russian People* (6 vols., 1829–33).

**Pol′hem′** (po͝ol′hĕm′), **Christopher.** 1661–1751. Swedish engineer and inventor; invented esp. machines used in transportation, mining, agriculture, and manufacturing; sometimes called "Father of Swedish Mechanics."

**Po′li** (pô′lē), **Giuseppe Saverio.** 1746–1825. Italian naturalist; author of work on testaceous mollusca.

**Po′li′gnac′** (pô′lē′nyȧk′). An ancient French family of nobility, including: **Melchior de Polignac** (1661–1742); diplomat under Louis XIV and XV; destined for the church; ambassador to Poland (1695–97); retired, but recalled to favor at court (1702); plenipotentiary at Congress of Utrecht (1712–13); cardinal (1713), minister at Rome (1725–32), archbishop of Auch (1726); member of French Academy. His grandnephew **Armand Jules François Polignac,** Duc **de Polignac** (1745–1817); m. (1767) **Yolande Martine Gabrielle de Po′las′tron′** [dē pô′lȧs′trôɴ′] (c. 1749–1793), intimate friend of Marie Antoinette. Through court favor they received huge pensions which aroused popular hatred; their extravagance a direct cause of the revolution; emigrated to the Ukraine (1789). Their son **Armand Jules Marie Héraclius,** Comte (*later* Duc) **de Polignac** (1771–1847); officer and émigré, b. Paris; took part in conspiracy against Napoleon (1804), imprisoned (1804–13); aide-de-camp and adherent of comte d'Artois (later Charles X). His brother **Auguste Jules Armand Marie,** Comte (*later* Prince) **de Polignac** (1780–1847); ultraroyalist politician, b. in Versailles; implicated in conspiracy against Napoleon (1804), imprisoned for two years; became intimate (1814) with comte d'Artois; held several offices under Bourbon restoration and was ambassador to London (1823–29); minister of foreign affairs under Charles X (1829–30); promulgated the Ordinances of July, 1830, that caused the revolution, driving out Charles; arrested and imprisoned at Ham (1830–36); wrote two works on current political history. His son **Charles Ludovic Marie,** Prince **de Polignac** (1827–1904), army officer in Tunis and Algeria.

**Poliorcetes, Demetrius.** See DEMETRIUS I of Macedonia.

**Po·li′tes** *or* **Po·li′tis** (pô·lyē′tēs), **Nikolaos Sokrates.** 1872–1942. Greek jurist and diplomat; associate of Venizelos and on staff of ministry of foreign affairs (1914–16); minister of foreign affairs (1916–20, 1922, 1936); delegate to Peace Conference at Paris (1919); Greek minister in Paris and Madrid (1924–36, 1938–40).

**Po·li′tian** (pô·lĭsh′ăn). *Lat.* **Angelus Po·li′ti·a′nus** (pô·lĭsh′ĭ·ā′nŭs). *Ital.* **Angelo Po′li·zia′no** (pō′lē-tsyä′nô). *Real name* **Angelo Am′bro·gi′ni** (äm′brô-jē′nē). 1454–1494. Italian Humanist and poet; protégé of Lorenzo de' Medici; canon of Florence Cathedral. Author of *Orfeo, Stanze per la Giostra di Giuliano de' Medici, Miscellanea* (critical essays), Latin translations, as of the *Iliad* (books 2–5), Herodian, Epictetus's *Enchiridion,* and Plato's *Charmides,* and Latin poems, as *Rusticus* and *Manto.*

**Po′lit·zer** (pō′lĭt·sẽr), **Adam.** 1835–1920. Austrian aurist; director of otological clinic (1873–1906), U. of Vienna; introduced new method (politzerization) of treating catarrh of inner ear.

**Polk** (pōk), **Frank Lyon.** 1871–1943. American lawyer and statesman; counselor for U.S. Department of State (1915–19); undersecretary of state (1919–20); head of American delegation to Peace Conference, Paris (1919).

**Polk, James Knox.** 1795–1849. Grandnephew of Thomas Polk. Eleventh president of the United States, b. in Mecklenburg County, N.C.; adm. to bar (1820); practiced, Columbia, Tenn.; member, U.S. House of Representatives (1825–39), and speaker (1835–39); governor of Tennessee (1839–41); president of the United States (1845–49).

**Polk, Thomas.** 1732?–1794. American Revolutionary leader; served in American Revolution; at Brandywine and Valley Forge; delegate to Continental Congress (1786). His son **William** (1758–1834) was a Revolutionary officer; served at Brandywine, Germantown, Valley Forge, and at Guilford Court House, and Eutaw Springs; managed Jackson's campaign in North Carolina (1824, 1828). William's son **Leonidas** (1806–1864) was a clergyman and Confederate army commander; grad. U.S.M.A., West Point (1827); resigned commission (1827) and studied theology; appointed Protestant Episcopal missionary bishop of the Southwest (1838) and bishop of Louisiana (1841); a founder of U. of the South, Sewanee, Tenn. (1860); entered Confederate army as major general (1861); in command of Mississippi River defenses (1861–62); lieutenant general (Oct., 1862); fought at Shiloh, Murfreesboro, Chickamauga; killed at Pine Mountain (June 14, 1864).

**Pol′lai·uo′lo** (pōl′lī·wô′lō), **Antonio.** 1429–1498. Florentine painter, goldsmith, sculptor, and engraver; protégé of the Medici and the Florentine signory; as an engraver, associate of Finiguerra; headed large atelier from which issued works in niello, sculptures, paintings, goldsmith's work, etc.; leading bronze sculptor after Verrocchio; pioneer in study of anatomy by dissection for artistic purposes; called to Rome (1484) by Innocent VIII. Works include tombs of Sixtus IV and Innocent VIII, bronze group *Hercules Strangling Cacus,* terra-cotta bust *The Young Warrior,* engraving *Ten Fighting Nudes,* and paintings, as *Martyrdom of St. Sebastian* and *Apollo and Daphne.* His brother **Piero** (1443–1496) collaborated with Antonio in painting; his own paintings include *Coronation of the Virgin, Three Saints, Prudence,* and *Annunciation.* Their nephew **Simone** (1454?–?1508), *called* **il Cro′na·ca** (ēl krô′nä·kä) [*i.e.* "the Chronicler"], was an architect; friend of Savonarola; admirer and describer of ancient works (hence his nickname); his masterpiece, the great cornice of Palazzo Strozzi.

**Pol′lard** (pŏl′ẽrd), **Albert Frederick.** 1869–1948. English historian; professor of English history, London (1903–27); director of Inst. of Historical Research and professor of constitutional history. Author of works on early Tudor period, lives of Thomas Cranmer (1904) and

Wolsey (1929); and *Factors in Modern History* (1907), *A Short History of the Great War* (1920), *Factors in American History* (1925), etc.

**Pollard, Alfred William.** 1859–1944. English bibliographer; assistant in department of printed books, British Museum (1883), asst. keeper (1909), keeper (1919–24); professor of English bibliography, King's Coll., London (1919); editor of the Globe *Chaucer* (1898); author of *Early Illustrated Books* (1893), *A Census of Shakespeare Quartos* (1916), the chapter on Shakespeare's text in *Cambridge Companion to Shakespeare Studies* (1934), etc.

**Pollard, Charles Louis.** 1872–1945. American botanist and entomologist, b. New York City; on staff of U.S. Department of Agriculture (1894–1903), and assistant curator of U.S. National Museum, Washington, D.C. (1895–1903); consulting botanist for *Webster's New International Dictionary* (1909); librarian, Martha Canfield Free Library, Arlington, Vt. (from 1937).

**Pollard, Edward Alfred.** 1831–1872. American journalist, b. in Albemarle County, Va.; editor, *Daily Richmond Examiner* (1861–67); founder and editor, *Southern Opinion*, a weekly journal (1867–69); writer of many books on the Civil War.

**Pol'len** (pŏl'ĕn), **John Hungerford.** 1820–1902. English artist and author; one of first to reintroduce fresco decoration into England; influential in reforming taste in domestic furniture and decoration. Two of his seven sons were: **John Hungerford** (1858–1925), who entered the Society of Jesus (1877) and was ordained priest (1891); made special study of history of Society of Jesus and lives of English, Scottish, and Irish Catholics after Reformation. **Arthur Joseph Hungerford** (1866–1937), expert in naval gunnery; pioneer in development of naval fire control.

**Pol'li·o** (pŏl'ĭ·ō), **Gaius A·sin'i·us** (ȧ·sĭn'ĭ·ŭs). 75 B.C.–5 A.D. Roman soldier, orator, and politician. Sided with Caesar in civil war; engaged at Pharsalus (48 B.C.) and against Sextus Pompeius in Spain. Later joined fortunes with Mark Antony; governor of part of Gaul; helped negotiate peace of Brundisium (40), reconciling Antony and Octavius for a time. Consul (40); campaigned in Illyria (39); constructed first public library in Rome. Patron of literature; author of tragedies and a history of civil wars; only few fragments of his orations extant. Vergil addressed fourth eclogue to him.

**Pol'lock** (pŏl'ŭk). Name of an illustrious English legal family descended from David Pollock, saddler to George III, and including:

His three sons: Sir **David** (1780–1847), chief justice of supreme court of Bombay. Sir **Jonathan Frederick** (1783–1870), judge; M.A., Cantab. (1809); attorney general (1834–35, 1841–44); chief baron of exchequer (1844–66). Sir **George** (1786–1872), military commander in India; commanded expedition sent to relief of Jalalabad, forced Khyber Pass, defeated Afghan chief at Tezín, and destroyed bazaar at Kabul (1842); senior government director of East India Company (1854); field marshal (1870).

Sir **William Frederick** (1815–1888); eldest son of Sir Jonathan Frederick; master of the Court of Exchequer (1846); queen's remembrancer (1874–86); translator of Dante's *Divina Commedia* into blank verse (1854). His brother **George Frederick** (1821–1915); master of the Court of Exchequer (1851); queen's remembrancer (1886); senior master of supreme court. Another brother, Sir **Charles Edward** (1823–1897); baron of exchequer (1873); justice of high court (1875–79); author of legal works.

Sir **Frederick** (1845–1937); eldest son of Sir William Frederick Pollock; professor of jurisprudence at University Coll., London (1882), and at Oxford (1883–1903); professor of common law, Inns of Court (1884–90); judge of admiralty court of Cinque Ports (from 1914); author of *Spinoza* (1880) and of authoritative texts on contracts, torts, partnership, fraud, jurisprudence, of *League of Nations* (1920), and with F. W. Maitland, of *History of English Law Before the Time of Edward I* (2 vols., 1895). His brother **Walter Herries** (1850–1926); M.A., Cantab.; editor of *Saturday Review* (1883–94); author of works on the French theater, French poets, of *Jane Austen and her Contemporaries*, etc.

Sir **Ernest Murray** (1861–1936); 4th son of George Frederick Pollock; M.A., Cantab. (1887); chairman of contraband committee (1915); solicitor general (1919–22); attorney general (1922); master of the rolls (1923).

Sir **John** (1878–1964), playwright; son of Sir Frederick Pollock (1845–1937); M.A., Cantab. (1903); called to bar (1906); turned to writing plays, including *The Invention of Dr. Metzler* (1905), *The Luck King* (1921), and *The Vulture* (1931); Red Cross commissioner in Russia (1915–18); translated and adapted plays from Ibsen and Brieux, *Anna Karénina* from Tolstoi's novel; author of books on Anatole France (1925, 1927) and historical writings; contributor to *Cambridge Modern History.*

**Pollock, Channing.** 1880–1946. American novelist, playwright, and lecturer, b. Washington, D.C.; dramatic critic (1905–19) for *Ainslee's Magazine*, *Smart Set*, *The Green Book*. Author of: fiction, *Behold the Man* (1900), *Stage Stories* (1901), *The Footlights—Fore and Aft* (1909), *Star Magic* (1933), *Winner Lose All* (1939), etc.; plays, *A Game of Hearts* (1900), *Clothes* (with Avery Hopwood, 1906), *The Traitor* (1908), *The Red Widow* (with Rennold Wolf, 1911), *A Perfect Lady* (with Rennold Wolf, 1914), *Ziegfeld Follies of 1915* (with Rennold Wolf, 1915), *Roads of Destiny* (1918), *The Crowded Hour* (with Edgar Selwyn, 1918), *The Fool* (1922), *Mr. Moneypenny* (1928), *Stranglehold* (1932), etc.; miscellaneous works including the autobiographical *Harvest of My Years* (1943).

**Pol'lok** (pŏl'ŭk), **Robert.** 1798–1827. Scottish poet; author of a long essay in blank verse, *The Course of Time* (1827), suggesting harmonies of Cowper and Young.

**Pol'lux** (pŏl'ŭks), **Julius.** Greek Sophist and lexicographer of 2d century A.D.; appointed professor of rhetoric at Athens by Emperor Commodus. Only extant work is *Onomasticon*, a Greek dictionary (10 books).

**Po'lo** (pō'lō), **Gaspar Gil.** See GIL POLO.

**Po'lo** (*Angl.* pō'lō; *Ital.* pô'-), **Marco.** 1254?–?1324. Italian traveler, b. in Venice; accompanied (1271 ff.) his father and uncle on a trip from Acre through Sivas, Mosul, Baghdad, Hormuz, Khurasan to the Oxus River (Amu Darya), up the Oxus to The Pamirs, and by way of Kashgar, Yarkand, and Khotan to Lop Nor, then across the Gobi desert to Tangut and Shangtu, where they found Kublai Khan (1275). Entered the diplomatic service of Kublai Khan and was used on missions to various parts of the Mongol empire. Left China (1292) and returned by way of Sumatra, India, and Persia to Venice (1295). Captured by Genoese and imprisoned for a year at Genoa (1298), where he dictated to a fellow prisoner the story of his travels, published under the title of *The Book of Marco Polo.*

**Po·lon'ski** (pŭ·lôn'skû·ĭ; *Angl.* -skĭ), **Yakov Petrovich.** 1820–1898. Russian poet; tutor to sons of Emperor Alexis Mikhailovich. Among his works are *The Grasshopper Musician*, *Discord*, *Poetical Works* (3 vols.), *Sheaves*, *Winter-Wheat*, *Evening Bells* (awarded Pushkin prize), and *At Sunset.*

**Pol'y·ae'nus** (pŏl'ĭ·ē'nŭs). Greek scholar of Macedonia in 2d century A.D.; lived in Rome as rhetorician. Author of *Strategica*, or *Strategemata*, a compilation of military stratagems written in Greek and presented in anecdotal form.

**Po·lyb′i·us** (pô·lĭb′ĭ·ŭs). 205?–?125 B.C. Greek historian, b. Megalopolis in Arcadia; in service in Achaean League; taken as political prisoner to Rome (168) and remained in exile about seventeen years; became friend of Scipio the Younger and, through him, an associate of leading literary figures in Rome; accompanied Scipio to Africa (147) and was present at destruction of Carthage (146); occupied himself thereafter with writing *Histories*, a general history of Rome and nearby countries from 266 to 146 B.C. (40 books, of which only first 5 and a few fragments are extant).

**Pol′y·carp** (pŏl′ĭ·kärp), Saint. 69?–?155. Christian martyr; one of the Apostolic Fathers; bishop of Smyrna; author of letter to the Philippians (extant); because of his sanctity of life and through his attacks on heresies, became very influential in Smyrna and neighboring regions; burned at stake on demand of mob during a period of persecutions of Christians in Asia.

**Pol′y·cli′tus** *or* **Pol′y·clei′tus** (pŏl′ĭ·klī′tŭs) *or* **Pol′y·cle′tus** (-klē′tŭs). Greek sculptor and architect of Sicyon, in 5th century B.C.; credited with developing to highest perfection the abstract proportion which characterizes Greek sculpture; carved a figure (*Doryphorus*), embodying athletic type in accepted correct proportions, which was called the "canon." Chief work, the chryselephantine *Hera* at Argos.

**Po·lyc′ra·tes** (pô·lĭk′rȧ·tēz). Tyrant of Samos (c. 535 B.C. ff.); collected and armed a fleet of 100 ships and made himself master of the Aegean basin; became notorious for acts of piracy. Lured to mainland by Oroetes, Persian satrap of Lydia, and crucified (c. 522 B.C.).

**Pol′y·do′rus** (pŏl′ĭ·dō′rŭs). Rhodian sculptor, of 1st century B.C.; collaborated with Agesander and Athenodorus in carving the Laocoön group.

**Pol′y·euc′tus** (pŏl′ĭ·ūk′tŭs). Greek sculptor; known to have executed bronze statue of Demosthenes (280 B.C.).

**Pol′yg·no′tus** (pŏl′ĭg·nō′tŭs). Greek painter of 5th century B.C., b. on island of Thasos; received Athenian citizenship as reward for his paintings in the Poecile and Theseum; associated with Cimon in rebuilding Athens. Regarded as leading representative of Greek painting of his century.

**Pol′y·sper′chon** (pŏl′ĭ·spûr′kŏn). Macedonian general; served under Alexander the Great; succeeded Antipater as regent of Macedonia (319 B.C.); superseded by Cassander (*q.v.*).

**Pom·bal′** (pōɴm·bäl′), Marquês **de** (cr. 1769). **Sebastião José de Car·va′lho e Mel′lo** (thĕ kĕr·vá′lyōō ē mâ′lōō). 1699–1782. Portuguese statesman, b. Soure, near Coimbra; envoy extraordinary to London (1738–45), to Vienna (1745–49). On accession of Joseph Emanuel, appointed minister for foreign affairs (1750–56); gained complete ascendancy over Joseph Emanuel that lasted till end of reign (1777); active in aid of sufferers from great earthquake at Lisbon (1755). Prime minister (1756–77); sought to strengthen commerce and industry; under him colonies developed, native slaves in Brazil liberated (1755); reduced power of Inquisition; engaged in long controversy with Jesuits (1754–59), who were finally expelled from all Portuguese dominions; reorganized finances and defenses. Was dismissed (1777) after Joseph Emanuel's death. See MARIA I of Portugal.

**Pomeranus.** See Johann BUGENHAGEN.

**Pom′er·ene** (pŏm′ẽr·ēn), **Atlee.** 1863–1937. American lawyer and legislator; began practice at Canton, Ohio; U.S. senator from Ohio (1911–23); cosponsor of the Webb-Pomerene Act (1918) permitting business combinations for foreign trade. Special prosecutor in Teapot Dome oil lease investigation (1924).

**Pom′er·oy** (pŏm′ẽr·oi; pŏm′roi; pŭm′ẽr·oi; pŭm′roi), **John Norton.** 1828–1885. American lawyer and educator; author of legal treatises.

**Pomeroy, Seth.** 1706–1777. American Revolutionary officer, b. Northampton, Mass.; volunteer at Bunker Hill (1775); commissioned brigadier general in Continental army (1775). His *Journals* are important for eighteenth-century Massachusetts history.

**Pom′fret** (pŭm′frĕt; -frĭt; pŏm′-), **John.** 1667–1702. English poet; his poems included in Dr. Johnson's *Lives of the Poets* (1779); the most popular, *The Choice* (1700), praised by Dr. Johnson.

**Pom′pa′dour′** (pôɴ′pȧ′dōōr′; *Angl.* pŏm′pȧ·dōōr, -dōr), Marquise **de. Jeanne Antoinette Pois′son′** (pwá′sôɴ′). 1721–1764. Mistress of Louis XV of France. Daughter of François Poisson and Madeleine de la Motte; educ. at charge of a wealthy financier, Lenormand de Tournehem; m. (1741) his nephew, Lenormand d'Étoiles. First met king (1744); established at Versailles as mistress (1745) and presented with estate of Pompadour; made duchess (1752). Completely controlled Louis XV and political situation (1745–64), esp. in internal affairs; in foreign policies changed Richelieu's purpose of weakening house of Austria to one of alliances with Austria, which brought on Seven Years' War (1756–63).

**Pom·pe′ia** (pŏm·pē′(y)ȧ). Second wife of Julius Caesar, who repudiated her on suspicion of adultery on the grounds that "Caesar's wife must be above suspicion."

**Pom·pe′ius** (pŏm·pē′(y)ŭs). *Eng.* **Pom′pey** (pŏm′pĭ). A Roman gens to which belonged several distinguished soldiers and politicians:

**Gnaeus Pompeius Stra′bo** (strā′bō). d. 87 B.C. Politician; father of Pompey the Great; quaestor in Sardinia (103 B.C.); praetor (94); propraetor in Sicily (93); consul (89); sponsored law conferring on inhabitants of Gallia Transpadana privileges accorded to Latin colonies.

**Gnaeus Pompeius Mag′nus** (măg′nŭs). *Eng.* **Pompey the Great.** 106–48 B.C. General and statesman; ally of Sulla against Marius (83 ff.); aided in crushing Servile Insurrection (71); consul with Crassus (70); cleared sea of pirates (67); took command in the East (66), where he defeated Mithridates and annexed Syria and Palestine; enjoyed a triumph (61). Organized, with Julius Caesar and Crassus, First Triumvirate (60); consul (55). Became champion of Senate and Conservative party; brought on civil war and was decisively defeated at Pharsalus (48); fled to Egypt for protection, but was murdered by order of Ptolemy.

**Gnaeus Pompeius Magnus.** 75?–45 B.C. Soldier; son of Pompey the Great; commanded his father's fleet in Adriatic (48); after battle of Pharsalus (48), went to Africa and then to Spain; defeated at Munda by Caesar (45), captured and executed.

**Sextus Pompeius Magnus.** *Called* **Pompey the Younger.** 75–35 B.C. Second son of Pompey the Great; Roman soldier; crossed into Spain after father's defeat at Thapsus (46); defeated by Caesar at Munda (45); proscribed by the triumvirate (43). Collected fleet and gained control of Sicily, whence he harassed shores of Italy. Defeated by Agrippa at Naulochus (36); fled to Asia Minor; captured and executed by Antony's troops.

**Pompeius Trogus, Gnaeus.** See TROGUS.

**Pom′pi′dou′** (pōɴ′pē′dōō′), **Georges Jean Raymond.** 1911–1974. French statesman. Prime minister (1962–68), and president (1969–74) ) of France.

**Pom′pi′gnan′** (pôɴ′pē′nyäɴ′), Marquis **de. Jean Jacques Le·franc′** (lē·fräɴ′). 1709–1784. French lawyer and poet; author of a translation of the *Psalms* of

David and the tragedies of Aeschylus, a volume of *Odes Chrétiennes et Philosophiques* (1771), and a tragedy, a comedy, and two operas.

**Pom·pi'li** (pôm·pē'lē), **Vittoria**, *nee* **A'ga·noor'** (ä'gä-nôr'). 1857–1910. Italian woman poet; author of *Leggenda Eterna* (1900) and *Nuove Liriche* (1909).

**Pom'po·naz'zi** (pōm'pō·nät'tsē), **Pietro**. *Lat.* **Petrus Pom'po·na'ti·us** (pŏm'pō·nā'shĭ·ŭs). 1462–1525. Italian philosopher; known chiefly for his anti-Thomistic *De Immortalitate Animi* (1516), which provoked controversy involving Thomists, Averroists, and followers of Alexander of Aphrodisias.

**Pom·po'ni·us** (pŏm·pō'nĭ·ŭs), **Lucius**. *Surnamed* **Bo-no'ni·en'sis** (bō·nō'nĭ·ĕn'sĭs), *i.e.* "of Bononia (Bologna)." fl. about 90 B.C. Latin writer; first (with Novius) to give literary form and expression to *Fabulae Atellanae*, rude popular farces of rural or urban life; only fragments of his works extant.

**Pomponius Mela.** See MELA.

**Pomuk,** Saint **John of.** See JOHN OF NEPOMUK.

**Pon'ce** (pôn'sā), **Manuel M.** 1886–1948. Mexican pianist and composer of symphonies, chamber music, rhapsodies, and songs.

**Pon'ce** (pôn'thā), **Pedro de.** 1520?–1584. French Benedictine monk, b. in Spain; first teacher of deaf mutes.

**Pon'ce de Le·ón'** (pôn'thā thā lā·ōn'; pôn'sā; *Angl.* pŏns' dē lē'ŭn), **Juan.** 1460?–1521. Spanish governor of Puerto Rico and discoverer of Florida, b. in León; went to America with Columbus on second voyage (1493); to Puerto Rico (1508); made governor (1510); founded San Juan (1511); with three ships set out (1513) to search for Bimini, a fabulous island on which was said to be located the Fountain of Youth; discovered Florida on Easter Sunday (Span. *Pascua Florida*) and coasted along east and west sides; visited Bahamas (1513). Made second expedition to Florida (1521); attempted settlement, but driven off by natives, and wounded; died on return to Cuba.

**Pon'ce de Le·ón'** (pôn'thā thā lā·ōn'), **Luis.** 1527–1591. Spanish Augustinian monk, scholar, and lyric poet; professor of Thomistic philosophy and of theology, U. of Salamanca; vicar-general of the Augustinian order, and (1591) provincial of the order in Castile. His works include lyrics, translations from Greek and Roman classics and from Italian authors, and translations of the Psalms, Proverbs, the Song of Solomon, the Book of Job.

**Pon'ce·let'** (pôns'lĕ'), **Jean Victor.** 1788–1867. French mathematician and engineer; published *Traité des Propriétés Projectives des Figures* (1822); developed principle of duality; named and vindicated geometrical continuity. Military engineer at Metz (1815–25); professor of mechanics, École de l'Application, Metz (1825–35); professor of applied mechanics, Paris (1838–48).

**Pon·chiel'li** (pông·kyĕl'lē), **Amilcare.** 1834–1886. Italian opera composer; best known among his operas are *I Promessi Sposi* (1856) and *La Gioconda* (1876).

**Pond** (pŏnd), **James Burton.** 1838–1903. American lecture manager, b. Cuba, N.Y.; served through Civil War; began managing lecturers (c. 1873); copurchaser of Redpath Lyceum Bureau, Boston (1875–79); opened independent office, New York (1879). Among lecturers under his management were Henry Ward Beecher, Samuel Clemens, Charles Sumner, Sir Arthur Conan Doyle, Henry M. Stanley, Matthew Arnold, Ian Maclaren, Anthony Hope.

**Pond, John.** 1767?–1836. English astronomer; demonstrated error in Greenwich mural quadrant (1806); astronomer royal (1811); installed mercury horizon (1821) and otherwise improved and modernized equipment; published catalogue of 1113 stars, determined with superior accuracy.

**Po'nia·tow'ski** (pô'nyä·tôf'skē). Name of Polish princely family of Italian origin, including: Prince **Stanisław Poniatowski** (1676–1762), general and diplomat; joined Charles XII of Sweden in support of Stanisław Leszczyński; fought at Poltava (1709); represented Charles XII at the Porte. His son **Stanisław** became king of Poland (see STANISLAS II AUGUSTUS). Another son, **Andrzej** (1735–1773), was a general in the Austrian army. Prince **Józef Antoni** (1763–1813), son of Andrzej, b. Warsaw; commander in Napoleon's army; fought against Russia and aided Kosciusko (1792–94); joined French army (1800); active against Russians, esp. as minister of war in duchy of Warsaw (1807) and in campaign against Moscow; wounded at Smolensk (1812) and showed great valor at Leipzig; marshal of France (1813). Prince **Józef Michał** (1816–1873), nephew of Józef Antoni; musical composer; naturalized Tuscan subject (1847); later, resided in Paris; made senator by Napoleon III. Wrote many operas (among them, *Don Desiderio*) and several masses.

**Pons** (pôɴs), **Jean Louis.** 1761–1831. French astronomer; director of Lucca (Italy) observatory (1819) and Florence observatory (1825); credited with discovery of 37 comets (1801–27).

**Pons, Li'ly'** (lē'lē'; *Angl.* lĭl'ĭ). 1904– . Operatic soprano, b. in Cannes, France; m. August Mesritz (1923; divorced 1933), Andre Kostelanetz (1938). Operatic debut, as Lakmé, at Mulhouse (France) Municipal Opera (1928); in New York, at Metropolitan Opera House, as Lucia (1931). Chief roles, Lucia in *Lucia di Lammermoor*, Rosina in *The Barber of Seville*, Gilda in *Rigoletto*.

**Pon'sard'** (pôɴ'sår'), **François.** 1814–1867. French poet and playwright; author of a translation of Byron's *Manfred*, and the plays *Lucrèce* (1843), *L'Honneur et l'Argent* (1853), *Lion Amoureux* (1866), etc.

**Pon·selle'** (pŏn·sĕl'), **Rosa Melba.** *Real surname* **Pon·zil'lo** (pôn·tsēl'lō). 1897– . American operatic soprano, b. Meriden, Conn.; m. Charles A. Jackson (1936); joined Metropolitan Opera Company, in role of Donna Leonora in *La Forza del Destino* (1918), singing opposite Caruso. London debut, as Norma in Bellini's *Norma* (1929). Other roles include Carmen and Aïda. Her sister **Car·mel'a** [kär·mĕl'*ȧ*] (1892– ), mezzo-soprano, joined Metropolitan Opera Company (1926); chief roles, Amneris in *Aïda*, Aldalgisa in *Norma*, Laura in *La Gioconda*.

**Pon'son·by** (pŭn's'n·bĭ). English family in Ireland, descended from Sir **John** (1608–1678), who as colonel of a regiment of cavalry accompanied Cromwell to Ireland (1649); received grants of land in Ireland; M.P. (1661). His son Sir **William** (1657–1724), member of Irish Parliament and of privy council (1715), became (1723) Baron **Bess'borough** [bĕz'brŭ] (Irish peerage) and 1st Viscount **Dun·can'non** (dŭn·kăn'ŭn). **John** (1713–1789), Irish political leader; great-grandson of Sir John (1608–1678); 2d son of Brabazon Ponsonby, 1st Earl of Bessborough; commissioner of revenue (1744–71); speaker of Irish House of Commons (1756–71); one of principal "undertakers," members of great families monopolizing government of Ireland; lost in contest for supremacy with adherents of marquis of Townshend, viceroy of Ireland (1767–72). **William Brabazon** (1744–1806), 1st Baron Ponsonby; eldest son of John Ponsonby; Whig leader; member of Irish and British parliaments; father of Sir **John** (1770?–1855), Viscount Ponsonby, diplomat, ambassador at Constantinople (1832–37) and at Vienna (1846–50), and of Sir **William** (1772–1815), major general, who led famous charge of Union brigade at Waterloo and was killed. **George** (1755–1817); brother of 1st Baron Ponsonby; educ. Cambridge; became a Whig leader; chancellor of Irish exchequer (1782); urged claims of Irish Catholics; led opposition to union of parliaments; lord chancellor of Ireland (1806); official leader of opposition in British House of Commons (1808–17). **John William** (1781–1847), 4th Earl of Bessborough and Viscount Duncannon; great-grandson of 1st earl; a Whig leader in House of Commons (1805–34); member of House of Lords (from 1834); home secretary under Lord Melbourne (1834–35); lord lieutenant of Ireland (1846–47). Sir **Henry Frederick** (1825–1895), nephew of 4th earl; served in Crimea (1855–56); major general (1868); private secretary to Queen Victoria (1870 ff.). His son **Arthur Augustus William Harry** (1871–1946), 1st Baron **Ponsonby of Shul'brede** (shŏŏl'brēd); page of honor to Queen Victoria (1882–87); educ. Oxford; in diplomatic service (1894–1902); private secretary to Campbell-Bannerman (1906–08); undersecretary for foreign affairs in Labor government (1924); parliamentary secretary, ministry of transport (1929–31); leader of opposition in House of Lords (1931–35); author of *The Camel and the Needle's Eye* (1909), *Democracy and Diplomacy* (1915), *Religion in Politics* (1921), *English Diaries* (1923), *Samuel Pepys* (1928), *Queen Victoria* (1933), *Life Here and Now* (1936), *Henry Ponsonby* (1942; James Tait Black memorial prize), etc. **Vere Brabazon** (1880–1956), 9th Earl of Bessborough and Viscount Duncannon; B.A., Cantab.; M.P. (1913–20); served in Gallipoli (1915) and on staff in France (1916–18); governor general of Canada (1931–35).

**Ponsonby, William.** 1546?–1604. English publisher.

**Pon'son' du Ter'rail'** (pôɴ'sôɴ' dü tĕ'rȧ'y'), Vicomte **Pierre Alexis.** 1829–1871. French novelist.

**Pon·ta'no** (pôn·tä'nô), **Giovanni,** *often called* **Gioviano.** *Lat.* **Jovianus Pon·ta'nus** (pŏn·tā'nŭs). 1426–1503. Italian humanist, poet, and statesman; held offices under Aragonese dynasty in Naples; state secretary to Ferdinand I of Naples (1486–94); author of Latin verse, inspired chiefly by his wife Stella, as *Eridanus,* also of a history of Ferdinand's reign, and didactic poems.

**Ponte, Jacopo da.** See Jacopo *or* Giacomo da BASSANO.

**Pon'té'cou'lant'** (pôɴ'tā'kōō'läɴ'), Comte **de. Louis Gustave Le Doul'cet'** (lē dōō'sĕ'). 1764–1853. French politician; member of National Convention (1792) and its president (1795); member of Council of Five Hundred (1795); senator (1805) and count of the Empire (1808); organized defense of northeastern frontier (1813). Member of House of Peers under the Restoration.

**Pon'ti·ac** (pŏn'tĭ·ăk). d. 1769. American Ottawa Indian chief; took part in a general Indian attack, historically known as Pontiac's War or Conspiracy, upon the British (1763), in which he led the Indians attacking Detroit; made peace (1766) and remained friendly with British.

**Pon'tian** (pŏn'shăn; -shĭ·ăn) *or* **Pon'ti·a'nus** (pŏn'shĭ·ā'nŭs), Saint. Pope (bishop of Rome; 230–235); banished to Sardinia by Emperor Maximinus.

**Pontius Pilate.** See PILATE.

**Pon'ton** (?pŏn't'n; -tŭn), **Mungo.** 1802–1880. Scottish inventor of method of permanent photography, based on discovery that sunlight renders potassium dichromate insoluble (1839).

**Pon·top'pi·dan** (pŏn·tŏp'ē·dän), **Erik.** 1698–1764. Danish theologian; bishop of Bergen (1747–55); vice-chancellor, U. of Copenhagen (1755). Among his works are *A Natural History of Norway* (1752–53) and *The Atlas of Denmark* (8 vols.).

**Pontoppidan, Henrik.** 1857–1943. Danish novelist; originally an engineer, began work in fiction (1881); shared with Karl Gjellerup the Nobel prize for literature (1917). Among his novels are *Soil* (1891), *The Promised Land* (1892), *Dommens Dag* (1895), *Lykke-Per* (3 vols., 1898–1905), and *Kingdom of the Dead* (5 parts, 1912–16).

**Pon·tor'mo** (pôn·tôr'mô), **Jacopo da.** *Real name* **Jacopo Car·ruc'ci** (kär·rōōt'chē). 1494–1557. Italian painter of Florentine school, b. Pontormo; pupil of Leonardo da Vinci, Piero di Cosimo, and Andrea del Sarto. His works include *Visitation, Deposition, Adam and Eve Driven from Paradise* (in Florence), *St. Sebastian* (Borghese Palace, Rome), *Venus and Cupid* (National Gallery, London), and portraits, as of Andrea del Sarto and Cosimo de' Medici.

**Pontus de Thiard** (*or* **Thyard** *or* **Tyard**). See THIARD.

**Pool, Jurian.** See under Rachel RUYSCH.

**Poole** (pōōl), **Ernest.** 1880–1950. American author, b. Chicago; newspaper correspondent in Germany and France (1915) and in Russia (1917). Author of the plays *None So Blind* and *A Man's Friends,* and the novels *The Harbor* (1915), *His Family* (1917; awarded Pulitzer prize, 1918), *Beggar's Gold* (1921), *Millions* (1922), *Danger* (1923), *Silent Storms* (1927), *Nurses on Horseback* (1932), *One of Us* (1934), *Giants Gone* (1942), etc.

**Poole, John.** 1786?–1872. English author of comedies and farces, including *Paul Pry* (1825) and *Lodgings for Single Gentlemen* (1829).

**Poole, Paul Falconer.** 1807–1879. English historical and genre painter.

**Poole, Reginald Lane, Reginald Stuart, Sophia,** and **Stanley Lane-.** See under Edward William LANE.

**Poole, William Frederick.** 1821–1894. American librarian, b. Salem, Mass.; assistant in Yale's Brothers in Unity Library (1847–49); began *Poole's Index to Periodical Literature* (1848; 3rd edition, 1882); librarian, Boston (1852–69), Cincinnati (1871–73), Chicago (1874–94); author of monographs on American colonial times.

**Poor** (pŏŏr; pōr), **Charles Lane.** 1866–1951. American astronomer, b. Hackensack, N.J.; lecturer and professor of astronomy (1903–10), professor of celestial mechanics (from 1910), Columbia. His works include *The Solar System* (1908), *Gravitation versus Relativity* (1922), *The Relativity Deflection of Light* (1926), *What Einstein Really Did* (1930), *Men Against the Rule* (1937).

**Poor, Henry Varnum.** 1812–1905. American economist, b. Andover, Me.; editor of *American Railroad Journal* (1849–62). With his son **Henry William** (1844–1915), began compilation and publication of railway statistics, the first "Poor's Manual," *Manual of the Railroads of the United States,* appearing in 1868; supplemented the manual with *Poor's Directory of Railway Officials* (1886–95), *Poor's Handbook of Investment Securities* (1890–92).

**Poor, Henry Varnum, III.** 1888–1970. American painter, b. Chapman, Kans.; painted twelve murals in fresco for U.S. Department of Justice building, and a large mural entitled *Conservation of American Wild Life* for U.S. Department of the Interior building.

**Poore** (pŏŏr; pōr), **Benjamin Andrew.** 1863–1940. American army officer; grad. U.S.M.A., West Point (1886); during World War I, commanded 7th infantry brigade, 4th division, in France (May–Nov., 1918); in Aisne-Marne, St.-Mihiel, and Meuse-Argonne offensives; served in army of occupation, Germany (1918–19).

**Poore, Benjamin Perley.** 1820–1887. American journalist, b. near Newburyport, Mass.; Washington correspondent for group of newspapers (from 1854), conducting column over name "Perley"; edited first issue of *Congressional Directory* (1869). Author of historical and biographical works.

**Poore, Henry Rankin.** 1859–1940. American painter; excelled in landscape and in figure and animal painting.

**Poor Richard.** See Benjamin FRANKLIN.

**Poor Robin.** Pseudonym of William WINSTANLEY.

**Poor′ten** (pōr′tĕn), **Hein ter.** 1887– . Commander in chief of the Royal Netherlands Indies' army at time of Japanese invasion (1942); b. in Java.

**Poorten-Schwartz, J. M. W. van der.** See Maarten MAARTENS.

**Poot** (pōt), **Huibert Cornelisz(oon).** 1689–1733. Dutch poet, of peasant birth; self-taught; published *Mengeldichten* (2 parts, 1716, 1727), and became known as "the Dutch Hesiod."

**Pope** (pōp), **Alexander.** 1688–1744. English poet, b. London, son of Roman Catholic linen draper; developed physical deformity as result of severe illness at age of 12; undermined health by overstudy. Attracted Wycherley's attention with his verse (1704); came to public notice on publication of *Pastorals* in Tonson's *Miscellany* (1709); won Addison's praise for the *Essay on Criticism* (1711) and a wide and sure reputation with brilliant mock-heroic poem *The Rape of the Lock* (1712); gained friendship of Swift with *Windsor Forest* (1713); with Swift and Arbuthnot, formed Scriblerus Club and collaborated on the *Memoirs of Martinus Scriblerus* (1741); earned independence with his translations of the *Iliad* (1715–20) and *Odyssey* (1725–26); removed (1719) with his mother to a villa at Twickenham. Jointly with Swift published *Miscellanies* (1727–32), parodies upon writers, which evoked storm of abusive and scurrilous retorts from those who thought themselves injured; answered these in famous lampoon the *Dunciad* (1728, 1742), keen and biting satire on dullness in general and on particular poetasters and wits, including Lewis Theobald, Colley Cibber, John Dennis, Richard Bentley, Aaron Hill. Under influence of his friend Lord Bolingbroke, attempted systematic survey of human nature, completing *Essay on Man* (1733), lines and couplets of which have become household quotations, and four *Moral Essays;* in his last works, *Imitations of Horace* (1733–39), became mouthpiece of his political friends in satirizing Walpole's adherents, indulged savage vindictiveness, as in attack upon his former friend, Lady Mary Wortley Montagu, and gross insult offered Lord Hervey. See also Thomas TICKELL.

**Pope, John Russell.** 1874–1937. American architect, b. New York City. Among buildings designed by him are: Scottish Rite Temple, in Washington, D.C.; Lincoln Memorial, in Hodgenville, Ky.; American Battle Monument, at Montfaucon, France; National Gallery of Art, Washington, D.C.

**Pope, Nathaniel.** 1784–1850. American jurist, b. Louisville, Ky.; adm. to bar; moved to Kaskaskia, Ill., to practice; U.S. district judge for Illinois (1819–50). His son **John** (1822–1892) was an army commander; grad. U.S.M.A., West Point (1842); brigadier general of volunteers (1861); commanded army of the Mississippi in operations to open up navigation (1862); major general of volunteers (1862); co-operated with Grant, Buell, and Halleck in move against Corinth, Miss. (1862); commanded army of Virginia, and was defeated at Second Manassas (Aug., 1862); relieved of command and sent to department of the Northwest; promoted major general, U.S. army (1882); retired (1886).

**Pope,** Sir **Thomas.** 1507?–1559. English court clerk; privy councilor in Queen Mary's reign; retained Queen Elizabeth's favor; bought Oxford house of abbey of Durham and with this initial site and building founded and endowed Trinity Coll., Oxford (chartered 1556).

**Pope,** Sir **William Jackson.** 1870–1939. English chemist; known for work in crystallography and in organic chemistry; prepared first optically active sulphur, tin, and selenium compounds; developed method for producing mustard gas in great quantities.

**Pope′-Hen′nes·sy** (pōp′hĕn′ĕ·sĭ), **Una,** *nee* **Birch** (bûrch). 1876–1949. English writer; D.B.E. (cr. 1920); author of *The Aristocratic Journey* (1931), *The Laird of Abbotsford* (1932), *Edgar Allen Poe* (1934), *The Closed City* (1938), *Agnes Strickland* (1940), *Durham Company* (1941).

**Pop′ham** (pŏp′ăm; pŏp″m), Sir **Henry Robert Moore Brooke-** (brŏŏk-). 1878–1953. British soldier; served in World War (1914–18); commandant, Royal Air Force Staff Coll. (1921–26); air officer in chief command of air defense of Great Britain (1933–35); inspector general, Royal Air Force (1935–36); governor and commander in chief, Kenya (1937–39); air chief marshal, in command of entire Far East area (1940–42).

**Popham,** Sir **John.** 1531?–1607. English judge; solicitor general (1579); speaker of House of Commons (1580); attorney general (1581); lord chief justice (1592); presided at trials of Sir Walter Raleigh and Guy Fawkes; advocate of transportation system for convicts.

**Po·pov′** (pŭ·pôf′), **Aleksandr Stepanovich.** 1859–1905. Russian pioneer in radio; constructed sensitive filings coherer for detecting signals sent out by hertzian waves (1895); first to use wire high in air as an antenna.

**Pop·pae′a Sa·bi′na** (pŏ·pē′ȧ sȧ·bī′nȧ). d. 65 or 66 A.D. Roman woman; wife of Rufius Crispinus; became mistress of Otho, divorced her husband, and married Otho; became mistress of Nero, divorced Otho, and married Nero; died as result of a kick from Nero.

**Pöp′pel·mann** (pûp′ĕl·män), **Matthäus Daniel.** 1662–1736. German architect; architect of Augustus the Strong (1705); regarded as one of greatest masters of baroque style. Chief work, pavilion of the Zwinger (unfinished) in Dresden.

**Poquelin, Jean Baptiste.** See MOLIÈRE.

**Porbus.** See POURBUS.

**Por′ché′** (pôr′shā′), **François.** 1877–1944. French poet and playwright.

**Por′ches·ter** (pôr′chĭs·tẽr; -chĕs-), Viscounts. See under HERBERT family, 3.

**Por′ci·a** (pôr′shĭ·ȧ; -shȧ). d. 42 B.C. Daughter of Cato of Utica; wife of Bibulus, then of Brutus, assassin of Julius Caesar; committed suicide after battle of Philippi. Introduced (under spelling **Por′ti·a** [pōr′shĭ·ȧ; -shȧ; pôr′-]) by Shakespeare in his *Julius Caesar.*

**Porcupine, Peter.** Pseudonym of William COBBETT.

**Por′de·no′ne** (pōr′dā·nō′nā), **Giovanni Antonio da.** *Real name* **Giovanni Antonio de' Sac′chi** (dā säk′kē), *erroneously* **Li·ci′nio** (lē·chē′nyō). *Also called* **Re·gil′lo** (rā·jēl′lō). 1483–1539. Venetian painter, b. at Pordenone, Friuli; employed at Venice, Cremona, Ferrara, and in Fiuli. Among his works are a series of frescoes from the New Testament in Church of Castel Colalto near Conegliano, frescoes in cathedrals at Treviso and Cremona, frescoes from the lives of the Virgin and St. Catherine in Church of Madonna di Campagna at Piacenza, and portraits.

**Por′phy·ry** (pôr′fĭ·rĭ). *Lat.* **Por·phyr′i·us** (pôr·fĭr′ĭ·ŭs). *Orig. name* **Mal′chus** (măl′kŭs). 232?–?304. Greek scholar and Neoplatonic philosopher, b. in Syria; studied under Cassius Longinus and, in Rome (262 A.D.), under Plotinus; lectured on philosophy in Rome; vigorously defended paganism and opposed Christianity. Author of *Adversus Christianos* (15 books, only fragments of which are extant), of lives of Plotinus and commentaries on Aristotle and on Homer, and of *Chronicles* (from capture of Troy down to 270 A.D.).

**Por′po·ra** (pōr′pō·rä), **Niccolo** *or* **Nicola.** 1686–1766. Italian composer and teacher of singing; teacher in

Naples (1719), Venice (1725, 1744), Vienna and Dresden (1728), London (1733–36), Vienna (1745–47). Composer of 53 operas, 6 oratorios, 6 chamber symphonies, 12 violin concertos, and much church music, but best known as a singing teacher.

**Por′ras** (pôr′räs), **Belisario.** 1856–1942. Panamanian jurist; minister to U.S. (1910); president of Panama (1912–16, 1920–24), acting president (1918–20).

**Por′rée′** (pô′rā′), **Gilbert de La.** *Lat.* **Gilbertus Por′re·ta′nus** (pŏr′ē·tā′nŭs). 1070–1154. French scholastic theologian; bishop of Poitiers (1142); considered as influential in introducing Aristotelian philosophy in France.

**Por′se·na** (pôr′sĕ·nȧ) *or* **Por·sen′na** (pôr·sĕn′ȧ), **Lars.** King of Clusium in late 6th century B.C.; according to tradition, attacked Rome in effort to restore Tarquinius Superbus as king of Rome and was prevented from entering the city by the heroism of Horatius Cocles (*q.v.*).

**Por′son** (pôr′s'n), **Richard.** 1759–1808. English classical scholar; became widely known by his *Letters to Archdeacon Travis* (1788–89), an acute piece of criticism in defense of Gibbon's position on the genuineness of *1 John* v. 7; regius professor of Greek, Cambridge (1792). Edited four plays of Euripides; edited Aeschylus (1795); made distinct contributions to knowledge of iambic and trochaic verse; by minute collations of Greek texts made valuable emendations.

**Por′ta** (pôr′tä), **Baccio della.** See Fra BARTOLOMMEO.

**Porta, Carlo.** 1775–1821. Italian poet; leading Milanese dialect poet; known esp. for dialect satires against nobility, clergy, and classicists.

**Porta, Giacomo della.** 1541–1604. Italian architect; pupil of Vignola; completed various works begun by Vignola, including the façades of the churches Santa Caterina de'Funari and Il Gesù; completed the cupola of St. Peter's (1588–90; according to Michelangelo's model) and the Palazzo Farnese (begun by Michelangelo). Other works include Villa Aldobrandini (near Frascati) and several fountains in Rome.

**Porta, Giambattista della.** 1538?–1615. Italian physicist; made important physical observations, although much of his work was from point of view of magic and alchemy; first to recognize heating effect of light rays; made improvements in the camera obscura, although he did not invent it.

**Porta,** Fra **Guglielmo della.** 1510?–1577. Italian sculptor; known esp. for tomb of Pope Paul III (in choir of St. Peter's).

**Por′taels** (pôr′tȧls), **Jean François. 1818–1895.** Belgian historical and portrait painter.

**Por′tal** (pōr′t'l; pôr′-), **Charles Frederick Algernon.** 1st Viscount **Portal of Hungerford.** 1893–1971. British air chief marshal; director of organization in air ministry (1937–38); chief of bomber command (1940); chief of air staff (1940–45).

**Por′ta·la′** (pôr′tä·lä′), **Gaspar de.** See PORTOLÁ.

**Por′ta′lis′** (pôr′tȧ′lēs′), **Jean Étienne Marie.** 1745–1807. French jurist and statesman; member of Council of Ancients (1795–97); aided in drafting the *Code Civil* (1800 ff.). His son Comte **Joseph Marie** (1778–1858) was a councilor of state and count of the Empire under Napoleon; a peer of France, guardian of the seals, and minister of foreign affairs under Louis XVIII; first president of Court of Cassation (1829–51); senator (1851).

**Porte Crayon.** Pseudonym of David Hunter STROTHER.

**Por′te·ous** (pōr′tē·ŭs; pôr′-; -tyŭs), **John.** d. 1736. Scottish captain of Edinburgh city guard who fired on crowd at execution of a smuggler, Andrew Wilson, killing or wounding nearly thirty persons (1736), was sentenced to death, reprieved by Queen Caroline, taken from prison and hanged by an armed group in disguise. Incident (frequently called the Porteous riots) developed in Scott's *Heart of Midlothian.*

**Por′ter** (pōr′tẽr; pôr′-), **Andrew.** 1743–1813. American Revolutionary officer; in action at Trenton, Princeton, Brandywine, and Germantown; with General Sullivan in central New York campaign against Indians (1779). A grandson, **Horace** (1837–1921), was an army officer and diplomat; grad. U.S.M.A., West Point (1860); served through Civil War, aide-de-camp to Gen. Grant (1864–65), awarded Congressional medal of honor for gallantry at Chicamauga; after war, continued as military secretary to President Grant (to 1872); railroad and street railway executive (1872–97); U.S. ambassador to France (1897–1905).

**Porter, Arthur Kingsley.** 1883–1933. American archaeologist; professor, Harvard (1920–33). Author of *Mediaeval Architecture* (2 vols., 1908), *Lombard Architecture* (4 vols., 1915–17; awarded Grande Médaille de Vermeil by Société Française d'Archéologie), *Spanish Romanesque Sculpture* (2 vols., 1928), etc.

**Porter, Charles Talbot.** 1826–1910. American mechanical engineer; made successful use of high rotative speed in stationary engines after calculating inertia forces of reciprocating engine mechanism; invented central counterpoise governor for steam engines and an isochronous centrifugal governor for marine engines.

**Porter, Cole.** 1893-1964. American composer and lyricist, b. Peru, Ind.; composer of songs and music for *See America First* (1916), *Hitchy-Koo* (1919), *Wake Up and Dream* (1929), *Nymph Errant* (1933), *Anything Goes* (1934), *Red Hot and Blue* (1936), *Dubarry Was a Lady* (1939), *Panama Hattie* (1940), *Let's Face It* (1941), *Something For the Boys* (1942), etc.

**Porter, David.** 1780–1843. American naval officer, b. Boston; in War of 1812, commanded the *Essex,* which raided British commerce along Atlantic coast and cruised in Pacific, first U.S. naval vessel in Pacific waters; was captured off Valparaiso, Chile (Mar. 28, 1813). Commander in chief, West India squadron suppressing piracy (1823–25); court-martialed and suspended from duty for retaliatory action against Spanish authorities in Puerto Rico (1825–26); resigned from U.S. navy (Aug. 18, 1826). In Mexican naval service (1826–29). U.S. consul general to Algiers (1830); U.S. chargé d'affaires at Constantinople and later (1839) U.S. minister to Turkey; died at Constantinople. His son **David Dixon** (1813–1891) was also a naval officer; served under his father in the West Indies and in the Mexican navy; in Mexican war, served at Vera Cruz and Tabasco; in Civil War, commanded mortar fleet under Farragut at New Orleans and on the Mississippi (1862), aided in reduction of Vicksburg (1863), promoted rear admiral (July 4, 1863), commanded naval forces in attack on Fort Fisher (Dec., 1864–Jan., 1865); superintendent of U.S. Naval Academy (1865–69) and greatly improved curriculum and methods of instruction there; vice-admiral (1866) and admiral (1870); chairman of naval board of inspection (1877–91).

**Porter, Edwin S.** 1870–1941. American inventor; collaborated with Thomas A. Edison in developing motion-picture camera; made for Edison (1899) first story film, *The Life of an American Fireman.*

**Porter, Eleanor,** *nee* **Hodg′man** (hŏj′măn). 1868–1920. American fiction writer, b. Littleton, N.H.; m. John Lyman Porter (1892). Author of many short stories, and the novels *Cross Currents* (1907), *The Story of Marco* (1911), *Pollyanna* (1913), *Just David* (1916), *The Tie that Binds* (1919), etc.

**Porter, Fitz-John.** 1822–1901. Nephew of David

Porter. American army commander, b. Portsmouth, N.H.; grad. U.S.M.A., West Point (1845); brigadier general of volunteers (May, 1861); served in Shenandoah Valley, Peninsular campaign (1862); at Second Manassas, accused by Gen. Pope of failure to carry out orders; court-martialed and cashiered from army (Jan. 21, 1863). On review of case (1879), procured favorable report. Police commissioner, New York City (1884–88).

**Porter, Gene,** *nee* **Strat′ton** (străt′'n). 1868–1924. American author, b. in Wabash County, Ind.; m. Charles Darwin Porter (1886). Author of *The Song of the Cardinal* (1902), *Freckles* (1904), *At the Foot of the Rainbow* (1908), *A Girl of the Limberlost* (1909), *The Harvester* (1911), *Laddie* (1913), *Friends in Feathers* (1917), *The White Flag* (1923), *The Keeper of the Bees* (1925), and a volume of poems, *The Fire Bird* (1922).

**Porter, George.** 1920– British chemist. At U. of Cambridge (1949–54), U. of Sheffield (1955–63), The Royal Inst., London (1963– ). Awarded Nobel prize in chemistry (1967) with M. Eigen and R. Norrish.

**Porter, Harold Everett.** *Pseudonym* **Hol′wor′thy Hall** (hŏl′wûr′thĭ hôl). 1887–1936. American writer, b. Boston; A.B., Harvard (1909); served in air corps (captain) in World War I. Author of *Pepper* (1915), *Dormie One* (1917), *The Man Nobody Knew* (1919), *Egan* (1920), *Rope* (1921), *Colossus* (1930), and many short stories.

**Porter, Henry.** fl. 1596–1599. English dramatist; wrote plays (1596–99) for Henslowe for the Admiral's Men (earl of Nottingham's players); associate of Henry Chettle; author of *The Two Angry Women of Abington* (1599).

**Porter, Horace.** See under Andrew PORTER.

**Porter, Jane.** 1776–1850. English novelist; gained popularity with first romance, *Thaddeus of Warsaw* (1803), and immense success with national romance, *The Scottish Chiefs* (1810), which was translated into German and Russian; later novels include *The Field of Forty Footsteps* (1828). Her sister **Anna Maria** (1780–1832), novelist, wrote a series of works including *The Lake of Killarney* (1804), *The Hungarian Brothers* (1807), and *Barony* (1830). Their brother Sir **Robert Ker** (1777–1842), painter of altarpieces and battle scenes, was historical painter to czar of Russia (1804–06); traveled to Persia and Baghdad (1817–20); British consul in Venezuela (1826–41); published accounts of travels, and graphic narrative of campaign in Russia during 1812.

**Porter, Jer·main′** (jûr·mān′) **Gildersleeve.** 1852–1933. American astronomer; director, Cincinnati observatory (1884–1930); known esp. for his work in astrometry.

**Porter, Katherine Anne.** 1890– . American writer, esp. of short stories, b. near San Antonio, Tex.; author of *Flowering Judas* (1930); *Pale Horse, Pale Rider* (1939); *The Leaning Tower* (1944); *Ship of Fools* (1962); *Collected Short Stories* (1965); etc.

**Porter, Noah.** 1811–1892. American Congregational clergyman and educator, b. Farmington, Conn.; president of Yale (1871–86). Editor in chief, *Webster's American Dictionary of the English Language*, popularly known as *Webster's Unabridged* (1864), and of *Webster's International Dictionary of the English Language* (1890). Author of *The Human Intellect* (1868), *The Sciences of Nature versus the Science of Man* (1871), *The Elements of Moral Science...* (1885), *Kant's Ethics* (1886), etc. His brother **Samuel** (1810–1901) was a successful teacher of the deaf, at Hartford, New York, and Washington. His sister **Sarah** (1813–1900) was founder (1843) of Miss Porter's School for Girls, at Farmington, Conn.

**Porter, Peter Buell.** 1773–1844. American political leader; practiced law, Canandaigua, N.Y. (1795), Buffalo (1809); member, U.S. House of Representatives (1809–13); served in War of 1812, with distinction at Chippewa, Lundy's Lane, and Fort Erie; again in U.S. House of Representatives (1815–16); U.S. secretary of war (1828–29).

**Porter, Robert Percival.** 1852–1917. Journalist, b. at Norwich, England; to U.S. as a boy; founded and edited New York *Press* (1887–94); superintendent, eleventh U.S. census (1889–93); with London *Times* (1904–17).

**Porter, Rodney Robert.** 1917– . English biochemist, educated at Liverpool and Cambridge universities; Whitley Prof. of Biochemistry, Oxford U. (1967). Shared 1972 Nobel prize for medicine and physiology with G. M. Edelman for work in immunology.

**Porter, Samuel.** See under Noah PORTER.

**Porter, Sarah.** See under Noah PORTER.

**Porter, William Sydney.** *Pseudonym* **O. Hen′ry** (ō′ hĕn′rĭ). 1862–1910. American short-story writer, b. Greensboro, N.C.; left school at fifteen; employed in drugstore (to 1882); moved to Texas; settled in Austin; employed as clerk and bookkeeper (1885–87), draftsman in a Texas land office (1887–91), and bank teller (1891–94). Failed in editorship of humorous weekly the *Rolling Stone* (1894–95); columnist on Houston *Daily Post* (1895–96). Tried, convicted, and imprisoned (1898) for three years and three months for embezzlement when he was bank teller in Austin. To New York (1902) and devoted himself to short-story writing, achieving great success. His stories, appearing mainly in current magazines, were collected in *Cabbages and Kings* (1904), *The Four Million* (1906), *Heart of the West* (1907), *The Trimmed Lamp* (1907), *The Gentle Grafter* (1908), *The Voice of the City* (1908), *Options* (1909), *Roads of Destiny* (1909), *Whirligigs* (1910), *Strictly Business* (1910), *Sixes and Sevens* (1911), *Rolling Stones* (1913), *Waifs and Strays* (1917), *Postscripts* (1923).

**Por′tes Gil** (pôr′tās hēl′), **Emilio.** 1891– . Mexican lawyer and political leader; minister of the interior under President Calles (1924–28); provisional president of Mexico on assassination of General Obregon (Dec., 1928–Feb., 1930); minister of foreign affairs under President Cárdenas (1935).

**Por′te·us** (pōr′tē·ŭs; pôr′-; -tyŭs), **Beilby.** 1731–1808. English prelate; B.A., Cantab. (1752); won Seatonian prize with poem *Death* (1759), including the familiar line, "War its thousands slays, Peace, its ten thousands"; chaplain to George III (1769); bishop of Chester (1776–87), of London (1787–1808).

**Por·than′** (pŏr·tän′), **Henrik Gabriel.** 1739–1804. Finnish scholar; regarded as founder of study of Finnish language and literature.

**Portia.** See PORCIA.

**Portinari, Beatrice.** See BEATRICE PORTINARI.

**Port′land** (pōrt′lănd; pôrt′-), Earls and dukes of. English earldom held (1633–88) by Weston family (see Richard WESTON), revived (1689) and bestowed by William III upon William Bentinck (*q.v.*); held by Bentinck family when merged (1716) with dukedom of Portland (see Henry BENTINCK).

**Portland,** Titular earl of. = Sir *Edward Herbert* (1648?–1698), under HERBERT family, 4.

**Por′to·gal′lo** (pōr′tō·gäl′lō), **Marcantonio.** *Italianized name of* **Marcos Antônio da Fon·se′ca Por·tu·gal′** (thȧ fōN·sā′kȧ pŏŏr·tōō·gäl′). *Erroneously called* **Marcos Antonio Si·mão′** (sē·mouN′). 1769?–?1829. Portuguese composer; conductor at Lisbon (1799–1810), Rio de Janeiro, Brazil (1810–13), Vera Cruz, Mexico (1813–15). Composed esp. operas, masses, and religious music.

**Por′to·lá′** (pôr′tō·lä′), **Gaspar de.** 1723?–?1784. Spanish soldier in America; appointed governor of the Californias (1767); made thousand-mile march from Velicatá in Lower California to Monterey in Upper California, founding San Diego and Monterey (1769); left region (1770); governor of Puebla (1776).

**Por'to'-Riche'** (pôr'tō'rēsh'), **Georges de.** 1849–1930. French playwright; author of psychological dramas, including *La Chance de Françoise* (1889), *Amoureuse* (1891), *Le Passé* (1897), *Le Vieil Homme* (1911), *Le Marchand d'Estampes* (1917).

**Portsmouth,** Duchess of. See Louise Renée de KÉROUALLE.

**Portugal, Marcos Antônio da Fonseca.** See Marcantonio PORTOGALLO.

**Po'rus** (pō'rŭs) *or* **Po'ros** (-rŏs). d. 321? B.C. Indian king who ruled a country in the Indus valley (in modern northern Punjab); opposed Alexander in his invasion of India; his great army, with 200 elephants, completely defeated (326 B.C.) in the battle of the Hydaspes by Alexander's small Macedonian force; his life spared and kingdom restored; later assassinated by a Macedonian satrap.

**Po'sching·er** (pôsh'ĭng·ẽr), **Heinrich von.** 1845–1911. German journalist and historian; in government service (1876–1901), at first as journalistic worker for Bismarck. Author of books on Bismarck and Bismarck's policies.

**Po'sey** (pō'zĭ), **Thomas.** 1750–1818. American Revolutionary officer and politician, b. in Fairfax County, Va.; served through the Revolution; at the battle of Saratoga and storming of Stony Point; brigadier general in war against Indians in the Northwest (1793–94); major general of volunteers (1809); U.S. senator from Louisiana (1812–13); governor of Indiana Territory (1813–16).

**Pos'i·do'ni·us** (pŏs'ĭ·dō'nĭ·ŭs) *or* **Pos'ei·do'ni·us** (pŏs'ī-). Greek Stoic philosopher of early 1st century B.C., b. in Syria; taught in Rhodes; wrote general history (52 books) of period 146–88 B.C., treatise on natural philosophy (15 books), essay on the gods (13 books), etc. None of his works is extant.

**Pos'se·vi'no** (pōs'sā·vē'nō), **Antonio.** 1534–1611. Italian writer and ecclesiastical diplomat; joined Jesuit order (1559); to Sweden (1577), Russia (1581), Poland, Hungary, and Germany as papal diplomatic representative.

**Post** (pōst), **Albert Hermann.** 1839–1895. German jurist; regarded as a founder of study of comparative law.

**Post** (pōst), **Emily,** *nee* **Price** (prīs). 1873–1960. American writer and columnist, b. Baltimore, Md.; contributor to newspapers and magazines, esp. of articles on manners and social etiquette; author of *Etiquette* (1st ed., 1922), and other books.

**Post, George Browne.** 1837–1913. American architect, b. New York City; served in Union army in Civil War (1861–65). Architect in New York City (from 1868); a pioneer in introducing elevators in buildings, using iron floor beams, supplying steam heating in business buildings. Examples of his work are New York Produce Exchange, Vanderbilt residence and Huntington residence, Manufactures and Liberal Arts building at Chicago World's Fair (1893), College of the City of New York buildings, Pulitzer building, St. Paul building (at the time, 1897–99, the tallest in New York), New York Stock Exchange, Wisconsin State Capitol.

**Post, George Edward.** 1838–1909. American medical missionary in Tripoli (1863–67); professor, Beirut (1868–1909); noted linguist and botanist; taught in Arabic and translated many English medical texts into Arabic; edited for five years Arabic medical journal *Al-Tabib.*

**Post, Melville Davisson.** 1871–1930. American lawyer and detective-story writer; author of *The Strange Schemes of Randolph Mason* (1896), *The Man of Last Resort* (1897), *The Mystery at the Blue Villa* (1919), *The Man Hunters* (1926), *The Bradmoor Murder* (1929), etc.

**Post, Wiley.** 1900–1935. American aviator; twice flew around the world; killed with Will Rogers (*q.v.*) in airplane crash.

**Postl, Karl Anton.** See Charles SEALSFIELD.

**Po·ta'nin** (pŭ·tá'nyĭn), **Grigori Nikolaevich.** 1835–?1914. Russian explorer of central Asia, esp. Mongolia and western Tibet.

**Po·te'khin** (pŭ·tyā'ĸyĭn), **Aleksei Antipovich.** 1829–1908. Russian novelist and playwright; among his novels are *The Peasant Woman of Kazan, Brother and Sister, The Noble Poor,* and *Vampire of the Village;* among his plays, *The Voice of the People is not the Voice of God* and *A Vacant Place.* His brother **Nikolai Antipovich** (1834–1896) was also a writer, notably of comedies.

**Po·tëm'kin** (pŭ·tyôm'kyĭn), **Grigori Aleksandrovich.** 1739–1791. Russian statesman; officer in Horse Guards; conspirator in plot against Peter III (1762); distinguished himself against Turks (1769) and became chief favorite of Catherine II (1771); created field marshal (1784); constructed fleet in Black Sea; planned colonization of south Russian steppes; annexed Crimea; built arsenal of Kherson and harbor of Sevastopol; commander in chief of Russian army against Turkey (1787–91); created prince of Tauris (1787).

**Pot'gie'ter** (pŏt'ĸē'tẽr), **Andries Hendrik.** 1800?–1853. Boer colonizer; led farmers in exodus (1836) to Vet River; expelled the Matabele (1837) with heavy losses and occupied the country across Vaal River; migrated (1838) to Mooi River and (1845) towards Delagoa Bay; after British annexation of Natal received more independent Boers; joined (1852) in pact with Pretorius (*q.v.*) for co-operation in uniting the Transvaal.

**Pot'gie'ter** (pŏt'gē'tẽr), **Everhardus Johannes.** 1808–1875. Dutch writer; cofounder of magazine *De Muzen* (1834–36), later superseded by *De Gids* (*The Guide*), which became leading literary monthly of the Netherlands; contributor to this periodical. Among his books are *Liedekens van Bontekoe* (verse, 1840), *Het Noorden in Omtrekken en Tafereelen* (prose, 2 parts, 1836–40), *Ter Gedachtenis* (verse, 1863), *Proza 1837–45* (2 parts, 1864), and *Poëzij 1827–74* (2 parts, 1868–74).

**Po'thier'** (pô'tyā'), Dom **Joseph.** 1835–1923. French music scholar; made special study of religious music and published *Les Mélodies Grégoriennes d'après la Tradition* (1880), *Liber Gradualis* (1883), etc.

**Pothier, Robert Joseph.** 1699–1772. French jurist and author of legal treatises.

**Pot'i·phar** (pŏt'ĭ·fẽr; -fär). *In Douay Version* **Put'i·phar** (pŭt'-). In Bible (*Genesis* xxxix), an Egyptian official to whom Joseph was sold as a slave and whose wife attempted to seduce Joseph.

**Po·toc'ka** (pô·tôts'kä), Countess **Anna,** *nee* **Tycz·kie'-wicz** (tĭch·kyĕ'vĕch). 1776–1867. Niece of Marshal Poniatowski (*q.v.*). Polish writer. Chief work, *Memoirs* (covering period 1794–1820; esp. notable for account of Napoleon's stay in Warsaw, 1806–07).

**Po·toc'ki** (pô·tôts'kē). Distinguished Polish family, including: **Ignacy** (1750?–1809), one of those who drafted constitution of May 3, 1791, and supported Kosciusko in his rebellion. **Stanisław Szczęsny** (1752–1805), commander of Polish artillery; enlisted aid of Catherine II of Russia in Poland (1793), but forced by insurrection (1794) to leave Poland; sentenced to death for treason; returned to Poland after Russian army under Suvorov suppressed insurrection, and was appointed Russian field marshal by Catherine (1795). Stanisław's wife, **Zofja** (1766?–1822), of Greek descent, m. 1st Count de Witt (c. 1787; divorced 1790), 2d Stanisław Szczęsny Potocki (1790), known widely for her beauty and wit. **Stanisław Kostka** (1757?–1821), brother of Ignacy; collaborated with Ignacy and others in drafting constitution of May 3, 1791; became head of educational system in duchy of Warsaw (1807) and minister of public instruction in kingdom of Poland (1815). **Jan** (1761–1815), historian and archaeologist. **Alfred** (1817–1889); Austrian minister of agriculture (1867–70) and premier (1870–71).

**Potocki, Wacław.** 1622?–?1697. Polish poet; author of devotional verse, epigrams, narrative poetry, and, most notably, an epic (*Wojna Chocimska*) on the victory over the Turks at Chocim (*Rumanian* Hotin).

**Pott** (pŏt), **August Friedrich.** 1802–1887. German philologist; professor, Halle (1833). Chief works, *Etymologische Forschungen* (2 vols., 1833–36), *Die Zigeuner in Europa und Asien* (2 vols., 1844–45), etc.

**Pott** (pŏt), **Percivall.** 1714–1788. English surgeon; introduced improvements making surgery more humane, took steps toward abolishing extensive use of escharotics and cautery; suffered a particular kind of fracture of ankle, still called *Pott's fracture;* gave clinical description of a spinal affection known as *Pott's disease.*

**Pot'ter** (pŏt'ẽr), **Alonzo.** 1800–1865. American Protestant Episcopal clergyman, b. in Dutchess County, N.Y.; consecrated bishop of Pennsylvania (1845); established Episcopal hospital (1860) and a divinity school (1863) in Philadelphia. His brother **Horatio** (1802–1887) was also a Protestant Episcopal clergyman; consecrated bishop of New York (1854). Alonzo's son **Robert Brown** (1829–1887) was a Union general in the Civil War. Another son of Alonzo, **Eliphalet Nott** (1836–1901), was a Protestant Episcopal clergyman and educator; president of Union Coll. (1871–84) and Hobart Coll. (1884–97). A third son of Alonzo, **Henry Codman** (1835–1908), was also a Protestant Episcopal clergyman; pastorates, Troy, N.Y. (1859–66), Trinity Church, Boston (1866–68), Grace Church, New York (1868–83); consecrated assistant bishop of New York (1883), to aid his uncle Bishop Horatio Potter; succeeded as bishop of New York on his uncle's death (1887); initiated work on Cathedral of St. John the Divine, protested to mayor of New York on vice and corruption in New York (1899) with resulting investigation by Committee of Fifteen and election of Seth Low as a mayor pledged to reform, established respectable places where poor could buy intoxicating liquors (1904), protected liberal churchmen in his diocese; author of *The Scholar and the State* (1897), *The Modern Man and His Fellow Man* (1903), etc.

**Potter, Edward Clark.** 1857–1923. American sculptor, b. New London, Conn.; collaborated with Daniel Chester French in sculptures for Chicago World's Fair (1893); also in statues of Grant in Philadelphia, Hooker in Boston, and Devens in Worcester, Mass. Best known as sculptor of animals, especially horses. Among his equestrian statues are McClellan in Philadelphia, General Kearny in Washington, D.C., Custer in Monroe, Mich., Slocum in Gettysburg, Pa. His *Sleeping Faun* is in the Chicago Art Institute; his *Lions* stand on either side of the entrance to New York Public Library.

**Potter, Louis McClellan.** 1873–1912. American sculptor, b. Troy, N.Y.; made studies of Tlingit Indians in southern Alaska, carving *The Hunter with his Dogs, The Spirit of the Night;* designed the Horace Wells Memorial, Hartford, Conn.; carved bust of Samuel Clemens.

**Pot'ter** (pŏt'ẽr), **Paul** *or* **Paulus.** 1625–1654. Dutch painter; famous for paintings of animals; best-known canvas, *The Young Bull* (in the museum at The Hague).

**Potter, Paul Meredith.** 1853–1921. Journalist and playwright, b. Brighton, England; on editorial staff, Chicago *Tribune* (1888). Author of *The Ugly Duckling* (1890), *The American Minister* (1892), *The Victoria Cross* (1894), *The Conquerors* (1898), the musical comedies *The Queen of the Moulin Rouge* and *The Girl from Rectors*, etc.

**Potter, Robert Brown.** See under Alonzo POTTER.

**Pott'hast** (pŏt'hăst), **Edward Henry.** 1857–1927. American landscape painter, b. Cincinnati.

**Pot'tier'** (pô'tyā'), **Edmond.** 1855–1934. French archaeologist; directed excavations at Myrina in Asia Minor (1877–1880).

**Pottier, Eugène.** 1816–1887. French song writer and politician; member of the Paris Commune (1871); his poems collected under title *Chants Révolutionnaires* (1887); among his songs is the *International* (1871; music by Adolphe Degeyter), adopted as the rallying song of Communism.

**Pot'tin·ger** (pŏt''n·jẽr; -ĭn·jẽr), Sir **Henry.** 1789–1856. British soldier and diplomat, b. in County Down, Ireland; served during Maratha War; political agent in Sindh (1836–40); served with distinction in Opium War; first British governor of Hong Kong (1843); governor of Cape of Good Hope (1846–47); governor of Madras (1847–54).

**Pou'chet'** (pōō'shĕ'), **Félix Archimède.** 1800–1872. French naturalist; author of works on the natural history of the nightshade, applied botany, and the anatomy and physiology of mollusks; his *Hétérogénie ou Traité de la Génération Spontanée* (1859), in which he advocated doctrine of spontaneous generation, gave rise to controversy with Pasteur. His son **Georges** (1833–1894) was professor of comparative anatomy at Muséum d'Histoire Naturelle (from 1879).

**Pou'gin'** (pōō'zhăN'), **Arthur.** *In full* **François Auguste Arthur Pa'roisse'–Pou'gin'** (pȧ'rwȧs'-). 1834–1921. French musician and music scholar; published studies of composers, as *Meyerbeer* (1864), *Bellini* (1867), *Rossini* (1871), *Rousseau* (1901); compiled *Dictionnaire Historique et Pittoresque du Théâtre* (1880); wrote treatises on musical history.

**Pouil'let'** (pōō'yĕ'), **Claude Servais Mathias.** 1791–1868. French physicist; professor of physics, the Sorbonne (1838); invented a pyrheliometer; studied electric currents and compressibility of gases. His nephew **Louis Marie Eugène Pouillet** (1835–1905) was a lawyer; authority in copyright, trade-mark, and patent law.

**Pou'jou'lat'** (pōō'zhōō'lȧ'), **Jean Joseph François.** 1808–1880. French writer; editor of *Quotidienne;* author of *Histoire de Jérusalem* (1840–42), *Histoire de la Révolution Française* (1847), etc.

**Pou'lenc'** (pōō'lăNk'), **Francis.** 1899–1963. French composer of sonatas, a one-act comédie-bouffe (*Le Gendarme Incompris*), a ballet, marche militaire, a number of piano works, and songs. **See Arthur** HONEGGER.

**Poulet.** Variant of PAULET.

**Poul'sen** (poul's'n), **Frederik. 1876–1950.** Danish archaeologist; director, section of antiques, in glyptotheca of Karlsburg (1926 ff.). Author of *Under Greek Skies* (1908), *The Oracle of Delphi* (1919), *Egyptian Art* (1924), *Crete-Mycenean Art* (1926), etc.

**Poulsen, Valdemar.** 1869–1942. Danish electrical engineer, b. Copenhagen; invented telegraphone, an instrument for recording and reproducing sound by local magnetization of a steel wire, disk, or ribbon (1898); invented an arc generator for high-frequency continuous electrical oscillations, used in wireless telegraphy and telephony (1903).

**Poul'son** (poul's'n), **Zachariah.** 1761–1844. American publisher, b. Philadelphia; editor and publisher, *Poulson's American Daily Advertiser*, Philadelphia (1800–39), successor to the *Pennsylvania Packet*, first daily newspaper in U.S.; published *Poulson's Town and Country*

*Almanac* (1788–1801) and *Minutes* of the Pennsylvania constitutional convention of 1789.

**Poul'ton** (pōl't'n; -tŭn) Sir **Edward Bagnall.** 1856–1943. English zoologist. Author of *The Colours of Animals* (1890), *Charles Darwin and the Theory of Natural Selection* (1896), *Essays on Evolution* (1908), etc.

**Pound** (pound), Sir **Dudley,** *in full* **Alfred Dudley Pickman Rogers.** 1877–1943. British admiral; commanded *Colossus* in battle of Jutland (May 31, 1916); commander in chief in the Mediterranean (1936–39); first sea lord and chief of naval staff (1939–43).

**Pound, Ezra Loomis.** 1885–1972. Poet, critic, and editor, b. Hailey, Idaho; educated Hamilton College and U. of Penna. Traveled in Spain, Italy, and France (1907–08); lived in London (1909–19), Paris (1920–24), Italy (1924–45; 1958–72). An editor with magazines *Poetry* and *The Little Review;* a major influence on twentieth century U.S. and English literature; associated with T. S. Eliot and James Joyce. During World War II, broadcast for Italian Fascist regime; brought to U.S. 1945, charged with treason; held in mental hospital until 1958, when allowed to return to Italy. Major poetical works include *Cantos*, a cycle written over many decades, and *Personae* (1909), *Exultations* (1909), *Ripostes* (1912; containing earliest examples of imagist verse), *Lustra* (1916), *Homage to Sextus Propertius* (1919). Literary executor of Ernest Fenollosa, U.S. Orientalist, with the aid of whose notes he produced *Cathay* (1915), *Certain Noble Plays of Japan* (1916), and *Noh, or Accomplishment* (1917). Major prose works include criticism and translations.

**Pound, Roscoe.** 1870–1964. American educator, b. Lincoln, Nebr.; taught law, U. of Nebraska (1898–1907); professor, Northwestern (1907–09), Chicago (1909–10), Harvard (1910–37); dean of Harvard Law School (1916–36). Author of *Readings on the History and System of the Common Law* (1904), *Readings on Roman Law* (1906), *Outlines of Lectures on Jurisprudence* (1914), *The Spirit of the Common Law* (1921), *Introduction to the Philosophy of Law* (1922), *Law and Morals* (1924), *Criminal Justice in America* (1930). His sister **Louise** (1872–1958), also an educator, teacher of English, U. of Nebraska (1897–1945); known as folklorist and authority on the English ballad; senior editor, *American Speech* (1925–33).

**Pounds** (poundz), **John.** 1766–1839. English shoemaker and teacher of poor children; crippled by accident (1781); proclaimed to be originator of the idea of ragged schools.

**Pou'part'** (po͞o'pȧr'), **François.** 1661–1709. French physician and naturalist; author of works on cantharis, leeches, and mussels, as well as on osteology. Poupart's ligament, of the abdomen, is named after him.

**Pour'bus** (po͞or'bûs) *or* **Por'bus** (pôr'bûs). Name of family of Dutch painters, including: **Pieter** (1510–1584), painter of religious pictures and portraits; his son **Frans** (1545–1581), noted esp. as portrait painter; Frans's son **Frans** (1570–1622), portrait painter, with studio at court in Mantua (to 1600) and king's court in Paris.

**Pour'ta'lès'** (po͞or'tȧ'lâs'), Count **Friedrich von.** 1853–1928. German diplomat; ambassador in St. Petersburg (1907–14), where he tried vainly to keep Russia from entering war against Germany and Austria (1914).

**Pour'ta'lès'** (po͞or'tȧ'lâs'), **Guy de.** 1884–1941. French writer; author of *Marins d'Eau Douce* (1919), *The Life of Franz Liszt* (1925), *Montclar* (novel; 1926), *Nietzsche in Italy* (1929), *La Pêche Miraculeuse* (1937), *Shadows Around the Lake* (1938), etc.

**Pourtalès, Louis François de.** 1823–1880. Swiss naturalist; to U.S. (1846) and on staff of U.S. Coast Survey (1848–73); keeper, Harvard Museum of Comparative Zoology (1873–80), associated with Alexander Agassiz; studied marine life dredged from great depths.

**Poushkin.** Variant of PUSHKIN.

**Pous'sin'** (po͞o'săɴ'), **Gaspard.** See Gaspard DUGHET.

**Poussin, Nicolas.** 1594–1665. French historical and landscape painter; regarded as a master of the classical school; painted chiefly at studio in Rome.

**Pouts'ma** (pouts'mȧ), **H.** 1856–1937. Dutch grammarian, b. Gorredijk, Friesland; taught English language and literature in Dutch high schools. Author of *A Grammar of Late Modern English* (4 vols., 1904–28) and studies of the English verb (1921, 1922, 1923).

**Pow'der·ly** (pou'dẽr·lĭ), **Terence Vincent.** 1849–1924. American labor leader, b. Carbondale, Pa.; machinist by trade; joined Knights of Labor (1874) and became general master workman (1883–93); instrumental in obtaining alien contract-labor law (1885), and in establishing labor bureaus and public arbitration systems in many states; pursued conciliatory policy in labor disputes and tried to reconcile differences between Knights of Labor organization and American Federation of Labor; mayor of Scranton, Pa. (1878–84); U.S. commissioner general of immigration (1897–1902); chief, Division of Information in Bureau of Immigration (1907–21). Author of *Thirty Years of Labor, 1859–1889* (1889).

**Pow'ell** (pou'ĕl), **Adam Clayton, Jr.** 1908–1972. American congressman, clergyman, and writer, b. New Haven, Conn. Member, U.S. House of Representatives (1945–67; 1969–71) from New York.

**Powell, Anthony Dymoke.** 1905– . British novelist. Wrote *Music of Time* series which included *A Question of Upbringing* (1951), *At Lady Molly's* (1957).

**Pow'ell** (pō'ĕl), **Baden.** See BADEN-POWELL.

**Pow'ell** (pou'ĕl), **Cecil Frank.** 1903–1969. British physicist. Prof., U. of Bristol (1948–63); awarded Nobel prize in physics (1950) for work on photography of nuclear processes.

**Pow'ell** (pou'ĕl), **Dawn.** 1897–1965. American writer, b. Mt. Gilead, Ohio; m. Joseph R. Gousha (1920). Author of *She Walks in Beauty* (1928), *Dance Night* (1930), *The Story of a Country Boy* (1934), *Turn, Magic Wheel* (1936); and the plays *Jig Saw* and *Big Night.*

**Pow'ell** (?pō'ĕl), **Frederick York.** 1850–1904. English historian and Icelandic scholar. Jointly with Professor Guthbrandur Vígfússon, compiled *Icelandic Prose Reader* (1879) and wrote *Origines Islandicae* (1905); helped to found *English Historical Review* (1885). Wrote articles in *Encyclopaedia Britannica* and *Dictionary of National Biography.*

**Pow'ell** (pou'ĕl), **John Wesley.** 1834–1902. American geologist, b. Mount Morris, N.Y.; served through Civil War; pioneer explorer of Green and Colorado rivers (1869–75); on staff of U.S. Geological Survey (1875–94); succeeded Clarence King as director (1880); inaugurated (1883) publication of bulletins and (1890) monographs, and series of folio atlases (from 1894) presenting geologic and topographic charts. Also interested himself in ethnological study; director, bureau of ethnology, in Smithsonian Institution (1879–1902); founded *Contributions to North American Ethnology* (1877). His niece **Maud** (1868–1920) was a violinist; played with New York Philharmonic, under Theodore Thomas (1885) and at Chicago World's Fair (1893); organized, and appeared with, Maud Powell String Quartet (1894–98); on tour in U.S. and abroad (from 1898).

**Powell, Lewis Franklin.** 1907– . American jurist, b. Suffolk, Va. Assoc. justice, U.S. Supreme Court (1972– ).

**Powell, Lyman Pierson.** 1866–1946. American Protestant Episcopal clergyman, b. Farmington, Del.; president, Hobart College and William Smith College, Geneva, N.Y. (1913–18); rector of St. Margaret's Church, New York (1926–35). Among his many books are *Christian Science...* (1907), *The Emmanuel Movement in a New England Town* (1909), *Heavenly Heretics* (1910), *Lafayette* (1918), *The Teaching of Democracy* (1919), *The Human Touch* (1925), *The House by the Side of the Road* (1933).

**Powell, William Henry.** 1823–1879. American historical and portrait painter, b. New York City. His *Discovery of the Mississippi River by De Soto* fills a panel in the rotunda of the Capitol, Washington, D.C.; his *Oliver Hazard Perry at the Battle of Lake Erie* is in the Ohio State capitol, and an enlarged replica hangs in the Capitol at Washington, D.C.; among his portraits were *Albert Gallatin, Washington Irving, Gen. George B. McClellan.*

**Pow'er** (pou'ẽr), **Eileen.** 1889–1940. English historian; director of studies in history, Girton Coll., Cambridge (1913–20); reader in economic history, U. of London (1924–31); professor of economic history, London School of Economics (1931–40). Among her works are *Medieval English Nunneries* (1922), *Medieval People* (1924), *The Goodman of Paris* (1928).

**Power, Frederick Belding.** 1853–1927. American chemist, b. Hudson, N.Y.; organized school of pharmacy, U. of Wisconsin, and was its dean and professor (1883–92); director, Wellcome Chemical Research Laboratories, London, England (1896–1914); chief, phytochemical laboratory, bureau of chemistry in U.S. Department of Agriculture (1916–27). Known for his researches in the constituents of plant products, and esp. for his study of chaulmoogra seeds, from which is expressed the oil used in treatment of leprosy.

**Power, Marguerite.** See BLESSINGTON.

**Power, Tyrone,** *in full* **William Grattan Tyrone.** 1797–1841. Irish comedian; b. in Waterford County; joined strolling players at age of 14; succeeded (1826) Charles Connor as leading Irish comedian at Drury Lane; went down in *President*, lost in storm en route from America. His grandson **Frederick Tyrone** (1869–1931), American actor, b. London, Eng., was member of Augustin Daly's company (1890–98); leading man successively of Mrs. Fiske, Mrs. Leslie Carter, Julia Marlowe; chief success in poetic drama or in heroic roles; player in moving pictures in Hollywood (after 1927). The latter's son **Tyrone Edmond** (1914–1958), motion-picture actor, was born in Cincinnati; appeared in Chicago in *Merchant of Venice* (1931), in *Romance* (1934); entered motion pictures (1932) in *Tom Brown of Culver;* player of leading parts (from 1936), appearing in *Lloyd's of London* (1936), *Alexander's Ragtime Band* (1938), *Suez* (1938), *Marie Antoinette* (1938), *The Rains Came* (1939), etc.

**Pow'ers** (pou'ẽrz), **Hiram.** 1805–1873. American sculptor, b. near Woodstock, Vt.; to Washington, D.C. (1834), and executed portrait busts of noted men, including Jackson, Calhoun, Webster, Marshall; established studio in Florence, Italy (1837). Among his important works are *Greek Slave, Eve Before the Fall, California, The Last of the Tribe, Fisher Boy;* statues of Franklin and Jefferson in the Capitol, Washington, D.C.; statue of Webster, now in Boston.

**Powers, James T.** 1862–1943. American actor and singer; best known in comedy roles in light operas, as Rats in *A Tin Soldier*, Wun-Hi in *The Geisha*, etc.

**Powers, Thomas E.** 1870–1939. American cartoonist, b. Milwaukee, Wis.; on staff of Hearst newspapers (1896–1937).

**Pow'ha·tan'** (pou'ȧ·tăn'). *Indian name* **Wa-hun-sen-a-cawh** *or* **Wahunsonacook.** 1550?–1618. American Indian chief, father of Pocahontas (*q.v.*); head of a federation of Algonquian tribes, known as Confederacy of Powhatan, in eastern Virginia.

**Pow'is** *or* **Pow'ys** (pō'ĭs; pou'ĭs), Barons, earls, marquises, and dukes of. See HERBERT family, 2.

**Powlett.** Variant of PAULET.

**Pow'nall** (pou'n'l), Sir **Henry Royds.** 1887–1961. British army officer; director of military operations and intelligence, War Office (1938–40); chief of general staff, B.E.F. (1940); lieutenant general (1940); commanded British troops in northern Ireland (1940–41); vice-chief of imperial general staff (1940–41); chief of staff (1942 ff.) to supreme commander of Allied forces in southwest Pacific, Gen. Wavell.

**Pownall, Thomas.** 1722–1805. English colonial administrator in America, b. Lincolnshire, Eng.; to New York as secretary to the governor (1753); lieutenant governor of New Jersey (1755); governor of Massachusetts (1757–60); urged vigorous measures toward driving French from America; led expedition to Penobscot (1759) to block French; unable to win confidence of Shirley party in Massachusetts. Returned to England (1760); M.P. (1767–80); urged government to treat with colonies (1775). Author of *The Administration of the Colonies* (1764), proposing union of all British possessions in America.

**Pow'ys** (pō'ĭs). Family of English brothers, authors, sons of Charles Francis Powys, clergyman, descended from ancient Welsh princes: (1) **John Cowper** (1872–1963), b. Shirley, Derbyshire; author of novels, including *Wood and Stone, Wolf Solent* (1929); poetry, including *Wolfsbane, Mandragora, Samphire;* philosophical works, including *The Religion of a Skeptic* and *In Defense of Sensuality* (1930); works of criticism, including *Visions and Revisions* and *The Meaning of Culture* (1930); also an autobiography (1934); *Morwyn* (1937) and *The Pleasures of Literature* (1938). (2) **Theodore Francis** (1875–1953), b. Shirley; author of realistic stories of rustic life in southern England, characterized by monotony and gloom. (3) **Llewelyn** (1884–1939), b. Dorchester; victim of recurrent attacks of tuberculosis (from 1909); lived 5 years in Switzerland; manager of stock farm in British East Africa (1914–19); author of *Ebony and Ivory* (stories and impressions of African life, 1922), *Thirteen Worthies* (dealing with such figures as Chaucer, Marlowe, Walton; 1923), *Black Laughter* (1924), *Skin for Skin* (1925), *The Verdict of Bridlegoose* (his judgment on America; 1926), *Henry Hudson* (1927), *Cradle of God* (1929), *A Pagan's Pilgrimage* (1931), *Apples Be Ripe* (novel, 1930), *Life and Death* (1939), and essays. Married an American, **A·lyse' Greg'o·ry** (ă·lēs' grĕg'ō·rĭ) 1883–1967, manager of *Dial*, author of *She Shall Have Music* (1926).

**Poy'dras'** (pwȧ'dräs'; *Angl.* poi'drȧs), **Julien de La'lande'** (lȧ'läNd'). 1746–1824. Poet and politician, b. near Nantes, France; arrived New Orleans, La. (c. 1768); successively, itinerant peddler, trader, storekeeper, and planter; celebrated French capture of English fort at Baton Rouge, La. (1779) with *La Prise du Morne du Baton Rouge*, first epic poem in Louisiana literature. Bequeathed liberal amounts to Poydras Female Orphan Asylum and the Charity Hospital, in New Orleans, and to parishes of Pointe Coupée and West Baton Rouge to provide dowries for poor girls, and to Pointe Coupée parish to found an academy or college.

**Poy'nings** (poi'nĭngz), Sir **Edward.** 1459–1521. English soldier and diplomat; took part in rebellion against Richard III; escaped and attached himself to earl of Richmond (Henry VII); governor of Calais (1493). As deputy to Prince Henry (Henry VIII), governor of Ireland, summoned Drogheda parliament (1494) that enacted Poynings's law providing that every act of parliament must be approved by English privy council to become valid; expelled Perkin Warbeck, the Pretender (1495). Warden of Cinque Ports (c. 1500); executed military undertakings in France and performed diplomatic missions.

**Poyn'ter** (poin'tẽr), Sir **Edward John.** 1836–1919. English historical painter; first Slade professor of fine art, University Coll., London (1871–75); director of National Gallery (1894–1904). Executed decorative designs in fresco, mosaic, stained glass, pottery; known for classic oil paintings, including *Israel in Egypt,* which established his fame (1867), *Atalanta's Race* (1876), *Lesbia and her Sparrow* (1907).

**Poyn'ting** (poin'tĭng), **John Henry.** 1852–1914. English physicist; professor, Mason Coll., which later became U. of Birmingham (from 1880); investigated gravitational constant and mean density of the earth. Works include papers on electrical phenomena and on radiation and the pressure of light; also *Text-Book of Physics* (with J. J. Thomson; 1899–1914) and *The Earth: Its Shape, Size, Weight, and Spin* (1913).

**Poz'zo** (pōt'tsō), **Andrea dal.** 1642–1709. Italian Jesuit, architect, and painter of the Milanese school; master of illusionism in painting; known chiefly for his decoration of the ceiling of the Church of Sant'Ignazio, Rome.

**Poz'zo di Bor'go** (pōt'tsô dē bōr'gô), Count **Carlo Andrea.** 1764–1842. Corsican-born diplomat in Russian service; opposed Napoleon in Corsican politics (from c. 1792); fled from Corsica to England; member of British embassy staff in Vienna (1798–1804); entered Russian diplomatic service (1804). Consistently opposed Napoleon; entered Paris with allied armies (1814) and became commissary general to provisional government. Russian ambassador to France (1814 ff.) and Great Britain (1835).

**Pra'dier'** (prȧ'dyā'), **James.** 1792–1852. French sculptor; among notable works are *Vénus, Psyché, Satyre et Bacchante, Phryné, Sapho,* and *Médée.*

**Pra·dil'la** (prä·thē'lyä), **Francisco.** 1848–1921. Spanish painter; director, Spanish Acad., Rome (1881), and the Prado, Madrid (1896); among works are *Doña Juana la Loca* (in the Prado), *Surrender of Granada, 1492* (at Madrid), and decorations in the Murga Palace at Madrid.

**Pra'do** (prä'thō), **Mariano Ignacio.** 1826–1901. Peruvian general and political leader; fought under Castilla in revolution of 1854; disagreed with President Juan Antonio Pezet's policy of compromise toward Spain (1865) and overthrew him; president (dictator) of Peru (1865–68); declared war against Spain (1865); Spanish fleet defeated off Callao (1866). Forced to leave country (1868); returned, and was elected president (1876–79); defeated in War of the Pacific (1879). Spent most of rest of life in Europe.

**Pra'don'** (prȧ'dôɴ'), **Nicolas.** 1632–1698. French dramatic poet; author of tragedies *Pyrame et Thisbé* and *Phèdre et Hippolyte,* the latter advanced by enemies of Racine as a worthy competitor with Racine's *Phèdre;* the rivalry produced the War of the Sonnets, waged in verse between friends of the two playwrights. Other plays by Pradon were *Tamerlan* and *Régulus.*

**Pra'do U'gar·te'che** (prä'thō ōō'gär·tā'chā), **Manuel.** 1889-1967. Peruvian statesman; president, Central Reserve Bank of Peru (from 1934); pres. of Republic of Peru (1939–45; 1956–62).

**Pradt** (prȧt), **Dominique de.** 1759–1837. French Roman Catholic prelate and diplomat; member of States-General (1789); an émigré (1791–99); personal chaplain to Napoleon (1800) and a negotiator of Treaty of Bayonne dethroning the Bourbon king of Spain (1808). Archbishop of Malines (1808); failed in diplomatic mission in Poland (1812). Turned from Napoleon to favor Bourbon restoration; appointed by Louis XVIII grand chancellor of Legion of Honor.

**Praed** (prād), **Rosa Caroline Mackworth,** *nee* **Pri'or** (prī'ẽr). 1851–1935. Australian novelist; m. (1872) Campbell Mackworth Praed (d. 1901), nephew of Winthrop Mackworth Praed (*q.v.*). Author of *An Australian Heroine* (1880), *Nadine* (1882), *Nyria* (1904), *Romance of Mlle. Aïssé* (1910), *Soul of Nyria* (1932).

**Praed, Winthrop Mackworth.** 1802–1839. English poet; great-great-grandson of Humphry Mackworth, whose son took the added name Praed on marriage with daughter of Cornishman John Praed; his mother one of the New England family of Winthrop. Author of bright, witty skits and satirical pieces; pre-eminent in vers de société; emulator of Hood in *The Red Fisherman* and *Sir Nicholas.*

**Prae·to'ri·us** (prâ·tō'rē·ōōs), **Michael.** *Real surname* **Schult'heiss** (shōōlt'hīs) *or* **Schulz** (shōōlts). 1571–1621. German composer and writer on music; in service of duke of Brunswick-Wolfenbüttel (from 1612). Among his compositions are *Musae Sioniae* (9 parts, 1605–10), *Hymnia Sionia* (1611), *Terpsichore* (1612), *Polyhymnia* (1619), and *Puericinium* (1621); chief among his writings on music is *Syntagma Musicum* (3 parts, 1615–20).

**Pra'ga** (prä'gä), **Emilio.** 1839–1874. Italian poet; wrote poetry influenced by Hugo, Baudelaire, Musset, Heine, and the Italian romantics, as *Tavolozza* (1862), *Penombre* (1864), *Fiabe e Leggende* (1867), and *Trasparenze* (pub. 1877); author also of drama *Le Madri Galanti* (1863). His son **Marco** (1862–1929) was a playwright, influenced at first by the French naturalist school and later by the realists; author of *L'Amico* (1886), *Le Vergini* (1889), *La Moglie Ideale* (1890), *Mamma* (1891), *Alleluia* (1892), *L'Ondina* (1902), *La Porta Chiusa* (1913), *Il Divorzio* (1918), etc.

**Pra·ja'dhi·pok** (prȧ·chä'tĭ·pŏk). *Rarely known as* **Ra'ma VII** (rä'mä). 1893–1941. King (1925–35) of Siam (Thailand), brother of Rama VI; set up a council of state to aid in government; brought consular courts to an end; visited U.S. (1931); temporarily dethroned by coup d'état (1932) of people's party which established constitutional government; agreed to the change but (1933) suspended the new constitution; again forced to submit to the supporters of constitutional government; left the country (1934); abdicated (1935), retiring to England. Succeeded by Ananda Mahidol.

**Prandtl** (prän't'l), **Ludwig.** 1875-1953. German physicist; considered a founder of modern hydrodynamics and aerodynamics; his researches have led to improvements in the structure of ships and airplanes.

**Prang** (prăng), **Louis.** 1824–1909. Lithographer and engraver, b. at Breslau, in Silesia; to U.S. (1850); partner in Boston lithograph firm Prang & Mayer (1856), known as L. Prang & Co. (from 1860); published reproductions of famous works of art (from 1865); founded Prang Educational Co., Boston (1882) to publish school drawing books (*A Course in Water Color, Art Education for High Schools,* etc.).

**Prantl** (prän't'l), **Karl von.** 1820–1888. German philosopher; chief work, *Geschichte der Logik im Abendlande* (4 vols., 1855–70). His son **Karl Prantl** (1849–1893) was a botanist; author of *Untersuchungen zur Morphologie der Gefässkryptogamen* (2 parts, 1875, 1881) and *Lehrbuch der Botanik* (1874).

**Pra·sad'** (prȧ·säd'), **Ra·jen'dra** (rä·jān'drȧ). 1884–1963.

Indian Nationalist leader; member of All-India Congress Committee (from 1912), four times congress president; left legal practice (1920) to follow Gandhi's non-co-operation movement; first president of Republic of India (1950–62); one of the most popular political leaders.

**Pra·tel'la** (prä·tĕl'lä), **Francesco Balilla.** 1880–1955. Italian composer; representative of extreme futurism in music. Works include operas, the orchestral poem *Romagna*, the orchestral dance *La Guerra*, and piano and organ works.

**Pra'ti** (prä'tē), **Giovanni.** 1815–1884. Italian poet; ardent partisan of house of Savoy in Italian unification movement; court poet to house of Savoy; senator (1876 ff.). Among his works are the Romantic epic *Edmenegarda* (5 cantos, 1841), *Canti Lirici*, *Canti del Popolo*, *Memorie e Lacrime* (1844), *Psiche* (1875; collection of 500 sonnets), and *Iside* (1878).

**Prat'i·nas** (prăt''n·ăs). Athenian tragic poet of late 6th and early 5th century B.C.; a rival of Aeschylus. Said to have first introduced satyric drama in Greek theater as a kind of play distinct from tragedy.

**Prä·to'ri·us** (prâ·tō'rē·ŏŏs). = PRAETORIUS.

**Pratt** (prăt), **Bela Lyon.** 1867–1917. American sculptor, b. Norwich, Conn.; teacher of modeling, Boston Museum of Fine Arts (1893–1917); opened studio in Boston. Among his works are portrait busts of Charles William Eliot, Phillips Brooks, Henry Lee Higginson, John C. Ropes; the Nathan Hale statue on Yale University grounds; *Andersonville Prisoner Boy*, in National Cemetery, at Andersonville, Ga.; *Whalemen's Monument*, New Bedford, Mass.; sculptures for the Library of Congress, Washington, D.C.; and many medals, relief portraits, and bronze busts.

**Pratt,** Sir **Charles.** 1st Earl **Cam'den** (kăm'dĕn). 1714–1794. English jurist and political leader; attorney general (1757); chief justice of court of common pleas (1761); in case of John Wilkes decided on illegality of general warrants; in House of Lords, opposed taxation of American colonies and Stamp Act as unconstitutional; lord chancellor (1766); in opposition till death of Chatham; president of council (1782, 1784–94). His son Sir **John Jeffreys** (1759–1840), 2d Earl and 1st Marquis of Camden; as lord lieutenant of Ireland, blocked remedial legislation and carried out cabinet's policy, which resulted in rebellion of 1798; appealed for military intervention and turned over control to Cornwallis; secretary of war (1804–05); president of council (1805–06, 1807–12).

**Pratt, Charles.** 1830–1891. American oil magnate, b. Watertown, Mass.; with Henry H. Rogers, founded Charles Pratt & Co. (1867) for refining crude oil; business acquired by John D. Rockefeller (1874); became executive in Standard Oil Company. Benefactor of Amherst College and U. of Rochester; founded Pratt Institute, Brooklyn, for training of skilled artisans and draftsmen (incorporated 1886, opened 1887); established Pratt Institute Free Library, first free public library in Brooklyn or New York City.

**Pratt, Edwin John.** 1883–1964. Canadian poet and educator; professor of English literature, Victoria Coll., U. of Toronto. Editor, *Canadian Poetry Magazine.* Among his books are *Newfoundland Verse* (1923), *The Witches' Brew* (1926), *The Iron Door* (1927), *Verses of the Sea* (1930), and *The Fables of the Goats and Other Poems* (1937; received governor general's annual award for poetry).

**Pratt, Eliza Anna,** *nee* **Far'man** (fär'măn). 1837–1907. American editor and fiction writer; m. Charles Stuart Pratt (1877). Author of many books for children.

**Pratt, Enoch.** 1808–1896. American financier and philanthropist, b. North Middleborough, Mass.; settled in Baltimore, Md. (1831); founded firm of E. Pratt & Brothers, dealers in nails and iron and steel products; extended interests to banking, fire insurance, and transportation. Established Enoch Pratt Free Library, Baltimore (opened 1886); founded House of Reformation and Instruction for Colored Children, Cheltenham, Md., and the Maryland School for the Deaf and Dumb, Frederick, Md.

**Pratt, Francis Ashbury.** 1827–1902. American inventor, b. Woodstock, Vt.; machinist by trade; with Amos Whitney, founded Pratt & Whitney Co., Hartford, Conn. (1865), for manufacture of machine tools; president of the company (1865–98). Initiated system of manufacturing interchangeable parts, as for rifles during the Civil War; instrumental in bringing about adoption of standard system of gauges; invented metal-planing machine (1869), gear cutter (1884), milling machine (1885).

**Pratt, Richard Henry.** 1840–1924. American army officer and Indian educator, b. Rushford, N.Y.; in Union army through Civil War; commissioned 2d lieutenant of cavalry in regular army (1867); on frontier duty (to 1875). With government aid and approval, organized first nonreservation Indian school at Carlisle Barracks, Carlisle, Pa. (1879), from which developed Carlisle Indian Industrial School; remained head of this school until retired (1904); brigadier general on retired list.

**Pratt, Silas Gamaliel.** 1846–1916. American pianist and composer, b. Addison, Vt.; general director, Chicago Grand Opera Festival (1884); founded Pratt Institute of Music and Art, Pittsburgh (1906) and was its president (1906–16). Composer of lyric opera *Antonio*, *Centennial Overture*, opera *Zenobia*, opera *Ollanta*, *Lincoln Symphony*, *Ode to Peace*, the cantatas *The Last Inca* and *The Triumph of Columbus*, and many songs and piano pieces.

**Pratt, Thomas Willis.** 1812–1875. American civil engineer, b. Boston; excelled as bridge builder; invented the bridge and roof truss known as "Pratt truss" (patented 1844), an improved type of wood and steel truss (patented 1873), a new process of hull construction for ships (patented 1875).

**Pratt, Waldo Selden.** 1857–1939. American musician and teacher, b. Philadelphia; professor of music and hymnology (1882–1917) and professor of public worship (1917–25) at Hartford Theol. Sem., Hartford, Conn. Musical editor for *Century Dictionary;* editor of American Supplement to Grove's *Dictionary of Music and Musicians* and *New Encyclopedia of Music and Musicians.* Author of *History of Music* (1907), *Music of the Pilgrims* (1921), etc.

**Pratt, William Veazie.** 1869–1957. American naval officer, b. Belfast, Me.; grad. U.S.N.A., Annapolis (1889); assistant chief of naval operations (1917–19); accompanied President Wilson to France (Dec., 1918); commander of battleship division four of battle fleet (1923–25); president, Naval War College (1925–27); vice-admiral (1927); commander in chief, U.S. fleet (1929–30), with rank of admiral; chief of naval operations (1930–33); retired (1933).

**Pravda, František.** Pseudonym of Vojtěch HLINKA.

**Prax·ag'o·ras** (prăk·săg'ō·răs). fl. 4th cent. B.C. Greek physician, b. on island of Cos; defender of doctrine of humoralism; supposed by some to have been first to point out distinction between arteries and veins.

**Prax'e·as** (prăk'sē·ăs). Heretic of late 2d century A.D., from Asia Minor; a leader of modalistic monarchians.

**Prax·it'e·les** (prăk·sĭt''l·ēz). Athenian sculptor of 4th century B.C.; regarded as greatest of sculptors of that century. Among his works were statues of Hermes, Dionysus, Aphrodite of Cnidus (for which Phryne is said to have been model), Apollo, and a number of satyrs. Hawthorne's *Marble Faun* has reference to a statue of a satyr preserved at the Capitol in Rome and believed to be a copy of a statue by Praxiteles.

**Pray** (prā), **Isaac Clark**. 1813–1869. American journalist, playwright, and actor, b. Boston; successful in conducting dramatic school in New York; on the stage in England (1846–47) as Hamlet, Othello, Sir Giles Overreach, etc. Author of *The Old Clock*, *Medea*, *Orestes*, *Virginius*, *The Hermit of Malta*, and many farces and burlesques.

**Pré'ault'** (prā'ō'), **Antoine Auguste**. 1809–1879. French sculptor; among his notable works are *Charlemagne*, *Hécube*, *Carthage*, *L'Abbé de l'Épée*, *Clémence Isaure*, *Douleur*, *Général Marceau*, *Aristide Ollivier*, *La Paix*, and *La Guerre*.

**Pre'ble** (prĕb''l), **Edward**. 1761–1807. American naval officer, b. Portland, Me.; commissioned captain (1799) and convoyed a merchant fleet to East Indies, being first American warship to enter waters beyond Cape of Good Hope; commander (1803) of third squadron sent to Mediterranean in war with Tripoli; unsuccessful in assault on Tripoli (1804). His nephew **George Henry Preble** (1816–1885) was also a naval officer; served in Mexican War; accompanied Perry to Japan (1853); commanded gunboat *Katahdin* at outbreak of Civil War, on blockade duty before Mobile, Ala. (1862); dismissed from service for allowing Confederate cruiser *Oreto* to break through blockade; restored to duty (1863) and commanded sloop *St. Louis* off Lisbon, Portugal, and (1864) on southeast American coast blockade; promoted commodore (1871) and rear admiral (1876); commanded south Pacific squadron until retired (1878); author of *Our Flag...* (1872) and a genealogy of the Preble family.

**Prechtl** (prĕκ't'l), **Johann Joseph von**. 1778–1854. Austrian chemist and physicist; editor of a technical encyclopedia (20 volumes, 1830–55) and the yearbooks of the Polytechnical Inst. (1819–39).

**Pre'dis** (prâ'dēs), **Giovanni Ambrogio de**. 1455?–1508. Italian painter of Milanese school; court painter to Lodovico Sforza (1482 ff.).

**Preece** (prēs), Sir **William Henry**. 1834–1913. British electrical engineer; did pioneer work in railway signaling and in wireless telegraphy and telephony.

**Preedy, George Runnell**. Pseudonym of Gabrielle Margaret LONG.

**Pregl** (prā'g'l), **Fritz**. 1869–1930. Austrian chemist; professor in Graz; developed method of quantitative microanalysis; awarded 1923 Nobel prize for chemistry.

**Prejevalsky**. Variant of PRZHEVALSKI.

**Prel** (prĕl), **Karl**. Baron **du Prel** (dü). 1839–1899. German philosopher; chief works, *Die Philosophie der Mystik* (1889), *Der Spiritismus* (1893), *Die Entdeckung der Seele durch die Geheimwissenschaften* (2 vols., 1894), *Der Tod, das Jenseits, das Leben im Jenseits* (1899).

**Prel'ler** (prĕl'ĕr), **Friedrich**. 1804–1878. German painter; chief work, a series of landscapes illustrating the story of the *Odyssey*, now in the corridor of the museum at Weimar. His son **Friedrich** (1838–1901) was also a landscape painter.

**Pre'log** (prĕl'ŏg), **Vladimir**. 1906– . Swiss chemist, b. Yugoslavia. At U. of Zagreb (1935–41), Swiss Federal Institute of Technology (1941– ); awarded (with John W. Cornforth) Nobel prize for chemistry (1975).

**Prence** (prĕns) *or* **Prince** (prĭns), **Thomas**. 1600–1673. British governor of Plymouth colony, Massachusetts (1634–35, 1638, 1657–73); advocated free public schools.

**Pren'der·gast** (prĕn'dĕr·gȧst), **Maurice Braz'il** (brăz''l). 1861–1924. American painter, b. Roxbury, Mass.; studio in New York (1914–24); excelled in genre pictures, as of street scenes in Boston and impressions of Venetian and Neapolitan life; his later work became more abstract and purely decorative, and he became a leader among the radicals in American art.

**Pren'tiss** (prĕn'tĭs), **George Lewis**. 1816–1903. American clergyman and educator; ordained in Congregational ministry (1845); professor, Union Theol. Sem. (1871–97). His brother **Seargent Smith** (1808–1850) was a lawyer and a legislator; practiced in Vicksburg, Miss. (1832–45); member of U.S. House of Representatives (1838–39); famed as an orator; practiced law in New Orleans, La. (from 1845).

**Pre·ra'do·vić** (prĕ·rä'dô·vēt'y'; *Angl.* -vĭch), **Petar**. 1818–1872. Croatian lyric and epic poet; officer in Austrian army, rising to rank of general (1866); wrote early verse in German, but later in Croat; regarded as one of the greatest of Croatian poets.

**Pres'cott** (prĕs'kŭt), **Samuel**. 1751–?1777. b. Concord, Mass. American patriot; with Paul Revere when Revere was captured on his famous ride (Apr. 18, 1775), escaped the British detachment, and carried the warning to Concord, where minutemen quickly gathered and hid military stores; served at Ticonderoga (1776); captured by British (1777) and died at Halifax.

**Prescott, William**. 1726–1795. American Revolutionary soldier, b. Groton, Mass.; a farmer in Pepperell, Mass. (to 1775); colonel of a regiment of minutemen (1775); fortified Breed's Hill (night of June 16, 1775) and commanded redoubt there the next day in battle known as the battle of Bunker Hill.

**Prescott, William Hickling**. 1796–1859. Grandson of William Prescott. American historian, b. Salem, Mass.; educ. Harvard (1811–14); during college course, an accident destroyed the sight of left eye, and subsequent inflammation so weakened right eye that he was nearly blind all his life. Though thus handicapped, determined upon literary career; devoted himself to study of Spanish history. Worked for twelve years on first of his books, *History of the Reign of Ferdinand and Isabella the Catholic* (3 vols., 1838), four years on *History of the Conquest of Mexico* (3 vols., 1843), four years on *History of the Conquest of Peru* (1847). Published three volumes of *History of the Reign of Philip the Second* (2 vols., 1855; 3d vol. 1858), but did not live to complete the work.

**Pres'sen'sé'** (prĕ'säɴ'sā'), **Edmond De·haut' de** (dĕ·ō' dē). 1824–1891. French Protestant clergyman in Paris, and politician; founded (1854) Protestant journal *Revue Chrétienne;* member of National Assembly (1871); senator for life (1883). Among his works are *L'Église et la Révolution Française* (1864) and *Histoire des Trois Premiers Siècles de l'Église Chrétienne* (1858–77). His son **Francis Dehaut de Pressensé** (1853–1914) was prominent in politics; a defender of Dreyfus and Picquart; Socialist member of Chamber of Deputies (from 1902).

**Pres'ser** (prĕs'ĕr), **Theodore**. 1848–1925. American music publisher; built up in Philadelphia one of largest music-publishing houses in U.S.; established (1916) Presser Foundation to aid musicians and provide scholarships for music students.

**Pre'stel** (prĕs'tĕl), **Johann Theophilus**. 1739–1808. German painter and engraver.

**Pres'ter John** (prĕs'tĕr jŏn'), *i.e.* Priest (*or* Presbyter) John. A legendary Christian king and priest of the Middle Ages, whose kingdom was believed to be either in Asia or Africa. (1) *Of Asia:* A king and priest first described in chronicle (1145) of Otto, Bishop of Freising, as dwelling in the Orient far beyond Persia and Armenia, a Nestorian Christian, who attempted to come to the aid of Jerusalem during the Crusades. His connection with India due to legends of earlier origin (c. 1122) applied to this later Nestorian ruler. Believed to have sent to Byzantine Emperor Manuel I (c. 1165) a letter, now held to be spurious, containing accounts of the many marvels of his kingdom. Later (c. 1221), his deeds ascribed to a great conqueror, generally identified with Genghis Khan. In Marco Polo's narrative known as **Un-khan** (ŏŏn′kän′), *or* **Wang Khan** (wäng′ kän′), a Tatar king overthrown (c. 1220) by Genghis Khan, whose niece married Tului, fourth son of Genghis, and was mother of Kublai Khan. Asiatic legends died out and, because of vague geographical knowledge of the times, legends and name were transferred to Africa by Portuguese explorers. (2) *Of Africa:* A king of Ethiopia (Abyssinia) of the 14th century or 15th century. Monarchs of Ethiopia had long possessed a chapel and altar at the Church of the Sepulcher in Jerusalem; one of these monarchs became known as Prester John and on the map of Fra Mauro, a Venetian monk (fl. 1459), his kingdom was located in Abyssinia; communication sought with him by King John II of Portugal (1481–95) when searching the route to the Indies; definitely so named in a book (pub. 1540) about Abyssinia by a Portuguese traveler, Francisco Alvarez, who had resided there (1520–26).

**Pres′ton** (prĕs′tŭn), **Harriet Waters.** 1836–1911. American writer, b. Danvers, Mass.; authority on Provençal literature; author of *Troubadours and Trouvères, New and Old* (1876). Translator of Frédéric Mistral's *Mirèio*, of several works of Sainte-Beuve and of Paul de Musset's biography of his brother Alfred (1877).

**Preston, John Smith.** 1809–1881. American Confederate leader, b. near Abingdon, Va.; planter in Louisiana; in Confederate service through Civil War; in command of prison camp at Columbia, S.C. (1862) and superintendent of bureau of conscription at Richmond, Va. (1863–65); brigadier general (June 10, 1864); known as orator; champion of secessionist cause until his death.

**Preston, Margaret,** *nee* **Jun′kin** (jŭng′kĭn). 1820–1897. American writer, b. Milton, Pa.; m. John T. L. Preston (1857). Author of *Silverwood* (a novel; 1856), and volumes of poetry, including *Beechenbrook* (1865), *Old Songs and New* (1870), *Colonial Ballads* (1887), etc.

**Preston, Thomas.** 1537–1598. English dramatist; author of... *the Life of Cambises, King of Percia* (1569), a bombastic tragedy of murder and bloodshed signalizing the beginning of historical drama.

**Preston, William Ballard.** 1805–1862. American politician, b. in Montgomery County, Va.; member of U.S. House of Representatives (1847–49); U.S. secretary of the navy (1849–50); senator in Confederate States Congress (1861–62).

**Prest′wich** (prĕst′wĭch), Sir **Joseph.** 1812–1896. English geologist; London wine merchant; studied Thames basin; published work on water-bearing strata round London (1851) which became standard authority; professor of geology, Oxford (1874–88).

**Pre′te** (prâ′tā), **Carlo P. del.** 1897–1928. Italian aviator; with Capt. Arturo Ferrarin, established record for nonstop flight (July 3–4, 1928), Rome to Brazil (over 4500 miles).

**Pre′ti** (prâ′tē), **Mattia.** 1613–1699. *Known as* **Il Ca′va·lie′re Ca′la·bre′se** (ēl kä′vä·lyâ′rā kä′lä·brā′sā) *or* **Il Calabrese.** Italian painter; works include frescoes in Church of Sant'Andrea della Valle (Rome), frescoes from the life of St. Catherine in Church of San Pietro a Maiella (Naples), *Belshazzar's Banquet, Clarinda Freeing Olindo and Sofronia*, and *Martyrdom of St. Bartholomew.*

**Pre·to′ri·us** (prĕ·tōō′rē·ŭs), **Andries Wilhelmus Jacobus.** 1799–1853. South African Dutch colonizer and soldier; one of leaders (1838) of the great trek for Natal; beat off attack of 10,000 Zulus (1838); led Natal Boers in opposition to British and crossed to north of Vaal River (1848) to be free of British sovereignty; led anti-British war in attempt to consolidate independent Boer states; defeated at Boomplaats; went to aid of malcontents of Orange River (1851); won from British acknowledgment of independence of Transvaal Boers (1852); reconciled to his rival, General A. H. Potgieter; new district and town of Pretoria named in his honor. His eldest son, **Marthinus Wessels** (1819–1901), succeeded him as commandant general (1853); led punitive expedition against Chief Makapan (1854); was elected first president of newly constituted South African Republic (1857, again 1864, 1869); president (1859–63) of Orange Free State, strove to reconcile Free State burghers to amalgamation with Transvaal; attempted annexation of Bechuanaland and Delagoa Bay (1868) but yielded to Portugal's claim upon Delagoa Bay; resigned when Volksraad refused to ratify arbitration award which deprived Boers of their claim to diamond fields of lower Vaal (1871); after first annexation of Orange Free State by Great Britain (1877), joined insurgent Boer leaders, winning recognition of independence of the republic (1880); member of the ruling triumvirate until election of Paul Kruger as president (1883); lived to see British reannexation of his country.

**Pretyman,** Sir **George.** See TOMLINE.

**Preuss** (prois), **Hugo.** 1860–1925. German jurist and politician; minister of interior in Scheidemann's cabinet (1919); member of Weimar National Assembly (1919–20) and chief author of republican constitution adopted by that assembly.

**Preuss, Johann David Erdmann.** 1785–1868. German historian; chief work, *Friedrich der Grosse. Eine Lebensgeschichte* (4 vols., 1832–34).

**Prev′ost** (prĕv′ō; prĕv′ŏst), Sir **George.** 1767–1816. British colonial administrator; governor general of British North America (1811); made unsuccessful attack on Sackets Harbor, N.Y. (1813); repulsed at Plattsburg, N.Y., by Americans under Macomb (1814).

**Pré′vost′** (prā′vō′), **Marcel.** 1862–1941. French novelist; civil engineer by profession (to 1890), then devoted himself to writing. Among his many novels are *Le Scorpion* (1887), *Les Demi-Vierges* (1894), *L'Heureux Ménage* (1900), *La Princesse d'Erminge* (1905), *M. et Mme Moloch* (1906), *L'Adjudant Benoît* (1916), *Mon Cher Tommy* (1920), *La Retraite Ardente* (1927), and *L'Homme Vierge* (1930). For the stage, he wrote *Les Demi-Vierges* (1895), *La Plus Faible* (1904), *Pierre et Thérèse* (1909).

**Prévost, Pierre.** 1751–1839. Swiss philosopher and physicist; known for work relating to heat and magnetism; formulated theory of exchanges dealing with radiation from one body to another.

**Prévost d'Ex′iles′** (dāg′zēl′), **Antoine François.** *Known as* **Abbé Prévost.** 1697–1763. French novelist; entered Benedictine order (1721); left the order for life of travel and adventure, supporting himself by his writings. Notable among his works are *Les Mémoires d'un Homme de Qualité* (1728) and *Histoire du Chevalier Des Grieux et de Manon Lescaut* (1731).

**Pré′vost′-Pa′ra′dol′** (-pȧ′rȧ′dôl′), **Lucien Anatole.** 1829–1870. French journalist, politician, and diplomat; on staff of *Journal des Débats*, and a founder of *Courrier du Dimanche;* opponent of Napoleon III until more liberal governmental policies developed; French ambassador at Washington, D.C., where he committed suicide

(July 20, 1870) just after outbreak of Franco-Prussian War.

**Prey'er** (prī'ĕr), **Wilhelm Thierry.** 1841–1897. German physiologist and psychologist; advocate of Darwinism. Publications include works on child psychology, *Die Seele des Kindes* (1882), and hypnotism, etc.

**Prez'zo·li'ni** (prāt'tsô·lē'nē), **Giuseppe.** 1882– . Italian writer; collaborated with Giovanni Papini in founding and managing the periodicals *Leonardo* (1903–07) and *La Voce* (1908–16) and in writing *La Cultura Italiana* (1906) and *Vecchio e Nuovo Nazionalismo* (1914); as a critic, exercised influence in contemporary Italian literature. Author also of *La Teoria Sindicalista* (1909), *Benedetto Croce* (1909), *Io Credo* (1923), *Benito Mussolini* (1924), and *La Vita di N. Macchiavelli* (1927).

**Pri·bi'će·vić** (prē·bē'tyĕ·vēt'y'; *Angl.* -chĕ·vĭch), **Svetozar.** 1875–1936. Jugoslav statesman; interned (1914–17) in Budapest; minister of interior (1919–20, 1921); minister of education (1920–21, 1924–26). During troubled years following, allied himself with Croatians under Radić and demanded Croatian autonomy; temporarily interned (1929), and then withdrew to France. Author of *La Dictature du Roi Alexandre* (1932).

**Pri'bram** (prē'bräm), **Alfred Francis.** 1859–1942. Austrian historian; author of *The Secret Political Treaties of Austro-Hungary 1879–1914* (1920), *England and the International Policy of the Great European Powers 1879–1914* (1931), etc.

**Pri·by·lov'** (prĭ·bĭ·lôf'; *Angl.* prĭb'ĭ·lŏf), **Gerasim.** Russian sea captain; discoverer (1786) of group of islands in Bering Sea, called Pribilof Islands in his honor.

**Price** (prīs), **Bonamy.** 1807–1888. English economist; advocate of free trade; author of tracts on currency and banking.

**Price, Bruce.** 1845–1903. American architect, b. Cumberland, Md. Among his works are Chateau Frontenac, Quebec; Banff Springs (Alberta) Hotel; Richard Morris Hunt Memorial, Central Park, New York; Royal Victoria College for Women, Montreal.

**Price, Byron.** 1891– . American newspaper man; with Associated Press (1912–41), executive news editor (1937–41). U.S. director of censorship (1941–45).

**Price, Ira Maurice.** 1856–1939. American Oriental scholar, b. near Newark, Ohio; professor of Semitic languages and literatures, U. of Chicago (1900–25). Wrote treatises on Biblical, esp. Old Testament, history.

**Price, Langford Lovell.** 1862–1950. English economist; author of *Industrial Peace...*(1887), *Money and Its Relations to Prices* (1896), *Co-operation and Copartnership* (1914), etc.

**Price, Leontyne.** *Orig. name* **Mary Leontine Price.** 1927– . American soprano, b. Laurel, Miss. Appeared, as Bess in *Porgy and Bess* (1952–54); with many opera companies including the Metropolitan Opera Co. (1961–62); etc.

**Price, Richard.** 1723–1791. Welsh moral and political philosopher; Unitarian minister in London; established reputation with his *Review of the Principal Questions in Morals* (1757), foreshadowing Kantian theories; advocated reduction of national debt (1771); attacked the justice and policy of American war in *Observations on Civil Liberty and War with America* (1776).

**Price, Sterling.** 1809–1867. American politician and army commander, b. in Prince Edward County, Va.; practiced law, Keytesville, Mo. (from 1831); governor of Missouri (1853–57); major general in Confederate army in Civil War, serving in Missouri, Arkansas, and Texas.

**Price, Thomas.** 1852–1909. Australian statesman, b. in North Wales; stonecutter in Liverpool and on parliament buildings in Adelaide; Labor member of house of assembly (1893); parliamentary leader of Labor party (1901); prime minister (1905–09).

**Price, William Thompson.** 1846–1920. American dramatic critic, b. in Jefferson County, Ky.; served in Civil War; dramatic critic, Louisville *Courier-Journal* (1875–80), New York *Star* (1885–86); founded American School of Playwriting, New York (1901). Author of *The Technique of the Drama* (1892), *The Analysis of Play Construction and Dramatic Principle* (1908), etc.

**Prich'ard** (prĭch'ĕrd), **James Cowles.** 1786–1848. English physician and ethnologist; published *Researches into the Physical History of Man*, upholding the primitive unity of the human species (1813), *Natural History of Man* (1843), *Treatise on Diseases of the Nervous System* (1822), and *Treatise on Insanity...*(1835).

**Prichard, Katharine Susannah.** 1884– . Austral. nov.; m. Hugo Vivian Hope Throssell (1919; d. 1933); author of *The Pioneers* (1915), *Windlestraws*, *Working Bullocks* (1926), *Coonardoo* (1929), *Haxby's Circus* (1930), *Intimate Strangers* (1937), *The Earth Lover* (verse), and *Brumly Innes* (play).

**Pride** (prīd), **Thomas.** d. 1658. English Parliamentarian commander; commanded regiment at Naseby (1645); conducted expulsion of about 130 Presbyterian and Royalist members of Long Parliament (Pride's Purge, 1648); one of judges in trial of Charles I and a signer of death warrant; commanded brigade at Dunbar (1650) and Worcester (1651); opposed Cromwell's appointment as king.

**Prid'eaux** (prĭd'ō; prē'dō), **Humphrey.** 1648–1724. English Orientalist; dean of Norwich (1702–24); author of *Old and New Testament connected in the History of the Jews* (1716).

**Prien** (prēn), **Günther.** 1908–1941. German submarine commander; commanded submarine that penetrated Scapa Flow (Oct., 1939) and sank British battleship *Royal Oak;* lost at sea.

**Priess'nitz** (prēs'nĭts), **Vincenz.** 1799–1851. Silesian farmer, b. Gräfenberg; founder of hydrotherapy; evolved system of treating ailments with cold water, receiving special authorization from Austrian government for practicing new system.

**Priest'ley** (prēst'lĭ), **Herbert Ingram.** 1875–1944. American historian, b. Fairfield, Mich.; professor of Mexican history, U. of California (from 1923); author of books on Mexican history.

**Priestley, John Boynton.** 1894– . English novelist, critic, and playwright, b. in Yorkshire; served through World War (1914–19). Author of *The English Comic Characters* (1925), *George Meredith* (1926) and *Peacock* (1927) for *English Men of Letters* series; novels including *The Good Companions* (1929; dramatized with E. Knoblock, 1931), *Angel Pavement* (1930), *Faraway* (1932), *Rain Upon Godshill* (1939), *Let the People Sing* (1939), *Black-out in Gretley* (1942); plays including *Dangerous Corner* (1932), *Time and the Conways* (1937), *I Have Been Here Before* (1937), *Music at Night* (1938), *The Long Mirror* (1940); books on contemporary England, as *English Journey* (1934) and *Out of the People* (1941).

**Priestley, Joseph.** 1733–1804. English clergyman and chemist, b. Fieldhead, near Leeds; tutor in belles-lettres in nonconformist academy of Warrington, where he also lectured on anatomy and astronomy and introduced teaching of modern history and practical instruction in sciences (1761); minister in Leeds (1767–1772); librarian to Lord Shelburne (1772–1780); minister in Birmingham (1780–1791), where his house and effects were burned because of his sympathy with French Revolution; emigrated to U.S. with his wife, settling at Northumberland, Pa. (1794). Published *The History and Present State* *of Electricity* (1767), in which he explained the rings (Priestley rings) formed by an electrical discharge on a metallic surface and proposed an explanation of the oscillatory character of the discharge from a Leyden jar. Began researches into "different kinds of airs" (1767); announced discovery of "dephlogisticated air," now called oxygen (1774); adhered to phlogistic theory of combustion; isolated and described properties of nitrous oxide, ammonia, sulphur dioxide, hydrogen sulphide, carbon monoxide, etc.; discovered decomposition of ammonia by electricity (1781). Early protagonist of Unitarianism in U.S.; his theological treatises include *A General History of the Christian Church* (4 vols., 1790–1802) and *Notes on All the Books of Scripture* (4 vols., 1803–04). His *Essay on the First Principles of Government* (1768) suggested to Jeremy Bentham "the greatest happiness of the greatest number" as the criterion of moral goodness.

**Pri·e'to** (prē·ā'tō), **Joaquín.** 1786–1854. Chilean soldier and political leader; led revolt of Conservatives (1829–30); defeated (1830) Freire, Liberal leader; president of Chile (1831–41); with aid of Diego Portales, minister of war, administration was an era of peace and progress; constitution was adopted (1833); revolt of Freire suppressed (1836); war with Peru successfully concluded (1839).

**Prieto, Manuel García.** See Marqués de ALHUCEMAS.

**Pri'eur'-Du'ver'nois'** (prē'ûr'dü'vĕr'nwȧ'), Comte **Claude Antoine.** *Called* **Prieur de la Côte'-d'Or'** (dē lȧ kōt'dôr'). 1763–1827. French scholar and politician; elected member of National Assembly (1791) and of National Convention; member of Committee of Public Safety (1793); in Council of Five Hundred under the Directory; a founder of École Polytechnique; responsible for adoption of metric system and foundation of bureau of longitude.

**Pri·go'gine** (prĭ·gô'zhĭn; -gô·zhēn'), **Ilya.** 1917– Belgian chemist, b. Russia. At Free U. of Brussels (1951– ); awarded Nobel prize for chemistry (1977).

**Pri'ma·tic'cio** (prē'mä·tēt'chô), **Francesco.** *Fr.* **Le Pri'ma'tice'** (lē prē'mȧ'tēs'). 1504–1570. Italian painter and architect; aided Giulio Romano in decoration of Palazzo del Tè, Mantua. Called to Fontainebleau by Francis I (1532), where he succeeded Il Rosso as head artist; appointed abbé of St. Martin of Troyes (1544) and court architect by Catherine de Médicis; decorated the Château de Fontainebleau.

**Prime** (prīm), **Benjamin Youngs.** 1733–1791. American physician and poet; practiced medicine, Easthampton, Long Island. Author of *The Patriot Muse...*(1764), *Columbia's Glory or British Pride Humbled...A Poem on the American Revolution* (1791). A grandson, **Samuel Irenaeus Prime** (1812–1885), was a Presbyterian clergyman; on editorial staff, New York *Observer*, a religious weekly (1840–49, 1851–85); wrote weekly letters over pseudonym "Irenaeus" in *Observer;* conducted "Editor's Drawer" in *Harper's Magazine* (1853–85); author of *The Old White Meeting House* (1845), *Travels in Europe and the East* (1855), *The Power of Prayer* (1859). Another grandson of Benjamin, and a brother of Samuel, **Edward Dorr Griffin Prime** (1814–1891), was also a Presbyterian clergyman; assistant editor of, and contributor to, New York *Observer* (from 1853); author of *Around the World ...*(1872). A third grandson of Benjamin, and brother of Samuel and Edward, **William Cowper Prime** (1825–1905), was a journalist and educator; purchased interest in New York *Journal of Commerce* (1861) and edited it (1861–69); professor of the history of art, Princeton (from 1884); author of *The Old House by the River* (1853), *Coins, Medals, and Seals* (1861), *Pottery and Porcelain* (1878), *Along New England Roads* (1892), etc.

**Primo de Rivera y Orbaneja, Miguel.** See RIVERA Y ORBANEJA.

**Prim'rose** (prĭm'rōz). Name of a Scottish family including the earls and viscounts of **Rose'ber·y** (rōz'bĕr·ĭ; rōz'brĭ).

Sir **Archibald Primrose** (1616–1679), Lord **Car'ring·ton** (kăr'ĭng·tŭn), supported Royalist cause in civil war; lord clerk register (1660–76), a privy councilor (1661); justice general (1676–78). His son **Archibald** (1661–1723), 1st Viscount and 1st Earl of Rosebery; Scottish representative peer (1707, 1708, 1710, 1713); a commissioner for union with England. Sir **Archibald John** (1783–1868), 4th earl; great-grandson of 1st earl; privy councilor (1831); supported Reform Bill of 1832.

**Archibald Philip** (1847–1929), 5th earl; grandson of 4th earl; left Oxford without degree on account of owning race horses; undersecretary for home department with special charge of Scottish affairs (1881–83); visited Australia (1883–84); member of board of works (1885); foreign secretary under Gladstone (1886, 1892–94), holding to policy of distrust of Russia, firmness with France during trouble in Egypt, consideration of common interests of Germany and Great Britain. Liberal prime minister after Gladstone (1894–95); sought curtailment of hereditary right to seat and other reforms in House of Lords, also Welsh and Scottish disestablishment; leader of Liberal opposition (1895–96); advocated imperialist policy during Boer War, leading imperialist school in split from insular school of Liberal party; alienation from his former party increased by his fear of socialism. Zealous sportsman, won classic turf events (including Derby three times: 1894, 1895, 1905). Eloquent orator, remembered for his rectorial addresses, as at Glasgow (1900) and St. Andrews (1911) and on Robert Burns (1896).

**Prim y Prats** (prēn' ē präts'), **Juan.** 1814–1870. Spanish soldier and statesman, b. Reus, Catalonia; lieutenant-colonel of Cristinos (see MARIA CHRISTINA) during Carlist war (1833–39); opposed dictatorship of Espartero; exiled (1839); defeated Espartero (1843); major general (1843); captain general of Puerto Rico (1847–48); deputy in Cortes (1850–56), supporting O'Donnell; led successful campaigns in Morocco (1859–60); made (1860) marqués **de los Cas'til·le'jos** (thā lōs käs'tē·lyĕ'hōs); performed valuable services in Mexico (1862); with Serrano y Domínguez started revolution that overthrew Isabella II and Narváez (1868); held four different ministries (1869–70); secured consent of duke of Aosta (Amedeo of Savoy; see AMADEUS) to be king of Spain under new constitution (1870); murdered by unknown assassins.

**Prince** (prĭns), **John Dyneley.** 1868–1945. American philologist and diplomat, b. New York City; professor of Semitic languages, N.Y.U. (1892–1902), Columbia (1902–15); professor of Slavonic languages, Columbia (1915–21); U.S. minister to Denmark (1921–26), Yugoslavia (1926–33); again professor at Columbia (1933–37). Author of grammars of Assyrian, Russian, Lettish, Serbo-Croatian languages.

**Prince, Morton.** 1854–1929. American neurologist and psychologist, b. Boston; American authority on abnormal psychology; founded and edited *Journal of Abnormal Psychology* (1906–29). Author of *The Nature of Mind and Human Automatism* (1885), *The Unconscious* (1913), *Clinical and Experimental Studies in Personality* (1929).

**Prince, Thomas.** 1600–1673. See PRENCE.

**Prince, Thomas.** 1687–1758. American clergyman and historian, b. Sandwich, Mass.; pastorate at Old South Church, Boston (1718–58). Author of *A Chronological*

*History of New England in the Form of Annals* (one vol., bringing history down to 1633, publ. 1736).

**Prince, Walter Franklin.** 1863–1934. American psychical research investigator, b. Detroit, Me. Author of *The Psychic in the House* (1925), *The Case of Patience Worth* (1927), *Noted Witnesses for Psychic Research* (1928), *The Enchanted Boundary* (1930), etc.

**Prince′–Smith′** (prĭns′smĭth′), **John.** 1809–1874. German economist and champion of free trade, b. London; founder of German Free Trade party.

**Prin′cip** (prēn′tsēp), **Gavrilo.** 1893?–1918. Serbian student who assassinated Archduke Francis Ferdinand and his wife at Sarajevo (June 28, 1914).

**Prin′gle** (prĭng′g'l), **Henry Fowles.** 1897–1958. American journalist and writer, b. New York City; professor of journalism, Columbia (from 1936). Author of *Alfred E. Smith...*(1927), *Theodore Roosevelt, a Biography* (1931; awarded Pulitzer prize), *The Life and Times of William Howard Taft* (2 vols., 1939), etc.

**Pringle,** Sir **John.** 1707–1782. British physician; physician general to forces in Flanders (1744), in London (from 1748); physician to George III (1774); effected reforms in military medicine and sanitation; wrote *Observations on the Diseases of the Army* (1752).

**Pringle, Thomas.** 1789–1834. Scottish poet; started (1817) magazine that became parent of *Blackwood's Magazine;* through friendship of Sir Walter Scott, obtained grant of land in South Africa for brothers (1819) and became government librarian at Cape Town. Author of *South African Sketches* (1834) and volume of poems, *Ephemerides* (1828).

**Pringle–Pattison, Andrew Seth.** See Andrew SETH.

**Prings′heim** (prĭngs′hīm), **Alfred.** 1850–1941. German mathematician; known for work on theory of functions; author of an encyclopedia of mathematics.

**Pringsheim, Ernst.** 1859–1917. German physicist; known for work with Otto Lummer on radiation of heat from black bodies. The results of this work led Max Planck to develop the quantum hypothesis.

**Pringsheim, Nathanael.** 1823–1894. German botanist; one of first to demonstrate sexual reproduction in algae; investigated algoid fungi; published paper on alternation of generations in mosses and thallophytes.

**Prin′sep** (prĭn′sĕp), **Henry Thoby.** 1793–1878. British civil servant in India; member of Council of India (1858–74); author of a history of India under the marquis of Hastings (1823). **Valentine Cameron** (1838–1904), artist, b. Calcutta, son of Henry Thoby; friend of Millais and Burne-Jones; attracted notice with portrait (1866) of General Gordon in Chinese costume; painted huge picture of Lord Lytton's Indian durbar at Delhi (1876); also *Bacchus and Ariadne* and *The Gleaners;* author of two plays and two novels; said to be original of Taffy in du Maurier's *Trilby.*

**Prinsterer.** See GROEN VAN PRINSTERER.

**Printz** (prĭns), **Johan Björnsson.** 1592–1663. Swedish administrator in America; governor of New Sweden, the Swedish colony on the Delaware River (1643–53); returned to Sweden (1653); governor of Jönköping Län (1658).

**Pri′or** (prī′ẽr), **Matthew,** *often called* **Matt** (măt). 1664–1721. English poet and diplomat; friend of Charles Montagu (afterwards earl of Halifax), with whom he wrote (1687) *The City Mouse and the Country Mouse* in ridicule of Dryden's *Hind and the Panther;* secretary to ambassador at The Hague; secretary in negotiations at Rijswijk (1697); went over to Tories (1702), allying himself with Harley and St. John; employed through Queen Anne's reign in negotiations with France; took leading part in framing Treaty of Utrecht (1713), called "Matt's Peace"; on Queen Anne's death impeached by Sir Robert Walpole and imprisoned (1715–17). In prison composed long humorous poem *Alma, or the Progress of the Mind* (1718). Known for his occasional poems, the most ambitious of which was *Solomon on the Vanity of the World* (1718); for his neat epigrams; for elegance and easy grace of his familiar verse, as in *To a Child of Quality, The Female Phaeton.*

**Prior, Rosa Caroline Murray.** See PRAED.

**Pri′scian** (prĭsh′ăn; prĭsh′ĭ·ăn). *Full Lat. name* **Pri′sci·a′nus Cae·sar′i·en′sis** (prĭsh′ĭ·ā′nŭs sē·zâr′ĭ·ĕn′sĭs). fl. 500 A.D. Latin grammarian at Constantinople; author of *Institutionis Grammaticae*, an exposition (18 books) of Latin grammar so widely used and so highly regarded during Middle Ages that phrase "to break Priscian's head" came into use with reference to a violation of rules of grammar.

**Priscilla.** See AQUILA.

**Pris·cil′lian** (prĭ·sĭl′yăn; -sĭl′ĭ·ăn). *Lat.* **Pris·cil′li·a′nus** (prĭ·sĭl′ĭ·ā′nŭs). d. 385. Spanish religious reformer; as layman, founded religious sect, now called Priscillianists; ordained priest and consecrated bishop of Ávila; excommunicated by synod of Saragossa (380) as heretic; condemned to death for sorcery and executed along with other Priscillianist leaders.

**Pritch′ard** (prĭch′ẽrd), **Charles.** 1808–1893. English astronomer; professor at Oxford (1870), where he established observatory; determined libration of the moon; used wedge photometer in stellar photometry, measuring brightness of numerous stars; used photography in determination of stellar parallax.

**Pritchard, Hannah,** *nee* **Vaughan** (vôn). 1711–1768. English actress; member of Garrick's company for twenty years; excelled in characters of intrigue, including Lady Betty Modish and Lady Townly; also in tragedy as the Queen in *Hamlet*, Cleopatra in *All for Love*, Zara in *The Mourning Bride*, and not surpassed as Lady Macbeth before Mrs. Siddons.

**Pritch′ett** (prĭch′ĕt; -ĭt), **Henry Smith.** 1857–1939. American astronomer and educator, b. Fayette, Mo.; astronomer of expedition to New Zealand to observe transit of Venus (1882); professor, and observatory director, Washington U., St. Louis (1883–97); superintendent, U.S. Coast and Geodetic Survey (1897–1900); president, M.I.T. (1900–06); president, Carnegie Foundation for Advancement of Teaching (1906–30).

**Pritchett, Victor Sawdon.** 1900– . English journalist and short-story writer.

**Pri′thi·raj** (prĭ′tĭ·räj). d. 1192. Last Rajput king of Delhi and Ajmer (1182?–1192); overwhelmed and killed in battle of Tarain (1192) by Mohammed of Ghor; subject of many legends (see CHAND BARDAI).

**Prjevalsky.** Variant of PRZHEVALSKI.

**Pro′bus** (prō′bŭs), **Marcus Aurelius.** d. 282. Roman emperor (276–282), b. in Sirmium, Pannonia; distinguished soldier under emperors Valerian, Claudius, and Aurelian; made governor of the East by Tacitus; proclaimed emperor by soldiers; waged successful wars in Gaul and Illyricum and put down usurpers; killed in mutiny of his soldiers.

**Probus, Marcus Valerius.** Latin grammarian and critic of late 1st century A.D.; prepared annotated editions of Roman classics, as of Vergil, Horace, Lucretius, et al.; wrote a biography of Persius.

**Pro′cac·ci′ni** (prō′kät·chē′nē). Family of Italian painters, including: **Ercole** (1520?–1591). His son **Camillo** (1546–1629), among whose works is *The Last Judgment* (Church of Saint Procolo, Reggio). Another son, **Giulio Cesare** (1560?–1626), among whose works are *Transfiguration* (Milan) and *St. Francis of Assisi* (the Louvre).

A nephew of the latter two, **Ercole** (1596–1676), among whose works are *Crucifixion* (the Brera) and *Assumption of the Virgin* (Church of Santa Maria Maggiore, Bergamo).

**Pro′clus** (prō′klŭs; prŏk′lŭs) *or* **Proc′u·lus** (prŏk′ū·lŭs). 410?–485. Greek Neoplatonic philosopher, b. Constantinople; regarded as last of great teachers of this school of philosophy; teacher in Athens (c. 450). Vigorously defended paganism and opposed Christianity. Chief works: commentaries on dialogues of Plato, a work on Platonic theology, a brief statement of principles of Neoplatonism, essays on *Providence and Fate*, *Doubts about Providence*, and *The Nature of Evil*, a compendium of part of Aristotle's works, and treatises in fields of mathematics and astronomy.

**Pro′cop** *or* **Pro′kop** (*Czech* prô′kôp; *Ger.* prō′kōp *or* prō·kōp′), Saint. d. 1053. Patron saint of Bohemia; builder (1039) of a monastery in Sazawa valley, of which he became abbot. Canonized (1804).

**Procop** *or* **Prokop, Andrew.** *Latinized name* **Pro·co′pi·us** (prō·kō′pĭ·ŭs). *Surnamed* **the Great.** 1380?–1434. Hussite commander; after victory at Aussig (1426) and invasion of Moravia, Austria, Hungary, Silesia, and Saxony, was defeated and killed in battle of Böhmisch-Brod (May 30, 1434). Another **Procop,** *known as* **Procop the Little,** a priest and Hussite leader, fell in the same battle.

**Pro′co·pé′** (prŏ′kŏ·pā′), **Hjalmar Johan.** 1889–1954. Finnish economist and diplomat; practiced law in Helsinki; minister of commerce and industry (1920), of foreign affairs (1924); Finnish minister to Poland (1926–27); Finnish representative at League of Nations Council (1927–33); Finnish minister to U.S. (1939–44).

**Pro·co′pi·us** (prō·kō′pĭ·ŭs). Byzantine historian, b. Caesarea in Palestine; private secretary to Belisarius (527 A.D.); accompanied him on his Persian, African, and Italian campaigns. Chief work, *Histories*, narratives of Persian, Vandal, and Gothic wars of time of Justinian. Reputed author also of *Anecdota*, a supplement to *Histories* but not included with them because of fear of Justinian and Theodora; *Anecdota* attacks Justinian, Theodora, Belisarius and his wife Antonina, and a number of high government officials.

**Procopius of Ga′za** (gä′zȧ). 465?–?528. Christian Sophist and rhetorician.

**Proc′ter** (prŏk′tẽr), **Bryan Waller.** *Pseudonym* **Barry Corn′wall** (kôrn′wŏl; -wôl). 1787–1874. English poet; practiced as conveyancer and barrister in London; metropolitan commissioner in lunacy (1832–61). Author of poetry, as *Dramatic Scenes* (1819), *A Sicilian Story* (1820), and *The Flood of Thessaly* (1823), many songs, the tragedy *Mirandola* (prod. 1821), and a biography of Charles Lamb (1864). His daughter **Adelaide Anne** (1825–1864), poet, contributed verses under pseudonym **Mary Ber′wick** (bĕr′ĭk) to Dickens's periodicals; author of *Legends and Lyrics* (1858), including *The Lost Chord* (set to music by Sir Arthur Sullivan), and of hymns.

**Proc′tor** (prŏk′tẽr), **Alexander Phimister.** 1862–1950. Sculptor and painter, b. Ontario, Canada; to U.S. as a child; known esp. for his animal sculptures and landscape paintings. His *Panthers* is in Prospect Park, Brooklyn, N.Y.; *Lions*, on McKinley Monument, Buffalo, N.Y.; statuettes *Puma, Dog With Bone, Fawn, Fate*, in Metropolitan Museum of Art, New York City.

**Proctor, Edna Dean.** 1829–1923. American writer, b. Henniker, N.H. Author of volumes of poetry, as *The Song of the Ancient People* (1892), *Mountain Maid and Other Poems of New Hampshire* (1900), *Songs of America* (1906); and of travel accounts, as *A Russian Journey*, *From the Narrows to the Golden Gate*.

**Proctor, Frederick Francis.** 1851?–1929. American theatrical manager, b. Dexter, Me.; developed chain of vaudeville houses in cities of eastern U.S. (from 1895); merged into Radio-Keith-Orpheum circuit (1929).

**Proctor, Henry Hugh.** 1868–1933. American Negro Congregational clergyman, b. near Fayetteville, Tenn.; pastorates in Atlanta, Ga. (1894–1920) and Brooklyn, N.Y. (1920–33). Author of *Sermons in Melody* (1916), *Between Black and White* (1925).

**Proctor, Redfield.** 1831–1908. American lawyer and politician, b. Proctorsville, Vt.; served in Civil War. Reorganized marble quarry business and became president, Vermont Marble Co. (from 1869). Governor of Vermont (1878–80); U.S. secretary of war (1889–91); U.S. senator (1891–1908).

**Proctor, Richard Anthony.** 1837–1888. English astronomer and writer on science; in U.S. (from 1881); founder of *Knowledge*, a popular scientific magazine (1881). His publications include *Saturn and His System* (1865), *Half-hours with the Telescope* (1868), *Other Worlds than Ours* (1870), *Mysteries of Time and Space* (1883), etc.

**Proc′u·lus** (prŏk′ū·lŭs). See PROCLUS.

**Proculus, Sempronius.** Roman jurist of middle 1st century A.D.; disciple of Marcus Antistius Labeo. Gave his name to school of Roman jurists (Proculian school) founded by Labeo in time of Augustus.

**Prod′i·cus of Ce′os** (prŏd′ĭ·kŭs, sē′ŏs). Greek Sophist of 5th century B.C.; taught in Athens, a contemporary of Socrates; only a few fragments of his works extant.

**Pro′gin′** (prô′zhăN′), **Xavier.** French inventor (1833) of the prototype of the modern typewriter, having bars of type. Cf. Christopher Latham SHOLES.

**Pro′kesch von O′sten** (prō′kĕsh fôn ŏs′tĕn, ō′stĕn), Count **Anton.** 1795–1876. Austrian diplomat; ambassador in Athens (1834–49) and Berlin (1849–52); opposed Bismarck in meeting of German states at Frankfurt (1853–55); ambassador in Constantinople (1855–71).

**Pro′kho·rov′** (prô′kə·rôf′), **Alexander Mikhailovich.** 1916– . Soviet physicist. Awarded Nobel prize in physics (1964) with N. Basov and C. Townes for work in the field of quantum electronics.

**Pro·kof′iev** (prŭ·kôf′yĕf), **Sergei Sergeevich.** 1891–1953. Russian composer, b. St. Petersburg. Awarded Rubinstein prize (1910) for his piano concerto. His *The Buffoon* played by Diaghilev's ballet in Paris (1921) and *The Love for Three Oranges* produced in Chicago (1921). Among his other orchestral works are *Scythian Suite*, *Symphonie Classique*, and *Overture on Yiddish Themes*.

**Prokop.** See PROCOP.

**Pro·ko·po′vich** (prŭ·kŭ·pô′vyĭch), **Feofan.** 1681–1736. Russian archbishop and statesman; an adviser of Peter the Great, who called him from Kiev to St. Petersburg (1716); bishop of Pskov (1718); archbishop of Novgorod (1724). Author of the spiritual regulation for the reform of the Russian Church; creator of the holy synod.

**Pro′kosch** (prō′kŏsh), **Frederic.** 1908– . American novelist and poet; author of *The Asiatics* (1935), *The Seven Who Fled* (1937), *The Carnival* (verse; 1938), *Night of the Poor* (1939), *The Skies of Europe* (1941), *The Conspirators* (1943), etc.

**Pro′ny′** (prô′nē′; *Angl.* prō′nĭ), Baron **de. Gaspard Clair François Marie Riche** (rēsh). 1755–1839. French engineer and mathematician; in charge of straightening course of Po River, improvement of harbors of Genoa, Ancona, Venice, etc., and drainage of Pontine marshes; invented a friction brake.

**Pro·per′tius** (prō·pûr′shŭs; -shĭ·ŭs), **Sextus.** 50?–?15 B.C. Roman elegiac poet, b. near Assisi, Italy; educ. Rome. His poems chiefly amatory; his first book (c. 25 B.C.), dedicated to his mistress Cynthia (real name

Hostia), gained him admission to literary circle centering about Maecenas, where he enjoyed friendship of Ovid and Vergil. Four books of his poems, containing altogether over 4000 lines, are extant.

**Pros'per of Aq'ui·taine'** (prŏs'pĕr, ăk'wĭ·tān'). *Also* **Prosper Ti'ro** (tī'rō). Christian writer; native of Aquitaine and disciple of Saint Augustine; in Rome, on staff of Pope Leo I (440). Author of polemical literature, including a poem (*Adversus Ingratos*) against Pelagians, a series of defenses of Saint Augustine, and a treatise against the *Collatio* of Cassianus. Also wrote *Epitoma Chronicon*, a chronicle valuable as source book, esp. for years 425–455 A.D.

**Pro·tag'o·ras** (prō·tăg'ō·răs). Greek philosopher of 5th century B.C., b. Abdera in Thrace; taught in Athens; known as first of the Sophists; friend of Pericles. One of his books, *On the Gods*, questioned existence of the gods and caused his banishment from Athens. His philosophy is epitomized in famous saying: "Man is the measure of all things: of those which are, that they are; of those which are not, that they are not." Credited with being first to systematize study of grammar, distinguishing parts of speech, tenses, and moods.

**Proth'er·o** (prŏth'ĕr·ō), **George Walter.** 1848–1922. English historian and editor; professor of history, Edinburgh (1894–99); succeeded his brother (see below) as editor of *Quarterly Review* (1899–1922); attended Peace Conference as historical adviser to foreign office (1919); coeditor of *Cambridge Modern History* (1902–12); general editor of handbooks for Peace Conference delegates. His brother **Rowland Edmund** (1851–1937), 1st Baron **Ern'le** (ûrn''l), grad. Oxford, fellow (1875–91), was editor of *Quarterly Review* (1894–99); M.P. (1914–19); president of board of agriculture (1916–19); published *Life and Correspondence of Dean Stanley* (1893), *Letters and Journals of Lord Byron* (1898–1901), etc.

**Pro'tić** (prō'tēt·y'; *Angl.* -tĭch), **Stojan.** 1857–1923. Jugoslav statesman; elected to Serbian legislature (1887); first premier of newly organized Yugoslavia (1920–21).

**Pro·tog'e·nes** (prō·tŏj'ē·nēz). Greek painter, of late 4th century B.C., b. in Asia Minor; studio later in Rhodes; rival of Apelles; noted for the extreme care which he devoted to every detail of his paintings. Among his notable works were *Ialysus* in Rhodes, *Resting Satyr* (painted during siege of Rhodes by Demetrius Poliorcetes, 305–304 B.C.), and portraits of King Antigonus and Aristotle's mother.

**Pro·to·po'pov** (prŭ·tŭ·pô'pôf), **Aleksandr Dmitrievich.** 1864–1918. Russian statesman; large landholder in Simbirsk (Ulyanovsk) province; member of 3d and 4th Dumas; minister of interior (1916); considered reactionary by his party colleagues and dismissed from Moderate Liberal party; said to have secretly furthered disturbances (Feb., 1917) which he planned to suppress by force, but which actually resulted in overthrow of government; arrested and executed.

**Prou** (proo), **Maurice.** 1861–1930. French historian; author of *La Gaule Mérovingienne* (1897), *Recueil des Actes de Philippe Ier* (1908), etc.

**Prou'dhon'** (proo'dôN'), **Pierre Joseph.** 1809–1865. French journalist and politician, regarded as father of anarchism; took active part in Socialist movement in Paris (1848); founded and edited radical journals *Le Peuple* (1848–49), *La Voix du Peuple* (1849–50), and *Le Peuple de 1850* (1850). Student and critic of all existent forms of political organization, he wrote *Qu'est-ce que la Propriété?* (1840), *Principes d'Organisation Politique ou la Création de l'Ordre dans l'Humanité* (1843), *Contradictions Économiques* (1846), *La Philosophie de la Misère* (1846), *Les Idées Révolutionnaires* (1849), *De la Justice dans la Révolution et dans l'Église* (1858), *La Guerre et la Paix* (1861), *La Capacité des Classes Ouvrières* (1863), etc.

**Proust** (proost), **Joseph Louis.** 1754–1826. French chemist; director of royal laboratory, Madrid (1789); lost position with fall of Charles IV, his patron, and returned to France (1808). Established law of definite proportions known also as *Proust's law;* a founder of the wet way in analysis; investigated sugar in vegetable juices; first to prepare sugar from grapes, proving its identity with that obtained from honey.

**Proust, Marcel.** 1871–1922. French novelist, b. Paris; author of a series of novels under the general title *À la Recherche du Temps Perdu* (trans. by C. K. M. Scott-Moncrieff as *Remembrance of Things Past*) including *Du Côté de Chez Swann* (1913), *À l'Ombre des Jeunes Filles en Fleurs* (1918; awarded Goncourt prize), *Le Côté de Guermantes* (1921), *Sodome et Gomorrhe* (1921), *La Prisonnière* (1924), *Albertine Disparue* (1926), *Le Temps Retrouvé* (1928); introduced exhaustive psychological analysis as a recognized element in fiction.

**Prout** (prout), Father. Pseudonym of Francis Sylvester MAHONY.

**Prout, Ebenezer.** 1835–1909. English musical theorist and composer; author of *Harmony* (1889), *Counterpoint* (1890), *Fugue* (1891), *The Orchestra* (1897).

**Prout, Samuel.** 1783–1852. English landscape and architectural water-colorist; known for series of paintings of Continental streets and market places.

**Prout, William.** 1785–1850. English chemist and physician; M.D., Edinburgh (1811). Practiced in London; discovered hydrochloric acid in stomach (1823); suggested that hydrogen is the fundamental unit from which all elements are built (1815–16).

**Prou'ty** (prou'tĭ), **Olive,** *nee* **Hig'gins** (hĭg'ĭnz). 1882–1974. American writer, b. Worcester, Mass.; m. Lewis I. Prouty (1907). Author of *Bobbie, General Manager* (1913), *Stella Dallas* (1922), *White Fawn* (1931), *Lisa Vale* (1938), etc.

**Pro'voost** (prō'vōst), **Samuel.** 1742?–1815. American Protestant Episcopal clergyman, b. New York City; minister in Trinity parish (from 1784); consecrated first bishop of New York (1787).

**Prud'den** (prood''n), **Theophil Mitchell.** 1849–1924. American pathologist, b. Middlebury, Conn.; member, board of scientific directors, Rockefeller Institute (from 1901). Made special study of bacteriology; first to make diphtheria antitoxin in U.S. Author of *Manual of Normal Histology* (1881), *Handbook of Pathological Anatomy and Histology* (with Francis Delafield, a revision of a former work by Delafield, 1885). Interested in study of remains of the cliff dwellers in American Southwest; published *On the Great American Plateau* (1906).

**Pru·den'ti·us** (proo·dĕn'shĭ·ŭs; -shŭs), **Aurelius Clemens.** 348–?410. Latin Christian poet, b. probably in Spain; held official position under Emperor Theodosius; retired to monastery (c. 405). Author of *Cathemerinon* (including twelve long hymns for devotional use), *Psychomachia* (depiction of the struggle between virtue and vice for the soul of a Christian), *Peri Stephanon* (hymns praising martyrs and martyrdom), *Hamartigenia* (on the origin of evil), and *Apotheosis* (defense of the doctrine of the divinity of Christ).

**Pru'd'homme'** (prü'dôm'), **John Francis Eugene.** 1800–1892. American engraver, b. on island of St. Thomas, West Indies; to U.S. as a boy; engaged in banknote engraving (1852–69); on staff of bureau of engraving and printing, Washington, D.C. (1869–85). Among his engravings are portraits of DeWitt Clinton, Alexander

Hamilton, John Paul Jones, Stephen Decatur, Dolly Madison, Oliver Cromwell, Horatio Nelson, George Washington.

**Pru'dhomme'** (prü'dôm'), **Sully.** See SULLY PRUDHOMME.

**Pru'd'hon'** (prü'dôN'), **Pierre-Paul.** *Pen name of* **Pierre Pru'don'** (prü'dôN'). 1758–1823. French historical and portrait painter; accepted ideas of French Revolution and, later, the rule of Napoleon; regarded as leading painter of the empire period.

**Pru'ette** (prōō'ĕt), **Lorine Livingston.** 1896– . Am. writer, b. Millersburg, Tenn.; on editorial staff of *Industrial Psychology.* Auth. of *Women and Leisure* (1924), *G. Stanley Hall, A Biography of a Mind* (1926), *Saint in Ivory* (a novel, 1927), *Private Life of Your Glands* (1936), etc.

**Pru'nières'** (prü'nyâr'), **Henry.** 1886–1942. French music scholar; founder (1919) of *Revue Musicale.*

**Prus** (prōōs), **Bolesław.** *Pseudonym of* **Aleksander Gło·wac'ki** (glô·väts'kē). 1847–1912. Polish novelist; regarded as second only to Sienkiewicz. Among his chief works are *Warsaw Sketches, Chronicles, The Puppet, The Emancipated Woman, The Outpost, The Pharoah.*

**Pru'si·as** (prōō'shĭ·ăs). Name of two kings of Bithynia: **Prusias I,** *known as* **the Lame** (reigned 237–192 B.C.), warred with Attalus I of Pergamum, married the sister of Philip of Macedon, and aided Philip in fighting the Romans. His son **Prusias II,** *known as* **the Horseman** (reigned 192–148 B.C.), summoned Hannibal to his court and planned under Roman influence to assassinate him, but Hannibal discovered the plan and committed suicide (183); was forced by the Romans to return (154) conquests he had made of territory in Pergamum.

**Prus'sia** (prŭsh'ȧ), House of. For earlier rulers of Prussia, see house of BRANDENBURG. The Hohenzollerns (*q.v.*) became ruling family of Prussia when Frederick, Burgrave of Nuremberg and head of house of Hohenzollern, was granted sovereignty over mark of Brandenburg and became prince elector (1417). He was succeeded by electors Frederick II (ruled 1440–70), Albert III Achilles (1470–86), John (1486–99), Joachim I (1499–1535), Joachim II (1535–71), John George (1571–98), Joachim Friedrich (1598–1608), John Sigismund (1608–19; who became first duke, 1618), and dukes George William (1619–40), Frederick William, the Great Elector (1640–88), and Frederick III (1688–1713; who became king, 1701). For list of other rulers of Prussia (1701–1918), see HOHENZOLLERN.

**Prutz** (prōōts), **Robert.** 1816–1872. German writer; professor, Halle (1849–59). Among his works are *Gedichte* (1841), the plays *Karl von Bourbon, Moritz von Sachsen, Die Politische Wochenstube,* the novels *Die Schwägerin* (1851), *Das Engelchen* (3 vols., 1851), *Oberndorf* (1862), and the literary histories *Geschichte des Deutschen Theaters* (1847), *Die Deutsche Literatur der Gegenwart 1848–58* (1859), etc. His son **Hans** (1843–1929) made special study of the period of the crusades and wrote *Kulturgeschichte der Kreuzzüge* (1883), *Entwicklung und Untergang des Tempelherrenordens* (1888), etc.

**Pryce** (prīs), **Richard.** 1864–1942. Welsh novelist and playwright; among his novels are *An Evil Spirit* (1887), *Jezebel* (1900), *Morgan's Yard* (1932); among his plays, *Helen with the High Hand* (from Arnold Bennett's novel of same name, 1914), *Frolic Wind* (from Richard Oke's novel of same name, 1935).

**Prynne** (prĭn), **William.** 1600–1669. English Puritan pamphleteer; wrote controversial pamphlets assailing Arminianism and ceremonialism; attacked popular amusements and particularly stage plays in *Histriomastix* (1632); sentenced to life imprisonment and loss of his ears in pillory for supposed aspersion upon Charles I and Queen Henrietta Maria in *Histriomastix* (1634). Assailed Wren and the bishops in pamphlets written in Tower of London; deprived of stumps of his ears and branded on cheeks SL (*Seditious Libeler,* but interpreted by Prynne *Stigmata Laudis,* i.e. of Archbishop Laud). Released from prison by Long Parliament; attacked Laud with vindictiveness (1644); M.P. (1648); opposed Independents and execution of Charles I; expelled by Pride's Purge; readmitted to parliament as a Royalist (1661); published *Brevia Parliamentaria Rediviva* (1662), most valuable of his compilations of constitutional history.

**Pry'or** (prī'ẽr), **Roger Atkinson.** 1828–1919. American lawyer, legislator, and army officer, b. near Petersburg, Va.; member, U.S. House of Representatives (1859–61); served in Confederate army in Civil War. On staff, New York *Daily News* (1866); and practiced law in New York City (1866–90); judge, court of common pleas of New York (1890–94); justice, New York supreme court (1894–99).

**Przerwa–Tetmajer.** See TETMAJER.

**Przes·myc'ki** (pshĕs·mĭts'kē), **Zenon.** *Pseudonym* **Mi'riam** (mē'ryäm). 1861–1944. Polish man of letters; editor of weekly magazine *The Life,* Warsaw (1887–88), and monthly *Chimera* (1901–08); through these periodicals, exercised strong influence on development of Polish literature. Author of verse, and translations from Leconte de Lisle, Verlaine, Maeterlinck, et al.

**Przhe·val'ski** (pĕr·zhĕ·väl'y'·skû·ĭ; *Angl.* -skĭ), **Nikolai Mikhailovich.** 1839–1888. Russian explorer; traveled to west central China (1870–73); rediscovered (1876–77) Lake Lop Nor, formerly visited by Marco Polo; explored (1879–80) eastern Tibet and sources of Hwang Ho; on last trip (1883–85), crossed Gobi desert and located watershed between Hwang Ho and Yangtze. Among his discoveries were a wild camel and an early type of horse, now known as *Przhevalski's horse.*

**Przy'by·szew'ski** (pshĭ'bĭ·shĕf'skē), **Stanisław.** 1868–1927. Polish writer; among his essays are *Chopin and Nietzsche* and *Ola Hannson;* among his novels, *Die Todtenmesse* (1895) and *Homo Sapiens* (1895–98); among his prose poems, *De Profundis* (1900) and *Androgyne* (1901); among his plays, *Das Grosse Glück* (1902) and the cycle *Tanz der Liebe und des Todtes* (1901–03).

**Przy·wa'ra** (pshü·vä'rä), **Erich.** 1889– German Jesuit theologian and philosopher.

**Psal'ma·naz'ar** (săl'mȧ·năz'ẽr), **George** (jôrj). 1679?–1763. French literary impostor in London; real name unknown; posed as a pagan Formosan; imposed upon many in London, including bishop of London, for whom he translated the catechism into "Formosan"; confessed to his imposture after serious illness (1728); became a Hebraist and worked as hack writer; highly esteemed by Dr. Johnson.

**Psam'tik** (săm'tĭk). *Libyan* **Psam'a·tik** (săm'ȧ·tĭk). *Gr.* **Psam·met'i·chos** (sȧ·mĕt'ĭ·kŏs). Name of three kings of ancient Egypt of XXVIth (Saite) dynasty: **Psamtik I,** founder of dynasty; son of Necho I and father of Necho II; reigned 663–609 B.C.; established as regent of Egypt under Assyrians by Ashurbanipal (663); renounced allegiance to Assyria (c. 660) and, gaining control, restored independence of Egypt; made capital at Saïs; introduced Greek and Carian mercenaries into armies and permitted Greeks to settle in the delta; seized Thebes (654); strengthened frontiers; promoted commerce; reign marked by extraordinary renascence in art. **Psamtik II;** son of Necho II and father of Apries; reigned 593–588 B.C.; invaded Lower Nubia; reign remarkable for inscriptions of Greek and other mercenaries on colossi of temple at Abu-Simbel. **Psamtik III;** son of Ahmose II; reigned about six months in 525 B.C.; defeated by Cambyses II at Pelusium, Egypt becoming Persian province.

**Psel'lus** (sĕl'ŭs), **Michael Constantine.** Byzantine philosopher, politician, and writer of the 11th century; professor of philosophy, Constantinople; wielded great influence under Constantine Monomachus, Isaac Comnenus, and Constantine Ducas; prime minister during regency of Eudocia Macrembolitissa and the reign (1071–1078) of Michael VII Ducas. Revived study of Plato; wrote voluminously in many fields of human knowledge.

**Pseudo-Areopagite** *or* **Pseudo-Dionysius.** See DIONYSIUS THE AREOPAGITE (2).

**Pseudo-Demetrius.** See DEMETRIUS I of Russia.

**Psi'cha'ri'** (psē'kȧ'rē'), **Jean.** 1854–1929. French philologian, of Greek descent; leader among writers in modern Greek; author of novel (*The Dream of Yanniri*, 1897) and collection of plays (1901–02) in this language.

**Psou·sen'nes I** (sōō·sĕn'ēz). Ruler of XXIst (Tanite) dynasty of Egypt in 11th century B.C.; tomb discovered 1940.

**Ptah·ho'tep** ([p']tä·hō'tĕp; [p']täк-). fl. 2650 B.C. Sage and vizier of Vth (Memphite) dynasty of Egypt; author of *The Proverbs of Ptahhotep*, oldest monument of Egyptian literature extant, used in later reigns as school book.

**Ptol'e·my** (tŏl'ĕ·mĭ). *Lat.* **Ptol'e·mae'us** (tŏl'ĕ·mē'ŭs). Name of fifteen (fourteen or sixteen, according to others) kings of Egypt, the **Ptolemies** (323–30 B.C.), comprising the Macedonian (or XXXIst) dynasty.

**Ptolemy I.** *Called* **Ptolemy So'ter** (sō'tēr), *i.e.* "preserver." 367?–283 B.C. King (323–285 B.C.), founder of the dynasty; reputed son of Lagus and Arsinoë, a concubine of Philip II of Macedon; m. his half sister Berenice. General of army of Alexander the Great and one of his successors (Diadochi) in partition of his empire (323), receiving Egypt and Libya. Nominally satrap (323–306) but from the first actual ruler; defended his province in continuous wars with Alexander's generals; formed alliance with Antipater against Perdiccas, who was killed (321) by his own soldiers when he invaded Egypt; lost Syria to Antigonus (315), but won back southern Syria by victory over Demetrius at Gaza (312). Assumed title of king (305); supported Rhodians against Demetrius I (304)—whence the title *Soter;* concluded alliance with Cassander, Seleucus, and Lysimachus against Antigonus, who was defeated and killed at Ipsus (301). Made Alexandria his capital and foremost city in world; founded its library and museum and made it a haven for scholars; extended boundaries of kingdom; wrote a life of Alexander the Great. Resigned (285) in favor of his son Ptolemy Philadelphus.

**Ptolemy II.** *Called* **Ptolemy Phil'a·del'phus** (fĭl'ȧ·dĕl'fŭs). 309–246 B.C. King (285–246 B.C.), son of Ptolemy I and brother of Ptolemy Keraunos (see below); m. 1st Arsinoë I, daughter of Lysimachus of Thrace, 2d (276) his own sister Arsinoë II. Except for wars with Antiochus I and II of Syria, enjoyed peaceful reign; encouraged commerce, gaining maritime supremacy in Mediterranean and developing trade in Red Sea; built canal from Red Sea to Nile; established colony of Ptolemaïs Epitheras (near modern Suakin); encouraged literature (the Pleiad) and arts; made Alexandria center of Hellenistic culture; built lighthouse on Pharos. According to tradition, caused translation (Septuagint) of Hebrew Scriptures into Greek to be begun by 72 elders from Jerusalem and encouraged Manetho to write his history of Egypt.

**Ptolemy III.** *Called* **Ptolemy Eu·er'ge·tes** (ū·ûr'jĕ·tēz), *i.e.* "benefactor." 282?–221 (or 222) B.C. King (246–221 B.C.), son of Ptolemy II; m. Berenice II of Cyrene (*q.v.*). To avenge death of his sister Berenice, fought war (246–245) with Seleucus II of Syria and invaded Seleucid dominions; captured Babylon and Susa; recalled (243) by revolt in Egypt; reign for next twenty years generally one of peace; controlled eastern Mediterranean but allowed army to decline. Liberal patron of arts; added many books to great library in Alexandria; began temple at Idfu and erected many buildings elsewhere.

**Ptolemy IV.** *Called* **Ptolemy Phi·lop'a·tor** (fĭ·lŏp'ȧ·tôr), *i.e.* "loving his father." 244?–203 B.C. King (221–203 B.C.), son of Ptolemy III; m. his sister Arsinoë III. Weak ruler, under influence of court favorites; his army defeated by Antiochus III of Syria (218), but won decisive victory over Antiochus at Rafah (217). Composed a tragedy; built a temple to Homer.

**Ptolemy V.** *Called* **Ptolemy E·piph'a·nes** (ē·pĭf'ȧ·nēz), *i.e.* "illustrious." 210?–181 B.C. King (203–181 B.C.), son of Ptolemy IV. Kingdom attacked by Antiochus III: Coele-Syria (El Bika) and Palestine seized, and Egypt threatened, but saved by intervention of Rome; betrothed (198; m. 193) to Cleopatra I, daughter of Antiochus; declared of age (196), celebrated in a decree inscribed (195) by the Egyptian priesthood on the Rosetta stone; joined Rome in war against Antiochus; poisoned by members of his court.

**Ptolemy VI.** *Called* **Ptolemy Phil'o·me'tor** (fĭl'ō·mē'tôr), *i.e.* "loving his mother." 186?–145 B.C. King (181–145 B.C.), son of Ptolemy V; m. his own sister Cleopatra II. During his minority, country ruled by his mother; crowned king (173); defeated and made prisoner (170) by Antiochus IV; restored by Rome as joint ruler (170–164) with his brother Ptolemy VIII; quarreled and obliged to flee; restored by Rome (163), but secured Cyrene only; supported Demetrius II of Syria against Alexander Balas (147–145); killed in battle. See CLEOPATRA THEA (his daughter).

**Ptolemy VII.** *Called* **Ptolemy Ne'os Phi·lop'a·tor** (nē'ŏs fĭ·lŏp'ȧ·tôr), i.e. "New Philopator." 161–144. King (145–144), son of Ptolemy VI. Killed by his uncle, Ptolemy VIII.

**Ptolemy VIII** (*or* **VII** *or* **IX**). *Called* **Ptolemy Euergetes II.** *Nicknamed* **Phys'con** (fĭs'kŏn), *i.e.* "fat paunch." 184?–116 B.C. King (144–116 B.C.), brother of Ptolemy VI; m. 1st his own sister Cleopatra II, widow of Ptolemy VI, 2d his niece Cleopatra III. Joint ruler with Ptolemy VI (170–164); represented as extremely vicious and dissolute; expelled from Egypt by revolution led by his wife (131–129), but returned. Friendly to culture; improved Alexandrian library; restored many temples. See also PTOLEMY EUPATOR, below.

**Ptolemy IX** (*or* **VIII** *or* **X**). *Called* **Ptolemy Soter II,** *also* **La·thy'rus** (lȧ·thī'rŭs). d. 81 B.C. King (116–108, 88–80 B.C.), son of Ptolemy VIII; twice married, both times to his own sisters, Cleopatra IV and Cleopatra V Selene. Ruled jointly (116–108) with his mother, Cleopatra III; expelled by her, fled to Cyprus, where he reigned 108–88; on death of his brother Ptolemy X, recalled to rule in Egypt (88–80), a reign of civil strife.

**Ptolemy X** (*or* **IX** *or* **XI**). *Called* **Ptolemy Alexander I.** d. 88 B.C. King (108–88 B.C.), brother of Ptolemy IX; ruled with his mother after expulsion of Ptolemy IX; caused mother's death (101); driven from Egypt (88) and killed in unsuccessful attack on Cyprus.

**Ptolemy XI** (*or* **X** *or* **XII**). *Called* **Ptolemy Alexander II.** 105?–80 B.C. King (80 B.C.), son of Ptolemy X; m. Berenice, his stepmother; murdered her after 20 days' reign; killed by enraged populace; last of legitimate male line of Ptolemies.

**Ptolemy XII** (*or* **XI** *or* **XIII**). *Called* **Ptolemy Phi·lop′a·tor Ne′os Di′o·ny′sos** (fĭ·lŏp′*ȧ*·tôr nē′ŏs dī′ō·nī′sŏs). *Nicknamed* **Au·le′tes** (ô·lē′tēz), *i.e.* "flute player." 95?–51 B.C. King (80–51 B.C.), natural son of Ptolemy IX; m. his own sister Cleopatra VI Tryphaena. Vicious and debauched; friendly to Rome; driven into exile (58–55) but restored by Rome; bequeathed kingdom to his eldest son, Ptolemy XIII, and daughter Cleopatra VII (*q.v.*).

**Ptolemy XIII** (*or* **XII** *or* **XIV**). 61–48 B.C. King (51–48 B.C.); m. his sister Cleopatra VII; ruled jointly with her (51–49); expelled her (49); defeated by Caesar and drowned during flight.

**Ptolemy XIV** (*or* **XIII** *or* **XV**). 58?–44 B.C. King (47–44 B.C.); younger brother of Cleopatra VII; coregent with her; murdered by her to make room for her son Cesarion.

**Ptolemy XV** (*or* **XIV** *or* **XVI**). *Called* **Ptolemy Philopator Philometor Caesar,** *or commonly* **Ce·sar′i·on** (sē·zâr′ĭ·ŏn). 47-30 B.C. Son of Cleopatra VII by Julius Caesar; coregent with his mother (44?–30 B.C.); after Actium, put to death by Octavianus.

OTHER PTOLEMIES: **Ptolemy Ap′i·on** (ăp′ĭ·ŏn; ā′pĭ·ŏn). d. 96 B.C. Natural son of Ptolemy VIII; half brother of Ptolemy IX Lathyrus and Ptolemy X Alexander I; king of Cyrene (116–96 B.C.); ruled under protection of Rome, Cyrene becoming after his death part of Roman dominions.

**Ptolemy Ke·rau′nos** (kē·rô′nŏs) *or, Lat.,* **Ce·rau′nus** (sē·rô′n*ŭ*s), *i.e.* (Gr. *keraunos*) "thunderbolt." d. 279 B.C. King of Macedonia (280–279 B.C.); eldest son of Ptolemy I Soter of Egypt; repudiated for succession in Egypt by his father (Ptolemy Philadelphus being chosen instead); attached to court of Lysimachus of Thrace (283); killed Seleucus I (280); defeated Antigonus; slain by Gauls.

**Ptolemy of Mau′re·ta′ni·a** (mô′rē·tā′nĭ·*ȧ*). Grandson of Cleopatra and Antony; last of the dynastic line. See CLEOPATRA SELENE (2).

**Ptolemy** (tŏl′ē·mĭ). *Lat.* **Claudius Ptol′e·mae′us** (tŏl′ē·mē′*ŭ*s). Astronomer, mathematician, and geographer of Alexandria, of 2d century A.D. His *Megalē Syntaxis tēs Astronomias*, commonly known as *Almagest* from title of Arabic translation, described a system (Ptolemaic system) of astronomy and geography based on theory that the sun, planets, and stars revolve around the earth; this system was generally accepted until displaced by Copernican system (during 16th and 17th centuries). His *Geography* contains an estimate of size of the earth, description of its surface, and list of places located by latitude and longitude.

**Publicola, Publius Valerius.** See VALERIUS.

**Pub·lil′i·us** (pŭb·lĭl′ĭ·*ŭ*s), **Volero.** Roman politician; sponsor (471 B.C.) of legislation (Publilian laws) increasing the powers of the plebeians.

**Publilius Philo, Q.** See PHILO.

**Publilius Sy′rus** (sī′r*ŭ*s), *i.e.* "the Syrian." *Less correctly* **Pub′li·us Syrus** (pŭb′lĭ·*ŭ*s). fl. 1st century B.C. Latin writer of mimes, in which he acted with great success; little of his work extant.

**Puc·ci′ni** (po͞ot·chē′nē; *Angl.* po͞o·chē′-), **Giacomo.** 1858–1924. Italian operatic composer, b. Lucca; studied at Milan conservatory. Among his works are *Le Villi* (1884), *Edgar* (1889), *Manon Lescaut* (1893), *La Bohème* (1896), *Tosca* (1900), *Madame Butterfly* (1900), *La Fanciulla del West* (Eng. *Girl of the Golden West;* 1910), and the one-act opera *Gianni Schicchi* (1918; part of a trilogy). See Franco ALFANO.

**Pucelle d'Orléans, la.** See JOAN OF ARC.

**Puch′ta** (po͝oκ′tä), **Georg Friedrich.** 1798–1846. German jurist.

**Pück′ler–Mus′kau** (pük′lĕr·mo͝os′kou), Prince **Hermann von.** 1785–1871. German soldier, traveler, and writer; served in Prussian army (to 1804), Russian army (1813), and as adjutant with duke of Saxe-Weimar; retired (1815). Among his works are *Briefe eines Verstorbenen* (4 vols., 1830, 1832), *Tutti Frutti, aus den Papieren des Verstorbenen* (5 vols., 1834), *Jugendwanderungen* (1835), *Semilassos Vorletzter Weltgang...* (3 vols., 1835), *Semilasso in Afrika* (5 vols., 1836), and *Die Rückkehr* (3 vols., 1846–48).

**Pudsey, Hugh de.** See PUISET.

**Pu′ech′** (pü′ĕk′), **Aimé.** 1860–1940. French Greek scholar, at the Sorbonne (from 1893).

**Puech, Denys Pierre.** 1854–1942. French sculptor; among his notable works are monuments to Leconte de Lisle, King Edward VII, Doumergue, Mussolini.

**Pu′fen·dorf** (po͞o′fĕn·dôrf), Baron **Samuel von.** 1632–1694. German jurist and historian; chief works, *De Statu Imperii Germanici* (under pseudonym **Se′ve·ri′nus de Mon′zam·ba′no** [zā′vâ·rē′no͞os dȧ môn′tsäm·bä′nō]; 1667) and *De Jure Naturae et Gentium* (1672).

**Pu·ga·chev′** (po͞o·gŭ·chôf′), **Emelyan Ivanovich.** d. 1775. Russian Cossack soldier who (1773) proclaimed himself Peter III and led rebellion against Catherine II; after initial victories, he was decisively defeated and captured (Sept. 14, 1774), taken to Moscow in an iron cage, and executed (Jan. 11).

**Pu′get′** (pü′zhĕ′), **Pierre.** 1622–1694. French architect and sculptor, b. Marseilles; designed the portico of the Hôtel de Ville at Toulon (1656–57) and the Halle au Poisson and Hospice de Charité in Marseilles. Other works include statues *Hercule Gaulois* (now in the Louvre), *Persée Délivrant Andromède*, *Milon de Crotone*, and the bas-relief *Alexandre et Diogène*.

**Pughe** (pū), **William Owen.** *Orig. name* **William Ow′en** (ō′ĕn; -ĭn). 1759–1835. Welsh antiquarian and lexicographer; assumed surname Pughe (1806); published Welsh-English dictionary, work of twenty years (1783–1803).

**Pu′gin** (pū′jĭn; *Fr.* pü′zhăɴ′), **Augustus Charles.** 1762–1832. French architectural draftsman and archaeologist in London; known for his works on medieval architecture, esp. *Architectural Antiquities of Normandy* (1827). His son **Augustus Welby Northmore** (1812–1852), English architect and designer, was employed (1836–43) by Sir Charles Barry upon detail drawings for houses of Parliament; had extensive practice in designing Roman Catholic churches; instrumental in reviving Gothic architecture in England in 19th century. Many of his designs of churches completed by his son **Edward Welby** (1837–1875), who built cathedral at Cóbh, Ireland.

**Pu·gna′ni** (po͞o·nyä′nē), **Gaetano.** 1731–1798. Italian violinist and composer of operas, ballets, oratorios, orchestral overtures, and violin pieces.

**Pu′gno′** (pü′nyō′), **Raoul.** 1852–1914. French piano virtuoso; professor, Conservatory of Music, Paris (1892–1901).

**Pui′set′** (pü·ē′zĕ′) *or* **Pud′sey** (pŭd′zĭ), **Hugh de.** 1125?–1195. English prelate, b. in France; nephew of King Stephen; archdeacon to his uncle Henry of Blois, bishop of Winchester; through ecclesiastical politics in north of England, assisted by his mistress, Adelaide de la Percy, became bishop of Durham (1153); tried to join rebellion against Henry II (1174); on accession of Richard I, purchased earldom of Northumberland; worsted in struggle with Longchamps for the justiciarship; compelled to make submission to Geoffrey, archbishop of York (1192), and surrendered earldom (1194). Patron of learning, ordered survey of rents and customs recorded in the Durham Domesday Book, popularly known as the *Boldon Buke.*

**Pui′seux′** (pü·ē′zû′), **Victor Alexandre.** 1820–1883. French mathematician and astronomer; introduced new methods in algebraic functions; worked on celestial mechanics. His son **Pierre Henri** (1855–1928), astronomer, studied the secular acceleration of the moon's motion, and asteroids; made determination of the constant of aberration; collaborated on map of the moon; published work on kinematics.

**Pu′jo′** (pü′zhō′), **Ar′sène′** (år′sân′) **Pau′lin′** (pô′lăN′). 1861–1939. American lawyer and legislator; member, U.S. House of Representatives (1903–13); chairman, Committee on Banking and Currency (1911–13), and thus head of the so-called "money trust" investigation.

**Pu′jo′** (pü′zhō′), **Maurice.** 1872–1955. French journalist and politician; identified with French royalist group; editor in chief, *L'Action Française.* Author of a book on the Dreyfus case, *Après l'Affaire* (1899), two volumes of literary criticism, and a political drama *Les Nuées.*

**Pul.** See TIGLATH-PILESER III.

**Pulakesin II.** A Chalukya (*q.v.*) king.

**Pu·las′ki** (pụ̈·lăs′kĭ; -kī), **Casimir.** *Polish* **Kazimierz Pu·łas′ki** (pōō·läs′kē). 1748?–1779. Polish nobleman in American Revolutionary army, b. Podolia, Poland; involved in rebellion in Poland (1768–72); fled to Turkey (1772), France (1775). To America with letter of introduction from Franklin to Washington (1777); served as volunteer at Brandywine and Germantown; commissioned by Congress to organize independent cavalry corps (1778); ordered (Feb. 2, 1779) to support Gen. Lincoln in South Carolina; mortally wounded (Oct. 9, 1779) at siege of Savannah.

**Pul·che′ri·a** (pŭl·kẽr′ĭ·ȧ), Saint. *In full* **Ae′li·a** (ē′lĭ·ȧ) **Pulcheria Au·gus′ta** (ô·gŭs′tȧ). 399–453. Byzantine empress, daughter of Emperor Arcadius; reigned conjointly (414–450) with her brother Theodosius II; advised Theodosius to marry Eudocia (*q.v.*) who later became a rival for power and was exiled to Jerusalem (441?). On death of Theodosius (450) married Marcianus, who became her colleague on the throne. (See THEODOSIUS II and MARCIANUS, for events of reigns.) An enemy of Nestorianism and Monophysitism; a saint of the Eastern Church.

**Pul′ci** (pōōl′chē), **Luigi.** 1432–1484. Italian poet, b. Florence; protégé of Cosimo and Piero de' Medici; friend of Lorenzo il Magnifico; known particularly for his romantic chivalric epic *Il Morgante Maggiore* (28 cantos, 1483).

**Pul·gar′** (pōōl·gär′), **Hernando del.** 1436?–?1499. Spanish historian; author of a chronicle of Castilian rulers, chief source of material concerning Ferdinand and Isabella.

**Pul′itz·er** (pōōl′ĭt·sẽr), **Joseph.** 1847–1911. Journalist, b. at Makó, Hungary; to U.S. (1864) and enlisted in 1st New York Cavalry; mustered out of service (July, 1865), found work as reporter on *Westliche Post,* a German-language daily of St. Louis (1868); naturalized American citizen (1867); elected to Missouri legislature (1869); campaigned for Greeley (1872) and Tilden (1876); studied law; adm. to bar (1876); purchased St. Louis *Dispatch* (1878) and merged it with the *Post* to form the St. Louis *Post-Dispatch,* first of the Pulitzer journals. Moved to New York and bought New York *World* (1883). Member of U.S. House of Representatives from New York (1885–86); founded New York *Evening World* (1887). Retained control of and personal interest in these papers, though during his last years he was a nervous invalid and almost totally blind. Founded (1903) and endowed by bequest in his will a school of journalism at Columbia; also established the Pulitzer prizes "for the encouragement of public service, public morals, American literature, and the advancement of education." His son **Ralph** (1879–1939) was also a journalist; president of Press Publishing Co., publishers of New York *World* and New York *Evening World* (1911–30); accomplished sale of papers to Scripps-Howard chain (1931). Another son, **Joseph** (1885–1955), succeeded his father as president of Pulitzer Publishing Co., publisher of St. Louis *Post-Dispatch* (from 1912).

**Pull′man** (pōōl′măn), **George Mortimer.** 1831–1897. American inventor, b. Brocton, N.Y.; cabinetmaker in Albion, N.Y. (1848–55); contractor in Chicago (1855–59); storekeeper in Colorado mining town (1859–63). Again in Chicago, with his friend Ben Field designed Pullman car with folding upper berth (patented 1864) and extensible seat cushions to make lower berth (patented 1865). When railroads began accepting these cars, organized Pullman Palace Car Co. (1867). Also devised dining cars (1868), chair cars (1875), and vestibule cars (1887).

**Pulsz′ky** (pōōls′kĭ), **Ferencz.** 1814–1897. Hungarian politician and writer; accompanied Kossuth to England and U.S., giving account of trip in *White, Red, and Black* (1852); joined Garibaldi in his Calabrian expedition (1862); returned to Hungary (1866); became member of Diet and director of national museum at Pest.

**Pulte′ney** (pŭlt′nĭ; pōlt′-), **William.** Earl of **Bath.** 1684–1764. English political leader; Whig M.P. (from 1705); secretary at war (1714–17) under Walpole; alienated from Walpole on failure to receive cabinet position (1721); antagonist of Walpole in speeches and journalistic war; by fanning agitation against Spain (1739), contributed to downfall of Walpole government. Requested to form a government but refused (1742); failed of appointment as first lord of the treasury on death of Wilmington (1743); failed to form cabinet excluding Pitt (1746); retired. Remembered for oratorical eloquence.

**Pulteney,** Sir **William.** 1861–1941. English lieutenant general, commander of 3d Army Corps, British Expeditionary Force (1914–18); gentleman-usher of black rod to House of Lords (1920–41).

**Pum·pel′ly** (pŭm·pĕl′ĭ), **Raphael.** 1837–1923. American geologist, b. Owego, N.Y.; made trip up Yangtze Kiang and overland through Siberia to St. Petersburg (1864–65); engaged in exploration of copper and iron resources in Michigan and Lake Superior region (1865–70); made study of mineral resources of United States for the tenth U.S. census (1875–80); conducted expeditions under Carnegie Institution auspices in Central Asia (1903, 1904).

**Pun′nett** (pŭn′ĕt; -ĭt), **Reginald Crundall.** 1875–1967. English geneticist; educ. Clifton Coll. and Cambridge; professor of biology (1910–12) and genetics (1912–40), Cambridge; originated sex-linked method in poultry breeding.

**Pu′pi·e′nus Max′i·mus** (pū′pĭ·ē′nŭs măk′sĭ·mŭs), **Marcus Clodius.** d. 238. Roman emperor (238), joint ruler with Balbinus (*q.v.*), appointed by Senate; murdered by praetorians. See GORDIANUS III.

**Pu′pin** (pōō′pēn; *Angl.* pụ̈·pēn′), **Michael Id·vor′sky** (ēd·vōr′skē). 1858–1935. American physicist and inventor, b. in Yugoslavia; to U.S. (1874); professor of electromechanics, Columbia (1901–31). His inventions include: a system of multiplex telegraphy accomplished by electrical tuning (1894); the Pupin coil, which extended range of long-distance telephony; a means of overcoming static resistance to wireless telegraphy. Developed method for short-exposure X-ray photography by means of a fluorescent screen and discovered secondary X-ray radiations. Wrote *Electro-Magnetic Theory* (1895), *Immigrant to Inventor* (1923).

**Pupper, Johann.** See JOHANNES VON GOCH.

**Pur′bach** (po͞or′bäκ) *or* **Peu′er·bach** (poi′ẽr·bäκ), **Georg.** 1423–1461. Austrian mathematician and astronomer; professor in Vienna; taught Johann Müller (Regiomontanus); credited with early Occidental use of sines in trigonometry; compiled table of sines.

**Pur·cell′** (pẽr·sĕl′; pûr-), **Edward Mills.** 1912– . American physicist, b. Taylorville, Ill. At Harvard U. (1938–40; 1946– ), M.I.T. (1941–45). Awarded Nobel prize in physics (1952) with F. Bloch.

**Pur′cell** (pûr′s'l; -sĕl), **Henry.** 1659–1695. English composer, son of Henry Purcell, who, with his brother Thomas, sang at coronation of Charles II. Chorister of Chapel Royal, London (1664); succeeded Dr. John Blow as organist at Westminster Abbey (1680); organist to Chapel Royal (from 1682); composer in ordinary to king, composed ode or anthem for every public event. Wrote incidental music for series of dramas, beginning with Lee's *Theodosius* (1680); began composition of chamber music (1683); produced opera *Dido and Aeneas* (1689?), written to libretto by Nahum Tate, with no spoken dialogue, only recitative; composed music to Betterton's opera *Diocletian* (1690), adapted from Beaumont and Fletcher's *Prophetess*, and to *The Fairy Queen* (1693), an adaptation of Shakespeare's *The Tempest;* composed *Te Deum and Jubilate* for St. Cecilia's Day (1694).

**Pur′chas** (pûr′chăs), **Samuel.** 1575?–1626. English compiler of travel books, including *Purchas, his Pilgrimage* (1616), treating religions of all ages; *Purchas, his Pilgrim. Microcosmus or the Histories of Man* (1619); *Hakluytus Posthumus or Purchas his Pilgrimes* (4 vols., 1625), based in part upon manuscripts left by Hakluyt, narratives by Will Adams of his voyage to Japan, by William Hawkins of his visit to court of Great Mogul at Agra, and often, the only source of information upon explorations.

**Pur·due′** (pẽr·dū′; pûr-), **John.** 1802–1876. American merchant, b. Huntingdon County, Pa.; merchant in Lafayette, Ind.; benefactor of a land-grant college located at Lafayette (1869); thereafter named Purdue U.

**Pur′kin·je** (*Ger.* po͝or′kĭn·yā), **Johannes E′van·ge·li′sta** (*Ger.* ā′väng·gā·lĭs′tä). *Czech* **Jan E′van·ge·li′sta** (ĕ′vàng·gĕ·lĭs′tà) **Pur′ky·ně** (po͝or′kĭ·nyĕ). 1787–1869. Czech physiologist; professor in Breslau (1823) and Prague (1850). Known for observations and discoveries in physiology and microscopic anatomy, esp. relating to ophthalmology and embryology; credited with discovery of subjective visual figures and recurrent images, germinal vesicle in birds' eggs, sudoriferous glands of the skin and their ducts, ciliary movement in vertebrates, pear-shaped cells in middle layer of cerebellar cortex known as *Purkinje's cells*, network of fibers made up of large muscle cells in cardiac muscles of children, etc., known as *Purkinje's network, system,* or *tissue*, ganglionic bodies in the brain, the lumen of the axis cylinder in nerves. Made improvements in microtechnic. Proposed word "protoplasm" for formative material of young animal embryos.

**Pur·nell′** (pûr·nĕl′), **Benjamin.** 1860?–1927. American organizer (c. 1903) and head (known as "king") of a communistic religious colony called the House of David, established at Benton Harbor, Mich.

**Pursh** (pûrsh), **Frederick.** *Orig.* **Friedrich Traugott Pursch** (po͝orsh). 1774–1820. Botanist and horticulturist, b. in Saxony; to U.S. (1799) and curator of botanical gardens at Baltimore (1799–1802), near Philadelphia (1802–05), New York (1806–10); returned to England (c. 1812). Author of *Flora Americae Septentrionalis* (1814), *Journal of a Botanical Excursion in the Northeastern Parts of the States of Pennsylvania and New York* (publ. 1869).

**Pur′vits** (po͝or′vĭts), **Vilhelms.** 1872–1945. Latvian landscape painter; introduced western European art into eastern Europe.

**Pu′sey** (pū′zĭ), **Edward Bouverie.** 1800–1882. English Anglican theologian; son of Philip Bouverie, who took name Pusey on succeeding to manor of that name. M.A., Oxon. (1825); fellow of Oriel (1822), joining Keble and Newman; studied oriental languages and Biblical criticism, Göttingen (1825–27); regius professor of Hebrew, Oxford, and canon of Christ Church (from 1828). Alarmed by prevalence of rationalism in Anglican church, made common cause with Keble and Newman on *Tracts for the Times* (1833); produced tracts on baptism (1835) and on the Holy Eucharist (1836); supported Newman's interpretation of the Thirty-nine Articles in Tract 90 and became henceforth leader of Oxford Movement; suspended as university preacher on charge of heresy (1843); strove to hinder supporters from seceding to Church of Rome; influential in revival of confession in Church of England through sermons on *Absolution* (1846) and the *Presence of Christ in the Holy Eucharist* (1853) and books *The Doctrine of the Real Presence* (1855) and *The Real Presence* (1857); endeavored to bring about union of English and Roman churches (from 1865), as in *Eirenicon* (1865, 1869, 1870); opposed university reform.

**Pusey, Nathan Marsh.** 1907– . American educator; president of Harvard University (1953–71).

**Push′kin** (po͞osh′kyĭn; *Angl.* po͝osh′kĭn), **Aleksander Sergeevich.** 1799–1837. Russian poet, b. Moscow; on staff of ministry of foreign affairs (1817 ff.); his *Ode to Liberty* (1820) caused his exile to south Russia, but he continued to hold government office. Studied Byron's verse; visited Caucasus region; finally dismissed from public service because of liberality of views. Involved in Decembrist uprising (1825), but escaped punishment; later, restored to staff of ministry of foreign affairs (1832). Mortally wounded in duel. Among his works are *Ruslan and Lyudmila* (1820), *The Captive of the Caucasus* (1822), *Boris Godunov* (completed 1825; pub. 1831), *Fountain of Bakhchisarai* (1827), *Ode to Napoleon* (c. 1827), *Gipsies* (1827), *Poltava* (1829), *Evgeni Onegin* (1832), *History of the Revolt of Pugachev of 1773* (1834), *Pique Dame* (*The Queen of Spades;* 1834), and *The Captain's Daughter* (1836).

**Putiphar.** See POTIPHAR.

**Put′litz** (po͝ot′lĭts), **Gustav Heinrich Gans zu** (gäns′ tso͞o). 1821–1890. German man of letters; manager, Court Theater, Schwerin (1863–67) and Karlsruhe (1873–89). Among his volumes of verse are *Was Sich der Wald Erzählt* (1850) and *Vergissmeinnicht* (1853); among his plays, *Das Testament des Grossen Kurfürsten* (1859) and *Don Juan d'Austria* (1863); among his novels, *Das Frölenhaus* (1881) and *Das Maler-Majorle* (1883).

**Put′nam** (pŭt′năm), **Anne.** 1680?–1716. American woman of Salem, Mass., who, as a child of 12, figured prominently in witchcraft trials and by her testimony caused conviction of several persons.

**Putnam, Arthur.** 1873–1930. American sculptor, b. Waveland, Miss.; established foundry (1909) and cast bronzes by the cire-perdue method. Best known for his animal sculptures, as *Sneaking Coyote, Leopard and Gnu, Resting Puma, Crouching Wildcat, Snarling Jaguar,* etc.

**Putnam, Brenda.** 1890– . American sculptor, b. Minneapolis; studio in New York. Among her works are *Memorial Angel*, in Rock Creek Cemetery, Washington, D.C.; portrait bust of Harriet Beecher Stowe, in American Hall of Fame.

**Putnam, Charles Pickering.** 1844–1914. American physician and philanthropist, b. Boston; practiced in Boston; first president, Boston board of charities (1879) and active in its work (1879–1914). His brother **James Jackson** (1846–1918) was a neurologist; instituted one of first U.S. neurological clinics (1872); took special interest in psychoneuroses.

**Putnam, Frederic Ward.** 1839–1915. American anthropologist, b. Salem, Mass.; curator, Peabody Museum of American Archaeology and Ethnology, Harvard (from 1874); also, curator of anthropology, American Museum of Natural History, New York City (from 1894), and professor at Harvard (from 1887).

**Putnam, George Palmer.** 1814–1872. American publisher, b. Brunswick, Me.; settled in London, Eng. (1841) and opened store selling American books in English market (1841–48); returning to New York (1848), started a book-publishing business; established business as G. P. Putnam & Son (1866) and G. P. Putnam & Sons (1871); founded and published *Putnam's Monthly Magazine* (1853–57, 1868–70). Conducted campaign for international copyright agreements (from 1837). His son **George Haven** (1844–1930), b. London, Eng., served in Union army through Civil War; became partner in G. P. Putnam & Son (1866), and president (1872–1930); continued international copyright struggle, organized American Publishers' Copyright League (1886), and was instrumental in securing copyright act of 1909; author of *Books and Their Makers During the Middle Ages* (2 vols., 1896–97), *A Prisoner of War in Virginia 1864–65* (1912), and two volumes of *Memoirs.* George Palmer Putnam's daughter **Ruth** (1856–1931), b. Yonkers, N.Y., was a writer; author of *William the Silent, Prince of Orange* (2 vols., 1895), *Charles the Bold* (1908), *Alsace and Lorraine from Caesar to Kaiser* (1915), *Luxemburg and Her Neighbors* (1918), etc. For George Palmer Putnam's daughter **Mary Corinna**, see under Abraham JACOBI.

**Putnam, George Palmer.** 1887–1950. Grandson of George Palmer Putnam (1814–1872). American publisher and writer, b. Rye, N.Y.; served in World War; treasurer, G. P. Putnam's Sons, publishers (1919–30); m. (1931) as 2d wife Amelia Earhart (*q.v.*); chairman of editorial board, Paramount Productions (1932–35). Author of *In the Oregon Country...* (1918), *Soaring Wings* (1939), etc.

**Putnam, Herbert.** 1861–1955. American librarian, b. New York City; librarian of Congress (1899–1939); president, American Library Association (1898, 1904).

**Putnam, Israel.** 1718–1790. American Revolutionary commander, b. Danvers, Mass.; to Brooklyn, Conn. (c. 1739); served through French and Indian War (1754–63) and in Pontiac's War (1764); active in pre-Revolutionary agitation; volunteered (April, 1775) after news of Lexington. Appointed major general, Continental army; engaged at Bunker Hill; in chief command at New York just before Washington's arrival and during defeat in battle of Long Island (1776); commanded at Philadelphia (1776), in the highlands of the Hudson (1777), in Connecticut recruiting service (1778–79); incapacitated by paralytic stroke (1779).

**Putnam, James Jackson.** See under Charles Pickering PUTNAM.

**Putnam, Nina,** *nee* **Wil′cox** (wĭl′kŏks). 1888–1962. American writer, b. New Haven, Conn.; m. Robert Faulkner Putnam (1907; d. 1918), R. J. Sanderson (1919), Arthur James Ogle (1931; divorced), Christian Eliot (1933). Among her many books are *In Search of Arcady* (1912), *Adam's Garden* (1916), *Sunny Bunny* (1918), *Laughter, Ltd.* (1922), *Easy* (1924), *Laughing Through* (1930), *Paris Love* (1931), etc.

**Putnam, Rufus.** 1738–1824. Cousin of Israel Putnam. American Revolutionary officer and pioneer in Ohio country, b. Sutton, Mass.; served in French and Indian War; in command of defensive works around Boston (1775), and around New York (1776); served under Gates against Burgoyne; reconstructed West Point redoubts (1779); engaged at Stony Point; commissioned brigadier general (Jan., 1783). One of organizers of Ohio Company to colonize tract on north bank of Ohio River; led colony to Marietta (1788), and laid out the town, first organized settlement in Northwest Territory; judge, Northwest Territory (1790–96). Surveyor general of United States (1796–1803).

**Putnam, Ruth.** See under George Palmer PUTNAM.

**Put′nik** (po͝ot′nēk), **Radomir.** 1847–1917. Serbian general; commanded Serbian army at beginning (1914) of World War; defeated Austrians on the Jadar (Aug. 16–20, 1914), the Drina (Sept. 8–19, 1914), and at Rudnik Mountains (Dec., 1914); continued in command during defense of Serbia (1915), but was retired when armies of Central Powers overran Serbia (1915–16).

**Put′ten·ham** (pŭt″n·ăm), **George** (d. 1590) and his brother **Richard** (1520?–?1601). Sons of Robert Puttenham, country gentleman, and of Margery, sister of Sir Thomas Elyot. To one of the brothers is ascribed by the historian Edmund Bolton, in a note on contemporary poets, authorship of the anonymous *Arte of English Poesie* (1589), an important early treatise of English literary criticism.

**Püt′ter** (püt′ẽr), **Johann Stephan.** 1725–1807. German jurist.

**Putt′ka′mer** (po͝ot′kä′mẽr), **Robert von.** 1828–1900. Prussian statesman; minister of education (1879); introduced an improved orthography (known as *Puttkamer orthography*) into schools; minister of interior and vice-president of Prussian ministry (1881); dismissed from office by Emperor Frederick III (1888); lord lieutenant of Pomerania (1891–99).

**Pu′vis′ de Cha′vannes′** (pü′vē′ dẽ shȧ′vȧn′), **Pierre.** 1824–1898. French decorative painter, b. Lyons; best known for his murals for the museums of Amiens, Marseilles, and Lyons, the amphitheater of the Sorbonne, and Boston (U.S.A.) public library.

**P′u-yi, Henry.** See HSÜAN T'UNG.

**Pyat** (pyȧ), **Félix.** 1810–1889. French playwright and politician; member of Constituent Assembly (1848) and Legislative Assembly (1849); signed appeal to arms (1849) and was forced to flee France; returned to France (1870) and became a leader of Commune of Paris (1871); again had to flee France, not to return until the amnesty (1880); Revolutionary Socialist member of Chamber of Deputies (1888). Author of *Mathilde, Diogène,* and *Le Chiffonnier de Paris.*

**Pya·ta·kov′** (pyĭ·tŭ·kôf′), **Grigori L.** 1890–1937. Russian Soviet politician; assistant commissar for heavy industries (1931–37); reported executed for treason after conviction of having conspired with Trotsky for overthrow of government (Jan. 31, 1937).

**Pye** (pī), **Henry James.** 1745–1813. English poet; justice of peace at Westminster; poet laureate (1790) through favor of Pitt; author of ludicrously tame patriotic verses and one ambitious epic *Alfred* (1801).

**Pye, John.** 1782–1874. English landscape engraver; known as first to render adequately effects of light and atmosphere.

**Pyle** (pīl), **Howard**. 1853–1911. American illustrator and author, b. Wilmington, Del.; studio in New York (1876–80) and Wilmington (from 1880). Best known for illustrations of characters and events in early American history; excelled in pen-and-ink drawings. Wrote and illustrated a number of books for children, as *The Merry Adventures of Robin Hood* (1883), *The Wonder Clock* (1888), *Twilight Land* (1895), *Stolen Treasure* (1907).

**Pym** (pĭm), **John**. 1584–1643. English Parliamentary statesman; made his first important speech in Parliament (1621) against relinquishing disabilities of Roman Catholics; took stand in opposition to monopolies, papistry, absolutism; took leading part in impeachment of Buckingham (1626); second to Sir John Eliot in support of Petition of Right (1628). As acknowledged leader, opened Short Parliament (1640) with speech on national grievances and urged Parliament to withhold supplies pending removal of grievances; petitioned king to make terms with Scots, thus provoking king to dissolve Parliament. By petitioning, caused king to open Long Parliament (1640); rode with Hampden through England, urging voters to their duty; assumed leadership in attack upon government; moved impeachment of Strafford and of Laud; declined to be diverted by offer of chancellorship of exchequer; decided Strafford's fate by revealing to Parliament plot to bring army up to Westminster to overawe parliament; voted for Root and Branch Bill (1641) providing abolition of bishops as instruments of arbitrary government; promoted the Grand Remonstrance (1641); thwarted king's attempt to get control of Tower by calling up trainbands to guard Parliament; evaded king's attempt to capture him and others of the Five Members in House of Commons (1642); at opening of Civil War, a member of committee of safety (1642); took up matter of impeachment of Queen Henrietta Maria to House of Lords; led Parliament in seizing power of taxation and instituting an unprecedented excise tax and in rejecting peace negotiations; urged Essex to relief of Gloucester; persuaded Parliament to accept Scottish alliance (1643).

**Pyn'chon** (pĭn'chŭn), **William**. 1590?–1662. Pioneer in America; sailed from England (1630), and settled at Dorchester, in Massachusetts colony; treasurer, Massachusetts colony (1632–34); one of first settlers of Springfield, Mass. (1636); magistrate of Springfield (1639); member, Massachusetts Board of Assistants (1642–51). Returned to England (1652), after church authorities denounced him as a heretic because of views expressed in a tract *The Meritorious Price of Our Redemption* (1650). His son **John** (1626?–1703) was a merchant and trader; received his father's land and business interests when William went back to England (1652); held important elective and appointive offices in Springfield and in Massachusetts colony; built, at Springfield, first brick house in Connecticut Valley; at time of Indian attack (1675) during King Philip's War, hurried troops from Hadley and saved inhabitants, who had herded in his brick house for safety. The towns Northampton, Hadley, and Deerfield were built on lands owned by him.

**Pyn'son** (pĭn's'n), **Richard**. d. 1530. Norman printer in London; successor to the Belgian immigrant William de Machlinia as printer of English law books (c. 1490); introduced roman type into England (1509).

**Py'pin** (pĭ'pyĭn), **Aleksandr Nikolaevich**. 1833–1904. Russian literary critic and historian; author of *History of Slavic Literatures*, etc.

**Pyr'rho** (pĭr'ō). 365?–?275 B.C. Greek philosopher, of Elis; studied in India and Persia; taught skepticism (Pyrrhonism); founded a skeptic school in Elis.

**Pyr'rhus** (pĭr'ŭs). 318?–272 B.C. King of Epirus; succeeded to the throne (306); lost his throne temporarily, but was restored to it (295) with the aid of Ptolemy Soter. Went to Italy (281) to aid Tarentum against the Romans; proved himself a military genius, defeating the Romans at Heraclea (280) and Asculum (279). On being congratulated for his victory at Asculum, in which his losses had been heavy, he remarked: "One more such victory over the Romans, and we are utterly undone"; hence the phrase, "a Pyrrhic victory." Defeated by the Romans at Beneventum (275); killed in battle at Argos, Greece (272 B.C.).

**Py·thag'o·ras** (pĭ·thăg'ô·răs; pī-). Greek philosopher and mathematician, b. in Samos (hence known as "the Samian Sage"); said to have traveled widely in search of wisdom; settled (c. 530 B.C.) in Crotona, Greek colony in southern Italy. Around him, inspired by his teaching, developed an association devoted to reformation of political, moral, and social life; Pythagoreanism maintained its organization until middle of 4th century B.C. To Pythagoras are ascribed the doctrine of metempsychosis and the teaching that earthly life is only a purification of the soul. Pythagoras left no writings; all that is known of his doctrines comes from his disciples. Pythagoreans are known to have made considerable advances in mathematics and astronomy.

**Pythagoras of Rhe'gi·um** (rē'jĭ·ŭm). Greek sculptor of early 5th century B.C.; noted for his statues of athletes. None of his work survives.

**Pyth'e·as** (pĭth'ê·ăs). Greek navigator and geographer of late 4th century B.C., of Massilia (Marseilles); explored coasts of western Spain, Gaul, and British Isles; first Greek to formulate a correct theory of tides, their periodical fluctuation, and their relation with the moon.

**Pythias**. See DAMON AND PYTHIAS.

# Q

**Q.** Pen name of Sir Arthur QUILLER-COUCH.

**Qa'li, al-** (ăl·kä'lĭ). *Arab.* **abu-'Ali al-Qāli.** 901–967 A.D. Philologist in Spain, b. Armenia; educ. Baghdad; settled in Córdoba (942); known esp. for his *Amāli* ("Dictations"), lectures delivered in Córdoba; regarded as founder of Spanish school of philology.

**Qif'ti, al-** (ăl·kĭf'tĭ). *Arab.* **'Ali ibn-Yūsuf al-Qifṭi.** 1172–1248. Arab historian; vizier in Aleppo; author of *Ikhbār al-'Ulamā'*, an important source for history of the exact sciences in the East.

**Quad, M.** Pseudonym of Charles Bertrand LEWIS.

**Quain** (kwān), **Jones**. 1796–1865. British anatomist; known for his *Elements of Anatomy* (1828). His brother **Richard** (1800–1887) was also an anatomist and surgeon. Their cousin Sir **Richard Quain** (1816–1898) was specialist in diseases of the chest; physician extraordinary to Queen Victoria (1890); edited *Dictionary of Medicine* (1882).

**Quan'trill** (kwŏn'trĭl), **William Clarke**. 1837–1865. American Confederate guerrilla commander, b. Canal

Dover, Ohio; farmer, gambler, schoolteacher, desperado, in Kansas region (to 1861); chief of irregular guerrilla band operating in Kansas and Missouri (1861–62); mustered into Confederate service (1862); defeated federal cavalry unit (Oct., 1863) and brutally slaughtered those captured.

**Quantz** (kvänts), **Johann Joachim.** 1697–1773. German flutist and composer; flutist, teacher (1728) and court composer (1741) to Frederick the Great, Berlin; composed about 500 pieces, including about 300 concertos, for the flute; wrote *Versuch einer Anweisung die Flöte Traversière zu Spielen* (1752).

**Quar'itch** (kwŏr'ĭch), **Bernard.** 1819–1899. London bookseller, b. in Prussian Saxony; started bookseller's business near Leicester Square (1847), moved to Picadilly (1860). Published among catalogues of foreign and English books his valuable *General Catalogue of Old Books and Manuscripts* (12 vols., 1887–97).

**Quarles** (kwôrlz; kwärlz), **Francis.** 1592–1644. English poet, b. Romford, Essex; secretary to Archbishop Ussher in Ireland (1629?); chronologer to city of London (1639). Took Royalist side; wrote pamphlets (1644) in defense of Charles I; plundered by Parliamentary soldiers of his books and rare manuscripts (1644). Author of poetical works in the artificial style of the day, full of conceits, but with genuine wit and fancy, felicity of expression, and occasional poetic fire, including *Divine Poems* (1633) and other religious verse, also secular verse, as *Argalus and Parthenia* (1629), and *Emblems* (1635).

**Qua'si·mo'do** (kwä'zē·mô'dō), **Salvatore.** 1901–1968. Italian poet and writer. Awarded Nobel prize in literature (1959) for his lyrical poetry; wrote *La Vita Non E' Un Sogno* (1949), *La Terra Imparrigiable* (1958).

**Quas'si** *or* **Cois'si** (kwäs'ĭ), **Graman.** 18th-century Negro slave of Surinam, who discovered the value of the bark and wood of certain trees in treatment of malignant fevers common in Surinam, in honor of whom Linnaeus gave the name *Quassia* to the genus.

**Qua'tre·fages' de Bré'au'** (kȧ'trē·fȧzh' dē brā'ō'), **Jean Louis Armand de.** 1810–1892. French naturalist and ethnologist. Author of *Histoire de l'Homme* (1867), *Charles Darwin et ses Précurseurs Français* (1870), *Histoire Générale des Races Humaines* (1886–89), etc.

**Qua'tre·mère'** (kȧ'trē·mâr'), **Antoine Chrysostome.** 1755–1849. French archaeologist and politician; condemned to death during the Terror, but finally acquitted; member of Council of Five Hundred. Editor of *Dictionnaire d'Architecture;* author of *Jupiter Olympien, Canova et ses Ouvrages,* and studies on Raphael and Michelangelo.

**Quatremère, Étienne Marc.** 1782–1857. French Orientalist; professor of Persian at École des Langues Orientales (1827). Author of *Recherches sur la Langue et la Littérature de l'Égypte* (1808); editor of Rashīd al-Dīn's *History of the Mongols of Persia.*

**Quay** (kwā), **Matthew Stanley.** 1833–1904. American politician, b. Dillsburg, Pa.; served through Civil War; awarded Congressional Medal of Honor for heroism at Fredericksburg; secretary of Pennsylvania (1872–78, 1879–82), treasurer (1885–87); political boss of the State (from 1885); U.S. senator (1887–99; 1901–04).

**Quayle** (kwāl), **William Alfred.** 1860–1925. American Methodist Episcopal clergyman; elected bishop (1908) and resided in Oklahoma City (1908–12), St. Paul, Minn. (1912–16), St. Louis (1916–24).

**Queen** (kwēn), **Ellery.** *Pseudonym of* **Frederic Dan'nay** [dăn'ā] (1905– ) *and* **Manfred B. Lee** [lē] (1905–1971). American authors of detective fiction.

**Queens'ber'ry** (kwēnz'bĕr'ĭ; -bĕr·ĭ; -brĭ), Earls, marquises, and dukes of. See DOUGLAS family.

**Quei'po de Lla'no** (kĕ'ē·pō thā lyä'nō), **Gonzalo.** 1875?–1951. Spanish army officer; sided with Franco during civil war; military governor of Andalusia (to 1939); known for his propaganda broadcasts during civil war; said to have originated the phrase "fifth column."

**Quei·rós'** (kȧ·ē·rôsh') *or* **Qui·rós'** (kē·rôsh'), **Pedro Fernandes de.** 1560?–1614. Portuguese navigator; succeeded Mendaña as commander of Pacific exploring expedition; discovered New Hebrides.

**Quei·roz'** (kȧ·ē·rôsh'). Variant of QUEIRÓS.

**Queiroz, José Maria Eça de.** See EÇA DE QUEIROZ.

**Quelch** (kwĕlch), **John.** 1665?–1704. Pirate, b. London, England; captured and looted Portuguese vessels off Brazilian coast (1703–04); returned to Marblehead with booty (1704); caught, tried, convicted by testimony of accomplices, and hanged (June 30, 1704). Execution was later declared officially to have been a case of judicial murder.

**Quel·li'nus** (kvĕ·lē'nûs), **Artus.** 1609–1668. Flemish baroque sculptor, b. Antwerp; works include architectural decorations, notably reliefs and caryatids for the town hall, now the royal palace, in Amsterdam (1648–55).

**Quen'stedt** (kvĕn'shtĕt), **Friedrich August.** 1809–1889. German paleontologist, mineralogist, and geologist; authority on the Jurassic formations in Swabia.

**Quen·tal'** (kāɴn·täl'), **Antero Tarquinio de.** 1842–1891. Portuguese poet; among his works, darkly pessimistic in tone, are *Odes Modernas* (1865, 1875), *Primaveras Românticas* (1872), *Os Sonetos Completos* (1886).

**Qué'rard'** (kā'rȧr'), **Joseph Marie.** 1797–1865. French bibliographer; compiler of *La France Littéraire...,* a bibliography of 18th- and 19th-century French authors (10 vols., 1826–42; and a 2-volume supplement, 1854–64), and the 1st volume of *La Littérature Française Contemporaine* (1839), etc.

**Quercetanus, Andreas.** = André DUCHESNE.

**Quer'cia** (kwĕr'chä), **Jacopo della.** 1378?–1438. Sienese sculptor; chief master of Early Renaissance Sienese sculpture. Among his works are the tomb of Ilaria del Carretto (in cathedral at Lucca), *Fonte Gaia* (in the public square at Siena), bronze relief *Zacharias in the Temple* (in the baptistery at Siena), and the tomb of Antonio Galeazzo Bentivoglio (in Church of San Giacomo Maggiore, Bologna).

**Que'ri·do** (kvā'rē·dō), **Israel.** 1874–1932. Dutch writer, author esp. of realistic and socialistic novels and stories.

**Que·sa'da** (kā·sä'thä), **Ernesto.** 1858–1934. Argentine jurist and writer. Among his works are *Goethe* (1881), *San Martín* (1900), *The Social Evolution of the Argentine Republic* (1911), *La Evolución del Panamericanismo* (1919), and *Spengler* (1921).

**Quesada, Gonzalo de.** 1868–1915. Cuban diplomat; minister to U.S. (to 1912) and, later, to Germany.

**Quesada, Gonzalo Jiménez de.** See JIMÉNEZ DE QUESADA.

**Ques'nay'** (kĕ'nā'), **François.** 1694–1774. French physician and economist; physician to the duc de Villeroi, and later to the king of France. In economics, a contributor to the *Encyclopédie,* where his articles formulated the basis of the theory of the physiocrats; author also of *Tableau Économique* (1758), *Maximes* (1758), *Physiocratie* (1768).

**Quesnay de Beau're·paire'** (dē bōr'pâr'), **Jules.** 1837–1923. French jurist and writer; prepared the accusation against General Boulanger before the High Court; president of the Court of Cassation (1893–1899); resigned and campaigned against Dreyfus and his friends. Author of *Le Panama et la République* (1899), *Français* *et Cosmopolites* (1901), and under the pseudonym **Jules de Glou'vet'** (dĕ glōō'vĕ') the novels *Le Forestier* (1880), *Le Berger* (1881), *La Famille Bourgeois* (1883), *Le Père* (1886), etc.

**Quesne** (kân), **Jacques Salbigoton.** 1778–1859. French philosopher; originator of the theory, known as psychism, that there is a fluid universally diffused and equally animating all living beings.

**Ques'nel'** (kĕ'nĕl'), **Pasquier.** 1634–1719. French theologian; member of the Oratory (1657), and director of its Paris congregation. His edition of Leo the Great's *Opera Omnia* (1675), with his annotations, was put on the *Index Expurgatorius*, and Quesnel was attacked for Gallicanism. His refusal to condemn Jansenism led to further attacks on him, esp. by the Jesuits; fled to Brussels (1685) and published *Réflexions Morales* (1687–94); identified as a Jansenist, he was imprisoned (1703), but escaped to Amsterdam. Before his death, he had established a Jansenist church in the Netherlands.

**Qué'te·let'** (kā'tlĕ'), **Lambert Adolphe Jacques.** 1796–1874. Belgian statistician and astronomer; director of the new royal observatory (1828); conducted statistical researches on the development of the physical and intellectual qualities of man, formulating a theory of the "average man" as a basic type.

**Que·ve'do** (kā·vā'thō), **José Heriberto García de.** See GARCIA DE QUEVEDO.

**Quevedo y Vil·le'gas** (ē vē·lyā'gäs), **Francisco Gó'mez de** (gō'māth thā). 1580–1645. Spanish writer; minister of finance under duke of Osuna, viceroy of Naples; imprisoned after fall of Osuna (1620–23); a secretary to Philip II (1632); imprisoned (1639–42) for his political attacks. Known chiefly as a prose satirist; his works include the picaresque novel *Historia y Vida del Buscón* (1626; also called *El Gran Tacaño* and *Pablo de Segovia*) and *Los Sueños* (1607 ff.).

**Que'zon y Mo·li'na** (kā'sôn ē mō·lē'nä), **Manuel Luis.** 1878–1944. Philippine statesman; educ. Santo Tomás U.; member of Philippine assembly (1907–09); Philippine commissioner in Congress of U.S.A. (1909–16); president of Philippine Senate (1916–35); president of Commonwealth of the Philippines (from 1935). Following Japanese conquest of the Philippine Islands, became head of the Philippine government in exile, with headquarters in Australia (Mar.–May, 1942) and U.S. (from May, 1942).

**Qui'che·rat'** (kēsh'rà'), **Louis Marie.** 1799–1884. French philologist; author of *Traité de Versification Latine* (1826), *Thesaurus Poeticus Linguae Latinae* (1836), *Dictionnaire Latin-Français* (1844) and *Français-Latin* (1858). His brother **Jules Étienne Joseph** (1814–1882), archaeologist on staff of Bibliothèque Nationale, is regarded as one of the founders of archaeology in France.

**Quick** (kwĭk), **Herbert,** *in full* **John Herbert.** 1861–1925. American lawyer, editor, and author, b. in Grundy County, Iowa; practiced at Sioux City, Iowa (1890–1909). Author of *In the Fairyland of America* (1902), *Aladdin & Co.* (1904), *On Board the Good Ship Earth* (1913), *Vandemark's Folly* (1922), etc.

**Quid'de** (kvĭd'ĕ), **Ludwig.** 1858–1941. German historian and politician, a leader in the German peace movement (from 1892); founded and edited (1889–95) *Deutsche Zeitschrift für Geschichtswissenschaft;* imprisoned briefly (1896) on charge of lese majesty for writing *Caligula* (1894). President, German Peace Society (1914–29) and German Peace Cartel (1920–29); awarded, with Ferdinand Buisson, Nobel peace prize for 1927. Author of *Völkerbund und Demokratie* (1920), *Völkerbund und Friedensbewegung* (1920), *Die Schuldfrage* (1922), etc.

**Qui·dor'** (?kē·dôr'), **John.** 1801–1881. American painter; studio in New York (from 1851). Known esp. for series of imaginative paintings suggested by his friend Washington Irving's *History of New York by Diedrich Knickerbocker* and *Rip Van Winkle.*

**Quil'lard'** (kē'yàr'), **Pierre.** 1864–1912. French journalist and poet; author of books on the Armenian problem; author also of books of verse, as *La Gloire du Verbe* (1891), *La Lyre Héroïque et Dolente* (1898).

**Quil'ler-Couch'** (kwĭl'ēr·kōōch'), Sir **Arthur Thomas.** *Pen name* **Q.** 1863–1944. English man of letters, b. in Cornwall; son of Thomas Quiller-Couch and grandson of the ichthyologist **Jonathan Couch** (1789–1870) of Polperro. Graduate, and lecturer in classics, Oxford; at Oxford, published *Dead Man's Rock* (1887), a romance; journalist in London and contributor to *The Speaker.* Settled at Fowey, Cornwall (1891); commissioned to complete R. L. Stevenson's *St. Ives* (1898); King Edward VII professor of English literature, Cambridge (since 1912); mayor of Fowey (1937). Published most of his poetical work in *Poems and Ballads* (1896); edited *Oxford Book of English Verse* (1900), *Oxford Book of Ballads* (1910), *Oxford Book of Victorian Verse* (1912), and *Oxford Book of English Prose* (1925). Author of many romances, short stories, and novels, including *The Splendid Spur* (1889), *Noughts and Crosses* (1891), *I Saw Three Ships* (1892), *The Delectable Duchy* (1893), *The Ship of Stars* (1899), *The Westcotes* (1902), *Hetty Wesley* (1903), *Fort Amity* (novel, 1904), *Poison Island* (novel, 1907), *Lady Good-for-Nothing* (novel, 1910), *Corporal Sam and other Stories* (1910), *Hocken and Hunken* (1912), *Foe-Farrell* (novel, 1918), *Q's Mystery Stories* (1937); author also of several volumes of criticism, including *Adventures in Criticism* (1896), *On the Art of Writing* (1916), *On the Art of Reading* (1920), *Charles Dickens and other Victorians* (1925), *The Poet as Citizen* (1934).

**Quil'ter** (kwĭl'tēr), **Roger.** 1877–1953. English composer of songs and settings of English lyrics, including *Song Cycle to Julia* (1905), *Seven Elizabethan Lyrics* (1908), and settings of Tennyson; composed also orchestral music, as *Serenade* (1907), *Three English Dances,* and *A Children's Overture,* and the operetta *Julia* (1936).

**Quim'by** (kwĭm'bĭ), **Phineas Parkhurst.** 1802–1866. American mental healer, b. Lebanon, N.H.; clockmaker by trade; lacked formal education; gave hypnotic exhibitions (1838–47); devoted himself to mental healing (from 1847); office, Portland, Me. (from 1859). In later years, endeavored to work out religious philosophy and a science of health and happiness to account for results achieved by mental healing. Among his consultants was Mary Baker Eddy (in 1862 and 1864); some have advanced theory that from him Mrs. Eddy gained basic ideas of her system of Christian Science. After his death (Jan. 16, 1866), his patients Warren F. Evans and Julius Dresser tried to continue his work; from their efforts sprang the New Thought movement.

**Quin** (kwĭn), **James.** 1693–1766. Irish actor, b. London; appeared first in Dublin; played small parts at Drury Lane, London, before first success as Bajazet in Rowe's *Tamerlane* (1715); rival to Garrick in such parts as Richard III and Falstaff; retired (1751) to gay life in Bath.

**Quin, Wyndham-.** See Earls of DUNRAVEN.

**Qui'nault'** (kē'nō'). Family of French actors, including: **Jean Baptiste Maurice** (1687–1745); his brother **Abraham Alexis,** called **Qui'nault'-Du'fresne'** [-dü'frân'] (1693–1767), who married the actress **Catherine Marie Jeanne Du'pré'** [dü'prā'] (1705–1767); his sisters **Marie Anne Catherine** (1695–1791), who married secretly the duc de Nevers, and **Jeanne Françoise** (1699–1783).

**Quinault, Philippe.** 1635–1688. French poet and playwright, b. Paris; wrote (between 1653 and 1666) many verse tragedies, tragicomedies, comedies; turned to writing librettos, esp. for operas of Jean Baptiste Lully (*q.v.*); credited with creating the lyric tragedy.

**Quinck'e** (kvĭng'kĕ), **Georg Hermann.** 1834–1924. German physicist; investigated molecular forces of fluids, esp. capillary phenomena, also optical properties of metals and acoustics; constructed an apparatus for measuring the length of sound waves by means of interference. His brother **Heinrich Irenäus** (1842–1922), physician, was the originator of lumbar puncture (1891).

**Quin'cy** (kwĭn'zĭ; -sĭ), **Josiah.** 1744–1775. American lawyer and political leader, b. Boston; practiced in Boston; active as pamphleteer in pre-Revolutionary agitation; on mission to England to argue the cause of the colonies (1774–75); died at sea (Apr. 26, 1775) on his return trip. His son **Josiah** (1772–1864) was a statesman and educator; adm. to bar, Boston (1793); member of U.S. House of Representatives (1805–13); opposed the Embargo Act, admission of Louisiana, and War of 1812; member of Massachusetts State senate (1804–05, 1813–20); mayor of Boston (1823–29); president of Harvard (1829–45); author of *The History of Harvard University* (2 vols., 1840), *A Municipal History...of Boston* (1852), etc. A son of Josiah (1772–1864), **Edmund** (1808–1877), was engaged in the antislavery movement (from 1837); editor of the *Abolitionist* (1839), the *Anti-Slavery Standard* (1844), and, in Garrison's absence, of the *Liberator* (1843, 1846, 1847). Edmund's nephew **Josiah Phillips** (1829–1910), grandson of Josiah (1772–1864), was a lawyer and writer; author of dramatic poems *Lyteria* (1854) and *Charicles* (1856), *The Peckster Professorship* (satirical novel; 1888), etc.

**Quine** (kwīn), **Willard Van Orman.** 1908– . American philosopher, b. Akron, Ohio. At Harvard U. (1936– ); wrote *Elementary Logic* (1941), *From a Logical Point of View* (1953), *Selected Logic Papers* (1966), etc.

**Qui'net'** (kē'nĕ'), **Edgar.** 1803–1875. French writer and politician; studied philosophy in Germany and made French translation (1827) of Herder's *Ideen zur Philosophie der Geschichte der Menschheit;* traveled widely in Greece, Italy, and Spain, and wrote of his observations in these countries. Author of two epic poems (*Napoléon*, 1836, and *Prométhée*, 1838) and a prose drama (*Ahasvérus*, 1833). Was involved in revolutionary activities (1848) and banished from France (1852); again in France (after 1870). Other books by him were *Les Révolutions d'Italie* (1848–52), *Les Esclaves* (verse, 1853), *Histoire de la Campagne de 1815* (1862), *L'Esprit Nouveau* (1874).

**Quinn** (kwĭn), **Edmond Thomas.** 1868–1929. American sculptor and painter, b. Philadelphia; among his works are a bronze statue of Edwin Booth as "Hamlet," in Gramercy Park, New York; *Nymph*, in Metropolitan Museum of Art, etc.

**Quiñónez Molina, Alfonso.** See MOLINA.

**Quin·ta'na** (kēn·tä'nä), **Manuel José.** 1772–1857. Spanish writer and statesman; practiced law, Madrid; secretary of the Cortes and regency; imprisoned (1814–20); president of public instruction (1821); tutor to Queen Isabella (1833); senator (1835). Known particularly for his *Vidas de Españoles Célebres* (3 vols., 1807–34); also wrote patriotic odes, and tragedies, as *El Duque de Viseo* (1801) and *El Pelayo* (1805).

**Quin'tard** (kwĭn'tärd), **George William.** 1822–1913. American manufacturer, b. Stamford, Conn.; manufactured marine engines, notably for U.S. naval ships during Civil War (1861–65); with James Murphy, founded (1869) Quintard Iron Works, manufacturers of marine engines. His brother **Charles Todd** (1824–1898) was a physician and clergyman; served with Confederate army through Civil War; elected bishop of Tennessee (1865); instrumental in founding University of the South (opened 1868) and its vice-chancellor (1868–72).

**Quin·te'ro** (kēn·tā'rō), **Serafín Ál'va·rez** [äl'vä·rāth] (1871–1938) and his brother **Joaquín Álvarez** (1873–1944). Spanish dramatists in collaboration. Their plays, dealing chiefly with Andalusian life, include *El Patio* (1900), *Malvaloca* (1912), and *La Calumniada* (1919). Their plays, translated titles, including *The Women Have Their Way*, *A Hundred Years Old*, *Fortunato*, and *The Lady from Alfaqueque*, have long been popular.

**Quin·til'ian** (kwĭn·tĭl'yăn). *Full Lat. name* **Marcus Fabius Quin·til'i·a'nus** (kwĭn·tĭl'ĭ·ā'nŭs). Roman rhetorician, b. in Spain; taught oratory in Rome (from 68 A.D.). Author of *Institutio Oratoria* (12 books) containing, in addition to principles of rhetoric, a practical exposition of the whole education of a Roman and a description of methods used in the best Roman schools.

**Quintus Icilius.** See GUICHARD.

**Qui·ri'ni** (kwē·rē'nē), **Angelo Maria.** 1680–1755. Italian prelate and scholar; joined Benedictine order (1696); archbishop of Corfu (1723), cardinal (1726), bishop of Brescia (1727); prefect of Vatican library (1730); prefect of Congregation of the Index (1740). Author of *Orthodoxa Veteris Graeciae Officia* (2 vols., 1721), *Enchiridion Graecorum* (1725), *Imago Pauli III* (1745).

**Qui·ri'nus** (kvē·rē'nōōs). Pseudonym of J. J. I. von DÖLLINGER.

**Qui·ri'nus** (kwĭ·rī'nŭs), **Publius Sulpicius.** *In Authorized Version of Bible* **Cy·re'ni·us** (sī·rē'nĭ·ŭs). *In Douay Version* **Cy·ri'nus** (sĭ·rī'nŭs). d. 21 A.D. Roman governor of Syria (probably twice: 4–1 B.C. and from 5 A.D.); during his administration, the census of the Jews for tax purposes was taken at time of Jesus's birth.

**Qui·roz'** (kē·rōsh'). Variant of *Quirós* (see QUEIRÓS).

**Quis'ling** (kvĭs'lĭng; *Angl.* kwĭz'-), **Vidkun.** 1887–1945. Norwegian politician and official; in diplomatic and intelligence service (1918 ff.), esp. in Russia; minister of defense (1931–32); resigned to found own political party (the National Union) with a platform calling for the suppression of Communism and the freeing of Norwegian labor from unionism. Actively collaborated in German conquest of Norway (1940); proclaimed sole political head of Norway (1940), as head of State Council of thirteen Nazi-dominated commissioners. His name has become a synonym for *traitor;* shot.

**Qui'ta** (kē'tȧ), **Domingo dos Reis** (thōōzh rā'ēsh). 1728–1770. Portuguese poet; author of pastorals, idylls, sonnets, odes, and dramas, as *Inês de Castro.*

**Quit'man** (kwĭt'măn), **John Anthony.** 1798–1858. American lawyer and politician, b. Rhinebeck, N.Y.; defended North Carolina's nullification doctrine (1834); in Mexican War, as brigadier general of volunteers, served under Gen. Taylor; governor of Mexico City (1847); governor of Mississippi (1850–51); member, U.S. House of Representatives (1855–58).

**Quo Tai-chi** (gwô' tī'chē'). 1889–1952. Chinese diplomat; educ. U. of Pennsylvania; counselor to Dr. Sun Yat-sen (1921–22); vice-minister for foreign affairs, at Canton (1923–24) and at Nanking; minister (1932–35) and ambassador (1935–41) to Great Britain; delegate to League of Nations Assembly, and representative in League of Nations Council (1936 ff.); foreign minister (1941–42); member UN Security Council (from 1946).

**Qus'ta ibn-Lu'qa** (kōōs'tä ĭb''n·lōō'kä). *Arab.* **Qusṭa ibn-Lūqa.** d. 923? Arab scientist and translator, b. Baalbek; translated works of Aristotle, and the *Mechanica* of Hero of Alexandria; also wrote more than 30 original works on science.

# R

**Raa'be** (rä'bĕ) *or* **Nie'mann–Raa'be** (nē'män-), **Hedwig.** 1844–1905. German actress; m. (1871) Albert Niemann (*q.v.*); portrayer chiefly of naïve roles.

**Raabe, Wilhelm.** *Pseudonym* **Jakob Cor·vi'nus** (kôr-vē'nŏŏs; *Angl.* kôr·vī'nŭs). 1831–1910. German poet and novelist. Author of *Die Chronik der Sperlingsgasse* (an idyl, 1856), *Halb Mär, Halb Mehr* (5 tales, 1859), *Der Hungerpastor* (1864), *Abu Talfan* (1868), *Der Schüdderump* (1870), *Deutscher Mondschein* (4 tales, 1873), *Horacker* (1876), *Alte Nester* (1880), *Odfeld* (1889), *Stopfkuchen* (1891), etc.

**Rab.** See ABBA ARIKA.

**Ra'bah Zo·beir'** (rá'bĭ zōō·bīr'). d. 1900. African chieftain; originally a slave or follower of Zobeir Rahama Pasha (*q.v.*); overthrew sultan of Bornu (1893); attacked sultan of Bagirmi (1897).

**Ra·ba'nus Mau'rus** (rä·bä'nŏŏs mou'rŏŏs). *Also* **Hra·ba'nus** (rä·bä'nŏŏs) *or* **Rha·ba'nus** (rä·bä'nŏŏs) **Maurus.** 776?–856. Frankish theologian, scholar, and teacher, b. Mainz; educ. at Fulda and at Tours (802) under Alcuin, who surnamed him "Maurus." Head of school at Fulda (803); abbot of Fulda (822–842); archbishop of Mainz (from 847); helped spread Romance learning in Germany; opposed Gottschalk's theories of predestination. Author of poems and of many commentaries and theological and pedagogical writings.

**Ra'baud'** (rá'bō'), **Henri Benjamin.** 1873–1949. French conductor and composer of two symphonies, an oratorio (*Job*), operas (*Fille de Roland*, *Mârouf*, *Miracle des Loups*), and many instrumental and choral pieces.

**Rabbi.** = JUDAH HA-NASI.

**Ra'be·lais'** (răb'ĕ·lā'; răb'ĕ·lā; *Fr.* rá'blĕ'), **François.** 1494?–1553. French humorist and satirist, b. near Chinon. Became monk; member of Cordelier convent of Fontenay-le-Comte (1509–24). Studied medicine at Montpellier (1530); practiced at Lyons (1532). Wandered widely in France and Italy; returned to take parish of Meudon (1550–52). Edited various medical treatises. Fame rests on two novels, published under pseudonym **Al'co'fri'bas' Na'sier'** [ál'kô'frē'bás' ná'-zyā'] (an anagram of *François Rabelais*), *Pantagruel* (1533) and *Gargantua* (1535), noted for their broad and racy humor and grotesque invention.

**Ra'be·ner** (rä'bĕ·nĕr), **Gottlieb Wilhelm.** 1714–1771. German satirist; contributed, chiefly to *Bremer Beiträge* (from 1741), prose satires on middle-class life.

**Ra'bi** (rä'bĭ), **Isidor Isaac.** 1898– . American physicist, b. in Austria; to U.S. in infancy; at Columbia U. (1929–67); known esp. for study of radio-frequency spectra of atoms and molecules. Awarded Nobel prize in physics (1944).

**Ra'bi·ah** (rä'bĭ·ă). *Arab.* **Rābi'ah al-'Adawīyah.** *Known as* **Rabiah of Bas'ra** (bŭs'rá). 717?–801 A.D. Arab mystic and poetess; became chief saint of Sunnite hagiology.

**Ra'bi·no'witz** *or* **Ra'bi·no'vitz** (rä'bĭ·nô'vĭts; rá·bĭn'-ô·vĭts), **Solomon.** *Pseudonym* **Sha·lom'** (shä·lōm') *or* **Sho'lem** (shō'lĕm) **A·lei'chem** (á·lā'kĕm). 1859–1916. Yiddish humorist, b. Kiev, Russia; to U.S. (1906).

**Raby,** Baron. See earls of STRAFFORD.

**Ra'can'** (rá'käN'), Marquis **de. Honoré de Bu·eil'** (dē bü·ā'y'). 1589–1670. French poet. His one significant work is a pastoral dramatic elegy, *Arthénice ou les Bergeries* (1619).

**Ra'chel** (rā'chĕl). In the Bible, a daughter of Laban and wife of her cousin Jacob (*q.v.*).

**Ra'chel'** (rá'shĕl'), Mlle. *Stage name of* **Elisa Fé'lix'** (fā'lēks'). 1820–1858. French actress; excelled in tragic roles, as Camille, Roxane, Phèdre, Lucrèce, Cléopâtre.

**Rach'ford** (răsh'fĕrd), **Benjamin Knox.** 1857–1929. American physician, b. Alexandria, Ky. Inaugurated Babies Milk Fund, in Cincinnati (1909). Conducted important investigations in digestive action of the bile and pancreatic juice, in auto-intoxication, and in the activity of various toxins in the body.

**Rachilde.** Pseudonym of Marguerite VALLETTE.

**Rach·ma'ni·noff** (rŭκ·má'nyĭ·nôf), **Sergei Wassilievitch.** 1873–1943. Russian composer, pianist, and conductor, b. in Novgorod government. Professor of piano, Marzinsky Institute for Girls, Moscow (1893 ff.); conductor of a private opera (1897–98) and Moscow Imperial Theater (1904–06); appeared as pianist and conductor in principal European and American cities; resident in Dresden (1907–18) and New York (from 1918). His compositions include piano concertos and other piano pieces, notably the prelude in C sharp minor, short operas (*Aleko*, 1893; *The Miser Knight*, 1906; *Francesca da Rimini*, 1906), symphonies, a symphonic poem (*The Isle of Death*), the cantata *The Bells* (1914), choruses, songs, chamber music, etc.

**Ra'cine'** (rá'sēn'; *Angl.* rá·sēn'), **Jean Baptiste.** 1639–1699. French dramatic poet, b. at La Ferté-Milon. At court (from 1663), member of group including La Fontaine, Boileau, and Molière; had his first two plays, *La Thébaïde* (1664) and *Alexandre* (1665), produced by Molière's company at the Palais Royal; dissatisfied with production, submitted plays thenceforth to rival company, the Hôtel de Bourgogne, which successfully played his masterpieces of tragedy, *Andromaque* (1667), *Britannicus* (1669), *Bérénice* (1670), *Bajazet* (1672), *Mithridate* (1673), *Iphigénie* (1674), *Phèdre* (1677). After the War of the Sonnets (see Nicolas PRADON), wrote two religious tragedies, *Esther* (1689) and *Athalie* (1691). His biography was written by his son **Louis** (1692–1763).

**Rack'ham** (răk'ăm), **Arthur.** 1867–1939. British artist and illustrator; best known for illustrations of children's classics, as *The Legend of Sleepy Hollow*, Andersen's *Fairy Tales*, *The Pied Piper of Hamelin*, *Peer Gynt*.

**Racz·kie'wicz** (räch·kyĕ'vēch), **Władysław.** 1885–1947. Polish lawyer; in Russian army (1914–17), later organizing Polish forces on Eastern front; Polish minister of interior; president of senate (1930–35); president of Polish government in exile (1939–45).

**Ra·czyń'ski** (rä·chĭn'y'·skē), Count **Edward.** 1786–1845. Polish scholar; author of *Poland and the Poles* (1840), *Memories of Great Poland* (1842–43), etc.

**Ra'da** (rä'thä) *or* **Her·ra'da** (ĕr·rä'thä), **Juan de.** 1490?–1542. Spanish soldier, b. in Castile; in Chile with Diego de Almagro (1535–36); led conspiracy against Pizarro (1541); reputed slayer of Pizarro (June 26, 1541); set up Almagro's son Diego as governor of Peru.

**Rad'a·gai'sus** (răd'á·gī'sŭs) *or* **Rad'a·gais** (răd'á·gīs). d. 406. Germanic chieftain; invaded Italy (405 A.D.) and besieged Florence, where he was defeated by Stilicho; surrounded at Faesulae (Fiesole) and captured.

**Rad'cliffe** (răd'klĭf), **Ann,** *nee* **Ward** (wôrd). 1764–1823. English romantic novelist, b. London; m., at age of 23, William Radcliffe, law student, later proprietor and editor of *The English Chronicle*. Traveled and described scenery and medieval ruins in journal; laid scene of first novel (1789) in Scotland. Originator of school of romance characterized by vivid scenic description and by startling events and horrors seemingly supernatural but ultimately traced to natural causes. Author of *A Sicilian Romance* (1790), *The Romance of the Forest* (1791), *The Mysteries of Udolpho* (1794), and *The Italian* (1797).

**Rad'cliffe** *or* **Rad'clyffe** (răd'klĭf), Sir **James.** 3d Earl of **Der'went·wa'ter** (dûr'wĕnt·wô'tẽr; -wŏt'ẽr). 1689–1716. English Jacobite nobleman; grandson of Sir **Francis Radcliffe** (d. 1697), 1st earl (cr. 1688), and son of **Edward Radcliffe** (1655–1705), 2d earl, and Lady Mary Tudor, daughter of Charles II by the actress Moll Davis. Brought up as companion of Prince James Edward, Old Pretender, in France (till 1710); leader in Stuart rising (1715), taken prisoner at Preston, attainted, beheaded.

**Radcliffe, John.** 1650–1714. English physician; attended William III, Queen Mary, and Princess Anne, despite his Jacobitism; M.P. (1713); bequeathed property to Radcliffe Library, Infirmary, and Observatory, Oxford.

**Rad'cliffe** *or* **Rad'clyffe** (răd'klĭf) *or* **Rat'clyffe** (răt'klĭf), Sir **Thomas.** 3d Earl of **Sus'sex** (sŭs'ĕks; -ĭks). 1526?–1583. English lord deputy of Ireland (1556–64); vigorously subjugated various parts of island and reintroduced spiritual supremacy of the crown and the English liturgy; failed to subdue O'Neill.

**Ra'de** (rä'dĕ), **Paul Martin.** *Pseudonym* **Paul Mar'tin** (mär'tēn). 1857–1940. German Lutheran theologian, b. in Silesia; champion of evangelical freedom.

**Ra'dek** (rȧ'dyĕk), **Karl Bernardovich.** 1885–?1939. Russian Communist politician, b. Lwów; educ. Cracow and Bern. Joined Social Democratic party (1904), and was in prison for a year (1905). Journalist on Social Democratic papers in Poland and Germany (1906–14); in Switzerland during early part of World War. After Russian Revolution (1917), accompanied Lenin, Zinoviev, and others across Germany. Took part in Brest Litovsk peace negotiations; after German Revolution (1918), went to Germany and aided in reorganizing German Communist party; imprisoned in Germany (1919). To Russia (1920), and rose to leadership in the Communist International, but lost his influence (c. 1923); charged with being an adherent of Trotsky, and dismissed from the party (1925; readmitted 1930); tried in Moscow (1937) for treasonable activities and condemned to ten years' imprisonment.

**Ra·dets'ki** (rŭ·dyāts'kû·ĭ; *Angl.* rȧ·dĕts'kĭ), **Fëdor Fëdorovich.** 1820–1890. Russian general; noted for his defense of Shipka Pass (Aug.–Sept., 1877) during the war with Turkey.

**Ra·detz'ky** (rä·dĕts'kē), **Joseph Wenzel.** Count **Radetzky von Ra'detz** (fōn rä'dĕts). 1766–1858. Austrian soldier; served against Napoleon at Hohenlinden, Aspern, Wagram; chief of staff for Prince Schwarzenberg (1813–14, 1815). Created field marshal (1836). Commanded Austrian army which defeated Sardinians at Custoza (1848) and Novara (1849) and captured Venice (1849). Governor general of Lombardy-Venetia (1849–57).

**Ra'dha·krish'nan** (rä'dŭ·krĭsh'nŭɴ), Sir **Sar've·pal'li** (sŭr'vē·pŭl'lĭ). 1888–1975. East Indian philosopher and educator in England; professor of Eastern religions and ethics, Oxford (1936–52). Among his many works are *The Hindu View of Life* (1927), *Eastern Religions and Western Thought* (1939); president of India (1962–67).

**Ra'dić** (rä'dĕt·y'; *Angl.* -dĭch), **Stefan.** 1871–1928. Croat politician; organized (1904) and headed Croatian Peasant party. Member of legislature in newly organized Yugoslavia and for a short time (1925–26) minister of education; assassinated in parliament.

**Ra'di'guet'** (rȧ'dē'gĕ'), **Raymond.** 1903–1923. French poet and novelist; author of *Les Joues en Feu* (verse; 1920), *Devoirs de Vacances* (verse; 1921), *Le Diable au Corps* (novel; 1923), *Le Bal du Comte d'Orgel* (novel; 1924).

**Ra·di'shchev** (rŭ·dyē'shchĕf), **Aleksandr Nikolaevich.** 1749–1802. Russian writer; best known for his *Voyage from Petersburg to Moscow* (1790), in which he criticized serfdom, absolutism in government, and religion; exiled to Siberia.

**Ra'dis'son'** (rȧ'dē'sôɴ'), **Pierre Esprit.** 1636–?1710. Fur trader and explorer; b. prob. Paris, France; to Canada (c. 1651). Captured and adopted by Iroquois Indians (1651–54); escaped (1654). Made fur-trading trips to western country (1657, 1659), perhaps reaching Upper Mississippi waters. Entered English service (c. 1660); made expedition to Hudson Bay Region; inspired organization of Hudson's Bay Company (chartered 1670) for fur trade in this region. His accounts of his voyages were published as *Voyages of Peter Esprit Radisson* (1885).

**Raditch.** = Radić.

**Rad'loff** (rät'lôf), **Wilhelm.** 1837–1918. German-Russian philologist, b. Berlin. Teacher, Barnaul, Siberia (1859–70); inspector of Mohammedan schools in Kazan (1871–84); curator of Asiatic museum, St. Petersburg (1884 ff.); did research work in dialects in Crimea (1886) and Lithuania (1887).

**Ra'do·sla'vov** (rȧ'dô·slȧ'vôf), **Vasil.** 1854–1929. Bulgarian statesman; premier of Bulgaria (1913–18) and largely instrumental in causing Bulgaria to enter World War I on side of Central Powers. Fled to Berlin (1918).

**Ra'do·witz** (rä'dō·vĭts), **Joseph Maria von.** 1797–1853. Prussian general and statesman; friend and adviser of crown prince (later Frederick William IV). Leader of ultraconservatives in Frankfurt National Assembly (1848); lieutenant general (1849). At Erfurt Parliament (1850), championed a union of German states under Prussian leadership; foreign minister (1850); director of military education (1852).

**Ră·du·le'scu** (rȧ·dōō·lĕ'skōō), **Ioan Heliade.** 1802–1872. Rumanian writer; founded and edited first Rumanian periodical in Bucharest, the literary journal *Curierul Românesc* (1829–48). Involved in revolutionary activities (1848); lived abroad, but returned (1859). Author of plays, literary history and criticism, a national epic poem (*Mihaida*, 1846), and translations from works of Dante, Tasso, Molière, Lamartine, Byron, etc.

**Radvanyi, Netty.** See Anna Seghers.

**Ra·dzi'will.** *Pol.* **Ra·dzi'wiłł** (rä·jē'vēl). Lithuanian-Polish family raised to rank of princes of the realm in 16th century, including notably: **Nicholas** (1515–1565), called "the Black," voivode of Vilna; received from the emperor the title of prince of Nieswiez; an ardent Calvinist, published a translation of the Bible into Polish. The eccentric and enormously wealthy **Charles Stanislas** (1734–1790). The musician and composer Prince **Anthony Henry** (1775–1833); married the daughter of Prince Ferdinand of Prussia; composed a musical adaptation of Goethe's *Faust*. Anthony's grandson Prince **Ferdinand** (1834–1926), member of the German Reichstag (1874–1918) and head of the Polish group therein. Ferdinand's son Prince **Janusz** (1880–1967) supported Piłsudski after his coup d'état (1926) and served as chairman of the committee of foreign affairs in the Diet (after 1930).

**Radziwill,** Princess **Catherine.** *Russ.* **Ekaterina Rad·zi·vil'** (rŭt·zyĭ·vyēl'). *Pseudonym* Count **Paul Vas·si'li** (vŭ·syē'lyû·ĭ). 1858–1941. Russian writer; m. Prince Adam Radziwill; and 2d, Charles Danvin. Among her many works are *Behind the Veil of the Russian Court,*

*Confessions of the Czarina, The Firebrand of Bolshevism, Nicholas II, the Last of the Tsars, The Taint of the Romanovs.*

**Rae** (rā), **John.** 1813–1893. Scottish Arctic explorer, b. in Orkney Islands. Doctor to Hudson's Bay Co.; joined expedition of Sir John Richardson in search of Sir John Franklin (1847); on several exploring expeditions (between 1846 and 1864); proved King William's Land to be an island and learned fate of Franklin from natives of west coast of Boothia (1853–54).

**Rae′burn** (rā′bẽrn; -bûrn), Sir **Henry.** 1756–1823. Scottish portrait painter; called the Scottish Reynolds. Fashionable Edinburgh portrait painter (from 1787), including among his sitters Scott, Hume, Boswell, Christopher North, Lord Melville, Henry Mackenzie, and Dugald Stewart.

**Rae′der** (râ′dẽr), **Erich.** 1876–1960. German admiral; chief of staff under Admiral von Hipper during World War; took part in fighting at Dogger Bank and Jutland, bombardments along the English coast, etc.; admiral (1928); grand admiral (1939); commander in chief of navy (1935–43); sentenced to life imprisonment (1946).

**Raedwald.** See REDWALD.

**Rae′mae′kers** (rá′má′kẽrs), **Louis.** 1869–1956. Dutch political cartoonist and artist, b. in Roermond. His works include landscapes, portraits, posters, and esp., anti-German cartoons which appeared chiefly in the Amsterdam *Telegraaf* during and after the World War, and were published in *The Great War in 1916, The Great War in 1917, Devant l'Histoire* (1918), *Cartoon History of the War* (1919).

**Rafael, Raffael, Raffaello, Raffaelo.** See RAPHAEL.

**Raff** (räf), **Joseph Joachim.** 1822–1882. German composer, b. in Switzerland; director, Hoch Conservatory, Frankfurt am Main (from 1877). Composer of chamber music, works for piano, symphonies, operas, orchestral suites, overtures, concertos, string quartets, violin sonatas, songs, stage music, etc.

**Raf′fa·e·li′no del Gar′bo** (räf′fä·å·lē′nō däl gär′bō). *Real name* **Raffaello Cap·po′ni** (käp·pō′nē). 1466–1524. Florentine painter; pupil of Botticelli and Filippino Lippi.

**Raf′fa′el′li′** (rá′fá′ĕ′lē′), **Jean François.** 1850–1924. French painter, of Italian descent, b. Paris; identified with impressionists; painter esp. of scenes in the streets and suburbs of Paris.

**Raffaellino.** See Raffaello dal COLLE.

**Raf′fet′** (rá′fĕ′), **Denis Auguste Marie.** 1804–1860. French lithographer and illustrator. Among books illustrated by him were Béranger's *Chansons*, Chateaubriand's *Œuvres*, Thiers's *Histoire de la Révolution Française*. Best known for his lithographs of battle scenes.

**Raf′fles** (răf′'lz), Sir **Thomas Stamford.** 1781–1826. English colonial administrator; founder of Singapore. Sent to Penang as asst. secretary to first governor (1805). Persuaded Lord Minto of necessity of taking Java from French and accompanied expedition; as lieutenant governor of Java (1811–16), introduced new system of land tenure and removed fetters imposed on trade. As lieutenant governor of Benkulen in Sumatra (1818–23), by acquisition and founding of Singapore (1819), checked threatened control by Dutch of Eastern Archipelago.

**Ra′fi′nesque′** (rá′fē′nĕsk′), **Constantine Samuel.** *Called himself* **Ra′fi′nesque′-Schmaltz′** (-shmälts′) *to 1814.* 1783–1840. Naturalist, b. Constantinople, of French parentage. In U.S. (1802–04); Palermo, Sicily (1804–14); again U.S. (1815–40); traveled throughout U.S. on collecting trips; described many new species of plants and fishes. Author of *Ichthyologia Ohioensis* (1820), *Medical Flora of the United States* (1828–30), etc.

**Rafn** (räv′'n; räf′'n), **Carl Christian.** 1795–1864. Danish philologist and antiquary; published works on Norse sagas and antiquities, as *Antiquitates Americanae* (1837) on the discovery of America by the Scandinavians in the 10th century.

**Ra′ghu·nath′ Rao** (rŭ′gŏŏ·nät′ rä′ŏŏ) *or* **Ra′go·ba** (rŭ′gō·bä). d. 1783. Maratha leader, brother of Balaji Baji Rao. Seized Lahore and control of the Punjab (1758); defeated Mogul forces (1763); was seized and imprisoned (1768) by Madhu Rao I; caused murder of Narayan Rao (1773), the fifth peshwa; became involved in civil war (1773–74); asked aid of British at Bombay, promising cession of Salsette and Bassein (1774); signed Treaty of Surat (1775); received pension.

**Rag′lan** (răg′lăn), 1st Baron. **Fitzroy James Henry Som′er·set** (sŭm′ẽr·sĕt; -sĭt). 1788–1855. British field marshal; 8th son of 5th duke of Beaufort (cf. SOMERSET family). Aide-de-camp to duke of Wellington in Peninsular War (1808–12), military secretary (1812–14); lost his sword arm at Waterloo. Military secretary to Wellington (1827–52); succeeded Wellington as commander of forces and was created Baron Raglan of Raglan (1852). Commanded British troops in Crimean War; won battle of Alma (1854); blamed Lucan for loss of light brigade at Balaklava (1854); made field marshal for victory at Inkerman (1854); made scapegoat for failure of commissariat during winter (1854–55); died ten days after repulse at Malakoff and Redan. The raglan overcoat was named for him.

**Ra·guet′** (?rä·gā′), **Con′dy** (?kŏn′dĭ). 1784–1842. American economist, b. Philadelphia. Founded *Free Trade Advocate, and Journal of Political Economy* (1829), which changed to *Banner of the Constitution* (1830) and was succeeded by *The Examiner, and Journal of Political Economy* (1833–35). Proprietor, Philadelphia *Gazette* (1835). Author of *The Principles of Free Trade*... (1835), *A Treatise on Currency and Banking* (1839), etc.

**Ra′hab** (rā′hăb). In the Bible (*Joshua* ii and vi. 22–25), a harlot of Jericho who hid Joshua's spies and helped them to escape.

**Rah′bek** (rä′bĕk), **Knud Lyne.** 1760–1830. Danish poet, writer, and literary critic. Directed literary periodical *Minerva* (1785–1809) and edited (1791–1808, 1815–22) *Den Danske Tilskuer*, modeled after the English *Spectator;* published editions of Scandinavian poets, esp. Holberg, dramatic and literary criticisms, stories, dramas, lyric poetry, etc.

**Rahl** (räl), **Karl.** 1812–1865. Austrian historical and portrait painter.

**Raibolini, Francesco.** See FRANCIA.

**Raiff′ei′sen** (rīf′ī′zĕn), **Friedrich Wilhelm.** 1818–1888. German economist; founder of German agricultural cooperative credit societies following agricultural crisis of 1846–47; retired to Neuwied (1865) and founded the system of agricultural co-operative banks (Raiffeisen bank).

**Raikes** (rāks), **Robert.** 1735–1811. English publisher and founder of Sunday schools.

**Raimond, C. E.** Pseudonym of Elizabeth ROBINS.

**Rai·mon′di** (rī·mōn′dē), **Marcantonio.** *Often called* **Marc′an·to′ni·o** (märk′än·tô′nyō). 1475?–?1534. Italian engraver, b. Bologna; reputedly a pupil of Francia; leading Italian line engraver of the Renaissance; employed at Rome (1510–27). Among his works are *The Climbers* (after Michelangelo), and *Poetry, Massacre of the Innocents, Quos Ego, Judgment of Paris, Death of Dido* (all after Raphael).

**Raimondi, Pietro.** 1786–1853. Italian composer, known esp. for compositions in counterpoint; composer of operas, ballets, and religious music.

**Raimond Lulle.** See Raymond LULLY.

**Rai'mund** (rī'mŏŏnt), **Ferdinand.** *Orig. surname* **Rai'mann** (rī'män). 1790–1836. Austrian actor and playwright; appeared chiefly in local comedy roles at the Leopoldstädter Theater, Vienna (1817–30), where he was director (1828–30); committed suicide (1836). Author of romantic dramas and comedies.

**Raimundus Lullus.** See Raymond LULLY.

**Rainalducci, Pietro.** See Antipope NICHOLAS V.

**Raine** (rān), **William MacLeod.** 1871–1954. Journalist and writer of adventure stories, especially westerns; b. in London, Eng.; to U.S. (1881). His books include *A Texas Ranger* (1911), *The Yukon Trail* (1917), *Ironheart* (1923), *Border Breed* (1935), *Sons of the Saddle* (1938), *The River Bend Feud* (1939), *Riders of the Rim Rocks* (1940).

**Raines** (rānz), **John.** 1840–1909. American legislator; member, New York State Assembly (1881–83, 1885), New York State Senate (1886–89, 1895–1909), U.S. House of Representatives (1889–93). Chiefly remembered as author of Raines Law (1896) providing that no liquor should be sold on Sunday except in licensed hotels having no less than ten bedrooms; saloons thereupon added rooms to qualify for right to serve liquor and these "Raines Law Hotels" soon gained bad reputation.

**Rai'ney** (rā'nĭ), **Paul J.** 1877–1923. American explorer and hunter; made motion pictures of African wild animals in their native environment.

**Rai'nis** (rä'ē·nĭs), **Jan.** *Pseudonym of* **Jan Pliek'šans** (plē'ĕk·shäns). 1865–1929. Latvian writer; in exile (1905–20); returned to Latvia after its establishment as independent republic. Among his works are the symbolical dramas *Fire and Night*, *Induls and Arija*, and *The Sons of Jacob*, and translations of Goethe's *Faust*, Shakespeare's *King Lear*, etc.

**Rain'olds** *or* **Reyn'olds** (rĕn''ldz), **John.** 1549–1607. English Biblical scholar; president of Corpus Christi Coll., Oxford (1598–1607). Representing Puritan party at Hampton Court Conference, urged upon king need for authorized version of the Bible; assisted in translation of the Prophets.

**Rain'wa'ter** (rān'wô'tẽr; -wŏt'ẽr), **L. James,** *in full* **Leo James.** 1917– . American physicist. At Columbia U. (1939– ); awarded (with Aage N. Bohr and Ben Roy Mottelson) Nobel prize for physics (1975).

**Rai'ny** (rā'nĭ), **Robert.** 1826–1906. Scottish Presbyterian leader; principal (1874–1901), Free Church Coll. Combated Dean Stanley's Broad-Church views and William Robertson Smith's views on use of hymns and instrumental music; as champion of liberal party, carried union of the Free and United Presbyterian churches (1900); first moderator of United Free Church of Scotland.

**Rais** *or* **Raiz.** See Baron de RETZ.

**Rai San·yo** (rä·ē sän·yō). 1780–1833. Japanese historian; author of *Nihon-gwaishi*, written in Chinese (22 vols.) and of *Nihon-seiki*, also written in Chinese (16 vols.); works credited with inspiring Samurai to overthrow the power of the Shoguns in the revolution of 1868.

**Rai·su'li** (rä·sōō'lĭ), **Ah'med ibn–Mu·ham'med** (ä'măd ĭb''n mōō·hăm'măd). 1875?–1925. Moroccan brigand; kidnaped Walter Harris, London *Times* correspondent in Tangier, Ion Perdicaris, naturalized American citizen (1904), and Sir Harry Maclean (1907); his demands for ransom met by his superior, the sultan of Morocco, in order to avoid disastrous war with other nations.

**Ra'ja·go·pa'la·cha'ri** (rä'jȧ·gō·pä'lä·chä'rē), **Cha'kra·var'ti** (chŭ'krȧ·vŭr'tĭ). 1879–1972. Called "C. R."; also "the Tamil Ma·hat'ma (mȧ·hät'mȧ; *Angl.* -hăt'-)." Indian Nationalist leader. An ascetic Brahman; lawyer and politician; closely associated with Gandhi (from 1918); prime minister of Madras (1937–39); governor general of India (1948–50); founder of conservative *Swatantra* ("Freedom") party (1959).

**Rajaraja I.** See CHOLA.

**Rajendra Choladeva I.** See CHOLA.

**Rajendralala Mitra.** See MITRA.

**Raj'na** (rī'nä), **Pio.** 1847–1930. Italian philologist; author of *Le Origini dell'Epopea Francese* (1884), etc.

**Rá'kó·czy** (rä'kō·tsĭ). Name of a distinguished Transylvanian family, including notably: **George I** (1591–1648), prince of Transylvania (1631–48); allied himself with the Swedes and French in invading Austria (1644–45) and won important political concessions. **Francis II** (1676–1735), a Protestant; headed insurrection in Hungary (1703) and extended his power over Hungary and Transylvania, but was defeated by the Austrians (1708) and lived thereafter in exile.

**Rá'ko·si** (rä'kô·shĭ), **Jenő.** 1842–1929. Hungarian journalist, poet, dramatist, and writer. Edited radical and reform journals. Author of the comedy *Aesop* (1866), the tragedies *Magdalene* (1884) and *Andrew and Joanna* (1885), the novel *The Greatest Fool*, translations of Shakespeare, etc.

**Ra·kov'ski** (rŭ·kôf'skû·ĭ; *Angl.* -skĭ), **Khristian Georgievich.** 1873–194?. Bulgarian-born Russian politician and diplomat, of Rumanian descent; during early years of World War I, was arrested and imprisoned for his subversive activities. After the Russian Revolution (1917), became (1919) member of the Central Committee of the Communist Party. President, Soviet of People's Commissars of the Ukraine (1919 ff.). Soviet chargé d'affaires in London (1924); Soviet ambassador to France (1926–27). In struggle between Trotsky and Stalin, opposed Stalin; was expelled from the Communist party and exiled to Stalingrad.

**Ra'leigh** *or* **Ra'legh** (rô'lĭ; rä'lĭ; răl'ĭ), Sir **Walter.** *Spelled his name consistently* **Ralegh** *(from 1581) but never* **Raleigh,** *the prevailing modern form.* 1552?–1618. English courtier, navigator, historian, and poet. Joined his half brother Sir Humphrey Gilbert in piratical expedition against Spaniards (1578); active and cruel in suppression of Desmonds in Munster (1580). At court as protégé of Leicester, caught Queen Elizabeth's fancy; given estates, a license for exporting woolen goods, made warden of the stannaries. Granted patent to take unknown lands in America in queen's name; sent expedition which explored coast from Florida to North Carolina (1584) and named coast north of Florida "Virginia"; sent settlers (1585) who occupied Roanoke Island, North Carolina, but deserted colony (1586); made later unsuccessful attempts to colonize Virginia. Succeeded in introducing potatoes and tobacco into England, also into Ireland, where he set about repeopling his estates and where he became friend of poet Spenser; eclipsed as favorite by Essex and banished for four years from queen's presence because of intrigue and secret marriage with one of her maids, Elizabeth Throckmorton. Fitted out bootless expedition to seek fabulous wealth of Guiana, explored coasts of Trinidad and sailed up the Orinoco (1595); took brilliant part in expedition against Cádiz (1596) and attack on the Azores (1597). On death of Elizabeth (1603) was stripped of his offices and estates; on charge of conspiring against James I, sent to Tower of London, where he lived with wife and son (till 1616) and composed his *History of the World* (1614; carried down to 130 B.C.). Released in order to seek gold along the Orinoco, under promise not to entrench on Spanish possessions; set out on ill-fated expedition; lost his fleet by storms, lost men by desertion and disease, stricken with fever, lost his son Walter, returned (1618). On demand of Spanish minister, angered by destruction of new Spanish town San Tomás, beheaded at Whitehall under the old sentence against him. Author of poems, of which only about thirty fragments survive, including *Cynthia, the Lady of the Sea; Methought I saw the Grave where Laura lay; The Lie; The Pilgrimage;* prose works on the fight over the Azores and the discovery of Guiana; and political essays.

**Ra'leigh** (rô'lĭ), Sir **Walter Alexander.** 1861–1922. English critic and essayist; professor of modern literature, University Coll., Liverpool (1889), of English literature, Glasgow (1900) and Oxford (1904). Author of *The English Novel* (1894), *Style* (1897), *Milton* (1900), *Wordsworth* (1903), *Shakespeare* (1907), *Six Essays on Johnson* (1910), *Romance* (1917), and *War in the Air* (first volume of official history of Royal Air Force, 1922).

**Ralles** *or* **Rallis.** See RHALLES.

**Ralph** (rălf), **James.** 1695?–1762. American writer in England; b. probably in New Jersey; accompanied Benjamin Franklin to London (1724). Imitated James Thomson in blank-verse poems *The Tempest* and *Night* (1727); attacked Pope in *Sawney;* staged ballad-opera *The Fashionable Lady*, first play by an American on London stage (1730); in employ of George Bubb Dodington and Frederick Louis, Prince of Wales, as political writer and liaison officer; given pension by Pelham ministry to purchase his silence. Author of *The History of England*, from the Restoration through reign of William III (2 vols., 1744, 1746), and *The Case of Authors by Profession*, a defense of the professional writer under system of patronage (1758).

**Ralph, Julian.** 1853–1903. American journalist, b. New York City. On staff of New York *World* (1872), New York *Daily Graphic* (1873–75), New York *Sun* (1875–95). London correspondent for New York *Journal* (1895); accompanied Turkish army in war against Greece (1897). War correspondent for London *Daily Mail* (1899), accompanying Lord Roberts expedition to Bloemfontein.

**Ral'ston** (rôl'stŭn), **James Layton.** 1881–1948. Canadian statesman, b. Amherst, Nova Scotia; practiced law (1903–26; 1930–39); Canadian minister of national defense (1926–30), of finance (1939–40), again of national defense (1940–44).

**Ra'ma** (rä'mä). Name of seven kings of Siam (Thailand) of the Chakri dynasty:

**Rama I.** *Full name* **Chao P'ya Chakri.** King (1782–1809); terminated war with Burma (1793); established control over petty chieftains and secured part of Cambodia (1809); made Bangkok capital.

**Rama II.** King (1809–24).

**Rama III.** King (1824–51); established relations with western nations; signed treaties of commerce with Britain (1826) and U.S. (1833).

**Rama IV.** King (1851–68); a monk; began work of modernizing Siam; made new treaties with Britain (1855) and U.S. (1856) and similar treaties with nine other countries; relinquished Cambodia to French (1867).

**Rama V.** *Better known as* **Chu'la'long'korn'** (cho͝o'lä'lông'kôn'). *Full name* **Somdeth Phra Paraminda Maha Chulalongkorn.** 1853–1910. Son of Rama IV; b. Bangkok; king (1868–1910; under regency 1868–73); abolished feudal system and slavery; improved education, laws, and communications; introduced telegraph (1883); opened first railway (1893); in controversy with France forced to yield territory by the Franco-Siamese treaty (1893); visited European capitals (1897); signed later agreements with France by which (1904, 1907) further rearrangement of boundaries was made.

**Rama VI.** *Full name* **Chao Fa Maha Vajiravudh.** 1881–1925. Son of Rama V; educ. in England (1893–1901); held position in government administration (1902–10); king (1910–25); continued progressive policy of father; revised the calendar; instituted reforms in taxation; started many irrigation projects; declared war on Germany and Austria (1917); made treaty with U.S. (1920), abolishing extraterritorial rights for Americans; signed treaty with France (1925). Succeeded by his brother Prajadhipok (*q.v.*), rarely referred to as **Rama VII.**

**Ra'ma·krish'na** (rä'mȧ·krĭsh'nȧ). 1834–1886. Hindu yogi; spent adult life in service of a temple to the goddess Kali on the banks of the Ganges near Calcutta; averse to books and western ideas; looked upon as a sainted wise man by Hindus. The Ramakrishna Mission (a Vedantic order) founded (1897) by his followers.

**Ra'man** (rä'mȧn), Sir **Chan'dra·se'kha·ra** (chŭn'drȧ-shā'kȧ·rȧ) **Ven'ka·ta** (vāng'kȧ·tȧ). 1888–1970. Indian physicist; professor, Calcutta U. (1917–33); special university lecturer at Madras and other cities of India (1914–30); research associate, California Institute of Technology (1924); general president of Indian Science Congress (1928); knighted (1929); awarded Nobel prize in physics (1930) for important discovery in diffusion of light, especially the Raman effect (first announced, 1928); president, Indian Academy of Sciences (1934); author of many scientific papers.

**Ra'ma·nand'** (rä'mä·nŭnd'). fl. 14th century. Hindu teacher from the south of India who settled at Benares; wandered about India preaching in Hindi; appealed to people of all castes or of no caste; one of his disciples was Kabir (*q.v.*).

**Ra·ma'nu·ja** (rä·mä'no͝o·jȧ). d. about 1150 A.D. South Indian religious teacher, founder of the Vaishnava sect, and commentator on the Upanishads, etc. Lived at Srirangam; driven out by hostile king, fled to Mysore; converted ruler of Mysore and is said to have founded 700 monasteries; taught a monistic philosophy based on a belief in the incarnation of Vishnu.

**Ra·ma'nu·jan** (rä·mä'no͝o·jŭN), **Sri'ni·va'sa** (shrē'nĭ-vä'sȧ; srē'-). *Properly* **Srinivasa Ra·ma'nu·ja** (rä·mä'-no͝o·jȧ) **Ai·yen'gar** (ī·yŭN'gär). 1887–1920. East Indian mathematician; educ. Madras U. To England (1914), where he engaged in original research. Best known for studies on theory of numbers, theory of partitions, and theory of continued fractions.

**Ra'ma Ti'bo·ti'** (rä'mä tĭ'bô·tē') *or* **Thi'bo·di'** (tĭ'-bô·dē'). Founder of the Siamese monarchy (c. 1350); set up new Thaï state with capital at Ayuthia.

**RaMBaM.** See MAIMONIDES.

**Ram'baud'** (räN'bō'), **Alfred Nicolas.** 1842–1905. French historian; author of *L'Empire Grec au X^e Siècle ...* (1870), *L'Allemagne sous Napoléon I^er* (1874), *Histoire de la Révolution Française* (1883), *La France Coloniale* (1886), etc.

**Ramboldini** *or* **de' Ramboldoni, Vittorino.** See VITTORINO DA FELTRE.

**Ram'bouil'let'** (räN'bo͞o'yĕ'), Marquise **de. Catherine de Vi'vonne' de Sa'vel'li'** (dē vē'vôn' dē sȧ'vĕ'lē'). 1588–1665. French social leader; m. Charles d'Angennes, Marquis de Rambouillet (1600); established literary center at her salon in her home, Hôtel de Rambouillet, in Paris.

**Ra'meau'** (rȧ'mō'), **Jean.** *Pseudonym of* **Laurent La'baigt'** (lȧ'bĕ'). 1859–1942. French poet and novelist.

**Rameau, Jean Philippe.** 1683–1764. French organist and composer, esp. of operas and ballets.

**Ra·mée′, Marie Louise de la** (dĕl′ȧ·rȧ·mā′). *Pseudonym* **Oui′da** ([wē′dȧ]: *nursery pron. of Louise*). 1839–1908. English novelist. Published romances of fashionable life, including *Held in Bondage* (1863), *Under Two Flags* (1867), *Tricotrin* (1869), *Puck* (1870), *Moths* (1880), *Street Dust* (1901). To Florence (1874); depicted Italian peasant life, as in *A Village Commune* (1881); wrote also animal stories, esp. *A Dog of Flanders* (1872), and children's stories, as *Bimbi* (1882).

**Ramée, Pierre La.** See Petrus RAMUS.

**Ra′mek** (rä′mĕk), **Rudolf.** 1881–1941. Austrian statesman; member of Christian Socialist party, National Assembly (1919); succeeded Seipel as Bund chancellor (1924–26); second president of National Council (1930).

**Ramenghi, Bartolommeo.** See Il BAGNACAVALLO.

**Rameses.** Variant of RAMSES.

**Ram′es·sides** (răm′ĕ·sīdz; -sĭdz). The kings of ancient Egypt named Ramses, esp. those of XXth dynasty, Ramses III–XII, from about 1198 to 1090 B.C.

**Ra·mí′rez** (rä·mē′rās), **Pedro.** 1884–1962. Argentine cavalry officer; major general, commander of cavalry (1942); minister of war (Nov., 1942); resigned to join Arturo Rawson (*q.v.*) in coup that overthrew Castillo government (June 4, 1943); president (1943–44).

**Ra·mi′ro** (rä·mē′rō). Name of five kings of early Spain: (1) *Of León:* **Ramiro I** (791?–850); king (842–850). **Ramiro II** (923?–950); king (930–950); won great victory at Simancas over the Caliph Abd-er-Rahman. **Ramiro III** (962–982); king (967–982). (2) *Of Aragon:* **Ramiro I** (d. 1063); son of Sancho the Great of Navarre; first king of Aragon (1035–63); increased by conquest the territories of his kingdom. **Ramiro II,** *called* **the Monk,** *Span.* **el Mon′je** [ĕl mông′hā] (d. 1147); brother of Alfonso I; king (1134–37).

**Ram′ler** (räm′lẽr), **Karl Wilhelm.** 1725–1798. German poet; master of poetic diction. Wrote odes, the cantata *Der Tod Jesu* (1755; music by Graun), etc.

**Ram′mels·berg** (räm′ĕls·bĕrk), **Karl Friedrich.** 1813–1899. German chemist and mineralogist.

**Ram Mo′han Roy** *or* **Ram′mo′hun Roy** (räm′ mō′hŏn rō′ĭ; rä′ĭ), Raja. 1774–1833. Hindu religious reformer and founder of the Brahmo Samaj, b. near Murshidabad, Bengal, of Brahman parentage. Published (1790) a tract against idolatry; settled in Calcutta (1814) and devoted himself to religious reform; formed Spiritual Society (1816) which later (1830) developed into the Brahmo Samaj, a Hindu theistic society (cf. KESHUB CHUNDER SEN); active in abolishing suttee (1830); granted title of raja by emperor of Delhi; a scholar in several Oriental languages; wrote works in Bengali on the Vedanta philosophy.

**Ra·món′** (rä·môn′). See Ramon GOMEZ DE LA SERNA.

**Ra′mon′** (rá′môɴ′), **Gaston.** 1886–1963. French bacteriologist; with Pasteur Inst., Paris (from 1911); developed antitoxins for vaccination against diphtheria and tetanus, and a process achieving several immunities with a single vaccination.

**Ra·món′ Berenguer** (rä·môn′). See BERENGUER.

**Ramón Lull.** See Raymond LULLY.

**Ra·món′ y Ca·jal′** (rä·môn′ ē kä·häl′), **Santiago.** 1852–1934. Spanish histologist; educ. Saragossa; professor of anatomy, Valencia (1881–86), of histology, Barcelona (1886–92) and Madrid (1892–1922). With Camillo Golgi, awarded Nobel prize for medicine (1906). Known esp. for work on histology of brain and nerves; isolated the neuron; discovered (1889) laws governing structure and connection of nerve cells in gray matter of brain and spinal cord; discovered (1890) primary changes in neurons as functional units; devised new staining method for histological research on nervous system. Author of *Manual de Histología...*(1889), *Textura del Sistema Nervioso de Hombre y de los Vertebrados* (2 vols., 1899–1905), and *Estudios sobra la Degeneratión del Sistema Nervioso* (2 vols., 1913–14).

**Ra′mo·ri′no** (rä′mô·rē′nō), **Girolamo.** 1790–1849. Italian soldier; participated in Italian national movement (1821); associated with Mazzini; general (1848); active in military campaigns of 1848 and 1849; held responsible for defeat at Novara and executed.

**Ram·pol′la** (räm·pōl′lä), **Mariano.** Marchese **del Tin′da·ro** (dâl tēn′dä·rō). 1843–1913. Italian prelate; entered diplomatic service of Roman Curia (1869); created cardinal (1887); papal secretary of state (1887–1903); championed temporal power of pope against restrictions of Italian government.

**Ram′say** (răm′zĭ). Name of a Scottish family holding titles of earl and marquis of **Dal·hou′sie** (dăl·hōō′zĭ; -hou′zĭ) in peerage of Scotland, including among its chief members: **William Ramsay** (d. 1674), 2d Baron Ramsay and 1st Earl of Dalhousie (cr. 1633); aided Argyll against Montrose and supported Charles II (1651).

**George** (1770–1838), 9th earl, one of Wellington's generals, governor in chief of Canadian colonies (1819–28), commander in chief in India.

His third son, **James Andrew Broun** (1812–1860), 10th Earl and 1st Marquis of Dalhousie; British colonial administrator; B.A., Oxon. (1833); entered House of Lords (1838); succeeded Gladstone as president of Board of Trade (1845); youngest governor general of India ever appointed (1847–56), was successful in acquiring territory, developing Indian resources, reforming administration; after Second Sikh War, annexed the Punjab (1849); annexed province of Pegu, Lower Burma (1853); by application of doctrine of lapse, annexed Satara, Jaitpur, Sambalpur (1849), Jhansi, Nagpur (1853); established public works and engineering colleges; built railways (first link, 1855), metaled roads and bridges; installed imperial system of telegraph and post offices, of irrigation; opened Ganges Canal; improved civil service by leave and pension rules and by opening service to natural-born British subjects, black and white; took action against suttee, thuggee, dacoity, slave trade, crime of meriahs; annexed Oudh (1856) and returned to England, broken in health; declined to defend his policy from attack.

**Fox Maule** (1801–1874), 2d Baron **Pan·mure′** (?păn·mūr′) and 11th Earl of Dalhousie; grandson of 8th earl; served in army (1820–32); M.P. (1835); undersecretary for home affairs (1835–41); secretary for war (1846–52, 1855–58), censured for management of Crimean War; assumed surname Ramsay (1861).

His cousin **George** (1806–1880), 12th earl; naval officer; created Baron Ramsay in British peerage (1875); admiral (1875); father of Sir **John William** (1847–1887), 13th earl, retired from navy (1879), secretary for Scotland (1886). Sir **Alexander Robert Maule** (1881–1960), 3d son of 13th earl, served Dardanelles (D.S.O., 1916); m. (1919) Princess Patricia, daughter of duke of Connaught; rear admiral, aircraft carriers (1933–36); commander in chief, East Indies (1936); 5th sea lord and chief of naval air service (1938–39); admiral (1939).

**Ramsay, Allan.** 1686–1758. Scottish poet; wigmaker in Edinburgh; as original member of Easy Club, was inspired to write verses and became club laureate (1715). Turned bookseller; published additional canto to *Christ's Kirk on the Green* (1718), his collected poems (1721), and Scots songs to old melodies in *Tea-Table Miscellany*

(1724–27); edited old Scots poems in *Ever Green* (1724–27); produced his dramatic pastoral *The Gentle Shepherd* (1725), a popular success; first to introduce circulating library in Scotland. His eldest son, **Allan** (1713–1784), painted portraits in Edinburgh, including duke of Argyll; to London (c. 1756); court painter to George III (1767), having as subjects king, queen, Lord Bute, Gibbon, Chesterfield, and Hume.

**Ramsay,** Sir **Andrew Crombie.** 1814–1891. Scottish geologist; director-general of geological survey (1871). Author of *Physical Geology and Geography of Great Britain*, etc.

**Ramsay, Andrew Michael.** *Known as* **Che·va'lier' de Ramsay** (shĕ·vȧ'lyā' dē). 1686–1743. Scottish writer in French; converted to Roman Catholicism; tutor to two sons of Prince James Edward in Rome (1724–25). Author of *Les Voyages de Cyrus* (1727).

**Ramsay,** Sir **John.** Viscount **Had'ding·ton** (hăd'ĭng-tŭn) *and* Earl of **Hol'der·ness'** (hōl'dēr·nĕs'). 1580?–1626. Scottish conspirator and court favorite; assisted in rescuing James VI from Gowrie conspirators by killing earl of Gowrie and his brother (1600); accompanied James VI to England.

**Ramsay, Nathaniel.** 1741–1817. American Revolutionary officer; joined Continental army (1776); rallied troops retreating after battle of Monmouth (1778) and was wounded and captured. Member of Continental Congress (1785–87). U.S. marshal, district of Maryland (1790–98); naval officer, port of Baltimore (1794–1817). His brother **David** (1749–1815) was a physician and historian; practiced, Charleston, S.C. (from 1773); member of Continental Congress (1782–86); author of *History of the American Revolution* (2 vols., 1789), *History of the United States* (3 vols., 1816–17), etc.

**Ramsay,** Sir **William.** 1852–1916. British chemist; investigated determination of molecular complexity of pure liquids; discovered chemically inert elementary gases, argon (with Baron Rayleigh), neon, krypton, and xenon (with Morris W. Travers), and helium; advanced proof that emanation of radium produces helium during its atomic disintegration. Awarded Nobel prize for chemistry (1904). Author of *The Gases of the Atmosphere, Elements and Electrons*, etc.

**Ramsay,** Sir **William Mitchell.** 1851–1939. Scottish classicist and archaeologist; author of works on geography of Asia Minor and on early Christian history.

**Rams'den** (rămz'dĕn), **Jesse.** 1735–1800. English astronomical instrument maker; took out patents for improvements in the sextant, theodolite, equatorial, barometer, micrometer; specialized in divided circles; devised the mural circle.

**Ram'ses** (răm'sēz) *or* **Ram'e·ses** (răm'ē·sēz). Name of twelve kings of XIXth and XXth (Diospolite) dynasties of ancient Egypt:

**Ramses I.** Second king (c. 1315–1314 B.C.) of XIXth dynasty, beginning reign at advanced age; named his son Seti I as coregent; planned and began great hypostyle hall at Karnak.

**Ramses II.** Fourth king of XIXth dynasty (1292–1225 B.C.). Son of Seti I. In early years of reign, engaged in important campaign against Hittites; fought (1288 or 1287) indecisive battle at Kadesh on the Orontes in Syria; saved from destruction by personal bravery; after several more years of war with Hittites in Palestine and Syria, arranged treaty of permanent peace (1272); m. daughter of Hittite king; remainder of long reign peaceful. Completed Seti's temple at Abydos; added to temples at Karnak and Luxor; constructed at Thebes great mortuary temple of the Rameseum with its colossal statues of himself; built the rock-cut temple at Abu-Simbel. By most Egyptologists held to be the pharaoh of the oppression (*Genesis* and *Exodus*); with forced labor of Israelites, built treasure cities of Pithom and Ramses. See SESOSTRIS (last ¶).

**Ramses III.** *Known to the Greeks as* **Rhamp'si·ni'tus** (rămp'sĭ·nī'tŭs). Second king (1198–1167 B.C.) of XXth dynasty, first of the Ramessides proper. Engaged in wars with Libya and Syria; later in his reign, built many public edifices and made rich gifts to temples.

**Ramses IV–XII.** Remaining Ramessides, reigning from 1167 to 1090 B.C., all weaklings; only two kings reigned any considerable period, **Ramses IX** (1142–1123 B.C.) and **Ramses XII** (1118–1090 B.C.); empire declined rapidly; all power centered in high priest.

**Ram'sey** (răm'zĭ), **Alexander.** 1815–1903. American politician; governor, Territory of Minnesota (1849–53), State of Minnesota (1859–63); U.S. senator (1863–75); U.S. secretary of war (1879–81).

**Ramsey, Arthur Michael.** 1904– . Anglican prelate, ordained (1928); canon and professor of divinity (1940–50); bishop of Durham (1952–56); archbishop of York (1956–61); archbishop of Canterbury (from 1961).

**Ra'mus** (rā'mŭs; *Fr.* rȧ'mü'), **Petrus.** *Lat. form of* **Pierre de La Ra'mée'** (lȧ rȧ'mā'). 1515–1572. French philosopher and mathematician best known as a critic of Aristotelianism. His system of philosophy was known as *Ramism*, and his followers as *Ramists*.

**Ra·mu'sio** (rä·mōō'zyō), **Giambattista.** 1485–1557. Italian scholar and traveler; known chiefly for collection of accounts of explorations and travels, *Delle Navigazioni e Viaggi* (3 vols., 1550–69).

**Ra'muz'** (rȧ'müz'), **Charles Ferdinand.** 1878–1947. Swiss writer; resident in Paris (1902–14).

**Ra'na·de** (rä'nȧ·dāɴ; -dā), **Ma'ha·de'o** (mŭ'hä·dā'ō) **Go·vind'** (gō·vĭnd'). 1842–1901. Indian Brahman lawyer and reformer; founder of the social conference movement, and one of originators of Indian National Congress.

**Ranc** (räɴk), **Arthur.** 1831–1908. French politician; in exile (1853–59; 1873–79). Member of Chamber of Deputies (1881) and of Senate (1891–1900, 1903 ff.). Editor of the *Radical* (1900); succeeded Clemenceau as editor of *Aurore* (1905). Author of treatises on contemporary French history and politics.

**Ran'cé'** (räɴ'sā'), **Armand Jean Le Bou'thil'lier' de** (zhäɴ' lē bōō'tē'yā' dē). 1626–1700. French monk; abbot of La Trappe monastery (until retirement, 1695); instituted reforms and strict discipline in his order; known as founder of the Trappists (since 1892 united with the Cistercians).

**Rand** (rănd), **Ayn** (īn). 1905– . Amer. writer, b. Russia. To U.S. (1926). Author of *The Fountainhead, Atlas Shrugged*, etc.

**Rand** (rănd), **Edward Ken'nard** (kĕn'ärd; -ērd). 1871–1945. American educator, b. Boston; A.B., Harvard (1894); Ph.D., Munich (1900); professor of Latin, Harvard (1909–42); author of *Ovid and His Influence, Founders of the Middle Ages, A Walk to Horace's Farm, The Magical Art of Virgil*, etc.

**Ran'da** (rän'dä), Ritter **Anton von.** 1834–1914. Austrian jurist and politician; authority on Austrian civil law.

**Ran'dall** (răn'd'l), **Harrison McAllister.** 1870–1969. American physicist, b. Burr Oak, Mich.; Ph.B. (1893), Ph.D. (1902), Mich.; at U. of Michigan (1899–1941); known for work relating to high temperatures and for measurements in the infrared spectral region.

**Randall, James Ryder.** 1839–1908. American journalist and song writer, b. Baltimore. Intensely southern in sympathy, wrote *Maryland, My Maryland* (April, 1861) upon hearing of Baltimore mob resistance to the passage of Union troops through the city. In journalistic and secretarial work (from 1866).

**Randall, John Herman.** 1871–1946. American Baptist clergyman; pastor in New York City (1906–27); director of World Unity Foundation (1927); author of *A New Philosophy of Life* (1910), *Religion and the Modern World*, etc. His son **John Herman** (1899–    ), teacher of philosophy, Columbia (from 1925; professor from 1935); author of *The Making of the Modern Mind* (1926), *Our Changing Civilization* (1929), etc.

**Randall, Robert Richard.** 1750?–1801. American privateer and merchant, b. prob. in New Jersey. Bequeathed his fortune to found an asylum and hospital for aged and decrepit seamen, the institution to be called Sailors' Snug Harbor. His statue, carved by St. Gaudens (1884), stands on the Sailors' Snug Harbor grounds, Staten Island, N.Y.

**Randall, Samuel Jackson.** 1828–1890. American legislator, b. Philadelphia; member, U.S. House of Representatives (1863–90), and speaker of the house (1876–81). Codified rules of the House of Representatives and largely strengthened speaker's power.

**Ran′deg·ger** (*Ital.* rän′dā·gĕr; *Ger.* rän′dĕg′ĕr; *Angl.* răn′dĭ·jẽr), **Alberto.** 1832–1911. Composer and conductor in England; b. Trieste, Italy; settled in London (1854); conductor of Carl Rosa Opera Co. (1879–85) and Norwich Musical Festival (1881–1905); composer of operettas and cantatas; author of well-known *Primer of Singing.*

**Ran′dolph** (răn′dŏlf; -d'lf), **Edmund Jennings** *or* **Jenings.** 1753–1813. Son of John Randolph (1727?–1784), grandson of Sir John Randolph, and great-grandson of William Randolph. American statesman, b. Williamsburg, Va. Aide-de-camp to Gen. Washington (1775–76). Attorney general of Virginia (1776). Member, Continental Congress (1779–82). Governor of Virginia (1786–88). Delegate to Constitutional Convention (1787) and proposer of famous Virginia Plan; refused to sign constitution because of belief it was not adequately republican in its provisions, but advocated acceptance in Virginia ratification convention (1788). U.S. attorney general (1789–94); U.S. secretary of state (1794–95). Practiced law, Richmond, Va. (from 1795); was chief counsel for Aaron Burr when Burr was tried for treason (1807).

**Randolph, Edward.** 1632–1703. British agent in America, b. Canterbury, Eng. In Massachusetts colony (1676); appointed by king collector of customs in New England (1678); in constant trouble with colonial authorities. As a result of his reports, Massachusetts charter was declared forfeited (1684) and he was commissioned secretary and register of the Dominion of New England (1685). Arrested (1689) after rebellion had overthrown government of the "Dominion," and sent to England; freed and appointed surveyor general of customs for North America (1691). Again in colonies (1692–97) and in conflict with colonial authorities; imprisoned in Bermuda (1699–1700); in England (1700) made bitter attack on both charter and proprietary colonies for violations of the laws of trade.

**Randolph, George Wythe.** See under Thomas Mann RANDOLPH.

**Randolph, John.** d. 1346. See under Sir Thomas RANDOLPH.

**Randolph,** Sir **John.** 1693?–1737. Son of William Randolph. American colonial administrator, b. in Henrico County, Va.; clerk of Virginia House of Burgesses (1718–34); speaker, House of Burgesses (1734–37). His son **Peyton** (1721?–1775) was a lawyer and political leader; king's attorney for Virginia (1748–66); member of Virginia House of Burgesses (1748–49, 1752–75); on Virginia committee of correspondence (1759–67), and chairman of the committee (1773); first president, Continental Congress (1774, 1775). Another son, **John** (1727?–1784), was also a political leader; clerk, Virginia House of Burgesses (1752–56); king's attorney for Virginia (1756–75); loyalist at outbreak of American Revolution and fled to England (1775); lived on pension from the crown. Edmund Jennings Randolph (*q.v.*) was his son.

**Randolph, John.** 1773–1833. Known as John Randolph of Roanoke. Great-grandson of William Randolph. American statesman, b. in Prince George County, Va. Member, U.S. House of Representatives (1799–1813, 1815–17, 1819–25, 1827–29), and U.S. Senate (1825–27). Chairman, house ways and means committee, and administration leader (1801–05); opposed Jefferson (after 1805); brilliant orator and master of biting invective; bitter opponent of War of 1812, Missouri Compromise; stigmatized northern members of Congress who voted for Missouri Compromise as "Doughfaces"; marked eccentricities in speech and act (after 1818) indicated mental abnormality, which in last years passed into actual insanity. Fought harmless duel with Henry Clay (Apr. 8, 1826). U.S. minister to Russia (1830).

**Randolph,** Sir **Thomas.** 1st Earl of **Mor′ay** (mûr′ĭ) *or* **Mur′ray.** d. 1332. Scottish statesman. Nephew through his mother of King Robert Bruce. Captured at Methven; saved his life by deserting Bruce (1306). Captured by Sir James Douglas (1308); made submission to Bruce; created earl of Moray (one of seven original earldoms of Scotland) and became Bruce's most trusted adviser. Captured Edinburgh Castle by escalade (1314); commanded a division at Bannockburn (1314); took part in Edward Bruce's expedition into Ireland (1315); with Sir James Douglas, raided northern English counties and secured truce with Edward II; concluded offensive and defensive alliance with France (1326); became regent on death of Bruce (1329). His son **John** (d. 1346), 3d earl, defeated Edward de Baliol at Annan (1332); joint regent (c. 1334); liberated rest of country by subduing Edward de Baliol's lieutenant in Scotland; captive of English (1335–41); killed at battle of Neville's Cross (1346).

**Randolph, Thomas.** 1523–1590. English courtier and diplomat; the confidential agent of Elizabeth I in Scotland, Germany, and Russia. Banished from court of Mary, Queen of Scots, for complicity in Moray's rebellion (1566); failed in attempt to save Morton (1581); successfully concluded treaty with James VI (1586).

**Randolph, Thomas.** 1605–1635. English poet and dramatist; writer of English and Latin verse; friend of Ben Jonson; author of six plays, including *Aristippus, or the Joviall Philosopher* (1630), *The Jealous Lovers* (comedy; 1632), *The Muses' Looking-Glasse* (witty comedy; pub. 1638), *Amyntas* (pastoral drama; pub. 1638).

**Randolph, Thomas Mann.** 1768–1828. Great-great-grandson of William Randolph. American political leader, b. in Goochland County, Va.; m. Martha Jefferson, dau. of Thomas Jefferson (1790) and lived at Monticello with Jefferson. Member, U.S. House of Representatives (1803–07). Governor of Virginia (1819–22). His son **Thomas Jefferson Randolph** (1792–1875) was a financier; managed Thomas Jefferson's financial affairs (1816–26) and served as executor of Jefferson's estate after his death (1826); published *Memoir, Correspondence, and Miscellanies from the Papers of Thomas Jefferson* (4 vols., 1829). Another son of Thomas Mann Randolph, **George Wythe** [wĭth] (1818–1867), was a lawyer; practiced in Richmond, Va. (from c. 1849); served in Confederate army (1861–62), brigadier general; Confederate States secretary of war (1862).

**Randolph, William.** 1651?–1711. Planter and administrator in America, b. in Warwickshire, Eng.; to America (c. 1673) and settled in Virginia, on James River below Richmond. Became large landowner and slaveowner, and one of leading planters of Virginia. Attorney general for the crown in Virginia (1694–98); a founder of College of William and Mary. Among notable descendants of the same name are: Sir John Randolph, Edmund Jennings Randolph, John Randolph, Thomas Mann Randolph. See individual biographies.

**Randulf de Blundevill** and **Randulf de Gernons.** See earl of CHESTER.

**Ran'ga'bé'** (*Fr.* räN'gȧ'bā'), **Alexandre Rizos.** *Gr.* **Alexandros Rizos Rhan'ga·ves'** (räng'gä·vēs'). 1810–1892. Greek writer and statesman; professor of archaeology, Athens (1844), and associated with Bursian in excavations and discoveries among the ruins of the temple of Juno, near Argos. Among his verse and plays are *Phrosyne*, *The Vigil*, and *The Thirty Tyrants*.

**Ran'ger** (rān'jẽr), **Henry Ward.** 1858–1916. American landscape painter, b. Syracuse, N.Y.

**Rang'ström** (ràng'strûm), **Ture.** 1884–1947. Swedish composer, conductor, music critic, and singing teacher, b. Stockholm.

**Ra·nie'ri** (rä·nyâ'rē), **Antonio.** 1809–1888. Italian writer; friend of Leopardi (*q.v.*); professor of history, Naples. Works include biography of Leopardi, the novel *Ginevra* (1839), a history *I Primi Cinque Secoli della Storia d'Italia* (1841).

**Ran'jit Singh** (rŭn'jĭt sĭN'hȧ) *or* **Run'jit Singh,** Maharaja. 1780–1839. Called "the Lion of the Punjab." Founder of the Sikh kingdom. Succeeded his father (1792) as head of a Sikh confederacy; appointed governor of Lahore (1799) by the Afghan king; annexed Amritsar (1802); his ambition clashed with British claims but war was avoided; treaty as to boundaries signed (1809) with Charles Metcalfe, English agent; organized powerful army; added Multan (1818), Kashmir (1819), and Peshawar (1823); consolidated most of Punjab into a Sikh kingdom; always loyally supported British. His son and successor, **Dhu·leep'** (dŭ·lēp') **Singh** (1837–1893), under regency of his mother, was deposed (1849) as result of two anti-British outbreaks and pensioned; lived in Suffolk, England.

**Ran'jit·sinh'ji Vi'bha·ji** (rŭN'jĭt·sĭN'h'·jē vē'bȧ·jē), Sri Sir. Maharaja Jam Sahib of **Na'wa·na'gar** (nŭ'-väN·nŭg'ẽr). 1872–1933. Rajput nobleman, b. Sarodar, province of Kathiawar, India; adopted by his uncle Jam Sri Sir Vibhaji, Jam Sahib of Nawanagar, and succeeded a cousin as maharaja (1906). Educ. Cambridge. Won renown in England as a cricketer; champion batsman for All England (1896, 1900); went with Stoddart's All England XI to Australia (1897–98).

**Rank** (rängk), **Joseph.** 1816–1896. Novelist, b. in Bohemia; author of tales chiefly of Bohemian village life.

**Ran'ke** (räng'kĕ), **Leopold von.** 1795–1886. German historian, b. in Thuringia; a founder of the modern school of history; champion of objective writing based on source material rather than on legend and tradition. Professor, Berlin (1825–71). Historiographer of Prussia (1841); chancellor of the order Pour le Mérite (1867). His works include *Geschichte der Romanischen und Germanischen Völker von 1494–1535* (1824; containing a criticism of contemporary historians), *Die Römischen Päpste* (3 vols., 1834–39), *Deutsche Geschichte im Zeitalter der Reformation* (6 vols., 1839–47), *Neun Bücher Preussischer Geschichte* (3 vols., 1847–48), *Französische Geschichte* (5 vols., 1852–61), *Englische Geschichte* (7 vols., 1859–68), *Geschichte Wallensteins* (1869), *Weltgeschichte* (9 parts, 1881–88; completed by his assistants). Some of his works have been translated into English, notably the *History of the Popes*, Mrs. Sarah Austin's translation of which (1840) was the subject of a well-known essay by Macaulay.

**Ran'kin** (răng'kĭn), **Jeannette.** 1880–1973. Pacifist, woman suffragist, and legislator, b. near Missoula, Mont.; active in woman-suffrage work (from 1910); first woman member of U.S. House of Representatives (1917–19; 1941–43); only member of the house to vote against declaration of war (Dec., 1941).

**Ran'kine** (răng'kĭn), **William John Macquorn.** 1820–1872. Scottish civil engineer and physicist; best known for researches in molecular physics. Author of manuals *The Steam Engine*, *Civil Engineering*, etc. The Rankine cycle is named after him.

**Ran'som** (răn'sŭm), **John Crowe.** 1888–1974. Critic and poet, b. Pulaski, Tenn. Rhodes scholar at Oxford (1910–13). Teacher of English, Vanderbilt (1914–37); professor of poetry, Kenyon Coll. (from 1937); a founder of *Kenyon Review* (1939). Author of volumes of verse *Poems about God* (1919), *Chills and Fever* (1924), *Grace After Meat* (1924), *Two Gentlemen in Bonds* (1926), *Selected Poems* (1945; revised 1963). Critical works include *God Without Thunder* (1930), *The World's Body* (1938), *New Criticism* (1941), and *Poems and Essays* (1955).

**Ran'some** (răn'sŭm), **Arthur.** 1884–1967. English author of *The Hoofmarks of the Faun* (1911), *The Elixir of Life* (1915), *Six Weeks in Russia* (1919), *The Chinese Puzzle* (1927), *Winter Holiday* (1933), *Secret Water* (1939), *The Big Six* (1940), etc.

**Ransome, Frederick Leslie.** 1868–1935. Geologist, b. Greenwich, England. On staff, U.S. Geological Survey (1897–1923) and geologist (from 1900). Professor of economic geology, U. of Arizona (1923–27) and Calif. Inst. Tech. (1927–35).

**Rant'zau, von** (fōn rän'tsou). Noble family originating in Holstein and including: **Johann** (1492–1565), Danish soldier and statesman; influenced Frederick I to accept the crown of Denmark; spread the principles of the Reformation through the country; became governor of Schleswig and Holstein. His son **Heinrich** (1526–1598) succeeded him as governor of Schleswig-Holstein (1566). Johann's great-grandson **Josias** (1609–1650) served in the armies of the prince of Orange, King Christian IV of Denmark, Gustavus Adolphus, Emperor Ferdinand II; entered French service (1635) and was promoted lieutenant general (1644) and marshal of France (1645).

**Ranulf de Blundevill.** See earl of CHESTER.

**Ran'vier'** (räN'vyā'), **Louis Antoine.** 1835–1922. French histologist; director of histological laboratory and professor of general anatomy, Collège de France (1875).

**Raoul.** See RUDOLF (d. 936 A.D.).

**Ra'oul'** (rȧ'ōōl'), **Étienne Fiacre Louis.** French naval surgeon; collected plant specimens in New Zealand and New Caledonia (c. 1840). The genus *Raoulia* is named for him.

**Ra'oult'** (rȧ'ōōl'), **François Marie.** 1830–1901. French physicist and chemist; known esp. for work on the freezing point and vapor pressure of solutions in relation to the concentration and molecular weight of the dissolved substance.

**Rapagnetta.** See *note* under Gabriele D'ANNUNZIO.

**Raph'a·el** (răf'ȧ·ĕl; -ĭ·ĕl; rā'fā·ĕl; -fĭ·ĕl). *Ital.* **Raf'fa·el'lo** (räf'fä·ĕl'lō). *In full* **Raffaello San'ti** (sän'tē) *or* **San'zio** (sän'tsyō). *Also* **Raf'fa·el** (răf'ȧ·ĕl; -ĭ·ĕl) *or* **Raf'a·el** (răf'ȧ·ĕl; -ĭ·ĕl; rā'fā·ĕl; -fĭ·ĕl) *or* **Raf'fa·e'lo**

(räf′fä·ȧ′lô). 1483–1520. Italian painter, b. Urbino; studied first under his father, Giovanni Santi, later, reputedly under Timoteo Viti; assistant to Perugino (c. 1500 ff.). To Florence (1504) and Rome (after 1508); in service of Pope Julius II; later, protégé of Leo X; appointed chief architect of St. Peter's (1514); conservator of excavations at Rome (1515). Works include *St. Michael, Apollo and Marsyas, St. George and the Dragon* (all in the Louvre), *Coronation of the Virgin* (Vatican gallery), *Marriage of the Virgin* or *Sposalizio* (the Brera), *La Belle Jardinière* (Paris), *Holy Family* (Madrid, Munich, St. Petersburg), *Adoration of the Trinity* (Church of San Severo, Perugia), *Entombment* (Borghese Gallery, Rome), *The Knight's Dream* and *St. Catharine* (National Gallery, London), frescoes in the Vatican, including *Theology, Philosophy, Poetry, Justice, Disputa,* cartoons for tapestries in Sistine Chapel, frescoes in Villa Farnesina, portraits, as *Donna Velata* (Pitti Palace), and other easel paintings, as *Madonna della Sedia* (in the Pitti Palace), *Sistine Madonna* (Dresden gallery), etc. As architect, designed Palazzo Pandolfi (in Florence) and Villa Madama (in Rome), etc.

**Raphael of Cats.** See Gottfried MIND.

**Ra′pin′ de Thoy′ras′** (rȧ′păɴ′ dẽ twȧ′räs′), **Paul de.** 1661–1725. French historian; author of *Histoire d'Angleterre* (to accession of William and Mary; 8 vols., 1723).

**Ra′pi·sar′di** (rä′pē·zär′dē), **Mario.** 1844–1912. Italian poet; literary opponent of Carducci. Among his works are *Lucifero* (1877), *Giobbe* (1884), *Atlantide* (1892), and translations, as of Shelley's *Prometheus Unbound.*

**Rapp** (räp; *Angl.* răp), **George,** *orig.* **Johann Georg.** 1757–1847. Religious leader, b. in Württemberg. As head of group of separatists, emigrated to U.S. (1803) and settled town of Harmony, in Butler County, Pa. Moved to Indiana and settled new town called Harmony in Wabash Valley (1814–24). Moved again and settled town called Economy, in Beaver County, Pa., on Ohio River, below Pittsburgh (from 1825). Members of this religious communistic society called Harmonites, or sometimes Economites. Colony successful under Rapp's guidance. Rule of celibacy finally led to its extinction (1903).

**Rapp** (rȧp), **Comte Jean.** 1772–1821. French general; aide-de-camp to Desaix de Veygoux and later to Napoleon; distinguished himself at Leipzig and Wagram, and in the Russian campaign, esp. in the defense of Danzig (1813–14); rallied to Napoleon during the Hundred Days; in exile (1815–17).

**Rap′pold** (?răp′ōld), **Marie,** *nee* **Win′te·roth** (?wĭn′tĕ·rōth). 1880–1957. American operatic soprano, b. Brooklyn, N.Y.; m. Julius Rappold (divorced, 1913), Rudolph Berger (1913); member of Metropolitan Opera Company, New York City (from 1905).

**Rap′po·port** (răp′ō·pōrt; -pôrt), **Angelo Solomon.** 1871–1950. British editor and writer, b. in Little Russia; to England, and became naturalized (1898). On editorial staff of *Encyclopedia Britannica* (1906); editor of *Twentieth Century Russia* (1915–16), *New Gresham Encyclopaedia* (1918–24), *Illustrated Palestine* (1927–29); coeditor, *British Encyclopaedia* (1933). Among his many books are *Primer of Philosophy* (1903), *Russian History* (1905), *Home Life in Russia* (1913), *History of Poland* (1915), *Dictionary of Socialism* (1926), *Myths and Legends of Ancient Israel* (3 vols., 1928), *Mediaeval Legends of Christ* (1934), and *The Folklore of the Jews* (1937).

**Ra′schig** (räsh′ĭĸ), **Fritz.** 1863–1928. German chemist and industrialist; authority on the distillation of coal tar and the resulting products.

**Ras′coe** (răs′kō), **Arthur Burton.** 1892–1957. American editor, anthologist, and writer, b. Fulton, Ky.; author of *Theodore Dreiser* (1925), *Titans of Literature* (1932), *Prometheans* (1933), *The Joys of Reading* (1937), *Belle Starr: "The Bandit Queen"* (1941), etc.

**Ra′shi** (rä′shē). d. 1105. Medieval French-Jewish commentator on the Bible and Babylonian Talmud, whose Hebrew name Rabbi She′lo·moh′ ben Yis·haq′ (shĕ′lō-mō′ bĕn yĭs·häk′) forms the acrostic Rashi, by which name he is popularly known.

**Ra·shīd′ al–Dīn′** (ră·shēd′ ăd·dēn′). *Called* **al–Ta·bīb′** (ăt′tă·bēb′), *i.e.* "the physician." 1250?–1318. Arabic historian, b. at Hamadan; physician to the Mongol sovereigns of Iran; vizier of the empire; composed encyclopedic *History of the Mongols of Persia.*

**Rasis.** See RHAZES.

**Rask** (räsk), **Rasmus Christian.** 1787–1832. Danish philologist and Orientalist; a founder of modern science of comparative philology; professor of literary history (1825) and of Oriental languages (1831), and librarian (1829), U. of Copenhagen. In a work (1818) on the origin of Old Norse, showed its relationship to other European languages and set forth principle of consonantal sound shifting in Germanic languages, later formulated as a law by Jacob Grimm. Wrote grammars of Icelandic (1811), Anglo-Saxon (in Swedish, 1817), Spanish (1824), Frisian (1825), Danish (1830), Old Norse (1832), and other languages; essays on ancient Egyptian (1827) and ancient Jewish (1828) chronology; a work on the Zend-Avesta, etc.

**Ra·sko′va** (rŭ·skô′vŭ), **Marina.** 1912–1943. Russian aviatrix, b. Moscow; grad. from flying school (1935); made several noteworthy long-distance flights; major in Soviet air force; killed at her post.

**Ras′mus·sen** (räs′mo͝o·s′n), **Knud Johan Victor.** 1879–1933. Danish arctic explorer and ethnologist, b. in Greenland of an Eskimo mother. Authority on the Greenland Eskimo; held theory that Eskimos spring from same stock as North American Indians. Took part in Danish literary Greenland expedition (1902–04) under Mylius-Erichsen; studied the Eskimo of North Greenland, and made first sledge crossing on record across Melville Bay; made ethnological expeditions to North Greenland (1906–08, 1909, 1910–11) and established (1910) Cape York station at Thule; led several Thule expeditions (from 1912) to North and East Greenland and the American Arctic. Author of *Lapland* (1907), *The People of the Polar North* (1908), *Myths and Legends from Greenland* (3 vols., 1921–25), *In the Home of the Polar Eskimos* (1923), *Across Arctic America* (1927), *The Eagle's Gift* (1932), etc.

**Ras′pail′** (rȧs′pȧ′y′), **François Vincent.** 1794–1878. French scientist and politician; involved in revolutionary activities (1830 and 1848), was arrested and banished (1848); returned to France after amnesty (1859). Among his books are *Mémoire sur les Graminées, Nouveau Système de Chimie Organique* (1833), *Nouvelles Études Scientifiques* (1864), etc.

**Ra′spe** (räs′pĕ), **Henry.** See HENRY RASPE.

**Raspe, Rudolph Erich.** 1737–1794. German mineralogist and author of *Baron Munchausen's Narrative of His Marvellous Travels and Campaigns in Russia* (1785), constituting original of chapters ii to vi of current version of Munchausen stories. Professor of archaeology and curator of museum at Kassel; charged with stealing and selling medals, fled to England (1775); masquerading as mining expert, swindled Sir John Sinclair by pretending to discover gold and silver on his estate (1791); original of Douster-swivel in Scott's *Antiquary.* Revealed as author of *Munchausen* only in 1824 by biographer of Bürger (editor of first German version, 1786). See MÜNCHHAUSEN.

**Ras·pu′tin** (rŭs·pōō′tyĭn), **Grigori Efimovich.** 1871?–1916. Russian holy man and court favorite, b. prov. of Tobolsk, Siberia, son of a poor peasant. Received little education; m. Olga Chanigov and lived as a peasant in his native village (until 1904). Left family (1904) and devoted himself to religion; gained reputation as a holy man among the peasantry. In St. Petersburg (1907 ff.), gained ascendancy over the czar and czarina; interfered in church politics as well as in secular politics; notorious for debauchery and ignorance. Assassinated by a group of Russian noblemen (Dec. 31, 1916) in a patriotic endeavor to rid Russia of his baneful influence.

**Ras·sam′** (räs·säm′), **Hor·muzd′** (hŏr·mōōzd′). 1826–1910. Turkish Assyriologist, b. Mosul in Asiatic Turkey, of native Christian parents. Assisted Sir A. H. Layard in archaeological excavations near Nineveh (1845–47, 1849–51) and succeeded him as British agent in excavations; discovered palace of Ashurbanipal at Nimroud (Calah). Sent to Abyssinia (1864), there imprisoned (1866) by Theodore until released by Sir Robert Napier (1868); made important investigations in Assyria and Babylonia (1876–82).

**Ra·strel′li** (räs·trĕl′lē), **Carlo Bartolomeo.** d. 1744. Florentine sculptor; called to Russia (1715) by Peter the Great. His son **Francesco** [*or* **Bartolomeo**] (1700–1771) was an architect in Russia; works include Ruhenthal Palace (Kurland), Church of Saint Andrew (Kiev), Peterhof and Winter palaces (Leningrad), and Tsarskoe-Selo Palace.

**Ratclyffe,** Sir **Thomas.** See RADCLIFFE.

**Rat′dolt** (rät′dôlt), **Erhard.** 1442?–1528. German printer and type cutter; b. Augsburg; printed chiefly liturgical, mathematical, and astronomical works with ornamental borders and initial letters, including an edition of Euclid (1482) containing over 400 wood engravings and over 200 diagrams; originated the decorated title page, and was among first to use several colors on one page.

**Ra′teau′** (rȧ′tō′), **Camille Edmond Auguste.** 1863–1930. French engineer, specializing in manufacture of turbines (as multicellular turbines) and in study of the use of turbines in aviation.

**Rath** (rät), **Gerhard vom.** 1830–1888. German mineralogist; professor, U. of Bonn (1863).

**Ra′the·nau** (rä′tĕ·nou), **Emil.** 1838–1915. German-Jewish electrotechnician and industrialist, b. Berlin; a founder of the German Edison Company (1883), forerunner of the Allgemeine Elektrizitäts-Gesellschaft, or A. E. G. (1887), of which he was general director. His son **Walther** (1867–1922) became director of electrochemical enterprises, Bitterfeld (1893), a director of A. E. G. (1899), and president of A. E. G. (1915); directed distribution of war raw materials in Prussian war ministry (1914–15); participated in preliminary preparations for Versailles Peace Conference (1919); took part in preparations for London Conference (1921); minister of reconstruction in Wirth's first cabinet (1921); represented Germany at Cannes Conference (1922) and secured diminution of reparation payment of 1922; as foreign minister in Wirth's second cabinet (1922), participated in conference at Genoa, and signed Rapallo Treaty with Russia (1922); assassinated by reactionaries (1922).

**Rath′ke** (rät′kĕ), **Martin Heinrich.** 1793–1860. German anatomist.

**Ra·ti′chi·us** (rä·tĭκ′ē·ŏŏs) *or* **Rat′ke** (rät′kĕ) *or* **Ra′tich** (rä′tĭκ), **Wolfgang.** 1571–1635. German educational reformer, b. in Holstein. In Holland (1603–11), devised new system of teaching languages, based on Baconian theory of induction; attempted to introduce system in Augsburg, Kassel, Hanau, Frankfurt, and Basel.

**Ra′tis′bonne′** (rȧ′tēz′bôn′), **Louis Fortuné Gustave.** *Pseudonym* **Trim** (trēm). 1827–1900. French man of letters; on editorial staff of *Journal des Débats* (1853–76); librarian of Château de Fontainebleau (1871) and of the Senate (1875). Author of *Au Printemps de la Vie* (1857), a one-act play *Héro et Léandre* (1859), *Albums* (over pseudonym); translator of Dante's *Divina Commedia.*

**Ratke, Wolfgang.** German form of RATICHIUS.

**Ratramnus.** See under Johannes Scotus ERIGENA.

**Rat′sey** (răt′sĭ), **Gamaliel.** d. 1605. English highwayman of Northamptonshire; robbed in mask and indulged in rough humor; hanged at Bedford.

**Rat·taz′zi** (rät·tät′tsē), **Urbano.** 1808–1873. Italian statesman; joined with Cavour (1851); president, Chamber of Deputies (1852–53); minister of justice and cults (1853–54) and interior (1854–58, 1858–60); prime minister (Mar.–Dec., 1862; Apr.–Oct., 1867); leader of the opposition (1867 ff.).

**Ratti, Achille.** See Pope PIUS XI.

**Rat′zel** (rät′sĕl), **Friedrich.** 1844–1904. German geographer; professor, Munich (1876), Leipzig (from 1886); a founder of anthropogeography; made important contributions to political geography. Author of *Städte und Kulturbilder aus Nordamerika* (2 vols., 1876), *Die Vereinigten Staaten von Nordamerika* (2 vols., 1878–80), *Die Erde und das Leben* (2 vols., 1901–02), etc.

**Rat′zen·ho′fer** (rät′sĕn·hō′fĕr), **Gustav.** 1842–1904. Austrian general, philosopher, and sociologist. Lieutenant general and president of the military supreme court (1898). Author of *Wesen und Zweck der Politik* (3 vols., 1893; on the relationship of politics and sociology), *Die Soziologische Erkenntnis* (1898), *Der Positive Monismus* (1899), *Positive Ethik* (1901), etc.

**Rau** (rou), **Karl Heinrich.** 1792–1870. German political economist; helped introduce into Germany the economic theories of Adam Smith and Ricardo; author of *Lehrbuch der Politischen Ökonomie* (3 vols., 1826–37), etc.

**Rauch** (rouκ), **Christian Daniel.** 1777–1857. German sculptor, founder of Berlin school of sculpture. His works include the reclining marble statue for the sarcophagus of Queen Louise of Prussia (in Charlottenburg), many portrait busts including life-size marble bust of Goethe (in Leipzig), statues of Scharnhorst and von Bülow (in Berlin) and Dürer (in Nuremberg), and six marble *Victories* for the Valhalla near Regensburg.

**Rauch, Frederick Augustus.** 1806–1841. Educator, b. in Prussia; to U.S. (1831). Organizer and first president, Marshall College (1836–41), merged (1853) in Franklin and Marshall College at Lancaster, Pa. Colleague of John W. Nevin, and collaborator with him in laying basis of Mercersburg theology.

**Rau′mer** (rou′mĕr), **Friedrich Ludwig Georg von.** 1781–1873. German scholar; traveled extensively in Europe and America (1815–41); member, German National Assembly, Frankfurt (1848) and Prussian Upper Assembly. Founded (1830; with F. A. Brockhaus Co.) and edited *Historisches Taschenbuch;* author of works on history, literary history, law, and economics, including *Geschichte der Hohenstaufen* (6 vols., 1823–25), *Geschichte Europas* (8 vols., 1832–50), *Die Vereinigten Staaten von Nordamerika* (2 vols., 1845), *Handbuch zur Geschichte der Literatur* (4 vols., 1864–66). His brother **Karl Georg** (1783–1865), geologist, was professor (1811) and on government board of mines, Breslau; professor (1819) and (until 1823) on board of mines, Halle; professor of mineralogy and pedagogy, Erlangen (1827); author of *Lehrbuch der Allgemeinen Geographie* (1832), *Geschichte der Pädagogik* (4 vols., 1843–54), etc. Karl's son **Rudolf**

(1815–1876), philologist, was professor at Erlangen (from 1846), champion of a reformed German phonetic spelling, and author of *Geschichte der Germanischen Philologie* (1870), etc. A grandnephew of Friedrich, **Hans** (1870– ), an economist, was business manager of German electrochemical industries (1918); member of German People's party in Reichstag (1920–30); minister of the treasury (1920–21); minister of economics in Stresemann's first cabinet (1923).

**Raun'kiær** (roun'kâr), **Christen.** 1860–1938. Danish botanist; collection of his papers published (in English trans., 1934) as *Life Forms of Plants and Statistical Plant Geography.*

**Rau'pach** (rou'päκ), **Ernst Benjamin Salomo.** 1784–1852. German dramatist; author of the tragedy *Die Leibeigenen, oder Isidor und Olga* (1826), the popular play *Der Müller und Sein Kind* (1835), the cycle *Die Hohenstaufen* (16 parts), *Der Nibelungen Hort.*

**Rau'schen·busch** (rou'shĕn·bo͝osh), **Walter.** 1861–1918. American Baptist clergyman, b. Rochester, N.Y.; leader in social interpretation and application of Christianity. Author of *Christianity and the Social Crisis* (1907), *The Social Principles of Jesus* (1916), etc.

**Rau'scher** (rou'shẽr), **Joseph Othmar von.** 1797–1875. Prince-archbishop of Vienna and Austrian cardinal (from 1855). Participated in concordat of 1855; at first opposed dogma of papal infallibility in Vatican Council (1870) and favored a liberal government.

**Rausch'ning** (roush'nĭng), **Hermann.** 1887– . Anti-Nazi politician and writer; pres., Danzig Landbund (1932) and the senate and foreign and personnel depts. (1933–34); fled to Eng. (1940), to U.S. (1940) and naturalized (1948). Among his books are *The Revolution of Nihilism, The Beast from the Abyss* (1941), *The Conservative Revolution* (1941), *Makers of Destruction,* etc.

**Rau'sen·ber'ger** (rou'zĕn·bĕr'gẽr), **Fritz.** 1868–1926. German inventor of artillery; with Krupp works (from 1928), director (1910); designed long-range gun used by the Germans to bombard Paris in World War.

**Rau'ten·berg** (rou'tĕn·bĕrκ; *Angl.* -t'n·bûrg), **Robert.** 1858–1940. Sculptor, b. Silesia, Ger.; to U.S. (1887) and became naturalized citizen. Specialist in ecclesiastical work.

**Rau'zan'** (rō'zäɴ'), **Jean Baptiste.** 1757–1847. French priest; chaplain of Louis XVIII; founder of the Society of the Priests of Mercy, approved by the pope (1834); members of the society are known as Fathers, or Priests, of Mercy.

**Ra'vail'lac'** (rȧ'vȧ'yȧk'), **François.** 1578–1610. Murderer of King Henry IV of France; b. of poor parents near Angoulême.

**Ra'vais'son'-Mol'lien'** (rȧ'vĕ'sôɴ'mô'lyăɴ'), **Jean Gaspard Félix Lacher.** 1813–1900. French philosopher and archaeologist; author of *Rapport sur la Philosophie en France au XIX^e Siècle* (1868), *La Vénus de Milo* (1871).

**Ra'vel'** (rȧ'vĕl'), **Maurice Joseph.** 1875–1937. French composer, b. at Ciboure. Among his notable works are *Myrrha* (cantata; 1901), *Shéhérazade* (set of songs; 1903), *Gaspard de la Nuit* (piano piece; 1908), *L'Heure Espagnole* (one-act opera; 1910), *Daphnis et Chloé* (ballet; 1912), *La Valse, Rhapsodie Espagnole, Tzigane* (1915), *L'Enfant et les Sortilèges* (1925), *Boléro* (ballet; 1928), and a concerto for piano and orchestra (1932).

**Ra'ven-Hill'** (rā'vĕn·hĭl'), **Leonard.** 1867–1942. English cartoonist and painter; on staff of *Punch* (1896–1936).

**Ra'vens·croft** (rā'vĕnz·krŏft), **Thomas.** 1592?–?1635. English composer; author of *Pammelia,* earliest collection of rounds and catches printed in England (1609), and supplementary collections *Deuteromelia* (1609; including "Three Blind Mice"), *Melismata* (1611), and *The Whole Booke of Psalmes* (1621).

**Ra'ven·stein** (*Eng.* rā'vĕn·stīn; *Ger.* rä'vĕn·shtīn), **Ernst Georg.** 1834–1913. Cartographer; b. Frankfort, Germany; to England and member of staff of topographical department of war office (1855–75); first recipient of Victoria gold medal of Royal Geographical Society (1902). Published *Systematic Atlas* (1884), *Map of Equatorial Africa* (1884), *Atlas of the World* (1911), etc.

**Ra've·steyn** (rȧ'vĕ·stīn), **Jan Anthonisz van.** 1572?–1657. Dutch portrait painter.

**Raw'don-Has'tings** (rô'd'n·hās'tĭngz), **Francis.** See Hastings.

**Raw'lings** (rô'lĭngz), **Marjorie,** *nee* **Kin·nan'** (kĭ·năn'). 1896–1953. American novelist, b. Washington, D.C.; m. Charles A. Rawlings (1919; div. 1933), Norton S. Baskin (1941). Author of *South Moon Under* (1933), *Golden Apples* (1935), *The Yearling* (1938; Pulitzer prize), *Cross Creek* (1942), *Cross Creek Cookery* (1942), etc.

**Raw'lins** (rô'lĭnz), **John Aaron.** 1831–1869. American lawyer and army officer, b. Galena, Ill.; chief of staff, U.S. army (1865). U.S. secretary of war (1869).

**Raw'lin·son** (rô'lĭn·s'n), Sir **Henry Creswicke.** 1810–1895. English Assyriologist. In East India Company's military service, studied Persian and the Indian vernaculars; as political agent at Kandahar (1840–42) and Baghdad (1844), completed transcript of cuneiform inscription of Darius I Hystaspis at Behistun, which he deciphered and interpreted (1846); received grant from British Museum to continue Assyrian and Babylonian excavations begun by Layard; director of East India Co. (1856); M.P. (1858); British minister in Persia (1859–60); member of India Council (1858, 1868–95), favored forward policy in Afghanistan. See Edward Hincks and William H. F. Talbot.

His brother **George** (1812–1902), Orientalist, was Camden professor of ancient history, Oxford (1861–89); canon of Canterbury (1872); edited *The History of Herodotus* (with his brother; 4 vols., 1858–60); author of *The Five Great Monarchies of the Ancient Eastern World* (4 vols., 1862–67), *The Sixth Great Oriental Monarchy—Parthia* (1873), *The Seventh Great Oriental Monarchy—the Sassanian or New Persian Empire* (1876), and histories of Egypt and Phoenicia.

**Henry Seymour Rawlinson** (1864–1925), 1st Baron Rawlinson; soldier; elder son of Sir Henry Creswicke Rawlinson; served with Roberts in India (1887–90), in Sudan with Kitchener (1898), and through Boer War; in World War I commanded forces sent to aid Antwerp (1914), and 4th army in battle of the Somme (1916); British representative on Supreme War Council (Feb., Mar., 1918); commanded forces in northern Russia (1919); commander in chief in India (1920).

**Rawns'ley** (rônz'lĭ), **Hardwicke Drummond.** 1851–1920. Anglican clergyman and writer; vicar of Crosthwaite (1883–1917); canon of Carlisle. Author of several volumes of verse and a number of books about the English Lake District and its literary associations.

**Raw'son** (rou'sôn), **Arturo.** 1884–1952. Argentine cavalry officer; succeeded Pedro Ramírez (*q.v.*) as commander of cavalry (1942); led military coup that overthrew Castillo government (June 4, 1943); turned over government to Ramírez (June 7).

**Ray** (rā), **Edward.** 1877–1943. British golf champion. Won British open championship, at Muirfield (1912).

**Ray, Isaac.** 1807–1881. American physician, b. Beverly, Mass. Specialist in mental diseases. Author of *Mental Hygiene* (1863), *Contributions to Mental Pathology* (1873), etc.

**Ray, John.** *Wrote his name* **Wray** *till 1670.* 1627?–1705. English naturalist; often called "father of English natural history." M.A., Cantab. (1651); with a pupil, **Francis Wil'lugh·by** [wĭl'ŭ·bĭ] (1635–1672; M.A., Cantab., 1659), toured England, Wales, Low Countries, Germany, Italy, and France, making collections on which to base complete systematic descriptions of animal and vegetable life; first demonstrated nature of buds and made division of flowering plants into dicotyledons and monocotyledons in *Methodus Plantarum Nova* (1682); first introduced a feasible limitation of term *species;* provided foundation of the Natural System in his classification of plants, using the fruit, later the flower, in classifying; after issuing *Historia Generalis Plantarum* (3 vols., 1686, 1688, 1704), took over zoological classification, which Willughby had completed at his death only for ornithology and ichthyology, devoted himself to insects (1690), and practically attained modern division into Metabola and Ametabola; wrote, besides botanical and zoological works, some theological works and a collection of proverbs (1670).

**Ray, Man** (măn). 1890–1976. American painter and photographer; studio in Paris (from 1921). Prominent among the surrealists; author of the surrealist films *Emak Bakia* (1926), *L'Étoile de Mer* (1928).

**Ray'burn** (rā'bẽrn), **Sam Taliaferro.** 1882–1961. American lawyer, b. in Roane Co., Tenn.; moved to Tex. (1887); member, U.S. House of Representatives (1913–61), speaker (1940–46; 1949–53; 1955–61).

**Ra'yet'** (rȧ'yĕ'), **Georges Antoine Pons.** 1839–1906. French astronomer; discovered, in collaboration with C. J. E. Wolf, three small stars, the first of a class of white or yellowish stars (Wolf-Rayet stars), whose spectrum indicates hydrogen, helium, etc.

**Ray'leigh** (rā'lĭ), 3d Baron. **John William Strutt** (strŭt). 1842–1919. English mathematician and physicist; educ. Cambridge. Professor of experimental physics, Cambridge (1879–84), of natural philosophy, Royal Institution (1887–1905); chancellor of Cambridge (1908). Published first scientific paper *Some Electro-magnetic Phenomena Considered in Connexion with the Dynamical Theory* (1869); investigated theory of sound, concerning which he published a textbook; directed work on redetermination of absolute electric units; work on determination of densities of gases led him to discovery (with Sir William Ramsay) of element argon (1894); made researches in physical optics. An original member of Order of Merit (1902); awarded 1904 Nobel prize for physics.

**Ray'mond'** (rā'môɴ'). Name of counts of **Tou'louse'** (tōō'lōōz'), including: **Raymond IV** *called* **Raymond de Saint'-Gilles'** [dē săɴ'zhēl'] (d. 1105), succeeded his older brother (1088), commanded a large army in the First Crusade (1096) and besieged Tripoli (1104). **Raymond VI** (1156–1222) succeeded his father Raymond V (1196); m. (1196) Joan, Queen of Sicily; fought with the Albigenses against the Crusaders under Simon de Montfort, was decisively defeated in the battle of Muret (1213) and had his possessions handed over to Montfort by the Fourth Lateran Council; resumed war against Montfort; gained back most of his territory.

**Ray'mond** (rā'mŭnd), **An'to·nín** (ăn'tô·nyēn). 1889– . Architect, b. in Prague, Czechoslovakia; to U.S. (c. 1914); accompanied Frank Lloyd Wright (*q.v.*) to Japan; remained there to practice (1921–37); pioneer of modern architecture in Orient.

**Ray'mond'** (rā'môɴ'), **Fulgence.** 1844–1910. French neurologist; author of works on tabes dorsalis, poliomyelitis, muscular atrophy in syphilis, neurasthenia, etc.

**Ray'mond** (rā'mŭnd), **George Lansing.** 1839–1929. American educator; professor, Williams (1874–80), Princeton (1880–1905), George Washington U. (1905–12). Author of a novel (*Modern Fishers of Men*, 1879), poetry, a few plays, and many works on aesthetics.

**Raymond, Henry Jarvis.** 1820–1869. American journalist and politician, b. Lima, N.Y. With George Jones, founded New York *Times* (1851) and was its editor (1851–69). Lieutenant governor of New York (1855–57). Member of meeting that founded Republican party (1856) and drafted statement of its principles. Supported Lincoln vigorously through Civil War. Member, U.S. House of Representatives (1865–67). Author of *A Life of Daniel Webster* (1853), *A History of the Administration of President Lincoln* (1864), etc.

**Raymond, John Howard.** 1814–1878. American educator, b. New York City. Professor, Colgate (1838–50); an organizer and professor, U. of Rochester (1850–55); first president, Brooklyn Collegiate and Polytechnic Institute (1855–64); president, Vassar College (1865–78). His nephew **Rossiter Worthington Raymond** (1840–1918) was a mining engineer; aide-de-camp to Gen. Frémont (1861–64); U.S. commissioner of mining statistics (1868–76); president, American Institute of Mining Engineers (1872–75) and secretary (1884–1911); author of essays on U.S. mining legislation, *A Glossary of Mining and Metallurgical Terms* (1881), and a *Life of Peter Cooper* (1901).

**Raymond, John T.** *Assumed name of* **John O'Brien** (legalized 1881). 1836–1887. American comedian, b. Buffalo, N.Y. Professional debut (1853); best-known roles, Asa Trenchard in *Our American Cousin*, Tony Lumpkin in *She Stoops to Conquer*, Crabtree in *The School for Scandal*, Colonel Mulberry Sellers in *The Gilded Age*.

**Raymond Lully.** See LULLY.

**Ray'mond of Pe'ña·fort'** (rā'mŭnd, pā'nyä·fôrt'), Saint. *Span.* San **Rai·mun'do de Peñafort** (sän rī·mōōn'dō thā). 1176?–1275. Spanish Dominican monk and theologian; canon of Barcelona (1219); aided Peter Nolasco (*q.v.*) in founding order for ransom of Christian captives; zealous supporter of the Inquisition and of a crusade against the Moors (1229); called to Rome by Pope Gregory IX (1230); codified canon law; his *Decretalium Gregorii P. IX* forms volume V of *Corpus Juris Canonici;* bishop of Tarragona (1235) and general of the Dominican order (1238–40).

**Ray'mond of Sa·bun'de** (rā'mŭnd, sä·bōōn'dā). *Span.* **Rai·mun'do Sabunde** (rī·mōōn'dō). d. ?1437. Spanish theologian; chiefly remembered for his treatise on natural theology, translated by Montaigne into French.

**Ray'nal'** (rā'nȧl'), **Guillaume Thomas François.** 1713–1796. French historian and philosopher, regarded as a leader among the French freethinkers; educated for priesthood. Collaborator in *Histoire Philosophique et Politique des Établissements et du Commerce des Européens dans les Deux Indes* (1770), which was publicly burned (1781) by order of the parliament because of its attacks on the clergy and on European civilized peoples for their conduct and policies toward the natives in the Indies.

**Raynal, Paul.** 1890– . French playwright; author of the love comedy *Le Maître de son Cœur* (1921), the war tragedy *Le Tombeau sous l'Arc de Triomphe* (1924), and the battle drama *La Francerie* (1933).

**Ray'nou·ard'** (rā'nwȧr'), **François Just Marie.** 1761–1836. French scholar and playwright; author of the plays *Caton d'Utique* (1794), *Templiers* (1805); best known for his studies in Provençal language and literature, as his collection of troubadour poetry *Choix de Poésies Originales des Troubadours* (1816–21), his *Lexique Roman* (1838–44), etc.

**Ray′ski** (rī′skē), **Louis Ferdinand von.** 1806–1890. German painter; best known for his portraits.

**Ra·zi′ya** (ră·zē′yȧ) *or* **Ra·ziy′yat–ud–din′** (ră·zĭy′-yă·to͝od·dēn′). d. 1240. Queen of Delhi of the Slave dynasty (1236–40), the only woman ruler of Mohammedan India. Daughter of Altamsh and sister of Firuz Shah I. Appointed by Altamsh as his successor; according to Moslem sources, a wise and just ruler and benefactor to her realm, but her reign disturbed by revolts; slain by Hindu followers.

**Rea** (rā), **Samuel.** 1855–1929. American railroad executive, b. Hollidaysburg, Pa. Rose from rodman (1871) to president (1912) of Pennsylvania Railroad; retired (1925). Awarded Franklin medal by Franklin Institute for outstanding engineering accomplishments (1926).

**Read** (rēd), **George.** 1733–1798. American lawyer and Revolutionary leader, b. in Cecil County, Md.; practiced, New Castle, Del. Member, Continental Congress (1774–77) and signer of Declaration of Independence. Presiding officer, Delaware constitutional convention (1776). Judge, U.S. court of appeals in admiralty cases (1782–86). Delegate to Constitutional Convention (1787) and vigorous upholder of rights of the smaller states. Instrumental in causing Delaware to be first state to ratify the Constitution. U.S. senator from Delaware (1789–93). Chief justice of Delaware (1793–98). Among his descendants were John Read, John Meredith Read (1797–1874), John Meredith Read (1837–1896). See under John READ (1769–1854).

**Read, Herbert.** 1893–1968. English editor, critic, poet, and museum curator, b. in Yorkshire. Served in World War (1914–18); captain (1917). Director of Museum of Modern Art, in London. Author of *Naked Warriors* (1919), *Eclogues* (1919), *Mutations of the Phoenix* (1923), *Phases of English Poetry* (1928), *The Sense of Glory* (1929), *The Meaning of Art* (1931), *The Innocent Eye* (1933), *Poems, 1914–1934* (1935), *Art and Society* (1936), *Poetry and Anarchism; Collected Essays* (1938).

**Read, John.** 1769–1854. Son of George Read. American lawyer, b. New Castle, Del.; practiced, Philadelphia (from 1792); president, Philadelphia Bank (1819–41). His son **John Meredith** (1797–1874) was a jurist; attorney general of Pennsylvania (1846); justice, Pennsylvania supreme court (1858–74) and chief justice (from 1872). John Meredith Read's son **John Meredith** (1837–1896) was a lawyer and diplomat; practiced, Albany; U.S. consul general, Paris, France (1869–73); U.S. minister to Greece (1873–79); resident in Paris (from 1881).

**Read, Nathan.** 1759–1849. American inventor and industrialist, b. Warren, Mass. Designed multitubular steam boiler, double-acting steam engine, and a chain-wheel device for propelling boats (all patented 1791); a machine for cutting and heading nails (patented 1798). Member, U.S. House of Representatives (1800–03).

**Read, Opie.** 1852–1939. American writer, b. Nashville, Tenn.; founded and edited the humorous journal *Arkansas Traveler* (1883–91); engaged in literary work in Chicago (1891–1939); author of many adventure stories, including *A Tennessee Judge* (1893), *The Jucklins* (1895), *The Starbucks* (1902), *Old Lim Jucklin* (1905), *Gold Gauze Veil* (1927).

**Read, Thomas Buchanan.** 1822–1872. American poet and painter, b. near Guthriesville, Pa. Tailor's apprentice, grocer's assistant, cigarmaker, sculptor of tombstones, sign painter (to c. 1842). Opened studio in Boston (c. 1842); moved to Philadelphia (1846). Painted portraits of Longfellow, Mrs. Browning, William Henry Harrison; his portrait of George Peabody hangs in Peabody Institute, Baltimore. Published several volumes of poetry and was regarded by contemporaries as one of America's leading poets. Best known of his poems, *Drifting* and *Sheridan's Ride.*

**Reade** (rēd), **Charles.** 1814–1884. English novelist and dramatist, b. Ipsden, son of an Oxfordshire squire. Fellow of Magdalen Coll., Oxford (1835), M.A. (1838); barrister (1843) but did not practice. Began career by writing plays, the most successful being *Masks and Faces* (with Tom Taylor; 1852), *Gold* (1853), *The Courier of Lyons* (melodrama; 1854), *Sera Nunquam* (1865), *Drink* (1879). On advice of actress Laura Seymour rewrote *Masks and Faces* as a novel, *Peg Woffington* (1852); depicted Scottish fisherfolk in *Christie Johnstone* (1853); employed fiction to expose social abuses in *It Is Never too Late to Mend* (1856); followed five lesser novels with his masterpiece, the historical novel about the father of Erasmus, *The Cloister and the Hearth* (1861). Drew attention to abuses in private asylums for insane in *Hard Cash* (1863), to the marriage problem in *Griffith Gaunt* (1866), to the abuse by trade-unions called "rattening" in *Put Yourself in His Place* (1870); scandalized American reviewers with his autobiographical *A Terrible Temptation* (1871), revealing his methods of documentation; failed in health after death (1879) of Laura Seymour, the platonic friend who had kept his house (from 1854); pictured degrading features of village life in *A Woman Hater* (1877); left behind at death a completed novel, *A Perilous Secret.*

**Read′ing** (rĕd′ĭng), 1st Marquis of. **Rufus Daniel I′saacs** (ī′zȧks; -zĭks). 1860–1935. British statesman; Liberal M.P. (1904–13); solicitor general (1910); attorney general (1910–13), first attorney general to be member of cabinet; lord chief justice of England (1913–21); created Baron Reading (1914) and Viscount Reading (1916); special envoy to U.S. (1918–19); created Viscount **Er′leigh** [ûr′lĭ] (1917); viceroy and governor general of India (1921–26); created marquis of Reading (1926); foreign secretary in first national government (1931).

**Reading, John.** 1677–1764. English organist at Lincoln Cathedral and (after 1707) in London; composer of tune *Adeste Fideles.*

**Ré′al′ del Sarte** (rā′ȧl′ dĕl sȧrt′), **Louis Maxime.** 1888–1954. French sculptor; executed monuments to Edward VII, King Alexander of Yugoslavia, Marshal Joffre; statues of Clemenceau and General Mangin; monuments *Morts de Compiègne* and *Morts des Armées de Champagne.*

**Ré′au′mur′** (rā′ō′mür′), **René Antoine Fer′chault′ de** (fĕr′shō′ dĕ). 1683–1757. French naturalist and physicist; constructed a thermometer (Reaumur thermometer) so graduated that 0° marks the freezing point and 80° the boiling point of water; invented an opaque white glass known as Reaumur porcelain, also a method of tinning steel; worked on the production of steel and improvements in the manufacture of iron; investigated the action of the electric ray, regeneration of lost parts in crustaceans, artificial incubation of eggs, auriferous rivers, turquoise mines, etc. Author of *Mémoires pour Servir à l'Histoire des Insectes* (6 vols., 1734–42).

**Re·bek′ah** *or* **Re·bec′ca** (rē·bĕk′ȧ). In the Bible, the wife of Isaac (*Genesis* xxiv) and mother of Esau and Jacob (*Genesis* xxv. 20 ff.).

**Re′ber** (rā′bẽr), **Franz von.** 1834–1919. German art scholar; director, Royal Gallery (1875–1907).

**Re·ber′** (rē·bâr′), **Napoléon Henri.** 1807–1880. French composer of symphonies, chamber music, a suite of orchestral pieces, comic operas (as *La Nuit de Noël,* 1848, *Le Père Gaillard,* 1852, *Le Ménétrier à la Cour,* etc.), ballets, and songs.

**Re′bi·kov** (ryā′byĭ·kôf), **Vladimir Ivanovich.** 1866–

1920. Russian composer; settled in Vienna and devoted himself to composition; identified with ultramodern school of music; composer of operas (*The Storm* and *Narcissus*), orchestral suites, symphonic poems, and choral works.

**Reb'mann** (rāp'män), **Johannes.** 1820–1876. German missionary, traveler, and explorer in East Africa; discovered Mt. Kilimanjaro with Krapf (1848) and investigated Swahili and other native languages.

**Re·boul'** (rē·bōōl'), **Jean.** *Called* **Le Bou'lan'ger' de Nîmes** (lē bōō'läN'zhā' dē nēm'), *i.e.* the baker of Nîmes. 1796–1864. French poet, much admired by Lamartine, Dumas père, and others of his time; his most noted work is *L'Ange et l'Enfant* (1828); among his volumes of verse are *Poésies* (1836) and *Les Traditionnelles* (1857).

**Re·boux'** (rē·bōō'), **Paul.** 1877– . French writer; author of books of verse, but best known for his exotic novels, as *Josette* (1902), *La Petite Papacoda* (1910), *Le Phare* (1911), *Chouchou* (1919), *Trio* (1924), *Bamboulina* (1929), etc.

**Re·brea'nu** (rē·bryä'nōō), **Liviu.** 1885–1944. Rumanian writer; reputed founder of the modern novel in Rumanian literature; author of *Jon* (2 vols., 1920), *Adam and Eve* (1925), etc.

**Ré'ca'mier'** (rā'kà'myā'), **Jeanne Françoise Julie Adélaïde,** *nee* **Ber'nard'** (bĕr'nàr'). 1777–1849. French society beauty and wit; m. Jacques Récamier, Paris banker (1793). Her salon attracted the notables of the day during the Consulate and the Empire; after the Restoration, she retired to Abbaye-aux-Bois, where she maintained close friendship with Chateaubriand. Her *Souvenirs et Correspondance* were edited and published (1852) by her niece and adopted daughter, Mme. Lenormand.

**Rech'berg und Ro'then·lö'wen** (rĕK'bĕrK ŏŏnt rō'tĕn·lû'vĕn), Count **Johann Bernhard von.** 1806–1899. Austrian statesman; ambassador in Stockholm (1841) and Rio de Janeiro (1843); helped Metternich in Revolution of 1848; represented Austria at Frankfurt (1849); associate of Radetzky in government of Lombardy-Venetia (1853); Austrian representative and president, Federal Council (1855), where he opposed Bismarck; foreign minister (1859–64) and minister president (until 1860).

**Reck'ling·hau'sen** (rĕk'lĭng·hou'zĕn), **Friedrich Daniel von.** 1833–1910. German pathologist; known for work on inflammatory conditions; discovered the leucocyte known as the wandering cell.

**Re·clus'** (rē·klü'), **Jean Jacques Élisée.** 1830–1905. French geographer; author of many books of travel and description, including *La Terre...* (1867–68), *Géographie Universelle* (1875–94), *L'Afrique Australe* (in collaboration; 1901).

**Rec'orde** (?rĕk'ôrd), **Robert.** 1510?–1558. English mathematician; B.A., Oxon.; taught mathematics at Oxford and Cambridge; physician to Edward VI and Queen Mary. Early writer of English textbooks of arithmetic, geometry, astronomy; discovered method of extracting square root of multinomial algebraic expressions; first to use sign = with modern meaning (1557).

**Re·cou'ly'** (rē·kōō'lē'), **Raymond.** 1876–1950. French journalist and historian; served in World War (captain) and wrote *Foch le Vainqueur* (1919), *La Barrière du Rhin* (1923), *Joffre* (1931), etc.

**ReDaK.** See under Kimchi.

**Red Cloud** (rĕd' kloud'). 1822–1909. American Indian chief, b. in Nebraska; chief of the Oglalas and leader of Sioux and Cheyenne bands (1866), warred against whites (1866–68); deposed by government Indian agent (1881).

**Red Eagle.** See William Weatherford.

**Redesdale,** Barons. See under William Mitford.

**Red'field** (rĕd'fēld), **Edward Willis.** 1869–1965. American landscape painter; known esp. for his winter scenes in the Delaware River region.

**Redfield, William C.** 1789–1857. American entrepreneur and meteorologist, b. Middletown, Conn.; saddler and harness maker by trade. Projected railway lines, esp. one between New York and Albany and one connecting the Hudson and Mississippi rivers (from 1829). Made study of gales and hurricanes, demonstrating that violent gales are whirlwinds, having a rotary and progressive movement, that the direction of revolution is uniform, and that the velocity of rotation increases from the outer edge toward the center. A founder and first president, American Association for the Advancement of Science (1848).

**Redfield, William Cox.** 1858–1932. Grandson of William C Redfield. American industrialist and politician, b. Albany, N.Y.; steel manufacturer and exporter, New York City (1883–1913); member, U.S. House of Representatives (1911–13); U.S. secretary of commerce (1913–19).

**Red'grave** (rĕd'grāv), **Richard.** 1804–1888. English genre and landscape painter; author, with his brother **Samuel** (1802–1876), writer on art, of *A Century of Painters of the English School* (1866).

**Re'di** (râ'dē), **Francesco.** 1626?–1697 or 1698. Italian physician, naturalist, and poet; one of first to test scientifically the theory of spontaneous generation; showed that no maggots developed in meat protected so that flies could not lay their eggs on it (1668). Author of the dithyrambic *Bacco in Toscana* (1685), etc.

**Red' Jack'et** (rĕd' jăk'ĕt; -ĭt). *Indian name* **Sagoyewatha.** 1758?–1830. American Indian chief, b. in Seneca County, N.Y. A chief of the Senecas; known as an orator. Pursued policy of friendship with whites, but opposed cession of Indian lands to U.S. and efforts to train Indians in white man's civilization.

**Red'lich** (rāt'lĭK), **Joseph.** 1869–1936. Austrian jurist and politician, b. in Moravia; authority on English government; member, Austrian Parliament (1907–18) and German Progressive party, Moravian Diet; minister of finance in last imperial cabinet of Lammasch (1918); professor of comparative law, Harvard U. (1926–31); again minister of finance (1931). Author of *Local Government in England* (1901), *The Procedure of the House of Commons* (1905), etc.

**Red'man** (rĕd'măn), **Ben Ray.** 1896–1961. American journalist and writer, b. Brooklyn, N.Y.; editor of "Old Wine in New Bottles" book column in New York *Herald-Tribune* (1926–37); on producing staff of Universal Pictures (from 1937). Translator of many modern French works; author of *Masquerade* (verse; 1923), *Marriage for Three* (comedy; 1929), *The Perfect Crime* (detective story; 1929), *The Bannerman Case* (detective story, under pseudonym **Jeremy Lord** [lôrd]; 1935), etc.

**Red'mayne** (rĕd'mān), Sir **Richard Augustine Studdert.** 1865–1955. English mining and civil engineer; government chief inspector of mines (1908–20). Chairman governor, Imperial Mineral Resources Bureau (1918–25); chairman, Advisory Council on Minerals to Imperial Institute (1925–35).

**Red'mond** (rĕd'mŭnd), **John Edward.** 1856–1918. Irish political leader, b. Ballytrent, Wexford. M.P. (1881); prominent organizer of home-rule propaganda; leader of Parnellite group on death of Parnell (1891). Adopted conciliatory attitude toward government and anti-Parnellites, and brought about amalgamation of the two

Irish Nationalist parties (1900), aiming at a free Ireland within British Empire. As chairman of united party used balance of power in House of Commons to force through constitutional resolutions removing veto power of House of Lords (1909–11); procured Irish acceptance of home-rule bill (1912); opposed attempted separation of Ulster; opposed Sinn Feiners and other extremists. Supported Great Britain in World War and promoted recruiting in Ireland but declined place in Asquith's coalition cabinet (1915); expressed detestation of Easter Rebellion (1916); played conciliatory role in Irish convention of devising scheme of self-government for Ireland but lost control to de Valera and extreme nationalists.

**Re·don′** (rē·dôN′), **Odilon**. 1840–1916. French painter and engraver; identified with the postimpressionist school; as a painter, best known for his paintings of flowers.

**Re·dou′té′** (rē·do͞o′tā′), **Pierre Joseph**. 1759–1840. French painter of flowers.

**Red′path** (rĕd′päth), **James**. 1833–1891. Journalist, b. Berwick upon Tweed, Scotland; to U.S. (c. 1850). On staff, New York *Tribune* (1852–82). Vigorous abolitionist; aided in transporting ex-slaves to Haiti and in securing U.S. recognition of independence of Haiti; war correspondent with Union armies in Civil War. Established lecture bureau (1868); editor, *North American Review* (1886–87). Author of *The Roving Editor, or Talks with Slaves in the Southern States* (1859), *The Public Life of Captain John Brown* (1860), *Talks about Ireland* (1881), etc.

**Red′vers** (rĕd′vẽrz). Name of Norman family holding lands in Devonshire, including **Baldwin of Redvers**, 1st Earl of **Dev′on** [dĕv′ŭn] (d. 1155), who raised revolts against King Stephen.

**Red′wald** (rĕd′wôld) *or* **Raed′wald** (răd′-). d. 627? King of East Angles; gained independence of control of Ethelbert, King of Kent, and became fourth Bretwalda; defeated Æthelfrith (617) and set Edwin on throne of Northumberland.

**Red Wing** (rĕd′ wĭng′). 1750?–?1825. American Indian chief, b. near present Red Wing, Minn.; became chief among Sioux Indians through prowess in war; aided British in War of 1812; adopted policy of friendship with Americans (from 1814).

**Red′witz** (rĕt′vĭts), Baron **Oskar von**. 1823–1891. German poet, dramatist, and novelist; author of *Amaranth* (romantic poem; 1849), *Das Lied vom Neuen Deutschen Reich* (cycle of about 600 patriotic sonnets; 1871), *Odilo* (epic; 1878), *Ein Deutsches Hausbuch* (epic-lyrical poem; 1883), dramas *Thomas Morus* (1856) and *Philippine Welser* (1859), *Hermann Stark* (novel; 1868), etc.

**Red′wood** (rĕd′wo͝od), Sir **Bo′ver·ton** (?bō′vẽr·t′n; -tŭn). 1846–1919. English chemist; authority on petroleum.

**Reed** (rēd), **Douglas**. 1895– . British writer, b. London; served in World War (1914–18); newspaper editor and correspondent (1921–39); author of *The Burning of the Reichstag* (1934), *Insanity Fair* (1938), *Nemesis?* (1940), *A Prophet at Home* (1941), *All Our To-morrows* (1942), etc.

**Reed**, Sir **Edward James**. 1830–1906. English naval architect; employed by navy to convert wooden vessels into armorclads (1862); as chief constructor of navy (1863–70), instituted entirely new construction, designed and launched the *Bellerophon;* Liberal M.P. (1874); a lord of treasury (1886). Author of *Our Ironclad Ships* (1869), *The Stability of Ships* (1884).

**Reed, Ezekiel**. fl. 18th century. American inventor; resident of Bridgewater, Mass.; invented nailmaking machine (patented 1786).

**Reed, Florence**. 1883–1967. American actress, b. Philadelphia; m. Malcolm Williams; appeared in *The Typhoon*, *The Yellow Ticket*, *Chu-Chin-Chow*, etc.

**Reed, Henry Hope**. 1808–1854. Grandson of Joseph Reed. American literary critic and educator; best known for introducing Wordsworth favorably to American public.

**Reed, Isaac**. 1742–1807. English Shakespearean editor; practiced as conveyancer; devoted himself to literature and archaeology; revised Dr. Johnson and George Steevens's edition of Shakespeare (1785); edited the "first variorum" Shakespeare from Steevens's notes (21 vols., 1803).

**Reed, James A.** 1861–1944. American lawyer and politician, b. in Ohio; practiced in Kansas City, Mo. (from 1887). U.S. senator from Missouri (1911–29).

**Reed, John**. 1887–1920. American journalist and poet, b. Portland, Ore.; grad. Harvard (1910). On staff of radical magazine *The Masses* (1913). War correspondent (1914) for *Metropolitan Magazine* with Pancho Villa in Mexico and (1914–16) with armies on eastern front in Europe in World War I. In Russia in time to observe revolution of October, 1917; associated with Lenin. Expelled from National Socialist Convention, in U.S. (1919); organized and led Communist Labor party, and edited its journal *The Voice of Labor*. Indicted for sedition, escaped to Russia and identified himself with Russian Communist authorities. Died of typhus; buried in the Kremlin, Moscow. Author of *Sangar* (in *Poetry*, 1912), *The Day in Bohemia* (1913), *Insurgent Mexico* (1914), *The War in Eastern Europe* (with Boardman Robinson; 1916), *Tamburlaine and Other Poems* (1916), *Red Russia* (1919), *Ten Days that Shook the World* (1919).

**Reed, Joseph**. 1741–1785. American Revolutionary commander and statesman, b. Trenton, N.J. President, second Provincial Congress, Philadelphia (1775). Military secretary for Gen. Washington (1775), and adjutant general of Continental army. Member, Continental Congress (1777, 1778). President, supreme executive council of Pennsylvania (1778–81).

**Reed, Stanley Forman**. 1884– . American jurist, b. in Mason Co., Ky.; A.B., Kentucky Wesleyan (1902) and Yale (1906); began law practice in Maysville, Ky. (1910); general counsel, Federal Farm Board (1929–32), Reconstruction Finance Corp. (1932–35); solicitor general of U.S. (1935–38); associate justice, U.S. Supreme Court (1938–57).

**Reed, Thomas Brackett**. 1839–1902. American lawyer and legislator, b. Portland, Me. Member, U.S. House of Representatives (1877–99) and speaker of the house (1889–91, 1895–99); responsible for adoption by the house of a series of rules, Reed's Rules (Feb. 14, 1890), increasing speaker's power to expedite legislation favored by majority party.

**Reed, Walter**. 1851–1902. American army surgeon, b. Belroi, Va. M.D., Virginia (1869), and also, Bellevue Hospital Medical College (1870). Entered army medical corps (1875). On frontier duty (1875–90). Curator, Army Medical Museum, and professor of bacteriology and microscopy at Army Medical College, Washington, D.C. (1893), promoted major (1893). Head of commission (including James Carroll, Jesse Lazear, Aristides Agramonte) to investigate cause and mode of transmission of yellow fever (1900); proved by controlled experiments that yellow fever is transmitted by the mosquito known as *Aëdes aegypti*, and also proved the method of transmission. With this knowledge, it was possible to eradicate the disease by destroying the carriers. The Walter Reed Hospital, Washington, D.C., was named in his honor. Elected to American Hall of Fame (1945).

**Ree'der** (rē'dẽr), **Andrew Horatio.** 1807–1864. American lawyer, b. Easton, Pa. First governor, Kansas Territory (1854–55); removed by president. Became leader of Free State party in Kansas; elected to U.S. Senate, but not allowed to take his seat. Resumed practice of law, Easton, Pa.

**Ree'dy** (rē'dĭ), **William Marion.** 1862–1920. American journalist, b. St. Louis, Mo. Editor, *Sunday Mirror*, St. Louis (from 1893), and proprietor (from 1896), the weekly journal becoming known as *Reedy's Mirror.*

**Rees** (rēs), **John Krom.** 1851–1907. American astronomer, b. New York City; professor, Columbia (1881–1907). Investigated variation of terrestrial latitudes and the constant of aberration; did important work in celestial photography.

**Reese** (rēs), **Lizette Woodworth.** 1856–1935. American writer, b. in Baltimore County, Md.; author of autobiographical works and volumes of poetry, including *A Handful of Lavender* (1891), *Wayside Lute* (1909), *Spicewood* (1920), *Wild Cherry* (1923), *White April* (1930), *Pastures* (1933).

**Reeve** (rēv), **Arthur Benjamin.** 1880–1936. American author of detective fiction, including *Adventures of Craig Kennedy, Scientific Detective* (series in *Cosmopolitan Magazine*, 1910–18), *The Clutching Hand* (1934).

**Reeve, Clara.** 1729–1807. English novelist; translator of Barclay's *Argenis* (1772) and author of novels, including *The Champion of Virtue, a Gothic Story* (1777), renamed *The Old English Baron*, avowedly in imitation of Sir Horace Walpole's *Castle of Otranto.*

**Reeve, Henry.** 1813–1895. English man of letters; member of staff of the *Times* (1840), guided its foreign policy for 15 years; editor of *Edinburgh Review* (1855–95), of *Greville Memoirs* (1865), and author of historical essays.

**Reeve, Richard Andrews.** 1842–1919. Canadian physician; specialist in ophthalmology and otology.

**Reeve, Tapping.** 1744–1823. American lawyer and educator, b. Brookhaven, Long Island, N.Y.; practiced, Litchfield, Conn.; opened Litchfield Law School (1784) and was its sole teacher (1784–98).

**Reeves** (rēvz), **Arthur Middleton.** 1856–1891. American philologist and historian; devoted himself to study of languages, Icelandic culture, Old Norse manuscripts. Published *The Finding of Wineland the Good*, with phototype plates of the original vellum manuscripts of the saga treating the Norse discoveries of America (1890).

**Reeves, Helen Buckingham**, *nee* **Ma'thers** (?mā'thẽrz; măth'ẽrz). *Pseudonym* **David Ly'all** (lī'ăl). 1853–1920. English novelist; m. (1876) Henry Albert Reeves (d. 1914); author of *Comin' thro' the Rye* (1875), *Cherry Ripe* (1877), *The Story of a Sin* (1881), *A Man of the Time* (1894), *Bam Wildfire* (1897), etc.

**Reeves, John Sims.** 1818–1900. English tenor singer; appeared at Drury Lane under Macready as tenor in Purcell's *King Arthur*, and in *Der Freischütz*, and *Acis and Galatea* (1841–43); after study in Paris and Milan appeared with success on English operatic stage (1847) and in oratorio (1848); premier English tenor, for whom tenor parts were written in Costa's *Eli* and *Naaman.*

**Reeves, William Pember.** 1857–1932. British journalist, politician, and economist, b. Canterbury, New Zealand. Editor, Canterbury *Times*, Lyttelton *Times*. Member of New Zealand Parliament (1887–96); minister of education, labor, and justice (1891–96). Agent general for New Zealand (1896–1905), and high commissioner (1905–08). Director, London School of Economics (1908–19). Author of *State Experiments in Australia and New Zealand; The Long White Cloud, a History of New Zealand; An Introduction to the History of Communism and Socialism;* compiler of a volume of New Zealand verse.

**Re'ga·la'do** (rā'gä·lä'thō), **Tomás.** 1864– . Salvadoran general and political leader; president of El Salvador (1899–1903). Attempted to form new Central American union; brought El Salvador into a commanding position in Central American affairs.

**Re'ge·ner** (rā'gĕ·nẽr), **Erich.** 1881–1955. German physicist; known for investigations on elementary charges of electricity, cosmic rays at great depths in water, oxygen in the stratosphere, etc.

**Re'ger** (rā'gẽr), **Max.** 1873–1916. German composer and contrapuntist; director of court orchestra (1911–14) and general music director (1913), Meiningen. Composer of organ music, piano and violin concertos, choral works, chamber music, church music, songs, etc.

**Reggio,** Ducs **de.** See Nicolas Charles OUDINOT.

**Regillo.** See Giovanni Antonio da PORDENONE.

**Re'gi·no of Prüm** (rā'gē·nō, prüm'). *Also* **Re'gi·non** (rā'gē·nôn). d. 915. German monk and chronicler; educ. in the monastery of Prüm, of which he was abbot (892–899); abbot of St. Martin's, at Trier (899–915). Author of a *Chronicon* (a history of the world from the dawn of the Christian era to 906).

**Regiomontanus.** See Johann MÜLLER (1436–1476).

**Reg'nal** (rĕg'n'l), **F.** Pseudonym of Baron Frederic A. D'ERLANGER.

**Re·gnard'** (rẽ·nyȧr'), **Jean François.** 1655–1709. French playwright; noted esp. as writer of comedies.

**Re·gnault'** (rẽ·nyō'), **Henri Victor.** 1810–1878. French chemist and physicist; made determinations of coefficients of expansion, specific heats, and vapor pressures of mixtures; conducted researches on the halogen and other derivatives of unsaturated hydrocarbons. His son **Alexandre Georges Henri** (1843–1871) was a genre and figure painter; paintings include *Thetis Giving to Achilles the Arms of Vulcan*, an equestrian portrait of General Prim, the *Lady in Red* and *Automedon Taming the Horses of Achilles, Judith and Holofernes*, and *Salome.*

**Regnault,** Baron **Jean Baptiste.** 1754–1829. French historical painter.

**Ré'gnier'** (rā'nyā'), **Claude Ambroise.** Duc **de Mas'sa'** (dē mȧ'sȧ'). 1746–1814. French statesman; member of States-General (1789) and Council of Ancients (1796); appointed by Napoleon councilor of state, minister of justice (1802–13), president of the Corps Législatif (1813). Created duc de Massa (1809).

**Régnier, Henri de.** 1864–1936. French poet, critic, and novelist, b. Honfleur. Regarded as one of the leaders of the symbolists. Among his volumes of verse are *Lendemains* (1885), *Sites* (1887), *Aréthuse* (1895), and *Flamma Tenax* (1922–28). Among his critical works are *Sujets et Paysages* (1906), *Portraits et Souvenirs* (1913), and *Nos Rencontres* (1931). Among his novels are *La Double Maîtresse* (1900), *Le Passé Vivant* (1905), *La Pécheresse* (1920), and *L'Escapade* (1926).

**Régnier, Mathurin.** 1573–1613. Nephew of the poet Philippe Desportes. French poet; private secretary to Cardinal de Joyeuse, in Rome (1593–1604); a canon of Chartres cathedral (1609). Best known for his satires, as *Le Goût Décide de Tout, La Folie est Générale, Le Mauvais Repas, Le Mauvais Lieu.*

**Regula,** Saint. See Saint FELIX.

**Reg'u·lus** (rĕg'ū·lŭs), **Marcus Atilius.** d. about 250 B.C. Roman hero; consul (267 and 256). Defeated Carthaginian fleet, invaded Africa, and defeated Carthaginian army (256); defeated and captured by the Carthaginians (255). On his promise to return to Carthage, he was sent with an embassy to Rome (250) to negotiate peace, or the exchange of prisoners; failed in his mission, and, true to his promise, returned to Carthage, where he was tortured to death.

**Re'han** (rē'ăn), **Ada.** *Orig. surname* **Cre'han** (krē'ăn). 1857–1916. Actress, b. Limerick, Ireland; to U.S. (1865) and settled in Brooklyn, N.Y. In Augustin Daly's company, New York (1879–99); excelled in comedy roles.

**Rehn** (rĕn), **Frank Knox Morton.** 1848–1914. American painter; best known for his marines.

**Rehn'quist** (rĕn'kwĭst), **William Hubbs.** 1924– American jurist, b. Milwaukee, Wis. Associate justice, U.S. Supreme Court (1972– ).

**Re'ho·bo'am** (rē'(h)ô·bō'ăm). King of Judah (c. 933–917 B.C.); son of King Solomon. During the early years of his reign (*1 Kings* xii. 1–24) the northern tribes revolted under Jeroboam and succeeded in dividing the Hebrews into two kingdoms, two tribes comprising the Kingdom of Judah and ten tribes the Kingdom of Israel; both kingdoms invaded by Sheshonk of Egypt (c. 926).

**Rei'cha** (rī'кä), **Anton.** 1770–1836. Composer and music theorist, b. Prague. Studied with his uncle **Joseph Reicha** (1746–1795), cellist, Kapellmeister, and composer. In Vienna (1802–08), to Paris (1808). Composed operas and instrumental music; wrote *Traité de Mélodie* (1814), *Traité de Haute Composition Musicale* (2 vols., 1824–25), *L'Art du Compositeur Dramatique* (1833).

**Rei'chardt** (rī'кärt), **Johann Friedrich.** 1752–1814. German composer, conductor, and writer on music; Kapellmeister and court composer to Frederick the Great (1775); dismissed by Frederick William II for sympathy with French Revolution (1794). His compositions include the first German Liederspiel *Liebe und Treue* (1800), Singspiele, settings for many of Goethe's poems, operas, chamber music, symphonies, etc.

**Rei'che·nau** (rī'кĕ·nou), **Walther von.** 1884–1942. German field marshal, b. Karlsruhe. Commanded German army which captured Warsaw (1939); commanded army on southern sector of Russian front (1941).

**Rei'chen·bach** (rī'кĕn·bäк), **Heinrich Gottlieb Ludwig.** 1793–1879. German botanist and zoologist; professor of natural history, Dresden (from 1820). Author of *Iconographia Botanica seu Plantae Criticae* (1823–32; with 1000 plates), *Handbuch des Natürlichen Pflanzensystems* (1837), etc. His son **Heinrich Gustav** (1824–1889) was authority on orchids, and professor and director of the botanical gardens, Hamburg (from 1864).

**Reichenbach,** Baron **Karl von.** 1788–1869. German natural philosopher and industrialist. Discovered creosote and paraffin in wood tar; later, conducted researches on what he designated as "od," an alleged force or natural power supposed to produce the phenomena of hypnotism.

**Rei'che·now** (rī'кĕ·nō), **Anton.** 1847–1941. German ornithologist. His son **Eduard** (1883–1960), protozoologist; investigator of sleeping sickness in Africa and of the animal parasites of man and domestic animals.

**Rei'chens·per'ger** (rī'кĕns·pĕr'gẽr), **August.** 1808–1895. German politician and writer on art. Member of Frankfurt National Assembly (1848–49), Prussian Chamber of Deputies (1850–63, 1870–76), and Reichstag (1867–84); a founder and leader of Catholic group and Center party (1852). Wrote *Die Christlich-Germanische Baukunst* (1845), *Phrasen und Schlagwörter* (1862).

**Reichstadt,** Duc **de.** See NAPOLEON II.

**Reich'stein** (rīk'stīn; rīк'shtīn), **Tadeus.** 1897– Swiss (Polish-born) chemist. Awarded Nobel prize in physiology and medicine (1950) with E. Kendall and P. Hench for hormone research.

**Reid** (rēd), **Alexander Peter.** 1836–1920. Canadian physician; helped found Halifax Medical College, Halifax, Nova Scotia.

**Reid, E. Emmet.** 1872– American chemist; on teaching staff, Johns Hopkins (from 1914; professor of organic chemistry, 1916–37).

**Reid, Elizabeth.** See under Whitelaw REID.

**Reid, Forrest.** 1876–1947. British novelist, poet, and critic, b. Belfast. Author of *The Bracknels, a Family Chronicle* (1911), *The Gentle Lover* (1913), *W. B. Yeats, a Critical Study* (1915), *A Garden by the Sea* (1918), *Brian Westby* (1934), *Peter Waring* (1937), etc.

**Reid,** Sir **George.** 1841–1913. Scottish painter and illustrator; best known for his portraits.

**Reid, George Agnew.** 1860–1947. Canadian painter; head of the Ontario Coll. of Art, Toronto (1912–29).

**Reid,** Sir **George Houston.** 1845–1918. Australian political leader, b. in Renfrewshire, Scotland; emigrated to Australia (1852). Premier of New South Wales (1894–99); member of first Commonwealth parliament and leader of free traders (1901); prime minister of Commonwealth (1904) through coalition with Labor party; high commissioner in London (1910–15).

**Reid, Harry Fielding.** 1859–1944. American geologist; professor, Johns Hopkins (1901–30); authority on dynamic geology, seismology, and glaciology.

**Reid,** Sir **James.** 1849–1923. British surgeon, b. in Scotland; resident physician to Queen Victoria (1881–1901) and physician in ordinary (1889–1901); also, physician in ordinary to Edward, Prince of Wales (1899–1901) and King Edward VII (1901–10), and to King George V (1910–23).

**Reid, James L.** 1844–1910. American agriculturist in central Illinois. By chance mixture of seeds in his cornfields, bred variety, known as *Reid's yellow dent,* widely publicized at World's Columbian Exposition, Chicago (1893), which became leading variety in U.S. corn belt. Established seed business to meet demands for seed corn.

**Reid, Mayne.** See Thomas Mayne REID.

**Reid, Ogden Mills.** See under Whitelaw REID.

**Reid, Robert.** 1862–1929. American painter, b. Stockbridge, Mass. Studio in New York (from 1889). Examples of his work: *The Open Fire* and *The Japanese Screen,* in Corcoran Art Gallery, Washington, D.C.; *Fleur de Lys,* in Metropolitan Museum of Art, New York City; also murals and stained-glass windows.

**Reid,** Sir **Robert Gillespie.** 1842–1908. Canadian railway contractor, b. Perthshire, Scotland; settled in Montreal (1871). Had charge of building international bridge over Niagara River, international railway bridge over the Rio Grande, Lachine bridge over the St. Lawrence, and heaviest section of Canadian Pacific Railway north of Lake Superior.

**Reid, Robert Threshie.** 1st Earl of **Lore'burn** (lōr'bẽrn; lôr'-). 1846–1923. British jurist, b. at Corfu, of Scottish parents. Liberal M.P. (1880–1905); supporter of Gladstone's Irish policy; solicitor general (May, 1894), attorney general (Oct., 1894–95). Successful as arbitrator of boundary dispute between Venezuela and British Guiana (1899); supported Boer cause (1899–1902); lord chancellor (1905–12), instrumental in establishment of Court of Criminal Appeal (1907); as Liberal presided over almost entirely hostile House of Lords; supported Parliament Bill (1911); created earl (1911).

**Reid, Samuel Chester.** 1783–1861. American naval officer, b. Norwich, Conn. Commanded privateer in War of 1812, and in Fayal harbor in the Azores repulsed three attacks from British warships; finally scuttled his ship to escape capture. Designed U.S. flag in its present form, and the first one, made by his wife Mary, was raised on the Capitol Apr. 12, 1818.

**Reid, Thomas.** 1710–1796. Scottish philosopher, founder of the so-called Scottish or common-sense school; professor, Aberdeen (1751); made reply to Hume in *Inquiry into the Human Mind on the Principles of Common Sense* (1763); chief of a philosophical school aiming to deliver philosophy from skepticism. Succeeded Adam Smith as professor of moral philosophy at Glasgow (1764–81). Published *Essays on the Intellectual Powers of Man* (1785), *Essays on the Active Powers of Man* (1788).

**Reid, Thomas Mayne,** *known as* **Mayne.** 1818–1883. Fiction writer, b. Ballyroney, Ireland; to U.S. (c. 1838). Served in Mexican War. To England (1849) and devoted himself to writing. Among his many romances and adventure stories are: *The Rifle Rangers* (1850), *The War Trail* (1857), *Afloat in the Forest* (1865), *The Castaways* (1870), *Free Lances* (1881). His *The Quadroon* (1856) was dramatized and became basis of Boucicault's successful play, *The Octoroon.*

**Reid,** Sir **Thomas Wemyss.** 1842–1905. Scottish journalist and biographer. Edited *Leeds Mercury* (1870–87); manager of Cassell's publishing firm (1887–1905); biographer of Charlotte Brontë, Lord Houghton; author of two novels, *Gladys Fane* (1884), *Mauleverer's Millions* (1886).

**Reid, Whitelaw.** 1837–1912. American journalist and diplomat, b. near Xenia, Ohio. On staff, Cincinnati *Gazette* (1861–65); made reputation as war correspondent with Union armies. On staff, New York *Tribune* (1868); managing editor (1869); editor (1872–1905). U.S. minister to France (1889–92); member, American commission to negotiate peace with Spain (1898); U.S. ambassador to Great Britain (1905–12). His son **Ogden Mills** (1882–1947) became associated with New York *Tribune* (1908); managing editor (1912); editor (from 1913). Whitelaw Reid's wife, **Elizabeth** (1858–1931), dau. of Darius Ogden Mills, was acting head of nursing division, American Red Cross, in Spanish War (1898), and chairman of American Red Cross in London during World War; benefactor of humanitarian projects including Dr. Trudeau's sanitarium at Saranac Lake; established the D. O. Mills training school for nurses, Saranac Lake (1912).

**Reid,** Sir **William.** 1791–1858. British meteorologist, soldier, and colonial administrator; served as engineer in Peninsular War (1810–14), in expeditions against New Orleans (1815) and against Algiers (1816). Governor of Bermuda (1839–46), Windward Islands (1846–48), Malta (1851–58); major general (1856). Contributed to development of circular theory of hurricanes.

**Reil** (rīl), **Johann Christian.** 1759–1813. German physician; published works on the anatomy of the nervous system, fever, and mental diseases.

**Reille** (râ'y'), **Honoré Charles Michel Joseph.** 1775–1860. French soldier under Napoleon at Jena and Friedland (1806); aide-de-camp to Napoleon (1808). Distinguished himself at Essling and Wagram (1809) and in Napoleon's service at Waterloo (1815). Created peer of France (1819) and marshal of France (1847); supported the coup d'état (Dec. 2, 1851); senator (1852).

**Rei·ma'rus** (rī·mä'rōōs), **Hermann Samuel.** 1694–1768. German theologian and naturalistic philosopher. Author of the rationalistic *Apologie oder Schutzschrift für die Vernünftigen Verehrer Gottes*, a series of anonymous critical essays on the gospel history, fragments of which were published (1774 ff.) by Lessing (*q.v.*) in Brunswick as the "Wolfenbüttel fragments."

**Rein** (rīn), **Wilhelm.** 1847–1929. German educator and writer on pedagogy, exponent of Herbartianism; edited *Enzyklopädisches Handbuch der Pädagogik* (1st ed., 7 vols., 1894–1903), and wrote *Theorie und Praxis des Volksschulunterrichts* (with others, 8 vols., 1878–85), *Pädagogik im Grundriss* (1890), etc.

**Reina Barrios, José María.** See Barrios.

**Rei'nach'** (rĕ'nȧk'), **Joseph.** 1856–1921. French journalist and politician; member of Chamber of Deputies (1889–98, 1906–14); conducted journalistic campaigns against Boulangism (1889), for proving innocence of Capt. Dreyfus (1897–1906), and against loss of morale and defeatism during the World War (1914–18). His brother **Salomon** (1858–1932) was an archaeologist; director of Musée de Saint-Germain (from 1902); among his many notable treatises are *Apollo: Histoire Générale des Arts Plastiques* (1904), *Orpheus, Histoire Générale des Religions* (1909), and *Répertoire de la Statuaire Grecque et Romaine* (5 vols., 1897–1924). Another brother, **Théodore** (1860–1928), was professor of numismatics at Collège de France (1924), and author of books on ancient history, archaeology, numismatics, Greek music.

**Rei'na'cher** (rī'nä'kẽr), **Eduard.** 1892– . German poet; author of *Todes-Tanz* (1923), *Elsaesser Idyllen und Elegien* (1924), *Im Blauen Dunste* (1932), *An den Schlaf* (1936), etc.

**Rei'neck·e** (rī'nĕ·kĕ), **Karl.** 1824–1910. German pianist, composer, conductor, and music teacher, b. Altona; interpreter of Mozart. Conductor of Gewandhaus concerts (1860–95) and teacher at Conservatory (until 1902), Leipzig. Composed about 250 pieces, including operas and operettas, as *König Manfred* (1867), choral works, as the oratorio *Belsazar*, much chamber music, symphonies, orchestral overtures, children's songs, etc.

**Rei'ner** (rī'nẽr), **Fritz.** 1888–1963. Hungarian conductor; to U.S., and conductor of Cincinnati Symphony Orchestra (1922–31); musical director of Pittsburgh Symphony Orchestra (1938); orchestra leader, and head of opera department, Curtis Inst. of Music, Philadelphia (from 1934).

**Rein'hardt** (rīn'härt), **Max.** *Orig. surname* **Gold'mann** (gôlt'män). 1873–1943. Austrian theatrical director and stage manager, b. near Vienna; specialist in impressionistic mass effects. Director of the Deutsches Theater (1905–20, 1924–32) and the Kammerspiele (1906); produced (1902–12) plays of Shakespeare, Molière, Gorki, Wilde, Strindberg, Hofmannsthal, Wedeking, Shaw, and others, *Oedipus Rex*, *Sumurun* (seen in New York, 1912), *The Miracle* (London, 1911), etc. Produced the Salzburg Festspiele (1920 ff.); toured United States (1923) and produced the pageant spectacle *The Miracle;* opened (1924) the Komödie in Berlin and the Theater in der Josefstadt in Vienna; active in Kurfürstendamm Theater, Berlin (1925–26) and Berlin Theater (1928–29); guest producer, New York (1927–28). Gave up theaters in Berlin (1932) and withdrew as director (1933).

**Reinhardt, Walther.** 1872–1930. German soldier; distinguished himself in Verdun offensive (1916); Prussian minister of war (1919). Commander in chief of the newly organized republican Reichswehr (1919).

**Rein'hart** (rīn'härt), **Benjamin Franklin.** 1829–1885. American portrait and historical painter; studio in New York (1853–61), London (1861–68), and New York (1868–85). His nephew **Charles Stanley Reinhart** (1844–1896) was also a painter; studio in New York (1870–80), engaged in making illustrations for Harper's (1870–77); studio in Paris (1880–91); continued illustration work for Harper's, and also for Scribner's, Appleton's, and others; his *High Tide at Gettysburg* was exhibited in the Paris Exposition (1900); his *Washed Ashore* hangs in Corcoran Art Gallery, Washington, D.C.

**Rein'hold** (rīn'hôlt), **C.** Pseudonym of Christian Reinhold Köstlin.

**Reinhold, Karl Leonhard.** 1758–1823. German philosopher; son-in-law of Wieland; professor, Jena (1787) and

Kiel (from 1794). Author of *Briefe über die Kantsche Philosophie* (1786–87), *Über die Paradoxien der Neuesten Philosophie* (1799), etc. His son **Christian Ernst** (1793–1855) was professor of philosophy at Jena.

**Rei′nick** (rī′nĭk), **Robert**. 1805–1852. German painter and poet; settled in Dresden (1844); published *Liederbuch für Deutsche Künstler* (with Kugler, 1833) and Hebel's *Allemannische Gedichte* (with illustrations by A. L. Richter, 1851), which he translated into High German; and wrote *Lieder* (1844), *Deutscher Jugendkalender* (1849–52), etc.

**Rei′nisch** (rī′nĭsh), **Leo**. 1832–1919. Austrian Egyptologist and philologist; traveled (1865–80) in Egypt and N. E. Africa; author of several works on Egyptology and of grammars, dictionaries, and philological studies of languages of northern Africa.

**Rein′ke** (rīng′kĕ), **Johannes**. 1849–1931. German botanist and philosopher; engaged in research on sea algae and on the roots of phanerogams; advocate of vitalism; opposed Haeckel's theories.

**Rein′ken** (rīng′kĕn), **Jan** *or* **Johann**. 1623–1722. Organist and composer, b. in Alsace; compositions include *Partite Diverse* for organ, *Hortus Musicus* for 2 violins, viola, and thorough bass (1687), variations for the clavier, arrangements for the organ, etc.

**Rein′kens** (rīng′kĕns), **Joseph Hubert**. 1821–1896. German Old Catholic theologian and bishop; became associated with Old Catholic movement (1870), and was suspended (1870) because of opposition to dogma of papal infallibility; excommunicated (1872). Chosen first Old Catholic bishop of Germany (1873); resident thereafter in Bonn. Author of works on ecclesiastical history, etc.

**Rein′mar von Ha′ge·nau** (rīn′mär fôn hä′gĕ·nou). *Called also* **Reinmar der Al′te** (dĕr äl′tĕ). d. 1210? Minnesinger and knight of Alsatian or Upper Austrian descent; active at court in Vienna, where Walther von der Vogelweide came under his influence; accompanied Leopold V on crusade (1190). His songs appear in Haupt's *Des Minnesangs Frühling*, etc.

**Reinsch** (rīnsh), **Paul Samuel**. 1869–1923. American educator and diplomat, b. Milwaukee, Wis. Taught political science, U. of Wisconsin (1898–1913); professor (from 1901). An organizer of American Political Science Association (1904); an editor, *American Political Science Review* (1906–17). U.S. minister to China (1913–19). Legal adviser to Chinese government (1919–23). Died at Shanghai (Jan. 24, 1923). Author of *World Politics at the End of the Nineteenth Century* (1900), *Colonial Administration* (1905), *American Legislatures and Legislative Methods* (1907), *An American Diplomat in China* (1922).

**Reis** (rīs), **Johann Philipp**. 1834–1874. German physicist; first described publicly an electrical telephone (1861). The first telephone of practical use was invented by Alexander Graham Bell (*q.v.*)

**Rei′se·nau′er** (rī′zĕ·nou′ĕr), **Alfred**. 1863–1907. German concert pianist.

**Reis′ke** (rīs′kĕ), **Johann Jakob**. 1716–1774. German classical philologist and Arabic scholar, authority on Greek literature. Edited Theocritus (2 vols., 1765–66), the Greek orators (12 vols., 1770–75), Plutarch (12 vols., 1774–82), Dionysius of Halicarnassus (6 vols., 1774–77), and Libanius (4 vols., 1791–97).

**Reis′ner** (rīs′nĕr), **George Andrew**. 1867–1942. American Egyptologist, b. Indianapolis; A.B. (1889), Ph.D. (1893), Harvard; director, Egyptian expedition of Harvard and Boston Museum of Fine Arts (from 1905); curator, Egyptian dept., Boston Museum of Fine Arts (1910–42); asst. professor (1905–14), professor (1914–42), Harvard.

**Reiss** (rīs), **Albert**. 1870–1940. German operatic tenor; member of Metropolitan Opera Company of New York (1901–17).

**Reiss, Wilhelm**. 1838–1908. German explorer, in Colombia, Ecuador, Peru, and Brazil (1868–76); with Alphons Stübel, made first ascent of Mount Cotopaxi; author of *Das Totenfeld von Ancon in Peru* (with Stübel; 3 vols., 1880–87), etc.

**Reis′si·ger** (rīs′ĭ·gĕr), **Karl Gottlieb**. 1798–1859. German composer of operas, masses and church music, orchestral and chamber music, piano pieces, and many songs.

**Reiss′ner** (rīs′nĕr), **Ernst**. 1824–1878. German anatomist; known for work on the structure of the ear.

**Reith** (rēth), Sir **John Charles Walsham**. 1889–1971. British government official; engineer by profession; served during World War I. Chairman, Imperial Airways (1938–39); first chairman, British Overseas Airways Corp. (1939–40). Minister of information (1940); minister of transport (1940); minister of works and buildings, and first commissioner of works (1940–42).

**Reitz** (rāts), **Francis William**. 1844–1934. South African statesman, b. in Cape Colony. President, Orange Free State (1889–96). State secretary, South African Republic (1898–1902). President of the Senate, Union of South Africa (1911–18).

**Reit′zen·stein** (rī′tsĕn·shtīn), **Richard**. 1861–1931. German classical scholar; author of works chiefly on Greek etymology and philology and ancient religion.

**Rej** (rā), **Mikołaj**. *Also* **Nicholas Rey** (rā). 1505–1569. Polish writer, b. in Ukraine; one of first to use Polish as literary language. Chief poetical work, *The Mirror* (1567); author also of biblical drama *Zywot Józefa* and metrical translations of the Psalms into Polish.

**Ré′jane′** (rā′zhän′). *Stage name of* **Gabrielle Charlotte Ré′ju′** (rā′zhü′). 1856–1920. French emotional actress; m. M. Porel, director of the Vaudeville Theater, Paris (1893); divorced (1905). Founded and managed Théâtre Réjane (1905). Among her most successful roles were Madame Sans Gêne, Sappho, Zaza, Lysistrata.

**Rej′mont** (rā′mônt). = REYMONT.

**Re·lan′der** (rĕ·län′dĕr), **Lauri Kristian**. 1883–1942. Finnish statesman; president of Finland (1925–31).

**Rel′ly** (rĕl′ĭ), **James**. 1722?–1778. British Universalist; co-worker of George Whitefield but broke away because of his belief in salvation for all men; regarded by Whitefield as antinomian (c. 1761); preached Universalism in London till death; his convert John Murray was the founder of Universalist churches in America.

**Re′mak** (rā′mäk), **Robert**. 1815–1865. German physician and physiologist; discovered the nonmedullated nerve fibers with a neurilemma (hence called fibers of Remak) found esp. in the sympathetic nervous system; also, worked in embryology; pioneered in electrotherapy.

**Re·marque′** (rĕ·märk′), **Erich Maria**. 1898–1970. German antimilitaristic novelist, b. in Westphalia; served in World War I; lived in Switzerland (1929–39); to U.S. (1939), naturalized; author of the war novel *Im Westen Nichts Neues* (transl. *All Quiet on the Western Front;* 1929), *The Road Back* (on postwar problems; 1931), *Three Comrades* (1937), *Flotsam* (1941).

**Rem′brandt** (rĕm′brănt; *Du.* rĕm′bränt). *In full* **Rembrandt Har′mensz** [*or* **Har′mens·zoon**] **van Rijn** *or* **Ryn** (här′mĕns [här′mĕn·sŭn, -sŏn, -sōn] vän rīn′). 1606–1669. Dutch painter and etcher, b. Leiden; leading representative of the Dutch school of painting and master of light and shadow. Settled in Amsterdam (1631) as portrait painter and teacher; m. (1634) the wealthy **Saskia van Uij′len·burgh** [oi′lĕm·bûrk] (d. 1642), mother of his son Titus (1641–1668). Suffered financial reverses, was declared bankrupt (1656). Was employed in art shop set up (1660) by his housekeeper **Hendrickje Stof'fels** (stô'fĕls) and his son Titus; spent last years in poverty and semiseclusion. His many paintings, etchings, drawings, and prints include chiefly group and single portraits, also Biblical and mythical representations, landscapes, still lifes, genre pictures. Among his portraits are a portrait of himself and his wife, his son Titus, Hendrickje Stoffels, scores of self-portraits, studies of old women and of Jewish rabbis, the groups *The Anatomy Lesson of Dr. Tulp, The Sortie of the Banning Cocq Company*, known as *The Night Watch*, and *The Syndics;* among his religious and mythological subjects, *Simeon in the Temple, Danaë, Angel Leaving Tobit, Christ as the Gardener*, the Samson series; among his landscapes, *The Repose of the Holy Family, The Windmill;* among his still lifes, *Carcass of Beef.* Miscellaneous works, *The Woman Taken in Adultery, The Auctioneer, Old Woman Cutting her Nails, Lady with a Pink, Toilet of Bathsheba;* etchings and engravings, *Descent from the Cross, The Three Crosses, Christ Healing the Sick*, called the "Hundred-Guilder Print," *Christ Preaching, Burgomaster Jan Six.*

**Re'mé·nyi** (rĕ'mā·nyĭ), **Ede.** *Orig. surname* **Hoff'mann** (hôf'män). 1830–1898. Hungarian violinist; in U.S. (1849), Weimar (1853), and England, where he was violinist to Queen Victoria; again in U.S. (1855); returned to Hungary (1860); settled in Paris (1875) and toured in many parts of the world.

**Re'mi'** *or* **Re'my'** (rā'mē'), Saint. *Lat.* **Re·mig'i·us** (rē·mĭj'ĭ·ŭs). 437?–?533. Frankish prelate; archbishop of Reims (459); baptized Clovis in the Christian faith, and became known as "the Apostle of the Franks."

**Rem'ing·ton** (rĕm'ĭng·tŭn), **Eliphalet.** 1793–1861. American firearms manufacturer, b. Suffield, Conn.; established factory for making rifles, at what is now Ilion, N.Y. (c. 1828). Purchased arms manufactory of Ames & Co., Springfield, Mass. (1845); contracted for government work. Marketed Remington pistol (from 1847). Expanded into manufacture of agricultural implements (from 1856). His son **Philo** (1816–1889), b. Litchfield, N.Y., was associated with his father in gun-manufacturing business; president of company (1861–65); reorganized factory (1865), separating agricultural implement works from gun factory, and becoming president of E. Remington & Sons, gun manufacturers (1865–89). Expanded operations to include manufacture of Remington sewing machines (from 1870) and Remington typewriters (from 1873); forced by financial conditions to sell sewing-machine business (1882), typewriter plant (1886), and agricultural implement factory (1887).

**Remington, Frederic.** 1861–1909. American painter, illustrator, and sculptor, b. Canton, N.Y. Traveled in western U.S. and worked as cowboy; was artist and correspondent in Cuba in Spanish-American War (1898). Known as animal painter and illustrator of scenes from the American West. His bronze sculptures *Broncho Buster* and *Wounded Bunkie* are in Metropolitan Museum of Art, New York City, as is also his painting *Cavalry Charge on the Southern Plains.* Other well-known paintings, *A Dash for the Timber, The Last Stand, The Emigrants, Conjuring the Buffalo Back.* Author and illustrator of *Pony Tracks* (1895), *Crooked Trails* (1898), *The Way of an Indian* (1906), etc.

**Re'mi·zov** (ryā'myĭ·zôf), **Aleksei Mikhailovich.** 1877–1957. Russian novelist and short-story writer, b. Moscow; left Russia (1921), resided in Paris (1923 ff.); among his works are *The Fifth Pestilence, Tales of the Russian People, The Chronicle of 1917, On a Field Azure.*

**Re'mo·ri'no** (rā'mô·rē'nō). = RAMORINO.

**Rem'sen** (rĕm's'n), **Ira.** 1846–1927. American chemist and educator, b. New York City; first professor of chemistry, Johns Hopkins U. (1876–1913). President, Johns Hopkins U. (1901–13). Founded *American Chemical Journal* (1879) and edited it (1879–1927). Conducted investigations both in organic and in inorganic chemistry; discovered saccharin. Author of many textbooks in organic and inorganic chemistry.

**Remus.** See ROMULUS.

**Ré'mu'sat'** (rā'mü'zȧ'), Comtesse **de. Claire Élisabeth Gra'vier' de Ver'gennes'** (grȧ'vyā' dē vĕr'zhĕn'). 1780–1821. French writer; lady in waiting to the Empress Joséphine; best known for her letters, published (1881) by her grandson. Her son Comte **François Marie Charles de Rémusat** (1797–1875) was a politician and writer; minister of the interior (1840) and of foreign affairs (1871–73); author of *Essais de Philosophie* (1842), *Abélard* (1845), *Passé et Présent* (1847), *Saint Anselme* (1853), *L'Angleterre au XVIII^e^ Siècle* (1856), *John Wesley et le Méthodisme* (1870), etc.

**Rémusat, Jean Pierre Abel.** 1788–1832. French physician and Sinologue; author of *Essai sur la Langue et la Littérature Chinoises* (1811), *Éléments de la Grammaire Chinoise* (1822), *Histoire du Buddhisme* (1836), etc.

**Remy,** Saint. See REMI.

**Re·nan'** (rē·näN'), **Joseph Ernest.** 1823–1892. French philologist and historian; a leader of the school of critical philosophy in France. Among his earlier books are *Averroès et l'Averroïsme* (1852), *Études d'Histoire Religieuse* (1857), and *De l'Origine du Langage* (1858). His most famous works are those in the series entitled *Histoire des Origines du Christianisme*, including *La Vie de Jésus* (1863), *Les Apôtres* (1866), *Les Évangiles et la Seconde Génération Chrétienne* (1877), *L'Église Chrétienne* (1879), *Marc Aurèle et la Fin du Monde Antique* (1880). Among other works are *Histoire du Peuple d'Israël* (1887–94), *Drames Philosophiques* (1888), etc.

**Re·nard'** (rē·nȧr'), **Alphonse François.** 1842–1903. Belgian geologist; reported (with Sir John Murray, 1891) on the rock specimens and oceanic deposits collected by the *Challenger* expedition.

**Renard, Jules.** 1864–1910. French writer; one of founders of *Mercure de France* (1890); among his many works are *Crime de Village* (1888), *Poil de Carotte* (1894), *Bucoliques* (1898), and the plays *Le Plaisir de Rompre* (1897), *Le Pain de Ménage* (1899), *La Bigote* (1909).

**Re·naud'** (rē·nō'). *Professional name of* **Maurice Arnold Cros'neau'** (krō'nō'). 1861–1933. French baritone singer; sang in New York (1905–12).

**Re·nau'dot'** (rē·nō'dō'), **Théophraste.** 1586–1653. French physician and journalist; physician to the king; received appointment as commissary general of the poor, and established an information and publicity agency on their behalf; began publishing news, and thus established a regular journal, called the *Gazette* (1631). Opened first free medical clinic for the poor (1635); also, first pawnshop.

**Re·nault'** (rē·nō'), **Louis.** 1843–1918. French jurist; professor at Dijon and (from 1873) at Paris; professor of international law (from 1881). Counselor to the ministry of foreign affairs (1890). France's representative at international conferences, notably at The Hague (1907); awarded, with Ernesto T. Moneta, Nobel peace prize (1907). Among his many legal treatises are *Introduction à l'Étude du Droit International* (1879), *Précis de Droit Commercial* (1879–82).

**Ren'dall** (rĕn'd'l), **Gerald Henry.** 1851–1945. Anglican clergyman and educator; headmaster, Charterhouse School (1897–1911). Among his books are *Cradle of the Aryans* (1889), *Charterhouse Sermons* (1911), and treatises on Shakespeare.

**Re·né′ I** (rē·nā′). *Lat.* **Re·na′tus** (rē·nā′tŭs). *Called* **the Good.** *Fr.* **le Bon** (lē bôN′). 1409–1480. Duke of Anjou (1434–80) and Lorraine (1434–53); see ANJOU, LORRAINE; b. Angers, son of Louis II of Anjou. Duke of Bar (1430–56), count of Provence and Piedmont (1431–80), and titular king of Naples (1435–42); m. Isabella of Lorraine (1420); claimed succession to duchy of Lorraine (1431) but defeated by count of Vaudémont and held as prisoner (1431–32, 1435–38); confirmed as duke of Lorraine by the emperor (1434). Inherited Naples from his brother Louis III (1435); joined Isabella there (1438) but driven out by Alfonso of Aragon (1442). Retired to Provence (1442); his court at Aix a resort of poets and artists. Author of poems, romances, etc.; called the "last of the troubadours." His daughter Margaret married Henry VI of England. His grandson **René II** (1451–1508) was duke of Lorraine (1473–1508).

**René.** 1518–1544. Prince of Orange and Count of Nassau. See NASSAU, 2a; ORANGE.

**Re·née′** (rē·nā′) of France. 1510–1575. Daughter of Louis XII of France; m. Ercole II, Duke of Ferrara (1527), member of Este family. Accepted Calvinism; imprisoned during Inquisition (1554), confessed and attended mass; returned to Protestantism when released from prison. Received letters of advice from Calvin.

**Re′ni** (râ′nē), **Guido.** 1575–1642. Italian painter of Eclectic school, b. near Bologna; employed at Rome (c. 1602–22); forced by intrigues of jealous rivals to return to Bologna (1622); chief master of Eclectics (1622–42). Among his works are *Crucifixion of St. Peter, Madonna della Pietà, Concert of Angels, Aurora,* also called *Triumph of Phoebus, St. Paul Reproaching St. Peter, Massacre of the Innocents, Apotheosis of St. Dominic, Myth of Hercules, Triumph of Samson over the Philistines, Fortuna, Rape of Helen, St. Sebastian, Nativity, Ecce Homo,* and, reputedly, *Beatrice Cenci.*

**Ren′nell** (rĕn′'l), 1st Baron. **James Rennell Rodd** (rŏd). 1858–1941. English diplomat and writer; secretary of legation at Cairo (1894–1901); councilor of embassy at Rome (1901–04); British minister to Sweden (1904–08); ambassador to Italy (1908–19); British delegate to the League of Nations (1921; 1923). Author of *Frederick, Emperor and Crown Prince; Customs and Lore of Modern Greece; Sir Walter Raleigh; Rome of the Renaissance and Today* (1932), and three series of *Memoirs;* also, author of volumes of verse.

**Rennell, James.** 1742–1830. English geographer; surveyor general of Bengal for East India Co.; published his *Bengal Atlas* (1779). Mapped India, turned to Western Asia and Africa. Author of works on hydrography; a pioneer in oceanography, after whom Rennell's current was named.

**Ren·nen·kampf′** (ryĕn·nĕn·kåmpf′), **Pavel Karlovich.** 1854–1918. Russian general of cavalry; served in Russo-Japanese War (1904–05) and in World War (1914–18); defeated Germans at Insterburg (Aug. 7, 1914), but was defeated by Hindenburg at Tannenberg (Aug. 26–30, 1914). Governor of St. Petersburg (1915); commander in chief on the northern front (1916). Shot by the Bolsheviks (1918).

**Ren′ner** (rĕn′ēr), **Karl.** 1870–1950. Austrian statesman; headed Austrian delegation at peace negotiations (1919); chancellor (1919–20); minister of foreign affairs (1920); member, national council (1920–34), president (1931–33); imprisoned following Social Democratic revolt (1934); president, 2d republic (from 1945); author (sometimes under pseudonyms **Sy·nop′ti·cus** [zü·nŏp′tē·ko͞os] and **Rudolf Spring′er** [shprĭng′ēr]) of works chiefly on economics, government, law, and socialism.

**Ren′nie** (rĕn′ĭ), **John.** 1761–1821. Scottish civil engineer; designed Waterloo, Southwark, and London bridges (the last completed by his sons); designed London dock and East India dock on Thames among others, and Plymouth breakwater. His sons **George** (1791–1866) and Sir **John** (1794–1874), civil engineers, carried on their father's business; George built the *Dwarf,* first screw vessel in British navy; John was knighted on completion of London Bridge (1831).

**Re′no** (rē′nō), **Jesse Lee.** 1823–1862. American army officer, b. Wheeling, W.Va.; grad. U.S.M.A., West Point (1846); brigadier general of volunteers (Nov., 1861); major general (July, 1862); engaged at Manassas and Chantilly; killed in action at South Mountain (Sept. 14, 1862). His son **Jesse Wilford** (1861–1947), engineer, invented moving stairway (1892).

**Re·noir′** (rē·nwȧr′), **Pierre Auguste.** 1841–1919. French painter, b. Limoges; regarded as a leader among the impressionists. Best known for his figure paintings, landscapes, and flower pictures. Among his notable canvases are *Lise, Femme à l'Éventail, Le Moulin de la Galette, Madame Charpentier et ses Enfants, Dans la Loge, Baigneuses, La Balançoire,* and portraits of Monet, Sisley, Wagner.

**Re·nouf′** (?rē·no͞of′), Sir **Peter le Page** (?lē pȧzh′). 1822–1897. British Egyptologist, b. in Guernsey; keeper of Oriental antiquities in British Museum (1885–91); contributed to proceedings of Society of Biblical Archaeology among other papers a translation of *The Book of the Dead.*

**Re·nou′vier′** (rē·no͞o′vyā′), **Charles Bernard.** 1815–1903. French idealistic philosopher; a leader in neocriticism; founded *Critique Philosophique* (1872) and *Critique Religieuse* (1878). Among his many books are *Manuel de Philosophie Moderne* (1842), *Manuel de Philosophie Ancienne* (1844), *Les Dilemmes de la Métaphysique* (1900), *Le Personnalisme* (1902).

**Rensselaer, Van.** See VAN RENSSELAER.

**Rentsch′ler** (rĕnch′lēr), **Harvey Clayton.** 1881–1949. American physicist; developed (with Dr. Robert F. James) a lamp whose ultraviolet rays kill disease germs, microorganisms causing decay, molds, etc.

**Ren′wick** (rĕn′(w)ĭk), **James.** 1662–1688. Scottish Covenanter; joined Cameronians (1681); proclaimed Lanark declaration (1682); ordained (1683); field preacher; outlawed for his *Apologetic Declaration* (1684), disowning authority of Charles II; refused to join rising under earl of Argyll (1685); captured and hanged (1688), last of Covenanting martyrs.

**Ren′wick** (rĕn′wĭk), **James.** 1792–1863. Physicist, b. Liverpool, England; to U.S. as a child. Professor, Columbia (1820–53). Author of *Outlines of Natural Philosophy* (2 vols., 1822–23), *Treatise on the Steam-Engine* (1830), *Applications of the Science of Mechanics to Practical Purposes* (1840). His son **Henry Bre·voort′** [brē·vōrt′] (1817–1895) was an engineer in government service (1837–40); on northeastern U.S. boundary survey (1840–47); examiner in U.S. Patent Office (1848–53); first U.S. inspector of steam vessels, New York City (1853); patent expert (from c. 1860). A second son, **James** (1818–1895), was an architect; won competition for design of Grace Church, New York City (1843); also designed Calvary Church, Church of the Covenant, Saint Bartholomew's, Saint Patrick's Cathedral; other works, Smithsonian Institution, Washington, D.C., Bank of the State of New York, the original structure for Vassar College at Poughkeepsie, N.Y., Corcoran Art Gallery, Washington, D.C. A third son, **Edward Sa′bine** [sā′bĭn] (1823–1912), was an inventor, patent expert, and consulting engineer, in Washington, D.C. (1849–55) and New York (from 1855); inventor of breech-loading firearm, grain harvester and binder, chicken incubator and chicken brooder.

**Repgow** *or* **Repkow, Eike von.** See EIKE VON REPGOW.

**Re'pin** (ryā'pyĭn), **Ilya Efimovich.** 1844–1930. Russian painter; among his canvases are *Mist over the Volga, The Nihilists, The Return from Siberia, The Cossacks.*

**Rep'ing·ton** (rĕp'ĭng·tŭn), **Charles A'Court** (ȧ·kōrt'; ȧ·kôrt'). 1858–1925. British soldier and journalist; served in Afghanistan (1878–79), Burma (1888–89), Sudan (1898), South Africa (1899–1900). Military correspondent for London *Times* (1904–18), London *Morning Post* (1918–19), London *Daily Telegraph* (1919–25). Author of *Vestigia* (1919), *Diary* (1920), *After the War* (1922).

**Rep·nin'** (ryĕp·nyēn'), **Anikita Ivanovich.** 1668–1726. Russian general under Peter the Great; defeated by Charles XII of Sweden; commanded Russian center in victory at Poltava (1709); governor general of Riga; created field marshal by Catherine I. His grandson Prince **Nikolai Vasilievich Repnin** (1734–1801) was a general (from 1762); resident in Poland (1763–69), which became a virtual Russian protectorate; engaged in the war with Turkey and the subsequent peace negotiations (1774); appointed ambassador to Turkey; engaged in second war with Turkey (1790); negotiated partition of Poland (1792); governor general of Estonia and Livonia.

**Rep'plier** (rĕp'lẽr), **Agnes.** 1855–1950. American author, b. Philadelphia. Author esp. of essays, as in *Books and Men* (1888), *Points of View* (1891), *Essays in Miniature* (1892), *Essays in Idleness* (1893), *Varia* (1897), *Compromises* (1904), *Americans and Others* (1912), *Counter-Currents* (1915), *Points of Friction* (1920), *Under Dispute* (1924), *In Pursuit of Laughter* (1936), *Eight Decades* (1937), etc.

**Re'que·séns'** (rā'kȧ·sāns'), **Luis de Zú'ñi·ga y** (thȧ thōō'nyē·gä ē). d. 1576. Spanish soldier and statesman; succeeded duke of Alva as governor of the Low Countries, then (1573) in revolt; promised an amnesty and remission of taxes, but could not grant religious freedom to the Dutch people; failed in attempts to capture Leiden or conquer Holland.

**Re·quier'** (rē·kyā'), **Augustus Julian.** 1825–1887. American lawyer and poet, b. Charleston, S.C. U.S. district attorney for Alabama (1853–61); continued as district attorney for the Confederacy (1861–65). Practiced law, New York City (from 1866). Author of *The Spanish Exile* (a blank-verse drama, 1842), *Poems* (1860), *Ode to Shakespeare* (1862), *The Legend of Tremaine* (1864), and a number of war lyrics written in the Southern cause.

**Re·sen'de** (rĕ·zäɴn'dĕ), **Garcia de.** 1470–1536. Portuguese poet; author of the collection of contemporary verse *Cancioneiro Geral* (1516), the chronicle *Vida e Feitos de D. João II* (1545), and a supplement to the latter, *Miscelânea*, a rhymed chronicle of contemporary events.

**Re·shev'sky** (rĕ·shĕf'skĭ), **Samuel.** 1911– . American chess master, b. Poland; toured U.S. as a child chess marvel (1920); naturalized; American national champion (1936–44).

**Re·shid' Pa·sha'** (rĕ·shēd' pä·shä'), **Mustafa Mehmet.** 1802–1858. Turkish statesman, b. Constantinople; grand vizier (1837–38); envoy to London, Berlin, Paris; minister of foreign affairs (1839); chief adviser to young sultan Abdul-Medjid I (from 1839); Turkish representative in Paris (1841–45). Again minister of foreign affairs (1845), and grand vizier (1846 ff., with several interruptions), serving through the early part of the Crimean War (1854–55).

**Re·spi'ghi** (rȧ·spē'gē), **Ottorino.** 1879–1936. Italian composer; appeared in the U.S. as pianist and conductor. His works include the operas *Re Enzo, Semirama, Maria Vittoria, La Campana Sommersa, La Fiamma, Belfagor*, symphonic poems, as *Pini di Roma* and *Ballata delle Gnomidi*, an opera-oratorio *Maria Egiziaca*, and *Sinfonia Drammatica.*

**Res'tif'** (rā'tēf'; rĕs'tēf'), **Nicolas Edme.** *Known as* **Restif de La Bre·tonne'** (dē lȧ brē·tôn'). 1734–1806. French novelist. The nature of his subject matter caused him to be nicknamed the "Rousseau of the Gutter" and the "Voltaire of Chambermaids."

**Res'ton** (rĕs'tŭn), **James Barrett.** 1909– . American journalist, b. Scotland. To U.S. (1910); with *New York Times.*

**Res'tout'** (rĕs'tōō'), **Jean.** 1692–1768. French painter; best known for his religious pictures; his *Ananie Impose les Mains à Saint Paul* hangs in the Louvre.

**Res·tre'po** (rȧs·trā'pō), **Carlos E.** 1867–1937. Colombian political leader and diplomat; president of Colombia (1910–14); minister of interior (1930–34); ambassador to Vatican City (1934).

**Restrepo, José Manuel.** 1775?–?1860. Colombian historian; friend of Bolívar and other leaders in struggle for independence; chief work, *Historia de la Revolución de la República de Colombia* (10 vols., 1827).

**Resz'ke** (rĕsh'kĕ), **Jean de** (zhäɴ' dē). *Real name* **Jan Mie·czi'sław** (myĕ·chē'släf). 1850–1925. Polish operatic tenor; sang at the Théâtre Française, the Théâtre Italien, and the Opéra, in Paris (until 1889); on tour (1889 ff.), singing in United States (1892, 1893–94, 1895–96, 1896–97, 1898–99, 1900–01); teacher of singing, studio in Paris (from c. 1901); among his chief roles were Faust in *Faust*, Romeo in *Romeo and Juliet*, Radames in *Aïda*, Ascanio in *Benvenuto Cellini.* His brother **Édouard de Reszke** (1855–1917) was an operatic basso; sang at Théâtre Italien, Paris (1876), and at the Opéra (1885–89); on tour (after 1889) in Europe and United States, interpreting, with special success, Wagnerian roles; opened school of singing, London (1907). Their sister **Joséphine** (1855–1891), a coloratura soprano, sang at the Paris Opéra (1875–79); withdrew from the stage after her marriage to baron von Kronenburg.

**Reth'berg** (*Angl.* rĕth'bûrg; *Ger.* rĕt'bĕrk), **Elisabeth.** *Stage name of* **Lisbeth Sätt'ler** (zĕt'lĕr). 1894– . Operatic soprano, b. in Saxony; American debut, Metropolitan Opera Company, New York City, in role of Aïda (1922).

**Re'thel** (rā'tĕl), **Alfred.** 1816–1859. German historical painter and graphic artist; works include drawings of episodes from the life of St. Boniface; portraits of emperors Maximilian I and II, Charles V, and others, *Daniel in the Lions' Den, Saints Peter and John Healing the Lame*, fresco designs for the Aachen Rathaus representing the life of Charlemagne (1847–51), series of 6 water colors depicting *Hannibal Crossing the Alps* (1842–44), drawings for woodcuts *Death the Destroyer* and *Death the Friend* (1847–51), and for woodcut illustrations to *The Dance of Death*, etc.

**Re·tief'** (rĕ·tēf'), **Pieter**, *called* **Piet.** d. 1838. South African Boer leader in the Great Trek (1836).

**Ré'tif' de La Bretonne** (rā'tēf'). = RESTIF DE LA BRETONNE.

**Ret'té'** (rĕ'tā'), **Adolphe.** 1863–1930. French poet and writer; identified with the symbolist group. Among his books of verse are *Cloches en la Nuit* (1889), *Une Belle Dame Passa!* (1893), and *Sous l'Étoile du Matin* (1910); among his prose works, *Réflexions sur l'Anarchie* (1894), *La Seule Nuit* (a novel, 1899), *Les Rubis du Calice* (1927), *Oraisons du Silence* (1930).

**Retz** (rĕts) *or* **Rais** (rĕs) *or* **Raiz** (rĕts), Baron **de. Gilles de La′val′** (dē lȧ′vȧl′). 1404?–1440. Marshal of France; distinguished himself in wars against English; notorious for cruelties, esp. to children. His story is reputed to have some connection with tale of Bluebeard, immortalized by Charles Perrault (*q.v.*).

**Retz** (rĕts), Cardinal **de. Jean François Paul de Gon′di′** (dĕ gôɴ′dē′). 1614–1679. French ecclesiastic and politician, of Florentine descent. Conspicuous for riotous life and frequent duels as young man. Became deeply involved in first war of the Fronde (1648–49), at first on side of court, later on people's side; determined opponent of Cardinal Mazarin; created cardinal (1651); imprisoned (1652) but escaped. Archbishop of Paris (1654–62); resigned archbishopric (1662) in return for rich benefices. Retired to private life in Lorraine, where he wrote his *Mémoires*, valuable as source of information on contemporary court life.

**Ret′zi·us** (rĕt′sĭ·ŭs), **Anders Johan.** 1742–1821. Swedish botanist; pupil of Linnaeus. His son **Anders Adolf** (1796–1860), anatomist and anthropologist, was a pioneer in craniometry. The latter's son **Gustaf Magnus** (1842–1919), anthropologist and anatomist, professor of histology (1877) and of anatomy (1889–91) at Stockholm, is known for researches on the nervous systems of men and animals and on cranial anthropology.

**Retzsch** (rĕch), **Moritz.** 1779–1857. German painter, etcher, and designer. His works include etchings in outline illustrating Goethe, Schiller, Shakespeare, etc.

**Reubell, Jean François.** See REWBELL.

**Reu′ben** (rōō′bĕn). *In Douay Version* **Ru′ben** (rōō′-). In the Bible, Jacob's eldest son (*Genesis* xxix. 32), ancestor of one of the twelve tribes of Israel.

**Reuch′lin** (roiĸ′lēn; roiĸ·lēn′), **Johann.** *Grecized form* **Cap′ni·o** (kăp′nĭ·ō; *Ger.* käp′nē·ō). 1455–1522. Granduncle of Melanchthon (*q.v.*). German humanist; promoter of Greek and Hebrew studies in Germany, and champion of modern (Reuchlinian) pronunciation of Greek. In service of Duke Eberhard of Württemberg (1481); count of German Empire (1492); judge in Swabian League (1502–13); in controversy (1510–16) with Dominicans of Cologne and the obscurantists; taught Greek and Hebrew, Ingolstadt (1519) and Tübingen. Author of various editions and Latin translations of Greek texts, works on Latin, Greek, and Hebrew, including the first Hebrew grammar *Rudimenta Linguae Hebraicae* (1506), an edition of the seven penitential psalms (1512; one of the first Hebrew books printed in Germany), *De Accentibus et Orthographia Linguae Hebraicae* (1518), Latin satirical comedies *Sergius* (1496) and *Henno* (1497), cabalistic works *De Verbo Mirifico* (1494) and *De Arte Cabbalistica* (1517), etc.

**Reu′mont′** (rû′môɴ′), **Alfred von.** 1808–1887. German diplomat, and author of works on Italian history and Renaissance art, and biographies of Michelangelo (1834) and Benvenuto Cellini (1847), etc.

**Reusch** (roish), **Franz Heinrich.** 1825–1900. German Old Catholic theologian; friend and pupil of Döllinger. Author of *Lehrbuch der Einleitung in das Alte Testament* (1859), *Geschichte der Moralstreitigkeiten in der Römisch-Katholischen Kirche...* (with Döllinger; 2 vols., 1889).

**Reuss** (rois). Two former German principalities, now in Thuringia, and their two ruling houses; originated with Erkenbert (1122?), who was appointed by the emperor as imperial bailiff of Gera and Weida, and whose descendants called themselves "lords of Weida"; house named Reuss (1300?); made princely house (1426); divided (1564) into three branches: **Reuss Elder Line,** *or* **Reuss′-Greiz′** (-grīts′); **Reuss Younger Line,** *or* **Reuss′-Schleiz′-Ge′ra** (-shlīts′ gā′rä); and a middle line (became extinct 1616); male members of both surviving branches always named Henry (Heinrich) in honor of Holy Roman emperor Henry VI (1165–1197), individuals being distinguished by numbers. Lords became counts (1673); head of Elder Line became prince of the empire (1778) and head of the Younger Line became prince (1806). Recent rulers: *Elder Line:* Henry XXII (1846–1902; ruled 1859–1902; his daughter Hermine, 1887– , m. 1922 as second wife ex-kaiser William II of Germany) and his son Henry XXIV (1878–1927; heir to throne but forbidden to rule; see HENRY XXVII, below). *Younger Line:* Henry XIV (1832–1913; ruled 1867–1908, regent for Elder Line 1902–08) and his son Henry XXVII (1858–1928; ruled in both principalities, 1908–13; as prince, 1913–18, abdicated).

**Reuss** (rois), **Édouard Guillaume Eugène.** 1804–1891. Alsatian-French Protestant theologian; best known for his translation of the Bible (1874–81), with an introduction and commentaries.

**Reu′ter** (roi′tēr), **Christian.** 1665–?1712. German dramatist and novelist; author of satirical comedies, the satirical novel, forerunner of the Münchhausen style, *Schelmuffskys Reisebeschreibung* (1696), and festival plays for the court at Berlin (1703–10).

**Reuter, Fritz.** 1810–1874. German dialect (Plattdeutsch) humorous prose writer and poet. Author of tales and poems chiefly of village life, the epic *Kein Hüsung* (1858), *Hanne Nüte* (1859), and *Schurr-Murr* (1861), the collection of largely autobiographical stories *Olle Kamellen* containing *Ut de Franzosentid* (1859), *Ut Mine Festungstid* (1862), and *Ut Mine Stromtid* (1864).

**Reuter, Gabriele.** 1859–1941. German novelist in Weimar, b. in Egypt; author of novels dealing largely with the emancipation of women.

**Reuter, Ludwig von.** 1869–1943. German vice-admiral; engaged in battle of Jutland (1916); in command of German fleet interned after war at Scapa Flow and there scuttled by Germans under his orders.

**Reuter,** Baron **Paul Julius von.** *Orig. name* **Israel Beer** (bâr) **Jo′sa·phat** (yō′zä·fät). 1816–1899. German pioneer newsgatherer, b. Kassel; founded in Aachen (1849) a central telegraphic and pigeon-post bureau for collecting and transmitting news, forerunner of Reuter's News Agency with headquarters in London (from 1851); removed to England (1851) and became naturalized British subject; created baron (1871) by duke of Saxe-Coburg-Gotha.

**Reu′ter·dahl** (*Swed.* rĕ′ōō·tēr·däl), **Henry.** 1871–1925. Painter, b. Malmö, Sweden; to U.S. (1893) on commission to make illustrations of Chicago Columbian Exposition. Newspaper correspondent during Spanish-American War. Settled in Weehawken, N.J. (1899). Noted for his naval paintings and illustrations. Illustrated J. D. Long's *New American Navy* (1903). His *Combat between the Monitor and the Merrimac* hangs in the National Gallery of Art, Washington, D.C.

**Reu′ther** (rōō′thēr), **Walter Philip.** 1907–1970. American labor leader, b. Wheeling, W. Va. Pres., United Automobile Workers (1946–70), Congress of Industrial Organizations (1952–55).

**Ré′vai** (rā′voi), **Miklós.** 1750?–1807. Hungarian philologist and poet; founder of science of historical philology in Hungary; author of *Antiquitates Literaturae Hungaricae* (vol. 1, 1803), *Elaboratior Grammatica Hungarica* (2 vols., 1803–06).

**Revellière–Lépeaux, La.** See LAREVELLIÈRE-LÉPEAUX.

**Revelstoke,** 1st Baron. See BARING family.

**Re′vent·low** (rā′vĕnt·lō), Count **Ernst zu.** 1869–1943.

German journalist and Pan-Germanist; on staff of *Deutsche Tageszeitung* during World War (1914–18); vigorously supported von Tirpitz's policy of unrestricted submarine warfare. Among his works are *Der Russisch-Japanische Krieg* (3 vols., 1904–06), *Weltfrieden oder Weltkrieg* (1907), *Nationaler Sozialismus im Neuen Deutschland* (1932), etc.

**Re·ver'din'** (rē·vĕr'dăN'), **Jacques Louis.** 1842–1928. Swiss surgeon; devised the epidermic graft and a suture needle; investigated goiter.

**Re've·re** (rā'vā·rā), **Giuseppe.** 1812–1889. Italian poet; wrote for revolutionary journal *La Concordia* (Turin); participated in five-day insurrection (Milan, 1848). Among his works are *Sdegno ed Affetto* (1845), *Marine e Paesi* (1858), and historical dramas.

**Re·vere'** (rē·vēr'), **Paul.** 1735–1818. American patriot, b. Boston; silversmith and engraver by trade. Took part in famous Boston Tea Party (1773). Appointed official courier for Massachusetts Provincial Assembly (1774). Rode from Boston to Lexington to warn countryside that the British were on the march (Apr. 18, 1775), a ride celebrated by Longfellow in his poem *The Midnight Ride of Paul Revere.* Designed and printed first issue of Continental money; designed and engraved first official seal for the colonies, and the State seal for Massachusetts. Member, committee of correspondence (1776). In command at Castle William (1778–79); took part in unsuccessful Penobscot expedition (1779). Discovered process for rolling sheet copper. His grandson **Joseph Warren Revere** (1812–1880) was a naval and army officer; served in conquest of California (1846–48); resigned from navy (1850); at outbreak of Civil War, entered Union army as colonel of New Jersey volunteer regiment; served in Peninsular campaign, at Seven Pines and Antietam; brigadier general (Oct., 1862); at Fredericksburg and Chancellorsville; court-martialed and dismissed for withdrawal without orders at Chancellorsville, but sentence was revoked and his resignation accepted (Sept., 1864).

**Revilla Gigedo,** Condes **de.** See Juan Francisco GÜEMEZ DE HORCASITAS.

**Ré'ville'** (rā'vēl'), **Albert.** 1826–1906. French Protestant clergyman; pastor of the Walloon church, Rotterdam (1851); author of *Histoire des Religions* (1889).

**Re·vil'lout'** (rē·vē'yōō'), **Eugène.** 1843–1913. French Egyptologist; specialist in study of Coptic and demotic Egyptian; author of *Chrestomathie Démotique* (1880), *Les Origines Égyptiennes du Droit Civil Romain* (1912), etc.

**Rew'bell'** *or* **Reu'bell'** (rû'bĕl'), **Jean François.** 1747–1807. French Revolutionary politician; member of the States-General (1789); president of the Constituent Assembly (1791); member of the National Convention (1792), the Council of Five Hundred (1795), and president of the Directory (1796–99). Member of Council of Ancients (1799).

**Rewi Alley.** See ALLEY.

**Rey, Jacobus Hercules De La.** See DE LA REY.

**Rey, Louis É. E.** See REYER.

**Rey, Nicholas.** See Mikołaj REJ.

**Rey'baud'** (rā'bō'), **Louis.** 1799–1879. French journalist and politician; member of Chamber of Deputies (1846–48); author of satirical novels *Jérôme Paturot à la Recherche d'une Position Sociale* (1843) and *Jérôme Paturot à la Recherche de la Meilleure des Républiques* (1848), ridiculing modern manners and institutions.

**Rey'er'** (rā'yâr'), **Louis Étienne Ernest.** *Orig. surname* **Rey** (rā). 1823–1909. French composer and music critic; among his compositions the most notable are the operas *La Statue* (1861), *Sigurd* (1884), and *Salammbô* (1890).

**Re'yes** (rā'yās), **Rafael.** 1850?–1921. Colombian explorer, soldier, author, and political leader. With his brothers Enrique and Nestor explored the tributaries of the Amazon in southeast Colombia; made commander in chief of Colombian army; Colombian representative in Washington (1903) in relation to loss of Panama. President of Colombia (1904–09); assumed dictatorial power; made many improvements, but lost popularity; resigned (1909) when his treaty with U.S. recognizing independence of Panama was not approved.

**Rey'mont** (rā'mônt), **Władysław Stanisław.** 1867–1925. Polish novelist; awarded Nobel prize for literature (1924) for *The Peasants* (4 vols., 1904–10). Other works are *The Beloved Land* (1898), *Before Sunrise* (1902), and *The Last Polish Parliament* (1917).

**Rey'naud'** (rā'nō'), **Jean.** 1806–1863. French philosopher; associated for a time with philosophy and policies of Saint Simon; author of *Terre et Ciel* (1854), a book condemned by a council of bishops assembled at Périgueux.

**Reynaud, Paul.** 1878–1966. French politician; minister of finance (1930), for colonies (1931–32), of justice (1932 and 1938), of finance (1938–40); premier (1940) at the period of the French defeat and France's surrender to Germany; interned by Pétain government (1940); a principal defendant in trial at Riom (1942); imprisoned by Germans (1943–45); member, constituent assembly (1946).

**Rey'nier'** (rā'nyā'), Comte. **Jean Louis E'ben'e'zer'** (ā'bĕn'ā'zâr'). 1771–1814. French soldier; accompanied Napoleon to Egypt (1798) and distinguished himself at Heliopolis (1800). Held responsible for defeat at Alexandria (1801) and sent back to France in disgrace. Distinguished himself in the Italian campaign (1805) and became secretary of war under Murat, King of Naples. Again joined Napoleon's army and was engaged at Wagram (1809); captured at Leipzig (1814).

**Rey'nold' de Cres'sier'** (rā'nôl' dē krĕ'syā'), Baron. **Frédéric Gon'zague'** (gôN'zȧg'). 1880– . Swiss historian; author of *La Démocratie et la Suisse* (1929), *L'Europe Tragique* (1934), *Portugal* (awarded Camoëns prize, 1938), etc.

**Reyn'olds** (rĕn''ldz), **Edwin.** 1831–1909. American engineer, b. Mansfield, Conn. Inventor of the Reynolds-Corliss engine; built (1888) first triple expansion pumping engine for waterworks use; invented improvements in boilers, air compressors, ore crushers, and hoisting machines; patented (1888) a blowing engine for blast furnaces.

**Reynolds, Jackson Eli.** 1873–1958. American banker, b. Woodstock, Ill.; president, First National Bank of City of New York (1922–37). See Melvin A. TRAYLOR.

**Reynolds, John.** 1549–1607. See RAINOLDS.

**Reynolds, John Fulton.** 1820–1863. American army officer, b. Lancaster, Pa.; grad. U.S.M.A., West Point (1841); brigadier general of volunteers (Aug., 1861), and major general (Nov., 1862). Engaged at Fredericksburg and Chancellorsville; killed in first day's fighting at Gettysburg (July 1, 1863).

**Reynolds,** Sir **Joshua.** 1723–1792. English portrait painter, b. at Plympton near Plymouth. Gained attention with portrait of Captain the Hon. John Hamilton; taken as guest by Commodore Augustus Keppel to Mediterranean; studied three years in Italy. On return to London (1752) became foremost fashionable portrait painter. Suggested founding (1764) of Literary Club, of which Dr. Johnson, Garrick, Goldsmith, Burke, Boswell, and Sheridan were members. Painter to king (1784). Executed portraits of Lord Heathfield, Johnson, Sterne, Goldsmith, Gibbon, Burke, Fox, Garrick, and of Mrs.

Siddons as the Tragic Muse (1784); admired for his studies of women and children, including *Viscountess Crosbie, Master Bunbury, The Strawberry Girl, Lady Penelope Boothby, Duchess of Devonshire and her Baby, The Age of Innocence, Three Ladies Waldegrave;* compelled to cease painting because of partial failure of eyesight (1790); buried in crypt of St. Paul's Cathedral.

**Reynolds, Walter.** d. 1327. English prelate; bishop of Worcester, and (1310) chancellor of England; appointed (1313) archbishop of Canterbury by Pope Clement V on urging of Edward II despite previous election of Thomas de Cobham by Canterbury monks; carried on struggle for precedence between archbishops of York and Canterbury; introduced ecclesiastical reform; supported Edward II until 1324, when he took part of Adam of Orlton, Bishop of Hereford; declared for Edward III, whom he crowned (1327).

**Reyn'olds–Ste'phens** (-stē'vĕnz), Sir **William.** *Orig. surname* **Stephens.** 1862–1943. British sculptor; assumed name Reynolds-Stephens (1890). Among his notable sculptures are the *Davidson Memorial* in Lambeth Palace, centenary memorial to Charles Lamb outside of Christ Church in London, *Sir Lancelot and the Nestling; Guinevere and the Nestling,* and a number of portrait busts.

**Re·za'nov** (ryĕ·zȧ'nôf), **Nikolai Petrovich.** 1764–1807. Russian entrepreneur in Alaska, b. St. Petersburg. An organizer of a fur-trading company, Russian-American Co. (1801), granted administration of, and a monopoly in, the coast of northwest America and the chain of islands off this coast.

**Reza Shah Pahlavi.** Variant of RIZA SHAH PAHLAVI.

**Rez'ni·cek** (rĕz'nē·chĕk), Baron **Emil Nikolaus von.** 1860–1945. Composer, conductor, and teacher, b. Vienna. Teacher, Hochschule für Musik, Berlin (from 1920). Composer chiefly of operas, including *Donna Diana* (1894) *Till Eulenspiegel* (1901), *Ritter Blaubart* (1920), and *Das Opfer* (1932), also of incidental music to Strindberg's *Dream Play* (1915), symphonies, symphonic suites, the symphonic poem *Schlemihl* (1912), variations for orchestra, a violin concerto (1925), overtures, string quartets, piano pieces, choral works, a requiem (1894), a mass (1898), songs, etc.

**Rhal'les, Rhal'lis, Ral'les,** *or* **Ral'lis** (rä'lyēs), **Demetrios.** 1844–1921. Greek statesman; premier of Greece (1897, 1903, 1905, 1920–21); during World War (1914–18), supported policies of Constantine against Venizelos.

**Rhampsinitus.** See RAMSES III.

**Rhangaves, Alexandros Rizos.** See RANGABÉ.

**Rhä'ti·cus** (râ'tē·ko͞os) *or* **Rhe'ti·cus** (rā'-). *Real name* **Georg Joachim von Lau'chen** (fôn lou'kĕn). 1514–1576. German astronomer and mathematician; pupil and associate of Copernicus at Frauenburg; instrumental in publishing Copernicus's *De Revolutionibus Orbium Coelestium;* to disseminate the Copernican theory.

**Rha'zes** (rā'zēz) *or* **Ra'sis** (rā'sĭs). *Lat. forms of* **Rāzi.** *Full Arab. name* **abu-Bakr Muḥammad ibn-Zakarīyā' al-Rāzi.** 850–923 A.D. Persian-born Mohammedan physician; chief physician of great hospital in Baghdad. Author of more than 140 medical works, including a general treatise (in 10 books, transl. into Latin c. 1485). His important works, translated into Latin, had great influence on medical science in Middle Ages.

**Rhe'gas, Re'gas, Rhi'gas,** *or* **Ri'gas** (rē'gäs), **Konstantinos.** 1754?–1798. Greek lyric poet and patriot; best known for patriotic hymns or chants, including a paraphrase of the *Marseillaise.*

**Rhein'ber'ger** (rīn'bĕr'gēr), **Joseph Gabriel von.** 1839–1901. German composer, organist, conductor, and teacher; director of court church music (1877), Munich; composer of organ pieces, operas, symphonies, overtures, chamber music, piano pieces, choruses, songs, etc.

**Rhe·na'nus** (rē·nā'nŭs; *Ger.* râ·nä'no͞os), **Be·a'tus** (bē·ā'tŭs; *Ger.* bā·ä'to͞os). 1485–1547. German humanist, b. in Alsace; became intimate with Erasmus and superintended printing of his works; published editions of Pliny the Younger (1514), Tacitus (1519), the editio princeps of Velleius Paterculus, whose manuscript he discovered (1520), and the historical *Rerum Germanicarum Libri Tres* (1531).

**Rhe·né'–Ba'ton'** (rē·nā'bȧ'tôN'). ***Professional name of*** **René Baton.** 1879–1940. French composer and orchestra conductor. His compositions include variations for piano and orchestra, songs, piano pieces, etc.

**Rheticus.** See RHÄTICUS.

**Rhi·a'nus** (rī·ā'nŭs). Greek scholar and poet of 3d century B.C., b. in Crete; long resident in Alexandria. Prepared edition of Homer; wrote epigrams, an epic (*Heraclaeid*), etc.

**Rhind** (?rĭnd), **Massey,** ***in full*** **John Massey.** 1860–1936. British sculptor; to U.S. (1899) and established studio in New York. Among his works are the bust of Henry Ward Beecher in the American Hall of Fame, the McKinley Memorial at Niles, Ohio, statue of George Washington in Washington, D.C.

**Rhine** (rīn), **Joseph Banks.** 1895– . American psychologist; known for investigations in parapsychology.

**Rhins, Dutreuil de.** See DUTREUIL DE RHINS.

**Rhin'thon** (rĭn'thŏn). Greek playwright of late 4th and early 3d century B.C. Invented the comic burlesque of tragedy, known as hilaro-tragedy. Only the titles of a few of his plays are extant.

**Rhode, John.** Pseudonym of C. J. C. STREET.

**Rhodes** (rōdz), **Cecil John.** 1853–1902. British administrator and financier in South Africa. Sent to Natal for his health (1870); moved to Orange Free State on discovery of diamonds and worked prosperous claim with his brother; acquired fortune in Kimberley diamond fields. Entered Cape House of Assembly (1881); energetic in establishing cordial relations between British and Dutch in colony and in bringing about annexation of Bechuanaland (1884); obtained by cession from Lobengula, King of the Matabele, territory north of Bechuanaland, named Rhodesia, and made sole manager (till 1896) of company incorporated with rights of sovereignty over the territory. Amalgamated diamond mines about Kimberley under corporation, the De Beers Consolidated Mines (1888). Prime minister of Cape Colony (1890–96); aimed at establishment of a Federal South African dominion under British flag; in interest of imperial federation contributed £10,000 to home-rule party in England (1880); advanced project for Cape-to-Cairo railway; directed suppression of Matabeles (1893–94); plotted overthrow of South African Republic by encouraging Uitlander population in Transvaal to have recourse to armed insurrection; on failure of premature Jameson Raid (Dec., 1895) into Transvaal was disclosed as instigator of attack upon government of a friendly nation; forced to resign premiership (1896). Devoted himself to development of Rhodesia and northward extension of railway and telegraph lines; through personal influence established permanent peace with Matabeles after outbreak (1896); re-entered Cape parliament (1898); during Boer War, besieged at Kimberley (Oct., 1899–Feb., 1900); failed to find health in Egypt; succumbed to heart disease; buried among Matoppo Hills. Left by will £6,000,000 to public service, endowed 170 scholarships for education at Oxford of youth of British Empire, U.S., and Germany.

**Rhodes, Harrison Garfield.** 1871–1929. American writer; author of *The Lady and the Ladder* (1906), *High Life* (1920), and the plays *Ruggles of Red Gap* (from Harry Leon Wilson's novel; 1915), *Mr. Barnum* (with Thos. A. Wise, 1918), *Her Friend the King* (with A. E. Thomas, 1922), etc.

**Rhodes, James Ford.** 1848–1927. American historian, b. Cleveland. In coal and iron business (1874–85); devoted himself to historical study and writing (from 1885). Author of *History of the United States from the Compromise of 1850* (7 vols., 1893–1906), *The History of the Civil War, 1861–1865* (1917), *History of the United States from Hayes to McKinley, 1877–1896* (1919), etc.

**Rhodes, William Barnes.** 1772–1826. English dramatist; author of burlesque tragic opera *Bombastes Furioso.*

**Rhodogune.** See RODOGUNE.

**Rho·do'pis** (rō·dō'pĭs). *Real name* **Dor'i·cha** (dŏr'ĭ·kȧ). Greek courtesan of 6th century B.C.; native of Thrace; attacked by Sappho in a poem.

**Rhon'dda** (rŏn'dȧ; *Welsh* r'hŏn'thȧ), Viscount. **David Alfred Thom'as** (tŏm'ăs). 1856–1918. Welsh colliery owner and British food controller in World War. Gladstonian Liberal in parliament (1888–1910); aided Lloyd George by organizing British industry (1914 ff.). President of local-government board in Lloyd George's cabinet (1916); as food controller stopped speculation, fixed prices, set up system of compulsory food rationing.

**Rhouphos.** See RUFUS OF EPHESUS.

**Rhyndacenus.** Sobriquet of Andreas J. LASCARIS.

**Rhys** (rēs), **Ernest.** 1859–1946. English editor and writer, b. London. Editor of *The Camelot Series* (1886–91), *The Lyric Poets* (1894–99), *Everyman's Library.* Author of verse, as *Welsh Ballads* (1898), *Lays of the Round Table* (1908), *Song of the Sun* (1937), the novels *The Fiddler of Carne* (1896), *Black Horse Pit* (1295), autobiographical works *Everyman Remembers* (1931) and *Wales England Wed* (1940), etc.

**Rhŷs** (rēs), Sir **John.** 1840–1915. British Celtic scholar, b. in Wales; first professor of Celtic at Oxford (1877); principal of Jesus Coll. (1895–1915). Author of numerous works on Celtic philology, inscriptions, history, religion; editor of Welsh texts.

**Ri·az' Pa'sha** (rĭ·yäz' pȧ'shä). 1835?–1911. Egyptian statesman; prime minister (1879–81; 1888–91; 1892–94). Political rival of Nubar Pasha (*q.v.*).

**Ri'ba·de·nei'ra** *or* **Ri'ba·de·ney'ra** (rē'bä·thā·nē'ē·rä), **Pedro de.** 1527–1611. Spanish hagiologist; follower of St. Ignatius of Loyola; joined Society of Jesus, Rome (1540); active in promulgation of Jesuit order. Author of *Vita Ignatii Loiolae* (1572), etc.

**Ri·bal'ta** (rē·bäl'tä), **Francisco de.** 1555?–1628. Spanish painter of the Valencian school; known esp. for his chiaroscuro work in his own independently created "light and dark style," also called "tenebroso."

**Ri'bault'** (rē'bō'), **Jan** (zhäN). 1520?–1565. French naval officer and colonizer in America; under patronage of Admiral Coligny, established French colony (1562) at what is now Port Royal, S.C.; colony abandoned later in same year. Coligny sent out second expedition under Laudonnière (1564) and Ribault carried reinforcements (1565). Spaniards attacked colony and Ribault sailed with fleet to meet Spaniards. In his absence, Spaniards marched overland and destroyed the colony (1565). Ribault's fleet was wrecked in storm; he was captured by Spaniards and killed (Oct. 12, 1565).

**Rib'beck** (rĭb'ĕk), **Otto,** *in full* **Johann Carl Otto.** 1827–1898. German classical scholar, philologist, and critic; published a critical edition of Vergil with prolegomena (5 vols., 1859–67), editions of Juvenal (1859) and of Horace's *Epistles* (1869).

**Rib'ben·trop** (rĭb'ĕn·trôp), **Joachim von.** 1893–1946. German diplomat; served in World War (1914–18); in business as wine merchant after the war. Conducted negotiations between Adolf Hitler and the German government (1930). Identified himself with Hitler movement, and aided in organizing Nazi government (1933). Ambassador at large (1935), to Great Britain (1936–38). Minister of foreign affairs (1938–45); negotiated Anglo-German naval agreement (1935), German-Japanese anti-Comintern agreement (1936), Russo-German Nonaggression Pact (1939), and Italo-German-Japanese alliance (1940). Hanged as war criminal.

**Ri·bei'ro** (rē·bā'ē·rōō), **Bernardim.** 1482–1552. Portuguese poet; author of the pastoral *Saudades,* better known by its opening words *Menina e Moça* (publ. 1554).

**Ri·bei'ro–Fer·rei'ra** (-fĕr·rā'ē·rȧ), **Tomaz Antônio.** 1831–1901. Portuguese poet, lawyer, and statesman; minister of colonies (1878), interior (1881), public works (1885, 1890); minister to Brazil (1895, 1896). Author of collections of lyrics *Sons Que Passam* (1854) and *Vésperas* (1858), the epic *Dom Jaime* (1861), the narrative *Delfina do Mal* (1868), *Dissonâncias* (verse; 1891), etc.

**Ri·be'ra** (rē·bā'rä). Variant of RIVERA.

**Ribera, José,** *Ital.* **Giuseppe,** *whence Span.* **Jusepe, de.** *Called in Italy* **Lo Spa'gno·let'to** (lō spä'nyô·lāt'tô). 1588–1652. Spanish painter and etcher; one of leading painters of the Neapolitan school; known esp. as a colorist and representative of the tenebrosi. Among his works are *Martyrdom of St. Bartholomew, Immaculate Conception, Descent from the Cross, Adoration of the Shepherds, Pietà, Magdalen, Lucretia, Assumption.*

**Ri'bot'** (rē'bō'), **Alexandre Félix Joseph.** 1842–1923. French statesman; minister of foreign affairs (1890); premier of France (1892–93, 1895); finance minister (1914–17), and again premier (1917).

**Ribot, Théodule Armand.** 1839–1916. French psychologist; pioneer in experimental psychology; conducted psychopathological studies.

**Ribot, Théodule Augustin.** 1823–1891. French genre, historical, and portrait painter and etcher.

**Ri'card'** (rē'kȧr'), **Louis Xavier de.** 1843–1911. French poet; imprisoned (1863) and in exile (1871) for republican activities; founded *L'Art* (1865) and, with C. Mendès, *Le Parnasse Contemporain* (1866); author of *Les Chants de l'Aube* (1862), *Ciel, Rue, Terre et Foyer* (1865).

**Ri·car'do** (rĭ·kär'dō), **David.** 1772–1823. English economist; founder of classical school of economics; b. London, son of a Dutch Jew. Followed his father in stock exchange; renounced by father on his entry into Church of England; succeeded as a broker. Having read *Wealth of Nations,* devoted himself to economic studies; created stir by pamphlet *The High Price of Bullion a Proof of the Depreciation of Bank-notes* (1809), which influenced report of Bullion Committee (1811); attempted systematic exposition of his theories in *Principles of Political Economy and Taxation* (1817), developing his theory of rent, profit, and wages, and presenting clear statement of the quantity theory of money. M.P. (1819–23); accepted as authority on financial matters.

**Ri·ca'so·li** (rē·kä'sô·lē), **Bettino.** Baron of **Bro'lio** (brô'lyô). 1809–1880. Italian statesman; participated in Tuscan liberal movements (1848–49); retired to private life (1849–59). Assumed leadership in Tuscan liberal movements (1859); made dictator of Tuscany (1859–60); secured union of Tuscany and Sardinia (March, 1860); governor general of Tuscany (1860–61); prime minister of Italy (June, 1861–March, 1862; June, 1866–April, 1867).

**Ric·car'di** (rēk·kär'dē), **Arturo.** 1878– . Italian admiral; chief of staff and undersecretary of the navy (1940).

**Ric·ca′ti** (rē̇k·kä′tē̇), Count **Jacopo Francesco.** 1676–1754. Italian mathematician; concerned chiefly with depression of differential equations, proposing the equation which bears his name.

**Ric′ci** (rēt′chē̇), **Corrado.** 1858–1934. Italian art scholar; general director of antiquities and works of art in Italy (1906–19). His works include *L'Ultimo Rifugio di Dante* (1891), *Il Correggio* (1896), *Michelangiolo* (1900), *Raffaello* (1920), *Beatrice Cenci* (12 vols., 1923), *Roma* (1924), *La Pittura del Cinquecento nell' Alta Italia* (1929).

**Ricci, Curbastro Gregorio.** 1853–1925. Italian mathematician.

**Ricci, Federigo.** 1809–1877. Italian operatic composer. His brother **Luigi** (1805–59) was also an operatic composer, and often collaborated with him.

**Ric′ci** (rĭch′ĭ), **L. A. da Costa.** See Lewis RITCHIE.

**Ric′ci** (rēt′chē̇), **Matteo.** 1552–1610. Italian missionary; joined Jesuit order (1571); missionary to India (1578); settled in China (1583); permitted to found mission at Peking (1601); as a favorite of the emperor, succeeded in introducing Christianity into Chinese cities. Author of a work on Chinese geography and history and of several works in Chinese, as *On the Nature of God*, now a Chinese classic.

**Ricci, Scipione de'.** 1741–1810. Italian prelate; bishop of Pistoia and Prato (1780–91); attempted ecclesiastical reforms (condemned by Pius VI, 1794); imprisoned (1799) until his retraction of the condemned propositions (1805).

**Ricci, Sebastiano.** 1660–1734. Italian painter of Venetian school; works include decorations in Chelsea hospital chapel, chapel at Bulstrode, and hall of Burlington House (all in England), and in Palazzo Maruccelli (in Florence).

**Ricciarelli, Daniele.** See VOLTERRA.

**Ric′cio** (rēt′chō̇), **Andrea.** *Real surname* **Bri·o′sco** (brē̇·ôs′kō̇). 1470?–1532. Italian sculptor and architect, b. Padua.

**Ric′cio** (rēt′chō̇; *Angl.* rĭch′ĭ·ō), **David.** See RIZZIO.

**Ric′cio** (rēt′chō̇), **Domenico.** *Called* **Il Bru′sa·sor′ci** (ēl brōō′zä·sōr′chē̇). 1494–1567. Italian painter of Veronese school; among his works are *Vision of the Madonna*, *Entry of Charles V and Clement VII into Bologna*, *Annunciation*, and *Fable of Phaëthon.*

**Ric·cio′li** (rē̇t·chô′lē̇), **Giovanni Battista.** 1598–1671. Italian Jesuit astronomer; rejected Copernican theory; made (with P. Grimaldi) a detailed telescopic study of the moon, introducing nomenclature for lunar features still used. Author of *Almagestum Novum* (2 vols., Bologna, 1651).

**Ric′co·bo′ni** (rēk′kō̇·bô′nē̇), **Lodovico,** *known as* **Lelio.** 1675?–1753. Italian-born actor and playwright in Paris; made success as comedian at Comédie Italienne. His wife, **Helena Virginia,** *nee* **Bal·let′ti** [bäl·lāt′tē̇] (1686–1771), and his son **Antonio Francesco** (1707–1772) were also connected with the stage. Antonio's wife, a Frenchwoman, **Marie Jeanne,** *nee* **La′bo′ras′ de Mé′zières′** [lȧ′bô′rȧ′ dẽ mā′zyâr′] (1714–1792), was also an actress, but is best known as a novelist; author of *Ernestine*, *L'Histoire de Miss Jenny Level*, etc.

**Rice** (rīs), **Cale Young.** 1872–1943. American poet and dramatist, b. Dixon, Ky. A.M., Harvard (1896). Author of: poetry, *From Dusk to Dusk* (1898), *With Omar* (1900), *Nirvana Days* (1908), *Many Gods* (1910), *Far Quests* (1912), *Trails Sunward* (1917), *Shadowy Thresholds* (1919), *Sea Poems* (1921), *Bitter Brew* (1925), *Seed of the Moon* (1929), *High Perils* (1933); plays, *Charles di Toca* (1903), *David* (1904), *The Immortal Lure* (1911), *Porzia* (1913); novels, *Youth's Way* (1923), *Early Reaping* (1929). His wife (m. 1902), **Alice Caldwell,** *nee* **He′gan** [hē′gӑn] (1870–1942), also a writer; author of *Mrs. Wiggs of the Cabbage Patch* (1901), *Lovey Mary* (1903), *Mr. Opp* (1909), *A Romance of Billy Goat Hill* (1912), *The Buffer* (1929), *Mr. Pete & Co.* (1933), *My Pillow Book* (1937), etc.

**Rice, Edmund Ignatius.** 1762–1844. Irish philanthropist; founder of the Irish Christian Brothers. Abandoned provision merchant business, joined nine others in taking religious vows, assumed a habit, and, as Christian Brothers (order sanctioned by pope, 1820), established schools in Cork, Dublin, Thurles, and Limerick; superior general of the order (1822–38).

**Rice, Elmer L.** *Orig.* **Rei′zen·stein** (rī′z'n·stīn). 1892–1967. American playwright, b. New York City. Author of: plays, *On Trial* (1914), *Iron Cross* (1917), *Home of the Free* (1917), *For the Defense* (1919), *Close Harmony* (1924; with Dorothy Parker), *Cock Robin* (1927), *Street Scene* (awarded Pulitzer prize, 1929), *Counsellor-at-Law* (1931), *We, the People* (1933), *Between Two Worlds* (1934), *Not for Children* (1936), etc.; and the novels *A Voyage to Purilia* (1930) and *Imperial City* (1937).

**Rice, James.** 1843–1882. English novelist; collaborator with Sir Walter Besant in *Ready-Money Mortiboy* (1872), *The Golden Butterfly* (1876), and *The Seamy Side* (1881), etc.

**Rice, Richard Henry.** 1863–1922. American engineer; designed first turboblower for blast furnaces in America; expert on steam turbines.

**Rice, Thomas Dartmouth.** 1808–1860. American minstrel-show pioneer, b. New York City; introduced *Jim Crow*, a song and dance number (c. 1830) with sensational success; known as "Father of American Minstrelsy."

**Rice, William Marsh.** 1816–1900. American merchant and philanthropist, b. Springfield, Mass. Opened store in Houston, Tex. (1838); developed large exporting, importing, and retail business; bequeathed his fortune for educational institution at Houston, Tex. Rice Institute was opened in 1912.

**Rich** (rĭch), **Barnabe.** 1540?–1617. English soldier and writer of fiction; under patronage of Sir Christopher Hatton; author of euphuistic tales *The Strange and Wonderful Adventures of Don Simonides* (1581) and *The Adventures of Brusanus* (1592). His story *Apolonius and Silla* (in *Riche His Farewell to Militarie Profession*, 1581) was Shakespeare's source for plot of *Twelfth Night.*

**Rich, Edmund** (1175?–1240). See Saint EDMUND RICH.

**Rich,** Sir **Henry.** 1st Baron **Ken′sing·ton** (kĕn′zĭng·tŭn) and 1st Earl of **Hol′land** (hŏl′ӑnd). 1590–1649. Son of Robert Rich, 1st Earl of Warwick, and Penelope Rich (Sir Philip Sidney's Stella: see *Penelope Devereux* at DEVEREUX family). Educ. Cambridge; M.P. (1610); courtier favored by James I; sent to Paris (1624) to negotiate marriage of Prince Charles and Henrietta Maria, again (1625) to arrange treaty between Louis XIII and Huguenots. Deserted cause of Charles I (1641), joined Parliamentary party; member of committee of safety; shifted allegiance three times; captured by Parliamentarians and beheaded.

His elder brother, Sir **Robert** (1587–1658), 2d Earl of **War′wick** [wŏr′ĭk] (from 1619), naval commander and Puritan colonial administrator. Educ. Cambridge; M.P. (1610); conducted unsuccessful privateering expedition against Spaniards (1627). Procured patent for Massachusetts colony (1628); granted Saybrook patent in Connecticut (1631); managed Bermudas Co.; councilor of New England Co.; friend of Thomas Hooker, founder of Hartford. Estranged from court, opposed forced loan (1626), payment of ship money, and Laud's church policy; lord high admiral (1643–49), intercepted king's ships and relieved ports; attempted to win back revolted fleet (1648); organized new fleet until removed from post on dissolution of House of Lords. As head of commission for government of colonies, aided in incorporation of Providence Plantations (later Rhode Island).

**Rich, John.** 1692–1761. English actor, father of English pantomime; son of **Christopher Rich,** manager of Drury Lane. On father's death (1714) opened new theater in Lincoln's Inn Fields; introduced the pantomime, playing part of Harlequin (1716); produced a pantomime annually (till 1760); opened Covent Garden (1732).

**Rich,** Lady **Penelope.** = Penelope DEVEREUX.

**Rich,** Sir **Richard.** 1st Baron **Rich** (cr. 1547). 1496?–1567. English chancery officer, b. London; solicitor general (1533); acted basely in trial of Bishop Fisher and perjured himself in trial of Sir Thomas More; profited by suppression of monasteries and disposal of their revenues; lord chancellor of England (1548–51), supported Protector Somerset (1548–49); deserted to Warwick and effected overthrow of Somerset; signed proclamation in favor of Lady Jane Grey (1553) and immediately after declared for Mary, during whose reign he was active in persecution of protestants.

**Rich, Richard.** fl. 1610. English soldier and adventurer; sailed for Virginia with Captain Christopher Newport (1609); on return published *Newes from Virginia,* narrating shipwreck on Bermudas, probably suggesting scenes in Shakespeare's *Tempest.*

**Rich'ard** (rĭch'ẽrd). Name of three kings of England:

**Richard I.** *Surnamed* **Cœur' de Li'on** (kûr' dẽ lē'ŏn; *Fr.* kûr' dẽ lyôN') *or* **Lion-Hearted.** 1157–1199. King (1189–99), of house of Anjou, or Plantagenet; third son of Henry II. Leagued against his father twice (1173–74; 1188–89); succeeded to throne of England, the duchy of Normandy, and county of Anjou (1189). Started on Third Crusade (1189), joining Philip II of France (1190); conquered Cyprus (1191); aided in capture of Acre (1191); recaptured Jaffa from Saladin (1192). On his return, was captured in Austria (1192) and held for ransom; was ransomed and returned to England (1194). Wounded by an arrow near Limoges, France, and died (Apr. 6, 1199).

**Richard II.** 1367–1400. King (1377–99), of house of Anjou, or Plantagenet; son of Edward the Black Prince, and grandson of Edward III. Succeeded Edward III as king (1377); during his minority, government administered by duke of Lancaster and duke of Gloucester. Economic distress caused rebellion of peasants under Wat Tyler (1381). Assumed control of government (1389); banished Henry of Bolingbroke, Duke of Hereford, and confiscated his Lancastrian estates (1398–99); defeated by Henry of Bolingbroke (later, Henry IV), captured, deposed by Parliament (1399), imprisoned, and probably murdered in prison (1400).

**Richard III.** 1452–1485. King (1483–85), of house of York. Duke of Gloucester; third son of Richard Plantagenet, 3d Duke of York, and younger brother of Edward IV. Nicknamed "Crouchback." Quarreled with brother, duke of Clarence. On death of Edward IV, Richard seized the young successor, Edward V, and secured appointment of himself as protector; assumed the crown (June 26, 1483), and shortly afterward announced the deaths of Edward V and Edward's younger brother Richard, the duke of York. Suppressed rebellion led by duke of Buckingham (1483), but was defeated and killed in the battle of Bosworth Field (Aug. 22, 1485) by the earl of Richmond, who became Henry VII, first of the Tudor family.

**Richard I** of Normandy. *Known as* **Richard the Fearless.** d. 996 A.D. Duke of Normandy; warred against the last of the Carolingians; supported Hugh Capet and the Capetian dynasty. His son **Richard II,** *known as* **Richard the Good** (d. 1027), succeeded his father (996), remained loyal to the Capetian dynasty, waged successful war against the English and Swedes, and brought Normandy to the height of its power.

**Richard.** Earl of **Corn'wall** (kôrn'wôl; *Brit. usu.* -wăl) and King of the Romans. 1209–1272. Second son of King John of England. Commanded expedition that recovered Gascony (1225–26); having quarreled with his brother Henry III and married daughter of 1st earl of Pembroke, joined baronial opposition and opposed foreigners brought over by Henry; went on crusade (1240–41); having married (1243) Sancha, sister of Queen Eleanor, became for a time peacemaker between barons and king, then ally of his brother against Simon de Montfort; elected king of the Romans during interregnum of Holy Roman Empire, crowned at Aachen (1257), established authority in Rhine Valley until funds exhausted; in aiding brother, taken prisoner at battle of Lewes (1264); released after Evesham (1265); died of paralysis after murder by de Montfort's sons of his eldest son, **Henry of Cornwall** *or* **of Al'maine** [ăl'-mān] (1235–1271), who had witnessed father's coronation at Aachen, fought for royalists at Lewes (1264), and mediated between Henry III and Gloucester (1267).

**Richard de Bury.** See BURY.

**Richard of Ci'ren·ces'ter** (sī'rĕn·sĕs'tẽr; sĭs'ĭ·tẽr; sĭs'ĭs·tẽr; sĭz'ĭ·tẽr). c. 1335–c. 1401. English chronicler; Benedictine monk; compiler of *Speculum Historiale de Gestis Regum Angliae 447–1066.* Had forgery *De Situ Britanniae* fathered upon him by the literary impostor Charles Julius Bertram, Copenhagen teacher (1758).

**Richard of De·vi'zes** (dē·vī'zĭz). fl. 1189–1192. English chronicler; known for *Chronicon de rebus gestis Ricardi Primi,* an account of events in England and Holy Land during 3d crusade.

**Richard Plantagenet.** See Duke of YORK.

**Richard Strongbow.** 2d Earl of **Pembroke.** See under family de CLARE.

**Rich'ards** (rĭch'ẽrdz), **Charles Brinkerhoff.** 1833–1919. American mechanical engineer, b. Brooklyn, N.Y. Invented Richards's indicator (1860), first steam-engine indicator suitable for use on high-speed engines; invented machine for testing strength of metals; became authority on heating and ventilation. Professor of engineering, Sheffield Scientific School, Yale (1884–1909).

**Richards, Dickinson Woodruff.** 1895–1973. American physician, b. Orange, N.J. At Columbia U. (1928–61); awarded Nobel prize in physiology or medicine (1956) with W. Forssmann and A. Cournand.

**Richards, Ellen Henrietta,** *nee* **Swal'low** (swŏl'ō). 1842–1911. American chemist, b. Dunstable, Mass.; m. Robert Hallowell Richards (1875). Instructor in sanitary chemistry, M.I.T. (1884–1911). An organizer, and first president, of American Home Economics Association (1908). Author of *Chemistry of Cooking and Cleaning* (1882), *The Cost of Food* (1901), *Sanitation in Daily Life* (1907), *Euthenics* (1910), etc.

**Richards, Grant,** *in full* **Franklin Thomas Grant.** 1872–1948. English publisher and writer; author of *Caviare* (1912), *Bittersweet* (1915), *Double Life* (1920), *Vain Pursuit* (1931), *Memories of a Misspent Youth* (1932), *Housman: 1859–1936* (1940).

**Richards, Henry Brinley.** 1819–1885. Welsh pianist and composer of piano pieces, part songs, choruses, including *Her Bright Smile Haunts Me Still* and *God Bless the Prince of Wales* (the Welsh national anthem; 1862).

**Richards, Ivor Armstrong.** 1893–1979. English literary critic; author of *Foundations of Aesthetics* (with C.K.

Ogden and James Wood; 1921), *The Meaning of Meaning* (with C. K. Ogden; 1923), *Principles of Literary Criticism* (1924), *Science and Poetry* (1925), *Mencius on the Mind* (1931), *Basic Rules of Reason* (1933), and *Interpretation in Teaching* (1938).

**Richards, Laura Elizabeth,** *nee* **Howe** (hou). 1850–1943. Daughter of Samuel Gridley Howe and Julia Ward Howe. American writer, b. Boston; m. Henry Richards (1871). Author of many juveniles, from *Five Mice* (1881) to *Harry in England* (1937), and of biographies of Julia Ward Howe (with her sister Maud Howe Elliott, 1916; awarded Pulitzer prize), Elizabeth Fry (1916), Abigail Adams (1917), Joan of Arc (1919), Laura Bridgman (1928), Samuel Gridley Howe (1935).

**Richards, Theodore William.** 1868–1928. American chemist, b. Germantown, Pa. Teacher of chemistry, Harvard (1889–1928), professor (from 1901). Best known for his determination of the atomic weights of chemical elements with an accuracy theretofore unapproached. Also conducted important investigations in physical chemistry, especially thermochemistry and thermodynamics, thermometry, etc. Awarded the 1914 Nobel prize in chemistry. His father, **William Trost** (trōst) **Richards** (1833–1905), b. Philadelphia, was a landscape and marine painter.

**Richards, Thomas Addison.** 1820–1900. Landscape painter and illustrator, b. London, Eng.; to U.S. as a boy. Known as a member of Hudson River school. Professor of art, N.Y.U. (1867–87). Author and illustrator of *American Scenery* (1854) and *Appletons' Illustrated Hand-book of American Travel* (1857).

**Richards, William.** 1793–1847. American Congregational clergyman; in Hawaiian Islands as missionary (1822–38). In service of native Hawaiian government (from 1838); secured recognition of Hawaiian independence by U.S., Great Britain, and France (1842).

**Richards,** Sir **William Buell.** 1815–1889. Canadian jurist; first chief justice of Supreme Court of Canada (1875–79). Knighted (1878).

**Rich'ard·son** (rĭch'ẽrd·s'n), Sir **Benjamin Ward.** 1828–1896. English physician; experimented with new anesthetics and invented pieces of medical apparatus and embalming methods.

**Richardson, Charles.** 1775–1865. English lexicographer; teacher of school on Clapham Common (till 1827); developed his lexicon published in *The Encyclopaedia Metropolitana* (1818) into *A New Dictionary of the English Language* (2 vols., 1836–37), presenting etymologies designed to explain the basic, radical meaning of each word and illustrative passages to show how derived meanings developed.

**Richardson, Dorothy M.** Mrs. **Alan O'dle** (ō'd'l). 1872–1957. English novelist; introduced stream-of-consciousness technique into English fiction. Author of *Pilgrimage*, a sequence of novels.

**Richardson, Henry Handel.** *Pseud. of* **Ethel Florence Lindesay Richardson.** 1870–1946. Australian novelist, b. Melbourne. Author of *Maurice Guest* (1908), *The Getting of Wisdom* (1910), *The Fortunes of Richard Mahony* (1930; a trilogy), *The End of Childhood* (1934), *The Young Cosima* (1939).

**Richardson, Henry Hobson.** 1838–1886. American architect, b. in St. James Parish, La. Won competition for the Church of the Unity, Springfield, Mass. (1866), for an Episcopal church, West Medford, Mass. (1866), for Brattle Street Church, Boston (1870), and for Trinity Church, Boston (1872). Designed Sever Hall (1878) and Austin Hall (1881) at Harvard; Marshall Field building, Chicago (1885); and many private residences.

**Richardson,** Sir **John.** 1787–1865. Scottish naturalist and Arctic explorer; surgeon and naturalist to Sir John Franklin's polar expeditions (1819–22, 1825–27); separating from Franklin, explored coast to the Coppermine River and Great Slave Lake (1826); conducted search expedition for Franklin (1847). Author of *Fauna Boreali-Americana* (1829–37) and works on ichthyology and polar exploration.

**Richardson,** Sir **Owen Wil'lans** (wĭl'ănz). 1879–1959. English physicist; B.A., Cantab. (1900), D.Sc., U. of London (1904); professor, Princeton, U.S.A. (1906–14), King's College, London (1914–24; director of research from 1924). Known especially for work on thermionic emission (Richardson effect). Awarded 1928 Nobel prize for physics (1929). Author of *The Ionisation Produced by Hot Platinum in Different Gases* (1906), *The Electron Theory of Matter* (1914), *The Emission of Electricity from Hot Bodies* (1916), *Molecular Hydrogen and Its Spectrum* (1933).

**Richardson, Rufus By'am** (bī'ăm). 1845–1914. American classical archaeologist; professor of Greek, Dartmouth (1882–93). Director, American School of Classical Studies, Athens, Greece (1893–1903). In charge of excavation work at Eretria (1894–95) and ancient Corinth (1896–1902).

**Richardson, Samuel.** 1689–1761. English novelist, b. Derbyshire. Set up printing establishment in London; prospered and became printer of journals of the House of Commons; purchased moiety of patent of king's printer (1760). Author of *Pamela: or Virtue Rewarded* (1740), a novel of a maidservant's defense of her virtue told in form of correspondence, which attained phenomenal popularity; worked eight years at his masterpiece, *Clarissa; or the History of a Young Lady*, usually called *Clarissa Harlowe*, which won him European fame (7 vols., 1747–48); embodied his ideal of a Christian gentleman in *Sir Charles Grandison* (1753); left seven folio volumes of correspondence, chiefly with women friends.

**Rich'berg** (rĭch'bûrg), **Donald Randall.** 1881–1960. American lawyer, b. Knoxville, Tenn.; practiced in Chicago (1904–33); general counsel for National Recovery Administration (1933–35); also, executive director of National Emergency Council (1934–35); in practice in Washington, D.C. (from 1936); author of *Tents of the Mighty* (1930), *The Rainbow* (1936), etc.

**Ri'che·lieu'** (rē'shẽ·lyû'; *Angl.* rĭsh'ẽ·lo͞o), Duc **de. Armand Jean du Ples'sis'** (dü plĕ'sē'). *Known as* **É'mi'nence' Rouge** (ā'mē'näNs' ro͞ozh'), *i.e.* "red eminence," *from the color of his habit.* 1585–1642. French statesman and cardinal, b. Paris. Bishop of Luçon (1606–14). Elected member of the States-General (1614). Favored by Concini (Marquis d'Ancre) and Marie de Médicis (1614–19). Cardinal (1622); chief minister of Louis XIII (1624–42), who was completely under his control; actually directed domestic and foreign policies of France. *Domestic:* Rising of Huguenots in south (1622–28); defeat of Soubise (1625); La Rochelle besieged and captured (1627–28); Huguenots deprived of power. Officially appointed prime minister (1629). Suppressed plots of Gaston d'Orléans (1626), Henri, Duc de Montmorency (1632), and Cinq Mars (1642). Foiled attempt of Marie de Médicis to dismiss him (Day of Dupes, Nov. 11, 1630). Influence of nobility reduced. *Foreign:* Life aim was to humble Hapsburgs; in Thirty Years' War, intervened by subsidizing (1631) Gustavus Adolphus of Sweden to fight the emperor. After Treaty of Prague (1635), led Catholic France to join with Swedish and German Protestants in war against Catholic Imperialist armies, made alliances with Oxenstierna and Bernhard of Saxe-Weimar, sent armies into Spain and Italy. Laid down principles upon which Peace of Westphalia was later (1648) made; Bourbons had gained balance of power from Hapsburgs.

**Richelieu,** Duc **de. Louis François Armand de Vi′gne·rot′ du Ples′sis′** (dē vēn′y′·rō′ dü plĕ′sē′). 1696–1788. French soldier and diplomat; grandnephew of Cardinal Richelieu. Distinguished himself in the War of the Polish Succession, at the siege of Philippsburg (1733); promoted field marshal, and lieutenant general in Languedoc (1738). Engaged also in the War of the Austrian Succession, at Fontenoy, Ravenna, and Lawfeld; freed Genoa from Austrian siege (1748); created marshal of France (1748). His influence at court, esp. with regard to his hostility toward Austria, markedly affected by Pompadour's support of alliance with Austria, an alliance that brought France into Seven Years' War; commanded campaign in Hanover, ending in capitulation of Closterseven (1757). His grandson **Armand Emmanuel du Plessis,** Duc **de Richelieu** (1766–1822), was a politician; an émigré (1789 or 1790), served in Russian army during most of the revolutionary and Napoleonic period; at the Restoration, became Louis XVIII's chief minister (1815–18) after the fall of Talleyrand-Périgord and Fouché (1815); represented France at the Congress of Aix-la-Chapelle (1818); again premier (1820–21) after death of duc de Berry.

**Ri′che·pin′** (rēsh′păN′), **Jean.** 1849–1930. French writer, b. in Algeria. In Paris, contributed to various journals; published *La Chanson des Gueux* (verse; 1876), for which he was imprisoned and fined; followed this with other verse, *Les Caresses* (a verse drama; 1877), *Les Blasphèmes* (1884), *La Mer* (1886), etc. For the stage he wrote *Nana Sahib* (1883), *Le Flibustier* (comedy; 1888), *Le Mage* (opera; 1891), *Par le Glaive* (heroic drama; 1894). Author also of a number of psychological novels, as *Madame André* (1874), *Le Pavé* (1883), *Les Braves Gens* (1886), *La Clique* (1917), etc.

**Ri′cher′** (rē′shā′), **Edmond.** 1559–1633. French Gallican theologian; opposed Jesuit policies and influence; forced to resign his various offices and to retract his doctrines; appointed canon of Paris.

**Ri·che′rus** (rĭ·kē′rŭs). *Fr.* **Ri′cher′** (rē′shā′). 10th-century French monk and chronicler of Reims; author of a continuation of Hincmar's *Annales.*

**Ri′chet′** (rē′shĕ′), **Charles Robert.** 1850–1935. French physiologist; professor, U. of Paris (1887–1927). Conducted researches in serum therapy; discovered the phenomenon of anaphylaxis; awarded the 1913 Nobel prize for physiology and medicine; studied psychical phenomena.

**Ri′chier′** (rē′shyā′), **Ligier.** 1500?–1567. French sculptor; among his notable works are the sepulcher of the Church of Saint-Étienne, the *Virgin and Saint John* at Saint-Mihiel, the mausoleum of René de Châlons with its remarkable skeleton which formerly bore in its hand a small casket of silver gilt enclosing the heart of the prince of Orange.

**Rich′man** (rĭch′măn), **Arthur.** 1886–1944. American playwright, b. New York City; author of *Ambush* (1921), *The Awful Truth* (1922), *All Dressed Up* (1925), *A Proud Woman* (1927), *The Season Changes* (1936), etc.

**Rich′mond** (rĭch′mŭnd). *Duke of Richmond:* English title borne (1623–72) by members of Stewart family (*q.v.*) and (1675 to present) by members of Lennox family (*q.v.*). *Duchess of Richmond:* title borne by Frances Teresa Stuart (see STEWART family). *Earl of Richmond:* English title borne by Peter of Savoy (*q.v.*) and (from 1453) by Edmund Tudor (1430?–1456) and by his son Henry VII (*q.v.*) until his accession. *Countess of Richmond and Derby:* title borne by wife of Edmund Tudor, Margaret Beaufort (*q.v.*).

**Richmond,** Sir **Bruce Lyttelton.** 1871–1964. English journalist; member, editorial staff of London *Times* (1899–1938); editor of *Times Literary Supplement.*

**Richmond, Grace Louise,** *nee* **Smith.** 1866–1959. American fiction writer; m. Nelson Guernsey Richmond (1887); among her many tales are *The Indifference of Juliet* (1905), *Red Pepper Burns* (1910), *Red and Black* (1919), *Lights Up* (1927), *Bachelor's Bounty* (1931).

**Richmond, Legh.** 1772–1827. English clergyman; writer of popular evangelical tracts.

**Richmond, Mary Ellen.** 1861–1928. American social worker; on staff, Charity Organization Department of Russell Sage Foundation (1909–28).

**Richmond,** Sir **William Blake.** 1842–1921. English painter and decorator; painted portraits and mythological themes; designed mosaic decorations of choir of St. Paul's Cathedral. His father, **George** (1809–1896), portrait painter, achieved fame by his water color of William Wilberforce.

**Rich′ter** (rĭK′tẽr), **Adrian Ludwig.** 1803–1884. German painter, graphic artist, and illustrator. His works include paintings, illustrations for Goldsmith's *Vicar of Wakefield,* Andersen's fairy tales (1851), etc., and many etchings.

**Richter, Ämilius Ludwig.** 1808–1864. German jurist; introduced historical treatment of church law.

**Rich′ter** (rĭk′tẽr), **Burton.** 1931– . American physicist. At Stanford U. (1956– ); awarded (with Samuel C. C. Ting) Nobel prize for physics (1976).

**Rich′ter** (rĭK′tẽr), **Ernst Friedrich.** 1808–1879. German music theorist and composer of an oratorio (1849), church vocal music, organ pieces, chamber music, piano sonatas, and songs.

**Richter, Eugen.** 1838–1906. German politician; entered Reichstag (1867) and Prussian House of Deputies (1869), and became leader of Progressists, later of German Liberals, finally of radical People's party; opposed esp. Bismarck's conservative economic and social policy, government control of railroads, and Social Democrats.

**Richter, Franz Xaver.** 1709–1789. German composer, b. in Moravia; representative of the Mannheim school; composed many symphonies, string quartets, sonata trios, and other chamber music, piano concertos, an oratorio, masses, requiems, motets, psalms, passions, and other church music; introduced (with Stamitz) a new instrumental style represented by Haydn, Mozart, and Beethoven.

**Richter, Gustav.** 1823–1884. German portrait and historical painter.

**Richter, Hans.** 1843–1916. Musical conductor, b. in Hungary; court opera conductor (1875–1900), Vienna; conducted first complete performance of his friend Wagner's *Ring des Nibelungen,* Bayreuth (1876) and was one of chief conductors of Bayreuth Festspiele. Conducted Hallé concerts, Manchester, Eng. (1900–10); directed German opera, London (from 1904); returned to Bayreuth (1912).

**Richter, Helene.** 1861–1944 or 1945. Viennese Anglicist and historian of the theater; translator of Shelley's *Prometheus Bound* (1895), and author of biographies of Mary Wollstonecraft (1897), Shelly (1898), William Blake (1906), and Byron (1929).

**Rich′ter** (rĭK′tẽr), **Jean** (zhäN) **Paul** (poul) **Friedrich.** *Pseudonym* **Jean Paul.** 1763–1825. German humorist and prose writer, b. in Bavaria; studied theology, U. of Leipzig (1781–84) and attempted to support himself by writing, etc.; fled creditors (1784); to Hof, where he lived in poverty; tutor near Hof (1787–94); met Charlotte von Kalb (*q.v.*) in Weimar; settled in Bayreuth (1804); received government pension (1808). His novels and romances include *Die Unsichtbare Loge* (1792), *Hesperus* (1795), *Leben des Quintus Fixleins* (1796), *Blumen-, Frucht-, und Dornenstücke, oder...Siebenkäs* (3 vols., 1796–97), *Titan* (6 vols., 1800–03), *Die Flegeljahre* (4 vols., 1804–05), *Des Feldpredigers Schmelzle Reise nach Flätz* (1809), and *Der Komet* (3 vols., 1820–22; incomplete); author also of *Levana oder Erziehungslehre* (a classic work on pedagogy, 1807), *Vorschule der Ästhetik* (reflections on art, 1804), and patriotic, philosophical, and political writings.

**Richter, Jeremias Benjamin.** 1762–1807. German chemist; pioneer in stoichiometry; discovered the law (Richter's law of proportionality) that acids and alkalies unite in constant proportions to form salts.

**Richter, Theodor,** *in full* **Hieronymus Theodor.** 1824–1898. German metallurgical chemist; codiscoverer, with Ferdinand Reich, of the element indium (1863).

**Richt'ho'fen** (rĭKt'hō'fĕn), Baron **Ferdinand von.** 1833–1905. German geographer and geologist; with Prussian mission to eastern Asia (1860–62); worked as geologist in California; traveled in China and Japan (1868–72); professor, Berlin (1886).

**Richthofen,** Baron **Manfred von.** 1892–1918. German military aviator in World War; credited with destroying 80 enemy planes; killed in action (Apr. 21, 1918). His cousin Frieda married (1914) D. H. Lawrence (*q.v.*).

**Richthofen,** Baron **Oswald von.** 1847–1906. German statesman; aide of von Bülow, whom he succeeded (1900) as foreign secretary of state; Prussian state minister (1905). His son Baron **Hartmann** (1878–1953) represented National Liberals in Reichstag (1912–18); helped found German Democratic party; member of Weimar National Assembly (1919–20), Prussian People's Assembly (1919–21), Reichstag (1924–28).

**Richt'my'er** (?rĭkt'mī'ẽr), **Floyd Karker.** 1881–1939. American physicist; known for work relating to X rays and their absorption.

**Ric'i·mer** (rĭs'ĭ·mẽr). d. 472. Roman general, of Suevian birth; destroyed the fleet of the Vandals (456); deposed Emperor Avitus and elevated Majorian to the throne (456); remained thereafter real sovereign of the Western Roman Empire, deposing and elevating emperors at his will but not himself aspiring to the purple because of his Suevian birth.

**Rick'ard** (rĭk'ẽrd), **George Lewis,** *known as* **Tex** (tĕks). 1871–1929. American prize-fight promoter, from 1906, when he promoted Gans-Nelson fight, Goldfield, Nev.

**Rickard, Thomas Arthur.** 1864–1953. American mining engineer and author, b. Pertusola, Italy, of English parentage; to U.S. (1885); mining engineer in Colorado, California, Canada, Australia, and New Zealand; edited various technical journals in U.S. and England. Author of *Journeys of Observation* (1908), *Man and Metals* (1932), *A History of American Mining* (1932).

**Rick'en·back'er** (rĭk'ĕn·băk'ẽr), **Edward Vernon,** *known as* **Eddie.** 1890–1973. American aviator, b. in Columbus, Ohio. Engaged in automobile racing (to 1917). Served in U.S. army air corps (1917–19); commanded 94th Aero Pursuit squadron, credited with 69 victories in World War, 26 credited to him personally; awarded Congressional Medal of Honor. Author of *Fighting the Flying Circus* (1919). After World War I, organizer and vice-president of Rickenbacker Motor Co., Detroit (to 1926); on staff of General Motors Corp., Fokker Aircraft Corp., American Airways, Inc., Aviation Corp., and (1933–38) North American Aviation, Inc.; president and general manager, Eastern Air Lines. Rescued after three weeks on raft in Pacific Ocean (Nov., 1942) following special flight for U.S. government; described experience in *Seven Came Through* (1943).

**Rick'ert** (rĭk'ẽrt), **Edith,** *in full* **Martha Edith.** 1871–1938. American educator; at U. of Chicago (1924–38). Wrote *Out of the Cypress Swamp* (1902), *Folly* (1906), *The Golden Hawk* (1907), *The Greedy Goroo* (1929), *Severn Woods* (1929), etc. Collaborator with John Matthews Manly (*q.v.*) in *The Writing of English* (1919), *Contemporary British Literature* (1921), *Contemporary American Literature* (1922), *The Text of the Canterbury Tales* (publ. 1940), etc.

**Rick'ert** (rĭk'ẽrt), **Heinrich.** 1863–1936. German philosopher; disciple of Windelband and leader of so-called southwestern German or Baden school of philosophy.

**Rick'etts** (rĭk'ĕts; -ĭts), **Charles.** 1866–1931. British painter, sculptor, art critic, and stage-set designer. Designed stage settings for *King Lear, St. Joan, Henry VIII, Canterbury Mystery.* Coeditor of *The Dial* (1889–97).

**Ricketts, Howard Taylor.** 1871–1910. American pathologist; discovered that ticks transmit Rocky Mountain spotted fever and that body lice transmit typhus fever.

**Rick'man** (rĭk'măn), **Thomas.** 1776–1841. English architect; designer esp. of churches in Gothic style; author of *Attempt to Discriminate the Styles of Architecture in England* (1817), which was of influence in revival of medievalism.

**Rick'o'ver** (rĭk'ō'vẽr), **Hyman George.** 1900– . American naval officer, b. in Poland. A developer of first nuclear-powered submarine. Received Enrico Fermi Award (1965) for contributions to atomic science.

**Ri'cord'** (rē'kôr'), **Philippe.** 1800–1889. Physician, b. Baltimore, of French parentage. Personal physician to Napoleon III (from 1852). Specialized in treatment of venereal diseases; discovered and demonstrated that syphilis and gonorrhea are distinct diseases; devised special technique in urethroplasty.

**Ri·cor'di** (rē·kôr'dē). Family of Italian music publishers, including **Giovanni** (1788–1853), founder of publishing house Stabilimento Ricordi (1808); his son **Tito** (1811–1888), pianist; Tito's son **Giulio** (1840–1912), composer under the pseudonym **Burg'mein** (bo͝orK'-mīn); and Giulio's brother **Enrico** (d. 1887).

**Ric'tus'** (rēk'tüs'), **Jehan.** *Pseudonym of* **Gabriel Randon de Saint' A'mand'** (dē săN'-tà'mäN'). 1867–1933. French poet; author of frank verses dealing with the miseries and complaints of the poor.

**Rid'dell** (rĭd''l), 1st Baron. **George Allardice Riddell.** 1865–1934. English newspaper proprietor; practiced law in Cardiff, Wales. To London and gained control of Sunday paper *The News of the World.* Close friend of Lloyd George; during World War I, became chief intermediary between government and press.

**Riddell, Charlotte Eliza Lawson,** *nee* **Cow'an** (kou'ăn). *Known as* Mrs. **J. H. Riddell.** *Early pseudonym* **F. G. Traf'ford** (trăf'ẽrd). 1832–1906. Irish novelist; coproprietor and editor of *St. James's Magazine* (1867); wrote *The Moors and the Fens* (1858), *George Geith of Fen Court* (1864), *Footfall of Fate* (1900), etc.

**Riddell, Henry Scott.** 1798–1870. Scottish author of popular songs, as *The Crook and Plaid* and *Scotland Yet.*

**Rid'der** (rĭd'ẽr), **Herman.** 1851–1915. American journalist, b. New York City. Founded (1878) and edited (1878–86) *Katholisches Volksblatt,* New York City, a weekly Catholic paper. Founded *Catholic News* (1886), a similar journal published in English. Manager (from 1890) and president (from 1907) of company publishing *New-Yorker Staats-Zeitung,* German-language daily.

**Rid'dle** (rĭd''l), **Matthew Brown.** 1836–1916. American Reformed Dutch Church clergyman, b. Pittsburgh. Member, American committee on the revision of the New Testament; an editor of the American version.

**Riddle, Oscar.** 1877–1968. American zoologist. Investigations include work on the physiology of development and reproduction, the basis of sex, heredity, and internal secretions.

**Ride′out** (rīd′out), **Henry Milner.** 1877–1927. American writer; author of English textbooks, anthologies, and several novels and volumes of short stories.

**Ri′der** (rī′dẽr), **Fre′mont** (frē′mŏnt), *in full* **Arthur Fremont.** 1885–1962. American editor of *Monthly Book Review* (1909–17), *Publishers' Weekly* (1910–17), *American Library Annual* (1912–17), *Library Journal* (1914–17). President of The Rider Press, magazine publishers (1914–33), and Cumulative Digest Corp. (1915–31). Librarian, Wesleyan U. (1933–53).

**Ridge** (rĭj), **Lola.** 1883–1941. American poet, b. Dublin, Ireland; to Australia in childhood; to U.S. (1907), settled in New York; m. David Lawson. Author of *The Ghetto* (1918), *Sun-up* (1920), *Red Flag* (1927), *Firehead* (1929), *Dance of Fire* (1935).

**Ridge, William Pett.** 1860?–1930. English novelist.

**Ridge′way** (rĭj′wā), Sir **William.** 1853–1926. British archaeologist, b. in Ireland; author of *Origin of Metallic Currency and Weight Standards* (1892), *The Early Age of Greece* (1901), *The Origin of Tragedy* (1910), etc.

**Ridg′way** (rĭj′wā), **Robert.** 1850–1929. American ornithologist, b. Mount Carmel, Ill. On staff of Smithsonian Institution, in charge of bird collections (1869–80); curator of birds, U.S. National Museum (1880–1929). Devised Ridgway color system to aid in describing accurately bird coloration. Author of *A History of North American Birds* (with S. F. Baird and T. M. Brewer, 5 vols., I–III, 1874, IV–V, 1884), *Color Standards and Nomenclature* (1886), *The Birds of North and Middle America* (8 vols., 1901–19), etc.

**Ri′ding** (rī′dĭng), **Laura.** 1901– . American writer, b. New York City; m. (1941) Schuyler B. Jackson (d. 1968). Her poetry is represented in *Collected Poems* (1938); among her prose works are *Anarchism Is Not Enough* (1928), *Contemporaries and Snobs* (1928), *Experts Are Puzzled* (1930), *A Trojan Ending* (1937). Collaborated with Robert Graves in *A Survey of Modernist Poetry* (1927), *A Pamphlet against Anthologies* (1928).

**Ri′ding·er** *or* **Rie′ding·er** (rē′dĭng·ẽr), **Johann Elias.** 1698–1767. German painter, engraver, and etcher; best known for his depiction of animals.

**Rid′ley** (rĭd′lĭ), **Nicholas.** 1500?–1555. English reformer and Protestant martyr. Chaplain to Henry VIII and canon of Canterbury (1541); bishop of Rochester (1547). Pronounced in favor of reformed opinions; appointed as one of visitors to establish Protestantism in Cambridge U.; helped Cranmer with compilation of English prayer book and Thirty-nine Articles; succeeded Bonner as bishop of London on latter's deprivation (1550); active in propagation of reformed opinions. Denounced queens Mary and Elizabeth as illegitimate and espoused cause of Lady Jane Grey; on Mary's accession declared a heretic and excommunicated; condemned and burned alive, with Latimer.

**Ri·dol′fi** (rē·dôl′fē) *or* **Ri·dol′fo** (-fō), **Roberto di.** 1531–1612. Florentine conspirator in England; settled in London (c. 1555); plotted (from c. 1569) to marry Mary, Queen of Scots, to duke of Norfolk and set her on English throne; sought co-operation of duke of Alva, Pius V, and Philip II to overthrow Elizabeth; failed when his emissary Charles Baillie was seized (1571) and Norfolk and Leslie were arrested.

**Rid′path** (rĭd′påth), **John Clark.** 1840–1900. American historian, b. in Putnam County, Ind.; author of popular histories and historical textbooks, including *A Popular History of the United States of America* (1876), *Cyclopedia of Universal History* (4 vols., 1880–85), *Great Races of Mankind* (4 vols., 1884–94). Editor in chief, *The Ridpath Library of Universal Literature* (25 vols., 1898).

**Rie′beeck** (rē′bāk) *or* **Rie′beek** (-bāk) *or* **Rie′beck** (-bĕk), **Jan van.** b. 1634. Dutch naval surgeon and pioneer in South Africa; founded Cape Town (1652) and remained in South Africa (to 1662). Later, governor of Malacca and secretary to council of India.

**Rieck′e** (rē′kĕ), **Carl Viktor Eduard.** 1845–1915. German physicist; worked on the physics of crystals and on electrical conduction in metals in accordance with the electron theory.

**Rie′de′sel** (rē′dā′zĕl), Baron **Friedrich Adolph von.** 1738–1800. German army officer, b. in Hesse; commanded Brunswick contingent in British army serving against the Americans in the Revolution; captured at Saratoga (1777), exchanged (1779), in command on Long Island (1779–80); left memoirs, letters, etc. translated by W. L. Stone (1868).

**Riedinger, Johann Elias.** See Ridinger.

**Rie′ger** (rē′gẽr), Baron **Franz Ladislaus von.** 1818–1903. Czech statesman and party leader. Leader of Czech movement in Prague revolution (1848); coleader (with father-in-law, Palacký) of Czech National party of conservative Old Czechs (1860); took part in Bohemian Declaration demanding Czech rights and Bohemian autonomy (1868); lost seat in Reichsrat following supremacy of radical Young Czechs (1891); member, Austrian House of Lords (1897); created baron (1898).

**Riegl** (rē′g'l), **Alois.** 1858–1905. Austrian art scholar; carried on researches in relationship between Oriental and ancient art and in medieval western European art.

**Rie′go y Nú′ñez** (ryā′gō ē nōō′nyāth), **Rafael del.** 1785–1823. Spanish patriot; active in Peninsular War against Napoleonic domination; military leader of Revolution of 1820; president of the Cortes (1822–23); captured while resisting intervention of Holy Alliance, Málaga (1823); executed as traitor.

**Riehl** (rēl), **Alois.** 1844–1924. German positivist neo-Kantian philosopher, logician, and critic; author of *Der Philosophische Kritizismus* (3 vols., 1876–87), *Friedrich Nietzsche* (1897), *Zur Einführung in die Philosophie der Gegenwart* (1903), etc.

**Riehl, Wilhelm Heinrich von.** 1823–1897. German historian of culture and novelist; professor of political economy (1854) and history of culture (from 1859), Munich, and (1885) director of Bavarian National Museum. Author of works on history of culture, and the stories *Geschichten aus Alter Zeit* (1862–64), *Neues Novellenbuch* (1867), etc.

**Riel** (ryĕl), **Louis.** 1844–1885. Canadian insurgent leader, b. Manitoba, a French half-breed with Indian and Irish ancestors. Succeeded father as leader of métis, or French half-breeds, who became alarmed lest they lose rights and titles to land through incorporation of Northwest Territories into Canadian Dominion; headed rebels who captured Fort Garry (Winnipeg) and set up provisional government in valley of Red River; decamped on capture of Fort Garry by Col. Garnet Wolseley (Sept., 1870). Established second rebel government in Manitoba, bent on redressing wrongs of métis; began active warfare; surrendered after fall of Batoche (1885); found guilty of treason and hanged.

**Rie′mann** (rē′män), **Georg Friedrich Bernhard.** 1826–1866. German mathematician; originated a non-Euclidean system of geometry; contributed to the development of the theory of functions; imagined Riemann's surface; applied theory of potential to pure mathematics. Worked in mathematical physics.

**Riemann, Hugo,** *in full* **Karl Wilhelm Julius Hugo.**

1849–1919. German musical historian and critic. Composed technical studies and exercises for piano, chamber music, songs, and choruses. Author of musical textbooks, reference books, and historical studies, including *Musiklexikon* (1882; 11th ed., 1929).

**Rie′men·schnei′der** (rē′mĕn·shnī′dẽr), **Tilman** *or* **Till** *or* **Dill.** 1460?–1531. German sculptor and woodcarver. Settled in Würzburg (1483); imprisoned (1525) and tortured for siding against bishop in Peasants' War; lived subsequently in retirement. His works include stone figures of Adam and Eve, tomb of Bishop Rudolf von Scherenberg, tomb of Henry II and his wife, and altars.

**Rie′mer** (rē′mẽr), **Friedrich Wilhelm.** 1774–1845. German scholar and literary historian; teacher of Goethe's son (1803) and literary assistant to Goethe (until 1812); librarian, Weimar. Compiled a Greek-German dictionary (1802–04), wrote *Gedichte* (2 vols., 1826), and *Mitteilungen über Goethe* (2 vols., 1841), and edited many of Goethe's works.

**Rien′zi** (ryĕn′tsē) *or* **Rien′zo** (-tsō), **Cola di.** *Real name* **Niccolo Ga·bri′ni** (gä·brē′nē). 1313–1354. Italian patriot, called "last of the Romans." Led revolution in Rome (1347), overthrew the aristocratic government, and promulgated a new constitution. Became head of the Roman state, with title of tribune; antagonized the people by his arbitrary policies and the pope by his territorial ambitions; expelled from Rome (1348). Returned to Rome (1354) and again assumed dictatorial attitude and powers; murdered in a riot (Oct. 8, 1354). Hero of an opera by Wagner and a novel by Bulwer-Lytton.

**Rie′pen·hau′sen** (rē′pĕn·hou′zĕn), **Franz,** *orig.* **Friedrich** (1786–1831), and his brother **Johannes,** *orig.* **Christian** (1789–1860). German painters, designers, and etchers; resident in Rome (from 1805).

**Ries** (rēs). A family of German musicians, including: **Ferdinand** (1784–1838), pianist and composer; pupil of Beethoven (1801–05); resident in London (1813–24); coauthor of *Biographische Notizen über Ludwig van Beethoven* (1838); composer of operas, oratorios, symphonies, overtures, piano concertos, and much piano and chamber music. His brother **Hubert** (1802–1886), violinist and composer of violin studies, was imperial concertmeister, Berlin (1836–72). Hubert's son **Franz** (1846–1932), violinist, composer, and music publisher, was co-owner (from 1881) and manager (until 1924) of Ries and Erler, music publishers in Berlin; composed orchestral and chamber music, songs, and piano pieces.

**Rie′se** (rē′zĕ) *or* **Ries** (rēs), **Adam.** 1492–1559. German arithmetician; reputed originator of the radical sign commonly used today.

**Rie′sen·berg** (rē′z'n·bûrg), **Felix.** 1879–1939. American engineer and writer, b. Milwaukee, Wis.; with Wellman polar expedition (1906–07); navigator of airship *America* in first attempt to reach North Pole by dirigible (Sept., 1907). In engineering work, New York City (1911–39). Author of many books of the sea.

**Rie′se·ner** (rē′zĕ·nẽr; *Fr.* rēz′nâr′), **Jean Henri.** 1734–1806. Cabinetmaker in Paris, b. in Prussia; master of marquetry. In Paris (1767); ebonist to the king (1782).

**Ries′man** (rēs′măn), **David.** 1909– . American social scientist, b. Philadelphia, Pa. At U. of Chicago (1946–58); Harvard U. (1958– ). Wrote *The Lonely Crowd.*

**Riet′schel** (rē′chĕl), **Ernst.** 1804–1861. German sculptor of the Dresden school. His works include bronze statues of Frederick Augustus I of Saxony, Lessing, Goethe, and Schiller, gable groups for Leipzig U. and for the Berlin Opera House, memorials to Luther, etc.

**Rietz** (rēts), **Julius.** 1812–1877. German composer, violoncellist, and conductor; succeeded Mendelssohn as chief conductor, Düsseldorf opera (1835); later, director in Leipzig and Dresden; composed operas, symphonies, overtures, incidental music to works of Goethe and others, choruses, chamber music, piano pieces, and songs; edited chief operas of Mozart and complete works of Mendelssohn (1874–77).

**Rigas.** See RHEGAS.

**Ri′gaud′** (rē′gō′), **André.** 1761–1811. Haitian general, b. Cayes, Haiti; opposed Toussaint L'Ouverture; was defeated and withdrew to France; returned to Haiti with Leclerc; imprisoned with Toussaint L'Ouverture; escaped and aroused Haitians in rebellion against Pétion (1810) but was defeated.

**Rigaud, Hyacinthe.** *Real name* **Hyacinthe François Honorat Mathias Pierre Martyr André Jean Ri·gau′ y Ros′** (rē·gou′ ē rōs′). 1659–1743. French portrait painter.

**Ri′gault′** (rē′gō′), **Ange Hippolyte.** 1821–1858. French writer; author of *Histoire de la Querelle des Anciens et des Modernes* (1856), etc.

**Rig′don** (rĭg′dŭn), **Sidney.** 1793–1876. American Mormon leader, b. in Allegheny County, Pa. In Baptist ministry (1819); identified with Campbellite movement (1828–30), and with Mormons (from 1830). Became first counselor to Joseph Smith, founder of Mormonism, and official spokesman for Smith and the Mormon Church. After Smith's assassination (1844), was excommunicated from Mormon Church by Brigham Young. Rallied group of Mormons who proclaimed him first president, prophet, seer; new group gradually disintegrated, and Rigdon spent last years in Friendship, N.Y.

**Rigg** (rĭg), **James Harrison.** 1821–1909. English Wesleyan clergyman and writer in exposition and defense of Methodism.

**Riggs** (rĭgz), **Elias.** 1810–1901. American missionary in Greece, Asia Minor, and Turkey (1832–1901); made Armenian translation of the Scriptures (publ. 1853), Bulgarian translation (publ. 1871), and was member of committee preparing standard Turkish text (publ. 1878).

**Riggs, John Mankey.** 1810–1885. American dentist; studied dentistry with Dr. Horace Wells of Hartford, Conn.; practiced, Hartford (from 1840). Stressed hygienic care of mouth for prevention of tooth decay; originated treatment for pyorrhea alveolaris, which became widely known as Riggs' disease. Aided Dr. Horace Wells and G. Q. Colton in first use of nitrous oxide gas (laughing gas) as an anesthetic, extracting one of Dr. Wells's teeth after Wells had been anesthetized by Colton (Dec. 11, 1844).

**Riggs, William Henry.** 1837–1924. American collector (from 1857) of medieval armor, arms, and art; donor of collection (1913) to Metropolitan Museum of Art, New York City, where it is exhibited in Riggs Armor Hall.

**Ri′ghi** (rē′gē), **Augusto.** 1850–1920. Italian physicist; known for researches on electricity; designed an electrical oscillator.

**Riis** (rēs), **Jacob August.** 1849–1914. Journalist and writer, b. in Ribe, Denmark; to U.S. (1870). Police reporter on staff of New York *Tribune* (1877–88) and New York *Evening Sun* (1888–99). Active in improving conditions in schools and tenements of lower New York; introduced parks and playgrounds in congested districts; established Jacob A. Riis Neighborhood House for social work in former Mulberry Bend block (1888–89). Intimate friend of and co-worker with Theodore Roosevelt. Author of *How the Other Half Lives* (1890), *The Children of the Poor* (1892), *The Making of an American* (1901), *Children of the Tenements* (1903), *Theodore Roosevelt the Citizen* (1904), *Neighbors: Life Stories of the Other Half* (1914), etc.

**Ri'ley** (rī'lĭ), **Charles Valentine.** 1843–1895. Entomologist, b. London, Eng.; to U.S. (1860). First chief, U.S. Entomological Commission (1877–78); entomologist to U.S. Department of Agriculture (1878–79, 1881–94). Published *Insect Life* (1889–94).

**Riley, James Whitcomb.** 1849–1916. American poet, b. Greenfield, Ind. On staff of Indianapolis *Journal* (1877–85); by contributions of verse to this paper established his fame. Wrote many dialect poems dealing with scenes of simple life and marked by kindly humor, pathos, sincerity, and naturalness; gained sobriquet of "Hoosier poet"; has also been called "the poet laureate of democracy." Among his works are *The Old Swimmin' Hole and 'Leven More Poems* (under pseudonym "Benj. F. Johnson, of Boone," 1883), *Old Fashioned Roses* (1888), *Rhymes of Childhood* (1890), *Green Fields and Running Brooks* (1892), *Book of Joyous Children* (1902), *Out to Old Aunt Mary's* (1904), *The Raggedy Man* (1907), *The Little Orfant Annie Book* (1908), *When the Frost is on the Punkin* (1911), *Old Times* (1915), etc.

**Ril'ke** (rĭl'kĕ), **Rainer Maria.** 1875–1926. German lyric poet and writer, b. in Prague; resident in Paris (1902 ff.), where he was secretary to Auguste Rodin, and in Italy, Scandinavia, Austria, and Switzerland. Author of lyric collections, tales, the lyrical prayer book *Stundenbuch* (1905), the narrative poem *Die Weise von Liebe und Tod des Cornets Christoph Rilke* (1906), the introspective novel *Aufzeichnungen des Malte Laurids Brigge* (2 vols., 1910), etc.

**Rim'baud'** (răN'bō'), **Arthur,** *in full* **Jean Nicolas Arthur.** 1854–1891. French poet; identified with the symbolists and associated for a time with Verlaine. Wrote his verse chiefly before the age of 20; led vagabond life for several years (from 1873); went into business as merchant and trader in North Africa, and amassed a fortune (1880–91); author of *Le Dormeur du Val, Le Bateau Ivre, Une Saison en Enfer, Les Illuminations* (published by Verlaine, and containing his very original *Sonnet des Voyelles*).

**Rimini, Francesca da.** See FRANCESCA DA RIMINI.

**Rim'mer** (rĭm'ẽr), **William.** 1816–1879. Sculptor, b. Liverpool, Eng.; to America (1818). Stonecutter, sculptor, and painter, East Milton, Mass., where a patron brought his work to public attention. Studio in Boston (from 1870). Among his best-known sculptures are *Alexander Hamilton, Chaldean Shepherd, Endymion, Osiris.* His *St. Stephen* is in Boston Museum; *The Falling Gladiator, Fighting Lions,* and *The Dying Centaur,* in Metropolitan Museum of Art, New York.

**Rim'ski–Kor·sa·kov'** (ryĕm'skû·ĭ·kŭr·sŭ·kôf'; *Angl.* rĭm'skĭ·kôr'sȧ·kŏf), **Nikolai Andreevich.** 1844–1908. Russian composer, b. Tikhvin; grad. Naval Academy, St. Petersburg, and served a few years in the Russian navy; professor, St. Petersburg Conservatory of Music (1871); inspector of naval bands (1873–84). Among his operas are *The Maid of Pskov* (*Pskovitianka*), *The Snow Maiden* (*Snegurochka*), *Mlada, The Czar's Betrothed, The Immortal Koshchei, Mozart and Salieri, Pan Voevoda, Le Coq d'Or;* among his symphonic poems, *Sadko, Fairy Tales,* and *Scheherazade;* also composed symphonies, overtures, choral works, and piano pieces.

**Rin·cón'** (rĕng·kōn'), **Antonio del.** 1446–1500. Spanish painter, b. Guadalajara; considered by some as founder of Spanish school of painting; first to abandon Gothic style. Among his works are portraits of Ferdinand and Isabella, and the seventeen-panel altarpiece *Life of the Virgin* (in Church of Robledo de Chevala, Toledo).

**Rine'hart** (rīn'härt), **Mary,** *nee* **Roberts.** 1876–1958. American fiction writer and playwright, b. Pittsburgh; m. Stanley Marshall Rinehart (1896; d. 1932). Her works include: *The Circular Staircase* (1908), *Amazing Adventures of Letitia Carberry* (1911), *Tish* (1916), *The Amazing Interlude* (1917), *The Breaking Point* (1922), *Lost Ecstasy* (1927), *The Romantics* (1929), *The Door* (1930), *Miss Pinkerton* (1932), *Married People* (1937), *The Wall* (1938), *Double Life* (play; 1907), *Seven Days* (farce; with Avery Hopwood, 1909), *Cheer Up* (farce; 1913), *Tish* (play; 1919), *Spanish Love* and *The Bat* (plays; with Avery Hopwood, 1920), *The Breaking Point* (play; 1923).

**Rinehart, Stanley M., Jr.** 1897–1969. Son of Mary Roberts Rinehart. American publisher, b. Pittsburgh, Pa. Served in World War (1917–19). On staff of George H. Doran Co. and Doubleday, Doran & Co. (1919–29). With his brother **Frederick R.** (1902–    ), and with John Farrar, founded publishing house Farrar and Rinehart, Stanley becoming president and Frederick secretary-treasurer of the firm.

**Rinehart, William Henry.** 1825–1874. American sculptor, b. near Union Bridge, Md. Studio in Italy (from 1855). Among his well-known works are *Latona and Her Children* and *Rebecca,* in Metropolitan Museum of Art, New York City; *Clytie, Hero, Day, Night, Strewing Flowers,* in Corcoran Gallery, Washington, D.C. He completed Thomas Crawford's work on the bronze doors for the Capitol, Washington, D.C.

**Ring'er** (rĭng'ẽr), **Sydney.** 1835–1910. English physician; known for work in clinical medicine and for physiological researches, esp. on the influence of organic salts on the circulation and heart beat.

**Ring'ling** (rĭng'lĭng). Name of five brothers, American circus owners: **Albert C.** (1852–1916), **Otto** (1858–1911), **Alfred T.** (1861–1919), **Charles** (1863–1926), and **John** (1866–1936). Organized their first circus (1884); acquired Forepaugh-Sells circus (1906) and Barnum and Bailey circus (1907).

**Ringuet.** Pseudonym of Philippe PANNETON.

**Rin'te·len** (rĭn'tĕ·lĕn), **Anton.** 1876–1946. Austrian jurist and politician; involved in Nazi Putsch in Austria (1934); sentenced to life imprisonment (1935); amnestied (1936).

**Ri'nuc·ci'ni** (rē'nōōt·chē'nē), **Ottavio.** 1562–1621. Italian poet; author of first Italian melodrama, *Dafne* (1594; music by Jacopo Peri), based on the Greek recitative.

**Rio'ja** (ryō'hä), **Francisco de.** 1586?–1659. Spanish poet; follower of Herrera; known esp. for lyric poems, including sonnets, canciones, and silvas (verse of peculiar metrical arrangement).

**Ríos, José Amador de los.** See AMADOR DE LOS RÍOS.

**Ríos** (rē'ōs), **Juan Antonio.** 1888–1946. Chilean lawyer and statesman, b. Cañete; minister of the interior (1932), of justice (1932); president of Chile (1942–46).

**Rip'ley** (rĭp'lĭ), **Eleazar Wheelock.** 1782–1839. American army officer in War of 1812; engaged at Fort George and took part in Wilkinson's unsuccessful invasion of Canada (1813); brigadier general (Apr. 15, 1814); engaged at Fort Erie, Lundy's Lane (1814); member, U.S. House of Representatives (1835–39).

**Ripley, George.** 1802–1880. American literary critic and social reformer, b. Greenfield, Mass. Ordained in Unitarian ministry (1826); pastor, Purchase Street Church, Boston (1826–41); withdrew from Unitarian ministry (1841). Associated with Emerson, Alcott, Margaret Fuller, and others in what has become known as the transcendental school (from 1836); founded the *Dial* (1840) and aided Margaret Fuller in editing it. Organized and headed Brook Farm, officially known as The Brook Farm Institute of Agriculture and Education (1841–47), where a group tried the experiment of communal living; made it a phalanx of Fourier socialism by new constitution (1844). Edited the *Harbinger*, a Fourierite magazine (1845–49). Literary critic, New York *Tribune* (1849–80). Founder (1850) and literary editor, *Harper's New Monthly Magazine*. With Charles A. Dana, edited *New American Cyclopaedia* (16 vols., 1858–63).

**Ripley, William Ze·bi′na** (zĕ·bī′nȧ). 1867–1941. American economist, b. Medford, Mass.; professor, M.I.T. (1895–1901), Harvard (1901–33). Expert on transportation problems for U.S. Industrial Commission (1900–01). Author of *Financial History of Virginia* (1890), *Races of Europe* (1899), *Trusts, Pools and Corporations* (1905), *Railway Problems* (1907), *Main Street and Wall Street* (1927).

**Rip′man** (rĭp′măn), **Walter.** *Orig.* **Ripp′mann.** 1869–1947. English educator, b. London; among his many books are *Elements of Phonetics* (1899), *The Sounds of Spoken English* (1906), *German Grammar* (1909), *Dictionary of English Rhymes* (1932), and many textbooks in French and German.

**Ripon,** Earl of, and marquis of. See Frederick John ROBINSON.

**Rip′per·da** (rĭp′ẽr·dȧ), **Jan Willem,** Duke of. 1680–1737. Dutch-born adventurer; Dutch ambassador to Spain (1715); became a Roman Catholic and entered Spanish diplomatic service; represented Spain at Vienna (1724–25) and concluded treaty of alliance between Spain and Emperor Charles VI; was created duke and prime minister of Spain (1725–26). On failure of the alliance, was imprisoned (1726–28), escaped to Holland, and again became a Protestant. Later, served under the sultan of Morocco; became a Mohammedan; adopted name **Os·man′ Pa′sha** (ŏŏs·mȧn′ [ŏŏth·män′] pȧ′shä); commanded army defeated at Ceuta (1733); spent last years in exile at Tetuán.

**Rippl–Ró′nai** (rĭp″'l·rō′noi), **József.** 1861–1927. Hungarian painter and graphic artist; exponent of modern Hungarian art; works include portraits (*My Mother*), pastels, etchings, lithographs, and designs for glass paintings, gobelins, and bookbindings.

**Ri′quet′** (rē′kĕ′), **Pierre Paul de.** 1604–1680. French engineer; planned Languedoc Canal to connect Atlantic Ocean and Mediterranean Sea; brought plan to Colbert (1662) and received approval of Colbert and Louis XIV; spent rest of his life and his personal fortune building the canal which was carried to completion six months after his death.

**Ri′sing** (rē′sĭng), **Johan Classon.** 1617–1672. Swedish colonial governor in America; governor of New Sweden, Swedish colony on Delaware River (1654–55); colony conquered by Dutch under Stuyvesant (Aug., 1655).

**Ris′ler′** (rēz′lâr′), **Joseph Édouard.** 1873–1929. French pianist; interpreter of Liszt and Beethoven.

**Ris′ley** (rĭz′lĭ), Sir **Herbert Hope.** 1851–1911. English civil servant in India and anthropologist; author of *Anthropometric Data* (2 vols., 1891), *Ethnographical Glossary* (2 vols., 1892), and *The People of India* (1908).

**Ris′so** (rēs′sō), **Giovanni Antonio.** 1777–1845. Italian naturalist; known for work on the mollusks of the Mediterranean.

**Rist** (rēst), **Charles.** 1873–1955. French economist, b. Lausanne, Switzerland. Subgovernor, Bank of France (1926–29); financial adviser to national banks of Rumania and, later, Austria (1931). Among works are *Histoire des Doctrines Économiques depuis les Physiocrates jusqu'à nos jours* (with Gide; 1909), *History of Monetary and Credit Theory* (trans. 1940), etc.

**Rist** (rĭst), **Johann von.** 1607–1667. German poet and writer; wrote words and some of the music for many sacred and secular songs, including the hymn *O Ewigkeit, Du Donnerwort;* also, allegorical musical plays.

**Ris′tić** (rēs′tēt·y′; *Angl.* rĭs′tĭch), **Jovan.** 1831–1899. Serbian statesman; premier of Serbia (1872–73, 1875, 1876–80, 1887–88); chief of council of regency (1889–93).

**Ri·sto′ri** (rē·stô′rē), **Adelaide.** 1822–1906. Italian actress; m. Marchese Capranica del Grillo (1847); one of leading tragediennes of European stage; played principally in Paris. Among her notable roles were Francesca da Rimini, Maria Stuart, Medea, Phaedra, Lady Macbeth, and Pia dei Tolomei.

**Ritch′ey** (rĭch′ĭ), **George Willis. 1864–1945.** American astronomer; on staff of Yerkes Observatory (1896–1904), solar observatory in Carnegie Institution (1905–09), Mt. Wilson Observatory; director of astrophotographic laboratory at Observatoire de Paris (1924–30). Coinventor of an aplanatic reflecting telescope; inventor of fixed vertical universal type of reflecting telescope, and of cellular type of optical mirrors; designer (1931) and constructor of a 40-in. reflecting telescope, at the U.S. naval observatory in Washington, D.C.

**Ritch′ie** (rĭch′ĭ), **Anna Cora Mowatt.** See MOWATT.

**Ritchie, Anne Isabella,** *nee* **Thack′er·ay** (thăk′ẽr·ĭ). 1837–1919. English novelist; eldest daughter of William Makepeace Thackeray; m. (1877) her second cousin Sir **Richmond Thackeray Willoughby Ritchie** (1854–1912; secretary in political and secret department of India Office, 1902; permanent undersecretary of state, 1909). Wrote novels, including *The Village on the Cliff* (1867), *Old Kensington* (1873), and several volumes of essays.

**Ritchie, Charles Thomson.** 1st Baron **Ritchie.** 1838–1906. British legislator; Conservative M.P. (1874); president of local government board (1886–92), in Lord Salisbury's cabinet (from 1887); carried revolutionary local government bill for England and Wales (1888); president of Board of Trade (1895–1900); home secretary (1900–02); chancellor of exchequer in Balfour's cabinet (1902); resigned because of opposition to Chamberlain's proposals for a preferential tariff (1903).

**Ritchie,** Sir **Lewis.** *Formerly* **L. A. da Costa Ric′ci** (rĭch′ĭ). *Pseudonym* **Bar′ti·me′us** (bär′tĭ·mē′ŭs). 1886–1967. British naval paymaster and writer. Author of *Naval Occasions* (1914), *The Long Trick* (1917), *Seaways* (1923), *An Off-Shore Wind* (1936), and *Under Sealed Orders* (1938).

**Ritchie, Neil Methuen.** 1897– . British army commander, b. in Hampshire, Eng., of Scottish ancestry; served through World War (1914–18); member of General Auchinleck's staff (1940); deputy chief of staff in Middle East (1941); commander of 8th army in Libya (1941–42), of East Asia land forces (1947); lieutenant general (1945).

**Ritchie, Thomas.** 1778–1854. American journalist, b. Tappahannock, Va.; founded (1804) and edited (1804–45), Richmond *Enquirer*, establishing it as one of leading papers in U.S.; edited *Union*, Washington, D.C. (1845–51).

**Ritchie,** Sir **William Johnstone.** 1813–1892. Canadian jurist; chief justice of Canada (1879–92).

**Rit′schl** (rĭch′ĕl), **Albrecht.** 1822–1889. German Protestant theologian; founded Ritschlian school or movement, emphasizing the ethical-social content of theology and holding that Christian theology should rest mainly on an appreciation of the inner life of Christ.

**Ritschl, Friedrich Wilhelm.** 1806–1876. Cousin of Albrecht Ritschl. German classical philologist; edited *Priscae Latinitatis Monumenta Epigraphica* (1862); author of works on Plautus, and studies on linguistic history, metrics, and epigraphy, collected in *Opuscula Philologica* (5 vols., 1867–79), etc.

**Rit'son** (rĭt's'n), **Joseph.** 1752–1803. English literary antiquary; made savage onslaught on Warton's *History of English Poetry;* assailed Johnson and Steevens for their texts of Shakespeare; made strictures on Percy's *Reliques;* detected antiquary John Pinkerton's forgeries in *Select Scottish Ballads* (1784) and the Ireland forgeries (1795).

**Rit'ten·house** (rĭt''n·hous), **David.** 1732–1796. Great-grandson of William Rittenhouse. American astronomer, b. near Germantown, Pa. Gained reputation by building two orreries, one for Princeton U. (c. 1767) and one for the U. of Pennsylvania. Built observatory and a transit telescope, believed to be first telescope made in America, to observe the transit of Venus (1769). Inventor of a collimating telescope (1785); one of earliest to use spider webs in the eyepiece of a telescope. During Revolutionary War, served as member of Pennsylvania assembly (1776) and president of the council of safety (1777); treasurer of Pennsylvania (1777–89). First director, U.S. Mint (1792–95). President, succeeding Benjamin Franklin, American Philosophical Society (1791–96).

**Rittenhouse, Jessie Belle.** 1869–1948. American critic and poet, b. Mount Morris, N.Y.; m. Clinton Scollard (1924). A founder, Poetry Society of America. Edited, *The Rubáiyát of Omar Khayyám* (1900), and several anthologies of poetry. Author of *The Younger American Poets* (1904), verse including *The Door of Dreams* (1918), *The Lifted Cup* (1921), *The Secret Bird* (1930), and an autobiography, *My House of Life* (1934).

**Rittenhouse, William.** 1644–1708. Clergyman and industrialist, b. Mülheim an der Ruhr, Prussia. Became Mennonite clergyman and paper manufacturer. To America (1688) and settled in Germantown, Pa.; chosen first pastor of the Mennonite group there; elected bishop (1703) of first Mennonite church in America. Organized paper-manufacturing company and built (1690) first paper mill in America.

**Rit'ter** (rĭt'ẽr), **Alexander.** 1833–1896. German violinist and composer; disciple of Liszt and Wagner, and champion of the modern German school. His works include chiefly operas, symphonies, and songs.

**Rit'ter** (rĭt'ẽr), **Frédéric Louis.** 1834–1891. Composer and educator, b. in Alsace; to U.S. (1856); conductor, Sacred Harmonic Society, and Arion male chorus. Professor of music, Vassar College (1867–91). Composer of symphonies, concertos for piano and violoncello, chamber music, organ music, choral pieces, and songs.

**Ritter, Gerhard.** 1888–1967. German historian; author of *Stein...Biographie* (1931), *Friedrich der Grosse...* (1936), and treatises on medieval history.

**Ritter, Heinrich.** 1791–1869. German philosopher; author of *Geschichte der Philosophie* (12 vols., 1829–53), *Historia Philosophiae Graeco-Romanae* (with Preller; 1838), *Enzyklopädie der Philosophischen Wissenschaften* (3 vols., 1862–64), and other works on logic, metaphysics, and ethics.

**Ritter, Johann Wilhelm.** 1776–1810. German physicist; discovered existence of ultraviolet rays through their photochemical action; conducted researches in electricity, anticipating subsequent discoveries.

**Ritter, Joseph Elmer.** 1891–1967. American Roman Catholic prelate, b. New Albany, Ind. Ordained (1917); archbishop of Indianapolis (1944–46), of St. Louis (1946–61); cardinal (1961).

**Ritter, Karl.** 1779–1859. German geographer; one of the founders of modern scientific geography; showed the influence of geographical features on the course of history and the relationship between man and nature.

**Rit'ters·haus'** (rĭt'ẽrs·hous'), **Emil.** 1834–1897. German lyric poet and insurance agent.

**Ritt'ner** (rĭt'nẽr), **Thaddäus.** 1873?–1921. German-Polish playwright and novelist.

**Ritz** (rĭts), **César.** 1850–1918. Swiss-born hotelkeeper and restaurateur.

**Ri'va A·güe'ro** (rē'vä ä·gwā'rō), **José de la.** 1783–1858. Peruvian soldier and politician, b. Lima; one of early leaders for independence of Peru; joined army of San Martín (1821) and twice imprisoned; first president of Peru republic (Feb. to June, 1823) but compelled by Bolívar and Sucre to resign.

**Ri'va·da'via** (rē'vä·thä'vyä), **Bernardino.** 1780–1845. Argentine statesman; active in struggle for independence (1811–14); Argentine envoy in London, Paris, and Madrid (1814–20); governor of Buenos Aires (1820–23); president of the Argentine Confederation (1826–27); resigned (June 27, 1827) to avert civil war. Spent most of his later years in exile.

**Ri'va·de·nei'ra** (rē'vä·thā·nĕ'ē·rä). Variant of RIBADENEIRA.

**Ri'va·ro'la** (rē'vä·rō'lä), **Cirilo.** d. 1871. Paraguayan political leader; fought in war against Argentina (1865–70); first president of republic of Paraguay (1870–71; retired); killed.

**Ri'va·ro'li** (rē'vä·rô'lē), **An'toine'** (äN'twȧn'). *Called* Comte **de Ri'va'rol'** (dẽ rē'vȧ'rôl'). 1753–1801. French journalist of Italian descent; settled in Paris (c. 1780). At outbreak of French Revolution, took royalist side; an émigré (from 1792) in Brussels, London, and Hamburg. Best known for his epigrams, collected under the title *L'Esprit de Rivarol.*

**Ri'vas** (rē'väs), Duque **de. Ángel de Sa'a·ve'dra** (thä sä'ä·vā'thrä). 1791–1865. Spanish politician and man of letters, b. Córdoba. Fought in war of independence and was condemned to death (1823), but escaped; lived in exile until the amnesty (1834). Minister of interior (1835) and shortly thereafter again forced into exile. Returned to Spain, became premier and, later, ambassador in Naples, Paris (1856), and Florence (1860). Author of *Ensayos Poéticos* (1813), *Florinda* (an epic; 1825), *El Moro Expósito* (epic; 1834), *Don Álvaro* (play; 1835), *La Morisca de Alajuar* (1842), etc. Credited with introducing romanticism in Spanish literature.

**Ri·ve'ra** (rē·vā'rä). Variant of RIBERA.

**Rivera, Diego.** 1886–1957. Mexican painter, esp. of murals. His communist sympathies are reflected in his paintings; his murals in Rockefeller Center, New York City, were removed as a result of a controversy over their political implications.

**Rivera, José Fructuoso.** 1790?–1854. Uruguayan general and statesman, b. Paysandú, of Gaucho descent. Served under Artigas and was one of "the Thirty-three Immortals" who freed Uruguay (after 1825); led revolution (1830) and became first president of Uruguay (1830–35); at first supported Oribe, but later (1838) led revolt that deposed him; again president (1838–42); participated in nine-year Civil War (1842–51), leader of Colorados, besieged in Montevideo; defeated by Urquiza at the battle of India Muerta (1845) and fled to Brazil; chosen as one of three to administer provisional government of Uruguay (1853) but died the next year.

**Rivera y Or'ba·ne'ja** (ē ôr'bä·nĕ'hä), **Miguel Pri'mo de** (prē'mō thā). Marqués **de Es·tel'la** (thā ās·tā'lyä). 1870–1930. Spanish general and dictator, b. Cádiz. In Spanish-American War, served in Cuba and Philippines (1898); in Morocco (1909–13); military governor of Cádiz (1915–17), of Barcelona (1922). After bloodless revolution became dictator and proclaimed martial law (1923); led in person campaign in Morocco (1924) against Abd-el-Krim, but only partly successful; premier (actually dictator) of reconstituted government (1925–

30). Secured surrender of Abd-el-Krim in war in Morocco, with aid of France (1926). At first supported by king and army officers but finally forced by them to retire (1930); died suddenly in Paris. His son **José Antonio Primo de Rivera** (d. 1939) was founder of Fascist (Falangist) movement in Spain; killed by Loyalists in civil war.

**Riv'ers** (rĭv'ẽrz), Earl. See (1) Richard and Anthony WOODVILLE; (2) Richard SAVAGE.

**Rivers, William Halse Rivers.** 1864–1922. English physiologist and anthropologist; founder of Cambridge school of experimental psychology; on anthropological expedition to Torres Straits (1898), to Melanesia (1908); psychopathologist during World War. Author of *History of Melanesian Society* (2 vols., 1914), *Instinct and the Unconscious* (1920), *Psychology and Politics* (published posthumously, 1923), etc.

**Riverton, Stein.** Pseudonym of Sven ELVESTAD.

**Rives** (rēvz), **A'mé'lie'** (ȧ'mā'lē'). Princess **Trou'betz·koy** (trōō'bĕts·koi; *Russ.* trŏŏ·byĕts·koi'). 1863–1945. American novelist and playwright, b. Richmond, Va.; m. John Armstrong Chanler (1888; divorced), Prince Pierre Troubetzkoy (1896; d. 1936). Author of *The Quick or the Dead* (1888), *Barbara Dering* (1892), *Athelwold* (1893), *Selené* (a poem, 1905), *Trix and Over-the-Moon* (1909), *World's End* (1913), *As the Wind Blew* (poems, 1922), *Firedamp* (1930); and the plays *Herod and Mariamne* (1888), *The Fear Market* (1916), *Allegiance* (1918), *Love-in-a-Mist* (with Gilbert Emery, 1926), *The Young Elizabeth* (1937), etc.

**Rives, William Cabell.** 1793–1868. American political leader, b. in Amherst County, Va.; member, U.S. House of Representatives (1823–29); U.S. minister to France (1829–32); U.S. senator (1832–34, 1836–39, 1841–45); again, U.S. minister to France (1849–53); member of Confederate Congress (1861–62).

**Riv'i·ere'** (?rĭv'ĭ·âr'), **Briton.** 1840–1920. English painter; son and pupil of **William Riviere** (1806–1876), painter and drawing master of Huguenot ancestry. Passed from Pre-Raphaelite to Scottish influence; contributor to *Punch;* made specialty of animal and figure paintings. An uncle, **Robert** (1808–1882), was a bookseller and noted bookbinder, in Bath (1829–40) and London (from 1840), binding books for collectors, including duke of Devonshire.

**Ri'vière'** (rē'vyâr'), **Henri Laurent.** 1827–1883. French naval officer; ambushed and killed by pirates near Hanoï (May 19, 1883). Author of novels, comedies, and the historical study *La Marine Française sous Louis XV* (1859).

**Rivière, Jacques.** 1886–1925. French journalist; editor of *Nouvelle Revue Française* (1919–25).

**Riv'ing·ton** (rĭv'ĭng·tŭn). Name of a family of English publishers including: **Charles** (1688–1742), b. in Derbyshire; took over (1711) trade of Richard Chiswell, London publisher and bookseller, and became leading publisher of theological books. Charles's son **James** (1724–1803) continued in publishing business (to 1756); emigrated to Philadelphia (1760); set up bookshops in Philadelphia, New York, and Boston; confined business to Wall Street, New York (1765); Tory journalist; publisher of *Rivington's New York Gazetteer* (1773–75), bitterly attacked American Revolutionary movement; deprived of press by Sons of Liberty (1775), returned to England for new press, and set up *Rivington's New York Loyal Gazette* (later called *Royal Gazette,* 1777–83); turned spy for Washington (1781). The London business was carried on by John's sons **Francis** (1745–1822) and **Charles** (1754–1831), and by Francis's son **John** (1779–1841) and Charles's son **Francis** (1805–1885), and by the younger John's son **John** (1812–1886), until absorbed by Longmans, Green & Co. (1890), only to be revived (1897) under headship of **Septimus** (1846–1926), author of *The House of Rivington* (1894).

**Ri·vi'nus** (rē·vē'nŏŏs; *as Lat.,* rĭ·vī'nŭs), **August Quirinus.** *Orig. surname* **Bach'mann** (bäĸ'män). 1652–1723. German botanist; author of *Ordo Plantarum* (1690–99), in which he set forth a new system of botanical classification based on the corolla.

**Ri'voire'** (rē'vwȧr'), **André.** 1871–1930. French poet and playwright.

**Rivoli,** Duc **de.** See André MASSÉNA.

**Rix** (rĭks), **Julian Walbridge.** 1850–1903. American landscape painter, b. Peacham, Vt. To San Francisco; began paintings and black-and-white sketches of California landscapes (1875). Opened studio in New York City (c. 1888).

**Riza Bey.** See AHMED RIZA BEY.

**Ri·zal'** (rē·säl'), **José.** 1861–1896. National hero of the Filipinos, b. on island of Luzon. Studied at U. of Madrid. His political tale *Noli me Tangere* (1886) caused his exile by Spanish government; wrote, while in exile, second political novel, *El Filibusterismo* (1891). On return to Philippines (1896), was arrested, charged with instigating native insurrection, condemned and shot.

**Ri·za' Shah Pah'la·vi** *or* **Pah'le·vi** (rĭ·zä' shä' pă'lȧ·vē). *Orig.* **Riza Khan** (kän) **Pahlavi.** 1877–1944. Shah (or king, 1925–41) of Iran (Persia), b. in Mazanderan province. Soldier; at head of Persian Cossack force, expelled all Russian officers (1921); made commander of Persian army; reorganized it (1921–24); prime minister (1923–25). Chosen shah by National Assembly after deposition (1925) of Ahmed Shah (*q.v.*); crowned (1926); abolished capitulations (1928); strengthened finances and improved transportation; abdicated (1941); succeeded by his son Mohammed Riza Pahlavi.

**Riz'zio** (rēt'tsyō; *Angl.* rĭt'sĭ·ō) *or* **Ric'cio** (rēt'chō; *Angl.* rĭch'ĭ·ō), **David.** 1533?–1566. Italian musician and favorite of Mary, Queen of Scots. Accompanied Piedmontese ambassador to Scotland (1561); entered Mary's service as musician and bass singer, became valet de chambre and (1564) private foreign secretary; arranged marriage with Darnley; became virtual secretary of state, haughty and overbearing, excluding Darnley from political power; was dragged from Mary's supper chamber at Holyrood Palace by armed band, including Darnley, Morton, and Lindsay, and hacked to death with daggers.

**Riz'zo** (rēt'tsō) *or* **Riz'zi** (rēt'tsē) *or* **Ri'zo** (rē'tsō), **Antonio.** 1430?–?1498. Italian sculptor; employed at Vicenza and Venice (1467–98); known esp. for his tomb of Doge Niccolò Trono in Venice.

**R. L. S.** See Robert Louis STEVENSON.

**Roach** (rōch), **John.** *Orig. surname* **Roche** (rōch). 1813–1887. Ironmaster and shipbuilder, b. in County Cork, Ireland; to U.S. (1829); naturalized (1842) as Roach; built marine engines and iron steamships, including several war vessels; sometimes called "father of iron shipbuilding in America."

**Rob'bia** (rōb'byä), **Luca della.** 1400?–1482. Florentine sculptor; began career as goldsmith; known chiefly as originator of Robbia work; his works in Florence include ten panels in high relief known as the *Singing Galleries* (now in cathedral museum), bronze sacristy door with reliefs of the church fathers and the Evangelists (in cathedral), and reliefs as *Liberal Arts* (on campanile), *Resurrection, Ascension* (in cathedral), *Evangelists* (in church of Santa Croce); other works include tomb of Benozzo Federighi (in church of San Francesco di Paolo, near Florence), *Virtues* (in Portogallo chapel, San

Miniato), and a *Madonna* (Metropolitan Museum, N.Y.). Luca's nephew **Andrea della Robbia** (1437–1528) succeeded him as a terra-cotta sculptor; his works in Florence include the fourteen bambini medallions on façade of Ospedale degl'Innocenti, *Meeting of St. Francis and St. Dominic* (relief in Ospedale di San Paolo), a *Madonna* (church of Santa Maria Maggiore), *Assumption of the Virgin* (Metropolitan Museum, N.Y.). Andrea's son **Giovanni** (1469?–?1529) was also a terra-cotta sculptor; his works include the sacristy fountain (Santa Maria Novella, Florence), the reliefs *Seven Works of Mercy* (on façade of Ospedale del Ceppo, Prato in Toscana), and a lunette *Resurrection* (in Brooklyn Institute museum). Another of Andrea's sons, **Girolamo** (1488–1566), was a terra-cotta sculptor and architect; employed chiefly in France for kings of the house of Valois; built Château de Madrid (in Bois de Boulogne).

**Rob'bins** (rŏb'ĭnz), **Frederick Chapman.** 1916– . American physician, b. Auburn, Ala. Awarded Nobel prize in physiology and medicine (1954) with J. F. Enders and T. Weller for discoveries concerning the virus of poliomyelitis.

**Robbins, Jerome.** 1918– . American dancer and choreographer, b. New York City. Director and choreographer of ballets, films, and plays, including *West Side Story* (1957) and *Fiddler on the Roof* (1964).

**Robert.** Name of two kings of France:

**Robert I.** 865?–923. King (922–923) but by some not counted in regular line of kings of France. Son of Robert the Strong and brother of Eudes. Did not claim crown of France on death of Eudes (898); recognized by Charles III as duke of the Franks; revolted against Charles; elected king by the nobles (922) but defeated by Charles.

**Robert II.** *Called* **the Pious.** *Fr.* **le Pieux** (lẽ pyû'). 970?–1031. King (996–1031); son of Hugh Capet, b. Orléans; sometimes known as Robert I; m. (996) as second wife, his cousin Bertha of Burgundy (b. 962?). Excommunicated (998) by Pope Gregory V, because of marriage. Last year of reign troubled by revolt of sons by his third marriage, incited by their mother, **Constance of Arles** [ȧrl] (d. 1032).

**Robert I** and **II.** Dukes of Burgundy. See BURGUNDY.

**Rob'ert** (rŏb'ẽrt). Name of three counts of Flanders:

**Robert I,** the Frisian. 1013?–1093. Made expeditions against Moors in Galicia and against Byzantines; regent of Flanders (1070) but forced to leave; made pilgrimage to Palestine (1085–91).

**Robert II,** of Jerusalem. d. 1111. Count (1093–1111); son of Robert I. Took part in First Crusade (1096–99); fought with Louis VI against Henry I of England.

**Robert III,** of Béthune. 1240–1322. Son of Guy de Dampierre. Fought against King Philip IV of France (1297); held as prisoner at Chinon (1304–05); refused to grant lands to Philip; defeated (1319) by Philip.

**Robert.** Name of two dukes of Normandy:

**Robert I.** *Called* **the Devil.** *Fr.* **le Dia'ble** (lẽ dyä'bl'). d. 1035. Son of Duke Richard II; father of William the Conqueror. Duke (1028–35). An unscrupulous and cruel ruler, but energetic and bold; aided nephews in England against Canute; made pilgrimage to Palestine; died at Nicaea on his return. Subject of many legends and of Meyerbeer's opera *Robert le Diable.*

**Robert II.** *Called* **Curt-hose.** *Fr.* **Courte'-Heuse'** (ko͝or'tûz'). 1054?–1134. Eldest son of William the Conqueror. Duke (1087–1134). Rebelled against his father (1077, 1080, 1082). Disputed over Normandy with his brother William II (1089, 1091, 1094); took important part in First Crusade (1096–99); delayed in Italy on his return (1100); invaded England (1101) in attempt to take throne from his younger brother, Henry I; retired to Normandy; at war again with Henry (1105–06); defeated at Tinchebray (Sept. 28, 1106); imprisoned at Cardiff (1106–34).

**Robert.** Count of Paris. Sometimes known as **Robert I** of France. See CAPETIAN dynasty.

**Robert.** Name of three kings of Scotland:

**Robert I,** called "the Bruce." King (1306–1329). See Robert de Bruce VIII (1274–1329) under BRUCE family.

**Robert II.** 1316–1390. King (1371–1390), founder of Stuart dynasty (see STEWART family). Succeeded to father's office as high steward and to estates (1326); led second division of Scottish army at Halidon Hill (1333); regent during David II's absence in France (1334–41) and after David II's capture at Neville's Cross (1346).

**Robert III.** *Originally* **John Stewart** of Kyle (kīl). 1340?–1406. King (1390–1406). Created earl of **Ath'oll** [ăth'ŭl] (1367) and earl of **Car'rick** [kăr'ĭk] (1368); never capable of governing personally because of disability from accident; forced to delegate power of administration to ambitious younger brother, Robert Stewart, 1st Duke of Albany (see STEWART family); gave over guardianship of his elder son, **David Stewart** (1378?–1402), Duke of **Rothe'say** (rŏth'sĭ; -sā), to Albany, who presumably starved him to death at Falkland; succumbed to grief on receipt of news of capture by English of his younger son, James, en route to France.

**Robert.** Earl of **Glouces'ter** (glŏs'tẽr; glôs'-). d. 1147. Illegitimate son of Henry I of England and half brother of Empress Matilda. Received by marriage large possessions in Normandy, Wales, and England; quarreled with his cousin Stephen (king of England), who confiscated his Welsh and English lands (1137); joined with Matilda in invasion (1139) and for eight years contested royal title; with aid of son-in-law earl of Chester, captured Stephen (1141); was captured at Stockbridge and exchanged for Stephen.

**Ro'bert** (rō'bẽrt), **Carl.** 1850–1922. German archaeologist and classical philologist.

**Rob'ert** (rŏb'ẽrt), **Christopher Rhinelander.** 1802–1878. American philanthropist; founded (1835) firm of Robert and Williams, sugar, cotton, and tea importers, New York City. Financed foundation of Robert College, at Bebek, a suburb of Constantinople (opened by Cyrus Hamlin, missionary, 1863), supported the institution during his lifetime, and bequeathed it a substantial amount in his will. Also a benefactor of Beloit College, Hamilton College, and Auburn Theological Seminary.

**Robert, Henry Martyn.** 1837–1923. American army officer and parliamentarian. Military engineer, on defenses of Washington (1861), at Philadelphia (1861–62). Chief of engineers, U.S. army (1901). Author of *Robert's Rules of Order* (1876; revised edition, 1915).

**Ro'bert'** (rô'bâr'), **Hubert.** 1733–1808. French painter; best known for paintings of architectural works.

**Ro'bert'** (rô'bâr'), **Louis Léopold.** 1794–1835. Swiss painter, best known for scenes of Italian life.

**Ro'bert' de Mo'lesmes'** (rô'bâr' dẽ mô'lâm'), Saint. 1029?–1111. French ecclesiastic; a founder of the Cistercian order (1098). See Saint Stephen HARDING.

**Robert Guiscard.** See GUISCARD.

**Rob'ert of An'jou** (rŏb'ẽrt, ăn'jo͞o; *Fr.* rô'bâr', äɴ'-zho͞o'). 1275–1343. Duke of Anjou and king of Naples (1309–43); second son of Charles II; crowned by Pope Clement V at Avignon; leader of Guelph or papal faction in Italy, esp. as opponent of Emperor Henry VII; waged unsuccessful war against Sicily (1325–41). A man of learning and patron of literary men, esp. Petrarch.

**Rob'ert of Cour'te·nay'** (rŏb'ẽrt, ko͞or'tẽ·nā'). d. 1228. Emperor of the Eastern Roman Empire (1221–28);

younger son of Emperor Peter of Courtenay (*q.v.*). A weak sovereign, unable to resist encroachments of the Greeks, esp. of John Ducas, the Nicaean emperor.

**Robert of Geneva.** See Antipope CLEMENT VII.

**Robert of Glouces'ter** (glŏs'tẽr; glôs'-). fl. 1260–1300. English chronicler, reputed author of vernacular history of England from days of legendary Brut to 1270, written in rhymed couplets; contemporary authority only from 1256–1270; one of last chroniclers to write in Old English.

**Robert of Ju'mièges'** (zhü'myâzh'). fl. 1037–1052. English prelate. Norman abbot of Jumièges (1037); crossed to England with Edward the Confessor (1041); bishop of London (1044). Leader of party hostile to Earl Godwin; archbishop of Canterbury (1051), drove Earl Godwin into exile; fled to Normandy on Godwin's return (1052); deposed by witan.

**Robert the Strong.** Count of Anjou. See CAPETIAN.

**Ro'bert'–Fleu'ry'** (rô'bâr'flû'rē'). *Real name* **Joseph Nicolas Robert Fleury.** 1797–1890. French painter; professor (1855) and director (1863), École des Beaux-Arts (Paris). Among his canvases are *Scène de la Saint Barthélemy*, *Le Connétable Albert de Luynes*, *Entrée Triomphale de Clovis à Tours*, *Benvenuto Cellini dans son Atelier*, *Jane Shore*, etc. His son **Tony Robert–Fleury** (1837–1911) was also a painter.

**Rob'erts** (rŏb'ẽrts), **Benjamin Titus.** 1823–1893. American Methodist Episcopal clergyman; criticized conditions in the church (1857); expelled from the church (1858). Became first general superintendent (1860–93) of Free Methodist Church, organized (1860) as a result of the schism caused by his expulsion.

**Roberts, Brigham Henry.** 1857–1933. Mormon leader, b. Warrington, Eng.; to U.S. (1866). Mormon missionary in U.S. (1880–86) and England (1886–88). Member, First Council of Seventy, Mormon Church (1888). Elected to U.S. House of Representatives (1898) but was refused seat because of his plural marriages. Served as chaplain in France (1918–19). Author of *A Comprehensive History of the Church of Jesus Christ of Latter Day Saints, Century I* (6 vols., 1930), etc.

**Roberts, Cecil Edric Mornington.** 1892–1976. British journalist, poet, and fiction writer. Among his books are *Phyllistrata and Other Poems* (1913), *Collected War Poems* (1916), *The Chelsea Cherub* (novel; 1917), *A Tale of Young Lovers* (poetic drama; 1922), *Little Mrs. Manington* (1926), *The Right to Kiss* (comedy; 1926), *Havana Bound* (1930), *Victoria Four-Thirty* (1937), *They Wanted to Live* (1938), *And so to Bath* (1939), *One Small Candle* (1942), *Here Comes Sylvia* (1943), etc.

**Roberts,** Sir **Charles George Douglas.** 1860–1943. Canadian writer; served in World War (captain, 1915; major, 1917). Among his books of verse are *Orion and Other Poems* (1880), *In Divers Tones* (1887), *Ave...*(1892), *Songs of the Common Day* (1893), *New York Nocturnes* (1898), *The Book of the Rose* (1903), *The Vagrant of Time* (1927), and *Twilight over Shangamauk...*(1937). Among his prose works are many nature and animal stories.

**Roberts, David.** 1796–1864. Scottish landscape and architectural painter.

**Roberts, Elizabeth Madox.** 1881–1941. American poet and novelist, b. near Springfield, Ky. Author of *Under the Tree* (verse; 1922), *The Time of Man* (1926), *Jingling in the Wind* (1928), *The Great Meadow* (1930), *A Buried Treasure* (1931), *The Haunted Mirror* (short stories; 1932), *He Sent Forth a Raven* (1935), *Black is my Truelove's Hair* (1938), *Song in the Meadow* (verse; 1940), *Not by Strange Gods* (short stories; 1941).

**Roberts, Frederick Sleigh.** 1st Earl **Roberts of Kan'da·har', Pre·to'ri·a, and Wa'ter·ford** (kăn'dȧ·här', prē̇·tō'rĭ·ȧ, wô'tẽr·fẽrd). *Nicknamed by soldiers* **Bobs** *or* **Bobs Ba·ha'dur** (bŏbz bȧ·hô'dōōr; -hä'-). 1832–1914. British soldier, b. Cawnpore, India, son of General Sir Abraham Roberts. Served in Sepoy Mutiny (1857–58), winning Victoria Cross for heroism at Khudaganj; aided in siege and capture of Delhi, relief of Lucknow, and battle of Cawnpore. Asst. quartermaster general in Abyssinian and Lushai campaigns. In Second Afghan War, forced Afghan position at Peiwar Kotal, took Kabul, and re-entered Afghan capital (1879); performed memorable march from Kabul to relief of Kandahar, achieving pacification of Afghanistan (1880). Commander in chief in India (1885–93); field marshal (1895); commander in chief in Ireland (1895–99). Held supreme command in South Africa (from 1899); relieved Kimberley; compelled Boers under Cronjé to surrender at Paardeberg (1900); annexed Orange Free State; occupied Pretoria; annexed Transvaal; handed over command to Lord Kitchener; created earl. Devoted himself after retiring (1904) to creation of a citizen army. Author of *The Rise of Wellington* (1895) and *Forty-One Years in India* (1897).

**Roberts, Howard.** 1843–1900. American sculptor; his life-size statue of Robert Fulton is in National Hall of Statuary, Washington, D.C.

**Roberts, Kenneth.** 1885–1957. American novelist, b. Kennebunk, Me. Captain, intelligence department, American Siberian expeditionary force (1918–19). Staff correspondent, *Saturday Evening Post* (from 1919). Author of *Europe's Morning After* (1921), *Black Magic* (1924), *Arundel* (1930), *Northwest Passage* (1937), *Oliver Wiswell* (1940), etc.

**Roberts, Morley.** 1857–1942. English fiction writer, b. London. Led roving life (1876–86) as ranchman, railroader, and sailor in various parts of the world. Among his many tales are *The Western Avernus* (1887), *King Billy of Ballarat* (1891), *Red Earth* (1894), *The Adventure of the Broad Arrow* (1897), *Immortal Youth* (1902), *Lady Penelope* (1905), *Captain Spink* (1908), *Sea Dogs* (1910), *Hearts of Women* (1919), *Followers of the Sea* (1923), *The Serpent's Fang* (1930), etc.

**Roberts, Owen Josephus.** 1875–1955. American jurist, b. Philadelphia; A.B. (1895), LL.B. (1898), teacher of law (1898–1918), U. of Penn.; special counsel for U.S. in prosecuting "oil cases" (1924); associate justice, U.S. Supreme Court (1930–1945).

**Rob'erts–Aus'ten** (rŏb'ẽrts·ôs'tĕn; -tĭn), Sir **William Chan'dler** (*Brit.* chăn'dlẽr). 1843–1902. English metallurgist; initiated alloys research; invented automatic recording pyrometer (1891).

**Rob'ert·son** (rŏb'ẽrt·s'n), Sir **Charles Grant.** 1869–1948. British historian; principal (1920–38) and vice-chancellor (1927–38), Birmingham U. Author of *The Rise of the English Nation* (1895), *England under the Hanoverians* (1911), *A Historical Atlas of Modern Europe* (1915), *The Evolution of Prussia* (with J. A. R. Marriott), *Bismarck* (1918), etc.

**Robertson, E. Arnot.** *Pen name of* Mrs. **Henry Ernest Tur'ner** (tûr'nẽr), *nee* **Eileen Arbuthnot Robertson.** 1903–1961. English novelist; m. H. E. Turner (1927). Author of *Cullum* (1928), *Three Came Unarmed* (1929), *Four Frightened People* (1931), *Thames Portrait* (1937), *Summer's Lease* (1940), etc.

**Robertson, Frederick William.** 1816–1853. English clergyman of Anglican Church; gained reputation as earnest preacher and Broad Churchman, emphasizing not theology but principles of spiritual life; his sermons (5 vols.) known throughout English-speaking world.

**Robertson, George Croom.** 1842–1892. Scottish philosopher allied to school of Mills and Bain; started and edited *Mind* (1876).

**Robertson,** James Logie. *Pseudonym* **Hugh Hal′i·bur′ton** (hăl′ĭ·bûr′t′n). 1846–1922. Scottish writer, b. in Kinross-shire. On teaching staff of Edinburgh Ladies' Coll. (from 1876). Among his books of verse are *Poems* (1878), *Horace in Homespun* (1886), and *Ochil Idylls* (1891); among his prose works, *The White Angel and Other Stories* (1886), *For Puir Auld Scotland* (1887), *In Scottish Fields* (1890), and *A History of English Literature* (1894).

**Robertson, John Mackinnon.** 1856–1933. British journalist, politician, and Shakespearean scholar, b. on Isle of Arran. M.P. (1906–18); parliamentary secretary to Board of Trade (1911–15). Among his many books are *The Baconian Heresy, Shakespeare and Chapman* (1917), *The Problem of Hamlet* (1919), *The Problems of the Shakespeare Sonnets* (1926), *The Political Economy of Free Trade* (1928), *History of Free Thought in the Nineteenth Century* (1929), etc.

**Robertson, Margaret Brunton.** See Dame Madge KENDAL.

**Robertson, Thomas William.** 1829–1871. English dramatist; bro. of Dame Madge Kendal (*q.v.*). Actor, prompter, stage manager in London (from 1848); produced (1851) first play, *A Night's Adventure;* married (1856), and acted with, Elizabeth Burton (d. 1865); retired from stage and scored first writing success with *David Garrick* (1864), which, with Sothern acting, had long run; established reputation with *Society* (1865), a new kind of realistic comedy, dubbed "cup and saucer comedy"; sustained success with series of comedies *Caste* (1867), *Play* (1868), *School* (1869), *M.P.* (1870).

**Robertson, William.** 1721–1793. Scottish historian; principal, U. of Edinburgh (1762); king's historiographer (1763); author of *History of Scotland 1542–1603* (2 vols., 1759), *History of the Reign of Emperor Charles V* (1769), which was praised by Voltaire and Gibbon and established his reputation on the Continent, and *History of America* (1777).

**Robertson,** Sir **William Robert.** 1860–1933. British soldier; entered army as private soldier (1877) and advanced through grades to field marshal (1920). During World War (1914–18), quartermaster general of British Expeditionary Force (1914), chief of the general staff of B.E.F. (1915), chief of imperial general staff (1915–18), commander in chief of British army on the Rhine (1919–20). Author of *From Private to Field Marshal* (1921) and *Soldiers and Statesmen, 1914–18* (1926).

**Ro·ber′ty de la Cer′da** (rŭ·byār′tyĭ dyĕ lŭ tsâr′dŭ), **Evgeni de** (dyĕ). 1843–1915. Russian sociologist of Spanish descent; among his works are *Sociology* (1880), *The Unknowable, its Metaphysics, its Psychology* (1889), *Ethics* (1896), *New Program of Sociology* (1904).

**Ro′ber′val′** (rô′bĕr′vȧl′), **Gilles Per′sonne′** (pĕr′sôn′) **de** *or* **Per′so′nier′** (pĕr′sô′nyā′) **de.** 1602–1675. French mathematician; originated methods for constructing tangents and for determining the area of a cycloid; invented the balance which bears his name.

**Robe′son** (rōb′s′n), **George Maxwell.** 1829–1897. American lawyer and politician, b. Oxford Furnace, N.J.; U.S. secretary of the navy (1869–77).

**Robeson, Paul.** 1898–1976. American Negro actor and singer, b. Princeton, N.J.; A.B., Rutgers (1919), LL.B., Columbia (1923). On American stage in *Emperor Jones* (1923), *All God's Chillun, Porgy, Black Boy.* Made first concert appearance, singing Negro spirituals, in New York City (1925); on concert tours in Europe (1926–28, 1931, 1938), America (1929), and Russia (1936). On stage in London, England, in *Othello* (1930), *The Hairy Ape* (1931), *Stevedore* (1933). Starred or featured in motion pictures.

**Ro′bes′pierre′** (rô′bĕs′pyâr′; *Angl.* rōbz′pēr), **Maximilien François Marie Isidore de.** 1758–1794. Known as "the Incorruptible." French revolutionist, b. Arras. Advocate at Arras (1781–89). Elected to States-General (1789). Acquired notoriety as a radical in Constituent Assembly (1789–91); opposed Girondists; leader in Jacobin Club (1791–92); with Pétion de Villeneuve, crowned by people of Paris as "incorruptible patriots" (1791). Not active in mob instigation and prison massacres (1792); elected first deputy from Paris to National Convention; became recognized leader of radical popular party (Montagnards). Demanded death of king (1793). Chosen member of second Committee of Public Safety (July, 1793). For one yea '1793–94) virtually prime minister of the committee, i. ideal patriot but not its dictator. Responsible for m·ch of the Reign of Terror; attacked Hébert; sent his friends, Desmoulins and Danton, to guillotine (1794). Inaugurated worship of the Supreme Being (May–June, 1794). Overthrown by Revolution of 9th Thermidor (July 27); arrested and guillotined the next day by Revolutionary Tribunal. Death ended Reign of Terror.

**Ro′bey** (rō′bĭ), **George.** *Stage name of* **George Edward Wade** (wād). 1869–1954. English actor, esp. comic actor on variety stage; also in motion pictures, including *Don Quixote, Chu Chin Chow, Southern Roses.*

**Ro′bin′** (rô′băɴ′), **Charles.** 1821–1885. French anatomist; professor of histology (from 1862). Compiler of *Dictionnaire de Médecine et de Chirurgie* (with Littré).

**Rob′in Hood** (rŏb′ĭn hŏŏd′). Legendary English outlaw, hero of a cycle of ballads. Name thought to be variant of **Hö′de·ken** (hû′dĕ·kĕn), elf of Germanic folk tales. First mentioned in second version of *Piers Plowman* (c. 1377); recorded historically in Wyntoun's chronicle of Scotland (c. 1420); treated fully in *Lytell Geste of Robyn Hoode* (printed c. 1495 by Wynkyn de Worde); celebrated in Ben Jonson's pastoral drama *The Sad Shepherd* (1641); figures in Scott's *Ivanhoe;* hero of a comic opera by Reginald De Koven, of a play *Sherwood* by Alfred Noyes, and of Tennyson's *The Foresters.* According to various conjectures identified as: a Saxon chief resisting Normans (by Augustin Thierry and by Sir Walter Scott); one of proscribed followers of Simon de Montfort; an adherent of earl of Lancaster in insurrection of 1322; an early earl of Huntingdon (by playwright Anthony Munday in 1601).

**Rob′ins** (rŏb′ĭnz; rō′bĭnz), **Benjamin.** 1707–1751. English mathematician and military engineer; invented ballistic pendulum, first described in his *New Principles of Gunnery* (1742); made discoveries regarding rifling of gun barrels.

**Rob′ins** (rŏb′ĭnz), **Elizabeth.** *Pseudonym* **C. E. Rai′mond** (rā′mŭnd). 1862?–1952. American actress and writer, b. Louisville, Ky.; m. George Richmond Parks (1885). Successful on stage as interpreter of Ibsen; advocate of woman suffrage. Author of *George Mandeville's Husband* (1894), *The Convert* (1907), *Come and Find Me* (1908), *Way Stations* (1913), *Camilla* (1918), *Ibsen and the Actress* (1928), *Theatre and Friendship* (1932), etc.

**Robins, Raymond.** 1873–1954. American social economist. With American Red Cross mission in Russia (1917–18); studied economic and educational conditions in Russia (1933); married (1905) **Margaret Drei′er** [drī′ĕr] (1869–1945), also a social economist; as president of International Congress of Working Women, convened congress in Vienna (1923); associated with many organizations for defending and promoting the interests of working women.

**Rob′in·son** (rŏb′ĭn·s′n), **Anastasia.** See MORDAUNT family.

**Robinson, Benjamin Lincoln.** See under James H. ROBINSON.

**Robinson, Boardman.** 1876–1952. Painter and illustrator, b. in Somerset, Nova Scotia; settled in New York; instructor in Art Students' League (1918–29); director of Colorado Springs Fine Arts Center (from 1930). Painted murals in Radio City, New York City, and U.S. Department of Justice building, Washington, D.C. Coauthor with John Reed, whom he accompanied (1915) to Russia and the Balkans, of *The War in Eastern Europe* (1916).

**Robinson, Charles.** 1818–1894. American pioneer and politician, b. Hardwick, Mass. To California (1849); engaged in aiding antislavery forces; returned to Massachusetts (1851). Kansas agent of New England Emigrant Aid Company (1854), sent out to help save Kansas from becoming a slave state; leader of Free State faction in Kansas; elected governor of the territory by this faction (1856). First governor of the State of Kansas (1861–63).

**Robinson, Charles Mulford.** 1869–1917. American journalist and authority on city planning, b. Ramapo, N.Y. Consultant upon city planning, Buffalo, N.Y. (1902), and later in other cities (Detroit, Omaha, Denver, Oakland, Los Angeles). Author of *The Improvement of Towns and Cities...* (1901), *City Planning* (1916), *The City Sleeps* (a book of essays and poetry, 1920).

**Robinson, Christopher.** See under John Beverley ROBINSON.

**Robinson, Corinne, *nee* Roosevelt.** 1861–1933. Sister of President Theodore Roosevelt. American philanthropist and writer, b. New York City; m. Douglas Robinson (1882; d. 1918). Active in Red Cross and social-service work, notably during World War. Author of *The Call of Brotherhood* (verse; 1912), *One Woman to Another* (1914), *My Brother, Theodore Roosevelt* (1921), *Out of Nymph* (verse; 1930), etc.

**Robinson, David Moore.** 1880–1958. American educator; professor of archaeology and epigraphy, Johns Hopkins (from 1912) and lecturer in Greek literature (from 1915). Director of excavations, at Pisidian Antioch and Sizma for U. of Michigan (1924), at Olynthus (1928–38). Editor in chief, Johns Hopkins *Studies in Archaeology.* Author of many treatises in fields of archaeology and epigraphy and Greek literature.

**Robinson, Edward.** 1794–1863. American Biblical scholar; professor, Andover (1830–33), Union Theol. Sem. (1837–63). Explored Palestine with Eli Smith, American missionary and Arabic scholar, who aided greatly in Robinson's masterpiece, *Biblical Researches in Palestine, Mount Sinai and Arabia Petraea* (3 vols., 1841). Founded (1831) and edited (1831–35) *American Biblical Repository;* founded (1843) *Bibliotheca Sacra.* Compiled *A Hebrew and English Lexicon of the Old Testament* (1836), *A Greek and English Lexicon of the New Testament* (1836). He married, as second wife, **The·re'se** (tā·rā'zĕ) **Al'ber·ti'ne** (äl'bĕr·tē'nĕ) **Lou·i'se** (lo͞o·ē'zĕ) **von Ja'kob** [fôn yä'kôp] (1797–1870), pseudonym, from initials of her name, **Tal'vj** (täl'vē); b. Halle, Saxony, philologist and author; student of Slavic languages and literature; author of *Volkslieder der Serben* (1825), *Historical View of the Slavic Language* (1834), etc., and the novels *Heloise* (1850) and *Die Auswanderer* (1852; in English, *The Exiles,* 1853).

**Robinson, Edward.** 1858–1931. American archaeologist, b. Boston. Curator of classical antiquities, Boston Museum of Fine Arts (1885–1902) and director of the museum (1902–05). Assistant director, Metropolitan Museum of Art, New York City (1905–10) and director (1910–31).

**Robinson, Edward Mott.** 1800–1865. American merchant and financier; leader in whaling industry, New Bedford, Mass. (1831?–60); member of firm owning line of packet ships plying between New York and California (1860–65); his fortune was the basis of that amassed by his daughter, Hetty Green (*q.v.*).

**Robinson, Edwin Arlington.** 1869–1935. American poet, b. Head Tide, Me. Resident in Gardiner, Me. (1870–97) and New York City (from 1897). Associated with summer colony at Peterboro, N.H. (from 1911) and did much of his writing there. His books include *The Torrent and the Night Before* (1896), *The Children of the Night* (1897), *Captain Craig* (1902), *The Town Down the River* (1910), *The Man Against the Sky* (1916), *Merlin* (1917), *The Three Taverns* (1920), *Lancelot* (1920), *Avon's Harvest* (1921), *Collected Poems* (awarded Pulitzer prize, 1921), *Roman Bartholomew* (1923), *The Man Who Died Twice* (1924, awarded Pulitzer prize, 1925), *Dionysus in Doubt* (1925), *Tristram* (awarded Pulitzer prize, 1927), *Sonnets* (1928), *Cavender's House* (1929), *The Glory of the Nightingales* (1930), *Matthias at the Door* (1931), *Nicodemus* (1932), *Talifer* (1933), and two plays (*Van Zorn,* 1914; *The Porcupine,* 1915).

**Robinson, Ezekiel Gilman.** 1815–1894. American Baptist clergyman and educator; after several pastorates, became professor of Biblical theology, Rochester Theol. Sem. (1853–60) and president (1860–72). President, Brown U. (1872–89).

**Robinson, Frederick Bertrand.** 1883–1941. American educator, b. Brooklyn, N.Y.; president, C.C.N.Y. (from 1927).

**Robinson, Frederick John.** Viscount **Gode'rich** (gōd'rĭch) *and* 1st Earl of **Rip'on** (rĭp'ŭn). 1782–1859. English statesman. M.P. (1806); undersecretary for colonies (1809); joint paymaster general of forces (1813–17); chancellor of exchequer (1823–27); introduced fiscal reforms; secretary for war, commissioner for Indian affairs, leader of House of Lords (1827); prime minister for seven months (1827–28); secretary for war and colonies (1830); lord privy seal (1833); created earl (1833); president of Board of Trade (1841) and of board of control for Indian affairs (1843–46).

**George Frederick Samuel Robinson** (1827–1909), 1st Marquis of **Ripon,** *known as* Viscount **Goderich** (1833–59), his son; statesman; Liberal M.P. (1852); joined Christian Socialist movement and pleaded for democracy in tract *The Duty of the Age,* suppressed by F. D. Maurice as too radical (1852); succeeded father as earl of Ripon and uncle as earl de Grey (1859); secretary for war (1863) and for India (1866); lord president of council in Gladstone's administration (1868–73); chairman of joint high commission on Alabama claims (1871); resigned as grand master of Freemasons, became a convert to Roman Catholicism (1874); governor general of India (1880–84); reversed Afghan policy of Lord Lytton; repealed restrictions on vernacular press; encouraged development of self-government; first lord of admiralty (1886); colonial secretary (1892–95); lord privy seal and Liberal leader in House of Lords (1905–08).

**Robinson, Geoffrey.** 1874–?1918. English journalist; educ. Oxford; secretary to Lord Milner in South Africa (1901–05); editor, Johannesburg *Star* (1905–10); South African correspondent (1910–12) and editor (1912 ff.), London *Times.*

**Robinson, Heath,** *in full* **William Heath.** 1872–1944. English illustrator and cartoonist. On staff of *Penny Illustrated Paper* and contributor of humorous sketches to *The Sketch, The Graphic, Strand Magazine,* etc. Also, designer of comedy sets for productions at Alhambra and Empire theaters in London.

**Robinson, Henry Crabb.** 1775–1867. English journalist and diarist; friend of Lamb, Coleridge, Wordsworth, Southey; kept a diary (35 vols.), journals (30 vols.), and letters and reminiscences (36 vols.), of which selections have been published by the divine Thomas Sadler (1869) and Edith J. Morley (1927).

**Robinson,** Sir **Hercules George Robert.** 1st Baron **Ros'mead** (?rŏz'mēd). 1824–1897. British colonial governor; 2d son of Admiral **Hercules Robinson** (1789–1864). Administrator in Ireland during famine (1848); governor of Cape of Good Hope (1880–89, 1895–97); negotiated terms of peace with Boers (1881) and for release of Jameson raiders (1896).

**Robinson, Jackie** *in full* **John Roosevelt.** 1919–1972. Athlete, b. Cairo, Ga.; first black baseball player in major leagues. Joined (Brooklyn) Dodgers (1947); rookie of the year (1947), most valuable player award (1949); lifetime batting average .311. Retired from baseball (1956) and entered business.

**Robinson, James Harvey.** 1863–1936. American historian and educator, b. Bloomington, Ill. Professor, Columbia (1892–1919). Organizer of, and lecturer in, New School for Social Research, New York City (1919–21). A pioneer in new methods and content of history teaching, supplementing the former narrative of politics and war with a story of social, scientific, intellectual, and artistic progress. His books include: *Introduction to the History of Western Europe* (1903), *The Development of Modern Europe* (with C. A. Beard, 2 vols., 1907), *The New History* (1911), *The Mind in the Making* (1921), *The Ordeal of Civilization* (1926). His brother **Benjamin Lincoln** (1864–1935) was a botanist; professor, Harvard (from 1899); editor of Gray's *Synoptical Flora of North America* (1892–97) and 7th edition of *Gray's New Manual of Botany* (with M. L. Fernald).

**Robinson, John.** 1576?–1625. English clergyman and minister to Pilgrim Fathers. Moved with section of the community to Leiden and was ordained pastor (1609); with Brewster, Bradford, and Cushman, organized Pilgrims' emigration to America and effected their removal to Plymouth, Eng. (1920), whence they sailed in the *Mayflower;* intended to follow but died in Leiden.

**Robinson,** Sir **John Beverley.** 1791–1863. Canadian jurist; in struggle for responsible government, chief opponent of reformers; opponent of union of Upper and Lower Canada (1841). His son **Christopher** (1828–1905), leading counsel for crown in prosecution of Louis Riel for treason (1885); one of counsel for British government in Bering Sea controversy with U.S. (1893).

**Robinson, John Cleveland.** 1817–1897. American army officer, b. Binghamton, N.Y.; educ. U.S.M.A., West Point (1835–38). Commanded Fort McHenry (1861) and by firmness cowed rioters in Baltimore (Apr., 1861); engaged at Fredericksburg, Chancellorsville, Gettysburg, and lost leg at Spotsylvania. Awarded Medal of Honor. His statue stands on the battlefield of Gettysburg where he successfully defended his position against Confederate attacks.

**Robinson,** Sir **Joseph Benjamin.** 1840–1929. South African mine owner and operator.

**Robinson, Joseph Taylor.** 1872–1937. American lawyer and legislator, b. Lonoke, Ark. Member, U.S. House of Representatives (1903–13); U.S. senator (1913–37) and Democratic leader in Senate (1923–37). Cosponsor of Robinson-Patman Act or Fair-Trade Agreement (1936).

**Robinson, Lennox.** 1886–1958. British playwright, novelist, and theater manager, b. in County Cork, Ireland. Manager of Abbey Theatre in Dublin (1910–14, 1919–23), and director (from 1923). Author of short stories and novels including *A Young Man from the South* (1917); of many plays, most of them produced originally at Abbey Theatre, including *The Clancy Name* (1908), *Patriots* (1912), *The Whiteheaded Boy* (1916), *The Lost Leader* (1918), *The Big House* (1926), *Church Street* (1934), and *Killycreggs in Twilight* (1937); and of the autobiographical *Curtain Up* (1942).

**Robinson, Mary,** *nee* **Dar'by** (där'bĭ). *Known as* **Per'di·ta** (pûr'dĭ·tȧ). 1758–1800. English actress, b. Bristol, of Irish descent. As Perdita in Garrick's production of *Winter's Tale* and in other Shakespearean roles at Drury Lane (1776–80), captivated (1778) prince of Wales, the future George IV, whose mistress she became on receipt of a bond for £20,000 (never paid). Deserted by the prince, devoted herself to writing poems, plays, novels under pen name of Perdita. Painted by Reynolds, Romney, Hoppner, Gainsborough.

**Robinson, Mary.** 1857–1944. See DARMESTETER.

**Robinson,** Sir **Robert.** 1886–1975. British chemist. At Oxford U. (1930–55); awarded Nobel prize in chemistry (1947) for studies on plant pigments.

**Robinson, Samuel Murray.** 1882–1972. U.S. naval officer, b. Eulogy, Texas; grad. (1903) U.S.N.A.; chief of bureau of engineering (1931–35, 1939–40), bureau of ships (1940–42), office of procurement and material (1942–46). Retired (1946); administrator, Webb Institute of Naval Architecture (1946–52).

**Robinson, Theodore.** 1852–1896. American landscape painter of impressionistic school, b. Irasburg, Vt.

**Robinson, Therese Albertine Louise.** See under Edward ROBINSON (1794–1863).

**Robinson, Thomas Romney.** 1792–1882. British astronomer; astronomer of Armagh observatory (1823); inventor of cup anemometer (1846).

**Robinson, William.** 1840–1921. Engineer, b. in County Tyrone, Ireland; to U.S. as a child. Invented system of automatic electric signaling (patented 1872), the basis of all modern automatic block signaling systems.

**Ro'bi'quet'** (rô'bē'kĕ'), **Pierre Jean.** 1780–1840. French chemist; with Vauquelin, discovered asparagine; found codeine in opium; investigated meconic acid.

**Robles Quiñones, José María Gil.** See GIL ROBLES QUIÑONES.

**Rob'lin** (rŏb'lĭn), **Richard Owen.** 1907– . American chemist, b. Rochester, N.Y.; known for research in chemotherapy, esp. sulfa drugs; announced (1940) discovery of sulfadiazine.

**Rob Roy.** (1) Nickname of Robert MACGREGOR, 1671–1734. (2) Pseudonym of John MACGREGOR, 1825–1892.

**Robsart, Amy.** See under Robert DUDLEY, Earl of Leicester.

**Rob'son** (?rŏb's'n), **Eleanor Elsie.** 1879– . Actress, b. Wigan, Lancashire, Eng.; to U.S. while very young. Greatest success as Mary Ann in Zangwill's play *Merely Mary Ann* (1903–05). Retired after marriage (1910) to August Belmont (*q.v.*).

**Rob'son** (rōb's'n), **May.** *Real name* **Mary Rob'i·son** (rŏb'ĭ·s'n). 1865–1942. Actress, b. Australia; to U.S. (1879); m. Augustus H. Brown (1889). Member of Daniel Frohman's company and Lyceum Theatre company (1886–93) and Charles Frohman's company (1893–1906); esp. successful in comedy roles. In motion pictures (from c. 1932).

**Rob'son** (rŏb's'n), **Stuart.** 1836–1903. American actor, b. Annapolis, Md.; excelled as comedian; joint star with William H. Crane (1877–89).

**Robusti, Jacopo.** See TINTORETTO.

**Ro'by** (rō'bĭ), **Henry John.** 1830–1915. English legal and classical scholar. Known for his *Grammar of the Latin Language from Plautus to Suetonius* (1871–74) and writings on Roman law.

**Ro'byn** (rō'bĭn), **Alfred George.** 1860–1935. American comic opera composer (*Yankee Consul, Gypsy Girl, Yankee Tourist, The Girl from Frisco,* etc.).

**Ro'ca** (rô'kä), **Julio Argentino.** 1843–1914. Argentine general; president of Argentina (1880–86; 1898–1904). His son **Julio Argentino** (1873–1942) was vice-president of Argentina (1932–38), ambassador to Brazil (1938–42).

**Roca, Vicente Ramón.** 1790?–1850. Provisional president and (1845–1850) president of Ecuador.

**Ro'ca·fuer'te** (rô'kä·fwĕr'tā), **Vicente.** 1783–1847. Ecuadorian educator; president of Ecuador (1835–39).

**Roc'co** (rôk'kō), **Alfredo.** 1875–1935. Italian jurist and statesman; minister of justice (1925–32); carried through reform in Italian penal, civil, and commercial law.

**Roch** (rôk), Saint. *Lat.* **Ro'chus** (rō'kŭs). 1295?–?1327. French Franciscan monk who devoted himself to tending the sick and plague-stricken.

**Roch** (rôk), **Madeleine.** 1885–1930. French actress; best known for interpretation of tragic roles.

**Ro'cham'beau'** (rô'shäN'bō'), Comte **de. Jean Baptiste Donatien de Vi'meur'** (dē vē'mûr'). 1725–1807. French soldier; served in War of Austrian Succession and Seven Years' War; brigadier general (1761). Commanded French force dispatched (1780) to aid Americans in Revolutionary War; joined Washington's Continental army at White Plains, N.Y. (July, 1781). The joint forces marched southward, besieged Cornwallis at Yorktown, and with French fleet preventing an escape by sea forced Cornwallis to capitulate (Oct. 19, 1781). Returned to France (Jan., 1783). Marshal of France (1791).

**Roche** (rōch), **Alexander.** 1861–1921. Scottish painter.

**Roche** (rōsh), **Arthur Somers.** 1883–1935. American fiction writer.

**Roche** (rōch), **James Jeffrey.** 1847–1908. Journalist and author, b. in Queen's County, Ireland; to Prince Edward Island as a boy. Settled in Boston (1866). Author of *Songs and Satires* (1886), *Ballads of Blue Water and Other Poems* (1895), *The V-a-s-e and Other Bric-à-Brac* (1900), *The Sorrows of Sap'ed* (1904).

**Roche** (rôsh), **Mazo de la.** See DE LA ROCHE.

**Roche'fort'** (rôsh'fôr'), **Henri,** *in full* **Victor Henri.** Marquis **de Roche'fort'-Lu'çay'** (-lü'sā'). 1830–1913. French journalist, politician, and playwright; on staff of *Figaro;* founded and edited *La Lanterne* (1868), *L'Intransigeant* (1880–1907), and *La Patrie* (1907 ff.). In politics, attacked empire of Napoleon III; involved in communist uprising in Paris (1871) and banished (1873); returned after amnesty (1880). Among his many works are *Les Français de la Décadence* (1866), *La Grande Bohème* (1867), *Les Dépravés* (1875), *Les Naufrageurs* (1876), *L'Évadé* (1880).

**Rochefoucauld, La.** See LA ROCHEFOUCAULD.

**Roche'grosse'** (rôsh'grōs'), **Georges Antoine.** 1859–1938. French painter.

**Rochejacquelein** *or* **Rochejaquelein, La.** See LA ROCHEJACQUELEIN.

**Roch'es'ter** (rŏch'ĕs'tēr; *Brit. usu.* -ĭs·tēr), 1st Earl of. (1) See Lawrence HYDE.
(2) **Henry Wil'mot** (wĭl'mŏt). 1612?–1658. English Royalist soldier and courtier. His son **John** (1647–1680), 2d earl, poet, became a favorite courtier and boon companion of Charles II, and one of most dissolute; patron of Elizabeth Barry (*q.v.*) and of several poets; repented on deathbed, according to popular pamphlet by Bishop Burnet; author of graceful amorous lyrics, mordant satires in verse, and a tragedy, *Valentinian* (produced 1685), adapted from Beaumont and Fletcher.

**Rochester,** Viscount. See Robert CARR (d. 1645).

**Rochester, Nathaniel.** 1752–1831. American pioneer in Genesee region, upper New York State (from 1800); purchased land there, on part of which was founded the city of Rochester (1812), named in his honor.

**Ro'chet'** (rô'shĕ'), **Louis.** 1813–1878. French sculptor; among his works are *Guillaume le Conquérant,* marble statue of Napoleon Bonaparte, and a colossal statue of Charlemagne (Paris) executed in collaboration with his brother **Charles** (1815–1900), sculptor and painter.

**Rochus,** Saint. See ROCH.

**Rock'e·fel'ler** (rŏk'ĕ·fĕl'ēr; rŏk'fĕl'ēr), **John Davison.** 1839–1937. American oil magnate, b. Richford, N.Y.; moved to Cleveland, Ohio (1853). In oil-refining business (from 1862). Organized Standard Oil Co. (1870) and became its president; gained monopoly of oil business. Organized Standard Oil trust (1882); dissolved by court decree (1892). Remained dominant in oil business until his retirement (1911). Established four great charitable corporations, Rockefeller Foundation, General Education Board, Laura Spelman Rockefeller Memorial, Rockefeller Institute for Medical Research, each of which he endowed with large amounts. His brother **William** (1841–1922) was associated with him in development of oil business. John Davison's son **John Davison** (1874–1960) became associated with his father's business interests (1897), and later interested in the philanthropic corporations established by his father; planned and built real-estate development in New York known as Rockefeller Center. His son **John Davison** (1906–1978) also associated with Rockefeller interests. Another son, **Nelson Aldrich** (1908–1979), asst. sec. of state (1944–45); gov. of N.Y. (1959–73); U.S. vice-president (1974–77).

**Rock'hill** (rŏk'hĭl), **William Woodville.** 1854–1914. American diplomat, b. Philadelphia. U.S. secretary of legation, Peking, China (1884–86); chargé d'affaires, Seoul, Korea (1886–87). Made two expeditions into Mongolia and Tibet under auspices of Smithsonian Institution (1888–89, 1891–92). U.S. assistant secretary of state (1894–97). U.S. minister to Greece, Rumania, and Serbia (1897–99). U.S. special agent in China after Boxer rebellion (1900). U.S. minister to China (1905–09); U.S. ambassador to Russia (1909–11), and to Turkey (1911–13). Appointed special adviser to Yüan Shih-k'ai (1914), but died on way to China.

**Rock'ing·ham** (rŏk'ĭng·ăm), 2d Marquis of. **Charles Wat'son-Went'worth** (wŏt's'n·wĕnt'wûrth; -wērth). 1730–1782. English statesman. Grandson of Thomas Watson and Anne, daughter of Thomas Wentworth, Earl of Strafford; son of **Thomas Watson-Wentworth** (1690?–1750), who was created earl of Malton (1733), Viscount Higham (1734), and marquis of Rockingham (1746). Styled in courtesy in father's lifetime Viscount **High'am** (hī'ăm) and Earl of **Mal'ton** (môl't'n; -tŭn). Educ. Cambridge; lord of bedchamber (1751–62); dismissed as lord lieutenant of North and East Ridings of Yorkshire (1751–62) because of Whig opinions in opposition to earl of Bute; called on to form coalition ministry (July, 1765); repealed Stamp Act and opposed grants to king's brothers, to mortification of George III; dismissed on duke of Grafton's secession from government (1766); leader in House of Lords of opposition to Lord North's American policy (1768–81); favored independence for American colonies; again prime minister (1782), with Fox and Shelburne (afterwards marquis of Lansdowne) as secretaries of state, but died after three months.

**Rock'ne** (rŏk'nē), **Knute** (no͞ot) **Kenneth.** 1888–1931. Football player and coach, b. at Voss, Norway; to U.S. (1893) and settled in Chicago. B.S., Notre Dame (1914). Captain, Notre Dame football team (1913); assistant coach (1914–18); head coach (1918–31). Killed in airplane crash (Mar. 31, 1931).

**Rock′well** (rŏk′wĕl; -wĕl), **Alphonso David.** 1840–1933. American physician; practiced, New York City (from 1865). Associated with Dr. George M. Beard as pioneer in electrotherapeutics.

**Rockwell, Kiffin Yates.** 1892–1916. American World War aviator, b. Newport, Tenn. Enlisted in French Foreign Legion soon after outbreak of World War (1914); one of original members of Escadrille Lafayette (Apr., 1916). Killed in action (Sept. 23, 1916).

**Rockwell, Norman.** 1894–1978. American painter and illustrator, b. New York City; known esp. for his paintings of boys, often appearing on covers of *Saturday Evening Post, Life*, etc.

**Rod** (rôd), **Édouard.** 1857–1910. Swiss novelist, resident many years in Paris. Professor of comparative literature, Geneva (1886–93). Author of *Le Sens de la Vie* (1889), *Le Ménage de Pasteur Nandié* (1898), *L'Inutile Effort* (1903), and *Le Glaive et le Bandeau* (1909).

**Ro′da Ro′da** (rō′dä rō′dä), **Alexander Friedrich Ladislaus.** *Real surname* **Ro′sen·feld** (rō′zĕn·fĕlt). 1872–1945. Humorous writer and journalist, b. in Slavonia; author of many humorous stories, the comedy *Der Feldherrnhügel* (with Carl Rössler; 1910), the autobiographical novel *Roda Rodas Roman* (1925), etc.

**Rod·ber′tus** (rôt·bĕr′to͝os), **Johann Karl.** 1805–1875. German economist and politician; leader of Left Center and member, Lower House (1849); accepted the constitution during a gradual evolution of socialism; held that united labor produces the national income of rent, profit, and wages, and championed a society organized on a communistic basis.

**Rod′chen·ko** (rôt′chĭn·kô), **Aleksandr.** 1891– . Russian painter, photographer, and typographer; identified with ultramodern school of art; member of group practicing constructivism (1917–22); repudiated art to devote himself to "useful" activities (1922), such as typography, furniture designing, and theater sets.

**Rodd, James Rennell.** See Baron RENNELL.

**Rod′dick** (rŏd′ĭk), Sir **Thomas George.** 1846–1923. Canadian physician; as a Conservative member of the Dominion House of Commons (1896–1904), introduced the *Roddick Bill*, to establish a central national registration, and uniform standards, for all licensed medical practitioners throughout Canada, and was instrumental in securing its passage (1902) as the Canada Medical Act.

**Ro′de** (rō′dĕ), **Christian Bernhard.** 1725–1797. German painter and engraver.

**Ro′de** (rō′thĕ), **Helge.** 1870–1937. Danish lyric poet, dramatist, novelist, and literary critic; opponent of materialism and Darwinism, and champion of a modern mysticism.

**Rode** (rôd), **Jacques Pierre Joseph.** 1774–1830. French violinist. Beethoven wrote expressly for him Opus 50 for violin and orchestra. Composer of many violin pieces, including a series of 24 caprices.

**Ro′den·bach** (*Flem.* rō′dĕn·bäK; *Fr.* rô′dĕn′bȧk′), **Georges.** 1855–1898. Belgian poet, of symbolist group, associated with 19th-century Belgian literary revival.

**Ro′den·berg** (rō′dĕn·bĕrK), **Julius.** *Real surname* **Le′vy** (lā′vē). 1831–1914. German poet and writer; edited in Berlin the belletristic journal *Der Salon* (with Dohm; 1867–74) and founded and edited (from 1874) the monthly review *Deutsche Rundschau.* Author of poems, realistic novels, and sketches of life and travels.

**Rod′er·ick** *or* **Rod′er·ic** (rŏd′ẽr·ĭk). *Span.* **Ro·dri′go** (rô·thrē′gō). d. ?711 A.D. Last king of the Visigoths in Spain; succeeded to the throne (c. 710); was defeated, and probably slain, by the Moslems under Tariq in the battle of Rio Barbate (not Jerez, as generally stated). According to some, lived to continue losing fight, retiring into Portugal (d. 713). Many legends have gathered about the name of this "last of the Goths" (in writings of Washington Irving, Southey, and Landor).

**Roderic O'Connor.** See O'CONNOR.

**Rodg′ers** (rŏj′ẽrz). Name of a family celebrated in American naval history, including: **John Rodgers** (1773–1838), captain (1799); in Mediterranean, engaged with Barbary pirates (1802–06); ranking officer in active service in War of 1812. His brother **George Washington** (1787–1832), served through War of 1812; in Mediterranean (1816–19) and New York navy yard (1819–25). John's son **John** (1812–1882), with North Pacific Exploring and Surveying Expedition (1852–56); aide to Admiral Du Pont at battle of Port Royal (1861); commanded flagship of fleet operating on James River (1862); engaged in attack on Fort Sumter (1863) and later captured Confederate ironclad *Atlanta;* rear admiral commanding Asiatic squadron (1870–72). **William Ledyard** (1860–1944), son of John Rodgers (1812–1882), grad. U.S.N.A., Annapolis (1878); held command in Atlantic fleet in World War (1916–18); commanded Asiatic fleet (1918–19); retired as rear admiral (1924). A great-grandson of John (1773–1838), **John** (1881–1926), grad. U.S.N.A., Annapolis (1903); on submarine and mine barrage duty in North Sea during World War; commanded naval air station, Pearl Harbor, Hawaii (1922–25); killed in airplane crash (Aug. 27, 1926). George Washington Rodgers's son **Christopher Raymond Perry** (1819–1892) served in Seminole War (1839–42) and Mexican War (1846–48); commanded flagship of Admiral Du Pont in attack on Port Royal (1861); fleet captain, South Atlantic blockading squadron (1862–63); engaged in attack on Charleston (Apr., 1863); rear admiral (1874); superintendent, U.S. Naval Academy (1874–78); commander in chief, Pacific squadron (1878–80). Another son of George Washington Rodgers, **George Washington** (1822–1863), served in Mexican War (1846–48); killed in attack on Charleston.

**Rodgers, Richard.** 1902– . American composer, producer; b. N.Y.C.; collab. with Lorenz Hart, lyricist, in writing musical comedies: *Dearest Enemy, Connecticut Yankee, On Your Toes, I'd Rather Be Right, Babes in Arms*, etc.; with Oscar Hammerstein (b. 1895): *Oklahoma!, Allegro, Carousel, South Pacific, The King and I.*

**Ro′din′** (rô′dăN′), **François Auguste René.** 1840–1917. French sculptor, b. Paris. First exhibited at the Paris Salon (1877) his figure called *L'Âge d'Airain*, which expressed his idea of the proper construction of a statue, but which was so unusual that it raised a storm of criticism. Among his other notable works are *Saint Jean Baptiste Prêchant*, portrait busts of Laurens, Carrier-Belleuse, Victor Hugo, Proust, Bernard Shaw, Gustav Mahler, Clemenceau, and others, monument of Claude Lorrain, statue of Balzac, sculptures *Le Baiser, Le Penseur, L'Homme qui Marche*, etc.

**Rod′man** (rŏd′măn), **Hugh.** 1859–1940. American naval officer, b. Frankfort, Ky.; grad. U.S.N.A., Annapolis (1880). Rear admiral (1917), admiral (1919); retired (1923). Commanded division 9, U.S. battleship force, on duty with British grand fleet (Nov., 1917); commander of U.S. battleships (Apr., 1918); commanded 6th battle squadron in North Sea, co-operating with British grand fleet (1918–19). Commander in chief of Pacific fleet (1919).

**Rodman, Thomas Jackson.** 1815–1871. American army officer, b. near Salem, Ind.; grad. U.S.M.A., West Point (1841); served in ordnance department. Invented Rodman gun, made by casting successive layers of metal around a hollow core.

**Rod'ney** (rŏd'nĭ), **Caesar.** 1728–1784. American Revolutionary statesman, b. near Dover, Del. Member of Continental Congress (1774–76, 1777, 1778), and signer of Declaration of Independence. Major general in Delaware militia in American Revolution. President of Delaware (1778–82). His brother **Thomas** (1744–1811) was colonel in Delaware militia in American Revolution, engaged at Trenton and Princeton; member, Continental Congress (1781–83, 1785–87); U.S. judge, Territory of Mississippi (1803–11). Thomas's son **Caesar Augustus** (1772–1824) was a lawyer and legislator; member of U.S. House of Representatives (1803–05) and strong supporter of Jefferson's policies; attorney general of the United States (1807–11); first U.S. minister to Argentina (1823–24); died at Buenos Aires.

**Rodney, George Brydges.** 1st Baron **Rodney.** 1719–1792. English admiral; governor of Newfoundland (1748–52); M.P. (1751); rear admiral (1759); reduced Martinique and took St. Lucia, Grenada, St. Vincent (1762); vice-admiral (1763); commander in chief at Jamaica (1771–74) and Leeward Islands (1779); admiral (1778); captured Spanish convoy off Cape Finisterre (1780), and off Cape St. Vincent took seven ships out of eleven (1780); seized Dutch settlements in West Indies (1781); captured seven ships and de Grasse himself in brilliant victory off Dominica (Apr. 12, 1782); raised to peerage, pensioned, lived in retirement.

**Ro·dó'** (rô·thō'), **José.** 1872–1917. Uruguayan prose writer; among his works are *Ariel*, *Motivos de Proteo*, and *El Mirador de Próspero.*

**Rod'o·gu'ne** (rŏd'ô·gū'nē) *or* **Rhod'o·gu'ne** (rŏd'-). fl. 2d century B.C. Parthian princess, daughter of Mithridates I; m. (c. 140 B.C.) Demetrius II Nicator of Syria while he was a prisoner of Mithridates; on his return, quarreled violently with Cleopatra Thea, first wife of Demetrius. Subject of Corneille's *Rodogune* (1644 or 1645).

**Rodolphe.** See RUDOLF.

**Rodrigo Díaz de Bivar.** See the CID.

**Ro·dri'gues Al'ves** (rōō·thrē'gēs äl'vēs), **Francisco de Paula.** 1848–1919. Brazilian statesman; president of São Paulo (1900–02, 1912–16); president of Brazil (1902–06). Elected president again (1918) but did not serve, because of sickness.

**Ro·drí'guez** (rô·thrē'gās), **Abelardo L.** 1889–1967. Mexican general and political leader; active in various revolutions; provisional president of Mexico (1932–34) on Ortiz Rubio's resignation; dominated by Calles.

**Ro·drí'guez** (rô·thrē'gāth), **Pedro.** See Conde de CAMPOMANES.

**Ro·drí'guez A'rias** (rô·thrē'gāth [-gās] ä'ryäs), **Alejandro.** Spanish governor of Cuba (1892–93).

**Ro·drí'guez Ca·bril'lo** (rô·thrē'gāth [-gās] kä·brē'(l)yō), **Juan.** See CABRILLO.

**Ro·drí'guez Car'ra·ci'do** (rô·thrē'gāth kär'rä·thē'thō), **José.** 1856–1928. Spanish chemist and scholar; professor of pharmacy (1881–98) and biological chemistry (1898–1926), U. of Madrid, and rector of the university (1916–28).

**Ro·drí'guez de Fon·se'ca** (rô·thrē'gāth thā fôn·sā'kä), **Juan.** 1451–1524. Spanish prelate; principal chaplain to Isabella, later to Ferdinand. Head of department of affairs in the Indies (1493 ff.); enemy of Columbus; sent Bobadilla to New World to investigate Columbus's administration; later opposed Cortes; organized Council of the Indies with himself as chief (1511).

**Ro·drí'guez Ma·rín'** (rô·thrē'gāth mä·rēn'), **Francisco.** 1855–1943. Spanish scholar; known esp. as a Cervantes scholar; author of numerous lexicographic and critical works and of several editions of *Don Quixote.*

**Rod·zian'ko** (rŭt·zyån'kô), **Mikhail.** 1859–1924. Russian politician; deputy in the 3d and 4th Dumas, and president of the Duma (1911–16). During the Revolution, head of Committee of the Duma (March 11–16, 1917). Author of *The Fall of Czarism* (1925).

**Ro·dzin'ski** (rô·jĭn'skĭ; *Pol.* rô·jēn'y'·skē), **Artur.** 1894–1958. Musician and conductor, b. at Spalato, in Dalmatia. To U.S. (1926), naturalized (1933); assistant conductor, under Stokowski, of Philadelphia orchestra (1926–29); conductor of Los Angeles Philharmonic orchestra (1929–33), Cleveland orchestra (1933–42), New York Philharmonic orchestra (1943–47), Chicago Symphony orchestra (1947–48).

**Roe** (rō), **Edward Payson.** 1838–1888. American Presbyterian clergyman and novelist, b. New Windsor, N.Y. Pastorate, Highland Falls, N.Y. (1866–74). Author of *Barriers Burned Away* (1872), *Opening a Chestnut Burr* (1874), *From Jest to Earnest* (1875), *Without a Home* (1881), *He Fell in Love with His Wife* (1886), etc.

**Roe, Francis Asbury.** 1823–1901. American naval officer; executive officer of the *Pensacola* when it ran down Potomac past Confederate batteries (1861); commanded gunboat *Katahdin* in operations opening Mississippi River from New Orleans to Port Hudson (1862–63). Engaged Confederate ironclad *Albemarle* and forced its retreat (1864). Rear admiral (1884). Author of *Naval Duties and Discipline* (1865).

**Roe** *or* **Row** (rō), Sir **Thomas.** 1581?–1644. English diplomat; won reputation by successful mission to court of great mogul, Jahangir, at Agra to gain commercial treaty (1615–18); secured further privileges for English merchants as ambassador to Ottoman Porte (1621–28); took part in peace conferences at Hamburg, Regensburg, and Vienna (1638–42); left diplomatic memoirs.

**Roeb'ling** (rōb'lĭng; *Ger.* rûb'-), **John Augustus.** 1806–1869. Civil engineer and industrialist, b. Mühlhausen, Ger. To U.S. (1831); naturalized (1837). Established factory manufacturing first wire rope made in America (1841). Designed suspension bridges, including one over Niagara River at Niagara Falls (opened 1855), over Ohio River between Cincinnati and Covington (opened 1867); suggested and made preliminary plans for Brooklyn Bridge (plans approved, 1869). His son **Washington Augustus** (1837–1926) associated with him (from 1857); served in Union army through Civil War; succeeded father as chief engineer in construction of Brooklyn Bridge (1869) and carried it to completion (1883).

**Roe'buck** (rō'bŭk), **John.** 1718–1794. English inventor; introduced leaden condensing chambers in manufacture of sulphuric acid; set up manufactory of sulphuric acid at Prestonpans (1749) and ironworks at Carron (c. 1760), later famous for production of ordnance; patented (1762) process of converting cast iron into malleable iron by use of pit coal with artificial blast. **John Arthur Roebuck** (1801–1879), his grandson, radical member of Parliament, brought up in Canada; protested at bar of House of Commons against suspension of Canadian constitution (1838); by carrying motion for inquiry into conduct of Crimean War, brought about resignation of Aberdeen's government; chairman of Sevastopol committee (1855); supported Lord Beaconsfield's policy during Eastern crisis (1877–78).

**Rœ'de·rer'** (rē'drâr'), Comte **Pierre Louis.** 1754–1835. French economist and politician; member of Constituent Assembly (1789), where he was prominent in consideration of financial and judicial legislation. President, department of the interior, in the Council of State (1799); senator (1802). Minister of finance for King Joseph, at Naples (1806). Supported Napoleon during the Hundred

Days, and entered the Chamber of Peers (1815). Lost his honors at the Second Restoration, but was again admitted to the Chamber of Peers (1832).

**Roe'di·ger** (rû'dĭ·gẽr), **Emil.** 1801–1874. German Semitic scholar.

**Roehm.** Variant of Röhm.

**Ro·e'las** (rô·ā'läs) *or* **Rue'las** (rwā'-), **Juan de las.** *Called* **El Clé'ri·go** (ĕl klā'rē·gō). 1560?–1625. Spanish painter of Andalusian school.

**Roe'lofs** (rōō'lôfs), **Willem.** 1822–1897. Dutch landscape painter, etcher, and naturalist; pioneer of modern Dutch emotional landscape.

**Roe'mer** (rû'mẽr), **Friedrich Adolf.** 1809–1869. German geologist; authority on the mountains of northwestern Germany. His brother **Ferdinand** (1818–1891) investigated and wrote on the geology of Texas and Tennessee.

**Roe'mer** (rû'mẽr), **Olaus** *or* **Ole.** 1644–1710. Danish astronomer; professor of astronomy at Copenhagen; discovered that light is not transmitted instantaneously; estimated the velocity of light from his observations of the variations in the time of eclipse of Jupiter's satellites according to the earth's distance from that planet; erected first transit instrument of value.

**Roent'gen** (rûnt'gĕn), **David.** 1743–1807. German cabinetmaker, expert in marquetry and metal mountings. Son and pupil of **Abraham Roentgen** (1711–1793), whom he succeeded (1772) in the furniture shop at Neuwied; helped influence development of ornamental furniture in Germany and France (1785–90).

**Roent'gen** *or* **Rönt'gen** (rûnt'gĕn; *Angl.* rĕnt'-, rŭnt'-, -yĕn), **Wilhelm Conrad.** 1845–1923. German physicist, b. Lennep, Prussia; educ. U. of Zurich. Professor, Strassburg (1876), Giessen (1879), Würzburg (1888), Munich (1900–20). Discovered X rays, frequently called Roentgen, or Röntgen, rays (1895); awarded the 1901 Nobel prize for physics.

**Roe'rich** (rû'rĭk), **Nicholas Konstantin.** 1874–1947. Russian painter; made pilgrimage through Russia, painting (1901–04), and through central Asia (1923–28). The Roerich Museum in New York City was built for display of his paintings and collections.

**Rog'er I** of Sicily (rŏj'ẽr). **Ro'ger' Guis'card'** (*Fr.* rô'zhā' gēs'kȧr'). 1031–1101. Norman conqueror in Sicily; aided his brother Robert Guiscard (from c. 1060), capturing Messina (1061), Palermo (1072), Catania, Girgenti, etc.; assumed title count of Sicily (c. 1071); captured island of Malta from the Saracens (1090). His son **Roger II** of Sicily (1095–1154) succeeded him (1101) and assumed title grand count of Sicily (1101–30) and king of Sicily (1130–54); waged successful war upon the Byzantine emperor Manuel Comnenus, pillaging cities on the Greek peninsula and capturing territory along the North African coast.

**Roger Bernard I.** Count of **Foix** (1012–35). See Foix.

**Roger di Flor.** See Flor.

**Roger–Ducasse.** See Ducasse.

**Rog'er of Hove'den** (rŏj'ẽr, hŏv'dĕn) *or* **How'den** (hou'd'n). fl. 1174–1201. English chronicler; compiled *Chronica 732–1201* (1192–1201), informative (from 1192) on foreign affairs and domestic policy and on constitutional history.

**Roger of Salis'bur·y** (sôlz'bẽr·ĭ; -brĭ). d. 1139. English prelate and political and judicial officer; chancellor under Henry I (1101); bishop of Salisbury (1102; consecrated 1107); remodeled administrative system of secular government; created exchequer system, the management of which was kept in his family over a century; justiciar of England, next in power to king; ruled in Henry I's absence; went over to Stephen, taking royal treasure and administrative system (1135); excited enmity of barons by avarice and acquisition of castles; forced to surrender castles and power (1139).

**Roger of Wen'do'ver** (wĕn'dō'vẽr). d. 1236. English chronicler; Benedictine monk, St. Albans; in scriptorium at St. Albans compiled *Flores Historiarum*, extending from creation to 1235, valuable from 1202 as firsthand authority.

**Rog'ers** (rŏj'ẽrz), **Bruce.** 1870–1957. American printer and book designer, b. Lafayette, Ind.; B.S., Purdue (1890). On staff, Riverside Press, Cambridge, Mass. (1895–1912). Printing adviser, University Press, Cambridge, Eng. (1917–19), and Harvard U. Press, Cambridge, Mass. (from 1919). Also associated with William Edwin Rudge, printer, Mt. Vernon, N.Y. (1920–28) and with Emery Walker, Ltd., London, Eng. (1928).

**Rogers, Edith,** *nee* **Nourse** (nûrs). 1881–1960. American legislator, b. Saco, Me.; m. (1907) John Jacob Rogers (d. 1925); American Red Cross worker in France (1917); member, from Massachusetts (succeeding her husband), U.S. House of Representatives (from 1925); presidential representative in care of disabled soldiers (from 1922).

**Rogers, Henry Huttleston** (*or* **Huddleston**). 1840–1909. American financier, b. Mattapoisett, Mass.; went into oil business in Pennsylvania (1861); associated with Charles Pratt in oil refinery, Brooklyn, N.Y. (1867); devised and patented (1871) machinery for separating naphtha from crude oil. With Pratt, joined Standard Oil Co. organization (1874); vice-president (1890); originated idea of pipe-line transportation; known as chief executive officer of Standard Oil interests. His son **Henry Huddleston** (1879–1935) succeeded to his business interests; also, served in New York National Guard and in National Army during World War; took part in Aisne-Marne and Oise offensives in France.

**Rogers, James Blythe.** 1802–1852. American chemist, b. Philadelphia; coauthor with his brother Robert of *A Text Book on Chemistry* (1846). A brother, **William Barton** (1804–1882), was a geologist; first president, M.I.T. (1862–70, 1878–81); results of his geological survey work with his brother Henry, published in *Annual Reports...on the Geology of the Virginias* (1884). Another brother, **Henry Darwin** (1808–1866), was also a geologist; director, geological survey of New Jersey (1835) and Pennsylvania (1836); professor of natural history, U. of Glasgow, Scotland (1858–66). A third brother, **Robert Empie** (1813–1884), was a chemist; professor of medical chemistry and toxicology, Jefferson Medical College, Philadelphia (1877–84).

**Rogers, James Edwin Thorold.** 1823–1890. English economist; first Tooke professor of statistics and economic science, King's Coll., London (1859–90); adopted Cobden's views; advanced Liberal M.P. (1880 ff.). Author of *History of Agriculture and Prices in England*, record of period 1259–1793 (8 vols., 1866–93), *Economic Interpretation of History* (1888), *Industrial History of England* (1892), etc.

**Rogers, James Gamble.** 1867–1947. American architect; practiced in New York City (from 1905). Designed buildings at Yale (Sterling Memorial Library, Harkness Memorial Quadrangle, etc.), Columbia-Presbyterian Medical Center in New York City, Northwestern University professional group in Chicago, etc.

**Rogers, James Harris.** 1856–1929. American electrical engineer and inventor, b. Franklin, Tenn.; patented various inventions in multiplex telegraphy, high-frequency current, underground and undersea radio transmission.

**Rogers, James Hotchkiss.** 1857–1940. American pianist and composer; author of cantatas (*The Man of Nazareth, The Mystery of Bethlehem*), anthems, piano pieces, and many songs.

**Rogers, John.** 1500?–1555. English Protestant martyr; continued Tyndale's English version of Old Testament, using also Coverdale's translation; published complete Bible under pseudonym **Thomas Mat'thew** [măth'ū] (1537); prebendary of St. Pauls (1551). Preached, on accession of Mary, doctrine as taught in King Edward's days, warning against popery; imprisoned in Newgate by order of new bishop of London; brought before commission appointed by Cardinal Pole, sentenced to death as heretic by Gardiner for denying Christian character of Church of Rome and the real presence in the Sacrament.

**Rogers, John.** 1627–?1665. English preacher, a Fifth Monarchy Man; sided with army against Parliament; one of first to join Fifth Monarchy movement; antagonized by establishment of Protectorate, addressed warning letter to Cromwell and denounced him from pulpit (1654); imprisoned (1655), released (1657), sent to Tower on charges of conspiracy (1658). At Restoration, studied medicine at Leiden and Utrecht; M.D. (1662).

**Rogers, John.** 1829–1904. American sculptor, b. Salem, Mass. Successful with *The Slave Auction*, exhibited in New York (1859–60). Studio in New York; home in New Canaan, Conn. (from 1877). Best known for his statuette groups illustrating Civil War scenes, literary and dramatic figures, and scenes from country life.

**Rogers, Moses.** 1779?–1821. American mariner, b. New London, Conn.; commanded steamer *Phoenix* on its initial trip around Sandy Hook and Cape May to the Delaware River (1809), first ocean voyage of a steamship; commanded steamer *Savannah* on first transatlantic voyage (1819).

**Rogers, Randolph.** 1825–1892. American sculptor, b. Waterloo, N.Y. Sculptor of the bronze Columbus doors in the Capitol, Washington, D.C.; *Ruth* in Metropolitan Museum of Art, New York City; *John Adams* in Mount Auburn Cemetery, Cambridge, Mass.; *Lincoln* in Philadelphia; *Genius of Connecticut*, State Capitol, Hartford, Conn., etc.

**Rogers, Robert.** 1731–1795. American frontier soldier, b. Methuen, Mass.; captain of company of rangers (1756) and promoted major by Gen. Abercromby (1758). Rogers's Rangers became famous for raids. At outbreak of Revolutionary War, negotiated with both British and Continentals (1775–76); imprisoned by Washington on suspicion of espionage; escaped and organized royalist force, the Queen's Rangers; defeated and deprived of his command, near White Plains, N.Y. Fled to England (1780); lived there on half-pay pension from British government.

**Rogers, Robert Cameron.** 1862–1912. American poet, b. Buffalo, N.Y. Among his works are *Wind in the Clearing, and Other Poems, Will o' the Wisp, The Rosary, and Other Poems.*

**Rogers, Robert Empie.** See under James Blythe ROGERS.

**Rogers, Robert William.** 1864–1930. American Orientalist; professor of ancient Oriental literature, Princeton (1919–29).

**Rogers, Samuel.** 1763–1855. English poet; published (1792) *The Pleasures of Memory*, on which his poetical reputation is based. Patron of artists and men of letters; friend of Wordsworth, Scott, and Byron; long a literary dictator; kept notebook of conversations with friends, which was edited by his nephew William Sharpe (1859). Declined laureateship on Wordsworth's death.

**Rogers, Will,** *in full* **William Penn Adair.** 1879–1935. American actor, lecturer, and humorist, b. Oologah, Indian Territory, now Oklahoma. In vaudeville with lasso act at Hammerstein's Roof Garden, New York (1905); developed successful accompanying monologue (c. 1912). Associated with Ziegfeld Follies (from 1914). Starred in motion pictures, as in *They Had to See Paris, Happy Days, State Fair, David Harum, Judge Priest, The County Chairman, Life Begins at Forty, Steamboat Round the Bend.* Wrote syndicated newspaper articles, in New York *Times* daily (from 1926), filled with shrewd satire, comment on news of the day, and homely philosophy. Killed in airplane crash with Wiley Post (*q.v.*). Author of *The Cowboy Philosopher on Prohibition* (1919), *What We Laugh At* (1920), *Illiterate Digest* (1924), *Letters of a Self-Made Diplomat to His President* (1927), *Will Rogers's Political Follies* (1929), etc.

**Rogers, William Augustus.** 1832–1898. American astronomer and physicist; best known for researches in micrometry, establishing accurate values of the yard and the meter, and observations of exact positions of catalogued stars between 50° and 55° north declination.

**Rogers, William Pierce.** 1913– . American lawyer; U.S. secretary of state (from 1969).

**Rogers, Woodes.** d. 1732. English seaman and colonial governor. Commander of privateering expedition against Spaniards in South Seas (1708–11); with William Dampier as pilot, reached Juan Fernández (1709), sent Thomas Dover and landing party ashore, and rescued Alexander Selkirk; sacked Guayaquil; published journal of voyage (1712). Rented Bahama Islands from lords proprietors and was commissioned as governor (1718–21, 1729–32); suppressed piracy.

**Ro·get'** (rō·zhā'; *Brit. also* rŏzh'ā), **Peter Mark.** 1779–1869. English physician and scholar; instrumental in establishing U. of London; author of *On Animal and Vegetable Physiology*, a Bridgewater treatise (1834), and *Thesaurus of English Words and Phrases* (1852), which reached 28th edition during his lifetime.

**Ro'gier'** (rô'zhyā'), **Charles Latour.** 1800–1885. Belgian statesman; opposed union with the Low Countries; took part in revolutionary movements (1830) and became member of provisional government; premier of Belgium (1847–52).

**Rogier van der Weyden** *or* **Roger de La Pasture.** See WEYDEN.

**Ro'han'** (rô'äɴ'). Name of a feudal family of France derived from that of a small town in Morbihan, Brittany. The family claimed connection with early kings of Brittany and after the 15th century developed many branches, esp. the seigneurs of Gié, the princes of Soubise and Guéménée, and the dukes of Rohan-Chabot and Montbazon. The Rohan family included: **Hercule de Rohan,** Duc **de Mont'ba'zon'** [dẽ môɴ'bȧ'zôɴ'] (1568–1654), who fought under Henry III and Henry IV against the Holy League; made governor of Paris. **René de Rohan** (1550–1586), a descendant of the marshal of Gié, led a Calvinist army (1570) and defended Lusignan against the Catholics (1574–75). His son **Henri,** Duc **de Rohan** (1579–1638), Huguenot leader and author, b. Blain; favorite of Henry IV; created duke (1603); fought as leader of Huguenots in Bearnese revolts (1622, 1625–26, 1627–29). Lived in Venice (1629–32). Again in service of France (1632–33). Retired to Geneva and enlisted under Bernhard of Saxe-Weimar; killed at Rheinfelden. Author of celebrated *Mémoires* and of a book on the history and art of war, *Le Parfait Capitaine* (1631). **Louis René Édouard,** Cardinal **de Rohan** (1734–1803), of the Guéménée branch, b. Paris; took orders at Strasbourg (1760); ambassador to Vienna (1772), where Empress Maria Theresa was hostile to him; recalled (1774); made grand almoner of France (1777) and cardinal (1778); became archbishop of Strasbourg (1779); involved in the mysterious "affair of the diamond necklace" (1784–86) in which he was duped by the

Comtesse de La Motte (*q.v.*) and others; arrested, tried, and acquitted. Deprived of public office and exiled (1786). Refused to take oath to the constitution and went to Ettenheim, Baden (1791).

**Roh′de** (rō′dĕ), **Erwin.** 1845–1898. German classical scholar and philologist; pupil of Friedrich Ritschl and friend of Nietzsche.

**Roh′de** (rō′thĕ), **Ruth,** *nee* **Bry′an** (brī′ăn). 1885–1954. Daughter of William Jennings Bryan (*q.v.*). American diplomat; m. 1st Reginald Owen (1910; d. 1927), 2d Börge Rohde (1936). Member, from Florida, U.S. House of Representatives (1929–33). U.S. minister to Denmark (1933–36), first U.S. woman diplomat.

**Rohlfs** (rōlfs), **Charles.** 1853–1936. American furniture designer, b. New York City; m. (1884) Anna Katharine Green (*q.v.*); credited with first designing type of furniture known as *mission furniture* or *Rohlf's furniture.*

**Rohlfs** (rōlfs), **Friedrich Gerhard.** 1831–1896. German explorer; explored Morocco disguised as a Mohammedan (1861–62); crossed Africa from Tripoli to Lagos (1865–66); visited Abyssinia and the oases between Tripoli and Egypt (1868), the Libyan desert (1873–74), etc.

**Röhm** (rûm), **Ernst.** 1887–1934. German soldier and National Socialist leader; follower of Hitler in National Socialist Workers' party, took part in Hitler Putsch in Munich (1923), and was arrested as a ringleader; as chief of staff, took over organization and command of the Brown Shirts and Black Shirts in Germany (1931); led national revolution in Bavaria (1933) and became state commissar and Reich's secretary of state in Bavaria. Charged with conspiracy to overthrow Hitler as chancellor; executed in purge (June, 1934).

**Roh′mer** (rō′mẽr), **Sax.** *Pseudonym of* **Arthur Sarsfield Ward** (wôrd) or **Wade.** 1883–1959. English author of mystery thrillers, esp. a series centering about fictional character Dr. Fu Manchu.

**Rohr′bach** (rōr′bäk), **Paul.** 1869– . German journalist and writer on world politics and geography.

**Rohr′ba′cher′** (rōr′bȧ′shâr′), **René François.** 1789–1856. French historian; chief work, *Histoire Universelle de l'Église Catholique* (1842–49).

**Ro′jas** (rô′häs), **Fernando de.** 1475?–?1538. Spanish writer; reputed author of dramatic prose romance *Tragicomedia de Calisto y Melibea,* better known as *La Celestina,* chief contribution to development of the national drama in the 15th century.

**Rojas Vil′lan·dran′do** (vē′lyän·drän′dō), **Augustín de.** 1572?–1612. Spanish dramatist and actor.

**Ro′jas–Zor·ril′la** (-thôr·rē′lyä), **Francisco de.** 1607–1648. Spanish dramatist; author of widely imitated plays, both tragedies and comedies.

**Ro′ki·tan′sky** (rō′kē·tän′skē), Baron **Karl von.** 1804–1878. Austrian physician; professor of pathological anatomy, Vienna (from 1834); one of the founders of modern pathological anatomy. Author of *Handbuch der Pathologischen Anatomie* (3 vols., 1842–46).

**Ro·kos·sov′ski** (rŭ·kŭ·sôf′skû·ĭ; *Angl.* -skĭ), **Konstantin.** 1896–1968. Russian army officer; major in World War I; joined Red Guards (1917); lieutenant general, in command of central sector in defense of Moscow in World War II; as commander of the Don front, launched (1943) attack resulting in crushing of German resistance before Stalingrad.

**Ro′land′ de La Pla′tière′** (rô′läɴ′ dẽ lȧ plȧ′tyâr′), **Jean Marie.** 1734–1793. French revolutionary statesman; became leader among the Girondists (1791); minister of interior (1792, 1793). Attacked Robespierre and members of the Mountain and attempted to save life of Louis XVI; forced to flee Paris into Normandy; committed suicide (Nov. 15, 1793) when he learned of sentence and execution of his wife, **Jeanne Manon,** *nee* **Phli′pon′** [flē′pôɴ′] (1754–1793), commonly known as Mme. Roland; her salon in Paris was headquarters for Republicans and Girondists (1791–93); after fall of Girondists, she was arrested, tried before the Revolutionary Tribunal, condemned, and guillotined (Nov. 8, 1793); according to popular report, her last words were, "O Liberty, what crimes are committed in thy name!"

**Ro·lan′do** (rō·län′dō), **Luigi.** 1773–1831. Italian anatomist; known for discoveries concerning the structure and function of the nervous system, esp. the brain.

**Rolf.** See Rollo.

**Rolfe** (rŏlf), **John.** 1585–1622. English colonist in America, b. in Norfolk, Eng.; to Jamestown, Va. (1610). Experimented until he discovered method of curing tobacco, thus making it an article of export and laying basis of Virginia's trade and prosperity during colonial period. Married (1614) Pocahontas (d. 1617), daughter of Indian chief Powhatan. Probably killed by Indians in his Virginia home (1622).

**Rolfe, Robert Mon′sey** (?mŭn′zĭ). Baron **Cran′worth** (krăn′wûrth). 1790–1868. English lawyer and judge; lord chancellor in Aberdeen's ministry (1852) and Palmerston's (till 1857), and again 1865–66; remembered for a measure for shortening of conveyances (1860).

**Rolfe, William James.** 1827–1910. American educator, b. Newburyport, Mass.; introduced teaching of English literature in Massachusetts schools (1848–68). Author and editor of many school texts and editions of standard authors, notably the poems of Tennyson and Scott. Edited Shakespeare's works in forty volumes (1871–84; wholly revised, 1903–06), establishing reputation as Shakespearean scholar. Also wrote *A Life of William Shakespeare* (1904).

**Roll** (rôl), **Alfred Philippe.** 1846–1919. French painter; associated with plein-air school.

**Rol′land′** (rô′läɴ′), **Romain.** 1866–1944. French man of letters, b. Clamecy. Author of many biographical and critical studies, dramas, and novels; in later years, evinced sympathy for ideas advanced by the Third International. Awarded Nobel prize in literature (1915). Among his works on or for the theater are *Les Origines du Théâtre Lyrique Moderne* (1895), *Morituri ou les Loups, Danton* (1901), *Le 14 Juillet* (1902), and *Le Théâtre du Peuple* (1903); among his biographical and critical works are *Beethoven* (1903), *Michel-Ange* (1905), *Vie de Tolstoï* (1911), and *Mahatma Gandhi* (1926); his outstanding work in fiction is *Jean Christophe* (10 vols., 1904–12), huge novel portraying life of a musician of genius in the contemporary world.

**Rolle de Ham′pole** (rōl′ dĕ hăm′pōl), **Richard.** 1290?–1349. English hermit, known as "the Hermit of Hampole." Indifferent to scholastic philosophy; studied religion. At Dalton, later at Hampole, led the contemplative life. Author of religious treatises in Latin and English, including *De Emendatione Vitae* and *De Incendio Amoris,* and a poem *The Pricke of Conscience,* in seven books, protesting papal pretensions (printed 1863).

**Rolle′ston** (rōl′stŭn), **Thomas William.** 1857–1920. Irish journalist and writer; editor of *Treasury of Irish Poetry* (with Stopford Brooke; 1900); author of *Sea Spray* (verse, 1909), *Myths and Legends of the Celtic Race* (1911), etc.

**Rol′lier′** (rô′lyā′), **Auguste.** 1874–1954. Swiss physician; pioneer in heliotherapy for tuberculous bones and joints, for which he established a clinic in the Alps.

**Rol′lin′** (rô′lăɴ′), **Charles.** 1661–1741. French educator; rector of U. of Paris (1694–95); coadjutor of Collège de Beauvais (1699–1711) and removed because of Jansenist sympathies; again rector, U. of Paris (1720), but removed as a Jansenist. Chief work is *Traité des Études* (1726–31), book on the duties of a college head.

**Rol'li'nat'** (rô'lē'nȧ'), **Maurice.** 1846–1903. French poet.

**Rol'lins** (rŏl'ĭnz), **Hyder Edward.** 1889–1958. American educator; professor, Harvard (from 1926). Editor of *Old English Ballads* (1920), *The Pepys Ballads* (8 vols., 1929–32), *England's Helicon* (2 vols., 1935), *Shakespeare's Poems* (in *New Variorum Shakespeare;* 1938), etc.

**Rol'lo** (rŏl'ō) *or* **Rolf** (rŏlf) *or* **Hrolf** (rŏlf). *Called* **the Gang'er** (găng'ẽr) *or* **Walker.** 860?–?931. Norse chieftain and Viking leader; invaded northwestern France (c. 890–910); received Rouen and adjacent territory (911) by treaty with Charles the Simple of France—the beginning of Normandy; lands increased later by conquests. Ancestor of Norman dukes, kings, and crusaders.

**Rol'lock** (rŏl'ŭk), **Robert.** 1555?–1599. Scottish theologian; first principal of newly-founded college, afterwards Edinburgh U. (1583–99).

**Rolls** (rōlz), **Charles Stewart.** 1877–1910. English motorcar manufacturer and aviator; pioneer of automobiles in England; organized C. S. Rolls & Co., automobile manufacturers, which merged with Royce, Ltd., to form Rolls-Royce, Ltd. (1904). Crossed and recrossed English Channel in airplane (June, 1910), killed, first English victim of aviation.

**Rolph** (rŏlf), **James, Jr.** 1869–1934. American shipowner, merchant, and politician, b. San Francisco; mayor of San Francisco (1911–32); governor of California (1931–34).

**Rolshoven, Julius.** 1858–1930. American painter, b. Detroit; in group associated with Frank Duveneck (1879).

**Röl'vaag** (rōl'väg), **Ole Edvart.** 1876–1931. Educator and novelist, b. in Norway; to America (1896). Professor of Norwegian, St. Olaf College, Northfield, Minn. (1906–31). Achieved fame with *Giants in the Earth* (1927; English translation of his two Norwegian novels *I de Dage* ["In These Days"] and *Riket Grundlaegges* ["The Kingdom is Founded"], novels of Norwegian settlers in South Dakota in the 1870's); also wrote *Peder Seier* (Eng. trans. *Peder Victorious*, 1929) and *Den Signede Dag* ("The Blessed Day"; Eng. trans. *Their Fathers' God*, 1931).

**Ro'ma·gno'li** (rō'mä·nyô'lē), **Ettore.** 1871–1938. Italian Hellenic scholar and philologist; engaged chiefly in revival of Greek classic drama, making modern verse translations of plays and staging them.

**Ro'ma·gno'si** (rō'mä·nyō'sē), **Giovanni Domenico.** 1761–1835. Italian jurist and philosopher; as a philosopher, influenced by Condillac's sensualism. Works include *Genesi del Diritto Penale* (1791), *Che Cosa è la Mente Sana* (1827), *Della Natura e dei Fattori dell'Incivilimento* (1832), etc.

**Ro'mains'** (rô'măɴ'), **Jules.** *Pseudonym of* **Louis Fa'ri'goule'** (fȧ'rē'gōōl'). 1885–1972. French writer; sponsor and chief exponent of the doctrine of unanimism, that the unifying principles in human groups are more significant, as for literary treatment, than are personal individualities; to U.S. after capitulation of France (1940). Author of novels, including *Le Bourg Régénéré* (1906), *Mort de Quelqu'un* (1911), *Lucienne* (1922), a series of interconnected novels under general title *Les Hommes de Bonne Volonté* (27 vols., 1932–46), and *Salsette Discovers America* (1942); verse, *L'Âme des Hommes* (1904), *Odes et Prières* (1913), *Chants des Dix Années 1914–1924* (1928); plays, *L'Armée dans la Ville* (1911), *Le Dictateur* (1926), *Le Roi Masqué* (1931).

**Ro'man** (rōō'mȧn), **Johan Helmich.** 1694–1758. Swedish violinist and composer; called "Father of Swedish Music." Composed symphonies, suites, festival and church music, violin concertos, sonatas, cantatas, etc.

**Ro·ma'ña** (rô·mä'nyä), **Eduardo López de.** Peruvian civil engineer and political leader; president of Peru (1899–1903).

**Ro·ma'nes** (rō·mä'nēz), **George John.** 1848–1894. British biologist, b. Kingston, Canada; early an intimate friend of Charles Darwin; at University College, London, began research on nervous and locomotor systems of medusae and echinoderms, reported in *Jelly-fish, Star-fish, and Sea-urchins* (1885); showed parallelism in development of mental faculties of animals and man in *Animal Intelligence* (1881) and *Mental Evolution in Animals* (1883), and further applied Darwin's theory of evolution to development of mind in *Mental Evolution in Man* (1888); professor of physiology at Royal Institution of London (1888–91); upheld hereditability of acquired characteristics in *Examination of Weismannism* (1892); founded (1891) Romanes lecture at Oxford to be delivered annually on scientific or literary topic; developed in *Darwin and after Darwin* his theory of physiological selection hypothesizing possible evolution of a distinct species from an isolated group of an original species (3 vols., 1892–97); originally a skeptic, latterly a Christian.

**Ro'ma·ni'no, Il** (ēl rō'mä·nē'nō). *Real name* **Girolamo Ro·ma'ni** (rō·mä'nē). 1485–1566. Italian painter of Brescian school; studied in Padua and Venice.

**Ro·ma'no** (rō·mä'nō), **Emanuel.** *Real family name* **Gli'cen·stein** (glē'chĕn·stān). 1904– . Painter, b. Rome, Italy; to U.S. (1928). Executed murals for Metropolitan Life Insurance Co., New York; his genre pictures are well known, including many dealing with circus life and scenes.

**Romano, Enotrio.** See Giosuè CARDUCCI.

**Ro·ma'no** (rō·mä'nō), **Giulio.** *Real name* **Giulio Pip'pi de' Gia·nuz'zi** (pēp'pē dā jä·nōōt'tsē), *a contraction of* **Giulio di Pietro di Filippo de' Gianuzzi.** 1499–1546. Italian painter and architect, b. Rome; after Raphael, chief master of the Roman school. Pupil and heir of Raphael; assisted Raphael at Rome, and with Penni (*q.v.*), continued his uncompleted work; called to Mantua (1524) as chief artist to Duke Federigo Gonzaga. His works include *Madonna* (in the Louvre), frescoes in the Stanza d'Eliodoro, Stanza dell'Incendio, and the Loggie (all in the Vatican), *Apollo and the Muses* (in the Pitti Palace), frescoes representing the *Story of Psyche* and *Fall of the Titans* (in the Palazzo del Tè, Mantua), and scenes from the Trojan War (in ducal palace at Mantua). As an architect, designed and built the ducal palace at Mantua, church of San Benedetto (near Mantua), the Palazzo del Tè at Mantua.

**Romano, Giulio.** 1550?–1618. See Giulio CACCINI.

**Ro'ma·no'nes** (rô'mä·nō'nās), **Conde de. Álvaro de Fi'gue·ro'a y de Tor'res** (thȧ fē'gā·rō'ä ē thȧ tôr'rās). 1863–1950. Spanish statesman; premier of Spain (1915, 1917, 1918–19); remained loyal to the king and head of the Monarchist party at outbreak of Revolution (1931).

**Ro·ma'nov** *or* **Ro·ma'noff** (rŭ·mȧ'nôf). Name of a Russian dynasty (1613–1917) which began with Michael Romanov, grandnephew of Ivan IV and son of Philaret, patriarch (1619–33). The family originated with a German nobleman, Andrew Kobyla, who emigrated (14th century) from Prussia to Moscow; his descendants became prominent at Russian court, one member, Roman Yurievich (d. 1543) taking the name *Romanov;* his daughter Anastasia Romanovna married (1547) Czar Ivan IV as his first wife; their son Fëdor I (or Theodore; d. 1598), last of Rurik (*q.v.*) dynasty. Nikita, brother of

Anastasia, chosen chairman of council acting as regent during reign of Fëdor I (1584–98); Nikita's son Fëdor (Theodore), better known by his monastic name Philaret, became metropolitan of Rostov after Boris Godunov's death (1605); his son Michael Romanov was chosen (1613) by boyars as new czar, but actually Philaret was real ruler (1613–33). Michael was succeeded by his son Alexis I (1645–76), whose three sons were in turn czars: Fëdor III (1676–82), Ivan V (1682–89), and Peter I the Great (1689–1725). Peter was followed by his wife Catherine I (1725–27), his grandson by his first wife, Peter II (last representative of direct male line, 1727–30), then by Anna Ivanovna (1730–40), daughter of Ivan V, then Ivan VI (1740–41), a descendant of Ivan V through Anthony Ulrich of Brunswick, who married Anna Leopoldovna (*q.v.*). Line of succession returned (1741) to female side of house in Elizabeth (empress, 1741–62), daughter of Peter I and Catherine I. Elizabeth's sister Anna (d. 1728) married Charles Frederick of Holstein-Gottorp (see OLDENBURG, 3a) and their son Peter III succeeded (1762) his aunt, establishing the so-called **Hol′stein–Got′torp–Ro·ma′nov** (hôl′shtīn-gŏt′ôrp-) line (1762–1917). Peter III was followed by his wife Catherine II the Great (1762–96) and Paul I (1796–1801), son of Peter III and Catherine. Later rulers were: Alexander I (1801–25), eldest son of Paul; Nicholas I (1825–55), brother of Alexander I; Alexander II (1855–81), son of Nicholas I; Alexander III (1881–94), son of Alexander II; and Nicholas II (1894–1917), son of Alexander III. Nicholas II abdicated (Mar. 15, 1917) in favor of his brother Michael, who resigned the next day in favor of the provisional government. Nicholas II, his wife (Alexandra Feodorovna), and children were all executed (July 16, 1918) at Ekaterinburg by the Bolsheviks, ending the dynasty. Maria, daughter of Nicholas I, married duke of Leuchtenberg (see ROMANOVSKI). See *Table (in Appendix)* for RUSSIA.

**Romanov, Panteleimon.** 1884–1936. Russian novelist; a naturalist of school of Tolstoi and Gorki; author of the prose epic *Rus'*, short stories, and dramas.

**Ro·ma·nov′ski** (rŭ·mŭ·nôf′skû·ĭ; *Angl.* -skĭ), Prince. Russian title granted (1852) descendants of Maximilien, Duke of Leuchtenberg (see LEUCHTENBERG), Russian general. He had six children, among them several Russian officers: **Nikolai,** *Ger.* **Nikolaus** (1843–1891) and **Georgi,** *Ger.* **Georg** (1852–1912). **Aleksandr** (1881– ), son of Georgi, was 6th duke of Leuchtenberg; in France after Revolution (1917).

**Ro·ma′nus** (rō·mā′nŭs). Pope (897).

**Romanus.** Name of four rulers of the Eastern Roman Empire: **Romanus I Lec′a·pe′nus** [lĕk′ȧ·pē′nŭs] (d. 948); regent of the empire for Constantine VII (919–944); a common soldier of Armenian birth; seized control during minority of his stepson Constantine; crowned himself emperor (919); ignorant, but an able administrator; tried to establish a new dynasty but deposed by Constantine (944). **Romanus II** (939–963); son of Constantine VII; emperor (959–963); sent Nicephorus on successful expedition against Saracens of Crete; one of his daughters, Theophano, became wife of Otto II of Germany. **Romanus III Ar′gy·rus** [är′jĭ·rŭs] (968?–1034); emperor (1028–34); married Zoë, daughter of Constantine VIII; supposed to have been murdered by Zoë and Michael IV. **Romanus IV Di·og′e·nes** [dī·ŏj′ĕ·nēz] (d. 1071); married (1067) Eudocia Macrembolitissa, widow of Constantine X; emperor and coregent with her (1067–71), during minority of Michael VII Ducas; an able general, won many victories against Seljuks (1067–71), but completely defeated by them under Alp Arslan (1071) at Manzikert, Armenia; taken prisoner, but released and killed by Michael's uncle.

**Rom′berg** (rôm′bĕrĸ). A family of German musicians, including: **Anton** (1742–1814), bassoonist. His son **Bernhard** (1767–1841), violoncellist and composer, exponent of modern school of German violoncellists; on many concert tours, some with his cousin **Andreas Jakob** (1767–1821), violinist, conductor, and composer of sacred music, operas, a children's symphony, and, esp., of music for Schiller's *Lied von der Glocke.*

**Romberg, Moritz Heinrich.** 1795–1873. German pathologist and neurologist; founder of scientific neurotherapy in Germany.

**Rom′berg** (rŏm′bûrg), **Sig′mund** (sĭg′mŭnd). 1887–1951. Hungarian composer; to U.S., and composed music for light operas, as *Maytime* (1917), *Student Prince* (1924), *Blossom Time* (1926), *Desert Song* (1926), *New Moon* (1927).

**Rom′bouts** (rôm′bouts), **Theodoor.** 1597–1637. Dutch painter of conversation and genre pieces and engraver.

**Ro′mé′ de Lisle** (rô′mā′ dē lēl′), **Jean Baptiste Louis.** 1736–1790. French mineralogist, discoverer of the law (law of constant angles) that the angles between the various faces of a crystal remain unchanged throughout its growth; author of *Cristallographie* (1783), etc.

**Ro·mei′ke** (rō·mī′kē), **Henry.** 1855–1903. Originator of press-clipping bureau, b. Riga, Russia. Bureau begun in Paris (c. 1883), established in London (c. 1884) and in New York City (c. 1885).

**Römer.** Variant of ROEMER.

**Ro·me′ro** (rô·mā′rō), **Carlos Orozco.** 1898– . Mexican caricaturist, engraver, and portrait painter; one of organizers of Gallery of Mexican Modern Art.

**Romero, Matías.** 1837–1898. Mexican lawyer and diplomat; minister to U.S. (1863–68, 1882–92, 1892–98).

**Ro′mier′** (rô′myā′), **Lucien.** 1885–1944. French journalist and historian; editor, *Journée Industrielle* (1920–24), *Figaro* (1924–26, 1934 ff.). Author of *L'Homme Nouveau* (1928), *Plaisir de France* (1932), etc.

**Rom′il·ly** (rŏm′ĭ·lĭ), Sir **Samuel.** 1757–1818. English lawyer and law reformer; practiced mainly on chancery side; early adopted Rousseauistic views; became friendly with Mirabeau; met Pierre Dumont, Genevese preacher; published pamphlet on French Revolution (1790); solicitor general in All-the-Talents Administration (1806); made labor of his life (from 1807) reform of the criminal law of England; secured repeal of Elizabethan statute making it a capital offense to steal from the person (1808); persevered in efforts to mitigate harsh and irrational laws; shared in antislavery agitation; favored Roman Catholic emancipation.

**Rom′mel** (rôm′ĕl), **Erwin.** 1891–1944. German general; served in World War (1914–18); member of National Socialist party, attached to bodyguard of Adolf Hitler (1933); commanded Hitler's headquarters staff in Austrian, Sudetenland, and Prague occupations, and in Polish campaign (1939); commanded a Panzer division in invasion of France (1940); commander of German forces in Africa (1941–43); recaptured Tobruk (June, 1942) and drove British back to El Alamein, Egypt; promoted to rank of general field marshal; defeated by British at El Alamein (Nov., 1942) and forced out of Egypt, Libya, and Tripolitania; dislodged from Mareth Line in Tunisia (Mar., 1943); recalled; held defense posts in Italy and Balkans, and in Western Europe at time of Allied invasion of Normandy (June, 1944); died apparently as a result of Hitler's orders.

**Rom′ney** (rŏm′nĭ; rŭm′-), Earl of. See *Henry Sidney* (1641–1704), under SIDNEY family.

**Romney, George.** 1734–1802. English historical and

portrait painter, b. Lancashire; set up as portrait painter in London (1762); gained attention with *Death of General Wolfe* (1763); took studio in Cavendish Square; rival of Reynolds for patronage of aristocracy; gradually devoted more time to painting ideal subjects, including *Milton and his Daughters, Newton Making Experiments with the Prism.*

**Rom′u·ald** (rŏm′ū·ăld), Saint. 950?–1027. Italian Benedictine monk; founder (1012) at Camaldoli, near Florence, of a barefooted order of hermit Benedictines, known as *Camaldolites.*

**Rom′u·lus** (rŏm′ū·lŭs). First legendary king (753–716 B.C.) of early Rome, a Latin, son of Rhea Silvia. According to legend, he, with twin brother **Re′mus** (rē′mŭs), founded city of Rome on Palatine Hill (753 B.C.); slew Remus in a quarrel; established three classes of knights (equites); led in rape of the Sabine women and in war with Sabines that followed; with **Titus Ta′ti·us** (tā′shĭ·ŭs; -shŭs) ruled united Romans and Sabines. By later Romans worshiped as war god Quirinus.

**Romulus Au·gus′tu·lus** (ô·gŭs′tū·lŭs). b. 461? Last Roman emperor of the West (475–476); son of Orestes; crowned by his father, but a puppet ruler only; deposed by Odoacer; retired to Campania.

**Ron′ald** (rŏn′ld), Sir **Landon.** 1873–1938. English conductor, composer, and music critic; conductor for Madame Melba on tour in U.S. (1894); conductor, Royal Albert Hall Orchestra (1908–38).

**Ron′alds** (rŏn′ldz), Sir **Francis.** 1788–1873. English inventor of telegraphic and meteorological instruments.

**Ronaldshay,** Earls of. See Lawrence DUNDAS, Marquis of Zetland.

**Ron·co′ni** (rông·kō′nē), **Domenico.** 1772–1839. Italian tenor; sang in principal cities of Europe, notably St. Petersburg (1801–05) and Munich (1819–29).

**Ron′de·let′** (rôN′dlĕ′), **Guillaume.** 1507–1566. French naturalist and physician; known esp. for investigation of the fishes of the Mediterranean.

**Rong′e** (rông′ĕ), **Johannes.** 1813–1887. German priest and reformer; Roman Catholic chaplain, Grottkau (1840); excommunicated (1844) following his open letter denouncing exhibition of the Holy Coat of Treves. Stirred up agitation resulting in formation of German Catholic church, of which he became pastor in Breslau (1845); fugitive in London (1849–61) as result of political activities as democratic leader.

**Ron′sard′** (rôN′sȧr′), **Pierre de.** 1524–1585. French poet; page to Charles, Duc d'Orléans, third son of Francis I of France, and, for a time, to James V of Scotland. Becoming deaf (c. 1542), gave up hope of preferment at court and devoted himself to study and writing; became chief of famous group of poets known as the Pléiade devoted to revivifying French language and its use in the noblest literature. His *Odes* (c. 1550) was followed by *Amours de Cassandre* (1552), *Hymnes* (1555–56), and *Élégies, Mascarades, et Bergeries* (1565); became great favorite of Charles IX and attached to his court until Charles's death (1574). Labored long on an epic, *La Franciade*, but failed to finish it. Regarded as father of lyric poetry in France.

**Röntgen, Wilhelm Conrad.** See ROENTGEN.

**Rood** (rōōd), **Ogden Nicholas.** 1831–1902. American physicist, b. Danbury, Conn. Conducted researches in mechanics, electricity, acoustics, and optics; devised improvement of Sprengel air pump to produce higher vacuums; developed a flicker photometer for comparing brightness of light of different colors; invented process for measuring huge electrical resistances.

**Rooke** (rōōk), Sir **George.** 1650–1709. English naval commander; supported revolution of 1688; rear admiral (1690); took part in battles of Beachy Head (1690) and La Hogue (1692), in the latter burning thirteen French ships in night attack; commanded unsuccessful expedition against Cádiz (1702) but destroyed French and Spanish fleet at Vigo; commander in chief of grand fleet (1703); with Sir Cloudesley Shovell captured Gibraltar (1704) and few days later fought indecisive battle with superior French fleet off Málaga.

**Roon** (rōn), Count **Albrecht Theodor Emil von.** 1803–1879. Prussian soldier and statesman; minister of war (1859–73) of marine (1861–71); field marshal (1873); president of Prussian cabinet (Jan. 1–Nov. 9, 1873). Famous for effective organization of Prussian army which made possible its speedy mobilization leading to decisive victories in wars of 1866 and 1870–71.

**Roos** (rōs). Family of German landscape and animal painters: **Johann Heinrich** (1631–1685) and his sons **Philipp Peter** (1657–1705), called **Ro′sa di Ti′vo·li** (rô′zä dē tē′vō·lē), and **Johann Melchior** (1659–1731).

**Roos** (rōs), **Sjoerd H. de.** See DE ROOS.

**Roo′se·velt** (rō′zĕ·vĕlt; -vĕlt; *formerly often, and still sometimes,* rōō′zĕ·vĕlt; *the usual pron. in both branches of the family is* rō′zĕ·vĕlt), **Franklin Del′a·no** (dĕl′ȧ·nō). 1882–1945. Thirty-second president of the United States, b. Hyde Park, N.Y.; distant cousin of Theodore Roosevelt; A.B., Harvard (1904); studied law at Columbia (1904–07); with law firm of Carter, Ledyard & Milburn, New York (1907–10); member of firm of Roosevelt & O'Connor, New York (1924–33); member, New York State Senate (1910–13); asst. secretary of the navy (1913–20); governor of New York (1929–33). President of the United States (1933–45), first president to be re-elected for a third term. Initiated administrative and legislative reforms known collectively as the New Deal; met at sea with Winston Churchill (Aug., 1941) to draw up joint statement of American-British international policy known as the Atlantic Charter. Under emergency powers delegated by Congress established (1942–45) agencies to supervise military production and regulate civilian economy. Conferred on war strategy and international affairs with Churchill at Washington (June, 1942 and May, 1943), Casablanca, Morocco (Jan., 1943), and Quebec (Aug., 1943 and Sept., 1944), with President Vargas at Natal, Brazil (Jan., 1943), President Ávila Camacho at Monterrey, Mexico (Apr., 1943), Churchill and Chiang Kai-shek at Cairo (Nov., 1943), Churchill and Stalin at Tehran (Dec., 1943), and again at Yalta, Crimea (Feb., 1945), and Admiral Nimitz and General MacArthur at Pearl Harbor (July, 1944); died at Warm Springs, Ga. (Apr. 12, 1945) of cerebral hemorrhage. Author of *Whither Bound* (1926), *Looking Forward* (1933), *On Our Way* (1934), etc. His wife, **Anna Eleanor,** *nee* **Roosevelt** (1884–1962), lecturer and writer; author of *When You Grow Up to Vote* (1932), *It's Up to the Women* (1933), *This Is My Story* (1937), *My Days* (1938), *The Moral Basis of Democracy* (1940).

**Roosevelt, Kermit.** 1889–1943. Son of President Theodore Roosevelt (*q.v.*), and brother of Theodore Roosevelt, Jr., Quentin Roosevelt, and Alice Lee Roosevelt Longworth, wife of Nicholas Longworth. American soldier, explorer, businessman, and writer, b. Oyster Bay, N.Y. Served in World War, in British service (captain) and, later, in U.S. service. Accompanied father on hunting trip in Africa (1909–10) and on exploration of so-called "River of Doubt" in Brazil (1914). President, Roosevelt Steamship Co.; vice-president, U.S. Lines. Author of *War in the Garden of Eden* (1919), *The Happy Hunting Grounds* (1920), *American Backlogs* (1928), etc. Major in British army (1939–41); transferred to U.S. army; died on active service in Alaska.

**Roosevelt, Nicholas.** 1893– . American journalist, soldier, diplomat, and writer, b. New York City. Captain of infantry, U.S. army (1917–19), during World War I. On staff of New York *Tribune* (1921–23), New York *Times* (1923–30), New York *Herald Tribune* (1933–42). Vice-governor of the Philippines (1930); U.S. minister to Hungary (1930–33). Author of *The Philippines, a Treasure and a Problem* (1926), *The Restless Pacific* (1928), *America and England?* (1930), *The Townsend Plan* (1936), *A New Birth of Freedom* (1938).

**Roosevelt, Nicholas J.** 1767–1854. American inventor, b. New York City; experimented unsuccessfully with building steamboats (1797–1809). Associated with Robert Fulton (1809) in project for introducing steamboats on western rivers; built steamboat *New Orleans* at Pittsburgh (1811) and steamed in it to New Orleans in fourteen days. Granted patent for invention of vertical paddle wheels (1814). His grandnephew **Robert Barnwell Roosevelt** (1829–1906) was an author and politician; adm. to bar (1850); an organizer of Committee of Seventy in New York City which was instrumental in overthrowing the Tweed Ring; member of U.S. House of Representatives (1871–73); U.S. minister to the Netherlands (1888–89); vigorous advocate of conservation measures; author esp. of books on fishing and hunting.

**Roosevelt, Quentin.** 1897–1918. Youngest son of President Theodore Roosevelt (*q.v.*), and brother of Theodore Roosevelt, Jr., Kermit Roosevelt, and Alice Lee Roosevelt Longworth. American aviator in World War I; killed in action over German lines (July 14).

**Roosevelt, Theodore.** 1858–1919. Great-grandnephew of Nicholas J. Roosevelt, and nephew of Robert Barnwell Roosevelt. Distant cousin of Franklin Delano Roosevelt. Twenty-sixth president of the United States, b. New York City. Grad. Harvard (1880). Studied law (1880–81). Member, New York State legislature (1882–84). Lived outdoor life on North Dakota ranch (1884–86). Unsuccessful candidate for mayor of New York (1886). Member, U.S. Civil Service Commission (1889–95). President, New York City Board of Police Commissioners (1895–97). U.S. assistant secretary of the navy (1897–98). With Leonard Wood, organized first volunteer cavalry regiment, popularly known as Roosevelt's Rough Riders, and as its lieutenant colonel, and later as colonel, served with it in Cuba (1898). Governor of New York (1899, 1900). Vice-president of the United States (1901), succeeding to the presidency on death of McKinley (Sept. 14, 1901); elected to the presidency (1904) and served altogether 1901–09. Notable during his administration were his recognition of Republic of Panama when it revolted (Nov. 3, 1903) from Colombia, and the beginning of construction of Panama Canal; his services in bringing representatives of Russia and Japan together at Portsmouth, N.H., with the resulting Treaty of Portsmouth (Sept. 5, 1905) ending Russo-Japanese War; his receipt of Nobel prize for peace (1906); his aggressive policies in curbing trusts and regulating business; his efforts to conserve national resources, with appointment of conservation commission headed by Gifford Pinchot (1908). Successfully maneuvered nomination of Taft for president (1908). After leaving White House, led big-game hunting expedition to East Africa (1909–10), returning home through Europe where he was highly honored. Dissatisfied with Taft policies, organized Progressive party and was its candidate for president (1912); result was defeat of both Roosevelt and Taft, and election of Woodrow Wilson. Conducted exploring expedition in South America (1914) and discovered a tributary of the Madeira River. Sympathized vigorously with Allied Powers in World War I; sought military command (1917–18), but was not commissioned. Author of *The Naval War of 1812* (1882), *Hunting Trips of a Ranchman* (1885), *Thomas Hart Benton* (1886), *Gouverneur Morris* (1888), *Ranch Life and the Hunting-Trail* (1888), *Essays on Practical Politics* (1888), *The Winning of the West* (4 vols., 1889–96), *The Wilderness Hunter* (1893), *The Rough Riders* (1899), *Life of Oliver Cromwell* (1900), *The Strenuous Life* (1900), *Hunting the Grizzly* (1905), *African Game Trails* (1910), *True Americanism* (1910), *Through the Brazilian Wilderness* (1914), *Life Histories of African Game Animals* (1914), *America and the World War* (1915). Elected to American Hall of Fame (1950).

**Roosevelt, Theodore,** Jr. 1887–1944. Son of President Theodore Roosevelt (*q.v.*), and brother of Quentin Roosevelt, Kermit Roosevelt, and Alice Lee Roosevelt Longworth, wife of Nicholas Longworth. American writer, soldier, explorer, and politician, b. Oyster Bay, N.Y. B.A., Harvard (1908). Served in A.E.F. in France in World War I (major, lieutenant colonel); engaged at Cantigny, Soissons, Meuse-Argonne offensive, St.-Mihiel offensive; an organizer of American Legion (1919). Asst. secretary of the navy (1921–24); unsuccessful candidate for governor of New York (1924). Leader of Field Museum expeditions to Asia (1925, 1928–29). Governor of Puerto Rico (1929–32); governor general of the Philippines (1932–33). Editor, Doubleday Doran & Co. (from 1935). Brigadier general (Dec., 1941); took part in campaigns in North Africa (1942–43), Italy (1943), and France (1944). Author of *Average Americans* (1919), *Rank and File* (1928), *All in the Family* (1929), *Colonial Policies of the United States* (1937), etc.

**Root** (rōōt), **Elihu.** 1845–1937. American lawyer and statesman, b. Clinton, N.Y. Grad. Hamilton (1864); LL.B., N.Y.U. (1867). Adm. to bar (1867); practiced, New York City. U.S. secretary of war (1899–1904); reorganized administrative system in War Department. U.S. secretary of state (1905–09); strengthened friendly relations between U.S. and South American countries. U.S. senator from New York (1909–15). Counsel for U.S. in North Atlantic Fisheries Arbitration (1910); member, Hague Tribunal (1910); president, Carnegie Endowment for International Peace (1910). Awarded Nobel prize for peace (1912). Headed special U.S. diplomatic mission to Russia (1917). U.S. commissioner plenipotentiary at Washington Conference on Limitation of Armaments (1921–22). Author of *Experiment in Government and the Essentials of the Constitution*, *Addresses on Government and Citizenship*, *Military and Colonial Policy of the United States*, *Latin America and the United States*, *Russia and the United States*.

**Root, George Frederick.** 1820–1895. American composer and teacher, b. Sheffield, Mass. Founded (1853) New York Normal Institute, esp. for training teachers of music. Composer of cantatas, sacred music, and a number of popular songs, including *Rosalie, the Prairie Flower*, the hymn *The Shining Shore*, and the battle songs *The Battle Cry of Freedom; Tramp, Tramp, Tramp, the Boys are Marching; Just Before the Battle, Mother*.

**Root, John Wellborn.** 1850–1891. American architect, b. Lumpkin, Ga.; in partnership (Chicago) with Daniel H. Burnham, Burnham & Root (1873–91). Designer of the Montauk building and Monadnock building, Chicago. Consulting architect, World's Columbian Exposition (1890–91). See John A. HOLABIRD.

**Root, Robert Kilburn.** 1877–1950. American educator; teacher of English, Yale (1903–05), Princeton (1905–46), professor (1916–46) and dean of the faculty (1933–46). Author of *Classical Mythology in Shake-*

*speare* (1903), *The Poetry of Chaucer* (1906), *Manuscripts of Chaucer's Troilus* (1914), etc.

**Root′haan** (rōt′hän), **Johannes Philipp.** 1785–1853. Jesuit priest, b. Amsterdam; general of the Jesuit order (from 1829).

**Roo′ze·boom** (rō′zĕ·bōm), **Hendrik Willem Bakhuis.** 1854–1907. Dutch physical chemist; known for practical applications of the phase rule.

**Ro′partz′** (rô′pȧr′), **Joseph Guy Marie.** 1864–1955. French musician and composer of symphonic poems (*La Cloche des Morts*, *Les Landes*, etc.), symphonies, chamber music, sonatas, and some church music (*Messe de Sainte Odile*, etc.).

**Ro′per** (rō′pẽr), **Daniel Cal·houn′** (kăl·hōōn′). 1867–1943. American lawyer and politician, b. in Marlboro County, S.C.; first assistant postmaster general (1913–16); commissioner of internal revenue (1917–20); secretary of commerce (1933–38); minister to Canada (1939).

**Ropes** (rōps), **Arthur Reed.** *Pseudonym, for stage works,* **Adrian Ross** (rŏs). 1859–1933. English writer, b. London. Author of lyrics and librettos for many musical comedies, including *San Toy* (1899), *The Merry Widow* (1907), *King of Cadonia* (1908), *Monsieur Beaucaire* (1919), *Lilac Time* (1922), *The Beloved Vagabond* (1927). Published also *Poems* (1884) and *Short History of Europe* (1889).

**Ropes, John Codman.** 1836–1899. Historian, b. St. Petersburg, Russia, of American parentage; practiced law, Boston. Author of *The Army under Pope* (1881), *The First Napoleon* (1885), *The Campaign of Waterloo* (1892), *Story of the Civil War* (2 vols., 1894–98), etc.

**Rops** (rôps), **Félicien.** 1833–1898. Belgian-French painter, engraver, and lithographer.

**Ropshin.** Pseudonym of Boris SAVINKOV.

**Ro·quette′** (rô·kĕt′), **Otto.** 1824–1896. German poet and writer; author of the narrative poem *Waldmeisters Brautfahrt* (1851), *Liederbuch*, including the song *Noch ist die Blühende Goldene Zeit* (1852), the novel *Heinrich Falk* (3 vols., 1858), a history of German literature (2 vols., 1862–63), etc.

**Rör′dam** (rûr′dȧm), **Valdemar.** 1872–1946. Danish author of verse narratives *Bjovulf* (1899), *Gudrun Dyre* (1902), and *Jens Hvas til Ulvborg* (1922–23), and idylls, lyrics, and dramas.

**Ro′re** (rō′rĕ), **Cyprien de** *or* **Cipriano da.** 1516–1565. Flemish composer of the Venetian school; composed several books of 4-part and 5-part madrigals; also motets, masses, psalms, a Passion (1557), etc.

**Ro′rer** (rōr′ẽr), **Sarah Tyson,** *nee* **Hes′ton** (hĕs′tŭn). 1849–1937. American domestic-science teacher and writer; m. W. Albert Rorer (1871). Principal, Philadelphia School of Domestic Science. On staff, *Ladies' Home Journal* (1897–1911). Author of various books on cookery, notably *Mrs. Rorer's New Cook Book.*

**Ro′sa** (rō′zä), **Carl August Nicholas.** *Orig. surname* **Ro′se** (rō′zĕ). 1843–1889. German operatic impresario in England; m. operatic soprano Madame Parepa (1867); started Carl Rosa Opera Company (1875); popularized opera in English and encouraged native English composers of opera.

**Ro·sa′** (rô·zä′), **Edward Bennett.** 1861–1921. American physicist; best known for his investigations of electrical measurements; had share in establishment of existing international system of electrical units.

**Ro′sa** (rô′zä), **Salvator.** *Also called* **Sal′va·to·riel′lo** (säl′vä·tô·ryĕl′lō). 1615–1673. Italian painter and poet; leading painter of Neapolitan school; known chiefly for landscapes and battle scenes. As a poet, wrote satires in terza rima, as *La Musica*, *La Poesia*, *La Guerra*, and *L'Invidia.*

**Ro′sa·li′a,** San′ta (sän′tä rō′zä·lē′ä). *Eng.* Saint **Ros′a·lie** (rŏz′ȧ·lē; rō′zȧ·lē). d. 1160. Italian religious; niece of King William II of Sicily; patron saint of Palermo; lived as hermit in grotto on Monte Pellegrino.

**Rosamund, Fair.** See *Rosamund Clifford,* under CLIFFORD family.

**Ro′sa of Li′ma** (rō′zȧ, lē′mȧ), Saint. See Saint ROSE OF LIMA.

**Ro′sas** (rō′säs), **Juan Manuel de.** 1793–1877. Argentine dictator, b. Buenos Aires. Chief of Federalist party (from 1828); governor of Buenos Aires (1829–31, 1835–52). After other Argentine provinces joined Buenos Aires in a loose union, wielded supreme power over them all, though continuing nominally as merely governor of Buenos Aires. Waged war in alliance with Oribe, exiled president of Uruguay, to subjugate all Uruguay (1842–51), but was unable to capture Montevideo. Finally defeated (Feb. 3, 1852) by Brazil in alliance with certain of the Argentine provinces; fled to England and lived there in exile (1852–77).

**Ros′cel·li′nus** (rŏs′ĕ·lī′nŭs) *or* **Ru′ce·li′nus** (rōō′sĕ·lī′nŭs). *Also known as* **Ros′ce·lin′ de Com′piègne′** (rôs′lăN′ dē kôN′pyân′y′). *Also* **Ros′cel′lin′** (rô′sĕ′lăN′). d. after 1120. Scholastic philosopher; canon at Loches where Abelard was his pupil; founder of nominalism; forced by a council at Soissons (1092) to abjure his doctrine of the Trinity, by which he taught that the three persons of the Godhead were three Gods.

**Ro′scher** (rôsh′ẽr), **Wilhelm.** 1817–1894. German economist, a founder of historical school of political economy; professor, Göttingen (1843) and Leipzig (from 1848). His son **Wilhelm Heinrich** (1845–1923), classical philologist and scholar, wrote chiefly on Greek and Roman mythology, cults, and symbolism of numbers.

**Ros′ci·us** (rŏsh′ĭ·ŭs; rŏsh′ŭs), **Quintus.** 126?–?62 B.C. Roman actor, regarded as greatest of Roman comic actors. Friend of Cicero, by whom he was defended when sued (76 B.C.) by Chaerea for 50,000 sesterces. Honored by Sulla, who presented him with a gold ring, symbol of equestrian rank.

**Ros′coe** (rŏs′kō), **William.** 1753–1831. English historian; practiced as attorney (from 1774), meanwhile studying the classics and Italian; author of *Life of Lorenzo de' Medici* (1795), *Life and Pontificate of Leo the Tenth* (1805), and a children's classic *The Butterfly's Ball and the Grasshopper's Feast* (1807). His grandson Sir **Henry Enfield Roscoe** (1833–1915), chemist, with Bunsen laid foundations of photochemistry and formulated the reciprocity law; made elaborate investigation of vanadium and compounds and devised process for preparing pure vanadium; did research on niobium, tungsten, uranium, perchloric acid.

**Ros·com′mon** (rŏs·kŏm′ŭn), 4th Earl of. **Wentworth Dil′lon** (dĭl′ŭn). 1633?–1685. British poet, b. in Ireland; nephew of earl of Strafford. After Restoration received lands formerly belonging to his family. Chief works: blank-verse translation of Horace's *Ars Poetica* (1680) and an essay on translated verse, defining poetic diction (1684). First critic to avow admiration for *Paradise Lost.*

**Rose** (rōz), **Edward Everett.** 1862–1939. Playwright, b. in Province of Quebec, Canada; best known for his dramatizations of novels, including *David Harum*, *Richard Carvel*, *Eben Holden*, *Rupert of Hentzau*, *Gentleman from Indiana.*

**Rose, George.** *Pseudonym* **Arthur Sketch′ley** (skĕch′lĭ). 1817–1882. English humorous writer and entertainer; Anglican curate; joined Roman Catholic Church (1855); wrote nearly thirty books on fictitious Mrs. Brown.

**Rose, Hugh Henry.** Baron **Strath·nairn′** (străth-nârn′). 1801–1885. British military commander; commissioner at French headquarters in Crimean War; in Sepoy Mutiny (1857–58), gained victory over Tantia Topi, captured fortress of Jhansi, and virtually reconquered Central India; commander in chief in India (1860); commander in Ireland, kept Fenians under control (1865–70); general (1867) and field marshal (1877).

**Rose, John Holland.** 1855–1942. English historian, b. Bedford; educ. Cambridge. Reader in modern history (1911–19) and professor of naval history (1919–33), Cambridge. Among his many books are *The Rise of Democracy* (1897), *The Life of Napoleon I* (1902), *The Development of the European Nations, 1870–1921* (1923), and *The Mediterranean in the Ancient World* (1933).

**Rose, Joseph Nelson.** 1862–1928. American botanist, b. near Liberty, Ind. Assistant curator, U.S. National Museum (1896–1905) and associate curator (1905–12, 1923–28). Research associate, Carnegie Institution, Washington, D.C. (1912–23). Author of a four-volume monograph, *The Cactaceae* (with N. L. Britton, 1919–23).

**Ro′se** (rō′zĕ), **Valentin.** 1736–1771. German apothecary; discoverer of a fusible alloy (Rose's alloy). His son **Valentin** (1762–1807), also an apothecary, first prepared inulin and sodium bicarbonate. **Heinrich** (1795–1864), son of the younger Valentin, apothecary and chemist, rediscovered columbium which he called niobium (1844); wrote a handbook of analytical chemistry (2 vols., 1851). **Gustav** (1798–1873), mineralogist, brother of Heinrich, was explorer of southern Asia, Vesuvius, Etna, and the extinct volcanoes of the Auvergne; pioneer in petrography; originator of a system of crystallography.

**Rosebery,** Earls of. See Primrose family.

**Rose′crans** (rōz′krăns), **William Starke.** 1819–1898. American army commander, b. Kingston, Ohio; grad. U.S.M.A., West Point (1842). Resigned from army (1854) to go into business. Volunteered at outbreak of Civil War; commissioned brigadier general, U.S. army (1861). Succeeded McClellan in command of Department of the Ohio (1861). Commanding Department of West Virginia, expelled Confederates, thus making possible formation of State of West Virginia (1861). Succeeded Pope in command of army of the Mississippi (1862); engaged successfully at Iuka (Sept., 1862) and Corinth (Oct., 1862). Promoted major general of volunteers (1862). Commanded army of the Cumberland; defeated Confederates at Murfreesboro (Jan., 1863) but was defeated at Chickamauga (Sept., 1863) and relieved of his command. Commanded Department of the Missouri (1864). Resigned from army (1867). U.S. minister to Mexico (1868–69). Member of U.S. House of Representatives, from California (1881–85). U.S. register of the treasury (1885–93).

**Ro′seg′ger** (rō′zĕg′ĕr; rōs′ĕg′ĕr), **Peter,** *known until 1894 as* **P. K.** (**Petri Ket′ten·fei′er** [kĕt′ĕn·fī′ĕr]). 1843–1918. Austrian poet and novelist; founded in Graz monthly journal *Der Heimgarten* (1876). Author of Styrian dialect verse *Zither und Hackbrett* (1870), of tales and novels dealing with religious, social, and economic problems, and of philosophical and autobiographical works.

**Ro′sel·li′ni** (rō′zäl·lē′nē), **Ippolito.** 1800–1843. Italian Orientalist and archaeologist.

**Ro′sel′ly′ de Lorgues** (rô′zĕ′lē′ dĕ lôrg′), Comte **Antoine François Félix.** 1805–1898. French writer; best known for books in defense of Roman Catholicism and on life of Columbus.

**Ro′sen** (rō′zĕn). Family of German Orientalists, including: **Friedrich August** (1805–1837), author of *Radices Sanscritae* (1827). His brother **Georg** (1820–1891) wrote Persian grammar *Elementa Persica* (1843), *Über die Sprache der Lazen* (1844), *Ossetische Grammatik* (1846), a history of Turkey, and translated Bulgarian folk poems (1879). Georg's son **Friedrich** (1856–1935) concluded German-Abyssinian agreement (1904); ambassador at Tangiers (1905), at Algeciras Conference (1906); ambassador at Teheran (1908), Bucharest (1910), Lisbon (1912), The Hague (1916), Madrid (1920); foreign minister (May–Oct., 1921); author of a revision of his father's *Elementa Persica* (1915), translations from modern Indian and Persian, etc.

**Ro′sen** (rō′z'n), **Charles.** 1878–1950. American landscape painter.

**Ro′sen** (rô′zyĭn), Baron **Roman Romanovich.** 1847–1921. Russian diplomat; minister to Japan (1897; 1903–04); ambassador to U.S. (1905) and one of Russia's plenipotentiaries at peace negotiations (1905) at Portsmouth, N.H., following Russo-Japanese War (1904–05). Fled from Russia after the Revolution (1917) and lived as journalist in New York.

**Ro′se·nau** (rō′zĕ·nou), **Milton Joseph.** 1869–1946. American sanitarian, b. Philadelphia; surgeon, U.S. Public and Marine Hospital Service (1890–1909); professor of preventive medicine and hygiene, Harvard Medical School (1909–35), and of epidemiology, Harvard School of Public Health (1922–35).

**Ro′sen·bach** (rō′z'n·băk), **Abraham S. Wolf.** 1876–1952. American bibliophile, b. Philadelphia. Author of *The Unpublishable Memoirs* (1917), *The All-Embracing Doctor Franklin* (1932), *A Book Hunter's Holiday* (1936), etc.

**Ro′sen·berg** (rō′zĕn·bĕrk), **Alfred.** 1893–1946. German Nazi leader and writer; editor in chief of *Völkischer Beobachter* (1921 ff.) and editor of *Nationalsozialistische Monatshefte* (1930); entered Reichstag (1930); director of newly established foreign policy office of Nazi party (1933); founder and leader of Kampfbund for German culture; author of *Die Spur der Juden im Wandel der Zeiten* (1920), *Wesen, Grundsätze, und Ziele der N.S.D.A.P.* (1922), *Der Mythus des 20. Jahrhunderts* (1930), *Das Wesensgefüge des Nationalsozialismus* (1932), *Blut und Ehre* (1934), etc.; hanged as war criminal.

**Rosenberg, Arthur.** 1889–1943. German historian; lived in U.S. (1933–43); author of *Geschichte des Bolschewismus* (1932), *Demokratie und Sozialismus* (1938), etc.

**Ro′sen·berg** (rō′z'n·bûrg), **Frederick.** English inventor, who took out (1843) first American patent for a machine for distributing type after use. Cf. Etienne Robert Gaudens.

**Ro′sen·busch** (rō′zĕn·bo͝osh), **Harry,** *in full* **Karl Heinrich Ferdinand.** 1836–1914. German geologist; worked esp. in microscopic and classificatory petrography.

**Ro′sen·feld** (rō′z'n·fĕld), **Morris.** 1862–1923. Poet, b. at Bokscha, then in Russian Poland; to U.S. (1886) and employed as tailor in New York (1886–1900). His verse expresses the miseries of the poor and oppressed, as in the volumes *Die Glocke* (1888), *Die Blumenkette* (1890), *Songs from the Ghetto* (a selection made by Professor Leo Wiener, *q.v.*, and translated with notes, 1898), *Dos Liderbuch* (1917).

**Rosenfeld, Paul.** 1890–1946. American music critic and writer; music critic of *The Dial* (1920–27). Coeditor, *The American Caravan* (from 1927). Author of *Musical Portraits* (1920), *The Boy in the Sun* (novel; 1928), *By Way of Art* (essays; 1928), etc.

**Ro′sen·kranz** (rō′zĕn·kränts), **Karl,** *in full* **Johann Karl Friedrich.** 1805–1879. German Hegelian philosopher. Works include *Enzyklopädie der Theologischen Wissenschaften* (1831), *Handbuch einer Allgemeinen Geschichte der Poesie* (3 vols., 1832–33), *Psychologie* (1837), *Hegels Leben* (1844), *Die Wissenschaft der Logischen Idee*

(2 vols., 1858–59), and *Diderots Leben und Werke* (2 vols., 1866).

**Ro′sen·kreutz** (rō′zĕn·kroits), **Christian.** *Lat.* Fra′ter **Ro′sae Cru′cis** (frā′tēr rō′zē krōō′sĭs). Reputed 15th-century founder of the secret Rosicrucian Society, the name of which is due to two anonymous pamphlets (1641) now generally attributed to the German theologian Johann Valentin Andreä purporting to give information about the society.

**Ro′sen·man** (rō′z′n·măn), **Samuel Irving.** 1896–1973. American jurist, b. San Antonio, Texas; justice, supreme court of N.Y. (1932–43); special counsel to Roosevelt and Truman (1943–45).

**Ro′sen·mül′ler** (rō′zĕn·mül′ēr), **Johann Christian.** 1771–1820. German physician and anatomist.

**Ro′sen·thal** (rō′zĕn·täl), **Moriz.** 1862–1946. Austrian concert pianist, b. Lemberg. In concert work, Vienna (1884) and, subsequently, in principal cities of Europe and America; became pianist to Austrian emperor (1912). Works include original compositions for piano.

**Ro′sen·wald** (rō′z′n·wôld), **Julius.** 1862–1932. American merchant and philanthropist, b. Springfield, Ill. Vice-president and treasurer, Sears, Roebuck & Co. (1895–1910) and president (1910–25). Creator (1917) of Julius Rosenwald Fund for the "well-being of mankind." Did much to aid Negro education in the South, and to alleviate Jewish distress in the Near East. Presented Chicago (1929) with Museum of Science and Industry.

**Rose of Li′ma** (rōz, lē′mȧ), Saint. 1586–1617. Peruvian ascetic, b. Lima; led life of unusual austerity; took veil as sister of Third Order of St. Dominic (1606); canonized by Pope Clement X (1671), the first native-born American saint.

**Ro·si′ni** (rô·zē′nē), **Giovanni.** 1776–1855. Italian writer; author of poems, a history of Italian painting (1839–42), and historical novels and plays, as *Luisa Strozzi* (1833).

**Ros·lin′** (rôs·lēn′), **Alexander.** 1718–1793. Swedish portrait painter; at courts of Bayreuth and Parma (until 1752); settled in Paris (1752).

**Rosmead,** Baron. See Sir Hercules G. R. ROBINSON.

**Rosmer, Ernst.** Pseudonym of Elsa BERNSTEIN.

**Ros·mi′ni–Ser·ba′ti** (rôz·mē′nē·sâr·bä′tē), **Antonio.** 1797–1855. Italian philosopher; founded religious order, Institute of Charity (1828); adviser to Pius IX. Influenced politically by Gioberti; worked in interest of Italian confederation (1848); fell into pope's disfavor through influence of Cardinal Antonelli; retired to Stresa after condemnation of his works by Congregation of the Index (1849); his philosophical system is known as Rosminianism. Author of *Nuovo Saggio sull'Origine delle Idee* (1830), *Il Rinnovamento della Filosofia in Italia* (2 vols., 1836), *Delle Cinque Piaghe della Santa Chiesa* (1848; on Index, 1849–54), and *La Costituzione secondo la Giustizia Sociale*. . . (1848; on Index, 1849–54).

**Ros′ny′** (rō′nē′), Baron **de.** See SULLY.

**Rosny, J. H.** *Pseudonym of the brothers* **Joseph Henri Honoré Bo′ëx′** [bô′ĕks′] (1856–1940) *and* **Séraphin Justin François Boëx** (1859–1948). French novelists and collaborators (to 1909). Among their novels are *Nell Horn* (1886), *Daniel Valgraive* (1891), *Le Crime du Docteur* (1903), *Le Fardeau* (1906). Joseph published *Marthe Baraquin* (1909), *La Force Mystérieuse* (1914), *Le Pluraliste* . . . (1919), *Les Sciences et le Pluralisme* (1930); and Séraphin published *L'Affaire Dérive* (1909), *Sépulcres Blanchis* (1913), *La Carapace* (1914), *Les Beaux Yeux de Paris* (1927), etc.

**Rosny, Léon Louis Lucien Pru′nol′ de** (prü′nôl′ dẽ). 1837–1916. French Orientalist and ethnographer; professor of Japanese, Paris (1868); asst. director of École des Hautes Études, Paris (1886).

**Ross** (rŏs), **Adrian.** Pseudonym of Arthur Reed ROPES.

**Ross, Alexander.** 1783–1856. Canadian pioneer, b. in Scotland; to Canada (1805); accompanied John Jacob Astor's expedition to Oregon (1810–12) and described first settlement on Columbia River; served Hudson's Bay Co. (from 1821); helped organize and chronicle Red River settlement (from 1825).

**Ross, Betsy,** *nee* **Gris′com** (grĭs′kŭm). **1752–1836.** Maker of first American flag, b. Philadelphia; m. John Ross (1773, d. 1776), Joseph Ashburn (1777, d. 1782), John Claypoole (1783). Reputed to have made the flag at request of George Washington, Robert Morris, and George Ross. The stars-and-stripes flag was voted the national emblem by Continental Congress (June 14, 1777).

**Ross, Charles Griffith.** 1885–1950. American journalist, b. Independence, Mo.; taught journalism, U. of Mo. (1908–18); with St. Louis *Post-Dispatch* (1918–45); press secretary to President Truman (from 1945).

**Ross,** Sir **Denison,** *in full* **Edward Denison.** 1871–1940. English Oriental scholar; professor of Persian, U. of London (1896–1937).

**Ross, Edward Als′worth** (ălz′wûrth). 1866–1951. American sociologist; professor, Stanford (1893–1900), Nebraska (1901–06), Wisconsin (1906–37). Author of *Honest Dollars* (1896), *The Foundations of Sociology* (1905), *Sin and Society* (1907), *Social Psychology* (1908), *Russia in Upheaval* (1918), *Civic Sociology* (1925), *World Drift* (1928), etc.

**Ross,** Sir **Frederick Leith–.** See LEITH-ROSS.

**Ross, George.** 1730–1779. American jurist, b. New Castle, Del.; member, Continental Congress (1774–77), and a signer of Declaration of Independence.

**Ross,** Sir **James Clark.** 1800–1862. Scottish polar explorer; made four Arctic expeditions under Parry (1819–27); with his uncle (1829–33), determined position of North Magnetic Pole (1831); worked on magnetic survey of Great Britain (1838); commanded Antarctic expedition for geographical discovery (1839–43); published *Voyage of Discovery* (1847); made voyage to Baffin Bay in search of Sir John Franklin (1848–49). For him are named Ross Sea, Ross Island, and other parts of Antarctica. His uncle Sir **John Ross** (1777–1856), Arctic explorer, made expeditions in search of the Northwest Passage (1818, 1829–33), surveying Boothia Peninsula, King William Land, and Gulf of Boothia; published narratives of the two voyages; undertook third voyage in search of Franklin (1850); rear admiral.

**Ross, Janet Anne.** See under Lucie DUFF-GORDON.

**Ross, John.** *Indian name* **Coo′wes·coo·we′** *or* **Koo′wes·koo·we′** (kōō′wĕs·kōō·wē′). 1790–1866. American Indian chieftain, half-breed son of Scotch father and part Cherokee Indian mother, b. near Lookout Mountain, Tenn. Served with Andrew Jackson against the Creeks (1812). President, national council of Cherokees (1819–26); chief of eastern Cherokee (1828–39); resisted policy of moving Cherokee nation to Indian Territory. Chief, United Cherokee Nation (1839–66).

**Ross** (rŏs), **Ludwig.** 1806–1859. German archaeologist; directed excavations and restorations, notably of Temple of Nike, Athens (1835–36); professor, Halle (from 1845).

**Ross** (rŏs), **Martin.** See Violet Florence MARTIN.

**Ross, Nellie,** *nee* **Tay′loe** (tā′lō). 1876–1977. American politician; m. William Bradford Ross (1902; d. 1924); elected governor of Wyoming to complete deceased husband's term (1925–27), first woman governor of a state; first woman director of U.S. Mint (1933–53).

**Ross, Robert.** 1766–1814. English soldier; served with Sir John Moore in La Coruña campaign (1808), and again in Iberian Peninsula (1812); commanded expeditionary force in co-operation with Admiral Sir Alexander Cochrane against coasts of U.S. (1814); won battle of Bladensburg and burned Washington (1814); killed at North Point, Md.

**Ross,** Sir **Ronald.** 1857–1932. British physician, b. in India. Entered Indian medical service (1881); began study of malaria (1892); discovered life history of the malarial parasite in mosquitoes (1897–98); found malarial mosquito in West Africa (1899); awarded 1902 Nobel prize for physiology and medicine. Professor of tropical sanitation, U. of Liverpool and Liverpool School of Tropical Medicine; physician for tropical diseases, King's College Hospital, London (1913); director in chief, Ross Institute and Hospital for Tropical Diseases, Putney Heath, London. Author of: *The Prevention of Malaria* (1910) and other medical works; five mathematical works, a novel, etc.

**Ross,** Sir **William Charles.** 1794–1860. English miniature painter; executed over 2000 miniatures on ivory.

**Rosse,** Earls of. See William PARSONS.

**Ros·sel'li** (rô·sĕl'lê), **Cosimo di Lo·ren'zo Fi·lip'pi** (dê lô·rĕn'tsô fê·lēp'pê). 1439–1507. Florentine painter; assisted in decoration of Sistine Chapel (1840 ff.). Works include *The Last Supper, The Tables of the Law,* and *Christ Preaching from the Lake* (in Sistine Chapel).

**Ros'sel·li'no** (rōs'sâl·lē'nô) *or* **Ros'sel·li'ni** (-nê), **Bernardo.** 1409–1464. Florentine sculptor and architect; son of **Matteo di Do·me'ni·co Gam'ba·rel'li** (dê dô·mā'nê·kō gäm'bä·rĕl'lê). Among his works are tomb of Leonardo Bruni, tomb of Beata Villana (in Florence), tomb of Filippo Lazzari (in Pistoia); as an architect, built Palazzo Ruccellai (at Florence), façade of church of the Misericordia (at Arezzo), the Palazzo Piccolomini (at Pienza), the Pienza cathedral, and was employed at the Vatican. His brother and pupil **Antonio Rossellino** (1427–?1479) was also a sculptor; his works include the sarcophagus of St. Marcolinus (in the Forlì museum), the tomb of the cardinal of Portugal (in church of San Miniato, Florence), the group *Nativity* (in Metropolitan Museum, N.Y.).

**Ros·set'ti** (rô·sĕt'ĭ; -zĕt'ĭ), **Dante Gabriel,** *orig.* **Gabriel Charles Dante.** 1828–1882. English painter and poet, b. London; with Holman Hunt, Millais, and others, founded Pre-Raphaelite school of painting (1848). Expressed the Pre-Raphaelite motive in *Ecce Ancilla Domini;* turned to water colors of legendary or romantic cast, including illustrations of Browning's poem *The Laboratory,* also *Dante Drawing the Angel* (1852), *Found* (begun 1853); with patronage of Ruskin and friendship of William Morris, Swinburne, and Burne-Jones, executed some of his best paintings, including the triptych for Llandaff Cathedral; took part in revival of stained-glass painting as an art; m. (1860) Elizabeth Eleanor Siddal, whom he painted innumerable times before her death from tuberculosis (1862); in grief buried his manuscript poems in her coffin. Executed a triptych of Paolo and Francesca (c. 1860), *Beata Beatrix* (1865), *Monna Vanna* (1866), *Pandora* (1871), *Proserpina in Hades* (1874), *La Ghirlandata* (1878), and the famous *Dante's Dream;* replied in *The Stealthy School of Criticism* (in *Athenaeum,* 1871) to Robert Buchanan's attack from a moral point of view on *The Fleshly School of Poetry* (in *Contemporary Review*). As poet contributed *The Blessed Damozel,* six sonnets, and four lyrics to *The Germ,* organ of the Pre-Raphaelite Brotherhood; also wrote *Retro me Sathanas, The Portrait, The Choice;* translated early Italian poetry (1861), later revised as *Dante and his Circle* (1874); published *Ballads and Sonnets* (1881), containing the completed sonnet sequence *House of Life,* and *Rose Mary, The White Ship, The King's Tragedy.* His brother **William Michael** (1829–1919), art critic; assistant secretary to Board of Inland Revenue (1869–94); m. (1874) **Lucy,** daughter of Ford Madox Brown and herself a painter; a founder of Pre-Raphaelite Brotherhood, and editor of its organ, *The Germ;* contributed to *The Spectator* (from 1850); biographer of Shelley and Keats; editor of poetical works of Coleridge, Milton, Campbell, Blake, Whitman; edited collected works of his brother and sister.

Their sister **Christina Georgina** (1830–1894), poet; lived all her life in London; contributed seven lyric poems to *The Germ* under pseudonym of **Ellen Al·leyne'** [ă·lān'; ăl'ĭn] (1850); model to her brother, also to Holman Hunt, Ford Madox Brown, and Millais; published her best verse in *Goblin Market* (1862); afflicted with Graves' disease (1871); from religious scruples twice declined proposals of marriage; long attended her mother and devoted herself to religious disquisition; author of *Sing-Song* (book of children's poems; 1872), *Time Flies* (a collection of homilies; 1885), *The Face of the Deep* (a commentary on the *Apocalypse;* 1892), besides further poetical works, *The Prince's Progress* (1866), *A Pageant* (1881), *New Poems* (1896).

Their older sister, **Maria Francesca** (1827–1876); author of *A Shadow of Dante* (1871); entered an Anglican sisterhood (1874).

Their father, **Gabriele Rossetti** (1783–1854), Italian poet and political refugee from Naples; early renounced painting for literature; as member of secret society of Carbonari took part in Napoleonic revolution of 1820 and saluted it with patriotic odes; fled on return to power of King Ferdinand; professor of Italian, King's Coll., London (1831); eccentric commentator on Dante, showing the *Inferno* chiefly political and antipapal.

**Ros'si** (rōs'sê), Countess. See Henriette SONTAG.

**Ros'si** (rōs'sê; *Angl.* rŏs'ĭ), **Bruno.** 1905– . Physicist, b. in Italy; professor, Padua (1932–38); research associate in cosmic rays, Chicago (from 1939); known for investigations of cosmic rays.

**Ros'si** (rōs'sê), **Ernesto.** 1829–1896. Italian actor; known particularly for Shakespearean roles; accompanied Adelaide Ristori to Paris (1855); played in Spain, Portugal, South America, U.S. (1881), London. Author of plays, as *Adèle, La Prière d'un Soldat,* and *Les Hyènes.*

**Rossi, Francesco de'.** See Cecco di SALVIATI.

**Rossi, Giovanni Battista de'.** 1494–1540. See Il Rosso.

**Rossi, Giovanni Battista de'.** 1822–1894. Italian archaeologist and epigraphist; known chiefly as discoverer of the catacombs of St. Calixtus; regarded as founder of Christian archaeology; mapped Roman catacombs.

**Rossi,** Count **Pellegrino.** 1787–1848. Italian statesman and economist; called to professorship of political economy at Collège de France by Louis Philippe (1834); in diplomatic service of French government (1840–45). Appointed prime minister of Papal States by Pius IX (1848); attempted Italian confederation under leadership of Papal States; assassinated.

**Rossi, Salomone.** *Sometimes called* **L'E·bre'o** (lā·brâ'ô). c. 1565–c. 1628. Rabbi, and one of leading instrumental composers of the Renaissance, b. Mantua; composer at Mantuan court (1587–1628). His works include four books of sonatas (1607–22), seven books of madrigals, a religious drama *Maddalena* (1617), and synagogal music.

**Ros·si'ni** (rôs·sē'nê), **Gioacchino Antonio.** 1792–1868. Italian operatic composer, b. Pesaro; leading representative of bel canto school of opera; one of last masters of opera buffa. Director of San Carlo and Del Fondo theaters (Naples, 1815) and Théâtre Italien (Paris). Among his 39 operas are *Tancredi* (1813), *Il Barbiere* *di Siviglia* (1816), *Otello* (1816), *Il Califfo di Bagdad* (1818), *Mosè in Egitto* (1818), *Semiramide* (1823), and *Guillaume Tell* (1829); nonoperatic compositions include the celebrated *Stabat Mater* (1842), cantatas, religious music, and many pieces for piano.

**Ros′si·ter** (rŏs′ĭ·tẽr), **Thomas Prichard.** 1818–1871. American painter, b. New Haven, Conn. Excelled in portraiture and historical paintings. His *Washington and Lafayette at Mount Vernon* hangs in Metropolitan Museum of Art, New York City; *The Prince of Wales and President Buchanan*...in National Gallery of Art, Washington, D.C.; *Rebecca at the Well* in Corcoran Gallery of Art, Washington, D.C.

**Rosslyn,** Earl of. See Alexander WEDDERBURN.

**Ros′so, Il** (ēl rōs′sō). *Also called* **Il Rosso Fio′ren·ti′no** (fyō′rân·tē′nō). *Real name* **Giovanni Battista de′Ros′si** (dâ·rōs′sē). 1494–1540. Florentine painter; pupil of Andrea del Sarto; called to Fontainebleau as chief artist by Francis I (1530). His works include frescoes from the life of Francis I and mythological subjects.

**Ros′tand′** (rôs′täɴ′), **Edmond.** 1868–1918. French poet and playwright, b. Marseilles. Made literary debut with volume of verse, *Les Musardises* (1890); then turned to the stage and wrote *Les Romanesques* (1894), *La Princesse Lointaine* (1895), *La Samaritaine* (1897), and his great successes *Cyrano de Bergerac* (1898), *L'Aiglon* (1900), and *Chantecler* (1910); m. **Louise Rose Étiennette,** *called* **Rosemonde, Gé′rard′** [zhā′rår′] (1871–1953), poet, author of *Les Pipeaux* (1889), *L'Arc en Ciel*, *Les Féeries du Cœur*, etc. Their son **Maurice** (1891–1968) collaborated with his mother on some plays, as *Un Bon Petit Diable* (1912) and *La Marchande d'Allumettes* (1914), and himself wrote verse and fiction, as *Les Insomnies* (verse, 1924), *Morbidezza* (verse, 1928), *Le Cercueil de Cristal* (1920), *Le Second Werther* (1927).

**Ro·stop·chin′** (rŭ·stŭp·chēn′), Count **Fëdor Vasilievich.** 1763–1826. Russian soldier, politician, and writer. Aide-de-camp to Czar Paul I; promoted general and grand marshal of the court; appointed minister of foreign affairs. Governor of Moscow (1812); organized its defense against Napoleon; believed to have ordered the burning of the city when its fall became inevitable.

**Ro·stov′tzeff** (rŭ·stôf′tsĕf), **Michael Ivanovich.** 1870–1952. American historian, b. in Russia; educ. Kiev and St. Petersburg Univs.; professor of classical philology and ancient history, St. Petersburg (1901–18); professor of ancient history, U. of Wisconsin (1920–25), Yale (1925–39); director of archaeological studies (1939–44). Among his works are *History of the Ancient World* (1924–26), *Social and Economic History of the Roman Empire* (1926), *Social and Economic History of the Hellenistic World* (1941).

**Ros′wey′de** (rŏs′vī′dĕ), **Heribert.** 1569–1629. Jesuit scholar and hagiographer, b. Utrecht; laid plan for collection of sources known as *Acta Sanctorum*, or *Lives of the Saints*, carried out by Jean de Bolland and his followers.

**Ros·wi′tha** (rôs·vē′tä). Also **Hrot·svi′tha** *or* **Hrot·swi′tha** (hrôt·svē′tä). 10th-century German Benedictine nun, poet, and chronicler; author of chronicles of Otto I (in verse) and six Latin comedies.

**Rotch** (rŏch), **Abbott Lawrence.** 1861–1912. American meteorologist; first professor of meteorology in Harvard (1906–12). Interested in development of aeronautics. Author of *Sounding the Ocean of Air* (1900), *The Conquest of the Air* (1909), *Charts of the Atmosphere for Aeronauts and Aviators* (with Andrew Henry Palmer, 1911), etc.

**Roth** (rōt), **Justus Ludwig Adolf.** 1818–1892. German geologist and mineralogist.

**Roth, Rudolf von.** 1821–1895. German Sanskrit scholar; helped introduce Vedic studies into Germany; author, with Otto von Böhtlingk, of *Sanskrit Wörterbuch* (3 vols., 1855–75).

**Ro′the** (rō′tĕ), **Richard.** 1799–1867. German Protestant theologian; author of *Theologische Ethick* (system of speculative theology, 3 vols., 1845–48), *Theologische Enzyklopädie* (pub. 1880), etc.

**Ro′then·stein** (rō′thĕn·stīn), Sir **William.** 1872–1945. English painter, b. Bradford, Yorkshire. An official artist with English and Canadian armies during World War I. Principal of Royal Coll. of Art (1920–35). Published several series of portrait drawings; author of interesting volumes of reminiscences.

**Roth′er·ham** (rŏth′ẽr·ăm), **Thomas.** *Known as* **Thomas Scott** (skŏt). 1423–1500. English prelate; became bishop of Rochester (1468–71) and of Lincoln (1471–80), and chancellor of England (1474–83); archbishop of York (1480).

**Roth′er·mel** (rŏth′ẽr·mĕl), **Peter Frederick.** 1817–1895. American artist; known esp. for historical paintings. His *Battle of Gettysburg* now hangs in the State Capitol, Harrisburg, Pa.

**Rothermere,** Viscount. See Harold Sidney HARMSWORTH.

**Rothes,** Earls and duke of. See LESLIE family.

**Rothesay,** Duke of. See *David Stewart*, under ROBERT III of Scotland.

**Roth′ko** (rŏth′kō), **Mark.** *Orig. name* **Marcus Rothkovich.** 1903–1970. American (Russian-born) painter. A pioneer abstract expressionist.

**Rothmaler, Karl von.** See Karl von EINEM.

**Roth′schild** (*Ger.* rōt′shĭlt; *Eng.* rŏth(s)′chīld, rŏs′chīld; *Fr.* rôt′shēld′). Family of Jewish financiers, including: **Meyer Amschel** (1743–1812), founder, a moneylender at Frankfort on the Main; financial adviser (1801) to the landgrave of Hesse-Cassel; agent of the British government in subsidizing European sovereigns in wars against Napoleon. His five sons: **Meyer Amschel** (1773–1855), who succeeded his father as head of the Frankfort establishment; **Salomon** (1774–1855), who founded a branch at Vienna; **Nathan Meyer** (1777–1836), who founded a branch at London; **Karl** (1788–1855), who founded a branch at Naples; and **James** (1792–1868), who founded a branch at Paris.

Meyer Amschel (the second) died childless, and the Frankfort business passed to nephews, sons of Karl, and was liquidated (1901) after the death of Karl's son **Wilhelm Karl** (1828–1901).

Salomon was succeeded in the Vienna branch by his son **Amschel Salomon** (1803–1874), who in turn was succeeded by his son **Albert** (1844–1911).

Nathan Meyer was succeeded by his son **Lionel Nathan** (1808–1879), elected to Parliament (1847, 1849, 1852, 1857) but not allowed to take his seat because he could not take the oath "in the true faith of a Christian"; instrumental in securing removal of ban on Jews (1858) and sat in Parliament (1858–68; 1869–74). Lionel Nathan's brother **Sir Anthony de Rothschild** (1810–1876) was Austrian consul general (1858), and first president of the new United Synagogue, in London (1870). Another brother, **Meyer Amschel de Rothschild** (1818–1874), was a noted sportsman and art collector, and member of Parliament (1859–74). Lionel Nathan was succeeded as head of the London banking house by his son Sir **Nathan Meyer,** 1st Baron **Rothschild** (1840–1915), member of Parliament (1865–85) and of the House of Lords (from 1885), first person of the Jewish faith to be admitted to the House of Lords. Nathan Meyer's son **Lionel Walter,** 2d Baron **Rothschild**

(1868–1937), M.P. (1899–1910), wrote zoological treatises. The branch of Naples, founded by Karl, was discontinued (c. 1861). James, youngest son of the founder, gave influential support to the Restoration government and to the administration of Louis Philippe; he was succeeded as head of the Paris branch by his son **Alphonse** (1827–1905), who became a regent of the Bank of France, and president of the board of directors of the Chemins de Fer du Nord.

**Ro′trou′** (rô′trōō′), **Jean de.** 1609–1650. French playwright; associated with Corneille, Guillaume Colletet, Boisrobert, and L'Étoile to form group of Richelieu's "Five Poets" who composed together according to plans laid down by the cardinal. Wrote *Saint Genest* (1646) and *Venceslas* (1647). Praised by Voltaire, who called him "le véritable fondateur du théâtre Français."

**Röt′scher** (rûch′ẽr), **Heinrich Theodor.** 1803–1871. German aesthetician and drama critic.

**Rot′teck** (rôt′ĕk), **Karl Wenzeslaus von.** 1775–1840. German historian and politician; champion of liberalism. Edited, with Welcker, *Staatslexikon. Enzyklopädie der Staatswissenschaften* (15 vols., 1834–43; 3 suppl., 1846–48); wrote *Allgemeine Geschichte* (6 vols., 1812–18), etc.

**Rot′ten·ham′mer** (rôt′ĕn·häm′ẽr), **Johann.** 1564–1625. German painter; works include small mythological and religious scenes with landscape, painted on copper, some large paintings, as *Death of Adonis* (in the Louvre), altarpieces in Augsburg and frescoes for chapels and ducal palaces.

**Rott′mann** (rôt′män), **Karl.** 1797–1850. German landscape painter; painted 28 frescoes of Italian scenes for arcades of the Munich Hofgarten and 23 Greek landscapes for the New Pinakothek.

**Ro′ty′** (rô′tē′), **Louis Oscar.** 1846–1911. French sculptor and engraver of coins, medals, etc.

**Rou·ault′** (rwō), **Georges.** 1871–1958. French painter of ultramodern school, identified with Fauvists; studied under Gustave Moreau; curator of Musée Gustave Moreau.

**Rou′bil′lac′** (rōō′bē′yȧk′), **Louis François.** 1695–1762. French sculptor; studio in England (from 1744); protégé of Walpole family; executed statue of Shakespeare now in British Museum, etc.

**Rouërie** *or* **Rouarie,** Marquis **de La.** See Charles ARMAND.

**Rou′gé′** (rōō′zhā′), Vicomte **Emmanuel de.** 1811–1872. French Egyptologist; discoverer of prototypes of Semitic alphabet in early Egyptian hieratic.

**Rou′get′ de Lisle** (rōō′zhĕ′ dē lēl′), **Claude Joseph.** 1760–1836. French army officer and composer of songs; known as composer of words and music of *Marseillaise* (1792), originally published under title *Chant de Guerre pour l'Armée du Rhin.*

**Rough′ead** (rŭf′ĕd), **William.** 1870–1952. Scottish lawyer and writer; educ. Edinburgh U.; wrote books under series title *Notable British Trials* (1906–32), and *Knaves' Looking-Glass* (1935), *Rascals Revived* (1940), *Reprobates Reviewed* (1941), *The Art of Murder* (1943).

**Rou·her′** (rwâr), **Eugène.** 1814–1884. French statesman; member of Constituent Assembly (1848) and Legislative Assembly (1849). Premier of France and minister of justice (1849–51); minister of justice (1851–52), and of agriculture, commerce, and public works (1855). Again premier (minister of state, 1863–69). President of Senate (1869–70) and a leader of Bonapartists (1871).

**Rou′ma′nille′** (rōō′mȧ′nē′y′), **Joseph.** 1818–1891. French Provençal writer; leader of the Félibrige; a founder and editor of the Félibrige journal, *Armana Prouvençau* (1854). Among his works are *Li Margarideto* (1847), *Lis Oubreto en Vers* (1862), *Lis Oubreto en Prose* (1859), *Li Conte Prouvençau, Li Cascareleto* (1883), etc.

**Rourke** (rŏŏrk), **Constance M.** 1885–1941. American author; educ. Vassar College and the Sorbonne; instructor in English, Vassar (1910–15); author of *Trumpets of Jubilee* (1927), *American Humor* (1931), *Davy Crockett* (1934), *Audubon* (1936), *Charles Sheeler* (1938), etc.

**Rous** (rous), **Francis.** 1579–1659. English Puritan and hymnologist. Author of *The Arte of Happiness* (1619) and *Testis Veritatis* (1626). Known esp. for his metrical version of *Psalms* (1643).

**Rous, Francis Peyton.** 1879–1970. American pathologist, b. Baltimore, Md. At Rockefeller Inst. (1910–45; emeritus 1945); awarded Nobel prize in physiology and medicine (1966) with C. B. Huggins for discovery of tumor-inducing viruses.

**Rouse** (rous), **William Henry Denham.** 1863–1950. British educator and writer, b. Calcutta. Wrote *An Echo of Greek Song* (1899), *Gods, Heroes, and Men of Greece* (1934), *Homer* (1939), and a number of translations from Indian literature and legend.

**Rous′seau′** (?rōō′sō′), **Harry Harwood.** 1870–1930. American naval officer; member, Isthmian Canal Commission (1907–14); associated with Gen. George W. Goethals in building Panama Canal (to 1916).

**Rous′seau′** (rōō′sō′), **Henri.** *Known as* **Le Dou·a′nier′** (lē dwȧ′nyā′). 1844–1910. French painter, esp. of scenes of everyday life in France and in Mexico. His *La Charmeuse de Serpents* hangs in the Louvre.

**Rousseau, Jacques.** 1626–1694. French painter of interiors and architectural views.

**Rousseau, Jean Baptiste.** 1671–1741. French poet, b. Paris. Banished from France (c. 1712) because of satirical couplets ascribed to him, attacking certain prominent men of letters. Best known for his *Cantates, Psaumes,* and *Ode à la Fortune.*

**Rousseau, Jean Jacques.** 1712–1778. Familiarly known as "Jean Jacques." French philosopher and author, b. Geneva. Ran away to Italy and Savoy; lived with Mme. de Warens at Annecy (1731), later at Chambéry (1732–41), but with several periods of wandering during these years. Lived chiefly in Paris (from 1741); associated with Diderot; wrote an opera, *Les Muses Galantes* (1747) and articles (on music and political economy) for the *Encyclopédie;* took as mistress (c. 1743) Thérèse le Vasseur, an illiterate inn servant, by whom he had five children, all placed in a foundling hospital. Acquired fame as a writer by his essay *Discours sur les Arts et Sciences* (1750), developing the paradox that the savage state is superior to the civilized; produced an operetta, *Le Devin du Village* (1752). Established by Mme. d'Épinay in a cottage, the Hermitage, near Montmorency (1756–57); here wrote *Julie, ou la Nouvelle Héloïse* (1761), a sentimental and moralizing romance, written in the form of letters; quarreled with Grimm, Diderot, and Mme. d'Épinay (1758); attacked Voltaire. Published *Le Contrat Social* (1762), a discussion of the principles of political right, upholding that the rightful authority is the general will, and *Émile, ou Traité de l'Éducation* (1762), the simple romance of a child, Émile, reared apart from other children by methods of experimentation, a book that formed the basis of modern elementary education; for its antimonarchic views, *Émile*...was condemned by Parliament of Paris (1762). Threatened by Jesuits, fled to Switzerland (1762), then to London (1766); invited by David Hume to live at Wootton, Derbyshire; quarreled with Hume and fled to France (1767); undoubtedly partly insane during last 10 or 15 years of his life; in Paris (1770–78) writing *Confessions* (pub. 1781 and 1788), *Dialogues,* and *Rêveries du Promeneur Solitaire* (1782).

**Rousseau, Philippe.** 1816–1887. French painter; best known for pictures of animals, flowers, fruits, etc.

**Rousseau, Théodore.** *In full* **Pierre Etienne Theodore Rousseau.** 1812–1867. French landscape painter; identified with the Barbizon school; studio at Barbizon during later years.

**Rousseau, Victor.** 1865–1954. Belgian sculptor.

**Rous'sel'** (rōō'sĕl'), **Albert Charles Paul Marie.** 1869–1937. French composer of symphonies, concertos, operas (*Padmâvati*, 1923; *La Naissance de la Lyre*, 1925), ballets, serenades, etc.

**Rous'se·lot'** (rōōs'lō'), Abbé **Jean Pierre.** 1846–1924. French pioneer in experimental phonetics and in study of dialect as related to geography and genealogy. Author of *Principes de Phonétique Expérimentale* (1897–1909) and *Précis de Prononciation Française* (1902; with F. Laclotte).

**Routh** (routh), **Edward John.** 1831–1907. British mathematician, b. Quebec; author of classic works on dynamics and statics, including *Rigid Dynamics* (1860), *Essay on the Stability of a Given State of Motion* (1877), *Statics* (2 vols., 1891).

**Routh, Martin Joseph.** 1755–1854. English patristic scholar; edited *Reliquiae Sacrae*, collection of ecclesiastical writings of second and third centuries (1814–48).

**Rout'ledge** (rŭt'lĭj; rout'-), **George.** 1812–1888. English publisher in London (from 1843); made success of publishing classics at one shilling each, the "Railway Library" (1848); followed with "Routledge's Universal Library," edited by Henry Morley (60 vols., 1883); established branch in New York (1854).

**Rou'vier'** (rōō'vyā'), **Pierre Maurice.** 1842–1911. French statesman; member of National Assembly (1871), of Chamber of Deputies (1876–1902), and of Senate (1903–05). Minister of commerce and colonies (1881–82, 1884–85); premier of France (1887); minister of finance (1887, 1889–92, 1902–05); again premier (1905–06).

**Roux** (rōō), **Pierre Paul Émile.** 1853–1933. French physician and bacteriologist. With Pasteur Institute (from 1888), director (1904–18). Worked with Pasteur on the etiology and treatment of various infectious diseases, including anthrax, tetanus, and hydrophobia; conducted researches (with Nocard) leading to the discovery of the pneumococcus; demonstrated (with Yersin, 1889) that the diphtheria bacillus produces a toxin, a discovery which led to the development of a diphtheria antitoxin by Emil von Behring.

**Roux** (rōō), **Wilhelm.** 1850–1924. German anatomist; reputed founder of modern experimental embryology; known for researches on the early development of the fertilized egg.

**Rovere.** See duke of URBINO.

**Ro·vi'go** (rô·vē'gô), Duc **de. Anne Jean Marie René Sa'va'ry'** (så'vá'rē'). 1774–1833. French soldier in Napoleonic armies; aide-de-camp to Napoleon (1800). Appointed head of secret service when Napoleon was first consul (1802). General of brigade (1803); supervised process leading to execution of duc d'Enghien (1804); general of division (1805); distinguished himself at battle of Ostrołęnka (1807). Succeeded Fouché as minister of police (1810–14); was loyal to Napoleon during Hundred Days and tried vainly to accompany him to St. Helena.

**Row.** See also ROE.

**Row'an** (rō'ăn), **Stephen Clegg.** 1808–1890. American naval officer, b. near Dublin, Ireland; to U.S. (1818). In command of sloop *Pawnee*, defending Washington, at outbreak of Civil War; took part in first naval action of the war at Aquia Creek (May 25, 1861). Co-operated with Gen. Burnside in seizing Roanoke Island (Feb., 1862), and destroyed Confederate ships. Commanded *New Ironsides;* engaged in Charleston Harbor (1863). Rear admiral (1866); vice-admiral (1870).

**Rowe** (rō), **Leo Stanton.** 1871–1946. American political scientist; professor, Pennsylvania (1904–17); director-general, Pan American Union (from 1920); president, American Acad. of Political and Social Science (1902–30).

**Rowe, Nicholas.** 1674–1718. English poet and dramatist; produced (1700–15) eight plays, including *The Ambitious Stepmother* (1700), *Tamerlane* (1702), *The Fair Penitent*, an adaptation in which appears Lothario, said to have suggested Lovelace to Samuel Richardson (1703), *The Tragedy of Jane Shore* (1714), *The Tragedy of Lady Jane Grey* (1715). First modern editor of Shakespeare; published edition of plays from fourth folio with biography containing collection of Shakespearean traditions made at Stratford by Thomas Betterton (6 vols., 1709); divided and numbered acts and scenes, noted entrances and exits, modernized grammar, spelling, and punctuation, prefixed the *dramatis personae*. Praised by Dr. Johnson for his translation of Lucan; poet laureate (1715).

**Row'ell** (rou'ĕl), **Newton Wesley.** 1867–1941. Canadian lawyer and politician; member of Dominion parliament (1917–21); member of Imperial War Cabinet and Imperial War Conference (1918); Canadian delegate at first Assembly of League of Nations (1920). Author of *Canada a Nation* (1923), etc.

**Row'land** (rō'lănd), **Henry Augustus.** 1848–1901. American physicist; first professor of physics, Johns Hopkins (1875–1901). Invented the concave grating for the spectroscope. Determined mechanical equivalent of heat and of the ohm. Discovered magnetic effect of electric convection. Conducted researches on the solar spectrum. Also investigated alternating currents.

**Row'land·son** (rō'lănd·s'n), **Thomas.** 1756–1827. English caricaturist; settled in London as portrait painter (1777), soon turning to caricature and illustration; designed and engraved a series of plates entitled *Tours of Dr. Syntax* (1812, 1820, 1821), with verses by Dr. William Combe, also *The English Dance of Death* (1815–16), *The Dance of Life* (1816). Illustrated works of Smollett, Goldsmith, and Sterne, and *Baron Munchausen.*

**Row'ley** (rō'lĭ), **Samuel.** d. 1633? English dramatist; author of two extant plays, *When you see me, You know me. Or the famous Chronicle Historie of King Henry VIII* (1605) and *The Noble Souldier* (1634).

**Rowley, Thomas.** See Thomas CHATTERTON.

**Rowley, William.** 1585?–?1642. English actor and dramatist; collaborator with Dekker, Middleton, Thomas Heywood, Webster, Massinger, and Ford. Played under Philip Henslowe's management at the *Hope;* retired (c. 1627). Sole author of *A New Wonder, A Woman Never Vext* (1632), *A Match at Midnight* (1633), *A Shoomaker a Gentleman* (1637). Collaborated with Thomas Dekker and John Ford in *The Witch of Edmonton* (publ. 1658); with Middleton in *A Faire Quarrell* (1617) and *The Changeling* (performed 1621; publ. 1653); with Heywood in *Fortune by Land and Sea* (printed 1655).

**Rown'tree** (roun'trē; -trē), **Joseph.** 1836–1925. English cocoa manufacturer and philanthropist; improved conditions in his factory, established social-welfare organizations, founded model village (New Earswick, 1904), and wrote (with Arthur Sherwell) books on temperance. His son **Benjamin Seebohm** (1871–1954) continued his interests.

**Row'son** (rou'z'n), **Susanna,** *nee* **Has'well** (hăz'wĕl; -wĕl). 1762–1824. Author, actress, and educator, b. Portsmouth, England; to America as a child; m. William Rowson (1787). On English stage (1792) and American stage (1793–97). Author of novels, including

*Charlotte, a Tale of Truth,* better known as *Charlotte Temple* (1791), *Reuben and Rachel* (1798), *Charlotte's Daughter,* better known as *Lucy Temple* (1828), etc.

**Rowton,** Baron. See Montagu William Lowry CORRY.

**Rox·an'a** (rŏk·săn'ȧ; -sä'nȧ) *or* **Rox·an'e** (rŏk·săn'ē; -sä'nē). d. 310 B.C. Daughter of a Bactrian prince, and wife (m. 327) of Alexander the Great. With her son Alexander IV, placed under regency of Perdiccas after Alexander's death (323); later went to Macedonia; with her son, imprisoned at Amphipolis and murdered by order of Cassander (*q.v.*). See STATIRA.

**Ro'xas** (rô'häs). Variant of ROJAS.

**Ro'xas y A·cu'ña** (rô'häs ē ä·kōō'nyä), **Manuel.** 1892–1948. Philippine statesman; educ. U. of the Philippines. Speaker, Philippine House of Representatives (1922–34); member of National Assembly (1935–38); secretary of finance (1938–41); brig. general, World War II; president (1946–48).

**Roxburgh,** Earls and dukes of. See KERR family.

**Roy** (roi), **William.** 1726–1790. British military engineer and geodesist.

**Roy'all** (roi'ăl), **Kenneth Claiborne.** 1894–1971. American lawyer, b. Goldsboro, N.C.; served in World War I and II; brigadier general (1943); undersecretary of war (1945–47); secretary of war (1947–49).

**Roy'bet'** (rwȧ'bĕ'), **Ferdinand.** 1840–1920. French painter and engraver.

**Royce** (rois), Sir **Henry,** *in full* **Frederick Henry.** 1863–1933. British engineer; founded (1884) Royce, Ltd., in Manchester, and joined with C. S. Rolls (1904) in founding Rolls-Royce, Ltd., of Derby and London.

**Royce, Josiah.** 1855–1916. American philosopher, b. Grass Valley, Calif. Taught philosophy, Harvard (1882–1916; professor from 1892). A noted metaphysician, developed philosophy of idealism emphasizing individuality and will rather than intellect. His philosophical writings include *The Religious Aspect of Philosophy* (1885), *The Spirit of Modern Philosophy* (1892), *The Conception of God* (1897), *The World and the Individual* (1900), *Sources of Religious Insight* (1912), *The Problem of Christianity* (2 vols., 1913), *The Hope of the Great Community* (1916).

**Royce, Ralph.** 1890–1965. American army officer, b. Marquette, Mich.; grad. U.S.M.A., West Point (1914); served in World War I (1917–18); air attaché, London (1941); flight commander in southwest Pacific area (1942); major general; commander, air training at Maxwell Field (1942–43), 1st air force (1943), U.S. forces in Middle East (1943), tactical air forces in Europe (1944).

**Roy'croft** (roi'krŏft), **Thomas.** d. 1677. English printer; appointed by Charles II king's printer of Oriental languages; among books printed by him are a polyglot Bible (1654–57) and editions of the classics.

**Roy'den** (roi'd'n), **Agnes Maude.** 1876–1956. English social worker and evangelist, educ. Oxford. Active in woman-suffrage movement (1908–14) and editor of *The Common Cause.* Asst. preacher at City Temple, first woman in Great Britain to occupy pulpit of regular place of worship (1917–20).

**Royde–Smith, Naomi Gwladys.** 1875–1964. English novelist; m. Ernest Milton (1926): *John Fanning's Legacy* (1927), *The Mother* (1931), *Private Room* (play, 1934), *The Altar-Piece* (1939), *Jane Fairfax* (1940), etc.

**Roy'er'–Col'lard'** (rwȧ'yā'kô'lȧr'), **Pierre Paul.** 1763–1845. French philosopher and politician; accepted the French Revolution; elected to Council of Five Hundred (1797); after the Restoration, a leader of the Doctrinaires, advocates of constitutional monarchy; member (president, 1828) of Chamber of Deputies.

**Royle** (roil), **Edwin Milton.** 1862–1942. American actor and playwright, b. Lexington, Mo. Author of *Friends, The Squaw Man, The Unwritten Law, The Winning of Barbara Worth* (from Harold Bell Wright's novel), *The Conqueror, My Wife's Husbands, Marrying Mary, Her Way Out,* etc.

**Ro·zhde'stven·ski** (rŭ·zhdyā'stvyĕn·skû·ĭ; *Angl.* -skĭ), **Zinovi Petrovich.** 1848–1909. Russian admiral; commanded Baltic fleet in the Russo-Japanese War (1904–05); decisively defeated at the battle of Tsushima, in the Sea of Japan, by the Japanese fleet under Admiral Togo (May 27–28, 1905).

**Roz'wa·dow'ski** (rôz'vä·dôf'skē), **Jan.** 1867–1935. Polish philologist; author of *Linguistic Phenomena and Development* (1913), *Phonetic History of the Polish Language* (1915), etc.

**Ruben.** See REUBEN.

**Ru'bens** (*Angl.* rōō'bĕnz; *Flem.* rü'bĕns), **Peter Paul.** 1577–1640. Flemish painter; m. **Isabella Brandt** [bränt] (d. 1626). Was called to Paris (1622) to decorate the Luxembourg for Marie de Médicis; was sent to Madrid in a diplomatic capacity (1628), met Velázquez and painted five portraits of Philip V. To London (1629); m. **Helena Four'ment'** [fōōr'mäN'] (1630), a niece of Isabella Brandt. Painted landscapes, portraits, and esp. historical and sacred subjects; renowned for excellence of his coloring. Among his most notable works are *The Descent from the Cross* (in the cathedral at Antwerp), *The Fall of the Damned* (at Munich), *The Rape of the Sabines* (at London).

**Rubianus, Crotus.** See CROTUS RUBIANUS.

**Ru·bi'ni** (rōō·bē'nē), **Giovanni Battista.** 1795–1854. Italian tenor singer; sang in principal cities of Europe; director of singing, St. Petersburg.

**Ru'bin·stein** (*Angl.* rōō'bĭn·stīn; *Pol.* rōō'bēn-), **Akiba.** 1882–1961. Polish chess master, b. Łódź. Winner of first prize in international tournaments at Carlsbad (1907), San Sebastián, Piešt'any, and Breslau (1912), and Vienna (1922).

**Ru'bin·stein** (*Angl.* rōō'bĭn·stīn; *Russ.* rōō·byĭn·shtīn'), **Anton.** 1829–1894. Russian Jewish pianist and composer, b. Kherson, Ukraine; made many concert tours in Europe and (1872–73) U.S.; settled in St. Petersburg (1848), became court pianist and imperial concert director (1858), founded and directed (1862–67; 1887–90) St. Petersburg Conservatory of Music; spent last years principally in Berlin (1890–92) and Dresden. Compositions include operas, as *Feramors* (1863), *The Demon* (1875), *The Maccabees* (1875), *Nero* (1879), and *Sulamith* (1883); oratorios, as *Paradise Lost* (1855), *The Tower of Babel* (1872), *Moses* (1887); *The Ocean Symphony* and other orchestral works; piano concertos and piano pieces, chamber music, songs, etc.

**Ru'bin·stein** (*Angl.* rōō'bĭn·stīn; *Pol.* rōō'bēn-), **Arthur.** 1889– . American (Polish-born) concert pianist; on concert tours around the world.

**Rub'ner** (rōōb'nẽr), **Max.** 1854–1932. German physiologist and hygienist; worked esp. on effect of climate on man, application of law of conservation of energy to animal metabolism, and nutrition.

**Ru'bru'quis'** (rü'brü'kē'), **Guillaume.** *Also* **William of Ruys'broeck** (rois'brōōk) *or* **Ru'brouck'** (rü'-brōōk') *or* **Ru'bruck** (rōō'brōōk) *or* **Ru'bruk** (rōō'-brōōk). 1220?–?1293. Franciscan missionary and traveler, b. in Brabant. In the Holy Land (c. 1248–53); sent by Saint Louis of France on mission (1253) to the Tartar chief; traversed the Crimea and steppes between Don and Volga rivers, and country eastward to Mongolia. Wrote for Saint Louis an account of his trip (*Itinerarium*), which was published in part by Hakluyt

(1598–99) and by Purchas (1625), and complete by Paris Société de Géographie (1839).

**Rucelinus.** See ROSCELLINUS.

**Ru'cel·la'i** (rōō'chĕl·lä'ē), **Giovanni.** 1475–1525. Italian poet and dramatist; cousin of Leo X (Giovanni de' Medici); appointed apostolic prothonotary; governor of Castel Sant' Angelo. One of first to use blank verse (*versi sciolti*), as in poem *Le Api* (1524), in imitation of Vergil's *Georgics* (Book IV); known esp. as an initiator of Italian classic tragedy with plays *Rosmunda* (1515) and *Oreste* (1525; in imitation of Euripides's *Iphigenia*). His father, **Bernardo Rucellai** (1449–1514), was an Italian humanist; brother-in-law of Lorenzo the Magnificent; after death of Lorenzo, leader of Platonic Academy whose garden meeting place was named after him Orti Oricellari.

**Ruchrath** *or* **Ruchrad, Johannes.** Real name of JOHN OF WESEL.

**Ruck, Berta.** See under Oliver ONIONS.

**Rück'ert** (rük'ĕrt), **Friedrich.** 1788–1866. German poet; professor of Oriental languages, Erlangen (1826–41) and Berlin (1841–48); retired to estate at Neuses, near Coburg (1848). Works include *Deutsche Gedichte* (containing anti-Napoleonic *Geharnischte Sonette* under pseudonym **Frei'mund Rai'mar** [frī'mōōnt rī'mär], 1814), *Kranz der Zeit* (1817), *Liebesfrühling* (love poems; 1823), *Die Weisheit des Brahmanen* (6 vols., 1836–39), historical dramas, and translations and imitations of famous literature of the East.

**Ruck'stull** (rŭk'stŭl), **Frederic Wellington.** 1853–1942. Sculptor, b. in Alsace; to U.S. as a child. Studio in New York. Among his works: *Evening*, a life-size female statue now in Metropolitan Museum of Art, New York City; *Solon*, a heroic bronze statue in Library of Congress, Washington, D.C.; statue of John C. Calhoun in Capitol, Washington, D.C.; and various memorial monuments.

**Rū'da·gī'** *or* **Rū'da·kī'** (rōō'dă·gē'). d. 954 A.D. Persian poet. Only fragments of his works are extant.

**Rud'beck** (rōōd'bĕk), **Olof.** 1630–1702. Swedish scientist; discovered the lymphatic system; attempted in his *Atland eller Manheim*, or *Atlantikan* (1675–98), to prove that the cradle of human culture and Plato's Atlantis were in Sweden. The botanical genus *Rudbeckia* is named for him.

**Rud'di·man** (rŭd'ĭ·măn), **Thomas.** 1674–1757. Scottish classical scholar; editor of Livy (1751); author of a Latin grammar that superseded all others (1714) and a philological work, *Grammaticae Latinae Institutiones* (1725–32).

**Rude** (rüd), **François.** 1784–1855. French sculptor; studio in Brussels (1815–27) and Paris (from 1827). Among his notable works are *Petit Pêcheur Napolitain Jouant avec une Tortue* (in the Louvre), *Départ des Volontaires en 1792* (high relief on Arc de Triomphe), *Jeanne d'Arc Écoutant ses Voix*, and various portrait busts and statues.

**Rudge** (rŭj), **William Edwin.** 1876–1931. American printer, b. Brooklyn, N.Y. Founder and head of "The Printing House of William Edwin Rudge," specialist in artistic printing and book designing.

**Ru'di·ger** (rōō'dyĭ·gyĕr), Count **Fëdor Vasilievich.** 1784–1856. Russian general in wars against Napoleon (1812–14) and in Russo-Turkish War (1828–29); aided in suppressing rebellion in Poland (1830–31). Received surrender of Görgey at Világos (1849), ending the Hungarian rebellion.

**Ru'di·nì'** (rōō'dē·nē'), **Antonio.** Marchese **di Starab'ba** (dē stä·räb'bä). 1839–1908. Italian statesman; minister of interior (1869); premier (1891–92, 1896–98); during premiership, sought rapprochement with France to insure maintenance of Triple Alliance.

**Rud'mose–Brown'** (rŭd'mōz·broun'), **Thomas Brown.** 1878–1942. English educator; author of *French Literary Studies* (1917), *Walled Gardens* (verse, 1918), and *A Short History of French Literature* (1923). His brother **Robert Neal** (1879–1957), scientist and polar explorer, was surveyor and naturalist on Scottish arctic expeditions (1909, 1914, 1919), visiting Spitsbergen; author of *A Naturalist at the Poles* (1923), and *The Polar Regions* (1927).

**Ru'dolf** *or* **Ru'dolph** of Haps'burg (rōō'dŏlf, hăps'bûrg; *Ger.* rōō'dôlf, häps'bŏŏrk). 1858–1889. Archduke and crown prince of Austria; only son of Emperor Francis Joseph. Patron of literature and the arts; collaborated in preparing *Die Österreichisch-Ungarische Monarchie in Wort und Bild* (1886–1902); m. (1881) Princess Stephanie of Belgium (d. 1945); developed romantic attachment for Baroness **Marie Ve'tse·ra** (vĕ'chĕ·rä); resulted in tragedy when the bodies of the two were found (Jan., 1889) together in Rudolf's hunting lodge of Mayerling, near Vienna. It was officially announced that the two had committed suicide; all investigation and further information were suppressed.

**Rudolf** *or* **Rudolph.** *Fr.* **Ro'dolphe'** (rô'dôlf'). Name of three kings of Burgundy:

**Rudolf I.** d. 912. Son of Conrad, Count of Auxerre; first king of Transjurane Burgundy (888–912); recognized by Emperor Arnulf.

**Rudolf II.** d. 937. Son of Rudolf I and father of Empress Adelaide; king of Burgundy (912–937); contested crown of Italy with Hugh of Provence (922–926); received ancient kingdom of Provence (933) and established new kingdom of Arles.

**Rudolf III.** d. 1032. Last independent king of Burgundy (993–1032); at his death lands bequeathed to Emperor Conrad II.

**Ru'dolf** (rōō'dŏlf; *Ger.* -dôlf) *or* **Ra'oul'** (rȧ'ōōl'). d. 936 A.D. King of the Franks and duke of Burgundy; son of Richard, Duke of Burgundy. Succeeded his father in the dukedom (921); m. Emma, daughter of Robert, Count of Paris. Leagued with Robert, drove Charles III (Charles the Simple) from his throne; supported Robert as king of the Franks until his death (923); and succeeded Robert on the throne (923–936).

**Rudolf.** d. 1080. Duke of Swabia (1057–80). Chosen king of Germany (1077) in opposition to Henry IV, who had been excommunicated; at first successful in conflict with Henry, but slain in battle (1080).

**Rudolf.** Name of two Holy Roman emperors:

**Rudolf I of Hapsburg.** 1218–1291. Son of Albert IV, Count of Hapsburg. Landgrave of Alsace (1239–91); elected king of Germany (1273) and Holy Roman emperor (1273–91), first of the Hapsburg line (*q.v.*); recognized by Pope Gregory X on his promise to renounce imperial rights in Rome, the papal territories, and Sicily, and to lead a new crusade. Consolidated his power in Austria; invested his sons Albert and Rudolf with the duchies of Austria and Styria; defeated and killed Ottokar of Bohemia at Marchfeld (1278).

**Rudolf II.** 1552–1612. Holy Roman emperor (1576–1612); son of Maximilian II; educated at Spanish court by Jesuits. Scholarly, but an impractical ruler and intolerant toward Protestants. Successful insurrection in Hungary forced him (1608) to make his brother Matthias king of Hungary and governor of Austria and Moravia; in *Majestätsbrief* (*Letter of Majesty*), granted Bohemians religious freedom (1609); transferred Bohemia to Matthias (1611).

**Rudolf of** [*Ger.* **von**] **Ems** (āms; ĕms). d. about 1254.

Middle High German epic poet of Swiss descent. Successively in service of Simon de Montfort and Conrad IV, whom he accompanied to Italy; author of legendary poems *Der Gute Gerhard* and *Barlaam und Josaphat*, historical dramatic poems *Wilhelm von Orlens* and *Alexander*, and *Weltchronik*, based on Old Testament.

**Rudolph.** Variant of RUDOLF.

**Ru'dolph** (rōō'dŏlf), **Paul.** 1858–1935. German physicist; worked in Zeiss factory at Jena with Ernst Abbe; devised many types of lenses including first commercially successful anastigmatic lenses.

**Rue, Warren de la.** See DE LA RUE.

**Rue'da** (rwā'thä), **Lope de.** 1510?–1565. Spanish dramatist; author of four comedies adapted from the Italian, bucolic dialogues, etc.

**Rue'de·mann** (rōō'dĕ·măn; *Ger.* rü'dĕ·män), **Rudolf.** 1864–1956. American geologist and paleontologist, b. in Germany; to U.S. (1892). Authority on graptolites.

**Ruelas, Juan de las.** See ROELAS.

**Ruf'fin** (rŭf'ĭn), **Edmund.** 1794–1865. American agriculturist, b. in Prince George County, Va. Conducted experiments for restoring fertility of Virginia soil; founded and edited *Farmer's Register* (1833), a journal that helped to arouse interest in scientific farming.

**Ruf·fi'ni** (rōōf·fē'nē), **Giovanni.** 1807–1881. Italian writer in England; joined Mazzini's Young Italy party (1833) and had to flee from Austrian persecution (1836); again in Italy (1848–49) and involved in revolutionary activities; fled to England (1849). Lived in England (1836–42, 1849 ff.). Author of several English novels including *Doctor Antonio* (1855), *Lavinia* (1860), *Vincenzo* (1863), *Dear Experience* (1878).

**Ruf'fo** (rōōf'fō), **Fabrizio.** 1744–1827. Italian prelate and soldier; cardinal (1794); as general in Neapolitan army, led royalists against invading French forces under Championnet; with Fra Diavolo (*q.v.*), restored Ferdinand I to throne of Naples (1799).

**Ruffo, Titta.** 1878–1953. Italian baritone; debut at Teatro Costanzi, Rome (1898); sang at Rio de Janeiro, Vienna, Paris, throughout Italy, and in U.S.

**Ru·fi'nus** (rōō·fī'nŭs), **Flavius.** d. 395. Roman statesman, b. in Gaul; praetorian prefect of the East under Theodosius the Great (392) and under Arcadius (395); became known for persecutions and other cruel practices; engaged in disloyal intrigue with the Visigoth Alaric and was murdered in Constantinople on instigation of Gainas, friend of his rival Stilicho.

**Rufinus, Tyrannius.** 345?–410. Latin theologian and presbyter, b. near Aquileia. Lived as monk in Egypt, on Mount of Olives near Jerusalem (375), and in Aquileia (from 398); opposed his former friend St. Jerome in bitter controversy over doctrines of Origen; translated into Latin the Greek Christian writers, Eusebius of Caesarea, the *Clementine Recognitions*, Origen's *Principia* and *Homilies*, and *Historia Monachorum in Aegypto.*

**Rufus, Lucius Varius.** See VARIUS RUFUS.

**Ru'fus of Eph'e·sus** (rōō'fŭs, ĕf'ĕ·sŭs). *Greek* **Rhou'phos** (rōō'fŏs). fl. early part 2d century A.D. Greek anatomist and physician; author of a treatise on the nomenclature of parts of the human body, which indicates the state of anatomical knowledge preceding Galen, and of a work on diseases, an extant fragment of which contains the first historical mention of bubonic plague.

**Ru'ge** (rōō'gĕ), **Arnold.** 1803–1880. German writer on philosophy and politics; edited various radical journals; taught at Halle (1830); with Ernst Echtermeyer founded (1838) *Hallesche, Jahrbücher für Deutsche Wissenschaft und Kunst*, organ of Young German Hegelians, continued in Dresden (1840–43) as *Deutsche Jahrbücher*, and condemned by government censorship. Extreme leftist member of Frankfurt National Assembly (1848); fled to London (1849), where he helped found European Democratic Committee. Settled in Brighton as teacher and writer (from 1850).

**Ru'ger** (rōō'gẽr), **Thomas Howard.** 1833–1907. American army officer; brigadier general of volunteers (Nov., 1862). Commanded Union division at Gettysburg (July 1–3, 1863); suppressed draft riots, New York City (Aug., 1863). Commanded division in Tennessee campaign against Hood, and in North Carolina campaign (1865); brevetted major general.

**Rugg** (rŭg), **Harold Ordway.** 1886–1960. American educator, b. Fitchburg, Mass.; B.S., Dartmouth (1908); Ph.D., Illinois (1915); professor of education, Teachers College, Columbia (from 1920); author of *Introduction to American Civilization* (1929), *Culture and Education in America* (1931), *Changing Governments and Changing Cultures* (1932), etc.

**Rug'gles–Brise'** (rŭg''lz·brīs'), Sir **Evelyn John.** 1857–1935. English penologist; chairman of Prison Commission (1895–1921); originator of Borstal system whereby juvenile delinquents are dealt with in a special institution (Borstal Institution) under supervision of a special association (Borstal Association) established (1908) by act of Parliament.

**Ruhm'korff** (rōōm'kôrf), **Heinrich Daniel.** 1803–1877. German physicist and maker of electrical instruments; invented (1851) an induction coil which bears his name.

**Ruhn'ken** (rōōng'kĕn), **David.** 1723–1798. German classical philologist and scholar; author of *Epistolae Criticae* (1749–51) and editions of Timaeus's lexicon to Plato's works, entitled *Timaei Sophistae Lexicon Vocum Platonicarum* (Leiden, 1754, and again in 1789), of works of the Roman rhetorician Rutilius Lupus (1768), and of Muret (4 vols., 1789).

**Ruisbroe(c)k, Jan van.** See RUYSBROEK.

**Ruis'dael** *or* **Ruys'dael** *or* **Ruijs'dael, van** (vän rois'däl). Surname of two Dutch painters, Jacob van Ruisdael (usual spelling) and his uncle Salomon van Ruysdael (usual spelling). **Jacob** (1628?–1682), landscape painter and etcher, b. Haarlem; moved to Amsterdam (1657); traveled in Holland and Germany in search of material; returned to Haarlem (1681), where he died in the almshouse. Works represent chiefly forest scenery, waterfalls, and shore and mountain scenes, with figures painted by others. **Salomon** (1600?–1670), naturalistic landscape painter; member of Dutch school; painted chiefly village, river, and canal scenes.

**Ruiter, Michel Adriaanszoon de.** See RUYTER.

**Ru·iz'** (rōō·ēth'), **José Martínez.** *Pseudonym* **A'zo·rín'** (ä'thō·rēn'). 1874–1967. Spanish writer; leading representative of "generation of 1898." Author of novels, as *Don Juan* (1922), and *Doña Inés* (1925), short stories, dramas, literary studies, as *La Ruta de Don Quijote* (1905) and *Al Margen de los Clásicos* (1915), and especially essays on Castilian life, as *El Alma Castellana 1600–1800* (1900), *Los Pueblos* (1904), and *Madrid: Guía Sentimental* (1918).

**Ruiz, Juan.** 1283?–?1351. Called "Archpriest of Hita." Spanish poet; known particularly for *Libro de Buen Amor*, a miscellany of fables, legends, amorous stories, satire, devotion, attacks on the church, etc.

**Ruiz Aguilera, Ventura.** See AGUILERA.

**Ru·iz' de Alarcón y Mendoza** (rōō·ēs'; -ēth'), **Juan.** See ALARCÓN Y MENDOZA.

**Ru·iz' Gui'ña·zú'** (rōō·ēs' gē'nyä·sōō'), **Enrique.** 1884–1967. Argentinian lawyer and statesman, b. Buenos Aires; minister to Switzerland (1931); permanent delegate to League of Nations (1935); foreign minister (1941–43); ambassador to Spain (1943–44).

**Ru·iz′ Zorrilla** (rōō·ēth′), **Manuel.** See ZORRILLA.

**Rul′hière′** (rül′yâr′), **Claude Carloman de.** 1735–1791. French historian and poet; author of verse, stories, epistles (as the *Disputes*), and a historical study, *Causes de la Révocation de l'Édit de Nantes et sur l'État des Protestants en France depuis le Commencement du Règne de Louis XIV* (1788).

**Rul′lus** (rŭl′ŭs), **Publius Servilius.** Roman politician; tribune of the people (64 B.C.); under secret encouragement by Julius Caesar, sponsored an agrarian law (providing for wide distribution of land among poorer citizens and the founding of colonies) against which Cicero delivered four speeches in the Senate, the bill being withdrawn before a vote was taken.

**Rum′bold** (rŭm′bōld), Sir **Horace George Montagu.** 1869–1941. British diplomat; chargé d'affaires at Tokyo (1909, 1911, 1912–13) and Berlin (July, 1914); minister to Switzerland (1916–19) and Poland (1919–20); ambassador to Turkey (1920–24), Spain (1924–28), Germany (1928–33; retired).

**Rumford,** Count. See Benjamin THOMPSON.

**Rumford, Robert Kennerley.** 1870–1957. See under Dame Clara BUTT.

**Rumi.** See JALAL-UD-DIN RUMI.

**Ru·mian′tsev** (rōō·myán′tsĕf), Count **Pëtr Aleksandrovich.** 1725–1796. Russian general; distinguished himself in the Seven Years' War (1756–63); commanded Russian army against the Turks (1768–74) and aided in directing the campaign against the Turks (1787–91); directed Suvorov's campaign against the Poles (1794). His son Count **Nikolai Petrovich** (1754–1826) was Russian minister of foreign affairs (1807), and later grand chancellor of Russia.

**Rüm′ker** (rüm′kĕr), **Karl Ludwig Christian.** 1788–1862. German astronomer; author of a catalogue of 12,000 fixed stars.

**Ruml** (rŏŏm′'l), **Beards′ley** (bẽrdz′lĭ). 1894–1960. American business executive, b. Cedar Rapids, Iowa; chairman, Federal Reserve Bank of N.Y. (1947); presented to U.S. Senate (1942) pay-as-you-go plan of Federal taxation which was adopted (1943).

**Rum′sey** (rŭm′zĭ), **Charles Cary.** 1879–1922. American sculptor. Captain of cavalry in World War I. His equestrian statue of *Pizarro* is now in Lima, Peru; *Dying Indian*, in Brooklyn Museum of Art.

**Rumsey, James.** 1743–1792. American mechanical engineer, b. in Cecil County, Md. Known for experiments in building a steamboat; demonstrated on the Potomac (Dec., 1787) with a boat driven by streams of water forced through the stern by a steam pump; also invented improved steam boiler. Received patents in England and U.S. (1791) on his steamboat and steam boiler. Died before his second demonstration steamboat was finished.

**Run′ci·man** (rŭn′sĭ·măn), **Walter.** 1st Viscount **Runciman.** 1870–1949. English politician; M.P. (1899–1900, 1902–18, 1924–37); parliamentary secretary to local government board (1905–07); financial secretary to the treasury (1907–08); president of board of education (1908–11) and board of agriculture (1911–14); president of board of trade (1914–16, 1931–37). Head of British mission to Czechoslovakia (1938). Lord president of the council (1938–39). Created viscount (1937). His father, Sir **Walter Runciman** (1847–1937), was a shipping magnate; wrote a number of books on ships.

**Rund′stedt** (rŏŏnt′shtĕt), **Karl Rudolf Gerd von.** 1875–1953. German field marshal. Chief of the general staff in World War I; commanded armies in Poland (1939), France (1940), and Russia (1941–42); commander in chief on western front (1942–45).

**Ru′ne·berg′** (rōō′nĕ·băr′y'), **Johan Ludvig.** 1804–1877. Finnish poet writing in Swedish, b. Finland; national poet of Finland. Author of 3 volumes of lyric poems (1830, 1833, 1843), translations of Serbian folk songs (1830), *The Elk Hunters* (epic of Finnish village life written in hexameters, 1832), idyls *Hanna* (1836) and *Christmas Eve* (1841), romantic tale in verse *Nadeschda* (1841), romantic Norse epic *King Fjalar* (1844), *Ensign Stål's Stories* (a series of ballads, romances, and tales dealing with war of independence of 1808 and containing national hymn of Finland *Vårt Land*, 1848, 1860), prose tales, and dramatic works.

**Rung′e** (rŏŏng′ĕ), **Carl David Tol·mé′** (tôl·mā′). 1856–1927. German mathematician; worked on the spectra of various elements.

**Runge, Friedlieb Ferdinand.** 1795–1867. German chemist; credited with the discovery of aniline in coal tar (1834).

**Runjit Singh.** = RANJIT SINGH.

**Run′kle** (rŭng′k'l), **Bertha.** d. 1958. Am. novelist; m. (1904) Louis H. Bash (1872–1952), Am. army officer; author of *Straight down the Crooked Lane* (1915), etc.

**Runkle, John Daniel.** 1822–1902. American mathematician and educator; professor, M.I.T. (1865–68; 1880–1902), acting president (1868–70) and president (1870–78).

**Run′ny·mede** (rŭn′ĭ·mēd). Early pseudonym of Benjamin DISRAELI.

**Run′yon** (rŭn′yŭn), **Damon,** *in full* **Alfred Damon.** 1880–1946. American journalist and writer; feature writer, King Features, International News Service (from 1918). Author of *Tents of Trouble* (verse; 1911), *Rhymes of the Firing Line* (1912), short stories, and the play *A Slight Case of Murder* (with Howard Lindsay; 1935), etc.

**Ru′pert** (rōō′pĕrt; *Ger.* -pĕrt) *or* **Ru·per′tus** (rōō·pûr′tŭs; *Ger.* -pĕr′tōōs) *or* **Ru′precht** (rōō′prĕKt), Saint. 650?–after 715. Called "Apostle of the Bavarians." Bishop of Worms and patron saint of Bavaria, of royal Frankish descent; did missionary work in Bavaria (after 694) on invitation of Duke Theodor II, and founded St. Peter's abbey in Salzburg.

**Rupert,** Prince. Count Palatine of **Rhine** *and* Duke of **Bavaria.** Duke of **Cum′ber·land** (kŭm′bĕr·lănd) *and* Earl of **Hol′der·ness′** (hōl′dĕr·nĕs′). 1619–1682. Born in Prague; son of Elector Palatine Frederick V and Elizabeth, daughter of James I of England; hence nephew of Charles I. Known as "the Mad Cavalier." Served against Imperialists in Thirty Years' War (1637–38); captured and imprisoned (1638–41). Appointed general of horse by Charles I (1642), became dominant figure of Royalist forces in English Civil War; appointed generalissimo of king's army (1644); distinguished himself in defeat at Naseby; recognizing Charles's cause as both bad and lost, surrendered Bristol to Fairfax (1645); was dismissed from all offices; cleared by court-martial; on surrender of Oxford, ordered to leave England (1646). Commanded Royalist fleet (1648–50) in unprofitable campaign; escaped to West Indies after breaking up of squadron by Blake in mouth of Tagus (1650); retired to Germany (1654–60). At Restoration, privy councilor; admiral of the white under duke of York in war against Dutch, and shared command (1666) with Monck (duke of Albemarle); vice-admiral of England in second Dutch war (1672); admiral of fleet (1673); first lord of admiralty (1673–79). Improved processes of mezzotint; experimented with making of gunpowder, boring of guns; invented a brasslike alloy, Prince Rupert's metal or Prince's metal.

**Rupert** of the Palatinate. *Ger.* **Ruprecht.** 1352–1410.

King of Germany (1400–10); count palatine of the Rhine (1398–1410) of the Wittelsbach line; made unsuccessful expedition to Italy (1401–02).

**Ru'pert** (ro͞o'pĕrt; *Ger.* -pĕrt) *or* **Rup'precht** (ro͝op'-rĕKt) of Bavaria. 1869–1955. Crown prince of Bavaria; son of King Louis III of Bavaria. In World War I, commanded Bavarian troops in Lorraine campaign (1914); commanded German front in Artois and southern Flanders (1914). Chief commander (1917) of northern group of armies on western front.

**Rupp** (ro͝op), **Julius.** 1809–1884. German Protestant theologian. Removed from pastorate (1845) for opposition to Athanasian Creed; founded at Königsberg (1846) a Free Protestant congregation.

**Rup'pert** (ro͞o'pĕrt), **Jacob.** 1867–1939. American brewer; co-owner (1914–23) and sole owner (1923–39), New York American League baseball team.

**Rup'pin** (ro͝op'ĭn), **Arthur.** 1876–1943. Economist and authority on Jewish demography, b. Posen; to Palestine (1908); sociology prof., Hebrew U. of Jerusalem (1926); director of Zionist colonization (from 1929).

**Rupprecht** *or* **Ruprecht.** German forms of RUPERT.

**Ru'rik** (ro͝or'ĭk). *Russ.* **Ryu'rik** (ryo͞o'ryĭk). d. 879 A.D. Reputed founder of the Russian empire; said to have been a Scandinavian chief who conquered Novgorod and established himself as grand prince of Novgorod (c. 862). The house of Rurik was a Russian royal family, descended from Rurik, extinct at the death of Fëdor Ivanovich (1598).

**Rusbroek, Jan van.** See RUYSBROEK.

**Rush** (rŭsh), **Benjamin.** 1745?–1813. American physician and political leader, b. near Philadelphia. Practiced, Philadelphia (from 1769). Professor of chemistry, College of Philadelphia (1769–91) and at U. of Pennsylvania after merger of College of Philadelphia into U. of Pennsylvania (1791). Member, Continental Congress (1776, 1777) and signer of Declaration of Independence. Surgeon in Continental army (1777–78). Established first free dispensary in U.S. (1786). Member, Pennsylvania constitutional ratification convention (1787). Treasurer, U.S. Mint (1797–1813). Author of *Medical Inquiries and Observations* (5 vols., 1789–98), *Medical Inquiries and Observations upon the Diseases of the Mind* (1812), etc. His son **Richard** (1780–1859) was a lawyer and statesman; comptroller, U.S. Treasury (1811); attorney general of the United States (1814–17); secretary of state (1817); U.S. minister to Great Britain (1817–25); had a part in persuading Monroe and John Q. Adams to proclaim the Monroe Doctrine; U.S. secretary of the treasury (1825–28); U.S. minister to France (1847–49). Another son, **James** (1786–1869), was a physician and psychologist.

**Rush, William.** 1756–1833. American sculptor, b. Philadelphia; renowned esp. for his figureheads carved to adorn the prows of ships; his life-sized statue of Washington is in Independence Hall, Philadelphia; known as first native-born American sculptor.

**Rush'di Pa'sha** (ro͝osh'dĭ pä'shä). 1864?–1928. Egyptian statesman; prime minister through difficult period of World War I and its immediate aftermath (1914–19).

**Rush'worth** (rŭsh'wûrth), **John.** 1612?–1690. English historian; sat in five parliaments, for Berwick; secretary to council of state (1660); secretary to lord keeper (1667). Author of *Historical Collections* covering period 1618 to 1648 (8 vols., 1659–1701).

**Ru'si·ñol' y Prats** (ro͞o'sē·nyôl' ē präts'), **Santiago.** 1861–1931. Spanish painter; wrote plays and prose.

**Rusk** (rŭsk), **David Dean.** 1909– . Am. statesman, b. Georgia; pres., Rockefeller Foundation (1952–60); U.S. secy. of state (1961–69).

**Rusk, Jeremiah McLain.** 1830–1893. American businessman and political leader; stage driver, railroad construction foreman, tavern keeper, sheriff, coroner (to 1861); army officer in Civil War; brevetted brigadier general (1865); member, U.S. House of Representatives (1871–77); governor of Wisconsin (1882–89); U.S. secretary of agriculture (1889–93).

**Rusk, Thomas Jefferson.** 1803–1857. American jurist and legislator; to Texas (1835); secretary of war, provisional government of Texas (1836). Fought in battle of San Jacinto (1836); commanded Houston's army after Houston was wounded. First chief justice, Texas supreme court (1840). Active in furthering annexation of Texas to U.S.; president of Texas convention which confirmed annexation and drew up constitution (1845). U.S. senator from Texas (1846–57).

**Rus'kin** (rŭs'kĭn), **John.** 1819–1900. English art critic and sociological writer, b. London. Won Newdigate prize at Oxford with a poem *Salsette and Elephanta* (1839). Met Turner (1840); set out to establish superiority of modern landscape painters, esp. Turner, over the old masters, in first volume of *Modern Painters* (1843), which in four later volumes (1846, 1856, 1856, 1860) expanded into discursive treatment of his views of the principles of true art, revolutionary in spirit and splendid in prose style. Published *Seven Lamps of Architecture*, stimulating Gothic revival (1849), and *Stones of Venice* (3 vols., 1851–53), both presenting poetical aspect of architecture and both illustrated by the author; defended Pre-Raphaelites (1851). Delivered at Edinburgh lectures on architecture and painting (1854), at Manchester lectures on the political economy of art (1857); issued treatises on drawing and perspective. Influenced by Carlyle, devoted writings toward impressing nation with necessity for a radical change in attitude to art, religion, and economics, developing heterodox views and urging social reform in *Unto this Last* (in *Cornhill Magazine*, 1860), *Munera Pulveris* (in *Fraser's Magazine*, 1862), *Sesame and Lilies* (1865), *The Crown of Wild Olive* (1866), *Time and Tide, by Weare and Tyne* (1867); advocated national system of education, in countrywide lectures (1855–70). First Slade professor of fine arts, Oxford (1869–79; 1883–84); gave £5000 for endowment of school of drawing in Oxford (1871); after death of mother lived rest of life at Brantwood, Coniston Lake; issued at irregular intervals a sort of periodical, *Fors Clavigera* (*i.e.*, "Fortune bearing a club"), 96 essays in form of letters to workmen and laborers on remedies for poverty and misery, one of practical applications of which was founding of guild of St. George, each member to give a tithe to philanthropy; revived handmade linen industry in Langdale; dispersed whole of large fortune in philanthropy, living himself on income from his books. Brought out in 24 monthly parts his last work, his autobiography (up to 1864) *Praeterita;* suffered at times from brain fever (after 1878). Other well-known works include *The King of the Golden River* (a fairy tale, 1851), *Ethics of the Dust* (on crystallization, 1866), *The Queen of the Air* (on Greek cloud myths, 1869), *Val d'Arno* (on Florentine art, 1874), *Proserpina* (studies of wayside flowers, 1875–86), *Bible of Amiens* (on history of Christendom, 1885) *The Art of England* (1884).

**Rus'sell** (rŭs''l). English family holding the earldom of **Bed'ford** [bĕd'fẽrd] (from 1550), dukedom of Bedford (from 1694), and barony of **Ampt'hill** [ăm(p)t'(h)ĭl] (from 1881), and tracing descent from **Henry Russell,** Weymouth wine merchant, probably of Gascon origin, who sat in four parliaments (1425–42).

**John Russell** (1486?–1555), 1st Earl of **Bedford;** great-grandson of Henry; saw military service in France;

one of Henry VIII's executors; lord privy seal (1542, 1547, 1553); for his part in suppressing western rebellion, created earl (1550); joint ambassador to Philip of Spain (1554); left to descendants abbey lands of Tavistock, and in Bedfordshire the Cistercian house of Woburn, chief seat of family. His son **Francis** (1527?–1585), 2d earl, took part in Wyatt's insurrection but escaped to Geneva (1554); warden of east marches; governor of Berwick; lord lieutenant of northern counties under Queen Elizabeth.

Sir **William** (1558?–1613), 1st Baron **Russell of Thorn'haugh** (thôrn'hô); 4th son of 2d earl; fought beside Sir Philip Sidney at Zutphen; governor of Flushing (1587–88); lord deputy of Ireland (1594–97); with Sir John Norris reduced Tyrone (1597). His son **Francis** (1593–1641), 4th earl; built square of Covent Garden (c. 1631); led in undertaking project of draining the great Fen Level; died of smallpox.

**William** (1613–1700), 5th Earl and 1st Duke of Bedford; son of 4th earl; as general of horse in Parliamentary army, fought at Edge Hill and Newbury; continued his father's work of draining the Fens (1649); created duke of Bedford and marquis of **Tav'is·tock** [tăv'ĭs·tŏk] (1694).

**William** (1639–1683); Lord Russell (courtesy title); 3d son of 1st duke; Whig parliamentary leader, known as "the Patriot"; educ. Cambridge; M.P. (1660); as active member of the "country party" (1673), attacked Buckingham and Danby; dallied with temporary alliance with Louis of France; proposed address to king to remove duke of York from his councils (1678); attacked Lauderdale in full council (1680); presented duke of York as popish recusant; again seconded motion for exclusion of duke of York (1681); attended only one meeting, with Monmouth, Essex, Hampden, Algernon Sidney, for discussion of resistance to government; accused by informers, along with Algernon Sidney, of complicity in Rye House Plot; charged with high treason, and through perjury by Lord Howard and a packed jury, found guilty and beheaded; his attainder reversed on accession of William and Mary. His wife (m. 1669) **Rachel** (1636–1723); Lady Russell; 2d daughter of Thomas Wriothesley, 4th Earl of Southampton; tireless in her efforts to save his life; partly responsible for Princess Anne's cohesion to regime of William III; correspondent of Tillotson.

**Edward** (1653–1727), Earl of **Or'ford** (ôr'fẽrd); naval commander; nephew of 1st duke of Bedford; served as agent of prince of Orange (before 1688); later, a correspondent of exiled James; admiral of the blue under Torrington, whom he succeeded (1690); held chief command of English and Dutch fleets in victory of La Hogue over French, off Point Barfleur (1692); first lord of admiralty (1694–99, 1709–10, 1714–17).

**John** (1710–1771); 4th duke; great-grandson of 1st duke; Whig leader; opposed Sir Robert Walpole; first lord of the admiralty in Pelham's administration; secretary for southern department on Chesterfield's resignation (1748–51); lord lieutenant of Ireland in duke of Devonshire's administration (1756–57); ambassador for negotiating treaty of peace with France (1762–63); president of council (1763–67). His grandson **Francis** (1765–1802); 5th duke; attached himself to Fox's party; assailed by Burke as "the leviathan among the creatures of the crown"; tore down Bedford House, designed by Inigo Jones, and built Russell and Tavistock squares, London (c. 1800). Francis's brother **John** (1766–1839); 6th duke; lord lieutenant of Ireland (1806–07); rebuilt Covent Garden market, London (1830). Lord **George William** (1790–1846); 2d son of 6th duke; aide-de-camp to Wellington (1812, 1817); major general (1841); ambassador at Berlin (1835–41).

**Odo William Leopold** (1829–1884), 1st Baron **Ampthill**; diplomat, b. in Florence; son of Lord George; held posts in Vienna, Paris, Constantinople, and Florence; unofficial representative at Vatican (1858–70); ambassador at Berlin (1871–84). His son **Arthur Oliver Villiers** (1869–1935); 2d baron; private secretary to Joseph Chamberlain (1895–99); governor of Madras (1899–1906); one of founders of National party (1918).

For the earls Russell, descendants of 6th duke of Bedford, see Lord John Russell, John Francis Stanley Russell, and Bertrand Russell.

**Russell, Annie.** 1869–1936. Actress, b. Liverpool, Eng.; to Canada as a child; later to U.S.; m. (1st) Eugene Presbrey, (2d) Oswald Yorke. Under Charles Frohman's management (1896), starred in *Sue*, play by T. E. Pemberton and Bret Harte. In London (1898 and again 1905); created title role in Shaw's *Major Barbara* (1906). Joined New Theatre Company (1910) playing especially Viola and Lady Teazle. Under own management (1912–14) produced theater classics, including *Much Ado About Nothing, The Rivals, The School for Scandal, She Stoops to Conquer;* retired. Again on stage (1917–18).

**Russell, Bertrand Arthur William.** 3d Earl **Russell.** 1872–1970. English mathematician and philosopher, b. Trelleck. Grandson of 1st earl (see Lord John Russell) and younger brother of 2d earl (see John Francis Stanley Russell). Fellow of Trinity Coll., Cambridge (to 1916); dismissed because of pacifist beliefs and opposition to World War I. Professor of philosophy, U. of California in Los Angeles. Awarded Nobel prize in literature (1950). Among his many books are *Essay on the Foundations of Geometry* (1897), *Principles of Mathematics* (1903), *Introduction to Mathematical Philosophy* (1919), *The A B C of Atoms* (1923), *The A B C of Relativity* (1925), *The Analysis of Matter* (1927); author also of *Philosophical Essays* (1910), *The Analysis of Mind* (1921), *The Prospects of Industrial Civilization* (1923), *Marriage and Morals* (1929), *Education and the Social Order* (1932), *In Praise of Idleness* (1935), *Power: A New Social Analysis* (1938), etc.

**Russell, Charles.** 1st Baron **Russell of Kil·low'en** (?kĭ·lō'ĕn). 1832–1900. British judge, b. in County Down, Ireland, of a Roman Catholic family. M.P. (1880); attorney general (1886, 1892–94); sought establishment of a subordinate parliament in Ireland; leading counsel for Parnell in Parnell Commission (1888–89); with Sir Richard Webster, represented Great Britain in Bering Sea arbitration (1893); lord chief justice of England (1894), presided at trial of leaders of Jameson Raid (1896); one of arbitrators of British Guiana-Venezuela boundary (1899).

**Russell, Charles Edward.** 1860–1941. American journalist and writer, b. Davenport, Iowa; city editor, New York *World* (1894–97); managing editor, New York *American* (1897–99); publisher, Chicago *American* (1900–02). Socialist candidate for governor of New York (1910, 1912) and for U.S. senator (1914); declined Socialist nomination for presidency of U.S. (1916). Author of *Such Stuff as Dreams* (1902), *Thomas Chatterton, the Marvelous Boy* (1908), *Songs of Democracy* (1909), *Why I Am a Socialist* (1910), *The American Orchestra and Theodore Thomas* (1927; awarded Pulitzer prize for biography), *Haym Salomon and the Revolution* (1930), *Bare Hands and Stone Walls* (1933), etc.

**Russell, Charles Taze** (tāz). 1852–1916. Known as "Pastor Russell." American religious leader, b. Pittsburgh. Originally Congregationalist, became pastor of independent church, Pittsburgh (1878). Preached doctrine that second coming of Christ occurred invisibly in 1874, that since then the world has been in the "Millennial Age," that the end of this age would come in 1914 to be followed by social revolution, chaos, resurrection of the dead, and finally establishment of Christ's kingdom on earth. His followers (Russellites) became organized in a society called International Bible Students' Association. See Joseph Franklin RUTHERFORD.

**Russell, Elizabeth Mary.** Countess **Russell.** *Nee* **Mary Annette Beau′champ** (bē′chăm). *Pen name* **Elizabeth.** 1866–1941. Novelist, b. Sydney, Australia; cousin of Katherine Mansfield (*q.v.*); m. Count Henning August von Arnim (d. 1910); spent nearly twenty years on his East Prussian estate, where she wrote *Elizabeth and her German Garden* (1898), *The Solitary Summer* (1899), *The Caravaners* (1910), *The Pastor's Wife* (1914), etc. Returned to England for education of her children; m. (1916) as 2d husband John Francis Stanley Russell (*q.v.*), 2d Earl Russell; separated (1919); resumed writing of novels, including *The Enchanted April* (1922), *Father* (1931), *All the Dogs of My Life* (1936), *Mr. Skeffington* (1940).

**Russell, George William.** *Pseudonym* **Æ** (ā′ē′). 1867–1935. Irish man of letters, b. Lurgan, County Armagh. Editor of *The Irish Homestead* (1904–23) and *The Irish Statesman* (from 1923). Author of *Homeward: Songs by the Way* (1894), *The Earth Breath* (1897), *The Divine Vision* (1904), *New Poems* (1904), *Irish Essays* (1906), *Deirdre* (play; 1907), *The Renewal of Youth* (1911), *Gods of War* (1915), *The National Being, some Thought on an Irish Policy* (1917), *The Candle of Vision* (1919), *Midsummer Eve* (1928), *Vale and other Poems* (1931), *House of the Titans and Other Poems* (1934), etc.

**Russell, Henry.** 1812–1900. English singer and song composer, b. in Kent; composer of nearly 800 songs, including *A Life on the Ocean Wave; I'm Afloat; Cheer, Boys, Cheer;* and *There's a Good Time Coming.* His son **William Clark** (1844–1911), novelist, b. New York, shipped at early age in British merchant service (1858–66); settled in London as journalist; author of long series of nautical tales of adventure, and also lives of Dampier (1889), Nelson (1890), and Collingwood (1891).

**Russell, Henry Norris.** 1877–1957. American astronomer; authority on sidereal astronomy and astrophysics.

**Russell, Howard Hyde.** 1855–1946. American lawyer, clergyman, and prohibitionist; ordained in Congregational ministry (1885); initiated Anti-Saloon League movement in Ohio (1893); an organizer and first general superintendent of Anti-Saloon League of America (1895–1903); superintendent, New York Anti-Saloon League (1901–09).

**Russell, Irwin.** 1853–1879. American poet, b. Port Gibson, Miss.; author of Negro dialect poems, collected and published posthumously as *Poems by Irwin Russell* (1888), with preface by Joel Chandler Harris.

**Russell, Israel Cook.** 1852–1906. American geologist; on staff, U.S. Geological Survey (from 1880); author of *Lakes of North America* (1895), *Glaciers of North America* (1897), *Volcanoes of North America* (1897), *Rivers of North America* (1898), *North America* (1904).

**Russell, James Earl.** 1864–1945. American educator; professor of education and dean (1897–1927), Teachers Coll., Columbia.

**Russell, John.** 1745–1806. English portrait painter, esp. in pastel; painter to George III, prince of Wales, and duke of York; described his methods in *The Elements of Painting in Crayon* (1772).

**Russell,** Lord **John.** 1st Earl **Russell of King′ston Russell** (kĭng′stŭn). 1792–1878. British statesman, b. London; 3d son of 6th duke of Bedford (see RUSSELL family). Whig M.P. (1813); strenuous advocate of parliamentary reform, of repeal of Test and Corporation acts; supported Catholic Emancipation Act (passed 1829). One of four framers of Reform Act of 1832; moved its first reading (1831); introduced it second and third time; championed it till passage (1832). Leader of Whigs in House of Commons (1834); home secretary (1835); colonial secretary (1839) under Melbourne; committed himself to repeal of corn laws, helping protectionists to force Peel out of office. Prime minister and first lord of treasury (1846–52); quieted Ireland by combination of coercive and relief measures; sought to adapt free-trade policy to British commerce; dismissed Lord Palmerston from post of foreign secretary for recognizing Napoleon's coup d'état (1851); defeated by Palmerston, resigned (1852). In Lord Aberdeen's coalition ministry as foreign secretary (1852–53), president of council (1854–55); lost popularity and was out of office (till 1859). Foreign secretary in Palmerston's ministry; advocated "Italy for the Italians"; created earl (1861); influential in maintaining British neutrality during Civil War in U.S. Again prime minister (1865–66) on death of Palmerston; on defeat of his new reform bill, retired. Author of a *Life of William Lord Russell* (1819), *Memoirs of Affairs of Europe* (1824–29), memoirs of Thomas Moore (8 vols., 1853–56) and of C. J. Fox (1853–57; 3 vols., 1859–66), *Recollections and Suggestions* (1875).

**Russell, John Francis Stanley.** 2d Earl **Russell.** 1865–1931. English electrical engineer, barrister, agnostic, Fabian; grandson of Lord John Russell (*q.v.*), 1st earl; older brother of Bertrand Russell (*q.v.*), 3d earl; m. (1916) as 3d wife the novelist Elizabeth (see Elizabeth Mary RUSSELL). Parliamentary secretary to ministry of transport (1929). Author of *Lay Sermons, Divorce,* and *My Life and Adventures* (1923).

**Russell, John Scott.** 1808–1882. Scottish naval architect; discovered wave of translation and developed wave-line system of designing ships (c. 1840); constructed the prodigious *Great Eastern,* the failure of which forced him to abandon shipbuilding, and the armored frigate *Warrior,* first seagoing vessel of its kind.

**Russell, Lillian.** *Real name* **Helen Louise Leon′ard** (lĕn′ẽrd). 1861–1922. American singer and actress, b. Clinton, Iowa; m. Harry Braham (1880, divorced 1884); Edward Solomon (1884, annulled 1893); John Haley Augustin Chatterton, stage name Signor Perugini (1894, divorced 1898); Alexander Pollock Moore (1912). Sang in Tony Pastor's Bowery variety theater (1880). Rose to stardom in Edmond Audran's *The Great Mogul* (1881); excelled in comic-opera roles. Joined Weber and Fields burlesque company (1899), sang in popular pieces as *Fiddle-dee-dee* and *Whoop-dee-doo.* Left stage (1912).

**Russell, Thomas.** 1767–1803. Irish revolutionist; volunteered for army service in India (1782); held commission in Ireland (till 1791); librarian of Belfast library (1794). Organized with Wolfe Tone and Napper Tandy the United Irish Society in Dublin (1791); arrested with other United Irishmen (1796) and imprisoned (till 1798); with Robert Emmet attempted to incite rising in Ireland (1803); executed for high treason.

**Russell,** Lord **William.** 1639–1683. See under RUSSELL family.

**Russell, William Clark.** See under Henry RUSSELL.

**Russell, William Fletcher.** 1890–1956. American educator; professor of education, Teachers College, Columbia (1923–27); dean (1927–49); president (1949–54).

**Russell, William Hepburn.** 1812–1872. American pioneer in express business; founded pony express, between St. Joseph, Mo., and Sacramento, Calif. (1860), carrying mail across the West in ten days.

**Russell,** Sir **William Howard.** 1820–1907. British war correspondent; reported for *The Times* (from 1841); published *The War, 1855–56;* exposed mismanagement of Crimean War, inspired Florence Nightingale's work, applied phrase "thin red line" to infantry at Balaklava. Founder of *Army and Navy Gazette* (1860).

**Rus'ski** (rōōs'skû·ĭ; *Angl.* rōōs'kĭ), **Nikolai Vladimirovich.** 1854–1918. Russian general in World War I; commanded army which invested Lemberg, the army of Niemen, and (1917) the armies of the north.

**Rust** (rōōst), **Bernhard.** 1883–1945. German National Socialist (Nazi) politician. Reich minister of science, education, and popular instruction (1934 ff.).

**Rust** (rŭst), **John Daniel** (1892–1954) and his brother **Mack Donald** (1900–1966). American inventors of Rust cotton picker.

**Rus'tin** (rŭs'tĭn), **Bayard.** 1910– . American civil rights leader, b. West Chester, Pa. Helped organize first freedom rides into the South (1947); organizer of March on Washington (1963); executive director, A. Philip Randolph Inst., New York City (1966– ).

**Rüs'tow** (rüs'tō), **Wilhelm Friedrich.** 1821–1878. German army officer and author of works on military history, strategy, Napoleonic campaigns, etc.

**Ru'ta** (rōō'tä), **Michele.** 1827–1896. Italian composer and writer on music.

**Ru'te·beuf'** (rüt'bûf'). d. about 1285. 13th-century French trouvère; author of various lyrics and didactic poems, many barbed with satire; author also of various fabliaux and a drama of the old miracle-play type.

**Rut'gers** (rŭt'gẽrz), **Henry.** 1745–1830. American landed proprietor and philanthropist; benefactor of Queen's College, New Brunswick, N.J., which changed its name (1825) to Rutgers College in his honor.

**Ruth** (rōōth). Chief character in the Old Testament book of *Ruth;* a Moabitess who, after the death of her husband, accompanied her mother-in-law, Naomi, to Bethlehem, where she became wife of Boaz, a relative of her first husband, and through him ancestress of David.

**Ruth, George Herman.** *Known as* **Babe** (bāb) **Ruth** *or* **the Bam·bi'no** (băm·bē'nō). 1895–1948. American professional baseball player, b. Baltimore; member of Boston American League Club (1915), New York American League Club (1920–35); voted most valuable player in American League (1923); retired (1935).

**Ruth'er·ford** (rŭth'ẽr·fẽrd), **Daniel.** 1749–1819. Scottish physician; M.D., Edinburgh (1772), with dissertation showing nitrogen a gas distinguishable from carbon dioxide.

**Rutherford, Ernest.** 1st Baron **Rutherford of Nel'son** (nĕl's'n). 1871–1937. British physicist, b. Nelson, New Zealand; educ. New Zealand U. and Cambridge. Professor of physics, McGill U., Montreal (1898–1907); professor and director of the physical laboratories, U. of Manchester (1907–19); professor of experimental physics and director of Cavendish Laboratory, Cambridge (from 1919); professor of natural philosophy, Royal Institution. Investigated the nature of radioactive transformations and the nature of the atom; disintegrated the nucleus of the nitrogen atom with alpha particles from radium; enunciated theory that the atom is not indivisible and consists of a small impenetrable nucleus surrounded by electrons revolving in planetary orbits. Awarded 1908 Nobel prize for chemistry. Author of *Radio-activity* (1904), *Radio-active Substances and Their Radiations* (1912), *The Newer Alchemy* (1937), etc.

**Rutherford, Joseph Franklin.** 1869–1942. Known as "Judge Rutherford." American sectarian leader, b. in Missouri. Joined Russellites; became (c. 1907) legal adviser for this sect; succeeded Pastor Charles Taze Russell (*q.v.*) as its head (1916). Imprisoned (1917–19) in federal penitentiary at Atlanta because of his stand against military service and his encouragement to conscientious objectors. Russellites under his guidance changed their name to Jehovah's Witnesses (1931), with slogan "Millions now living will never die."

**Rutherford, Mark.** Pseudonym of William Hale WHITE.

**Rutherford, Samuel.** 1600–1661. Scottish theologian; banished (1636) from pastorate for nonconformity to Acts of Episcopacy in his *Exercitationes pro Divina Gratia* directed against Arminianism. One of commissioners to Westminster Assembly (1643); engaged in controversies with non-Covenanters; author of *Lex Rex* (1644), which was burned by the hangman (1661); remembered for letters written during banishment.

**Ruth'er·furd** (rŭth'ẽr·fẽrd), **Lewis Morris.** 1816–1892. American astronomer and physicist; set up small observatory at his home in New York (1856) and started photographing celestial bodies. Interested himself also in spectroscopy (from 1862). Designed ruling engine (1870) enabling him to construct finest interference gratings made up to that time for use in spectroscopic work. Retired (1883).

**Ruth'er·ston** (rŭth'ẽr·stŭn), **Albert Daniel.** 1881–1953. English painter, illustrator, and stage designer. Designed stage sets for *The Winter's Tale, Androcles and the Lion, Le Mariage Forcé,* etc.

**Ruth'ven** (rōōth'vĕn; rĭv'ĕn). Name of a noble Scottish family bearing titles Baron **Ruthven,** Baron **Gow'rie** (gou'rĭ), and Earl of **Gowrie,** and including:

**Patrick Ruthven** (1520?–1566), 3d Baron Ruthven, was annually elected provost of Perth (1553–66); Protestant privy councilor of Mary, Queen of Scots; advocate of Darnley marriage; assistant in Rizzio murder (1566). His second son, **William** (1541?–1584), 4th Baron Ruthven and 1st Earl of Gowrie, joined conspiracy against Rizzio; took active part, with his father, in intrigues on side of the kirk; custodian of Mary, Queen of Scots, at Lochleven; lord high treasurer for life (1571); chief conspirator in "Raid of Ruthven," for carrying off the boy king James VI and keeping him virtual prisoner (1582); pardoned, continued to plot with Angus, Mar, and others; beheaded for high treason. His son **John** (1577?–1600), 3d Earl of Gowrie, M.A., Edinburgh (1593), extreme Protestant, continued family practices of intrigue and treason, first by joining Atholl and Montrose in offer to serve Queen Elizabeth; studied in Padua (1594–99); headed opposition to James VI; killed, with his brother **Alexander** (1580?–1600), in his own house at Perth in the so-called Gowrie conspiracy, whether as result of the foiling of a kidnaping plot to make away with James VI or to obtain from him a settlement of his debt to Gowrie, or by veiled assassination by James VI and retainers, there is still doubt.

**Walter Patrick Hore'–Ruth'ven** [hōr'-; hôr'-] (1870–1956), 9th Baron Ruthven, British soldier in Boer and World wars, was lieutenant governor of Guernsey and commander of troops there (1929–34). His brother Sir **Alexander Gore Arkwright Hore–Ruthven** (1872–1955), 1st Baron Gowrie of Canberra and of Dirleton, soldier, received Victoria Cross for bravery as commander of camel corps in the Sudan; distinguished himself in White Nile (1899); military secretary to governor general of Australia (1908); severely wounded at Gallipoli; D.S.O.; governor of South Australia (1928–34); governor of New South Wales (1935); governor general of Australia (1936–45).

**Ruth'ven** (rōōth'vĕn), **Alexander Grant.** 1882–1971.

American educator, b. Hull, Iowa; B.S., Morningside College (1903); Ph.D., Michigan (1906); teacher of zoology, Michigan (1906–29), chairman of department (1927–29); president, U. of Michigan (1929–51).

**Ruth'ven** (rōōth'vĕn; rĭv'ĕn), **Patrick.** Earl of **Forth** (fōrth; fôrth) *and* of **Brent'ford** (brĕnt'fērd). 1573?–1651. Scottish soldier in English Royalist army; descended from collateral line of noble family of Ruthven (*q.v.*); knighted by Gustavus Adolphus for service in Swedish army (1627), major general (1632). Gathered Royalist forces in Scotland (1638); surrendered Berwick to Covenanters (1640); led left wing at Edge Hill; general in chief of Charles I's army; declared traitor by Scottish parliament (1644); forced surrender of Essex's army at Lostwithiel (1644); superseded by Prince Rupert (1644).

**Ru·til'i·us Na·ma'ti·a'nus** (rōō·tĭl'ĭ·ŭs nā·mā'shĭ·ā'nŭs), **Claudius.** Roman poet of early 5th century A.D.; author of *De Reditu Suo*, long poem in two books, describing a coastal voyage from Rome to Gaul, of which about 700 lines are extant.

**Rutilius Ru'fus** (rōō'fŭs), **Publius.** b. about 150 B.C. Roman jurist and general; participated with Scipio Aemilianus in siege of Numantia (133); praetor (c. 118); extended praetorian law; as legate, aided Metellus in victory over Jugurtha and Bomilcar in Numidia (109); consul (105); incurred hostility of equestrian order and was tried and condemned on trumped-up charge of corruption in office. Withdrew to Smyrna and devoted himself to writing his memoirs.

**Rü'ti·mey'er** (rü'tē·mī'ēr), **Ludwig.** 1825–1895. Swiss naturalist; known for work in craniology and investigations in the mammalian paleontology of Switzerland.

**Rutland,** Earls and dukes of. See MANNERS family.

**Rut'ledge** (rŭt'lĭj), **Ann.** 1816–1835. Daughter of Abraham Lincoln's landlord at New Salem, Ill.; fiancée of Abraham Lincoln; died suddenly of malarial fever.

**Rutledge, John.** 1739–1800. American statesman, b. Charleston, S.C.; practiced law, Charleston, S.C. (from 1761); member of Continental Congress (1774–76; 1782–83); president of South Carolina (1776–78); governor (1779–82); member, State constitutional ratification convention (1788); associate justice, U.S. Supreme Court (1789–91); appointed chief justice (1795) and served one term, but not confirmed by U.S. Senate. His brother **Edward** (1749–1800), lawyer; member of Continental Congress (1774–77) and a signer of Declaration of Independence; member, South Carolina legislature (1782–96); governor of South Carolina (1798–1800).

**Rutledge, Wiley Blount.** 1894–1949. American jurist, b. Cloverport, Ky.; A.B., Wisconsin (1914); high-school teacher (1915–22); LL.B., Colorado (1922); professor of law, Colorado (1924–26), Washington U. (1926–35; dean 1931–35); dean of law, Iowa (1935–39); associate justice, U.S. Court of Appeals for D.C. (1939–43); associate justice, U.S. Supreme Court (1943–49).

**Rut'ter** (rŭt'ēr), **Owen.** 1889–1944. English journalist and writer; British civil servant, stationed in North Borneo; served in World War (1914–18); traveled widely in Far East. Among his many books are *Through Formosa* (1923), *White Rajah* (1931), *The True Story of the Mutiny in the Bounty* (1936), *Regent of Hungary... Admiral, Nicholas Horthy* (1939), *Through the Land of St. Joan* (1940), *Violation* (1941).

**Ruvigny,** Marquis **de.** See Henri de MASSUE.

**Ru'ville** (rü'vĭl), **Albert von.** 1855–1934. German historian; author of a biography of William Pitt (3 vols., 1905), *Zurück zur Heiligen Kirche* (1910), *Der Goldgrund der Weltgeschichte* (1912–13), *Die Kreuzzüge* (1920), etc.

**Ruwi Alley.** Variant of *Rewi Alley* (see ALLEY).

**Ruy Díaz de Bivar.** See the CID.

**Ruy Ló'pez de Si·gu'ra** (rwē' lō'pāth thā sē·gōō'rä). 16th-century Spanish writer on chess, from whom the Ruy Lopez chess opening was named.

**Ruys'broeck** (rois'brōōk) *or* **Ruis'broeck** (rois'brōōk) *or* **Rus'broek** (rûs'brōōk), **Jan van.** 1293–1381. Called "the Ecstatic Doctor." Flemish mystical theologian, b. Ruysbroek; precursor of the Reformation. Vicar of St. Gudule, Brussels (1318); retired (1343) to Augustinian monastery of Groenendael, near Waterloo, where he became prior; influenced Tauler, Gerhard Groote, and other mystics, and helped found the Brothers of the Common Life; beatified (1908); author of mystic works in Flemish and Latin.

**Ruysbroeck, William of.** See RUBRUQUIS.

**Ruysch** (rois), **Fredrik.** 1638–1731. Dutch anatomist.

**Ruysch, Rachel.** 1664–1750. Dutch painter; m. **Jurian Pool** (pōl), portrait painter (1695); appointed court painter to elector palatine (1708); noted as painter of flowers and fruits.

**Ruysdael, Jacob** and **Salomon van.** See RUISDAEL.

**Ruys de Bee'ren·brouck** (rois' dē bā'rĕn·brouk), **Joseph Marie.** See BEERENBROUCK.

**Ruy'ter** *or* **Rui'ter** (roi'tēr), **Michel Adriaanszoon de.** 1607–1676. Dutch admiral and naval hero; rear admiral in expedition to aid Portugal against Spain (1641); distinguished himself under Tromp in First Dutch-English War (1652–53); commanded Dutch squadron in support of Denmark against Sweden (1659). Defeated English fleet under Monck in four-day battle off Dunkirk (1666) during Second Dutch-English War (1665–67), but suffered subsequent defeat at North Foreland (1666); sailed up the Thames, and helped in concluding Peace of Breda (1667). Commanded against combined English and French fleets at Sole (Southwold) Bay, Schoeneveld, and Texel during Third Dutch-English War (1672 ff.); named general lieutenant admiral; commanded Dutch-Spanish squadron in Mediterranean against French and Sicilians (1676) and was mortally wounded in battle off coast of Sicily.

**Ru'žič'ka** (rōō'zhēch'kä), **Le'o·pold** (lā'ō·pôlt), *orig.* **La'vo·slav** (lä'vô·släv). 1887–1976. Chemist, b. Vukovar, Yugoslavia; teacher of chemistry at Zurich (from 1918); became known first for his synthesis of musk; awarded (with Adolph Butenandt, *q.v.*) 1939 Nobel prize for work on sex hormones.

**Ruz·zan'te, Il** (ēl rōōd·dzän'tā). *Real name* **Angelo Be·ol'co** (bā·ôl'kō). 1502–1542. Italian playwright and actor; reputed inventor of the masked comedy.

**Ryall, William Bolitho.** See William BOLITHO.

**Ry'an** (rī'ăn), **Abram Joseph.** 1838–1886. American Roman Catholic priest and poet, b. Hagerstown, Md.; chaplain in Confederate army (1862–65); pastor at Mobile, Ala. (1870–83). His lyrics endeared him to the South and caused him to be called "the Poet of the Confederacy." His collected poems (publ. 1879), included such favorites as *The Conquered Banner, The Sword of Robert E. Lee, Gather The Sacred Dust, The Lost Cause, March of the Deathless Dead, In Memoriam.*

**Ryan, Patrick John.** 1831–1911. Roman Catholic clergyman, b. Thurles, Ireland; to U.S. (1852); noted as preacher and orator; titular archbishop of Salamis (1884) and transferred to see of Philadelphia.

**Ryan, Thomas Fortune.** 1851–1928. American financier, b. in Nelson County, Va.; organized brokerage firm (1873); acquired New York City street-railway franchise and extended properties until (by 1900) his group controlled transportation lines in the city; consolidated his interests with August Belmont's subway interests (1905); withdrew from traction field (1906). Organized American Tobacco Co., later (1911) ordered dissolved by the government as a monopoly. Also acquired extensive interests in New York banks, Seaboard Air Line Railroad, Equitable Life Assurance Society, rubber and mining properties in Belgian Congo, and coal deposits in Ohio and West Virginia.

**Ryd′berg** (rüd′băr·y′), **Abraham Viktor.** 1828–1895. Swedish poet, writer, and critic; champion of liberalism and tolerance; professor of history of civilization, Stockholm (from 1884); author of tales, historical novels, volumes of lyrics, the controversial work *The Teachings of the Bible about Christ* (1862), critical writings on *Faust* (1867) and a translation of *Faust* (1876), art history (*Roman Days*, 1877), Germanic mythology (2 vols., 1886–89), etc.

**Ryd′berg** (rĭd′bûrg), **Per** (pûr) **Ax′el** (ăk′s'l). 1860–1931. Botanist, b. in Odh, Sweden; to U.S. (1882); on staff, New York Botanical Garden (1899–1931); author of *Flora of the Sand Hills of Nebraska* (1895), *Flora of Colorado* (1906), *Flora of the Prairies and Plains* (1932).

**Ry′der** (rī′dẽr), **Albert Pinkham.** 1847–1917. American painter, b. New Bedford, Mass. Studio, New York City. Excelled in landscapes, marines, and figure paintings. His *Toilers of the Sea*, *The Curfew Hour*, and *The Bridge* now hang in Metropolitan Museum of Art, New York City; *Moonlight at Sea* in National Gallery of Art, Washington, D.C.

**Ryder, Charles Wolcott.** 1892–1960. American army officer, b. Topeka, Kans.; grad. (1915) U.S.M.A., West Point; served in France (1917–18); major general, and chief of staff, 6th army corps (1941); in command of U.S. forces landing at Algiers (Nov., 1942) and subsequently engaged in Tunisian campaign.

**Ryder,** Sir **Dudley.** 1691–1756. English judge; educ. Edinburgh and Leiden; M.P. (1733); solicitor general (1733); attorney general (1737); prosecutor of rebels of 1745; lord chief justice of King's Bench (1754); kept diaries and records, the earliest, for period 1715–16, being first to appear in print (pub. 1939). His son **Nathaniel** (1735–1803) was 1st Baron **Har′row·by** (hăr′ō·bĭ). The 1st baron's son **Dudley** (1762–1847), 1st Earl of **Harrowby** and Viscount **San′don** (săn′-dŭn), and 2d Baron **Harrowby,** statesman, M.A., Cantab. (1782), M.P. (1784), was undersecretary for foreign affairs (1789); treasurer of navy (1800–01); foreign secretary in Pitt's cabinet (1804) and chancellor of duchy of Lancaster (1805); sent on mission to emperors of Austria and Russia and king of Prussia; lord president of council (1812–27); refused premiership (1827). The 2d baron's son **Dudley** (1798–1882), 2d Earl of **Harrowby,** M.P. (1831), supported Peel in advocacy of free trade; chancellor of duchy of Lancaster and privy councilor (1855); lord privy seal (1855–57); proposed first standing committee of cabinet. The 2d earl's 2d son, **Dudley Francis Stuart** (1831–1900), 3d Earl of **Harrowby,** M.A., Oxon. (1878), M.P. (1856), was supporter of Palmerston; as Viscount **Sandon,** sat for Liverpool (1868–82); member of first London school board; active in promoting legislation on matters of education and social reform; president of Board of Trade (1878–80); lord privy seal (1885–86).

**Rydz–Śmigły.** = Śmigły-Rydz.

**Ryepin.** Variant of Repin.

**Ry′er·son** (rī′ẽr·s'n), **Adolphus Egerton.** 1803–1882. Canadian clergyman; Methodist minister on Niagara circuit (c. 1824); cofounder and first editor of *Christian Guardian*, Methodist organ (1829); one of originators and first president of Victoria Coll., Cobourg, Ontario (1841); superintendent of public schools, Upper Canada (1844–76), resisted Anglican effort to control university training and restrict benefits of public endowments to one church.

**Ryerson, Martin An′toine′** (äɴ′twȧn′). 1856–1932. American businessman and philanthropist, b. Grand Rapids, Mich. Trustee, Chicago Art Institute (1890–1932); built and endowed Ryerson Library for study of art. An incorporator, Field Museum of Natural History (1893).

**Ry′kov** (rĭ′kôf), **Aleksei Ivanovich.** 1881–1938. Russian politician and Soviet government official; often arrested, imprisoned, and exiled under the Czarist regime. Associated with Lenin (1917) in and after the Russian Revolution; became head of Supreme Economic Council and a member of the Politburo. After Lenin's death (1924), served as president of the Soviet of People's Commissars (1924–30); opposed Stalin's policies and was dismissed from office; reinstated in office after publicly recanting his opposition (1931–36). Involved in plot to assassinate Stalin (1936); executed for treason (Mar. 14, 1938).

**Ry′land** (rī′lănd), **Henry.** 1856–1924. English painter; best known for his water colors.

**Ry′lands** (rī′lăndz), **John.** 1801–1888. English textile manufacturer; one of original financiers of Manchester ship canal; benefactor of many charities. The John Rylands Library, Manchester, was founded by his wife as a memorial.

**Ryle** (rīl), Sir **Martin.** 1918– . British astronomer. At Cambridge U. (1948– ); appointed astronomer royal (1972); awarded (with Antony Hewish) Nobel prize for physics (1974).

**Ry·le′ev** (rĭ·lyā′yĕf), **Kondrati Fëdorovich.** 1795–1826. Russian lyric poet; involved in Decembrist plot (1825) and executed.

**Ry′mer** (rī′mẽr), **Thomas.** 1641–1713. English archaeologist and critic; succeeded Shadwell as court historiographer (1692); published collection of documents concerning treaties and alliances of Great Britain with other powers (from 1101–1654), under title *Foedera* (20 vols., 1704–35; vols. XVI–XX edited by the historian Robert Sanderson). Author of play in rhymed verse, *Edgar, or the English Monarch* (1678), of poems in memory of Waller, and of translations and critical discussions of poetry and drama; in *Tragedies of the Last Age Considered* passed unfavorable judgments on Beaumont and Fletcher's plays (1678); in *Short View of Tragedy* condemned Shakespeare's failure to preserve the unities in *Othello* (1692).

**Rys′kind** (rĭs′kĭnd), **Morris.** 1895– . American playwright, b. New York City; collaborator with George Kaufman in *Animal Crackers* (1928), *Strike Up the Band* (1930), *Of Thee I Sing* (also with George and Ira Gershwin, 1931; awarded Pulitzer prize), *Let 'Em Eat Cake* (1933), and the film version of *Stage Door* (1937), and with Irving Berlin in *Louisiana Purchase* (1940).

**Ry′ti** (rü′tĭ), **Rysto Heikki.** 1889–1956. Finnish lawyer; minister of finance (1921–24); governor of Bank of Finland (1923–45); president (1940–44); sentenced (1946) as war criminal to 10 years imprisonment.

**Rytter, Poul.** Pseudonym of Parmo Carl Ploug.

**Ryurik.** See Rurik.

**Rze·wu′ski** (zhĕ·vo͞o′skē). Distinguished Polish family, including: **Stanisław**, who fought against Turks (1698) and Swedes (1706), and was given title "Grand Hetman of the Crown"; **Wacław** (1706?–1779), palatine of Podolia and later of Cracow, and author of verse and plays; **Henryk** (1791–1866), poet and novelist, distinguished himself in 1809 campaign, wrote *Memoirs of Severin Soplica* (1839), *November* (1845), *Imaginary Voyages* (1851), etc.

# S

**Sá** (sȧ), **Men de** *or* **Mem de.** 1500?–1572. Governor general of Brazil (1556–72); founder (1566–67) of city of Rio de Janeiro, in collaboration with his nephew **Estacio de Sá** (1520?–1567), who died of wounds received in action against French and Indians besieging the city.

**Saa·di′** *or* **Sa·di′** (sä·dē′). *Real name* **Muslih-ud-Din.** 1184?–1291. Persian poet, b. in Shiraz; little is known of his life history. Chief works, *Būstān* (*Fruit Garden*, 1257), *Gulistān* (*Rose Garden*, 1258), and *Dīwān* (collection of lyrics).

**Saa′di·a ben Jo′seph** (sȧ′dē·ȧ bĕn jō′zĕf; -zĭf). *Arab.* **Sa'īd al-Fayyūmi.** 892–942 A.D. Jewish commentator and scholar; as Gaon of Sura, brought the school to the peak of its reputation among Jewish communities; translated most of the Bible into Arabic; wrote a commentary on *Sefer Yezīra* (a mystical treatise ascribed to Abraham), *Book of Beliefs and Convictions*, poetry, works on the liturgy, a grammatical treatise, and polemical works.

**Saar** (zär), **Ferdinand von.** 1833–1906. Austrian poet and playwright.

**Saa′ri·nen** (sä′rĭ·nĕn), **Gottlieb Eliel.** 1873–1950. Finnish architect; with his partners **Herman Gesellius** and **A. Lindgren** designed Finnish Pavilion at Paris Exposition of 1900 and national museum in Helsinki. To U.S. (c. 1927) and built Cranbrook School, Bloomfield Hills, Mich.; director, Cranbrook School. His son **Eero** (1910–1961) was also an architect.

**Sa′a·ve′dra** (sä′ä·vā′thrä), **Ángel de.** See **Duque de** RIVAS.

**Saavedra, Juan Bautista.** 1870–1939. Bolivian jurist; president of Bolivia (1921–25).

**Saavedra La′mas** (lä′mäs), **Carlos.** 1880–1959. Argentine lawyer, diplomat, and statesman, b. Buenos Aires; minister of foreign affairs (from 1932); president, Assembly of the League of Nations (1936). Presided over conference in Buenos Aires (1935) which ended the long Chaco war. Awarded Nobel peace prize (1936).

**Saavedra y Fa·jar′do** (ē fä·här′thō), **Diego.** 1584–1648. Spanish diplomat and writer; chief works, *Idea de un Príncipe Político Cristiano* and *República Literaria.*

**Sabacon.** See SHABAKA.

**Sa′ba′tier′** (sȧ′bȧ′tyā′), **Auguste.** 1839–1901. French Protestant theologian; known as representative of liberalism in theology.

**Sabatier, Paul.** 1854–1941. French chemist; engaged in researches on catalytic action; originated method of hydrogenating organic compounds in presence of finely divided metals. With Victor Grignard, awarded the 1912 Nobel prize for chemistry.

**Sabatier, Paul.** 1858–1928. French historian and Protestant clergyman; made special study of Saint Francis of Assisi.

**Sa′ba·ti′ni** (sä′bä·tē′nē; săb′ȧ·tē′nē), **Rafael.** 1875–1950. Italian author and dramatist; writer in English, chiefly of historical romances; among his works are *The Lion's Skin* (1911), *The Life of Cesare Borgia* (1912), *Torquemada and the Spanish Inquisition* (1913), *The Gates of Doom* (1914), *The Sea Hawk* (1915), *The Snare* (1917), *Scaramouche* (1921), *Captain Blood* (1922), *Fortune's Fool* (1923), *The Carolinian* (1925), *Chivalry* (1935), *The Fortunes of Captain Blood* (1936), *The Lost King* (1937), *Columbus* (1942), and several plays.

**Sabbah, ibn-al-.** See HASAN IBN-AL-SABBAH.

**Sab·bat′a·i Ze·bi′** *or* **Ze·vi′** (să·băt′ā·ī tsĕ·vē′). *Also* **Shab·bet′ha·i** (shă·bĕt′ā·ī). 1626–1676. Hebrew mystic, b. in Smyrna, of Spanish descent; proclaimed himself the Messiah (1648), and gathered about him a large following among the Jews of eastern Europe; moved upon Constantinople, but was captured and imprisoned (1666). When brought before Sultan Mohammed IV for a hearing, he accepted Islamic faith in order to save his life.

**Sab′ba·ti′ni** (säb′bä·tē′nē), **Andrea.** *Called* **Andrea da Sa·ler′no** (dä sä·lĕr′nō). 1480?–1545. Italian painter; pupil of Raphael and known as a skillful imitator of his master.

**Sa·bel′li·us** (sȧ·bĕl′ĭ·ŭs). Roman Christian prelate and theologian; became a leader of modalistic monarchians; excommunicated (c. 220) by Pope Calixtus. His followers were known as Sabellians.

**Sa′bin** (sā′bĭn), **Florence Re′na** (rē′nȧ). 1871–1953. American anatomist; B.S., Smith (1893); M.D., Johns Hopkins (1900). Teacher of anatomy, Johns Hopkins (1902–17), and professor of histology (1917–25); on staff, Rockefeller Institute for Medical Research (1925–38). Recipient of National Achievement award (1932).

**Sab′in** (?săb′ĭn), **Joseph.** 1821–1881. Bibliographer, b. in Northamptonshire, Eng.; to U.S. (1848); established himself in New York as dealer in rare books and prints (c. 1865). Chief work, *Dictionary of Books Relating to America, from its Discovery to the Present Time*, better known as *Bibliotheca Americana* (14 vols., 1868–84; vols. 15–20, ed. by Wilberforce Eames, 1885–92).

**Sab′ine** (săb′ĭn), Sir **Edward.** 1788–1883. British physicist, soldier, and explorer; astronomer to expeditions of John Ross (1818) and William Edward Parry in search of the Northwest Passage (1819–20); at Spitsbergen and in tropical Africa, conducted pendulum experiments for determining shape of earth; devoted most of life to researches on terrestrial magnetism; discovered (1852) interrelation between periodic variation of sunspots and magnetic disturbances on the earth; president of Royal Society (1861–71); general (1870).

**Sa′bine** (sā′bĭn), **Wallace Clement Ware.** 1868–1919. American physicist; known for researches in acoustics.

**Sa·bin′i·a′nus** (sȧ·bĭn′ĭ·ā′nŭs). d. 606. Pope (604–606).

**Sa·bi′nus** (sȧ·bī′nŭs), **Massurius.** Roman jurist of 1st century A.D.; head of Sabinian school.

**Sabuktagin.** Variant of SUBUKTIGIN.

**Sabunde, Raimundo.** See RAYMOND OF SABUNDE.

**Sabutai.** Variant of SUBOTAI.

**Sac′a·ga·we′a** (săk′ȧ·gȧ·wē′ȧ), *i.e.* Bird Woman. Also **Sac′a·ja·we′a** *or* **Sak′a·ja·we′a** (săk′ȧ·jȧ·wē′ȧ). 1787?–1812. American Indian woman interpreter; member of Shoshone tribe; captured by Hidatsas and sold to a Canadian trapper, Toussaint Charbonneau, whom she married by Indian rites and later accompanied as guide to Lewis and Clark expedition (1805).

**Sa·ca′sa** (sä·kä′sä), **Juan Bautista.** 1874–1946. Nicaraguan political leader; president of Nicaragua (1933–36); attempted reconciliation with Sandino forces (1933) that resulted in assassination of Sandino (Feb. 21, 1934) by National Guard; forced to resign (June 6, 1936); took refuge in the U.S.

**Sac·chet′ti** (säk·kāt′tē), **Franco.** 1335?–1400. Italian poet and writer of novelle; author of *Trecento Novelle* in style of Boccaccio, burlesque and serious poetry, and *Sermoni.*

**Sac′chi** (säk′kē), **Andrea.** 1599–1661. Italian painter; his *Miracle of St. Gregory* and *Vision of St. Romuald* hang in the Vatican.

**Sacchi, Bartolommeo de'.** *Called in Latin* **Pla·ti'na** (plȧ·tī'nȧ). 1421–1481. Italian humanist and historian; appointed Vatican librarian by Sixtus IV (1475). Wrote *Historia de Vitis Pontificum Romanorum* ... (1479).

**Sacchi, Giovanni Antonio de'.** See Giovanni Antonio da PORDENONE.

**Sac·chi'ni** (säk·kē'nē), **Antonio Maria Gasparo.** 1734–1786. Italian composer, esp. of operas.

**Sac'co** (säk'kō; *Angl.* săk'ō), **Ni·co'la** [nē·kô'lä] (1891–1927) and **Bar'to·lo·me'o** (bär'tō·lō·mâ'ō) **Van·zet'ti** [vän·dzāt'tē; *Angl.* văn·zĕt'ĭ] (1888–1927). Political radicals, b. in Italy; to U.S. (1908); arrested on charge of murder of a shoe-factory paymaster and guard at South Braintree, Mass. (Apr. 15, 1920) and theft of $16,000 payroll; tried and convicted (July 14, 1921); on appeal of their case, doubt of their guilt led to widespread support and world-wide protests; electrocuted (Aug. 23, 1927) after special committee (A. Lawrence Lowell of Harvard, Samuel W. Stratton of M.I.T., and Judge Robert Grant) appointed (June 1, 1927) by governor of Massachusetts to review case had found trial fair.

**Sacharissa.** See *Lady Dorothy Sidney*, under SIDNEY family.

**Sa'chau** (zä'ĸou), **Eduard.** 1845–1930. German Oriental scholar; director, Seminary of Oriental Languages, Berlin.

**Sa'cher–Ma'soch** (zä'ĸēr·mä'zōĸ), **Leopold von.** 1836–1895. German novelist; author of *Das Vermächtnis Kains* (4 vols., 1870–77), *Die Messalinen Wiens* (1874), *Polnische Judengeschichten* (1886), etc. The term *masochism* has become used for a form of abnormality depicted in some of his novels.

**Sa·chev'er·ell** (sȧ·shĕv'ẽr·ĕl), **Henry.** 1674?–1724. English political preacher; preached two sermons (1709) attacking Whig ministry for neglect of the interests of the church and condemning toleration and occasional conformity, becoming thereby idol of Tory party; impeached at instigation of Godolphin and suspended from preaching for three years; on fall of Godolphin ministry, selected to preach Restoration sermon and presented to rich rectory by new Tory ministry (1713).

**Sacheverell, William.** 1638–1691. English political leader; opponent of court party; M.P. (1670); member of committee preparing Test Act (1673); a manager of impeachment of five Catholic peers and impeachment of Thomas Osborne, 1st Earl of Danby; took prominent part in investigation of Oates's pretended Popish Plot; made first suggestion of excluding James, Duke of York, from the succession (1678) and promoted Exclusion Bill. After retirement during reign of James II, returned to Parliament; helped draw up Bill of Rights.

**Sachs** (săks), **Bernard.** 1858–1944. American neurologist; professor, Columbia.

**Sachs** (zäks), **Hans.** 1494–1576. German Meistersinger, b. Nürnberg. An itinerant shoemaker, he studied the art of Meistergesang (c. 1511–15); began writing (1514) and composed altogether over 6000 works, including tragedies, comedies, songs, fables, allegories, and narratives. At the Reformation, accepted the doctrines of Luther. Depicted as central figure in Wagner's opera *Die Meistersinger von Nürnberg* (1868).

**Sachs, Julius von.** 1832–1897. German botanist; known for investigations of metabolism of plants, influence of heat and light on growth of plants, mechanics of growth, formation of flowers, etc.

**Sachs, Karl Ernst August.** 1829–1909. German Romance language scholar and lexicographer; with the lexicographer Césaire Villatte, prepared *Enzyklopädisches Wörterbuch der Französischen und Deutschen Sprache* (4 vols., 1869–80).

**Sachs, Michael.** 1808–1864. German rabbi and scholar; rabbi of congregations in Prague (1836) and Berlin (1844); a leader among the conservative rabbis.

**Sachs, Nelly.** 1891–1970. German-Jewish poet and dramatist; to Sweden (1940). Shared Nobel prize in literature (1966) with S. Y. Agnon. Known for lyrical and dramatic works; wrote *Eclipse of the Stars* (1949), *Flight and Metamorphosis* (1959), etc.

**Sach'sen** (zäk'sĕn). German form of SAXE.

**Sack'ville** (săk'vĭl). Name of an English family possessing earldom and dukedom of **Dor'set** (dôr'sĕt; -sĭt), and including: Sir **Richard** (d. 1566), of Buckhurst, Sussex; first cousin of Anne Boleyn; barrister; M.P. (1529); induced Roger Ascham to write *The Scholemaster*. He was father of the poet Thomas Sackville (*q.v.*), 1st Earl of Dorset, whose eldest son, **Robert** (1561–1609), 2d earl, M.P. (1585), endowed Sackville Coll. for the Poor, Sussex. **Sir Edward** (1591–1652), 4th earl; son of 2d earl; M.P. (1614); held minor command at battle of Prague (1620); ambassador to Louis XIII (1621); interested in Bermuda Islands and Virginia; privy councilor (1626) and lord chamberlain to Henrietta Maria (1628); joined Charles I at outbreak of Civil War; commissioner of treasury (1643); lord chamberlain to king and lord president of council (1644). His grandson **Charles** (1638–1706), 6th Earl of Dorset and 1st Earl of **Mid'dle·sex** (mĭd''l·sĕks); poet and courtier; M.P. (1660); notorious for riotous and dissipated life, often roistering with Sir Charles Sedley; served as volunteer in fleet against Dutch (1665); retired from court during James II's reign; made privy councilor and lord chamberlain (1689–97) by William of Orange; thrice regent during William III's absences; generous patron of men of letters, including Prior, Wycherley, Dryden; author of song *To all you ladies now on land* (1665). **Lionel Cranfield Sackville** (1688–1765), 1st Duke of Dorset (cr. 1720); son of 6th earl; lord warden of Cinque Ports (1708–17, 1728, 1757–65); twice lord steward of the household; twice lord lieutenant of Ireland; lord president of the council (1745–51); often acting lord justice of Great Britain; father of **Charles** (1711–1769), 2d duke; M.A., Oxon. (1730); intimate of Frederick, Prince of Wales; a lord of the treasury under Henry Pelham (1743–47).

**George Sackville Ger'main** [jûr'măn; -mān] (1716–1785), 1st Viscount **Sackville** (cr. 1782); 3d son of 1st duke; known as Lord George Sackville (till 1770); M.A., Dublin (1734); second in command of St.-Malo expedition (1758); failed to lead cavalry charge needed to complete victory at Minden; dismissed from service; chief secretary to his father (1751–56); assumed name Germain (1770); as secretary of state for colonies (1775–82), virtually directed war in America; erroneously credited with authorship of *Letters of Junius* (cf. Sir Philip FRANCIS). With his son **Charles** (1767–1843), 5th duke, the titles became extinct.

**Sackville, Thomas.** 1st Earl of **Dor'set** (dôr'sĕt; -sĭt) and Baron **Buck'hurst** (bŭk'hûrst). 1536–1608. English poet and diplomat; planned and wrote *Induction* for *A Myrrovre for Magistrates*, elevated and allegoric poetry (1559–63); collaborated with Thomas Norton (*q.v.*) in blank-verse *Tragedy of Gorboduc*, the earliest English tragedy (1561), probably writing last two acts. Grand master of freemasons (1561–67); raised to peerage as Baron Buckhurst (1567); announced her death sentence to Mary, Queen of Scots (1586); diplomat in France and Low Countries (1587–98); lord treasurer (1599–1608); presided at Essex's trial (1601); created earl (1604). See also SACKVILLE family.

**Sack'ville–West'** (-wĕst'). Name of an English family

originating in the union of a branch of the West family, including the Earls and Barons **De La Warr** (dĕl′ȧ·wẽr), with a branch of the Sackville family, including the dukes and earls of **Dor′set** (dôr′sĕt; -sĭt). Its members include:

**George John Sackville West** (1791–1869), 5th Earl De La Warr; lord chamberlain (1841, 1858–59); m. Elizabeth, daughter of John Frederick Sackville, 3d Duke of Dorset; assumed additional name of Sackville (1843).

His 5th son, **Lionel Sackville Sackville–West** (1827–1908), 2d Baron **Sackville of Knole** (nōl); diplomat; served under Lord Lyons at Paris through Franco-Prussian War; minister to Argentine Republic (1872–78), Spain (1878–81), U.S. (1881–88); member of commission settling U.S.–Canadian differences over fishing rights (1887–88); dismissed by Pres. Cleveland for recommending, in his answer to the Murchison letter, that the inquirer, a fictitious Charles F. Murchison, vote Democratic ticket as advantageous to British interests (1888).

**Lionel Edward Sackville–West** (1867–1928), 3d Baron Sackville; nephew to 2d baron; M.A., Oxon.; served at Gallipoli, in Egypt, Palestine, and France (1914–18); m. (1890) his cousin **Victoria Sackville–West** (1864–1936).

Their daughter **Victoria Mary Sackville–West** (1892–1962); poet and novelist, b. Knole Castle, Sevenoaks, a gift of Queen Elizabeth to her lord treasurer, Thomas Sackville; m. (1913) the journalist and diplomat Harold Nicolson (*q.v.*), with whom she traveled in Persia, Hungary, Bulgaria, and Morocco; published (1919–24) four novels, including *Heritage* (1919), and two volumes of short stories, gaining attention with *The Heir* (short stories; 1922); published a personal narrative of her ancestors, *Knole and the Sackvilles* (1923), and an account of her travels, *Passenger to Teheran* (1926); established reputation as a poet with *The Land*, giving the year's cycle of an English farmer, interspersed with lyrics (1926; awarded Hawthornden prize 1927). Author of biographies of Aphra Behn and Andrew Marvell; of novels, including *The Edwardians* (1930), *All Passion Spent* (1931), *The Dark Island* (1934), *Saint Joan of Arc* (1936), *Pepita* (1937), *Grand Canyon* (1942); of poetry, including *King's Daughter* (1930), *Collected Poems* (1933), *Solitude* (1938); of *Country Notes* (essays; 1939).

Sir **Charles John Sackville–West** (1870–1962), 4th baron; military officer; brother of 3d baron; served at Manipur (1891), Burma (1891–92), in Boer War (1899–1900), World War (1914–18); member of Allied Military Committee of Versailles (1918); major general (1919); military attaché, Paris (1920–24). His son **Edward Charles** (1901–1965), 5th Baron; author of *Piano Quintet* (1925), *The Ruin* (a Gothic novel, 1926), *The Sun in Capricorn* (1934), and *Flame in Sunlight* (a life of De Quincey, 1936).

**Sac′ro·bos′co** (săk′rō·bŏs′kō), **Johannes de.** *Also* **John of Hol′y·wood** (hŏl′ĭ·wŏŏd) *or* **of Hal′i·fax** (hăl′ĭ·făks). fl. 1230. English mathematician; professor, Paris; one of first to use mathematical writings of Arabians; paraphrased part of Ptolemy's *Almagest* as a treatise, *Tractatus de Sphaera Mundi;* author of *Algorismus*, on arithmetic.

**Sa′cy′** (sȧ′sē′), Baron **Antoine Isaac Sil′ves′tre de** (sēl′vĕs′tr′ dē). 1758–1838. French Oriental scholar; rector, U. of Paris (1815); peer of France (1832). Regarded as founder of Arabic study in France. His son **Samuel Ustazade** (1801–1879) was editor of *Journal des Débats* (1828–79).

**Sá da Ban·dei′ra** (sȧ′ thȧ bäNn·dā′ē·rȧ), **Bernardo de.** 1795–1876. Portuguese politician; premier of Portugal (1865, 1868–69, 1870–71).

**Sa·dat′** (sȧ·dat′; -dät′), **Anwar el-** 1918– . Egyptian leader. President of Egypt (1970– ). Awarded (with Menahem Begin) Nobel prize for peace (1978).

**Sade** (sȧd), Comte **Donatien Alphonse François de.** *Better known as* Marquis **de Sade.** 1740–1814. French soldier and writer; confined much of his life in various prisons; died in an insane asylum; author of two erotic novels, *Justine* (1791) and *Juliette* (1798). Sadism, a form of sexual activity in which gratification is obtained by inflicting pain upon the person loved, was described by him and receives its name from him.

**Sá de Mi·ran′da** (sȧ′ thē mē·răNn′dȧ), **Francisco de.** 1485?–1558. Portuguese poet and playwright. His *Os Estrangeiros* (1527) was Portugal's first prose comedy, and *Cleopatra* (c. 1550) Portugal's first classical tragedy. Credited with introducing Renaissance into Portugal.

**Sadi.** See SAADI.

**Sad′leir** (săd′lẽr). Variant of SADLER.

**Sad′ler** (săd′lẽr), Sir **Michael Ernest.** 1861–1943. English educator; professor of history and administration of education, Victoria U., Manchester (1903–11), vice-chancellor of Leeds U. (1911–23). His son **Michael Sad′leir** [săd′lẽr] (1888–1957), author and publisher, entered office of Constable & Co. Ltd., London publishers (1912), director (1920); member of British delegation to Paris Peace Conference (1919); member of secretariat, League of Nations; author of five novels (1918–25), a biography (1927) and a bibliography (1928) of Anthony Trollope, and *Bulwer and his Wife* (1931), *The Strange Life of Lady Blessington* (1933), *These Foolish Things* (1937), *Fanny by Gaslight* (1940).

**Sad′ler** *or* **Sad′leir** *or* **Sad′leyer** (săd′lẽr), Sir **Ralph.** 1507–1587. English diplomat, mostly engaged in Scottish affairs. One of Henry VIII's principal secretaries of state (c. 1537); sent to Edinburgh to restrain influence of Cardinal Beaton (1542); helped arrange treaty of Leith (1560); one of commissioners to treat with Scots on flight of Mary, Queen of Scots (1568); guardian of Mary, Queen of Scots (1580–84).

**Sad′li·er** (săd′lĭ·ẽr), **Denis.** 1817–1885. Book publisher, b. in County Tipperary, Ireland; to U.S. (1830). With his brother **James** (d. 1869), founded a bookbinding and publishing business, D. & J. Sadlier & Co., New York City (1836); became principal publisher of Catholic books in America. James Sadlier's wife (m. 1846), **Mary Anne**, *nee* **Mad′den** [măd′'n] (1820–1903), b. Ireland; to U.S. (1844), was a short-story writer and novelist.

**Sadoc.** See ZADOC.

**Sa′do·le′to** (sä′dō·lā′tō), **Jacopo.** 1477–1547. Italian prelate; bishop of Carpentras (1517); cardinal (1536); papal legate to France (1542); active in Council of Trent (1545 ff.); sought reunion of Roman Catholic and Protestant churches.

**Sadt′ler** (săd′lẽr; săt′lẽr), **John Philip Benjamin.** 1823–1901. American Lutheran clergyman and educator, b. Baltimore; president, Muhlenberg College, Allentown, Pa. (1877–85). His son **Samuel Philip** (1847–1923) was a chemist; professor, U. of Pennsylvania (1874–91); chemical editor, *The Dispensatory of the United States* (1883–1923); author of *A Text-book of Chemistry for... Pharmaceutical and Medical Students* (with Henry Trimble, 1892), etc.

**Sadyk Pasha.** See Michał CZAJKOWSKI.

**Sæ′mund** (sī′mŭnd). *Known as* **Sæmund the Wise.** 1056–1133. Icelandic scholar; author of works on the history of Iceland. Bishop Brynjolf Sveinsson, discoverer (1643) of the *Elder*, or *Poetic, Edda*, erroneously attributed it to Sæmund, and it became also known as the *Edda of Sæmund the Wise.* Cf. SNORRI STURLUSON.

**Sá'enz Pe'ña** (sä'āns pā'nyä), **Luis.** 1823–1907. Argentine politician; president of Argentina (1892–95). His son **Roque** (1851–1914) was president of Argentina (1910–14); author of electoral reform bill (passed 1912).

**Saerch'ing·er** (sûrch'ĭng·ẽr), **Cé'sar'** (sā'zȧr'; sē'zẽr) **Victor Charles.** 1884–1971. Music editor and journalist, b. Aachen, Ger.; to U.S. (1898); edited *The Art of Music* (14 vols., 1913–17) and *International Who's Who in Music* (1918); foreign correspondent in Berlin (1919–21) and London (1925–26); in London (1930–37) as European director, Columbia Broadcasting System; conductor of radio series "The Story behind the Headlines" (1938–48). Author of *Hello, America!* (1938), *The Way out of War* (1940), etc.

**Ša'fa·řík** *or* **Schaf'fa·rik** (shȧ'fȧr·zhēk), **Pavel Josef.** 1795–1861. Czech Slavic scholar; professor of Slavic philology at U. of Prague (from 1848).

**Sa·fa'wid** (să·fä'wĭd) *or* **Sa'fa·vid'** (să'fă·vĭd'). A Moslem Persian dynasty (1502–1736) founded by Shah Ismail and named after an ancestor, **Sa·fi'–al–Din'** [să·fĭ'yăd·dēn'] (1252–1334) of Ardebil, a Persian saint who claimed descent from Ali, the fourth caliph. Its last ruler was Abbas III, who was succeeded by Nadir Shah.

**Saffāḥ, al–.** See abu-al-ABBAS.

**Saf·far'id** (să·fär'ĭd). A Mohammedan dynasty of Persia (867–903), established in the eastern part (Seistan); named from Yaqub ibn-al-Layth, nicknamed **al–Saf·far'** (ăs'săf·fär'), *i.e.* "the coppersmith." It was nominally dependent on the caliphs of Baghdad; became subordinate to the Samanids.

**Saf'ford** (săf'ẽrd), **Truman Henry.** 1836–1901. American mathematician and astronomer; professor of astronomy, U. of Chicago (1866–71), Williams (1876–1901); author of *Mathematical Teaching and Its Modern Methods* (1887), *The Development of Astronomy in the United States* (1888), etc.

**Sa·gas'ta** (sä·gäs'tä), **Práxedes Mateo.** 1827–1903. Spanish statesman; editor of progressist journal and member of Cortes (1859–63); took part against reactionary government of Isabella II (1859–68); became member of provisional government attached to Prim (1869–70); prime minister (1872–74); in Serrano ministry (1874); leader of Liberals in Cortes (1875–83); again prime minister after death of Alfonso XII (1885–90 and 1893–95); resigned because of trouble in Cuba but during critical period (war with United States) again conducted government (1897–99); prime minister (1901–02).

**Sage** (sāj), **Henry Williams.** 1814–1897. American merchant and philanthropist; in transportation and lumber business, Ithaca, N.Y. (1832–57; 1880–97); member, board of trustees, Cornell U. (1870–97) and president of board (1875–97); liberal benefactor of Cornell.

**Sage, Russell.** 1816–1906. American financier, b. in Oneida County, N.Y. Grocery clerk, Troy, N.Y.; acquired interest in wholesale grocery firm (1839–57). Moved to New York (1863); bought New York Stock Exchange seat (1874). Associated with Jay Gould in extensive stock-market operations and security promotion. His second wife, **Margaret Olivia,** *nee* **Slo'cum** [slō'kŭm] (1828–1918), inherited unconditionally his $70,000,000 fortune and became known for her philanthropies; established Russell Sage Foundation for improving social and living conditions in the United States, with gift of $10,000,000 (1907); gave liberally to Emma Willard School, Rensselaer Polytechnic Institute, Cornell, Princeton, and Russell Sage Institute of Pathology.

**Sagittarius.** See Heinrich SCHÜTZ.

**Sa'ha** (sä'hä), **Meghnad N.** 1893–1956. Indian physicist; professor, Allahabad U. (1923–39), Calcutta U. (from 1939); known for work on radiation and ionization.

**Sa'ha·gún'** (sä'ä·gōōn'), **Bernardino de.** 1499?–1590. Spanish Franciscan missionary and historian in Mexico; wrote treatises on the Aztecs and Spanish conquest of Mexico.

**Sai·cho** (sī·chō). *Known also by posthumous title* **Dengyo Dai·shi** (dĕn·gyō dī·shē). 767–822. Japanese bonze, b. in Omi. Became bonze at twelve; convinced of truth of Tendai doctrine, built monastery for its propagation on Hiei-zan Mountain (c. 788); ordered by emperor to go to China (802), visited many Buddhist temples; after return (805) to Japan, established Tendai sect; did much to spread Buddhism in Japan; is said to have first (805) brought tea from China to Japan.

**Sa·id' Ha·lim' Pa·sha'** (sä·ēd' hä·lĭm' pä·shä'), **Mehmet.** 1863–1921. Turkish statesman; member of Young Turks party. After Turkish Revolution (1908), became successively senator, president of the Council of State, and (1914) grand vizier. In early years of World War, endeavored to keep Turkey neutral; resigned (Feb., 1917). Imprisoned by British in Malta (1918–21); assassinated in Rome (Dec. 6, 1921).

**Sa·id' Mo·ham'med Pa'sha** (să·ēd' mŏŏ·hăm'măd pȧ'shä). d. 1928. Egyptian statesman; succeeded Boutros Pasha as prime minister (1910); worked with British for administrative reforms (1910–14); again prime minister (1919) at time when revolutionary spirit was rife; barely escaped assassination; cabinet minister under Zaghlul Pasha.

**Sa·id' Pa'sha** (să·ēd' pȧ'shä). 1822–1863. Viceroy of Egypt (1854–63); fourth son of Mehemet Ali (*q.v.*) and uncle of Abbas I; under French influence; granted (1854) concession to de Lesseps for construction of Suez Canal (work begun 1859).

**Sai·go Ta·ka·mo·ri** (sī·gō tä·kä·mō·rē). 1827–1877. Japanese general and patriot; influential in revolution (1868) overthrowing the power of the shoguns and restoring the rule of the emperor; leader of the Satsuma rebellion (1877); killed in action (Sept. 14, 1877).

**Saint** (sānt), **Thomas.** English inventor (1790) of a machine for stitching which anticipated most features of a modern sewing machine except the eye-pointed needle. Cf. Elias HOWE.

**St. Albans,** 1st Earl of. See Henry JERMYN.

**St. Aldwyn,** 1st Earl. See HICKS BEACH.

**Saint'–A'mant'** (săN'-tȧ'mäN'), **Marc Antoine Gi'rard' de** (zhē'rȧr' dē). 1594–1661. French poet; called by Gautier the creator, along with Scarron and Théophile de Viau, of burlesque poetry in France.

**Saint'–Ar'naud'** (săN'-tȧr'nō'), **Armand Jacques Le·roy' de** (lē·rwȧ' dē). 1801–1854. French soldier; marshal of France (1852) and commander in chief of the French army in the Crimean War. Co-operated with Lord Raglan of the British army in winning the battle of Alma (Sept., 1854); died shortly afterwards.

**Saint'–Au'bain'** (săN'-tō'băN'), **Andreas Nicolai de** (dē). *Pseudonym* **Karl Bern'hard** (bĕrn'härt). 1798–1865. Danish novelist and chronicler.

**Saint'–Au'bin', de** (dē săN'-tō'băN'). French family of artists, consisting of three brothers: **Charles Germain** (1721–1786), engraver and illustrator; **Gabriel Jacques** (1724–1780), painter, illustrator, engraver, and etcher; **Augustin** (1737–1807), painter and engraver.

**Saint Carilef** *or* **Saint Calais.** See WILLIAM OF SAINT CARILEF.

**Saint Clair.** See SINCLAIR family.

**St. Clair** (sănt klâr'; sĭng'klâr; sĭn'klâr), **Arthur.** 1736?–1818. Soldier in America, b. Thurso, Scotland; bought estate in western Pennsylvania; served in Continental army, brigadier general, at battles of Trenton and Princeton; major general (1777), evacuated Fort Ticonderoga before Burgoyne's advance; court-martialed (1778) and fully exonerated. Member of Continental Congress (1785–87) and president (1787). First governor of Northwest Territory (1787–1802). As major general of federal troops, suffered defeat by Indians near Fort Wayne (Nov. 4, 1791), and resigned from his army command (1792). Removed from his governorship by Jefferson (1802) for criticism of congressional legislation creating the State of Ohio.

**Saint-Cyr** (săN'sēr'), Marquis **Laurent de Gou'vion'** (dē gōō'vyôN'). 1764–1830. French marshal; entered army (1792); served in Rhine campaign, and in Germany and Italy; created marshal for victory at Polotsk (1812), in Russian campaign; minister of war (1815, 1817–19).

**St. Den'is** (sânt dĕn'ĭs), **Ruth.** 1878–1968. *Originally* **Ruth Dennis.** American dancer and teacher of dancing; m. Ted Shawn (1914; separated 1930); with Ted Shawn (*q.v.*), organized Den'i·shawn' (dĕn'ĭ·shôn') School of Dancing, in Los Angeles, later in New York, and the Denishawn Dancers, with whom she toured U.S. and England (1922–25) and the Orient (1925–26).

**Sainte'-Beuve'** (săNt'bûv'), **Charles Augustin.** 1804–1869. French man of letters, b. Boulogne. Studied medicine in Paris (1823), but gave it up for writing. Literary critic for *Le Globe;* later, contributor also to *Le Constitutionnel, Le Moniteur,* and *Le Temps.* Among his works are *Vie, Poésies et Pensées de Joseph Delorme* (verse, 1829), *Les Consolations* (verse, 1831), *Volupté* (a novel, 1834), *Pensées d'Août* (verse, 1837), *Portraits Littéraires* (1832–39), and the famous series *Causeries du Lundi* (15 vols., 1849–61) and *Nouveaux Lundis* (13 vols., 1861–66), made up from his newspaper and periodical articles.

**Sainte-Claire De·ville'** (săNt'klâr' dē·vēl'), **Henri Étienne.** 1818–1881. French chemist. Devised method for commercial production of aluminum (1854); one of first to prepare toluene; discovered nitrogen pentoxide; studied metallurgy of platinum and platinum metals; investigated thermal dissociation; devised method of analyzing minerals.

**Sainte-Hélène,** Sieur **de. Jacques Lemoyne.** See under Charles LEMOYNE.

**Sainte-Maure** *or* **Sainte-More, Benoît de.** See BENOÎT DE SAINTE-MAURE.

**Sainte'-Pa'laye'** (săNt' pȧ'lā'), **Jean Baptiste de La Curne de** (dē lȧ kürn' dē). 1697–1781. French scholar; authority on Provençal; compiled *Dictionnaire Historique de l'Ancien Langage Français.*

**Saint'-É'vre·mond'** (săN'-tā'vrē·môN'), Seigneur **de. Charles de Mar'gue·tel' de Saint'-De·nis'** (dē mȧr'gē·tĕl' dē săN'dē·nē'). 1610?–1703. French courtier, wit, and littérateur, an exile in England (1662–65, 1670–1703). Served through large part of Thirty Years' War; royalist during Fronde; involved in fall of Fouquet; on discovery of letter to Créqui attacking Mazarin and his policy (1661), fled to England. Warmly received by Charles II; intimate with Grammont. In Low Countries (1664–70); attached himself to Hortense Mancini, Duchess of Mazarin, an attractive niece of Mazarin, who set up in London a salon for lovemaking, gambling, and witty conversation. Author of critical essays, including one on English comedy, dialogues, reflections, and occasional poems, none published during his life.

**Saint'-Ex'u'pé'ry'** (săN'-tăg'zü'pā'rē'), **Antoine de.** 1900–1944. French aviator and writer; author of *Night Flight* (1932), *Wind, Sand and Stars* (1939), *Flight to Arras* (1942), *The Little Prince* (1943).

**Saint-Gau'dens** (sânt·gô'd'nz), **Augustus.** 1848–1907. Sculptor, b. Dublin, Ireland; to U.S. in infancy. Studio in New York (1873–85) and Cornish, N.H. (1885–1907). Among his important works are: *Lincoln,* now in Lincoln Park, Chicago; *Farragut,* in Madison Square, New York City; *Shaw Memorial,* on Boston Common; *Deacon Chapin,* also called *The Puritan,* in Springfield, Mass.; equestrian statues of *General Sherman* in New York and *General Logan* in Chicago; *Amor Caritas,* in the Luxembourg, Paris. Elected to American Hall of Fame (1920).

**Saint'-Ge·lais'** (săN'zhē·lĕ'), **Mellin de.** 1491–1558. French poet of the court of Francis I; identified with the school of Clément Marot; author of lyrics, rondeaux, epigrams, and other short pieces; said to have introduced the sonnet from Italy into France.

**Saint'-Ger'main'** (săN'zhĕr'măN'), Comte **de.** d. about 1784. Adventurer in Paris (from c. 1750); claimed to possess philosophers' stone and elixir of life; employed by Louis XV as a diplomat on confidential missions; involved in many political intrigues of the day; retired to Schleswig-Holstein (c. 1775) and studied occult sciences in association with Landgrave Charles of Hesse.

**Saint-Germain,** Comte **Claude Louis de.** 1707–1778. French general; in French army during early years of Seven Years' War; passed into service of Denmark (1760); retired (1766). Appointed (1775) minister of war by Louis XVI, but his efforts to economize and introduce Prussian discipline into the French service forced his resignation (1777).

**Saint'-Hi'laire'** (săN'-tē'lâr'), **Auguste de.** *In full* **Augustin François César Prou'ven'çal'** (prōō'văN'sȧl') **de Saint-Hilaire.** 1799–1853. French botanist; engaged in explorations and botanical researches in Brazil (1816–22); published a work in three volumes on flora of Brazil (1824–25).

**Saint-Hilaire, Étienne Geoffroy** and **Isidore Geoffroy.** See GEOFFROY SAINT-HILAIRE.

**Saint-Hilaire, Jules Barthélemy.** See BARTHÉLEMY SAINT-HILAIRE.

**Saint-Hilaire, Marco de.** *Real name* **Émile Marc Hi'laire'** (ē'lâr'). 1793–1887. French writer; a page in Napoleon I's court; author of *Mémoires d'un Page de la Cour Impériale* (1830).

**Sain'tine'** (săN'tēn'), **Xavier.** *Real name* **Joseph Xavier Bo'ni'face'** (bô'nē'fȧs'). 1798–1865. French fiction writer and playwright; author of the story *Picciola,* telling of the love of a prisoner for a flower (1836); author or coauthor of many comedies and vaudeville sketches.

**St. John** (sĭn'jŭn), **Henry.** See 1st Viscount BOLINGBROKE.

**St. John** (sânt jŏn'), **J. Hector.** See M.-G. Jean de CRÈVECŒUR.

**St. John** (sĭn'jŭn), **Oliver.** 1598?–1673. English judge; consul for Lord Saye and John Hampden in resistance to payment of ship money (1637); married cousin of Oliver Cromwell; member of Short and Long parliaments; solicitor general (1641–43); supported bill for Strafford's attainder; drew up Root and Branch and Militia bills; performed duties of attorney general (1644); one of peace commissioners at Uxbridge (1645); chief justice, Court of Common Pleas (1648); member of council of state (1659, 1660). Published *Case of Oliver St. John* (1660) to disclaim any share in Charles I's execution and explain relations with Cromwells.

**Saint'-Just'** (săN'zhüst'), **Louis Antoine Léon de.** 1767–1794. French revolutionary leader; member of the National Convention (1792) and intimate associate of Robespierre. Member of Committee of Public Safety (1793); active in overthrow of the Girondists and in bringing on the Reign of Terror. Arrested with Robespierre and guillotined (July 28, 1794).

**Saint'-Lam'bert'** (săN'lăN'bâr'), Marquis **Jean François de.** 1716–1803. French poet and philosopher.

**St. Laurent** (săn' lô'räɴ'), **Louis Stephen.** 1882–1973. Canadian lawyer; prime minister of Canada (1948–57).

**St. Leg'er** (sânt lĕj'ẽr; sĕl'ĭn·jẽr), Sir **Anthony.** 1496?–1559. English administrator; lord deputy of Ireland (1540); by severe measures subdued chief families, finally even Con O'Neill; recalled on charge of falsifying accounts (1556) and died while investigation was in progress.

**St. Leger, Barry.** 1737–1789. British officer in American Revolution; took part under General Abercrombie in siege of Louisburg (1758); with Wolfe at Quebec; commanded expedition intended to join General Burgoyne in Hudson Valley, but stopped at battle of Oriskany (1777). Founded (1776) the St. Leger, a horse race at Doncaster, England.

**Saint'–Lé'on'** (săɴ'lā'ôɴ'), **Charles Victor Arthur Michel.** 1821–1870. French violinist, dancer, and choregrapher; ballet master in Munich and Paris. His wife, **Fan'ny'** (*Fr.* fȧ'nē'), *nee* **Francesca Cer·ri'to** [chĕr·rē'tō] (1821–after 1895), Italian-born dancer, appeared, until their separation (c. 1850), in a number of his ballets.

**St. Leon'ards** (sânt lĕn'ẽrdz), Baron. **Edward Burtenshaw Sug'den** (sŭg'dĕn). 1781–1875. English jurist; gained reputation with treatise on law of vendors and purchasers (1805) and learned edition of Sir Geoffrey Gilbert's *Law of Uses and Trusts* (1808). Tory M.P. (1828), opposed Reform Bill of 1832; solicitor general (1829); lord chancellor of Ireland (1834–35, 1841–46); lord chancellor of Great Britain (1852).

**St.-Leu,** Comte **de.** See Louis BONAPARTE.

**St. Lus'son'** (săɴ' lü'sôɴ'), Sieur **de. Simon François Dau'mont'** (dō'môɴ'). d. 1674. French explorer in America. In Canada (1663–68; 1670–74). Headed expedition (1670–71) to region around upper Great Lakes. Conducted ceremonies at Sault Ste. Marie (June 14, 1671) in presence of Jesuit missionaries and representatives of Indian tribes, taking possession of the country in the name of Louis XIV.

**Saint'–Mar'ceaux'** (săɴ'mȧr'sō'), **Charles René de.** 1845–1915. French sculptor; a leader in the Academical school of sculpture.

**Saint–Marc Gi'rar'din'** (săɴ'mȧrk' zhē'rȧr'dăɴ'), **François Auguste.** *Orig.* **Marc Girardin.** 1801–1873. French politician and man of letters; contributed political articles to *Journal des Débats* (from 1828); professor of poetry, Sorbonne (1834); member of Chamber of Deputies (1835–48); author of literary criticism, esp. a *Cours de Littérature Dramatique* (1843–63), originally given as lectures at the Sorbonne.

**Saint'–Mar'tin'** (săɴ'mȧr'tăɴ'), **Louis Claude de.** 1743–1803. French mystic philosopher; one of the Illuminati; at first under influence of Martínez Pasqualis (*q.v.*); later devoted himself to the philosophical speculations of Jakob Böhme. His followers were known as Martinists.

**St. Maur.** See SEYMOUR family.

**Saint'–Mé'min'** (săɴ'mā'măɴ'), **Charles Balthazar Julien Fe'vret' de** (fā'vrĕ' dẽ). 1770–1852. French engraver, b. Dijon, France; to America (1793); began engraving (c. 1796); engraved profile portraits of many distinguished Americans of early nineteenth century.

**Saint'–Pierre'** (săɴ'pyâr'), Abbé **de.** *Real name* **Charles Irénée Cas'tel'** (kȧs'tĕl'). 1658–1743. French writer; abbot of Tiron (1695); accompanied Cardinal de Polignac to Congress of Utrecht (1712) and published *Projet de Paix Perpétuelle* (1713); wrote other studies on contemporary social, political, and economic problems.

**Saint–Pierre.** 1737–1814. See Jacques Henri BERNARDIN DE SAINT-PIERRE.

**Saint'–Ré'al'** (săɴ'rā'ȧl'), Abbé **de. César Vi'chard'** (vē'shȧr'). d. 1692. French historian; author of *La Conjuration des Espagnols contre Venise* (1674), *Vie de Jésus-Christ* (1678), etc.

**Saint–Rémy de Valois, Jeanne de.** See under Marc Antoine de LA MOTTE.

**Saint'–Saëns'** (săɴ'säɴs'), **Camille,** *in full* **Charles Camille.** 1835–1921. French pianist, organist, and composer; organist at the Madeleine (1858–77). Composer of operas, symphonies and symphonic poems, chamber music, choral works, and much piano and church music. Among his best-known compositions are the opera *Samson et Dalila,* the symphonic poems *Phaëton, Le Rouet d'Omphale, La Danse Macabre, La Jeunesse d'Hercule,* symphonies in A minor and C minor, a G minor piano concerto, and the humorous suite *Le Carnaval des Animaux.*

**Saints'bur·y** (sānts'bẽr·ĭ; -brĭ), **George Edward Bateman.** 1845–1933. English critic, journalist, and educator, b. Southampton. Journalist in London (1876–95); professor of English, Edinburgh (1895–1915). Among his many books are *Short History of French Literature, and French Lyrics* (1882), *Essays in English Literature* (1890; 2d series, 1895), *Nineteenth Century Literature* (1896), *Sir Walter Scott* (1897), *Matthew Arnold* (1899), *A History of Criticism* (3 vols., 1900–04), *Minor Caroline Poets* (3 vols., 1905–21), *A History of English Prosody* (3 vols., 1906–10), *The Later Nineteenth Century* (1908), *History of English Criticism* (1911), *History of English Prose Rhythm* (1912), *The English Novel* (1913), *A History of the French Novel* (vol. I, 1917; II, 1919), etc.

**Saint'–Si'mon'** (săɴ'sē'môɴ'), Duc **de. Louis de Rou'vroy'** (dẽ rōō'vrwȧ'). 1675–1755. French soldier, statesman, and writer, b. Paris. Served in Louis XIV's armies; distinguished himself at Namur and Neerwinden, and at the royal court. Member of the council of regency at beginning of reign of Louis XV; ambassador to Spain (1721). His fame rests on his *Mémoires* in which he described and commented on French affairs and the French court over a period of about thirty years, during reigns of Louis XIV and Louis XV.

**Saint–Simon,** Comte **de. Claude Henri de Rou'vroy'** (dẽ rōō'vrwȧ'). 1760–1825. French philosopher and social scientist, b. Paris; served (1777–83) as volunteer in French troops fighting with Americans in American Revolution. On return to France (1783), amassed fortune by land speculation and then lost it all in his various experiments. Developed his social theories in a series of treatises, including *L'Industrie ou Discussions Politiques, Morales et Philosophiques...*(1817), *Système Industriel* (1820–23), *Nouveau Christianisme* (1825). His theories were developed by his disciples into a system known as Saint-Simonianism. He is regarded as founder of French socialism.

**St. Victor, Hugh** *or* **Hugo of.** See HUGH OF ST. VICTOR.

**Saint–Victor, Niepce de.** See NIEPCE DE SAINT-VICTOR.

**Saint'–Vic'tor'** (săɴ'vēk'tôr'), **Paul de.** *In full* **Paul Bins** (băɴs), Comte **de Saint–Victor.** 1825–1881. French literary critic.

**St. Vincent,** Earl of. See John JERVIS.

**Sai·on·ji** (sī·ôn·jē), Prince **Kimmochi.** 1849–1940. Japanese statesman, b. Kyoto; began official career as vice-senator and senator (1881–84); worked with Ito on the constitution; minister to Austria (1885–87), to Germany (1887–91); vice-president of House of Peers (1893); privy councilor, minister of education, and acting prime minister for varying periods (1892–1906); leader of the Seiyukai (1903); twice prime minister, forming his own cabinet (1906–08; 1911–12); retired from politics (1914); represented Japan at Paris Peace Conference (1919); granted title of prince (1922); last surviving member of the genro; a statesman of genuine liberal and democratic views.

**Sais'set'** (sĕ'sĕ'), **Émile Edmond.** 1814–1863. French philosopher.

**Sa'ite** (sā'īt) *or* **Sa·it'ic** (sȧ·ĭt'ĭk). Name of two dynasties, XXIVth (718–712 B.C.) and XXVIth (663–525 B.C.), of Egyptian kings from ancient city of Sais in the Nile delta, capital of XXVIth dynasty. See *Table (in Appendix)* for EGYPT.

**Sai·to** (sī·tō), **Hiroshi.** 1886–1939. Japanese diplomat; minister to Netherlands (1933) and U.S. (1934–38).

**Saito, Jiro.** 1893– . Japanese army officer, regarded as one of chief agents of Japanese fifth-column activities in Hawaii, Philippines, Netherlands Indies, Malaya, etc.; in Manchuria at time of "Mukden incident" (1931); to Bangkok to reorganize Siamese army (1934); later (1940–41) active in Indo-China and Thailand.

**Saito,** Viscount **Makoto.** 1858–1936. Japanese admiral and administrator; naval aide-de-camp to the emperor in the Chinese-Japanese War (1894–95); served in Russo-Japanese War (1904–05); minister for the navy (1913–14); governor general of Chosen (1919–27, 1929–31); prime minister of Japan (1932–34); keeper of privy seal (1935–36); assassinated in February mutiny.

**Sa·jous'** (sȧ·zhōō'), **Charles Eu'cha·riste de Mé'di·cis** (chärlz ū'kȧ·rĭst dē mĕd'ĭ·sē). 1852–1929. French-born physician in U.S.; son of Charles de Médicis-Jodoigne; assumed name of his stepfather, Charles Sajous. Professor of therapeutics, Temple U. (1909–22); professor of applied endocrinology, Pennsylvania Post Graduate School (1921–29). Edited *Annual and Analytical Cyclopaedia of Practical Medicine,* later titled *Sajous's Analytic Cyclopaedia...* (from 1898); managing editor, *New York Medical Journal* (1911–19). Author of *The Internal Secretions and the Principles of Medicine* (2 vols., 1903–07).

**Sakajawea.** Variant of SACAGAWEA.

**Sa'kel** (zä'kĕl), **Manfred.** 1906–1957. Psychiatrist, b. in Austria; to U.S. (1937). Announced before the Vienna Medical Society his discovery of the method of treating schizophrenic patients with overdoses of insulin to produce shock (1933).

**Sa'kha·rov'** (säk'ă·rôf'; säk'-; -rôv'), **Andrei Dimitrievich.** 1921– . Russian physicist and civil libertarian. Awarded Nobel prize for peace (1975).

**Saki.** Pseudonym of Hector Hugh MUNRO.

**Saklatvala, Shapurji.** 1874–1936. Merchant, lawyer, and politician, b. Bombay, India; joined family mercantile firm of Tata Sons in Bombay; a founder of Tata Iron and Steel Works in India. To London (1905) and became associated with Labor and Socialist organizations; joined British Communist party; first Communist M.P. (1922–23, 1914–29).

**Sakyamuni.** See GAUTAMA BUDDHA.

**Sal'a** (săl'ȧ), **George Augustus Henry.** 1828–1895. English writer; correspondent of London *Daily Telegraph* in U.S. during Civil War, in France (1870–71), Russia (1876), Australia (1885); author of books of travel, social satire, novels, including *Quite Alone* (1864), and an autobiography, *Life and Adventures* (1895).

**Sal'a·din** (săl'ȧ·dĭn). *Arab.* **Ṣa·lāḥ'–al–Dīn'** (sȧ·lä'-hōōd·dēn') **Yūsuf ibn–Ayyūb.** 1138–1193. Sultan of Egypt and Syria; vizier in Egypt (c. 1169); suppressed Fatimid dynasty (1171) and was proclaimed sultan (1174); conquered most of Syria; campaigned to drive the Christians from Palestine, and defeated them in a battle near Tiberias (1187); went on to capture Acre, Jerusalem, Ashkelon, and other towns. Fought an army of crusaders (Third Crusade, 1189–92) under Richard I of England and Philip II of France; lost Caesarea and Jaffa, and was forced (1192) to accept a three-year truce. Renowned for courage and magnanimity.

**Sa'la·man'ca** (sä'lä·mäng'kä), **Daniel.** 1869–1935. Bolivian political leader; president of Bolivia (1931–34); broke off diplomatic relations with Paraguay (1931); declared war (1933). Forced to resign (1934).

**Salamanca y Ne·gre'te** (ē nȧ·grā'tā), **Manuel.** 1831–1891. Spanish general; commanded in civil war (1873); governor of Cuba (1889–90).

**Sa·lan'dra** (sä·län'drä), **Antonio.** 1853–1931. Italian statesman; minister of agriculture (1899–1900) and finance (1906, 1909–10); premier (1914–16); declared neutrality of Italy (Aug., 1914); formed alliance with Triple Entente; declared war on Austria (May, 1915); representative at Paris Peace Conference (1919). Opposed to Fascism (to 1926); senator (1928 ff.).

**Sa'las Bar'ba·dil'lo** (sä'läs bär'bä·thē'lyō), **Alonso Jerónimo de.** 1581–1635. Spanish writer; friend of Cervantes; known esp. for picaresque novels and short stories.

**Sa'la·ver'ry** (sä'lä·vĕr'rē), **Felipe Santiago.** 1806–1836. Peruvian general; led a force against Gamarra (1834); proclaimed himself chief of Peru (1835–36); defeated in battle, captured, and shot by Santa Cruz of Bolivia (1836).

**Sa·la·zar'** (sȧ·lȧ·zär'), **Antonio de O·li·vei'ra** (thē ō·lē·vā'ē·rȧ). 1889–1970. Portuguese statesman; prime minister and minister of finance (from 1932) and minister of war and foreign affairs (from 1936), virtual dictator of Portugal. Chiefly responsible for draft of new Portuguese constitution (1933).

**Sa'la·zar' y Tor'res** (sä'lä·thär' ē tôr'rās), **Agustín de.** 1642–1675. Spanish poet and playwright; author of a number of comedies, of which *Segunda Celestina* has survived to the present day.

**Sal·da'nha** (säl·dä'nyȧ), Duque **de. João Carlos de O·li·vei'ra e Daun** (thē ō·lē·vā'ē·rȧ ē thouN'). 1791–1876. Portuguese soldier and statesman; grandson of Pombal. Held military and diplomatic posts in Brazil (about 1810–22). Minister of foreign affairs (1825); governor of Oporto (1826–27); supported Dom Pedro against usurper Dom Miguel; appointed marshal (1834); minister of war and president of the council (1835); exiled (1836–46) after instigating counterrevolution against Septembrists; premier (1846–49, 1851–56, 1870).

**Sale** (sāl), **George.** 1697?–1736. English Orientalist; published highly paraphrastic English translation of the Koran (1734).

**Sale,** Sir **Robert Henry.** 1782–1845. British soldier; renowned for his defense of Jalalabad (1841–42).

**Salerno, Masuccio di.** See MASUCCIO DI SALERNO.

**Sales'bur·y** (sālz'bĕr·ĭ; -brĭ) *or* **Salis'bur·y** (sôlz'-), **William.** 1520?–?1600. Welsh scholar; edited collection of Welsh proverbs, probably first book printed in Welsh (c. 1546); compiler of *Dictionary in Englyshe and Welshe* (1547). Translated New Testament into Welsh, with assistance of Richard Davies, Bishop of St. Davids, and Thomas Huet (printed 1567).

**Salian** house. See FRANCONIAN house.

**Sa·lie'ri** (sä·lyâ'rē), **Antonio.** 1750–1825. Italian composer; court Kapellmeister in Vienna (1788–1824); composer esp. of church music and operas.

**Sa'lim·be'ne** (sä'lēm·bâ'nâ), Fra. *Also* **Ognibene di Gui'do d'A·da'mo** (dē gwē'dō dä·dä'mō). 1221–?1289. Italian monk and chronicler; known chiefly for his chronicle dealing with the period 1168–1287.

**Sa·li'nas** (sä·lē'näs), **Pedro.** 1892–1951. Spanish poet and educator; professor, Johns Hopkins (1940). English translations (by Eleanor Turnbull) from his selected verse published as *Lost Angel and Other Poems* (1938) and *Truth of Two and Other Poems* (1940).

**Sal′in·ger** (săl′ĭn·jẽr), **Jerome David.** 1919– . American author. Works include *Catcher in the Rye* (1951), *Nine Stories* (1953), *Franny and Zooey* (1961), *Seymour: An Introduction* (1963), etc.

**Sa′lis** (zä′lĭs), **Johann Gaudenz.** Baron **von Sa′lis-See′wis** (-zā′vĭs). 1762–1834. Swiss soldier and poet. Some of his songs were translated by Longfellow.

**Salis′bur·y** (sôlz′bẽr·ĭ; -brĭ). See also SALESBURY.

**Salisbury.** (1) Earls of. See William LONGSWORD; MONTACUTE family; NEVILLE family. (2) Earls and marquises of. See CECIL family. (3) Countess of. See *Margaret Pole*, under POLE family.

**Salisbury, Frank O.** 1874–1962. English portrait, historical, and figure painter.

**Salisbury, John of.** See JOHN OF SALISBURY.

**Salisbury, Roger of.** See ROGER OF SALISBURY.

**Salisbury, Rollin D.** 1858–1922. American geologist; professor, Chicago (1892–1922), authority on glacial and Pleistocene deposits; author of *Geology* (with Thomas C. Chamberlin, 1906).

**Salk** (sô[l]k), **Jonas Edward.** 1914– . American physician, b. New York City. Developed vaccine (the Salk vaccine) for prevention of poliomyelitis (1954); director, Salk Inst. for Biological studies (1963– ).

**Sal′lust** (săl′ŭst). *Full Latin name* **Gaius Sal·lus′ti·us Cris′pus** (să·lŭs′chĭ·ŭs [-tĭ·ŭs] krĭs′pŭs). 86–34 B.C. Roman historian and politician; tribune of the people (52 B.C.). Partisan of Julius Caesar; quaestor (49); praetor (46); accompanied Caesar to Africa and was present at defeat of Pompeian army at Thapsus (46). Governor of Numidia, where he amassed great fortune. On return to Rome, devoted himself to historical writing. His *History of the Jugurthine War* and *Conspiracy of Catiline* are extant; only fragments of his *History of the Roman Republic* have survived.

**Sal·ma′si·us** (săl·mā′zhĭ·ŭs; -zhŭs; -shĭ·ŭs; -shŭs), **Claudius.** *Latinized form of* **Claude de Sau′maise′** (dē sō′mâz′). 1588–1653. French classical scholar; professor at Leiden (1631 ff.). Chiefly remembered for his *Defensio Regia pro Carolo I* (1649), which occasioned Milton's *Pro Populo Anglicano Defensio* (1650) in rebuttal. Reputation as a scholar rests upon his publication of Casaubon's notes on *Augustan History* with many original notes of his own and his commentary (1629) on Solinus's *Polyhistor*.

**Sal′mi·nen** (säl′mĭ·nĕn), **Sally.** 1906– . Finnish author; to U.S. (1930); m. Johannes Dyrkopp (1940); author of *Katrina* (1936) and *Mariana* (1940).

**Salm′on** (săm′ŭn), **Daniel Elmer.** 1850–1914. American veterinarian; investigator, U.S. Department of Agriculture (1879–84); chief, Bureau of Animal Industry (1884–1905). Inaugurated meat-inspection system, quarantine period for imported livestock, and methods for suppression of contagious diseases of cattle.

**Salm′on** (săm′ŭn), **George.** 1819–1904. Irish mathematician and theological writer; prof. of divinity (1866–88), provost (1888–1902), Trinity Coll., Dublin.

**Sal′mon** (săl′mŭn), **Thomas William.** 1876–1927. American psychiatrist; on staff, U.S. Public Health Service (1903–15); had much to do with regulations to bar mentally unfit immigrants from entering U.S. With American army in France during World War; consultant in controlling shell shock among troops.

**Salm′-Salm′** (zälm′zälm′), Princess **Agnes Elisabeth Wi·no′na** (wĭ·nō′nȧ) **Le·clercq′** (lē·klâr′), *nee* **Joy** (joi). 1840–1912. Wife of German soldier of fortune Felix Nepomuk, Prince Salm-Salm (m. 1862); b. Franklin County, Vt., or, possibly, Philipsburg, Quebec. Accompanied husband in American Civil War service (1862–65) and to Mexico (1866), where Salm-Salm became aide to Emperor Maximilian. Salm-Salm killed at Gravelotte (1870); Princess Salm-Salm organized hospital brigade and served through Franco-Prussian War; resident in Germany thereafter; m. Charles Heneage (1876). Author of *Ten Years of My Life* (2 vols., 1876).

**Sa·lo′me** (sȧ·lō′mē). In the Bible, wife of Zebedee and mother of the apostles James and John; one of the women who watched the crucifixion of Jesus (*Matthew* xxvii. 56; *Mark* xv. 40) and went to the sepulcher on the resurrection morning (*Mark* xvi. 1).

**Salome.** 14? A.D.–before 62 A.D. Daughter of Herodias (*q.v.*) and Herod Philip, granddaughter of Herod the Great. Instructed by her mother, asked Herod Antipas for the head of John the Baptist as a reward for her dancing (*Mark* vi. 21–28). Married (1) Philip the Tetrarch, and (2) Aristobulus, son of Herod of Chalcis and king of Lesser Armenia. Subject of many famous paintings, of a poem by Oscar Wilde and an opera (1905) by Richard Strauss.

**Salomon.** Variant of SOLOMON.

**Sal′o·mon** (săl′ō·mŭn), **Haym** (hīm). 1740?–1785. Merchant and financier, b. at Lissa, Poland; to America (1772); founded mercantile and brokerage business in New York City. Imprisoned by British in New York as a spy (1776, again 1778); condemned to death (1778) but escaped to American lines. Opened brokerage business, Philadelphia; paymaster general of French forces in America; handled war subsidies advanced by French and Dutch governments; aided in maintaining American credit by extending large cash advances to American treasury. Also gave financial aid to many patriot leaders, including Jefferson, Madison, and Randolph.

**Sa′lo′mon′** (sȧ′lô′mōN′), **Louis Étienne Félicité.** 1820–1888. Haitian general and politician; commander in chief of the Haitian army (1855–59); in exile (1859–79); president of Haiti (1879–88).

**Salt** (sôlt), Sir **Titus.** 1803–1876. English manufacturer; wool stapler; started wool spinning (1834), devising machinery for using coarse Russian wool or donskoi; discovered method of manufacturing alpaca (1836); opened model manufacturing town of Saltaire (1853); Liberal M.P. (1859).

**Sal′ten** (zäl′tĕn), **Fe′lix** (fā′lĭks). *Pseudonym of* **Felix Salz′mann** (zälts′män). 1869–1945. Hungarian writer; author of essays, plays, and works of fiction, including *Bambi, City Jungle, Fifteen Rabbits, Hound of Florence, Samson and Delilah, Florian, the Emperor's Stallion, Bambi's Son, Good Comrades, A Forest World.*

**Sal′ter** (sôl′tẽr), 1st Baron **James Arthur.** 1881– English economist; secretary of Allied Maritime Transport Council (1918); member of Supreme Economic Council (1919); general secretary of Reparation Commission (1920–22); director of economic and finance section, League of Nations (1919–20; 1922–31), and member of advisory council of League (from 1932); professor of political theory and institutions, Oxford (1934–44), M.P. (1937–50).

**Sal′ton·stall** (sôl′t′n·stôl), **Gurdon.** 1666–1724. American clergyman, b. Haverhill, Mass. Governor of Connecticut (1707–24). Established system of ecclesiastical discipline embodied by the Saybrook Synod in the Saybrook Platform (1708). Influenced chartering of Yale College and its removal from Saybrook to New Haven. His grandfather **Richard Saltonstall** (1610?–1694) came to America (1630) and was one of original settlers of Watertown, Mass. A descendant, **Leverett Saltonstall** (1892–1979), b. Chestnut Hill, Mass.; A.B. (1914),

LL.B. (1917), Harvard; lawyer; governor of Massachusetts (1939–44); U.S. senator (from (1944–67).

**Sal'tus** (sôl'tŭs), **Edgar Evertson.** 1855–1921. American author, b. New York City; LL.B., Columbia; author of *The Philosophy of Disenchantment* (1885), *The Anatomy of Negation* (1886), *Mr. Incoul's Misadventure* (1887), *The Pace That Kills* (1889), *Vanity Square* (1906), *The Monster* (1912), *The Imperial Orgy* (1920), etc.

**Saltykov, Mikhail Evgrafovich.** See N. SHCHEDRIN.

**Sal·ty·kov'** (sŭl·tĭ·kôf'), Count **Pëtr Semënovich.** 1698?–1772. Russian field marshal; commanded Russian army in the Seven Years' War (1756–63), and notably in the victory at Kunersdorf (1759).

**Saltz'mann** (zälts'män), **Karl.** 1847–1923. German painter.

**Sal'va·to're** (säl'vä·tō'rȧ), **Vic'tor** (vĭk'tẽr). 1884–1965. Sculptor, b. in Tivoli, Italy; to U.S. (1886); among his portrait busts is one of James Fenimore Cooper in American Hall of Fame.

**Salvator Rosa** *or* **Salvatoriello.** See Salvator ROSA.

**Sal·ve'mi·ni** (säl·vā'mē·nē), **Gaetano.** 1873–1957. Italian historian; member, Chamber of Deputies (1919–21); arrested as anti-Fascist (1925); settled in London; visiting professor, Harvard (1930) and Yale (1932); lecturer, history of Italian civilization, Harvard (1933–48). Author of *Mazzini* (1915), *The Fascist Dictatorship in Italy* (1927), *Under the Axe of Fascism* (1936), *Italian Fascism* (1938), etc.

**Salvi, Giovanni Battista.** See Il SASSOFERRATO.

**Sal'vi·a'nus** (săl'vĭ·ā'nŭs). Ecclesiastic; ordained priest (c. 428 A.D.); author of *De Gubernatione Dei.*

**Sal·via'ti** (säl·vyä'tē), **Antonio.** 1816–1900. Italian mosaicist; his mosaic works are in Westminster Abbey, St. Paul's Cathedral (London), cathedrals at Erfurt, Aachen, etc.

**Salviati, Cecco di.** *Real name* **Francesco de' Ros'si** (dā rōs'sē). 1510–1563. Italian painter; protégé of Cardinal Giovanni Salviati; assisted Primaticcio in decoration of Fontainebleau.

**Salviati, Leonardo.** *Academic name* **In'fa·ri·na'to** (ēn'fä·rē·nä'tō). 1540–1589. Italian humanist; attacked work of Tasso; known chiefly for *Avvertimenti della Lingua sopra il Decamerone* (1584, 1586).

**Sal·vi'ni** (säl·vē'nē), **Tommaso.** 1829–1916. Italian tragedian; achieved distinction in Niccolini's *Edipo* and Alfieri's *Saul.* First appeared in U.S. (1873). Played title role in *Othello* with Edwin Booth as Iago (1886). Other roles were Paolo in *Francesca da Rimini*, Orosmane in Voltaire's *Zaïre*, and Samson, Hamlet, Macbeth, King Lear. His son **Alessandro** (1861–1896) was also an actor; best-known role, D'Artagnan in *The Three Guardsmen.*

**Sal'vi·us Ju'li·a'nus** (săl'vĭ·ŭs jōō'lĭ·ā'nŭs). fl. 2d century A.D. Roman jurist under Hadrian and the Antonines; twice elected consul; drew up the *Perpetual Edict* (edictum perpetuum), or *Praetor's Edict* (131 A.D.).

**Salz'mann** (zälts'män), **Christian Gotthilf.** 1744–1811. German educator, and author of many pedagogical works.

**Salzmann, Felix.** See Felix SALTEN.

**Sam** (sȧm), **Vilbrun Guillaume.** d. 1915. President of Haiti; led revolution (Jan., 1915); seized presidency for few months; overthrown and murdered by mob; his regime led to American intervention (Aug.–Sept., 1915).

**Sa'main'** (sȧ'măɴ'), **Albert Victor.** 1858–1900. French poet; one of founders of *Mercure de France* (1890) and contributor to *La Revue des Deux Mondes.* His verse is found in *Au Jardin de l'Infante* (1893), *Aux Flancs du Vase* (1898), and *Le Chariot d'Or* (1901).

**Sa·man'id** (sä·män'ĭd). A Persian native dynasty ruling from Bokhara (874–999), named after **Sa·man'** (sä·män'), a Persian noble of Balkh, whose great-grandson became its first ruler. It overthrew the Saffarids; fostered Persian literature and art; nominally subject to caliphs of Baghdad; conquered by Ghaznevids.

**Sa'mas·sum·u'kin** (sä'mäs·sŏŏm·ōō'kēn). Variant of SHAMASH-SHUM-UKIN.

**Sam'bha·ji** (sŭm'bä·jē), Raja. d. 1689. Maratha leader; son of Sivaji, whom he succeeded as Maratha ruler (1680–89); captured by Aurangzeb and executed.

**Sam'bourne** (săm'bẽrn; -bōrn), **Edward Linley.** 1844–1910. English draftsman and illustrator; member of staff (1871) and cartoonist in chief (1900–10), *Punch;* illustrator of Kingsley's *Water Babies* (1885).

**Sammu-ramat.** See SEMIRAMIS.

**Sam'o·set** (săm'ō·sĕt; sȧ·mŏs'ĕt, -ĭt). An early 17th-century Indian chief who became a firm friend of the Pilgrims settled at Plymouth.

**Sam'ple** (sȧm'p'l), **Paul Starrett.** 1896–    . American painter; artist in residence, Dartmouth College (from 1938).

**Samp'son** (săm(p)'s'n), **Emma,** *nee* **Speed** (spēd). 1868–1947. American writer, b. Louisville, Ky.; m. Henry Aylett Sampson (1896; d. 1920); best known as author of a series of "Miss Minerva" books.

**Sampson, William Thomas.** 1840–1902. American naval officer; grad. U.S.N.A., Annapolis (1861); president, board of inquiry into the destruction of battleship *Maine* (1898); commander in chief, North Atlantic Squadron, in Spanish-American War; the fleet under his command destroyed Spanish fleet under Cervera when it tried to escape from harbor of Santiago de Cuba (July 3, 1898). Controversy ensued when press credited W. S. Schley with the victory, because at beginning of the battle Sampson was several miles away in conference with General Shafter, and Schley's cruiser, the *Brooklyn*, was conspicuous in the engagement. Rear admiral (1899).

**Samsi-Adad.** See SHAMSHI-ADAD.

**Sam'son** (săm's'n). In the Bible, one of the Hebrew judges, a man of prodigious strength, who performed heroic deeds against the Philistines, but through the treachery of his paramour Delilah (*q.v.*) was finally captured by his enemies and his eyes put out (*Judges* xiii–xvi).

**Samson, George.** See Sir George ALEXANDER.

**Sam'son'** (säɴ'sôɴ'), **Joseph Isidore.** 1793–1871. French actor and playwright; excelled as comedian, head of the company at the Comédie Française (1832–64).

**Sam'son of Tot'ting·ton** (săm's'n, tŏt'ĭng·tŭn). 1135–1211. English ecclesiastic; mitred abbot of abbey of Bury St. Edmunds (1182–1211) and appointed by pope judge delegate in ecclesiastical cases; fought at siege of Windsor (1193); built up abbey materially and morally. The original of Carlyle's rhetorical essay on Abbot Samson in *Past and Present.* See JOCELIN DE BRAKELOND.

**Sam·so'nov** (sŭm·sô'nôf), **Aleksandr Vasilievich.** 1859–1914. Russian general who commanded the army which invaded East Prussia (Aug., 1914); decisively defeated in great battle of Tannenberg (Aug. 26–31, 1914); committed suicide.

**Sa·mu'dra·gup'ta** (sȧ·mŏŏ'drȧ·gŏŏp'tȧ). Second king (330?–?375) of Gupta dynasty in India; son of Chandragupta I; brought all Ganges valley and northern part of Deccan under his control; greater part of his long reign marked by prosperity, flourishing of literature and art, and religious tolerance.

**Sam'u·el** (săm'ū·ĕl). In the Bible, a Hebrew judge and

first of the great prophets, brought up under the high priest Eli, whom he succeeded as judge. The story of his life and ministry is recorded in the Old Testament book of *1 Samuel* (in Douay Bible named *1 Kings*), chapters i to xxv.

**Samuel, Harold.** 1879–1937. British pianist; best known as interpreter of Bach.

**Samuel,** Sir **Herbert Louis.** 1st Viscount **Samuel.** 1870–1963. English Liberal leader; chancellor of duchy of Lancaster, with seat in cabinet (1909–10, 1915–16); postmaster general (1910–14, 1915–16); home secretary (1916, 1931–32); special commissioner to Belgium (1919); first high commissioner to Palestine (1920–25); leader of Liberal party (1931–35). Author of *Liberalism: its Principles and Proposals* (1902), *The War and Liberty* (1917), *Belief and Action* (1937).

**Samuel, Marcus.** See Bearsted.

**Sam'u·els** (săm'ū·ĕlz), **Samuel.** 1823–1908. American ship captain, b. Philadelphia; in U.S. service during Civil War, commanding *G. B. McClellan* at capture of Fort Fischer (1865); won first transatlantic yacht race (1866) in James Gordon Bennett's *Henrietta.*

**Sam'u·el·son** (săm'ū·ĕl·sŭn), **Paul Anthony.** 1915– . American economist, b. Gary, Ind. At M.I.T. (1940– ); awarded Nobel prize in economic science (1970); wrote *Foundations of Economic Analysis* (1947); *Economics: An Introductory Analysis* (7th ed., 1967).

**Sämund.** = Sæmund.

**San'born** (săn'bẽrn; -bôrn), **Franklin Benjamin.** 1831–1917. American journalist and humanitarian; associated with John Brown and cognizant of his plans for seizure of Harpers Ferry; editor, Boston *Commonwealth* (1863–67), Springfield *Republican* (1868–72); associated with William T. Harris in establishing Concord School of Philosophy (1879–88). Wrote biographies or recollections of Thoreau (1882), John Brown (1885), S. G. Howe (1891), A. Bronson Alcott (with W. T. Harris, 2 vols., 1893), Pliny Earle (1898), Ralph Waldo Emerson (1901), Hawthorne (1908).

**Sanborn, James S.** 1835–1903. American businessman; joined staff of spice firm in Boston (1868); organized firm of Chase & Sanborn (1878).

**Sanborn, Walter Henry.** 1845–1928. American jurist; practiced, St. Paul, Minn. Judge, U.S. circuit court of appeals, eighth circuit (1892–1928).

**Sán'chez Cer'ro** (sän'chās sĕr'rō), **Luis M.** 1889–1933. Peruvian soldier and political leader, b. Piura, of Indian parentage; led revolt in Arequipa against Leguía y Salcedo (Aug., 1930) and forced his resignation; provisional president of Peru (1930–31); forced to resign by naval junta (Mar., 1931); elected president (1931–33).

**Sán'chez Co·el'lo** (sän'chāth kō·ā'lyō), **Alonso.** 1531?–1588. Spanish painter; employed at Madrid and Lisbon; succeeded Antonio Moro as court painter to Philip II.

**Sán'chez de Bus'ta·man'te y Sir·vén'** (sän'chās thā bōōs'tä·män'tā ē sēr·vān'), **Antonio.** 1865–1951. Cuban jurist, b. Havana; professor of international law, U. of Havana (1884 ff.); senator (1902–18). Cuban delegate plenipotentiary, second Hague Peace Conference (1907); to Paris Peace Conference (1919); member, Hague Tribunal (1908 ff.); judge, World Court (1921–39). Wrote numerous books on international law.

**San'cho** (săN'shōō). Name of two kings of Portugal of the house of Burgundy (*q.v.*): **Sancho I** (1154–1211); king (1185–1211); called "the City-Builder"; son of Alfonso I; waged war with Moors; built cities and roads. His grandson **Sancho II,** called **Ca·pê'lo** [kȧ·pā'lōō] (1208–1248); king (1223–48); son of Alfonso II; deposed by Pope Innocent IV (1245); waged civil war (1246–48) against his brother Alfonso (see Alfonso III).

**San'cho** (sän'chō). Name of six kings of early Spain: (1) *Of Asturias and León:* **Sancho I** (d. 967); king (955–967). (2) *Of Aragon:* **Sancho I** *or* **Sancho Ra·mí'rez** (rä·mē'rāth). = Sancho V of Navarre. (3) *Of Castile:* **Sancho I** (970–1035), called "the Great"; king (1027–35); see Sancho III of Navarre. **Sancho II,** called **el Fuer'te** (ĕl fwĕr'tā), *i.e.* the Strong (d. 1072); son of Ferdinand I; king (1065–72); at war with Sancho IV of Navarre; defeated (1071) and assassinated at siege of Zamora. **Sancho III** (d. 1158); king (1157–58). **Sancho IV** called **el Bra'vo** [ĕl brä'vō] (1258–1295); son of Alfonso X; king (1284–95); reign a period of continuous strife and violence.

**San'cho** (sän'chō). Name of seven kings of Navarre: **Sancho I** *or* **Sancho Gar·cés'** [gär·thās'] (d. 925); first king of Navarre (905–925); allied with Ordoño III of León, but defeated by the Moslems (920). **Sancho II** (d. 994); king (970–994). **Sancho III** *or* **Sancho Garcés el Ma·yor'** [ĕl mä·yôr'] (970–1035); grandson of Sancho I; king (1000–35); held lordship of Aragon; conquered Castile and León; king of Castile, as Sancho I (1027–35); proclaimed himself "King of Spain," but by his will divided kingdom among four sons. **Sancho IV,** called **el No'ble** [ĕl nō'blā] (d. 1076); son of García; king (1054–76); waged war against the king of Castile and fought the Moors; assassinated by his brother Ramiro; a scholar and author. **Sancho V** *or* **Sancho Ra·mí'rez** [rä·mē'rāth] (d. 1094); son of Ramiro I of Aragon and grandson of Sancho the Great; king (1076–94) and, as Sancho I, king of Aragon (1063–94); fought Moorish kings of Saragossa and Huesca (1080–89); killed at siege of Huesca. **Sancho VI,** called **el Sa'bio** (ĕl sä'byō), *i.e.* the Wise (d. 1194); king (1150–94); war with Aragon and Castile (1173–80), terminated by a truce (1180–90) and an alliance with Aragon. **Sancho VII,** called **el Fuer'te** (ĕl fwĕr'tā), *i.e.* the Strong (d. 1234); brother of Berengaria; king (1194–1234); spent three years in Africa (1199–1202) fighting in the service of the Almoravides; took part in the battle of Navas de Tolosa (1212); devoted himself to internal administration (1212–34); last of the direct line of Navarrese kings.

**Sancho Gar·cés'** (gär·thās'). (1) See Sancho I and III of Navarre. (2) d. 1021. King of Castile (995–1021).

**San'croft** (săn'krŏft; săng'-), **William.** 1617–1693. English prelate; dean of St. Paul's, London (1664); archbishop of Canterbury (1678); crowned James II (1685). Refused to read James II's Declaration of Indulgence (1688) exempting Catholics and dissenters from penal statutes and with six bishops, Ken, Lake, White, Turner, Lloyd, and Trelawny, petitioned against it; acquitted, with the bishops, of seditious libel; deprived of his see (1690).

**Sanctis, Francesco De.** See De Sanctis.

**Sanc·to'ri·us** (săngk·tō'rĭ·ŭs). *Latin name of* **Santorio San·to'rio** (sän·tô'ryō). 1561–1636. Italian professor of medicine at Padua (1611–24); conducted experiments on insensible perspiration; invented a clinical thermometer and an apparatus for measuring the pulse.

**Sand** (sănd; *Fr.* säNd), **George.** *Pseudonym of* **Amandine Aurore Lucie,** *nee* **Du'pin'** (dü'păN'). Baronne **Du'de·vant'** (düd'väN'). 1804–1876. French writer, b. Paris; m. Casimir Dudevant (1822; separated, 1831). Became intimate (1831–33) with Jules Sandeau (*q.v.*), with whom she collaborated in contributions to *Figaro.* Formed close attachment with Alfred de Musset, whom she accompanied to Italy (1833–34), where they became estranged; returned to Paris. Became one of artistic group including Chopin (with whom she had a liaison, 1838–47), Liszt, Balzac, Delacroix, and Lamennais.

Among her best-known works are *Indiana* (1832), *Valentine* (1832), *Mauprat* (1837), *Lélia* (1839), *Consuelo* (1842), *La Comtesse de Rudolstadt* (1843), *Jeanne* (1844), *La Mare au Diable* (1846), *Jean de la Roche* (1859), *Le Marquis de Villemer* (1860), *Lettres d'un Voyageur*, and her long *L'Histoire de ma Vie* (begun in 1847). Her son **Maurice Dudevant**, *known as* **Maurice Sand** (1823–1889), painter and writer, illustrated several of his own works, including *Masques et Buffons* (1859), a study of actors and types of the Italian comedy.

**Sand** (zänt), **Karl Ludwig.** 1795–1820. German university student; murdered August Friedrich von Kotzebue (Mar. 23, 1819), whom he believed to be a Russian spy and an enemy to German popular liberties; beheaded (May 20, 1820). The incident brought on the Carlsbad decrees restricting academic liberties, etc.

**San'day** (săn'dā; -dĭ), **William.** 1843–1920. English theologian; specialized in scientific study of New Testament.

**Sand'burg** (săn(d)'bûrg), **Carl.** 1878–1967. American author, b. Galesburg, Ill.; served in Puerto Rico during Spanish-American War. On staff of the magazine *System* (Chicago, 1913), Chicago *Daily News* (1917); won poetry prize offered by the magazine *Poetry* (Chicago, 1914); devoted himself to writing, lecturing, reading from his own works, singing folk songs, and collecting old ballads. Awarded half of poetry prize offered by Poetry Society of America (1919 and 1921). His poetry, mostly in free verse, includes *Chicago Poems* (1915), *Corn Huskers* (1918), *Smoke and Steel* (1920), *Slabs of the Sunburnt West* (1922), *Good Morning, America* (1928), *Early Moon* (1930), *The People, Yes* (1936); awarded Pulitzer prize for poetry for *Complete Poems* (1951). Author also of books for children, including *Rootabaga Stories* (1922) and *Potato Face* (1930), of biographies, *Abraham Lincoln—The Prairie Years* (1926), *Steichen the Photographer* (1929), *Mary Lincoln, Wife and Widow* (with Paul M. Angle; 1932); awarded Pulitzer prize for history for *Abraham Lincoln—The War Years* (1939).

**Sand'by** (săn(d)'bĭ), **Paul.** 1725–1809. English engraver and water-color painter; known as father of water-color art; an original member of Royal Acad. (1768); introduced aquatint process of engraving into England.

**San'deau'** (säN'dō'), **Jules,** *in full* **Léonard Sylvain Jules.** 1811–1883. French novelist and playwright; intimate with George Sand (1831–33), with whom he collaborated in contributions to *Figaro*, including the novel *Rose et Blanche* (1831). Librarian (1853) and curator (1859) of the Mazarin Library, Paris. Collaborator with Émile Augier in the play *Le Gendre de Monsieur Poirier* (1854).

**San'de·man** (săn'dē·măn), **Robert.** 1718–1771. Religious sectarian, b. Perth, Scotland; linen manufacturer in Scotland (1736–44); associated with John Glass, founder (c. 1730) of Glassites, a Scottish sect teaching that there is no authority in the New Testament for giving civil magistrates any jurisdiction in ecclesiastical matters; m. John Glass's daughter, Catherine (1737, d. 1746); served as elder in Glassite churches in Scotland and in London (1744–64). To America (1764) and organized congregations of Glassites or Sandemanians in New England cities and towns.

**Sander, Nicholas.** See SANDERS.

**Sanders.** See also SAUNDERS.

**San'ders** (zän'dērs), **Daniel.** 1819–1897. German philologist; compiled *Wörterbuch der Deutschen Sprache* (2 vols., 1860–65); edited *Zeitschrift für Deutsche Sprache* (1888–97); collaborated with Eduard Muret on *Enzyklopädisches Wörterbuch der Englischen und Deutschen Sprache* (4 vols., 1891–1901).

**San'ders** (sän'dērz) *or* **San'der** (-dēr), **Nicholas.** 1530?–1581. English Roman Catholic controversialist and historian; employed by Cardinal Hosius in checking spread of heresy; in Madrid, strove to effect Roman Catholic conquest of England; sent to Ireland (1579) as papal agent to stir up rebellion; after annihilation of his Spanish and Italian supporters by Lord Grey (1580), died of cold and starvation in woods. Author of *De Origine ac Progressu Schismatis Anglicani* (completed by Edward Rishton), basis of Roman Catholic accounts of English Reformation.

**San'ders** (zän'dērs), **Otto Liman von.** See LIMAN VON SANDERS.

**Sanderson.** See also SAUNDERSON.

**Sanderson, J. S. Burdon-.** See BURDON-SANDERSON.

**San'der·son** (sän'dēr·s'n), **Robert.** 1587–1663. English prelate and casuist; regius professor of divinity, Oxford (1642–48); deposed by Parliament (1648), and reinstated (1660); bishop of Lincoln (1660–63).

**Sanderson, Thomas James Cobden-.** See COBDEN-SANDERSON.

**Sand'ham** (săn'dăm), **Henry.** 1842–1910. Painter and illustrator, b. Montreal, Can.; studio in Boston (1880–1901), London, Eng. (1901–10); known esp. for illustrations of Poe's *Lenore*, Helen Hunt Jackson's *Ramona*, and *Glimpses of California and the Missions*.

**San·di'no** (sän·dē'nō), **Augusto César.** 1893–1934. Nicaraguan guerrilla leader; supported a liberal insurrection (1926) in Nicaragua and seized American property; proclaimed an outlaw by U.S. state department (1927); waged guerrilla warfare (1927–32) against U.S. marines, declaring that attacks were motivated solely by his patriotic aim to end U.S. intervention in Nicaraguan affairs. U.S. withdrew last of its marines from Nicaragua (1933) and Sandino agreed to amnesty terms. Assassinated in Managua.

**Sand'ler** (sänd'lēr), **Rickard J.** 1884–1964. Swedish statesman; cabinet official (1920, 1921, 1924); prime minister (1925); delegate to League of Nations (1927, 1929, 1931–39); minister of foreign affairs (1932–40).

**Sandon,** Viscounts. See under Sir Dudley RYDER.

**San'dow** (săn'dō; *Ger.* zän'-), **Eugene.** 1867–1925. Professional strong man and exponent of physical culture, b. Königsberg, Ger.; exhibited at Chicago World's Fair (1893).

**San'drart** (zän'drärt), **Joachim von.** 1606–1688. German painter, engraver, and art scholar; known esp. for his portraits, but painted also altarpieces, Biblical scenes, etc.

**Sandre, Thierry.** See Charles MOULIÉ.

**Sandrocottus** *or* **Sandracottus.** See CHANDRAGUPTA (MAURYA).

**Sands** (săndz), **Comfort.** 1748–1834. American merchant; in West Indian trade (to 1776); escaped from New York at time of British occupation; a founder and director, Bank of New York, the city's first bank (1784); president, New York chamber of commerce (1794–98). His son **Robert Charles** (1799–1832) was a writer; associated with William Cullen Bryant and Gulian Crommelin Verplanck in publishing an annual, *The Talisman* (from 1828), in which appeared his best work.

**Sandwich,** Earls of. See MONTAGU.

**Sandys** (săndz), **Edwin.** 1516?–1588. Anglican bishop of Worcester (1559–70) and London (1570–76); archbishop of York (1576–88); one of translators of the Bishops' Bible (1565). His second son, Sir **Edwin** (1561–1629), colonial organizer, leader in House of Commons (1604), assailed great monopolies, served on East India Co. committee (1619–23, 1625–29); member of council for Virginia (1607); joint manager of Virginia colony (1617), treasurer (1619–20), organized government of colony (1619); assisted in obtaining charter for the *Mayflower;* accused of attempt to establish republican, Puritan state in America, and imprisoned (1621). Sir Edwin's youngest brother, **George** (1578–1644), colonist and poet, treasurer of Virginia Co. (1621); resident in Virginia (1621–28); member of governor's council (1624, 1626, 1628); after return to England (1628?), represented Virginia (1640) when its assembly petitioned for restoration of its charter rights; also wrote *Ovid's Metamorphoses Englished . . . by G. S.* (1626), *A Paraphrase Upon the Psalmes of David and Upon the Hymns Dispersed throughout the Old and New Testaments* (1638), *A Paraphrase Upon the Song of Solomon* (1641).

**Sandys, Frederick,** *in full* **Anthony Frederick Augustus.** 1829–1904. English artist; associate of Pre-Raphaelite group; attracted attention with *A Nightmare* (1857), a lithographic caricature of Millais's *Sir Isumbras at the Ford;* for magazines, executed woodcuts from Scandinavian mythology and medieval legends; known chiefly for crayon portraits of Tennyson, Matthew Arnold, Browning, John Morley, John Richard Green, and others.

**Sandys,** Sir **John Edwin.** 1844–1922. English classical scholar; editor of many Greek classics.

**Sandys, Oliver.** *Real name* **Marguerite Florence Hé′lène** (hā′lĕn) **Ev′ans** (ĕv′ănz), *nee* **Jer′vis** (jûr′vĭs). 1894–1964. British writer, b. Burma; m. Caradoc Evans (*q.v.*). Author (under pseudonym Oliver Sandys) of *The Garment of Gold, Jinks, Mops, Whatagirl,* etc., and (as **Countess Bar·cyn′ska** [?bär·sĭn′skȧ]) of *Honeypot, Tesha, Under the Big Top, God and Mr. Aaranson, That Trouble Piece,* etc.

**San′ford** (săn′fẽrd), **Edward Terry.** 1865–1930. American jurist, b. Knoxville, Tenn.; practiced, Knoxville; associate justice, U.S. Supreme Court (1923–30).

**Sanford, Francis Hugh.** 1887–1926. British naval officer in World War I; engaged in raids at Zeebrugge and Ostend (1918).

**San·fuen′tes An′do·na·e′gui** (sän·fwān′tās än′dō·nä·ā′gē), **Juan Luis.** 1858–1930. President of Chile (1915–20).

**San·gal′lo** (säng·gäl′lō), **Giuliano da.** *Orig.* **Giuliano Giam·ber′ti** (jäm·bĕr′tē). 1445–1516. Florentine architect, sculptor, and military engineer; assisted Raphael in designing and building Saint Peter's; distinguished himself as military engineer in Florentine army, against Naples (1478). After accession of Julius II, joined with Michelangelo in competition with Raphael and Bramante for work on St. Peter's; after accession of Leo X, joined Raphael in continuation of this work. His brother **Antonio** (1455–1534), also an architect and military engineer, built a number of churches and palaces, and fortifications for Pope Alexander VI. A son of Giuliano, **Francesco** (1494–1576), was a sculptor. A nephew of Giuliano and Antonio, **Antonio Picconi da Sangallo,** *orig.* **Antonio Cor·dia′ni** [kôr·dyä′nē] (1483?–1546), architect and military engineer, worked with Raphael in directing building of St. Peter's; constructed many important fortifications for the pope. Another nephew, **Bastiano da Sangallo** (1484–1551), painter; painted chiefly Madonnas.

**Sang′er** (săng·ẽr), **Frederick.** 1918–     . British biochemist. At Cambridge U. (1940–     ); awarded Nobel prize in chemistry (1958) for work on the structure of proteins, especially insulin.

**Sanger, John** (1816–1889) and his brother **George** (1825–1911). Latterly known as Lord **John** and Lord **George.** English circus proprietors (from 1853); purchased Astley's amphitheater and exhibited an equestrian pantomime each winter, touring summers.

**Sanger, Margaret,** *nee* **Hig′gins** (hĭg′ĭnz). 1883–1966. American leader of birth-control movement; m. William Sanger (1900), J. Noah H. Slee (1922). A trained nurse by profession; indicted (1915) for sending pleas for birth control through the mails. Organized first American Birth Control Conference, New York (1921); made world tour on behalf of movement (1922); founder and first president, American Birth Control League. Author of books and pamphlets on birth control.

**San Giu·lia′no** (sän′ jōō·lyä′nō), Marchese **di. Antonino Pa′ter·nò′ Ca·stel′li** (pä′târ·nô′ kä·stĕl′lē). 1852–1914. Italian statesman; ambassador to London and Paris (1906–10); minister of foreign affairs (1910–14); stanch supporter of Triple Alliance.

**Sang′ster** (săng′stẽr), **Margaret Elizabeth,** *nee* **Mun′son** (mŭn′s'n). 1838–1912. American writer; m. George Sangster (1858, d. 1871); editor, *Harper's Bazaar* (1889–99); wrote novels and published collections from her magazine verse and prose contributions.

**Sangster, Margaret Elizabeth.** 1894?–     . American writer; granddaughter of Margaret Elizabeth Sangster (1838–1912); m. Gerrit Van Deth; contributing editor, *Christian Herald* (from 1913). Among her many books are *Cross Roads* (verse; 1919), *The Island of Faith* (novel; 1921), *Love Lightly* (novel; 1932), *Singing on the Road* (1936), *Little Letter to God* (1938).

**San′ka·ran Na′ir** (sŭng′kȧ·rȧn nä′yẽr), Sir **Chettur.** 1857–1934. Indian jurist and statesman; puisne judge, Madras high court (1908). Founder and editor, *Madras Review* and *The Madras Law Journal;* supporter of the Indian National Congress; member of Council of State of India (1925).

**San′key** (săng′kĭ), **Ira David.** 1840–1908. American evangelist and hymn writer; associated with Dwight L. Moody in evangelistic work (from 1870); toured U.S., England, Scotland, and Ireland (from 1873). Compiled collections of popular hymns used in evangelistic meetings, including *Sacred Songs and Solos* (1873), *Gospel Hymns* (a series, 1875–91).

**Sankey, John.** 1st Viscount **Sankey.** 1866–1948. English jurist; king's counsel (1909); judge, King's Bench Division of High Court of Justice (1914–28); lord chancellor of England (1929–35); British representative on Hague Tribunal (from 1930).

**San Mar·tín′** (sän′ mär·tēn′), **José de.** 1778–1850. South American soldier and statesman, b. Yapeyú, now in Argentina, on the Uruguay River. Offered his services to Buenos Aires in its fight for independence (1812); defeated Spaniards (1813) and succeeded Belgrano as commander in chief (1814). Organized army in Cuyo province, Argentina (1814–16), crossed the Andes and, with Gen. O'Higgins, defeated the Spanish at Chacabuco (1817) and Maipo (1818) in Chile; established independence of Chile; with aid of Lord Cochrane, developed a Chilean fleet and left with it for Peru (1820). Won over Peruvians and entered Lima (July, 1821) as Spanish withdrew; proclaimed independence of Peru; assumed title of "Protector of Peru." Resigned (Sept. 20, 1822), refusing to oppose Bolívar's ambition, but his work had made possible Bolívar's later victories over the Spanish at Junín and Ayacucho (1824). Regarded as an able soldier, and a farsighted and upright statesman.

**San′mi·che′li** (säm′mē·kâ′lē), **Michele.** 1484–1559. Italian architect and military engineer; associated with Antonio da Sangallo in work on fortifications; reputedly first to employ bastionary system of fortification and inventor of the pentagonal bastion.

**San Mi·guel′** (sän′ mē·gĕl′), Duque **Evaristo.** 1785–1862. Spanish soldier and statesman; active in uprising (1820) of Riego y Núñez (*q.v.*); minister of foreign affairs

(1823); to London (1824–30) and Paris (1830–34) as exile. On return (1834), was promoted field marshal; minister of war; organized reserve army; retired (1843). President, Madrid defense junta (1854 ff.)

**San'na·za'ro** (sän'nä·dzä'rō), **Jacopo.** *Academic name* **Ac'ti·us Sin·ce'rus** (ăk'shĭ·ŭs sĭn·sēr'ŭs). 1458–1530. Italian writer; author of *Arcadia* (1504), prototype of modern prose pastoral; also of Latin elegies, eclogues, epigrams, and the religious poem *De Partu Virginis* (1526); and, in Italian, *Rime, Farse,* and monologues.

**Sa'no di Pie'tro** (sä'nō dē pyâ'trō). *In full* **An·sa'no di Pie'tro di Men'cio** (än·sä'nō dē pyâ'trō dē mān'-chō). 1405–1481. Italian painter; notable as miniaturist.

**San·ra·ku** (sän·rä·kōō), **Kano.** *Professional name of* **Kimura Mi·tsu·yo·ri** (mē·tsōō·yō·rē). 1559–1635. Japanese decorative painter.

**San'som** (săn'sŭm), Sir **George Bailey.** 1883–1965. English diplomat and scholar; on consular duties in Japan (from 1904); professor, Columbia U., 1935–53. Author of *Historical Grammar of the Japanese Language* (1928), *A Short Cultural History of Japan* (1931), *A History of Japan* (3 vols.; 1958–63).

**San'son'** (säN'sôN'), **Charles Henri.** 1740–1795. Public executioner in Paris (1788–93); presided at execution of Louis XVI; succeeded in office by his son **Henri** (d. 1840), executioner of Marie Antoinette, and others.

**San'so·vi'no** (sän'sō·vē'nō), **Andrea.** *Real name* **Andrea Con·tuc'ci** (kōn·tōōt'chē). 1460–1529. Italian sculptor and architect; employed at Lisbon (1491–1500), Florence (1500–09), Rome (1509–13), and Loreto (1513). His works include a marble group *Baptism of Christ,* tombs of Cardinal Ascanio Sforza and Cardinal Girolamo Basso della Rovere, *Annunciation, Coronation of the Virgin.*

**Sansovino, Jacopo.** *Real name* **Jacopo Tat'ti** (tät'tē). 1486–1570. Italian sculptor and architect; pupil of Andrea Sansovino, whose surname he assumed; employed at Florence, Rome (to 1527), and Venice; Venetian state architect (1529). Among his Venetian architectural works are Cornaro Palace, library of St. Mark, churches of San Giorgio dei Grechi, San Francesco della Vigna, and San Martino, and the Zecca (mint); sculptural works include *St. John, Madonna,* monument to Doge Venier, and statues *Apollo, Athene, Mercury,* and *Peace* (in the campanile, Venice).

**San'ta An'na** (sän'tä ä'nä) *or* **San'ta A'na, Antonio López de.** 1795?–1876. Mexican general, revolutionist, president, and dictator, b. Jalapa. Led revolts against Iturbide (1822), against Guerrero (1828), and against Bustamante (1832). President of Mexico (1833–36); attempted to crush Texan Revolution, seized the Alamo (1836) but was defeated and captured by Sam Houston at San Jacinto (Apr. 21, 1836). Practically in control (1839–42), and made dictator (1844) by the constitution of 1843; deposed and exiled (1845); recalled and made provisional president (1847); commanded army against U.S. (1846–47), defeated at Buena Vista, Cerro Gordo, and Puebla, and driven out of Mexico City by Gen. Scott. Exiled (1848) but recalled and made president (1853–55); again exiled (1855; revolution of Ayutla). Lived in Cuba, Venezuela, St. Thomas, and U.S. (1855–74); returned to Mexico City (1874) and died in poverty and neglect.

**San'ta Cruz** (krōōth'), 1st Marquis of. **Álvaro de Ba·zán'** (thā bä·thän'). 1526–1588. Spanish admiral; distinguished himself in victory over Turks at Lepanto (1571) and in battle of Terceira against the Portuguese pretender (1583); credited with suggesting to Philip II the Spanish Armada.

**San'ta Cruz** (krōōs'), **Andrés.** 1792?–1865. Bolivian general and political leader; active in revolution of Peru against Spain (1820–23). President of Bolivia (1829–39); head (1836–39) of Peru-Bolivian Confederation, a union he had long planned; overthrown (1839) at battle of Yungay by Gen. Manuel Bulnes of Chile; exile in Europe.

**San'ta Ma·rí'a** (mä·rē'ä), **Domingo.** 1825–1889. President of Chile (1881–86); brought war with Peru and Bolivia to successful conclusion (1883).

**San·ta'na** (sän·tä'nä), **Pedro.** 1801–1864. Leader of revolution by which Santo Domingo separated from Haiti (1844); president, Republic of Santo Domingo (1844–48; 1853–56; 1858–61).

**San'tan·der'** (sän'tän·dĕr'), **Francisco de Paula.** 1792–1840. General and politician of New Granada (Colombia); served in the revolutionary war, and was promoted general of division at the battle of Boyacá (Aug. 7, 1819). Vice-president (1821–28), and acting president in Bolívar's absence (1821–26; 1827). Political activities led to banishment (1829–32). President of New Granada (1832–37). Regarded as founder of New Granada (Colombia).

**San'ta·rem'** (säNN'tȧ·rāēN'), Visconde **de. Manuel Francisco de Bar'ros e Sou'sa** (thĕ bär'rōōz ē sō'zȧ). 1791–1856. Portuguese statesman and scholar; minister of state (1827–33); author of works on early Portuguese history, maps, voyages of discovery, etc.

**San'ta Rit'ta Du·rão'** (säNN'tȧ rē'tȧ thōō·rouN'), **José de.** 1737–1784. Brazilian Augustinian monk and poet; chief work, *Caramurú* (epic on discovery and colonization of Bahia).

**San'ta·ro'sa,** Conte **San·tor're di** (sän·tôr'râ dē sän'-tä·rō'zä). **Annibale de' Ros'si di Po'ma·ro'lo** (dā rōs'sē dē pō'mä·rô'lō). 1783–1825. Italian patriot; subprefect of La Spezia under Napoleon (1812–14); captain in Sardinian army (1815); a leader in Piedmontese liberal movement; organized conspiracy against Austrians (1821); condemned to death, fled into exile; killed at Sphakteria while fighting for Greek independence.

**San'ta·ya'na** (sän'tä·yä'nä), **George** (jôrj). 1863–1952. Poet and philosopher, b. Madrid, Spain; to U.S. (1872); teacher of philosophy, Harvard (1889–1912; professor 1907–12); resident in Europe, chiefly in France and Italy (from 1912). Author of several volumes of verse, of philosophical works including *The Sense of Beauty* (1896), *The Life of Reason* (5 vols., 1905–06), *Winds of Doctrine* (1913), *Character and Opinion in the United States* (1920), *Soliloquies in England* (1922), *Scepticism and Animal Faith* (1923), *Dialogues in Limbo* (1925), *Platonism and the Spiritual Life* (1927), *The Realm of Essence* (1928), *The Realm of Matter* (1930), *The Genteel Tradition at Bay* (1931), *The Last Puritan* (1935), *The Realm of Truth* (1937), *The Realm of Spirit* (1940), and of the autobiographical *Persons and Places* (1943).

**San'terre'** (säN'târ'), **Antoine Joseph.** 1752–1809. French revolutionary politician and general; took part in storming of the Bastille (1789); commander in chief of the Parisian Garde Nationale (1792), protected royal family from the mob; appointed field marshal, guarded the royal prisoners up to the moment of their execution; a general of division, commanded a volunteer army against the Vendeans (1793) but without success; was arrested and imprisoned (1793–94); released after fall of Robespierre.

**Santerre, Jean Baptiste.** 1658–1717. French historical and portrait painter.

**San'ti** (sän'tē), **Giovanni.** 1435?–1494. Italian painter and poet; father of Raphael; court painter to duke of Urbino; author of a rhymed chronicle of art.

**Santi, Raffaello.** See RAPHAEL.

**San'til·la'na** (sän'tē·lyä'nä), Marqués **de. Íñigo Ló'pez de Men·do'za** (lō'pāth thā mān·dō'thä). 1398–1458. Spanish poet, nephew of Pedro López de Ayala. Prominent at court of John II of Castile; known particularly for contributions to Spanish versification; considered first to compose Spanish sonnets in imitation of Petrarch. Works include lyric poetry, didactic poetry, a collection of 100 proverbs in 8-verse stanzas (1449), 42 sonnets marking advent of Italianate epoch in Spanish versification, a Dantesque allegorical poem treating of the Genoese victory over Alfonso V (1444), and prose works.

**Sant'ley** (sănt'lĭ), Sir **Charles.** 1834–1922. English concert and operatic baritone; toured U.S. (1871, 1891), Australia (1889–90), and South Africa (1893, 1903).

**San'to·ri'ni** (sän'tō·rē'nē), **Giovanni Domenico.** 1681–?1737. Italian physician and anatomist.

**Santorio, Santorio.** See SANCTORIUS.

**San'tos** (sän'tōs), **Eduardo.** 1888–1974. Colombian politician, b. Bogotá; LL.D., National University of Bolivia; journalist, owner of *El Tiempo* (1913–37); served as member and president of the House of Representatives, and later as senator and president of the Senate; president of Colombia (1938–42).

**Santos, Máximo.** 1836–1887. President of Uruguay (1882–86).

**San'tos-Du'mont'** (säɴn'tōōz·dü'môɴ'), **Al·ber'to** (äl·bâr'tōō). 1873–1932. Brazilian aeronaut in France; built and flew (1898) cylindrical balloon with gasoline engine and (1901) airship that won prize for making first flight from St.-Cloud around Eiffel Tower and return; erected (1903) at Neuilly first airship station, where he kept his dirigibles; flew 715 feet in box-kitelike airplane (1906); constructed monoplane weighing 260 lbs. (1909).

**Sa·nu'do** (sä·nōō'dō) *or* **Sa·nu'to** (-tō), **Marino.** 1466–1535. Venetian chronicler and statesman; known chiefly for his *Diaries* (58 vols., pub. 1872–1902), a chronicle of period 1496–1533, invaluable as historical source material.

**Sanzio, Raffaello.** See RAPHAEL.

**Sa'phir** (zäf'ĭr), **Moritz Gottlieb.** 1795–1858. Austrian journalist and humorist; editor, *Berliner Schnellpost* (1826–29) and *Berliner Kurier* (1827–29), in Berlin, and *Der Humorist* (1837–58), in Vienna.

**Saphira.** See ANANIAS.

**Sa·pir'** (sȧ·pĭr'), **Edward.** 1884–1939. American anthropologist and linguist, b. in Pomerania; to U.S. (1889); professor of anthropology and linguistics, Chicago (1927–31), Yale (from 1931). Known esp. for studies on ethnology and linguistics of various Indians of northwestern U.S. Author of ***Language, an Introduction to the Study of Speech*** (1921), etc.

**Sapor.** Variant of SHAPUR.

**Sapper.** See Cyril MCNEILE.

**Sapphira.** See ANANIAS.

**Sap'pho** (săf'ō). fl. about 600 B.C. Greek lyric poet, of Lesbos. Little is known of her life history. Of her nine books of lyric poems, all are lost except one ode to Aphrodite and a few fragments. Among the ancients, she was ranked with Homer and Archilochus; Plato (in *Phaedrus*) refers to her as the "tenth Muse." The story that she threw herself from the Leucadian rock because of unrequited love for Phaon, a boatman of Mytilene, is legendary.

**Sapru,** Sir **Tej Bahadur.** 1875–1949. Indian jurist and Liberal leader; represented government of India at British Imperial Conference in London (1923), Round Table conferences (1930, 1931, 1932), and on Joint Parliamentary Committee (1933).

**Sa·rac'o·ğlu'** (sä·räj'ō·glōō'), **Şükrü.** d. 1953. Turkish statesman; minister of justice (1934–37) and foreign affairs (1937 ff.); prime minister (1942–46).

**Sar'ah** *or* **Sar'a** (sâr'ȧ; sā'rȧ) *or* **Sa'rai** (sā'rī; sâr'ā·ī). In the Bible, the wife of Abraham (*Genesis* xi. 29) and mother of Isaac (*Genesis* xvii. 15; xxi. 1–5).

**Sarapion.** See SERAPION.

**Sa'ra·sa'te y Na'vas·cués'** (sä'rä·sä'tā ē nä'väs-kwās'), **Pablo de.** 1844–1908. Spanish violin virtuoso and composer of pieces for the violin, as Spanish dances, fantasias, etc.

**Sa'ras·va'ti** (sŭ'rȧs·vŭ'tē), **Da·ya'nan'da** (dȧ·yä'nŭn'dȧ). 1827–1883. Brahman, founder of a native reform church of the Vedic religion, known as Arya Samaj, teaching that there are three eternal substances, God, spirit, and matter, that Vedic hymns are the only inspired scriptures, and advocating reform of caste system, abolition of child marriage, and spread of education.

**Sarawak,** Raja of. See Sir James BROOKE.

**Sa'ra·zen** (sär'ȧ·z'n), **Gene.** 1901– . American golfer, b. Rye, N.Y.; winner of U.S. national open championship (1922, 1932) and professional championship (1923, 1924, 1933) and British open championship (1932).

**Sar·biew'ski** (sär·byĕf'skē), **Maciej Kazimierz.** 1595–?1640. Polish Jesuit and poet, whose epigrams and lyrics gained him title of the Sarmatian, or Polish, Horace.

**Sar'cey'** (sȧr'sā'), **Francisque.** *Pseudonym* **Sa'ta'né' Bi'net'** (sȧ'tȧ'nā' bē'nĕ'). 1827–1899. French journalist and dramatic critic; contributor to *Figaro, L'Opinion Nationale, Le Temps*, and other Paris journals.

**Sar'da·na·pa'lus** (sär'd'n·ȧ·pā'lŭs). *Gr.* **Sar'da·na·pal'los** (-păl'ŏs) *or* **Sar'da·na·pa'los** (-pā'lŏs). Apparently the Greek form of Ashurbanipal (*q.v.*). An effeminate and immoral sovereign, ruler of Assyria (c. 822 B.C.); according to legend (account of Ctesias), burned himself, queen, and treasures with his palace when capture of Nineveh threatened; by some, but probably erroneously, identified with Ashurbanipal (reigned 669–626 B.C.); a similar fate actually befell Shamash-shum-ukin (c. 648 B.C.), Ashurbanipal's brother. Story treated by Byron in drama *Sardanapalus* (pub. 1821).

**Sar'dou'** (sȧr'dōō'), **Victorien.** 1831–1908. French playwright, b. Paris; achieved first success with *Les Premières Armes de Figaro* (1859) and *Les Pattes de Mouche* (1860), followed by long series of comedies and dramas, including *Nos Intimes* (1861), *Les Diables Noirs* (1863), *La Famille Benoîton* (1865), *Rabagas* (1872), *Divorçons* (1880), *La Tosca* (1887), *Cléopâtre* (1890; with Émile Moreau), *Thermidor* (1891), *Madame Sans-Gêne* (1893; with Émile Moreau), *Gismonda* (1894), *Spiritisme* (1897), *Robespierre* (1899), *La Sorcière* (1903), *La Piste* (1906).

**Sa·rett'** (sär·ĕt'), **Lew.** 1888–1954. American educator and poet, b. Chicago; professor of speech, Northwestern U. (from 1921). Among his volumes of verse are *Many, Many Moons* (1920), *The Box of God* (1922), *Ode to Illinois* (1924), *Slow Smoke* (1925), *Wings Against the Moon* (1931).

**Sar·fat'ti** (sär·fät'tē), **Margherita,** *nee* **Gras·si'ni** (gräs·sē'nē). *Pseudonyms* **Ci·diè'** (chē·dyâ') *and* **El Se·re'no** (āl sā·rā'nō). 1886–1961. Italian writer; art critic on staff of *Il Popolo d'Italia*, and literary critic on *La Stampa*. Author of a biography of Mussolini, a volume of verse, a novel, an essay (*America, or the Pursuit of Happiness*, 1937), and works on art and artists.

**Sarg** (särg), **Tony,** *in full* **Anthony Frederick.** 1882–1942. American illustrator and marionette maker, b. in Guatemala, of a German father and English mother; educated in Germany and served as officer in German army (to 1905). Illustrator in London (1905); to U.S. (1915) and naturalized (1921); creator of "Tony Sarg's Marionettes" (1915) and proprietor of marionette shows. Author and illustrator of *Tony Sarg's Animal Book* (1925), *Tony Sarg's Wonder Zoo* (1927), *Tony Sarg's Wonder Book* (1941), etc.

**Sar'gent** (sär'jĕnt), **Charles Sprague.** 1841–1927. American dendrologist, b. Boston; professor of horticulture, Harvard (1872–73), and of arboriculture (1879–1927). First director, Arnold Arboretum, Harvard (1873–1927). Edited *Garden and Forest* (1888–97); gathered the Jesup collection of woods of North America, now in American Museum of Natural History, New York City. Author of *The Silva of North America* (14 vols., 1891–1902), *Manual of the Trees of North America* (1905), etc.

**Sargent, Dudley Allen.** 1849–1924. American physical culturist; opened Hygienic Institute and School of Physical Culture, New York (1878). Also, organized in Cambridge (1881) Sargent School for Physical Education, designed to train physical-culture teachers.

**Sargent, Epes.** 1813–1880. American writer, b. Gloucester, Mass.; editor, Boston *Transcript* (1847–53). Author of plays, fiction, adventure books, verse, and miscellaneous works, notably books on spiritualism. His brother **John Osborne** (1811–1891) was a lawyer and writer; practiced law, New York (from 1841); best known work, *Horatian Echoes* (1893), with introduction by Oliver Wendell Holmes.

**Sargent, John Gar'i·bal'di** (găr'ĭ·bôl'dĭ). 1860–1939. American lawyer and public official, b. Ludlow, Vt.; attorney general of the United States (1925–29).

**Sargent, John Osborne.** See under Epes SARGENT.

**Sargent, John Sing'er** (sĭng'ẽr). 1856–1925. Painter, b. in Florence, Italy, of American parentage. Painted in Italy, Spain, and England; studio in London (1885); visited and painted in U.S. (1876, 1887, 1890, and almost annually from 1895); established studio in Boston (1903). Refused English knighthood (1907) on ground that he was an American citizen. Among his best-known works are mural decorations in the Boston Public Library; *Gitana, Hermit, Padre Sebastiano, The Wyndham Sisters*, and portraits of *W. M. Chase* and *Henry Marquand*, now in Metropolitan Museum of Art, New York City; *El Jaleo*, in Boston Museum of Art; *Carnation, Lily, Lily, Rose*, in Tate Gallery, London; *Carmencita*, in the Luxembourg, Paris; *Lake O'Hara*, in Fogg Art Museum of Harvard University.

**Sargent, Winthrop.** 1753–1820. American soldier in Continental army through American Revolution; active in affairs of Ohio Company; aided in founding Marietta, Ohio (1788). Appointed, by Congress, secretary of "Territory Northwest of the River Ohio" (1787–98). First governor, Mississippi territory (1798–1801). His grandson **Winthrop Sargent** (1825–1870) was a lawyer and historian; author of *The History of an Expedition Against Fort Du Quesne, in 1775; Under Major-General Edward Braddock* (1855), *Life and Career of Major John André* (1861).

**Sar'gon** (sär'gŏn). *Akkadian and Assyrian* **Sharrukin,** *i.e.* "the righteous king." Name of two kings:

**Sargon I.** King of Babylon (c. 2637–2582 B.C.; according to some, fl. 2872 B.C.); founder of Semitic dynasty of Akkad; unified Sumerian territory with capital at Agade; conquered Elam and Syria; favorite subject of later legends; succeeded by his (supposed) son Naram-Sin.

**Sargon II.** King of Assyria (722–705 B.C.), succeeding Shalmaneser V (*q.v.*); founder of Sargonid dynasty. Origin not known, but probably of the nobility. Consolidated the empire, putting down rebellions that continually broke out in various parts; conquered Samaria and destroyed northern kingdom of Israel (722–721), carrying people away to Assyria (*2 Kings* xvii); defeated Hama and Damascus (720); ravaged Armenia; seized Carchemish (717); carried out successful expeditions against Urartu, Philistia, etc.; received homage of Cyprus (709); separated Elam from Babylon; engaged in great war against Merodach-baladan of Babylon, whom he completely defeated; made himself king of Babylon (710); developed policy of transporting peoples of conquered regions to distant parts of empire; built, as royal residence, Dur-Sharrukin (modern Khorsabad) in mountains north of Nineveh; killed in expedition against Cimmerians in Asia Minor. Succeeded by his son Sennacherib.

**Sar'gon·id** (sär'gŏn·ĭd). Name of two dynasties: (1) The Semitic dynasty of Akkad (c. 2500 B.C.) of King Shar-galisharri. (2) An Assyrian dynasty (722–612 B.C.) founded by Sargon II (722–705), who was followed by Sennacherib (705–681), Esarhaddon (681–669), and Ashurbanipal (669–626); terminated by fall of Nineveh (612).

**Sar'is** (săr'ĭs), **John.** d. 1646. English merchant and sea captain who made first voyage of Englishmen to Japan (1612) and obtained emperor's commission to settle and trade in Japan. Cf. Richard COCKS.

**Sar'ment'** (sȧr'mäɴ'), **Jean.** 1897– . French actor and playwright; author of *Pêcheur d'Ombres* (1921), *Madelon* (1925), *Léopold le Bien-Aimé* (1927), *Bobard* (1930), etc.

**Sar·mien'to** (sär·myān'tō), **Domingo Faustino.** 1811–1888. Argentine political leader; exiled to Chile (1835–52) during Rosas regime; helped Urquiza defeat Rosas. President of Argentina (1868–74); terminated war of Triple Alliance against Paraguay; with help of Avellaneda, reorganized school system of Argentina (1875–88). Author of educational works.

**Sarmiento de Acuña, Diego.** See GONDOMAR.

**Sarmiento de Gam·bo'a** (thā gäm·bō'ä), **Pedro.** 1530?–after 1589. Spanish sea captain; sent (1579) to explore Strait of Magellan; made second voyage in attempt to settle a colony on Strait of Magellan (1583); captured by English on return trip and held prisoner (1583–88); all but two of colonists died of starvation; wrote report of his expedition (pub. 1708).

**Sar'noff** (sär'nŏf), **Da'vid** (dā'vĭd). 1891–1971. American radio executive, b. in Uzlian, Minsk, Russia; to U.S. (1900); president, Radio Corporation of America (1930–49), also of R.C.A. Communications, Inc., and allied companies; chairman of the board (1947–70).

**Sa·ro'lea** (sȧ·rōl'yȧ), **Charles.** 1870–1953. Scholar and publicist, b. Tongres, Belgium; lecturer and head of French and Romance department, Edinburgh (1894–1931). During World War I, traveled in Great Britain and United States lecturing and raising funds for Belgian relief. Among his many books are *H. Ibsen* (1891), *The Balkan Question* (1906), *Victor Hugo* (1911), *Europe's Debt to Russia* (1916), *The Russian Revolution* (1917), *Modern Brazil* (1921), *Impressions of Soviet Russia* (1924).

**Sa·ro'yan** (sä·rō'yän), **William.** 1908– . American fiction writer and playwright, b. Fresno, Calif. Author of short stories, as in *The Daring Young Man on the Flying Trapeze* (1934), *Little Children* (1937), *Love, Here is My Hat* (1938), *The Trouble with Tigers* (1938), *My Name is Aram* (1940), of plays, as *My Heart's in the Highlands* (1939), *The Time of Your Life* (1939), *Love's Old Sweet Song* (1939), *The Beautiful People*

(1941), *Razzle Dazzle* (1942; short plays), of *The Human Comedy* (1943; novel, originally written as a scenario).

**Sar′pi** (sär′pē), **Paolo,** *orig.* **Pietro.** *Also called* **Fra Paolo** *or* **Pau′lus Ven′e·tus** (pô′lŭs vĕn′ē·tŭs) *or* **Paulus Ser·vi′ta** (sûr·vī′tȧ) *or* **Brother Paul.** 1552–1623. Italian prelate, historian, scientist, and statesman; entered Servite order (1565), of which he became provincial (1579). Devoted himself to scientific and philosophical studies (from 1588); credited with discovery of contractility of the iris; opposed temporal power of pope; counselor of state to Venetian republic in its conflict with Paul V; counseled banishment of Jesuits from Venice. Known for his history of Council of Trent.

**Sar′rail′** (sȧ′rȧ′y′), **Maurice Paul Emmanuel.** 1856–1929. French general in World War I (1914–18); defended Verdun in first year of the war; commanded French army at Salonika (1915–18), captured Monastir (1916), dethroned Constantine I, King of Greece (1917). French high commissioner in Syria (1924).

**Sar′raut′** (sȧ′rō′), **Albert.** 1872–1962. French colonial administrator; governor general of Indo-China (1911–14, 1916–19); minister of colonies (1922, 1932); minister of interior (1927).

**Sar′ra′zin′** (sȧ′rȧ′zăN′), **Jacques.** 1588–1660. French sculptor; carved four statues for the high altar in Church of Saint Nicholas des Champs, Paris; decorated the central pavilion of the Louvre.

**Sar′re** (zär′ĕ), **Friedrich.** 1865–1945. German archaeologist and art scholar; founded (1904) Mohammedan art section in Berlin Museum, and was its curator (1904–31) and director (from 1922).

**Sar′rette′** (sȧ′rĕt′), **Bernard.** 1765–1858. French musician; founder (1789–95) and director (1797–1814), French Conservatory of Music, Paris.

**Sars** (särs), **Michael.** 1805–1869. Norwegian zoologist; known for work on metamorphosis of marine mollusks and on alternation of generations; established relation between living and fossil crinoids. His son **Johan Ernst** (1835–1917), historian and politician, described Norwegian life under Danish rule; influenced, by his writings, development of national spirit among Norwegians.

**Sars′field** (särs′fēld), **Patrick.** Titular Earl of **Lu′can** (lū′kăn). d. 1693. Irish Jacobite and soldier, descendant of Anglo-Norman family. Served against Monmouth at Sedgemoor (1685); assisted in James II's reorganization of Irish forces into a Roman Catholic army; fled with James II to France and returned with him to Ireland (1689); present at battle of the Boyne (1690) and caused William III to raise siege of Limerick (1690); after Limerick, joined French service with his troops.

**Sar′tain** (sär′tān), **John.** 1808–1897. Engraver, b. London, Eng.; to U.S. (1830). On staff of *Graham's Magazine* (1841); introduced pictorial illustration as a characteristic feature in American periodicals. A founder and proprietor of *Sartain's Union Magazine of Literature and Art* (1849–52), to which the leading literary figures of the day contributed. His son **Samuel** (1830–1906) was also an engraver; best known for his plates of Biblical subjects. John's daughter **Emily** (1841–1927) was an engraver and painter. Another son of John Sartain, **William** (1843–1924), was a painter; excelled in landscapes and genre paintings.

**Sar′ti** (sär′tē), **Giuseppe.** 1729–1802. Italian composer, in Venice, Milan, and St. Petersburg; composer esp. of operas and sacred music.

**Sar′to** (sär′tō), **Andrea del.** *Real name* **Andrea Domenico d'A′gno·lo di Fran·ce′sco** (dä′nyō·lō dē frän·chās′kō). *Family name* **Van·nuc′chi** (vän·no͝ok′kē). 1486–1531. Florentine painter; associated with Franciabigio (c. 1508–c. 1512); at court of Francis I, Paris (1518–19); known particularly as colorist and as master of chiaroscuro. Works include the frescoes *Adoration of the Kings* and *Birth of the Virgin* (in cloister of Church of Sant'Annunziata, Florence), frescoes from life of St. John the Baptist (in cloister of the Scalzi, Florence), and easel paintings, as *Annunciation, Holy Family, Pietà, Adoration of the Virgin,* and *Descent from the Cross* (all in Pitti Palace), *Madonna of the Harpies* (Uffizi Gallery), *Holy Family* (National Gallery, London), and portraits.

**Sarto, Giuseppe Melchiorre.** See Pope Pius X.

**Sar′ton** (sär′t'n), **George Alfred Leon.** 1884–1956. American scholar, b. Ghent, Belgium; to U.S. (1915), naturalized (1924); lecturer on history of science, Harvard (1916–18 and 1920–51), professor (1940–51); author of books and papers on the history of science.

**Sar·to′ri·us von Wal′ters·hau′sen** (zär·tō′rē·o͝os fōn väl′tĕrs·hou′zĕn), Barons: **August** (1852–1938), German economist; author of treatises on American economic conditions and problems and on conditions in Germany after World War I; his grandfather **Georg** (1765–1828), historian; his father, **Wolfgang** (1809–1876), geologist; and his son **Hermann Wolfgang** (1882–1954), musician and composer.

**Sar′tre** (sȧr′tr'), **Jean-Paul.** 1905– . French author, playwright, and philosopher. Awarded Nobel prize in literature (1964); wrote *Being and Nothingness* (1943), *No Exit* (1945), *Critique of Dialectical Reason* (1964), etc.

**Sar′wat Pa′sha** (sŭr′wăt [thăr′wăt] pȧ′shä), **Abd·el′ Kha′lek** (ȧb·do͞ol′ κä′lĭk). 1873–1928. Egyptian statesman; prime minister (1922, 1927–28).

**Sas·san′i·dae** (să·săn′ĭ·dē) *or* **Sas′sa·nids** (săs′ȧ·nĭdz) *or* **Sas·sa′ni·ans** (să·sā′nĭ·ănz). Name of last native dynasty (226–641 A.D.) of Persian kings, successors of the Arsacidae. Founded by Ardashir I, grandson of Sassan (hence the name) and overthrown by Arabs under Omar; it numbered about 25 kings, chief among them after Ardashir I being Shapur II, Yazdegerd I, Kavadh I, Khosru I and II; last sovereign was Yazdegerd III. See individual biographies for the kings; see also Bahram, Ormizd, and Narses.

**Sas′so·fer·ra′to, Il** (ēl säs′sō·fâr·rä′tō). *Real name* **Giovanni Battista Sal′vi** (säl′vē). 1605–1685. Italian painter; known particularly as painter of religious subjects, esp. Madonnas.

**Sas·soon′** (să·so͞on′). Name of a wealthy family of Spanish-Jewish origin attaining prominence in 19th century in Bombay, India, where **David Sassoon** (b. 1792), a Baghdad merchant, established a banking and mercantile business, carried on (from 1864) by his son Sir **Albert Abdullah David** (1818–1893), who contributed generously to philanthropies in Bombay and England and built (1872–75) as a gift to Bombay the Sassoon dock at Colaba. Sir Albert's grandson Sir **Philip,** *in full* **Philip Albert Gustave David** (1888–1939), art connoisseur; M.P. (from 1912); secretary to Sir Douglas Haig during World War I (1915–18); undersecretary of state for air (1924–29; 1931–37); first commissioner of works (from 1937). Other members of the family include Siegfried Sassoon (*q.v.*).

**Sassoon, Siegfried.** 1886–1967. English writer; served in World War. Author of verse, including *The Old Huntsman* (1917), *Counter Attack* (1918), *Satirical Poems* (1926), *The Heart's Journey* (1928), *Vigils* (1935), *Rhymed Ruminations* (1940), and of autobiographical prose works, *Memoirs of George Sherston* (originally published as three separate volumes: *Memoirs of a Fox-Hunting Man*, 1928, awarded Hawthornden prize and James Tait Black memorial prize; *Memoirs of an Infantry Officer*, 1930; *Sherston's Progress*, 1936), *The Old*

*Century and Seven More Years* (1938), *The Weald of Youth* (1942).

**Sas'tri** (shäs'trē; säs'-), **V. S. Sri'ni·va'sa** (shrē'nĭ·vä'sȧ; srē'-). 1869–1946. Indian statesman; member, viceroy's legislative council (1916–20), council of state (1920). Indian representative at British Imperial Conference in London (1921) and League of Nations Assembly (1921).

**Sa'tie'** (sȧ'tē'), **Erik.** *In full* **Alfred Erik Les'lie'–Sa'tie'** (lĕs'lē'-). 1866–1925. French composer; identified with ultramodern school of music; composed chiefly piano works.

**Sa·to** (sä·tō), **Eisaku.** 1901–1975. Japanese statesman. Prime minister of Japan (1964–72); awarded (with Sean MacBride) Nobel prize for peace (1974).

**Sato, Naotake.** 1882–1971. Japanese diplomat; minister to Poland and League of Nations; ambassador to Belgium and delegate to League (1931–32); ambassador to France (1933–36); minister of foreign affairs (1937–38); adviser to foreign office (1938–42); ambassador to Russia (1942–45).

**Sa'tow** (sä'tō), Sir **Ernest Mason.** 1843–1929. British diplomat; minister to Uruguay (1888), Morocco (1893), Japan (1895), China (1900–06). Author of *Murray's Handbook for Japan* (with A. G. S. Hawes), *English-Japanese Dictionary* (with M. Ishibashi), *A Guide to Diplomatic Practice*, etc.

**Sa·tsu·ma** (sä·tso͞o·mä). One of the four powerful clans of Japan, named from its early home in southwestern Kyushu; it supported the emperor at the time of the Restoration (1867–68). See SAIGO TAKAMORI.

**Sat'ter·lee** (săt'ĕr·lē), **Francis Le Roy.** 1881–1935. American roentgenologist, b. New York City. At age of fifteen, took first X-ray photograph in America; invented protective shield for X-ray operators; first to X-ray mouth and teeth.

**Satterlee, Henry Yates.** 1843–1908. American Protestant Episcopal clergyman; bishop, diocese of Washington (1896); planned and began Washington Cathedral.

**Sat'ur·ni'nus** (săt'ĕr·nī'nŭs), **Lucius Appuleius.** d. 100 B.C. Roman politician; partisan of Marius; quaestor (104 B.C.); tribune (103, 100). Sponsored law providing for distribution of land among veterans who served with Marius and for founding colonies to which Italians should be admitted. During year-end elections, his partisans clubbed the senatorial candidate to death; he was declared a public enemy and defeated in fight in the forum; stoned to death by members of opposition party.

**Sauck'el** (zou'kĕl), **Fritz.** 1894–1946. German newspaper publisher; Nazi official in Thuringia (1925), governor (1933); commissioner general of man power in occupied territories; hanged as war criminal.

**Sau'er** (zou'ĕr), **Emil.** Ritter **von Aich'ried** (fōn ĭκ'rēt). 1862–1942. German concert pianist; composer of concertos, sonatas, and études for the piano.

**Sauer'wein'** (sôr'wĕn'), **Jules.** 1880– . French journalist; foreign editor of *Le Matin* (1909–31) and *Paris-Soir* (1931 ff.); special correspondent of the New York *Times.*

**Saul** (sôl). First king of Israel (*1 Samuel* x–xxxi); a Benjamite, son of Kish; anointed as king by Samuel (c. 1025 B.C.); protector, later rival, of David (see also JONATHAN); defeated and killed by the Philistines in battle of Mount Gilboa; succeeded by David.

**Saul of Tar'sus** (sôl, tär'sŭs). = Saint PAUL.

**Saul'cy'** (sōl'sē'), **Louis Frédéric Joseph Cai'gnart'** (kĕ'nyȧr') **de.** 1807–1880. French archaeologist and numismatist.

**Saumaise, Claude de.** See Claudius SALMASIUS.

**Sau'ma·rez** (?sō'mȧ·rĕz; ?sō'mȧ'rā'), **James.** Baron **de Saumarez.** 1757–1836. British naval commander; made commander for gallantry off Dogger Bank (1781); distinguished himself at battle of Cape St. Vincent; wounded at battle of the Nile (1798); routed French and Spanish fleet at Algeciras (1801); commanded squadron in Baltic in war with Russia (1809–13); admiral (1814).

**Saun'ders** (sôn'dĕrz; sän'-). See also SANDERS.

**Saunders, Frederick.** 1807–1902. Author and librarian, b. London, Eng.; to U.S. (1837). Assistant librarian (1859–76) and librarian (1876–96), Astor Library, N.Y.; helped negotiate consolidation (1895) of Astor and Lennox Libraries and Tilden Trust into N.Y. Public Library.

**Saunders, Hilary Aidan St. George.** 1898–1951. British writer; educ. Oxford; served in World War (1916–18); asst. librarian, House of Commons (1938–45); librarian (1946–50); coauthor of novels (with John Leslie Palmer, *q.v.*); author of *The Battle of Britain* (1940), *Bomber Command* (1941), *Coastal Command* (1942), etc.

**Saunders, Richard.** See Benjamin FRANKLIN.

**Saunders, William.** 1836–1914. Canadian agriculturist and horticulturist, b. in Devonshire, Eng.; to Canada (1848); manufacturing chemist in London, Ontario; commissioned by Dominion government to establish government experimental farms (in Ottawa, Nova Scotia, Manitoba, and British Columbia); directed activities in crossbreeding of cereals and fruits to produce hardy, early-ripening, and rust-resistant varieties. A son, Sir **Charles Edward** (1867–1937), was a wheat expert; one of group directed by his father that developed, by crossbreeding, the Marquis variety of wheat, maturing in 110 days and thus esp. adapted for growth in Canadian climate. See Angus MACKAY.

**Saunderson.** See also SANDERSON.

**Saun'der·son** (sôn'dĕr·s'n; sän'-) *or* **San'der·son** (săn'-), **Nicholas.** 1682–1739. English mathematician; lost his sight at one year of age through smallpox; lectured on Newtonian philosophy at Cambridge (1707); professor of mathematics (1711); fellow of Royal Society.

**Sau'ret'** (sō'rĕ'), **Émile.** 1852–1920. French violinist.

**Sa'ush·shat'tar** (sä'o͝osh·shät'tär). Founder of the Mitanni empire (c. 1475 B.C.).

**Saus'sier'** (sō'syā'), **Félix Gustave.** 1828–1905. French general; engaged (1870) at Metz in Franco-Prussian War; was captured, escaped, and commanded a brigade in the army of the Loire (1871); commanded expeditionary force in Tunis (1881); military governor of Paris (1884–86).

**Saus'sure', de** (dē sō'sür'). Name of a distinguished Swiss family including: **Nicolas** (1709–1790), agriculturist. His son **Horace Bénédict** (1740–1799), professor of philosophy at Geneva (1762–86); made many researches in geology, physics, meteorology. Horace's daughter **Albertine Adrienne;** see under Jacques NECKER. Horace's son **Nicolas Théodore** (1767–1845), chemist and naturalist; pioneer in experimental physiology; known for work on nutrition and respiration in plants, on fermentation, germination, composition of alcohol, transformation of starch into sugar, etc. Horace's grandson **Henri** (1829–1905), entomologist, authority on Orthoptera and Hymenoptera. Henri's son **Ferdinand** (1857–1913), professor of Sanskrit at Geneva (from 1906); his *Cours de Linguistique Générale* (1916), posthumously edited from his students' lecture notes, is one of the foremost works giving stimulus and direction to modern linguistics.

**Saus'sure'** (sō'sür'), **René de.** *Pseudonym* **An·ti'do** (ăn·tē'dō). Swiss-French philologist; student of Esperanto and translator of Ramuz's *Aline* (1911); edited language project *Antido* (1907) as a compromise between the conflicting systems of Esperanto and Ido; published *Esperantido* (1917) and *Nov-Esperanto* (1925).

**Sau′ter** (?sou′tẽr), **George.** 1866–1937. Portrait painter, b. in Bavaria; studio in London (1895–1915).

**Sau′vage′** (sō′vȧzh′), **Pierre Louis Frédéric.** 1785–1857. French shipbuilder and inventor; designed and patented (1832) an early screw propeller, the design of which was plagiarized by others.

**Sau′veur′** (sō′vûr′), **Joseph.** 1653–1716. French geometrician and physicist; professor, Collège de France (1686); engaged at siege of Mons to apply his principles of fortification (1691); credited with first calculation of absolute vibration numbers and with first scientific explanation of overtones.

**Sa′va** (sä′vä), Saint. d. 1236 or 1237. Organizer of the Serbian church; first bishop of Serbia (1219–34).

**Sa′va** (sä′vȧ), **George,** *pseudonym.* 1903– . Surgeon and novelist; naturalized British subject: *The Healing Knife* (1938), *A Surgeon's Destiny* (1939), *Twice the Clock Round* (1940), *A Ring at the Door* (1940), *Valley of Forgotten People* (1941), *A Tale of Ten Cities* (1942), *School for War* (1942).

**Sav′age** (săv′ĭj), **Arthur William.** 1857–1938. American arms manufacturer and inventor, b. Kingston, Jamaica, B.W.I.; to U.S. (1886; naturalized 1895). Founder, Savage Arms Co., Utica, N.Y. (1893); inventor of a dirigible torpedo and improvements in magazine rifles.

**Savage, Augusta Christine.** 1910–1962. American Negro sculptress, b. West Palm Beach, Fla.; studied at Cooper Union, N.Y., and in Paris (1931–33); best known for her studies of Negro heads; among individual works are *Woman of Martinique, The Martyr;* one of four women sculptors commissioned to do work for the World's Fair in New York (1939–40).

**Savage, Edward.** 1761–1817. American painter and engraver, b. Princeton, Mass.; studio in Philadelphia (1794–1801), and New York (from 1801). His portraits of George and Martha Washington are now in Boston Museum of Fine Arts.

**Savage, Eugene Francis.** 1883– . American figure, landscape, mural, and portrait painter, and sculptor; professor in Yale Art School (from 1923).

**Savage, Henry Wilson.** 1859–1927. American theatrical producer; in real-estate business, Boston (1880–95); organized Castle Square Opera Company (1895), to present opera in English at moderate prices; played *The Bohemian Girl, Martha, Faust, Romeo and Juliet.* Expanded to New York and Chicago; introduced light operas, as *The Prince of Pilsen* (1903), *The Yankee Consul* (1903), *The County Chairman* (1903), *The College Widow* (1904). His grand opera company presented Wagner's *Parsifal* (1904) and Puccini's *Madame Butterfly* (1906) for the first time in English. Made great success in producing Lehár's *The Merry Widow* (1907).

**Savage, James.** 1784–1873. American antiquary, b. Boston; secured legislative incorporation of the Provident Institution for Savings, Boston (1816), one of first savings banks incorporated in U.S., of which he became president. A founder of Boston Athenaeum. Edited John Winthrop's *The History of New England from 1630 to 1649* (2 vols., 1825–26); published *Genealogical Dictionary of the First Settlers of New England...on the Basis of Farmer's Register* (4 vols., 1860–62).

**Savage, John.** 1828–1888. Journalist, poet, and playwright, b. Dublin, Ireland; to U.S. (1848). Served in Union army in Civil War; wrote a number of war songs, including *The Starry Flag.* Identified with Fenians (1867); lectured, wrote, and toured the country for Fenian cause. Author of *'98 and '48: the Modern Revolutionary History and Literature of Ireland* (1856), *Faith and Fancy* (a collection of verse, 1864), *Poems* (1867), *Fenian Heroes and Martyrs* (1868).

**Savage, Michael Joseph.** 1872–1940. New Zealand labor leader and politician; prime minister of New Zealand (1935–40).

**Savage, Richard.** 4th Earl **Riv′ers** (rĭv′ẽrz). 1660?–1712. English soldier and rake; M.P. (1681), as Viscount Colchester; joined William of Orange when he landed in England; accompanied him to Flanders (1691, 1692); commanded force, originally intended to join Camisards against France, sent to Lisbon (1706–07); superseded in command; courted Tory party and made constable of Tower of London (1709); plenipotentiary to elector of Hanover (1710); general (1712).

**Savage, Richard.** 1697?–1743. English poet; put forward, but did not substantiate, claim that he was son of Richard Savage, 4th Earl Rivers, by countess of Macclesfield. Friend of Dr. Johnson, who shared poverty with him and wrote his biography (1744; later included in *The Lives of the Poets*). Had plays acted at Drury Lane, including *Love in a Veil* (1718; comedy) and *Sir Thomas Overbury* (1723), in which he played title role. Barely escaped death penalty for killing a gentleman in tavern brawl (1727); pensioned for a time on condition of writing yearly ode on Queen Caroline's birthday; alienated friends who aided him, of whom Pope was the most persevering; died in prison for debt. Author of poems *The Bastard* (1728) and, his masterpiece, *The Wanderer* (1729).

**Savage, Thomas Staughton.** 1804–1880. American Protestant Episcopal clergyman and naturalist, b. Cromwell, Conn. First missionary sent to Africa by Protestant Episcopal Church; established mission station in Liberia (1836–46). On return to U.S. (1847), wrote paper on the gorilla, previously unknown to scientists, on the habits of the chimpanzee, and on the termites of western Africa.

**Sa′vart′** (sȧ′vȧr′), **Félix.** 1791–1841. French physician and physicist; invented acoustical instrument (Savart's wheel) for determining number of vibrations per second corresponding to a tone, and a quartz plate (Savart plate) for studying polarized light; made investigations on resonance, esp. in stringed instruments.

**Savary, Anne Jean Marie René.** See Duc de ROVIGO.

**Sa′ver·y** (sā′vẽr·ĭ), **Thomas.** 1650?–1715. English military engineer; invented machine for polishing glass; patented first commercially successful steam engine, an atmospheric engine for pumping water (1698).

**Savery, William.** 1721–1787. American cabinetmaker, resident of Philadelphia. Examples of his work (highboys, lowboys, tables, and a desk) are in the Palmer Collection in the Metropolitan Museum of Art, New York City.

**Sa′vi′gnon′** (sȧ′vē′nyôɴ′), **André.** 1880– . French novelist, author of *Les Filles de la Pluie, Scènes de la Vie Ouessantine* (Goncourt prize, 1912), *Une Femme dans chaque Port, Au Petit Bateau, Douze Nuits de Londres,* etc.

**Sa′vi·gny** (säv′ĭn·yē), **Friedrich Karl von.** 1779–1861. Prussian jurist and statesman; regarded as one of the founders of the historical school of jurisprudence. Among his works are *Das Recht des Besitzes* (1806), *Geschichte des Römischen Rechts im Mittelalter* (6 vols., 1815–31), *System des Heutigen Römischen Rechts* (8 vols., 1840–49), *Das Obligationenrecht* (2 vols., 1851–53). His son **Karl Friedrich** (1814–1875) was a Prussian diplomat and politician.

**Sav′ile** (săv′ĭl), Sir **George.** Marquis of **Hal′i·fax** (hăl′ĭ-făks). 1633–1695. English statesman; opposed test acts; brought about rejection of bill for exclusion of James from succession (1679–81); lord privy seal (1682–85, 1689–90); president of council (1685), dismissed for opposition to repeal of test and habeas corpus acts. Sent by James II with Godolphin and Nottingham to arrange compromise with William of Orange; gave allegiance to William. One of first writers of political pamphlets; in his *Character of a Trimmer* (1688), urged Charles II to free himself from his brother James's influence; author of essays. The prototype of Jotham in Dryden's *Absalom and Achitophel.*

**Savile,** Sir **George.** 1726–1784. English political leader; M.P. (1759–83); tried unsuccessfully to bring in bill safeguarding rights of electors (1771); called for relief from subscription to Thirty-nine Articles (1772); justified resistance of American colonies (1775); advocated relief of Roman Catholics from obsolete penalties and disabilities (1778); proposed bill to secure Protestantism from popish encroachment.

**Savile,** Sir **Henry.** 1549–1622. English classical scholar; tutor in Greek to Queen Elizabeth; warden of Merton Coll., Oxford (1585–1622); translated four books of the *Historiae* of Tacitus (1591). One of scholars appointed to prepare Authorized Version of the Bible, assigned parts of Gospels, Acts, and Book of Revelation (1604 ff.). Published edition of St. Chrysostom (8 vols., 1610–13; printed by king's printer) and edition of *Cyropaedia* (1613). Founded and endowed Savile professorships of geometry and astronomy, Oxford.

**Sa·ville'** (sȧ·vĭl'), **Marshall Howard.** 1867–1935. American archaeologist; explored Mexican and Central and South American sites for Aztec, Zapotec, and Mayan remains; professor, Columbia (from 1903).

**Sa'vin·kov** (sá'vyĭn·kôf), **Boris Viktorovich.** *Pseudonym* **Rop'shin** (rôp'shĭn). 1879–1925. Russian politician; joined Social Democratic party, and became a leader in terrorist activities; organized assassination of Grand Duke Sergius (1905); arrested and condemned to death, but escaped to Switzerland (1906). To Russia (1917), and became vice-minister of war in the Kerenski government. Opposed Bolsheviks, first in Russia, then in Poland, and later in Paris. Returned to Russia (1924) and was arrested and condemned to death; sentence commuted to life imprisonment; committed suicide in prison. Author of terrorist novels *The Pale Horse* (1909) and *That Which Never Happened* (1913).

**Sa'vo·na·ro'la** (sä'vô·nä·rô'lä; *Angl.* săv'ō·nȧ·rō'lȧ), **Girolamo.** 1452–1498. Italian reformer, b. Ferrara; joined Dominican order (1475). To Florence (1482); prior of St. Mark's, Florence (1491); denounced in vehement sermons corruption of secular life, licentiousness of ruling class, and worldliness of clergy. As spiritual leader of the Piagnoni (democratic party), drove Pietro de' Medici from power (1494); exercised virtual dictatorship in Florence, preaching crusade for establishment of an ideal Christian state; denounced Pope Alexander VI, whose enmity he incurred. Lost hold on Florentine republic as the Arrabbiati (aristocratic party) regained power; excommunicated (1497); openly rebelled against pope; captured by the Arrabbiati in attack on convent of St. Mark, imprisoned, and tried for sedition and heresy (1498); tortured, hanged, with two other Dominicans, and burned (May 23).

**Savorgnani, Brazza.** See BRAZZA.

**Sa'vov** (sá'vôf), **Mikhail.** 1857–1928. Bulgarian soldier and statesman; commanded wing of Bulgarian army in its victory over Serbians at Slivnica (1885); minister of war (1891–97, 1902–08); commander in chief of Bulgarian army in 1st and 2d Balkan Wars (1912–13); Bulgarian minister to France (1922–23).

**Sa·voy'** (sȧ·voi'). *Fr.* **Sa'voie'** (sá'vwá'). *Ital.* **Sa·vo'ia** (sä·vô'yä). The oldest reigning family in Europe, founded by **Humbert I** (970?–?1050), constable of Emperor Conrad II and count of Savoy, a small state in the Alps between France and Italy (modern Savoy and Piedmont). Possessions increased in 11th century; made duchy (1416) by Emperor Sigismund. In the main line most important rulers were:
*Counts:* **Philippe I** (1207–1285, reigned 1268–85); **Amadeus V** (*Fr.* **Amédée**), *called* **the Great** (1249–1323, reigned 1285–1323); **Amadeus VI** (1334–1383, reigned 1343–83), founder of the Order of the Annunziata; **Amadeus VII** (1360–1391, reigned 1383–91), secured Nice; **Amadeus VIII** (1383–1451, reigned 1391–1440), first duke (1416), later (1439–49) antipope (see FELIX V).
*Dukes:* **Philibert I,** *called* **the Hunter** (1464–1482, reigned 1472–82), under regency of his mother, Yolande of France; **Charles I** (1468–1490, reigned 1482–90); Emmanuel Philibert (*q.v.*). Emmanuel Philibert's son **Charles Emmanuel I, the Great** (reigned 1580–1630) married Catherine of Spain; from them descended the two chief modern houses of Savoy: (1) Main line (1630–1831) included: **Victor Amadeus I; Charles Emmanuel II; Victor Amadeus II** (d. 1732), by Treaty of Utrecht (1713) made king of Sicily (1713–20), and king of Sardinia (1720) when Sicily was ceded to Emperor Charles VI. Subsequent Savoy kings of Sardinia were: Charles Emmanuel III, Victor Amadeus III, Charles Emmanuel IV, Victor Emmanuel I, and Charles Felix (see separate biogs.). Succession to throne of Sardinia passed (1831) to Charles Albert of the Savoy-Carignan (Carignano) line (see 2). (2) Cadet branch (Savoy-Carignan) originated with **Thomas François** (1596–1656), *Ital.* **Tommaso Francesco,** Prince of **Ca'ri'gnan'** [ká'rē'nyäN'] (anc. Yvois, town in Ardennes, near Mézières), 4th son of Charles Emmanuel I (d. 1630). Sixth prince was Charles Emmanuel (d. 1800); seventh prince was Charles Albert, King of Sardinia, whose son was Victor Emmanuel II, first king of modern Italy, succeeded by Humbert I and Victor Emmanuel III. (See separate biogs.; see also AMADEUS, King of Spain, and *Tables in Appendix* for ITALY and SPAIN.) There were two collateral branches of the Savoy-Carignan line, descended from Thomas François: (a) Counts of Soissons, from Eugène Maurice de Savoie-Carignan (1633–1673), soldier, extinct (1736) in his son Prince Eugene of Savoy (*q.v.*); (b) Counts of Villafranca, who later (1888) took the title Villafranca-Soissons. An early branch of the main line was ducal house of Nemours (1528–1659) established by marriage of Charlotte, direct descendant of Amadeus VIII in fourth generation, and Philippe, Duke of Nemours.

**Savoy, Peter of.** See PETER OF SAVOY.

**Saw'yer** (sô'yẽr), **Ruth.** 1880– . American writer of juveniles, b. Boston; m. Albert C. Durand (1911); professional storyteller (from 1908); awarded Newbery medal for contribution to children's literature (1937).

**Sax** (sȧks), **Charles Joseph.** 1791–1865. Belgian maker of musical instruments. His son **Antoine Joseph,** *known as* **Adolphe** (1814–1894), also a maker of musical instruments, invented the saxhorn, the saxotromba, and the saxophone.

**Saxe** (*Angl.* săks; *Fr.* sȧks). French name of Saxony, used in English chiefly in names of former duchies in Thuringia, which (1485–1547) was in electorate of Saxony. See WETTIN, ERNESTINE LINE, ALBERTINE LINE.

**Saxe** (sȧks), Comte **Hermann Maurice de.** *Known as* **Marshal Saxe** *or* **Marshal de Saxe.** 1696–1750. French marshal, natural son of Augustus II of Saxony. Served under Marlborough and Prince Eugene; captured Prague (1741) and Eger (1742); created marshal of France (1744); victor at Fontenoy (1745) and Rocourt

(1746); created marshal general (1747); captured Maastricht (1748).

**Saxe** (săks), **John Godfrey.** 1816–1887. American poet, b. Highgate, Vt.; proprietor and editor, Burlington (Vt.) *Sentinel* (1850–56); best known for his humorous verse.

**Saxe′–Al′ten·burg** (săks′ăl′tĕn·bo͝ork). A former German duchy (now part of Thuringia) and its ruling house, which formed a branch of the Ernestine line (*q.v.*) of Saxony. District, a part of the Wettin lands (from 1250), fell at their division (1485) to Ernestine line, then passed to Albertine line (1547–54); family branch founded 1603, became extinct 1672; land then made part of Saxe-Gotha. **Saxe′–Go′tha–Al′ten·burg** [-gō′thȧ-; -tȧ-; *Ger.* -tä-] (1672–1825); made a duchy (1826) under duke of Hildburghausen, who became Duke Frederick (1763–1834) of the new line of Saxe-Altenburg; *Gotha* exchanged for *Saalfeld* (1826; see SAXE-COBURG-GOTHA). Recent rulers: Duke Joseph (1789–1868; ruled 1834–48, abdicated); his brother George (1848–53); George's son Ernest I (1853–1908); Ernest's nephew Ernest II (1871–1955); ruled 1908–18, abdicated).

**Saxe′–Co′burg** (săks′kō′bûrg). (1) A German duchy, early (1247–1485) a possession of the Wettin family (*q.v.*), later (1485) fell to Ernestine line (*q.v.*). See SAXE-COBURG-GOTHA. (2) A royal house (1901–10) of Great Britain, whose sole representative as ruler was Edward VII, eldest son of Victoria. See WINDSOR.

**Saxe–Coburg,** Prince of. See Friedrich JOSIAS.

**Saxe′–Co′burg–Go′tha** (-gō′thȧ; -tȧ; *Ger.* -tä) *or* **Saxe–Coburg and Gotha.** A former German duchy (now a part of Thuringia) and its ruling house, which formed a branch of the Ernestine line (*q.v.*) of Saxony. The elder line (a branch of the Ernestine line) became extinct (1633). New line founded (1680) by Duke Albert, second son of Ernest the Pious (see SAXE-GOTHA and ERNEST I, Duke of Saxe-Gotha); inherited (1699) by his brother John Ernest (1658–1729); by acquisition of Saalfeld (1735) duchy became **Saxe′–Co′burg–Saal′feld** (-zäl′fĕlt); on extinction of Saxe-Gotha-Altenburg line (1825; see SAXE-ALTENBURG), Duke Ernest I exchanged *Saalfeld* for *Gotha* (1826). Recent rulers: Ernest Frederick (1764–1800), Ernest III (1806–44; became Ernest I after 1826), Ernest II (1844–93), Alfred (1893–1900), Charles Edward (1884–1958; ruled 1900–18, abdicated).

Connections with other ruling houses, through Duke Francis Frederick (1750–1806) of Saxe-Coburg-Saalfeld, father of Duke Ernest I of Saxe-Coburg-Gotha: (1) Princess Victoria Mary Louisa, daughter of Duke Francis, m. (1818) as second husband, duke of Kent; their daughter was Queen Victoria of England. See houses of HANOVER, SAXE-COBURG, and WINDSOR. (2) Leopold (*q.v.*), youngest son of Duke Francis, who became king of the Belgians (1831). (3) Ferdinand (*q.v.*), eldest son of Duke Ferdinand (second son of Duke Francis), m. (1836) Queen Maria II of Portugal and became king consort. (4) Albert (*q.v.*), second son of Duke Ernest I and brother of Duke Ernest II, m. (1840) Queen Victoria of England. (5) Ferdinand (*q.v.*), Prince of Bulgaria, son of Prince Augustus of Saxe-Coburg, who was a brother of Ferdinand (3) and second son of Duke Ferdinand; elected prince (1887); granted title of "king," or czar (1908).

**Saxe–Gotha.** Early name (before acquisition of Coburg, 1672) of ducal house of Saxe-Coburg-Gotha (*q.v.*). See ERNEST I, Duke of Saxe-Gotha.

**Saxe′–Hild′burg·hau′sen** (săks′hĭlt′bo͝ork·hou′zĕn). District around city of Hildburghausen; established (1683) as minor duchy by Ernest, sixth son of Ernest the Pious of Saxe-Gotha; became part of Saxe-Altenburg (1826), when its ruler Duke Frederick (1763–1834) founded new line of Saxe-Altenburg (*q.v.*).

**Saxe′–Mei′ning·en** (săks′mī′nĭng·ĕn). A former German duchy (now a part of Thuringia) and its ruling house, which formed a branch of the Ernestine line (*q.v.*) of Saxony. It was founded (1680) by Bernhard, third son of Ernest the Pious of Saxe-Gotha; duchy increased (1826) by addition of part of lands (including Saalfeld) of Saxe-Gotha-Altenburg on its extinction (see SAXE-ALTENBURG). Recent rulers: Bernhard Erich Freund (ruled 1803–21, under regent; 1821–66), his son George (1866–1914), his son Bernhard (1914–18, abdicated).

**Saxe′–Wei′mar–Ei′se·nach** (săks′vī′mär·ī′zĕ·näk). A former German duchy (now a part of Thuringia) and its ruling house. District came (1373) into possession of Wettin family (*q.v.*), from them (1485) to the Ernestine line (*q.v.*); formed (1547) one of the small duchies in Thuringia and (1640) a principality, Saxe-Weimar, which added Eisenach (1644); again divided but united (1741) under Ernest Augustus I (ruled 1728–48); especially prosperous under rule (1758–1828) of Charles Augustus (*q.v.*); became grand duchy (1815). Rulers since Ernest Augustus I: Ernest Augustus Constantine (1748–58), Charles Augustus (1758–1828), Charles Frederick (1828–53), Charles Alexander (1853–1901), William Ernest (1901–18, abdicated). See also Duke BERNHARD (1604–1639). Since 1877 officially known as *Grand Dukes of Saxony;* chief of the Ernestine line of the twentieth century.

**Saxe–Wittenberg.** See WETTIN.

**Saxe–Zeitz** (săks′tsīts′). *Ger.* **Sach′sen–Zeitz′** (zäk′sĕn·tsīts′). A branch line (1656–1746) of the electoral house of Saxony, founded by Maurice, fourth son of Elector John George I (*q.v.*).

**Sax′o Gram·mat′i·cus** (săk′sō grȧ·măt′ĭ·kŭs). 1150?–?1220. Danish historian; probably secretary to Archbishop Absalon of Lund. Author of *Gesta Danorum,* or *Historia Danica,* a history of Denmark down to 1186, written in Latin, and containing the Amleth (Hamlet) legend.

**Sax′on** (săk′s'n), **Lyle.** 1891–1946. American journalist and writer, b. Baton Rouge, La.; author of *Father Mississippi* (1927), *Old Louisiana* (1929), *La Fitte, the Pirate* (1930), *Children of Strangers* (1937), etc.

**Saxony,** House of. See ALBERTINE LINE.

**Sax′ton** (săks′tŭn), **Joseph.** 1799–1873. American inventor, b. Huntington, Pa. Experimented with magnetoelectric machines and patented several inventions (a locomotive differential pulley, a fountain pen, etc.). Curator, standard weighing machinery, U.S. Mint (1837–43); designed and built balances used to check standard weights of U.S. government's assay and coining offices. Superintendent of weights and measures, U.S. Coast Survey (1843–73); invented a deep-sea thermometer, a self-registering tide gauge, an immersed hydrometer, an ever-pointed pencil.

**Say** (sā). Family of French economists, including: **Jean Baptiste** (1767–1832), author of *Traité d'Économie Politique* (1803), *Lettres à Malthus* (1820), and *Cours Complet d'Économie Politique Pratique* (1828–30). His grandson **Léon,** *in full* **Jean Baptiste Léon** (1826–1896), active opponent of socialism; finance minister (1872–73, 1875–76, 1876–79, 1882); author of *Le Socialisme d'État* (1884), *Les Solutions Démocratiques de la Question des Impôts* (1886), etc.

**Say** (sā), **Thomas.** 1787–1834. American entomologist, b. Philadelphia; zoologist on Long's exploring expedition to the Rocky Mountain region (1819–20, 1823); member of Robert Owen's utopian colony at New Harmony, Ind. (1825–27); called the father of descriptive entomology in America, as author of *American Entomology; or Descriptions of the Insects of North America* (3 vols., 1824–28).

**Sayaji Rao III,** Sir. See Maharaja Gaekwar of BARODA.

**Sa'ya·na** (sä'yȧ·nȧ). d. 1387. Hindu scholar, brother of Madhava and minister at court of king of Vijayanagar. With his brother, author of great commentary on the *Rig-Veda* and other Vedic works.

**Sayce** (sās), **Archibald Henry.** 1845–1933. English divine and philologist; professor of Assyriology, Oxford (1891–1919); author of *Assyrian Grammar for Comparative Purposes* (1872), *The Monuments of the Hittites* (1881), *The Races of the Old Testament* (1891), *Egyptian and Babylonian Religion* (1903), etc.

**Saye and Sele,** Viscount and Baron. See FIENNES.

**Say'ers** (sā'ẽrz; sârz), **Dorothy Leigh.** 1893–1957. English writer; m. (1926) Oswald Atherton Fleming. Author of detective fiction, including *Whose Body?* (1923), *Strong Poison* (1930), *Murder Must Advertise* (1933), *Gaudy Night* (1935), *Busman's Honeymoon* (1937), *In the Teeth of the Evidence* (1939); of verse; and of essays, as *Begin Here* (1940), *The Mind of the Maker* (1941).

**Sayf'-al-Daw'lah** (sī'fo͝od·dou'lă). 915?–967 A.D. Shiite sovereign in northern Syria; established himself in Aleppo (944); patron of learning. During his reign Aleppo reached its peak of culture and prosperity.

**Sayre** (sâr), **Francis Bowes.** 1885–1972. American lawyer and administrator, b. South Bethlehem, Pa.; A.B., Williams (1909), LL.B., Harvard (1912); m. (1st) Jessie Woodrow Wilson (1913; d. 1933), dau. of President Wilson, (2d) Elizabeth Evans Graves (1937); adviser to Siamese government (1923–30); U.S. asst. secretary of state (1933–39); U.S. high commissioner to Philippines (1939–42); deputy director (1943) and diplomatic adviser (from 1944) of foreign relief.

**Sayre, Lewis Albert.** 1820–1900. American surgeon; aided in organizing Bellevue Hospital Med. Coll. (1861), and professor of orthopedic surgery there (1861–98), the first such professor in U.S. Renowned as orthopedic surgeon; first American surgeon to perform a resection of the hip for hip-joint disease; developed original treatment of lateral curvature of the spine.

**Say'yid Ah'mad Khan** (sī'yĭd ä'măd kän'), Sir. 1817–1898. Moslem educator and reformer, b. Delhi, India; maintained friendly relations with the British, and aided in saving British residents during the Sepoy Mutiny (1857–58); member, legislative councils of India and Allahabad.

**Say'yids** (sī'yĭdz) [*Arabic, literally,* "princes" *or* "lords"]. A weak dynasty (1414–1450) of Mohammedan rulers of a small territory around Delhi, after the invasions of Tamerlane; driven out by the Lodi Afghans.

**Sa·zo'nov** (sŭ·zô'nôf), **Sergei Dmitrievich.** 1866–1927. Russian diplomat; minister of foreign affairs (1910–16); promoted Russian-English entente (1912) and defeated (1914–16) all attempts to have Russia make separate peace with the Central Powers. Escaped from Russia after the Bolsheviks seized power (Nov. 6–7, 1917); became minister of foreign affairs for Kolchak, who was fighting the Bolsheviks; retired to private life (1920).

**Scae'vo·la** (sē'vō·lȧ; sĕv'ō-), **Gaius Mucius.** Roman hero. According to legend, volunteered to assassinate Lars Porsena when he was beseiging Rome (509 B.C.); penetrated to Porsena's camp, but mistook Porsena's secretary for Porsena and killed him. Threatened with being burnt alive if he refused to divulge details of plot, he thrust right hand into fire nearby and held it there until it was burned off. Porsena, impressed with his courage, released him and negotiated peace with Rome.

**Scaevola, Publius Mucius.** Roman jurist and orator. Consul (133 B.C.) during disorders caused by reforms sponsored by the Gracchi; opposed Scipio Africanus, the Younger; pontifex maximus (130); published a digest (80 books) of annals of the office of pontifex maximus. His son **Quintus Mucius** was consul (95 B.C.); with his colleague, Lucius Licinius Crassus, sponsored law denying Roman citizenship to allies in the future, legislation which caused the Social War; governor of Asia; later, pontifex maximus; proscribed by Marian party in civil turmoil (82) and murdered.

**Sca'la, del'la** (dāl'lä skä'lä). Italian noble family; ruled Verona (1260–1387). Its members include: **Mastino I della Scala** (d. 1277), Ghibelline leader; podesta of Verona (1260 ff.); later appointed perpetual captain of Verona and imperial vicar. **Can** (kän) **Francesco della Scala,** *called* **Ca'ne Gran'de** (kä'nā grän'dā) **della Scala** *or, simply,* **Can Grande** (1291–1329); appointed imperial vicar of Verona by Emperor Henry VII of Germany; elected by Ghibellines (1318) captain general of Lombardy; known esp. as patron of the arts, and as patron of Dante during latter's exile from Florence. Can Grande's nephew **Mastino II della Scala** (d. 1351); extended his power over Brescia (1332), Parma (1335), and Lucca (1335). **Antonio della Scala** (d. 1388); driven from power by Gian Galeazzo Visconti (1387).

**Scales,** Baron. See Anthony WOODVILLE.

**Scal'i·ger** (skăl'ĭ·jẽr), **Julius Caesar.** 1484–1558. Italian physician and scholar, b. Padua. Practiced medicine in Verona (to 1525), in Agen, France (from 1526). Writings include Latin verse, a treatise on poetics, a treatise on the meters of comedy, and a Latin grammar on scientific principles, *De Causis Linguae Latinae* (1540). Best known for his philosophical and scientific writings, including commentaries on works of Aristotle, Hippocrates, Theophrastus, and esp. his *Exercitationes* on Jerome Cardan's *De Subtilitate*. His son **Joseph Justus** (1540–1609) was one of the most renowned scholars of his time; became a Protestant (c. 1562); studied jurisprudence at Valence (1570–72); professor, Geneva (1572–74), Leiden (from 1593). His pre-eminent position as a scholar led to violent attacks by the Jesuits, culminating in a personal philippic by Kaspar Scioppius (1607). He laid down and applied in his editions of *Catalecta*, of Festus, Catullus, Tibullus, and Propertius, rules of criticism and of textual emendation that laid the foundation for modern textual criticism. His edition of Manilius (1579) and his *De Emendatione Temporum* (1583) revolutionized accepted ideas on ancient chronology and laid the foundation of the modern study of the subject; in his *Thesaurus Temporum* (1606) he collected, often restoring defective texts, all available extant chronological writings of classic Greek and Latin.

**Sca·moz'zi** (skä·môt'tsē), **Vincenzo.** 1552–1616. Italian architect; representative of the transition from late Renaissance to baroque style. Among his works are Palazzo Trissino-Barton (at Vicenza), Barbari monument (in Church of the Carità, Venice), and plans for the reconstruction of the cathedral at Salzburg.

**Scan'der·beg** (skăn'dẽr·bĕg). *Turkish* **Is·ken·der' Bey** (ĭs·kĕn·dĕr' bā'). *Real name* **George Cas'tri·o'ta** (kăs'trĭ·ō'tȧ). 1403?–1468. Albanian chief and national hero. Educ. in Constantinople as a Moslem; served in Turkish army (to 1443). Inspired by news of Albanian insurrection against Turks (1443), returned to Albania, proclaimed himself Christian, gathered Albanian chiefs around him, and began determined struggle for Albanian independence. Gained alliance of Venice, Naples, and the Papacy; concluded ten-year armistice with Turks

(1461). Broke armistice and attacked Turks; deserted by his allies; at his death (1468) left Albania in such desperate straits that it was soon conquered. Known as "the Albanian Alexander," and "the Athlete of Christendom." See ZOG I.

**Scanderbeg III.** See ZOG I.

**Scarfoglio,** Signora **Eduardo.** See Matilda SERAO.

**Scar·lat′ti** (skär·lät′tē), **Alessandro.** 1659–1725. Italian composer; regarded as founder of the modern opera. Composer of operas, masses, oratorios, and cantatas, and reputed inventor of recitatives and the "da capo." His son **Domenico** (1683–1757) was a harpsichord and organ player, and composer esp. of music for the harpsichord.

**Scar′lett** (skär′lĕt; -lĭt), **James.** 1st Baron **Ab′in·ger** (ăb′ĭn·jẽr). 1769–1844. English judge, b. in Jamaica; attorney general under Canning and Wellington; appointed Lord Chief Baron of the Exchequer (1834); instrumental in effecting reforms in administration of justice. His son Sir **James Yorke** (1799–1871), cavalry commander, held regimental command (1840–54); commanded heavy brigade in successful charge against Russian cavalry at Balaklava (Oct. 25, 1854); commanded entire British cavalry in Crimea (1855); adjutant general (1860–65).

**Scar′pa** (skär′pä), **Antonio.** 1747–1832. Italian anatomist and surgeon; known esp. for work on the anatomy of the ear, nerve ganglia, and bones.

**Scar′ron′** (skȧ′rôN′), **Paul.** 1610–1660. French comic poet, novelist, and dramatist, b. Paris. Became an abbé (1629); entered service of Charles de Beaumanoir, Bishop of Le Mans (1633); a paralytic last part of his life (1638–60); m. (1652) Françoise d'Aubigné, who later was Mme. de Maintenon. Among his works are *Le Typhon,* (a burlesque poem, 1644), the plays *Jodelet ou le Maître Valet* (1645) and *Don Japhet d'Arménie* (1652), the burlesque epic *Virgile Travesti* (1648–53), and esp. the picaresque novel *Roman Comique* (1651–57).

**Scar′taz·zi′ni** (skär′tät·tsē′nē), **Giovanni Andrea.** 1837–1901. Swiss clergyman and Dante scholar; edited the *Divina Commedia,* with commentaries (4 vols., 1874–90).

**Scau′rus** (skô′rŭs), **Marcus Aemilius.** 163?–88 B.C. Roman politician; curule aedile, praetor, and consul (115); censor (109); in charge of grain supply at Ostia (104). His son **Marcus Aemilius** served during Third Mithridatic War (74–64 B.C.) as quaestor to Pompey; governor of Sardinia (55); accused of extortion in his province (54), defended by Cicero, Quintus Hortensius, and others, and acquitted.

**Scève** (sâv), **Maurice.** 16th-century French poet; author of *Délie Objet de Plus Haute Vertu* (1544), a poem which set the fashion (followed later by Ronsard and du Bellay) for a series of poems addressed to a real or an imaginary mistress.

**Schacht** (shäKt), **Hjal′mar** (yäl′mär), *in full* **Hor′ace** (hŏr′ĭs) **Gree′ley** (grē′lĭ) **Hjalmar.** 1877–1970. German financier; director, Deutsche Bank (1908–15); director, Nationalbank für Deutschland (1916 ff.) and partner in Darmstädter und Nationalbank. Commissioner of currency for Germany (1923); president of the Reichsbank (1923–30; 1933–39); acting minister of national economy (1934–37). Took part in Dawes Committee discussions (1924) and Reparations Commission deliberations (1929). Acquitted (1946) as war criminal.

**Schack** (shäk), **Adolf Friedrich.** 1815–1894. German man of letters; settled in Munich (1855); accumulated art collection (Schack Gallery) which he willed to the German emperor, who presented it to the city of Munich. Best known for his translations and critical works, including *Geschichte der Dramatischen Literatur und Kunst in Spanien* (3 vols., 1845–46), *Spanisches Theater* (2 vols., 1845), *Epische Dichtungen aus dem Persischen des Firdusi* (2 vols., 1853), *Poesie und Kunst der Araber in Spanien und Sicilien* (1865), etc.

**Scha′dow** (shä′dō), **Johann Gottfried.** 1764–1850. Prussian court sculptor (1788); rector (1805) and director (1816–50), Acad. of Art, Berlin. Regarded as founder of the modern Berlin school of sculptors. Among his works are a statue of Frederick the Great in Stettin, a group entitled *Quadriga of Victory* for the Brandenburger Tor in Berlin, a group *Crown Princess Louise and her Sister* in the palace in Berlin, a statue of Blücher in Rostock, and many portrait busts. His son **Rudolf** (1786–1822) was also a sculptor. Another son, **Wilhelm von Scha′dow-Go′den·haus** [-gō′dĕn·hous] (1789–1862), was a painter; professor, Acad. of Art, Berlin (1819); director, Acad. of Art, Düsseldorf (1826); considered virtual founder of the old Düsseldorf school of painting; best known for his historical and religious canvases.

**Schae′ber·le** (shā′bẽr·lē), **John Martin.** 1853–1924. Astronomer, b. in Württemberg, Ger.; to U.S. in infancy. Member, original staff of Lick Observatory, Mount Hamilton, Calif. (1888–97); observed solar eclipses there (1889) and in French Guiana (1889), Chile (1893).

**Schae′fer** (shâ′fẽr), **Clemens.** 1878– . German physicist; known for researches on infrared rays and the structure of molecules and crystals.

**Schä′fer** (shâ′fẽr), **Dietrich.** 1845–1929. German historian; among his many works are *Die Deutsche Hanse* (1903), *Kolonialgeschichte* (1903), *Weltgeschichte der Neuzeit* (2 vols., 1907), *Deutsche Geschichte* (2 vols., 1910), *Bismarck...* (2 vols., 1917).

**Scha′fer** (shā′fẽr), Sir **Edward Albert Sharpey–.** See SHARPEY-SCHAFER.

**Schä′fer** (shâ′fẽr), **Heinrich.** 1868–1957. German Egyptologist.

**Schäfer, Wilhelm.** 1868–1952. German writer; founded (1900) and edited the monthly *Rheinlande.* Author of collections of *Anekdoten* (1908, 1911, 1929, 1938), novels, including *Karl Stauffers Lebensgang* (1912), *Der Hauptmann von Köpenick* (1930), *Der Fabrikant Anton Beilharz und das Therеslc* (1933), and the biographical *Meine Eltern* (1938).

**Schaff** (shâf), **Morris.** 1840–1929. American army officer; grad. U.S.M.A., West Point (1862); served in Civil War; author of *Spirit of Old West Point* (1907), *Sunset of the Confederacy* (1912), etc.

**Schaff, Philip.** 1819–1893. Church historian, b. at Chur, Switzerland; to U.S. (1844) as professor in Mercersburg Theological Seminary (1844–65). Affiliated with Presbyterian Church (from 1870); professor, Union Theological Seminary (1870–93). President of American Committee in work of revising the English Bible (1881–85). His works include *History of the Christian Church* (7 vols., 1858–90), *The Creeds of Christendom* (1877). Edited American translation of Johann J. Herzog's *Realenzyklopädie* (1882–84; now known as *The Schaff-Herzog Encyclopedia of Religious Knowledge*).

**Schaffarik.** See ŠAFAŘÍK.

**Schäff′le** (shĕf′lĕ), **Albert Eberhard Friedrich.** 1831–1903. German economist and sociologist; Austrian minister of commerce (1871); later, settled in Stuttgart. Among his works are *Kapitalismus und Sozialismus* (1870), *Bau und Leben des Sozialen Körpers* (4 parts, 1875–78), *Abriss der Soziologie* (1906).

**Schaff′ner** (shäf′nẽr), **Jakob.** 1875–1944. Swiss-born novelist in Germany.

**Schalck′en** (sKäl′kĕn), **Godfried.** 1643–1706. Dutch portrait and genre painter.

**Schall von Bell** (shăl′ fôn bĕl′), **Johann Adam.** 1591–1666. German Jesuit missionary in China (from 1622); revised Chinese calendar; directed (1645 ff.) the mathematical-astronomical bureau; was created a mandarin by the emperor of China. Later under the Ch'ing emperor K'ang-hsi, the imperial policy changed; Schall von Bell was imprisoned (to 1665) and many of his reforms nullified.

**Schal′ly** (shăl′ē), **Andrew Victor.** 1926– . American physiologist, b. Poland. To England (1939); at Baylor College of Medicine (1957–62); with Veterans Administration hospital, New Orleans (1962– ); awarded (with Roger Guillemin and Rosalyn S. Yalow) Nobel prize for physiology or medicine (1977).

**Scham′berg** (shăm′bûrg), **Jay Frank.** 1870–1934. American dermatologist, b. Philadelphia; associated in discovery of synthesis of arsphenamine and neoarsphenamine, making possible supplies of the drugs for treatment of syphilis during World War.

**Schamyl.** Variant of SHAMYL.

**Scha′per** (shä′pẽr), **Friedrich.** 1841–1919. German sculptor; among his works are a bronze statue of Bismarck in Cologne, a marble statue of Goethe in Berlin, a monument to Luther in Erfurt.

**Scharf** (shärf), **John Thomas.** 1843–1898. American Confederate soldier and historian, b. Baltimore. Captured within Federal lines (1864) and about to be tried as a spy when war ended; pardoned by President Johnson (Sept., 1865). On editorial staff, Baltimore *News, Sunday Telegram, Morning Herald;* Maryland land-office commissioner (1884–92); U.S. inspector of Chinese immigration at New York (1893–97). Collector of Americana, presented (1891) to library of Johns Hopkins U. Author of *History of Maryland* (3 vols., 1879), *History of the Confederate States Navy* (1887), etc.

**Schar′lieb** (?shär′lēb), Dame **Mary Ann Dacomb,** *nee* **Bird.** 1845–1930. English gynecologist; m. William Mason Scharlieb (1865; d. 1891); in Madras (1866 ff.); aided in founding Royal Victoria Hospital for Caste and Gosha Women in Madras, and practiced in Madras (to 1887) and, later, in London. Grad. M.D., London U. (1888), first woman to obtain this degree at London U. Appointed gynecologist at Royal Free Hospital, London (1902), first woman to hold staff appointment in a London general hospital.

**Scharn′horst** (shärn′hôrst), **Gerhard Johann David von.** 1755–1813. Prussian general; chief of staff in war against Napoleon (1806–07). Began reorganization of Prussian army (1807), working with Stein, Gneisenau, Hardenberg, and others; forced by Napoleon to leave Prussian service (1810), but on French defeat in Russia (1812) became chief of staff to Blücher; fought in War of Liberation; badly wounded at Lützen, died at Prague a month later (June 8).

**Schar·wen′ka** (shär·vĕng′kä), **Philipp.** 1847–1917. German composer of orchestral, choral, and chamber music, piano and violin pieces, and songs. His brother **Xaver** (1850–1924) was a piano virtuoso and composer; founded (1881) Scharwenka Conservatory of Music, Berlin; directed (1891–98) Scharwenka Music School in New York; assoc. director (from 1898) of his conservatory in Berlin (merged, 1893, with Klindworth Conservatory into Klindworth-Scharwenka Conservatory); composer of piano concertos, an opera, a symphony, chamber music, and piano pieces.

**Schau′dinn** (shou′dĭn), **Fritz.** 1871–1906. German zoologist; on expedition to Arctic Ocean (1898); compiled *Fauna Artica* (1900); director of department of protozoological research, Inst. for Tropical Diseases, Hamburg (1906). Investigated free-living and parasitic rhizopods, coccidians, trypanosomes, etc.; discovered the organism (*Spirochaeta pallida*) causing syphilis (1905); proved that tropical dysentery is caused by a certain amoeba (*Endamoeba histolytica*).

**Schäu′fe·lein** *or* **Schäuf′fe·lein** *or* **Scheu′fe·lein** (shoi′fĕ·līn), **Hans Leonard.** 1480?–?1539. German painter, illustrator, and wood engraver; municipal painter of Nördlingen (from 1515).

**Schauff′ler** (shôf′lẽr; *Ger.* shouf′-), **William Gott′lieb** (gŏt′lēb; *Ger.* gôt′lēp). 1798–1883. Missionary, b. in Stuttgart, Ger.; to U.S. (1826); ordained in Congregational ministry (1831). Missionary in Turkey and Armenia (1831–74); translated the Old Testament into the Sephardi tongue, the Armeno-Turkish Bible into Turkish, and the New Testament into Turkish. Author of *Meditations on the Last Days of Christ* (1837). His son **Henry Albert** (1837–1905) was also a Congregationalist clergyman and missionary. His grandson **Robert Haven Schauffler** (1879–1964), American writer, b. Brünn, Austria; officer in World War, in France (1918–19); m. as 2d wife Margaret Widdemer (1919; divorced); widely known as lecturer. Among his many books are *The Musical Amateur* (1911), *Scum o' the Earth and Other Poems* (1912), *The White Comrade and Other Poems* (1920), *Magic Flame and Other Poems* (1923), *Music as a Social Force in America* (1927), *The Days We Celebrate* (4 vols., 1940).

**Schaumburg, Paul.** Real name of Paul BURG.

**Schaum′burg-Lip′pe** (shoum′bŏŏrk·lĭp′ĕ). A former German principality and its ruling family, founded (1643) by a younger member (Count Philip, 1601–1681) of the Lippe-Alverdissen branch, who inherited the county of Schaumburg (see LIPPE); became a principality (1807). Recent rulers: Count William (1724–1777), and princes George William (1787–1860; ruled 1807–60), Adolf George (1817–1893; ruled 1860–93), George (ruled 1893–1911), and his son Adolf (1883–1936; the last ruler, 1911–abdicated 1918).

**Schech′ter** (shĕk′tẽr), **Solomon.** 1850–1915. Hebraist, b. in Focşani, Rumania; in England (1882–1901); reader in Talmud and rabbinical literature, Cambridge U. (1890–1901); professor of Hebrew, U. of London (1899–1901). President, Jewish Theological Seminary, New York City (1901–15). Founded United Synagogue of America. An editor, *Jewish Quarterly Review* and *The Jewish Encyclopedia.* Collected from the Genizah of Fostat, near Cairo, Egypt, store of about 50,000 manuscripts and fragments, chiefly in Hebrew and Arabic, which he contributed to Cambridge U. Discovered among the manuscripts lost chapters of Ecclesiasticus, which he published (1899) as *The Wisdom of Ben Sira....* Also wrote *Studies in Judaism* (1908), *Some Aspects of Rabbinic Theology* (1909), etc.

**Schee′le** (shā′lĕ), **Karl Wilhelm.** 1742–1786. Swedish chemist; credited with discovery of chlorine, barium, manganese, oxygen (independently of Priestley), also numerous compounds, including ammonia, glycerin, tartaric acid, prussic acid, and a yellowish-green copper arsenite pigment known as Scheele's green.

**Scheer** (shār), **Reinhard.** 1863–1928. German naval commander; chief of staff of high-sea fleet under von Holtzendorff (1910); commander of German high-sea fleet (Jan., 1916); led fleet in battle off Jutland (May 31, 1916); retired (1918).

**Scheff** (shĕf), **Frit′zi** (frĭt′sē). 1882?–1954. Actress and singer, b. in Vienna; m. Baron Fritz von Bardeleben, John Fox, Jr. (1908), George Anderson (1913). Operatic debut, in Munich (1900); joined Metropolitan Opera Company, in New York (1902); sang in comic opera (1903–13) and in vaudeville (1913–18).

**Schef'fel** (shĕf'ĕl), **Josef Victor von.** 1826–1886. German poet and novelist; resident in Karlsruhe (from 1864). Among his works are the lyric-epic poem *Der Trompeter von Säkkingen* (1854), the historical novel *Ekkehard* (1855), and books of lyric verse.

**Schef'fer'** (shĕ'fâr'), **Ary.** 1795–1858. Dutch-born French figure and portrait painter. His brother **Henry** (1798–1862) was a historical and genre painter.

**Scheffler, Johannes.** Real name of ANGELUS SILESIUS.

**Schei'bler** (shī'blẽr), **Johann Heinrich.** 1777–1838. German physicist; devised a standard of musical pitch (known as Stuttgart, or Scheibler's, pitch, with a' at 440 vibrations) adopted by Stuttgart congress of physicists (1834).

**Scheibler, Karl.** 1827–1899. German chemist; established laboratory for sugar industry at Berlin (1861); devised method of extracting sugar from molasses and made other important contributions to development of sugar industry.

**Schei'de·mann** (shī'dĕ·män), **Philipp.** 1865–1939. German political leader, printer by trade. Editor of Socialist newspaper (1895); member of Reichstag (from 1898). During World War (1914–18), consistently but futilely urged a compromise peace. Member of cabinet formed by Prince Max of Baden (Oct., 1918). After emperor had fled to Netherlands, Scheidemann, as people's commissioner, proclaimed establishment of the republic and was elected first prime minister; resigned office when National Assembly accepted terms of Treaty of Versailles (1919). When Nazis came to power, Scheidemann fled into exile; died in Copenhagen.

**Schei'ner** (shī'nẽr), **Christoph.** 1579?–1650. German Jesuit astronomer; rector of Jesuit college at Neisse (1622). Discovered existence of sunspots independently of Galileo (1611); adhered to theory of a stable earth with a moving sun; invented a pantograph.

**Scheiner, Julius.** 1858–1913. German astrophysicist; known esp. for spectroscopic work in determining motion of stars in the line of sight; devised a sensitometer for measurement of sensitivity of photographic plates.

**Sche'le de Vere** (shā'lē dĕ vẽr'), **Max'i·mil'i·an** (măk'sĭ·mĭl'ĭ·ăn; -mĭl'yăn). 1820–1898. Philologist, b. in Wexiö, Sweden; to U.S. (1843); professor of modern languages, U. of Virginia (1844–95); pioneer in teaching comparative philology, and in systematic instruction in Anglo-Saxon.

**Sche'ler** (shā'lẽr), **Max.** 1874–1928. German philosopher; professor, Cologne (1919) and Frankfort (1928).

**Schel'ling** (shĕl'ĭng), **Ernest Henry.** 1876–1939. American pianist, composer, and conductor, b. Belvidere, N.J.; bro. of Felix Emanuel Schelling. Toured widely in U.S., Europe, and South America (from 1903). Conductor, New York Philharmonic Society Orchestra; also, in Boston, Philadelphia, Baltimore, San Francisco, Los Angeles, and Cincinnati; conductor, Baltimore Symphony Orchestra (1936, 1937, 1938). Captain of cavalry, A.E.F. (1917); major (Nov. 10, 1918); awarded D.S.M. (1923).

**Schelling, Felix Emanuel.** 1858–1945. American educator, b. New Albany, Ind.; bro. of Ernest Henry Schelling. Professor of English literature, Pennsylvania (from 1893); editor of a number of Elizabethan plays, and author of many books on Elizabethan literature, including *History of Elizabethan Drama* (1908), *English Literature During the Lifetime of Shakespeare* (1910), *The English Lyric* (1913), *Foreign Influences in Elizabethan Plays* (1923), *Elizabethan Playwrights* (1925). Also wrote "The Restoration Drama" for *The Cambridge History of Literature* (1912).

**Schel'ling** (shĕl'ĭng), **Friedrich Wilhelm Joseph von.** 1775–1854. German philosopher; professor, Jena (1798), Würzburg (1803), Munich (1827); lecturer, U. of Berlin (1841–46). Among his works are *Ideen zu einer Philosophie der Natur* (1907), *Der Erste Entwurf eines Systems der Naturphilosophie* (1799), *System des Transzendentalen Idealismus* (1800), *Bruno oder über das Natürliche und Göttliche Prinzip der Dinge* (1802), *Philosophie und Religion* (1804), *Untersuchungen über das Wesen der Menschlichen Freiheit* (1809).

**Schem** (shĕm), **Alexander Jacob.** 1826–1881. Educator and statistician, b. in Westphalia, Ger.; ordained Roman Catholic priest (1849), but left church and emigrated to U.S. (1851). Editor in chief, *Deutsch-amerikanisches Conversations-lexikon* (11 vols., 1869–74). Assistant superintendent, New York City public schools (1874–81). Published *The American Ecclesiastical and Educational Almanac* (1869), etc.

**Schenck** ( skĕngk), **James Findlay.** 1807–1882. American naval officer in Civil War; took part in attack on Fort Fisher; rear admiral (1868); retired (1869). His brother **Robert Cumming** (1809–1890) was a politician and army officer; member of U.S. House of Representatives (1843–51); U.S. minister to Brazil (1851–53); brigadier general of volunteers (May, 1861), engaged at First Bull Run and wounded at Second Bull Run; major general (Aug., 1862), in command at Baltimore; resigned (1863) and again member of U.S. House of Representatives (1863–71); U.S. minister to Great Britain (1871–76).

**Schen'kel** (shĕng'kĕl), **Daniel.** 1813–1885. German Protestant theologian; a founder of the German Protestant Union. Author of *Das Wesen des Protestantismus* (3 vols., 1845–51), *Christliche Dogmatik, vom Standpunkt des Gewissens* (2 vols., 1858–59), etc.

**Schen'ken·dorf** (shĕng'kĕn·dôrf), **Max von.** 1783–1817. German lawyer and poet; served in Prussian army (1813) at battle of Leipzig; counselor at Coblenz (1815–17). His lyrics include a number of patriotic songs.

**Schep'pe·grell** (shĕp'ĕ·grĕl), **William.** 1860–1928. American laryngologist; authority on hay fever, b. Hanover, Germany, of American parents. Practiced in New Orleans, La. (from 1890); invented many appliances for use in the ear, nose, and throat.

**Sché'rer'** (shā'râr'), **Barthélemy Louis Joseph.** 1747–1804. French Revolutionary general; distinguished himself at Valmy (1791); commanded army of Italy and won battle of Loano (Nov. 24, 1795); minister of war (1797–99); was defeated by the Austrians in Italy (1799) and resigned.

**Schérer, Edmond.** 1815–1889. French journalist; Protestant clergyman (1843) and professor at Geneva (1845); resigned (1849) and edited at Strasbourg *Revue de Théologie et de Philosophie Chrétienne* (1850–60). Member of editorial staff and, later, editor of *Le Temps* (from 1860). Most distinguished as literary critic.

**Sche'rer** (shā'rẽr), **Wilhelm.** 1841–1886. Austrian-born German philologist; professor, Vienna (1868), Strassburg (1872), Berlin (1877). Among his works are *Zur Geschichte der Deutschen Sprache* (1868) and *Geschichte der Deutschen Literatur* (1883).

**Scher'man** (shûr'măn), **Harry.** 1887–1969. Writer, b. Montreal, Canada; to U.S. (1889); in newspaper work in New York (1907–12); an originator of the Book-of-the-Month Club; author of *The Promises Men Live By* (a work on economics, 1938).

**Scher'man** (shär'män), **Lucian.** 1864–1946. German ethnographer and Orientalist.

**Scherr** (shĕr), **Johannes.** 1817–1886. German literary historian; a leader of Democratic party in south Germany; involved in revolutionary activities (1848–49) and forced into exile; professor in Polytechnikum, Zurich (from 1860). Among his works are *Deutsche Kultur- und Sittengeschichte* (3 vols., 1852–53), *Allgemeine Geschichte der Literatur* (2 vols., 1851), *Geschichte der Religion* (3 vols., 1855–57), and the satirical novel *Michel* (1858).

**Scher'rer** (shĕr'ĕr), **Paul.** 1890–1969. Swiss physicist; known for investigations in magnetism and (with Debye) on the physics of X rays and the structure of matter.

**Scheufelein.** See SCHÄUFELEIN.

**Scheu'rer'–Kest'ner'** (shû'râr'kĕst'nâr'), **Auguste.** 1833–1899. French chemist and politician; founded co-operative society for workingmen (1865); elected to Chamber of Deputies (1871) and Senate (1875; vice-president, 1896). Published *Principes Élémentaires de la Théorie Chimique des Types Appliquée aux Combinaisons Organiques* (1862), etc.

**Schia'pa·rel'li** (skyä'pä·rĕl'lē), **Elsa.** 1890?–1973. French dress designer, of Italian descent, b. Rome, Italy; established gown salon in Paris (c. 1927); in U.S. (1939–45).

**Schia'pa·rel'li** (skyä'pä·rĕl'lē), **Giovanni Virginio.** 1835–1910. Italian astronomer; asst. observer (1860) and director (1862–1900), Milan observatory. Discovered asteroid Hesperia (1861); showed that meteor swarms travel in cometary orbits; observed numerous double stars; observed markings on Mars which he called canals (1877); believed that Mercury and Venus rotate on their axes in the same time as they revolve around the sun.

**Schia·vo'ne** (skyä·vō'nā), **Andrea.** *Real name* **Andrea Me·dol'la** (mā·dōl'lä) *or* **Mel·dol'la** (māl-). 1522?–1582. Italian painter; employed at Venice. Among his works are *Adoration of the Magi* (in the Ambrosiana, Milan), *Flight to Emmaus* (in Church of San Sebastiano, Venice), *Holy Family* (in Dresden gallery).

**Schi'chau** (shĭĸ'ou), **Ferdinand.** 1814–1896. German engineer and shipbuilder; constructed first screw vessel in Germany (1855); built torpedo boats and destroyers for Germany, Russia, Italy, and China; established shipyard at Danzig.

**Schicht** (shĭĸt), **Johann Gottfried.** 1753–1823. German conductor, and composer of oratorios, masses, Te Deums, and motets.

**Schick** (shĭk), **Bé'la** (bā'lȯ). 1877–1967. Pediatrician, b. Boglár, Hungary; connected with U. of Vienna (1902–23); professor of pediatrics (1918–23). To U.S. (1923; naturalized 1929); pediatrician in chief, Mt. Sinai Hospital, N.Y. (from 1923); clinical professor of diseases of children, Columbia (from 1936). Discovered Schick test for determining susceptibility to diphtheria (1913). Known also for writings on scarlet fever, tuberculosis, nutrition of newborn children, concentrated feeding in childhood, etc.

**Schick'e·le** (shĭk'ĕ·lĕ), **René.** 1885–1940. German writer, b. in Alsace; on staff of *Strassburger Neue Zeitung;* edited *Weisse Blätter* (1916–20); author of *Hans im Schnakenloch* (play; 1916), *Das Erbe am Rhein* (trilogy of novels), etc.

**Schicklgruber.** See Adolf HITLER.

**Schief'ner** (shēf'nĕr), **Franz Anton.** 1817–1879. Russian philologist; specialized in the study of Mongolian, East Turkish, and Tibetan languages.

**Schie'mann** (shē'män), **Theodor.** 1847–1921. German historian, b. in Kurland, a province of Russia; professor of eastern European history, Berlin (1892–1920).

**Schiff** (shĭf), **Jacob Henry.** 1847–1920. Banker, b. Frankfurt am Main; to U.S. (1865); naturalized (1870); partner in Kuhn, Loeb & Co. (from 1875) and head of firm (1885). Associated with E. H. Harriman against J. J. Hill and J. P. Morgan & Co. in struggle for control of Northern Pacific Railroad, bringing on stock-market panic of May 9, 1901; active in floating Japanese bonds in U.S. during Russo-Japanese War (1904), and in marketing Chinese loan (1911). Recipients of his philanthropies include the Montefiore Hospital; Henry Street Settlement; Columbia U.; Harvard U., where he established a Semitic Museum; Cornell, where he founded a chair for study of German culture; Tuskegee Institute; Jewish Theological Seminary in New York; the American Red Cross. His son **Mortimer Leo** (1877–1931) succeeded him as head of Kuhn, Loeb & Co.

**Schiff** (shĭf), **Moriz.** 1823–1896. German physiologist; known for work on the physiology of the nervous system.

**Schiff, Sydney.** See Stephen HUDSON.

**Schi'ka·ne'der** (shē'kä·nā'dĕr), **Emanuel.** 1751–1812. German theater manager and librettist; among his librettos was that of *Die Zauberflöte,* with music by Mozart (1791).

**Schild'kraut** (shĭlt'krout), **Rudolph.** 1862–1930. German actor; stage debut in Vienna (1893); acted in Hamburg and Berlin, with special success in Shakespearean roles; to U.S. (1911, 1920, and 1922); associated with motion pictures in Hollywood (from 1926). Especially notable for his interpretations of Shylock and Mephistopheles; interpreted also plays of Hauptmann, Sudermann, Pinero, Shaw, and other moderns. His son **Joseph** (1896–1964) also an actor; played in Berlin and Vienna (1913–20); on U.S. stage (from 1920); played in *Liliom, Peer Gynt,* etc., and in motion pictures *Orphans of the Storm, Song of Love, Émile Zola* (in role of Dreyfus), etc.

**Schil'ler** (shĭl'ĕr), **Ferdinand Canning Scott.** 1864–1937. English philosopher; tutor, Oxford (1903–26); professor, U. of Southern California (from 1929). Among his books are *Riddles of the Sphinx* (1891), *Humanism* (1903), *Cassandra, or the Future of the British Empire* (1926), *Social Decay and Eugenical Reform* (1932).

**Schil'ler** (shĭl'ĕr), **Johann Christoph Friedrich von.** 1759–1805. German poet and playwright, b. Marbach, Württemberg. Surgeon in a Württemberg regiment (1780); went absent without leave to witness performance of his first play, *Die Räuber* (1781), was arrested by duke of Württemberg, and condemned to publish nothing except medical treatises. Escaped from Württemberg and spent years outside of the country (the Wanderjahre, 1782–91); in Mannheim (1783–85), where his drama *Kabale und Liebe* was successfully produced (1784); in Weimar (1787), where his blank verse *Don Carlos* appeared, as well as his historical work *Geschichte des Abfalls der Vereinigten Niederlande.* Professor of history, Jena (1789), where he completed his *Geschichte des Dreissigjährigen Krieges* (1791–93) and published several philosophical essays; formed friendship with Goethe and was inspired thereby to produce more poetry; with Johann Friedrich Cotta, founded (1795) literary journal *Die Horen;* founded (1796) *Musenalmanach* and contributed to it *Das Ideal und des Leben, Die Macht des Gesanges, Würde der Frauen, Der Spaziergang, Der Ring des Polykrates, Der Handschuh, Der Taucher, Das Lied von der Glocke;* also, completed his trilogy *Wallenstein.* Settled in Weimar (1799–1805) to be near Goethe and to devote himself completely to writing; during this last period of his life wrote the dramas *Maria Stuart* (1800), *Die Jungfrau von Orleans* (1801), *Die Braut von Messina* (1803), *Wilhelm Tell* (1804), and translated *Macbeth,* Gozzi's *Turandot,* and Racine's *Phèdre.* During later years worked under the handicap of continuous ill health. Regarded as second only to Goethe in field of German literature, and as first among German dramatists.

**Schil'ling** (shĭl'ĭng), **Johannes.** 1828–1910. German sculptor; among his works are a group of four statues on the Brühl terrace in Dresden, the equestrian monument to King John in Dresden, the statue of Schiller in Vienna, and statue of Emperor William I for Hamburg.

**Schil'ling-Cann'stadt** (shĭl'ĭng·kän'shtät), **Paul von.** 1786–1837. Electrician, b. Revel (Tallinn), Russia; credited with developing first practical electromagnetic telegraph, in which he utilized the positive or negative positions of two or more of the needles of five galvanometers to indicate the letters of the alphabet (1832).

**Schil'lings** (shĭl'ĭngs), **Max von.** 1868–1933. German conductor, and composer of operas, symphonic fantasies, a rhapsody, a string quartet, and songs.

**Schim'mel** (sKĭm'ĕl), **Hendrik Jan.** 1823–1906. Dutch journalist and writer; editor of the newspaper *De Gids* (1851–57) and of the monthly magazine *Nederland* (from 1854). Among his dramas are *Joan Wouters* (1848), *Struensee* (1868); among his novels, *Mary Hollis* (1860), *Mylady Carlisle* (2 parts, 1864).

**Schim'per** (shĭm'pẽr). Name of a family of German scientists including: **Karl Friedrich** (1803–1867), pioneer in modern plant morphology; formulated theory of phyllotaxis. His cousin **Wilhelm Philipp** (1808–1880), paleontologist and botanist, and authority on mosses. The latter's son **Andreas Franz Wilhelm** (1856–1901), botanist; wrote on plant geography.

**Schin'dler** (shĭn'dlẽr), **Anton.** 1795–1864. German conductor; close friend and biographer of Beethoven (*Biographie von L. van Beethoven,* 1840).

**Schin'dler** (shĭn'dlẽr), **Kurt** (ko͝ort). 1882–1935. Music conductor and editor, b. Berlin; to U.S. (1905); assistant conductor at Metropolitan Opera House in New York (1905–08); organized (1909) McDowell Chorus, which became Schola Cantorum (1912–26); edited compilations of Russian, Finnish, and Spanish songs.

**Schin'kel** (shĭng'kĕl), **Karl Friedrich.** 1781–1841. German architect and painter; in architecture, endeavored to adapt classical Grecian forms to purposes of modern structures. Designed Royal Theater, School of Artillery and Engineering, and the Old Museum (all in Berlin).

**Schi'pa** (skē'pä), **Tito.** 1890–1965. Operatic tenor, b. in Lecce, Italy; to U.S. (1919); member of Chicago Opera Association (1919–32) and Metropolitan Opera Company in New York (from 1932).

**Schip'per** (shĭp'ẽr), **Jakob.** 1842–1915. German English scholar; among his works are *Englische Metrik* (2 parts, 1881–88), and editions of Dunbar's *Poems* and of W. Kennedy's *Poems;* treated also the Shakespeare-Bacon controversy.

**Schi'rach** (shē'räK), **Baldur von.** 1907–1974. German Nazi politician; leader (1930 ff.) of the Nazi Youth organization; gauleiter in Vienna (1940–45); sentenced (1946) as war criminal to 20 years imprisonment.

**Schir'mer** (shĭr'mẽr), **Gus'tave** (go͝os'täv). 1829–1893. Music publisher, b. Königsee, Saxony; to U.S. (1840); head of G. Schirmer, music publishers (from 1866). His son **Rudolph Edward** (1859–1919) was associated with him in the music publishing house (from 1885) and became president of the firm as reorganized after Gustave Schirmer's death.

**Schirmer, Johann Wilhelm.** 1807–1863. German painter, esp. of landscapes and Biblical scenes; pupil of Schadow and Lessing in Düsseldorf, where he later (1839) became professor at the academy; director of new art school, Karlsruhe (1853).

**Schjel'de·rup** (shĕl'dro͝op), **Gerhard.** 1859–1933. Norwegian composer of music dramas, tone poems, chamber music, and songs.

**Schlaf** (shläf), **Johannes.** 1862–1941. German writer; collaborated with Arno Holz in naturalistic sketches, as *Papa Hamlet* (1889) and *Neue Gleise* (1892), and is regarded therefore as a joint founder of the naturalistic school in Germany. Later, wrote novels, plays, philosophical essays, some poetry, and studies on and translations of Whitman, Verhaeren, Maeterlinck, Novalis.

**Schla'gint·weit** (shlä'gĭnt·vīt). Family name of six brothers, German explorers, naturalists, and writers: **Hermann von Schlagintweit** (1826–1882); explored the Alps (1846–53) with **Adolf Schlagintweit** (1829–1857), making first ascent of Monte Rosa (1851); explored India and Central Asia (1854–57) with Adolf and Robert. **Robert von Schlagintweit** (1833–1885), professor of geography at Giessen (from 1864). **Eduard Schlagintweit** (1831–1866), soldier; wrote on the Spanish invasion of Morocco. **Emil Schlagintweit** (1835–1904), known for works on Tibet. **Max Schlagintweit** (1849–1935), soldier and explorer; traveled in Greece, Turkey, and Asia Minor.

**Schle'gel** (shlā'gĕl), **August Wilhelm von.** 1767–1845. German man of letters, b. in Hanover; professor, Bonn (1818–45). With his brother Friedrich, founded the literary journal *Athenaeum,* which became the organ of the romantic school of writers in Germany. Closely associated for a number of years (from 1804) with Madame de Staël. Made special study (1818 ff.) of Oriental languages and literature; published (1823–30) the journal *Indische Bibliothek,* and edited the *Bhagavad-Gīta* (1823, with a Latin translation) and the *Rāmāyana* (1829). Among his other works are a poetical translation of *Shakespeare* (1798 ff.), a tragedy *Ion* (1803), *Spanisches Theater* (2 vols., 1803–09), *Über Dramatische Kunst und Literatur* (1809–11). His brother **Friedrich** (1772–1829) studied Oriental languages in Paris (1802–04); adopted Roman Catholic faith (1803); secretary to the state chancery in Vienna (1808), and Austrian counselor of legation at Frankfurt am Main (1815–18); his literary works include lyric poems, the novel *Lucinde* (1799), the drama *Alarcos* (1802), the essay *Von der Sprache und Weisheit der Indier* (1808), *Geschichte der Alten und Neuen Literatur* (2 vols., 1815), *Philosophie des Lebens* (1828), *Philosophie der Geschichte* (2 vols., 1829). Friedrich's wife, **Dorothea,** *nee* **Mendelssohn** (1763–1839), was the daughter of Moses Mendelssohn (*q.v.*); m. (1st) Simon Veit (1783), by whom she had a son, the painter Philipp Veit (*q.v.*), and (2d) Friedrich von Schlegel; translated Madame de Staël's *Corinne* (1807) and wrote some fiction.

**Schlei'cher** (shlī'Kẽr), **August.** 1821–1868. German philologist; author of *Die Sprachen Europas* (1850), and treatises on Lithuanian and Slavic tongues.

**Schleicher, Kurt von.** 1882–1934. German soldier and statesman; on staff of the quartermaster general during World War (1914–18); major general (1929); lieutenant general (1931). Appointed minister of defense (1932) and chancellor of Germany (Dec. 2, 1932–Jan. 28, 1933) until succeeded by Adolf Hitler and the Nazi regime. Murdered during Nazi purge (June 30, 1934) on charge that he was involved in conspiracy to overthrow Hitler regime.

**Schlei'den** (shlī'dĕn), **Matthias Jakob.** 1804–1881. German botanist, b. Hamburg; contributed to development of the cell theory, recognized the nucleus as an essential part of the cell.

**Schlei'er·ma'cher** (shlī'ẽr·mä'Kẽr), **Friedrich Ernst Daniel.** 1768–1834. German Protestant theologian and philosopher, b. Breslau; professor of theology, Berlin (1810–34). Among his works are *Reden über die Religion* (1799), *Grundlinien einer Kritik der Bisherigen Sittenlehre* (1803), *Kurze Darstellung des Theologischen Studiums* (1810), *Der Christliche Glaube nach den Grundsätzen der Evangelischen Kirche* (1821–22; 2d edition, revised 1830–31), and a translation of Plato's works (1804–28).

**Schlemihl,** Peter. Pseudonym of Ludwig THOMA.

**Schlem'mer** (shlĕm'ẽr), **Oskar.** 1888–1943. German painter of ultramodern school; an instructor at the Bauhaus (to 1933).

**Schle'sing·er** (shlā'zĭng·ẽr). See Bruno WALTER.

**Schle'sing·er** (shlā'zĭng·ẽr), **Arthur Mei'er** (mī'ẽr). 1888–1965. American historian, b. Xenia, Ohio; professor, Harvard (from 1925); author of *The Colonial Merchants and the American Revolution, 1763–1776* (1918; awarded Justin Winsor prize by American Historical Assoc.), *Political and Social History of the United States, 1829–1925* (1925), etc. His son, **Arthur Meier, Jr.,** (1917– ) historian, educator, and author.

**Schles'in·ger** (slĕs'ĭng·gẽr), **Frank.** 1871–1943. American astronomer, at Yerkes Observatory, U. of Chicago (1903–05); director, Allegheny Observatory, U. of Pittsburgh (1905–20); director, Yale observatory (1920–41). Investigated stellar parallax, motion in the line of sight, solar rotation, spectroscopic binaries, etc.

**Schleswig–Holstein–Sönderborg–Glücksburg.** See OLDENBURG, 4.

**Schley** (slī), **Winfield Scott.** 1839–1911. American naval officer; grad. U.S.N.A., Annapolis (1860). Commanded rescue expedition in Arctic (1884) searching for Lieut. Greely. Second to Admiral William T. Sampson in commanding naval force blockading Santiago de Cuba (1898); because of Sampson's absence from the spot at time of emergence of Spanish fleet, directed action resulting in destruction of that fleet (July 3, 1898); central figure in unfortunate controversy over assignment of credit for American victory. Rear admiral (1899); retired (1901).

**Schley'er** (shlī'ẽr), **Johann Martin.** 1831–1912. German Roman Catholic clergyman and linguistic scholar; inventor of Volapük (first published 1880).

**Schlich** (shlĭk), Sir **William.** 1840–1925. English forester, of German descent; naturalized in England (1886); inspector general of forests to government of India (1881); organized first school of forestry in England (1885), transferred to Oxford U. (1905); professor of forestry, Oxford (1905–19); author of *A Manual of Forestry* (5 vols.), *Forestry in the United Kingdom*, etc.

**Schlief'fen** (shlē'fĕn), Count **Alfred von.** 1833–1913. German soldier; chief of general staff (1891–1905); promoted field marshal (1911); drew up what was known as the "swinging door" plan (Schlieffen plan) for a war against France, by which a northern army and a southern army were to swing around a central "hinge" and crush French resistance.

**Schlie'mann** (shlē'män), **Heinrich.** 1822–1890. German traveler and archaeologist; in business (until c. 1863); amassed large fortune; in California at time it entered the Union (1850) and thus acquired American citizenship. Devoted himself to study of Homeric sites (from 1868); conducted excavations in Asia Minor and opened up what he believed to be ruins of ancient Troy; later excavated and explored remains in Mycenae (1876), Orchomenus (1881), Tiryns (1884). Among his works are *Ithaka, der Peloponnes und Troja* (1869), *Trojanische Altertümer* (1874), *Mykenä* (1878), *Ilios* (1881), *Orchomenos* (1881), *Troja* (1883), *Tiryns* (1886).

**Schlik** *or* **Schlick** (shlĭk), Count **Franz von.** 1789–1862. Austrian general; commanded 2d army at battle of Solferino (1859).

**Schlos'ser** (shlŏs'ẽr), **Friedrich Christoph.** 1776–1861. German historian; author of *Geschichte des 18. Jahrhunderts* (2 vols, 1823), *Weltgeschichte für das Deutsche Volk* (19 vols., 1843–57).

**Schlö'zer** (shlû'tsẽr), **August Ludwig von.** 1735–1809. German historian; chief works are *Vorstellung der Universalhistorie* (1772), *Vorbereitung zur Weltgeschichte für Kinder* (1779).

**Schlü'ter** (shlü'tẽr), **Andreas.** 1664–1714. German sculptor and architect; chief architect (1699–1706) of the royal palace in Berlin; among his sculptures are the equestrian statue of the great elector in Berlin, tomb of Frederick I and his consort.

**Schma'len·bach** (shmä'lĕn·bäk), **Eugen.** 1873–1955. German economist; specialized in study of business organization and management.

**Schmauk** (shmouk), **Theodore Emanuel.** 1860–1920. American Lutheran clergyman, b. Lancaster, Pa.; president, General Council of the Evangelical Lutheran Church in North America (1903); author of *A History of the Lutheran Church in Pennsylvania* (1902–03), etc.

**Schmauss** (shmous), **August.** 1877–1954. German meteorologist.

**Schme'ling** (shmā'lĭng), **Max.** 1905– . German professional pugilist and soldier; world heavyweight champion (1930–32).

**Schmer'ling** (shmĕr'lĭng), **Anton von.** 1805–1893. Austrian jurist and statesman; premier of Austria (1860–65); first president of Austrian supreme court (1865–91).

**Schmet'tow** (shmĕt'ō), Count **Eberhard von.** 1861–1935. German soldier; lieutenant general, cavalry commander, in World War (1914–18).

**Schmidt** (shmĭt), **Adolf Wilhelm.** 1812–1887. German historian; professor, Zurich (1851) and Jena (1860); member of Frankfort parliament (1848) and Reichstag (1874–76).

**Schmidt, Eduard.** See Kasimir EDSCHMID.

**Schmidt, Georg Friedrich.** 1712–1775. German engraver and etcher; among his engravings are portraits of Empress Elizabeth, after Louis Tocqué, Pierre Mignard, after Rigaud, Frederick the Great, after Pesne; among his etchings, 25 plates after Rembrandt.

**Schmidt, Isaac Jakob.** 1779–1847. German philologist; authority on Mongolian and Tibetan languages.

**Schmidt, Johannes.** 1843–1901. German philologist; made special study of Indo-Germanic.

**Schmidt, Julian,** *in full* **Heinrich Julian.** 1818–1886. German journalist and historian of literature.

**Schmidt, Kaspar.** See Max STIRNER.

**Schmidt, Nathaniel.** 1862–1939. Orientalist, b. in Sweden; professor of Semitic languages and literatures, Colgate U. (1888–96), Cornell U. (1896–1932).

**Schmidt, Oskar.** 1823–1886. German zoologist; investigated flatworms and sponges.

**Schmidt, Otto Ernst.** *Pseudonym* **Otto Ernst** (ĕrnst). 1862–1926. German writer of novels, plays, and essays. His plays include *Die Grösste Sünde* (1895), *Jugend von Heute* (1899), *Bannermann* (1904); his fiction, *Kartäusergeschichten* (1895), *Semper der Jüngling* (1907), *Semper der Mann* (1916); his essays, *Neitzsche, der Falsche Prophet* (1914), etc.

**Schmidt, Wilhelm.** 1868–1954. Austrian philologist and ethnographer.

**Schmidt'bonn** (shmĭt'bôn), **Wilhelm.** *Pseudonym of* **Wilhelm Schmidt.** 1876–1952. German writer; director of the Düsseldorf theater (1906–08); author of plays, short stories, novels, fairy tales, and poetry.

**Schmidt'–Rott'luff** (shmĭt'rŏt'lo͝of), **Karl.** 1884– . German painter of landscapes and portraits; associated with ultramodern development toward abstractionism in German art. See Erich HECKEL.

**Schmitt** (shmĭt), **Aloys.** 1788–1866. German pianist; composer of operas, oratorios, masses, overtures, and chamber music.

**Schmitt** (shmĭt), **Bernadotte Everly.** 1886–1969. American historian, b. Strasburg, Va.; professor, U. of Chicago (from 1925); editor, *Journal of Modern History* (from 1929); author of *England and Germany, 1740–1914* (1916), *Triple Alliance and Triple Entente* (1934), etc. Awarded Pulitzer prize for history (1931) for his *The Coming of the War, 1914.* Editor for Reference History section of *Webster's New International Dictionary, Second Edition.*

**Schmitt, Carl.** 1888– . German legal scholar.

**Schmitt** (shmēt), **Florent.** 1870–1958. French composer of an opera, *Antony et Cléopâtre* (1920), three ballets, symphonic poems, orchestral works, chamber music, and piano pieces.

**Schmitz, Ettore.** See Italo Svevo.

**Schmol'ler** (shmôl'ẽr), **Gustav.** 1838–1917. German economist and historian; leader of younger German school of economic thought. Among his works are *Grundriss der Allgemeinen Volkswirtschaftslehre* (2 vols., 1900–04), *Die Soziale Frage* (1918).

**Schmuck'er** (shmŭk'ẽr; *Ger.* shmo͝ok'ẽr). Name of a family of Lutheran clergymen in U.S., including: **John George** (1771–1854), b. Michelstadt, Ger.; to U.S. (1785); ordained in Pennsylvania (1800); pastorates at Hagerstown, Md. (1794–1809), York Pa. (1809–36), and in York County (1836–52). His son **Samuel Simon** (1799–1873) was a founder of, and first professor in, Gettysburg Theol. Sem. (1826–64); a founder and first president of Gettysburg College (1832–34); leader of the low-church Lutheran party in America. Samuel Simon's son **Beale Melanchthon** (1827–1888) was leader of high-church party in Lutheran church and renowned liturgical scholar; collaborated with A. T. Geissenhainer in *A Liturgy for the Use of the Evangelical Lutheran Church* (1860).

**Schna'bel** (shnä'bĕl), **Artur.** 1882–1951. Concert pianist, b. in Austria. Composed numerous works for piano, orchestra, voice; his later work atonal. Edited and recorded Beethoven's piano works. Lecturer, U. of Chicago (1940, 1945); U. of Michigan (1943).

**Schnabel, Johann Gottfried.** *Pseudonym* **Gi·san'der** (gē·zän'dẽr). 1690?–?1750. German writer; known esp. for his imitations of *Robinson Crusoe,* as in *Die Insel Felsenburg* (4 vols., 1731–43).

**Schneck'en·bur'ger** (shnĕk'ĕn·bo͝or'gẽr), **Max.** 1819–1849. German poet; author of the words of the German patriotic song *Die Wacht am Rhein* (1840; music by Karl Wilhelm).

**Schnee** (shnā), **Heinrich.** 1871–1949. German colonial administrator; governor, German East Africa (1912–19); author of *German East Africa in the World War* (1919), *German Colonial Encyclopaedia* (1920), etc.

**Schnee'voigt** (shnā'fōt), **Georg.** 1872–1947. Finnish violoncellist and orchestra conductor.

**Schnei'der** (shnī'dẽr), **Friedrich.** 1786–1853. German conductor, and composer of 7 operas, 16 oratorios, 25 cantatas, 13 psalms, 5 hymns, 23 symphonies, many overtures, piano sonatas, choral works, and songs.

**Schneider, Hermann.** 1886– . German literary historian; author of *Heldendichtung, Geistlichendichtung, Ritterdichtung* (1925), *Germanische Altertumskunde* (1938), etc.

**Schneider, Johann Gottlob.** 1750–1822. German lexicographer; chief work, a Greek-German dictionary (pub. 1797–98), which became the foundation of all later Greek-German dictionaries.

**Schnei'der'** (shnā'dâr'; *Angl.* shnī'dẽr), **Joseph Eugène.** 1805–1875. French industrialist; with his brother **Adolphe** (d. 1845), organized company and bought (1836) ironworks at Le Creusot, which he later developed into largest steel-manufacturing and munitions plant in the world; the Schneider gun was so named in his honor. Supported coup d'état of Louis Napoleon (Dec. 2, 1851); titular president of Corps Législatif (1867–70).

**Schnei'der** (shnī'dẽr), **Louis.** *Pseudonym* **L. W. Both** (bōt). 1805–1878. German actor and writer; comedian at Royal Theater, Berlin; stage compositions include *Die Schöne Müllerin, Der Schauspieldirektor, Der Kurmärker und die Picarde;* historical writings include *Geschichte der Oper und des Königlichen Opernhauses in Berlin* (1852), *König Wilhelm* (1869).

**Schnei'de·win** (shnī'dĕ·vĭn), **Friedrich Wilhelm.** 1810–1856. German classical scholar; best known for his edition of Sophocles (7 vols., 1849–54).

**Schnitter.** See Johannes Agricola.

**Schnitzer, Eduard.** Real name of Emin Pasha.

**Schnitz'ler** (shnĭts'lẽr), **Arthur.** 1862–1931. Austrian physician, playwright, and novelist, b. Vienna; practiced in Vienna (from 1885). Among his plays are *Anatol* (1893), *Paracelsus* (1899), *Der Einsame Weg* (1904), *Die Grosse Scene* (1915); among works of fiction, *Die Frau des Weisen* (1898), *Leutnant Gustl* (1901), *Frau Bertha Garlan* (1901), *Doktor Gräsler, Badearzt* (1916), *Casanovas Heimkehr* (1918), *Fräulein Else* (1924), *Traumnovelle* (1926).

**Schnorr von Ca'rols·feld** (shnôr' fôn kä'rôls·fĕlt), **Julius.** 1795–1872. German painter; works include frescoes in Villa Massimi in Rome and in Königsbau and Festsaalbau in Munich. Published *Bibel in Bildern,* with over 200 illustrations (1852–60). His son **Ludwig** (1836–1865) was an operatic tenor; known esp. as an interpreter of Wagnerian roles.

**Scho'ber** (shō'bẽr), **Johann.** 1874–1932. Austrian statesman; in Austrian imperial police service (from 1898); president of Vienna police (1914, 1922–29). Chancellor of Austria (June, 1921–May, 1922; Sept., 1929–Sept., 1930); vice-chancellor and minister of foreign affairs (Dec., 1930–Feb., 1932).

**Scho'bert** (shō'bẽrt), **Johann.** d. 1767. German pianist, and composer of sonatas, concertos, and chamber symphonies.

**Schoef'fel** (?shĕf'ĕl), **John B.** 1846–1918. American impresario, associated with Henry Eugene Abbey (*q.v.*). See also Agnes Booth.

**Schoel'cher'** (shĕl'shâr'), **Victor.** 1804–1893. French politician; journalist on liberal papers in Paris; devoted efforts chiefly to emancipation of slaves in French possessions, finally achieving success (1848). Expelled from France after the coup d'état (Dec. 2, 1851); an exile in England (to 1870); elected senator for life (1875).

**Schoen** (shûn), Baron **Wilhelm Eduard von.** 1851–1933. German diplomat; ambassador to Russia (1906) and France (1910–14); transmitted declaration of war, Germany against France (Aug. 3, 1914).

**Schoenberg.** = Schönberg.

**Schoe'ne·feld** (shû'nĕ·fĕld), **Henry.** 1857–1936. American musician and director, b. Milwaukee; teacher and director in Chicago (1879–1902); musical director of Germania Turnverein, Los Angeles (from 1911), and of the Woman's Symphony Orchestra of Los Angeles.

**Schoen'hof** (shûn'hōf), **Jacob.** 1839–1903. Merchant and economist, b. at Oppenheim, Ger.; to U.S. (1861); wholesale lace merchant in New York (1861–84); retired (1884); in U.S. consular service in England (1885); given special mission by Secretary of State Bayard to study industrial conditions abroad; strong advocate of free trade.

**Schoe'ten·sack** (shû'tĕn·zäk), **Otto.** 1850–1912. German prehistorian and anthropologist; investigated neolithic beds of the middle Rhine; discovered (1907) lower jaw of a fossil man in the sands at Mauer near Heidelberg, regarded as belonging to an extinct species of man which he called "Heidelberg man."

**Schöf'fer** (shûf'ĕr), **Peter.** 1425?–1502 (or 1503). German printer; an assistant to Johann Fust, and Fust's successor (1466); gained reputation as an inventor of matrices and the type mold, and as father of letter founders, largely as a result of his own unjustified claims that he perfected the art of printing.

**Scho'field** (skō'fēld), **John McAllister.** 1831–1906. American army officer; grad. U.S.M.A., West Point (1853). Brigadier general of volunteers (Nov., 1861); major general (May, 1863); an army commander in Sherman's Atlanta campaign (1864); defeated Hood in battles of Franklin and Nashville; commander, department of North Carolina (1865). U.S. secretary of war (1868–69). Major general, U.S. army, commanding department of the Missouri (1869), division of the Pacific (1870–76, 1882–83), division of the Missouri (1883–86), division of the Atlantic (1886–88). Superintendent, U.S.M.A., West Point (1876–81). General in chief, U.S. army (1888–95). Lieutenant general, U.S. army (1895); retired (1895). Author of an autobiography, *Forty-Six Years in the Army* (1897).

**Schofield, Walter Elmer.** 1867–1944. American painter, b. Philadelphia.

**Schofield, William Henry.** 1870–1920. Scholar and educator, b. Brockville, Ontario, Canada; professor, Harvard (from 1906). Author of *English Literature, from the Norman Conquest to Chaucer* (1906), *Chivalry in English Literature* (1912), etc.

**Schokalsky.** See SHOKALSKI.

**Scholarios, Georgios.** See GENNADIUS II.

**Scholes** (skōlz), **Percy Alfred.** 1877–1958. English musicologist; music critic, London *Evening Standard* and British Broadcasting Corp.; extension lecturer at Oxford, Cambridge, Manchester, and London U.

**Schöll** (shûl), **Adolf.** 1805–1882. German archaeologist and critic; among his works are *Beiträge zur Kenntnis der Tragischen Poesie der Griechen* (1839), *Sophokles* (1840), and *Goethe in Hauptzügen seines Lebens und Wirkens* (1882).

**Schol'laert** (skŏl'ärt), **François.** 1851–1917. Belgian statesman; prime minister (1908–11); took over Congo Free State and made it a province of Belgium under name of Belgian Congo.

**Schol'ten** (skŏl'tĕn), **Jan Hendrik.** 1811–1885. Dutch Protestant theologian; leader of school of theological criticism in the Netherlands.

**Scholtz** (shōlts), **Friedrich von.** 1851–1927. German artillery general in World War (1914–18).

**Scholz** (shōlts), **Wilhelm von.** 1874– . German writer; dramaturgist and play director, Court Theater, Stuttgart (1910–23); author of verse, plays, and fiction.

**Schö'mann** (shû'män), **Georg Friedrich.** 1793–1879. German classical scholar.

**Schom'berg** (shōm'bĕrk; *Angl.* shŏm'bûrg), **Friedrich Hermann.** Duke of **Schomberg** (*cr.* 1689, *in English peerage*). 1615?–1690. Soldier of fortune, b. Heidelberg; served under prince of Orange (1633), in Swedish army in Germany (1634), in Dutch army (1639–50), in French army (from 1650), in Portuguese service (1660–68). Naturalized in France (1668); French marshal (1675), left France after revocation of Edict of Nantes (1685); general in chief of Brandenburg army (1687). Accompanied William of Orange to England (1688) as second in command; naturalized in England (1689); commanded expedition to Ireland against James II (1689–90); killed at battle of the Boyne (1690).

**Schom'berg'** (*Fr.* shôn'bĕrg'), **Gaspard de.** 1540–1599. German-born French soldier; naturalized in France (1570). Distinguished himself at Moncontour (1569) and Dormans (1575); honored by Henry III and Henry IV; councilor in charge of administration of finance under Henry IV. His son Comte **Henri** (1575–1632), marshal of France (1625), aided in siege of La Rochelle (1628) and fought in Lorraine (1631). Henri's son **Charles,** Duc **d'Hal'lu·in'** [dȧ'lü·ăN'] (1601–1656), was governor of Languedoc (1632–44), marshal of France (1637), viceroy of Catalonia (1648).

**Schom'burgk** (shŏm'bûrk; *Ger.* shōm'bŏŏrk), Sir **Robert Hermann.** 1804–1865. British traveler and explorer, b. Freiburg; with assistance of Royal Geographical Society, made geographical and botanical exploration of British Guiana, on which he discovered the victoria regia lily; surveyed boundaries of British Guiana, establishing Schomburgk line (1841–43); consul to Santo Domingo (1848) and Bangkok (1857–64). His brother **Moritz Richard** (1811–1890), botanist, accompanied him in exploration of British Guiana (1840–42); was director of botanical garden at Adelaide, Australia (1866–90).

**Schön** (shûn), **Martin.** See Martin SCHONGAUER.

**Schön, Theodor von.** 1772–1856. Prussian statesman; associated with Stein and Hardenberg in carrying out reforms in Prussian government after Treaty of Tilsit (1807); urged liberal reforms upon Frederick William IV (1840).

**Schön'bach** (shûn'bäk), **Anton Emanuel.** 1848–1911. Austrian philologist; made special study of old German literature, esp. theological literature.

**Schön'bein** (shûn'bīn), **Christian Friedrich.** 1799–1868. German chemist; discovered ozone (1839); first to produce guncotton (1845) and from it collodion.

**Schön'berg** (shûn'bĕrk), **Arnold.** 1874–1951. Austrian composer; identified with ultramodern school of music by his departure from accepted forms of composition; to U.S. (1933; citizen, 1940) as teacher, conductor; prof., U.C.L.A. (1936–44). Works include string sextet *Verklärte Nacht* (1899), *Gurrelieder* (a large work for solo voices, chorus, and orchestra; performed 1913), the symphonic poem *Pelleas and Melisande*, dramatic works, as *Erwartung* and *Die Glückliche Hand* (both performed 1924), the cycle *Pierrot Lunaire* (1912), pieces for mixed chorus, songs, chamber music, orchestral and piano works, etc.

**Schö'ne·mann** (shû'nĕ·män), **Lili,** *really* **Anna Elisabeth.** 1758–1817. German woman beloved by Goethe (c. 1774) and central figure, under name Lili, in Goethe's lyrics of this period; later married the Strasbourg banker Bernhard Friedrich von Türckheim (d. 1831).

**Schö'ner** (shû'nĕr), **Johannes.** 1477–1547. German astronomer and geographer; author of numerous mathematical, astronomical, and geographical works; made terrestrial globes, including the first bearing the name *America.*

**Schön'feld** (shûn'fĕlt), **Eduard.** 1828–1891. German astronomer; assisted Argelander (*q.v.*) in the preparation of Durchmusterung, a catalogue of stars of the Northern Hemisphere to the 9–10th magnitude, and later extended the catalogue to 23°, south declination; catalogued 489 nebulae.

**Schon'gau'er** (shōn'gou'ĕr), **Martin.** *Also known as* **Martin Schön** (shûn) *and* **Hipsch** *or* **Hübsch Mar'tin** (mär'tēn). 1445?–1491. German engraver and painter, b. in Colmar; established a school of painting in Colmar, which became the most important center of late Gothic art in Upper Germany; chief painting, a picture of the Madonna and Child, known as *Madonna of the Rose-hedge,* now at Colmar. He is best known as an engraver, reputed the greatest of the 15th century.

**Schön'herr** (shûn'hĕr), **Karl.** 1867–1943. Austrian playwright; author of *Judas von Tirol* (1897), *Erde* (1908), *Glaube und Heimat* (1911), *Volk in Not* (1916), *Es* (1923), *Herr Doktor, Haben Sie Zu Essen* (1930), etc.

**Schön'lein** (shûn'līn), **Johann Lukas.** 1793–1864. German physician; pioneer in clinical method of teaching medicine; discovered the vegetable parasite causing favus; described purpura rheumatica, hence also called Schönlein's disease.

**Schön'than** (shûn'tän), **Franz von.** 1849–1913. Austrian playwright; chief director, Vienna municipal theater (1883); collaborated with his brother **Paul** (1853–1905) and other playwrights in a number of stage compositions.

**School'craft** (sko͞ol'kràft), **Henry Rowe.** 1793–1864. American ethnologist; explored mineral deposits of southern Missouri and Arkansas (1817–18); with Cass exploring expedition to Lake Superior region (1820). Indian agent in Lake Superior region (1822–36); superintendent of Indian affairs for Michigan (1836–41).

**Schoorle.** See SCOREL.

**Scho'pen·hau'er** (shō'pĕn·hou'ẽr), **Arthur.** 1788–1860. German philosopher; resident in Frankfort (from 1831); chief expounder of pessimism. Among his works are *Über die Vierfache Wurzel des Satzes vom Zureichenden Grunde* (1813), *Die Welt als Wille und Vorstellung* (1819), *Über den Willen in der Natur* (1836), *Die Beiden Grundprobleme der Ethik* (1841). His mother, **Johanna,** *nee* **Tro'sie'ner** [trō'zē'nẽr] (1766–1838), was a writer of short stories, novels, and books of travel.

**Schop'fer'** (shôp'fâr'), **Jean.** *Pseudonym* **Claude A'net'** (à'nĕ'). 1868–1931. French novelist and essayist; author of *Petite Ville* (1901), *Les Bergeries* (1904), *La Révolution Russe* (4 vols., 1917–19), *Quand la Terre Trembla* (1921), *Mademoiselle Bourrat* (1923; play), *La Fille Perdue* (1924; play).

**Schoppe.** See SCIOPPIUS.

**Schorel.** See SCOREL.

**Schor'lem'mer** (shôr'lĕm'ẽr), **Carl.** 1834–1892. Chemist, b. in Darmstadt, Germany; naturalized as British subject (1879); showed that normal paraffins form a single instead of double series; made important observations on the valence of carbon.

**Schorr** (shôr), **Friedrich.** 1888–1953. Operatic baritone, b. in Hungary; American debut, as Hans Sachs in *Die Meistersinger*, in Baltimore (1923); joined Metropolitan Opera Company (1925); known for Wagnerian roles.

**Schott** (shŏt), **Charles Anthony.** 1826–1901. Civil engineer and geodesist, b. Mannheim, Baden, Germany; to U.S. (1848); naturalized (1853); on staff of U.S. Coast Survey (1848–1900); known esp. for researches in geodesy and terrestrial magnetism.

**Schott** (shôt), **Walter.** 1861–1938. German sculptor.

**Schott'ky** (shôt'kē), **Friedrich Hermann.** 1851–1935. German mathematician; worked on problems concerning the theory of functions. His son Walter (1886–1976), physicist, was known for researches dealing with the theory of electrons, the theory of ions, and the problem of electroacoustics; invented the screen-grid tube (1915); discovered an irregularity in the emission of thermions in a vacuum tube, the shot, or Schottky, effect.

**Schou'ler** (sko͞o'lẽr), **William.** 1814–1872. Journalist and historian, b. near Glasgow, Scotland; to U.S. (1816); editor, *Ohio State Journal*, Columbus, Ohio (1856–58), Boston *Atlas and Daily Bee* (from 1858); author of *A History of Massachusetts in the Civil War* (2 vols., 1868–71). His son **James** (1839–1920) was a lawyer and historian; served in Union army in Civil War; practiced law in Boston and Washington; noted for his *History of the United States of America under the Constitution* (7 vols., 1880–1913).

**Schou'ten** (sкou'tĕn), **Willem Cornelis.** 1567?–1625. Dutch mariner in service of the East India Co.; sailed west to the East Indies, the first to double Cape Horn (1616), which he named after his birthplace (Hoorn).

**Schra'der** (shrä'dẽr), **Eberhard.** 1836–1908. German Protestant theologian and Assyriologist; author of works of Biblical criticism and treatises on Oriental philology, ethnology, and history.

**Schrader, Otto.** 1855–1919. German philologist; chief works, *Sprachvergleichung und Urgeschichte* (1883), *Reallexikon der Indogermanischen Altertumskunde* (1901).

**Schrau'dolph** (shrou'dôlf), **Johannes von.** 1808–1879. German painter; assisted Hess in decorating All Saints Chapel in the Basilica, Munich; also, decorated the interior of the cathedral at Spires (with his brother **Claudius,** 1813–1891). Johannes's son **Claudius** (1843–1902) was also a painter.

**Schreiber,** Lady **Charlotte Elizabeth.** = Lady Charlotte GUEST.

**Schrei'ber** (shrī'bẽr), **Georges** (zhôrzh). 1904– . American painter, b. Brussels; educ. in Brussels and elsewhere in Europe; to U.S. (1928), naturalized (1938); editor and compiler of *Portraits and Self Portraits* (1936); represented in Metropolitan and Whitney Museums, N.Y. City, and museums in Brooklyn, Syracuse, Terre Haute, Los Angeles, etc.

**Schrei'ner** (shrī'nẽr), **Ol'ive** (ŏl'ĭv) **Em'i·lie** (ĕm'ĭ·lĭ; *Ger.* â·mē'lē·ĕ) **Al'ber·ti'na** (ăl'bẽr·tē'nȧ). *Pseudonym* **Ralph I'ron** (ī'ẽrn; ī'rŭn). 1855–1920. British author and feminist; b. in Basutoland, daughter of a Lutheran missionary. Governess in South Africa; scored success with *The Story of an African Farm* (1883), depicting life on a Boer farm and the spiritual problems of an imaginative spirit; author also of works on politics and emancipation of women, and the unfinished novel *From Man to Man* (1926); correspondent of Havelock Ellis (1884–1917). M. (1894) **Samuel Cron Cronwright** (1863–1936), a mem. of the Cape parliament and her biographer, who took name **Cron'wright-Schrei'ner** (krŏn'rīt-). Her brother **William Philip Schreiner** (1857–1919) was a South African statesman; prime minister of Cape Colony (1898–1900); high commissioner for Union of South Africa, in London (1914–19).

**Schre'ker** (shrā'kẽr), **Franz.** 1878–1934. Austrian composer of operas (both music and librettos), including *Der Ferne Klang* (1912), *Der Singende Teufel* (1928), *Der Schmied von Gent* (1932).

**Schre·ve'li·us** (sкrâ·vā'lē·ŭs), **Cornelis.** 1615?–?1664. Dutch classical scholar.

**Schrey'er** (shrī'ẽr), **Adolf.** 1828–1899. German painter, esp. of Austrian military scenes and travel scenes in Asia Minor and Algeria.

**Schrief'fer** (shrē'fẽr), **John Robert.** 1931– . Physicist, b. Oak Park, Ill. Ph.D., U. of Ill. Shared 1972 Nobel prize for physics with John Bardeen and Leon Cooper for studies of superconductivity of metals.

**Schrö'der** (shrû'dẽr), **Alwin.** 1855–1928. German violoncellist; played in Boston, Mass., U.S.A. (from 1886). His brother **Carl** (1848–1935) was solo cellist, Gewandhaus Orchestra, Leipzig (1874–81); court Kapellmeister, Sondershausen (1881), and founder of a conservatory of music there; instructor in Stern Conservatory of Music, Berlin (1911–21); composer of operas, symphonies, and vocal, piano, and violoncello pieces.

**Schröder, Friedrich Ludwig.** 1744–1816. German actor, theater manager, and playwright; as an actor, esp. successful in tragic roles.

**Schröder, Ludwig von.** 1854–1933. German admiral in command of the German end of the North Sea during World War (1914–18).

**Schröder,** Sophie, *nee* **Bür'ger** (bür'gẽr). 1781–1868. German actress; wife (1804–18) of the singer Friedrich Schröder; excelled in tragic roles. Her daughter **Wilhelmine Schrö'der–De·vri'ent'** [-dē·vrē'äɴ'; -dĕ·vrēnt'] (1804–1860) was an operatic soprano; m. 1st, Karl Devrient (*q.v.;* 1823; divorced or separated, 1828), 2d, Herr von Döring (later divorced), and 3d, Herr von Bock (1850); member of Dresden opera company (1823–47); lieder singer in Berlin until she retired (c. 1856).

**Schrö'ding·er** (shrû'dĭng·ẽr), **Erwin.** 1887–1961. Austrian physicist; known for work on the wave theory of matter and on the new quantum theory; developed a concept of atomic structure based on wave mechanics; shared with Paul Dirac the 1933 Nobel prize for physics. Also made important contributions to the theory of color and investigated radium.

**Schrödter, Adolf.** = Adolf Schroedter.

**Schroe'der** (shrû'dẽr), **Leopold von.** 1851–1920. German Sanskrit scholar.

**Schroe'der** (?shrō'dẽr), **Seaton.** 1849–1922. American naval officer; grad. U.S.N.A., Annapolis (1868); with Lieut. William H. Driggs, developed the Driggs-Schroeder gun (1888–89).

**Schroed'ter** (shrût'ẽr), **Adolf.** 1805–1875. German painter, esp. of humorous genre scenes and representations of Don Quixote and Falstaff.

**Schu'bart** (shōō'bärt), **Christian Friedrich Daniel.** 1739–1791. German musician and poet; founded *Deutsche Chronik,* Augsburg (1774); imprisoned by duke of Württemberg (1777–87); under patronage of Frederick the Great (1787); music director of the court and theater in Stuttgart. Among his best poems are *Die Fürstengruft, Kaplied, Friedrich der Grosse.*

**Schu'bert** (shōō'bẽrt), **Franz Peter.** 1797–1828. Austrian composer, b. Vienna. Music teacher in Vienna; began writing songs at the age of fourteen; wrote *The Erlking* at the age of eighteen; during his short life wrote about 600 songs; recognized as one of the greatest masters of song in musical history; others of his famous songs are *Who is Sylvia?* and *Hark, Hark, the Lark.* Among other compositions are a symphony in C major, a symphony in B minor (unfinished), sixteen sonatas, and chamber music.

**Schubert, Gotthilf Heinrich von.** 1780–1860. German naturalist and writer on philosophy; influenced at first by the natural philosophy of Schelling; later devoted himself to mysticism; chief work, *Die Geschichte der Seele* (1830).

**Schubert, Hermann.** 1848–1911. German mathematician; professor in Hamburg (1876–1908); known for work on the characteristics of a system of curves.

**Schu'chardt** (shōōĸ'ärt), **Hugo.** 1842–1927. German Romance philologist.

**Schuch'ert** (shŏŏk'ẽrt), **Charles.** 1858–1942. American paleontologist; professor of historical geology, Yale (1904–23; emeritus); author of *Text-book of Historical Geological Paleogeography of North America, The Earth and Its Rhythms.*

**Schück** (shük), **Johan Henrik Emil.** 1855–1947. Swedish historian of literature; professor, Lund (1890–98); Uppsala (1898–1920); president, Nobel Foundation (from 1918); chief works, *Svensk Litteraturhistoria* (1886–90), *Svenska Folkets Historia* (1915).

**Schück'ing** (shük'ĭng), **Levin.** 1814–1883. German journalist and novelist; among his novels are *Die Ritterbürtigen* (3 vols., 1846), *Ein Sohn des Volks* (2 vols., 1849), *Der Bauernfürst* (2 vols., 1851), *Paul Bronkhorst* (3 vols., 1858). His grandson **Walther Schücking** (1875–1935) was a jurist and political leader; member of Reichstag (1919–28); member of Permanent Court of International Justice (1930), first German to be seated on this court.

**Schu'len·burg, von der** (fôn dẽr shōō'lĕn·bŏŏrĸ). German noble family, including: Count **Johann Matthias** (1661–1747), general; served under Marlborough and Prince Eugene against the French, and later (1715) entered the Venetian service to fight against the Turks. Count **Friedrich Wilhelm** (1742–1815), Prussian government official; dismissed after Treaty of Tilsit (1807), he became a general in service of Jerome of Westphalia. Count **Friedrich** (1865–1939), German major general; served in crown prince's army in World War (1914–18). Count **Werner** (1875–1944), diplomat; German ambassador to Russia (1934–41).

**Schu'ler** (shōō'lẽr), **Hans.** 1874–1951. Sculptor, b. in Germany; to U.S. (1880); studio in Baltimore, Md. Among his works are: *Ariadne,* in Walters's Gallery, Baltimore; Buchanan Memorial in Washington, D.C.; portrait bust of George Peabody, in American Hall of Fame.

**Schul'te** (shŏŏl'tĕ), **Aloys.** 1857–1941. German historian; author of *Die Fugger in Rom* (1904), *Tausend Jahre Deutscher Geschichte und Deutscher Kultur am Rhein* (1925), etc.

**Schulte, Johann Friedrich von.** 1827–1914. German Roman Catholic scholar; opposed doctrine of papal infallibility and became (from 1870); a leader among Old Catholics; regarded as an authority on canon law.

**Schulte, Karl Joseph.** 1871–1941. German Roman Catholic prelate; archbishop of Cologne (1920); cardinal (1921). Consistent opponent of Hitlerism and Nazi policies.

**Schul'tens** (sĸûl'tĕns), **Albert.** 1686–1750. Dutch Hebrew and Arabic scholar.

**Schultheiss, Michael.** See Praetorius.

**Schult'hess** (shŏŏlt'hĕs), **Edmund.** 1868–1944. Swiss statesman; president of Swiss Confederation for regular one-year terms (1917, 1921, 1928, 1933).

**Schult'ze** (?shōōlt'sē), **Carl Emil.** *Pseudonym* **Bun'ny** (bŭn'ĭ). 1866–1939. American cartoonist, b. Lexington, Ky.; originated "Foxy Grandpa" comic strip, which appeared in New York *Herald* (1900–02) and in New York *American* (from 1902); on staff of New York *Evening Journal* and International Feature Service, Inc. (1923–27).

**Schult'ze** (shŏŏl'tsĕ), **Johann F. E.** Prussian artillery officer; one of the first to make smokeless powder (c. 1862).

**Schultze, Max Johann Sigismund.** 1825–1874. German anatomist; known esp. for researches in microscopic anatomy; altered the conception of the cell, emphasizing the living protoplasm and not the membrane; demonstrated minute nerve endings in the nose, ear, and retina; investigated life histories of various lower animals.

**Schult'ze–Naum'burg** (-noum'bŏŏrĸ), **Paul.** 1869–1949. German architect and writer; author of *Kunst und Rasse* (1927), *Die Kunst der Deutschen* (1934), *Bauten Schultze-Naumburg* (1939), etc.

**Schulz** (shŏŏlts), **Albert.** 1802–1893. German literary scholar; interested himself in study of old German poetry, esp. that associated with the Arthurian cycle.

**Schulz** (shŏŏlts), **Le'o** (lē'ō). 1865–1944. Cellist, b. in Posen, Poland; to U.S. (1889); soloist and first cellist with New York Philharmonic Society (for thirty years, to 1929), and with New York Symphony Orchestra; also, professor of music at Yale; composer of many works for the violoncello.

**Schulz, Michael.** See Praetorius.

**Schul'ze** (shŏŏl'tsĕ), **Gottlob Ernst.** *Also* **Ä'ne·si·dem'–Schul'ze** (â'nâ·zē·dām'-). 1761–1833. German skeptic and philosopher; author of *Grundriss der Philosophischen Wissenschaften* (2 vols., 1788–90), *Psychische Anthropologie* (1815), *Über die Menschliche Erkenntnis* (1832), etc.

**Schul'ze-De'litzsch** (-dā'lĭch), **Hermann**, *in full* **Franz Hermann**. 1808–1883. German lawyer, economist, and sociologist; member of Prussian legislature (1849–51; 1861 ff.); devoted himself to furthering organization of co-operative societies and people's banks; regarded as founder of workingmen's co-operative associations in Germany.

**Schu'ma'cher** (shōō'mä'ĸẽr), **Heinrich Christian**. 1780–1850. Danish astronomer; professor and director, Copenhagen observatory (1815); directed a triangulation of Holstein and a geodetic survey of Denmark.

**Schumacher, Peder**. See Count GRIFFENFELD.

**Schu'man** (shōō'măn), **Frederick Lewis**. 1904– . American political scientist and writer, b. Chicago; author of *International Politics* (1933), *The Nazi Dictatorship* (1935), *Europe on the Eve* (1939), *Night over Europe* (1941), etc.

**Schuman, William**. 1910– . American composer, b. N.Y. City; at Sarah Lawrence Coll. (1935–45); president, Juilliard Sch. of Music (1945–62), Lincoln Center of Performing Arts (1962–69). Composed symphonies, string quartets, orchestral and choral music, including *American Festival Overture, This Is Our Time* (cantata), and the choral works *Holiday Song, Requiescat*, and *Pioneers;* awarded first Pulitzer prize in music for *Secular Cantata No. 2, A Free Song* (1942).

**Schu'mann** (shōō'män), **Georg**. 1866–1952. German conductor, and composer of symphonies, symphonic poems, overtures, choral works, chamber music, organ and piano pieces, and songs.

**Schumann, Robert**. 1810–1856. German composer, b. Zwickau, in Saxony; studied in Leipzig; founded (1834) and edited (1834–44) the musical journal *Die Neue Zeitschrift für Musik;* settled in Dresden (1844); director of music, Düsseldorf (1850–53); became mentally unbalanced; committed to an asylum (1854). Composer of an opera (*Genoveva*), symphonies, overtures, choral works (as *Paradise and the Peri*), piano pieces (including a piano quintet), and esp. songs; regarded as one of the greatest of Schubert's successors in the art of song writing. His wife (m. 1840), **Clara Josephine**, *nee* **Wieck** [vēk] (1819–1896), was a pianist; renowned for her interpretation of Chopin's works and the piano pieces of her husband; teacher in the conservatory of music, Frankfurt a.M. (1878–92).

**Schumann, Viktor**. 1841–1913. German physicist; investigated that portion of the ultraviolet spectrum lying approximately between 1850 and 1200 angstrom units, developing a plate for photographing it.

**Schu'mann-Heink'** (shōō'măn·hīngk'; *Ger.* shōō'-män-), **Er'nes·ti'ne** (ĕr'nĕs·tē'nĕ), *nee* **Roess'ler** (rûs'-lẽr). 1861–1936. Operatic contralto, b. near Prague, then in Austria; m. Ernst Heink (1882), Paul Schumann (1893), William Rapp, Jr. (1905; divorced 1914). Sang for several seasons (from 1898) with Metropolitan Opera Company in New York, and reappeared with the Metropolitan in *Das Rheingold* at the age of 64 (1926); known also as concert singer, esp. of German lieder.

**Schum'pe'ter** (shŏŏm'pā'tẽr), **Joseph Alois**. 1883–1950. German economist; professor, Harvard (from 1932); author of *Die Sozialen Klassen* (1927), *Business Cycles* (1939), etc.

**Schu'ré'** (shü'rā'), **Édouard**. 1841–1929. French writer; author of books on musical history and on mysticism, novels, verse, as *La Vie Mystique* (1893) and *L'Âme des Temps Nouveaux* (1909), dramas, as *Les Enfants de Lucifer* (1900) and *Léonard de Vinci* (1905), and critical works.

**Schü'rer** (shü'rẽr), **Emil**. 1844–1910. German Protestant theologian; founder and associate editor (1876–81, 1887–1910), *Theologische Literaturzeitung*.

**Schur'man** (shŏŏr'măn), **Jacob Gould**. 1854–1942. American educator and diplomat, b. Freetown, Prince Edward Island, Canada. Professor of philosophy, Cornell (1886–92); president, Cornell (1892–1920). President, first U.S. Philippine commission (1899). U.S. minister to Greece and Montenegro (1912–13); U.S. ambassador to China (1921–25) and to Germany (1925–30). Author of *Kantian Ethics and the Ethics of Evolution* (1881), *Agnosticism and Religion* (1886), *The Ethical Import of Darwinism* (1888), *Why America is in the War* (1917), etc.

**Schurz** (shŏŏrts), **Carl**. 1829–1906. Army officer and politician, b. near Cologne, Germany; involved in revolutionary movement (1848–49); forced to flee Germany; to U.S. (1852); adm. to bar (1859); practiced in Milwaukee; campaigned for Lincoln (1860); U.S. minister to Spain (1861–62). Brigadier general of volunteers (June, 1862); engaged at Second Bull Run, Chancellorsville, Gettysburg; major general (1863). Journalist (1865–68). U.S. senator from Missouri (1869–75); U.S. secretary of the interior (1877–81). An editor, New York *Evening Post* (1881–83); editorial writer for *Harper's Weekly* (1892–98). Resident of New York (from 1881). Author of *Life of Henry Clay* (2 vols., 1887) and volumes of speeches and reminiscences.

**Schusch'nigg** (shŏŏsh'nĭk), **Kurt von**. 1897–1977. Austrian statesman; served in World War I (1914–18). Entered parliament (1927); founded and headed Ostmärkische Sturmscharen, patriotic organization to defend Austria's independence. Minister of justice (1932–34) and education (1933–34); federal chancellor (1934–38) and minister of public security (1937); leader of "Patriotic Front" (1936–38). After Nazi occupation of Austria, was arrested and held in prison and in a concentration camp; liberated (1945). At St. Louis U. (1948–68).

**Schus'sele** (shōō's'l), **Christian**. 1826–1879. French painter; to U.S. (1848). Sartain's engravings of many of Schussele's paintings made the artist widely known.

**Schu'ster** (shōō'stẽr), Sir **Arthur**. 1851–1934. British physicist; led Royal Society eclipse expedition to Siam (1875); professor of physics, U. of Manchester (1888–1907); made researches in spectroscopy, esp. relating to the spectra of the solar corona and of the stars, also in calorimetry, radiometry, seismology, and terrestrial magnetism; author of *A Theory of Optics* (1904), *The Progress of Physics* (1911), etc. His brother Sir **Felix** (1854–1936), financier, was governor, Union of London and Smith's Bank (1895–1918); member, Council of India (1906–16).

**Schuster, Max Lincoln**. 1897–1971. American publisher, b. in Austria of American parents; to U.S. as infant; B.Litt., Columbia (1917); engaged in journalism; cofounder (1924; with Richard Leo Simon, *q.v.*) and partner, Simon and Schuster, book publishers, N.Y. City; editor of *A Treasury of the World's Great Letters* (1940).

**Schütz** (shüts), **Heinrich**. *Known also as* **Sa'git·ta'ri·us** (zä'gĭ·tä'rē·ŏŏs). 1585–1672. German composer, esp. of church music, as sacred songs and symphonies, psalms, passion music, and choral works, and of the first German opera, *Daphne* (1627). See Martin OPITZ.

**Schut'zen'ber'ger'** (shüt'sĕn'bĕr'zhâr'), **Paul**. 1827?–1897. French chemist, known for work in physiological chemistry, researches on dyestuffs, fermentation, etc.;

author of *Traité des Matières Colorantes* (1867), *Les Fermentations* (1875), *Traité de Chimie Générale* (1879–90; his most important work), etc.

**Schuy'ler** (skī'lẽr), **Philip John.** 1733–1804. American statesman, b. Albany, N.Y. Served (1755–60) in French and Indian War. Delegate to Continental Congress (1775). Major general, Continental army, commanding northern department; organized expedition (1775–76) to attack Canada; after disagreements with Gen. David Wooster and Gen. Horatio Gates, superseded in his command by Gates (1777); resigned (1779). Member, Continental Congress (1778–81); one of first two U.S. senators from New York (1789–91, 1797–98); aggressive supporter of financial program of Alexander Hamilton, his son-in-law. A great-granddaughter of his, **Louisa Lee Schuyler** (1837–1926), was a prominent social-welfare worker.

**Schwab** (shwŏb), **Charles Michael.** 1862–1939. American industrialist, b. Williamsburg, Pa.; educ. St. Francis College. In employ of Carnegie Steel Co., beginning as stake driver in engineering gang; president, Carnegie Steel Co. (1897–1901), U.S. Steel Corp. (1901–03), Bethlehem Steel Corp. (1903–13) and chairman of the board (from 1913). During World War I, served as director-general of shipbuilding for U.S. Shipping Board Emergency Fleet Corp. (1918).

**Schwab** (shväp), **Gustav.** 1792–1850. German writer; published *Der Bodensee* (verse; 1827), a life of Schiller (1840), anthologies of German prose and lyric poetry, and *Schönste Sagen des Klassischen Altertums* (3 vols., 1838–40), *Deutsche Volksbücher* (3 vols., 1836 ff.).

**Schwa'be** (shvä'bĕ), **Heinrich Samuel.** 1789–1875. German astronomer of Dessau; discovered the eleven-year periodicity of sunspots (1843).

**Schwal'be** (shväl'bĕ), **Gustav.** 1844–1917. German anatomist and anthropologist; known for researches on the racial development of man, esp. in connection with fossil remains, as the Neanderthal skull and skull remains from South America.

**Schwann** (shvän), **Theodor.** 1810–1882. German naturalist; professor of anatomy (1848) and physiology (1858), Liége. Discovered pepsin; made researches on artificial digestion, conduction in nerves, the laws of muscular contraction, spontaneous generation, putrefaction and fermentation; commonly credited with founding the cell theory.

**Schwan'tha'ler** (shvän'tä'lẽr), **Ludwig von.** 1802–1848. German sculptor; studio in Munich. Among his works are the colossal statue *Bavaria*, sculptures for the royal palace, the glyptotheca, and the Old Pinakothek (all in Munich).

**Schwartz** (shwȧrts), **Marie Sophie,** *nee* **Bi'rath** (*prob.* bē'rät). 1819–1894. Swedish novelist; among her works are *A Man of Rank and a Woman of the People* (1858), *David Waldner* (1866), *The Grandson* (1872).

**Schwartz** (shvärts), **Wilhelm.** 1821–1899. German scholar; a founder of the study of comparative mythology.

**Schwarz** (shvärts), **Berthold.** German monk and alchemist, of 13th or 14th century; reputed inventor of gunpowder. His identity with the Franciscan, Meister **Ber'thold** (bĕr'tōlt), *real name* **Konstantin Anck'lit'zer** (ängk'lĭt'sẽr) *or* **Ank'lit'zen** (ängk'lĭt'sĕn) *or* **An'ge·li'sen** (äng'gĕ·lē'zĕn), who lived in Freiburg (c. 1250), has not been definitely established.

**Schwarz** (shwôrts), **Eugene A·man'dus** (ȧ·măn'dŭs). 1844–1928. Entomologist, b. at Liegnitz, Silesia, Germany; to U.S. (1872); on staff, U.S. Department of Agriculture (1878–1926), in bureau of entomology (from 1881); custodian of collection of Coleoptera in U.S. National Museum, Washington, D.C. (1898–1926).

**Schwarz** (shvärts), **Hermann.** 1864–1952. German philosopher.

**Schwarz, Hermann Amandus.** 1843–1921. German mathematician; worked on the theory of minimal surfaces and on the theory of functions.

**Schwarz, Karl.** 1812–1885. German Protestant theologian; a founder of, and a leader in, the German Protestant Union.

**Schwar'zen·berg, von** (fōn shvär'tsĕn·bĕrk). Princely Austrian family, including: Prince **Karl Philipp** (1771–1820); served with distinction in battles of Hohenlinden (1800) and Wagram (1809); commanded Austrian contingent in Russia (1812) and made field marshal; commanded allied armies opposing Napoleon (1813–14) and won victory at Leipzig (1813). Prince **Felix** (1800–1852), diplomat; prime minister of Austria (1848–52), suppressed insurrections in Italy and Hungary, restored (1850) old federal diet, and caused Emperor Francis Joseph to suspend entirely the constitution (Dec. 31, 1851). Prince **Friedrich** (1809–1885), ordained priest (1833); consecrated archbishop of Salzburg (1835), cardinal (1842), and archbishop of Prague (1849).

**Schwarzert, Philipp.** See MELANCHTHON.

**Schwat'ka** (shwŏt'kȧ), **Frederick.** 1849–1892. American army officer and arctic explorer; grad. U.S.M.A., West Point (1871). With William Henry Gilder, commanded arctic expedition in search of Sir John Franklin (1878–80), discovering wreckage of one of Franklin's ships and graves of members of his party. Resigned from army (1885); explored course of Yukon River (1883–84); headed New York *Times's* Alaskan expedition (1886); also visited northern Mexico. Author of *Along Alaska's Great River* (1885), *Nimrod in the North* (1885), *The Children of the Cold* (1886), *In the Land of Cave and Cliff Dweller* (1893).

**Schwe'gler** (shvā'glẽr), **Albert.** 1819–1857. German theologian and philosopher.

**Schweig'ger** (shvī'gẽr), **Johann Salomo Christoph.** 1779–1857. German physicist; professor at Erlangen (1817) and Halle (1819); invented the needle galvanometer (1820).

**Schwein'furth** (shvīn'fo͝ort), **Georg August.** 1836–1925. German traveler in Africa (1863–88); discovered Uele River (1870); proved existence of pygmies in Africa by discovery of Akka dwarfs. Author of *Im Herzen von Afrika* (1874), etc.

**Schwei'nitz** (shwī'nĭts), **George Edmund de** (dĕ). 1858–1938. American ophthalmologist, b. Philadelphia, Pa.; served with A.E.F. in France (1917–18); known for work on the prevention of blindness; author of *Diseases of the Eye* (1892), *Toxic Amblyopias* (1896).

**Schweinitz, Lewis David von** (vŏn). 1780–1834. American Moravian clergyman and mycologist, b. Bethlehem, Pa.; in Germany (1798–1812); general agent of Moravian Church at Salem, N.C. (1812–21); administrator, northern province of Moravian Church, headquarters at Bethlehem, Pa. (1821–34). Made notable studies of fungi, publishing *The Fungi of Lusatia* (1805), *The Fungi of North Carolina* (1818), *A Synopsis of North American Fungi* (1831).

**Schweit'zer** (shvī'tsẽr), **Albert.** 1875–1965. French Protestant clergyman, philosopher, physician, and music scholar; missionary physician and founder of Lambaréné Hospital in French Equatorial Africa (1913). Author of *Kant's Philosophy of Religion* (1899), *The Mysticism of the Apostle Paul* (1930), *On the Edge of the Primeval Forest* (1922). In the field of music, wrote a monograph on John Sebastian Bach and (with Widor) published a critical edition of Bach's organ works. Received Nobel Peace Prize (1952).

**Schweit'zer** (shvī'tsẽr), **Johann Baptist von.** 1834–1875. German politician and writer; succeeded Ferdinand Lassalle as president of Der Allgemeine Deutsche Arbeiterverein (1864); member of North German Federation legislature (1867–71). Author of plays.

**Schwel'len·bach** (shwĕl'ĕn·bäk), **Lewis Baxter.** 1894–1948. American lawyer, b. Superior, Wis.; U.S. senator (1935–40); judge, eastern district of Washington (1940–45); U.S. secretary of labor (1945–48).

**Schwen'de·ner** (shvĕn'dĕ·nẽr), **Simon.** 1829–1919. Botanist, b. in Switzerland; maintained that lichens are a connecting link between fungi and algae; set forth a mechanical theory of the development and arrangement of plant tissues.

**Schwenk'feld** *or* **Schwenck'feld** (shvĕngk'fĕlt), **Kaspar.** 1489–1561. German Silesian nobleman and Protestant mystic; followers known as Schwenkfeldians.

**Schwe·rin'** (shvâ·rēn'), Count **Kurt Christoph von.** 1684–1757. German soldier; created field marshal by Frederick the Great; won battle of Mollwitz (1741); distinguished himself in the Second Silesian War (1744–45) and the beginning of the Seven Years' War.

**Schwick'er** (shvĭk'ẽr), **Johann Heinrich.** 1839–1902. Hungarian historian.

**Schwind** (shvĭnt), **Moritz von.** 1804–1871. German painter, a master of the German late-romantic school. Among his works are decorations of the new art hall in Karlsruhe, decorations of the Tieck room in the royal palace in Munich, and three great water-color cycles.

**Schwing'er** (shwĭng'ẽr), **Julian Seymore.** 1918– . American physicist, b. New York City. At Harvard U. (1945– ); awarded Nobel prize in physics (1965) with S. Tomonaga and R. Feynman for work on quantum electrodynamics.

**Schwit'ters** (shvĭt'ẽrs), **Kurt.** 1887–1948. German artist and writer; identified with ultramodern movements, notably Dadaism; edited *Merz* (1923–27). Author of *Anna Blume* (1919), *Die Blume Anna* (1924), etc. Produced collages and plastic work.

**Schyn'se** (shĭn'zĕ), **August.** 1857–1891. German Catholic missionary; accompanied Stanley and Emin Pasha from East Africa to the coast (1889); traveled with the latter to Lake Victoria and return (1890); explored Uganda (1891).

**Schyt'te** (shüt'ĕ), **Ludwig.** 1848?–1909. Danish pianist, and composer of an opera (*Hero*, 1898), operettas, a concerto, and many piano pieces and songs.

**Scia·lo'ia** (shä·lō'yä), **Antonio.** 1817–1877. Italian economist and statesman; active in national movement; minister of finance (1865–67) and public instruction (1872). His son **Vittorio** (1856–1933) was also a statesman; minister of justice (1909–10), without portfolio (1916–17), of foreign affairs (1919–20); representative to Paris Peace Conference (1919–20); aided in framing covenant of League of Nations; Italian representative, Council of League of Nations (1925–31).

**Scid'more** (sĭd'mōr), **Eliza Ru'ha·mah** (ro͞o'ȧ·mä). 1856–1928. American traveler and writer; author of *Alaska...*(1885), *Jinrikisha Days in Japan* (1891), *Java, the Garden of the East* (1897), *China, the Long-Lived Empire* (1900), *Winter India* (1903), etc.

**Sci·op'pi·us** (sī·ŏp'ĭ·ŭs; *Ger.* shŏp'ē·o͞os), **Kaspar.** *Latinized form of* **Kaspar Schop'pe** (shŏp'ĕ). 1576–1649. German classical scholar and controversialist. Among objects of his attacks were Scaliger and King James I of England. Published some Latin verse and prose writings, works on Latin grammar and composition, and editions of some Latin authors.

**Scip'i·o** (sĭp'ĭ·ō), **Gnaeus Cornelius.** d. 212 (or 211) B.C. Brother of Publius Cornelius Scipio. Roman general; consul (222 B.C.) and co-operated with Marcus Claudius Marcellus in subduing Cisalpine Gaul; campaigned with his brother in Spain against the Carthaginians (from 218) and with him was defeated and slain.

**Scipio, Lucius Cornelius.** *Surnamed* **Bar·ba'tus** (bär·bā'tŭs). Roman consul (298 B.C.); campaigned against Etruscans. His son **Lucius Cornelius,** consul (259 B.C.), subjugated Corsica and Sardinia.

**Scipio, Publius Cornelius.** d. 212 (or 211) B.C. Father of Scipio Africanus. Roman general; consul (218 B.C.) with Sempronius Longus (*q.v.*); defeated by Hannibal at the Ticino and the Trebbia. Gained naval supremacy (217) by victory off the Iberus (Ebro). Campaigned in Spain with brother Gnaeus Cornelius Scipio (*q.v.*); defeated by Carthaginians and killed.

**Scipio Ae·mil'i·a'nus Af'ri·ca'nus Nu'man·ti'nus** (ē·mĭl'ĭ·ā'nŭs ăf'rĭ·kā'nŭs nū'măn·tī'nŭs), **Publius Cornelius.** 185–129 B.C. Roman general; known as "Scipio the Younger"; grandson by adoption of Scipio Africanus the Elder. Served in Spain as military tribune (151 B.C.), and in Africa at outbreak of Third Punic War (149); commanded army against Carthage (147) and captured Carthage (146); censor (142); consul, with governorship of Spain (134); seized Numantia (133). Headed aristocratic party in Rome (132) in opposition to popular reforms; died suddenly, perhaps killed.

**Scipio Af'ri·ca'nus** (ăf'rĭ·kā'nŭs), **Publius Cornelius.** 237–183 B.C. Roman general; known as "Scipio the Elder"; father of Cornelia (*q.v.*); aedile (212 B.C.); proconsul, with command in Spain (211). Consul (205) and commanded Roman invasion of Carthage, his successes there causing Carthage to recall Hannibal from Italy; crushed Hannibal in great battle of Zama (202). Later (190), went to Syria as legate with his brother **Lucius Cornelius Scipio,** who was consul and commander of expedition against Antiochus III; co-operated with brother in winning battle of Magnesia (190). Regarded as Rome's greatest general up to time of Julius Caesar.

**Scipio Na·si'ca** (nȧ·sī'kȧ), **Publius Cornelius.** Roman politician; consul (138 B.C.); pontifex maximus. Violently opposed to reforms of Tiberius Gracchus; with his partisans, attacked and murdered Gracchus (133).

**Scog'an** (skŏg'ăn) *or* **Scog'gin** (skŏg'ĭn), **Henry.** 1361?–1407. English poet; generally regarded as subject of Chaucer's humorous *Envoy to Scogan.*

**Scogan** *or* **Scoggin, John** (*or* **Thomas?**). fl. 1480–1500. Jester at court of Edward IV of England; M.A., Oxon. Alleged author of *Jests,* said to have been compiled by Andrew Boorde.

**Scol'lard** (skŏl'ẽrd), **Clinton.** 1860–1932. American poet, b. Clinton, N.Y.; m. (1924) as second wife Jessie Rittenhouse (*q.v.*). Professor of English, Hamilton (1888–96; 1911–12). Author of *Pictures in Song* (1884), *Old and New World Lyrics* (1888), *Songs of Sunrise Lands* (1892), *The Hills of Song* (1895), *Skenendoa* (1896), *The Lyric Bough* (1904), *Odes and Elegies* (1905), *Songs of a Syrian Lover* (1911), *Lyrics from a Library* (1913), *Italy in Arms* (1915), etc.

**Sco'pas** (skō'păs). Greek sculptor, native of island of Paros; long resident in Athens (from c. 377 B.C.). Carved decorations for mausoleum of Halicarnassus and for temple of Athena Alea at Tegea. The Apollo Citharoedus in the Vatican is supposed to be a copy of a statue by him.

**Scopes** (skōps), **John Thomas.** 1900–1970. American educator, b. Salem, Ill. As teacher in Rhea County High School, Dayton, Tenn., taught theory of evolution in defiance of a state law against such teaching in tax-supported schools, thus precipitating famous Dayton, or Scopes, trial (July, 1925) in which the state's case was upheld by William Jennings Bryan and the defense by Clarence Darrow of Chicago; convicted and fined a nominal sum ($100), but conviction was reversed on technical grounds by the Tennessee supreme court.

**Sco'po·li** (skô'pô·lē), **Giovanni Antonio.** 1723–1788. Italian naturalist; professor of mineralogy, Schemnitz (1766), of natural history, Pavia (1777); friend of Linnaeus, who named after him the genus *Scopolia*, which in turn gave its name to *scopolamine*, an alkaloid occurring in roots of herbs of this genus.

**Sco'rel** (skō'rĕl), **Jan van.** *Also* **Scho'rel** (skō'rĕl) *or* **Schoor'le** (skōr'lĕ). 1495–1562. Dutch painter; Roman Catholic canon at Utrecht; best known for portraits.

**Scores'by** (skōrz'bĭ), **William.** 1789–1857. English Arctic explorer; son of **William Scoresby** (1760–1829), whaling captain and explorer, whom he accompanied on the *Resolution* on trip to Greenland Sea, reaching 81°30′ N. latitude. Demonstrated that polar ocean is warmer at great depths than at surface; surveyed and charted 400 miles of east coast of Greenland; entered church (1825); carried on investigations in natural history, meteorology, magnetism; made voyage to Australia to gather data on terrestrial magnetism (1856).

**Scot.** See also Scott.

**Scot** *or* **Scott** (skŏt), **Michael.** 1175?–?1234. Scottish translator and astrologer with posthumous fame as a magician. Learned Arabic at Toledo; at court of Emperor Frederick II, worked with other scholars on translation of Aristotle's works and Averroës's commentaries from Arabic into Latin; sent by Frederick to communicate this version of Aristotle to universities of Europe. Through his original works dealing with astrology, alchemy, and occult sciences, became known as a wizard; credited with magical exploits and, in popular legend, possessor of a demon horse and a demon ship and foreteller of own death.

**Scott** (skŏt). Family name of earls and dukes of Buccleuch and dukes of Queensberry. See Buccleuch.

**Scott, Alexander.** 1525?–?1584. Scottish poet; author of short poems (1545–68) preserved only in Bannatyne MS. and brought forward by Allan Ramsay.

**Scott, Charles.** 1739?–1813. American Revolutionary officer, b. in Powhatan County, Va. Served in American contingent under Washington in Braddock's campaign against the Indians (1755). Commanded Virginia regiment (1775–77); brigadier general, Continental army (Apr., 1777); brevetted major general (1783). Moved to Kentucky (1785); served under Gen. St. Clair in Indian fighting (1791) and under Gen. Wayne at battle of Fallen Timbers (1794). Governor of Kentucky (1808–12).

**Scott, Charles Prestwich.** 1846–1932. English journalist; held long connection (1871–1929) with Manchester *Guardian*, of which he became editor (1872) and chief proprietor (1905). An advanced liberal, advocated home rule, opposed tariffs and Boer War; M.P. (1895–1906).

**Scott, Clement William.** 1841–1904. English dramatic critic; pioneer of picturesque dramatic criticism; adapted French dramas; author of sentimental verse, collected in *Lays of a Londoner* (1882) and *Lays and Lyrics* (1888).

**Scott, Cyril Meir** (mēr). 1879–1970. English pianist and composer; wrote *Heroic Suite* (c. 1900; produced by Hans Richter at Liverpool) and overture to *Pelléas and Mélisande* (played at Frankfurt), both later withdrawn because of their immaturity. Turned to writing music with no key signature; advanced the cyclic sonata form. Known chiefly for songs and piano compositions, also for chamber music and several operas, including *Alchemist* (1925) and *The Shrine* (1925). Author of *My Years of Indiscretion* (1924), *Music: Its Secret Influence throughout the Ages, An Outline of Modern Occultism*, etc.

**Scott, David.** 1806–1849. Scottish painter and engraver; designed 25 illustrations to *Ancient Mariner* (1837) and 40 to *Pilgrim's Progress* (1850), and astronomical designs in Nichol's *Architecture of the Heavens* (1850); works characterized by bold imaginative quality and originality. His brother **William Bell** (1811–1890), poet and painter, was known for a series of paintings of Northumbrian history; author of five volumes of poetry, modeled on Blake and Shelley.

**Scott, Dred.** 1795?–1858. American Negro, b. of slave parents in Southampton County, Va. Central figure in the Dred Scott Case, inaugurated by his suit (1848) to obtain his freedom on ground that he had resided in free territory. The U.S. Supreme Court held (1857) that he was not a citizen and not entitled to any standing in court; and further declared that the Missouri Compromise was unconstitutional, that Congress could not prohibit a citizen of any state from carrying slaves or other property into any territory, and that Congress could not impair the constitutional protection of such slaves or property in the territory.

**Scott, Duncan Campbell.** 1862–1947. Canadian poet, b. Ottawa, of English and Scottish parents; deputy superintendent general, department of Indian affairs (1913–32); joint editor with Pelham Edgar of "Makers of Canada" series. Author of *The Magic House and Other Poems* (1893), *Labor and the Angel* (1898), *New World Lyrics and Ballads* (1905), *Lundy's Lane* (1916), and *Beauty and Life* (1921).

**Scott, Evelyn.** 1893–1963. American writer of novels, books of verse, and juveniles. Among her works are *The Narrow House* (a novel, 1921), *The Golden Door* (a novel, 1927), *The Wave* (1929), *The Winter Alone* (verse, 1930), *Bread and a Sword* (1937), *The Shadow of the Hawk* (a novel, 1941).

**Scott, Fred Newton.** 1860–1931. American educator; teacher of English, U. of Michigan; professor (from 1901), head of department of rhetoric (1903–21), and of department of rhetoric and journalism (1921–27). Author of *Paragraph-Writing* (with J. V. Denney, 1891), *An Introduction to the Methods and Materials of Literary Criticism* (with C. M. Gayley, 1899), *The Standard of American Speech and Other Papers* (1926), etc.

**Scott, Frederick George.** 1861–1944. Canadian Anglican clergyman and poet; chaplain, 1st Canadian division, B.E.F. (1914–18), senior chaplain (from 1915); archdeacon of Quebec (1925). Author of *Soul's Quest* (1888), *My Lattice* (1894), *The Hymn of Empire* (1906), *In the Battle Silences* (1916), *The Great War as I Saw It* (1922), *In Sun and Shade* (1926).

**Scott, Geoffrey.** 1885–1929. English critic; author of *The Architecture of Humanism* (1914) and *Portrait of Zélide* (1925); editor of Boswell's private papers from Malahide Castle (pub. 1928–32).

**Scott,** Sir **George Gilbert.** 1811–1878. English architect; stimulated by study of Pugin's works on medieval architecture, led Gothic revival, notably in England; built or restored cathedrals, churches, schools, monuments, college and public buildings; builder or designer of new government domestic offices (London), Albert Memorial (Glasgow U.), and Episcopal cathedral (Edinburgh). Grandson of **Thomas Scott** (1747–1821), theologian and Biblical commentator.

Sir George's grandson Sir **Giles Gilbert Scott** (1880–1960), architect, designed Liverpool Cathedral (consecrated 1924), a revival of Gothic architecture; designed or restored ecclesiastical buildings, built war memorials, and the new library at Cambridge U.

**Scott, George Herbert.** 1888–1930. English airship commander; took on patrol first British rigid airship (1917); devised system of mooring airships at head of a mast; navigated rigid airship *R34* on first transatlantic airship flight (1919); victim of crash of *R101* over France.

**Scott,** Sir **Giles Gilbert.** 1880–1960. English architect especially of ecclesiastical and academic buildings, including Liverpool Cathedral, restoration work on Chester Cathedral, new buildings for Clare College and the new library at Cambridge, and at Oxford additions to Magdalen College and extensions to Bodleian Library.

**Scott, Hugh.** 1885–1960. English entomologist and writer; educ. Cambridge, where he became curator of entomology (1909–28); on natural history expeditions to Seychelles (1908–09), Abyssinia (1926–27), Yemen (1937–38), etc.

**Scott, Hugh Lenox.** 1853–1934. American army officer; grad. U.S.M.A., West Point (1876); served in Indian campaigns; studied Indian sign language and became a negotiator with various Indian tribes. Chief of staff, U.S. army (1914–17); retired for age (1917) but kept on active duty (to May, 1919).

**Scott, Hugh Stowell.** *Pseudonym* **Henry Seton Mer′ri·man** (mĕr′ĭ·măn). 1862–1903. English novelist; underwriter in Lloyd's. Author of *Young Mistley* (his first novel; 1888), *The Slave of the Lamp* (1892), *The Sowers* (1896), and *Barlasch of the Guard* (1902).

**Scott, Irving Murray.** 1837–1903. American shipbuilder, b. Hebron Mills, Md.; moved to San Francisco (1860) and worked in Union Iron Works; partner in this company (1865–1903). Added shipbuilding plant to Union Iron Works (1883); built warship *Charleston* (1889), first battleship built on Pacific coast; later, the *Olympia, San Francisco, Oregon, Wisconsin, Ohio.*

**Scott, James Brown.** 1866–1943. Lawyer, b. in Ontario, Can.; solicitor, U.S. Department of State (1906–10); trustee and secretary, Carnegie Endowment for International Peace (from 1910); editor in chief, *American Journal of International Law* (1907–24); authority on international law.

**Scott, John.** 1630?–1696. English adventurer, b. prob. at Ashford, Kent. Had a part in English seizure of New Amsterdam; became "president" of Long Island; fled to West Indies to escape arrest on charges of dishonest dealings in land. Served under Lord Francis Willoughby against the French at St. Kitts (1665–66); court-martialed and cashiered for cowardice (1667). Held commission in Dutch service, but was dismissed for dishonesty; appeared as a witness in the Popish Plot and against Samuel Pepys, but Pepys was cleared and Scott thoroughly discredited.

**Scott** of Am′well (ăm′wĕl; -wĕl), **John.** 1730–1783. Scottish Quaker poet; friend of Dr. Johnson and frequenter of Mrs. Elizabeth Montagu's parties.

**Scott, John.** 1st Earl of **Eldon.** 1751–1838. See ELDON.

**Scott, John Morin.** 1730?–1784. American politician and Revolutionary officer, b. New York City; brigadier general (1776); engaged in battle of Long Island; resigned (1777); secretary of state, New York (1778–84); member, Continental Congress (1779–83).

**Scott, John Prindle.** 1877–1932. American composer, concert singer, and singing teacher. Composer of many sacred anthems and popular songs, including *The Lord Is My Shepherd, Come Ye Blessed, The Old Road, The Dearest Place, Even Song.*

**Scott, Michael.** 1175?–?1234. See Michael SCOT.

**Scott, Michael.** 1789–1835. Scottish novelist; in business in Jamaica (1810). Author of *Tom Cringle's Log* and *The Cruise of the Midge.*

**Scott, Orange.** 1800–1847. American clergyman and abolitionist; because of church opposition to his abolitionist views, withdrew (1841) from Methodist Episcopal Church and with his supporters founded (1843) Wesleyan Methodist Connection of America.

**Scott,** Sir **Percy Moreton.** 1853–1924. English naval officer and gunnery expert; invented two devices improving accuracy of naval gunnery (1896); in Boer War, carried naval guns to Ladysmith; in Boxer Rebellion, aided International Brigade (1900); retired as admiral (1913); took charge of air defenses of London during World War. Vigorous advocate of substitution of submarines and aircraft for battleships.

**Scott** *or* **Scot** (skŏt), **Reginald** *or* **Reynold.** 1538?–1599. English author of first practical treatise on hop culture in England and of *The Discouerie of Witchcraft* (1584), a brilliant attack upon witch superstition.

**Scott, Robert.** 1811–1887. English clergyman and lexicographer; master of Balliol (1854–70); dean of Rochester (1870–87). Collaborator with H. G. Liddell (*q.v.*) in *Greek-English Lexicon* (1843).

**Scott, Robert Falcon.** 1868–1912. English antarctic explorer; entered navy (1882); commander of antarctic expedition in the *Discovery* (1901–04); surveyed South Victoria Land and interior of Antarctic Continent, discovered King Edward VII Land, sounded Ross Sea; served in navy (till 1909). Commanded antarctic expedition in the *Terra Nova* (1910); began southern sledge journey (Nov., 1911) with four companions and reached South Pole (Jan. 18, 1912) shortly after Roald Amundsen's expedition; with companions, perished on return trip as result of bad weather and insufficient food; his records and diaries found by searching party (Nov., 1912). His widow (see Lady KENNET) granted rank and precedence of wife of a K.C.B. His son **Peter Markham** (1909–    ), artist, exhibiting paintings at Royal Acad.; illustrator of Lord Kennet's *A Bird in the Bush;* specialist in bird paintings, esp. ducks and geese, and in portraits; author of *Morning Flight* (1935) and *Wild Chorus* (1938).

**Scott** *or* **Scot, Thomas.** See ROTHERHAM.

**Scott,** Sir **Walter.** 1771–1832. Scottish poet, novelist, historian, and biographer, at first under various pseudonyms, including: **Jedediah Cleish′both′am** (klēsh′bōth′ăm), **Chrystal Croft′an′gry** (krôft′ăng′grĭ), Captain **Cuthbert Clut′ter·buck′** (klŭt′ẽr·bŭk′), **Peter Pat′tie·son** (păt′ĭ·s′n). Known as "the Border Minstrel," "the Wizard of the North," and "the Great Magician"; born in Edinburgh, son of a scion of the Scotts of Harden, **Walter** (1729–99), and Anne Rutherford, daughter of John Rutherford, a medical professor in Edinburgh U. (see BUCCLEUCH family). Insatiable reader of ballads and romances, collector of chapbooks; acquired French and Italian to read Dante and Ariosto. Called to bar (1792), sheriff of Selkirk (1799); a principal clerk to court of session (1812). Published anonymously (1796) translation of Bürger's *Lenore* and *Der Wilde Jäger* (*Wild Huntsman*) and a translation of Goethe's *Götz von Berlichingen* (1799); contributed ballads *Glenfinlas, The Eve of St. John,* and *The Gray Brother* to Matthew Gregory Lewis's *Tales of Wonder* (1801); m. (1797) Charlotte Margaret Charpentier, daughter of French émigré. Published first important work, *Minstrelsy of the Scottish Border* (3 vols., 1802–03), and first considerable original work, *The Lay of the Last Minstrel* (narrative poem; 1805); decided on literary career; commenced novel *Waverley* (1804), but laid it aside on adverse comment of friend (1805); on appointment as clerk of session, withdrew from bar (1806). Formed secret partnership (1805) with Ballantyne in printing business; increased reputation with *Marmion* (1808); started *Quarterly Review* (1809); edited Dryden's works, with a *Life* (1808); had rupture with Jeffrey of *Edinburgh Review;* began relations (1808) with new firm of John Ballantyne and Co., for which he furnished half the capital; surpassed earlier triumphs with publication of *Lady of the Lake* (1810); published *Vision of Don Roderick* (1811); built home, Abbotsford on the Tweed (1812). Published poems *Rokeby* (1812) and *The Bridal of Triermain* (1813); declined laureateship in favor of Southey (1813); published *Life and Works of Swift* (19 vols., 1814). Began series of historical novels with *Waverley* (1814), enormously popular; published *Lord of the Isles* (1815; dealing with Robert Bruce), *Harold the Dauntless* (his last long poem; 1817), and novels *Guy Mannering* and *The Antiquary* (1815), *The Black Dwarf* and *Old Mortality* (1816; first of four series of novels under collective title *Tales of My Landlord*), and *Rob Roy* (1817). Despite painful illnesses, completed *The Heart of Midlothian* and *The Bride of Lammermoor* (1818), *The Legend of Montrose* and *Ivanhoe* (1819), *The Monastery* (1820). Made baronet (1820). Continued novels with *The Abbot* (1820), *Kenilworth* and *The Pirate* (1821), *The Fortunes of Nigel* (1822), *Peveril of the Peak, Quentin Durward,* and *St. Ronan's Well* (1824), *Redgauntlet* (1824), *Tales of the Crusaders, The Betrothed,* and *The Talisman* (1825). At pinnacle of fame as man of letters, but failing in health, found himself with liabilities of £130,000 when Constable and Co. and Ballantyne and Co. (publishing and printing firms in which he was partner) failed (Jan., 1826); lost his wife (1826). Set to work as novelist and historical writer, no longer under pseudonyms, to pay off indebtedness, producing *Woodstock* (1826), *The Two Drovers, The Highland Widow, The Surgeon's Daughter,* and nine-volume *Life of Napoleon* (1827), *Fair Maid of Perth* (1828), *Tales of a Grandfather* (1828, 1829, 1830, 1831), *Anne of Geierstein* (1829), *History of Scotland* (2 vols., 1830), and his best play, *Auchindrane, or the Ayrshire Tragedy* (1830). Suffered apoplectic strokes (1830) from which he never recovered; produced two more novels, *Count Robert of Paris* and *Castle Dangerous* (1831; 4th series of *Tales of My Landlord*); cruised on government vessel in Mediterranean for recovery of health, but returned across Europe to die at Abbotsford; buried in Dryburgh Abbey; balance of his debts paid off with funds realized through disposal of copyrights. His daughter Charlotte Sophia's husband, John Gibson Lockhart (*q.v.*), was his biographer; his great-granddaughter **Mary Monica Maxwell Scott** (1852–1920) was author of *The Tragedy of Fotheringay* (1895), a history of Abbotsford (1897), *Joan of Arc* (1905), and *St. Francis de Sales and his Friends* (1913).

**Scott, Walter.** 1867–1938. Canadian statesman, b. London, Ontario, of Scottish parents; printer and journalist; member of House of Commons for Assiniboia West (1900, 1904); instrumental in creation of provinces of Saskatchewan and Alberta (1905); formed first Saskatchewan ministry (1905); retired on account of ill health (1916).

**Scott, Walter Dill.** 1869–1955. American educator; professor of psychology, Northwestern (1901–20); president, Northwestern (1920–39). Author of *The Psychology of Public Speaking* (1907), *The Psychology of Advertising* (1908), *Increasing Human Efficiency* (1911), *Stabilizing Business* (1923), *Man and His Universe* (1929), etc.

**Scott, William.** Baron **Stow'ell** (stō'ĕl). 1745–1836. English jurist; brother of John Scott, 1st Earl of Eldon. Intimate with Dr. Johnson; advocate general for lord high admiral (1782); judge of consistory court (1788–1821); privy councilor (1798); judge of high court of admiralty (1798–1828). Highest English authority on maritime and international law.

**Scott, William Am'a·sa** (ăm'ȧ·sȧ). 1862–1944. American economist; author of *Money and Banking, Development of Economics* (1933), etc.

**Scott, William Bell.** See under David SCOTT.

**Scott, William Berryman.** 1858–1947. American geologist; professor, Princeton (1884–1930; emeritus); known for work on vertebrate paleontology and on extinct mammalian fauna of North and South America.

**Scott, Winfield.** 1786–1866. American army officer, b. near Petersburg, Va. Engaged at Queenstown Heights (1812); brigadier general (Mar., 1814); engaged at battles of Chippewa and Lundy's Lane (1814); brevetted major general (1814). On duty in South Carolina (1832), pacifying the nullifiers. On duty on Canadian border (1838–39), preventing conflict with Canada over boundary line. General in chief, U.S. army (1841); commander in Mexican War; captured Vera Cruz (Mar., 1847); defeated Mexicans at Cerro Gordo (Apr., 1847), Contreras and Churubusco (Aug., 1847), Molino del Rey and Chapultepec (Sept., 1847), and occupied Mexico City (Sept. 14, 1847); promoted lieutenant general (1852). Whig candidate for presidency (1852); defeated by Franklin Pierce; retired (1861).

**Scott-Gatty, Alfred Scott.** See under Juliana Horatia EWING.

**Scot'ti** (skôt'tē), **Antonio.** 1866–1936. Italian operatic basso; joined Metropolitan Opera Company, New York (1899), and remained there until retirement (1933).

**Scott'-Mon·crieff'** (skŏt'mŏn·krēf'; mŭn-), **Charles Kenneth Michael.** 1889–1930. Scottish translator; captain in Scottish Borderers (1914); translator of *Song of Roland* (1919), *Beowulf* (1921), Stendhal's works; authorized translator of Proust (*Remembrance of Things Past*) and Pirandello; author of *Austria's Peace Offer* (1921).

**Scott-Moncreiff,** Sir **Colin Campbell.** 1836–1916. British engineer; in charge of irrigation department, Egypt (1883–92); supervised construction of Nile Barrage, making possible irrigation of Egypt; undersecretary for Scotland (1892–1902).

**Scott-Moncrieff,** Sir **George Kenneth.** 1855–1924. British military engineer; commanded Royal Engineers, China expeditionary force (1900–01); served on Waziristan expedition (1901); director of fortifications and works, war office (1911–18; retired).

**Scott-Paine** (skŏt'pān'), **Hubert.** 1891–1954. English aircraft and motorboat builder; built first circular flying-boat hull (1913), first quadruplane and one of the first twin-engined land machines (1915); built motor torpedo boat flotilla, anti-submarine vessels, and wireless-controlled motor vessel for admiralty.

**Scotus, Adam.** See ADAM SCOTUS.

**Scotus, Duns.** See John DUNS SCOTUS.

**Scotus, Johannes.** See Johannes Scotus ERIGENA.

**Scria'bin** *or* **Scria'bine** (skryȧ'byĭn), **Alexander.** *Russ.* **Aleksandr Nikolaevich Skryabin.** 1872–1915. Russian composer; piano instructor, Conservatory of Music, Moscow (1898–1903). Among his orchestral works are three symphonies, and two tone poems (*Le Poème de l'Extase* and *Le Poème du Feu*, or *Prometheus*); among his piano works are ten sonatas, études, preludes, and a number of dances.

**Scribe** (skrēb), **Augustin Eugène.** 1791–1861. French playwright, b. Paris; catered to public taste in over 350 plays of which he was author or coauthor. Among the best of his plays are *L'Ours et le Pacha* (1820), *Mon*

*Oncle César* (1821), *Valérie* (1822), *Le Mariage d'Argent* (1827), *Bertrand et Raton* (1833), *L'Ambitieuse* (1834), *La Camaraderie* (1836), *Les Indépendants* (1837), *La Calomnie* (1840), *Le Verre d'Eau* (1840), *Une Chaîne* (1841), *Le Puff* (1848), *Adrienne Lecouvreur* (with Legouvé; 1849), *Bataille des Dames* (1851), etc. Author also of various opera and comic-opera librettos.

**Scri·ble'rus** (skrĭ·blẹr'ŭs), **Martinus.** Joint pseudonym of Pope, Swift, and Arbuthnot in *Memoirs of Martinus Scriblerus*, published with Pope's works (1751).

**Scrib'ner** (skrĭb'nẽr), **Charles.** 1821–1871. American publisher, b. New York City. A founder with Isaac D. Baker of Baker & Scribner, publishers (1846), the beginning of Charles Scribner's Sons (incorporated, 1878). Founder and publisher, *Scribner's Monthly* (1870–81). His three sons, **John Blair** (1850–1879), **Charles** (1854–1930), and **Arthur Hawley** (1859–1932), continued the business which started a new *Scribner's Magazine* (1887). A son of Charles (1854–1930), **Charles** (1890–1952), succeeded to the presidency of the company in 1933. See Roswell SMITH.

**Scribner, Frank Lamson–.** See LAMSON-SCRIBNER.

**Scri·bo'ni·a** (skrĭ·bō'nĭ·ȧ). Second wife of Emperor Augustus (*q.v.*); mother of Julia (*q.v.*); divorced (39 B.C.).

**Scripps** (skrĭps). Name of a family of American newspaper publishers, including: **James Edmund** (1835–1906), b. London, England; to U.S. (1844); founded and edited *Evening News*, Detroit (from 1873); associated with his half brother Edward in founding or acquiring newspapers in Cleveland, St. Louis, and Cincinnati; purchased Detroit *Tribune* (1891). His sister **Ellen Browning** (1836–1932), b. London, England; to U.S. (1844); on staff of Detroit *Evening News* (from 1873), Cleveland *Penny Press* (from 1878), Cincinnati *Post* (from 1882). Their half brother **Edward Wyllis** (1854–1926), on staff of Detroit *Evening News* (1873); with financial aid from family, founded (1878) and edited Cleveland *Penny Press*, purchased *Evening Chronicle*, St. Louis (1880) and *Penny Post*, Cincinnati (1882); in partnership (from 1889) with Milton Alexander McRae, organized Scripps-McRae League of Newspapers (1895) and Scripps-McRae Press Association (1897); purchased Publishers' Press (1904) and merged it with Scripps-McRae Press into United Press (1907); organized (1902) Newspaper Enterprise Association to supply cartoons and feature articles to papers of his chain and to other papers, origin of modern syndicated matter; bought interest in San Diego *Sun* (1893) and added other newspapers to form a West Coast chain. **Robert Paine** (1895–1938), son of Edward Wyllis, editorial director of the Scripps-McRae (now Scripps-Howard) newspapers (from 1917); associate editorial director (from 1925) with Roy Wilson Howard (*q.v.*).

**Scrip'ture** (skrĭp'tūr), **Edward Wheeler.** 1864–1943. American psychologist and phonetician; lecturer in psychiatry, Columbia (from 1909); professor of experimental phonetics and director of the phonetic institute, Vienna (1923–33). Author of *Thinking, Feeling, and Doing* (1895), *The New Psychology* (1897), *Elements of Experimental Phonetics* (1902), *Researches in Experimental Phonetics* (1906), *Stuttering and Lisping* (1912).

**Scrive'ner** (skrĭv'nẽr), **Frederick Henry Ambrose.** 1813–1891. English Biblical critic; one of revisers of New Testament (1870–82).

**Scroggs** (skrŏgz), Sir **William.** 1623?–1683. English judge; fought on Royalist side in Civil War; justice of common pleas (1676); lord chief justice of England (1678). Presiding in trial of victims of Titus Oates's plot (Popish Plot), intimidated defense witnesses but disparaged evidence of accusers to save George Wakeman, queen's physician, and adjourned grand jury to forestall indictment of duke of York (later James II); impeached but never tried; removed from office (1681).

**Scrope, le** (lĕ skrōōp'). Name of distinguished north of England family of judges including: Sir **Henry** (d. 1336) and his brother Sir **Geoffrey** (d. 1340), judges. Henry's son **Richard** (1327?–1403), 1st Baron **Scrope of Bol'ton** (bōl't'n; -tŭn), lawyer; warden of West March; chancellor (1378–80, 1381–82). Geoffrey's son Sir **Henry** (1315–1391), 1st Baron **Scrope of Mas'ham** (măs'ăm), soldier under Edward III and warden of West March. **Richard** (1350?–1405), prelate; son of 1st Baron Scrope of Masham; grad. and chancellor of Cambridge; bishop of Coventry and Lichfield (1386) and archbishop of York (1398–1405); supporter of revolution of 1399; leader, with Northumberland and Bardolf, of rebellion beyond Tyne (1404); executed at York. Richard's nephew **Henry** (1376?–1415), 3d Baron Scrope of Masham; grandson of 1st baron; treasurer of kingdom (1410–11); entrusted by Henry IV and Henry V with foreign negotiations; executed for complicity in plot to dethrone Henry V. **William** (1351?–1399), Earl of **Wilt'shire** (wĭlt'shĭr; -shẽr); son of 1st Baron Scrope of Bolton; served under John of Gaunt in France; captain of Cherbourg and Brest; chamberlain of Richard II's household; ambassador to Scotland (1398); treasurer of England (1398); executed by Henry IV.

**Scrope, George Julius Poulett.** *Orig. surname* **Thomson.** 1797–1876. English geologist; brother of Charles Edward Poulett Thomson, Baron Sydenham (see THOMSON); m. (1821) daughter and heiress of the artist and sportsman William Scrope (1772–1852) and assumed her name. Eyewitness of eruption of Vesuvius (1822); with Sir Charles Lyell sought to replace Wernerian theory of neptunism with uniformitarianism. Liberal M.P. (1833–68); defender of free trade; advocate of reform of the poor law. Author of *Geology of the Extinct Volcanoes of Central France* (1827) and *Principles of Political Economy* (1833).

**Scud'der** (skŭd'ẽr), **Horace Elisha.** See under Samuel H. SCUDDER.

**Scudder, Janet.** 1873–1940. American sculptor and painter; among her works are *Frog Fountain*, in Metropolitan Museum of Art in New York; *Fighting Boys' Fountain* in Art Institute of Chicago; *Little Lady of the Sea.*

**Scudder, John Milton.** 1829–1894. American eclectic physician.

**Scudder, Samuel Hubbard.** 1837–1911. American naturalist, b. Boston; best known for his studies of butterflies and Orthoptera. His brother **Horace Elisha** (1838–1902) was a writer; editor of *Riverside Magazine for Young People* (1867–70), and of *Atlantic Monthly* (1890–98); author of *Dream Children* (1864), *The Dwellers in Five-Sisters Court* (1876), *A History of the United States* (1884), and biographies of *Noah Webster* (1882), *Bayard Taylor* (with Marie Hansen-Taylor, 1884), *George Washington* (1890), and *James Russell Lowell* (2 vols., 1901).

**Scudder, Vi'da** (vē'dȧ) **Dutton.** 1861–1954. American educator; assoc. professor of English (1892–1910) and professor (1910–27), Wellesley College. Among her books are *The Life of the Spirit in the Modern English Poets* (1895), *Social Ideals in English Letters* (1898), *The Disciple of a Saint* (1907), *Socialism and Character* (1912), *The Franciscan Adventure* (1931).

**Scu'dé'ry'** *or* **Scu'dé'ri'** (skü'dā'rē'), **Georges de.** 1601–1667. French writer; among works are tragedies, tragicomedies, and comedies, a critical work directed against Corneille, a book of verse, and an epic poem;

best-known play is the tragicomedy *L'Amour Tyrannique* (1638); his epic *Alaric ou Rome Vaincue* (1654) drew trenchant satire of Boileau. His sister **Magdeleine de Scudéry** *or* **Scudéri** (1607–1701), often known as **Sa'pho'** (sȧ'fō'), was a poet, novelist, and lady of fashion whose Saturday salons were frequented by notable persons of the day; best-known works are *Artamène ou le Grand Cyrus* (10 vols., 1649–53) and *Clélie* (1656).

**Scul'lin** (skŭl'ĭn), **James Henry**. 1876–1953. Australian statesman; leader of Federal Parliamentary Labor party (1928–35); prime minister of Australia (1929–31).

**Scy'lax of Car'y·an'da** (sī'lăks, kăr'ĭ·ăn'dȧ). Greek historian and geographer of 6th century B.C.; sent by Darius I Hystaspis to explore course of Indus River; sailed down it to sea and westward through Indian Ocean to Red Sea; wrote account (now lost) of journey.

**Scyl'lis** and **Di·poe'nus** (sĭl'ĭs, dī·pē'nŭs). Greek sculptors (collaborators) of 6th century B.C.; worked in wood, ebony, ivory, and, probably, marble; their studio, according to Pliny, was in Sicyon.

**Sea'borg** (sē'bôrg), **Glenn Theodore**. 1912– . American chemist, b. Ishpeming, Mich. At U. of Calif. (1937–42; 1946–61; 1971– ); awarded Nobel prize in chemistry (1951) with E. McMillan; Fermi award (1959); chairman, Atomic Energy Comm. (1961–71). Aided in disc. of 9 new elements (elements 94–102).

**Sea'bur·y** (sē'bẽr·ĭ; -bĕr'ĭ), **Samuel**. 1729–1796. American Protestant Episcopal clergyman, b. Groton, Conn.; B.A., Yale (1748); loyalist during American Revolution; chosen bishop by Protestant Episcopal clergy of Connecticut (1783) and consecrated in Scotland by nonjuring Scottish prelates (Nov. 14, 1784); first bishop of the Protestant Episcopal Church in America. His grandson **Samuel** (1801–1872), clergyman; a leader of the high-church party. The bishop's great great-grandson **Samuel** (1873–1958), lawyer, b. New York City; justice, N.Y. Supreme Court (1906–14); associate judge, N.Y. Court of Appeals (1914–16).

**Seadiah.** Variant of SAADIA.

**Sea'ger** (sē'gẽr), **Henry Rogers**. 1870–1930. American economist; professor, Columbia (1902–30).

**Seals'field** (sēlz'fēld; *in German, also* zēls'fēlt), **Charles**. *Orig. name* **Karl Anton Postl** (pôs't'l). 1793–1864. Novelist, b. in Poppitz, Moravia; educated for priesthood but fled from the monastery where he was undergoing his novitiate. Traveled in U.S. (1823–26; 1827–32) and became American citizen; resident in Switzerland (after 1832), but retained his American citizenship. Author of *Tokeah; or the Wild Rose* (2 vols., 1828), *Der Virey und die Aristokraten; oder Mexiko im Jahre 1812* (3 vols., 1834), *Lebensbilder aus der Westlichen Hemisphäre* (5 vols., 1846), etc. His identity with the escaped monk Karl Anton Postl was not made known until after his death.

**Sea'man** (sē'măn), **Augusta**, *nee* **Hui'ell** (hū'ĕl). 1879–1950. American writer; m. Robert Reece Seaman (1906; d. 1927), Francis Parkman Freeman (1928). Author esp. of juveniles, as *Little Mamselle of the Wilderness* (1913), and mystery stories.

**Seaman, Elizabeth**, *nee* **Coch'rane** (kŏk'răn). *Pseudonym* **Nellie Bly** (blī). 1867–1922. American journalist; m. (1895) Robert L. Seaman (d. 1904). On staff, Pittsburgh *Dispatch*, New York *World*, and at the close of her life, New York *Journal*. Wrote about treatment of the insane (1888); made trip around world in the then record time of 72 days, 6 hours, and 11 minutes. Author of *Ten Days in a Madhouse* (1888), *Nellie Bly's Book: Around the World in Seventy-Two Days* (1890).

**Seaman, Sir Owen**. 1861–1936. English editor and humorist; on staff of *Punch* (from 1897), its editor (1906–32). Among his books are *Oedipus the Wreck* (1888), *Cap and Bells* (1899), *Borrowed Plumes* (1902), and *Interludes of an Editor* (1929).

**Seares** (sērz), **Frederick Hanley**. 1873–1964. American astronomer, b. Cassopolis, Mich.; B.S., Calif. (1895); professor, U. of Missouri (1901–09); on staff of Mount Wilson Observatory as superintendent of computing division and editor of publications (1909–25), assistant director (1925–40), research associate (1940 ff.).

**Sears** (sērz), **Barnas**. 1802–1880. American Baptist clergyman and educator; professor of Christian theology, Newton Theological Institution (1836–48), president (1839–48); president, Brown U. (1855–67). General agent (1867–80) for administration of Peabody Education Fund (see George PEABODY).

**Sears, Edmund Hamilton**. 1810–1876. American Unitarian clergyman; author of *Regeneration* (1853), *Athanasia; or Foregleams of Immortality* (1858), and a number of hymns, including *Calm on the Listening Ear of Night* and *It Came Upon a Midnight Clear*.

**Sears, Isaac**. 1730–1786. American colonial merchant; leader of radical elements in New York City opposing British policy. On receiving news of Lexington and Concord, seized New York arsenal and customhouse and controlled city until arrival of Washington's army (1775). Resident in Boston (1777–83), esp. engaged in sending out privateers to prey on British commerce.

**Sears, Paul Bigelow**. 1891– . American botanist, b. Bucyrus, Ohio; B.S., Ohio Wesleyan (1913), Ph.D., Chicago (1922); taught at U. of Nebraska (1919–27); professor of botany, U. of Oklahoma (1927–38), Oberlin (from 1938); authority on pollens, applied ecology, and history of climate; author of *Deserts on the March* (1935), *Life and Environment* (1939), *This Useful World* (1941), etc.

**Sears, Richard D.** 1862–1943. American tennis player, b. Boston; first American amateur champion at lawn tennis (1881–87) and court tennis (1892).

**Sears, Richard Warren**. 1863–1914. American merchant, b. Stewartville, Minn.; established mail-order business in Minneapolis (1886); moved to Chicago (1887); sold business (1889). Again opened mail-order business, with A. C. Roebuck, in Minneapolis; moved to Chicago (1893) and firm became Sears, Roebuck & Co., with Sears as president (to 1909; retired). Roebuck's interest purchased by Julius Rosenwald (1895).

**Sears, Taber**. 1870–1950. American mural painter and designer of stained-glass windows, b. Boston.

**Sea'shore** (sē'shōr), **Carl E'mil** (ā'mĭl). 1866–1949. Psychologist and educator, b. Mörlunda, Sweden; to U.S. as a boy; professor of psychology (1902–08), dean of graduate college (1908–36), State U. of Iowa. Invented apparatus for use in psychological laboratory work. Author of *Elementary Experiments in Psychology* (1908), *Introduction to Psychology* (1922), *Psychology of Music* (1938), etc.

**Sea'ton** (sē't'n), 1st Baron. See Sir John COLBORNE.

**Seaton, William Winston**. 1785–1866. American journalist; associate editor, with Joseph Gales, of the *National Intelligencer*, Washington, D.C. (1812–64). With Gales, made shorthand reports of congressional debates (1812–29), afterwards published by authority of Congress, together with earlier reports, as *The Debates and Proceedings in the Congress of the United States* (42 vols., 1834–56). Gales and Seaton also published *Register of Debates in Congress*, covering years 1824–37 (14 vols., 1825–37), and *American State Papers* (38 vols., 1832–61).

**Seatoun.** See SETON.

**Se·at'tle** (sē·ăt''l). 1786?–1866. Indian chief, b. near Seattle, Washington; friendly to early white settlers;

signed treaty (1855) ceding land to the whites. The city of Seattle is named after him.

**Sea'well** (?sōō'ĕl), **Molly Elliot.** 1860–1916. American novelist; author of *The Sprightly Romance of Marsac* (1896), *John Mainwaring, Financier* (1908), *The Diary of a Beauty* (1915), etc.

**Se·bas'tian** (sē·băs'chăn), Saint. Third-century Christian martyr; soldier by profession; served under emperors Maximian and Diocletian; made many converts to Christianity. Ordered by Diocletian to desist from proselyting; refused and was executed.

**Sebastian.** *Port.* **Sebastião.** 1554–1578. King of Portugal (1557–78); son of Dom John (1537–1554), only son of John III; during his minority (1557–68), government under his grandmother Catherine of Austria, and later his uncle Cardinal Henry (see HENRY, King of Portugal); educated by Jesuits; led expedition to Morocco; defeated and slain at the battle of Alcázarquivir; last important ruler of House of Aviz (*q.v.*); subject of later legends.

**Sé'bas'tia'ni'** (sā'bȧs'tyȧ'nē'), Comte **Horace François Bastien.** 1772–1851. French general and diplomat; distinguished himself at Marengo, Austerlitz, and in the Spanish and Russian campaigns; ambassador at Constantinople (1802, 1806–07); ambassador to Naples (1834) and London (1835–40); marshal of France (1840).

**Se'ba·stia'no del Piom'bo** (sā'bäs·tyä'nō dāl pyōm'bō). *Real name* **Sebastiano Lu·cia'ni** (lōō·chä'nē). 1485?–1547. Italian painter, b. Venice; to Rome (1509) to aid Agostino Chigi in decoration of Villa Farnese; friend and associate of Michelangelo (1512 ff.); to Venice (1527–29); appointed keeper of papal seals (whence his surname; 1531). Among his works are an altarpiece in the Church of San Giovanni Crisostomo, Venice, *Resurrection of Lazarus*, now in National Gallery, London, *Martyrdom of St. Agatha*, now in Pitti Palace, and portraits.

**Sec'chi** (sāk'kē), **Pietro Angelo.** 1818–1878. Italian astronomer; joined Jesuit order (1833); director of observatory, Roman Coll., Rome (1849). Known for spectroscopic work on the sun and fixed stars; classified stars according to color of their spectra; made meteorological and magnetic observations.

**Sec'combe** (sĕk'ŭm), **Thomas.** 1866–1923. English critic and biographer; on editorial staff, *Dictionary of National Biography* (1891–1901). Author of *The Age of Johnson* (1900), *George Meredith* (1913), *Dr. Johnson and Mrs. Thrale*, etc.

**Sé'ché'** (sā'shā'), **Léon.** 1848–1914. French writer; among his books of verse are *Les Griffes du Lion* (1871), *Amour et Patrie* (1875), and *La Chanson de la Vie* (1888); among his prose works, *Alfred de Vigny* (1902), *Alfred de Musset* (1906), etc.

**Séchelles, Marie Jean Hérault de.** See HÉRAULT DE SÉCHELLES.

**Sechten, von.** See Ludwig von SIEGEN.

**Seck'en·dorff** (zĕk'ĕn·dôrf), **Veit Ludwig von.** 1626–1692. German statesman and historian; chief work, *Teutscher Fürstenstaat* (1656). His nephew Count **Friedrich Heinrich von Seckendorff** (1673–1763) was an Austrian soldier and diplomat; represented Austria in Berlin (1726); engaged in War of the Polish Succession; defeated French at Klausen (1735); created field marshal, and commanded army against Turks (1737); served in Bavarian army (1740–45) during War of the Austrian Succession.

**Se'cord** (sē'kôrd), **Laura.** 1775–1868. Canadian heroine, who carried (1813) news to the British at Beaver Dams (between Stony Creek and Niagara River) of an intended American surprise attack and enabled the British force to capture the American contingent.

**Se·cre'tan'** (sē·krā'täN'), **Marc Louis François.** 1804–1867. Swiss optical instrument maker; in Paris (from 1844). His son **Auguste** (1833–1874) succeeded him (1867) as director of the business, was succeeded (1874) by his cousin **Georges Emmanuel Secretan** (b. 1837), who constructed the great telescope in the Paris observatory.

**Se·cun'dus** (*as Lat.*, sē·kŭn'dŭs), **Johannes.** *Real name* **Jan Nicolai E've·raerts** (ā'vē·rȧrts). 1511–1536. Dutch poet; author of a volume of Latin love poems *Basia*, and a number of elegies, odes, epistles, and epigrams, collected and published (1541) as *Opera Poetica.*

**Secydianus.** See SOGDIANUS.

**Se·daine'** (sē·dân'), **Michel Jean.** 1719–1797. French playwright; author of *Épître à mon Habit* (1745), *Le Diable à Quatre* (1756), *Blaise le Savetier* (1759), *Philosophe sans le Savoir* (1765), *Gageure Imprévue* (1768), and librettos for several of Monsigny's operas.

**Sed'don** (sĕd''n), **James Alexander.** 1815–1880. American politician, b. Fredericksburg, Va.; Confederate States secretary of war (1862–65).

**Seddon, Richard John.** 1845–1906. New Zealand statesman, b. in Lancashire, England; to Melbourne, Australia (1863), New Zealand (1866); member of New Zealand parliament (1879); advocate of state ownership and state socialism. Premier (1893–1906); carried through old-age pensions (1898); arranged universal penny postage (1901); nationalized coal mines and fire insurance; in late years known as a British imperialist.

**Sedg'wick** (sĕj'wĭk), **Adam.** 1785–1873. English geologist; prebendary of Norwich (1834). Studied geology of Cornwall and Devon, red sandstone of northern half of England, geology of Lake District and of Wales; with Murchison, introduced term Devonian for slates, etc., in West Somerset, Devon, and Cornwall.

**Sedgwick, Anne Douglas.** 1873–1935. American novelist, b. Englewood, N.J.; lived chiefly in Paris and London (from 1882); m. Basil de Selincourt (1908). Studied painting, Paris (1891–96). Among her novels are *The Dull Miss Archinard* (1898), *Tante* (1911), *The Encounter* (1914), *Adrienne Toner* (1922), *The Little French Girl* (1924), *The Old Countess* (1927), *Dark Hester* (1929), *Philippa* (1930).

**Sedgwick, Ellery.** 1872–1960. American editor, b. New York City; editor, *Atlantic Monthly* (1908–38). His brother **Henry Dwight** (1861–1957), lawyer and writer, practiced in New York (to 1898); author of *Essays on Great Writers* (1902), *The New American Type and Other Essays* (1908), *An Apology for Old Maids and Other Essays* (1917), *Dante* (1919), *Marcus Aurelius* (1921), *Pro Vita Monastica* (1923), *The Art of Happiness* (1933), *In Praise of Gentlemen* (1935), *The House of Guise* (1937), etc.

**Sedgwick, John.** 1813–1864. American army officer; grad. U.S.M.A., West Point (1837); brigadier general of volunteers (1861); served in Peninsular campaign; major general (1862); engaged at Antietam, Chancellorsville, Fredericksburg, Gettysburg, The Wilderness. Killed in action at Spotsylvania (May 9, 1864).

**Sedgwick, Theodore.** 1746–1813. American jurist, b. West Hartford, Conn.; military secretary to Gen. John Thomas (1776); member, Continental Congress (1785–88). In Massachusetts constitutional ratification convention (1788), advocated ratification. Member, U.S. House of Representatives (1789–96, 1799–1801), speaker (1799–1801); U.S. senator (1796–99); justice, Massachusetts supreme court (1802–13). His son **Theodore** (1780–1839) was a lawyer; practiced in Albany; author of *Public and Private Economy* (3 vols., 1836–39). A daughter of the first Theodore, **Catharine Ma·ri'a**

[mȧ·rī′ȧ] (1789–1867), was a writer; author of *A New-England Tale* (1822), *Hope Leslie* (1827), *The Linwoods ...* (1835), *Means and Ends...* (1839), *Married or Single?* (1857), etc. A son of the second Theodore, **Theodore** (1811–1859), was a lawyer; author of legal and political treatises. This third Theodore's son **Arthur George** (1844–1915) was also a lawyer; assistant editor of the *Nation* (1872–1905) and *Evening Post* (1881–85); author of legal treatises.

**Sedgwick, William Thompson.** 1855–1921. American biologist and sanitarian; at M.I.T. (1883–1921). Wrote *General Biology* (with E. B. Wilson, 1886), *Principles of Sanitary Science and the Public Health* (1902), *The Human Mechanism* (with T. Hough, 1906).

**Sed′ley** (sĕd′lĭ), Sir **Charles.** 1639?–1701. English wit and dramatist of the Restoration; notorious man of fashion and profligate; known for his bons mots; wrote tragedies *Antony and Cleopatra* (1677) and *The Tyrant King of Crete* (1702); comedies including *Bellamira* (1687); society verse and songs, including *Phyllis Is My Only Joy.* His daughter **Catherine** (1657–1717) was mistress of James II; countess of Dorchester (1686).

**Se·du′li·us** (sē·dū′lĭ·ŭs), **Coelius** *or* **Caelius.** Fifth-century Roman Christian poet; chief work, *Carmen Paschale,* a poetic version of the Gospels.

**Sée** (sā), **Henri Eugène.** 1864–1936. French historian; author of *Les Idées Politiques en France au 18ᵉ Siècle* (1920), *La Vie Économique et les Classes Sociales en France au 18ᵉ Siècle* (1924), *Les Origines du Capitalisme* (1926), etc.

**See** (sē), Sir **John.** 1844–1907. Australian statesman, b. in England; to New South Wales (1853); member of colonial parliament, New South Wales (1880–1904); premier of New South Wales (1901–04).

**See, Thomas Jefferson Jackson.** 1866–1962. American astronomer and mathematician; head of department of astronomy, and assistant in organizing Yerkes Observatory, U. of Chicago (1893–96); astronomer at Lowell Observatory, Flagstaff, Ariz. (1896–98); professor of mathematics, U.S. navy (from 1899), in charge of U.S. Naval Observatory (1899–1902), and of naval observatory on Mare Island, Calif. (from 1903). Known esp. for investigations of double stars, the ether, the cause of universal gravitation and magnetism, cosmic evolution, and earthquakes. Discovered precession of earth's magnetic poles in 540 years under action of sun's like poles. Established wave theory of solid bodies and of the cosmic ray.

**See′bach** (zā′bäκ) *or* **Nie′mann–See′bach** (nē′män-), **Marie.** 1829–1897. German actress; m. (1859; div. 1868) Albert Niemann (*q.v.*). Among her most successful roles were Ophelia, Desdemona, Maria Stuart, Jane Eyre, Lady Macbeth.

**See′beck** (zā′bĕk), **Thomas Johann.** 1770–1831. German physicist; worked with Goethe on theory of color, esp. on effect of colored light; credited with discovery of thermoelectricity, whose laws he studied; demonstrated use of thermoelement for measuring temperature; studied heat radiation and the rotary effect of sugar solutions on plane-polarized light; constructed a polariscope.

**See′bohm** (sē′bōm), **Frederic.** 1833–1912. English economic historian; author of works on the Reformation, and three works upsetting prevailing view of Anglo-Saxon communal groups of freemen, *The English Village Community* (1883), *The Tribal System in Wales* (1895), *Tribal Custom in Anglo-Saxon Law* (1902); traced English open-field manorial system of farming to an amalgamation of the Roman villa with the Celtic tribal system. His brother **Henry** (1832–1895) was an ornithologist.

**Seeckt** (zākt), **Hans von.** 1866–1936. German soldier; chief of general staff of Mackensen's armies on eastern front (1915–16); chief of general staff of Turkish field army (1917–18). In China as military adviser to Chiang Kai-shek, helping with reorganization of Chinese army (1932–35). Author of military treatises.

**Seed** (sēd), **Miles Ainscough.** 1843–1913. Inventor and industrialist, b. Preston, England; to U.S. (1865). Perfected process for making photographic dry plate and organized company (1882) to manufacture it. Sold out to Eastman Kodak Co. (1902).

**See′ger** (sē′gẽr), **Alan.** 1888–1916. American poet, b. New York City; grad. Harvard (1910). To Paris (1912); enlisted in French Foreign Legion at outbreak of World War I. Author of poems collected in *Juvenilia* and *Later Poems.* Best-known individual poems: *I Have a Rendezvous With Death* and *Ode in Memory of the American Volunteers Fallen for France.*

**Seeger, Peter.** *Known as* **Pete Seeger.** 1919– American folk singer and composer, b. New York City. Wrote many ballads, work songs, dance tunes, etc., including *Where Have All the Flowers Gone* (1961).

**See′ley** (sē′lĭ), Sir **John Robert.** 1834–1895. English historian and essayist; professor of Latin, University Coll., London (1863); caused storm of religious controversy by essay *Ecce Homo* (1865), and in *Natural Religion* (1882) contended that supernaturalism is not essential to religion; professor of modern history, Cambridge (1869–95). Author of *Life and Times of Stein,* on anti-Napoleonic revolt (1878), *The Expansion of England* (1883), and *The Growth of British Policy* (1895).

**See′ly** (sē′lĭ), **John Edward Bernard.** 1st Baron **Mot′ti·stone** (mŏt′ĭ·stŭn). 1868–1947. English political leader; conservative M.P. (1900–06); Liberal M.P. (1906); undersecretary for colonies (1908–10); secretary of state for war (1912–14), resigned after Curragh incident, when he initialed without authority from cabinet an army-council minute freeing certain army officers from service against threatened Ulster rebellion against home rule. Commanded brigade of Canadian cavalry in World War I; deputy minister of munitions (1918); undersecretary of state for air and president of air council (1919); lord lieutenant of Hampshire (from 1918); elevated to peerage (1933). Wrote *Adventure* (1930), *My Horse Warrior* (1934), and *Paths of Happiness* (1938).

**See′lye** (sē′lĭ), **Julius Hawley.** 1824–1895. American clergyman and educator; professor of philosophy, Amherst (1858–76); president, Amherst (1876–90). Author of *The Way, the Truth, and the Life* (1873), *Duty* (1891), *Citizenship* (1894). His brother **Lau·re′nus** (lô·rē′nŭs) **Clark** (1837–1924) was a Congregational minister; first president, Smith College (1873–1910).

**Se′fe·ria′des** (sĕf′ẽr·yä′thēs), **Giorgos Stylianou.** *Pseud.* **George Se·fe′ris** (sĕ·fĕr′ēs). 1900–1971. Greek poet and diplomat. Amb. to Great Britain (1957–62). Awarded Nobel prize in literature (1963).

**Sef′ström′** (sâv′strûm′), **Nils Gabriel.** 1787–1854. Swedish chemist and mineralogist; rediscovered and named the element vanadium (1830).

**Se′gan·ti′ni** (sā′gän·tē′nē), **Giovanni.** 1858–1899. Italian painter; influenced by French impressionists. Among works are *At the Tether* (in National Gallery, Rome), *Dark Hours* (in Berlin gallery), *Unnatural Mothers* (in Vienna gallery), and an unfinished triptych *Alpine World* (in Segantini Museum, St. Moritz).

**Se′gar** (sē′gär), **Elzie Cris′ler** (krĭs′lẽr). 1894–1938. American cartoonist, b. Chester, Ill.; originator of "Popeye the Sailor" (from c. 1930) and other comic strips.

**Se'ga·rel'li** (sā'gä·rĕl'lē), **Gherardo.** 13th-century Italian ecclesiastic; founder of Apostolic Brothers.

**Se'ghers** (zā'gĕrs), **Anna.** Pseudonym of **Netty Rad'vá·nyi** (rŏd'vä·nyĭ), *nee* **Rei'ling** (rī'lĭng). 1900– . German novelist; wrote *Aufstand der Fischer von St. Barbara* (1929; Eng. transl. *The Revolt of the Fishermen*, 1929), volume of short stories (1930) and *Die Gefährten* (1932); fled to Paris (1933); wrote *Der Kopflohn* (1933) and *Die Retting* (1934); after fall of France, to U.S.; published *The Seventh Cross* (1942).

**Segonzac, André Dunoyer de.** See DUNOYER DE SEGONZAC.

**Se·go'via** (sā·gō'vyä), **Andrés.** 1894– . Spanish guitarist, composer and arranger of works for classical guitar.

**Se·grais'** (sẽ·grĕ'), **Jean Regnault de.** 1624–1701. French poet; secretary to duchesse de Montpensier and collaborator with her in *Relation de l'Isle Imaginaire* and *La Princesse de Paphlagonie* (1659). Among his own works are *Bérénice* (a novel, 1648–51), *Athis* (verse, 1653), *Poésies Diverses* (1658), and verse translations of Vergil's *Aeneid* and *Georgics*.

**Se·grè'** (sâ·grā'), **Emilio.** 1905– . American physicist, b. in Italy. To U.S. (1938); at U. of Calif. (1938– ). Awarded Nobel prize in physics (1959) with O. Chamberlain for discovery of the antiproton.

**Sé'guier'** (sā'gyā'), **Pierre.** Duc **de Ville'mor'** (dē vēl'môr'). 1588–1672. French statesman; chancellor of France (1635); suppressed rebellion in Normandy (1639); active in securing recognition of Anne of Austria as regent after death of Louis XIII. One of founders of Académie Française.

**Se'guin** (sā'gwĭn), **É'douard'** (ā'dwȧr'). 1812–1880. Physician, b. Clamecy, France; to U.S. (1850); specialist in mental disease, esp. in treatment of idiots. His son **Edward Con'stant** [kŏn'stănt] (1843–1898) was also a physician; in U.S. army medical corps (to 1869); specialized in neurology; known esp. for his belief in the value of drugs, properly administered, and for his use of iodides in large doses in stubborn cases.

**Sé'gur'** (sā'gür'). Prominent French family, including: Comte **Henri François de Ségur** (1689–1751), lieutenant general (1738); distinguished himself at Raucoux (Roucourt) and Lawfeld (1746). His son Marquis **Philippe Henri** (1724–1801), marshal of France, and minister of war (1781–87), signed ordinance restricting officers to those having at least four heraldic quarters of nobility. Philippe's son Comte **Louis Philippe** (1753–1830), served with Rochambeau in America; ambassador to St. Petersburg; appointed by Napoleon councilor of state; created peer of France at the Restoration. Louis's brother Vicomte **Joseph Alexandre** (1756–1805), deputy of Paris nobility in States-General (1789); author of *Réflexions sur l'Armée* (1789), *Les Femmes*...(1801), and several stage productions. Louis's son Comte **Philippe Paul** (1780–1873) served in Napoleon's armies and was general of brigade (1811); wrote *Histoire de Napoléon et de la Grande Armée en 1812* (1824), *Histoire de Charles VIII*, etc.

**Sei'del** (sī'd'l), **E'mil** (ē'mĭl). 1864–1947. American Socialist leader; mayor of Milwaukee (1910–12), first Socialist to be elected to such office in an important American city.

**Seidl** (zī'd'l), **An'ton** (ăn'tŏn). 1850–1898. Musician, b. Pest, Hungary; assisted Richard Wagner (1872–78). To Metropolitan Opera House, New York City (1885), to succeed Leopold Damrosch as conductor of German opera; naturalized American citizen (1891); succeeded Theodore Thomas as conductor, New York Philharmonic Society (1891–98). Noted for his conducting of Wagnerian operas and for presenting (1893) the American première of Dvořák's *New World Symphony*.

**Seidl, Johann Gabriel.** 1804–1875. Austrian journalist and poet; wrote *Bifolien* (1836), *Gedichte in Niederösterreichischer Mundart* (1844), and *Natur und Herz* (1853). His text *Gott erhalte Franz den Kaiser*, to music by Haydn, became Austria's national anthem.

**Seignelay,** Marquis **de.** See Jean Baptiste COLBERT (1651–1690).

**Sei'gno'bos'** (sā'nyô'bôs'), **Charles.** 1854–1942. French historian; professor at the Sorbonne, Paris (from 1890). Among his works are *Le Régime Féodal en Bourgogne* (1882), *Histoire de la Civilisation* (1884–86), *Histoire Politique de l'Europe Contemporaine* (1897), etc.

**Seil'lière'** (sĕ'yâr'), Baron **Ernest Antoine Aimé Léon.** 1866–1955. French author of philosophical, critical, and historical studies.

**Sei'pel** (zī'pĕl), **Ignaz.** 1876–1932. Austrian Roman Catholic prelate and statesman; apostolic prothonotary (1921). Entered Austro-Hungarian cabinet (1918), last under the monarchy; head of Christian Socialist party; chancellor of Austria (1922–24, 1926–29); minister of foreign affairs (1930).

**Seitz** (zīts), **Adalbert.** German naturalist; published (beginning 1906) an important work on butterflies, *Die Gross-Schmetterlinge der Erde* (Eng. title *The Macrolepidoptera of the World*).

**Seitz, Anton.** 1829–1900. German painter, esp. of genre scenes.

**Seitz, Karl.** 1869–1950. Austrian politician; president of Provisional National Assembly and member of the State Council (1918–19); member of the Constituent National Assembly and the Nationalrat (1920). President of Nationalrat and acting president of Republic of Austria (1919–20); burgomaster and governor of Vienna (1923–34); under arrest after the rebellion (Feb., 1934) and again after German occupation of Austria (1938).

**Se·ja'nus** (sē·jā'nŭs), **Lucius Aelius.** d. 31 A.D. Roman politician and conspirator; favorite of Emperor Tiberius, who made him commander of praetorian guard. Conceiving ambition to usurp throne, poisoned emperor's son Drusus Caesar (23 A.D.) and persuaded emperor to banish Agrippina, widow of Germanicus Caesar; the death, under suspicious circumstances, of Agrippina followed. On discovery of his intrigues, he was executed by order of Tiberius. Subject of a play, *Sejanus*, by Ben Jonson.

**Sé'jour'** (sā'zhōōr'), **Vic'tor'** (vēk'tôr'). *Full name* **Juan** (zhwäɴ) **Victor Séjour Mar'cou' et Fer'rand'** (mȧr'kōō' ā fĕ'räɴ'). 1817–1874. Playwright, b. New Orleans, La., natural son of a Santo Domingan Negro and a New Orleans quadroon; resided in Paris most of his life. Author of verse dramas and melodramas, notable for magnificence of stage setting and costumes.

**Se·ki** (sĕ·kē), **Kowa.** 1642?–1708. Japanese mathematician.

**Selborne,** Earls of. See Sir Roundell PALMER.

**Sel'den** (sĕl'dĕn), **George Baldwin.** 1846–1922. American lawyer and inventor; specialized in patent law; applied for patent on gasoline motor-propelled vehicle (1879) and was granted patent (Nov. 5, 1895) for a "road engine," the first American patent for a gasoline-driven car (cf. C. E. DURYEA). Sold rights to his patent on royalty basis; protracted litigation followed, the Ford Motor Company refusing to pay royalties and finally gaining decision (1911) that its engine was of a different fundamental type from the Selden engine.

**Selden, John.** 1584–1654. English jurist, antiquary, Orientalist, and statesman; acquired European reputation as scholar by his writings, including a treatise

*Duello, or Single Combat* (1610); a collection of records of civil government of Britain before Norman conquest (1615); the authoritative *Titles of Honour* (1614). Won fame as Orientalist by a Latin treatise inquiring into polytheism, *De Diis Syris* (1617), and expositions of rabbinical law; collected Oriental manuscripts. Incurred indignation of clergy by his *History of Tythes* (1618), denying tithes as divine institution; imprisoned (1621) for part in repudiation by Parliament of king's doctrine that privileges of Parliament were originally royal grants. M.P. (1623); took part in impeachment of Buckingham (1626); helped to draw up Petition of Right (1628); imprisoned with Eliot and Holles after discussion of tonnage and poundage (1629); opposed crown on question of ship money. Member of Long Parliament; aided in drawing articles of impeachment of Laud (1641); keeper of records of Tower of London (1643); lay member of Westminster Assembly (1643), sought to moderate fanaticism of his colleagues; disapproved execution of Charles I and took no further part in public affairs. His best-known work, *Table Talk* (1689), consisting of reports of his utterances over twenty years, composed by his secretary.

**Sel'des** (sĕl'dĕs), **George.** 1890–1970. American journalist and writer, b. Alliance, N.J. Author of *The Truth Behind the News* (1929), *Sawdust Caesar* (1932), *Iron, Blood and Profits* (1934), *Lords of the Press* (1938). Proprietor and editor, *In Fact* (1940). His brother **Gilbert Vivian** (1893– ), also a journalist and writer; on editorial staff of *Collier's* (1919), *The Dial* (1920–23), New York *Journal* (1931–37); author of *The Wise-Crackers* (a play, 1925), *Lysistrata* (a play, 1930), *The Wings of the Eagle* (fiction, 1929), *Against Revolution* (1932), *Your Money and Your Life* (1937), and some murder mysteries under the pseudonym of **Foster Johns** (jŏnz).

**Seld'te** (zĕl'tĕ), **Franz.** 1882–1947. German politician; served in World War I (1914–18); founder (1918) and first Reich leader of the Stahlhelm; Reich minister of labor (1933–45).

**Se'ler** (zā'lĕr), **Eduard Georg.** 1849–1922. German authority on American anthropology; studied Mayan works of art, Mexican picture writing, and ancient Indian astronomy, mythology, and calendar system.

**Se·leu'ci·dae** (sē·lū'sĭ·dē). A dynasty (312–64 B.C.) which, at height of its power, ruled over Bactria (Balkh), Persia, Babylonia, Syria, and part of Asia Minor. Founded by Seleucus I Nicator; included about 26 sovereigns; gave its name to an era (Seleucidan Era) long used in Western Asia and by the scattered Jews; last remaining region (Syria) of empire made a Roman province by Pompey (64 B.C.). See individual biographies under SELEUCUS, ANTIOCHUS, DEMETRIUS.

**Se·leu'cus** (sē·lū'kŭs). Name of six kings of the Seleucidae (*q.v.*):

**Seleucus I.** *Surnamed* **Ni·ca'tor** (nī·kā'tôr; -tĕr). 358?–280 B.C. Macedonian general under Alexander the Great, and founder of Seleucid dynasty; satrap of Babylon (321–312), king of Babylon (312–280), and ruler of Seleucid empire (306–280). Fought in Alexander's campaigns (333–323); commander under Perdiccas (323) and, later (321), one of those responsible for his death; given satrapy of Babylon (321); founded Seleucia on the Tigris; joined coalition of Ptolemy, Lysimachus, and Cassander against Antigonus; after defeat of Antigonus at Gaza (312), made Babylon independent; conquered eastern regions as far as the Indus (311–302); with Lysimachus won decisive victory (301) at Ipsus over Antigonus I; received Syria and Asia Minor as parts of new empire (301); made Antioch his capital; m. (300?) Stratonice (*q.v.*); took prisoner (285) Demetrius I of Macedonia; defeated Lysimachus (281); proclaimed himself king of Macedon; assassinated by Ptolemy Keraunos. Succeeded by his son Antiochus I Soter.

**Seleucus II.** *Surnamed* **Cal'li·ni'cus** (kăl'ĭ·nī'kŭs). d. 226 B.C. King (247–226 B.C.); son of Antiochus II, and father of Seleucus III and Antiochus III; raised to throne by his mother, Laodice; at war (246–245) with Ptolemy III Euergetes of Egypt; defeated in a war (241?–236) by his brother Antiochus Hierax, to whom he gave Asia Minor as independent kingdom; lost Parthia to rising Arsacid dynasty (227?).

**Seleucus III.** *Surnamed* **So'ter** (sō'tĕr). d. 223 B.C. King (226–223 B.C.); son of Seleucus II; failed in attempt to recover Asia Minor from Attalus.

**Seleucus IV.** *Surnamed* **Phi·lop'a·tor** (fĭ·lŏp'ȧ·tôr). 217?–175 B.C. King (187–175 B.C.); son of Antiochus III; left helpless by Roman defeat of his father; assassinated; throne seized by his brother Antiochus IV.

**Seleucus V.** d. 125 B.C. King (125 B.C.). Son of Demetrius II and brother of Antiochus VIII; killed by his mother, Cleopatra Thea.

**Seleucus VI.** *Surnamed* **E·piph'a·nes Nicator** (ē·pĭf'ȧ·nēz). d. 95 B.C. King (96–95 B.C.); son of Antiochus VIII.

**Sel'fridge** (sĕl'frĭj), **Harry Gordon.** 1857–1947. Merchant, b. Ripon, Wis.; on staff of Marshall Field & Co., Chicago (to 1904). To London, Eng. (1906) and organized Selfridge & Co., Ltd., and developed it into one of the largest department stores in Europe; became naturalized British subject (1937).

**Selfridge, Thomas Oliver.** 1836–1924. American naval officer, b. Charlestown, Mass.; grad. U.S.N.A., Annapolis (1854). Served in Union navy through Civil War; on the *Cumberland* when it was sunk by the *Merrimac*, in command of gunboat *Cairo* attacking Vicksburg, took part in Red River expedition, served under Admiral Porter in attacks on Fort Fisher. Surveyed and explored Isthmus of Darien region for interoceanic canal; surveyed Amazon and Madeira rivers (1878). Captain (1881); commodore (1894); rear admiral (1896); retired (1898).

**Sel'ig·man** (sĕl'ĭg·măn), **Charles Gabriel.** 1873–1940. English ethnologist; author of *The Melanesians of British New Guinea* (1910), *The Races of Africa* (1930), etc.

**Seligman, Joseph.** 1819–1880. Financier, b. Baiersdorf, Bavaria; to U.S. (1837); established J. & W. Seligman & Co., New York, international banking house (1864), with branches later at San Francisco, New Orleans, London, Paris, and Frankfurt am Main; aided Union cause during Civil War by marketing bonds abroad; co-operated with U.S. treasury in handling conversion operations of U.S. bonds and resumption of specie payments (1874–79). Member, Committee of Seventy, which exposed the Tweed Ring in New York; chairman, New York City Rapid Transit Commission. A brother, **Jesse** (1827–1894), was also a financier, associated with Joseph in banking firm of J. & W. Seligman & Co. (from 1864) and its president (1880–94). A son of Joseph, **Isaac Newton** (1855–1917), was also a banker; associated with J. & W. Seligman & Co. (from 1876), and president of the firm (1894–1917). Another son of Joseph, **Edwin Robert Anderson** (1861–1939), was an economist; taught at Columbia (1885–1931), professor (from 1891); author of *Essays in Taxation, Economic Interpretation of History, Principles of Economics, Studies in Public Finance*, etc.

**Se·lim'** (sĕ·lēm'). Name of three Turkish sultans:

**Selim I** (1467–1520), son of Bajazet II, whom he dethroned in order to seize power (1512); executed 40,000

Shiites in order to assure Sunnite uniformity in the Mohammedan faith; conquered sections of Persia (1514), and annexed Syria (1516) and Egypt (1517). **Selim II** (1524?–1574); succeeded his father Suleiman the Magnificent (1566); conquered Cyprus (1570) and lost the naval battle of Lepanto (1571). **Selim III** (1761–1808); succeeded his uncle Abdul-Hamid I (1789); attempted to reorganize his army on western European models (1805); aroused a revolt among the Janizaries (1807).

**Sel′in·court** (?sĕl′ĭn·kōrt; -kôrt), **Ernest de.** 1870–1943. English educator; professor of English language and literature, Birmingham (1908–35), and vice-principal of the university (1931–35). Edited critical editions of a number of English classics; published *Oxford Lectures on Poetry* (1934) and *Letters of William and Dorothy Wordsworth* (1935 ff.). His brother **Hugh** (1878–1951), novelist and playwright, wrote the novels *A Boy's Marriage* (1907), *The High Adventure* (1908), *Realms of Day* (1915), *One Little Boy* (1923), *Mr. Buffum* (1930), *Studies from Life* (1934), and plays *Loyalty* (1909), *Getting What You Want* (1913), etc. Another brother, **Basil** (1876– ), m. (1908) Anne Douglas Sedgwick (*q.v.*), wrote *The English Secret and Other Essays*, etc.

**Sel·juk′** (sĕl·jōōk′; sĕl′jōōk). Name of several Turkish dynasties which ruled over large sections of western Asia in 11th, 12th, and 13th centuries; derived from Seljuk, of Turkish tribe of the Ghuz, who early in 11th century began conquests of territories ruled by members of the dynasties.

**Selkirk,** Earls of. See DOUGLAS family.

**Sel′kirk** (sĕl′kûrk) *or* **Sel′craig** (-krāg), **Alexander.** 1676–1721. Scottish sailor; the original of Defoe's hero Robinson Crusoe. Joined William Dampier in privateering expedition to South Seas; quarreled with his captain; was set ashore (Oct., 1704) at his own request on Mas-a-Tierra, one of Juan Fernández islets, and remained there alone until taken off (Feb., 1709) by Thomas Dover, captain of one of prizes of a privateering expedition under Woodes Rogers and Dampier. Probably known to Defoe only through accounts by Woodes Rogers, Edward Cooke, and Richard Steele.

**Sel′la** (sĕl′lä), **Quintino.** 1827–1884. Italian statesman, engineer, and mineralogist; minister of finance (1862, 1864–65, 1869–73).

**Sel′lar** (sĕl′ẽr), **William Young.** 1825–1890. Scottish classical scholar; author of *Roman Poets of the Republic* (1863)...*of the Augustan Age* (1877), and *Horace and the Elegiac Poets* (1892).

**Sel′lers** (sĕl′ẽrz), **Isaiah.** 1802?–1864. Mississippi River steamboat pilot, b. in Iredell County, N.C. Under pseudonym of **Mark Twain** (twān), later used by Samuel L. Clemens, contributor to New Orleans *Daily Picayune;* for a long time held record for run from New Orleans to St. Louis (May 4, 1844).

**Sellers, Matthew Bacon.** 1869–1932. American airplane engineer; conducted research work in aerodynamics (from 1900); built wind tunnel for testing dynamic air pressure on arched surfaces. Patented aerial apparatus, a quadruplane (1911), improvements in steering and running gear of airplanes. Technical editor, *Aeronautics* (1911–32).

**Sellers, William.** 1824–1905. American industrialist and inventor; founded and headed machine-tool manufacturing works in Philadelphia (1848). Patented various machine tools, rifling machines, riveters, steam injectors, steam hammers, hydraulic machinery, spiral-geared planer. President, Franklin Institute (1864–67), to which he presented the paper *A System of Screw Threads and Nuts,* proposing a standard system of screw threads; his system was adopted by U.S. government (1868).

**Se·lous′** (sĕ·lōōs′), **Frederick Courteney.** 1851–1917. English hunter and explorer in South Africa.

**Sels′don** (sĕlz′dŭn), 1st Baron. **William Mitch′ell–Thom′son** (mĭch′ĕl·tŏm′s'n). 1877–1938. British politician; M.P. (1906–32); member of supreme economic council, in Paris (1919); postmaster general (1924–29).

**Sel′wyn** (sĕl′wĭn), **George Augustus.** 1809–1878. English missionary; first bishop to New Zealand (1841); studied Maori and gained confidence of natives. While in England attending Pan-Anglican synod, accepted bishopric of Lichfield (1868); honored by erection of Selwyn Coll., Cambridge, as memorial.

**Selz′nick** (sĕlz′nĭk), **David Oliver.** 1902–1965. American motion-picture producer, b. Pittsburgh. On staff of Metro-Goldwyn-Mayer Corp. (1926–27), Paramount Pictures Corp. (1927–31), RKO Radio Pictures, Inc. (1931–33), and Metro-Goldwyn-Mayer (1933–35). Organized Selznick International Pictures, Inc. (1935–36) and produced *Little Lord Fauntleroy* (1936), *Garden of Allah* (1936), *Prisoner of Zenda* (1937), *Tom Sawyer* (1937), *Gone with the Wind* (1939), etc. His father, **Lewis J. Selznick** (1871–1933), was a pioneer in the motion-picture producing business.

**Sem′bach** (zĕm′bäĸ), **Johannes.** 1881– . Operatic tenor, b. Berlin, Ger.; to U.S. (1914) and naturalized (1921). Member of Metropolitan Opera Company in New York (from 1914). Excelled in Wagnerian roles.

**Sem′brich** (zĕm′brĭĸ; *Angl.* sĕm′brĭk), **Mar·cel′la** (mär·tsĕl′ä; *Angl.* -sĕl′ȧ). *Real name* **Pra·xe′de** (prä·ksā′dĕ) **Mar′cel·li′ne** (mär′tsĕ·lē′nĕ) **Ko·chań′ska** (kô·ĸän′y'·skä). 1858–1935. Operatic soprano, b. Lemberg, Austria; adopted mother's family name, Sembrich; m. Wilhelm Stengel. Operatic debut as Elvira, in Athens, Greece (1877). Sang at Dresden Opera (1878), Covent Garden in London (1880). American debut as Lucia in *Lucia di Lammermoor,* with Metropolitan Opera Company in New York (1883). Retired (from opera, 1909; from concert stage, 1916). Director of vocal department at Curtis Institute in Philadelphia (from 1924).

**Se·më′nov** (syĭ·myô′nôf), **Grigori.** 1890?–1946. Russian Cossack hetman, and general in eastern Siberia; fought the Bolsheviks (1918–21); designated by Kolchak commander in chief of Transbaikalia (1920); occupied Vladivostok (1920); driven from Siberia (1921).

**Semenov, Nikolai Nikolaevich.** 1896– Soviet chemist. Awarded Nobel prize in chemistry (1956) with C. N. Hinshelwood for studies on chemical reaction.

**Semënov, Pëtr Petrovich.** *Also* **Semënov–Tian-shan′ski** (-tyȧn·shȧn′skû·ĭ; *Angl.* -skĭ). 1827–1914. Russian traveler and geographer; made extensive explorations in Dzungaria and Central Asia (1846–56); authorized by Czar Alexander III to add Tianshanski to his surname because of his explorations among the Tian Shan (Tien Shan) mountains.

**Se·mir′a·mis** (sē·mĭr′ȧ·mĭs). Greek name of legendary queen of Assyria, wife of Ninus, founder of Nineveh. Noted for her great beauty, wisdom, and voluptuousness; reputed to have built many cities, including Babylon with its hanging gardens, temples, etc.; conquered many countries but unsuccessful in invasion of India; said to have reigned 42 years. Identified in some legends with the goddess Ishtar. Historically, there is reason to believe that Queen **Sam′mu–ra′mat** (säm′-mōō·rä′mät), wife of Shamshi-Adad V and mother of Adadnirari III, queen regent for her son (811–808 B.C.), is the original of the Semiramis legend.

**Sem′ler** (zĕm′lẽr), **Johann Salomo.** 1725–1791. German Protestant theologian; professor, Halle (1753); sometimes called "Father of German Rationalism."

**Sem′mel·weis** (zĕm′ĕl·vīs), **Ignaz Philipp.** 1818–1865.

Hungarian obstetrician; proved that puerperal fever is contagious (1847–49); became pioneer of antisepsis in obstetrics.

**Semmes** (sĕmz), **Raphael.** 1809–1877. American naval officer, b. in Charles County, Md.; resigned from U.S. navy to enter Confederate States navy (1861); commanded Confederate commerce destroyers *Sumter* (1861–62) and *Alabama* (1862–64), which under his command became one of most famous of commerce destroyers; *Alabama* sunk by U.S. ship *Kearsarge* off Cherbourg (June 19, 1864). Commissioned rear admiral and put in command of James River squadron (1865). Practiced law, Mobile, Ala. (from 1867).

**Se'mon** (sē'mŭn), **Waldo Lonsbury.** 1898– . American chemist, b. Demopolis, Ala.; B.S. (1920), Ph.D. (1923), U. of Washington; research chemist, B. F. Goodrich Co., Akron, Ohio (from 1926), director of synthetic research department (from 1937); known esp. for researches and writings on synthetic rubber.

**Se·mon'i·des** (sê·mŏn'ĭ·dēz). = SIMONIDES (of Amorgos).

**Sem'per** (zĕm'pẽr), **Gottfried.** 1803–1879. German architect; made adaptations of Italian Renaissance style. Works include opera house (1837–41, burned; rebuilt 1871–78) and synagogue (1838–40), Dresden; Polytechnicum, railroad station, and observatory, Zurich; imperial palace, imperial museums, and theaters, Vienna. His nephew **Karl Semper** (1832–1893), naturalist, wrote on travels in the Philippines, also on natural conditions affecting animal life.

**Sem'pill** (sĕm'pĭl) *or* **Sem'ple** (-p'l). Name of a Scottish family of hereditary sheriffs of Renfrewshire, including: **Robert Sempill,** 3d Lord Sempill (1505?–1572); governor and constable of castle of Douglas (1533); supporter of Mary of Guise and of Mary, Queen of Scots, until murder of Darnley (1567); fought against Mary at Carberry Hill and Langside. His son John by his second wife was ancestor of the Sempills of Beltrees; Sir **James Sempill** of Beltrees (1566–1625), John's son, who was educated with young James VI and assisted him in preparing *Basilicon Doron* (1599); Sir James's son **Robert Sempill** of Beltrees (1595?–?1668), poet, wrote *Life and Death of Habbie Simson;* and Robert's son **Francis** (1616?–1682), ballad writer and wit, credited with *Maggie Lauder* and *Blythsome Wedding.* **Robert Sempill** (1530?–1595); soldier and ballad writer; doubtless a cadet of the house of Sempill, probably illegitimate son of Robert, 3d Lord Sempill; bitter antagonist of Mary, Queen of Scots, and Roman Catholic Church; fled from Paris at Massacre of St. Bartholomew (1572); author of coarse ballads and political poems, as *The Regentis Tragedie,* a broadside (1570).

**Sem'ple** (sĕm'p'l), **Ellen Churchill.** 1863–1932. American geographer; lecturer in anthropogeography, U. of Chicago (1906–23); professor, school of geography, Clark U., Worcester, Mass. (1921–32).

**Sempronius Gracchus.** See GRACCHUS.

**Sem·pro'ni·us Lon'gus** (sĕm·prō'nĭ·ŭs lŏng'gŭs), **Tiberius.** Roman general and politician; consul (218 B.C.); with his colleague, Publius Cornelius Scipio (*q.v.*), defeated (218) by Hannibal at the River Trebbia.

**Sé'nan'cour'** (sā'näɴ'ko͞or'), **Étienne Pi'vert' de** (pē'vâr' dẽ). 1770–1846. French writer; admirer of Jean Jacques Rousseau; author of several works marked by deep pessimism, as *Rêveries sur la Nature Primitive de l'Homme* (1799), *Obermann* (novel; 1804), *Observations sur le Génie du Christianisme* (1816), etc.

**Sen·der'** (sān·dĕr'), **Ramón José.** 1902– . Spanish radical writer; studied law in Madrid (1919 ff.); involved in demonstrations against dictator Primo de Rivera; served in army in Morocco; to Mexico (1939); naturalized (1941). Author of *Imán* (trans. as *Pro Patria,* 1935), *Counter-attack in Spain* (trans. 1937), *Mr. Witt Among the Rebels* (trans. 1938), *A Man's Place* (1940), *Dark Wedding* (1943), etc.

**Sen'e·ca** (sĕn'ê·kȧ), **Marcus** (*or* **Lucius**) **Annaeus.** 54 B.C.?–39 A.D. Roman rhetorician, b. Córdoba, Spain. Author of *Controversiae* (10 books; a discussion of 74 imaginary legal cases and methods of presenting them), *Suasoriae* (1 book), and a historical work (now lost). His second son, **Lucius Annaeus** (4 B.C.?–65 A.D.), statesman and philosopher, b. Córdoba, Spain; studied in Rome; entered legal profession. Summoned (49 A.D.) to tutor Domitius, who later became emperor under name Nero; influential councilor of Nero in early years of his power. In later years, Nero turned against him; finally accused him of complicity in conspiracy of Piso; by order of Nero, took own life. Most important works are philosophic essays, including *Ad Marciam de Consolatione, De Ira, Ad Helviam de Consolatione, De Brevitate Vitae, De Constantia Sapientis, De Clementia, De Vita Beata, De Beneficiis, De Tranquillitate Animi, De Otio, De Providentia.* Known also as author of nine tragedies, *Hercules Furens, Thyestes, Phoenissae, Phaedra* (or *Hippolytus*), *Oedipus, Troades, Medea, Agamemnon, Hercules Oetaeus.*

**Se'ne·fel'der** (zā'nĕ·fĕl'dẽr), **Aloys.** 1771–1834. Inventor of lithography (about 1796); inspector of maps at royal printing office, Munich (1806); invented process of lithographing in colors (1826); pensioned by king of Bavaria.

**Sengi.** Variant of ZANGI.

**Sen'ior** (sēn'yẽr), **Nassau William.** 1790–1864. English economist; barrister, Lincoln's Inn (1819); professor of political economy, Oxford (1825–30, 1847–52); author of *An Outline of the Science of Political Economy* (1836), etc.

**Senn** (sĕn), **Nicholas.** 1844–1908. Surgeon, b. in Switzerland; to U.S. (1852); practiced in Milwaukee (1874–93), Chicago (from 1893). Noted as military surgeon; chief surgeon, 6th army corps, in Cuba (1898). Author of *Experimental Surgery* (1889), *Medico-Surgical Aspects of the Spanish-American War* (1900), etc.

**Sen·nach'er·ib** (sĕ·năk'ẽr·ĭb). A Sargonid king of Assyria (705–681 B.C.); son of Sargon II. Continued wars of his father against Merodach-baladan (*q.v.*) and alliance of Babylon and Elam; drove Merodach-baladan out of Babylon (703) and assumed its kingship; made campaign in the west (701); captured Sidon and secured submission of Ashdod, Ammon, Moab, and Edom; failed to take Tyre; defied by Hezekiah; invaded Palestine and captured many cities of Judah (*2 Kings* xviii. 13); had fleet built by Phoenician captives and with it destroyed Babylonian colony in Elam (694); fought a great indecisive battle with Elamites (691) at Khalule (on the Diyala); destroyed Babylon (689). A second campaign against Jerusalem (*2 Kings* xix) and conflict with Taharka of Egypt (c. 683) uncertain and unconfirmed by Assyrian records; account of destruction of his army by pestilence probably legendary. Active in building, esp. in restoring Nineveh to great splendor. Killed by one of his sons. See ESARHADDON.

**Sen'nett** (sĕn'ĕt; -ĭt), **George Burritt.** 1840–1900. American industrialist and ornithologist; manufacturer of oil-well machinery; deposited large ornithological collection in American Museum of Natural History, New York (1883).

**Še·no'a** (shĕ·nō'ä), **August.** 1838–1881. Croatian writer; regarded as a creator of modern Croatian prose. In addition to lyrics and ballads, wrote novels, including *The Goldsmith's Treasure* (1871) and *Diogenes* (1878).

**Se·nu'si, al-** *or* **al-Se·nus'si** (ăs'sǎ·nōō'sē). *Arab.* **Muḥammad ibn-'Ali al-Sanūsi.** 1791–1851. Moslem religious reformer; organized (1837) a brotherhood (Senusian, or Senussian, sect) for the purification and propagation of Islam. Members of the order are famous for their fanaticism and belligerency.

**Senusret** *or* **Senusrit** *or* **Senusert.** See SESOSTRIS.

**Septimius Severus, Lucius.** See SEVERUS.

**Se·púl've·da** (sâ·pōōl'vâ·thä), **Juan Gi·nés' de** (hĕ·nās' thā). 1490?–1574. Spanish theologian and historian; royal historiographer (from 1536); wrote (in Latin) theological treatises and histories of Charles V and Philip II.

**Se·quoy'a** *or* **Se·quoy'ah** (sē·kwoi'ȧ; -kwō'yȧ). 1770?–1843. Took name **George Guess** (gĕs) at maturity, from American trader he believed to be his father. American Indian scholar, b. in Tennessee; made study of his own Cherokee language and succeeded in forming syllabary (1809–21) approved by Cherokee council (1821) and effective in teaching thousands of his people to read and write. Name perpetuated in *Sequoia* a genus of coniferous trees, and in Sequoia National Park.

**Se'ra·fin'** (sā'rä·fēn'), **Tullio.** 1878–1968. Italian operatic conductor; succeeded Toscanini as conductor at La Scala, Milan (1908); conductor at Metropolitan Opera Co., New York (1924).

**Se·ra'o** (sâ·rä'ō), **Matilda.** Signora **Eduardo Scar·fo'glio** (skär·fô'lyō). 1856–1927. Italian novelist, b. Patras, Greece; lived in Naples (1859 ff.); to Rome (1882); m. journalist Eduardo Scarfoglio (1885); founded, with Scarfoglio, *Il Corriere di Napoli* (1891). As a novelist, known chiefly for her psychological novels. Among her works are *Ventre di Napoli* (1885), *Il Paese di Cuccagna* (1891), *La Ballerina* (2 vols., 1899), *Storia di Due Anime* (1904), *Ella Non Rispose* (1914), *Mors Tua* (1926).

**Se·ra'pi·on** (sĕ·rā'pĭ·ŏn) *or* **Sa·ra'pi·on** (sȧ-). Fourth-century Christian prelate; bishop of Thmuis in the Nile delta. Supported Athanasius in his attacks on Arian heresy. Reputed author of a Sacramentary, discovered in 1894 and valued as one of earliest large liturgical compilations.

**Serbati.** See ROSMINI-SERBATI.

**Sereno, El.** See SARFATTI.

**Se·re'nus of An·tis'sa** (sĕ·rē'nŭs, ăn·tĭs'ȧ). Greek geometer of Egypt, probably of 4th century A.D.

**Ser'geant** (sär'jănt), **Jonathan Dickinson.** 1746–1793. American lawyer, b. Newark, N.J. Member, Continental Congress from New Jersey (1776 and 1777); attorney general of Pennsylvania (1777–80). His son **John** (1779–1852) was also a lawyer; member of U.S. House of Representatives (1815–23, 1827–29, 1837–41); national Republican candidate for vice-president (1832). Another son, **Thomas** (1782–1860), was also a lawyer; secretary of Pennsylvania (1817–19); attorney general of Pennsylvania (1819–20); associate justice, Pennsylvania supreme court (1834–46); author of legal treatises.

**Ser'gel** (sĕr'gĕl), **Johan Tobias von.** 1740–1814. Swedish sculptor; chief Swedish sculptor of classical school. Among his works are *Gustavus III*, *Faun*, *Diomedes Stealing the Palladium*, colossal *Muse of History Recording the Deeds of Gustavus Adolphus*, and many portrait busts.

**Ser'gi** (sĕr'jē), **Giuseppe.** 1841–1936. Italian anthropologist; known esp. for work on origin and spread of the Mediterranean race, origin of the Aryans, and distribution of races.

**Sergiev, Joann.** See JOHN OF KRONSHTADT.

**Ser'gi·us** (sûr'jĭ·ŭs), Saint. 1314?–?1392. A saint of the Eastern Church, esp. popular in Russia.

**Sergius.** Name of four popes (see *Table of Popes*, Nos. 84, 102, 120, 144), especially:

**Sergius I,** Saint. d. 701. Pope (687–701), b. Palermo; rejected provisions of the Quinisext, or 2d Trullan, Council (692); protected by Roman soldiers from arrest by the Emperor Justinian II; interested in English missions; consecrated St. Willibrord as apostle to the Frisians.

**Sergius II.** d. 847. Pope (844–847); crowned Emperor Louis II as king of the Lombards (844); during his pontificate, Rome plundered (846) by the Saracens.

**Sergius.** Patriarch of Constantinople (610–638) and chief minister and adviser to Emperor Heraclius; defended Constantinople against the Avars (626). Wrote edict "Ecthesis" (638) and caused its promulgation by Heraclius, thus inaugurating Monothelete controversy.

**Sergius.** *Russ.* **Sergei Aleksandrovich.** 1857–1905. Russian grand duke, son of Czar Alexander II; commander in chief of the military district of Moscow; used his influence at court to oppose liberalism; killed by a bomb (Feb. 17, 1905).

**Sérigny,** Sieur **de. Joseph Lemoyne.** See under Charles LEMOYNE.

**Se'ring** (zā'rĭng), **Max.** 1857–1939. German economist; professor, U. of Berlin (from 1897).

**Ser'kin** (sĕr'kĭn), **Rudolf.** 1903– . Bohemian-born pianist in U.S.; studied under Arnold Schönberg; on concert tour in Europe (1920); debut in U.S. (1933); annual concert tours in U.S. (from 1934); on faculty of Curtis Institute of Music, Philadelphia (1939– ).

**Ser'lio** (sĕr'lyō), **Sebastiano.** 1475–1554. Italian architect and writer on art; appointed architect at palace of Fontainebleau by French king, Francis I. Author of *Opere di Architettura.*

**Se·rov'** (syĕ·rôf'), **Aleksandr Nikolaevich.** 1820–1871. Russian composer; wrote both libretto and music for his operas *Judith*, *Rogneda*, and *The Malign Influence* (called also *The Power of Evil*); composer also of symphonies, religious music, etc.

**Ser'pa Pin'to** (sĕr'pȧ pēɴn'tōō), **Alexandre Alberto da Ro'cha** (thȧ rô'shȧ). 1846–1900. Portuguese explorer in Africa; crossed Africa from west to east (1877–79); governor of Mozambique (1889); author of *How I Crossed Africa* (2 vols., 1881).

**Ser'ra** (sĕr'rä), **Junípero,** *orig.* **Miguel José.** 1713–1784. Spanish missionary in America; entered Franciscan order (1730); to Mexico City (1749); missionary to Indians northeast of Querétaro (1750–59). Sent to Lower California (1767); co-operated with government in plans to establish missions in Upper California; founded mission at San Diego (July 16, 1769), first European settlement in Upper California; continued as leader in white occupation of California, establishing missions of San Carlos de Monterey (1770), San Antonio de Padua and San Gabriel (1771), San Luis Obispo (1772), San Francisco de Assisi and San Juan Capistrano (1776), Santa Clara (1777), and San Buenaventura.

**Ser·ra'no Su·ñer'** (sĕr·rä'nō sōō·nyĕr'), **Ramón.** 1901– . Spanish lawyer and politician; brother-in-law of Francisco Franco (*q.v.*). Member of the Cortes (1933–36); minister of interior (1937–40); minister of foreign affairs in Franco government (1940–42). Strongly Falangist and pro-Nazi in sympathy. Head of Junta Politica, a body of twenty members exercising dominant authority in post-civil-war Spain.

**Serrano y Do·mín'guez** (ē thō·mēng'gāth), **Francisco.** Duque **de la Tor're** (thā lä tôr'rā). 1810–1885. Spanish general and statesman; served in Carlist wars under Queen Isabella (1834–39); field marshal and captain general of Valencia (1840) and of Granada (1848); took part in the O'Donnell uprising (1856); governor of Cuba (1859–62). After death of O'Donnell (1867), became leader of Union Liberal party; with Prim dethroned the queen (1868) and later became regent (1869–71); military leader under King Amadeus; after re-establishment of monarchy (1874), retired to France, but returned to Spain (1881).

**Ser·ra′to** (sĕr·rä′tō), **José**. 1868–1960. President of Uruguay (1923–27).

**Ser′rell** (sĕr′ĕl), **Edward Wellman**. 1826–1906. Engineer, b. London, Eng.; to U.S. as a child; railroad and bridge engineer (1845–61); during Civil War, military engineer in Union army, notably chief engineer and chief of staff of the army of the James; designed and superintended building of battery in a swamp near Charleston, S.C., battery known as "Swamp Angel"; brevetted brigadier general (1865).

**Sert** (sĕrt), **José Maria**. 1876–1945. Spanish painter, esp. of murals.

**Ser·to′ri·us** (sûr·tō′rĭ·ŭs), **Quintus**. d. 72 B.C. Roman general and statesman; served under, and remained a partisan of, Marius. Quaestor (91 B.C.); praetor (83); held command for Marius in Spain (82) and captured Tangier. Waged war against partisans of Sulla; fought Metellus and Pompey in Spain. Joined (77) by Marcus Perperna (or Perpenna), who undermined his power in Spain and finally caused his assassination.

**Ser′van·do′ni** (sĕr′vän·dō′nē), **Giovanni Niccolò**. *Fr.* **Jean Nicolas Ser′van′do′ni′** (sĕr′väɴ′dô′nē′). 1695–1766. Italian architect and painter, b. Florence; to Paris (1724); architect to the king (1732). Among his works are the façade of the Church of Saint-Sulpice (Paris), altar of the Church of the Chartreux (Lyons), and the altar of the cathedral at Sens.

**Ser·ve′tus** (sûr·vē′tŭs), **Michael**. *Span.* **Miguel Ser·ve′to** (sĕr·vā′tō). 1511–1553. Spanish theologian and physician; opposed doctrine of the Trinity in *De Trinitatis Erroribus* (1531). Went to Paris to study medicine (1536); believed by some to have discovered circulation of the blood; lectured on geometry and astrology; went to Louvain to study theology and Hebrew; practiced medicine at Avignon and Charlieu; studied at medical school of Montpellier (1540); practiced in Vienne (1541–53). Opponent of Trinitarianism and infant baptism; published *Christianismi Restitutio* (1553), for which he was arrested and brought to trial before Inquisition at Vienne; escaped, but was apprehended at Geneva; imprisoned at Calvin's request and burned at the stake as a heretic.

**Ser′vice** (sûr′vĭs), **Robert William**. 1874–1958. Canadian writer, b. in England; emigrated to Canada and settled on Vancouver Island, B.C.; traveled widely in the subarctic region. Best known for his verse, such as *The Shooting of Dan McGrew*, collected in volumes including *Songs of a Sourdough* (1907), *Ballads of a Cheechako*, *Rhymes of a Rolling Stone*, *Ballads of a Bohemian;* author also of novels, as *The House of Fear*.

**Servilius Rullus, Publius**. See RULLUS.

**Ser′viss** (sûr′vĭs), **Garrett Putnam**. 1851–1929. American journalist and author of popular books on scientific subjects, as *Astronomy with an Opera Glass* (1888), *Curiosities of the Sky* (1909), *The Moon Maiden* (1915), etc.

**Ser′vi·us** (sûr′vĭ·ŭs). *In full* **Servius Marius** (*or* **Maurus**) **Hon′o·ra′tus** ([h]ŏn′ō·rā′tŭs). Latin grammarian and scholar of late 4th and early 5th century A.D.; author of commentary on Vergil.

**Servius Tul′li·us** (tŭl′ĭ·ŭs). Sixth legendary king (578–534 B.C.) of the early Romans; an Etruscan, son-in-law of Tarquinius Priscus.

**Se·sos′tris** (sē·sŏs′trĭs). *Greek corruption of Egyptian* **Sen·us′ret** (sĕn·ŭs′rĕt) *or* **Sen·us′rit** (-rĭt) *or* **Sen·u′sert** (sĕn·ōō′sĕrt). *Also transliterated* **U′sert·sen′** (ōō′sĕrt·sĕn′) *or* **U′sert·e·sen′** (ōō′sĕrt·ĕ·sĕn′) *or* **U′sirt·e·sen′** (ōō′sĭrt·ĕ·sĕn′). Name of three kings of ancient Egypt of XIIth (Theban) dynasty:

**Sesostris I.** Second king of the dynasty (c. 1980–1935 B.C.). Son of Amenemhet I and father of Amenemhet II; ruled as coregent with his father (1980–1970); led expeditions against Nubia and the Libyans; sole ruler (1970); completed conquest of Nubia and penetrated into Cush; erected red granite obelisk in Faiyum region.

**Sesostris II.** Fourth king of the dynasty (c. 1906–1887 B.C.); son of Amenemhet II; ruled as coregent with father (1906–1903); built town (now Illahun) and pyramid near Faiyum.

**Sesostris III.** Fifth king of the dynasty (c. 1887–1849 B.C.); son of Sesostris II and father of Amenemhet III; had canal dug through first cataract of the Nile; conducted campaigns in Nubia, reaching second cataract; invaded Syria; built pyramid at Dashur; raised Egypt to state of great power, embracing thousand miles of Nile Valley.

Name **Sesostris** also given to a mythical king of Ptolemaic Egypt, whose exploits are founded on deeds of Ramses II and others.

**Ses·shu** (sĕs·shōō). 1419–1506. Japanese Zen priest and landscape artist. One of his chief works is a landscape scroll in the Prince Mori Motoaki collection in Tokyo.

**Ses′sions** (sĕsh′ŭnz), **Roger Huntington**. 1896– . American composer, b. Brooklyn, N.Y. At Princeton U. (1953–65); wrote symphonies, chamber music, concertos, the opera *Trial of Lucullus* (1947), etc.

**Ses·son** (sĕs·sŏn). 1485?–?1570. Japanese priest and artist.

**Se·sti′ni** (sā·stē′nē; sĕs·tē′nĭ), **Benedict**. 1816–1890. Roman Catholic clergyman and mathematician, b. Florence, Italy; entered Society of Jesus (1836). To U.S. (1848) and on staff of Georgetown U., Washington, D.C. (1848–69), Jesuit Seminary, Woodstock, Md. (1869–85). Founded and edited *Messenger of the Sacred Heart* (1866–85). Author of mathematical treatises.

**Ses′ti·us** (sĕs′chĭ·ŭs) *or* **Sex′ti·us** (sĕks′tĭ·ŭs), **Publius**. Roman politician; quaestor (63 B.C.), supported Cicero in crushing Catiline's conspiracy; tribune (57), aided in recall of Cicero from exile; defended (56) by Cicero, Hortensius, and Crassus on charge of using illegal force as tribune, and acquitted; praetor (53); during civil war, supported Pompey at first, but later joined Caesar.

**Se′tä·lä** (sĕ′tä·lä), **Emil Nestor**. 1864–1935. Finnish philologist; professor, Helsinki (1893–1929); minister of education (1917–18, 1925) and foreign affairs (1926); chancellor, Åbo (Turku) U. (from 1926).

**Seth** (sĕth), **Andrew**. 1856–1931. Scottish philosopher, b. Edinburgh; on succeeding to Haining estate (1898), assumed additional surname **Prin′gle–Pat′ti·son** (prĭng′g'l·păt′ĭ·s'n); professor, Edinburgh (1891–1919). Wrote *Hegelianism and Personality* (1887), *Man's Place in the Cosmos* (1897), *The Idea of Immortality* (1922).

**Seth, James**. 1860–1924. Philosopher and educator, b. Scotland; professor, Brown U. (1892–96), Cornell (1896–98), Edinburgh (1898–1924). Wrote *English Philosophers and Schools of Philosophy* (1912).

**Se′the** (zā′tĕ), **Kurt**. 1869–1934. German Egyptologist.

**Se′ti** (sē′tē). *Gr.* **Se′thos** (sē′thŏs). Name of two kings of XIXth (Diospolite) dynasty of ancient Egypt:

**Seti I.** King (1313–1292 B.C.); son of Ramses I and father of Ramses II; coregent with his father (1314); reorganized government of kingdom; overran Palestine; fought successful war with Libyans west of Nile delta;

engaged in indecisive conflict with Hittites in Syria, ultimately making treaty of peace. Completed colonnaded hall at Karnak begun by his father; built splendid sanctuary at Abydos dedicated to great gods of the empire. Many of his battle and other reliefs have survived.

**Seti II.** Last king (1209?–1205 B.C.) of XIXth dynasty.

**Se'ton** *or also* **Sey'ton** *or* **Sea'toun** (sē't'n). Name of an old Scottish family dating from reign of Alexander I and holding among its honors the earldoms of **Win'ton** [wĭn't'n; -tŭn] (cr. 1600), of **Dun·ferm'line** [dŭn-fûrm'lĭn] (cr. 1606), and of **Eg'lin·ton** (ĕg'lĭn·tŭn), by marriage (see 6th earl of Eglinton under MONTGOMERIE family). Through marriage (c. 1408) with heiress Elizabeth Gordon and reversion to ancestral name Gordon, **Alexander** became ancestor of earls and marquises of Huntley and dukes of Gordon (see GORDON family). Members of Seton family include: **George** (1530?–1585), 5th Baron Seton; Roman Catholic, master of household of Mary, Queen of Scots (1561); assisted her in escape from Loch Leven (1568); entrusted with mission to duke of Alva, seeking military aid (c. 1571); one of Morton's (James Douglas) judges (1581); appears in Scott's *Abbot.* His son **Robert** (d. 1603), a favorite of James VI, was 1st earl of Winton. Another son, Sir **Alexander** (1555?–1622), 1st Earl of Dunfermline; prior of Pluscarden (1565); studied law in France; lord president of court of session (1593); chief of the Octavians (1596); guardian of Prince Charles (who became Charles I of England); commissioner for union with England (1604); member of English privy council (1609). His son **Charles** (d. 1673), 2d Earl of Dunfermline; one of leaders of Scottish Covenanting army opposing Charles I (1639); privy councilor in England (1640); supported the Engagement for attempted rescue of the king (1647); privy councilor (1660); extraordinary lord of session (1667); lord privy seal (1671).

**Se'ton** (sē't'n), Saint **Elizabeth Ann,** *nee* **Bay'ley** (bā'lĭ). 1774–1821. American religious, b. New York City; m. William Magee Seton (1794). A founder (1797) of Society for Relief of Poor Widows with Small Children, first charitable organization in New York. After death of husband (1803), joined Roman Catholic Church (1805); founded order (1809), which became known as Sisters of Charity of St. Joseph, or briefly, Sisters of Charity, and served as first superior of the order (1809–21); canonized (1975). Her grandson **William Seton** (1835–1905) was a writer; served in Union army through Civil War; author of *Nat Gregory, or the Old Maid's Secret* (1867), *Romance of the Charter Oak* (1871), *The Pride of Lexington* (1873), etc. A brother of William, **Robert** (1839–1927), was a Roman Catholic clergyman; consecrated (1903) titular archbishop of Heliopolis; author of *Essays on Various Subjects Chiefly Roman* (1862), and a book of reminiscences.

**Seton, Ernest Thompson.** *Orig. surname* **Thompson.** 1860–1946. Writer and illustrator, b. in England; lived in backwoods of Canada (1866–70) and on western plains (1882–87). Published *Mammals of Manitoba* (1886) and *Birds of Manitoba* (1891). Founder, Woodcraft Indians (1902); chief scout, Boy Scouts of America (1910–15). Author of many nature stories, usually illustrated by himself, including *Wild Animals I Have Known* (1898), *The Biography of a Grizzly* (1900), *Lobo, Rag and Vixen* (1900), *Lives of the Hunted* (1901), *Wild Animals at Home* (1913), *Biography of an Arctic Fox* (1937).

**Se'ton–Wat'son** (-wŏt's'n), **Robert William.** 1879–1951. British historian; specialist in study of central European and Balkan history and politics. Among his many books are *The Southern Slav Question* (1911), *Europe in the Melting Pot* (1919), *Slovakia Then and Now* (1931), *Treaty Revision* (1934), *Britain in Europe, 1789–1914* (1937).

**Set'tem·bri'ni** (sāt'tām·brē'nē), **Luigi.** 1813–1877. Italian writer and patriot; imprisoned because of political activities (1839–42, 1849–58); escaped to England (1858); returned to Naples (1860); known esp. for *Lezioni di Letteratura Italiana* (3 vols., 1866–72).

**Set'tle** (sĕt''l), **Elkanah.** 1648–1724. English playwright and poetaster, memorable chiefly through ridicule of Dryden and Pope. Author of the tragedy *Cambyses* (1666), first of series of bombastic dramas that annoyed Dryden as offering rivalry to his popularity; gained success with *Empress of Morocco* (1671); pilloried as Doeg by Dryden in second part of *Absalom and Achitophel* (1682).

**Seu'rat'** (sû'rà'), **Georges.** 1859–1891. French painter; a founder of neoimpressionism. Cf. Paul SIGNAC.

**Seuse, Heinrich.** See Heinrich SUSO.

**Seuss, Dr.** Pseudonym of T. S. GEISEL.

**Šev'čík** (shĕf'chēk), **Otakar** *or* **Ottokar.** 1852–1934. Bohemian violin virtuoso; famous as a teacher; author of *School of Intonation* (1922), *School of the Virtuoso* (1926).

**Sé've·rin'** (sā'vrăN'), **Fernand.** 1867–1931. Belgian poet; author of *Le Lys* (1888), *Le Don d'Enfance* (1899), *La Solitude Heureuse* (1905), etc.

**Se've·ring** (zā'vĕ·rĭng), **Carl.** 1875–1952. German statesman; Socialist Democratic member of Reichstag (1907–11); member of Weimar national assembly (1919); member of Reichstag (1920–33) and Prussian Landtag (1921–33); Prussian minister of interior (1920–21, 1921–25, 1930–33); German minister of interior (1928–30).

**Se've·ri'ni** (sā'vā·rē'nē), **Gino.** 1883–1966. Italian painter; joined futurist movement (1910); abandoned futurism for classicism (1918); author of *Du Cubisme au Classicisme* (1921).

**Sev'er·i'nus** (sĕv'ĕr·ī'nŭs). d. 640. Pope (640); elected (638), but unable for more than a year to secure imperial confirmation because of his refusal to acknowledge the Ecthesis (638).

**Sev'ern** (sĕv'ĕrn), **Joseph.** 1793–1879. English portrait and subject painter; friend of Keats; known esp. for his *Spectre Ship* (*The Ancient Mariner*).

**Seversky, Alexander Procofieff de.** See DE SEVERSKY.

**Se·ve'rus** (sē·vēr'ŭs). Name of four Roman emperors: (1) **Flavius Valerius Severus.** d. 307. Emperor (306–307); created Caesar (305) and Augustus (306) by Galerius; sent against Maxentius, but unsuccessful. (2) **Livius** *or* **Vibius Severus.** d. 465. Emperor (461–465), b. in Lucania; made emperor by Ricimer on death of Majorian; a puppet ruler; reign marked by inroads of Vandals, Goths, and other barbarians in the empire. (3) **Lucius Septimius Severus.** 146–211. Emperor (193–211), b. near Leptis in Africa; m. (187) Julia Domna. Quaestor and praetor under Marcus Aurelius; commander in chief of army in Pannonia and Illyria; proclaimed emperor by the soldiers; overcame his rivals Didius Julianus at Rome (193), Pescennius Niger in northern Syria (194) and Albinus in Gaul (197); waged successful war against the Parthians (197–202); for this victory memorial arch erected by the Senate (205–207); spent last years (208–211) in Britain; died at Eboracum (York); his reign the golden age of jurists, esp. Papinian, Ulpian, and Paulus. (4) **Marcus Aurelius Alexander Severus.** See ALEXANDER SEVERUS.

**Severus, Sulpicius.** See SULPICIUS SEVERUS.

**Se·vier'** (sē·vēr'), **John.** 1745–1815. American soldier and politician, b. near New Market, Va.; emigrated toward Tennessee (from 1772); member, local committee of safety (Knoxville, Tenn., 1776); led force across Smoky Mountains to win victory over British at battle of King's Mountain (Oct. 7, 1780). Governor of the temporary State of Franklin (1785–88); member, U.S. House of Representatives (1789–91); first governor of Tennessee (1796–1801, 1803–09); again, member of U.S. House of Representatives (1811–15).

**Sé'vi'gné'** (sā'vē'nyā'), Marquise **de.** *Nee* **Marie de Ra'bu'tin'-Chan'tal'** (dē rȧ'bü'tăN'shäN'tȧl'). 1626–1696. French writer and lady of fashion; m. Marquis Henri de Sévigné (1644; killed in a duel 1651); famed for her letters, *Lettres de Mme de Sévigné*, written to her daughter **Françoise Marguerite,** Comtesse **de Gri'-gnan'** (dē grē'nyäN'), who lived in Provence, where her husband was lieutenant governor. The letters record in faultless French events of daily interest in her life in Paris or at her country seat in Brittany.

**Sew'all** (sū'ăl), **Arthur.** 1835–1900. American shipbuilder and banker, b. Bath, Me.; specialized in building wooden full-rigged ships (to c. 1892) and steel sailing vessels (from c. 1892). President, Bath National Bank (1871–1900); democratic vice-presidential nominee (1896).

**Sewall, Samuel.** 1652–1730. Colonial American jurist, b. Bishopstoke, Eng.; to America (1661) and settled in Boston. Member, governor's council (1684–86, 1689–1725); judge, presiding at Salem over witchcraft cases, condemning 19 persons to be executed (1692); later (1697), publicly confessed error and guilt for his part in the trials. Justice, Massachusetts superior court (1692–1728) and chief justice (1718–28). His diary, covering period 1674–77 and 1685–1729, was published by Massachusetts Historical Society (3 vols., 1878–82). His grandnephew **Jonathan Mitchell Sewall** (1748–1808) was a lawyer and poet; author of *Eulogy on the Late General Washington* (1800), *Miscellaneous Poems* (1801), etc.

**Se'ward** (sē'wērd), **Anna.** 1742–1809. English poet; known as "the Swan of Lich'field" (lĭch'fēld); supplied Boswell with particulars about Dr. Johnson, whom she imitated in her letters (6 vols., 1811–13); published poetical novel *Louisa* (1782); bequeathed her poetical works, including elegies and sonnets, to Sir Walter Scott, who published them, with a memoir (3 vols., 1810).

**Sew'ard** (sū'ērd), **William Henry.** 1801–1872. American statesman; practiced law in Auburn, N.Y. (from 1823); governor of New York (1839–43); U.S. senator (1849–61); prominent antislavery advocate, and famous for declaration in speech at Rochester (1858) that the antagonism between freedom and slavery was an "irrepressible conflict" between opposing and enduring forces. U.S. secretary of state (1861–69), conducting delicate negotiations with foreign nations during Civil War period and immediately thereafter.

**Sew'ell** (sū'ĕl), **Anna.** 1820–1878. English author of *Black Beauty; The Autobiography of a Horse* (1877).

**Sextius, Publius.** See SESTIUS.

**Sex'tus Em·pir'i·cus** (sĕks'tŭs ĕm·pĭr'ĭ·kŭs). Greek physician and skeptic philosopher of late 2d and early 3d centuries A.D. Author of *Pyrrhonic Sketches* (containing doctrines of Skeptics) and *Against the Mathematici.*

**Sey'dlitz** (zī'dlĭts), **Friedrich Wilhelm von.** 1721–1773. Prussian cavalry commander; distinguished himself under Frederick the Great in Seven Years' War (1756–63) and gained reputation as one of greatest cavalry commanders in history; appointed general of cavalry (1767).

**Seyf'fert** (sī'fērt), **Leopold.** 1887–1956. American painter, b. California, Mo.

**Sey'mour** (sē'mōr; -môr; -mēr) *or* **St. Maur** (sānt [sĭnt] môr'). Name of historic English family originally from St. Maur, Normandy, that obtained land in Monmouthshire in 13th century and, by marriage, in Somersetshire in 14th century, and in which were created earldom and marquisate of **Hert'ford** (här'fērd; härt'-) and dukedom of **Som'er·set** (sŭm'ēr·sĕt; -sĭt).

DUKES OF SOMERSET: **Edward Seymour** (1506?–1552), 1st Earl of Hertford (second creation 1537) and Duke of Somerset (created 1547), known as "the Protector." Accompanied Wolsey (1527) and Henry VIII (1532) to meetings with Francis I; with Cranmer and Audley, managed affairs in Henry's absence (1541); warden of Scottish marches (1542); lord great chamberlain (1543); sacked Edinburgh (1544); commanded army in France (1546); managed to conceal news of Henry VIII's death until he had gained consent of Edward VI permitting him to assume protectorate of England with power to act with or without advice of council (1547), king in all but name; crushed Scottish resistance in battle of Pinkie (1547); provoked rebellion by religious innovations and Protestant reforms; lost prestige through attainder of his brother Thomas (1549); differed with majority of his council over constitutional liberty; indicted by Warwick and deposed from protectorate (1550); pardoned and readmitted to privy council; condemned on charge of conspiring with Arundel and Paget to murder Warwick and, despite flimsy evidence, beheaded on charge of felony; buried in Tower of London.

His brother **Thomas** (1508?–1549), Baron **Seymour of Sude'ley** (sūd'lĭ); employed on diplomatic missions to European courts; marshal of English army in Netherlands (1543); admiral of fleet guarding Channel (1544); lord high admiral (1547); m. (1547) queen dowager, Catherine Parr; schemed to displace his brother the protector as guardian of young king, Edward VI, and to marry Edward VI to Lady Jane Grey; bargained with pirates on west coast for their support; renewed attempts to marry Princess Elizabeth; for fomenting opposition to brother's authority, executed on charge of treason.

Their sister **Jane** (1509?–1537); lady in waiting to Catherine of Aragon and Anne Boleyn; m. Henry VIII (as 3d wife) the day after execution of Anne Boleyn; died a few days after giving birth to Edward VI. Another sister, **Elizabeth,** m. Thomas Cromwell's son.

**Edward Seymour** (1539?–1621), Earl of Hertford; son of Protector Somerset by his 2d marriage; *de jure* duke of Somerset (1552), but deprived of title and estates by father's attainder; created (1559) Baron **Beau'champ** (bē'chăm) and earl of Hertford by Queen Elizabeth; secretly m. (1560) Lady Catherine Grey, sister of Lady Jane Grey, for which he was imprisoned (1561–71) and fined £15,000; lord lieutenant of Somerset and Wiltshire (1602, 1608); high steward of revenue to Queen Anne (1612–19).

Edward's (1539?–1621) son **Edward Seymour** (1561–1612), Baron Beauchamp, was supported by Cecil, Raleigh, Lord Howard of Effingham, and others in attempts to establish his legitimacy through his mother, Catherine Grey Seymour, as heir to throne on death of Queen Elizabeth.

Edward's (1561–1612) son **William Seymour** (1588–1660), 2d Earl and 1st Marquis of Hertford, and 2d Duke of Somerset, fell into disgrace for privately marrying (1610) Arabella Stuart, daughter of earl of Lennox and heir to English throne after James I; escaped to Paris (until 1616); entered House of Lords as Baron Beauchamp (1621); succeeded his grandfather as earl of Hertford (1621); created marquis of Hertford (1640); took conspicuous part in Royalist cause in Civil War (1642–43), taking Hereford, reducing Cirencester, defeating Sir William Waller at Lansdown, and capturing Bristol; took seat in House of Peers (1660) as Baron Seymour and duke of Somerset. On death of 4th duke (1675), the marquisate of Hertford became extinct.

**Charles Seymour** (1662–1748), 6th Duke of Somerset; great-grandson of Edward, Baron Beauchamp, through the barons **Seymour of Trow′bridge** (trō′brĭj); known as "the Proud Duke of Somerset"; m. Elizabeth Percy, daughter of last earl of Northumberland (1682); refused to introduce papal nuncio at St. James's (1687); fought on side of prince of Orange (1688); speaker of House of Lords (1690); joint regent (1701); enjoyed confidence of Queen Anne, as did his wife, who replaced duchess of Marlborough (1711).

With death of their son **Algernon Seymour** (1684–1750), 7th duke, one of Marlborough's officers, the baronies of Beauchamp and of Seymour of Trowbridge and earldom of Hertford became extinct, and dukedom of Somerset and barony of Seymour passed to a distant cousin, Sir **Edward Seymour** (1695–1757), 8th Duke of Somerset, whose grandfather Sir **Edward Seymour** (1633–1708), speaker of House of Commons in reign of Charles II, was a member of elder branch of family, the Seymours of Berry Pomeroy, descended from Protector Somerset by the protector's first marriage.

Edward's (1695–1757) grandson **Edward Adolphus Seymour** (1775–1855), 11th Duke of Somerset, was fellow of Royal Society (1797), Society of Antiquaries (1816), Linnean Society (1820), and author of mathematical treatises. His son **Edward Adolphus Seymour** (1804–1885), 12th duke, married a granddaughter of Richard Brinsley Sheridan; held minor offices in Lord Melbourne's administration (1835–41); first commissioner of works under Lord John Russell (1851); first lord of admiralty (1859–66); created earl of St. Maur of Ber′ry Pom′e·roy [bĕr′ĭ pŏm′ē·roi] (1863); his successors still head of family.

See also Sir Michael SEYMOUR, of younger branch.

MARQUISES OF HERTFORD (2d creation): **Francis Sey′mour-Con′way** [-kŏn′wā] (1719–1794), 1st Marquis of Hertford (2d creation); son of Francis Seymour, 1st Lord Conway; nephew of Sir Robert Walpole and 1st cousin of 8th duke of Somerset; created Viscount Beauchamp and earl of Hertford (1750), marquis of Hertford (1793); lord lieutenant of Ireland (1765–66); lord chamberlain (1766–82).

His son **Francis Ingram Seymour** (1743–1822), 2d Marquis of Hertford; M.A. Oxon. (1762); member of Irish House of Commons (1761–68); English M.P. (1766); opponent of repeal of American tea duty (1774) and advocate of union of Great Britain and Ireland; ambassador extraordinary to Berlin and Vienna (1793–94); lord chamberlain of household (1812–21).

Francis' (1743–1822) son **Francis Charles Seymour-Conway** (1777–1842), 3d Marquis of Hertford, vice-chamberlain to George, prince regent, was the original of marquis of Steyne in Thackeray's *Vanity Fair* and of Lord Monmouth in Disraeli's *Coningsby*.

**George Hamilton Seymour** (1797–1880); diplomat; grandson of 1st marquis of Hertford; minister at Florence (1830); envoy extraordinary to Brussels (1836) and St. Petersburg (1851–54); through him, Czar Nicholas proposed (1853) that Turkey, the "Sick Man of the East," be dismembered.

**Frederick Beauchamp Paget Seymour** (1821–1895), 1st Baron **Alces′ter** (ôls′tẽr); naval commander; great-grandson of 1st marquis of Hertford; took *Meteor* floating battery out to Crimea and back to Portsmouth (1855–56); commanded naval brigade in New Zealand during Maori War (1860–61); rear admiral (1870) and vice-admiral (1876); commander in chief in Mediterranean (1880–83), commanding bombardment of Alexandria (1882).

**Seymour, Beatrice Kean.** See under William Kean SEYMOUR.

**Seymour,** Lady **Catherine.** Countess of **Hert′ford** (här′fẽrd; härt′-). 1538?–1568. Daughter of Henry Grey, Duke of Suffolk and sister of Lady Jane Grey, also great-granddaughter of Henry VII; m. (1553) Henry Herbert, 2d Earl of Pembroke; divorced; m. (1560) Edward Seymour, Earl of Hertford, secretly and without royal consent; charged with treason, died a prisoner.

**Seymour, Charles.** See under Thomas Day SEYMOUR.

**Seymour, Horatio.** 1810–1886. American politician; member of New York assembly (1842, 1844, 1845); instrumental in obtaining legislative sanction for construction of Erie Canal. Governor of New York (1853–55); again governor (1863–65). Assisted in quelling draft riots in New York (July, 1863), but provoked bitter criticism for speech from City Hall construed as sympathetic with the rioters. Presided over Democratic national conventions (1864, 1868); was Democratic candidate for president of the United States (1868). Aided Governor Tilden in driving Boss Tweed from power (after 1868).

**Seymour,** Sir **Michael.** 1768–1834. British naval commander; b. in Limerick, Ireland, of a younger branch of the family of the dukes of Somerset settled in Ireland; rear admiral and commander in chief in South America (1832–34). His son Sir **Michael** (1802–1887) entered navy (1813); rear admiral (1854); commander on China station, captured Canton and forced passage of Pei (1856–58); admiral (1864) and vice-admiral of United Kingdom (1875). Sir **Edward Hobart Seymour** (1840–1929); naval commander; nephew of the admiral; served in Black Sea in Crimean War (1854–56) and in capture of Canton and Taku forts (1857–63); guarded Suez Canal (1882); vice-admiral (1895); commander in chief on China station through Boxer Rebellion (1897–1901); member, Order of Merit (1902); admiral of fleet (1905).

**Seymour, Robert.** 1800?–1836. English caricaturist and book illustrator; produced plates for first part of *Pickwick Papers* (1836).

**Seymour, Thomas Day.** 1848–1907. American classical scholar; professor of Greek, Yale (1880–1907). Author of *Introduction to the Language and Verse of Homer* (1885), *Life in the Homeric Age* (1907). His son **Charles** (1885–1963), historian and educator; teacher of history, Yale (from 1911); professor (1918–37); president of Yale (1937–50). Chief of Austro-Hungarian division of American commission to negotiate peace (1918–19). Author of *Electoral Reform in England and Wales* (1915), *The Diplomatic Background of the War* (1916), *Woodrow Wilson and the World War* (1921), *The Intimate Papers of Colonel House* (4 vols., 1926–28), *American Diplomacy During the World War* (1934), *American Neutrality, 1914–1917* (1935), etc.

**Seymour, William Kean.** 1887– . English poet; author of *The Street of Dreams* (1914), *Swords and Flutes* (1919), *Chinese Crackers* (1938). His wife, **Beatrice Kean,** *nee* **Stapleton** (d. 1955), novelist, is author of *Invisible Tides* (1919), *False Spring* (1929), *The Happier Eden* (1937), etc.

**Seyss′-In′quart** (zīs′ĭng′kvärt), **Artur von.** 1892–1946. German politician, born a Sudeten German at Stannern in Czechoslovakia; Austrian minister of interior and of security in Schuschnigg cabinet (Feb.–Mar., 1938); chancellor and minister of defense in Austria after German occupation (1938); appointed by Hitler governor of Austrian territory (1938); admitted to German cabinet as minister without portfolio (1939); deputy governor of occupied German territory in Poland (1939–40); German high commissioner of the Netherlands (1940–45); hanged as war criminal.

**Seyton.** See SETON.

**Sfor′za** (sfôr′tsä). Name of Italian family that ruled Milan (1450–1535), including: **Giacomuzzo,** *or* **Muzio, At·ten′do·lo** (ät·tĕn′dô·lō). 1369–1424. Founder of family; peasant from Romagna; leader of condottieri; later, constable under Joanna II of Naples (1416), taking name *Sforza* (Ital. *sforzare,* to force); soldier in service of Pope Martin V. **Francesco Sforza** (1401–1466); natural son of G. Attendolo; Italian condottiere; won fame as soldier; m. (1441) Bianca Maria (1423–1468), natural daughter of Filippo Maria Visconti, Duke of Milan; overthrew Ambrosian republic (1447) and obtained dukedom by force and strategy; ruled Lombardy and other parts of north Italy (1450–66). **Galeazzo Maria Sforza** (1444–1476); son of Francesco; duke of Milan (1466–76); dissolute and cruel; assassinated. **Giangaleazzo Sforza** (1469–1494); son of Galeazzo; duke of Milan (1476–81) under regency of mother and uncle; expelled by Lodovico (1481). **Lodovico,** *or* **Ludovico, Sforza** (1451–1508); called **Il Mo′ro** (ēl mô′rô), *i.e.* "the Moor"; son of Francesco; duke of Milan (1481–99); regent for Giangaleazzo (1476–81); usurped government (1481); joined league against French (1495); defeated by Louis XII (1499); imprisoned (1500); died in France; patron of Leonardo da Vinci. **Caterina Sforza** (1463–1509); natural daughter of Galeazzo Maria; countess of **For·lì′** (fôr·lē′); three times married; third husband was Giovanni de' Medici (1467–1498); see MEDICI family; notorious for intrigues, cruelty, and courage. **Massimiliano Sforza** (1491–1530); son of Lodovico; duke of Milan (1512–15); defeated by Francis I of France at Melegnano (1515). **Francesco Maria Sforza** (1492–1535); son of Lodovico; duke of Milan (1522–35); last of main line; duchy passed to Emperor Charles V. For Giovanni Sforza, husband of Lucrezia Borgia, see BORGIA.

**Sforza,** Count **Carlo.** 1873–1952. Italian statesman, b. Lucca; in diplomatic service (1896–1919); minister for foreign affairs (1920–21 and from 1947); senator (1919–26); ambassador to France (1922), and a leader of anti-Fascist opposition (1922 ff.); resident in Belgium (1926 ff.), U.S. (1940 ff.); named head of "Free Italians" at meeting at Montevideo (Aug., 1942); author of *The Chinese Enigma* (1927), *Makers of Modern Europe* (1930), *European Dictatorships* (1931), *Europe and Europeans* (1936), *Fifty Years of War and Diplomacy in the Balkans* (1941), *The Real Italians* (1942), etc.

**Sgam·ba′ti** (zgäm·bä′tē), **Giovanni.** 1841–1914. Italian piano virtuoso, conductor, and composer of symphonies, overtures, concertos, piano quartet, string quintet and string quartet, piano pieces, and songs.

**Shab′a·ka** (shăb′ȧ·kȧ). *Greek* **Sab′a·con** (săb′ȧ·kŏn). First king (712–700 B.C.) of XXVth (Ethiopian) dynasty of Egypt; brother of Piankhi; supreme in Egypt, but failed to be aid to Jews against Assyria; probably not the So of the Bible (see *2 Kings* xvii. 4). His successor, **Shab′a·ta′ka** (shăb′ȧ·tä′kȧ), who was probably his son, reigned (c. 700–688 B.C.) and was succeeded in turn by Shabaka's nephew Taharka (*q.v.*).

**Shabbethai Zebi** *or* **Zevi.** See SABBATAI ZEBI.

**Shack′le·ton** (shăk′'l·tŭn; -t'n), Sir **Ernest Henry.** 1874–1922. British explorer, b. Kilkee, Ireland. Junior officer on national Antarctic expedition under Robert F. Scott in the *Discovery* (1901); accompanied Scott on sledge journey over Ross Shelf Ice. Sailed (1907) in *Nimrod* in command of expedition which reached point about 97 miles from South Pole (1909) and which sent parties to summit of Mt. Erebus and to South Magnetic Pole; commanded trans-Antarctic expedition in the *Endurance* (set out in 1914); when ship was crushed in ice, made trip of 800 miles with five companions to north coast of South Georgia to get help (1916); organized winter equipment of British North Russian expeditionary force (1918–19); died at South Georgia Island while on third expedition to the Antarctic. Author of *Heart of the Antarctic* (1909) and *South* (1919), which give accounts of his expeditions.

**Sha′drach** (shā′drăk) and **Me′shach** (mē′shăk) and **A·bed′ne·go** (ȧ·bĕd′nē·gō). *Or in Douay Version* **Si′drach** (sī′drăk) and **Mi′sach** (mī′săk) and **Ab·den′a·go** (ăb·dĕn′ȧ·gō). In the Bible, three faithful Hebrews miraculously saved from burning in a fiery furnace (*Daniel* i. 7, iii. 12–30). Their song for deliverance from the fiery furnace is contained in the Old Testament apocryphal book *Song of the Three Children.*

**Shad′well** (shăd′wĕl; -wĕl), **Thomas.** 1642?–1692. English dramatist and poet; scored hit with *The Sullen Lovers* (1668; based on Molière's *Les Fâcheux*); produced twelve other comedies, including *Epsom Wells* (1672) and *Squire of Alsatia* (1688), also an opera based on Shakespeare's *Tempest,* and three tragedies. Became champion of true-blue Protestants, attacking, in *The Medal of John Bayes* (1682), Dryden and the court party; immortalized as Og in Dryden's retort, *Mac Flecknoe* (1682); attempted reply in version of tenth satire of Juvenal; superseded Dryden as poet laureate and historiographer royal.

**Shaf′fer** (shā′fẽr), **Philip Anderson.** 1881–1960. American biochemist; known for researches on diet, treatment of typhoid fever, metabolism in diabetes, velocities of chemical reactions, etc.

**Sha′fi′i, al-** (ăsh·shä′fĭ·ē). *Arab.* **Muḥammad ibn-Idrīs al-Shāfi′i.** 767–820. Arabic scholar and religious leader; founder of Shafiite school of canon law. Shafiites constitute one of four Sunnite sects in Moslem world.

**Shaf′ter** (shȧf′tẽr), **William Rufus.** 1835–1906. American army officer, b. in Kalamazoo County, Mich.; served in Civil War; brevetted brigadier general, and awarded medal of honor for gallantry at Fair Oaks. Major general of volunteers (1898), commanding expeditionary force to Santiago de Cuba; received surrender of the city (July 17, 1898). Retired (1899).

**Shaftes′bur·y** (shȧfts′bẽr·ĭ; -brĭ), Earls of:

**Anthony Ashley Coo′per** (kōō′pẽr; ko͝op′ẽr). 1st Baron **Ash′ley** (ăsh′lĭ) and 1st Earl of **Shaftesbury.** 1621–1683. English statesman, son of John Cooper, Hampshire baronet, and Anne Ashley, dau. of Sir Anthony Ashley, of Dorset. Educ. Oxford; elected to Short Parliament (1640); raised foot and horse for Charles I (1643); changed views and became Roundhead, and received command of Parliamentary forces in Dorset (1644); member of Cromwell's council of state (1653–54); one of commissioners sent to bring back Charles II; suffered accident causing lifelong internal abscess; privy councilor (1660); created Baron Ashley (1661); chancellor of exchequer (1661–72); member of the Cabal Ministry (1667); a judge of integrity as lord chancellor (1672), dismissed for supporting Test Act (1673); incited fear of Romanist uprising (1674); imprisoned one year for protesting against prorogation of Parliament (1677); encouraged terror incited by Titus Oates and persecuted Roman Catholics (1678–80), bringing about death of his enemy William Howard, Viscount Stafford; president of privy council (1679); secured passage of Habeas Corpus

Act (1679); first to introduce bill for making judges independent of the crown; endeavored to give succession to duke of Monmouth, the king's bastard son; indicted duke of York as a popish recusant (1680); charges of high treason (1681) dismissed by Whig grand jury; on hesitation of Monmouth and Russell to rebel openly, forced to flee to Holland, where he died. Characterized in Part III of Butler's *Hudibras*, and the Achitophel of Dryden's *Absalom and Achitophel.*

His grandson **Anthony Ashley Cooper** (1671–1713), 3d earl, styled "Lord Ashley" (1683–99); moral philosopher; author of *Characteristics of Men, Manners, Opinions, Times* (1711), his collected treatises.

**Anthony Ashley Cooper** (1801–1885), 7th earl, philanthropist, styled "Lord Ashley" (1811–51); lord of the admiralty (1834); m. (1830) Lady Emily, dau. of 5th Earl Cowper; chairman of lunacy commission (1828–85); secured reform of lunacy laws (1845); urged 10-hour law for factory workers (1833–44), which was passed (1847); obtained abolition of apprenticeships and employment of women and children in coal mines (1842); secured passage of Climbing Boys Act preventing employment of chimney sweeps (1840), and an act for improving lodginghouses (1851); brought about erection of model tenements; active in organization of ragged schools (from 1843).

**Shah** (shä). For many names beginning with *Shah* (a title of ruler in eastern countries, esp. Persia), see the first element following *Shah.*

**Shah A'lam** (ä'lȧm). 1728–1806. Mogul emperor (1759–1806); fled to protection of British in Bengal (1759); restored to throne (1764) as pensioner of the East India Company; titular emperor only; became prisoner and tool of Marathas (1771); payment of pension stopped by Warren Hastings (1773).

**Shah Ja·han'** *or* **Shah'ja·han'** (shä'jȧ·hän'). *Also* **Shah Je·han'** (shä'jĕ·hän'). *Known in youth as* Prince **Khurram.** 1592–1666. Fifth emperor of Hindustan (1628–58) of Mogul dynasty; son of Jahangir; m. (1612) **Ar'ju·mand' Ba·nu'** [är'jo͝o·mănd' bä·no͞o'] (1592–1631), his favorite wife, better known as **Mum·taz' Ma·hall'** (mo͝om·täz' mȧ·häl'), *i.e.* "the ornament, or distinguished one, of the palace." Rebelled against his father (1622–26). In his reign Mogul power reached its highest point; lost Afghan province of Kandahar (1653) but added parts of the Deccan (1636, 1655). His age the golden period of Mohammedan architecture in India; famous especially were the Taj Mahal at Agra erected (1632–45) as a mausoleum for his favorite wife, the Pearl Mosque in the Agra fort, the palace and Great Mosque at Delhi, and the celebrated Peacock Throne (1628–35). Founded (1639–48) modern city of Delhi (Hindu name, Shahjahanabad). Deposed by his son Aurangzeb (1658); kept prisoner in the fort at Agra (1658–66).

**Shah Shu·ja'** (sho͞o·jä'). 1780?–1842. King of Afghanistan (1803–10); grandson of Ahmad Shah; deposed his brother Mahmud Shah (1803); his rule unpopular, himself deposed by Mahmud Shah (1810); became pensioner of Indian government; defeated in battle by Dost Mohammed (1834); put forward by Lord Auckland (1838–39) during First Afghan War (1838–42) as ruler of Afghanistan in place of Dost Mohammed; escorted to Kabul (1839); killed by followers of Dost Mohammed.

**Sha'han** (shā'ăn), **Thomas Joseph.** 1857–1932. American Roman Catholic clergyman, b. Manchester, N.H. Domestic prelate of the pontifical court, and rector of Catholic U. (1909–28). A founder and an editor of the *Catholic Encyclopedia* (1907–13).

**Shah'ji Bhons'la** (shä'jē bōNs'lăN). 1594–1664. Maratha soldier of fortune, father of Sivaji; joined imperial army (1629); entered service of Bijapur (1637); seized by Bijapur as hostage for Sivaji (1649) but released; governor of Poona and Bangalore.

**Shairp** (shârp; shärp), **John Campbell.** 1819–1885. Scottish teacher and author; professor of poetry, Oxford (1877–87). Author of *Kilmahoe and Other Poems* (1864), *Studies in Poetry and Philosophy* (1868), *Culture and Religion* (1870), and life of Burns in "English Men of Letters" series.

**Shake'speare** *or* **Shak'spere** (shāk'spēr), **William.** *Family records show 44 different spellings of the surname.* 1564–1616. English dramatist and poet, b. Stratford upon Avon. Son of John Shakespeare, a glover and dealer in farm produce; m. Anne Hathaway (1582). Established in London as actor-playwright (1592); member of chamberlain's players (formed 1594; became king's players, 1603). Prospered financially; grant of family arms made to his father (1596); purchased (1597) New Place, largest house in Stratford, and acquired other property in Stratford; continued to live chiefly in London (till 1610); moved to Stratford, but continued occasional playwriting and visits to London. Individual plays published first in quarto form (19 of them, some reprinted, appearing from 1594 to 1622); first folio, containing 36 plays, grouped as comedies, histories, tragedies (pub. 1623); second folio (1632); third folio (1663); fourth folio (1685); quartos and folios following 1623 of little value for textual criticism. Plays [dates for the most part conjectural]: *Henry VI* (part 1, 1591–92; parts 2 and 3, 1590–91), *Comedy of Errors* (1591–92), *Two Gentlemen of Verona* (1592), *Richard III* (1592–93), *Titus Andronicus* (1593), *Love's Labour's Lost* (1594), *King John* (1594), *Romeo and Juliet* (1594–95), *Richard II* (1595), *A Midsummer Night's Dream* (1595), *Taming of the Shrew* (in collab.; 1596), *Merchant of Venice* (1596), 1 & 2 *Henry IV* (1597–98), *Much Ado about Nothing* (1598–99), *Henry V* (1599), *Julius Caesar* (1599–1600), *As You Like It* (1599–1600), *Merry Wives of Windsor* (1599–1600), *Hamlet* (1600–01), *Twelfth Night* (1601), *Troilus and Cressida* (1602), *All's Well That Ends Well* (1602), *Measure for Measure* (1604), *Othello* (1604), *King Lear* (1605–06), *Macbeth* (1605–06), *Antony and Cleopatra* (1607), *Timon of Athens* (1607–08), *Pericles* (in collab.; 1608), *Coriolanus* (1608–09), *Cymbeline* (1610), *A Winter's Tale* (1611), *The Tempest* (1611), *Henry VIII* (in collab.; 1612–13), *The Two Noble Kinsmen* (in collab.; 1612–13). Poems: *Venus and Adonis* (pub. 1593), *The Rape of Lucrece* (pub. 1594), *The Passionate Pilgrim* (in small part his; pub. 1599), *Sonnets* (pub. 1609).

**Sha'ler** (shā'lẽr), **Nathaniel Southgate.** 1841–1906. American geologist, b. Newport, Ky.; professor of paleontology, Harvard (1869–88) and geology (1888–1906), and dean of Lawrence Scientific School (1891–1906). Author of *A First Book in Geology* (1884), *Aspects of the Earth* (1889), *The Interpretation of Nature* (1893), *The Individual: A Study of Life and Death* (1900), *Man and the Earth* (1905), etc.

**Shal'ma·ne'ser** (shăl'mȧ·nē'zẽr). Name of five kings of Assyria:

**Shalmaneser I.** Reigned c. 1276–57 B.C.; son of Adadnirari I; conquered northern Mesopotamia; probably invaded northern Syria; removed capital from Ashur (Assyria) to Calah; succeeded by his son Tukulti-Ninurta I.

**Shalmaneser II.** *Also known as* **Shulmanu-asharid.** Reigned 1019–08 B.C.

**Shalmaneser III** (*or* **II**). Reigned 859–825 B.C.; son of Ashurnasirpal II; embarked on campaign of conquest west of Euphrates, esp. against Damascus and Urartu; defeated Hittites; opposed by Damascus and Ahab of Israel; fought inconclusive battle of Karkar (854); again opposed by league (851); plundered Hama; broke power of alliance and received submission (842) of Damascus, Tyre and Sidon, and of Jehu of Israel.

**Shalmaneser IV** (*or* **III**). Reigned 782–772 B.C.; made many expeditions against Chaldeans.

**Shalmaneser V** (*or* **IV**). Reigned 727–722 B.C.; overran Phoenicia (725); defeated in naval battle by Tyrians; resisted by Hoshea, last king of Israel; defeated Israelites and their ally, So of Egypt; besieged and caused capture of Samaria (724–722), but probably city actually surrendered to his successor, Sargon II.

**Shalom Aleichem.** See Solomon RABINOWITZ.

**Shalyapin, Feodor Ivanovich.** See CHALIAPIN.

**Sha'mash–shum–u'kin** (shä'mäsh-shōōm·ōō'kēn). d. 648? B.C. Ruler of Babylon (668–648? B.C.) under his younger brother, Ashurbanipal, King of Assyria; led revolt (654–648?); committed suicide in manner described in legend of Sardanapalus (*q.v.*).

**Sham'shi–A'dad** (shäm'shē·ä'däd) *or* **Sam'si–A'dad** (säm'sē-). Name of five kings of Assyria, about whom little more than names and dates of reign is known.

**Shamshi–Adad I** (reigned c. 2113 B.C.); **II** (c. 1716–1687 B.C.); **III** (1661–36 B.C.); **IV** (d. 1039 B.C.), restored temple of Ishtar at Nineveh; **V** (824–811 B.C.), had long wars with Urartu to the north and Babylon to the south; see SEMIRAMIS.

**Sha'myl** *or* **Scha'myl** (shä'mĭl). 1797–1871. Caucasian leader; imam of the Lezghians (from 1834); dominant power in Dagestan; led tribes of Dagestan in long war to maintain independence from Russia; defeated and captured (1859).

**Shang** (shäng) *or* **Yin** (yĭn). A dynasty of early China (1766–1122 B.C.) supposed to have had 28 rulers. Gradually subdued aborigines, and several times removed their capital; rulers at first capable, but dynasty degenerated until its last member, Chou Hsin (1154–1122), was overthrown and the Chou dynasty set up. See KI TSE.

**Shan'ka·ra·char'ya** (shŭng'kȧ·rä·chär'yȧ). *Also* **Shan'ka·ra** *or* **San'ka·ra** (shŭng'kȧ·rä). fl. 800 A.D. (788?–?820). Hindu philosopher, one of the most famous of Indian theologians. Probably a native of Malabar; wandered about India, finally reached Kashmir, and died at Kedarnath in the Himalayas; wrote great commentaries on the Vedanta philosophy, still held as authoritative in India; his doctrine the ancient and orthodox monism.

**Shank'lin** (shăngk'lĭn), **William Arnold.** 1862–1924. American Methodist Episcopal clergyman and educator; president, Wesleyan U., Middletown, Conn. (1909–23).

**Shanks** (shăngks), **Edward Richard Buxton.** 1892–1953. English writer; on staff of London *Evening Standard* (1928–35). Author of *Queen of China and Other Poems* (1919; awarded Hawthornden prize), *The Island of Youth and Other Poems* (1921), *First Essays on Literature* (1923), *Bernard Shaw* (1924), *Queer Street* (1932), *My England* (1938), and *Rudyard Kipling* (1939).

**Shan'non** (shăn'ŭn), **Charles.** 1863–1937. English painter and lithographer.

**Shannon, Fred Albert.** 1893–1963. American historian; associate professor (1939–41) and professor (from 1941), Univ. of Illinois. Author of *The Organization and Administration of the Union Army 1861–1865* (1928; awarded Justin Winsor prize by American Historical Assoc., and Pulitzer prize in history).

**Shannon, James Jebusa.** 1862–1923. Portrait and figure painter, b. Auburn, N.Y.; to London (c. 1880).

**Shantz** (shänts), **Homer Le·Roy'** (lĕ·roi'). 1876–1958. American botanist; plant physiologist, bureau of plant industry, U.S. Department of Agriculture (1910–26); president, U. of Arizona (1928–36); chief, division of wild-life management, forest service, U.S. Department of Agriculture (1936–44).

**Sha·pir'o** (shȧ·pĭr'ō), **Karl Jay.** 1913– American poet, b. Baltimore, Md. Wrote *Person, Place and Thing* (1942), *V-Letter and Other Poems* (1945), *The Bourgeois Poet* (1964), *Selected Poems* (1968), etc.

**Shap'ley** (shăp'lĭ), **Harlow.** 1885–1972. American astronomer, at Mt. Wilson Observatory, Calif. (1914–21); professor, Harvard, and director of Harvard Coll. observatory (from 1921). Known for researches in photometry, spectroscopy, and cosmogony.

**Sha'posh·ni·kov** (shȧ'pôsh·nyĭ·kôf), **Boris Mikhailovich.** 1882–1945. Russian army officer; author of works on strategy used as textbooks in Russian military schools. Colonel during World War I; credited with devising most of Bolshevik military strategy during Civil War; chief of general staff of Red army (1928–31, 1937–43); made marshal of Red army, following successful attack on Mannerheim line (Finland, 1940); commander in chief of Russian army and air force (1942–43).

**Sha·pur'** (shä·pōōr') *or, Lat.,* **Sa'por** (sā'pôr). Name of three kings of the Sassanidae of Persia:

**Shapur I.** King (241–272); son of Ardashir I (*q.v.*) and father of Narses (*q.v.*); resumed contest of his father with Rome; invaded Syria; defeated and driven back by Roman general Timesitheus (243); concluded peace with Emperor Philip (244); renewed war against Rome (252); seized (254) Nisibis (Nusaybin); defeated and took prisoner Emperor Valerian in battle near Edessa (260); held emperor captive until his death; overcome by Odenathus (262), Prince of Palmyra; lost Ctesiphon and Armenia. In his reign, Manichaeism founded.

**Shapur II,** *surnamed* "the Great." Son of Ormizd II. King (309–379). Born king; in early years of reign, country governed by nobles; on becoming of age showed remarkable strength and independence; one of greatest of Sassanian kings; waged war against Arabs; at first only partially successful in long war (337–363) against Romans; defeated Emperor Constantius II; attacked by nomadic tribes on the east; finally, after capturing Amida (Diyarbekir) and Singara, was attacked (363) by great Roman army under Emperor Julian; near Ctesiphon, repulsed Julian; made peace (363) with Jovian, disgraceful to Romans; conquered Armenia; transferred great numbers of inhabitants from western lands to Susiana (Khuzistan); rebuilt Susa and founded Nishapur. His son **Shapur III,** king (383–388), brother of Bahram IV and uncle of Yazdegerd I.

**Sharett, Moshe.** See SHERTOK.

**Shar'ga·li·shar'ri** (shär'gä·lē·shär'ē) *or* **Shar'ka·li·shar'ri** (shär'kä-). c. 2500 B.C. King of the Semitic dynasty of Akkad known as the Sargonid dynasty.

**Shar'low** (shär'lō), **Myrna Do'cia** (dō'shȧ). 1893?– American operatic soprano; m. Edward Bering Hitchcock (1921). Member of Boston Opera Company (1912–14), Chicago Opera Association (1915–21 and 1923 ff.), and Metropolitan Opera Company of New York.

**Sharp** (shärp), **Abraham.** 1651–1742. English mathematician. Aided John Flamsteed at Greenwich Observatory in constructing large mural arc (1676–90); known for mathematical writings and for skill in graduating instruments and making astronomical instruments.

**Sharp, Cecil James.** 1859–1924. British musician, music teacher, and anthologist; wrote *A Book of British Song, English Folk-Carols, English Folk-Chanteys.*

**Sharp, Dallas Lore.** 1870–1929. American educator and

naturalist; teacher of English, Boston U. (1900–22), professor (from 1909). Author of many popular nature books, including *A Watcher in the Woods* (1903), *Beyond the Pasture Bars* (1914).

**Sharp, Granville.** 1735–1813. English philanthropist; zealous in cause of liberating slaves in England; through lawsuits, obtained formulation of principle that as soon as a slave set foot on English soil he was free (1772); founded society for abolition of slavery (1787); advocated cause of American colonies; agitated against press gangs.

**Sharp, James.** 1618?–1679. Scottish prelate; leader of Resolutioners against the Protesters, chosen to plead cause of moderate party before Cromwell (1657); sent to London again (1660); corrupted by Charles and Clarendon, betrayed interests of the Kirk and served interests of English bishops in re-establishment of episcopacy in Scotland; rewarded with archbishopric of St. Andrews (1661); severe in repression of covenanting principles; became tool of Lauderdale; murdered on Magus Moor in revenge by Covenanters.

**Sharp, Margery.** 1905– . Eng. nov.; m. Geoffrey Castle. Among her books are *Rhododendron Pie*, *The Flowering Thorn*, *The Nutmeg Tree* (1937), *Harlequin House* (1939), *The Stone of Chastity* (1940).

**Sharp, William.** 1749–1824. English engraver; executed plates after Guido Reni, Domenichino, Dolci, West, Trumbull, Reynolds.

**Sharp, William.** *Pseudonym* **Fiona Mac·leod′** (măk-loud′). 1856?–1905. Scottish poet and man of letters, promoter of Celtic revival; b. at Paisley; educ. Glasgow; traveled in Australia for his health (1876–78); bank clerk; intimate of the Rossettis; d. in Sicily. Author under his own name of several volumes of poems, including *Earth's Voices* (1884), *Romantic Ballads and Poems of Phantasy* (1888), biographies of D. G. Rossetti, Shelley, Heine, Browning, Sainte-Beuve, and romances, including *The Children of Tomorrow* (1889), *The Gypsy Christ* (1895); a few novels, including *Silence Farm* (1899); edited *Canterbury Poets;* published anthologies of sonnets. Under the pseudonym Fiona Macleod, kept secret until after his death, published (from 1893) series of mystical stories and poetical prose works about the primitive Celtic world, beginning with *Pharais* (1894), and including *The Mountain Lovers*, *The Sin-eater* (1895), *Green Fire* (1896), *Drostan and Iseult* (1902), and the dramas *The House of Usna*, *The Immortal Hour* (1900), *Deirdre* (1903), *The Winged Destiny* (1904).

**Sharp, William Graves.** 1859–1922. American lawyer and diplomat; practiced Elyria, Ohio; developed Lake Superior Iron and Chemical Co.; U. S. ambassador to France (1914–19).

**Sharpe** (shärp), **Alexander John.** See A. J. Ellis.

**Sharpe** (shärp), **Henry Granville.** 1858–1947. American army officer; quartermaster general, U. S. army (1916), and major general (1918); retired (1920). Author of *The Art of Subsisting Armies in War*, *The Provisioning of the Modern Army in the Field*, etc.

**Sharpe, Richard Bowdler.** 1847–1909. English ornithologist; asst. keeper of vertebrates, British Museum (1895); prepared its *Catalogue of Birds* (27 cols., 1874–98), of which he wrote thirteen volumes; contributed *Birds of Great Britain* (4 vols., 1894–97) to Allen's *Naturalists' Library*.

**Sharpe, Samuel.** 1799–1881. English Egyptologist; author of works on Egyptian hieroglyphics and inscriptions; published revised translations of Old and New Testaments (1840, 1865).

**Shar′pey–Scha′fer** (shär′pĭ·shā′fẽr), Sir **Edward Albert.** 1850–1935. English physiologist; studied muscular action, also hormones; devised prone pressure method (sometimes called Schafer method) of artificial respiration (1903). Author of *The Endocrine Organs*, etc.

**Shar′ples** (shär′p'lz; shärp′lĕs, -lĭs), **James.** 1751?–1811. Portrait painter, b. in England; to U.S. (1793); settled in Philadelphia (1796), and in New York (1798). Made portraits of George and Martha Washington. His wife, **Ellen,** *nee* **Wallace,** and his children **Felix Thomas, James** (b. 1788), and **Rolinda** (b. 1793) were also painters and their work is often confused with his.

**Sharp′less** (shärp′lĕs; -lĭs), **Isaac.** 1848–1920. American educator; professor of mathematics and astronomy (1879–84), dean (1884–87), and president (1887–1917), Haverford College. Author of *Story of a Small College* (1918), etc.

**Sharrukin.** See Sargon.

**Shars′wood** (shärz′wo͝od), **George.** 1810–1883. American jurist, b. Philadelphia; author of legal treatises.

**Shas′tri** (shäs′trē) **Shri Lal** (läl) **Bahadur.** 1904–1966. Indian politician; prime minister of India (1964–66).

**Shat′tuck** (shăt′ŭk). Family of American physicians, including: **George Cheyne** [chēn] (1783–1854); practiced in Boston. His son **George Cheyne** (1813–1893) practiced in Boston (from 1840); founded St. Paul's School, Concord, N.H. (1855). The latter's two sons, **George Brune** [bro͞on] (1844–1923) and **Frederick Cheever** (1847–1929).

**Shattuck, Aaron Draper.** 1832–1928. American painter; best known for his landscapes, chiefly of scenes in the White Mountains and the Housatonic Valley.

**Shaugh′nes·sy** (shô′nĕ·sĭ), **Thomas George.** 1st Baron **Shaughnessy.** 1853–1923. Railroad official; b. Milwaukee, Wis.; employee of Chicago, Milwaukee and Saint Paul R.R. (1869–82). To Canada as general purchasing agent for Canadian Pacific Ry. (1882); advanced through grades to president of Canadian Pacific (from 1898) and of associated companies.

**Shaw** (shô), **Albert.** 1857–1947. American editor, b. Shandon, Ohio; founded (1891) and edited (1891–1937) *American Review of Reviews;* editor, *Literary Digest* (1937–39). Author of *Municipal Government in Great Britain* (1894), *Municipal Government in Continental Europe* (1895), *Political Problems of American Development* (1907), *Abraham Lincoln* (2 vols., 1929), etc.

**Shaw, Anna Howard.** 1847–1919. Woman-suffrage leader, b. Newcastle upon Tyne, England; to U.S. (1851). Licensed in Methodist ministry; M.D., Boston U. Medical School (1886). Prominent as lecturer advocating woman suffrage (from 1885); president of National American Woman Suffrage Association (1904–15).

**Shaw, George Bernard.** 1856–1950. British playwright, novelist, and critic, b. Dublin; to London to devote himself to writing (c. 1876). Art, music, and dramatic critic on London journals; established reputation by sympathetic criticisms of Whistler, painters of impressionist school, Wagnerian music, Ibsen and the drama of ideas; prominent as a Socialist. Began writing plays (c. 1892); first popular success was *John Bull's Other Island* (1904); later plays established him as leading British playwright of his time. Among his plays are *The Philanderer*, *Mrs. Warren's Profession*, and *The Man of Destiny* (contained in *Plays: Pleasant and Unpleasant*, 1898), *The Devil's Disciple* and *Caesar and Cleopatra* (contained in *Three Plays for Puritans*, 1900), *Man and Superman* (1903), *How he Lied to her Husband* (1904), *Major Barbara...* (1905), *The Doctor's Dilemma* (1906), *Getting Married* (1908), *The Shewing-up of Blanco Posnet* (1909), *Misalliance* (1910), *Fanny's First Play* (1911), *Androcles and the Lion* (1912), *Pygmalion* (1912), *Great Catherine* (1913), *The Music-Cure* (1914),

*Augustus Does His Bit* (1916), *Heartbreak House* (1917), *Back to Methuselah* (cycle of 5 plays, 1921), *Saint Joan of Arc* (1923), *The Apple Cart* (1929), *Too True to be Good* (1932), *Geneva* (1938), and *King Charles's Golden Days* (1939). Among other works are novels *The Irrational Knot*, *Love among the Artists*, *Cashel Byron's Profession*, and *An Unsocial Socialist* (all written between 1879 and 1883). Author of various tracts and books on socialism, including *Fabianism and the Empire* (1900) and *The Intelligent Woman's Guide to Socialism and Capitalism* (1928). Many of his music and dramatic criticisms have been collected and published, as *Music in London, 1890–94* (1931) and *Our Theatres in the Nineties* (3 vols., 1931). Awarded Nobel prize for literature (1925).

**Shaw, Henry Wheeler.** *Pseudonyms* **Josh Bil'lings** (bĭl'ĭngz) *and* **Uncle E'sek** (ē'sĕk). 1818–1885. American humorist, b. Lanesboro, Mass.; settled in Poughkeepsie, N.Y., as auctioneer and real-estate dealer. First humorous sketches appeared in local newspapers; attracted wider notice by *An Essa on the Muel, bi Josh Billings*, published in a New York paper (1860). Among his most successful books are *Josh Billings, His Sayings* (1865), *Josh Billings' Farmers' Allminax* (pub. annually, 1870–80), *Josh Billings Struggling With Things* (1881).

**Shaw, Irwin.** 1913– . American writer, b. Brooklyn, N.Y. Author of plays *Bury the Dead* (1936; one-act play), *The Gentle People* (1939; scenarized as *Out of the Fog*), *Retreat to Pleasure* (1940); short stories, as in *Sailor Off the Bremen* (1939), *Welcome to the City* (1942); and novels, *The Young Lions* (1948), *Two Weeks in Another Town* (1960).

**Shaw, Lemuel.** 1781–1861. American jurist; practiced in Boston; drafted first charter of City of Boston (1822), which remained in effect until 1913; chief justice, Massachusetts supreme court (1830–60).

**Shaw, Leslie Mortier.** 1848–1932. American lawyer, banker, and politician; practiced law at Denison, Iowa; organized bank and mortgage-loan business (1880); governor of Iowa (1898–1902); U.S. secretary of the treasury (1902–07).

**Shaw, Richard Norman.** 1831–1912. British architect, b. Edinburgh; started practice as partner of William Eden Nesfield (1862); broke from academic tradition in designing country houses on grand scale; his greatest achievement, New Scotland Yard on Thames Embankment (1891).

**Shaw, Robert Gould.** 1837–1863. American soldier, b. Boston; commissioned colonel of 54th Massachusetts volunteers, the first regiment of colored troops from a free state mustered into United States service; killed at head of his troops in assault on Fort Wagner, S.C. (July 18, 1863). A monument by Augustus Saint-Gaudens stands in his memory on Boston Common.

**Shaw, Thomas Edward.** See Thomas Edward LAWRENCE.

**Shaw, Tom.** 1872–1938. British labor leader, b. in Lancashire; M.P. (1918–31); minister of labor (1924); secretary of state for war (1929–31).

**Shaw,** Sir **William Napier.** 1854–1945. English meteorologist; director, Meteorological Office (1905–20); professor, Royal Coll. of Science (1920–24).

**Shaw'–Le·fe'vre** (shô'lĕ·fē'vẽr), **Charles.** 1st Viscount **Ev'ers·ley** (ĕv'ẽrz·lĭ). 1794–1888. English Whig leader; M.P. (1830); speaker of House of Commons (1839–57); raised to peerage (1857); ecclesiastical commissioner (1859). His brother Sir **John George** (1797–1879) practiced as conveyancer; member of commissions, including ecclesiastical commission (1847) and civil service commission (1855); clerk of the parliaments (1855–75, deputy from 1848). The latter's only son, **George John** (1831–1928), 1st Baron **Eversley,** Liberal M.P. (1863–85, 1886–95); in maiden speech, urged stopping in port of Confederate privateer *Alabama;* commissioner of works (1880–83, 1892–94); postmaster general (1883); member of London County Council (1897–1901); raised to peerage (1906).

**Shawn** (shôn), **Ted,** *really* **Edwin M.** 1891–1972. American dancer, b. Kansas City, Mo.; m. (1914) Ruth St. Denis (*q.v.*). His company of men dancers (organized 1933) toured U.S. and England.

**Shay** (shā), **Frank.** 1888–1954. American bookdealer, editor, and writer; proprietor of Frank Shay's Bookshop, New York and Provincetown, Mass.; originator of the Caravan Theatre, Frank Shay's Traveling Bookshop. Compiler or editor of many books on plays, the theater, and stagecraft; writer of *Iron Men and Wooden Ships* (1923), *My Pious Friends and Drunken Companions* (1927), *Incredible Pizarro—Conqueror of Peru* (1932), *The Best Men are Cooks* (1938), etc.

**Shays** (shāz), **Daniel.** 1747?–1825. American Revolutionary officer and insurrectionary leader, b. prob. in Hopkinton, Mass.; in the Revolution, engaged at Bunker Hill, Ticonderoga, Saratoga, and Stony Point; commissioned captain (1777); prominent in the insurrection in western Massachusetts (1786–87), commonly called Shays' Rebellion; attacked U.S. government arsenal at Springfield, Mass., and was repulsed by militia (Jan., 1787); routed at Petersham (Feb. 2, 1787); fled to Vermont. Condemned to death by Massachusetts supreme court, but pardoned (June 13, 1788). Resident of Sparta, N.Y., until his death.

**Shche'drin** (shchā'drĭn), **N.** *Real name* **Mikhail Evgrafovich Sal·ty·kov'** (sŭl·tĭ·kôf'). 1826–1889. Russian writer; his novel *Contradictions* (1847) caused his exile (1847–55); later he was governor of Ryazan, and then of Tver; among his other works, many of them characterized by extreme melancholy, are *Provincial Sketches*, *Story of a City*, *Satires in Prose* (1863), and *The Messieurs Golovlev* (1881).

**Shea** (shā), **John Dawson Gilmary.** 1824–1892. American historian, b. New York City. Chief among his works are *Discovery and Exploration of the Mississippi Valley* (1852), *History of the Catholic Church in the United States* (4 vols., 1886–92).

**Sheaf'fer** (shā'fẽr), **Walter A.** 1867–1946. American fountain-pen manufacturer, b. Bloomfield, Iowa; jeweler in Bloomfield (1883–1906) and Fort Madison, Iowa (1906–13); founder (in Fort Madison, 1913), president (1913–38), then board chairman of Sheaffer Pen Co.

**Shean** (shēn), **Al.** 1868–1949. German-born comedian on American stage; organized Manhattan Comedy Four, familiar in vaudeville for 15 years; on legitimate stage in *The County Fair*, *The Prisoner of Zenda*, *Too Hot to Handle*, *The Great Waltz*. Best known in vaudeville as partner of **Ed Gal'la·gher** [găl'ȧ·gẽr; găl'ĭ-] (d. 1929) in comedy team of "Gallagher and Shean."

**Shear** (shẹr), **Cornelius Lott.** 1865–1956. American plant pathologist; asst. agrostologist (1898–1901), pathologist (1902–25), in charge of office of mycology and disease survey (1925–35; retired, 1935), U.S. Dept. of Agriculture. Worked on diseases of cranberries, grapes, cotton, etc.

**Shear, Theodore Leslie.** 1880–1945. American archaeologist; lecturer on art and archaeology (1921–27) and professor of classical archaeology (from 1928), Princeton. Director of excavation of Athenian agora; conducted excavations at Corinth (1925–31) and Athens (from 1931).

**Shedd** (shĕd), **William Greenough Thayer.** 1820–1894.

American theologian, b. Acton, Mass.; professor, Union Theol. Sem. (1863–93). A conservative theologian, opposed to higher criticism as expounded by his colleague Charles A. Briggs.

**Shee** (shē), Sir **Martin Archer.** 1769–1850. Irish portrait painter.

**Shee′an** (shē′ăn), **Vincent,** *in full* **James Vincent.** 1899–1975. American foreign correspondent and writer, b. in Christian County, Ill.; m. (1935) Diana Forbes-Robertson. Author of *An American Among the Riffi* (1926), *Gog and Magog* (1929), *Personal History* (1935), *Between the Thunder and the Sun* (1943), the novels *Sanfelice* (1936), *A Day of Battle* (1938), *Not Peace But a Sword* (1939), *Bird of the Wilderness* (1941), etc.

**Shee′ler** (shē′lēr), **Charles.** 1883–1965. American photographer (to 1931) and painter, b. Philadelphia; influenced by French modernists Picasso, Matisse, and Braque; painter of colonial American subjects and, later, of the contemporary industrial scene.

**Sheep′shanks′** (shēp′shăngks′), **Richard.** 1794–1855. English astronomer; engaged in controversies with Charles Babbage and others; had his reconstructed standard of length adopted (1855); devised method of driving an equatorial by clockwork. His brother **John** (1787–1863), art collector, presented his collection of modern British art to the nation (1857).

**Shef′field** (shĕf′ēld), **John.** 3d Earl of **Mul′grave** (mŭl′grāv). 1st Duke of **Buck′ing·ham and Nor′man·by** [bŭk′ĭng·ăm, nôr′măn·bĭ] (cr. 1703). 1648–1721. English political leader and poet; patron of Dryden, friend of Pope. Great-grandson of Sir **Edmund** (1564?–1646), 1st Earl of Mulgrave, who was granted manor of Mulgrave for services against Spanish Armada (1588). Served with fleet and army against Dutch under Charles II; privy councilor (1685), joined opposition to William III, dismissed (1696); on accession of Queen Anne lord of privy seal (1702), deprived of office by Whigs (1705); lord president of council (1710–14). Author of *Essay on Poetry*, praised by Pope; *Essay on Satire*, often attributed to Dryden, who accordingly received a beating at hands of bravoes of John Wilmot, Earl of Rochester; and a recast of Shakespeare's *Julius Caesar* in two plays. His son **Edmund** (1716–1735) succeeded to titles, which became extinct with his death.

**Sheffield, Joseph Earl.** 1793–1882. American merchant and philanthropist; cotton commission merchant in Mobile, Ala. (1817–35); settled in New Haven, Conn. (1835). Made large gifts to Yale's scientific department, which had been founded in 1847 and made a separate school in 1854; this school was named Sheffield Scientific School in his honor (1861).

**She′han** (shē′ăn), **Lawrence Joseph.** 1898– American Roman Catholic churchman, b. Baltimore, Md. Ordained (1922); bishop (1945); archbishop of Baltimore (1961– ); cardinal (1965).

**Sheil** (shēl), **Richard Lalor.** 1791–1851. Irish dramatist and politician; author of *Adelaide, or the Emigrants* (1814; at Dublin), *Apostate* (1817; London), *Bellamira* (1818), *Evadue* (1819). Joined Catholic Assoc. (1823) and aided O'Connell with impassioned speeches until granting of Catholic emancipation (1829); M.P. (1829), aided O'Connell in agitation for repeal of union of Great Britain and Ireland; after defeat of repeal, took office under Melbourne ministry (1838–41), first Roman Catholic to be privy councilor; master of mint (1846–50); ambassador at Florence (1850).

**Shelburne,** 2d Earl of. Sir **William Petty.** See Marquises of LANSDOWNE.

**Shel′by** (shĕl′bĭ), **Evan.** 1719–1794. Frontiersman and military leader in America, b. Tregaron, Wales; to America (c. 1734). Served in Braddock's campaign (1755); in force under Gen. Forbes that captured Fort Duquesne (1758). Moved to southwest Virginia (1773); colonel of militia in Washington County. Thanked by Continental Congress for expedition against Chickamauga Indian towns on lower Tennessee River (1779). Brigadier general of militia in North Carolina (1786); resigned (1787). His son **Isaac** (1750–1826) was also a soldier; colonel of militia in Virginia (1780). Organized a colonial force after fall of Charleston (1780) and defeated British at Kings Mountain (Oct. 7, 1780); served in North Carolina legislature (1781, 1782); settled in Kentucky region (1783); first governor of State of Kentucky (1792–96, 1812–16); led Kentucky volunteers who joined General Harrison and defeated British at battle of the Thames (Oct. 5, 1813).

**Shelby, Joseph Orville.** 1830–1897. Of same family as Evan and Isaac Shelby. American Confederate soldier, b. Lexington, Ky. Joined Confederate army (1861) and became prominent cavalry commander; brigadier general (1864), co-operating with General Price in campaigns in the western area.

**Shel′don** (shĕl′dŭn), **Charles Monroe.** 1857–1946. American clergyman and author, b. Wellsville, N.Y. Ordained in Congregational ministry (1886); pastorates, Waterbury, Vt. (1886–88), Topeka, Kans. (1889–1912). Editor, *Christian Herald*, New York City (from 1920). Author of *Richard Bruce* (1891), *In His Steps* (1896; dramatized, 1923), *The Narrow Gate* (1902), *All the World* (1918), *In His Steps Today* (1921), etc.

**Sheldon, Edward Brewster.** 1886–1946. American playwright, b. Chicago; author of *Salvation Nell* (1908), *The Nigger* (1909), *The Boss* (1911), *Romance* (1913), *Song of Songs* (1914), *Lulu Belle* (with C. MacArthur; 1926), *Dishonored Lady* (with M. A. Barnes; 1930).

**Sheldon, Edward Stevens.** 1851–1925. American philologist; instructor in modern languages (1877–84), assistant professor (1884–94) and professor (1894–1921) of Romance philology, Harvard. Etymologist for *Webster's International Dictionary* (1890) and *Webster's New International Dictionary* (1909). His brother **Henry Newton** (1843–1926) was a jurist; practiced in Boston (1866–94); judge of Massachusetts superior court (1894–1905) and of supreme court (1905–15).

**Sheldon, Gilbert.** 1598–1677. English prelate; warden of All Souls Coll., Oxford (1626–48), ejected by Parliament for Royalist activities; bishop of London (1660) and, during Juxon's old age, virtual primate; archbishop of Canterbury (1663–77), severe against Dissenters; built Sheldonian Theatre at Oxford (1669).

**Sheldon, Walter Lorenzo.** 1858–1907. Ethical culture leader, b. West Rutland, Vt. Organized Ethical Society of St. Louis (1886), and Self-Culture Hall Association (1888), a social-settlement center. Also, organized classes for teaching Negroes; busied himself with the training of children; established a current-problems discussion club. The building of the Ethical Society of St. Louis (1912) was named Sheldon Memorial in his honor.

**She′le·khov** (shā′lyĕ·κôf), **Grigori Ivanovich.** 1747–1795. Russian merchant; organized (1783) trading and exploring expedition to Alaska; founded (Aug. 14, 1784) first Russian colony in Alaska on Kodiak Island; expanded trade and influence to Alaskan mainland. His company became nucleus after his death of famous Russian-American Company (1799).

**Shel′ford** (shĕl′fērd), **Victor Ernest.** 1877– . American zoologist; professor (from 1927), U. of Illinois. Author of *Animal Communities in Temperate America* (1913), *Laboratory and Field Ecology* (1929), etc.; compiler of *Naturalist's Guide to the Americas* (1925).

**Shel'ley** (shĕl'ĭ), **Harry Rowe.** 1858–1947. American organist and composer, b. New Haven, Conn. Organist in Fifth Avenue Baptist Church, New York City (from 1899). Composer of two symphonies, an overture, an orchestral suite (*Souvenir de Baden-Baden*), a violin concerto, cantatas (*Vexilla Regis, Death and Life*, etc.), and many anthems, songs, and other organ pieces.

**Shelley, Mary Wollstonecraft,** *nee* **God'win** (gŏd'wĭn). 1797–1851. English novelist; only child of William Godwin and Mary Wollstonecraft Godwin (*qq.v.*). Accompanied P. B. Shelley to Continent (1814) and married him (1816); much in company of Byron, Trelawny, and Leigh Hunt. Author of *Frankenstein* (ghastly novel of a monster; 1818), *The Last Man* (story of destruction of human race by an epidemic; 1826), and the autobiographical *Lodore* (1835).

**Shelley, Percy Bysshe.** 1792–1822. English poet, b. Warnham, near Horsham, Sussex, grandson of Sir Bysshe Shelley (1713–1815); educ. Eton and University Coll., Oxford, whence he was expelled, with his friend Thomas Jefferson Hogg, for circulating pamphlet *The Necessity of Atheism* (1811); m. Harriet Westbrook, daughter of retired innkeeper (1811); filled with revolutionary ardor, visited Ireland and addressed Dublin popular assembly held by O'Connell; driven from Tanyrallt, Wales, by supposed attempt on his life. Became disciple of philosophical radical William Godwin; abandoned Harriet (later making a settlement on her) and eloped to Switzerland with Godwin's daughter Mary (see Mary Wollstonecraft SHELLEY), whom he married (1816) after Harriet's suicide; refused custody of his two children by decision of Lord Eldon on ground of his atheism; visited Byron in Switzerland (1816). After pulmonary attack, left England never to return (1818); spent rest of life in company of Byron, Edward Trelawny, and the ex-cavalry officer Edward Williams in Italy; lived (1818–19) at Byron's villa near Este, and in Venice, Rome, Leghorn, and Florence; settled in Pisa (1820); worked on last poems at Lerici on Gulf of Spezia (1822); visited Leigh Hunt at Pisa and was lost in a storm while sailing back with Edward Williams; his body, washed ashore, was burnt on a pyre. Works include antireligious poem *Queen Mab* (privately printed, 1813), *Alastor, or the Spirit of Solitude, Hymn to Intellectual Beauty*, and *Mont Blanc* (all written in 1816), *Revolt of Islam* (written in 6 months under title *Laon and Cynthia*, 1817), *Rosalind and Helen* (completed in Italy), *Lines on the Euganean Hills, Julian and Maddalo* (record of a discussion with Byron), *Prometheus Unbound*, tragedy *The Cenci, Stanzas written in Dejection near Naples* (typical lyric; 1818), *The Masque of Anarchy*, the satire on Wordsworth *Peter Bell the Third, Ode to the West Wind* (1819), *Epistle to Maria Gisborne*, the fantasy *The Witch of Atlas*, satirical drama *Oedipus Tyrannus*, lyrics, including *The Sensitive Plant* and *The Skylark* (1820), *Epipsychidion* (in homage to ideal womanhood; completed after meeting in Pisa a young Italian noblewoman, Emilia Viviani), the prose *Defence of Poetry* in answer to Peacock, the elegy *Adonais* (on death of Keats), lyric drama *Hellas* (1821), *Charles I*, and *The Triumph of Life* (1822).

**Shel'ton** (shĕl't'n; -tŭn), **Thomas.** fl. 1612–1620. First English translator of *Don Quixote* (part i, 1612; part ii, 1620).

**Shêng-tsu.** See K'ANG-HSI.

**Shenshin, Afanasi.** See FET.

**Shen'stone** (shĕn'stŭn; -stōn), **William.** 1714–1763. English poet; author of *The Schoolmistress* (1742, a poem describing in Spenserian stanzas his own teacher), *Pastoral Ballad* (1755), etc.

**Shên Tsung.** See WAN LI.

**Shep'ard** (shĕp'ẽrd). See also SHEPHERD, SHEPPARD.

**Shepard, Alan Bartlett.** 1923– . American astronaut, b. East Derry, N.H. First American in space (suborbital flight; May 5, 1961); fifth man on the moon (Apollo 14 flight, 1971).

**Shepard, Helen Miller,** *nee* **Gould** (gōōld). 1868–1938. American philanthropist, b. New York City, daughter of Jay Gould. Among her gifts were a library building and hall of fame building to New York U., a building for the naval branch of the Brooklyn Y.M.C.A. Her husband (m. 1913), **Finley Johnson Shepard** (1867–1942), was an executive of the Missouri Pacific Ry.

**Shepard, Thomas.** 1605?–1649. Clergyman in colonial New England, b. Towcester, Eng. To America (1635) and became pastor at Cambridge, Massachusetts. Friend of John Harvard and influential in establishing Harvard College at Cambridge (1636). His diary (publ. 1747) records vividly life in the colony during his time.

**Shep'herd** (shĕp'ẽrd). See also SHEPARD, SHEPPARD.

**Shepherd, William Robert.** 1871–1934. American historian; wrote *Historical Atlas, The Hispanic Nations of the New World, The Story of New Amsterdam*, etc.

**Shepherd Kings.** See HYKSOS.

**Shep'pard** (shĕp'ẽrd). See also SHEPARD, SHEPHERD.

**Sheppard, Hugh Richard,** *known as* **Dick.** 1880–1937. Anglican prelate; canon and precentor of St. Paul's Cathedral (1934–37); prominent as a pacifist. Author of *If I were Dictator*, etc.

**Sheppard, John,** *known as* **Jack.** 1702–1724. English robber; incited to crime by a woman named Bess Lyon (called "Edgeworth Bess"); committed almost daily robbery in or near London; captured through Jonathan Wild, whose enmity he had aroused, and condemned to death. Escaped from condemned cell through aid of Edgeworth Bess; rearrested, but escaped from strongest part of Newgate; finally captured while drunk. Subject of painting by Sir James Thornhill, a narrative by Defoe, and a novel, *Jack Sheppard*, by Ainsworth.

**Sheppard, Morris.** 1875–1941. American lawyer and legislator, b. Wheatville, Tex.; member, U.S. Congress (1902–13), U.S. Senate (from 1913). Ardent prohibitionist; cosponsor of the Sheppard-Towner Act (1921) providing for federal and state co-operation to assure maternal and infant welfare and hygiene.

**Shep'stone** (shĕp'stŭn; -stōn), Sir **Theophilus.** 1817–1893. British South African statesman; secretary for native affairs (1856–77); secured recognition of Cetewayo as king (1872), but on his failure to keep peace (1876), received discretionary powers from 4th earl of Carnarvon and annexed Transvaal (1877); administrator of Transvaal (1877–79) and Zululand (1883).

**Sher'a·ton** (shĕr'ȧ·t'n; -tŭn), **Thomas.** 1751–1806. English furniture maker and designer, in London (c. 1790); never had shop of his own; gave drawing lessons; published *The Cabinet-Maker and Upholsterer's Drawing Book* (1791) and *The Cabinet Dictionary*, with engravings, advocating a severe style (1803). Showed tendency to the tortured and bizarre in later designs and in *The Cabinet Maker, Upholsterer and General Artists' Encyclopaedia*, with plates in color (beginning 1804).

**Sher'brooke** (shûr'brŏŏk), Viscount. See Robert LOWE.

**Sherbrooke,** Sir **John Coape.** 1764–1830. English soldier; second in command to Wellesley (afterward duke of Wellington) in Peninsular War (1809); governor general of Canada (1816–18).

**Shere A'li** *or* **Sher A'li** (shär' ŭ'lē). *Also* **Shere Ali Khan** (kän). 1825–1879. Amir of Afghanistan (1863–78); son of Dost Mohammed Khan; forced into contests with brothers and nephew for throne (1866–69) but overcame all; aided by his son Yakub Khan whom, however, he later seized and imprisoned; became unfriendly to British (1878) through their failure to guarantee his sovereignty; action led to Second Afghan War (1878–81); lost Kandahar (1878), fled to Turkestan, and died a fugitive; succeeded by his son Yakub Khan.

**Sher'i·dan** (shĕr'ĭ·d'n). Name of Irish family that forfeited Quilcagh House, County Cavan, as result of adherence to James II, including among its members: **William** (1636–1711), bishop of Kilmore (1682–93), a Nonjuror, and his brother **Thomas** (fl. 1661–1688), chief secretary for Ireland (1687) and secretary to James II in exile. Their nephew **Thomas Sheridan** (1687–1738), schoolmaster; married heiress of Charles MacFadden, thereby recovering Quilcagh House, where Swift confided in him the project of *Drapier's Letters* and prepared *Gulliver's Travels* for the press; translated *Philoctetes* of Sophocles and the satires of Persius and Juvenal. Thomas's son **Thomas** (1719–1788), actor and teacher of elocution; actor at Covent Garden and Drury Lane, London (1744), and later under Garrick (1760); manager of Theatre Royal, Dublin (1747–57); gained pensions for Dr. Johnson and himself; published, after working twenty years on pronunciation and orthoëpy, his *General Dictionary of the English Language* (1780); editor and biographer of Swift. His wife (m. 1747), **Frances**, *nee* **Cham'ber·laine** [chām'bẽr·lĭn; -lān] (1724–1766), novelist and dramatist; author of *Memoirs of Miss Sidney Bidulph* (1761, 1767), written by Richardson's advice; had two plays produced (1763), of which *The Discovery* became one of Garrick's stock pieces; left behind an Oriental tale, *Nourjahad* (pub. 1767). Their third son was Richard Brinsley SHERIDAN (*q.v.*).

**Sheridan, Clare Con·sue'lo** (kŏn·swē'lō), *nee* **Frew'en** (frōō'ĕn; -ĭn). 1885-1970. English sculptor and writer; m. Wilfred Sheridan, killed in France in World War; executed portrait busts of Princess Patricia, Asquith, Marconi, Lenin, Trotsky, Gandhi, and other notables; author of *Russian Portraits* (1921), *My American Diary* (1922), *Stella Defiant* (1924), *Make Believe* (1926), *The Substitute Bride* (1931), *Arab Interlude* (1936), *Redskin Interlude* (1938), *The Mask* (novel; 1942), etc.

**Sheridan, Lady Helen Selina.** See under Frederick BLACKWOOD.

**Sheridan, Philip Henry.** 1831–1888. American army commander, b. Albany, N.Y.; grad. U.S.M.A., West Point (1853). Ranked as captain at outbreak of Civil War; appointed colonel of a Michigan cavalry regiment (1862); brigadier general (June, 1862); major general (Dec., 1862). Engaged at Chickamauga; commanded cavalry of the Army of the Potomac; engaged in the Wilderness, Spotsylvania, Cold Harbor; raided (May, 1864) Confederate communication lines around Richmond; commanded Army of the Shenandoah in drive through the Shenandoah Valley (1864); made famous ride from Winchester to rally his troops after their repulse at Cedar Creek (Oct. 19, 1864), a ride celebrated in verse (*Sheridan's Ride*) by Thomas Buchanan Read; again engaged in cavalry raids from Winchester to Petersburg (Feb.–Mar., 1865); deployed his army across Confederate line of retreat from Appomattox and thus forced Lee's surrender to Grant. Commanded military division of the Gulf (1865–67); military governor of 5th military district (Louisiana and Texas, 1867); severity of his administration led to his transfer to department of the Missouri; lieutenant general (Mar. 4, 1869). In Europe (1870–71) accompanying German armies in the field. Succeeded Sherman as commander in chief, U.S. army (1884); general (1888). Author of *Personal Memoirs of P. H. Sheridan* (2 vols., 1888).

**Sheridan, Richard Brinsley.** 1751–1816. Irish dramatist and parliamentary orator, b. Dublin; son of Thomas and Frances Sheridan (see SHERIDAN family) and cousin of James Sheridan Knowles (*q.v.*). Collaborated with N. B. Halhed, student in Oxford, in metrical translation of Aristaenetus (1771) and in a farce, *Jupiter*, which foreshadows *The Critic*. Eloped (1772) to France with Elizabeth Ann Linley (see under Thomas LINLEY); married her (1773). Settled in London (1773) and turned to dramatic composition; rose to first place among writers of comedies of manners by his three great comedies, *The Rivals* (1775), *The School for Scandal* (1777), and *The Critic* (1779). Bought Garrick's share in Drury Lane Theatre, London, and became manager (1776); besides a poor farce, *St. Patrick's Day*, a comic opera, *The Duenna* (1775), and a comedy, *A Trip to Scarborough* (1777), produced only one other play, a patriotic melodrama adapted from Kotzebue, *Pizarro* (1799); lost his new theatre (opened 1794) by fire (1809). M.P. (1780), as ally of Charles James Fox; undersecretary for foreign affairs (1782); secretary to treasury (1783); confidential adviser to George, Prince of Wales; declined gift from Continental Congress for opposing British war in America; made two great speeches in impeachment of Warren Hastings, one moving adoption of Oudh charge (1787) and one as manager of impeachment (1788); electrified House of Commons with reply to Mornington's speech against French republic (1794); opposed Irish union (1799); treasurer of navy in All-the-Talents ministry (1806–07); given magnificent funeral in Westminster Abbey. His son **Thomas** (1775–1817), poet, became colonial treasurer at Cape of Good Hope; m. (1805) **Caroline Henrietta Cal'lan·der** [kăl'ăn·dẽr] (1779–1851), author of *Carwell, or Crime and Sorrow* (1830) and two other novels. Their daughters were the three famous beauties Lady Dufferin (see under Frederick BLACKWOOD), Hon. Mrs. Norton (see Caroline Elizabeth Sarah NORTON), and Lady Seymour, later duchess of Somerset (see *Edward Adolphus Seymour*, under SEYMOUR family).

**Sher'iff** (shĕr'ĭf), **Laurence.** d. 1567. London grocer and founder of Rugby School.

**Sher'ley** *or* **Shir'ley** (shûr'lĭ). Name of English family of Wiston, Sussex, founded by **Ralph Sherley** *or* **Shirley** (d. 1510), sheriff of Surrey and Sussex. His great-grandson Sir **Thomas Sherley** (1542–1612), sheriff of Surrey and Sussex (1578), as treasurer-at-war to English army in Netherlands involved himself in debts to the crown; said to have suggested creation of baronets. The three sons of Sir Thomas were travelers and adventurers: Sir **Thomas** (1564?–?1630) served in Netherlands and Ireland; tried to retrieve family fortunes by privateering expeditions in the Levant (1598–1602); captured by Turks (1603) and imprisoned two years. Sir **Anthony** (1565–?1635) served in Netherlands (1586) and Normandy (1591); commanded expedition against Caribbean settlements (1596); sent as ambassador to seek alliance between England and Shah Abbas of Persia (1599); having failed, sent by shah to arrange military alliances in Europe against Turks; failed, incurred debts, got involved in intrigue; went off to squander Emperor Rudolph II's money in Morocco on pretext of setting Arabs against Turks (1605–06); general in Mediterranean under Philip of Spain (1609). **Robert** (1581?–1628) accompanied Sir Anthony to Persia; distinguished himself in wars against Turks; married a Persian wife, a noble Circassian; sent by Shah Abbas of Persia to negotiate European alliances against Turks, royally received by Sigismund III of Poland, Emperor Rudolph II, and Pope Paul V, but returned to England (1611), distrusted by all parties; on second mission from shah, offering Persian silk trade, was ejected from Spain after five years' negotiation (1617–22) and dismissed in England after opposition by East India Co.; died in disgrace in Persia.

**Sher′lock** (shûr′lŏk), **William.** 1641?–1707. Nonjuror; dean of St. Paul's, London (1691–1707); author of *A Vindication of the Doctrine of the Trinity* (1690), which brought forth Robert South's *Animadversions on Dr. Sherlock's Book...*(1693) and later an accusation of tritheism (1695).

**Sher′man** (shûr′măn), **Frank Dempster.** 1860–1916. American poet and educator; adjunct professor (1891–1904), and professor (1904–16), of graphics, Columbia. Author of several books of poetry, including *Madrigals and Catches* (1887), *Lyrics for a Lute* (1890), *Lyrics of Joy* (1904), and *A Southern Flight* (with Clinton Scollard, 1905).

**Sherman, Henry Clapp.** 1875–1955. American chemist; professor of organic analysis (1907–11), of food chemistry (1911–24), and of chemistry (from 1924), Columbia. Author of *Chemistry of Food and Nutrition* (1911), *The Vitamins* (with Sybil Laura Smith; 1922), etc.

**Sherman, James Schoolcraft.** 1855–1912. Vice-president of the United States, b. Utica, N.Y.; practiced law in Utica; member of U.S. House of Representatives (1887–91, 1893–1909); vice-president of the U.S. (1909–12).

**Sherman, John.** 1823–1900. American statesman, b. Lancaster, Ohio; bro. of William Tecumseh Sherman; practiced law in Mansfield, Ohio (1844–53) and Cleveland (from 1853). Member, U.S. House of Representatives (1855–61) and U.S. Senate (1861–77); chairman, U.S. Senate finance committee (1867–77); supported vigorously measures for prosecution of Civil War and for reconstruction of the South; defended protective tariff; prominent in securing passage of legislation for restoring specie payments and for refunding the national debt. U.S. secretary of the treasury (1877–81); again, U.S. senator (1881–97); author of the Sherman Antitrust Act (1890) and Sherman Act for keeping up price of silver (in force, 1890–93); U.S. secretary of state (1897–98).

**Sherman, Roger.** 1721–1793. American jurist and statesman, b. Newton, Mass. Settled in New Milford, Conn. (1743); member of Connecticut legislature (1755, 1756, 1758–61, 1764–66). Moved to New Haven (1761); member, Connecticut State senate (1766–85); judge, Connecticut superior court (1766, 1767, 1773–88). Member of Continental Congress (1774–81, 1783, 1784) and a signer of the Declaration of Independence; also signed Articles of Association (1774), Articles of Confederation, and the Federal Constitution, only person to sign all four state papers. Mayor of New Haven (1784–93). Member, Constitutional Convention in Philadelphia (1787), U.S. House of Representatives (1789–91), U.S. Senate (1791–93).

**Sherman, Stuart Pratt.** 1881–1926. American critic and educator, b. Anita, Iowa; professor (from 1911) and permanent chairman of the English department (from 1914), U. of Illinois. His works include *Matthew Arnold: How to Know Him* (1917), *On Contemporary Literature* (1917), *Americans* (1922), *The Genius of America* (1923), *Points of View* (1924), *Critical Woodcuts* (1926), etc.

**Sherman, William Tecumseh.** 1820–1891. American army commander, b. Lancaster, Ohio; bro. of John Sherman (1823–1900); grad. U.S.M.A., West Point (1840). Brigadier general of volunteers (Aug., 1861); engaged at Bull Run; served under Grant at Shiloh and Corinth; promoted major general (May, 1862); took part in capture of Vicksburg (July 4, 1863). Commanded Army of the Tennessee (1863) and the military division of the Mississippi (1864). Started from Chattanooga (May 6, 1864) for his famous march through Georgia and reached Atlanta after a series of engagements (Sept. 2, 1864); left Atlanta on the "March to the Sea" (Nov. 15, 1864) and entered Savannah (Dec. 21, 1864); marched northward through South Carolina and North Carolina (1865), and received the surrender of Johnston's army (April 26, 1865). Commanded military division of the Mississippi (1865), and the division of the Missouri (1866); lieutenant general (1866) and succeeded Grant as general and commander of the army (1869). Retired (1884). Elected to American Hall of Fame (1905).

**Sher′riff** (shĕr′ĭf), **Robert Cedric.** 1896– . English writer; among his plays are *Journey's End* (1929), *Windfall* (1933), *St. Helena* (with Jeanne de Casalis; 1934); among his novels, *The Fortnight in September* (1931), *Greengates* (1936), *The Hopkins Manuscript* (1939). Also wrote adaptations for motion pictures.

**Sher′rill** (shĕr′ĭl), **Charles Hitchcock.** 1867–1936. American diplomat; practiced law in New York (1891–1909); U.S. minister to Argentina (1909–11); U.S. ambassador to Turkey (1932–33). Author of *Stained Glass Tours in France* (1908), *Modernizing the Monroe Doctrine* (1916), *Bismarck and Mussolini* (1931), etc.

**Sher′ring·ton** (shĕr′ĭng·tŭn), Sir **Charles Scott.** 1861–1952. English physiologist; educ. Cambridge; professor of physiology, Liverpool (1895–1913), Royal Institution of Great Britain (1914–17), and Oxford (to 1936). Civil member, Order of Merit (1924); shared with Edgar Douglas Adrian, 1932 Nobel prize for physiology and medicine, awarded for their discoveries regarding function of the neuron. Author of *The Integrative Action of the Nervous System* (1906), *Mammalian Physiology* (1916), *Man on His Nature* (1941), etc.

**Sher Shah** (shār shä). *Also known as* **Sher Khan** (kän). d. 1545. Afghan king of Bengal (1539–40) and of Delhi (1540–45); defeated the Mogul emperor Humayun (1539, 1540) and forced him to flee to Persia.

**Sher·tok′** (shĕr·tŏk′), **Moshe.** 1894–1965. Jewish Zionist leader, b. in Russian Ukraine; long resident in Palestine; became (1933) head of political department of Zionist organization; changed name to **Sha·rett′** (shä·rĕt′; shă-) after establishment of Israel; prime minister (1954–55).

**Sher′wood** (shûr′wŏŏd), **Mary Martha,** *nee* **Butt** (bŭt). 1775–1851. English writer of juvenile books; m. (1803) Captain Henry Sherwood and accompanied him to India; author of *Little Henry and his Bearer*, *Susan Gray* (1802), etc.

**Sherwood, Robert Emmet.** 1896–1955. American playwright; served in Canadian expeditionary force (1917–19); on editorial staff of *Life* magazine (1920–28). Author of *The Road to Rome* (1927), *Waterloo Bridge* (1930), *The Petrified Forest* (1934), *Idiot's Delight* (1936; awarded Pulitzer prize), *Abe Lincoln in Illinois* (1938), *There shall be no Night* (1940); wrote also the novel *The Virtuous Knight* (1931).

**Sherwood, William Hall.** 1854–1911. American pianist and music teacher; influenced development of musical appreciation in U.S. by his teaching and by his interpretation of work of the masters.

**She′shonk** (shē′shŏngk) *or* **Sho′shenk** (shō′shĕngk). Name of four kings of XXIId (Bubastite) dynasty of ancient Egypt: **Sheshonk I.** *In the Bible* **Shi′shak** (shī′shăk). Founder of the dynasty; reigned c. 945–924 B.C.; member of Libyan family settled in the delta; usurped throne and established new capital at Bubastis; set up sort of feudal state; maintained close relations with high priests; invaded Palestine (c. 926 B.C.) in reign of Rehoboam; plundered many towns, including Jerusalem, in the two Jewish kingdoms (*1 Kings* xi and xiv); built temples and halls, esp. at Bubastis and Thebes. **Sheshonk II.** Son of Osorkon II; died (c. 877 B.C.), probably while coregent with father who (c. 880–874) was ruling crown prince. **Sheshonk III** (reigned c. 834–784 B.C.). **Sheshonk IV** (reigned c. 782–745 B.C.).

**Shev·chen'ko** (shĕf·chăn'kô), **Taras Grigorievich.** 1814–1861. Ukrainian poet; professor, U. of Kiev (1845); founded (1846) an organization (Brotherhood of Cyril and Methodius) to further great social reforms, as abolition of slavery, social equality, etc.; exiled, and his organization suppressed by the government (1847); pardoned by Czar Alexander II (1857). Published collection of poetry in Ukrainian language, *Kobzar* (1840), and many popular poems (as *Kateryna*, *Naïnichka*, *Maria*), which gained him fame as the father of Ukrainian national literature.

**Shi·ba·ta** (shē·bä·tä), **Zeshin.** 1807–1891. Japanese lacquer artist and painter.

**Shibe** (shīb), **Thomas S.** 1866–1936. American sportsman; president of Philadelphia American League Baseball Club, whose home grounds are called Shibe Park in his honor.

**Shi·bu·sa·wa** (shē·bōō·sä·wä), Viscount **Ei-ichi.** 1840–1931. Japanese banker.

**Shi·de·ha·ra** (shē·dĕ·hä·rä), Baron **Kijuro.** 1872–1951. Japanese diplomat; ambassador to U.S. (1919–22); foreign minister (1924–27; 1929–31); premier (1945–46).

**Shiel** (shēl), **Matthew Phipps.** 1865–1947. British journalist and fiction writer, b. in West Indies, of Irish descent. Author of *Shapes in the Fire*, *The Dragon* (1913), *Children of the Wind* (1924), *Dr. Krasinski's Secret* (1930), *Poems* (1936), etc.

**Shield** (shēld), **William.** 1748–1829. English viola player at Italian opera, London, and composer of songs and operatic music at Covent Garden, London.

**Shields** (shēldz), **Charles Woodruff.** 1825–1904. American theologian; ordained in Presbyterian ministry (1849); pastorate in Philadelphia (1850–65). Professor of the harmony of science and religion, Princeton (1865–1903); ordained deacon, Protestant Episcopal Church (1898) and priest (1899).

**Shields, James.** 1806?–1879. American army officer and politician, b. Altmore, Ireland; to U.S. (1823) and settled in Kaskaskia, Ill. At Cerro Gordo in Mexican War. Governor of Oregon Territory (1849); U.S. senator from Illinois (1849–55). Moved to Minnesota Territory (1855); U.S. senator from Minnesota (1858–59); moved to California (1859). Volunteered at outbreak of Civil War; engaged in Shenandoah Valley campaign. Moved to Carrollton, Mo.; U.S. senator from Missouri (1879).

**Shi·ga** (shē·gä), **Kiyoshi.** 1870–1957. Japanese bacteriologist; collaborator with Paul Ehrlich in his experiments; discovered cause of endemic dysentery; carried on experiments in leprosy, beriberi, and tuberculosis.

**Shi·ge·mi·tsu** (shē·gĕ·mē·tsōō), **Ma·mo·ru** (mä·mō·rōō). 1887–1957. Japanese diplomat; member, Paris Peace Conference (1919); minister to China (1931–33); amb. to Russia (1936–38), Britain (1938–41), Nanking government (1941–43); foreign minister (1943–45).

**Shih Huang Ti** (shĭr' hwäng' tē'). *Sometimes* **Ch'in Shih Huang Ti** (chĭn'). 259–210 B.C. Chinese emperor (247 or 246–210 B.C.; under regency until 221), fourth monarch of Ch'in dynasty. Assumed title of Shih Huang Ti, *i.e.* "the First Emperor." Greatly extended limits of empire and united all under single rule; drove back the Hsiung-Nu on northwest; built Great Wall (completed 204 B.C.) to keep out barbarian hordes; established capital at Hsien-yang (now Sian); in order to insure absolute power for himself and successors, decreed that all historical writings be destroyed (see LI SSŬ); hence the burning (212) of the books (*i.e.* the classics).

**Shil'la'ber** (shĭl'ā'bĕr), **Benjamin Pen·hal'low** (?pĕn·hăl'ō). 1814–1890. American humorist, b. Portsmouth, N.H.; best known as author of *Life and Sayings of Mrs. Partington* (1854).

**Shi·ma·da** (shē·mä·dä), **Shigetaro.** 1883– . Japanese admiral; commander in chief of Japanese fleet in Chinese waters (1940–41); minister for the navy in the Tojo cabinet (1941–44).

**Shi'mer** (shī'mĕr), **Porter William.** 1857–1938. American chemist and metallurgist; discovered titanium carbide; invented a combustion crucible, a new process for casehardening iron and steel, etc.

**Shinn** (shĭn), **Asa.** 1781–1853. American Methodist Episcopal clergyman; circuit preacher (1801–25); one of organizers of separate Methodist Protestant Church (1830).

**Shinn, Everett.** 1876–1953. American painter, esp. of murals. His wife (m. 1898; d. 1940), **Florence,** *nee* **Sco'vel** (?skō'vĕl), was an illustrator of works of fiction, as *Lovey Mary*, *Mrs. Wiggs of the Cabbage Patch*, *Coniston*, etc.

**Shin-ran-Sho·nin** (shēn·rän·shō·nēn). 1173–1262. Japanese Buddhist theologian; founder of the Buddhist sect Shin-shu.

**Shinso.** See SOAMI.

**Shin'well** (shĭn'wĕl; -wĕl), **Emanuel.** 1884– . British Laborite politician, b. London; active in trade-union movement in Glasgow; M.P. (1922–24, 1928–31, 1935 ff.); national organizer (1920) of Amalgamated Marine Workers' Union; secretary to department of mines (1924, 1930–31); financial secretary, War Office (1929–30); minister of fuel and power (from 1945).

**Ship'ley** (shĭp'lĭ), Sir **Arthur Everett.** 1861–1927. English zoologist.

**Ship'man** (shĭp'măn), **Samuel.** 1883–1937. American dramatist; collaborator with John B. Hymer in writing *East is West* and *First is Last*, and with Aaron Hoffmann in *Friendly Enemies*. Author of *Love and Art*, *A Social Outcast*, *It Depends on the Woman*, *Sweethearts*, *The Good-for-Nothing*, etc.

**Ship'pen** (shĭp'ĕn), **Edward.** 1639–1712. Colonial administrator in America, b. Methley, Yorkshire, Eng.; to America (1668). Joined Society of Friends (1671); settled in Philadelphia (c. 1694). Mayor of Philadelphia (1701–03) and city treasurer (1705–12). His great-grandson **Edward Shippen** (1729–1806) was a jurist; associate justice (1791–99) and chief justice (1799–1805), Pennsylvania supreme court. His daughter **Margaret,** *known as* **Peggy** (1760–1804), married Benedict Arnold (1779). Another great-grandson, **William Shippen** (1736–1808), was a physician; taught anatomy and midwifery, Philadelphia (from 1762); chief of medical department, Continental army (1777–81); a founder and president (1805–08) of Coll. of Physicians of Philadelphia; first professor of anatomy, surgery, and midwifery, U. of Pennsylvania (1791).

**Ship'stead** (shĭp'stĕd), **Hen'rik** (hĕn'rĭk). 1881–1960. American dentist and politician; U.S. senator from Minnesota (1923–47).

**Ship'ton** (shĭp'tŭn), Mother. Reputed witch and prophetess of Yorkshire, England, in Tudor times, probably wholly mythical creation of a tract of 1641, the earliest reference extant, magnified by imaginary biography (1677) by Richard Head, an anonymous history (1686), innumerable chapbooks, and a pretended biography (1862) as if of 1448 by **Charles Hind'ley** (hīnd'lĭ), a bookseller. Traditionally, indentified as one **Ursula South'ill** [south'ĭl] *or* **South'iel** [south'ēl] (b. about

1486–88); made extraordinary prophecies, of death of Cardinal Wolsey, civil war, London fire of 1666, invention of steam engine and telegraph, end of world in 1881; lived to be over seventy years of age.

**Shi'ras** (shī'rȧs), **George.** 1832–1924. American jurist, b. Pittsburgh, Pa.; associate justice, U.S. Supreme Court (1892–1903).

**Shi·ra·to·ri** (shē·rä·tō·rē), **Toshio.** 1887–1949. Japanese diplomat and politician; joined Japanese foreign service (1914); minister to Sweden, Norway, Denmark, and Finland (1933–36); ambassador to Italy (1938); member of the national council (1942); known as an extremist Fascist in his sympathies and policies.

**Shi'rer** (shī'rĕr), **William Lawrence.** 1904– . American journalist and radio commentator, b. Chicago; A.B., Coe College (1925); foreign correspondent for Chicago *Tribune* (1925–33) and Universal News Service (1935–37); continental European representative of Columbia Broadcasting System (1937–40); returned to U.S. (Dec., 1940). Author of *Berlin Diary* (1941).

**Shir'law** (shûr'lô), **Walter.** 1838–1909. Painter and engraver, b. Paisley, Scotland; to U.S. as a child; best known for his genre paintings and mural work.

**Shir'ley** (shûr'lĭ). See also SHERLEY.

**Shirley, James.** 1596–1666. English dramatist; settled in London (1625) and wrote about forty plays; stopped by Puritan edict (1642). Bore arms on Royalist side; burnt out in great fire of 1666. Author of tragedies, including *The Maid's Revenge* (1626), *Love's Cruelty* (1631), *The Traitor* (1631), and *The Cardinal* (1641), comedies, including *Changes, or Love in a Maze* (1632), *Hyde Park* (1632), *The Gamester* (1633), *Coronation* (1635), and *The Lady of Pleasure* (1635), and masques second only to those of Jonson, including *The Contention of Ajax and Ulysses* (1659), containing the dirge "The glories of our blood and state."

**Shirley, Laurence.** See FERRERS family.

**Shirley, William.** 1694–1771. Colonial governor in America, b. Preston, Sussex, Eng. To America (1731) and settled in Boston; governor of Massachusetts (1741–49); planned the successful expedition against Louisburg (1745). In England (1749–53), member of commission in Paris to determine boundary between New England and French North America. Again governor (1753–56); appointed major general (1755) at outbreak of French and Indian War; planned attack on Niagara (1755); was criticized for failure of expedition; relieved of governorship (1756). Governor of the Bahama Islands (1761–67).

**Shishak.** See SHESHONK I.

**Shish·man'** (shēsh·män') *or* **Shish·ma'nid** (shĭsh-mä'nĭd). A dynasty of Bulgarian kings of the 10th to 14th centuries.

**Shivaji.** See SIVAJI.

**Shock'ley** (shŏk'lĭ), **William Bradford.** 1910– American physicist, b. England. Awarded Nobel prize in physics (1956) with J. Bardeen and W. Brattain for discoveries of the transistor effect.

**Sho'ghi Ef·fen'di** (shou'ē ĕf·fĕn'dĭ). **1896–1957.** Head of Bahai faith (from 1921); grandson of Abdul Baha; resident at Haifa, Palestine.

**Sho·kal'ski** (shŭ·kál'y'·skû·ĭ; *Angl.* shō·kăl'skĭ), **Yuli Mikhailovich.** *Also, often in English,* **Scho·kal'sky.** 1856–1940. Russian geographer; professor, Leningrad (1910 ff.); conducted investigations of Black Sea (1924–27). Author of *Oceanography* (1917).

**Sholem Aleichem.** See Solomon RABINOWITZ.

**Sholes** (shōlz), **Christopher Latham.** 1819–1890. American inventor, b. Mooresburg, Pa.; printer by trade; experimented with numbering machines and letter-writing machines (from 1864); concentrated on invention of typewriter (from 1867); with **Carlos Glid'den** (glĭd''n) and **Samuel W. Sou'lé** (sōō'lā; sōō·lā') received patent for a typewriter (1868); after Glidden and Soulé relinquished their rights, sold his own rights to Remington Arms Co. for $12,000 (1873), the Remington typewriter being later perfected on basis of this patent. Cf. Xavier PROGIN.

**Sho'lo·khov** (shô'lŭ·kôf), **Mikhail Aleksandrovich.** 1905– . Russian author; awarded Nobel prize in literature (1965); wrote *And Quiet Flows the Don* (4 vols., 1928–40), *Virgin Soil Upturned* (2 vols., 1932, 1960); also *The Mortal Enemy, The Colt,* etc.

**Shonts** (shŏnts), **Theodore Perry.** 1856–1919. American transportation executive; chairman, Second Isthmian Canal Commission (1905–07); president, Interborough Rapid Transit Co., New York City (1907–19).

**Shook** (shŏŏk), **Alfred Montgomery.** 1845–1923. American industrialist, b. near Winchester, Tenn.; associated (1866–1901) with Tennesee Coal, Iron, & Railroad Co. in exploiting iron-ore resources of Tennessee and Alabama and steel-manufacturing industry in the Birmingham district.

**Shore** (shōr), **Jane.** 1445?–?1527. Mistress of Edward IV of England; daughter of London mercer; m. William Shore, Lombard Street goldsmith. Exercised influence over Edward IV by wit and beauty, never to any man's hurt, says Sir Thomas More (from 1470 to king's death, 1483). Mistress of marquis of Dorset; accused of sorcery and robbed by Richard III, and made to do penance (1483).

**Sho'rey** (shō'rĭ), **Paul.** 1857–1934. American classical scholar; professor of Greek, U. of Chicago (1892–1933), and head of the department (1896–1927). Among his most notable works were *The Idea of Good in Plato's Republic* (1895), *The Unity of Plato's Thought* (1903), *What Plato Said* (1933).

**Short** (shôrt), Sir **Frank,** ***in full* Francis Job. 1857–1945.** English engraver.

**Short, Sidney Howe.** 1858–1902. American electrical engineer and inventor, b. Columbus, Ohio; recognized authority on electric-railway construction and continuous-current motors.

**Short, Walter Campbell.** 1880–1949. American army officer, b. Fillmore, Ill.; A.B., U. of Illinois (1901); commissioned 2d lieutenant (1902); served in World War I (1917–18); commander of Hawaiian department at the time of the Japanese attack (Dec. 7, 1941).

**Shor'ter** (shôr'tĕr), **Clement King.** 1857–1926. English journalist and literary critic; editor, *Illustrated London News* (1891–1900), and founder and editor, *The Sketch* (1893–1900); editor of *The Sphere* (1900–26). Among his books are *Charlotte Brontë and her Circle* (1896), *Sixty Years of Victorian Literature* (1897), *Napoleon's Fellow Travellers* (1909), and *George Borrow* (1913). He married (1896) **Dora Sig'er·son** [sĭg'ĕr·s'n] (1866–1918), poet and novelist, b. Dublin; associated with Irish literary revival; among her works are *The Fairy Changeling and Other Poems* (1897), *Ballads and Poems* (1899), *The Woman who Went to Hell* (1902), *The Country House Party* (1905), and *Madge Lindsley and Other Poems* (1913).

**Short'house'** (shôrt'hous'), **Joseph Henry.** 1834–1903. English novelist; wrote (1866–76) psychological romance *John Inglesant,* kept it three years in manuscript, printed 100 copies (1880), and became suddenly famous when Gladstone praised it (1881).

**Shoshenk.** Variant of SHESHONK.

**Sho·sta·ko'vich** (shŭ·stŭ·kô'vyĭch), **Dimitri Dimitrievich.** 1906–1975. Russian composer, b. St. Petersburg (Leningrad); studied at Leningrad Conservatory (1919–

25); works include symphonies, esp. the fifth, commemorating the 20th anniversary of the October Revolution (1937), and the seventh, depicting from first-hand information the battle of Leningrad (1942); the operas *The Nose* (1929) and *Katerina Ismailova* (1934); ballets; piano pieces.

**Sho·sta·kov'ski** (shŭ·stŭ·kôf'skû·ĭ; *Angl.* -skĭ), **Pëtr Adamovich.** 1853– . Russian pianist.

**Shot'well** (shŏt'wĕl; -wĕl), **James Thomson.** 1874-1965. Historian, b. Strathroy, Ontario; B.A., Toronto (1898). Ph.D., Columbia (1903); professor, Columbia (from 1908); chief of division of history and member of International Labor Commission, Paris Peace Conference (1918–19); chairman of Commission to Study the Organization of Peace (formed 1939), often called "Shotwell commission." Author of *The Religious Revolution of Today* (1913), *War As an Instrument of National Policy* (1929), *The Heritage of Freedom* (1934), *What Germany Forgot* (1940), etc.

**Shoup** (shōōp), **George Laird.** 1836–1904. American merchant and politician; original settler of Salmon, Idaho; governor of Idaho Territory (1889); first governor of State of Idaho (Oct.–Dec., 1890), and first U.S. senator from Idaho (1890–1901).

**Shov'ell** (shŭv'ĕl), Sir **Cloudesley** *or* **Clowdisley.** 1650–1707. English naval commander; burned four men of war belonging to Tripolitan pirates (1676); captain of the *Edgar* at Bantry Bay (1689); took part at Beachy Head (1690); at La Hogue (1692), burned twenty enemy ships; M.P. (1698); took part in capture of Gibraltar and action off Málaga (1704); admiral and commander in chief of fleet (1705); failed in attack on Toulon (1707); lost on return trip when ship struck rock in fog.

**Showa.** See HIROHITO.

**Shra'dy** (shrā'dĭ), **George Frederick.** 1837–1907. American surgeon; editor, *Medical Record* (1866–1904); specialist in plastic surgery. A son, **Henry Merwin** (1871–1922), was a sculptor; among his best-known works are the Grant memorial in Union Square, Washington, D.C.; an equestrian statue of William the Silent on Riverside Drive, New York City.

**Shrap'nel** (shrăp'n'l), **Henry.** 1761–1842. English artillery officer; inventor of shrapnel shell, successfully used at Surinam (1804); improved construction of howitzers and mortars.

**Shreve** (shrēv), **Henry Miller.** 1785–1851. American Mississippi River steamboat captain; owned interest in one of first steamboats on Mississippi River (1814); established practicability of steam navigation on Mississippi and Ohio rivers; devised shallow-draft boats with high-pressure engines mounted on deck for river traffic. Defended successfully against Fulton-Livingston interests, who claimed right to a monopoly of river traffic, his right to navigate the river; his success in this suit opened up Mississippi River navigation to competitive enterprise. Shreveport, La., is named after him.

**Shrews'bur·y** (shrōōz'bĕr·ĭ; shrōz'-; -brĭ), Earls and duke of. See (1) Robert of BELESME; (2) TALBOT family.

**Shrewsbury,** Countess of. See Elizabeth TALBOT.

**Shri'dha·ra'ni** (shrē'dȧ·rä'nĭ), **Krish'na·lal'** (krĭsh'nȧ·läl'). 1911–1960. East Indian author in U.S., b. in Umrala, India. Educ. at Gandhi's national university at Ahmedabad, and participated as a follower of Gandhi in the march to the sea (to break the salt law); imprisoned; delegate to the Indian National Congress (1933). To New York (1934); M.A., New York U. (1935); M.S. (1936) and Ph.D. (1940), Columbia. Author of *The Banyan Tree; I Shall Kill the Human in You* (1932); *War Without Violence* (1939); *My India, My America* (1941); *Warning to the West* (1942), etc.

**Shu** *or* **Shu Han.** See HAN (dynasty), 2.

**Shu'brick** (shōō'brĭk), **John Templer.** 1788–1815. American naval officer; on the *Constitution* in its battle with the *Guerrière* (Aug. 19, 1812) and with the *Java* (Dec. 29, 1812); and on the *Hornet* when it captured the *Peacock* (Feb. 24, 1813). Lost at sea (1815). His brother **William Branford** (1790–1874) was also a naval officer; commanded Pacific squadron in Mexican War; commanded fleet (1858–59) sent to Paraguay to obtain satisfaction after a U.S. steamer had been fired on, and succeeded in obtaining a treaty settling the matter and all other matters then in dispute.

**Shu·bun** (shōō·bōōn). fl. 1st half of 15th century. Chinese painter naturalized as Japanese; used Chinese models and linked Chinese and Japanese art more closely; his pupil Kano Masanobu founded Kano school.

**Shudi, Burkat.** See John BROADWOOD.

**Shu'feldt** (shōō'fĕlt), **Robert Wilson.** 1850–1934. American army physician and ornithologist; served with Merritt, Crook, and Sheridan on the frontier (1876–81); curator of Army Medical Museum, Washington (1882).

**Shu·ja'-ud-din'** (shōō·jä'ōōd·dēn'). d. 1739. Nawab of Bengal (1725–39); subject to Delhi.

**Shul'gi** (shōōl'gē). Second king (2456?–?2409 B.C.) of Sumerian dynasty of Ur; son of Ur-Engur. His capital at Ur; consolidated empire; built many temples, some of which still exist.

**Shull** (shŭl). Family name of four American brothers, biologists: **James Marion** (1872–1948), artist-botanist. **George Harrison** (1874–1954), botanist; professor, Princeton (from 1915); known for work on variation, heredity, and plant breeding; founder and managing editor, *Genetics* (1916–25). **Charles Albert** (1879–1962), plant physiologist. **Aaron Franklin** (1881–1961), zoologist; known for work on sex determination, heredity, and evolution.

**Shulmanu-asharid.** = SHALMANESER II.

**Shun Chih** (shōōn' jĭr'). 1638–1661. Chinese emperor (1644–61), first of the Ch'ing, or Manchu, dynasty. Son of **Ch'ung Te** (chōōng' dŭ'), ruler of Manchuria (1627–35), who called himself emperor (1636–43). Placed on throne at Peking at age of six under regency of Prince Hwai; devoted his efforts to consolidating new realm; established Manchu supremacy but kept Chinese to assist in administration.

**Shurt'leff** (shûrt'lĕf; -lĭf), **Nathaniel Bradstreet.** 1810–1874. American antiquary, b. Boston; practiced medicine in Boston; mayor of Boston (1868–70); edited *Records of the Governor and Company of the Massachusetts Bay in New England* (1853–54), *Records of the Colony of New Plymouth in New England* (1855–57).

**Shurtleff, Roswell Morse.** 1838–1915. American landscape painter.

**Shu'ster** (shōō'stẽr), **George Nau'man** (nou'män). 1894– . American educator and writer; on editorial staff, *The Commonweal* (1925–39); president, Hunter Coll., New York (1940–60). Author of *English Literature* (1926), *The Catholic Church and Current Literature* (1929), *The Germans* (1932), *Like a Mighty Army* (1935); edited Hitler's *Mein Kampf* (1939).

**Shuster, William Morgan.** 1877–1960. American lawyer, financier, and publisher; treasurer general and financial adviser, Persia (1911–12); president, The Century Co. (1915–33), Appleton-Century Co. (from 1933).

**Shute** (shōōt), **Henry Augustus.** 1856–1943. American humorist; judge of police court, Exeter, N.H. (1883–1926); author of *The Real Diary of a Real Boy* (1902) and other books about boys, in most of which the hero is the autobiographical character "Plupy Shute."

**Shute, Nevil.** *Professional name used by* **Nevil Shute**

**Nor'way** (nôr'wā). 1899–1960. English aeronautical engineer and writer; served in World War I; entered airship construction company (1924). Founded airplane factory and served as its managing director. Author of *So Disdained* (U.S. title *The Mysterious Aviator;* 1928), *Lonely Road* (1932), *Ordeal* (1939), *Landfall* (1940), *The Pied Piper* (1942).

**Shute, Samuel.** 1662–1742. Colonial administrator in America; governor of Massachusetts Bay and New Hampshire (1716–27); engaged in continuous dispute with the assembly over his rights and policies.

**Shu·va'lov** (shŏŏ·vȧ'lôf), Count **Pëtr Andreevich.** 1827–1889. Russian diplomat; ambassador to Great Britain (1874–79). His brother Count **Pavel Andreevich** (1830–1908) was a general and diplomat; served in Crimean War (1854–56) and in Russo-Turkish War (1878–79); ambassador to Germany (1885–94).

**Shver'nik** (shvyăr'nyĭk), **Nikolai Mikhailovich.** 1888–1970. Soviet politician; member of central committee of Bolshevik party (from 1925); gen. secretary of all-union soviet of trade-unions (1930–44); chairman of presidium (1944–46), president (1946–53).

**Si'ba·wayh'** (sē'bă·wī'). *Arab.* **Sībawayh.** 750?–?793 A.D. Arab grammarian, b. in Persia; studied at Basra; resident at Baghdad; author of a treatise on grammar, commonly referred to as *al-Kitāb* ("The Book"), which settled the principles of Arabic grammar and is still recognized as authoritative.

**Sib'bern** (sĭb'ĕrn), **Frederik Christian.** 1785–1872. Danish philosopher.

**Si·be'li·us** (sĭ·bā'lĭ·ŏŏs), **Jean.** 1865–1957. Finnish composer; studied under Albert Becker in Berlin. Composer of symphonies, a violin concerto in D minor, choral works, tone poems, piano, violin, and violoncello pieces, and songs. Wrote the tone poems *The Swan of Tuonela, Lemminkäinen's Homecoming, Finlandia,* and waltzes *Valse Romantique* and *Valse Triste.*

**Si'bert** (sī'bĕrt), **William Luther.** 1860–1935. American army officer; grad. U.S.M.A., West Point (1884). Member, Isthmian Canal Commission (1907–14), in charge of construction of a large part of the Panama Canal. Commanded 1st division, A.E.F. (June, 1917); organized and directed chemical warfare service, U.S. army (1918–20).

**Sib'ley** (sĭb'lĭ), **Henry Hastings.** 1811–1891. American pioneer and politician; agent of American Fur Co. in trading with the Sioux; established himself at Mendota, near Fort Snelling, Minn. (1835); first governor of State of Minnesota (1858); led militia in suppressing Indian uprisings (1862, 1863, 1864).

**Sibley, Hiram.** 1807–1888. American businessman, b. North Adams, Mass.; became interested in possibilities of the telegraph; with Ezra Cornell, organized Western Union Telegraph Co. (chartered 1856); president of the company (1856–69); projected and carried through a transcontinental line, amalgamated (1864) with Western Union. Established extensive seed and nursery business. An incorporator (with Ezra Cornell) and benefactor of Cornell U.; contributed to foundation of Sibley College of Mechanical Engineering at Cornell; presented Sibley Hall to U. of Rochester.

**Sibley, John Langdon.** 1804–1885. American librarian; librarian of Harvard U. (1856–77).

**Sib'thorp** (sĭb'thôrp), **John.** 1758–1796. English botanist; professor of botany, Oxford (1784); studied flora of Mediterranean region.

**Si'card'** (sē'kȧr'), **Roche Ambroise Cucurron.** 1742–1822. Known as "Abbé Sicard." French educator of deaf mutes.

**Sick'el** (zĭk'ĕl), **Theodor von.** 1826–1908. German historian; professor, Vienna (1867); founded (1881) and directed (1881–1901) Austrian Historical Inst. in Rome.

**Sick'ert** (sĭk'ĕrt), **Walter Richard.** 1860–1942. British painter and etcher, b. Munich, of German descent. Among his canvases are *Noctes Ambrosianae, Ennui, Baccarat at Dieppe, Supper at the Casino.*

**Sick'ing·en** (zĭk'ĭng·ĕn), **Franz von.** 1481–1523. German knight; inherited estates on the Rhine; aided in election of Charles V as emperor (1519) and was made imperial chamberlain and councilor. Favored Reformation and headed a league (1522–23) for spreading Reformation throughout the German states and overthrowing hostile princes and ecclesiastical rulers; was defeated by alliance of archbishop of Trier, landgrave of Hesse, and count palatine of the Rhine.

**Sick'les** (sĭk''lz), **Daniel Edgar.** 1825–1914. American army officer and politician; practiced law in New York. Member, U.S. House of Representatives (1857–61). Shot and killed Philip Barton Key, son of Francis Scott Key, because of Key's attentions to Mrs. Sickles; tried and acquitted on plea of temporary mental aberration. At outbreak of Civil War, organized brigade in New York and commanded it in the Peninsular campaign. Promoted major general (1863); engaged at Chancellorsville and Gettysburg, where he lost his right leg in defense of his position on the famous Peach Orchard salient (July 2, 1863). Military governor of the Carolinas (1865–67). Retired as major general (1869). U.S. minister to Spain (1869–73). Again, member of U.S. House of Representatives (1893–95). Instrumental in obtaining Central Park for New York City.

**Siculus.** See CALPURNIUS SICULUS.

**Sid'dal** (sĭd''l), **Elizabeth Eleanor.** d. 1862. English milliner's assistant, and Dante Gabriel Rossetti's model; sat to Rossetti for most of his Beatrices; became engaged to Rossetti (1851); showed ability in verse and water colors; m. Rossetti (1860); victim of tuberculosis; died of overdose of laudanum taken to relieve neuralgia; buried with Rossetti's manuscript poems entombed in her coffin (afterwards opened for recovery of poems, 1869).

**Siddhartha,** Prince. See GAUTAMA BUDDHA.

**Sid'dons** (sĭd''nz), **Sarah,** *nee* **Kem'ble** (kĕm'b'l). 1755–1831. English tragic actress, b. in Wales; member of her father's traveling theatrical company (see KEMBLE family); m. (1773) her fellow actor William Siddons; attracted attention as Belvidera (1774); appeared first at Drury Lane as Portia (1775); after success in provinces returned to Drury Lane (1782) as Isabella in Garrick's version of Southerne's *Fatal Marriage,* scoring a triumph, and becoming acknowledged queen of the stage; played Shakespearean parts, including Lady Macbeth, her greatest role (from 1785), Volumnia in her brother John's version of *Coriolanus,* Desdemona, Rosalind, Ophelia; made great impression as Queen Catherine in her brother John's revival of *Henry VIII* (1788); gave her farewell performance as Lady Macbeth (1812); appeared in occasional benefit performances (the last in 1819). Created among all her parts only Elvira in *Pizzaro* (1799). Painted by Reynolds as the Tragic Muse, and by Gainsborough, among others.

**Sidetes.** See ANTIOCHUS VII of Syria.

**Sidg'wick** (sĭj'wĭk), **Henry.** 1838–1900. English philosopher; professor, Cambridge (1883–1900). One of founders and first president (1882–85, 1888–93) of Society for Psychical Research and member of Metaphysical Society. In philosophy a follower of John Stuart Mill; made his chief contribution in ethics; rejected intuitionism and egoistic hedonism, adopted a utilitarianism with intuitional basis in prudence, benevolence, and justice as axioms of practical reason. Author of *Methods of Ethics* (1874; on which his reputation chiefly rests),

*Principles of Political Economy* (1883), *Practical Ethics* (1898), etc.

His wife (m. 1876), **Eleanor Mildred** (1845–1936), sister of A. J. Balfour, actively supported movement for higher education for women and emancipation of women; became principal of Newnham Coll. (1892–1910).

**Arthur Sidgwick** (1840–1920), classical scholar and essayist; brother of Henry Sidgwick; edited works of Vergil and Aeschylus; author of Greek textbooks. His daughter **Ethel** (1877–1970), novelist and author of plays for children.

**Si′di Mo·ham′med** (sē′dĭ mo͝o·hăm′măd). Name of several rulers of Morocco, esp.: **Sidi Mohammed** (1712?–1789); sultan (1757–89); sought to introduce western European culture into Morocco; cultivated peaceful relations with Christian nations; founded Mogador (1760); abolished Christian slavery (1777). **Sidi Mohammed** (1803–1873); emperor of Morocco (1859–73); defeated by Spain (1859), and forced by the peace treaty following (1860) to pay large indemnity and cede territory. Extended to Europeans (1864) freedom of trade in his country. **Sidi Mohammed III** (1911–1961); sultan (1927–61) under French protectorate; 18th of the dynasty.

**Si′dis** (sĭ′dĭs), **Bo′ris** (bō′rĭs). 1867–1923. Psychologist and psychopathologist, b. Kiev, Russia; to U.S. (1887); established Sidis Psychotherapeutic Institute, Portsmouth, N.H. (1909) and practiced there (1909–23). Author of *An Experimental Study of Sleep* (1909), *The Psychology of Laughter* (1913), *The Causation and Treatment of Psychopathic Diseases* (1916), etc.

**Sid·ky′ Pa′sha, Ba·kir′** (bă·kēr′ sĭd·kē′ pá′shä). *Arab.* **al-Fa·rīq′** (ăl′fă·rēk′) **Bakīr Ṣidqi.** 1890–1937. Dictator of Iraq, b. in Kurdistan; served in Turkish army (1908–18), and in the army of King Faisal (1919 ff.); seized power by a coup d'état (1936); assassinated (Aug. 11, 1937).

**Sidmouth,** 1st Viscount. See Henry ADDINGTON.

**Sid′ney** (sĭd′nĭ). Name of a distinguished English family including: Sir **William** (1482?–1554); commanded English right at Flodden (1513); attended Henry VIII at Field of Cloth of Gold (1520); received manor of Penshurst in Kent (1552).

His son Sir **Henry** (1529–1586), administrator in Ireland; brought up at court as companion of Prince Edward; accompanied his brother-in-law, the earl of Sussex, lord deputy, to Ireland (1556); served as vice-treasurer, and in absences of Sussex, as lord justice (1558); president of Welsh marches (1559–86); lord deputy of Ireland (1565–71, 1575–78); restored Calvagh O'Donnell and crushed Shane O'Neill in Ulster; favored earl of Ormonde in Munster, arrested Desmond, leaving government to Desmond's brother, who was arrested later; forced to reverse his policy in Munster; reduced rebellious Butlers (brothers of earl of Ormonde) in Munster (1569); returned to Ireland (1575) after four years at English court and in Wales; once more pacified Ulster and southern Ireland; effected shire divisions on English model; suppressed rebellion of earl of Clanricarde and his sons (1576) and hunted Rory O'More to his death (1578); recalled by Queen Elizabeth because of discontent with his expenditures. His eldest son was Sir Philip Sidney (*q.v.*); a daughter, Mary, m. Henry Herbert, 2d Earl of Pembroke (see PEMBROKE).

Sir Henry's second son, **Robert** (1563–1626), Viscount **Lisle** (lĭl; lēl) and 1st Earl of **Leices′ter** [lĕs′tẽr] (fifth creation, 1618); accompanied his brother Sir Philip to Flushing and fought at Zutphen and Arnhem (1586); wounded at Steenwijck (1592), distinguished himself at Turnhout (1598); liaison officer between court and Essex during Essex's rebellion (1601); member of Virginia, East India, and Northwest Passage companies; wrote words for Dowland's songs. See Lady Mary WROTH.

Robert's son **Robert** (1595–1677), 2d earl; ambassador to Denmark and to France; m. (1616) Dorothy Percy; father of Algernon Sidney (*q.v.*) and the following:

Lady **Dorothy Sidney** (1617–1684), *later* Countess of **Sun′der·land** (sŭn′dẽr·lănd), celebrated as **Sach′a·ris′sa** (săk′ȧ·rĭs′ȧ) in poems of Edmund Waller (*q.v.*), who paid literary court to her (1634?–38); m. (1639) Henry Spencer (1620–1643; see SPENCER family), who was created earl of Sunderland (1643); benefactress of distressed clergy and Royalists.

**Philip Sidney** (1619–1698), 3d Earl of **Leicester,** styled Lord Lisle (till 1677), member of Short and Long parliaments, lord lieutenant of Ireland (1646–47), member of republican councils of state and of two Protectorate councils.

**Henry Sidney** *or* **Sydney** (1641–1704), Earl of **Rom′ney** (rŏm′nĭ; rŭm′-); envoy to France (1672), to The Hague (1679–81); commander in Dutch service (1681–85); accompanied William of Orange to England and Ireland; lord lieutenant of Ireland (1692); a lord justice (1697).

**Sid′ney** *or* **Syd′ney** (sĭd′nĭ), **Algernon.** 1622–1683. English republican leader and martyr. Son of Robert Sidney (1595–1677), 2d Earl of Leicester (see SIDNEY family), whom he accompanied on embassies to Denmark and France; served under his brother Philip, Lord Lisle, against Irish rebels (1641–43); wounded at Marston Moor, fighting on Parliamentary side (1644); governor of Colchester (1645), of Dover (1648–50); M.P. (1646); as commissioner for trial of Charles I, took no part in trial; a severe republican, retired (1653–59) on account of Cromwell's usurpation of power; member of council of state (1659), dispatched to Denmark and Sweden as mediator (1659–60). Pardoned by Charles II, returned to England (1677); as a republican, favored duke of Monmouth as successor to Charles II; negotiated with Louis XIV to secure aid for support of Monmouth, received moneys from French ambassador; discussed insurrection with Whig leaders (1683); on discovery of Rye House Plot sent to Tower of London, tried before Lord Jeffreys, convicted of treason, executed. Author of *Discourses Concerning Government* (1698); may have helped Penn with liberal provisions of Pennsylvanian constitution.

**Sidney, Margaret.** Pseudonym of Harriet Mulford Stone LOTHROP.

**Sidney,** Sir **Philip.** 1554–1586. English poet, statesman, and soldier, b. in Penshurst, Kent; eldest son of Sir Henry Sidney (see SIDNEY family) and Mary Dudley, sister of Queen Elizabeth's favorite, the earl of Leicester. With his father in Ireland (1576); ambassador to Emperor Rudolf and to prince of Orange (1577); presented defense of his father's Irish policy to Queen Elizabeth (1577). Saw much of Spenser (from 1578) and received dedication of *The Shepheardes Calender* (1579); member of the Areopagus, a group interested in writing English verse in classical meters; wrote masque, *Lady of May,* with which his uncle Leicester entertained the queen (1578). Fell out of favor of Queen Elizabeth after remonstrating against her proposed marriage with the duc d'Alençon; retired to Wilton, home of his sister Mary, Countess of Pembroke (see PEMBROKE). His pastoral romance *Arcadia,* in melodious and elaborate prose, much of it euphuistic, interspersed with poems (written 1580–81, for amusement of his sister Mary), was popular for a century, as well as influential in literature. Addressed to Penelope Devereux, daughter of earl of Essex (see DEVEREUX family), impassioned sonnets (1580–84), over 100 of which were later published with eleven songs as *Astrophel and Stella;* replied vigorously in *Defence of Poesie* (originally *Apologie for Poetrie*) to abusive Puritan pamphlet by Gosson, with discussion of essential nature and kinds of poetry and status of poetry in his own time. M.P. (1581); m. (1583) Frances, daughter of Sir Francis Walsingham, but continued to write sonnets to "Stella"; desired active part in enterprises of Frobisher, Hakluyt, and Raleigh, and in advancing Protestant cause against Spain; tricked out of going with Drake's buccaneering expedition, sent with Leicester to support Netherlanders against Spain (1585); with Prince Maurice made successful raid on Axel (1586); in attack on a convoy of provisions at Zutphen (1586) wounded in thigh and died 26 days after at Arnhem. Commemorated in Spenser's *Astrophel,* and in elegies by James VI, Breton, Drayton.

**Sidonius Apollinaris.** See APOLLINARIS SIDONIUS.

**Sidrach.** See SHADRACH.

**Sie′be** (zē′bĕ), **Augustus.** 1788–1872. German inventor in England; invented (1819) the modern diving suit.

**Sie′beck** (zē′bĕk), **Hermann.** 1842–1920. German philosopher.

**Sie′bold, von** (fôn zē′bôlt). Family of German scientists including: **Karl Kaspar** (1736–1807), anatomist, surgeon, and obstetrician. His son **Adam Elias** (1775–1828), obstetrician. Adam's son **Eduard Kaspar Jakob** (1801–1861), obstetrician. Another son of Adam, **Karl Theodor Ernst** (1804–1885), zoologist; rediscovered parthenogenesis in insects; worked on the intestines of worms and fish and on the development of the jellyfish. Another grandson of Karl Kaspar, **Philipp Franz van** (vän; fän) **Siebold** (1796–1866), Bavarian naturalist and traveler; with Dutch mission in Japan (1823–30); mediator between Japan and European countries (1859); wrote on Japanese flora, fauna, language, etc.

**Sie′den·topf** (zē′dĕn·tôpf), **Henry Friedrich Wilhelm.** 1872– . German physicist; chief of the microscope division of the Zeiss works and professor of microscopy at U. of Jena; with Richard Zsigmondy invented the ultramicroscope (1903).

**Sieg′bahn** (sēg′bän), **Karl Manne Georg.** 1886– . Swedish physicist; professor, U. of Lund (1920–23), Uppsala (1923–26), and at Royal Acad. of Sciences, Stockholm (from 1937); known for investigations in X-ray spectroscopy; discovered the M series in the X-ray spectrum; awarded the 1924 Nobel prize for physics (1925).

**Sie′gen** (zē′gĕn), **Ludwig von.** *Called* **von Sech′ten** (zĕκ′tĕn). 1609–after 1676. German engraver; discoverer of the art of mezzotint engraving.

**Sieg′fried′** (sĕg′frēd′), **André.** 1875–1959. French economist and historian; professor of economic geography, École des Sciences Politiques, Paris (1911) and Collège de France (1933); author of *Le Canada, les Deux Races* (1906), *L'Angleterre d'Aujourd'hui* (1924), *Les États-Unis d'Aujourd'hui* (1927; transl. as *America Comes of Age*), *Amérique Latine* (1933), *Le Canada, Puissance Internationale* (1937), *Suez and Panama* (transl. 1940), etc.

**Sieg′fried** (zēκ′frēt), **Hermann.** 1819–1879. Swiss cartographer; prepared atlas (known as *Siegfriedkarte*) of Switzerland, on the scale of 1 to 25,000.

**Sieg′lin** (zēκ′lĭn), **Wilhelm.** 1855–1935. German historian and geographer; author of *Schulatlas zur Geschichte des Altertums* (1899), etc.

**Sie′mens** (zē′mĕns; *Angl.* sē′mĕnz). Family of German electrical engineers and industrialists, including: **Werner von Siemens** (1816–1892); invented the dial telegraph (1846); first to suggest use of gutta-percha for insulation of conductors; with J. G. Halske founded at Berlin firm of Siemens & Halske for manufacture of telegraphic equipment (1847), subsequent expansion embracing manufacture of electrical apparatus and handling of electrical engineering projects; constructed first telegraph line in Germany (Berlin to Frankfurt am Main); proposed Siemens's mercury unit of resistance; invented the shuttle winding for the dynamo (1856); constructed a selenium photometer.

His brother **Wilhelm,** *later* Sir **William, Siemens** (1823–1883), b. in Lenthe; to England (1844), and naturalized (1859); invented a regenerative steam engine (1847); improved the regenerative furnace applied in Siemens process of making steel; designed ship *Faraday* which laid the Atlantic cable (1874); invented a pyrometer and the bathometer; laid electric tramway at Portrush, Ireland, one of first in United Kingdom (opened 1883).

Other brothers, b. in Menzendorf: **Friedrich Siemens** (1826–1904); worked at Wilhelm's firm in England; invented a regenerative smelting oven (1856), widely used in the glassmaking industry. **Karl von Siemens** (1829–1906); organized (1853–67) and was director (1880–94) of Russian branch of Siemens & Halske.

Werner's sons: **Wilhelm von Siemens** (1855–1919), b. in Berlin; director of Siemens & Halske after his father's death; contributed to development of incandescent lamp. **Carl Friedrich von Siemens** (1872–1941), b. in Charlottenburg; directed (1902–08) London division of firm and held various executive positions in German divisions of firm.

**Sie′me·ring** (zē′mĕ·rĭng), **Rudolf.** 1835–1905. German sculptor; executed monuments to Frederick the Great in Marienburg, Luther in Eisleben, and Emperor Frederick William I in Berlin, and the equestrian statue of George Washington in Philadelphia.

**Sie·mień′ski** (shĕ·myĕn′y′·skē), **Lucjan.** 1809–1877. Polish man of letters; best known as translator of Homer's *Odyssey* into Polish.

**Sien·kie′wicz** (shĕn·kyĕ′vēch), **Henryk.** 1846–1916. Polish novelist; educ. Warsaw. Among his notable novels are *With Fire and Sword* (1884), *The Deluge* (1886), *Without Dogma* (1891), *Children of the Soil* (Polish title *Rodzina Polanieckich;* 1893), *Quo Vadis?* (1896), and *The Crusaders* (4 vols., 1900). Awarded Nobel prize for literature (1905).

**Sierra, Gregorio Martínez.** See MARTÍNEZ SIERRA.

**Sie′ve·king** (zē′vĕ·kĭng), **Heinrich.** 1871–1946. German economist.

**Sieve′king** (sēv′kĭng), **Lancelot de Gi·berne′** (dĕ jĭ·bûrn′), *known as* **Lance** (låns). 1896– . English writer and playwright; educ. Cambridge; aviator in World War (prisoner, 1918–19); owner and editor, *The New Cambridge* (1919–22); joined British Broadcasting Co. (1924), and began production of radio plays; first to produce a television play. Author of *Dressing Gowns and Glue* (1919), *Gladstone Bags and Marmalade* (1920), *The Cud* (1922), *Stampede* (1924), *The Perfect Witch* (1935), *Silence in Heaven* (1936), etc.

**Sie′vers** (zē′fērs; -vērs), **Eduard.** 1850–1932. German philologist; professor, Jena (1871), Tübingen (1883), Halle (1887), Leipzig (1892). Among his works are *Grundzüge der Lautphysiologie* (1876), *Der Heliand und die Angelsächsiche Genesis* (1875), *Angelsächsische Grammatik* (1881; translated into English by A. S. Cook), and *Metrische Studien* (4 vols., 1901–19).

**Sie′vers** (sē′vērz), **Frederick William.** 1872–1966. American sculptor; studio in Richmond, Va. Among his works are portrait busts of James Madison and Zachary Taylor, in the Capitol, Richmond, Va.; portrait bust of Matthew Fontaine Maury, in American Hall of Fame; an equestrian statue of Gen. Robert E. Lee with group of Confederate soldiers, at Gettysburg, Pa.

**Sie′vers** (*Russ.* syē′vyẽrs; *Ger.* zē′fẽrs, -vẽrs), Count **Yakov Efimovich,** *Ger. names* **Jakob Johann.** 1731–1808. Russian statesman, of German origin; governor of Novgorod (1764) and later of Novgorod, Tver, and Pskov; retired (1781). Ambassador to Poland (1789), and had share in negotiating partitions of that country; recalled (1794). Director of water communications (1797); the canal between the Volkhov and Msta rivers was built under his direction and bears his name.

**Sie′yès′** (syā′yâs′), **Emmanuel Joseph.** 1748–1836. Generally known as "Abbé Sieyès." French Revolutionary leader; canon of Tréguier (1775) and, later, vicar-general of the bishop of Chartres. Sympathized with reform movement preceding French Revolution and became prominent with publication of pamphlet on the third estate, *Qu'est-ce que le Tiers État?* (1789). Member of the States-General (1789), National Assembly, National Convention (1792–95), Council of Five Hundred (1795–99), and the Directory (1799); one of chief organizers of coup d'état (1799) which raised Napoleon to first consul. Appointed senator and count of the empire by Napoleon. Exiled at the Restoration; returned to France (1830).

**Sifadda, Siful.** See Henrik Arnold WERGELAND.

**Sif′ton** (sĭf′tŭn), Sir **Clifford.** 1861–1929. Canadian statesman; member of Dominion legislature (1896–1911); Canadian minister of the interior and superintendent general of Indian affairs (1896–1905).

**Si′ge·bert** (*Ger.* zē′gĕ·bĕrt; *Fr.* sēzh′bâr′). Name of three kings of the Franks, especially: **Sigebert I** (535–575), youngest son of Clotaire; king of Austrasia (561–575); m. (561) Brunhilde (*q.v.*); defeated Avars (562); later (567) held prisoner by them; spent last part of reign in civil wars with brothers Guntran and Chilperic; assassinated.

**Si′ge·bert′ of Gem′bloux′** (sēzh′bâr′, zhäɴ′blōō′). 1030?–1112. Belgian chronicler; chief work, a chronicle of the years 381–1111.

**Si′gel** (sē′gĕl; *Ger.* zē′-), **Franz.** 1824–1902. Union army commander in American Civil War, b. in Sinsheim, Baden, Germany; to U.S. (1852) and settled in New York City (1852–57) and St. Louis (1857–61). Served through Civil War; organized infantry regiment and became its colonel; brigadier general of volunteers (May 17, 1861), major general (Mar. 21, 1862); resigned commission (1865). Publisher and editor, *New Yorker Deutsches Volksblatt.* A bronze equestrian statue of Sigel (by Karl Bitter) stands on Riverside Drive, New York City.

**Si′ger′ de Bra′bant′** (sē′zhā′ dẽ brȧ′bäɴ′). 1235?–?1281. French philosopher; a follower of Averroism and, as such, opposed by Thomas Aquinas and Albertus Magnus and condemned by Bishop Tempier of Paris (1270 and 1277). Immortalized by Dante in canto X of *Il Paradiso.*

**Sig′e·rist** (sĭg′ĕ·rĭst; *Ger.* zē′gĕ-), **Henry Ernest.** 1891–1957. Authority on the history of medicine, b. Paris; educ. in Zurich, London, Munich; M.D., Zurich (1917); professor of history of medicine, Leipzig (1925–32), Johns Hopkins (1932–47). His many works (in German and English) include: *Antike Heilkunde* (1927), *Man and Medicine* (1932), *The Great Doctors* (1933), *American Medicine* (1934), *Socialized Medicine in the Soviet Union* (1937), *Medicine and Human Welfare* (1941).

**Sig′er·son** (sĭg′ẽr·s'n), **Dora.** See Clement SHORTER.

**Sigerson, George.** c. 1833–1925. Irish physician and Gaelic scholar; president of Irish Literary Society; one of those promoting the Celtic revival.

**Sig′is·mund** (sĭj′ĭs·mŭnd; sĭg′-; *Ger.* zē′gĭs·mo͝ont). *Fr.* **Si′gis′mond′** (sē′zhēs′môɴ′). d. 524. King of Burgundy (516–524), succeeding his father, Gundobad; defeated and made prisoner (523) by Clodomir, King of the Franks.

**Sigismund.** 1368–1437. King of Hungary (1387–1437) and of Bohemia (1419–37); Holy Roman emperor (1411–37; crowned 1433) of the house of Luxemburg; son of Charles IV; m. (1387) Mary, Queen of Hungary, after rescuing her from prison; undertook crusade against the Turks (1396) but badly defeated at Nicopolis (Nikopol) by Bajazet I; inaugurated Council of Constance (1414); implicated in the death of John Huss (1415); defeated in war with Bohemia (1420–22).

**Sigismund.** Name of three kings of Poland:

**Sigismund I.** 1467–1548. Son of Casimir IV. Grand duke of Lithuania (1505–48) and king of Poland (1506–48). Waged war, generally with success, against Russia, Walachia, and Moldavia (1508–28); encouraged reform of currency; concluded war with Teutonic Order (1525); aided Hungary against the Turks at Mohács (1526) and siege of Vienna (1529); Lutheranism introduced.

**Sigismund II Au·gus′tus** (ô·gŭs′tŭs). 1520–1572. King (1548–72). Son of Sigismund I. Continued struggles with landowning nobility; during his reign influence of Reformation extended and Lithuania and Ukraine united to Poland (1569); last of the Jagellons.

**Sigismund III** *or* **Sigismund Va′sa′** (vä′sȧ′). 1566–1632. Son of John III of Sweden. King of Poland (1587–1632) and king of Sweden (1592–1604; crowned 1594). In constant struggle with Jan Zamojski, Polish chancellor (1587–1605); lost crown of Sweden to his uncle (later, 1604, Charles IX) by defeat at Stångebro (1598); left Sweden but never relinquished claim to its throne; state of anarchy in Poland (1606–10); at outbreak of Thirty Years' War (1618) joined the emperor against the Protestants.

**Sigismund.** 1566–1632. King of Sweden (1592–1604). See SIGISMUND III, King of Poland.

**Si′gnac′** (sē′nyȧk′), **Paul.** 1863–1935. French painter, esp. of landscapes and marines; with Georges Seurat (*q.v.*) regarded as a founder of neoimpressionism.

**Signorelli, Luca.** *In full* **Luca d'E·gi′dio di Ven·tu′ra de' Si′gno·rel′li** (dā·jē′dyō dē vān·to͞o′rä dā sē′nyō-rĕl′lē). *Also called* **Luca da Cor·to′na** (dä kôr·tō′nä). 1441–1523. Italian painter; notable as first Italian artist to use nude figures as means of pictorial expression. His frescoes include *Life of Moses* (Sistine Chapel, Vatican) and *Conversion of St. Paul* (church at Loreto).

**Si·go′nio** (sē·gô′nyō), **Carlo.** *Lat.* **Si·go′ni·us** (sĭ·gō′-nĭ·ŭs). 1524–1584. Italian humanist.

**Sig′our·ney** (sĭg′ẽr·nĭ), **Lydia Howard,** *nee* **Hunt′ley** (hŭnt′lĭ). 1791–1865. American author; m. Charles Sigourney (1819; d. 1854). Contributed verse and miscellaneous articles to current periodicals (from c. 1820); immensely popular in her day; produced more than sixty volumes, as *Moral Pieces in Prose and Verse, How to be Happy, Letters to Young Ladies, Pocahontas and Other Poems, Poems Religious and Elegiac, The Faded Hope.*

**Sigs′bee** (sĭgz′bē), **Charles Dwight.** 1845–1923. American naval officer; grad. U.S.N.A., Annapolis (1863). Commanded coast survey steamer *Blake* and co-operated with Alexander Agassiz in deep-sea exploration in Gulf of Mexico (1875–78); invented special apparatus for this work. Commanded U.S. battleship *Maine* at time it was blown up in Havana harbor (Feb. 15, 1898); commanded the *St. Paul* in Spanish-American War; defeated Spanish destroyer *Terror* and Spanish cruiser *Isabella II* off San Juan, Puerto Rico. Promoted rear admiral (1903); retired (1907).

**Si'gurd** (sĭg'gŏŏrd). Name of two rulers of Norway: **Sigurd I.** 1089?–1130. Called "the Crusader." King (1103–30). One of the three sons of Magnus III; ruled jointly with Eystein (1103–22) and Olaf (1103–15) and alone after their deaths; made expedition to Holy Land (1107–11), having many adventures in Spain, Sicily, and at Constantinople; quarreled with Eystein but civil war avoided; invaded Sweden (1123).

**Sigurd II.** *Called* **Sigurd Mund** (mŏŏn), *i.e.* Mouth. 1134–1155. King (1137–55). A son of Harold Gille; joint ruler with his brother Inge.

**Si'gurd** (sē'gŭrd). Pseudonym of Alfred, Baron HEDENSTIERNA.

**Si'gurds·son** (sĭ'gûrths·sŏn), **Jón.** 1811–1879. Icelandic man of letters and statesman; archivist and librarian of Royal Norse Archaeological Society (1847–65). Published *Icelandic Sagas* (2 vols., 1843–47), *Edda Snorra Sturlusonar* (2 vols., 1848–52), *Diplomatarium Islandicum* (vol. I, period 874–1264, pub. 1857–76). In political field, leader in long struggle to gain liberal reforms from Danish government; regarded as chiefly responsible for Denmark's grant of a constitution to Iceland (1874).

**Si'gur·jóns'son** (sĭ'gûr·yōns'sŏn), **Jóhann.** 1880–1919. Icelandic poet and playwright; his plays include *Dr. Rung* (1905), *The Hraun Farm* (1908), *Eyvind of the Hills* (1911), *The Liar* (1917), *The Story of Burnt Njal.*

**Sij'mons** (sī'mōns), **Barend.** 1853–1935. Dutch philologian; authority on Norse sagas.

**Si·kan'dar II** (sĭ·kŭn'dẽr). d. 1517. Second Lodi sultan of Delhi (1489–1517); conquered Bihar (1492); ruled extensive but weakly governed kingdom.

**Si·kor'ski** (sē̇·kôr'skē̇), **Władysław.** 1881–1943. Polish general, statesman, and writer, esp. on military matters; grad. Univ. Technical Coll., Lwów (1908); a leader of Piłsudski's Polish legions (1914–18); commanded an army against Russia (1920); prime minister of Poland (Dec., 1922–May, 1923); minister of war (Feb., 1924–Nov., 1925); opposed Piłsudski's coup d'état (1926); to Paris (1928); after German conquest of Poland (1939), became commander in chief of the Polish army in France and prime minister of Polish government in exile.

**Si·kor'sky** (sĭ·kôr'skĭ; *Russ.* syĭ·kôr'skû·ĭ), **Igor Ivan.** 1889–1972. Aeronautical engineer, b. in Kiev, Russia; to U.S. (1919) and naturalized (1928). Interested in airplane design from youth. Built and flew first multimotor airplane (1913); produced first commercial amphibian airplane (1928); developed practical helicopter (1939). Organized companies to manufacture planes of his design (1923ff.), merged into United Aircraft corporation (1929) as a subsidiary of which he remained head until his retirement (1957).

**Si'las** (sī'lăs). In the Bible, a worker in the early Christian church at Jerusalem, companion of Paul on his second missionary journey (*Acts* xv. 40 ff.); generally regarded as the **Sil·va'nus** [sĭl·vā'nŭs] (*in Douay Bible* **Syl·va'nus** [sĭl-]) of the Pauline epistles.

**Sil'cher** (zĭl'кẽr), **Friedrich.** 1789–1860. German composer; wrote music for many German popular songs, including *Annchen von Tharau, Ich weiss nicht was soll es bedeuten, Morgen muss ich fort von hier.*

**Si'les** (sē'lās), **Hernando.** 1881–1942. Bolivian jurist and Nationalist party leader; president of Bolivia (1926–30); deposed by revolution.

**Sil'hou·ette'** (sē'lwĕt'; *Angl.* sĭl'ŏŏ·ĕt'), **Étienne de.** 1709–1767. French controller general of finances (1759); introduced reforms but incurred ridicule and hostility on the part of the nobility by economies and attempts to reduce pensions and privileges. It was by way of ridicule that the nobles applied his name to a mere outline profile drawing, "silhouette."

**Sil'i·us I·tal'i·cus** (sĭl'ĭ·ŭs ĭ·tăl'ĭ·kŭs), **Tiberius Catius.** 25 (or 26)–101 A.D. Latin epic poet and politician; consul (68 A.D.); proconsul in Asia; withdrew to private life; acquired Cicero's villa at Tusculum; became patron of letters; author of an epic, *Punica* (17 books, about 14,000 lines), on the Second Punic War.

**Sill** (sĭl), **Edward Rowland.** 1841–1887. American poet and essayist, b. Windsor, Conn.; professor of English, U. of California (1874–82). His essays and poems have been collected and published (*The Prose of Edward Rowland Sill*, 1900; *The Poems of Edward Rowland Sill*, 1902). Among his better known single poems are *The Fool's Prayer* and *Opportunity.*

**Sil'lan·pää'** (sĭl'lån·pă'), **Frans Eemil.** 1888–1964. Finnish writer, b. in southwestern Finland; grad. U. of Helsinki; author of *Life and the Sun* (1916), *The Maid Silja* (transl. 1933), *Meek Heritage* (1919; transl. 1938), and other novels and collections of short stories; awarded Nobel prize for literature (1939).

**Sil'li·man** (sĭl'ĭ·măn), **Benjamin.** 1779–1864. American chemist and geologist; professor, Yale (1802–53). Founded (1818) and edited *The American Journal of Science and Arts*, usually called *Silliman's Journal;* active in organization of Yale medical school. His son **Benjamin** (1816–1885), chemist, became his father's teaching assistant; associate editor (1838) and later editor, *American Journal of Science;* with John P. Norton, established at Yale a school of applied chemistry which later became the Sheffield Scientific School; professor of chemistry, Yale (from 1853). Both father and son were original members of National Acad. of Sciences (1863).

**Sills** (sĭlz), **Kenneth Charles Morton.** 1879–1954. American educator, b. Halifax, Nova Scotia; president of Bowdoin (from 1918); author of *The First American and Other Poems* (1911).

**Si'lo·é'** (sē'lō̇·ā'), **Gil de.** fl. 1475?–?1505. Spanish sculptor; one of the last exponents of Gothic sculpture in Spain. His son **Diego** (d. 1563) was a sculptor and architect; leading Spanish representative of Italian High Renaissance decorative art.

**Si·lo'ne** (sē̇·lō'nā), **Ignazio.** 1900–1978. Italian writer; opponent of Fascism, living in exile at Zurich; author of *Fontamara, Bread and Wine, School for Dictators, The Fox and the Camellias*, etc.

**Sil'va** (sĭl'vȧ), **Antônio José da.** *Called* **O Ju·de'u** (ŏŏ zhŏŏ·thā'ŏŏ). 1705–1739. Portuguese playwright; imprisoned by Inquisition (1726, 1737–39); burned at stake (Oct. 19, 1739); author of burlesque comedies, parodies of mythological and classical subjects, and comedies of manners.

**Silva, Inocêncio Francisco da.** 1810–1876. Portuguese bibliographer.

**Silva Carvalho, José da.** See CARVALHO.

**Silva Guimarães, Bernardo Joaquin da.** See GUIMARÃES.

**Silva Leitão, João Baptista da.** See ALMEIDA-GARRETT.

**Silvanus.** See SILAS.

**Sil·ve'la** (sē̇l·vā'lä), **Francisco.** 1843–1905. Spanish lawyer and statesman; as minister of justice (1883–84), sponsored legislation providing for new civil and criminal codes; premier of Spain (1899–1900, 1902–03).

**Sil'ver** (sĭl'vẽr), **Ab'ba** (ăb'ȧ) **Hil'lel** (hĭl'ĕl). 1893–1963. Rabbi, b. in Lithuania; to U.S. in youth; rabbi of The Temple, Cleveland, Ohio (from 1917); author of *Religion in a Changing World* (1930), etc.

**Sil·ve'ri·us** (sĭl·vẽr'ĭ·ŭs), **Saint.** d. 538? Pope (536–?538). Elected through influence of Theodat, King of the Ostrogoths; arrested by Belisarius (537) and exiled; restored by Justinian but soon again exiled.

**Sil'ver·man** (sĭl'vẽr·măn), **Joseph.** 1860–1930. American rabbi, b. Cincinnati, Ohio; junior rabbi (1888–97) and rabbi (1897–1922), emeritus (1922–30), Temple Emanu-El, New York City; active in social-service work and in forwarding the Zionist movement; contributing editor to the *Jewish Encyclopedia.*

**Silvester.** See SYLVESTER, popes and antipopes.

**Sil'ves'tre** (sēl'vĕs'tr'), **Louis de.** 1675–1760. French painter; director, Dresden Acad. of Art (1716); returned to Paris (1748).

**Silvestre, Paul Armand.** 1837–1901. French writer; on staff of *Gil Blas* (from 1879); his early work chiefly in verse; for *Gil Blas* wrote humorous and somewhat Rabelaisian tales, as *Les Farces de mon Ami Jacques* (1881), *Les Bêtises de mon Oncle* (1883), *Fabliaux Gaillards* (1888); also composed librettos for several operas, including Saint-Saëns's *Henry VIII* and Godard's *Jocelyn.*

**Silvestre de Sacy,** Baron. See SACY.

**Sim'coe** (sĭm'kō), **John Graves.** 1752–1806. English soldier; first lieutenant governor of Upper Canada (1792–94); clashed with colonists over military methods; virtual founder of Toronto as capital.

**Si'me·non'** (sēm'nôN'), **Georges.** *Pen name of* **Georges Sim** (sēm). 1903– . Novelist, b. in Liège, of Breton father and Belgian mother; lived in France (1933–40); author of numerous popular novels (under a variety of pseudonyms), a series of detective stories centered about the fictional Inspector Maigret (many of them translated into English), and other fiction, as *In Two Latitudes, Affairs of Destiny, Tropic Moon.*

**Sim'e·on** (sĭm'ē·ŭn). In the Bible: (1) Jacob's second son (*Genesis* xxix. 33), ancestor of one of the twelve tribes of Israel. (2) *In R.V.* **Sym'e·on** (sĭm'ē·ŭn). A devout Jew who, when he saw the infant Jesus in the temple, uttered the song now known as the *Nunc Dimittis.*

**Sim'e·on** (sĭm'ē·ŭn; *Bulg.* sĭ·mâ·ôn') *or* **Sym'e·on** (sĭm'ē·ŭn; *Old Bulg.* sōō·mâ·ôn'). d. 927 A.D. Bulgarian sovereign; succeeded his father, Boris, as prince of Bulgaria (893); at war with Byzantine Empire (894–897); secured a peace (897) by which Constantinople paid tribute; defeated Magyars; after death of Leo VI (912) again waged war with Byzantines (913–14, 919–24); assumed title (925) of czar (emperor) of the Romans and Bulgars; educated as a monk, made his court a cultural center.

**Sim'e·on** (sĭm'ē·ŭn), **Charles.** 1759–1836. English evangelical preacher; perpetual curate of Trinity Church, Cambridge (1783–1836); leader of evangelical revival in Church of England.

**Sim'e·on** *or* **Sym'e·on of Dur'ham** (sĭm'ē·ŭn, dûr'ăm). fl. 1130. English chronicler; precentor of Durham; compiler of a history of the church of Durham (printed 1732) and a history of the kings of Northumbria.

**Sim'e·on Sty·li'tes** (sĭm'ē·ŭn stī·lī'tēz; stĭ-), Saint. 390?–459. Syrian ascetic; first and most widely known pillar saint, or stylite (Greek *stylites,* from *stylos,* pillar); passed the last 30 years of his life on top of a pillar, about 60 feet high. From this perch he preached, made many converts, and exercised through his disciples a considerable influence.

**Sim'mel** (zĭm'ĕl), **Georg.** 1858–1918. German philosopher and sociologist.

**Sim'mons** (sĭm'ŭnz), **Edward,** *orig.* **Edward Emerson.** 1852–1931. American painter, b. Concord, Mass.; best known for his murals as in the Library of Congress in Washington, and the Massachusetts State House in Boston.

**Simmons, Franklin.** 1839–1913. American sculptor; studio in Lewiston, Me., later in Waterville, Brunswick, and Portland, and in Rome, Italy (from 1867). Among his works are equestrian statue of John Alexander Logan, in Washington; bronze statue of Longfellow, Portland, Me.; and portrait busts of Grant, Sherman, etc.

**Simmons, Furnifold McLendell.** 1854–1940. American lawyer and legislator; member, U.S. House of Representatives (1887–89), and Senate (1901–31); chairman, Senate Finance Committee (1913–19), and cosponsor with Representative O. W. Underwood of Underwood-Simmons Tariff Act (1913).

**Simms** (sĭmz), **William Gilmore.** 1806–1870. American writer, b. Charleston, S.C.; author of novels, books of poetry, histories (*A History of South Carolina,* 1840; *South Carolina in the Revolution,* 1854; etc.), and biographies (*Marion, Nathanael Greene,* etc.).

**Sim'nel** (sĭm'nĕl; -n'l), **Lambert.** 1477?–?1534. English impostor; educated and put forward by young Oxford priest as personator of the duke of Clarence's son Edward (1475–1499), Earl of Warwick, who was imprisoned in Tower; taken to Ireland (1487), backed by his pretended aunt, Margaret, Duchess of Burgundy, sister of Edward IV, gained powerful following, crowned as King Edward VI in Dublin Cathedral (1487); landed in Lancashire with force of Germans and ill-armed Irish levies; defeated at Stoke (1487); pardoned and became royal falconer.

**Si'mon** (sī'mŭn). In the Bible, name of two of the twelve apostles: (1) **Simon Peter.** = PETER. (2) **Simon Ze·lo'tes** (zē·lō'tēz), *i.e.* the zealot *or* the Cananaean, *D.V.* Cananean, *A.V.* Canaanite (*Matthew* x. 4; *Mark* iii. 18; *Luke* vi. 15; *Acts* i. 13).

**Si'mon'** (sē'môN'), **André Louis.** 1877–1970. French wine authority, b. in Paris; editor of *Wine and Food Quarterly.* Among his many books are a history of the wine trade in England, *The Art of Good Living* (1929), *Madeira Wine* (1933), *Champagne* (1934), *A Dictionary of Wine* (1936), *André Simon's French Cook Book* (1939).

**Si'mon** (sī'mŭn), **Herbert Alexander.** 1916– . American economist. At Carnegie-Mellon U. (1949– ); awarded Nobel prize for economics (1978).

**Si'mon** (sī'mŭn), Sir **John Allse'brook** (?ôls'brŏŏk). Viscount **Simon** (cr. 1940). 1873–1954. British lawyer and politician; grad. Oxford; called to bar (1899); junior counsel for British government in Alaska Boundary Arbitration (1903); M.P. (1906–18; 1922–40); solicitor general (1910); attorney general (1913); home secretary (1915–16); chairman of Indian statutory commission (1927–30); foreign secretary (1931–35); home secretary, and deputy leader of House of Commons (1935–37); chancellor of the exchequer (1937–40); lord chancellor (1940–45).

**Si'mon'** (sē'môN'), **Jules François Simon Suisse** (sü·ēs'). 1814–1896. French philosopher and statesman; succeeded Cousin as professor at the Sorbonne, Paris (1839); member of the Constituent Assembly (1848–50); lost his professorship because of refusal to take oath required by the emperor (1852). Member of Corps Législatif (1863–70) and steadily opposed the government; minister of public instruction in the government of national defense (1870–71, 1871–73); senator for life (1875); premier of France (1876–77).

**Simon, Richard.** 1638–1712. French Roman Catholic theologian, member of the Congregation of the Oratory (to 1678). Among his works are *Histoire Critique du Vieux Testament* (1678) which brought violent criticism from both Roman Catholics and Protestants, *Histoire Critique du Texte du "Nouveau Testament"* (1683), etc.

**Si'mon** (sī'mŭn), **Richard Leo.** 1899–1960. American publisher, b. New York City; A.B., Columbia (1920); cofounder (1924; with Max L. Schuster, *q.v.*) and partner, Simon and Schuster, book publishers.

**Si'mon'** (sē'môN'), **Théodore.** 1873–1961. French psychologist; authority on the mental development of children; collaborated with Alfred Binet in devising the Binet-Simon intelligence test.

**Si'mon de Mont'fort** (sī'mŭn dē mŏnt'fērt; *Fr.* sē'-môN' dē môN'fôr'). See MONTFORT.

**Si'mon Ma'gus** (sī'mŭn mā'gŭs). In the Bible, a Samaritan sorcerer, converted by Philip (*Acts* viii. 9–24) and severely rebuked by Peter for offering money to purchase the power of giving the Holy Ghost—hence the term *simony*, applied in ecclesiastical law to traffic in sacred things, esp. the buying and selling of benefices.

**Si'monds** (sī'mŭn(d)z), **Frank Herbert.** 1878–1936. American journalist, b. Concord, Mass.; assoc. editor, New York *Tribune* (1915–18); contributing editor, *Review of Reviews* magazine (1914–33). Attained distinction as war correspondent. Among his books are *They Shall Not Pass—Verdun* (1916), *History of the World War* (5 vols., 1917), *Can Europe Keep the Peace?* (1931), *Can America Stay at Home?* (1932).

**Simonds, George Sherwin.** 1874–1938. American army officer; grad. U.S.M.A., West Point (1899). Brigadier general, National Army, in World War (1917–19); commanded infantry brigade in Canal Zone (1925–27); deputy chief of staff, U.S. army (1935–36).

**Si'mone'** (sē'môn'). *Real name* **Pauline Ben'da'** (băN'dȧ'). 1880– . French actress; made debut in Bernstein's *Le Détour* (1902); appeared in several plays by Bernstein, by Rostand (*Chantecler*, *L'Aiglon*), and others.

**Si·mo'ne Mar·ti'ni** (sē·mō'nȧ mär·tē'nē). See MARTINI.

**Si·mon'i·des of A·mor'gos** (sī·mŏn'ĭ·dēz, ȧ·môr'gŏs). Greek poet of 7th century B.C.; native of Samos; founder of a colony on island of Amorgos; wrote esp. in iambics; only fragments of his work extant.

**Simonides of Ce'os** (sē'ŏs). Greek poet of late 6th and early 5th centuries B.C., b. on island of Ceos; resident in court of Hipparchus at Athens (to 514 B.C.), in Thessaly, and later in life in court of Hiero of Syracuse; author especially of lyric verse, including odes, elegies, dirges, epigrams, and hymns to the gods; only fragments of his works extant.

**Si'mo'nis'** (sē'mô'nēs'), **Eugène.** 1810–1882. Belgian sculptor; among his works are the equestrian statue of Godfrey of Bouillon in Brussels, and bas-reliefs for the Théâtre de la Monnaie in Brussels.

**Simons, Menno.** See MENNO SIMONS.

**Si'mo·vić** (sē'mō·vēt'y'; *Angl.* -vĭch), **Dušan.** 1882–1962. Yugoslav general and politician; premier of Yugoslavia (1941–1942); cabinet official in Yugoslav government in London (1942).

**Sim·pli'ci·us** (sĭm·plĭsh'ĭ·ŭs; -plĭsh'ŭs), **Saint.** Pope (468–483). During his pontificate Western Empire fell before barbarians.

**Simplicius.** Greek Neoplatonic philosopher of early 6th century A.D.; native of Cilicia; disciple of Ammonius and Damascius; author of commentaries on some of Aristotle's works, and on the *Enchiridion* of Epictetus.

**Simp'son** (sĭm(p)'s'n), **Bertram Lenox.** See Putnam WEALE.

**Simpson, Edmund Shaw.** 1784–1848. Actor and theater manager, b. in England; to U.S. (1809) and made success in comedy roles; acting manager (1812–40) and sole lessee and manager (1840–48) of the Park Theater, New York City. His son **Edward** (1824–1888) was a naval officer; first head of department of ordnance at U.S.N.A., Annapolis (1858–62); on ironclad *Passaic* in attacks on Fort Wagner and Fort Sumter (1863); rear admiral (1884); retired (1886).

**Simpson, Evan John.** *Pseudonym* **Evan John.** 1901–1953. British playwright and novelist; author of *Stranger's Gold*, *King's March*, *Crippled Splendor* (novel), *Prelude to Massacre*, *King-at-arms*, *King's Masque* (historical romance, 1941).

**Simpson,** Sir **George.** 1792–1860. Canadian explorer, b. in Scotland; administrator (1821–56) of Hudson's Bay Company's territory; crossed North American continent (1828); sent out northwestern expedition (1837); made overland journey round the world (1841–42); Simpson's Falls and Cape George Simpson named after him.

**Simpson, Helen de Guer'ry** (dē gĕr'ĭ). 1897–1940. English novelist; m. Denis Browne (1927); author of *Acquittal* (1925), *Boomerang* (1932; awarded James Tait Black memorial prize), *Henry VIII* (1934), *Saraband for Dead Lovers* (1935), *Maid No More* (1940), etc.; collaborated with Clemence Dane in *Enter Sir John* (1929), *Printer's Devil* (1930), *Re-enter Sir John* (1932).

**Simpson, James Hervey.** 1813–1883. American army officer; served in Seminole War (1837–38); on topographical engineering duty (1838–61); served through Civil War; brevetted brigadier general (1865); on survey and engineering duty until retirement (1880); author of *The Shortest Route to California* (1869), *Coronado's March in Search of the Seven Cities of Cibola* (1871), *Exploration... of Utah* (1876), etc.

**Simpson,** Sir **James Young.** 1811–1870. Scottish physician; first to use ether as anesthetic in obstetric practice (1847); discovered anesthetic property of chloroform (1847), the use of which he also introduced in obstetric practice; originated means of diagnosis.

**Simpson, Matthew.** 1811–1884. American Methodist Episcopal clergyman; bishop (1852); spoke widely in support of Union cause during Civil War; delivered eulogy at Lincoln's burial in Springfield, Ill.

**Simpson, Thomas.** 1710–1761. English mathematician; author of *New Treatise on Fluxions* (1737).

**Simpson,** Sir **William John Ritchie.** 1855–1931. British physician; on government commissions to South Africa, Hong Kong, etc. to investigate causes of plague; director of tropical hygiene, Ross Institute and Hospital for Tropical Medicine.

**Sim'rock** (zĭm'rŏk), **Karl.** 1802–1876. German writer and language scholar; studied old German legends and literature; translated the *Nibelungenlied*, the *Edda*, and several poems of the Arthurian cycle; compiled *Heldenbuch* (6 vols., 1843–49), *Deutsche Volksbücher* (13 vols., 1845–66), and *Handbuch der Deutschen Mythologie...* (1853–55).

**Sims** (sĭmz), **George Robert.** 1847–1922. English journalist and playwright, b. London; under pseudonym **Dag'o·net** (dăg'ō·nĕt; -nĭt) wrote "Mustard and Cress" columns in the *Referee*. Among his books and plays are *The Dagonet Ballads*, *Rogues and Vagabonds*, *Dorcas Dene, Detective* (1897), *Anna of the Underworld*, *Harbour Lights*, *Little Christopher Columbus*, *Two Little Vagabonds*, *The Romany Rye*, *Gipsy Earl*, *Puss in Boots*, *In Gay Piccadilly*, *A Scarlet Sin*, etc.

**Sims, William Sow'den** (sou'd'n). 1858–1936. American naval officer, b. Port Hope, Ont., Canada, of United States parents; to U.S. as a child. Grad. U.S.N.A., Annapolis (1880). Commissioned rear admiral (Jan., 1917), vice-admiral (May, 1917), admiral (Dec., 1918), reverting to permanent rank of rear admiral after World War (Mar., 1919). Commanded American naval operations in European waters (Apr., 1917–Mar., 1919). Submitted lengthy report (1920) charging that serious errors had been made by U.S. Navy Department in management of naval operations during World War. Retired (Oct., 1922). Coauthor, with Burton Jesse Hendrick, of *The*

*Victory at Sea* (awarded Pulitzer prize for history, 1920).

**Sims, Winfield Scott.** 1844–1918. American inventor; invented electrically propelled torpedo (patented 1882), a pneumatic gun used by American troops in Cuba during Spanish-American War, a wireless dirigible torpedo, and a dynamite gun.

**Si·nan′** (sĭ·nän′). 1489?–1587. Turkish architect; designed more than 300 buildings, including the Suleiman mosque in Constantinople and the Selim mosque in Adrianople.

**Sin′clair** (sĭng′klâr; sĭn′-; sĭn·klâr′). Name (variant of Saint Clair) of Scottish family descended from Anglo-Norman barons, members of which have held the earldoms of **Ork′ney** [ôrk′nĭ] (1379–1471) and of **Caith′ness** [kăth′nĕs; kăth·nĕs′], including: Sir **William Sinclair** *or* **Saint Clair** [sĭng′klâr; sĭn′-; sĭn·klâr′] (1240–?1303), Baron of **Ross′lyn** [rŏs′lĭn]; partisan of Baliol and leader of Scots in revolt against Edward I of England. His grandson Sir **William Sinclair;** accompanied Sir James Douglas, bearer of heart of Bruce, to Palestine, and was slain with him by Saracens in Andalusia. The latter's son Sir **Henry** (d. 1400?), Earl or Prince of Orkney (created by Haakon VI of Norway, 1379); aided by the Venetian navigators Niccolò and Antonio Zeno conquered (1391) Faeroes Islands (Frislanda) and Shetland; later voyaged with Antonio Zeno to "Engroeneland" (probably Greenland).

Sir Henry's grandson Sir **William Sinclair** (1404?–1480), 3d Earl of Orkney and 1st Earl of Caithness (1455), assisted in repelling English invasion (1448); chancellor of Scotland (1454–56); one of regents and ambassador to England (1461); on cession of Orkney isles by Norway to King James III (1470), resigned his rights in favor of sovereign. Sir William's (1404?–1480) great-grandson **George Sinclair** (d. 1582), 4th Earl of Caithness; Roman Catholic supporter of Mary, Queen of Scots; implicated in Darnley murder; presided at trial of Bothwell; instigated acts of violence in northern Scotland. George's grandson **George Sinclair** (1566?–1643), 5th Earl of Caithness; won pension for putting down rebellion of son of Patrick Stewart, 2d Earl of Orkney (1615); for outrages and debt, was driven to Shetland by commission of fire and sword (1623). **James Sinclair** (1821–1881), 14th Earl of Caithness; invented steam vehicle for use on macadamized roads, a gravitating compass, and a tape loom; created Baron **Bar′ro·gill** (?băr′ō·gĭl) in British peerage (1866).

Sir **John Sinclair** (1754–1835), writer on finance and agriculture; M.P. (1780–1811); first president of board of agriculture (1793–98), introduced improved methods of tillage and new breeds of livestock; gained reputation as financier with *History of the Public Revenue of British Empire* (1784); prevented extension of financial crisis by plan for issue of exchequer bills (1793); supervised compilation of *Statistical Account of Scotland* (21 vols., 1791–99); superintended publication of Gaelic versions of poems of Ossian left by James Macpherson (1807). His fourth daughter, **Catherine** (1800–1864), was supervisor of home for widows of officers of army and navy; author of tales and descriptive works.

**Sinclair,** Sir **Archibald.** 1890–1970. British army officer and statesman; entered army (1910) and served through World War (1914–18); chief whip of the Liberal party in House of Commons (1930–31), and leader of the Liberal party in Parliament (1935); Lord Rector of Glasgow U. (1938); secretary of state for air (1940–45).

**Sin′clair** (sĭn′klâr), **Harry Ford.** 1876–1956. American businessman; in oil production and refining business (from 1901). Leased from U.S. government through Albert B. Fall (*q.v.*), secretary of the interior, oil properties in Teapot Dome; congressional investigation (1923–24) led to demand for annulment of leases; found guilty (1927) of contempt of U.S. Senate in refusing to testify on Teapot Dome leases and served three months in federal prison. Acquitted (Apr. 21, 1928) of charges of conspiracy with Fall to defraud the government.

**Sin′clair** (sĭng′klâr; sĭn′-; sĭn·klâr′), **May.** 1865?–1946. English novelist, b. in Cheshire; author of *The Divine Fire* (1904), *The Tree of Heaven* (1917), *Mary Olivier: A Life* (1919), *Mr. Waddington of Wyck* (1921), *A Cure of Souls* (1923), *The Rector of Wyck* (1925), *The Intercessor and Other Stories* (1931), etc.

**Sin·clair′** (sĭn·klâr′), **Upton Beall** (bĕl). 1878–1968. American writer and politician, b. Baltimore, Md.; A.B., C.C.N.Y. (1897); Socialist candidate for U.S. House of Representatives from a New Jersey district (1906); moved to California; Socialist candidate for U.S. House of Representatives (1920), for U.S. Senate (1922), for governor of California (1926, 1930); received Democratic nomination for governor (1934), running on a platform promising to "end poverty in California" (EPIC [*pronounced* ĕp′ĭk]) by a system of old-age assistance; founded American Civil Liberties Union in California. Author of novels, including *The Jungle* (1906), *The Money Changers* (1908), *King Coal* (1917), *The Brass Check* (1919), *The Goose-step—A Study of American Education* (1923), *Oil* (1927), *Boston* (1928), *The Way Out* (1933), and a series about a contemporary American, "Lanny Budd," beginning with *World's End* (1940) and including *Dragon's Teeth* (1942; Pulitzer prize), and *Presidential Mission* (1947).

**Sin′ding** (sĭn′dĭng), **Otto.** 1842–1909. Norwegian painter; best known for religious, historical, and genre pictures. A brother, **Stephen** (1846–1922), was a sculptor; studio in Paris (from 1911). Another brother, **Christian** (1856–1941), was a composer of opera, symphonies, concertos, violin sonatas, piano pieces, and songs.

**Sing′er** (sĭng′ẽr), **Isaac Bashevis.** 1904–    . American writer in Yiddish, b. Poland. To U.S. (1935); wrote *Gimpel the Fool* (1957), *Spinoza of Market Street* (1961), *In My Father's Court* (1966); awarded Nobel prize for literature (1978).

**Sing′er** (sĭng′ẽr), **Isaac Merrit.** 1811–1875. American inventor, b. Pittstown, N.Y. Invented sewing machine (patented 1851) and organized I. M. Singer & Co. to manufacture it; patented twenty improvements in his machine (between 1851 and 1863). Sued by Elias Howe for patent infringement (1851–54) and lost case, but success of machine made penalty harmless; took lead in merging sewing-machine manufacturers and pooling patents. Retired from business (1863).

**Sing′er** (sĭng′ẽr; *Ger.* zĭng′ẽr), **Isidore.** 1859–1939. Austrian-born journalist; to France (1887), Italy (1891), and U.S. (1895); managing editor of *Jewish Encyclopaedia* (12 vols., 1901–05); author of *La Question Juive* (1893), *Christ or God* (1908), etc.

**Sing′er** (sĭng′ẽr), **Israel Joshua.** 1893–1944. Polish-born writer; in U.S. (from 1934); naturalized (1939). His works (orig. written in Yiddish) include *Pearls* (short stories, 1922), *Iron and Steel, The New Russia, Yoshe Kalb* (1932; later dramatized), *Savinkoff* (a play, 1933), *The Brothers Ashkenazi* (a novel, 1936), *The River Breaks Up* (1938), *East of Eden* (1939).

**Sing′er** (zĭng′ẽr), **Paul.** 1844–1911. German politician; member of Reichstag (from 1884) and a leader of the Social Democratic party.

**Sing′er** (sĭng′ẽr), **William H., Jr.** 1868–1943. American landscape painter, b. Pittsburgh, Pa.; his *Mysterious North* hangs in Metropolitan Museum of Art in New York; *Solitude*, in the Luxembourg in Paris.

**Singh,** Sir **Bhupindar.** See Maharaja of PATIALA.

**Singh,** Sir **Pertab.** See PERTAB SINGH.

**Singleton, Mary.** See Mary Montgomerie CURRIE.

**Sing'mas'ter** (sĭng'màs'tẽr), **Elsie.** 1879–1958. American writer; m. Harold Lewars (1912; d. 1915); author of *Gettysburg—Stories of the Red Harvest and the Aftermath* (1913), *Virginia's Bandit* (1929), *Rifles for Washington* (1938), etc.

**Sin'ha** (sĭɴ'hȧ), Sir **Satyendra Prasanno.** 1st Baron of **Rai'pur** (rī'po͝or). 1864–1928. Indian lawyer and statesman; practiced at Calcutta. Representative of India at Imperial War Conference in London (1917); undersecretary of state for India (1919–20); governor of Bihar and Orissa (1920–21). First Indian member of viceroy's executive council.

**Sinibaldi, Guittoncino de'.** See CINO DA PISTOIA.

**Sinjohn, John.** Pseudonym of John GALSWORTHY.

**Sinz'hei'mer** (zĭnts'hī'mẽr), **Hugo.** 1875–1945. German jurist.

**Si·quei'ros** (sē·kē'ē·rōs), **David Alfaro.** 1896–1974. Mexican mural painter, b. Chihuahua; went to Spain and published *Vida Americana*, with a *Manifesto to the Painters of America.* In Mexico (1922), identified himself with revolutionary agitation among Mexican workers; imprisoned (1930) for radical activities. Later, expelled from U.S. for incorporating radical political views in his frescoes on public buildings; worked in Motevideo and Buenos Aires (1932) and Brazil (1934). Considered largely instrumental in reviving true fresco painting in America.

**Si·raj'–ud–dau'la** (sĭ·räj'o͞od·dou'lȧ). *Also* **Su·ra'jah Dow'lah** (sŭ·rä'jȧ dou'lȧ). 1728?–1757. Nawab of Bengal (1756–57); sought to seize wealth of foreign merchants; with large force captured Calcutta (June, 1756); responsible for tragedy of Black Hole; driven out of Calcutta by Clive; sided with the French in their contest with Clive; plotted against by Mir Jafar (*q.v.*); his large army totally defeated by small force of Clive at Plassey (June 23, 1757); killed by Mir Jafar's son. See OMICHUND.

**Si·rén'** (sĭ·rān'), **Osvald.** 1879–1966. Swedish art critic and educator; author of studies of Giotto, Leonardo da Vinci, and a number of articles and treatises on Chinese art.

**Si·ri'ci·us** (sĭ·rĭsh'ĭ·ŭs; -rĭsh'ŭs), Saint. Pope (bishop of Rome; 384–398). Convened council of Capua (391); much occupied with doctrines of heretics; several of his papal decretals still extant.

**Si·rin'go** (sĭ·rĭng'gō), **Charles A.** 1855–1928. American cowboy, detective, and author of racy adventure fiction, as *A Texas Cowboy*...(1885), *History of "Billy the Kid"* (1920), *Riata and Spurs* (1927).

**Sirlin.** See SYRLIN.

**Si·sen'na** (sĭ·sĕn'ȧ), **Lucius Cornelius.** 120?–67 B.C. Roman politician and historian; quaestor in Sicily (77 B.C.); governor of Achaia; author of a history of Rome, of which only fragments are extant.

**Sis'er·a** (sĭs'ẽr·ȧ). *In Douay Version* **Sis'a·ra** (-ȧ·rȧ). In the Bible, the general of the Canaanite king Jabin who was defeated by the Israelites under Barak and killed by Jael (*Judges* iv).

**Si·sin'ni·us** (sĭ·sĭn'ĭ·ŭs; -sĭn'yŭs). Pope (708).

**Sis'ler** (sĭs'lẽr), **George Harold.** 1893–1973. American professional baseball player, b. Manchester, Ohio; first baseman, St. Louis, American League (1915 ff.).

**Sis'ley'** (sēs'lā'), **Alfred.** 1839–1899. French landscape painter, of English descent; a leader of the impressionistic school.

**Sis'mon'di'** (sēs'môɴ'dē'; *Angl.* sĭs·mŏn'dĭ), **Jean Charles Léonard Si'monde' de** (sē'môɴd' dē). 1773–1842. Swiss historian and economist, of Italian descent; author of *Histoire des Républiques Italiennes au Moyen Âge* (16 vols., 1803–18), *Nouveaux Principes d'Économie Politique* (1819), *Histoire des Français* (31 vols., 1821–44), etc.

**Sit'ter** (sĭt'ẽr), **Willem de.** 1872–1934. Dutch astronomer; studied distribution, motion, and parallax of stars; professor, Leiden (1908). Made researches on Galilean satellites of Jupiter, at Cape (South Africa), Greenwich, and Leiden observatories; director, Leiden observatory (1919); made cosmological deductions from Einstein's theory of relativity; studied question of recession of spiral nebulae from the sun; made calculation of radius of the universe based on the mean density of matter; enunciated theory of an expanding universe.

**Sittewald, Philander von.** Pen name of Johann Michael MOSCHEROSCH.

**Sit'ting Bull** (sĭt'ĭng bo͝ol'). 1834–1890. Am. Indian leader and medicine man, b. on Grand River, S.Dak. Head of Sioux Indian war council (1875); a leader in Sioux war (1876–77), and with Gall and Crazy Horse at battle of the Little Big Horn, where Custer and all his men were slain (June 25, 1876); forced to retreat across Canadian border (1877). Returned to surrender at Fort Buford (1881); was located on Standing Rock Indian reservation. Again active in Indian agitation (1890); arrested and shot by Indian guards. His prominence made him central figure in a number of legends.

**Sit'well** (sĭt'wĕl; -wĕl). English literary family, including: Sir **George Reresby Sitwell** (1860–1943), author of *The First Whig, Country Life in the 17th Century, Tales of My Native Village* (1934), *Idle Fancies in Prose and Verse* (1938); and his children: (1) Dame **Edith** (1887–1964), poet, critic, and novelist; author of *The Mother and Other Poems* (1915), *Elegy on Dead Fashion* (1926), *Gold Coast Customs* (1929), *Alexander Pope* (1930), *The English Eccentrics* (1933), *Aspects of Modern Poetry* (1934), *I Live Under a Black Sun* (novel; 1937), *Look! The Sun* (anthology; 1941), etc. (2) Sir **Osbert** (1892–1969), poet, playwright, and novelist; served in World War (1914–18); author of *Argonaut and Juggernaut* (1919), *Who Killed Cock Robin?* (1921), *Out of the Flame* (1923), *Triple Fugue, and Other Stories* (1924), *England Reclaimed* (1927), *The Man Who Lost Himself* (1929), *Dumb Animal and Other Stories* (1930), *Dickens* (1932), *Miracle on Sinai* (1933), *Penny Foolish* (1935), *Those Were the Days* (1938), *Two Generations* (1940), *A Place of One's Own* (1942). (3) **Sacheverell** (1897–    ), poet and critic; author of volumes of verse and of *Southern Baroque Art* (1924), *German Baroque Art* (1927), *Mozart* (1932), *Canons of Giant Art* (1933), *Dance of the Quick and the Dead* (1936), *Narrative Pictures* (1937), *Old Fashioned Flowers* (1939), *Poltergeists* (1940), *Valse des Fleurs* (1941), etc.

**Si'va·ji** (sĭ'vä·jē) *or* **Shi'va·ji** (shĭ'-). 1627–1680. Founder of the Maratha power in India; organized bands of horsemen and secured forts in Western Ghats; carried on war with Bijapur; seized Poona (1663) and declared himself independent (1664); at war with Aurangzeb; was captured and imprisoned but escaped (1666); sacked Surat (1670); crowned as independent king (1674); successfully extended his dominions to the south (1676); weakened rule of Mogul and greatly strengthened power of Marathas.

**Sivertsen, Cort.** Original name of ADELAER.

**Si'vo·ri** (sē'vō·rē), **Camillo.** 1815–1894. Italian violinist, and composer of a number of violin works.

**Si'ward** (sū'ẽrd). Earl of **North·um'ber·land** (nôr·thŭm'bẽr·lănd). *Called* **the Strong.** d. 1055. Danish warrior in England. Became earl of all Northumberland by murdering his wife's uncle (1041); supported Edward the Confessor against Godwin (1051); invaded Scotland in interests of his kinsman Malcolm Canmore, routed King Macbeth (1054), and established Malcolm III as king of Cumbria.

**Six'tus** (sĭks'tŭs) *or* (esp. for I to III) **Xys'tus** (zĭs'tŭs). *Ital.* **Si'sto** (sēs'tō). Name of five popes (see *Table of Popes*, Nos. 7, 24, 44, 214, 229): **Sixtus I;** saint; pope (116?–?125) during the reign of Hadrian. **Sixtus II;** saint; pope (257–258); reconciled churches of North Africa and Rome; died a martyr under Valerian. **Sixtus III;** saint; pope (432–440); restored Basilica of Liberius. **Sixtus IV,** *real name* **Francesco del'la Ro've·re** [dāl'lä rō'vā·rā] (1414–1484); pope (1471–84); b. at Celle Ligure, near Savona, Italy. General of the Franciscan order (1464). After becoming pope confined attention to Italian politics; involved in conspiracy against the Medici which resulted in a war with Florence (1478–80); urged Venetians to attack Ferrara and then abandoned them (1480–84); had Sistine Chapel built (1473) and the Sistine Bridge across the Tiber, but became unpopular because of heavy taxations for these structures, and for his extreme nepotism. **Sixtus V,** *real name* **Felice Pe·ret'ti** [pā·rāt'tē] (1521–1590); pope (1585–90); b. at Grottammare, The Marches. Became cardinal (1570). As pope, brought order in the Papal States; revised regulations for the college of cardinals, restricting number to 70; a patron of art, built Lateran Palace, erected Vatican Library, and completed or restored other structures; authorized new edition of the Septuagint (1587); published new edition of the Vulgate (1590).

**Sixt von Ar·min'** (zĭkst' fōn är·mēn'), **Friedrich.** 1851–1936. Prussian general of infantry; served through World War; commander of fourth army in Flanders (1917–18).

**Sjö'berg'** (shû'băr'y'), **Erik.** *Pseudonym* **Vi·ta'lis** (vĭ·tä'lĭs). 1794–1828. Swedish poet.

**Skan'da·gup'ta** (skŭn'dȧ·gŏŏp'tȧ). d. ?480 A.D. Last of the great Gupta dynasty (455–480) of India; son of Kumaragupta I; repulsed inroad of Huns from Central Asia (c. 455); took title *Vikramaditya* (*q.v.*). At time of his death Huns came again in great numbers and broke up Gupta empire (480–490).

**Skanderbeg.** Variant of SCANDERBEG.

**Skar'bek** (skär'bĕk), **Fryderyk.** 1792–1866. Polish writer of works on economics, and humorous novels depicting contemporary Polish society.

**Skeat** (skēt), **Walter William.** 1835–1912. English philologist; Elrington and Bosworth professor of Anglo-Saxon, Cambridge (1878–1912). Edited three parallel texts of *Piers Plowman* (1886) and Oxford edition of Chaucer (7 vols., 1894–97); compiled *Etymological English Dictionary* (1879–82). Founded English Dialect Society (1873); wrote textbooks and prepared texts for Early English Text Society and Scottish Text Society; popularized philology.

**Skel'ton** (skĕl't'n; -tŭn), **John.** 1460?–1529. English poet, b. prob. in Norfolk; educ. Oxford and Cambridge; created poet laureate by both universities, and perhaps by king; produced translations and elegies (1489); became rector of Diss, Norfolk (1498). Turned to development of an original vein of caustic satire replete with slang, grotesque words, Latin quotations, and unrestrained jocularity, in short doggerel rhymed lines in a meter of his own invention; attacked abuses in church and state. Author of *The Bowge of Courte*, allegorical poem printed by Wynkyn de Worde, also *Why come ye nat to Courte, Colyn Cloute*, and *Speke, Parrot*, attacking the clergy and Wolsey; *The Tunnyng of Elynor Rummynge*, a coarse Hogarthian picture of low life; *The Boke of Phyllyp Sparowe*, tender and fanciful lament over a pet bird.

**Skene** (skēn), **William Forbes.** 1809–1892. Scottish historian and antiquary; historiographer royal for Scotland (1881). Author of *The Highlanders of Scotland* (1837) and *Celtic Scotland* (3 vols., 1876–80).

**Sketchley, Arthur.** Pseudonym of George ROSE.

**Skin'ner** (skĭn'ẽr), **Constance Lindsay.** 1879–1939. Writer, b. in northern British Columbia; among her many books are *Songs of the Coast Dwellers* (verse), *Pioneers of the Old Southwest* and *Adventurers of Oregon* in Yale U. series of *Chronicles of America;* plays, *David* (1910), *Good Morning, Rosamond* (1917); a number of novels and juveniles.

**Skinner, Halcyon.** 1824–1900. American inventor, esp. of power looms to weave different types of carpets.

**Skinner, John.** 1721–1807. Scottish song writer. Episcopalian minister at Longside, Aberdeenshire (1742–1807); corresponded with Burns who secured some of his best songs for James Johnson's *Scots Musical Museum.* Author of *Tullochgorum, Ewie wi' the Crookit Horn*, and other favorite songs.

**Skinner, Otis.** 1858–1942. American actor, b. Cambridge, Mass. Starred in *Hamlet* (1896), *Francesca da Rimini* (1902), *Kismet* (1911–14), *Cock o' the Walk* (1915–16), *Mister Antonio* (1916–18), *The Honor of the Family* (1918–19), *Blood and Sand* (1921–22), *Sancho Panza* (1923–25), *Merry Wives of Windsor* (1927–28), *Merchant of Venice* (1931–32), etc. His daughter **Cornelia Otis** (1901–1979), actress and monologuist, m. Alden S. Blodgett (1928); appeared in *Will Shakespeare, Blood and Sand, The Wild Westcotts*, etc.; author, producer, and actor of *Edna His Wife* (a monodrama, from the novel by Margaret Ayer Barnes), *The Wives of Henry VIII, The Empress Eugénie*, and of many shorter sketches; author of the play *Captain Fury*, and books of light essays, as *Excuse It, Please* (1936).

**Skinner, Stephen.** 1623–1667. English physician and philologist; M.D., Heidelberg (1654). Author of *Etymologicon Linguae Anglicanae* (pub. 1671), which includes botanical, forensic, and Old English words, also proper names, and which made a distinct contribution to etymology.

**Skip'sey** (skĭp'sĭ), **Joseph.** 1832–1903. English collier poet; pitman in Northumberland coalpits from age of seven; self-taught; edited *Canterbury Poets* (1884–85); custodian of Shakespeare's birthplace, Stratford upon Avon (1889–91). Author of *The Collier Lad* and *Carols from the Coalfields.*

**Sko'be·lev** (skô'byĭ·lyĕf), **Mikhail Dmitrievich.** 1843–1882. Russian soldier; distinguished himself in Russo-Turkish War (1877–78) at Pleven, Shipka Pass, and Adrianople; stormed Geok-Tepe and conquered the Tekke Turkomans (1881); governor of Minsk (1881).

**Sko'da** (skō'dä), **Emil von.** *Czech* **Škoda** (shkô'dȧ). 1839–1900. Nephew of Joseph Skoda. Czech engineer and industrialist; took over machine works in Pilsen and founded Skoda Works (1866), which he developed into famous factory for manufacture of military equipment, esp. large cannon and other artillery. His son **Karl** (1879–1929) was director of firm (from 1909).

**Skoda, Joseph.** *Czech* **Škoda.** 1805–1881. Czech physician; known for diagnostic work, esp. in connection with percussion and auscultation.

**Sko·ro·pad'ski** (skŭ·rŭ·pȧt'skû·ĭ; *Angl.* -skĭ), **Pavel Petrovich.** 1873–1945. Russian general in World War (1914–18); commanded a cavalry division in invasion of East Prussia (1914). Of Ukrainian birth, he headed a Ukrainian corps after the Russian Bolshevik coup d'état

(Nov., 1917), and had himself proclaimed hetman of the Ukraine; overthrown by a democratic coalition in the Ukraine (Nov., 1918); fled to Germany.

**Skou·lou′des** *or* **Skou·lou′dis** (skōō·lōō′thēs), **Stephanos.** 1836–1928. Greek statesman; minister of marine (1892) and foreign affairs (1897); prime minister (1915–16).

**Skram** (skräm), **Erik.** 1847–1923. Danish novelist; author of *Gertrude Colbjörnsen* (1897) and *Agnes Vittrup* (1897). His wife, **Amalie,** *nee* **Al′ver** [äl′vẽr] (1847–1908), b. Bergen, Norway, was also a novelist; author of *Constance Ring* (1885), a series about the Hellemyr family, *Professor Hieronymus* (1895), etc.

**Skrine** (skrēn), **Agnes,** *nee* **Hig′gin·son** (hĭg′ĭn·s'n). *Pseudonym* **Moira O'Neill′** (ō·nēl′). Irish poet; m. Walter C. Skrine; author of *Songs from the Glens of Antrim* (1900). Mother of **Mary Nesta Skrine** (1905– ), *pseudonym* **M. J. Far′rell** (făr′ĕl); m. Robert Keane; author of *Young Entry, Mad Puppettstown, Full House, The Rising Tide,* etc.

**Skryabin.** See SCRIABIN.

**Skrzy·nec′ki** (skshĭ·nĕts′kē), **Jan.** 1787–1860. Polish general; commander in chief (Feb.–Aug., 1831) of Polish army in rebellion against Russia; was defeated (May 26, 1831) at Ostrolenka; relieved of command (Aug., 1831).

**Skrzyń′ski** (skshĭn′y'·skē), Count **Aleksander.** 1882–1931. Polish statesman; prime minister (1925–26). Played important part in organization of League of Nations, and in negotiations resulting in Locarno Pact (1925).

**Slade** (slād), **Felix.** 1790–1868. English collector of books, engravings, and glass; bequeathed collection to British Museum; endowed art professorships at Oxford, Cambridge, and University Coll., London.

**Sla′den** (slā′d'n), **Douglas Brooke Wheelton.** 1856–1947. English writer, b. London; to Australia (1879), and became first professor of history in U. of Sydney. Returned to England (c. 1886) and devoted himself to writing. Editor of *Who's Who* (1897–99) and *The Green Book* (1910–11). Published *Australian Lyrics* (1882), *The Spanish Armada* (1888), *The Japs at Home* (1892), *The Secrets of the Vatican* (1907), *The Confessions of Frederick the Great* (1915), *The Douglas Romance* (1916), *The Shadow of a Great Light* (1917), *Eve, an Artist's Model* (1932), etc.

**Sla′ter** (slā′tẽr), **Samuel.** 1768–1835. Industrialist, b. in Derbyshire, Eng. Apprenticed to partner of Richard Arkwright, inventor of cotton-spinning machinery (1783). Familiarized himself with this machinery, and machines invented by James Hargreaves and Samuel Crompton. To America (1789) and contracted with firm of Almy & Brown, Providence, R.I., to reproduce for them Arkwright's cotton machinery; this he did from memory. Established factory in Pawtucket under firm name of Almy, Brown & Slater (1793). Regarded as founder of American cotton industry. His nephew **John Fox Slater** (1815–1884) was also a cotton manufacturer; developed factories in partnership with his brother **William S.**; established (1882) the John F. Slater Fund of $1,000,000 to be used for the education of freedmen in the South.

**Sla′tin Pa′sha** (slä′tēn pä′shä), Baron **Rudolf Carl.** 1857–1932. Austrian-born soldier in Egyptian and British service; served in Egypt under General Gordon (1878 ff.); was appointed governor general of Darfur (1881). Captured by the Mahdi Mohammed Ahmed (*q.v.*) and held prisoner (1884–95); escaped to Cairo and was made pasha by the khedive (1895). British inspector general of the Sudan (1900–14). Author of *Fire and Sword in the Sudan* (1896).

**Slat′ter·y** (slăt′ẽr·ĭ), **Charles Lewis.** 1867–1930. American Protestant Episcopal clergyman; rector of Grace Church, New York (1910–22); bishop coadjutor of Massachusetts (1922–27) and bishop (from 1927).

**Slave dynasty** (slāv). Name of a dynasty of Mohammedan (chiefly Turki) kings of Delhi (1206–90) in northern India, founded by Kutb-ud-din Aibak, a slave; most of its members were either fanatics or worthless debauchees; see ALTAMSH and BALBAN.

**Sła′wek** (slä′vĕk), **Walery.** 1879–1939. Polish patriot and statesman; assisted Piłsudski; prime minister of Poland (1930; 1930–31; 1935).

**Slei·da′nus** (slī·dä′nŏŏs), **Johannes.** *Also* **Slei·dan′** (slī·dän′). *Real name* **Phi·lip′pi** (fē·lĭp′ē) *or* **Phi′lipp·son** (fē′lĭp·zōn). 1506?–1556. German historian; diplomatic representative of Francis I of France in negotiations with the Schmalkaldic League (1537); represented Strasbourg at the Council of Trent (1551). Chief work, *De Statu Religionis et Reipublicae Carolo V. Caesare Commentarii* (1555).

**Slem′mer** (slĕm′ẽr), **Adam J.** 1828–1868. American army officer; defended Fort Pickens in Pensacola Harbor, Florida, against Confederate attacks (Jan.–Apr., 1861), thus keeping the key to the Gulf of Mexico in Union hands.

**Slep′i·an** (slĕp′ĭ·ăn), **Joseph.** 1891–1969. American electrical engineer; investigated conduction of electricity in gases.

**Sles′in·ger** (slĕs′ĭn·jẽr), **Tess.** 1905–1945. American fiction writer; author of *Unpossessed* (1934) and *Time: the present* (short stories; 1935).

**Sle′vogt** (slā′fōкt), **Max.** 1868–1932. German painter; associated with impressionistic school.

**Slick, Sam.** Pseudonym of Thomas Chandler HALIBURTON.

**Sli′dell** (slī′d'l; *popularly* slī·dĕl′), **John.** 1793–1871. American politician and diplomat, b. New York City; brother of Alexander Slidell Mackenzie (*q.v.*). Practiced law, New Orleans (1819–35); member, U.S. House of Representatives (1843–45) and U.S. Senate (1853–61); wielded great political influence in Buchanan's administration; withdrew from U.S. Senate and joined Confederacy (Feb., 1861); appointed to represent the Confederacy in France (1861). With James M. Mason took passage on British steamer *Trent* en route to Paris; was arrested by Captain Wilkes of U.S.S. *San Jacinto* and taken to Boston (Nov., 1861); released after strong British protests and returned to British ship (Jan., 1862). Failed to gain recognition of Confederacy by France. Lived abroad (from 1862).

**Sling′e·land** (slĭng′ĕ·länt), **Pietr Cornelisz van.** 1640–1691. Dutch painter of still life, portraits, and genre scenes.

**Sli′pher** (slī′fẽr), **Vesto Melvin.** 1875–1969. American astronomer; known for investigations in astronomical spectroscopy, esp. relating to the rotations and atmospheres of the planets; directed research leading to discovery of the planet Pluto; discovered rapid rotation and great space velocities of the nebulae.

**Sloan** (slōn), **Alfred Pritchard.** 1875–1966. American industrialist; president (14 yrs.) and chairman of board of directors (from 1937), General Motors Corp.

**Sloan, James Forman,** *known as* **Tod.** 1874–1933. American jockey, b. near Kokomo, Ind.; popularized the crouching, forward seat now universal in flat racing.

**Sloan, John.** 1871–1951. American painter, etcher, and illustrator, b. Lock Haven, Pa.; etched plates illustrating novels by Paul de Kock; illustrated for *Harper's, Collier's, Scribner's,* and other magazines; painter of landscapes, figure paintings, and portraits.

**Sloan, Matthew Scott.** 1881–1945. American electrical engineer and industrialist; president, Brooklyn Edison Co., Inc. (1919–32), Edison Construction Co., Inc. (1923–32), and New York Edison Co. (1928–32).

**Sloan, Samuel.** 1817–1907. Businessman and railroad executive, b. Lisburn, Ireland; to U.S. as an infant; president, Delaware, Lackawanna & Western Railroad (1867–99), and chairman of board of directors (1899–1907).

**Sloane** (slōn), Sir **Hans.** 1660–1753. British physician and naturalist; physician to governor of Jamaica (1687–89), collected 800 new species of plants; succeeded Sir Isaac Newton as president, Royal Society (1727–41); first physician to George II (1727); founded Botanic Garden (1721). Acquired by bequest (1702) collection of William Courten, naturalist; bequeathed to nation library of 50,000 volumes, several thousand manuscripts, pictures, coins, and curiosities, which formed nucleus of British Museum.

**Sloane, Thomas O'Conor.** 1851–1940. American physicist and writer on science; on editorial staff of *Scientific American*, *Youth's Companion*, etc.; author of *Home Experiments in Science* (1888), *Standard Electrical Dictionary* (1892), *Motion Picture Projection* (1921), etc.

**Sloane, William Milligan.** 1850–1928. American historian and educator; professor, Columbia (1896–1916). Author of *Life of Napoleon Bonaparte* (1894–96), *The Balkans: A Laboratory of History* (1914), *Greater France in Africa* (1924), etc.

**Sloat** (slōt), **John Drake.** 1781–1867. American naval officer; commanded Pacific Squadron (1844); took over California from Mexico on outbreak of Mexican War (July 7, 1845); act commended by U.S. secretary of war. His statue stands at the Presidio, Monterey, Calif.

**Slo'combe** (slō'kŭm), **George Edward.** 1894–1963. English journalist; chief foreign correspondent, *Daily Herald* (1920–31); foreign editor, *Evening Standard* (1932–34); foreign-affairs commentator, *Sunday Express* (from 1940); author of *A History of Poland* (1916; reprinted 1939), *Paris in Profile* (1928), *Henry of Navarre* (1931), *Crisis in Europe* (1934), *Don John of Austria* (1935), *The Tumult and the Shouting* (1936; autobiography), *The Dangerous Sea* (1936), *Rebels of Art: Manet to Matisse* (1939), etc.

**Slo'cum** (slō'kŭm), **Frances.** 1773–1847. b. Warwick, R.I.; captured by Delaware Indians (1778), adopted and brought up by them, married into the tribe, and preferred to remain with them after her identity had been established (1835) and her relatives made known to her.

**Slocum, Henry Warner.** 1827–1894. American army officer; grad. U.S.M.A., West Point (1852); brigadier general of volunteers (1861); major general (July, 1862). Commanded extreme right of Union line at Gettysburg (July 2–4, 1863); with Sherman on march to the sea and northward through the Carolinas (1864–65); resigned commission (1865) and practiced law in Brooklyn (1866); member, U.S. House of Representatives (1869–73; 1883–85).

**Slos'son** (slŏs''n), **Edwin Emery.** 1865–1929. American chemist; best known as an interpreter of sciences to nontechnical readers and audiences, as in *Creative Chemistry* (1919), *Easy Lessons in Einstein* (1920), *Snapshots of Science* (1928), etc.

**Sło·wac'ki** (slô·väts'kē), **Juliusz.** 1809–1849. Polish poet and playwright.

**Slu'ter** (slü'tẽr), **Claus.** d. 1406. Dutch-Burgundian sculptor; in service (1389) of Philip the Bold of Burgundy. Chief work, tomb of Philip the Bold, now preserved in museum at Dijon.

**Slye** (slī), **Maud.** 1879–1954. American pathologist; educ. Brown U., U. of Chicago, U. of Minnesota. Associate professor of pathology and director of the cancer laboratory, Chicago (1919–44). Known esp. for her researches in cancer; published 42 brochures on cancer.

**Small** (smôl), **Albion Woodbury.** 1854–1926. American educator; head of department of sociology, U. of Chicago (1892–1924); founder (1895) and editor (1895–1926), *American Journal of Sociology.*

**Small, John Kun'kel** (?kŭng'kĕl; ?kŏŏng'-). 1869–1938. American botanist; investigated native palms, irises, flowering epiphytes, cacti, and ferns of southeastern U.S., and wrote on the flora of that region.

**Smal'ley** (smôl'ĭ), **George Washburn.** 1833–1916. American journalist; practiced law in Boston (to 1861). On staff, New York *Tribune* (1861); war correspondent in Shenandoah Valley and with army of the Potomac; war correspondent with Prussian army in Austro-Prussian War (1866); organized London bureau of New York *Tribune* (1867). Excelled in telegraphing reports of Franco-Prussian War (1870–71). Remained abroad as the *Tribune's* European correspondent (to 1895). American correspondent of London *Times* (1895–1905).

**Small'wood** (smôl'wŏŏd), **William.** 1732–1792. American Revolutionary officer, b. in Charles County, Md.; commanded Maryland regiment (1776); engaged at battle of Long Island and covered Washington's retreat; engaged at White Plains; commissioned brigadier general (Oct., 1776), and major general (Sept., 1780); engaged in battle of Camden and received thanks of Congress. Governor of Maryland (1785–88).

**Smart** (smärt), **Benjamin Humphrey.** 1786?–1872. English teacher of elocution; author of manuals on English pronunciation and grammar, and of a pronouncing dictionary based on Walker's.

**Smart, Christopher.** 1722–1771. English poet, b. in Kent; published *Poems on Several Occasions*, including *The Hop Garden* (1752), and replied to pseudoscientific compiler John Hill's criticism of it in his satire *Hilliad* (1753). After symptoms of mental aberration (1751) developed religious mania, confined to asylum; in confinement, produced his one original and powerful poem, *A Song to David* (1763).

**Smart,** Sir **George Thomas.** 1776–1867. English violinist, organist, and orchestral conductor; produced in England Beethoven's *Mount of Olives* (1814), Mendelssohn's *St. Paul* (1836), Weber's *Oberon;* composed church music and glees. His brother **Henry** (1778–1823) was a violinist and piano maker. Henry's son **Henry Thomas** (1813–1879) was a London church organist, and composer.

**Smart, John.** 1741?–1811. English miniature painter of late 18th and early 19th centuries.

**Smart, William.** 1853–1915. Scottish political economist; author of *An Introduction to the Theory of Value* (1891), *Studies in Economics* (1895), etc.

**Smartt** (smärt), Sir **Thomas William.** 1858–1929. Physician and politician in South Africa, b. in County Meath, Ireland; to South Africa (1880). Associated with Cecil Rhodes (1899–1902) and pledged to carry out his plans for South Africa. Leader of Unionist party in legislature of Union of South Africa, succeeding Jameson (1912), and negotiated union (1920) with party led by General Smuts; secretary of agriculture (1921–24).

**Smea'ton** (smē't'n), **John.** 1724–1792. English civil engineer; improved instruments used in navigation and astronomy; rediscovered (1756) hydraulic cement, unknown since fall of Rome; awarded gold medal for improvements on windmills and watermills (1759); rebuilt Eddystone lighthouse (1759); constructed Ramsgate harbor (1774), Forth and Clyde Canal, and Perth, Banff, and Coldstream bridges.

**Smec·tym'nu·us** (smĕk·tĭm'nū·ŭs). A composite acrostic pseudonym of five English authors (Presbyterian clergymen) of a pamphlet (1641) assailing Bishop Joseph Hall's claim of divine right for the episcopacy: *S*tephen *M*arshall, *E*dmund *C*alamy, *T*homas *Y*oung, *M*atthew *N*ewcomen, *W*illiam *S*purstow.

**Smed'ley** (smĕd'lĭ), **Frank**, *in full* **Francis Edward**. 1818–1864. English novelist; author of *Frank Fairleigh* (1850), *Lewis Arundel* (1852), and *Harry Coverdale's Courtship* (1855), which were illustrated by Cruikshank and Phiz.

**Smedley, William Thomas.** 1858–1920. American painter and illustrator.

**Smel'fun'gus** (smĕl'fŭng'gŭs; smĕl·fŭng'gŭs). Epithet applied to Tobias Smollett by Laurence Sterne in *A Sentimental Journey.*

**Smel'lie** (smĕl'ĭ), **William.** 1745–1795. Scottish printer and antiquary; chief compiler and printer of 1st edition of *Encyclopedia Britannica* (3 vols., 1771).

**Smer'dis** (smûr'dĭs). *Pers.* **Bar'di·ya** (bär'dĭ·yȧ). d. about 525 B.C. Persian noble; younger son of Cyrus the Great and brother of Cambyses II; appointed governor of an eastern province; secretly murdered by Cambyses on his departure for Egypt. Since his death was not generally known, **Gau·ma'ta** (gou·mä'tȧ), known as "the False Smerdis," a Magian priest from Media, usurped throne (522 B.C.); killed by Darius (521). Story told by Ctesias and Herodotus.

**Sme'ta·na** (smĕ'tȧ·nȧ), **Augustin.** 1814–1851. Czech philosopher; author of *The Meaning of the Present Age* (1848) and *The Spirit, its Beginning and its End* (pub. 1865).

**Smetana, Bedřich.** 1824–1884. Czech pianist, conductor, and composer; regarded as founder of modern Czechoslovak music. His opera, *The Bartered Bride* (1866), typifying Bohemian life, became widely popular. Composer also of symphonies, chamber music, piano pieces, choral works, and songs.

**Smet de Nae'yer** (smĕt' dē nȧ'yẽr), Count **Paul de.** 1843–1913. Belgian statesman; premier of Belgium (1896–99, 1899–1907); member of the senate (1910).

**Sme'to·na'** (smĕ'tô·nä'), **Antanas.** 1874–1944. Lithuanian statesman; first president, Lithuanian state council and Republic of Lithuania (1920–21); re-elected president (1926, 1931, 1938).

**Smi'bert** (smī'bẽrt), **John.** 1688–1751. Painter, b. Edinburgh, Scotland; accompanied George Berkeley to America (1728); opened studio in Boston (1730) and painted portraits of the most eminent personages in the colony, the earliest of painters in America.

**Smid'dy** (smĭd'ĭ), **Timothy A.** 1877–1962. Irish economist, b. Cork; professor, University Coll., Cork. Economic adviser to Irish plenipotentiaries negotiating Anglo-Irish treaty (1921); envoy and fiscal agent of Dail Eireann to U.S. (1922–24). Irish Free State's first minister to United States (1924–29). Irish Free State high commissioner in London (1929–30). Member, Irish Free State tariff commission (from 1930).

**Smig'ly-Rydz'** (symēg'lĭ·rĭts'), **Edward.** 1886–1941. Polish general; served in Pilsudski's Polish legions (1914–17). Inspector general of Polish army, succeeding Piłsudski (1935); marshal of Poland, and most powerful man in country (1936–39). After German occupation of Poland, took refuge in Rumania (1939).

**Smiles** (smīlz), **Samuel.** 1812–1904. Scottish biographical author; began series of biographies of leaders in industry with *Life of George Stephenson* (1857), and *Lives of the Engineers* (3 vols., 1861–62); scored popular success with *Self-Help* (1859); also wrote *Character* (1871), *Thrift* (1875), *Duty* (1880), *Life and Labour* (1887).

**Smil'lie** (smĭ'lĭ), **James.** 1807–1885. Engraver, b. Edinburgh, Scotland; to Quebec, Canada (1821) and New York (c. 1829). Engaged in bank-note engraving (1830) and line engraving after paintings by leading contemporary artists; esp. successful as engraver of landscapes. A son, **James David** (1833–1909), was an engraver, painter, and etcher. Another son, **George Henry** (1840–1921), was a landscape painter.

**Smillie, Robert.** 1859–1940. British labor leader, b. Belfast; miner in Lanarkshire (1875–91); president, Miners' Federation of Great Britain (1912–21); chairman, General Council of Trade Unions (1924–25); M.P. (1923–29). Author of *My Life for Labour* (1924).

**Smirke** (smûrk), **Robert.** 1752–1845. English historical painter and book illustrator, R.A. (1793). Father of: Sir **Robert** (1781–1867), architect; designed in classic style Covent Garden theatre (1809), College of Physicians, the Post Office, the Mint, the British Museum, and in Gothic style, library and dining hall of Inner Temple and restoration of York minster. **Sydney** (1798–1877) assisted his brother Robert; designed reading room of British Museum (1854–57).

**Smith** (smĭth). See also SMYTH, SMYTHE.

**Smith, Adam.** 1723–1790. Scottish economist, b. in Kirkcaldy, Fifeshire; at Edinburgh (1748) joined brilliant group comprising David Hume, John Home, Dr. Hugh Blair, Lord Hailes, Principal Robertson; professor of logic, Glasgow (1751), and of moral philosophy (1752–64), lecturing on theology, ethics, jurisprudence, political institutions; won reputation with his *Theory of Moral Sentiments* (1759); as tutor to the young duke of Buccleuch (1763–65), met wits and philosophers of Louis XV in France, conversed with Turgot and other physiocrats, saw Voltaire at Geneva. Retired to Kirkcaldy for study (1767–76), worked out theory of division of labor, money, prices, wages, and distribution, produced *Inquiry into the Nature and Causes of the Wealth of Nations* (1776), which laid foundation of science of political economy, setting up system of natural liberty of trade and commerce, and which became authoritative in politics as well as economics, exerting influence through world equaled by few other books. In London, member of literary club of Garrick, Reynolds, Dr. Johnson; commissioner of customs, Edinburgh (1778); lord rector of Glasgow U. (1787).

**Smith, Alan Penniman.** See under Nathan SMITH.

**Smith, Albert Holmes.** 1835–1885. American obstetrician and gynecologist.

**Smith, Albert Richard.** 1816–1860. English lecturer and humorous writer; one of original contributors to *Punch.*

**Smith, Alexander.** Alias of John ADAMS (1760?–1829).

**Smith, Alexander.** 1830–1867. Scottish poet; one of chief representatives of the spasmodic school (see under Sidney DOBELL); collaborated with Sidney Dobell in *War Sonnets* (1855), inspired by Crimean War; after publishing *City Poems* (1857), *Edwin of Deira* (1861), turned to prose with *Dreamthorp* (essays; 1863), *A Summer in Skye,* and two novels.

**Smith, Alexander.** 1865–1922. Chemist, b. Edinburgh, Scotland; to U.S. (1890); professor (1904–11), U. of Chicago. Distinguished for studies in physical chemistry, esp. on forms of sulphur and on vapor-pressure measurements at high temperatures.

**Smith, Alfred Emanuel.** 1873–1944. American political leader, b. New York City; member of New York State legislature (1903–15), and democratic leader of the Assembly (1911) and speaker (1913); sheriff of New York County (1915–17); president, New York Board of Aldermen (1917); governor of New York for four terms (1919–20; 1923–28); democratic candidate for president of the

United States (1928); president, Empire State, Inc., managing the Empire State Building in New York City.

**Smith, Alfred Holland.** 1863–1924. American railroad executive; president, New York Central (1914–24).

**Smith, Andrew Jackson.** 1815–1897. American army officer; grad. U.S.M.A., West Point (1838). Chief of cavalry under Halleck in Corinth campaign (1862); brigadier general of volunteers (Mar., 1862); major general (May, 1864). Defeated Forrest at Tupelo, Miss. (July 14, 1864); engaged at Nashville (Dec., 1864) and at Mobile (Mar.–Apr., 1865).

**Smith, Arthur Henderson.** 1845–1932. American Congregational missionary in China (1872–1925); author of a number of books on China.

**Smith, Asa Dodge.** 1804–1877. American Presbyterian clergyman and educator; pastorate, New York City (1834–63); president, Dartmouth (1863–77).

**Smith, Ashbel.** 1805–1886. American physician and politician, b. Hartford, Conn.; practiced in Salisbury, N.C. (to 1837); surgeon general, Republic of Texas (1837); Texas minister to England and France (1842–44); secretary of State of Texas (1845); negotiated treaty with Mexico by which Texan independence was acknowledged by Mexico (1845); served with Texas troops in Civil War. Author of *Reminiscences of the Texas Republic* (1876).

**Smith, Azariah.** 1817–1851. American medical missionary; Presbyterian missionary in Armenia and Turkey (1842–51). A cousin, **Judson Smith** (1837–1906), was also engaged in missionary work; ordained in Congregational ministry (1866); professor, Oberlin (1866–84); secretary, American Board of Commissioners for Foreign Missions (1884–1906). A nephew of Judson Smith, **Gerald Birney Smith** (1868–1929), was a theologian; ordained in Baptist ministry (1902); taught at U. of Chicago divinity school (1900–29).

**Smith, Benjamin Eli.** See under Eli SMITH.

**Smith, Buckingham.** 1810–1871. American antiquarian; U.S. secretary of legation, Mexico City (1850–52), and Madrid (1855–58). Specialized in study of early Spanish explorations in America.

**Smith, Charles Alphonso.** 1864–1924. American educator, b. Greensboro, N.C.; professor, U. of Virginia (1909–17); head of English department, U.S.N.A., Annapolis (1917–24). Author of *What Can Literature Do for Me?* (1913), and works on Anglo-Saxon and English grammar and philology.

**Smith,** Sir **Charles E. Kingsford–.** See KINGSFORD-SMITH.

**Smith, Charles Ferguson.** 1807–1862. American army officer; grad. U.S.M.A., West Point (1825); commanded Red River expedition (1856); served with Utah expedition (1857–60); commanded department of Utah (1860–61). Engaged under Grant in operations against Fort Henry, Tenn., Fort Heiman, Ky., Fort Donelson, Tenn.; major general (Mar., 1862).

**Smith, Charles Henry.** *Pseudonym* **Bill Arp** (ärp). 1826–1903. American humorist, b. Lawrenceville, Ga. Contributor to Atlanta (Ga.) *Constitution;* author of *Bill Arp, So Called* (1866), *Bill Arp: From the Uncivil War to Date* (1903), etc.

**Smith, Charles Sprague.** 1853–1910. American educator; founded (1897) People's Institute at Cooper Union, which developed into a notable community center.

**Smith, Charlotte,** *nee* **Turner.** 1749–1806. English poet and novelist; author of *Elegiac Sonnets and Other Essays* (1784), a poem *Beachy Head,* and successful novels, including *Emmeline* (1788), *Celestina* (1792), *The Old Manor House* (1793).

**Smith, David Eugene.** 1860–1944. American mathematician; professor, Teachers Coll., Columbia (1901–26; emeritus); mathematical editor, *New International Encyclopaedia* (1902–16), *Encyclopaedia Britannica* (1927). Author of *History of Modern Mathematics* (1896), *Our Indebtedness to Greece and Rome in Mathematics* (1922), *The Rubáiyát of Omar Khayyám* (metrical version; 1933), *Poetry of Mathematics and Other Essays* (1934), etc.

**Smith, David Nichol.** 1875–1962. British educator, b. Edinburgh; professor of English, Oxford (from 1929). Author of *Shakespeare Criticism* (1916), *Some Observations on Eighteenth Century Poetry* (1937), etc.

**Smith, David Stanley.** 1877–1949. American music educator; professor of music, Yale (from 1916), and dean of the school of music (1920–40); conductor, New Haven Symphony Orchestra (from 1919); composer of symphonic, chamber, and church music, and choral works with orchestra.

**Smith, Dodie.** *Pseud.* (*to 1935*) **C. L. An′tho·ny** (ăn′tō·nĭ; -thō·nĭ). 1896– . Eng. playwright; m. (1939) Alec Macbeth Beesley. Author of *Autumn Crocus* (1930), *Service* (1932), *Touch Wood* (1933), *Call It a Day* (1935), *Dear Octopus* (1938), etc.

**Smith, Donald Alexander.** 1st Baron **Strath·co′na and Mount Roy′al** (străth·kō′nȧ, mount roi′ăl). 1820–1914. Canadian administrator, b. in Scotland; head of Montreal department, Hudson's Bay Co. (1868); sent by Canadian government to negotiate with Louis Riel; member of dominion parliament (1871–79, 1887); with his cousin George Stephen, completed greater part of Great Northern Railway (1879) and Canadian Pacific Railway (1885); governor of Hudson's Bay Co. (1889); high commissioner for Canada (1896).

**Smith, Edgar Fahs** (fäz). 1854–1928. American chemist and educator; professor, U. of Pennsylvania (1888–1920). Author of textbooks of chemistry and treatises upon the history of chemistry.

**Smith, Edgar McPhail.** 1857–1938. American playwright and librettist; script writer for Weber and Fields (1896–1904); writer and adapter of many plays, musical comedies, operas, burlesques.

**Smith, Edmund Kirby.** See KIRBY-SMITH.

**Smith, Edmund Munroe.** See under Henry Boynton SMITH.

**Smith,** Lady **Eleanor Furneaux.** 1902–1945. English novelist, daughter of 1st earl of Birkenhead (*q.v.*). Author of *Red Wagon* (1930), *Flamenco* (1931), *Ballerina* (1932), *Tzigane, or Romany* (1935), *Portrait of a Lady* (1936), *Life's a Circus* (an autobiography; 1939), *The Man in Grey* (1941), and short stories.

**Smith, Eli.** 1801–1857. American Congregational clergyman and missionary, b. Northford, Conn. Made exploratory trip through Armenia (1830–31), resulting in founding of important mission at Rezaieh. Devoted himself (from c. 1847) to translating Bible into Arabic. His son **Benjamin Eli** (1857–1913) was a lexicographer; managing editor of *The Century Dictionary and Cyclopedia* (1882–94) and editor in chief (from 1894); also in charge of *The Century Cyclopedia of Names, The Century Atlas.*

**Smith, Elizabeth Oakes.** See under Seba SMITH.

**Smith, Ellison DuRant.** 1864–1944. Known as "Cotton Ed Smith." American planter and politician, b. Lynchburg, S.C.; U.S. senator (1909–44).

**Smith, Elmer Boyd.** 1860–1943. Painter and illustrator, b. in St. John, New Brunswick; known esp. for his illustrations of children's books.

**Smith, Er·min′nie** (?ûr·mĭn′ĭ) **Adelle,** *nee* **Platt** (plăt). 1836–1886. American ethnologist, b. Marcellus, N.Y.; m. Simeon H. Smith (1853); interested herself in American Indian culture; made an Iroquois-English dictionary and wrote *Myths of the Iroquois* (1883).

**Smith, Ernest Bramah.** See Ernest BRAMAH.

**Smith, Francis Henney.** 1812–1890. American army officer and educator, b. Norfolk, Va.; first superintendent, Virginia Military Institute (1839–89). In Confederate service during Civil War.

**Smith, Francis Hopkinson.** 1838–1915. American author, painter, and engineer, b. Baltimore, Md.; construction engineer (from c. 1864). Also known as a water-color and black-and-white artist; illustrated his own travel sketches in Spain, the Netherlands, Italy, and Mexico, and his own *Charcoals of New and Old New York* (1912), *In Thackeray's London* (1913), *In Dickens's London* (1914). Among his well-known novels are: *Colonel Carter of Cartersville* (1891), *Caleb West, Master Diver* (1898), *The Fortunes of Oliver Horn* (1902), *The Tides of Barnegat* (1906), *Kennedy Square* (1911).

**Smith, Francis Marion.** 1846–1931. American prospector and financier, b. Richmond, Wis.; with partner W. T. Coleman (*q.v.*), discovered borax deposits in Nevada; organized Pacific Coast Borax Co.; monopolized borax market; acquired additional deposits in Death Valley, Calif.

**Smith,** Sir **Francis Pettit.** 1808–1874. English inventor; took out patent on a screw propeller (1836), six weeks ahead of John Ericsson; constructed screw steamer, the *Archimedes,* for British navy (1839), after success of which the first war screw steamer in British navy, the *Rattler,* was constructed (1841–43).

**Smith, Frederick.** See BIRKENHEAD.

**Smith, George.** 1789–1846. Scottish founder of firm of Smith, Elder & Co., booksellers and stationers, and (from 1819) publishers. His son **George** (1824–1901) joined firm (1838), took charge of business (1843), became head of firm (1846); published early works of John Ruskin, Charlotte Brontë's *Jane Eyre* (1848), Thackeray's *Henry Esmond* (1852); founded *Cornhill Magazine* (1859) with Thackeray as editor and, with Frederick Greenwood, *Pall Mall Gazette* (1865), a literary newspaper; published works of Browning, Arnold, Leslie Stephen, among others. Projected and published *Dictionary of National Biography* (63 vols., 1885–1900), edited by Sir Leslie Stephen and Sir Sidney Lee, with supplementary volumes (1901) and carried on after his death in successive supplements.

**Smith, George.** 1840–1876. English Assyriologist; deciphered (1872) Chaldean account of Deluge from Layard's tablets; by excavations (1873) in Nineveh discovered missing fragments of the tablets and fragments on duration of Babylonian dynasties; made two other expeditions in behalf of British Museum.

**Smith,** Sir **George Adam.** 1856–1942. Scottish Biblical scholar and educator, b. Calcutta; author of many religious treatises, including *The Book of Isaiah* (2 vols., 1888–90), *The Twelve Prophets* (2 vols., 1896–97), *The Early Poetry of Israel* (1912), etc.

**Smith, George Gregory.** See GREGORY SMITH.

**Smith, George Otis.** 1871–1944. American geologist; with U.S. Geological Survey (from 1896), director (1907–30); chairman, Federal Power Commission (1930–33); retired. Authority on the economics of mineral and power resources.

**Smith, Gerald Birney.** See under Azariah SMITH.

**Smith, Gerrit.** 1797–1874. American philanthropist, b. Utica, N.Y. Active in various movements, as strict Sunday observance, antitobacco and prohibition agitation, dress reform and woman's suffrage, prison reform. Associated with William Lloyd Garrison in abolitionist movement; aided John Brown and knew something of his plans against Harpers Ferry.

**Smith, Giles Alexander.** See Morgan Lewis SMITH.

**Smith, Goldwin.** 1823–1910. British historian and publicist; regius professor of history, Oxford (1858–66); championed Northern cause in American Civil War; professor of English and constitutional history, Cornell U. (1868–71); settled in Canada; edited *Canadian Monthly* (1872–74); founded and edited *The Week* and *The (Toronto) Bystander.* Distrusted imperialism; deprecated orthodox religion; declared himself in favor of John Bright's views, rather than Gladstone's; opposed home rule for Ireland; maintained that Canada was destined to unite with U.S.; denounced by Disraeli as a social parasite in *Lothair* (1870); opposed Boer War. Author of numerous works on history and politics.

**Smith,** Sir **Grafton Elliot.** 1871–1937. British anthropologist, b. New South Wales; professor of anatomy (1919–36), University Coll., London. Authority on early inhabitants of Nile valley; investigated Peking man; made researches in comparative anatomy of the brain and the evolution of man.

**Smith, Hamilton Othanel.** 1931– . American geneticist. At Johns Hopkins U. (1967– ); awarded (with Werner Arber and Daniel Nathans) Nobel prize for physiology or medicine (1978).

**Smith, Hannah,** *nee* **Whi'tall** (hwĭ't'l). 1832–1911. American religious leader, b. Philadelphia; m. (1851) Robert Pearsall Smith (d. 1898), brother of Lloyd Pearsall Smith. As a result of successive religious experiences, finally devoted herself to preaching a life of "absolute consecration, entire obedience, and simple trust"; resident in England from 1886. Her son **Logan Pear'sall** (pēr'sôl) **Smith** (1865–1946), essayist, b. Philadelphia; author of *The Youth of Parnassus* (1895), *Life and Letters of Sir Henry Wotton* (1907), *Songs and Sonnets* (1909), *The English Language* (1912), *Trivia* (1918), *Words and Idioms* (1925), *On Reading Shakespeare* (1933), *Unforgotten Years* (1938), *Milton and His Modern Critics* (1940), etc. See also Bernard BERENSON.

**Smith, Harry Bache.** 1860–1936. American librettist, b. Buffalo, N.Y.; collaborated at different times with Reginald De Koven, Victor Herbert, Irving Berlin, Jerome Kern. Also wrote *The Girl from Montmartre, Countess Maritza,* etc.

**Smith,** Sir **Harry George Wakelyn.** 1787–1860. English soldier; took leading part in subduing Kaffirs (1836) and in Sikh campaigns (1842–46); by his strategy won battle of Aliwal (Punjab) against Sikhs (1846); governor of Cape of Good Hope (1847); routed Boers under Pretorius at Boomplaats (1848); put down Kaffir rebellion (1850).

**Smith, Henry Boynton.** 1815–1877. American Presbyterian clergyman; professor of church history (1850–54) and theology (1854–74), Union Theol. Sem.; editor, *American Theological Review* (from 1859). His nephew **Edmund Munroe Smith** (1854–1926) was an educator; professor of Roman law and comparative jurisprudence (1891–1922) and Bryce professor of European legal history (1922–24), Columbia; author of *Bismarck and German Unity* (1898), *A General View of European Legal History* (1927), etc.

**Smith, Henry John Stephen.** 1826–1883. British mathematician; leading authority of his day on theory of numbers; devoted himself (after 1864) to elliptic functions.

**Smith, Henry Preserved.** 1847–1927. Brother of Richmond Mayo-Smith (*q.v.*). American clergyman; ordained in Presbyterian ministry (1875); tried for heresy (1892–94) and suspended from ministry. Professor of Biblical literature, Amherst (1898–1906); professor of history of religions, Meadville Theol. School (1907–13); librarian, Union Theol. Sem. (1913–25). A pioneer in modern Biblical criticism in U.S.

**Smith, Henry Welles.** Original name of Henry Fowle DURANT.

**Smith, Hezekiah.** 1737–1805. American Baptist clergyman; regimental chaplain (1775–78) and brigade chaplain (1778–80) in Continental army, and generally known as Chaplain Smith.

**Smith, Hoke.** 1855–1931. American lawyer and politician, b. Newton, N.C.; proprietor, Atlanta (Ga.) *Journal* (1887–1900); U.S. secretary of the interior (1893–96); governor of Georgia (1907–09; 1911); U.S. senator (1911–21); opposed President Wilson's stand on U.S. entrance into League of Nations.

**Smith, Horace.** 1808–1893. American inventor and manufacturer; associated with Daniel Baird Wesson (from 1853); patented with Wesson a revolver (Aug. 8, 1854); began manufacture of Smith & Wesson revolvers in Springfield, Mass. (1857).

**Smith, James.** 1719?–1806. Lawyer and legislator, b. in northern Ireland; to America as a boy; member of Continental Congress (1776–78); a signer of the Declaration of Independence.

**Smith, James** (1775–1839) and his brother **Horatio,** *generally known as* **Horace** (1779–1849). English humorous poets; joint authors of *Rejected Addresses,* a classic of parody composed on occasion of reopening of Drury Lane Theatre (1812), James, the gay conversationalist, parodying Wordsworth, Southey, Coleridge, Crabbe, and Cobbett, while Horatio parodied Scott, Byron, Monk Lewis, and Moore. James also wrote successful skits for Charles Mathews, *Country Cousins, A Trip to Paris, A Trip to America;* Horatio wrote historical novels, including *Brambletye House* (1826; in imitation of Scott) and *Gaieties and Gravities* (3 vols., 1826).

**Smith, James Francis.** 1859–1928. American army officer and jurist, b. San Francisco, Calif.; practiced law in San Francisco. Served in Philippines through Spanish-American War; brigadier general of volunteers (Apr., 1899). Military governor of Negros and later of Visayas (1899–1900). Associate justice, Philippines supreme court (1901–03); governor general of the Philippines (1906–09). Associate justice, U.S. court of customs appeals (1910–28).

**Smith, Jeremiah.** 1759–1842. American jurist, b. Peterborough, N.H.; practiced law in Peterborough. Governor of New Hampshire (1809–10); chief justice, New Hampshire supreme court (1802–09; 1813–16); associated with Daniel Webster and Jeremiah Mason as counsel for Dartmouth College trustees in famous Dartmouth College case (1816–20). His son **Jeremiah** (1837–1921) and his grandson **Jeremiah** (1870–1935) were also jurists of distinction.

**Smith, Jessie Willcox.** d. 1935. American portrait painter and illustrator; excelled in painting portraits of children, and in illustrating children's books.

**Smith** *or* **Smyth** (smĭth), **John.** 1570?–1612. English nonconformist clergyman; called the "Se-baptist" (self-baptizer). Influenced by Brownists, left Established Church and became pastor of independent congregation at Gainsborough (1606); migrated to Amsterdam to escape persecution; became a Baptist under Mennonite influence; wrote some of first expositions of principles of General Baptists.

**Smith, John.** 1580–1631. English colonist in America, b. Willoughby, Lincs, Eng.; military adventurer in wars against the Turks (to 1604?). To America (1606) and arrived at Jamestown, Va. (May 24, 1607); on governing council of colony; made prisoner by Indians, condemned to death, and, according to his story, rescued by Pocahontas, daughter of the chieftain Powhatan. Led exploring expeditions up the Potomac and Rappahannock rivers and around Chesapeake Bay. President of the colony (1608–09); returned to England (1609). Explored New England coast (1614) and attempted a second voyage there but was captured by the French (1615). Author of *A True Relation of... Virginia Since the First Planting of That Collony* (1608), *A Map of Virginia...* (1612), *A Description of New England* (1616), *New England Trials* (1620), *The Generall Historie of Virginia, New-England, and the Summer Isles* (1624), *The True Travels, Adventures, and Observations of Captaine John Smith...*(1630), etc.

**Smith, John Merlin Pow'is** (pō'ĭs). 1866–1932. Theologian, b. London, Eng.; to America (1883); professor, U. of Chicago (from 1915); editor, *American Journal of Semitic Languages* (1915–32); author of critical commentaries on books of the Old Testament.

**Smith, John Raphael.** 1752–1812. English portrait painter and mezzotint engraver.

**Smith, John Stafford.** 1750–1836. English musical antiquary and composer of anthems and glees, and probably of the tune of the song *To Anacreon in Heaven,* which was later used as tune of *The Star-Spangled Banner.* Cf. Francis Scott KEY.

**Smith, Joseph.** 1805–1844. Founder of the Mormon Church, b. Sharon, Vt. According to his own account, began to have visions in 1820 telling him that the church of Christ had been withdrawn from the earth and that God had chosen him to restore it; received (Sept. 22, 1827) from an angel a book written in strange hieroglyphics on golden plates, telling the history of the true church in America; with miraculous aid translated the book and published it at Palmyra, N.Y., as *The Book of Mormon* (1830). Founded Church of Jesus Christ of Latter-day Saints at Fayette, N.Y. (Apr. 6, 1830). *The Book of Mormon,* with *A Book of Commandments* (1833) and *Doctrine and Covenants* (1835), provide the basis for the church's doctrine and organization. Moved his small congregation to Kirtland, Ohio (1831), then to Missouri (1838), and to Commerce, Ill., renamed Nauvoo; governed the Mormon colony despotically, with aid of small group of advisers. Opposition to polygamy (1843) created schism in church; opposition expressed in *Nauvoo Expositor* (June 7, 1844); put his opponents to flight and destroyed their printing press. Arrested and jailed by non-Mormons in neighboring towns and villages; taken from jail at Carthage, Ill., by a mob (June 27, 1844) and shot. Claim made (1852) that he received revelation (1843) authorizing polygamy; claim later controverted. See Brigham YOUNG. His son **Joseph** (1832–1914), b. Kirtland, Ohio, accepted (1860) presidency of Reorganized Church of Jesus Christ of Latter-day Saints, an offshoot from the original Mormon Church; opposed polygamy; moved to Lamoni, Iowa (1881); by wise leadership, increased membership in his church to over 70,000; moved (1906) to Independence, Mo., still the headquarters of this sect; author of *History of the Church* (with H. C. Smith; 1897 ff.). A nephew of Joseph Smith (1805–1844), **Joseph Fielding Smith** (1838–1918), was taken to Utah with the Mormons under the leadership of Brigham Young (1848); served in so-called Utah War; missionary to Great Britain (1860–63) and to Hawaii (1864–65); made an apostle of the Mormon Church (1866); president of European mission with headquarters in England (1874–75, 1877); second counselor to the president of his church (1880–1901) and first counselor (1901); president of the Mormon Church (1901–18); appeared before U.S. Senate committee (1904) investigating qualifications of Reed Smoot for a seat in the senate and declared that the Mormon Church no longer sanctioned plural marriages; did much during his administration to strengthen his church organization and to foster friendly relations with non-Mormons.

**Smith, Joseph Lindon.** 1863–1950. American painter, b. Pawtucket, R.I. Among his works are murals in the Boston Public Library and the Horticultural Hall in Philadelphia. On staff of archaeological expeditions to Egypt; present at discovery of important tombs in the Valley of the Kings at Luxor. Has painted many of the architectural treasures of antiquity.

**Smith, Judson.** See under Azariah SMITH.

**Smith, Justin Harvey.** 1857–1930. American historian, b. Boscawen, N.H.; professor of modern history, Dartmouth (1898–1908). Author of *The Troubadours at Home* (1899), *The Annexation of Texas* (1911), *The War With Mexico* (2 vols., 1919; awarded Pulitzer prize in 1920), etc.

**Smith** (smĭt), **Kaj Birket–.** See BIRKET-SMITH.

**Smith** (smĭth), **Lloyd Pear′sall** (pẽr′sôl). 1822–1886. American librarian, b. Philadelphia; brother-in-law of Hannah Whitall Smith. Assistant librarian (1849–51) and librarian (1851–86), Library Company of Philadelphia; first editor of *Lippincott's Magazine* (1868–69); one of original editorial staff of *American Library Journal* (1876).

**Smith, Logan Pearsall.** See under Hannah Whitall SMITH.

**Smith, Marcus.** See under Solomon F. SMITH.

**Smith, May,** *nee* **Ri′ley** (rī′lĭ). 1842–1927. American poet, b. Rochester, N.Y.; m. Albert Smith (1869; d. 1919); author of *The Gift of Gentians* (1882), *The Inn of Rest* (1888), *Sometime and Other Poems* (1892), etc.; remembered esp. for poems *Sometime*, *Tired Mother*, *The Child in Me*.

**Smith, Melancton.** 1744–1798. American Revolutionary patriot; organized and captained first company of rangers organized in Dutchess County. In business in New York City (from 1785). Member of Continental Congress (1785–88) and of constitutional ratification convention (1788). His grandson **Melancton Smith** (1810–1893) was a naval officer; served under Farragut in attack on New Orleans (1862) and Port Hudson (1863); served under Porter in attack on Fort Fisher (1864–65); rear admiral (1870).

**Smith, Morgan Lewis.** 1821–1874. American army officer; organized and commanded Missouri infantry regiment (1861); engaged at Fort Donelson, and in Shiloh and Corinth campaigns; brigadier general of volunteers (July, 1862); engaged at Vicksburg, Missionary Ridge. His brother **Giles Alexander** (1829–1876) served as officer in his brother's regiment and succeeded to colonelcy when brother became brigadier general (July, 1862); engaged against Vicksburg; brigadier general (Aug., 1863); served under Sherman in march through the Carolinas; major general (Nov., 1865); mustered out (1865).

**Smith, Naomi Gwladys Royde–.** See ROYDE-SMITH.

**Smith, Nathan.** 1762–1829. American physician, b. Rehoboth, Mass.; introduced teaching of anatomy, surgery, and medicine at Dartmouth; professor, Yale (1813–29); founder of Yale Medical School. Author of *Practical Essay on Typhous Fever* (1824). A son, **Nathan Ry′no** [rī′nō] (1797–1877), was also a physician; first professor of anatomy at Jefferson Medical School, Philadelphia (1826–27); professor of anatomy (1827–29) and surgery (1829–77) at U. of Maryland. A son of Nathan Ryno Smith, **Alan Penniman** (1840–1898), was a surgeon in Baltimore, largely instrumental in influencing Johns Hopkins to found and endow Johns Hopkins Hospital.

**Smith, Norman Kemp.** 1872–1958. British philosopher; professor of logic and metaphysics, Edinburgh (1919–45).

**Smith, Paul.** 1825–1912. American huntsman and guide, b. Milton, Vt.; established a hunter's lodge in the Adirondacks, first at Loon Lake (1852) and later at St. Regis Lake (1858), where he expanded the lodge to a large hotel. He was largely responsible for development of the Adirondack region.

**Smith, Pauline.** South African writer of novels and short stories, b. Little Karoo, Cape of Good Hope; educ. in England and long resident there. Among her books are *Little Karoo* (1925), *Beadle* (1927), *A.B.* (1933), and *Platkops Children* (1935).

**Smith, Percey Franklyn.** 1867–1956. American mathematician; professor, Sheffield Scientific School, Yale (1900–36; emeritus). Known for work in analytic geometry.

**Smith, Preserved.** 1880–1941. American historian; B.A., Amherst (1901); Ph.D., Columbia (1907); professor of history, Cornell (1922–41); author of *Life and Letters of Martin Luther* (1911), *The Age of the Reformation* (1920), *Erasmus* (1923), *A History of Modern Culture* (vol. I, 1930; vol. II, 1934).

**Smith, Richard.** 1735–1803. American lawyer, b. Burlington, N.J.; adm. to bar (c. 1760); member of Continental Congress (1774–76); writer of a detailed diary of proceedings of the congress (Sept. 12–Oct. 1, 1775 and Dec. 12, 1775–Mar. 30, 1776), valuable as historical source material.

**Smith, Richard Penn.** See under William SMITH (1727–1803).

**Smith, Robert.** 1689–1768. English mathematician; Plumian professor of astronomy (1716–60) and master of Trinity College, Cambridge (1742).

**Smith, Robert.** 1722?–1777. Architect, b. prob. Glasgow, Scotland; to America (c. 1750); offices in Philadelphia; designed Nassau Hall at Princeton U., St. Peter's Church in Philadelphia, etc.

**Smith, Robert.** 1757–1842. See under Samuel SMITH.

**Smith, Robert Payne.** See PAYNE SMITH.

**Smith,** Sir **Ross Macpherson.** 1892–1922. British aviator, b. Adelaide, South Australia; served in World War (1914–18), in Royal Flying Corps (1916–18). After World War, with his brother made first long-distance flight from England to Australia (Nov. 12–Dec. 10, 1919) and won £10,000 prize offered by Commonwealth of Australia for achievement of such a flight within 720 consecutive hours. Killed in airplane accident.

**Smith, Roswell.** 1829–1892. American publisher, b. Lebanon, Conn. With Josiah Gilbert Holland, joined Charles Scribner in publishing business (1870). Purchased interests of Holland and Scribner (1881), and founded and headed The Century Co.; continued *Scribner's Monthly* under name of *Century Magazine;* published *The Century Dictionary and Cyclopedia* (1891).

**Smith, Samuel.** 1752–1839. American politician, b. Carlisle, Pa. Organized volunteer company (1775); engaged in battle of Long Island and battle of Monmouth; commanded Maryland contingent sent to suppress Whisky Insurrection (1791). Commissioned brigadier general of Maryland militia (1794); major general commanding defense of Baltimore (1812); member of U.S. House of Representatives (1793–1803; 1816–22), and U.S. Senate (1803–15; 1835–38). His brother **Robert** (1757–1842) was a lawyer and statesman; U.S. secretary of the navy (1801–09); U.S. secretary of state (1809–11).

**Smith, Samuel Francis.** 1808–1895. American Baptist clergyman and poet, b. Boston; editorial secretary, American Baptist Missionary Union (from 1854). His poetry was collected and published as *Poems of Home and Country* (1895). He is best known as author of *My Country, 'tis of Thee* (first published in Mason's *The*

*Choir*, 1832) and the missionary hymn *The morning light is breaking*.

**Smith, Samuel Stanhope.** 1750–1819. American Presbyterian clergyman and educator; taught classics at Princeton (1770–73), moral philosophy (1779–1812); president of Princeton (1795–1812).

**Smith, Sarah.** See Hesba STRETTON.

**Smith, Seba.** *Pseudonym* Major **Jack Dow′ning** (dou′nĭng). 1792–1868. American satirist, b. Buckfield, Me.; founded and edited first daily newspaper in Maine, the Portland *Courier* (1829), and contributed to it a series of letters written by a supposed Major Jack Downing and satirizing humorously politics of the Andrew Jackson period; contributed a second series to the *Daily National Intelligencer*, Washington, D.C. (from 1847). His wife, **Elizabeth Oakes**, *nee* **Prince** [prĭns] (1806–1893), was author of many novels.

**Smith, Sheila Kaye–.** See KAYE-SMITH.

**Smith,** Sir **Sidney.** 1764–1840. = Sir William Sidney SMITH.

**Smith, Sidney.** 1877–1935. American cartoonist; on staff of Chicago *Tribune* (1911–35); creator of "The Gumps."

**Smith, Solomon Franklin,** *known as* **Sol.** 1801–1869. American comedian and theater manager; partner in theater management firm of Ludlow & Smith (1835–53), controlling theaters in St. Louis, Mobile, and New Orleans. A son, **Marcus,** *known as* **Mark** (1829–1874), was also a comedian; excelled in portrayal of old gentlemen.

**Smith, Sophia.** 1796–1870. American philanthropist, b. Hatfield, Mass.; inherited fortune from brother Austin Smith (d. 1861). On advice of her pastor, John Morton Greene, bequeathed fortune for founding a college for women, Smith College, Northampton, Mass., opened in 1875.

**Smith, S. S.** Pseudonym of Thames Ross WILLIAMSON.

**Smith, Sydney.** 1771–1845. English clergyman, essayist, and wit; took orders (1794); with Jeffrey and Brougham, started *Edinburgh Review* (1802). Preacher in Foundling Hospital and lecturer on moral philosophy at Royal Institution in London (1804–06); a favorite among Whigs at Holland House because of his drollery and wit and cogent political reasoning; spent twenty years as village parson and village doctor in Yorkshire (1809–28); canon of St. Paul's, London (1831–45); follower of Paley in theology, took secular view of religious obligations. Champion of parliamentary reform but opposed the ballot; denouncer of everything American. Author of sixty-five articles in *Edinburgh Review;* produced *Peter Plymley Letters* in defense of Catholic emancipation (1807). Originator of the character Mrs. Partington, later made famous by Shillaber.

**Smith,** Sir **Sydney Armitage–.** See ARMITAGE-SMITH.

**Smith, Theobald.** 1859–1934. American pathologist, b. Albany, N.Y.; professor, Harvard (1896–1915); director, department of animal pathology, Rockefeller Institute for Medical Research (1915–29). Known for work in the cause and nature of infectious and parasitic diseases; developed a theory of immunization; discovered the organism causing Texas fever, demonstrating that it was transmitted by a cattle tick; announced that there was distinction between human and bovine types of tubercle bacilli; announced results of successful experiments on immunizing effects of neutral toxin-antitoxin mixtures in diphtheria (1909).

**Smith, Theodore Clarke.** 1870–1960. American educator; professor of American history, Williams (1903–38). Author of *Political Reconstruction* (1903, in *Cambridge Modern History*), *Parties and Slavery, 1851–59* (1906), *Wars Between England and America* (1914).

**Smith,** Sir **Thomas.** 1513–1577. English statesman and scholar; regius professor of civil law and vice-chancellor, Cambridge (1544); one of two secretaries of state (1548–49, 1572–76). In Elizabeth's reign sent on diplomatic missions; negotiated peace of Troyes (1564).

**Smith, Thorne.** 1892–1934. American humorist; author of a number of ribald and whimsical tales, including *Topper* (1926), *The Night Life of the Gods* (1931), *The Bishop's Jaegers* (1932), *Skin and Bones* (1933).

**Smith, Walter Be·dell′** (bĕ·dĕl′). 1895–1961. American army officer, b. Indianapolis; chief of staff to General Eisenhower (1942–46); ambassador to Russia (1946–49); under sec'y of state (1953–54).

**Smith, Walter Chalmers.** 1824–1908. Scottish poet and preacher; Free Church minister, Edinburgh (1876–94). Wrote *The Bishop's Walk* (1861), *Olrig Grange* (1872), *Raban* (1880), *Kildrostan* (1884), etc.

**Smith, Walter Granville–.** See GRANVILLE-SMITH.

**Smith, William.** 1697–1769. Jurist, b. in Buckinghamshire, Eng.; to America (1715); practiced law, New York City; conspicuous as counsel in cases in which he sought to restrict the governor's prerogative. One of counsel for defense of John Peter Zenger (*q.v.*) when tried for seditious libel (1735). Associate justice, New York supreme court (1763–69). A son, **William** (1728–1793), was also a jurist; chief justice of New York (1780) and member of the provincial council (from 1767); refused (1777, 1778) to take oath of allegiance to the revolutionary state; when New York was evacuated by British (1783), he went to England; chief justice of Canada (1786–93).

**Smith, William.** 1727–1803. Clergyman and educator, b. Aberdeen, Scotland; to New York (1751). Teacher of logic, rhetoric, and moral philosophy in the Academy and Charitable School in Philadelphia, which developed into U. of Pennsylvania (1754); first provost of the institution (1755–91). His grandson **Richard Penn Smith** (1799–1854) was a lawyer and playwright; purchased and edited Philadelphia *Aurora* (1822–27); author of a number of plays (1825–35), most of them adapted from or inspired by French originals.

**Smith, William.** 1769–1839. English geologist; founder of stratigraphical geology; known as the "father of English geology." As mineral surveyor and civil engineer, noted regularity and inclination of strata; became authority on drainage and irrigation. Won fame with large *Geological Map of England and Wales* (1815), which formed basis for 21 separate county geological maps, constituting a *Geological Atlas of England and Wales;* first recipient of Wollaston Medal (1831).

**Smith, William.** 1797–1887. American politician, b. in King George County, Va.; member, U.S. House of Representatives (1841–43; 1853–61); governor of Virginia (1846–49). In Confederate army through Civil War. Again governor of Virginia (1864–65).

**Smith,** Sir **William.** 1813–1893. English classical and Biblical lexicographer; editor of *Dictionary of Greek and Roman Antiquities* (1842), of which he himself wrote greater part, *Dictionary of Greek and Roman Biography* (1849), and *Greek and Roman Geography* (1857); edited Gibbon (1854); editor of dictionaries of the Bible (1860–65), of Christian antiquities (1875–80), of Christian biography (1877–87). Editor of *Quarterly Review* (1867–93). His brother **Philip** (1817–1885), historian, was his coadjutor in compilation of classical dictionaries.

**Smith, William Benjamin.** 1850–1934. American educator, b. Stanford, Ky.; at Tulane U. (1893–1915). Wrote *The Color Line* (1905), *Der Vorchristliche Jesus* (1906), *The Merman and the Seraph* (1906), *Ecce Deus* (1911), *Push? or Pull?* (1912), *Mors Mortis* (1915), and mathematical textbooks.

**Smith, William Farrar.** 1824–1903. American army officer, b. St. Albans, Vt.; grad. U.S.M.A., West Point (1845). Commanded corps at Antietam and Fredericksburg; chief engineer in operations around Chattanooga, Tenn. (1863); engaged at Cold Harbor and Petersburg; resigned from U.S. army (1867). President, board of police commissioners, New York City (1875–81). In U.S. army engineer work (from 1881).

**Smith, William Henry.** 1825–1891. English news agent, bookseller, and cabinet minister; early became partner in father's news agency; M.P. (1868); first lord of admiralty (1877–80) in Disraeli's cabinet; first lord of treasury and leader of House of Commons (from 1886).

**Smith, William Robertson.** 1846–1894. Scottish Biblical critic and Orientalist; professor of Oriental languages and Old Testament exegesis at Free Church College, Aberdeen (1870–81); dismissed (1881) because of heterodoxy of his Biblical articles in ninth edition of *Encyclopaedia Britannica*, after trial that popularized his scholarly views and methods. Coeditor with Thomas Spencer Baynes of *Encyclopaedia Britannica* (from 1880), editor in chief (1887–88); professor of Arabic, Cambridge (1883–86, 1889–94).

**Smith,** Sir **William Sidney.** 1764–1840. English naval commander. While plenipotentiary at Constantinople, went to relief of Acre, and compelled Napoleon to raise siege (1799); destroyed Turkish fleet off Abydos (1807); blockaded the Tagus River; vice-admiral (1810), admiral (1821).

**Smith, William Stephens.** 1755–1816. American Revolutionary officer, b. New York City. Major, and aide-de-camp to General Sullivan (Aug., 1776); aide-de-camp to Washington (July, 1781). A founder of Society of the Cincinnati; succeeded von Steuben as its president.

**Smith, Winchell.** 1871–1933. American playwright, b. Hartford, Conn. Associated with Arnold Daly (1904) in producing G. B. Shaw's plays on New York stage; dramatized George Barr McCutcheon's *Brewster's Millions* (1906), and with its success devoted himself entirely to playwriting. Author of *The Fortune Hunter, The Only Son;* coauthor of *Via Wireless* (1908; with Paul Armstrong), *The New Henrietta* (1913; with Victor Mapes), *Turn to the Right* (1916; with J. E. Hazzard), *Lightnin'* (1918; with Frank Bacon).

**Smith, Xanthus Russell.** 1839–1929. American painter, b. Philadelphia; served in Civil War; after the war, painted many battle scenes; also painted landscapes, marines, and portraits (Washington, Whitman, Lincoln).

**Smith'-Dor'ri·en** (smĭth'dŏr'ĭ·ĕn), Sir **Horace Lockwood.** 1858–1930. British soldier; served in Zulu War (1879), Egyptian War (1882), Nile expedition (1884), Sudan campaign (1885), in Bengal (1893–94) and the Punjab (1894–96), Boer War (1899–1901), again in India (1901–07); promoted major general (1899), lieutenant general (1906), general (1912). In World War, commanded 2d army corps, then 2d army, in British expeditionary force (1914–15); commanded East African forces (1915–16). Governor of Gibraltar (1918–23).

**Smith'son** (smĭth's'n), **Harriet Constance.** *Later* Madame **Ber'lioz'** (bĕr'lyôz'). 1800–1854. Irish actress; made first appearance as Lady Teazle, Dublin (1815); engaged by Elliston; accompanied Macready to Paris (1828); again in Paris (1832) playing Shakespearean parts; m. (1833) Hector Berlioz (*q.v.*); separated (1840).

**Smithson,** Sir **Hugh.** 1715–1786. See PERCY family.

**Smithson, James.** 1765–1829. Known in his youth as **James Lewis** (*or* **Louis**) **Ma'cie** (mā'sĭ) after his mother, Elizabeth Keate Macie. Illegitimate son of Hugh Smithson Percy, 1st Duke of Northumberland. British chemist and mineralogist; author of many scientific papers, including one on calamines, the mineral smithsonite (calamine) being named after him. Bequeathed over £100,000 to the United States to found at Washington, D.C., the Smithsonian Institution, which was established by act of Congress (1846).

**Smo·hal'la** (smô·hăl'*ȧ*). 1815?–1907. American Indian religious leader, chief of the Wanapûm, a tribe living in Yakima County, Washington; famed as medicine man (1850); wandered down Pacific coast to Mexico and back through Arizona, Utah, and Nevada (1856?–?60); appeared among his own tribe as one miraculously returned from the spirit world. Gained wide following for his Dreamer religion; his teaching responsible for much of Indian hostility to the whites in period from 1870, esp. that culminating in the Nez Percé War (1877).

**Smol'lett** (smŏl'ĕt; -ĭt), **Tobias George.** 1721–1771. British novelist, b. Dalquhurn, Dumbartonshire, Scotland; grandson of Sir James Smollett, a Whig judge and promoter of Union of 1707; educ. at Glasgow. Sailed as surgeon's mate on Cartagena expedition (1741–43); married a Jamaica heiress (1747) and settled as surgeon in Downing Street, London; M.D. (1750). After success of *The Adventures of Roderick Random*, a picaresque novel (1748, anonymously), and *The Adventures of Peregrine Pickle* (1751), gave up practice of medicine at Bath, to live by his pen; settled at Chelsea; published *Ferdinand Count Fathom* (1753), prototype of later schools of mystery and horror stories. Translated *Don Quixote* (1755); edited the Tory *Critical Review* (1756); broke his health producing a standard library *History of England* (1756–57); attempted a vast *Universal History;* translated Voltaire in 38 volumes; edited the unsuccessful *Briton* (1762). Ridiculed, abused, and imprisoned for political articles supporting Lord Bute; traveled abroad for his health and published his excellent *Travels through France and Italy* (1766), which provoked Sterne's portrait of "Smelfungus" (in *A Sentimental Journey*); left England again (1768), an invalid, to live in Italy; embittered, launched Rabelaisian satire upon English public affairs in *The Adventures of an Atom* (1769); accomplished his best character drawing in his last novel, *The Expedition of Humphry Clinker* (1770); died at Leghorn. Author also of a farce, *The Reprisal, or the Tars of Old England* (produced 1757), a mediocre novel, *Adventures of Sir Launcelot Greaves* (1760–62), and poems including *The Tears of Scotland* and *Ode to Independence.*

**Smoot** (smōōt), **Reed.** 1862–1941. American politician and Mormon leader, b. Salt Lake City. Elected an apostle of the Church of Jesus Christ of Latter-day Saints (1900); U.S. senator (1903–33); chairman of finance committee, U.S. Senate; member of World War Foreign Debt Commission (1922); sponsor in Senate of tariff act of 1930, known as Smoot-Hawley Tariff Act. See Joseph Fielding SMITH.

**Smreczyński, Franciszek.** See Władysław ORKAN.

**Smuts** (smŭts; *Sou. Afr. Du.* smûts), **Jan Christiaan.** 1870–1950. South African soldier and statesman, b. Cape Town; practiced law first at Cape Town and later at Johannesburg. A Boer leader in Boer War (1899–1902); commander in chief of Republican forces in Cape of Good Hope (1901–02). Largely instrumental in effecting the Union of South Africa. During World War, organized South African forces and co-operated with General Botha in suppressing a rebellion in South Africa and in conquering Southwest Africa (1914–15); later (1916), commanded British troops in British East Africa. Representative of Union of South Africa in Imperial War Cabinet (1917; 1918) and (with General Botha) at the

Peace Conference in Paris. Prime minister of the Union of South Africa (1919–24; 1939 ff.); minister of justice (1933–39). Made field marshal (1941).

**Smy′bert** (smī′bẽrt), **John.** = John SMIBERT.

**Smyth** (smĭth; smīth). See also SMITH, SMYTHE.

**Smyth** (smīth), Dame **Ethel Mary.** 1858–1944. English composer, writer; militant suffragist; composed *The March of the Women* (1911), battle song of the Women's Social and Political Union. Composer of symphonies, operas, choral works, instrumental pieces, and songs.

**Smyth** (smīth), **Herbert Weir.** 1857–1937. American Greek scholar; professor, Harvard (1901–25).

**Smyth** (?smĭth; ?smīth), Sir **Nevill Maskelyne.** 1868–1941. British army officer; educ. Sandhurst; served in Sudan campaign (V.C., 1898); assisted in Sudan surveys; chartered Nile cataracts from Wadi Halfa to Ethiopia; in World War commanded Australian infantry brigade in Dardanelles (1915) and in France (1916–18); major general (1918); retired (1924).

**Smyth** (smīth), **William.** 1797–1868. American educator; professor of mathematics, Bowdoin (from 1828). A son, **Egbert Coffin Smyth** [smīth] (1829–1904), was a Congregational clergyman; professor of ecclesiastical history, Andover Sem. (1863–1904) and president of the faculty (1878–96). Another son, **Newman Smyth** [smīth] (1843–1925), was also a Congregational clergyman; pastorate in New Haven, Conn. (1882–1908); author of *Old Faiths in New Light* (1878), *The Place of Death in Evolution* (1897), *Modern Belief in Immortality* (1910), etc.

**Smyth** (?smĭth; ?smīth), **William Henry.** 1788–1865. English naval officer and hydrographer; surveyed coasts of Sicily and adjacent shores of Adriatic and Sardinia; published his results (1828); a founder of Royal Geographical Society (1830); admiral (1863). Author of *The Mediterranean* (1854) and *The Sailor's Word-book* (1867). His son **Charles Piazzi** (1819–1900) was astronomer royal for Scotland (1845–88); author of *Our Inheritance in the Great Pyramid* (1864) and *On the Antiquity of Intellectual Man* (1868).

**Smythe** (smīth; smīth). See also SMITH, SMYTH.

**Smythe,** Sir **Thomas.** *Orig. surname* **Smith.** 1558?–1625. English merchant; elected first governor of East India Co. (1600), and re-elected (1603); journeyed to Jarosław and obtained trading privileges from Russian czar for Muscovy Co., of which his maternal grandfather was a founder (1604–05); obtained charter for Virginia Co., of which he was treasurer (1609–20); resigned because of charges of undue self-enrichment; devoted fortune to endowment of school founded by his grandfather and other charities.

From his elder brother Sir **John Smith** of Ostenhanger, now Westenhanger, Kent (d. 1635), descended the family comprising Viscounts **Strang′ford** (străng′fẽrd) in Irish peerage (cr. 1628) and Barons **Pens′hurst** (pĕnz′hûrst) of Penshurst in peerage of United Kingdom (cr. 1825), including:

**Percy Clinton Sydney Smythe** (1780–1855), 6th Viscount Strangford and 1st Baron Penshurst; diplomat; as secretary of legation at Lisbon, published *Poems from the Portuguese of Camoëns* (1803); ambassador to Portugal (1806), Sweden (1817), Turkey (1820), Russia (1825); special emissary to Brazil (1828).

His eldest son, **George Augustus Frederick Percy Sydney Smythe** (1818–1857), 7th viscount and 2d baron; b. Stockholm; M.P. (1841–52); one of the Young England party from whom Disraeli drew his portrait of the hero of *Coningsby;* foreign undersecretary (1845–46); brilliant journalist (1847–52); fought with Colonel Frederick Romilly last duel in England (1852).

Another son, **Percy Ellen Frederick William Smythe** (1826–1869), 8th viscount and 3d baron; philologist; as student attaché at Constantinople, mastered Persian, Greek, Turkish, Arabic, Hindustani; Oriental secretary during Crimean War; devoted himself to philological studies and writing of articles on Near East; contributed chapters to *Eastern Shores of the Adriatic* (1863), written by his wife, **Emily Anne,** *nee* **Beau′fort** [bō′fẽrt] (d. 1887), a descendant of Beauforts of the crusades, who personally superintended hospital in Turkey established by her for Turkish soldiers.

**Snef′ru** (snĕf′ro͞o) *or* **Sne′fe·ru** (snĕ′fĕ·ro͞o). fl. about 2920 B.C. Last king of IIId (Memphite) dynasty of kings of ancient Egypt; brought Egypt to high level of prosperity; built large ships and increased sea trade; built two pyramids; developed copper mines in Sinai.

**Sneider.** See Johannes AGRICOLA.

**Snell** (snĕl), **Foster Dee.** 1898– . American chemist, b. Binghamton, N.Y.; B.S., Colgate (1919), Ph.D., Columbia (1923); consulting chemist in Brooklyn (from 1923); author of technical papers and (with his wife) of *Colorimetric Methods of Analysis* (2 vols., 1936–37) and *Chemicals of Commerce* (1939).

**Snell, Henry Bayley.** 1858–1943. American marine and landscape painter, b. Richmond, Eng.

**Snel′laert** (snĕl′ärt), **Ferdinand Augustin.** 1809–1872. Flemish writer; founder (1836) at Ghent of the Flemish society La Langue est tout le Peuple, which began the Flemish movement in modern literature.

**Snel′len** (snĕl′ĕn), **Herman.** 1834–1908. Dutch ophthalmologist; originated Snellen's test type for determining acuteness of vision.

**Snel′ling** (snĕl′ĭng), **Josiah.** 1782–1828. American army officer; established military fort near St. Paul and Minneapolis (1820), now known as Fort Snelling, and commanded there (to 1828). A son, **William Joseph** (1804–1848), was first a trapper in region around Fort Snelling and later a journalist in Boston; best known for his social satires; author also of *Tales of the Northwest...*(1830), *The Rat-Trap; or, Cogitations of A Convict in the House of Correction* (1837). Another son, **Henry Hunt** (1817–1897), b. Plattsburg, N.Y., was an expert in photography; author of *A Dictionary of the Photographic Art* (1854), etc.

**Snel′li·us** (snĕl′ĭ·ŭs; *Du.* snĕl′ē·ûs), **Willebrord.** *Also* **Snell van Ro′yen** (snĕl′ vän rō′yĕn). 1591–1626. Dutch mathematician; discoverer of law of refraction.

**Sneth′en** (snĕth′'n), **Nicholas.** 1769–1845. American clergyman; entered Methodist Episcopal ministry (1794); a founder of Methodist Protestant church (1828).

**Sni′der** (snī′dẽr), **Denton Jaques** (*prob.* zhȧk). 1841–1925. American philosopher; taught in St. Louis schools (1867–77); lectured through the Middle West (1884–97); author of several volumes of verse (*Delphic Days,* 1880, *Homer in Chios,* 1891, etc.), volumes of commentaries on Shakespeare, Dante, Goethe, Homer, and books on philosophy.

**Snider, Jacob.** d. 1866. American inventor of a breech-loading rifle (Snider rifle) adopted (after 1859) by the British government.

**Snof′ru** (snŏf′ro͞o). Variant of SNEFRU.

**Snoil′sky** (snoil′skü), Count **Carl.** 1841–1903. Swedish lyric poet.

**Snor′ri Stur′lu·son** (snŏr′rĭ stûr′lû·sŏn). 1178–1241. Icelandic statesman and historian; head of legislative assembly and of highest court in Iceland; became involved in political intrigues and was assassinated (Sept. 23, 1241). Author of the *Heimskringla* (a poetic chronicle of Norse mythology and early history), and the *Younger, or Prose, Edda,* also known as the *Edda of Snorri Sturluson* (a prose work treating of Norse mythology and the language and modes of composition of the scalds).

**Snow** (snō), Baron **Charles Percy**. 1905–    . British writer, physicist, and diplomat. Wrote series of novels *Strangers and Brothers* (11 vols., 1940–70).

**Snow, Edgar Parks**. 1905–1972. American journalist, b. Kansas City, Mo.; chief Far Eastern correspondent, London *Daily Herald* (1937), etc. Author of *Far Eastern Front* (1934), *Red Star Over China* (1937), *The Battle for Asia* (1941), etc.

**Snow, Francis Huntington**. 1840–1908. American naturalist; professor, U. of Kansas (from 1866), and chancellor (1890–1901). Snow Hall of Natural History at U. of Kansas is named in his honor.

**Snow, John**. 1813–1858. English physician; discovered that cholera is transmitted by contaminated water; introduced use of ether as anesthetic into English surgical practice (1846–47).

**Snow, Lorenzo**. 1814–1901. American Mormon leader, b. Mantua, Ohio. Went with Brigham Young to Salt Lake City (arriving 1848); made an apostle of the church (1849); leader of Mormon colony settled in Brigham City, Utah (from 1853). After passage of Edmunds Act (1882) making polygamy a punishable offense, Snow was convicted of unlawful cohabitation and sent to prison (1886); decision reversed by U.S. Supreme Court (1887). Chosen president of the Mormon church (Sept. 13, 1898). First to enunciate the doctrine of eternal progression in the aphorism, "As man now is, God once was; as God now is, man may be." His sister **Eliza Roxey** (1804–1887), also a Mormon, was a poet; went to Utah with group led by Brigham Young (1847); became one of the plural wives of the prophet Joseph Smith (1842) and also of Brigham Young (1849); author esp. of hymns.

**Snow, Wilbert**, *in full*, **Charles Wilbert**. 1884–    . American poet; author of *Maine Coast* (1923), *The Inner Harbor* (1926), *Down East* (1932), *Before the Wind* (1938), *Maine Tides* (1940).

**Snow′den** (snō′d'n), **Philip**. 1st Viscount **Snowden of Ick′orn·shaw** (ĭk′ôrn·shô). 1864–1937. English politician; Socialist (from 1893); chairman of Independent Labor party (1903–06; 1917–20); M.P. (1906–18; 1922–31); chancellor of the exchequer (1924; 1929–31); lord privy seal (1931–32); became bitter critic of the government. Author of *Socialism and Syndicalism*, *Socialism and the Drink Question*, *The Living Wage*, *Labour and Finance*, *Labour and the New World*.

**Snowdon**, Earl of. See Antony ARMSTRONG-JONES.

**Sny′der** (snī′dẽr), **John Francis**. 1830–1921. American physician and archaeologist, b. near Cahokia, Ill.; best known for his survey and investigation of the Cahokia mounds in Illinois.

**Snyder, John Wesley**. 1895–    . American banker, b. Jonesboro, Ark.; national bank receiver (1930–36); federal loan administrator and director of War Mobilization (1945); secretary of the treasury (1946–53).

**Snyder, Virgil**. 1869–1950. American mathematician.

**Sny′ders** (snī′dẽrs), **Frans**. 1579–1657. Dutch painter, esp. of animals; friend of and co-worker with Rubens.

**So** (sō). See SHABAKA.

**So·a·mi** (sō·ä·mē). *Real name* **Shin·so** (shēn·sō). 1460?–?1530. Japanese landscape painter.

**Soane** (sōn), Sir **John**. 1753–1837. English architect, son of a mason named Swan; enlarged and rebuilt Bank of England in Roman Corinthian style; presented to nation (1833) antiquarian collection of paintings, sculpture, drawings, and gems.

**Sobieski, John**. See JOHN III SOBIESKI.

**So·bre′ro** (sō·brâ′rō), **Ascanio**. 1812–1888. Italian chemist; discovered nitroglycerin (1847).

**So′cin** (zō′tsēn), **Albert**. 1844–1899. German Oriental scholar.

**So·ci′nus** (sō·sī′nŭs), **Laelius**. *Latin form of* **Lelio Soz·zi′ni** (sōt·tsē′nē). 1525–1562. Italian theologian; author of an anti-Trinitarian doctrine developed by his nephew **Faustus Socinus** *or* **Fausto Sozzini** (1539–1604) into the doctrinal system known as Socinianism. Faustus was denounced by the Inquisition (1559); took refuge in Zurich (1559–62) and under protection of the grand duke of Tuscany in Florence (1562–74); went to Poland (c. 1579) and at Synod of Brześć (1587) established an understanding among his followers (Socinians) and organized a church. Among his works are *De Jesu Christo Servatore*, *De Auctoritate S. Scripturae*.

**Soc′ra·tes** (sŏk′rȧ·tēz). 470?–399 B.C. Greek philosopher, b. in Athens, son of a sculptor, Sophroniscus. In early life himself a sculptor; later devoted himself wholly to philosophy. Developed and used with his pupils, who included Plato, Xenophon, and Alcibiades, an original method (still known as the Socratic method) of inquiry and instruction, consisting of a series of questionings the object of which is to elicit a clear and consistent expression of something supposed to be implicitly known by all rational beings. Attacked by Aristophanes as a Sophist and innovator; his contempt for conventional ideas and ways of life brought him many enemies; accused of impiety and of corrupting youth, defended himself in a speech intentionally angering instead of conciliating the judges; condemned; drank hemlock in prison, with his disciples grouped about him (399). Left no writings of his own; his philosophy known through the writings of his disciple Plato (*q.v.*). His doctrines are the basis of idealistic philosophy, and have profoundly influenced philosophic thought through succeeding centuries. See XANTHIPPE.

**Socrates**. *Surnamed* **Scho·las′ti·cus** (skō·lăs′tĭ·kŭs). Greek church historian of 5th century A.D.; author of an ecclesiastical history of the period from 306 to 439.

**Sod′du** (sôd′dōō), **Ubaldo**. 1883–    . Italian army commander; served in World War I. Appointed by Mussolini commander of Italian forces in Albania in effort to stop Greek advance (1940); gave up command after failure to halt Greeks (1941).

**Sod′dy** (sŏd′ĭ), **Frederick**. 1877–1956. English chemist; demonstrator in chemistry at McGill U., Montreal (1900–02), where he did research in radioactivity with Rutherford; lecturer, U. of Glasgow (1904–14); professor, Aberdeen U. (1914–19), Oxford (1919–36; retired). With Rutherford developed theory of atomic disintegration of radioactive elements; investigated origin and nature of isotopes; awarded 1921 Nobel prize for chemistry (1922). Author of *Radioactivity* (1904), *The Interpretation of Radium* (1909), *Matter and Energy* (1912), *Science and Life* (1920), *Cartesian Economics* (1922), *The Wrecking of a Scientific Age* (1927), *Money versus Man* (1931), *Interpretation of the Atom* (1932), *Rôle of Money* (1934), *British Budget* (1938), etc.

**Sö′der·berg′** (sû′dẽr·băr′y'), **Hjalmar**. 1869–1941. Swedish novelist and short-story writer.

**Sö′der·blom′** (sû′dẽr·blōōm′), **Nathan**. 1866–1931. Swedish Protestant theologian; professor, Uppsala (1901) and Leipzig (1912); archbishop of Uppsala (1914); chief works, *The Religions of the World* (1905), *Introduction to the History of Religion* (1920), *Christian Fellowship* (1923); awarded Nobel peace prize (1930).

**Sö′der·wall′** (sû′dẽr·väl′), **Knut Fredrik**. 1842–1924. Swedish philologist; published a history of the Swedish language and a dictionary of Old Swedish.

**So′do·ma, Il** (ēl sô′dō·mä). *Real name* **Giovanni Antonio de′ Baz′zi** (dā bät′tsē). 1477?–1549. Italian painter of Sienese school; employed chiefly at Siena (1501–c. 1507, 1515 ff.), and at Rome (c. 1507–15); associate of Agostino Chigi at Rome. Works include *Alexander in the Tent of Darius*, *Flagellation of Christ*, *Nativity*, *St. Catharine*, *Leda and the Swan*.

**Soem'mer·ring** (zûm'ĕ·rĭng), **Samuel Thomas von.** 1755–1830. German anatomist and naturalist; established the number and names of the cranial nerves; invented an electric telegraph (1809); made researches on improvement of wine, on fossil animals, on sunspots, etc.

**Sog'di·a'nus** (sŏg'dĭ·ā'nŭs) *or* **Se·cyd'i·a'nus** (sē·sĭd'ĭ·ā'nŭs). d. 424 B.C. Natural son of Artaxerxes I of Persia; murdered his half brother Xerxes II; after reign of few months, was killed by another brother, Ochus (Darius II).

**Sohn** (zōn). Name of family of German painters, including: **Carl Ferdinand** (1805–1867), known esp. for mythological scenes, portraits, and paintings of female figures; his son **Karl Rudolf** (1845–1908), painter of portraits and genre scenes; Carl Ferdinand's nephew **Wilhelm** (1830–1899), painter of Biblical pictures and genre scenes.

**Soiaro, il.** See Bernardino GATTI.

**Sois'sons'** (swȧ'sôɴ'), Counts of. A collateral branch of the Savoy-Carignan line of the house of Savoy (see SAVOY); especially, **Eugène Maurice de Sa'voie'-Ca'ri'gnan'** [dē sȧ'vwȧ'kȧ'rē'nyäɴ'] (1633–1673), French soldier; father of Prince Eugene of Savoy.

**Sojo, Toba.** See TOBA SOJO.

**So·kol'ni·kov** (sŭ·kôl'y'·nyĭ·kôf), **Grigori Yakovlevich.** 1888– . Russian Communist politician; member of Bolshevik faction (from 1905); arrested (1907) and exiled to Siberia (1909), but escaped and lived abroad (to 1917). Member of Russian delegation which negotiated treaty with Germany at Brest Litovsk (1918). Asst. people's commissar of finance (1922); chairman of oil syndicate (1928); ambassador to Britain (1929–32); asst. commissar for timber industry until arrest (1937) for Trotskyist activities; sentenced to ten years' imprisonment.

**So·ko·loff'** (sŭ·kŭ·lôf'), **Nikolai.** 1886–1965. Violinist and orchestra conductor, b. near Kiev, Russia; to U.S. as a boy; conductor, Cleveland Symphony Orchestra (1918–33); conductor in Seattle, Wash. (1938).

**So'ko·low** (sō'kō·lōv), **Na'hum** (nā'(h)ŭm). 1861–1936. Polish-born Jewish writer and Zionist leader; editor of *History of Zionism. 1600–1918* (2 vols., 1919).

**So·lan'der** (*Angl.* sō·lăn'dẽr; *Swed.* sōō·lăn'dẽr), **Daniel Charles.** 1736–1782. Botanist, b. in Sweden; to England (1760); instructed English botanists in Linnaean system; given charge of cataloguing natural history collections of British Museum; accompanied Sir Joseph Banks on Cook's voyage in *Endeavour* (1768–71) and to Iceland (1772); curator of natural history, British Museum (1773 ff.).

**So·la'ri** (sō·lä'rē) *or* **So·la'rio** (-ryō), **Antonio.** *Called* **lo Zin'ga·ro** (lō tsĕng'gä·rō), *i.e.* the Gypsy. 1382–1455. Italian painter; painted frescoes in the Benedictine monastery at Naples.

**Solari** *or* **Solario, Christoforo.** *Known as* **il Gob'bo** (ēl gôb'bō), *i.e.* the Hunchback. Italian sculptor and architect of the second half of the 15th century; carved many statues for the cathedral of Milan. His brother **Andrea,** *also known as* **Andrea del Gobbo** (1458–after 1509), was a painter; his *Virgin Nourishing the Infant Jesus* and portrait of Charles d'Amboise hang in the Louvre.

**Solf** (zōlf), **Wilhelm.** 1862–1936. German statesman; as foreign secretary (Oct.–Dec., 1918), negotiated the armistice with the Allies; ambassador to Tokyo (1920).

**Sol'ger** (zōl'gẽr), **Karl Wilhelm Ferdinand.** 1780–1819. German philosopher.

**Sol'i·man** (sŏl'ĭ·măn). Variant of SULEIMAN.

**So·li'nus** (sō·lī'nŭs), **Gaius Julius.** Latin grammarian and writer, probably of early 3d century A.D.; author of *Collectanea Rerum Memorabilium* (revised in 6th century under title *Polyhistor*), a description of the world of his day with comments on historical, social, religious, and natural history topics.

**So·lís'** (sō·lēs'), **Juan Di'az de** (dē'äth thā). 1470?–1516. Spanish navigator and discoverer; made two voyages with Vicente Yáñez Pinzón along Atlantic coast of South America (1497–98, 1508–09); appointed pilot major of Spain, on death of Vespucci (1512); made voyage to South America (1515–16), entering great estuary of La Plata; landed near mouth of Paraná and was ambushed and killed by Guarani Indians (1516).

**Solís y Ri'ba·de·nei'ra** (ē rē'bä·thā·nē'ē·rä), **Antonio de.** 1610–1686. Spanish historian, dramatist, and statesman; private secretary to Philip IV; historiographer of the Indies (1665); ordained priest (1667); known esp. for his *Historia de la Conquista de Méjico, Población, y Progresos de la América Septentrional* (1684); author also of the plays *Amor y Obligación*, *El Amor al Uso*, *Un Bobo Hace Ciento*, *El Doctor Carlino*, and *La Gitanilla de Madrid*.

**Solitario, El.** See Serafín ESTÉBANEZ CALDERÓN.

**Sol·lo·hub'** (sŭ·lŭ·gōōp') *or* **Sol·lo·gub',** Count **Vladimir Aleksandrovich.** 1814–1882. Russian writer of novels, short stories, and plays.

**Solms** (zōlms). Name of an ancient German family settled at Schloss Braunfels as early as 946, including: **Heinrich Maastricht Solms** (1636–1693), Count of **Solms'-Braun'fels** (-broun'fĕls), general in Dutch army; accompanied William of Orange and led Dutch guards into Westminster; distinguished himself at the Boyne; censured after Steenkerke.

**So·lo·gub'** (sŭ·lŭ·gōōp'), **Fëdor.** *Pseudonym of* **Fëdor Kuzmich Te·ter'ni·kov** (tyĕ·tyār'nyĭ·kôf). 1863–1927. Russian writer, identified with symbolist school; author of poetry, novels, essays, short stories, and plays.

**Sol'o·mon** (sŏl'ō·mŭn). King of Israel (c. 973–c. 933 B.C.); son of David and Bath-sheba. Under his rule Israel rose to the height of its greatness; noted for his wealth and his wisdom; builder of the temple (Solomon's Temple) in Jerusalem and many public buildings; made alliance with Hiram of Tyre. Reputed author of *Proverbs*, *The Song of Solomon*, *Ecclesiastes*, and *Wisdom of Solomon*.

**Solomon, Iz'ler** (ĭz'lẽr). 1910– . American orchestra conductor; conductor of Illinois Symphony Orchestra, Chicago (1936–42), etc.

**Solomon, Solomon Joseph.** 1860–1927. English painter, notably of portraits and murals; served in World War; called attention to need for camouflage in modern warfare, and initiated it in British army.

**So·lo·mos'** (sô·lô·môs'), **Dionysios.** 1798–1857. Greek poet; author of *Hymn to Liberty*, which, with music by Mantzaros, has become the Greek national anthem.

**So'lon** (sō'lŏn; -lŭn). 638?–?559 B.C. Athenian lawgiver; one of the Seven Wise Men of Greece. Distinguished himself first by his success in wresting Salamis from the Megarians (c. 596 B.C.). In period of acute economic distress, elected archon (c. 594) and given full powers to initiate economic and constitutional reforms: reorganized the boule (senate), popular assembly, and council of the Areopagus, improved the lot of the debtors, and divided the population into four "classes." The reforms were bitterly opposed by some elements in the city and Solon, to escape the turmoil, left Athens for ten years, traveling in Egypt, Cyprus, and Lydia. Shortly after his return, Pisistratus (*q.v.*) made himself tyrant of the city.

**So·lov·iëv'** (sŭ·lŭv·yôf'), **Sergei Mikhailovich.** 1820–

1879. Russian historian; professor, and later rector, U. of Moscow; author of *History of Russia* (29 vols., 1851–79), *Political and Diplomatic History of Alexander I* (1877). His son **Vladimir Sergeevich** (1853–1900) was philosopher, critic, and poet; *The Crisis of Western Philosophy* (1875), *Russia and the Universal Church* (1889), *History of Materialism* (1894), *History of Ethics* (1896–98), *The Justification of the Good* (1898), *War, Progress, and the End of History . . .* (1900).

**Sol·ti·kov′** (sŭl·tĭ·kôf′). Variant of SALTYKOV.

**Sol′vay′** (sôl′vā′; *Angl.* sŏl′vā), **Ernest.** 1838–1922. Belgian industrial chemist. Invented a process (Solvay process) for making soda from common salt; erected (1863) at Couillet, near Charleroi, Belgium, first plant for utilizing the process; improved the process and established plants in all parts of the world.

**Solway,** Earl of. See *3d duke of Queensberry,* under DOUGLAS family.

**Solyman.** See SULEIMAN.

**Sol′zhe·ni′tsyn** (sôl′zhĕ·nēt′sĭn), **Alexander Isayevich.** 1918– . Russian author. Awarded Nobel prize in literature (1970); wrote *One Day in the Life of Ivan Denisovich* (1962), *The First Circle* (1968), *Cancer Ward* (1968), etc.

**So′ma·de′va** (sō′mȧ·dā′vȧ). fl. 11th century A.D. Sanskrit author; native Brahman of Kashmir; wrote *Kathasarit-sagara* ("Ocean of Streams of Story"), a collection of tales and romances, mainly Brahmanistic, but containing much that is Buddhist in character.

**Som′bart** (zôm′bärt), **Werner.** 1863–1941. German political economist; advocate of liberal social reforms favoring the working classes. Wrote *Der Moderne Kapitalismus* (2 vols., 1902; vol. III, 1928), *Die Juden und das Wirtschaftsleben* (1911; translated by M. Epstein as *The Jews and Modern Capitalism*).

**Som′ers** (sŭm′ẽrz). See also SUMMERS.

**Som′ers** *or* **Sum′mers** (sŭm′ẽrz), Sir **George.** 1554–1610. English navigator; one of founders of South Virginia Company; commanded fleet carrying settlers which was wrecked on Bermudas or Somers Islands; took possession of islands for king of England.

**Som′ers** *or* **Som′mers** (sŭm′ẽrz), **John.** Baron **Somers.** 1651–1716. English lawyer and statesman; intimate with leaders of country party, Essex, William Russell, and Algernon Sidney; junior counsel for defense in trial of the Seven Bishops (see William SANCROFT); chairman of committee that drew up Declaration of Rights; solicitor general (1689); attorney general (1692); lord keeper of great seal (1693); lord chancellor and Baron Somers of Evesham (1697). Member of the junto, second only to Sunderland in influence with William III; one of council of regency during William III's absence in Holland. Compelled to resign the seal under repeated attacks by the country party (1700); retired (1702) but active in settling terms of union with Scotland (1707); president of council (1708–10).

**Som′er·set** (sŭm′ẽr·sĕt; -sĭt), Dukes of. See BEAUFORT and SEYMOUR families.

**Somerset,** Earls of. See (1) *John Beaufort* (1373?–1410), under BEAUFORT family; (2) Robert CARR (d. 1645).

**Somerset.** An English family holding earldom, later marquisate, of **Worces′ter** (wo͝os′tẽr), merged (1682) with dukedom of **Beau′fort** (bō′fẽrt). Its founder, **Charles Somerset** (1460?–1520), Earl of Worcester, illegitimate son of Henry Beaufort, 3d Duke of Somerset (see BEAUFORT family), assumed name Somerset; m. daughter of William Herbert, Earl of Huntingdon; sent on diplomatic missions by Henry VII (1490–1505) and by Henry VIII (1515–18); created Baron **Her′bert of Rag′lan** [hûr′bẽrt, răg′lăn] (1506) and earl of Worcester (1514), which titles descended in direct line to **Henry Somerset** (1577–1646), 5th Earl and 1st Marquis of Worcester, provider of funds to Charles I at outbreak of Civil War.

Henry's son **Edward Somerset** (1601–1667), 6th Earl and 2d Marquis of Worcester, and titular Earl of **Gla·mor′gan** [glȧ·môr′găn] (conferred 1644), inventor, began mechanical experimentation (1628); at outbreak of Civil War defending South Wales for Charles I, defeated by Waller at Highnam (1643); sent to Ireland to raise troops (1645); succeeding father (1646), went into exile (1648); restored to portion of estates (1660), devoted himself to experiments; author of *Century of Inventions* (1655; pub. 1663), describing ciphers, automata, calculating machine, and a steam-driven hydraulic machine capable of raising column of water forty feet.

Edward's son **Henry Somerset** (1629–1700), 3d Marquis of Worcester, 1st Duke of Beaufort (created 1682), renounced Catholicism and was member of Parliament; on Cromwell's death demanded free parliament and favored Restoration; defended Bristol against Monmouth's forces (1685) but surrendered it (1688) to William of Orange; lived in state at ducal residence of Badminton in Gloucestershire, whence the game badminton received its name.

The 2d duke, **Henry Somerset** (1684–1714), was prominent Tory leader and member of Swift's Brothers' Club. The 5th duke was father of Lord Raglan (*q.v.*), British field marshal. The 7th duke, **Henry Somerset** (1792–1853), aide-de-camp to duke of Wellington in Peninsular War (1812–14), was prominent sportsman, promoter of Badminton Hunt. The 8th duke, **Henry Charles Fitzroy Somerset** (1824–1899), was one of editors of Badminton Library; his 2d son, Lord **Henry Somerset** (1840–1932), song composer, m. (1872) daughter of Earl Somers (see Lady Isabella Caroline SOMERSET).

**Somerset, Fitzroy James Henry.** Baron **Raglan.** See RAGLAN.

**Somerset, Henry Richard Charles,** *known as* Lord **Henry.** 1849–1932. English song writer; author of *All Through the Night, The First Spring Day, Echo, Where'er You Go, A Song of Sleep,* etc.

**Somerset, Isabella Caroline.** *Known also as* Lady **Henry Somerset.** 1851–1921. English philanthropist, daughter and coheiress of 3d and last Earl Somers; m. (1872) Lord Henry Somerset, 2d son of 8th duke of Beaufort (see SOMERSET family). Devoted herself to temperance work; president of World's W.C.T.U. (1898–1906); founded farm colony for inebriate women (1895); founded and edited *Woman's Signal* (1894).

**Som′er·vell** (sŭm′ẽr·vĕl; -vĕl), Sir **Arthur.** 1863–1937. English composer; known esp. for his operettas, as *The Enchanted Palace, Princess Zara,* the cantata *The Forsaken Merman,* the symphony in D minor *Thalassa,* and the settings for lyrics of English poets.

**Somervell, Brehon Burke.** 1892–1955. American army officer, b. Little Rock, Ark.; district engineer, D.C. (1926–30); chief of construction division, Quartermaster Corps (1940–41); assistant chief of staff (1941–42); chief Army Service Forces (1942–46).

**Somervell,** Sir **Donald Bradley.** 1889–1960. British lawyer; educ. Oxford; M.P. (1931–45); solicitor general (1933–36); attorney general (1936–45); home secretary (1945); lord justice of appeal (1946–54).

**Som′er·ville** (sŭm′ẽr·vĭl), **Edith Anna Œnone.** 1861–1949. Irish novelist; began (1887) long collaboration with her cousin Violet Florence Martin (*q.v.*), producing vivid tales of Irish life. After cousin's death (1915), published several works as products of collaboration, including *Stray-Aways* (1920); author also of *The Big*

*House of Inver* (novel, 1925), *The States through Irish Eyes* (1930), and *An Incorruptible Irishman* (a life of Charles Kendal Bushe, Chief Justice of Ireland, great-grandfather of the two cousins).

**Somerville,** Sir **James Fownes.** 1882–1949. British naval officer; in World War (1914–18); commander in chief in East Indies (1938–39; retired because of health); as vice-admiral in Mediterranean (1940–42), attacked French ships at Oran (July, 1940), shelled Genoa (Feb., 1941), aided in sinking of *Bismarck* (May, 1941), escorted convoy to Malta in 3-day battle (Oct., 1941); appointed (Apr., 1942) commander in chief in Indian waters.

**Somerville, Mary,** *nee* **Fair′fax** (fâr′făks). 1780–1872. Scottish writer on mathematics and physical science; m. (1812) her cousin Dr. William Somerville; on invitation of Lord Brougham, turned Laplace's *Mécanique Céleste* into popularized English version *Celestial Mechanism of the Heavens* (1831). Author of *The Connection of the Physical Sciences* (1834), *Molecular and Microscopic Science* (1866). Somerville Coll., Oxford, is named after her.

**Somerville, William.** 1675–1742. English poet; author of *The Two Springs* (a fable, 1725), *The Chase* (four books of Miltonic blank verse on hunting, 1735), *Hobbinol* (a burlesque of rural games, 1740), and *Field Sports* (on hawking, 1742).

**Som′mer·feld** (zôm′ẽr·fĕlt), **Arnold.** 1868–1951. German physicist; with F. Klein, developed a theory of the gyroscope; contributed to development of quantum theory, Bohr atomic theory, quantum theory of spectral lines, theory of metallic electrons, etc.

**Som′mers** (sŭm′ẽrz). See SOMERS and SUMMERS.

**Somodevilla, Zenón** *or* **Cenón de.** See Marqués de la ENSENADA.

**So·mo′za** (sô·mō′sä), **Anastasio.** 1896–1956. President of Nicaragua (1937–47).

**Sönderborg–Augustenburg.** See OLDENBURG, 4.

**Son′neck** (sŭn′ĕk), **Oscar George Theodore.** 1873–1928. American musician and librarian; first chief of the music division, Library of Congress (1902–17); on staff of G. Schirmer Co., music publishers, New York City (1917–28), and vice-president (from 1921); edited *The Musical Quarterly* (1914–28); published treatises on American musical history.

**Son′nen·schein** (sŏn′ĕn·shīn), **Edward Adolf.** 1851–1929. English classical scholar and grammarian, of Austrian descent; professor, Birmingham (1883–1918); author of *A New Latin Grammar* (1912), *A New French Grammar* (1912), *A New English Grammar* (1916), etc. His brother **William Swan** (1855–1931), publisher in London (1878 ff.); compiled list of *The Best Books* (1887), and *A Reader's Guide to Contemporary Literature* (1894); prepared a dictionary of phrases.

**Son·ni′no** (sôn·nē′nō), Baron **Sidney.** 1847–1921. Italian statesman; minister of finance (1893–94), of treasury (1894–96); premier (Feb.–May, 1906; Dec., 1909–March, 1910); minister of foreign affairs (1914–19); representative at Paris Peace Conference (1919). Known also as a Dante scholar.

**Sonora,** Marqués **de la.** See José GÁLVEZ.

**Son′tag** (zôn′täк), **Henriette.** *Ennobled* (1826) *as* **Henriette Sontag von Lau′en·stein** (fôn lou′ĕn-shtīn). 1806–1854. German operatic coloratura soprano; m. Count Rossi (1828).

**Soong** (so͝ong). Influential Chinese family including: **Charles Jones Soong.** d. 1927. Merchant, a native of Hainan Island. To United States (c. 1880); became a Christian at Wilmington, N.C., and received at baptism name of Charles Jones after an American sea captain who befriended him; educ. at Vanderbilt U. Returned to China as Southern Methodist Episcopal missionary; helped organize first Y.M.C.A. in Shanghai; became Bible manufacturer and salesman; m. Miss Ni (d. 1931), of a cultured family of Shanghai. Their six children, all educated in America, include three daughters and three sons. The daughters, **Ai-ling** (ī′lĭng′), **Ch'ing-ling** (chĭng′lĭng′), and **Mei-ling** *or* **Mayling** (mā′lĭng′), married H. H. Kung, Sun Yat-sen, and Chiang Kai-shek, respectively. For biographies, see under husbands' names. The sons are:

**Tse-ven** *or* **Tsu-ven** *or, better,* **Tsŭ-wên** (tso͝o′wŭn′) **Soong.** *Better known by Anglicized name* **T. V. Soong.** 1894–1971. Studied at Harvard (1915) and Columbia. English secretary of Canton government (1923); president, Central Bank, Canton (from 1924); minister of finance, Nationalist government, Canton (1925–27) and at Nanking (1928–33); member of executive committee of Kuomintang; chief delegate, World Economic Conference, London (1933); chairman of board, Bank of China (1935–42); foreign minister (1941–45); acting president, Executive Yuan (1932–33; 1944–47).

**Tsŭ-liang** (tso͝o′lĭ·äng′) **Soong.** *Anglicized* **T. L. Soong.** Educ. at Vanderbilt. During war with Japan, in charge of transportation of war materials and supplies in southern China; director of Southwest Import and Export Bureau; director of Central Bank of China.

**Tsŭ-an** (tso͝o′än′) **Soong.** *Anglicized* **T. A. Soong.** Educ. at Harvard.

**Soothill, Dorothea.** See under Sir Alexander HOSIE.

**So·phi′a** (sô·fī′ȧ; sō′fĭ·ȧ). d. after 578. Niece of Empress Theodora. Byzantine empress, wife of Justin II (565–578); administered affairs of the empire (574–578) jointly with Tiberius II Constantinus.

**So·phi′a** (*Ger.* zô·fē′ä). 1630–1714. Electress of Hanover. See ERNEST AUGUSTUS.

**So·phi′a** (*Ger.* zô·fē′ä). d. 1284. German duchess, founder of the landgraviate of Hesse. Daughter of St. Elizabeth of Hungary and niece of Henry Raspe (*q.v.*); m. Henry of Brabant; mother of Henry I, first male ruler of Hesse (*q.v.*).

**Soph′ia** (*Russ.* sôf′yȧ). Russian empress. See under IVAN III VASILIEVICH.

**Sophia A·le·kse′ev·na** (ŭ·lyĕ·ksyā′yĕv·nŭ). 1657–1704. Regent of Russia; third daughter of Czar Alexis. Upon death of her brother Czar Fëdor III (1682), she instigated an uprising among the Strelitzi; they invaded the Kremlin and murdered the supporters of Peter (later Peter I, known as "the Great"); Sophia took the regency for her half brothers Ivan and Peter, and ruled Russia (1682–89). Forced by Peter into a convent at Moscow (1689), and later imprisoned (from 1698) on suspicion of again inciting rebellion among the Strelitzi.

**So·phi′a Char′lotte** (*Eng.* sô·fī′ȧ [sō′fĭ·ȧ] shär′lŏt). *Ger.* **So·phi′e Char·lot′te** (zô·fē′ĕ [zô·fē′] shär·lôt′ĕ). 1668–1705. Daughter of Ernest Augustus, 1st Elector of Hanover (see HANOVER), and sister of George I of England. Queen of Prussia (1701–05); spent early years in Paris; m. (1684), as 2d wife, Prince Frederick of Prussia (later King Frederick I); patron of arts and letters and special friend of Leibnitz; Charlottenburg named for her.

**So·phi′a Dor′o·the′a** (*Eng.* sô·fī′ȧ [sō′fĭ·ȧ] dŏr′ō-thē′ȧ). *Ger.* **So·phi′e Do′ro·the′a** (zô·fē′ĕ [zô·fē′] dō′rô·tā′ä). 1666–1726. Daughter of Duke George William of the Brunswick-Lüneburg line (see BRUNSWICK); m. (1682) George Louis, Crown Prince of Hanover (later George I of England); made victim of court intrigues; accused of liaison with young Swedish nobleman, Count Philipp Christoph von Königsmark, colonel of the guards at Hanover; after his death (1694), arrested and tried;

marriage annulled and imprisoned for 32 years at Castle of Ahlden; known as **Princess of Ahl'den** (äl'dĕn). Her children were George II of England, and **Sophia Dorothea** (1687–1757), wife (m. 1706) of Frederick William I of Prussia, by whom she was mother of Frederick the Great.

**So·phi'e** (*Ger.* zō·fē'ĕ, zō·fē'). 1805–1872. Archduchess of Austria; daughter of King Maximilian I Joseph of Bavaria, b. Munich; m. (1824) Archduke Francis Charles of Austria. Mother of Emperor Francis Joseph, whom she was active in placing on throne at time of 1848 Revolution.

**Sophie.** *In full* **Sophie Dorothea Ulrike Alice.** 1870–1932. Princess of Prussia and queen of Greece (1913–17, 1920–22); third daughter of Frederick III, Emperor of Germany, and sister of William II; b. Potsdam; m. (1889) Prince Constantine, who succeeded to throne of Greece (1913) on assassination of his father, George I; left Greece (1917) at his abdication; after return (1920) left a second time when Constantine was forced to abdicate (Sept., 1922); lived in Florence. Mother of Alexander I and George II, kings of Greece, and of Helen, who married Carol II (*q.v.*) of Rumania.

**Soph'o·cles** (sŏf'ō·klēz). 496?–406 B.C. Greek tragic playwright; ranked with Aeschylus and Euripides as greatest among Greek dramatists. Defeated Aeschylus for the prize for tragedy (468 B.C.); defeated by Euripides (441); won altogether 18 or 20 times. Wrote about 120 plays, of which 7 are extant, *Oedipus Tyrannus* (or *Oedipus Rex*), *Oedipus at Colonus*, *Antigone*, *Electra*, *Philoctetes*, *Ajax*, *Maidens of Trachis*. See IOPHON.

**Soph'o·cles** (sŏf'ō·klēz), **E·van'ge·li'nus** (ē·văn'jĕ·lī'nŭs) **Ap'os·tol'i·des** (ăp'ŏs·tŏl'ĭ·dēz). 1805?–1883. Classical philologist, b. in Thessaly, Greece; to U.S. (c. 1827); teacher of Greek, Harvard (from 1842), professor (from 1860). Author of *A Romaic Grammar* (1842), *History of the Greek Alphabet* (1848), *Greek Lexicon of the Roman and Byzantine Periods* (1870), etc.

**Sophonias.** See ZEPHANIAH.

**Soph'o·nis'ba** (sŏf'ō·nĭz'bȧ). *Properly* **Soph'o·ni'ba** (-nī'bȧ). d. about 204 B.C. Daughter of Hasdrubal of Carthage. Originally betrothed to the Numidian prince Masinissa, but married (for political reasons) to Masinissa's rival, Syphax. Masinissa defeated Syphax, captured Sophonisba, and married her, but was compelled by his Roman allies to discard her; sent her poison to commit suicide in order not to fall into the hands of the Romans. Her story is the theme of a number of tragedies, including ones by Marston, Corneille, Voltaire, and Alfieri.

**So'phron** (sō'frŏn). fl. about 430 B.C. Greek playwright, of Syracuse; best known as writer of mimes, a form of play apparently originated by him; only fragments of his work have survived.

**Sop'with** (sŏp'wĭth), **Thomas Octave Murdoch.** 1888– . British aeronaut and industrialist; flew from England to Continent by airplane (1910); founded Sopwith Aviation Co., Ltd., Kingston-on-Thames (1912); chairman, Hawker Siddeley Aircraft, Ltd. Active in yacht racing; competed unsuccessfully for the *America's* Cup (1934, 1937), losing both times to Harold Stirling Vanderbilt (*q.v.*).

**So·rab'ji** (sō·räb'jē), **Cornelia.** 1866?–1954. East Indian woman lawyer and writer; author of *Love and Life Behind the Purdah* (1902), *Sun-Babies* (1904), *The Purdahnashin* (1917), *Therefore* (1924), *Gold Mohur Time* (1930), *India Calling* (1934), *India Recalled* (1936), etc.

**So·ra'nus** (sō·rā'nŭs). Greek physician, of Ephesus, in early 2d century A.D.; practiced in Alexandria, and later in Rome; head of the "methodist school."

**Sor'bon'** (sôr'bôɴ'), **Robert de.** 1201–1274. French theologian; chaplain and confessor of Saint Louis (Louis IX); founded (1257) the Maison de Sorbonne, a foundation for poor theological students, forerunner of the modern Sorbonne.

**Sor'by** (sôr'bĭ), **Henry Clifton.** 1826–1908. English geologist; pioneer of microscopic petrology; devoted himself to independent investigations in spectroscopy, microscopy, biology, geology, archaeology; studied architecture and Egyptian hieroglyphics; invented method of making thin slices of rock for microscopic inspection; aided in founding of Sheffield U.

**Sor·del'lo** (sôr·dĕl'lō; *Angl.* sôr·dĕl'ō). 13th-century Italian troubadour; lived chiefly in Provence. Among his works, written in Provençal, are love songs, sirventes, and a didactic poem *Documentum Honoris;* known chiefly through Dante's account in *Purgatorio* VI and VII; subject also of Browning's *Sordello.*

**So'rel'** (sô'rĕl'), **Agnès.** 1422?–1450. Mistress of King Charles VII of France (1444–50).

**Sorel, Albert.** 1842–1906. French historian; author of *Histoire Diplomatique de la Guerre Franco-Allemande* (1875), *L'Europe et la Révolution Française* (1885–1903), etc.

**Sorel, Charles.** Sieur **de Sou'vi'gny'** (dē sōō'vē'nyē'). 1597?–1674. French writer; historiographer of France (1635); best known for a novel (*La Vraie Histoire Comique de Francion*, 1622) burlesquing the pastoral and chivalric romances so popular in his time.

**Sorel, Georges.** 1847–1922. French journalist; a leader in proclaiming the philosophy of revolutionary syndicalism. Among his notable books are *L'Avenir Socialiste des Syndicats* (1898), *Réflexions sur la Violence* (1908), and *De l'Utilité du Pragmatisme* (1921).

**Sö'ren·sen** (sû'rĕn·s'n), **Sören Peter Lauritz.** 1868–1939. Danish chemist; suggested the symbol *p*H to denote the negative logarithm of the concentration of the hydrogen ion in a scale (Sörensen scale) to express acidity or alkalinity of a solution; investigated protein solutions.

**Sor'ge** (zôr'gĕ), **Reinhard Johannes.** 1892–1916. German playwright and poet; associated with ultramodern expressionist group. Author of *Bettler* (play, 1912), *Guntwar, die Schule eines Propheten* (dramatic poem, 1914), *Metanoeite* (Christmas mystery play, 1915), *König David* (play, 1916).

**Soriano, Francesco.** See Francesco SURIANO.

**So'rin** (sō'rĭn; *Fr.* sô'răɴ'), **Edward Frederick.** 1814–1893. Roman Catholic clergyman and educator, b. near Laval, France; to Vincennes, Ind., as missionary (1841); founded Notre Dame U. (chartered 1844) and served as its first president (1844–65); superior general, Congregation of Holy Cross (from 1868).

**Sor'ley** (sôr'lĭ), **William Ritchie.** 1855–1935. British philosopher; professor, Cambridge (1900–33). Author of *Recent Tendencies in Ethics* (1904), *The Interpretation of Evolution* (1910), *The Moral Life* (1911), *A History of English Philosophy* (1920), etc.

**So'ro·kin** (sô'rŭ·kyĭn), **Pitirim Alexandrovich.** 1889–1968. Russian-born sociologist in U.S.; educ. St. Petersburg U.; professor of sociology, St. Petersburg (1919–22); to U.S. (1923); professor of sociology, U. of Minnesota (1924–30), Harvard (from 1930; emeritus from 1964); author of *Sociology of Revolution* (1925), *A Source Book in Rural Sociology* (1930–31), *Social and Cultural Dynamics* (1937–41), *Man and Society in Calamity* (1943), etc.

**So·rol'la y Bas·ti'da** (sō·rō'lyä ē bäs·tē'thä), **Joaquín.** 1863–1923. Spanish painter; winner of Grand Prix, Paris Exposition (1900); exhibited in the U.S. (1909); one of foremost modern impressionists; known particularly for his treatment of sunlight. His *Swimmers, Beaching the Boat,* and *After the Bath* are in Metropolitan Museum, New York; a number of his portraits, as of Blasco-Ibáñez and other writers, are in Hispanic Society, New York.

**Sorzano, José Luis Tejada.** See TEJADA SORZANO.

**So·sen** (sō·sĕn), **Mori.** 1747–1821. Japanese painter; best known for his paintings of monkeys.

**So·sib′i·us** (sō·sĭb′ĭ·ŭs). Greek sculptor of the time of Augustus; known esp. for his reliefs; identified with the Neo-Attic, or New Attic, school of sculpture.

**So·sig′e·nes** (sō·sĭj′ĕ·nēz). Greek astronomer and mathematician, in Alexandria; commissioned by Julius Caesar (c. 46 B.C.) to reform the Roman calendar; author of *Revolving Spheres*, only fragments of which are extant.

**Sosn·kow′ski** (sôs′′n·kôf′skē), **Kazimierz.** 1885–1969. Polish soldier; chief of staff, 1st brigade, Piłsudski legion (1914); arrested, with Piłsudski, by Germans (1917). General and commander of Warsaw district; minister of war (1920–24); commander of army corps, province of Poznań (1925–27), of Polish armed forces (1943–44).

**Sos′tra·tus** (sŏs′trȧ·tŭs). Greek architect of 3d century B.C. Built for Ptolemy Philadelphus at Alexandria the Pharos (lighthouse), which became model of structures of this kind.

**So′ta·des** (sō′tȧ·dēz). Greek satirist of 3d century B.C.; known esp. as composer of scurrilous and licentious verse; lampooned Ptolemy II Philadelphus; was captured, sealed up in chest of lead, and cast into sea.

**So·ta·tsu** (sō·tä·tso͝o). 17th-century Japanese painter; introduced combination of gold dust and Chinese ink in his work; considered precursor of Ogata Korin.

**So′ter** (sō′tĕr), **Saint.** Pope (bishop of Rome; 165?–174).

**Soter.** See ANTIOCHUS I of Syria, ATTALUS I of Pergamum, DEMETRIUS I of Syria, PTOLEMY I and VIII, SELEUCUS III.

**Soth′e·by** (sŭth′ĕ·bĭ; sŏth′-). Family of English auctioneers and antiquaries, including: **John**, founder (1744) of Covent Garden auction room for books and prints, moving business to Strand (1817); his nephew **Samuel** (1771–1842); and Samuel's son **Samuel Leigh** (1805–1861), specialist in cataloguing, author of works on early printing, block books, and on Milton's autograph.

**Soth′ern** (sŭth′ērn), **Edward Askew.** 1826–1881. Actor, b. Liverpool, Eng.; to U.S. (1852); success in role of Lord Dundreary in *Our American Cousin* (from 1858). His son **Edward Hugh** (1859–1933), b. New Orleans, was leading man in Daniel Frohman's stock company at Lyceum Theater in New York (1886–1900), acting with success in romantic adventure plays; presented Shakespearean drama with Julia Marlowe (1904–07 and 1909–16); author of a volume of reminiscences. Cf. Virginia HARNED and Julia MARLOWE.

**Soto, Hernando** (*or* **Fernando**) **de.** See DE SOTO.

**So′to** (sō′tō), **Marco Aurelio.** 1846–1908. President of Honduras (1874–75 and re-elected for two terms 1877–83); administration marked by civil order and many progressive acts; new constitution promulgated (1880).

**Sou′bei′ran′** (so͞o′bā′räN′), **Eugène.** 1797–1858. French apothecary; professor in the school of pharmacy, Paris; one of the discoverers of chloroform (1831).

**Soubirous, Bernadette.** See BERNADETTE OF LOURDES.

**Sou′bise′** (so͞o′bēz′). A princely branch of the Rohan family of France, deriving its name from the village of Soubise (an ancient seigneury) near Rochefort. Allied with the Guéménée branch; made principality (1667). Its members included: **Benjamin de Rohan** (1583–1642), Seigneur **de Soubise,** b. La Rochelle; brother of Henri de Rohan (see under ROHAN); Protestant leader against Louis XIII in Huguenot wars (1621–29); unsuccessfully defended La Rochelle against Richelieu (1627–28); died in England. **Charles de Rohan** (1715–87), Prince **de Soubise;** entered military service (1734); lieutenant general (1748); in command during Seven Years' War; defeated at Rossbach (1757); won battles of Sondershausen and Lutterberg (1758); made marshal of France through influence of Mme. Pompadour (1758); retired (1763); a prominent personage in court of Louis XVI. Line became extinct at his death. See ROHAN.

**Sou·blette′** (so͞o·blĕt′), **Carlos.** 1790–1870. Secretary of war of Venezuela (1836–39); president (1843–47); in exile (1848–58).

**Souf′flot′** (so͞o′flō′), **Jacques Germain.** 1713–1780. French architect; best known as architect of the Panthéon, Paris; designed also Hôtel de Ville in Bordeaux and the cathedral in Rennes.

**Soukhomlinov.** Variant of SUKHOMLINOV.

**Sou′las′** (so͞o′lȧs′), **Josias de.** Sieur **de Prime′fosse′** (dẽ prēm′fôs′). *Pseudonym* **Flo′ri′dor′** (flô′rē′dôr′). 1608?–1672. French actor, at the Hôtel de Bourgogne; created roles in plays of Corneille and Racine.

**Soule** (sōl), **George Henry, Jr.** 1887–1970. American editor and writer; editor of *The New Republic* (from 1924). Author of *The Useful Art of Economics* (1929), *A Planned Society* (1932), *The Future of Liberty* (1936), etc.

**Sou′lé′** (so͞o′lā′), **Pierre.** 1801–1870. Jurist and politician; involved in intrigues against King Charles X of France, escaped to England and thence to U.S. (1825). Settled in New Orleans and practiced law there; U.S. senator (1847; 1849–53); U.S. minister to Spain (1853–55); there engaged in intrigues to detach Cuba from Spain and attach it to U.S. Associated with James Buchanan and John Y. Mason in framing the Ostend Manifesto (Oct. 18, 1854) proposing the purchase of Cuba from Spain; manifesto repudiated by U.S. Secretary of State William L. Marcy and Soulé was made scapegoat for the administration. Joined Confederacy in Civil War.

**Sou′lé** (so͞o′lā; so͞o·lā′), **Samuel W.** See Christopher Latham SHOLES.

**Sou′louque′** (so͞o′lo͝ok′), **Faustin Élie.** 1785–1867. Haitian Negro general and politician; elected president of Haiti (1847); proclaimed himself emperor of Haiti, under the title Faustin I (1849). Deposed (1858) and lived in exile (from Jan., 1859).

**Soult** (so͞olt), **Nicolas Jean de Dieu** (dẽ dyû′). Duke of **Dalmatia.** 1769–1851. Marshal of France; won distinction under Masséna at Zurich (1799) and in defense of Genoa (1800); created marshal by Napoleon (1804). Engaged at Austerlitz, Jena, Pułtusk, Preussisch-Eylau; created duke of Dalmatia (1807). Served in Spain (1808–11) and French commander in chief there (1809–11); conquered Andalusia (1810) but suffered defeat at La Albuera (1811); engaged at Lützen and Bautzen (1813); minister of war under Louis XVIII (Dec., 1814–Mar., 1815); rallied to Napoleon on his return from Elba. Lived in exile (1815–19); recalled to France (1819) and again appointed marshal (1820); minister of war (1830–34, 1840–44).

**Sou′met′** (so͞o′mĕ′), **Alexandre.** 1788–1845. French poet and playwright; author of the dramas *Clytemnestre* (1822), *Saül* (1822), *Cléopâtre* (1824), *Jeanne d'Arc* (1825), *Les Macchabées* (1827), *Émilia* (1827), and several long poems, including *L'Incrédulité*, celebrating the renaissance of Catholicism in France (1810), and *La Divine Épopée* (1840).

**Sou′pault′** (so͞o′pō′), **Philippe.** 1897– . French poet, novelist, and biographer; author of poetry, *Wertwego*

(1922), *Georgia* (1929); fiction, *Le Bon Apôtre* (1923), *En Jouet* (1926), *Le Nègre*, etc.; biography, *Henri Rousseau, Charles Baudelaire, William Blake.*

**Sou′riau′** (sōō′ryō′), **Maurice.** 1856–? . French scholar; professor of Norman literature, Caen (1895). Among his works are *L'Évolution du Vers Français au XVII^e Siècle* (1893), *Pascal* (1897), *Moralistes et Poètes* (1907), *Histoire du Romantisme en France* (1927 ff.).

**Sou′sa** (sōō′sȧ; *popularly* -zȧ), **John Philip.** 1854–1932. Known as "the March King." American bandmaster and composer, b. Washington, D.C.; bandmaster of U.S. Marine Band (1880–92); organized his own band and toured U.S. and foreign countries with great success (from 1892). Notable among his marches are *Semper Fidelis* (1888), *Washington Post March* (1889), *Liberty Bell* (1893), *King Cotton* (1897), *Stars and Stripes Forever* (1897), *Hands Across the Sea* (1899). Among his comic operas were *El Capitan* (1896), *The Bride-Elect* (1897), *The Free Lance* (1906).

**Sou′sa** (sō′zȧ), Frei **Luiz de** (thē). *Orig. name* **Manoel de Sousa Cou·ti′nho** (kō·tē′nyōō). 1555–1632. Portuguese Dominican monk and writer; author of *História de São Domingo* and *Anaes do Rei Dom João III;* subject of a drama (1844) by Almeida-Garrett.

**Sousa, Martim Affonso de.** 1500?–1564. Portuguese admiral; commanded first colonizing expedition sent to Brazil (1530–33) and founded first Portuguese settlement there at São Vicente (Jan., 1532).

**Sou′tar** (sōō′tẽr), **Andrew.** 1879–1941. British novelist; during World War (1914–18), served in British air force. Author also of many motion-picture scenarios, and of a play, *If We But Knew.*

**Sou′ter** (sōō′tẽr), **Alexander.** 1873–1949. British classical and Biblical scholar; published editions of classical and Biblical texts, Pelagius's *Expositions of Thirteen Epistles of St. Paul* (3 parts; 1922, 1926, 1931), also *Text and Canon of the New Testament* (1913), etc.

**South** (south), **Robert.** 1634–1716. English court preacher; waged verbal war against both Romanism and Puritanism; chaplain to duke of York (1667); canon in Oxford (1670); accompanied embassy to Polish court (1676); chaplain to Charles II; declined preferment. Acquiesced in the Revolution (1688); carried on (from 1693) literary controversy on the Trinity with William Sherlock (*q.v.*). As a preacher supported doctrine of passive obedience and divine right of kings. Best known for his sermons, masterpieces of clearness in vigorous pithy English.

**South′ack** (?sŭth′ăk), **Cyprian.** 1662–1745. Cartographer in colonial New England, b. London; to Boston, Mass. (1685). Commissioned by Admiralty board to protect New England coast from pirates and privateers; in pursuance of duties, charted northeast coast of North America.

**South·amp′ton** (south·(h)ăm(p)′tŭn), Duke of. See *Charles Fitzroy*, under Barbara VILLIERS.

**Southampton,** Earl of. A title held by members of the English family of **Wriothes′ley** (*pron. prob.* rĭz′lĭ), including: Sir **John Wriothesley,** *more correctly* **Writh** *or* **Wrythe** (rĭth), Garter king-of-arms (1479), head of College of Heralds (1483).

His grandson **Thomas Wriothesley** (1505–1550), 1st Baron **Wriothesley of Titch′field** (tĭch′fēld) and 1st Earl of Southampton (cr. 1547); statesman; ambassador to Mary of Hungary (1538); one of king's chief secretaries (1540); formulated offensive and defensive league between Charles V and Henry VIII (1543); lord chancellor of England (1544); deprived of office for commissioning four civilians to hear chancery cases in his absence (1547); readmitted to council, arranged fall of Somerset.

Thomas's grandson **Henry Wriothesley** (1573–1624), 3d earl, soldier and Shakespeare's patron. M.A., Cantab. (1589); at court received marks of Queen Elizabeth's favor; liberal patron of poets, received dedications of Thomas Nash's *Jack Wilton*, Gervase Markham's poem on Sir Richard Grenville, Shakespeare's *Venus and Adonis* (1593) and *The Rape of Lucrece* (1594). Accompanied Essex on expeditions to Cádiz and to the Azores (1596, 1597); made hasty marriage with Elizabeth Vernon, cousin of Essex, incurring anger of queen (1598); took part in Essex's rebellion and tried to excite public feeling by effecting revival of Shakespeare's *Richard II*, portraying deposition of a king; sentenced to death (1601), but released by James I (1603); entertained James's queen (Anne) with performance of *Love's Labour's Lost* by Burbage and his company, of which Shakespeare was a member (1603). Helped to equip expedition to Virginia (1605), member of Virginia Company's council (1609) and treasurer (1620–24); incorporator of other companies. Volunteered, with his eldest son, for service of United Provinces of Netherlands against Spain but succumbed to fever at Bergen op Zoom.

Henry's second son, **Thomas** (1607–1667), 4th earl, supported resolution in House of Commons that redress of grievances should precede supply, but later joined Charles I as one of his closest advisers; adviser to Charles II; lord high treasurer of England (1660–67).

**South′ard** (sŭth′ẽrd), **Samuel Lewis.** 1787–1842. American lawyer and politician, b. Basking Ridge, N.J.; U.S. senator (1821–23; 1833–42); U.S. secretary of the navy (1823–29); governor of New Jersey (1832–33).

**South′cott** (south′kŭt), **Joanna.** 1750–1814. English religious fanatic; domestic servant, originally a Methodist; declared herself the woman of *Revelation* xii, announced that she was to be delivered of Shiloh, a second messiah, on Oct. 19, 1814; died of brain disease (Dec. 27, 1814), leaving followers said to number 100,000. Author of several works of Biblical interpretation and prophecy, including *The Book of Wonders* (1813–14).

**South′erne** (sŭth′ẽrn), **Thomas.** 1660–1746. British dramatist, b. near Dublin. Known for two successful tragedies, *The Fatal Marriage* (1694), renamed by Garrick *Isabella, or the Fatal Marriage*, and *Oroonoko, or the Royal Slave* (1696), both plots being adapted from novels by Aphra Behn.

**Sou′they** (sou′thĭ; sŭth′ĭ), **Robert.** 1774–1843. English poet and man of letters, b. Bristol. Spent two years at Oxford, where he met Coleridge; with Coleridge and Robert Lovell, formed visionary socialistic scheme of a pantisocracy on banks of Susquehanna River in America; m. (1795) Edith Fricker (d. 1837). On trips to Spain and Portugal, studied history and literature of Iberian Peninsula; settled at Greta Hall, Keswick, in Lake District (1803). Became as strongly Tory as he had been Republican and received government pension. Contributed for thirty years (from 1808) to *Quarterly Review;* expanded an article into his classic *Life of Nelson* (1813); accepted poet laureateship (1813); chief events of period the surreptitious publication (1817) of revolutionary drama *Wat Tyler* (written 1794), Peel's offer of a baronetcy, Byron's parody in *The Vision of Judgment* (1822) of his apotheosis of George III. Remembered not for epic poems *Thalaba* (1801), *Madoc* (1805), *The Curse of Kehama* (1810), and *Roderick, the Last of the Goths* (1821), as he hoped, but for shorter poems, *The Holly Tree, My days among the dead are past, The Inchcape Rock, The Battle of Blenheim, Stanzas Written in My Library*, and for his vigorous and graceful prose in *Letters of Espriella* (1807), *The Doctor*, his *Commonplace Book* (1849–51),

his biographical and historical works, including lives of Wesley (1820), Cowper (1833–37), histories of Brazil (1810–19), Peninsular War (1823–32), and esp. his *Letters* (1856).
His second wife, **Caroline Ann**, *nee* **Bowles** [bōlz] (1786–1854), poet, sent anonymously ms. of narrative poem *Ellen Fitzarthur* (1820) to him, initiated regular correspondence that culminated in marriage (1839); wrote also *The Widow's Tale* (1822), *Tales of Factories*, and, in prose, *Chapters on Churchyards*.

**South'well** (south'wĕl; -wĕl), **Robert.** 1561–1595. English poet and Jesuit martyr, b. in Norfolk; domestic chaplain to countess of Arundel; composed his *Consolations for Catholics;* betrayed to authorities as native-born subject ordained to Roman Catholic priesthood; imprisoned and tortured for three years (1592–95); executed. Author of choice verses, including *St. Peter's Complaint* (1595), *Burning Babe*, and other devotional poems, and prose religious works.

**South'wold** (south'wōld), **Stephen.** *Pseudonym* **Neil Bell** (bĕl). 1887–1964. English novelist; author of *Precious Porcelain, Strange Melody, The Son of Richard Carden, Winding Road, Bredon and Sons, Spice of Life* (short stories).

**South'worth** (south'wûrth; -wẽrth), **Emma Dorothy Eliza**, *nee* **Nev'itte** (nĕv'ĭt). 1819–1899. American novelist; m. Frederick H. Southworth (1840). Author of *Retribution* (1849), *The Missing Bride* (1855), *The Hidden Hand* (1859), *The Fatal Marriage* (1869), *The Maiden Widow* (1870), etc.

**Sou'tine'** (?sōō'tēn'), **Haim** *or* **Chaim.** 1894–1943. Lithuanian painter in Paris (1913 ff.).

**Sou'za'** (sōō'zä'), **Robert de.** 1865– . French writer, identified with the symbolist movement in literature; author of volumes of verse, literary criticism, and the science of poetry.

**Sou'za Bo·te'lho** (sō'zȧ bōō·tā'lyōō), **Marquês José Maria de.** 1758–1825. Portuguese diplomat and writer; Portuguese ambassador at Paris (1802). His wife (m. 1802) **Adèle Marie Émilie Fil'leul'** [fē'yûl'] (1761–1836), widow of Comte **de Fla'haut'** [dē flȧ'ō'] (guillotined, 1793), was author of novels, including *Adèle de Sénanges* (1794), *Eugène De Bothelin* (1808), *Eugénie et Mathilde* (1811), *La Comtesse de Fargy* (1822), etc.

**So'va** (sô'vȧ), **Antonín.** 1864–1928. Czech lyric poet and novelist.

**Sow'er** (sō'ẽr), **Christopher.** 1693–1758. Printer and publisher, b. in Germany; to America (1724); settled in Germantown, Pa., and became (1738) first German printer and publisher in the colonies. Published an edition of the Bible (1743). His son **Christopher** (1721–1784) inherited the business (1758); published second (1763) and third (1776) editions of the Sower, or Germantown, Bible; arrested on suspicion of treason, maltreated, and despoiled of all his property (1778). A son of the second Christopher, **Christopher** (1754–1799), took over the publishing business (1774); was a loyalist during the American Revolution; fled to England (c. 1783); to New Brunswick (1785) and became deputy postmaster general and king's printer, also publisher of the *Royal Gazette and Weekly Advertiser*.

**Sow'er·by** (sō'ẽr·bĭ), **James.** 1757–1822. English artist; portraitist and miniaturist; turned to illustration of botanical and conchological works; compiled and illustrated *English Botany* (36 vols., 1790–1814) and *British Mineralogy* (5 vols., 1804–17); his *Mineral Conchology of Great Britain* (7 vols., 1812–46) completed by his eldest son, **James de Carle** [dē kärl'] (1787–1871).

**Sowerby, Katherine Githa.** d. 1970. English playwright and author; m. John Kaye Kendall. Author of *Rutherford & Son* (1912), *Sheila* (1917), *The Stepmother* (1924), *The Policeman's Whistle* (1934), etc. Collaborator with her younger sister, **Amy Millicent**, painter and illustrator, in a number of books for children. Amy Sowerby is also known for her illustrations of *Alice in Wonderland, Child's Garden of Verses*, etc.

**Soxh'let** (zôks'lĕt; *Angl.* sŏks'-), **Franz von.** 1848–1926. German agricultural chemist; devised method of sterilizing milk; made investigation to determine differences between human and bovine milk; devised an apparatus (Soxhlet apparatus) used in extracting fatty material with ether or other volatile solvent.

**Soy'er'** (swȧ'yā'), **Alexis Benoît.** 1809–1858. French cook and writer on cookery.

**Soy'er** (soi'ẽr), **Raphael.** 1899– . Painter, b. Russia; to U.S. (c. 1913) and settled in New York City. Known esp. for his paintings of New York City's unfortunates.

**So'zo·men** (sō'zō·mĕn). *In full* **Her'mi·as So·zom'e·nus** (hûr'mĭ·ȧs [hûr·mī'ȧs] sō·zŏm'ē·nŭs). Greek church historian of early 5th century A.D., b. in Palestine; author of an ecclesiastical history modeled upon and closely paralleling that of Socrates Scholasticus (*q.v.*), and dealing with the period 324 to 415 A.D.

**Sozzini, Fausto** and **Lelio.** See SOCINUS.

**Spaak** (spȧk), **Paul-Henri.** 1899–1972. Belgian statesman, b. Brussels; advocate of European unity; min of foreign affairs (1936–38; 1939–45; 1946–50; 1954–57; 1961–66); premier (1938–39; 1946; 1947–50); first pres., UN general assembly (1946); secy. general of NATO (1957–61).

**Spaatz** (späts), **Carl.** 1891–1974. American army officer, b. Boyertown, Pa. Grad. U.S.M.A. (1914); mil. observer in Eng. (1940); chief of air staff (1941), of U.S. air force in Europe (1942); deputy allied air commander in Mediterranean (1943); chief, U.S. bombing force in Germany (1944) and Japan (1945); first chief of staff of independent U.S. Air Force (1947).

**Spa'da** (spä'dä), **Leonello.** 1576–1622. Italian painter; among his works are frescoes in Church of San Michele in Bosco (at Bologna), and in Church of Madonna della Chiara (at Reggio).

**Spaeth** (spāth), **Sigmund.** 1885–1965. American musician, lecturer, and writer, b. Philadelphia; A.B., Haverford (1905), Ph.D., Princeton (1910); music editor on various newspapers and magazines (from 1913); author of *The Common Sense of Music* (1924), *The Art of Enjoying Music* (1933), *Great Symphonies* (1936), etc.

**Spa'gna, Lo** (lō spä'nyä). *Real name* **Giovanni di Pie'tro** (dē pyâ'trō). fl. 1500–1530. Italian painter of the Umbrian school, b. in Spain.

**Spagnoletto, Lo.** See José de RIBERA.

**Spagnuolo, Lo.** See Giuseppe Maria CRESPI.

**Spahn** (shpän), **Peter.** 1846–1925. German jurist and politician; member of German Reichstag (1884–1917, 1920–25); Prussian minister of justice (Aug., 1917–Nov., 1918); member of Weimar National Assembly (1919–20).

**Spa'la·tin'** (shpä'lä·tēn'; shpä'lä·tēn), **Georg.** *Real surname* **Burck'hardt** (bŏŏrk'härt). 1484–1545. German reformer; associate of Luther in advancing cause of Protestant Reformation. Translator of Latin writings of Luther, Melanchthon, and Erasmus, and biographer of electors Frederick, John, and John Frederick of Saxony.

**Spal'ding** (spôl'dĭng), **Albert.** 1888–1953. American violinist, b. Chicago; concert debut, Paris (1905), and in New York with New York Symphony Orchestra (1908); officer in aviation corps signal service through World War I. Composer of many violin pieces.

**Spalding, Albert Goodwill.** 1850–1915. American sportsman and businessman, b. in Ogle County, Ill.; played professional baseball, with Boston team (1871–

75) and Chicago team (1876); was successively manager, secretary, and president of the Chicago club (to 1891). Organized with his brother a sporting-goods business (1876); edited *Spalding's Official Baseball Guide* (1878–80).

**Spalding, John.** c. 1609–c. 1670. Scottish historian; author of the annalistic *Memorials of the Troubles in Scotland and England*, covering period from 1624–1645.

**Spalding, Lyman.** 1775–1821. American physician, b. Cornish, N.H.; practiced in Portsmouth, N.H., and later in New York City. Investigated yellow fever, vaccination, and hydrophobia; founded the U.S. Pharmacopoeia (1820).

**Spalding, Martin John.** 1810–1872. American Roman Catholic clergyman; bishop of Louisville (1848); archbishop of Baltimore (1864). His nephew **John Lancaster Spalding** (1840–1916), bishop of Peoria, Ill. (1877); wrote a number of books on religion, philosophy, education, and social issues, and volumes of verse, including *America and Other Poems* (1885), *The Poet's Praise* (1887); resigned his see (1908); created titular archbishop of Scythopolis (1909).

**Spal'lan·za'ni** (späl'län·tsä'nē), **Lazzaro.** 1729–1799. Italian naturalist; professor, Pavia (from 1769). Known for experiments on digestion, circulation of the blood, fertilization in animals, the senses of bats, regeneration of the legs in salamanders; disproved the theory of spontaneous generation.

**Spang'en·berg** (shpäng'ĕn·bĕrк; *Angl.* spăng'ĕn·bûrg), **Augustus Gottlieb.** 1704–1792. Moravian church clergyman, b. in Prussia; assistant to Count Zinzendorf at Herrnhut (1733) and allied himself with the Unitas Fratrum. To America (1735) and labored for Moravian church in Georgia and Pennsylvania. Bishop (1744); organized and directed Moravian settlement at Bethlehem, Pa. (1744–50) and on land grant in North Carolina (1752–62). Returned to Herrnhut (1762); dominating figure in his church (1762–92). Author of a life of Zinzendorf, a history of the Unitas Fratrum, and *Idea Fidei Fratrum*, a compendium of the Christian faith of the Unitas Fratrum (1779).

**Span'heim** (shpän'hīm), Baron **Ezechiel von.** 1629–1710. Swiss-born German scholar and statesman; represented Brandenburg in negotiations leading to Treaty of Ryswick (1697); first Prussian minister in London (1702).

**Spann** (shpän), **Othmar.** 1878–1950. Austrian economist and sociologist.

**Spar'go** (spär'gō), **John.** 1876–1966. Socialist and author, b. Stithians, Cornwall, Eng.; to U.S. (1901); active as lecturer, writer, and worker in the socialist cause (1901–17); resigned from Socialist party (1917) because of its attitude on issues involved in World War. With Samuel Gompers, founded American Alliance for Labor and Democracy (1917); also active in founding the Nationalist party (1917); became vigorous critic of Bolshevism. A founder of Prospect House Social Settlement, Yonkers, N.Y. Resident of Bennington, Vt. (from c. 1920). Author of many books on socialism and social reform.

**Sparks** (spärks), **Edwin Erle.** 1860–1924. American educator; professor of American history, U. of Chicago (1904–08); president, Pennsylvania State College (1908–20). Author of *The United States of America* (2 vols., 1904), *National Development, 1877–1885* (1907), etc.

**Sparks, Jared.** 1789–1866. American historian, b. Willington, Conn.; bought and edited *North American Review* (1823–29). Published *The Diplomatic Correspondence of the American Revolution* (12 vols., 1829–30), *The Life of Gouverneur Morris* (3 vols., 1832), *The Writings of George Washington* (12 vols., 1834–37), *The Works of Benjamin Franklin* (10 vols., 1836–40), *The Library of American Biography* (10 vols., 1834–38). Professor of history, Harvard (1839–49); president of Harvard (1849–53).

**Spar'ta·cus** (spär'tȧ·kŭs). d. 71 B.C. Roman slave and gladiator, from Thrace; leader of a slave insurrection (Servile War, 73–71 B.C.). After several times defeating Roman armies sent against him, he was finally beaten by Crassus, and killed in action.

**Spaul'ding** (spôl'dĭng), **Edward Gleason.** 1873–1940. American educator; professor of philosophy, Princeton (from 1914). Author of *The New Rationalism* (1918), *What Am I?* (1928), *A World of Chance* (1936).

**Spaulding, Elbridge Gerry.** 1809–1897. American banker and legislator; member, U.S. House of Representatives (1849–51; 1859–63); introduced (Dec. 30, 1861) bill for issue of legal-tender treasury notes payable on demand to relieve U.S. Treasury situation; known as "Father of Greenbacks." Organized and headed Farmers' and Mechanics' National Bank, Buffalo (from 1864).

**Spaulding, Levi.** 1791–1873. American Congregational missionary in Ceylon (1820–73); noted as a Tamil linguist and compiler of a Tamil dictionary, and as a reviser (1865–71) of the Tamil Old Testament.

**Spaulding, Solomon.** 1761–1816. American clergyman, b. Ashford, Conn.; preached in New England pastorates; withdrew from ministry (1795) and went into business. Author of a romance entitled *The Manuscript Found*, which purported to be an account of the original people in America, and to have been dug up from an ancient mound. It was later charged that the *Book of Mormon* was compiled by Joseph Smith and Sidney Rigdon from a manuscript copy of this unpublished romance.

**Spea'ker** (spē'kẽr), **Tristram E.**, *known as* **Tris** (trĭs). 1888–1958. American professional baseball player, b. Hubbard City, Texas; center fielder in American League, with Boston (1909–15), Cleveland (1916–26), Washington (1927), Philadelphia (1928).

**Speaks** (spēks), **Oley.** 1876–1948. American concert baritone and composer; among the songs composed by him are *Sylvia, On the Road to Mandalay, When the Boys Come Home, Fuzzy Wuzzy.*

**Spears** (spērz), **John Randolph.** 1850–1936. American writer, b. in Ohio; wrote on naval subjects, as *The History of Our Navy* (1897), *Story of the American Merchant Marine* (1910), *Master Mariners* (1911), etc.

**Speck'ba'cher** (shpĕk'bä'kẽr), **Joseph.** 1767–1820. Tirolese insurrectionary leader in uprisings against French (1797, 1800, 1805, 1809).

**Speck von Stern'burg** (shpĕk' fôn shtĕrn'bo͝ork), Baron **Hermann.** 1852–1908. German diplomat; served through Franco-Prussian War (1870–71); military attaché, German embassy at Washington, D.C. (1885–90); German ambassador to U.S. (1903–08).

**Sped'ding** (spĕd'ĭng), **James.** 1808–1881. English editor of Bacon's works; educ. Trinity Coll., Cambridge, where he was member of brilliant circle including Tennyson and Thackeray. Published *Works of Francis Bacon* (7 vols., 1857–59), *Life and Letters* (7 vols., 1861–74); author of *Life and Times of Bacon* (1878).

**Spee** (shpā), Count (*Ger.* Graf) **Maximilian von.** 1861–1914. German vice-admiral; surprised and defeated British squadron under Admiral Cradock at Coronel off the Chilean coast (Nov. 1, 1914); sank with his flagship *Scharnhorst* when his fleet was destroyed by the British under Rear Admiral Sturdee near the Falkland Islands (Dec. 8, 1914).

**Speed** (spēd), **John.** 1552–1629. English antiquarian and cartographer; published a series of 54 maps of various parts of England and Wales (1608–10). Author of a *History of Great Britain* (1611).

**Speer** (spēr), **Robert Elliott.** 1867–1947. American religious leader; secretary, Presbyterian Board of Foreign Missions (1891–1937); author of *The Man Christ Jesus* (1896), *Missionary Principles and Practice* (1902), *Missions and Modern History* (1904), *Race and Race Relations* (1924), *Christian Realities* (1935), etc.

**Speght** (spāt), **Thomas.** fl. 1598. English schoolmaster; published an edition of Chaucer's works (1598) and, with assistance of Francis Thynne, a second edition (1602).

**Spei′cher** (spī′kẽr), **Eugene Edward.** 1883–1962. American painter; best known as a portrait painter, with studio at Woodstock, N.Y., in summer, and New York City in winter. His *Katharine Cornell as Candida* is in the Whitney Museum of Modern Art in New York; *The Blue Necklace* in Toledo (Ohio) Museum of Art.

**Spei′ser** (spī′zẽr), **Ephraim A′vig·dor** (ä′vĕg·dôr). 1902–1965. Archaeologist and Semitic scholar, b. Skalat, Galicia; to U.S. (1920); naturalized (1926). M.A., Pennsylvania (1923), Ph.D., Dropsie College, Philadelphia (1924). Research scholar, U. of Pennsylvania (1924–26); Guggenheim fellow for study in Mesopotamia (1926–28); discovered site of city of Tepe Gawra; professor of Semitics, U. of Pennsylvania (from 1931); field director of excavations in Mesopotamia (1930–32, 1936–37). Editorial consultant for *Webster's New International Dictionary, Second Edition.* Author of *Mesopotamian Origins* (1930), *Excavations at Tepe Gawra* (1935), and many monographs on archaeological, philological, and historical subjects.

**Speke** (spēk), **John Hanning.** 1827–1864. English African explorer; accompanied Richard Burton in expedition into Somaliland (1854); in expedition under Burton to investigate Lake Nyasa (1856), discovered lakes Tanganyika and Victoria; confirmed his theory of the latter as source of the Nile (1862); published *Journal of the Discovery of the Source of the Nile* (1863); furnished information to Samuel Baker that enabled him to discover Lake Albert (1864).

**Spell′man** (spĕl′măn), **Francis Joseph.** 1889-1967. American Roman Catholic clergyman, b. Whitman, Mass.; consecrated bishop (1932), and archbishop of New York (1939); elevated to cardinalate (1946).

**Spel′man** (spĕl′măn), **Sir Henry.** 1564?–1641. English antiquary; prepared as preliminary to his learned works on English law, a glossary of obsolete Latin and Old English terms (2 vols., 1626; completed by his son, 1664); author of *Concilia, Decreta, Leges, Constitutiones* (2 vols., 1639–64), an attempt to document ecclesiastical history.

**Spe′mann** (shpā′män), **Hans.** 1869–1941. German zoologist; professor at Rostock (1908); director, Kaiser Wilhelm Institute of Biology (1914); professor at Freiburg (from 1919). Worked esp. on the mechanics of embryologic development, discovering the directive function (organizer effect) of certain tissues. Awarded 1935 Nobel prize for physiology and medicine.

**Spence** (spĕns), **Joseph.** 1699–1768. English anecdotist. His *Essay on Pope's Odyssey* (1727) won him a professorship of poetry at Oxford (1728) and the friendship of Pope. Recorded anecdotes from conversations of Pope and his friends (publ. 1820).

**Spence, Thomas.** 1750–1814. London bookseller and inventor of Spencean system of land nationalization; proposed (1775) establishment of self-contained communities organized on semisocialistic principles, with a single-tax system; persecuted for his views. Author of pamphlets on the millennium, the natural state of man, and the like.

**Spen′cer** (spĕn′sẽr). Name of old English family taking origin from Robert Despencer, steward to William the Conqueror, and from the Hugh Despensers, favorites of Edward II, and descending through Sir John Spencer (d. 1522) to his great-great-grandson **Robert Spencer** (d. 1627), 5th knight in succession, 1st Baron **Spencer of Worm·leigh′ton** (wûrm·lā′t'n), sheep breeder, active opponent of Bacon, supporter of Southampton (*q.v.*) and Virginia colonization, reputed wealthiest man in England. The Spencer family, having family seat at Althorp in Northamptonshire, has been honored with earldom of Sunderland, earldom of Spencer, and dukedom of Marlborough, including among its members:

EARLS OF SUN′DER·LAND (sŭn′dẽr·lănd): **Henry Spencer** (1620–1643), 1st Earl of **Sunderland,** 3d Baron Spencer; grandson of Robert, 1st Baron Spencer; m. (1639) Lady Dorothy Sidney, known as **Sach′a·ris′sa** [săk′*ȧ*·rĭs′*ȧ*] (see SIDNEY family); killed at battle of Newbury, fighting for Charles I.

His son **Robert** (1640–1702), 2d earl; crafty politician; educ. Oxford; m. (1665) Anne Digby, rich heiress; by paying court to Charles II's mistresses, appointed ambassador at Madrid, Paris, and Cologne (1671–78); secretary of state for northern department (1679) and member of inner cabinet (1679–81); with Essex and Halifax, opposed Shaftsbury, who favored Monmouth; worked for exclusion bill, excluding duke of York from succession, and thereby lost his place in privy council; regained royal favor through intercession of duchess of Portland, mistress of Charles II; advocated disgraceful arrangement whereby Charles II, in return for French pension, agreed to assemble no parliament for three years; increased his influence under James II as lord president of council and principal secretary of state; effected dismissal of his rival, Rochester, after professing Roman Catholicism (1687); accepting French pension, deceived James II and French by sending William of Orange information; on arrival of William in England fled to Holland, convinced William of his indispensability, returned (1691), entertained William a week at Althorp; made lord chamberlain and one of lord justices; induced William to choose all his ministers from one party, the modern system; virtual head of government until forced by popular indignation to resign (1697).

His second son, **Charles** (1674–1722), 3d earl; statesman and bibliophile; Lord Spencer on death of brother (1688); m. (1700) Lady Anne Churchill, daughter of famous duke of Marlborough; envoy extraordinary to Vienna (1705); through Marlborough's influence named secretary of state for southern department (1706), and one of five Whigs, called the junto, who dominated government (1708–10). During last years of Queen Anne, in constant communication with Hanover; on accession of George I, relegated to Ireland as viceroy; joined cabinet as lord keeper of privy seal (1715); intrigued with Stanhope to secure dismissal of Townshend (1716) and Walpole (1717); became first lord of treasury (1718); having taken some part in promoting South Sea Bubble (1720), accused of taking bribe of £50,000 and forced to resign (1721); retained influence with George I. Collector of rare books; patron of Addison and other men of letters.

DUKES OF MARL′BOR·OUGH (märl′b*ŭ*·r*ŭ*; -br*ŭ*; môl′-): **Charles Spencer** (1706–1758), 3d Duke of **Marlborough** and 5th Earl of **Sunderland;** 3d son of 3d earl; succeeded his brother (1729) and succeeded (1733) to dukedom of Marlborough on death of maternal aunt, Marlborough's eldest daughter, duchess in her own right, thus merging two titles; commanded brigade at Dettingen (1743) and in expedition against St.-Malo (1758). His eldest son, **George** (1739–1817), 4th duke; lord privy seal in Grenville ministry (1763–65). George's

eldest son, **George** (1766–1840), 5th duke; M.A. Oxon. (1786); M.P. (1790); spent enormous sums on his gardens and library of early printing; took additional name of **Church′ill** (chûrch′(h)ĭl) by royal license (1817).
George's (1766–1840) grandson **John Winston Spencer Churchill** (1822–1883), 7th duke; prominent Conservative; as marquis of **Bland′ford** (blăn(d)′fẽrd), M.P. (1844), brought about carriage of Blandford Act (1856) for dividing parishes for purposes of church work; lord lieutenant of Ireland (1876–80); his 3d son was Lord Randolph Churchill (*q.v.*), statesman, whose son Winston Leonard Spencer Churchill (*q.v.*, at CHURCHILL) became prime minister (May, 1940).
**William Robert Spencer** (1769–1834); poet and wit; younger son of 2d son of 3d duke of Marlborough; educ. Oxford; belonged to Whig set of Fox and Sheridan; wrote graceful society verse, that attracted Byron, and ballads including *Beth Gélert*, that attracted Christopher North.

EARLS SPENCER: Branch of Spencer family including earls Spencer founded by **John Spencer,** 3d and youngest son of Charles Spencer, 3d Earl of Sunderland, by Anne, daughter of great duke of Marlborough. John succeeded to Sunderland property and inherited property from his grandmother the duchess. His only son, **John Spencer** (1734–1783), 1st Earl **Spencer** (created 1765) was father of Georgiana, beautiful duchess of Devonshire (see under CAVENDISH family).
**George John** (1758–1834), 2d earl; by courtesy, Viscount **Al′thorp** (ôl′trŭp; ôl′thôrp); son of 1st earl; M.A., Cantab. (1778); deserted extreme Whig faction; became Pitt's first lord of admiralty (1794–1801); showed organizing skill and supervised putting down of mutinies of Spithead and The Nore; singled out Nelson to command in Mediterranean; home secretary in All-the-Talents Administration (1806–07); helped form Roxburghe Club (1812); collected books in rehabilitation of Althorp Library, which became nucleus of Rylands Library at Manchester.
George's eldest son, **John Charles** (1782–1845), 3d earl, best known as Lord **Althorp;** M.A., Cantab. (1802); M.P. (1804), joined advanced Whig party; junior lord of treasury (1806–07); leader of Whig opposition (1830); chancellor of exchequer and leader in House of Commons (Dec., 1830); industrious leader, played important part in preparing and carrying Reform Bill after one rejection by House of Lords (1832); carried bill for reforming Irish Church; withdrew after succession to earldom; returned to pronounce in favor of repeal of corn laws (1841); first president of Royal Agricultural Society and a notable cattle breeder.
John Charles's nephew **John Poyntz Spencer** (1835–1910), 5th earl; statesman; son of 4th earl and Elizabeth Poyntz; M.A., Cantab. (1857); succeeded to earldom (1857); ardent sportsman, helped form National Rifle Assoc. (1860); began long career as Liberal politician as lord lieutenant of Ireland under Gladstone (1868–74); lord president of council, with seat in cabinet (1880–82); reappointed lord lieutenant of Ireland (1882–85), forced to adopt repressive measures after murder of his Irish secretary, Lord Frederick Cavendish (1882); having embraced Gladstone's home-rule policy, again president of council (1886); first lord of admiralty (1892–95); Liberal leader in House of Lords (1902–05); often suggested as best-fitted for prime minister, but incapacitated by illness (after 1905).
**Charles Robert** (1857–1922), 6th earl, Viscount **Althorp;** only son of 4th earl by second wife; parliamentary groom in waiting to queen (1886) and vice-chamberlain (1892–95).

**Spencer, Ambrose.** 1765–1848. American lawyer and politician; associated with DeWitt Clinton in controlling Republican politics in New York State (1800–12); in sole control (1812–16); power then waned and ended (1823). Chief justice (1819–23), New York supreme court; member, U.S. House of Representatives (1829–31). His son **John Canfield** (1788–1855) was member of U.S. House of Representatives (1817–19); practiced law in Albany (from 1837); U.S. secretary of war (1841–43); U.S. secretary of the treasury (1843–44).

**Spencer, Charles Albert.** 1813–1881. American optical instrument maker, b. Lennox, N.Y.; founded company to manufacture first American microscopes (1847), the Spencer Lens Company developing from this organization.

**Spencer,** Lady **Diana.** See under Topham BEAUCLERK.

**Spencer, Dorothy.** Countess of Sunderland. See under SIDNEY family.

**Spencer, Herbert.** 1820–1903. English philosopher, b. at Derby. As subeditor of the *Economist* in London (1848–53), made acquaintance of Huxley and Tyndall, George Eliot and John Stuart Mill, and developed the ethical and social views of his first important work, *Social Statics* (1851), advocating extreme individualism; thereafter absorbed in study of development of doctrine of evolution as applied to sociology; began to apply the doctrine of evolution in *Principles of Psychology* (1855); sought to develop the organizing principle that all organic development is change from state of indefinite homogeneity to state of definite heterogeneity; provided by Darwin's *Origin of Species* (1859) with documentary evidence of what had been speculation. Announced (1860) a *System of Synthetic Philosophy* covering metaphysics, biology, psychology, sociology, and ethics, of which he published *First Principles* (1862), *Principles of Biology* (2 vols., 1864, 1867), *Principles of Sociology* (3 vols., 1876, 1882, 1896), *Data of Ethics* (1879), *Principles of Ethics* (2 vols., 1892, 1893, of which *Data of Ethics* constitutes part one). Author also of *Education* (a leading textbook; 1861), *The Man versus the State* (again urging limitation of functions of government; 1884), three volumes of essays, and *Autobiography* (1904). One of few modern thinkers to attempt systematic account of all cosmic phenomena, including mental and social principles; influenced contemporary philosophy, psychology, and ethics throughout Europe and America, India and Japan.

**Spencer, Platt Rogers.** 1800–1864. American calligrapher, b. East Fishkill, N.Y.; originator of Spencerian style of handwriting; teacher of penmanship in schools and business colleges; author of copybooks and textbooks on penmanship.

**Spencer, Robert.** 1879–1931. American painter; his *Repairing the Bridge* hangs in Metropolitan Museum of Art, New York City; *Mountebanks and Thieves*, *Day in March*, *The Auction*, in Phillips Memorial Gallery, Washington, D.C.

**Spencer,** Sir **Walter Baldwin.** 1860–1929. English ethnographer, b. Stretford, Lancashire; to Melbourne, Australia (1887), to become professor of biology, U. of Melbourne (1887–1919); made special study of the Australian aborigines. Author of *Native Tribes of the Northern Territory of Australia* (1914), *Wanderings in Wild Australia* (1928), and, with Francis James Gillen (d. 1912), of *Native Tribes of Central Australia* (1889), *Northern Tribes of Central Australia* (1904), *Across Australia* (1912), *The Arunta, a Study of a Stone Age People* (pub. 1927).

**Spen′der** (spĕn′dẽr), **John Alfred.** 1862–1942. English journalist; son of Dr. J. K. Spender of Bath and **Lilian**

Headland **Spender** (1838–1895), novelist; assistant editor (1893), editor (1896–1922), *Westminster Gazette;* member of special Milner mission to Egypt (1919–20); author of *The Comments of Bagshot* (1914), biography of Sir Henry Campbell-Bannerman (1923), *The Changing East* (1926), *A Short History of Our Times* (1934), *New Lamps and Ancient Lights* (1490), etc. His brother **Edward Harold** (1864–1926), journalist and novelist; author of *Story of the Home Rule Session* (1893), *One Man Returns* (1914), *The Man Who Went* (1919), biographies of Herbert Henry Asquith (1915), General Botha (1916), David Lloyd George (1920), *The Cauldron of Europe* (1925). Edward's son **Stephen** (1909– ), poet and critic; author of *Poems, The Destructive Element, Vienna, The Burning Cactus* (1936), *Forward from Liberalism* (1937), *Trial of a Judge* (tragedy; 1938), *Poems for Spain* (1939), *The Still Centre* (1939), *Ruins and Visions* (1941), *Life and the Poet* (1942).

**Spe′ner** (shpā′nẽr), **Philipp Jacob.** 1635–1705. German Protestant theologian; leader of Lutheran Pietism. Also known as a genealogist and heraldic scholar; author of *Opus Heraldicum* (2 vols., 1680, 1690).

**Speng′ler** (shpĕng′lẽr), **Oswald.** 1880–1936. German writer on philosophy of history; chief work, *Der Untergang des Abendlandes. Umrisse einer Morphologie der Weltgeschichte* (2 vols., 1918–22; trans. into English under title *Decline of the West*), in which he predicted the eclipse of Western civilization.

**Spen′love–Spen′love** (spĕn′lŭv·spĕn′lŭv), **Frank.** 1868–1933. English landscape and figure painter; founded Spenlove School of Modern Art, known as Yellow Door School (1896).

**Spen′ser** (spĕn′sẽr). See also DESPENSER and SPENCER.

**Spenser, Edmund.** 1552–1599. English poet, b. London; claimed kinship with Spencer family of Althorp and had claim allowed. Grad. Cambridge (B.A., 1572; M.A., 1576), where he profited by friendship of Gabriel Harvey. After a reputed sojourn in the north where he prob. met and fell in love with the "Rosalind" of his *Shepheardes Calender*, he secured place through Harvey in Leicester's household in London, and became acquainted with Leicester's nephew Sir Philip Sidney (1578); with Sidney, Dyer, and others formed a literary club, Areopagus; at suggestion of Harvey and Edward Kirke experimented in classical measures. Launched first work of Elizabethan literature, *The Shepheardes Calender*, comprising 12 eclogues, with archaic glossary, and dedicated to Sidney, friend and patron (1579). As secretary accompanied Arthur Grey, Lord Grey de Wilton, lord deputy, to Ireland (1580); began writing *Faerie Queene*, an imaginative allegorical presentation and vindication of Protestantism and Puritanism; received grant of Kilcolman Castle, near Cork, part of forfeited estates of earl of Desmond; commemorated death of Sidney in a pastoral elegy, *Astrophel* (1586); published three books of *Faerie Queene* (1590), which won him such a reputation that the printer brought out minor poems, partly rewritten, as *Complaints* (1590). Married (1594) Elizabeth Boyle, whom he had courted in *Amoretti*, and commemorated the marriage in *Epithalamion*. Published *Colin Clouts come home againe* (1595), written (1591) after he was presented to Queen Elizabeth by Sir Walter Raleigh; published second installment of three books of *Faerie Queene* (1596) and *Foure Hymnes* (on love and beauty and heavenly love) showing Platonic influence (1596); showed strong bias for relentless subjugation in his prose *View of the Present State of Ireland* (1596). Returned from second visit to England, depressed in spirits and in health; sheriff of Cork (1598); in burning of Kilcolman castle by Irish insurrectionists (1598), lost his youngest child and perhaps additional books of *Faerie Queene*, barely saved wife and other children; died on mission to London with dispatches; buried in Westminster Abbey near Chaucer. Called "the Poet's Poet"; excelled in richness and beauty of imagination; enriched poetry with invention of Spenserian stanza (rhyme scheme *ababbcbcc*).

**Spe·ran′ski** (spyĕ·rȧn′skû·ĭ; *Angl.* spĕ·răn′skĭ), Count **Mikhail Mikhailovich.** 1772–1839. Russian statesman; accompanied Czar Alexander I to the conference with Napoleon at Erfurt (1806), and was described by Napoleon as "the only clear head in Russia." Minister of state (1809–12); governor general of Siberia; member of the council of state (1821).

**Sperl** (shpĕrl), **Hans.** 1861– . Austrian jurist.

**Sper′ry** (spĕr′ĭ), **Charles Stillman.** 1847–1911. American naval officer; commanded battleship fleet in cruise around the world (1908–09).

**Sperry, Elmer Ambrose.** 1860–1930. American electrical engineer and inventor, b. Cortland, N.Y. Invented improved dynamo and new type of arc lamp (1879); organized Sperry Electric Company, Chicago (1880), Sperry Electric Mining Machine Company (1888), Sperry Electric Railway Company (1890) and National Battery Company. Founded (1900) electrochemical research laboratory in Washington, D.C., where (with his associate, C. P. Townsend) he developed process for making pure caustic soda from salt, a chlorine detinning process for recovering tin from old cans and scrap. Also experimented with design of an internal-combustion engine of the Diesel type. Most notable inventions were gyroscopic compasses and stabilizers for ships and airplanes; organized Sperry Gyroscope Company, Brooklyn, N.Y. (1910) for manufacturing these instruments, and remained at its head until 1929. Also invented high-intensity arc searchlight (1918), now standard searchlight in military and naval use.

**Speu·sip′pus** (spū·sĭp′ŭs). Greek philosopher; nephew and disciple of Plato at Athens; accompanied Plato to Sicily (361 B.C.), and named by Plato on his deathbed as his successor (347). Only a fragment of one of his works, *On Pythagorean Numbers*, is extant.

**Spe′wack** (spē′wăk), **Samuel** (1899–1971) **and** his wife **Bella,** *nee* **Co′hen** [kō′ĕn] (1899– ). Playwrights; Samuel, b. in Russia, came to U.S., 1904; Bella, b. in Hungary, came to U.S., 1903. After journalistic experience, collaborated in the plays *The Solitaire Man* (1926), *Poppa* (1928), *The War Song* (1928), *Clear All Wires* (1932), *Spring Song* (1934), *Boy Meets Girl* (1935).

**Spey′er** (spī′ẽr), **James.** 1861–1941. American banker, b. New York City; partner in Speyer & Co.; senior partner (from 1899). His brother **Edgar** (1862–1932) was also a banker, associated (from 1886) with English firm of Speyer Brothers, London; also, consolidated London Underground Ry., of which he was chairman (retired, 1915); resided in U.S. (1915–32) and devoted himself esp. to art and music; Richard Strauss's opera *Salome* is dedicated to him in recognition of his interest and assistance. Edgar's wife, **Leonora,** *nee* **Von Stosch** [vŏn stŏsh′] (1872–1956), American poet, b. Washington, D.C.; m. (2d) Edgar Speyer (1902); author of *Canopic Jar* (1921), *Fiddler's Farewell* (1926; awarded Pulitzer prize for poetry), *Naked Heel* (1931), *Slow Wall* (1939).

**Spie′gel** (shpē′gĕl), **Friedrich von.** 1820–1905. German Orientalist; by his editions of *Kammavāka* (1841) and *Anecdota Pālica* (1845), founded study of Pali in Germany. Edited also *Avesta*, with a translation and commentary; published *Eranische Altertumskunde* (3 vols., 1871–78).

**Spie′gel** (shpē′gĕl; spē′-), **Shalom.** 1899– . Rumanian-born American Jewish scholar; to U.S. (1928), and became professor of Hebrew language and literature, and librarian, Jewish Institute of Religion, New York.

**Spie'ghel** (spē'gĕl), **Adriaan van den.** *Lat.* **Spi·ge'li·us** (spĭ·jē'lĭ·ŭs). 1578–1625. Flemish botanist and anatomist, b. in Brussels.

**Spiel'ha'gen** (shpēl'hä'gĕn), **Friedrich.** 1829–1911. German novelist; author of *Clara Vere* (1856), *Durch Nacht zum Licht* (4 vols., 1862), *In Reih und Glied* (5 vols., 1867), *Hammer und Amboss* (5 vols., 1869), and *Sturmflut* (3 vols., 1877). Author also of plays, including *Liebe für Liebe* (1875) and *Hans und Grete* (1876), etc.

**Spiess** (shpēs), **Adolf.** 1810–1858. German founder of gymnastic schools.

**Spigelius.** See Adriaan van den SPIEGHEL.

**Spill'man** (spĭl'măn), **William Jasper.** 1863–1931. American agricultural scientist; on staff of U.S. Department of Agriculture (1902–18; 1921–31).

**Spin'den** (spĭn'dĕn), **Herbert Joseph.** 1879–1967. American anthropologist; curator of American Indian art and primitive cultures, Brooklyn Museum (from 1929). Authority on ancient art and ancient American history; worked out chronology of Mayan inscriptions, the Mayan civil and Venus calendars, etc.

**Spind'ler** (shpĭnd'lẽr), **Karl.** 1796–1855. German novelist; author of *Der Jude* (1827), *Der Jesuit* (1829), etc.

**Spi·nel'lo A're·ti'no** (spē·nĕl'lō ä'rā·tē'nō). *Real name* **Luca Spinello.** 1330?–1410. Florentine painter; among his works are frescoes in sacristy of San Miniato at Florence, in the Campo Santo at Pisa, at Casentino, and at Arezzo.

**Spi·net'ti** (spē·nāt'tē), **Giovanni.** fl. 1500. Venetian manufacturer of musical instruments; inventor of the spinet.

**Spin'garn** (spĭn'gärn), **Joel Elias.** 1875–1939. American author, b. New York City. A founder and literary adviser of Harcourt, Brace & Co., publishers (1919–32); chairman of board of directors, National Association for the Advancement of Colored People (1913–19), treasurer (1919–30), president (1930–39); founded Spingarn medal (1913). Author of *A History of Literary Criticism in the Renaissance* (1899), *The New Criticism* (1911), *The New Hesperides and Other Poems* (1911), *Poems* (1924), *Creative Criticism and Other Essays* (1931), etc. His brother **Arthur Barnett** (1878–1971) was president of the National Association for the Advancement of Colored People (1940–65).

**Spin'ner** (spĭn'ẽr), **Francis Elias.** 1802–1890. American banker and politician; member, U.S. Congress (1855–61); treasurer of the United States (1861–75).

**Spí'no·la** (spē'nō·lä), **Ambrogio di** (dē). *Span.* **Ambrosio de Spí'no·la** (thā spē'nō·lä). Marqués **de los Bal·ba'ses** (thā lōs bäl·bä'sās). 1569–1630. Italian general in Spanish service; led army to Netherlands against Maurice of Nassau (1602–09); commander of Spanish army there; captured Ostend (1604); conquered Palatinate (1620); dissolved Protestant Union (1621); captured Jülich (1622), Breda (1625).

**Spi·no'za** (spĭ·nō'zȧ), **Baruch** *or* **Benedict.** 1632–1677. Dutch philosopher, b. Amsterdam, of Portuguese-Jewish parentage. Excommunicated from the synagogue (1656); supported himself by grinding lenses; devoted himself chiefly to study of philosophy, esp. system expounded by Descartes. Offered chair of philosophy at Heidelberg, but refused it because of possibility it might in some way curb his complete independence of thought. Now regarded as most eminent expounder of pantheism. Among his works are *Tractatus Theologico-Politicus* (1670) and *Ethica Ordine Geometrico Demonstrata* (finished 1674, but pub. posthumously).

**Spire** (spēr), **André.** 1868–1966. French writer; vigorous advocate of Zionism and associate of Weizmann and Sokolow in negotiations for Jewish home in Palestine after the World War.

**Spi·ta'ler** (shpē·tä'lẽr), **Rudolf.** 1859– . Austrian astronomer, geophysicist, and meteorologist.

**Spit'ta** (shpĭt'ä), **Karl Johann Philipp.** 1801–1859. German Protestant clergyman and poet; author esp. of religious verse. One son, **Philipp** (1841–1894), was a music scholar; wrote studies of Bach, Schumann, etc. Another son of Karl, **Friedrich** (1852–1924), was a Protestant clergyman; author of *Luther und der Evangelische Gottesdienst* (1884), *Zur Geschichte und Literatur des Urchristentums* (3 vols., 1893–1907), etc.

**Spit'te·ler** (shpĭt'ĕ·lẽr), **Carl.** *Pseudonym* **Felix Tan'dem** (tän'dĕm). 1845–1924. Swiss writer; among his works (written in German) are *Prometheus und Epimetheus* (epic in rhythmical prose; 1881), *Extramundana* (verse; 1883), *Schmetterlinge* (short poems; 1889), *Die Mädchenfeinde* (child's story; 1892), *Der Olympische Frühling* (epic; 4 vols., 1900–06), *Glockenlieder* (1906), *Imago* (novel; 1906), *Meine Frühesten Erlebnisse* (story of his boyhood; 1914), and *Prometheus der Dulder* (epic; 1924). Awarded Nobel prize for literature (1919).

**Spit'zer** (shpĭt'sẽr), **Leo.** 1887–1960. Austrian philologist and literary historian; to Johns Hopkins (1936).

**Spitz'ka** (spĭts'kȧ), **Edward Charles.** 1852–1914. American psychiatrist; specialized in nervous and mental cases. His son **Edward Anthony** (1876–1922) was also a physician; specialized in nervous and mental cases; made studies of the human brain.

**Spitz'mül'ler** (shpĭts'mül'ẽr), Baron **Alexander.** 1862– . Austrian financier; general manager of Austrian Creditanstalt, largest bank of old Hapsburg monarchy (1910). Minister of commerce (1915), of finance (Dec., 1916–June, 1917; Apr.–Nov., 1918); governor of Austro-Hungarian bank (1919–23), engaged in efforts to reconstruct bankrupt Austrian Creditanstalt (1931).

**Spitz'weg** (shpĭts'vāк), **Carl.** 1808–1885. German painter of landscapes and genre scenes.

**Splawn** (splôn), **Walter Marshall William.** 1883– . American lawyer, economist, and educator; professor of economics (1919–28), and president (1924–27), U. of Texas. Member, Interstate Commerce Commission (1934) and chairman (1938). Author of *Consolidation of Railroads* (1924), *Government Ownership and Operation of Railroads* (1928).

**Spock** (spŏk), **Benjamin McLane.** 1903– . American physician, b. New Haven, Conn. Author of books on child care, including *Common Sense Book of Baby and Child Care* (1946), *Baby's First Year* (1955), etc.

**Spode** (spōd), **Josiah.** 1754–1827. English potter, of Stoke in Staffordshire; improved the old willow pattern; made porcelain with paste made of bones as well as feldspar (1800).

**Spof'ford** (spŏf'ẽrd), **Ainsworth Rand.** 1825–1908. American librarian; librarian (1864–97), Library of Congress, Washington, D.C.

**Spofford, Harriet Elizabeth,** *nee* **Prescott.** 1835–1921. American novelist and poet; m. Richard Smith Spofford (1865). Among her works are *Sir Rohan's Ghost* (1860), *The Amber Gods* (1863), *Azarian* (1864), *New England Legends* (1871), *Poems* (1881), *In Titian's Garden and Other Poems* (1897), *A Little Book of Friends* (1916), etc.

**Spof'forth** (spŏf'ẽrth; -ōrth; -ôrth), **Frederick Robert.** 1853–1926. Known as "the Demon." Australian cricketer; renowned as a bowler in the Australian team's tours of 1878 and 1882 in England.

**Spohr** (shpōr), **Louis.** 1784–1859. German violin virtuoso and composer. Among his many works are operas, oratorios, symphonies, concert overtures, and piano, violin, and harp pieces; operas include *Faust* (1816), *Zemire und Azor* (1818), *Jessonda* (1822), *Der Alchimist* (1830), and *Die Kreuzfahrer* (1845).

**Spon·ti′ni** (spôn·tē′nē), **Gasparo.** Conte **di Sant′ An·dre′a** (dē sän′tän·drâ′ä). 1774–1851. Italian composer, chiefly of operas, including *La Vestale* (1807), *Ferdinand Cortez* (1809), *Olympia* (1819), *Agnes von Hohenstaufen* (1829).

**Spoo′ner** (spōō′nẽr), **She′ar·ja′shub** (shē′ẽr·jā′shŭb). 1809–1859. American dentist and art connoisseur; withdrew from practice (c. 1840) to devote himself to promotion of art appreciation in U.S. Published *Anecdotes of Painters, Engravers, Sculptors and Architects* (1853).

**Spooner, William Archibald.** 1844–1930. Anglican clergyman and educator; dean (1876–89), and warden (1903–24), of New College, Oxford. An occasional lapse of speech, whereby he transposed sounds in two or more words (as *a blushing crow*, for *a crushing blow*), led to coinage of the word *spoonerism* in the English language.

**Spö′rer** (shpû′rẽr), **Gustav Friedrich Wilhelm.** 1822–1895. German astronomer; studied sunspots; determined rotation period for various zones of the sun and position of sun's equator; formulated law (Spörer's law) expressing the latitude variation of the zones of sunspots.

**Spots′wood** (spŏts′wŏŏd), **Alexander.** 1676–1740. English colonial governor in America; lieutenant governor of Virginia (1710–22); improved production of tobacco and favored making tobacco notes legal tender; encouraged better relations with Indians; in conflict with his legislature over executive prerogatives. Deputy postmaster general of the American colonies (1730–39).

**Spot′ted Tail** (spŏt′ĕd tāl′; spŏt′ĭd). 1833?–1881. American Sioux Indian chief, b. near Fort Laramie, Wyo.; favored whites after 1866. Instrumental in causing surrender of Crazy Horse (1877).

**Spot′tis·woode** (spŏt′ĭs·wŏŏd), **Alicia Ann.** 1811–1900. Scottish composer of songs; m. (1836) Lord John Douglas Scott (1809–1860), son of duke of Buccleuch; resumed her maiden name (1870) on succeeding to estate of Spottiswoode, Berwickshire. Set to music William Douglas's song *Annie Laurie.*

**Spottiswoode** *or* **Spot′tis·wood** *or* **Spot′is·wood** (spŏt′ĭs·wŏŏd) *or* **Spots′wood** (spŏts′wŏŏd), **John.** 1565–1639. Scottish prelate; archbishop of Glasgow (1603) and member of Scots privy council (1605); James I's compliant agent in subjugating the kirk; archbishop of St. Andrews (1615); secured passage of Five Articles of Perth (1618) in interests of confirming episcopal government; chancellor of Scotland (1635–38); deposed and excommunicated by Glasgow General Assembly. Author of *History of Church of Scotland* (1655). He was son of **John Spottiswoode** (1510–1585), reformer, intimate of Knox, ecclesiastical superintendent of Lothian. A descendant of the same family, **William Spottiswoode** (1825–1883), English mathematician and physicist; took his father's place (1846) as queen's printer and head of Eyre & Spottiswoode's printing business; studied contact of curves and surfaces, determinants, polarization of light, electrical discharges in gases.

**Sprague** (sprāg), **Charles.** 1791–1875. American banker and poet, b. Boston. Among individual poems are *Curiosity, Ode to Shakspere, The Funeral, The Brothers.*

**Sprague, Frank Julian.** 1857–1934. American electrical engineer and inventor; organized (1884) Sprague Electric Railway & Motor Co. to manufacture electric motors. Recognized as pioneer in modern electric trolley system as a result of his installation of first modern trolley at Richmond, Va. (1887); devised and installed high-speed and automatic electric elevators, making tall buildings practicable; invented multiple-unit system of electric train control, now in general use; developed high-tension direct-current electric railway system, automatic electric signal and train brake control. Considered the "father of electric traction."

**Sprague, William Buell.** 1795–1876. American Congregational clergyman; known as a collector of pamphlets, manuscripts, and autographs; completed three full sets of autographs of the signers of the Declaration of Independence.

**Sprat** (sprăt), **Thomas.** 1635–1713. English prelate; author of poem on death of Cromwell published with others by Dryden and Waller (1659); author of a history of Royal Society, which he helped to found; bishop of Rochester (1684) and dean of Westminster (1683).

**Spreck′els** (sprĕk′ĕlz), **Claus** (klous). 1828–1908. Sugar manufacturer, known as the "Sugar King," b. Lamstedt, Hanover, Ger.; to U.S. (1846), and San Francisco (1856); in sugar business (from 1863); secured virtual monopoly of manufacture and sale of sugar on Pacific coast; developed sugar plantations in Hawaiian Islands. His oldest son, **John Die′drich** [dē′drĭk] (1853–1926), superintended family sugar properties in Hawaii (1876); founded J. D. Spreckels & Brothers Company, shipping and commission merchants (1880), operating Oceanic Steamship Co. between Hawaii and U.S.; settled at San Diego (1887) and interested himself in its development. Associated in business with J. D. Spreckels were two of his brothers, **Adolph Bernard** (1857–1924) and **Rudolph** (1872–1958). The latter was member of committee of fifty at time of San Francisco fire and earthquake (1906); organized and financed investigation into political corruption in San Francisco (1906).

**Spreng′el** (shprĕng′ĕl), **Christian Konrad.** 1750–1816. German botanist; first to point out (1793) the part played by insects in fertilization of flowers. His nephew **Kurt Polykarp Joachim Sprengel** (1766–1833), physician and botanist, was author of histories of medicine, surgery, and botany, a handbook of pathology, etc.

**Sprengel, Herman Johann Philipp.** 1834–1906. German chemist, b. near Hanover; naturalized as British subject. His inventions include safety explosives and the Sprengel pump, an air pump using mercury or other liquid.

**Spreng′er** (shprĕng′ẽr), **Aloys.** 1813–1893. Austrian Oriental scholar; in India (1843–57); professor, Bern (1858–81). Author of *Das Leben und die Lehre des Mohammed* (3 vols., 1861–65), etc.

**Sprigg** (sprĭg), Sir **John Gordon.** 1830–1913. South African statesman, b. Ipswich, England; settled in Cape Colony (1861); prime minister of Cape Colony (1878–81, 1886–90, 1896–98, 1900–04).

**Spring** (sprĭng), **Howard.** 1889–1965. British novelist, b. Cardiff, Wales; author of *Shabby Tiger* (1934), *O Absalom* (1938; American title *My Son, My Son*), *Fame is the Spur* (1940), and of the autobiographical *Heaven Lies About Us* (1939) and *In the Meantime* (1942).

**Spring, Samuel.** 1747–1819. American Congregational clergyman; pastor in Newburyport, Mass. (1777–1819). Extreme Calvinist in theology; instrumental in the founding of the American Board of Commissioners for Foreign Missions (1810); leader in establishing Andover Sem. (opened 1808).

**Spring′er** (sprĭng′ẽr), **Alfred.** 1854–1946. American chemist; coinventor and patentee of the torsion balance; patentee of aluminum soundboards for musical instruments.

**Springer, Frank.** 1848–1927. American lawyer and paleontologist; settled in Cimarron, N. Mex. (1873) and Las Vegas, N. Mex. (from 1883). Made study of fossil crinoids; associated with Charles Wachsmuth (*q.v.*) in building up the Wachsmuth-Springer collection of over 100,000 specimens, now in the National Museum, Washington, D.C.

**Spring-Rice** (sprĭng'rīs'), Sir **Cecil Arthur**. 1859–1918. British diplomat; minister to Persia (1906–08), to Sweden (1908–13); ambassador to U.S. (1913–18).

**Sproul** (sproul), **Robert Gordon.** 1891–1975. American educator; controller and secretary of board of regents, U. of California (1920–30); president (1930–1958).

**Spru'ance** (sprōō'ăns), **Raymond Ames**. 1886–1969. American admiral, b. Baltimore; grad. U.S.N.A. (1907); task force commander at Midway (June, 1942); chief of staff to Admiral Nimitz; head of Central Pacific command (1943–44), in charge of conquest of Gilbert and Marshall Islands; admiral (Feb., 1944); commander of U.S. 5th Fleet (Apr., 1944–Nov., 1945); commander in chief of U.S. Pacific fleet (1945–46).

**Spru'ner von Merz** (shprōō'nẽr fôn mĕrts'), **Karl.** 1803–1892. Bavarian general, historian, and geographer.

**Spur'geon** (spûr'jŭn), **Caroline F. E.** 1869–1942. English educator; B.A., Oxon. (1899); on staff of Bedford Coll. for Women (lecturer; 1901–06; head of English literature dept., 1913–29) and U. of London (lecturer, 1906–13; professor, 1913–29—first woman to hold a professorship in an English university); while visiting professor at Barnard Coll., N.Y. City (1920–21) helped organize International Federation of University Women, and was its first president (1920–24); because of health lived in Tucson, Ariz. (from 1939). Authority on Chaucer and Shakespeare; author of *Five Hundred Years of Chaucer Criticism and Allusion* (1920–25), *Keats's Shakespeare* (1928), *Shakespeare's Imagery, and What It Tells Us* (1935), etc.

**Spurgeon, Charles Haddon.** 1834–1892. English Baptist preacher; at New Park Street Chapel, London (1854); Metropolitan Tabernacle, seating 6000, built for him (1859–61), providing him a pulpit until his death. A decided Calvinist, distrusted modern Biblical criticism, repudiated baptismal regeneration; published sermons weekly (collected into 50 volumes). Author of books of sayings, *John Ploughman's Talks* (1869), *John Ploughman's Pictures* (1880).

**Spurr** (spûr), **Josiah Edward.** 1870–1950. American geologist; author of *Through the Yukon Gold Diggings* (1900), etc. Mt. Spurr in Alaska is named in honor of his Alaskan explorations (1896, 1898).

**Spur'stow** (spûr'stō), **William.** See SMECTYMNUUS.

**Spurz'heim** (shpŏŏrts'hīm), **Johann Kaspar.** 1776–1832. German physician; cofounder with Franz Gall (*q.v.*) of phrenology.

**Spy.** Pseudonym of Sir Leslie WARD.

**Spynie,** Baron. See *Alexander Lindsay* (d. 1607), under LINDSAY family.

**Spy'ri** (shpē'rē), **Johanna,** *nee* **Heus'ser** (hoi'sẽr). 1827–1901. Swiss writer of books for children; author of *Heidis Lehr- und Wanderjahre* (1881), *Heidi kann brauchen, was es gelernt hat* (1881), etc., which have been translated into a single book entitled *Heidi.*

**Squan'to** (skwŏn'tō). d. 1622. American Indian of the Pawtuxet tribe; friendly to the whites of Plymouth colony; aided colonists by teaching them Indian methods of planting and fertilizing corn.

**Squar·cio'ne** (skwär·chō'nā), **Francesco.** 1394–1474. Italian painter; founder of the Paduan school; notable chiefly as a teacher of painting; as such, exerted influence on northern Italian art; known particularly as the teacher of Andrea Mantegna.

**Squibb** (skwĭb), **Edward Robinson.** 1819–1900. American pharmacist; founded Squibb chemical and pharmaceutical laboratory, Brooklyn, N.Y. (1858); admitted sons to partnership and changed firm name to E. R. Squibb & Sons (1892).

**Squibob.** See George Horatio DERBY.

**Squier** (?skwīr), **Ephraim George.** 1821–1888. American archaeologist, b. Bethlehem, N.Y.; studied esp. archaeological ruins in Central and South American countries; published *Nicaragua...*(2 vols., 1852), *The States of Central America* (1858), *Peru...*(1877), etc. See Edwin H. DAVIS.

**Squier** (skwâr), **George Owen.** 1865–1934. American military and electrical engineer; grad. U.S.M.A., West Point (1887). Specialized in signal communications; chief signal officer, U.S. army, with rank of brigadier general (Feb., 1917); promoted major general (Oct., 1917); retired (1923). First passenger with Orville Wright in test flights of army airplane (1907). Among his notable inventions were the polarizing chronophotograph, the sine-wave system of cable telegraphy, multiplex telephony and telegraphy over open-circuit bare wires laid in earth or sea, and esp. the line radio system permitting simultaneously as many as five telephone conversations and forty telegraph messages over a single wire.

**Squire** (skwīr), Sir **John Collings.** *Early pseudonym* **Solomon Ea'gle** (ē'g'l). 1884–1958. British journalist and miscellaneous writer, b. Plymouth; founder and editor (1919–34) of London *Mercury.* Author of *Imaginary Speeches* (1912), *The Three Hills and Other Poems* (1913), *The Birds, and Other Poems* (1919), *Collected Parodies* (1921), *Essays on Poetry* (1924), *Apes and Parrots* (1928), *Sunday Mornings* (1930), *The Honeysuckle and the Bee* (1937), *Water Music* (1939), etc.

**Squire, William Barclay.** 1855–1927. English music critic and antiquarian; librarian, Royal College of Music, at British Museum (1912–20). Contributor to *Grove's Dictionary of Music, Encyclopaedia Britannica, Dictionary of National Biography.*

**Sr'bik** (sûr'bĭk), **Heinrich von.** 1878–1951. Austrian historian.

**Ssŭ-ma Ch'ien** *or* **Sze-ma Ts'ien** (sŏŏ'mä' chĭ·yĕn'). 145–?87 B.C. First great historian of China; son of Ssŭ-ma T'an; spent many years in compiling the *Shih Chi* ("Historical Memoirs"), a model for all later dynastic histories of China; also reformed the Chinese calendar, determining the system of chronology still in use.

**Ssŭ-ma Kuang** (sŏŏ'mä' gwäng'). 1019–1086. Chinese historian, living under the Sung dynasty; minister of state for some years; retired to Lo-yang; spent later years of his life (1066–84) compiling his great history of China from the 5th century B.C. to the 10th century A.D., popularly called *The Mirror of History.*

**Ssŭ-ma T'an** (sŏŏ'mä' tän'). d. 110 B.C. Chinese scholar; ardent Taoist; became grand astrologer; collected much of the material used by his son Ssŭ-ma Ch'ien, the historian.

**Staal de Lau'nay'** (stál' dẽ lō'nā'), Baronne **de. Marguerite Jeanne,** *nee* **Cor'dier'** (kôr'dyā'). 1684–1750. French writer; lady in waiting to the duchesse du Maine (1711); m. baron de Staal (1735); best known for her *Mémoires* (publ. 1755).

**Stabili, Francesco degli.** See CECCO D'ASCOLI.

**Stachouwer.** See STARKENBORGH STACHOUWER.

**Stack** (stăk), Sir **Lee Oliver Fitzmaurice.** 1868–1924. British soldier and colonial administrator; retired from British army to join Sudan service; acting sirdar of Egyptian army and governor general of the Sudan (1917). Assassinated in Cairo.

**Stac'poole** (stăk'pōōl), **Henry de Vere Stacpoole.** 1863–1951. British physician and author of many popular novels, including *Pierrot, Pierrette, The Blue Lagoon,*

*The Drums of War, The Street of the Flute Player* (1912), *The Pearl Fishers* (1915), *The Starlit Garden* (1918), *The Beach of Dreams* (1919), *Men, Women, and Beasts* (1922), *Green Coral* (1935), *High-Yaller* (1938), *Old Sailors Never Lie* (1939), and of *Men and Mice* (1942; autobiography).

**Sta′di·on** (shtä′dē·ôn), Count **Johann Philipp von.** 1763–1824. Austrian statesman; minister of foreign affairs (1805–09), of finance (from 1815). His son Count **Franz** (1806–1853) was Austrian minister of interior (Nov., 1848–July, 1849).

**Staël** (stäl), Mme. **de.** *In full* **Anne Louise Germaine,** *nee* **Nec′ker′** (nĕ′kâr′; *Angl.* nĕk′ẽr). Baronne **de Staël–Hols′tein′** (-ôls′tĕn′). 1766–1817. French writer; daughter of Jacques and Suzanne Necker (*q.v.*); m. (1786) baron de Stael-Holstein, Swedish minister to Paris (d. 1802). Fled from France during the Revolution; was exiled by Napoleon; returned to France after the fall of the empire (1815). Among her works are *Lettres sur le Caractère et les Écrits de J. J. Rousseau* (1788), *De l'Influence des Passions sur le Bonheur des Individus et des Nations* (1796), *Delphine* (1803), *Corinne ou l'Italie* (1807), *De l'Allemagne* (1810), *Dix Années d'Exil* (1821).

**Staff** (stäf), **Leopold.** 1878–1957. Polish poet and playwright.

**Staf′ford** (stăf′ẽrd), Marquises of. See LEVESON-GOWER family.

**Stafford,** Viscount. See *William Howard* (1614–1680), under HOWARD family.

**Stafford,** Sir **Edward William.** 1819–1901. New Zealand statesman, b. in Edinburgh; educ. Trinity College, Dublin; to N.Z. (1843); prime minister and colonial secretary (1856–61); created three new provinces; established itinerant courts and native juries; again prime minister (1865–69 and Sept.–Oct., 1872); returned to live in England (1874).

**Stafford, Humphrey.** 1st Duke of **Buck′ing·ham** (bŭk′ĭng·ăm). 1402–1460. English soldier; captain of Calais (1442); created duke (1444); warden of Cinque Ports (1450); killed at battle of Northampton. His grandson **Henry** (1454?–1483), 2d duke, pronounced sentence on Clarence (1478); acted as great chamberlain at coronation of Richard III; raised force against Richard but was captured and executed as Salisbury. **Edward** (1478–1521), 3d duke; eldest son of Henry; privy councilor (1509); condemned and executed on trumped-up charges of disloyalty to Henry VIII.

**Stafford, Humphrey.** Earl of **Dev′on** (dĕv′ŭn). 1439–1469. English knight; privy councilor (1469). Sent by Edward IV against the Yorkshire rebel known as Robin of Redesdale; after quarrel with earl of Pembroke, withdrew with his troops; executed.

**Stafford, Wendell Philips.** 1861– . American jurist and poet; practiced law at St. Johnsbury, Vt.; associate justice, supreme court of District of Columbia (1904–31). Author of *North Flowers* (verse, 1902), *Voices, a Dramatic Ode* (1915), *The Land We Love* (verse, 1916), *War Poems* (1917). Poet laureate of Vermont.

**Stag·ne′li·us** (stăng·nā′lĭ·ŭs), **Erik Johan.** 1793–1823. Swedish poet; author of *Wladimir the Great* (epic, 1817), *The Lilies of Sharon* (verse cycle, 1821–22), *The Martyrs* (dramatic poem, 1821–22), and *The Bacchanals* (tragedy, 1822).

**Stahl** (shtäl), **Friedrich Julius.** 1802–1861. German lawyer, philosopher, and politician; chief work, *Die Philosophie des Rechts nach geschichtlicher Ansicht* (1830–37).

**Stahl, Georg Ernst.** 1660–1734. German physician and chemist; with Johann Joachim Becher, originated phlogiston theory to explain combustion; enunciated in *Theoria Medica Vera* (1707) doctrine of animism which holds that the soul is the vital principle and is responsible for every organic development.

**Stahl, Heinrich.** Pseudonym of J. D. H. TEMME.

**Stahl, Karl.** Pseudonym of Karl GOEDEKE.

**Stahl** (stål), **P. J.** Pseudonym of Pierre Jules HETZEL.

**Ståhl′berg′** (stôl′bĕr′y′), **Kaarlo Juho.** 1865–1952. Finnish statesman; president of Finnish Diet at outbreak (1914) of World War. After Finland gained its independence, elected (1919) first president of the republic; retired at end of presidential term (1925).

**Stahr** (shtär), **Adolf Wilhelm Theodor.** 1805–1876. German scholar; author of *Aristotelia* (1830–32), *Die preussische Revolution* (1850), *Lessing . . .* (1858), and *Bilder aus dem Altertum* (1863–66).

**Stahr, Fanny Lewald.** See LEWALD.

**Stain′back** (stān′băk), **Ingram Macklin.** 1883–1961. American lawyer and administrator, b. Somerville, Tenn.; A.B., Princeton (1907); J.D., Chicago (1912). Began practice of law in Honolulu (1912); attorney general, Territory of Hawaii (1914–17); served in army during World War. U.S. attorney, District of Hawaii (1934–40); U.S. district judge, District of Hawaii (1940–42); governor of Hawaii (1942–50).

**Stai′ner** (shtī′nẽr), **Jakob.** 1621–1683. See STEINER.

**Stai′ner** (stā′nẽr), Sir **John.** 1840–1901. English organist and composer; organist, St. Paul's Cathedral (1872–88); professor of music, Oxford (1889–99). Composer of oratorios, cantatas, anthems, church services, hymn tunes, madrigals, and songs. Author, with W. A. Barrett, of dictionary of musical terms (1870).

**Stair** (stâr), Viscounts and earls of. Titles in the English peerage named for an Ayrshire village and long held by members of the Scottish family of Dalrymple (*q.v.*).

**Sta·kha′nov** (stŭ·κá′nôf), **Aleksei Grigorievich.** 1905–1977. Russian coal miner; initiated (1935) a movement (Stakhanov movement) for speeding up production by encouraging individual initiative and by increased pay for notable efficiency.

**Sta′lin** (stá′lyĭn), **Joseph.** *Real name* **Iosif Vissarionovich Dzhu′ga·shvi′li** (jo͞o′gá·shvē′lē). 1879–1953. Russian political leader, b. near Tiflis, Georgia; son of a shoemaker. Attended theological seminary near Tiflis; expelled for Marxist propaganda. Joined Social Democratic party (1896); sided with Bolsheviks after party split (1903); repeatedly exiled to Siberia for political activity (1904–13), but always escaped; imprisoned (1913–17); freed after February revolution (1917); became close associate of Lenin; took part in October revolution (1917). Member of revolutionary military council (1920–23); people's commissar for nationalities (1921–23); general secretary of central committee of Communist party (1922 ff.), and member of Comintern executive committee. After Lenin's death (1924), eliminated opposition of Trotsky, Zinoviev, Kamenev, Bukharin, Rykov, and others (1926–27), and established himself as virtual dictator. Important events under his leadership include: development of Russian industry and agriculture under the "Five-Year plans" (1st, 1928; 2d, 1934; 3d, 1937); exile of Trotsky (1929); nonaggression pacts with Poland and France (1932), Italy (1933), Outer Mongolia (1934); Russian acceptance of membership in League of Nations (1934); "purges" of Communist party (1936–37) and Russian army (1937); nonaggression pact with Germany (Aug., 1939); annexation of eastern Poland after German invasion of Poland (1939); war with Finland (1939–40); annexation of Latvia, Estonia, Lithuania, and Bessarabia (1940). Following German invasion of Russia (June, 1941), became commissar for defense and chairman of the Council of People's Commissars, thus taking over supreme direction of military operations; created marshal of the Soviet Union (Mar., 1943). Conferred on war strategy and international affairs with Roosevelt and Churchill at Tehran (Dec., 1943) and Yalta, Crimea (Feb., 1945) and with Truman, Churchill, and Attlee at Potsdam, Ger. (July, 1945).

**Stal'lings** (stôl'ĭngz), **Laurence.** 1894–1968. American novelist and playwright, b. Macon, Ga.; with Metro-Goldwyn-Mayer motion-picture studios in Hollywood, Calif. (from 1936). Author of *Plumes* (a novel; 1924), the plays *What Price Glory?* (with Maxwell Anderson; 1924), *The Buccaneer* (1925), *First Flight* (1925), *Deep River* (1926), and motion pictures.

**Stam'bo·li'ski** (stȧm'bô·lē'skē) *or* **Stam'bu·li'ski** (stȧm'bo͝o-), **Aleksandr.** 1879–1923. Bulgarian statesman; a founder and leader of the Peasants' party. During World War (1914–18), opposed Bulgarian participation on side of Central Powers; imprisoned for three years. After World War, headed insurrection which seized government in name of the peasants; premier of Bulgaria (1920–23), exercising virtual dictatorship; assassinated.

**Stam'bo·lov'** (stȧm'bô·lôf') *or* **Stam'bu·lov'** (stȧm'bo͝o-), **Stefan.** 1855–1895. Bulgarian statesman; president of the Sobranje (1884–86); member of board of regency (1886–87); premier (1887–94); assassinated.

**Sta'mitz** (shtä'mĭts), **Johann.** 1717–1757. Bohemian violinist and composer; founder of so-called Mannheim school; contributed to development of sonata and symphony forms; composer of symphonies, concertos, sonatas, violin works, and harpsichord music.

**Stamm'ler** (shtäm'lẽr), **Rudolf.** 1856–1938. German legal philosopher; professor, Berlin (from 1916). His son **Wolfgang** (1886– ), German philologist and literary historian.

**Stamp** (stămp), **Josiah Charles.** 1st Baron **Stamp.** 1880–1941. British economist and banker; British member of commissions drafting Dawes Plan (1924) and Young Plan (1929); chairman, London Midland & Scottish Ry.; director of the Bank of England.

**Stan'ber'y** (stăn'bĕr'ĭ; -bẽr·ĭ), **Henry.** 1803–1881. American lawyer; practiced in Lancaster, Ohio, and in Cincinnati. U.S. attorney general (1866–68). Resigned (Mar. 12, 1868) to serve as chief counsel for Andrew Johnson in the impeachment proceedings.

**Standaert.** See Pieter van BLOEMEN.

**Stan'dish** (stăn'dĭsh), **Burt L.** See Gilbert PATTEN.

**Standish, Myles** *or* **Miles.** 1584?–1656. Colonist in America, b. in Lancashire, Eng.; accompanied Pilgrims to America on the *Mayflower* (1620); appointed captain, treated with the Indians, and superintended defenses of the colony. Served as agent in England for the colonists (1625–26), negotiating for ownership of their land and for supplies. Rose to place of leadership in colony; treasurer for nine years, and a member of the governor's council for 29 years. With John Alden, founded Duxbury (1631), and resided there until his death. No historical basis exists for the tale of John Alden's proposal to Priscilla Mullens on behalf of Captain Standish, as narrated in Longfellow's *The Courtship of Miles Standish.*

**Stand'ley** (stănd'lĭ), **William Harrison.** 1872–1963. American naval officer, b. Ukiah, Calif.; grad. U.S.N.A., Annapolis (1895); served in Spanish-American War (1898) and in World War (1917–18); chief of naval operations (1933–37) with rank of admiral; retired (1937); recalled to active duty (1941); United States ambassador to Russia (1942–43).

**Stan'field** (stăn'fēld), **Clarkson.** 1793–1867. English marine painter; executed some of best pictures at Hampstead, including *The Battle of Trafalgar* (1836) and *The Abandoned* (1856).

**Stan'ford** (stăn'fẽrd), **Alfred Boller.** 1900– . American writer; officer in American merchant marine. Author of *The Ground Swell* (1923), *Navigator—The Story of Nathaniel Bowditch of Salem* (1927), *Invitation to Danger* (1929), *Men, Fish, and Boats* (1934), etc.

**Stanford,** Sir **Charles Villiers.** 1852–1924. British composer, conductor, and teacher, b. at Dublin; organist of Trinity Coll., Cambridge; conductor of Bach Choir (1885–1902), Leeds Philharmonic Society, and Leeds Music Festival (1901–10). Composer of operas, symphonies, orchestral works, cantatas, song cycles, etc.

**Stanford, Leland,** *in full* **Amasa Leland.** 1824–1893. American capitalist and politician, b. Watervliet, N.Y.; to California (1852); engaged in selling miners' supplies and other merchandise; governor of California (1861–63). Identified especially with promoting and financing Central Pacific Railroad (built 1863–69), western link in transcontinental line; president and director, Central Pacific Railroad (1863–93) and Southern Pacific (1885–90); U.S. senator (1885–93). In memory of his son **Leland, Jr.** (1869–1884), founded Leland Stanford Junior University, now Stanford Univ. (1885; opened 1891).

**Stangeland, Karin Michaelis–.** See under Sophus MICHAELIS.

**Stan'hope** (stăn'ŭp). Name of English family descended from 1st earl of Chesterfield, ancestor of Philip Dormer, famous 4th earl (see CHESTERFIELD), and including among its members the Earls Stanhope:

**James** (1673–1721), 1st earl; soldier and statesman; educ. Oxford; volunteer in Italy and Flanders against France (1694–95); M.P. (1701); served under Marlborough (1703); assisted Peterborough at Barcelona (1705); minister to Spain (1706); commander in chief in Spain (1708); won cavalry action at Almenar and victory at Saragossa (1710); forced to capitulate at Brihuega (1710). Leader of Whig opposition in House of Commons (1712); secretary of state for southern department (1714, 1718); directed suppression of Jacobite uprising (1715); first lord of treasury and chancellor of exchequer (1717); created Viscount Stanhope of **Ma·hon'** [mȧ·ho͞on'; -hōn'] (1717) and Earl Stanhope (1718); negotiated quadruple alliance against Spain (1718) and compelled Spain to abandon plan of conquest (1719); partly responsible for South Sea Bubble, but did not profit from it.

His grandson **Charles** (1753–1816), 3d earl; democratic political leader and scientist; educ. Eton and Geneva; M.P. (1780), supported administration of 2d William Pitt, whose sister, Lady Hester Pitt, he married (1774); advocated discontinuance of war against American colonies and parliamentary reform (1781); broke with Pitt over French Revolution; chairman of Revolution Society, favoring French republicans; introduced motions against interferences in French affairs (1794, 1795), on which he was a "minority of one," a sobriquet that stuck; retired for five years; caricatured; house fired by rioters (1794); proposed peace with Napoleon (1800). Spent great deal on scientific research and experimentation; constructed calculating machines (c. 1777); perfected a process of stereotyping acquired by Clarendon Press, Oxford (1805); invented a monochord for tuning musical instruments, first hand-operated iron printing press (1798), and a microscopic lens bearing his name. Author of *Principles of Electricity* (1779); reply to Burke's *Reflections on the French Revolution* (1790); essay on rights of juries (1792).

Charles's eldest daughter by his first wife, Lady **Hester Lucy** (1776–1839); housekeeper and secretary of her uncle William Pitt (1803–06); left England forever (1810); made pilgrimage to Jerusalem; camped with Bedouins, Palmyra (1813); settled among Druses on Mt. Lebanon (1814); adopted eastern manners, practiced astrology, held imperious ascendancy over rude tribes as a prophetess, coming to believe herself possessed of gift of divination; incited Druses against Ibrahim Pasha; intrigued against British consuls; visited by Lamartine, Kinglake, and others; recklessly liberal, deserted by followers and robbed, finished life in wretchedness.

**Philip Henry** (1805–1875), 5th earl; better known by courtesy title Lord **Mahon**; historian; grandson of 3d earl; B.A., Oxon. (1827); M.P. (1830); held minor official appointments under Peel; secured passage of bill amending copyright law (1842); obtained parliamentary grant for founding national portrait gallery, subsequently created by his executors; aided establishment of Historical Manuscripts Commission; president of Society of Antiquaries (from 1846). Author of *History of War of Succession in Spain* (1832), *History of England from Peace of Utrecht to the Peace of Versailles* (1836–53), *Life of William Pitt* (1861–62), and *Reign of Queen Anne* (1870). See Kaspar HAUSER.

**Edward** (1840–1893); political leader and war office administrator; 2d son of 5th earl; educ. Oxford; barrister (1865); M.P. (1874); after holding minor offices, member of Lord Salisbury's cabinet (1885); colonial secretary (1886); as secretary for war (1887–92), put into full effect (1887) modern army system inaugurated by Viscount Cardwell, gave volunteers place in defense, decentralized stores, encouraged private armament firms, reorganized manufacturing departments and services of supply and transport, established army service corps, adopted magazine rifle.

**James Richard** (1880–1967), 7th earl, political leader; grandson of 5th earl; served in Boer War (1902) and World War (1914–18); undersecretary of state for war (1931–34); parliamentary undersecretary of state for foreign affairs (1934–36); first commissioner of works and member of British cabinet (1936–37); president of Board of Education (1937–38); first lord of the admiralty (1938–39); lord president of the council (1939–40) and leader of the House of Lords (1938–40).

**Stanhope, Fitzroy.** 1787–1864. British clergyman, after whom the stanhope buggy was named.

**Stan'is·las** (stăn'ĭs·lăs; -läs) *or* **Stan'is·laus** (-lôs), Saint. 1030–1079. Polish Roman Catholic prelate; bishop of Cracow (1071); denounced excesses of King Boleslav II of Poland, and finally excommunicated him; murdered by king's order; canonized (1253), and known as patron saint of Poland.

**Stanislas II Au·gus'tus** (ô·gŭs'tŭs). *Pol.* **Stanisław II Po'nia·tow'ski** (pô'nyä·tôf'skē). 1732–1798. Son of Prince Stanisław Poniatowski. Last king of independent Poland (1764–95). Elected to Diet (1752); representative at Russian court (1755); gained favor of future Catherine II, through her influence made king (1764); well-educated and well-meaning, but without strength of character. Condition of country became anarchic; three partitions carried out by Russia, Austria, and Prussia (1772, 1793, 1795); resigned at third partition.

**Stanislas I** (*Pol.* **Stanisław**) **Lesz·czyń'ski** (lĕsh-chĭn'y'·skē). 1677–1766. Son of Rafael Leszczysńki, of an old family of Polish nobility, b. Lemberg. King of Poland (1704–09, 1733–35); opposed Augustus II of Saxony and Poland; secured support of Charles XII of Sweden, who had him chosen king (1704–09); defeated by Augustus after Charles lost battle of Poltava (1709); governor of Zweibrücken in Palatinate (1718–25). Daughter Maria became wife of Louis XV of France (1725); through this alliance restored to throne of Poland at death of Augustus II (1733); War of Polish Succession (1733–35) followed; driven out (1735–36) by Augustus III, supported by Russia; received duchies of Lorraine and Bar (1737) from Francis Stephen (Francis I) in exchange for Tuscany and received pension from France; maintained court at Lunéville and Nancy; encouraged letters. Wrote *Œuvres du Philosophe Bienfaisant* (publ. 1767).

**Stanislaus.** = STANISLAS.

**Sta·ni·slav'ski** (stŭ·nyĭ·slăf'skû·ĭ; *Angl.* stăn'ĭ·slăf'skĭ). *Professional name of* **Konstantin Sergeevich A·le·kse'ev** (ŭ·lyĭ·ksyā'yĕf). 1863–1938. Russian actor and producer; cofounder and director (1898–1938), Moscow Art Theater.

**Stan'ley** (stăn'lĭ). Family name of earls of **Der'by** (*Brit. usu.* där'bĭ). The family, descended from Adam de Aldithley, one of William the Conqueror's companions, was founded by Sir **John Stanley** (1350?–1414), lieutenant in Ireland under Richard II, Henry IV, Henry V, who married Isabel Lathom, heiress of West Derby, Lancashire, and was granted Isle of Man (1405; held in family till 1736). Their grandson **Thomas** (1406?–1459), 1st Baron Stanley (cr. 1456), was lieutenant governor of Ireland (1431–37), lord chamberlain and privy councilor (1455). Members include:

**Thomas Stanley** (1435?–1504), 2d Baron Stanley and 1st Earl of Derby; son of 1st baron; m. Eleanor Neville, daughter of Yorkist leader; made chief justice of Cheshire and Flint by Edward IV (1461); held commands in France (1475) and Scotland (1482); m. (c. 1482) Margaret Beaufort, Countess of Richmond and Derby; confirmed in all his offices and created earl of Derby (1485) by his wife's son Henry VII, despite his remaining neutral at Bosworth, where his brother Sir **William** (d. 1495), justiciar of North Wales, saved the day for Richmond (Henry VII), later becoming lord chamberlain (1485).

**Edward Stanley** (1508–1572), 3d earl; grandson of 1st earl; helped to quell Pilgrimage of Grace (1536); commissioner for trial of Lady Jane Grey; privy councilor under Elizabeth; lord lieutenant of Cheshire and Lancashire. His son **Henry** (1531?–1593), 4th earl, styled Lord **Strange** [strānj] (till 1572); lord lieutenant of Lancashire, one of commissioners who tried Mary, Queen of Scots (1586), emissary to Spain.

**James Stanley** (1607–1651), 7th earl, styled Lord Strange (till 1642), known as the "Martyr Earl"; grandson of 4th earl; fought on Royalist side through Civil War; took part in Prince Rupert's campaign (1644), bringing relief to Lathom House, which his wife, **Charlotte de la Tré'moille'** [dē là trā'mwàl'] (1599–1664), Countess of Derby, had heroically defended against Parliamentary besiegers (Feb. to May); withdrew with wife to Isle of Man; joined Charles II at Worcester (1651); captured and executed.

**Edward George Geoffrey Smith Stanley** (1799–1869), 14th earl, styled Lord Stanley (till 1851); statesman, known as the "Rupert of debate"; won Latin verse prize at Oxford (1819); M.P. (1820); as chief secretary for Ireland (1830–33), supported Reform Bill and carried first national education bill; as colonial secretary (1833–34, 1841–44) carried act freeing slaves in West Indies; forced Whigs to modify proposals for Irish disendowment (1835); became leader of Protectionist party in House of Lords upon Peel's declaration in favor of immediate free trade (1846); formed Protectionist ministry (Feb., 1852), but resigned after defeat on budget (Dec.); opposed Palmerston's foreign policy (1855–58); as prime minister again (1858–59), settled disputes with France and Naples and difficulties with America over right of search;

refused crown of Greece (1863); instrumental in preventing English intervention in German-Danish war (1864); as prime minister a third time (1866–68), carried parliamentary Reform Act of 1867; resigned in favor of Disraeli; made last speech in opposition to Irish disestablishment; an accomplished classical scholar, translated the *Iliad* into blank verse (1864).

**Edward Henry Smith Stanley** (1826–1893), 15th earl; eldest son of 14th earl; statesman; took double first at Cambridge; Conservative M.P. (1848); undersecretary for foreign affairs (1852); as secretary for India (1858–59), carried measure transferring government of India to the crown; foreign secretary in his father's third administration and Disraeli's first and second (1866–68, 1874–78); postponed war between France and Prussia by collective guarantee of the neutrality of Luxemburg (1867), admitted arbitration in Alabama case, accepted purchase of Suez Canal shares, demanded punishment for perpetrators of Bulgarian atrocities, paved way for Constantinople Conference on Turkish reform; resigned when Disraeli ordered British fleet to Dardanelles; opposed acquisition of Cyprus and First Afghan War (1879); joined Liberal party (1880); colonial secretary under Gladstone (1882–85), seceding on home rule; joined Liberal Unionist party (1886); its leader in House of Lords (1886–91).

His brother **Frederick Arthur Stanley** (1841–1908), 16th earl; secretary of state for war (1878–80); colonial secretary (1885–86); president of board of trade (1886–88); created Baron Stanley of Pres'ton [prĕs'tŭn] (1886); governor general of Canada (1888–93); first lord mayor of Liverpool (1895–96). His son **Edward George Villiers** (1865–1948), 17th earl; financial secretary to War Office (1900–03); postmaster general (1903–05); director of recruiting (1915–16); war secretary (1916–18, 1922–24); ambassador to France (1918–20). See also separate entries for other members, as Edward STANLEY, James STANLEY, Oliver STANLEY.

**Stanley, Edward.** 1779–1849. English prelate of Anglican church; descendant of John Stanley, brother of 1st earl of Derby (see STANLEY family). Bishop of Norwich (1837–49); advocate of church reform, of admission of nonconformists to national schools, of ragged schools, of temperance. His son **Arthur Penrhyn** (1815–1881); B.A., Oxon. (1837); canon of Canterbury (1851); and dean of Westminster (1864–81); representative of broadest theology of Church of England; offended High Church Anglicans by championship of Colenso and preaching in Scottish Presbyterian pulpits; voluminous writer on ecclesiastical history; also, author of biographies of Arnold and Bishop Stanley. See Edward John STANLEY.

**Stanley, Edward John.** 2nd Baron **Stanley of Al'der·ley** (ôl'dẽr·lĭ). 1802–1869. English statesman; son of John Thomas Stanley, 1st baron, who was brother of Edward Stanley (*q.v.*), Bishop of Norwich; privy councilor and Liberal whip; president of board of trade (1855–58); postmaster general (1860–66). His son **Henry Edward John** (1827–1903), 3d baron, diplomat; secretary to special mission to Danubian provinces (1856–58); convert to Moslem religion; total abstainer; translator of Spanish and Portuguese works of travel.

**Edward Lyulph Stanley** (1839–1925), 4th Baron **Shef'field** [shĕf'ēld] (in Irish peerage), 4th Baron Stanley of Alderley, educationalist; 3d son of 2d baron; as a member of London school board (1876–85, 1888–1904), took active part in development of public education; opponent of denominational influences. His son **Arthur Lyulph** (1875–1931), 5th baron, was governor of Victoria (1914–20).

**Stanley, Edward Montagu Cavendish.** Lord **Stanley.** 1894–1938. British politician; eldest son of 17th earl of Derby (see STANLEY family); educ. Oxford; served in World War I; M.P. (1922); junior lord of treasury (1924–27); parliamentary and financial secretary to admiralty (1931–35, 1935–37); undersecretary of state, India Office and Burma Office (1937–38).

**Stanley, Francis Edgar.** 1849–1918. American inventor and manufacturer; invented photographic dry plate, steam-driven automobile (1897).

**Stanley,** Sir **Henry Morton.** *Orig. name* **John Row'lands** (rō'lăndz). 1841–1904. Explorer in Africa, b. Denbigh, Wales; adopted by New Orleans merchant, Henry Morton Stanley, and given his name (1859); brought up in a workhouse; ran away (1856) and finally shipped as cabin boy from Liverpool to New Orleans (1859). Served in Confederate army (1861–62); captured at Shiloh; enlisted in U.S. navy (1864); engaged at Fort Fisher. Newspaper correspondent (from 1865), in Asia Minor (1866), Abyssinia and Crete (1868), Spain (1869). Commissioned (1869) by James Gordon Bennett of the New York *Herald* to lead expedition into central Africa to find David Livingstone (*q.v.*); started Mar. 21, 1871, and after great difficulties reached Livingstone Nov. 10, 1871, greeting him with the famous remark "Dr. Livingstone, I presume?" Published *How I Found Livingstone* (1872). Led exploring expedition into Africa (1874–77); traced southern sources of the Nile River, circumnavigated Lake Victoria, discovered Lake Edward, surveyed Lake Tanganyika, and descended the Congo from Nyangwe to its mouth at Boma. Published *Through the Dark Continent* (2 vols., 1878). In service of King Leopold of Belgium, again went to Africa (1879–84) and opened up Congo region, establishing trading stations and building communication lines; on basis of his work Congo Free State was organized. Published *The Congo and the Founding of its Free State* (2 vols., 1885). Led final expedition to Africa (1887–89) to rescue Emin Pasha (*q.v.*); discovered the "Mountains of the Moon" (Ruwenzori) and traced the Semliki River to its source in Lake Edward. Published *In Darkest Africa* (2 vols., 1890). Became repatriated British subject (1892), and an M.P. (1895). Additional works: *My Early Travels and Adventures in America and Asia* (2 vols., 1895), *Through South Africa* (1898).

**Stanley,** Sir **Herbert James.** 1872–1955. English colonial administrator; M.A., Oxon.; resident commissioner in Rhodesia (1915–18); imperial secretary, Union of South Africa (1918–24); governor of Northern Rhodesia (1924–27), of Ceylon (1927–31); high commissioner for South Africa (1931–35); governor of Southern Rhodesia (1935–42).

**Stanley, James.** 1465?–1515. Sixth son of 1st earl of Derby (see STANLEY family). Bishop of Ely (1506); cofounder of St. John's and Christ's Coll., Cambridge.

**Stanley, Oliver Frederick George.** 1896–1950. British politician; son of 17th earl of Derby (see STANLEY family); educ. Oxford; served in World War I, M.P. (1924); minister of transport (1933–34); minister of labor (1934–35); president of board of education (1935–37); of board of trade (1937–40); war secretary (1940); colonial secretary (1942–45).

**Stanley, Thomas.** 1625–1678. English classical scholar; descendant of 3d earl of Derby (see STANLEY family); M.A., Cantab. (1641); published translations of Tasso, Petrarch, Lope de Vega, and Greek and Latin poets; author of *History of Philosophy* (4 vols., 1655–62); edited Aeschylus with Latin translation and commentary (1663–64).

**Stanley, Wendell Meredith.** 1904–1971. American biochemist; with Rockefeller Inst. for Med. Research (from 1931); corecipient (see John H. NORTHROP) of 1946 Nobel prize for chemistry.

**Stanley**, Sir **William.** d. 1495. See at *1st earl of Derby*, under STANLEY family.

**Stanley, William.** 1858–1916. American electrical engineer and inventor; research assistant to Hiram Stevens Maxim, and later to Edward Weston; established his own research laboratory, Englewood, N.J. (1883–85); experimented especially on storage batteries and incandescent lamps. Best known for his invention of the transformer; also, invented two-phase motors, generators, and a type of alternating-current watt-hour meter using magnetic suspension of its moving parts.

**Stanmore,** Barons. See GORDON family.

**Stan'nard** (stăn'ẽrd), **Henrietta Eliza Vaughan,** *nee* **Palmer.** 1856–1911. English novelist; contributed short stories of military life to *Family Herald* (1874–84), under pseudonym **Violet Whyte** (hwīt); m. Arthur Stannard (1884). Author under pseudonym **John Strange Win'ter** (wĭn'tẽr) of *Houp-la* (1885), *Bootles' Baby, Beautiful Jim* (1888), and *The Ivory Box* (1909).

**Stan'ton** (stăn't'n; -tŭn; *Brit. also* stän'-), Sir **Ambrose Thomas.** 1875–1938. British physician, b. in Canada; director of government laboratories, Federated Malay States (1920); chief medical adviser to secretary of state for the colonies (from 1926). Known for researches on cause and control of beriberi.

**Stanton, Edwin McMasters.** 1814–1869. American lawyer, b. Steubenville, Ohio; U.S. attorney general (1860–61); U.S. secretary of war (1862–68), guiding the war department through the Civil War. After death of Lincoln, opposed Johnson and Johnson's policies; intrigued with congressional groups against the president. Suspended by Johnson (Aug., 1867); restored by act of U.S. Senate (Jan., 1868); dismissed by Johnson (Feb. 21, 1868); refused to leave office, and was supported in his act by the Senate. Impeachment charges were brought against President Johnson because of his dismissal of Stanton; when these charges failed, Stanton resigned (May, 1868). Appointed associate justice, U.S. Supreme Court (1869), but died before he could take his seat.

**Stanton, Elizabeth,** *nee* **Ca'dy** (kā'dĭ). 1815–1902. American woman-suffrage leader, b. Johnstown, N.Y.; m. **Henry Brewster Stanton** (1805–87), a lawyer, journalist, and abolitionist orator (1840). Organized first woman's rights convention, Seneca Falls, N.Y. (July 19–20, 1848), thus launching the woman's suffrage movement. Associated with Susan B. Anthony in the movement (from 1851). First president, National Woman Suffrage Association (1869–90). Compiler, with Susan B. Anthony and Matilda Joslyn Gage, of *History of Woman Suffrage* (3 vols., 1881–86). See Harriot BLATCH.

**Stanton, Frank Lebby.** 1857–1927. American journalist and poet; on staff of Atlanta (Ga.) *Constitution* (from 1889). In the *Constitution* started daily column, "Just from Georgia," one of the first "columns" in American newspapers. Published *Songs of a Day and Songs of the Soil* (1892), *Songs from Dixie Land* (1900), *Up from Georgia* (1902), *Frank L. Stanton's Just from Georgia* (1927), etc. Sometimes called the "Poet Laureate of Georgia." Among his best-known poems are *Mighty Lak' a Rose, Going Home, Georgia Land.*

**Stan'y·hurst** (stăn'ĭ·hûrst), **Richard.** 1547–1618. Translator of Vergil, b. Dublin; contributed *Description of Ireland* and *History of Ireland* to Holinshed's *Chronicles* (1577); translated first four books of *Aeneid* into grotesque English hexameters (Leiden, 1582) in accordance with Gabriel Harvey's theory that English verse could be based on quantity after manner of classical prosody.

**Stap'fer'** (stȧp'fâr'), **Paul.** 1840–1917. French essayist; author of *Shakspeare et l'Antiquité* (1879–80), *Molière et Shakspeare* (1886), *Rabelais* (1889), *Montaigne* (1894), *Études sur Goethe* (1906), etc.

**Sta'ple·ton** (stā'p'l·t'n; -tŭn), **Thomas.** 1535–1598. English Roman Catholic theologian and controversialist in Latin; remembered for his English prose translations of Bede's works and for his life of Thomas More (in *Tres Thomas*, 1588; reprinted separately, 1689).

**Stap'pen** (stäp'ĕn), **Charles** (shȧrl) **van der.** 1843–1910. Belgian sculptor; regarded as a founder of modern Belgian realism in sculpture.

**Sta·ra'ce** (stä·rä'chā), **Achille.** 1889–1945. Italian politician; took part in Mussolini's march on Rome (1922); secretary general of Fascist party (1932–39); chief of staff of militia (1939–41); executed.

**Star'hem·berg** (shtä'rĕm·bĕrĸ), Count **Ernst Rüdiger von.** 1635–1701. Austrian field marshal; in command of defense of Vienna during its siege by Turks (1683). His cousin Count **Guido von Starhemberg** (1654?–1737) was also a soldier; commanded jointly with Stanhope in Spain during War of the Spanish Succession and won victories at Almenara and Saragossa (1710).

**Starhemberg,** Prince **Ernst Rüdiger von.** 1899–1956. Austrian statesman; vice-chancellor under Dollfuss and Schuschnigg (1934–36), and minister for security (1934–35). Escaped after Nazi occupation of Austria and went to France to raise an Austrian legion to fight with France against Germany (1939).

**Stark** (stärk), **Frey'a** (frā'ȧ) **Madeleine.** 1893– . English writer and traveler in Arabia; author of *Bagdad Sketches* (1933), *The Southern Gates of Arabia* (1936), *A Winter in Arabia* (1940), *Letters from Syria* (pub. 1942).

**Stark, Harold Raynsford.** 1880–1972. American naval officer, b. Wilkes-Barre, Pa.; grad. U.S.N.A., Annapolis (1903); aide on staff of Admiral Sims (1917–19); chief, Bureau of Ordnance (1934–37); commander, cruiser division of U.S. fleet (1937–39); chief of naval operations (1939–42); commander in European waters (1942–45).

**Stark, James.** 1794–1859. English landscape painter, b. Norwich. His son **Arthur James** (1831–1902), one of last artists of Norwich school, perfected animal painting, and portrayed homely English scenes, as in *Dartmoor Drift* (1877).

**Stark** (shtärk), **Johannes.** 1874–1957. German physicist, b. Schickenhof, Bavaria. Discovered Doppler effect in canal rays (1905) and effect (Stark effect) produced on spectrum lines by subjecting source of light to intense electric field. Awarded 1919 Nobel prize for physics.

**Stark** (stärk), **John.** 1728–1822. American Revolutionary officer, b. Londonderry, N.H.; m. **Molly,** *really* **Elizabeth, Page** [pāj] (1737?–1814). Served in French and Indian War; engaged (colonel) at Bunker Hill (1775), in Canadian expedition (1776), at Trenton and Princeton; resigned commission (Mar., 1777); commissioned brigadier general of New Hampshire troops to aid Vermont in resisting Burgoyne; won battle of Bennington (Aug. 16, 1777); brigadier general in Continental army (Oct., 1777); commanded Northern Department; member of court-martial that condemned Major André; brevetted major general (Sept., 1783).

**Star'ken·borgh Stach'ou'wer** (stär'kĕm·bôrĸ stäĸ'-ou'wẽr), **Alidius Warmoldus Lambertus Tjar'da van** (chär'dȧ vän). 1888– . Dutch diplomat and administrator; grad. U. of Groningen; practiced law in The Hague; entered diplomatic service; on legation staff in Washington (1915–19), Paris (1919–24), Berlin (1924–25); commissioner of the queen for province of Groningen

(1925–33); ambassador to Belgium (1933–36); governor general of Netherlands East Indies (1936–45); captured by invading Japanese (1942).

**Star′key** (stär′kĭ), **Geoffrey.** See GEOFFREY THE GRAMMARIAN.

**Starkey, James Sullivan.** *Pseudonym* **Seumas O'Sul′li·van** (ō·sŭl′ĭ·văn). 1879–1958. Irish poet; editor of *Dublin Magazine;* author of *The Twilight People* (1905) and other volumes of poems.

**Star′kie** (stär′kĭ), **William Joseph Myles.** 1860–1920. British educator, b. Sligo, Ireland; resident commissioner of national education in Ireland (1899–1920), and chairman of board of intermediate education (1911–20).

**Star′ley** (stär′lĭ), **James.** 1830–1881. English inventor; invented a sewing machine; engaged in manufacture of sewing machines and bicycles at Coventry, his improvements rendering the bicycle suitable for general use.

**Star′ling** (stär′lĭng), **Ernest Henry.** 1866–1927. English physiologist; professor, University Coll., London (1899–1923). Codiscoverer with Sir William M. Bayliss (*q.v.*) of secretin (1902). Chief work, *Principles of Human Physiology* (1912).

**Starr** (stär), **Ellen Gates.** 1860–1940. American social-service worker; cofounder with Jane Addams of Hull House, in Chicago.

**Starr, Frederick.** 1858–1933. American anthropologist; assistant professor (1892–95), associate professor (1895–1923), U. of Chicago. Author of *Some First Steps in Human Progress* (1895), *American Indians* (1898), *The Truth About the Congo* (1907), *In Indian Mexico* (1908), *Philippine Studies* (1909), etc.

**Star′rett** (stăr′ĕt; -ĭt), **Laroy S.** 1836–1922. American inventor, esp. of carpenters' tools and precision instruments.

**Starrett, Paul.** 1866–1957. American building contractor; with his brothers **Ralph** and **William Aiken** (1877–1932), founded Starrett Bros., Inc., New York City (1922), and assumed its presidency. Among buildings erected under his supervision are the Flatiron building and the Empire State building.

**Starrett, Vincent,** *in full* **Charles Vincent Emerson.** 1886– . American writer, b. Toronto, Canada; journalist (to 1916); author esp. of detective fiction and bibliophilic works, including *Estrays* (1918), *Banners in the Dawn* (1922), *Buried Caesars* (1923), *The Great Hotel Murder* (1934), *Books Alive* (1940), *Bookman's Holiday* (1942), *Autolycus in Limbo* (verse, 1943), etc.

**Star·zyń′ski** (stär·zĭn′y′·skē), **Stefan.** 1893–?1940. Polish hero; mayor of Warsaw (1937–39); directed defense of Warsaw against German invaders (1939); seized by Nazis and imprisoned in concentration camp (1939), and later shot.

**Stas** (stȧs), **Jean Servais.** 1813–1891. Belgian chemist; known for determinations of atomic weights; devised method for detection of vegetable alkaloids.

**Sta·si′nus** (stȧ·sī′nŭs). fl. 7th(?) century B.C. Greek epic poet, of Cyprus; reputed author of *Cypria* (11 books), poem dealing with events leading up to Trojan War.

**Sta′sov** (stȧ′sôf), **Vladimir Vasilievich.** 1824–1906. Russian music and art critic; champion of new school of Russian composers inaugurated by Balakirev.

**Stas′sen** (stăs′'n), **Harold Edward.** 1907– . American politician, b. West St. Paul, Minn.; practiced law in St. Paul; governor of Minnesota (1938–43); director for mutual security (1953).

**Sta·ti′ra** (stȧ·tī′rȧ). Persian queen of late 4th century B.C.; wife of Darius III, King of Persia. In Nathaniel Lee's tragedy, *The Rival Queens, or the Death of Alexander the Great,* both Roxana (*q.v.*) and Statira are represented as wives of Alexander the Great.

**Sta′ti·us** (stā′shĭ·ŭs; -shŭs), **Publius Papinius.** 45?–?96 A.D. Roman poet in court of Emperor Domitian; author of lyric verse, including elegies, odes, and poems in praise of the emperor, and of the epics *Thebaid* or *Thebais* (12 books) and *Achilleid* or *Achilleis* (of which only fragments are extant).

**Statius Caecilius.** See CAECILIUS STATIUS.

**Stat′ler** (stăt′lẽr), **Ellsworth Milton.** 1863–1928. American hotel proprietor, b. in Somerset County, Pa.; started (1905) chain of Statler luxury hotels, with hotels in Buffalo, St. Louis, Cleveland, Detroit, Boston, and took over management of Hotel Pennsylvania in New York.

**Stau′ding·er** (shtou′dĭng·ẽr), **Hermann.** 1881–1965. German chemist. Awarded Nobel prize in chemistry (1953) for studies of macromolecular chemistry.

**Stauf′fer** (stou′fẽr), **David McNeely.** 1845–1913. American civil engineer; part proprietor and associate editor, *Engineering News* (1883–1907). Known as a collector of Americana, pen-and-ink and water-color drawings, and engravings. Author of *American Engravers Upon Copper and Steel* (2 vols., 1907).

**Stau′ning** (stou′nĭng), **Thorvald.** 1873–1942. Danish statesman; president, Socialist Democratic party (1910); premier of Denmark (1924–26, 1929–40).

**Staun′ton** (stôn′t'n; -tŭn; stän′-), Sir **George Leonard.** 1737–1801. English diplomat; friend of Dr. Johnson and Burke; undertook mission to Warren Hastings (1782) and negotiated treaty with Tipu Sahib (1784); secretary of Macartney's embassy to China (1792). His son Sir **George Thomas** (1781–1859) accompanied Macartney's embassy (1792); remained at Canton (1798–1817) as interpreter, as chief of East India Co. factory, etc.; cofounder of Royal Asiatic Society (1823); translated from Chinese *Fundamental Laws of China* (1810).

**Staunton, Howard.** 1810–1874. English chess player and Shakespearean scholar; reputed son of Frederick Howard, 5th Earl of Carlisle (see HOWARD family). World's chess champion (1843–52). Published edition of Shakespeare (1857–60), showing mastery of Elizabethan literature; edited photolithographic facsimile of Shakespeare folio of 1623 (1866).

**Stau·ra′ci·us** (stô·rā′shĭ·ŭs; -shŭs). d. 811. Son of Nicephorus I. Emperor of the Eastern Roman Empire for few months only (811).

**Sta′vis′ky′** (stȧ′vēs′kē′), **Serge Alexandre.** 1886?–1934. French swindler, b. near Kiev, Russia; to Paris (1900); became French citizen (1914). Sold worthless bonds to workers of poorer classes to amount of 40,000,000 francs; gigantic fraud discovered (Dec., 1933); fled to Chamonix. Disclosure of frauds caused sensation in French politics, downfall of two ministries; trial ended (Jan., 1936) with conviction of nine persons.

**Stead** (stĕd), **William Thomas.** 1849–1912. English journalist; founded English *Review of Reviews* (1890). Forced Gladstone government to send Gordon to Khartoum (1884); as result of his exposure in *The Maiden Tribute of Modern Babylon* of outrages against women and children permitted by law, was imprisoned, but instrumental in obtaining enactment of Criminal Law Amendment Act (1885). Devoted himself to advocacy of international peace and friendship with Russia and to psychic research; victim of *Titanic* disaster. Author of *If Christ came to Chicago* (1893) and *The Americanization of the World* (1902).

**Stea′gall** (stē′gôl), **Henry Bascom.** 1873–1943. American lawyer, b. Clopton, Ala. Member, U.S. House of Representatives (1915–41); cosponsor with Carter Glass of Glass-Steagall Banking Reform Act (June 16, 1933).

**Steb′bing** (stĕb′ĭng), **Thomas Roscoe Rede.** 1835–1926. English naturalist; specialized in study of Crustacea.

**Steb'bins** (stĕb'ĭnz), **George Coles.** 1846–1945. American hymn writer; co-operated with Dwight L. Moody in evangelistic work (from 1876), and collaborated with Ira D. Sankey in publishing books of hymns. Composer of over 1500 hymns, including *There is a green hill far away*, and *True-hearted, whole-hearted.*

**Stebbins, Joel.** 1878–1966. American astronomer; director of Washburn Observatory and professor of astronomy, Wisconsin (from 1922). Known for work on stellar photometry.

**Stecchetti, Lorenzo.** See Olindo GUERRINI.

**Sted'man** (stĕd'măn), **Charles.** 1753–1812. British military historian, b. Philadelphia; served with British at Lexington and Bunker Hill; commissary to army of Sir William Howe; settled in England (1783). Author of *History of the Origin, Progress, and Termination of the American War* (2 vols., 1794), best contemporary British account.

**Stedman, Edmund Clarence.** 1833–1908. American poet and businessman, b. Hartford, Conn.; on staff of New York *World* (1860), and one of its war correspondents (1861); opened brokerage office in New York City (1865); member of New York Stock Exchange (1869–1900). Published *Poems Lyrical and Idyllic* (1860), *The Nature and Elements of Poetry* (1892), etc.; compiled anthologies, *A Library of American Literature...*(11 vols., 1889–90; with Ellen Mackay Cortissoz), *A Victorian Anthology, 1837–1895* (1895), *An American Anthology, 1787–1899* (1900).

**Stedman, Thomas Lathrop.** 1853–1938. American physician and editor; compiler and editor of *A Practical Medical Dictionary* (1911); editor of *The Twentieth Century Practice of Medicine* (21 vols., 1895–1903), *Dunglison's Medical Dictionary* (23d ed.; 1904), *Reference Handbook of the Medical Sciences* (4th ed.; 8 vols., 1923), etc.

**Steed** (stēd), **Henry Wickham.** 1871–1956. English journalist; foreign correspondent of London *Times*, at Rome (1897–1902), Vienna (1902–13); foreign editor of the *Times* (1914–19), editor (1919–22); also, proprietor and editor of *Review of Reviews* (1923–30); author of *The Hapsburg Monarchy* (1913), *Through Thirty Years* (1924), *Hitler: Whence and Whither?* (1934), *The Doom of the Hapsburgs* (1937), *Our War Aims* (1939), *The Fifth Arm* (1940), *That Bad Man* (1942), etc.

**Steeg** (stĕg), **Jules.** 1836–1898. French clergyman and journalist; author of *L'Édit de Nantes* (1880), *La Vie Morale* (1888), etc. His son **Théodore** (1868–1950) was a politician; member of Chamber of Deputies (1905–14) and the Senate (1914–21; 1929–30); minister of education (1911–12; 1913; 1917) and of the interior (1912–13; 1917; 1920; 1920–21); governor general of Algeria (1921–25) and resident general of France in Morocco (1925–29); premier of France for a short period (1930).

**Steel** (stēl), **Flora Annie,** *nee* **Webster.** 1847–1929. English novelist; m. Henry William Steel (1867) of Indian civil service, and lived in India (1868–89). Author of books dealing with Anglo-Indian life, including *The Potter's Thumb* (1894), *On the Face of the Waters* (story of Sepoy Mutiny, 1896), *In the Permanent Way* (1897), *Hosts of the Lord* (1900).

**Steele** (stēl), Sir **Richard.** 1672–1729. British essayist and dramatist, b. Dublin. Schoolfellow at Charterhouse of Joseph Addison (*q.v.*). Left Oxford and enlisted in life guards (1694); became captain and secretary to Baron John Cutts (1696–97). Produced devotional manual *The Christian Hero* (1701), and three comedies, *The Funeral, or Grief à la Mode* (1701), *The Lying Lover* (1703), and *The Tender Husband* (1705). Gentleman waiter to Prince George of Denmark (1706); appointed gazetteer by Harley (1707); m. (1707) Mary Scurlock, his "dear Prue." Started (1709) the *Tatler*, triweekly journal of politics and society into which, under name of **Isaac Bick'er·staff** (bĭk'ẽr·ståf), he inserted essays on manners and morality; received contributions by Addison; in conjunction with Addison, carried on the *Spectator*, in which appeared the *Sir Roger de Coverley* papers (1711–12); projected a number of other periodicals, chief among them the *Guardian* (1713) and the *Plebeian* (1718). Zealous Whig; lost office of gazetteer (1710) and expelled from House of Commons (1714). Favored Hanoverian succession, received honors and substantial rewards, made governor of royal company of comedians, and knighted (1715); appointed one of commissioners of forfeited estates in Scotland, welcomed by literati of Edinburgh (1716). Denounced, in the *Plebeian*, Lord Sunderland's Peerage Bill limiting the prerogative of the sovereign to create peers (1718); answered by Addison in the *Old Whig.* Quarreled with Addison; deprived of Drury Lane patent in consequence (restored by Walpole, 1721). Illustrated views on dueling and respect for women in last play, *Conscious Lovers* (1722).

**Steele, Wilbur Daniel.** 1886–1970. American writer of fiction, esp. short stories, b. Greensboro, N.C. Four times awarded O. Henry prize for his short stories (*For They Know Not What They Do, The Man Who Saw Through Heaven, Bubbles, Can't Cross Jordan*).

**Steen** (stān), **Jan.** 1626–1679. Dutch genre painter.

**Steen** (stēn), **Marguerite.** 1894–1975. English writer; successively teacher, dancing mistress, actress, and novelist. Author of *Gilt Cage* (1927), *The Reluctant Madonna* (1929), *Unicorn* (1931), *The Wise and the Foolish Virgins* (1932), *The Tavern* (1935), *The Lost One* (1937), *Family Ties* (1939), *The Sun Is My Undoing* (1941), etc.

**Steen'bock** (stēn'bŏk), **Harry.** 1886–1967. American biochemist; at U. of Wisc. (1908–67). Studied human and animal nutrition; synthesized Vitamin D.

**Steen'strup** (stēn'stro͝op), **Johann Japetus Smith.** 1813–1897. Danish zoologist, archaeologist. His son **Johannes** (1844–1935), historian; author esp. of works on early Norman history.

**Steen'wijk** *or* **Steen'wyk** (stān'vīk), **Hendrik van.** 1550?–?1603. Dutch painter in Germany; known esp. for paintings of interiors of Gothic churches. His son **Hendrik** (1580?–?1649) was also a painter; said to have been often employed by Vandyke to paint in architectural backgrounds of Vandyke's portraits.

**Steer** (stēr), **Philip Wilson.** 1860–1942. English painter, b. Birkenhead. Among his canvases are *Richmond Castle, Yorkshire* (in the Metropolitan Museum), *Chepstow Castle, The Music Room,* and *The Golden Valley.* Member, Order of Merit (1931).

**Stee'vens** (stē'vĕnz), **George.** 1736–1800. English Shakespearean commentator; collected library of Elizabethan literature; published reprint from original quartos, *Twenty of the Plays of Shakespeare* (1766). Collaborated with Johnson in ten-volume edition (1773). Prompted by jealousy of Edmund Malone, who brought out an edition (1790), prepared 15-volume edition (1793) in which he made reckless emendations, and which was reissued (1803) by Isaac Reed in 21 volumes, with additional notes by Steevens, as the "first variorum." Detected forgeries of Chatterton and Ireland.

**Steevens, George Warrington.** 1869–1900. English journalist; special correspondent of London *Daily Mail* in U.S., Greece, Germany, Egypt, India, South Africa, and at Dreyfus trial; died of enteric fever at siege of Ladysmith.

**Stefan.** Polish form of STEPHEN.

**Ste'fan** (shtĕ'fän), **Josef.** 1835–1893. Austrian physicist; first stated law (Stefan's, or Stefan-Boltzmann, law) that the total radiation from a black body is proportional to the fourth power of its absolute temperature; investigated hydrodynamics, kinetic theory of gases, and theory of electricity.

**Stefani, Alberto De.** See DE STEFANI.

**Ste'fans·son** (stĕ'făns·sŏn; *Angl.* stĕf''n·s'n), **Vil'hjal'-mur** (vĭl'hyoul'mẽr). 1879–1962. Arctic explorer, b. Arnes, Manitoba, Canada, of Icelandic parents. On trip to Iceland (1904), archaeological expedition of Peabody Museum of Harvard to Iceland (1905), Harvard-Toronto U. ethnological expedition to Eskimos of Mackenzie Delta (1906–07), 2nd expedition to Mackenzie Delta, under auspices of American Museum of Natural History and Canadian government (53 months, 1908–12). In command of Canadian Arctic Expedition to explore Canadian and Alaskan regions of the arctic (1913–18). Author of *My Life with the Eskimo* (1913), *Friendly Arctic* (1921), *The Northward Course of Empire* (1922), *Hunters of the Great North* (1922), *The Adventure of Wrangell Island* (1925), *The Three Voyages of Martin Frobisher* (1938), *Iceland: The First American Republic* (1939), *Ultima Thule* (1940), *Greenland* (1942), etc.

**Stef'fen** (shtĕf'ĕn), **Albert.** 1884–1963. Swiss novelist and playwright.

**Stef'fens** (shtĕf'ĕns), **Henrik.** 1773–1845. German philosopher, b. in Norway.

**Stef'fens** (stĕf'ĕnz), **Lincoln,** *in full* **Joseph Lincoln.** 1866–1936. American journalist, b. San Francisco. City editor, New York *Commercial Advertiser* (1898–1902); managing editor, *McClure's Magazine* (1902–06); associate editor, *American Magazine* and *Everybody's Magazine* (1906–11). Author of *The Shame of the Cities* (1904), *The Struggle for Self-Government* (1906), *Upbuilders* (1909), *The Least of These* (1910), and an autobiography (1931).

**Stei'chen** (stī'kĕn), **Edward.** 1879–1972. Photographer, b. Luxembourg, to U.S. (1880); pioneer in photography as art form. In World War I, led photo division of air service; in World War II, headed navy photo unit. Director, photo department, Museum of Modern Art (New York), 1947–1962. Author of *A Life in Photography* (1968).

**Stein** (shtīn), Baroness **von. Charlotte Albertine Ernestine,** *nee* **von Schardt** (fôn shärt'). 1742–1827. German lady in waiting, in court of duchess of Weimar; m. Baron von Stein (1764). Beloved by Goethe (1775–89). To her, Goethe addressed *Briefe aus der Schweiz* (1779) and many love letters, later published (1848).

**Stein** (stīn), Sir **Au'rel** (ô'rĕl), *in full* **Mark Aurel.** 1862–1943. British archaeologist, b. Budapest; made archaeological explorations in Chinese Turkestan, central Asia and west China, central Asia and Persia, upper Swat, Baluchistan, and Makran, south Persia, western Iran, and Iraq and Trans-Jordan. Author of *Chronicle of Kings of Kashmir* (1900), *Ancient Khotan* (1907), *Ruins of Desert Cathary* (1912), *The Thousand Buddhas* (1921), *Innermost Asia* (4 vols.), *On Alexander's Track to the Indus* (1929), *Archaeological Reconnaissances in S. E. Iran* (1937), *An Old Routes of Western Iran* (1940), etc.

**Stein, Gertrude.** 1874–1946. American writer, b. Allegheny, Pa.; long resident in France; author of *Three Lives* (1908), *Tender Buttons* (1915), *Making of Americans* (1925), *Lucy Church Amiably* (1930), *Matisse, Picasso and Gertrude Stein* (1932), *The Autobiography of Alice B. Toklas* (1933), *Four Saints in Three Acts* (1934), *Everybody's Autobiography* (1937), *Picasso* (1938), *The World Is Round* (1939), *Ida* (1941), etc.

**Stein** (shtīn), Baron **Heinrich von.** 1857–1887. German philosopher and poet; tutor of Siegfried Wagner (1879–80), and friend of Richard Wagner. Chief philosophical work, *Die Entstehung der Neuren Ästhetik* (1886); chief literary work, *Helden und Welt* (1883), to which Wagner wrote an introduction. Collaborated with Glasenapp in a *Wagner-Lexikon* (1883).

**Stein,** Baron **Heinrich Friedrich Karl vom und zum** (fôm ŏŏnt tsŏŏm; tsōōm). 1757–1831. Prussian statesman, b. Nassau; as Prussian minister of foreign affairs (1807–08), accomplished many reforms in administration, taxation, and civil service; serfdom abolished; assisted Scharnhorst and Gneisenau in army reorganization; forced to resign by Napoleon (1808). Fled to Austria; lived there (1809–12); summoned to Russia to act as counselor to czar (1812–13); after battle of Leipzig (1813), head of the council of administration of reconquered German territory and leader in military diplomacy (1813–15); frustrated in plans for Germany by Metternich and Hardenberg at Congress of Vienna (1814–15), retired (1815).

**Stein, Lorenz von.** 1815–1890. German political scientist; professor, Vienna (1855–85).

**Stein, William Howard.** 1911– . Biochemist, b. New York City. Ph.D., Columbia, 1938. Shared 1972 Nobel prize for chemistry with C. B. Anfinsen and Stanford Moore for work on enzymes.

**Stei'nach** (shtī'näĸ), **Eugen.** 1861–1944. Austrian physiologist and biologist; known for experiments in rejuvenation of men and animals by grafting the sexual glands of young animals.

**Stein'beck** (stīn'bĕk), **John Ernst** (ûrnst). 1902–1968. American novelist, b. Salinas, Calif.; educ. Stanford U. Author of *Cup of Gold* (1929), *Pastures of Heaven* (1932), *To a God Unknown* (1933), *Tortilla Flat* (1935), *In Dubious Battle* (1936), *Of Mice and Men* (1937), *The Grapes of Wrath* (1939), *The Moon Is Down* (1942), *East of Eden* (1952), *Travels with Charlie* (1962). Awarded Nobel prize for literature (1962).

**Stein'berg** (stīn'bûrg), **Milton.** 1903–1950. American rabbi and writer, b. Rochester, N.Y.

**Steindl** (shtīn'd'l), **Emmerich von.** 1839–1902. Hungarian architect; designed the parliament building in Budapest (1883–1902).

**Stein'dorff** (shtīn'dôrf), **Georg.** 1861–1951. German Egyptologist; professor, Leipzig (1893); engaged in explorations in Nubia and Egypt (from 1899); to U.S. (1939); author of many books on Egypt and Egyptology including *Religion of the Ancient Egyptians* (1905), *Art of the Egyptians* (1928), *When Egypt Ruled the East* (1942).

**Stei'nen** (shtī'nĕn), **Karl von den.** 1855–1929. German ethnologist; professor of ethnology, Berlin (1900), and director of the Ethnological Museum (1904–28).

**Stei'ner** (stī'nẽr), **Edward Alfred.** 1866–1956. Clergyman and sociologist, b. in Czechoslovakia; to U.S. and ordained in Congregational ministry (1891); lecturer on sociological questions, esp. immigration problems. Author of *The Immigrant Tide* (1909), *From Alien to Citizen* (1914), *The Making of a Great Race* (1929), etc.

**Stei'ner** *or* **Stai'ner** (shtī'nẽr), **Jakob.** 1621–1683. German violinmaker, b. in the Tirol; learned the art under the masters in Cremona.

**Stei'ner** (shtī'nẽr), **Jakob.** 1796–1863. Swiss mathematician; known for work in synthetic geometry.

**Steiner, Rudolf.** 1861–1925. Austrian social philosopher; founder of the spiritualistic and mystical doctrine known as anthroposophy. Became associated with theosophy movement (from 1902); met Annie Besant, the leader of the movement, and was strongly influenced by her; founded (1912) Der Anthroposophische Bund, and a number of institutions for the teaching of his doctrines, as the Goetheanum at Dornach, near Basel. In later life, opposed theosophy but continued to expound his own anthroposophy.

**Stein'hardt** (stīn'härt), **Laurence Adolph.** 1892–1950. American lawyer and diplomat, b. New York City; A.B. (1913), LL.B. (1915), Columbia; practiced law in New York; U.S. minister to Sweden (1933–37); ambassador to Peru (1937–39), Russia (1939–41), Turkey (1942–44), Czechoslovakia (1944–48), Canada (1948–50).

**Stein'heil** (shtīn'hīl), **Carl August von.** 1801–1870. German physicist; organized Austrian telegraph system (1849 ff.); credited with discovering possibility of using the earth for a return conductor in telegraphy.

**Stei'nitz** (shtī'nĭts; *Angl.* stī'-), **William,** *orig.* **Wilhelm.** 1836–1900. Chess master, b. Prague, Bohemia; recognized as champion of the world (1866–1894); defeated by Emanuel Lasker in championship matches (1894 and 1896); to U.S. (1883) and naturalized (1884).

**Stein'le** (shtīn'lĕ), **Edward.** 1810–1886. Austrian painter in Germany; a member of Nazarene circle of painters under leadership of Overbeck, Rome (1828 ff.); painter of religious and mythological subjects and portraits.

**Stein'len'** (stĕn'lĕn'), **Théophile Alexandre.** 1859–1923. French artist, b. in Switzerland; naturalized (1901). Settled in Paris (1878) and contributed drawings to the *Chat Noir*, *Gil Blas Illustré*, etc.; well known for his posters and lithographs. Illustrated a number of books, including Bruant's *Dans la Rue*, Delmet's *Chansons de Femme*, Anatole France's *Crainquebille*, etc.

**Stein'man** (stīn'măn), **David Barnard.** 1886–1960. American civil engineer; authority on bridge building; b. New York City; B.S., C.C.N.Y. (1906), C.E. (1909), Ph.D. (1911), Columbia; in consulting practice (from 1920). Designer or consulting engineer for suspension bridge at Florianopolis, Brazil, largest bridge in South America (1922–26), Carquinez Strait Bridge in California, longest cantilever bridge in U.S. (1923–27), St. John's Bridge, Portland, Oregon (1929–31), Cologne-Mühlheim Bridge over Rhine in Germany, Tri-Borough and Henry Hudson bridges, New York City. Author of many technical books, esp. on suspension bridges.

**Stein'metz** (stīn'mĕts; *Ger.* shtīn'-), **Charles Pro'teus** (prō'tūs; -tē·ŭs), *orig.* **Karl August Rudolf.** 1865–1923. American electrical engineer, b. Breslau, Germany; forced to leave Germany because of socialistic editorial written for a Breslau paper (1888); to U.S. (1889); consulting engineer, General Electric Co., Schenectady, N.Y. (from 1893); professor, Union Coll. (from 1902). Derived mathematically the law of hysteresis; worked on theory and calculation of alternating-current phenomena; investigated electrical phenomena duplicating those of lightning; developed lightning arresters for high-power transmission lines; patented over 100 inventions, including improvements on generators and motors. Author of *Engineering Mathematics* (1910), *Radiation, Light and Illumination* (1909), *America and the New Epoch* (1916), etc. See Rudolf EICKEMEYER.

**Stein'metz** (shtīn'mĕts), **Karl Friedrich von.** 1796–1877. Prussian soldier; defeated Austrians at Náchod and Skalitz (1866); in Franco-Prussian War, commanded 1st army in battles at Spichern, Colombey-Nouilly, and Gravelotte (1870); removed (Sept., 1870) and appointed governor general of Posen and Silesia; field marshal (1871).

**Stein'metz** (stīn'mĕts), **Sebald Rudolf.** 1862–1940. Dutch ethnologist and social philosopher; author of *Philosophy of War* (1907), *Sociology of War* (1929), etc.

**Stein'thal** (shtīn'täl), **Heymann.** 1823–1899. German philologist; with Moritz Lazarus, credited with establishing science of ethnopsychology.

**Stein'way** (stīn'wā), **Henry En'gel·hard** (ĕng'gĕl·härd; *Ger.* ĕng'ĕl·härt). *Orig.* **Heinrich Engelhard Stein'weg** (shtīn'vāK); *name legally changed (1864).* 1797–1871. Piano manufacturer, b. Wolfhagen, Ger.; engaged in making of pianos (from 1820); to U.S. (1851); with several sons, founded piano factory in New York (1853). His son **Christian Friedrich Theodore** (1825–1889), in piano manufacture in Germany (to 1865), joined American firm of Steinway & Sons (1865); returned to Germany (1870) but continued to give American firm benefit of his researches and experiments. Another son, **William** (1835–1896), president of Steinway & Sons (1876–96), was first chairman of Rapid Transit Commission of New York City, which planned building of New York's first subway; subway under East River from 42d Street to Long Island City is named Steinway Tunnel in his honor.

**Ste'kel** (shtā'kĕl), **Wilhelm.** 1868–1940. Viennese psychiatrist; disciple of Freud; credited with psychoanalyzing over 10,000 individuals.

**Stel'la** (stĕl'ȧ). Name associated in literature with (1) Lady Penelope DEVEREUX and (2) Esther JOHNSON.

**Stel'la'** (stĕ'lȧ'), **Jacques.** 1596–1657. French painter; appointed by Richelieu painter to the king; executed many canvases for the queen, the cardinal, and for the churches of Paris.

**Stel'la** (stĕl'ȧ; *Ital.* stāl'lä), **Joseph.** 1880–1946. American painter, b. in Italy; to U.S. (1896); works include crayon and pastel drawings of miners and steel-mill workers, and paintings, as *Old Man*, *Brooklyn Bridge*, *Tree of My Life*, *Factory*, *Dance of Spring*, *Lotus.*

**Stel'ler** (shtĕl'ĕr; *Angl.* stĕl'-) *or* **Stoel'ler** (shtûl'ĕr), **Georg Wilhelm.** 1709–1746. German naturalist; on expedition to north Asia led by Vitus Bering (1737); explored Kamchatka (1740–41, 1742–44); accompanied Bering (*q.v.*) to coast of Alaska, wintering on Bering Island (1741–42). Wrote accounts of his travels and described birds and animals, including Steller's sea cow (now extinct) and Steller's sea lion, both named after him.

**Stelz'le** (stĕlz'lē), **Charles.** 1869–1941. American Presbyterian clergyman and sociologist, b. New York City; a leader in effort to bring about adjustments within the church to meet modern economic conditions. Author of *The Workingman and Social Problems* (1903), *Boys of the Street* (1904), *Gospel of Labor* (1912), etc.

**Sten'bock** (stān'bôk). Swedish noble family, including: Count **Gustaf Otto Gustafsson Stenbock** (1614–1685); served in Thirty Years' War; general of infantry (1648); fought in Polish war, and against Danes (1657) and Norwegians (1658); admiral (1666). Count **Magnus Gustafsson** (1665–1717); distinguished himself at Narva (1700); defeated Danes at Hälsingborg (1710); field marshal; invaded Holstein; defeated and forced to surrender at Tönning (1713).

**Sten'dhal'** (stăN'dȧl'). *Pseudonym of* **Marie Henri Beyle** (bāl). 1783–1842. French writer, b. Grenoble; settled in Paris (1821). French consul at Trieste (1830) and Civitavecchia (from 1831). Author of several biographical studies, as *Haydn* (1814), *Rossini* (1824), *Napoléon* (pub. 1876), and a few enormously popular romantic novels, including *Armance* (1823) and his best-known works, *Le Rouge et le Noir* (1831) and *La Chartreuse de Parme* (1839).

**Steng'el** (shtĕng'ĕl), **Edmund Max.** 1845– . German philologist.

**Stengel,** Mme. **Wilhelm.** See Marcella SEMBRICH.

**Sten'kil'** (stān'chēl'). Name of early Swedish dynasty (1060–1125), founded by Stenkil Ragnvaldsson (d. 1066), Earl of West Götaland.

**Ste'no** (*Dan.* stē̜'nō̇), **Nicolaus.** *Latinized from* **Niels** (*or* **Nicolas**) **Sten'sen** (stē̜n's'n). 1638–1687. Danish anatomist; discoverer of the "duct of Steno," the duct of the parotid gland.

**Stenvall, Alexis.** See KIVI.

**Ste'phan** (shtĕ'fän), **Heinrich von.** 1831–1897. German statesman; first postmaster general of the German Empire; promoted Universal Postal Union.

**Ste·pha'ni** (shtȧ·fä'nē), **Franz von.** 1876–1939. German National Socialist (Nazi) leader; took part in Kapp Putsch (1920); district leader of Stahlhelm (1924–33); member of Reichstag (from 1930); supreme commander of Sturmabteilung reserves.

**Stephanus.** See ESTIENNE family.

**Steph'a·nus Byz'an·ti'nus** (stĕf'ȧ·nŭs bĭz'ăn·tī'nŭs). Byzantine geographer, probably of early 6th century A.D.; author of a geographical dictionary, *Ethnika*, only fragments of which are extant.

**Ste'phen** (stē'vĕn), Saint. In the Bible, the first Christian martyr, accused of blasphemy and stoned to death (*Acts* vi. 5–vii. 60).

**Stephen.** Name of nine popes (see note below, and see *Table of Popes*, Nos. 23, 92, 94, 97, 110, 113, 125, 128, 153), including:

**Stephen I,** Saint; pope (bishop of Rome; 254–257); defended the validity of heretic baptism.

**Stephen II;** pope (752–757); crowned Pepin the Short king of the Franks (754), confirming recognition by Pope Zacharias; received Donation of Pepin (755), *i.e.* temporal power over the exarchate of Ravenna and over the Pentapolis.

**Stephen IX;** 1000?–1058; pope (1057–58); son of the duke of Lorraine; died as he was beginning campaign of reform.

☞ Some lists give ten popes named Stephen; a doubtful pope, Stephen II, died a few days after election (752), before his consecration.

**Stephen.** *Sometimes* **Stephen of Blois** (blwä). 1097?–1154. King of England (1135–54). 3d son of Stephen Henry, Count of Blois and Chartres, and Adela, daughter of William the Conqueror. Brought up at court of uncle Henry I of England, married Matilda of Boulogne, and regarded (to 1125) as heir to English throne; forced to swear, with lay barons, acknowledgment of widowed Empress Matilda of Germany, Henry I's daughter, as future ruler and of ultimate claims of Matilda's son Henry of Anjou. On Henry I's death, claimed throne, declaring Matilda, daughter of a nun, illegitimate; enthroned by Londoners and crowned at Westminster (1135); granted two charters of liberties; drove back Scots (1138); opposed by Empress Matilda's half brother Robert, Earl of Gloucester; as result of quarrel with Bishop Roger of Salisbury, brought clergy against him. Taken prisoner (1141) by forces of Empress Matilda (who had landed 1139) and Gloucester; released in exchange for Gloucester and again crowned (1141) after reign of six months by Matilda; strove through five years of anarchic conditions in England to expel Matilda; quarreled with papacy and failed to obtain papal sanction for coronation of son Eustace (1151); submitted on Eustace's death and acknowledged as his heir (1153) Matilda's son Henry, Duke of Normandy (later Henry II).

**Stephen.** *Hung.* **István.** Name of five kings of Hungary, especially:

**Stephen I** *or* Saint **Stephen.** 975?–1038. First king of Árpád dynasty (997–1038); called "the Apostle of Hungary." Son of Duke Geza; m. Gisela, sister of Emperor Henry II; succeeded his father (997) as duke of Hungary; crowned king (1001) with crown sent by pope; given title of "Apostolic King," held thereafter (to 1918) by sovereigns of Hungary; continued Christianizing policy of his father and suppressed paganism; called in foreign priests, endowed abbeys, and formed a council of nobles and high churchmen; encouraged agriculture and trade; became patron saint of Hungary; canonized (1087).

**Stephen V.** 1239–1272. King (1270–72); son of Béla IV. As prince ruled duchy of Styria (1254–59) and invaded Bulgaria (1268); defeated Ottokar II of Bohemia (1271).

**Stephen.** *Serb.* **Ste'van** (stĕ'vän). Name of rulers of Serbia, including: **Stephen Ne'ma·nya** *or*, *Serb.*, **Ne'ma·nja** [nĕ'mä·nyä] (1114–1200), founder of Nemanyich dynasty (1190–1371); **Stephen Nemanya I** (d. 1228), first king of Serbia; **Stephen Nemanya VIII** (d. 1334), honored as a saint by Serbian church because of piety and philanthropies; **Stephen Nemanya IX,** *named* **Stephen Du'shan** *or*, *Serb.*, **Du'šan** [dōō'shän] (1308?–1355), rebelled against father and seized power (1331), king of Serbia (1335–46), had himself crowned emperor of the Serbs, Greeks, Bulgars, and Albanians (1346), drew up legal code known as Code of Dushan (1349–54), conquered Bosnia (1350), Macedonia (1353), and was marching on Constantinople at time of death; **Stephen** (d. 1427), Despot of Serbia, forced to become tributary of Turks. See NEMANYA.

**Stephen, George.** 1st Baron **Mount Stephen** (mount'). 1829–1921. Canadian financier, b. in Scotland; merchant in Canada (from 1850); president of Bank of Montreal; instrumental in completion of Canadian Pacific Railway, of which he was president (1880–88); lived in England (from 1898). With his cousin Donald Alexander Smith (*q.v.*), Baron Strathcona and Mount Royal, chief founder of Royal Victoria Hospital, Montreal.

**Stephen, James.** 1758–1832. English lawyer and abolitionist, b. in Dorsetshire; practiced in St. Kitts in West Indies (1783–94); M.P. (1808–15); having seen brutality to Negroes in St. Kitts, sent information on slave trade to abolitionist Wilberforce; m. (1800) Wilberforce's sister; master in chancery (1811–31); author of *Slavery in the British West India Colonies* (2 vols., 1824, 1830). Grandfather of Sir Leslie Stephen (*q.v.*) and his brother Sir **James Fitzjames Stephen** (1829–1894), judge; became lifelong friend of Sir Henry Maine; as legal member of council in India (1869–72), chiefly responsible for Indian Evidence Act (1872); professor of common law at Inns of Court (1875–79); judge of High Court of Justice (1879–91); author of *General View of the Criminal Law of England* (1863), first attempt made since Blackstone to explain principles of English law, and *History of the Criminal Law* (1883); father of **James Kenneth** (1859–1892), known as **J.K.S.,** author of light verse collected in *Lapsus Calami* and *Quo Musa Tendis.*

**Stephen,** Sir **Leslie.** 1832–1904. English philosopher, critic, and biographer; grandson of James Stephen (*q.v.*); m. Thackeray's younger daughter (1867). Abandoned orthodox religious views, resigned college tutorship (1862), relinquished holy orders (1875); defined his agnostic position in *Essays on Free Thinking and Plain Speaking* (1873). Visited United States (1863) and, after investigating Civil War, supported slave emancipation and cause of the North; on second visit (1868), became close friend of J. R. Lowell, C. E. Norton, Emerson, and Holmes. Contributed to *Saturday Review*, *Fraser's Magazine*, and *Nation;* co-operated in founding of *Pall Mall Gazette;* editor, *Cornhill Magazine* (1871–82); collected critical essays from *Cornhill Magazine* (from 1866) and issued them as *Hours in a Library* (1874, 1876, 1879). Reviewed positions of writers of deist controversy and of utilitarian and intuitional philosophers in his chief work, *History of English Thought in the Eighteenth Century* (1876), and in *The English Utilitarians* (3 vols., 1900); published *Science of Ethics* (1882). Inaugurated "English Men of Letters" series with biography of Samuel Johnson (1878); contributed biographies of Alexander Pope (1880), Jonathan Swift (1882), George Eliot (1902), and Thomas Hobbes (1904). First editor (1882–91) of *Dictionary of National Biography;* contributed many of most important biographies of 18th and 19th centuries; saw completion of twenty-six volumes before forced by ill health to retire (1891). Author also of *An Agnostic's Apology* (1893), *Social Rights and Duties* (1896), *Studies of a Biographer* (1899–1902), *English Literature and Society in the Eighteenth Century* (1904), and *Collected Essays* (10 vols., 1907). He was the original of Meredith's portrait of Vernon Whitford in *The Egoist.* For his two daughters, Vanessa and Virginia, see under Clive BELL and Leonard WOOLF.

**Ste′phen Bá′tho·ry** (stē′vĕn bä′tô·rĭ). *Hungarian* **István Báthory.** 1533–1586. Prince of Transylvania (1571–76) and king of Poland (1575–86); won renown as soldier with John Zápolya; under influence of Jan Zamojski, was elected king of Poland (1575) by nobility; overcame revolt of Danzig (1577); in war with Russia (1579–82) gained victory over Ivan the Terrible. See BÁTHORY.

**Stephen of Blois.** See STEPHEN, King of England.

**Stephen of By·zan′ti·um** (bĭ·zăn′shĭ·ŭm; bī-; -tĭ·ŭm). = STEPHANUS BYZANTINUS.

**Stephen of Mol·da′vi·a** (mŏl·dā′vĭ·ȧ). *Known as* **Stephen the Great.** 1433?–1504. Prince of Moldavia (1457–1504); noted especially for his victory over a strong Turkish army at Racova (1475). Under his administration Moldavia reached the peak of its power.

**Stephen of Mu′ret′** (mü′rĕ′), Saint. 1046?–1124. Founder of Order of Grammont, an order of hermit monks established near Limoges.

**Ste′phens** (stē′vĕnz), **Alexander Hamilton.** 1812–1883. American politician, b. near Crawfordville, Ga.; practiced law at Crawfordville. Member, U.S. House of Representatives (1843–59), allying himself first with the Whigs and later with the Democrats. Though disapproving immediate secession, remained loyal to his state when it voted to secede (1861). Vice-president of the Confederacy (1861–65); head of Confederate mission at Hampton Roads Conference (Feb., 1865). At end of war, was imprisoned (May–Oct., 1865) at Fort Warren, Boston; paroled (Oct. 12, 1865). Elected U.S. senator (1866), but was refused a seat; member, U.S. House of Representatives (1873–82); governor of Georgia (1883). Author of *A Constitutional View of the Late War Between the States* (2 vols., 1868–70).

**Stephens, Alice Barber.** 1858–1932. American artist; m. Charles Hallowell Stephens (1890). Illustrated George Eliot's *Middlemarch*, D. M. Craik's *John Halifax, Gentleman*, Hawthorne's *Marble Faun*, etc.

**Stephens, Frederic George.** 1828–1907. English art critic and member of Pre-Raphaelite Brotherhood. Art critic to *Athenaeum* (1861–1901); author of *The Private Collections of England.* See Holman HUNT.

**Stephens, George.** 1813–1895. English archaeologist and philologist; author of *The Old Northern Runic Monuments of Scandinavia and England* (1866, 1868, 1884).

**Stephens, Henry Morse.** 1857–1919. Historian, b. Edinburgh, Scotland; to U.S. (1894); professor, Cornell (1894–1902), and head of history department, U. of California (1902–19). Among his works are *History of the French Revolution* (2 vols., 1886, 1891), *Europe, 1789–1815* (1893). A founder (1895) and an editor (1895–1905), *American Historical Review.*

**Stephens, James.** 1825–1901. Irish agitator; civil engineer by profession; active in Young Ireland movement. Inaugurated Irish Republican Brotherhood (founded in New York as Fenian Brotherhood) on military basis (1858); founded *Irish People* as organ of party (1863); arrested in Dublin (1865), escaped to New York, where he was deposed by Fenians; expelled from France (1885).

**Stephens, James.** 1882–1950. Irish poet and novelist. Author of *Insurrections* (verse, 1909), *The Hill of Vision* (verse, 1912), *The Charwoman's Daughter* (novel, 1912; American title *Mary, Mary*), *The Crock of Gold* (novel, 1912), *Here Are Ladies* (1913), *The Demi-Gods* (1914), *The Rocky Road to Dublin* (1915), *Songs from the Clay* (1915), *Reincarnation* (1918), *Deirdre* (1923), *In the Land of Youth* (1924), *Etched in Moonlight* (1928), *Strict Joy* (poems, 1931), *Kings and the Moon* (1938).

**Stephens, John Lloyd.** 1805–1852. American traveler and author, b. Shrewsbury, N.J.; practiced law in New York (1826–34); traveled in eastern Mediterranean and eastern Europe (1834–36), in Central America (1839 and 1841). Author of *Travel in Egypt, Arabia Petraea, and the Holy Land* (2 vols., 1837), *Travel in Greece, Turkey, Russia, and Poland* (2 vols., 1838), *Travel in Central America, Chiapas, and Yucatán* (2 vols., 1841), *Travel in Yucatán* (1843).

**Stephens, Uriah Smith.** 1821–1882. American labor leader; tailor by trade; a founder (1869) of the Noble Order of the Knights of Labor.

**Stephens, William.** See Sir William REYNOLDS-STEPHENS.

**Ste′phen·son** (stē′vĕn·s'n), **Benjamin Franklin.** 1823–1871. American physician; regimental surgeon, 14th Illinois Volunteers (1861–64). Designer and founder of Grand Army of the Republic.

**Stephenson, George.** 1781–1848. English inventor and founder of railways, b. Wylam, near Newcastle. Devised miner's safety lamp, claiming priority over Sir Humphry Davy for its invention (1815); built locomotive tried successfully on Killingworth colliery railway (1814); patented locomotive engine with steam blast (1815); directed construction of railway eight miles long for Hetton colliery (opened 1822); with brother and cousin, established locomotive works at Newcastle (1823); construction engineer for Stockton and Darlington Ry. (opened 1825) and Liverpool and Manchester Ry. (opened 1830), winning contest to determine suitable engine for latter with his locomotive, "the Rocket," having tubular boiler (1829); engaged in building various other railways. His only son, **Robert** (1803–1859), was also an engineer; manager of Newcastle locomotive works; made improvements in locomotives and assisted his father in construction of locomotive "Rocket" and of railways; construction engineer for Birmingham and London Ry., first railway into London (completed 1838); known for his bridges, including one over the Tyne at Newcastle, Victoria Bridge at Berwick, Menai tubular-girder bridge, and bridge over the St. Lawrence at Montreal. **George Robert Stephenson** (1819–1905), civil engineer, employed by his uncle George Stephenson, directed construction of railways in Kent, Schleswig-Holstein, Jutland, and New Zealand; constructed fixed as well as swinging bridges in England and abroad; proprietor of Newcastle locomotive works (1859–86).

**Step·nyak′** (styĭp·nyȧk′), **Sergei Mikhailovich.** *Pseudonym of* **Sergei Mikhailovich Krav·chin′ski** (krŭf·chēn′skû·ĭ; *Angl.* -skĭ). 1852–1895. Russian writer; joined

Nihilists (1872); forced to flee from Russia. Chosen by his associates to murder General Mezentsev, he stabbed the general (Aug. 16, 1878); wrote a vindication of his act under the title *Life for Life.* Lived chiefly in Switzerland and Italy (1879–83), and settled in London (1884). Among his works are *Underground Russia* (1882), *Russia under the Tsars* (1885), *Andrei Kozhukhov* (1889; translated into English under the title *The Career of a Nihilist*), *King Stork and King Log* (1895).

**Ster'ling** (stûr'lĭng), **George.** 1869–1926. American poet, b. Sag Harbor, N.Y.; leader in artist colony at Carmel, Calif. (1908–15); committed suicide (Nov. 17, 1926). Published ten volumes of verse (after 1903) and a number of separate poems; among his better-known lyrics are *Spring in Carmel, Autumn in Carmel, The Last Days, Beyond the Breakers.*

**Sterling, John.** 1806–1844. British essayist and poet, b. in Ireland, of a family of Scottish origin; founded literary club (1838), later known as *The Sterling Club,* including as members Carlyle, Tennyson, John Stuart Mill, Sir Francis Palgrave. Author of *Essays and Tales* (1848), *The Election* (humorous poem, 1841), and *Strafford* (tragedy, 1843). Rendered famous by Carlyle's biography *Life of Sterling* (1851). His father, **Edward Sterling** (1773–1847), contributed as editorial writer to London *Times* powerful articles that won for the paper the popular name "the Thunderer."

**Sterling, John William.** 1844–1918. American lawyer and philanthropist; practiced in New York City; bequeathed his large fortune to Yale U. Sterling Memorial Library is named in his honor.

**Stern, Daniel.** Pseudonym of Marie, Comtesse d'AGOULT.

**Stern** (stûrn), **Gladys Bertha.** 1890–1973. English novelist, b. London; m. Geoffrey Lisle Holdsworth; author of *Pantomime* (1914), *The Back Seat* (1923), *Tents of Israel* (1924; American title *The Matriarch;* later dramatized), *Thunderstorm* (1925), *Debonair* (1928; later dramatized), *Mosaic* (1930), *Monogram* (1936), *The Woman in the Hall* (1939), *Another Part of the Forest* (1941), *The Young Matriarch* (1942), etc.

**Stern, Joseph William.** 1870–1934. American song writer and publisher; a founder of Joseph W. Stern & Co., music publishers (1894); wrote *The Little Lost Child, My Mother Was a Lady,* etc.

**Stern** (shtĕrn), **Julius.** 1820–1883. German musician; cofounder (1850; with Adolf B. Marx and Theodor Kullak) of the Berlin (later Stern) Conservatory.

**Stern** (shtĕrn; *Angl.* stûrn), **Louis William.** 1871–1938. German psychologist; to U.S. as professor at Duke U., N.C. (1934–38); a pioneer in field of intelligence tests.

**Stern, Otto.** 1888–1969. American physicist, b. Sohrau, Germany; taught at U. of Frankfurt (1914–21) and U. of Hamburg (1923–33); professor, Carnegie Tech. (from 1933); awarded 1943 Nobel prize for physics, for work on atomic structure.

**Stern'berg** (shtĕrn'bĕrĸ), **Alexander von.** See UNGERN-STERNBERG.

**Stern'berg** (shtĕrn'bĕrĸ; *Angl.* stûrn'bûrg), Baron **Constantin Ivanovich von.** 1852–1924. Pianist, b. St. Petersburg, Russia; to U.S. and became naturalized citizen. Founded Sternberg School of Music, Philadelphia, conducted this school (1890–1924).

**Stern'berg** (stûrn'bûrg), **George Miller.** 1838–1915. American physician; in Medical Corps, U.S. army (from 1861); detailed (1879) to duty with Havana Yellow Fever Commission. Engaged in bacteriological study (from 1880); first to demonstrate the plasmodium of malaria (1885) and the bacilli of tuberculosis and of typhoid fever (1886). As U.S. surgeon general (1893–1902), established Army Medical School, Dental Corps, Nurse Corps, and founded Army Tuberculosis Hospital at Fort Bayard, N.Mex. Organized Yellow Fever Commission, headed by Major Reed, which discovered transmission of yellow fever by a certain species of mosquito. Retired in 1902. Renowned as American pioneer in field of bacteriology.

**Sternburg, Hermann Speck von.** See SPECK VON STERNBURG.

**Sterne** (stûrn), **Laurence.** 1713–1768. British novelist, b. Clonmel, Ireland; great-grandson of **Richard Sterne** (1596?–1683; Cavalier churchman imprisoned for Royalism, 1642–45; a reviser of Book of Common Prayer; archbishop of York, 1664–83). Vicar of Sutton-in-the-Forest (1738) and prebendary of York (1741); m. Elizabeth Lumley (1741), who was disturbed by his "small quiet attentions" to other women and became insane (1758); dabbled in painting and music; took part in orgies of "demoniacks" at Crazy Castle, house of John Hall-Stevenson (*q.v.*); carried on flirtation and correspondence (publ. 1855–56) with Mlle. Fourmantelle. Created sensation with first two volumes of novel *The Life and Opinions of Tristram Shandy* (1760), partly because of its eccentric humor and whimsicality, partly because of its unconventionality and indecorum; after *Sermons of Mr. Yorick* (1760), published third and fourth volumes of *Tristram Shandy* (1761), fifth and sixth (1762), seventh and eighth (1765), and last (1767). Abroad for his health (1762–64); met in London Mrs. Elizabeth Draper, for whom he kept *The Bramine's Journal* (Apr.–Aug., 1767); separated from his wife (1767). Spent most of 1767 writing *A Sentimental Journey through France and Italy* (2 vols. of projected 4 vols., 1768), in which humor of *Tristram Shandy* is replaced by sentimental enjoyment of travels from Calais to Lyons, contrasted by author with the distaste of French and Italian customs expressed by Smelfungus, *i.e.* Tobias Smollett. Publication of his *Letters of Yorick to Eliza* (1766–67), authorized by Mrs. Draper (1775).

**Sterne** (stûrn), **Maurice.** 1878–1957. Painter and sculptor, b. Libau, Russia; to U.S. (1890). Studio in San Francisco. See Mabel LUHAN.

**Sterne** (stûrn), **Simon.** 1839–1901. American lawyer and reformer, b. Philadelphia; practiced in New York (from 1860). Editor, *New York Social Science Review* (1865). Founded Personal Representation Society, which advocated adoption of the Hare system of proportional representation. Secretary of the committee of seventy which overthrew the Tweed Ring. Lectured in behalf of free trade (1876–88). Drafted New York State Railroad Commission Act (1882) and the federal Interstate Commerce Act (1887).

**Ster'ner** (stûr'nẽr), **Albert.** 1863–1946. Painter, b. London, Eng., of American parentage; studio in Chicago (1879–84) and New York (from 1885).

**Stern'heim** (shtĕrn'hīm), **Carl.** 1881–1943. German playwright and fiction writer.

**Stern'hold** (stûrn'hōld), **Thomas.** d. 1549. English versifier; joint author with **John Hopkins** (d. 1570) of metrical versions of the Psalms formerly attached to the Prayer Book; designated as author of forty Psalms, to sixty by John Hopkins, in the complete book of Psalms (1562), known (after 1696) as the Old Version.

**Ster'rett** (stĕr'ĕt; -ĭt), **John Robert Sitlington.** 1851–1914. American classical scholar and archaeologist; conducted archaeological research expeditions in Asia Minor and Babylonia.

**Stë'sel** (shtyô'sĕl·y'), **Anatoli Mikhailovich.** 1848–1915. Russian general, descended from German family named **Stös'sel** (shtû'sĕl); commanded garrison at Port Arthur (1904); defeated by Japanese under Oku (May 26–27,

1904); surrendered Port Arthur to General Nogi (Jan. 1, 1905). Court-martialed (1906); condemned to death, but sentence commuted to 10 years' imprisonment (1908); pardoned (1909).

**Ste·sich'o·rus** (stē·sĭk'ō·rŭs). 640?–?550 B.C. Greek lyric poet, of Himera in Sicily; only fragments of his works extant.

**Stet'son** (stĕt's'n), **Augusta Emma,** *nee* **Sim'mons** (sĭm'ŭnz). 1842?–1928. American Christian Science leader, b. Waldoboro, Me.; m. Frederick J. Stetson, shipwright (1864). Joined Christian Science movement, and began practice as a Christian Science healer; sent by Mrs. Eddy to New York City (1886) and there organized (1888) First Church of Christ, Scientist, and served as its pastor (1888–1909). Investigated by directors of the Mother Church in Boston (1909), found guilty of insubordination and false teaching, and officially excommunicated. Continued to proclaim Mrs. Eddy's semidivinity, and after Mrs. Eddy's death (1910) prophesied her resurrection.

**Stetson, Francis Lynde.** 1846–1920. American lawyer; handled legal work in organization of U.S. Steel Co.

**Stetson, Grace Ellery Channing.** See under William Ellery CHANNING.

**Stetson, John Batterson.** 1830–1906. American hat manufacturer, b. Orange, N.J.; in family hat business as a boy; opened his own factory in Philadelphia (1865).

**Stet·tin'i·us** (stĕ·tĭn'ĭ·ŭs; -tĭn'yŭs), **Edward Reil'ley** (rī'lĭ). 1865–1925. American industrialist and financier; joined J. P. Morgan & Co. (1915); acted as chief purchasing agent in U.S. for the allied governments during World War I; partner in J. P. Morgan & Co. (1916–25). His son **Edward Reilley** (1900–1949), also an industrialist, chairman of finance committee, U.S. Steel Corp. (1935–39), and president (1939). Chairman, War Resources Board (1939–40); director of priorities division, Office of Production Management (Jan.–Sept., 1941); administrator of lend lease (1941–43); undersecretary of state (1943–44); secretary of state (Dec., 1944–June, 1945) and chairman of U.S. delegation to United Nations conference at San Francisco; U.S. representative to UN Preparatory Commission and delegate (1945–46); rector of U. of Va. (1946–47).

**Steu'art** (stū'ērt). See STEWART and STUART.

**Steu'ben** (stū'bĕn; *Ger.* shtoi'bĕn), Baron **Friedrich Wilhelm Ludolf Gerhard Augustin von.** 1730–1794. Soldier, b. Magdeburg, Prussia; officer in Prussian army under Frederick the Great in the Seven Years' War (1756–63); aide-de-camp to the king (1762–63). To America (1777), recommended to Washington by Franklin; reported to Washington at Valley Forge (Feb. 23, 1778); designated inspector general, Continental army, and given the task of training the army. Reorganized and drilled the army with marked success; commissioned major general in Continental army; engaged at Monmouth and Yorktown; became trusted adviser to Washington. After the war, one of the organizers of the Society of the Cincinnati. Honorably discharged from the army (1784). Naturalized American citizen (Pennsylvania, 1783; New York, 1786); made his home in New York (1784–94). Prepared *Regulations for the Order and Discipline of the Troops of the United States* (1778–79).

**Steu'ben** (shtoi'bĕn), Baron **Karl** (*or* **Charles**) **Wilhelm von.** 1788–1856. German painter; studio chiefly in Paris, where he had a share in decorating the Palais Royal, the palace of Versailles, and a hall in the Louvre; went to St. Petersburg, where he painted several family groups.

**Steuben, Kuno von.** 1855–1935. German general in World War I (1914–18).

**Stevan.** Serbian form of STEPHEN.

**Ste'vens** (stē'vĕnz), **Abel.** 1815–1897. American Methodist Episcopal clergyman, b. Philadelphia. Author of *History of the Religious Movement of the Eighteenth Century, Called Methodism* (3 vols., 1858–61), *History of the Methodist Episcopal Church in the United States* (4 vols., 1864–67), *Madame De Staël...* (2 vols., 1881), etc.

**Stevens, Albert William.** 1886–1949. American aerial photographer and stratosphere investigator; made air maps of upper Amazon (1924); made first photograph showing laterally earth's curvature (1930) and first photographs of moon's shadow on earth during sun eclipse (1932); made balloon ascensions into stratosphere (60,600 ft., 1934; with Capt. O. A. Anderson, 72,395 feet, 1935).

**Stevens, Alfred George.** 1817–1875. English sculptor; designed vases and lions at British Museum; worked (from 1856) on monument of duke of Wellington in St. Paul's Cathedral.

**Stevens, Alfred.** 1828–1906. Belgian painter; best known for small canvases depicting Parisian ladies and genre scenes of Parisian society life. His brother **Joseph** (1826–1892) painted animals, esp. dogs.

**Stevens, Benjamin Franklin.** See under Henry STEVENS.

**Stevens, Edwin Augustus.** See under John STEVENS.

**Stevens, Henry.** 1819–1886. American bibliophile, b. Barnet, Vt.; to London, Eng. (1845) and established himself as a bookdealer; collected Americana for the British Museum, and acted as London agent for many American libraries. Authority on the bibliographical history of the English Bible, and on early Americana. His brother **Benjamin Franklin** (1833–1902) was also a bibliophile; joined Henry in London as a partner (1860–64); established independent bookshop (1866–99), and acted as agent in London for many American libraries and private buyers.

**Stevens, James Floyd.** 1892–1971. American writer; author of tales built around the legendary character "Paul Bunyan," as in *Paul Bunyan* (1925), *Saginaw Paul Bunyan* (1932), etc.

**Stevens, John.** 1749–1838. American inventor, b. New York City; became interested in steamboat development by John Fitch and James Rumsey (1788); to protect inventors, secured federal legislation (1790) establishing first patent laws in U.S.; secured patents (1791) on a vertical steam boiler and an improved type of steam engine. In partnership (1800) with Nicholas J. Roosevelt and Robert R. Livingston to carry on experiments in steam navigation and transportation. Patented multitubular boiler (1803). Succeeded in building a practical steamship, the *Phoenix* (1808), and sent it from New York to Philadelphia (1809), thus making it the first seagoing steamboat in the world. Interested himself in rail transportation; organized company, The Pennsylvania Railroad (1823), but could not raise funds to build road. A son, **Robert Livingston** (1787–1856), was an engineer and inventor; served under Moses Rogers in handling the *Phoenix* on the sea trip from New York to Philadelphia (1809) and operated the *Phoenix* as a ferry between Philadelphia and Trenton; became naval architect; also interested himself in rail transportation; president and chief engineer of the Camden and Amboy Railroad and Transportation Company (1830). Invented the T-rail, a hook-headed spike, and a metal plate to cover the joint between rails. Imported locomotive from England and with it began (Nov. 12, 1831) first steam railway service in New Jersey. Another son of John, **Edwin Augustus** (1795–1868), was also an engineer and inventor; treasurer and manager, Camden & Amboy Railroad and Transportation Company (1830); bequeathed land and money to found Stevens Institute of Technology, Hoboken, N.J.

**Stevens, John Harrington.** 1820–1900. Pioneer in Minnesota region; built (1849) first house in what became site of Minneapolis.

**Stevens, John Leavitt.** 1820–1895. American diplomat; U.S. minister to Paraguay and Uruguay (1870–74), Norway and Sweden (1877–83), Hawaii (1889–93). Had part in overthrow of Queen Liliuokalani (Jan., 1893) by acknowledging Dole's provisional government and requesting landing of force from U.S. cruiser *Boston* in Honolulu harbor to protect U.S. citizens and property.

**Stevens, John Paul.** 1920– . American jurist. Associate justice of U.S. Supreme Court (1975– ).

**Stevens, Robert Livingston.** See under John STEVENS.

**Stevens, Thaddeus.** 1792–1868. American lawyer and legislator; practiced at Gettysburg, Pa. (1816); member, U.S. House of Representatives (1849–53; 1859–68). Vigorously opposed slavery; supported financial measures but opposed many other administration policies. Leader in Congressional reconstruction plan; proposed impeachment of President Johnson and managed the trial.

**Stevens, Wallace.** 1879–1955. Poet, b. Reading, Pa. Trained as lawyer; worked as insurance executive. Poems published in *Harmonium* (1923; 1931), *Ideas of Order* (1935), *The Man with the Blue Guitar* (1937), etc.; *Collected Poems* (1954; awarded Pulitzer prize, 1955).

**Ste′ven·son** (stē′vĕn·s'n), **Adlai Ewing.** 1835–1914. American politician, b. in Christian County, Ky.; member (from Ill.), U.S. House of Representatives (1875–77; 1879–81); first asst. postmaster general (1885–89); vice-president of the U.S. (1893–97). His grandson **Adlai Ewing Stevenson** (1900–1965), lawyer, b. Los Angeles; asst. to secy. of the navy (1941–44), to secy. of state (1945); U.S. delegate to UN General Assembly; governor of Illinois (1949–53); Democratic candidate for U.S. president (1952, 1956), U.S. amb. to UN (1961–65).

**Stevenson, Andrew.** 1784–1857. American politician, b. in Culpeper County, Va.; member, U.S. House of Representatives (1821–34) and speaker of the house (1827–34); U.S. minister to Great Britain (1836–41).

**Stevenson, Burton Egbert.** 1872–1962. American writer and anthologist, b. Chillicothe, Ohio; compiler esp. of anthologies of poetry; author of novels.

**Stevenson, Edward Luther.** 1858–1944. American historian and cartographer; professor, Rutgers (1891–1911); author of *Maps Illustrating Early Discovery and Exploration in America, 1502–1530* (1903–06), *The Derotero of Alonso de Chavis* (1929), *Geography of Claudius Ptolemy* (1930), etc.

**Stevenson, John Hall–.** *Orig.* **John Hall.** 1718–1785. English poetaster; friend and imitator of Laurence Sterne. Assumed wife's surname (c. 1738); inherited from maternal aunt the dilapidated Skelton Castle, Yorkshire, in which, as "Crazy Castle," he formed a club of "demoniacks" and entertained Sterne. Author of *Crazy Tales* (1762), and political pamphlets in verse; also of a continuation of *A Sentimental Journey* (1769). The original of Eugenius in *Tristram Shandy*.

**Stevenson, Robert.** 1772–1850. Scottish civil engineer, b. Glasgow; designed and built lighthouses (1797–1843), inventing intermittent and flashing lights; invented the hydrophore; author of *Account of the Bell Rock Lighthouse* (1824). Three of his four sons were engineers: **Alan** (1807–1865) designed ten lighthouses, introducing prismatic rings. **David** (1815–1886) executed works for improvement of rivers in Scotland and northern England, and constructed beacons and lighthouses, introducing use of paraffin (1870) and aseismatic arrangement. **Thomas** (1818–1887) invented azimuthal condensing system; devised Stevenson screen for thermometers (1864) and made other meteorological contributions; m. Margaret Isabella, daughter of Rev. James Balfour; father of Robert Louis Stevenson (*q.v.*).

**Stevenson, Robert Louis Balfour.** *Known in literary connections as* **R. L. S.** 1850–1894. Scottish essayist, novelist, and poet, b. Edinburgh; grandson of Robert Stevenson (*q.v.*). Frail in health from infancy and victim of gastric fever (1858). Began study for family profession of civil engineering, but later turned to letters, and made study of literary style; contributed essays to *Cornhill Magazine* and other periodicals; described canoe trip in France and Belgium (1876) in *An Inland Voyage* (1878) and foot journey in *Travels with a Donkey in the Cévennes* (1879). Traveled (1879) as steerage passenger across Atlantic and on immigrant train across America to San Francisco to join Mrs. Osbourne, whom he had met at Fontainebleau (1876); m. Mrs. Osbourne (1880) and took her to mining camp, Calistoga, pictured in *The Silverado Squatters;* returned to Scotland. Produced series of essays and stories, including *Virginibus Puerisque* (1881), *New Arabian Nights* (1882), *Treasure Island* (1883), *A Child's Garden of Verses* (1885), *Prince Otto* (1885), *Dr. Jekyll and Mr. Hyde* (1886), *Kidnapped* (1886), *The Merry Men* (1887), *The Black Arrow* (1888). After death of father, Thomas Stevenson (1887), published lyric poems called *Underwoods* (1887) and left Scotland with wife, mother, and stepson for America; at Saranac Lake (winter 1887–88), wrote greater part of *Master of Ballantrae* and essays; expressed his attitude to life in *Pulvis et Umbra* (1888); set out from San Francisco on pleasure cruise to Marquesas Islands, Tahiti, Honolulu, leper colony Molokai, and Gilbert Islands, which terminated in voluntary exile at Samoa (from Christmas, 1889) lasting till his death, except for voyage to Sydney (1890), where he published *Father Damien: An Open Letter to the Rev. Dr. Hyde* (see Joseph DAMIEN DE VEUSTER); lived at Vailima, 500 feet above the sea; acknowledged by Samoans as chief with name **Tu′si·ta′la** (tōō′sē·tä′lä) ["teller of tales"], temporarily recovered health; wrote three Pacific tales, *Island Nights' Entertainments* (1893), and romances of Scottish life, including *Catriona* (1893); began *The Justice Clerk*, afterwards called *Weir of Hermiston* (unfinished), and *St. Ives* (completed by A. T. Quiller-Couch). Collaborated with W. E. Henley in several unsuccessful dramas; collaborated with wife in *The Dynamiter* (1885) and with his stepson Lloyd Osbourne in *The Wrong Box* (1889), *The Wrecker* (1892), and *The Ebb Tide* (1894). His *Vailima Letters* edited by Sidney Colvin (1895).

**Stevenson, Walter Clegg.** 1877–1931. British physician, b. in Calcutta; educ. Dublin U.; author of treatises on radium treatment and orthopedic surgery.

**Stevenson, William.** d. 1575. English clergyman and probable author of *Gammer Gurton's Needle*, early English comedy (acted 1566); prebendary of Durham (1561). See also John BRIDGES (d. 1618) and Bishop John STILL.

**Ste·vin′** (stē·vĭn′) *or* **Ste·vi′nus** (-vē′nŭs), **Simon.** 1548–1620. Dutch mathematician, b. Bruges; military and civil engineer under Maurice of Nassau; invented system of sluices as means of defense; enunciated theorem of the triangle of forces; discovered fact that downward pressure of a liquid is independent of shape of its container; introduced decimal fractions into common use.

**Stew′ard·son** (stū′ẽrd·s'n), **John.** 1858–1896. American architect; in partnership with Walter Cope in Philadelphia (1886–96); firm designed buildings for U. of Pennsylvania, Bryn Mawr, and Princeton.

**Stew'art** (stū'ẽrt). See also STUART.

**Stewart,** Scottish and English royal house. See STUART.

**Stew'art** *or* **Stu'art** *or* **Steu'art** (stū'ẽrt). Surname of a family descended from a Breton immigrant to Norfolk, **Alan Fitzflaald** (d. 1114?), and a daughter of a Domesday baron, which inherited the Scottish and ultimately the English throne. Alan's elder son, **William**, was ancestor of earls of Arundel. **Walter Stewart** (d. 1177), Alan's younger son, went to Scotland, where he received from David I lands in Renfrew, including Paisley, and the hereditary dignity of high steward or seneschal of Scotland, whence the surname *Stewart* (modified by some branches to *Steuart* or to French form *Stuart*) took origin in reign (1153–65) of Malcolm IV. His grandson **Walter** (d. 1246), 3d steward, was appointed justiciary of Scotland by Alexander II. **Alexander** (1214–1283), 4th steward, inherited by marriage isles of Bute and Arran and led Scots against Haakon IV of Norway at Largs (1263). **James** (1243–1309), 5th steward, distinguished himself in wars of Wallace and of Bruce; compelled by Edward I of England to swear fealty on the Black Rood; one of regents (1285). **Walter** (1293–1326), 6th steward, was joint commander with Sir James Douglas of left wing at battle of Bannockburn (1314); by marriage (1315) with Marjory, daughter of Robert the Bruce, brought Scottish crown to family, his son **Robert** (1316–1390), 7th steward, ascending throne (1371) as Robert II (*q.v.*) and his grandson **John**, Lord of Kyle, known as Earl of Carrick, succeeding as Robert III (*q.v.*). Robert II's younger son by Elizabeth Mure, **Alexander** (1343?–?1405), Earl of **Buch'an** [bŭk'ăn; *Scot.* bŭk'ăn] (by marriage) and Lord of **Bad'e·noch** (băd'ĕ·nŏk), on being censured by bishops of Moray and Ross for deserting his wife, burned Forres and Elgin (1390); excommunicated; called "the Wolf of Badenoch." An illegitimate son of his, **Alexander Stewart** (1375?–1435), Earl of **Mar** (mär), forced Isabel, Countess of Mar, after murdering her husband, to marry him and make him heir to Douglas estates; ambassador to England (1406–07); warden of marches (1424). A great-grandson of another illegitimate son of earl of Buchan was **William Stewart** (1481?–?1550), chronicler and versifier, who produced metrical translation of Hector Boece's *Historia Scotorum* at request of James V.

DUKES OF AL'BA·NY (ôl'bȧ·nĭ), BARONS A'VAN·DALE (ā'văn·dāl; ăv'ăn-) AND O'CHIL·TREE (ō'kĭl·trē; ō'kĭl-; ŏ'kĭl; ŏ'kĭl-), AND EARLS OF AR'RAN (ăr'ăn):

**Robert Stewart** (1340?–1420), 1st Duke of Albany; 3d son of Robert II; hostage in England (1360); hereditary governor of Stirling (1373); chamberlain of Scotland (1382–1407); led invasion of England (1388); governor of Scotland because of physical disability of brother Robert III (1389–99); plotted to gain throne of Scotland; defeated by English (1402); probably made away with David Stewart, Duke of Rothesay (see under ROBERT III of Scotland); regent of Scotland on capture of Prince James and death of Robert III (1406); prosecuted war with England; crushed revolt of Donald MacDonald, second lord of the isles (1411).

**Alexander** (1454?–1485), Duke of Albany and Earl of March (märch); 2d son of James II of Scotland; received lordship of Isle of Man; high admiral of Scotland; warden of the marches; governor of Berwick; lieutenant of Scotland (1472); having pretensions to throne, intrigued with Edward IV of England, surrendered Berwick, and attempted to seize his brother James III (1482); after death of Edward IV, indicted and outlawed (1483).

**John** (1481–1536), Duke of Albany; only son of Alexander Stewart (1454?–1485) by his second wife; brought up in France; inaugurated regent of Scotland (1515); declared heir to throne (1516); negotiated at Rouen (1517) treaty with France against England; on return found disorder caused by rivalry between Angus and Arran; reconciled himself with Margaret Tudor, queen dowager, and aided her to obtain divorce from Angus (see under DOUGLAS family); accused by Henry VIII and Wolsey of ambition to marry queen dowager; attempted to invade England with large army, but on refusal of Scots to fight outside Scotland, returned to France (1522); made final fruitless attempt to storm Wark with French troops (1523); dismissed from regency on declaration of James V as king (1524); negotiated marriages of Henry, Duke of Orleans, with Catherine de Médicis (1533), and of James V.

**Andrew** (d. 1488), 1st Baron Avandale; great-grandson of Robert, 1st Duke of Albany; chancellor of Scotland (1460–82); obtained cession of Orkney and Shetland from Denmark; ambassador to France (1484); succeeded by two nephews, the second created (1543) Baron Ochiltree.

**Andrew** (fl. 1548–1598), 2d Baron Ochiltree; son of 1st baron; accompanied Knox to Holyrood (1563); took part in Moray's uprising against Mary on her marriage to Darnley (1565) and in conspiracy against Rizzio; member of Morton's privy council (1578).

**James Stewart** of Both'well·muir' [bŏth'wĕl·mūr'; bŏth'-] (d. 1596), Earl of Arran; second son of 2d Baron Ochiltree; served as soldier of fortune against Spanish in Low Countries; on behalf of Esmé Stuart, 1st Duke of Lennox, accused James Douglas, 4th Earl of Morton, of murder of Darnley (1580); became privy councilor (1581); recognized as head of the Hamiltons and earl of Arran in place of his cousin James Hamilton, 3d earl, pronounced insane; rival of Lennox; by his action toward the Kirk in Montgomerie case caused Ruthven raid (1582), but after James VI's escape from Protestant lords, gained influence over him, obtained custody of Stirling and Edinburgh castles, and became lord chancellor (1584); alienated supporters by use of power; undermined in his negotiations with English by his agent; himself banished (1586) on return of banished lords; on return as Captain James Stewart, murdered in revenge by nephew of Morton.

EARLS AND DUKES OF LEN'NOX (lĕn'ŭks); Stewarts of Darnley, Lennox, and Aubigny, springing from marriage of Sir John Stewart, 2d son of Alexander (1214–1283), 4th steward, with heiress of Bonkil, through their son Sir Alan of Dreghorn, and including:

Sir **John Stewart** *or* **Stuart** of Darn'ley [därn'lĭ] (1365?–1429), Seigneur of Au'bi'gny' (ō'bē'nyē'); one of commanders in defeat of English at Beaugé (1421); married Elizabeth, daughter of Duncan, Earl of Lennox. His grandson Sir **John** (d. 1495), Lord Darnley, 1st Earl of Lennox (of Stewart line); joined conspiracy of 1482 against James III; headed rising in favor of James IV but surprised and defeated at Tallymoss (1488); allowed by agreement with two rival claimants to retain earldom, his by no new creation and by no legal decision; his eldest son, **Matthew Stewart,** 2d earl, was slain at Flodden while commanding Scottish right wing (1513).

**Matthew Stewart** (1516–1571), 4th Earl of Lennox; grandson of 2d earl and heir male of Stuarts of Scotland at death of James V; keeper of Dumbarton Castle (1531); returned from France as rival claimant to James Hamilton, 2d Earl of Arran (1543); seized Mary of Guise, queen dowager, and Princess Mary at Edinburgh in fruitless attempt at marriage with Mary of Guise (1543); after treasonable negotiations with Henry VIII, joined

English party, surrendered Dumbarton and Bute, won hand of Lady Margaret Douglas (*q.v.*), niece of Henry VIII, and became governor of Scotland (1544); outlawed in Scotland (1545); returned to Scotland, restored to title and lands (1564); arranged marriage (1565) between his eldest son, Henry Stewart, Lord Darnley (see DARNLEY) and Mary, Queen of Scots (*q.v.*); after Darnley's murder, took part in imprisonment of Mary at Loch Leven; provisional regent in behalf of his infant grandson, afterward James VI; confirmed in regency (1570) after assassination of Lord James Stewart, Earl of Moray; fought against queen's supporters, Huntly and the Hamiltons; captured at Stirling; mortally wounded in skirmish. His second son, **Charles**, succeeded as earl of Lennox. Charles's daughter Lady **Arabella Stuart** (1575–1615) was first cousin of James VI of Scotland and next in succession to him to both Scottish and English thrones after Queen Elizabeth; center of intrigues aimed at eliminating James VI as Elizabeth's successor; closely guarded because of Elizabeth's suspicion, made ineffectual attempts to escape in order to marry successive suitors; secretly married (1610) William Seymour (see SEYMOUR family), also of royal descent, younger brother of Edward Seymour, heir to throne after Queen Elizabeth by Henry VIII's will; imprisoned, died insane in Tower.

**Esmé Stuart** *or* **Stewart** (1542?–1583), 6th Seigneur of Aubigny and 1st Duke of Lennox; nephew of Matthew, 4th Earl of Lennox; sent to Scotland as agent of Guises to restore Roman Catholicism; became favorite of James VI, by whom he was made earl of Darnley and (1581) duke of Lennox; secured condemnation of James Douglas, 4th Earl of Morton, for murder of Darnley; expelled from Scotland for plotting invasion of England by a Spanish army (1582). His son **Ludovick Stuart** (1574–1624), 2d Duke of Lennox and Duke of Rich′mond (rĭch′mŭnd), was naturalized in England on accession of James VI and made privy councilor; steward of the household (1616). The latter's nephew **James Stuart** (1612–1655), 4th Duke of Lennox and Duke of Richmond, supplied Charles I with large sums of money during the Civil War; warden of Cinque Ports (1640).

**Charles Stuart** (1639–1672), 6th Duke of Lennox, 3d Duke of Richmond, and 10th Seigneur of Aubigny; nephew of James, 4th Duke of Lennox; returned to England from France with Charles II. His wife (m. 1667) **Frances Teresa Stuart** *or* **Stewart** (1647–1702), Duchess of Richmond and Lennox, was a granddaughter of Walter Stewart or Stuart, 1st Lord **Blan·tyre′** (blăn·tīr′); remarkable beauty; known as **La Belle** (lȧ bĕl′) **Stuart**; maid of honor to Queen Catherine of Braganza; mistress of Charles II; the original of the figure of Britannia on reverse side of the halfpenny (1672) and on medals.

EARLS OF MOR′AY (mûr′ĭ) OR MURRAY:

**James Stewart** *or* **Stuart** (1499?–1544), Earl of Moray; natural son of James IV; guardian of James V and lieutenant general of French forces in Scotland; suppressed insurrection of isles (1531); member of council of state (1543).

Lord **James Stewart** *or* **Stuart** (1531?–1570), Earl of Mar and Earl of Moray; natural son of James V; half brother of Mary, Queen of Scots, whom he accompanied to France (1548) and whom he annoyed by joining the Reformers (1556); negotiated with Queen Elizabeth for help against French; with English help reoccupied Edinburgh (1560); dispatched (1561) by Scottish estates to France to invite Mary Stuart to return to her kingdom; on her arrival became virtually her home secretary, or prime minister, and tried to dissuade her from Romanizing Scotland; defeated Huntly for her; supported projected Spanish alliance for Mary; opposed Darnley match by appeal to arms and, lacking full Protestant support, had to seek asylum in England (1565); returned after assassination of Rizzio (1566), nominally reconciled to Mary; left for France immediately after Darnley's murder (1567); recalled as regent (1567) after Mary's abdication at Loch Leven; took no steps against principals in murder of Darnley; defeated Mary's forces at Langside (1568); proposed to Queen Elizabeth imprisonment of Mary in Scotland; secured peace in the realm; assassinated at Linlithgow by James Hamilton of Bothwellhaugh at instigation of Mary's adherents. **James Stewart** *or* **Stuart** (d. 1592), 2d Earl of Moray; son-in-law of the preceding; called "the bonny earl"; slain by Huntly's men on James VI's warrant, perhaps because of his favor with the queen, and long left unburied, as related in popular ballads. See ***George Gordon***, 1st Marquis of Huntly, under GORDON family. His great-grandson **Alexander Stewart** (d. 1701), 5th Earl of Moray, was Scottish secretary of state (1680–88).

EARLS OF ORK′NEY (ôrk′nĭ):

Lord **Robert Stewart** (d. 1592), Earl of Orkney; natural son of James V; half brother of regent Moray. Abbot of Holyrood (1539); joined lords of the congregation; had knowledge of plot against Darnley and said to have warned him; imprisoned by Morton on charge of offering Orkney Islands to Denmark (1575); one of chief conspirers bringing about Morton's ruin (1580–81). His son **Patrick** (d. 1614), 2d Earl of Orkney, virtual independent sovereign of the Orkneys and Zetland, was deprived of justiciarship and imprisoned on charge of tyranny and cruelty.

EARLS OF ATH′OLL (ăth′ŭl):

Sir **John Stewart** of Balveny (1440?–1512), 1st Earl of Atholl (of a new Stewart line); son of Sir James Stewart, the black knight of Lorne; a descendant of Alexander, 4th steward (see above); aided in subjugation of Angus of the Isles (1480); one of James III's generals (1488).

**John** (d. 1578), 4th Earl of Atholl; great-grandson of 1st earl; at first supported Protestant party in adhering to movement in favor of Queen Elizabeth's marriage to Arran, but soon after joined with Huntly in attempt to seize Edinburgh for papists; member of Queen Mary's first council (1561), at first in harmony with Lord James Stewart (afterward regent Moray); leader of Scottish Catholic nobles after fall of Huntly; Mary's chief counselor after Darnley marriage, but not connected with Rizzio's or Darnley's murder; said to have been witness of opening of Casket Letters; member of council of regency during Moray's absence (1567); after Moray's assassination (1570) joined league against James VI's party and supported Mary's restoration; joined (1578) Argyll against Morton and became chancellor; reconciled with Morton through English mediation; died under suspicion of poison.

EARLS AND MARQUISES OF BUTE (būt):

**John Stuart** (1713–1792), 3d Earl of Bute; Scottish favorite of George III and British prime minister; grandson of Sir James Stuart (d. 1710), 1st Earl of Bute, who was descended from a natural son of one of the Stuart kings; lived retired life; student of agriculture, botany, and architecture; m. daughter of Lady Mary Wortley Montague; gained favor of Frederick Louis, Prince of Wales, through chance meeting (1747); as privy councilor and groom of the stole inculcated in George III Bolingbroke's doctrine of absolute monarchy; prime minister (May, 1762), after ejection of Pitt; aroused increased popular hostility by negotiation for peace and Treaty of Paris (1763) and by cider tax; resigned (April, 1763); failing in intrigue against Grenville, forced to withdraw from court (1765); voted against repeal of Stamp Act (1766); devoted himself to scientific pursuits, esp. botany, and patronage of arts; gave Dr. Johnson a pension of £300 a year. **John Patrick Crich'ton–Stuart** [krī't'n-] (1847–1900), 3d Marquis of Bute; fourth descendant of 3d earl; educ. Christ Church, Oxford; renounced Presbyterianism and entered Roman Catholic Church (1868); became president of University College, Cardiff; lord lieutenant of county of Bute (1892); author of a translation of Roman Catholic breviary (1879). **James Archibald Stuart–Wort'ley–Mac·ken'zie** [-wûrt'lĭ·mȧ·kĕn'zĭ] (1776–1845), 1st Baron Wharn'cliffe (hwôrn'klĭf); grandson of 3d earl of Bute; nephew of 1st marquis of Bute; dropped in time second of two surnames assumed by his father on succeeding to estates in Yorkshire and in Scotland; served in army (1790–1801); Tory M.P. (1797); advocated freeing of wool from export duties, opposed further protection to agriculture, and advocated amendment of corn laws; supported Catholic emancipation; opposing parliamentary reform, sought to effect compromise (1831–32); lord privy seal in Peel's ministry (1834) and president of council (1841). His youngest son, **James Archibald Stuart–Wortley** (1805–1881), became solicitor general under Lord Palmerston (1856–57). Lady **Emmeline Charlotte Elizabeth Stuart–Wortley** (1806–1855), daughter of 5th duke of Rutland and wife of 1st baron's second son, published volumes of poems, some relating her travels, some sonnets; edited *Keepsake* (1837, 1840).

**Stewart, Alexander Turney.** 1803–1876. Merchant, b. in Lisburn, Ireland; to U.S. (c. 1820) and settled in New York. Opened small dry-goods store (1823), which developed into great retail store of A. T. Stewart & Co. See John WANAMAKER.

**Stewart, Alfred Walter.** 1880–1947. Irish chemist, and writer (under pseudonym **John Jervis Con'ning·ton** [kŏn'ĭng·tŭn]) of detective fiction; professor of chemistry, Queen's U., Belfast. Author of *Stereochemistry*, *Recent Advances in Physical and Inorganic Chemistry*, etc.; also of *Dangerfield Talisman*, *Murder in the Maze*, etc.

**Stewart** *or* **Steuart, Archibald James Edward.** See *Marquises and Duke of Douglas and Barons Douglas of Douglas*, under DOUGLAS family.

**Stewart, Balfour.** 1828–1887. Scottish physicist and meteorologist; director of Kew observatory (1859–71); professor of natural philosophy, Owens Coll., Manchester (1870–87). His researches on radiant heat contributed to foundation of spectrum analysis; turned to meteorology, making special study of terrestrial magnetism; investigated sunspots. Author of *The Unseen Universe* (1875; with Peter Guthrie Tait) and works on physics and sunspots.

**Stewart, Charles.** 1778–1869. American naval officer, b. Philadelphia; commanded schooner *Experiment* (1800) and captured two French privateers; commanded brig *Siren* in war against Tripolitan pirates (1804). In War of 1812, commanded the *Constitution*, preying on British commerce (1813–14) and capturing two British warships, *Cyane* and *Levant* (1815). Created senior flag officer by act of congress (1859); commissioned rear admiral on the retired list (1862).

**Stewart, Charles William.** See under Robert STEWART.

**Stewart,** Sir **Donald Martin.** 1824–1900. British field marshal, b. in Elginshire, Scotland; entered Bengal army (1840); commanded Abyssinian expedition (1867–68); commanded Kandahar field force in Afghan War (1878); sent Roberts on famous march from Kabul to Kandahar while he himself led rest of army through Khyber Pass to India; commander in chief in India (1880–85); field marshal (1894).

**Stewart, Donald Ogden.** 1894– . American writer and actor, b. Columbus, Ohio; served in U.S. navy during World War (1917–19). On stage, in Philip Barry's play, *Holiday* (1929), and in his own play, *Rebound* (1930). Author of *A Parody Outline of History* (1921), *Perfect Behavior* (1922), *Mr. and Mrs. Haddock Abroad* (1924), *Mr. and Mrs. Haddock in Paris, France* (1926), *Father William* (1929), etc.

**Stewart, Dugald.** 1753–1828. Scottish philosopher, son of **Matthew Stewart** (1717–1785; Edinburgh professor of mathematics, 1747–85; author of *Tracts, Physical and Mathematical*, 1761). Professor of moral philosophy, Edinburgh (1785–1820; inactive from 1809). One of the Scottish school, holding doctrine of natural realism, professed the Baconian empirical method, but disavowed its developments and retained intuitionism. Author of *Elements of the Philosophy of the Human Mind* (3 vols., 1792, 1814, 1827) and *The Philosophy of the Active and Moral Powers* (1828).

**Stewart, George Neil.** 1860–1930. Physiologist, b. London, Ontario; head of laboratory of experimental medicine, Western Reserve U. (1907–30). Invented calorimetric method of measuring blood flow; investigated epinephrine output of adrenal glands; established efficacy of extracts of adrenal cortex.

**Stewart,** Sir **Herbert.** 1843–1885. English soldier; took possession of Cairo after Tell el-Kebir (1882); commanded cavalry at Suakin (1884); on expedition for relief of Khartoum, led relief column sent across desert of Metemma and repulsed Arabian attack near Abuklea; three days later, mortally wounded; made major general on deathbed.

**Stewart, Herbert Leslie.** 1882–1953. Canadian philosopher; professor, Dalhousie U., Halifax (from 1913). Author of *Nietzsche and the Ideals of Modern Germany* (1915), *Modernism Past and Recent* (1932), *From a Library Window* (1941), etc.

**Stewart,** Sir **James Pur'ves–** (pûr'vĕs [-vĭs]-). 1869–1949. Scottish neurologist; author of *Diagnosis of Nervous Diseases* (trans. into French, Spanish, German, and Arabic), *Intracranial Tumours* (trans. into Russian), *Healing of Nerves* (with Sir C. Ballance), *Sands of Time* (1939), etc.

**Stewart, John.** 1749–1822. British traveler, known as "Walking Stewart," b. London, of Scottish parents. General in Haidar Ali's army; in service of nabob of Arcot, rose to position of prime minister. Traveled into interior of India, through Persia, Ethiopia, crossed desert of Arabia, walked through France and Spain (1783); walked from Calais to Vienna (1784); in North America (1791).

**Stewart, John Aikman.** 1822–1926. American banker, b. New York City; originator and organizer of United States Trust Co. (1853); its secretary (1853–64), president (1864–1902), and chairman of its board of trustees (1902–26). Trustee of Princeton U. (1868–1926) and president pro tempore (1910–12).

**Stewart, John Alexander.** 1846–1933. British philosopher; professor, Oxford. Author of *Notes on the Nicomachean Ethics of Aristotle* (2 vols., 1892), *Plato's Doctrine of Ideas* (1909), *Platonism in English Poetry, in English Literature and the Classics* (1912), etc.

**Stewart, Philo Penfield.** 1798–1868. American missionary, b. Sherman, Conn.; joined John J. Shipherd in Elyria, Ohio (1832), and with him founded Oberlin College (opened 1833), about nine miles from Elyria. Invented Oberlin cookstove.

**Stewart, Potter,** 1915– . American lawyer; b. Jackson, Mich.; assoc. justice, U.S. Supreme Court (from 1958).

**Stewart, Robert.** 2d Marquis of **Lon′don·der′ry** (lŭn′dŭn·dĕr′ĭ; -dĕr·ĭ; -drĭ). *Known generally as* Viscount **Cas′tle·reagh** (kȧs′'l·rā). 1769–1822. English statesman, eldest son of **Robert Stewart** (1739–1821; Ulster proprietor who was created Viscount Castlereagh 1795, and marquis of Londonderry 1816); educ. Cambridge. Member of Irish Parliament (1790); keeper of Irish privy seal (1797–98); chief secretary for Ireland (1799–1801), responsible for passage through Irish Parliament (1800) of Pitt's measure for immediate union; resigned on George III's refusal to allow introduction of Irish Catholic emancipation bill (1801). President of East India board of control at Pitt's request (1802); appointed also war secretary by Pitt (1805–06, 1807–09); responsible for Elbe expedition (1805); seized Danish fleet, extended war to Iberian Peninsula, selected Wellesley as general; made scapegoat of failure of Walcheren expedition; challenged his rival Canning to duel, wounded him slightly (1809). As foreign secretary and leader of House of Commons (1812–22), led coalition against Napoleon; prevented allies from treating separately with France; by threat of withdrawal of British subsidy, forced Bernadotte to send re-enforcements to Blücher, whereupon battle of Laon was won (1814). As British representative at Congress of Vienna (1814), thwarted ambitions of Russia in Poland and Prussia in Saxony by secret treaties with France and Austria; after Waterloo, secured Napoleon's removal to St. Helena and settled terms of confinement; in opposition to Metternich, restrained allies from retaliation on France and minimized penalties exacted (1815). Defeated in House of Commons on income tax (1816); vainly opposed resumption of cash payment by Bank of England (1819); blamed for Six Acts (1819) impairing civil liberties; opposed Metternich's policy of intervention by Continental powers in revolutionary movement in Spain; in dread of Russian attack upon Turkey (1821), forced by Greek insurrection to co-operate with Metternich; wrote instructions to himself for conference at Verona (1822), which were carried out by Canning. Mentally disordered by overwork and responsibility; cut his own throat; buried in Westminster Abbey.

His half brother **Charles William Stewart** *afterward* **Vane** [vān] (1778–1854), 3d Marquis of Londonderry, soldier and diplomat; served in Netherlands (1794), on Rhine and Danube (1795), in Irish rebellion (1798), in Holland (1799); undersecretary for war (1807); cavalry commander (1808), adjutant general to Wellington in Iberian Peninsula until invalided home (1811); British minister to Berlin, seconding his brother's diplomacy; ambassador in Vienna (1814); took surname Vane in place of Stewart on second marriage (1819) to heiress of Sir Harry Vane-Tempest.

**Stewart, William Downie.** 1878–1949. New Zealand publicist and political leader, b. Dunedin; member of New Zealand Parliament (1914–35); minister of internal affairs (1921–24), of customs (1921–28), of industries and commerce (1923–26); attorney general of New Zealand (1926); minister of finance (1926–28; 1931–33); resigned from ministry (1933). Author of *State Socialism in New Zealand* (with J. E. Le Rossignol; 1910), etc.

**Stewart, William Morris.** 1827–1909. American lawyer and legislator; to California in gold rush; in law partnership with Henry S. Foote in San Francisco (1854). To Nevada (1859) and practiced in Virginia City and Carson City; specialist in mining law; U.S. senator from Nevada (1864–75; 1887–1905); author (1869) of the 15th amendment to the Constitution in the form in which it was finally adopted; vigorous advocate of remonetization of silver (1888–1900).

**Stewart, William Rhinelander.** 1852–1929. American financier and philanthropist; member, New York State Board of Charities (1882–1929), and president of the board (1894–1903; 1907–23); member of committee of seventy (1894) opposed to Tammany Hall and working for election of reform administration in New York City. Organized New York State Conference of Charities and Corrections (1900) and a similar conference for New York City (1910).

**Stewart–Murray.** Family name of dukes of ATHOLL.

**Steyn** (stān), **Martinus Theunis.** 1857–1916. South African lawyer and statesman, b. Winburg, Orange River Colony; practiced in Bloemfontein (1883–89). Second puisne judge (1889–93), first puisne judge (1893–96). President of Orange Free State (1896–1900); negotiated union of Orange Free State with the Transvaal in war against Great Britain (1899); representative at peace conference (1902).

**Stick′ney** (stĭk′nĭ), **Trumbull.** 1874–1904. American poet; author of *Dramatic Verses* (1902) and *The Poems of Trumbull Stickney* (1905).

**Stie′gel** (stē′gĕl; *Ger.* shtē′-), **Henry William.** 1729–1785. Jocularly spoken of as "Baron von Stiegel." Glassmaker, b. near Cologne, Ger.; to America (1750); became British subject (1760). Employed in iron foundry in Lancaster County, Pa. (1751); with partners, bought the foundry (1758); founded town of Manheim (1762) in Lancaster County. Brought glassmakers from England and established glass factory at Manheim (1764–65). Collections of Stiegel glassware are in Metropolitan Museum of Art, N.Y., and Pennsylvania Museum of Art, Philadelphia.

**Stieg′litz** (stēg′lĭts), **Alfred.** 1864–1946. American photographer and editor, b. Hoboken, N.J.; photoengraver in New York, esp. interested in experiments with three-color work (1890–93); editor, *American Amateur Photographer* (1892–96); founder and editor, *Camera Notes* (1897–1903); editor and publisher, *Camera Work* (from 1903). See Georgia O'KEEFFE. His brother **Julius Oscar** (1867–1937), b. Hoboken; educ. Germany (Ph.D., Berlin, 1889); taught chemistry at U. of Chicago (1892–1933; professor 1905–33; chairman of department 1915–33).

**Stie′ler** (shtē′lẽr), **Adolf.** 1775–1836. German cartographer, known for his *Handatlas* (1817–22) and a school atlas (1821).

**Stiern′hielm′** (shârn′yĕlm′), **Georg.** *Original name* **Georgius O·la′i′** (ōō·lä′ĭ′). 1598–1672. Swedish poet and scholar; known as "the Father of Swedish Poetry." Chief work, the epic *Hercules* (c. 1647).

**Stie′ve** (shtē′vĕ), **Friedrich.** 1884– . German diplomat and writer; director, cultural department, German foreign office (from 1933). Author of *Gedichte* (1908), *Deutschland und Europa* (1926), *Geschichte des Deutschen Volkes* (1934), *Vom Volksstumm zum Volksstaat* (1937).

**Sti′fel** (shtē′fĕl), **Michael.** *Also* **Sty′fel** (shtē′fĕl) *or* **Stief′fel** (shtē′fĕl). 1487–1567. German mathematician; Augustinian monk converted to Protestantism (1523) through Luther's influence; professor, Jena (from 1559); regarded as first German authority on the theory of numbers.

**Stig′and** (stĭg′ănd). d. 1072. English prelate; chaplain to Canute; chief adviser to Queen Emma after death of Canute; bishop of Elmham (1038; consecrated 1043) and Winchester (1047); supported Earl Godwin against Edward the Confessor, and arranged peace between them (1052); appointed archbishop of Canterbury (1052), but unrecognized by popes except briefly by Benedict X; submitted to William I (1066); deposed by papal legates and imprisoned till death for usurpation and plurality.

**Stigl′may′er** *or* **Stigl′mai′er** (shtē′g'l·mī′ēr), **Johann Baptist.** 1791–1844. German founder; head of a bronze foundry in Munich (1824).

**Stiles** (stīlz), **Charles War·dell′** (wôr·dĕl′). 1867–1941. American medical zoologist; professor of zoology (1902–30) and medical director (1930–31), U.S. Public Health Service; also, lecturer on medical zoology, Johns Hopkins (1897–1937); scientific secretary, Rockefeller Commission for Eradication of Hookworm Disease (1909–14). Author of *Trichinosis in Germany* (1901), *Report on Hookworm Disease (Uncinariasis) in the United States* (1903), *Key-Catalogue of the Protozoa, Worms, Crustacea, Arachnoids, and Insects of Man, Primates, Chiroptera, Insectivora, Carnivora* (1925–32), etc.

**Stiles, Ezra.** 1727–1795. American clergyman and scholar, b. North Haven, Conn.; pastor of Second Congregational Church, Newport, R.I. (1755–76 actively; 1776–86 in absentia); president, Yale (1778–95); also, professor of ecclesiastical history, and gave instruction in Hebrew, theology, and the sciences.

**Stiles, Henry Reed.** 1832–1909. American physician and historian, b. New York City; proprietor and manager of sanitarium on Lake George, in New York State (1888–1909). Interested himself in antiquarian research; published *The History of Ancient Windsor, Connecticut* (1859), *A History of the City of Brooklyn* (3 vols., 1867–70), *The Stiles Family in America...*(1895), *The History of Ancient Wethersfield, Connecticut* (2 vols., 1904), *Joutel's Journal of La Salle's Last Voyage, 1686–87* (1906).

**Stil′i·cho** (stĭl′ĭ·kō), **Flavius.** 359?–408 A.D. Roman general and statesman; son of Vandal chieftain in Roman service; commander in chief of army under Emperor Theodosius; guardian and chief minister of Honorius. Repelled Alaric (403 A.D.) and defeated barbarian armies under Radagaisus (405 or 406). Suspected of being involved in conspiracy against Honorius; abandoned by own troops and executed by order of Honorius.

**Still** (stĭl), **Andrew Taylor.** 1828–1917. Founder of osteopathy, b. Jonesboro, Va.; moved to Kansas (1853); busied with farming, doctoring Indians, and studying anatomy. Lost three children in epidemic of spinal meningitis (1864); soon thereafter devised the treatment known as osteopathy. Moved to Kirksville, Mo. (1875) and developed large practice. Incorporated American School of Osteopathy, Kirksville, Mo. (1894), and founded *Journal of Osteopathy.*

**Still,** Sir **George Frederic.** 1868–1941. English pediatrician; author of works on diseases of children. Still's disease, a variety of polyarthritis affecting children, is named after him.

**Still, John.** 1543?–1608. English prelate; master of St. John's Coll. (1574–77), of Trinity (1577–1608), Cambridge; bishop of Bath and Wells (1593–1608). Advanced by Isaac Reed, on inconclusive evidence, as author of *Gammer Gurton's Needle,* early English comedy (see also William STEVENSON and John BRIDGES, d. 1618).

**Stil·lé′** (stĭ·lē′), **Alfred.** 1813–1900. American physician; practiced in Philadelphia; professor, U. of Pennsylvania (1864–83). Author of *Elements of General Pathology* (1848), *Therapeutics and Materia Medica* (1860), *National Dispensatory* (with John M. Maisch, 1879). A founder and first secretary, American Medical Association, and its president (1871). His brother **Charles Janeway** (1819–1899) was professor of English literature and belles lettres, U. of Pennsylvania (1866–81) and provost of the university (1868–80); author of *How a Free People Conduct a Long War* (1862), *Studies in Mediaeval History* (1882), *The Life and Times of John Dickinson* (1891), *Major-General Anthony Wayne and the Pennsylvania Line* (1893).

**Stil′le** (shtĭl′ĕ), **Hans.** 1876– . German geologist.

**Stille, Karl.** Pseudonym of H. C. G. DEMME.

**Stilling, Heinrich.** See JUNG-STILLING.

**Stil′ling·fleet′** (stĭl′ĭng·flēt′), **Edward.** 1635–1699. English prelate; rector of Sutton, Bedfordshire; wrote *Irenicum* (1659), suggesting compromise in struggle between Episcopacy and Presbyterianism; received rapid promotion after writing *Origines Sacrae* (1662) and a defense of Church of England against charge of schism (1664); chaplain to Charles II (1667), canon of Canterbury (1669), archdeacon of London (1677), dean of St. Paul's, London (1678), bishop of Worcester (1689–99); engaged in ceaseless controversy with Nonconformists, Romanists, Deists, and Socinians; reported historical investigation of antiquities of British church in *Origines Britannicae* (1685); resisted proposed Declaration of Indulgence (1688); had controversy with Locke on the Trinity (1696–97).

His grandson **Benjamin Stillingfleet** (1702–1771), botanist after whom euphorbiaceous genus *Stillingia* was named, explored Mer-de-Glace, Chamonix (1741); popular conversationalist at assemblies of Mrs. Agmondesham Vesey at Bath, always wearing blue stockings and thus originating term *bluestocking* applied to a woman affecting literary taste and learning (c. 1748); first to propose English names for grasses; in preface of one of his works, introduced Linnaean principles into England (1759).

**Still′man** (stĭl′măn), **James.** 1850–1918. American financier; associate and friend of William Rockefeller (from 1884); president, National City Bank (1891–1909); allied with Standard Oil group of financiers, and later with E. H. Harriman.

**Stillman, William James.** 1828–1901. American artist and journalist; studio in New York; art critic for New York *Evening Post;* U.S. consul at Rome, Italy (1862–65) and Crete (1865–68); special correspondent of London *Times* in Herzegovina, Montenegro, Albania, and Italy (1875–98).

**Still′well** (stĭl′wĕl; -wĕl), **Lewis Buckley.** 1863–1941. American electrical engineer, b. Scranton, Pa. Among projects with which he was concerned are electrification of elevated lines in New York City (1899–1906), of Hoosac Tunnel (1910–11), and of Holland Vehicular Tunnels (1924–27).

**Sti′lo** (stī′lō), **Lucius Aelius Praeconinus.** 154?–74 B.C. Roman philologist; teacher of Varro and Cicero. Only fragments of his works are extant.

**Stil′well** (stĭl′wĕl; -wĕl), **Joseph W.** 1883–1946. American army officer, b. Palatka, Fla. Grad. U.S.M.A., West Point (1904); served in World War (1917–18) in France; studied Chinese in China (1920–23; 1926–28; 1932–39); on mission to China (1942) lieutenant general; appointed by Chiang Kai-shek chief of staff in China war theater; in command of all American forces in China-Burma-India theater (1942–44); general (1944); commander of U.S. Army ground forces (Jan.–June, 1945); commander of U.S. 10th Army in Pacific (1945–46).

**Stim′son** (stĭm′s'n), **Frederic Jesup.** *Pseudonym* **J. S. of Dale** (dāl). 1855–1943. American lawyer and writer; practiced law in Boston; professor, Harvard (1903–14). U.S. ambassador to Argentina (1914–21) and special ambassador to Brazil (1919). Author of several legal treatises and a number of novels, including *The Crime of Henry Vane* (1884), *Mrs. Knollys and Other Stories* (1894), *In Cure of Her Soul* (1906), also of works on U.S. constitution.

**Stimson, Henry Lewis.** 1867–1950. American statesman, b. New York City; practiced law in New York City; U.S. secretary of war (1911–13); colonel of field artillery with A.E.F. in France (1917–18); governor general, Philippine Islands (1927–29); U.S. secretary of state (1929–33), secretary of war (1940–45).

**Stimson, John Ward.** 1850–1930. American landscape painter and art teacher, b. Paterson, N.J.; founded (1888) and directed Artist-Artisan Institute in New York.

**Stine** (stīn), **Charles Milton Altland.** 1882–1954. American chemist, b. Norwich, Conn.; A.B. (1901), B.S. (1903), M.S. (1905), Gettysburg Coll.; with E. I. Du Pont de Nemours & Co. (from 1907); known for numerous patents including processes and products connected with propellant powder, high explosives, dyes, artificial leather, and paints.

**Stin'nes** (shtĭn'ĕs), **Matthias.** 1790–1845. German industrialist; built up a coal-mining and river-transportation business in the Ruhr region. His grandson **Hugo Stinnes** (1870–1924) was trained as a mining engineer and had two years' experience (1890–92) in the business established by Matthias; an advocate of "vertical trust" building, he founded a firm of his own in same region, which expanded to form Stinnes Combine and included control of river and ocean barges and steamers, coal and iron mines, factories, power plants, etc. in Europe and South America; during World War (1914–18), served as head of industrial production in Germany and occupied Belgium; organized (1920) the Rhine-Elbe Union (see E. KIRDORF); further expanded his interests to include timberlands, insurance companies, as well as paper-manufacturing plants and newspapers, in order to extend political influence; member of the Reichstag (1920–24).

**Stires** (stīrz), **Ernest Milmore.** 1866–1951. American Protestant Episcopal clergyman, b. Norfolk, Va.; rector of St. Thomas's Church in New York (1901–25); bishop of Long Island (1925).

**Stir'ling** (stûr'lĭng). (1) Earl of. See Sir William ALEXANDER (1567?–1640). (2) Lord. See William ALEXANDER (1726–1783).

**Stirling, James.** 1692–1770. Scottish mathematician, called "the Venetian." Studied mathematics at Venice (1715–25), where he discovered secret of Venetian glassmaking; friend of Newton; author of *Methodus Differentialis* (1730).

**Stirling, James Hutchison.** 1820–1909. Scottish philosopher; revealed Hegel to English readers in *The Secret of Hegel* (2 vols., 1865); attacked Sir William Hamilton's doctrine of perception (1865); sought to refute Huxley's theory of protoplasm (1869).

**Stirling, Yates.** 1843–1929. American naval officer; rear admiral (1902); commanded Philippine squadron (1903–04); commander in chief of U.S. fleet (1904–05); retired (1905). His son **Yates, Jr.** (1872–1948), also a naval officer, grad. U.S.N.A., Annapolis (1892); chief of staff of naval district of New York (1918–19); commanded battleship *Connecticut* (1919) and *New Mexico* (1922–24); promoted rear admiral (1926); chief of staff, U.S. fleet (1927); retired (1936).

**Stir'ling-Max'well** (-măks'wĕl; -wĕl), Sir **William.** 1818–1878. Scottish historical writer; assumed surname Maxwell on succeeding to baronetcy and estates of maternal uncle (1865). Rector of St. Andrews (1863) and Edinburgh (1871); chancellor of Glasgow (1875). Author of *Annals of the Artists of Spain* (1848) and the standard works *The Cloister Life of the Emperor Charles V* (1852) and *Don John of Austria* (1883). See Caroline NORTON.

**Stir'ner** (shtĭr'nẽr), **Max.** *Pseudonym of* **Kaspar Schmidt** (shmĭt). 1806–1856. German philosopher; author of *Der Einziger und sein Eigentum* (1845), expounding views of philosophical anarchists, and *Die Geschichte der Reaktion* (2 parts, 1852), and translations of Adam Smith's *Wealth of Nations* and J. B. Say's *Traité d'Économie Politique.*

**Sto·bae'us** (stô·bē'ŭs), **Joannes.** Greek anthologist, probably of late 5th century A.D.; compiled an anthology of extracts from more than 500 Greek authors.

**Sto'bo** (stō'bō), **Robert.** 1727–?1772. Soldier in America, b. in Glasgow, Scotland; served (captain) with George Washington at Fort Necessity (July 3, 1754); held as hostage by the French; escaped from Quebec down the St. Lawrence (1759); joined British at Louisburg; assisted Wolfe in attack on Quebec (1759), pointing out spot where Wolfe could land troops for climbing up to the Plains of Abraham. Captain in 15th regiment of foot (c. 1760), and served with it in Canada, West Indies, and England (to 1770). Has been used as prototype of fictional characters, as Robert Moray in Gilbert Parker's *The Seats of the Mighty*, and Lismahago in Smollett's *The Expedition of Humphry Clinker.*

**Stock** (stŏk), **Frederick Au'gust** (ô'gŭst). 1872–1942. Musical conductor, b. in Jülich, Ger.; to Chicago (1895); succeeded Theodore Thomas as director of Chicago Symphony Orchestra, then (1905) known as Theodore Thomas Orchestra; general music director, Century of Progress Exposition, Chicago (1933). Composer of a symphony, concerto, *March and Hymn to Democracy*, and a number of string quartets and songs.

**Stock'ard** (stŏk'ẽrd), **Charles Rupert.** 1879–1939. American biologist and anatomist; professor of anatomy (from 1911) and long head of department, Cornell U. Medical Coll. Investigated origin of the blood, relation between hormones and structural development, physical basis of personality, experimental production of monstrosities such as cyclopean monsters, influence of chemicals on embryonic development, regeneration and growth, the oestrous cycle, cancer, etc.

**Stöck'er** (shtûk'ẽr), **Adolf.** = Adolf STOECKER.

**Stock'mar** (*Ger.* shtŏk'mär; *Angl.* stŏk'-), Baron **Christian Friedrich von.** 1787–1863. Anglo-Belgian statesman, b. Coburg, of Swedish descent. Physician, then secretary, adviser, and political agent to Duke Leopold of Saxe-Coburg and continued as his confidential adviser when he became king of Belgians (from 1831); sent by Leopold (1837) as adviser to Queen Victoria; accompanied Prince Albert, afterwards prince consort, on tour of Italy (1838); unofficial counselor of Victoria and Albert, dividing time between England and the Continent (1840); representative of Ernest, Duke of Saxe-Coburg-Gotha, at Frankfurt Diet (1848).

**Stock'ton** (stŏk'tŭn), **Charles Herbert.** 1845–1924. American naval officer; rear admiral (1906); president, George Washington U. (1910–18); made special study of international law, and published *International Law: A Manual...* (1898), *Outlines of International Law* (1914), etc.

**Stockton, Frank R.**, *in full* **Francis Richard.** 1834–1902. American fiction writer, b. Philadelphia; wood engraver in Philadelphia and New York (1852–c. 66); assistant editor of *St. Nicholas* (1873–81); made first outstanding success with *Rudder Grange* (1879); among his noteworthy novels, mostly humorous, are *The Lady or the Tiger?* (a short story, 1882), *The Rudder Grangers Abroad* (1884), *The Casting Away of Mrs. Lecks and Mrs. Aleshine* (1886) and its sequel *The Dusantes* (1888), *The Squirrel Inn* (1891), *The Adventures of Captain Horn* (1895), *Mrs. Cliff's Yacht* (1896).

**Stockton, Richard.** 1730–1781. American lawyer, b. Princeton, N.J.; member of executive council of New

Jersey (1768–76); associate justice, New Jersey supreme court (1774–76); member of Continental Congress (1776) and a signer of the Declaration of Independence. His son **Richard** (1764–1828) was also a lawyer; U.S. senator (1796–99), and representative (1813–15). A son of this second Richard, **Robert Field** (1795–1866), was a naval officer; in command on Pacific coast of N. America (1845–47); co-operated with army in conquering California; prematurely proclaimed California a territory of United States (Aug. 17, 1846) and assumed title of governor and commander in chief; forced to retake parts of territory with aid of army under Stephen W. Kearny (*q.v.*), with whom he later quarreled over questions of authority; resigned from U.S. navy (1850); U.S. senator from New Jersey (1851–53). Robert Field Stockton's son **John Potter** (1826–1900) was a lawyer and politician; U.S. minister to the Papal States (1858–61); U.S. senator (1869–75); attorney general of New Jersey (1877–92).

**Stod'dard** (stŏd'ẽrd), **Amos.** 1762–1813. See Solomon STODDARD. American soldier; served in American Revolution (1779–83); practiced law in Hallowell, in District of Maine; commissioned captain (1798) and major (1807), U.S. army; appointed first civil and military commandant of Upper Louisiana (1804); in War of 1812, served in defense of Fort Meigs. Author of *Sketches... of Louisiana* (1812).

**Stoddard, Charles Warren.** 1843–1909. See Solomon STODDARD. American traveler and author, b. Rochester, N.Y.; moved to San Francisco (1855). Published poems in *Golden Era*, San Francisco, over pseudonym **Pip Pep'per·pod'** [pĭp pĕp'ẽr·pŏd'] (from 1861). Among his books are *South-Sea Idyls* (1873), *Mashallah!* (1881), *The Lepers of Molokai* (1885), *Hawaiian Life* (1894), *In the Footprints of the Padres* (1902), *The Island of Tranquil Delights* (1904), *The Dream Lady* (1907).

**Stoddard, Elizabeth Drew.** See under Richard Henry STODDARD.

**Stoddard, Frederick Lincoln.** 1861–1940. Mural painter, b. in Province of Quebec, Canada; studio in New York (1906–22) and Gloucester, Mass. (1922–40); designed murals for St. Louis City Hall, Memorial Church in Baltimore, Md.

**Stoddard, John Fair.** 1825–1873. See Solomon STODDARD. American educator, b. Greenfield, N.Y.; published *The American Intellectual Arithmetic* (1849), first of a series of his widely used textbooks in mathematics.

**Stoddard, John Lawson.** 1850–1931. See Solomon STODDARD. American traveler and author, b. Brookline, Mass.; traveled widely (from 1874) and made success as lecturer on travel subjects; published *Red-Letter Days Abroad* (1884), *Glimpses of the World* (1892), *John L. Stoddard's Lectures* (10 vols., 1897–98; 5 additional volumes, 1901); selected and edited *The Stoddard Library: A Thousand Hours of Entertainment with the World's Great Writers* (12 vols., 1910).

**Stoddard, John Tappan.** 1852–1919. See Solomon STODDARD. American chemist; head of chemistry department, Smith College (1897–1919); inaugurated technical laboratory training at Smith.

**Stoddard, Lothrop,** *in full* **Theodore Lothrop.** 1883–1950. American writer, b. Brookline, Mass.; author of *Present-Day Europe—Its National States of Mind* (1917), *The Rising Tide of Color Against White World-Supremacy* (1920), *The Revolt Against Civilization* (1922), *Racial Realities in Europe* (1924), *Scientific Humanism* (1926), *Europe and Our Money* (1932), *Clashing Tides of Color* (1935), etc.

**Stoddard, Richard Henry.** 1825–1903. American poet and literary critic, b. Hingham, Mass.; inspector of customs, New York City (1853–70); also, literary reviewer for New York *World* (1860–70); literary editor, New York *Mail and Express* (1880–1903). Collections of his verse are: *The Poems of Richard Henry Stoddard* (1880), *The Lion's Cub; With Other Verse* (1890). Among his poems the following are especially well known: *A Hymn to the Beautiful, A Household Dirge, Leonatus, The Burden of Unrest, Invocation to Sleep, Spring, Autumn, The Two Brides, The Dead Master* (a tribute to William Cullen Bryant), *Abraham Lincoln: An Horation Ode.* His wife, **Elizabeth Drew,** *nee* **Bar'stow** [bär'stō] (1823–1902), was a novelist and poet.

**Stoddard, Solomon.** 1643–1729. American Congregational clergyman, b. Boston; grad. Harvard (1662); first librarian of Harvard (1667–74); pastor in Northampton, Mass. (1672–1729); progenitor of Amos Stoddard, Charles Warren Stoddard, John Fair Stoddard, John Lawson Stoddard, John Tappan Stoddard. See also Jonathan EDWARDS.

**Stoddard, William Osborn.** 1835–1925. American journalist, b. Homer, N.Y.; coeditor, *Central Illinois Gazette* (1858); met and admired Abraham Lincoln; worked for his election in senatorial campaign of 1858; in columns of the *Gazette* proposed Lincoln for the presidency (1859); active on Lincoln's behalf in presidential campaign of 1860; private secretary to President Lincoln (1861–64); U.S. marshal of Arkansas (1864–66). Among his many books were *Abraham Lincoln* (1884), *Inside the White House in War Times* (1890), *The Table Talk of Lincoln* (1894), and more than 75 juveniles.

**Stod'dert** (stŏd'ẽrt), **Benjamin.** 1751–1813. American businessman and politician, b. in Charles County, Md.; served (captain) in Revolutionary War (1777–79); secretary to the board of war (1779–81); acted as confidential agent for the government in securing tracts of land on which the federal capital city was to be established; on creation of U.S. Navy Department (1798), became first U.S. secretary of the navy (1798–1801). See Richard S. EWELL.

**Stoeck'el** (stĕk'ĕl), **Carl.** 1858–1925. American music patron, b. New Haven, Conn.; settled in Norfolk, Conn. (from 1895); instrumental in organizing the Litchfield County Choral Union (1899), which gave annual music festivals at Norfolk (1899–1923), for which (from 1908) distinguished composers contributed original compositions.

**Stoeck'er** (shtûk'ẽr), **Adolf.** 1835–1909. German Protestant clergyman; court and cathedral preacher in Berlin (1874); dismissed as court pastor (1890) because of his Socialist party activities; a leader of the Christian Socialist party.

**Stoeller, Georg Wilhelm.** See STELLER.

**Stoessel.** = STÖSSEL (see STĔSEL).

**Stoes'sel** (stĕs''l), **Albert.** 1894–1943. American violinist and choral and symphony conductor; conductor, New York Oratorio Society (from 1921).

**Stoffels, Hendrickje.** See REMBRANDT.

**Sto'ja·di'no·vić** (stō'yä·dē'nô·vēt'y'; *Angl.* -vĭch), **Milan.** 1888– . Yugoslav statesman; prime minister and minister of foreign affairs (1935–39).

**Sto'ker** (stō'kẽr), **Bram.** 1847–1912. British writer, b. Dublin; business adviser and secretary to Sir Henry Irving (from 1878); wrote *Personal Reminiscences of Henry Irving* and several novels, including the mystery thriller *Dracula.*

**Stokes** (stōks), **Anson Phelps.** 1838–1913. American financier, b. New York City; in employ of Phelps, Dodge & Co., mercantile concern founded by his grandfather Anson Greene Phelps; partner in this concern (1861–79); successful in New York building construction and management concerns (The Woodbridge Co., organized 1895; Haynes Co., 1902); aided in founding Metropolitan Museum of Art, New York City. Two of his sisters, **Olivia Egleston Phelps** (1847–1927) and **Caroline Phelps** (1854–1909), were widely known for their philanthropies. A brother, **William Earl Dodge** (1852–1926), built and operated Hotel Ansonia, New York City (1906–26). A son of Anson Phelps Stokes, **Anson Phelps** (1874–1958), clergyman, was secretary of Yale U. (1899–1921); canon of Washington (D.C.) Cathedral (from 1924). Another son of Anson Phelps Stokes, **Isaac Newton Phelps** (1867–1944), architect, designed St. Paul's Chapel at Columbia U., Woodbridge Hall at Yale, Music School at Harvard, Title Guarantee and Trust building in New York, University Settlement in New York; author of *The Iconography of Manhattan Island* (6 vols., 1915–28). A third son, **Harold Phelps** (1887–1970), journalist, was on staff of New York *Evening Post* (1911–23) and its correspondent in Albany (1913–17), at Peace Conference in Paris (1919), in Washington (1919–23); secretary to Herbert Hoover (1924–26); on editorial staff of New York *Times* (since 1926); served overseas with A.E.F. in World War, and engaged in Oise-Aisne and Meuse-Argonne campaigns. A fourth son, **James Graham Phelps** (1872–1960), humanitarian and political scientist, joined Socialist party (1906); president of Intercollegiate Socialist Society (1907–18); member of national executive committee of Socialist party (1908); withdrew from Socialist party (1917) and became secretary-treasurer of Social Democratic League of America; treasurer of American Alliance for Labor and Democracy (1917–19); on governing boards of many educational and philanthropic organizations. The first wife of J. G. Phelps Stokes, **Rose Harriet Pas'tor** (pȧs'tẽr), *nee* **Wieslander** (1879–1933); took stepfather's name Pastor; b. in Russian Poland; a political radical; lived in London (1882–90) and in U.S. (from 1890); worked in cigar factory in Cleveland (to 1903); on staff of *Jewish Daily News*, New York (1903–05); m. J. G. Phelps Stokes (1905) but was estranged (from 1917) over questions arising from the World War; became identified with radical socialist groups that later became communistic; was divorced by J. G. Phelps Stokes (Oct. 17, 1925); m. Isaac Romaine (1927); died of cancer at Frankfurt am Main (June 20, 1933).

**Stokes, Frederick Abbot.** 1857–1939. American publisher, b. Brooklyn, N.Y.; founder (1881) Frederick A. Stokes Co., publishers, and its president (1890–1939).

**Stokes,** Sir **Frederick Wilfrid Scott.** 1860–1927. English civil engineer and inventor; received patents on improvements in breakdown cranes, railway, hydraulic, and refrigerating machinery, and ordnance; responsible for design of sluice and lock gates of Aswan dam (1901) and Sennar dam (1926); invented (1915) Stokes trench mortar for firing high-explosive bombs and gas, smoke, and incendiary bombs. His elder brother, **Adrian** (1854–1935), was a landscape painter.

**Stokes,** Sir **George Gabriel.** 1819–1903. British mathematician and physicist, b. in Ireland; friend of Lord Kelvin. Professor of mathematics, Cambridge (from 1849); developed modern theory of motion of viscous fluids; made investigations in optics, esp. on undulatory theory of light; published *The Dynamical Theory of Diffraction* (1849); pioneer in spectrum analysis; discovered nature of fluorescence; investigated ultraviolet spectrum; considered a founder of geodesy for his study of variations in gravity.

**Stokes, William.** 1804–1878. Irish physician and clinician; son of **Whitley Stokes** (1763–1845; regius professor of medicine, Dublin [1830–43], who was grandson of Gabriel Stokes, engineer and first of family to settle in Ireland). Published one of earliest treatises in English on use of stethoscope (1825); edited *Dublin Journal of Medical Science;* founded Pathological Society (1838); physician to Queen Victoria in Ireland (1861); author of treatises on typhus fever, cholera, and diseases of the heart and lungs.

William's eldest son, **Whitley** (1830–1909), became barrister and went to India (1862); legal member of viceroy's council (1877–82); drafted Anglo-Indian civil and criminal codes (1887); author of works on Indian law (1865–91); returned to England and the study of Celtic; one of editors of *Irische Texte*, Leipzig (1880–1900); collaborator in *Urkeltischer Sprachschatz* (1894); author of Irish translations and glossaries and Cornish and Breton works. See John STRACHAN.

**Margaret M'Nair Stokes** (1832–1900), archaeologist; sister of Whitley Stokes (1830–1909); edited and contributed drawings to earl of Dunraven's *Notes on Irish Architecture* (1875–77); wrote *The High Crosses of Ireland* (incomplete; 1898).

Sir **William** (1839–1900), surgeon, a younger son of William Stokes; consulting surgeon to British forces in South Africa (1900).

**Adrian** (1887–1927), pathologist, son of Henry John Stokes (Irish civil servant, a younger son of the elder William Stokes); as officer in royal army medical corps (1914–19), performed invaluable service on tetanus, typhoid, jaundice, and other diseases, and invented method of administering oxygen to gas victims by nasal catheter.

**Sto·kow'ski** (stô·kôf'skē; *Pol.* stô-), **Le'o·pold** (lē'ô·pōld) **An·to'ni** (än·tô'nē) **Sta·ni'slaw** (stä·nē'släf). 1882–1977. Orchestra conductor, b. London; grad. Oxford U.; conductor of Cincinnati Symphony Orchestra (1909–12), Philadelphia Symphony Orchestra (1914–36), and N.Y. Symphony Orchestra (1944–45).

**Stol'berg** (shtôl'bĕrk), Count **Christian zu.** 1748–1821. German poet; his poems and stage works were published jointly with those of his brother Count **Friedrich Leopold** (1750–1819), under the title *Der Brüder Christian und Friedrich Leopold Grafen zu Stolberg Gesammelte Werke* (20 vols., 1820–25).

**Stoll** (stōl), **Elmer Edgar.** 1874–1959. American Shakespearean scholar; professor, Minnesota (from 1915); author of *John Webster* (1905), *Shakespeare Studies* (1927), *Art and Artifice in Shakespeare* (1933), *Shakespeare's Young Lovers* (1937), etc.

**Stolo, Licinius Calvus.** See LICINIUS CALVUS STOLO.

**Sto·ly'pin** (stŭ·lĭ'pyĭn), **Pëtr Arkadevich.** 1863–1911. Russian lawyer and statesman; president, provincial court, government of Kovno (Kaunas); governor of Grodno (1902) and of Saratov (1903); minister of the interior (May, 1906) and premier of Russia (July, 1906); pursued policy of liberal pacification; assassinated.

**Stone** (stōn), **Edward James.** 1831–1897. English astronomer at Cape of Good Hope (1870–79); observer at Oxford (from 1879); produced *Cape Catalogue*, which lists 12,441 stars to 7th magnitude (1880), later extending catalogue to include stars from 25° S. declination to the equator.

**Stone, Ellen Maria.** 1846–1927. American missionary in Bulgaria (1878–1902); with a companion, kidnaped by Bulgarian brigands (Sept. 3, 1901); ransomed by payment of about $66,000 (Feb., 1902); thereafter, lectured on her captivity, and in the cause of temperance.

**Stone, Frank.** See under Marcus STONE.

**Stone, Grace,** *nee* **Zar'ing** (zâr'ĭng). 1896– . American writer, b. New York City; m. Ellis S. Stone (1917). Author of *Letters to a Djinn* (1922), *The Bitter Tea of General Yen* (1930), *The Cold Journey*, dealing with the

Deerfield (Mass.) massacre (1934), and (under pseudonym **Ethel Vance**) of *Escape* (1939), *Reprisal* (1942).

**Stone, Harlan Fiske.** 1872–1946. American jurist; professor of law (1902–05), and dean (1910–23), Columbia Law School; U.S. attorney general (1924–25); associate justice, U.S. Supreme Court (1925–41), chief justice (from 1941).

**Stone, Horatio.** 1808–1875. American sculptor, b. Jackson, N.Y.; studio in Washington, D.C. (from 1848). Among his works are a marble bust of Roger Brooke Taney, marble statues of Alexander Hamilton, John Hancock, a statue of Jefferson.

**Stone, Irving.** *Family name orig.* **Ten′nen·baum** (tĕn′ĕn·bŏm). 1903– . American writer, b. San Francisco; author of *Pageant of Youth* (1933), *Lust for Life* (biography of Vincent van Gogh; 1934), *Sailor on Horseback* (biography of Jack London; 1938), *Clarence Darrow for the Defense* (biography; 1941), *They Also Ran* (1943), etc.

**Stone, John Marshall.** 1830–1900. American Confederate army officer and politician; governor of Mississippi (1876–82; 1890–96); reorganized State government in way to assure political control by native white people.

**Stone, Lucy.** Mrs. **Henry Brown Black′well** (blăk′wĕl; -wĕl). 1818–1893. American woman suffragist, b. near West Brookfield, Mass.; m. (1855) Henry Brown Blackwell, but retained her maiden name as an indication she had not lost her individuality by her marriage. Lectured on woman's rights and against slavery. Sent out call for first national woman's-rights convention at Worcester, Mass. (1850); arranged for annual conventions thereafter. Called attention to her cause by letting her goods be sold for unpaid taxes (in New Jersey, 1858) and protesting the taxes as levied without giving her representation; aided in organizing New Jersey Woman Suffrage Association; became its president (1867); aided in forming American Woman Suffrage Association (1869). Raised money for founding *Woman's Journal* (1870); coeditor with her husband (1872–93).

**Stone, Marcus.** 1840–1921. Son of the artist **Frank Stone** (1800–1859). English historical and genre painter; among his canvases are *Nell Gwynne, Interrupted Duel, Post Bag, Bad News, Gambler's Wife.*

**Stone, Melville Elijah.** 1848–1929. American journalist, b. Hudson, Ill.; founded in Chicago the first penny (one-cent) daily newspaper, Chicago *Daily News* (1875); added a morning edition (1881); sold his interests in the papers (1888); organized and became president of Globe National Bank, Chicago (1891); general manager, Associated Press of Illinois (1893–1900), and Associated Press, incorporated in New York (1900–23).

**Stone, Nicholas.** 1587–1647. English sculptor and architect; executed designs of Inigo Jones in Renaissance architecture and rejuvenated art in England; executed tombs of Bodley at Oxford and of Donne at St. Paul's, London.

**Stone, Samuel.** 1602–1663. Puritan clergyman in America, b. Hertford, Eng.; emigrated with Thomas Hooker to New England (1633); pastor, Cambridge, Mass. (1633–36); purchased site of Hartford, Conn., from the Indians and settled there (1636); minister of the church in Hartford (1636–63).

**Stone, Walter King.** 1875–1949. American muralist and illustrator.

**Stone, Warren Sanford.** 1860–1925. American labor-union leader, b. near Ainsworth, Iowa; grand chief, Brotherhood of Locomotive Engineers (1903–25); obtained important agreements with western railroads (1906), southeastern railroads (1908), and eastern railroads (1912); leader in struggle for passage of Adamson Act (1916); instrumental in founding *Labor* (1919), weekly organ of the railway unions, and in putting his Brotherhood into the banking business (1920); favored co-operative ownership of the railroads.

**Stone, William.** 1603?–?1660. English colonial administrator in America, b. in Northamptonshire, Eng.; to Virginia (before 1628). Governor of Maryland, appointed by Lord Baltimore, the proprietor (1648); had trouble with a Puritan parliamentary commission from England (1652 and 1654); forced by commission to resign (1654). Under orders from Lord Baltimore, rallied force and fought his Puritan opponents at battle of Severn (Mar. 25, 1655); was defeated, wounded, captured, tried, and sentenced to death, but not executed. Member of governor's council (1657). His great-great-grandson **Thomas Stone** (1743–1787) was a lawyer; began practice in Frederick, Md.; member of Continental Congress (1775–78) and a signer of the Declaration of Independence; member of the Congress of the Confederation (1784–85).

**Stone, William Joel.** 1848–1918. American politician; practiced law at Nevada, Mo. (from 1871); member, U.S. House of Representatives (1885–91); governor of Missouri (1893–97); U.S. senator (1903–18). Controlled Democratic party in Missouri; nicknamed "Gum-Shoe Bill" because of his skill in avoiding charges of political corruption (1902–03). Chairman, senate committee on foreign relations (1914–18); was one of "little group of willful men" who blocked President Wilson's armed-ship bill (1917).

**Stone, William Leete.** 1792–1844. American journalist and historian; one of proprietors of New York *Commercial Advertiser* (1821–44); interested himself in the Iroquois Indians and gathered materials for their history; instrumental in creating New York State Historical Agency for obtaining transcripts of documents on American history to be found in European archives. See Maria MONK. His son **William Leete** (1835–1908) was also a journalist and historian; city editor, New York *Journal of Commerce* (1864–67); on staff of New York customhouse (from 1872); devoted himself chiefly to historical research and writing, publishing works dealing with the American Revolutionary period.

**Stone, William Oliver.** 1830–1875. American portrait painter, b. Derby, Conn.; studio in New York (from 1854).

**Stone, Witmer.** 1866–1939. American naturalist, authority on ornithology, b. Philadelphia, Pa.; curator (1908–24), director of museum (1925–28), vice-president (1927), director emeritus (from 1929), Acad. of Natural Sciences of Philadelphia; editor, *The Auk* (1912–36); author of *Birds of Eastern Pennsylvania and New Jersey* (1894), *Mammals of New Jersey* (1908), etc.

**Stonehaven,** Baron. See John Lawrence BAIRD.

**Stone′man** (stōn′măn), **George.** 1822–1894. American army officer and politician, b. Busti, N.Y.; grad. U.S.M.A., West Point (1846). Brigadier general, chief of cavalry in the Army of the Potomac, under General McClellan; served in Peninsular campaign (1861–62). Major general of volunteers (Nov., 1862); engaged at Fredericksburg; under orders from General Hooker, led great raid (Apr. 13–May 2, 1863) toward Richmond; chief of cavalry bureau, Washington, D.C. (1863); engaged in Atlanta campaign under Sherman (1864); captured at Clinton, Ga. (Aug., 1864) and exchanged (Oct., 1864); led raids in southwestern Virginia, eastern Tennessee, and the Carolinas (1864–65); retired (1871). Governor of California (1883–87).

**Sto′ney** (stō′nĭ), **George Johnstone.** 1826–1911. Irish physicist; educ. Trinity Coll., Dublin; professor of natural philosophy, Queen's Coll., Galway (1852–57); secretary, Queen's U. (1857–82). His work includes investigations relating to physical optics, molecular physics, kinetic theory of gases, and the conditions limiting planetary atmospheres; introduced word *electron* to designate the elementary charge of electricity.

**Stong** (stŏng), **Phil**, *in full* **Philip Duffield.** 1899–1957. American writer, b. Keosauqua, Iowa; A.B., Drake (1919); teacher (1919–23); in newspaper work (1923–31). Author of many juvenile stories, and of novels including *State Fair* (1932), *Stranger's Return* (1933), *Village Tale* (1934), *Farmer in the Dell* (1935), *The Rebellion of Lennie Barlow* (1937), *The Long Lane* (1939), *The Iron Mountain* (1942), *One Destiny* (1942).

**Stopes** (stōps), **Marie Carmichael.** 1880–1958. English paleobotanist, birth-control advocate, and author. Investigated coal mines and fossil plants; lectured on paleobotany at University Coll. (London) and at U. of Manchester. After annulment (1916) of marriage with R. R. Gates, m. (1918) Humphrey Verdon Roe (1878–1949), with whom she founded Mothers' Clinic for Constructive Birth Control (1921); pres.; Society for Constructive Birth Control and Racial Progress. Author of *The Study of Plant Life for Young People*, *Plays of Old Japan* (with Professor Sakurai), *Conquest*, *Married Love* (1918), *Radiant Motherhood* (1920), *Contraception: its Theory, History and Practice* (1923), *Sex and the Young* (1926), *Enduring Passion* (1928), *Sex and Religion* (1929), *Love Songs for Young Lovers* (verse; 1939), etc.

**Sto·ra′ce** (stô·rä′châ), **Stephen.** 1763–1796. English composer; as composer to Drury Lane Theatre (from 1787), made impression with Singspiel *The Doctor and the Apothecary*, and attained success with *The Haunted Tower* (opera; 1789); introduced grand finale into English opera in *The Pirates* (1792); with Colman, produced *The Iron Chest* (1796). His sister **Anna** (*or* **Ann**) **Selina** (1766–1817), coloratura singer, was the original Susanna in Mozart's *Nozze di Figaro*, Vienna (1786); m. John Abraham Fisher, violinist and composer; the original Margaretta in her brother's *No Song No Supper* (1790) and Barbara in *Iron Chest* (1796); sang with John Braham (*q.v.*) on the Continent and in London (1797–1808).

**Sto′rer** (stōr′ẽr), **David Humphreys.** 1804–1891. American physician and naturalist; practiced in Boston; specialized in obstetrics; professor in Harvard Medical School (1854–68), and dean (1854–64). Also, interested himself in natural history; published *A Synopsis of the Fishes of North America* (1846), *A History of Fishes in Massachusetts* (1867). A son, **Horatio Robinson** (1830–1922), b. Boston, was also a physician; introduced specialism in gynecology and founded (1869) *Journal of the Gynecological Society of Boston*, first journal devoted exclusively to diseases of women; carried on vigorous campaign against criminal abortions. Another son, **Francis Humphreys** (1832–1914), was a chemist; professor, M.I.T. (1865–1907); associate of Charles W. Eliot and coauthor with him of *A Manual of Inorganic Chemistry* (1867) and *The Compendious Manual of Qualitative Chemical Analysis* (1868); conducted important researches in agricultural chemistry. A nephew of David H. Storer, **Bellamy Storer** (1847–1922), was a politician; practiced law in Cincinnati; member of U.S. House of Representatives (1891–95); U.S. minister to Belgium (1897–99), to Spain (1899–1902), and to Austria-Hungary (1902–06).

**Sto′rey** (stō′rĭ), **Moor′field** (mōr′fēld). 1845–1929. American lawyer and publicist, b. Roxbury, Mass.; practiced in Boston. Vigorous opponent of political corruption; leader in Anti-Imperialist League, opposing U.S. ownership of the Philippine Islands; defended rights of American Indians; published numerous pamphlets, books, and letters in newspapers, on current issues.

**Stork** (stôrk), **Charles Wharton.** 1881– . American educator and writer, b. Philadelphia. His volumes of verse include *Day Dreams of Greece* (1908), *The Queen of Orplede* (1910), *Sea and Bay* (1916), *Sunset Harbor* (1933).

**Storm** (shtôrm), **Theodor.** 1817–1888. German fiction writer; lawyer by profession; entered Prussian government service (1853); held judicial posts until his retirement (1880). Among his many works are *Immensee* (1852), *Im Sonnenschein* (1854), *Abseits* (1863), *Viola Tricolor* (1873), *Der Spiegel des Cyprianus*, *Pole Poppenspäler* (1874), *Carsten Curator* (1878), *Renate* (1878), *Die Söhne des Senators* (1880), *Der Schimmelreiter* (1888).

**Stör′mer** (stûr′mẽr), **Fredrik Carl Mülertz.** 1874–1957. Norwegian mathematician; developed mathematical basis of polar light theory; invented an apparatus for photographing aurora borealis; worked on integration of differential equations.

**Stor′month** (stôr′mŭnth), **James.** 1825–1882. British clergyman and lexicographer; compiled *Etymological and Pronouncing Dictionary of the English Language* (1871), *English Spellings and Spelling Rules* (1876), etc.

**Storr** (shtôr), **Gottlob Christian.** fl. 1777–1797. German Protestant theologian; professor, Tübingen (1777–97), and founder of the Tübingen school of theology.

**Storrs** (stôrz). A family of American Congregational clergymen, including: **John** (1735–1799), a chaplain in the American Revolution; his son **Richard Salter** (1763–1819), pastor in Longmeadow, Mass., for almost 34 years; his son **Richard Salter** (1787–1873), pastor in Braintree, Mass., for 62 years (1811–73); and his son **Richard Salter** (1821–1900), pastor of the Church of the Pilgrims, Brooklyn, N.Y., for over 50 years (1846–1900).

**Storrs,** Sir **Ronald.** 1881–1955. British administrator and historian; military governor of Jerusalem (1917–20) and, later, civil governor; governor and commander in chief, Cyprus (1926–32) and Northern Rhodesia (1932–34). Author of *A Quarterly Record of the War* (1939 ff.), etc.

**Sto′ry** (stō′rĭ), **Isaac.** 1774–1803. Cousin of Joseph Story. American poet, b. Marblehead, Mass.; grad. Harvard (1793) and studied for law. Known for his political satire and wit in verses first published in Newburyport (Mass.) *Political Gazette* over the pseudonym **Peter Quince** (kwĭns), and later collected in *A Parnassian Shop, Opened in the Pindaric Stile; by Peter Quince, Esq.* (1801).

**Story, John.** 1510?–1571. English Roman Catholic martyr; lecturer on civil law, Oxford (1535), and first regius professor (1544). M.P. (1547), opposed Act of Uniformity (1548); returned from exile (1553) and served as Queen Mary's prosecutor of Protestant heretics and as Queen's proctor at trial of Cranmer (1555). Pensioner of Philip II of Spain (1563); agent of duke of Alva in establishing Inquisition in Netherlands. Kidnaped by English and executed for high treason.

**Story, Joseph.** 1779–1845. American jurist, b. Marblehead, Mass.; began practice in Salem, Mass. Member, U.S. House of Representatives (1808–09); associate justice, U.S. Supreme Court (1811–45); also, professor of law, Harvard (1829–45); a pioneer in organizing and directing teaching in Harvard Law School. Author of a famous series of commentaries, including *Commentaries on the Law of Bailments* (1832), *Commentaries on the Constitution of the United States* (3 vols., 1833), *The Con-*

*flict of Laws* (1834), *On Equity Jurisprudence* (2 vols., 1836), *Equity Pleading* (1838), *Law of Agency* (1839), *Law of Partnership* (1841), *Law of Bills of Exchange* (1843), *Law of Promissory Notes* (1845). Elected to American Hall of Fame (1900). His son **William Wetmore** (1819–1895) was a sculptor and man of letters; practiced law in Boston and wrote legal treatises; studied painting, sculpture, and music; settled in Rome (1856) and thereafter devoted himself to sculpture; became intimate friend of Robert and Elizabeth Barrett Browning, Nathaniel Hawthorne, Charles Eliot Norton, Walter Savage Landor, John Lothrop Motley, in Rome; his *Libyan Sibyl* is in the National Academy of Art in Washington, his *Medea* and a replica of his *Cleopatra*, in Metropolitan Museum of Art in New York, his statues of John Marshall and Joseph Henry in Washington, D.C.; author of a volume of poetry and several volumes of essays. His grandson **Julian Russell Story** (1857–1919), b. Walton-on-Thames, in Surrey, Eng., was a portrait painter; his portrait of Madame Emma Eames, his first wife (m. 1891; divorced 1907), hangs in Cincinnati (Ohio) Art Museum.

**Stoss** (shtōs), **Veit.** 1440?–1533. German sculptor and wood carver; carved high altar for the Marienkirche, Cracow, tomb of Casimir IV, Cracow, tombstone of Archbishop Olesnicki in Gniezno cathedral, altarpieces at Schwabach and Bamberg. Regarded as master of wood carving in Germany.

**Stössel.** See STĔSEL.

**Stoth′ard** (stŏth′ẽrd), **Thomas.** 1755–1834. English illustrator and painter; engraved plates for *Poems of Ossian;* executed graceful illustrations for *Pilgrim's Progress, Don Quixote, Robinson Crusoe, Peregrine Pickle, Clarissa Harlowe, Gulliver's Travels,* and other classics; decorated Burghley House (1799–1803). His son **Charles Alfred** (1786–1821), historical draftsman, exhibited oil painting *The Death of Richard II* at the Royal Academy (1811), drew Bayeux tapestry for Society of Antiquaries; prepared a history of costumes, *Monumental Effigies of Great Britain* (10 parts, 1811–21), completed (1832) by other artists employed by his wife (see Anna Eliza BRAY), with letterpress by her brother.

**Stough′ton** (stō′t'n), **Israel.** d. 1645? British colonist in America; founder of Dorchester, Mass. (1630); commander of Massachusetts troops in Pequot War (1637). His son **William** (1630?–1701) was assistant on Massachusetts council (1671–86), lieutenant governor (1692–1701); presided at trial of Salem witches (1692); founder of Stoughton Hall, Harvard.

**Stout** (stout), **George Frederick. 1860–1944.** English philosopher and psychologist; professor of logic and metaphysics, St. Andrews U. (1903–36; retired). Editor of *Mind* (1891–1920); author of *Analytic Psychology* (1896), *Manual of Psychology* (1898; 5th ed. 1938), *Studies in Philosophy and Psychology* (1930), etc.

**Stout, Rex Todhunter.** 1886–1975. American writer, b. Noblesville, Ind.; author of detective fiction, esp. stories centering around the detective "Nero Wolfe."

**Stout,** Sir **Robert.** 1844–1930. New Zealand jurist and statesman, b. in Shetland Islands; to New Zealand (1863). Attorney general (1878–79); prime minister, attorney general, and minister of education (1884–87); chief justice of New Zealand (1899–1926); member of Legislative Council (1926–30).

**Stout, William Bushnell.** 1880–1956. American engineer, b. Quincy, Ill.; engineer for automotive companies; founder and president (from 1919) of Stout Engineering Laboratories; built first all-metal airplane in U.S. (1922); formed company to build metal commercial planes (1922–25; sold to Ford Motor Co.); founded passenger air line (1926–29; sold to United Aircraft and Transport Co.); engaged in transportation research in airplane, railroad, and automotive fields; active in development of stainless-steel airplanes and welded-steel aircraft engines.

**Stow** (stō), **John.** 1525?–1605. English historian and antiquary; devoted himself (from c. 1565) to collecting and transcribing manuscripts and producing histories. Published *The Woorkes of Geffrey Chaucer* (1561), *A Summarie of Englyshe Chronicles* (1565), *The Annales of England* (1580), and *A Survay of London* (1598, 1603), a standard authority on Old London.

**Stowe** (stō), **Harriet Elizabeth,** *nee* **Bee′cher** (bē′chẽr). 1811–1896. Daughter of Lyman Beecher; sister of Henry Ward Beecher. American author, b. Litchfield, Conn.; m. Calvin Ellis Stowe (1836). During residence in Cincinnati (1833–50), became ardent abolitionist; encouraged by her brother and husband, wrote *Uncle Tom's Cabin, or Life Among the Lowly,* first published (as a serial, 1851–52) in an antislavery paper, the *National Era,* Washington, D.C., and in book form (2 vols., 1852). Book became important factor in solidifying sentiment in the North against slavery, and making the issue a moral one; had much to do with bringing on the Civil War. Among her other novels were: *Dred, A Tale of the Great Dismal Swamp* (1856), *The Minister's Wooing* (1859), *The Pearl of Orr's Island* (1862), *Oldtown Folks* (1869). Aroused storm of criticism by *Atlantic Monthly* article (Sept., 1869) entitled *The True Story of Lady Byron's Life,* in which, on basis of information given her by Lady Byron, she charged Lord Byron with incest with his sister Augusta. Her collected works, *The Writings of Harriet Beecher Stowe,* appeared in 1896 (16 vols.). She was elected to the American Hall of Fame (1910).

**Stowe, Leland.** 1899– . American journalist, b. Southbury, Conn.; A.B., Wesleyan (1921); on staff of Worcester *Telegram,* N.Y. *Herald Tribune, Pathé News* (1921–26); Paris correspondent, N.Y. *Herald Tribune* (1926–35); roving reporter in North and South America (1936–39); on foreign staff of Chicago *Daily News* (from 1939); awarded Pulitzer prize (1930); author of *Nazi Means War* (1933), *No Other Road to Freedom* (1941).

**Stowell,** Baron. See William SCOTT.

**Stow′ell** (stō′ĕl), **Ellery Cory.** 1875–1958. American jurist; professor of international law, American U., Washington, D.C. (from 1922). Author of *The Diplomacy of the War of 1914* (1915), *Intervention in International Law* (1921), *International Law* (1931).

**Stoyadinovitch.** Variant of STOJADINOVIĆ.

**Strabane,** Baron and viscount. See under earls, marquises, and dukes of ABERCORN.

**Stra′bo** (strā′bō). 63 B.C.?–?24 A.D. Greek geographer, b. Amasya, in Pontus; settled in Rome (c. 20 B.C.); traveled widely and wrote *Geography* (17 books) describing Europe, Asia, Egypt, and Libya. Author also of a history of Rome (now lost).

**Strabo, Gaius Fannius.** See FANNIUS.

**Strabolgi,** Barons. See Joseph Montague KENWORTHY.

**Strachan** (strôn), **John.** 1778–1867. Canadian Anglican bishop. b. Aberdeen, Scotland; to Canada (1799); ordained deacon (1803) and archdeacon of Toronto (1827); as member of executive council (1815) and legislative council (1820), strove to establish ecclesiastical control of higher education; obtained royal charter for King's Coll. (1826–27); first bishop of Toronto (1839). Faced popular resentment over exclusive endowment of Episcopal education; energetically opposed division of Clergy Reserves; finally established King's Coll. (1843), with modifications of its charter; when King's Coll. reorganized as U. of Toronto, founded Trinity U., entirely under control of Episcopal Church (1852).

**Strachan, John.** 1862–1907. British classical and Celtic scholar, b. in Banffshire, Scotland; professor of Greek, Owens Coll., Manchester (1885–1907); with Kuno Meyer, founded Summer School of Irish Learning at Dublin (1903); with Whitley Stokes, produced *Thesaurus Palaeohibernicus* (2 vols., 1901–03). Author of memoirs on Irish philology and *Introduction to Early Welsh* (pub. 1909).

**Stra'chey** (strā'chĭ), **John St. Loe.** 1860–1927. English journalist; editor of *Cornhill Magazine* (1896–97), and proprietor and editor of *Spectator* (1898–1925). Among his books are *The Manufacture of Paupers, Problems and Perils of Socialism, A New Way of Life* (1909), and *The Adventure of Living* (1922). His son **Evelyn John St. Loe** (1901–1963), Socialist writer and politician; author of *Revolution by Reason* (1925), *The Menace of Fascism* (1933), *The Nature of Capitalist Crisis* (1935), *The Theory and Practice of Socialism* (1936), *The Economics of Progress* (1939); minister of food (from 1946).

**Strachey, Lytton,** *in full* **Giles Lytton.** 1880–1932. English writer; educ. Cambridge; among his books are *Landmarks in French Literature* (1912), *Eminent Victorians* (1918), *Queen Victoria* (1921), *Books and Characters* (1922), *Pope* (1925), and *Elizabeth and Essex* (1928).

**Strachey,** Sir **Richard.** 1817–1908. Anglo-Indian administrator, b. in Somersetshire; member, Council of India (1875–89); fellow of Royal Society (1854) for his investigations in Indian geology, botany, and meteorology. His older brother, Sir **Edward** (1812–1901), was student of Oriental languages and Biblical criticism; author of *Jewish History and Politics* (1874) and *Miracles and Science* (1854). Their younger brother, Sir **John** (1823–1907), Anglo-Indian administrator, was chief commissioner of Oudh (1866); lieutenant governor of North-West Provinces (1874–76); member of Council of India (1885–95).

**Strachey, William.** An English colonist in Virginia; secretary and recorder of Virginia under Lord De La Warr (1610–11); author of *The Historie of Travaile into Virginia Britannia...* (first publ. by Hakluyt Society, 1849), etc.

**Strack** (shträk), **Hermann.** 1848–1922. German Protestant theologian and Orientalist.

**Stra·del'la** (strä·dĕl'lä), **Alessandro.** 1645?–1682. Italian singer and composer, a master of the aria; composer of operas, oratorios, cantatas, and sonatas, all still in manuscript. He figured in a love affair which served as subject of Flotow's opera *Alessandro Stradella.*

**Stra'di·va'ri** (strä'dē·vä'rē), **Antonio.** *Lat.* **Antonius Strad'i·var'i·us** (străd'ĭ·vâr'ĭ·ŭs). 1644–1737. Italian violinmaker, b. Cremona; pupil and associate of Nicolò Amati; worked independently (1669 ff.); made Cremonas, violas, and violoncellos; assisted in later work by his sons **Francesco** (1671–1743), who carried on father's art, and **Omobono** (1679–1742), known esp. for skill in repairing stringed instruments.

**Stradonitz, Kekule von.** See KEKULE VON STRADONITZ.

**Straf'ford** (străf'ẽrd), 1st Earl of. Sir **Thomas Went'worth** (wĕnt'wûrth; -wẽrth). 1st Baron **Ra'by** (rā'bĭ). 1593–1641. English statesman; M.P. (1614); opposed agitation for war against Spain (1625); anti-Puritan and supporter of royal prerogative; imprisoned for failure to contribute to forced loan (1627); virtual leader of House of Commons, introduced bill for securing liberties of subjects from forced loans, billeting of soldiers, arbitrary imprisonment, but on its nonacceptance by Charles, relinquished leadership to Eliot and Coke (1628); did not oppose Petition of Right, which replaced his moderate bill. Taken into court favor; made president of council of the north (Dec. 25, 1628) and as royal executive checked insubordination; privy councilor (1629). As lord deputy of Ireland (1632–38), adopted "Thorough" policy, coerced country into obedience and order. Chief adviser to Charles I (1639); created Baron Raby and earl of Strafford (1640); lord lieutenant of Ireland (1640); advocated invasion of Scotland to crush Presbyterian insurgents and force adoption of the English liturgy; obtained £180,000 in subsidies from Irish parliament and prepared to lead Irish troops against Scots (1640); urged Charles to various despotic actions; commanded forces in Yorkshire against invading Scots. Impeached for treason by Pym and followers in Commons, who accused him of subverting the law of the kingdom by plotting to coerce parliament with a northern army; imprisoned, tried (1641) under a bill of attainder, substituted for impeachment and passed by commons and lords, and unwillingly assented to by Charles I; beheaded on Tower Hill. His grandnephew **Thomas Wentworth** (1672–1739), 3d Baron Raby and 3d Earl of Strafford, diplomatist, was ambassador at Berlin (1703–11), at The Hague (1711–14); one of negotiators of the peace of Utrecht (1711–13).

**Straight** (strāt), **Willard Dickerman.** 1880–1918. American diplomat and financier; in Chinese customs service (1901–04); U.S. vice-consul at Seoul, Korea (1905); U.S. consul general at Mukden (1906). Acting chief, division of Far Eastern Affairs, U.S. Department of State (1908–09). Again in China (1909–12), acting for American business and financial interests. Volunteered at entrance of U.S. into World War; died of pneumonia contracted in line of duty, Paris (Dec. 1, 1918).

**Stran'a·han** (străn'ȧ·hăn), **James Samuel Thomas.** 1808–1898. American civic leader, b. Peterboro, N.Y.; moved to Brooklyn, N.Y. (1844); identified himself with municipal development of Brooklyn, as in building of harbor improvements, docks and piers, and in East River ferry lines; president, Brooklyn park board (1860–82) and largely responsible for development of Prospect Park; supported project for East River Bridge (opened 1883); advocated consolidation of Brooklyn with New York City (accomplished 1898). A statue of him by Frederick William MacMonnies is in Prospect Park.

**Strand'berg'** (strȧnd'băr'y'), **Carl Vilhelm August.** *Pseudonym* **Ta'lis Qua'lis** (tä'lĭs kvä'lĭs). 1818–1877. Swedish poet and journalist; published *Poems of Passion* (1845), *Wild Roses* (1848), etc.

**Strand'man** (strȧnd'mȧn), **Otto.** 1875– . Estonian statesman; prime minister of Estonia (1919); president of parliament (1920–22); minister of foreign affairs and of finance (1924); minister to Poland (1927–29); chief of state and prime minister (1929–31); minister to France (1933 ff.).

**Strang** (străng), **William.** 1859–1921. Scottish painter and etcher.

**Strange** (strānj), Earl. See 4th duke of ATHOLL.

**Strange,** Sir **Robert.** 1721–1792. Scottish line engraver; executed historical engravings in London (from 1751), chiefly after Italian masters; knighted by George III for engraving of West's *Apotheosis of the Royal Children* (1786).

**Strangford,** Viscounts. See under Sir Thomas SMYTHE (1558?–1625).

**Stra'pa·ro'la** (strä'pä·rô'lä), **Giovanni Francesco.** d. about 1557. Italian writer, b. in Caravaggio; known for his collection of 73 novelle and tales *Tredici Piacevoli Notti* (vol. 1, 1550; vol. 2, 1553; called in Eng. *Facetious Nights*), notable as source material for Shakespeare, Molière, et al., and containing such tales as *Beauty and the Beast* and *Puss in Boots.*

**Stras′bur′ger** (shträs′bo͝or′gẽr), **Eduard.** 1844–1912. German botanist; known for researches in the history of development of plants and in cytology.

**Stras′ser** (shträs′ẽr), **Artur.** 1854–1927. Austrian sculptor; chief work, a bronze group, *Antony in his Triumphal Chariot*, before the Secession Building in Vienna.

**Strasser, Otto Johan Maximilian.** 1897–1974. German writer, b. in Bavaria; served in World War I; edited newspapers in northern Germany; joined Nazi party (1925), whose northern leader was his brother **Gregor** (1892–1934); broke with Hitler (1930); exiled (1933); lived in Vienna, Prague (where he edited *Die Deutsche Revolution*, 1934–39), Zurich, Paris; founder (1941) of "Free German Movement"; to Canada (1940). Wrote *Hitler and I* (1940), *History in My Time* (1941), *Flight from Terror* (with Michael Stern, 1942).

**Strass′mann** (shträs′män), **Fritz.** 1902– . German chemist. Shared Enrico Fermi Award (1966) with O.H. Hahn and L. Meitner for studies of nuclear fission.

**Strat′e·mey′er** (străt′ĕ·mī′ẽr), **Edward.** 1862–1930. American writer of juveniles, b. Elizabeth, N.J. Author of the *Bound to Win* and *Old Glory* series; under pseudonym **Arthur M. Win′field** (wĭn′fēld), the *Rover Boys* series (1899–1926); under pseudonym Capt. **Ralph Bone′hill** (bōn′hĭl), the *Flag of Freedom* (1899–1902), *Mexican War* (1900–02), *Frontier* (1903–07) series; founded Stratemeyer Literary Syndicate (1906), produced *Tom Swift* series under pseudonym **Victor Appleton.**

**Stratemeyer, George E.** 1890–1969. American army officer; served in World War I; chief of staff of air forces (1942–43); chief U.S. air officer in India-Burma-China theater (1943–45).

**Strat′ford** (străt′fẽrd), **John de.** d. 1348. English prelate; made bishop of Winchester (1323) by pope against wishes of Edward II; sided with Queen Isabella, drew up six articles comprising reasons for deposition of Edward II, and obtained his abdication (1327). Member of royal council of Edward III; chancellor (1330–34; 1335–37; Apr., 1340) and chief adviser to Edward III (1330–40); archbishop of Canterbury (1333); president of council during Edward's absence (1345, 1346).

**Stratford de Redcliffe,** Viscount. See Sir Stratford Canning.

**Strathcona and Mount Royal,** Baron. See Donald Alexander Smith.

**Strathnairn,** Baron. See Hugh Henry Rose.

**Stra′to** (strā′tō) *or* **Stra′ton** (-tŏn) **of Lamp′sa·cus** (lămp′sȧ·kŭs). Greek peripatetic philosopher; successor of Theophrastus as head of the Lyceum (288 B.C.).

**Stra′ton** (strā′t′n), **John Roach.** 1875–1929. American Baptist clergyman; in New York City (1918–29); became renowned as religious zealot, denouncing from his pulpit cabaret life, liquor, dancing, and prize fighting.

**Strat′o·ni′ce** (străt′ō·nī′sē). fl. about 300 B.C. Daughter of Demetrius I Poliorcetes of Macedonia. When quite young, married (c. 300) Seleucus I Nicator; given up by him (292) to become wife of his son (her stepson) Antiochus I, Satrap of Bactria and, later, King of Syria; mother of Antiochus II.

**Strat′ton** (străt′′n), **Charles Sherwood.** *Known as* General **Tom Thumb** (thŭm). 1838–1883. American midget, b. Bridgeport, Conn. Joined P. T. Barnum's organization (1842), and was on exhibition in New York, England, and on the continent of Europe (1844–47). Married (1863) **Mercy Lavinia Warren Bum′pus** (bŭm′pŭs), *known as* **Lavinia Warren** (1841–1919), a dwarf in Barnum's organization. Until he was in his teens, he was only 2′1″ tall and weighed about fifteen pounds; at maturity, he was 3′4″ tall and weighed about seventy pounds.

**Stratton, George Malcolm.** 1865–1957. American psychologist, b. Oakland, Calif.; professor, Johns Hopkins (1904–08), California (1908–35).

**Stratton, Samuel Wesley.** 1861–1931. American physicist, b. Litchfield, Ill. By request of U.S. secretary of the treasury, prepared report on a proposed bureau of standards, drafted bill establishing bureau (passed by Congress, 1901), and became first director of the bureau (1901–23). President, M.I.T. (1923–30). See Nicola Sacco.

**Stratton Porter, Gene.** See Porter.

**Straus** (strous), **Isidor.** 1845–1912. Merchant, b. in Rhenish Bavaria; to U.S. (1854); with his father, **Lazarus Straus,** organized crockery firm of L. Straus & Son, in New York (1865); took over crockery and glassware department of R. H. Macy & Co. (1874); partner in Macy & Co., with his brother Nathan (1888), purchasing full ownership in 1896; also, developed Abraham & Straus, a department store in Brooklyn, N.Y.; member of U.S. House of Representatives (1894–95); lost in the *Titanic* disaster (Apr. 15, 1912). His brother **Nathan** (1848–1931), joined L. Straus & Son (1866); with Isidor became member (1888) and owner (1896) of R. H. Macy & Co.; New York City park commissioner (1889–93); president of board of health (1898); led campaign for pasteurized milk (from 1892) and established milk stations in New York and other large cities; retired from business (1914); chosen by popular vote (1923) as the citizen who had done most for public welfare in the first quarter century of greater New York history. Another brother, **Oscar Solomon** (1850–1926), lawyer and diplomat, joined L. Straus & Sons (1881); U.S. minister to Turkey (1887–89; 1898–1900); member of Permanent Court of Arbitration at The Hague (1902–26); U.S. secretary of commerce and labor (1906–09); first American ambassador to Turkey (1909–10). Isidor's son **Jesse Isidor** (1872–1936), merchant and diplomat; president of R. H. Macy & Co. (1919); minister to France (1933–36). Another son, **Percy Selden** (1876–1944), also became president of R. H. Macy & Co. (to 1940). Nathan's son **Nathan** (1889–1961), on staff of R. H. Macy & Co. (1910–13), edited and published humorous weekly, *Puck* (1914–17); administrator of the United States Housing Authority (1937 ff.). Jesse Isidor's son **Jack Isidor** (1900– ), president of R. H. Macy & Co. (1940–56).

**Straus** (shtrous), **Oscar.** 1870–1954. Composer, b. Vienna, Austria; became naturalized French citizen (1939). Best known as composer of operettas and comic operas; resident (since 1927) in U.S., Vienna, and Paris. Among his many compositions are *Die Lustigen Nibelungen* (1904), *Walzertraum* (1907), *Der Tapfere Soldat* (1908; produced in New York as *The Chocolate Soldier;* adapted from Shaw's play *Arms and the Man*), *Der Letzte Walzer* (1920), *Die Teresina* (1925).

**Strauss** (shtrous), **David Friedrich.** 1808–1874. German theologian and philosopher; called to professorship in Zurich (1839), but strong opposition to his doctrines forced him to leave the city. Endeavored to prove the Bible history to be mythical. Among his books are *Das Leben Jesu, Kritisch Bearbeitet* (2 vols., 1835–36), *Die Christliche Glaubenslehre in ihrer Geschichtlichen Entwicklung und im Kampfe mit der Modernen Wissenschaft* (2 vols., 1840–41), *Der Alte und der Neue Glaube* (1872), and a number of biographical studies.

**Strauss, Johann.** 1804–1849. Austrian composer and orchestra conductor in Vienna (1825); on tour in Germany (1833); in Paris and London (1837). Appointed court dance music director (1835). Among his compositions are 150 waltzes, 14 polkas, 28 galops, 35 quadrilles, and 19 marches. His son **Johann** (1825–1899) succeeded to leadership of his orchestra and with it toured widely and successfully; devoted himself chiefly to composition (after 1863); among his operettas are *Indigo* (1871), *Die Fledermaus* (1874), *Cagliostro* (1875), *Prinz Methusalem* (1877), *Eine Nacht in Venedig* (1883), *Waldmeister* (1895); among his waltzes are *An der Schönen Blauen Donau* (trans. as *The Blue Danube*), *Wiener Blut*, *Morgenblätter*, *Rosen aus dem Süden*. Johann's brother **Josef** (1827–1870) succeeded him as conductor of the orchestra (1863); composed many dances; another brother, **Eduard** (1835–1916), succeeded to leadership of the orchestra on Josef's death (1870); appointed court dance music conductor; composed more than 200 dance pieces.

**Strauss** (strous), **Joseph Baermann.** 1870–1938. American bridge engineer, specializing in building long-span bridges. Among bridges designed by him are Columbia River Bridge at Longview, Wash.; George Washington Memorial Bridge across Hudson River from upper New York City; the Golden Gate Bridge in San Francisco.

**Strauss** (shtrous), **Richard.** 1864–1949. German conductor and composer. Son of the horn virtuoso and chamber musician **Franz Strauss** (1822–1905). Chief Kapellmeister, Weimar (1889–94), Munich (1894–98), Berlin (1898–1919); head of an advanced school of composition at the Acad. of Arts (1917–20); collaborator with Franz Schalk as head of the State Opera, Vienna (1919–24); president of the Reich's music department (1933). As composer, regarded as leader of the New Romantic school. Among his many notable works are operas: *Guntram* (1894), *Feuersnot* (1901), *Salome* (1905), *Elektra* (1909), *Der Rosenkavalier* (1911), *Ariadne auf Naxos* (1912), *Die Frau ohne Schatten* (1919), *Arabella* (1933); tone poems: *Don Juan* (1889), *Macbeth* (1890), *Tod und Verklärung* (1891), *Till Eulenspiegels Lustige Streiche* (1895), *Also Sprach Zarathustra* (1896), *Don Quichote* (1898), *Ein Heldenleben* (1899), *Sinfonia Domestica* (1904); and ballets, symphonies, chamber music, choral works, and songs.

**Straussenburg,** Baron **Artur Arz von.** See ARZ VON STRAUSSENBURG.

**Strauss und Tor'ney** (shtrous' o͝ont tôr'nī), **Victor Friedrich von.** 1809–1899. German diplomat and writer; a leader of Conservative party during revolutionary period (1848–49); representative in Bundestag (1850–66). Translated, with commentary, works of Chinese philosopher Lao-tzu, and collection of ancient Chinese poems *Schi-King;* wrote *Altägyptische Göttergläuben* (2 parts, 1889–91), plays, poetry, and novels.

**Stra·vin'sky** (*Angl.* strȧ·vĭn'skĭ; *Russ.* strŭ·vyēn'-skû·ĭ), **Igor Fëdorovich.** 1882–1971. Russian composer, b. Oranienbaum; studied composition with Rimski-Korsakov (1902). Lived in France (1910 ff.), later in U.S.; naturalized (1946). Regarded as leader of futurist group in modern music. Among his works are a symphonic fantasy *Fireworks*, the ballets *L'Oiseau de Feu*, *Petrouchka*, *Le Sacre du Printemps*, *Les Noces*, *Pulcinella*, the opera *Le Rossignol*, the scenic oratorio *Oedipus Rex*, a string quartet, piano concerto, burlesque (*Renard*), etc.

**Straw** (strô), **Jack.** Name or nickname of one of the leaders in Wat Tyler's rebellion (1381).

**Strawn** (strôn), **Silas Hardy.** 1866–1946. American lawyer and diplomat, b. near Ottawa, Ill.; practiced in Chicago (from 1891). U.S. delegate to special conference at Peking on Chinese customs tariffs; American member, and chairman, Chinese Extraterritoriality Commission.

**Streck'fuss** (shtrĕk'fo͞os), **Karl.** 1778–1844. German man of letters; best known for his translations of Ariosto's *Orlando Furioso* (5 vols., 1818–20), Tasso's *Jerusalem Delivered* (2 vols., 1822), and Dante's *Divina Commedia* (3 vols., 1824).

**Street** (strēt), **Alfred Billings.** 1811–1881. American author, b. Poughkeepsie, N.Y.; director, New York State Library, Albany (1848–62). His collected poems were published in 1845. Among the better-known individual poems are *The Gray Forest Eagle*, *The Settler*, *Lost Hunter*, *Frontenac*.

**Street, Cecil John Charles.** *Pseudonym* **John Rhode** (rōd). 1884– . British detective-story writer; creator of the fictional crime detector Dr. Priestley.

**Street, George Edmund.** 1824–1881. English architect; as assistant of Sir George Gilbert Scott, developed partiality for Gothic style and ability in restoring medieval monuments; restored cathedrals of Salisbury and Carlisle, and Christ Church, Dublin; designed nave of Bristol Cathedral and Crimean Memorial Church in Constantinople.

**Street, Julian.** 1879–1947. American writer, b. Chicago. Author of *My Enemy the Motor* (1908), *The Need of Change* (1909), *Paris à la Carte* (1911), *American Adventures* (1917), *After Thirty* (1919), *Cross-Sections* (1923), *The Country Cousin* (a comedy with Booth Tarkington), etc.

**Stree'ter** (strē'tẽr), **Edward.** 1891– . American humorist, b. New York City; served on Mexican border (1916–17) and in France and Germany (1918–19); author of *Dere Mable* (1918), *That's Me All Over, Mable* (1919), and *Daily Except Sundays* (1938; illust. by Gluyas Williams).

**Strei'cher** (shtrī'ĸẽr), **Julius.** 1885–1946. German journalist and politician; after World War (1914–18), became notorious for his anti-Semitic campaign (from 1919). Joined Nazi movement and took part with Hitler in Munich beer-hall Putsch (1923); arrested and imprisoned (1924); managing editor, *Der Stürmer* (1923–45); gauleiter of Franconia; hanged as war criminal.

**Streit** (strīt), **Clarence Kirsh'man** (kûrsh'măn). 1896– . American journalist and author, b. California, Mo. A.B., Montana State U. (1919); Rhodes scholar at Oxford (1920–21). On staff of Philadelphia *Public Ledger* (1920–24) and New York *Times* (1925–39). Author of *Where Iron Is, There is the Fatherland* (1920), *Hafiz—The Tongue of the Hidden* [Rubáiyát] (1928), *Union Now* (1939), *Union Now with Britain* (1941).

**Streit'berg** (shtrīt'bĕrĸ), **Wilhelm.** 1864–1925. German philologist; chief works, *Urgermanische Grammatik* (1896), *Gotisches Elementarbuch* (1896), *Gotische Bibel* (2 parts, 1908, 1910).

**Stre'se·mann** (shtrā'zē·män), **Gustav.** 1878–1929. German statesman; member of Reichstag (from 1907); chancellor of Germany (1923); minister of foreign affairs (1923–29). Pursued postwar conciliatory policy; negotiated mutual security pact with France, the Locarno Pact, and secured Germany's admission to League of Nations on an equal status with other great nations; sponsored Germany's adoption of Dawes plan (1924) and Young plan (1929). Shared Nobel peace prize with Aristide Briand (1926).

**Stret'ton** (strĕt''n), **Hesba.** *Pseudonym of* **Sarah Smith.** 1832–1911. Novelist and writer of juveniles; contributor of short stories to Dickens's magazines, *Household Words* and *All the Year Round;* author of *Jessica's First Prayer* (1866), translated into all European and most African and Asian languages. See Benjamin WAUGH.

**Streu'vels** (strû'vĕls), **Stijn.** *Pseudonym of* **Frank La·teur'** (lȧ·tûr'). 1871?–1969. Flemish writer; pastry cook (to 1905); known esp. for his realistic stories of peasant life.

**Strib'ling** (strĭb'lĭng), **Thomas Sig'is·mund** (sĭj'ĭs-mŭnd). 1881–1965. American novelist, b. Clifton, Tenn. Author of *Birthright* (1921), *Fombombo* (1922), *Red Sand* (1923), *Teeftallow* (1926), *Bright Metal* (1928), *Strange Moon* (1929), *Clues of the Caribbees* (1929), *Backwater* (1930), *The Forge* (1931), *The Store* (1932; awarded Pulitzer prize 1933), *Cathedral* (1933). Coauthor of *Rope*, a dramatization of *Teeftallow*, produced in New York (1928).

**Strich** (shtrĭκ), **Fritz**. 1882?– . German literary historian.

**Strick'er, Der** (dĕr shtrĭk'ĕr). 13th-century Middle High German poet; author of epics, fables, and tales, as *Daniel vom Blühenden Tal*, *Pfaffen Amis*, etc.

**Strick'land** (strĭk'lănd), **Agnes**. 1796–1874. English historical writer; collaborated with her older sister **Elizabeth** (1794–1875) in *Lives of the Queens of England* (12 vols., 1840–48) and *Lives of the Queens of Scotland and English Princesses* (8 vols., 1850–59); sole author of *Lives of the Last Four Stuart Princesses* (1872) and novels, including *How Will It End?* (1865); biographized by her sister **Jane Margaret** (1800–1888), author of *Rome* (1854).

**Strickland, Hugh Edwin**. 1811–1853. English geologist. Grandson of Edmund Cartwright, inventor of power loom. Made geological tour of Asia Minor, Thracian Bosporus, Italy, and Switzerland (1835); associated with Sir Roderick I. Murchison in study of Silurian system; drew up rules of zoological nomenclature (1841–42), accepted with few modifications; a founder of Ray Society for publishing natural history works.

**Strickland, William**. 1787?–1854. American engraver, architect, and engineer, b. in Philadelphia. In architecture, leader in the Greek revival in America; designed the Masonic Temple, the customhouse, and the Merchants' Exchange, in Philadelphia, the marble sarcophagus of Washington at Mount Vernon, and the capitol of Tennessee at Nashville.

**Strig'ul** *or* **Strig'uil** (?strĭg'ŭl), Earls of. See (1) *Richard de Clare* (d. 1176), under family de CLARE. (2) MARSHAL family.

**Strind'berg'** (strĭn'băr'y'), **August**. 1849–1912. Swedish playwright and novelist; engaged variously as schoolteacher, private tutor, actor, and journalist; on staff of Royal Library, Stockholm (1874). Regarded as greatest modern writer in Sweden, sometimes called "the Shakespeare of Sweden." Among his plays are *Master Olof* (1874), *The Secret of the Guild* (1880), *Sir Bengt's Wife* (1882), *The Father* (1887), *Lady Julia* (1888), *To Damascus* (in 3 parts, 1898–1904), *Crimes and Crimes* (1899), *Gustavus Vasa* (1899), *Gustavus Adolphus* (1900), *The Dance of Death* (1901), *A Dream Play* (1902). Among his novels and tales are *The Red Room* (1879), *Swedish Fates and Adventures* (1882–83), *Realized Utopias* (1885), *Married* (1884–86), *The People of Hemsö* (1887), *In the Outer Skerries* (1890), *A Blue Book* (1907–08 ff.).

**String'er** (strĭng'ĕr), **Arthur John Ar·buth'nott** (är-bûrth'nŭt [*sic*]). 1874–1950. Fiction writer, b. in Chatham, Province of Ontario, Canada; author of *Watchers of Twilight* (1894), *Gun Runner* (1912), *City of Peril* (1923), *Dark Soil* (1933), *Heather of the High Hand* (1937), and several volumes of verse.

**Strobl** (shtrō'b'l), **Karl Hans**. 1877–1946. Austrian fiction writer.

**Strode** (strōd), **Ralph**. fl. 1350–1400. English schoolman; teacher of logic and philosophy, Oxford; against his colleague John Wycliffe, defended possession of wealth by clergy; dedicatee, with John Gower, of Chaucer's *Troilus and Criseyde;* listed as a *nobilis poeta* in fifteenth-century list of fellows of Merton Coll. Suggested by I. Gollancz as author of *The Pearl*.

**Strode, William**. 1599?–1645. English parliamentary leader, one of the Five Members; M.P. (1624–45); one of leaders holding John Finch, speaker of House of Commons, in his chair after his refusal to put Sir John Eliot's resolutions to vote (1629); imprisoned (till 1640); member of Short Parliament; in Long Parliament, proposed parliamentary control over ministerial appointments; supported Grand Remonstrance (1641); zealous in prosecution of Strafford and of Laud and bitter opponent of any compromise with Charles; one of five members impeached by Charles for high treason (1642).

**Strode, William**. 1602–1645. English poet; canon of Christ Church, Oxford (1638). Author of *The Floating Island*, a tragicomedy acted before Charles I and his queen (1636), and of lyrics and elegies.

**Stro'ga·nov** (strô'gŭ·nôf). Family of Russian nobles, descended from **Anika Stroganov**, an early 16th-century merchant and owner of salt pits and ironworks in the Ural Mountains. His three sons, **Yakov**, **Grigori**, and **Semën**, continued the business, Semën with Cossack help conquering western Siberia and annexing it to Russia (after 1581). Peter the Great abolished the privileges held by the members of the family then living, **Aleksandr**, **Nikolai**, and **Sergei**, but conferred upon them the title of baron. Nikolai's great-grandson **Sergei Grigorievich** (1794–1882) financed archaeological researches on the shore of the Black Sea, founded and endowed a school of design in Moscow, and served as curator of the Moscow educational district (1835–47), greatly improving conditions in the U. of Moscow.

**Stroh'mey'er** (shtrō'mī'ĕr), **Friedrich**. 1776–1835. German chemist; discovered the element cadmium (1817).

**Ström'gren'** (strûm'grān'), **Elis**. 1870–1947. Swedish astronomer; professor, Copenhagen (1907).

**Strong** (strŏng), **Anna Louise**. 1885–1970. American writer, b. Friend, Nebr.; m. (1932) Joel Shubin, of Moscow, U.S.S.R. In child-welfare work (1911–18), and newspaper and magazine work (1918–25); correspondent in Russia (1921–25). Author of *Songs of the City* (1906), *Children of Revolution* (1925), *China's Millions* (1928), *Red Star in Samarkand* (1929), *This Soviet World* (1936), *Spain in Arms* (1937), *One Fifth of Mankind* (on China; 1938), *My Native Land* (1940), *The Soviets Expected It* (1941), etc.

**Strong, Caleb**. 1745–1819. American politician, b. Northampton, Mass.; member of Constitutional Convention of 1787; one of first two U.S. senators from Massachusetts (1789–96); governor of Massachusetts (1800–07; 1812–16).

**Strong, Charles Augustus**. 1862–1940. American psychologist; professor, Columbia (1903–12); resided in Italy (from 1912). Author of *Why the Mind Has a Body* (1903), *The Origin of Consciousness* (1918), *The Wisdom of the Beasts* (1921), and *A Theory of Knowledge* (1923).

**Strong, Eugénie,** *nee* **Sel'lers** (sĕl'ĕrz). 1860–1943. Eng. classical scholar; educ. Girton Coll., Cambridge, of which she became (1910) first "life fellow"; m. (1897) S. Arthur Strong, librarian to House of Lords; asst. director, British School of Archaeology, Rome (1909–25); lecturer and editor of works on classical art and archaeology; author of *Roman Sculpture from Augustus to Constantine* (1907), *Apotheosis and After Life* (1915), *Art in Ancient Rome* (1929).

**Strong, George Veazey**. 1880–1946. American army officer, b. Chicago; grad. U.S.M.A., West Point (1904); LL.B., Northwestern (1916); lieut. col. during World War; military adviser to Disarmament Conference (1913–34); brigadier general (1938); assistant chief of staff (Oct., 1938); major general, commanding 8th army corps (May, 1941); appointed head of military intelligence branch (June, 1942).

**Strong, James.** 1822–1894. American educator, b. New York City; professor of exegetical theology, Drew Theol. Sem. (1867–93). Compiler of *Cyclopaedia of Biblical, Theological, and Ecclesiastical Literature* (with John M'Clintock, 10 vols., 1867–81), *The Exhaustive Concordance of the Bible* (1890). Author of *Irenics* (1883), *The Doctrine of a Future Life* (1891), etc.

**Strong, James Hooker.** 1814–1882. American naval officer; on *Monongahela* in battle of Mobile Bay (Aug. 5, 1864), rammed Confederate ironclad *Tennessee* and forced its surrender. Rear admiral (1873); commanded South Atlantic squadron (1873–75); retired (1876).

**Strong, Josiah.** 1847–1916. American clergyman; published *Our Country* (1885), which attracted wide attention because it emphasized evils and dangers in our social and economic life, followed by *The New Era* (1893), defining function of Christian Church to extend the kingdom of Christ on earth. Founded League for Social Service (1898), reorganized as American Institute for Social Service (1902), to carry on Christian work.

**Strong, Leonard Alfred George.** 1896–1958. English writer, of partly Irish descent; B.A., Oxon. (1920); schoolmaster for twelve years; director of Methuen Ltd. (1938 ff.). Author of verse including *Dublin Days, The Lowery Road, Difficult Love, Call to the Swan,* fiction including *Dewer Rides, The Jealous Ghost, The Garden, The Brothers, Sea Wall, Tuesday Afternoon, The Open Sky, They Went to the Island, The Bay,* and other prose works including *Common Sense about Poetry, The Minstrel Boy, John McCormack.*

**Strong, Richard Pearson.** 1872–1948. American physician in medical corps, U.S. army; established, and served as director of, army pathological laboratory; served as director of government biological laboratory, Manila, P.I. (1901–13); professor of tropical medicine, Harvard (1913–28; emeritus).

**Strong, William.** 1808–1895. American jurist; practiced law in Reading, Pa.; member, U.S. House of Representatives (1847–51); associate justice, U.S. Supreme Court (1870–80); chief figure in the Supreme Court's reversal of its decision declaring the Legal Tender Act of 1862 unconstitutional (decision rendered Feb. 7, 1870; decision reversed May 1, 1871, Strong writing the majority opinion).

**Strongbow, Richard.** 2d Earl of **Pembroke.** See under de CLARE family.

**Stross'may'er** (shtrŏs'mī'ẽr), **Joseph Georg.** 1815–1905. South Slavonic Roman Catholic prelate; ordained priest (1838); consecrated bishop of Djakovo (1850). Became leader of Croatian National party and promoter of pan-Slavism.

**Stro'ther** (strŏ'thẽr), **David Hunter.** 1816–1888. American illustrator and army officer, b. Martinsburg, Va. (now W.Va.). Did magazine illustrations, esp. a series of sketches (beginning 1853) of Southern life and scenes for *Harper's New Monthly Magazine* under pseudonym **Porte Cray'on** (pōrt' krā'ŏn). Served in Union army in Civil War; brevetted brigadier general (1865); U.S. consul general in Mexico City (1879–85). Contributed to *Harper's Magazine* series of articles, *Personal Recollections of the War* (1866–68), and *The Mountains* (1872–75), all illustrated by his own drawings.

**Stroud** (stroud), **William.** 1860–1938. English inventor and industrialist; professor of physics, Leeds (1885–1909); co-inventor (see Archibald BARR) of range finders and other instruments; chairman of Barr & Stroud, Ltd. (from 1931).

**Strow'ski' de Rob'ko'wa'** (strôv'skē' dẽ rôb'kô'vȧ'), **Fortunat.** 1866–1952. French educator; author of works on literary criticism; one of the group of French writers constituting the so-called "Jury."

**Stroz'zi** (strôt'tsē). Noble Florentine family, including: **Filippo** (1426–1491), known as The Elder; a banker; commenced (1489) construction of Strozzi Palace (completed 1553). His son **Giambattista** (1488–1538), known as Filippo II; became involved in intrigues against the Medicis; led attacks of Florentine exiles against Florence; defeated and captured, committed suicide in prison. Giambattista's son **Piero** (d. 1558) also fought the Medicis; fled to France and, after suicide of his father, entered French service; campaigned in Italy (1544, 1551, 1554); created marshal of France (1556); mortally wounded in action before Thionville (1558). Piero's brother **Leone** (1515–1554) entered Order of Malta; served in French navy against English and Spanish (1545–51); returned to command naval force of Order of Malta (1551); died of wounds received in action.

**Stroz'zi** (strôt'tsē) *or* **Stroz'za** (-tsä), **Bernardo.** 1581–1644. Italian painter and engraver, b. Genoa; known as **Il Ca'puc·ci'no** (ēl kä'po͞ot·chē'nō) *or* **Il Pre'te Ge'no·ve'se** (ēl prā'tā jā'nō·vā'sā), because he was for a time member of a Capuchin monastery, from which he escaped and fled to Venice.

**Strub'berg** (shtro͝ob'ĕrк), **Friedrich Armand.** *Pseudonym* **Ar'mand** (är'mänt). 1806–1889. Novelist, b. in Kassel, Germany; to U.S. (1826–29), agent for various mercantile houses. Settled in America (c. 1839); killed man in a duel in New York, assumed name of **Schub'bert** (sho͝ob'ẽrt) and fled to live on Texas frontier (c. 1841). Physician and director for Mainzer Adelsverein, a German organization to aid and transport German emigrants to Texas (1843). Practiced medicine in Arkansas during epidemic of smallpox and cholera (c. 1850–54). Resident in Germany (after 1854). Wrote series of more than fifty novels based on his experiences in the United States.

**Stru'be** (shtro͞o'bĕ), **Gu'stav** (go͝os'täf). 1867–1953. Violinist, conductor, and composer, b. Ballenstedt, Ger.; to U.S. (1890) and naturalized (1896). Organizer and conductor of Baltimore Symphony Orchestra (1915–30). Composer of symphonies, symphonic poems, concertos, sonatas, violin and piano pieces, etc.

**Stru'en·see'** (shtro͞o'ĕn·zā'), Count **Johann Friedrich von.** 1737–1772. German-Danish statesman and philosopher, b. Halle; educ. as a physician; became follower of Encyclopedists; appointed (1768) court physician to Christian VII of Denmark (*q.v.*); gained political authority as minister of state (1770); made extensive changes and reforms that often conflicted with national customs, but which in many cases were beneficial; absolute in power for about 10 months (1771–72); connected with scandal concerning Queen Caroline Matilda; forced out of office by conspiracy of nobles; condemned to death, tortured, and beheaded.

**Strug** (stro͞ok, **Andrzej.** *Pseudonym of* **Tadeusz Ga·lec'ki** (gä·lĕts'kē). 1873–1937. Polish novelist; author of *Story of a Bomb* (1910), *The Tomb of the Unknown Soldier* (1922), *The Fortune of Treasurer Spiewankiewicz* (1928), etc.

**Strun'sky** (strŭn'skĭ), **Simeon.** 1879–1948. Editor and essayist, b. Vitebsk, Russia; to U.S. in his youth. On staff of *New International Encyclopedia* (1900–06), New York *Evening Post* (1906–20); editor, New York *Evening Post* (1920–24); on editorial staff, New York *Times* (from 1924). Among his books are *The Patient Observer* (1911), *Post-Impressions* (1914), *King Akhnaton* (1928), *The Rediscovery of Jones* (1931), etc.

**Strupp** (shtrōōp), **Karl.** 1886–1940. German jurist.

**Struth'er** (strŭth'ẽr), **Jan.** *Pseudonym of* **Joyce Max'tone Gra'ham** (măks'tŭn grā'ăm; grâ'ăm), *nee* **An'struth'er** (ăn'strŭth'ẽr). 1901–1953. English writer; m. Anthony Maxtone Graham (1923). Among her books are *Betsinda Dances and Other Poems* (1931), *The Modern Struwwelpeter* (1936), *Try Anything Twice* (1938), *Mrs. Miniver* (1939), *The Glassblower and Other Poems* (1940).

**Strutt** (strŭt), **Jedediah.** 1726–1797. English cotton spinner; inventor of machine to be fixed to a stocking frame for producing ribbed goods, for which he, with his brother-in-law William Woollatt, took out patents (1758, 1759); entered partnership with Sir Richard Arkwright and erected cotton mill at Nottingham. His eldest son, **William** (1756–1830), invented the Belper stove (1806).

**Strutt, John William.** See 3d Baron RAYLEIGH.

**Strutt, Joseph.** 1749–1802. English antiquary; author of *A Complete View of the Dress and Habits of the People of England* (2 vols., 1796–99) and *The Sports and Pastimes of the People of England* (1801).

**Stru've** (*Ger.* shtrōō'vĕ). Name of a family of astronomers including: **Friedrich Georg Wilhelm von Struve** (1793–1864), b. Altona, Germany; educ. Dorpat (Tartu), Russia; observer (1813) and director (1817), Dorpat observatory; director, Pulkovo observatory (1839); known for investigations of double stars; one of first to measure stellar parallax; made geodetic survey of Livonia (1816–19); measured an arc of the meridian (1822–27). His son **Otto Wilhelm von Struve** (1819–1905), b. Dorpat; director, Pulkovo observatory (1862–89); discovered about 500 new double stars; made a new determination of the constant of precession; investigated rings of Saturn; made a determination of the mass of Neptune. Otto's son **Ludwig von Struve** (1858–1920), professor and director of the observatory, U. of Kharkov (1894), professor, Simferopol (1919), known for work on determination of the constant of precession and on proper motion of the solar system. Ludwig's son **Otto Stru've** [*Angl.* strōō'vē] (1897–1963), b. Kharkov, Russia; educ. Kharkov and Chicago (Ph.D., 1923); to U.S. (1921), naturalized (1927); assistant, Yerkes Observatory (1921–23); teacher (from 1924) and professor of astrophysics (from 1932), Chicago; director, Yerkes Observatory (from 1932) and McDonald Observatory of U. of Texas (from 1932).

**Stru've** (shtrōō'vĕ), **Gustav.** 1805–1870. Political agitator, b. in Munich, Ger.; practiced law in Mannheim; founded and edited *Deutscher Zuschauer*, a radical journal agitating for establishment of a republic (1846–48); took active part in revolutionary movement of 1848. On its failure, fled from Germany; to U.S. (1851); edited *Die Sociale Republik*, New York City (1858–59); served in Union army (1861–62). Resided in Germany from 1863.

**Strype** (strīp), **John.** 1643–1737. English ecclesiastical historian and biographer; collected original documents, esp. of Tudor period. Author of *Ecclesiastical Memorials 1513–1558* (3 vols., 1721) and of biographies of Cranmer (1694), Sir John Cheke (1705), Matthew Parker (1711), Whitgift (1718).

**Strzy·gow'ski** (schĭ·gôf'skē), **Josef.** 1862–1941. Austrian art critic and historian.

**Stu'art** (stū'ẽrt). See also STEWART.

**Stuart.** For members of family other than Scottish and English sovereigns and royal pretenders see STEWART family.

**Stu'art** *or* **Stew'art** *or* **Steu'art** (stū'ẽrt). Name of Scottish and English royal house tracing descent from a follower of William the Conqueror (see STEWART family), which provided several regents of Scotland, the sovereigns of Scotland from 1371 to 1688, the last four (from accession of James VI of Scotland as James I of England in 1603) being also sovereigns of England (see ROBERT II and III, JAMES I to V, and MARY, QUEEN OF SCOTS; JAMES I, CHARLES I and II, JAMES II, MARY II, and ANNE, of England). The title of James I to the English throne was through his great-grandmother Margaret (wife of James IV of Scotland), who was a daughter of Henry VII of England. After deposition of James II in 1688, the Jacobites long upheld the Stuart claim to British throne (see James Francis Edward STUART, Charles Edward STUART, and Henry Benedict Maria Clement Stuart, Cardinal YORK, the Jacobite Henry IX). See also *Tables* (*in Appendix*) for ENGLAND and GREAT BRITAIN.

**Stuart, Archibald.** 1757–1832. American politician, b. near Staunton, Va.; served in American Revolution; became leader of conservative branch of Jeffersonian Democrats in Virginia; judge of the general court of Virginia (1800–31). His son **Alexander Hugh Holmes** (1807–1891) was also a politician; member of U.S. House of Representatives (1841–43); U.S. secretary of the interior (1850–53); remained loyal to his state in Civil War; rector, U. of Virginia (1876–82; 1884–86).

**Stuart, Charles.** 1783–1865. Abolitionist, b. in Jamaica, B.W.I.; lieutenant in British East India Company's service (1801–14); to Canada and later to U.S. To England, lecturing against slavery in the British West Indies (1828); published tract, *The West India Question: Immediate Emancipation Safe and Practical* (1832). Lecturer for American Anti-Slavery Society in Ohio, Vermont, and New York (1834–38). Visited West Indies (1838–40) to study effects of emancipation. Honored at antislavery convention (1842).

**Stuart, Charles Edward Louis Philip Casimir.** *Often called* **Charles Edward.** 1720–1788. English prince, b. Rome. Known as the "Young Pretender" or "Young Chevalier" or "Bonnie Prince Charlie." Elder son of James Francis Edward Stuart, the Old Pretender; grandson of James II. Fought at siege of Gaeta (1734); sent by Marshal Saxe (1744) to head a quickly thwarted French invasion of England; landed in Hebrides unsupported (1745) and raised his father's standard in Scotland, heading the Forty-five, famous Jacobite uprising; after success at Prestonpans, crushed by duke of Cumberland at Culloden Moor (1746); after five months in hiding escaped to Brittany; expelled from France by terms of Treaty of Aix-la-Chapelle (1748), wandered incognito as count of **Al'ba·ny** (ôl'bȧ·nĭ); alienated supporters by illicit relations with Scottish mistress, Clementina Walkinshaw, by whom he had daughter, Charlotte Stuart, and by his imperious temper and drunken habits; m. (1772; separated 1784) Louisa von Stolberg (see countess of ALBANY); tended by his daughter till his death.

**Stuart, Gilbert Charles.** 1755–1828. American painter, b. in Rhode Island; studied under Benjamin West in London (1776). Studio in London (to 1787) and Dublin, Ireland (to 1793); gained distinction as portrait painter, ranked by contemporaries with Ramsay, Romney, Gainsborough, Reynolds. Studio in New York (1793), Philadelphia (1794–96), Germantown (1796–1803), Washington, D.C. (1803–05), and Boston (1805–28). Best known for his portraits of Washington, including five full-length portrayals. The so-called Athenaeum head of Washington, with its pendant the portrait of Martha Washington, is in the Boston Athenaeum; the so-called Gibbs-Channing portrait is now in the Metropolitan Museum of Art in New York City. He also painted John Adams, John Quincy Adams, Jefferson, Madison, Joseph Story, Judge Stephen Jones, F. S. Richards of Boston. During his residence in England he painted George III, George IV (as Prince of Wales), Mrs. Siddons, Sir Joshua Reynolds, Benjamin West. Elected to American Hall of Fame (1900). See Gilbert Stuart NEWTON.

**Stuart, Isaac William.** See under Moses STUART.

**Stuart, James.** 1713–1788. British painter and architect, known as "Athenian Stuart," b. London; son of Scottish mariner. Painter of fans for Lewis Goupy; after visits to Rome (1741) and Athens (1751), published with the architect Nicholas Revett (1720–1804) *The Antiquities of Athens* (1762), which, as first accurate account of monuments of Athens, led to introduction of Greek architecture in London.

**Stuart,** Sir **James.** 1780–1853. Canadian jurist; solicitor general of Lower Canada (1801); represented Montreal in House of Assembly (1808–17), leader of English party aiming at union of two provinces. Attorney general of Lower Canada (1825), suspended on account of independent attitude (1831); as chief justice of Lower Canada (1838), drafted Act of Union which became law (1841).

**Stuart, James Ewell Brown,** *known as* **Jeb.** 1833–1864. American army officer; grad. U.S.M.A., West Point (1854); resigned from U.S. army (1861) to join the Confederate service; brigadier general (Sept., 1861). Made spectacular raid completely around McClellan's army (June, 1862); engaged in Seven Days' Battles; promoted major general (Sept., 1862); engaged at Manassas. Led raid into Pennsylvania, reaching Chambersburg and again encircling Union army (Oct., 1862); commanded Confederate right at Fredericksburg; succeeded Jackson as corps commander at Chancellorsville; commanded cavalry force at Gettysburg (July 2–4, 1863). Mortally wounded in action (May 11, 1864) and died following day.

**Stuart, James Francis Edward.** *Often called* **James Edward.** 1688–1766. Known to Jacobites as "James III," to Hanoverians as the "Old Pretender," also as the "Chevalier de St. George." English prince of Wales; only son of James II by Mary of Modena. Carried by fugitive mother to court of St.-Germain, where proclaimed by Louis XIV (1701) successor to his father; attainted (1702); made futile attempt to land in Scotland (1708); served with French in Low Countries; landed at Peterhead during Mar's rebellion in his favor (1715) but fled before duke of Argyll; m. (1719) Princess Clementina Sobieski (1702–1735), granddaughter of king of Poland; had by her two sons, Charles Edward Stuart (*q.v.*) and Henry Benedict Stuart, known as Cardinal York. Presented with allowance and palace at Rome by Pope Clement XI.

**Stuart, Jesse Hilton.** 1907– . American writer, b. near Riverton, Ky. Awarded Guggenheim Fellowship (1937). Among his works are *Man with a Bull-Tongue Plow* (verse; 1934), *Head o'W-Hollow* (short stories; 1936), *Beyond Dark Hills* (autobiography; 1938), *Trees of Heaven* (novel; 1940), *Men of the Mountains* (stories; 1941).

**Stuart, John McDouall.** 1815–1866. South Australian explorer, b. in Fifeshire, Scotland; accompanied Captain Sturt's expedition (1844–45) as draftsman; made six expeditions (1858–62) into interior, the last bringing him to Van Diemen's Gulf on Indian Ocean.

**Stuart, John Todd.** 1807–1885. American lawyer, b. near Lexington, Ky.; grad. Centre College, Danville, Ky. (1826); practiced law in Springfield, Ill. (from 1828); in partnership with Abraham Lincoln in firm of Stuart and Lincoln (1837–41); member, U.S. House of Representatives (1839–43; 1863–65). He was a cousin of Mary Todd Lincoln (*q.v.*).

**Stuart, Mary.** See MARY, QUEEN OF SCOTS.

**Stuart, Moses.** 1780–1852. American theologian and educator, b. Wilton, Conn.; professor of sacred literature, Andover Sem. (1810–48); made himself an authority on Hebrew; forced recognition of German scholarship in U.S. Translator of many German works, including a Hebrew grammar and a Greek grammar of the New Testament. Author of series of commentaries on books of the Old Testament showing importance of German scholarship in Biblical criticism. Author of *Critical History and Defence of the Old Testament Canon* (1845). His son **Isaac William** (1809–1861), b. New Haven, Conn., was a historian; author of *Life of Captain Nathan Hale ...*(1856), *Life of Jonathan Trumbull...*(1859), etc.

**Stuart, Ruth,** *nee* **Mc·En'er·y** (măk·ĕn'ẽr·ĭ). 1849–1917. American writer, b. Marksville, in Avoyelles Parish, La.; m. Alfred Oden Stuart (1879; d. 1883). Her stories, chiefly of Southern life, include *A Golden Wedding and Other Tales* (1893), *Sonny* (1896), *In Simpkinsville ...*(1897), *The Second Wooing of Salina Sue...*(1905), *The Unlived Life of Little Mary Ellen* (1910), *Daddy Do-Funny's Wisdom Jingles* (1913).

**Stu'art-Jones'** (-jōnz'), Sir **Henry.** 1867–1939. English classical scholar, b. Leeds; professor of ancient history, Oxford (1920–27); principal, University Coll. of Wales, Aberystwyth (1927–34). Author of *The Roman Empire* (1908), *Classical Rome* (1910), and *Fresh Light on Roman Bureaucracy* (1920); reviser of Liddell and Scott's *Greek-English Lexicon* (1925; 9th ed.).

**Stuart-Wortley.** See *earls of Bute* under STEWART family.

**Stubbs** (stŭbz), **George.** 1724–1806. English animal painter; published *The Anatomy of the Horse* (1766), for which he drew and engraved all plates; executed pictures in enamel (1771). Known chiefly for accurate paintings of horses.

**Stubbs** *or* **Stubbes** (stŭbz), **John.** 1543?–1591. English Puritan; author of pamphlet *The Discoverie of a Gaping Gulf* (1579), condemning Queen Elizabeth's proposed marriage with Henry, Duke of Anjou, for which he and his printer had their right hands struck off. His kinsman **Philip Stubbs** *or* **Stubbes** (fl. 1583–1591), Puritan pamphleteer, denounced luxuries and evils of the times in *The Anatomie of Abuses* (1583), answered by Thomas Nash.

**Stubbs, William.** 1825–1901. English historian and prelate; vicar of Navestock, Essex (1850–66), where he began historical researches and published such early works as *Registrum Sacrum Anglicanum,* calendar of English bishops from Augustine (1858). As Oxford regius professor of modern history (1866–84), published his chief work, *The Constitutional History of England* (down to 1485; 3 vols., 1874–78), a standard authority. Canon of St. Paul's (1879); bishop of Chester (1884) and Oxford (1889); mostly abandoned historical researches with edition of William of Malmesbury's works (2 vols., 1887–89); actively interested in education and archaeology.

**Stuck** (shto͝ok), **Franz von.** 1863–1928. German painter and sculptor; contributed humorous illustrations to *Fliegende Blätter;* painted (from 1889) religious and allegorical subjects and portraits. Among his sculptures are a bronze statue of an athlete and a bronze statue of an Amazon on horseback.

**Stuck** (stŭk), **Hudson.** 1863–1920. Protestant Episcopal clergyman and author, b. in London, Eng.; to U.S. (1885). Dean of the cathedral at Dallas, Tex. (1894–1904); archdeacon of the Yukon (1904–20). One of group of four who made first ascent of Mount McKinley, Alaska (1913).

**Stuck′en·berg** (stŏŏk′ĕn·bûrg), **John Henry Wil′brandt** (wĭl′brănt). 1835–1903. Lutheran clergyman, b. at Bramsche, in Hanover, Ger.; to U.S. as a child. Professor of exegesis, Wittenberg (1873–80); pastor of American Church in Berlin, Ger. (1880–94). Among his notable books are *Ninety-five Theses* (1868), *History of the Augsburg Confession* (1869), *The Life of Immanuel Kant* (1882), *Introduction to the Study of Philosophy* (1888). Also specialized in study of sociology, and wrote *Introduction to the Study of Sociology* (1898) and *Sociology, the Science of Human Society* (2 vols., 1903).

**Stuc′ley** (stŭk′lĭ) *or* **Stuke′ly, Thomas.** 1525?–1578. English adventurer; sent by Henry II of France to England for information, revealed French plans for capture of Calais; imprisoned instead of being rewarded. Buccaneer (from 1558–65); engaged by Sir Henry Sidney in Ireland and by French ambassador in London; in service of Philip II of Spain, commanded three galleys at battle of Lepanto; concocted plots against England; joined expedition by King Sebastian of Portugal against Morocco; commanded center in battle of Alcázar, in which he was killed.

**Stu′de·ba′ker** (stū′dĕ·bā′kẽr), **Clement.** 1831–1901. American wagon manufacturer, b. near Gettysburg, Pa. With older brother Henry, founded firm of H. & C. Studebaker, South Bend, Ind. (1852). Other brothers entered the business, **John M.**, **Peter E.**, and **Jacob F.**; organized Studebaker Brothers Manufacturing Co. (1868), with Clement as president; developed largest wagon and carriage manufacturing company in the world. Manufacture of Studebaker automobiles begun after his death.

**Stud′nicz·ka** (shtŏŏt′nĭts·kä), **Franz.** 1860–1929. Austrian archaeologist and classical scholar.

**Stuer′mer** (shtür′mẽr). = STÜRMER.

**Stuke′ley** (stŭk′lĭ), **William.** 1687–1765. English antiquary, known as "The Arch-Druid"; wrote copiously on Druid remains, his chief work being on Stonehenge (1740).

**Stukely, Thomas.** See STUCLEY.

**Stü′ler** (shtü′lẽr), **Friedrich August.** 1800–1865. German architect; designer of the New Museum, several churches, and portions of the royal palace in Berlin, the Cologne Museum, the University of Königsberg, etc.

**Stülp′na′gel** (shtülp′nä′gĕl), **Otto von.** 1880–1948. German army officer; educ. at Potsdam Military College; served in World War (1914–18); on the general staff as quartermaster general (1938); chairman, German-French Armistice Commission, Wiesbaden (1940); commander of occupied France (1940 ff.).

**Stumm** (shtŏŏm), **Karl.** *Ennobled* (1888) *as* Baron **von Stumm′–Hal′berg** (-häl′bĕrk). 1836–1901. German industrialist and politician; succeeded to proprietorship of family ironworks at Neunkirchen (1858). Member of Reichstag (1867–81; 1889–1901); vigorous opponent of Socialism.

**Stumpf** (shtŏŏmpf), **Carl.** 1848–1936. German philosopher and psychologist; investigated the sensation of tone and wrote *Tonpsychologie* (2 vols., 1883–90), *Beiträge zur Akustik und Musikwissenschaft* (9 parts, 1898–1924), *Die Sprachlaute* (1926), etc.; founded archives of phonograph records of primitive music (1901).

**Stumpf, Johannes.** 1500–1577 (or 1578). Swiss historian; collaborated with Aegidius Tschudi (*q.v.*) and others in preparing *Gemeiner Loblicher Eidgenossenschaft Städten, Landen und Völkern Chronikwürdiger Taten Beschreibung* (13 books, 1546).

**Stur′dee** (stûr′dē), Sir **Doveton,** *in full* **Frederick Charles Doveton.** 1859–1925. British naval commander; rear admiral (1908), admiral (1917), and admiral of the fleet (1921). Commanded the *Invincible* in the naval action off Falkland Islands (Dec. 8, 1914) during which the German raiding squadron under Admiral von Spee was destroyed; commanded 4th battle squadron in battle of Jutland (May 31, 1916).

**Sturdee, Vernon Ashton Hobart.** 1890–1966. Australian soldier; served in Middle East during World War (1914–18); director of military operations and intelligence (1933–37), of staff duties at army headquarters (1937–39); commander of Eastern Command, Australia (1939–40), of 8th Division, Australian Imperial Force (1940); lieutenant general (1941); chief of general staff, Australia (1940–42); appointed (Mar., 1942) chief of staff to Sir T. A. Blamey (*q.v.*).

**Stur′dza** (stŏŏr′dzä) *or* **Stur′za** (stŏŏr′zä). Ancient Rumanian family, including: **Alexander** (1791–1854), journalist and diplomat in Russian service; **Michael** (1795–1884), Prince of **Mol·da′vi·a** [mŏl·dā′vĭ·ȧ] (1834–49), who improved country's educational system and general economic conditions; **Ioan**, Prince of Moldavia (1822–28), who suppressed Greek irregular troops roaming through Moldavia after Greek revolution, improved educational conditions, was captured by Russians (1828) and died in exile; **Dimitrie** (1833–1914), who was a statesman, and four times premier of Rumania (1895–96, 1897–99, 1901–06, 1907–09), and wrote on current national and international issues.

**Stu′re′** (stŏŏ′rĕ′). Name of family of Swedish nobility, especially: **Sten** the Elder (1440?–1503); son of half sister of King Charles VIII. On death of Charles, appointed regent of Sweden (1470–1503); led Swedes against Danish rule; defeated Christian I at Brunkeberg (1471); aided in founding U. of Uppsala (1477); encouraged printing of first books in Sweden (1483); compelled by nobles to acknowledge rule (1497–1501) of King John of Denmark over Sweden. Succeeded as regent by **Svante** (d. 1512; regent 1503–12). Svante succeeded by his son **Sten** the Younger (1493?–1520); regent (1512–20); conducted long feud (1513–17) with archbishop of Uppsala; fought against Danish army (1518–20) under Christian II, who besieged Stockholm; mortally wounded at Bogesund.

**Stur′geon** (stûr′jŭn), **William.** 1783–1850. English electrician and inventor; devised first electromagnet (1823); described process of amalgamating zinc plate of battery with film of mercury (1830); constructed electromagnetic rotary engine; established *Annals of Electricity*, first electrical journal in England (1836); invented first moving-coil galvanometer (1836).

**Stur′gis** (stûr′jĭs), **Russell.** 1836–1909. American architect, b. Baltimore; among buildings designed by him are Flower Hospital in New York Farmers' & Mechanics' Bank building in Albany, and Battell Chapel, Farnam, Durfee, and Lawrance halls at Yale College. Devoted himself largely to writing (from c. 1885). Editor for art and archaeology for *Webster's International Dictionary*, *Century Dictionary*, *Johnson's Universal Encyclopedia*. Edited "The Field of Art" in *Scribner's Magazine* (1897–1909). Editor in chief of *A Dictionary of Architecture and Building* (3 vols., 1901–02), *Outlines of the History of Art* (2 vols., 1904). Author of first two volumes of *A History of Architecture* (4 vols., 1906–15; vols. III & IV by Arthur L. Frothingham). Wrote a series of books on art appreciation. His son **Richard Clipston** (1860–1951), also an architect, practiced in Boston (from 1887); among buildings of his design are Public Library of Brookline, Mass., Cathedral of Manila, Philippine Islands, Federal Reserve Bank building of Boston.

**Stürgkh** (shtürk), Count **Karl von.** 1859–1916. Austrian prime minister (1911–16); assassinated by Friedrich Adler.

**Sturleson** *or* **Sturluson, Snorri.** See SNORRI STURLUSON.

**Sturm** (stürm), **Jacques Charles François.** 1803–1855. French mathematician, b. Geneva, Switzerland; known for work on differential equations, optics, and mechanics; originated a theorem (Sturm's theorem) for determining the number and position of the real roots, between given limits, of an algebraic equation.

**Sturm** (shtŏŏrm), **Johannes.** 1507–1589. German educator; head of a school in Strasbourg (1538 ff.) emphasizing maintenance of strict discipline and thorough mastery of the classics. Author of treatises on educational organization and methods.

**Sturm, Julius.** 1816–1896. German clergyman and lyric poet; published *Fromme Lieder* (3 parts, 1852, 1858, 1892), *Israelitische Lieder* (1867), *Gott Grüsse Dich* (1876), *Palmen und Krone* (1888). His son **August** (1852–1923) practiced law at Naumburg (from 1884); published epic poems, volumes of lyrics, plays, etc.

**Stür'mer** (*Ger.* shtür'mẽr; *Russ.* shtyōō r'myẽr), **Boris Vladimirovich.** 1849–1917. Russian politician, of German descent; governor of Novgorod (1894), and later of Yaroslavl province; premier of Russia (Jan.–Nov., 1916); suspected of having treasonable relations with Germany; arrested after the Russian Revolution (1917), and died in prison.

**Sturm von Stur'meck** (shtŏŏrm' fôn shtŏŏr'mĕk), **Jakob.** 1489–1553. Strasbourg statesman and Reformation leader; represented Strasbourg at Spires (1526) and later, at second Diet of Spires (1529); signed the "protest" presented to the assembly and thus became one of the original "Protestants." Founded the Protestant Gymnasium in Strasbourg (1538), which later developed into the University of Strasbourg.

**Štur'sa** (shtŏŏr'sȧ), **Jan.** 1880–1925. Czech sculptor; regarded as a leader of the modern Czech school of sculpture; among his works are *Eve, Hetaira, Wounded Man*, and many portrait busts.

**Sturt** (stûrt), **Charles.** 1795–1869. English explorer in Australia; secretary to Sir Ralph Darling, governor of New South Wales (1827); led several expeditions into interior of Australia; discovered Darling River (1828); surveyor general, South Australia (1833); returned from third expedition quite blind (1846); colonial secretary (1849–51); died in England.

**Stur'te·vant** (stûr'tĕ·vănt), **Edgar Howard.** 1875–1952. American educator and philologist, b. Jacksonville, Ill.; A.B., Indiana (1898); Ph.D., Chicago (1901); taught Latin at Indiana U. (1901–02, 1905–07), classical philology at Columbia (1907–20); clerk in N.Y. City bank (1920–23); on teaching staff, Yale (from 1923; professor of linguistics, from 1927); author of *Studies in Greek Noun Formation* (4 parts; 1910–13), *Linguistic Change* (1917), *The Pronunciation of Latin and Greek* (1920; 2d ed., 1940), *Hittite Glossary* (1931; 2d ed., 1937), *A Comparative Grammar of the Hittite Language* (1933), *Hittite Chrestomathy* (1935).

**Sturza.** See STURDZA.

**Stur'zo** (stŏŏr'tsō), **Luigi.** 1871–1959. Italian priest and political leader; founded Popular party in Italy (1919); as opponent of Fascism, fled to England (1926). Author of *Italy and Fascism* (1926), *The International Community and the Right of War* (1929), etc.

**Stutz** (shtōōts), **Ulrich.** 1868–1938. German legal scholar.

**Stuy've·sant** (stī'vĕ·s'nt; *Du.* stoi'vĕ·sänt), **Peter,** *orig.* **Petrus.** 1592–1672. Dutch administrator in America, b. in West Friesland, the Netherlands. Served in Dutch army, and in employ of Dutch West India Company (1635). Governor of Curaçao and adjacent islands (1643); lost his right leg in campaign against island of St. Martin (1644). Appointed director-general of New Netherland and adjacent regions (1646); arrived in New Amsterdam (May, 1647). Conciliated the Indians; arranged a boundary line with Hartford settlers (1650); expelled the Swedes from Delaware (1655); aroused great discontent in colony by dictatorial measures. Forced to surrender New Netherlands to the English (Sept., 1664); defended himself in the Netherlands against charges (1665). Returned to New York and lived on his farm on the "Bouwerij" (Bowery).

**Stylites,** Saint **Simeon.** See SIMEON STYLITES.

**Suar'di** (swär'dē), **Bartolommeo.** *Called* **Il Bra'man·ti'no** (ēl brä'män·tē'nō). c. 1460–c. 1536. Italian painter and architect of the Lombard school; court architect to Duke Francesco Sforza (1525 ff.). His works include *St. Martin* and *Crucifixion* (the Brera, Milan), *Adoration of the Magi* (Venice), and *Ecce Homo* (the Certosa, Pavia).

**Suá'rez** (swä'rāth), **Francisco.** 1548–1617. Spanish Jesuit theologian and scholastic philosopher, b. in Granada. Taught philosophy at Segovia (1572–74) and theology at Valladolid (1576 ff.), Collegium Romanum at Rome (1580–85), and at Alcalá, Salamanca, and Coimbra (1585 ff.). Considered foremost Jesuit theologian; adherent of Thomas Aquinas; opposed by strict Dominican Thomists for tending toward Molinism. Author of a commentary on Thomas Aquinas's *Summa Theologica* (5 vols., 1590–1603), *Disputationes Metaphysicae* (2 vols., 1597), *De Virtute et Statu Religionis* (4 vols., 1608–25), *Defensio Fidei* (1613), and *De Divina Gratia* (3 parts, 1620).

**Sub'lette** (sŭb'lĕt; -lĭt), **William Lewis.** 1799?–1845. American soldier and fur trader, b. in Lincoln County, Ky. Member of Ashley's expedition to the Rocky Mountains (1823); led his own expedition to that region for trading (1828, 1832) and to Santa Fe (1831); part of Oregon Trail became known first as "Sublette's cut-off" and "Sublette's trace." Was first to drive wagons over the trail to the Rockies.

**Sub'o·tai'** (sŭb'ō·tī') *or* **Sab'u·tai'** (sŭb'ōō·tī'). *Called* **Ba'ga·tur'** (bä'gȧ·tōōr'), *i.e.* the Valiant. 1172?–1245. Mongol general, a master strategist; chief of staff of Genghis Khan; led Mongol armies under Genghis and Ogadai in many campaigns in Asia; planned and aided Batu Khan's conquests in Europe (1237–41). See BATU KHAN.

**Su·buk'ti·gin'** (sōō·bŏŏk'tĭ·gēn') *or* **Sa·buk'ta·gin'** (să·bŏŏk'tă·gēn'). d. 997. Moslem sultan of Ghazni (977–997) and founder of Ghaznevid dynasty; father of Mahmud of Ghazni. A Turk slave; by marriage, obtained rule in Ghazni (977); extended territory over all Afghanistan and into India.

**Su'cher** (zōō'kẽr), **Rosa,** *nee* **Has'sel·beck** *or* **Ha'sl·beck** (häs'ĕl·bĕk). 1849–1927. German operatic soprano; m. (1877) **Josef Sucher** (1843–1908), conductor, known for his interpretation of Wagnerian music. She sang in opera in Hamburg (1879–88) and Berlin (1888–99), notably in Wagnerian roles.

**Su'chet'** (sü'shĕ'), **Louis Gabriel.** 1772–1826. French soldier, b. at Lyons; volunteered for service (1792); general in chief of the army of Italy (1800); commanded a division in the battles of Austerlitz (1805), Jena (1806), and Pultusk (1806); served in Peninsular War (1808–14). Created marshal of France and duc d'Albufera (1811).

**Suck'ling** (sŭk'lĭng), Sir **John.** 1609–1642. English Cavalier poet, son of Sir **John Suckling** (1569–1627;

comptroller of the household and secretary of state, descendant of an old Norfolk family). Inherited large estates from father (1627); traveled in France and Italy (1628–30); volunteered under Gustavus Adolphus (1631–32). Became famous for wit and prodigality; inventor of game of cribbage; retired to his estates (1635) and wrote *A Session of the Poets* (1637), poem descriptive of his contemporaries, a tract on Socinianism, and four plays valuable only for their good lyrics: *Aglaura*, produced at his own expense (1637), containing the lyric "Why so pale and wan, fond lover?," *The Goblins* (1638), *Brennoralt, or the Discontented Colonel* (1639), reflecting his own character, and *The Sad One* (unfinished). At outbreak of Civil War raised troop of one hundred horse, accompanied Charles on Scottish expedition (1639); was returned to Long Parliament; took part in plot to rescue Strafford from Tower (1641) and had to flee to Continent; said by John Aubrey to have poisoned himself in Paris in fear of poverty.

**Suck′ow** (sōō′kō), **Ruth.** 1892–1960. American writer, b. Hawarden, Iowa; m. Ferner Nuhn (1929). Author of *The Odyssey of a Nice Girl* (1925), *The Folks* (1934), *Carry-Over* (1936), *New Hope* (1941), etc.

**Su′cre** (sōō′krā), **Antonio José de.** 1795–1830. South American liberator and general, b. Cumaná, Venezuela. Bolívar's chief lieutenant in campaign (1821) against Spain in Quito (Ecuador); won battle of Pichincha (1822). Served under Bolívar in Peru (1823–25) and with him defeated Spanish at Junín; won battle of Ayacucho (1824). Convened deliberative assembly in Upper Peru, now Bolivia (1825). First president of new republic (1826–28); resigned because of opposition of native Bolivians. Assassinated near Pasto, Colombia (June 4, 1830).

**Sud′bur·y** (sŭd′bĕr·ĭ; -bĕr′ĭ), **Simon of.** *Sometimes* **Simon The′o·bald** (thē′ô·bôld; tĭb′ăld) *or* **Tyb′ald** (tĭb′ăld). d. 1381. English prelate; one of chaplains of Pope Innocent VI, who made him bishop of London (1361); archbishop of Canterbury (1375); crowned Richard II; tried Wycliffe at Lambeth (1378); chancellor of England (from 1380); imprisoned John Ball, who was released by rebellious mob; held accountable by insurgents for their distress, dragged from Tower and beheaded.

**Su′der·mann** (zōō′dĕr·män), **Hermann.** 1857–1928. German playwright and novelist; educ. Königsberg and Berlin. Among his plays are *Ehre* (1889), *Sodoms Ende* (1891), *Heimat* (1893), *Schmetterlingsschlacht* (1895), *Das Glück im Winkel* (1895), *Johannes* (1898), *Drei Reiherfedern* (1899), *Stein unter Steinen* (1905), *Blumenboot* (1905). Among his novels are *Frau Sorge* (1887), *Der Katzensteg* (1891), *Es War* (1894), *Der Tolle Professor* (1926), *Die Frau des Steffen Tromholt* (1927).

**Südfeld, Max Simon.** See Max NORDAU.

**Sue** (sü; *Angl.* sōō), **Eugène,** *really* **Marie Joseph.** 1804–1857. French novelist, b. at Paris. Took name *Eugène* from his patron Prince Eugène de Beauharnais. Studied painting and medicine; served six years as naval surgeon. Among his works are *Plick et Plock* (1831), *La Coucaratcha* (1832–34), *Arthur* (1838), *Mathilde* (1841), *Le Morne au Diable* (1842), the enormously popular *Mystères de Paris* (1842–43), and the classic *Juif Errant* (*Wandering Jew*, 1844–45). Lived in exile after the coup d'état of Napoleon III on Dec. 2, 1851.

**Suess** (züs), **Eduard.** 1831–1914. Austrian geologist and paleontologist, b. London; authority on structural geology, esp. of mountains.

**Suesse, Dana Nadine.** 1911–    . American composer, b. Shreveport, La. In addition to many song hits, she composed *Concerto in Three Rhythms*, *Young Man with a Harp* (performed by Philadelphia Symphony orchestra, July, 1939), *Evening in Harlem*, *Jazz Nocturne*, etc.

**Sue·to′ni·us** (swē·tō′nĭ·ŭs). *In full* **Gaius Suetonius Tran·quil′lus** (trăng·kwĭl′ŭs). Roman biographer and historian; accompanied younger Pliny to Bithynia (112 A.D.); private secretary to Emperor Hadrian (c. 119–121 A.D.). Chief work, *Lives of the Caesars*. Only fragments of his other works are extant.

**Su·e·tsu·gu** (sōō·ĕ·tsōō·gōō), **Nobumasa.** 1881–1944. Japanese naval officer; grad. naval academy (1899); held many naval posts including chief of staff of 1st fleet, commander of submarine squadron, director of education bureau of navy, commander in chief of 2d fleet, then of 1st fleet; supreme war councilor; admiral, on reserve list (1937); home minister in Konoye cabinet; member of cabinet advisory council.

**Suf′folk** (sŭf′ŭk), Dukes of. See POLE family; Charles BRANDON; *Henry Grey* (d. 1554), under GREY family.

**Suffolk,** Earls of. See Robert and William de UFFORD; de la POLE family; HOWARD family.

**Suffolk,** Countess of. See Henrietta HOWARD.

**Sugden, Edward Burtenshaw.** See Baron ST. LEONARDS.

**Su′ger′** (sü′zhâr′). 1081?–1151. French churchman and statesman; became abbé of Saint-Denis (1122); counselor of Louis VI (from 1124); official minister (1130–37); minister to Louis VII (1137–51); regent of France (1147–49) while the king was away on the Second Crusade. Increased wealth of Saint-Denis; given title (1149) by Louis VII of "Père de la Patrie." An able administrator and author of several historical works.

**Su·gi·ya·ma** (sōō·gē·yä·mä), **Hajime.** 1880–1945. Japanese army officer; educ., Military College; attended Disarmament Conference, Geneva (1926–28); vice-chief of the general staff (1934); member of Supreme War Council (1935); minister of war (1937–38; 1944–45); commander in North China (1938–39); chief of general staff (1940–44); field marshal (1943); committed suicide.

**Sui** (swē). A Chinese dynasty (589–618 A.D.), uniting China after several centuries of confusion; followed by the T'ang dynasty.

**Su′i·das** (sū′ĭ·dăs). Greek lexicographer of Constantinople, probably of late 10th century A.D.; compiler of an encyclopedic Greek lexicon.

**Suk** (sōōk), **Josef.** 1874–1935. Czech violinist and composer of symphonies, symphonic poems, choral works, chamber music, and piano pieces.

**Su·khom·li′nov** (sōō·kŭm·lyē′nôf), **Vladimir Aleksandrovich.** 1848–1926. Russian general; chief of the general staff (1908); minister of war (1909); held responsible for Russian military unpreparedness at the outbreak (1914) of the World War. Convicted of treason by the provisional government (1917) and sentenced to life imprisonment; amnestied by the Soviet government (1918) and took refuge in Germany.

**Su·lei·man′** (sü·lā·män′). *Arab.* **Su·lay·mān′** (sōō·lī·măn′). d. 717. Ommiad caliph (715–717); besieged Constantinople (716–717); forced by Emperor Leo III to give up siege.

**Su·lei·man′** (sü·lā·män′). d. 1108. = Sultan KILIJ ARSLAN I.

**Su·lei·man′** (sü·lā·män′) *or* **Sol′y·man** (sŏl′ĭ·măn). Name of three Turkish rulers: **Suleiman,** *sometimes called* **Suleiman I** (d. 1411), eldest son of Bajazet I, was an independent ruler (1403–11) in Adrianople. **Suleiman I** (*or* **II**), *known as* **the Magnificent** (1496?–1566), succeeded his father, Selim I, as sultan (1520); added to his territories Belgrade, Budapest, Rhodes, Tabriz, Baghdad, Aden, Algiers; organized the ulema, or clerical class, in hierarchical order with Sheikh ul Islam at its head; reformed and improved administration of the country, and encouraged arts and sciences.

**Suleiman II** [*or* **III**] (1641–1691) succeeded his brother Mohammed IV as sultan (1687); faced disturbed conditions within Turkey and an unsuccessful war with Austria; entrusted administration to his minister Mustafa Kuprili, who introduced numerous liberal reforms.

**Suleiman Pa·sha'** (pä·shä'). 1840–1892. Turkish general and politician; involved in deposition of Sultan Abdul-Aziz (1876); in Russo-Turkish War (1877–78), held command in Bulgaria, and was forced to retreat to Constantinople; charged with treason and imprisoned (1878), but later pardoned.

**Sul'la** (sŭl'ȧ), **Lucius Cornelius.** *Surnamed* **Fe'lix** (fē'lĭks). 138–78 B.C. Roman general and politician; served as quaestor in army of Marius against Jugurtha (107–106 B.C.), and captured Jugurtha; served successfully against the Cimbri and Teutones (104–101). Praetor (93); propraetor in Cilicia (92); served in Social War (90–89); consul (88). Aspired to dictatorial power; opened civil war against Marius (88), and captured Rome. Campaigned against Mithridates (87–83). Returned to Italy (83) and defeated the younger Marius (82). Dictator of Rome (82–79); proscribed great numbers of the leaders among the Marian party, most of whom were killed. During his dictatorship, reorganized the senate and the judiciary, and founded military colonies throughout Italy.

**Sul'li·van** (sŭl'ĭ·văn), **Alan.** *Pseudonym* **Sinclair Murray.** 1868–1947. Canadian novelist, author esp. of adventure stories, many of them set along the Gulf of St. Lawrence; author of *Rapids* (1920), *Jade God* (1925; dramatized 1930), *Broken Marriage* (1929), *Ironmaster* (1931), *Cornish Interlude* (1932), *Man at Lone Tree* (1933), *Great Divide* (1935), *Money Spinners* (1936), *With Love from Rachel* (1937), *Cycle of the North* (1938), *Three Came to Ville Marie* (1941), etc.

**Sullivan,** Sir **Arthur Seymour.** 1842–1900. English composer, b. London; organist and choirmaster, St. Michael's, Chester Square, London (1861–72); gained reputation by performance of his *Tempest* music at Crystal Palace (1862); produced the cantata *Kenilworth* (1864), the comic opera *Cox and Box* (in collaboration with F. C. Burnand; produced 1867), overtures *In Memoriam* (1866) and *Marmion* (1867), two oratorios, *The Prodigal Son* (1869) and *The Light of the World* (1873), *Te Deum* (1871) in celebration of recovery of prince of Wales, later Edward VII; conductor of a number of orchestras and festivals. Collaborated with W. S. Gilbert first in *Thespis* (1871), then in memorable series of comic operas (for which see William Schwenck GILBERT). First principal of National Training School of Music (1876–81); produced incidental music to *Henry VIII* (1877), sacred cantata *The Martyr of Antioch* (1880), setting to Longfellow's *Golden Legend* (1886), and a serious opera, *Ivanhoe* (1891). During disagreement with Gilbert over financial arrangements produced opera *Haddon Hall* (1892); resumed collaboration with Gilbert in *Utopia, Limited* (1893). Best known, outside of comic operas, for his songs, including "Orpheus with his Lute," "Thou'rt Passing Hence," "The Lost Chord," and for the hymn tune "Onward, Christian Soldiers."

**Sullivan, Edmund J.** 1869–1933. English illustrator of *Tom Brown's Schooldays, The Rivals, Sartor Resartus, Natural History of Selborne, Omar Khayyam,* etc.

**Sullivan, Frank,** *in full* **Francis John.** 1892– . American humorist; author of *Life and Times of Martha Hepplethwaite* (1926), *Broccoli and Old Lace* (1931), *In One Ear* (1933), *Sullivan at Bay* (1939), etc.

**Sullivan, George.** See under John SULLIVAN.

**Sullivan, James Edward.** 1860–1914. American sports promoter, b. New York City; organized Amateur Athletic Union of the United States (1888); did much to revive Olympic games; served as American director at the games, and was personal representative of two presidents, Theodore Roosevelt (1906 and 1908) and William H. Taft (1912), at the games. Did much to maintain true standards of amateurism in sports.

**Sullivan, John.** 1740–1795. American Revolutionary officer; practiced law in Durham, N.H. (from 1760); member of Continental Congress (1774, 1775, 1780, 1781); commissioned brigadier general (June, 1775); served through siege of Boston (1775–76); promoted major general (Aug., 1776); engaged and was captured at battle of Long Island (Aug. 27, 1776) and was exchanged. Led unsuccessful expedition against British on Staten Island (Aug., 1777); engaged at Germantown; spent winter at Valley Forge (1777–78). Commanded American forces besieging Newport (1778) but failed because of lack of co-operation by French fleet. With Gen. James Clinton (Sullivan-Clinton expedition) defeated combined Indian-Loyalist contingent near Elmira, N.Y. (Aug. 29, 1779) and ravaged the country. Resigned commission (Nov. 30, 1779). Attorney general of New Hampshire (1782–86); president of New Hampshire (1786, 1787, 1789); U.S. district judge of New Hampshire (1789–95). His brother **James** (1744–1808) was a lawyer; practiced at Limerick, Me. (to 1778) and Groton, Mass. (from 1778); member of Continental Congress (1782); governor of Massachusetts (1807, 1808); author of *The History of the District of Maine* (1795), etc. A son of John Sullivan, **George** (1771–1838), was a lawyer and politician; represented New Hampshire in famous Dartmouth College Case (1817).

**Sullivan, John Lawrence.** 1858–1918. American heavyweight pugilist, b. Boston. Won championship by defeat of Paddy Ryan at Mississippi City, Miss., fighting with bare knuckles and on the turf (Feb. 7, 1882); lost championship to James J. Corbett (Sept. 7, 1892).

**Sullivan, Louis Henri.** 1856–1924. American architect, b. Boston; in independent practice (from 1900). Notable among buildings designed by him are Auditorium Building, Chicago; Transportation Building at World's Columbian Exposition (1893); the Wainwright Building and Union Trust Building in St. Louis; the Gage Building and Stock Exchange Building in Chicago; the Bayard Building in New York. Regarded as the father of modernism in architecture, esp. as adapting architecture to modern needs by his designs of the skyscraper.

**Sullivan, Mark.** 1874–1952. American journalist, b. Avondale, Pa.; columnist and commentator, New York *Herald-Tribune;* author of *Our Times—the United States* (6 vols., 1900–25), *The Education of an American* (1938), etc.

**Sul'li·vant** (sŭl'ĭ·vănt), **William Starling.** 1803–1873. American botanist; surveyor and civil engineer in Ohio; interested himself in botany (from c. 1833); specialized in study of mosses. Author of *Musci Alleghanienses* (2 vols., 1845–46), *Musci Boreali-Americani* (with Leo Lesquereux, 1856), *Icones Muscorum* (1864), etc.

**Sul'ly'** (sü'lē'; *Angl.* sŭl'ĭ), Duc **de. Maximilien de Bé'thune'** (dē bā'tün'). Baron **de Ros'ny'** (rō'nē'). 1560–1641. French statesman, b. near Mantes-sur-Seine; brought up a Protestant; friend of young Henry at court of Navarre; accompanied Henry in his flight from French court (1576); fought in campaigns against Holy League (1576–90). Appointed minister of finance by Henry IV (1597); held many high offices during remainder of reign (1597–1610); reorganized finances of

France, replenished the treasury, promoted agriculture, construction of roads and bridges, etc. Created duc de Sully (1606). At Henry's death forced to resign; lived in retirement (1610–41). Wrote *Mémoires* (1638), a dry but valuable account of contemporary events.

**Sul'ly** (sŭl'ĭ), **James.** 1842–1923. English psychologist and philosopher; professor, University Coll., London. Author of *Sensation and Intuition* (1874), *Pessimism* (1877), *The Human Mind* (1892), *Children's Ways* (1897), *An Essay on Laughter* (1902), etc.

**Sully, Thomas.** 1783–1872. Painter, b. Horncastle, in Lincolnshire, Eng.; to U.S. as a boy (1792). Studied with his brother **Lawrence** (d. 1803); opened studio in New York (1806), and Philadelphia (1808); known to have painted more than 2600 works. Among his best-known works are *Washington Crossing the Delaware*, now in Boston Museum of Art; *Marquis de Lafayette*, in Independence Hall, Philadelphia; and *Jefferson, Madison, Jackson*, etc.

**Sul'ly' Pru'dhomme'** (sü'lē' prü'dôm'), **René François Armand.** 1839–1907. French poet and literary critic, b. Paris. Among his volumes of verse are *Stances et Poèmes* (1865), *Les Épreuves* (1866), *Les Solitudes* (1869), *Les Destins* (1872), *Les Vaines Tendresses* (1875), *La Justice* (1878), *Le Prisme* (1886), *Le Bonheur* (1888); among his critical works, *De l'Expression dans les Beaux Arts* (1884) and *Réflexion sur l'Art des Vers* (1892). First to be awarded Nobel prize in literature (1901).

**Sul·pi'ci·us** (sŭl·pĭsh'ĭ·ŭs; -pĭsh'ŭs), **Servius Rufus.** d. 43 B.C. Roman jurist and orator, to whom Cicero devoted several chapters of his *Brutus;* consul (51 B.C.) and proconsul of Achaia after the battle of Pharsalus (46 B.C.).

**Sulpicius Ru'fus** (rōō'fŭs), **Publius.** 121?–88 B.C. Roman statesman; tribune of the plebs (88 B.C.). At outbreak of civil war between Sulla and Marius, declared himself in favor of Marius; captured by Sulla when Sulla seized Rome (88) and immediately executed. He is introduced as an interlocutor in Cicero's *De Oratore.*

**Sulpicius Se·ve'rus** (sē·vḗr'ŭs). 360?–?410. Latin Christian writer, b. in Aquitaine. In early life, a lawyer; later, attached himself to Saint Martin of Tours, gave his goods to the poor, and devoted himself to religion. Chief work, *Chronicle*, a concise résumé of world history.

**Sulte** (sült), **Benjamin.** 1841–1923. Canadian writer, b. at Three Rivers, Quebec; government clerk (1867–1903; retired). Author of *Les Laurentiennes* (verse, 1870), *Les Chants Nouveaux* (verse, 1876), *Histoire des Canadiens-Français* (8 vols., 1882–84), *History of Quebec* (1908), *Mélanges Historiques* (10 vols., 1918–22).

**Sulz'ber'ger** (sŭlz'bûr'gēr; sŏŏlz'-), **Cyrus Lin'dau'er** (lĭn'dou'ēr). 1858–1932. Cousin of Mayer Sulzberger. American merchant and philanthropist, b. Philadelphia. In employ of textile-importing firm of N. Erlanger, Blumgart & Co., New York City (from 1877); president of the firm (1902) and chairman of its board of directors (1929). Student of problems of Jewish immigration into U.S.; aided in distributing Jewish immigrants in localities outside of New York City; president (1903–09; 1919–21) of Jewish Agricultural and Industrial Aid Society. His son **Arthur Hays** (1891-1968), journalist, president and director, New York Times Co. (1935–57); publisher of the New York *Times* (1935–61).

**Sulzberger, May'er** (mī'ēr). 1843–1923. Cousin of Cyrus L. Sulzberger. Jurist, b. Heidelsheim, in Baden, Ger.; to U.S. as a boy, and settled in Philadelphia. Judge, court of common pleas (1895–1916). Collector of Hebrew manuscripts and incunabula, which he presented (1902) to the Jewish Theol. Sem. of America. Published studies on ancient Hebrew law and economy.

**Sul'zer** (zŏŏl'tsēr), **Johann Georg.** 1720–1779. Swiss philosopher and writer on aesthetics.

**Su·ma·ro'kov** (sŏŏ·mŭ·rô'kôf), **Aleksandr Petrovich.** 1718–1777. Russian writer; director, first permanent theater in St. Petersburg (1756); later, moved to Moscow and presented his plays there. Author of comedies *The Guardian* (1765), *The Usurer* (1768), satires, and miscellaneous works; best-known drama, *The False Demetrius.*

**Sum·ba'tov** (sŏŏm·bȧ'tôf), Prince **Aleksandr Ivanovich.** 1853–1927. Russian actor and playwright; member of the Imperial Little Theater company in Moscow, and known for his interpretation of classical roles; director of the theater (from 1909). Among his plays are *The Elbow Is Near, but You Cannot Bite It, Rustling Leaves, Chains, The Gentleman, The Sunset, The Power of Women.*

**Sum'mer·all** (sŭm'ēr·ôl), **Charles Pe·lot'** (pē·lōt'). 1867–1955. American army officer; grad. U.S.M.A., West Point (1892); brigadier general (1919), major general (1920); served with A.E.F. in France (1917–18) commanding 1st division (July–Oct., 1918) and later the 5th, 9th, and 4th army corps; chief of staff, U.S. army (1926–30); appointed general (1929); retired (1930); president of The Citadel (1931–53).

**Sum'mers** (sŭm'ērz). See also SOMERS.

**Summers, Montague,** *in full* **Alphonsus Joseph-Mary Augustus Montague.** 1880–1948. English man of letters; authority on Restoration drama and on demonology; author of *Jane Austen, An Appreciation* (1919), *History of Witchcraft and Demonology* (1926), *The Vampire, His Kith and Kin* (1928), *The Werewolf* (1933), *A Popular History of Witchcraft* (1937), *The Gothic Achievement* (1939), *A Bibliography of the Gothic Novel* (1940), etc.

**Sum'ner** (sŭm'nēr), **Charles.** 1811–1874. American statesman, b. Boston. U.S. senator (1851–74); a leader in Congress among the opponents of slavery. His vitriolic attacks upon slavery and its defenders brought a physical assault on him by Representative Preston S. Brooks of South Carolina (May 22, 1856), inflicting injuries from which he never fully recovered. First prominent statesman to urge emancipation (Oct., 1861). Chairman of committee on foreign affairs, U.S. Senate (1861–71). Took prominent part in impeachment proceedings against President Johnson; opposed President Grant on question of annexing Santo Domingo (1871); and opposed Grant's re-election (1872). *The Works of Charles Sumner* (15 vols.) published between 1870 and 1883.

**Sumner, Edwin Vose.** 1797–1863. American army officer, b. Boston; acting governor of New Mexico (1852); commander at Fort Leavenworth, Kans., during free-soil and proslavery struggle (1856); brigadier general (Mar., 1861); served in Peninsular Campaign at South Mountain and Antietam; major general (July, 1862); commanded the right at Fredericksburg.

**Sumner, Increase.** 1746–1799. American jurist, b. Roxbury, Mass.; associate justice, Massachusetts supreme court (1782–97); governor of Massachusetts (1797, 1798, 1799).

**Sumner, James Batcheller.** 1887-1955. American biochemist, b. Canton, Mass.; Ph.D., Harvard (1914); professor, Cornell (from 1929); corecipient (see John H. NORTHROP) of 1946 Nobel prize for chemistry.

**Sumner, William Graham.** 1840–1910. American economist and sociologist, b. Paterson, N.J.; ordained deacon, Protestant Episcopal Church (1867) and priest (1869); professor of political and social science, Yale (1872–1910). Noted as inspiring teacher and brilliant lecturer; prominent in advocating free trade, sound currency, development of "big business," civil-service reform; strongly opposed Socialism, interference in business by the government, U.S. imperialistic policy. Author of *A History of American Currency* (1874), *American Finance* (1875), *What Social Classes Owe to Each Other* (1883), *The Financier and Finances of the American Revolution* (2 vols., 1891), and biographies of *Andrew Jackson as a Public Man* (1882), *Alexander Hamilton* (1890), *Robert Morris* (1892). During his last years, devoted himself to a study of social groups and their characteristics; his *Folkways* was published in 1907; his *Science of Society* was completed, edited, and published by A. G. Keller (4 vols., 1927). Among the most notable volumes of his essays are: *War and Other Essays* (1911), *Earth Hunger and Other Essays* (1913), *The Challenge of Facts and Other Essays* (1914), *The Forgotten Man and Other Essays* (1919).

**Sum′ter** (sŭm′tẽr), **Thomas.** 1734–1832. American Revolutionary officer, b. near Charlottesville, Va.; lieutenant colonel of South Carolina troops (1776–78); commissioned brigadier (Oct. 6, 1780); raised troops and campaigned in South Carolina against the British under Tarleton. Member, U.S. House of Representatives (1789–93; 1797–1801), U.S. Senate (1801–10).

**Sun′day** (sŭn′dĭ), **William Ashley,** *popularly called* **Billy.** 1862–1935. American evangelist, b. Ames, Iowa; professional baseball player (1883–90); engaged in Y.M.C.A. work (1891–95) and evangelistic work (from 1896); ordained in Presbyterian ministry (1903).

**Sun′der·land** (sŭn′dẽr·lȧnd), Earls of. See SPENCER family.

**Sunderland,** Countess of. See under SIDNEY family.

**Suñer, Ramón Serrano.** See SERRANO SUÑER.

**Sun Fo** (so͝on′ fô′). *Pekingese form* **Sun K'o** (kŭ′). 1891– . Chinese government official, b. in Kwangtung; son of Sun Yat-sen by his first wife; educ. in Hawaii and at U. of California (B.A., 1916) and Columbia (M.S., 1917); aided his father as secretary (1917–21); mayor of Canton (1921–24, 1926–27); member of Kuomintang Central Executive Committee (1926– ); minister of communications (1926–27); state councilor of Nationalist government (1928–31); president of Executive Yuan (1932–33); of Legislative Yuan (from 1933); anti-Japanese.

**Sung** (so͝ong). Name of two Chinese dynasties: (1) A minor dynasty (420–479 A.D.) with capital at Nanking, known (after its founder, Liu Yu) as **Liu Sung** (lē·o͞o′), to distinguish it from the later and more famous dynasty. (2) A dynasty of eighteen sovereigns (960–1280), generally divided into the Sung dynasty proper (960–1127; founded by Chao K'uang-yin), sometimes called **Northern Sung** because its capital, Kaifeng, was north of the Yangtze, and the **Southern Sung** (1127–1280), after the Kin Tatars carried the emperor of the north away from Kaifeng, leaving independent the provinces south of the Yangtze. The dynasties were notable for progress in reforms, for high achievement in literature and arts, for development of the art of printing, and especially for painting and ceramics. In 13th century Mongols began overrunning territory of Southern Sung, which yielded (1280) to Kublai Khan, who established the Yüan dynasty. Coexistent with it in the north was the Kin Tatar dynasty. See WANG AN-SHIH, SSŬ-MA KUANG, CHU HSI.

**Sun Yat-sen** (so͝on′ yät′sĕn′). *Also known as* **Sun Wen** (so͝on′ wŭn′) *and* **Chung Shan** (jo͝ong′ shän′). 1866–1925. Chinese statesman and revolutionary leader, b. near Macao; called "father of the Revolution." Learned English early; first graduate (1894) of new Coll. of Medicine, Hong Kong (hence title "Doctor"). Implicated in secret revolution (1895) in Canton, forced to flee; during long exile (1895–1911) lived in Hawaii, U.S., England, and Japan; kidnaped for ten days by Chinese legation in London (1896). Planned revolution against the Manchus, which was finally brought about (1911); founded Kuomintang (1912), establishing his three great principles (nationalism, democracy, people's livelihood); elected provisional president of new Chinese Republic (1911) but retired (1912) to allow Yüan Shih-k'ai to become provisional president of entire country. Appointed director of national railways; disagreed with policy of Yüan (1913–16); elected president of Southern Chinese Republic (1921); expelled by Gen. Chen Chiung-ming (1922); influenced by, but did not fully accept, Communist doctrines of Mikhail Borodin (1922–23); fled to Shanghai; re-established himself in Canton (1923); declared war against Gen. Ts'ao K'un (1923); gained in influence after Feng Yu-hsiang's defeat of Wu P'ei-fu in the north (1924); went to conference of leaders at Peking (1925); died of cancer. Great mausoleum erected to his honor at Nanking and remains transferred there by state (1929). Cf. SUN FO, his son by his first wife (divorced). His second wife (m. 1916), **Ch'ing-ling** (chĭng′lĭng′) **Soong** (1890– ), usually known as Madame **Sun** (so͝on), second daughter of C. J. Soong (see SOONG family). Educ. at Shanghai and at Wesleyan Coll., Macon, Ga. (grad. 1913); on return to China became secretary to Sun Yat-sen, working with him until his death (1925). Left her family to join left-wing group at Hankow (1926–27); lived in Moscow (1927–31); returned briefly (1929) to attend state burial of Sun at Nanking; withdrew from affairs for some years but remained powerful influence; resident at Hong Kong; supported National Salvation group (a left-wing movement of Kuomintang); during war with Japan (1937 ff.) again active, because of her anti-Japanese convictions.

**Su′pan** (zo͞o′pän), **Alexander.** 1847–1920. Austrian geographer; editor of *Petermanns Geographische Mitteilungen,* in Gotha (1884–1909); author of *Grundzüge der Physischen Erdkunde* (1884), etc.

**Su′per′vielle′** (sü′pĕr′vyĕl′), **Jules.** 1884–1960. French poet, playwright, and fiction writer.

**Sup′pé** (zo͝op′ā), **Franz von.** 1819–1895. Austrian composer of operettas, ballet music, symphonies, overtures, masses and songs. Among his operettas are *Leichte Kavallerie* (1866), *Fatinitza* (1876), *Boccaccio* (1879), *Donna Juanita* (1880).

**Surajah Dowlah.** See SIRAJ-UD-DAULA.

**Sur′couf′** (sür′ko͞of′), **Robert.** 1773–1827. French corsair; preyed upon English commerce in the Indian Ocean (from 1795); created baron of the empire.

**Sur Das** (so͞or däs). c. 1483–1563. Hindu poet; lived at Mathura (modern Muttra) on the Jumna River; wrote some 75,000 verses in Hindi; best-known work *Sur Sagar.*

**Surfaceman.** Pseudonym of Alexander ANDERSON.

**Su·ria′no** (so͞o·ryä′nō) *or* **So·ria′no** (sō-), **Francesco.** 1549–after 1621. Italian composer, esp. of church music.

**Su′ri·kov** (so͞o′ryĭ·kôf), **Vasili Ivanovich.** 1848–1916. Russian painter, esp. of historical subjects, as *The Execution of the Streltsi, Suvorov at the St. Gothard.*

**Sürlin.** See SYRLIN.

**Sur·ratt′** (sŭ·răt′), **Mary E.** 1820–1865. American woman, keeper of boardinghouse in Washington, D.C., which served as meeting place of John Wilkes Booth and his conspirators; hanged (July 7), probably on insufficient evidence, for complicity in assassination of President Lincoln. Her son **John H.** (b. 1844), educated for Roman Catholic priesthood, became secret dispatch rider for the Confederacy; as friend of Booth, took active part in his plot; after Lincoln's assassination, arrested

(1866) and tried (1867), but released (1868) on failure of government to secure indictment.

**Sur′rey** (sûr′ĭ), Earl of. *Called commonly* Earl **Warenne.** English title held first (1088?–1148) by members of WARENNE family, next (till 1347) by a family descended from the daughter and heiress of Earl William, Isabel de Warenne, and her husband, Hamelin Plantagenet; then (from 1353), united with the earldom of Arundel, by the Fitzalans (see earls of ARUNDEL), beginning with Richard (1307?–1376); by John Mowbray (1451–1476); finally (from 1483) by the dukes of Norfolk (see HOWARD family), and by Henry HOWARD (1517?–1547).

**Sur′tees** (sûr′tēz), **Robert.** 1779–1834. English antiquary and topographer; spent his life gathering remains of antiquity for his *History and Antiquities of the County of Durham* (4 vols., 1816–40); author of a spurious ballad, "The Death of Featherstonhaugh," and perhaps of "Barthram's Dirge," included in Scott's *Minstrelsy of the Scottish Border.*

**Surtees, Robert Smith.** 1803-1864. English novelist and sporting writer; published *The Horseman's Manual* (1831); cofounder with Rudolph Ackermann of the *New Sporting Magazine* (1832), to which he contributed sketches of the humorous character Mr. John Jorrocks, sporting cockney grocer, later collected as *Jorrocks's Jaunts and Jollities* (1838) and followed by sequels *Handley Cross* (1843) and *Hillingdon Hall* (1845). Author also of *Mr. Facey Romford's Hounds* (1864), etc.

**Su·san′na** *or* **Su·san′nah** (sū̇·zăn′ȧ). In the Apocryphal book of *Susanna* or *History of Susanna*, the beautiful and virtuous wife of Joachim who was proved innocent by Daniel of the charge of adultery brought against her by certain Jewish elders who had vainly attempted her chastity. Her accusers were put to death.

**Su Shih.** See SU TUNG-P'O.

**Süs′kind** (züs′kĭnt), **Wilhelm Emanuel.** 1901– . German novelist and translator; editor of magazine *Die Literatur* (from 1933); author of *Tordis* (1927), *Jugend* (1930), *Mary und ihr Knecht* (1932).

**Su′so** (zōō′zō) *or* **Seu′se** (zoi′zĕ), **Heinrich.** *Real surname* **Berg** (bĕrK). 1300?–1366. German mystic, a disciple of Eckhart; wandered through Swabia as an itinerant preacher (c. 1335–48); settled in Ulm (c. 1348). Author of two books on mystic faith, *Das Büchlein der Wahrheit* and *Das Büchlein der Ewigen Weisheit* (translated by Suso into Latin as *Horologium Sapientiae*).

**Süss, Hans.** Real name of Hans von KULMBACH.

**Sussex,** Earl of. See Sir Thomas RADCLIFFE.

**Süss′–Op′pen·hei′mer** (züs′ŏp′ĕn·hī′mẽr), **Joseph.** 1698–1738. German Jewish financier in service of Duke Charles I of Württemberg; arrested and hanged after the duke's death (1737). He is the subject of a novel *Jud Süss* (1925; American title *Power*) by Feuchtwanger.

**Suth′er·land** (sŭth′ẽr·lănd). (1) Duke of. See *George Granville Leveson-Gower,* under LEVESON-GOWER family. (2) Earls of. See GORDON family.

**Sutherland, Earl Wilbur.** 1915–1974. American physiologist, b. Burlingame, Kans. At Vanderbilt U. (1963– ); awarded Nobel prize in physiology and medicine (1971) for his research on hormones.

**Sutherland, George.** 1862–1942. Jurist, b. in England; to U.S. as a boy. Member, U.S. House of Representatives (1901–03) and U.S. Senate (1905–17) from Utah; associate justice, U.S. Supreme Court (1922–38).

**Sutherland, Richard K.** 1893–1966. American army officer, b. Hancock, Md.; chief of staff to military missions to Philippine commonwealth (1938–41), to U.S. army forces in Far East (1941–45).

**Su′tro** (sōō′trō), **Adolph Heinrich Joseph.** 1830–1898. Mining engineer, b. Aachen, Prussia; to U.S. (1850); to California (1851) and Nevada (1860). Planned tunnel (over 20,000 feet long) into Mount Davidson to reach the rich Comstock lode; superintended construction (1869–78) of this tunnel, known as Sutro Tunnel. Sold his interest in Sutro Tunnel and invested in San Francisco real estate. Mayor of San Francisco (1894–96).

**Su′tro** (sōō′trō), **Alfred.** 1863–1933. English playwright, b. London. Author of *The Cave of Illusion* (1900), *Arethusa* (1903), *The Walls of Jericho* (1904), *The Perfect Lover* (1905), *The Fascinating Mr. Vanderveldt* (1906), *John Glayde's Honour* (1907), *The Laughing Lady* (1922), *The Desperate Lovers* (1927), *Living Together* (1929), etc. Translator of Maeterlinck's *Wisdom and Destiny* and *Life of the Bee,* etc.

**Sut′ter** (sōō′tẽr), **John Augustus.** 1803–1880. Pioneer in California, b. in Kandern, Baden; to U.S. (1834). With trading parties to Santa Fe (1835, 1836) and to Oregon region (1838). Landed in San Francisco Bay (1839); founded colony on site of what is now Sacramento; became Mexican citizen (1841) and received from Governor Alvarado a grant of land. Gold was discovered on his property (Jan. 24, 1848); in the subsequent rush, his workmen deserted, his sheep and cattle were stolen, and his land occupied by squatters; became bankrupt (1852). Given pension of $250 a month by State of California (1864–78). See James W. MARSHALL.

**Sutt′ner** (zo͝ot′nẽr), **Bertha von.** *Nee* Countess **Kin′sky** (kĭn′skē). 1843–1914. Austrian writer; m. (1876) the novelist Baron Arthur Gundaccar von Suttner (1850–1902). Took active part in movement for international peace; founded (1891) Austrian Society of Friends of Peace, and attended peace congresses in Bern (1892), Antwerp (1894), Hamburg (1897); awarded the Nobel peace prize (1905). Among her chief works are *Inventarium einer Seele* (1883), *Die Waffen Nieder* (1889), *Trente et Quarante* (1893), *Einsam und Arm* (2 vols., 1896), *Das Maschinenzeitalter* (1899).

**Sut′ton** (sŭt′'n), Sir **John Bland–.** See BLAND-SUTTON.

**Sutton, Thomas.** 1532?–1611. English mine owner and founder of the Charterhouse school; leased coal lands in Durham; estimated the richest commoner in England. Purchased (1611) former Carthusian monastery of Thomas Howard, Earl of Suffolk, and on site built Charterhouse school and hospital.

**Su Tung–p'o** (sōō′ do͝ong′pô′). *Real name* **Su Shih** (sōō′ shĭr′). 1036–1101. Chinese poet of distinction and statesman, under the Sung dynasty. Several times banished for political reasons.

**Suvarov** *or* **Suvaroff.** Incorrect variants of SUVOROV.

**Su·vo′rin** (sŏŏ·vô′ryĭn), **Aleksei Sergeevich.** 1834–1912. Russian journalist; founder (1876) of Russian daily newspaper *Novoe Vremya.* Began publishing *Suvorin Calendar* (1872) and the monthly *Istoricheski Vestnik* (1881). Published reference works and "libraries" of Russian and foreign classics. Promoted Moscow Little Theater, and wrote plays for it.

**Su·vo′rov** (sŏŏ·vô′rôf), Count **Aleksandr Vasilievich.** 1729–1800. Russian field marshal, b. in Finland of Swedish descent; served in Seven Years' War (1756–63), Russo-Turkish War (1773–74); commanded Russian army against the Turks (1787–92), winning the battle of Kinburn by bayonet charge (1787) and gaining surname **Rym′nik·ski** (rĭm′nyĭk·skû·ĭ) for his victory at Rimnik (1789). Created field marshal (1794); defeated the French at Cassano d'Adda, the Trebbia River, and Novi (1799), gaining additional surname **I·ta·li′ski** (ĭ·tŭ·lyē′ĭ·skû·ĭ). Commander in chief of Russian armies (1800).

**Su·yu′ti** (sŏŏ·yōō′tĭ). *Arab.* **Jalāl–al–Dīn al–Suyūṭi.** 1445–1505. Arabic writer, son of a Turkish slave woman. Precocious student; made pilgrimage to Mecca (1464); promoted to chair in the mosque of Bibars (1486–1501). Prolific writer; 561 titles of works by him are known, and more than 300 are extant; wrote on nearly every branch of Moslem science and literature.

**Suz'zal·lo** (sōō'z'l·ō), **Henry**, *orig.* **Anthony Henry.** 1875–1933. American educator, b. San Jose, Calif.; president, U. of Washington (1915–26); president, Carnegie Foundation for the Advancement of Teaching (1930–33); editor in chief, *The National Encyclopedia* (10 vols., 1932).

**Svärd** (svărd), **Lotta.** Finnish woman of late 18th century, possibly a creation of the imagination; reputed to have lost her husband in the war of 1788–90 and thereafter to have followed the army as sutler, selling tobacco, coffee, liquor, etc., to the soldiers. Subject of many legends, and central figure in Runeberg's poem *Lotta Svärd.* A modern Finnish women's organization is called The Lotta Svärd Organization.

**Sva'to·pluk** (svȧ'tô·plŏŏk). d. 894. Prince of Moravia (870–894); united Moravia, Slovakia, and Bohemia under name of Great Moravia against emperor of Germany; finally overcome by Magyars under Árpád. During his reign western Slavs converted by Greek missionaries, saints Cyril and Methodius (*qq.v.*).

**Sved'berg'** (svād'băr'y'), **The**, *in full*, **Theodor.** 1884–1971. Swedish chemist; educ. U. of Uppsala; lecturer (1907), professor (1912–49), U. of Uppsala; director, Institute of Physical Chemistry. Known for research in colloid chemistry, especially on disperse systems. Awarded 1926 Nobel prize for chemistry.

**Šveh'la** (shvĕκ'lȧ), **Antonín.** 1873–1933. Czech statesman; leader of Agrarian party in the legislature; first minister of interior in new Czechoslovak state (1919–20); premier of Czechoslovakia (1922–29).

**Sveins'son** (svāns'sŏn), **Brynjolf.** fl. 17th century. Icelandic bishop; discoverer (1643) of the *Elder*, or *Poetic*, *Edda*, which he mistakenly attributed to the historian Sæmund (*q.v.*).

**Sven** *or* **Svend.** See Sweyn.

**Svend'sen** (svĕn'sĕn), **Johan.** 1840–1911. Norwegian composer of symphonies, Norwegian rhapsodies, tone poems, overtures, chamber music, choral works, and songs.

**Svens'son** (svĕns'sŏn), **Jón.** 1857–1944. Icelandic writer, esp. of adventure tales.

**Sver'drup** (svăr'drŏŏp), **Harald Ulrik.** 1888–1957. Meteorologist and oceanographer, b. in Sogndal, Norway; head of scientific work on Maud expedition in Arctic (1917–25), and on Wilkins-Ellsworth submarine Arctic expedition on board *Nautilus* (1931). To U.S. (1936); professor of oceanography and director of Scripps Institution of Oceanography, U. of California (1936–48). Returned to Norway (1948).

**Sverdrup, Johan.** 1816–1892. Norwegian statesman; president of the Storting (1871–81); prime minister (1884–89).

**Sverdrup, Otto Neumann.** 1855–1930. Norwegian arctic explorer. On Nansen's expedition to Greenland (1888) and polar expedition (1893–96), returning the ship *Fram* to Norway after Nansen left it in an attempt to reach North Pole over the ice; leader of expedition that unsuccessfully attempted to circumnavigate Greenland (1898–1902); leader of Arctic expeditions in 1914 and 1920 to search for lost Russian explorers and in 1928 to search for crew of Italian dirigible *Italia.*

**Sver'ker** *or* **Swer'ker** (svĕr'kẽr). d. 1156. King of Sweden (1130–50); deposed.

**Sver're** (svăr'rĕ) *or* **Swer'ro** (swĕr'ō). *Known as* **Sverre Si'gurds·son** (sĭg'gŏŏrts·sŏn). 1152?–1202. King of Norway (1184–1202); supposed son of Sigurd Mund, b. Faeroes. Became leader of robber band; claimed throne of Norway; fought and often defeated Magnus Erlingsson (1179–84), finally at Norefjord, where Magnus was killed; weakened the aristocracy; built strong monarchy with support of peasantry; one of Norway's greatest kings.

**Sve'vo** (zvā'vô), **Italo.** *Pseudonym of* **Ettore Schmitz** (shmēts). 1861–1928. Italian fiction writer; known esp. for three novels, *Una Vita* (1883), *Senilità* (1898), *La Coscienza di Zeno* (1923).

**Svin'huf·vud** (svēn'hōō·vōōd), **Pehr Evind.** 1861–1944. Finnish statesman; member of the legislature (1907–17), banished to Siberia by Russian government (1914–17). Head of Finnish government (1917–18); member of supreme court (1919 ff.), again of legislature; premier (1930); president (1931–37).

**Swain** (swān), **Charles.** 1801–1874. English poet, called "the Manchester Poet." Author of *The Mind and Other Poems* (1832) and songs, including "I cannot mind my wheel, mother" and "Somebody's waiting for somebody."

**Swain'son** (swān's'n), **William.** 1789–1855. English naturalist; emigrated to New Zealand, where he became attorney general; expounded the quinary system of classification. Author of eleven volumes in Lardner's *Cabinet Cyclopaedia* and three volumes in Sir William Jardine's *Naturalists' Library.*

**Swam'mer·dam** (svăm'ẽr·dăm), **Jan.** 1637–1680. Dutch naturalist; known for his biological researches with the microscope; first to describe the red blood cells (1658); discovered the valves of the lymph vessels (1664); studied the anatomy of insects, which he classified on the basis of development.

**Swan** (swŏn), **John Macallan.** 1847–1910. English painter and sculptor; won reputation with oil painting *The Prodigal Son* (1889); made special study of animals and frequently included felines in his sculptures and pictures.

**Swan,** Sir **Joseph Wilson.** 1828–1914. English chemist and electrician; patented carbon, or autotype, process of photographic printing; made improvement in bromide photographic paper; produced carbon-filament incandescent electric lamp, working independently of Thomas A. Edison (1879–80); invented cellular-surfaced lead-plate storage battery.

**Swann** (swŏn), **William Francis Gray.** 1884–1962. Physicist, b. in England; B.Sc. (1905), D.Sc. (1910), U. of London; to U.S. (1913); chief of physical division, department of terrestrial magnetism, Carnegie Institution, Washington (1913–18); professor, Minn. (1918–23), Chicago (1923–24), Yale (1924–27); director, Bartol Research Foundation, Franklin Institute (1927–59). Known especially for work on cosmic rays, also on thermal measurements, electroconductivity, relativity, atmospheric electricity, and atomic structure.

**Swan'son** (swŏn's'n), **Claude Augustus.** 1862–1939. American politician, b. Swansonville, Va.; practiced law in Chatham, Va.; member, U.S. House of Representatives (1893–1905); governor of Virginia (1906–10); U.S. senator from Virginia (1910–33); U.S. secretary of the navy (1933–39).

**Swan'wick** (swŏn'ĭk), **Anna.** 1813–1899. English translator and feminist; translator of Aeschylus, Schiller, and Goethe. Her *Faust* (1850–78) in blank verse is one of the best existing translations.

**Swarth, Hélène.** See Lapidoth-Swarth.

**Swar'thout** (swôr'thout), **Gladys.** 1904–1969. American operatic mezzo-soprano, b. Deepwater, Mo.; m. Harry Richmond Kern (1925; d. 1931), Frank M. Chapman, Jr. (1932). Member of Chicago Civic Opera Company (1924–25), Ravinia Company, Chicago (1927–29), Metropolitan Opera Company of New York (from 1929).

**Swa′sey** (swā′zĭ), **Ambrose.** 1846–1937. American industrialist, b. Exeter, N.H. Partner with Worcester R. Warner in Warner & Swasey (1881), incorporated as The Warner & Swasey Co. (1900), manufacturers of machine tools and astronomical instruments. Among instruments made by this firm were the 36-inch Lick telescope, the 40-inch Yerkes telescope, the 72-inch reflecting telescope for Canadian government, the 60-inch telescope for Argentine National Observatory. Swasey himself invented a range and position finder adopted by U.S. government.

**Swayne** (swān), **Noah Haynes.** 1804–1884. American jurist, b. in Frederick County, Va.; practiced in Coshocton, Ohio. Associate justice, U.S. Supreme Court (1862–81). His son **Wager** (1834–1902) was a lawyer and army officer; practiced at Columbus, Ohio; served in Union army through Civil War; awarded Medal of Honor for heroism in battle of Corinth (Oct. 4, 1862); brigadier general of volunteers (Mar., 1865), and major general (May, 1866); assistant commissioner of the Freedman's Bureau, in charge of its operations in Alabama (1865–68); retired from U.S. army (1870); practiced law in New York (from 1870).

**Swaythling,** Baron. See Samuel MONTAGU.

**Swe′den·borg′** (svā′dĕn·bôr′y′; *Angl.* swē′d'n·bôrg), **Emanuel.** *Surname orig.* **Sved′berg′** (svād′băr′y′). 1688–1772. Swedish scientist, philosopher, and religious writer, b. Stockholm. Assessor on Swedish board of mines (1716). Distinguished himself at siege of Fredrikshall (1718) by inventing machines for carrying boats overland from Stromstadt to Iddefjord; ennobled by Queen Ulrika Eleonora (1719) and took seat in House of Peers. Devoted himself to scientific research, and published *Prodromus Principiorum Rerum Naturalium* (1721), *Opera Philosophica et Mineralia* (3 vols., 1734), *Prodromus Philosophiae Ratiocinantis de Infinito et Causa Finali Creationis* (1734), *Oeconomia Regni Animalis* (1740–41), and *Regnum Animale* (1744–45). Began having visions (c. 1743); resigned position as assessor of mines (1747) and devoted himself thereafter to psychical and spiritual research; began voluminous works on interpretation of the Scriptures as immediate voice of God. Chief theological works are *Arcana Coelestia* (1749–56), *Heaven and Hell*, *The Divine Providence*, and *The Divine Love and Wisdom*. Although he himself never tried to preach or to found a religious sect, his followers, Swedenborgians, constitute a considerable society with a regular ecclesiastical organization, known as New Jerusalem Church, Church of the New Jerusalem, or, simply, New Church.

**Swee′linck** *or* **Swe′linck** (svā′lĭngk), **Jan Pieters.** *Also known as* **Jan Pie′ters·zoon** (pē′tēr·sŭn; -sōn; -sōn). 1562–1621. Dutch organist and composer; organist of the Old Church, Amsterdam (1581?–1621). Composer of organ and piano works, and *Cantiones Sacrae* (for 5 voices; 1619).

**Swee′ny** (swē′nĭ), **Peter Barr.** 1825–1911. American politician; district attorney of New York (1857). Close associate of William M. Tweed in control of Tammany Hall; member of Tweed Ring; city chamberlain (1866); New York park commissioner (1869). Fled to Canada when Tweed Ring was overthrown (1871) and later to France; allowed to escape prosecution by returning $400,000 to New York.

**Sweeny, Thomas William.** 1820–1892. Soldier, b. in County Cork, Ireland; to U.S. (1832). With General Franz Sigel in operations in southwest Missouri (1861); with Grant at capture of Fort Donelson, and with Sherman at Shiloh; brigadier general of volunteers (Nov., 1862); engaged at Kennesaw Mountain and Atlanta (1864). Dismissed from army (Dec., 1865) but reinstated (Nov., 1866). In interval when out of army, led futile Fenian raid on Canada. Retired from army (1870).

**Sweet** (swēt), **Henry.** 1845–1912. English phonetician and comparative philologist, b. London; published *History of English Sounds from the Earliest Period* (1874), *Anglo-Saxon Reader* (1876), *Handbook of Phonetics* (1877); chief founder of modern phonetics; applied phonetic method in *A New English Grammar* (1892, 1898) and *The History of Language* (1900); reader in phonetics, Oxford (1901), a position created for him. Other works: *The Sounds of English* (1908; his last work in phonetics), Old and Middle English texts, primers of speech, an Anglo-Saxon dictionary, a historical English grammar.

**Swe′gen** (svĕ′ĭn) *or* **Swein** (svĕ′ĭn). Variants of SWEYN.

**Swerker.** See SVERKER.

**Swerro.** See SVERRE.

**Swert, Jules De.** See DE SWERT.

**Swe·tchine′** (svyĕ·chēn′), **Anne Sophie,** *nee* **Soy·ma′·nov** (sŭ·ĭ·mä′nôf). 1782–1857. Russian-French writer, b. Moscow; m. General Swetchine (1799). Converted to Roman Catholicism (1815) and moved to Paris; maintained salon noted for its social courtesy, intellectual brilliance, and religious feeling. Her works are marked by mysticism, as in *Old Age* and *Resignation*.

**Swete** (swēt), **Henry Barclay.** 1835–1917. English theologian; regius professor of divinity, Cambridge (1890–1915); distinguished for work in criticism of Biblical texts, exegesis of New Testament, patristic studies, and interpretation of Apostles' Creed.

**Swet′ten·ham** (swĕt′'n·ăm; swĕt′năm), Sir **Alexander.** 1846–1933. British colonial administrator; in Ceylon civil service (1868–83); auditor general, Ceylon (1891–95); acting governor, Straits Settlements (1898, 1900). Captain general and governor in chief, Jamaica (1904–07). His brother Sir **Frank Athelstane** (1850–1946) was British resident in Perak (1889–95), and resident general in Federated Malay States (1896–1901); governor and commander in chief, Straits Settlements (1901–04); author of *Malay-English Vocabulary* (1880), *Malay Sketches* (1895), *The Real Malay* (1899), *British Malaya* (1906), etc.

**Sweyn** (svĕ′ĭn) *or* **Sven** (svĕn) *or* **Svend** (svĕn). Name of three kings of Denmark:

**Sweyn I.** *Known as* **Sweyn Fork′beard′** (fôrk′bērd′). d. 1014. Son of Harold Bluetooth and father of Canute the Great. King (985?–1014). In early years a viking; led large fleet to England which did great damage (994) but assaulted London unsuccessfully; at war with Olaf Tryggvesson of Norway (1000), who was defeated and killed; after massacre of Danes in England (1002), led or sent plundering expeditions annually (1003–14) that ravaged the land and exacted tribute; died suddenly at Gainsborough.

**Sweyn II.** *Sometimes* **Sweyn Es′trith·son** (ĕs′trĕth·sŏn). d. 1075. Son of Earl Ulf and of Estrith, daughter of Sweyn Forkbeard. King (1047–75), first of Estrith dynasty (*q.v.*). Born in England; lived in Sweden after murder of his father; made an earl by King Magnus the Good; became king (1047); at war with Harold III of Norway (1047–64); usually defeated, but finally won peace; attempted twice to conquer England (1069, 1075), but driven away by Canute; succeeded by five of his sons as kings of Denmark.

**Sweyn III.** d. 1157. Natural son of Eric the Memorable. King of part of Denmark (1147–57); waged civil war against Canute V, whom he assassinated; defeated and killed in battle by Waldemar I.

**Swift** (swĭft), **Gustavus Franklin.** 1839–1903. American meat packer, b. near Sandwich, Mass.; established himself at Chicago (1875). Made first shipment of dressed beef to eastern market (1877); developed refrigerator car; profited by utilization of by-products to make oleomargarine, soap, glue, fertilizer, etc. Incorporated business as Swift & Co. (1885). Developed overseas markets for American beef; established additional packing houses in other cities. His sons: **Louis Franklin** (1861–1937), president of Swift & Co. (1903–31) and chairman of its board of directors (1931–32), **Charles Henry** (1872–1948), chairman of the board of directors of Swift & Co., **Gustavus Franklin** (1881–1943) and **Harold Higgins** (1885-1962), both vice-chairmen of the board and **George Hastings** (1878–1951), director of Swift & Co., chairman of board of A. C. Laurence Leather Co. and Consolidated Rendering Co., and president of John P. Squire Co.

**Swift, Jonathan.** 1667–1745. English satirist, b. Dublin; cousin of John Dryden. To England (1688) and became secretary to Sir William Temple; in rebellion against subserviency and delay in advancement, returned to Ireland, took orders (1694), and obtained small living of Kilroot, near Belfast. Returned to Sir William Temple in Surrey (1696–99), where he wrote *A Tale of a Tub*, on corruption in religion and learning, and *The Battle of the Books*, a travesty on the controversy over ancient and modern learning (both pub. 1704); supervised education of Esther Johnson (*q.v.*), the Stella of his correspondence and journal. After publication of Temple's works, returned to Ireland where the lord deputy (earl of Berkeley) obtained for him some small preferments (1702–10); visited frequently by Stella, who came to live in Dublin; on frequent visits to London, became friend of Addison, Steele, Halifax, Congreve and other Whig writers; wrote ecclesiastical pamphlets, narrative poem *Baucis and Philemon*, and, under pseudonym **Isaac Bick′er·staff** (bĭk′ẽr·stȧf), squibs on Partridge the almanac maker (1708). Made futile appeals to Godolphin administration on behalf of Irish clergy (1708–09); turned from Whigs to Tory party (1710); filled the *Examiner* with political invective and statements of policy, guided public opinion through these articles and masterly pamphlets (including *The Conduct of the Allies*, 1711), and became a power in the state, contributing to overthrow of Marlborough and to peace of Utrecht (1713). Made dean of St. Patrick's, Dublin (1713), despite dislike of Queen Anne, who would not consent to a bishopric; on death of queen and return of Whigs to office, retired to Ireland an embittered man (1715). During the four years in London, had been active in literary circles: contributed to *Tatler*, *Spectator*, and *Intelligencer;* aided Pope and Arbuthnot in forming Scriblerus Club and contributed to *Memoirs of Martinus Scriblerus;* proposed an English academy for regulation of the English tongue. In London, became object of passionate devotion of Esther Van·hom′righ (văn·ŭm′rĭ; -hŏm′rĭg) (1690–1723), the Vanessa of *Cadenus and Vanessa*, who followed him to Ireland; began (1710) his *Journal to Stella*, intimate letters largely in baby language; evaded Vanessa; may have married Stella, but was apparently prevented from marrying by some mysterious obstacle. Devoted himself to exposing unfair treatment of Ireland and the Englishry in Ireland by Whigs; successfully urged cancellation of "Wood's halfpence" in Ireland by his *Drapier's Letters* (1724); visited Pope and Gay (1726) and made ineffectual remonstrance to Walpole on Irish affairs. Published most famous work, *Gulliver's Travels* (1726), a keen satire upon cant and sham of courts, parties, statesmen, the only work for which he received payment (£200); paid last visit to England (1727). A popular idol in Ireland as champion of people's grievances in ironical tracts, such as the *Modest Proposal* to utilize children by fattening and eating them (1729); spent a third of his income on charities; was increasingly lonely and haunted by dread of insanity (from 1738); produced trivial, bitter, sometimes indecent works, among them *Directions to Servants* (1745), *Polite Conversation*, *Hamilton's Bawn*, *Rhapsody on Poetry*, and *Verses on the Death of Dr. Swift.*

**Swift, Joseph Gardner.** 1783–1865. American army officer, b. on island of Nantucket, Mass. Appointed cadet in corps of artillerists and engineers, Newport, R.I. (1800); transferred to West Point, N.Y. (1801), where United States Military Academy was formally established (Mar. 16, 1802); received his commission with one other officer (Oct. 12, 1802) and is regarded as member of first class graduated from U.S.M.A. Promoted rapidly to rank of colonel and chief engineer of the army (1812); for service in War of 1812 was brevetted brigadier general (Feb., 1814). Head of the U.S.M.A., West Point (1816–18). Resigned from army (Nov. 12, 1818). Civil engineer in charge of harbor improvement on Great Lakes (1829–45).

**Swift, Lewis.** 1820–1913. American astronomer, b. Clarkson, N.Y. Country storekeeper in Cortland County, N.Y. (1851–72); in hardware business, Rochester, N.Y. (1872). Interested in astronomy (from 1855); director of Warner Observatory, Rochester (1884–93) and the Lowe Observatory on Echo Mountain, Calif. (1893–1901). Discovered twelve comets, over 1200 nebulae; observed three total eclipses of the sun (1869, 1878, 1889).

**Swin′burne** (swĭn′bûrn; -bẽrn), **Algernon Charles.** 1837–1909. English poet, b. London. Associated with Dante Gabriel Rossetti and William Morris (from 1857); recognized as lyric poet of high order on publication of *Atalanta in Calydon* (1865), a drama in classical form with choruses; not so successful in a trilogy relating to Mary, Queen of Scots, *Chastelard* (1865), *Bothwell* (1874), *Mary Stuart* (1881); evoked censure by paganism and revolt from convention in *Poems and Ballads* (first series, 1866). Spent some time with Mazzini, whom he met at house of George Howard, later Earl of Carlisle, and his circle; issued republican songs, *A Song of Italy* (1867) and *Songs before Sunrise* (1871); returned to Greek model in *Erechtheus* (1876), lyric drama showing extraordinary metrical power; subdued subject matter of *Poems and Ballads* (second series, 1878); in alarming state of health, spent rest of life (from 1879) in house of Watts-Dunton, Putney. Expressed his passion for the sea in *Songs of the Springtides* and *Studies in Song* (1880); executed perhaps his most perfect work in *Tristram of Lyonesse* (1882), a romantic poem in heroic couplets; treated theme already treated by Byron in tragedy, *Marino Faliero* (1885); published another drama, *Locrine* (1887), a third series of *Poems and Ballads* (1889), and his last volumes of poems, *Astrophel* (1894), *A Tale of Balen* (1896), *A Channel Passage* (1899); showed decline of power in last plays, *The Sisters* (1892), in prose, and *Rosamund, Queen of the Lombards* (1899), and his last work, *The Duke of Gandia* (1908). In prose wrote chiefly essays in literary criticism.

**Swing** (swĭng), **Raymond Gram.** 1887–1968. American journalist and radio news commentator, b. Cortland, N.Y. War correspondent in Berlin for Chicago *Daily News* (1914–17), New York *Herald* (1919–22); later, foreign correspondent for Philadelphia *Public Ledger* and New York *Evening Post.* News commentator, first (1935) on American affairs for British Broadcasting Corporation, and later for American and Canadian networks.

**Swin′gle** (swĭng′g'l), **Walter Tennyson.** 1871–1952. American agricultural botanist; in charge of crop physiology and breeding researches, U.S. Dept. of Agriculture (1902–34); chief physiologist, Division of Plant Exploration and Introduction (from 1934). Introduced fig insect into U.S., thereby making possible culture in Calif. of Smyrna type figs; instrumental in establishing commercial culture of date palms in the U.S. and of Egyptian cotton in Arizona; with Lyman J. Briggs, produced by hybridization new citrus fruits; invented improvements in high-power microscopes; first to prove existence of centrosomes in plants; originated theory of metaxenia dealing with the direct effect of pollen on fruit (1928).

**Swin′ner·ton** (swĭn′ẽr·t'n; -tŭn), **Frank Arthur.** 1884– . English novelist and critic; author of *The Merry Heart* (1909), *R. L. Stevenson: a Critical Study* (1914), *Nocturne* (1917), *Coquette* (1921), *A Brood of Ducklings* (1928), *The Georgian House* (1932), *The Georgian Literary Scene* (1935), *Swinnerton: an Autobiography* (1936), *The Two Wives* (1940), *The Fortunate Lady* (1941), *Thankless Child* (1942).

**Swin′ton** (swĭn′t'n; -tŭn), 1st Earl of (cr. 1955). **Philip Cun′liffe–Lis′ter** (kŭn′lĭf·lĭs′tẽr). *Orig. family name* **Lloyd–Greame** (loid′grām′). 1884–1972. English soldier and statesman; educ. Oxford; called to bar (1908); in army (1914–17); joint secretary, ministry of national service (1917–18); M.P. (1918–35); president of the board of trade (1922–23; 1924–29; 1931); secretary of state for the colonies (1931–35), for air (1935–38); minister resident in West Africa (1942–44); first minister for civil aviation (1944–45).

**Swinton,** Sir **Ernest Dunlop.** 1868–1951. British soldier and writer; entered army (1888); served in Boer War and World War; inventor of the tank (1914); colonel commandant, Royal Tanks Corps (1934–38); became major general. Professor of military history, Oxford (1925–39). Author of *The Defence of Duffer's Drift* (1904) under pseudonym **Backsight–Forethought,** of *The Green Curve* (1909), *The Great Tab Dope* (1915), and other stories under pseudonym **O′le Luk–Oie** [ŏl′ē lo͝ok′oi′] ("Olaf Shut-eye"), also of *The Study of War* (1926), and *An Eastern Odyssey* (1935).

**Swinton, William.** 1833–1892. War correspondent and military historian, b. near Edinburgh, Scotland; to Canada (1843) and U.S. (1853). On staff of New York *Times* (1858), and its war correspondent (1861–64); professor of English, U. of California (1869–74). Author of numerous widely used textbooks, and *Campaigns of the Army of the Potomac* (1866), *The Twelve Decisive Battles of the War* (1867), etc.

**Swith′un** (swĭth′ŭn; swĭth′-) *or* **Swith′in** (-ĭn), Saint. d. 862. English ecclesiastic; appointed by Ethelwulf, on his accession, bishop of Winchester (852?–862); one of king's chief counselors in ecclesiastical matters; buried outside north wall of Winchester Minster; on being moved inside cathedral (July 15, 971), accomplished miracles, according to contemporary writers. Popularly associated with myth that if it rains on July 15, it will rain the forty succeeding days.

**Swope** (swōp), **Ge·rard′** (jĕ·rärd′). 1872–1957. American electrical engineer and executive, b. St. Louis, Mo. B.S., M.I.T. (1895); entered employ of General Electric Co. as helper (1893); rose to presidency of the corporation (1922–39; 1942–44). Member of first National Labor Board (1933), Advisory Council on Economic Security (1934), Advisory Council on Social Security (1937–38), etc.

**Swope, Herbert Bayard.** 1882–1958. American journalist and publicist, b. St. Louis, Mo.; war correspondent of New York *World* with German armies (1914–16); awarded Pulitzer prize for his reports (1917); newspaper correspondent at Paris Peace Conference (1919); executive editor, New York *World* (1920–29; retired). Author of *Inside the German Empire; Journalism—An Instrument of Civilization; France, England and Germany After the War,* etc.

**Swyn′ford** (swĭn′fẽrd), **Catherine.** Duchess of **Lan′cas·ter** (lăng′kăs·tẽr). 1350?–1403. John of Gaunt's mistress and third wife, daughter of a knight from Hainaut attendant upon Philippa of Hainaut, queen of Edward III; m. Sir Hugh Swynford of Lincolnshire; became mistress of John of Gaunt, Duke of Lancaster (c. 1372) and wife (1396) on death of his second wife. Mother by John of Gaunt of four children, who took name Beaufort and were legitimized by parliament (1397); ancestress of Henry VII of England.

**Sy·ag′ri·us** (sī·ăg′rĭ·ŭs). 430?–486. Last Roman governor in Gaul; defeated by Clovis (486).

**Sy′bel** (zē′bĕl), **Heinrich von.** 1817–1895. German historian; at Munich, founded first history seminar in Germany; also, founded *Historische Zeitschrift* (1859). Director of the Prussian government archives (from 1875). His works include *Geschichte der Revolutionszeit 1789–95* (3 vols., 1853–60), *Die Begründung des Deutschen Reichs durch Wilhelm I* (7 vols., 1889–94).

**Syd′en·ham** (sĭd′'n·ăm; sĭd′năm), Baron. See Charles Edward Poulett THOMSON.

**Sydenham, Thomas.** 1624–1689. English physician; served in parliamentary forces in civil war. Introduced cooling method of treating smallpox and use of Peruvian bark in agues; described chorea, hysteria, malaria, smallpox, and gout; studied epidemics in relation to different seasons, years, and ages; insisted on clinical observation instead of theory; friend of John Locke and Robert Boyle; often called "the English Hippocrates."

**Sydenham of Combe,** Baron. See George Sydenham CLARKE.

**Sy′den·strick′er** (sī′d'n·strĭk′ẽr), **Edgar.** 1881–1936. Brother of Pearl Buck (*q.v.*). American economist and statistician, b. Shanghai, China; to U.S. (1896). First public health statistician, in U.S. Public Health Service (from 1915); director of research, Milbank Memorial Fund (from 1928); lecturer, George Washington U. (1921–23), Columbia (from 1929). Author of *Health and Environment,* etc.

**Syd′ney** (sĭd′nĭ). See also SIDNEY.

**Sydney,** Viscount. See *Thomas Townshend,* under TOWNSHEND family.

**Sy′fret** (sē′frĕt; -frĭt), **Edward Neville.** 1889– . British naval officer, b. in South Africa; entered navy (1904); rear admiral (1940); naval secretary to first lord of admiralty (1939–41); in command of cruiser squadron (1941–43); executed British invasion of Madagascar (1942); acting admiral; appointed (Mar., 1943) a lord commissioner of admiralty, and vice-chief of naval staff.

**Sykes** (sīks), Sir **Frederick Hugh.** 1878–1954. English soldier and administrator; commanded Royal Flying Corps, military wing (1912–14); commanded Royal Naval Air Service in Eastern Mediterranean (1915–16); chief of air staff (1918–19); chief of air section, Peace Conference, Paris; controller general of civil aviation (1919–22); M.P. (1922–28; 1940); governor of Bombay (1928–33).

**Sykes, George.** 1822–1880. American army officer; grad. U.S.M.A., West Point (1842); brigadier general of volunteers (1861); major general (1862); engaged at Gettysburg (July 2–4, 1863), commanding V corps defending Little Round Top and Big Round Top. On duty in Kansas (1864–65).

**Sykes,** Sir **Mark.** 1879–1919. English traveler and foreign office adviser; grandson of Sir **Tatton Sykes** (1772–1863), breeder of sheep and horses, owner of race horses, master of foxhounds. In World War I sent on missions to Near East; advocate of Arab independence and pro-Zionist; instrumental in concluding of Sykes-Picot Agreement (1916), assigning spheres of interest in Near East to Russia, France, and Britain; sought to reconcile aims of French and Arabs at Aleppo (1918).

**Sykes,** Sir **Percy Molesworth.** 1867–1945. English soldier; in Persia and Baluchistan (1893–1918); member, intelligence department in Boer War; consul general, Khurasan (1905–13), Chinese Turkestan (1915); appointed to organize South Persia Rifles for restoring order in southern Persia (1916–18). Wrote *Ten Thousand Miles in Persia* (1902), and with his sister **Ella,** *Through Deserts and Oases of Central Asia* (1920).

**Syl'la** (sĭl'ȧ). = SULLA.

**Sylva, Carmen.** See ELIZABETH, Queen of Rumania.

**Sylvanus.** See SILAS.

**Syl·ves'ter** *or* **Sil·ves'ter** (sĭl·vĕs'tẽr). Name of two popes (see *Table of Popes*) and two antipopes:

**Sylvester I,** Saint. d. 335. Pope (bishop of Rome; 314–335), b. Rome; story of his baptizing Constantine the Great a pure legend.

**Sylvester II.** *Real name* **Ger'bert'** (zhĕr'bâr'). 940?–1003. Pope (999–1003), b. near Aurillac, Auvergne, France; an eminent scholar, esp. in mathematics and natural science; teacher at Reims; later (991), archbishop of Reims; befriended by emperors Otto II and III; as tutor, influenced the youth Otto III by his ideas of a restored empire; made archbishop of Ravenna (998); took interest in affairs in all parts of central Europe; made Prague archbishopric for Slavs; reputed to have sent golden crown to St. Stephen, King of Hungary. Wrote textbooks and advanced learning, esp. music and the sciences; wrote letters, theological works, and two works on mathematics.

**Sylvester III.** Antipope (1045); elevated on expulsion from Rome of Benedict IX.

**Sylvester IV.** Antipope (1105–1111) in opposition to Paschal II.

**Sylvester, Frederick Oakes.** 1869–1915. American artist; painted esp. scenes along the Mississippi River. Also published two books of poetry.

**Sylvester, James Joseph.** *Orig. surname* **Joseph.** 1814–1897. Mathematician, b. London, Eng.; professor, U. of Virginia (1841–42); in actuarial work in London (1844–56); professor, Royal Military Academy, Woolwich (1855–70), and Johns Hopkins U., Baltimore (1876–83); Savilian professor of geometry, Oxford (1883–97). First editor, *American Journal of Mathematics* (1878–84). Did original work in the theory of numbers, in higher algebra, and esp. in the theory of invariants.

**Sylvester, Josuah.** 1563–1618. English poet; translated scriptural epics of the Gascon Huguenot, Seigneur Du Bartas, in rhymed decasyllabic couplets (*Canticle,* 1590; *La Semaine,* 1592). Also wrote *The Divine Weeks of the World's Birth* (1604).

**Syl·ves'ter Goz'zo·li'ni** (sĭl·vĕs'tẽr gŏt'tsṓ·lē'nē), Saint. 1177–1267. Italian Roman Catholic abbot; founder (1231) of the Sylvestrian Order, approved by Pope Innocent IV (1247).

**Syl'vi·us** (sĭl'vĭ·ŭs). Latinized form of surname of **Jacques Dubois** (1478–1555), French anatomist.

**Syl'vi·us** (sĭl'vĭ·ŭs), **Franciscus.** *Real name* **Franz de le Bo·ë'** (dĕ lĕ bṓ·ā'). 1614–1672. Physician and anatomist, b. Hanau, Prussia; professor, Leiden. Leader in iatrochemistry; first to indicate significance of nodules in lungs in pulmonary tuberculosis.

**Syme** (sīm), **James.** 1799–1870. Scottish surgeon; established private surgical hospital where he inaugurated his own system of instruction (1829). Known for work on the nature of inflammation and on the function of the periosteum in the repair of bone; treated wounds by leaving them open until blood stopped oozing; introduced into Britain excision of the elbow, and amputation of the ankle joint, known as Syme's operation; contributed to knowledge of diseases of the rectum; treated stricture of urethra by external division.

**Symeon.** Variant of SIMEON.

**Sy'ming·ton** (sī'mĭng·tŭn), **Stuart.** *In Full* **William Stuart Symington.** 1901– . American politician, b. Amherst, Mass. First U.S. secy. of the air force (1947–50); member, U.S. Senate (1953– ) from Missouri.

**Sy'ming·ton** (sī'mĭng·tŭn; sĭm'ĭng-), **William.** 1763–1831. Scottish engineer and inventor; with brother built working model of steam road carriage (1786); patented steam engine in which rotary motion was obtained by chains and ratchet wheels (1787), an engine of this type being used successfully to propel a boat on Dalswinton loch (1788); supervised construction of larger engine which propelled a boat seven miles per hour (1789); patented engine with piston rod guided by rollers in a straight path, connected by a rod to a crank attached directly to the paddle-wheel shaft (1801), used to propel the tugboat *Charlotte Dundas* which towed two barges 19½ miles in six hours. Robert Fulton made a trip on this boat.

**Sym'ma·chus** (sĭm'ȧ·kŭs), Saint. Pope (498–514); opposed by Antipope Laurentius; expelled Manichaeans from Rome.

**Symmachus.** Bible translator of late 2d century A.D.; lived in Samaria. Translated Old Testament into Greek; only fragments of this work are extant.

**Symmachus, Quintus Aurelius.** Roman orator and statesman; champion of paganism; proconsul of Africa (373 A.D.); pontifex maximus; prefect of Rome (384); consul (391); protested (382) against removal of statue and altar of Victory from senate building, and later (384) wrote to Emperor Valentinian II asking that these symbols be restored to their former place.

**Symmes** (sĭmz), **John Cleves.** 1742–1814. American Revolutionary soldier, b. Southold, Long Island, N.Y.; colonel of militia (1775); engaged at Monmouth and Short Hills; member of Continental Congress (1785, 1786); received (1788) grant of land between Miami and Little Miami rivers (the Miami Purchase); founded colony centered around present Cincinnati, Ohio.

**Sym'onds** (sĭm'ŭn(d)z), **John Addington.** 1840–1893. English poet, essayist, and literary historian; son of **John Addington Symonds** (1807–1871), Bristol physician. Published his *Renaissance in Italy* (7 vols., 1875–86), a classic authority on subject; interrupted by illness, settled for rest of life at Davos Platz, Switzerland; published excellent translations of *Autobiography of Benvenuto Cellini* (1887) and of sonnets of Michelangelo and Campanella; biographer of Shelley (1878), Sir Philip Sidney (1886), Ben Jonson (1886), Walt Whitman (1893). See Dame Katharine FURSE.

**Sy'mons** (?sī'mŭnz; ?sĭm'ŭnz), **Arthur.** 1865–1945. British poet and literary critic, b. in Wales. Among his many works are *An Introduction to the Study of Browning* (1886), *Days and Nights* (1889), *Silhouettes* (1892), *London Nights* (1895), *Amoris Victima* (1897), *The Symbolist Movement in Literature* (1899), *Images of Good and Evil* (1900), *The Fool of the World, and Other Poems* (1906), *The Romantic Movement in English Poetry* (1909), *Knave of Hearts* (1913), *Studies in Elizabethan Drama*

(1920), *Dramatis Personae* (1926), *Confessions* (1930), *Jezebel Mort, and Other Poems* (1931); author also of translations of Baudelaire's *Letters* (1927) and *The Woman and the Puppet* by Pierre Louÿs (1936).

**Symons, Gardner,** *in full* **George Gardner.** 1865–1930. American painter, esp. of winter landscapes, b. Chicago.

**Symons, Thomas William.** 1849–1920. American military engineer; advocated building of New York State Barge Canal, consulting engineer during construction (1904–08); known as "Father of the Barge Canal."

**Sy·ne'si·us** (sī·nē'zhĭ·ŭs; -zhŭs). Christian prelate and Neoplatonic philosopher; bishop of Ptolemais (c. 410 A.D.). Among his extant works are *Dio, sive de suo ipsius Instituto, De Providentia, De Insomniis,* and *Epistolae.*

**Syng** (sĭng), **Philip.** 1703–1789. Silversmith in colonial America, b. Ireland; shop in Philadelphia (from c. 1720); one of original organizers of U. of Pennsylvania (1750); treasurer of Philadelphia (1759–69).

**Synge** (sĭng), **John Millington.** 1871–1909. Irish dramatist and promoter of Celtic revival of 1890's; settled in Paris (1895); visited Aran Isles annually (1898–1902) and following suggestion of W. B. Yeats, abandoned literary criticism in order to portray primitive life of Aran islanders; wrote two plays, *The Shadow of the Glen* and *Riders to the Sea* (performed 1903, 1904). Took up residence in Ireland (1903) and devoted himself to interests of the Abbey Theatre, Dublin, contributing to its fame by *The Well of the Saints* (three acts; 1905), and his masterpiece, *The Playboy of the Western World* (1907); author of descriptive essays, *In Wicklow* and *In West Kerry;* all but finished his tragedy, *Deirdre of the Sorrows* (produced 1910).

**Synge, Richard Laurence Millington.** 1914– . British biochemist. Awarded Nobel prize in chemistry (1952) with A. J. Martin for their development of partition chromatography.

**Syntax,** Doctor. See William Combe.

**Sy'phax** (sī'făks). d. about 201 B.C. Numidian king; rival of Masinissa and husband of Sophonisba (*q.v.*); defeated by the Romans under Scipio Africanus.

**Syr'lin** *or* **Sür'lin** (zür'lĭn) *or* **Sir'lin** (zĭr'lĭn), **Jörg.** 1425?–1491. German cabinetmaker, sculptor, and wood carver; works include double row of choir stalls in cathedral at Ulm and stone fountain in its market place.

**Syrokomla, Władysław.** See L. W. Kondratowicz.

**Sza'bó** (sŏ'bō), **István.** *Known as* **Sza'bó–Nagy'a'tád** (-nŏd'y'·ŏ'täd). 1863–1924. Hungarian politician; founder and leader of the Peasants' party; minister of agriculture (1919; 1924); member of the counterrevolutionary administration (1919–21; 1922–24).

**Szárvady, Wilhelmine Clauss–.** See Clauss-Szárvady.

**Szász** (säs), **Károly.** 1829–1905. Hungarian ecclesiastic, poet, and translator; Protestant bishop in Budapest (from 1884); author of epics, lyrics, and plays.

**Szatkowska, Zofja de.** = Zofia Kossak-Szczucka.

**Sze** (sōō). Variant of *Ssŭ,* in Ssŭ-ma Ch'ien, etc.

**Sze** (sōō; *Angl.* zē), **Sao-ke** (sou'kē') **Alfred.** *Orig.* **Shih Chao–chi** (shĭr' jou'jē'). 1877–1958. Chinese diplomat, b. at Hangchow; educ. in U.S. at Cornell (B.A., 1901; M.A., 1902). Minister of communications in first cabinet of Chinese Republic (1912); minister to Great Britain (1914–21, 1929–32) and to the United States (1921–29, 1932–35); delegate to Paris Peace Conference (1918–19); chief representative of China at Washington Conference (1922–23); delegate to Geneva opium conferences (1924–25); delegate to League of Nations Assembly (1931); ambassador to the United States (1935–37).

**Szé'che·nyi** (sā'chĕ·nyĭ). Distinguished Hungarian family, including: Count **István Széchenyi** (1791–1860), soldier and statesman; rode through French lines on eve of battle of Leipzig to carry orders to Blücher and Bernadotte (Oct. 16–17, 1813); led cavalry charge which scattered Murat's bodyguard at battle of Tolentino (1815); took initiative in projects to open the Danube from Buda to the Black Sea; introduced steamboats on the Danube, the Theiss (Tisza), and Lake Balaton; opposed radicalism of Kossuth; minister of ways and communications (1848). His son Count **Béla** (1837–1918) traveled widely, notably in western and southwestern China; collaborated with Lájos Lóczy and Gustav Kreitner in writing *Wissenschaftliche Ergebnisse der Reise in Ostasien, 1877–80* (1890–97). A nephew of István, Count **Imre Széchenyi** (1825–1898), a diplomat, was ambassador in Berlin (1878–92). Count **László Széchenyi** (1879–1938), diplomat; m. (1908) Gladys Moore Vanderbilt, dau. of Cornelius Vanderbilt (1843–1899); minister to U.S. (1922–33) and Great Britain (1933–35).

**Széll** (sāl), **Kálmán von.** 1845–1915. Hungarian statesman; prime minister (1899–1903).

**Szent–Györ'gyi von Nagy'ra'polt** (sĕnt·dyûr'dyĭ fôn nŏd'y'·rŏ'pôlt), **Albert.** 1893– . Hungarian chemist, b. Budapest; educ. Budapest. Lecturer, Groningen (1922–26); worked at Cambridge U. in England; professor, U. of Szeged, Hungary (from 1930); known esp. for work on biological combustion; isolated vitamin C. Awarded 1937 Nobel prize for physiology and medicine. To U.S. (1947).

**Szeps** (sĕps), **Berta.** Austrian writer and diplomat. Daughter of Moritz Szeps, editor of *Neues Wiener Tagblatt;* m. Emil Zuckerkandl, professor of anatomy, Vienna. In Switzerland (1917) as confidential agent of Austria to establish contact with French government and seek terms of peace, and again after the war to seek aid for Austria. Furthered social reforms in postwar Austria. Published memoirs, translated as *My Life and History* (1939), covering the period from 1878.

**Szi'ge·ti** (sĭ'gĕ·tĭ; *Angl.* -gĕ·tĭ), **Joseph.** 1892–1973. Violinist, b. Budapest, Hungary; professor, Geneva Conservatory of Music (1917–24); to U.S. (1925), naturalized (1951); retired (1960).

**Szig'li·ge'ti** (sĭg'lĭ·gĕ'tĭ), **Ede.** 1814–1878. Hungarian playwright; his plays depict Hungarian folk life.

**Szi'lá·gyi** (sĭ'lä·dyĭ), **Sándor.** 1827–1899. Hungarian historian.

**Szi·lard'** (zĭ·lärd'; sĭl'ärd), **Leo.** 1898–1964. American physicist, b. in Hungary. To U.S. (1937); with E. Fermi devised a chain reaction system (1942).

**Szí'nyei** (sē'nyĕ·ĭ), **Paul Mer'se** (mĕr'sĕ) **von.** 1845–1920. Hungarian painter.

**Szold** (zōld), **Henrietta.** 1860–1945. American Jewish Zionist leader, b. Baltimore, Md. With Jewish Publishing Society of America (1892–1916); associated with Zionist movement (1916). Founder and president (1912–26) of Hadassah, U.S. women's Zionist organization.

**Szuj'ski** (shōō'ē·skē), **Józef.** 1835–1883. Polish historian, poet, and playwright; author of historical dramas, as *Halszka z Ostroga* (1858), *Jerzy Lubomirski* (1863), etc.

**Szumowska, Antoinette.** See Timothée Adamowski.

**Szy'ma·now'ski** (shĭ'mä·nôf'skē), **Karol.** 1883–1937. Polish composer; composed the operas *Hagith* and *Le Roi Roger,* ballet *Harnasie,* chorals *Stabat Mater, Demeter,* and *Agave,* masques *Scheherezade, Tantris the Fool,* and *Don Juan's Serenade,* symphonies, orchestral works, chamber music, and songs.

**Szy'mo·no'wicz** (shĭ'mô·nô'vēch), **Szymon.** 1558–1629. Polish poet; known as "the Polish Pindar." Author of *Castus Joseph* (1587), *Epithalamium Sigismondi III* (1592), *Idylles* (1614), and *Penthesilea* (1618).

# T

**Taaf'fe** (tä'fĕ), Count **Eduard von.** 1833–1895. Austrian statesman, of Irish descent; premier of Austria (1868–70; 1879–93).

**Ta·ba'ri, al-** (ăt'tȧ·bȧ'rē). *Arab.* **abu-ja'far Muḥammad ibn-Jarīr al-Ṭabarī.** 838–923. Arab historian and theologian, b. in northern Persia; best-known work, *History of the Prophets and Kings*, commonly known as the *Annals*, a history of the world from the creation to 915 A.D.

**Tabb** (tăb), **John Banister.** 1845–1909. American Roman Catholic priest and poet, b. in Amelia County, Va. Served with Confederate forces in Civil War; ordained priest (1884); teacher of English, Saint Charles' College, Ellicott City, Md. (1884–1909); author of *Poems* (1894), *Lyrics* (1897), *Later Lyrics* (1902), *The Rosary in Rhyme* (1904).

**Ta·ber'nae·mon·ta'nus** (tä·bĕr'nâ·mŏn·tä'no͝os; *Angl.* tȧ·bûr'nē·mŏn·tā'nŭs), **Johann Teodor.** c. 1515–1590. German physician and botanist.

**Tab'i·tha** (tăb'ĭ·thȧ). = DORCAS.

**Tabley,** Baron **de.** See John Byrne Leicester WARREN.

**Ta'bou·is'** (tȧ'bwē'), **Geneviève R.,** *nee* **Le Quesne** (lẽ kân'). 1892– . French journalist; niece of Jules Cambon; m. Robert Tabouis (1916); free-lance correspondent, esp. in field of international politics (1924–32); foreign news editor of *L'Œuvre*, Paris (from 1932); author of *They Called Me Cassandra* (1941).

**Tac·chi'ni** (täk·kē'nē), **Pietro.** 1838–1905. Italian astronomer; known for observations of total solar eclipses and of solar prominences.

**Ta'ché'** (tȧ'shā'), Sir **Étienne Pascal.** 1795–1865. Canadian statesman; practiced as physician; member of legislative assembly, Quebec (1841), speaker (1856); premier in Taché-Macdonald ministries (1856–57; 1864–65); presided over intercolonial conference held at Ottawa to discuss federation (1864). His nephew **Alexandre Antonin Taché** (1823–1894), Canadian missionary and prelate; missionary to Indians of Great Lakes and Northwest; bishop (1853) and archbishop (1871) of St. Boniface, Manitoba; defended Louis Riel in Saskatchewan rebellion (1870).

**Ta Ch'ing.** = CH'ING (dynasty).

**Tac'i·tus** (tăs'ĭ·tŭs), **Cornelius.** 55?–after 117 A.D. Roman orator, politician, and historian; quaestor (79 A.D.); praetor (88); consul (97). Chief work, *Historiae*, an account of the reigns of emperors Galba, Otho, Vitellius, Vespasian, Titus, and Domitian; other works, *Dialogue on Orators*, *Life of Agricola*, *Germania*, *Annales* (history of the Julian emperors from the death of Augustus).

**Tacitus, Marcus Claudius.** 200?–276. Roman emperor (275–276), b. in Umbria; elected by the Senate after death of Aurelian; ruled only about half a year; instituted reforms and favored restoration of power to the Senate; won victory over Goths in Asia Minor; killed by his soldiers.

**Ta·cón'** (tä·kôn'), **Miguel de.** Marqués **de la U·nión' de Cu'ba** (thā lä o͞o·nyôn' dā ko͞o'bä). 1777–1855. Spanish sailor and soldier; military governor of Popayán, Colombia (1806); led Spanish forces in uprisings in South America (1809–14); fought in civil war in Spain (1823); captain general of Cuba (1834–38); suppressed Cuban constitution of 1834; excluded Cuban deputies from Spanish Cortes (1837).

**Tad.** Pseudonym of Thomas Aloysius DORGAN.

**Tadema.** See ALMA-TADEMA.

**Taffari** *or* **Tafari.** See HAILE SELASSIE.

**Taft** (tăft), **Alphonso.** 1810–1891. American jurist and politician, b. Townshend, Vt. Began practice in Cincinnati, Ohio; judge, Cincinnati superior court (1865–72). U.S. secretary of war (1876); U.S. attorney general (1876–77); U.S. minister to Austria-Hungary (1882–84) and to Russia (1884–85). A son, **Charles Phelps** (1843–1929), lawyer and publisher, was proprietor and editor of Cincinnati *Times-Star* (from 1880). Another son, **William Howard** (1857–1930), was twenty-seventh president of the U.S. See William Howard TAFT. Another son, **Henry Waters** (1859–1945), lawyer, practiced in New York City; special assistant to U.S. attorney general in prosecuting Tobacco Trust; member of charter-revision commission of New York City (1901); author of *Law Reform...* (1926), *An Essay on Conversation* (1927), *Japan and America...* (1932), *Opinions—Literary and Otherwise* (1934), etc. Another son, **Horace Dutton** (1861–1943), educator, was founder (1890) and headmaster (1890–1936) of The Taft School, Watertown, Conn.

**Taft, Lo·ra'do** (lō·rā'dō). 1860–1936. American sculptor, b. Elmwood, Ill.; studio in Chicago (from 1883); exercised important influence on development of sculpture in the Middle West. In addition to many portrait busts, he has executed *Solitude of the Soul*, now in Art Institute of Chicago; *Black Hawk*, a heroic statue in Oregon, Ill.; bust of Frances E. Willard in American Hall of Fame; *Columbus Memorial Fountain* in Washington, D.C.; *Ferguson Fountain of the Great Lakes* and the colossal *Fountain of Time* in Chicago; the Victor Lawson memorial, *The Crusader*, in Graceland Cemetery, Chicago.

**Taft, William Howard.** 1857–1930. Twenty-seventh president of the United States, b. Cincinnati, Ohio. Son of Alphonso Taft. Grad. Yale (1878), Cincinnati Law School (1880); adm. to bar (1880); practiced in Cincinnati; judge, Ohio superior court (1887–90); U.S. solicitor general (1890–92); U.S. circuit court judge (1892–1900). President, U.S. Philippine Commission (1900–01) and first civil governor of the Philippine Islands under American control (1901–04). U.S. secretary of war (1904–08). Provisional governor of Cuba (Sept. 29–Oct. 13, 1906). President of the United States (1909–13). Lost popularity by his defense of the Payne-Aldrich Tariff Act (1909) and his dismissal of Gifford Pinchot because of Pinchot's charges against the secretary of the interior, Richard A. Ballinger. Lost political support of Theodore Roosevelt and was defeated for second term election (1912). Professor of constitutional law, Yale (1913–21). Chief justice, U.S. Supreme Court (1921–30). His biography, *The Life and Times of William Howard Taft* (1939), was written by Henry F. Pringle. His son **Robert Alphonso** (1889–1953), lawyer; B.A., Yale (1910), LL.B., Harvard (1913); practiced in Cincinnati; U.S. senator from Ohio (1939–53). Another son, **Charles Phelps** (1897– ), lawyer; practiced in Cincinnati; served with A.E.F. in France in World War; member of Cincinnati City Council (1938–42); director of U.S. Community War Services (1941–43), of Wartime Economic Affairs, Dept. of State (1944).

**Tag'gard** (tăg'ẽrd), **Genevieve.** 1894–1948. American poet, b. Waitsburg, Wash.; m. Robert Wolf (1921), Kenneth Durant (1935); a founder (1920) and an editor (1920–26) of *The Measure, a Journal of Verse;* teacher of English, Sarah Lawrence College (from 1935). Author of *For Eager Lovers* (1922), *Hawaiian Hilltop* (1923),

*Words for the Chisel* (1926), *Traveling Standing Still* (1928), *Not Mine to Finish* (1934), *Calling Western Union* (1936), *Long View* (1942); also wrote a biography of Emily Dickinson (1930).

**Tag'gart** (tăg'ẽrt), **Thomas.** 1856–1929. Politician, b. in County Monaghan, Ireland; to U.S. as a child (1861); originally a restaurant worker; later, operated various hotels in Indiana. Democratic national committeeman (1904–16); instrumental in securing nomination of Woodrow Wilson for presidency (1912); U.S. senator from Indiana (1916).

**Taghlak.** See TUGHLAK.

**Ta'glia·coz'zi** (tä'lyä·kôt'tsē), **Gasparo.** 1546–1599. Italian surgeon, b. Bologna; developed a method of grafting flesh from one part of a body to repair an injury of another part, esp. of the nose, ears, or lips.

**Ta·glio'ni** (tä·lyō'nē). Italian family of ballet dancers including: **Filippo** (1777–1871), ballet master at Stockholm, Kassel, Vienna (1805–10, 1819–27), Warsaw, etc., and composer of many ballets, as *La Sylphide.* His daughter **Maria** (1804–1884), m. (1832) Count Gilbert de Voisins, known esp. for her dancing in *La Sylphide.* His son **Paul** (1808–1884), ballet master (1849 ff.) and ballet director (1869 ff.) at Royal Theater, Berlin, and composer of ballets, as *Flick und Flock.* Paul's daughter **Maria** (1833–1891), m. Prince Joseph Windisch-Graetz (1866), particularly successful at London (1847), at Berlin Royal Theater, and at San Carlos in Naples.

**Ta'gore** (tä'gôr; *freq. Angl.* tȧ·gōr'), Sir **Ra·bin'dra·nath'** (rȧ·bēn'drȧ·nät'). *Written also* **Ra·vīn'dra·nā'tha Thā'ku·ra** (rȧ·vēn'drȧ·nä'tȧ tä'kŏŏ·rȧ). 1861–1941. Hindu poet, b. Calcutta; studied law in England (1877). Established (1901) school at Santiniketan, Bolpur, Bengal, which developed into an international university called Visva-Bharati; translated some of his Bengali works into English (1912); visited Europe, Japan, China, Russia, America; awarded Nobel prize for literature (1913), utilized the £8000 for upkeep of his school; resigned his knighthood (1919) in protest against repressive measures in Punjab. Delivered Hibbert lectures, *Religion of Man,* London (1930); exhibited in European capitals and New York paintings executed after age of 68; set to music over 3000 songs. Author of about 60 poetical works besides volumes of stories, such as *Mashi* (1918), *Broken Ties* (1925), plays, including *The Post Office* (1914), *Sacrifice* (1917), *Red Oleander* (1924), novels, including *The Home and the World* (1919), *Gora* (1924). Among his best-known works are: *Gitanjali* (1912), *The Gardener, The Crescent Moon, Chitra* (1913), *Sādhanā* (1914), *Songs of Kabir* (1915), *Fruit Gathering, Stray Birds, Hungry Stones* (1916), *Nationalism* (1917), *Lover's Gift, Parrot's Training* (1918), *The Wreck, Thought Relics, The Fugitive* (1921), *Creative Unity* (1922), *Fireflies* (1928).

**Ta·har'ka** (tȧ·här'kȧ). *In the Bible (2 Kings* xix. 9) **Tir·ha'kah** (tĭr·hā'kȧ). Third king of the XXVth (Ethiopian) dynasty of Egypt, reigned 688–663 B.C.; nephew of Shabaka. As general of Shabaka's army, defeated (701) by Sennacherib (*q.v.*); on accession, ruled in peace (688–675); defeated Esarhaddon of Assyria in great battle (675), but later (761) overwhelmed and his army scattered by Assyrians (668–667); driven back to Upper Egypt by Ashurbanipal (667); reigned there until his death.

**Tah-gah-jute.** See James (or John) LOGAN.

**Tah·masp'** (tä·mäsp'). Name of two kings of Persia: **Tahmasp I** (1514–1576); son and successor of Ismail I; king (1524–76); seized Baghdad (1529) but lost it (1534) in war with Turks; annexed Shirvan (1538); made peace with Turkey (1555); left Persia weaker than he found it. **Tahmasp II** (d. 1739); son and successor of Husein; king (1722–32); at first aided by Nadir Shah (*q.v.*), but later deposed by him.

**Tahmasp Kuli Khan.** See NADIR SHAH.

**Tai Chin** (dī' jĭn') *or* **Tai Wên-chin** (dī' wŭn'jĭn'). fl. 1450. Chinese painter; one of the foremost of the Ming dynasty; developed a new school of landscape technique in ink.

**Tai'lhade'** (tȧ'yȧd'), **Laurent.** 1854–1919. French poet; author esp. of ballads, lyrics, and satirical verse.

**Tail'lan'dier'** (tä'yäɴ'dyā'), **René Gaspard Ernest.** *Known as* **Saint Re·né'** (săɴ' rē·nā') **Taillandier.** 1817–1879. French journalist and scholar; on staff of *Revue des Deux Mondes;* author of *Scot Érigène et la Philosophie Scolastique* (1843), *Michel Lermontoff* (1856), *Corneille et ses Contemporains* (1864), *Boursault* (1881).

**Tail'le·fer'** (tī'[ē·]fâr'). d. 1066. Norman trouvère; said to have preceded the Norman army invading England (1066), singing of Charlemagne and Roland at Roncesvalles; permitted by William to strike first blow; killed at Hastings; depicted in Bayeux tapestry.

**Tail'le·ferre'** (tī'[ē·]fâr'), **Germaine.** 1892– Fr. composer of ultramodern school; originally a member of "The Six" (see A. HONEGGER); works include a piano concerto in D, a violin sonata, chamber works, and songs.

**Taine** (tĕn), **Hippolyte Adolphe.** 1828–1893. French philosopher and critic, b. at Vouziers; contributor to *Journal des Débats* and *Revue des Deux Mondes;* examiner at Saint-Cyr (1864); professor of aesthetics and history of art, École des Beaux-Arts (1864 ff.); honored with LL.D. degree by Oxford (1871). Among his most notable works are *Essai sur les Fables de La Fontaine* (1853), *Essai sur Tite-Live* (1854), *Voyage aux Pyrénées* (1855), *Essais de Critique et d'Histoire* (1855), *Idéalisme Anglais* (1864), *Histoire de la Littérature Anglaise* (1865), *Philosophie de l'Art* (1865), *Vie et Opinions de Thomas Graindorge* (1867), *De l'Intelligence* (1870), *Origines de la France Contemporaine* (in three parts, *L'Ancien Régime, La Révolution, Le Régime Moderne,* 1871–94).

**Tain'ter** (tān'tẽr), **Charles Sumner.** 1854–1940. American inventor, b. Watertown, Mass.; inventor of various sound-recording instruments, including the Graphophone and the Dictaphone.

**Ta·i·ra** (tä·ē·rä). *Also known, esp. contemporaneously, by its Chinese name,* **Hei·ke** (hā·kĕ). Japanese military clan or family (in control 1160–85). Originated with a prince of the 9th century, son of Emperor Kwammu; reached height of its power in 11th and 12th centuries; rivals of the Minamoto; its great leader, Kiyomori (*q.v.*), placed clan in control of affairs (1160); his death (1181) a signal for rising of the Minamoto; totally defeated by Yoshitsune (1185) at Dan no Ura.

**Taisho.** See YOSHIHITO.

**Tait** (tāt), **Archibald Campbell.** 1811–1882. Anglican prelate, b. Edinburgh; reared a Presbyterian; educ. Glasgow and Oxford; in Glasgow resolved upon entry into ministry of Church of England. Headmaster of Rugby (1842); dean of Carlisle (1849); bishop of London (1856). Made archbishop of Canterbury by Disraeli (1869) to quiet strife over Irish disestablishment; accepted the inevitable, withdrew opposition to Irish Church bill, by forbearance aided settlement; aroused resentment by trying to solve problems of ritualism by Public Worship Regulation Act, providing deprivation of recalcitrant clergy (1874).

**Tait, Arthur Fitzwilliam.** 1819–1905. Painter, b. near Liverpool, Eng.; to U.S. (1850) and opened studio in New York; best known for his animal and bird paintings.

**Tait, Charles.** 1768–1835. American jurist and politician, b. in Louisa County, Va.; practiced in Lexington,

Ga. (from 1798). U.S. senator (1809–19); chairman of committee on naval affairs (1814–18) and did much to strengthen the U.S. navy. Moved to Claiborne, Ala. (1819); made notable contribution to scientific knowledge by revealing the famous Claiborne formation, a Middle Eocene formation around the Gulf of Mexico, containing many well-preserved fossil shells.

**Tait, Peter Guthrie.** 1831–1901. Scottish physicist and mathematician; professor, Edinburgh (from 1860). Investigated properties of ozone, the foundations of the kinetic theory of gases, the latent heat of electricity, etc. His publications include *Dynamics of a Particle* (with William J. Steele, 1856), *Elementary Treatise on Quaternions* (1867), *Introduction to Quaternions* (with Philip Kelland, 1873), *Natural Philosophy* (vol. 1 with Lord Kelvin, 1867), *The Unseen Universe* (with Balfour Stewart, 1875), *Heat* (1884), *Light* (1884), *Properties of Matter* (1885), etc.

**T'ai Tsung** (tī' dzŏŏng'). 597–649. Chinese emperor (627–649) of the T'ang dynasty; son of Li Yüan. Strengthened army; conquered the Eastern Turks (624–630); controlled petty states of Turkestan and established contacts with Persia and India; received Nestorian missionaries and Mohammedans; strongly supported arts and literature; welcomed (645) Hsüan Tsang (*q.v.*) back from his pilgrimage to India.

**Tai Wên–chin.** = Tai Chin.

**Ta·ka·ha·shi** (tä·kä·hä·shē), Viscount **Korekiyo.** *Original surname,* **Ka·wa·mu·ra** (kä·wä·mōō·rä). 1854–1936. Adopted into Takahashi family and assumed that name. Japanese financier; governor of Bank of Japan (1911 ff.); minister of finance (1913–14, 1918); premier of Japan (1921–22); again minister of finance (1927, 1931–34, 1934–36); assassinated.

**Ta·ka·hi·ra** (tä·kä·hē·rä), Baron **Kogoro.** 1854–1926. Japanese diplomat; minister to the Netherlands (1892), Italy (1894), Austria-Hungary (1895), U.S. (1900–05); member of Japanese staff at signing of Treaty of Portsmouth (1905); ambassador to Italy (1907–08) and U.S. (1908–09).

**Ta·ka·mi·ne** (tä·kä·mē·nĕ), **Jokichi.** 1854–1922. Japanese chemist in America; to U.S. (1890) to apply in the distilling industry the starch-digesting enzyme Takadiastase that he had developed; established laboratory at Clifton, N.J.; isolated adrenalin from the suprarenal gland (1901); consulting chemist, Parke, Davis & Co., Detroit.

**Ta·ka·u·ji** (tä·kä·ōō·jē). 1305–1358. Founder of Ashikaga shogunate of Japan and first shogun (1338–58). Minamoto warrior serving under the Hojos at time of the imperial restoration of Daigo II (1333–36); terminated Hojo rule (1333); at first supported Daigo, then revolted (1335), driving emperor out of Kyoto (1336); virtual dictator of the government; appointed shogun (1338); his rule part of period of civil wars between Northern and Southern dynasties.

**Tak'e·lot** (tăk'ĕ·lŏt). Name of three kings of Egypt: **Takelot I;** third king (895–874 B.C.) of XXIId (Bubastite) dynasty; son of Osorkon I. **Takelot II;** king (860–834 B.C.) of XXIId dynasty; son of Osorkon II, with whom he was coregent (860–853 B.C.); reign a period of decline. **Takelot III;** third and last king of XXIIId (Tanite) dynasty, reigned probably as coregent; overcome by Ethiopians (718 B.C.).

**Ta·la·at' Pa·sha'** (tä·lä·ät' pä·shä'), **Mehmet.** *Earlier name* **Talaat Bey** (bā'). 1872–1921. Turkish politician; leader of Young Turks; after Turkish revolution (1908), became successively minister of the interior, postmaster general, again minister of the interior; succeeded Said Halim Pasha as grand vizier of Turkey (Feb. 10, 1917) but was forced into retirement (Oct., 1918); assassinated by an Armenian student (Mar. 15, 1921).

**Tal'bot** (tôl'bŭt). Name of a Norman family of the English aristocracy named in *Domesday Book,* descended from **Richard Talbot,** who obtained from Henry II the lordship of Linton in Herefordshire and from Richard I custody of Ludlow Castle, and including for several generations wardens of the Welsh border, in later generations earls and one duke of Shrewsbury. Prominent members include:

**Gilbert** (1277?–1346), 1st Baron Talbot; head of house under Edward II; took part in invasion of Scotland (1319); later took side of Thomas of Lancaster against king; pardoned by Edward III, confirmed in manor of Linton; summoned to parliament as baron (1331).

**John** (1388?–1453), 1st Earl of **Shrews'bur·y** [shrōōz'bĕr·ĭ; -brĭ; shrōz'-] (cr. 1442); 2d son of 4th Baron Talbot; summoned to parliament (1409–21); served in Welsh wars; lord lieutenant of Ireland (1414–19); hero of forty fights in France during Henry VI's reign before he was checked at Orléans by Joan of Arc and at Patay taken prisoner (1429); on release was for five years mainstay of English cause in France, reconquering lost territory, defeating Burgundians (1437), and recovering Harfleur (1440); sent again to govern Ireland (1445) and created earl of **Wa'ter·ford** [wô'tĕr·fĕrd; wŏt'ĕr-] (1446); sent to aid of Gascons (1452), took Bordeaux but was defeated and killed at Castillon. His younger brother **Richard** (d. 1449) was archbishop of Dublin (1417), lord chancellor of Ireland (1423), and deputy in viceroy's absences. **John** (1413–1460), 2d Earl of Shrewsbury, was chancellor of Ireland (1446) and treasurer of England (1456), fell at Northampton, fighting on king's side.

**George** (1468–1538), 4th Earl of Shrewsbury and Earl of Waterford; grandson of 2d earl; ambassador to Pope Julius II (1511) and to Ferdinand of Aragon (1512) in interests of alliance against France; present at Field of the Cloth of Gold (1520); sent by Henry VIII against rebels in the Pilgrimage of Grace (1536). His grandson **George** (1528?–1590), 6th earl; took part in Somerset's invasion of Scotland and was entrusted by Queen Elizabeth with custody of Mary, Queen of Scots (1569–84), chiefly at Sheffield Manor, a task made difficult by the machinations of his wife, the redoubtable Bess of Hardwick, builder of Chatsworth (see Elizabeth Talbot).

**Charles** (1660–1718), 12th Earl and only Duke of Shrewsbury; godson of Charles II; became a Protestant (1679); one of seven signatories to letter of invitation to William of Orange (1688), whom he supported with £12,000; a secretary of state (1689–90, 1694–1700); one of regents during king's absences (1695, 1696); lived abroad (1700–07); became lord chamberlain (1710) in Tory administration; lord lieutenant of Ireland (1713); as lord high treasurer (1714) at great crisis on death of Queen Anne courageously promoted peaceful accession of George I and assured Hanoverian succession; lord chamberlain (1714–15); succeeded in earldom by a cousin, **Gilbert,** a Roman Catholic priest.

On death (1856) of the 17th earl, the earldom of Shrewsbury passed to **Henry John Chetwynd Talbot** (1803–1868), 3d Earl Talbot, head of a branch of Talbot family descended from the 3d son of 2d earl of Shrewsbury. Other members of this branch included: **William** (1659?–1730), bishop of Durham; his son **Charles** (1685–1737), Baron **Talbot of Hen'sol** (?hĕn'sŏl), a patron of the poet Thomson, solicitor general (1726), lord chancellor (1733); Charles's son **William** (1710–1782), steward of royal household, created Earl Talbot (1761); his nephew

**John Chetwynd Talbot,** who succeeded him as baron, was created (1782) 1st Earl Talbot of Hensol, and was grandfather of 18th earl of Shrewsbury. The earl of Shrewsbury and Talbot is the premier earl on the rolls of England and Ireland.

**Talbot, Elizabeth.** Countess of **Shrews′bur·y** (shro͞oz′-bĕr·ĭ; -brĭ; shrōz′-). *Known as* **Bess of Hard′wick** (bĕs, härd′wĭk). 1518–1608. Daughter and coheiress of John Hardwick of Hardwick, Derbyshire; inherited estates of her four husbands: the second (1549), Sir William Cavendish; the fourth, George Talbot, 6th Earl of Shrewsbury; built Chatsworth on the Cavendish estates; entrusted with care of Mary, Queen of Scots (1569–84) at Tutbury.

**Talbot, Richard.** Earl and titular Duke of **Tyr·con′nel** (tĭr·kŏn′'l). 1630–1691. Irish Jacobite; served in Royalist forces in Civil War; plotted in London for upset of Commonwealth. At Restoration employed in household of duke of York (James II); spokesman of Irish Roman Catholics in opposing Ormonde (1670); schemed to injure character of Anne Hyde, duke's wife; accused of complicity in Popish Plot (1678), went into exile. Made commander in chief in Ireland and earl of Tyrconnel by James II (1685); lord deputy in Ireland (1687); foreseeing revolution in England, endeavored to turn over Ireland to France; after battle of the Boyne fled to France; created duke of Tyrconnel (1689) by James II.

**Talbot, Silas.** 1751–1813. American naval officer, b. Dighton, Mass.; commissioned captain in Continental navy (Sept., 1779); captured by British and held as prisoner of war (1779–81); named by Washington third in list of six captains in U.S. navy (June, 1794); commanded the *Constitution* during the war with France.

**Talbot, William Henry Fox.** 1800–1877. English pioneer in photography; invented and described (1839) "photogenic drawing," contemporaneously with invention of the daguerreotype; process later improved and known as the calotype or Talbotype process (patented 1841); discovered method of instantaneous photography (1851). With Rawlinson and Hincks, one of earliest to decipher cuneiform inscriptions of Nineveh. See also L. J. M. Daguerre.

**Tal′fourd** (tăl′fẽrd; tôl′-), Sir **Thomas Noon.** 1795–1854. English judge, dramatic poet, and editor of the letters (1837) and memorials (1848) of Charles Lamb. M.P. (1835); introduced and championed international copyright bill (1837); sergeant-at-law (1833); judge of common pleas (1849); made famous speech as advocate of Edward Moxon, prosecuted for publishing Shelley's *Queen Mab.* Known for his tragedy *Ion* (1835), in Greek manner, performed by Macready.

**Ta·li·e·sin** (tăl′ĭ·ĕ′sĭn; *Welsh* tȧ′lĭ-). Welsh bard of 6th century, perhaps a mythical personage, to whom were formerly ascribed poems and legends collected in the 14th century *Book of Taliesin.*

**Talis Qualis.** Pseudonym of Carl Vilhelm August Strandberg.

**Tal′lard′** (tȧ′lȧr′), Comte **Camille de.** Duc **d'Hos′tun′** (dôs′tûɴ′). 1652–1728. French soldier; defeated the imperialists at Speyer (1703) in the War of the Spanish Succession, and was created marshal of France; was defeated and captured by Marlborough at Blenheim (1704).

**Tal′ley′rand′** (tȧ′lā′räɴ′; *Angl.* tăl′ĭ·rănd). Distinguished French family, including notably four brothers and their descendants: **Gabriel Marie de Talleyrand,** Comte **de Pé′ri′gord′** [dē pā′rē′gôr′] (1726–1795), governor of Picardy (1770) and lieutenant general (1780). Comte **Charles Daniel de Talleyrand** (1734–1788), lieutenant general (1784), father of Charles Maurice de Talleyrand-Périgord (*q.v.*). **Alexandre Angelique de Talleyrand-Périgord** (1736–1821), cardinal (1817) and archbishop of Paris. Baron **Louis Marie Anne de Talleyrand** (1738–1799), ambassador to Naples (1788). Gabriel's son **Élie Charles de Talleyrand,** Prince **de Cha′lais′** (shȧ′lĕ′), Duc **de Périgord** (1754–1829), field marshal (1791) and émigré (1792–1800), created peer of France (1814). Elie's son **Augustin Marie Élie Charles de Talleyrand,** Duc **de Périgord** (1788–1879), fought in Wagram campaign, in Russia (1812), and in defense of France (1814), created field marshal (1816), and succeeded his father in house of peers. Louis's two sons, Comte **Auguste Louis de Talleyrand-Périgord** (1770–1832), minister to Switzerland (1808–23) and peer of France (1825), and Baron **Alexandre de Talleyrand** (1776–1839), politician, minister to Florence and then to Copenhagen, created peer of France (1838).

**Tal′ley′rand′-Pé′ri′gord′** (-pā′rē′gôr′), **Charles Maurice de.** Prince **de Bé′né′vent′** (dē bā′nā′väɴ′). 1754–1838. French statesman, b. Paris. Took orders (1775); became abbé of Saint-Denis and (1789) bishop of Autun. Member of States-General (1789), representing clergy of Autun; member of Constituent Assembly (1789); proposed confiscation of church property for raising funds to meet expenses of government; became a leader in financial discussions. Excommunicated by the pope (1791). Envoy to England (1792); minister of foreign affairs (1797–1807); created grand chamberlain by Napoleon (1804) and prince de Bénévent (1806). Quarreled with Napoleon (1809) and opposed the emperor's Russian and Spanish policy. At Napoleon's fall, was instrumental in securing restoration of the Bourbons and became Louis XVIII's minister of foreign affairs (1814) and, for a short time, prime minister (1815); after Napoleon's return from Elba and defeat at Waterloo (June 18, 1815), was forced by hostility of nobles at court to resign his post (Sept., 1815). Was involved in Revolution of 1830 and served as ambassador to Great Britain (1830–34); instrumental in organizing Quadruple Alliance (1834). His *Mémoires* were edited by the duc de Broglie (1891).

**Tal′lien′** (tȧ′lyăɴ′), **Jean Lambert.** 1767–1820. French revolutionist; secretary of Commune of Paris (1792); member of National Convention (1792) and of Committee of Public Safety; sent by convention to Bordeaux, he increased the convictions and executions there during Reign of Terror (1793). Leader in the overthrow of Robespierre (1794) and thereafter a leader in more moderate policies; suppressed Jacobins and the Revolutionary Tribunal; member of the Council of Five Hundred. Taken on Egyptian expedition as a savant; later, served as consul at Alicante.

**Tallien, Jeanne Marie Ignace Thérésa,** *nee* **Ca′bar·rús′** (kä′bär·ro͞os′). 1773–1835. French lady of fashion and politician in the revolutionary period; dau. of Conde de Cabarrús (*q.v.*); m. Marquis J. J. de Fontenay (1789; divorced 1793), Jean Lambert Tallien (1794; divorced), comte de Caraman (1805), who later became prince de Chimay. Exerted strong influence over Tallien's policies in the National Convention.

**Tal′lis** *or* **Tal′lys** *or* **Tal′ys** (tăl′ĭs), **Thomas.** 1510?–1585. English organist and composer; father of English cathedral music. Organist to Queen Elizabeth; with William Byrd, granted a monopoly of music printing for 21 years by Queen Elizabeth (1575). Composed five anthems (published 1560), eight tunes for Archbishop Parker's *Psalter* (1567), others for different collections, many still in manuscript; with Byrd, contributed motets to *Cantiones Sacrae* (1575). One of first to compose settings for Anglican service.

**Tal′ma′** (tȧl′mȧ′), **François Joseph.** 1763–1826. French tragedian; debut at Comédie Française (1787); triumphed in Chénier's *Charles IX* (1789). One of founders of the Théâtre Français de la Rue Richelieu (1791), where he played some of his greatest roles, as Henry VIII, Nero, Aegisthus in *Agamemnon*, Othello, Macbeth, Hamlet. He was a favorite with Napoleon, and later with Louis XVIII.

**Tal'mage** (tăl'mĭj), **James Edward.** 1862–1933. Geologist and Mormon leader, b. in Hungerford, Berkshire, Eng.; to U.S. (1876) and settled in Provo, Utah. President, Latter-day Saints' College (1888–93), U. of Utah (1894–97); professor of geology, U. of Utah (1897–1907). Appointed to the Council of the Twelve Apostles (1911) and thereafter devoted himself to the work of the Mormon Church, becoming an authority on technical theological questions. Author of *First Book of Nature* (1888), *Tables for Blowpipe Determination of Minerals* (1899), *The Great Salt Lake, Present and Past* (1900), and religious books, including *The Articles of Faith* (1899), *The Story of "Mormonism"* (1907), *The House of the Lord* (1912), *Jesus the Christ* (1915), *The Vitality of "Mormonism"* (1919). Special editor for Mormon Church terms, *Webster's New International Dictionary, Second Edition.*

**Talmage, John Van Nest.** 1819–1902. American missionary; ordained in Dutch Reformed Church (1846); missionary to the Chinese, resident on island of Kulangsu opposite Amoy (1847–89). His brother **Thomas de Witt** (1832–1902) was also a clergyman in Dutch Reformed Church; notable pastorates in Brooklyn, N.Y. (1869–94), Washington, D.C. (1894–99). Editor, *Christian Herald* (1890–1902). Known as brilliant preacher, though criticized by some for sensationalism.

**Talvj.** See under Edward ROBINSON (1794–1863).

**Ta·ma'gno** (tä·mä'nyō), **Francesco.** 1851–1905. Italian operatic tenor; creator of the title role in Verdi's *Otello*, reputedly written especially for him.

**Ta·mai** (tä·mī), **Katsunori.** *Pseudonym* **Ashihei Hi·no** (hē·nō). 1903–1960. Japanese soldier and writer; served in the war in China (1937); author of *Wheat and Soldiers* (1939) and *War and Soldier* (1940) glorifying the courage and endurance of Japanese troops.

**Ta·ma'ra** (tŭ·mä'rŭ) *or* **Tha'mar** (tä'mär). Before 1160–1212. Queen of Georgia, in Asia (1184–1212); by her statesmanship raised Georgia to peak of its political power.

**Ta·ma'yo** (tä·mä'yō), **Rufino.** 1899– . Mexican painter; among his works are frescoes in the National Conservatory of Music and in the National Museum, Mexico City.

**Tamayo y Baus** (ē bous'), **Manuel.** 1829–1898. Spanish dramatist; works mark transition from Romanticism in the drama. Among his plays are *Virginia* (1853, verse), *La Ricahembra* (with Aureliano Fernández Guerra y Orbe; 1854, verse), *La Locura de Amor*, treating of Juana la Loca (1855), *La Esperanza de la Patria* (with M. Cañete), *La Bola de Nieve* (1856, verse), *Lo Positivo* (1862), *Lances de Honor* (1863), *Un Drama Nuevo* (his masterpiece, 1867), *No Hay Mal Que por Bien No Venga* (1869), and *Los Hombres de Bien* (1870).

**Tam'er·lane** (tăm'ĕr·lān) *or* **Tam'bur·laine** (tăm'bĕr·lān). *English corrupted forms of* **Ti·mur' Lenk** (tĭ·mōōr' lĕngk'), *i.e.* "Timur the Lame." *Called also* **Ti·mour'** (tĭ·mōōr') *or* **Timur.** 1336?–1405. Eastern conqueror, b. near Samarkand; nicknamed "Prince of Destruction." Through house of Jagatai (*q.v.*) descendant of Genghis Khan. Succeeded father as chief of a Turkish tribe (1360); made himself lord of Turkestan (1370) with capital at Samarkand; conquered Persia, Central Asia, and penetrated Russia (1381) as far as Moscow; led his armies through passes into India (1398); captured and destroyed Delhi; invaded Asia Minor and Syria; defeated Turks in great battle at Angora (1402), capturing Sultan Bajazet I and compelling him to raise siege of Constantinople.

**Tamm** (tăm; tȧm), **Igor Yevgenyevich.** 1895–1971. Soviet physicist. Awarded Nobel prize in physics (1958) with P. Cherenkov and I. Frank for nuclear studies.

**Tam'ma·ny** (tăm'ȧ·nĭ). fl. 1685. An American Indian chief of the Delaware tribe, invested by legend with many noble characteristics; adopted after American Revolution as patron saint of various political organizations, as the Sons of King Tammany, later Sons of Saint Tammany, in Philadelphia (1772), and the Society of Tammany in New York (founded 1786, reorganized 1789).

**Tamm'saa're** (tȧm'sä'rĕ), **Anton.** *Pseudonym of* **Anton Han'sen** (hän'zĕn). 1878–1940. Estonian novelist and playwright; best-known work, *Tode ja Õigus* (*Truth and Right*, 5 vols., 1916–33).

**Tamo.** See BODHIDHARMA.

**Tan.** See Vladimir BOGORAZ.

**Ta·na·ka** (tä·nä·kä), Baron **Gi·ichi.** 1863–1929. Japanese soldier and statesman; vice-chief of the general staff (1915); leader of Seiyukai party (1925); prime minister of Japan and minister of foreign affairs (1927–29); reputed author (c. 1927) of *Tanaka Memorial*, a restatement of Japan's blueprint of world conquest.

**Tanaquillus Faber.** See Tannegui LEFEBVRE.

**Tan'chelm** (tän'kĕlm) *or* **Tan'quelm'** (täN'kĕlm') *or* **Tan'que·lin'** (täN'klăN'). *Lat.* **Tan·quel'mus** (tăng·kwĕl'mŭs) *or* **Tan·de'mus** (tăn·dē'mŭs). d. 1115? Flemish heretic; denounced the sacraments of the church, and gained many followers, known as *Tanchelmians.*

**Tan'cred** (tăng'krĕd; -krĭd). d. 1194. King of Sicily; natural son of Roger, Duke of Apulia; crowned king of Sicily (1190); right to throne challenged by Emperor Henry VI of Germany; reign marked by prolonged struggle to maintain power.

**Tancred.** 1078?–1112. Norman hero, son of Otto the Good and Emma, sister of Robert Guiscard; joined First Crusade (1096–99) and distinguished himself at capture of Nicaea and Tarsus, siege of Antioch, capture of Jerusalem, and battle of Ashkelon; became prince of Galilee and, later, of Edessa. His deeds are celebrated in Tasso's *Jerusalem Delivered.*

**Tandem, Felix.** Pseudonym of Carl SPITTELER.

**Tandemus.** See TANCHELM.

**Tan'drup** (tȧn'trōōp), **Harald Konrad Nils.** 1874– . Danish novelist and playwright; author of more than forty works, including a humorous treatment of the Jonah story translated into English as *Jonah and the Voice* (1938; republished as *Reluctant Prophet*, 1939).

**Tan'dy** (tăn'dĭ), **James Napper.** 1740–1803. Irish revolutionary agitator; cofounder, with Wolfe Tone and Thomas Russell, and first secretary of Society of United Irishmen (1791); raised two battalions of a national guard and on its failure fled to America. Given command by French government of a corvette and soldiers, ineffectually invaded Donegal; later taken by British and convicted, but released on intercession by Napoleon. Remembered as hero of *The Wearing of the Green.*

**Ta·ne'ev** (tŭ·nyā'yĕf), **Sergei Ivanovich.** 1856–1915. Russian composer of a trilogy of operas, seven symphonies, six string quartets, chamber music, choral works, piano pieces, and songs.

**Ta'ney** (tô'nĭ), **Roger Brooke.** 1777–1864. American jurist, b. in Calvert County, Md. U.S. attorney general (1831–33); adviser of President Jackson in the Bank of the United States contest. U.S. secretary of the treasury

(1833–34); removed government deposits from Bank of the United States; appointment as secretary of the treasury not confirmed by U.S. Senate (June 24, 1834). Nominated for associate justice, U.S. Supreme Court (1835), but rejected by U.S. Senate. Nominated (Dec. 28, 1835) and confirmed (Mar. 15, 1836) as chief justice, U.S. Supreme Court, succeeding John Marshall. Name always associated with the decision in the Dred Scott (*q.v.*) case (1857).

**T'ang** *or* **Tang** (tăng). A Chinese dynasty (618–907 A.D.), one of the most glorious in history of China. It followed the Sui dynasty, was founded by Li Yüan, and had twenty sovereigns, of whom the chief were T'ai Tsung, Kao Tsung, and Hsüan Tsung, and the usurping Empress Wu Hou. Foreign commerce was encouraged, and Nestorianism and Mohammedanism secured a foothold in China. Under its prosperity China attained its golden age of literature and arts; cf. LI PO, TU FU, WU TAO-TZŬ, WANG WEI, and HSÜAN TSANG. One of the Five Dynasties (*q.v.*) is known as the **Later T'ang** (923–936), during which was begun (932) the block printing of the Confucian classics (see FÊNG TAO).

**T'ang Shao-i** *or* **T'ang Shao-yi** (tăng' shou'ē'). 1860–1938. Chinese statesman, b. in Kwangtung. One of the first group (1873–81) of Chinese government students to be educated in the United States (at Columbia); special envoy to Europe and United States (1908). Active in Revolution (1911–12); first prime minister (1912), subsequently holding various government positions; one of four directors of Canton government (1919–22); official in Nationalist government (from 1928).

**T'ang Yin** (tăng' yĭn'). 1470–1523. Chinese figure and landscape painter of the Ming dynasty.

**Ta·ni** (tä·nē), **Masayuki.** 1889–1962. Japanese politician; educ. Tokyo Univ.; entered diplomatic service (1914), serving in France (1918–23), U.S. (1927–30), Manchukuo (1933–36), etc., and in various posts in Japan; in Tojo cabinet as president of board of information (1941–42), foreign minister (1942–43); ambassador to Nanking govt. (1943–45).

**Ta'nite** (tā'nīt). Name of two dynasties of kings of Egypt, the XXIst (1090–945 B.C.) and the XXIIId (745–718 B.C.), derived from Tanis, their capital city, in the delta. See *Table (in Appendix)* for EGYPT.

**Tan'na·hill** (tăn'ȧ·hĭl), **Robert.** 1774–1810. Scottish song writer; author of such favorite songs as "Gloomy Winter's Noo Awa," "Jessie the Flower o' Dunblane," "The Braes o' Gleniffer," "The Midges Dance Aboon the Burn."

**Tannegui Lefebvre.** See Tannegui LEFEBVRE.

**Tan'ner** (tăn'ẽr), **Henry Os'sa·wa** (?ŏs'ȧ·wȧ). 1859–1937. American Negro painter, b. Pittsburgh, Pa.; chief works are of a religious nature; his *Destruction of Sodom and Gomorrah* hangs in Metropolitan Museum of Art in New York City.

**Tanner, James.** 1844–1927. Known as "Corporal Tanner." American soldier and politician; enlisted in Union army at outbreak of Civil War; promoted corporal; at Second Bull Run was so wounded that both legs were amputated. U.S. commissioner of pensions (1889); largely increased pension payments to veterans without making proper investigation into their claims; resignation accepted (Sept., 1889) with no suspicion of any personal dishonesty on his part. Commander in chief, Grand Army of the Republic (1905–06).

**Tann'häu'ser** (tän'hoi'zẽr; *Angl.* tăn'-). 13th-century Middle High German lyric poet; central figure of a legend used by Richard Wagner in his opera of the same name.

**Tanquelin.** See TANCHELM.

**Tanquelm.** *Latin* **Tanquelmus.** See TANCHELM.

**Tan·sil'lo** (tän·sēl'lō), **Luigi.** 1510–1568. Italian poet in service of viceroy of Naples. Among his works are didactic poems, as *La Balia* and *Il Podere*, the religious epic *Le Lagrime di San Pietro*, lyrics, etc.

**Tan'tia To'pi** (tän'tyä tō'pē). 1819?–1859. Hindu rebel. A Maratha Brahman, in service of Nana Sahib; leader in the Sepoy Mutiny; responsible for Cawnpore massacre (1857); defeated at Bithur; led Gwalior contingent that defeated British at Cawnpore (1857), but was routed by Sir Colin Campbell a few days later; joined forces with Rani of Jhansi; beaten at siege of Jhansi by Sir Hugh Henry Rose (1858); fled to jungles of Rajputana; captured by General R. C. Napier's forces and hanged.

**Ta·nuc'ci** (tä·nōōt'chē), Marchese **Bernardo di.** 1698–1783. Italian statesman and jurist, b. in Tuscany. Minister and regent during minority (1759–67) of Ferdinand I, King of Naples. After Maria Carolina became queen (1768), influence reduced; finally dismissed (1776).

**Tanyu** *or* **Tannyu.** See KANO.

**Tao Kuang** (dou' gwäng'). 1782–1850. Chinese emperor (1821–50), sixth of the Ch'ing dynasty. Son of Chia Ch'ing. Had a disturbed reign: trouble over opium (1836–42); first war (Opium War, 1839–42) with Great Britain (see LIN TSÊ-HSÜ); Treaty of Nanking (1842) opening first five treaty ports for general trade (Canton, Amoy, Foochow, Ningpo, and Shanghai) and ceding Hong Kong to Great Britain; Treaty of Wanghsia (1844), secured by Caleb Cushing, granted extraterritorial rights to United States citizens.

**Taparelli, Massimo.** See AZEGLIO.

**Tap'pan** (tăp'ăn), **Arthur.** 1786–1865. American silk merchant and philanthropist, b. Northampton, Mass.; prominent in abolitionist movement; at first associated with William Lloyd Garrison but later withdrew from American Anti-Slavery Society (1840) and organized and headed new American and Foreign Anti-Slavery Society. His brother **Benjamin** (1773–1857) was a lawyer; judge, 5th Ohio circuit court of common pleas (1816–23); U.S. senator from Ohio (1839–45); opposed to Bank of the United States, zealous antislavery member, sound-money advocate. Another brother, **Lewis** (1788–1873), was partner with Arthur Tappan in silk business in New York (1828–37); founded The Mercantile Agency (1841), first commercial credit-rating agency in U.S.; one of founders of American Anti-Slavery Society (1833); at first associated with William Lloyd Garrison but later associated with brother Arthur in organizing American and Foreign Anti-Slavery Society (1840) and became its treasurer; author of *Is It Right To Be Rich?* (1869) and *The Life of Arthur Tappan* (1870). A son of Benjamin Tappan, **Eli Todd** (1824–1888), was an educator; president, Kenyon College (1869–75) and professor of mathematics and economics (1875–87).

**Ta·ra·fa'** (tă·ră·fă'). *Arab.* **Ṭarafah ibn-al-'Abd.** d. about 560. Arab poet; executed by order of the king for his satires on royalty; author of one of the seven poems entitled *Mu'allaqāt* which are still regarded as classic models of Arabic poetry.

**Tar'bell** (tär'bĕl; -bĕl), **Edmund C.** 1862–1938. American painter; work is impressionistic in style. His *Josephine and Mercié* hangs in the Corcoran Art Gallery in Washington, D.C.; his *Girl Reading* and *My Children in the Woods* in Boston Art Museum.

**Tarbell, Ida Minerva.** 1857–1944. American author, b. in Erie County, Pa.; on editorial staff of *McClure's Magazine* (1894–1906) and *American Magazine* (1906–15). Author of *Short Life of Napoleon Bonaparte* (1895),

*History of the Standard Oil Company* (2 vols., 1904), *He Knew Lincoln* (1907), *The Business of Being a Woman* (1912), *New Ideals in Business* (1916), *The Rising of the Tide* (1919), *Owen D. Young—A New Type of Industrial Leader* (1932), the autobiographical *All in the Day's Work* (1939), etc.

**Tarde** (tȧrd), **Gabriel.** 1843–1904. French sociologist and criminologist; professor of modern philosophy, Collège de France (from 1899). Regarded man as an agent striving to realize ends suggested by the social environment and either sanctioned or rejected by it; developed a theory of imitation, holding that the inferior copy the superior, the lower class the upper class. Author of *Criminalité Comparée* (1886), *Les Lois de l'Imitation* (1890), *Études Pénales et Sociales* (1892), *Les Lois Sociales* (1898), etc.

**Tar'dieu'** (tȧr'dyû'). Family of French engravers, including: **Nicolas Henri** (1674–1749); his nephew and pupil **Pierre François** (1711–?1774) and his son **Jacques Nicolas** (1716–1791); Jacques's son **Charles Jean,** *called* **Tar'dieu'-Co'chin'** [-kô'shăɴ'] (1765–1830), a painter; **Pierre Alexandre** (1756–1844); Pierre's brother **Antoine François,** *called* **de l'Es'tra'pade'** [dẽ lĕs'trȧ'pȧd'] (1757–1822); and Antoine's son **Ambroise** (1788–1841). See also Auguste Ambroise TARDIEU.

**Tardieu, André Pierre Gabriel Amédée.** 1876–1945. French politician, b. at Paris; son of Eugène Amédée Tardieu (*q.v.*). Journalist, on staff of *Le Figaro* (1901) and (writing sometimes under the pseudonym **George Vil'liers'** [vē'lyā']) of *Le Temps* (1903). Member of Chamber of Deputies (1914–24); high commissioner of France in U.S. (1917–18); member of the Paris Peace Conference (1918–19) and supporter of Clemenceau; minister of the liberated regions (1919–20). Again member of the Chamber of Deputies (1926) and minister of public works and the liberated regions (1926–28); minister of the interior (1928); premier of France (1929–30); minister of agriculture (1931); again premier (1932).

**Tardieu, Auguste Ambroise.** 1818–1879. Son of Pierre Alexandre Tardieu (see TARDIEU family). French physician and authority on forensic medicine. His brother **Eugène Amédée** (1822–1893) was a geographer on the staff of the ministry of foreign affairs; father of André Tardieu (*q.v.*).

**Tardivaux, René.** See René BOYLESVE.

**Ta'riq** *or* **Ta'rik** (tä'rĭk). *Arab.* **Ṭāriq ibn-Ziyād.** d. about 720. Moslem general; led first Moslem (Berber) invasion of Spain, landing (711) with army of 7000 at Gibraltar (name derived from *jabal* [Arabic for *mount*] and *Tariq*). Defeated Visigoths under King Roderick (*q.v.*) near Rio Barbate (July 19, 711); conquered Córdoba, Toledo, and other parts of Iberian Peninsula.

**Tar'king·ton** (tär'kĭng·tŭn), **Booth,** *in full* **Newton Booth.** 1869–1946. American novelist, b. Indianapolis; grad. Princeton (1893); author of *The Gentleman from Indiana* (1899), *Monsieur Beaucaire* (1900), *The Conquest of Canaan* (1905), *Guest of Quesnay* (1908), *Penrod* (1914) and other stories centering about this boy character (*Penrod and Sam,* 1916; *Penrod Jashber,* 1931; *The Complete Penrod,* 1932), *Seventeen* (1917), *The Magnificent Ambersons* (1918; awarded Pulitzer prize), *Alice Adams* (1921; Pulitzer prize), *Women* (1925), *The Plutocrat* (1927), *Young Mrs. Greeley* (1929), *Mirthful Haven* (1930), *Little Orvie* (1934), *Rumbin Galleries* (1937), *The Heritage of Hatcher Ide* (1940), *The Fighting Littles* (1941), *Kate Fennigate* (1943), etc. Author or co-author of a number of plays, including *Up from Nowhere, Clarence, Colonel Satan.*

**Tarle'ton** (tärl'tŭn), Sir **Banastre.** 1754–1833. English soldier; accompanied Cornwallis to America (1776); aided Clinton in capture of Charleston (1780); defeated Colonel Abraham Buford at Waxhaw Creek (1780); routed part of General Gates's force at Camden; defeated General Sumter at Catawba Fords; was defeated by General Morgan at Cowpens; with Cornwallis at surrender. Acquired reputation for barbaric cruelty; general (1812).

**Tarl'ton** (tärl'tŭn), **Richard.** d. 1588. English comedian; one of original company of Queen Elizabeth's players (1583–88), for whom he wrote *The Seven Deadly Sins;* Elizabeth's favorite clown; known for his improvisations of doggerel verse; reputed author of anecdotes collected as *Tarlton's Jests* (1592?–?1611). Probable original of Spenser's Pleasant Willy and Shakespeare's Yorick.

**Tar'nier'** (tȧr'nyā'), **Stéphane.** 1828–1897. French obstetrician; one of the first to apply the ideas of Pasteur and Lister to obstetrics; inventor of a type of obstetrical forceps.

**Tar·quin'i·us** (tär·kwĭn'ĭ·ŭs). *Eng.* **Tar'quin** (tär'kwĭn). Name of two legendary kings (the Tarquins) and of two legendary characters of the early Romans: (1) **Lucius Tarquinius Pris'cus** (prĭs'kŭs), *i.e.* "old, ancient." Fifth of the legendary kings (616–578 B.C.), reputedly a Corinthian adventurer, who began Temple of Jupiter on Capitoline Hill, waged successful war against Sabines, Latins, and Etruscans, and was murdered by sons of Ancus Marcius. (2) **Lucius Tarquinius Su·per'bus** (sū·pûr'bŭs), *i.e.* "proud." Seventh and last of the legendary kings (534–510 B.C.) of early Rome. Son of Tarquinius Priscus and son-in-law of Servius Tullius. By tradition a cruel despot; abolished certain rights of Romans but made city powerful among neighbors; acquired Sibylline Books; driven into exile by people aroused and led by L. Junius Brutus because of crime of his son Tarquinius Sextus; failed in attempt to recover Rome with aid of Lars Porsena of Clusium through heroic defense of Horatius Cocles (subject of Macaulay's *Horatius*); with his exile Roman monarchy abolished (510 B.C.). (3) **Lucius Tarquinius Col'la·ti'nus** (kŏl'ȧ·tī'nŭs). Legendary early Roman, cousin of sons of King Tarquinius Superbus; m. Lucretia (*q.v.*); one of the first two consuls of Rome (509 B.C.). (4) **Tarquinius Sex'tus** (sĕks'tŭs). d. 496? B.C. Legendary early Roman, son of Tarquinius Superbus; involved in death of Lucretia, wife of Tarquinius Collatinus; driven from Rome with his father. See LUCRETIA.

**Tarr** (tär), **Ralph Stockman.** 1864–1912. American geologist and educator, b. Gloucester, Mass. Professor and head of department of physical geography, Cornell (1906–12). Organized Cornell Greenland expedition (1896); led National Geographic Society expeditions to Alaska (1909, 1911). Investigated geological formations of the Finger Lake region in upper New York State. Made significant contributions to knowledge of glacial erosion, the nature of ablation moraine, and the part played by earthquakes in the progress and course of glaciers.

**Tar'rasch** (tär'äsh), **Siegbert.** 1862–1934. German chess master.

**Tar·ta'glia** (tär·tä'lyä), **Niccolò.** *Orig.* **Nicola Fon·ta'na** (fōn·tä'nä). 1500?–1557. Italian mathematician; credited with discovery (1541) of the solution of the cubic equation, later published by G. Cardano (*q.v.*) as his own (1545); wrote on fortifications, the raising of sunken ships, and the diving bell; claimed invention of the gunner's quadrant.

**Tar·ti'ni** (tär·tē'nē), **Giuseppe.** 1692–1770. Italian violinist and composer; concertmaster at Padua (from 1721); composer of many violin concertos and sonatas.

**Ta′sche·reau′** (tȧsh′rō′), **Elzéar Alexandre.** 1820–1898. Canadian prelate; archbishop of Quebec (1871–98); first Canadian cardinal (1886). His nephew Sir **Henri Elzéar Taschereau** (1836–1911), Canadian jurist, judge of superior court (1871–78), of supreme court (1878–1906), chief justice (1902–06); member imperial privy council (1904); author of works on Canadian criminal and civil law. Henri's first cousin Sir **Henri Thomas Taschereau** (1841–1909), judge of superior court of Quebec (1878–1907), chief justice of King's Bench (1907–09). His brother **Louis Alexandre Taschereau** (1867–1952), minister of public works and labor, Quebec (1907–19), prime minister of Province of Quebec (1920–36).

**Taschereau, Jules Antoine.** 1801–1874. French journalist and librarian; founded *Revue Rétrospective* (1832); editor of Molière's works, Boufflers's works, and of *Correspondance Littéraire de Grimm et de Diderot* (1829–30); author of *Histoire de la Vie et des Ouvrages de Corneille* (1829), etc.

**Ta·shi·ro** (tä·shē·rō), **Shiro.** 1883–1963. Biochemist, b. in Kagoshima, Japan; to U.S. (1901); taught at U. of Chicago (1914–18), and at Cincinnati U. (from 1919; professor from 1921). Inventor of the biometer, an instrument for measuring minute quantities of carbon dioxide as given off by small masses of tissue, etc.

**Tas′man** (täs′män; *Angl.* tăz′măn), **Abel Janszoon.** 1603–1659. Dutch mariner; sent by Van Diemen, governor general of Dutch East Indies, on exploring expedition to Australian waters (Aug., 1642); discovered Tasmania (which he named Van Diemen's Land), New Zealand (Dec., 1642), and some of the Friendly Islands (1643); on second voyage (1644), discovered Gulf of Carpentaria.

**Tas′saert** (täs′ärt), **Nicolas François Octave.** 1800–1874. Flemish-born painter in France; known for historical works and genre scenes.

**Tassaert, Pierre Antoine.** 1729–1788. Dutch sculptor; court sculptor of Frederick the Great (from 1775).

**Tas′sie** (tăs′ĭ), **James.** 1735–1799. Scottish gem engraver and modeler; in London produced reproductions of gems of richest cabinets in Europe; executed large profile medallion portraits of contemporaries.

**Tas′so** (täs′sō; *Angl.* tăs′ō), **Torquato.** 1544–1595. Italian poet, b. at Sorrento; studied under Jesuits at Naples. Protégé of Scipione Gonzaga, patriarch of Jerusalem, and later of Vicenzo Gonzaga; sometime in service of Cardinal Luigi d'Este. To Paris (1570); met French Pleiad; in retinue of Alfonso II d'Este, Duke of Ferrara (1572 ff.); lecturer in astronomy and mathematics, U. of Ferrara (1574 ff.). Beset by delusory fears of persecution (c. 1575); began series of mad wanderings (1577 ff.); committed to insane asylum of Sant' Anna, Ferrara (1579–86). Known esp. for his *Jerusalem Delivered* (*Gerusalemme Liberata*, 1575), an heroic epic poem dealing with the capture of Jerusalem during First Crusade; his other works include the Carolingian epic *Rinaldo* (1562), the pastoral dramatic poem *Aminta* (1573), the tragedies *Galealto di Norvegia* and *Il Re Torrismondo*, the religious epic *Il Mondo Creato* (all completed c. 1590), and three *Discorsi dell'Arte Poetica*. His father, **Bernardo Tasso** (1493–1569), was also a poet; in service of Ferrante Sanseverino, Prince of Salerno, and later (1563 ff.) of Guglielmo Gonzaga, Duke of Mantua; known particularly for his *L'Amadigi di Gaula* (1542–60; based on Ordóñez de Montalvo's *Amadís de Gaula*, a Spanish prose version of *Amadis of Gaul*), a romantic epic in 100 cantos; his other works include the chivalric epic *Il Floridante* (completed by Torquato Tasso, 1587) and *Rime, Odi, e Salmi* (1560).

**Tas·so′ni** (täs·sō′nē), **Alessandro.** 1565–1635. Italian poet and writer; in service of Charles Emanuel of Savoy (1613–22); counselor and chamberlain to Francesco de' Medici, Duke of Modena (1632). Known particularly for his mock heroic epic *La Secchia Rapita* (12 cantos, 1614; pub. 1622).

**Tas′tu′** (tȧs′tü′), **Sabine Casimire Amable,** *nee* **Vo′ïart′** (vô′yȧr′). 1798–1885. French poet; m. Joseph Tastu (1816; d. 1849); achieved success with her *Oiseaux du Sacre* (1825).

**Ta·ta,** Sir **Jam·set′ji** (jŭm·sāt′jē). 1839–1904. Indian Parsi merchant and industrialist; established Empress Mill at Nagpur (1877), Svadeshi Mill at Bombay (1887). Under his son and successor, Sir **Do·rab′ji** (dä·räb′jē) **Jamsetji** (1859–1932), business was organized under firm name Tata and Sons, and expanded to include Tata Iron and Steel Company. Another son, Sir **Ra′tan·ji′** (rŭ′-tȧn·jē′) **Jamsetji** (1871–1918), also associated with the business, was known as a financier and philanthropist.

**Tate** (tāt), **Allen,** *in full* **John Orley Allen.** 1899–1979. American poet, critic, and biographer, b. in Clarke County, Ky. One of group of founders of and contributors to *The Fugitive*, a literary magazine (1922–25). Author of biographies, *Stonewall Jackson...*(1928), *Jefferson Davis...*(1929), and *Robert E. Lee* (1932); a volume of essays (1936); volumes of verse, including *Mr. Pope and Other Poems* (1928), *Three Poems* (1930), *The Mediterranean and Other Poems* (1935); the novel *The Fathers* (1938); critical essays, *Reason in Madness* (1941); etc. Married (1924) **Caroline Gor′don** [gôr′d'n] (1895– ), winner of O. Henry memorial prize (1934); author of *Penhally* (1931), *The Garden of Adonis* (1937), etc.

**Tate,** Sir **Henry.** 1819–1899. English sugar refiner and philanthropist; gave large sums to Liverpool University Coll. and Liverpool hospitals; gave to the nation his collection of modern paintings, and the Tate Gallery to house the collection (opened 1897).

**Tate, Nahum.** 1652–1715. British poet and playwright, b. and educ. in Ireland. Wrote plays, mostly adaptations from Shakespeare and other Elizabethan dramatists; commissioned by Dryden to write second part of *Absalom and Achitophel* (1682); poet laureate (1692); collaborated with Nicholas Brady in the *New Version of the Psalms of David* (1696), in meter; credited with hymns "While shepherds watched" and "As pants the hart"; author of the libretto of Purcell's opera *Dido and Aeneas*. Pilloried in the *Dunciad*.

**Tate, Ralph.** 1840–1901. English geologist and paleontologist; professor of natural sciences, U. of Adelaide, Australia (1875–1901); accompanied Horn expedition to central Australia as geologist (1894); author of a *Handbook of the Flora of Extratropical Australia* (1890).

**Ta′tian** (tā′shăn; -shĭ·ăn). *Latin* **Ta′ti·a′nus** (tā′shĭ-ā′nŭs). Christian writer, originally from Syria; to Rome (c. 152 A.D.); studied under Justin, after whose death (c. 165 A.D.) he adopted heretical doctrines of the Encratites. Among his many writings only two are extant, *Oratio ad Graecos* (an apology for Christianity) and *Diatessaron* (a harmony of the Gospels).

**Tatius, Achilles.** See ACHILLES TATIUS.

**Tatius, Titus.** See ROMULUS.

**Tat′lock** (tăt′lŏk), **John Strong Perry.** 1876–1948. American educator; known as a Chaucer scholar; professor of English, U. of Michigan (1905–15), Stanford (1915–25), Harvard (1925–29), U. of California (from 1929). Compiler (with Arthur G. Kennedy, 1927) of *Concordance to Chaucer*.

**Tat′tam** (tăt′ăm), **Henry.** 1789–1868. British Orientalist and Coptic scholar.

**Tat′ter·sall** (tăt′ẽr·sôl; -s'l), **Richard.** 1724–1795. English horseman; founder (1766) of Tattersall's, London horse-auction mart. Stud groom to 2d duke of Kingston; horse auctioneer at Hyde Park corner (1766).

**Tatti, Jacopo.** See Jacopo SANSOVINO.

**Tatt'nall** (tăt'n'l), **Josiah.** 1795–1871. American naval officer, b. near Savannah, Ga. Served in War of 1812, against Algerian pirates (1815), and in Mexican War. Commander of squadron in Asiatic waters (1857–60); aided British naval force after its repulse at the mouth of the Pei-ho (1859), violating thereby American neutrality, with remark, "Blood is thicker than water." Captain in Confederate navy, commanding naval defenses of Georgia and South Carolina (1861–62), Virginia (1862) where he commanded the ironclad *Virginia* (the former *Merrimack*) and destroyed it to prevent it from falling into Union hands, and again Georgia (1863–64).

**Ta'tum** (tāt'ŭm), **Edward Lawrie.** 1909–1975. American biochemist, b. Boulder, Colo. At Stanford U. (1937–45; 1948–56), Yale U. (1945–48), Rockefeller U. (1957–75); awarded Nobel prize in physiology or medicine (1958) with G. Beadle and J. Lederberg.

**Tau'bes** (tou'bĕs), **Frederic.** 1900– . American painter (portraits, landscapes, still lifes) and teacher, b. Lwów; to U.S. (1930); studio in New York; author of *Technique of Oil Painting* (1941).

**Tauch'nitz** (touκ'nĭts; *Angl.* touk'-), **Karl Christoph Traugott.** 1761–1836. German printer and publisher; known esp. for editions of the classics printed at his press in Leipzig. His son **Karl Christian Philipp** (1798–1884) continued the business until it was bought by O. Holtze (1865). Karl Christoph's nephew **Christian Bernhard Tauchnitz** (1816–1895) founded (1837) a printing and publishing house in Leipzig; began publication (1841) of the highly successful "Tauchnitz Edition" of a *Collection of British and American Authors.*

**Tau'ent·zien** (tou'ĕn·tsēn), **Friedrich Bogislaw von.** 1710–1791. Prussian general; distinguished himself at Kolín (1757); commanded fortress of Breslau (1758–91). Employed G. E. Lessing (*q.v.*) as secretary (1760–65).

**Tau'ler** (tou'lẽr), **Johannes.** 1300?–1361. Known as "the Illuminated Doctor." German mystic and preacher; member of Dominican Order; expelled from Strasbourg (1339), settled in Basel; associated for a time with the "Friends of God"; returned to Strasbourg (1352).

**Tau'nay'** (tō'nā'), Visconde **de. Alfredo d'Es'cra'gnolle'** (dĕs'krȧ'nyôl'). 1843–1899. Brazilian military engineer, politician, and writer; served in war against Paraguay (1865–70); author of novels, essays, poems, and historical sketches.

**Tau·ris'cus of Tral'les** (tô·rĭs'kŭs, trăl'ēz). Greek sculptor, probably of the 1st century B.C.; said to have collaborated with his brother Apollonius of Tralles (*q.v.*) in carving the group of statuary known as the *Farnese Bull*, now in the National Museum at Naples.

**Tau'sen** (tou's'n), **Hans.** 1494–1561. Danish religious reformer; originally a monk, studied under Luther in Wittenberg (1523–25) and thereafter preached the doctrines of the Reformation in Viborg and Copenhagen; became Protestant bishop in Ribe (1542); translated the Pentateuch into Danish.

**Taus'sig** (tou'sĭg), **Frank William.** 1859–1940. American economist and educator; taught at Harvard (1882–1935); author of *Tariff History of the United States* (1888), *Wages and Capital* (1896), *Principles of Economics* (1911), *Free Trade, the Tariff, and Reciprocity* (1919), *International Trade* (1927), etc.

**Ta'vannes'** (tȧ'vȧn'), Seigneur **de. Gaspard de Saulx** (dē sō'). 1509–1573. French soldier; distinguished himself at siege of Metz (1552) and capture of Calais (1558); marshal of France (1570); one of those chiefly responsible for Massacre of St. Bartholomew (1572).

**Ta'vast·stjer'na** (tȧ'vȧst·shâr'nȧ), **Karl August.** 1860–1898. Finnish poet, novelist, and playwright.

**Tav'er·ner** (tăv'ẽr·nẽr), **John.** 1495?–1545. English composer, chiefly of church music.

**Taverner, Richard.** 1505?–1575. English religious reformer; wrote in support of Reformation; prepared revision of Matthew's Bible, known as Taverner's Bible (1539), and commentary on epistles and gospels (1540); translator of Erasmus.

**Ta'ver'nier'** (tȧ'vĕr'nyā'), **Jean Baptiste.** 1605–1689. French traveler, notably in Turkey, Persia, central Asia, and the East Indies.

**Tavistock,** Marquis of. See RUSSELL family.

**Tay'lor** (tā'lẽr). Name of an English family, the Taylors of Ongar, eminent in art and literature, including: **Isaac** (1730–1807), engraver and portrait painter, illustrator of Chambers's *Cyclopaedia* and Richardson's *Sir Charles Grandison* (1778). His sons **Charles** (1756–1823), engraver, and **Isaac** (1759–1829), engraver, nonconformist pastor of Ongar (1810), author of books for children, such as *Advice to the Teens* (1818), whose wife (m. 1781), **Ann,** *nee* **Martin** (1757–1830), wrote manuals of conduct, such as *Practical Hints to Young Females* (1815). Children of Isaac and Ann: **Ann** (1782–1866, m. 1813 Joseph Gilbert) and **Jane** (1783–1824), known as authors of *The Minor's Pocket Book*, the immensely popular *Original Poems for Infant Minds* (2 vols., 1804–05) and *Rhymes for the Nursery* (1806; including Jane's poem "Twinkle, twinkle, little star"). **Isaac** (1787–1865), artist, author, and inventor, admired as engraver by Rossetti; author of *The Elements of Thought* (1823), *Spiritual Despotism* (1835), *Ultimate Civilisation* (1860); inventor of machine for engraving upon copper, important to manufacture of calico. **Jefferys** (1792–1853), inventor of a ruling machine for engravers; author of fanciful stories for children.

**Isaac** (1829–1901), archaeologist and philologist; eldest son of Isaac (1787–1865); canon of York (1885); advocated revision of the Prayer Book in *The Liturgy and the Dissenters* (1860); published works in philology, including *Words and Places* (1864) and *The Alphabet* (2 vols., 1883), and in archaeology, including *Etruscan Researches* (1874), *The Origin of the Aryans* (1889).

**Taylor, Alfred Alexander.** See under Robert Love TAYLOR.

**Taylor, Alfred Edward.** 1869–1945. English philosopher; professor, McGill U. (1903–08), St. Andrew's (1908–24), Edinburgh (1924–41). Among his many books are *The Problem of Conduct* (1901), *Elements of Metaphysics* (1903), *The Faith of a Moralist* (1930), *The Christian Hope of Immortality* (1938), etc.

**Taylor, Bayard,** *sometimes called* **James Bayard.** 1825–1878. American writer, b. Kennett Square, Pa. Commissioned by *Saturday Evening Post, United States Gazette,* and New York *Tribune* to take a trip in Europe, sending back letters from place to place (1844–46); published *Views Afoot* (1846). On staff of New York *Tribune* (1848); took trip to California during the gold rush (1849–50); published *Eldorado* (1850). Traveled in Egypt, Asia Minor, Syria, and Europe (1851–52), and in India, China, and Japan (1852–53); published *A Journey to Central Africa* (1854), *The Lands of the Saracen* (1855), *A Visit to India, China, and Japan...* (1855), and lectured widely on his travels. Devoted himself (1863–70) to translation of Goethe's *Faust* (2 vols., 1870–71). U.S. minister to Germany (1878). In addition to works mentioned above, published three novels and a number of volumes of verse.

**Taylor, Bert Leston.** 1866–1921. American journalist, b. Goshen, Mass.; editor of column called "A Line o'

Type or Two," over his initials B.L.T., in Chicago *Daily Tribune* (1901–03; 1909–21).

**Taylor, Brook.** 1685–1731. English mathematician; obtained solution of problem of center of oscillation (1708; published 1714); became founder of the calculus of finite differences through his *Methodus Incrementorum Directa et Inversa* (1715) in which he also set forth Taylor's theorem, a fundamental theorem concerning functions; published *Linear Perspective* (1715).

**Taylor, Charles A.** 1864–1942. American dramatist; author esp. of melodramas, as *From Rags to Riches, The Queen of White Slaves*, etc. See Laurette TAYLOR.

**Taylor, Charles Fayette.** 1827–1899. American orthopedic surgeon, b. Williston, Vt.

**Taylor, Deems,** *in full* **Joseph Deems.** 1885–1966. American composer and music critic, b. New York City; A.B., N.Y.U. (1906); music critic, New York *World* (1921–25); editor, *Musical America* (1927–29); music critic, New York *American* (1931–32); music consultant for Columbia Broadcasting System (from 1936). Composer of *The Siren Song* (a symphonic poem, 1912), *The Chambered Nautilus* (a cantata, 1914), *Through the Looking Glass* (a suite for orchestra, 1918), *The King's Henchman* (grand opera with libretto by Edna St. Vincent Millay, produced at Metropolitan Opera House, New York, 1927), *Peter Ibbetson* (grand opera, 1931), and various choral pieces and piano compositions.

**Taylor, Francis Henry.** 1903–1957. American art-museum director, b. Philadelphia; director, Metropolitan Museum of Art, New York (from 1940).

**Taylor, Frank Walter.** 1874–1921. American portrait painter and illustrator; studio in Philadelphia (from 1898).

**Taylor,** Sir **Frederick Williams–.** See WILLIAMS-TAYLOR.

**Taylor, Frederick Winslow.** 1856–1915. American efficiency engineer, b. Germantown, Pa. Opened office in Philadelphia as consulting engineer, prepared to systematize shop management and study reduction of manufacturing costs. Made remarkable success in applying his ideas of scientific management. Developed (1899), with Maunsel White, Taylor-White process for heat-treating high-speed tool steels, increasing cutting capacities 200 or 300 per cent. From 1901, devoted himself to expounding the so-called Taylor system, or scientific management. Author of *The Principles of Scientific Management* (1911), etc.

**Taylor, George.** 1716–1781. Iron manufacturer, b. prob. in northern Ireland; to America (c. 1736); operated furnace in Bucks County, Pa.; member of Committee of Correspondence (1774–76), and of Continental Congress (1776–77); a signer of the Declaration of Independence.

**Taylor, George.** 1837–1909. Pseudonym of Adolf HAUSRATH.

**Taylor, Graham.** 1851–1938. American clergyman and educator; ordained in Dutch Reformed ministry (1873); pastorate, Hartford, Conn. (1880–92). Founder and resident warden, Chicago Commons Social Settlement (from 1894), which became one of most widely known social settlements in U.S.

**Taylor, Hannis.** 1851–1922. American lawyer; practiced at Mobile, Ala. (1870–92); U.S. minister to Spain (1893–97); special counsel for United States before Spanish Treaty Claims Commission (1902); junior counsel for United States before Alaska Boundary Tribunal (1903).

**Taylor,** Sir **Henry.** 1800–1886. English poet; wrote articles for *Quarterly Review* and *London Magazine;* held appointments in Colonial office (1824–72); author of verse dramas, including *Philip van Artevelde* (1834), a great success, and of lyrical poetry, one lyric, "If I had the wings of a dove," appearing in many anthologies.

**Taylor, Henry Osborn.** 1856–1941. American author, b. New York City; A.B., Harvard (1878); LL.B., Columbia (1881); author of *Ancient Ideals, a Study of Intellectual and Spiritual Growth from Early Times to the Establishment of Christianity* (2 vols., 1900), *The Mediaeval Mind* (2 vols., 1911), *Deliverance—The Freeing of the Spirit in the Ancient World* (1915), *Freedom of Mind in History* (1922), *Human Values and Verities* (1928), *A Historian's Creed* (1939).

**Tay'lor'** (tā'lôr'), Baron **Isidore Justin Séverin.** 1789–1879. French writer, of English ancestry, b. at Brussels; royal administrator of the Théâtre Français; inspector of fine arts (1838). Best known for his *Voyages Pittoresques et Romantiques de l'Ancienne France* (1820–63), a 24-volume work illustrated by his own drawings and by Isabey, Géricault, Ingres, Vernet, Fragonard, Viollet-le-Duc.

**Tay'lor** (tā'lẽr), **James Monroe.** 1848–1916. American Baptist clergyman and educator; president of Vassar College (1886–1914).

**Taylor, Jeremy.** 1613–1667. English prelate and author; chaplain to Laud and Charles I; received D.D. on publication of *Episcopacy Asserted* (1642). After downfall of Royalist cause took refuge in Wales, kept a school, had as patron Richard Vaughan, Earl of Carbery, whose mansion, Golden Grove, immortalized in *The Golden Grove*, a manual of devotion (1655), provided Taylor with seclusion for producing his enduring literary monuments (1646–60), including the *Liberty of Prophesying* (1646), *Holy Living* (1650), *Holy Dying* (1651), *Worthy Communicant* (1660). Received from Charles I, shortly before his execution, his watch and some jewels; published *Ductor Dubitantium* (1660), a piece of casuistry dedicated to Charles II; as bishop of Down and Connor (1661) and administrator of Dromore diocese, involved in conflicts with Presbyterian clergy, and built cathedral of Dromore; undertook his last great work, *Dissuasive from Popery* (1664, 1667); buried in cathedral of Dromore.

**Taylor, John.** 1580–1653. English pamphleteer; known as "the Water Poet." A Thames waterman and collector of perquisites for lieutenant of Tower; published odd-titled booklets describing harebrained journeys undertaken for self-advertisement, for example, a journey from London to Edinburgh on foot in *Penniless Pilgrimage* (1618), a voyage in a brown-paper boat from London to Queensborough in *Praise of Hempseed* (1620). Journeyed to Prague, where he was entertained by queen of Bohemia (1620). Kept public house at Oxford (1642); returned to London and took over Crown public house in Phoenix Alley, Longacre.

**Taylor, John.** 1753–1824. Known as "John Taylor of Car'o·line (kăr'ō·līn)." American politician and agriculturist, b. in Virginia; served in Continental army (1775–79; 1781); U.S. senator from Virginia (1792–94; 1803; 1822–24); author of *An Inquiry into the Principles and Policy of the Government of the United States* (1814), *Tyranny Unmasked* (1822), etc.

**Taylor, John.** 1808–1887. Mormon leader; baptized in Mormon Church (1836); created apostle (1838). After death of Joseph Smith (1844), sided with Brigham Young in struggle for succession; accompanied Young to Utah and settled there; member of legislature of Territory of Utah (1857–76). After Brigham Young's death (1877), was acting head of the church; chosen president (1880). Accepted polygamy and had seven wives; forced into exile (1884) to escape arrest by U.S. government; managed affairs of church from his retreat (1884–87).

**Taylor, John Edward.** 1791–1844. English liberal journalist; founded the Manchester *Guardian* (1821).

**Taylor, Joseph Wright.** 1810–1880. American physician, businessman, and philanthropist; founder and benefactor of Bryn Mawr College, where the main building, Taylor Hall, is named in his honor.

**Taylor, Laurette,** *nee* **Coo′ney** (kōō′nĭ). 1884–1946. American actress, b. New York City; m. (1st) Charles A. Taylor (*q.v.*), (2d) J. Hartley Manners (1912; d. 1928); success in *Peg O' My Heart, Alice Sit by the Fire, The Old Lady Shows Her Medals,* and as Juliet, Portia, etc.

**Taylor, Maxwell Davenport.** 1901– . American army officer and diplomat, b. Keytesville, Mo. Division commander, Europe (1944–45); chairman, Joint Chiefs of Staff (1962–64); amb. to South Vietnam (1964–65).

**Taylor, Meadows,** *in full* **Philip Meadows.** 1808–1876. Anglo-Indian administrator and novelist; author of *Confessions of a Thug* (1839) and other novels of Indian life and about the Sepoy Mutiny.

**Taylor, Moses.** 1806–1882. American financier, b. New York City; in importing business (1832–55); president, City Bank of New York (1855–82); acquired controlling interest in Delaware, Lackawanna & Western Railroad in panic of 1857; associated with Cyrus W. Field in the first Atlantic cable attempt.

**Taylor, Myron Charles.** 1874–1959. American lawyer and businessman, b. Lyons, N.Y.; chairman of board of directors and chief executive of U.S. Steel Corp. (1932–38); appointed (1939) personal representative of President F. D. Roosevelt at Vatican City.

**Taylor, Nathaniel William.** 1786–1858. American theologian; ordained in Congregational ministry (1812); professor of didactic theology, Yale Divinity School (1822–58). Developed elaborate system of theology, involving freedom of will (Taylorism) which aroused controversy, dividing New England churches into Taylorites and Tylerites (adherents of doctrine taught by Bennet Tyler, Taylor's opponent).

**Taylor, Norman.** 1883–1967. American botanist, b. England; to U.S. (1889). Curator of plants, Brooklyn Botanic Garden (1911–29). On expeditions to Bahamas (1904), Haiti (1905), Cuba (1906), Santo Domingo (1909), Yucatán (1928), Brazil (1929). Editor, *Torreya* (1911–21), *The Garden Dictionary* (1933–36). Author of *Botany, the Science of Plant Life* (1924), *Guide to the Wild Flowers* (1928), etc.

**Taylor, Phoebe Atwood.** *Pseudonym* **Alice Til′ton** (tĭl′t'n; -tŭn). 1909– . American detective-story writer, b. Boston; many of her novels have a Cape Cod background; creator of the fictional crime detectors Leonidas Witherall (*Cold Steal,* 1939; *Left Leg,* 1940; etc.) and Asey Mayo (*Deadly Sunshade,* 1940; etc.).

**Taylor, Richard.** 1826–1879. Son of Zachary Taylor. American army officer; sugar planter in Saint Charles Parish, La. (from 1849). Brigadier general, Confederate army (Oct., 1861); served under Stonewall Jackson in Shenandoah Valley campaign. Promoted major general (July, 1862); commanded District of West Louisiana; checked Banks at Pleasant Hill and Sabine Crossroads (Apr., 1864). Promoted lieutenant general (Aug., 1864); succeeded to command of Gen. J. B. Hood's army (Nov., 1864); surrendered to Gen. Canby at Citronelle, Ala. (May 4, 1865).

**Taylor, Robert Love.** 1850–1912. American politician, b. Happy Valley, Tenn. Governor of Tennessee (1887–91; 1897–99); U.S. senator from Tennessee (1907–12). His brother **Alfred Alexander** (1848–1931) was also a politician; campaigned for governorship against his brother Robert (1886) in famous campaign in which the brothers appeared on the same platform and amused the crowds by fiddling, droll stories, and quick repartee; governor of Tennessee (1921–23).

**Taylor, Robert Tunstall.** 1867–1929. American orthopedic surgeon.

**Taylor, Rowland.** d. 1555. English Protestant martyr; chaplain to Cranmer (1540); archdeacon of Exeter (1552); advocated cause of Lady Jane Grey; resisted restoration of the Mass under Mary; burnt for heresy near Hadleigh.

**Taylor, Samuel Coleridge.** = Samuel COLERIDGE-TAYLOR.

**Taylor, Thomas.** 1758–1835. English classical scholar; known as "the Platonist." Clerk in Lubbock's bank; left desk to translate and expound Plato, Aristotle, and Neo-Platonists and Pythagoreans without scholarly training or critical ability; author of translations and dissertations and *The Spirit of All Religions* (1790).

**Taylor, Tom.** 1817–1880. English dramatist. Barrister (1846); secretary to board of health (1850–72); editor of *Punch* (1874–80). Made his first hit with *To Parents and Guardians* (1845); wrote or adapted over one hundred dramatic pieces, including *Our American Cousin* (1858), produced in New York, in which E. A. Sothern created role of Lord Dundreary, *Still Waters Run Deep* (1855), *Victims* (1857), *The Overland Route* (1860), *The Ticket of Leave Man* (1863), in which the detective Hawkshaw appears, and *Masks and Faces* (with Charles Reade; 1852). Author also of biography of Benjamin Robert Haydon (3 vols., 1853) and of *Leicester Square* (1874).

**Taylor, William.** 1765–1836. English man of letters; known as William Taylor of Norwich; introduced to English readers the poetry and drama of Germany; translated Bürger's *Lenore* into English ballad meter (1790), Lessing's *Nathan der Weise* (1790), and Goethe's *Iphigenie* (1793). Author of *Tales of Yore* (3 vols., 1810), *English Synonyms Discriminated* (1813), and *Historic Survey of German Poetry* (3 vols., 1828–30).

**Taylor, William.** 1821–1902. American Methodist Episcopal clergyman; in evangelistic and missionary work in California (1849–56), cities of the U.S. and Canada (1856–61), Australia, Tasmania, and New Zealand (1861–64), South Africa (1866), England and Scotland (1867), India (1870–77), Peru and Chile (1877–78). Elected missionary bishop for Africa (1884) and served from 1884 to 1896.

**Taylor, William Rogers.** 1811–1889. American naval officer; fleet captain under Admiral Dahlgren in operations against Morris Island (July, 1863); commanded *Juniata* in first attack on Fort Fisher (Dec., 1864). Rear admiral (1871); retired (1873). His father, **William Vi′gner·on** (vĭn′yẽr·ŭn) **Taylor** (1780–1858), was also a naval officer; sailing master of Perry's flagship, the *Lawrence,* in the battle of Lake Erie (Sept. 10, 1813).

**Taylor, Zachary.** 1784–1850. Nicknamed "Old Rough-and-Ready." Twelfth president of the United States, b. in Orange co., Va. Entered U.S. army as 1st lieutenant (1808). After years of Indian fighting and routine frontier duty, took command of the army in Texas (1845); defeated Mexicans at Palo Alto (May 8, 1846), Resaca de la Palma (May 9, 1846); occupied Matamoros (May 18, 1846); brevetted major general and named commander of the army of the Rio Grande. Captured Monterrey (Sept. 24, 1846); defeated Santa Anna at Buena Vista (Feb. 22–23, 1847), ending the war in northern Mexico. President of the United States (1849–50); died July 9, 1850, after only a year and four months in office.

**Ta Yü.** See YÜ.

**Taze′well** (tăz′wĕl; -wĕl), **Henry.** 1753–1799. American lawyer; judge, Virginia supreme court (1785–93) and chief justice (1789–93); judge, Virginia court of appeals (1793); U.S. senator (1794–99). His son **Littleton Waller**

(1774–1860) was also a lawyer and politician; practiced in Norfolk, Va. (1802–22); U.S. senator (1824–32); governor of Virginia (1834–36); in retirement, honored as Virginia's first citizen (1836–60).

**Tch-, Tsch-.** For many Russian names beginning *Tch-*, *Tsch-*, see Ch-.

**Tchai·kov′sky** *or, Russian,* **Chai·kov′ski** (chī·kôf′skĭ; *Russ.* -skû·ĭ), **Pëtr Ilich.** 1840–1893. Russian composer, b. in Ural region; studied law in St. Petersburg; devoted himself to music (from 1862); visited England (1881, 1889) and U.S. (1891). Among his best-known works are *Fifth Symphony in E Minor*, *Fourth Symphony in F Minor*, the symphonic poem *Francesca da Rimini*, overtures to *Hamlet* and *Romeo and Juliet*, *March Slave* and *1812 Overture*, the ballets *Swan Lake*, *The Sleeping Beauty*, and *Nutcracker*, and several operas, including *Eugene Onegin* and *Queen of Spades*. His *Sixth Symphony*, known as *Symphonie Pathétique*, was first performed and conducted by him in St. Petersburg nine days before his death, but its first successful presentation (conducted by Nápravník, *q.v.*) occurred later.

**Tcher·no′witz** (chĕr·nō′wĭts), **Chaim** (kī·ĭm′). 1871–1949. Russian-born Talmudist in New York; rabbi in Odessa (1897), where he organized a Yeshibah (1905); called to New York; became (1923) professor of Talmud, Jewish Institute of Religion.

**Teach** (tēch) *or* **Thatch** (thăch), **Edward.** *Known as* **Black′beard′** (blăk′bẹrd′). d. 1718. English pirate; privateer in West Indies during War of Spanish Succession; turned pirate after cessation of hostilities (1713). Cruised along Spanish Main, among Bahamas, and north to the Carolinas; captured large French merchantman, equipped her with 40 guns, renamed her *Queen Anne's Revenge*, and preyed on shipping off Carolina and Virginia coasts; protected by corrupt governor of North Carolina; killed in attack (Nov. 22, 1718) by two naval sloops sent by governor of Virginia.

**Teas′dale** (tēz′dāl), **Sara.** 1884–1933. American poet, b. St. Louis, Mo.; m. Ernst B. Filsinger (1914; divorced 1929). Her best-known work is found in *Rivers to the Sea* (1915), *Love Songs* (awarded Columbia University prize of $500, 1917), *Flame and Shadow* (1920), *Dark of the Moon* (1926), *Strange Victory* (1933).

**Teck** (tĕk), Duke and prince of. German titles of royal house of Württemberg (from 14th century), which was allied by marriage with British royal house, including: **Francis Paul Louis Alexander** (1830?–1900), Duke of Teck, soldier in Austrian and British armies; educ. in Imperial Austrian Academy of Engineers (1849–53); accompanied Field Marshal Wimpffen to Italy; distinguished himself in battle of Solferino (1859); married Princess Mary Adelaide of Great Britain (1866); made duke of Teck (1871) by his cousin King Charles of Württemberg; served on staff of Sir Garnet Wolseley in Egyptian campaign; distinguished himself at Tell el-Kebir (1882); British colonel (1882), major general (1892). His children: (1) Princess **Victoria Mary** of Teck (1867–1953), became Queen Mary, consort of George V of Great Britain. (2) **Adolphus Charles** (1868–1927), Duke of Teck, Marquis of **Cam′bridge** (kām′brĭj), b. at Kensington Palace; served in Boer War; military attaché in Vienna (1904–09); in World War, assistant military secretary in war office and military secretary to commander in chief in France; abandoned German title and created marquis of Cambridge (1917); m. daughter of 1st duke of Westminster (1894). (3) Prince **Francis Joseph Leopold Frederick** of Teck (1870–1910); served in Egyptian army (1897–98), and in Boer War (1899–1900); retired (1902). (4) Prince **Alexander** of Teck (1874–1957); see 1st Earl of Athlone.

**Te·cum′seh** (tē·kŭm′sĕ; -sē) *or* **Te·cum′tha** (-thȧ) *or* **Te·cum′the** (-thĕ; -thē) *or* **Ti·kam′thi** (tĭ·kăm′thĭ). 1768?–1813. American Indian chief of the Shawnee tribe; joined his brother Tenskwatawa in effort to unite western Indians against the Whites; during his temporary absence, his brother was maneuvered into battle with an American army under William Henry Harrison, and utterly defeated (battle of Tippecanoe, Nov. 7, 1811). Threw in his lot with the British in War of 1812; killed in action at the battle of the Thames (Oct. 5, 1813). His brother, perhaps his twin brother, **Ten·skwa′ta·wa** [tĕn·skwä′tä·wä] (1768?–?1834), known as "the Prophet," original name **Lalawethika,** *sometimes called* **Elskwatawa,** gained fame as an Indian religious mystic and revivalist; after defeat in battle of Tippecanoe, lost all his prestige; lived on British pension (to 1826), and thereafter in U.S.

**Ted′der** (tĕd′ẽr), **Arthur William.** 1st Baron **Tedder.** 1890–1967. British air chief marshal; B.A., Cantab. (1912); served in World War I in France (1915–17) and Egypt (1918–19), in air service from 1916; held posts in air ministry (1926–27) and in connection with R.A.F. training and development; R.A.F. commander in Far East (1936–38); director-general of research in air ministry (1938–40); R.A.F. deputy commander (1940–41) and commander in chief in Middle East (1940–41); coordinated air-force activities in campaign that drove Rommel from Egypt and Libya; vice-chief of staff, R.A.F. (Nov., 1942); allied air commander in chief in Mediterranean theater (Feb., 1943); deputy supreme commander (1943–45); chief of air staff ′46–50).

**Teg′art** (tĕg′ẽrt), Sir **Charles Augustus.** 1881–1945. British official in India; member of Indian police (1901–31), council of India (1932–36); to Palestine (1937) as adviser to government on police organization; built barrier of electrically charged barbed wire ("Tegart's Wall") along Palestinian-Syrian border.

**Teg′et·mei′er** (tĕg′ĕt·mī′ẽr; tā′gĕt-), **William Bernhard.** 1816–1912. English naturalist, of German origin; coworker with Darwin on variation in animals; quoted in the *Origin of Species;* editor and editorial writer for fifty years of *The Field.*

**Te′gett·hoff** (tā′gĕt·hôf), **Wilhelm von.** 1827–1871. Austrian admiral; commanded Austrian squadron which took part in Austro-Prussian victory over Danish fleet off Helgoland (1864); defeated Italian fleet in battle of Vis (1866).

**Teg·nér′** (tĕng·nār′), **Esaias.** 1782–1846. Swedish poet; professor of Greek, Lund (1812); bishop of Vexiö (1824); leading representative of so-called Gothic school in Swedish literature; recognized as one of greatest Swedish poets; among his works are *War Song for the Militia of Scania* (1808), *Sweden* (*Svea*, 1811), *The Children of the Lord's Supper* (1820), *Axel* (1822), *Frithjofs Saga* (a romance cycle; 1825), etc.

**Teich′man** (tīch′măn), Sir **Eric.** 1884–1944. British consular official and writer; on duty in China (1907–17; 1919–20; 1922–36; 1942–44); author of *Travels of a Consular Officer in North-West China* (1921), *Journey to Turkistan* (1937), *Affairs of China* (1938).

**Teil′hard′ de Char′din′** (tā′yȧr′ dē shȧr′dăN′), **Pierre.** 1881–1955. French paleontologist and explorer; on geological expedition to region of the Ordos, along Great Wall of China (1923); also on later expeditions into interior of Asia; known for work on Cenozoic geology and on history of early man in eastern Asia.

**Teir′linck** (tĭr′lĭngk), **Herman.** 1879– . Flemish writer; one of leading representatives of young Flemish school; author of verse, novels (esp. *Mijnheer Serjanszoon*, 1908), and plays.

**Teispes.** Persian ruler. See ACHAEMENIDAE.

**Teis'se·renc' de Bort** (tĕs'räɴ' dē bôr'), **Léon Philippe.** 1855–1913. French meteorologist; investigated upper atmosphere by means of balloons; one of the discoverers of the stratosphere, or isothermal layer.

**Tei·xei'ra** (tā̂ē·shā̂ē'rȧ), **Pedro.** 1575?–1640. Portuguese soldier in Brazil; governor of Pará (1620–21; 1640); commanded expedition (1637–39) which carefully explored the Amazon, ascending that river and the Napo and crossing the mountains to Quito, and returning by the same route.

**Tei·xei'ra de Mat'tos** (?tā̂ē·shā̂ē'rȧ thē mȧ'tōosh), **Alexander Louis.** 1865–1921. English journalist and translator, b. Amsterdam; resident in England (from 1874); editor of *Dramatic Opinions* (1891), *Candid Friend* (1901–02); best known for translations from works of Dutch, Belgian, and French authors.

**Teixeira Gomes, Manuel.** See GOMES.

**Te·ja'da Sor·za'no** (tĕ·hä'thä sôr·sä'nō), **José Luis.** 1881–1938. President of Bolivia (1934–36); concluded the war in the Chaco by a peace treaty with Paraguay (signed June 12, 1935); deposed.

**Tek'a·kwith'a** (tĕk'ȧ·kwĭth'ȧ), **Ka'te·ri** (kä'tĕ·rĭ). 1656–1680. Known as "Lily of the Mohawks." American Indian maiden; instructed by Jesuits and baptized; lived a life of sanctity; venerated (1943).

**Te'le·ki** (tĕ'lĕ·kĭ). Noted Hungarian family, including: **Mihály** (1634–1690), who received title of count for his services in Transylvania; **József** (1790–1855), historian and statesman, governor of Transylvania (1841–48); Count **Paul** *or* **Pál** (1879–1941), geographer and statesman, member of Szeged counterrevolutionary government (1920–21), foreign minister (1920), minister of education (1938), premier of Hungary (1920, 1926, 1939–41).

**Te'le·mann** (tā'lĕ·män), **Georg Philipp.** 1681–1767. German composer of operas, cantatas, oratorios, and chamber music.

**Te·le'sio** (tâ·lâ'zyô), **Bernardino.** 1509–1588. Italian philosopher; founded *Accademia Telesiana* or *Cosentina;* known particularly for his *De Rerum Natura juxta Propria Principia* (1565; 2 vols., 1910–13); revolted against medieval Aristotelianism; advocated empirical method.

**Te·les'pho·rus** (tē·lĕs'fō·rŭs), Saint. Pope (bishop of Rome; 125?–?136).

**Tel'ford** (tĕl'fērd), **Thomas.** 1757–1834. Scottish civil engineer. His numerous works include the Ellesmere canal (1793), Caledonian canal, 920 miles of roads and 20 bridges in northern Scotland, improvements in Scottish harbors, Gotha canal between Baltic Sea and North Sea (1808–10), and the Menai Strait suspension bridge (begun, 1819).

**Tel'ler** (tĕl'ēr), **Edward.** 1908– . American (Hungarian-born) physicist; Ph.D., Leipzig (1930); professor, George Washington U. (1936–41), Chicago U. (1946–49), Calif. U. (from 1953); received Enrico Fermi prize (1962).

**Tel'ler** (tĕl'ēr), **Henry Moore.** 1830–1914. American lawyer and politician; practiced at Central City, Colo. (from 1861); first U.S. senator from Colorado (1876–82); U.S. secretary of the interior (1882–85); again U.S. senator (1885–1909). Advocate of remonetization of silver, fought repeal of Sherman Silver Purchase Act (1893).

**Téllez, Gabriel.** See TIRSO DE MOLINA.

**Téllez y Girón, Pedro.** See duke of OSUNA.

**Tel'lier'** (tĕ'lyā'), **Charles Albert Abel.** 1828–1913. French engineer; pioneer in the cold-storage industry; conceived refrigerating machines for preserving meats, etc. (1868–69); transported foods across the Atlantic Ocean in a ship equipped with a refrigerating plant (1876).

**Telmann, Konrad.** Pseudonym of Konrad ZITELMANN.

**Tem'in** (tem'ĭn), **Howard Martin.** 1934– . American oncologist. At U. of Wisconsin (1960– ); awarded (with David Baltimore and Renato Dulbecco) Nobel prize for physiology or medicine (1975).

**Tem'me** (tĕm'ĕ), **Jodocus Donatus Hubertus.** *Pseudonym* **Heinrich Stahl** (shtäl). 1798–1881. German jurist, criminologist, and novelist. In Prussian judiciary (1839–49); political activities as a pronounced liberal caused his dismissal and trial for treason (1849; acquitted).

**Tem'pel** (tĕm'pĕl), **Ernst Wilhelm Leberecht.** 1821–1889. German astronomer; discovered 6 planetoids, almost 60 nebulae, and 20 comets (1856–77).

**Tem'per·ley** (tĕm'pēr·lĭ), **Harold William Va·zeille'** (vă·zĕl'). 1879–1939. English historian; served in World War (1914–18); member of British staff at Paris Peace Conference (1919). Editor, with George P. Gooch, of British documents *The Origins of the War* (10 vols., 1928–36). Author of *Life of George Canning* (1905), *Frederic the Great and Kaiser Joseph* (1915), *History of Europe in the Nineteenth and Twentieth Centuries* (with A. J. Grant, 1932), *Europe: The Revolutionary and Napoleonic Eras* (with A. J. Grant, 1935), *England and the Near East: The Crimea* (1936).

**Tem'pest** (tĕm'pĕst; -pĭst), Dame **Mary Susan,** *nee* **Eth'er·ing·ton** (ĕth'ēr·ĭng·tŭn; ĕth'rĭng-). *Known as* **Marie Tempest.** 1866–1942. English actress; m. Cosmo Charles Gordon-Lennox (1898; d. 1921), and W. Graham Browne (1921; d. 1937). Early stage career in musical comedy; later, left musical comedy and created role of Nell Gwyn in *English Nell* and title role in *Becky Sharp.* In U.S., starred under management of Charles Frohman. Theater manager (from 1911), producing and appearing in Arnold Bennett's *The Honeymoon,* Anthony Wharton's *At the Barn,* Jerome K. Jerome's *Esther Castways,* Henry Arthur Jones's *Mary Goes First,* etc. Dame of the British Empire (1937).

**Tempesta,** Cavaliere. See Pieter MULIER.

**Tem'ple** (tĕm'p'l), Earls of. See GRENVILLE family.

**Temple, Frederick.** 1821–1902. English prelate and primate. As headmaster of Rugby (1857–69), enlarged school and modernized curriculum. Bishop of Exeter (1869); bishop of London (1885–96); archbishop of Canterbury (1896–1902). His son **William** (1881–1944) was headmaster of Repton (1910–14); chaplain to king (1915–21); canon of Westminster (1919–21); bishop of Manchester (1921–29); archbishop of York (1929–42); archbishop of Canterbury (1942–44).

**Temple, Henry John.** 3d Viscount **Palmerston.** See PALMERSTON.

**Temple,** Sir **Richard.** 1826–1902. Anglo-Indian administrator. Chief commissioner of Central Provinces (1862–67); finance minister of India (1868–74); lieutenant governor of Bengal (1874–77); governor of Bombay (1877–80); returned to England; M.P. (1885–95). Author of *India in 1880* (1880), *Cosmopolitan Essays* (1886), *Memoir of John Lawrence* (1889), a life of James Thomason, lieutenant governor of the North-West Provinces (1893), and an autobiography (1896).

**Temple,** Sir **Richard Carnac.** 1850–1931. British soldier and Orientalist; served in Afghan campaign (1878–79), Burma war (1887–89); chief commissioner of Andaman and Nicobar Islands (1894). Founded and edited *Panjab (Indian) Notes and Queries* (1883–87); proprietor and editor of *Indian Antiquary* (from 1884). Among his works are *Andamanese Language* (with Edward Horace Man, 1877), *Legends of the Panjab* (3 vols., 1883–90), *Anthropology as a Practical Science* (1914).

**Temple,** Sir **William.** 1628–1699. English diplomat, statesman, and essayist, b. London. Envoy at Brussels (1666); effected Triple Alliance (1668) of England, Holland, and Sweden against France, for protection of Spain; as ambassador at The Hague, thwarted by Charles II's secret understanding with Louis XIV, which reversed policy of Triple Alliance; retired to his villa at Sheen. Recalled to negotiate treaty of Westminster (1674); twice declined secretaryship of state; again ambassador at The Hague, brought about marriage of William of Orange and Princess Mary (1677); took part in conference at Nijmegen (1679), which made treaty bringing about general pacification. Tried ineffectually to reform privy council and for a time was one of an inner council of four; retired (1681) to Sheen, then (1686) to Moor Park in Surrey, where Swift was his secretary (1689) and assisted with his *Memoirs*, treating affairs of the periods 1672–79, 1679–81. Took no part in the revolution; declined office on William III's invitation but was consulted frequently. Author of an *Essay upon the Present State of Ireland* (1668), three volumes of *Miscellanea* (1680, 1692, 1701), including his best-known essay, *Of Ancient and Modern Learning*, which by considering the *Epistles of Phalaris* genuine precipitated a controversy with Bentley, and essays on government, gardening, trade, long life, heroic virtue, and poetry.

**Temple, William.** 1881–1944. See under Frederick TEMPLE.

**Tem′ple·ton** (tĕm′p'l·t'n; -tŭn), **Alec Andrew.** 1910–1963. Welsh blind pianist, composer, and entertainer, b. in Cardiff, Wales; has played on tour in England and United States.

**Temujin** *or* **Temuchin.** See GENGHIS KHAN.

**ten Brink.** See BRINK.

**Ten Broeck** (tĕn bro͝ok′; tĕn), **Abraham.** 1734–1810. American Revolutionary leader; brigadier general of militia of Albany County; contributed to American success by participating in battle of Bemis Heights (1777), forcing retreat of General Burgoyne. Mayor of Albany (1779–83, 1796–99).

**Ten·chi** (tĕn·chē) *or* **Ten·ji** (tĕn·jē). 626–671. Japanese emperor (662–671). As prince, much interested in reforms; granted (669) Nakatomi Kamatari the name of Fujiwara (*q.v.*); as emperor, published code of laws (670); in his reign Japanese expedition withdrew from Korea.

**Ten′cin′** (täɴ′săɴ′), **Claudine Alexandrine Gué′rin′ de** (gā′răɴ′ dẽ). 1685–1749. French writer and society leader in the reign of Louis XV; mother of d'Alembert, through a liaison with Louis Camus, Chevalier Destouches. Author of *Le Siège de Calais* (1739), *Les Mémoires du Comte de Comminges* (1735), *Les Malheurs de l'Amour* (1747), *Lettres au Duc de Richelieu* (publ. 1806).

**Ten′dron′** (täɴ′drôɴ′), **Marcel.** *Pseudonym* **Marc El′der′** (ĕl′dâr′). 1884– . French novelist, b. Nantes; author of *Une Crise* (1905), *Marthe Rouchard, Fille du Peuple* (1912), *Le Peuple de la Mer* (awarded Goncourt prize, 1913), *Jacques et Jean* (1931).

**Te′ne·ra′ni** (tā′nā·rä′nē), **Pietro.** 1789–1869. Italian sculptor; one of chief representatives of classicism in sculpture; among his works are *Deposition from the Cross* (in the Lateran, Rome), Bolívar's monument (for Colombia), tomb of Pius VIII (in St. Peter's Rome), and portrait busts.

**Ten Eyck** (tĕn īk′; tĕn), **James A.** 1851–1938. American oarsman; crew coach at Syracuse U. for 35 years (1903–38).

**Teng′bom** (tĕng′bo͝om), **Ivar.** 1878–1968. Swedish architect; designed the royal palaces at Stockholm and Drottningholm.

**Te·niers′** (*Flem.* tĕ·nērs′; *Angl.* tĕn′yẽrz; *often, as Fr.,* tā′nyā′), **David,** known as "the Elder." 1582–1649. Flemish painter; known for his historical, genre, and landscape paintings, as *The Temptation of St. Anthony, Dutch Kitchen,* etc. His son **David,** known as "the Younger" (1610–1690), studied under him and became renowned as a genre, landscape, and portrait painter; among his many notable canvases are *The Denial of St. Peter, The Prodigal Son, Judith, Archers of Antwerp, Village Festival, A Merry Repast, Flemish Tap-Room, Backgammon Players, The Barber Shop, Guard Room, Cow Stable.*

**Ten′i·son** (tĕn′ĭ·s'n), **Thomas.** 1636–1715. English prelate and primate; championed Protestantism in reign of James II; ministered to Monmouth before execution (1685); preached charitable funeral sermon on Nell Gwyn (1687); bishop of Lincoln (1691); archbishop of Canterbury (1694). One of seven lords justices in authority during William's absence (1695); a commissioner for union with Scotland (1706); one of three officers entrusted with choice of regent until arrival of George I, whom he crowned (1714); one of founders of Society for Propagation of the Gospel; established at St. Martin-in-the-fields first public library in London (1695).

**ten Kate, Jan Jacob Lodewijk.** See J. J. L. ten KATE.

**Ten′nant** (tĕn′ănt), **Smithson.** 1761–1815. English chemist; discovered elements osmium (1803) and iridium (1804).

**Tennant, William.** 1784–1848. Scottish linguist and poet. A lifelong cripple; professor of Oriental languages, St. Andrews (1834–48). Author of verse including *Anster Fair,* a mock heroic poem in ottava rima, which brought him reputation (1812), *The Thane of Fife* (1822), and *Papistry Storm'd* (1827), two tragedies *Cardinal Beaton* (1823) and *John Baliol* (1825), and *Syriac and Chaldee Grammar* (1840).

**Ten′nent** (tĕn′ĕnt), **William.** 1673–1745. Clergyman, b. in Ireland; to America (c. 1717) and joined Presbyterian ministry (1718); pastorates in Bedford, N.Y. (1720–26) and Neshaminy, Pa. (1726–45); built a "log college" (1736) where he lived, and taught and trained many for the Presbyterian ministry; college ceased at his death, and its supporters joined with others in organizing Princeton. His son **Gilbert** (1703–1764) was also a Presbyterian clergyman; trained in his father's "log cabin"; by his fervor and zeal prepared the way for the Great Awakening under George Whitefield's leadership; carried his evangelistic preaching into Boston and New England region (1740–41); is regarded as one of the leaders of the Great Awakening. Another son, **William** (1705–1777), was also a Presbyterian clergyman; trained in his father's "log college"; pastorate at Freehold, N.J. (1733–77).

**Ten′ney** (tĕn′ĭ), **Charles Daniel.** 1857–1930. American missionary in China; selected by Chinese government to be first president of Imperial Chinese U., Tientsin (1895–1906); performed valuable services both for Chinese and for foreigners during Boxer Rebellion (1900).

**Ten′niel** (tĕn′yĕl), Sir **John.** 1820–1914. English cartoonist and illustrator; cartoonist on staff of *Punch* (1850–1901), notable for dignity, geniality of satire, and good taste; illustrator of Lewis Carroll's *Alice's Adventures in Wonderland* (1865) and *Through the Looking Glass* (1872).

**Ten′ny·son** (tĕn′ĭ·s'n), **Alfred.** 1st Baron **Tennyson.** *Commonly known as* **Alfred,** Lord **Tennyson.** 1809–1892. English poet, b. at Somersby, Lincolnshire, fourth of eight sons of rector **George Clayton Tennyson** (1778–1831). Published with his brother Charles *Poems by Two Brothers* (1827); at Trinity College, Cambridge, one of a gifted group known as "the Apostles." Won chancellor's medal with poem *Timbuctoo* (1829) in blank verse and published *Poems, Chiefly Lyrical* (1830). Left Cambridge without a degree (Feb., 1831); traveled with Arthur Henry Hallam in the Pyrenees and on the Rhine (1832); met scant success with *Poems* (1832), including *The Lady of Shalott, The Palace of Art, The Lotos-Eaters, A Dream of Fair Women*, brutally reviewed by Lockhart in the *Quarterly Review*. On death (1833) of Arthur Hallam, his sister's fiancé, wrote *Two Voices* and began *In Memoriam*. Spent nine years reading and meditating before publishing *Poems* (2 vols., 1842: including *Morte d'Arthur; Ulysses; Locksley Hall; Godiva; Break, Break, Break*), which secured his place as a great poet; added to his reputation with *The Princess* (1847), a jeu d'esprit on women's rights, interspersed with lyrics. In the eventful year of 1850 published *In Memoriam*, one of the great English elegies, married Emily Sellwood, and was appointed poet laureate on the death of Wordsworth. Traveled in Italy, settled at Twickenham, wrote *Ode* on death of Wellington; moved to Farringford in Isle of Wight (1853), where he lived part of each year for rest of his life. Wrote *Charge of the Light Brigade* (1854); puzzled the public with *Maud* (1855); awakened public to enthusiasm by returning to Arthurian legend with *The Idylls of the King* (1859; added to, 1869, 1872; completed, 1885). After the narrative poems *Enoch Arden* and *Aylmer's Field* (1864), turned to a series of historical dramas, *Queen Mary* (1875), *Harold* (1876), *Becket* (1884), and lesser plays, of which *The Cup* (1881) met some success when acted. Built Aldworth, his second residence, near Haslemere (1868–70); raised to peerage as Baron Tennyson of Fresh'wa'ter and Ald'worth [frĕsh'wô'tẽr (-wŏt'ẽr), ôld'wûrth] (1884). Showed active imagination and mature art during his last years in *The Revenge, Defence of Lucknow*, and other ballads, tales in dialect, narratives idyllic and lyrical, as *Rizpah*, classical pieces including *Tiresias and Other Poems* (1885), and *Demeter and Other Poems* (1889), containing *Merlin and the Gleam* and *Crossing the Bar;* shortly before death, corrected proof of *Death of Œnone and Other Poems;* buried in Westminster Abbey.

His two elder brothers were poets: **Frederick** (1807–1898) contributed to *Poems by Two Brothers* (1827), spent most of his life in Italy and Jersey; author of *Days and Hours* (lyrics, 1854), *The Isles of Greece* (1890), *Daphne* (1891), and *Poems of the Day and Year* (1895). **Charles Tennyson Tur'ner** [tûr'nẽr] (1808–1879) entered the church, took name Turner under will of a great-uncle (1830); besides contributing to *Poems by Two Brothers* (1827), published over 300 sonnets (1830–80).

Alfred's eldest son, **Hallam** (1852–1928), 2d baron, was governor and commander in chief of South Australia (1899–1902); governor general of Commonwealth of Australia (1902–04); author of *Alfred, Lord Tennyson: a Memoir* (1897); editor of Eversley edition of his father's works, with notes (1908). Hallam's eldest son, **Lionel Hallam** (1889–1951), 3d baron, served with distinction in the World War and in antiaircraft brigade, Territorial Artillery; author of *From Verse to Worse* (1933).

See also Fryniwyd Tennyson JESSE.

**Ten'ny·son-D'Eyn'court** (-dān'kûrt; -kōrt; -kôrt), Sir **Eustace Henry William**. 1868–1951. British naval architect; second cousin of Alfred, Lord Tennyson. As director of naval construction, admiralty (1912–24), designed and constructed ships and was head of committee that produced first tank.

**Tenskwatawa.** See under TECUMSEH.

**Teoscopoli** *or* **Teoscopuli, Domenico.** See GRECO.

**Teotocópuli** *or* **Teotocopulo.** See GRECO.

**Te·ra·u·chi** (tĕ·rä·ōō·chē), Count **Hisaichi**. 1879–1946. Japanese army officer; grad. military academy (1900) and military staff college (1909); further training in Germany; major general (1924); held commands in Chosen, Manchuria, and (1932) Taiwan; general (1935); minister of war (1936–37); commander in North China (1938); member of supreme war council (1938 ff.); commander of Japanese forces in Southwest Pacific (1942).

**Terauchi, Masatake.** 1853–1919. Japanese general and statesman; lieutenant general (1892); minister of war (1902); governor general of Korea (1910); premier of Japan (1916–18). His administration of Korea (Chosen) led to its annexation to Japan.

**Ter·borch'** *or* **Ter Borch** (tẽr·bôrk'), **Gerard.** 1617–1681. Dutch genre and portrait painter; studied under his father, **Gerard Terborch** (1584–1662), and under Molyn. Among his notable canvases are *Peace Congress of Münster, The Reading Lesson, The Concert, Paternal Admonition, Guitar Lesson, The Letter, The Smoker, The Toilet, A Lady Playing the Theorbo.*

**Ter·bo'ven** (tĕr·bō'vĕn), **Josef.** 1898–1945. German politician and administrator; member of National Socialist German Workers' (Nazi) party; member of Reichstag (1933 ff.); commissioner in Norway (1940 ff.).

**Terëmin, Lev.** See Leo THEREMIN.

**Ter'ence** (tĕr'ĕns). *Full Latin name* **Publius Te·ren'ti·us A'fer** (tē·rĕn'shĭ·ŭs [-shŭs] ā'fẽr). 185–159 B.C. Roman playwright, b. Carthage; taken to Rome as slave of a Roman senator; finally freed. Regarded as a master of Latin comedy; much of his work modeled upon material taken from Greek playwrights Menander and Apollodorus; his extant plays include *Andria, Hecyra, Heautontimoroumenos, Eunuchus, Phormio*, and *Adelphi.*

**Te·ren'ti·a'nus Mau'rus** (tē·rĕn'shĭ·ā'nŭs mô'rŭs). Roman prosodist, probably of late 2d century A.D.; author of hexameter treatise on prosody (4 books).

**Terentius.** = TERENCE.

**Terentius Varro,** (1) **Gaius,** (2) **Marcus,** (3) **Publius.** See VARRO.

**Teresa.** See also THERESA, THÉRÈSE.

**Te·resh'ko'va** (tĭ·rĕsh'kô·və), **Valentina Vladimirovna.** 1937– . Soviet cosmonaut. First woman in space (June 16–19, 1963).

**Ter·hune'** (tûr·hūn'), **Edward Payson.** 1830–1907. American clergyman. His wife (m. 1856), **Mary Virginia,** *nee* **Hawes** [hôz] (1830–1922), *pseudonym* **Marion Har'land** (här'lănd), was an author; published her first novel, *Alone*, in 1854; followed this with over twenty-five more novels, and with travel books, biographies, and works on household management. Their son **Albert Payson** (1872–1942), also a writer, was on staff of New York *Evening World* (1894–1916); author of many novels and short stories; esp. successful in writing about dogs, as in *Lad: A Dog* (1919), *The Heart of a Dog* (1926), *The Way of a Dog* (1934). His sisters also writers: **Christine** (see C. T. HERRICK) and **Virginia Belle** (1865–1945), m. (1889) Frederic Franklyn Van de Water (d. 1917); author of *Everyday Etiquette* (in collaboration with her mother, 1905), *Little Talks with Mothers of Little People* (1911), *The Shears of Delilah* (1914), *The Heart of a Child* (1927), etc. The wife of Albert P., **Anice Morris,** *nee* **Stock'ton** (stŏk'tŭn) (1873–1964), concert pianist, composer, and writer, composed the score for comic opera *Nero* and operetta *The Woodland Princess*, etc.

**Ter'man** (tûr'măn), **Lewis Madison.** 1877–1956. American psychologist; at Stanford U. (1910–42); known for his work on intelligence tests.

**Ter'naux'-Com'pans'** (tĕr'nō'kôN'päN'), **Henri.** 1807–1864. French bibliographer; collector of early Americana; published (in 20 vols.) translations from his collection, entitled *Voyages, Relations et Mémoires Originaux pour Servir a l'Histoire de la Découverte de l'Amérique* (1836–40).

**Ter·pan'der** (tûr·păn'dẽr; tẽr-). Greek musician and poet of 7th century B.C.; native of Lesbos; long resident in Sparta; known as "Father of Greek music" and regarded by some as founder of Greek lyrical poetry; said to have improved the lyre by increasing the number of its strings from 4 to 7, thus inventing the heptachord. Of his hymns to the gods, only a few lines are extant.

**ter Poorten, Hein.** See POORTEN.

**Ter'ra** (tĕr'rä), **Gabriel.** 1873–1942. Uruguayan lawyer and political leader; president of Uruguay (two terms: 1931–38); made himself dictator (1933).

**Ter'ry** (tĕr'ĭ), **Alfred Howe.** 1827–1890. American army officer in the Civil War; engaged (colonel) at First Bull Run, capture of Port Royal, S.C. (Nov., 1861) and Fort Pulaski, Ga. (Apr., 1862). Brigadier general (Apr. 25, 1862); engaged against Richmond and Petersburg (1864); brevetted major general (Aug. 26, 1864). Commanded land forces assaulting and capturing Fort Fisher (Dec., 1864–Jan., 1865); major general of volunteers (Apr. 20, 1865). Remained in regular army after Civil War.

**Terry, Charles Sanford.** 1864–1936. British historian and authority on the life and music of Bach; professor, Aberdeen (1903–30); author of *The Young Pretender* (1903), *A History of Scotland* (1920), and of *Johann Sebastian Bach* (1920), *Bach, a Biography* (1928), etc.

**Terry, Eli.** 1772–1852. American clock manufacturer, b. South Windsor, Conn.; devoted himself to making shelf clocks with wooden works, perfecting (c. 1814), a short shelf clock with light pillars and a scrolled top, known as the "Terry clock"; sold these in large quantities.

**Terry, Ellen Alicia** *or* **Alice.** 1847–1928. English actress; professional debut at Haymarket (1863); m. George Frederick Watts, painter (1864; separated 1865). Acted Katharine to Sir Henry Irving's Petruchio (1867); lived in retirement with the architect and theatrical designer E. W. Godwin (1868–74); bore daughter Edith Craig and son Edward Gordon Craig (*q.v.*). Success on stage as Portia (1875), and again as Olivia in W. G. Wills's adaptation of *Vicar of Wakefield* (1878); m. Charles Clavering Wardell, actor under name of Charles Kelly (1877; separated 1881). Irving's leading lady in Shakespearean roles and in plays by Wills, Tennyson, Charles Reade, Sardou (1878–1902); received public tribute in jubilee (1906); in Pittsburgh, m. (1907) James Usselmann (1876–1938), young American actor under name of James Carew, with whom she lived till 1910. Lectured on Shakespearean subjects in U.S., England, and Australia (1910–15); last appearance at Hammersmith in Walter de la Mare's *Crossings* (1925); created Dame Grand Cross, Order of British Empire (1925).

Her brother **Fred** (1863–1933), actor manager, played in all principal cities of United Kingdom, Canada, and U.S.; with his wife (see Julia NEILSON) assumed managership of Haymarket Theatre, London (1900), and Strand (1915). His daughter **Phyllis Neil'son–Ter'ry** [nēl's'n-] (1892–1977), actress, played Viola in *Twelfth Night* (1910), other leading Shakespearean roles, a revival of *London Assurance* (1913), Trilby in an all-star revival in New York City (1915); managed Apollo Theatre, London; toured South Africa (1927).

**Terry,** Sir **Richard Runciman.** 1865–1938. British organist and choirmaster; organist of Westminster Cathedral (1901–24).

**Ter·tul'lian** (tûr·tŭl'yăn; tẽr-). *Full Latin name* **Quintus Septimius Florens Ter·tul'li·a'nus** (tûr·tŭl'ĭ·ā'nŭs; tẽr-). 160?–?230 A.D. Latin ecclesiastical writer, of Carthage; one of the fathers of the church. Educated for the law. Converted to Christianity (c. 190 A.D.); devoted himself to mastery of the Scriptures and of Christian literature; became a presbyter in Carthage. Accepted Montanist doctrines; withdrew (c. 207) from the orthodox church and became head of a small Montanist group in Carthage. Among his many works are *Apologeticus* (a defense of Christianity inspired by persecutions under Emperor Septimius Severus), *Ad Martyres, De Baptismo, De Poenitentia, De Monogamia.*

**Tes'la** (tĕs'lȧ), **Nikola.** 1856–1943. American electrician and inventor, b. in Austria-Hungary of Serbian (Yugoslav) parents; to U.S. (1884); naturalized. Employed by Edison Co., West Orange, N.J., for several years. Applied the principle of the rotating magnetic field, which he had conceived, to an induction motor; his other inventions include a system of arc lighting, the Tesla motor and a system of alternating-current transmission, generators of high-frequency currents, a transformer, wireless systems of communication and of power transmission.

**Tes·sin'** (tĕs·sēn'), **Nicodemus** (1615–1681) and his son **Nicodemus** (1654–1728). Swedish architects. Nicodemus the elder was royal architect (1646). Nicodemus the younger was royal architect (1676); designer of royal castle at Stockholm.

**Teternikov, Fëdor Kuzmich.** See Fëdor SOLOGUB.

**Tet·ma'jer** (tĕt·mä'yĕr), **Kazimierz.** *Also* **Przer'wa–Tet·ma'jer** (pshĕr'vä-). 1865–1940. Polish writer; among his works are lyrics (publ. in 8 vols., 1891–1925), novels, and plays.

**Te'traz·zi'ni** (tā'trät·tsē'nē), **Luisa.** 1874–1940. Italian coloratura soprano; m. (1st) J. G. Bazelli, (2d) Pietro Vernati. Operatic debut as Inez in Meyerbeer's *L'Africaine*, at Florence (1895). Appeared at Covent Garden, London (1907) and Metropolitan Opera House, New York (1908); toured U.S. (1910–13); member of Chicago Opera Company (1913–14); resident chiefly in Italy (after 1914); sang notably in *Rigoletto, Lucia di Lammermoor, La Traviata, Les Huguenots.*

**Tet'ri·cus** (tĕt'rĭ·kŭs), **Gaius Pius Esuvius.** d. 276? Roman senator; master of Gaul, Britain, and northern Spain (269?–274); pretender to throne of Western Roman Empire; defeated by Aurelian at Châlons (274).

**Tet'zel** *or* **Te'zel** (tĕt'sĕl), **Johann.** 1465?–1519. German Dominican monk; appointed (1517) by Archbishop Albert of Mainz to sell indulgences. His preaching aroused Luther to publish his 95 theses at Wittenberg (1517); answered Luther with 106 theses, but was disowned and rebuked by Catholics.

**Teub'ner** (toib'nẽr), **Benediktus Gotthelf.** 1784–1856. German publisher; founded publishing house of B. G. Teubner, Leipzig (1811); known esp. as publisher of scholarly low-priced editions of Greek and Latin classics.

**Teuf'fel** (toi'fĕl), **Wilhelm Sigismund.** 1820–1878. German classical philologist; professor, Tübingen (1849). Chief work, *Geschichte der Römischen Literatur* (1869–70).

**Tew·fik' Pa·sha'** (*Turk.* tĕv·fēk' pä·shä'), **Ahmed.** *New Turkish* **Ahmet Tevfik Paşa.** 1845–1936. Turkish statesman; minister of foreign affairs (1885–1909); grand vizier (1909, 1914–19); ambassador at London (1909–14); head of Turkish delegation at London Conference (1921); fled to Egypt (1922) on deposition of sultan.

**Tew·fik' Pa'sha** (*Arab.* tou·fēk' pȧ'shä), **Mohammed.** 1852–1892. Khedive of Egypt (1879–92). Eldest son of Ismail Pasha (*q.v.*). On deposition of Ismail by Great Powers (1879), appointed khedive by sultan; found Egypt greatly embarrassed financially; yielded to joint British and French control of finances of Egypt (1880), bringing about revolt (1881) of Nationalists under Arabi Pasha (*q.v.*); Alexandria bombarded by British fleet and Arabi defeated by British at Tell el-Kebir (1882); forced to admit establishment by British of virtual protectorate (1883); lost Sudan to the Mahdi, Mohammed Ahmed (1884–85); forced to relinquish control of administration to Lord Cromer. Succeeded by son Abbas (II).

**Tewfik Rushdi Aras.** See ARAS.

**Te·xei'ra** *or* **Te·xey'ra** (tĕ·shā'rȧ). = TEIXEIRA.

**Teyte** (tāt), Dame **Maggie.** 1889–1976. English operatic and concert lyric soprano; member, Opéra Comique, Paris, T. Beecham Opera Co. and Covent Garden Opera Co. Sang in U.S. (1911–14; 1915–18; 1945).

**Tha'a'li·bi, al–** (ăl'thă·ä'lĭ·bĭ). *Arab.* **abu–Manṣūr 'Abd–al–Malik al–Tha'ālibī.** 961–1038. Arab philologist and man of letters, b. Nishapur, Persia; chief work, *Yatīmat al-dahr*, valuable source of information on Moslem poets.

**Thach'er** (thăch'ẽr), **James.** 1754–1844. American physician and historian, b. Barnstable, Mass. In army medical service through American Revolution; present at Yorktown and surrender of Lord Cornwallis. Practiced at Plymouth, Mass. (from 1784). Author of a diary, *A Military Journal during the American Revolutionary War* (pub. 1823); compiler of *American Medical Biography* (1828).

**Thacher, Thomas Anthony.** 1815–1886. American educator; taught classics at Yale (from 1838), professor of Latin (from 1851); one of editors of *Webster's Dictionary of the English Language* (1847–64).

**Thack'er·ay** (thăk'ẽr·ĭ), **William Makepeace.** *Pseudonyms:* **Michael Angelo Tit'marsh** (tĭt'märsh), **Charles James Yel'low·plush'** (yĕl'ō·plŭsh'), **George Savage Fitz·boo'dle** (fĭts·bōō'd'l), **Jeames** (jēmz), **Mr. Brown, Théophile Wag'staff** (wăg'stăf). 1811–1863. English novelist. Educ. Trinity Coll., Cambridge (1829–30), where he was a member of the circle including Spedding, Tennyson, FitzGerald, Monckton Milnes. Entered Middle Temple but turned to journalism; contributed regularly (from 1837) to periodicals in London; published his first book, *Paris Sketch-Book* (1840), followed by *Irish Sketch-Book* (1843); contributed *The Yellowplush Papers*, *The Great Hoggarty Diamond*, *Catherine*, *A Shabby Genteel Story*, and *Barry Lyndon* to *Fraser's Magazine;* as contributor to *Punch* (1842–54), with pen and pencil, proved master of burlesque and gained wide recognition with *Jeames's Diary*, and *The Book of Snobs*, among nearly 400 contributions; parodied novels of Bulwer-Lytton, Lever, and Disraeli in a series *Mr. Punch's Prize Novelists* (1847). Reached turning point in career with publication of *Vanity Fair* (1847–48) and maintained reputation as novelist of first rank with *Pendennis* (1848–50), largely autobiographical. Lecturer in England and (1852–53, 1854–55) America, taking as subjects *The English Humorists of the Eighteenth Century* (1851) and the *Four Georges* (1855). Reached height of his powers in *Henry Esmond* (1852) and *The Newcomes* (1853–55), showing a falling off in *The Virginians* (1857–59), a sequel to *Esmond.* As editor of *Cornhill Magazine* (1859–62) contributed *Lovel the Widower*, *The Adventures of Philip*, *Roundabout Papers* (essays), and *Denis Duval* (left unfinished at his death). Author also of *The Fitzboodle Papers* (1842–43), *Notes of a Journey from Cornhill to Grand Cairo* (1846), *The Kickleburys on the Rhine* (1850), *Rebecca and Rowena* (a reprint; 1850), *The Rose and the Ring* (1855), and ballads. Father of Anne Isabella Thackeray Ritchie (*q.v.*).

**Thad·dae'us** (thă·dē'ŭs) *or* **Thad'de·us** (thăd'ē·ŭs). In Bible, one of the twelve apostles. See JUDAS, 2.

**Tha'is** (thā'ĭs). Greek hetaera of late 4th century B.C.; mistress of Alexander the Great. According to tradition, incited Alexander to burn down the Persian palace at Persepolis.

**Thal'berg** (täl'bĕrk), **Sigismund.** 1812–1871. Swiss-born piano virtuoso, natural son of Prince von Dietrichstein; professional debut (1827); composer of a concerto, a sonata, études, fantasies, and variations on opera themes.

**Tha'les** (thā'lēz). 640?–546 B.C. Greek philosopher and scientist, of Miletus; one of the Seven Wise Men of Greece. Recognized as founder of Greek geometry, astronomy, and philosophy. Gained fame in his own day by predicting an eclipse of the sun for May 28, 585 B.C. In mathematics, he founded the geometry of lines, and thus is credited with introducing abstract geometry. In philosophy, he taught that water, or moisture, was the one element from which the world was formed.

**Thäl'mann** (tâl'män), **Ernst.** 1886–1944. German Communist leader; member of the Reichstag (1924); first leader (1925) of newly founded Red Front combat group; arrested and imprisoned during National Socialist revolution (1933).

**Thamar.** See TAMARA.

**Thane** (thān), **Elswyth.** American author; m. (as 2d wife; 1927) C. W. Beebe (*q.v.*); author of *Riders of the Wind* (1925), *The Tudor Wench* (1933), *Young Mr. Disraeli* (1935), *From This Day Forward* (1942), etc.

**Thanet, Octave.** Pseudonym of Alice FRENCH.

**Thant** (thȧnt), **U** (ōō). 1909–1974. Burmese official; secretary-general of United Nations (1961–71).

**Tha'raud'** (tȧ'rō'), **Jérôme** (1874–1953) and his brother **Jean** (1877–1952). French novelists; collaborators; authors of *Dingley, l'Illustre Écrivain* (1902; awarded Goncourt prize, 1906), *La Fête Arabe* (1912), *Le Maroc* (1924), *Les Bien-Aimées* (1932), etc.

**Thatch, Edward.** See TEACH.

**Thatch'er** (thăch'ẽr), **Henry Knox.** 1806–1880. American naval officer; commanded first division of Admiral David Porter's fleet in attacks on Fort Fisher (Dec., 1864–Jan., 1865); co-operated with army in capture of Mobile, Ala., and received surrender of Confederate fleet on the Tombigbee River (1865).

**Thatcher, Margaret Hilda** *nee* **Roberts.** 1925– . British politician, b. Grantham, Lincolnshire; m. Denis Thatcher (1951). Member of parliament (1959– ); secretary of state for education and science (1970–74); leader of Conservative party (1975– ); prime minister (1979– ).

**Thaw** (thô), **Harry Kendall.** See under Stanford WHITE.

**Thax'ter** (thăks'tẽr), **Celia,** *nee* **Laigh'ton** (lā't'n). 1835–1894. American poet; m. (1851) Levi Lincoln Thaxter (d. 1884). Among the volumes of her verse are: *Poems* (1872), *Driftweed* (1879), *Poems for Children* (1884), *Idyls and Pastorals* (1886). Author also of a volume of prose sketches, *Among the Isles of Shoals* (1873). Her son **Roland** (1858–1932) was a botanist; specialist in cryptogamic botany.

**Thayendanegea.** Indian name of Joseph BRANT.

**Thayer** (thâr), **Abbott Handerson.** 1849–1921. American painter; studio in New York (1879–1901) and at foot of Mount Monadnock in New Hampshire (1901–21). His *Caritas* is in the Boston Museum of Fine Arts; *Self-Portrait*, in the Corcoran Gallery of Art, Washington, D.C.; *Winter Sunrise, Monadnock*, in the Metropolitan Museum of Art in New York City.

**Thayer, Alexander Wheelock.** 1817–1897. American author and diplomat, b. South Natick, Mass. Devoted himself to study of materials for a life of Beethoven. U.S. consul at Trieste (1864–82). His *Life of Ludwig van Beethoven* appeared in three volumes (1866, 1872,

1879) but was incomplete; an edition completed by Hugo Riemann appeared in five volumes (1901–11); an edition prepared by Henry E. Krehbiel appeared in three volumes, published by the Beethoven Association (1921).

**Thayer, Eli.** 1819–1899. American educator and politician, b. Mendon, Mass. Interested himself in promoting emigration from the East into the undeveloped West (from c. 1852), esp. to Kansas, where the settlers influenced the final admission of Kansas as a Free State. Author of *A History of the Kansas Crusade, Its Friends and Its Foes* (1889), etc.

**Thayer, Ernest Lawrence.** 1863–1940. American ballad writer, b. Lawrence, Mass.; author of the song *Casey at the Bat* (1888).

**Thayer, James Bradley.** 1831–1902. American lawyer and educator, b. Haverhill, Mass.; professor, Harvard Law School (1874–1902); associated with Christopher C. Langdell, John C. Gray, and James B. Ames in introducing case method of teaching law. Authority on constitutional law and the law of evidence. His son **William Sydney** (1864–1932), b. Milton, Mass., was a physician; professor in Johns Hopkins Medical School (1897–1921); in Army Medical Corps (major, colonel, brigadier general) in World War I; president of American Medical Association (1928–29). Another son, **Ezra Ripley** (1866–1915), was a lawyer and educator; dean of Harvard Law School (1910–15).

**Thayer, John Milton.** 1820–1906. American army officer and politician, b. Bellingham, Mass.; served in Union army in Civil War; one of first U.S. senators from State of Nebraska (1867–71); governor of Territory of Wyoming (1875–79); governor of Nebraska (1887–91).

**Thayer, Sylvanus.** 1785–1872. American army officer and educator, b. Braintree, Mass.; grad. U.S.M.A., West Point (1808). In Corps of Engineers; sent to Europe to study military schools there, and European armies and fortifications (1815–17). Superintendent, U.S.M.A., West Point (1817–33); established military organization and academic standards and methods of instruction which in their essential principles have been maintained since his superintendency; has become known as "Father of the Military Academy." Served on harbor fortifications and improvements (1833–63). Est. (1867) and endowed Thayer School of Engineering at Dartmouth College. Elected to American Hall of Fame (1965).

**Thayer, Whitney Eugene.** 1838–1889. American organist and composer, b. Mendon, Mass.; noted as teacher of the organ, with studio in Boston (1875–81) and New York (1881–89); author of *The Art of Organ Playing...* (1874).

**Thayer, William Roscoe.** 1859–1923. American author, b. Boston; devoted himself to study of Italian history, and published *The Dawn of Italian Independence* (2 vols., 1893), *A Short History of Venice* (1905), *The Life and Times of Cavour* (1911); also published *The Life and Letters of John Hay* (2 vols., 1915), *Theodore Roosevelt; an Intimate Biography* (1919), *The Art of Biography* (1920).

**Thayer, William Sydney.** See under James B. THAYER.

**The·ag'e·nes** (thē·ăj'ĕ·nēz). Greek tyrant of Megara in late 7th century B.C.; credited with construction of an aqueduct for the city.

**The'ban** (thē'băn). Name of XIth (2160–2000 B.C.), XIIth (2000–1788 B.C.), XIIIth and XVIIth (between c. 1788 and 1580 B.C.) dynasties of ancient Egypt; derived from city of Thebes on the Nile, their capital. See *Table (in Appendix)* for EGYPT.

**The'baw** *or* **Thi'baw** (thē'bô). 1858–1916. Last king of Burma (1878–85). Showed open hostility toward British; intrigued with French for railway contracts; defied British ultimatum; defeated in Third Burmese War and deposed (1885), Burma being annexed to India (1886).

**Thec'la** (thĕk'lȧ), Saint. First-century Christian saint of Asia Minor; reputedly a disciple of Saint Paul. She is one of the most famous saints of the Greek Church.

**Thei'ler** (tī'lẽr), **Max.** 1899–1972. American physician and bacteriologist, b. South Africa. To U.S. (1922); awarded Nobel prize in physiology and medicine (1951) for discoveries concerning yellow fever and a vaccine (1937) to combat it.

**The·mis'ti·us** (thē·mĭs'chĭ·ŭs; -tĭ·ŭs). Greek rhetorician and statesman, b. in Paphlagonia and long resident in Constantinople; prefect of Constantinople (384 A.D.); author of panegyrics addressed to successive emperors of the East, and of paraphrases of some of Aristotle's works.

**The·mis'to·cles** (thē·mĭs'tō·klēz). 527?–?460 B.C. Athenian statesman and general; in politics, led party opposed to Aristides (*q.v.*); induced Athenians to increase their naval strength. Commanded Athenian fleet in the victory over Persians at Salamis (480 B.C.). Continued urging measures for Athens' safety, including expansion of the fleet and land fortifications, but was ostracized (c. 470). Accused of complicity in the treason of Pausanias, he was exiled; finally went to Persia, was received and pensioned by Artaxerxes.

**Thé'nard'** (tā'nȧr'), Baron **Louis Jacques.** 1777–1857. French chemist; author of a textbook, *Traité Élémentaire de Chimie Théorique et Practique* (4 vols., 1813–16), which was standard for 25 years; with his friend Gay-Lussac (*q.v.*), carried on many researches; credited with discovery of hydrogen peroxide (1818); first prepared Thénard's blue, a coloring matter used for porcelain.

**The'o·bald** (thē'ō·bôld; tĭb'ăld) *or* **Ted·bal'dus** (tĕd-bôl'dŭs; -băl'dŭs). d. 1161. Anglo-Norman prelate. Prior of abbey of Bec (1127); archbishop of Canterbury (1138); after brief allegiance to Empress Matilda, crowned Stephen king. Refused to consecrate king's nephew to see of York and attended papal council of Reims in defiance of Stephen's prohibition (1148); refused to crown Count Eustace, Stephen's son; effected reconciliation (1153) between Stephen and Henry, Duke of Normandy, who became Henry II (1154); crowned Henry II. Made his archdeacon Thomas à Becket chancellor to succeed him (1155) but was disappointed when Becket switched to co-operate with Henry II's ecclesiastical policy. Resisted efforts of monasteries to throw off episcopal control; introduced study of civil law, and established canonical jurisprudence in England.

**The'o·bald** (thē'ō·bôld; tĭb'ăld), **Lewis.** 1688–1744. English playwright and Shakespearean critic. Translated from Plato, the Greek dramatists, and Homer; wrote essays, biographies, and poems; charged with plagiarism in his play *The Perfidious Brother* (1716). In a pamphlet, *Shakespeare Restored* (1726), criticized Pope's edition; immortalized as hero of Pope's *Dunciad* (1728, 1742). Published edition of Shakespeare (7 vols., 1734) that placed him in front rank of Shakespearean commentators.

**The'o·bald** (thē'ō·bôld), **Samuel.** 1846–1930. American ophthalmologist, b. Baltimore, Md.; a founder of Baltimore Eye and Ear Dispensary (1874) and Baltimore Eye, Ear, and Throat Charity Hospital (1882); on Johns Hopkins Hospital staff (1889–1925); introduced use of boric acid in treatment of eye diseases.

**The'o·bald** (thē'ō·bôld; tĭb'ăld), **Simon.** See Simon of SUDBURY.

**The·oc'ri·tus** (thē·ŏk'rĭ·tŭs). Greek pastoral poet of 3d century B.C.; reputedly native of Syracuse. Regarded as creator of pastoral poetry; of his work about 30 idyls and a number of epigrams are extant.

**The'o·dat** (thē'ô·dăt). d. 536. King of the Ostrogoths (534–536); attacked by armies of Justinian under Mundus, Prince of the Gepidae, and Belisarius; was defeated; assassinated by an officer of his own army. His life is subject of a tragedy (*Théodat*) by Thomas Corneille (1672).

**The'o·do'ra** (thē'ô·dō'rȧ). Name of three empresses of the Eastern Roman Empire: **Theodora** (508?–548); in early life an actress noted for her beauty; married Justinian I (523); exerted for 20 years a great influence over him and over the political and religious events of the empire; at time of Nika riot (532) prevented emperor from fleeing. **Theodora** (d. ?867); second wife of Emperor Theophilus (829); on his death (842), made regent for their son Michael III; devoted iconodule, caused iconoclasts to be expelled from office and brought back image worship; forced to retire to a convent (858). **Theodora** (980–1056); daughter of Constantine VIII and elder sister of Zoë; plotted against Zoë (1031); crowned coempress (1042); joint ruler with Zoë (1042–50) and Constantine IX (1042–55); on latter's death became sole empress (1055–56), last of Macedonian dynasty.

**Theodora.** fl. 1st half of 10th century. Member of Roman nobility, wife of Theophylact, a prominent senator; granted title of "Senatrix" because of her influence in Roman and papal affairs; much profligacy, probably exaggerated, attributed to her and her daughter Marozia (*q.v.*), who later achieved similar influence.

**The'o·dore** (thē'ô·dōr). Name of two popes (see *Table of Popes*, Nos. 73, 115), especially: **Theodore I.** d. 649. Pope (642–649); a Greek of Jerusalem; opposed the Monotheletes; condemned the Ecthesis of the emperor Heraclius.

**The'o·dore** (thē'ô·dōr) of Abyssinia. *Originally* **Kasa** *or* **Kassa.** 1818?–1868. King of Abyssinia; proclaimed king in 1855. Conquered Shoa and warred against the Gallas; imprisoned British consul Charles Duncan Cameron (1864). British under Napier invaded Abyssinia (1868); Theodore committed suicide (Apr. 13, 1868).

**Theodore.** Name of two Nicaean emperors of the Eastern Roman Empire: **Theodore I Lascaris** (d. 1222), son-in-law of Alexius III (see LASCARIS); first Nicaean emperor (1206–22); soldier, fought against Franks when Constantinople fell (1204); rallied Greeks and Byzantines and founded new empire in Asia; crowned at Nicaea (1206); able general and administrator; defeated Latins, emperors of Trebizond, and Seljuk Turks. **Theodore II Lascaris,** *also* **Ducas** (1221–1258); son of John III Ducas; emperor (1254–58); repulsed (1256) Bulgarians; well-educated and an author of many works; afflicted with a mental disease.

**Theodore I.** King of Corsica. See Theodor von NEUHOF.

**Theodore.** Name of three czars of Russia. See FËDOR.

**Theodore, Edward Granville.** 1884–1950. Australian publisher, gold-mine operator, and politician, b. in Port Adelaide, South Australia; in politics, leader of Labor party, and premier of South Australia (1919–25); treasurer of the Commonwealth of Australia (1929–30; 1931).

**Theodore of Mop'su·es'ti·a** (mŏp'sū·ĕs'chĭ·ȧ). 350?–?428 A.D. Greek Christian theologian of the Antioch school; disciple of Diodorus of Tarsus. Became presbyter in Antioch (c. 383 A.D.); bishop of Mopsuestia, in Cilicia (c. 392). Author of commentaries on books of the Bible. He and his writings were included in the Three Chapters naming persons and works condemned by Emperor Justinian in his edict (543 A.D.) attempting to reconcile the Monophysites to the church.

**Theodore of Tar'sus** (tär'sŭs). 602?–690. Prelate and ecclesiastical organizer in England, b. at Tarsus in Cilicia; studied at Athens. Consecrated archbishop of Canterbury by Pope Vitalian (668); to England (669) and founded a Greek school at Canterbury; gained submission of heterogeneous churches of several English kingdoms and established ecclesiastical unity; held first synod of clergy at Hertford (673), and later synods; divided diocese of Wilfrid into four, appointed bishops to them, who were displaced by Pope Agatho for Wilfrid's appointees; divided Mercia into five dioceses; reconciled to Wilfrid (686); supervised, and wrote in part, a penitential (still extant).

**The·od'o·ret of Cyr'rhus** (thē·ŏd'ô·rĕt, sĭr'ŭs). 390?–?457 A.D. Greek Christian theologian of the Antioch school. Bishop of Cyrrhus (423 A.D.); deposed (c. 448–451); restored by Council of Chalcedon (451). Author of a church history, commentaries, exegeses, controversial treatises, biographies, etc. His writings in defense of Nestorius were included in the Three Chapters naming persons and works condemned by Emperor Justinian in his edict (543 A.D.) attempting to reconcile the Monophysites to the church.

**Thé'o'do'ric'** (tā'ô'dô'rēk'). Same as THIERRY, especially Thierry I–IV, Frankish kings of the Merovingian dynasty.

**The·od'o·ric** (thē·ŏd'ô·rĭk). *Late Lat.* **The·od'o·ri'cus** (thē·ŏd'ô·rī'kŭs; thē'ô·dô-). *Ger.* **Die'trich** (dē'trĭk). *Often called* **Theodoric the Great.** 454?–526. King of the Ostrogoths and founder of the Ostrogothic kingdom in Italy. Son of a chieftain of the Amalings, b. in Pannonia. Succeeded father as king (474); engaged in series of wars, sometimes against Emperor Zeno, sometimes in his service (474–487); began invasion of Italy (488); defeated Odoacer at Aquileia and Verona (489); completed conquest (489–493); caused death of Odoacer in violation of treaty and became sole ruler of Italy (493); issued Edict of Theodoric (506); made Ravenna his capital; defeated Franks and Bulgarians in minor wars and consolidated empire to include Sicily, Dalmatia, and part of the German lands. In Teutonic legends, esp. in the *Nibelungenlied,* known as **Dietrich von Bern** (fōn bĕrn'), *i.e.* "Theodoric of Verona." See AMALASUNTHA.

**Theodoric I.** d. 451. Son of Alaric. King of the Visigoths (419–451). Killed at battle of Châlons-sur-Marne while fighting with Romans against Huns under Attila. His son **Theodoric II** (426–466), King of the Visigoths (453–466); assassinated his brother King Thorismond (*q.v.*); invaded Spain and made conquests on Iberian Peninsula; assassinated by his brother Euric.

**The'o·do'rus Stu·di'ta** (thē'ô·dō'rŭs stū·dī'tȧ). *Eng.* **Theodore the Stu'dite** (stū'dīt). 759–826 A.D. Monk of the Eastern Church; abbot of the monastery of the Studium, Constantinople, where he put in effect a policy of asceticism and monastic reform. Forced (824) to leave Constantinople; passed remaining years in various monasteries. Known for penmanship and industry in copying manuscripts; author of hymns and controversial treatises.

**The'o·do'si·us I** (thē'ô·dō'shĭ·ŭs; -shŭs). *In full* **Fla'vi·us** (flā'vĭ·ŭs) **Theodosius.** *Called* "the Great." 346?–395. Roman general and emperor (379–395), b. in Spain. Son of Theodosius (d. 376). Accompanied his father into Britain (368); defeated Sarmatians in Moesia (374); summoned by Gratian to share empire (378); made Augustus at Sirmium (379); given Egypt and the East and entrusted with their protection against Goths; made peace with Visigoths and Ostrogoths along the Danube (379–386); allowed Goths to settle within the empire; gave son Arcadius title of Augustus (383); accepted Maximus as colleague in the West (383–388); finally overthrew him (388) at Aquileia; at Milan (388–391), with short visit to Rome (389); humiliated himself publicly before Bishop Ambrose (390) as penance for cruel vengeance upon Thessalonica; aroused by murder of coemperor Valentinian II, led army against Eugenius and Arbogast and defeated them at Frigidus near Aquileia (394); caused second son, Honorius, to be proclaimed emperor of the West under guardianship of Stilicho (395); died at Milan.

**Theodosius.** Name of two rulers of the Eastern Roman Empire (see also THEODOSIUS I, Roman emperor before the division):

**Theodosius II.** 401–450. Son of Arcadius; emperor (408–450); during minority (408–421) empire ably ruled by praetorian prefect Anthemius (d. 414) and emperor's sister Pulcheria, who ruled jointly with him (414–450); married (421) Eudocia, daughter of an Athenian philosopher; during reign: his generals fought two wars against Persia (421 and 441); sent great fleet that ended piracies of Vandals (431); repulsed Huns (408), but later paid large tributes to keep Attila and armies out of the Balkans; Council of Ephesus (431); publication (438) of the Theodosian Code, a collection of imperial constitutions.

**Theodosius III.** d. after 717. Emperor (716–717), an obscure and incapable tax official, raised to the throne; forced to retire when Leo III chosen.

**Theodosius.** Greek geometer and astronomer of 1st century B.C. (or earlier); chief work, *Sphaerica* (3 books, on the geometry of the sphere).

**Theodosius.** d. 376 A.D. Father of Emperor Theodosius I (*q.v.*). Roman general; campaigned in Britain against Picts and Scots; suppressed revolt in Mauretania (370); suspected of conspiracy by Emperor Valens; executed at Carthage.

**The′o·dulf** (thē′ō·dŭlf). d. 821. Ecclesiastic and scholar; bishop of Orléans; renowned as one of cultural leaders in Carolingian renaissance.

**The·og′nis** (thė·ŏg′nĭs). Greek elegiac poet of Megara, of 6th century B.C.; one of the chief gnomic poets. About 1400 lines ascribed to him are extant.

**The·oph′a·nes** (thė·ŏf′ȧ·nēz), Saint. *Called* "the Confessor." 758?–818 A.D. Greek monk and chronicler; founded a monastery at Sigriano near Cyzicus; opposed iconoclastic policy of Leo V, and died in prison. Continued chronicle of George Syncellus, and covered the period 284 to 813 A.D.

**The·oph′a·no** (thė·ŏf′ȧ·nō). (1) Saint. 866–893. First wife (880) of Byzantine emperor Leo VI; famed for virtues and miracles. (2) Empress (d. after 976); second wife (956) of Byzantine emperor Romanus II; of low birth but very beautiful; empress (959–963); mother of emperors Basil II and Constantine VIII; regent alone (963); wife of regent-emperor Nicephorus (969); exiled (970). (3) Empress. 955?–991. See OTTO II, Holy Roman Emperor.

**The·oph′i·lus** (thė·ŏf′ĭ·lŭs). d. 842. Emperor of the Eastern Roman Empire (829–842); son of Michael II; a strong iconoclast; also a great builder and lover of pomp and display; in long war with Saracens (829–838), at first victorious but later (838) suffered severe defeat at Amorium in Phrygia, his chief ancestral city.

**Theophilus.** Early Christian to whom the Gospel of Luke and the Acts of the Apostles are addressed (*Luke* i. 3; *Acts* i. 1).

**Theophilus.** Christian prelate of 2d century A.D.; bishop of Antioch (169); one of the fathers of the church; author of a defense of Christian religion.

**Theophilus.** Sixth-century jurist of Constantinople; one of compilers of the *Institutes* of Justinian (see DOROTHEUS); author of a Greek paraphrase of the *Institutes*, much used in the East.

**Theophorus.** See Saint IGNATIUS.

**The′o·phras′tus** (thē′ō·frăs′tŭs). d. about 287 B.C. Greek philosopher and scientist; disciple of Aristotle, and his successor as head of Peripatetic school; continued teachings of Aristotle; distinguished in field of natural science with *History of Plants* and *Theoretical Botany;* wrote character sketches (*Characters*), as of *The Flatterer, The Grumbler, The Man of Petty Ambition,* etc.

**The′o·pom′pus of Chi′os** (thē′ō·pŏm′pŭs, kī′ŏs). b. about 380 B.C. Greek historian; studied in Athens under Isocrates; chief works, extant only in fragments, *Hellenics* (12 books; a history of Greece from 411 to 394), and *History of Philip* (58 books).

**The′o·rell′** (tā′ō·rĕl′), **Axel Hugo Theodor.** 1903– Swedish biochemist. Awarded Nobel prize in physiology and medicine (1955) for his studies on enzymes.

**Theos.** See ANTIOCHUS II of Syria.

**Theotocópuli** *or* **Theotokopoulos.** See GRECO.

**The·ram′e·nes** (thė·răm′ĕ·nēz). Athenian statesman and general; became one of the Thirty Tyrants (404 B.C.); accused of treason by Critias and required to drink hemlock (404 B.C.).

**Ther′e·min** (*Angl.* thĕr′ĕ·mĭn), **Leo.** *Russ.* **Lev Te·rë′min** (tyĕ·ryô′myĭn). 1896– . Russian engineer; inventor of instruments, including the theremin, producing electrical, or so-called ether-wave, music.

**The·re′sa** *or* **Te·re′sa** (tĕ·rē′sȧ; -zȧ; *Span.* tā·rā′sä), Saint. 1515–1582. Spanish saint; Carmelite nun (from 1534); founded reformed (discalced) order of Carmelites (1562); famous for her mystical visions; author of *El Camino de la Perfección* and *El Castillo Interior.* See St. JOHN OF THE CROSS.

**Thé′rèse′ de Li′sieux′** (tā′râz′ dē lē′zyû′) *or* **Te·re′sa of Lisieux** (tĕ·rē′sȧ; -zȧ), Saint. *Real name* **Thérèse Mar′tin′** (mȧr′tăN′). 1873–1897. Known as "Little Flower of Jesus." French Carmelite nun; member of the Carmelite convent at Lisieux; canonized (1925) as Saint Thérèse, the Little Flower.

**Thé′roigne′ de Mé′ri′court′** (tā′rwȧn′y′ dē mā′rē′-kōōr′). *Pseudonym of* **Anne Joseph Ter′wagne′** (tĕr′wȧn′y′). 1762–1817. Heroine of French Revolutionary period; a leader in assault on the Bastille (July 14, 1789) and in later mob demonstrations; called by crowd "the Amazon of Liberty."

**Thesiger.** See Viscounts and Barons CHELMSFORD.

**Thes′pis** (thĕs′pĭs). Greek poet of 6th century B.C.; reputed founder of the tragic drama (hence the word Thespian, an actor); said to have introduced monologues, and perhaps dialogues, in the existing dithyrambic choruses of hymns to Bacchus and other deities.

**Theu′nis′** (tû′nēs′), **Georges.** 1873–1966. Belgian statesman; premier of Belgium (1921–25).

**Theu′riet′** (tû′ryĕ′), **André,** *in full* **Claude Adhémar André.** 1833–1907. French writer; on staff of ministry of finances; author of a few volumes of verse, as *Chemin des Bois* (1857) and *Le Bleu et le Noir* (1873), and many novels, including *Le Mariage de Gérard* (1875), *Sauvageonne* (1880), *Reine des Bois* (1890), *La Sœur de Lait* (1902), *Mon Oncle Flo* (1906).

**Thévenin, Denis.** Pseudonym of Georges DUHAMEL.

**Thiard** *or* **Thyard** *or* **Tyard** (tyȧr), **Pontus de.** 1521–1605. French poet; almoner of Henry III of France, and bishop of Chalon-sur-Saône; regarded as one of the leaders in the poetic renaissance in France; one of the seven poets composing the Pleiad; among his works are *Erreurs Amoureuses* (1549–55), *Le Livre des Vers Lyriques* (1555), treatises on theology, grammar, etc.

**Thi'baud'** (tē'bō'), **Jacques.** 1880–1953. French violin virtuoso.

**Thi'bau'deau'** (tē'bō'dō'), Comte **Antoine Clair.** 1765–1854. French politician; member of the National Convention (1792); president of the Council of Five Hundred (1796); ennobled by Napoleon I; exiled (1816–30); appointed to the Senate by Napoleon III (1852).

**Thi'bau'det'** (tē'bō'dě'), **Albert.** 1874–1936. French literary critic.

**Thibault, Jacques Anatole François.** Real name of Anatole FRANCE.

**Thi'baut' IV** (tē'bō'). 1201–1253. Count of Champagne (1201–53) and king of Navarre (1234–53); known as lyric poet.

**Thi'baut'** (tē'bō'), **Anton Friedrich Justus.** 1772–1840. German jurist; wrote *System des Pandektenrechts* (1803).

**Thibaw.** See THEBAW.

**Thiel'mann** (tēl'män), Baron **Johann Adolf von.** 1765–1824. German soldier; commanded brigade of Saxon cuirassiers in Russian army (1812); commandant of fortress of Torgau (1813); commanded 3d Prussian army corps (1815) and was engaged at Ligny and Wavre, contributing to final allied victory at Waterloo.

**Thier'ry'** (tyě'rē'). Name of four Frankish kings of the Merovingian dynasty (*q.v.*): **Thierry I** (ruled 511–534), **II** (596–613), **III** (673–?691), **IV** (720–737).

**Thierry, Augustin,** *in full* **Jacques Nicolas Augustin.** 1795–1856. French historian; renown rests on two works, *Conquête de l'Angleterre par les Normands* (1825) and *Lettres sur l'Histoire de France* (1827). His brother **Amédée,** *in full* **Simon Dominique Amédée** (1797–1873), author of *Histoire des Gaulois* (1828), *Histoire de la Gaule sous l'Administration Romaine* (1840–47), etc.; prefect (1830), master of requests (1838), councilor of state (1853), senator (1860).

**Thiers** (tyâr), **Louis Adolphe.** 1797–1877. French statesman and historian; formed lifelong friendship with Mignet (*q.v.*). To Paris (1821); identified himself with opposition; fought Polignac ministry (1829–30). Under Louis Philippe held various cabinet offices (1832–36); minister of foreign affairs (1836; 1840); urged French support of Mehemet Ali in Syria; spent five years in travel and writing (1840–45). In Revolution of 1848, a moderate, friendly to Republic; banished (1851–52); occupied in historical writing (1853–63); leader of Liberal opposition (1863–70), attacking Napoleon III's imperial policies. After Franco-Prussian War, led in rehabilitation of France and negotiated peace treaty with Germany (1871); crushed Paris Commune (1871); elected first president of Third Republic (1871–73); resigned (Mar. 24, 1873), defeated by Monarchists and Clericals; retired from public life (1873). Wrote *Histoire de la Révolution Française* (1823–27; 10 vols.) and *Histoire du Consulat et de l'Empire* (pub. 1845–62; 19 vols.).

**Thiersch** (tērsh), **Friedrich.** 1784–1860. German philologist; engaged in research in Greece (1830–31); published *De l'État Actuel de la Grèce et des Moyens d'Arriver à sa Restauration* (2 vols., 1833).

**Thiess** (tēs), **Frank.** 1890– . German novelist.

**Thiet'mar** (tēt'mär) *or* **Diet'mar** (dēt'mär) *or* **Dith'mar** (dĭt'mär). 975–1018. German chronicler; bishop of Merseburg (1009–18); author of history (*Chronicon*) of Saxon sovereigns.

**Thi'mon'nier'** (tē'mô'nyā'), **Barthélemy.** 1793–1859. French tailor; patented in France (1830) first sewing machine put to practical use. Cf. Elias HOWE.

**Thi'nite** (thī'nīt). Name of Ist and IId dynasties (from c. 3400 to 2980 B.C.) of kings of ancient Egypt, derived from native town, Thinis or This, of these rulers, probably near Abydos. See *Table* (*in Appendix*) for EGYPT.

**Thir'kell** (thûr'kěl), **Angela Margaret,** *nee* **Mac·kail'** (mȧ·kāl'). 1890–1961. English novelist; m. J. Campbell McInnes (1911; divorced 1917), then G. L. Thirkell; author of *August Folly* (1936), *The Brandons* (1939), *Cheerfulness Breaks In* (1940), *Northbridge Rectory* (1942), *Marling Hall* (1942), etc.

**Thirl'by** (thûrl'bĭ), **Thomas.** 1506?–1570. English prelate and diplomat; signed decree of annulment of Henry VIII's marriage with Anne of Cleves (1540); bishop of Westminster (1540), Norwich (1550), Ely (1554).

**Thirlestane,** Baron **Maitland of.** See MAITLAND.

**Thirl'wall** (thûrl'wôl), **Connop.** 1797–1875. English prelate and historian. With Julius Charles Hare, translated first volume of Niebuhr's *Römische Geschichte* as *Rome* (1828) and essays; completed *History of Greece* (1835–44). Bishop of St. David's (1840), built churches, learned to preach in Welsh; one of four prelates who refused to inhibit Bishop Colenso from preaching; supported abolition of Jewish disabilities (1848) and Irish disestablishment (1869); chairman of revisers of Old Testament.

**This'el·ton-Dy'er** (thĭs''l·tŭn·dī'ẽr), Sir **William Turner.** 1843–1928. English botanist, b. Westminster; B.A., Oxon. (1867); assistant director, Royal Botanic Gardens at Kew (1875–85); dealt chiefly with colonial matters and had much to do with development of cocoa production in Ceylon and rubber cultivation in Far East; founded *Kew Bulletin* (1887); as director at Kew (1885–1905; retired) developed the work of its laboratory and edited several of its important publications, as *Flora Capensis;* devoted last years to research and writing on classical Greek and Latin plant names.

**This'tle·wood'** (thĭs''l·wo͝od'), **Arthur.** 1770–1820. English conspirator; plotted assassination of Castlereagh and other cabinet ministers at the earl of Harrowby's house, but (probably on information of one conspirator) was captured and hanged.

**Tho'burn** (thō'bẽrn), **James Mills.** 1836–1922. American Methodist Episcopal clergyman; to India as missionary (1859–1908); missionary bishop for India (1888–1908). His sister **Isabella** (1840–1901) was also a missionary in India (from 1870); Isabella Thoburn College, woman's college of Lucknow Univ., is named for her.

**Thö'köly** (tû'kûl·y'), Count **Imre.** *Also* **Tö'köly** (tû'kûl·y') *or* **Tö'kö·lyi** (-kû·lyĭ) *or* **Tö'kö·li** (-kû·lĭ). 1657–1705. Hungarian patriot; led insurrections against Austria (from 1678) with Turkish aid; continued campaigns against Austria until Treaty of Karlowitz (1699); created by sultan prince of Widdin; resided thereafter in Constantinople.

**Thom** (tŏm), **William.** 1798?–1848. Scottish weaver and poet; attracted attention with *The Blind Boy's Pranks* (1841); published *Rhymes and Recollections* (1844), including graphic poems out of his own experience, such as *The Mitherless Bairn.*

**Tho'ma** (tō'mä), **Hans.** 1839–1924. German painter; a leader in modern German school; painter of landscapes, genre scenes, portraits, religious and allegorical subjects; also known as lithographer, etcher, and illustrator.

**Thoma, Ludwig.** *Pseudonym* **Peter Schle·mihl'** (shlā·mēl'). 1867–1921. German journalist and writer; editor of *Simplizissimus* (1899); known esp. as author of humorous sketches of Bavarian life, dramas, and satires.

**Thoma,** Ritter **Wilhelm von.** 1891–1948. German general; served in World War (1914–18); led German tank forces in Spanish civil war; tank commander under Guderian in France (1940), at Sedan, Calais, Dunkirk; field commander of Afrika Korps; captured by British (Nov. 4, 1942) after El Alamein battle.

**Thom'as** (tŏm'ăs). In Bible, one of the twelve apostles (*Matt.* x. 3; *Mark* iii. 18; *Luke* vi. 15; *Acts* i. 13), referred to also (*John* xi. 16 and xx. 24) as **Did'y·mus** (dĭd'ĭ-mŭs), who (according to *John* xx. 24–29) doubted, until he had proof of, Jesus's resurrection.

**Thomas,** Earl of **Lancaster.** See LANCASTER.

**Tho'mas'** (tô'mä'), **Albert.** 1878–1932. French politician; Socialist member of Chamber of Deputies (1910); appointed to organize production of munitions of war (1914); minister of armaments (1915–17); director of the International Labor Bureau of the League of Nations, at Geneva, until his death.

**Thom'as** (tŏm'ăs), **Albert Ellsworth.** 1872–1947. American playwright, b. Chester, Mass.; journalist in New York (1895–1909); author of *Her Husband's Wife* (1910), *Come Out of the Kitchen* (1916), *The Champion* (1920), *Her Friend the King* (with H. G. Rhodes, 1922), *Merely Murder* (1937), etc.

**Tho'mas'** (tô'mä'), **Ambroise,** *in full* **Charles Louis Ambroise.** 1811–1896. French composer, esp. of operas and stage music, including *La Double Échelle* (1837), *Le Panier Fleuri* (1839), *Le Comte de Carmagnole* (1841), *Le Songe d'une Nuit d'Été* (1850), *Le Carnaval de Venise* (1857), *Mignon* (1866), *Hamlet* (1868), *Françoise de Rimini* (1882); author also of masses, cantatas, a Requiem, motets, and choral works.

**Thom'as** (tŏm'ăs), **Amos Russell.** 1826–1895. American homeopathic physician and educator.

**Tho'mas'** (tô'mä'), **André Antoine.** 1857–1935. French philologist; collaborator in compilation of *Dictionnaire Général de la Langue Française*...(1889–1900).

**Thom'as** (tŏm'ăs), **Arthur Goring.** 1850–1892. English composer of operas, including *Esmeralda* (1883) and *Nadeshda* (1885), the choral ode *The Sun Worshippers* (1881), and songs.

**Thomas, Augustus.** 1857–1934. American dramatist, b. St. Louis, Mo.; made first success with *Alabama* (1891); among his plays were *In Mizzoura* (1893), *The Hoosier Doctor* (1897), *Arizona* (1899), *The Earl of Pawtucket* (1903), *Mrs. Leffingwell's Boots* (1905), *The Witching Hour* (1907), *The Harvest Moon* (1909), *As a Man Thinks* (1911), *The Copperhead* (1918).

**Thomas, Brandon.** 1856–1914. English actor and playwright; author of *Charley's Aunt* (1892), *Women Are So Serious* (1901), *A Judge's Memory* (1906).

**Thomas, Calvin.** 1854–1919. American educator; professor of Germanic languages and literatures, Columbia (1896–1919); known especially as a Goethe scholar; editor of Goethe's *Faust* (2 vols., 1892–97), and author of *Goethe* (1917).

**Thomas, Cyrus.** 1825–1910. American ethnologist; on staff of Bureau of American Ethnology (from 1882); directed explorations of mounds in the central U.S.; also, a pioneer in investigation and study of Maya culture.

**Thomas, David Alfred.** See Viscount RHONDDA.

**Thomas, Dylan.** 1914–1953. British poet, b. in South Wales; joined British army (1940); author of *Map of Love* (1939), *World I Breathe* (1939), *Portrait of the Artist as a Young Dog* (1940).

**Thomas, Edith Matilda.** 1854–1925. American poet, b. Chatham, Ohio; resident in New York (from 1887); among her volumes of verse are *A New Year's Masque* ...(1885), *Lyrics and Sonnets* (1887), *The Inverted Torch* (1890), *In Sunshine Land* (1895), *The Dancers*...(1903), *The Flower from the Ashes* (1915).

**Thomas, Edward,** *in full* **Philip Edward.** 1878–1917. British poet and critic; recorded nature observations in his first book, *The Woodland Life* (1897); published essays, *Horae Solitariae* (1902), and twenty-odd travel books and critical biographies. Began to write poetry after forming friendship with Robert Frost (1912); enlisted in Artists' Rifles (1915), wrote poems in camp and on furloughs; killed in action in battle of Arras, Easter Monday (1917). Author of *The South County* (1909), *Light and Twilight* (1911), *The Happy-Go-Lucky Morgans* (1913), and a volume of short stories, *Four-and-Twenty Blackbirds* (1915). His first book of *Poems* (1917) published under pseudonym **Edward Eas'ta·way** (ēs'-tȧ·wā). His wife, **Helen,** *nee* **No'ble** (nō'b'l), recounted their courtship in *As It Was* (1926) and their married life in *World Without End* (1930).

**Thomas, Frederick William.** 1867–1956. British Orientalist; professor of Sanskrit, Oxford (1927–38); author of *Mutual Influence of Muhammadans and Hindus in India* (1892).

**Thomas, George Henry.** 1816–1870. American army commander, b. in Southampton County, Va.; grad. U.S.M.A., West Point (1840). Remained loyal to Union during the Civil War; brigadier general of volunteers (Aug., 1861), and major general (Apr., 1862); engaged at Perryville, and gained fame and the nickname "the Rock of Chickamauga" by his defense of his position in the battle of Chickamauga (Sept. 19–20, 1863). Commanded Army of the Cumberland in battle of Chattanooga (Nov. 24–25, 1863) and in Sherman's Atlanta campaign (1864). Sent to Tennessee to repel Hood's army (Sept., 1864) and won battle of Nashville (Dec. 15–16, 1864); promoted major general in the regular army. Commanded Military Division of the Pacific (1869–70).

**Thomas, George Holt.** 1869–1929. English aircraft manufacturer; founded Aircraft Manufacturing Co. (c. 1912), which produced many of the British planes used during World War.

**Thomas, Isaiah.** 1750–1831. American printer, b. Boston. Founded *Massachusetts Spy* and printed it in Boston (1770–75) and Worcester, Mass. (1775–1802); set up printing business in Worcester; later, established branches in other colonial cities. In addition to printing a number of the magazines of the day, he published many books notable for beauty of typography, including a folio Bible (first Bible printed in English in U.S.), Perry's dictionary (first dictionary printed in U.S.), Perry's speller, Blackstone's *Commentaries*, and textbooks, lawbooks, etc. Also, was first publisher in U.S. to do a large amount of printing of music type. Known, too, for publication of children's books. Author of *The History of Printing in America* (2 vols., 1810). Founded and incorporated American Antiquarian Society (1812) and was its first president.

**Thomas, James Henry.** 1874–1949. English labor leader and politician; successively, errand boy, locomotive wiper, railroad fireman, engineer. General secretary, National Union of Railwaymen (1918–24; 1925–31). M.P. (1910–36); secretary of state for colonies (1924; 1931; 1935–36); Lord Privy Seal and minister of employment (1929–30); secretary of state for the dominions (1930–35). Author of *When Labour Rules* (1920), etc.

**Thomas, Jesse Burgess.** 1777–1853. American lawyer and politician, b. Shepherdstown, Va. (now W.Va.); U.S. senator from Illinois (1818–29); introduced (1820) measure prohibiting slavery north of 36°30' except for area in proposed State of Missouri, this measure being later embodied in famous "Missouri Compromise."

**Thomas, John.** 1724–1776. American physician and Revolutionary officer, b. Marshfield, Mass. In army medical service (1746–60). Commissioned brigadier general in Continental army (June, 1775); at Gen. Washington's request remained in command at Roxbury (1775–76); ordered by Gen. A. Ward to seize Dorchester Heights (Mar. 4, 1776) and thereby forced British evacuation of Boston. Promoted major general (Mar., 1776) and commander of American army operating against Quebec; died of smallpox (June 2, 1776).

**Thomas, John.** 1805–1871. Physician and religious leader, b. in England; to U.S. (1844); founder of the Christadelphian sect (c. 1850).

**Thomas, John Jacobs.** 1810–1895. American agriculturist; editor, *Rural Affairs* (1869–81); author of *The Fruit Culturist* (1846), later expanded and entitled *The American Fruit Culturist* (1849), which marks beginning of systematic pomology in U.S. His brother **Joseph** (1811–1891) was a physician and lexicographer; on staff of J. B. Lippincott & Co., Philadelphia (1854–71), engaged in *Gazetteer of the United States* (1854), *A Comprehensive Medical Dictionary* (1864), *Dictionary of Biography and Mythology* (2 vols., 1870); also, contributed biographical and geographical sections to *Webster's American Dictionary of the English Language* (1867).

**Thomas, Lorenzo.** 1804–1875. American army officer; grad. U.S.M.A., West Point (1823). Served in Mexican War. Adjutant general, U.S. army (1861–63); on duty in Mississippi Valley organizing Negro regiments (1863–65); brevetted major general (Mar., 1865). At height of conflict between President Andrew Johnson and Secretary of War Stanton, Johnson dismissed Stanton (Feb. 21, 1868) and appointed Thomas ad interim secretary of war; Stanton resisted removal, and Thomas was unable to take office; the impeachment trial of Johnson followed. Retired (1869).

**Thomas, Lowell.** 1892– . American author and radio news commentator, b. Woodington, Ohio. Chief of mission sent to Europe by President Wilson to prepare historical record of World War I; attached in turn to Belgian, French, Italian, Serbian, American, British, and Arabian armies; prepared historical and pictorial record of German revolution. Made 25,000-mile flight by airplane over Europe, northern Africa, and Asia to study international development in aviation (1926–27). News commentator on the radio (from 1930). Author of many books of travel, comment, and adventure.

**Thomas, Martha Carey.** 1857–1935. American educator, b. Baltimore, Md. Dean, professor of English (1884–94) and president (1894–1922), Bryn Mawr College. Also, co-operated with Mary Elizabeth Garrett in founding (1885) Bryn Mawr School for Girls, Baltimore; founded (1910) first graduate school of social economy and research connected with an American college; founded (1922) first school on college campus for workers in industry. Prominent woman suffragist. Author of *The Higher Education of Women* (1900).

**Thomas, Norman Mattoon.** 1884–1968. American Socialist politician, b. Marion, Ohio. Ordained in Presbyterian ministry (1911); resigned from ministry (1931). Founder and editor, *World To-Morrow* (1918–21); assoc. editor, *The Nation* (1921–22); director, League for Industrial Democracy (1922). Socialist candidate for president of the United States (1928, 1932, 1936, 1940, 1944, 1948). Author of *America's Way Out—A Program for Democracy* (1930), *As I See It* (with Paul Blanshard, 1932), *War—No Profit, No Glory, No Need* (1935), etc.

**Thomas, Philip Evan.** 1776–1861. American pioneer railroad promoter and executive; promoted Baltimore and Ohio Railroad (incorporated Apr. 24, 1827), second railroad in U.S. chartered to carry passengers; served as its president (1827–36), during a major part of its construction.

**Thomas, Robert Bailey.** 1766–1846. American publisher, b. Grafton, Mass.; founded (1792), edited, and published *The Farmer's Almanac* (1792–1846).

**Thomas, Seth.** 1785–1859. American clock manufacturer, b. Wolcott, Conn. Associated with Eli Terry and Silas Hoadley in firm of Terry, Thomas & Hoadley to manufacture clocks by mass production methods (1807). Founded clock factory of his own at Plymouth Hollow, Conn. (1812); organized Seth Thomas Clock Co. (1853). His son **Seth** (1816–1888) continued the business at Plymouth Hollow, renamed (c. 1860) Thomaston, Conn.

**Thomas, Sidney Gilchrist.** 1850–1885. English metallurgist and inventor; discovered method for eliminating phosphorus from iron in Bessemer converter (1875); the method, now known as the Thomas-Gilchrist process, Thomas process, or basic open-hearth process, was proved to be effective by his cousin Percy Carlyle Gilchrist (1851–1935).

**Tho′mas** (tŏm′ăs), **Theodore**, *in full* **Christian Friedrich Theodore.** 1835–1905. Orchestra conductor, b. at Esens, Ger.; to U.S. (1845) and settled in New York. Organized orchestra (1862); conducted symphony concerts in New York City (1864–69; 1872–78) and on tour (esp. between 1869 and 1878). Conductor, Chicago Symphony Orchestra (1891–1905). Exercised great influence on development of a knowledge and appreciation of symphonic music.

**Thomas, Theodore Gail·lard′** (gĭl·yärd′). 1831–1903. American gynecologist; originated operation of laparoelytrotomy, use of the incubator (1867); first to remove small ovarian tumor by cutting through the vagina. Author of *Practical Treatise on the Diseases of Women* (1868).

**Thomas à Becket.** See Becket.

**Thom′as a Kem′pis** (tŏm′ăs ȧ[ȧ, ä] kĕm′pĭs). *Properly* **Thomas Ha′mer·ken** (hä′mẽr·kĕn), *or* **He′mer·ken** (hā′mẽr·kĕn), **von Kem′pen** (fôn kĕm′pĕn). *Also* **Thomas Häm′mer·lein** (hĕm′ẽr·līn). 1380–1471. German ecclesiastic and writer, b. Kempen, Prussia; entered Augustinian monastery near Zwolle (1407); ordained (1413); chosen subprior of monastery (1425, 1447). Famed as reputed author of the religious classic *De Imitatione Christi* (*Imitation of Christ*).

**Thomas Aquinas,** Saint. See Aquinas.

**Thomas de Cantelupe.** See Cantelupe.

**Thomas de Marleberge** *or* **of Marlborough.** See Marleberge.

**Thomas François.** *Ital.* **Tommaso Francesco.** Prince of **Carignan.** See Savoy.

**Thom′as of Ba·yeux′** (tŏm′ăs; bȧ·yōō′, *Fr.* bȧ′yû′). d. 1100. English prelate; appointed archbishop of York by William the Conqueror (1070); forced by council of bishops to yield obedience to Canterbury (1072).

**Thomas of Broth′er·ton** (brŏth′ẽr·t′n; -tŭn). Earl of **Nor′folk** (nôr′fŭk). 1300–1338. Marshal of England; son of Edward I, King of England; joined Queen Isabella upon her landing in England (1326) and was active in group that forced deposition of Edward II.

**Thomas of Can′ter·bur′y** (kăn′tẽr·bẽr′ĭ; -bẽr·ĭ; -brĭ). = Thomas à Becket.

**Thomas of Ce·la′no** (chå·lä′nō). 1200?–?1255. Italian Franciscan monk, b. Celano, Abruzzi e Molise; follower of Francis of Assisi (c. 1214 ff.); author of biographical sketches of St. Francis, as *First Legend* (1229), *Second Legend* (1247), and *Tract on the Miracles of St. Francis;* reputed author of hymn *Dies Irae.*

**Thomas of Erceldoune.** See Erceldoune.

**Thomas of Her′e·ford** (hĕr′ē·fẽrd). = Thomas de Cantelupe.

**Thomas of Wood′stock** (wŏŏd′stŏk). Earl of **Buck′·ing·ham** (bŭk′ĭng·ăm; -hăm). Duke of **Glouces′ter** (glŏs′tẽr; glôs′-). 1355–1397. Youngest son of Edward III of Windsor, King of England. Virtual ruler of

England (1386–89). m. Eleanor de Bohun, heiress of earl of Hereford, Essex, and Northampton; aided in repelling French and Spanish at Dover (1380), in futile expedition to subdue Brittany (1380), and in suppression of peasant uprising in Essex (1381). In absence of his brother John of Gaunt, headed opposition to his nephew Richard II; one of judges condemning Michael de la Pole, Earl of Suffolk (1386); joined other lords in routing Robert de Vere at Radcot Bridge (1387); as leader of lords appellant in Wonderful Parliament, guilty of vindictive cruelty (1388). Arrested by Richard II after reported plot to seize king (1397); taken to Calais and probably murdered.

**Thomas the Bastard.** See FAUCONBERG.

**Thomas the Rhymer** *or* **Thomas Rhymer.** = Thomas of ERCELDOUNE.

**Thom'a·shef'sky** (tŏm'ȧ·shĕf'skĭ), **Boris.** 1864–1939. Russian-born Yiddish actor and producer in U.S.; b. in Kiev; to U.S. (1877). Credited with introducing the Yiddish theater into U.S.; acted and produced plays in New York, where he established the National Theater. Translated Shakespeare's plays into Yiddish; wrote many original sketches and operettas.

**Tho·ma'si·us** (tō·mä'zē·ōōs), **Christian.** *Latinized from* **Tho'mas** (tō'mäs). 1655–1728. German jurist and philosopher; among his works are *Institutiones Jurisprudentiae Divinae* (1688), *Introductio ad Philosophiam Aulicam* (1688), and *Fundamenta Juris Naturae ac Gentium* (1705).

**Thom'a·son** (tŏm'ȧ·s'n), **John William, Jr.** 1893–1944. American marine corps officer and writer; served in World War; author of *Fix Bayonets* (1926), *Red Pants* (1927), *Marines and Others* (1929), *Salt Winds and Gobi Dust* (1934), *Lone Star Preacher* (1940).

**Tho'mé'** (tô'mā'), **Francis,** *in full* **François Luc Joseph.** 1850–1909. French pianist, and composer of many ballets and pantomimes, operettas, including *Barbe Bleuette* and *La Conversion de Pierrot*, and piano pieces, including the well-known *Simple Aveu.*

**Thomond,** Earls and marquises of. Titles borne by O'Brien family (*q.v.*).

**Thomp'son** (tŏm(p)'s'n). See also THOMSON.

**Thompson, Alfred Wordsworth.** 1840–1896. American landscape and historical painter; studio in New York (1868).

**Thompson, Benjamin.** Count **Rum'ford** (rŭm'fẽrd). 1753–1814. Physicist and adventurer, b. Woburn, Mass. Loyalist during American Revolution; knighted (Feb. 23, 1784). In service of elector of Bavaria (1784–95), who created him a count of the Holy Roman Empire (1791). In England (1795), introduced improvements in heating and cooking equipment for houses. Returned to Bavaria (1796) and headed council of regency; appointed Bavarian minister to Great Britain, but not received as such in London because he was a British subject. Instrumental in organization of the Royal Institution (1799); planned (1801) organization of Bavarian Academy of Arts and Sciences, at Munich. Resident chiefly in Paris and Anteuil (from 1802); developed a calorimeter and a photometer, devised improvements in lighting.

**Thompson, Carmi Alderman.** 1870–1942. American lawyer and public official; treasurer of the United States (1912–13); special commissioner sent by President Coolidge to survey conditions in the Philippines (1926).

**Thompson, Charles Miner.** 1864–1941. American editor and author; editor in chief (1911–25), *Youth's Companion;* on staff of Harvard U. Press (1925–36); author of juveniles, including *The Calico Cat* (1908).

**Thompson, Daniel Pierce.** 1795–1868. American lawyer and author; practiced in Montpelier, Vt.; author of a number of romances framed against the background of Vermont history, including *The Green Mountain Boys* (1839), *Centeola* (1864).

**Thompson, David.** 1770–1857. Explorer and fur trader, b. London, Eng.; apprenticed to Hudson's Bay Co. (1784); served in western Canada (1789–1812), keeping careful journals and field notes of his travels; prepared large map of northern U.S. and Canada, made by use of his own survey figures (1812–14); head of British commission for fixing and marking U.S.-Canadian boundary (1816–26).

**Thompson, Denman,** *orig.* **Henry Denman.** 1833–1911. American actor and playwright; author and star ("Josh Whitcomb") of *The Old Homestead,* first presented in Boston (1886).

**Thompson, Dorothy.** 1894–1961. American journalist, b. Lancaster, N.Y.; m. Josef Bard (1923; divorced), Sinclair Lewis (1928; divorced 1942), Maxim Kopf (1943); correspondent in Vienna (1920–24), Berlin (1924–28); columnist, syndicated through New York Herald-Tribune Syndicate (1936–41), Bell Syndicate (1941 ff.); author of *New Russia* (1928), *Political Guide* (1938), *Let the Record Speak* (1939), *Listen, Hans* (1942).

**Thompson, Edward Herbert.** 1860–1935. American archaeologist; U.S. consul in Yucatán (1885–1909). Made study of remains of Maya civilization; discovered "Hidden City" ruins in interior of Yucatán; uncovered "Maya Venus," a high priest's mausoleum, the "Temple of the Painted Columns," and obtained many objects of archaeological significance.

**Thompson,** Sir **Edward Maunde.** 1840–1929. British librarian and paleographer, b. in Jamaica, W.I. On staff of British Museum (from 1861); director and principal librarian of the museum (1888–1909). Author of *Handbook of Greek and Latin Palaeography* (1893), *An Introduction to Greek and Latin Palaeography* (1912); edited and published a number of manuscripts from the British Museum.

**Thompson, Elizabeth Southerden.** See under Sir William Francis BUTLER.

**Thompson, Ernest Seton.** = Ernest Thompson SETON.

**Thompson, Francis.** 1859–1907. English poet. In London (1885); in destitution and ill health, fell prey to opium; working in bootmaker's shop, wrote his first poems, which he sent to Wilfrid Meynell (*q.v.*), editor of *Merry England;* hospitalized and nurtured by the Meynells (1888–93). Gained acclaim of critics with *Poems* (1893; including *The Hound of Heaven*), *Sister Songs* (1895) and *New Poems* (1897); author also of literary criticism, a life of Loyola (1909), and *Essay on Shelley* (1909).

**Thompson, George.** 1804–1878. English abolitionist; associated with Garrison and Whittier in antislavery movement in U.S. (from 1834); denounced by President Jackson and forced to leave U.S. (1835).

**Thompson,** Sir **Henry.** 1820–1904. English surgeon; specialist in surgery of the urogenital tract; his publications include *Stricture of the Urethra* (1854), *Practical Lithotomy and Rithotrity* (1863).

**Thompson, Jacob.** 1810–1885. American politician, b. Leasburg, N.C. U.S. secretary of the interior (1857–61); resigned to serve in Confederate army; secret agent of the Confederacy in Canada; held responsible for attacks upon United States planned along Canadian-American border.

**Thompson, John.** 1802–1891. American banker, b. Peru, Mass.; founded First National Bank, New York City (chartered 1863); served as its president; sold controlling interest (1873), founded Chase National Bank, New York City (1877).

**Thompson,** **John Reuben.** 1823–1873. American journalist and poet, b. Richmond, Va.; editor, *The Southern Literary Messenger* (1847–60); literary editor, New York *Evening Post* (1867–73); regarded as a poet expressing the Virginia tradition.

**Thompson,** Sir **John Sparrow David.** 1844–1894. Canadian statesman; minister of justice for Canada (1885), defended hanging of Louis Riel; negotiated fisheries treaty with U.S. (1887); prime minister (1892–94); one of arbitrators of Bering Sea Controversy (1893).

**Thompson,** **John Taliaferro.** 1860–1940. American army officer, and inventor of firearms and airplane devices; with Commander John N. Blish, U.S. navy, invented the Thompson submachine gun.

**Thompson,** **Joseph Osgood.** 1863–1953. American physicist; established law of elastic lengthening in metals.

**Thompson,** **Joseph Parrish.** 1819–1879. American Congregational clergyman; a founder of the *New Englander;* on editorial board of the *Independent* (1848–62); resident in Berlin (from 1871). His son **William Gilman** (1856–1927) was a physician; specialist in industrial and occupational diseases and in diseases resulting from or associated with war conditions.

**Thompson,** **Launt.** 1833–1894. Sculptor, b. in Ireland; to U.S. (1847); studio, New York City (1857–75; 1881–94) and in Italy (1875–81). His bronze statue of Abraham Pierson is on the Yale campus; of Gen. Winfield Scott, on the grounds of the Old Soldiers' Home in Washington, D.C.

**Thompson,** **Martin E.** 1786?–1877. American architect, partner of Ithiel Town (1827–28) and one of the founders (1826) of the National Academy of Design.

**Thompson,** **Maurice,** *in full* **James Maurice.** 1844–1901. American writer; practiced law in Crawfordsville, Ind. (1871–84); a literary editor of the *Independent* (1889–1901); author of two volumes of poetry (*Songs of Fair Weather,* 1883; *Poems,* 1892), books of nature sketches, books on archery, juveniles, and several historical romances, including the popular *Alice of Old Vincennes* (1900).

**Thompson,** **Randall.** 1899– . American composer, b. New York City. Director, Curtis Institute of Music, Philadelphia (1939–41). Noted esp. for choral works, as *The Peaceable Kingdom* (1936), *The Testament of Freedom* (1943, based on writings of Thomas Jefferson).

**Thompson,** **Reginald Campbell.** 1876–1941. English archaeologist; conducted excavations for British Museum at Nineveh (1904, 1927, 1929, 1930, 1931), Carchemish (1911), Abu Shahrain (1918). During World War served with intelligence department in Mesopotamia. Among his works are *Reports of the Magicians and Astrologers of Nineveh and Babylon* (2 vols., 1900), *The Devils and Evil Spirits of Babylonia* (2 vols., 1903–04), *Semitic Magic* (1908), *Assyrian Medical Texts* (1923), *The Epic of Gilgamish* (translation, 1928; text, 1930), etc.

**Thompson,** **Richard Wigginton.** 1809–1900. American politician; practiced law in Bedford, Ind. U.S. secretary of the navy (1877–80).

**Thompson,** **Silvanus Phillips.** 1851–1916. English physicist; author of works on electricity and magnetism, and on lives of scientists.

**Thompson,** **Smith.** 1768–1843. American jurist; U.S. secretary of the navy (1819–23); associate justice, U.S. Supreme Court (1823–43).

**Thompson,** **Sylvia.** 1902–1968. English novelist and lecturer; m. Theodore Dunham Luling (1926); author of *The Hounds of Spring* (1925), *Golden Arrow* (1935), *Recapture the Moon* (1937), *The Adventure of Christopher Columin* (1939), *The Gulls Fly Inland* (1941).

**Thompson,** **Will Henry.** 1848–1918. American Confederate soldier and writer; engaged in the Wilderness, Spotsylvania, Cold Harbor, Petersburg, Virginia; practiced law at Crawfordsville, Ind. (1872–89) and Seattle, Wash. (from 1889); author of *High Tide at Gettysburg* (1888), etc.

**Thompson,** **Will Lam′ar·tine** (lăm′ẽr·tēn). 1847–1909. American song writer, b. in Beaver County, Pa.; author of *The Old Tramp, My Home on the Old Ohio, My Sweetheart and I Went Fishing, Come Where the Lilies Bloom,* etc.; also wrote many hymns.

**Thompson,** **William.** 1785?–1833. Irish landowner and political economist; student of Bentham's utilitarianism; enthusiastic supporter of Robert Owen's co-operative system; author of *An Inquiry into the Principles of the Distribution of Wealth* (1824), laying foundation of scientific socialism.

**Thompson,** **William Boyce.** 1869–1930. American mining operator, b. Virginia City, Mont. Accompanied American Red Cross mission to Russia (1917–18); tried to get American aid for Kerenski regime, and after Kerenski's fall urged recognition of Soviet government. Founded and financed Boyce Thompson Institute for Plant Research (1919), established at Yonkers, N.Y., and dedicated in 1924.

**Thompson,** **William Gilman.** See under Joseph P. THOMPSON.

**Thoms** (tŏmz), **William John.** 1803–1885. English antiquary; clerk of House of Lords (from 1845) and (1863–1882) its deputy librarian; published *Lays and Legends of Various Nations* (2 vols., 1834), *The Book of the Court* (1838), and other antiquarian works; founder (1849) and editor (till 1872) of *Notes and Queries.*

**Thom′sen** (tŏm′s'n), **Julius,** *in full* **Hans Peter Jörgen Julius.** 1826–1909. Danish chemist; known esp. for research on the heat changes involved in chemical reactions; invented (c. 1853) process for the manufacture of soda from cryolite.

**Thomsen, Vilhelm Ludvig Peter.** 1842–1927. Danish philologist; author of *The Relations between Ancient Russia and Scandinavia and the Origin of the Russian State* (1878); decipherer of the Orkhon inscriptions (1893).

**Thom′son** (tŏm′s'n). See also THOMPSON.

**Thomson,** Sir **Basil Home** (hūm). 1861–1939. English police commissioner, prison warden, and writer; governor of Dartmoor Prison (to 1907); director of Intelligence at Scotland Yard (1919–21); author of *South Sea Yarns* (1894), *The Story of Dartmoor Prison* (1907), *The Skene Papers* (1909), *Queer People* (1922), *Mr. Pepper, Investigator* (1925), *The Story of Scotland Yard* (1935), etc.

**Thomson,** **Charles.** 1729–1824. Politician and patriot in American Revolution, b. in Ireland; to America, an orphan (1739); merchant in Philadelphia (from 1760); secretary of the Continental Congress (1774–89); messenger of the congress to notify Gen. Washington of his election to the presidency.

**Thomson,** **Charles Edward Poulett.** Baron **Syd′en·ham** (sĭd′'n·ăm; sĭd′năm). 1799–1841. British economic expert. Brother of George Julius Poulett Scrope (*q.v.*). Liberal M.P. (1826); vice-president of board of trade (1830), president (1834); effected tariff changes in direction of free trade; advocated legislation on usury, banking, and factory management; negotiated commercial treaties. Governor general of Canada (1839–41); assisted in union of Upper and Lower Canada and established responsible government.

**Thomson,** Sir **Charles Wyville.** 1830–1882. Scottish naturalist; made special study of deep-sea life; described sounding and dredging expeditions in *The Depths of the*

*Sea* (1873) and his circumnavigating expedition in *The Voyage of the Challenger* (1877).

**Thomson, Christopher Birdwood.** 1st Baron **Thomson.** 1875–1930. British soldier and statesman; served in Boer War (1899–1902) and World War I (1914–18); secretary of state for air (1924; 1929–30).

**Thomson, Elihu.** 1853–1937. Electrician and inventor, b. Manchester, England; to U.S. as a boy. An organizer (1883) of the Thomson-Houston Electric Co., which was merged (1892) with Thomas Edison's company to form the General Electric Co., which manufactured and operated under his inventions, for which he obtained more than 700 patents. Inventor of electric welding, the standard three-phase alternating-current generator, the centrifugal cream separator, the common watt meter, the street arc lamp. See E. J. HOUSTON.

**Thomson,** Sir **George Paget.** 1892– . Son of Sir Joseph John Thomson. English physicist; served in Royal Air Force (1915–19); professor of natural philosophy, U. of Aberdeen (1922–30); professor of physics, Imperial College of Science and Technology, London U. (1930–52). Shared 1937 Nobel prize for physics with Clinton Joseph Davisson (*q.v.*) for their discovery (independently and by different methods) of the diffraction of electrons by crystals (1927). Author of *Applied Aerodynamics* (1919), *The Atom, Wave Mechanics of the Free Electron.*

**Thomson, Hugh.** 1860–1920. English illustrator; known esp. for his black-and-white illustrations for works of Goldsmith, Miss Mitford, Jane Austen, Thackeray, and George Eliot; executed illustrations in colors of Shakespeare's *As You Like It, The Merry Wives of Windsor,* Barrie's *Quality Street,* and others.

**Thomson, James.** 1700–1748. Scottish poet; to London (1725); tutor to Thomas Hamilton, who became 7th earl of Haddington; introduced to Pope, Arbuthnot, Gay; published blank-verse poems *Winter* (1726), *Summer* (1727), *Spring* (1728), *Autumn* (1730), brought together as *The Seasons,* for first time giving description of nature the leading place, and paving the way for the emotional treatment of nature by the Romantic poets. Author of dramas *Sophonisba* (1730), *Agamemnon* (1738), *Edward and Eleanora* (1739). Pensioned (1738) after dedicating poem *Liberty* (1735–36) to prince of Wales; author, with David Mallet (*q.v.*), of *The Masque of Alfred* (1740; containing song *Rule Britannia;* music by T. A. Arne). Deputized duties as surveyor general of Leeward Islands (1744); produced most successful of his dramas, *Tancred and Sigismunda* (1745), and his final tragedy, *Coriolanus* (1749). Completed his one long work in rhyme, the allegorical poem *The Castle of Indolence* (1748), in Spenserian stanzas, generally considered his masterpiece.

**Thomson, James.** *Known by his signature* **B. V.** *for* **Bysshe Va·no′lis** (bĭsh vȧ·nō′lĭs). 1834–1882. Scottish poet of despair. Army school master, near Cork; loved daughter of armorer-sergeant in garrison and was precipitated into pessimism by her illness and death. Published *To Our Ladies of Death* (1861) and *The City of Dreadful Night* (1874; pub. as book, 1880); contributed long poem *Sunday up the River* to *Fraser's Magazine* (1869). Lived in poverty and misery, victim of narcotics and dipsomania; wrote chiefly in despairing and atheistic mood, but occasionally in happier mood, as in *Give a man a horse he can ride;* published *Vane's Story, Weddah and Om-el-Bonain, and Other Poems* (1881) and collected prose writings as *Essays and Phantasies* (1881).

**Thomson, John.** 1765–1846. Scottish physician and surgeon. His son **Allen** (1809–1884), biologist and anatomist, was an early exponent of embryology.

**Thomson, John.** 1778–1840. Scottish landscape painter; first to depict ruggedness of Scottish scenery.

**Thomson, John Arthur.** 1861–1933. Scottish biologist; regius professor of natural history, U. of Aberdeen (from 1899); attempted in lectures and writings to popularize biology and to correlate science and religion; author of *Outlines of Zoology, The Wonder of Life* (1914), *What is Man?* (1923), *Science and Religion* (1925), etc.

**Thomson, Joseph.** 1858–1895. Scottish explorer in Africa; geologist of expedition under Alexander Keith Johnston to Central Africa, succeeding as leader on death of Johnston (1879); reached Lake Tanganyika, discovered Lake Rukwa; headed expedition through the Masai country (1882), reached Lake Victoria (1883). By expedition for Royal Niger Co. to Sokoto gained part of central Sudan for Great Britain (1885); explored Atlas Mountains, Morocco (1888). Wrote travel records.

**Thomson,** Sir **Joseph John.** 1856–1940. English physicist, b. near Manchester; professor, Cambridge (1884–1918), Royal Institution, London (1905–18); master, Trinity College, Cambridge (1918); developed research laboratory (Cavendish laboratory) at Cambridge. Investigated conduction of electricity through gases, the mass and charge of the electron, and radioactivity. Awarded 1906 Nobel prize for physics. Author of *The Application of Dynamics to Physics and Chemistry* (1888), *Elements of the Mathematical Theory of Electricity and Magnetism* (1895), *Rays of Positive Electricity and Their Application to Chemical Analysis* (1913), *The Electron in Chemistry* (1923). See George Paget THOMSON.

**Thomson, Mortimer Neal.** *Pseudonym* **Q. K. Philander Doe′sticks** (dō′stĭks), **P.B.** 1831–1875. American humorist; on staff of New York *Tribune* (1855); editor, *Frank Leslie's Illustrated Weekly* (1873–75). Created "Doesticks," assumed writer of a series of letters later collected and published as *Doesticks: What He Says* (1855). Wrote *Plu-ri-bus-tah, a Song That's-by-No-Author* (a mock-heroic parody of *Hiawatha,* 1856), *Nothing to Say,* etc.

**Thomson, Robert William.** 1822–1873. Invented the pneumatic tire, the principle of which he patented in England (1845); equipped a horse-drawn brougham with pneumatic tires. See John Boyd DUNLOP.

**Thomson,** Sir **StClair.** 1859–1943. British physician; M.D., Lausanne (1891); pioneer in laryngology, and authority on diseases of ear, nose, and throat.

**Thomson, Thomas.** 1773–1852. Scottish chemist; published *System of Chemistry* (1802), the third edition (1807) of which contained first detailed account of John Dalton's atomic theory; at Glasgow U. (1818); founded first chemical laboratory for students in Britain.

**Thomson, Virgil.** 1896– . American composer and music critic, b. Kansas City, Mo. Music critic for N.Y. *Herald Tribune* (1940–54). Composed operas, including *Four Saints in Three Acts* (1928); ballet and chamber music; also music for orchestra and movies, including *Louisiana Story* (1948), etc.

**Thomson, William.** See Baron KELVIN.

**Thor′beck′e** (tôr′bĕk′ĕ), **Jan Rudolf.** 1798–1872. Dutch statesman; leader of liberal group; premier (1849–53, 1862–66, 1871–72).

**Thor′borg′** (tōōr′bôr′y'), **Kerstin.** 1906–1970. Swedish operatic contralto; m. Gustav Bergman; operatic debut in Wagner's *Ring* cycle, at Covent Garden, London (May, 1936), and in Wagner's *Die Walküre,* at Metropolitan Opera House, New York (Dec., 1936).

**Tho′reau** (thôr′ō; thô·rō′), **Henry David.** 1817–1862. American writer, b. Concord, Mass. Grad. Harvard (1837); schoolteacher in Concord (1839–41); lived in home of Ralph Waldo Emerson (1841–43) where he was associated with such transcendentalists as Bronson Alcott, George Ripley, and Margaret Fuller. Retired to a hut beside Walden Pond, at Concord (July 4, 1845–Sept. 6, 1847), where he devoted himself to a study of nature and to writing. After another year in the Emerson household (1847–48), lived in his father's house (1849–62), with occasional excursions to Cape Cod and into Maine. Published during his lifetime only two books, *A Week on the Concord and Merrimack Rivers* (1849) and *Walden, or Life in the Woods* (1854), and a few magazine articles. From his journals, manuscripts, and letters his friends have published *The Writings of Henry David Thoreau* (20 vols., 1906). His life has been written by H. S. Canby (1939). Elected to Am. Hall of Fame (1960).

**Thor'finn Karl'sef'ni** (thôr'fĭn kärl'sĕv'nĭ). Icelandic sailor and explorer of beginning of 11th century; said to have headed an expedition from Greenland which sailed along the coast of what is now New England and attempted to plant a colony in what is now southeastern Massachusetts (1004–05); project abandoned (1006).

**Tho'rild** (tōō'rĭld), **Thomas**. 1759–1808. Swedish journalist and poet; engaged in literary controversies with Kellgren and Leopold; sympathy with principles of French Revolution caused his banishment for four years (1793); published *Passionerna* (in unrhymed dactylic verse, 1781), *Sermon of Sermons* (1789), *True Heavenly Religion Restored* (1790), and *The Freedom of the Public Spirit* (1792).

**Thor'is·mond** *or* **Thor'is·mund** (thŏr'ĭz·mŭnd). d. 453. Son of Theodoric I; king of the Visigoths (451–453); ruled in Provence; joined Romans in defeat of Attila (451); assassinated by his brother Theodoric II.

**Thorn'bur·y** (thôrn'bĕr·ĭ), **George Walter**. 1828–1876. English journalist and man of letters; on staff of *Athenaeum;* a contributor to Dickens's periodicals *Household Words* and *All the Year Round;* author of art criticisms, historical and topographical sketches, several novels, poems, a biography of J. M. W. Turner, and a popular descriptive history of London, *Old and New London* (2 vols., 1872, 1876).

**Thorn'dike** (thôrn'dīk), **Ashley Horace**. 1871–1933. American educator, b. Houlton, Me.; professor of English, Columbia (1906–33); known as an authority on Elizabethan drama. Author of *Tragedy* (1908), *The Facts About Shakespeare* (with William Allan Neilson; 1913), *Shakespeare's Theatre* (1916), *English Comedy* (1929), etc. His brother **Edward Lee** (1874–1949), psychologist; professor, Teachers Coll., Columbia (1904–40). Author of *Animal Intelligence* (1911), *The Psychology of Learning* (1914), *The Measurement of Intelligence* (1926), *Fundamentals of Learning* (1932), etc. Another brother, **Lynn** (1882–1965), historian; taught history at Western Reserve U. (1909–24), professor, Columbia (from 1924); author of *The History of Medieval Europe* (1917), *A History of Magic and Experimental Science* (vol. I to 1327 A.D., 1923; vols. II & III, 14th and 15th centuries, 1934), *A Short History of Civilization* (1926), etc.

**Thorndike,** Dame **Sybil**. 1882– . English actress; m. Lewis Thomas Casson (1908); played Shakespearean leads at Old Vic (1914–18); took over management of New Theatre (1922) and Criterion Theatre (1923), and later Regent Theatre, Empire Theatre, Lyceum Theatre, Princess Theatre; toured Egypt, Palestine, Australia, and New Zealand (1932–33). Created Dame of the British Empire (1931).

**Thorn'hill** (thôrn'hĭl), Sir **James**. 1675–1734. English historical painter; designed series of paintings for interior of dome of St. Paul's; painted portraits of Sir Isaac Newton, Steele, Bentley.

**Thorn'ton** (thôrn't'n; -tŭn), Sir **Edward**. 1817–1906. English diplomat. Son of Sir **Edward Thornton** (1766–1852), diplomat. Envoy at Washington (1867–81), aided in settlement of boundary and fishing disputes between Canada and U.S.; arbitrator of Mexican and U.S. claims (1873–76); ambassador at St. Petersburg (1881–84), at Constantinople (1884); retired (1886).

**Thornton, Henry Worth**. 1871–1933. Railroad executive, b. Logansport, Ind.; in employ of Pennsylvania Railroad (1894–1914); general manager, Great Eastern Railway, England (1914–22); naturalized British subject (1919); president and chairman of the board, Canadian National Railways (1922–32).

**Thornton, James**. 1862–1938. English-born vaudeville actor in U.S.; composer of popular songs, as *When You Were Sweet Sixteen, My Sweetheart's the Man in the Moon,* etc.

**Thornton, John Wingate**. 1818–1878. American author of pamphlets and books on early American history.

**Thornton, Matthew**. 1714?–1803. Physician and patriot in American Revolution, b. in Ireland; to America as a child; practiced medicine in Londonderry, N.H. (from 1740); active in pre-Revolutionary agitation; member of Continental Congress (1776) and a signer of the Declaration of Independence.

**Thornton, Richard Hopwood**. 1845–1925. Lawyer and philologist, b. in Lancashire, Eng. In London mercantile house (1863–71); to Canada (1871) and U.S. (1874; naturalized, 1881). First dean, Oregon Law School, Portland, Ore. (1884–1903). Compiler of *An American Glossary, Being an Attempt to Illustrate Certain Americanisms Upon Historical Principles* (2 vols., 1912).

**Thornton, William**. 1759–1828. American architect, b. in the West Indies; to U.S. (c. 1787) and naturalized in Delaware (1788); settled in Philadelphia. Though not trained as an architect, won competition for design of building for the Library Company of Philadelphia (1789). Associated with John Fitch in his steamboat experiments (1788–90). Won competition for design of National Capitol at Washington, D.C. (1792); design revised by Étienne S. Hallet (*q.v.*). Commissioner of the District of Columbia (1794–1802); supervised construction of Capitol until replaced by Latrobe, who was appointed surveyor of public buildings (1803). Also designed a number of houses in Washington for private individuals.

**Thor'ny·croft** (thôr'nĭ·krŏft), Sir **Hamo**, *in full* **William Hamo**. 1850–1925. English sculptor; won recognition with *Warrior Bearing a Wounded Youth* (1876); known esp. for *The Mower* (1884), *A Sower* (1886), and statues of General Gordon (1888), Oliver Cromwell (1899), and King Alfred (1901). His father, **Thomas Thornycroft** (1815–1885), his mother, **Mary Francis** (1814–1895), and her father, **John Francis** (1780–1861), were all sculptors.

**Thornycroft,** Sir **John Isaac**. 1843–1928. English naval architect; brother of Sir Hamo Thornycroft. Established shipbuilding works at Chiswick (1866); successful in producing high-speed launches and torpedo boats, later torpedo-boat destroyers; constructed first torpedo boat for English navy (1877) and, during World War, developed a coastal torpedo speedboat known as "scooter."

**Thór'odd·sen** (thōr'ŏd·sĕn), **Jón Thórdarson**. 1819–1868. Icelandic novelist and poet; studied law, U. of Copenhagen; district judge in Iceland (from 1850). Regarded as master of Icelandic prose; his *Lad and Lass* (1850) earliest true novel produced in Iceland; other works include *Man and Wife* (novel pub. 1876) and poems, mostly satirical (pub. 1871).

**Thóroddsen, Thorvaldur**. 1855–1921. Icelandic geologist and geographer; educ. U. of Copenhagen; schoolmaster in Iceland (from 1880); made numerous geological explorations (1876–98), esp. into little-known interior to investigate volcanic structure and history of the island. Works (written in Icelandic, Danish, and German) include a history of Icelandic geography (2 vols., 1898) and several volumes on the volcanoes of Iceland.

**Thorpe** (thôrp), **Benjamin.** 1782–1870. English philologist; pioneer in Old English translation, philology, and history; published *Cædman's Metrical Paraphrase of Scriptures* (1832), *Anglo-Saxon Poems of Beowulf* (1855), *The Anglo-Saxon Chronicle* (1861), and *A Collection of English Charters* (1865).

**Thorpe,** Sir **Edward,** *in full* **Thomas Edward.** 1845–1925. English chemist; government chemist (1894–1909); author of *Chemical Problems* (1870), *Qualitative Analysis* (1873), *Inorganic Chemistry* (2 vols., 1874), *Quantitative Analysis* (1874), *A Dictionary of Applied Chemistry* (7 vols.), *A History of Chemistry* (2 vols.), etc.

**Thorpe, James Francis.** *Known as* **Jim Thorpe.** 1888–1953. American athlete, b. Prague, Okla. Won decathlon and pentathlon in Olympic Games (1912; later disqualified for previous loss of amateur status); also played baseball and football.

**Thorpe, Rose Hartwick.** 1850–1939. American writer; m. E. Carson Thorpe (1871; d. 1916); author of fiction and verse. Her most famous poem is *Curfew Must Not Ring Tonight.*

**Thor'vald'sen** *or* **Thor'wald'sen** (to͝or'väl's'n), **Bertel.** 1768–1844. Danish sculptor. Designed the colossal statue of a lion at Lucerne; statues of various figures of classical mythology, including Jason, Ganymede, Venus, Psyche, and the Graces; bas-reliefs *Triumphal Entry of Alexander into Babylon* and *Night and Morning:* and *Christ and the Twelve Apostles.* Regarded as a leader in the classical revival.

**Thothmes.** Variant of THUTMOSE.

**Thou** (to͞o). Distinguished French family, including: **Christophe de** (1508–1582), magistrate, president of the Parliament of Paris at the time of the Massacre of Saint Bartholomew (1572). His brother **Nicolas de** (1528–1598), bishop of Chartres, selected to instruct Henry IV in the Roman Catholic faith. Christophe's son **Jacques Auguste de** (1553–1617), lawyer, magistrate, and historian, councilor of state (1588), one of those who drafted the Edict of Nantes (1598), one of the chief successors to Sully in the councils of the regent Marie de Medicis, and author of *Historia sui Temporis* (1604–08).

**Thrale,** Mrs. See Hester Lynch PIOZZI.

**Thras'y·bu'lus** (thrăs'ĭ·bū'lŭs). Athenian general and statesman. Quelled an oligarchic insurrection in Samos (411 B.C.); aided Alcibiades in victories over Spartans at sea, at Cynossema (411), and Cyzicus (410). Exiled from Athens by the Thirty Tyrants (404); instrumental in effecting a return of democratic government in Athens (403). Induced Athens to join Theban League against Sparta (395); commanded fleet against Spartans (389).

**Throck·mor'ton** (thrŏk·môr't'n; thrŏk'môr't'n) *or* **Throg·mor'ton** (thrŏg·môr'-; thrŏg'môr'-), Sir **Nicholas.** 1515–1571. English diplomat; M.P. (1545–67); fought at battle of Pinkie (1547) and siege of Boulogne (1549–50); managed to secure favor of Mary Tudor despite signing document giving crown to Lady Jane Grey (1553); acquitted of complicity in Wyatt's rebellion (1554). Rose rapidly under Queen Elizabeth; ambassador to France (1560). Became personal friend of Mary, Queen of Scots, and supporter of her claim to be Elizabeth's successor; repeatedly ambassador to Scotland (1561–67) on futile missions; imprisoned (1569) on suspicion of participating in duke of Norfolk's conspiracy in favor of Mary, Queen of Scots. His daughter **Elizabeth** married Sir Walter Raleigh (*q.v.*). His nephew **Francis Throckmorton** *or* **Throgmorton** (1554–1584) was always a zealous Roman Catholic and engaged in plots against English government; agent of conspiracy between agents of Mary, Queen of Scots, and Spanish ambassador.

**Thu·cyd'i·des** (thū·sĭd'ĭ·dēz). 471?–?400 B.C. Greek historian, b. Athens; during Peloponnesian War, commanded expedition sent (424 B.C.) to aid Amphipolis, but failed to prevent capture of city by Brasidas; thereupon, went into exile (423–403), during which he wrote *History of the Peloponnesian War* (an account which carries war down to 411). Regarded as first critical historian; ranked as greatest historian of antiquity.

**Thucydides.** fl. 5th cent. B.C. Athenian statesman; after death of Cimon (449 B.C.) became leader of aristocratic party in opposition to Pericles; ostracized (441).

**Thu'gut** (to͞o'go͞ot), Baron **Franz de Pau'la** (dȧ pou'lä) **von.** 1736–1818. Austrian minister of foreign affairs (1793–1800).

**Thuil'le** (tvĭl'ĕ), **Ludwig.** 1861–1907. German composer of operas *Theuerdank* (1897), *Lobetanz* (1898), etc.

**Thul'den** (tûl'dĕn), **Theodor van.** 1606–1676. Dutch painter; studied under Rubens.

**Thul'strup** (?tŭl'strŭp), **Thure,** *in full* **Bror Thure.** 1848–1930. Artist, b. Stockholm, Sweden; to U.S. (c. 1878); self-taught as an illustrator and painter; freelance contributor to *Frank Leslie's Illustrated Weekly Newspaper* and *Harper's Weekly* (in the 1880's); excelled in historical and battle pictures.

**Thumb,** General **Tom.** See Charles Sherwood STRATTON.

**Thun'berg'** (to͞on'băr'y'), **Carl Peter.** 1743–1828. Swedish botanist; studied under Linnaeus at Uppsala; professor, U. of Uppsala (1781), succeeding Linnaeus; author esp. of works on the flora of the Cape of Good Hope and of Japan.

**Thur'ber** (thûr'bẽr), **Charles.** 1803–1886. American inventor, b. East Brookfield, Mass. In partnership with brother-in-law Ethan Allen, firm of Allen & Thurber, manufacturing firearms in Worcester, Mass. (1836–56). Patented a hand printing machine (1843) which bears a resemblance to a modern typewriter, and which contains a device for letter spacing by means of a cylinder moving longitudinally.

**Thurber, George.** 1821–1890. American botanist; botanist and commissary on the U.S.-Mexico boundary survey (1850); editor, *American Agriculturist* (1863–85); specialized in study of American grasses.

**Thurber, James Grover.** 1894–1961. American artist and writer, b. Columbus, Ohio; managing editor of the *New Yorker,* to which he contributed humorous drawings and essays. Author of *Is Sex Necessary?* (with E. B. White; 1929), *The Owl in the Attic* (1931), *The Seal in the Bedroom* (1932), *My Life and Hard Times* (1934), *The Middle-aged Man on the Flying Trapeze* (1935), *Let Your Mind Alone* (1937), *The Last Flower* (1939), and the play *The Male Animal* (with Elliott Nugent, 1940).

**Thu'reau'-Dan'gin'** (tü'rō'dän'zhăn'), **Paul.** 1837–1913. French journalist and historian; author of *Histoire de la Monarchie de Juillet* (1884–92), *Histoire de la Renaissance Catholique en Angleterre* (1899 ff.), etc. His son **François** (1872–1944), an Assyriologist on the staff of the Louvre museum (from 1895).

**Thu'ret'** (tü'rĕ'), **Gustave Adolphe.** 1817–1875. French botanist; authority on marine algae; with Édouard Bornet, made discoveries relating to sexual reproduction in seaweed, esp. the Fucaceae and Floridae.

**Thur'loe** (thûr'lō), **John.** 1616–1668. English secretary of state under the Commonwealth; M.P. (1654); member of Cromwell's second council (1657); efficient in direction of intelligence and postal department; kept Cromwell informed of plans of foreign powers; favored Cromwell's acceptance of crown; supported government of Richard Cromwell. At Restoration, liberated from charge of high treason on condition of counseling secretaries of state. His correspondence (7 vols., 1742) provides chief source of information of the Protectorate.

**Thur'low** (thûr'lō), **Edward.** 1st Baron **Thurlow.** 1731–1806. English judge; barrister (1754); M.P. (1765); made greatest speech of his life in Douglas v. Hamilton peerage case (1769). Solicitor general (1770); attorney general (1771); overthrew Lord Mansfield's doctrine of perpetual copyright in case before House of Lords (1774); favored coercion of American colonies. Lord chancellor (1778–83); autocratic in House of Lords; worked in opposition to Burke's proposals of reform and against Rockingham government; presided at trial of Warren Hastings (1788); dismissed (1792) on insistence of Pitt. Defender of royal prerogatives and interests of slave traders; patron of Dr. Johnson and Crabbe.

**Thur'man** (thûr'măn), **Allen Granberry.** 1813–1895. American politician, b. Lynchburg, Va.; practiced law in Chillicothe, Ohio; member, U.S. House of Representatives (1845–47); U.S. senator (1869–81); was candidate for Democratic presidential nomination in conventions of 1876, 1880, 1884, and for vice-president of the United States (1888).

**Thurmayr, Johannes.** See Johannes AVENTINUS.

**Thurn** (to͝orn), Count **Heinrich Matthias von.** 1567–1640. Bohemian Protestant leader; gave signal for Protestant uprising by defenestration of imperial legates at Prague (May 23, 1618), and took command of rebel troops; invaded Austria and besieged Vienna (1619); later, joined Swedish army under Gustavus Adolphus and fought at Leipzig (1631) and Lützen (1632); surrendered to Wallenstein (1633).

**Thur'ney'sen** (to͝or'nī'zĕn), **Rudolf.** 1857–1940. German philologist and Celtic scholar; published *Handbuch des Altirischen* (1909), *Die Irische Helden- und Königssage bis zum 17. Jahrhundert* (1921), *Irisches Recht* (1931), etc.

**Thurn'wald** (to͝orn'vält), **Richard.** 1869–1954. German sociologist; made research expeditions to the Solomon Islands, New Guinea, and East Africa; author of *Ethnopsychologische Studien an Südsee-Völkern* (1913), *Primitive Psychologie* (1922), *Lehrbuch für Völkerkunde* (1939), etc.

**Thurs'by** (thûrz'bĭ), **Emma Cecilia.** 1845–1931. American soprano singer and vocal teacher, b. Brooklyn, N.Y.; toured U.S. and Europe with marked success; principal soloist with Theodore Thomas and his orchestra (1884); devoted herself chiefly to teaching (from 1898). Regarded as greatest interpreter of Mozart of her time.

**Thurs'field** (thûrs'fēld; thûrz'-), Sir **James Richard.** 1840–1923. English journalist and naval expert; author of *Peel, The Navy and the Nation* (with Sir George S. Clarke, later Lord Sydenham), *Nelson and other Naval Studies, Naval Warfare.*

**Thurs'tan** (thûrs'tăn) *or* **Turs'tin** (tûrs'tĭn). d. 1140. English prelate, native of Bayeux; clerk of William Rufus; secretary of Henry I; archbishop of York (1114), but was refused consecration by Archbishop Ralph de Turbine of Canterbury unless he professed obedience; crowned by Pope Calixtus at Reims (1119); carried on negotiations between King Henry and France and became reconciled with Henry (1120). Refused to acknowledge new archbishop of Canterbury, William of Corbeil, as primate (1123), and continued controversy; took active part in gathering army that defeated Scots at battle of the Standard (1138); entered order of Cluniacs (1140); founder of large number of monasteries in north of England.

**Thurs'ton** (thûrs'tŭn), **Ernest Temple.** 1879–1933. English novelist and playwright; author of novels of poetic quality, including *Traffic* (1906), *The City of Beautiful Nonsense* (1909), *The Passionate Crime* (1915), *Charmeuse* (1924), *Mr. Bottleby Does Something* (1925), *Man in a Black Hat* (1930), *A Hank of Hair* (1932); plays, including *The Greatest Wish* (1912), *Driven* (1914), *The Wandering Jew* (1920), *The Blue Peter* (1924), *Charmeuse* (1930); and volumes of poems. His first wife (m. 1901, divorced 1910), **Katherine Cecil,** *nee* **Mad'den** [măd''n] (1875–1911), novelist, was author of *John Chilcote, M.P.* (1904), dramatized by her husband as *The Masquerader* (1905).

**Thurston, Howard.** 1869–1936. American magician, b. Columbus, Ohio; made tour of the world (1904–07); starred with Harry Kellar (1907–08); author of *My Life of Magic* (1929).

**Thurston, Lorrin Andrews.** 1858–1931. Hawaiian lawyer and politician, b. Honolulu; one of leaders in successful revolutionary movement (1887); minister of the interior in new constitutional government (1887–90); again, leader in revolution of 1893, in which Queen Lilinokalani was dethroned; Hawaiian envoy to U.S. (1893–94); aided in framing constitution of Republic of Hawaii (1894); headed commission that negotiated treaty of annexation to U.S. (1897).

**Thurston, Robert Lawton.** 1800–1874. American steam-engine manufacturer. His son **Robert Henry** (1839–1903) was a mechanical engineer and educator; naval engineer in Union navy through Civil War; professor of mechanical engineering, Stevens Tech. (1871–85); director of Sibley College, Cornell U. (1885–1903); author of many books and articles on mechanical engineering.

**Thut·mo'se** (tho͞ot·mō'sĕ) *or* **Thoth'mes** (thōth'mēs). Name of four kings of XVIIIth (Diospolite) dynasty of Egypt:

**Thutmose I.** Reigned (c. 1540–1501, 1496–1493 B.C.). Of unknown, but not royal, birth; proclaimed successor to Amenhotep I; conquered Nubia; led successful expedition into Asia as far as the Euphrates; spent much of reign in building operations; built two pylons and hypostyle halls at Karnak and erected two obelisks; restored temple of Osiris at Abydos; had record of his deeds preserved in an inscription on rocks near third cataract of Nile; period of confusion at end of reign; probably deposed by Thutmose III (c. 1501), but regained throne temporarily (c. 1496–1493).

**Thutmose II.** Son of Thutmose I, reigned jointly (c. 1496 to 1493 B.C.) with father after deposition of Thutmose III and Hatshepsut (c. 1496); a weak ruler.

**Thutmose III.** Son of Thutmose I and a concubine, Isis; father of Amenhotep II. Reigned jointly (c. 1501–1496, 1493–1481 B.C.) with wife and half sister, Queen Hatshepsut (*q.v.*); ruled alone (c. 1481–1447 B.C.). One of greatest of Egyptian kings; began rule by deposing father, but with his queen was temporarily set aside by revolution of Thutmose I and II (see above); regained control, but his influence secondary to that of queen until her death (1481). Invaded Syria with great army; won battle of Megiddo (1479); came into conflict with powerful state of Mitanni; ravaged its territory, capturing several cities including Carchemish on the Euphrates; made seventeen campaigns into Asia, using booty and tribute to adorn Egyptian temples; devoted much time to building; enlarged great temple of Amen at Karnak and had his annals inscribed on its walls; built or restored many temples in Egyptian cities (Heliopolis,

Memphis, Abydos, etc.) and in Nubia; erected many obelisks (including two known as Cleopatra's Needles, one now in New York, the other in London).

**Thutmose IV.** King (c. 1420–1411 B.C.). Grandson of Thutmose III. Son of Amenhotep II and father of Amenhotep III; m. a Mitannian princess; contracted friendly alliances with Babylonia and the Mitanni; led military expeditions into Phoenicia and Nubia; finished last obelisk of Thutmose III in his honor (it now stands before the Lateran in Rome).

**Thwaites** (thwāts), **Reuben Gold.** 1853–1913. American historian, b. Dorchester, Mass.; secretary, State Historical Society of Wisconsin (1887–1913); collected and translated, with assistants, Jesuit material dealing with Wisconsin history, *Jesuit Relations and Allied Documents* (73 vols., 1896–1901). Edited *Original Journals of the Lewis and Clark Expedition* (8 vols., 1904–05), Hennepin's *New Discovery* (1903), *Early Western Travels* (32 vols., 1904–07), etc.; author of *Father Marquette* (1902), *Daniel Boone* (1902), *France in America* (1905), etc.

**Thwing** (twĭng), **Charles Franklin.** 1853–1937. American educator, b. New Sharon, Me.; ordained in Congregational ministry (1879); president, Western Reserve U. and Adelbert Coll. (1890–1921); also, secretary, Carnegie Foundation for the Advancement of Teaching (1905–21); author of *American Colleges...*(1878), *College Administration* (1900), *Letters from a Father to His Son Entering College* (1912), *The College President* (1925), *The American College and University—A Human Fellowship* (1935), etc.

**Thyard, Pontus de.** See THIARD.

**Thynne** (thĭn), **Thomas.** 3d Viscount **Wey′mouth** (wā′mŭth). 1st Marquis of **Bath** (bȧth). 1734–1796. English secretary of state (1768–70, 1775–79); gained favor of George III by vigor in repressing Wilkes riots; resigned (1770) on imminence of war with Spain over claims to Falkland Islands; weak in conduct of war against France and American colonies; accused of cherishing policy of peace at any price; showed unreliability and personal ambition; not invited to join Pitt's cabinet (1783).

**Thynne, William.** *Alternative family surname* **Bote′ville** (bŏt′vĭl). d. 1546. English student of Chaucer and first editor of Chaucer's works (1532); father of **Francis** (1545?–1608), who with others revised and continued Holinshed's *Chronicle*, criticized Speght's 1st edition of Chaucer and assisted him with his 2d edition (1602).

**Thys′sen** (tĭs′ĕn), **Fritz.** 1873–1951. German industrialist; inherited control of great iron- and steel-manufacturing plants (Thyssen Combine) upon death of his father, **August Thyssen** (1842–1926), and upon organization of gigantic Vereinigte Stahlwerke (United Steel Works) became chairman of board of directors (1926). Joined Nazis in 1923 and aided in Hitler's rise to power; after Hitler's accession to the chancellorship (1933), Thyssen became economic dictator of the Ruhr industrial region; disagreements with Hitler's policies (beginning 1936) caused his flight to Switzerland (Sept., 1939); the German government confiscated all his property (Dec., 1939). Author of *I Paid Hitler* (1941).

**Ti·bal′di** (tē·bäl′dē), **Pellegrino.** *In full* **Pellegrino Tibaldi,** *or* **di Ti·bal′do** (dē tē·bäl′dō), **de′ Pel′le·gri′ni** (dā pāl′lā·grē′nē). *Also called* **Pellegrino da Bo·lo′gna** (dä bō·lō′nyä). 1527–1596. Italian painter and architect; municipal architect, Milan (1561); head architect, Milan cathedral (1567); to Spain (1586) in service of Philip II. Works include frescoes in Palazzo Poggi and Church of San Giacomo Maggiore at Bologna and in the Escorial at Madrid; easel pictures, as *Adoration of the Shepherds* (in Borghese Gallery, Rome), *St. Jerome* (in Dresden Gallery); and architectural works, as churches of San Fedele and San Sebastiano at Milan and San Gaudenzio at Novara. His brother **Domenico** (1541–1582) was painter, engraver, and architect.

**Tib′bett** (tĭb′ĕt; -ĭt), **Lawrence Mervil.** 1896–1960. American operatic baritone, b. Bakersfield, Calif.; debut on concert stage (1917); in opera, at Metropolitan Opera House, New York City (Nov., 1923); has also sung over the radio and in motion pictures.

**Ti·be′ri·us** (tī·bēr′ĭ·ŭs). *In full* **Tiberius Claudius Ne′ro Cae′sar** (nē′rō [nēr′ō] sē′zēr). 42 B.C.–37 A.D. Second emperor of Rome (14–37 A.D.). Son of Tiberius Claudius Nero and Livia Drusilla; adopted by Emperor Augustus when the latter married his mother (38 B.C.); carefully educated. Commanded expedition to Armenia (20 B.C.) and with brother Nero Claudius Drusus against the Rhaetians (15 B.C.); consul (13 B.C.); on death of Drusus recalled to Germany (9 B.C.); again consul (7 B.C.); tribune (6 B.C.); forced by Augustus to divorce his wife Vipsania Agrippina (11 B.C.) and to marry Julia, daughter of Augustus; retired to Rhodes for seven years (6 B.C.–2 A.D.); made his heir by Augustus (4 A.D.); led Roman armies in many campaigns in Germany, Dalmatia, and Pannonia (4–14 A.D.). Became emperor (14 A.D.); at first wise and beneficent; later, esp. under influence of Lucius Aelius Sejanus, vicious, cruel, and tyrannical; prob. caused death of his nephew Germanicus Caesar (19 A.D.), and of his only son, Drusus Caesar (23 A.D.); freedom abolished in Rome; went to Campania (26 A.D.); had Sejanus killed (31 A.D.); spent rest of his life (27–37 A.D.) at Capri.

**Tiberius.** Name of two rulers of Eastern Roman Empire (see also TIBERIUS, Roman emperor before division): **Tiberius II Con′stan·ti′nus** [kŏn′stăn·tī′nŭs] (d. 582); court officer, adopted by Justin II (574) and in control jointly with Sophia (574–578); emperor (578–582); reign troubled by conflicts with Persians and Avars. **Tiberius III Ap′si·mar** [ăp′sĭ·mär] (d. 705); commander of the fleet; overthrew Leontius (698); emperor (698–705); gained military successes over Saracens; seized when Justinian II was restored; beheaded.

**Tiberius Claudius Drusus Nero Germanicus.** See CLAUDIUS I.

**Tiberius Claudius Nero.** See Tiberius Claudius NERO.

**Ti·bul′lus** (tĭ·bŭl′ŭs), **Albius.** 54?–?18 B.C. Roman elegiac poet; enjoyed patronage of Messala (Marcus Valerius Messala Corvinus) and may have accompanied him (c. 30 B.C.) on his campaign to put down an insurrection in Aquitania. Little of his life history known; two books of his verse are extant.

**Tich′borne Claimant** (tĭch′bôrn; -bērn). See Arthur ORTON, impersonator of **Roger Charles Tichborne** (1829–1854), presumptive heir to estates of Tichborne family of Hampshire, who was lost at sea.

**Tick′ell** (tĭk′ĕl), **Thomas.** 1686–1740. English poet; contributed verses to *Guardian* and *Spectator;* accompanied Joseph Addison to Ireland when latter was secretary to lord lieutenant (1714); published translation of first book of *Iliad* (1715), which because of Addison's praise Pope assumed to be Addison's, designed to eclipse his own version, thus occasioning the quarrel between Addison and Pope; undersecretary to Addison, secretary of state (1717); secretary to lords justices of Ireland (from 1724). Collected and edited Addison's works (1721); author of *Kensington Gardens* (1722), the ballad *Colin and Lucy* (1725), and *Elegy on Addison*, an ode.

**Tick′nor** (tĭk′nẽr; -nôr), **Elisha.** 1757–1821. American educator and businessman, b. Lebanon, Conn.; schoolteacher in Boston (1785–95); an organizer of Massachusetts Mutual Fire Insurance Co. (1798); a founder of Provident Institution for Savings, Boston, one of first savings banks in U.S. (1816). His son **George** (1791–1871), b. Boston, was an educator and historian; professor of French and Spanish and belles-lettres, Harvard (1819–35); a founder of Boston Public Library (1852); notable among his works are *History of Spanish Literature* (1849), *Life of William Hickling Prescott* (1864).

**Ticknor, William Davis.** 1810–1864. American publisher, b. Lebanon, N.H. Established bookstore and publishing house in Boston, Mass. (1832), which later, under firm name of Ticknor & Fields, became one of chief publishing houses in the U.S. Published the *Atlantic Monthly* and works by Hawthorne, Thoreau, Emerson, Longfellow, Holmes, Whittier, and Lowell, and by the English authors Browning, Tennyson, De Quincey, and Leigh Hunt, being among the first American publishers to make payments for rights to publish editions of works by English or other foreign authors. See also James T. FIELDS.

**Tieck** (tēk), **Ludwig.** 1773–1853. German writer; settled in Dresden (1819) and became literary adviser to court theater there (1825); invited to Berlin (1841) by Frederick William IV of Prussia, and granted a pension for rest of his life; among his many works are the novels *Abdallah* (1796), *William Lovell* (3 vols., 1795–96), *Dichterleben* (1826), *Der Tod des Dichters* (1834), *Der Junge Tischlermeister* (1836), *Vittoria Accorombona* (1840); several volumes of short stories; the comedies *Blaubart* (*Bluebeard*), *Der Gestiefelte Kater* (*Puss in Boots*), *Prinz Zerbino;* the dramas *Leben und Tod der Heiligen Genoveva* and *Fortunat;* volumes of dramatic and literary criticism; a translation of *Don Quixote;* and many lyric poems. His brother **Christian Friedrich** (1776–1851) was a sculptor; lived in Weimar in association with Goethe and his circle (1801); modeled a number of portrait busts, including Goethe, Schelling, Humboldt, Prince Ludwig of Bavaria.

**Tie'de·mann** (tē'dĕ·män), **Dietrich.** 1748–1803. German philosopher; among his notable works are *Untersuchungen über den Menschen* (3 parts, 1777–98) and *Geist der Spekulativen Philosophie* (6 vols., 1790–97). His son **Friedrich** (1781–1861) was an anatomist and physiologist.

**Tied'ge** (tēt'gĕ), **Christoph August.** 1752–1841. German poet; author of the didactic poem *Urania* (1801), the songs *An Alexis send ich dich* and *Schöne Minka, ich muss scheiden,* etc.

**Tief'fen·bruck'er** (tē'fĕn·brŏŏk'ẽr), **Kaspar.** 1514?–?1570. Bavarian-born lute maker and violinmaker; naturalized French citizen (1559); reputed one of earliest known makers of violins.

**Tie'le** (tē'lĕ), **Cornelius Petrus.** 1830–1902. Dutch theologian; author of a compendium of religious history.

**Tie'mann** (tē'män), **Ferdinand.** 1848–1899. German organic chemist; investigated terpenes and camphors; produced vanillin artificially; discovered ionone.

**T'ien-wang.** See HUNG HSIU-CH'ÜAN.

**Tie'po·lo** (tyâ'pô·lō), **Giovanni Battista.** 1696–1770. Italian painter; master of Venetian school; employed at Venice, Würzburg (1750–53), and in Spain (1763–70); director, Venetian Acad. (1754). Among his works are frescoes in Villa Valmerana at Vicenza, Church of Santa Maria del Rosario at Venice, royal palace at Würzburg, and royal palace at Madrid; easel pictures, as *Adoration of the Kings* (in Munich Pinakotek); and etchings, as *Scherzi di Fantasia.* His son and pupil **Giovanni Domenico** (1727–1804) was also a painter; works include esp. decorations in royal palace at Würzburg.

**Tier'ney** (tẽr'nĭ), **George.** 1761–1830. English political leader; M.P. (1788), leading opponent of Pitt's policy; accused by Pitt of obstruction, fought bloodless duel with Pitt; treasurer of navy in Addington's ministry (1802); president of board of control (1806); leader of Whigs in opposition (1817–21); master of mint in Canning's ministry (1827–28).

**Tiet'jens** (tē'jĕns), **Eunice,** *nee* **Ham'mond** (hăm'ŭnd). 1884–1944. American author, b. Chicago; m. 1st, Paul Tietjens (1904; divorced 1914); 2d, Cloyd Head (1920); on editorial staff of magazine *Poetry,* Chicago (from 1913); lecturer on poetry, U. of Miami (1933–35); author of a play (*Arabesque,* with Cloyd Head, 1925), a few novels and juveniles, books of verse, including *Profiles from China* (1917), *Body and Raiment* (1919), *Profiles from Home* (1925), *Leaves in Windy Weather* (1929), and the autobiographical *The World at My Shoulder* (1938). See Laurens HAMMOND.

**Tiet'ze** (tē'tsĕ), **Hans.** 1880–1954. Austrian art scholar; professor of history of art, Vienna.

**Tif'fa·ny** (tĭf'ȧ·nĭ), **Charles Lewis.** 1812–1902. American jeweler, b. Killingly, Conn.; opened store in New York City (1837); began manufacturing own jewelry (1848); established branch in Paris (1850) and London (1868); adopted firm name, Tiffany & Co. (1853); incorporated (1868). His son **Louis Comfort** (1848–1933) was a painter and stained-glass artist; among his paintings were *The Dock Scene; Study of Quimper, Brittany; Market Day at Nuremberg;* developed original process by which he manufactured peculiarly beautiful opalescent glass; established and endowed Louis Comfort Tiffany Foundation, for art students (1919), deeding to it an estate at Oyster Bay, Long Island, N.Y., and his collection of paintings, glassware, and objets d'art.

**Tig'el·li'nus** (tĭj'ĕ·lī'nŭs), **Ofonius.** Roman politician; a favorite of Nero, who made him prefect of praetorian guard (62 A.D.); accompanied Nero to Greece (67); later deserted Nero and carried praetorian guard with him; committed suicide (69) when he learned, shortly after accession of Otho, that Otho had decided to execute him.

**Ti'gert** (tī'gẽrt), **John James.** 1856–1906. American Methodist Episcopal clergyman; elected bishop (1906); author of *A Constitutional History of American Episcopal Methodism* (1894). His son **John James** (1882–1965), an educator; first Rhodes scholar from Tennessee; professor of philosophy and psychology, U. of Kentucky (1911–21); U.S. Commissioner of Education (1921–28); president of U. of Florida (1928–47).

**Tighe** (tī), **Mary,** *nee* **Blach'ford** (blăsh'fẽrd). 1772–1810. Irish poet; m. (1793) her cousin Henry Tighe; admired for her beauty and for her poem *Psyche* (1805), in Spenserian stanzas, which attracted Moore and Keats.

**Tig'lath-pi·le'ser** (tĭg'lăth·pī·lē'zẽr; -pĭ·lē'zẽr). Name of three kings of Assyria.

**Tiglath-pileser I.** Reigned (c. 1115–1102, or according to some c. 1116–1093 B.C.). Extended Assyrian dominions, esp. to northwest in regions of old Hittite empire on upper Euphrates; led campaign to seacoast of Mediterranean; defeated king of Babylonia, Marduk-nadin-akhē; renowned as mighty hunter.

**Tiglath-pileser II.** Reigned (c. 956–934 B.C.).

**Tiglath-pileser III.** *In Bible* (*1 Chron.* v. 26) **Til'gath-pil·ne'ser** (tĭl'găth·pĭl·nē'zẽr). *Also known as* **Pul** (pŭl). Reigned (745–727 B.C.). Gained throne as result of revolt in Calah; made headquarters in northern Syria (742–740); subjugated Israel and Samaria; led campaigns in far east and in north; again in west (734), joined in alliance with Ahaz of Judah; defeated Philistines; captured many cities, including Gaza and Damascus (733–732); crushed revolt in Babylon (729) and made himself king in name as well as fact (see NABONASSAR).

**Ti·gra'nes** (tĭ·grā'nēz). Name of several kings of Armenia, of whom the most notable was **Tigranes the Great** (140?–55 B.C.); reigned (95 or 94–55 B.C.); extended territories by conquest of northern Mesopotamia, Syria, Cappadocia; founded new royal city, Tigranocerta (Siirt); attacked and defeated by Romans under Lucullus (69 and 68); surrendered to Pompey (66) and ruled thereafter as vassal of Rome.

**Tikamthi.** See TECUMSEH.

**Ti'khon** (tyē'κôn). *Real name* **Vasili Ivanovich Be·lya'vin** (byĕ·lyȧ'vyĭn). 1865?–1925. Patriarch of Moscow and head of Russian Orthodox Church. Elected patriarch during Russian Revolution (1917); took determined stand against Bolsheviks; issued pastoral letter (1919) denouncing Bolshevik cruelty, suppression of liberty and faith, and blasphemy and sacrilege. Arrested and held in prison; released (June, 1923), perhaps under influence of protests from the pope, archbishop of Canterbury, and church leaders all over world. Retired to monastery.

**Til'den** (tĭl'dĕn), **Samuel Jones.** 1814–1886. American politician, b. New Lebanon, N.Y.; practiced law in New York City. Leader of Democratic faction nicknamed the "Barnburners" (1845); identified with Free-Soil movement (from 1848); leader in attack on and destruction of Tweed Ring (1868–72). Governor of New York (1875–76). Democratic candidate for president of the United States (1876); received about 250,000 more votes than the Republican candidate, Rutherford B. Hayes, and 184 uncontested electoral votes against 163 for Hayes, with returns from Oregon, Louisiana, South Carolina, and Florida (carrying 22 electoral votes altogether) missing and not counted; an electoral commission was created by Congress (Jan. 29, 1877) to examine and report upon the contested returns in these states; the commission reported all the states in favor of Hayes, electing him president by one electoral vote. Tilden accepted the result to avoid civil war, but always maintained that he was wrongfully deprived of the election. Bequeathed his fortune to a Tilden Trust, to be used for establishing a free public library in New York City.

**Tilden,** Sir **William Augustus.** 1842–1926. English chemist; known for researches in organic chemistry on organic bases, alkaloids, terpenes, etc., and in physical chemistry on specific heats of elements.

**Tilden, William Tatem, Jr.** 1893–1953. American tennis player, b. Philadelphia; A.B., Pennsylvania (1922); tennis champion of the world (1920–25); member of U.S. Davis Cup team (1920 ff.); became professional tennis player (1931); led troupe of players on exhibition tour in U.S.; author of books on lawn tennis.

**Tilgath-pilneser.** See TIGLATH-PILESER III.

**Tilgh'man** (tĭl'măn), **Benjamin Chew.** 1821–1901. American inventor; perfected the production of steel shot chilled to hardness, used for sawing, polishing and grinding stone; invented sulphite process for producing wood pulp for papermaking (1867); also invented the sandblast (c. 1871). Cf. Hugh BURGESS.

**Tilghman, Matthew.** 1718–1790. American Revolutionary leader, b. in Queen Anne County, Md.; chairman, Committee of Correspondence for Talbot County; president of Council of Safety; head of Maryland delegations to Continental Congress (1774–76).

**Tilghman, Tench.** 1744–1786. American Revolutionary officer, b. in Talbot County, Md.; grad. Pennsylvania (1761); aide-de-camp and military secretary to General Washington (1776–83).

**Tilghman, William Matthew.** 1854–1924. American frontiersman, b. Fort Dodge, Iowa; scout, buffalo hunter, deputy sheriff, U.S. marshal; at opening of Oklahoma (1889), secured location at Guthrie; deputy U.S. marshal (1891–1910); marshal, Cromwell, Okla. (1924); assassinated (Nov. 1, 1924).

**Tilg'ner** (tĭlg'nẽr), **Victor.** 1844–1896. Austrian sculptor; designed many monuments and statues for public buildings and parks, as for the Volksgarten and Tiergarten near Vienna; also, carved portrait busts.

**Til'le·mont'** (tē'y'·môɴ'), **Sébastien Le Nain de** (lẽ năɴ' dẽ). 1637–1698. French historian; took orders (1676). His most notable works are *Histoire des Empereurs et des Autres Princes qui ont Régné pendant les Six Premiers Siècles de l'Église* (1690–1738) and *Mémoires pour Servir à l'Histoire Ecclésiastique des Six Premiers Siècles* (1693–1712).

**Til'lett** (tĭl'ĕt; -ĭt), **Benjamin.** 1860–1943. English labor leader; secretary of Dock, Wharf, Riverside, and General Workers' Union from its beginning (1887) to its amalgamation (1922) with Transport and General Workers' Union; a leader of 1889 dock strike; Laborite M.P. (1917–24, 1929–31).

**Til'ley** (tĭl'ĭ), Sir **Samuel Leonard.** 1818–1896. Canadian politician, b. in New Brunswick; merchant; premier of New Brunswick (1860–65); powerful influence in cause of confederation; carried cause for union of maritime provinces (1866); member of Dominion House of Commons and of Macdonald ministries (1868–73, 1878–85); lieutenant governor of New Brunswick (1873–78, 1885–93); formulator of national policy of protective tariff.

**Til'lich** (tĭl'ĭκ), **Paul.** 1886–1965. German Protestant theologian and philosopher.

**Til'lier'** (tē'lyā'), **Claude.** 1801–1844. French journalist and novelist; best known for his novel *Mon Oncle Benjamin* (1841).

**Till'man** (tĭl'măn), **Benjamin Ryan.** 1847–1918. American politician, b. in Edgefield County, S.C.; governor of South Carolina (1890–94); U.S. senator (1895–1918); opponent of Grover Cleveland and Theodore Roosevelt.

**Till'man** (tĭl'män), **Fritz.** 1874–1953. German Roman Catholic theologian.

**Til'lo** (tyĕl'lô), **Aleksei Andreevich.** 1839–1900. Russian scientist; general in Russian army; known esp. for work in geodesy, meteorology, terrestrial magnetism, and hypsometry, and for his atlases of isobars of Russia and Asia.

**Til'lot·son** (tĭl'ŭt·s'n), **John.** 1630–1694. English prelate, primate, and preacher; auditor on Presbyterian side at Savoy conference (1661); submitted to Act of Uniformity (1662); preacher at Lincoln's Inn (1664); attempted to wean hearers away from Puritanism; preached against atheism and against Roman Catholicism; chaplain to Charles II. Dean of Canterbury (1670); canon of St. Paul's, London (1675), dean (1689); reluctantly accepted appointment as archbishop of Canterbury (1691), after deposition of nonjuror Sancroft. Pursued relentlessly by nonjurors; defended himself, in four lectures on Socinian controversy, against charge of unorthodoxy (1679–80).

**Til'ly** (tĭl'ē), Count of. **Johan Tser·claes'** (tsẽr·klȧs'). 1559–1632. Flemish field marshal; appointed (1610) by Maximilian, Duke of Bavaria, to reorganize his armies. On outbreak of Thirty Years' War (1618) made commander in chief of field forces of Catholic League; won battle of White Mountain (1620). Successfully conducted campaign in the Palatinate (1621–23). Made count of the empire. Defeated Christian IV of Denmark and Norway at Lutter am Barenberge (1626); replaced Wallenstein in command of Imperial forces (1630); took Magdeburg by storm (1631) but could not restrain his army from terrible atrocities; completely defeated by Gustavus II at Breitenfeld (1631) and at the Lech (1632) where he was mortally wounded.

**Til'ney** (tĭl'nĭ), **Frederick.** 1875–1938. American neurologist, b. Brooklyn, N.Y.; practiced in New York City (from 1905); author of *The Brain from Ape to Man* (2 vols., 1928), and technical works on the nervous system.

**Tilpin.** See TURPIN.

**Til'ton** (tĭl't'n; -tŭn), **Alice.** Pseudonym of Phoebe Atwood TAYLOR.

**Tilton, James.** 1745–1822. American physician; regimental surgeon of a Delaware regiment (1776–77); in charge of hospitals (1777–80); senior hospital physician and surgeon (1780–83). Member of Continental Congress (1783–85). Physician and surgeon general of the U.S. army (1813–15); issued *Regulations for the Medical Department* (Dec., 1814), defining clearly for the first time duties of medical officers and the sanitary staff.

**Tilton, Theodore.** 1835–1907. American journalist; on editorial staff of the *Independent*, a Congregational journal (1856–71); one of central figures in famous case of Tilton vs. Beecher (1875), in which he sued Henry Ward Beecher, pastor of Plymouth Church, Brooklyn, N.Y., for criminal conversation with his wife, Elizabeth Tilton, and demanded large damages; trial resulted in a disagreement of the jury (1875); lived in Paris (from c. 1883).

**Ti·mae'us** (tī·mē'ŭs). fl. c. 400 B.C. Greek Pythagorean philosopher, of Locri in Italy. His name is attached to one of Plato's dialogues, which embodies a theory of the universe and contains, incidentally, the story of the lost Atlantis.

**Timaeus.** 345?–?250 B.C. Greek historian, of Tauromenium (Taormina) in Sicily; exiled by Agathocles; lived in Athens for fifty years. His chief work, extant only in fragments, was a history of Italy and Sicily from earliest times to 264 B.C.

**Timaeus.** Sophist, probably of 3d century A.D., who wrote a short Greek lexicon to Plato (still extant, in part) which is valued for its excellent explanations of words and has been edited many times (see D. RUHNKEN).

**Ti·mag'e·nes** (tĭ·măj'ē·nēz; tī-). Greek historian of 1st century B.C., originally from Alexandria; captured and taken as slave to Rome; when freed, opened school of rhetoric in Rome; gained favor of Emperor Augustus. Author of *History of Augustus* and *History of the Diadochi.*

**Ti·man'thes** (tĭ·măn'thēz; tī-). fl. c. 400 B.C. Greek painter, of Sicyon; his chief work, *Sacrifice of Iphigenia*, regarded as one of the great paintings of antiquity.

**Ti·mar'chus** (tĭ·mär'kŭs; tī-). d. after 258 B.C. Tyrant of Miletus, native of Aetolia; seized Samos (c. 260 B.C.); made himself tyrant; overthrown by Antiochus II of Syria.

**Timarchus.** d. about 160 B.C. Satrap of Babylon; a favorite of Antiochus IV; appointed by him as satrap; declared himself "Great King of Babylonia and Media"; overthrown by Demetrius I of Syria, and put to death.

**Tim'by** (tĭm'bĭ), **Theodore Ruggles.** 1822–1909. American inventor of revolving turret for a battery of guns (patented 1862), first used as a distinctive feature of John Ericsson's *Monitor.*

**Ti'me·sith'e·us** (tī'mē·sĭth'ē·ŭs; tĭm'ē-). *Full name* **Gaius Furius Sabinus Aquila Timesitheus.** *Also corrupted form* **Mi·sith'e·us** (mī·sĭth'ē·ŭs). d. 243 A.D. Roman general; father-in-law of Emperor Gordianus III; able official in many provinces of empire; praetorian prefect (241–243); in Persian war defeated Shapur I (243).

**Tim'ken** (tĭm'kĕn), **Henry.** 1831–1909. Inventor and manufacturer, b. near Bremen, Ger.; to U.S. as a boy; established carriage manufacturing works, St. Louis (1855); invented special type of carriage spring (patented 1877) and a tapered roller bearing (patented 1898); organized Timken Roller Bearing Axle Co. (1898).

**Ti·mo'le·on** (tĭ·mō'lē·ŏn; tī-). d. about 337 B.C. Greek statesman and general, of Corinth; disapproved act of his brother **Ti·moph'a·nes** (tĭ·mŏf'ȧ·nēz; tī-) in making himself tyrant of Corinth, and acquiesced in his brother's execution; forced into exile by wrath of his family. Sent to aid Greek cities in Sicily against tyrants of Syracuse (c. 343 B.C.); defeated and removed Hicetas, who had made himself master of that city; reorganized government; successfully defended Syracuse against attacks by Hicetas and a Carthaginian army (c. 338); withdrew to private life (337–336).

**Ti·mom'a·chus** (tĭ·mŏm'ȧ·kŭs; tī-). Byzantine painter of about 1st century B.C.; among known paintings are *Ajax, Medea, A Gorgon, Iphigenia in Tauris.*

**Ti'mon** (tī'mŏn). Athenian misanthrope of late 5th century B.C.; subject of Shakespeare's play *Timon of Athens.*

**Timon of Phli'us** (flī'ŭs). fl. c. 280 B.C. Greek skeptic, author of satirical poems (known as *silloi;* hence the designation *sillograph* for a satirical poet, esp. Timon) against dogmatic philosophers; also said to have written dramas and epic poems; only fragments of his works are extant.

**Timophanes.** See TIMOLEON.

**Ti·mo·shen'ko** (tyĭ·mŭ·shân'kô), **Semën Konstantinovich.** 1895–1970. Russian army commander, b. in Bessarabia; served in World War (1914–18); cavalry commander under Bolshevik regime (1917–18); friend of Joseph Stalin (from 1919); commander of North Caucasus area (1937) and Kiev area (1938); directed occupation of eastern Poland (1939) and part of operations against Finland (1939–40); created marshal (1940); appointed people's commissar for defense (1940), succeeding Voroshilov (*q.v.*); assigned to defense of central area (Smolensk and Moscow) against German invaders (1941); commander in chief on southwestern front, directing defense of Stalingrad and the Caucasus (1941–42), on northwestern front, directing winter offensive (1942–43).

**Ti·moth'e·us** (tĭ·mŏth'ē·ŭs; tī-). 446?–?357 B.C. Greek poet and musician, b. Miletus; wrote many poems, of which only fragments are extant; introduced the 11-string cithara.

**Timotheus.** d. about 354 B.C. Athenian statesman and general; captured Corcyra [Corfu] (375 B.C.) and Samos (366–365). During Social War (357–355), held joint command of fleet, with Chares and Iphicrates; with Iphicrates, refused to engage enemy fleet because of weather conditions, Chares leading his division of fleet into action with disastrous results; subsequently tried, on Chares' complaint, and condemned to pay a large fine; withdrew from Athens, and shortly afterward died.

**Timotheus.** Greek sculptor of 4th century B.C.; collaborator with Scopas, Bryaxis, and Leochares in decorating Mausoleum of Halicarnassus.

**Tim'o·thy** (tĭm'ō·thĭ). *In A.V. usually* **Ti·moth'e·us** (tĭ·mŏth'ē·ŭs; tī-). A convert and, later, colleague of St. Paul (*Acts* xvi. 1 ff.; xvii. 14; xviii. 5; xix. 22; xx. 4; etc.) to whom are addressed two New Testament pastoral epistles (*1* and *2 Timothy*).

**Timour** *or* **Timur** *or* **Timur Lenk.** See TAMERLANE.

**Tim'rod** (tĭm'rŏd), **Henry.** 1828–1867. American poet, b. Charleston, S.C.; gained fame as "laureate of the Confederacy" with a series of impassioned poems inspired by outbreak of the Civil War. Among his best-known poems are: *Charleston, The Cotton-Boll, Katie, A Cry to Arms, Carolina, Carmen Triumphale, Magnolia Cemetery.*

**Ti·mur′ Shah** (tē·mo͞or′ shä′) *or* **Tai·mur′ Shah** (tī-). 1746–1793. Amir of Afghanistan (1773–93); son of Ahmad Shah; removed capital to Kabul.

**Ti′nayre′** (tē′nâr′), **Marcelle**, *nee* **Chas′teau′** (shä′tō′). 1872–1948. French novelist; m. Julien Tinayre (1889; d. 1923); wrote *Avant l'Amour* (1897), *Maison du Péché* (1899), *La Rebelle* (1905), *Perséphone* (1920), *Un Drame de Famille* (1925), *L'Ennemi Intime* (1931).

**Tin′ber·gen** (tĭn′bĕr′κē[n]), **Jan.** 1903– Dutch economist. At Netherlands School of Economics (1933– ); awarded the first Nobel prize in economic science (1969) with R. Frisch. His brother **Nikolaas** (1907– ), an ethologist, was at Oxford U. (1949–77); awarded Nobel prize for physiology or medicine (1973) with Karl von Frisch and Konrad Lorenz.

**Tinc·to′ris** (tĭngk·tō′rĭs), **Johannes.** 1446?–1511. Dutch musician and writer on music; edited earliest music dictionary, *Terminorum Musicae Diffinitorium* (c. 1475).

**Tin′dal** (tĭn′d'l), **Matthew.** 1657–1733. English deist; a Roman Catholic under James II, reverted to rationalism (1688); raised storm with his *The Rights of the Christian Church Asserted* (1706), disputing possession by Romish or other priests of any independent power over the church and defending theory of state control, which work was proscribed (1707) and burnt by order of House of Commons (1710), and with *Christianity as Old as the Creation* (1730), divesting religion of the miraculous element and setting up morality as alone giving religion its claim to reverence.

**Tindal** *or* **Tindale, William.** See TYNDALE.

**Tindaro,** Marchese **del.** See Mariano RAMPOLLA.

**Ti′nel′** (tē′nĕl′), **Edgar.** 1854–1912. Belgian pianist, and composer of an opera (*Katharina*), oratorios (including *Franciscus*, 1898), a mass for five voices, cantatas, etc.

**Ting** (tĭng), **Samuel Chao Chung.** 1936– . American physicist. At Columbia U. (1964–67), Massachusetts Institute of Technology (1967– ); awarded (with Burton Richter) Nobel prize for physics (1976).

**Ting′ley** (tĭng′lĭ), **Katherine Augusta,** *nee* **West′cott** (wĕs′kŭt). 1847–1929. American theosophist leader, b. Newbury, Mass.; m. Philo Buchanan Tingley, her third husband (1888). Was spiritualist medium in New York City (c. 1888). Introduced into theosophical movement by William Quan Judge (d. 1896) and succeeded in merging the Theosophical Society into a new organization, Universal Brotherhood, of which she was the head, with headquarters at Point Loma, Calif.

**Tin′ker** (tĭng′kĕr), **Chauncey Brewster.** 1876–1963. American educator; teacher of English, Yale (1903–45) and professor (1913–45); authority on Dr. Samuel Johnson and his period in English literature.

**Tin′ne** (tĭn′ĕ), **Alexandrine** *or* **Alexine.** 1839–1869. Dutch traveler in Africa; explored course of the White Nile to Gondokoro (1862); murdered by Tuaregs at beginning of another expedition (Aug. 1, 1869).

**Tin′to·ret′to** (tĭn′tō·rĕt′ō; *Ital.* ēl tēn′tō·rāt′tō), **Il.** *Real name* **Jacopo Ro·bu′sti** (rō·bo͞os′tē). 1518–1594. Italian painter of Venetian school; employed almost exclusively at Venice; sought Michelangelo's design and Titian's coloring as ideal of painting. Among his works are *Circumcision* (in Church of Santa Maria del Carmine, Venice), *Last Judgment* (in Church of Madonna dell'Orto, Venice), *Crucifixion* (in Church of San Cassiano, Venice), *Ecce Homo* (in Scuola di San Rocco, Venice), *Marriage of St. Catharine* (Venice); easel pictures, as *Abraham's Sacrifice* (in the Uffizi Gallery), *St. George and the Dragon* (in National Gallery, London); and portraits, as *Self-Portrait*, *Tommaso Contarini*, *Doge Niccolò da Ponte Sebastiano Venier*. His son **Domenico** (1565–1637), *called* **Tintoretto the Younger,** and his daughter **Marietta** (1560–1590), *called* **La Tin′to·ret′ta** (lä tēn′tō·rāt′tä), were also painters.

**Ti′poo Tib** *or* **Tip** (tē′po͞o tĭp′). *Nickname of* **Hamidi bin Muhammad.** 1837?–1905. Trader and slave merchant in equatorial Africa, of mixed Arab and African blood; gave up slave trade (c. 1866) and tried to establish himself in power over upper Congo region; aided Cameron (1874) and Stanley (1876); finally forced out by Belgians of Congo Free State and retired to Zanzibar.

**Tippoo Sahib.** = TIPU SAHIB.

**Tip′toft** (tĭp′tŏft), **John.** Earl of **Worces′ter** (wo͝os′tĕr). 1427?–1470. English humanist and Yorkist administrator. Called "the butcher of England." Created earl of Worcester (1449); lifelong supporter of house of York. Treasurer of exchequer (1452); ambassador to council of Mantua (1459); advanced by Edward IV to high office, first as lord high constable (1462–67, 1470); gained evil reputation for cruelty by executions of earl of Oxford, of Lancastrians, and of twenty of Clarence's party taken at sea (1470); virtually Edward IV's prime minister (1470) until the latter's flight; captured, tried, and executed.

**Ti′pu Sa′hib** *or* **Tip′poo Sa′hib** (tē′po͞o sä′hĭb). 1751–1799. Sultan of Mysore (1782–99). Son of Haidar Ali (*q.v.*). Crowned sultan (1782); built up powerful court at Seringapatam. Felt bitter hatred against British and wished to drive them out; invaded protected state of Travancore (1789); opposed by alliance of British with the Marathas and the nizam in Third Mysore War (1790–92); was defeated and forced by treaty of Seringapatam (1792) to cede half his domain; killed in action at storming of Seringapatam in Fourth Mysore War (1799); his dominions partitioned.

**Ti′ra·bo′schi** (tē′rä·bôs′kē), **Girolamo.** 1731–1794. Italian scholar; librarian to duke of Modena; chief work, *Storia della Letteratura Italiana* (13 vols., 1771–82).

**Ti′rard′** (tē′rár′), **Pierre Emmanuel.** 1827–1893. French politician; prime minister (1887–88, 1889–90); had to deal with Boulangist movement.

**Tirhakah.** See TAHARKA.

**Tir′i·da′tes** (tĭr′ĭ·dā′tēz). Name of several kings of Armenia: **Tiridates I** (d. 73? A.D.); king (51–60; 63–73? A.D.); brother of an Arsacid king of Parthia; driven out (60) by Corbulo, a Roman general; restored (63); went to Rome and received (66) Armenian crown from Nero. **Tiridates III,** *called* "the Great" (238?–314); king (259–314); driven out of Armenia by Persians (252); educ. Rome; became king (259); after defeat by Persians, again secured throne (286) with aid of Diocletian; made wide conquests; baptized (303) by Saint Gregory and established Christianity.

**Tiridates.** Name of three kings of Parthia of the Arsacid (*q.v.*) dynasty, esp.: **Tiridates I** *or* **Ar′sa·ces II** (är′sȧ·sēz). King (248 or 247–210 B.C.); established independence of Parthia; defeated Seleucus Callinicus of Syria. By some considered as Arsaces, real founder of the dynasty, and not as brother of the legendary Arsaces (I); little known about him or his immediate successors.

**Ti′ro** (tī′rō), **Marcus Tullius.** Roman freedman of 1st century B.C.; private secretary to Cicero; said to have introduced a system (Tironian system) of shorthand into ancient Rome.

**Tiro, Prosper.** See PROSPER OF AQUITAINE.

**Tir′pitz** (tĭr′pĭts), **Alfred von.** 1849–1930. German naval commander; admiral (1903) and high admiral (1911); as state secretary of navy and Prussian minister of state (1898–1916) credited with creating modern German navy. Responsible during World War for German declaration of a war zone, a submarine blockade, and unrestricted submarine warfare, policies which as applied drew U.S. into war (1917). After fall of German Empire (1918), took refuge in Switzerland, where he published *Erinnerungen* (1919). Later, returned to Germany and became member of Reichstag (1924–28).

**Tir′so de Mo·li′na** (tēr′sō thā mō·lē′nä). *Pseudonym of* **Gabriel Tél′lez** (tā′lyāth). 1571?–1648. Spanish dramatist; cleric (1601 ff.); superior, Mercenarian monastery, Soria (1645 ff.); friend of Lope de Vega. Works include collections of tales, verse, and plays, and a history of the Order of Mercy (1639); among individual plays are *El Burlador de Sevilla* (first dramatic presentation of Don Juan, 1630), *La Prudencia en la Mujer*, *Marta la Piadosa*, *La Celosa de Sí Misma*, and *La Villana de Vallecas*.

**Ti′ru·val′lu·var** (tĭ′rŏŏ·vŭ′lŏŏ·vēr). fl. between 800 and 1000 A.D. Greatest of Tamil poets, author of the *Kural* (made up of 1330 couplets and treating of virtue, wealth, and pleasure); probably lived near Madras.

**Tisch′bein** (tĭsh′bīn), **Johann Heinrich.** 1722–1789. German painter; court painter to William VIII of Hesse-Cassel; known esp. for his portraits of German princes and princesses. A nephew, **Johann Friedrich August Tischbein** (1750–1812), was also a painter, known esp. for his portraits. Another nephew, **Johann Heinrich Wilhelm Tischbein,** *known as* **Goe′the–Tisch′bein** (gû′tĕ-), *or as* "the Neapolitan" (1751–1829), was also a painter; a friend of Goethe; court painter to the duke of Oldenburg (1809).

**Ti′schen·dorf** (tĭsh′ĕn·dôrf), **Konstantin von.** 1815–1874. German Protestant theologian and Biblical scholar; traveled in Palestine and Near East, and brought back many manuscripts, including *Codex Sinaiticus* (which he edited, 1862).

**Ti·se′li·us** (tĭ·sā′lĭ·ŭs), **Arne Wilhelm Kaurin.** 1902–1971. Swedish biochemist. At U. of Uppsala (1925–68); awarded Nobel prize in chemistry (1948) for his studies concerning the nature of serum proteins.

**Tishbi, Elijah.** See Elijah LEVITA.

**Tisi** *or* **Tisio, Benvenuto.** See Benvenuto da GAROFALO.

**Ti′so** (tyĭ′sô), **Josef.** 1887–1947. Slovak clergyman and politician; ordained priest (1909); member of Slovak People's party (from 1921); succeeded Hlinka as its leader (1938); prime minister of Slovakia (Oct., 1938); made by Hitler president of Slovakia (Oct., 1939); signed pact of adherence to Axis (Nov., 1940), hanged.

**Tis′san′dier′** (tē′säN′dyā′), **Gaston.** 1843–1899. French aeronaut; made numerous balloon ascensions (from 1868); devised first model of a dirigible propelled by electricity.

**Tis′sa·pher′nes** (tĭs′ȧ·fûr′nēz). Persian satrap in Asia Minor (414 B.C.); opposed Cyrus the Younger, and revealed his intrigues to Artaxerxes II; engaged in battle of Cunaxa (401 B.C.); pursued the Greek Ten Thousand on their return march; appointed by Artaxerxes chief ruler in western Asia; defeated by Agesilaus near Sardis (395), and executed by order of the king.

**Tis′se·rand′** (tēs′räN′), **François Félix.** 1845–1896. French astronomer; professor of celestial mechanics at the Sorbonne (1883); director, Paris observatory (1892); on French expedition to Japan (1874) and to Santo Domingo (1882) to observe transits of Venus.

**Tis′sot′** (tē′sō′), **James Joseph Jacques.** 1836–1902. French painter, engraver, and enameler; studio in London (c. 1870–80); traveled in Palestine (1887) and made studies for a set of 300 water-color paintings, exhibited (1894) under the title *Vie de Notre Seigneur Jésus Christ*.

**Ti′sza** (tĭ′sŏ), **Kálmán.** 1830–1902. Hungarian statesman; prime minister of Hungary (1875–90). His son **István** (1861–1918) was also a Hungarian statesman; prime minister of Hungary (1903–05, 1913–17); murdered by terrorists, who charged him with responsibility for bringing on World War.

**Titch′e·ner** (tĭch′′n·ēr), **Edward Bradford.** 1867–1927. Psychologist, b. Chichester, Eng.; professor (1895–1909), Cornell; research professor in Cornell graduate school (from 1909); known as a leader in the structuralist school of philosophy; author of *Experimental Psychology* (2 vols., 1901–05), *A Textbook of Psychology* (2 vols., 1909–10), etc.

**Titcomb, Timothy.** Pseudonym of Josiah Gilbert HOLLAND.

**Tite** (tīt), Sir **William.** 1798–1873. English architect; rebuilder of Royal Exchange (1841–44).

**Ti′tian** (tĭsh′ăn). *Ital.* **Ti·zia′no** (tē·tsyä′nō) **Ve·cel′li** (vā·chĕl′lē) *or* **Ve·cel′lio** (-lyō). 1477–1576. Italian painter; chief master of Venetian school; succeeded Giovanni Bellini as painter to Venetian state; protégé of Alfonso d'Este, Duke of Ferrara, and Emperor Charles V; court painter to Charles V (1532 ff.). Among his works are frescoes; portraits, as *Alfonso d'Este and Laura Dianti* (in the Louvre), *Alessandro de' Medici* (at Hampton Court), *Maltese Knight* (at Madrid), etc.; religious pictures, as *Holy Family* (in National Gallery, London), *Assumption of the Virgin* (altarpiece in San Nicolò dei Frari, Venice), *Ecce Homo* (at Vienna), etc.; and mythological pictures, as *Medea and Venus*, *Worship of Venus*, *Bacchus and Ariadne*, *Danaë*, *Venus and Cupid*, and *Rape of Europa*. See also VECELLI.

**Titl** (tē′t′l), **Anton Emil.** 1809–1882. Austrian composer of operas, overtures, a mass, and several songs.

**Titmarsh, Michael Angelo.** Pseudonym of William Makepeace THACKERAY.

**Tito.** Marshal. See Josip BROZ.

**Ti′to** (tē′tō), **Ettore.** 1860–1941. Italian painter; painted frescoes in Villa Berlingieri at Rome, and Venetian scenes.

**Tit·to′ni** (tēt·tō′nē), **Tommaso.** 1855–1931. Italian statesman; deputy (1886); senator (1901); minister of foreign affairs (1903–05, 1906–09, June–Nov., 1919); ambassador to London (1905–06) and France (1910–16); senate president (1919–28).

**Ti′tu·le′scu** (tē′tōō·lĕ′skōō), **Nicolae.** 1883–1941. Rumanian diplomat and statesman; minister of finance (1917, 1920–22); Rumanian representative at peace negotiations at St. Germain and Trianon (1919–20); Rumanian minister in London (1922–27, 1928–32); minister of foreign affairs (1927–28; 1932–36).

**Ti′tus** (tī′tŭs). A companion of St. Paul, not mentioned in Acts but referred to in several of the epistles, to whom, as superintendent of the churches in Crete, is addressed a New Testament pastoral epistle (*Titus*).

**Titus.** *In full* **Titus Flavius Sa·bi′nus Ves·pa′si·a′nus** (sȧ·bī′nŭs vĕs·pā′zhĭ·ā′nŭs). 40?–81 A.D. Second of the Flavian emperors of Rome (79–81). Eldest son of Emperor Vespasian and Flavia Domitilla, b. Rome. Served in campaigns in Germany and Britain; later entrusted by his father with command of legion in Judea (69–70); besieged and captured Jerusalem (70); granted joint triumph with Vespasian at Rome (71) and arch (Arch of Titus) erected by Domitian (81) to commemorate taking of Jerusalem. Received title of Caesar, but for a time (c. 72–79) lived a dissolute life; reign marked by great beneficence and by solicitude for welfare of people (hence called the "Delight of Mankind").

**Tiy** *or* **Tii** (tē). fl. 1400 B.C. Queen of Egypt; reputed wife of Amenhotep III and mother of Ikhnaton; supposed by some to be a Syrian princess, daughter of Tushratta, King of the Mitanni; influenced both husband and son in religious ideas.

**Tiz′ard** (tĭz′ärd), Sir **Henry Thomas.** 1885–1959. English scientist; educ. Oxford; lecturer at Oriel College, Oxford (1911–21); served in World War I (in air service from 1915); rector of Imperial Coll. of Science and Technology (1929–42); chairman of Aeronautical Research Committee (1933–43); elected president of Magdalen Coll. (1942), first scientist to hold such a position at Oxford; member of British Air Council and of advisory council, Ministry of Aircraft Production (1941–43).

**Tiziano Vecelli** *or* **Vecellio.** See TITIAN.

**To·ba′ni** (tô·bä′nē), **Theodore Moses.** 1855–1933. Composer, b. Hamburg, Ger.; to U.S. as a child; wrote *Hearts and Flowers, The Spanish Patrol, Moonlight on the Hudson, Land of My Dreams.*

**To·ba So·jo** (tô·bä sō·jō). 1053–1114. Japanese painter; best known for satires, using animals to represent human activities, foibles, etc.

**Tobias.** See TOBIT.

**To′bit** (tō′bĭt). *In Douay Bible* **To·bi′as** (tô·bī′ăs). A pious Jew whose story is related in the Apocryphal book of Tobit, which corresponds to the canonical book of Tobias, in Douay Bible. In both Apocryphal and Douay books, his son's name is spelled **Tobias.**

**To′bler** (tō′blẽr), **Ludwig.** (1827–1895), a Swiss philologist and **Adolf** (1835–1910), a Romance philologist.

**Toby, M.P.** Pseudonym of Sir Henry LUCY.

**Tocque′ville′** (tôk′vēl′), **Alexis Charles Henri Maurice Clé′rel′ de** (klā′rĕl′ dē). 1805–1859. French writer; sent on mission (1831) to U.S. to study American penitentiaries; published, with Gustave de Beaumont de La Bonninière, *Du Système Pénitentiaire aux États-Unis et de son Application en France* (1833). To England (1832) and wrote his most notable work, *La Démocratie en Amérique* (2 vols., 1835, 1840). Member of Constituent Assembly (1848) and Legislative Assembly (1849); minister of foreign affairs (1849); opposed the coup d'état (Dec. 2, 1851) and was for a short time imprisoned. His *L'Ancien Régime et la Révolution* (vol. 1, 1856) was incomplete at his death.

**To′dar Mall** (tō′dẽr mŭl′), Raja. d. 1589. Hindu general and able finance minister under Akbar; caused survey of empire to be made and a taxation system established; led army that subjugated Bengal (1575); restored order in Bihar (1580) and Badakhshan (1586).

**Todd** (tŏd), Lord **Alexander Robertus.** 1907– . British chemist. At Cambridge U. (1944– ); awarded Nobel prize in chemistry (1957) for work on nucleotides and nucleotide co-enzymes.

**Todd,** Sir **Charles.** 1826–1910. English astronomer in Australia; director, colonial observatory, Adelaide (1855–1906); organized meteorological service; also, postmaster general, South Australia (1870–1905).

**Todd, David.** 1855–1939. American astronomer, b. Lake Ridge, N.Y. Teacher of astronomy (1881), professor (from 1892), Amherst; professor of astronomy and higher mathematics, Smith (1882–87). Designed and erected observatory at Smith (1886–87), Amherst (1903–05). In charge of expeditions to observe solar eclipses in Japan (1887; 1896), West Africa (1889–90), Tripoli (1900; 1905), Dutch East Indies (1901), Russia (1914), Florida (1918), South America (1919). First to photograph the solar corona from an airplane (1925); inventor of an automatic device for photographing eclipses. Author of *A New Astronomy* (1897), *Astronomy Today* (1924), etc.

**Todd, Henry Alfred.** 1854–1925. American philologist; professor at Columbia (1893–1925); editor of a number of old and medieval French manuscripts.

**Todd, Henry John.** 1763–1845. English clergyman and editor; edited Milton and Spenser; improved Johnson's etymologies and brought number of dictionary entries up to about 58,000 words in his edition of *Johnson's Dictionary* (1818).

**Todd, Mary.** See Mary Todd LINCOLN.

**Todd, Thomas.** 1765–1826. American jurist; associate justice, U.S. Supreme Court (1807–26).

**Todd, Thomas Wingate.** 1885–1938. American anatomist, b. Sheffield, England; to U.S.; professor, Western Reserve (from 1912); made study of growth and maturation of children.

**Tod′hun′ter** (tŏd′hŭn′tẽr; *Brit. also* -(h)ŭn·tẽr), **Isaac.** 1820–1884. English mathematician; author of standard textbooks in mathematics, and treatises on the history of mathematical theories of probability, attraction, elasticity.

**Todhunter, John.** 1839–1916. Irish writer; practiced medicine in Dublin; later settled in London. Author of poetical works, including *Laurella* (1876), *Forest Songs* (1881), *The Banshee and Other Poems* (1888), *Sounds and Sweet Airs* (1905); and dramas, including *Alcestis* (1879), *Rienzi* (1881), *The Poison Flower* (1891), *A Comedy of Sighs* (1895).

**Todleben.** See TOTLEBEN.

**Todt** (tōt), **Fritz.** 1891–1942. German military engineer; served in World War (1914–18); joined National Socialist party (1923); as inspector general of roads in Hitler's cabinet (1933), responsible for building network of high-speed highways suitable for military or commercial transportation; major general (1938) and builder of the Siegfried line of defenses in the West (Westwall); credited also with construction of chain of submarine bases along the north French coast (1940–42).

**Toep′ler** (tûp′lẽr), **August Joseph Ignaz.** 1836–1912. German physicist; worked in acoustics; invented an air pump for producing a high vacuum; increased the power of the induction machine.

**To·go** (tō·gō), Marquis **Heihachiro.** 1847–1934. Japanese admiral; studied at Greenwich, Eng. (1871–78); served in Chino-Japanese War (1894–95). Commanded Japanese fleet in Russo-Japanese War (1904–05); attacked Port Arthur (Feb. 8, 1904); scattered Russian Port Arthur squadron in battle (Aug. 10, 1904); won great battle of Tsushima, annihilating Russian fleet under Rozhdestvenski (May 27–28, 1905). Member of supreme military council (1909); created count (1907) and marquis (1934).

**Togo, Shigenori.** 1882–1950. Japanese diplomat; ambassador to Germany (1937–39) and Russia (1939–40); minister of foreign affairs (1941–42); sentenced (1948) as war criminal to 20 years' imprisonment.

**To·jo** (tō·jō), **Eiki** *or, from 1941,* **Hideki.** 1885–1948. Japanese lieutenant general; military attaché in Germany (1919); head of secret police; chief of staff of Kwantung army (1937–40); minister of war in Konoye cabinet (1940–41); prime minister (1941–44); hanged as war criminal.

**To·ki·ma·sa** (tô·kē·mä·sä), **Hojo.** 1138–1215. First great leader of Hojo family of Japan; father-in-law of Yoritomo. See HOJO.

**Tököly** *or* **Tökölyi** *or* **Tököli.** See THÖKÖLY.

**To·ku·ga·wa** (tô·kōō·gä·wä). Famous Japanese noble family, branch of the Minamoto clan and the shogunate held by it (1603–1867). Its founder was Iyeyasu (*q.v.*) and its capital was at Yedo (Tokyo); its shoguns had control over emperors until court revolution led by leaders of Western clans forced resignation of its last representative (1867).

**Tokugawa, Iyesato.** 1863–1940. Japanese prince; entered House of Peers (1890); president, House of Peers (1903); delegate to Conference on Limitation of Armaments, Washington (1921).

**To'land** (tō'lănd), **Hugh Hu'ger** (hū'gẽr). 1806–1880. American surgeon; practiced in Columbia, S.C. Known for operations for clubfoot and strabismus, and use of the lithotomy forceps. To San Francisco (1853). Founded Toland Medical College there at his own expense (1864), and later placed the college in charge of the U. of Calif. of which it became a part (1873).

**Toland, John,** *orig.* **Junius Janus.** 1670–1722. Irish deist and literary adventurer; brought up as Roman Catholic, but became Protestant at early age. Living at Oxford, launched warfare between deists and the orthodox with *Christianity not Mysterious* (1696), which, because of its resemblance to John Locke's *Reasonableness of Christianity,* caused Bishop Stillingfleet to couple him and Locke as Socinians. Turned to political and literary subjects with *Life of Milton* (1698), which led to charges of heresy, answered in his *Amyntor* (1699), debating comparative evidence for canonical and apocryphal scriptures. By pamphlet *Anglia Libera* (1701), on succession of Hanoverian house, won favorable reception at court of Electress Sophia, to whose daughter Sophia Charlotte he addressed *Letters to Serena* (1704); sent by Harley on missions to Holland and Germany (1707), defended Harley and Marlborough in pamphlets (until 1714); later, wrote partisan pamphlets for Harley's enemies. Returned to theological works in *Nazarenus* (1718) and *Tetradymus* (1720), and parodied Anglican liturgy in *Pantheisticon* (1720).

**Tol'bert** (tōl'bẽrt; tȯl'-), **William Richard.** 1913– . Liberian statesman. Vice-president (1951–71), president of the Republic of Liberia (1971– ).

**Tol'dy** (tôl'dĭ), **Ferencz.** *Real surname* **Sche'del** (shā'dĕl). 1805–1875. Hungarian historian of literature. Edited first systematic history of Hungarian literature in German language, *Handbuch der Ungarischen Poesie* (2 vols., 1828).

**To·le'do** (tō·lā'thō), **Francisco de.** 1515?–1584. Spanish administrator in Peru; viceroy of Peru (1569–81); allowed execution of the young Inca Tupac Amaru (*q.v.*); introduced the Inquisition into Peru; and promulgated new code of laws.

**Tolentino de Almeida, Nicolão.** See ALMEIDA.

**Tol'kien** (tŏl'kēn), **John Ronald Reuel.** 1892–1973. British writer, b. South Africa. At Oxford U. (1925–59); wrote fantasies, including *The Hobbit* (1937), *The Lord of the Rings* (3 vols., 1954–56), etc.

**Toll** (tôl), Baron **Eduard von.** 1858–1902. Russian Arctic explorer; made expeditions to New Siberian Islands (1885–86, 1892–94, 1900–02); discovered layers of fossil ice along southern coast of Bolshoi Island containing preserved mammoth remains, rhinoceros, etc.

**Toll** (tôl), Count **Johan Kristoffer.** 1743–1817. Swedish soldier and statesman. Head of commission of national defense (1783); marshal of the Diet, and leader of Royalist party (1800); aided in defense of Stralsund (1807); created marshal of Sweden (1807).

**Tol'lens** (tŏl'ĕns), **Hendrik.** 1780–1856. Dutch poet; among his works are the comedies *The Wedding* (1799) and *Avarice and Covetousness* (1801), and the verse *Idylls and Love Songs* (1801–05), *Poems* (1808–15), *Romances, Ballads, and Legends* (1818–19), and *Last Poems* (1848, 1853). Author of the national anthem, *Wien Neerlands Bloed.*

**Tol'ler** (tôl'ẽr), **Ernst.** 1893–1939. German poet, playwright, and political agitator; leader of social revolutionary movements in Germany following World War I. Sentenced to five years in prison (1919) for political activities; banished from Germany by Nazis (1933); committed suicide in New York. In addition to several volumes of verse, he wrote the plays *Die Wandlung* (1919), *Masse Mensch* (1921), *Die Maschinenstürmer* (1922), *Hinkemann* (1923), *Hoppla, Wir Leben* (1927), *Feuer aus den Kesseln* (1930), *Die Blinde Göttin* (1936), and *Die Nacht ist Vorgerücht* (1938); also wrote *I Was a German* (autobiography; Eng. translation, 1934).

**Tol'ler** (tŏl'ẽr), **Thomas Northcote.** 1845–1930. See under Joseph BOSWORTH.

**Tol'man** (tōl'măn), **Richard Chace.** 1881–1948. American physicist; professor (from 1922), dean of the Graduate School (from 1935), Calif. Inst. Tech.; known for studies on the theory of colloids, theory of relativity, quantum theory, statistical mechanics, thermodynamics, etc.

**Tol·stoi'** (tŭl·stoi'; *Angl.* tŏl·stoi', tŏl'stoi), Count **Aleksei Konstantinovich.** 1817–1875. Russian writer; served in Crimean War (1854–56); author of lyric poetry, novels, and plays. His best-known novel is the historical romance *Prince Serebryany* (1863); among his plays are *The Death of Ivan the Terrible* (1866), *Czar Fëdor Ivanovich* (1868), and *Czar Boris* (1870).

**Tolstoi,** Count **Aleksei Nikolaevich.** 1882–1945. Russian novelist and dramatist; left Russia during Russian Revolution (1917), but returned (1922). Among his many novels are *Nikita's Childhood* (1922), *The Way Through Hell* (1922), *Aelita* (1923), *Seven Days...* (1925), *The Year 1918* (1928), and *Peter the Great* (1930).

**Tolstoi,** Count **Dmitri Aleksandrovich.** 1823–1889. Russian minister of public instruction (1866–80); minister of interior (1883 ff.).

**Tolstoi,** Count **Lev** (*Eng.* **Leo**) **Lvovich.** 1869–1945. Son of Count L. N. Tolstoi (1828–1910). Russian novelist; author of *For the Children* and *Years of Famine,* and *Prelude of Chopin* (revealing blessings of marriage and intended as reply to his father's *Kreutzer Sonata*).

**Tolstoi,** Count **Lev** (*Eng.* **Leo**) **Nikolaevich.** 1828–1910. Russian novelist, social and moral philosopher, and religious mystic, b. in province of Tula. Educ. Kazan; entered army and served in the Caucasus and in Crimean War (1854–56), commanding battery at Sevastopol (1855). Retired from army after Crimean War to devote himself to study and writing; emancipated his serfs in accordance with provisions of Emancipation Act (1861) and lived on his country estate, Yasnaya Polyana; m. (1862) Sofya Andreevna Behrs. Underwent spiritual transformation (after 1876) which led him to renounce Russian Orthodox Church and evolve new Christianity whose central creed was nonresistance to evil; Tolstoyism became an organized sect and began (c. 1884) to gain proselytes; meanwhile, Tolstoi, in a series of notable works, recorded his conversion and new beliefs. Among his many works are *Childhood* (1852), *The Cossacks* (1854; pub. 1862), *Two Hussars* (1856), *Three Deaths* (1859), *Kholstomer* (1861), *War and Peace* (1866), *Anna Karenina* (1875–77), *A Confession* (1879; pub. 1884), *The Death of Ivan Ilyich* (1886), *The Kreutzer Sonata* (1889), *The Power of Darkness* (play; 1889), *The Fruits of Enlightenment* (play; 1891), *Master and Man* (1895), *What is Art?* (1896), *Resurrection* (1899–1900), and *The Living Corpse* (play; 1911).

**Tolstoi,** Count **Pëtr Andreevich.** 1645–1729. Russian statesman; sent to Turkey by Peter the Great as ambassador (1702); imprisoned by Turks during Russo-Turkish War (1711 ff.); accompanied Peter the Great to western Europe (1716); member of supreme privy council under Czarina Catherine I.

**Tolstoy.** Variant of TOLSTOI.

**Tomás, Tomás Navarro.** See Tomás NAVARRO.

**Tom'baugh** (tŏm'bô), **Clyde William.** 1906– . American astronomer, b. Streator, Ill.; assistant (1929–38), assistant astronomer (1938), Lowell Observatory,

Flagstaff, Ariz.; discovered planet Pluto (1930). See also Percival LOWELL.

**Tombs** (tōōmz), Sir **Henry**. 1824–1874. British commander in India. Distinguished himself in both Sikh wars (1845–49); during Sepoy Mutiny, won Victoria Cross by gallantry at siege of Delhi (1857); commanded troop at Lucknow (1858); served as brigadier general in subsequent operations (1863, 1864).

**Tomes** (tōmz), Sir **John**. 1815–1895. English dental surgeon.

**Tom'kis** *or* **Tom'kys** (tŏm'kĭs), **Thomas**. fl. 1604–1615. English author of comedy *Albumazar* (1615), about an Arabian astronomer, acted before James I on visit to Cambridge, revived by Dryden and by Garrick.

**Tom'line** (tŏm'lĭn), Sir **George Pretyman**. 1750–1827. English prelate; tutor to the younger Pitt (1774) and his private secretary (1783–87); dean of St. Paul's and bishop of Lincoln (1787), bishop of Winchester (1820). Assumed additional surname Tomline (1803) on receipt of estate. Advised Pitt against relationship with Addington and in favor of guarantee to George III not to bring forward Roman Catholic emancipation.

**Tom'lin·son** (tŏm'lĭn·s'n), **Henry Major**. 1873–1958. English journalist, novelist, and miscellaneous writer; war correspondent in France (1914–17); literary editor, *Nation* and *Athenaeum* (1917–23). Author of *The Sea and the Jungle* (1912), *Old Junk* (1918), *London River* (1921), *Tidemarks* (1924), *Gallions Reach* (1927), *Between the Lines* (1928), *All Our Yesterdays* (1930), *Mars His Idiot* (1935), *All Hands* (1937), *The Day Before* (1939).

**Tom'ma·se'o** (tōm'mä·zâ'ō), **Niccolò**. *Real surname* **To'ma·šić** (*Croatian* tō'mä·shēt'y'; *Angl.* -shĭch). 1802–1874. Italian writer, b. in Dalmatia; minister of public instruction, Venice (1848); fled to Corfu after Manin insurrection (1849); settled at Florence (1861). Works include *Dizionario dei Sinonimi della Lingua Italiana* (1832), *Dell'Italia* (1835), *La Commedia di Dante* (1837), *Canti Popolari Corsi, Toscani, Greci, e Illirici* (1841), *Bellezza e Civiltà* (1857), *Ispirazione e Arte* (1858), and *Dizionario della Lingua Italiana* (with B. Bellini; 4 vols., 1861–79).

**Tom'ma·si'ni** (tōm'mä·zē'nē), **Vicenzo**. 1880–1950. Italian composer; representative of impressionism in music. Works include operas *Medea*, *Amore di Terra Lontana*, and *Uguale Fortuna;* ballet *Le Donne di Buon Umore;* symphonic poems, as *Poema Erotico* and *Il Beato Regno;* instrumental and vocal compositions.

**To'mo·na'ga** (tō'mō·nä'gȧ), **Shinichiro**. 1906–1979. Japanese physicist. Awarded Nobel prize in physics (1965) with R. Feynman and J. Schwinger for their work on quantum electrodynamics.

**Tom'pi·on** (tŏm'pĭ·ŭn), **Thomas**. 1639–1713. English clockmaker, known as "father of English watchmaking." Clockmaker for royal observatory (1676); with Robert Hooke (*q.v.*), made one of first English watches with balance spring (1675); with William Houghton and Edward Barlow, patented cylinder escapement (1695). Maker of barometers and sundials for William III.

**Tomp'kins** (tŏm(p)'kĭnz), **Daniel Augustus**. 1851–1914 American industrialist; promoted industrial development of the South; author of *Cotton Mill Processes and Calculations* (1899), *Cotton and Cotton Oil* (1901), etc.

**Tompkins, Daniel D.** 1774–1825. American politician, b. Scarsdale, N.Y.; associate justice, New York State supreme court (1804–07); governor of New York (1807–17); vice-president of the United States (1817–25).

**Tompkins, Sally Louisa.** 1833–1916. American Confederate hospital head; outfitted and maintained at her own expense hospital in Richmond (1861–65); commissioned by Jefferson Davis a captain in Confederate army (Sept. 9, 1861), only woman commissioned in Confederate service.

**Tom'ski** (tôm'skû·ĭ; *Angl.* tŏm'skĭ), **Mikhail Pavlovich**. 1880–1936. Russian Communist leader; joined Bolsheviks (1904); in prison and exile (1909–17); active in Bolshevik coup d'état (Nov., 1917); member of Union Central Executive Committee, U.S.S.R. (from 1923). Opposed Stalin's policies for industrialization of Russia and was dismissed from Communist party (1928); recanted (1929) and became director-general of Soviet chemical industries and member of presidium of Supreme Economic Council. Involved in plot to overthrow Stalin, committed suicide.

**Ton'dorf** (tŏn'dôrf), **Francis Anthony**. 1870–1929. American Roman Catholic clergyman and scientist, b. Boston; on teaching staff of Georgetown U. (1904–29); founded Georgetown seismological observatory (opened, 1911) and served as its director.

**Tone** (tōn), **Wolfe**, *in full* **Theobald Wolfe**. 1763–1798. Irish revolutionist, a founder of United Irishmen. Attracted attention with *Hibernicus*, asserting Irish independence, and pamphlet promoting union of dissenters with Roman Catholics against British government (1791); with Thomas Russell and Napper Tandy, founded Society of United Irishmen (1791); asst. secretary of Catholic Committee (1792). In memorandum for William Jackson, French spy, described Ireland as ripe for revolution; allowed by government to emigrate to America (1795), whence he went to Paris to promote landing of a French force for invasion of Ireland; adjutant general of expedition under Hoche, consisting of 43 sail and 15,000 men, which was dispersed by a storm (1796). Embarked in small French squadron under General Hardy and Admiral Bompard, which was captured by British after fight off Lough Swilly (1798).

**To'ner** (tō'nẽr), **Joseph Meredith**. 1825–1896. American physician; practiced in Washington, D.C. (from 1855). Wrote on medical history and biography; also, made special study of events in life of George Washington, and edited several of his *Journals*. Collected library of material on American medical history and biography, which he presented (1882) to the Library of Congress.

**Tong'er·loo** (tông'ẽr·lō), **Georges van**. 1886– . Belgian sculptor and painter, b. Antwerp; served in World War I (1914–18); collaborated with Theo van Doesburg and Pieter Mondriaan in founding the Dutch de Stijl group; edited *De Sikkel* (1924).

**To'ni** (tô'nē), **Giovanni Battista de**. 1864–1924. Italian botanist; authority on algae.

**Tonks** (tŏngks), **Henry**. 1862–1937. English painter, b. in Warwickshire; Slade professor of fine art, London (1917–30).

**Ton'son** (tŏn's'n), **Jacob**. 1656?–1736. English publisher. Purchased copyright of *Paradise Lost;* published plays for Dryden, his translation of Vergil (1697), and *The Fables* (1699); aided by Dryden in starting *Miscellany* (1684–1708); secretary of Kit-cat Club; published works for Addison, Dryden's *Alexander's Feast* (1707), Pope's *Pastorals* (1709), and Rowe's *Shakespeare* (1709); moved (1710) to a shop in Strand, where Swift met Addison and Steele (1711); publisher of Addison's *Drummer* (1715), Tickell's *Iliad* (1715), Steele's *Conscious Lovers*, Pope's *Shakespeare* (1725). Succeeded in publishing business by his nephew and grandnephew, both named Jacob Tonson.

**Tonstall, Cuthbert.** See TUNSTALL.

**Ton'ti** (tōn'tē), **Lorenzo**. A 17th-century Italian-born banker in Paris (1653), who originated the tontine system of life insurance. His son **Henry de Ton'ti'** *or*

**Ton'ty'** [*Fr.* dē tôɴ'tē'; *Angl.* tŏn'tĭ] (1650–1704) was a companion of La Salle in his Mississippi Valley explorations (1678–83); built fort and trading post in Illinois region and lived there (until c. 1699), bringing in colonists and missionaries from Canada; moved to French settlement near mouth of the Mississippi (1700) and aided the Louisiana colony in exploration and trade (1700–04).

**Tooke** (tŏŏk), **Horne,** *in full* **John Horne.** 1736–1812. English political radical and philologist; called "philosopher of Wimbledon." Son of John Horne, poulterer; added name of friend William Tooke of Purley to his own (1782). B.A., Cantab. (1758); ordained to a curacy (1760); traveling abroad as tutor, met Voltaire and John Wilkes; became energetic supporter of Wilkes (1767) until their epistolary quarrel (1771); supposed author or part author of addresses to George III (1770); by spirited opposition to an enclosure bill (1774), earned gratitude of William Tooke of Purley in Surrey; for promoting subscription for relief of relatives of Americans "murdered" at Lexington and Concord, fined and imprisoned for year (1778); refused admission to bar. During imprisonment, commenced a treatise on etymology of English words and witty divagations into metaphysics and politics, *Ἔπεα πτερόεντα, or The Diversions of Purley* (1786; expanded 1798), in which he was one of first to insist upon necessity of studying Gothic and Anglo-Saxon for philology. Supported Pitt (1782–90) in pamphlets; tried for high treason, but acquitted (1794); M.P. (1801), but excluded by special act rendering clergymen ineligible.

**Tooke, William.** 1744–1820. English historian; author of Russian histories, including *A History of Russia from Rurik to Catherine II* (1800). His son **Thomas** (1774–1858), economist, became early advocate of free trade and authority on finance and banking; combated view that fall of prices was result of return to cash payments; author of *History of Prices* (6 vols., 1838–57).

**Toole** (tōōl), **John Lawrence.** 1830–1906. English comedian; son of James Toole, civic toastmaster commemorated by Dickens and Thackeray. First acted in London as Samuel Pepys in *The King's Rival* and as Weazel in *My Friend the Major* (1854); close friend of Henry Irving (from 1857); established character as comedian at Adelphi (1858–67); played in *Thespis*, first Gilbert and Sullivan collaboration (1871). Lessee of Folly (also known as Toole's) Theatre, London (1879–95); toured America (1874) and Australia (1890–91).

**Toombs** (tōōmz), **Robert,** *in full* **Robert Augustus.** 1810–1885. American statesman, b. in Wilkes County, Ga.; practiced law in Washington, Ga.; member, U.S. House of Representatives (1845–53); known for aggressively defending Southern position on slavery question; U.S. senator (1853–61); withdrew (1861) to join Confederacy. Secretary of state of the Confederate States (1861); brigadier general (July, 1861); escaped arrest (1865) by fleeing to London (1865–67). Resumed law practice in Washington, Ga. (1867), but never asked for pardon to regain U.S. citizenship under the Reconstruction laws.

**Too'mer** (tōō'mẽr), **Jean.** 1894–1967. American Negro writer, and lecturer on psychology, literature, etc.; author of *Cane* (1923), *Essentials* (1931), *Portage Potential* (1932).

**Too'rop** (tō'rŏp), **Jan.** 1858–1928. Dutch painter, b. on island of Java; associated in later work (from c. 1900) with the pointillists.

**To·pe'li·us** (tŏŏ·pā'lĭ·ŭs), **Zachris.** 1818–1898. Swedish-Finnish journalist, educator, and writer; among his books of verse are lyric collections entitled *Heath Blossoms* (1845, 1850, 1854, 1860) and *New Leaves* (1870); among his plays, *Titian's First Love, After Fifty Years, The Princess of Cyprus;* among his novels, a series of six picturing life in 17th and 18th centuries in Sweden and Finland under general title *The Surgeon's Stories* (1872–74).

**To·pe'te y Car·bal'lo** (tō·pā'tā ē kär·bä'lyō), **Juan Bautista.** 1821–1885. Spanish admiral and politician; chief of staff during Morocco war (1859). Joined Liberals under O'Donnell; sent to Pacific station in war with Peru and Chile (1865–66); wounded at Callao. Returned to Spain and took active part in revolution of 1868 which drove Isabella II from Spain; joined by Prim y Prats and Sagasta in winning over Cádiz and in provisional government that followed; in ministries of Serrano y Domínguez (1872, 1874); retired from active politics (1879).

**Töpf'fer'** (tûp'fâr'), **Rodolphe.** 1799–1846. Swiss artist, educator, and writer; professor of belles-lettres, Geneva (1832–46); among his short stories (*Nouvelles Genevoises*, 1841) is the well-known *La Bibliothèque de mon Oncle* (written in 1833); published series of humorous drawings, collected in *Histoires en Estampes* (1846–47).

**To'pi'nard'** (tō'pē'nȧr'), **Paul.** 1830–1911. French anthropologist; professor, École d'Anthropologie (1876); succeeded Broca as secretary-general of the Anthropological Society (1880).

**Top'la'dy** (tŏp'lā'dĭ), **Augustus Montague.** 1740–1778. English clergyman and champion of the doctrinal Calvinism of the Church of England; bitter antagonist of Wesley and Methodism; author of *Rock of Ages* (1775), *Deathless principle, arise*, and other hymns.

**Töp'ler** (tûp'lẽr). See TOEPLER.

**Tor'bert** (tôr'bẽrt), **Alfred Thomas Archimedes.** 1833–1880. American army officer; brigadier general of volunteers (as of Nov. 29, 1862); commanded cavalry division in Sherman's army (1864); brevetted major general (Mar., 1865).

**Tor'den·skjold** (*Norw.* tŏr'd'n·shŏl; *Dan.* -skyŏl), **Peder.** *Real surname* **Wes'sel** (vĕs'sĕl). 1691–1720. Norwegian naval officer, b. Trondheim; served in Dano-Norwegian navy making daring and successful attacks upon Swedish naval forces; ennobled under title of Tordenskjold (Thunder Shield, 1716); promoted rear admiral (1718) and vice-admiral (1719); killed in duel (1720).

**Tordesillas, Antonio de Herrera y.** See Antonio de HERRERA Y TORDESILLAS.

**To·rell'** (tŏŏ·rĕl'), **Otto Martin.** 1828–1900. Swedish geologist; traveled in Scandinavia, Switzerland, and Iceland studying glaciology; accompanied Nordenskjöld on two expeditions to Spitsbergen (1858 and 1861); chief of Swedish Geological Survey (1870–97); showed that drift deposits of northern Europe were chiefly of glacial origin.

**To·rel'li** (tō·rĕl'lē), **Achille.** 1841–1922. Italian dramatist; works include *I Mariti* (1867), *Fragilità* (1869), *Triste Realtà* (1871); also, comedies in Neapolitan dialect, a novel, and critical works.

**Torelli, Giuseppe.** 1650?–1708. Italian violinist, and composer of concertos and symphonies; reputed one of earliest composers of the concerto grosso.

**To·re'no** (tō·rā'nō), Conde **de. José María Quei'po de Lla'no y Ruiz de Sa·ra'bia** (kĕ'ē·pō thā lyä'nō ē rōō·ēth' thā sä·rä'byä). 1786–1843. Spanish statesman and historian; participated in revolution (1808); deputy in Cortes (1811–14, 1820–23); helped frame constitution of 1812; exiled (1814–20, 1823–32); prime minister (1834) in regency of Maria Christina; author of *Historia del Levantamiento, Guerra, y Revolución de España* (1836–38).

**To·ri·i** (tō·rē·ē). Family of Japanese painters of 18th century of the ukiyoye school, including: **Ki·yo·no·bu** [kē·yō·nō·bōō] (1664–1729); began as print master and painter of theatrical posters, later depicted actors. **Ki·yo·ma·su** [kē·yō·mä·sōō] (1702?–1763); painter and printer; depicted women and actors, and illustrated books. **Ki·yo·mi·tsu** [kē·yō·mē·tsōō] (1735–1785); son and pupil of Kiyomasu; perfected a two-color process. **Ki·yo·na·ga** [kē·yō·nä·gä] (1752–1815); painter and printer, most brilliant representative of the school, esp. skillful in line and color; had great influence on later artists.

**Tor·lo'nia** (tôr·lô'nyä). Distinguished Italian family of Rome, including: **Giovanni** (1754–1829), banker, created duke of Bracciano by the pope; his eldest son, **Marino** (1796–1865), who succeeded to the dukedom; Marino's brother **Alessandro** (1800–1886), known as art collector, created prince of **Ci'vi·tel'la–Ce'si** (chē'vē·tĕl'lä·châ'zē).

**Torquatus, Titus Manlius.** See MANLIUS.

**Tor'que·ma'da, Juan de** (dā tôr'kā·mä'thä). *Latin* **Johannes de Tur're·cre·ma'ta** (dē tûr'ē·krē·mā'tȧ). 1388–1468. Spanish Dominican monk and prelate; ably supported papal policies at the council of Basel (1431–35); created cardinal (1439); author of many theological works.

**Torquemada, Juan de.** 1545?–after 1617. Spanish Franciscan monk and historian in Mexico; provincial of the Franciscan order in Mexico (1614–17); chief work *Monarquía Indiana* (3 vols., 1615).

**Torquemada, Tomás de.** 1420?–1498. Spanish Dominican monk, nephew of Cardinal Juan de Torquemada; appointed by Ferdinand and Isabella first inquisitor general for all the Spanish possessions (1483); made grand inquisitor by Innocent VIII (1487); organized the Inquisition in Spain; became notorious for the severity of his judgments and the cruelty of his punishments.

**Torre,** Duque **de la.** See Francisco SERRANO Y DOMÍNGUEZ.

**Tor'rence** (tŏr'ĕns), **Ridgely,** *in full* **Frederic Ridgely.** 1875–1950. American author, b. Xenia, Ohio; librarian, New York Public Library (1897–1903); editor, *The Critic* (1903); assoc. editor, *The Cosmopolitan* (1905–07), *The New Republic* (1920–34); poet in residence, Antioch (Ohio) Coll. (from 1938). Author of volumes of verse including *The House of a Hundred Lights* (1900), *Abelard and Heloise* (poetic drama, 1907), *Hesperides* (1925), the plays *El Dorado* (1903) and *The Undefended Line* (1938), and plays of Negro life presented on the stage by Negroes, including *Granny Maumee, The Rider of Dreams, Simon the Cyrenian.*

**Tor'rens** (tŏr'ĕnz), Sir **Henry.** 1779–1828. British army officer, of Irish birth; military secretary to Wellesley (afterward duke of Wellington) in Portugal (1808); major general (1814); adjutant general of the forces (1820). **Robert Torrens** (1780–1864), soldier and economist; 2d cousin of Sir Henry Torrens; fought in Peninsula War; M.P. (1831); one of first economists to attribute production of wealth to joint action of land, labor, and capital, and to state law of diminishing return; advocate of colonization of South Australia and of repeal of corn laws. His son Sir **Robert Richard** (1814–1884) emigrated to Australia (1840), became first premier and colonial treasurer of South Australia (1857), originated Torrens land-title system. **William Torrens Mc·Cul'lagh** (mȧ·kŭl'ȧ) **Torrens** (1813–1894), social reformer; son of James McCullagh, Irish mathematician, and Jane Torrens, niece of Robert Torrens (1780–1864); commissioner of Irish poor relief (1835); joined Anti-Corn-Law League; independent liberal M.P. (1847); facilitated clearing of slums by his Artisans' Dwellings Act (1868); established London school board by his amendment of Education Act (1870); author of *The Industrial History of Free Nations* (1846), *History of Cabinets* (1894).

**Tor'res** (tôr'rās), **Luis Va·ez' de** (vä·āth' thā). Spanish navigator of the early 17th century; sailed around New Guinea and discovered (1606) the strait that bears his name (Torres Strait).

**Tor'res Na·har'ro** (tôr'rās nä·är'rō), **Bartolomé de.** d. about 1531. Spanish poet and dramatist; lived at Rome (c. 1513) and Naples; known esp. for his part in developing Spanish comedy; first to designate acts as *jornadas;* author of *Propaladia,* a collection of dramatic works including the comedies *Comedia Himenea* and *Aquilana* (1517).

**Tor'rey** (tŏr'ĭ), **Bradford.** 1843–1912. American ornithologist, b. Weymouth, Mass.; on editorial staff, *Youth's Companion* (1886–1901); author of *Birds in the Bush* (1885), *Everyday Birds* (1901), *Field Days in California* (1913), etc.

**Torrey, Charles Cutler.** 1863–1956. American Semitic scholar; professor, Yale (1900–32).

**Torrey, Charles Turner.** 1813–1846. American abolitionist, b. Scituate, Mass.; settled in Baltimore and aided escaping slaves; arrested, tried (1844), and sentenced to six years' imprisonment in Maryland State penitentiary; died in prison.

**Torrey, John.** 1796–1873. American botanist and chemist, b. New York City; professor of chemistry, Coll. of Phys. & Surg., New York (1827–55), and also professor of chemistry and natural history, Princeton (1830–54); U.S. assayer, in New York Assay Office (1854–73). Collaborated with Asa Gray in preparation of first two volumes of *Flora of North America* (1838–43). Issued monograph on the Cyperaceae (1836); collaborated with Asa Gray in issuing revision of the Eriogoneae (1870). His botanical library and herbarium were deposited with Columbia (1860) and transferred to New York Botanical Garden (1899).

**Torrey, Reuben Archer.** 1856–1928. American evangelist; ordained in Congregational ministry (1878); associated with Dwight L. Moody; superintendent, Moody Bible Institute (1889–1908); dean, Bible Institute, Los Angeles (1912–24); also, pastor of Church of the Open Door, Los Angeles (1915–24).

**Tor'ri·cel'li** (tŏr'rē·chĕl'lē), **Evangelista.** 1608–1647. Italian mathematician and physicist; served at Florence as amanuensis to Galileo who had become blind (1641); after death of Galileo, succeeded him as mathematician to grand duke of Tuscany and professor at Florentine Academy. Made improvements on the telescope; discovered principle of the barometer and devised earliest form of the instrument (1643); constructed a simple microscope; worked on the cycloid.

**Tor'ri·gia'no** (tōr'rē·jä'nō), **Pietro.** 1472–1522. Florentine sculptor; under patronage of Lorenzo the Magnificent; said by Cellini to have broken nose of Michelangelo in a quarrel; soldier in papal army; executed tomb for Henry VII and his queen in Westminster Abbey (1518), and allegedly tomb of Margaret, Countess of Richmond; died in prison of the Inquisition in Spain.

**Tor'ring·ton** (tŏr'ĭng·tŭn). (1) Earl of. = *Arthur Herbert* (1647–1716), under HERBERT family, 4. (2) Viscount. See George BYNG.

**Tor'sten·son'** *or* **Tor'stens·son'** (tôr'stĕn·sôn'), **Lennart.** Count of **Or'ta'la** (ōōr'tä'lȧ). 1603–1651. Swedish soldier; served under Gustavus II in Germany (1630–32); commander in chief of Swedish army in Germany (1641); won battles of Schweidnitz (1642),

Breitenfeld (1642), Jüterbog (1644), Jankau (1645); joined Rákóczy, conquered Moravia and invaded Austria (1645); resigned command because of ill health (1646).

**To'ry'** (tô'rē'), **Geoffroy.** 1480?–?1533. French typographer and type designer; royal printer (1530); designed types for Simon de Colines and Robert Estienne; encouraged use of roman letters instead of gothic, and introduced in French printing the accent, the apostrophe, and the cedilla; also, engraved many vignettes and decorated letters for books he published.

**To'ry** (tō'rĭ), **Henry Marshall.** 1864–1947. Canadian physicist and educator; president, U. of Alberta (1908–28); also, president of National Research Council of Canada (1923–35) and director of the National Research Laboratories (1927–35).

**To'sca·nel'li** (tōs'kä·nĕl'lē), **Paolo dal Poz'zo** (däl pōt'tsō). 1397–1482. Italian physician and cosmographer of Florence; reputed to have given Columbus suggestions by letter and map for a westward voyage to the Far East.

**To'sca·ni'ni** (tōs'kä·nē'nē; *Angl.* tŏs'kȧ·nē'nĭ), **Arturo.** 1867–1957. Italian operatic and symphonic conductor; conductor at La Scala, Milan (1898–1907; 1921–31), Metropolitan Opera Co. (1907–21), N.Y. Philharmonic-Symphony Orchestra (1928–33), guest conductor Philadelphia Orchestra (1930–31; 1941–42), at Bayreuth Festival (1930–32), Salzburg Festival (1934–36). Organizer and conductor, National Broadcasting Co. symphony orchestra (1937–54).

**To·sel'li** (tō·zĕl'lē), **Enrico.** 1883–1926. Italian pianist, and composer of piano pieces, chamber music, a symphonic poem, two operettas, and a widely known *Serenade.*

**Tosorthros.** See ZOSER.

**To'sti** (tôs'tē), Sir **Francesco Paolo.** 1847–1916. Italian-born song composer in England; to London (1875) and became singing teacher to royal family (1880); lived in Rome (from 1913); among his many songs are *Good-bye, At Vespers, Amore, Mattinata, Serenata.*

**Tos'tig** (tŏs'tĭg). Earl of **North·um'bri·a** (nôr·thŭm'brĭ·ȧ). d. 1066. Saxon ruler, son of Earl Godwin and brother of Harold (II); m. Judith, daughter of Count Baldwin IV of Flanders (1051); made earl of Northumbria, Northamptonshire, and Huntingdonshire by his brother-in-law King Edward the Confessor (1055); his severity caused revolt of Northumbrians and setting up of Morcar in his place (1065); outlawed and exiled; joined Harold III Haardraade, King of Norway, in invasion (1066) of northern England, where they defeated Morcar at York, but were defeated by Harold II at Stamford Bridge and slain.

**Tóth** (tōt), **Kálmán.** 1831–1881. Hungarian poet and playwright.

**Tot'i·la** (tŏt''l·ȧ). *Real name* **Bad'ui·la** (băd'wĭ·lȧ). d. 552. King of the Ostrogoths in Italy (541–552); waged successful war against forces of Eastern Roman Empire; overran southern Italy (541–545); captured Rome (546); ravaged Sicily, Sardinia, and Corsica, and attacked Greece (546–551); took Rome a second time (549). Defeated and killed at Taginae by Byzantine general Narses.

**Tot'le·ben** *or* **Tod'le·ben** (tôt'lyĕ·byĕn), Count **Frants Eduard Ivanovich.** 1818–1884. Russian military engineer; distinguished himself during Crimean War (1854–56) by engineering skill in providing for defense of Sevastopol. Promoted general and appointed (1869) chief of department of engineers. During Russo-Turkish War (1877–78), planned successful siege (1877) of Plevna (Pleven) and of Bulgarian fortresses (1878). Appointed to command of entire Russian army (1878); created count. Successively governor of Odessa and governor of Vilna.

**Totnes,** Earl of. See George CAREW.

**Tot'tel** (tŏt''l), **Richard.** 1525?–1594. English publisher and compiler of first English anthology of poetry, known as *Tottel's Miscellany* (1557), including previously unpublished poems by Surrey, Wyatt, Grimald, Heywood, and others. Charter member of Stationers' Co. (1557); published mostly law books, but also More's *Dialogue of Comfort* (1553), Lydgate's *Falls of Princes* (1554), and Hawes's *Passetyme of Pleasure* (1555).

**Tot'ten** (tŏt''n), **Joe Byron.** 1875–1946. American playwright and stage director, b. Brooklyn, N.Y.; dramatized Kauffman's *The House of Bondage,* MacGrath's *Arms and the Woman,* Zane Grey's *Riders of the Purple Sage,* Jack London's *John Barleycorn,* Rives's *The Valiants of Virginia.* Author of a number of farces.

**Totten, Joseph Gilbert.** 1788–1864. American military engineer, b. New Haven, Conn.; grad. U.S.M.A., West Point (1805). Engaged on harbor defenses and river and harbor improvements (1808–38). Served with Gen. Scott in Mexican War; originated plan of operations against Vera Cruz; brevetted brigadier general (Mar., 1847). Promoted brigadier general (Mar., 1863); brevetted major general (1864). Fort Totten, in New York Harbor, is named in his honor.

**Tottington.** See SAMSON OF TOTTINGTON.

**Tou'cey** (?tou'sĭ), **Isaac.** 1792–1869. American politician, b. Newtown, Conn.; member, U.S. House of Representatives (1835–39); governor of Connecticut (1846–47); U.S. attorney general (1848–49); U.S. senator (1852–57); U.S. secretary of the navy (1857–61). Suspected, possibly without reason, of arranging U.S. naval forces in 1860 so as to aid the South in its secession.

**Tou'let'** (tōō'lĕ'), **Paul Jean.** 1867–1920. French writer; by his collection of short lyric poems in an unusual verse form, *Contrerimes,* published (1921) after his death, he exercised considerable influence on a select group of French writers.

**Tou'louse'–Lau'trec'.** *In full* **Henri Marie Raymond de Tou'louse'–Lau'trec' Mon'fa'** (tōō'lōōz'lō'trĕk' môɴ'fá'). 1864–1901. French painter; studied under Cormon. Grotesquely misshapen physically and given to periods of dissipation, he yet left a number of notable paintings, esp. of life and characters in Paris, as *Le Promenoir, Les Femmes qui Dansent,* etc. Excelled also as a designer of posters, an illustrator, and a lithographer.

**Tou'mey** (tōō'mĭ), **James William.** 1865–1932. American forester; professor of forestry (1903–09), dean of school of forestry (1910–22), professor of silviculture (1922–32), Yale.

**Touraine.** French countship. See BLOIS.

**Touraine,** Dukes of. See *earls of Douglas,* under DOUGLAS family.

**Tour·gée'** (tōōr·zhā'), **Albion Wi'ne·gar** (?wĭ'nē·gēr). 1838–1905. American politician and author, b. Williamsfield, Ohio; served in Civil War; judge, North Carolina superior court (1868–74); showed political partisanship and was branded as a carpetbagger; moved to Mayville, N.Y. (1881). Author of novels based on his experience during the Reconstruction period, including *Toinette* (1874, over pseudonym **Henry Chur'ton** [chûr't'n]), *A Fool's Errand* (1879), *An Appeal to Caesar* (1884).

**Tourguenieff** *or* **Tourgueneff.** Variants of TURGENEV.

**Tour·jée'** (tōōr·zhā'), **Eben.** 1834–1891. American musician, b. Warwick, R.I.; with Robert Goldbeck, founded (1867) New England Conservatory of Music in Boston.

**Tournachon, Félix.** See NADAR.

**Tournebu, Adrien.** See TURNÈBE.

**Tour'ne·fort'** (to͞or'nĕ·fôr'), **Joseph Pitton de.** 1656–1708. French botanist; one of the founders of modern systematic botany; credited with being first to group plants into genera; author of *Éléments de Botanique ou Méthode pour Connaître les Plantes*, of *Institutiones Rei Herbariae* (3 vols., 1700), etc.

**Tour'ne·mire'** (to͞or'nĕ·mēr'), **Charles.** 1870–1939. French organist, and composer of sacred and lyric dramas, symphonies, chamber music, etc.

**Tour'neur** *or* **Tur'nour** *or* **Tur'ner** (tûr'nẽr), **Cyril.** 1575?–1626. English dramatist; served in Low Countries; served as Sir Edward Cecil's secretary on disastrous expedition to Cádiz (1625); on return trip, put ashore among sick in Ireland and died there; author of two tragedies, *The Revenger's Tragedy* (1607) and *The Atheist's Tragedy* (1611), and an allegorical lament on political and ecclesiastical corruption (1600).

**Tourte** (to͞ort), **François.** 1747–1835. French manufacturer of violin bows; devised the bow known as the *Tourte bow.*

**Tour'ville'** (to͞or'vēl'), Comte **de. Anne Hilarion de Co'ten'tin'** (dĕ kô'tăN'tăN'). 1642–1701. French naval officer; chief of squadron (1676) and second in command under Duquesne in clearing the Mediterranean of Algerian and Tripolitan pirates (1683); vice-admiral (1689); defeated Anglo-Dutch fleet off the Isle of Wight (1690), but was defeated at La Hogue (May 29, 1692); created marshal of France (1693); triumphed over Anglo-Dutch fleet off Cape St. Vincent (May 26–27, 1693).

**Tou'sard'** (to͞o'zȧr'), **Anne** (än) **Louis de.** 1749–1817. Army officer, b. Paris, France; to America (1777); engaged at Brandywine and Germantown; lost right arm in action (Aug. 28, 1778). Commissioned major of artillery in U.S. army; colonel (1798); planned and supervised construction of defenses at Fort Mifflin, Pa., West Point, N.Y., and Newport, R.I. Reorganized garrison at West Point as a military school (1801–02). To France, and pensioned by Napoleon (1802–05). French agent at New Orleans (1805) and later vice-consul at Philadelphia, Baltimore, and New Orleans (to 1816). Died in Paris.

**Toussaint, Anna Louisa Geertruida.** See BOSBOOM-TOUSSAINT.

**Tous'saint' L'Ou'ver'ture'** (to͞o'săN' lo͞o'vĕr'tür'), **Pierre Dominique.** 1743–1803. Haitian Negro general and liberator, b. near Cape François, Haiti, of African slave parents. Took prominent part in slave insurrection (1791); after slaves were freed (1793), joined French republicans; became their recognized leader; forced British to evacuate island (1798); defeated Rigaud, leader of mulattoes, in civil war (1799); master of entire island (1801); gave just and firm administration (1801–02); resisted Napoleon's attempt to re-establish slavery; overcome by French forces under Gen. Leclerc (1802); charged with conspiracy and sent as prisoner to France; died in prison.

**Tout** ( tout), **Thomas Frederick.** 1855–1929. English historian; author of *Analysis of English History* (1891), *Edward the First* (1893), *The Empire and the Papacy* (1898), *History of England, 1216–1377* (1905, constituting vol. III of Longman's *Political History of England*), *France and England...* (1922), etc.

**To'vey** (tō'vĭ), Sir **Donald Francis.** 1875–1940. English composer and writer on music; Reid professor of music, Edinburgh (from 1914); composer of a symphony, a concerto for violoncello and orchestra (1934), an opera, *The Bride of Dionysus* (to R. C. Trevelyan's text), and chamber music; author of *Essays in Musical Analysis* (5 vols. of program notes), etc.

**Tov'ey** (tŭv'ĭ), **John Cronyn.** 1st baron. 1885–1971. British naval officer; in command of destroyer flotillas in Mediterranean (1938–40); commander in chief of home fleet (1940–43), of the Nore (1943–46).

**Tow'er** (tou'ẽr), **Charlemagne.** 1848–1923. American businessman and diplomat, b. Philadelphia; U.S. minister to Austria-Hungary (1897–99), ambassador to Russia (1899–1902), and to Germany (1902–08).

**Tow'ers** (tou'ẽrz), **John Henry.** 1885–1955. American naval officer, b. Rome, Ga.; grad. (1906) U.S.N.A., Annapolis; in naval aviation service (from 1911); asst. chief, Bureau of Aeronautics (1929–31, 1938–39), chief (1939–42); commander, air force, Pacific Fleet (1942–44); deputy commander, Pacific area (1944–45).

**Towle** (tōl), **George Makepeace.** 1841–1893. American journalist, lecturer, and author of *Pizarro* (1879), *Beaconsfield* (1879), *Marco Polo* (1880), *Ralegh...* (1881), *Drake* (1883), etc.

**Town** (toun), **Ithiel.** 1784–1844. American architect, b. Thompson, Conn.; designed Center Church and Trinity Church on New Haven, Conn., green, Christ Church in Hartford, Conn., the U.S. Custom House in New York City; in partnership with Martin E. Thompson (1827–28) and with Alexander J. Davis (in firm of Town & Davis, 1829–43); patented design for truss bridge (1820) and received many commissions for building bridges.

**Towne** (toun), **Charles Hanson.** 1877–1949. American poet; editor of *Harper's Bazaar* (1926–31); columnist on New York *American* (1931–37); author of *The Quiet Singer and Other Poems, Youth and Other Poems, An April Song,* English lyrics for Offenbach's opera *La Belle Hélène,* etc.

**Townes** (tounz), **Charles Hard.** 1915– . American physicist, b. Greenville, S.C. At Columbia U. (1948–61), M.I.T. (1961–67), U. of Calif. (1967– ). Awarded Nobel prize in physics (1964) with N. Basov and A. Prokhorov for development of the maser.

**Town'ley** (toun'lĭ), **James.** 1714–1778. English dramatist; headmaster (1760) of Merchant Taylors' school; author of *High Life below Stairs* (produced 1759).

**Town'send** (toun'zĕnd), **Edward Davis.** 1817–1893. American army officer; adjutant general, U.S. army (1862–80); under his direction was begun collection of material on Civil War, later published as *War of the Rebellion: Official Records.*

**Townsend, Edward Waterman.** 1855–1942. American journalist, legislator, and writer, b. Cleveland, Ohio; on staff of New York newspapers; made success by sketches of Bowery life in the slang of New York's East Side; created fictional character Chimmie Fadden.

**Townsend, Francis Everett.** 1867–1960. American physician, b. Fairbury, Ill.; originator and head of the Townsend Recovery Plan, officially Old-Age Revolving Pensions, Ltd., proposing monthly pensions of $200 to U.S. citizens over 60, funds to be provided by a 2 per cent transaction tax.

**Townsend, John Kirk.** 1809–1851. American ornithologist, b. Philadelphia; member of expedition under one Nathaniel J. Wyeth from Independence, Mo., to the Oregon region (1834). Birds from his collection were painted for last volume of Audubon's *Birds of America* (1844); and his mammals were described and painted by Audubon and John Bachman in *The Viviparous Quadrupeds of North America.*

**Townsend, John Sealy Edward.** 1868–1957. Irish physicist; first to determine the electrical charge on one ion in a gas (1897).

**Townsend, Meredith White.** 1831–1911. English journalist; with Richard Holt Hutton (*q.v.*), bought and edited *Spectator*, London (1861–97), specializing on foreign politics and India; collaborated with the historical writer John Langton Sanford in *The Great Governing Families of England* (2 vols., 1865).

**Town'shend** (toun'zĕnd). Name of English family including distinguished statesmen and soldiers:

**Charles Townshend** (1674–1738), 2d Viscount Townshend of Rayn'ham (răn'ăm); statesman. Son of Sir **Horatio**, 1st viscount (1630?–1687), of old Norfolk family, promoter of Restoration; educ. Cambridge. In House of Lords, went over from Tories to Whigs; a commissioner for union with Scotland (1706); plenipotentiary in negotiations preceding Treaty of Utrecht (1709); voted enemy of his country (1712) for having exceeded authority in Barrier treaty. Secretary of state for northern department on accession of George I, with power to name colleagues to form ministry (1714); married Sir Robert Walpole's sister (1713); prompt and severe in suppressing Jacobite rising (1715); promoted defensive alliances with emperor and with France; dismissed through Stanhope's intrigues, on charge of plotting to place prince of Wales on throne (1716). After break of South Sea Bubble, again secretary of state for northern department (1721), with Walpole as first lord of treasury and chancellor of exchequer, through reign of George I; obtained dismissal of rival John Carteret, but overshadowed by Walpole's financial ability and superior influence in House of Commons; dissatisfied with working of Quadruple Alliance, forced separation of emperor from Spain in order to break up Austrian dominions; won Hanoverian League to side of Spain (1729); prepared way for alliance between Spain and France; on threat of Prussian majesty to join emperor, urged campaign against empire; opposed by Walpole and Queen Caroline, resigned (1730) and devoted himself to agriculture, improving cultivation of turnips and crop rotation.

His grandson **Charles Townshend** (1725–1767), cabinet minister; sometimes called "the Weathercock"; educ. Leiden and Oxford; M.P. (1747); a lord of admiralty (1754–55). On accession of George III, transferred support from Pitt to Bute and became secretary-at-war (1761–62); paymaster general (1765); chancellor of exchequer (1766) in Chatham's ministry and, on impairment of Chatham's mind, controlled the ministry; sought to find in America revenue lost by reduction of land tax; delivered in House of Commons witty and eloquent but reckless speeches, including so-called "champagne" speech (1767); suspended activities of New York assembly; as last official act, passed through Parliament measure taxing glass, paper, and tea on importation into American colonies, which led toward separation of colonies.

Charles's brother **George** (1724–1807), 4th Viscount and 1st Marquis Townshend; soldier; M.A., Cantab. (1749). Served in Netherlands and at Culloden Moor (1746) and Laufeld (1747); drafted militia bill (1757); as brigadier general under Wolfe, commanded left wing on Heights of Abraham in Quebec expedition, and on death of Wolfe succeeded to chief command (1759); as lord lieutenant of Ireland (1767–72), sought to break down government by introduction of settlers called undertakers, obtained parliamentary majority by corruption; created marquis (1786) and field marshal (1796).

Sir **Charles Vere Ferrers Townshend** (1861–1924), soldier; great-grandson of 1st marquis; served in Sudan expedition (1884–85); distinguished himself by holding Chitral fort, India (1895); served in Boer War; major general (1911); drove Turks from Al Qurna on Tigris and pursued them to Amara (1915); defeated Turks and took Kut-el-Amara, but failed to capture Baghdad, and finally surrendered Kut (1916); wrote *Life of Field-Marshal 1st Marquis Townshend.*

**Thomas Townshend** (1733–1800), 1st Viscount **Syd'ney** (sĭd'nĭ), cabinet minister; son of a teller of the exchequer (1701–1780), who was son of Charles Townshend, 2d viscount. A lord of the treasury under Rockingham (1765); joint paymaster of the forces (1767–68); war secretary in Rockingham's administration (1782), and home secretary in Shelburne's and again in Pitt's; created Baron Sydney (1783). Sydney, Australia, was named for him.

**Toy** (toi), **Crawford Howell.** 1836–1919. American Oriental scholar; professor of Hebrew and other Oriental languages, Harvard (1880–1909); author of *History of the Religion of Israel* (1882), *Judaism and Christianity* (1890), *Introduction to the History of Religions* (1913), etc.

**Toyn'bee** (toin'bē), **Arnold.** 1852–1883. English sociologist and economist; pioneer in social settlement movement in district of Whitechapel, where two years after his death, Toynbee Hall, first social settlement in the world, was erected in his honor.

His brother **Paget** (1855–1932), philologist and Dante scholar; published *Life of Dante* (1900), and translations, critical texts of letters of Dante (1912–17, 1920), dictionary of proper names in Dante (1914), *Dante in English Art* (1920); editor of *Oxford Dante* (1924); also, supplemented edition of *Letters of Horace Walpole* (3 vols., 1912; 3 vols., 1919–25) by his wife, **Helen,** *nee* **Wrigley** (d. 1910), continued her work with Walpole's *Journals* (1923, 1928) and *Reminiscences* (1924).

Their nephew **Arnold Joseph Toynbee** (1889–1975), historian; son-in-law of Gilbert Murray; during World War, in political intelligence department of foreign office; delegate to Paris Peace Conference (1919); professor of Byzantine and modern Greek language, literature, and history, U. of London (1919–24); professor of international history, U. of London (1925–55); author of works on Greek history and civilization, etc.

**To·yo·ku·ni** (tō·yō·kōō·nē), **Utagawa.** 1769–1825. Japanese painter and print maker; best known for delineations of contemporary actors and life in the theater.

**To·yo·to·mi** (tō·yō·tō·mē). Family name given (1585) to Hideyoshi (*q.v.*) after he became kwampaku (official representative of emperor). Also held by his son Hideyori, and applied to a period (1573–1602) of Japanese painting.

**T. P.** = Thomas Power O'CONNOR.

**Tra'cy'** (trȧ'sē'), Marquis **de. Alexandre de Prou'ville'** (dē prōō'vēl'). 1603–1670. French soldier; lieutenant general of French possessions in North America; in Quebec (1665), led expedition against Mohawks (1666), forcing them to sue for peace.

**Tracy, Antoine Louis Claude Destutt de.** See DESTUTT DE TRACY.

**Tra'cy** (trā'sĭ), **Benjamin Franklin.** 1830–1915. American lawyer, b. near Owego, N.Y.; counsel for defense in case of Tilton vs. Beecher (1875); judge, New York court of appeals (1881–82); U.S. secretary of the navy (1889–93); increased number of battleships and raised standards of service; sometimes referred to as "Father of the American Navy."

**Tragus.** See Hieronymus BOCK.

**Tra·herne'** (trȧ·hûrn'), **Thomas.** 1637?–1674. English poet and religious writer; chaplain of Sir Orlando Bridgeman, lord keeper of the seals, at Teddington. Author of *Roman Forgeries* (1673), *Christian Ethicks* (1675), *Centuries of Meditations,* in prose, and original imaginative poems of metaphysical type once mistaken for the work of Henry Vaughan. See Bertram DOBELL.

**Traill** (trāl), **Henry Duff.** 1842–1900. English journalist and writer of biographical and critical studies. Editorial writer of *Daily Telegraph* (1882–97); directed editing of *Social England* (6 vols., 1893–97); first editor of *Literature* (1897–1900). Author of *The New Lucian* (1884; series of "dialogues of the dead") and a successful play, *Glaucus, a Tale of a Fish* (1865); collaborator with Robert Hichens in *The Medicine Man* (played 1898).

**Traill, Peter.** See Guy Mainwaring MORTON.

**Train** (trān), **Arthur.** 1875–1945. American lawyer and writer, b. Boston; A.B. (1896), LL.B. (1899), Harvard; practiced in New York; author of stories involving courts and legal matters, many of them with the fictional lawyer Ephraim Tutt as central character.

**Tra'jan** (trā'jăn). *Lat.* **Marcus Ulpius Tra·ja'nus** (trȧ·jā'nŭs). 52 or 53–117. Roman emperor (98–117), b. near Seville, Spain. Early began career of soldier; military tribune for ten years; served in Syria and Spain; consul (91); adopted as successor by Nerva (97). On accession took title *Imperator Caesar Nerva Trajanus Augustus;* completed fortifications on Rhine (98–99); conducted first Dacian campaign (101–103), in which Decebalus was defeated; in second campaign (104–106) completely defeated Dacians and made Dacia a Roman province; famous triumphal column (Trajan's Column) erected (114) to commemorate event; period of peace (107–114); conducted successful wars against Armenians and Parthians (114–116); died on return in Cilicia; improved and constructed many buildings (especially Trajan's Forum); also built many roads and bridges throughout the empire.

**Trall** (trôl), **Russell Thacker.** 1812–1877. American physician, b. in Tolland County, Conn.; founded water-cure establishment (1843) and New York Hygeio-Therapeutic Coll., New York City.

**Trapassi, Pietro.** See METASTASIO.

**Trask** (trăsk), **Spencer.** 1844–1909. American banker and philanthropist. His wife **Kate,** *nee* **Nich'ols** [nĭk'ŭlz] (1853–1922), was a writer under pen name **Katrina Trask;** published *Sonnets and Lyrics* (1895), *Lessons in Love* (1900), *In My Lady's Garden* (1907), *King Alfred's Jewel* (1909), etc.

**Trau'be** (trou'bĕ), **Isidor.** 1860–1943. German physical chemist; known especially for work on atomic and molecular covolumes.

**Traube, Ludwig.** 1818–1876. German clinician and pathologist; introduced experimentation with animals into the study of pathology; promoted use of percussion and auscultation, and of thermometry in physical diagnosis.

**Trau'bel** (trou'bĕl), **Helen.** 1903–1972. Am. operatic and concert soprano, b. St. Louis, Mo.; member of Metropolitan Opera Co. (1940–53), known esp. for Wagnerian roles; first transcontinental concert tour (1940–41).

**Traubel, Horace L.** 1858–1919. American author; Marxian Socialist and follower of Eugene V. Debs; close associate, friend, and a literary executor, of Walt Whitman; published *With Walt Whitman in Camden* (3 vols., 1906–14); also wrote *Chants Communal* (1904), *Optimos* (1910), *Collects* (1915).

**Traut'mann** (trout'män), **Reinhold.** 1883–1951. German philologist; author of *Baltisch-Slawisches Wörterbuch* (1923), *Die Volksdichtung der Grossrussen...* (1935), etc.

**Trautt'mans·dorff** (trout'mäns·dôrf), Count **Maximilian von und zu.** 1584–1650. Austrian diplomat and statesman; concluded peace of Nikolsburg (1622) and Treaty of Prague (1635); took part in peace congresses at Münster and Osnabrück (1645–48), preliminary to Treaty of Westphalia (1648); prime minister of Austria (1648–50).

**Traut'wine** (trout'wīn), **John Cresson.** 1810–1883. American engineer, b. Philadelphia; engaged in railroad engineering (1831–43), canal building in Colombia (1844–49), transisthmian railroad survey at Panama (1849–51), transisthmian canal survey at Panama (1852–54), interoceanic railway survey in Honduras (1857), dock construction in Montreal (1858), etc.; author of *Engineers' Pocket Book* (1871).

**Trav'ers** (trăv'ẽrz), **Jerome Dunstan.** 1887–1951. American golf player; winner of U.S. amateur championship (1907, 1908, 1912, 1913) and the open championship (1915).

**Travers, Morris William.** 1872-1961. English chemist; professor, University College, Bristol (from 1904). With Sir William Ramsay, discovered the elements neon, krypton, and xenon (1898); known also for researches relating to low temperatures.

**Travers, Pamela.** 1906– . Australian writer in England, b. in North Queensland; best known for her "Mary Poppins" books, as *Mary Poppins* (1934) and *Mary Poppins Comes Back* (1935).

**Tra'viès' de Vil'lers'** (trȧ'vyâs' dẽ vē'lâr'), **Charles Joseph.** 1804–1859. French painter and caricaturist; a founder of *Charivari* (1831) and of *Caricature* (1838), where most of his work appeared; one of the illustrators (1848–55) of Balzac's novels.

**Trav'is** (trăv'ĭs), **Walter Jeremiah.** 1862–1927. Golf champion, b. in Maldon, Victoria, Australia; to U.S. as a young man; amateur champion of U.S. three times (1900, 1901, 1903) and British amateur champion (1904).

**Travis, William Barret.** 1809–1836. Lawyer and soldier, b. near Red Banks, S.C.; went to Texas (1831); rose to leadership among the aggressive Texans ready to resist Mexican authority; commanded Texas force of 188 men at the Alamo, completely destroyed by Mexican army under Santa Anna (Mar. 6, 1836).

**Tray'lor** (trā'lẽr), **Melvin Alvah.** 1878–1934. American banker, b. Breeding, Ky.; president, First National Bank, Chicago (1931–34); with Jackson Reynolds, represented the United States in organizing the Bank for International Settlements, at Basel, Switzerland (1929).

**Tre·bo'ni·us** (trē·bō'nĭ·ŭs), **Gaius.** d. 43 B.C. Roman general; held command in Spain (46 B.C.); consul (45); an accomplice in assassination of Caesar (44) and received governorship of Asia; killed at Smyrna by Dolabella.

**Tré'cul'** (trā'kül'), **Auguste Adolphe Lucien.** 1818–1896. French botanist; specialist in morphology.

**Tree** (trē), **Ellen.** 1805–1880. English actress. See Charles John KEAN.

**Tree,** Sir **Herbert Beer'bohm** (bēr'bōm). 1853–1917. English actor-manager; son of Julius Beerbohm, naturalized English grain merchant of German origin; half brother of Max Beerbohm (*q.v.*). Made stage debut (1876) as Beerbohm Tree (surname *Tree* being a translation of the second element of his orig. surname *Beerbohm,* "pear tree"); won first success as curate in *The Private Secretary* (1884); lessee and manager Haymarket Theatre (1887–97), playing in Ibsen, Wilde, Maeterlinck, and as Iago, Hamlet, Henry VIII, and Falstaff; as manager of Her Majesty's Theatre (from 1897), played wide range of parts, attempted to revive poetic drama with Stephen Phillips's plays *Herod* (1900), *Ulysses* (1902), and *Nero* (1906), and staged overelaborate productions of Shakespeare; filled motion-picture contract, Los Angeles (1915). Author of *Thoughts and Afterthoughts* (1913). His wife (m. 1883), **Maud Holt** [hōlt] (1864–1937), actress under name of Mrs. Beerbohm Tree, was well known in her chief parts, Ophelia and Lady Teazle.

**Treece** (trēs), **Henry.** 1912–1966. British poet, of Irish-

Welsh extraction; pilot officer in R.A.F.; poems collected in *Towards a Personal Armageddon* (1941), *Invitation and Warning* (1942).

**Tréfouret, Jeanne Alfrédine.** See Jane HADING.

**Tre·gel′les** (trē·gĕl′ĭs), **Samuel Prideaux.** 1813–1875. English Biblical scholar; ironworker; largely self-educated in Greek, Hebrew, Chaldee, and Welsh; prepared a critical edition of Greek Testament (1857–72).

**Treil′hard′** (trĕ′yȧr′), Comte **Jean Baptiste.** 1742–1810. French politician; member of the States-General (1789), National Convention (1792), Council of Five Hundred, Court of Cassation; represented France at congress of Rastatt (1798); member of the Directory; appointed by Napoleon president of court of appeal in Paris, and member of Council of State; played important part in drafting various legal codes.

**Treitsch′ke** (trīch′kĕ), **Heinrich von.** 1834–1896. German historian and publicist, b. Dresden; professor, Kiel (1866), Heidelberg (1867), Berlin (1874); succeeded Ranke as historiographer of Prussia (1886); strong supporter of Hohenzollern dynasty; advocated colonial expansion; largely responsible for growth of anti-British feeling in Germany; chief work, *Deutsche Geschichte im 19. Jahrhundert* (5 vols., 1879–94).

**Tre·law′ny** (trē·lô′nĭ), **Edward John.** 1792–1881. English sailor and adventurer; son of army officer; entered navy at thirteen; deserted at Bombay because of hard treatment, led adventurous career in Eastern Archipelago; companion of Shelley and Byron in Italy (1821); present at Leghorn on occasion of Shelley and Williams's drowning, superintended recovery and cremation of bodies (1822); with Byron, aided in Greek struggle for independence; became social favorite in London; buried beside Shelley. Portrayed as the old seaman in Millais's *Northwest Passage.* Author of the autobiographical *Adventures of a Younger Son* (1831) and *Recollections of the Last Days of Shelley and Byron* (1858; recast as *Records of Shelley, Byron and the Author*, 1878).

**Trelawny,** Sir **Jonathan.** 1650–1721. Bishop of Bristol (1685); one of the Seven Bishops (see William SANCROFT) who petitioned against James II's Declaration of Indulgence (1688), but were acquitted of charge of seditious libel.

**Tre·lease′** (trē·lēs′), **William.** 1857–1945. American botanist, b. Mt. Vernon, N.Y. B.S., Cornell (1880), Sc.D., Harvard (1884); professor, Washington U. (1885–1913), Illinois (1913–26); author of *Agave in the West Indies* (1913), *The Genus Phoradendron* (1916), *The American Oaks* (1925), etc.

**Tre·main′** (trē·mān′), **Henry Edwin.** 1840–1910. American army officer and lawyer, b. New York City; served through Civil War; aide-de-camp to Gen. Sickles at Fredericksburg, Chancellorsville, Gettysburg; on staff duty with Army of the Potomac (1864–65); brigadier general (Nov., 1865); awarded Congressional Medal of Honor; practiced law in New York City (1868 ff.).

**Trem′bley′** (träɴ′blā′), **Abraham.** 1700–1784. Swiss naturalist; while working in Holland, discovered regeneration of lost parts in hydras.

**Trench** (trĕnch), **Frederic Herbert.** 1865–1923. British poet, b. in Ireland; educ. Oxford; examiner for board of education (1891–1909); artistic director, Haymarket Theatre, London (1909–11); resident chiefly in Italy (from 1911); author of volumes of verse, *Napoleon* (play; 1919), etc.

**Trench, Richard Chen′e·vix** (shĕn′ĕ·vē). 1807–1886. English poet and Anglican prelate, b. Dublin; M.A., Cantab. (1833); intimate with members of the Apostles' Club, including Tennyson; curate (1841) and chaplain (1845) to Samuel Wilberforce; professor of divinity, King's Coll., London (1846–58); dean of Westminster (1856); archbishop of Dublin (1863–84); took lead in opposing Irish disestablishment; author of sonnets, lyrics, and hymns; edited *Sacred Latin Poetry*, medieval church hymns (1849); promoted scientific study of language with his philological works, as *On the Study of Words* (1851), *English Past and Present* (1855); suggested resolution passed by Philological Society (1857) that originated scheme of Oxford *New English Dictionary;* author of erudite but popular *Notes on the Parables* (1841) and *Notes on the Miracles* (1846).

**Tren′chard** (trĕn′chärd; -chẽrd), **Hugh Montague.** 1st Viscount **Trenchard.** 1873–1956. Marshal of the Royal Air Force. Entered army (1893); served in Boer War (1899–1902), World War (1914–18); major general (1916); chief of air staff (1918–29); air marshal (1919), air chief marshal (1922), marshal of the R.A.F. (from 1927); commissioner, metropolitan police (1931–35).

**Trenck** (trĕngk), Baron **Franz von der.** 1711–1749. Austrian soldier; commanded regiment of Croatian peasants known as pandours and notorious for cruelty and pillage; joined army of Maria Theresa with his regiment; court-martialed (1746) and condemned to death, but sentence commuted to imprisonment; spent last years in prison at Spielberg. His cousin Baron **Friedrich von der Trenck** (1726–1794), military adventurer, served in Prussian army of Frederick the Great (1742); imprisoned on charges of plotting against king; escaped (1747); entered Austrian service (1749); captured by Frederick and again imprisoned (to 1763); in Paris during French Revolution, arrested by Robespierre, convicted of being a foreign secret agent, and executed.

**Tren′de·len·burg** (trĕn′dĕ·lĕn·bo͝orĸ), **Friedrich Adolf.** 1802–1872. German philosopher; professor, Berlin; adherent of Aristotelianism and opponent of Hegelianism.

**Tre′pov** (tryâ′pôf), **Dmitri Fëdorovich.** 1855–1906. Russian general and government official; chief of imperial police in Moscow (fr. 1896); placed in command of St. Petersburg to suppress public disturbances (1905); severity of his measures caused a number of strikes throughout Russia. His brother **Aleksandr Fëdorovich** (1863–1928) was Russian prime minister (Nov., 1916–Jan., 1917).

**Tres′cot** (trĕs′kŭt), **William Henry.** 1822–1898. American lawyer, historian, and diplomat, b. Charleston, S.C.; asst. secretary of state (1860–61); resigned to join Confederacy (1861); a counselor for U.S. government in hearing before Halifax Fishery Commission (1877); one of three commissioners sent (1880) to China to negotiate changes in Burlingame Treaty on Chinese immigration; author of *Diplomacy of the Revolution* (1852); *The Diplomatic History of the Administrations of Washington and Adams* (1857), etc.

**Tres′ham** (?trĕs′ăm), **Francis.** 1567?–1605. English conspirator; initiated into Gunpowder Plot, disapproved of it and revealed it to his brother-in-law Lord Monteagle.

**Tre′sić Pa′vi·čić** (trĕ′sēt·y′ [*Angl.* -sĭch] pä′vē·chēt′y′ [*Angl.* -chĭch]), **Ante.** 1867– . Croatian writer and diplomat; Yugoslav representative (1920–27) successively in Madrid, Lisbon, and Washington; author of volumes of verse and of plays including *Czar Simeon* (1897), *Herodes* (1910), *Cato of Utica* (1911).

**Treu** (troi), **Georg.** 1843–1921. German archaeologist; took part in excavations at Olympia (1877–81).

**Treub** (trûp), **Melchior.** 1851–1910. Dutch botanist; director of department of agriculture, Netherlands East Indies (1885 ff.); author of works on plant physiology.

**Tre·vel′yan** (trē·vĕl′yăn; -vĭl′yăn). Name of English family of Cornish origin including: Sir **Charles Edward**

(1807–1886), member of Bengal civil service (from 1826); wrote *On the Education of the People of India* (1838); asst. secretary to treasury, London (1840–59); governor of Madras (1859), recalled for opposing financial policy of Calcutta (1860); Indian finance minister (1862), carried out reforms; in conjunction with his cousin Sir **Walter Calverley Trevelyan** (1797–1879), geologist, edited *Trevelyan Papers.*

Sir **George Otto** (1838–1928), historian; only son of Charles Edward by his first wife, Hannah More Macaulay, sister of Lord Macaulay; grad. Cambridge (1861); private secretary to his father in India; wrote humorous books, including comedy *The Dawk Bungalow* (1863) and *Letters of a Competition Wallah* (1864), and a serious book, *Cawnpore* (1865); M.P. (1865); secretary to admiralty (1880–82); chief secretary for Ireland (1882–84); advocate of extension of household suffrage to the counties; secretary for Scotland (1886, 1892–95); member of Order of Merit (1911); author of biography of his uncle, *The Life and Letters of Lord Macaulay* (2 vols., 1876), *The Early History of Charles James Fox* (1880), *The American Revolution* (6 vols., 1899–1914).

George Otto's eldest son, Sir **Charles Philips** (1870–1958), Liberal M.P. (1899); parliamentary secretary of board of education (1908–14), resigned in protest against war policy; minister for education in Macdonald cabinets (1924, 1929–31).

**Robert Calverley** (1872–1951), 2d son of George Otto; author of verse translations of Greek dramas and Lucretius, also of volumes of original verse and plays in verse, including *Cecilia Gonzaga* (1903), *Sisyphus* (1908), *The Pearl Tree* (1917), *Rimeless Numbers* (1932), *Beelzebub* (1935), and a prose work, *Thamyris, or the Future of Poetry* (1925).

**George Macaulay** (1876–1962, 3d son of George Otto, historian; educ. Cambridge; served in World War (1915–18), commanding British ambulance unit in Italy; regius professor of modern history, Cambridge (1927–40); member of Order of Merit (1930); author of a trilogy on Garibaldi (1907, 1909, 1911), *British History in the Nineteenth Century, 1782–1901* (1922), *History of England* (1926), *England under Queen Anne* (3 vols., 1930–34), *The English Revolution, 1688* (1938), *English Social History* (1942), biographies of John Bright, Lord Grey, Sir George Otto Trevelyan, etc. His wife, **Janet Penrose,** *nee* **Ward** [wôrd] (1879–1956), daughter of Humphry and Mary Ward; assisted at Passmore Edwards Settlement, founded by her mother; started school treatment centers, London; worked for Belgian refugees; author of *Evening Play Centres for Children* (1920), *A Short History of the Italian People* (1920), *The Life of Mrs. Humphry Ward* (1923), etc.

**Tre·ven′a** (?trē·vĕn′ȧ), **John.** *Pseudonym of* **Ernest George Hen′ham** (hĕn′ăm). 1870– . English poet and novelist in Canada.

**Treves** (trēvz), Sir **Frederick.** 1853–1923. English physician; a founder of British Red Cross Society, and first chairman of its executive committee; sergeant surgeon to King Edward VII and George V; surgeon extraordinary to Queen Victoria (1900–01); surgeon in ordinary to Queen Alexandra. Compiled *German-English Dictionary of Medical Terms;* author of books on surgery, and *The Other Side of the Lantern* (1905), *Highways and Byways in Dorset* (1906), *Cradle of the Deep* (1908), *The Country of the Ring and the Book* (1913), *The Riviera of the Corniche Road* (1921), etc.

**Trevet, Nicholas.** See TRIVET.

**Trevethin,** Baron. See Sir Alfred Tristram LAWRENCE.

**Tre′vi·ra′nus** (trā′vē·rä′no͝os), **Gottfried Reinhold.** 1776–1837. German naturalist; known esp. for histological and anatomical studies on invertebrates; credited with coining the term *biology* in his *Biologie oder Philosophie der Lebenden Natur* (6 vols., 1802–22). His brother **Ludolph Christian** (1779–1864), physician and botanist, discovered the intercellular spaces.

**Tre·vi′sa** (trĕ·vē′sȧ), **John de.** 1326–1412. English translator, a Cornishman; fellow at Oxford (Exeter 1362–69; Queen's 1369–79); vicar of Berkeley; translator of Higden's *Polychronicon* (1387), with added introduction and continuation, and *De Proprietatibus Rerum* of Bartholomaeus Anglicus (1398).

**Trev′i·thick** (trĕv′ĭ·thĭk), **Richard.** 1771–1833. English engineer and inventor; engineer in Cornish mine; improved plunger pump for deep mining, later developing it into a water-pressure engine; built high-pressure steam engine (1800); completed steam road carriage, first vehicle to convey passengers by force of steam (Christmas Eve, 1801); built first steam locomotive to be tried on a railway, hauling ten tons of iron, seventy men, and five wagons 9½ miles at nearly five miles an hour (Feb., 1804); first to use exhaust steam to increase draft in chimney; proved that friction of smooth wheels on track is adequate traction for ordinary grades; applied high-pressure steam engines to rock boring, dredging, and agriculture.

**Tri′bo·lo, Il** (ēl trē′bô·lō). *Real name* **Niccolò Pe·ri′co·li** (pâ·rē′kô·lē). 1485–1550. Italian sculptor and architect; architect to Grand Duke Cosimo I of Tuscany; works include marble statues *Sibyls,* and *Assumption of the Virgin* (Bologna), and tomb of Adrian VI (with Michelangelo, at Pisa).

**Tri·bo′ni·an** (trĭ·bō′nĭ·ăn). *Lat.* **Tri·bo′ni·a′nus** (trĭ·bō′nĭ·ā′nŭs). d. ?545. Roman jurist, b. in Pamphylia; chief legal minister of Justinian, who appointed him (528) one of ten commissioners to prepare the *Codex* of imperial constitutions; chief of various commissions (530–534) that prepared under Justinian's orders the *Institutes,* the *Digest* (or *Pandects,* 533), and revised *Codex* (see JUSTINIAN I); held office of quaestor most of the time till his death.

**Triboulet.** See FEVRIAL.

**Trie′pel** (trē′pĕl), **Heinrich.** 1868–1946. German jurist.

**Tri′go** (trē′gō), **Felipe.** 1864–1916. Spanish novelist; author of *Las Ingenuas* (1901), *En la Carrera* (1909), *El Médico Rural* (1912), *Murió de un Beso* (1925), etc.

**Tri·kou′pes** *or* **Tri·kou′pis** *or* **Tri·cou′pis** (trē·ko͞o′pēs), **Spyridon.** 1788–1873. Greek statesman; served in revolution at Missolonghi (1821); head of the ministry (1832); Greek ambassador to Great Britain (1835–38, 1841–43, and 1850), and to France (1849); author of a history of the Greek revolution. His son **Kharilaos** (1832–1896) was minister of foreign affairs (1866 and 1877–78) and prime minister (1875, 1880, 1882, 1883, 1885, 1886–90, 1892–95).

**Trim.** Pseudonym of Louis F. G. RATISBONNE.

**Trim′ble** (trĭm′b'l), **Isaac Ridgeway.** 1802–1888. American army officer; Confederate brigadier general under Jackson in Shenandoah Valley campaign (1862); major general (Oct., 1862); commanded division at Gettysburg (July, 1863), captured.

**Trimble, Robert.** 1777–1828. American jurist, b. in Augusta County, Va.; associate justice, U.S. Supreme Court (1826–28).

**Trine** (trīn), **Ralph Waldo.** 1866–1958. American writer; author of a series entitled *The Life Books,* including *In Tune With the Infinite, In the Hollow of His Hand,* etc.

**Trinqueau.** See NEPVEU.

**Tris′si·no** (trēs′sē·nō), **Giovanni Giorgio** *or* **Giangiorgio.** 1478–1550. Italian writer and scholar; protégé of Popes Leo X, Clement VII, and Paul III; served papacy as nuncio; propounded formation of an "Italian language" by a synthesis of Italian dialects; ardent neo-Aristotelian; known esp. for his *Sofonisba* (1515), first regular tragedy of modern literature, and his *Italia Liberata dai Goti* (1547–48), first regular epic poem; first to use the verso sciolto (unrhymed hendecasyllabic verse).

**Trist** (trĭst), **Nicholas Philip.** 1800–1874. American lawyer and diplomat, b. Charlottesville, Va.; sent to Mexico as special agent to negotiate peace; although recalled (Nov., 1847), remained and signed Treaty of Guadalupe Hidalgo (Feb. 2, 1848), which was later accepted by both U.S. and Mexico.

**Tristan L'Hermite.** See François L'HERMITE.

**Tris'tan' L'Her'mite'** *or* **L'Er'mite'** (trēs'tän' lĕr'-mēt'), **Louis.** 15th-century French government official; served Charles VI and Charles VII; one of chief councilors of Louis XI; suppressed brigandage in parts of France; acquired reputation for extreme cruelty.

**Trit'heim** (trĭt'hīm), **Johannes.** *Latinized form* **Trit·he'mi·us** (trĭt·hē'mĭ·ŭs; trĭ·thē'-). *Real name* **Hei'den·berg** (hī'dĕn·bĕrk). 1462–1516. German humanist; abbot of monastery of Sponheim near Bad Kreuznach (1485), and later of Scottish monastery of St. James at Würzburg; author of *Annales Hirsaugienses* (1514), etc.

**Triv'et** (trĭv'ĕt; -ĭt) *or* **Trev'et** (trĕv'-), **Nicholas.** 1258?–?1328. English chronicler; Dominican friar; studied at Oxford and Paris; taught at Oxford; author of theological and philological works and of *Annales Sex Regum Angliae* (covering period, 1136–1307).

**Tri·vul'zio** (trē·vōōl'tsyō). Name of an ancient noble family of Milan, including notably: **Gian Giacomo** (1440?–1518) and his nephew **Teodoro** (1456?–1531), both in service of France and marshals of France. Teodoro's brother **Antonio** (1449–1508) and nephew **Augustino** (d. 1548), Gian Giacomo's nephew **Scaramuccia** (d. 1527), and Scaramuccia's nephew **Antonio** (d. 1559), Italian cardinals, and **Gian Giacomo Teodoro** (1597–1656), cardinal (from 1629) and governor and captain general of Milan (1655–56).

**Tro'chu'** (trô'shü'), **Louis Jules.** 1815–1896. French army officer; served in Algeria, Crimean War (1854–56), and Italian War (1859); during Franco-Prussian War, governor of Paris (Aug., 1870), and head of government of national defense; forced out of office by failure of his defense measures (Jan., 1871); resigned from army (1873); author of works on siege of Paris, defending his policies and actions.

**Troels-Lund.** See Troels Frederik LUND.

**Troel'stra** (trōōl'strȧ), **Pieter Jelles.** 1860–1930. Dutch Socialist; founder of Social Democratic Workers' party (1894), editor of its official organ *Het Volk* (1900), and its leader in the national legislature (1897–1925).

**Tro'gus** (trō'gŭs), **Gnaeus Pom·pe'ius** (pŏm·pē'(y)ŭs). fl. 1st cent. B.C.–1st cent. A.D. Roman historian; author of a general history, partly preserved in abridged version by Justin.

**Tro'land** (trō'lănd), **Leonard Thompson.** 1889–1932. American psychologist, physicist, and inventor, b. Norwich, Conn.; B.S., M.I.T. (1912); Ph.D., Harvard (1915); taught psychology, Harvard (1916–29); also, chief engineer of Technicolor Motion Picture Corp.; invented and perfected modern multicolor process for motion pictures; conducted important experiments in the psychology and physiology of vision; author of *The Mystery of Mind* (1926), *The Principles of Psychophysiology* (1929–30), etc.

**Trol'lope** (trŏl'ŭp), **Anthony.** 1815–1882. English novelist, b. London; day boy at Winchester and Harrow; in service of post office (1834–67): inspector in Ireland (1841–59); sent on missions to West Indies (giving him material for *The West Indies and the Spanish Main*, 1859), Egypt, U.S., Australia, New Zealand, South Africa; transferred to England (1859–67). Author of some 50 novels, including: the series of "Barsetshire Chronicles," *The Warden* (1855), *Barchester Towers* (1857), *Doctor Thorne* (1858), *Framley Parsonage* (1861), *The Small House at Allington* (1864), *The Last Chronicle of Barset* (1867), all dealing with the social life of a small cathedral city; the "Parliamentary series" of political novels beginning with *Phineas Finn* (1869) and including *Phineas Redux* (1874), *The Prime Minister* (1876), and *The Duke's Children* (1880); *The Three Clerks* (1858), *Orley Farm* (1862), *The Belton Estate* (1865), *The Claverings* (1867), *The Eustace Diamonds* (1873), *Ayala's Angel* (1881), *Dr. Wortle's School* (1881).

His father, **Thomas Anthony Trollope** (1774–1835), barrister, ruined himself by giving up law for a farm and by a disastrous attempt to run a fancy-goods shop in Cincinnati, Ohio; worked hard on an *Encyclopaedia Ecclesiastica.* His wife, **Frances,** *nee* **Milton** (1780–1863; m. 1809), novelist, accompanied him to Cincinnati and on their return published *Domestic Manners of the Americans* (1832), arousing considerable resentment in U.S.; supported family through her writings, including books of travel on Belgium, Paris, Vienna, and many novels, including *The Vicar of Wrexhill* (1837), *The Widow Barnaby* (1839), and *The Widow Married* (1840).

Anthony's older brother **Thomas Adolphus** (1810–1892), contributed to Dickens's *Household Words;* settled in Florence (1843); entertained English and foreign authors and supported Italian revolutionary movement; author of *The Girlhood of Catherine de Medici, History of Florence, Life of Pius IX,* and novels, such as *La Beata, Marietta, The Dream Numbers.* His second wife, **Frances Eleanor,** *nee* **Ter'nan** (tûr'năn), was author of *Aunt Margaret's Trouble* (1866), *Black Spirits and White* (1877), *That Unfortunate Marriage* (1888), and, with her husband, *Homes and Haunts of the Italian Poets* (1881).

Sir **Henry Trollope** (1756–1839), naval officer, second cousin of Thomas Anthony Trollope, was on duty in the boats sent to cover retreat after battle of Lexington and at Bunker Hill (1775); defeated seven French vessels off Hellevoetsluis (1796); took part in battle of Camperdown (1797); admiral (1812).

**Trom·bet'ti** (trôm·bāt'tē), **Alfredo.** 1866–1929. Italian linguistic scholar; championed theory of single origin of language; author of *L'Unità d'Origine del Linguaggio* (1905), *Elementi di Glottologia* (1922), etc.

**Tromlitz, A. von.** Pseudonym of Karl August Friedrich von WITZLEBEN.

**Tromp** (trômp), **Maarten Harpertszoon.** 1597–1653. Dutch admiral; defeated Spanish fleet off Gravelines (Feb., 1639) and combined Spanish-Portuguese fleet off English coast (Sept., 1639). Engaged British fleet off Dover (May, 1652) and was defeated, but won victory over British fleet under Blake later in same year (Nov., 1652). Killed in engagement against British under Monck off Texel Island. His son **Cornelis** (1629–1691) was also an admiral; defeated by British at Southwold Bay (1665); won victories over allied British-French fleet (June 7 and June 14, 1673); lieutenant admiral of United Provinces (1676).

**Tro'tha** (trō'tä), **Adolf von.** 1868–1940. German vice-admiral; chief of staff of high-sea fleet (1916–18); engaged at Jutland; as chief of admiralty (1919–20), laid groundwork for new German navy.

**Trots'ky** *or* **Trots'ki** (trôts'kû·ĭ; *Angl.* trŏt'skĭ), **Le'on** (lē'ŏn). *Real name* **Leib** (*or* **Lev**) **Davydovich Bron·stein'** (brŭn·shtīn'). 1879–1940. Russian Communist leader, b. near Elisavetgrad, of Jewish parents; educ. U. of Odessa. Became revolutionist; arrested (1898) and exiled to Siberia; escaped to England (1902) and became associated with Plekhanov and Lenin. On return to Russia (1905) promptly exiled again to Siberia; escaped to Vienna; on staff of *Arbeiter Zeitung* and *Pravda.* Took strong stand against World War I (1914) and was imprisoned in Germany; expelled from France (1916). After Russian revolution (March, 1917), returned to Russia and became people's commissar for foreign affairs in Soviet government (1917); negotiated with Germans at Brest-Litovsk. Transferred to commissariat of war (1918) and organized armies that repelled attacks on four fronts; organized (1920) labor battalions to save Russian economic life; remained loyal associate of Lenin, though several times differing from Lenin on matters of policy. After Lenin's death (1924), was defeated in contest with Stalin for control of the Communist party, relegated to minor governmental posts, then expelled from party (Nov., 1927) on charge that he had engaged in antiparty activities; banished from Russia (1929). Found haven in Mexico (1937), where he lived until murdered (Aug. 21, 1940). Author of *The Defense of Terrorism* (1921), *Literature and Revolution* (1925), *My Life* (1930), *History of the Russian Revolution* (3 vols., 1932), *Stalin* (1946), etc.

**Trott** (trŏt), **Benjamin.** 1770?–?1841. American miniaturist and portrait painter.

**Trot'ter** (trŏt'ẽr), **Wilfred.** 1872–1939. English surgeon; educ. U. of London; honorary surgeon to the king (1928–32), sergeant surgeon (1932–39); professor, University College Hospital Medical School (from 1935).

**Trot'zen·dorf** (trôt'sĕn·dôrf), **Valentin.** *Real name* **Valentin Fried'land** (frēt'länt). *Named* Trotzendorf *from his birthplace.* 1490–1556. German educator; rector of a Latin school in Goldberg (from 1523) which gained European reputation for efficiency and advanced methods.

**Trou·betz·koy'** (trōō·byĕts·koi'; *Angl.* trōō'bĕts·koi), Prince **Pierre** (pyâr). 1864–1936. Portrait painter, b. Milan, Italy; to U.S. (1896); m. Amélie Rives (*q.v.*); his portrait of Gladstone hangs in the National Gallery at Edinburgh. His brother Prince **Paul** [pôl] (1866–1938) was a sculptor; studio in Moscow (1897–1905) and Paris (from 1905); among his works are portrait busts of George Bernard Shaw, Anatole France, Paul Helleu, an equestrian monument to Alexander III of Russia, and many genre statuette groups of children, dogs, etc. See also TRUBETSKOI.

**Trou'bridge** (trōō'brĭj), Sir **Ernest Charles Thomas.** 1862–1926. British naval officer; entered navy (1875); rear admiral (1911); commander of cruiser squadron in Mediterranean (1913); failed to intercept German cruisers *Goeben* and *Breslau* on way to Dardanelles (1914); exonerated by court-martial; headed naval mission to Serbia (1915–16); superintended evacuation of Serbian army and refugees; vice-admiral (1916); admiral (1919).

**Trous'seau'** (trōō'sō'), **Armand.** 1801–1867. French physician; credited with first tracheotomy for the relief of croup.

**Trow'bridge** (trō'brĭj), **Augustus.** 1870–1934. American physicist, b. New York City; educ. Columbia and Berlin (Ph.D., 1898); professor of physics, Princeton (1906–33); intelligence officer on Pershing's staff (1918); developed range-finding devices using flash or sound of enemy guns as means of locating enemy batteries.

**Trowbridge, Edmund.** 1709–1793. American jurist, b. Cambridge, Mass.; attorney general of Massachusetts (1749–67); judge, Massachusetts superior court (1767–75); presided with strict impartiality in Boston Massacre trial (1771); remained neutral through American Revolution.

**Trowbridge, John.** 1843–1923. American physicist, b. Boston; S.B., Harvard (1865); taught at Harvard (1870–1910); instrumental in securing physics laboratory building (1884); originated laboratory methods of instruction and student research; investigated esp. spectrum analysis and conduction of electricity through gases; author of *The New Physics* (1884), *What Is Electricity?* (1896), etc.

**Trowbridge, John Townsend.** *Pseudonym* **Paul Crey'ton** (krā't'n). 1827–1916. American writer, b. Ogden, N.Y.; lived in Boston (from 1848); author of novels, books for boys (including the *Jack Hazard*, the *Tide Mill*, the *Toby Trafford*, and the *Start in Life* series), a few plays adapted from his stories, verse (including *Darius Green and His Flying Machine*), some descriptive work, and an autobiography.

**Troy** (trwä). Name of a family of French painters, of the 17th and 18th centuries, of whom the most distinguished was **Jean François de Troy** (1679–1752), director of Académie de France at Rome (1738–52) and painter of *Cérémonie de l'Ordre du Saint-Esprit Faite par Henri IV* (in the Louvre) and a series of seven canvases reproduced by the Gobelins.

**Troy'at'** (trwȧ'yȧ'), **Henri.** 1911– . French novelist; awarded Goncourt prize (1938) for *L'Araignée.*

**Troy'on'** (trwȧ'yôɴ'), **Constant.** 1813–1865. French landscape and animal painter, b. at Sèvres; member of the Barbizon group, associate of Rousseau, Diaz de La Peña, and Dupré; visited the Netherlands (1847) and studied works of Potter and Cuyp; became renowned as an animal painter. Among his many notable canvases are *Fête Champêtre en Limousin*, *Baigneuses*, *Forêt de Fontainebleau*, *Marché d'Animaux*, *Vache Blanche*, *Le Retour à la Ferme.*

**Tru·bets·koi'** (trōō·byĕts·koi'). Name of princely Russian family, including: **Sergei Petrovich** (1790–1859); involved in Decembrist plot (1825) and exiled to Siberia. Three brothers, **Sergei Nikolaevich** (1862–1905), philospher and politician, **Evgeni Nikolaevich** (1863–1920), jurist, philosopher, and politician, and **Grigori Nikolaevich** (1873–1930), diplomat and author. Sergei's son **Nikolai Sergeevich** (1890–1938), linguist. See also Prince Pierre TROUBETZKOY.

**Trüb'ner** (trüb'nẽr; *Angl.* trōōb'nẽr), **Nikolaus.** 1817–1884. London publisher and scholar, b. Heidelberg, Germany. Clerk in London (1843); entered partnership with Thomas Delf (1851), later with David Nutt, as Trübner & Co.; developed American trade and published *Bibliographical Guide to American Literature* (1855); studied Sanskrit, Hebrew, and Basque; published works rejected by ordinary publishers, for example, *Trübner's Oriental Series;* publisher for Early English Text Society and Royal Asiatic Society. See Kegan PAUL. His nephew **Karl Trübner** (1846–1907) was a bookseller and publisher in Stuttgart. Karl's brother **Wilhelm** (1851–1917), German painter, came early under influence of Leibl and the impressionist group; executed Heidelberg landscapes (1889), a later series at Amorbach and Neuburg (1913), and portraits.

**Tru'deau** (trōō'dō), **Edward Livingston.** 1848–1915. American physician, b. New York City; developed tuberculosis (1873) and resided in the Adirondacks for his health; made special study of tuberculosis; founded (1884) Adirondack Cottage Sanatorium, now the Trudeau Sanatorium, first American institution to try the open-air treatment; also established a laboratory in his home, replaced (1894) with the Saranac Laboratory, first laboratory in U.S. devoted to study of tuberculosis.

**Trudeau, Pierre Elliott.** 1919– . Canadian statesman, b. Montreal. Member, House of Commons (1965– ); minister of justice and attorney-general (1967–68); prime minister of Canada (1968–79).

**True** (trōō), **Alfred Charles.** 1853–1929. American educator, b. Middletown, Conn.; on staff of U.S. Department of Agriculture (1889–1929); dean of first graduate school of agriculture in U.S., at Ohio State U. (1902).

**True′ba y la Quin·ta na** (trwä′bä ē lä kēn·tä′nä), **Antonio de.** 1819?–1889. Spanish poet and novelist; author of *El Libro de los Cantares* (1852) and *El Libro de las Montañas* (1868), historical novels, as *El Cid Campeador* and *Las Hijas del Cid*, and Basque tales.

**Truinet.** See NUITTER.

**Tru·jil′lo** (trōō·hē′yō), **Julián.** 1829–1884. President of Colombia (1878–80).

**Trujillo Mo·li′na** (mō·lē′nä), **Rafael Leonidas.** 1891–1961. Dominican army officer and politician; president (1930–38; 1942–52); generalissimo (1932).

**Tru′man** (trōō′măn), **Harry S** 1884–1972. Thirty-third president of the United States, b. Lamar, Mo.; artillery officer in World War I; studied law in Kansas City, Mo. (1923–25); presiding judge, Jackson County Court, Mo. (1926–34); U.S. senator (1935–45); vice-president of the U.S. (1945); became president at death of F. D. Roosevelt (April, 1945); attended Potsdam conference (July, 1945); elected president of U.S. (1948) on "Fair Deal" platform. Published *Memoirs* (2 vols., 1955–56).

**Trum′bić** (trōōm′bēt·y′; *Angl.* -bĭch), **Ante.** 1864–1938. Croatian politician; during World War I, president of Yugoslav committee in London; concluded Declaration of Corfu with Serbia (July, 1917), which led to organization of Yugoslavia; foreign minister (1918–20); represented Yugoslavia at Peace Conference (1919).

**Trum′bull** (trŭm′bŭl), **Benjamin.** 1735–1820. American Congregational clergyman and historian; author of *A Complete History of Connecticut...MDCXXX, to MDCCXIII* (1797), and vol. I of projected *A General History of the United States of America..,1492–1792* (1810). His grandson **Lyman Trumbull** (1813–1896) was a jurist and legislator; U.S. senator from Ill. (1855–73); introduced resolution (1864) which became basis of 13th amendment to U.S. Constitution.

**Trumbull, James Hammond.** 1821–1897. American philologist and historian, b. Stonington, Conn.; secretary of state of Connecticut (1861–66); made special study of Indian history in colonial times, Connecticut Indian languages, and Indian place names; also edited *The Memorial History of Hartford County, Connecticut, 1633–1884* (2 vols., 1886). His brother **Henry Clay** (1830–1903), Congregational clergyman; chaplain in Civil War; editor and part owner, *Sunday School Times* (1875–1903); influential in promoting Sunday-school improvement.

**Trumbull, John.** 1750–1831. American lawyer and poet, b. Watertown, Conn. Practiced in Boston (1773–74), New Haven (1774–77), and Hartford (from 1781); judge of the Connecticut superior court (1801–19), and of the supreme court of errors (1808–19). Satirized collegiate instruction of his day in a 1700-line poem, *The Progress of Dulness* (1772–73); satirized British blunders of the period of the American Revolution in the burlesque epic poem *M'Fingal* (1782), an immensely popular imitation of *Hudibras.* Gave some assistance to Noah Webster in Webster's preparation of his dictionary.

**Trumbull, John.** 1756–1843. Son of Jonathan Trumbull (1710–1785). American painter, b. Lebanon, Conn. Served in Revolutionary War. Studied painting in London under Benjamin West (1780; 1782–83; 1784–85). Began his famous historical paintings in West's studio with *Battle of Bunker's Hill* and the *Death of General Montgomery in the Attack of Quebec* (both completed in 1786). Followed these with *Declaration of Independence, Surrender of Lord Cornwallis at Yorktown, Death of General Mercer at the Battle of Princeton*, and *Capture of the Hessians at Trenton.* Studio in New York (1789) and Philadelphia (1792); George Washington sat for him a number of times. In diplomatic service and business speculation (1793–1804). Again opened studio in New York (1804); painted portraits of notables of the day, including Timothy Dwight and Stephen Van Rensselaer. Again in Europe (1808–15); on return to U.S. was commissioned by Congress (Mar., 1817) to paint four large pictures for the rotunda of the Capitol at Washington (*Surrender of General Burgoyne at Saratoga, Surrender of Lord Cornwallis at Yorktown, Declaration of Independence, Resignation of Washington*). Turned over collection of his paintings to Yale College; Trumbull Gallery, first art museum in America connected with an educational institution, was built to hold his collection (opened 1832).

**Trumbull, Jonathan.** 1710–1785. American statesman, b. Lebanon, Conn. Entered father's mercantile house (1731). Deputy governor of Connecticut (1766–69), and governor (1769–84). Vigorous supporter of colonial cause during the Revolution; guided and encouraged Connecticut industry in supplying Continental army with food and munitions; maintained frequent contacts with Washington to learn the army's needs; Washington is said to have referred to him as "Brother Jonathan," origin of the phrase used to describe a typical American. His son **Joseph** (1737–1778) was a businessman; in father's mercantile firm (1756–67); in Connecticut legislature (1767–73); member of Continental Congress (1774); commissary general of Continental army (1775–77); member of the board of war (1777–78). Another son, **Jonathan** (1740–1809), was a soldier and politician; in Connecticut legislature (1774, 1775, 1779, 1780, 1788); first comptroller of the U.S. Treasury (1778–79); secretary on George Washington's staff (1781–83); member of U.S. House of Representatives (1789–95) and Speaker of the House (1791–93); U.S. senator (1795–96); governor of Connecticut (1797–1809). For his third son, John (1756–1843), see separate biography.

**Trumbull, Lyman.** See under Benjamin TRUMBULL.

**Truro,** Baron. See under Thomas WILDE.

**Trux′tun** (trŭks′tŭn), **Thomas.** 1755–1822. American naval officer; privateersman during American Revolution. In merchant marine (1783–94). Commissioned captain, U.S. navy (1794); commanded a squadron in West Indian waters during the war with France; captured French frigate *Insurgente* (Feb. 9, 1799) and defeated *La Vengeance* in night battle (Feb. 1–2, 1800). Influential in setting standards of discipline and in maintaining high morale in new U.S. navy. His grandson **William Talbot Truxtun** (1824–1887) commanded gunboat *Tacony* in attacks on Fort Fisher (Dec., 1864 and Jan., 1865); commissioned commodore (1882); retired (1886).

**Try′on** (trī′ŭn), **Dwight William.** 1849–1925. American landscape painter; studio in New York (1881); many of his paintings are in Freer Gallery, Washington, D.C.

**Tryon,** Sir **George.** 1832–1893. British naval officer; commander of first British seagoing ironclad (1861); vice-admiral (1889); commander of Mediterranean fleet (1891–93); responsible for fatal order sending the *Camperdown* into collision with his flagship, *Victoria*, in which he went down, along with 358 officers and men.

**Tryon, George Washington.** 1838–1888. American conchologist; author of *Manual of Conchology...*(from 1879; 9 vols. on marine shells and 3 vols. on land shells completed by time of his death).

**Tryon, William.** 1729–1788. British colonial governor (1765–71) of North Carolina, where he took measures to suppress the Regulators' revolt (1771); governor of New York (1771–78); speculated in land in district west of Schenectady, called Tryon County; commanded (1778–80) force of loyalists raiding Connecticut and destroying supplies intended for the Continental army.

**Ts'ai Lun** (tsī' lo͝on'). 50?–?118 A.D. Chinese eunuch at the Later Han court. According to official history of Han dynasty, invented (105) paper from tree bark, hemp, rags, and fish nets.

**Tsai Ting-kai** (tsī' tĭng'gī'). *Cantonese* **Ts'ai T'ing-ch'ieh** (tsī' tĭng'chĭ·ĕ'). 1892–1968. Chinese general; commander of famous Nineteenth Route army that defended Shanghai against Japanese (1932); led retreat to Fukien and there set up brief independent government (1936); strong supporter of Chiang Kai-shek in Chino-Japanese War (1937 ff.).

**Ts'ai T'ing-kan** (tsī' tĭng'găn'). 1861–1935. Chinese admiral, b. in Kwangtung. One of the first group (1873–81) of Chinese government students to be educated in the United States; took course in naval training; made commodore of torpedo fleet (1892); in Chinese-Japanese War (1894–95); chief English secretary of Yüan Shih-k'ai; vice-admiral (1924–26); minister for foreign affairs (1926–27). Published several volumes of English translations of Chinese poetry.

**Tsai Yuan-pei** (tsī' yü·än'pā'). 1867–1940. Chinese author and statesman; joined revolutionary party of Sun Yat-sen (1905); minister of education (1912); chancellor of Peking National Univ. (1917–23); member of central supervisory (1924) and political (1926) councils of Kuomintang; state councilor of the national government (1928). Author of *The History of Chinese Ethics, The Red Tower Dream,* etc.

**Tsal·da'res** *or* **Tsal·da'ris** (tsäl·thä'rēs), **Panages** *or* **Panagis.** 1868–1936. Greek statesman; a leader of Popular party in chamber of deputies; opposed Venizelos. Organized a government (Nov., 1932) which was replaced by Venizelos (Jan., 1933); defeated Venizelos at polls (March, 1933); premier (1933–35); forced out of office by Kondyles coup d'état (Oct. 10, 1935).

**Tsan'kov** (tsän'kôf), **Aleksandr.** 1879–1959. Bulgarian statesman; premier (1923–26); suppressed Communism with severe loss of life (Sept., 1923), and endeavored to further economic reconstruction in Bulgaria; tried unsuccessfully to form a coalition cabinet (1931).

**Tsankov, Dragan.** 1827–1911. Bulgarian statesman; premier (1880; 1883–84); active in coup d'état (Aug., 1886); head of provisional government then organized; imprisoned on return of Alexander (to 1894); member, and (1902) president, of the Sobranje.

**Ts'ao K'un** (tsou' ko͝on'). 1862 (or 1865)–1938. Chinese president (1923–24). Served in Chinese-Japanese War (1894); took part in Revolution (1911) that overthrew Manchu dynasty; tuchun of Chihli (1917–23); supported President Li Yüan-hung (1917); opposed Sun Yat-sen (1918); became marshal and gained control of Peking deposing President Li Yüan-hung (1923); at war with southern forces under Sun Yat-sen (1923); president of China for about 13 months; forced by Marshal Tuan Ch'i-jui to resign; entered Japanese puppet government (1937).

**Ts'ao Ts'ao** (tsou' tsou'). 155–220 A.D. Chinese general; minister of state (208); held real power over Hsien Ti, last emperor of the Later Han dynasty; set up the new Wei dynasty (220) of which his son Ts'ao P'ei was first ruler.

**Tsch-** *or* **Tch-.** For many Russian names beginning *Tsch-* or *Tch-*, see CH-.

**Tschaikovsky.** Variant of TCHAIKOVSKY.

**Tschakste.** Variant of ČAKSTE.

**Tscher'mak von Sey'se·negg** (chĕr'mäk fôn zī'zĕ·nĕk), **Gustav.** 1836–1927. Austrian mineralogist; known esp. for work in petrography, crystallography, and the study of meteorites. His son **Erich** (1871– ), botanist, is one of several who independently and almost simultaneously rediscovered Mendel's laws (1900). Another son, **Armin** (1870–1952), professor of physiology in the German University in Prague (1913), is known esp. for work on the nervous system and on heredity.

**Tschir'ky** (chĭr'kē), **Os'car** (ŏs'kẽr). *Known as* **Oscar of the Wal'dorf** (wôl'dôrf). 1866–1950. Maître d'hôtel, b. in Canton of Neuchâtel, Switzerland; to U.S. (1883) and naturalized (1888); first with the Hoffman House in New York City, then with Delmonico's; actively identified with Waldorf-Astoria Hotel from its opening (1893).

**Tschirn'haus** *or* **Tschirn'hauss** (chĭrn'hous), Count **Ehrenfried Walter von.** *Incorrectly* **Tschirn'hau'sen** (-hou'zĕn). 1651–1708. German mathematician, physicist, and philosopher; educ. at Leiden. Erected three glassworks and a mill for grinding burning glasses near Görlitz; made discoveries in the production of porcelain (see J. F. BÖTTGER). In algebra, introduced a general transformation for simplifying algebraic equations. Author of the philosophical works *Medicina Mentis et Corporis* (1687) and *Anleitung zu Nützlichen Wissenschaften, absonderlich zu der Mathesis und Physik* (1708).

**Tschu'di** (cho͞o'dē), **Aegidius** *or* **Gilg von.** 1505–1572. Swiss historian; chief magistrate (Landamman) of Glarus (1558); regarded as the "father of Swiss history"; chief work, posthumously published, *Chronicon Helveticum,* a chronicle of Swiss history from 1000 to 1470.

**Tschudi, Burkhard.** See John BROADWOOD.

**Tschudi, Johann Jakob von.** 1818–1889. Swiss naturalist and traveler in South America; ambassador to Brazil (1860–62), Vienna (1868–83). His brother **Friedrich** (1820–1886), statesman and writer, opposed Catholic clergy during Sonderbund War; author of *Das Tierleben der Alpenwelt* (1853), etc.

**Tsêng Chi-tsê** (dzŭng' jĕ'dzĕ'). 1839–1890. Chinese diplomat and statesman, known as "Marquis Tsêng." Son of Tsêng Kuo-fan. Minister to Great Britain and France (1878–80); envoy to Russia (1880–81), where he negotiated treaty restoring Kulja region to China; arranged convention (1885) with Great Britain concerning opium traffic; member of the Tsung-li Yamen (1886–87).

**Tsêng Kuo-fan** (dzŭng' gwô'făn'). 1811–1872. Chinese soldier and statesman; father of Tsêng Chi-tsê. In Taiping rebellion (1850–64) led in defense of Changsha, the capture of Wuchang and Hanyang, and in final years (1861–64), with the aid of Ward and Gordon, in the concluding victories around Nanking; less successful in Shantung against revolt (1865–68); viceroy of Chihli (1870). Author of many works (156 books, ed. by Li Hung-chang).

**Tsi.** = CH'I (dynasty).

**Tsin.** = CHIN (dynasties).

**Ts'in.** = CH'IN (dynasty).

**Tso-ch'iu Ming** (dzō'ō·chĭ·o͞o' mĭng'). fl. 5th century or 4th century B.C. Chinese author; probably disciple of Confucius; author of *Tso Chüan,* a commentary on the *Ch'un Ch'iu* (one of the Five Classics) and an interesting detailed account of China's feudal age.

**Tsong-kha-pa** (tsông'k'hä'pä'). c. 1357–1419. Tibetan reformer. After long period of study and preparation, including eight years as hermit, began reform of Lamaism; built (1409) new monastery about 25 miles east of Lhasa; at his death had more than 30,000 followers.

**Tso Tsung-t'ang** (dzō'ô dzŏŏng'täng'). 1812–1885. Chinese general and official; served in earlier years of Taiping rebellion against rebels; greatly aided Gen. Tsêng Kuo-fan (1861–64) in final years of rebellion, esp. in Chekiang province; governor general of Shensi and Kansu (1866–73), where he put down Mohammedan rebellion and captured Suchow in Kansu. In a later campaign (1875–78) conquered regions north and south of the Tien Shan mountains and added them as one province (Sinkiang) to China. Granted rank of marquis; became a member of the Tsung-li Yamen (1881); took part in war with French in Foochow (1884).

**Tsou'de·ros'** (tsōō'thâ·rôs'), **Emmanuel.** 1882-1956. Greek financier and statesman; technical adviser to Greek delegation at Paris Peace Conference (1919); minister of finance (1924–25); governor, Bank of Greece (1931–39); premier (1941–44).

**Tsoun'tas** (tsōōn'däs), **Chrestos.** 1857–1934. Greek archaeologist; commissioned (c. 1886) to continue exploration of ruins of Mycenae, begun by Schliemann, and made important discoveries there.

**Tsu·ne·ta·ka** (tsōō·nĕ·tä·kä), **Tosa.** Japanese painter of 13th century, founder of native Tosa school.

**Tuan Ch'i-jui** (dōō·än' chē'rā'). 1864–1936. Chinese marshal and politician; largely responsible for reorganization of northern army (1911); one of the military leaders who signed memorial to the throne, urging abdication (1911); appointed minister of war (1912); acting premier (1913); minister of war (1914); premier (1916–17, 1918); resigned and lived in retirement (1918–24); succeeded Ts'ao K'un as provisional president (1924–26).

**Tub'man** (tŭb'măn), **William Vacanarat Shadrach.** 1895–1971. Liberian lawyer and statesman. Assoc. justice of Liberian Supreme Court (1937–44); president of the Republic of Liberia (1944–71).

**Tuck** (tŭk), **Amos.** 1810–1879. American lawyer and politician, b. Parsonfield, Me.; grad. Dartmouth (1835); adm. to bar (1838) and practiced at Exeter, N.H.; member U.S. House of Representatives (1847–53); trustee (1857–66) of Dartmouth, where the Amos Tuck School of Administration and Finance, established (1900) by his son **Edward** (1842–1938), was named in his honor.

**Tuck'er** (tŭk'ẽr), **Abraham.** 1705–1774. English moralist; author of *The Light of Nature Pursued* (7 vols., 1768–78), on metaphysics, theology, and morals.

**Tucker, Benjamin Ricketson.** 1854–1939. American anarchist; founded *The Radical Review* (1877) and *Liberty* (1881); author of *State Socialism and Anarchism* (1899).

**Tucker, Beverley Dandridge.** 1846–1930. American Protestant Episcopal clergyman, b. Richmond, Va.; consecrated bishop coadjutor of southern Virginia (1906); author of Confederate memorial verses and essays. His son **Beverley Dandridge** (1882–1969), also a Protestant Episcopal clergyman, was consecrated bishop coadjutor of Ohio (1938).

**Tucker, Charlotte Maria.** *Pseudonym* **A. L. O. E.** 1821–1893. English writer; missionary in India (1875); wrote books for children, allegories and parables.

**Tucker, George.** 1775–1861. Educator and political economist, b. in Bermuda; to U.S. Member, U.S. Congress (1819–25). Wrote *Life of Thomas Jefferson* (2 vols., 1837), *The Theory of Money and Banks Investigated* (1839), *The History of the United States* (4 vols., 1856–57), *Political Economy for the People* (1859).

**Tucker, Josiah.** 1712–1799. English economist; dean of Gloucester (1758); author of tract deprecating war for sake of trade (1763), pamphlets setting forth advisability of separation from American colonies; forerunner of Adam Smith in his arguments against monopolies.

**Tucker, Luther.** 1802–1873. American journalist, b. Brandon, Vt.; bought and published Albany (N.Y.) *Cultivator* (1839), merging *Genesee Farmer* with it (1840); founded (1846), and published (1846–52), the *Horticulturist;* began issue of *Country Gentleman* (1853) with which he merged the *Cultivator* (1866) under title of *Cultivator and Country Gentleman;* author of *American Husbandry* (with Willis Gaylord, 1840). His son **Gilbert Milligan** (1847–1932) was associated with him in publishing the *Cultivator and Country Gentleman* (from 1867); editor in chief of the *Country Gentleman,* its successor (1897–1911); author of *Our Common Speech* (1895), *American English* (1921), etc.

**Tucker, Nathaniel Beverley.** 1820–1890. Son of Henry St. George Tucker (*q.v.* under St. George TUCKER). American planter and politician, b. Winchester, Va.; succeeded Hawthorne as U.S. consul at Liverpool (1858); joined Confederate service (1861); agent of Confederacy in France (1862–63) and Canada (1864); accused wrongfully of complicity in plot to murder Lincoln (1865); resident of Washington, D.C. (1872–90). His brother **John Randolph** (1823–1897) was a jurist and politician; practiced law at Winchester, Va. (1845–57); attorney general of Virginia (1857–65); member of U.S. House of Representatives (1875–87); author of *The Constitution of the United States* (2 vols., 1899). John Randolph Tucker's son **Henry St. George** (1853–1932) was a lawyer and politician; practiced law at Staunton, Va. (1876–89); member of U.S. House of Representatives (1889–97; 1922–32).

**Tucker, St. George.** 1752–1827. Jurist in America, b. in Bermuda; to America as a boy. Practiced law in Williamsburg, Va.; served in Colonial army in American Revolution; judge, Virginia general court (1788–1803), and supreme court of appeals (1803–11); judge, U.S. district court, district of Virginia (1813–27); prepared and published an annotated edition of *Blackstone's Commentaries* (5 vols., 1803). His son **Henry St. George** (1780–1848), b. in Chesterfield County, Va., was also a jurist; practiced at Winchester, Va.; member of U.S. House of Representatives (1815–19); judge of superior courts of chancery in Virginia (1824–31); president, supreme court of appeals of Virginia (1831–41); author of *Commentaries on the Laws of Virginia* (2 vols., 1836–37), *Lectures on Constitutional Law* (1843), etc. Another son, **Nathaniel Beverley** (1784–1851), was also a jurist; practiced in Charlotte County, Va.; circuit court judge in Missouri (1830–33); author of three novels (*George Balcombe,* 1836; *The Partisan Leader,* 2 vols., 1836; *Gertrude,* 1844–45), and many treatises on political economy and law. See also biographies under Nathaniel Beverley TUCKER (1820–1890).

**Tucker, Samuel.** 1747–1833. American naval officer, b. Marblehead, Mass.; in merchant marine service (1758–75); as captain of the *Franklin* and *Hancock,* preyed on British ships (1775–76); commissioned by Congress captain in Continental navy (Mar. 15, 1777); commanded frigate *Boston* carrying John Adams to his post as commissioner to France (1778); continued attacks on British commerce (1778–80).

**Tucker, Stephen Davis.** 1818–1902. American inventor and manufacturer, b. Bloomfield, N.J.; in employ of R. Hoe & Co., New York City (1834–93); received nearly 100 patents for improvements in printing presses; partner in R. Hoe & Co. (from 1860).

**Tucker, William Jewett.** 1839–1926. American Congregational clergyman and educator, b. Griswold, Conn.; professor, Andover Sem. (1880–93); president, Dartmouth College (1893–1909).

**Tuck'er·man** (tŭk'ẽr·măn), **Edward.** 1817–1886.

Nephew of Joseph Tuckerman. American lichenologist, b. Boston; professor of botany, Amherst (1858–86); authority on lichenology; author of *A Synopsis of the North American Lichens* (part I, 1882; part II, completed by Henry Willey, 1888), etc. His brother **Frederick Goddard** (1821–1873) wrote verse: *Poems* (1860), and *The Sonnets of Frederick Goddard Tuckerman* (edited by Witter Bynner; 1931).

**Tuckerman, Henry Theodore.** 1813–1871. Nephew of Joseph Tuckerman. American essayist and poet, b. Boston; author of *The Italian Sketch Book* (1835), *Isabel, or Sicily, a Pilgrimage* (a romance, 1839), *Thoughts on the Poets* (1846), *Characteristics of Literature* (2 series, 1849, 1851), *Mental Portraits* (1853), and a volume of verse, *Poems* (1851). The conventionality of his Petrarchan sonnets gave rise to word "tuckermanity."

**Tuckerman, Joseph.** 1778–1840. American Unitarian clergyman, b. Boston; became minister at large (1826), devoting himself chiefly to missionary work in Boston; founder (1812), Boston Society for the Religious and Moral Improvement of Seamen, first sailors' aid society in U.S. His grandson **Bay'ard** (bī'ärd) **Tuckerman** (1855–1923) was author of *A History of English Prose Fiction*...(1882), *Life of General Lafayette* (2 vols., 1889), *William Jay*...(1894), *Life of General Philip Schuyler, 1733–1804* (1903).

**Tudela, Benjamin of.** See BENJAMIN OF TUDELA.

**Tu'dor** (tū'dẽr). Name of an English house and of the dynasty occupying throne of England (1485–1603), founded by **Owen Tudor** (d. 1461), squire of an old Welsh family, who had three sons and a daughter by Catherine of Valois (*q.v.*), widow of Henry V, to whom he may have been legally married; had annuity from Henry VI; fought at Mortimer's Cross on side of Lancastrians; captured by Yorkists and beheaded. His eldest son, **Edmund Tudor** of Han'dam [hăn'dăm] (1430?–1456), Earl of **Rich'mond** [rĭch'mŭnd] (cr. 1453), married the heiress of John of Gaunt, Margaret Beaufort (*q.v.*), by whom he was father of Henry VII. Henry VII by marriage (1486) with Elizabeth, eldest daughter of Edward IV, united houses of York and Lancaster, a union symbolized by the Tudor rose.

**Jasper Tudor** of Hat'field [hăt'fēld] (1431?–1495), Earl of **Pem'broke** (pĕm'brŏŏk) and Duke of **Bed'ford** (bĕd'fẽrd), second son of Owen Tudor; fought for Henry VI at first battle of St. Albans (1455); defeated by Edward IV at Mortimer's Cross (1461) and retired to Scotland (1462); made attack on Wales (1468) only to be driven off by William Herbert; returned with Warwick (1470) but after battle of Tewkesbury fled with his nephew Henry (later Henry VII) to Paris, till their return to victory at Bosworth over Richard III (1485); created duke of Bedford (1485), earl marshal (1492).

The Tudor monarchs were: Henry VII (1485–1509) and VIII (1509–47), Edward VI (1547–53), Mary I (1553–58), Elizabeth (1558–1603). See these entries.

Other members of Tudor house include Henry VII's daughters Mary Tudor (1496–1533), queen of Louis XII of France (see MARY OF FRANCE), and Margaret Tudor (1489–1541), queen of James IV of Scotland (see MARGARET TUDOR), through whom the Stuart dynasty derived its title to throne of England (1603). See *Table (in Appendix)* for ENGLAND.

**Tudor, William.** 1779–1830. American author, b. Boston, Mass.; founder (1815) and first editor, *North American Review;* helped found Boston Athenaeum (1807); first to suggest erection of Bunker Hill Monument.

**Tuf'fier'** (tü'fyā'), **Théodore.** 1857–1929. French surgeon; pioneer in surgery of the lungs, heart, and blood vessels; advocate of spinal anesthesia.

**Tufts** (tŭfts), **Charles.** 1781–1876. American farmer and brick manufacturer, b. Somerville, Mass.; deeded land for establishment of Tufts College, Medford, Mass., with provision that its name should never be changed; trustee, Tufts College (1856–76).

**Tufts, John.** 1689–1752. American Congregational clergyman; author of *A Very Plain and Easy Introduction to the Art of Singing Psalm Tunes*...(1714 or 1715), a book which had considerable influence on development of church singing in New England. His nephew **Cotton Tufts** (1732–1815) was a physician; practiced in Weymouth, Mass. (from 1752); an organizer of Massachusetts Medical Society (1781) and its president (1787).

**Tu Fu** (dōō' fōō'). 712–770 A.D. Chinese poet of the T'ang dynasty, b. in Shensi province; second only to Li Po in fame; esp. admired for his beautiful lyrics.

**Tugh·lak'** (tŭg·lăk') *or* **Tagh·lak'** (tăg-). A Mohammedan dynasty of the kings of Delhi (1321–1414), founded by **Ghi·yas'-ud-din' Tughlak** (gĭ·yä'-thŏŏd·dēn') *or* **Tughlak Shah** (shä'), king (1321–25), who led a rebellion overthrowing the Khiljis and removing the capital from Delhi to a new city, Tughlakabad, four miles east; dynasty overthrown by the Sayyids (1414).

**Tug'well** (tŭg'wĕl; -wĕl), **Rexford Guy.** 1891–1979. American economist, b. Sinclairville, N.Y.; taught, Columbia U. (1920–37); adviser to F. D. Roosevelt (from 1933); undersecretary of agriculture (1934–37); chairman, N.Y. City Planning Commission (1938–41); governor of Puerto Rico (1941–46); professor, Chicago U. (from 1946). Author of *Industry's Coming of Age* (1927), *The Industrial Discipline* (1933), *Battle for Democracy* (1935), etc.

**Tukaji Rao Holkar I** and **III.** See HOLKAR.

**Tu'ka·ram'** (tŏŏ'kä·räm'). 1608–1649. Marathi poet; retired from worldly life to a Krishna temple; wrote many poems and religious songs (English translation of complete poems pub. 1869).

**Tuke** (tūk). Name of an English family active in philanthropy, including: **William Tuke** (1732–1822), Quaker merchant; pioneer in England, contemporary with Pinel in France, of humane care of the insane. His son **Henry** (1755–1814), Quaker minister. Henry's son **Samuel** (1784–1857) continued his grandfather's system for the insane. Samuel's son **James Hack** (1819–1896) devoted himself to distributing relief in Ireland (from 1880); instrumental through *The Condition of Donegal* (1889) in passage of Irish Land Act (1891). His brother **Daniel Hack** (1827–1895), physician; London specialist in mental diseases (1875); author of *A Manual of Psychological Medicine* (with Sir John C. Bucknill; 1858) and of works on insanity. Daniel's younger son, **Henry Scott** (1858–1929), painter; settled in Cornwall; painted chiefly youthful nudes against marine backgrounds; created stir with *August Blue* (1894; now in Tate Gallery).

**Tuke,** Sir **Samuel.** d. 1674. English Royalist and playwright; in Royalist army commanded at Lincoln, fought at Marston Moor (1644); defended Colchester (1648); under Restoration sent on missions to French court; author of *The Adventures of Five Hours* (1663), a tragicomedy lauded by Pepys.

**Tu·kha·chev'ski** (tŏŏ·kŭ·chăf'skû·ĭ; *Angl.* tŏŏk'ȧ-chĕf'skĭ), **Mikhail Nikolaevich.** 1893–1937. Russian general and politician; lieutenant in World War (1914–18); joined Bolshevik army; served against Poland (1920) and against generals Kolchak and Denikin. Commanded western military district (1925) and Leningrad military district (1928); member of Union Central Executive Committee; created marshal of the Soviet Union. Tried before military tribunal, and convicted, on charge of treason; executed (June 12, 1937).

**Tu·kul′ti–Nin·ur′ta** (to͞o·ko͝ol′tē·nēn·o͝or′tä) *or, less correctly,* **Tu·kul′ti–Ni′nib** (-nē′nĕb). Name of two kings of Assyria: **Tukulti–Ninurta I;** son of Shalmaneser I; king (1256–1233 B.C.); made conquests in northwest, esp. against Hittites; built new capital; captured Babylon. **Tukulti–Ninurta II;** son of Adad-nirari II; king (889–884 B.C.); restored Assyrian prestige; increased prosperity of people.

**Tu·lane′** (to͞o·lān′; tû-), **Paul.** 1801–1887. American merchant, b. near Princeton, N.J.; established dry-goods and clothing business, New Orleans, La. (from 1822); gave liberally (from 1882) to U. of Louisiana, founded at New Orleans (1834); its name changed to Tulane U. of Louisiana (1884) in his honor.

**Tu′lasne′** (tü′làn′), **Louis René.** 1815–1885. French botanist, sometimes called the founder of modern mycology; discovered polymorphism in fungi.

**Tull** (tŭl), **Jethro.** 1674–1741. English agriculturist; invented and perfected machine drill for sowing seed (c. 1701); introduced system of sowing in drills; confirmed his theories of use of manure and importance of pulverizing soil.

**Tullius, Servius.** See SERVIUS TULLIUS.

**Tul′loch** (tŭl′ŭK; -ŭk), **John.** 1823–1886. Scottish liberal theologian; principal and professor of theology, St. Mary's Coll., St. Andrews (1854), lectured on comparative religion; chaplain to Queen Victoria for Scotland (1859); moderator of general assembly of Church of Scotland (1878), founder of liberal church party; active in reorganization of education in Scottish schools and universities. Author of works on religious and philosophical thought of 17th, 18th, and 19th centuries.

**Tul′lus Hos·til′i·us** (tŭl′ŭs hŏs·tĭl′ĭ·ŭs). Third legendary king (673–641 B.C.) of the early Romans.

**Tul′ly** (tŭl′ĭ). Anglicized form of *Tullius*, once commonly used in reference to Marcus Tullius CICERO (106–43 B.C.).

**Tul′ly** (tŭl′ĭ), **Jim.** 1891–1947. American writer, b. near St. Marys, Ohio. Orphaned (1902); worked at odd jobs, farm and factory laborer, tramp, circus roustabout, pugilist, newspaper reporter, and often jailed for vagrancy. His verse first appeared in Cleveland *Plain Dealer* (1911). Among his many books are *Beggars of Life* (1924), *Circus Parade* (1927), *Blood on the Moon* (1931), *The Bruiser* (1936), *A Hollywood Decameron* (1937), *Biddy Brogan's Boy* (1942).

**Tully, Richard Walton.** 1877–1945. American playwright and producer, b. Nevada City, Calif.; author of *My Cinderella Girl*, *Rose of the Rancho*, *Omar the Tentmaker*, *The Flame*. See Eleanor GATES.

**Tully, William.** 1785–1859. American physician, b. Saybrook Point, Conn.; professor, Yale (1829–42); compiler of *Materia Medica, or, Pharmacology and Therapeutics* (2 vols., 1857–58). Tully's powder, a modification of Dover's powder, is named after him.

**Tulp** (tûlp), **Claes Pieterszoon.** *Orig. name* **Nicolaes Pie′ters·zoon** (pē′tĕr·sŭn; -sōn; -sŏn), *the name* Tulp *being added because of the tulip* (*Dutch* tulp) *carved on the façade of his house.* 1593?–?1674. Dutch anatomist; professor, Surgeons' Guild, Amsterdam (1628–53); commissioned Rembrandt to paint (1632) *The Anatomy Lesson*, which shows Dr. Tulp demonstrating the structure of the human body to a group of his contemporaries.

**Tul′si Das** (to͝ol′sē däs′). 1532–1623. Hindu poet and reformer, called the greatest poet of medieval Hindustan. Converted by his wife to worship of Rama, made his headquarters at Ajodhya; wrote in the reign of Akbar; composed a version in Awadhi, the literary dialect of Eastern Hindi, of the Ramayana epic entitled *Rām-charit-mānas* ("The Lake of Rama's deeds") which is today sometimes called the "Bible of Northern India"; also the author of five other long works consisting of history, hymns, prayers, etc., of the Rama legend, and a number of shorter works.

**Tu′lui** (to͞o′lo͞o·ē) *or* **Tu′lē** (to͞o′lē). Youngest son of Genghis Khan (*q.v.*).

**Tu·lu′nid** (to͞o·lo͞o′nĭd). Short-lived Mohammedan dynasty in Egypt (868–905), of Turkish origin, founded by Ahmed ibn-Tulun (*q.v.*). It made Egypt independent of Baghdad and it conquered Syria, but was overcome (905) by forces of Caliph al-Muktafi.

**Tum′ul·ty** (tŭm′ŭl·tĭ), **Joseph Patrick.** 1879–1954. American lawyer, b. Jersey City, N.J.; private secretary to Woodrow Wilson as governor (1910–13), and as president of the United States (1913–21); author of *Woodrow Wilson as I Know Him* (1921).

**T'ung Chih** (to͝ong′ jĭr′). *Personal name* **Tsai Ch'un** (dzī′ cho͞on′). 1856–1875. Chinese emperor (1862–75), eighth of the Ch'ing (Manchu) dynasty. Son of Hsien Fêng and his concubine Yehonala (see TZU HSI). Ruled under regency of his mother and Prince Kung (1862–73). During his reign Robert Hart began establishment of maritime customs service (1863) and Anson Burlingame and his mission visited China (1868–70).

**Tun′ney** (tŭn′ĭ), **Gene,** *really* **James Joseph,** 1898–1978). American pugilist, b. New York City. Won heavyweight championship of the world by defeating Jack Dempsey (Sept. 23, 1926); retained it by defeating Dempsey again (1927); retired from the ring undefeated (1928).

**Tun′stall** (tŭn′st'l), **Brian,** *in full* **William Cuthbert Brian.** 1900–1970. English naval historian; educ. Cambridge; lecturer in history and English, Royal Naval Coll., Greenwich (1925–37); author of *Admiral Byng and the Loss of Minorca* (1928), *The Byng Papers* (1930–33), *Nelson* (1933), *The Realities of Naval History* (1936), *William Pitt, Earl of Chatham* (1939), *World War at Sea* (1942), etc.

**Tun′stall** *or* **Ton′stall** (tŭn′st'l), **Cuthbert.** 1474–1559. English prelate and scholar. Learned in Greek, Hebrew, mathematics, and civil law; friend of Erasmus and More; employed by Henry VIII and Wolsey on diplomatic missions to emperor (1515–21); negotiated treaty of Cambrai (1529); master of rolls (1516–22); bishop of London (1522–30); keeper of privy seal (1523); succeeded Wolsey as bishop of Durham (1530). Adhered to Roman Catholic dogma, prohibited Tyndale's *New Testament*, but acquiesced in royal supremacy, publicly defending Henry VIII's headship of church. Alarmed at sweeping reforms under Edward VI, voted against first act of uniformity (1549); accused of inciting to rebellion and deprived (1552); restored under Mary (1553), refrained from persecution of Protestants. On accession of Elizabeth, refused oath of supremacy and declined to consecrate Matthew Parker as archbishop of Canterbury, and was deprived (1559).

**Tu·pac′ A·ma′ru** (to͞o·päk′ ä·mä′ro͞o). 1544?–1571. Inca chieftain, last of the male line. Youngest son of Manco Inca; offered no opposition to Spaniards; ordered seized by Viceroy Francisco de Toledo, and beheaded.

**Tupac Amaru.** *Name assumed* (*1771*) *by* **José Gabriel Con′dor·can′qui** (kôn′dôr·käng′kē). 1742–1781. Peruvian revolutionist, direct descendant of the early Incas; known as "the Last of the Incas." Headed a rebellion of Indians against Spanish government (1780); defeated and captured (March, 1781); tortured and killed (May 18, 1781).

**Tupac Yu·pan′qui** (yo͞o·päng′kē). d. about 1487. Tenth Inca ruler of Peru (middle of 15th century); father of Huayna Capac; noted for his wide conquests, which extended Inca kingdom north into modern Ecuador, south into Chile, and covered large sections of Amazon Valley.

**Tup'per** (tŭp'ĕr), **Benjamin.** 1738–1792. American Revolutionary officer, b. Stoughton, Mass. Served (lieutenant colonel and colonel) through American Revolution; defended Springfield, Mass., in time of Shays' Rebellion (1786); influential in organization of Ohio Company to settle the Northwest Territory; a pioneer in settling Marietta, Ohio.

**Tupper,** Sir **Charles.** 1821–1915. Canadian statesman; premier of Nova Scotia (1864–67); strong advocate of Canadian federation. Held various portfolios under Sir John A. Macdonald in Dominion ministries (1872–73, 1878–84, 1887–88); first minister of railways and canals (1879–84); chiefly responsible for completion of Canadian Pacific Railway; Canadian high commissioner in London (1884–96); prime minister of Canada (Apr.–June, 1896); urged adoption of preferential tariff with Great Britain and sister colonies.

**Tupper,** Sir **Charles Hibbert.** 1855–1927. Canadian lawyer and statesman, b. in Amherst, Nova Scotia. Member of Canadian House of Commons (1882–1904); Canadian minister of marine and fisheries (1888–95); attorney general for Canada (1895–96); represented Canadian and British interests in Bering Sea fisheries arbitration at Paris (1892).

**Tupper, Martin Farquhar.** 1810–1889. English versifier, b. London; gained world-wide success with *Proverbial Philosophy* (1838), a series of didactic and moralizing commonplaces, seemingly in verse but without rhyme or meter; author also of books of ballads, novels, and a naïve autobiography.

**Tu'ra** (to͞o'rä), **Cosimo.** 1430?–1495. Italian painter, b. in Ferrara; founder of the Ferrarese school; among his works are *Pietà* (in the Louvre and at Venice), *Annunciation* (in Ferrara cathedral), *Christ Crucified* (in the Brera), and *Madonna with Saints* (in Berlin Museum).

**Tu·ra'ti** (to͞o·rä'tē), **Augusto.** 1888– . Italian Fascist politician; journalist (to 1922); participated in Mussolini's march on Rome (1922), and became general secretary of the Fascist party (1926–30); resigned from the party and his offices (1932).

**Turati, Filippo.** 1857–1932. Italian Socialist leader; founder and manager of the socialist periodicals *Critica Sociale* (1890 ff.) and *La Lotta di Classe* (1898 ff.). Effected Mussolini's appointment as editor in chief of *Avanti* (1912); opposed Italy's intervention in World War (1915); as opponent of Fascism, forced to flee into exile (1926).

**Tur'ber·ville** *or* **Tur'ber·vile** (tûr'bĕr·vĭl), **George.** 1540?–?1610. English poet, pioneer in use of blank verse; author of three metrical letters on Russia in Hakluyt's *Voyages*, of *Epitaphs, Epigrams, Songs and Sonnets* (1567), translations from Ovid, and *The Booke of Faulconrie, or Hawking* (1575), and probably *Noble Art of Venerie* (1575).

**Turck** (tûrk), **Fenton Benedict.** 1857–1932. American surgeon; director of research laboratory, Turck Foundation; invented the gyromele (1893); conducted research on gastritis, peptic ulcer, traumatic shock, etc.

**Tu'renne'** (tü'rĕn'; *Angl.* tū·rĕn'), Vicomte **de. Henri de La Tour d'Au'vergne'** (dē là to͞or' dô'vĕrn'y'). 1611–1675. Son of Henri, Duc de Bouillon. French marshal, b. Sedan. Brought up in Protestant faith. Served in Dutch War of Independence (1625–30). Entered French army (1630); served with distinction in campaigns of Thirty Years' War against Imperial army in France and Italy (1635–40); victorious over Spaniards at Casale Monferrato (1640) and conquered Roussillon (1642); appointed marshal (1643); given command of French army in Germany (1643–45); joined Swedes in conquering Bavaria (1645–48); with Condé won battle of Nördlingen (1645). These campaigns hastened end of Thirty Years' War (1648). Joined the Fronde (1649) but later was reconciled with the court (1651). Commanded royal armies against Condé in third civil war of the Fronde (1651–58), finally, by the victory of the Dunes (1658), completely defeating him. Commanded armies of Louis XIV in French invasion of Spanish Netherlands (1667). Induced by Louis to become a Catholic (1668). Commanded French armies in war in Holland, the Palatinate, and Alsace against the Empire (1672–75) until killed in action near Offenburg, Baden. Considered by Napoleon the greatest of all military leaders.

**Tur·ge'nev** (to͝or·gyā'nyĕf), **Aleksandr Ivanovich.** 1784?–1846. Russian historian; published *Historica Russiae Monumenta* (2 vols., 1841–42). His brother **Nikolai Ivanovich** (1790–1871) was involved in Decembrist plot (1825) and took refuge in Paris; author of *Russia and the Russians* (1847).

**Turgenev, Ivan Sergeevich.** 1818–1883. Russian novelist, b. Orel; educ. Moscow, St. Petersburg, and Berlin. Accepted minor government post (c. 1840) but soon resigned to devote himself to writing. Inherited large fortune (1850). Among his works are *Annals of a Sportsman* (sometimes translated as *A Sportsman's Sketches;* 1852), the short stories *A Quiet Backwater, Asya*, and *First Love*, and the novels *Rudin* (1855), *A Nest of Gentlefolk* (1858), *Helene* (1860; translated as *On the Eve*), *Fathers and Sons* (1862; here term *nihilist* is introduced and defined), *Smoke* (1867), *Virgin Soil* (1876), *A Lear of the Steppes* (1870), *Clara Milich* (1882).

**Tur'got'** (tür'gō'), **Anne Robert Jacques.** Baron **de l'Aulne** (dē lōn'). 1727–1781. French statesman and economist. Intendant of Limoges (1761–74); minister of marine under Louis XVI (1774); controller general of finance (1774–76). Removed because of opposition to his reforms by the queen, Malesherbes, Maurepas, and the nobles, clergy, rich bourgeoisie. Retired to devote himself to scientific and literary studies (1776–81). As intendant, imbued with physiocratic theories, abolished the corvée, constructed roads and bridges, reformed interest rates, and distributed the burden of taxation more justly. As finance minister, policy based on the guiding principles: "No bankruptcy, no increase in taxation, no borrowing"; in spite of tremendous financial difficulties then facing France, introduced a rigid economy, abolished certain feudal privileges, and attempted to restore free trade in grain between the provinces. One of the founders of the science of political economy. Best known works are *Lettres sur la Tolérance* (1753–54), *Réflexions sur la Formation et la Distribution des Richesses* (1766), *Mémoire sur les Prêts à Intérêt* (1769), *Les Six Édits* (1776).

**Tu·ri'na** (to͞o·rē'nä), **Joaquín.** 1882–1949. Spanish pianist, and composer of operas, symphonic poems, a string quartet, and many piano works.

**Turmair, Johannes.** See Johannes Aventinus.

**Turn'bull** (tûrn'bo͝ol), **Robert James.** 1775–1833. American lawyer and writer, b. New Smyrna, Fla. Practiced in Charleston, S.C. (1794–1810); thereafter, lived on his plantation. Author of a series of papers (1827) in the Charleston *Mercury* over the pseudonym "Brutus," and collected in book form in *The Crisis: or, Essays on the Usurpations of the Federal Government* (1827); vigorous advocate of nullification policy. A member of the South Carolina nullification convention (1832) and framer of its *Address* to the people.

**Tur'nèbe'** (tür'nĕb'), **Adrien.** *Real surname* **Tour'ne·bu'** (to͞or'nē·bü'). *Lat.* **Adrianus Tur·ne'bus**

(tûr·nē′bŭs). 1512–1565. French Hellenic scholar; translator and editor of many Greek works; regarded as one of the leaders in the French literary renaissance.

**Tur′ner** (tûr′nẽr), **Charles Root**. 1875–1947. American dentist and educator, b. Raleigh, N.C.; professor of prosthetic dentistry, Pennsylvania (from 1902) and dean of the school of dentistry (from 1917); author of *American Text Book of Prosthetic Dentistry* (1932); special editor for dentistry, *Webster's New International Dictionary, Second Edition*.

**Turner, Charles Tennyson**. See under Alfred TENNYSON.

**Turner, Charles Yardley**. 1850–1918. American painter, b. Baltimore, Md.; studio in New York (from 1881); best known for his figure paintings and murals; his *Bridal Procession* hangs in the Metropolitan Museum of Art in New York City.

**Turner, Cyril**. See Cyril TOURNEUR.

**Turner, Edward Raymond**. 1881–1929. American historian, b. Baltimore, Md.; professor of European history, Johns Hopkins (1925–29); authority on English constitutional history.

**Turner, Francis**. 1638?–1700. English prelate; bishop of Rochester (1683), of Ely (1684); one of the Seven Bishops (see William SANCROFT) who petitioned against James II's Declaration of Indulgence (1688), but were acquitted of charge of seditious libel; refused to take oath of allegiance to William and Mary; deprived of his see (1690).

**Turner, Frederick Jackson**. 1861–1932. American historian, b. Portage, Wis.; professor of history, Harvard (1910–24); influenced treatment of American history by emphasis on significance of the frontier in American national development; author of *Rise of the New West* (1906), *The Frontier in American History* (1920), *The Significance of Sections in American History* (1932; awarded Pulitzer prize, 1933).

**Turner,** Mrs. **G. D.** See Margaret WILSON.

**Turner,** Mrs. **Henry E.** See E. Arnot ROBERTSON.

**Turner, Herbert Hall**. 1861–1930. English astronomer; author of *Modern Astronomy*, *Astronomical Discovery*, *The Great Star Map*, and *A Voyage in Space*.

**Turner, John Hastings**. 1892–1956. English novelist and playwright.

**Turner, John Roscoe**. 1882–1960. Am. econ. and educ.; pres., West Virginia U. (1928–35); dean of men, C.C.N.Y. (1935–42), prof. of economics (1942–44); author of *Ricardian Rent in American Economics*, *Introduction to Economics*, *Economics—The Science of Business*.

**Turner, Joseph Mallord William**. 1775–1851. English landscape painter, chiefly a water-colorist. Exhibited first picture of naval engagement, *Battle of the Nile* (1799). In period of his first style (1800–20) introduced historical and mythological subjects and imitated van de Velde and Poussin; included Alpine scenes after first tour abroad (1802); painted *Garden of the Hesperides* (1806) in rivalry with Poussin, *Sun Rising in the Mist* (1807) in rivalry with Claude Lorrain; etched plates for his *Liber Studiorum* (1807–19); executed also in this period *Shipwreck* (1805), *Apollo and Python* (1811), *Dido Building Carthage* (1815), *Crossing the Brook* (1815). Began period of his second style (1820–35) with visit to Italy; ceased to imitate, idealized scenery, showed heightened scale of color; painted the *Bay of Baiae* (1823), *Harbours of England* (1824), *Dido Directing the Equipment of the Fleet* (1828), and the imaginative *Ulysses Deriding Polyphemus* (1829), called by some his masterpiece; idealized Italy in *Childe Harold's Pilgrimage* (1832); exhibited the poetical picture *The Golden Bough* (1834) and a collection of water colors on Venetian subjects, as well as *Grand Canal* in oil. In his third period (1835–45), sought to convey his impressions of nature, gained more poetic and dreamlike effects and even more brilliant color and light, as in the sea pieces *The Fighting Téméraire* (1839), *The Slave Ship* (1840), *Peace: Burial at Sea* (1842), in the later Venetian pictures, *The Sun of Venice Going to Sea* (1843), *The Approach to Venice* (1844), and in vague thoughts in color, such as *War, The Exile* (1842). His reputation increased by praise in Ruskin's *Modern Painters* (1843); after 1845 failed in mind and sight; exhibited for last time (1850). As an illustrator executed drawings for Thomas Dunham Whitaker's *History of Richmondshire* (1823), for *The Rivers of England* (1824), *The Provincial Antiquities of Scotland* (1825), *The Rivers of France* (1833–35); under his supervision line engravers brought the art to new perfection.

**Turner, Josiah**. 1821–1901. American politician and journalist, b. Hillsboro, N.C. Opposed secession, but loyal to his state when it seceded; representative in Confederate Congress (1863–65); advocated early peace. Owner and editor, Raleigh (N.C.) *Sentinel* (1868–76); attacked "carpetbag" government in North Carolina and largely responsible for overthrow of reconstruction in the state.

**Turner, Nat**. 1800–1831. American slave leader, b. in Southampton County, Va.; became religious fanatic; sought to convince his fellow slaves of his divine inspiration and leadership; plotted uprising of slaves (Nat Turner's Insurrection, 1831); murdered his master's entire family, aroused neighboring slaves and murdered a number of other whites in the vicinity; captured, tried, convicted, and hanged (Nov. 11, 1831).

**Turner,** Sir **Richard Ernest William**. 1871–1961. British soldier; served in Boer War (V.C., 1900); major general in World War I, commanded Canadian brigade of infantry, and later 2d Canadian division; after World War promoted lieutenant general.

**Turner, Ross Sterling**. 1847–1915. American painter and art teacher, b. Westport, N.Y.; studio in Boston (from 1882); master of water colors; also, successful in re-creating the illuminated manuscript of medieval times.

**Turner, Samuel Hulbeart**. 1790–1861. American Protestant Episcopal clergyman and Biblical critic, b. Philadelphia. Professor, General Theol. Sem., New York (1818–61); also, professor of Hebrew language and literature, Columbia (from 1830); author of a series of commentaries on books of the Bible, beginning with *A Companion to the Book of Genesis* (1841).

**Turner, Sharon**. 1768–1847. English historian; author of *History of the Anglo-Saxons* (4 vols., 1799–1805), extended through reign of Elizabeth and issued in collective edition (12 vols., 1839).

**Turner, Walter James Redfern**. 1889–1946. Australian poet and music critic. Served in World War. Music critic, *New Statesman* (from 1916); dramatic critic, London *Mercury* (1919–23). Among his books are *The Hunter, and Other Poems* (1916), *Paris and Helen* (1921), *Music and Life* (1921), *Smaragda's Lover* (1924), *Orpheus, or the Music of the Future* (1926), *Music, a Short History* (1932), *Songs and Incantations* (1936), *The Duchess of Popocatapetl* (1939).

**Turner, Walter Victor**. 1866–1919. Engineer and inventor, b. in Essex, Eng.; to U.S. (1888); granted over 400 patents, chiefly for air-brake devices; authority on pneumatic engineering.

**Turner, William**. 1510–1568. English clergyman, physician, and pioneer botanist. At Cambridge published botanical essay *Libellus de Re Herbaria Novus*

(1538); became intimate with Konrad Gesner in Zurich, collected plants in Rhine country, and wrote his *Newe Herball*, first essay on scientific botany in England (pub. 1551). Dean of Wells (1550–53); restored (1560) after living abroad through reign of Mary.

**Tur′pain′** (tür′pǎn′), **Albert Camille Léopold.** 1867– . French physicist; pioneer in experiments in wireless telegraphy.

**Tur′pin** (tûr′pĭn; *Fr.* tür′pǎn′) *or* **Til′pin** (tĭl′pĭn; *Fr.* tēl′pǎn′). French ecclesiastic of the 8th century; archbishop of Reims (c. 753). The so-called *Chronicle of Turpin*, once ascribed to him, has been proved by internal evidence to have been written in the 12th century.

**Tur′pin** (tûr′pĭn), **Richard,** *known as* **Dick.** 1706–1739. English robber. Son of an alehouse keeper; apprentice to butcher; cattle thief; deer stealer; smuggler; partner of a highwayman, Tom King, whom he accidentally killed when firing at a constable; at York assizes convicted of horse stealing; hanged. In legend and fiction (as Ainsworth's *Rookwood*), hero of ride from London to York on Black Bess, to establish an alibi.

**Turrecremata, Johannes de.** See Juan de TORQUEMADA (1388–1468).

**Tur′re·ti′ni** (too͝′rā·tē′nē), **Franz** (1623–1687) and his son **Johann Alfons** (1671–1737). Swiss Protestant theologians; both professors in Geneva.

**Turstin.** See THURSTAN.

**Tu′sar** (too͝′sär), **Vlastimil.** Prime minister at Czechoslovakia (1919–20).

**Tush·rat′ta** (too͝sh·răt′ȧ). A king of the Mitanni (c. 1400 B.C.); repelled Hittite invasion; in close contact with Egypt; reputed to have had a daughter, Tiy (*q.v.*), who married Amenhotep III of Egypt.

**Tusitala.** Epithet applied in Samoa to Robert Louis STEVENSON.

**Tus·saud′** (tŭ·sō′; too͝-; *Fr.* tü′sō′), **Marie,** *nee* **Gres′holtz** (grĕs′hōlts) *or* **Gros′holtz** (grōs′-). *Known as* **Madame Tussaud.** 1760–1850. Swiss modeler in wax; founder of Madame Tussaud's Exhibition in London. Modeled heads of leaders and victims of French Revolution; married a winegrower Tussaud (1794); moved to London and transferred her collection of figures (1802); finally settled it in Baker Street (1833), and connected with it a Chamber of Horrors, containing relics of criminals and instruments of torture.

**Tus′ser** (tŭs′ẽr), **Thomas.** 1524?–1580. English versifier on agriculture; settled as farmer at Cattiwade in Suffolk; introduced culture of barley. Author of *Hundredth Good Pointes of Husbandrie* (1557) in lively verse, furnishing instruction in farming, and wise maxims giving rise to many proverbs.

**Tut′ankh·a′men** (too͞t′ängk·ä′mĕn) *or* **Tut′enkh·a′mon** (too͞t′ĕngk·ä′mŏn). fl. about 1358 B.C. One of last kings of XVIIIth (Diospolite) dynasty of Egypt. At first followed new cult of his wife and father-in-law (see IKHNATON); later, returned to religion of priests of Amen (hence last element in his name); changed capital from Akhetaton back to Thebes; ruled but a few years; his tomb discovered (1922) in the Valley of the Kings near Luxor by George E. S. M. Herbert, Earl of Carnarvon, and Howard Carter.

**Tut′hill** (tŭt′hĭl), **William Bur′net** (bûr′nĕt). 1855–1929. American architect, b. New York City; office in New York (1877). Among buildings designed by him are: Carnegie Hall, Post Graduate Medical School and Hospital, Columbia Yacht Club, all in New York City; Princeton Inn, at Princeton, N.J.; Carnegie Library, at Pittsburgh, Pa.

**Tut′tle** (tŭt′'l), **Daniel Sylvester.** 1837–1923. American Protestant Episcopal clergyman; consecrated (1867) missionary bishop of Montana, home at Salt Lake City (1869–86); bishop of Missouri, with home at St. Louis (1886–1923); presiding bishop of his church (1903–23).

**Tuttle, Margaretta Muh′len·berg** (mū′lĕn·bûrg), *nee* **Perkins.** American writer; m. Frederic Crosby Tuttle (1907); author of *Feet of Clay* (a novel, 1923; later dramatized for motion pictures), *The Unguarded Hour* (a motion picture), and *Kingdoms of the World* (a novel, 1927).

**Tut′wi′ler** (tŭt′wī′lẽr), **Henry.** 1807–1884. American educator; opened Greene Springs School for Boys, at Greene Springs, near Havana, Ala. (1847) and remained its headmaster (1847–84). His daughter **Julia Strudwick Tutwiler** (1841–1916) was also an educator; coprincipal (1883–88) and sole principal (1888–1910), Alabama Normal College; instrumental in securing state grant for founding Alabama Girls Industrial School (opened 1896); gained admission (1896) for graduates of Alabama Normal College to U. of Alabama, thus inaugurating coeducation in the University; also interested herself in reform of prison conditions in Alabama; composer of *Alabama* adopted as the state song.

**Tuyll, Isabella van.** See Isabelle de CHARRIÈRE.

**Twacht′man** (twäkt′măn), **John Henry.** 1853–1902. American painter, b. Cincinnati, Ohio; studio in his home near Greenwich, Conn. (from 1889); noteworthy among American painters of the impressionist school. His work is represented in Metropolitan Art Museum in New York City, Boston Museum of Fine Arts, National Gallery of Art in Washington, D.C., etc.

**Twad′dell** (twŏd′'l; twŏ·dĕl′), **William.** d. about 1840. Scottish inventor of a hydrometer (Twaddell's hydrometer) for liquids heavier than water (c. 1830).

**Twain** (twān), **Mark.** Pseudonym of Samuel Langhorne CLEMENS and Isaiah SELLERS.

**Tweed** (twēd), **John.** 1869–1933. British sculptor, of Scottish ancestry. Among his works are the national memorial to Earl Kitchener, London, marble bust of Lord Curzon of Kedleston for Oxford Union, the Lord Beresford memorial in St. Paul's, statues of Cecil J. Rhodes at Bulawayo, Queen Victoria at Aden and Madras, Alfred Beit at Salisbury in South Africa, Lord Clive at London and Calcutta.

**Tweed, William Marcy.** 1823–1878. American politician, b. New York City. New York City Democratic alderman (1852–56) and also member of U.S. House of Representatives (1853–55). New York City school commissioner (1856–57); member of board of supervisors, designed to stop election corruption (1856). A sachem in Tammany organization and powerful political boss (1859); grand sachem (1868). Opened law office (1860); bought control of a printing company (1864), which thereafter gained contracts for city printing; organized a marble company and supplied New York with marble for new county courthouse; dictated Democratic nominations for mayor of New York City and for governor of the state. New York State senator (1867–71); commissioner of public works, New York City (1870). Became head of a group of New York City politicians, including Comptroller Connolly, City Chamberlain Peter B. Sweeny, Mayor A. Oakey Hall, and others, known as the Tweed Ring, which gained control of New York City finances and swindled the treasury of many millions of dollars. Charges of corruption brought by *Harper's Weekly*, with powerful cartoons by Thomas Nast (1870), and by the New York *Times* (1870). Actual destruction of ring due to efforts of chairman of Democratic State committee, S. J. Tilden (*q.v.*). Tweed arrested in a civil suit (Oct. 26, 1871) and in a criminal action (Dec. 16, 1871). On first criminal trial, jury disagreed; on second trial, Tweed was convicted (Nov.,

1873) and imprisoned on Blackwell's Island. On his release (Jan., 1875), he was arrested in civil action brought by state of New York to recover his stealings; escaped and fled to Spain; arrested there and returned to New York (Nov., 1876). Died in Ludlow Street Jail, New York City.

**Tweeddale,** Earl and marquis of. See John HAY.

**Tweedmouth,** Baron. See Edward MARJORIBANKS.

**Tweedsmuir,** Baron. See Sir John BUCHAN.

**Twen·ho′fel** (twĕn·hō′fĕl), **William Henry.** 1875–1957. American geologist, b. Covington, Ky.; B.A. (1908), Ph.D. (1912), Yale; taught in rural schools, Ky. (1896–1902), at Univs. of Kansas (1910–16) and Wisconsin (1916 ff.; professor from 1921); author of *Treatise on Sedimentation* (1926; revised ed., with others, 1932); *Invertebrate Paleontology* (with R. R. Schrock, 1935), *Principles of Sedimentation* (1939), *Methods of Study of Sediments* (1941), etc.

**Twich′ell** (twĭch′ĕl), **Joseph Hopkins.** 1838–1918. American Congregational clergyman; pastorate, Hartford, Conn. (1865–1918). Close friend of Samuel L. Clemens, Charles Dudley Warner, Harriet Beecher Stowe. Figures as Harris in Mark Twain's *A Tramp Abroad.*

**Twiggs** (twĭgz), **David Emanuel.** 1790–1862. American army officer, b. in Richmond County, Ga. Served (colonel) under Gen. Zachary Taylor in Mexican War; promoted brigadier general (June, 1846); joined Gen. Scott at Vera Cruz; engaged at Cerro Gordo. At outbreak of Civil War, commanded Department of Texas; surrendered (Feb., 1861) to Confederate general McCulloch, and was dismissed from U.S. army (1861). Commissioned major general in Confederate army (May, 1861). Died July 15, 1862.

**Twiss** (twĭs), Sir **Travers.** 1809–1897. English jurist and juridical writer. Regius professor of civil law, Oxford (1855–70); retired to private life (1872) because of scandalous libel. Drafted for king of Belgium a constitution for Congo Free State (1884); counsel extraordinary to British Embassy during Berlin Conference (1884–85). Author of *The Law of Nations* (1861–63).

**Twitcher, Jemmy.** Nickname of John MONTAGU, 4th Earl of Sandwich.

**Twort** (twôrt), **Frederick William.** 1877–1950. English bacteriologist; first to describe bacteriophage (1915).

**Tyard, Pontus de.** See THIARD.

**Tybald, Simon.** See Simon of SUDBURY.

**Tych′sen** (tüκ′sĕn), **Olaus** (*or* **Oluf**) **Gerhard.** 1734–1805. German Orientalist.

**Tye** (tī), **Christopher.** 1497?–1572. English organist and composer; translated first half of Acts of Apostles into English verse set to music (1553), some of part songs of which became hymn tunes; under Queen Elizabeth organist to Chapel Royal; composer of anthems and church services.

**Ty′ler** (tī′lẽr), **Bennet.** 1783–1858. American theologian, b. Middlebury, Conn. Ordained in Congregational ministry (1808). President, Dartmouth (1822–28). Became leader (from 1828) of conservatively orthodox group of clergymen; his theology became known as "Tylerism" contrasted with "Taylorism," the doctrine of Nathaniel W. Taylor (*q.v.*). A founder, professor of Christian theology, and president, Theological Institute of Connecticut, now the Hartford Theological Seminary (1834–57).

**Tyler, John.** 1747–1813. Father of President John Tyler (*q.v.*). American jurist, b. in York County, Va.; judge, Virginia general court (1789–1808), one of first judges to maintain the overruling power of the judiciary; governor of Virginia (1808–11).

**Tyler, John.** 1790–1862. Son of John Tyler, the Virginia jurist. Tenth president of the United States, b. in Charles City County, Va. Grad. William and Mary (1807). Adm. to bar and began practice in Charles City County (1809). Member of U.S. House of Representatives (1817–21); governor of Virginia (1825–27); U.S. senator (1827–36). Vice-president of the United States (1841), succeeding to the presidency on death of President William Henry Harrison (Apr. 4, 1841); administration (1841–45) marked by party conflict, Tyler acting with the Democratic party although elected as a Whig, by negotiation of Webster-Ashburton Treaty, and by annexation of Texas to the Union. Remained loyal to Virginia when it seceded.

**Tyler, John Mason.** 1851–1929. American biologist, b. Amherst, Mass.; author of *Whence and Whither of Man* (1897), *Man in the Light of Evolution* (1908), *New Stone Age* (1921), *Coming of Man* (1923), etc.

**Tyler, Lyon Gar′di·ner** (gär′d'n·ẽr). 1853–1935. Son of John Tyler, President of the United States. American educator; president, Coll. of William and Mary (1888–1919); author of *Cradle of the Republic* (1900), *England in America* (1904), *Williamsburg, the Old Colonial Capital* (1907), etc.; editor, *Narratives of Early Virginia, 1606–1625* (1907), *Biographical Dictionary of Virginia* (5 vols., 1915).

**Tyler, Moses Coit.** 1835–1900. American educator, b. Griswold, Conn.; professor of rhetoric and English literature, U. of Michigan (1867–73; 1874–81); professor of American history, Cornell (1881–1900); a founder of American Historical Association (1884); author of *A History of American Literature During the Colonial Time, 1607–1765* (2 vols., 1878), *Three Men of Letters* (1895), *The Literary History of the American Revolution 1763–1783* (2 vols., 1897), etc.

**Tyler, Robert.** 1816–1877. American lawyer and politician; private secretary to his father, President Tyler (1841–44). Moved to Philadelphia (1844); prothonotary to Pennsylvania supreme court; at outbreak of Civil War, fled to Richmond, Va.; appointed register of Confederate treasury; editor, Montgomery (Ala.) *Mail and Advertiser* (1867–77); led in attacks on carpetbag government in Alabama.

**Tyler, Royall.** 1757–1826. American jurist and author, b. Boston. Major on Gen. Benjamin Lincoln's staff in suppression of Shays' Rebellion (1786). Chief justice, Vermont supreme court (1807–13); professor of jurisprudence, U. of Vermont (1811–14). Author of *The Contrast*, first comedy written by a native American and professionally produced (in New York, Apr. 16, 1787); also wrote a novel, *The Algerine Captive* (1797).

**Tyler, Wat** *or* **Walter.** *Last name also written* **Tegheler** *or* **Helier.** d. 1381. English leader of Peasants' Revolt. Perhaps a tiler of Essex; by confusion with John Tyler of Dartford, traditionally credited with killing tax collector who insulted his daughter, thereby giving signal for uprising in Kent; chosen leader of mob assembled (June, 1381) in protest against Statute of Laborers and imposition of poll tax, as well as economic distress, and led movement on London; presented to Richard II at Smithfield demands for abolition of serfdom, removal of restrictions upon freedom of labor and trade, and amnesty for rebels; on presenting fresh demands the following day (June 15, 1381) killed by Lord Mayor Walworth.

**Ty′lor** (tī′lẽr), Sir **Edward Burnett.** 1832–1917. English anthropologist; visited Mexico (1856), recorded visit in *Anahuac; or, Mexico and the Mexicans* (1861); made reputation with his *Researches into The Early History of Mankind* (1865); first professor of anthropology, Oxford (1896–1909); chief work, *Primitive Culture* (1871).

**Ty'nan** (tī'năn), **Katharine.** 1861–1931. Irish poet and novelist, b. in County Dublin; m. H. A. Hink'son [hĭngk's'n] (1893; d. 1919). One of leaders of Irish literary renaissance. Among her many works are *Shamrocks* (1887), *Ballads and Lyrics* (1890), *A Nun...* (1892), *Cuckoo Songs* (1894), *The Handsome Brandons* (1898), *The Honorable Mollie* (1903), *The Luck of the Fairfaxes* (1904), *Irish Poems* (1913), *The Story of Margery Dawe* (1915), *Herb o' Grace* (1918), *The Second Wife* (1920), *Wives* (1924), *The Wild Adventure* (1928), *A Fine Gentleman* (1929).

**Tyn'dale** *or* **Tin'dal** *or* **Tin'dale** (tĭn'd'l), **William.** 1492?–1536. English translator of New Testament and Pentateuch. Preaching in Gloucestershire, introduced New Learning, for which he was rebuked by William of Malvern, abbot of St. Peter's, Gloucester. Began translation of New Testament from Greek into the vernacular as a means of overcoming corruption of the church; got no help from Cuthbert Tunstall, bishop of London; finding publication impossible in England, left for Hamburg (1524); visited Luther at Wittenberg; began printing translation of Matthew and Mark at Cologne (1525); stopped by injunction after discovery by dean of Frankfurt and sending of warning to Henry VIII and Wolsey; completed printing at Worms of 3000 New Testaments in small octavo, which were smuggled into England and there suppressed by bishops (only five or six copies now extant). Escaping seizure ordered by Wolsey, found refuge with Philip the Magnanimous, Landgrave of Hesse, at Marburg; leaned on Luther in marginal notes of his version of the Pentateuch published at Marburg (1530); issued version of Jonah with prologue (1531); issued revised version of New Testament (1534); his version of the Bible the chief basis, with admixture of Wycliffe version, of the Authorized Version of 1611. Swung over to Zwinglian position on Eucharist; published tracts advocating principles of English Reformation, among them the sole authority of Scripture in the church, including *The Parable of the Wicked Mammon* (1528) and *The Obedience of a Christian Man* (1528). Lost favor of Henry VIII because of denunciation in *The Practyse of Prelates* (1536) of Henry's divorce, as well as of the Roman Catholic Church; at Antwerp conducted controversy with Sir Thomas More (1531). Betrayed in Flanders by Henry Phillips, a Roman Catholic zealot, to imperial officers; imprisoned at Vilvorde for sixteen months; strangled and burned at stake, in spite of intercession by Thomas Cromwell.

**Tyn'dall** (tĭn'd'l), **John.** 1820–1893. British physicist and popularizer of science, b. in Ireland. Professor of natural philosophy at Royal Institution (1853); colleague of Faraday whom he succeeded as scientific adviser to Trinity House and Board of Trade (1866) and as superintendent of the Royal Institution (1867); with T. H. Huxley studied glaciers in Switzerland; lectured in the U.S. (1872–73). Investigated transmission, radiation, and absorption of radiant heat by vapors and gases; attempted to determine proportion of luminous to nonluminous rays in light from various sources; studied the decomposition of vapors by light; showed that the blue of the sky is due to fine particles in the atmosphere; by experiments with pure air, verified fallacy of doctrine of spontaneous generation; discovered that the transmission of sound is effected by variations in density of the atmosphere. His publications include: *Heat Considered as a Mode of Motion* (1863), *On Sound* (1867), *Faraday as a Discoverer* (1868), *Contributions to Molecular Physics in the Domain of Radiant Heat* (1872), *Lessons in Electricity, at the Royal Institution* (1876), etc.

**Tyng** (tĭng), **Stephen Higginson.** 1800–1885. American Protestant Episcopal clergyman; pastorates, in Philadelphia (1829–45), and New York (1845–78); renowned as preacher; leader of the low-church party in Protestant Episcopal denomination.

**Tyrconnel,** Earl of. See (1) Rory O'DONNELL; (2) Richard TALBOT (1630–1691).

**Tyrone,** Earls of. See under O'NEILL family.

**Tyr'rell** (tĭr'ĕl), **George.** 1861–1909. Irish Roman Catholic theologian, b. Dublin; joined Roman Catholic Church (1879); entered Jesuit order (1880). Sought to reconcile conservative element of Catholicism with principle of development in *The Faith of the Millions, Hard Sayings, Nova et Vetera.* His modernism, revealed in his *Letter to a Professor of Anthropology* (pub. without his knowledge, 1906), caused his dismissal from Society of Jesus. Replied to Pius X's encyclical *Pascendi* against modernism (1907); answered Cardinal Mercier's attack on modernism in his *Medievalism* (1908); suffered minor excommunication, with reserved case at Rome. Author also of *Through Scylla and Charybdis* (an account of his religious development, 1907), *Christianity at the Cross-Roads* (1909), *Essays on Faith and Immortality* (1914), and *Autobiography* (2 vols., 1912). His first cousin **Robert Yelverton Tyrrell** (1844–1914) was a classical scholar; joint editor, with Louis Claude Purser, of commentary on *Correspondence of Cicero* (7 vols., 1879–1900).

**Tyr'rell** *or* **Tyr'ell** (tĭr'ĕl), Sir **James.** d. 1502. English Yorkist; supposed instrument of Richard III in murder of Edward V and his brother Richard, Duke of York (1483); beheaded on confession of murder of princes.

**Tyrrell, William George.** 1st Baron **Tyrrell** of A'von (ā'vŭn; ăv'ŭn). 1866–1947. British diplomat; ambassador to France (1928–34).

**Tyr·tae'us** (tûr·tē'ŭs). Greek elegiac poet of Sparta, of middle 7th century B.C. According to tradition, his martial verses inspired Spartans to victory over Messenians. Three complete poems and a few fragments of his works are extant.

**Tyr'whitt,** *later* **Tyr'whitt–Wil'son** (tĭr'ĭt·wĭl's'n), **Gerald Hugh.** 14th Baron **Ber'ners** (bûr'nẽrz). 1883–1950. English musical composer and painter; succeeded uncle as Lord Berners (1918). Composer of three funeral marches for piano, *Fantaisie Espagnole* for orchestra, a comic operatic version of Mérimée's *Le Carrosse du Saint Sacrement* (1923), and four ballets, *Triumph of Neptune* (1926), *Luna Park* (1930), *The Wedding Bouquet* (with text by Gertrude Stein, 1937), and *Cupid and Psyche* (1939). Author of *First Childhood* (1934), *The Camel* (1936), *The Girls of Radcliff Hall* (1937).

**Tyrwhitt,** Sir **Reginald Yorke.** 1870–1951. English naval commander; commanded destroyer flotilla in actions in Helgoland Bight (Aug. and Dec., 1914) and off Dogger Bank (1915); admiral (1929); admiral of the fleet (1934); commander in chief, China station (1927–29), The Nore (1930–33); retired (1939); restored to active list (1940).

**Tyrwhitt, Thomas.** 1730–1786. English classical scholar. Edited classical authors, of which Aristotle's *Poetics* was his chief work (pub., 1794). Author of *Observations upon Shakespeare* (1766); edited and exposed *Rowley Poems* as forgeries by Chatterton (1777–78); editor of Chaucer's *Canterbury Tales* (1775–78), contributing to elucidation of Chaucer's versification and fixing of the Chaucer canon.

**Ty'son** (tī's'n), **George Emory.** 1829–1906. American arctic whaler, b. Red Bank, N.J.; member of *Polaris* arctic expedition under Charles Francis Hall; assumed command of a group, 19 in all, accidentally left adrift on an ice floe (Oct. 15, 1872–Apr. 30, 1873) and by resourcefulness and seamanship kept up morale of members of the party until they were rescued, after drifting about 1800 miles, by a sealer off Labrador.

**Tyson, James.** 1841–1919. American physician, b. Philadelphia; on teaching staff, U. of Pennsylvania (1868–1910) and dean of the medical faculty (1888–92); author of *The Cell Doctrine...*(1870), *The Practice of Medicine* (1896), etc.

**Tyt'ler** (tĭt'lẽr), **James.** 1747–1805. Scottish literary hack and scientific dabbler. As editor, wrote large portions of second and third editions of *Encyclopaedia Britannica.* Constructed fire balloon, in which he was first person in Great Britain to navigate the air (1784); hence known as "Balloon Tytler." Expressed advanced views on reform in *The Historical Register* (1792); fled to Salem, Mass., to avoid arrest, and there published newspaper (till 1805). Author of verses, including *The Bonnie Bruckit Lassie.*

**Tytler, William.** 1711–1792. Scottish historian; writer to the signet; author of an exculpatory *Inquiry into the Evidence against Mary Queen of Scots* (1760) and editor of *Poetical Remains of James the First, King of Scotland* (1783). His son **Alexander Fraser** (1747–1813), Lord **Wood'house'lee** (?wo͝od'hous'lē), judge and historian, was judge advocate of Scotland (1790); judge of court of session as Lord Woodhouselee (1802); author of lives of Lord Kames and Petrarch, and *Elements of General History* (1801). Alexander's 4th son, **Patrick Fraser** (1791–1849), was a historian; devoted himself chiefly to biographical and historical works, including *Life of the Admirable Crichton* (1819), *Lives of Scottish Worthies* (1831–33), *History of Scotland* (1828–43), *England under Reigns of Edward VI and Mary* (1839).

**Tyut'chev** (tyo͞ot'chĕf), **Fëdor Ivanovich.** 1803–1873. Russian poet; ranked second only to Pushkin as a lyric poet in Russian literature; published volume (1854) including poems (translated later into English as *Nature, Spring, An Autumn Evening, The Deserted Villa, The Last Love*).

**Tza'ra** (tsä'rä), **Tri·stan'** (trē·stän'). 1896–1963. Rumanian-born poet, essayist, and editor in Paris; associated with ultramodern literary movements; a leader in founding Dadaism, and for a time (c. 1930) identified with the surrealists; editor of *Dada* (1916–20).

**Tze'tzes** (tsĕt'sēz; *Mod. Gr.* tsâ'tsēs), **Johannes** *or* **John.** 12th-century Byzantine poet and grammarian; author of *Book of Histories* (usually known as *Chiliades*), *Iliaca*, and commentaries on certain Greek authors.

**Tzu Hsi** *or* **Tze–hsi** (tso͞o' shē'). *More correctly,* **Tz'ŭ Hsi.** *Also known as* **Ye·ho·na·la** (yĕ·hŏ·nä·rä). 1835–1908. Called "the Old Buddha." Chinese empress dowager, regent (1862–73, 1875–89, 1898–1908). Concubine of Emperor Hsien Fêng and mother of T'ung Chih. Coregent with Prince Kung for T'ung Chih (1862–73); on T'ung Chih's death (1875) assumed regency for her nephew Kuang Hsü; retired (1889) but when the emperor attempted reforms (1898), again seized control, with assistance of Li Hung-chang; reactionary in her policies, encouraged the Boxers but on final success of treaty powers in capturing Tientsin and Peking, fled from the court to Sian (1900); remained in exile (1900–02); always hostile to foreign influence.

# U

**U'bal·di'ni** (o͞o'bäl·dē'nē), **Petruccio.** 1524?–?1600. Florentine illuminator and scholar; to England (1545); fought in Scottish wars (1549); wrote *Vita di Carlo Magno Imperatore* (first Italian book printed in England, 1581) and historical and biographical narratives.

**Ubaldini, Ruggiero.** Archbishop of Pisa (1276); Ghibelline leader; imprisoned (1288) and starved Ugolino della Gherardesca and Ugolino's two sons and two grandsons (Dante's *Divina Commedia*, Inferno XXXIII).

**Ubaldus.** See Hucbald.

**Ubaydullah.** See Fatimid dynasty.

**Uberti.** See (1) Farinata degli Uberti; (2) Fazio degli Uberti.

**U'ber·ti'ni** (o͞o'bâr·tē'nē), **Francesco.** *Called* **Il Bachiac'ca** (ēl bä·kyäk'kä). 1494?–1557. Italian painter; known esp. for historical paintings, executed on small scale and with many figures.

**Ü'ber·weg** (ü'bẽr·väk), **Friedrich.** 1826–1871. German philosopher; author of *Grundriss der Geschichte der Philosophie* (1862–66), etc.

**U·bi'co Cas'ta·ñe'da** (o͞o·bē'kō käs'tä·nyā'thä), **Jorge.** 1878–1946. President of Guatemala (1931–44).

**Uc·cel'lo** (o͞ot·chĕl'lō), **Paolo.** *Real name* **Paolo di Do'no** (dē dō'nō). 1397–1475. Florentine painter; known esp. for his experimental studies in foreshortening and linear perspective; known also as a mosaicist and designer of stained-glass windows. His works include an equestrian portrait of Sir John de Hawkwood, portraits of Giotto, Brunelleschi, Donatello, and a self-portrait, *Battle of San Romano, St. George and the Dragon*, and *Hunting Scene at Night.*

**U'chard'** (ü'shȧr'), **Mario.** 1824–1893. French novelist and playwright.

**U·cha'ti·us** (o͝o·кä'tsē·o͝os), Baron **Franz von.** 1811–1881. Austro-Hungarian general, inventor, and authority on artillery; introduced an improved process of manufacturing steel (1856) and invented ballistic apparatus, a steel bronze (called Uchatius bronze) for cannon, ring grenades (1875), etc.

**U·chi·da** (o͝o·chē·dä), Viscount **Yasuya.** 1865–1936. Japanese diplomat; minister to China (1901–06); ambassador to Austria-Hungary (1906) and U.S. (1908–12); minister of foreign affairs (1912–14, 1918–23, 1932–33); ambassador to Russia (1914–17); member of privy council (1924–29).

**U'dall** (ū'd'l) *or* **Uve'dale** (ūv'dāl), **John.** 1560?–1592. English Puritan preacher; suspected of complicity in *Martin Marprelate* tracts; imprisoned (1590) and sentenced to death (1591) for pamphlets attacking the episcopacy; died soon after being pardoned.

**Udall** *or* **Uvedale, Nicholas.** 1505–1556. English schoolmaster, Latin scholar, and playwright. Headmaster of Eton (1534); dismissed for misconduct (1541). Translated Erasmus's *Apophthegms* (1542), Peter Martyr's works on the Eucharist, and the Great Bible (1551); had his play *Ralph Roister Doister* produced (probably 1553), the earliest extant English comedy, modeled on Plautus's *Miles Gloriosus.* Playwriter to Queen Mary (1554); headmaster, Westminster (1554–56).

**U'det** (o͞o'dĕt), **Ernst.** 1896–1941. German aviator and army officer; served in air force in World War (1914–18); credited with destroying 62 enemy planes; chief of technical bureau of German air force, with rank of lieutenant general (1938).

**U'dr·žal** (ŏŏ'dĕr·zhȧl), **František.** 1866– . Czechoslovak statesman; premier of Czechoslovakia (1929–32).

**Uech'tritz** (üĸ'trĭts), **Friedrich von.** 1800–1875. German dramatist and novelist; author of tragedies, a dramatic poem, and religious novels.

**Uechtritz, Kuno von.** 1856–1908. German sculptor; works include monuments of Moltke and Elector George William of Brandenburg, the Hubertus Fountain in Berlin, decorative pieces, and portrait busts.

**Uex'küll** (üks'kül), Baron **Jakob Johann von.** 1864–1944. German biologist and comparative psychologist.

**Uf'er** (ŭf'ẽr), **Walter.** 1876–1936. American painter; studio at Taos, N.Mex., where he studied and painted esp. Pueblo Indian scenes.

**Uf'ford** (ŭf'ẽrd), **Edward Smith.** 1851–1929. American Baptist evangelist and hymn writer; wrote the revival hymn "Throw out the life line."

**Ufford, Robert de** (dĕ). 1st Earl of **Suf'folk** (sŭf'ŭk). 1298–1369. English soldier in France and chief counselor of Edward III; distinguished himself at Poitiers (1356). His second son, **William** (1339?–1382), 2d earl, accompanied John of Gaunt through France (1373); served in France and Brittany (1377–78) and in Scotland (1380); Richard II's chief commissioner of array for Norfolk and Suffolk (1377); played part in Peasants' Revolt under Wat Tyler (1381), at first sought as their leader, later active in suppressing revolt; a leader in opposition to John of Gaunt (1381).

**U·gar'te** (ōō·gär'tā), **Manuel.** 1874–1951. Argentine writer; regarded as one of initiators of modernism in Argentine literature, as in *Gardens of Illusion;* supporter of Spanish-American consolidation of interests to check U.S. enterprize, as in his *The Future of Latin America* and *The Destiny of a Continent.*

**Uggione, Marco da.** See Oggiono.

**U'go·li'ni** (ōō'gô·lē'nē), **Vincenzo.** d. 1626. Italian composer, esp., of church music and chorales.

**Ugolino.** Count of **Segni.** See Pope Gregory IX.

**Ugolino della Gherardesca** *or* **da Pisa.** See Gherardesca.

**Ugubaldus.** See Hucbald.

**U'guc·cio'ne da Pi'sa** (ōō'gōōt·chō'nā dä pē'sä). d. 1210. Italian canonist and lexicographer; bishop of Ferrara (1190); author of *Magnae Derivationes.*

**Uh'de** (ōō'dĕ), **Fritz von.** 1848–1911. German religious and genre painter; paintings include *Family Concert, The Sermon on the Mount, The Wise Men from the East, The Ascension, The Last Supper, Going Home,* and impressionistic portraits.

**Uh'land** (ōō'länt), **Johann Ludwig.** 1787–1862. German poet of the Swabian school, philologist, and literary historian. His works include poems, ballads, and songs, as *Der Gute Kamerad, Der Wirtin Töchterlein, Die Kapelle, Schäfers Sonntagslied, Taillefer, Das Schloss am Meer, Bertran de Born, Das Glück von Edenhall, Des Sängers Fluch, Schwäbische Kunde,* and *Der Schwarze Ritter,* the plays *Ernst, Herzog von Schwaben* (1818) and *Ludwig der Bayer* (1819); essays and treatises, as *Über das Altfranzösische Epos* (1812), *Walther von der Vogelweide* (1822), and *Der Mythus von Thôr* (1836), and the collection *Alte Hoch- und Niederdeutsche Volkslieder.*

**Uh'len·beck** (ü'lĕn·bĕk), **Christianus Cornelius.** 1866–1951. Dutch linguist and philologist; professor of Sanskrit and Indo-Germanic philology, Amsterdam (1892), of Old German languages, Leiden (1899–1926). Chief works, *Etymologisches Wörterbuch der Gotischen Sprache* (1896), *Etymologisches Wörterbuch der Altindischen Sprache* (2 vols., 1898–99).

**Uh'len·beck** (ōō'lĕn·bĕk), **George Eugene.** 1900– . Physicist, b. Batavia, Java; Ph.D., U. of Leiden (1927); to U.S. (1927); teacher (1927–35), professor (from 1939), U. of Michigan; professor of theoretical physics, Utrecht, Holland (1935–39).

**Uh'len·huth** (ōō'lĕn·hōōt), **Paul.** 1870–1957. German bacteriologist and hygienist. Discoveries credited to him include: a method for discriminating between human and animal blood; serums against hog cholera and (with Löffler) against foot-and-mouth disease; the cause of Weil's disease; and the modern treatment of syphilis with arsenicals.

**Uh'lich** (ōō'lĭĸ), **Leberecht.** 1799–1872. German Protestant rationalistic theologian; head of the "Friends of Light" or "Protestant Friends" (1841; suspended for heterodoxy, 1847); withdrew from Evangelical church and became preacher of the Free Congregation, Magdeburg.

**Uh'rich'** (ü'rēk'), **Jean Jacques Alexis.** 1802–1886. French army officer; in command at Strasbourg at the time of its surrender (Sept. 28, 1870).

**U·jej'ski** (ōō·yā'skē), **Kornel.** 1823–1897. Polish poet; among his works are *The Lamentations of Jeremiah* (1847), *Interpretations of Chopin* (1860). His *Choral Song* is known among Poles as the national anthem of Poland in mourning.

**Uj'fal'vy von Me'ző·kö'vesd** (ōō'y'·fŏl'vĭ fôn mĕ'zû-kû'vĕsht), **Karl Eugen.** 1842–1904. Austrian traveler and philologist; conducted three expeditions to Central Asia for French government (1876–82); author of *Expédition Scientifique Française en Russie, en Sibérie et dans le Turkestan* (1878–82), etc.

**U·krain'ka** (ōō·krīn'kŭ), **Lesya.** *Pseudonym of* **Laryssa Petrovna Kvit·ka'** (kvyĭt·kȧ'). 1781–1913. Ukrainian poetess; among her works are *On Wings of Song* (1893), *Thoughts and Dreams* (1899), and the plays *Isolde of the White Hands* and *Cassandra.*

**Ul'bach'** (ül'bȧk'), **Louis.** 1822–1889. French journalist and novelist.

**Ulenspiegel, Till.** See Eulenspiegel.

**Ul'fi·las** (ŭl'fĭ·lăs; -lȧs) *or* **Ul'fi·la** (-lȧ) *or* **Wul'fi·la** (wŏŏl'fĭ·lȧ). 311?–381 A.D. Bishop of the Goths, and translator of Bible into Gothic; consecrated bishop at Synod of Antioch (341 A.D.). Served as missionary bishop among Visigoths beyond Danube (341–348); then, with permission of Emperor Constantius, settled in Moesia, near Nicopolis (c. 348). From a Greek original, translated Bible into Moeso-Gothic, devising for purpose (it is said) a written alphabet based on Greek uncials supplemented from Gothic runes; extant fragments of his Bible constitute (with a few other scattered remains) earliest known specimen of Teutonic languages.

**Ull'mann** (ŏŏl'män), **Hermann.** 1884– . German political writer and propagandist.

**Ullmann, Karl.** 1796–1865. German Protestant evangelical theologian; prelate, Karlsruhe (1853–61), and president of the supreme ecclesiastical council.

**Ul·lo'a** (ōō·lyō'ä), **Antonio de.** 1716–1795. Spanish naval officer and scientist; with French scientific expedition to South America (1735–44) to measure an arc of the meridian; collaborated in secret report on conditions in Peru (c. 1749; pub. under title *Noticias Secretas de América,* 1826); made rear admiral (1760); governor of Louisiana (1766–68; driven out by Creole uprising); pioneer in many branches of science in Spain.

**Ulloa, Francisco de.** d. about 1540. Spanish soldier and explorer in America; accompanied Hernando Cortes in conquest of Mexico; sent north by Cortes (1539) to explore Gulf of California; established fact that Lower California is a peninsula.

**Ul·lo'a** (o͞ol·lô'ä), **Girolamo.** 1810–1891. Italian general and historian.

**Ul·lo'a** (o͞o·yō'ä), **Luis.** 1869–1936. Peruvian historian and librarian, b. Lima. Under commission from Peruvian government, collected from Europe and Peru documents on Peruvian history from the discovery by Pizarro (1527) until the year of Peruvian independence (1824); published (30 vols.) results of his researches.

**Ullswater,** Viscount. See LOWTHER family.

**Ul'ma·nis** (o͝ol'mä·nĭs), **Karl'is** (kär'lĭs). 1877–1940. Latvian statesman; first prime minister of newly-organized Latvia (1918); again prime minister (1931–32); prime minister, minister of foreign affairs, and virtual dictator (from 1934), and president (1936–40) until his country was annexed to Russia as a constituent republic.

**Ul'pi·an** (ŭl'pĭ·ăn). *Full Latin name* **Domitius Ul'pi·a'nus** (ŭl'pĭ·ā'nŭs). 170?–228 A.D. Roman jurist; member of the council under Emperor Lucius Septimius Severus; master of requests under Caracalla; banished from Rome by Heliogabalus, but recalled (222) by Alexander Severus and made chief adviser to the emperor. Author of many legal treatises, commentaries, etc.

**Ul'rich** (o͝ol'rĭk). 1487–1550. Duke of Württemberg, b. in Alsace. Succeeded to duchy (1498); assumed personal control (1503); won new territory (1504). Aroused rebellion of peasants because of oppressions (1514) and opposition of nobility because of murder of Hans von Hutten; expelled by Swabian League (1519). With aid of Philip of Hesse, recovered his dukedom (1534) but only as a fief of Austria. Introduced Reformation into Württemberg; joined Schmalkaldic League and fought against Charles V (1546); forced to accept Augsburg Interim; again threatened with deposition at time of death (1550).

**Ulrich von Lich'ten·stein** *or* **Liech'ten·stein** (fôn lĭk'tĕn·shtīn). 1200?–?1276. Middle High German lyric poet; author of *Frauendienst* (c. 1255), an autobiographical novel in verse containing minnesongs and dancing songs, and *Frauenbuch* (1257), descriptive of the customs and morals of his time.

**Ulrich von Tür'heim** (fôn tür'hīm). fl. 1236–1285. Middle High German epic poet and noble. He continued Gottfried von Strassburg's *Tristan und Isolde* (c. 1236) and completed (after 1243) Wolfram von Eschenbach's *Willehalm.*

**Ul·ri'ci** (o͝ol·rē'tsē), **Hermann.** 1806–1884. German theistic philosopher and critic; opponent of Hegel; professor, Halle (from 1834); author of *Über Shakespeares Dramatische Kunst* (1839), *Über Prinzip und Methode der Hegelschen Philosophie* (1841), *Glauben und Wissen* (1858), etc.; with Immanuel Fichte, edited a philosophical journal (from 1847).

**Ul·ri'ka E'le·o·no'ra** (ŭl·rē'kȧ ĕ'lĕ·ô·nō'rȧ). 1656–1693. Daughter of Frederick III of Denmark; m. (1680) Charles XI of Sweden. Her daughter **Ulrika Eleonora** (1688–1741) m. (1715) Frederick of Hesse; chosen queen of Sweden (1718) after death of her brother Charles XII; abdicated (1720) in favor of her husband who became king as Frederick I (*q.v.*).

**Ulster,** Earl of. Title held first by Hugh de LACY (d. 1242?) and later by MORTIMER family.

**U'lug-Beg'** (o͞o'lo͝og·bĕg'; -bā'). 1394–1449. Tatar prince; ruler of Turkestan (from 1447); founded an observatory at Samarkand; compiled astronomical tables.

**Ulyanov, Vladimir Ilyich.** See Nikolai LENIN.

**'Umar.** Arabic form of OMAR.

**'Umar ibn–al–Farid.** See IBN-AL-FARID.

**Umayyad.** See OMMIAD.

**Umberto.** See HUMBERT.

**Um'fra·ville, de** (dē ŭm'frȧ·vĭl). An English family of Norman descent, prominent in English-Scottish history in 13th and 14th centuries, including **Gilbert** (1244?–1307), styled Earl of **An'gus** (ăng'gŭs), who fought for Edward I against Baliol and Wallace (1296–98), his son **Robert** (1277–1325), and grandson **Gilbert** (1310–1381).

**U'na·mu'no y Ju'go** (o͞o'nä·mo͞o'nō ē ho͞o'gō), **Miguel de.** 1864–1936. Spanish philosopher and writer; professor of Greek (1891 ff.), rector and professor of Spanish literature (1901–14, 1930–36), U. of Salamanca. Partisan of republican form of government in Spain; deputy to the Cortes (c. 1921–24); banished to Fuerteventura, Canary Islands (1924); in voluntary exile at Paris (1924–30). His works include *Paz en Guerra* (1897), *Amor y Pedagogía* (1902), *Vida de Don Quijote y Sancho Panza* (1905), *Mi Religión y Otros Ensayos* (1910), *Rosario de Sonetos Líricos* (1911), *Contra Esto y Aquello* (1912), *Del Sentimiento Trágico de la Vida* (1913), *Niebla* (novel; 1914), *Ensayos* (7 vols., 1916–19), *El Cristo de Velázquez* (poem; 1920), *Tres Novelas Ejemplares* (1921), *De Fuerteventura a París* (volume of sonnets; 1925), and plays, as *Sombras de Sueño* (1931) and *El Otro* (1932).

**Un'cas** (ŭng'kăs). 1588?–?1683. American Indian sachem, son of a Pequot sachem, and ruler of the western division, known as Mohegans, of the Pequot tribe; engaged in series of wars with Indians of the Narragansett tribe (1643–47); attacked Massasoit (1661) but English intervened to force surrender of his prisoners and plunder; required (1675) to leave sons in English hands as pledge of his neutrality or aid in King Philip's War.

**Uncle Sam.** See Samuel WILSON (1766–1854).

**Un·dén'** (o͝on·dān'), **Bo Östen.** 1886– . Swedish jurist and statesman; delegate to League of Nations Assembly (1921–31) and conferences (1922); minister of foreign affairs (1924–26; from 1945); minister without portfolio (1932–36); chancellor, Swedish universities (from 1937); delegate to UN (from 1946).

**Un'der·hill** (ŭn'dẽr·hĭl), **Evelyn.** 1875–1941. English poet and writer upon mysticism; m. Hubert Stuart Moore, barrister; author of *A Barlamb's Ballad Book, Mysticism, Man and the Supernatural, The Rhythm of Sacrifice.*

**Underhill, John.** 1597?–1672. English military adventurer in America; in service of Saybrook Plantation in destroying the Pequots (1637); in employ of Dutch (c. 1644) to fight Indians on Long Island; later (1653) denounced Governor Stuyvesant; served as privateer out of Providence, R.I.; preying on Dutch commerce (1653); aided in reducing New Amsterdam Dutch to English control (1664–65); high constable and undersheriff of North Riding, Yorkshire, Long Island, N.Y. (1666).

**Un'der·wood** (ŭn'dẽr·wo͝od), **John Thomas.** 1857?–?1935. American industrialist; developed Underwood Typewriter Co. (incorp. 1895, and merged, 1910, into Underwood Elliot Fisher Co.) which developed and manufactured a typewriter invented by one Franz X. Wagner and patented by Wagner in U.S. (1893, 1896).

**Underwood, Joseph Rogers.** 1791–1876. American jurist and legislator, b. in Goochland County, Va.; associate justice, Kentucky court of appeals (1828–35); member, U.S. House of Representatives (1835–43), and U.S. Senate (1847–53). His grandson **Oscar Wilder Underwood** (1862–1929) was also a lawyer and legislator; practiced in Birmingham, Ala.; member, U.S. House of Representatives (1895–96; 1897–1915) and U.S. Senate (1915–27); Democratic floor leader in the House (1911–15) and chairman of the Committee on Ways and Means; one of leading candidates for Democratic presidential nomination at convention in 1912; with Senator F. M. Simmons sponsored tariff legislation (passed Oct. 3, 1913) known as Underwood-Simmons Tariff Act.

**Underwood, Lucien Marcus.** 1853–1907. American botanist; author of *Our Native Ferns and How to Study Them* (1881), *Moulds, Mildews, and Mushrooms* (1899), etc.

**Underwood, Sophie Kerr.** See Sophie KERR.

**Und'set** (ŏŏn'sĕt), **Sigrid.** 1882–1949. Norwegian novelist, b. in Denmark; m. (1912) Anders C. Svarstad; marriage annulled (1925). Secretary in Norway (1899–1909); converted to Roman Catholicism (1924); awarded Nobel prize in literature for 1928. Her novels include *Fru Marta Oulie* (a novel in diary form; 1907), modern novels, as *Jenny* (1911), *The Wild Orchid*, and *The Burning Bush* (1930), and the medieval romances *Kristin Lavransdatter* (1920–22), *The Master of Hestviken*, orig. title *Olav Audunsson* (1925–27), *Ida Elizabeth* (1932), *Saga of Saints* (1934), a trilogy (*The Bridal Wreath, The Mistress of Husaby*, and *The Cross*), and a tetralogy (*The Axe, The Snake Pit, In the Wilderness*, and *The Son Avenger*). Other works include short stories, essays on Roman Catholicism, translations of Icelandic sagas, and poems.

**Ung'er** (ŏŏng'ĕr), **Franz.** 1800–1870. Austrian botanist; pioneer in plant anatomy, physiology, and ecology, and in paleobotany.

**Unger, Gustav Hermann.** 1886– . German composer and writer on music.

**Unger, Hellmuth.** 1891–1953. German writer and physician; author of plays, novels, ballads, etc.

**Unger, Joseph.** 1828–1913. Austrian jurist and statesman; author of *System des Österreichischen Allgemeinen Privatrechts* (1856–59 ff.), *Handeln auf Eigene Gefahr* (1891), etc.

**Ung'ern–Stern'berg** (ŏŏng'ĕrn·shtĕrn'bĕrk), Baron **Alexander von.** *Pen name* **Alexander von Sternberg.** 1806–1868. Novelist, b. in Esthonia; resident in Germany (from 1830); author of social novels, the political novel *Die Royalisten* (1848), the biographical novel *Elisabeth Charlotte* (1861), works on art and artists, and memoirs (6 vols., 1855–60).

**Ung'ern–Stern'berg** (ŏŏng'ĕrn·shtĕrn'bĕrk), Baron **Roman Nikolaus von.** 1885–1921. Russian anti-Bolshevik general; served in World War I on Turkish front; after Bolshevik coup d'état (Nov., 1917), fought them in eastern Siberia; raided Urga (Jan., 1921); captured by Bolsheviks and shot (Sept. 18, 1921).

**Un–khan.** See PRESTER JOHN, 1.

**Un'na** (ŏŏn'ä), **Paul Gerson.** 1850–1929. German dermatologist; credited with discovery of plasma cell and of organism causing soft chancre; known also for work on biochemistry of the skin.

**Un'ruh** (ŏŏn'rōō), **Fritz von.** 1885–1970. German playwright, poet, and novelist; officer in World War I; author of plays opposing militarism, symbolical plays, comedies, a volume of poetry, and a war novel, *Der Opfergang* (1916).

**Un'ter·mey'er** (ŭn'tĕr·mī'ĕr), **Louis.** 1885–1977. American author and editor, b. New York City. Manufacturing jeweler (1902–23); devoted himself to study and writing (from 1923). Poetry editor, *The American Mercury* (1934–37). His many works include *The Younger Quire* (parodies; 1910), *First Love* (1911), *Challenge* (1914), *These Times* (1917), *The New Adam* (1920), *Roast Leviathan* (1923), *American Poetry Since 1900* (essays; 1923), *Forms of Poetry* (1926), *Burning Bush* (1928), *Food and Drink* (verse; 1932), *Heinrich Heine—Paradox and Poet* (2 vols., 1937), a number of translations, and anthologies of verse. His first wife, **Jean,** *nee* **Starr** [stär] (1886–1970; m. 1907; divorced), also a poet and anthologist; author of *Growing Pains* (1918), *Dreams Out of Darkness* (1921), *Winged Child* (1936), etc.

**Un'ter·my'er** (ŭn'tĕr·mī'ĕr), **Samuel.** 1858–1940. American lawyer, b. Lynchburg, Va.; practiced in New York City. Carried through merger of Utah Copper Co., Boston Consolidated Co., and Nevada Consolidated Co.; counsel for Rogers-Rockefeller-Lewisohn interests in struggle with F. Augustus Heinze over Montana Copper Mines; counsel for committee on banking and currency of U.S. House of Representatives in Pujo money-trust investigation. Chairman of board that framed income tax law and excess profits laws during World War I.

**Un'ver·dor'ben** (ŏŏn'fĕr·dôr'bĕn), **Otto.** 1806–1873. German chemist; discovered aniline among the products obtained in the destructive distillation of indigo (1826).

**Un'win** (ŭn'wĭn), **Mary,** *nee* **Caw'thorne** (kô'thôrn). 1724–1796. Friend and counselor of the English poet William Cowper; m. (1744) Morley Unwin (d. 1767); engagement to Cowper (1772) broken off because of his insanity.

**Unwin, Thomas Fisher.** 1848–1935. English publisher. Founder of the publishing house of T. Fisher Unwin (1882); joint founder of first council of the Publishers Association; "discoverer" of the novelist Joseph Conrad.

**Up'dike** (ŭp'dīk), **Daniel Berkeley.** 1860–1941. American printer and publisher, b. Providence, R.I.; founded the Merrymount Press, Boston (1893); instrumental in improving typography in U.S.; author of *Printing Types—Their History, Forms and Use* (2 vols., 1922).

**Updike, John Hoyer.** 1932– . American writer, b. Shillington, Pa. Author of *Rabbit, Run* (1960), *The Centaur* (1963), *Couples* (1968), *Rabbit Redux* (1971), etc.; also poetry and short stories.

**Up'ham** (ŭp'ăm), **Thomas Cogswell.** 1799–1872. American philosopher and educator, b. Deerfield, N.H.; professor, Bowdoin (1824–67); among his notable works are *A Philosophical and Practical Treatise on the Will* (1834), *Principles of the Interior or Hidden Life* (1843).

**Upham, Warren.** 1850–1934. American geologist and archaeologist, b. Amherst, N.H.; secretary and librarian, Minnesota Historical Society (1895–1914), and archaeologist (1914–33); made special study of glaciers.

**Up'john** (ŭp'jŏn), **Richard.** 1802–1878. Architect, b. Shaftesbury, Eng.; to U.S. (1829); opened architect's office in Boston (1834), and in New York (1839). One of founders of American Institute of Architects, and its first president (1857–76). Among his notable works are Trinity Church in New York (consecrated 1846); Church of the Pilgrims in Brooklyn, N.Y.; Grace Church in Newark, N.J.; St. Paul's Church in Buffalo, N.Y.; Bowdoin College Chapel; Trinity Chapel in New York City. His son **Richard Mi·chell'** [mĭ·shĕl'] (1828–1903) was also an architect; in partnership with father (from 1853); among notable buildings designed by him are the State Capitol of Connecticut at Hartford, Central Congregational Church of Boston, Madison Square Presbyterian Church of New York.

**Up'shur** (ŭp'shĕr), **Abel Parker.** 1791–1844. American jurist and statesman; U.S. secretary of the navy (1841–43), and U.S. secretary of state (1843–44).

**Up'son** (ŭp's'n), **Arthur Wheelock.** 1877–1908. American lyric poet; author of *Sonnets and Songs.*

**Upson, Ralph Hazlett.** 1888–1968. American aeronautical engineer, b. New York City. Winner of International Balloon Race (1913) and American National Balloon Race (1913, 1919, 1921); designed first successful metal-clad airship (1929); awarded Wright Brothers medal by Society of Automotive Engineers for his contribution to wing design (1930). His brother **William Hazlett** (1891–1975), fiction writer; served in field artillery in France (1917–19); employee of Caterpillar Tractor Co., Peoria, Ill. (1919–24); author of *The Piano Movers* (1927), *Me* *and Henry and the Artillery* (1928), *Alexander Botts—Earthworm Tractors* (1929), *Earthworms in Europe* (1931), and a motion picture, *Earthworm Tractors* (1936).

**Up'ton** (ŭp'tŭn), **Emory.** 1839–1881. American army officer and writer on tactics and military history; grad. U.S.M.A., West Point (1861). Distinguished service with Army of the Potomac and in the Tennessee, Alabama, Georgia campaign; brigadier general (1864), and brevetted major general. Author of *A New System of Infantry Tactics, Double and Single Rank, Adapted to American Topography and Improved Firearms* (1867, adopted by U.S. army, 1867), *The Military Policy of the United States* (1904), etc.

**Upton, Florence.** d. 1922. Portrait painter and illustrator, b. in Flushing, Long Island, N.Y., of English parentage; creator of the grotesque golliwogg dolls; author of *The Golliwogg Series, The Vegemen's Revenge, Borbee and the Wisp,* etc.

**Upton, George Putnam.** *Pseudonym* **Per'e·grine Pick'le** (pĕr'ĕ·grĭn pĭk''l). 1834–1919. American journalist and music critic; on staff, Chicago *Evening Journal* (1856–62); started first column of musical comment and criticism to appear in a Chicago newspaper; on staff, Chicago *Daily Tribune* (1862–1919); a founder and first president, Chicago Apollo Musical Club (1872). Author of *Letters of Peregrine Pickle* (1869), *Standard Operas* (1886), *Standard Oratorios* (1887), etc.

**Ur'bal'** (ür'bȧl'), **Victor Louis Lucien d'.** 1858–1943. French general; commanded (1917) the 10th army in Flanders.

**Ur'ban** (ûr'băn). Name of eight popes (see *Table of Popes,* Nos. 17, 159, 172, 182, 200, 202, 230, 237), especially:

**Urban II.** *Real name* **O'do** (ō'dō) *or* **U'do** (ōō'dō). 1042?–1099. Pope (1088–99), b. Châtillon-sur-Marne, France. A Benedictine; legate to Germany (1082–85); opposed (1088–97) by powerful antipope, Clement III; continued policy of Gregory VII in opposing Emperor Henry IV; excommunicated Henry IV and Philip I of France; convoked councils (1095) at Piacenza and Clermont; at latter preached First Crusade; died before news of capture of Jerusalem reached Italy.

**Urban IV.** *Real name* **Jacques Pan'ta'lé'on'** (päɴ'-tȧ'lā'ôɴ'). d. 1264. Pope (1261–64). Son of a shoemaker of Troyes, France. Excluded from Rome by Manfred of Sicily; incited Charles of Anjou to oppose Manfred; sided with Henry III of England against his barons; appointed many French cardinals, later a cause of Western Schism; instituted feast of Corpus Christi (1246).

**Urban V.** *Real name* **Guillaume de Gri'mo'ard'** (dẽ grē'mō'ȧr'). 1310–1370. Pope (1362–70), b. Grisac, France. Tried to return pontificate from Avignon to Rome (1367–70), but compelled to leave because of unsettled conditions; founded or aided several universities.

**Urban VI.** *Real name* **Bartolommeo Pri·gna'ni** (prē·nyä'nē). 1318–1389. Pope (1378–89), b. Naples. Archbishop of Bari; first pope at Rome of Western Schism, in opposition to Clement VII at Avignon; deposed Queen Joanna of Naples (1380); crowned Charles of Durazzo king of Naples (1381) but quarreled with him later (1384).

**Urban VIII.** *Real name* **Maffeo Bar'be·ri'ni** (bär'-bȧ·rē'nē). 1568–1644. Pope (1623–44), b. Florence. Held many high offices in the church before election as pope; acquired duchy of Urbino for the papacy (1631); published revision of breviary (1631); instituted College of Propaganda (1627); in Thirty Years' War, sided with France against emperor and Spain; denounced Jansenists (1644); built Barberini Palace, baldachin in St. Peter's, and other structures in Rome; a patron of foreign missions.

**Ur'ban** (ûr'băn), **Joseph.** 1872–1933. Architectural designer and interior decorator, b. Vienna, Austria; to America (1901 and 1911); art director for Boston Opera Company (1911–14); designed stage sets for the Ziegfeld Follies (1915), for the Metropolitan Opera, and for some of James K. Hackett's Shakespearean productions; became naturalized citizen (1917); opened studio at Yonkers.

**Urban, Sylvanus.** Pseudonym of Edward Cave (*q.v.*) and later editors of *Gentleman's Magazine.*

**Urban, Wilbur Marshall.** 1873–1952. American psychologist; author of *The Intelligible World—Metaphysics and Value* (1929), *Fundamentals of Ethics* (1930), etc.

**Urbina.** Variant of URVINA.

**Ur·bi'no** (ōōr·bē'nō), Duke of. **Giovanni del'la Ro've·re** (dāl'lä rō'vā·rā). 1458–1501. Brother of Pope Julius II; nephew of Pope Sixtus IV. Italian nobleman; m. daughter of Federigo da Montefeltro, Duke of Urbino; advanced through uncle's influence to be prefect of Rome. His son **Francesco Maria della Rovere,** Duke of **Urbino** (1490–1538), captain general of papal troops (1508), succeeded Guido Ubaldo da Montefeltro as duke of Urbino (1508); waged war upon Ferrara; captured Bologna (1512); temporarily disgraced (1516–21), but regained favor; became commander in chief of Venetian troops (1523) and fought vainly (1526–27) against advance of imperial army. Francesco's son **Guidubaldo della Rovere,** Duke of **Urbino** (1514–1574) was captain general of Venetian army (1540–52) and of papal troops (1553); prefect of Rome (1555). Guidubaldo's son **Francesco Maria della Rovere** (1549–1631), last duke of Urbino, agreed with Pope Urban VIII (1626) to allow his territory to pass to the papacy. See also Lorenzo de' MEDICI and MONTEFELTRO family.

**Urchard,** Sir **Thomas.** See URQUHART.

**Ure** (ūr), **Andrew.** 1778–1857. Scottish chemist; author of *Dictionary of Chemistry* (2 vols., 1821), *Dictionary of Arts, Manufactures, and Mines* (1837–39), etc.

**Ur–En'gur** (ŏŏr'ĕn'gŏŏr). *More correctly* **Ur–Nam'mu** (-näm'mōō). First king (ruled 18 years in the 23d or 22d century B.C.) of Third (Sumerian) dynasty of Ur; restored peace in southwestern Asia; author of Sumerian law code. Father of Shulgi.

**U·re'ta** (ōō·rā'tä), **Alberto.** 1887– . Peruvian lawyer and writer; director of the reviews *Mercurio Peruano* and *Nueva Revista Peruana;* author of *El Parnaso y el Simbolismo* (1915), *El Dolor Pensativo* (1917), *Las Tiendas del Desierto* (1933), *Elegías de la Cabeza Loca* (1939), etc.

**U'rey** (ū'rĭ), **Harold Clayton.** 1893– . American chemist, b. Walkerton, Ind.; on teaching staff, Columbia (from 1929), professor (from 1934). Awarded 1934 Nobel prize for chemistry for his discovery of heavy hydrogen; known also for work on other isotopes, the structure of atoms and molecules, thermodynamics of gases, and absorption spectra; professor, Chicago U. (from 1945).

**Ur'fé'** (ür'fā'), **Honoré d'.** 1568–1625. French writer; known esp. as author of the chivalric pastoral romance *L'Astrée,* whose characters (Céladon, Astrée, Silvandre, Hylas) became popular types in 17th-century romance. See Thomas D'URFEY.

**U·ri'ah** (ū·rī'ȧ). *In Douay Version* **U·ri'as** (-ăs). In Bible (*2 Samuel* xi), a Hittite captain in army of Israel whose death in battle was brought about by order of David so that David might take his wife Bath-sheba.

**U'ri·bu'ru** (ōō'rē·bōō'rōō), **José Evaristo.** 1835–1914. Argentine political leader; president of Argentina (1895–

98). His son **José Evaristo** (1880–1956), historian and diplomat; minister (1921–27) and ambassador (1927–31) to Great Britain.

**Uriburu, José Francisco.** 1868–1932. Argentine political leader; leader of Conservatives; led revolution that overthrew Irigoyen (1930); provisional president of Argentina (1930–32).

**U·riu** (ōō·ryōō), Baron **Sotokichi.** 1854–1937. Japanese vice-admiral; studied at U.S.N.A., Annapolis; rear admiral (1900); commanded squadron that attacked Russian ships in harbor of Chemulpho (Feb. 9, 1904); engaged in battle of Tsushima (May 27–28, 1905).

**Ur–Nammu.** See UR-ENGUR.

**Ur′quhart** (ûr′kĕrt; -kärt), **David.** 1805–1877. British diplomat, b. in Scotland. Served in Greek navy in Greek War of Independence (1827–28). Secretary of embassy, Constantinople (1836); recalled for hostility to Russia (1837). M.P. (1847–52); bitterly opposed foreign policy of Palmerston and British object, in Crimean War, of putting Christian Turkish subjects under European protectorate; retired (1864).

**Ur′quhart** (ûr′kĕrt; -kärt) *or* **Ur′chard** (ûr′kĕrd; -kärd), Sir **Thomas.** 1611–1660. Scottish author; translator of Rabelais. Fought on Royalist side in Civil War; wounded and taken prisoner at Worcester (1651); released on parole by Cromwell; died abroad. Author of *Epigrams* (1641), *Trissotetras,* a treatise on logarithms (1645), several quaint tracts, and the free translation of Rabelais, a masterpiece (books I & II, 1653; III, 1693; the translation, books IV and V, being completed by Peter Anthony Motteux, *q.v.*, in 1708).

**Ur·qui′za** (ōōr·kē′sä), **Justo José.** 1800–1870. Argentine general; governor of Entre Ríos province (1842–54); defeated Rivera (1845), Rosas (1852); first constitutional president of Argentina (1854–60); commander in chief of national forces and again governor of Entre Ríos (after 1860); defeated (1861) by Mitre; assassinated.

**Urrabieta Vierge, Daniel.** See VIERGE.

**Ur·ra′ca** (ōōr·rä′kä). 1081–1126. Queen of Castile and León (1109–26); m. 1st, Raymond of Burgundy; 2d, Alfonso I, the Battler, of Aragon and Navarre (her third cousin); quarreled with Alfonso; defeated in battle of Sepúlveda (1111); succeeded by her son Alfonso VII.

**Ur′ry** (ûr′ĭ) *or* **Hur′ry** (hûr′ĭ), Sir **John.** d. 1650. Scottish professional soldier; successively, in English Parliamentary army (1642), in Royalist army at Marston Moor (1644), in Scottish army (1645), in Royalist army again (1650); captured and beheaded at Edinburgh.

**Urry, John.** 1666–1715. English editor of Chaucer, of Scottish descent.

**Ur·si′nus** (ûr·sī′nŭs; *Ger.* ōōr·zē′nōōs), **Zacharias.** *Real surname* **Beer** (bār) *or* **Bär** (bâr). 1534–1583. German Reformed theologian and writer; with Olevianus and others, drew up Heidelberg Catechism (1563).

**Ur′su·la** (ûr′sŭ·lȧ), Saint. d. 238 or 283 or 451. Christian martyr, daughter of a British prince. Patroness and leader of virgins on a pilgrimage to Rome; put to death near Cologne by Huns, with her eleven thousand virgins, according to the ancient legend which received increase of detail in twelfth century and was popularized by Geoffrey of Monmouth.

**Urs′wick** (ûrz′wĭk), **Christopher.** 1448–1522. English ecclesiastic and diplomat; friend of Erasmus.

**Ur·vi′na** (ōōr·vē′nä), **José María.** *Also* **Ur·bi′na** (-bē′nä). 1808–1891. Ecuadorian political leader; president of Ecuador (1852–56); in exile in Peru (1856–76); commander in chief of Ecuadorian army (1876–78).

**U′se·dom** (ōō′zĕ·dŏm), **Guido von.** 1854–1925. German admiral; in World War, leader of Turkish mission and in defense of Dardanelles.

**U′se·ner** (ōō′zĕ·nĕr), **Hermann.** 1834–1905. German classical scholar; author of works on Greek philosophy, literature, rhetoric, and the history of religion.

**Usertsen** *or* **Usertesen** *or* **Usirtesen.** See SESOSTRIS.

**Ush′er** (ŭsh′ĕr), **John Palmer.** 1816–1889. American lawyer, b. Brookfield, N.Y.; practiced, Terre Haute, Ind. (from 1840); U.S. secretary of the interior (1863–65).

**Usher, Roland Greene.** 1880–1957. American historian; on teaching staff, Washington U., St. Louis, Mo. (from 1907), and professor (from 1914); author of *Pan-Germanism* (1913), *Pan-Americanism* (1915), *The Story of the Great War* (1919), etc.

**Usk** (ŭsk), **Thomas.** d. 1388. Secretary to John de Northampton, Wycliffite lord mayor of London; executed by order of Merciless Parliament (1388); author of allegorical prose work, *The Testament of Love,* formerly ascribed to Chaucer.

**U·spen′ski** (ōō·spyăn′skû·ĭ; *Angl.* ōō·spĕn′skĭ), **Gleb Ivanovich.** 1840?–1902. Russian writer; author of novels of small-town and peasant life.

**Ussh′er** (ŭsh′ĕr), **Henry.** 1550?–1613. Irish church dignitary; obtained charter for Trinity College, Dublin (1592); archbishop of Armagh (1595). His nephew **James Ussher** (1581–1656) was a theologian and scholar; archbishop of Armagh (1625); corresponded with Laud (1628–40); defeated attempt to make doctrinal standards of Irish church conform exactly to those of the English (1634); urged Charles I not to abandon Strafford; propounded a scheme of Biblical chronology long inserted in margin of editions of the Authorized Version, according to which the creation took place 4004 B.C.

**U·ta·ma·ro** (ōō·tä·mä·rō), **Kitagawa.** 1754?–1806. Japanese engraver and designer of color prints.

**U′ther Pen·drag′on** (ū′thĕr pĕn·drăg′ŭn). Legendary king of Britain; husband of Igraine and perhaps father of King Arthur.

**Uth′watt** (?ŭth′wŏt), Sir **Augustus Andrewes.** 1879–1949. British lawyer; educ. Ballarat Coll. (Victoria, Australia) and Oxford (B.C.L., 1904); legal adviser to ministry of food (1915–18); chairman of various governmental committees on war damage (1939 ff.).

**U′titz** (ōō′tĭts), **Emil.** 1883–1956. German philosopher and aesthetician; author of *Was ist Stil?* (1911), *Der Künstler* (1925), *Charakterologie* (1925), *Geschichte der Ästhetik* (1932), etc.

**U·tril′lo** (ōō·trē′lō), **Maurice.** 1883–1955. French painter; best known for his paintings of cathedrals, villages, and Parisian street scenes.

**Uvedale.** See UDALL.

**U′wins** (ū′wĭnz), **Thomas.** 1782–1857. English oil and water-color painter; miniature painter (from 1798).

**Uz** (ōōts; ōōts), **Johann Peter.** 1720–1796. German poet and jurist; author of *Lyrische Gedichte* (1749), a humorous epic, and a didactic poem. He is the subject of Jakob Wassermann's *Sturreganz* (1922).

**U′zanne′** (ü′zàn′), **Louis Octave.** 1852–1931. French journalist and bibliophile.

**U′zès′** (ü′zâs′), Duc **d′.** See under CRUSSOL.

**Uzès,** Duchesse **d′. Marie Clémentine de Ro′che-chouart′–Mor′te·mart′** (dĕ rô′shĕ·shwàr′môr′tĕ·màr′). 1847–1933. French sculptor and author, b. in Paris; m. Emmanuel, 12th Duc d'Uzès (1866; d. 1878). A social leader among the French nobility; exhibited sculpture at the Salon of French Artists under pseudonym **Ma′nu·e′la′** (mà′nü·ĕ′là′); author of two novels (*Pauvre Petite, Julien Masly*) and several plays.

**Uz·zi′ah** (ŭ·zī′ȧ) *or* **Az′a·ri′ah** (ăz′ȧ·rī′ȧ). *In Douay Bible,* **O·zi′as** (ō·zī′ăs) *or* **Az′a·ri′as** (ăz′ȧ·rī′ăs). King of Judah (780–740 B.C.); son of Amaziah; enjoyed long prosperous reign (*2 Kings* xv; *2 Chronicles* xxvi).

# V

**Vaca, Álvar Núñez Cabeza de.** See CABEZA DE VACA.

**Vaca de Castro, Cristóbal.** See CASTRO.

**Va′ca·re′scu** (vä′kä·rĕ′sko͞o). Name of a noble Walachian family, including: **Ionache** (1654–1714), grand treasurer of Walachia; his grandson **Ionache** (1730–1796), a scholar and poet, author of first Rumanian grammar written in the vernacular, and a history of Turkey; the younger Ionache's son **Alecu** (d. 1798), famed as a poet; Alecu's son **Iancu** (1786–1863), who inaugurated modern Rumanian poetry, aided in establishing the Rumanian theater, and translated German and French works into Rumanian; Alecu's niece **Elena** (1868–1947), author of novels and poems in Rumanian and in French, whose *Rumanian Ballads* were awarded the Jules Favre prize at the French Academy.

**Va·car′i·us** (vȧ·kâr′ĭ·ŭs). 1120–?1200. Italian civilian and canonist; to England as counselor to Archbishop Theobold (c. 1143); in service of Roger de Pont l'Évêque, archbishop of York (1154 ff.); prebendary of Southwell (1167).

**Va′chell** (vā′chĕl), **Horace Annesley.** 1861–1955. English writer; educ. Harrow and Sandhurst; author of many novels, including *Romance of Judge Ketchum* (1894), *Quinney's* (1914; dramatized 1915), *Whitewash* (1920), *Quinney's Adventures* (1924), *Vicar's Walk* (1933), *Quinneys for Quality* (1938); plays, including *Her Son* (1907; also pub. as novel), *Jelf's* (1912), *Count X* (1921), *Plus Fours* (1923); essays, as in *My Vagabondage* (1936), *Little Tyrannies* (1940); and *A Writer's Autobiography* (1937).

**Va′che·rot′** (vȧsh′rō′), **Étienne.** 1809–1897. French philosopher; succeeded Cousin as professor at the Sorbonne (1839); removed from his professorship for refusing to sign the oath of allegiance to the empire (1852). Among his works are *La Métaphysique et la Science* (1858), *La Religion* (1868), etc.

**Vac′que·rie′** (vȧ′krē′), **Auguste.** 1819–1895. French journalist and playwright; with François Paul Meurice and others, founded (1869) radical journal *Le Rappel.* His plays include *Tragaldabas* (melodrama, 1848), *Jean Baudry* (comedy, 1863), *Le Fils* (comedy, 1866), etc.

**Va′dász** (vŏ′däs), **Nicolaus.** 1884–1927. Hungarian painter.

**Va′dé′** (vȧ′dā′), **Jean Joseph.** 1720–1757. French burlesque song writer, librettist, and playwright; author of comedies, comic operas, and vaudeville sketches. Credited with introducing a literature expressing the manners and language of the market place; author of the chef-d'œuvre of this type of literature, *Pipe Cassée, Poème Épitragi-poissardi-héroï-comique.*

**Va′di·a′nus** (vä′dē·ä′no͝os), **Joachim.** *Real name* **von Watt** (fôn vät′). 1484–1551. Swiss humanist; friend of Zwingli, and supporter of Luther; regarded as founder of Protestant church in St. Gallen.

**Vaez de Torres, Luis.** See TORRES.

**Va′ga** (vä′gä), **Perino del.** *Real name* **Pietro Buo′nac·cor′si** (bwô′näk·kōr′sē). 1501–1547. Italian painter; pupil of Raphael; assisted Raphael in decoration of the loggia in the Vatican.

**Va·glie′ri** (vä·lyâ′rē), **Dante.** 1865–1914. Italian classical scholar, b. Trieste; known esp. for archaeological excavations at Ostia.

**Vah′len** (fä′lĕn), **Johannes.** 1830–1911. German classical scholar and philologist; author of critical studies of the works of Ennius, Aristotle, Cicero, and others, and of philosophical writings.

**Vahram.** Variant of BAHRAM.

**Vai′da–Voe·vod′** (vī′dä·voi·vŏd′), **Alexandru.** 1871–1950. Rumanian statesman; after Austria's collapse (1918), selected to represent Rumanian interests at Paris Peace Conference. Prime minister of Rumania (1919–20); succeeded in gaining recognition of incorporation of Bessarabia into Rumania.

**Vai′hing·er** (fī′ĭng·ẽr), **Hans.** 1852–1933. German philosopher; founder of the Kant Society (1904); cofounder (1919) and editor (1919–29) of *Annalen der Philosophie.* Author of *Die Philosophie des Als Ob...* (1911), a study of the "as if" philosophy first formulated by him (1876–78), and of *Der Mythus und das Als Ob* (1927), etc.

**Vail** (vāl), **Alfred.** 1807–1859. Cousin of Theodore Newton Vail. American pioneer in telegraphy, b. Morristown, N.J. Grad. N.Y.U. (1836). Financed Samuel F. B. Morse in later stages (1837–38) of development of the telegraph in return for a one-fourth interest in the American rights and a one-half interest in foreign patents. Collaborated with Morse in demonstrating instrument in New York, Philadelphia, and Washington (1837–38). Withdrew from further participation in the enterprise (c. 1848).

**Vail, Theodore Newton.** 1845–1920. Cousin of Alfred Vail. American telephone and telegraph executive, b. near Minerva, Ohio. Began as telegraph operator for Western Union Telegraph Co., in New York City (1864–66). General manager, Bell Telephone Co. (1878–87); incorporated American Telephone & Telegraph Co. (1885) through which he intended to unify the telephone industry and provide for exchanges by long-distance system; became first president of the A.T.&T. Co.; resigned (1889). Again president, A.T.&T. Co. (1907–19).

**Vail′lant′** (vȧ′yäɴ′), **Édouard.** 1840–1915. French Socialist politician; member of the Commune of Paris (1871); condemned to death (1871) but escaped to England; member of Chamber of Deputies (from 1893) and Socialist-party candidate for the presidency of France.

**Vaillant, Jean Baptiste Philibert.** 1790–1872. French army officer in Russian campaign (1812), and at Ligny and Waterloo; engineer officer at siege of Antwerp (1832) and at siege and capture of Rome (1849); created marshal of France (1851); minister of war (1854–59); commander in the Italian War (1859–61); minister of the emperor's household (1860–70).

**Vaj′da** (vī′dŏ), **Ernő.** 1887–1954. Hungarian playwright; author of *Fata Morgana, Harem,* etc.

**Valbert, G.** Pseudonym of Victor CHERBULIEZ.

**Val·bue′na** (väl·bwā′nä), **Antonio de.** 1844–1929. Spanish literary critic.

**Valck′e·naer** (väl′kĕ·när), **Lodewijk Kaspar.** 1715–1785. Dutch classical philologist and critic; prepared editions of Greek texts; author of *Diatribe de Aristobulo* (pub. 1806), etc.

**Valdemar.** See WALDEMAR.

**Valdemaras.** Variant of VOLDEMARAS.

**Val·dés′** (väl·dās′), **Armando Palacio.** See PALACIO VALDÉS.

**Valdés, Gabriel de la Con′cep·ción′** (dā lä kôn′sĕp·syôn′). *Pseudonym* **Plá′ci·do** (plä′sē·thō). 1809–1844. Cuban poet; known esp. for his poems about the slave trade and his apostrophes to liberty; executed by Spaniards.

**Valdés, Juan de.** 1500?–1541. Spanish theologian and reformer; one of first Spaniards to adopt in part ideas of German Reformation; resident in Italy (1530 ff.); author of *Diálogo de Mercurio y Carón* (a Spanish prose classic, 1528), and *Diálogo de la Lengua* (earliest philological treatise in Spain, 1533).

**Valdés, Juan Meléndez.** See MELÉNDEZ VALDÉS.

**Val′dès′** (vȧl′dâs′), **Pierre.** = Peter WALDO.

**Val·dés′ Le·al′** (väl·dās′ lā·äl′), **Juan de.** 1630–1691. Spanish painter and engraver; among his works are *The Two Cadavers, Death Surrounded by the Devices of Human Vanity,* and a series of three paintings on the life of St. Jerome.

**Val·di′via** (väl·dē′vyä), **Pedro de.** 1500?–1553. Spanish soldier; conqueror of Chile. To New World (c. 1534); served under Pizarro in battle at Las Salinas, Peru (1535); led expedition into Chile (1540); founded Santiago (1541); aided in suppressing rebellion of Gonzalo Pizarro in Peru (1547–48); resumed war against Araucanian Indians (1549); founded Concepción (1550) and Valdivia (1552); killed in battle.

**Valdo, Peter.** See WALDO.

**Va′lence′** (vȧ′läɴs′), **William de.** Titular Earl of **Pem′broke** (pĕm′bro͝ok). d. 1296. French soldier and diplomat in court of his half brother Henry III of England. Son of English King John's widow, Isabella of Angoulême, by her second marriage; m. granddaughter and heiress of 1st earl of Pembroke, assuming title. Fought on side of Henry III against Simon de Montfort, and at Lewes and Evesham; to Holy Land with Prince Edward (1270–73). His son **Ay′mer** [ā′mẽr] (1265?–1324), Earl of Pembroke, English soldier and ambassador, led van of Edward II's army against Bruce (1306); defeated Scots at Ruthven (1306); defeated by Bruce at Loudon Hill (1307); shared in king's defeat at Bannockburn (1314); arranged temporary peace (1318) between Thomas of Lancaster and Edward II (later broken, and Lancaster beheaded); his 3d wife, Mary of Chatillon, was foundress of Pembroke Hall at Cambridge.

**Valencia,** Duke of. See Ramón María NARVÁEZ.

**Va′len′ciennes′** (vȧ′läɴ′syĕn′), **Achille.** 1794–1865. French zoologist; author of *Histoire Naturelle des Poissons* (1828–49; the first 6 of the 11 volumes in collaboration with Georges Cuvier), etc.

**Va′lens** (vā′lĕnz). 328?–378 A.D. Roman emperor of the East (364–378), b. in Pannonia. Made emperor (364) by his brother Emperor Valentinian I of the West; waged successful war against Goths (367–369); made discreditable treaty of peace with Persia (376); allowed Visigoths, overwhelmed by the Huns, to settle south of the Danube in Thrace; his unwise treatment of them led to war (377–378); defeated and slain by Goths under Fritigern at Adrianople (worst rout of Romans since Cannae).

**Va′len·tin** (vä′lĕn·tēn), **Gabriel Gustav.** 1810–1883. German physiologist; credited with discovering the diastatic action of pancreatic juice and, with J. E. Purkinje, ciliary epithelial motion.

**Val′en·tine** (văl′ĕn·tīn), Saint. Christian martyr, probably of late 3d century. His festival is February 14th. The custom of sending valentines on this day originated in a heathen rite celebrating the worship of Juno; association of the custom with Saint Valentine is accidental.

**Val′en·tine** (văl′ĕn·tīn). *Lat.* **Val′en·ti′nus** (-tī′nŭs). Pope (827).

**Valentine, Edward Virginius.** 1838–1930. American sculptor; studio in Richmond, Va. (from 1865). Among his noteworthy works are recumbent figure of Robert E. Lee for the Lee Mausoleum at Washington and Lee U.; bronze statue of Robert E. Lee in Statuary Hall, Washington, D.C.; statue of Jefferson Davis in Richmond; statue of "Stonewall" Jackson in Lexington, Va.; statue of John J. Audubon in New Orleans.

**Va′len·ti′ni** (vä′lān·tē′nē), **Pierfrancesco.** d. 1654. Italian composer of the Roman school; composer esp. of madrigals, motets, litanies, canzonets, and monodic songs.

**Val′en·tin′i·an** (văl′ĕn·tĭn′ĭ·ăn; -tĭn′yăn). *Lat.* **Val′en·tin′i·a′nus** (văl′ĕn·tĭn′ĭ·ā′nŭs). Name of three Roman emperors:

**Valentinian I.** 321–375. Emperor (364–375), b. of humble parentage in Pannonia. Entered army at early age; advanced rapidly but degraded by Constantius (357) and banished by Julian (362); restored (363); fought in the East; on death of Jovian, chosen emperor; appointed his brother Valens as colleague; kept western lands for his own administration; forced to contend (365–370) with many barbarian invasions in Gaul, Illyricum, and Africa; brought about reforms in religion, legal practice, and education; succeeded by his sons Gratian (*q.v.*) and Valentinian II.

**Valentinian II.** 372–392. Emperor (375–392), jointly with his half brother Gratian (375–383). Received Italy, Illyricum, and Africa; during minority, government administered by Empress Justina; gave promise of becoming wise ruler; driven out of Italy (387) by Magnus Maximus; murdered by Arbogast, Frankish commander of his army.

**Valentinian III.** 419–455. Emperor (425–455) in the West. Son of Constantius and Galla Placidia; grandnephew of Valentinian I. Raised to the throne by Theodosius II but under mother's regency (425–c. 440) and never actually ruled; during his reign much of Western Empire seized or ravaged by Vandals, Visigoths, and Suevi (Africa conquered by Vandals under Genseric); Aëtius, his general, however, often defeated and drove back many barbarian armies, especially the Huns under Attila at Châlons (451); assassinated Aëtius (454); murdered by adherents of Aëtius.

**Val′en·ti′no** (văl′ĕn·tē′nō; *Ital.* vä′lān-), **Rudolph.** *Professional name of* **Rodolpho d′An′ton·guol′la** (dän′-tông·gwôl′lä). 1895–1926. Motion-picture actor, b. at Castellaneta, Italy; to U.S. (1913); took out citizenship papers (1925); made chief success in *Blood and Sand, The Four Horsemen of the Apocalypse, The Sheik.*

**Val′en·ti′nus** (văl′ĕn·tī′nŭs). Gnostic philosopher and teacher, b. probably in Egypt; educ. Alexandria. Went to Rome and taught (c. 135–160 A.D.), his disciples including Origen, Clement of Alexandria, and Heracleon; excommunicated because of heterodoxy of teachings; withdrew from Rome to Cyprus (c. 160) in hope of finding a more favorable reception for his doctrines. His interpretation of Gnostic doctrines was known as Valentinian Gnosticism, or Valentinianism.

**Valera, Eamon de.** See DE VALERA.

**Va·le′ra y Al′ca·lá′ Ga·lia′no** (vä·lā′rä ē äl′kä·lä′ gä·lyä′nō), **Juan.** 1824–1905. Spanish writer and statesman; member, editorial staff of liberal journal *El Contemporáneo* (1859); prominent in Unión Liberal. Minister to Frankfurt (1865); director of public instruction (1871 ff.); minister to Lisbon (1881–83), Washington (1883–86), Brussels (1886–88); ambassador to Vienna (1893–95). Works include novels, as *Pepita Jiménez* (1874), *Las Ilusiones del Doctor Faustino* (1875), *El Comendador Mendoza* (1877), *Doña Luz* (1879), and *Juanita la Larga,* shorter prose works, critical works, and verse translations of Goethe's *Faust,* Uhland's ballads, Thomas Moore's *Paradise and the Peri,* poems of Whittier, James Russell Lowell, etc.

**Va·le′ri·an** (vȧ·lēr′ĭ·ăn). *Lat.* **Publius Licinius Va·le′ri·a′nus** (vȧ·lēr′ĭ·ā′nŭs). d. ?269 A.D. Roman emperor (253–260), of noble birth. Loyal to Gallus, but arrived with legions from Gaul too late to save him; chosen emperor by soldiers; took his son Gallienus as colleague; lacked energy to meet onslaughts of barbarians in various parts of empire; tried to stop Persian conquest of Syria and Armenia; at first successful but was surprised and defeated by Shapur I at Edessa (260); held in captivity until his death.

**Va·le'ri·us An'ti·as** (vȧ·lēr'ĭ·ŭs ăn'tĭ·ăs; ăn'shĭ·ăs). fl. 1st century B.C. Roman historian; author of a (lost) history of Rome.

**Valerius Flac'cus** (flăk'ŭs), **Gaius.** fl. 1st century A.D. Roman poet; adapted an epic, *Argonautica* (more than half of which is extant), based on legend of quest of the golden fleece. Cf. APOLLONIUS OF RHODES.

**Valerius Max'i·mus** (măk'sĭ·mŭs). Latin writer; attached to retinue of Sextus Pompeius; consul (14 A.D.) and, later, proconsul of Asia; prepared a compilation of historical anecdotes, chiefly taken from Cicero, Livy, Sallust, and Trogus, apparently intended for use as a textbook in rhetoric classes.

**Valerius Potitus, Lucius.** See HORATIUS.

**Valerius Pub·lic'o·la** (pŭb·lĭk'ō·lȧ), **Publius.** Roman statesman; colleague of Brutus (*q.v.*) in first year (509 B.C.) of Roman Republic, hence credited with being a founder of the republic; said to have sponsored liberal measures (hence his surname Publicola, "friend of the people") and to have held consular office four times.

**Va'lé'ry'** (vȧ'lā'rē'), **Paul Ambroise.** 1871–1945. French man of letters, b. in Cette (Sète); settled in Paris (1892). Known as a poet and a philosopher; as a poet, associated with the symbolist group; among his books of verse are *La Jeune Parque* (1917), *Aurore* (1917), *Le Cimitière Marin* (1920), *Le Platane*, *L'Ébouche d'un Serpent*, etc. Among his prose writings are *Introduction à la Méthode de Léonard de Vinci*, *Soirée avec M. Teste* (1895), *L'Âme et la Danse* (1924), *Eupalinos ou l'Architecte* (1924), *Analecta* (1927), *Regards sur le Monde Actuel* (1931).

**Valette, Jean Parisot de La.** See LA VALETTE.

**Va'lin'** (vȧ'lăN'), **Martial Henri.** 1898– . French air officer; educ. St. Cyr; served in World War (cavalry) and Riff campaign; transferred to air force (1926); squadron commander in France (1938–39); air adviser in Brazil (1940–41); joined de Gaulle; chief of air forces (1941–46); delegate to UN (from 1946).

**Val'la** (väl'lä; *as Lat.*, văl'ȧ), **Lorenzo,** *Lat.* **Laurentius.** 1406–1457. Italian humanist; protégé of Popes Nicholas V and Calixtus VI; papal secretary (1455 ff.). Among his works are *De Elegantia Latinae Linguae* (6 books, 1471), Latin translations of Homer, Herodotus, and Thucydides, and critical and theological treatises.

**Val·lan'di·gham** (vă·lăn'dĭ·găm), **Clement Laird.** 1820–1871. American politician, b. New Lisbon, Ohio. Member, U.S. House of Representatives (1858–63); strongly opposed policies leading to Civil War. Became known as leader of the Peace Democrats, or "Copperheads," in the Northwest (from 1862). Defied Gen. Burnside's order warning peace party in military district of Ohio that declaration of sympathy with the enemy would not be tolerated; arrested (May 5, 1863), tried, convicted, and condemned to be confined at Fort Warren; sentence commuted by President Lincoln to banishment to the Confederacy. Returned to Ohio (June, 1864) and conducted speaking campaign against Lincoln and the prosecution of the war. His influence waned after the Civil War period.

**Val'le** (väl'lā), **Pietro della.** 1586–1652. Italian traveler in the Orient; studied languages and customs; chief work, *Viaggi in Turchia, Persia, ed India Descritti in 54 Lettere Famigliari* (2 vols., 1650–58).

**Val'le In·clán'** (vä'lyā ēng·klän'), **Ramón del.** 1869–1936. Spanish writer; at Madrid (1895 ff.); president of the Ateneo, Madrid (1932 ff.). His works, many with a Galician locale, include novels, as *Flor di Santidad: Historia Milenaria* (1913); poetry, as *Aromas de Legenda* (1907), *Las Mieles del Rosal* (1910), *La Media Noche* (1917), and *Cara de Plata* (1923); plays, as *El Embrujado* (1913), *La Marquesa Rosalinda* (1913), and *Romance de Lobos* (1915); and a series of studies on the spirit of the Spanish people in the 19th century (1928 ff.).

**Val·le'jo** (vä·yĕ'hō), **Mariano Guadalupe.** 1808–1890. Soldier and pioneer in California; in Mexican military service (from 1823). Supported his nephew Juan Bautista Alvarado in rebellion (1836) resulting in proclamation of the "free state" of California; lived at Sonoma as semi-independent chief, with Indian allies and Mexican troops devoted to his cause (1836–46). Aided in securing Californian submission to United States; state senator in California's first legislature.

**Val'len·tine** (văl'ĕn·tīn), **Benjamin Ben'na·ton** (bĕn'ȧ·tŭn; -t'n). 1843–1926. Journalist and playwright, b. London, Eng.; to U.S. (1871); a founder of *Puck*, and its first managing editor (1877–84); for *Puck* he wrote his famous series of letters from a "Lord Fitznoodle" narrating his strange adventures among the Americans.

**Val'lette'** (vȧ'lĕt'), **Marguerite,** *nee* **Ey'me·ry'** (ām'rē'). *Pseudonym* **Ra'childe'** (rȧ'shēld'). 1860?–1953. French novelist and critic; m. Alfred Vallette, founder of *Mercure de France;* author of realistic novels dealing esp. with abnormal psychology, as *Nono* (1885), *Monsieur Vénus* (1889), *L'Heure Sexuelle* (1898), *La Tour d'Amour* (1914), *La Maison Vierge* (1920), *Refaire l'Amour* (1928), *L'Homme au Bras de Feu* (1931).

**Val'lis·nie'ri** (väl'lēz·nyâ'rē), **Antonio.** 1661–1730. Italian physician and naturalist; investigated the life histories of insects, esp. reproduction.

**Val'lot'** (vȧ'lō'), **Joseph.** 1854–1925. French astronomer and geographer; founded observatory at Chamonix and one on Mont Blanc.

**Val·mi'ki** (väl·mē'kē). fl. 3d century B.C. Reputed author of the Sanskrit epic *Ramayana.*

**Valnay, Raoul.** Pseudonym of A. M. É. HERVÉ.

**Va'lois'** (vȧ'lwȧ'). Name of a royal house of France derived from an ancient district of Picardy, northeast of Paris, a county (10th to 12th century), united to crown by King Philip Augustus (1214), but soon detached. Granted by Philip III (1285) to his son Charles (see CHARLES DE VALOIS). On death of King Charles IV (last of main Capetian line), Charles de Valois's son Philip, Count of Valois and nephew of Philip IV, was called to throne as Philip VI (1328–50), first of house of Valois (1328–1589).

Three collateral branches of the house: (1) CAPETIAN (1328–1498)—Philip VI, John II, Charles V, VI, VII, Louis XI, Charles VIII. (2) ORLÉANS (1498–1515)—descended from Louis, Duc d'Orléans and Comte de Valois, a son of Charles V; represented by Louis XII. (3) ANGOULÊME (1515–1589)—descended from John, another son of Louis, Duc d'Orléans, and from Charles, son of John, both counts of Angoulême; represented by Francis I, Henry II, Francis II, Charles IX, Henry III. On death of Henry III (1589), Henry IV, first of the Bourbons (see BOURBON) succeeded.

County of Valois granted (1344) to Philippe, Duke of Orléans, son of Philip VI; made a duchy (1406), remained generally as property of dukes of Orléans until the Revolution (1789). See CAPETIAN, ORLÉANS, ALENÇON, ANGOULÊME, and the individual biographies of rulers; see also MARGARET OF NAVARRE. See *Table (in Appendix)* for FRANCE.

**Val·sal'va** (väl·säl'vä), **Antonio Maria.** 1666–1723. Italian anatomist; known for his researches on the ear.

**Vám'bé'ry** (väm'bā'rĭ), **Ármin.** *Real name* **Her'mann Bam'ber'ger** (hĕr'män bäm'bĕr'gẽr). 1832?–1913. Hungarian traveler and writer; author of *Travels in Central Asia* (1865), *My Wanderings and Adventures in Persia* (1868), *Etymological Dictionary of Turco-Tatar Languages* (1878), *The Origin of the Magyars* (1882), etc.

**van.** For many names containing *van*, see that part of the name following *van*.

**Van Al'len** (văn ăl'ĕn, -ĭn), **James Alfred.** 1914– . American physicist, b. Mt. Pleasant, Iowa. At U. of Iowa (1951– ); pioneer in high-altitude rocket research; discovered radiation belts around the earth (Van Allen Belt; 1958).

**Van Am'ringe** (văn ăm'rĭnj), **John Howard.** 1835–1915. American educator; teacher of mathematics, Columbia (1860–1910), dean (1894–1910).

**Van'brugh** (văn'brŭ), **Irene.** 1872–1949. English actress; toured Australia and New Zealand (1889, 1923–25, 1927–29); m. (1901) Dion Boucicault (d. 1929); created important roles in *The Liars* (1897), *Trelawny of the Wells, The Gay Lord Quex, Admirable Crichton;* played Queen in *Hamlet* (1931); toured with *Viceroy Sarah* (1937). Her older sister **Violet** (1867–1942), actress, known for Shakespearean roles; appeared first in London in *The Butler;* m. Arthur Bourchier (d. 1927), and played in his company; created roles in *The Ambassador, Hearts Are Trumps, The Wedding Guest.*

**Van·brugh'** (văn·brōō'; *in England commonly* văn'brŭ), Sir **John.** 1664–1726. English dramatist and architect, of Flemish descent. Wrote *The Provoked Wife* (1690–92; produced 1697), *The Relapse* (1696), followed by adaptations from the French including *Aesop* (1697; from Boursault's *Ésope*), and *The Confederacy* (1705; after F. C. Dancourt). Turned to architecture; designed (1701) Castle Howard (completed 1714) and other country mansions in English baroque style developed from the Palladian architecture introduced by Inigo Jones; commissioned (1705) by Queen Anne to design and build Blenheim Palace, Woodstock (completed by duchess of Marlborough); appointed Clarenceux king-of-arms, a sinecure (1704–26). His *Journey to London* completed by Cibber as *The Provoked Husband* (1728).

**Van Brunt** (văn brŭnt'), **Henry.** 1832–1903. American architect, b. Boston; grad. Harvard (1854); in partnership in Boston (1863–83) with W. R. Ware (*q.v.*), and in Kansas City (1883–1903) with F. M. Howe.

**Van Bu'ren** (văn bū'rĕn), **Martin.** 1782–1862. Eighth president of the United States, b. Kinderhook, N.Y. Adm. to bar (1803); attorney general of New York (1816–19). Resident of Albany (from 1816) and member of influential political group nicknamed the "Albany regency." U.S. senator from New York (1821–28); governor of New York (1829); resigned to become U.S. secretary of state (1829–31); nominated U.S. minister to Great Britain, but nomination not confirmed by U.S. Senate (Jan. 25, 1832); vice-president of the United States (1833–37); president of the United States (1837–41); unsuccessful Democratic candidate for presidency (1840) and Free-Soil party candidate (1848). Author of *Inquiry into the Origin and Course of Political Parties in the United States* (1867).

**Vance** (våns), **Alfred Glenville.** *Real name* **Alfred Peck Stevens.** 1838?–1888. English pantomimist and comic singer, called "the Great Vance."

**Vance, Ethel.** Pseudonym of Grace Z. STONE.

**Vance, Louis Joseph.** 1879–1933. American fiction writer; author of *Terence O'Rourke, Gentleman Adventurer* (1905), *The Fortune Hunter* (1910), *The Lone Wolf* (1914), *Linda Lee, Inc.* (1922), *They Call It Love* (1927), *The Lone Wolf's Son* (1931), etc.

**van Ceulen.** See Cornelius JANSSEN VAN CEULEN.

**Van Corlaer, Arendt.** See VAN CURLER.

**Van Cort'landt** (văn kôrt'lănt; -lănd; *Du.* vän kŏrt'-länt), **Oloff Stevenszen.** 1600–1684. Dutch businessman in New Amsterdam (from 1638); burgomaster (1655–60; 1662–63); one of commissioners treating with English to surrender city (1664); deputy mayor (1667); his name is perpetuated in Van Cortlandt Park, New York City, originally a part of his estate. His son **Stephanus** (1643–1700), b. in New York (then called New Amsterdam), was a businessman and politician; first native-born mayor of New York City (1677, 1686, 1687); associate justice (1691–1700) and chief justice (1700), New York supreme court. Another son, **Jacobus** (1658–1739), was a merchant; mayor of New York City (1719); heir to that part of his father's estate which is now Van Cortlandt Park. A grandson of Stephanus, **Pierre** [pyâr] (1721–1814), was a country gentleman and politician; resident (from 1749) at Croton, N.Y., where he inherited manorial estate; served in American Revolution (1775); president of council of safety (1777); member of second, third, fourth provincial congresses; first lieutenant governor of the State of New York (1777–95). Pierre's son **Philip** (1749–1831) was a soldier and politician; colonel of New York regiment in the Continental army (1775); assisted Gates's army at Saratoga (1777); co-operated with Sullivan-Clinton expedition; in command at Schenectady (1780); engaged in final campaign at Yorktown; brevetted brigadier general (1783); member of U.S. House of Representatives (1793–1809).

**Van·cou'ver** (văn·kōō'vẽr), **George.** 1757–1798. English navigator; commanded an expedition of exploration and discovery (1791–92) along coasts of Australia, New Zealand, Hawaiian Islands; circumnavigated Vancouver Island, and explored Pacific coast of North America (1792–94).

**Van'ču·ra** (vån'chŏŏ·rå), **Vladislav.** 1891–1942. Czech physician and novelist; executed by Nazis (June, 1942); author of *Jan Marhoul, Baker; Tilled Fields and Battle Fields; Marketa Lazarova; Flight to Budapest;* etc.

**Van Cur'ler** (văn kûr'lẽr), **Ar'ent** (âr'ĕnt). *Also* **A'rendt Van Cor'laer** (ä'rĕnt vän kŏr'lär). 1620–1667. Dutch settler in America (from 1638); purchased land (1661) on Mohawk River near its junction with the Hudson and settled there; founder of present city of Schenectady, N.Y.

**Van'dal'** (väɴ'dål'), **Albert.** 1853–1910. French historian; author of *Napoléon et Alexandre I$^{er}$* (3 vols., 1894–97), *L'Avènement de Bonaparte* (2 vols., 1902), etc.

**Van'damme'** (väɴ'dåm'), **Dominique René.** Comte **d'U'ne·bourg'** (dün'bōōr'). 1770–1830. French soldier; served in the Revolutionary and Napoleonic armies; created peer of France during the Hundred Days, and put in command of the 3d army corps; distinguished himself at Wavre in the battle of Waterloo (June 18, 1815).

**Van de Graaff** (văn' dĕ grăf'), **Robert Jemison.** 1901–1967. American physicist; known for development of a high-voltage electrostatic generator and for works in nuclear physics.

**Van'de·grift** (văn'dĕ·grĭft), **Alexander Archer.** 1887–1973. U.S. marine corps officer, b. Charlottesville, Va.; commissioned (1909); served in Nicaragua (1912), Mexico (1914), Haiti (1915–23 at various times), China (1927–29, 1935–37); brigadier general (1940); major general (1941); in charge of landing and subsequent operations on Guadalcanal (Aug.–Dec., 1942), Bougainville (Nov., 1943); lieutenant general (July, 1943); commandant of marine corps (1944–47).

**Vandegrift, Margaret.** See Thomas Allibone JANVIER.

**van den, van der.** For many names containing one of these elements, see that part of the name following the element.

**van den Bosch** (vän dĕn bŏs′), **Jan.** 1780–1844. Dutch governor general of Batavia (1830) and founder of Dutch system of civilizing the natives; minister of state for colonies (1833).

**Van′ De·poele′** (văn′ dĕ·po͞ol′), **Charles Joseph.** 1846–1892. Inventor, b. in Belgium; to America (1869); naturalized (1878). Demonstrated practicability of electric traction (1874) and patented his electric railway (1883); sold patents to Thomson-Houston Electric Co., Lynn, Mass. (1888), and entered their employ as electrician. Received patents also on an electric generator (1880), a carbon commutator brush (1888), an alternating-current electric reciprocating engine (1889), a telpher system (1890), a coal-mining machine (1891), a gearless electric locomotive (1894).

**Van′der·bilt** (văn′dẽr·bĭlt). Name of an American family prominent in transportation and finance, including: **Cornelius** (1794–1877), known as "Commodore Vanderbilt," founder of the family fortune; b. Port Richmond, Staten Island, N.Y.; founded (1810) freight and passenger ferry business between Staten Island and New York City; sold his vessels (1818) and became captain (1818–29) on ferry line between New Brunswick, N.J., and New York City; established his own shipping service on Hudson River (1829), running in successful competition with lines already there; financed and established a line to California via Nicaragua (1850), which he sold out (1858) to competitors operating via the Panama route; bought controlling interest in New York and Harlem Railroad (1862–63), the Hudson River Railroad, and the New York Central Railroad; engaged in bitter stock-market struggle with James Fisk and Daniel Drew for control of Erie Railroad (1867–68); consolidated railroads (1869) and extended the lines to Chicago. His son **William Henry** (1821–1885) inherited the bulk of his fortune; became (1877) president of New York Central Railroad.

William Henry Vanderbilt left four sons: (1) **Cornelius** (1843–1899), president, New York & Harlem Railroad (1886–99); chairman of board of New York Central & Hudson River and of Michigan Central; regarded as head of the Vanderbilt family (from 1885); in memory of his son **William Henry,** presented (1893) dormitory to Yale. (2) **William Kissam** (1849–1920), chairman of board of directors of Lake Shore & Michigan Southern Railroad (1883–1903); president of New York, Chicago & St. Louis Railway (1882–87); surrendered active management of Vanderbilt railroad interests to a Rockefeller-Morgan-Pennsylvania Railroad group (1903); enthusiastic yachtsman, owned and sailed the *Defender* in the international yacht races with England (1895). (3) **Frederick William** (1856–1938), expert in railroad management; noted as a yachtsman. (4) **George Washington** (1862–1914); interested himself in agriculture and forestry; acquired vast landed estate near Asheville, N.C., where he built magnificent country home, "Biltmore"; there he directed experiments in agriculture, forestry, and stockbreeding.

Cornelius Vanderbilt (1843–1899) was father of **Gertrude** (see William Collins WHITNEY), **Gladys** (see László SZÉCHENYANI), and sons: (1) **Cornelius III** (1873–1942), director of many railroad companies and banks; during World War served as colonel of engineers (1917) and brigadier general in the National army (July 6, 1918). (2) **Alfred Gwynne** (1877–1915), sportsman; lost in the *Lusitania* disaster. (3) **Reginald Claypoole** (1880–1925), sportsman, interested in horse shows.

William Kissam Vanderbilt left two sons: (1) **William Kissam** (1878–1944); entered service of New York Central & Hudson River Railroad (1903); vice-president (1912). (2) **Harold Stirling** (1884-1970 ); also associated with management of New York Central lines; in World War I, lieutenant in U.S. naval reserve; interested in yachting; skipper of the American yacht in three international cup contests, sailing the *Enterprise* (1930) to beat Sir Thomas Lipton's *Shamrock V*, the *Rainbow* (1934) to beat T. O. M. Sopwith's *Endeavour*, and the *Ranger* (1937) to beat T. O. M. Sopwith's *Endeavour II*. A son of Cornelius Vanderbilt III, **Cornelius Vanderbilt, Jr.** (1898–1974), journalist; founder (1923) and president of Vanderbilt Newspapers, Inc.; served in World War I as despatch driver of 27th division, A.E.F.; author of *Personal Experiences of a Cub Reporter* (1922), *Reno* (1929), *Park Avenue* (1930), *Palm Beach* (1931), *Farewell to Fifth Avenue* (1935), etc.

**Van′der·cook** (văn′dẽr·ko͝ok), **John Womack.** 1902–1963. Writer and editor, b. London, Eng.; educ. in U.S.; journalist (1921–25); explored in Dutch Guiana, Liberia, and South Sea Islands; news commentator for National Broadcasting Co.; author of *Tom-Tom* (1926), *Black Majesty* (1928), *Murder in Trinidad* (1933), *Caribbee Cruise* (1938), etc.

**Van der Donck** (vän′ dẽr dôngk′), **Adriaen.** 1620–?1655. Dutch lawyer and colonist in America; established colony on site of what is now Yonkers (1645); author of a description of New Netherland (publ. 1655).

**Van′der·lip** (văn′dẽr·lĭp), **Frank Arthur.** 1864–1937. American financier; vice-president (1901–09) and president (1909–19), National City Bank, New York City.

**Van′der·lyn** (văn′dẽr·lĭn), **John.** 1775–1852. American painter; attracted attention by his *Marius Amid the Ruins of Carthage* (1807); also portraits, of Zachary Taylor, John A. Sidell and Francis L. Waddell.

**Van′der′monde′** (väN′dẽr′môNd′), **Alexis Théophile.** 1735–1796. French mathematician.

**van der Poorten–Schwartz, J. M. W.** See Maarten MAARTENS.

**Van′der·vel′de** (vän′dẽr·vĕl′dĕ), **Émile.** 1866–1938. Belgian statesman; minister of state and member of the Belgian cabinet during World War I (1914–18); minister of justice (1919) and of foreign affairs (1925).

**Van De·van′ter** (văn′ dē·văn′tẽr), **Willis.** 1859–1941. American jurist, b. Marion, Ind.; practiced law at Cheyenne, Wyo. (from 1884); U.S. circuit judge, 8th judicial circuit (1903–10); associate justice, U.S. Supreme Court (1910–37).

**Vandevelde** *or* **van de Velde.** See VELDE.

**van Deventer,** Sir **Louis Jacob.** See DEVENTER.

**Van de Water, Virginia Belle Terhune.** See under Edward Payson TERHUNE.

**Van Die′men** (văn dē′mĕn; *Du.* vän), **Anton.** 1593–1645. Dutch statesman; member of high council of Dutch East India Co. (1625), general manager (1632); governor general of Dutch East Indies (1636). Sent out exploring expedition under Abel Tasman (Aug., 1642) which discovered (Dec., 1642) large island off southeastern Australia and named it Van Diemen's Land (now known as Tasmania).

**Van Dine, S. S.** Pseudonym of Willard Huntington WRIGHT.

**van Dong′en** (vän dông′ĕ[n]), **Kees.** *Orig. name* **Cornélius Théodorus Marie van Dongen.** 1877–1968. French (Dutch-born) Fauvist painter. To France (1897; naturalized 1929); to Monaco (c. 1945).

**Van Do′ren** (văn dō′rĕn), **Carl.** 1885–1950. American writer, b. Hope, Ill.; A.B., Illinois (1907), Ph.D., Columbia (1911); managing editor, *Cambridge History of Ameri-*

*can Literature* (1917–21); literary editor, *The Nation* (1919–22), *Century Magazine* (1922–25); editor, The Literary Guild (1926–34); author of *The American Novel* (1921; rev. ed. 1940), *Contemporary American Novelists* (1922), *James Branch Cabell* (1925), *Swift* (1930), *Sinclair Lewis* (1933), *Benjamin Franklin* (1938; Pulitzer prize), *Secret History of the American Revolution* (1941), *Mutiny in January* (1943), etc. His brother **Mark** (1894–1972), also a writer; literary editor (1924–28), motion-picture critic (1935–38), *The Nation;* author of verse, criticism, and novels, including *Collected Poems, 1922–1938* (1939; Pulitzer prize), *Shakespeare* (1939), *Windless Cabins* (1940), *The Transparent Tree* (1940), *The Mayfield Deer* (1941), *Tilda* (1943), *Liberal Education* (1943). Carl's wife (m. 1912; divorced), **I·ri′ta** [ī·rē′tȧ] (1891–1966), A.M. (1909), Florida State Coll. for Women; on editorial staff of *The Nation* (1919–24), New York *Herald Tribune* (from 1924; literary editor from 1926). Mark's wife (m. 1922), **Dorothy,** *nee* **Graffe** [grăf] (1896– ), writer; A.B., Barnard (1918); on editorial staff of *The Nation* (1919–36); author of *Strangers* (1926), *Flowering Quince* (1927), *Brother and Brother* (1928), *Those First Affections* (1938).

**Van Doren, Harold Livingston.** 1895–1957. American industrial designer; author of *Industrial Design—A Practical Guide* (1940); translated Ambroise Vollard's biographies of Cézanne (1923), Renoir (1925).

**Van Dorn** (văn dôrn′), **Earl.** 1820–1863. American army officer; grad. U.S.M.A., West Point (1842); resigned from U.S. service (1861) to enter Confederate army. Colonel of cavalry, stationed in Texas (1861); received surrender of Union troops there (Apr., 1861); promoted major general (Sept., 1861). Murdered (May 8, 1863).

**Van Dru′ten** (văn drōō′t'n), **John William.** 1901–1957. English playwright; LL.B., London U. (1922); author of *Young Woodley* (produced in N.Y. 1925; pub. as a novel 1929), *A Woman on Her Way* (novel; 1930), *There's Always Juliet* (1931), *The Distaff Side* (1933), *And Then You Wish* (novel; 1936), *Gertie Maude* (1937), *Old Acquaintance* (1939), *The Damask Cheek* (1942; with Lloyd Morris), etc.

**Van Dyck** (văn dīk′), **Cornelius Van Al′en** (văn ăl′ĕn). 1818–1895. American medical missionary in Syria (1840–93); noted for his command of Arabic; worked (1857–65) to complete translation of Bible into Arabic, begun (c. 1848) by Eli Smith. Exercised influence in modern renaissance of Arabic literature, his books proving possibility of writing idiomatic Arabic in easily comprehensible style.

**van Dyck** *or* **Dijk** (văn dīk′; *Du.* vän), **Philip.** See DYCK.

**Van·dyke′** *or* **Van Dyck** (văn dīk′; *Flem.* vän), Sir **Anthony.** 1599–1641. Flemish painter; studied under Rubens and was his assistant on some of his great canvases; studios in England (after 1632); knighted by Charles I of England (1632) and appointed court painter. Among his religious paintings are *Crucifixion* in the church at Malines, *Elevation of the Cross* at Courtrai, *St. Augustine in Ecstasy* at Antwerp. Best known for portraits of Charles I, members of English royal family, and English notables of the period.

**van Dyke** (văn dīk′), **Henry.** 1852–1933. American clergyman, educator, and writer; pastor, Brick Presbyterian Church, New York (1883–99); professor of English literature, Princeton (1899–1913; 1919–23). U.S. minister to the Netherlands and Luxembourg (1913–16). Chaplain (lieutenant commander), U.S. navy (1917–19). Author of *The Reality of Religion* (1884), *Little Rivers* (1895), *The Story of the Other Wise Man* (1896), *The Builders, and Other Poems* (1897), *Fisherman's Luck* (1899), *The Toiling of Felix, and Other Poems* (1900), *The Ruling Passion* (1901), *The Blue Flower* (1902), *Music, and Other Poems* (1904), *Out of Doors in the Holy Land* (1908), *The Unknown Quantity* (1912), *The Valley of Vision* (1919), *The Golden Key* (1926), *Gratitude* (1930), etc. His brother **Paul** (1859–1933) was a historian and educator; professor, Princeton (1898–1928); author of *The Age of the Renascence* (1897), *Catherine de Medicis* (2 vols., 1922), *George Washington*...(1931), etc.

**Van Dyke, John Charles.** 1856–1932. American educator; professor of history of art, Rutgers (from 1889); author of *Principles of Art* (1887), *American Art and Its Tradition* (1919), *Rembrandt and His School* (1923), *In Java* (1929), etc.

**Vane** (vān), **Charles William Stewart.** See under Robert STEWART.

**Vane,** Sir **Henry,** *or commonly* Sir **Harry.** 1613–1662. English Puritan statesman; to America (1635) and settled at Boston. Elected governor of Massachusetts (May 25, 1636); lost popularity by taking side of Anne Hutchinson in theological dispute; defeated for governor in election (1637), and returned to England. Joint treasurer of royal navy (1639); member of parliament (1640); knighted by Charles I (1640); one of commissioners who negotiated the Solemn League and Covenant with Scotland; approved the Self-Denying Ordinance and the New Model (1645); condemned Pride's Purge (1648). Member of council of state (1649); imprisoned (1656) for attack on Cromwell's Protectorate; was arrested after the Restoration (1660); held for two years in prison; tried, convicted, and executed (June 14, 1662) for treason.

**van Gogh, Vincent.** See GOGH.

**Van Hise** (văn hīs′), **Charles Richard.** 1857–1918. American geologist and educator; on teaching staff, U. of Wisconsin (1879–1903); president, U. of Wisconsin (1903–18). On U.S. Geological Survey staff (from 1883); prepared monographs on Wisconsin geology, esp. covering iron-producing sections in Lake Superior region.

**Van Hoog′stra′ten** (vän hōĸ′strȧ′tĕn), **Willem.** 1884–1965. Dutch orchestra conductor; American debut as conductor of New York Philharmonic Orchestra (1922–23); conductor of Portland (Oregon) Symphony Orchestra (1925 ff.).

**Van Horne** (văn hôrn′), Sir **William Cornelius.** 1843–1915. Railroad executive, b. in Will County, Ill. General manager (1881–84), vice-president (1884–88), and president (1888–99), Canadian Pacific Railway, superintending its construction (1881–86) and the first years of its operation. Projected and constructed railroad in Cuba (1900–02), and in Guatemala (1903–08). Naturalized Canadian citizen (from c. 1890).

**Van Ing′en** (văn ĭng′ĕn), **William Brantley.** 1858–1955. American muralist; painted murals in Congressional Library at Washington, D.C., in Pennsylvania State Capitol at Harrisburg, etc.

**Va·ni′ni** (vä·nē′nē), **Lucilio.** *Also called* **Giulio Cesare Vanini.** 1585–1619. Italian philosopher; ordained priest; advocated mechanistic philosophy of natural development; condemned as atheist and magician and burned at the stake.

**Van Len′nep** (văn lĕn′ĕp; -ĭp), **Henry John.** 1815–1889. American Congregational missionary in Smyrna, Constantinople, and Tokat, Turkey (1839–69); author of *Travels in Little-Known Parts of Asia Minor* (2 vols., 1870), *Bible Lands*...(1875).

**Van Loo** *or* **Van′loo′** (*Fr.* väɴ′lō′; *Du.* vän·lō′). Family of French painters, descended from the Dutch painter **Jan Van Loo** (1585?–?1630) and including his son **Jakob** *or* **Jacques** (1614–1670), who became a naturalized Frenchman; Jacques's sons **Abraham Louis,** *known as* **Louis** (1641–1713), and **Jean** (1650?–1700); Louis's sons **Jean Baptiste** (1684–1745) and **Charles André,** *known as* **Carle** (1705–1765); Jean Baptiste's sons **Louis Michel,** *known as* **Michel** (1707–1771), and **Charles Amédée Philippe** (1719–?1796); and Carle's son **Jules César Denis,** *known as* **César** (1743–1821).

**van Loon** (văn lōn′), **Hendrik Willem.** 1882–1944. Journalist, lecturer, and writer, b. Rotterdam, the Netherlands; to U.S. (1902); A.B., Cornell (1905); Ph.D., Munich (1911); newspaper correspondent Europe (1906, 1914, 1915–18); lecturer U.S. on hist. and hist. of art. Auth.: *The Story of Mankind* (1921; awarded Newbery medal, 1923), *The Story of the Bible* (1923), *America* (1927), *R.v.R., Life and Times of Rembrandt van Rijn* (1931), *Van Loon's Geography* (1932), *Ships* (1935), *Christmas Carols* (1937), *The Arts* (1937), *Van Loon's Lives* (1942), etc.

**Van Name** (văn nām′), **Addison.** 1835–1922. American librarian; librarian, Yale U. (1865–1905). His son **Willard Gibbs** (1872–1959), zoologist; consulting editor on *Webster's New International Dictionary* (1903–09); zoologist at New York State Museum in Albany (1910–16); on staff of American Museum of Natural History (from 1916) and associate curator (from 1926).

**Van′ni** (vän′nē), Cavaliere **Francesco.** 1563–1609. Italian painter, b. Siena. Among his works are *Simon the Magician Reprimanded by Saint Peter, Flagellation of Christ, Death of Saint Cecilia, The Dead Christ.*

**Vanni-Marcoux, Jean Émile.** = Vanni MARCOUX.

**Van Nos′trand** (văn nŏs′trănd), **David.** 1811–1886. American founder of publishing house of Van Nostrand & Co.; specialized in publishing technical and military works.

**Vannucci, Pietro.** See PERUGINO.

**Vanolis, Bysshe.** Pseudonym of James THOMSON (1834–1882).

**Van Paassen, Pierre.** See Pierre van PAASSEN.

**Van Rens′se·laer** (văn rĕn′sĕ·lär; *Angl.* văn rĕn′sĕ·lẽr, -lẽr), **Kiliaen.** 1595–1644. Dutch merchant; dealer in precious stones at Amsterdam; a founder and organizer of Dutch West India Company (chartered 1621). Through an agent, bought from American Indians huge tract comprising present counties of Albany, Columbia, and Rensselaer, in New York State, and received land patent for it (1635); colonized "Rensselaerswyck," as the area was named. Among his descendants in America were Stephen Van Rensselaer and Martha Van Rensselaer (*qq.v.*).

**Van Rens′se·laer** (văn rĕn′sĕ·lẽr; -lẽr), **Mariana,** *nee* **Griswold.** 1851–1934. American art critic; m. Schuyler Van Rensselaer (1873; d. 1884); author of *Book of American Figure Painters* (1886), *American Etchers* (1886), *English Cathedrals* (illustrated by Joseph Pennell, 1892), *History of the City of New York in the Seventeenth Century* (2 vols., 1909), *Poems* (1910), *Many Children* (1921), etc.

**Van Rensselaer, Martha.** 1864–1932. Descendant of Kiliaen Van Rensselaer. Schoolteacher; on Cornell U. staff as organizer and director of extension courses for farm women (1900); lecturer in newly organized department of home economics (1907), and professor of home economics, Cornell (1911). Director, New York State College of Home Economics (1925). Chosen (1923) by National League of Women Voters as one of twelve most distinguished women in the U.S.

**Van Rensselaer, Stephen.** 1764–1839. Descendant of Kiliaen Van Rensselaer. American army officer and politician, b. New York City. Inherited great Van Rensselaer estate in New York (1769); lieutenant governor of New York (1795–1801); major general of New York militia; in command (1812) of New York's northern frontier; attacked Queenstown, Canada, across Niagara River (Oct. 13, 1812) and met with disaster. Member, U.S. House of Representatives (1822–29). Advocated canal to connect Great Lakes with Hudson River; member of first canal commission (1810), and second canal commission (1816–39), serving as its president (1825–39). Founded Rensselaer Polytechnic Institute (incorporated as Rensselaer Institute, 1826). Member, board of regents, U. of the State of New York (1819–39), and chancellor (1835–39).

**Van Schaick** (văn skīk′), **Goo′se** (gō′sē) *or* **Go′sen** (gō′sĕn) *or* **Goo′sen** (gō′sĕn). 1736–1789. American Revolutionary army officer, b. Albany, N.Y.; campaigned in Cherry Valley against Joseph Brant (1775); wounded at Ticonderoga (1777); engaged at Monmouth; led detachment against Onondaga Indians (Apr., 1779), destroying their chief settlement and their supplies; brevetted brigadier general (Oct., 1783).

**Van·sit′tart** (văn·sĭt′ẽrt), **Henry.** 1732–1770. Anglo-Indian administrator; governor of Bengal (1760–64); waged war on Mir Kasim, the subahdar (1763). His younger son, **Nicholas** (1766–1851), 1st Baron **Bex′ley** (bĕks′lĭ), was chancellor of the exchequer (1812–23).

**Vansittart,** Sir **Robert Gilbert.** 1st Baron **Vansittart of Den′ham** [dĕn′ăm] (cr. 1941). 1881–1957. British diplomat; descendant of Henry Vansittart (*q.v.*); educ. Eton; secretary to foreign secretary Curzon (1920–24); permanent undersecretary of state for foreign affairs (1930–38); chief diplomatic adviser to foreign secretary (1938–41); author of novels, volumes of verse, and plays including *Les Pariahs* (1902), *Dead Heat* (1939), *Shy at the Moon.*

**Van Slyke** (văn slīk′), **Lucius Lincoln.** 1859–1931. American agricultural chemist; known esp. for his researches in the chemical composition of the constituents of milk and their relation to one another. His son **Donald Dexter** (1883–1971), research chemist on staff of Rockefeller Institute (1907–48), and chief chemist of the institute's hospital (1914); devised several chemical methods, as for the analysis of proteins, for determining the carbon-dioxide holding capacity of blood, etc.; known also for researches on diabetes and nephritis, in quantitative clinical chemistry, etc.

**Van So′mer** (văn sō′mẽr), **Paul.** 1576–1621. Dutch portrait painter at court of James I of England.

**van't Hoff** (vänt hŏf′), **Jacobus Hendricus.** 1852–1911. Dutch physical chemist, b. Rotterdam. Professor, Amsterdam (1878), Berlin (from 1896). Advanced theory of asymmetric carbon atom, laying foundation for stereochemistry; applied thermodynamics to chemistry; propounded theory that dissolved substances obey the laws of gases; investigated the formation and decomposition of double salts, esp. those occurring at Stassfurt, Saxony. Awarded 1901 Nobel prize in chemistry.

**Van Tie′ghem′** (vän′ tyā′gĕm′), **Philippe Édouard Léon.** 1839–1914. French botanist; known for his studies on myxomycetes, ascomycetes, and bacteria; proposed a new classification of plants.

**Van Twil′ler** (văn tvĭl′ẽr; *Angl.* văn twĭl′ẽr), **Wou′ter** (vou′tẽr) *or* **Wal′ter** (wôl′tẽr). 1580?–?1656. Nephew of Kiliaen Van Rensselaer. Dutch administrator in America; governor of New Netherland (1633–37).

**Van Tyne** (văn tīn′), **Claude Halstead.** 1869–1930. American historian; professor of American history (1906–30), U. of Michigan; author of *The American Revolution, 1776–1783* (1905), *The War of Independence, American Phase* (1929; awarded Pulitzer prize, 1930), etc.

**Van Vech′ten** (văn vĕk′tĕn), **Carl.** 1880–1964. American writer, b. Cedar Rapids, Iowa; on staff of New York *Times* (1906–13); author of *Music After the Great War* (1915), *In the Garret* (1920), *Peter Whiffle, His Life and Works* (1922), *The Blind Bow-Boy* (1923), *The Tattooed Countess* (1924), *Nigger Heaven* (1926), *Spider Boy* (1928), *Sacred and Profane Memories* (1932), etc.

**Van'vi·tel'li** (vän'vē·tĕl'lē), **Luigi.** 1700–1773. Italian architect; supervising architect, St. Peter's, Rome (1726 ff.).

**Van Vleck'** (văn vlĕk'), **John Hasbrouck.** 1899– . American physicist. At Harvard U. (1951–69); awarded (with Philip W. Anderson and Sir Nevill F. Mott) Nobel prize for physics (1977).

**Vanzetti, Bartolomeo.** See under Nicola SACCO.

**Va'pe·reau'** (vȧ'prō'), **Louis Gustave.** 1819–1906. French writer; compiler of *Dictionnaire Universel des Contemporains* (1858), *Dictionnaire Universel des Littératures* (1888); author of *L'Homme et la Vie* (1896).

**Va'quez'** (vȧ'kĕz'), **Louis Henri.** 1860–1936. French physician; specialist in diseases of the heart; first to describe (1892) erythremia, sometimes called Vaquez's disease, also known as Osler's (or Osler-Vaquez) disease.

**Varagine, Jacobus de.** See JACOBUS DE VARAGINE.

**Varahran** *or* **Varanes.** = BAHRAM.

**Var'chi** (vär'kē), **Benedetto.** 1503–1565. Italian scholar; known esp. for *Storia Fiorentina* (pub., 1721), a history of Florence in the period 1527–38.

**Var'da·man** (vär'dȧ·măn), **James Kimble.** 1861–1930. American politician; governor of Mississippi (1904–08); U.S. senator (1913–19); vigorously opposed President Wilson and his World War I policies.

**Vardhamāna Jñātiputra, Mahāvīra.** See MAHĀVĪRA.

**Var'don** (vär'd'n), **Harry.** 1870–1937. English golf player; professional (from 1903); won British open championship six times (1896, 1898, 1899, 1903, 1911, 1914), the American open (1900), and the German open (1911).

**Va·rè'** (vä·rĕ'), **Daniele.** 1880–1956. Italian diplomat and author; minister to China; author of *The Maker of Heavenly Trousers, Handbook of the Perfect Diplomat, Laughing Diplomat, The Gate of Happy Sparrows, The Last Empress.*

**Va'ren** (fä'rĕn), **Bernhard.** *Lat.* **Bern·har'dus** (bûrn-här'dŭs; *Ger.* bĕrn·här'dōōs) **Va·re'ni·us** (vȧ·rē'nĭ·ŭs; *Ger.* vä·rā'nē·ōōs). 1622–?1650. Geographer, b. in Hanover, Ger.; author of *Descriptio Regni Japoniae* (1649) and *Geographia Generalis* (his chief work, 1650).

**Va·rèse'** (vă·rāz; vȧ'râz'), **Edgard.** 1883–1965. American composer, b. France. To U.S. (1916); founder and director, International Composers' Guild (1921–27); works include *Arcana* (1927) and *Ionisation* (1931).

**Var'gas** (vȧr'gȧs), **Getulio Dornelles.** 1883–1954. Brazilian lawyer and political leader, b. São Borja; president of Rio Grande do Sul (1928–30); led successful revolution against President Washington Luiz (1930); provisional president of Brazil (1930–34); president (1934–45; 1951–54), elected under constitution of 1934, inaugurating second republic. Wrote political history of Brazil (1938).

**Var'gas** (vär'gäs), **José Maria.** 1786–1854. Venezuelan physician and statesman; vice-president (1834) and president (1835–36), Venezuela; senator (1838–46); councilor of state (1847–49). Resident in U.S. (from 1853).

**Vargas, Luis de.** 1502–1568. Spanish painter; among his works are *Nativity* and *Temporal Generation of Christ,* the latter popularly known as *La Gamba* (in Seville cathedral), and *Holy Family* (in the Louvre).

**Var'i·an** (vâr'ĭ·ăn), **Russell Harrison.** 1898–1959. American physicist, b. Washington, D.C.; A.M., Stanford (1927); known for research in microwaves and electronics; inventor, with his brother **Sig'urd** [sĭg'ērd] (1901–61), of the klystron, UHF resonator; research engineer, Sperry Gyroscope Co., Long Island (1940–46).

**Var'ick** (văr'ĭk), **Richard.** 1753–1831. American Revolutionary soldier and politician; military secretary to Gen. Philip J. Schuyler (1775); aide-de-camp to Gen. Benedict Arnold at West Point (1780) but in no way involved in Arnold's treason. Chosen by George Washington as recording secretary (1781) to arrange, classify, and copy all the correspondence and records of the headquarters of the Continental army; completed task in forty volumes of transcripts (1783). Mayor of New York City (1789–1801).

**Varinus.** See GUARINO DA VERONA.

**Var'i·us Ru'fus** (vâr'ĭ·ŭs rōō'fŭs), **Lucius.** Roman poet of 1st century B.C.; friend of Horace, Vergil, and Maecenas; author of a tragedy (*Thyestes*) and two epics; commissioned by Emperor Augustus to edit Vergil's *Aeneid.* Only fragments of works extant.

**Var'ley** (vär'lĭ), **John.** 1778–1842. English landscape painter and art teacher; one of founders of Royal Society of Painters in Water Colours, where he exhibited (1805–42); friend of William Blake.

**Varn'ha'gen von En'se** (färn'hä'gĕn fŏn ĕn'zĕ), **Karl August.** 1785–1858. German diplomat and writer. Entered Austrian army (1809) and Russian army (1813), and took part in War of Liberation; in Prussian diplomatic service (1814); minister president, Karlsruhe (1815–19); pensioned (1824). Author of *Biographische Denkmale* (5 vols., 1824–30), biographies of General Seydlitz (1834), Field Marshals Schwerin (1841) and Keith (1844), Queen Sophia Charlotte (1837), and others, *Denkwürdigkeiten* (7 vols., 1837–46), etc.

**Var'num** (vär'nŭm), **James Mitchell.** 1748–1789. American lawyer and Revolutionary officer, b. Dracut, Mass. Brigadier general, Continental army (1777); commanded defense of Forts Mercer and Mifflin on the Delaware River; commanded department of Rhode Island (1779). Member, Continental Congress (1780–82, 1786, 1787). U.S. judge, Northwest Territory (1787); aided in framing code of territorial laws.

**Va'ro·li** (vä·rō·lē), **Costanzo.** 1543?–1575. Italian surgeon and anatomist; described the broad mass of nerve fibers (the pons Varolii) on undersurface of the brain.

**Va'ro·ta'ri** (vä'rō·tä'rē), **Dario.** 1539–1596. Italian painter, b. Verona. His son **Alessandro,** *often called* **il Pa'do·va·ni'no** [ēl pä'dō·vä·nē'nō] (1590–1650), was also a painter; among his works are *Diana and Callisto, Minerva,* and *The Marriage at Cana.*

**Var'ro** (văr'ō), **Gaius Terentius.** Roman general and politician; consul with Lucius Aemilius Paulus (216 B.C.); impatient with Fabian strategy, gave battle to Hannibal; was defeated in battle of Cannae (216).

**Varro, Marcus Terentius.** 116–27 B.C. Roman scholar; studied in Rome and Athens. In civil war, joined Pompey, but after Pharsalus (48 B.C.), was reconciled with Caesar and appointed director of the library Caesar planned to found; after Caesar's assassination, was proscribed by Second Triumvirate but his life was saved by his friends. Wrote on various subjects, including languages, religion, law, customs, political institutions, philosophy, geography; chief work, *Rerum Humanarum et Divinarum Antiquitates,* portions of which have survived.

**Varro, Publius Terentius.** *Surnamed* **At'a·ci'nus** (ăt'ȧ·sī'nŭs). Roman poet of 1st century B.C.; wrote satires, didactic verse, and an epic, *Argonautica* or *Argonautae* (adapted from Apollonius of Rhodes).

**Var'rus** (văr'ŭs). = VARUS.

**Var'the·ma** (vär'tā·mä) *or* **Bar'the·ma** (bär'tā·mä), **Lodovico di.** *Lat.* **Var'to·ma'nus** (vär'tō·mā'nŭs) *or* **Ver'to·man'nus** (vûr'tō·măn'ŭs). 16th-century Italian traveler and writer; traveled through Egypt, countries of southwestern China, India, islands of Malay Archipelago, and as far east as the Moluccas (1502–07), returning home via Cape of Good Hope. Author of *Itinerario di Lodovico di Varthema Bolognese* (1st pub., 1510; 1st Eng. trans., 1576–77).

**Var'us** (vâr'ŭs), **Publius Quintilius.** d. 9 A.D. Roman general; consul (13 B.C.); governor of Syria (6–4 B.C.); commanded Roman army in Germany (6–9 A.D.); committed suicide when his army was destroyed by Germans under Arminius in battle of Teutoburger Wald (9 A.D.).

**Va'sa'** (vä'sȧ'). Name of dynasty of Swedish kings (1521–1720) derived from that of family estate in Uppland, region around Uppsala. Taken by Gustavus Eriksson, son of Eric Johansson, king (1523–60) as Gustavus (I) Vasa and founder of dynasty; his successors were: Eric XIV, John III, Sigismund, Charles IX, Gustavus (II) Adolphus, and Christina (ruled 1632–54). Next four sovereigns of Vasa dynasty are sometimes termed the Palatinate branch (1654–1720) because Charles (X) Gustavus, its first member, was son of count palatine of Zweibrücken and Catherine, sister of Gustavus Adolphus; his successors were Charles XI, Charles XII, and Ulrika Eleonora. The Holstein-Gottorp line (1751–1818) is considered by some as part of the Vasa dynasty. See OLDENBURG and *Table* (*in Appendix*) for SWEDEN.

**Va·sa'ri** (vä·zä'rē), **Giorgio. 1511–1574.** Italian painter, architect, and art historian; considered founder of modern art history and criticism; studied painting under Andrea del Sarto and Michelangelo; protégé of the de' Medici; known esp. for his series of biographies of Italian artists from Cimabue to Michelangelo, *Vite de' Più Eccelenti Pittori, Scultori, ed Architetti Italiani* (1550), chief source book for history of Italian Renaissance artists.

**Vasco da Gama.** See GAMA.

**Vas'con·cel'los** (vȧsh'kōN·sĕ'lo͞osh), **Joaquim Antônio da Fon·se'ca e** (thȧ fōN·sā'kȧ ē). 1849–1936. Portuguese critic; professor of German, Oporto (1883 ff.). His wife, **Karoline Wilhelma Mi'cha·e'lis de Vasconcellos** [mĭ'kä·ā'lĭs thĕ] (1851–1925), b. Berlin, was a Romance philologist; known esp. for studies of language and literature of Iberian Peninsula.

**Va'sey** (vā'zĭ), **George.** 1822–1893. Physician and botanist, b. near Scarborough, Eng.; to U.S. in infancy; botanist on Major Powell's exploring expedition to Colorado (1868); botanist, U.S. Dept. of Agriculture, in charge of U.S. National Herbarium, Washington, D.C. (from 1872). Specialized in study of grasses. Vasey grass is so named in his honor.

**Vash'ti** (văsh'tī). In Bible, queen of Ahasuerus (*q.v.*).

**Vasili.** Russian form of BASIL.

**Vas'mer** (fäs'mẽr), **Max.** 1886– . German Slavic scholar; author of *Griechisch-Slawische Studien*, etc.

**Vásquez de Ayllón, Lucas.** See AYLLÓN.

**Vásquez de Coronado.** See CORONADO.

**Vass** (vŏsh), **József.** 1877–1930. Hungarian Roman Catholic clergyman and statesman; a leader of the Christian National party; after collapse of Bolshevist regime of Béla Kun, aided in political reconstruction.

**Vas'sar** (văs'ẽr), **Matthew.** 1792–1868. Brewer and merchant, b. in Norfolk, Eng.; to America (1796) and settled in Dutchess County, N.Y.; operated brewery in Poughkeepsie, N.Y.; founded (1861) and endowed a college for women, later named Vassar College in his honor, at Poughkeepsie, N.Y.

**Vassili,** Count **Paul.** See Princess Catherine RADZIWILL.

**Vatatzes.** See *John III Vatatzes* (page 784).

**Va'ter** (fä'tẽr), **Abraham.** 1684–1751. German physician and anatomist.

**Vat'tel** (fät'ĕl), **Emmerich von.** 1714–1767. Swiss-born jurist in Saxon service; chief work, *Droit des Gens* (1758).

**Va·tu'tin** (vŭ·to͞o'tyĭn), **Nikolai.** 1900?–1944. Russian army officer; served in World War; army commander in Ukraine (1941); colonel general, commander of southwestern front forces in Stalingrad victory (1942); commander of 1st Ukrainian army; took part in capture of Kharkov and Kiev (1943), liberated Ukraine, advanced into Poland (1943–44); retired for ill health.

**Vau'ban'** (vō'bäN'), Marquis **de. Sébastien Le Pres'tre** (lẽ prâ'tr'). 1633–1707. French military engineer; in successive wars from 1655 conducted sieges of Gravelines, Ypres, Audenarde, Lille, Maastricht, Valenciennes, Cambrai, Luxemburg, Mons, Namur; commissary general of fortifications (1678); marshal of France (1703).

**Vau'caire'** (vō'kâr'), **Maurice.** 1865–1918. French writer; author of verse, novels, plays, and a number of librettos.

**Vau'can'son'** (vō'käN'sôN'), **Jacques de.** 1709–1782. French inventor of many improvements in silk-weaving machinery.

**Vau'cher'** (vō'shā'), **Jean Pierre Étienne.** 1763–1841. Swiss botanist; credited with discovering the function of spores.

**Vau'dreuil'** (vō'drû'y'; *Angl.* vô·droi'). Name of prominent French and French-Canadian family, including: **Philippe de Ri'gaud'** (dẽ rē'gō'), Marquis **de Vaudreuil** (1643–1725), commander of French army in Canada, and governor of Canada (1703). His son **Louis Philippe de Rigaud,** Comte **de Vaudreuil** (1691–1763), officer in French navy, serving in Canadian waters (to 1725); distinguished himself in battle off Cape Finisterre (1747); promoted chief of squadron (1753). Louis Philippe's brother **Pierre François de Rigaud,** Marquis **de Vaudreuil-Ca'va'gnal'** [-kȧ'vȧ'nyȧl'] (1698–1765), last French governor of Canada (1755–60); capitulated to the English (1760). Louis Philippe's son **Louis Philippe de Rigaud,** Marquis **de Vaudreuil** (1724–1802), French naval officer; served in wars against England (1778–83); commanded one division of de Grasse's fleet at Yorktown (1781); commanded detachment that protected French royal family from the mob at Versailles (Oct. 5–6, 1789); an émigré in England (1791–1800); retired and pensioned by Napoleon I. Another son of Louis Philippe, **Joseph Hyacinthe de Vaudreuil** (1740–1817), was an army officer; field marshal (1780); took part under comte d'Artois in siege of Gibraltar (1782); émigré in England (1789–99); created peer of France (1814) and commissioned lieutenant general; later, appointed governor of the Louvre.

**Vau'ge·las'** (vōzh'lä'), Seigneur **de. Claude Fa'vre** (fȧ'vr'). Baron **de Pé'roges'** (dẽ pā'rôzh'). 1595–1650. French philologist; author of *Remarques sur la Langue Française* (1647), a treatise credited with doing much to fix usage and purify French diction.

**Vaughan** (vôn), **Benjamin.** 1751–1835. British diplomat and colonist, b. in Jamaica. Acquainted with Benjamin Franklin, sided with American colonists, Irish conspirators, and French revolutionists; unofficially promoted conciliation in Anglo-American peace negotiations (1782). Accompanied his brother to America (1796) and settled at Hallowell, Maine; carried on agricultural experiments; corresponded with first six presidents of the U.S. and published collections of Franklin's works; left portions of his library to Harvard and Bowdoin.

**Vaughan, Henry.** 1622–1695. British mystic poet, known as **the Sil'u·rist** [sĭl'ū·rĭst] (because born in South Wales, home of the ancient Silures). Practiced medicine in South Wales. Author of sacred poems, *Silex*

*Scintillans* (first part 1650, second 1655), including the well-known poem *They are all gone into the world of light!;* nonreligious poems, *Olor Iscanus* (1651), *Thalia Rediviva* (1678); and translations.

**Vaughan, Herbert Alfred.** 1832–1903. English Roman Catholic prelate; bishop of Salford (1872–92); archbishop of Westminster (1892–1903); cardinal (1893); active in social and educational programs; largely responsible for passage of Education Act (1902) whereby British denominational schools became state-supported; built Westminster Cathedral. One of his brothers, **Roger William Bede** (1834–1883), entered Benedictine order (1854); archbishop of Sydney, Australia (1877–83); biographer of Thomas Aquinas. Another brother, **Bernard John** (1847–1922), was a Jesuit priest and popular preacher in Manchester for 16 years, and in London (from 1899). The youngest brother, **John Stephen** (1853–1925), was canon of Westminster (1898); bishop of Salford (1909–25).

**Vaughan, Hilda.** See under Charles Langbridge MORGAN.

**Vaughan, Robert.** 1795–1868. English Congregational clergyman and historian; editor of *British Quarterly* (1845–65); author of histories of Stuart and Commonwealth periods.

**Vaughan, William.** 1577–1641. British poet, b. South Wales; a colonizer of Newfoundland; purchased tract of land in Newfoundland (1616), to which he sent settlers (1617–18); author of *The Golden Grove* (a severe criticism of the manners of the age, 1600), *The Spirit of Detraction* (a mystical work, 1611), and *The Golden Fleece* (an allegory upon his colony, 1626).

**Vaughan Wil′liams** (vôn′ wĭl′yămz), **Ralph.** 1872–1958. English composer; among his compositions are *London Symphony, Sea Symphony, Flos Campi, Sir John in Love, Dona Nobis Pacem, Five Variants on Dives and Lazarus,* etc.

**Vau′que·lin′** (vō′klăN′), **Louis Nicolas.** 1763–1829. French chemist; assistant to Fourcroy (1783–91), and succeeded him on the faculty of medicine, Paris (1809); codiscoverer, with P. J. Robiquet, of asparagine.

**Vauquelin de La Fres′naye′** (dẽ lȧ frā′nā′), **Jean.** Sieur **des Yve′teaux′** (dā-zēv′tō′). 1536–?1608. French poet; admirer of Ronsard; author of *Foresteries, Idylles, Épîtres,* and five books of satires.

**Vau′tier′** (vō′tyā′), **Benjamin.** 1829–1898. Swiss genre painter and illustrator in Düsseldorf; his paintings, dealing chiefly with the life of the Swiss and Black Forest peasants, include *Peasants at Cards, The First Dancing Lesson, Toast to the Bride, Prodigal Son.*

**Vau′ve·nargues′** (vōv′nȧrg′), Marquis **de. Luc de Cla′piers′** (dẽ klȧ′pyā′). 1715–1747. French soldier and moralist; in army (1733–43); remembered for his *Introduction à la Connaissance de l'Esprit Humain,* with appended *Réflexions* and *Maximes.*

**Vaux** (vôks), **Calvert.** 1824–1895. Landscape architect, b. in London; assisted Andrew Jackson Downing (1850–52) with U.S. Capitol grounds, and Frederick Law Olmsted with various New York and Chicago parks.

**Vaux, Mary Morris.** See under Charles D. WALCOTT.

**Vaux, Roberts.** 1786–1836. American philanthropist, b. Philadelphia; interested himself in prison reform; instrumental in establishment (1826) of house of refuge for juvenile delinquents; had part in creation of Frankford Asylum for the Insane, and of institution for instruction of the blind, and another for the deaf and dumb; justice, court of common pleas (1835).

**Vaux** (vôz; vôks; vōks), **Thomas.** 2d Baron **Vaux of Har′row·den** (hăr′ō·dĕn; -d'n). 1510–1556. English poet; emulator of Wyatt and Surrey and contributor of two poems to *Tottel's Miscellany* (1557), and poems of chivalric love and religious poems to a popular anthology, *The Paradyse of Daynty Deuises* (1576). His granddaughter **Anne Vaux** (fl. 1605–1635), zealous Roman Catholic, harbored conspirators in the Gunpowder Plot.

**Va′zov** (vȧ′zôf), **Ivan.** 1850–1921. Bulgarian poet and novelist.

**Vázquez de Ayllón, Lucas.** See AYLLÓN.

**Vé′ber′** (vā′bâr′), **Jean.** 1864–1928. French painter and engraver. His brother **Pierre** (1869–1942), author of many comedies and novels and collaborator in many plays.

**Veb′len** (vĕb′lĕn), **Oswald.** 1880–1960. American mathematician; professor, Princeton (1910–32) and in the Institute for Advanced Study, Princeton (from 1932).

**Veblen, Thorstein Bunde.** 1857–1929. American social scientist, b. Cato, Wis. On teaching staff, U. of Chicago (1892–1906), Stanford (1906–09), U. of Missouri (1911–18), New School for Social Research, New York City (1919). His writings contain many keen criticisms of established social and economic institutions. Author of *The Theory of the Leisure Class* (1899), *The Theory of Business Enterprise* (1904), *Imperial Germany and the Industrial Revolution* (1915), *The Higher Learning in America* (1918), *The Vested Interests and the State of the Industrial Arts* (1919), *Absentee Ownership and Business Enterprise in Recent Times* (1923), etc.

**Vec′chi** (vĕk′kē), **Orazio.** 1550?–1605. Italian composer; known esp. for his *L'Amfiparnasso: Commedia Armonica,* a scenic representation in which individual roles are assumed by quartets or quintets singing in the style of the madrigal.

**Vecchio, Palma.** See Jacopo PALMA.

**Ve·cel′li** (vā·chĕl′lē) *or* **Ve·cel′lio** (-lyō). Family of Italian painters including **Tiziano Vecelli** (= TITIAN), his brother **Francesco** (1475–1560), cousin **Cesare** (1521?–1601), son **Orazio** (1528?–1575), also **Marco Vecelli,** *sometimes called* **Marco di Ti·zia′no** [dē tē·tsyä′nō] (1545–?1616), brought up by Titian, with whom he later collaborated, and Marco's son **Tiziano,** *called* **Il Ti′zia·nel′lo** [ēl tē′tsyä·nĕl′lō] (1579–after 1645).

**Ved′der** (vĕd′ẽr), **Elihu.** 1836–1923. American painter and illustrator; studio in Rome (from 1867). His *Minerva* and the accompanying murals are on walls of the Library of Congress, Washington, D.C.; his *The Lost Mind* and *African Sentinel* are in the Metropolitan Museum of Art, New York City. The best of his illustration work is found in his illustrations for the *Rubáiyát of Omar Khayyám.*

**Veen** (vān), **Otto van.** 1556–?1629. Dutch Biblical and historical painter, teacher of Rubens; worked chiefly at Antwerp and Brussels.

**Vefik Pasha.** See AHMED VEFIK PASHA.

**Vega, Garcilaso de la.** See GARCILASO DE LA VEGA.

**Ve′ga** (vā′gä), **Lope de.** *In full* **Lope Félix de Vega Car′pio** (kär′pyō). *Called* **El Fé′nix de Es·pa′ña** (ĕl fā′nēks thā ās·pä′nyä). *Pseudonyms* **El Li′cen·cia′do To·mé′ de Bur·guil′los** (ĕl lē′thān·thyä′thō tō·mā′ thā bōōr·gē′lyōs) *and* **Gabriel Pa′de·co·pe′o** (pä′thā-kō·pā′ō). 1562–1635. Spanish dramatic poet and founder of the Spanish national drama, b. Madrid. Banished from Castile (1588) as result of duel; served in Spanish Armada (1588); secretary to duke of Alba at Alba de Tormes; returned to Madrid (1596). Ordained priest (1614) after death of second wife; apostolic prothonotary (1616); doctor of theology (1627). Reputed author of about 1800 plays and several hundred autos and entremeses of which 431 plays and 50 autos are extant; developed comic character called the gracioso.

Works include the plays *El Castigo sin Venganza*, *Porfiar Hasta Morir*, *La Estrella de Sevilla*, *El Mejor Alcalde el Rey*, *El Acero de Madrid*, *La Noche Toledana*, *El Perro del Hortelano*, *El Hermano Honrado*, *Juana de Nápoles*, *Si No Vieran las Mujeres*, *El Príncipe Perfecto*, *Los Tellos de Meneses*, *La Boba para Otros y Discreta para Sí*, *La Fuente Ovejuna*, and *Los Hechos de Garcilaso de la Vega;* poems, as *La Hermosura de Angélica* (continuation of Ariosto's *Orlando Furioso;* 1602), *La Dragontea* (epic attacking Sir Francis Drake; 1598), *San Isidro* (1599), *Rimas* (collection of sonnets; 1602), and *Jerusalén Conquistada* (epic after Tasso; 1609); the prose-verse pastoral *Arcadia* (1598); prose romances, as *El Peregrino en Su Patria* (1604) and *Dorotea* (1632); and prose tales, as *Guzmán el Bravo* and *La Desdicha por la Honra.*

**Vega y Vargas, Sebastián Garcilaso de la.** See under GARCILASO DE LA VEGA (1539?–1616).

**Ve·ge'ti·us** (vḗ·jē'shĭ·ŭs; -shŭs). *In full* **Flavius Vegetius Re·na'tus** (rḗ·nā'tŭs). Roman writer of 4th century A.D.; author of a treatise on military science, *Epitoma Rei Militaris.*

**Ve'gi·us** (vē'jĭ·ŭs), **Mapheus.** *Ital.* **Maffeo Ve'gio** (vâ'jō). 1406–1458. Italian humanist.

**Veh'se** (fā'zĕ), **Karl Eduard.** 1802–1870. German historian; for political reasons, banished from Prussia; lived in Switzerland, Italy, Saxony; author of *Geschichte der Deutschen Höfe seit der Reformation* (48 vols., 1851–59).

**Veidt** (fīt), **Conrad.** 1893–1943. Actor, b. in Germany; character actor on Berlin stage (1913); motion-picture star in Hollywood and in England (since 1917); naturalized British subject (1938).

**Veiller, Bayard.** 1869?–1943. American journalist and playwright; esp. successful with melodramas, including *Within the Law* (1918), *The Thirteenth Chair* (1916; with Will Irwin), *Trial of Mary Dugan* (1928); author also of motion-picture scenarios.

**Vein'te·mil'la** (vĕ'ēn·tâ·mē'yä), **Ignacio de.** 1830–1909. Ecuadorian dictator and general, b. Cuenca. Led Liberal revolt that overthrew President Antonio Borrero; provisional president of Ecuador (1876–78); elected president (1878–83); abolished concordat with church of Rome (1878); deposed (1883) during a civil war and exiled.

**Veit** (fīt), **Philipp.** 1793–1877. Grandson of Moses Mendelssohn and son of Dorothea Schlegel. German religious painter, of Jewish parentage; converted to Catholicism (1809). A founder and member of the Nazarenes, Rome (1815–30); director of the Städel Art Institute, Frankfurt am Main (1830–43). Works include *Triumph of Religion*, *Immaculate Conception*, *Two Marys at the Sepulcher*, murals for Mainz cathedral, portraits, etc.

**Veitch** (vēch), **John.** 1829–1894. Scottish philosopher and historical writer; author of memoirs of Dugald Stewart and Sir W. Hamilton, poems, essays on Scottish border poetry, and *Dualism and Monism* (1895).

**Veitch, William.** 1794–1885. Scottish classical scholar; collaborated with Liddell and Scott on later editions of their *Greek-English Lexicon.*

**Ve'la** (vā'lä), **Vincenzo.** 1822–1891. Italian sculptor; among his works are a marble statue *Spartacus*, decorative figures for the tomb of Donizetti, *Primavera*, *Dying Napoleon*, and statues of Charles Albert and Cavour.

**Ve·las'co** (vâ·läs'kō), **Luis de.** 1500?–1564. Spanish viceroy of Mexico (1550–64); emancipated great numbers of native Indians; equipped López de Legazpe's expedition to Philippines. His son **Luis** (1539–?1617) was viceroy of Mexico (1590–95; 1607–11) and of Peru (1596–1604).

**Velásquez.** See VELÁZQUEZ.

**Ve·lás'quez** (vâ·läs'kāth; -kās) *or* **Ve·láz'quez** (vâ·läth'kāth; -läs'kās), **Diego.** 1465?–?1522. Spanish soldier and administrator; to Hispaniola with Columbus (1493); sent to conquer Cuba (1511); governor of Cuba (1511–22); founded Santiago (1514) and Havana (1515). Sent out expeditions under Córdoba (1517), Grijalva (1518), and Cortes (1519). Ordered Cortes to return (1520); on his refusal sent Narváez to arrest him (see NARVÁEZ).

**Ve·láz'quez** (vâ·läth'kāth) *or* **Ve·lás'quez** (vâ·läs'-), **Diego Ro·drí'guez de Sil'va y** (rō·thrē'gāth thā sēl'vä ē). 1599–1660. Spanish painter, b. Seville; leading painter of the Spanish school. To Madrid (1622); appointed court painter (1623); quartermaster general of king's household (1652 ff.). Considered leading representative of naturalism in painting. Works include genre and historical paintings, as *Water Carrier of Seville*, *Breakfast*, *Los Borrachos* (also called *Bacchus*), *Boar Hunt*, and *Surrender of Breda* (also called *Las Lanzas*); portraits, as of Philip IV, Infanta María, Olivares; Marianna of Austria; and court jesters, dwarfs, idiots, and beggars; equestrian portraits of Philip IV, the queen, Prince Balthazar, and Olivares, religious paintings, as *Adoration of the Magi*, *Christ in the House of Martha*, *Crucifixion*, and *Christ and the Pilgrims of Emmaus;* and mythological works, as *Mars*, *Mercury and Argus*, and *Venus with a Mirror.*

**Vel'de, van de** (vän dĕ vĕl'dĕ). A family of Dutch painters, including: **Esaias** (1590?–1630), painter of landscapes and of military and carnival scenes; his brothers **Jan** (1593?–?1641), whose works include portraits, historical and genre scenes, landscapes, and other views, and **Willem** (1611–1693), draftsman and painter, esp. of marines and naval battles, resident in London (from 1673) as court painter; Willem's sons **Willem** (1633–1707), painter, esp. of marines and Anglo-Dutch sea battles, resident in London (from 1673) and court painter (from 1677), and **Adriaen** (1636?–1672), painter of landscapes with animals and figures and of mythological and Biblical scenes, and etcher.

**Vel'de** (vĕl'dĕ), **Hen'ry** (hăng'rē) **van de.** 1863–1957. Belgian architect and craftsman; leader of a modern movement in architecture and arts; author of *Vom Neuen Stil* (1907), *Le Nouveau, son Apport à l'Architecture et aux Industries d'Art* (1929), etc.

**Vé'lez de Gue·va'ra** (vā'lāth thā gā·vä'rä), **Luis.** 1579–1644. Spanish lawyer, and author of plays, poetry, and novels, as *El Diablo Cojuelo*, source for Lesage's *Diable Boiteux.*

**Vel·le'ius Pa·ter'cu·lus** (vĕ·lē'yŭs pȧ·tûr'kŭ·lŭs), **Marcus,** *or perhaps* **Gaius.** c. 19 B.C.–30 A.D. Roman author of an abridgment of Roman history (two books).

**Ven'a·ble** (vĕn'ȧ·b'l), **Charles Scott.** 1827–1900. American Confederate army officer and educator, b. in Prince Edward County, Va.; aide-de-camp on staff of Gen. Robert E. Lee (1862–65); professor of mathematics, U. of Virginia (from 1865). His son **Francis Preston** (1856–1934) was professor of chemistry, U. of North Carolina (1881–1900); president, U. of North Carolina (1900–14); again professor of chemistry there (from 1914).

**Venantius Fortunatus.** See FORTUNATUS.

**Venceslas.** Variant of WENCESLAUS.

**Ven'dôme'** (väɴ'dōm'). Family of French nobility, holding countship of Vendôme from about 10th century. Vendôme made duchy (1515) by Francis I and bestowed on Charles de Bourbon; Charles's son Anthony de Bourbon married Jeanne of Navarre and was father of Henry IV of France who granted duchy to his natural son, César de Bourbon, Duc de Vendôme. Other sons of Charles de Bourbon were Cardinal Charles de Bourbon (see BOURBON) and Louis I de Bourbon, Prince de Condé (see CONDÉ).

**Vendôme,** Duc **de. César de Bour'bon'** (dĕ bōōr'bôN'). 1594–1665. French nobleman and soldier; natural son of Henri IV of France and Gabrielle d'Estrées; legitimized (1595); made governor of Brittany (1598); m. daughter of duc de Mercœur (*q.v.*); distinguished himself in war against Hugenots (1621); involved in intrigues against Richelieu and Mazarin; commanded royal army (1653) and recaptured Libourne and Bordeaux. His son **Louis de Vendôme** (1612–1669), *known also as* Duc **de Mer'cœur'** (dĕ mĕr'kûr'), married Laure Mancini, niece of Mazarin (1651); after her death, took orders (1657); appointed cardinal (1667). For César's younger son, François de Vendôme, see Duc de BEAUFORT. A son of Louis, **Louis Joseph,** Duc **de Vendôme,** *known also as* Duc **de Pen'thiè'vre** [dĕ pāN'tyâ'vr'] (1654–1712), was a French soldier; commander in Catalonia; created marshal of France; captured Barcelona (1697); commanded army against Prince Eugene of Savoy at Luzzara (1702); defeated at Oudenarde (1708); victorious over Austrians in Spain at Villaviciosa (1710). Louis Joseph's brother **Philippe de Vendôme,** *known as* **Le Pri'eur'** (lĕ prē'ûr') **de Vendôme** (1655–1727), was also a soldier; entered (1666) Knights of Malta (Hospitalers); grand prieur of France (1678), field marshal (1691), lieutenant general (1693); disgraced for inaction at battle of Cassano.

**Ve'ne·zia'no** (vā'nâ·tsyä'nô), **Agostino.** *Real name* **Agostino de' Mu'si** (dâ mōō'zē). 1490?–?1540. Italian copperplate engraver, b. at Venice; pupil of Raphael; engraved after works of Raphael, Giulio Romano, Michelangelo, Bandinelli, and the antique.

**Ven'ge·rov** (vyān'gyĕ·rôf), **Semën Afanasievich.** 1855–1920. Russian literary critic and historian.

**Ve'ni·ze'los** (vâ'nyĕ·zâ'lôs), **Eleutherios.** 1864–1936. Greek statesman, b. on the island of Crete. Called to Athens as political adviser (1909) and effected peaceable settlement between king and opposition leaders; appointed premier of Greece (Oct., 1910). Instrumental in organizing Balkan League (1912) and after First Balkan War (1912) in forming alliance against Bulgaria which participated in Second Balkan War (1913). During World War, vigorously championed cause of Allied Powers; when opposed by the pro-German king resigned premiership (Mar. 6, 1915). Aided Koundouriotes (*q.v.*) in establishing so-called provisional government of national defense at Salonika (1916), which received official recognition from Allied Powers. After forced abdication of King Constantine (1917), Venizelos formed a ministry (June 27, 1917) and took Greece into the war on the side of the Allies. Was successful in safeguarding Greek interests at Peace Conference in Paris (1919). Resigned as premier (Nov. 16, 1920); held premiership again for short time (1924); advocated formation of a republic (approved by plebiscite, Apr. 14, 1924). Again premier of Greece (1928–32; 1933). Leader of opposition to Tsaldares government (from 1933); instigated unsuccessful military and naval revolt (March, 1935); forced to flee into exile. During absence from Greece, courtmartialed and condemned to death; received amnesty on return of King George II to Greek throne (Nov., 1935).

**Venn** (vĕn), **Henry.** 1725–1797. English clergyman; rector of Yelling (1771–97); author of religious works, including *The Compleat Duty of Man* (1763).

**Venn, John.** 1834–1923. English logician and man of letters; teacher of logic and author of *The Logic of Chance* (1866), *Symbolic Logic* (1881), and *The Principles of Empirical Logic* (1889).

**Ven'ning** (vĕn'ĭng), Sir **Walter King.** 1882–1964. British army officer; served in World War (1914–18), in India (1929–34), at War Office (1934–38); quartermaster general (1939 ff.); appointed director-general of British supply mission in U.S. (Oct., 1942).

**Venosta,** Marchese **Emilio Visconti-.** See VISCONTI-VENOSTA.

**Venth** (vĕnt), **Carl.** 1860–1938. Musician, b. Cologne, Ger.; to U.S. (1880), naturalized (1885); concertmaster at Metropolitan Opera House, N.Y. (1884); conductor of Brooklyn Symphony Orchestra and, in Texas, of Dallas Symphony Orchestra (1911–13) and Fort Worth Symphony Orchestra (from 1913).

**Ven·tu'ri** (vān·tōō'rē), **Adolfo.** 1856–1941. Italian art historian and critic; author of *Storia dell'Arte Italiana* (19 vols., 1901 ff., still unfinished).

**Venturi, G. B.** 1746–1822. Italian physicist credited with first observing the phenomenon upon which the operation of the Venturi tube (later invented by Clemens Herschel) depends.

**Ve'ra** (vâ'rä), **Augusto.** 1813–1885. Italian Hegelian philosopher; introduced Hegelian philosophy into France and Italy. Works, in French, Italian, and English, include *Problème de la Certitude* (1845), *Philosophie de la Nature de Hegel* (3 vols., 1863–65), *Problema dell'Assoluto* (4 parts, 1872–82), etc.

**Ve'ra·ci'ni** (vā'rä·chē'nē), **Francesco Maria.** 1685?–1750. Italian violinist, and composer of violin sonatas, violin concertos, and symphonies for string orchestra.

**Veragua,** Duke of. See *Luis Columbus*, under Christopher COLUMBUS.

**Ver'beck** (vûr'bĕk), **Guido Herman Fridolin.** 1830–1898. Missionary in Japan, b. in the Netherlands; to U.S. (1852); missionary of Dutch Reformed Church, in Japan (1859–98). His son **William** (1861–1930) was head of Manlius School, then St. Johns School, at Manlius, N.Y. (from 1888); officer in New York National Guard, and adjutant general (1910–12).

**Ver·biest'** (vĕr·bēst'), **Ferdinand.** 1623–1688. Flemish Jesuit missionary and astronomer in China; head of imperial astronomical bureau, Peking (1669); instrumental in determining boundary between China and Russia.

**Ver'boeck·ho'ven** (vĕr'bōōk·hō'vĕn), **Eugène Joseph.** 1798–1881. Belgian painter; best known for his portrayal of animals.

**Ver·brug'ghen** (*Angl.* vĕr·brŏŏg'ĕn), **Hen'ri** (äN'rē). 1873–1934. Violinist and conductor, b. Brussels, Belgium; head, New South Wales Conservatory of Music, Sydney, Australia (1915–22); conductor, Minneapolis, Minn., Symphony Orchestra (1923–31).

**Ver'cel'** (vĕr'sĕl'), **Roger.** 1894–1957. French novelist; served in the World War; author of *Capitaine Conan* (1934; awarded Goncourt prize), the scene of which is laid in the Balkans just after the armistice.

**Ver'cin·get'o·rix** (vûr'sĭn·jĕt'ō·rĭks). Gallic chief of the Arverni; leader of rebellion which initiated Gallic War; after preliminary successes, was besieged by Caesar in Alesia and forced to surrender (52 B.C.); taken to Rome and exhibited in Caesar's triumph (46), then executed.

**Ver'da·guer'** (vĕr'thä·gĕr'), **Mosén Jacinto.** 1845–1902. Catalan poet; author of the epics *La Atlántida* (1876) and *Canigó* (1886), and many lyrics.

**Ver'di** (vār'dē; *Angl.* vâr'-), **Giuseppe.** 1813–1901. Italian operatic composer, b. Roncole, Parma. Among his works are the operas *Oberto* (1839), *Nabuccodonosor* (1842), *I Lombardi* (1843), *Ernani* (1844), *Giovanna d'Arco* (1845), *La Battaglia di Legnano* (1849), *Stiffelio* (1850), *Rigoletto* (1851), *Il Trovatore* (1852), *La Traviata* (1853), *Les Vêpres Siciliennes* (1855), *Simone Boccanegra* (1857), *Un Ballo in Maschera* (1859), *La Forza* *del Destino* (1862), *Don Carlos* (1867), *Aïda* (1871), *Otello* (1887), and *Falstaff* (1893); also the dramatic cantata *Inno delle Nazioni* (1862), the *Manzoni Requiem* (1874), and sacred music.

**Ver′dy′ du Ver′nois′** (vĕr′dē′ dü vĕr′nwȧ′), **Julius von.** 1832–1910. Prussian general, and writer on military strategy.

**Vere, de** (dĕ vēr′). Family name of the earls of **Ox′ford** [ŏks′fērd] (1st creation, 1142–1703), including: **Robert** (1170?–1221), 3d earl, one of the 25 executors of Magna Charta. **Robert** (1362–1392), 9th earl, Duke of Ireland, bosom friend of Richard II; granted regal powers in Ireland (1385); accused (1387) of treason by Thomas of Woodstock, Duke of Gloucester, at a time when the young king's authority had been suspended; escaped with Richard's connivance, fled northward, raised an army, and marched toward London; deserted by his troops and routed by enemy lords at Radcot Bridge, near Witney; escaped to Continent; attainted (1388); killed in a boar hunt. **John** (1443–1513), 13th earl, a Lancastrian; aided in restoration of Henry VI (1470); escaped from Barnet field to France (1471); fought for Henry Tudor (Henry VII) at Bosworth (1485) and was restored to his title, estates, and hereditary chamberlainship; led van of royal army at Stoke (1486); commanded expedition in Picardy (1492); defeated Cornish rebels (1497). **Edward** (1550–1604), 17th earl, *known as* Lord **Bul′beck** [bo͝ol′bĕk] (until 1562); courtier and lyric poet; ward of Lord Burghley; angered Queen Elizabeth by dueling and by insulting Sir Philip Sidney (1579); ran through his estates; sat as judge in trial of Mary, Queen of Scots; fought against Spanish Armada (1588); author of miscellanies of verse (1576–1600); held by so-called Oxfordian school to have been author of Shakespeare's dramatic works. The house became extinct on death of Aubrey, 20th earl, in 1703.

**Vere,** Sir **Aubrey de** and **Aubrey Thomas de.** See DE VERE.

**Vere** (vēr), Sir **Francis.** 1560–1609. English soldier, grandson of John de Vere, 15th Earl of Oxford. In command of English troops in Low Countries (1589); served in Cádiz expedition (1596); aided in victory at Turnhout (1598), Nieuport (1600), and defense of Ostend (1601–02). His brother **Sir Horace** (1565–1635), Baron Vere of Tilbury, took over command from Sir Francis (1604); in Thirty Years' War was forced to surrender at Mannheim to Tilly (1622).

**Vérendrye,** Sieur **de La.** See LA VÉRENDRYE.

**Ve·re·sa′ev** (vyĕ·ryĕ·sȧ′yĕf), **Vikenti.** *Pseudonym of* **Vikenti Vikentievich Smi·do′vich** (smyĭ·dô′vyĭch). 1867–1943. Russian physician and writer; author of *Memoirs of a Physician* (1901) and the novels *Astray* (1895), *At the Front* (1907), *The Deadlock* (1923), and *The End of Andrei Ivanovich.*

**Ve·re·shcha′gin** (vyĕ·ryĕ·shchȧ′gyĭn), **Vasili Vasilievich.** 1842–1904. Russian genre and battle painter; served in the Caucasus and in Russo-Turkish War (1877–78). Among his paintings is a cycle of twenty canvases from history of India, twenty from the Russian campaign in Turkestan, and twenty from the Russo-Turkish War. Sailed with the Russian fleet (1904) against Japan and was killed in explosion of battleship *Petropavlovsk* in harbor of Port Arthur (Apr. 13, 1904).

**Ver′ga** (vār′gä), **Giovanni.** 1840–1922. Italian writer; with Capuana, leader of Sicilian realists; known particularly for portrayals of Sicilian life and customs. Among his works are *I Malavoglia* (1881), *Mastro Don Gesnaldo* (1889), *Pane Nero* (1902), and short stories, as *Cavalleria Rusticana* (later dramatized; libretto for Mascagni's opera).

**Vergara,** Prince of. See Baldomero ESPARTERO.

**Ver′gennes′** (vĕr′zhĕn′), Comte **de. Charles Gra′vier′** (grȧ′vyā′). 1717–1787. French statesman; ambassador to Turkey (1755–68), Sweden (1771–74); minister of foreign affairs under Louis XVI (1774–87); policy of hatred toward England led to support of American colonies in their War of Independence; formed offensive and defensive alliance with new republic (1777–81); negotiated Treaty of Paris (1783).

**Ver′gil** *or* **Vir′gil** (vûr′jĭl). *Full Latin name* **Publius Ver·gil′i·us Ma′ro** (vûr·jĭl′ĭ·ŭs mā′rō). 70–19 B.C. Roman poet, b. near Mantua, in Cisalpine Gaul. Studied in Rome; friend of Horace; enjoyed patronage of Maecenas, Asinius Pollio, and Octavius (Augustus). Chief works, *Eclogues*, or *Bucolics* (pastoral poems), *Georgics* (didactic poems glorifying peasant life and duties), and *The Aeneid* (great epic built around legend of wanderings of Aeneas after fall of Troy and his settlement in Latium).

**Ver′gil** (vûr′jĭl), **Pol′y·dore** (pŏl′ĭ·dōr). 1470?–?1555. Italian-English ecclesiastic and historian. Sent by Pope Alexander VI to England as subcollector of Peter's pence (1502–15); naturalized (1510); edited Gildas (1525); published *Anglicae Historiae Libri XXVI*, an accurate history in elegant Latin, esp. valuable for Henry VII's reign, but with strong bias against Wolsey (1534)

**Ver′gniaud′** (vĕr′nyō′), **Pierre Victurnien.** 1753–1793. French lawyer and Revolutionary politician; president of the Legislative Assembly (1791); member of the National Convention, a leader of the Girondists; renowned for his oratory; guillotined (Oct. 31, 1793).

**Ver·hae′ren** (vĕr·hȧ′rĕn), **Émile.** 1855–1916. Belgian poet; one of the editors of *La Jeune Belgique;* identified with the symbolist group of poets. Author of *Les Flamandes* (1883), *Les Moines* (1886), *Les Soirs* (1887), *Les Débâcles* (1888), *Les Flambeaux Noirs* (1890), *Les Campagnes Hallucinées* (1893), *Les Heures Claires* (1896), *Les Aubes* (1898), *Tendresses Premières* (1904), *Les Ailes Rouges de la Guerre* (1916), and a few dramas.

**Ver–Huell′** *or* **Ver·huel′** (vĕr·hûl′), **Carel Hendrik.** 1760–1845. Admiral, b. in the Netherlands; rear admiral in Dutch navy (1803); defeated English at Walcheren; entered French service (1810) and fought against his own countrymen (1813–14); naturalized French citizen (1814); in chamber of peers (1819).

**Ve·ris′si·mo** (vĕ·rē′sē·mo͞o), **Erico.** 1905– . Brazilian novelist, b. in Cruz Alta (Rio Grande do Sul); resident of Porto Alegre, the setting of his novels; author of books for children, a fictionalized life of Joan of Arc (1935), and novels including *Música ao Longe* (1934), *Caminhos Cruzados* (1935; transl. as *Crossroads*, 1943), *Olhai os Lírios do Campo* (1938), *Saga* (1940).

**Ver′jus′** (vĕr′zhü′), **Louis.** Sieur, *later* Comte, **de Cré′cy′** (dē krā′sē′). 1629–1709. French diplomat; represented France at the signing of the Truce of Ratisbon (1684) and the Treaty of Ryswick (1697).

**Ver′laine′** (vĕr′lān′), **Paul.** 1844–1896. French poet, b. at Metz; at first associated with the Parnassians; later known as a leader among the symbolists; an originator of decadents (see also S. MALLARMÉ and C. BAUDELAIRE). Among his works are *Poèmes Saturniens* (1866), *Fêtes Galantes* (1869), *La Bonne Chanson* (1870), *Sagesse* (1881), *Les Poètes Maudits* (1884), *Jadis et Naguère* (1884), *Femmes* (1890), *Bonheur* (1891), *Élégies* (1893), *Mort* (1895).

**Ver·meer′** (vĕr·mār′), **Jan.** *Known also as* **Jan van der Meer van Delft** (vän dĕr mār′ vän dĕlft′). 1632–1675. Dutch genre, landscape, and portrait painter and colorist; painted about forty known pieces, mostly life-size figures and interiors, including *The Procuress, Christ with Mary and Martha, Diana at Her Toilet, The*

*Milk Woman*, *The Lace Maker*, and *Young Girl Asleep*.

**Vermeer van Haarlem, Jan.** See Jan van der MEER.

**Vermigli, Pietro Martire.** See PETER MARTYR.

**Verne** (vĕrn), **Jules.** 1828–1905. French writer, originally of plays and librettos, later of enormously popular semiscientific romances of adventure, in which many later technological developments are forecast with remarkable accuracy. Among his most widely read stories are *Cinq Semaines en Ballon* (1863), *Voyage au Centre de la Terre* (1864), *Vingt Mille Lieues sous les Mers* (1870), *Le Tour du Monde en Quatre-Vingts Jours* (1873), *Michel Strogoff* (1876), *César Cascabel* (1890), *Le Sphinx des Glaces* (1897).

**Ver′ner** (vĕr′nẽr), **Karl Adolph.** 1846–1896. Danish philologist; professor of Slavic philology, Copenhagen (from 1888); developed and revised Grimm's law, explaining certain apparent exceptions to this law by a statement (now known as *Verner's law*) propounded in his *Eine Ausnahme der Ersten Lautverschiebung*, on the position of the accent and the relations between Indo-European and early Teutonic consonants.

**Ver′net′** (vĕr′nĕ′). Family of French painters, including: **Antoine** (1689–1753); his son **Claude Joseph**, *known as* **Joseph** (1714–1789), painter of marines and landscapes; Joseph's son **Antoine Charles Horace**, *known as* **Carle** (1758–1835), historical and animal painter, who accompanied Napoleon to Italy and made many sketches later used in battle pictures (*Bataille de Marengo*, etc.); Carle's son **Horace** (1789–1863), painter of battle and genre scenes, chiefly of Arab life (after 1836); Carle's grandson **Émile Charles Hippolyte Ver′net′-Le·comte′** [-lẽ·kôɴt′] (1821–1900), painter of landscapes and genre scenes.

**Verneuil,** Marquise **de.** See Catherine Henriette de Balzac d'ENTRAGUES.

**Ver′nier′** (vĕr′nyā′; *Angl.* vûr′nĭ·ẽr), **Pierre.** 1580–1637. French mathematician; devised a scale (vernier, or vernier scale) for making accurate measurements of linear or angular magnitudes, described in his *Construction, Usage et Propriétés du Quadrant Nouveau de Mathématiques* (1631). Cf. Pedro NUNES.

**Ver′non** (vûr′nŭn). Original family name of HARCOURT family.

**Vernon, Edward.** 1684–1757. English admiral; nicknamed "Old Grog" [grŏg] (because he wore a grogram cloak in foul weather). Stormed Porto Bello (1739); failed in Cartagena expedition (1741); first to issue rum diluted with water, "grog" (1740); cashiered (1746) for pamphlets attacking admiralty.

**Vernon, Richard.** 1726–1800. English sportsman; called "Father of the Turf"; a founder of the Jockey Club.

**Vé′ron′** (vā′rôɴ′), **Louis Désiré.** *Known as* **Doc′teur′ Véron** (dôk′tûr′). 1798–1867. French journalist; founded *La Revue de Paris* (1829) and revived *Le Constitutionnel*, a journal in opposition to the government (1835).

**Ve·ro′na** (vȧ·rō′nä), **Guido.** *Pen name* **Guido da** (dä) **Verona.** 1881–1939. Italian novelist; known for realistic and erotic treatment of postwar social life.

**Ve′ro·ne′se** (vā′rō·nā′sȧ), **Paolo.** *Real name* **Paolo Ca·glia′ri** *or* **Ca·lia′ri** (kä·lyä′rē). 1528–1588. Italian painter of Venetian school; called "Painter of Pageants"; b. Verona. Employed chiefly at Venice (c. 1555 ff.); known esp. as a decorative artist; succeeded Giorgione and Titian as chief master of Venetian school. Works include *Temptation of St. Anthony*, *Coronation of the Virgin*, *Deposition from the Cross*, frescoes in Library of St. Mark at Venice, *Marriage at Cana*, *Supper at Emmaus*, *Venice Enthroned*, *Apotheosis of Venice*, and easel paintings, as *Holy Family*, *Raising of Lazarus*, and *Mars and Venus*. For his brother and sons, see CAGLIARI.

**Ve·ron′i·ca** (vĕ·rŏn′ĭ·kȧ), Saint. According to legend, a woman of Jerusalem who, as Christ bore the cross, wiped his face with a cloth which miraculously retained the imprint of his countenance.

**Ver′rall** (vĕr′ôl), **Arthur Woollgar.** 1851–1912. English classical scholar; editor of Aeschylus and Euripides.

**Ver′ra·za′no** (vār′rä·tsä′nō) *or* **Ver′raz·za′no** (-rät-tsä′-), **Giovanni da.** 1485?–?1528. Florentine navigator; explored coast of North America (1524) from Cape Fear northward, probably as far as Cape Breton, discovering New York and Narragansett bays.

**Ver′res** (vĕr′ēz), **Gaius.** d. 43 B.C. Roman politician; proquaestor in Cilicia under praetor Cn. Cornelius Dolabella (80 B.C.); praetor (74) and governor of Sicily. Made himself notorious (74–70) by extortion, excessive taxation, pillage, and disregard of civil rights of Roman citizens; brought to trial (70) and prosecuted by Cicero; went into exile to escape conviction. Executed by order of Mark Antony.

**Ver′rill** (vĕr′ĭl), **Addison Emery.** 1839–1926. American zoologist; professor, Yale (1864–1907); also, in charge of scientific work of U.S. Commission of Fish and Fisheries in southern New England (1871–87). Editor of zoological definitions for *Webster's International Dictionary* (1890). His son **Alpheus Hyatt** (1871–1954), naturalist, explorer, and author, made explorations in the West Indies, Guiana, Central America, and Panama (1889–1920); rediscovered supposedly extinct insectivorous mammal *Solenodon paradoxus* in Santo Domingo (1907); in Central America discovered remains of unknown prehistoric culture (1924–27); conducted explorations in Peru and Bolivia (1928–32); author of many adventure books for boys and books on natural history.

**Ver′ri·o** (vĕr′ĭ·ō), **An·to′ni·o** (ăn·tō′nĭ·ō; -nyō). 1639?–1707. Italian decorative painter in England; employed by Charles II and James II to decorate Windsor Castle, by William III and Queen Anne to decorate Hampton Court.

**Ver′ri·us Flac′cus** (vĕr′ĭ·ŭs flăk′ŭs), **Marcus.** fl. late 1st and early 2d century A.D. Roman grammarian and teacher; a freedman, called to court by Augustus to tutor his grandsons Gaius and Lucius; chief work, *De Verborum Significatu*.

**Ver·roc′chio** (vâr·rôk′kyō) *or* **Ve·roc′chio** (vâ·rôk′-), **Andrea del.** *Real name* **Andrea di Mi·che′le Cio′ne** (dē mē·kā′lā chō′nā). 1435–1488. Florentine sculptor and painter; after Donatello, leading sculptor of Tuscan school. His sculptures include the bronze statue *David*, sarcophagus of Piero de' Medici and brother Giovanni, *Christ and St. Thomas*, reliefs, and an equestrian statue of General Bartolommeo Colleoni (completed by A. Leopardi). His paintings include *Baptism of Christ*, *Madonna and Child*, and *Unknown Young Woman*.

**Ver·schaf′felt** (vẽr·skäf′ĕlt), **Pierre Antoine.** *Known also by Italian name of* **Pietro Fiam·min′go** (fyäm-mēng′gō), *i.e.* Peter the Fleming. 1710–1793. Flemish sculptor; executed marble statue of Pope Benedict XIV, in Rome (1737), and many sculptures in other Italian cities.

**Vertomannus.** See Lodovico di VARTHEMA.

**Ver′tot′** (vĕr′tō′), Abbé **de. René Au′bert′** (ō′bâr′). 1655–1735. French historian; historiographer of the Knights of Malta, or Hospitalers (1715); author of *Histoire des Révolutions de Portugal* (1689), *Histoire des Révolutions de la République Romaine* (1719), etc.

**Ver′tue** (vûr′tū), **George.** 1684–1756. English engraver and antiquary; his collected materials for history of art in England were purchased and used by Horace Walpole in *Anecdotes of Painting in England*.

**Verulam,** Baron. See Francis BACON.

**Ve'rus** (vēr'ŭs), **Annius.** See MARCUS AURELIUS.

**Verus, Lucius Aurelius.** *Orig. name* **Lucius Ceionius Com'mo·dus** (kŏm'ō·dŭs). 130–169. Roman emperor (161–169), colleague of Marcus Aurelius. Adopted as son by Emperor Hadrian (136) and later (138) by Emperor Antoninus Pius along with Marcus Aurelius; after death of emperor (161), made coruler with tribunitian and proconsular powers; led expedition to Parthia (162); took part in wars in northern Italy and Pannonia (167–168).

**Ver·wey'** (vĕr·vī'), **Albert.** 1865–1937. Dutch poet and critic, leader in "1880 movement" for revival of Dutch literature; author of lyric and dramatic poetry, literary essays and critical works, translations of Dante's *Divina Commedia* (1923) and of Sidney and Shelley.

**Ver·worn'** (fĕr·vōrn'), **Max.** 1863–1921. German physiologist; made researches on the physiology of cells.

**Ver'y** (vĕr'ĭ; vēr'ĭ), **Edward Wilson.** 1847–1910. American naval officer (1867–85) and ordnance expert; inventor (1877) of Very's night signals (Very lights).

**Very, Frank Washington.** 1852–1927. American astronomer, b. Salem, Mass.; chief assistant for 10 years to Professor Langley. Invented device to record accurate quantitative measurements of Fraunhofer lines in the solar spectrum; confirmed existence of water vapor and oxygen in atmosphere of Mars; advanced theory of the origin of matter; proved that the white nebulae are galaxies.

**Very, Jones.** 1813–1880. American transcendentalist poet and essayist, b. Salem, Mass. Composed religious sonnets which he alleged were communicated to him directly by the Holy Ghost (1837); was persuaded by friends to spend a month in an insane asylum (1838). Under patronage of Ralph Waldo Emerson, published *Essays and Poems* (1839), extravagantly praised by Channing, Bryant, and Emerson.

**Ve·sa'li·us** (vē·sā'lĭ·ŭs; -lyŭs; vē·zā'-), **An'dre·as** (ăn'drē·ăs). 1514–1564. Belgian anatomist, b. Brussels; one of the first to dissect the human body to study anatomy; lectured at Padua, Basel, Pisa, and Bologna. Made pilgrimage to Holy Land (1564) in fulfillment of condition of the commutation of his death sentence by the Inquisition for dissecting the human body. Author of *De Humani Corporis Fabrica* (7 books, and an *Epitome*, 1543).

**Ves'cy** *or* **Ves'ci** (vĕs'ĭ), **Eustace de.** Baron **Vesci.** 1170?–1216. English nobleman, one of the twenty-five executors of the Magna Charta.

**Ve'sey** (vē'zĭ), **Elizabeth,** *nee* **Vesey.** 1715?–1791. Irish leader of the bluestocking circle in London and Bath; m. Agmondesham Vesey, Irish M.P. and member of Dr. Johnson's club; her literary parties attained high repute (1780–84).

**Vesey, William.** 1674–1746. American Anglican clergyman; rector of Trinity Church, New York City (1697–1746). Vesey Street in New York is named after him.

**Ves·pa'sian** (vĕs·pā'zhăn; -zhĭ·ăn). *Lat.* **Titus Flavius Sabinus Ves·pa'si·a'nus** (vĕs·pā'zhĭ·ā'nŭs). 9–79 A.D. First of the Flavian emperors of Rome (69–79), b. at Reate in Latium. His father of humble origin, his mother, Vespasia Polla, sister of a senator. Held various public offices (military tribune, quaestor, aedile, and praetor); sent by Claudius in command of legion in Germany and later (43) in Britain; conquered Isle of Wight; consul (51); proconsul of Africa (63) under Nero; sent to conduct war against Jews (66); won favor of soldiers, who chose him emperor at Alexandria (69) as against Otho and Vitellius; left son Titus (*q.v.*) in command in Judea; reign marked by suppression of revolt of Batavians (69–70), triumph with Titus (71), beginning of erection of Colosseum, and conquests in Britain by Agricola (78–79).

**Ves·puc'ci** (vĕs·po͞o'chē; *Ital.* vā·spo͞ot'chē), **A'me·ri'go** (ä'mā·rē'gō). *Lat.* **A·mer'i·cus Ves·pu'cius** (ȧ·mĕr'ĭ·kŭs vĕs·pū'shŭs). 1454–1512. Italian navigator, b. Florence. Took part in several early voyages to New World (1497, 1499, 1501, 1503); claimed to have been member of expedition of Ojeda (1499–1500) that first discovered mainland; in last two voyages (1505, 1507), explored Darien region; made maps; appointed pilot major of Spain (1508); his accounts published (1507) by Martin Waldseemüller, German geographer, who suggested new lands be named "America."

**Vesque von Pütt'ling·en** (vĕsk' fōn püt'lĭng·ĕn), **Johann.** *Pseudonym* **J. Ho'ven** (hō'fĕn). 1803–1883. Austrian composer of operas, including *Turandot* (1838), *Jeanne d'Arc* (1840), *Der Liebeszauber* (1845), *Der Lustige Rath* (1852), etc.

**Vestris,** Madame. See *Lucia Elizabeth Mathews*, under Charles MATHEWS.

**Vetch** (vĕch), **Samuel.** 1668–1732. Soldier and trader in America, b. Edinburgh, Scotland; to New York (1699) and Boston (c. 1702); proposed to British authorities plan for ousting French from America; was empowered (1709) to raise troops for the purpose; conquered Port Royal and Acadia, renamed Annapolis Royal and Nova Scotia (1710), and was appointed military governor of Nova Scotia, and later (1715–17) civil governor.

**Vetsera,** Baroness **Marie.** See RUDOLF of Hapsburg (1858–1889).

**Vet'ter·li** (fĕt'ĕr·lē), **Friedrich.** 1822–1882. Swiss inventor; invented a magazine gun adopted by Switzerland (1868) and Italy (1870).

**Vet·to'ri** (vāt·tō'rē), **Piero.** *Lat.* **Petrus Vic·to'ri·us** (vĭk·tō'rĭ·ŭs). 1499–1585. Italian humanist; known esp. for editions of the classics, including Cicero's letters (*Epistulae*), Euripides's *Electra*, Aristotle's *Ethics*.

**Veturia.** Mother of Coriolanus (*q.v.*).

**Veuil'lot'** (vû'yō'), **Louis François.** 1813–1883. French journalist; editor of *L'Univers Religieux* (1843 ff.); author of *Çà et Là* (1859), *Le Pape et la Diplomatie* (1861), *Satires* (1863), *Les Odeurs de Paris* (1866), *Œuvres Poétiques* (1878), etc.

**Ve·zin'** (vē·zăn'; -zăN'; vē'zĭn), **Hermann.** 1829–1910. American actor, b. Philadelphia; acted in London (from 1852) except for one tour (1857–58) of U.S. Among his leading roles were Hamlet, Jaques in *As You Like It*, Sir Giles Overreach in *A New Way to Pay Old Debts*, Ford in *The Merry Wives of Windsor*. His wife (m. 1863), **Jane Elizabeth,** *nee* **Thom'son** [tŏm's'n] (1827–1902), m. Charles Frederick Young (1846; divorced 1862), was an actress on the English stage, appearing many times with Vezin.

**Via·da'na** (vyä·dä'nä), **Lodovico.** *Real name* **Lodovico Gros'si** (grôs'sē). 1564–1627. Italian composer; works include *Cento Concerti Ecclesiastici*, a cappella masses, requiems, motets, canzonets, and madrigals.

**Via'la'** (vyȧ'lȧ'), **Pierre.** 1859–1936. French viticulturist; instrumental in introducing grafts of American vines on French stocks after attack of the phylloxera in France.

**Vian'ney'** (vyȧ'nā'), Saint **Jean Baptiste Marie.** 1786–1859. Known as the "Curé of Ars" (ȧrs). Roman Catholic priest; famed for purity of life and intensity of faith, resulting in making Ars a place of pilgrimage during his life and after his death; beatified by Pius X (1905) and canonized by Pius XI (1925).

**Viar'dot'** (vyȧr'dō'), **Louis.** 1800–1883. French journalist; on staff of *Le Globe*, *Le Siècle*, etc.; aided George Sand and Pierre Leroux in founding *Revue Indépendante*

(1841); manager of Théâtre-Italien (1838–41); author of *Histoire des Arabes et des Maures d'Espagne* (1832), *Merveilles de la Peinture* (1868), etc. He married **Michelle Pauline Gar·cí'a** [gär·thē'ä] (1821–1910), mezzo-soprano operatic singer and actress. See also her father Manuel García, and her sister Malibran.

**Vi'a·tor** (vī'ȧ·tôr), Saint. *Fr.* **Via'teur'** (vyȧ'tûr'). 360?–389. Confessor and lector of Lyons cathedral; retired to penitential solitudes in Egypt with St. Just, bishop of Lyons (381); his name taken by the Roman Catholic order of Clerics of St. Viator, founded 1835.

**Viau** (vyō), **Théophile de.** 1590–1626. French poet; condemned to death for participation in the writing and publication of *Parnasse Satirique* (1622), but sentence commuted to banishment; author also of the tragedy *Pyrame et Thisbé* (1617), *Histoire Comique, Traité de l'Immortalité de l'Âme,* etc.

**Viaud, Louis Marie Julien.** See Pierre Loti.

**Vi'bert'** (vē'bâr'), **Jehan Georges.** 1840–1902. French painter, esp. of genre scenes.

**Vi'caire'** (vē'kâr'), **Gabriel.** 1848–1900. French poet; identified with the Parnassians.

**Vi·cen'te** (vė·sāɴ'tĕ), **Gil.** 1470?–?1536. Portuguese writer; regarded as a founder of Portuguese drama. Works include autos, as *Auto da Alma,* tragicomedies, as *Amadís de Gaula* and *Templo de Apolo,* comedies, and farces, as *O Fidalgo Pobre* and *O Viúvo.*

**Vi'cen·ti'no** (vē'chān·tē'nō), **Nicola.** 1511–1572. Italian composer and theorist; attempted to revive chromatic and enharmonic Greek modes; invented the archicembalo and archiorgano, musical instruments fitted with keyboards suitable for rendering Greek modes.

**Vick'ers** (vĭk'ẽrz), **Edward.** 1804–1897. English steel manufacturer. Joint founder (1828), with his father-in-law, George Naylor, of steel-manufacturing company for making tools, files, etc., at Sheffield and Wadsley, which became (1867) Vickers' Sons & Co. and developed (1888) into armament factory; absorbed (1896) into Vickers' Sons and Maxim (see Sir Hiram S. Maxim). Firm merged (1927) with Sir W. G. Armstrong, Whitworth and Co., Ltd., to form Vickers Armstrong, Ltd. See also William G. Armstrong.

**Vi'co** (vē'kō), **Giovanni Battista.** 1668–1744. Italian philosopher; known esp. for his *Principi di una Scienza Nuova d'intorno alla Comune Natura delle Nazioni* (1725, 1730, 1744), an attempt to discover and organize laws common to the evolution of all society.

**Vic'tor** (vĭk'tẽr). Name of three popes (see *Table of Popes,* Nos. 14, 152, 158) and two antipopes:

**Victor I,** Saint. Pope (bishop of Rome; 189–198); disputed with bishops of Asia over Easter usage.

**Victor II.** *Real name* **Geb'hard** (gĕp'härt). 1018–1057. Pope (1055–57), b. in Swabia. Became an adviser of Emperor Henry III; during pontificate, reformed the clergy; aided by Hildebrand; acted as regent for Henry IV.

**Victor III.** *Real name* **Dau·fe'ri·us** (dô·fẽr'ĭ·ŭs). 1027–1087. Pope (1086–87), b. Benevento. Abbot, under the name **Des'i·de'ri·us** (dĕs'ĭ·dẽr'ĭ·ŭs), in charge of the cloister Monte Cassino (1057–86); effected an alliance (1078) between Robert Guiscard and Pope Gregory VII; convened synod at Capua (1087); sent army to Tunis (1087), which defeated Saracens; excommunicated the antipope Clement III; esp. famous as abbot of Monte Cassino during its golden age, causing some 70 books to be copied.

*Antipopes:* **Victor IV.** *Real name* **Gregorio Con'ti** (kōn'tē). Antipope (1138) in opposition to Innocent II.

**Victor IV.** *Real name* **Oc·ta'vi·us** (ŏk·tā'vĭ·ŭs). Antipope (1159–64) in opposition to Alexander III.

**Vic'tor'** (vēk'tôr') *or* **Vic'tor'-Per'rin'** (-pĕ'răɴ'), **Claude.** *Really* **Claude Victor Perrin.** Duc **de Bel'lune'** (dē bĕ'lün'). 1766–1841. French soldier in Revolutionary, Napoleonic, and Restoration armies; distinguished himself in battle of Marengo (1800). Created marshal of France for his service in victory of Friedland (1807); created duke after Treaty of Tilsit. Commanded army corps in Spain in Peninsular War (1808 ff.); defeated by Wellington at Talavera (1809); served in Russia, Germany, and France (1812–14). Remained loyal to Bourbons during Hundred Days; commissioned major general of royal guard (1815). Presiding officer at trial of officers accused of treason during Hundred Days; voted for death of Ney. Minister of war (1821–23).

**Vic'tor** (vĭk'tẽr), **Orville James.** 1827–1910. American author and publisher; originated (c. 1860) idea of the "dime novel," a story of adventure intended to reach a wide market and to be sold profitably for ten cents; organized, trained, and directed corps of writers to turn out rapidly the kind of book he wanted.

**Vic'tor Am'a·de'us** (vĭk'tẽr ăm'ȧ·dē'ŭs). *Ital.* **Vit·to'rio A'me·de'o** (vėt·tô'ryō ä'mā·dâ'ō). *Also* **Am'e·de'us** (ăm'ė·dē'ŭs). Name of three dukes of Savoy:

**Victor Amadeus I.** 1587–1637. Son of Charles Emmanuel I. Duke (1630–37).

**Victor Amadeus II.** 1666–1732. Son of Charles Emmanuel II. Duke (1675–1732). At first under control of Louis XIV; defeated at Chiari (1701) by his cousin Prince Eugene of Savoy in command of army of alliance against France; joined the alliance (1704), but the French under Louis Joseph, Duc de Vendôme, controlled Savoy (1702–06); aided Eugene, who gained great victory at Turin (1706); by Treaty of Utrecht (1713) made king of Sicily (1713–20); ceded Sicily to Austria (1720) and received Sardinia in exchange. King of Sardinia (1720–30) as Victor Amadeus I. Abdicated (1730).

**Victor Amadeus III.** 1726–1796. Son of Charles Emmanuel III. Duke (1773–96); king of Sardinia (1773–96) as Victor Amadeus II. Joined First Coalition against France (1792–93); lost Nice, Savoy, and parts of Piedmont.

**Victor Em·man'u·el** (ĕ·măn'ū·ĕl; ĭ-). *Ital.* **Vit·to'rio E'ma·nue'le** (vėt·tô'ryō ā'mä·nwâ'lā). Name of three Italian rulers:

**Victor Emmanuel I.** 1759–1824. Son of Victor Amadeus III, Duke of Savoy, b. Turin. Duke of Aosta. Led Sardinian forces against French (1792–96); king of Sardinia (1802–21) on abdication of brother Charles Emmanuel IV; all dominions except Sardinia in possession of French (1802–14); kingdom restored (1814–15). Abdicated (1821) in favor of brother Charles Felix.

**Victor Emmanuel II.** 1820–1878. Son of Charles Albert, King of Sardinia, b. Turin. Took part in war against Austria (1848–49); after defeat at Novara (1849), became king of Sardinia (1849–61) on abdication of his father; chose d'Azeglio and Cavour as ministers to help in strengthening kingdom and bringing about unification of Italy; guided by Cavour, joined England and France in Crimean War (1854–56); formed closer alliance with France (1856–59); Austria defeated in brief war (1859–61); Lombardy, Modena, Parma, Two Sicilies, and other states annexed (1860–61), but Nice and Savoy ceded to France (1861); assumed title of 1st "King of Italy" (1861–78); joined Prussia against Austria (1866) and, as a result, acquired Venetia; Rome freed of French troops (1870) and made capital. His four children were: Humbert I, who succeeded him as king (1878–1900); Clotilde, m. Napoleon Joseph Charles Paul Bonaparte; Amadeus, King of Spain (1870–73); Maria Pia, m. King Louis of Portugal.

**Victor Emmanuel III.** 1869–1947. Son of Humbert I, b. Naples. Prince of Naples. Entered army (1887); m. (1896) Princess Elena, daughter of Prince (later King) Nicholas of Montenegro. King of Italy (1900–46). Active leader in World War (1915–19); territory of Italy increased: two districts added to Venezia by Treaty of St. Germain (1919), Zara and Adriatic islands annexed by Treaty of Rapallo (1920), Fiume added by Agreement of Rome (1924). Assumed title of "Emperor of Ethiopia" (1936) and "King of Albania" (1939); by concordat (1929), full independent sovereignty of Vatican City recognized; with rise of Fascism (from 1922), authority declined and Italy became totalitarian until Fascist party was dissolved (1943); abdicated (1946) and went into exile in Portugal, being succeeded by his son Humbert II (*q.v.*).

**Vic·to′ri·a** (vĭk·tō′rĭ·ȧ). *In full* **Al′ex·an·dri′na** (ăl′ĕg·zăn·drē′nȧ; ăl′ĭg-) **Victoria.** 1819–1901. Queen of the United Kingdom of Great Britain and Ireland (1837–1901), and (from 1876) empress of India, of the house of Hanover, b. London. Only child of George III's fourth son, Edward, Duke of Kent (*q.v.*), and Victoria Mary Louisa, daughter of duke of Saxe-Coburg. Educ. under tutorship of Fräulein Louise Lehzen; received fatherly counsel from mother's brother Leopold I, King of the Belgians. Succeeded uncle King William IV (June 20, 1837). First years as queen passed under guidance of Lord Melbourne, Whig prime minister. m. Prince Albert of Saxe-Coburg-Gotha (Feb., 1840); accepted guidance in state policies (from c. 1841) of Albert and his adviser Baron Stockmar. Achieved measure of personal authority by requiring of Lord Palmerston that he inform her of every proposed course of action and that he modify in no way measures once sanctioned by her (1850). During Crimean War, founded Victoria Cross, first conferred in 1857. Conferred title of Prince Consort on her husband, Albert (1857). Approved abolition of East India Co. and reorganization of Indian government (1858). Dissuaded Prussia from intervening in Franco-Sardinian war (1858). After death of prince consort, endeavored to carry on political duties as she believed he would have had her do. Used personal influence in passage of Disraeli's Reform Act (1867); accepted Irish Disestablishment Act and aided in its passage through House of Lords (1869). Welcomed Disraeli as prime minister (1874); accepted title of Empress of India (1876). Celebrated her golden jubilee (1887) and her diamond jubilee (1897). Supported vigorous prosecution of Boer War (1899), and passage of Australian Commonwealth bill (1900). At time of her death, recognized as symbolizing a new conception of British monarchy and a unified empire. Supervised preparation of a biography of the prince consort (1867, 1874–80). Author of *Leaves from the Journal of our Life in the Highlands* (1868), *More Leaves* (1883). Volumes of her letters appeared in 1907 and 1926–27.

**Vic·to′ri·a** (vĭk·tō′rĭ·ȧ; *Span.* vĕk·tō′ryä). *In full* **Victoria Eu·ge′ni·a** (ū·jē′nĭ·ȧ) **Jul′ia** (jōōl′yȧ) **E′na** (ē′nȧ). 1887–1969. Daughter of Prince Henry Maurice of Battenberg, b. at Balmoral; m. Alfonso XIII (1906); queen of Spain (1906–31).

**Vic·to′ria** (vĕk·tō′ryä), **Guadalupe.** *Real name* **Manuel Félix Fer·nán′dez** (fĕr·nän′dās). 1789–1843. Mexican soldier and political leader, b. Durango. Joined revolution under Hidalgo (1810); adhered to plan of Iguala (1821), but joined Santa Anna (1823) in revolt against Iturbide. First president of republic (1824–29).

**Vic·to′ria** (vĕk·tō′ryä), **Tomás Luis de.** *Ital.* **Tommaso Lodovico da Vit·to′ria** (dä vĕt·tô′ryä). 1540?–1611. Spanish composer of the Roman school; friend and follower of Palestrina; maestro di cappella, Collegium Germanicum (at Rome), later, Church of Sant' Apollinare (Rome); to Madrid (1589 ff.). Works include a notable Requiem for Empress Mary, masses, motets, hymns, psalms, and magnificats.

**Vic·to′ri·a Ad′e·laide Mar′y Lou·ise′** (vĭk·tō′rĭ·ȧ ăd′ĕ·lād mâr′ĭ lōō·ēz′). 1840–1901. Princess royal of Great Britain, and German empress, oldest child of Queen Victoria and Prince Albert, m. (1858) Prince Frederick William of Prussia (later became emperor, three months before death, 1888) and by him became mother of William, later Kaiser William II (*q.v.*); consistently opposed policies of Bismarck; resided at her country place, Friedrichshof, near Kronberg (from 1888).

**Vic′to·ri′nus** (vĭk′tô·rī′nŭs). *Also known as* **Vic·to′ri·us of Aq′ui·ta′ni·a** (vĭk·tō′rĭ·ŭs; ăk′wĭ·tā′nĭ·ȧ, -tān′yȧ). Astronomer; commissioned (c. 465 A.D.) by Pope Hilarius to correct the calendar and fix the date of Easter; combined Metonic cycle (19 years) with solar cycle (28 years) and thus derived a period of 532 Julian years (19 × 28), at end of which the Easter moon would come in same month and on same day of week. Dionysius Exiguus (*q.v.*) made a few changes and gave his name to the new period (Dionysian period).

**Victorinus, Gaius Marius.** Latin writer of 4th century A.D., b. in Africa; taught rhetoric in Rome; in later life, converted to Christianity; author of works on grammar, philology, and esp. philosophy.

**Victorius, Petrus.** See Piero VETTORI.

**Vi·cu′ña–Mac·ken′na** (vē·kōō′nyä·mä·kĕ′nä), **Benjamín.** 1831–1886. Chilean historian and politician; in exile (1851–56); journalist (1856–58) and again exiled (1858–63); unsuccessful candidate for presidency (1875); wrote works on history of Chile.

**Vi′da** (vē′dä), **Marco Girolamo.** 1480?–1566. Italian poet; bishop of Alba (1532 ff.); known particularly for his Latin epic *Christias* (6 books, 1535).

**Vi′dal′** (vē′dȧl′), **Paul Antonin.** 1863–1931. French conductor and composer, esp. of ballet music, orchestral suites, motets, and incidental music for pantomimes and marionette shows.

**Vidal, Peire.** fl. 1175–1215. Provençal troubadour; accompanied Richard Cœur de Lion on Third Crusade (1189–92).

**Vi′di′** *or* **Vi′die′** (vē′dē′), **Lucien.** 1805–1866. French scientist; inventor of the aneroid barometer (1844).

**Vi′docq′** (vē′dôk′), **François Eugène.** 1775–1857. French police officer and adventurer; rose to be chief of a small, specialized detective force in Paris (1809–27; 1832). Organized a daring robbery and was himself detailed to investigate it; his part in the robbery was discovered and he was dismissed from the police force. Died in poverty and obscurity.

**Vid′ya·sa′gar** (vĭd′yä·sä′gôr), **Is′war** (ēsh′vôr) **Chan′dra** (chŏn′drô). 1820–1891. Bengali writer and social reformer; obtained (1839) title of *Vidyasagar* (*i.e.* "ocean of learning"); appointed (1850) head pundit of Fort William Coll.; active in cause of female education and in establishing aided schools; secured legislation allowing remarriage of Hindu widows (1855–56); simplified method of learning Sanskrit. Author of *The Exile of Sita* (1862), etc.

**Vie′big** (fē′bĭĸ), **Clara.** 1860–1952. German novelist and short-story writer, of the naturalistic school; m. (1896) Fritz Cohn; author of *Kinder der Eifel* (1897), *Die Frau mit den Tausend Kindern* (1929), *Insel der Hoffnung* (1933), etc.

**Vieille** (vyâ′y′), **Paul Marie Eugène.** 1854–1934. French engineer, b. Paris; inventor (1887) of a smokeless powder (poudre B) adopted by the French army.

**Viei'ra** (vyā'ē·rȧ), **Antônio.** 1608–1697. Portuguese Jesuit preacher and missionary; to Brazil (1652) as director of missions in Maranhão; deported to Portugal by colonists (1661); imprisoned by the Inquisition (1665–67); to Rome (1670–75) as preacher; retired to Brazil (1681 ff.); Jesuit provincial, Brazil (1688 ff.). His works, among the earliest of Portuguese prose, include sermons (15 vols., 1679–1748), *Esperanças de Portugal,* etc.

**Vie'le** (vē'lĕ), **Egbert Lu'do·vic'us** (lū'dō·vĭk'ŭs). 1825–1902. American soldier and civil engineer, b. Waterford, N.Y.; grad. U.S.M.A., West Point (1847); brigadier general of volunteers (Aug., 1861); engaged in capture of Fort Pulaski and Norfolk, Va.; military governor of Norfolk (1862); resigned (1863). His son **Herman Knickerbocker Vie'lé** [vē'lĕ] (1856–1908) was a painter and novelist; author of *The Inn of the Silver Moon* (1900), *The Last of the Knickerbockers* (1901), *Myra of the Pines* (1902), *Random Verse* (1903), *Heartbreak Hill* (1908), and a drama, *The House of Silence* (1906). Another son, **Egbert Ludovicus Vielé,** who changed his name to **Francis Vie'lé–Grif'fin** [-grĭf'ĭn] (1864–1937), was a poet, brought up in France and writing in French; associated with the symbolist movement; author of *Les Cygnes* (1887), *Poèmes et Poésies* (1895), *Sainte Agnès* (1901), *Sapho* (1911), *La Rose au Flot* (1922), *La Sagesse d'Ulysse* (1925), *Saint François aux Poètes* (1927), etc.

**Vier'eck** (vēr'ĕk; *Ger.* fēr'-), **George Sylvester.** 1884–1962. Editor and writer, b. Munich, Ger.; to U.S. (1895); assoc. editor, *Current Literature* (1906–15); editor, *International* (1912–18), *American Monthly* (1914–27); author of *Nineveh and Other Poems* (1907), *Confessions of a Barbarian* (1910), *The Candle and the Flame* (1912), *Glimpses of the Great* (1930), *The Kaiser on Trial* (1937), *The Temptation of Jonathan* (1938), etc. Sentenced to prison (1942) for failure to register as a German agent in U.S.; freed (1947).

**Vier'ge** (vyĕr'hā), **Daniel.** *In full* **Daniel Ur'ra·bie'ta** (ōōr'rä·byā'tä) **Vierge.** 1851–1904. Spanish illustrator, b. Madrid; to Paris (1867); on staff principally of *Monde Illustré* and *La Vie Moderne:* known esp. for pen-and-ink drawings; illustrated works of Hugo, Zola, Poe, Michelet's *Histoire de France* (2d ed., 1878–79), Quevedo y Villegas's *Pablo de Segovia* (pub. 1882), and an English edition of *Don Quixote* (4 vols., 1907).

**Viète** (vyĕt) *or* **Vie'ta'** (vyā'tȧ'; *as Lat.,* vī·ē'tȧ), **François.** Seigneur **de la Bi'go'tière'** (dē lȧ bē'gô'tyâr'). 1540–1603. Called "the Father of Algebra." French mathematician; privy councilor under Henry IV; discovered key and decoded messages sent by Spain to Netherlands. Introduced use of letters for quantities in algebra; devised new solutions for equations of second, third, and fourth degrees; applied algebra to geometry and trigonometry.

**Vi'ë·tor** (fē'ā·tôr), **Wilhelm.** 1850–1918. German philologist; teacher in England (1872–74); professor of English philology, Marburg; founded and edited (1880–85) the *Zeitschrift für Orthographie, Orthoepie, und Sprachphysiologie,* later called *Phonetische Studien* and *Die Neueren Sprachen;* author of *Elemente der Phonetik des Deutschen, Englischen, und Französischen* (1884), *A Shakespeare Phonology* and *A Shakespeare Reader* (1906), *Deutsches Aussprachewörterbuch* (1911), etc.

**Vieus'sens'** (vyû'säɴs'), **Raymond.** 1641–1716. French physician and anatomist; known for his studies of the brain and spinal cord.

**Vieux'temps'** (vyû'täɴ'), **Henri François Joseph.** 1820–1881. Belgian violinist; professor, Brussels Conservatory of Music (1871); composer for the violin.

**Vieuzac, Bertrand Barère de.** See BARÈRE DE VIEUZAC.

**Vi'gée'–Le·brun'** (vē'zhā'lē·brûɴ'), **Marie Anne Élisabeth.** 1755–1842. French painter; m. (1776) J. B. P. Lebrun (*q.v.*); at outbreak of French Revolution, fled from France (1789). Best known for her portraits, including those of the English princesses Adelaide and Victoria, Lady Hamilton as a bacchante, Lord Byron, and more than twenty of Marie Antoinette.

**Vi'ge·land** (vē'gĕ·län), **Adolf Gustav.** 1869–1943. Norwegian sculptor, whose works include busts of Sophus Bugge, Björnson, and Ibsen, and wood engravings.

**Vi'ger'** (vē'zhā'), **De·nis'** (dē·nē') **Ben'ja'min'** (băɴ'zhȧ'măɴ'). 1774–1861. Canadian statesman, b. Montreal; cousin of Louis Joseph Papineau. Sent to England as exponent of French Canadian grievances (1828, 1830); imprisoned in Canada for seditious articles (1838–40); member of Canadian parliament (1841–55) and of ministry (1843–46); virtual prime minister (1843–44).

**Vig'fús·son** (vĭg'fōōs·sŏn), **Guth'bran'dur** (gûth'brän'dēr). *Eng.* **Gud'brand** (gûth'bränd) **Vig'fus·son** (vĭg'fōōs·sŏn). 1827–1889. Icelandic philologist and scholar; in Copenhagen (1849–64); called to London (1864) to complete Richard Cleasby's *Icelandic-English Dictionary* (pub. 1869–74); reader in Scandinavian language and literature, Oxford (from 1884).

**Vigil, Francisco de Paula González.** See GONZÁLEZ VIGIL.

**Vig'i·lan'ti·us** (vĭj'ĭ·lăn'shĭ·ŭs; -shŭs). Gallic Christian presbyter; author of a book (c. 403 A.D.; now lost) against superstitious practices, which drew forth from Jerome a bitter attack, *Contra Vigilantium.*

**Vi·gil'i·us** (vĭ·jĭl'ĭ·ŭs). Pope (538?–555). Papal representative at Constantinople (536–538?); elected under orders of Belisarius; summoned by Justinian to Constantinople (545); at first refused to condemn the Three Chapters, but finally (554) ratified action of Council of Constantinople in condemning them.

**Vigna, Pietro della.** *Or* **Pietro delle Vigne.** See PIETRO DELLA VIGNA.

**Vigne, de** (dē vēn'y'). Family of 19th-century Belgian artists, including: **Ignace** (1767–1840), painter; his three sons: **Félix** (1806–1862), painter, **Édouard** (1808–1866), painter, and **Pierre** (1812–1877), sculptor; Pierre's son **Paul** (1843–1901), sculptor.

**Vi'gné'** (vē'nyā'), **Paul.** *Known as* **Vigné d'Oc'ton'** (dôk'tôɴ'). *Pseudonym* **Gaétan Ker'hou·el'** (kĕ'rwĕl'). 1859–1943. French writer and politician; on editorial staff of *Le Figaro, Le Temps, Revue Bleue, L'Illustration,* etc.; made special study of colonial problems while member of the Chamber of Deputies (1893–1906); author of many novels.

**Vi·gno'la** (vē·nyô'lä), **Giacomo da.** *Real name* **Giacomo Ba·roc'chio** (bä·rôk'kyō) *or* **Ba·roz'zi** (bä·rôt'tsē). 1507–1573. Italian architect, b. Vignola, near Modena. Employed in France under commission from Primaticcio (1541–43), at Bologna (1543–46), and at Rome (1546 ff.); papal architect (1551 ff.); succeeded Michelangelo as chief architect of St. Peter's (1564); known esp. for writings of architectural theory, as *Regola delle Cinque Ordini d'Architettura* (1563) and *Le Due Regole della Prospettiva Prattica* (pub. 1583).

**Vi'gny'** (vē'nyē'), Comte **Alfred Victor de.** 1797–1863. French man of letters; officer in the French army (1814–28). In literature, was an admirer of Victor Hugo and rose to acknowledged position as a leader of the romantic school. Among his many notable works are *Poèmes Antiques et Modernes* (1822), *Éloa, ou la Sœur des Anges* (1824), *Cinq-Mars* (well-known historical novel, 1826), *La Maréchale d'Ancre* (prose drama, 1831), *Chatterton* (romantic play, 1835), and translations into French verse of Shakespeare's *Othello* and *Merchant of Venice.*

**Vi'go** (vē'gō; *Angl.* vī'-), **Joseph Maria Francesco,** *known as* **Francis.** 1747–1836. Italian-born fur trader and pioneer in American northwest; headquarters at St. Louis (1772); gave material aid to George Rogers Clark, esp. in campaign planned at Kaskaskia which ended British influence in the Northwest Territory (1779); resident of Vincennes, Ind. (from c. 1783) and a naturalized U.S. citizen.

**Vi'gou'roux'** (vē'gōō'rōō'), **Fulcran Grégoire.** 1837–1915. French Roman Catholic Biblical scholar.

**Vikelas.** = BIKELAS.

**Vik'ra·ma'dit·ya** (vĭk'rȧ·mä'dĭt·yȧ) [*literally,* "Sun of Power"]. *Also* **Vik'ra·ma** (vĭk'rȧ·mȧ). Title assumed by Chandragupta II (375?–413 A.D.) and Skandagupta (455–480), kings of the Gupta dynasty of India. Name was associated by tradition with an earlier legendary Hindu raja of Ujjain who established an era (Vikrama Era, 57 B.C.) and also with a king called Vikrama (c. 544 A.D.); but recent research has generally accepted the period of the Gupta kings for the era. **Vikramaditya II,** a Chalukya king (733–746), severely defeated the Pallavas (740). **Vikramaditya VI** (1075–1125), of the restored Kalyani branch, brought security to his kingdom.

**Vi'las** (vī'lȧs), **William Freeman.** 1840–1908. American lawyer and politician, b. Chelsea, Vt.; professor of law, U. of Wisconsin (1868–85; 1889–92); U.S. postmaster general (1885–88); U.S. secretary of the interior (1888–89); U.S. senator (1891–97).

**Vil'drac'** (vēl'dräk'), **Charles.** 1882–1971. French poet and playwright.

**Vilhelm.** Swedish form of WILLIAM.

**Vil'la** (vē'yä), **Francisco,** *known as* **Pancho.** *Real name* **Doroteo A·ran'go** (ä·räng'gō). 1877–1923. Mexican cattle thief, bandit, and revolutionary leader; active in Madero revolution (1910) and against Carranza (1914–15). Driven into mountains of northern Mexico; crossed American border and raided Columbus, New Mexico, killing 16 persons and partly burning town (Mar. 9, 1916); pursued by American troops under Pershing, who withdrew when President Carranza objected to their presence on Mexican soil; assassinated.

**Villafranca,** Counts of. Collateral branch of Savoy-Carignan branch of house of Savoy (*q.v.*).

**Vil'la·me·dia'na** (vē'lyä·mȧ·thyä'nä), Conde **de. Juan Tas'sis** (tä'sēs). 1580–1622. Spanish poet; known esp. for vitriolic satires; author also of lyrics, masques, etc.; murdered by Philip IV and Olivares.

**Vil·la'ni** (vēl·lä'nē), **Giovanni.** 1280?–1348. Italian historian; known esp. for his Italian chronicle of the city of Florence (to 1348, 12 books), written from the Guelph point of view and including the history of other countries (hence often called *Chronicon Universale*). His brother **Matteo** (d. about 1363) extended the chronicle to 1363, adding eleven books.

**Villanova, Arnold of.** *Lat.* **Arnaldus Villanovanus.** See ARNAUD DE VILLENEUVE.

**Vil'la·nue'va** (vē'lyä·nwā'vä), **Joaquín Lorenzo de.** 1757–1837. Spanish writer and patriot; court preacher and royal confessor; deputy to the Cortes (1810); imprisoned during restoration (1814–20); re-elected deputy (1820); refused audience as minister plenipotentiary to the Holy See (1822); on restoration of 1823, fled to England, later Ireland.

**Villanueva, Juan de.** 1739–1811. Spanish architect; royal architect to Charles IV; his works include Prado Museum, Madrid astronomical observatory, etc.

**Vil·lard'** (vĭ·lär'; -lärd'), **Henry.** *Orig. name* **Ferdinand Heinrich Gustav Hil'gard** (hĭl'gärt). 1835–1900. Journalist, railroad executive, and capitalist in U.S.; b. Speyer, in Bavaria, Germany; emigrated to U.S. (1853); changed his name to avoid being forced to return and undergo military service; on staff of New York *Staats-Zeitung* (1858); New York *Herald* and New York *Tribune* (1861–63). Decided to establish monopoly of transportation facilities in Pacific northwest (c. 1879); formed a pool and bought control of Northern Pacific Railroad; president of the road (1881–84) and chairman of its board of directors (1888–93). Though he failed in establishing a monopoly, he was for a period most important railroad promoter in U.S. Aided Thomas A. Edison financially, and founded (1889) the Edison General Electric Co. Maintained his interest in journalism by buying control of New York *Evening Post* (1881). His wife (m. 1866), **Helen Frances,** *nee* **Garrison** (1844–1928), only daughter of William Lloyd Garrison (*q.v.*), interested herself in social reform after death of her husband (1900); aided National Association for the Advancement of Colored People; founded and headed Women's Peace Society (1919–28). Their son **Oswald Garrison** (1872–1949), journalist; editor and president, New York *Evening Post* (1897–1918); editor and owner of *The Nation* (1918–32); author of *John Brown* (1910), *Germany Embattled* (1915), *Prophets True and False* (1928), *The German Phoenix* (1933), *Fighting Years* (1939; autobiographical), *Within Germany* (1940), etc.

**Vil'la'ret'** (vē'lȧ'rĕ'), **Étienne Godefroy Timoléon de.** 1854–1931. French general in World War (1914–18).

**Villaret de Joy'euse'** (dē zwȧ'yûz'), **Louis Thomas.** 1750–1812. French fleet commander in battle with English under Lord Howe, off Brest (May 28–June 1, 1794); commander of naval forces in the Santo Domingo expedition (1801–02); governor of Martinique and St. Lucia (1802–09).

**Vil'la·ri** (vēl'lä·rē), **Pasquale.** 1827–1917. Italian historian, statesman, and educator; known esp. for his *Storia di Girolamo Savonarola e de' Suoi Tempi* (2 vols., 1859–61) and *Niccolò Machiavelli e i Suoi Tempi* (3 vols., 1877–82); among his other works are *I Primi Due Secoli della Storia di Firenze* (2 vols., 1894–98) and *Le Invasioni Barbariche in Italia* (1901).

**Vil'lars'** (vē'lȧr'), Duc **Claude Louis Hector de.** 1653–1734. Marshal of France; served in Germany and Flanders (1672–83) under Turenne, Condé, and Luxembourg; also, later, in the wars of the League of Augsburg (1688–97). In chief command of army during War of the Spanish Succession (1701–14); defeated Louis William I of Baden at Friedlingen (1702); made marshal of France (1702); won battle of Höchstädt (1703); suppressed Camisards (1704); conducted successful campaign in Germany (1705–08); was defeated by Marlborough at Malplaquet (1709) but defeated the Dutch at Denain (1712). Member of council of regency under Louis XV.

**Vil·la'te y de la He'ra** (vē·(l)yä'tȧ ē thȧ lä ā'rä), **Blas.** Conde **de Bal'ma·se'da** (thȧ bäl'mä·sā'thä). 1825–1882. Spanish general; three times governor of Cuba (1867, 1870–72, 1875–76); general in command of Spanish forces against Cuban revolutionists (1867–70).

**Vil'la-Ur·ru'tia** (vē'lyä·ōōr·rōō'tyä), Marqués **de. Wenceslao Ra·mí'rez** (rä·mē'rāth). 1850–1933. Spanish statesman and scholar; Spanish plenipotentiary in negotiating Treaty of Paris between U.S. and Spain (1898); ambassador to Austria; minister of foreign affairs (1905); ambassador to England (1906–13), France (1913–14), and Italy (1916–23).

**Villedieu,** Mme. **de.** See Marie Catherine DESJARDINS.

**Vil·le'gas** (vē·lyā'gäs), **Esteban Manuel de.** 1596?–1669. Spanish poet; early abandoned literary career to practice law; author of *Las Eróticas o Amatorias* (a volume of poems in imitation of Anacreon, Horace, and Catullus; 1617) and a translation of Boethius's *De Consolatione Philosophiae* (1665).

**Villegas, José.** 1848–1921. Spanish genre painter; director, Prado Museum (1901 ff.).

**Ville'har'douin'** (vē'lär'dwăN'), **Geoffroi de.** 1150?–?1218. French nobleman who served in the Fourth Crusade (1198–1207) under Count Thibaut III of Champagne and wrote its history in his *Chronicles*, one of the oldest extant specimens of French prose.

**Vil'lèle'** (vē'lĕl'), Comte **Jean Baptiste Séraphin Joseph de.** 1773–1854. French statesman; leader of the ultra-Royalists after the Restoration; premier (1822–28).

**Ville'main'** (vēl'măN'), **Abel François.** 1790–1870. French writer and politician; minister of public instruction (1839–44); among his notable works are *Éloge de Montesquieu* (1816), *Cours de Littérature Française* (1828), *Essai sur le Génie de Pindare* (1859).

**Ville'mes'sant'** (vēl'mĕ'säN'), **Jean Hippolyte Auguste Car'tier' de** (kȧr'tyā' dē). 1812–1879. French journalist; founder of *Le Figaro*, first (1854) as a weekly and later (1866) as a daily journal.

**Vil·le'na** (vē·lyā'nä), Marqués **de. Juan Manuel Fer·nán'dez Pa·che'co** (fĕr·nän'dāth pä·chā'kō). d. 1725. Spanish scholar; a founder of Spanish Academy (1714) and its first director; guided preparation of academy's first dictionary, *Diccionario de Autoridades* (1726–39).

**Villena, Enrique de.** *Also* Enrique **de A'ra·gón'** (thā ä'rä·gōn'). 1384–1434. Spanish writer and scholar; first to translate Vergil's *Aeneid* and Dante's *Divina Commedia;* author of *Arte de Trobar*, *Arte Cisoria*, *Libro del Aojamiento*, and *Doce Trabojos de Hércules*.

**Ville'neuve'** (vēl'nûv'), **Arnaud de.** See ARNAUD DE VILLENEUVE.

**Villeneuve, Jean Marie Rodrigue.** 1883–1947. Cardinal archbishop of Quebec; archbishop (from 1931); cardinal (from 1933).

**Villeneuve, Pierre Charles Jean Baptiste Silvestre de.** 1763–1806. French vice-admiral; commander of fleet designed to invade England (1805); defeated by Nelson in the battle of Trafalgar (Oct. 21, 1805).

**Ville'roi'** (vēl'rwä'), Duc **de. François de Neuf'ville'** (dē nû'vēl'). 1644–1730. French general of brigade (1672), field marshal (1674), lieutenant general (1677), marshal of France (1693); commanded armies in the Low Countries (1695); defeated and captured by Prince Eugene of Savoy at Cremona (Feb. 1, 1702); defeated at Ramillies (May 23, 1706). A favorite of Louis XIV, he was member of council of regency under Louis XV.

**Vil'liers, de** (dē vĭl'yērz). See DE VILLIERS.

**Vil'liers** (vĭl'yērz), **Alan John.** 1903– . Australian author of maritime adventure and history, b. Melbourne; went to sea at fifteen; won grain race of windjammers from Australia to England in 83 days (1933); sailed school ship *Joseph Conrad* round the world (1934, 1935, 1936); author of *Whaling in the Frozen South* (1925), *Vanished Fleets* (1931), *Grain Race* (1933), *The Making of a Sailor* (1938), *Sons of Sinbad* (1940), etc.

**Vil'liers** (vĭl'ērz; vĭl'yērz), **Barbara.** Countess of **Cas'tle·maine'** (kȧs''l·mān'). Duchess of **Cleve'land** (klēv'lănd). 1641–1709. London beauty (1656); m. (1659) Roger Palmer (*q.v.*), later Earl of Castlemaine; mistress of Charles II (1660–74), with rooms in Whitehall; became Roman Catholic (1663); carried on traffic in sale of offices; instrumental in dismissal of ministers; was created duchess of Cleveland (1670); lived in Paris (1677–84). Mother by Charles II (acknowledged paternity) of Charles Fitzroy (1662–1730), Duke of Southampton (cr. 1675) and of Cleveland (1709); Henry Fitzroy, Duke of Grafton; George Fitzroy (1665–1716), Duke of Northumberland (cr. 1674); and two daughters.

**Villiers, Charles Pelham.** 1802–1898. English leader of corn-law and poor-law reform; M.P., Wolverhampton (1835–98), as a free trader; repeated resolution against corn laws annually till their abolition (1846); president of poor-law board (1859–66), holding cabinet rank.

**Vil'liers** (vĭl'ērz; vĭl'yērz), **Edward.** 1st Earl of **Jer'sey** (jûr'zĭ). 1656–1711. English diplomat. Grandson of Sir **Edward Villiers** (1585?–1626), master of the mint and president of Munster, who was half brother of George Villiers (*q.v.*), 1st Duke of Buckingham. Master of horse to Queen Mary II (1689); envoy to Holland (1695, 1697); English representative at Congress of Ryswick (1696); ambassador in Paris (1698–99); one of lords justices of England (1699, 1700, 1701); dismissed from office by Queen Anne; involved in Jacobite plots. His sister **Elizabeth Villiers** (1657?–1733), later Countess of **Ork'ney** (ôrk'nĭ), maid of honor to Princess Mary in Holland (1677), became mistress to Prince of Orange (till 1694); married (1695) Lord George Hamilton (*q.v.*). **George Bussy Villiers** (1735–1805), 4th Earl of Jersey and 7th Viscount **Gran'di·son** (grăn'dĭ·s'n), was the so-called "prince of Macaronis" at court of George III.

**Villiers, Frederic.** 1852–1922. English war correspondent and war artist; in Serbia (1876), with Russians in Turkey (1877), in Greek-Turkish war of 1897–98, taking first successful war motion pictures, through Boer War (1899–1902) for *Illustrated London News*, with Japanese (1905), with Bulgarians (1912–13), with French and British armies (1914–17). Author and illustrator of *Pictures of Many Wars* (1902), *Villiers: His Five Decades of Adventure* (1921).

**Villiers, George.** 1st Duke of **Buck'ing·ham** (bŭk'ĭng·ăm). 1592–1628. English courtier and royal favorite; successor to earl of Somerset (1615); created earl of Buckingham (1617), marquis (1618), duke (1623). As lord high admiral (1619), urged English assistance for Bohemian Protestants; later intrigued with Spanish ambassador for Spanish conquest of the Palatinate; bungled schemes to marry Prince Charles (later Charles I) first to infanta Maria of Spain (1623), later to Henrietta Maria, sister of Louis XIII of France; sent futile expeditions under a German soldier, Count Mansfeld, against Palatinate (1625) and under his favorite, Sir Edward Cecil, against Cádiz (1625); saved from impeachment by Charles's dissolution of first and second parliaments; personally led expedition to relieve Rochelle, failed miserably; dismissal demanded by House of Commons; assassinated.

His son **George** (1628–1687), 2d duke, joined Royalists (1640) and served under Prince Rupert; joined Lord Holland's rising in Surrey (1648); gained favor of Charles II and became member of Cabal (1667–69); engaged in series of intrigues and caused much scandal by his personal immorality; attacked in parliament as promoter of popery and arbitrary government; dismissed from offices (1674). Remembered as Zimri in Dryden's *Absalom and Achitophel* and a figure in Scott's *Peveril of the Peak*. Author of several comedies, including the burlesque *The Rehearsal* (1671).

**Villiers, George William Frederick.** 4th Earl of **Clar'en·don** (klăr'ĕn·dŭn) of the Villiers line, and 4th Baron **Hyde** (hīd). 1800–1870. English statesman. As ambassador at Madrid (1833–39), conducted negotiations over question of Spanish succession; lord privy seal in Melbourne's government (1839–41); lord lieutenant of Ireland (1847–52); foreign secretary (1853–58) through Crimean War, exerting much influence in drafting of

Declaration of Paris (1856) laying down international rules of maritime warfare; foreign secretary (1865–66, 1868–70), responsible for basis adopted in later settlement of Alabama claims. He was grandson of **Thomas Villiers** (1709–1786), Baron Hyde (1756), 1st Earl of Clarendon (1776), diplomat, whose wife was a granddaughter of Henry Hyde, last (4th) Earl of Clarendon of 1st creation (see under Edward HYDE).

His grandson **George Herbert Hyde Villiers** (1877–1955), 6th Earl of Clarendon, was chief government whip, House of Lords (1922–25); chairman, British Broadcasting Corp. (1927–30); governor general of Union of South Africa (1931–37); lord chamberlain of king's household (1938–52).

**Vil'liers' de L'Isle'-A'dam'** (vē'lyā' dē lēl'á'däN'), Comte **Philippe Auguste Mathias de.** 1838–1889. French writer; reputed originator of symbolist school in French literature; author of *Premières Poésies* (1856–58), *Isis* (a novel), and a number of short stories and plays, including *Élen*, *Morgane* (1862), *La Révolte* (1870), *Le Nouveau Monde* (1875), *Axel* (publ. 1890).

**Vil'loi'son'** (vē'lwȧ'zôN'), **Jean Baptiste Gaspard d'Ansse de** (däNs' dē). 1753–1805. French Hellenic scholar; discovered at Venice the *Codex Marcianus*, or *Codex Venetus*, on which F. A. Wolf based his study of Homer; published the *Iliad*, edited from the *Codex Marcianus* (1788).

**Vil'lon'** (vē'yôN'), **François.** *Real name perhaps* **François de Mont'cor'bier'** (dē môN'kôr'byā'). b. 1431. French poet of humble family, adopted by Guillaume de Villon, whose surname he assumed. Led irregular life; fatally stabbed a priest (1455); involved in robbery at the Collège de Navarre in Paris (1456); arrested for theft (1462) and for brawling (1462), and sentenced to death, the sentence being later commuted to banishment from Paris. His works include *Le Petit Testament* (a poem in 40 stanzas, 1456), *Le Grand Testament* (a poem in 173 stanzas, containing many ballads or rondeaux, 1461). He is regarded as the first and one of the greatest of French lyricists.

**Vil'mar** (fĭl'mär), **August Friedrich Christian.** 1800–1868. German theologian and literary historian.

**Vin·cennes'** (vĭn·sĕnz'; *Fr.* văN'sĕn'), Sieur **de. Jean Baptiste Bis'sot'** (bē'sō'). 1668–1719. French explorer in America, b. near Quebec, Canada; in command among Miami Indians (1696); accompanied Henry de Tonty on his western expedition (1698). His son **François Marie Bissot,** Sieur **de Vincennes** (1700–1736), b. Montreal, succeeded his father among the Miamis at what is now Fort Wayne, Ind. (1719); under sponsorship of Louisiana authorities, built fort on site of what is now Vincennes, Ind. (1731 or 1732); killed by Chickasaw Indians (Mar. 25, 1736).

**Vincens,** Mme. **Charles.** See ARVÈDE BARINE.

**Vin'cent** (vĭn'sĕnt), Saint. d. 304. Spanish martyr; ordained deacon to Bishop Valerius of Saragossa; tortured and executed at Valencia under Diocletian; patron of winegrowers.

**Vin'cent'** (văN'säN'), **Charles.** See Pierre MAËL.

**Vin'cent** (vĭn'sĕnt), **Edgar.** See D'ABERNON.

**Vincent,** Sir **Howard,** *in full* **Charles Edward Howard.** 1849–1908. English soldier and political leader; first director of criminal investigation, Scotland Yard (1878–84); Conservative M.P. (1885–1908); advocated legislation on alien immigration and appointment of public trustee (passed 1905 and 1906); author of *Police Code and Manual of Criminal Law* (1882).

**Vin'cent'** (văN'säN'; *Angl.* vĭn'sĕnt), **Jean Hyacinthe.** 1862–1950. French physician; discovered the bacteria producing the diseases known as Vincent's angina and Vincent's infection, or trench mouth; developed a vaccine for typhoid and paratyphoid fevers; discovered a serum for the treatment of gas gangrene.

**Vin'cent** (vĭn'sĕnt), **John Heyl.** 1832–1920. American Methodist Episcopal clergyman; originated improvements in Sunday-school teaching; originator, with Lewis Miller, of Chautauqua movement, beginning (1874) in a Sunday-school teachers' assembly. Elected bishop (1888), episcopal residence at Buffalo, N.Y. (1888–92), Topeka, Kans. (1892–1900), and Zurich, Switzerland (1900–04); retired (1904). Author of *The Chautauqua Movement* (1886), *Our Own Church* (1890), etc. His son **George Edgar** (1864–1941), educator; president, U. of Minnesota (1911–17); president, Rockefeller Foundation (1917–29); author of *An Introduction to the Study of Society* (with Albion W. Small; 1895), *Social Mind and Education* (1896).

**Vincent, Marvin Richardson.** 1834–1922. American theologian; professor of sacred literature, Union Theol. Sem., New York City (1887–1916); author of *The Age of Hildebrand* (1896), *Word Studies in the New Testament* (4 vols., 1887–1900), etc.

**Vin'cent'** (văN'säN'), **Sténio Joseph.** 1874–1959. President of Haiti (1930–41), b. Port-au-Prince; lawyer, diplomat, educational official; founded newspapers *L'Effort* (1902) and *Haïti-Journal* (1930).

**Vin'cent' de Paul** (văN'säN' dē pôl'; *Angl.* vĭn'sĕnt dē pôl'), Saint. 1581?–1660. French Roman Catholic priest; renowned for his benevolence, his zeal, and his genius for practical charitable organization; founded the Congregation of the Priests of the Mission (1625), known as Lazarists or Vincentians, the Sisters of Charity (1634), also known as Vincentians, and foundling hospitals in Paris. Beatified (1729) and canonized (1737). The Société de Saint Vincent de Paul (lay society for poor relief, active in U.S., etc.) was founded by Frédéric Ozanam (*q.v.*) and others in Paris (1833).

**Vin'cent Fer·rer'** (vĭn'sĕnt fĕr·rĕr'), Saint. *Span.* San **Vi·cen'te** (vē·thān'tā) **Ferrer.** 1350–1419. Spanish Dominican monk, b. in Valencia; adviser to King John of Aragon; renowned as itinerant preacher (from 1399).

**Vin'cent of Beau'vais'** (vĭn'sĕnt, bō'vĕ'). d. before 1264. French Dominican and scholar; best known for his *Speculum Majus* (in three parts: *Speculum Naturale*, *Speculum Doctrinale*, *Speculum Historiale*), the most complete scientific encyclopedia of the 13th century.

**Vin'cent of Lé'rins'** (vĭn'sĕnt, lā'răNs'), Saint. *Lat.* **Vin·cen'ti·us Ler'i·nen'sis** (vĭn·sĕn'shĭ·ŭs [-shŭs] lĕr'ĭ·nĕn'sĭs). d. 450? French Roman Catholic priest; best known for his *Commonitorium pro Catholicae Fidei Antiquitate et Universitate* (434), written under pseudonym **Per'e·gri'nus** (pĕr'ē·grī'nŭs) and directed against heretics, esp. Nestorians.

**Vin·cen'ti·us** (vĭn·sĕn'shĭ·ŭs; -shŭs). Latin form of VINCENT.

**Vin'ci** (vēn'chē), **Leonardo da.** 1452–1519. Florentine painter, sculptor, architect, engineer, and scientist, b. Vinci, Tuscany; natural son of Ser Piero d'Antonio, a Florentine notary. To Florence (1466); protégé of Lorenzo the Magnificent. At Milan as protégé of Lodovico Sforza (1482–99). To Mantua, Venice, and Florence (1500); military engineer to Cesare Borgia (1502); competed with Michelangelo for commission to decorate Palazzo Vecchio. Appointed court painter to Louis XII of France (Milan, 1506), to Francis I (1516); to France (1516). As scientist, originated science of hydraulics and made significant studies in meteorology, anatomy, and mathematics; as engineer, built Martesana Canal and numerous military constructions; employed as architect in construction of Milan cathedral; sculptor of colossal bronze monument to Francesco Sforza (uncompleted; Milan). Among his paintings are *Annunciation, Adoration of the Kings, St. Jerome, Virgin of the Grotto, Last Supper* (mural in refectory in monastery of Santa Maria della Grazie, Milan), *Madonna with the Christ Child in the Lap of St. Anne* and *Mona Lisa* (in the Louvre). Author of *Treatise on Painting.*

**Vinci, Leonardo.** 1690–1732. Italian composer, esp. of operas; b. in Calabria.

**Vin′dex** (vĭn′dĕks), **Gaius Julius.** d. 68 A.D. Roman propraetor of Gallia Celtica; first Roman governor to rebel against Nero; his revolt failed.

**Vinea** *or* **Vineis, Petrus de.** See PIETRO DELLA VIGNA.

**Vi′ner** (vī′nẽr), **Charles.** 1678–1756. English jurist and author; published *Abridgment of Law and Equity* (23 vols., 1742–53); founder of the Vinerian common-law professorship at Oxford.

**Vi′net′** (vē′nĕ′), **Alexandre.** 1797–1847. Swiss Protestant theologian; devoted himself (1845–47) to organization of free churches in Vaud. Among his works are *Études sur Blaise Pascal* (1848), *Études sur la Littérature Française au 19ᵉ Siècle* (3 vols., 1849–51), *Histoire de la Littérature Française au 18ᵉ Siècle* (2 vols., 1853).

**Vin′je** (vĭn′yĕ), **Aasmund Olafsson.** 1818–1870. Norwegian poet, journalist, and language reformer; took active part in Landsmaal movement (from 1851); author of *Ferdaminni fraa Sumaren 1860* (a description of Norwegian country life, 1861), *A Norseman's Views of Britain and the British* (1863), *Storegut* (an epic cycle, 1866). Some of his poems became popular songs.

**Vi·no·gra′doff** (vyĕ·nŭ·grȧ′dôf), Sir **Paul** (pôl) **Gavrilovitch.** 1854–1925. Russian jurist and medieval historian; to England (1902); professor of jurisprudence, Oxford (1903–25); authority on early laws and customs in England; author of *Villainage in England* (1892), *Historical Jurisprudence* (1920–22; uncompleted); contributed to *Encyclopaedia Britannica* (11th ed.) and *Cambridge Medieval History.*

**Vin′son** (vĭn′s′n), **Carl.** 1883– . American lawyer and politician, b. near Milledgeville, Ga.; member of U.S. House of Representatives (1914–64).

**Vin′son, Frederick Moore.** 1890–1953. American jurist, b. Louisa, Ky.; member, U.S. Congress (1923–29, 1931–37); associate justice, U.S. Court of Appeals for D.C. (1937–43); director, Office of Economic Stabilization (1943–45); secretary of the treasury (1945–46); chief justice, U.S. Supreme Court (1946–53).

**Vin′ton** (vĭn′t′n; -tŭn), **Frederic Porter.** 1846–1911. American portrait painter; studio in Boston (1878).

**Violle** (vyôl), **Jules.** 1841–1923. French physicist; proposed a photometric unit (Violle's standard, or Violle, 1881); did research on the exploration of the atmosphere by sounding balloons, and on solar radiation, the mechanical equivalent of heat.

**Viol′let′-le-Duc′** (vyô′lĕ′lē·dük′), **Eugène Emmanuel.** 1814–1879. French architect and authority on Gothic art; a leader in the Gothic revival in France; designed the restoration of many medieval buildings in France, including the cathedrals of Amiens, Laon, and Notre-Dame de Paris; restored the Cité de Carcassonne, the Château de Pierrefonds, Château d'Arragory. Compiler of the illustrated *Dictionnaire Raisonné de l'Architecture Française du XIᵉ au XVIᵉ Siècle* (10 vols., 1854–69) and *Dictionnaire du Mobilier Français* (1855).

**Viot′ti** (vyôt′tē), **Giovanni Battista.** 1755–1824. Italian violinist; lived at Paris (1782–89, 1819 ff.), London (1792–93, 1795–1819), Hamburg (1793–95); director of grand opera, Paris (1819–22); works include violin concertos, sonatas, and duets, string trios and quartets, and compositions for piano.

**Vip·sa′ni·a Ag′rip·pi′na** (vĭp·sā′nĭ·ȧ [-sān′yȧ] ăg′rĭ·pī′nȧ). (1) d. 20 A.D. Dau. of Marcus Vipsanius Agrippa by first wife Pomponia; m. (1st) Tiberius (later emperor); mother of Drusus Caesar; divorced (11 B.C.); m. (2d) Asinius Gallus. (2) Her half sister. See AGRIPPINA.

**Vir′chow** (fĭr′kō), **Rudolf.** 1821–1902. German pathologist and political leader, b. in Pomerania. Professor of pathological anatomy, Würzburg (1849); professor and director, Pathological Institute, Berlin (from 1856). Founded cellular pathology; carried on researches on blood (leukemia, etc.), phlebitis, tuberculosis, rickets, tumors, trichinosis, etc. Made sanitary reforms in Berlin; established farms utilizing sewage for fertilizing the land. Worked also in archaeology and anthropology. One of the leaders of the Fortschrittspartei (progressists) and later of the German Liberal party; member of Prussian National Assembly (from 1862) and of the German Reichstag (1880–93); opposed policies of Bismarck. Author of *Die Cellularpathologie* (1858), *Handbuch der Speziellen Pathologie und Therapie* (6 vols., 1854–76), etc.

**Vi′ret′** (vē′rĕ′), **Pierre.** 1511–1571. Swiss reformer; associate of Farel (*q.v.*); converted Lausanne to Protestant faith (1536); opposed by people of Bern, was deposed (1559); withdrew to Geneva.

**Virgil.** See VERGIL.

**Virginia.** Roman girl. See Appius CLAUDIUS.

**Vir′i·a′thus** (vĭr′ĭ·ā′thŭs) *or* **Vir′i·a′tus** (-tŭs). d. 139? B.C. Shepherd of Lusitania (Portugal) who conducted war (149–139 B.C.) against Romans; assassinated.

**Vir′ta·nen** (vĭr′tȧ·nĕn), **Art′tu·ri Il′ma·ri** (ärt′too·rĭ ĭl′mȧ·rĭ). 1895–1973. Finnish biochemist; director, Biochemical Inst., Helsinki; awarded 1945 Nobel prize for chemistry, for work on conservation of fodder.

**Vi·rués′** (vē·rwās′), **Cristóbal de.** 1550–1610. Spanish dramatic and epic poet; captain in Spanish army; friend and early rival of Lope de Vega.

**Vi′scher** (fĭsh′ẽr). A family of Nuremberg sculptors and brass founders, including: **Hermann** the elder (d. 1488), who established the foundry; his son **Peter** the elder (1460?–1529), whose works include the tomb of Archbishop Ernest of Saxony, the shrine of St. Sebald (a canopied Gothic structure enclosing the silver sarcophagus of the saint and ornamented with reliefs and statuettes, 1508–19), and bronze figures of Kings Arthur and Theodoric for the tomb of Emperor Maximilian; and Peter's sons and assistants **Hermann** the younger (1486?–1517), **Peter** the younger (1487–1528), **Paul** *or* **Paulus** (d. 1531), to whom is ascribed the wooden statue known as the Nuremberg Madonna (ab. 1525), and **Hans** (1489?–1550), whose works include the double monument of Electors Joachim I and Johann Cicero of Brandenburg in Berlin cathedral and the fountain figure Apollo in Nuremberg.

**Vischer, Friedrich Theodor.** 1807–1887. German poet, literary critic, and aesthetician of the Hegelian school; author of *Kritische Gänge* (1844; new series, 1860 ff.), *Ästhetik, oder Wissenschaft des Schönen* (6 vols., 1846–57), volumes of verse, etc. His *Vorträge* were published (1898–1905) by his son **Robert** (1847–1933), art historian.

**Vi·scon′ti** (vēs·kōn′tē). Name of powerful Lombard family in Milan, of Ghibelline faction (c. 1200–1447), furnishing ruling dukes (1311–1447). Most important were: **Ottone** (1207?–1295), archbishop of Milan (1262–95). **Matteo** (1250?–1322), grandnephew of Ottone; Ghibelline leader; first of family to gain control of Milan (1311–22). **Galeazzo I** (1277?–1328), son of Matteo; duke (1322–28). **Azzo** (1302–1339), son of Galeazzo I; duke (1328–39); followed by his uncles **Giovanni** (1290?–1354) and **Lucchino** (1287?–1349), sons of Matteo; ruled jointly; Giovanni was archbishop (from 1342) and sole ruler (from 1349) of Milan; annexed Genoa (1353);

friend of Petrarch. Giovanni was succeeded (c. 1354) by his two nephews **Galeazzo II** (1320–1378) and **Bernabò** (1323–1385), who held court at Pavia and ruled jointly. **Gian Galeazzo,** *also* **Giangaleazzo** *or* **Giovanni Galeazzo** (1351–1402), son of Galeazzo II; succeeded his father and held court at Pavia as joint ruler (1378–85) with his uncle Bernabò whom he put to death (1385); duke (1385–1402); became master of northern and central Italy; Milan acknowledged as duchy of Holy Roman Empire by Emperor Wenceslaus (1395); bought Pisa and seized Siena (1399); patron of literature and art; founder of Milan cathedral; died of plague. **Gianmaria,** *also* **Giovanni Maria** (1389–1412), son of Gian Galeazzo; duke (1402–12); assassinated. **Filippo Maria** (1392–1447), son of Gian Galeazzo; last Visconti to rule as duke (1412–47). For Filippo's natural daughter, **Bianca Maria,** see Francesco SFORZA. **Valentina** (1366–1408), daughter of Gian Galeazzo; m. (1387) Louis (I), Duc d'Orléans; mother of Charles d'Orléans (the poet) and grandmother of Louis XII of France. Through her, Louis based his claims to Milan. See ORLÉANS.

**Visconti.** Family of Italian archaeologists and architects: **Giovanni Battista** (1722–1784) succeeded Winckelmann as prefect of antiquities at Rome (1768); reorganized Museo Pio-Clementino in the Vatican; directed excavations leading to discovery of Scipio's tomb. His son **Ennio Quirino** (1751–1818) was conservator of Capitoline Museum (1787 ff.); fled to France (1799); appointed curator in the Louvre; professor of archaeology; author of *Iconographie Grecque* (1801), *Iconographie Romaine* (1817), etc. Ennio's son **Lodovico Tullio Gioacchino** (1791–1853) was an architect at Paris (1799 ff.); among his works are the mausoleum for Napoleon and designs for union of the Louvre and the Tuileries. Lodovico's nephew **Pietro Ercole Visconti** (1802–1880) was commissioner of antiquities at Rome and curator of Vatican art collections.

**Vi·scon'ti–Ve·no'sta** (vḗs·kōn'tḗ·vȧ·nôs'tä), Marchese **Emilio.** 1829–1914. Italian statesman; supporter of Mazzini (1848–49); as Piedmontese commissar, effected union of Parma and Modena with the new kingdom (1859–61); deputy (1860 ff.); minister of foreign affairs (1863–64, 1866–67, 1869–76, 1896–98, 1899–1901); senator (1886); Italian representative at Moroccan Conference at Algeciras (1906).

**Vi·sha'kha·dat'ta** (vĭ·shä'kȧ·dŭt'tȧ). fl. 8th century A.D. Sanskrit dramatist; author of *Mudrā-rākshasa* ("Signet Ring of Rākshasa"), with a plot based on a political intrigue in the time of Chandragupta (Sandrocottus).

**Vish'va·mi'tra** (vĭsh'vä·mĭ'trȧ). A semilegendary sage of ancient India; supposed author of hymns in the *Rig-Veda.* The story of his life and struggle for position of chief priest is told in the *Ramayana* and in the *Puranas.*

**Vis'scher** (vĭs'ẽr), **Cornelis.** 1625?–?1662. Dutch engraver and designer of portraits, Biblical and historical studies, landscapes, etc.

**Vi·tal'ian** (vĭ·tăl'yăn; -tā'lĭ·ăn), Saint. *Lat.* **Vi·ta'li·a'nus** (vĭ·tā'lĭ·ā'nŭs). Pope (657–672), b. Segni, Italy; opposed Monothelitism; received Emperor Constans II in visit at Rome.

**Vitalis.** Pseudonym of Erik SJÖBERG.

**Vitalis, Ordericus.** *Or* **Orderic Vital.** See ORDERICUS VITALIS.

**Vite, Giovanni della.** See Jan MIEL.

**Vite, Timoteo della.** See Timoteo VITI.

**Vitellio** *or* **Vitello, Erasmus.** See Erazm CIOŁEK.

**Vi·tel'li·us** (vĭ·tĕl'ĭ·ŭs), **Aulus.** 15–69 A.D. Roman emperor (Jan.–Dec., 69); consul (48); later, proconsul in Africa; given command (68) of legions in Germany by Galba; proclaimed emperor by his soldiers; his generals Valens and Caecina defeated Otho; opposed by Vespasian and his army under Antonius Primus; defeated by Primus and killed.

**Vi'tet'** (vē'tĕ'), **Louis,** *called* **Ludovic.** 1802–1873. French writer and politician; member of Chamber of Deputies (1834–38), Legislative Assembly (1849), and National Assembly (1871). Among his books are *Les Barricades* (1826), *Les États de Blois* (1827), and *La Mort d'Henri III à St. Cloud* (1829), all three published together (1844) as a trilogy under the title *La Ligue.*

**Vi'ti** (vē'tḗ) *or* **del'la Vi'te** (dāl'lä vē'tȧ), **Timoteo.** 1467–1523. Italian painter; lived at Urbino (1495–1523); reputed master of Raphael.

**Vitovt.** See WITOLD.

**Vi·tru'vi·us Pol'li·o** (vĭ·trōō'vĭ·ŭs pŏl'ĭ·ō), **Marcus.** Roman architect and engineer of 1st century B.C.; appointed military engineer by Emperor Augustus; little known of life history; author of *De Architectura* (10 books), dedicated to Augustus, and for many centuries accepted as final authority in field of architecture.

**Vi'try'** (vē'trē'), **Jacques de.** See JACQUES DE VITRY.

**Vitry, Philippe de.** 1290?–1361. French Roman Catholic prelate; bishop of Meaux; known as a poet, composer, and authority on musical theory.

**Vit·to're** (vêt·tō'rā), Fra. See Fra Vittore GHISLANDI.

**Vittoria, Tommaso Lodovico da.** See Tomás Luis de VICTORIA.

**Vittoria Colonna.** See COLONNA family.

**Vit'to·ri'no da Fel'tre** (vēt'tô·rē'nô dä fāl'trā). *Real name* **Vittorino Ram'bol·di'ni** (räm'bôl·dē'nē) *or* **de' Ram'bol·do'ni** (dā räm'bôl·dō'nē). 1378–1446. Italian educator, b. at Feltre; private tutor to children of Marchese Gian Francesco Gonzaga of Mantua (1423 ff.); founded school admitting both noble and poor children (1425); known esp. for the practicability of his methods of instruction.

**Vittorio.** Italian form for VICTOR.

**Vi'tus** (vī'tŭs), Saint. Christian child martyr of late 3d century. Invoked by sufferers from chorea, a nervous disease, his name has become attached to the disease itself (St. Vitus's dance).

**Vi·val'di** (vḗ·väl'dḗ), **Antonio.** 1675?–1741. Italian violinist, and composer of violin concertos, operas, and sonatas.

**Vi·van'ti** (vḗ·vän'tḗ), **Annie.** 1868–1942. Anglo-Italian poet and playwright, b. in London, dau. of Italian patriot; m. John S. Chartres; author of lyric poems, war plays, and psychological novels, including *Vae Victis* (1917).

**Vi'va·ri'ni** (vē'vä·rē'nē). Family of Venetian painters, including: **Antonio da Mu·ra'no** [dä mōō·rä'nō] (1415?–?1470), who collaborated with his brother-in-law Giovanni d'Alemannia (1440–47), and among whose joint works are *Madonna with Holy Fathers* and *Coronation of the Virgin.* Antonio's brother **Bartolommeo da Murano,** *later called* **Bartolommeo Vivarini** (1432–?1491), who collaborated with Antonio (1447–64), Antonio's son **Alvise Vivarini** (1446?–?1503), pupil of his uncle Bartolommeo; rival of Giovanni Bellini; painter of *Virgin and Child, Enthroned Madonna, Madonna with Saints,* and *Santa Clara.*

**Vi'ves** (vē'vās), **Juan Luis.** 1492–1540. Spanish humanist and philosopher; professor of humanities, Louvain (1519 ff.); friend of Erasmus. To England (1523) on invitation of Henry VIII; tutor to Princess Mary; lectured at Oxford; lost royal favor through opposition to divorce of Catherine of Aragon (1528); retired to Bruges (1529 ff.). Known esp. as a logician; opposed scholasticism; one of first to emphasize induction as a philosophical and psychological method. Works include *De Initiis, Sectis, et Laudibus Philosophiae* (1518), commentary on Augustine's *City of God* (1522), *De Disciplinis* (including *De Causis Corruptarum Artium*, his chief work and one of the outstanding medieval works on education, 1531), *De Anima et Vita* (one of first modern works on psychology, 1538), and *De Veritate Fidei Christianae* (1540).

**Viv'i·an** (vĭv'ĭ·ăn; vĭv'yăn), **Herbert.** 1865–1940. British writer and traveler; author of *Servia, the Poor Man's Paradise* (1897), *Kings in Waiting* (1933), *Fascist Italy* (1936), etc.

**Vi'via'ni'** (vē'vyȧ'nē'), **René Raphaël.** 1863–1925. French statesman; Socialist deputy for Paris (1893–1902, 1906–10); minister of labor (1906–10); responsible for workmen's pensions law; minister of public instruction (1913–14); premier and minister of foreign affairs (1914–15); minister of justice in Briand's cabinet (1915–17).

**Vi'vien' de Saint'-Mar'tin'** (vē'vyăN' dẽ săN'mȧr'tăN'), **Louis.** 1802–1897. French geographer; author of *Histoire de la Géographie et des Découvertes Géographiques* (1873); editor of *L'Année Géographique* (1863–76), *Nouveau Dictionnaire de Géographie Universelle* (completed by Louis Rousselet, 1876–95).

**Vivonne de Savelli, Catherine de.** See Marquise de RAMBOUILLET.

**Viz'ca·í'no** (vēth'kä·ē'nō; vēs'-), **Sebastián.** 1550?–1615. Spanish explorer; to Mexico (c. 1586); led expeditions on western coast of Mexico north from Acapulco to Lower California (1596–97), and along Californian coast as far as 43° N (1602–03), entered San Diego and Monterey bays, anchored (1603) in bay at Point Reyes, north of San Francisco; made voyage of discovery (1611–14) from Mexico into Pacific, attempting unsuccessfully to establish trade with Japan.

**Viz'e·tel'ly** (vĭz'ẽ·tĕl'ĭ), **Henry Richard.** 1820–1894. English engraver and publisher; correspondent of *Illustrated London News* in Paris (1865–72) and Berlin (1872), as was his brother **Frank** (1830–?1883) from 1859 to his death in the Sudan. Two sons, by his first wife, were journalists: **Edward Henry** (1847–1903), correspondent of New York *Times* and London *Daily News* during Franco-Prussian War, and commander of New York *Herald* relief expedition (1889) to find Stanley; and **Ernest Alfred** (1853–1922), correspondent during Franco-Prussian War, editor of bibliophilists' *Heptameron* (1894), author of three novels and (latterly under pseudonym "Le Petit Homme Rouge") of French biographies. Another son, by his second wife, was **Frank (Francis) Horace** (1864–1938), American lexicographer, settled in New York (1891); naturalized (1926); member of Funk & Wagnalls Co.'s editorial staff (from 1891); associate editor of *Standard Dictionary* (from 1891), editor (1914–38); editor of *New Standard Encyclopaedia of Universal Knowledge* (25 vols., 1931, 1935), of *New International Year Book* (1932–38), and of numerous other reference books; editor of "Lexicographer's Easy Chair" column in *Literary Digest* (1904–10, 1912–37); radio broadcaster (1924–31); author of numerous texts on lexicography, simplified spelling, correct usage.

**Vlacich, Matthias.** = Matthias FLACIUS ILLYRICUS.

**Vlacq** (vläk), **Adrian.** 1600?–1667. Dutch mathematician; published (1628, 1633) tables of common logarithms between 20,000 and 90,000, filling a gap left by previous tables.

**Vlad'i·mir I** (vlăd'ĭ·mĭr; *Russ.* vlŭ·dyē'myĭr). *Known as* **Vladimir the Great** *and* Saint **Vladimir.** 956?–1015. First Christian ruler of Russia (reigned 980–1015); converted to Christianity (989?) and extended Russian dominions. His greatgrandson **Vladimir II,** *surnamed* **Mo·nom'a·chus** (mŏ·nŏm'ȧ·kŭs), *Russ.* **Mo·no·makh'** [mŭ·nŭ·mȧK'] (1053–1125), was grand prince of Kiev (1113–25); renowned as ruler, warrior, and writer of works which depict internal conditions in contemporary Russia.

**Vladislav.** See LADISLAS (kings of Poland).

**Vla'minck'** (vlȧ'măNk'), **Maurice de.** 1876–1958. French painter, identified with the Fauvists.

**Voegt'lin** (vĕkt'lĭn), **Carl.** 1879–1960. American pharmacologist, b. in Switzerland; Ph.D., Freiburg (1903); to U.S. (1904); associate professor, Johns Hopkins Med. School (1906–13); chief of Division of Pharmacology, U.S. Public Health Service (1913–39); chief of National Cancer Institute (1938–42).

**Voet** (vo͞ot), **Gisbert,** *or* **Voe'ti·us** (vē'shĭ·ŭs; *as Du.,* vo͞o'tsē·ûs), **Gys·ber'tus** (jĭz·bûr'tŭs; *as Du.,* gĭs·bĕr'tûs). 1588–1676. Dutch Calvinist theologian; opposed Arminianism, Cocceianism, and Cartesianism.

**Vogau, Boris Andreevich.** See PILNYAK.

**Vo'gel'** (vô'gĕl'), **Charles Louis Adolphe.** 1808–1892. French composer of the music for the national song *Les Trois Couleurs* sung after the July revolution (1830), and a number of melodies popular in their day.

**Vo'gel** (fō'gĕl), **Eduard.** 1829–1856. German explorer; commissioned by English government to assist Barth in exploring the Sudan (1853); made successful explorations around Lake Chad; killed by natives. His brother **Hermann Karl** (1841–1907), astrophysicist, known esp. for his work in spectroscopy.

**Vogel, Hermann Wilhelm.** 1834–1898. German photochemist; discovered (1873) that the addition of certain dyes to photographic emulsions increased the color sensitivity; devised a photometer; carried on research in spectral photography.

**Vogel, Hugo.** 1855–1934. German historical, genre, and portrait painter.

**Vo'gel** (vō'gĕl), Sir **Julius.** 1835–1899. New Zealand statesman; head of New Zealand government (1869–76; premier 1873–75, 1876); agent general in London (1876–81).

**Vo'gel** (fō'gĕl), **Walther.** 1880– . German historian, geographer, and political scientist.

**Vo'gel von Falck'en·stein** (fō'gĕl fôn fäl'kĕn·shtīn), **Eduard.** 1797–1885. German general; general chief of staff under Wrangel in German-Danish War (1864), and governor of Jutland; defeated Hanoverians at Langensalza (1866); defeated southern German troops and besieged Frankfurt am Main; governor general of Bohemia; governor general of German coast provinces (1870–71).

**Vogelweide.** See WALTHER VON DER VOGELWEIDE.

**Vo'gl** (fō'gĕl), **Heinrich.** 1845–1900. German Wagnerian tenor and oratorio singer; composed the opera *Der Fremdling* (1899) and many songs and ballads.

**Vogl, Johann Nepomuk.** 1802–1866. Austrian poet; author of *Balladen und Romanzen* (1835), *Lyrische Gedichte* (1844), *Soldatenlieder* (1849), etc.

**Vö'gler** (fû'glẽr), **Albert.** 1877–1945. German industrialist; assisted Hugo Stinnes and others in building up (1920) the Rhine-Elbe Union later merged (1926) into the United Steel Works; first chairman of union of German ironworkers (1916) and member of government board of control of German industry; member, Weimar National Assembly (1919–20); represented German National party in Reichstag (1920–24). See also Fritz THYSSEN and Emil KIRDORF.

**Vo'gler** (fō'glẽr), **Georg Joseph.** *Usually called* **Abt** (äpt), *or* **Ab'bé** (ä'bā), **Vo'gler.** 1749–1814. German organist, composer, and writer on music; ordained priest, Rome (1773); court music director and head of music school, Stockholm (1786–99); court Kapellmeister,

Darmstadt (from 1807), where he founded music school; teacher of von Weber and Meyerbeer; composed operas, ballets, church music, organ pieces, a symphony, overtures, chamber music, piano pieces, etc.

**Vogt** (fōKt), **Hans.** 1890– . German electrical engineer; inventor (in collaboration with Joseph Massolle and Dr. J. Engl, 1918–25) of a film for sound motion pictures carrying the sound record on it.

**Vogt, Karl.** 1817–1895. German zoologist; associated with Agassiz in preparation of his works on fishes.

**Vogt** (fôkt), **Nils Collett.** 1864–1937. Norwegian journalist and poet.

**Vo'gü·é'** (vô'gü·ā'), Marquis **de. Charles Jean Mel'chior'** (mĕl'kyôr'). 1829–1916. French archaeologist and diplomat; explored Palestine and Syria (1853–54); ambassador at Constantinople (1871–75) and Vienna (1875–79); author of books on Palestine and Syria, and a few studies in modern history. Of the same family was **Eugène Melchior,** Vicomte **de Vogüé** (1848–1910), writer and diplomat; in diplomatic service (1871–82) at Constantinople, Cairo, St. Petersburg; on staff of *Revue des Deux Mondes* and *Journal des Débats;* among his many books are *Le Roman Russe* (1886), *Heures d'Histoire* (1893), *Les Morts qui Parlent* (1899), *Le Maître de la Mer* (1903), *Maxime Gorki* (1905).

**Voigt** (fōKt), **Johannes.** 1786–1863. German historian; author of *Geschichte Preussens* (9 vols., 1827–38), *Geschichte des Deutschen Ritterordens* (2 vols., 1857–59), etc. His son **Georg** (1827–1891), also a historian, was author of *Enea Sylvio de' Piccolomini als Papst Pius II* (3 vols., 1856–63), *Moritz von Sachsen 1541–47* (1876), etc.

**Voigt, Woldemar.** 1850–1919. German physicist; known esp. for work in crystallography, thermodynamics, magnetooptics, and electrooptics; also, writer on the music of Bach.

**Voi'sin'** (vwȧ'zăN'), **Gabriel.** 1880–1973. French manufacturer of airplanes; with Blériot established a factory (1904) into which business his brother **Charles** (1882–1912) entered (1905); constructed the biplanes (1907–08) used by the sculptor-aviator Léon Delagrange, and also by Henri Farman, in their first successful flights.

**Voi'sins'** (vwȧ'zăN'), Countess **de.** = Maria TAGLIONI.

**Voit** (foit), **Karl von.** 1831–1908. German physiologist; professor, Munich (1863–1908); founder, with Ludwig von Buhl and Max von Pettenkofer, of *Zeitschrift für Biologie* (1864), and contributor to it of articles on nutrition and metabolism; devised with Pettenkofer apparatus for experiments on respiration.

**Voi'ture'** (vwȧ'tür'), **Vincent.** 1597–1648. French court wit, poet, and man of letters.

**Vojtěch.** See Saint ADALBERT.

**Vokes** (vōks). A family of English actors in burlesque appearing first as "Vokes children" (1861), including: **Frederick Mortimer** (1846–1888), actor and dancer; **Jessie Catherine Biddulph** (1851–1884), actress and dancer; **Victoria** (1853–1894), actress and singer; and **Rosina** (1858–1894), actress.

**Vol'bach** (fôl'bäK), **Fritz.** 1861–1941. German director, composer, and writer on music; composed symphonic poems, a symphony, choral works, the comic opera *Die Kunst zu Lieben* (1910), chamber music, songs, etc.; author of biographies of Handel (1898) and Beethoven (1905), *Handbuch der Musikwissenschaft* (2 vols., 1926–30), etc.

**Vol'de·ma'ras** (vôl'dĕ·mä'räs), **Augustinas.** 1883–1946. Lithuanian statesman; premier (1918, 1926–29); governed in dictatorial fashion, and was overthrown (1929); attempting to regain power by force (June 6–7, 1934), was arrested and sentenced to twelve years' imprisonment at hard labor.

**Vol'i·va** (vŏl'ĭ·vȧ), **Wilbur Glenn.** 1870–1942. American religious leader, b. near Newton, Ind.; ordained in ministry of Christian Church (1889); transferred to Christian Catholic Church (1899), and became assistant to John Alexander Dowie at Zion, Ill. (1906–07); succeeded Dowie as general overseer of the church (1907).

**Volk** (vōlk), **Leonard Wells.** 1828–1895. American sculptor, b. Wells, N.Y.; studio in Chicago (from 1857); a founder (1867) and president, Chicago Academy of Design. Among his works are the Douglas monument at Chicago and a Douglas statue in the capitol at Springfield, Ill.; statue of Lincoln in capitol at Springfield, Ill.; a bronze statue of Gen. James Shields in Statuary Hall, Washington, D.C. His son **Douglas,** *in full* **Stephen Arnold Douglas** (1856–1935), was a painter; organizer of Minneapolis School of Fine Arts (1886–93); painted portraits of King Albert, General Pershing, and David Lloyd George.

**Vol'kelt** (fôl'kĕlt), **Johannes Immanuel.** 1848–1930. German philosopher; author of *Kants Erkenntnistheorie* (1879), *System der Ästhetik* (3 vols., 1905–14), *Das Problem der Individualität* (1928), etc.

**Volk'mann** (fôlk'män), **Richard von.** 1830–1889. German surgeon; pioneer in antiseptic methods and orthopedics; author of medical works, fairy tales, and poems, including *Träumereien an Französischen Kaminen* (1871), which appeared under the pen name **Richard Le·an'der** (lȧ·än'dĕr), with illustrations by his son **Hans von Volkmann** (1860–1927), a landscape painter, etcher, and lithographer. Richard's father, **Alfred Wilhelm Volkmann** (1801–1877), was a physiologist and professor at Halle (from 1843).

**Volkmann, Robert,** *in full* **Friedrich Robert.** 1815–1883. German composer of symphonies, overtures, serenades for string orchestra, a violoncello concerto, string quartets, piano pieces, choral works, songs, etc.

**Vol·kon'ski** (vŭl·kôn'skû·ĭ; *Angl.* vŏl·kŏn'skĭ), Prince **Pëtr Mikhailovich.** 1776–1852. Russian general; served against Napoleon (1812, 1813); first to advise the march on Paris.

**Vol'kov** (vôl'kôf), **Fëdor Grigorievich.** 1729–1763. Russian actor; organized (1755) first troupe of actors in Russia; called to St. Petersburg by Czarina Elizabeth; founded (1756) Moscow Theater by royal command.

**Voll'mar** (fôl'mär), **Georg Heinrich von.** 1850–1922. German Social Democratic leader; edited Socialist papers; member of Reichstag (1881–87; 1890–1918); a leader of conservative wing of Social Democrats and forerunner of revisionism.

**Voll'mer** (vŏl'mĕr), **Lula.** d. 1955. American writer, b. Keyser, N.C.; author of plays, esp. on N.C. mountain folk, including *Sunup* (prod. 1923), *The Shame Woman* (1923), *The Dunce Boy* (1925), *Sentinels* (1931), *The Hill Between* (1938), radio serials, short stories, etc.

**Voll'möl'ler** (fôl'mûl'ĕr), **Karl.** 1848–1922. German Romance philologist. His son **Karl Gustav Vollmöller** *or* **Vollmoeller** (1878–1948), author of poems, dramas, comedies, and translations and adaptations, as of D'Annunzio's *Francesca da Rimini* (1904) and Molière's *Georges Dandin* (1912).

**Vol'lon'** (vô'lôN'), **Antoine.** 1833–1900. French painter; best known for his still-life and genre pictures.

**Vol'ney'** (vôl'nā'), Comte **de. Constantin François de Chasse'bœuf'** (shȧs'bûf'). 1757–1820. French scholar; member of the States-General (1789) and the National Assembly, and of the Chamber of Peers under Louis XVIII; author of *Voyage en Égypt et en Syrie* (1787), *Recherches Nouvelles sur l'Histoire Ancienne* (1814), etc.

**Vol'o·ge'sus** (vŏl'ō·jē'sŭs) *or* **Vol'o·ga'ses** (-gā'sēz).

Name of five Parthian kings: **Vologesus I** (reigned 50–77 A.D.), fought long war with Rome (54–63). His son **Vologesus II** (reigned 130?–147), under whom the Parthian empire was divided by recurring civil wars. **Vologesus III** (reigned 147–191), united the kingdom but suffered from Roman attacks and was forced to cede western Mesopotamia. **Vologesus IV** (reigned 191–209), defended Parthia against Rome. His son **Vologesus V** (reigned 209–?222), lost most of dominions to an Arsacid king.

**Vol'pe** (vōl'pâ), **Gioacchino.** 1876– . Italian historian; Fascist deputy (1924–29); works include *Lo Sviluppo Storico del Fascismo* (1928), *Fascismo* (1932), and *Storia del Movimento Fascista* (1933).

**Vol'pi** (vōl'pē), **Giuseppe.** Conte **di Mi'su·ra'ta** (dē mē'zōō·rä'tä). 1877–1947. Italian statesman and financier; collaborated in establishment of Italo-Turkish peace (1912); member, Italian delegation to Paris Peace Conference (1919); governor of Tripolitana (1921–25); senator (1922 ff.); minister of finance (1925–29).

**Vol'stead** (vŏl'stĕd), **Andrew Joseph.** 1860–1947. American legislator; practiced law at Granite Falls, Minn.; member, U.S. House of Representatives (1903–23). Author of the so-called Volstead Act (passed Oct. 28, 1919), to enforce prohibition of manufacture, sale, and transportation of intoxicating liquors under the 18th Amendment to U.S. Constitution (see also Wayne B. WHEELER); author also of the Farmers' Co-operative Marketing Act.

**Vol'ta** (vôl'tä), Count **Alessandro.** 1745–1827. Italian physicist; pioneer in electricity, b. Como; professor, Pavia (1779–1804); invented the electrophorus (1775) and the voltaic pile (1800); did research on the composition of marsh gas; studied atmospheric electricity. The volt, an electrical unit, is named in his honor.

**Vol·taire'** (vŏl·târ'; vŏl'târ; *Fr.* vôl'târ'). *Assumed name of* **François Marie A'rou·et'** (à'rwĕ'). 1694–1778. French writer, b. at Paris. Educ. under Jesuits at Collège Louis le Grand; began writing at early age, his expert satire getting him into trouble from the first; imprisoned in Bastille (1717–18), where he finished his first tragedy, *Œdipe* (produced, 1718) and began an epic poem on Henry IV of France; again in Bastille (1726); released on condition of leaving France. To England (1726–29); returned with definitive edition of his epic *La Henriade* (printed secretly, 1723; 2d ed., 1728). His observations on English social and political institutions are contained in the *Lettres Anglaises ou Philosophiques* (1734), which caused an uproar making it necessary for him to seek seclusion; resided at Château de Cirey in Lorraine (1734–49) with Mme. du Châtelet, a woman of learning who exerted on him an important intellectual influence. After her death, accepted (1750) invitation to visit Frederick the Great at Prussian court, where he prepared and published (1751) his greatest historical work *Le Siècle de Louis XIV;* quarreled with Frederick and left Prussia (1753); spent last twenty years of life (1758–78) at Ferney, near Geneva. Gained fame as defender of victims of religious intolerance, but chiefly as master of satire. Among his works are the tragedies *Brutus* (1730), *Zaïre* (1732), *Alzire* (1736), *Mahomet* (1741), *Mérope* (1743); philosophical novels *Zadig* (1747) and *Candide* (1759; a satire on the philosophical optimism of Pope and Leibnitz); philosophical poems *Le Mondain* (1736), *Discours sur l'Homme* (1738), and *Le Désastre de Lisbonne* (1756); historical works *Charles XII* (1730) and *Essai sur les Mœurs* (1756); and the *Dictionnaire Philosophique* (1764).

**Vol·ter'ra** (vôl·tĕr'rä), **Daniele da.** *Real name* **Daniele Ric'cia·rel'li** (rēt'chä·rĕl'lē). *Sometimes called* **Il Brac'ca·to'ne** (ēl bräk'kä·tō'nâ). 1509–1566. Italian painter, b. Volterra, Tuscany; works include *Descent from the Cross* and frescoes from life of the Virgin (Church of Santissima Trinità de' Monti, Rome), *Baptism of Christ, David and Goliath, Massacre of Innocents,* and *Moses on Mt. Sinai.*

**Volterra, Vito.** 1860–1940. Italian physicist; known for work in analysis and mechanics.

**Volterrano, Il.** See Baldassare FRANCESCHINI.

**Volumnia.** Wife of Coriolanus (*q.v.*).

**von, von dem, von den, von der, von und zu.** For many names containing one of these elements, see that part of the name following the element.

**Von Braun, Werner.** See BRAUN.

**Von'del** (vôn'dĕl), **Joost van den.** 1587–1679. Dutch poet and dramatist; author of lyric, satirical, patriotic, historical, and religious poems, translations and adaptations from Ovid, Vergil, Seneca, Sophocles, and Euripides, translations of the Psalms, and over thirty dramas, mostly Biblical and historical.

**von Hügel,** Baron **Friedrich.** See HÜGEL.

**von Hutten,** Baroness. See HUTTEN ZUM STOLZENBERG.

**von Kármán, Theodor.** See KÁRMÁN

**Von·noh'** (vŏ·nō'), **Robert William.** 1858–1933. American painter; excelled in portraiture. His second wife (m. 1899), **Bessie,** *nee* **Pot'ter** [pŏt'ēr] (1872–1955), sculptor.

**Voragine, Jacobus de.** See JACOBUS DE VARAGINE.

**Vor'län'der** (fōr'lĕn'dēr), **Karl.** 1860–1928. German philosopher; attempted to combine Neo-Kantianism of the Marburg school and Marxian socialism; edited Kant's collected works (9 vols., 1901–24); wrote *Kant und der Sozialismus* (1900), *Kant und Marx* (1911), *Marx, Engels, und Lassalle als Philosophen* (1920), etc.

**Vo'ro'noff'** (vô'rô'nôf'; *Russ.* vŭ·rô'nôf *or* vô'rŭ·nôf), **Serge** (sĕrzh). 1866–1951. Russian physician in Paris; director of the laboratory of experimental surgery, Collège de France (1917); known for researches on the grafting of animal glands on human beings for rejuvenation.

**Vo·ro'nov** (vŭ·rô'nôf; vô'rŭ·nôf), **Nikolai.** 1899–1968. Soviet army officer; artillery specialist; colonel general, in charge of organization of artillery offensive at Stalingrad (1942); marshal of artillery (1943).

**Vo·ron·tsov'** (vŭ·rŭn·tsôf'). Distinguished Russian family, including: **Mikhail Ilarionovich** (1714–1767), aided Elizabeth in coup d'état (Dec. 6, 1741) by which she seized Russian throne; became vice-chancellor (1744) and chancellor (1758). **Aleksandr Romanovich** (1741–1805), imperial chancellor (1802–04) under Czar Alexander I. Aleksandr's brother **Semën Romanovich** (1744–1832), Russian minister at Vienna (1783–85) and London (1785–1806). Semën's son **Mikhail Semënovich** (1782–1856), served against Napoleon (1805–07, 1812–14), against Turks (1809–11); commanded corps of occupation in France (1815–18); governor general of new Russia (south Russia), where he built up city of Odessa and was first to introduce steamboats on Black Sea; became commander in chief and governor of the Caucasus (1844); succeeded in conquering most of Dagestan (by 1848) and improving Russian position in Caucasus; created prince and field marshal (1856).

**Vo·ro·shi'lov** (vŭ·rŭ·shĭ'lôf), **Kliment Efremovich.** 1881–1969. Soviet soldier and politician, b. in Ukraine; joined Social Democratic party (1903); banished from Russia (1907–14); in World War I (1914–18) supported Lenin's position; carried on guerrilla warfare against Germans in Ukraine (1918); commanded 14th Soviet army; member of Ukrainian Soviet government; associated with Budënny as member of revolutionary military council in 1st cavalry army; suppressed revolt in Leningrad (Mar., 1921); member of central committee of Communist party (1921); commander of north Caucasian military district (1921) and Moscow district (1924–25); member of Politburo (from 1926). As president of revolutionary military council and people's commissar for defense (1925–40), credited with reorganization of Russian general staff, mechanization of army, development of air force, and organization of self-sufficient armies in eastern Siberia; placed in command on Leningrad front at outbreak of war with Germany (1941); with Zhukov, directed operations that broke German siege of Leningrad (1943); pres. U.S.S.R. (1953–60).

**Vö'rös·marty'** (vû'rŭsh·mŏrt'y'), **Mihály.** 1800–1855. Hungarian poet; among his works are *Zalán Futása* (epic, 1824), *Cserhalom* (epic, 1825), *Két Szomszéd Vár* (epic, 1831), *Vérnász* (drama, 1833), and a number of volumes of lyric verse, including *Szózat*, which became a national anthem.

**Vorse** (vôrs), **Mary**, *nee* **Hea'ton** (hē't'n). 1881–1966. American writer, b. N.Y.C.; m. Albert White Vorse (1898), Joseph O'Brien (1912), Robert Minor (1920; divorced, 1922); author of *The Breaking In of a Yachtsman's Wife* (1908), *The Autobiography of an Elderly Woman* (1911), *The Prestons* (1918), *Men and Steel* (1921), *Labor's New Millions* (1938), *Time and the Town* (1942), etc., and many short stories.

**Vor'ster·mans** (vŏr'stẽr·mäns) *or* **Vor'ster·man** (-män), **Lucas.** 1595?–?1675. Flemish painter and engraver; studied under Rubens (1619–23); studio in England (1624–34); executed many plates for Charles I.

**Vor'ti·gern** (vôr'tĭ·gûrn). fl. 450. British prince reported by Gildas and Bede to have invited the Saxons to Britain to repel the Picts and Scots and to have married Rowena, daughter of Hengist.

**Vos** (vŏs), **Cornelis de.** 1585–1651. Flemish portrait and religious painter. His brother **Paul** (1590?–1678) was a painter; best known for his hunting scenes.

**Vos** (vŏs), **Geerhardus.** 1862–1949. Clergyman, b. in Netherlands; to U.S. as a young man; ordained in Presbyterian ministry (1894); professor of Biblical theology, Princeton Theol. Sem. (1893–1932).

**Vos** (vŏs), **Martin de.** 1532–1603. Flemish painter of portraits and religious subjects.

**Voss** (fôs), **Johann Heinrich.** 1751–1826. German poet, translator, and classical philologist; translated Homer, Vergil, Horace, Hesiod, Aristophanes, and, with his sons Heinrich and Abraham, Shakespeare's plays (9 vols., 1818–29); author of verse (collected in 6 vols., 1802) and critical and controversial works.

**Voss, Richard.** 1851–1918. German writer; his many works, largely psychological and pathological, include dramas, novels, and stories.

**Vos'si·us** (vŏs'ĕ·ŭs) *or* **Voss** (vŏs), **Gerhard Johannes.** 1577–1649. Classical scholar, philologist, and theologian, b. near Heidelberg, of Dutch parents; director of the theological college, Leiden (1615), resigned (1619) under suspicion of heresy caused by his *Historia Pelagiana* (1618); professor, U. of Leiden (1622) and Amsterdam Athenaeum (1631). Author of *Ars Rhetorica* (1620), *De Historicis Graecis* (1623–24), *De Historicis Latinis* (1627), *Grammatica Latina* (1626) and *Grammatica Graeca* (1627), etc. His son **Isaac Vossius** *or* **Voss** (1618–1689), scholar and man of letters, collected valuable manuscripts; librarian at court of Queen Christina of Sweden (1648–58); settled in England (1670); made canon of Windsor by Charles II (1673–89); edited works of the geographers Scylax of Caryander and Pomponius Mela, also epistles of Ignatius (1646), Justin, Pliny, Catullus, etc.

**Voss'ler** (fôs'lẽr), **Karl.** 1872–1949. German Romance philologist and critic.

**Vo·sto'kov** (vŭ·stô'kôf), **Aleksandr Khristoforovich.** 1781–1864. Russian philologist; author of a *Russian Grammar* (1831) and a comparative study of Slavic languages.

**Vou·et'** (vwĕ), **Simon.** 1590–1649. French painter; first painter of the court (1627); painted a portrait of Louis XIII; executed murals for Cardinal Richelieu, Marshal d'Effiat.

**Vought** (vôt), **Chance Milton.** 1890–1930. American aeronautical engineer and designer, b. New York City. With financial backing of Birdseye B. Lewis, founded Lewis & Vought Corporation (1917), which later became the Chance Vought Corporation, for manufacture of airplanes; merged with Pratt & Whitney Aircraft Co. and Boeing Airplane Co. to form United Aircraft & Transport Corp. (1929).

**Voulgares, Demetrios.** See BULGARIS.

**Voyer d'Argenson.** See ARGENSON.

**Voy'nich** (voi'nĭch), **Wilfrid Michael.** 1865–1930. Polish bibliophile; to England (1890); authority on medieval manuscripts. He married **Ethel Lilian Boole** [bo͞ol] (1864–1960), English novelist; translator of Russian tales and plays; author of *The Gadfly* (1897), *Six Lyrics from Schevchenko* (1911).

**Voy'sey** (voi'zĭ), **Charles.** 1828–1912. English preacher, founder of Theistic Church, upon ejection from Anglican Church for heterodoxy (1871).

**Voz·ne·sen'ski** (vŭz·nyĕ·syăn'skû·ĭ; *Angl.* vŏz'nĕ·sĕn'skĭ), **Nikolai.** 1904–1950. Russian economist and politician; joined Communist party (1919); drafted third Five-Year Plan (1938), organizing industry in interior sections of country; chairman of state planning committee (1938); vice-chairman of Council of People's Commissars; member of state defense committee (1942–49).

**Voz'ne·sen'sky** (väz'nĕ·sĕn'skĭ), **Andrei Andreevich.** 1933– . Soviet poet. Wrote *Parabola* (1960), *Mosaic* (1960), *Antiworlds* (1964), etc.

**Vraz** (vräz), **Stanko.** 1810–1851. Croatian poet, of Slovene origin; author of sonnets, ballads, satires, romances, etc.; compiled anthology of national songs of both Slovenes and Croats.

**Vrchlický, Jaroslav.** Pseudonym of Emil FRIDA.

**Vre'de·man** (vrā'dĕ·män), *or* **Fre'de·man** (frā'-), **de Vries** (dĕ vrēs'), **Hans** *or* **Jan.** 1527–after 1604. Dutch architect and painter, esp. of architectural pieces.

**Vree'se** (vrā'sĕ), **Willem de.** 1869–1932. Flemish philologist and literary historian; leader of the Flemish movement.

**Vrî'danc** (frē'dängk). Middle High German form of FREIDANK.

**Vriendt, Frans de.** See Frans FLORIS.

**Vries, De.** See DE VRIES.

**Vries** (vrēs) *or* **Fries** (frēs), **Adriaen de.** 1560?–1627. Dutch sculptor, esp. in bronze; his works include bronze groups *Mercury and Psyche* and *Adonis and Venus; Mercury Fountain* and *Hercules Fountain* (Augsburg); busts of Rudolf II (Vienna); *Triton* (New York City).

**Vries, Hans,** *or* **Jan, Vredeman,** *or* **Fredeman, de.** See VREDEMAN DE VRIES.

**Vries** (vrēs), **Matthijs de.** 1820–1892. Dutch philologist; his publications include *Groot Woordenboek der Nederlandsche Taal* (in part with L. A. te Winkel, 1864 ff.; continued by others) and other works on linguistic subjects. He introduced the modern system of Dutch orthography with L. A. te Winkel (*q.v.*).

**Vroom** (vrōm), **Hendrick Cornelisz.** 1566–1640. Dutch painter of sea pictures, naval battles, and ships, and of tapestry and faïence designs.

**Vuil'lard'** (vü·ē'yȧr'), **Jean Édouard.** 1868–1940. French painter, esp. of interiors, still life, and flowers.

**Vuil'laume'** (vü·ē'yōm'). Family of French violinmakers, of whom the best known is **Jean Baptiste** (1798–1875).

**Vu'jić** (vōō'yĕt·y'; *Angl.* -yĭch), **Joakim.** 1772–1847. Serbian playwright and theater director; credited with being founder of the Serbian theater.

**Vulgaris.** = BULGARIS.

**Vul'pi·us** (vŏŏl'pē·ŏŏs), **Christian August.** 1762–1827. German novelist and playwright; bro. of Goethe's wife Christiane (see J. W. GOETHE); wrote *Rinaldo Rinaldini* (a fantastic novel about robbers; 6 parts, 1797–1800) and many plays; published a collection of curiosities (10 vols., 1811–23).

**Vyv'y·an** (vĭv'ĭ·ăn; vĭv'yăn), **Sir Vyell.** 1875–1935. British soldier; in charge of co-ordination of naval, military, and air forces at the Dardanelles (1914–15); vice-marshal of Royal Air Force (1919–25); knighted (1923).

# W

**Waa'ge** (vô'gĕ), **Peter.** 1833–1900. Norwegian chemist; professor (from 1862), Royal Frederick U., Oslo; with C. M. Guldberg, established the law of mass action.

**Waa'gen** (vä'gĕn), **Gustav Friedrich.** 1794–1868. German art critic and art historian; author of *Kunstwerke und Künstler in Deutschland* (2 vols., 1843–45), *Treasures of Art in Great Britain* (3 vols., 1854), etc.

**Waals** (vȧls), **Johannes Diderik van der.** 1837–1923. Dutch physicist; known for his work on the continuity of the liquid and gaseous states (formulating van der Waals' equation), electrolytic dissociation, and the thermodynamic theory of capillarity; awarded 1910 Nobel prize for physics.

**Wace** (*Angl.* wăs, wās; *mod. Fr.* wȧs). *Erroneously* **Robert Wace.** Anglo-Norman poet of 12th century; author of two poetical chronicles written in Norman French, *Roman de Brut* and *Roman de Rou.*

**Wace** (wās), **Henry.** 1836–1924. English ecclesiastical scholar; dean of Canterbury (1903–24). Editor of Luther's primary works; joint-editor, with Sir William Smith, of *Dictionary of Christian Biography...during the first Eight Centuries* (4 vols., 1877–87).

**Wach** (väĸ), **Adolf.** 1843–1926. German jurist; authority on civil action.

**Wa'chen·hu'sen** (vä'ĸĕn·hōō'zĕn), **Hans.** 1823–1898. German war correspondent and author of war observations, travel books, and novels.

**Wach'ler** (väĸ'lẽr), **Ernst.** 1871– . German theater director and author of festival plays. studies on drama and culture, and novels.

**Wachs'muth** (väks'mōōt), **Charles.** 1829–1896. Paleontologist, b. Hanover, Ger.; to U.S. (1852); collected rare crinoids. His collection purchased (1873) by Museum of Comparative Zoology at Cambridge, Mass. Associate of Louis Agassiz (1873), and later of Frank Springer, with whom he wrote the large *North American Crinoidea Camerata* (1897), dedicated to Agassiz.

**Wack'en·ro'der** (väk'ĕn·rō'dẽr), **Wilhelm Heinrich.** 1773–1798. German romanticist; writer esp. on old German art and music; friend of Ludwig Tieck, who collaborated with him in writing *Phantasien über die Kunst* (1799).

**Wack'er** (väk'ẽr), **Alexander von.** 1846–1922. German industrialist; developed (esp. from 1892) the electrotechnical and electrochemical industry; founded (1914) the Dr. Alexander Wacker Company, Munich, and companies in Switzerland, Norway, and Bosnia.

**Wack'er·na'gel** (väk'ẽr·nä'gĕl), **Wilhelm.** 1806–1869. German Germanic scholar; author of *Geschichte der Deutschen Literatur* (1851–53), *Altdeutsches Wörterbuch* (1861), *Poetik, Rhetorik, Stilistik* (pub. 1873), etc.

**Wad·dell'** (wŏ·dĕl'), **Helen.** 1889–1965. British author, esp. on medieval subjects; author of *Peter Abelard* (1933) and *The Desert Fathers* (1936).

**Waddell, Hugh,** 1734?–1773. Soldier, b. Lisburn, Ireland; to U.S. when young; settled in North Carolina. General and commander in chief of North Carolina troops under Gov. Tryon in campaign to pacify the Regulators (1771). His great-grandson **James Iredell Waddell** (1824–1886) was a naval officer; commanded Confederate raider *Shenandoah* (1864–65), which continued operations until Aug., 1865, in ignorance of collapse of Confederacy.

**Wad'ding** (wŏd'ĭng), **Luke.** 1588–1657. Irish Franciscan friar and historian; compiled annals of his order, biographies of its illustrious members, and monumental edition of life and writings of Duns Scotus (16 vols., 1639).

**Wad'ding·ton** (wŏd'ĭng·tŭn), **William Henry.** 1826–1894. French archaeologist and statesman, son of an English manufacturer resident in France. Traveled and explored in Asia Minor, Greece, and Syria, and published his *Voyage Archéologique en Grèce et en Asie Mineure* (1866–77). Member of National Assembly (1871) and Senate (1876); minister of public instruction (1876–77) and foreign affairs (1877–79); premier (1879); French ambassador to Great Britain (1883–93).

**Wade** (wād), **Benjamin Franklin.** 1800–1878. American lawyer and politician; U.S. senator from Ohio (1851–69); a leader of antislavery group in Senate; vigorously supported prosecution of war against seceding States; worked in close co-operation with Secretary Stanton; failed to understand Lincoln's policies and was joint author of Wade-Davis Manifesto (Aug. 5, 1864), condemning Lincoln's usurpation of power and insisting that Congress was paramount in matters of reconstruction in the South. Bitterly opposed Johnson and voted for Johnson's conviction in impeachment trial.

**Wade, George.** 1673–1748. Irish officer in British army; field marshal (1743); commanded British forces in Flanders (1744–45); commander in chief in England (1745); failed to stop southward march of Prince Charles Edward; superseded by duke of Cumberland.

**Wade, Sir Thomas Francis.** 1818–1895. English soldier, diplomat, and Chinese scholar; ambassador at Peking (1871–83); Chinese professor, Cambridge (1888); introduced Wade system of transliterating Chinese (Mandarin) language.

**Wader, Ralph de.** See GUADER.

**Wads'worth** (wŏdz'wûrth; -wẽrth), **James.** 1768–1844. American pioneer in Genesee Valley, New York; b. Durham, Conn. Associated with his brother William as land agent for owners of large tracts along east bank of Genesee River, in what are now Geneseo and Avon townships; settled there (1790), cultivated holdings of his own, and acted as agent in bringing in settlers. His son **James Samuel** (1807–1864) was an army officer; commanded defenses of Washington (1862); occupied Culp's Hill at Gettysburg (1863); mortally wounded in battle of the Wilderness (May, 1864). James Samuel's son **James Wolcott** (1846–1926), politician, was member of U.S. House of Representatives (1881–85; 1891–1907). His son **James Wolcott, Jr.** (1877–1952), businessman and political leader; U.S. senator from New York (1915–27); member of U.S. House of Representatives (from 1933); cosponsor with Edward R. Burke of the Selective Training and Service Act (1940).

**Wadsworth, Jeremiah.** 1743–1804. American Revolutionary officer, b. Hartford, Conn.; commissary general of Continental army (1778–79), and commissary of French troops in America. Member, Connecticut State constitutional ratification convention (1788), and U.S. House of Representatives (1789–95). Member, Connecticut executive council (1795–1801). Established first partnership for insurance in Connecticut (1794).

**Wadsworth, Peleg.** 1748–1829. American Revolutionary officer, b. Duxbury, Mass. With Theophilus Cotton's regiment, as engineer laid out American lines at Roxbury and at Dorchester Heights (1775). Aide-de-camp of Artemas Ward (1776); served under Washington in New York and on Long Island (1776) and under Sullivan in Rhode Island (1778). Commanded eastern department, headquarters at Thomaston, Me. (1780–81). Member, U.S. House of Representatives (1793–1807).

**Waech'ter** (vĕκ'tẽr), **Karl Georg von.** 1797–1880. German jurist.

**Wa'fer** (wā'fẽr), **Lionel.** 1660?–?1705. British surgeon and buccaneer. At sea as surgeon's assistant (1677); deserted (1679) and joined party of buccaneers on foray across Isthmus of Panama; accidentally disabled (1681), left companions and lived with Indians; found by William Dampier (*q.v.*); voyaged with Dampier and others; settled in Virginia. Author of *A New Voyage* (1699, 1704), first good description in English of Indians of Isthmus of Panama.

**Wa'ge·naar** (vä'gĕ·när), **Johan.** 1862–1941. Dutch organist, and composer of operas, a musical play, a humorous cantata, choral works, overtures (*Cyrano de Bergerac*, 1905), a tone poem (*Saul und David*, 1906), and smaller works for orchestra and choirs.

**Wag'nalls** (wăg'n'lz), **Adam Willis.** 1843–1924. American publisher, b. Lithopolis, Ohio: one of original founders, and president, Funk & Wagnalls Co., New York City, publishers.

**Wag'ner** (wăg'nẽr), **Ho'nus** (hō'nŭs), *known as* **Hans.** 1874–1955. American professional baseball player, b. Carnegie, Pa.; called "the Flying Dutchman"; shortstop, in National League, with Louisville (1897–99), Pittsburgh (1900–17).

**Wag'ner** (väg'nẽr), **Johann Peter Alexander.** 1730–1809. German sculptor; representative of the rococo style; resident in Würzburg (from 1756), where he was court sculptor (from 1771). His son **Johann Martin von Wagner** (1777–1858) was a sculptor and painter.

**Wagner, Karl Willy.** 1883– . German electrical engineer.

**Wagner, Otto.** 1841–1918. Austrian architect of modern ("Secessionist") school; designed Vienna Kur-Salon (1862), Metropolitan Railway Stations (1894–97), Postal Savings Bank (1905), churches, hospitals, etc.

**Wagner, Richard,** *in full* **Wilhelm Richard.** 1813–1883. German tone poet, composer, and writer on music, b. Leipzig; originator of the music drama and pioneer in the development of the leitmotiv. Music director of theaters at Magdeburg (1834–36), Königsberg (1836), and Riga (1837–39); married Minna Planer (1836; separated 1861). In Paris (1839–42) trying to gain foothold in theater; studied music, esp. grand opera, and completed *Faust Overture* (1840) and operas *Rienzi* (1840) and *Der Fliegende Holländer* (1841). To Dresden, where *Rienzi* and *Der Fliegende Holländer* were successfully produced (1842, 1843); court Kapellmeister (1843–49). Following alleged participation in May Day uprising (1849), fled to Zurich, his chief residence until 1858; carried on affair with friend's wife, Mathilde Wesendonk; conducted Philharmonic concerts, London (1855). Returned to Germany following amnesty (1861) and lived in various cities. Married (1870) Liszt's daughter Cosima (see below); settled in Bayreuth (1872), where his theater was founded (1872) and opened (1876) with his *Der Ring des Nibelungen;* guest conductor in London (1877) and chief German cities; spent last years in Italy; died in Venice (1883). His operas include *Die Feen* (completed 1833, never performed), *Rienzi* (1840, performed 1842), *Der Fliegende Holländer* (*The Flying Dutchman*, 1841, performed 1843), *Tannhäuser* (1845, performed 1845), *Lohengrin* (1848, performed 1850), the tetralogy *Der Ring des Nibelungen* (written 1848–74: *Das Rheingold*, 1854, performed 1869; *Die Walküre*, 1856, performed 1870; *Siegfried*, 1871, performed 1876; *Götterdämmerung*, 1874, performed 1876), *Tristan und Isolde* (1859, performed 1865), *Die Meistersinger von Nürnberg* (1867, performed 1868), and *Parsifal* (1882, performed 1882); orchestral choral works include *An Webers Grabe* (performed 1844), several overtures including *Faust Overture* (performed 1844), the *Siegfried Idyll* (1870), cantatas, choruses, songs, piano pieces, and arrangements. His literary works include letters, poems, and critical writings on music. His wife **Cosima** (1837–1930), daughter of Franz Liszt, first married (1857) Hans von Bülow (divorced 1869); helped develop idea of Bayreuth Festival, and was art director of festival plays (until 1908). Their son **Siegfried** (1869–1930) was a composer and director; director (from 1896) and art director (from 1909) of Bayreuth Festival plays; compositions include dramatic works, symphonic poems, a violin concerto, and the orchestral scherzo *Und Wenn die Welt voll Teufel Wär* (1923). Their younger daughter **Eva** married Houston S. Chamberlain (*q.v.*). Richard's niece **Johanna Jach'mann–Wag'ner** [yäκ'män-] (1828–1894), operatic soprano and actress, was a member of Dresden (1844–46) and Berlin (1850–62) court operas; m. Jachmann (1859); on stage as tragedienne, Berlin Theater (1862–72).

**Wag'ner** (wăg'nẽr), **Robert Ferdinand.** 1877–1953. Lawyer and legislator, b. in Hesse-Nassau, Ger.; to U.S. in childhood; B.S. (1898), C.C.N.Y.; LL.B. (1900), N.Y. Law School; practiced in New York City; state senator (1909–18); supreme court justice, N.Y. (1919–26); as U.S. senator (1927–49), introduced social legislation, including National Industrial Recovery Act (NIRA), Social Security Act, National Labor Relations Act (Wagner Act), Railway Pension Law, U.S. Housing Act of 1937.

**Wag'ner** (väg'nẽr), **Rudolf.** 1805–1864. German anatomist and physiologist; discovered the germinal spot in the human ovum (1835) and, with Georg Meissner, the tactile end organs (1852) known as Meissner's corpuscles; later became opponent of materialism; also known as an anthropologist and archaeologist. His brother **Moritz Friedrich** (1813–1887), naturalist, traveled in Algeria (1836–38), Asia (1843–45), North and Central America (1852–55), Panama and Ecuador (1858–60); wrote on his travels; sought to supplement Darwinian theory with a theory of migrations. Rudolf's son **Adolph** (1835–

1917) was an economist; supporter of "doctrinaire socialism"; author of works on economics, banking and finance, and social reform. Adolph's brother **Hermann** (1840–1929) was a geographer and statistician.

**Wag′ner** (väg′nẽr), **Sándor,** *or* **Alexander, von.** 1838–1919. Hungarian painter; known esp. for frescoes and murals with subjects taken from Hungarian history.

**Wag′ner von Jau′regg** (väg′nẽr fôn you′rĕk), **Julius.** *Surname also* **Wag′ner–Jau′regg.** 1857–1940. Austrian neurologist and psychiatrist; introduced treatment of general paralysis by infection of patient with malaria (1917); awarded 1927 Nobel prize for physiology and medicine.

**Wagstaffe, Launcelot.** Pseudonym of Washington IRVING.

**Wahr′mund** (vär′mo͝ont), **Adolf.** 1827–1913. German Orientalist, b. Wiesbaden; instructor in Arabic (1871) and director (1885–97), Oriental Academy; works include grammars of modern Arabic (1861), Osmanli Turkish (1869), and Persian (1875), a modern Arabic-German dictionary (3 vols., 1874–77).

**Wai′bling·en** (vī′blĭng·ĕn). *Also* **Wei′bling** (vī′blĭng). A surname of Conrad III of Germany, derived from an estate (now a town in Württemberg) belonging to Hohenstaufen family of Swabia, which was later applied to his followers; corrupted by imperial supporters in Italy into *Ghibelline* (*q.v.*). See also HOHENSTAUFEN.

**Wail′ly′** (vȧ′yē′), **Noël François de.** 1724–1801. French philologist and educator; author of *Principes Généraux de Langue Française* (1754); coeditor of 1798 edition of the *Dictionnaire de l'Académie.* His grandson **Barthélemy Alfred de Wailly** (1800–1869), lexicographer, compiled *Nouveau Dictionnaire Latin-Français* (1829).

**Waine′wright** (wān′rīt), **Thomas Griffiths.** 1794–1852. English art connoisseur; wrote art criticisms for *London Magazine* under name of **Janus Weath′er·cock′** (wĕth′ẽr·kŏk′); committed forgery (1826), convicted, and transported to Tasmania (1837), where he died.

**Wainfleet, William of.** See WAYNFLETE.

**Wain′wright** (wān′rīt), **Jonathan Mayhew.** 1792–1854. Protestant Episcopal clergyman, b. Liverpool, Eng.; to U.S. (c. 1803); consecrated bishop of New York (1852). His son **Jonathan Mayhew** (1821–1863), naval officer, supported Farragut and Porter in attacks on forts Jackson and St. Philip on lower Mississippi; killed in action (Jan. 1, 1863). The latter's grandson **Jonathan Mayhew** (1883–1953), army officer, b. Walla Walla, Wash.; grad. U.S.M.A., West Point (1906); served in France (1918); major general (1940), sent to Philippines; after Japanese invasion (Dec., 1941), commanded northern front until he succeeded MacArthur as commander in chief; defended Bataan and Corregidor (1942); prisoner of war; rescued in Manchuria (1945); general (1945); commander, 4th army (1946–47).

**Wainwright, Richard.** 1817–1862. American naval officer; commanded the *Hartford,* Farragut's flagship (Dec., 1861–Aug., 1862); in action running past forts Jackson and St. Philip in lower Mississippi (Apr. 24, 1862), and later at Vicksburg; engaged Confederate ram *Arkansas* below Vicksburg (July 15, 1862). Died of remittent fever contracted in line of duty. His son **Richard** (1849–1926) was also a naval officer; executive officer, U.S. battleship *Maine* (1897–98), when the *Maine* was sunk in Havana harbor (Feb. 15, 1898); commanded the *Gloucester,* formerly J. P. Morgan's *Corsair,* in battle of Santiago Bay (July 3, 1898), attacking Spanish destroyers successfully; engaged also in naval action off Puerto Rico; captain (1903) and rear admiral (1908).

**Wait** (wāt), **William Bell.** 1839–1916. American educator of the blind, b. Amsterdam, N.Y.; devised New York point, a variation of Braille, for use in printed literature for the blind, and invented machines for printing and typing New York point characters.

**Waite** (wāt), **Morrison Remick.** 1816–1888. American jurist; one of American counsel in Geneva Arbitration on *Alabama* claims (1871–72); chief justice, U.S. Supreme Court (1874–88).

**Waitz** (vīts), **Georg.** 1813–1886. German historian; authority on medieval history; disciple of Ranke; professor, Kiel (1842), Göttingen (1849–75), where he founded a school of historians, and Berlin (1875), where he directed *Monumenta Germaniae Historica.*

**Waitz, Theodor.** 1821–1864. German philosopher and anthropologist; based his philosophy on that of Herbart; sought to make psychology the basis of philosophy.

**Wa·ka·tsu·ki** (wä·kä·tso͞o·kē), **Reijiro.** 1866–1949. Japanese statesman; minister of finance (1912, 1914–15); premier of Japan (1926–27); chief of delegation to London Naval Conference (1929–30).

**Wake** (wāk), **William.** 1657–1737. English ecclesiastic; archbishop of Canterbury (1716–37); negotiated with French Jansenists on proposed union with English church (1717–20).

**Wake′feld** (wāk′fēld), **Robert.** d. 1537. English Hebraist; professor at Louvain (1519), Tübingen (1520–23), Oxford (1530ff). His brother **Thomas** (d. 1575) was first regius professor of Hebrew at Cambridge.

**Wake′field** (wāk′fēld), **Edward Gibbon.** 1796–1862. English colonial statesman; organized association for colonizing South Australia (1834); organized and managed New Zealand Land Company (1839–49) from London; sent shipload of colonists to New Zealand in the *Tory* (1839), compelling British government to recognize it as a colony in time to forestall annexation to France; a founder of Church of England colony at Canterbury (1849). His brother **William Hayward** (1803–1848) sailed in the *Tory* and directed colonial operations in New Zealand; founded Wellington (1840). Another brother, **Arthur** (1799–1843), founded Nelson, N.Z. The youngest brother, **Felix** (1807–1875), an engineer, assisted in founding Canterbury Colony. **Edward Jerningham** (1820–1879), son of Edward Gibbon, published notes on the settlements in New Zealand.

**Wakefield, Gilbert.** 1756–1801. English classical scholar; ordained Anglican deacon (1778), left church, and became a nonsectarian; tutor, Warrington Academy, a Unitarian school (1779–83); edited Bion and Moschus, the *Georgics,* Horace, Lucretius, and Greek plays; author of *Silva Critica* (1789), critical comments on the Scriptures, based on classical sources.

**Wak′ley** (wăk′lĭ), **Thomas.** 1795–1862. English surgeon and medical reformer; founder (1823) of *The Lancet,* weekly medical paper, subsequently edited by his son **Thomas Henry** (1821–1907), surgeon and journalist, and grandson **Thomas** (1851–1909), physician.

**Waks′man** (wäks′măn; wăks′-), **Selman Abraham.** 1888–1973. American microbiologist, b. Russia. To U.S. (1910); at Rutgers U. (1918–58); awarded Nobel prize in physiology and medicine (1952) for discovery of streptomycin.

**Wal·bur′ga** (väl·bo͝or′gä) *or* **Wal·pur′ga** (-po͝or′gä) *or* **Wal·pur′gis** (-gĭs), Saint. 710?–779. English saint; said to have aided St. Boniface in converting the Germans to Christianity; died abbess of Heidenheim. Walpurgis Night is the eve of May Day, her feast day.

**Walch** (välk). A family of German Protestant theologians and scholars, including: **Johann Georg** (1693–1775), editor of Luther's works (24 vols., 1740–52), and author of works on religious controversies, esp. in the Lutheran Church; and his sons **Johann Ernst Immanuel**

(1725–1778), theologian at Jena and mineralogist, and **Christian Wilhelm Franz** (1726–1784), author of works on church history and heresies.

**Wal′cott** (wôl′kŭt), **Charles Doolittle.** 1850–1927. American geologist and paleontologist; director, U.S. Geological Survey (1894–1907); secretary, Smithsonian Institution (from 1907). He married (1914) **Mary Morris Vaux** [vôks] (1860–1940), glaciologist and painter of wild flowers. Mount Mary Vaux in the Canadian Rockies was named after her.

**Wald** (wôld), **George.** 1906– . American biologist, b. New York City. At Harvard U. (1934– ); awarded Nobel prize in physiology and medicine (1967) with R. Granit and H. Hartline for research on the eye.

**Wald, Lillian D.** 1867–1940. American social worker, b. in Ohio; founder (1893), president, and organizer of public-health nursing, Henry Street Settlement, New York City; suggested Federal Children's Bureau (established by U.S. Congress, 1908), and town and rural nursing service by American Red Cross; active in all branches of social work. Author of *The House on Henry Street* (1915), *Windows on Henry Street* (1934). Elected to American Hall of Fame (1970).

**Wal′de** (väl′dĕ), **Alois.** 1869–1924. German philologist.

**Wal′deck** (väl′dĕk). Former German principality whose ruling house originated about 12th century; lands increased through marriages and inheritances (1631–73); divided into two lines; last ruler of princely line: Frederick (1865–1932); began rule in 1904, abdicated in 1918.

**Wal′deck′-Rous′seau′** (vȧl′dĕk′rōō′sō′), **Pierre Marie René.** 1846–1904. French lawyer and statesman; counsel for de Lesseps in the Panama trial; premier of France (1899–1902).

**Walde′grave** (wôl′grāv), **Frances Elizabeth Anne,** *nee* **Bra′ham** (brā′ăm). Countess **Waldegrave.** 1821–1879. Leader and hostess of London society; inherited estates of her second husband, 7th Earl Waldegrave, including Strawberry Hill, which she restored.

**Waldegrave, Robert.** 1554?–1604. English puritan printer; printed John Penry's first *Martin Marprelate* tract (1588).

**Wal′de·mar** (wôl′dĕ·mär). *Dan.* **Val′de·mar** (vȧl′dĕ·mär). Name of four kings of Denmark:

**Waldemar I.** 1131–1182. *Called* "the Great." Son of Canute Lavard. King (1157–82). Born week after father's murder; became claimant to throne after death of Eric III (1147); defeated and killed Sweyn III (1157); sole male survivor of ancient line; made Absalon his minister (1158); waged war against Wendish pirates (1159–69); with Absalon overcame their stronghold in Rügen (1169) and converted them; acknowledged overlordship of Emperor Frederick Barbarossa (1162); later (1182), his two daughters married two sons of the emperor; put down rebellion in Swedish provinces.

**Waldemar II.** 1170–1241. *Called* "the Victorious." Second son of Waldemar I and brother of Canute VI. King (1202–41). Conquered Holstein and Hamburg; recognized by emperor as lord of territories in northwestern Germany; extended conquests to eastern shore of Baltic (1206–10), seizing island of Oesel off Estonia; undertook campaign against Estonians on appeal of bishop of Riga (1218); miraculously received (1219) red banner (the Dannebrog, now Danish national flag) at critical moment in battle near Reval (Tallinn); most powerful ruler in northern Europe; defeated at Bornhöved (1227); lost Estonia (1227) but recovered it (1238); last years spent in domestic reform; promulgated codification of laws, the *Jutland Code* (1241).

**Waldemar III.** d. 1231. Eldest son of Waldemar II; ruled as coregent with his father.

**Waldemar IV At′ter·dag** (ȧt′tĕr·dȧg). 1320?–1375. Youngest son of Christopher II. King (1340–75); last of the Estrith dynasty. Educated at court of Emperor Louis of Bavaria (1326–40); returned to rule (1340) a country largely held by foreign princes; recovered southern part (1340–49); sold Estonia to Teutonic Knights (1346); Black Death raged 1349–50; victorious over Holstein counts (1357); Skåne (Danish province in southern Sweden) recovered (1360); seized Visby in Gotland (1361), beat off fleet of Hanseatic League (1362), and overcame Sweden (1365); attacked (1367–68) by coalition of Hanse cities, Sweden, Mecklenburg, etc.; suddenly left Denmark to live in Germany (1367–71) leaving defense against league to royal council; returned after humiliating peace of Stralsund (1370); recovered nearly all of Schleswig (1375).

**Wal′de·mar** (wôl′dĕ·mär; *Ger.* väl′-) *or* **Val′de·mar** (văl′-). *Called* "the Great." 1281?–1319. Margrave of Brandenburg (1303–19), of the Ascanian line. Fought successfully (1314–19) against league of German princes led by kings of Denmark and Sweden, against Slavs, etc.; extended boundaries of his margraviate; succeeded by his cousin Henry the Child, whose death (1320) ended Ascanian line. A false **Waldemar** (d. 1356) arose (1347) claiming Brandenburg; accepted for a time; declared impostor by Emperor Charles IV (1350).

**Wal′de·mar** (wôl′dĕ·mär). *Swed.* **Val′de·mar** (vȧl′dĕ·mȧr). 1238?–?1302. King of Sweden (1250–75); son of the regent Birger of Bjälbo; fought civil war with brothers; deposed (1275); fled to Norway.

**Waldemaras.** Variant of Voldemaras.

**Wal′den** (väl′dĕn), **Herwarth.** 1878– . German writer, critic, and composer esp. for piano; champion of futurism and expressionism in art.

**Wal′den** (väl′dĕn), **Paul** (poul). 1863–1957. Russian organic chemist; discovered a type of optical inversion (Walden inversion); investigated electrical conductivity of solutions, dissociation constants, etc.

**Wal′der·see** (väl′dĕr·zā), Count **Alfred von.** 1832–1904. German soldier; chief of general staff to grand duke of Mecklenburg-Schwerin and to governor of Paris (1871); chief of staff (1888); commander of European forces in China during Boxer rebellion (1900–01).

**Wal′dey′er-Hartz′** (väl′dī′ĕr·härts′), **Wilhelm von.** *Orig. surname* **Waldeyer.** 1836–1921. German anatomist; known for his work on histology of the nervous system, the eye, ear, and ovaries, and on cancer.

**Wald′heim** (vält′hīm), **Kurt.** 1918– . Austrian diplomat. Ambassador to Canada (1958–60); secretary general of the United Nations (1972– ).

**Wal′dis** (väl′dĭs), **Burkard.** 1490?–?1556. German poet and writer of fables; Franciscan monk; embraced Lutheranism (1524); imprisoned during religious persecutions (1536–40). His works include *Die Parabel vom Verlorenen Sohn* (1527), *Esopus* (a translation and revision in verse of Aesop, 1548), a collection of 400 rhymed fables, and humorous pieces.

**Wald′mül′ler** (vält′mül′ĕr), **Ferdinand Georg.** 1793–1865. Viennese landscape, portrait, and genre painter.

**Waldmüller, Robert.** Pseudonym of Édouard Duboc.

**Wal′do** (wôl′dō; wŏl′-) *or* **Val′do** (văl′dō; *Fr.* vȧl′dō′), **Peter.** *Lat.* **Petrus Wal′dus** (wôl′dŭs). fl. in late 12th century. French heretic; originally a successful merchant, renounced the world (c. 1173), gave away all his property, and devoted himself to religious study. He preached and gathered a number of disciples, known as "the Poor Men of Lyons," and later as *Waldenses.* He was excommunicated after a vain appeal to the Third Lateran Council (1179), and his followers were persecuted.

**Wal'do** (wôl'dō; wŏl'-), **Samuel Lovett.** 1783–1861. American painter, b. Windham, Conn.; self-taught; studio in New York (1809–61); in partnership with William Jewett (from 1820); a founder, National Academy of Design; best known for portraits.

**Wald'see·mül'ler** (vält'zā·mül'ēr) *or* **Walt'ze·mül'ler** (väl'tsā-), **Martin.** *Lat.* **Hy'la·com'y·lus** (hī'lȧ·kŏm'ĭ-lŭs) *or* **I'la·com'i·lus** (ī'lȧ·kŏm'ĭ·lŭs). 1470?–?1518. German cartographer; credited with being first to call the New World *America*, applying the name to South America in his *Cosmographiae Introductio* (1507) containing a map of the world in 12 sheets. The only known copy of the first edition of this book is in the public library in New York City.

**Waldstein, Charles.** See Charles WALSTON.

**Wald'teu'fel'** (vȧl'tû'fĕl'), **Émile.** 1837–1915. French composer; best known for his waltzes, including *Je t'Aime, Les Sourires, Soir d'Amour.*

**Wales** (wālz), **William.** 1734?–1798. English mathematician and astronomer: sent by Royal Society to Hudson's Bay to view transit of Venus (1769); accompanied James Cook on his second and third voyages (1772–74, 1776–80).

**Wa·lew'ska** (vä·lĕf'skä), Countess **Ma'rie'** (mȧ'rē') **Laczyńska.** 1789–1817. Polish noblewoman; mistress of Napoleon, and mother by him of Comte Alexandre Florian Joseph Colonna Walewski (*q.v.*).

**Wa·lew'ski** (vä·lĕf'skē), Comte **Alexandre Flo'ri·an'** (flô'ryäɴ') **Joseph Co'lon'na'** (kô'lô'nȧ'). 1810–1868. Natural son of Napoleon and the Polish countess Marie Walewska. Diplomat, naturalized Frenchman; served in French army (to 1837) and engaged in journalism in Paris. Minister to Florence (1849), Naples (1850); ambassador to Spain (1851) and Great Britain (1851); minister of foreign affairs (1855–60); president of the legislature (1865).

**Wa'ley** (wā'lĭ), **Arthur David.** *Orig. surname* **Schloss** (shlŏs). 1889–1966. Asst. curator, dept. of prints and drawings, British Museum; translator of Chinese and Japanese literary works, as: *170 Chinese Poems* (1919), *Japanese Poetry* (1919), *The No Plays of Japan* (1922), Lady Murasaki's *Tale of Genji* (1925–32), *The Analects of Confucius* (1939), and Wu Ch'eng-en's *Monkey* (1942).

**Walid.** *Arab.* **al-Wa·līd'** (ăl'wȧ·lēd'). Name of two Ommiad caliphs: **Walid I** (675?–715); caliph (705–715); son of Abd-al-Malik; reign one of greatest in history of Islam; his generals completed conquests in western Asia and India, and one of them, Tariq, led (711) victorious army into Spain; noted for building schools, hospitals, and mosques, esp. the cathedral mosque at Damascus. **Walid II** (d. 744); caliph (743–744); son of Yazid II.

**Walke** (wôk), **Henry.** 1808–1896. American naval officer; served under Commodore Foote on upper Mississippi (1861–63) and under Porter in operations against Vicksburg (1863); commanded the *Sacramento* pursuing Confederate raiders in Atlantic (1863–65). Commodore (1866); rear admiral (1870).

**Wal'ke·lin'** (vou'kĕ·lēn') *or* **Wal'che·lin'** (vou'chyĕ-lēn'). d. 1098. Norman bishop of Winchester by appointment (1070) of his kinsman William the Conqueror; built new cathedral (1079–93); joint regent during absence of William Rufus (1097–98).

**Walk'er** (wôk'ēr), **Am'a·sa** (ăm'ȧ·sȧ). 1799–1875. American businessman and economist, b. Woodstock, Conn. Farmer, store clerk, manufacturer's agent, shoe-shop proprietor (to 1840). On teaching staff, Oberlin (1842–49), Harvard (1853–60), Amherst (1860–69). Member, U.S. House of Representatives (1862–63). Author of *The Science of Wealth...* (1866). His son **Francis Amasa** (1840–1897), economist and educator; served through Civil War, rising from private to brevet brigadier general; chief, U.S. Bureau of Statistics (1869–71); U.S. commissioner of Indian affairs (1871–72); superintendent of the 9th and 10th United States censuses (1870, 1880). Professor, Yale (1873–81); president, M.I.T. (1881–97). Widely known as advocate of international bimetallism. His investigations of wages and profits strongly influenced economic theory.

**Walker, Charles Howard.** 1857–1936. American architect, b. Boston; practiced in Boston (from 1884); designed plan of St. Louis Exposition (1904); director, School of Fine Arts, Boston (1913–36).

**Walker, Frederick.** 1840–1875. English painter and illustrator; wood engraver's apprentice (1858); an illustrator of Thackeray.

**Walker, George.** 1618–1690. Anglo-Irish Episcopal clergyman and defender of Londonderry; joint governor of Derry during 150-day siege (April–July, 1689) by troops of James II; nominated by William III to bishopric of Derry; killed at battle of the Boyne (1690).

**Walker, Henry Oliver.** 1843–1929. American painter, b. Boston; studio in Boston (1883–89) and New York (from 1889); best known for his mural paintings, as in the Library of Congress, Washington, D.C.

**Walker, Horatio.** 1858–1938. Canadian painter; to New York (1885); took as chief subjects French-Canadians and their pastures and farms.

**Walker, James.** 1794–1874. American clergyman and college president; one of organizers, American Unitarian Association (1825); editor, *The Christian Examiner* (1831–39); professor of natural religion, moral philosophy, and civil polity, Harvard (1839–53); president, Harvard (1853–60).

**Walker, James John.** 1881–1946. American politician; mayor of New York (1926–32); involved by state legislative investigation of New York's municipal government and summoned before governor, Franklin D. Roosevelt, to answer charges; resigned (Sept. 1, 1932).

**Walker, James Thomas.** 1826–1896. British army field engineer in India; served in Sepoy Mutiny (1857); superintendent of trigonometrical survey of India (1861–83); general (1884).

**Walker, John.** 1732–1807. English actor, elocutionist (hence sometimes called "Elocution Walker"), and lexicographer; actor at Drury Lane and in Dublin; quit stage (1768); professional lecturer on elocution (1771 ff.); enjoyed patronage of Dr. Johnson; compiler of *A Critical Pronouncing Dictionary* (1791), *A Rhyming Dictionary* (1775).

**Walker, John.** 1781?–1859. English druggist; inventor of the friction match (1827).

**Walker, John Brisben.** 1847–1931. American journalist and publisher; managing editor, Washington (D.C.) *Chronicle* (1876–79); owner and editor, *Cosmopolitan Magazine* (1889–1905). Active in movement to keep U.S. from entering World War.

**Walker, John Grimes.** 1835–1907. American naval officer; commanded ironclad *Baron De Kalb* in Admiral Porter's Mississippi squadron and the *Saco* (1864) and the *Shawmut* (1865) in Atlantic coast blockade squadron, chief, bureau of navigation, U.S. navy (1881–89); president, Isthmian Canal Commission (1899–1904).

**Walker, Joseph Reddeford.** 1798–1876. American trapper and guide; trading headquarters at Independence, Mo. (1820–32). Member of Bonneville's expedition to Rocky Mountains (1832); guided Frémont's third expedition to California (1845–46); to California (1849, 1861–62). Walker Lake and Walker Pass are named after him.

**Walker, Mary Edwards.** 1832–1919. American physician and advocate of woman's rights, b. Oswego, N.Y. Received physician's certificate from Syracuse (N.Y.) Medical College (1855); practiced in Rome, N.Y. From her youth, advocated woman's rights; called attention to herself and her propaganda by wearing male attire. Served as nurse with Union army (1861–64), and commissioned assistant surgeon (1864–65). Practiced medicine in Washington, D.C. (from 1865), continuing also agitation for woman's rights.

**Walker, Nellie Verne.** 1874– . American sculptor, b. Red Oak, Iowa; her statue *Chief Keokuk* overlooks the Mississippi River at Keokuk, Iowa.

**Walker, Robert.** d. 1658? English painter of frequently copied portraits of Cromwell, and of Admiral Blake and General Monk.

**Walker, Robert John** (*or* **James**). 1801–1869. American politician; practiced law in Pittsburgh, Pa. (1821–26) and Natchez, Miss. (from 1826); U.S. senator from Mississippi (1836–45); U.S. secretary of the treasury (1845–49); governor of Kansas Territory (1857–58); financial agent of U.S. government in Europe (1863–64).

**Walker, Sarah,** *nee* **Breed′love** (brĕd′lŭv). 1867–1919. American Negro businesswoman, b. Delta, La.; m. C. J. Walker (1881; d. 1887); invented (1905) and successfully exploited a preparation for straightening kinky hair; bequeathed fortune to educational institutions and charities.

**Walker, Sears Cook.** 1805–1853. American astronomer; on staff, U.S. Naval Observatory, Washington, D.C. (from 1845); and in charge of computations of geographical longitude in U.S. Coast Survey (from 1847). Introduced theory that electric telegraph provided best means for determining difference of longitude from place to place, and the longitude of any given place from a prime meridian. Originated the telegraphing of transits of stars, and the application of the graphic record of time results to the registering of time observations for general astronomical purposes.

**Walker, Sidney,** *in full* **William Sidney.** 1795–1846. English Shakespearean critic; author of *Shakespeare's Versification* (1854, edited by W. N. Lettsom) and *A Critical Examination of the Text of Shakespeare* (1860).

**Walker, Stuart.** 1888–1941. American playwright and theatrical producer; directed repertory company in Indianapolis (1917–23; 1926–28) and Cincinnati (1922–31); director for Paramount-Publix Corporation (1931–34); producer, Paramount (from 1936). Originated "portmanteau theater." Author of *Portmanteau Plays* (2 series, 1917, 1919), *Five Flights Up* (1922), *The Demi-Reds* (with Gladys Unger, 1936), etc.

**Walker, Thomas Barlow.** 1840–1928. American lumberman and art collector, b. Xenia, Ohio; acquired collection of paintings and objets d'art, which he housed in the Walker Art Gallery in Minneapolis, open to the public.

**Walker, William.** 1824–1860. American filibuster, b. Nashville, Tenn. To California with gold rush (1850). Interested in colonization scheme in Mexico; gathered force and invaded Lower California (1853); declared Lower California an independent republic, with himself as president; proclaimed annexation (Jan., 1854) of Mexican state of Sonora; forced by Mexican attacks out of Mexico; surrendered to American force at border; tried (May, 1854) in San Francisco for violation of neutrality laws, but acquitted. Led small band of adventurers to Nicaragua and joined a revolutionary faction there (1855); captured Granada (Sept., 1855); became commander in chief of army under new regime; elected president, and inaugurated (July, 1856); recognized by U.S. Incurred hostility of Cornelius Vanderbilt by arbitrary seizure of boats belonging to Vanderbilt interests; ousted by coalition of Central American powers inspired by Vanderbilt; fled (May, 1857) to protection of U.S. warship. Tried repeatedly to return to Nicaragua; arrested at San Juan del Norte (Nov., 1857) by Commodore Paulding and returned to U.S.; arrested (Sept., 1860) by British naval officer in Honduras and turned over to Honduran authorities; court-martialed, convicted, and shot.

**Walker, William Hultz.** 1869–1934. American industrial chemist and engineer; known for work in production of art glass and manufacture of sterling silver, and for researches on chemistry of cellulose and its applications and uses, on prevention of corrosion of iron and steel, and on technology of petroleum.

**Walk′ley** (wôk′lĭ), **Arthur Bingham.** 1855–1926. English dramatic critic, of London *Star* (1888–1900), of *Times* (1900–26); author of *Dramatic Criticism* (1903) and collections of essays.

**Wal′lace** (wŏl′ĭs), **Alfred Russel.** 1823–1913. English naturalist, b. Monmouthshire. Trained as surveyor and architect; devoted himself to natural history (from 1845); on collecting expedition to the Amazon (1848–52); visited Malay Archipelago (1854–62); while there originated independently the theory of natural selection (1858), an account of which he sent to Darwin; the accounts of both were published in a joint paper by the Linnaean Society of London (1858). Investigated the geographical distribution of animals and noted the dissimilar forms in the Oriental and Australian regions of the archipelago separated by an imaginary line (Wallace's line); denied that man's spiritual nature has evolved by a natural process as has his physical being; opposed vaccination. Author of *Travels on the Amazon and Rio Negro* (1853), *On the Tendency of Varieties to Depart Indefinitely from the Original Type* (1858), *The Malay Archipelago* (1869), *Contributions to the Theory of Natural Selection* (1870), *Miracles and Modern Spiritualism* (1875), *The Geographical Distribution of Animals* (1876), *Darwinism* (1889), *The Wonderful Century* (1898), *Man's Place in the Universe* (1903), *The World of Life* (1910).

**Wallace, Charles William.** 1865–1932. American scholar and educator; professor of English dramatic literature, U. of Nebraska (from 1912). Known for researches in Shakespearean and Tudor drama. Among his works are *Globe Theatre Apparel* (1909), *Keysar vs. Burbage and Others* (1910), *The Evolution of the English Drama Up to Shakespeare* (1912).

**Wallace, David.** 1799–1859. American politician; governor of Indiana (1837–40); member, U.S. House of Representatives (1841–43); judge, court of common pleas (1856–59). His son **Lewis,** *known as* **Lew** (1827–1905), was a lawyer, army officer, and author; practiced law in Indianapolis; adjutant general of Indiana at outbreak of Civil War; commissioned brigadier general (Sept., 1861) and major general (Mar., 1862); took part in capture of Fort Donelson and distinguished himself at Shiloh; saved Cincinnati from capture by Gen. Kirby Smith (1863); defeated by Early at the Monocacy (July, 1864); member of court-martial which tried those accused of complicity in the assassination of Lincoln, and president of court which tried and convicted Henry Wirz, commandant of Andersonville Prison; governor of New Mexico Territory (1878–81); U.S. minister to Turkey (1881–85). Author of *The Fair God* (1873), *Ben Hur; A Tale of the Christ* (1880), *The Prince of India* (1893).

**Wallace,** Sir **Donald Mackenzie.** 1841–1919. British

journalist, b. Scotland; visited Russia (1870–75); foreign correspondent of London *Times;* private secretary to two viceroys of India (1884–89); director, foreign department of *Times* (1891–99). Author of *Russia* (2 vols., 1877) and *Egypt and the Egyptian Question* (1883).

**Wallace, Edgar.** 1875–1932. English author of popular thrillers, such as *The Four Just Men* (1906), *Sanders of the River, The Green Archer,* and plays, such as *The Ringer, The Squeaker, On the Spot, The Flying Squad.* His son **Bryan** married Margaret Lane (*q.v.*).

**Wallace, Henry.** 1836–1916. American agricultural editor and author; owner and editor (1895–1906), *Wallaces' Farm and Dairy,* later called *Wallaces' Farmer;* author of *Uncle Henry's Letters to the Farm Boy* (1897), *Letters to the Farm Folks* (1915), etc. His son **Henry Cantwell** (1866–1924) was coeditor (1895–1924) with his father and a brother, **John P.**, of *Wallaces' Farm and Dairy,* later named *Wallaces' Farmer;* U.S. secretary of agriculture (1921–24). A son of Henry Cantwell, **Henry A'gard** [ā'gärd] (1888–1965), agriculturist and cabinet member; associate editor (1910–24) and editor (1924–29), *Wallaces' Farmer,* and editor of its successor *Iowa Homestead and Wallaces' Farmer* (1929–33); secretary of agriculture (1933–40); vice-president of the U.S. (1941–45); head (1941) of Economic Defense Board; secretary of commerce (1945–46); editor, *New Republic* (from 1946); author of *Agricultural Prices* (1920), *Corn and Corn Growing* (1923), *New Frontiers* (1934), *Technology, Corporations, and the General Welfare* (1937), *The American Choice* (1940), *Sixty Million Jobs* (1945), etc.

**Wallace, Hugh Campbell.** 1863–1931. American businessman and diplomat; accumulated fortune in banking and real-estate business, Tacoma, Wash. (1887 ff.); U.S. ambassador to France (1919–21).

**Wallace, John Findley.** 1852–1921. American civil engineer; first chief engineer, Panama Canal (1904–05); consulting engineer, offices in Chicago (from 1906).

**Wallace, Lewis** *or* **Lew.** See under David WALLACE.

**Wallace,** Sir **Richard.** 1818–1890. English art connoisseur; educ. in Paris as Richard Jackson, probably natural son either of 4th marquis of Hertford or of Maria, wife of 3d marquis; inherited collection of paintings and art objects, which he bequeathed as Hertford-Wallace collection to British nation (1897).

**Wallace, Robert Charles.** 1881–1955. Canadian geologist and educator, b. Orkney, Scotland; president, U. of Alberta (1928–36); principal, Queen's U., Kingston, Ont. (from 1936); specialist in physical chemistry of rock magmas, in petrology, and in crystallography.

**Wallace,** Sir **William.** *Also* **Wal'ays** (wŏl'ĭs) *or* **Wal·len'sis** (wŏ·lĕn'sĭs), *i.e.* Welshman. 1272?–1305. Scottish patriot, of Welsh extraction. Known as "the Hammer and Scourge of England." Led Scottish insurgents, drove English out of Perth, Stirling, and Lanark (1297); defeated English at Stirling (1297) and ravaged Northumberland, Westmorland, and Cumberland (1297); proclaimed warden of Scotland; suffered rout at hands of Edward I of England at Falkirk (1298); waged guerrilla warfare (1299); solicited intervention on behalf of Scotland by Norway, France, and Pope Boniface VIII (1299–1302); outlawed by Edward I (1304); betrayed to English at Glasgow (1305); tried, in Westminster Hall, London; found guilty, and hanged, drawn, and quartered.

**Wallace, William.** 1844–1897. Scottish philosopher; succeeded T. H. Green as professor of moral philosophy, Oxford (1882–97); expositor of Hegelianism.

**Wallace, William.** 1860–1940. Scottish ophthalmologist, and composer of orchestral works, symphonic poems, and songs.

**Wallace, William Ross.** 1819–1881. American poet; author of lyrical verse and patriotic songs.

**Wallace, William Stewart.** 1884–1970. Canadian historical writer; librarian, U. of Toronto (1923–54); editor of *Canadian Historical Review* (1920–30) and of *The Encyclopaedia of Canada* (6 vols., 1935–37); author of Canadian historical and biographical works.

**Wallace, William Vincent.** 1813–1865. Irish pianist, violinist, and composer; emigrated to Australia (1835); after adventurous tours of South Seas, India, and South America, settled in England and wrote operas, piano music, and orchestrations.

**Wal'lach** (väl'äĸ), **Otto.** 1847–1931. German chemist; professor, Göttingen (1889–1915); known for researches on chemical composition of camphors, perfumes, and essential oils. Awarded 1910 Nobel prize for chemistry.

**Wal'lack** (wŏl'ăk), **Henry John.** 1790–1870. Actor, b. London, Eng.; on English stage (to 1819); American debut in Baltimore (1819). Leading man, Chatham Garden Theatre, New York City (1824); leading man and stage manager at Covent Garden, London (1834–36); stage manager and actor, National Theatre, New York (1837); at New Chatham Theatre, New York (1839–40); rented Covent Garden, London (1843); acted Sir Peter Teazle in opening performance, Broadway Theater, New York (1847). His brother **James William** (1795?–1864) was an actor of melodrama and light comedy; stage manager and actor in alternate engagements in London and New York; settled in New York (1852); actor and manager, Lyceum Theatre, New York (1852–61); built and, with his son Lester (see below), opened Wallack's Theatre at Broadway and 13th Street, New York (1861); among his notable Shakespearean roles were Iago, Macbeth, Richard III, Romeo, Hamlet. A son of Henry John, **James William** (1818–1873), b. London, Eng., was an actor on stage in U.S. and England from childhood; in America (from 1855), and well known for Shakespearean roles Othello, Hotspur, Iago, Richard III; made great success (1867) as Fagin in *Oliver Twist.* A son of James William (1795?–1864), **Lester,** *real name* **John Johnstone** (1820–1888), b. New York City, was an actor and dramatist; educ. in England; stage debut in New York (1847); stage manager under his father (1852–61), at Wallack's Theatre, Broadway and 13th St., New York (1861–81), and at a new Wallack's Theatre at Broadway and 30th St., New York (1882–87); author of the plays *The Three Guardsmen* (1849), *The Four Musketeers...*(1849), *Two to One* (1854), *The Veteran* (1856), *Rosedale* (1863), and a volume of reminiscences, *Memories of Fifty Years* (1889).

**Wal'las** (wŏl'ăs), **Graham.** 1858–1932. English political scientist; lecturer, London School of Economics (1895–1923); professor, U. of London (1914–23); author of *Life of Francis Place* (1897), *Human Nature in Politics* (1908), *The Art of Thought* (1926).

**Wal'len·berg'** (väl'lĕn·băr'y'), **André Oscar.** 1816–1886. Swedish financier; founded (1856) and directed the Enskilda Bank of Stockholm until his death, when his sons **Knut Agathon** (1853–1938) and **Marcus** (1864–1943) succeeded him. Marcus was Swedish representative at Supreme Economic Council, Paris (1919), Amsterdam meeting (1919), and Brussels conference (1920); on finance committee, League of Nations (1924); chairman for taxing German industries under Dawes Plan.

**Wal'len·stein** (wŏl'ĕn·stīn; *Ger.* väl'ĕn·shtīn), **Albrecht Eusebius Wenzel von.** Duke of **Fried'land** (frēt'länt) and **Meck'len·burg** (mĕk'lĕn·bŏŏrĸ; mā'klĕn-). Prince of **Sa'gan** (zä'gän). 1583–1634. Austrian general, b. near Königgrätz. Served in campaigns in Hungary and against Venice (1617); in Thirty Years' War lost his estates when Bohemia became Protestant; created duke (1625). Given command of imperial armies (1625); won successes against Mansfeld and king of Denmark (1626–27); besieged Stralsund (1628) unsuccessfully. Because of jealousy of princes of the empire, removed at Diet of Ratisbon (1630); recalled (1632); defeated at Lützen (1632) by Gustavus Adolphus; again removed from command; assassinated by Irish and Scottish officers.

**Wal'ler** (wŏl'ẽr), **Augustus Volney.** 1816–1870. English physiologist; invented a method (Wallerian method) of identifying tracts of nerve fibers by observing the direction of degeneration after cutting. His son **Augustus Dé'si·ré** [?dā'zĭ·rā] (1856–1922) was also a physiologist.

**Waller, Edmund.** 1606–1687. English poet. Related to John Hampden, but a Royalist. Addressed verses to **"Sach'a·ris'sa"** (săk'ȧ·rĭs'ȧ), that is, Lady Dorothy Sidney; conducted (1641) impeachment of Sir Francis Crawley, judge in common pleas, for maintaining (1636) legality of ship money; detected in plot, known as "Waller's Plot," for seizing London for Charles I (1643); spared death on betrayal of associates; expelled from House of Commons, fined £10,000, and banished (1644). Permitted to return (1652); wrote panegyric of Cromwell (1655) and poem of rejoicing on his death (1659). On Restoration wrote eulogy of Charles II; M.P. (1661–87) and favorite at court. Author of *Poems* (1645), elegant and graceful but rather frigid and artificial, *St. James's Park* (1661), and *Divine Poems* (1685); made the heroic couplet fashionable.

**Waller,** Sir **William.** 1597?–1668. English Parliamentary general. Won successes over Royalists in west of England (1642–43); defeated by Sir Ralph Hopton at Lansdown and by earl of Rochester at Roundway Down (1643). Raised new troops in London; stopped Hopton's second advance at Cheriton (1644); defeated at Cropredy Bridge (1644); led expedition for relief of Taunton (1645); relieved from command by Self-denying Ordinance (1645). Suggested idea for army reform that led to the organization (April, 1645) of the New Model army; became a leader of Presbyterian-Royalist opposition to Commonwealth; imprisoned (1648–51); plotted Royalist rising (1659); recovered seat in parliament (1660).

**Wal·lin'** (väl·lēn'), **Johan Olof.** 1779–1839. Swedish poet, archbishop, and orator; archbishop of Uppsala (1837); wrote the hymn *Dödens Engel* (*The Angel of Death*) and other verse.

**Wal'ling** (wŏl'ĭng), **Robert Alfred John.** 1869–1949. English writer; best known for mystery stories; creator of the fictional detective Mr. Tolefree.

**Walling, William English.** 1877–1936. American social economist, b. Louisville, Ky. A founder of Intercollegiate Socialist Society (now named League for Industrial Democracy), Women's Trade Union League, and National Association for the Advancement of Colored People. Author of *Russia's Message* (1908), *Socialism as It Is* (1912), *The Socialism of Today* (1916), *Sovietism* (1920), *American Labor and American Democracy* (1927), etc. He married (1906) **Anna Strun'sky** [strŭn'skĭ] (1879–1964), social economist and lecturer on social and literary subjects; collaborator with Jack London in *The Kempton-Wace Letters* (1903); author of *Violette of Père Lachaise* (1915).

**Wal'lis** (wŏl'ĭs), **John.** 1616–1703. English mathematician; Savilian professor of geometry, Oxford (1649–1703); most important work, *Arithmetica Infinitorum* (1655), in which he reduced the idea of limit to arithmetic form and arrived at results from which the binomial theorem, the differential calculus, and the integral calculus were developed; first used symbol ∞ for infinity.

**Wallis, Samuel.** 1728–1795. English circumnavigator; discoverer of Tahiti and Wallis Islands in Pacific (1767).

**Wal'lon'** (wȧ'lôɴ'), **Henri Alexandre.** 1812–1904. French historian and politician; member of Legislative Assembly (1849–50) and National Assembly (1871–75); minister of public instruction (1875–76); elected senator for life (1875); author of *Du Monothéisme chez les Races Sémitiques* (1859), *Saint Louis et son Temps* (1875), etc.

**Wal'lot** (väl'ōt), **Paul.** 1841–1912. German architect, notably of Reichstag building (1884–94) in Berlin.

**Walms'ley** (wômz'lĭ), **Leo.** 1892–1966. English novelist, b. in Yorkshire; served as flyer in East Africa (1914–18); author of *The Silver Blimp* (1921) and *Toro of the Little People* (1926), juveniles, of *Three Fevers* (1932; scenarized as *Turn of the Tide*), *Love in the Sun* (autobiographical novel, 1939), *Fishermen at War* (1941), etc.

**Waln** (wôl), **Nora.** 1895–1964. American writer, b. Grampian, Pa.; m. George Edward Osland-Hill (1922); used material acquired by residence in China (1920–28) and Germany (1934–38) in *House of Exile* (1933) and *Reaching for the Stars* (1939), respectively.

**Wal'pole** (wôl'pōl; wŏl'-), **Horace,** *baptized* **Horatio.** 4th Earl of **Or'ford** (ôr'fẽrd). 1717–1797. English man of letters; 4th son of Sir Robert Walpole. Made grand tour with poet Thomas Gray (1739–41); M.P. (1741–68); purchased (1757) Strawberry Hill, a villa outside Twickenham, converted it into a small Gothic castle, decorated it with curios and works of art; established there (1757–89) a printing press upon which first editions of many of his works were printed, also Gray's *Odes;* friend and correspondent of Madame du Deffand and Lady Ossory; befriended Robert, Mary, and Agnes Berry (*q.v.*), to whom he left all his printed books and manuscripts on his death; unmarried. Author of *The Castle of Otranto* (1764), the forerunner of supernatural romances of Mrs. Radcliffe and Matthew Gregory Lewis, of *Mysterious Mother,* a horrible tragedy in verse (1768), and several antiquarian works including *Historic Doubts on Richard III* (1768), *Anecdotes of Painting in England* (1762–71), *Catalogue of Engravers in England* (1763). Owes literary reputation chiefly to his charming, vivacious, often brilliant letters (1732–97; about 2700 in number).

**Walpole,** Sir **Hugh Seymour.** 1884–1941. English novelist, b. New Zealand, son of **George Henry Somerset Walpole** (1854–1929), who was bishop of Edinburgh in Scottish Episcopal Church (1910–29). First novels, *The Wooden Horse* (1909) and *Maradick at Forty* (1910); won reputation with *Fortitude* (1913); served with Russian Red Cross in World War (1914–16); published *The Dark Forest* (1916), *The Green Mirror* (1918), and *The Secret City,* based upon Russian experience (1919), *The Cathedral,* reflecting his youth in Durham (1922), *Jeremy,* first of a series on life of the English boy (1919); biographized Anthony Trollope in *English Men of Letters Series* (1928); wrote a series of chronicles of English social history, *Rogue Herries* (1930), *Judith Paris* (1931), *The Fortress* (1932), *Vanessa* (1933), *The Bright Pavilions* (1940), and *Katherine Christian* (pub. 1943), and other novels including: *The Duchess of Wrexe* (1914), *Harmer John* (1926), *Captain Nicholas* (1934), *The Youthful Delaneys* (1938), *The Blind Man's House* (1941), *The Killer and the Slain* (pub. 1942).

**Walpole,** Sir **Robert.** 1st Earl of **Or'ford** (ôr'fẽrd). 1676–1745. English statesman. Father of Horace Walpole, the author. Whig M.P. (1701–42); secretary at war (1708–10); treasurer of navy (1710–11); expelled from House of Commons on political charge of venality in navy office (1712). Advocated Hanoverian succession; paymaster of forces on accession of George I (1714); conducted impeachment of Bolingbroke and Harley;

prime minister and chancellor of exchequer (1715–17; resigned); devised first general sinking fund for reducing national debt (1717). Again paymaster (1720); profited through speculation in South Sea Scheme; called by public demand after South Sea collapse to restore order in public affairs; first lord of treasury and chancellor of exchequer, and prime minister (1721), sharing power with Townshend, secretary of state; reduced import and export duties (1721) to encourage trade; crushed Jacobite plot and exiled Atterbury (1723); cultivated friendship of France, and opposed Austrian alliance; quarreled with Townshend and forced his retirement (1730); managed transfer of power from House of Lords to House of Commons; first to unify cabinet government in person of prime minister; strove to establish sound finance at home; said to have laid foundations of free trade and modern colonial policy; tried to keep free of foreign intrigue and war, but forced into hostilities with Spain (1739); defeated in House of Commons (Jan., 1742). His younger brother **Horatio** *or* **Horace**, 1st Baron **Walpole of Wolterton** (1678–1757), was secretary of treasury (1715–17, 1721), ambassador at Paris (1723–30), at The Hague (1733–40).

**Spencer Horatio** (1806–1898), political leader; great-grandson of Horatio; conservative M.P. (1846–82); home secretary (1852, 1858–59, 1866).

Sir **Spencer** (1839–1907), son of Spencer Horatio, was inspector of fisheries (1867); governor of Isle of Man (1882–93); secretary to post office (1893–99); author of biographies of his grandfather Spencer Perceval (1874) and Lord John Russell (1889), a history of England from 1815 to 1880 (1878–1908), and *Essays Political and Biographical* (1908).

**Walpurga** *or* **Walpurgis**, Saint. See WALBURGA.

**Walram I** and **II**. See NASSAU, 1.

**Wal'ras'** (vȧl'rȧ'), **Léon**. 1834–1910. French economist.

**Walsh** (wôlsh), **David Ignatius**. 1872–1947. American lawyer and politician, b. Leominster, Mass.; governor of Massachusetts (1914, 1915); U.S. senator from Massachusetts (1919–47).

**Walsh, James Joseph**. 1865–1942. American physician and author, b. Archbald, Pa.; professor of nervous diseases and dean, Fordham Medical School (1905–12); medical director, Fordham school of sociology (from 1917); author of *Religion and Health* (1921), *Psychotherapy* (1923), *Spiritualism a Fake* (1925), *Laughter and Health* (1927), *A Golden Treasury of Medieval Literature* (1931), *The Thirteenth, Greatest of Centuries* (10th ed., 1937).

**Walsh, Pearl**. See Pearl BUCK.

**Walsh, Robert**. 1784–1859. American journalist, b. Baltimore, Md.; founder and editor of *The American Review of History and Politics*, first American quarterly magazine (1811–12), *American Register* (1817), *National Gazette and Literary Register* (with William Fry, 1820), *American Quarterly Review* (1827–37); U.S. consul general in Paris (1844–51). His grandson **Henry Collins Walsh** (1863–1927) was a journalist and explorer; member of Dr. Frederick A. Cook's arctic exploring expedition (1894); traveled in Central America (1896), Morocco (1897), West Indies (1911); wrote many articles on his travels and experiences; associate editor of the *Smart Set* (1902–06), editor of *Travel Magazine* (1907–10), associate editor of *National Marine* (1919–21).

**Walsh, Stephen**. 1859–1929. English trade-unionist and political leader; miner at thirteen; M.P. (1906–29); war secretary in first British Labor government (1924).

**Walsh, Thomas James**. 1859–1933. American lawyer and legislator, b. Two Rivers, Wis.; practiced law at Helena, Mont. (from 1890); U.S. senator from Montana (1913–33). In charge (1922–23) of investigation of leasing of naval oil reserves in Wyoming and California, and uncovered Teapot Dome scandal (1923). Selected by President Franklin D. Roosevelt to be U.S. attorney general, but died (Mar. 2, 1933) before the president's inauguration.

**Wal'sing·ham** (wôl'sĭng·ăm), Sir **Francis**. 1530?–1590. English statesman; secretary of state (1573–90); frequently overruled by both Burghley and Elizabeth I; failed to secure Anglo-French alliance against Spain (1581); organized, largely at his own expense, efficient system of secret intelligence, by which he detected plots against Elizabeth, among them Anthony Babington's (1586); secured conviction and execution of Mary, Queen of Scots (1587); forewarned Elizabeth (1587) of preparations of Spanish Armada and vainly urged defensive measures; scantily recompensed by Queen Elizabeth; on death of son-in-law Sir Philip Sidney, at mercy of Sidney's creditors; died deep in debt.

**Walsingham, Thomas**. d. 1422? English monk and chronicler; chief authority for reigns of Richard II, Henry IV, and Henry V.

**Wal'ston** (wôl'stŭn), Sir **Charles**. *Orig. surname* **Wald'stein** (wôld'stīn). 1856–1927. Archaeologist, b. New York City; studied at Columbia, New York City, and U. of Heidelberg; director of American school of archaeology at Athens, Greece (1889–93); professor at Cambridge U. (1895–1901; 1904–11); naturalized British subject (1899); conducted archaeological research among ruins in Eretria, Plataea, and Argolis.

**Wal'ter** (väl'tẽr), **Bruno**. *Real surname* **Schle'sing·er** (shlā'zĭng·ẽr). 1876–1962. Opera and symphony conductor, b. Berlin, of Jewish parentage; educ. Stern Conservatory, Berlin; conductor, Imperial Opera, Vienna (1901–12), Munich Opera House (1913–23), Municipal Opera, Berlin (1925–29), Leipzig Gewandhaus Orchestra (1929–33), Vienna State Opera (1935–38); guest conductor each season in New York (1922–26, 1932–35) and London (1924–32); resident in U.S. (from 1939), guest conductor of various orchestras and conductor of N.Y. Philharmonic (1947–50).

**Wal'ter** (wôl'tẽr), **Eugene**. 1874–1941. American journalist and playwright, b. Cleveland, Ohio; author of *Paid in Full* (1907), *The Easiest Way* (1908), *The Knife* (1917), *The Toy Girl* (1921), etc.

**Walter, Hubert**. d. 1205. English ecclesiastic, justice, and statesman. As bishop of Salisbury, accompanied Richard I on Third Crusade, led army back to England; as archbishop of Canterbury and chief justiciar (1193), governed kingdom and raised Richard's ransom; levied land tax to be assessed by knights, or middle-class landowners, elected to represent townships and hundreds (1198); insisted upon elective character of kingship at coronation of John (1199); chancellor (1199–1205).

**Walter, John**. 1739–1812. English newspaperman; founder of *The* (London) *Times*. Coal merchant (1755–81); bankrupt by loss of shipping (1782). Bought patent for printing from logotypes, that is, fonts of whole words (1782); did logographic printing of books; started newspaper *The Daily Universal Register* (1785), which was renamed *The Times* (1788). Convicted several times for libel. His second son, **John** (1776–1847), became sole manager of *The Times* (1803), sole editor (1803–10); lost printing of government advertisements and customhouse papers by reason of opposition to Pitt; initiated sending of special foreign correspondents abroad (1805); adopted steam printing press (1814); M.P. (1832–37, 1841). John's son **John** (1818–1894), barrister (1847), became sole manager of *The Times* (1847), introduced the Walter press (1869); pioneer of modern newspaper printing presses; M.P. (1847–65, 1868–85). **Arthur Fraser** (1846–1910), son of John (1818–94), was chief proprietor of *The Times* (1894–1908), chairman of board of directors (1908–10), in which chairmanship he was succeeded (1910–23) by his son **John** (1873–1968).

**Wal′ter** (wôl′tẽr; *orig.* wô′tẽr), **Lucy.** *Incorrectly* **Wal′ters** (wô(l)′tẽrz) *and* **Wa′ters** (wô′tẽrz). *Known also as* Mrs. **Bar′low** (bär′lō). 1630?–1658. Welshwoman; mistress of Charles II (1648–51), and by him mother of James, Duke of Monmouth (b. 1649).

**Wal′ter** (wôl′tẽr), **Thomas Ustick.** 1804–1887. American architect. b. Philadelphia. Made great success with design of Girard College, Philadelphia (1833), regarded by some as finest example of classic architecture in U.S. By appointment of President Fillmore, succeeded Robert Mills as architect of Capitol, Washington, D.C. (1851); designed and supervised construction of wings added to central building, and of the dome (1851–65).

**Walter of Eve′sham** (ēv′shăm; ē′shăm; ē′săm) . *Or* Walter **Od′ing·ton** (ŏd′ĭng·tŭn). fl. 1320. English Benedictine monk; compiler of a calendar for Evesham Abbey, and author of compendium of medieval musical knowledge, *De Speculatione Musices.*

**Walter the Penniless.** *Fr.* **Gau′tier′ sans a′voir′** (gō′tyā′ säɴ′-zȧ′vwȧr′). 11th-century French knight; one of the leaders (with Peter the Hermit) of disorderly hordes which roamed through Europe in a movement known later as the Peasants' Crusade; killed in battle of Nicaea (1097).

**Wal′ters** (wôl′tẽrz), **John.** 1721–1797. Welsh clergyman, compiler of English-Welsh dictionary (1770–94). His son **John** (1759–1789) was a poet.

**Wal′ters** (wô(l)′tẽrz), **Lucy.** See Lucy WALTER.

**Wal′ters** (wôl′tẽrz), **William Thompson.** 1820–1894. American businessman and art collector. b. Liverpool, Pa. His son **Henry** (1848–1931) was a railroad executive and art collector; expanded art collection begun by his father, built gallery in Baltimore to house it; gave gallery and collection to Baltimore at his death.

**Waltershausen, Sartorius von.** See SARTORIUS VON WALTERSHAUSEN.

**Wal′theof** (wäl′thā′ŏf). *Lat.* **Wal·de′vus** (wôl·dē′vŭs) *or* **Gual·le′vus** (gwŏ·lē′vŭs). d. 1076. English earl, son of Siward the Strong. Submitted to William the Conqueror after battle of Hastings (1066); joined Danish invaders in massacre of French at York (1069); pardoned by William and married William's niece Judith; earl of Northumberland (1072); confessed share in plot of earl of Norfolk against king, forgiven; convicted, probably unjustly, of complicity in plot for Danish invasion of England (1076) and beheaded.

**Wal′ther** (väl′tẽr), **Augustin Friedrich.** 1688–1746. German anatomist; professor, Leipzig (1723).

**Wal′ther** (väl′tẽr), **Carl Ferdinand Wilhelm.** 1811–1887. Lutheran clergyman, b. in Saxony. To U.S. (1839) with religious colony of German settlers; founded (1839) theological school at Altenburg, which moved to St. Louis (1850) and was named Concordia Theological Seminary; professor of theology there (from 1850). An organizer (1847), German Evangelical Lutheran Synod of Missouri, Ohio, and other states, and its president (1847–50; 1864–78). Author of theological works in German.

**Walther, Johann.** 1496–1570. Protestant church musician and composer; friend of Martin Luther, whom he advised and assisted in musical questions, notably in framing the German Mass (1524); published *Geystlich Gesangk-Buchleyn* for four voices, the first Protestant songbook (1524); composed religious songs, church music, and instrumental pieces.

**Walther, Johannes.** 1860–1937. German geologist.

**Walther von der Vo′gel·wei′de** (fôn dẽr fō′gĕl·vī′dĕ). 1170?–?1230. Middle High German lyric poet and minnesinger, b. probably in Austria or the Tirol, of noble family. Educ. at Babenberg court of Duke Frederick, Vienna, notably under Reinmar von Hagenau; lived life of a wandering singer (after 1198) chiefly in courts of Philip of Swabia, Landgrave Hermann of Thuringia, Otto IV, and Frederick II, from whom he received a fief (c. 1215). His poems include love songs (*Unter der Linden*), and political songs ("Sprüche") and religious songs (*Kreuzlied*, c. 1227) in which he championed German independence and unity and opposed the extreme claims of the popes.

**Wal′ton** (wôl′t'n; -tŭn), **Brian** *or* **Bryan.** 1600?–1661. English Biblical scholar; issued, with help of scholars, the *London*, or *Walton's*, *Polyglot Bible* (6 vols., 1654–57) with all or parts in seven Oriental languages; bishop of Chester (1660).

**Walton, Ernest Thomas Sinton.** 1903– . Irish physicist. Awarded Nobel prize in physics (1951) with J. Crockcroft for work in nuclear physics.

**Walton, Frederick.** English inventor (1860) of a process for oxidizing linseed oil used in manufacture of a linoleum (trade-marked *Lincrusta-Walton*).

**Walton, George.** 1741–1804. American lawyer and political leader, b. near Farmville, Va.; member of Continental Congress (1776–81); a signer of the Declaration of Independence and the Articles of Confederation; governor of Georgia (1779–80, 1789); chief justice of Georgia (1783–89); judge, Georgia superior court (1790–92; 1793–95; 1799–1804); U.S. senator (1795–96).

**Walton, George Lincoln.** 1854–1941. American neurologist, b. Lawrence, Mass.; wrote *Why Worry?* (1908), *Those Nerves* (1909), *The Flower-Finder* (1914), *Peg Along* (1915), *Oscar Montagu—Paranoiac* (1919).

**Walton, Izaak.** 1593–1683. English biographer and author. Carried on ironmonger's business in London (from 1614); retired to Stafford after Royalist defeat at Marston Moor (1644). Published biographies of John Donne (1640), Sir Henry Wotton (1651), Richard Hooker (1665), George Herbert (1670), and Bishop Robert Sanderson (1678). His masterpiece is *The Compleat Angler, or the Contemplative Man's Recreation* (1st ed. 1653; 5th ed. 1676), made up of dialogues between Piscator (angler), Venator (hunter), and Auceps (falconer), with anecdotes, quotations, country scenery, snatches of verse, enlarged by additions over 25 years (from 13 chapters in 1st, to 21 in 5th, edition) and by appending of part two by Charles Cotton on fly-fishing and making flies.

**Walton, Valentine.** d. 1661? English Parliamentary commander; brother-in-law of Cromwell; one of judges at trial of Charles I and signer of the warrant for his execution (1649); fled to Germany (1660).

**Walton,** Sir **William Turner.** 1902– . English composer; won reputation (1923) with a string quartet selected by jury for international festival at Salzburg and with *Façade*, a setting for recitation of poems by Edith Sitwell (Aeolian Hall, 1923).

**Waltz, Jean Jacques.** See HANSI.

**Waltzemüller, Martin.** See Martin WALDSEEMÜLLER.

**Wal′worth** (wôl′wûrth; -wẽrth), **Reuben Hyde.** 1788–1867. American jurist, b. Bozrah, Conn.; began practice in Plattsburg, N.Y.; last chancellor of State of New York (1828–48; office abolished 1848).
His son **Clarence Augustus** (1820–1900) was a Roman Catholic missionary; entered Order of the Most Holy Redeemer, known as the Redemptorist Order (1846); released from Redemptorist vows, aided in founding

Congregation of the Missionary Priests of St. Paul the Apostle, known as the Paulists (1858); pastor of St. Mary's Church, Albany, N.Y. (1866–1900); author of *The Gentle Skeptic* (1863), *The Doctrine of Hell* (1873), *The Oxford Movement in America* (1895). See Isaac Thomas HECKER.

**Walworth,** Sir **William.** d. 1385. English fishmonger; sheriff (1370) and lord mayor (1374, 1381) of London; lent money to Richard II; defended London Bridge against Kentish peasants (1381) and at Smithfield, in Richard II's presence, killed their leader, Wat Tyler.

**Wan'a·ma'ker** (wŏn'ȧ·mā'kẽr), **John.** 1838–1922. American merchant, b. Philadelphia. With brother-in-law Nathan Brown (d. 1868), started men's clothing business (1861), which within ten years developed into largest retail men's clothing store in U.S.; expanded business into a department store (from 1877); bought A. T. Stewart's business in New York and made it his Wanamaker store in that city (1896). U.S. postmaster general (1889–93). Founder (1858), and for many years superintendent, of Bethany Sunday School in Philadelphia. Benefactor of Y.M.C.A. in U.S. and many foreign countries. Sent two relief ships to Belgium at outbreak of World War (1914). His son **Lewis Rodman** (1863–1928) was associated with him in the Wanamaker stores; adm. to firm (1902) and resident manager of New York Wanamaker store (1911); sole owner and director of Wanamaker stores (from 1922); noted as patron of art, aviation enthusiast, interested especially in advancing transatlantic flights; financial backer of exploration among Indian tribes in western U.S.

**Wang** (wäng), **C. T.** *Orig.* **Wang Chêng-t'ing** (wäng' jĕng'tĭng'). 1882–1961. Chinese politician, b. in Chekiang province. Educ. Michigan and Yale (B.A., 1912); took part in organizing new republican government (1912); vice-speaker of senate (1911–12 and 1916–17); delegate to Paris Peace Conference (1918–19); director of Sino-Japanese commission on Shantung question (1922); minister for foreign affairs (1922–23, 1925–26, 1927–31); director-general of Sino-Russian negotiations (1923–24); member of Kuomintang Central Executive Committee (since 1930); ambassador to the United States (1936–38); retired to private business.

**Wang An-shih** (wäng' än'shĭr'). 1021–1086. Chinese statesman and reformer. Studied and wrote commentaries on the Confucian classics; prime minister (1068–85) for the Sung emperor Shen Tsung; carried out many economic reforms; established financial bureau that made loans to farmers, instituted pay for labor, levied an income tax, organized a conscript militia.

**Wang Chên** (wäng' jŭn'). fl. 14th century. Chinese author and printer under the Yüan dynasty. Wrote *Nung-shu* (pub. 1314), a description of the invention and development of block printing, early forms of type, and a typesetting device perfected by himself.

**Wang Ching-wei** (wäng' jĭng'wā'). *Orig.* **Wang Chao-ming** (jou'mĭng'). 1884–1944. Chinese politician, b. in Canton. Educ. in Japan, at Tokyo Law Coll. Joined revolutionary party and attempted (1910) to assassinate prince regent; sentenced to imprisonment for life but released (1911) after establishment of the republic; one of Sun Yat-sen's chief assistants (1911–25); a leader of the Left in the Kuomintang (1927–29). Turned politically to the Right (1930); joined Chiang Kai-shek; president of administrative council (1932–35); shot and nearly killed (1935); changed allegiance several times (1930–37), unpopular with both Left and Right; deputy leader of Kuomintang (1937–38). Deserted Nationalist government (1938) and fled to Hong Kong; became strongly pro-Japanese; made puppet ruler of China (1939) by Japanese army; assassination again attempted (1939). Author of several essays and a volume of poems (pub. 1938).

**Wang Ch'ung** (wäng' chŏŏng'). 27–97 A.D. Chinese philosopher of the Later Han dynasty. Acquired great learning; held official positions for a few years but retired to write *Lun Hêng* ("Animadversions") in which he ridiculed current Chinese superstitions and criticized freely the teachings of Confucius and Mencius and the Taoist doctrines.

**Wang Khan.** See PRESTER JOHN, 1.

**Wang Mang** (wäng' mäng'). 33 B.C.–23 A.D. Chinese emperor (9–23 A.D.), known as "the Usurper." Through his aunt, wife of Yüan T'i, Han emperor (48–32 B.C.), he obtained influence and high position at court; regent for two child emperors (1–8 A.D.). Seized throne (9 A.D.), thus terminating the Earlier, or Western, Han dynasty; his reign called by some the **Hsin** (shĭn) dynasty; introduced many radical reforms, esp. with regard to taxes, usury, ownership of land, price levels, and business monopolies; his policies provoked revolts; assassinated in one of these by princes of the Han, who founded (25) the Later, or Eastern, Han dynasty.

**Wang Wei** (wäng' wā'). 699–759 A.D. Chinese poet and painter of the T'ang dynasty; founder of a monochrome school of painting; tradition says his poems contained pictures and all his pictures contained poems; an ardent Buddhist, spent latter part of life in a monastery.

**Wang Yang-ming** (wäng' yäng'mĭng'). *Real name* **Wang Shou-jên** (shō'rĕn'). 1472–1528 or 1529. Chinese philosopher, of the Ming dynasty. At first a Taoist but later (c. 1506) began to teach Confucianism in a new interpretation; accused (1523) of heterodoxy; his teachings marked by a lofty idealism in contrast with realism of Chu Hsi; sought to understand the universe by examining his own mind; much studied by Japanese.

**Wan Li** (wän' lē'). *Dynastic name* **Shên Tsung** (shŭn' dzŏŏng'). 1563–1620. Chinese emperor (1573–1620), of the late Ming dynasty; sustained high level of Ming culture, but weak in defense against the Manchus.

**Wan'tage** (wŏn'tĭj), Baron. **Robert James Lindsay,** *afterwards* **Loyd'-Lind'say** (loid'lĭn(d)'zĭ). 1832–1901. English soldier; for his services at Alma and Inkerman (1854) in Crimean War, received (1857) first Victoria Cross ever awarded; assumed name Loyd-Lindsay on marriage (1858) to Harriet Sarah Loyd, daughter of Baron Overstone (*q.v.*); pioneer organizer of local volunteer corps for defense (1859); a founder of Red Cross Aid Society (1870) and director of its operations in Franco-Prussian War; became agriculturist and patron of art; a founder of Reading University.

**Wap'pers** (väp'ẽrs), Baron **Égide Charles Gustave.** 1803–1874. Belgian painter; best known for historical paintings, executed in romantic as opposed to classical style.

**Wa'qi·di, al-** (ăl·wä'kĭ·dĭ). *Arab.* **abu-'Abdullāh Muḥammad ibn-'Umar al-Wāqidi.** 747–823. Arab historian, b. Medina; chief work, *Kitāb al-Maghāzi*, a history of Mohammed's military campaigns.

**War'beck** (wôr'bĕk), **Perkin.** 1474–1499. Walloon impostor; pretender to crown of England. Servant of Breton silk merchant in Ireland, mistaken by people for son of duke of Clarence or of Richard III; professed (1492) to be Richard, Duke of York, second of Edward IV's sons, murdered in Tower; acknowledged as nephew by Margaret, dowager Duchess of Burgundy, sister of Edward IV of England; supported by earls of Desmond and Kildare; entertained as Richard IV by Charles VIII of France; supplied with money by Emperor Maximilian I for unsuccessful invasion of Kent,

England, and Waterford, Ireland (1495); welcomed by James IV of Scotland and given Lady Catherine Gordon in marriage; landed in Cornwall, proclaiming himself king (1499); advanced to Exeter; taken prisoner, confessed imposture; imprisoned in Tower of London; hanged for endeavoring to escape.

**War'burg** (*Ger.* vär'bŏŏrk; *Eng.* wôr'bûrg), **A'by** (ä'bē). 1866–1929. German art historian, b. Hamburg; carried on researches in European Renaissance art.

His brother **Max** (1867–1946), banker in Hamburg; adviser to the Reichsbank (from 1924); author of works on finance. Another brother, **Paul Moritz** (1868–1932), b. Hamburg; also a banker; adm. as partner in M. M. Warburg & Co., Hamburg (1895); to U.S. (1902) and joined banking firm of Kuhn, Loeb & Co., New York; naturalized as American citizen (1911); aided in planning national banking reorganization (1907–14); member of first Federal Reserve Board (1914–18); gained prominence (Mar., 1929) by warning of disaster threatened by wild stock-market speculation, seven months before the panic (Oct., 1929); author of *The Federal Reserve System. Its Origin and Growth* (2 vols., 1930). Another brother, **Felix Moritz** (1871–1937), b. Hamburg; also a banker; to U.S. (1894) and naturalized (1900); member of banking firm, Kuhn, Loeb & Co., New York (from 1896); widely known for his philanthropies.

A son of Paul Moritz, **James Paul** (1896–1969), b. Hamburg; banker; to U.S. as a child; vice-president, International Acceptance Bank, New York City (1921–29); financial adviser to World Economic Conference in London (1933); author of *Acceptance Financing* (1922), *The Money Muddle* (1934), *Hell Bent for Election* (1935), etc. A son of Felix Moritz, **Frederick Marcus** (1897– ), b. New York City; banker; partner in Kuhn, Loeb & Co. (from 1931).

**Warburg, Carl.** 19th-century Austrian physician; inventor (c. 1840) of Warburg's tincture, used as an antiperiodic, esp. in treatment of malaria.

**Warburg, Otto.** 1859–1938. German botanist; specialist in geographical and systematic botany and the culture of tropical plants.

**Warburg, Otto Heinrich.** 1883-1970. German physiologist; member of Kaiser Wilhelm Institute for Biology (from 1914); known for researches on respiratory ferments, on the physical chemistry and respiration of living cells, and on cancer. Awarded 1931 Nobel prize for medicine. His father, **Emil Gabriel Warburg** (1846–1931), was an experimental physicist.

**War'bur·ton** (wôr'bẽr·t'n; -bûr't'n), **Bartholomew Elliot George,** *usually known as* **Eliot.** 1810–1852. Irish traveler and novelist; author of *The Crescent and the Cross* (1845), *Memoir of Prince Rupert and the Cavaliers* (1849), and historical novels.

**Warburton, John.** 1682–1759. English antiquary and collector of rare manuscripts.

**Warburton, Peter Egerton.** 1813–1889. British military officer and explorer in Australia.

**Warburton, William.** 1698–1779. English prelate, theologian, and controversialist. Gained court favor with *Alliance between Church and State* (1736); chaplain to Frederick Louis, Prince of Wales (1738); chaplain to king (1754); dean of Bristol (1757); bishop of Gloucester (1759). Gained friendship of Alexander Pope with a defense of his *Essay on Man* (1739); persuaded Pope to add a fourth book to *Dunciad;* Pope's literary executor (1744); brought out edition of Pope's works (1751). Published, after quarrel with Lewis Theobald, with whom he had formerly collaborated in a Shakespeare edition, edition of Shakespeare's works (1747) with notes, which was severely criticized as wanting in critical sagacity. Wrote (1742–55) in disputation with skeptical views of Bolingbroke; silenced in controversy with Robert Lowth over Book of Job by Lowth's raillery and pointed attack on his arrogance and want of scholarship (1765).

**Ward** (wôrd), **Aaron Montgomery.** 1843–1913. American merchant, b. Chatham, N.J.; with George R. Thorne established business (1872) which developed into great mail-order house of Montgomery Ward & Co.; retired (1901). His wife, **Elizabeth J.,** *nee* **Cobb** [kŏb] (1857–1926), established a medical and dental school (1923) at Northwestern U. in memory of her husband.

**Ward,** Sir **Adolphus William.** 1837–1924. English historian. Author of *History of English Dramatic Literature* (1875), lives of Chaucer (1879) and Dickens (1882) in *English Men of Letters Series;* edited Marlowe, Robert Greene, Thomas Heywood; editor in chief of *Cambridge Modern History* (1902–12); edited, with A. R. Waller, *Cambridge History of English Literature* (1907–16); edited, with G. P. Gooch, *Cambridge History of British Foreign Policy 1783–1919* (1922–23); author of *Great Britain and Hanover* (1899) and *History of Germany 1815–1890* (1916–18).

**Ward, Artemas.** 1727–1800. American Revolutionary commander, b. Shrewsbury, Mass. Justice (1762–75) and chief justice (1775), Worcester County court of common pleas. Served under Abercromby in attack on Ticonderoga (1758). Organized resistance to General Gage as governor of Massachusetts (1774–75). On news of battle of Lexington, assumed command of American forces; commissioned general and commander in chief of Massachusetts troops (May 19, 1775); directed siege of Boston until Gen. Washington's arrival. Named by Continental Congress as second in command (to Gen. Washington) in Continental army, and commissioned major general (June 17, 1775). Under his orders, Gen. John Thomas (*q.v.*) seized Dorchester Heights (Mar. 4, 1776) and thus forced British evacuation of Boston. Resigned from army (Mar. 22, 1776). Member of Massachusetts executive council (1777–80), Continental Congress (1780–81), and U.S. House of Representatives (1791–95).

**Ward, Artemus.** Pseudonym of Charles Farrar BROWNE.

**Ward, Arthur Sarsfield.** See Sax ROHMER.

**Ward, Barbara.** *Known as* **Lady Robert Jackson.** 1914– . British writer and economist. At Harvard U. (1957–68), Columbia U. (1968– ); wrote *Five Ideas that Change the World* (1959), *Spaceship Earth* (1966).

**Ward, Christopher Longstreth.** 1868–1943. American lawyer and humorist; practiced law in Wilmington, Del. Author of *The Triumph of the Nut* (1923), *Twisted Tales* (1924), *Sir Galahad and Other Rimes* (1936), etc.

**Ward, Edward,** *often* **Ned.** 1667–1731. English tavern keeper and humorist; writer of coarse Hudibrastic doggerel verse (1691–1734); author of *The London Spy* (1698–1709), a prose work containing sketches of social life and characters of Queen Anne's time, esp. in London, and *Hudibras Redivivus* (1705–07), vulgar satire upon Whigs and the Low Church party.

**Ward, Edward Matthew.** 1816–1879. English historical painter of 17th-century, French Revolution, and 18th-century social life.

**Ward, Elizabeth Stuart,** *nee* **Phelps** (fĕlps). 1844–1911. American author, b. Boston; m. (1888) Herbert Dickinson Ward (see under William Hayes WARD); author of *The Gates Ajar* (1868), *Poetic Studies* (1875), *Doctor Zay* (1882), *Songs of the Silent World* (1884), *The Madonna of the Tubs* (1886), *Jack, the Fisherman* (1887), *A Singular Life* (1894), *Within the Gates* (1901), *Though Life Do Us Part* (1908).

**Ward, Frederick Townsend.** 1831–1862. American military adventurer, b. Salem, Mass.; in China (1859–62); organized troops to aid Chinese government forces in suppressing Taiping rebellion; his command, called "the Ever-Victorious Army," won a number of successes; wounded in action (Sept. 20) and died (Sept. 21, 1862).

**Ward, Harry Frederick.** 1873–1966. Methodist Episcopal clergyman, b. London, Eng.; to U.S. (1891); A.B., Northwestern (1897). Ordained (1899); professor of Christian Ethics, Union Theol. Sem., New York (from 1918). Chairman, American Civil Liberties Union (1920–40), American League for Peace and Democracy (1934–40). Author of *Social Creed of the Churches* (1913), *Poverty and Wealth* (1915), *The New Social Order—Principles and Programs* (1919), *Our Economic Morality* (1929), *Which Way Religion?* (1931), *In Place of Profit* (1933), *Democracy and Social Change* (1940).

**Ward, Henry Augustus.** 1834–1906. American naturalist, b. Rochester, N.Y. Collector from boyhood; developed business of supplying collections, known as "Ward's cabinets," of natural-history relics, fossils, minerals, etc., to colleges, museums, and the like, on order. Developed his own collection, Ward's Natural Science Establishment, exhibited at Chicago World's Fair (1893) and bought by Marshall Field to become nucleus of Field Museum of Natural History, Chicago.

**Ward, Herbert Dickinson.** See under William Hayes WARD

**Ward, Herbert T.** 1863–1919. English sculptor; best known for his bronzes of African natives.

**Ward, Mrs. Humphry.** See Mary Augusta WARD.

**Ward, James.** 1843–1925. English philosopher and psychologist; fellow of Trinity Coll., Cambridge (1875); professor of mental philosophy (1897–1925); author of *Naturalism and Agnosticism* (1899), *The Realm of Ends, or Pluralism and Theism* (1911), *A Study of Kant* (1922).

**Ward, John Quincy Adams.** 1830–1910. American sculptor, b. near Urbana, Ohio. Studio in Washington, D.C. (c. 1857–59); sculptured busts of Alexander H. Stephens, Hannibal Hamlin, and others; studio in New York (from 1861). President, National Academy of Design (1874). Among his notable works are: *Indian Hunter and Pilgrim* (Central Park, New York); *Good Samaritan* (Public Gardens, Boston); equestrian statues of General Sheridan (Albany, N.Y.), Gen. George H. Thomas (Washington, D.C.), and General Hancock (Philadelphia); statues of Gen. John F. Reynolds (Gettysburg, Pa.), Henry Ward Beecher (Brooklyn, N.Y.); and many portrait busts.

**Ward, Joseph.** 1838–1889. American Congregational clergyman and educator, b. Perry Centre, N.Y. Grad. Brown (1865) and Andover Sem. (1868); missionary in Dakota Territory; established school which later became first public high school in Dakota; founded Yankton College, first college in upper Mississippi Valley, and was its first president (1881–89).

**Ward,** Sir **Joseph George.** 1856–1930. New Zealand statesman. Postmaster general (1891); colonial treasurer (1893); pioneered loans to settlers (1894); introduced inland penny postage (1901) and state fire insurance for N.Z. (1903); prime minister (1906–12); minister of finance and postmaster general (1915–19), and with prime minister Massey represented N.Z. at Imperial war cabinets (1917, 1918) and Paris Peace Conference (1919); again prime minister (1928–30).

**Ward,** Sir **Leslie.** 1851–1922. English caricaturist and portrait painter; caricaturist on *Vanity Fair* under pseudonym of **Spy** [spī] (1873–1909).

**Ward, Lester Frank.** 1841–1913. American sociologist, b. Joliet, Ill.; on staff, U.S. Treasury Department, Washington, D.C. (1865–81); geologist (1883–92), paleontologist (1892–1906); professor of sociology, Brown U. (1906–13); pioneer in field of sociology in U.S.; author of *Dynamic Sociology* (1883), *The Psychic Factors of Civilization* (1893), *Outlines of Sociology* (1898), *Glimpses of the Cosmos* (6 vols., 1913–18).

**Ward, Mary Augusta,** *nee* **Ar'nold** (är'n'ld). *Better known as* Mrs. **Humphry Ward.** 1851–1920. English novelist, b. Hobart, Tasmania; niece of Matthew Arnold; m. (1872) Thomas Humphry Ward (1845–1926), editor of *Men of the Reign* (1885) and *Men of the Time.* Contributed to *Dictionary of Christian Biography;* published child's story *Milly and Olly* (1881); translated Amiel's *Journal Intime* (1885); in her best-known novel, the spiritual romance *Robert Elsmere* (1888), envisioned a vigorous Christianity, divested of the miraculous element and fulfilling the social gospel. Founded (1890) settlement in London which developed into Passmore Edwards Settlement (1897); opponent of woman suffrage. Author of other novels, including *David Grieve* (1892), *Marcella* (1894), *Lady Rose's Daughter* (1903), *The Marriage of William Ashe* (1905), *Daphine* (1909), *The Case of Richard Meynell* (1911), *The Coryston Family* (1913), *Missing* (1917), *Harvest* (1920). For her daughter **Janet**, see under TREVELYAN family.

**Ward, Nathaniel.** 1578?–1652. Clergyman, b. Haverhill, England. Entered Anglican ministry, but was dismissed for nonconformity (1633); to America and became pastor at Agawam (now Ipswich), Mass. (1633–38). Prepared legal code for Massachusetts (enacted 1641), first code of laws to be established in New England. Over pseudonym **Theodore de la Guard** (dĕl'ȧ·gärd'), published *The Simple Cobler of Aggawam in America* (1645), a satirical work representing itself as the reflections of a cobbler on the political and religious issues in England and the American colonies. Pastor at Shenfield, England (1648–52).

**Ward, Nathaniel Bagshaw.** 1791–1868. English botanist; inventor of the Wardian case, for transporting moisture-loving plants.

**Ward, Ned.** See Edward WARD.

**Ward, Robert DeCourcy.** 1867–1931. American meteorologist, b. Boston; on Harvard teaching staff (from 1890); professor of climatology (from 1910), first such professor in U.S.; author of *Climate, Considered Especially in Relation to Man* (1908), *The Climates of the United States* (1925).

**Ward, Robert Plumer.** 1765–1846. English writer on international law and novelist; kept a political diary (from 1809); author of the novels *Tremaine, or the Man of Refinement* (1825), *De Vere, or the Man of Independence* (1827), and *De Clifford, or the Constant Man* (1841). His nephew **William Ward** (1787–1849), financier and advocate of bimetallic currency; cricketer (scored 278 in one innings in 1820); bought lease of Lord's cricket ground to save it from the builder (1825).
William's son **William George** (1812–1882), theologian; known as "Ideal Ward," after his treatise *The Ideal of a Christian Church* (1844), in praise of Roman Catholicism; disciple of J. H. Newman, entered Roman Catholic Church (1845); edited *Dublin Review* (1863–78). His son **Wilfrid Philip** (1856–1916), man of letters; editor of *Dublin Review* (1906); wrote biographies of his father and of Newman, and essays.

**Ward, Samuel.** d. 1643. English Puritan theologian; one of translators of Apocrypha for Authorized Version of the Bible (1611); master of Sidney Sussex College, Cambridge (1610–43); professor of divinity, Cambridge (1623–43).

**Ward, Samuel.** 1725–1776. Rhode Island farmer and

political leader. Son of **Richard** (1689–1763), merchant, b. Newport, governor of Rhode Island (1740–42). Farmer, Westerly (from 1745) and prominent, like his father, in Rhode Island politics; governor of Rhode Island (1762, 1765, 1766); vigorously supported colonial side in Stamp Act controversy (1765–66); member of first and second Continental Congresses (1774–76); proposed and aided appointment of George Washington as commander in chief of American forces.

Samuel's son **Samuel** (1756–1832), b. Westerly, R.I., American Revolutionary officer; founded mercantile house of Samuel Ward & Brother, New York City; delegate to Annapolis Convention (1786) and Hartford Convention (1814); father of **Samuel** (1786–1839), banker; a founder and first president, Bank of Commerce, New York City; father of **Julia**, wife of Samuel Gridley Howe and known in literature as Julia Ward Howe, and of **Samuel** (1814–1884), politician; prominent as lobbyist in Washington, D.C., for financiers interested in congressional legislation (c. 1865–77); well known as bon vivant and raconteur; original of Horace Bellingham in his nephew F. Marion Crawford's novel *Dr. Claudius.*

**Ward, Seth.** 1617–1689. English bishop and astronomer. Opponent of Solemn League and Covenant; professor of astronomy, Oxford (1649–61); bishop of Exeter (1662–67), of Salisbury (1667); propounded theory of planetary motion; engaged in philosophical controversy with Thomas Hobbes; an original member of Royal Society.

**Ward, William, William George,** and **Wilfrid Philip.** See under Robert Plumer WARD.

**Ward, William Hayes.** 1835–1916. American clergyman, Orientalist, and journalist, b. Abington, Mass. Assoc. editor (1868–70), superintending editor (1870–96), and editor (1896–1913), New York *Independent.* Led first American exploring expedition to Babylonia (1884–85); made surveys which directed U. of Pennsylvania's expedition in uncovering ancient Nippur (1888–1900). Authority on Assyrian and Babylonian seals. His son **Herbert Dickinson** (1861–1932) was an author, and husband (from 1888) of Elizabeth Stuart Phelps Ward (*q.v.*); author of short stories, and three novels written in collaboration with his wife (*Master of the Magicians,* 1890; *A Lost Hero,* 1891; *Come Forth,* 1891).

**Warde** (wôrd), **Frederick.** 1851–1935. Actor, b. in Oxfordshire, Eng.; to U.S. (1874); starred esp. in Shakespearean drama; author of *Shakespeare's Fools,* etc.

**Warde,** Sir **Henry.** 1766–1834. English soldier; took part in capture of Mauritius (1810) and acted as governor (1811–13); governor of Barbados (1821–27).

**Ward'law** (wôrd'lô), **Henry. d. 1440.** Scottish bishop, nephew of **Walter Wardlaw,** cardinal (d. 1390). Consecrated bishop of St. Andrews (1403); tutor to James I of Scotland; founded St. Andrews U., the first in Scotland (1411); completed restoration of St. Andrews Cathedral.

**Ware** (wâr), **Eugene Fitch.** *Pseudonym* **I'ron·quill'** (ī'ẽrn·kwĭl'). 1841–1911. American lawyer and poet, b. Hartford, Conn.; member of Kansas State senate (1879–84); U.S. commissioner of pensions (1902–05). His collected verse appeared under title *The Rhymes of Ironquill.*

**Ware, Harriet.** 1877?–1962. American pianist and composer; m. Hugh Montgomery Krumbhaar (1913). Best known for her songs.

**Ware, Henry.** 1764–1845. American clergyman, b. Sherborn, Mass. Hollis professor of divinity, Harvard (1805–40); from his courses developed Harvard Divinity School (organized 1816), in which he was professor of systematic theology and evidences of Christianity (1816–45); associated with the liberal or Unitarian, branch of Congregationalists.

His son **Henry** (1794–1843), Unitarian clergyman; professor, Harvard Divinity School (to 1842); author of *The Life of the Saviour* (1833), and a few poems, addresses, and volumes of sermons.

Another son, **John** (1795–1864), physician; professor, Harvard Medical School (from 1836); president, Massachusetts Medical Society (1848–52).

A third son, **William** (1797–1852), Unitarian clergyman and writer; pastor, New York City (1821–36); author of *Zenobia: or, The Fall of Palmyra: An Historical Romance* (orig., *Letters of Lucius M. Piso from Palmyra, to His Friend Marcus Curtius at Rome;* 1837), its sequel *Probus: or, Rome in the Third Century* (1838), *Julian: or, Scenes in Judea* (1841), *Sketches of European Capitals* (1851).

**Ashur** (1782–1873), editor and jurist; nephew of Henry (1764–1845); first secretary of state of State of Maine (1820–22); U.S. judge of district court in Maine (1822–66); authority on American maritime law.

**John Fothergill Waterhouse** (1818–1881), Unitarian clergyman, b. Boston; son of Henry (1794–1843); pastor, Cambridgeport, Mass. (1846–64), Baltimore, Md. (1864–72), Boston (1872–81); author of *The Silent Pastor, or Consolations for the Sick* (1848), *Home Life: What It Is and What It Needs* (1864).

**William Robert** (1832–1915), architect and educator; half brother of John Fothergill; offices in Boston (from 1860); formed partnership with Henry Van Brunt (1863) and among notable buildings designed by them are the First Church of Boston, the Episcopal Theological School of Cambridge, Mass., Memorial Hall at Harvard U.; appointed head (1865) of a projected school of architecture in M.I.T.; also, founder and head of a school of architecture established in School of Mines, Columbia U. (1881–1903); regarded as founder of architectural education in U.S.

**Wa·renne'** (wä·rĕn'; *Fr.* vȧ'rĕn') *or* **War'ren** (wŏr'ĕn; -ĭn), **de** (dĕ). Name (derived from Guarenne or Varenne River) of an Anglo-Norman family holding large estates in Surrey, Sussex, Norfolk, and Yorkshire, founded in England by **William de Warenne** (1030?–1088), 1st Earl of **Sur'rey** [sûr'ĭ] (more commonly styled, as were his successors, Earl **Warenne**); distant cousin of William the Conqueror; fought at Hastings; joint chief justiciar (1075); founder of Cluniac priories; fatally wounded at siege of Pevensey Castle. His son **William** (1071?–1138), 2d earl, took part in Duke Robert's invasion of England (1101); pardoned by Henry II; fought in Normandy (1106, 1119, 1135). The latter's son **William** (d. 1148), 3d earl, supported King Stephen; killed on a crusade. **Isabel** (d. 1199); heiress of 3d earl; m. **Hamelin Plantagenet** (d. 1202), illegitimate son of Geoffrey Plantagenet and Henry II's half brother, who took (from 1163) name de Warenne and title of Earl Warenne, denounced Thomas à Becket, supported Henry II and Richard I, opposed Prince John (1191–99), and built great keep at Conisbrough. Their son **William** (d. 1240), Earl of Surrey, sided with John against pope and against barons; warden of Cinque Ports (1216); m. (1225) Matilda, coheiress of William Marshal, 1st Earl of Pembroke; a regent (1230); member of council to prevent king from squandering subsidy (1238).

William's (d. 1240) son **John** (1231?–1304), Earl of **Surrey and Sus'sex** (sŭs'ĕks; -ĭks), took Henry III's side against barons (1258–59); fought under Prince Edward at Lewes, fled to France, and lost lands to barons (1264); pardoned (1268); took oaths to Edward I; served in Wales (1277, 1282–83); received earldom of Sussex on death of his sister (1282); led invasion of Scotland, took Dunbar Castle (1296); routed by Wallace (1297) at Stirling Bridge; commanded rear at Falkirk

(1298). His grandson **John** (1286–1347), succeeded him as earl (1304); joined barons' party, but alienated by execution of Piers Gaveston, went over to Edward II (1312) and received pardon; stripped of many estates by Lancaster (1317–19); supported Edward II against Lancaster and against Queen Isabella; made commissioner to Scots (1327); sheriff of Surrey and Sussex (1339).

**War′field** (wôr′fēld), **David.** 1866–1951. American actor, b. San Francisco; starred by David Belasco in *The Auctioneer* (1900–03) and *The Music Master* (1903–07); appeared also in *A Grand Army Man*, *The Return of Peter Grimm*, *The Flying Dutchman.*

**War′ham** (wôr′ăm), **William.** 1450?–1532. English prelate. Bishop of London (1502); lord chancellor (1504–15); archbishop of Canterbury (1504); crowned Henry VIII and Catherine of Aragon (1509); gradually withdrew in favor of Wolsey after controversy over legatine authority (1518); acquiesced in Henry VIII's petition for divorce. Friend of Erasmus, Colet, Grocyn, Linacre.

**War′hol** (wôr′hôl), **Andy.** 1930?– . American artist. Known as pop artist; also movie director; produced *The Chelsea Girls*, etc.

**War′ing** (wâr′ĭng), **George Edwin.** 1833–1898. American sanitary engineer, b. Poundridge, N.Y.; colonel in Union army in Civil War; made reputation for efficiency as street-cleaning commissioner of New York City (1895–98).

**Waring,** Sir **Holburt Jacob.** 1866–1953. English surgeon; author of *Manual of Operative Surgery.*

**War′ing·ton** (wâr′ĭng·tŭn), **Robert.** 1838–1907. English agricultural chemist; made researches on preparation of artificial fertilizers and nitrification of the soil.

**Warlock, Peter.** See Philip Arnold HESELTINE.

**War′man** (wôr′măn), **Cy.** 1855–1914. American journalist; author of two volumes of verse (*Mountain Melodies*, 1892; *Songs of Cy Warman*, 1911) and many volumes of tales dealing with railroads and their operation.

**War′ming** (vär′mēng), **Johannes Eugenius Bülow.** 1841–1924. Danish botanist; credited with founding of plant ecology; did research in morphology and taxonomy.

**Warne** (wôrn), **Frederick.** 1825–1901. English publisher; inaugurated *Chandos Classics* (1868); published nearly all Mrs. Frances Hodgson Burnett's novels; introduced American *Century*, *St. Nicholas*, *Scribners* to English public.

**War′ner** (wôr′nẽr), **Adoniram Judson.** 1834–1910. American politician, b. Wales, N.Y. In Marietta, Ohio (from 1865); member, U.S. House of Representatives (1879–81; 1883–87); attained national prominence as a leader in movement for free coinage of silver. Engaged in transportation and electric-power development in Georgia (from 1898).

**Warner, Anna Bartlett.** See under Susan Bogert WARNER.

**Warner, Anne Richmond.** Mrs. **Anne Warner French** (frĕnch). 1869–1913. American fiction writer; m. Charles Eltinge French (1888; d. 1912); attained great popularity with her "Susan Clegg" tales.

**Warner, Charles Dudley.** 1829–1900. American man of letters, b. Plainfield, Mass. Assoc. editor (1867–1900), Hartford (Conn.) *Courant;* also, contributing editor, *Harper's New Monthly Magazine* (1884–98) and coeditor of *Library of the World's Best Literature* (30 vols., 1896–97). Collaborated with Mark Twain in writing *The Gilded Age* (1873). Best known for his collections of familiar essays, including: *My Summer in a Garden* (1871), *Backlog Studies* (1873), *Being a Boy* (1878), *On Horseback* (1888), *Fashions in Literature* (1902).

**Warner, Edward Pearson.** 1894–1958. American aeronautical engineer, b. Pittsburgh, Pa.; asst. secretary, U.S. navy, for aeronautics (1926–29); editor of *Aviation* (1929–35); author of *Airplane Design—Aerodynamics* (1927).

**Warner, George Townsend.** 1865–1916. English historian; master at Harrow (1891 ff.); author of *Landmarks in English Industrial History* (1899; many subsequent editions); coauthor with Clarence H. K. Marten of *Groundwork of British History* (1912) and a series of school textbooks on British history. See Sylvia Townsend WARNER.

**Warner, Harry Morris** (1881–1958), **Samuel Louis** (1887–1927), **Albert** (1884–1967), and **Jack L.** (1892–1978). *Orig. surname* **Ei′chel·baum** (ī′kĕl·boum). Four brothers, sons of Russian immigrants (1890); associated in the motion-picture business in U.S., as exhibitors (1903–1912) and producers (from 1912); first notable production success was James W. Gerard's *My Four Years in Germany* (1918); business incorporated (1923) as Warner Brothers Pictures, with Harry M. Warner as president, and the other brothers as vice-presidents; pioneered in development of talking motion pictures.

**Warner, Henry Byron.** 1876–1958. Actor, b. in London, Eng.; to U.S. as leading man with Eleanor Robson (1905); toured U.S. in *Alias Jimmy Valentine*, *The Ghost Breaker*, etc.; also, actor in, and director of, motion pictures.

**Warner, Olin Levi.** 1844–1896. American sculptor, b. Suffield, Conn.: studio in New York (from 1872). Among his notable works are a bust of John Insley Blair (Metropolitan Museum of Art, New York), statues of Governor Buckingham of Connecticut (State Capitol, Hartford), William Lloyd Garrison (Commonwealth Avenue, Boston), Gen. Charles Devens (Boston), one of the great bronze doors of Library of Congress building (Washington, D.C.), and the idyllic figures *Twilight*, *Dancing Nymph*, *Cupid and Psyche.*

**Warner, Seth.** 1743–1784. American Revolutionary officer, b. Roxbury, Conn.; with Ethan Allen and Benedict Arnold at capture of Ticonderoga (May 10, 1775); led force that seized Crown Point (May 11, 1775); lieutenant colonel of a Vermont regiment (July 26, 1775); led regiment in battle of Bennington (Aug. 16, 1777). Commissioned brigadier general by Vermont assembly (Mar. 20, 1778).

**Warner, Susan Bogert.** *Pseudonym* **Elizabeth Weth′er·ell** (wĕth′ẽr·ĕl). 1819–1885. American novelist, b. New York City. Made great success with her first two books, *The Wide, Wide World* (1850) and *Queechy* (1852). Among her later novels were *Melbourne House* (1864), *Daisy* (1868), *Diana* (1877), *Nobody* (1882). Collaborated in many books with her sister **Anna Bartlett** (1827–1915), pseudonym **Amy Lo′throp** (lō′thrŭp), including *Say and Seal* (1860), *Wych Hazel* (1876). Anna Warner was author of *Stories of Vinegar Hill* (6 vols., 1872), *The Fourth Watch* (1872), and a number of books on gardening.

**Warner, Sylvia Townsend.** 1893–1978. English writer; dau. of George Townsend Warner (*q.v.*); author of verse, as in *The Espalier* (1925), *Time Importuned* (1928), *Opus 7* (novel in verse; 1931), *Whether a Dove or a Seagull* (with V. Ackland; 1934), of fiction including *Lolly Willowes* (1926), *Mr. Fortune's Maggot* (1927), *Elinor Barley* (1930), *The Salutation* (short stories; 1932), *After the Death of Don Juan* (1938).

**Warner,** Sir **Thomas.** d. 1649. English colonizer; founded colony of St. Kitts (1624), Nevis (1628), Antigua (1632), Montserrat (1632). His three sons became governors: **Edward,** first governor of Antigua (1632); **Thomas** (d. 1675), natural son of Carib mother and nicknamed "Indian Warner," governor of Dominica; **Philip** (d. 1689), governor of Antigua (1672).

**Warner, William.** 1558?–1609. English poet; published *Pan his Syrinx*, consisting of 7 prose tales (1585), and his chief work *Albion's England* (1st ed., 1586), in 14-syllabled verse, consisting of history, mythical tales, theology.

**Warner, Worcester Reed.** 1846–1929. American maker of telescopes; with Ambrose Swasey (*q.v.*), founded (1881) Warner & Swasey Co., Cleveland, Ohio.

**Warnerius.** See IRNERIUS.

**War'ren, de** (dĕ wŏr'ĕn; -ĭn). See WARENNE.

**War'ren** (wŏr'ĕn; -ĭn), Sir **Charles.** 1840–1927. British soldier and archaeologist, b. Bangor, Wales; excavated at Jerusalem (1867) and surveyed Palestine (1867–70); served in military operations in South Africa, Egypt, etc.; commanded 5th division in Boer War (1899–1900); general (1904).

**Warren, Charles.** 1868–1954. American lawyer and writer; practiced in Boston; asst. attorney general of the United States (1914–18); author of *History of the American Bar...*(1911), *The Supreme Court in United States History* (3 vols., 1922; awarded Pulitzer prize), *Congress, the Constitution and the Supreme Court* (1925), etc.

**Warren, Charles Beecher.** 1870–1936. American lawyer and diplomat; practiced in Detroit; U.S. ambassador to Japan (1921–23), Mexico (1924); appointed U.S. attorney general by President Coolidge, but not confirmed by U.S. Senate.

**Warren, Cyrus Moors.** 1824–1891. American chemist and industrialist; devoted himself to research into the hydrocarbon constituents of tars; developed process of fractional condensation to separate these constituents, and used process also for investigations of mixture of hydrocarbons in Pennsylvania petroleum.

**Warren, Earl.** 1891–1974. American jurist, b. Los Angeles. Governor of California (1943–53); chief justice, U.S. Supreme Court (1953–69).

**Warren, Francis Emroy.** 1844–1929. American politician, b. Hinsdale, Mass.; governor, Wyoming Territory (1885–86; 1889–90); first governor, State of Wyoming (1890); U.S. senator from Wyoming (1890–93; 1895–1929). Interested himself in reclamation of arid lands; known as "Father of Reclamation." His daughter **Helen** m. Gen. John J. Pershing (1905).

**Warren, George Frederick.** 1874–1938. American agricultural economist; financial adviser for President Franklin D. Roosevelt; advocate of a managed currency in the form of a commodity or compensated dollar.

**Warren, Gouverneur Kemble.** 1830–1882. American army officer, b. Cold Spring, N.Y.; grad. U.S.M.A., West Point (1850); served in engineer corps. Commissioned colonel of volunteers (Aug., 1861); brigadier general (Sept., 1862); chief topographical engineer, Army of the Potomac (from Feb., 1863). Major general of volunteers (June, 1863) and chief engineer of Army of the Potomac; at Gettysburg by prompt action in seizing and holding Little Round Top position saved the day (July 2, 1863) for Union army. Commanded fifth corps (Mar., 1864); engaged in the Wilderness, Spotsylvania, Cold Harbor, Five Forks; commanded department of Mississippi (May, 1865). On military engineering duty (1865–82). Commemorated by a bronze statue at Little Round Top on Gettysburg battlefield.

**Warren, Henry White.** 1831–1912. American Methodist Episcopal clergyman; elected bishop (1880). His brother **William Fairfield** (1833–1929) was also a Methodist Episcopal clergyman; president, Boston Theol. School (1867–73); associated with organization of Boston U., of which Boston Theol. School became a part; first president of Boston U. (1873–1903); instrumental in making Boston U. the first university to award Ph.D. degree to women (1878).

**Warren, Howard Crosby.** 1867–1934. American psychologist; professor, Princeton.

**Warren, James.** See under Mercy WARREN.

**Warren,** Sir **John Borlase.** 1753–1822. British naval officer (1777–82, 1793–1814); captured French squadron (1806); admiral (1810).

**Warren, John Byrne Leicester.** Baron **de Tab'ley** (dĕ tăb'lĭ). 1835–1895. English poet; author of the tragedies *Philoctetes* (1866) and *Orestes* (1868), *Guide-book to Bookplates* (1880), and *Poems Dramatic and Lyrical* (1893, 1895).

**Warren, Joseph.** 1741–1775. American physician and Revolutionary officer, b. Roxbury, Mass.; practiced medicine in Boston. Entered army; was man who (Apr. 18, 1775) sent Paul Revere and William Dawes to Lexington to warn Hancock and Adams of their danger; president pro tempore of provincial Congress (1775). Commissioned major general (June, 1775); killed at Breed's Hill (battle of Bunker Hill, June 17, 1775).

His brother **John** (1753–1815), physician, practiced in Salem, Mass.; active in Boston Tea Party (Dec. 18, 1773); joined army as surgeon; senior surgeon of hospital at Cambridge (1775–76) and later of that on Long Island (1776–77); drew up plans for Harvard Medical School (1782), and was its first professor of anatomy and surgery; a founder and president, Massachusetts Humane Society.

John's son **John Collins** (1778–1856), surgeon, practiced with his father in Boston (from 1802); professor, Harvard Medical School (1809–47); first surgeon, Massachusetts General Hospital, Boston (1821); best known as surgeon who gave first public demonstration of ether anesthesia (in operation performed Oct. 16, 1846, ether administered by W. T. G. Morton).

John Collins's grandson **John Collins Warren** (1842–1927), surgeon, practiced in Boston (from 1869); on teaching staff, Harvard Medical School; author of *American Text Book of Surgery* (with W. W. Keen, 1892), *Surgical Pathology and Therapeutics* (1895). His son **Joseph** (1876–1942), professor of law, Harvard (1914–42).

**Warren, Josiah.** 1798?–1874. American social reformer, b. Boston. Joined Owen socialist community at New Harmony, Ind. (1825); became extreme individualist. Developed theory of society in which interchanges of goods and services should be based solely on cost element; tried out theory in "equity store" in Cincinnati (1827–29). Established and maintained new social community, known as "Modern Times," on Long Island, N.Y. (1850?–?1862), which attracted a number of eccentrics. Regarded as founder of philosophical anarchism in America. Inventor (1837–40) of a cylinder press, self-inking and printing on a continuous roll of paper, but destroyed it after workmen persistently sabotaged it. Patented (1846) process for making stereotype plates easily and cheaply. Author of *Equitable Commerce* (1846), *True Civilization an Immediate Necessity* (1863).

**Warren, Lavinia.** See under Charles Sherwood STRATTON.

**Warren, Mercy,** *nee* **O'tis** (ō'tĭs). 1728–1814. American woman of letters, b. Barnstable, Mass.; sister of James Otis; friend and correspondent of leading political figures of her day, including John Adams, Samuel Adams, Thomas Jefferson, Elbridge Gerry. Author of political satires (notably, *The Adulateur*, 1773, and *The Group*, 1775), several plays, verse (*Poems Dramatic and Miscel-*

*laneous,* 1790), and *History of the Rise, Progress, and Termination of the American Revolution* (3 vols., 1805). Her husband, **James Warren** (1726–1808), Massachusetts political leader, was paymaster general of Continental army (1775–76), member of the navy board for the eastern department (1776–81), and member of the governor's council (1792, 1793, 1794).

**Warren,** Sir **Peter.** 1703–1752. British naval officer; resident in New York City (1730–47); commanded British naval force that captured French fortress of Louisbourg (1745); commanded British squadron that defeated French squadron off Cape Finisterre (1747); knighted and promoted vice-admiral (1747). Resident in England (from 1747).

**Warren, Robert Penn.** 1905– . American writer, b. in Todd County, Ky.; educ. Vanderbilt and Oxford (Rhodes scholar, 1928–30); assoc. professor of English, Louisiana State (from 1934); coeditor, *Southern Review;* author of *Thirty-six Poems* (1935), *Night Rider* (1939), *At Heaven's Gate* (1943), etc.

**Warren, Russell.** 1783–1860. American architect; offices in Bristol, R.I., and Providence; member of the Greek revival movement in architecture; designer of residences in Rhode Island, and of public buildings; said to be inventor of the Warren truss, used in steel bridge construction.

**Warren, Samuel.** 1807–1877. English lawyer and novelist; queen's counsel (1851); author of many legal textbooks and of *Ten Thousand a Year* (1839), a novel of Tittlebat Titmouse's sudden elevation to wealth. His father, Dr. **Samuel** (1781–1852), Wesleyan preacher, was founder of seceding "Warrenites," who formed United Methodist Free Churches.

**Warren, Whitney.** 1864–1943. American architect; practiced in New York (from 1894). Among buildings designed in whole or in part by him are Grand Central Station in New York, Ritz-Carlton Hotel in New York, John Paul Jones Crypt at U.S.N.A., Annapolis, Md., the bronze gates of the Cathedral of St. John the Divine in New York. He was chosen architect for rebuilding the Louvain Library in Belgium after the World War.

**Warren, William.** 1767–1832. Actor and theatrical manager; to U.S. (1796); excelled in old man comedy roles, as Sir Toby Belch and Falstaff. His son **William** (1812–1888) was also an actor; excelled as comedian in stock company at Boston Museum (from 1847 till retirement, 1883); regarded as one of most distinguished American actors.

**Warren, William Fairfield.** See under Henry White WARREN.

**Warrington,** Earl of. See under George BOOTH.

**War'ris·ton** (wŏr'ĭs·tŭn), Lord. **Archibald John'ston** (jŏn'stŭn; jŏn's'n). 1611–1663. Scottish judge and statesman. Framed, with Alexander Henderson, Scots National Covenant (1638) to defend Presbyterianism against Charles I's attempt to force episcopacy upon Scottish church; a judge, or lord of session, as Lord Warriston (1641); led resistance to "engagement" between Charles and Scottish parliament (1648); a leading "remonstrant" of the faction committed to exclusion of king. Member of Cromwell's House of Lords, of council of state under Rump Parliament, and president of committee of public safety. After Restoration, given up by Louis XIV of France, tried by Scots parliament, and hanged at Edinburgh.

**Wartenburg.** See YORCK VON WARTENBURG.

**War'thin** (wôr'thĭn), **Al'dred** (ăl'drĕd; -drĭd) **Scott.** 1866–1931. American pathologist; professor and director, department of pathology, U. of Michigan (1903–31); author of *Old Age—the Major Involution* (1929), *The Creed of a Biologist* (1930), *The Physician of the Dance of Death* (1931).

**War'ton** (wôr't'n), **Joseph.** 1722–1800. English literary critic. Headmaster (1766–93) of Winchester; revolted in his *Odes* (1744, 1746) against critical rules of Pope and the "correct" school of poetry, and displayed an unfashionable love of nature and natural scenery; edited Vergil and translated *Eclogues* and *Georgics* (1753); known chiefly for *Essay on the Genius and Writings of Pope* (1756, 1782). Edited Pope (1797); friend of Dr. Johnson and member of Literary Club.
His brother **Thomas** (1728–1790) was a literary historian and critic, and poet laureate; attracted attention with heroic poem in praise of Oxford *The Triumph of Isis* (1749); wrote humorous verse, and established reputation with the scholarly *Observations on the Faerie Queene of Spenser* (1754); brought to bear vast stores of learning in *The History of English Poetry* (3 vols., 1774–81), extending to end of Elizabethan age; annotated Milton's minor poems (1785); one of first to detect Chatterton forgeries (1782); poet laureate (1785–90); precursor of romantic revival; displayed even in early poems taste for Gothic architecture and ruins.
Their father, **Thomas** the elder (1688?–1745), wrote Jacobite verses (1717–18), was professor of poetry, Oxford (1718–28), vicar of Basingstoke (1723–45).

**Warville, de.** See Jacques Pierre BRISSOT.

**War'wick** (wŏr'ĭk). English earldom, created c. 1088, and held by various families, including the Beauchamps, Nevilles, Plantagenets, Dudleys, Riches, and (since 1759) Grevilles. The chief members, entered elsewhere, are: Richard and Thomas BEAUCHAMP, Richard NEVILLE, the Kingmaker (1428–1471), Edward Plantagenet (1475–1499; see under George, Duke of CLARENCE), John DUDLEY (1502?–1553), Robert RICH (1587–1658), Leopold Guy GREVILLE (1882–1928).

**Warwick,** Countess of. **Frances Evelyn,** *nee* **May'nard** (mā'nẽrd). 1861–1938. British humanitarian; m. (1881) 5th earl of Warwick; founder of welfare organizations, training school for girls in horticulture, apiculture, etc., home for the crippled; member of Labor party and an active Socialist.

**Wa'sa** (*Ger.* vä'zä). Variant of VASA.

**Wash'burn** (wŏsh'bẽrn; -bûrn), **Albert Henry.** 1866–1930. American lawyer and diplomat; counsel for U.S. Treasury in customs cases (1901–04); U.S. minister to Austria (1922–30).

**Washburn, Israel.** 1813–1883. American lawyer and politician; practiced in Orono, Me. (1834–63) and Portland (from 1863); member, U.S. House of Representatives (1851–61); called meeting (May 9, 1854) of antislavery representatives and took measures toward organizing new political party (called "Republican," probably at his suggestion); governor of Maine (1861–62); U.S. collector of customs, Portland, Me. (1863–77). A brother, **Elihu Benjamin** (1816–1887), who chose to spell his surname **Wash'burne** (wŏsh'bẽrn; -bûrn), lawyer and politician; member of U.S. House of Representatives (1853–69); U.S. secretary of state for a few days resigning to become U.S. minister to France (1869–77). Another brother, **Cadwallader Colden** (1818–1882), businessman, army officer, and politician; settled in Mineral Point, Wis., and amassed fortune in land; member of U.S. House of Representatives (1855–61, 1867–71); served in Union army in Civil War (major general, Nov., 1862); governor of Wisconsin (1872–74); organized Washburn, Crosby & Co., milling firm (1877); also widely interested in lumbering and transportation lines; donor of Washburn Observatory to U. of Wisconsin and a public library to city of La Crosse, Wis.

Another brother, **William Drew** (1831–1912), lawyer, businessman, and politician; began practice in Minneapolis, Minn.; active in lumbering, water-power development, and milling industry; member of U.S. House of Representatives (1879–85); U.S. Senator (1889–95).

**Washburn, Stanley.** 1878–1950. American war correspondent, with Russian army (1914–15), French at Verdun (1916) and Rumanian army (1916). Military aid to heads of railway and diplomatic missions to Russia (1917); member of American delegation to Disarmament Conference, Washington, D.C. (1921).

**Washburne, Elihu Benjamin.** See under Israel WASHBURN.

**Wash'ing·ton** (wŏsh'ĭng·tŭn), **Booker Tal'ia·ferro** (tŏl'ĭ·vẽr). 1856–1915. American Negro educator, born a slave in Franklin County, Va. After great hardships in his youth, gained an education at Hampton Institute (1872–75). Chosen (1881) to establish and head a school at Tuskegee, Ala., the Tuskegee Institute for practical training of Negroes in trades and professions, which at his death had over a hundred buildings, extensive real-estate holdings, a faculty of about 200, a student body of 1500, an endowment of $2,000,000, and an annual budget of about $300,000. Gained national recognition as educational leader of the Negro people in the United States. Author of *Up From Slavery* (1901). Elected to American Hall of Fame (1945).

**Washington, Bushrod.** 1762–1829. Nephew of George Washington. American jurist, b. Westmoreland County, Va.; served in Continental army in American Revolution; practiced law in Alexandria, Va. (to 1790) and Richmond (from 1790); associate justice, U.S. Supreme Court (1798–1829). Resided (after 1802) at Mount Vernon, which was bequeathed to him by George Washington, along with his library, and his public and private papers.

**Washington, George.** 1732–1799. First president of the United States, b. Westmoreland County, Va., eldest son of Augustine Washington (d. 1743), a Virginia planter, and his second wife, Mary Ball (1708–89). Privately educated, chiefly by his elder half brother, Lawrence. Gained experience as surveyor by assisting in survey of certain Fairfax holdings in Shenandoah Valley (1748); county surveyor, Culpeper County, Va. (1749). Inherited Mount Vernon after death of Lawrence (1752). Commissioned district adjutant by Gov. Dinwiddie (1752); sent to carry ultimatum (1753) to French who were encroaching on English territory in Ohio region; delivered message but received unconciliatory reply. Commissioned lieutenant colonel and sent with 150 men (1754) to establish outpost on site of present city of Pittsburgh; found French strongly entrenched there and in possession of Fort Duquesne; entrenched himself at Great Meadows, Pa., in Fort Necessity; surprised and defeated first French force sent against him (May 27, 1754); gained honorable terms from French after resisting a ten-hour attack (July 3). Served on General Braddock's staff (1755) in British expedition against Fort Duquesne; engaged in disastrous battle at the Monongahela. Commissioned colonel and commander in chief of Virginia troops (1755), charged with defense of frontier from French and Indian attacks; engaged in fighting (1755–58) until French abandoned Fort Duquesne and British occupied it (Nov., 1758). m. Martha Custis (Jan. 6, 1759), widow of Daniel Parke Custis (see below); retired to Mount Vernon to live life of Virginia gentleman-farmer. Member, Virginia House of Burgesses (1759–74); became one of leaders of Virginia and colonial opposition to British policies in America. Member of First and Second Continental Congresses (1774–75). Elected to command all Continental armies (June 15, 1775); assumed command at Cambridge, Mass. (July 3, 1775). Remained in Boston area until he forced British evacuation of city (Mar. 17, 1776); engaged in New York and Long Island area (1776), and conducted masterly retreat southward through New Jersey; surprised and defeated Hessians at Trenton (Dec. 26, 1776), won battle of Princeton and forced British retirement to Brunswick, N.J.; established headquarters at Morristown, N.J. (1777). Engaged at Brandywine (Sept. 11, 1777), Germantown (Oct. 3–4, 1777), and held army together at Valley Forge through bitter winter (1777–78), where the troops were drilled by Baron von Steuben. Heartened by French alliance (1778), attacked British at Monmouth (June 28, 1778) and held the field while British retired to New York. Enabled by co-operation of French fleet under de Grasse and French army under Rochambeau to march against Cornwallis at Yorktown, Va., and force his surrender (Oct. 19, 1781). With great difficulty, held army together before New York until British evacuated city (Apr. 19, 1783). Resigned commission (Dec. 23, 1783) and again retired to Mount Vernon to resume care of plantation. Called from retirement to preside at federal convention in Philadelphia (1787). Unanimously chosen president of the United States under the new constitution; took oath of office in New York City (Apr. 30, 1789). Unanimously re-elected (1793). Declined third term, and after a farewell address to the American people (Sept., 1796) retired from political life (Mar. 3, 1797). On threat of war with France (1798), accepted commission as lieutenant general and commander in chief of army (July 3, 1798) and retained this commission until his death (Dec. 14, 1799). Buried in tomb on his estate at Mount Vernon. Elected to American Hall of Fame (1900).

His wife (m. 1759), **Martha**, *nee* **Dan'dridge** [dăn'drĭj] (1732–1802), m. (1749) Daniel Parke Custis (d. 1757). Known as a gracious hostess in the first president's home. Through a son (John Parke Custis, d. 1781) by her first husband she had four grandchildren, the two younger of whom, Eleanor Parke Custis and George Washington Parke Custis, were adopted by Washington after the death of their father (1781).

**Washington, Henry Stephens.** 1867–1934. American geologist; associated with J. P. Iddings, L. V. Pirsson, and Whitman Cross in devising systematic classification of igneous rocks on basis of chemical composition; on staff of geophysical laboratory, Carnegie Institution, Washington, D.C. (from 1912).

**Washington, William.** 1752–1810. American Revolutionary officer, kinsman of George Washington.

**Wa'sie·lew'ski** (vä'shĕ·lĕf'skē), **Joseph Wilhelm von.** 1822–1896. German violinist, music director, and writer on music; town director of music, Bonn (1869–84). Author of *Robert Schumanns Biographie* (1858), *Die Violine und ihre Meister* (1869), *Beethoven* (1888), etc.

**Wa'sil ibn-A·ta'** (wä'sĭl ĭb'n·ă·tä'). *Arab.* **Wāṣil ibn-'Aṭā'.** d. 748. Arab scholar; founder at Basra of Mutazala sect of Shiites.

**Was'ser·mann** (väs'ẽr·män; *Angl.* wŏs'ẽr·măn), **August von.** 1866–1925. German bacteriologist; director of department of experimental therapy and biochemistry, Koch Institute for Infectious Diseases (1906); director of department of experimental therapy, Kaiser Wilhelm Institute in Berlin-Dahlem (1913); discovered a reaction used as a test (Wassermann test) for syphilis (1906).

**Wassermann, Jakob.** 1873–1934. German novelist, b. Bavaria of Jewish parents; long resident in Austria;

m. (1901) **Julie Spey′er** (shpī′ēr). Wrote *Die Juden von Zirndorf* (1897), *Caspar Hauser* (1909), *Christian Wahnschaffe* (1919; Eng. tr. *The World's Illusion*), *Der Fall Maurizius* (1928), and an autobiography, biographies of Columbus (1929) and Stanley (*Bula Matari*, 1932), short stories, essays, one-act plays.

**Wast, Hugo.** See Gustavo MARTÍNEZ ZUVIRÍA.

**Wa′ter·house′** (wô′tẽr·hous′; wŏt′ẽr-), **Alfred.** 1830–1905. English architect; designer of public buildings and champion of Gothic tradition by designing of Manchester assize courts and town hall, on competitive awards; designed Owens College, Manchester, Girton College, Cambridge, Natural History Museum, South Kensington (1868–80); used terra cotta and one of first to use structural ironwork freely. His son **Paul** (1861–1924), a partner (1891–1905), succeeded him; designed college and hospital buildings; a specialist in town planning.

**Waterhouse, Benjamin.** 1754–1846. American physician, b. Newport, R.I. First professor of theory and practice of physic, Harvard (1783–1812). Best known as pioneer in vaccination in America (from 1800); published report *A Prospect of Exterminating the Small Pox* (1800) and *Information Respecting the Origin, Progress, and Efficacy of the Kine Pock Inoculation* (1810). Suggested (1782), and drew up preliminary plans for (1785), a humane society. Published also a lecture against use of tobacco and liquors.

**Waterhouse, John William.** 1847–1917. English painter, four of whose works are in National Gallery: *Consulting the Oracle, St. Eulalia, The Lady of Shalott, The Magic Circle.*

**Wa′ter·land** (wô′tẽr·lănd; wŏt′ẽr-), **Daniel.** 1683–1740. English theological assailant of Arians and deists (1719–37); historian of Athanasian Creed.

**Wa′ter·loo′** (vä′tẽr·lō′), **Anthonie** *or* **Antony.** 1609?–after 1676. Dutch landscape painter and etcher.

**Wa′ter·low** (wô′tẽr·lō; wŏt′ẽr-), Sir **Ernest Albert.** 1850–1919. English landscape painter.

**Wa′ter·man** (wô′tẽr·măn; wŏt′ẽr-), **Lewis Edson.** 1837–1901. American inventor and manufacturer; perfected and patented (1884) an improved fountain pen.

**Wa′ters** (wô′tẽrz; wät′ẽrz), **Ethel.** 1896–1977. American singer and actress, b. Chester, Pa. Appeared on stage in *As Thousands Cheer, Mamba's Daughters, The Member of the Wedding*, etc.; in films (*Cabin in the Sky*, etc.). Wrote autobiography, *His Eye is on the Sparrow.*

**Waters, Lucy.** See Lucy WALTER.

**Wat′kin** (wŏt′kĭn), **Lawrence Edward.** 1901– . American novelist, b. Camden, N.Y.; A.B., Syracuse (1924), A.M., Harvard (1925); teacher of English, Washington and Lee (1927 ff.); author of *On Borrowed Time* (1937; dramatized by Paul Osborn), *Geese in the Forum* (1940), *The Gentleman from England* (1941), etc.

**Wa′trous** (wô′trŭs; wŏt′rŭs), **Harry Willson.** 1857–1940. American painter, b. San Francisco; known for genre paintings, often with small, delicately finished figures.

**Wat′son** (wŏt′s'n), **Benjamin Philip.** 1880– Gynecologist, b. in Scotland; he taught at Columbia (1926–46); also director, Sloane Hospital for Women); author of *Gynecological Pathology and Diagnosis, New System of Gynecology*, etc.

**Watson, Edmund Henry Lacon.** 1865–1948. English journalist and novelist; schoolmaster (7 yrs.); Reuter's correspondent (1917–19); author of *The Unconscious Humorist* (1896), *In the Days of His Youth* (1935), etc.

**Watson, Elkanah.** 1758–1842. American businessman and agriculturist, b. Plymouth, Mass.; promoted a cattle show (1810) which antedated incorporation of Berkshire Agricultural Society, sponsor of America's first county fair; hence regarded as father of the county fair in U.S.

**Watson, George Lennox.** 1851–1904. Scottish naval architect; designer of royal yacht *Britannia* and British yachts for international races (1887–1901).

**Watson, Henry Brereton Marriott.** 1863–1921. British journalist and novelist, b. Melbourne, Australia; to England (1885); writer of adventure stories. His wife, **Rosamund,** *nee* **Ball** [bôl] (1863–1911), was author of *Ballad of the Bird-Bride* (1889), etc.

**Watson, Homer Ransford.** 1855–1936. Canadian painter; his *The Pioneer Mill* hangs in Windsor Castle, *The Torrent* in Kensington Palace.

**Watson, James Craig.** 1838–1880. Astronomer, b. Fingal, Ontario, Canada; to U.S. (1850); at U. of Michigan (1857–60; 1863–79). Director, Washburn Observatory, U. of Wisconsin (1879–80). Devoted himself esp. to study of comets and asteroids; discovered 22 asteroids. In charge of expedition to China (1874) to observe transit of Venus.

**Watson, James Dewey.** 1928– . American biochemist, b. Chicago, Ill. At Harvard U. (1955– ); awarded Nobel prize in physiology and medicine (1962) with F. Crick and M. Wilkins for work on the structure of DNA; wrote *The Double Helix* (1968), etc.

**Watson, John.** 1807–1863. American physician, b. Londonderry, Ireland; a founder of American Medical Assoc.; credited with being first in U.S. to perform esophagotomy (1844).

**Watson, John.** 1847–1939. Philosopher, b. and educ. Glasgow; professor, Queen's U., Kingston, Canada (1872); author of *Kant and His English Critics* (1881) and other elucidations of Kant.

**Watson, John.** *Pseudonym* **Ian Mac·lar′en** (măk-lăr′ĕn). 1850–1907. Scottish clergyman and author. Presbyterian minister, Liverpool (1880–1905); won reputation with *Beside the Bonnie Brier Bush* (1894), followed by other portrayals of humble Scottish life, member of the kailyard school. Also wrote religious works, including *The Upper Room* (1896), *The Potter's Wheel* (1898), *Children of the Resurrection* (1912).

**Watson, John Broadus.** 1878–1958. American psychologist; exponent of behaviorism; professor, Johns Hopkins (1908–20). Wrote *Animal Education* (1903), *Behavior* (1914), *Behaviorism* (1925), *Ways of Behaviorism* (1928).

**Watson, John Christian.** 1867–1941. Australian Labor party politician; prime minister of Australia (1904).

**Watson, John Dawson.** 1832–1892. English watercolorist and book illustrator; known for illustrations of *The Pilgrim's Progress* and *Robinson Crusoe.*

**Watson, John Fanning.** 1779–1860. American antiquarian; conducted bookstore in Philadelphia (1809–14); bank cashier in Germantown (1814–47); treasurer and secretary of Philadelphia, Germantown & Norristown Railroad (1847–59); published *Annals of Philadelphia* (1830), *Annals . . . New York City and State* (1846), etc.

**Watson, Richard.** 1737–1816. English chemist and Christian apologist; regius professor of divinity (1771), Cambridge; bishop of Llandaff (1782). Made discovery (1772) leading to black-bulb thermometer; gave advice to government for improving gunpowder (1787); defended Christianity against Edward Gibbon and Bible against Tom Paine.

**Watson, Sereno.** 1826–1892. American botanist; joined Clarence King's exploring expedition, then surveying Great Basin (1867); became botanist of the expedition; classified collection and published *Botany* (1871), often called "Botany of the King Expedition." Curator of Gray Herbarium in Cambridge, Mass. (1873–92). Collaborated with Asa Gray and W. H. Brewer in *Botany of California* (2 vols., 1876–80). Revised Gray's *Manual of Botany* (with J. M. Coulter, 1889).

**Watson, Thomas.** 1513–1584. English humanist scholar; bishop of Lincoln (1557); Roman Catholic controversialist, disputed against Cranmer at Oxford (1554).

**Watson, Thomas.** 1557?–1592. English lyrical poet; wrote Latin poems; translated into Latin Sophocles's *Antigone* (1581) and Tasso's *Aminta* (1585); translated into English collection of Italian madrigals (1590); author of *Hecatompathia*, or *Passionate Century of Love*, a collection of 18-line artificial love poems in English (1582), and of *Tears of Fancy*, true sonnets (1593).

**Watson, Thomas Augustus.** 1854–1934. American telephone technician; assistant to Bell in his experiments (1874–77); became research and technical head of the Bell Telephone Co. (to 1881). Opened machine shop (with F. O. Wellington) at East Braintree, Mass.; received contracts for warships for U.S. navy (from 1896); incorporated business as Fore River Ship & Engine Co. (1901).

**Watson, Thomas Edward.** 1856–1922. American lawyer and politician, b. Columbia County, Ga. Political leader of Agrarian malcontents in Georgia; elected member of U.S. House of Representatives on Farmers' Alliance ticket (1890); declared himself a Populist during term in Congress (1891–93). Introduced first resolution ever passed providing for free delivery of rural mail. Populist nominee for vice-president of the United States (1896) and for president (1904); U.S. senator (1921–22).

**Watson,** Sir **William.** 1715–1787. English physician and scientific experimenter. Influential in introducing Linnaean system of botanical classification into England; awarded Copley medal (1745) for electrical research; developed theory of electricity similar to Franklin's (1746, 1748).

**Watson,** Sir **William.** 1858–1935. English poet. First book, *The Prince's Quest* (1880); gained recognition with *Wordsworth's Grave* (1890) and fine ode on death of Tennyson, *Lacrymae Musarum* (1892); expressed political convictions with passion in sonnets in *The Purple East* (1896), *The Year of Shame* (1896). Author of several volumes of contemplative verse.

**Watt** (wŏt), **Charles.** English inventor; with his partner Hugh Burgess invented soda process for wood pulp for paper (1851–54); handled business in England after Burgess went to U.S. to build manufacturing plant (1854).

**Watt, James.** 1736–1819. Scottish mechanical engineer and inventor, b. Greenock. Mathematical-instrument maker, U. of Glasgow (1757). Improvements on steam engine suggested to him by model of the Newcomen engine given to him to repair; invented modern condensing steam engine (1765, patented 1769) in which the exhaust steam from cylinder is condensed in separate chamber (condenser); invented the double-acting engine (1782); effected other improvements on the steam engine, including sun-and-planet wheels and other means for converting reciprocal motion into rotary motion, and the centrifugal governor for regulating speed. His other inventions include an ink for copying manuscripts (patented 1780) and apparatus for reproducing sculpture. Formed a partnership with Matthew Boulton and manufactured steam engines at Soho Engineering Works, Birmingham (1775–1800). Originated (with Boulton) the term *horsepower*. The watt, a unit of power, is named in his honor. Cf. Salomon de CAUS. His son **James** (1769–1848), marine engineer, fitted with engines the *Caledonia*, first steamship to leave an English port (1817).

**Watt** (vät), **Joachim von.** See VADIANUS.

**Watt** (wŏt), **John Mitchell.** 1892– . South African pharmacologist, b. Port Elizabeth, of Scottish parentage; M.B., Edinburgh (1916); professor, Univ. of the Witwatersrand (1921– ); author of many technical articles, esp. on South African medicinal and poisonous plants.

**Watt,** Sir **Robert Alexander Watson.** 1892– . Scottish physicist; educ. Dundee Univ. Coll. and St. Andrews; on staff of Univ. Coll., Dundee (1912–19); meteorologist-in-charge, Royal Aircraft Establishment (1917–21); superintendent of radio research stations of Dept. of Scientific and Industrial Research (1921–33), of radio dept. of National Physical Laboratory (1933–36), of Bawdsey Research Station (1936–38); director of British communications development (1938–40); adviser on telecommunications to air and aircraft-production ministries (1940– ); did research on mechanical radio direction finders (1919 ff.); began (1935) research in airplane radiolocation, responsible for development of British and U.S. radar systems.

**Wat'teau'** (vȧ'tō'; *Angl.* wŏ·tō'), **Jean Antoine.** 1684–1721. French painter; known esp. for his scenes of conventional shepherds and shepherdesses, fêtes champêtres, country dances.

**Wat'ten·bach** (vät'ĕn·bäk), **Wilhelm.** 1819–1897. German historian and paleographer; professor, Berlin (1873), where he directed (1875–88) the *Monumenta Germaniae Historica*.

**Wat'ter·son** (wŏt'ẽr·s'n), **Henry.** 1840–1921. American journalist and politician, b. Washington, D.C. Known as "Marse Henry." Served with Confederate army through Civil War. Editor, Louisville (Ky.) *Courier-Journal* (1868–1918); rose to eminence as one of the great editors of the United States. Fought for restoration of home rule in southern states; supported Samuel J. Tilden for presidency; opposed Cleveland (in 1892) and Bryan (in 1896); bitterly attacked Theodore Roosevelt; supported Wilson but opposed entrance into League of Nations; vigorously advocated Allied cause in World War. Member, U.S. House of Representatives (1876–77). Awarded Pulitzer prize for journalism (1917) for his editorials welcoming U.S. declaration of war against Central Powers. Author of *The Compromises of Life* (1903), *"Marse Henry": An Autobiography* (2 vols., 1919), etc.

**Wat'tles** (wŏt''lz), **Willard Austin.** 1888–1950. American poet, b. Bayneville, Kans.; author of *Lanterns in Gethsemane* (1918), *A Compass for Sailors* (1928), etc.

**Watts** (wŏts), **Alaric Alexander.** 1797–1864. English journalist and poet; initiated *Men of the Time* (1856), a biographical dictionary of contemporaries, incorporated with *Who's Who* (1901); author of *Lyrics of the Heart* (1850).

**Watts, George Frederic.** 1817–1904. English painter and sculptor. Exhibited *A Wounded Heron* and two portraits (1837); won prize (1842) for cartoon *Caractacus;* painted portraits in Rome (1843–47); won British competition in oils (1847) with *King Alfred;* commissioned to fresco *George and the Dragon* in Hall of Poets of the Houses of Parliament (1848–53). Painted series of about 300 portraits of distinguished contemporaries (1864–95), including Garibaldi, Thiers, Guizot; painted symbolical pictures and moral allegories including *Life's Illusions* (1849), *Watchman, What of the Night* (1880), *Love and Death* (1877, 1896), *Sic Transit* (1892); as sculptor executed monuments including bronze equestrian statues of Hugo Lupus (1884) and *Physical Energy*, the latter as part of monument to Cecil Rhodes at Matopo Hills, Southern Rhodesia (1902).

**Watts, Henry.** 1815–1884. English chemist and editor of chemical reference books.

**Watts, Hugh.** 1582?–1643. English bell founder in Leicester.

**Watts, Isaac.** 1674–1748. English theologian and hymn writer. Composed 600 hymns including "O God, our help in ages past," "When I survey the wondrous cross," "There is a land of pure delight." Author also of sacred poems, metrical psalms, and theological works showing Arian tendencies.

**Watts, Mary,** *nee* **Stan′ber′y** (stăn′bĕr′ĭ; -bĕr·ĭ). 1868–1958. American novelist; m. Miles Taylor Watts (1891); author of *The Tenants* (1908), *Nathan Burke* (1910), *Van Cleve* (1913), *The House of Rimman* (1922), *Luther Nichols* (1923), etc.

**Watts,** Sir **Philip.** 1846–1926. British naval architect; designed British warships used in World War, including the *Dreadnought* battleship class and *Indomitable* battle cruiser class.

**Watts′-Dun′ton** (wŏts′dŭn′t'n; -tŭn), **Walter Theodore.** 1832–1914. English critic and poet. Added to his surname mother's name Dunton (1897). Contributed to *Examiner* and *Athenæum* (from 1874); intimate friend of Rossetti; took A. C. Swinburne into his house, fostered his genius (1879–1909); from early life studied East Anglian and Welsh gypsies. Author of *The Coming of Love* (a narrative poem, 1897), *Aylwin* (novel, 1898), *The Renascence of Wonder* (critical interpretation of the romantic movement), sonnets, and essays.

**Wau′chope** (wô′kŭp), Sir **Arthur Grenfell.** 1874–1947. British general; high commissioner and commander in chief, Palestine and Trans-Jordan (1931–38).

**Waugh** (wô), **Arthur.** 1866–1943. English literary critic and editor; managing director (1902–30) and chairman (1926–36) of publishing house of Chapman & Hall, Ltd. Edited Johnson's *Lives of the Poets* (1896), Dickens (1902–03); biographer of Tennyson and Browning; author of *Reticence in Literature* (1915), *One Man's Road* (1931). His elder son, **Alec,** *in full* **Alexander Ra′ban** [rā′băn] (1898– ), traveler, publisher's literary adviser, and author; works include *The Loom of Youth,* novel of schoolboy life (1917), many other novels, short stories. His younger son, **Evelyn Arthur St. John** (1903–1966), author of *Rossetti: A Critical Biography* (1928), novels including *Decline and Fall* (1929) and *Vile Bodies* (1930), *Waugh in Abyssinia* (1936), *Put Out More Flags* (1942).

**Waugh, Benjamin.** 1839–1908. English philanthropist; Congregational minister (1865–87); cofounder, with Hesba Stretton, of London Society for Prevention of Cruelty to Children (1884).

**Waugh, Beverly.** 1789–1858. American Methodist Episcopal bishop (1836); senior bishop (1852).

**Waugh, Edwin.** 1817–1890. English poet; called "The Lancashire Burns"; author of prose sketches including the humorous *Besom Ben Stories,* and of *Poems and Songs* (1859) in Lancashire dialect.

**Waugh, Frank Albert.** 1869–1943. American landscape architect; b. Sheboygan Falls, Wis.; B.S., Kansas State (1891); graduate study at Cornell U. and in Germany and France; professor, Mass. State (from 1902); author of treatises on landscape gardening and architecture, fruit culture, etc.

**Waugh, Frederick Judd.** 1861–1940. American painter, b. Bordentown, N.J.; studio at Provincetown, Mass.; best known for his marines.

**Wau′ters** (wou′tĕrs), **Émile Charles Marie.** 1846–1933. Belgian portrait and historical painter; among his paintings are *The Battle of Hastings* (1868) and *Madness of Hugo van der Goes* (1872).

**Wa′vell** (wā′vĕl), **Archibald Percival.** 1st Earl. 1883–1950. British army officer; educ. Winchester and Royal Military College at Sandhurst, and the army staff college; served in South African War, on Indian frontier (1908), in World War (1914–18), with Egyptian Expeditionary Force (1917–20); major general (1933); lieutenant general (1938); commander in chief of British forces in the Middle East (1939–41); general (1940); commander in chief in India (1941); supreme commander of allied forces in southwest Pacific (1942), of allied forces in India and Burma (1942); field marshal (1942); viceroy of India (1943–47). Author of *The Palestine Campaigns* (1928), *Allenby* (1940), *Generals and Generalship* (1941), *Allenby in Egypt* (1943).

**Way′land** (wā′lănd), **Francis.** 1796–1865. American clergyman and educator; president, Brown U. (1827–55); effected during administration the liberalization of curriculum and enlargement of university equipment, faculty, and student body. His son **Francis** (1826–1904) was dean, Yale Law School (1873–1903); reorganized and raised standards of Yale Law School during his administration; author of legal treatises.

**Wayne** (wān), **Anthony.** 1745–1796. American Revolutionary officer, b. Waynesboro, Pa. Known as "Mad Anthony." A tanner by trade; commissioned colonel of Pennsylvania regiment in Continental army (Jan., 1776); covered retreat of American force from Canada to Fort Ticonderoga (1776). Brigadier general (Feb., 1777); joined Washington at Morristown; commanded center in battle of Brandywine (Sept. 11, 1777), distinguished himself at Germantown (Oct. 4, 1777), and led advance in battle of Monmouth (June 28, 1778). Led brilliant attack which surprised and captured British garrison at Stony Point on the Hudson (July 16, 1779). On news of Arnold's attempted treason, moved troops to reinforce West Point (Sept., 1780). Engaged in Yorktown campaign (1781); retired (1783) as brevet major general. Member, U.S. House of Representatives, from Georgia (1791–92). Appointed major general (1791) by Washington to lead Americans against the hostile Indians; decisively defeated Indians at battle of Fallen Timbers near present Toledo, Ohio (Aug. 20, 1794), and thereafter negotiated satisfactory treaty with them (1795).

**Wayne, James Moore.** 1790?–1867. American jurist, b. Savannah, Ga.; member, U.S. House of Representatives (1829–35); supported Jackson policies; associate justice, U.S. Supreme Court (1835–67).

**Wayn′flete** *or* **Wain′fleet** (wān′flēt), **William of.** *Orig. surname* **Pat′yn** (păt′ĭn). 1395?–1486. English prelate; a favorite of Henry VI. Bishop of Winchester (1447–86); lord chancellor (1456–60); founded Magdalen College, Oxford (1458); released Henry VI from Tower of London (1470); co-operated with Edward IV in restoring Eton College; founded a free school at Waynfleet (1484).

**Weale** (wēl), **Putnam.** *Pseudonym of* **Bertram Lenox Simpson.** 1877–1930. English publicist; educ. in Switzerland, Germany, France, Italy, and China. Joined Chinese customs service (1896–1901). With Peking legations during Boxer siege (1900) and served with British Expeditionary Force as interpreter. Author of *Manchu and Muscovite* (1904), *Indiscreet Letters from Peking* (1907), *The Conflict of Colour* (1910), *The Revolt* (1912), *The Truth about China and Japan* (1919), *China's Crucifixion* (1928), etc.

**Weare** (wâr), **Meshech.** 1713–1786. American jurist and political leader, b. Hampton Falls, N.H.; justice of superior court (1747–75); chief justice (1776–82); first president, State of New Hampshire (1784–85), under constitution of 1784.

**Weath′er·ford** (wĕth′ẽr·fẽrd), **William.** *Known also as* **Red′ Ea′gle.** 1780?–1824. American Creek Indian chief, b. near Montgomery, Ala.; led force in attack on Fort Mims (Aug. 30, 1813), massacring about 500 men, women, and children; defeated by Andrew Jackson in battle of Horseshoe Bend (Jan. 27, 1814), and surrendered to Jackson; lived at peace thereafter in Monroe County, Ala.

**Weath′er·ly** (wĕth′ẽr·lĭ), **Frederic Edward.** 1848–1929. English lawyer, and writer of popular songs, including *Nancy Lee*, *Darby and Joan*, *London Bridge*, *Danny Boy*, *Roses of Picardy*.

**Wea′ver** (wē′vẽr), **James Baird.** 1833–1912. American lawyer and politician, b. Dayton, Ohio; began practice at Bloomfield, Iowa. Served through Civil War; brevet brigadier general (Mar., 1864). Member, U.S. House of Representatives, from Iowa, elected as a Greenbacker (1879–81) and as a Democrat and Greenback-Labor candidate (1885–89). Candidate of Greenback-Labor for president of the U.S. (1880), and of the People's party (1892), in the latter year winning 22 electoral votes and a popular vote of more than 1,000,000.

**Weaver, John Van Alstyn.** 1893–1938. American writer, b. Charlotte, N.C.; literary editor of Brooklyn *Daily Eagle* (1920–24); m. (1924) actress Peggy Wood; scenario writer for Paramount-Famous-Lasky Corp. (1928–31). Author of verse, *Finders* (1923), *To Youth* (1927), *Trial Balance* (1931); a play, *Love 'Em and Leave 'Em* (with Gerorge Abbott; 1926); novels, *Margie Wins the Game* (1922), *Her Knight Comes Riding* (1928).

**Weaver, Robert Clifton.** 1907– . American economist; U.S. secy of housing & urban development (1966–69).

**Weaver, Walter Reed.** 1885–1944. American army officer, b. Charleston, S.C.; grad. U.S.M.A., West Point (1908); in air service (from 1917); major general (1941); commanding general, U.S.A.A.F. Tech. Training Command, Knollwood Field, N.C. (Mar., 1942–July, 1943).

**Webb** (wĕb), **Alexander Stewart.** See under James Watson WEBB.

**Webb,** Sir **Aston.** 1849–1930. English architect; designed principal block of Victoria and Albert Museum (1891), Royal College of Science (1900–06), Admiralty Arch (1911), eastern façade of Buckingham Palace (1913), etc.

**Webb, Beatrice Potter.** See under Sidney James WEBB.

**Webb, Charles Henry.** *Pseudonym* **John Paul** (pôl). 1834–1905. American journalist, b. Rouse's Point, N.Y. Sailor on a whaler (1851–55). Founder and first editor, the *Californian* (1864–66) in which, in addition to his own contributions, appeared work by Bret Harte and Mark Twain. In New York (1866) and published Mark Twain's first book, *The Celebrated Jumping Frog of Calaveras County* (1867). Contributed "John Paul" letters to New York *Tribune* (1873), collected and published as *John Paul's Book* (1874). Also wrote *Sea-Weed and What We Seed* (1876), *Parodies: Prose and Verse* (1876), *Vagrom Verses* (1889), *With Lead and Line* (1901).

**Webb, Edwin Yates.** 1872–1955. American lawyer, legislator, and judge, b. Shelby, N.C. Member of U.S. House of Representatives (1903–19); cosponsor of Webb-Kenyon Act (1913) prohibiting shipment of intoxicating liquors in interstate commerce, and Webb-Pomerene Act (1918) permitting industrial combinations to be formed for export trade.

**Webb, George James.** 1803–1887. Musician and composer, b. near Salisbury, Eng.; to U.S. (1830); organist of Old South Church, Boston (1830); often collaborated with Lowell Mason in developing musical enterprises and appreciation of music in Boston. Widely known as composer of the music to which the hymn *Stand up, stand up for Jesus* is commonly sung.

**Webb, James Watson.** 1802–1884. American journalist and diplomat; proprietor and editor, *Morning Courier and New York Enquirer*, New York City (1829–61); U.S. minister to Brazil (1861–69). His son **Alexander Stewart** (1835–1911) was a Civil War general; grad. U.S.M.A., West Point (1855); at Gettysburg his brigade held the Bloody Angle and was chiefly responsible for repulse of Pickett's charge; chief of staff to General Meade (1865); awarded Medal of Honor; president of C.C.N.Y. (1869–1902). Another son, half brother of Alexander Stewart, **William Seward** (1851–1926), m. Eliza Osgood Vanderbilt, daughter of William H. Vanderbilt (1883); builder and president, Mohawk & Malone Railroad; director, Lake Shore and Michigan Southern Railroad.

**Webb** *or* **Webbe** (wĕb), **John.** 1611–1672. English architect; pupil and executor of Inigo Jones and editor of his tract on Stonehenge.

**Webb, Mary.** *Nee* **Mary Gladys Mer′e·dith** (mĕr′ĕ·dĭth). 1881–1927. English novelist; m. Henry Bertram Law Webb, a schoolmaster (1912); author of five novels, including *The Golden Arrow* (1916) and *Precious Bane* (1924), of a collection of essays, and of poems and short stories.

**Webb, Matthew.** 1848–1883. English swimmer. Known as "Captain Webb." Followed sea (from 1862); master mariner (1875); professional swimmer (from 1875); swam English Channel, from Dover to Calais (Aug. 24, 1875) in 21¾ hours; drowned in attempt to swim rapids below Niagara Falls.

**Webb, Sidney James.** 1st Baron **Pass′field** (păs′fēld). 1859–1947. English economist, socialist, and statesman, b. London. Civil-service clerk in war office (1878), colonial office (1881–91). One of founders of Fabian Society; author of *Socialism in England* (1890); taught economics, U. of London (1912–27). Member, London County Council (1892–1910); member, royal commission on trade-union law (1903–06); comember of royal poor-law commission (1905–09) with his wife, **Beatrice,** *nee* **Pot′ter** [pŏt′ẽr] (1858–1943; m. 1892), writer on economics and sociology, author of *The Co-operative Movement in Great Britain* (1891), *Factory Acts* (1901), and *My Apprenticeship* (1926). Jointly with his wife, submitted minority report in favor of the Poor Law (1909), set up Socialist salon, provided intellectual leadership to British Labor party, helped found *New Statesman* (1913), promoted London School of Economics and Political Science; proposed nationalization of coal mines (1919); M.P. (1922–29); president of board of trade in first Labor cabinet (1924); secretary for colonies (1929–31), and dominions (1929–30); created Baron Passfield (1929). Joint author with Beatrice Webb of *History of Trade Unionism* (1894), *Industrial Democracy* (1897), *The State and the Doctor* (1910), *Consumers' Co-operative Movement* (1921), *Decay of Capitalist Civilisation* (1921), *English Poor Law History* (3 vols., 1927, 1929), *Soviet Communism: a New Civilisation?* (1935), *The Truth about Soviet Russia* (1942).

**Webb, William Seward.** See under James Watson WEBB.

**Webbe** (wĕb). See also WEBB.

**Web′ber** (wĕb′ẽr), **Herbert John.** 1865–1946. American plant physiologist; authority on breeding of economic plants, as oranges, cotton, corn, and pineapples.

**We′ber** (vā′bẽr), **Albrecht.** 1825–1901. German Indologist; professor, Berlin (1856–1901); edited and contributed largely to *Indische Studien* (18 vols., 1849–98).

**Weber, Ernst Heinrich.** See under Wilhelm Eduard WEBER.

**Weber, Friedrich Wilhelm.** 1813–1894. German physician and poet; author of *Dreizehnlinden* (an epic, 1878).

**Weber, Georg.** 1808–1888. German historian; author of *Allgemeine Weltgeschichte* (15 vols., 1857–80), and of works on Calvinism in Germany, the Reformation, and the origin of Christianity.

**Web'er** (wĕb'ĕr), **Joseph M.** (1867–1942) and **Fields** (fēldz), **Lew**, *in full* **Lewis Maurice** (1867–1941). American comedy team, both b. New York City. Appeared together first in juvenile Dutch skits (1877). Organized theatrical company, Weber and Fields (1885), managers of theatrical enterprises, including Broadway Music Hall (1895–1904). Lew Fields opened Lew Fields' Theater, New York City (1904) and acquired Herald Square Theater (1906). Joseph M. Weber was proprietor and manager of Weber's Theater (from 1904). Weber and Fields again teamed up for a tour (1914).

**We'ber** (vā'bĕr), **Karl Julius.** 1767–1832. German writer; author of critical works and satirical and humorous writings.

**Weber,** Baron **Karl Maria Friedrich Ernst von.** 1786–1826. German composer, opera conductor, and pianist; called the creator of German romantic opera. Son of Baron **Franz Anton von Weber** (1734–1812), army officer, violinist, theater manager, and adventurer, cousin of Mozart's wife, Constanze. Opera conductor, Breslau (1804–06); music director to Prince Eugen von Württemberg in Silesia (1806); conductor, Prague theater (1813–17); directed and helped rebuild German opera in Dresden (1817); director, London (1826), where he died. Composed operas *Die Macht der Liebe und des Weins* (1799; destroyed), *Das Waldmädchen* (1800; incorporated in *Silvana*, 1810), *Peter Schmoll* (1803), *Rübezahl* (begun 1804, unfinished), *Abu Hassan* (1811), *Der Freischütz* (1821; orig. *Des Jägers Braut*), *Euryanthe* (1823), and *Oberon* (1826); music to *Preciosa* (1821); instrumental works, including *Invitation to the Dance;* and chorals, cantatas, masses, mixed quartets, and songs.

**Weber, Max.** 1864–1920. Sociologist, b. Erfurt, Ger. Influential student of social organization, bureaucracy, etc. Major works include *The Protestant Ethic and the Spirit of Capitalism, Theory of Social and Economic Organization, Methodology of the Social Sciences.*

**Web'er** (wĕb'ĕr), **Max.** 1881–1961. American painter, b. Byelostok, Russia; to U.S. (1891); teacher of painting; lecturer on history of art; author of *Cubist Poems* (1914), *Essays on Art* (1916), *Primitives* (1927).

**We'ber** (vā'bĕr), **Theodor.** 1836–1906. German Old Catholic theologian; vicar-general of the Old Catholics, Bonn (1890) and bishop (from 1896).

**Weber, Wilhelm Eduard.** 1804–1891. German physicist; with Gauss, investigated terrestrial magnetism, and devised an electromagnetic telegraph (1833); introduced the absolute system of electrical units patterned after Gauss's system of magnetic units. The weber, formerly the coulomb but now a magnetic unit, is named in his honor. His brother **Ernst Heinrich** (1795–1878), physiologist and anatomist, was known for research on the sense organs, esp. the ear and the cutaneous organs of sensation; formulated the law (Weber's law) that the least noticeable increase of a stimulus is a constant proportional of the original stimulus.

**We'bern** (vā'bĕrn), **Anton von.** 1883–1945. Viennese composer of a passacaglia for orchestra, chamber music, and *Geistliche Lieder* for soprano with various solo instruments.

**Web'ster** (wĕb'stĕr), **Augusta,** *nee* **Davies.** 1837–1894. English poet. Daughter of Vice-admiral George Davies; m. Thomas Webster, solicitor. Author of *Dramatic Studies* (1866), *Portraits* (1870), the novel *Lesley's Guardians* (1864), and several dramas.

**Webster, Daniel.** 1782–1852. American lawyer and statesman, b. Salisbury, N.H. Grad. Dartmouth (1801). Adm. to bar in Boston (1805) and practiced at Portsmouth, N.H. (from 1807). Member, U.S. House of Representatives from New Hampshire (1813–17), from Massachusetts (1823–27); resident of Boston (from 1816), practiced law; achieved national recognition as lawyer for Dartmouth College trustees in famous Dartmouth College case (1818). Member, U.S. Senate (1827–41). Gained fame as orator for his constitutional speeches in reply to Hayne (1830) and in opposition to Calhoun (1833); opposed President Jackson on U.S. Bank issue. U.S. secretary of state (1841–43); negotiated Webster-Ashburton treaty with Great Britain (1842). Again U.S. senator from Massachusetts (1845–50); opposed Mexican War and annexation of Texas; supported compromise measures on slavery proposed by Clay (1850). Again U.S. secretary of state (1850–52). Unsuccessful candidate for Whig nomination for the presidency (1852). Elected to American Hall of Fame (1900).

**Webster, Henry Kitchell.** 1875–1932. American novelist.

**Webster, Herman Armour.** 1878– . American painter and etcher.

**Webster, Jean,** *in full* **Alice Jane Chandler.** 1876–1916. American writer, b. Fredonia, N.Y.; m. Glenn Ford McKinney (1915); A.B., Vassar (1901); author of series of stories about a fictional character, Patty, including *When Patty Went to College* (1903) and *Just Patty* (1911), and the very successful novel *Daddy-Long-Legs* (1912) and its sequel *Dear Enemy* (1914).

**Webster, John.** 1580?–?1625. English dramatist, son of London tailor. Collaborated (from 1602) with members of Philip Henslowe's company of dramatists; part author with Dekker of *Westward Hoe* and *Northward Hoe* (c. 1604); altered, and wrote introduction to, Marston's *Malcontent* (1604); perhaps collaborated with Heywood on *Appius and Virginia* (c. 1609); approached tragic power and poetic genius of Shakespeare in two plays incontestably his, *The White Devil or Vittoria Corombona* (produced c. 1610) and *The Duchess of Malfi* (c. 1614); brought out involved tragicomedy *Devil's Law Case* (1619 or 1620).

**Webster, Margaret.** 1905–1972. British actress and director, b. New York City; played with John Barrymore in *Hamlet* in her London debut and with Sybil Thorndike in *The Trojan Woman;* directed Shakespearean presentations of Maurice Evans in New York (1937–39); also staged, directed, and acted in, *Family Portrait* (1939); in Hollywood (1940). Author of *Shakespeare without Tears* (rev. 1955), *Same Only Different* (1969), *Don't Put your Daughter on the Stage* (1972).

**Webster, Noah.** 1758–1843. American lexicographer and author, b. West Hartford, Conn. Educ. Yale (grad. 1778); served in Revolutionary War (Burgoyne campaign, 1777); taught school in various places (1779–83); admitted to bar in Hartford (1781). While teaching in Goshen, N.Y., wrote (1782–83) part I of *Grammatical Institute of the English Language*, a spelling book, later known as *Webster's Spelling Book* or *Blue-Backed Speller*, which for more than 100 years had enormous sale; completed parts II (grammar; 1784) and III (reader; 1785) of the *Institute;* agitated (esp. 1782–89) for uniform copyright law. Became ardent Federalist; his *Sketches of American Policy* (1785) one of first publications advocating strong central government; gave lectures (1785–86) in leading cities on English language, resulting in publication (1789) of *Dissertations on the English Language;* these interests led to acquaintance and correspondence with Benjamin Franklin. In journalistic work in New York, editing *The American Magazine* (1787–88); m. (1789) Rebecca Greenleaf (1766–1847) of Boston; practiced law in Hartford (1788–93); published (1793–98) in New York *The Minerva* (later *The Commercial Advertiser*) and *The Herald* (later *The Spectator*), Federalist papers. To New Haven (1798); devoted himself to writing, esp. *A Brief History of Epidemic and Pestilential Diseases* (2 vols., 1799), for many years the standard work on the subject. Published his first dictionary, *A Compendious Dictionary of the English Language* (1806); began (1807) work on larger dictionary. Moved to Amherst (1812); represented Hampshire County in Massachusetts legislature (1815, 1819); trustee of Amherst Acad. (1816–21), and its president (1820–21); a founder (1819–21) of Amherst Coll. Returned to New Haven (1822); visited England and France (1824–25) for study necessary to complete his dictionary; published *An American Dictionary of the English Language* (2 vols., 1828). Compiled brief *History of the United States* (1832), widely used as a schoolbook; published (1833) a revision of Authorized Version of English Bible; with his son **William Greenleaf** (1805–1869) published second edition (2 vols., 1840) of *American Dictionary;* died at New Haven (May 28, 1843). Rights to his dictionary sold by his heirs (1843) to firm of G. & C. Merriam of Springfield, Mass. (see MERRIAM).

☞ Do not confuse Noah Webster with Daniel Webster.

**Webster, Pelatiah.** 1726–1795. American publicist, b. Lebanon, Conn. In Congregational ministry (1749–55); merchant in Philadelphia (from 1755). Published *A Dissertation on the Political Union and Constitution of the Thirteen United States of North America* (1783), regarded by some as original suggestion of plan of government later embodied in the Constitution of the United States (1787). Also contributed to the Philadelphia press articles on money, credit, taxation, and commerce.

**Webster, Richard Everard.** Viscount **Al'ver·stone** (ôl'vẽr·stŭn). 1842–1915. English judge; attorney general (1885–92, 1895–1900), appearing in Bering Sea and Venezuela arbitrations; lord chief justice (1900); arbitrator on Alaska-Canada boundary (1903).

**Wec'ker'lin'** (vā'kĕr'lăN'), **Jean Baptiste Théodore.** 1821–1910. French composer of a heroic symphony (*Roland*), an oratorio (*Le Jugement Dernier*), cantatas, and other choral and orchestral works; compiler of collections of songs.

**Weck'her·lin** (vĕk'ẽr·lēn), **Georg Rudolph.** 1584–1653. German lyric poet; in London (from 1620); secretary for foreign tongues to Parliament (1644–49); assistant to John Milton (1652). Helped to introduce into German literature Renaissance verse forms and feeling, as in the ode and sonnet.

**Weck'mann** (vĕk'män), **Matthias.** 1621–1674. German organist, clavierist, and composer of sacred concertos, clavier and organ works, and cantatas.

**Wed'dell** (wĕd''l), **James.** 1787–1834. English navigator; reached 74° 15' S. latitude (1822–24) in sealing ships; gave name to Weddell Sea.

**Wed'der·burn** (wĕd'ẽr·bûrn), **Alexander.** 1st Baron **Lough'bor·ough** (lŭf'bŭ·rŭ; -brŭ). 1st Earl of **Ross'lyn** (rŏs'lĭn). 1733–1805. English judge, b. in Scotland, son of a Scottish judge; member of Scottish bar (1754–57), of English bar (from 1757); chief justice of common pleas (1780–93); lord chancellor (1793–1801).

**Wedderburn, James** (1495?–1553) and his brothers **John** (1500?–1556) and **Robert** (1510?–?1557). Scottish poets, authors, esp. of anti-Romanist ballads.

**Wed'di·gen** (vĕd'ĭ·gĕn), **Otto.** 1882–1915. German U-boat commander in World War; sank British cruisers *Aboukir*, *Hogue*, and *Cressy* (Sept. 22, 1914), and the *Hawke* (Oct. 14, 1914); lost in action (Mar., 1915).

**Wed'dle** (wĕd''l), **Thomas.** 1817–1853. English mathematician.

**We'de·kind** (vā'dĕ·kĭnt), **Frank** (frängk). 1864–1918. German poet and playwright; author esp. of satirical and symbolical plays, including *The Awakening of Spring* (1891), *The Earth Spirit* (1895) and its sequel *Pandora's Box* (printed 1904), *The Love Potion* (1900), *The Marquis of Keith* (1901), *Such is Life* (1902), *Hidallah* (1904), *The Dance of Death* (1906), *Censorship* (1909), *The Philosopher's Stone* (1909), *Simson* (1914), and *Herakles* (1917).

**Wedg'wood** (wĕj'wo͝od), **Josiah.** 1730–1795. English potter; patented (1763) and perfected (1769) a glazed cream-colored domestic earthenware, queen's ware; improved vitreous black ware in form known as "basalt"; named new factory "Etruria" (1769; hence *Etruria ware* or *Wedgwood ware*). Improved marbled ware and invented jasper ware (1773–80); assisted by John Flaxman, who modeled delicate designs after remains of Pompeii and Greek vases from Campania. His eldest daughter was mother of Charles Darwin. His son **Thomas** (1771–1805), physicist and philanthropist, sensitized paper with moist silver nitrate and succeeded in retaining an image projected on its surface (hence called first photographer), but could find no way of fixing the image. Josiah's grandson **Hensleigh Wedgwood** (1803–1891), mathematician and philologist, compiled a *Dictionary of English Etymology* (1857), in which he challenged Max Müller's theory of language as originating in a series of irresoluble roots, by his own theory that it originates in imitation of natural sounds.

**Josiah Clement Wedgwood** (1872–1943), naval architect; great-great-grandson of Josiah (1730–1795); at Elswick shipyards (1896–1900); served with distinction in Boer War and World War and on Mesopotamia commission and Siberian mission; vice-chairman of Labor party (1921–24); chancellor of duchy of Lancaster in first Labor cabinet (1924); author of a history of Staffordshire pottery, a work on local taxation, and a history of parliament from 1439 to 1509. Created Baron Wedgwood of Bar'las·ton [?bär'lăs·tŭn] (1941).

**Weed** (wēd), **Thurlow.** 1797–1882. American journalist and politician, b. Greene Co., N.Y. Editor, Albany (N.Y.) *Evening Journal* (1830–62); became leader of Whig, and later of Republican, party; instrumental in nomination of Harrison (1836, 1840), Clay (1844), Taylor (1848), Scott (1852); associate of Seward and Greeley in political domination of New York State. Vigorously supported Lincoln and his war policies; sent by Lincoln abroad on unofficial mission (1861–62). To New York City (1863); editor, New York *Commercial Advertiser* (1867).

**Week'ley** (wēk'lĭ), **Ernest.** 1865–1954. English philologist; author of *The Romance of Words* (1912), *Something About Words* (1935); compiler of *An Etymological Dictionary of Modern English* (1921).

**Weeks** (wēks), **Edwin Lord.** 1849–1903. American painter, b. Boston, Mass.; best known for his paintings of Oriental scenes and subjects.

**Weeks, John Wingate.** 1860–1926. American broker and politician; partner in brokerage firm, Hornblower & Weeks, Boston; member, U.S. House of Representatives (1905–13) and U.S. Senate (1913–19); U.S. secretary of war (1921–25).

**Weelkes** (wēlks), **Thomas.** 1575?–1623. English madrigal composer; organist, Chichester Cathedral (1602–23).

**Weems** (wēmz), **Mason Locke.** 1759–1825. American clergyman and author, b. Anne Arundel Co., Md. Ordained deacon and priest in Anglican Church (1784); pastor in Maryland (1784–92); hence often called "Parson Weems." Itinerant bookseller (1794–1825) for Mathew Carey, publisher. Author of *The Life and*

*Memorable Actions of George Washington* (first pub. c. 1800; enlarged in later editions), which is responsible for popular stories about Washington, including that of the famous hatchet and cherry tree (first inserted in edition of 1806). Author of biographies *Francis Marion* (1809), *Benjamin Franklin* (1815), and *William Penn* (1822), and the moral tracts *The Drunkard's Looking Glass, God's Revenge Against Adultery, Bad Wife's Looking Glass*, etc.

**Wee'nix** (vā'nĭks), **Jan Baptist.** 1621–1660. Dutch painter. His son and pupil **Jan** (1640?–1719) was court painter in Düsseldorf (1702–12), later in Amsterdam. Father and son known chiefly as painters of landscapes, still life, dead game, and hunting scenes.

**Weert, Jean de.** See Johann von WERTH.

**Weerts** (vārts), **Jean Joseph.** 1847–1927. French painter of murals, portraits, and historical and religious canvases.

**We·ge'li·us** (vå·gā'lĭ·ōōs), **Martin.** 1846–1906. Finnish music director and composer; teacher of Sibelius, Melartin, Järnefelt, and Palmgren; composed orchestral works, cantatas, chamber music, and songs.

**We'ge·ner** (vā'gĕ·nĕr), **Alfred Lothar.** 1880–1930. German geophysicist and meteorologist. On expeditions to Greenland (1906–08, 1912–17, 1929, 1930). Worked on the thermodynamics of the atmosphere; originated hypothesis (Wegener hypothesis) of continental drift according to which the continents have drifted slowly apart from an original single land area.

**Wei** (wā). Name of several dynasties of China, esp.: (1) One ruling (220–264 A.D.) in the state of Wei, that one of the three kingdoms north of the Yangtze. Its first ruler was Ts'ao P'ei (see TS'AO TS'AO), with capital at Loyang, and it followed the Later Han dynasty. It absorbed Shu and in turn came (264) under the control of the Western Chin dynasty. (2) The **Northern Wei,** a dynasty (386–534 A.D.) in northern China of the Toba Tatars, with capital at Loyang (495–534), which divided (534) into two short-lived dynasties: the **Eastern Wei** (534–550) and the **Western Wei** (535–556).

**Weibling.** See WAIBLINGEN.

**Wei'den·reich** (vī'dĕn·rīĸ), **Franz.** 1873–1948. German anatomist and anthropologist; professor, Strassburg (1903–18), Heidelberg (1922–24), Institute for Physical Anthropology, Frankfurt (1928), Peiping Union Medical College; best known for his studies of fossil man, esp. Peking man.

**Weid'lein** (wīd'līn), **Edward Ray.** 1887– . American chemical engineer, b. Augusta, Kans.; M.A., Kansas (1910); on staff (1912 ff.), director (1921 ff.), Mellon Institute of Industrial Research, Pittsburgh; head of chemicals branch, Office of Production Management (1940 ff.).

**Weid'man** (wīd'măn), **Charles Edward.** 1901–1975. American dancer; with Denishawn group (1921–27); formed dance group with Doris Humphrey (*q.v.*).

**Wei'er·strass'** (vī'ĕr·shträs'), **Karl Theodor.** 1815–1897. German mathematician; developed modern theory of analytical functions in *Abhandlungen aus der Funktionenlehre* (1886).

**Wei'gall** (wī'gôl), **Arthur Edward Pearse Brome** (brōōm). 1880–1934. English Egyptologist and author; in Egypt (from 1901); excavated tombs at Thebes and elsewhere.

**Wei'gand** (vī'gänt), **Gustav.** 1860–1930. German philologist; author of Rumanian and Bulgarian grammars; compiler of Bulgarian and Albanian dictionaries.

**Wei'gl** (vī'g'l), **Josef.** 1766–1846. Austrian composer of German and Italian operas, and of ballets, oratorios, cantatas, masses, etc.

**Weil** (vīl), **Adolf.** 1848–1916. German physician after whom an acute infectious disease (Weil's disease) is named.

**Weil, Gustav.** 1808–1889. German Orientalist and historian; author of a translation of the *Arabian Nights* (1837–41), and of histories of the caliphs (5 vols., 1846–62) and the Islamic peoples (1866).

**Weil** (vīl), **Henri.** 1818–1909. Hellenist, of German birth; naturalized Frenchman (1848); author of *Études sur le Drame Antique* (1897), and editor of many Greek classics.

**Wei'len** (vī'lĕn), **Josef von.** *Orig. surname* **Weil** (vīl). 1828–1889. Poet and dramatist, b. in Bohemia of Jewish origin; author of lyric poems, as *Phantasien und Lieder* (1853), dramas, as *Tristan* (1860) and *Graf Horn* (1871), and several novels.

**Weill** (vil), **Kurt.** 1900–1950. Composer, esp. of operas, ballets, musical comedies; b. Dessau, Germany; to U.S. (1935). Best known musical comedies include *Knickerbocker Holiday, Lady in the Dark, One Touch of Venus, Street Scene, Lost in the Stars.*

**Weill, René.** See Romain COOLUS.

**Wein'gar'ten** (vīn'gär'tĕn), **Julius.** 1836–1910. German mathematician.

**Wein'gart'ner** (vīn'gärt'nĕr), **Felix von.** 1863–1942. Composer, conductor, and writer on music, b. in Dalmatia; naturalized Swiss (1931). Conductor of symphony concerts, Berlin and Munich (until 1908); director, Vienna Court Opera (1908–10), Vienna Volksoper (1919–24), conservatory and music society, Basel (1927). Composer of operas, as *Sakuntala* (1884), *Genesius* (1892), *Kain und Abel* (1914), *Dame Kobold* (1916), and *Meister Andrea* (1920), orchestral works, including symphonies and symphonic poems, and chamber music, incidental stage music, songs, piano pieces, choruses.

**Wein'he'ber** (vīn'hā'bĕr), **Josef.** 1892–1945. Aust. poet.

**Wein'hold** (vīn'hôlt), **Karl.** 1823–1901. German scholar and philologist; author of *Über Deutsche Dialektforschung* (1853), grammars of German and Middle High German, works on literary history; compiler of a collection of Christmas plays and songs of southern Germany and Silesia (1853).

**Wein'man** (wīn'măn), **Adolph Alexander.** 1870–1952. Sculptor, b. Karlsruhe, Ger.; to U.S. in youth. Works include Lincoln Memorial at Madison, Wis., monument to Mayor William Jay Gaynor in Brooklyn, N.Y., sculpture for façade of Post Office Department building in Washington, D.C., bust of Horace Mann in American Hall of Fame. Designed the dime and half dollar for 1916 issue.

**Weir** (wēr), **Harrison William.** 1824–1906. English painter and illustrator; wood engraver on *Illustrated London News* (from 1842); illustrator of natural history texts.

**Weir, Robert Stanley.** 1856–1926. Canadian lawyer and writer; practiced law in Montreal; author of various legal treatises, and the words of the Canadian national song, *O Canada.*

**Weir, Robert Walter.** 1803–1889. American portrait and historical painter and educator, b. New Rochelle, N.Y. On teaching staff, U.S.M.A., West Point (1834–76), and professor of drawing there (1846–76). A son, **John Ferguson** (1841–1926), was also an artist and educator; studio in New York City; associated in painting with Hudson River school; professor and first director, Yale U. School of Fine Arts (1869–1913); paintings include genre compositions, landscapes, portraits, and flowers. Another son, **Julian Alden** (1852–1919), was also a painter; studio in New York (from 1877); strongly influenced by French impressionists.

**Weis'bach** (vīs'bäĸ), **Julius.** 1806–1871. German mining engineer; known for researches in hydraulics and development of mine surveying.

**Wei'sen·thal** (?wī'z'n·thôl), **Charles F.** English inventor (1755) of double-pointed needle, fundamental principle of sewing machine. Cf. Elias HOWE.

**Weis'haupt** (vīs'houpt), **Adam.** 1748–1830. German mystic, philosopher, and religious leader; founder (1776) of the Illuminati, or Perfectibilists, a secret rationalistic anticlerical sect.

**Weis'mann** (vīs'män), **August.** 1834–1914. German biologist, b. Frankfurt am Main. Studied medicine at Göttingen; professor of zoology, Freiburg (1866–1912). Denied that acquired characters are transmitted to offspring; contended that only variations of the germ plasm are inherited. Author of *Die Entwicklung der Dipteren* (1864), *Studien zur Deszendenztheorie* (2 vols., 1875–76), *Das Keimplasma, eine Theorie der Vererbung* (1892).

**Weiss** (vīs), **Albert Maria.** *Pseudonym* **Heinrich von der Cla'na** (fôn dẽr klä'nä). 1844–1925. Roman Catholic Dominican theologian and writer, b. in Upper Bavaria; author of *Apologie des Christentums* (5 vols., 1878–89).

**Weiss** (vīs), **Amalie.** See Joseph JOACHIM.

**Weiss** (wīs), **André.** 1858–1928. French jurist; member of the Hague Tribunal (1920); judge of the Permanent Court of International Justice (1922).

**Weiss** (vīs), **Bernhard.** 1827–1918. German Protestant theologian; author of a life of Jesus (1882) and contributions to H. A. W. Meyer's New Testament commentaries.

**Weiss, Ernst.** 1884–1940. German novelist; refugee from Germany after establishment of Nazi regime; committed suicide.

**Weiss** (wīs), **Pierre.** 1865–1940. French physicist; professor in Zurich (1903), U. of Strasbourg (1918); investigated magnetism, determining a unit of magnetic moment known as the *Weiss magneton.*

**Weis'se** (vī'sĕ), **Christian Felix.** 1726–1804. German poet and dramatist; friend of Lessing. Author of lyrics, tragedies, comic operas, comedies, librettos, books and lyrics for children; editor of *Der Kinderfreund*, a weekly journal for children (24 vols., 1775–82). His grandson **Christian Hermann Weisse** (1801–1866), philosopher and university professor, helped found the system of speculative theism which opposed the pantheistic philosophy of Hegel.

**Wei Tao-Ming** (wā' dou'mĭng'). 1899– . Chinese lawyer and diplomat, b. in Kiangsi province; grad. in law, U. of Paris (1924); lawyer in Shanghai; minister of justice (1928–29); mayor of Nanking (1930–31); secretary-general of Executive Yuan (1937–41), also member of Supreme Council of National Defense (to 1941); ambassador to United States (1942–46). His wife, **Soumay Tcheng Wei** [sōō'mā' chĕng' wā' (1896?–1959)]; lawyer, grad. in law, U. of Paris (1924); delegate to Paris peace conference (1919); envoy extraordinary to France (1928); member of Legislative Yuan and of 5-member commission drafting new Chinese civil code (1929); practiced law in Shanghai (1930–41).

**Weit'zen·böck** (vī'tsĕn·bûk), **Roland.** 1885– . Austrian mathematician.

**Weit'zen·korn** (wīt's'n·kôrn), **Louis.** 1893–1943. American journalist and playwright; editor in chief, New York *Evening Graphic;* author of *First Mortgage* (1929), *Five Star Final* (1931), etc., and motion-picture scenarios.

**Weiz'mann** (vīts'män), **Chaim.** 1874–1952. Chemist, scholar, and Zionist leader, b. in Grodno province, Russia. Active on behalf of Jewish interests, and in securing Balfour Declaration (1917) in favor of Jewish national home in Palestine; president, World Zionist Organization (1920–31) and Jewish Agency for Palestine (1929–31; 1935–46); president, Hebrew U., Jerusalem (from 1932), and director, Daniel Sieff Research Inst.; provisional president of Israel (1948–49), first president (1949–52).

**Weiz'säck'er** (vīts'zĕk'ẽr), **Baron Ernst von.** 1882–1951. German naval officer (1900–20) and diplomat (1920 ff.); undersecretary for foreign affairs (1938–43); ambassador to the Vatican (1943–45).

**Weizsäcker, Karl von.** 1822–1899. German Protestant theologian.

**We'ker·le** (vĕ'kĕr·lĕ), **Sándor.** 1848–1921. Hungarian statesman; premier of Hungary (1892–95, 1906–10, 1917–18).

**Wel'by** (wĕl'bĭ), **Amelia Ball,** *nee* **Cop'puck** (kŏp'ŭk). 1819–1852. American poet, b. Saint Michaels, Md.; m. George Welby (1838); collected works are in *Poems* (1845; fourteen editions by 1855); best-known poems, *The Rainbow*, *The Bereaved*, and *I Know Thee Not* (addressed to Lord Byron).

**Welch** (wĕlch; wĕlsh), **William Henry.** 1850–1934. American pathologist, b. Norfolk, Conn. Opened first pathology laboratory in U.S., Bellevue Hospital Medical College (1878); professor, Johns Hopkins (1884–1916), and pathologist to Johns Hopkins Hospital (1889–1916); director, Johns Hopkins School of Hygiene and Public Health (1918–26), and professor of history of medicine (1926–31). Author of *General Pathology of Fever* (1888), *Bacteriology of Surgical Infections* (1895), *Thrombosis and Embolism* (1899).

**Welck'er** (vĕl'kẽr), **Friedrich Gottlieb.** 1784–1868. German classical philologist and archaeologist; author of works on Greek art and literature, as *Die Griechischen Tragödien* (3 vols., 1839–41), *Alte Denkmäler* (5 vols., 1849–64). His brother **Karl Theodor** (1790–1869) was a liberal politician; coeditor with Rotteck of the *Staatslexikon* (18 vols., 1834–48).

**Weld** (wĕld), **Theodore Dwight.** 1803–1895. American abolitionist; m. **Angelina Grim'ké** (grĭm'kē) of South Carolina, also a prominent abolitionist writer and lecturer.

**Weld** (wĕld) *or* **Welde** (wĕld) *or* **Wells** (wĕlz), **Thomas.** 1595–1661. English Puritan and minister in Massachusetts Bay Colony. First pastor of Church at Roxbury, Mass. (1632); overseer, Harvard (1638); with John Eliot and Richard Mather, prepared *Bay Psalm Book* (1640), first book printed in English in America; agent for Bay Colony in London (1641–46); remained in England.

**Welf** (vĕlf). A German princely family, taking its name from the original home in Altdorf, Swabia. Henry (IX) the Black, Duke of Bavaria and son of Welf IV, had three children: Henry the Proud (*q.v.*), Welf VI, and Judith, who married Frederick II, Duke of Swabia, thus uniting houses of Welf and Hohenstaufen. In 12th century, Welf VI, uncle of Henry the Lion, was defeated (1140) by Conrad III (first of the Hohenstaufen kings of Germany) at Weinsberg. Most famous Welf was Henry the Lion (*q.v.*), Duke of Saxony and Bavaria, who defied Emperor Frederick Barbarossa and lost his possessions (1180–81). In Italy, supporters of the Welfs were called *Guelphs* (Ital. *Guelfo*, pl. *Guelfi*). See GUELPH and HOHENSTAUFEN. The British house of Windsor, through the German houses of Hanover and Brunswick, are descendants of the Welfs.

**Wel'ha'ven** (vĕl'hä'vĕn), **Johan Sebastian Cammermeyer.** 1807–1873. Norwegian poet and critic; championed conservatism in literature; attacked ornate style of Henrik Wergeland; author of the satirical sonnet cycle *Norges Daemring* (1834), patriotic and lyrical poems, ballads, and critical works.

**Well'come** (wĕl'kŭm), Sir **Henry.** 1854–1936. Chemical manufacturer and explorer, b. in Wisconsin; grad. (1874), Philadelphia School of Pharmacy and Chemistry; cofounder (1880, in London, Eng.) of Burroughs, Wellcome & Co., manufacturers of chemical and pharmaceutical products; first to enter Sudan after Gordon (1900); conducted archaeological expeditions to Upper Nile (1901–10); founded laboratories and hospitals.

**Wel'ler** (wĕl'ẽr), **Thomas Huckle.** 1915– . American biologist, b. Ann Arbor, Mich. At Harvard U. (1940– ); awarded Nobel prize in physiology and medicine (1954) with J. Enders and F. Robbins for work on poliomyelitis viruses.

**Welles** (wĕlz). See also WELLS.

**Welles, Gideon.** 1802–1878. American politician, b. Glastonbury, Conn.; descendant of Thomas Welles (*q.v.*). Editor and part owner, Hartford *Times* (1826–36). Postmaster, Hartford (1836–41). Aided in organization of Republican party, and in founding (1856) a Republican newspaper, Hartford *Evening Press.* U.S. secretary of the navy (1861–69); supported both Lincoln and Johnson. Articles which he contributed to the *Galaxy* (1871–77) and his diary, *Diary of Gideon Welles* (3 vols., 1911), are important historical documents.

**Welles, Orson,** *in full* **George Orson.** 1915– . American actor and producer, b. Kenosha, Wis. First stage appearance, with Gate Theatre, Dublin (1931–32); founded Mercury Theatre (1937); directed production of *Julius Caesar* (1937), *Shoemakers' Holiday, Heartbreak House,* and *Danton's Death* (1938); director of, and actor in, radio programs (from 1938); wrote, produced, directed, and acted in motion picture *Citizen Kane* (1940).

**Welles, Roger.** 1862–1932. American naval officer, b. Newington, Conn., descendant of Thomas Welles (*q.v.*). Engaged in arctic exploration (1887–90); explored upper reaches of Orinoco River (1891). Director of naval intelligence during World War I; retired (1926). His wife (m. 1908), **Harriet Ogden,** *nee* **Deen** (dēn), b. New York City, is author of *Anchors Aweigh* (1919).

**Welles, Sumner.** 1892–1961. American diplomat, b. New York City. Asst. chief and chief, Latin American Affairs Division in Department of State (1920–22). In Dominican Republic (1922 and 1929), and in Honduras (1924), laid foundation for American "good-neighbor" policy. U.S. ambassador to Cuba (1933). Under-secretary of state (1933–43). On mission to Europe to discuss political and economic problems with European statesmen (1940). U.S. delegate to conference of 21 American republics, Rio de Janeiro (Jan., 1942).

**Welles, Thomas.** 1598–1660. New England colonial governor. Resided in Northamptonshire, Eng. (to 1634); to New England (1635) to escape persecution for Puritanism; cofounder of Hartford, Connecticut (1637).

**Welles'ley** (wĕlz'lĭ). Family name (orig. and until c. 1790 spelled **Wes'ley** [wĕs'lĭ; wĕz'-]) of the dukes of **Wel'ling·ton** [wĕl'ĭng·tŭn] (cr. 1814) and the earls Cowley (cr. 1857), descendants of a family named **Col'ley** (kŏl'ĭ) *or* **Cow'ley** (kou'lĭ), probably of English origin, that settled in Ireland in 16th century.

**Richard Colley Wellesley** (1690?–1758), **1st Baron Mor'ning·ton** (môr'nĭng·tŭn) (Irish peerage. cr. 1746), took surname *Wesley* on inheriting (1728) estates of a cousin (Garrett Wesley, who was a relative of John and Charles Wesley) but name later changed to *Wellesley;* founded (1748) charity school at Trim, County Meath. His son **Garrett** (1735–1781), 1st Viscount **Wellesley of Dangan** and 1st Earl of **Mornington** (Irish peerage, cr. 1760), musician and composer of glees, was father of six sons, the 4th of whom was Arthur, the great duke of Wellington (*q.v.*), victor at Waterloo.

**Richard Colley** (1760–1842), 1st Marquis **Wellesley** (Irish peerage, cr. 1799) and 2d Earl of Mornington; Indian administrator; eldest of Garrett's sons, b. Dangen Castle; educ. Oxford; M.P. (1784); a lord of the treasury (1786). As governor general of India (1797–1805) under Pitt, rendered British power in India supreme by replacing French with British soldiers in Hyderabad, replacing Mohammedan dynasty in Mysore with friendly Hindu dynasty, persuading Indian princes to cede territory and contribute to support of British forces, etc. Ambassador to Spain (1809); foreign secretary (1809–12); baffled in attempt to form coalition ministry (1812); advocate of free trade and Catholic emancipation; lord lieutenant of Ireland (1821–28, 1833–34); suppressed Whiteboy raids in Ireland; lord chamberlain (1835).

**William Wellesley–Pole** [-pōl] (1763–1845), 3d Earl of Mornington and 1st Baron **Mar'y·bor'ough** [mâr'ĭ-bûr'ŭ; -bŭ·rŭ] (peerage of United Kingdom, cr. 1821); naval officer; Garrett's 2d son; took additional name *Pole* on succeeding to a cousin's estates (1778); chief secretary for Ireland (1809–12); postmaster general (1834–35).

**Henry** (1773–1847), 1st Baron **Cowley** (peerage of U.K., cr. 1828); diplomat; Garrett's youngest son; ambassador to Spain (1809–22), to Vienna (1823–31), to Paris (1841–46). His son **Henry Richard Charles** (1804–1884), 1st Earl **Cowley** and Viscount **Dangan** (cr. 1857); ambassador to Paris (1852–67); conducted negotiations preceding and following Crimean War; negotiated peace with Persia (1857); assisted Cobden in negotiating commercial treaty with France (1860).

**Wel'lesz** (vĕl'ĕs), **Egon Joseph.** 1885–1974. Viennese musicologist and composer; in England (from 1938).

**Well'hau'sen** (vĕl'hou'zĕn), **Julius.** 1844–1918. German Protestant theologian, Biblical critic, and Orientalist.

**Wel'ling·ton** (wĕl'ĭng·tŭn), 1st Duke of. **Arthur Welles'ley** (wĕlz'lĭ). 1769–1852. Known as "the Iron Duke." British general and statesman, b. Ireland (see WELLESLEY family). Entered army (1787); Irish M.P. (1790–95); commanded a division in war with Tipu Sahib (1799); appointed by his brother (then governor general of India) to supreme military and political command in the Deccan (to 1805); defeated Maratha chiefs (1803); returned to England (1805); Irish secretary (1807–09). Given command as lieutenant general in Peninsular War (1808); on death of Sir John Moore, given chief command; defeated forces of King Joseph (Bonaparte) under Victor at Talavera (1809); forced French under Masséna to retreat from Portugal (1810–11), defeated them at Salamanca, and entered Madrid (1812); given supreme command in Spain, defeated King Joseph at Vitoria (1813) and drove French across Pyrenees (1814), pursuing as far as Toulouse; created duke (1814). Ambassador to France (1814) and representative at Congress of Vienna (1814–15). Entrusted with command of army in Netherlands; with aid of Prussian Blücher, crushed Napoleon in Waterloo campaign (1815); spoke strongly against cession of French territory to Prussia; commanded army of occupation in France (1815–18); master general of ordnance with seat in cabinet (1818–27); as English representative in Congress of Verona (1822), unsuccessfully argued against French armed intervention in Spain; failed in mission to Russia to induce czar not to threaten war with Turkey in behalf of Greek independence (1826); commander in chief (1827–28, 1842–52). Prime minister (Jan., 1828–Nov., 1830); opposed Catholic emancipation but became convinced that only way to avoid civil war in Ireland was to force Catholic Emancipation Act through parliament (1829); declared against any reform of parliamentary representation and caused ministry to be voted out of office (1830); stubbornly opposed Reform Bill (1831–32); foreign secretary under Peel (Dec., 1834–Apr., 1835); member of Peel's second cabinet only as commander in chief (1841–46); supported Peel in corn-law legislation; subordinated party spirit to national interest and regained position as popular idol; organized the military in protection of London during Chartist uprisings (1848).

**Well'man** (wĕl'măn), **Hiller Crowell.** 1871–1956. American librarian, b. Boston; librarian, Springfield, Mass. (1902–48); president, American Library Association (1914–15). Special editor for library terms, *Webster's New International Dictionary, Second Edition.*

**Wellman, Walter.** 1858–1934. American journalist and explorer, b. Mentor, Ohio. Founded (1879) Cincinnati *Post.* Washington correspondent, Chicago *Herald* and *Record-Herald* (1884–1911). Led expedition to Spitsbergen (1894) and to Franz Josef Land (1898–99); attempted flight in dirigible over North Pole, but failed (1906, 1907, and 1909); also, attempted flight in dirigible across Atlantic, and failed (1910), but broke existing world records for time and distance sailing by airship (1008 miles in 72 hours). Author of *The Aerial Age* (1911).

**Wells** (wĕlz). See also WELLES.

**Wells, Carolyn.** 1862–1942. Am. writer, b. Rahway, N.J.; m. Hadwin Houghton (1918). Writer of humorous sketches, parodies, juveniles, short stories, novels, and detective fiction, including *The Jingle Book* (1899), *A Nonsense Anthology* (1902), *Fluffy Ruffles* (1907), *The Maxwell Mystery* (1913), *Vicky Van* (1918), *Spooky Hollow* (1923), *The Skeleton at the Feast* (1931), *Fleming Stone Omnibus* (1933), *The Killer* (1938).

**Wells, Charles Jeremiah.** *Pseudonym* **H. L. How'ard** (hou'ẽrd). 1799?–1879. English poet. Friend of Hazlitt and Keats. Author of a pseudo-Jacobean drama in verse, *Joseph and His Brethren* (1824), praised by Horne (1844) and D. G. Rossetti (1863) and reviewed by Swinburne (1875). Left England (1840); taught English in Quimper, Brittany.

**Wells, David Ames.** 1828–1898. American economist, b. Springfield, Mass. His pamphlet *Our Burden and Our Strength* (1864) demonstrating economic strength of U.S. brought him into national prominence; special commissioner of U.S. revenue (1866–69). Leading advocate of free-trade policies (from 1868). Among his notable books are *The Silver Question* (1877), *Our Merchant Marine* (1882), *Practical Economics* (1885), *The Theory and Practice of Taxation* (1900).

**Wells, Frederic Lyman.** 1884–1964. American psychologist, b. Boston; author of *Mental Adjustments* (1917), *Pleasure and Behavior* (1924), etc.

**Wells, Henry.** 1805–1878. American express operator, b. Thetford, Vt.; in express business (from 1841) and merged competing companies into American Express Co. (1850), of which he was president (1850–68); organizer of Wells, Fargo & Co. (1852).

**Wells, Henry Tanworth.** 1828–1903. English portrait painter; most popular work *Victoria Regina* (1880), a study of Queen Victoria as princess receiving news of her accession.

**Wells, Herbert George.** *Occasional pseudonym* **Reginald Bliss** (blĭs). 1866–1946. English novelist, sociological writer and historian. B.Sc., London (1888); taught science; journalist (1893). Wrote series of fantastic scientific romances, *The Time Machine* (1895), *The Island of Doctor Moreau* (1896), *The Wheels of Chance* (1896), *The Invisible Man* (1897), *The War in the Air* (1908); developed, in combination with scientific speculation, a strain of sociological idealism in *The War of the Worlds* (1898), *The Food of the Gods* (1904), *A Modern Utopia* (1905); stated his social creed in *New Worlds for Old* (1908), *First and Last Things* (1908). Wrote novels of character and humor including *Love and Mr. Lewisham* (1900), *Kipps: The Story of a Simple Soul* (1905), *The History of Mr. Polly* (1910), *Ann Veronica*, promoting feminism (1909); novels of contemporary English life including *Tono-Bungay* (1909), *The New Machiavelli* (1911), *The Passionate Friends* (1913), *The Research Magnificent* (1915), *Mr. Britling Sees It Through* (1916), *Joan and Peter* (1918); novels of discussion, as *Christina Alberta's Father* (1925), *The World of William Clissold* (1926), *Mr. Blettsworthy on Rampole Island* (1928). His *Outline of History* (1920), intended to replace "narrow nationalist history by a general review of the human record," was paralleled by *The Science of Life* (1929; written in collaboration with his son **George Philip** and with Julian Huxley) and by *The Work, Wealth, and Happiness of Mankind* (1932). Published stories and poems by his wife, **Amy Catherine,** *nee* **Rob'bins** [rŏb'ĭnz] (d. 1927), in *The Book of Catherine Wells* (1928). Later works include several scenarios and *The Shape of Things to Come* (1933), *World Brain* (1938), *Fate of Homo Sapiens* (1939), *The New World Order* (1940), *Guide to the New World* (1941), *Phoenix* (1942).

**Wells, Horace.** 1815–1848. American dentist, b. Hartford, Vt. Interested (from 1840) in anesthetic effects of nitrous oxide, or laughing gas; learned from Gardner Q. Colton how to administer the gas (1844); attempted demonstration in dental case before Harvard medical class (1845) but with unsatisfactory result because of extraction before patient was completely anesthetized. His claim (Dec. 7, 1846) to priority in discovery of anesthesia was made about two months after Morton's demonstration of use of ether.

**Wells, Linton.** 1893– . American journalist and radio broadcaster.

**Wells, Thomas.** 1595–1661. See WELD.

**Wells,** Sir **Thomas Spencer.** 1818–1897. English surgeon; surgeon for Queen Victoria's household (1863–96); perfected the operation of ovariotomy.

**Wels'bach** (vĕls'bäκ; *Angl.* wĕlz'băk, -bäk), **Aloys Au'er von** (ou'ẽr fôn). 1813–1869. Austrian printer; director (1841–64), Imperial Press, Vienna. His son Baron **Carl Auer von Welsbach** (1858–1929) was a chemist; discoverer of rare-earth elements neodymium and praseodymium; inventor of gaslight appliances, Welsbach burner and Welsbach mantle.

**Wel'ser** (vĕl'zẽr). Name of a German family of Augsburg, including: **Bartholomäus** (1488–1561), wholesale merchant, cofounder and head (1518–53) of a banking and commercial firm which lent large sums to Charles V, was granted (1528) the right to conquer and colonize Venezuela as a commercial enterprise, and suffered great losses when the charter was revoked (1546). His niece **Philippine** (1527–1580), secret wife (1557) of Archduke Ferdinand, son of Emperor Ferdinand I. His grandnephew **Markus** (1558–1614), scholar, author of Latin works on the history of Augsburg and Bavaria, and editor of the so-called *Peutinger Tafel* (1591).

**Welsh** (wĕlsh). See also WELCH.

**Wemyss** (wēmz), Earl of. Title in Scottish peerage held by an ancient family of Fife from creation (1633) of Sir **John Wemyss** (d. 1649), 1st baronet, as Earl of **Wemyss** and Baron **El'cho** (ĕl'kō) **and Meth'el** (mĕth'ĕl). The 1st earl took sides with Scottish Parliamentarians against Charles I in Civil War. **David** (1610–1679), 2d earl, led a Lowland army as Lord Elcho; defeated by Montrose at Tippermuir (1644) and Kilsyth (1645). **James** (1699–1756), 4th earl, married Janet, daughter of Col. Francis Charteris. **David** (1721–1787), Lord Elcho, son of 4th earl, commanded Prince Charles Edward's lifeguards (1745–46); wrote a narrative of this Jacobite uprising and was attainted. His brother **Francis** took name Char′ter·is (chär′tẽr·ĭs; chär′tẽrz) on inheriting (1771) maternal grandfather's estate and assumed the title of earl, which was granted on reversal of attainder (1826) to his grandson **Francis Wemyss-Charteris-Douglas** (1772–1853), 7th earl, who had taken name Douglas on inheriting some Douglas estates and earldom of March and had been created (1821) Baron **Wemyss of Wemyss** in peerage of United Kingdom. **Francis Wemyss-Charteris-Douglas** (1818–1914), 9th Earl of Wemyss (according to Burke 10th earl) and 6th Earl of **March** (märch); political leader, b. Edinburgh; educ. Oxford; an organizer, sometimes called father, of the volunteer movement; M.P. (1841–83); supported Sir Robert Peel on repeal of corn laws; a lord of the treasury (1852–55); as Lord Elcho, led a secession group from Liberals, nicknamed the Cave of Adullam, which defeated the Reform Bill of 1866; author of *The New War Office* (1899).

**Wemyss**, Sir **Henry Colville Barclay**. 1891–1959. British army officer; grad. Royal Mil. Acad., Woolwich (1910); major general (1939); director of mobilization (1939); acting lieutenant general (1940); adjutant general (1940–41); appointed member of combined Anglo-American chiefs of staff (1942); general (1945).

**Wen′ces·laus** (wĕn′sĕs·lôs). *Ger.* **Wen′zel** (vĕn′tsĕl), **Wen′zes·laus** (vĕn′tsĕs·lous). Name of four kings of Bohemia: **Wenceslaus I** (d. 1253), king (1230–53); son of Ottokar I; usually supported Emperor Frederick II; opposed by nobility for encouragement of German immigration; succeeded by his son Ottokar II. His grandson **Wenceslaus II** (1271–1305), king (1278–1305); under German regency (1278–83); assumed full control (1290); reduced power of nobles; elected king of Poland (1300), but resigned (1305); in conflict with Hapsburgs; at war with Albert I (1304–05). His son and successor, **Wenceslaus III** (1289–1306), king of Hungary (1301–04), of Bohemia (1305–06). **Wenceslaus IV.** See WENCESLAUS, Holy Roman emperor.

**Wenceslaus.** *Ger.* **Wenzel.** 1361–1419. King of Germany and Holy Roman emperor (1378–1400). King of Bohemia (1378–1419) as Wenceslaus IV. Son of Charles IV and brother of Sigismund. Imprisoned by Bohemian nobles (1393–94); deposed by German electors (1400); imprisoned in Vienna (1402), but regained Bohemian throne (1404).

**Wen′dell** (wĕn′d'l), **Barrett.** 1855–1921. American man of letters and educator, b. Boston. Grad. Harvard (1877). Teacher of English at Harvard (1880–1921), professor (from 1898). Best remembered as a great teacher. Among his notable books are *Cotton Mather, the Puritan Priest* (1891), *English Composition* (1891), *William Shakspere* (1894), *A Literary History of America* (1900), *The France of Today* (1907), *The Privileged Classes* (1908), *The Mystery of Education* (1909), *The Traditions of European Literature, from Homer to Dante* (1920).

**Wendover, Roger of.** d. 1236. See ROGER OF WENDOVER.

**Wendt** (vĕnt), **Hans Hinrich.** 1853–1928. German evangelical theologian.

**Wen′ley** (wĕn′lĭ), **Robert Mark.** 1861–1929. Philosopher, b. Edinburgh, Scotland; professor, U. of Michigan (1896–1929); author of *Socrates and Christ* (1889), *The Anarchist Ideal* (1913), *Stoicism and its Influence* (1924).

**Wen′ner·berg′** (vĕn′nẽr·băr′y'), **Gunnar.** 1817–1901. Swedish poet, composer, and statesman; minister of education (1870–75, 1888–91); governor of Växjö (1875); composer of words and music for *Gluntarne*, duets for male voices descriptive of student life at Uppsala (1849–51), of patriotic songs and hymns, and of psalms, oratorios, a *Stabat Mater*.

**Wen′ner-Gren′** (vĕn′nẽr·grān′), **Axel.** 1881–1961. Swedish industrialist; educ. in Germany; worked in Berlin and in U.S.; salesman for Swedish electric-lamp company, gradually becoming majority stockholder; formed Electrolux Company to manufacture vacuum cleaners (1921) and, later, refrigerators; acquired large interests in many industries in Sweden, including Sweden's largest wood-pulp producing company and the Bofors munitions works; donated large sums to establish foundations for scientific research in Sweden and (1937) the Axel Wenner-Gren Foundation for Nordic Co-operation and Research.

**Went′worth** (wĕnt′wûrth; -wẽrth), **Benning.** 1696–1770. Colonial governor in America, b. Portsmouth, N.H. Active in movement to make New Hampshire independent of Massachusetts; first royal governor of New Hampshire (1741–67). Made (1761) extensive grants of land, known as New Hampshire grants, in area west and east of Connecticut River claimed by both New York and New Hampshire, causing long dispute between the two provinces settled only by creation of State of Vermont. His nephew **John Wentworth** (1737–1820) succeeded to the governorship (1767); loyalist on outbreak of American Revolution and forced to flee (1775); lieutenant governor of Nova Scotia (1792–1808); created baronet (1795).

**Wentworth, Cecile de.** 1853?–1933. American painter; best known for her portraits, including Pope Leo XIII, Theodore Roosevelt, William H. Taft, Queen Alexandra.

**Wentworth, George Albert.** 1835–1906. American educator; teacher at Phillips Exeter Academy (1858–91) and head of its mathematics department for over thirty years; acting principal of Phillips Exeter (1883–84; 1889–90). Widely known as writer of mathematical textbooks. His son **George** (1868– ) aided his father (from 1894) in preparation of textbooks and collaborated with David Eugene Smith in Wentworth-Smith series of graded mathematical textbooks (from 1906).

**Wentworth, Henrietta Maria.** Baroness **Wentworth.** See under duke of MONMOUTH.

**Wentworth, Thomas.** See earl of STRAFFORD.

**Wentworth, William Charles.** 1793–1872. Founder of Australian colonial self-government, b. Norfolk Island, Australia. Known as "the Australian patriot." Practiced law, Sydney, and started *The Australian*, a newspaper (1824) in which he advocated admission to politics of "emancipists" (ex-convicts) and discouraged the "exclusivists" (officials) and "interlopers" (voluntary immigrants); obtained recall of governor, Sir Ralph Darling (1831); his agitation largely responsible for Constitution Act (1842) which gave colonial self-government to Australia; led "pastoral" or "squatter" party in first legislature (1843); founder of Sydney University (1852); secured new colonial constitution (1854); settled in England (1862) but continued to work for a federal parliament for all Australia.

**Wên Wang** (wŭn′ wäng′). 1231?–?1135 B.C. Ruler of state of Chou, in north central China; imprisoned by Chou Hsin, last of the Shang dynasty; while in prison supposed to have written *I Ching* ("Canon of Changes"), one of the Five Classics; release secured by his son Wu Wang, who became first emperor of the Chou dynasty. Cf. FU HSI.

**Wenzel** *or* **Wenzeslaus.** See WENCESLAUS.

**Wer'der** (vĕr'dĕr), Count **August von.** 1808–1887. German infantry general; fought in Austro-Prussian War (1866) and in Franco-Prussian War (1870–71).

**Werdt, Johann von.** See WERTH.

**We'ren·skiold** (vâ'rĕn·shöl), **Erik.** 1855–1938. Norwegian illustrator and painter of portraits and of Norwegian landscapes and folk life.

**Wer'fel** (vĕr'fĕl), **Franz.** 1890–1945. Expressionist poet, dramatist, and novelist, b. in Prague of Jewish parents. Served in World War (1915–17); resident chiefly in Vienna (from 1918); to U.S. (1940). Author of volumes of verse, dramatic works, stories, and novels, largely psychological as *Nicht der Mörder, der Ermordete ist Schuldig* (1920), *Verdi* (1924), *Der Tod des Kleinbürgers* (1926; trans. *The Man Who Conquered Death*), *Der Abiturientenlag* (1928; trans. *The Class Reunion*), *Barbara oder die Frömmigkeit* (1929), *Die Geschwister von Neapel* (1931), *Die 40 Tage des Musa Dagh* (1933; trans. *The Forty Days of Musa Dagh*), *The Song of Bernadette* (Eng. trans., 1941), *Between Heaven and Earth* (1944).

**Werff** (vĕrf), **Adriaen van der.** 1659–1722. Dutch baroque painter of Biblical, mythological, and genre scenes; court painter, Rotterdam.

**Wer'ge·land** (văr'gĕ·län), **Henrik Arnold.** 1808–1845. Norwegian lyric poet, dramatist, editor, and patriot; championed modern school in literature, in opposition to Welhaven, whom he satirized under pseudonym of **Siful Si·fad'da** (sē·fäd'dä) in farces *Papegöien* (1833) and *Den Konstitutionelle* (1839); author also of *Skabelsen, Mennesket, og Messias* (a long philosophical dramatic poem, 1830), *Campbellerne* (a musical drama which brought to a head the feud in the theater, 1837), and *Jan van Huysums Blomsterstykke* (1840), *Jöden* (1842), *Jödinden* (1844), and *Den Engelske Lods* (1844). See Camilla COLLETT.

**Wer'ner** (vĕr'nĕr), **Abraham Gottlob.** 1750–1817. German geologist and mineralogist; proponent of neptunism, the now obsolete theory that all of the rocks of the earth's crust were formed by the agency of water; arranged geological formations into groups; classified minerals systematically.

**Werner, Alfred.** 1866–1919. Swiss chemist; professor, U. of Zurich (from 1893). Announced (1893) the coordination theory of chemical constitution, which led to discovery of many cases of isomerism. Awarded 1913 Nobel prize for chemistry. Author of *Lehrbuch der Stereochemie* (1904).

**Wer'ner** (wûr'nĕr), **Alice.** 1859–1935. English philologist. Educ. Cambridge; lived in Africa (1893–96; 1911–13); professor of Swahili and Bantu, London U. (from 1921). Author of books on races, mythology, and languages of central and southern Africa; also, poems and stories. Consultant in etymology (Bantu and other African languages), *Webster's New International Dictionary, Second Edition.*

**Wer'ner** (vĕr'nĕr), **Anton Alexander von.** 1843–1915. German illustrator and historical and portrait painter; painted portraits chiefly of German officers in the Franco-Prussian War, and genre and contemporary historical scenes.

**Werner, E.** *Pseudonym of* **Elisabeth Bür'sten·bin'der** (bür'stĕn·bĭn'dĕr). 1838–1918. German novelist; author of *Am Altar* (1873), *Glück Auf!* (1874), *Gesprengte Fesseln* (1875), *Wege des Schicksals* (1912).

**Werner, Franz von.** *Pseudonym* **Mu·rad' E·fen·di'** (mōō·räd' [-rät'] ĕ·fĕn·dĭ'). 1836–1881. Poet and dramatist, b. Vienna; in Austrian and (1853) Turkish military service; in Turkish diplomatic service (from 1856); author of collections of poems, dramas, etc.

**Werner, Karl.** 1808–1894. German water-color painter; paintings include aquarelle studies of Egypt and Palestine, and views of churches, palaces, etc.

**Wer'ner** (wûr'nĕr), **Morris Robert.** 1897– . American writer; author of *Barnum* (1923), *Brigham Young* (1925), *Tammany Hall* (1928), *Privileged Characters* (1935), etc.

**Wer'ner** (vĕr'nĕr), **Zacharias,** *in full* **Friedrich Ludwig Zacharias.** 1768–1823. German poet and romantic dramatist; in Rome (1809–13), where he embraced Catholicism (1810); became priest (1814) and preached mainly in Vienna. Author of the dramas *Die Söhne des Thales* (2 vols., 1803), *Das Kreuz an der Ostsee* (1806), *Attila* (1808), and *Wanda* (1810), of the one-act play *Der Vierundzwanzigste Februar* (1810; one of the first "fate tragedies"), and of poems, hymns, sermons, etc.

**Wern'her, Bru'der** (brōō'dĕr vĕrn'hĕr). Traveler and Middle High German aphoristic poet of 13th century; member of a brotherhood of pilgrims to the Holy Sepulcher, and one of the 12 founders of the Meistersinger guild.

**Wern'her** (?wûr'nĕr), Sir **Julius Charles.** 1850–1912. British financier, b. at Darmstadt, Germany. Developed large diamond-mining company at Kimberley, South Africa; assisted Alfred Beit and Cecil Rhodes to amalgamate diamond mines (1888); naturalized British subject (1898); endowed educational institutions.

**Wer'nick·e** (vĕr'nĭ·kĕ), **Carl.** 1848–1905. German neurologist; authority on aphasia and hemianopia.

**Wer'nick·e** *or* **Wer'ni·ke** (vĕr'nĭ·kĕ), **Christian.** 1661–1725. German poet and epigrammatist; resident minister of king of Denmark at French court (1708–23); author of *Überschriften oder Epigrammata* (1701) and the heroic poem *Hans Sachs.*

**Wer'ren·rath** (wĕr'ĕn·răth), **Rei'nald** (rī'n'ld). 1883–1953. American operatic baritone, b. Brooklyn, N.Y.; debut at Metropolitan Opera House, N.Y. (1919).

**Werth** (?wûrth), **Alexander.** 1901–1969. British journalist (naturalized 1929), b. St. Petersburg, of Russian father and English mother; educ. in St. Petersburg and at Glasgow U. (M.A., 1924); correspondent in Paris (1929–40), Moscow (1941); author of *France in Ferment* (1934), *The Destiny of France* (1937; U.S. title *Which Way France?*), *France and Munich* (1939), *The Last Days of Paris* (1940), *Moscow War Diary* (1942).

**Werth** (vĕrt) *or* **Werdt** (vĕrt), **Johann von.** *Also* **Jean de Weert** (dĕ vārt). 1600?–1652. German general in the Thirty Years' War, at first (1622) in Imperialist, later (1630) in Bavarian, service; distinguished himself at Nördlingen (1634).

**Wertheimer, Leo.** See Constantin BRUNNER.

**Wes'brook** (wĕs'brŏŏk), **Frank Fairchild.** 1868–1918. Canadian pathologist and bacteriologist; professor, (1895–1913), and dean (1906–13), U. of Minnesota medical school; first president, U. of British Columbia (1913–18).

**Wes'cott** (wĕs'kŭt), **Glenway.** 1901– . American fiction writer, b. Kewaskum, Wis.; author of *The Apple of the Eye* (1924), *The Grandmothers—A Family Portrait* (1927; winner of Harper's 1927–28 prize novel contest), *Good-bye Wisconsin* (1928), *Fear and Trembling* (1932), *A Calendar of Saints for Unbelievers* (1932), *The Pilgrim Hawk* (1940), *Apartment in Athens* (1945).

**Wes'ley** (wĕs'lĭ; wĕz'-). Name of a family (originally **West'ley** [wĕst'lĭ]) of English gentry and clergy, largely nonconformists, including: **Samuel** (1662–1735), clergyman; published a book of poems, *Maggots* (1685); trained as a nonconformist but became rector at Epworth (1695–1735); lost rectory by fire (1709); author of *A Life of Christ* in verse (1693), *Dissertations on the Book of Job*

(1735). His eldest son, **Samuel** (1691–1739), classical scholar and poet; usher at Westminster school (1713–33); headmaster of Blundell's school at Tiverton (1733–39); friend of Bishop Atterbury, Addison, Swift, and Prior.

**John** (1703–1791), 15th child of Samuel Wesley the elder, theologian, evangelist, and founder of Methodism. M.A., Oxon. (1727); ordained priest (1728); became leader of his brother Charles's Methodist society at Oxford (1729–34). Accompanied Governor Oglethorpe to Georgia as missionary among colonists and Indians (1735–38); on voyage, met and was influenced by German Moravian colonists; started a correspondence with the Moravian founder Zinzendorf (1737); translated German hymns; met Peter Boehler, by whom he was considerably influenced, in London (1738). Prompted by awakening of faith in experience at a prayer meeting in Aldersgate Street, London (1738), swept aside ecclesiastical and High Church views, including apostolic succession, appointed lay preachers to assist, began preaching in fields at Bristol (1739), bought deserted gun foundry near London for preaching (1739); organized class meetings with admissions by "society tickets" to exclude undesirables (1742); held love feasts after model of primitive church, held first conference of Methodists (1744); preached rejection of doctrine of election and caused temporary breach with Whitefield (1741) and later secession of Welsh Calvinistic Methodists (1743); journeyed on horseback organizing societies through England (1742), Ireland on 42 trips (from 1747), Scotland on 22 trips (from 1751); held bishops and presbyters essentially of one order (1745) and himself ordained ministers for colonies; appointed Francis Asbury (*q.v.*) general superintendent in America (1772). Gave away annual income from his cheap books (about £1400), in helping needy and unemployed, in loans to debtors and businessmen, and in opening dispensaries. Failed to persuade Calvinists to union (1764); prepared declaration (1784) providing regulation of Methodist chapels and preachers; ordained presbyters to administer sacraments (1784). Author of educational treatises, translations from Greek, Latin, and Hebrew, histories of Rome and England, an ecclesiastical history, Biblical commentaries; edited *Imitation of Christ*, Bunyan, Baxter, Edwards, Rutherford, Law; compiled an English dictionary; published 23 collections of hymns; recorded his itineraries and spiritual life in his *Journal* (1735–90).

John's youngest brother, **Charles** (1707–1788), called a "methodist" by fellow students from his methodical habits of study. Gathered together at Oxford (1729) a group of fellow students, including his brother John, James Hervey, and George Whitefield, who shared fanatical religious zeal for regularity of living and strict observance of weekly sacrament. Accompanied his brother to Georgia as secretary to Governor Oglethorpe (1735) but returned in failing health (1736); experienced evangelical conversion (1738); active itinerant Methodist preacher (1739–56); opposed separation from Anglican Church (1755) and disagreed with his brother John's advocacy of doctrine of perfection (1762) and his ordination of presbyters (1784). Author of 6500 hymns, including *Jesus, lover of my soul; Love divine, all love excelling.*

Charles's son **Charles** (1757–1834), organist and composer of concertos. Another son, **Samuel** (1766–1837), also an organist and lecturer on music. His natural son, **Samuel Sebastian** (1810–1876), a famous cathedral organist, professor of organ, Royal Academy of Music (1850), and composer of church music.

**Wes'ly** (wĕs'lĭ; wĕz'-) *or* **West'ley** (wĕst'lĭ). Variants of WESLEY.

**Wes'sel** *or* **Wes'sel Gans'fort** (vĕs'ĕl gäns'fôrt). *First name perhaps* **Johann** *or* **Johannes**. 1420?–1489. Pre-Reformation reformer, mystic, and philosopher, b. Groningen; author of *Farrago Rerum Theologicarum* (pub. by Luther, 1522).

**Wes'sel** (vĕs'ĕl), **Horst**. 1907–1930. German National Socialist storm-troop leader; author of the "Horst Wessel song," sung since 1933, after the national anthem, as the official Nazi rallying song.

**Wes'son** (wĕs''n), **Charles Macon**. 1878–1956. American army officer, b. St. Louis; grad. U.S.M.A., West Point (1900); served in France in World War; chief of ordnance (1938–42).

**Wesson, Daniel Baird**. 1825–1906. American inventor and manufacturer, b. Worcester, Mass. In partnership with Horace Smith, invented new type of repeating action for pistols and rifles (1854); organized Smith & Wesson Co., Springfield, Mass. (1857) to manufacture the new firearm.

**West** (wĕst). Name of English family that after union with De La Warr family of Sussex held barony and earldom of De La Warr (see Thomas, 1577–1618, Baron DE LA WARR) and after marriage of George John (1791–1869) with Elizabeth Sackville became Sackville-West family (*q.v.*).

**West, Andrew Fleming**. 1853–1943. American educator; professor of Latin (1883–1928) and dean of graduate school (1901–28), Princeton.

**West, Benjamin**. 1730–1813. American mathematician and almanac maker, b. Rehoboth, Mass.; self-educated. Observed transit of Venus (1769) and published *An Account of the Observation of Venus Upon the Sun the Third Day of June 1769* (1769); also, studied an eclipse of the sun (1781) and published an account of it. Professor of mathematics and astronomy, Brown U. (1788–99). Began preparation of almanacs with *An Almanack, for the Year of Our Lord Christ, 1763...*, later named *The New-England Almanack...* (publ. annually at Providence, R.I., 1765–81); also, *Bickerstaff's Boston Almanac for the Year of Our Lord 1768* (publ. in Boston; also publ. for years 1779 and 1783–93, being the first illustrated almanac in Massachusetts). Prepared *The North-American Calendar: or Rhode Island Almanac* (1781–87) and *The Rhode Island Almanac* (publ. at Newport, 1804–06).

**West, Benjamin**. 1738–1820. American painter, b. near Springfield, Pa. Self-taught; studio in Philadelphia (to 1759) and New York (1759–60). In Italy (1760–63), and London (1763–1820). Established studio in London and gained fame by his historical paintings; close friend of Sir Joshua Reynolds; appointed by George III a charter member of the Royal Academy (founded 1768) and historical painter to the king (from 1772). Succeeded Reynolds as president of the Royal Academy (1792–1820). Among his notable paintings are *The Death of Wolfe, Battle of La Hogue, Christ Healing the Sick, Death on the Pale Horse, Alexander the Great and his Physicians, Penn's Treaty with the Indians*, and many portraits, esp. of George III and members of the royal family.

**West,** Sir **Edward**. 1782–1828. English economist; in his *Essay on the Application of Capital to Land* (1815) stated the law of diminishing returns, and anticipated Ricardo's theory of rent.

**West, Edward William**. 1824–1905. English Oriental scholar; special student of Parsi religion and of Pahlavi language and literature; translator of Pahlavi texts for Max Müller's *Sacred Books of the East.*

**West, Francis**. 1586–?1634. Governor of Virginia Colony, b. in England; arrived in Virginia (1608); one of group deposing Captain Smith in favor of George Percy

(1609); succeeded Percy as commander at Jamestown (1612); succeeded Yeardley as governor (1627–29).

**West, Gilbert.** 1703–1756. English author of *Observations on the Resurrection* (1747) and translations of Pindar in verse; included in Johnson's *Lives of the Poets.*

**West, Joseph.** fl. 1669–1685. Governor of South Carolina Colony, b. in England; designated by the English proprietors commander of an expedition of three vessels to settle Carolina (1669); made settlement at Albemarle Point, under governorship of William Sayle; succeeded Sayle (d. 1671) and served as governor (1671–72; 1674–82; 1684–85); left the settlement (1685).

**West,** Dame **Rebecca.** *Pseud.* (from Ibsen's *Rosmersholm*) *of* **Cicily Isabel Fair′field** (fâr′fēld). 1892– . English critic and novelist, b. Kerry, Ireland; m. (1930) Henry Maxwell Andrews, London banker. First book, *Henry James* (1916); first novels, *The Return of the Soldier* (1918), *The Judge* (1922), *Harriet Hume* (1929); recently, *The Meaning of Treason* (1949), *A Train of Powder* (1955), *The Count and the Castle* (1958).

**Westbury,** 1st Baron. See Richard BETHELL.

**West′cott** (wĕs(t)′kŭt), **Brooke Foss.** 1825–1901. English prelate and New Testament scholar; regius professor of divinity, Cambridge (1870–90). One of revisionists of New Testament (1870–81); brought out, in conjunction with F. J. A. Hort, a new critical text of New Testament in Greek (2 vols., 1881). Canon of Westminster (1883–90); bishop of Durham (1890–1901).

**Westcott, Edward Noyes** (nois). 1846–1898. American banker and novelist, b. Syracuse, N.Y.; in banking business (from 1862); author of *David Harum, A Story of American Life* (written 1895–96; publ. posthumously, 1898), which achieved wide popularity, was dramatized (1900), and later presented as a motion picture.

**Westcott, Thompson.** 1820–1888. American journalist and historian, b. Philadelphia; practiced law in Philadelphia. Founder and editor (1848–84), Philadelphia *Sunday Dispatch,* for many years the only Sunday newspaper in Philadelphia. Author of *Life of John Fitch...* (1857), the well-known *History of Philadelphia* (with J. T. Scharf; 3 vols., 1884), etc.

**Wes′ter·gaard** (vĕs′tēr·gôr), **Niels Ludvig.** 1815–1878. Danish Orientalist and philologist; author of works on Indian philology, Persian cuneiform inscriptions, etc.

**Wes′ter′mann′** (vĕs′tĕr′măn′), **François Joseph.** 1751–1794. French army officer; distinguished himself in the Wars of the Vendée; was arrested with Danton and guillotined.

**Wes′ter·mann** (wĕs′tēr·măn), **William Linn.** 1873–1954. American historian; author of *Story of the Ancient Nations* (1912); editor of *Westermann's Classical and Historical Map Series* (1918). Collaborator in publishing three series of *Greek Papyri* (1926, 1931, 1933).

**Wes′ter·marck** (vĕs′tēr·märk; *Angl.* wĕs′tēr·märk), **Edward Alexander.** 1862–1939. Finnish philosopher and anthropologist. His works include *The History of Human Marriage* (1891), *The Origin and Development of the Moral Ideas* (2 vols., 1906–08), *Early Beliefs and Their Social Influence* (1932), *Christianity and Morals* (1939), etc.

**Wes′ting·house′** (wĕs′tĭng·hous′), **George.** 1846–1914. American inventor and manufacturer, b. Central Bridge, N.Y. Invented air brake (first used on passenger trains in 1868) and organized (1869) Westinghouse Air Brake Co. to manufacture it. Also invented automatic railroad signal devices and was one of organizers of Union Switch & Signal Co. (1882). Interested himself in use of electricity; became pioneer in introducing in America the high-voltage alternating-current single-phase system for transmission of electricity, and organized (1886) Westinghouse Electric Co. for manufacturing and marketing purposes. Also patented a number of devices for practicable and economical transmission of natural gas. Took out altogether more than 400 patents during his lifetime. Elected to American Hall of Fame (1955).

**Westley.** Variant of WESLEY.

**West′ma·cott** (wĕs(t)′mȧ·kŭt), Sir **Richard.** 1775–1856. English sculptor; executed monumental statues in St. Paul's Cathedral and Westminster Abbey. His son **Richard** (1799–1872), sculptor of portraits and monuments, followed him as professor of sculpture, Royal Academy (1857–67).

**West′min′ster** (wĕs(t)′mĭn′stēr), **Matthew of.** Name long accepted as that of author of *Flores Historiarum,* a Latin chronicle of England from creation to 1326 (first printed 1567), which was shown by Henry Richards Luard (1825–1891) to be a compilation by various writers at abbeys of St. Albans and Westminster.

**Westmorland.** (1) Barons of. See CLIFFORD family. (2) Earls of. See NEVILLE family; John FANE.

**Wes′ton** (wĕs′tŭn), **Edward.** 1850–1936. American electrical scientist, b. London, Eng. To U.S. (1870); built first successful dynamo for electroplating (1872); established at Newark, N.J., first factory in U.S. devoted to manufacture of dynamo-electric machinery (1875). Invented improved cell, known as *Weston cadmium cell,* which was adopted (1908) as official standard of electromotive force by International Electric Commission. Patented many devices in field of incandescent and arc electric lighting.

**Weston, Richard.** 1st Earl of **Port′land** (pōrt′lănd; pôrt′-). 1577–1635. English political leader; chancellor of exchequer (1621); lord high treasurer (1628–33).

**Weston, Thomas.** 1575?–?1644. English adventurer and colonist in America; sent out expedition to Plymouth (1622) and himself landed there (1623), organizing trading trips up and down New England coast; took his expedition to Virginia (1624) and later to Maryland; settled in Maryland and received grant of 1200 acres (1642) in that colony.

**Wes′to′ver** (wĕs′tō′vēr), **Oscar.** 1883–1938. American army officer; chief of air corps, U.S. army (1935–38); killed in airplane accident.

**West′phal** (vĕst′fäl), **Rudolf Georg Hermann.** 1826–1892. German classical philologist; author of works on Greek metrics, rhythm, and music, including *Metrik der Griechischen Dramatiker und Lyriker* (with August Rossbach; 3 vols., 1854–65).

**West′-Wat′son** (wĕst′wŏt′s'n), **Campbell West.** 1877–1953. Anglican prelate in New Zealand, b. Liverpool, Eng.; bishop of Christchurch, New Zealand (from 1926); installed as primate and archbishop of New Zealand (1940).

**West′wood** (wĕst′wŏŏd), **John Obadiah.** 1805–1893. English entomologist.

**Wetherell, Elizabeth.** Pseudonym of Susan Bogert WARNER.

**Weth′er·ill** (wĕth′ēr·ĭl), **Samuel.** 1736–1816. American industrialist and Quaker; took oath of allegiance to American colonies, and expressed approval of war in defense of their rights; thereupon was cut off from Quaker fellowship (1777); one of organizers of body called Free, or Fighting, Quakers; is portrayed as a character in S. Weir Mitchell's novel *Hugh Wynne, Free Quaker.* Founded chemical firm (1785); first to produce white lead in the U.S. (1790). His great-grandson **Samuel Wetherill** (1821–1890) was associated with Wetherill & Brother, chemical manufacturers, developed from the original business; joined New Jersey Zinc Co. (1850) and invented process (1852) for deriving white oxide of zinc directly from the ore. The latter's son **John Price** (1844–1906) invented the Wetherill furnace and the Wetherill magnetic concentrating process for the treatment of refractory ores.

**Wet'more** (wĕt'mōr), **Alexander.** 1886– . American biologist, b. North Freedom, Wis.; A.B., Kansas (1912), Ph.D., George Washington (1920); with Biological Survey, U.S. Dept. of Agriculture (1910–24); assistant secretary, Smithsonian Inst., in charge of U.S. National Museum (1925– ). Authority on bird migration; author of *The Migration of Birds* (1927), *Fossil Birds of North America* (1931), *Systematic Classification for Birds of the World* (1940), etc.

**Wette, De.** See DE WETTE.

**Wet'ter·bergh'** (vĕt'tẽr·băr'y'), **Carl Anton.** *Pseudonym* **On'kel A'dam'** (ông'kĕl ä'dȧm'). 1804–1889. Swedish author of humorous stories and sketches of everyday life, and of social tales and novels.

**Wet·tin'** (vĕ·tēn'). A German family of nobility, originated in the 10th century; later (c. 1104) took name from castle on the Saale near Halle; acquired additional lands, margraviate of Meissen (1130) and lower Lusatia (1135); sold lands (1288) to archbishop of Magdeburg; became very influential family (14th century); electoral duchy of Saxony (around Wittenberg; hence, **Saxe'-Wit'ten·berg** [săks'wĭt''n·bûrg; -vĭt'ĕn·bĕrk]) granted by emperor to Frederick of Wettin (1422); divided (1485) into Ernestine line and Albertine line (*qq.v.*). It had in later times in its various branches many members of European ruling houses.

**Wex'ley** (wĕks'lĭ), **John.** 1907– . American playwright, b. New York City; educ. N.Y.U.; author of *The Last Mile* (1930), *Steel* (1931), *They Shall Not Die* (1934).

**Wey'den** (vī'dĕn), **Rogier van der.** *Fr.* **Roger de La Pas'ture'** (dẽ lȧ pä'tür'). 1399?–1464. Flemish religious painter; studio at Brussels (c. 1425).

**Weyer, Johann.** See WIER.

**Weyer, Maurice Constantin-.** See CONSTANTIN-WEYER.

**Wey'er·haeu'ser** (wī'ẽr·hou'zẽr), **Frederick.** 1834–1914. Businessman, b. in Germany; to U.S. (1852); acquired vast timber holdings in Minnesota region; known as "the Lumber King."

**Wey'gand'** (vā'gäɴ'), **Maxime.** 1867–1965. French soldier, b. Brussels; grad. St. Cyr (1888); chief of Foch's general staff (1914–23); general (1916); reorganized Polish army to resist Bolshevik attack (1920); French high commissioner in Syria (1923); chief of army general staff (1930); vice-president of Higher Council of War (1931); commander in chief in Near East (1939); took over command in France during retreat (1940) but was unable to prevent German victory; under Vichy regime, military commander in North Africa (1940) and (July, 1941) governor general of Algeria; resigned both posts after conference with Pétain (Nov., 1941).

**Weyl** (vīl), **Hermann.** 1885–1955. Mathematician, b. in Germany. To U.S.; professor, Princeton (from 1933). Known for work on differential equations, relativity theory, quantum mechanics, philosophy of mathematics.

**Wey'ler y Ni'co·la'u** (wĕ'ē·lĕr [bĕ'-] ē nē'kō·lä'ōō), **Valeriano.** Marquis of **Te'ne·ri'fe** (tā'nȧ·rē'fä; *Angl.* tĕn'ẽr·ĭf', -ēf'). 1838–1930. Spanish soldier and statesman; governor and military commander of Cuba (1896–97); recalled (Oct., 1897) in response to American protest to his ruthless policy in Cuba. Minister of war (1901–02, 1905, 1906–07); captain general of Catalonia (1909); suppressed Ferrer riots (July, 1909); president, supreme war council (1910).

**Wey'man** (wā'măn), **Stanley John.** 1855–1928. English novelist; author of a series of popular cloak-and-sword romances with French historical background, including *The Red Cockade* (1895), *Under the Red Robe* (1896), *The Long Night* (1903), and of period novels with English setting, including *Chippinge* (1906), *Ovington's Bank* (1922), *The Lively Peggy* (1928).

**Wey'mouth** (wā'mŭth), 3d Viscount. See Thomas THYNNE.

**Weymouth, Richard Francis.** 1822–1902. English philologist and New Testament scholar; author of *Early English Pronunciation* (1874), *Resultant Greek Testament* (1886).

**Wey'precht** (vī'prĕkt), **Karl.** 1838–1881. German arctic explorer; on expedition with Payer to Spitsbergen and Novaya Zemlya (1871); with Payer, leader of Austro-Hungarian expedition (1872–74) which discovered Franz Josef Land.

**Weyr** (vīr), **Rudolf von.** 1847–1914. Viennese sculptor, chiefly in the baroque style.

**Whal'ley** (hwā'lĭ; hwô'lĭ), **Edward.** d. 1675? English regicide; served in Puritan army in the English Civil War, and engaged at Marston Moor and at Naseby; entrusted with care of King Charles I (1647); member of court that tried Charles I and a signer of the king's death warrant; at Restoration, fled to New England and remained in hiding the rest of his life.

**Wharncliffe,** Baron. See *earls of Bute*, under STEWART family.

**Whar'ton** (hwôr't'n). Name of an old north of England family, including: **Thomas** (1495?–1568), 1st Baron Wharton (cr. 1544), supporter of Henry VIII against Scottish insurgents. His descendant **Philip** (1613–1696), 4th Baron Wharton, a strong Puritan; opposed court party in House of Lords, Long Parliament (1640); discontinued army service on routing of his regiment at Edgehill (1642); declined part in public affairs during Commonwealth and Protectorate; declared for William of Orange (1688).

**Thomas** (1648–1715), 1st Marquis of Wharton (cr. 1715), son of 4th baron; author of *Lilli Burlero, Bullen-a-la* (1687), a doggerel ballad ridiculing Irish papists; controller of William of Orange's household (1689–1702); created earl (1706); lord lieutenant of Ireland (1708–10), with Addison as secretary; attacked by Swift in *Examiner* (No. 14); received dedication of Addison's *Spectator* (vol. 5); joined Whigs in proclaiming George I (1714).

**Philip** (1698–1731), Duke of Wharton, son of 1st marquis; supported government in Irish House of Peers; forced as result of profligacy to sell estates and pictures (1723–30); satirized by Pope in *Moral Essays* (i. 179); supported cause of Old Pretender; served with Spaniards against English at Gibraltar (1727); outlawed and shorn of title and estates (1729).

**Wharton, Anne Hollingsworth.** 1845–1928. American writer, known for books on American colonial customs and society, as *Colonial Days and Dames* (1895), *English Ancestral Homes of Noted Americans* (1915); also wrote *An English Honeymoon* (1908), *A Rose of Old Quebec* (1913).

**Wharton, Anthony.** Pseudonym of Alister MCALLISTER.

**Wharton, Edith Newbold,** *nee* **Jones.** 1862–1937. American novelist; m. Edward Wharton (1885). Author of *The Valley of Decision* (1902), *The House of Mirth* (1905), *Ethan Frome* (1911), *The Age of Innocence* (1920; awarded Pulitzer prize), *A Son at the Front* (1923), *Twilight Sleep* (1927), *The Children* (1928), *Hudson River Bracketed* (1929), *Certain People* (1930), and an autobiography.

**Wharton, Francis.** 1820–1889. American jurist and clergyman, b. Philadelphia; practiced law in Philadelphia; ordained deacon and priest in Protestant Episcopal

Church (1862); professor, Episcopal Theol. Sem., Cambridge, Mass. (1871–81); on staff of U.S. Department of State (1885–89); author of legal treatises and two books on religious topics.

**Wharton, Joseph.** 1826–1909. American industrialist; developed first commercially successful production of spelter in U.S. Bought a nickel mine in Pennsylvania (1864); for many years, only U.S. producer of refined nickel; developed process (1875) for making pure malleable nickel. A founder of Swarthmore College; benefactor of U. of Pennsylvania, which with his gifts established Wharton School of Finance and Commerce.

**Wharton, Thomas.** 1614–1673. English physician; discoverer of Wharton's duct (from the submaxillary gland into the mouth).

**Wharton, William H.** 1802–1839. Revolutionary leader in Texas, b. in Albemarle County, Va. Planter in eastern Texas (from 1827). President of convention (1833) which undertook task of writing constitution for Texas after it should become separated from Mexico. Sent to U.S. to get aid (Nov. 12, 1835) for Texas revolutionaries. Minister of the Republic of Texas to U.S. (1836), charged with negotiations for recognition of Texas and final annexation to U.S.

**Whate'ly** (hwāt'lĭ), **Richard.** 1787–1863. English logician and theologian. Author of *Logic* (the quintessence of his deductive analysis and rationalistic views, 1826), and *Rhetoric* (1828); satirized skepticism by reducing to absurdity the application of logic to the Scriptures in *Historic Doubts Relative to Napoleon Bonaparte* (1819). Archbishop of Dublin (1831–63). Opposed Tractarian movement, supported Roman Catholic emancipation, advocated state endowment of Catholic clergy; a founder of Broad-Church policy; exerted himself in favor of common unsectarian religious education for Protestant and Roman Catholic schools (1831–53), and wrote manuals suited to the purpose. Author of religious books; edited Bacon's *Essays* and Paley's *Evidences* and *Moral Philosophy;* edited *A Selection of English Synonyms* (1851), prepared by his daughter E. Jane Whately, who published his *Life and Correspondence...*(1866).

**Wheat'ley** (hwēt'lĭ), **Henry Benjamin.** 1838–1917. English scholar and bibliographer; one of founders of Early English Text Society; edited complete edition of Samuel Pepys's *Journal* (1893–97).

**Wheatley, John.** 1869–1930. British labor leader; joined Independent Labor party (1908); M.P. (1922); as minister for health in first Labor cabinet, responsible for housing act (1924) providing fifteen-year building program of low-rent houses.

**Wheatley, Phillis.** 1753?–1784. Poet, b. in Africa. Kidnaped and taken as slave to Boston (c. 1761); maidservant to wife of John Wheatley, Boston; m. John Peters, a free Negro (1778). At age of 13 began writing poetry, in English; regarded as a prodigy in Boston; to England (1773), where she achieved great popularity; published *Poems on Various Subjects, Religious and Moral* (1773).

**Wheatley, William.** 1816–1876. American actor and theatrical manager; played chiefly in Philadelphia (1842–52); theater manager in Philadelphia and New York (from 1852); greatest success came when he introduced *The Black Crook* (1866).

**Whea'ton** (hwē't'n), **Henry.** 1785–1848. American jurist and diplomat, b. Providence, R.I.; practiced law in Providence; U.S. minister to Prussia (1837–46); author most notably of *Elements of International Law* (1836, with succeeding editions published for nearly a century later).

**Wheat'stone** (hwēt'stōn; *Brit. usu.* -stŭn), Sir **Charles.** 1802–1875. English physicist and inventor, b. Gloucester. Carried on researches in electricity, light, and sound; suggested the stereoscope; demonstrated velocity of electricity in a conductor; with William F. Cooke, devised an electric telegraph for transmitting messages (patented 1837) and a single-needle apparatus (patented 1845); made improvements on the dynamo; invented the concertina (1829), an automatic telegraph, the kaleidophon, a device (Wheatstone's bridge) for measuring electrical resistances.

**Whe'don** (hwē'd'n), **Daniel Denison.** 1808–1885. American Methodist Episcopal clergyman; editor, *Methodist Quarterly Review* (1856–84); widely known for his work on Whedon's Bible commentaries, *Commentaries on the New Testament* (5 vols., 1860–80) and *Commentaries on the Old Testament* (9 vols., of which he supervised preparation of first four).

**Whee'ler** (hwē'lẽr), **Benjamin Ide.** 1854–1927. American educator, b. Randolph, Mass.; president, U. of California (1899–1919); guided large expansion.

**Wheeler, Burton Kendall.** 1882–1975. American lawyer and politician; began practice at Butte, Mont.; U.S. senator from Montana (1923–47); Progressive party candidate for vice-president of the United States, on ticket headed by Robert M. La Follette (1924).

**Wheeler, John Archibald.** 1911– . American physicist, b. Jacksonville, Fla. At Princeton U. (1938– ); recipient of Enrico Fermi award (1968) for his work on nuclear fission.

**Wheeler, Joseph.** 1836–1906. American army officer and politician, b. near Augusta, Ga.; grad. U.S.M.A., West Point (1859). Resigned from U.S. army to join Confederate service (1861); commander of the cavalry of the Army of the Mississippi (1862); lieutenant general (Feb., 1865). Cotton planter and lawyer, Wheeler, Ala. (from 1868). Member, U.S. House of Representatives (1881–82; 1883; 1885–1900). Widely known for his efforts to promote complete reconciliation between the North and the South. Commissioned major general of volunteers at outbreak of Spanish-American War; commanded cavalry division in Shafter's army, brought on engagement at Las Guasimas (June 24, 1898), and was present at San Juan Hill (July 1, 1898). Commanded brigade in the Philippines (1899). Retired (1900).

**Wheeler, Nathaniel.** 1820–1893. American industrialist, b. Watertown, Conn. Took over manufacture of Allen B. Wilson's newly invented sewing machine, engaging Wilson to superintend the factory (1850). Reorganized company (1851 and 1853), locating plant in Bridgeport, Conn. (1856); remained president of the company until his death.

**Wheeler, Post.** 1869–1956. American journalist, diplomat, and writer; U.S. minister to Paraguay (1929–33), Albania (1933–34); author of *Love-in-a-Mist* (verse; 1901), *Russian Wonder Tales* (1910), *Albanian Wonder Tales* (1936), *Ho-Dan-Fo* (12 vols., 1938), etc.

**Wheeler, Schuyler Skaats.** 1860–1923. American inventor and industrialist; founded (1888), with Francis B. Crocker, the Crocker-Wheeler Co., and served as its president (from 1889); author of *Practical Management of Dynamos and Motors* (with F. B. Crocker, 1894).

**Wheeler, Wayne Bidwell.** 1869–1927. American lawyer; general counsel, Anti-Saloon League of America (1915–27); leading figure in prohibition movement, reaching success in passage and ratification of the eighteenth amendment to the U.S. Constitution (1919). Claimed authorship of what is known as the Volstead Act.

**Wheeler, William Adolphus.** 1833–1874. American lexicographer; assistant (1856–60) to Joseph E. Worcester in preparing *Dictionary of the English Language*

(1860). On staff of G. & C. Merriam Co., publishers of *Webster's Dictionary* (from 1860), assisting in preparing an edition of the unabridged dictionary (1864) and various abridgments in the Merriam-Webster series. Compiled *A Manual of English Pronunciation and Spelling* (with Richard Soule, 1861), *Dictionary of the Noted Names of Fiction* (1865), etc.

**Wheeler, William Almon.** 1819–1887. American lawyer and politician, b. Malone, N.Y.; member, U.S. House of Representatives (1861–63; 1869–77); author of compromise agreement, known as the Wheeler Compromise, by which a disputed election in Louisiana (1874) was satisfactorily settled; vice-president of the United States (1877–81).

**Wheeler, William Morton.** 1865–1937. American zoologist; author of *Social Life among the Insects* (1923), *Demons of the Dust, a Study in Insect Behavior* (1930), etc.

**Whee′lock** (hwē′lŏk), **Eleazar.** 1711–1779. American Congregational clergyman and educator, b. Windham, Conn. Tutored American Indians (from 1743) and planned widespread system of education for these people; plans failed (c. 1768) because of governmental disapproval and unsatisfactory results among the Indian graduates of his school. Thereupon, obtained charter (Dec. 13, 1769) for new college, Dartmouth Coll., which he established, with funds originally raised for his Indian education scheme, in Hanover, N.H.; first president of Dartmouth (1770–79). His son **John** (1754–1817) succeeded him as president of Dartmouth (1779–1817); last twelve years of administration marked by dispute with trustees of the college, bringing legislative interference, the legislature passing a bill changing name of Dartmouth College to Dartmouth University and enlarging number of trustees to give Wheelock adherents control of the university; result was court action brought by trustees of the college to maintain their rights under the original charter, the famous Dartmouth College Case decided (1818) in favor of the college by the Supreme Court of the United States.

**Wheelock, John Hall.** 1886–1978. American editor and poet; author of *Verses by Two Undergraduates* (with Van Wyck Brooks; 1905), *The Human Fantasy* (1911), *The Beloved Adventure* (1912), *Love and Liberation* (1913), *The Black Panther* (1922), *The Bright Doom* (1927), etc.

**Wheelock, Warren.** 1880–1960. American painter and sculptor; best known for his paintings and sculptures of men famous in American history.

**Wheel′wright** (hwēl′rīt), **Edmund March.** 1854–1912. Descendant of John Wheelwright. American architect, b. Roxbury, Mass. Office in Boston (1883); Boston city architect (1891–95). Designed the Cambridge bridge over the Charles River, the bridge over the Connecticut at Hartford; consultant on the Boston Museum of Fine Arts building and the Cleveland Museum of Art building.

**Wheelwright, John.** 1592?–1679. Clergyman in America, b. in England. To America (1636); involved in Antinomian controversy, defending his sister-in-law Anne Hutchinson; arrested, tried, and found guilty of sedition and contempt of the civil authority (1637); disfranchised and banished from Massachusetts. Settled and became pastor at Exeter, N.H., later at Wells, Me. (to 1646). On his application, expressing repentance and asking remission of sentence, his sentence was reversed (1644). Pastor at Hampton, N.H. (1647–?55) and Salisbury, N.H. (1662–79).

**Wheelwright, William.** 1798–1873. Descendant of John Wheelwright. American enterpriser in South America; most notable achievement, the trans-Andean railroad linking Argentina on the Atlantic with Chile on the Pacific, planned and begun during his lifetime and finished in 1910.

**Whet′stone** (hwĕt′stōn), **George.** 1544?–?1587. English playwright and author; his *Promos and Cassandra* (1578), a tale in prose from Cynthius's *Hecatommithi*, was used by Shakespeare in *Measure for Measure.*

**Whew′ell** (hū′ĕl), **William.** 1794–1866. English philosopher and mathematician; professor of moral philosophy, Cambridge (1838–55), master of Trinity Coll. (1841–66), vice-chancellor of university (1843, 1856); instituted tripos of moral science and tripos of natural science (1848); author of *Astronomy and General Physics* (first of the Bridgewater Treatises, 1833), *History of the Inductive Sciences* (1837), *Plurality of Worlds* (1853).

**Whib′ley** (hwĭb′lĭ), **Charles.** 1859–1930. English scholar and critic; contributed for quarter century to *Blackwood's Magazine;* author of critical and historical essays, literary studies, political portraits.

**Which′cote** *or* **Whitch′cote** (hwĭch′kŭt), **Benjamin** 1609–1683. English philosophical theologian; member, probably founder, of Cambridge Platonists.

**Whip′ple** (hwĭp′'l), **Abraham.** 1733–1819. American naval officer, b. Providence, R.I. Commissioned captain in the Continental navy (1775); captured and brought to port eight East Indiamen, with cargoes worth over $1,000,000 (1779).

**Whipple, Edwin Percy.** 1819–1886. American critic and essayist, b. Gloucester, Mass.; author of *Essays and Reviews* (2 vols., 1848–49), *Lectures on...Literature and Life* (1850), *Character and Characteristic Men* (1866), *Success and Its Conditions* (1871), *American Literature ...*(1887), etc.

**Whipple, George Hoyt.** 1878–1976. American pathologist, b. Ashland, N.H. A.B., Yale (1900); M.D., Johns Hopkins (1905). Resident pathologist, Johns Hopkins Hospital (1910–14); professor, California (1914–21); professor of pathology, School of Medicine and Dentistry, U. of Rochester (1921–55; dean, 1921–53). Shared Nobel prize (1934) with Dr. George Minot and Dr. William P. Murphy. Known esp. for experiments proving that liver aided in cases of anemia in animals.

**Whipple, Guy Montrose.** 1876–1941. American author of books on educational psychology.

**Whipple, Henry Benjamin.** 1822–1901. American Protestant Episcopal clergyman; consecrated first bishop of Minnesota (1859). Became convinced of injustice and cruelty of government's system of handling the Indians, and by pleas to the government finally succeeded in obtaining much-needed reforms.

**Whipple, Squire.** 1804–1888. American civil engineer; known esp. as bridgebuilder, and inventor of a truss (the Whipple truss) of trapezoidal form used in bridge construction.

**Whipple, William.** 1730–1785. American Revolutionary leader, b. Kittery, Me. Shipmaster (c. 1750–60); merchant at Portsmouth, N.H. (1760–75). Member, Continental Congress (1776–79), and a signer of Declaration of Independence; commanded militia contingents in the Saratoga campaign (1777) and the Rhode Island campaign (1778). Associate justice of the superior court in New Hampshire (1782–85).

**Whis′tler** (hwĭs′lẽr), **James Abbott McNeill.** 1834–1903. American painter and etcher, b. Lowell, Mass. Cadet at U.S.M.A., West Point (1851–54); discharged for failure in chemistry. To Paris (1855) to continue study of painting, and never thereafter returned to U.S.; painted in studios in Paris and in London alternately. Published his first group of etchings in Paris (1858). Achieved recognition by series of great paintings, including *The White Girl* (rejected at the Royal Academy in 1863 and a sensation later in the Salon des Refusés), *Portrait of My Mother* (exhibited, 1872; now in Musée de Luxembourg), portraits of Carlyle, Miss Alexander, Rosa Corder, the *Peacock Room*, and a series, *Nocturnes*. Gained great notoriety by suing John Ruskin (1878) for slander because of criticisms by Ruskin of one of Whistler's paintings; won verdict and one farthing damages, wearing the coin thereafter as a watch charm. Recognition of his genius came slowly, somewhat retarded by his pugnacity and personal idiosyncrasies. Excelled also as an etcher; his *Thames Series* (1871) placed him in first rank; later published *First Venice Series* (1880) and *Second Venice Series* (1881). Author of *The Gentle Art of Making Enemies* (1890). Others among his notable paintings are *Rose Whistler; Lady in a Fur Jacket; At the Piano; Blue Wave, Biarritz; Trafalgar Square; Westminster Bridge*. Elected to American Hall of Fame (1930).

**Whistler, Laurence.** 1912– . English poet; author of *Four Walls*, awarded gold medal presented by the king for best volume of verse published in England in 1934.

**Whistler, Rex John.** 1905–1944. English painter and illustrator; known for murals in the Tate Gallery and in Haddon Hall in Derbyshire, and for book illustrations (*Gulliver's Travels, Desert Islands*, etc.).

**Whis'ton** (hwĭs'tŭn), **William.** 1667–1752. English theologian and mathematician. Succeeded Newton as Lucasian professor of mathematics, Cambridge (1701); expelled (1710) from university on account of his Arian views, later promulgated in *Primitive Christianity Revived* (1711–12); known for his translation of Josephus (1737). See Thomas CHUBB.

**Whit'a·ker** (hwĭt'ȧ·kẽr), Sir **Frederick.** 1812–1891. New Zealand political leader, b. in England; to N.Z. (1840); premier (1863–64; 1882–83).

**Whitaker, Joseph.** 1820–1895. English publisher; edited *Gentleman's Magazine* (1856–59); founded the *Bookseller* (1858); started (1868) *Whitaker's Almanack*, annual book of reference.

**Whitchcote, Benjamin.** See WHICHCOTE.

**Whit'church** *or* **Whyt'church** (hwĭt'chûrch), **Edward.** d. 1561. English publisher. With Richard Grafton published various editions of Bible and prayer book (see GRAFTON for titles).

**White** (hwīt), **Alma,** *nee* **Brid'well** (brĭd'wĕl; -wĕl). 1862–1946. American religious leader; m. (1887) Kent White, Methodist Episcopal clergyman, and became herself a Methodist evangelist. Founded (1901) and headed the Pillar of Fire Church, incorporated in Colorado (1902), headquarters in Zarephath, N.J. (from 1908).

**White, Andrew.** 1579–1656. Jesuit missionary in America, b. London, Eng.; sailed with Lord Baltimore's colonists (1633) as head of Jesuit mission; worked as missionary in Maryland colony.

**White, Andrew Dickson.** 1832–1918. American educator and diplomat, b. Homer, N.Y. With Ezra Cornell, organized Cornell U. (chartered 1865; opened 1868); president of Cornell (1868–85); also, U.S. minister to Germany (1879–81). U.S. minister to Russia (1892–94); U.S. ambassador to Germany (1897–1902). Chairman of United States delegation to the Hague Peace Conference (1899).

**White, Bouck** (bouk). 1874–1951. American Congregational clergyman, Socialist; dismissed by the church because of his Socialism. Pastor, Church of the Social Revolution, New York City (1913); sentenced to prison for political agitation (1914, 1916, and 1917). Author of *Quo Vaditis* (1913), *The Immorality of Being Rich* (1914), *Letters from Prison* (1915), *The Free City* (1919), etc.

**White, Byron R.** 1917– . American jurist, b. Fort Collins, Colo.; associate justice, U.S. Supreme Court (from 1962).

**White, Edward Douglass.** 1845–1921. American jurist, b. in La Fourche parish, La. In Confederate army (1861–63). U.S. senator (1891–94); associate justice, U.S. Supreme Court (1894–1910), chief justice (1910–21). Known for enunciation of the "rule of reason" for interpretation and application of antitrust laws.

**White, Elijah.** 1806–1879. American physician and pioneer in Oregon region; appointed (1842) government Indian agent for the Northwest. Gathered party of about 120 emigrants and (1842) led them to Oregon country, the first considerable overland migration to this region, antedating by a year the Whitman expedition.

**White, Elwyn Brooks.** *Known as* **E. B. White.** 1899– . American writer, b. Mount Vernon, N.Y. Wrote *Stuart Little* (1945), *Charlotte's Web* (1952), etc.

**White, Francis.** d. 1711. English proprietor of White's Chocolate House, in St. James's St., London, famous for meetings of White's Club (originated c. 1697).

**White, George Leonard.** 1838–1895. American music teacher and choral director, b. Cadiz, N.Y.; organized (1871) and conducted (1871–85) Jubilee Singers of Fisk U., who successfully toured U.S. and Great Britain.

**White,** Sir **George Stuart.** 1835–1912. British field marshal. Won V.C. in second Afghan war (1878–80); brought end to third Burmese war (1885–86); commander in chief in India (1893–97); commanded in Natal, South Africa, and defended Ladysmith through siege of 119 days (1899–1900).

**White, Gilbert.** 1720–1793. English clergyman and naturalist; curate at Selborne; author of *Natural History and Antiquities of Selborne* (1789).

**White, Henry.** 1850–1927. American diplomat, b. Baltimore, Md.; U.S. ambassador to Italy (1905–07) and to France (1907–09); member of U.S. Peace Commission (Nov., 1918). Labored for U.S. entry into League of Nations (1918–19).

**White, Henry Kirke.** 1785–1806. English poet; attracted approval of Southey with *Clifton Grove* (1803); chief poem *The Christiad*, a fragment; known for hymn *Oft in danger, oft in woe*.

**White, Horace.** 1834–1916. American journalist, b. Colebrook, N.H.; on staff of Chicago *Tribune* (1857–74), editor in chief (1865–74); on staff (1881–99), editor in chief (1899–1903), New York *Evening Post*.

**White, Howard Judson.** 1870–1936. American architect, b. Chicago.

**White, Hugh Lawson.** 1773–1840. American lawyer and politician; presiding judge, Tennessee supreme court of errors and appeals (1809–15). U.S. senator from Tennessee (1825–40); conducted political feud with Andrew Jackson (from 1834). Nominated for president of the United States (1836); in election failed to prevent election of Van Buren, Jackson's choice.

**White, Israel Charles.** 1848–1927. American geologist; formulated (c. 1883) what is known as the "anticlinal theory" for location of petroleum and gas deposits.

**White, John.** 1590–1645. Welsh lawyer and Puritan. Called "Century White" from his *First Century of Scandalous Malignant Priests* (1643), published as chairman's report of parliamentary committee of inquiry into clerical immorality. Helped Massachusetts Bay colonists procure charter (1629), perhaps drafted it himself.

**White, John.** 1826–1891. New Zealand government official; author of *Ancient History of the Maori* (1889).

**White, John Blake.** 1781–1859. American painter; best known for historical paintings, including four in the Capitol at Washington, D.C.

**White, John Williams.** 1849–1917. American Greek scholar, b. Cincinnati, Ohio.

**White, Joseph Blan′co** (blăng′kō). 1775–1841. British theological writer, b. in Spain, of Irish Roman Catholic father and Andalusian mother. Ordained priest (1800); abandoned priesthood (1810); conducted, from England, Spanish patriotic newspaper *Español* (1810–14); took orders in English church but later became Unitarian; tutor in Whately's family, Dublin (1832–35). Author of works on Spain, evidences against Roman Catholicism, and an autobiography; best known in literature for sonnet *Night and Death*, praised by Coleridge.

**White, Margaret Bourke–.** See under Erskine CALDWELL.

**White, Maunsel.** 1856–1912. Am. inventor; collaborator with Frederick W. Taylor (*q.v.*) in inventing a process (Taylor-White process) for heat-treating high-speed steels.

**White, Patrick Victor Martindale.** 1912– . Australian writer. Wrote *Happy Valley* (1939), *The Living and the Dead* (1941), *The Aunt's Story* (1946), *Voss* (1957), *The Eye of the Storm* (1973), etc.; awarded Nobel prize for literature (1973).

**White, Peregrine.** 1620–1704. Born on the ship *Mayflower*, in Cape Cod harbor, thus being the first child of English parentage born in New England.

**White, Richard Grant.** 1821–1885. American essayist and critic, b. New York City; musical critic, *Morning Courier and New-York Enquirer* (1846–59); clerk on staff of New York Custom House (1861–78). Editor of a twelve-volume edition of *The Works of William Shakespeare* (1857–66). Among his books are *Handbook of Christian Art* (1853), *Words and Their Uses* (1870), *Every-day English* (1880), *England Without and Within* (1881), *Studies in Shakespeare* (1886). See Stanford WHITE.

**White, Stanford.** 1853–1906. Son of Richard Grant White. American architect, b. New York City. Formed firm of McKim, Mead & White (1879), with C. F. McKim and W. R. Mead. Among buildings designed by him were the Madison Square Presbyterian Church (demolished 1919), Century Club, Players Club, and Metropolitan Club, all in New York; several buildings for U. of Virginia; Battle Monument at U.S.M.A., West Point. Murdered by Harry K. Thaw in Madison Square Garden Roof (June 25, 1906).

**White, Stewart Edward.** 1873–1946. American fiction writer, b. Grand Rapids, Mich. Ph.B., Michigan (1895); major of field artillery (1917–18); author chiefly of adventure stories against a western U.S. background, as *The Blazed Trail* (1902), *The Forest* (1903), *The Rules of the Game* (1909), *The Forty Niners* (1918), *Back of Beyond* (1927), *Ranchero* (1933), *Stampede* (1942).

**White,** Sir **Thomas.** 1492–1567. English merchant; founded St. John's College, Oxford (1560), and helped found Merchant Taylors' School, London; lord mayor of London (1553).

**White, Thomas.** 1628–1698. English prelate. Chaplain (1683) to Anne (later Queen Anne, dau. of duke of York); bishop of Peterborough (1685); one of the "seven bishops" (see William SANCROFT) who petitioned against James II's Declaration of Indulgence (1688) but were acquitted of charge of seditious libel; refused to take oath of allegiance to William and Mary (1689); deprived of his see (1690).

**White, Walter Francis.** 1893–1955. American author, b. Atlanta, Ga.; B.A., Atlanta U. (1916); author of *Fire in the Flint* (novel, 1924), *Flight* (novel, 1926), *Rope and Faggot—A Biography of Judge Lynch* (1929), *A Man Called White* (autobiography, 1948). Assistant secretary (1918–29), secretary (1931–55), National Association for the Advancement of Colored People (NAACP); recipient of Spingarn Medal (1937).

**White, William.** 1748–1836. American Protestant Episcopal clergyman, b. Philadelphia. Rector of Christ Church, Philadelphia (1776–1836). Instrumental in organization of Protestant Episcopal Church in the United States, introducing principle that laity should share with clergy in government of church; drafted original constitution of the church and secured its adoption; collaborated with the clergyman William Smith in preparing American revision of Book of Common Prayer. Consecrated (in England, by Anglican bishops) first bishop of Pennsylvania (1787); presiding bishop of the church (1796–1836).

**White, William Alanson.** 1870–1937. American neurologist and psychiatrist; professor, Georgetown U. (from 1903), George Washington U. (from 1904). Author of *Outlines of Psychiatry*, *Principles of Mental Hygiene* (1917), *Foundations of Psychiatry* (1921), *The Major Psychoses* (1928), *Crimes and Criminals* (1933), etc.

**White, William Allen.** 1868–1944. Known as "the Sage of Emporia." American miscellaneous writer and journalist, b. Emporia, Kans.; educ. U. of Kansas; editor and proprietor, Emporia *Gazette* (from 1895), which he developed into one of the most notable small papers of the United States, distinguished for its editorials and its policies. Author of *The Real Issue and Other Stories* (1896), *In Our Town* (1906), *A Certain Rich Man* (1909), *In the Heart of a Fool* (1918), *The Martial Adventures of Henry and Me* (1918), *A Puritan in Babylon* (1938), *The Changing West* (1939), etc. His son **William Lindsay** (1900–1973), b. Emporia; A.B., Harvard (1924); on staff. of Emporia *Gazette*, Washington *Post* (1935), *Fortune* (1937); war correspondent in Europe (1939–40), England (1940–41); author of *What People Said* (novel; 1938), *Journey for Margaret* (1941), *They Were Expendable* (1942), *Report on the Russians* (1945). Editor and publisher of the *Gazette* (from 1944).

**White, William Hale.** *Pseudonym* **Mark Ruth′er·ford** (rŭth′ẽr·fẽrd). 1831–1913. English novelist; author of a trilogy of novels, *Autobiography of Mark Rutherford* (1881), *Mark Rutherford's Deliverance* (1885), and *The Revolution in Tanner's Lane* (1887); translated Spinoza's *Ethica* (1883).

**White,** Sir **William Henry.** 1845–1913. English naval architect; director of naval construction at the admiralty (1885–1902), responsible for designing of two hundred British warships; author of a standard *Manual of Naval Architecture* (1877).

**White′field** (hwĭt′fēld), **George.** 1714–1770. English evangelist and founder of Calvinistic Methodists. Succeeded Wesleys as leader of Methodists in Oxford; ordained in Church of England (deacon 1736, priest 1739); followed Wesleys on missionary journey to Georgia (1738), appointed minister at Savannah. Returning to England to raise funds, began open-air preaching, Bristol (1739), winning audiences of all classes by reason of oratorical and histrionic gifts; returned to Georgia and began construction of an orphanage at Savannah (1740); made evangelical tour through Virginia, Pennsylvania, New York, to Boston (1740); parted company with Wesley over predestination, became leader of rigid Calvinists (c. 1741); soon reconciled personally with Wesley, but presented by his supporters (1741) with Moorfields Tabernacle, a wooden shed near Wesley's church in London (rebuilt of brick 1753). Toured America (1744–48); made evangelizing tours of Great Britain, Ireland, and America, preaching on an average forty hours a week; compiled hymnbook (1753);

returned to America for seventh time (1769); converted his Savannah orphanage into Bethesda Coll.; died and buried at Newburyport, Massachusetts.

**White'head** (hwīt'hĕd), **Alfred North.** 1861–1947. English mathematician and philosopher, b. Isle of Thanet. Lecturer on mathematics, Trinity College, Cambridge (1885–1911), University College, U. of London (1911–14); professor, Imperial College of Science and Technology, U. of London (1914–24); to U.S.; professor of philosophy, Harvard (1924–36). Author of *Principia Mathematica* (with Bertrand Russell, 1910), *The Principles of Natural Knowledge* (1919), *Science and the Modern World* (1925), *Adventures of Ideas* (1933), *Nature and Life* (1934), etc.

**Whitehead, Charles.** 1804–1862. English poet and novelist; published *The Solitary* (poem of reflection, 1831) and *Autobiography of Jack Ketch* (1834); also wrote plays, as *The Cavalier* (1836), in blank verse.

**Whitehead, George.** 1636?–1723. English Quaker itinerant preacher and public disputant; improved legal status of the Friends through audiences with successive sovereigns Charles II to George I.

**Whitehead, John.** 1740?–1804. English clergyman and physician; one of John Wesley's three literary executors; published life of Wesley (1793–96).

**Whitehead, John Boswell.** 1872–1954. American electrical engineer; known for researches on the magnetic effect of electric displacement, single-phase railway system, measurement of high alternating voltage, etc.

**Whitehead, Robert.** 1823–1905. English inventor; invented a self-projecting underwater torpedo (1866).

**Whitehead, William.** 1715–1785. English poet laureate; wrote tragedies for Drury Lane, *The Roman Father* (1750) and *Creusa* (1754); succeeded Colley Cibber as poet laureate (1757); replied to attacks on his productions with *A Charge to the Poets* (1762); produced (1762) his most successful play, the comedy *School for Lovers.*

**White'hill** (hwīt'hĭl), **Clarence Eugene.** 1871–1932. American operatic baritone, b. Marengo, Iowa; sang, chiefly in Wagnerian roles, at Metropolitan Opera House, New York (1909–11, 1915–32) and with Chicago Opera Company (1911–15); also appeared at Covent Garden (London), at the Bayreuth festivals, and at Munich.

**White'ing** (hwīt'ĭng), **Richard.** 1840–1928. English journalist and novelist. Contributed to London *Evening Star* satirical sketches later collected in book form as *Mr. Sprouts—His Opinions* (1867); known for *No. 5 John Street* (novel of London slum life, 1899) and *All Moonshine* (1907).

**White'ley** (hwīt'lĭ), **William.** 1831–1907. English founder of London's first department store. Known by self-applied epithet "Universal Provider," his boast being that there was nothing his stores could not supply.

**White'locke** (hwīt'lŏk), **Bulstrode.** 1605–1675. English lawyer and statesman. Member of Long Parliament; chairman of committee that prosecuted Strafford; one of four commissioners of Great Seal under Commonwealth (1648), one of three (1649, 1654–55), but dismissed on opposing Cromwell's changes in courts of chancery (1655); president of council of state in fall of Richard Cromwell, and member of the superseding committee of safety. Lived in retirement after Restoration.

**White'man** (hwīt'măn), **Paul.** 1891–1967. American jazz-orchestra conductor, b. Denver, Colo.; toured U.S. (1924, 1925) and England and the Continent (1926); author of *Jazz* (1926).

**White'side** (hwīt'sīd), **Walker.** 1869–1942. American actor, b. Logansport, Ind.; successful (from 1893) in Shakespearean and classical repertory; also appeared in *Mr. Wu, The Master of Ballantrae, The Royal Box,* etc.

**Whit'field** (hwĭt'fēld) *or* **Whit'feld** (-fĕld), **Henry.** 1597–?1657. English clergyman and pioneer in America, b. near London; to America (1639) and bought from Indians site of present Guilford, Conn.; settled there as pastor and worked among the Indians; returned to England (1650).

**Whit'gift** (hwĭt'gĭft), **John.** 1530?–1604. English prelate; vice-chancellor of Cambridge (1570, 1573); bishop of Worcester (1577); archbishop of Canterbury (1583–1604). Carried out Queen Elizabeth's policy of enforcing religious uniformity, giving rise to Marprelate tracts; got law passed (1593) making Puritanism an offense; one of drafters (1595) of Lambeth Articles, espousing Calvinistic views, which were disapproved by Queen Elizabeth and withdrawn; crowned James I.

**Whithals, John.** See WITHALS.

**Whit'ing** (hwīt'ĭng), **Arthur.** 1861–1936. American pianist, and composer of orchestral and chamber music, piano pieces, and songs.

**Whiting, William Fairfield.** 1864–1936. American paper manufacturer, b. Holyoke, Mass.; president of Whiting Paper Co., Holyoke; succeeded Herbert Hoover as U.S. secretary of commerce (1928).

**Whit'ley** (hwĭt'lĭ), **John Henry.** 1866–1935. English expert in employer-labor relations. Liberal M.P. (1900–28); deputy speaker of House of Commons (1911–21), speaker (1921–28); declined peerage (1928). Chairman of parliamentary committee (1917–18) proposing "Whitley councils" for employer-employee negotiations; chairman of royal commission on labor in India (1929–31); Chairman, British Broadcasting Corporation (1930–35).

**Whit'lock** (hwĭt'lŏk), **Brand.** 1869–1934. American journalist, politician, and diplomat, b. Urbana, Ohio. U.S. minister to Belgium (1913–22); after outbreak of World War (1914), gained international fame by his tact, vigor, and efficiency in handling difficult problems, and greatly aided work of Belgian relief. Author of *The 13th District* (1902), *Belgium: A Personal Record* (2 vols., 1919), *La Fayette* (2 vols., 1929), *The Stranger on the Island* (1933).

**Whitlock,** Mrs. **Elizabeth.** See Elizabeth KEMBLE.

**Whitlock, Herbert Percy.** 1868–1948. American mineralogist; curator of mineralogy, American Museum of Natural History (1918–41); author of *The Story of the Minerals* (1925), *The Story of the Gems* (1936), etc.; special editor for terms in mineralogy, *Webster's New International Dictionary, Second Edition.*

**Whit'man** (hwĭt'măn), **Al'ber·y** (?ôl'bẽr·ĭ) **Allson.** 1851–1901. American Negro clergyman of the African Methodist Episcopal Church, and poet; author of *Leelah Misled* (1873), *Not a Man and Yet a Man* (1877), *The Rape of Florida* (1884), *An Idyl of the South* (1901), etc.

**Whitman, Charles Otis.** 1842–1910. American zoologist; planned and directed Marine Biological Laboratory at Woods Hole, Mass., from its foundation (1888–1908).

**Whitman, Marcus.** 1802–1847. American missionary and pioneer, b. Rushville, N.Y. Went to Oregon region as missionary (1835, 1836–42). Returned to the East (1842–43); to Washington and conferred with the secretary of war; returning to the West, accompanied emigrants to the valley of the Columbia, Oregon (1843) and continued his work, esp. among the Indians; regarded as instrumental in securing the Oregon country for U.S. He, his wife, and twelve other persons were massacred by Indians (Nov. 29, 1847).

**Whitman, Sarah Helen,** *nee* **Pow'er** (pou'ẽr). 1803–1878. American poet, b. Providence, R.I.; m. John Winslow Whitman (1828; d. 1833). Fiancée of Edgar Allan Poe (1848), to whom Poe wrote the second of his poems entitled *To Helen;* published *Edgar Poe and His*

*Critics* (1860) in defense of Poe; *The Last Letters of Edgar Allan Poe to Sarah Helen Whitman* appeared in 1909. Her collected poems (1879) contained many associated with Poe and many closely imitating Poe's verse forms and cadences.

**Whitman, Walt** (wôlt), *in full* **Walter.** 1819–1892. American poet, b. West Hills, Long Island, N.Y.; moved to Brooklyn (1823). Variously, office boy, printer's devil, schoolteacher, typesetter, and journalist (1830?–46). Editor, Brooklyn *Eagle* (1846–48); on staff of New Orleans *Crescent* (1848); again journalist in Brooklyn (1848–54). Published volume of verse *Leaves of Grass* (1855), received unfavorably by American reviewers, revised and enlarged in later editions (1856, 1860, 1867, 1871, 1876, 1881–82, 1882, 1888–89, 1891–92). Served as hospital nurse in Washington, D.C. (1862–64). Clerk in U.S. Department of the Interior (1865); dismissed (June 30, 1865) by the secretary of the interior because of the nature of his poetry as published in *Leaves of Grass;* given position as clerk in office of attorney general of the United States (1865–73). Stricken with paralysis (Jan., 1873); lived thereafter in Camden, N.J. Appreciation of his genius came slowly, first abroad and later in U.S. Whitman conceived of himself as the great poet of democracy, but his poetry has never been popular with the masses. Others of his books are *Drum-Taps* (1865), *Passage to India* (1871), *Democratic Vistas* (1871), *Memoranda During the War* (1875), *Two Rivulets* (1876), *Specimen Days and Collect* (1883), *November Boughs* (1888), *Goodbye, My Fancy* (1891). Among famous single poems are: *Out of the Cradle Endlessly Rocking* and the poems in memory of Lincoln *When Lilacs Last in the Dooryard Bloom'd* and *O Captain! My Captain!* Elected to American Hall of Fame (1930).

**Whit′mer** (hwĭt′mẽr), **David.** 1805–1888. American Mormon leader; brought Joseph Smith to the Whitmer farm (1829) where the translation of the *Book of Mormon* was completed (June, 1829); baptized by Smith into the new religion and was one of the three witnesses privileged by divine oracle to examine the golden plates and give evidence as to their supernatural source but material nature. Accompanied Smith to Ohio and Missouri; president of the High Council of Zion (1834–36); had differences of opinion with Smith; excommunicated (Apr., 1838). Resided thereafter in Richmond, Mo. where (c. 1867), with a few followers, he revived the "Church of Christ," founded a journal, and began proselyting; had about 150 members of his church at time of his death.

**Whit′ney** (hwĭt′nĭ), **Ad′e·line** (ăd′ĕ·lĭn) **Dutton,** *nee* **Train** (trān). 1824–1906. American writer, b. Boston; m. Seth D. Whitney (1843); author chiefly of books for girls; also published volumes of verse.

**Whitney, Anne.** 1821–1915. American sculptor, b. Watertown, Mass. Studio in Watertown (1860), Boston (from 1872). Among her notable works are the heroic statue of Samuel Adams, in Statuary Hall, Capitol building, Washington, D.C.; Charles Sumner, in Harvard Square, Cambridge, Mass.; and the portrait busts of Harriet Beecher Stowe, Frances Willard, Lucy Stone, etc.

**Whitney, Eli.** 1765–1825. American inventor, b. Westboro, Mass. Grad. Yale (1792). Guest on plantation of Mrs. Nathanael Greene, in Georgia (1792–93); drawing-room conversation and a suggestion from his hostess led him to experiment with machine for cleaning seed from cotton fibers; invented cotton gin (1793; patented 1794); entered partnership with Phineas Miller, manager of Mrs. Greene's plantation, to manufacture cotton gins, but partners failed to profit because of infringements and long litigation. Importance of invention immediately manifest in enormous increase of cotton production. Turned attention to manufacture of firearms; obtained government contract for 10,000 stand of arms, deliverable within two years; devised the system of manufacturing interchangeable parts in production of guns, probably first instance of this important system; secured other firearms contracts and operated factory at Whitneyville, near New Haven, Conn. Elected to American Hall of Fame (1900).

**Whitney, Gertrude Vanderbilt.** See under William Collins WHITNEY.

**Whitney, Harry Payne.** See under William Collins WHITNEY.

**Whitney, Josiah Dwight.** 1819–1896. American scientist, b. Northampton, Mass. On geological survey work in Michigan (1847–49); geological consultant, offices in Cambridge (1850); state geologist of California (1860–74); professor, Lawrence Scientific School, Harvard (1875–96); discoverer of Calaveras skull (1886), in Calaveras, Calif. Author of *Metallic Wealth of the United States* (1854), *Climatic Changes of Later Geological Times* (1882), etc. On editorial staff of *Encyclopaedia Britannica,* 9th edition, and *The Century Dictionary and Cyclopedia.* His brother **William Dwight** (1827–1894) was a philologist; professor, Yale (1854–94); noted as a scholar in Sanskrit and in linguistic science, as a teacher of modern languages, and as a lexicographer; author of *Sanskrit Grammar* (1879), and a number of Sanskrit texts, *Language and the Study of Language* (1867), *Oriental and Linguistic Studies* (2 vols., 1873, 1874), *The Life and Growth of Language* (1875), *Essentials of English Grammar* (1877), *Max Müller and the Science of Language; a Criticism* (1892); editor of the 1864 edition of *Webster's Dictionary;* editor in chief of *The Century Dictionary and Cyclopedia* (6 vols., 1889–91).

**Whitney, Mary Watson.** 1847–1920. American astronomer; professor of astronomy and director of observatory (1888–1910), Vassar. Published observations on positions of comets and asteroids, on variable stars, and on the measurement of photographic plates.

**Whitney, Myron William.** 1836–1910. American concert and operatic basso.

**Whitney, William Collins.** 1841–1904. American financier and politician, b. Conway, Mass. Adm. to bar (1865); practiced in New York; corporation counsel, New York City (1875–82). Prominent in affairs of New York's street-railway system (1883–1902). U.S. secretary of the navy (1885–89). Widely known as a sportsman, owner of a stud farm and a racing stable, and interested in reviving horse racing at Saratoga, N.Y. A son, **Harry Payne** (1872–1930), grad. Yale (1894), was trained to take over his father's large financial interests; associated with Guggenheim interests in ownership of mining properties in western U.S. and Mexico; noted polo player, captain of American team which won international cup from England (1909) and defended it (1911, 1913); also, continued his father's interest in horse breeding and racing; financed expedition to the South Sea (1921–22), under sponsorship of American Museum of Natural History, to collect birds of Polynesia. His wife, **Gertrude,** *nee* **Van′der·bilt** [văn′dẽr·bĭlt] (1877?–1942), sculptor, daughter of Cornelius Vanderbilt, m. Harry Payne Whitney (1896); carved Aztec fountain in Pan-American building, and the *Titanic* memorial, in Washington, D.C., equestrian statue of Col. William F. Cody, etc.; opened Whitney Museum of American Art in New York City (1931); associate member, National Academy of Design (1942).

**Whitney, William Dwight.** See under Josiah Dwight WHITNEY.

**Whitney, Willis Rodney.** 1868–1958. American chemist; director, research laboratory, General Electric Co. (1900–28), vice-president in charge of research (1928–41); known for research on solubility, colloids, electrical fever therapy, etc.

**Whit'ta·ker** (hwĭt'ȧ·kẽr), **Charles Evans.** 1901–1973. American jurist, b. near Troy, Kans. Associate justice, U.S. Supreme Court (1957–62).

**Whittaker, Edmund Taylor.** 1873–1956. English mathematician, b. in Lancashire.

**Whit'ti·er** (hwĭt'ĭ·ẽr), **John Greenleaf.** 1807–1892. Known as "the Quaker Poet." American poet, b. Haverhill, Mass. Largely self-educated; vigorous abolitionist. Among his published books are *Legends of New England in Prose and Verse* (1831), *Moll Pitcher* (1832), *Mogg Megone* (1836), *Ballads* (1838), *Lays of My Home and Other Poems* (1843), *The Voices of Freedom* (1846), *Songs of Labor* (1850), *The Panorama and Other Poems* (1856), *Home Ballads* (1860), *In War Time and Other Poems* (1864), *Snow-Bound* (1866), *Miriam and Other Poems* (1871), *Hazel Blossoms* (1875), *The Vision of Echard* (1878), *At Sundown* (1890). Among widely known individual poems are *Snow-Bound, Barbara Frietchie, Maud Muller, The Barefoot Boy.* Elected to American Hall of Fame (1905).

**Whit'ting·ham** (hwĭt'ĭng·ăm), **Charles.** 1767–1840. English printer; founded (1811) Chiswick Press; one of first to put out classics in cheap reprints; first to print India-paper editions.

**Whit'ting·ham** (hwĭt'ĭng·ăm; hwĭt''n·jăm), **William.** 1524?–1579. English prelate; assisted in translation of Bible (Geneva Bible, 1560); dean of Durham (1563).

**Whit'ting·ton** (hwĭt'ĭng·tŭn), **Richard.** 1358?–1423. English mercer and philanthropist; alderman of London (1393) and lord mayor (1397–98, 1406–07, 1419–20); M.P. (1416); made loans to Henry IV and Henry V; left legacies for rebuilding Newgate Prison, founding an almshouse, organizing Whittington College (suppressed, 1548). Became the subject of several legends.

**Whittlesey, William.** See Simon ISLIP.

**Whit'tredge** (hwĭt'rĭj), **Worthington.** 1820–1910. American painter; studio in New York (from 1859); painted chiefly landscapes of New York and New England.

**Whit'worth** (hwĭt'wûrth; -wẽrth), Sir **Joseph.** 1803–1887. English mechanical engineer and inventor; discovered method of producing an absolutely plane surface of metal; secured standardization of screw threads (Whitworth thread); devised hexagonal bore for rifles, improving their accuracy and range; discovered new way of making ductile steel for guns.

**Whym'per** (hwĭm'pẽr), **Edward.** 1840–1911. English wood engraver and alpinist. First to ascend Pointe des Écrins (1864) and other peaks in Mont Blanc group; found route up the Matterhorn (1865); visited Greenland (1867, 1872); first to reach summit of Chimborazo (1880).

**Whytchurch.** See WHITCHURCH.

**Whyte** (hwīt), **Alexander.** 1836–1921. Scottish Free Kirk clergyman; moderator (1898) of general assembly and writer on Böhme, Bunyan, Law, and others.

**Whyte, Violet.** Pseudonym of Henrietta STANNARD.

**Whyte'–Mel'ville** (hwīt'mĕl'vĭl), **George John.** 1821–1878. British novelist, b. in Scotland; captain, Coldstream Guards (1846–49); served in Turkish cavalry in Crimean War (1854); author of novels of fox hunting and steeplechasing, including *Digby Grand* (1853) and *Tilbury Nogo* (1854), and of historical novels, the best known being *The Gladiators* (1863).

**Wiart, Henry Carton de.** See CARTON DE WIART.

**Wica, L.** Pseudonym of WILLIAM, Prince of Sweden.

**Wi'chern** (vĭκ'ẽrn), **Johann Hinrich.** 1808–1881. German evangelical theologian; founder of home missions in Germany.

**Wi'chert** (vĭκ'ẽrt), **Ernst.** 1831–1902. German jurist and author of novels, comedies, historic plays, etc.

**Wick'ard** (wĭk'ẽrd), **Claude Raymond.** 1893–1967. American administrator, b. in Carroll Co., Ind.; on staff of Department of Agriculture (1933–40); U.S. secretary of agriculture (1940–45).

**Wick'er·sham** (wĭk'ẽr·shăm), **George Woodward.** 1858–1936. American lawyer; attorney general of U.S. (1909–13); president of International Arbitral Tribunal under the Young-plan treaties (1932–36).

**Wick'ham** (wĭk'ăm), Sir **Henry.** 1846–1928. English explorer and pioneer in establishing rubber plantations; brought from Brazil seeds of rubber trees from which developed rubber industry in the Far East.

**Wickham, William of.** See William of WYKEHAM.

**Wiclif** *or* **Wickliffe.** See WYCLIFFE.

**Wi'dal'** (vē'dȧl'), **Fernand,** *in full* **Georges Fernand Isidore.** 1862–1929. French physician; known esp. for work on bacterial agglutination and its application (in Widal's test) to the diagnosis of typhoid fever; advocated vaccination against typhoid fever. See Max von GRUBER.

**Wid'de·mer** (wĭd'ĕ·mẽr), **Margaret.** 1880?– . American writer, b. Doylestown, Pa.; m. Robert Haven Schauffler (1919; divorced). Author of verse, as in *Factories* (1915), *Old Road to Paradise* (1918), *Ballads and Lyrics* (1925), *Road to Downderry* (1931), *Hill Garden* (1937), fiction including *The Board Walk* (1919), *Graven Image* (1923), *Years of Love* (short stories; 1933), *Ladies Go Masked* (short stories; 1939), *Lover's Alibi* (1941), *Angela Comes Home* (1942), etc.

**Wide'ner** (wīd'nẽr), **Peter Ar·rell'** (ă·rĕl') **Brown.** 1834–1915. American businessman, b. Philadelphia; engaged in meat business; became financially interested in street railways in Philadelphia, New York, and Chicago, and in other enterprises; collected paintings, Chinese porcelains, tapestries, antiques, and other objets d'art which he bequeathed to city of Philadelphia; built and endowed Widener Memorial Industrial Training School for Crippled Children (1906). His son **Joseph Early** (1872–1943), capitalist and turfman; presented his notable art collection to the National Gallery of Art (1942). Peter's grandson **Harry Elkins** (1885–1912), bibliophile; lost on the *Titanic* (Apr. 15, 1912); the Harry Elkins Widener Memorial Library at Harvard (opened 1915) was given to the university in his honor by his mother.

**Wid'forss'** (vēd'fôrs'; -fôsh'), **Gunnar Mauritz.** 1879–1934. Painter; b. Stockholm, Sweden; to U.S. (1921), naturalized citizen (1929). Devoted himself esp. to painting scenes in Yosemite National Park, the Grand Canyon, Crater Lake, Yellowstone National Park; sometimes known as the "painter of the national parks."

**Wid'mann** (vĭt'män), **Johann.** Late 15th-century German mathematician; possibly the first to introduce the signs + and − for plus and minus.

**Widmann, Joseph Viktor.** 1842–1911. Swiss writer of plays, novels, short stories, travel descriptions, and poems.

**Wido of Spoleto.** See GUY OF SPOLETO.

**Wi'dor'** (vē'dôr'), **Charles Marie.** 1845–1937. French organist and composer, b. at Lyons; organist at Saint Sulpice, in Paris (from 1869); succeeded César Franck at Paris conservatory of music (1891); composer of a ballet, comic opera, ten symphonies for the organ, chamber music, and other choral and orchestral works.

**Widukind.** See WITTEKIND.

**Wied** (vēt), Princess of. See ELIZABETH, Queen of Rumania.

**Wied,** Count of. See HERMANN OF WIED.

**Wied,** Prince **Maximilian zu.** 1782–1867. German naturalist; wrote *Reise Nach Brasilien...1815–17* (2 vols., 1819–20), *Reise in das Innere Nord-America...1832–34* (2 vols., 1839–41), etc.

**Wied,** Prince **William of.** 1876–1945. See Prince WILLIAM OF WIED.

**Wie'de·mann** (vē'dĕ·män), **Gustav Heinrich.** 1826–1899. German physicist and chemist; known for researches in electricity and magnetism. His son **Karl Alfred** (1856–1936), Egyptologist; author of *Ägyptische Geschichte* (2 vols., 1884–88), *Das Alte Ägypten* (1920), etc.

**Wie'gand** (vē'gänt), **Theodor.** 1864–1936. German archaeologist; led excavations at Priene (1895–98), at Miletus, Didyma, and Samos (1898–1914), and at Pergamum (from 1927).

**Wie'land** (vē'länt), **Christoph Martin.** 1733–1813. German poet, prose writer, and translator. Called "the German Voltaire." Brought up a Pietist; lived chiefly in Weimar (from 1772); friend of Goethe, Schiller, and Herder. Edited *Der Teutsche Merkur*, a monthly literary magazine (1773–1810); founded and edited (1796–1809) *Das Attische Museum.* His works (45 vols., 1794–1802) are largely satirical or didactic, and include: dramas, and epics and narratives in verse, as *Lady Johanna Gray*, earliest German blank-verse drama (1758), *Idris und Zenide*, which introduced the Italian stanza into German literature (1768), *Musarion* (1768), and *Oberon* (1780); novels and romances, as the comic *Don Sylvio von Rosalva* (1764), the satire *Die Abderiten* (1774), and the historical *Aristipp* (4 vols., 1800–01); a fantastic tale, *Dschinnistan*, on which Mozart based his *Magic Flute;* and the first German prose translations of Shakespeare's plays (22 plays, 1762–66), as well as translations of Horace, Lucian, and Cicero.

**Wieland, Heinrich.** 1877–1957. German chemist; known for research on bile acids, chlorophyll, and hemoglobin. Awarded 1927 Nobel prize for chemistry.

**Wien** (vēn), **Wilhelm.** 1864–1928. German physicist. Awarded 1911 Nobel prize in physics for research on the radiation of energy from black bodies; worked also on X rays, hydrodynamics, etc. His cousin **Max Wien** (1866–1938), also a physicist, is credited with discovery of impulse excitation (1906), of importance in the development of wireless telegraphy; constructed acoustical device for measuring strength of tones.

**Wien'barg** (vēn'bärk), **Ludolf.** 1802–1872. German writer, b. Altona; lecturer on aesthetics and literature, Kiel (1833); became a leading exponent, with Gutzkow and others, in the Young Germany group, which he named.

**Wie'ner** (wē'nĕr; vē'-), **Le'o** (lē'ō). 1862–1939. Slavic scholar, b. at Bialystok, Poland; to U.S. (1882). Taught Slavic languages and literature at Harvard (1896–1930; professor from 1911). Author of *An Interpretation of the Russian People* (1915), etc. Consultant in pronunciation (Slavic languages), *Webster's New International Dictionary, Second Edition.*

**Wie·niaw'ski** (vyĕ·nyäf'skē), **Hen'ri'** (äN'rē'). 1835–1880. Polish violinist, and composer of concertos, études, and genre pieces for the violin.

**Wi'er** (vē'ĕr) *or* **Wey'er** (vī'ĕr), **Johann.** 1515–1588. Belgian physician; one of the first to challenge, and ridicule as superstition, the then universal belief in witchcraft.

**Wiertz** (vyĕrs), **Antoine Joseph.** 1806–1865. Belgian painter of historical pictures, usually of colossal size. The Musée Wiertz at Brussels was originally a studio built esp. for him by the Belgian government.

**Wier·zyń'ski** (vyĕr·zĭn'y'·skē), **Kazimierz.** 1894–1969. Polish poet; author of *The Spring and Wine* (1919), *Olympic Laurel* (1927), *The Tragic Freedom* (1936); awarded Olympic prize for poetry (1928).

**Wie'se** (vē'zĕ), **Kurt** (kŏŏrt). 1887–1974. American (German-born) author and illustrator of children's books.

**Wie'ser** (vē'zĕr), **Friedrich von.** 1851–1926. Austrian political economist; champion of the Austrian school of economists.

**Wig'gin** (wĭg'ĭn), **James Henry.** 1836–1900. American clergyman, b. Boston. Ordained in Unitarian ministry (1862); held various pastorates in Massachusetts (to 1875); editor in New York and Boston; withdrew from ministry because of agnostic views (1881). Became music and dramatic critic, and publisher's book editor. At request of Mary Baker Eddy (1885) acted as literary critic of 16th edition of *Science and Health with Key to the Scriptures;* continued this service for the revised edition of *Science and Health* (1890) and *Retrospection and Introspection* (1891). On Mrs. Eddy's behalf wrote answers to certain hostile criticism and aided in editing *The Christian Science Journal* (1887–89).

**Wiggin, Kate Douglas,** *nee* **Smith.** 1856–1923. American writer and educator, b. Philadelphia; m. Samuel Bradley Wiggin (1881; d. 1889), George Christopher Riggs (1895). Studied kindergarten training methods (1877); organized in San Francisco first free kindergarten on Pacific coast (1878); founded, with her sister **Nora Archibald Smith** (1859?–1934), California Kindergarten Training School (1880). First literary success was *The Birds' Christmas Carol* (1887). Others of her books are *Timothy's Quest* (1890), *Polly Oliver's Problem*, a story for girls (1893), *Penelope's Progress* (1898), the enormously popular *Rebecca of Sunnybrook Farm* (1903), and an autobiography, *My Garden of Memory* (1923).

**Wig'gins** (wĭg'ĭnz), **Carleton.** 1848–1932. American painter; studio in New York (from 1881); best known for his landscape and animal paintings. His son **Guy Carleton** (1883–1962), also an artist; director (from 1916) of the Guy Wiggins Art School in Lyme, Conn.

**Wig'gles·worth** (wĭg''lz·wûrth), **Michael.** 1631–1705. Clergyman and poet, b. in England; to America as a boy (1638); pastor at Malden, Mass. (from 1656); author of *The Day of Doom*, a long poem written in ballad meter (1662), *Meat Out of the Eater or Meditations Concerning the Necessity, End, and Usefulness of Afflictions Unto God's Children* (1669), etc. His son **Edward** (1693?–1765) was first Hollis professor of divinity, Harvard (1722–65). Edward's son **Edward** (1732–1794) succeeded him as Hollis professor of divinity at Harvard (1765–91); acting president of Harvard (1780).

**Wig'more** (wĭg'mōr), Barons of. See MORTIMER family.

**Wigmore, John Henry.** 1863–1943. American legal scholar, b. San Francisco; practiced law in Boston (1887–89); professor at Keio U., Tokyo, Japan (1889–92), and at Northwestern U. (1893–1929) and dean of its faculty of law (1901–29); author and editor of legal treatises.

**Wig'ner** (wĭg'nĕr), **Eugene Paul.** 1902– . American physicist, b. in Hungary. To U.S. (1930); received Enrico Fermi award (1958); also Nobel prize in physics (1963) with M. Mayer and H. Jenson.

**Wiht'red** (wĭkt'rād). King of Kent (690–725); drew up code of laws (695?).

**Wijnants, Jan.** See WYNANTS.

**Wi'la·mo'witz-Moel'len·dorff** (vē'lä·mō'vĭts·mûl'ĕn·dôrf), **Ulrich von.** 1848–1931. German classical scholar; editor of *Philologische Untersuchungen* (1880–1925); author of *Zukunftsphilologie*, an attack on Nietzsche's *Geburt der Tragödie* (1872–73), and of critical works on Greek history, literature, and writers.

**Wil'ber·force** (wĭl'bẽr·fōrs), **William.** 1759–1833. English philanthropist and antislavery crusader. Converted to evangelical Christianity through Isaac Milner, his former schoolmaster, then dean of Carlisle. Led agitation in House of Commons against slave trade (1787); through support of Thomas Clarkson, Pitt, and Quakers, won abolition of slave trade (1807); a founder of Antislavery Society (1823), urging extinction of slavery itself. Leader of the "Clapham Sect" of evangelical Christians and a founder of its organ, *The Christian Observer* (1801); supported extension of missionary teaching in India, and Catholic emancipation; expended most of fortune in philanthropy; heard on deathbed of second reading of bill abolishing slavery, which became law a month later. Buried in Westminster Abbey. Author of *Practical View of Christianity* (1797). A son, **Samuel** (1805–1873), called "Soapy Sam" because of his versatile facility, was an Anglican prelate; bishop of Oxford (1845), of Winchester (1869); diverged from Tractarians, took a leading part in several controversies; secured restoration to convocation of Canterbury and York of some of ancient authority as synodical assembly; author of *Agathos* (1840) and *History of Protestant Episcopal Church in America* (1844).

**Wil'brandt** (vĭl'bränt), **Adolf von.** 1837–1911. German novelist, dramatist, and poet; author of historic iambic tragedies in the manner of Schiller, of modern dramas and comedies, of novels and stories, and of poems, literary histories, and biographies.

**Wilbrord** *or* **Wilbrod,** Saint. See WILLIBRORD.

**Wil'bur** (wĭl'bẽr), **Cressy Livingston.** 1865–1928. American pioneer in field of vital statistics.

**Wil'bur, Curtis Dwight.** 1867–1954. American jurist, b. Boonesboro, Iowa; practiced law, Los Angeles, Calif. (from 1890); U.S. secretary of the navy (1924–29); judge, 9th U.S. circuit court of appeals (from 1929) and senior circuit judge (from 1931). His brother **Ray Lyman** (1875–1949), educator; professor of medicine (1909–16), president (1916–43), chancellor (from 1943), Stanford U.; U.S. secretary of the interior (1929–33).

**Wilbur, Samuel.** 1585?–1656. American pioneer, b. in England; to America (c. 1633) and settled in Boston; involved in Antinomian controversy and banished (1637); became one of the 18 original purchasers of Aquidneck (Rhode Island) from the Narragansett Indians, and a signer of the Portsmouth Compact organizing a government for the colony.

**Wil'bye** (wĭl'bĭ), **John.** 1574?–1638. English madrigal composer.

**Wil'cox** (wĭl'kŏks), **Cadmus Marcellus.** 1824–1890. American army officer, b. in Wayne County, N.C.; grad. U.S.M.A., West Point (1846). Resigned from U.S. army to enter Confederate service (1861). With Lee's army from first Bull Run to Appomattox; brigadier general (Oct., 1861); major general (rank from Aug., 1863).

**Wilcox, Delos Franklin.** 1873–1928. American public-utility expert; consultant on utility rates and problems, in New York City (from 1917); author of *City Problems* (1899), *The American City* (1904), *Municipal Franchises* (2 vols., 1910–11), etc.

**Wilcox, Ella,** *nee* **Wheeler.** 1850–1919. American journalist and poet, b. near Madison, Wis.; m. Robert Marius Wilcox (1884; d. 1916); for many years wrote a daily poem for a syndicate of newspapers; published over twenty volumes of verse, including *Drops of Water* (1872), *Poems of Passion* (her best-known book; 1883), *Sweet Danger* (1902), *The Art of Being Alive* (1914).

**Wilcox, Stephen.** 1830–1893. American inventor, b. Westerly, R.I. Invented safety water-tube boiler with inclined tubes (patented 1856), steam generator of similar type (patented 1867); with George Herman Babcock, organized firm Babcock, Wilcox & Co. (1867) to manufacture his boilers and steam engines.

**Wil·czyn'ski** (wĭl·zĭn'skĭ), **Ernest Julius.** 1876–1932. Mathematician, b. Hamburg, Ger.; to U.S. as a child. Excelled in knowledge of projective differential geometry, a field largely created by him.

**Wild** (vĭlt), **Heinrich von.** 1833–1902. Swiss physicist and meteorologist; observatory director, St. Petersburg (1868–94). Invented the polaristrobometer, a polarization photometer, and a magnetic theodolite.

**Wild** (wīld), **Horace B.** 1879–1940. American pioneer airman, b. Chicago; professional balloonist and parachute jumper in the 1890's; set dirigible flight record of six hours (1906); founded flying school at Lincoln, Nebraska.

**Wild, Jonathan.** 1682?–1725. English criminal. During a term in a debtors' prison, became acquainted with thieves and their ways; built criminal organization for thieving and for disposal of stolen goods; arranged for apprehension and conviction of disobedient members and nonmember criminals; hanged at Tyburn. Subject of a story by Defoe (1725) and, remotely, of Fielding's satire *Jonathan Wild* (1743).

**Wilde** (wīld), **Henry.** 1833–1919. English electrical engineer; invented a dynamo-electric machine (1864–65) generating a powerful electric light, and an electric searchlight adopted (1875) by British navy. Discovered principle of indefinite increase of magnetic and electric forces from quantities indefinitely small (1864), and new multiple relations among atomic weights by which existence of undiscovered elements and their properties have been predicted (1878). Also carried on experiments in electrolysis and magnetism.

**Wilde, Oscar Fingal O'Flahertie Wills.** 1854–1900. Irish poet, wit, and dramatist; at Oxford won Newdigate prize and became apostle of a cult affecting the doctrine of art for art's sake; burlesqued in the character Bunthorne in Gilbert and Sullivan's comic opera *Patience* (1881). Lectured in U.S. (1882) on aesthetic philosophy, gaining notoriety by aesthetic eccentricities. Wrote works of fiction, including *The Picture of Dorian Gray* (1891); published *Collected Poems* (1892); followed up *The Duchess of Padua*, a tragedy in blank verse (1891), with a series of light comedies with dexterously conceived situations and sparkling dialogue, including *Lady Windermere's Fan* (1892), *A Woman of No Importance* (1893), *An Ideal Husband* (1895), *The Importance of Being Earnest* (1895); produced drama *Salomé* in French, staged in Paris by Sarah Bernhardt (1894), later made into libretto of an opera by Richard Strauss. Tried on charge of sodomy, convicted, and imprisoned (1895–97); wrote in prison a prose apologia, *De Profundis* (1905); lived in Paris under name of **Sebastian Mel'moth** (mĕl'mŭth); wrote anonymously *Ballad of Reading Gaol* (1898), reflecting his tragic experiences.

**Wilde, Percival.** 1887–1953. American writer and playwright; author of many plays, esp. one-act plays adapted for little-theater presentation, a few novels, and some critical works.

**Wilde, Richard Henry.** 1789–1847. American lawyer, scholar, and poet, b. in Dublin, Ireland, and brought to U.S. as a child. Attorney general of Georgia (1811); member, U.S. House of Representatives (1815–17; 1825; 1827–35). Made special study of Dante and Italian literature; author of the lyric *My life is like the summer rose*, set to music by Sidney Lanier and others.

**Wilde, Thomas.** Baron **Tru'ro** (trōōr'ō). 1782–1855. English judge; Whig M.P. (1831–32, 1835–41); solicitor general (1839); attorney general (1841, 1846); chief justice of common pleas (1846–50); lord chancellor of England (1850–52).

**Wil'den·bruch** (vĭl'dĕn·broŏk), **Ernst von.** 1845–1909. Grandson of Prince Louis Frederick Christian of Prussia. German author of verse, historical and social plays, novels, and juvenile stories.

**Wil'der** (wīl'dẽr), **Burt Green.** 1841–1925. American educator and author, b. Boston, Mass.; professor of neurology and vertebrate zoology, Cornell (1867–1910). Reeled silk from spiders (1863), this type of silk being later (1865) woven into ribbon on steam loom; made anatomical preparations of nearly 2000 vertebrate brains. Composer of hymns and songs including music for O. W. Holmes's *Old Ironsides* and for Joyce Kilmer's *Peacemaker.*

**Wilder, Harris Hawthorne.** 1864–1928. American zoologist; among his books are *History of the Human Body* (1909), *Man's Prehistoric Past* (1923), *The Pedigree of the Human Race* (1926).

**Wilder, Marshall Pinckney.** 1798–1886. American businessman and civic leader, b. Rindge, N.H.; one of founders (1861), vice-president (1865–70), and trustee (1870–86), of Massachusetts Institute of Technology; in his nursery carried on extensive horticultural experiments; a leader in forming Massachusetts Agricultural College, now Massachusetts State College.

**Wilder, Marshall Pinckney.** 1859–1915. American mimic and public entertainer.

**Wilder, Russell Morse.** 1885–1959. **Am.** phys.; B.S. (1907), Ph.D. (1912), M.D. (1912), Chicago; member of Mayo Clinic, Rochester, Minn., and teacher of medicine, U. of Minn. (1919–29; 1931–50); with U.S. Public Health Ser. (1951–53). Researches include work relating to typhus fever, diabetes, metabolism, and nutrition.

**Wilder, Thornton Niven.** 1897-1975. American novelist and playwright, b. Madison, Wis.; A.B., Yale (1920); instructor in English, Lawrenceville Acad. (1921–28), U. of Chicago (1930–36); author of novels, *The Cabala* (1925), *The Bridge of San Luis Rey* (1927; awarded Pulitzer prize), *The Woman of Andros* (1930), *Heaven's My Destination* (1935), etc., and plays, *The Angel That Troubled the Waters* (1928), *Our Town* (1938; Pulitzer prize), *The Skin of Our Teeth* (1942; Pulitzer prize), etc.

**Wil'der·muth** (vĭl'dẽr·mōōt), **Ottilie,** *nee* **Roo'schütz** (rō'shüts). 1817–1877. German novelist; author of stories of Swabian life and of fiction for women and children.

**Wild'gans** (vĭlt'gäns), **Anton.** 1881–1932. Austrian poet and dramatist; author of collections of lyrics, the satirical epic poem *Kirbisch* (1927), and of plays including *Liebe* (1916), *Dies Irae* (1918), and the Biblical tragedy *Kain* (1920).

**Wil'ding** (wĭl'dĭng), **Anthony Frederick,** *called* **Tony.** 1883–1915. New Zealand lawn-tennis player; member of Australasian Davis cup team (from 1905); all England singles champion (1910–14), doubles champion (1907, 1908, 1910, 1914); killed in action at Artois.

**Wi'ley** (wī'lĭ), **Harvey Washington.** 1844–1930. American chemist and food analyst, b. Kent, Ind. Professor of chemistry, Purdue (1874–83); also, Indiana State chemist and investigator of food adulteration. Chief chemist, U.S. Department of Agriculture (1883–1912); performed great public service in leading campaign against food adulteration; instrumental in securing passage of the Food and Drugs Act by U.S. Congress (1906), and in its effective administration. Director of bureau of foods, sanitation, and health for *Good Housekeeping* magazine (1912–30). Professor of agricultural chemistry, George Washington U. (1899–1914). Wrote *Principles and Practice of Agricultural Analysis* (3 vols., 1894–97), *Foods and Their Adulteration* (1907), *History of a Crime Against the Food Law* (1929), etc.

**Wiley, Hugh.** 1884–1968. American author of stories of American Negro characters and life, as in *The Wildcat* (1920), *Lily* (1923), *Here's Luck* (1928).

**Wil'fley** (wĭl'flĭ), **Arthur Redman.** 1860–1927. American mining engineer and inventor, b. Maryville, Mo.; invented the Wilfley table, a type of sand table used for concentrating ores.

**Wil'frid** (wĭl'frĭd) *or* **Wil'frith** (wĭl'frĭth), Saint. 634–709. English prelate. Determined by his argument at Whitby (664) overthrow of the Celtic or Columbite party by the Roman discipline in England. Bishop of York, taking over his see in 668 or 669; built churches of architectural splendor (669–678); journeyed to Rome to recover his divided bishopric, thus establishing a precedent.

**Wil'gus** (wĭl'gŭs), **William John.** 1865–1949. American engineer; consulting engineer (1908–30); chairman of board of consulting engineers for building vehicular tunnel under Hudson River connecting New York and New Jersey (1919–22).

**Wil'helm** (vĭl'hĕlm). German form of WILLIAM.

**Wilhelm.** Duke of Brunswick. See BRUNSWICK.

**Wilhelm, Karl.** 1815–1873. German director of the choral society, Krefeld (1840–65), and composer of the music to Max Schneckenburger's *Die Wacht am Rhein* (1854).

**Wil'helm** (vĭl'hĕlm), **Richard.** 1873–1930. German Sinologue and theologian; missionary and pastor, Tsingtao (1899–1921); councilor of German legation, Peking (1922).

**Wilhelm von Hir'sau** (fôn hĭr'zou) *or* **Hir'schau** (hĭr'shou). d. 1091. Bavarian abbot (from 1071) of Benedictine monastery at Hirsau in Black Forest; author of *Constitutiones Hirsaugienses* (pub. 1854), *De Musica* (a treatise on music theory; pub. 1883), legends, works on philosophy and astronomy, etc.

**Wil'hel·mi'na** (wĭl'hĕl·mē'nȧ; wĭl'ĕ·mē'nȧ; *Du.* vĭl'hĕl-mē'nȧ). *In full* **Wilhelmina Helena Pauline Maria.** 1880-1962. Queen of the Netherlands (1890–1948). Dau. of William III and Emma of Waldeck-Pyrmont; b. at The Hague. Government under her mother as regent (1890–98); declared of age (1898); m. (1901) Duke Henry of Mecklenburg-Schwerin; one daughter, Juliana (*q.v.*); abdicated.

**Wil·hel'mj** (vĭl·hĕl'mĕ), **August.** 1845–1908. German violin virtuoso, and composer of several pieces for the violin, transcriptions from Bach, Chopin, and Wagner, etc.

**Wilkes** (wĭlks), **Charles.** 1798–1877. American naval officer, b. New York City. Commanded exploring expedition (1838–42) to the antarctic islands of the Pacific, and northwest coast of America; Wilkes Land in the Antarctic Continent is named in his honor; published *Narrative of the United States Exploring Expedition* (5 vols., 1844). Commanded *San Jacinto* (1861), halted British mail steamer *Trent* near the Bahamas and took off by force two Confederate commissioners, James M. Mason and John Slidell (Nov. 8, 1861); after vigorous British protest, the "Trent affair" was settled by return of the Confederate commissioners to the British.

**Wilkes, John.** 1727–1797. English political reformer. Joined the "Mad Monks of Medmenham Abbey" (see Sir Francis DASHWOOD); M.P. (1757); led profligate life. Founded *The North Briton* (1762), in which he attacked Lord Bute and charged George III with falsehood (issue No. 45; 1763); prosecuted for libel but obtained verdict, with damages for illegal arrest, against the secretary of state (1769). Expelled from House of Commons (1764) for seditious libel; outlawed for failing to stand trial. Returned from Continent (1768) and elected M.P.; stood trial on the old libel charge and was fined and imprisoned. Expelled from house on taking his seat (1769) and immediately re-elected and re-expelled, a third election being declared by the house in favor of his opponent, who had polled fewer votes. Became idol of mob, rioting for "Wilkes and liberty," and supported by London merchants; championed program of parliamentary reform, including suppression of rotten boroughs, and safeguarding of individual liberty against ministerial autocracy; lord mayor of London (1774). Admitted to House of Commons (1774–90); championed colonial rights in American Revolution; chamberlain of city of London (1779–97); lost popularity by his part in suppressing Gordon Riots (1780). Secured to Britons abolition of general warrants, freedom of press in reporting debates in House of Commons, enfranchisement of artisans and middle class.

**Wil′kie** (wĭl′kĭ), Sir **David**. 1785–1841. Scottish genre and portrait painter; illustrated humble life in Scotland; painter in ordinary to king (1830); turned to historical paintings, two of best known being *Preaching of Knox* (1832) and *Columbus* (1835).

**Wil′kins** (wĭl′kĭnz), Sir **Charles**. 1749?–1836. English Orientalist; superintendent of an East India Company trading station; took leading part in inventing types for alphabets of Bengali and Persian and established printing press for Oriental languages. First Englishman to gain thorough grasp of Sanskrit and to translate Sanskrit inscriptions.

**Wilkins,** Sir **George Hubert**. 1888–1958. Australian polar explorer and aviator; on Stefansson's arctic expedition (1913–17); navigator, England-Australia flight (1919); second-in-command, British Imperial Antarctic Expedition (1920–21); naturalist, Shackleton's Antarctic Expedition (1921–22); leader, Wilkins Australia and Islands Expedition for British Museum (1923–25); commander, Detroit Arctic Expedition (1926–27), Wilkins Detroit-News Arctic Expedition (1928), Wilkins Hearst Antarctic Expedition (1928–29), Wilkins-Ellsworth Nautilus Arctic Submarine Expedition (1931); manager, Ellsworth Trans-Antarctic Expeditions (1933–39); flew from Point Barrow to Spitzbergen over polar regions (1928). Author of *Flying the Arctic* (1928), *Undiscovered Australia* (1928), *Under the North Pole* (1931), *Thoughts Through Space* (with H. M. Sherman; 1942).

**Wilkins, John**. 1614–1672. English bishop (of Chester) and scientist; one of the founders of the Royal Society; author of *The Discovery of a World in the Moone* (1638), *A Discourse Tending to Prove That 'Tis Probable Our Earth Is One of The Planets* (1640), *On the Principles and Duties of Natural Religion* (1678), etc.

**Wilkins, Mary Eleanor.** See Mary Eleanor Wilkins FREEMAN.

**Wilkins, Maurice Hugh Frederick**. 1916– . British biophysicist, b. New Zealand. Awarded Nobel prize in physiology and medicine (1962) with F. Crick and J. Watson for work on the structure of DNA.

**Wilkins, Roy**. 1901– . American civil rights worker, b. St. Louis, Mo. Joined National Association for the Advancement of Colored People (1931), executive secy. (1955–64), executive director (1965–77).

**Wil′kin·son** (wĭl′kĭn·s′n), **Ellen Cicely**. 1891–1947. English feminist and politician; active in labor movement (1912) and suffragism (1913); M.P. (1924–31, 1935–47); parliamentary secretary to ministry of home security (1940–45); minister of education (1945–47).

**Wilkinson,** Sir **Geoffrey.** 1921– . British chemist. At U. of California (1946–50), Harvard U. (1951–56), U. of London (1956– ); awarded (with Ernst Otto Fischer) Nobel prize for chemistry (1973).

**Wilkinson, James.** 1757–1825. American army officer and adventurer, b. in Calvert County, Md. Commissioned captain in Continental army (1776, to rank from Sept., 1775); with Arnold in retreat from Montreal to Albany (1776); engaged at Trenton and Princeton; promoted lieutenant colonel (1777) and brevetted brigadier general. Secretary of board of war (1778). Involved in Conway cabal and forced to resign commission (1778). Clothier general of Continental army (1779–81). Engaged in trade in Mississippi Valley region (1784); conspired with Esteban Miró, Spanish governor of Louisiana, to gain trade monopolies for himself and, it is charged, to separate Kentucky region from U.S. and turn it over to Spain. In military service against Indians (1791); lieutenant colonel, U.S. army (Oct., 1791), and brigadier general (Mar., 1792); took over Detroit from British (1796) and, on General Wayne's death (1796), became ranking officer of U.S. army. With Colonel William C. C. Claiborne, represented U.S. in taking over Louisiana Purchase (1803) from French; governor of Louisiana (1805–06). Implicated in Aaron Burr's conspiracy and chief witness at Burr's trial; acquitted by court of inquiry and, later (1811), by court-martial. Commissioned major general (1813) and commanded American forces on Canadian frontier; failed in campaign against Montreal (1813); again brought before court of inquiry and acquitted (1815); honorably discharged from U.S. army (1815).

**Wilkinson, Jemima**. 1752–1819. American religious zealot, b. Cumberland, R.I. Emerged from a trance suffered in course of a fever convinced that she was resurrected from death and that her body was inhabited by the "Spirit of Life" sent by God to warn the world to flee from the wrath to come. Her preaching led to establishment of churches in Rhode Island and Connecticut, and founding of a colony near Seneca Lake in western New York (1790; dissolved, 1819).

**Wilkinson, John**. 1728–1808. English ironmaster. Invented machine for accurate boxing of cylinders; built first iron barge (1787); patented process for making lead pipe (1790); designed and cast first iron bridge in England (1779).

**Wilkinson, John**. 1821–1891. American naval officer. Resigned from U.S. navy (1861) to enter Confederate service. Famed as commander of blockade runner *Robert E. Lee* (1863). Led unsuccessful attempt to capture a steamer on Lake Erie and free Confederate prisoners held on Johnson's Island in the lake (1863–64).

**Wilkinson,** Sir **John Gardner**. 1797–1875. English traveler and Egyptologist; in Egypt and Nubia (1821–33); author of *Materia Hieroglyphica* (1828), *Manners and Customs of the Ancient Egyptians* (1837), etc.

**Wilkinson, Marguerite Ogden,** *nee* **Big′e·low** (bĭg′ĕ·lō). 1883–1928. Author, b. in Halifax, Nova Scotia; m. James G. Wilkinson (1909); compiler of the poetry anthologies *New Voices*, etc., and author of *The Great Dream* (1923), *Yule Fire* (1925), etc.

**Wilkinson,** Sir **Nevile Rodwell.** 1869–1940. British soldier, architect, and author; b. Ireland. Served in South African War, World War I; architect of the miniature masterpiece, Titania's Palace. Author of *Yvette in Italy* (1922), *Yvette in Venice* (1923), *Yvette in the U.S.A. with Titania's Palace* (1928), etc.

**Wilkinson, Tate**. 1739–1803. English actor; manager of Yorkshire circuit for 30 years; wrote memoirs.

**Wilks** (wĭlks), **Robert.** 1665?–1732. English actor, esp. in comedy, b. Dublin; associated in managership of Haymarket and Drury Lane theaters (from 1709).

**Wil'laert** (vĭl'ärt), **Adrian.** 1480?–1562. Flemish musician; originated style of writing music for two choirs; composer of two masses for from four to seven voices, many motets, psalms, hymns, and madrigals.

**Wil'lard** (wĭl'ẽrd), **Daniel.** 1861–1942. American railroad executive; president (from 1910), Baltimore & Ohio R.R.; chairman of advisory commission of Council of National Defense (1917–18) and chairman of War Industries Board (1917–18).

**Willard, Emma,** *nee* **Hart** (härt). 1787–1870. American educator, b. Berlin, Conn.; m. John Willard (1809; d. 1825) and Christopher Yates (1838; divorced 1843). Established Middlebury Female Sem. (1814–19), Waterford (N.Y.) Acad. (1819–21), Troy (N.Y.) Female Sem., now known as Emma Willard School (1821–38); retired (1838). Pioneer in field of higher education for women; published textbooks in history and a volume of poems (including notably *Rocked in the Cradle of the Deep*). Elected to American Hall of Fame (1905).

**Willard, Frances Elizabeth Caroline.** 1839–1898. Descendant of Simon Willard. American educator and reformer, b. Churchville, N.Y. Devoted life to temperance movement (from 1874), appearing on lecture platform and for a time conducting prayer groups on streets and in saloons; president, National W.C.T.U. (1879) and World's W.C.T.U. (1891); also, aided in organizing Prohibition party (1882). Elected to American Hall of Fame (1910).

**Willard, Jess.** 1883–1968. American heavyweight pugilist; won championship from Jack Johnson (Apr. 5, 1915); lost championship to Jack Dempsey (1919).

**Willard, Joseph.** 1738–1804. Great-grandson of Samuel Willard (1640–1707). American educator; president of Harvard (1781–1804).

**Willard, Joseph Edward.** 1865–1924. Descendant of Simon Willard. American lawyer and diplomat; practiced in Richmond, Va.; served in Spanish-American War, in Cuba (1898–99); U.S. minister (1913), and first U.S. ambassador (1913–21), to Spain.

**Willard, Josiah Flynt.** *Pen name* **Josiah Flynt** (flĭnt). 1869–1907. American sociologist; pursued life of a vagrant and wrote sociological study *Tramping with Tramps* (1899); also wrote *Notes of an Itinerant Policeman* (1900), *The World of Graft* (1901), and a novel, *The Little Brother* (1902).

**Willard, Simon.** 1605–1676. Colonist and trader in America, b. Kent, Eng. To America (1634) and settled in Cambridge, Mass. With Peter Bulkeley, founded town of Concord (1635). Member of General Court of Massachusetts nearly every year (1636–54) and an assistant on the governor's council (1654–76). Served as commander of colonial forces in Indian fighting on various occasions, notably in King Philip's War (1675). His son **Samuel** (1640–1707) was pastor of Old South Church in Boston (1678–1707); vice-president of Harvard (1700–07) and, in the absence of the president Increase Mather, actual head of the college.

**Willard, Simon.** 1753–1848. Descendant of Simon Willard (1605–1676). American clockmaker; settled in Roxbury (c. 1778) and manufactured clocks, specializing in church, hall, and gallery clocks (1778–1839). Patented (Feb. 8, 1802) a new timepiece, the Willard Patent Timepiece, which came to be known as the banjo clock.

**Will'cocks** (wĭl'kŏks), **Mary Patricia.** 1869– . English novelist; made reputation with *The Wingless Victory* (1907); other novels are *Eyes of the Blind* (1917), *The Cup and the Lip* (1929), *Madame Roland* (1936).

**Willcocks,** Sir **William.** 1852–1932. British engineer and irrigationist, b. in India. With irrigation department, Indian public works (1872–83) and Egyptian public works, reservoirs (1883–97); designed and built the dam at Aswan, Egypt (1898–1902); undertook irrigation work in Mesopotamia (1911).

**Will'cox** (wĭl'kŏks), **Walter Francis.** 1861–1964. American statistician; professor of economics and statistics, Cornell U. (1891–1931); also, chief statistician of 12th U.S. census (1899–1901), and special agent of the U.S. census bureau (1902–31). Author of *Introduction to the Vital Statistics of the United States, 1900–1930* (1933), etc.

**Wil'le·brandt** (wĭl'ĕ·brănt), **Mabel,** *nee* **Walker.** 1889–1963. American lawyer and public official; practiced at Los Angeles, Calif. Asst. attorney general of United States, in charge of cases arising out of federal tax laws, prohibition, and the bureau of federal prisons (1921–29).

**Willem.** Dutch form of WILLIAM.

**Wil'le·mer** (vĭl'ĕ·mẽr), **Marianne von,** *nee* **Jung** (yŏŏng). 1784–1860. German lady; wife of banker **Johann Jakob von Willemer** (1760–1838). Renowned for her friendship with Goethe, who wrote of her (under poetic name "Zuleika") in a number of his poems.

**Wil'lems** (vĭl'ĕms), **Flo·rent'** (flô·rĕnt'). 1812?–1905. Belgian painter; studio in Paris (from c. 1844).

**Willems, Jan Frans.** 1793–1846. Flemish scholar; archivist at Antwerp (to 1830) and at Ghent (1835–46); edited medieval works.

**Wil'let** (wĭl'ĕt), **William.** 1867–1921. American stained-glass artist; founded Willet Stained Glass and Decorating Co., in Pittsburgh (1899); moved offices to Philadelphia (1913). Among his notable works are chancel window in Calvary Church, Pittsburgh; windows in Cadet Chapel, West Point; the west window in the graduate-school building of Princeton U. He married (1895) **Anne Lee** (1867–1943), b. Bristol, Pa., who collaborated with him in the windows for Cadet Chapel, West Point, carrying project to completion after his death. She is also represented by work in many churches, much of it in collaboration with her son **Henry Lee Willet** (1899– ).

**Wil'lett** (wĭl'ĕt), **Marinus.** 1740–1830. American Revolutionary officer; served with distinction through the Revolution. Mayor of New York (1807–11).

**Willett, William.** 1856–1915. English builder; first promoter of the system of daylight saving.

**Wil'lette'** (vē'lĕt'), **Adolphe Léon.** 1857–1926. French painter and illustrator on staff of *Chat Noir, Courrier Français, Triboulet, Boulevard, Rire,* and other illustrated periodicals; founded *Pierrot* and *Pied-de-Nez.*

**Wil'liam** (wĭl'yăm). Name of four kings of England:

**William I.** *Called* **William the Conqueror.** 1027–1087. King of England (1066–87). Bastard son of Robert the Devil, Duke of Normandy; accepted by nobles as William II, Duke of Normandy (1035); with help of his feudal superior, Henry I of France, suppressed rebellion of nobles (1047); visited his cousin Edward the Confessor, and probably received promise that he should succeed Edward as king of England; married (c. 1053) Matilda, daughter of the count of Flanders, and a descendant of King Alfred, in defiance of a prohibition by the church on ground of consanguinity, but received papal dispensation (1059); instituted by decree (1061) custom later introduced into England as curfew; repulsed two invasions (1054, 1058) by French king and annexed county of Maine; exacted promise (1064) from Harold, Earl of Wessex, shipwrecked off Norman coast, to support his claim to English throne. Invaded England on death of Edward and accession of Harold (1066), bearing a consecrated banner signifying pope's approval of his claim; aided by invasion of northern England by Tostig, Harold's banished brother; encamped at Hastings; defeated Harold (Oct. 14) at a place called by a chronicler Senlac, later called Battle; crowned at Westminster on Christmas Day. Quelled insurrections in west and north (1068); repelled Danish invasion; completed conquest of England (1070); appointed Lanfranc archbishop of Canterbury (1070); compelled Malcolm, the Scottish king, to do him homage (1072). Conquered Maine (1073); returned to England (1075) to settle punishment of rebels under earls of Hereford and Norfolk, who had been defeated by Lanfranc; beheaded Waltheof, Earl of Northumberland, his only execution for a political offense. Strengthened power of the crown by building castles; gave confiscated land of rebels to his followers; caused all titles to land to be derived from his grant; established feudal system; ordered Domesday Book to be compiled (1085); organized church as department of government; separated spiritual from temporal courts; asserted supremacy of his own authority and refused homage to the pope. Engaged in wars in France; quelled uprisings led by his son Robert, Duke of Normandy (1080, 1082); in war with Philip I of France (1087), received fatal injury when his horse stumbled entering the captured town of Mantes; buried in abbey that he had built at Caen.

**William II.** c. 1056–1100. King of England (1087–1100); called **Ru′fus** (rōō′fŭs) from his fiery complexion. Second surviving son of William the Conqueror. Bore arms with father against brother Robert (1079); designated king of England by the witan, according to father's dying request; crowned at Westminster (1087). By ruthless, shortsighted, rapacious rule provoked barons under his uncle Odo, Bishop of Bayeux, to insurrection in favor of Robert; quelled insurrection by promises, never fulfilled, of good laws, reduction of taxes, redress for losses from William I's afforestments (1088). Appointed Anselm archbishop of Canterbury (1093); quarreled with him for maintaining church liberties (1097). Invaded Normandy (1089, 1091, 1094); received mortgage upon Normandy when brother Robert required funds for a crusade (1096); recovered Maine and failed to recover Vexin; invaded Wales three times without success. Slain by an arrow from an unknown hand (traditionally, that of Walter Tirel, a Norman) while hunting in New Forest; his body refused religious rites by clergy of Winchester.

**William III.** 1650–1702. King of England, Scotland, and Ireland (1689–1702). See WILLIAM III, Count of Nassau (p. 1577).

**William IV.** 1765–1837. Called "the Sailor-King," also "Silly Billy." King of Great Britain and Ireland (1830–37), of house of Hanover; also, king of Hanover (1830–37); 3d son of George III. As midshipman served in action off Cape St. Vincent (1780); captain of frigate (1785) and stationed in West Indies; rear admiral (1790). Duke of Clarence (1789); sat in House of Lords and opposed emancipation of slaves; sustained a connection with Dorothea Jordan, the actress (1791?–1811), which he was forced to break off in order to marry Adelaide of Saxe-Meiningen (1818); became heir to throne and lord high admiral (1827). Succeeded George IV as king (1830); by declining to accept resignation of Tory ministry and to create new peers, caused long political crisis and obstructed passage of second Reform Bill; brought about its passage (1832) by appeal in circular letter to peers, one hundred of whom absented themselves. As king of Hanover gave new constitution to that country (1833). Last English sovereign to attempt to force a ministry (the ministry of Sir Robert Peel, 1834) upon an unwilling majority in Parliament; buried at Windsor. Succeeded on British throne by his niece Victoria (*q.v.*) and on Hanoverian throne by his brother Ernest Augustus (*q.v.*) as Ernest I.

**William.** *Fr.* **Guillaume.** Name of ten dukes of Aq′ui-taine′ [ăk′wĭ·tān′] (886–1137), including: **William I** (886–918), called "the Pious," who founded Abbey of Cluny (c. 910). **William V** (960?–1030), called "the Great," patron of arts and literature. **William IX** (1071–1127), also count of Poitou; duke (1087–1127); spent most of his life in warfare; led unsuccessful crusade (1100–03); twice excommunicated for his licentiousness; first Provençal poet whose works have come down to us. **William X** (1099–1137); his daughter Eleanor m. (1137) Louis VII of France, uniting Aquitaine with Capetian line.

**William.** *Fr.* **Guillaume.** Name of five dukes of Normandy:

**William I.** *Called* **Long′sword′** (lŏng′sōrd′). *Fr.* **Longue′-É′pée′** (lôNg′ā′pā′) d. 943. Son of Rollo. Duke (927–943). Secured control over Rennes and Vannes; treacherously assassinated by count of Flanders.

**William II.** 1027 (or 1028)–1087. Son of Robert. Duke (1035–87) and king of England (1066–87); see WILLIAM I of England.

**William III.** 1056?–1100. Third son of Duke William II. Duke (1087–91). See WILLIAM II of England.

**William Ath′e·ling** (ăth′ĕ·lĭng; ăth′-). 1103–1120. Only son of Henry I of England. Duke (1120). Received homage of Norman barons (1115); m. (1119) Matilda, daughter of Fulk V, Count of Anjou; sailed for England from Point Barfleur in *White Ship* (Nov. 25, 1120); drowned.

**William Cli′to** (klī′tō). 1102?–1128. Son of Robert II; grandson of William the Conqueror. Made count of Flanders (1127–28); defeated by Thierry d'Alsace, Count of Flanders, and killed at siege of Alost.

**William.** 1227–1256. King of Germany. See WILLIAM OF HOLLAND.

**William.** Name of two German emperors (and kings of Prussia):

**William I.** *Full Ger. name* **Wilhelm Friedrich Ludwig.** 1797–1888. King of Prussia (1861–88) and German emperor (1871–88). Second son of Frederick William III of Prussia and Louise; b. Berlin. Fought against Napoleon (1814–15); m. (1829) Augusta (1811–1890), daughter of Charles Frederick, Duke of Saxe-Weimar; on accession of his brother (1840; see FREDERICK WILLIAM IV), became prince of Prussia; became very unpopular because of absolutist ideas and suppression of insurrections; fled to England (1848); made regent (1858–61) when king became insane. On becoming king (1861), declared that he "ruled by the favor of God, and of no one else"; his reign a continuous struggle with liberals; aided by Bismarck (appointed minister of foreign affairs, 1862), esp. in bringing about war with Austria (1866); commanded at Sadowa (1866); head of the North German Confederation (1867); led German armies in Franco-Prussian War (1870–71), personally commanding at Gravelotte and Sedan; proclaimed German emperor at Versailles (Jan. 18, 1871); Prussian government by its severe laws against Catholics broke off relations with Vatican (1872–87); two attempts made at assassination (1878); severe legislation against Socialists (1878); anti-Semitic movement (1880); alliance with Austria-Hungary and Italy (1882; renewed 1887); supported Bismarck and his generals in strengthening control of Germany by Prussia.

**William II.** *Full Ger. name* **Friedrich Wilhelm Viktor Albert.** 1859–1941. Emperor of Germany and king of Prussia (1888–1918). Grandson of William I; son of Frederick III and Victoria; b. Berlin. Educ. Bonn; m. (1881) Princess Augusta Victoria (1858–1921) of Schleswig-Holstein-Sonderburg-Augustenburg. On accession (1888), asserted divine mission of house of Hohenzollern (*q.v.*) to rule; visited Turkey (1888); dismissed Bismarck (1890); maintained Triple Alliance; sought friendly relations with Turkey; interested in social questions; began development of strong German fleet; aided transformation of Germany from an agricultural to an industrial state; unsuccessfully opposed growth of Socialism (1893–1912); expressed friendship to President Kruger of the South African Republic (1896); directed policy of seizing territory (Kiaochow) for indemnity in China (1897); played prominent part in Boxer Rebellion (1900–01); controversy with France over Morocco (1904–11); severely criticized at home for impetuous speech on friendship for Great Britain (1908). Sided with Austria-Hungary in crisis with Serbia (1914); dominant force of Central Powers at beginning of World War (1914); prestige gradually declined as Germany failed to win a decision; made offer of peace (1916); frequently visited battle fronts, but his control over army greatly reduced; toward the end (1918) saw inevitable defeat but refused to surrender; was denied support of army and navy; fled to Holland; abdicated (Nov. 28, 1918). Resident at chateau in Doorn, near Utrecht (from 1920); after Kaiserin Augusta Victoria's death (1921), m. (1922) as 2d wife, Princess Hermine of Schönaich-Carolath (b. 1887); granted payment (1926) by Prussian government for confiscated property. See also Crown Prince WILLIAM.

**William.** *Full Ger. name* **Friedrich Wilhelm Viktor August Ernst.** 1882–1951. Crown prince of Germany (1888–1918). Son of Emperor William II of Germany; b. Potsdam. Educ. Bonn; m. (1905) Cecilie Auguste Marie (b. 1886) of Mecklenburg-Schwerin; traveled in Orient and Italy (1903) and in India (1910–11); often quarreled with kaiser; removed from command of Death's Head Hussars (1913); in World War commanded 5th army (1914); in charge of unsuccessful attack on Verdun (1916); fled to Holland with kaiser (1918); renounced rights to crowns of Prussia and German Empire (1918); returned to Germany (1923).

**William.** Name of six landgraves and two electors of Hesse-Cassel, esp.:

**William IV.** 1532–1592. Called "the Wise." Founder of the elder line of the house of Hesse (see HESSE-CASSEL). Son of Philip the Magnanimous. Administered government (1547–52) during imprisonment of father; landgrave (1567–92), receiving Hesse and Kassel on division of landgraviate (1567); a Protestant, and wise ruler; a pioneer astronomer; built first observatory with revolving dome, at Kassel (1561).

**William VIII.** 1682–1760. Landgrave (1751–60).

**William IX.** 1743–1821. Landgrave (1785–1803); elector as **William I** (1803–21). Furnished the Hessian mercenary troops to Great Britain for use in the American Revolution; joined coalition against France (1792); lost his lands to the French (1806–13); restored by Congress of Vienna (1814–15).

**William II.** 1777–1847. Elector (1821–47). Son of William I. Served in Prussian army against Napoleon (1813); caused unrest by his conservatism (1830–31); forced to grant a new constitution (1831).

**William.** 1785–1831. Duke of Schles'wig-Hol'stein-Sön'der·borg'-Glücks'burg (shlās'vĭκ[shlĕs'vĭκ]·hôl'-shtīn·sûn'ẽr·bŏr[g]'·glüks'bo͝orκ); m. Princess Louise of Hesse-Cassel; father of Christian IX of Denmark.

**William.** Name of two kings of Würt'tem·berg (vür'-tĕm·bĕrκ):

**William I.** 1781–1864. King (1816–64). Son of Frederick I, King of Württemberg. Commanded troops of his kingdom in Napoleon's campaign against Russia (1812); led an army corps of the anti-Napoleonic allies (1813–15); granted a liberal constitution (1819); defender of rights of small German states; feared esp. domination of Prussia; worked for Germanic union by helping form the Zollverein (1828–30); his liberal policies weakened after 1848. Three times married.

**William II.** 1848–1921. King (1891–1918); grandson of William I and nephew of Charles I. Fought on side of Austria against Prussia (1866) and of Germany against France (1870–71); took no prominent part in German politics during his reign; forced to abdicate (1918).

**William IV.** 1852–1912. Son of Adolf of Nassau. Grand duke of Lux'em·burg [lo͝ok'sĕm·bo͝orκ] (1905–12); made family statute (1907) enabling daughters to succeed to the throne; succeeded by his daughter Marie Adélaïde.

**William.** *Dutch* **Willem.** Name of five counts of Nassau (princes of Orange), stadholders of Holland:

**William I.** *Known as* **William the Silent.** 1533–1584. Founder of Dutch Republic and first stadholder (1579–84). Son of William, Count of Nassau, and Juliana of Stolberg; b. at Dillenburg. Succeeded to principality of Orange (1544); page to Emperor Charles V (1548); m. (1551) Anna van Buren (d. 1558), of the Egmont family; appointed by Charles commander of imperial army (1555) and governor of northern Holland provinces; served in war of Philip II against Henry II of France (1556–59); became count of Nassau (1559); opposed Philip II (1559–67) in his persecution of Protestants in Orange and Holland; m. (1561) as second wife, Anna of Saxony; forced to flee to Germany (1567); refused to appear before Council of Blood (1567); led revolt (1568–76), the "War of Liberation," against duke of Alva and Spanish armies; lost help of French Huguenots (after 1572); Leiden relieved (1574); suffered several defeats, especially at Gembloux (1578); by Pacification of Ghent (1576) united southern provinces against Spain, and by Union of Utrecht (1579) seven northern provinces, which formally declared their independence of Spain; became first stadholder (1579–84); made hereditary (1581); m. (1583), as fourth wife, Louise de Coligny, dau. of Gaspard II de Coligny; assassinated at Delft by Balthasar Gérard. His eldest son, Philip William (d. 1618), was held as prisoner in Spain. Other sons were Maurice of Nassau (see MAURICE) and Frederick Henry (*q.v.*).

**William II.** 1626–1650. Stadholder (1647–50). Son of Frederick Henry and grandson of William the Silent; b. at The Hague; m. (1641) Mary, dau. of Charles I of England. Established peace with Spain (1648) which recognized independence of United Provinces; negotiated treaty with France (1650); attempted to make himself sovereign; after his death, stadholdership temporarily suspended (1650–72). See Jan DE WITT.

**William III.** 1650–1702. Stadholder of Holland (1672–1702) and king of England (1689–1702). Posthumous son of William II; b. at The Hague. Became leader, opposed to Jan De Witt; placed in command in war against France; proclaimed stadholder (1672); formed coalition, including England, against Louis XIV; forced Louis to make Treaty of Nijmegen (1678); m. (1677) Mary, dau. of duke of York, later James II of England; after Glorious Revolution in England (1688) appealed to by both Whigs and Tories to be English king; landed at Torbay, Devonshire, with Dutch army (1688); invited by Parliament to accept throne; crowned (1689) as joint sovereign with Mary; accepted Declaration of Rights (1689); Act of Toleration passed (1689); went to Ireland, defeated James at battle of the Boyne (1690); reigned as sole sovereign after death of Mary (1694); plot to assassinate him (1696) discovered and conspirators executed; joined first Grand Alliance against France (1689) which led to war (1689–97), concluded by Treaty of Ryswick (1697); Act of Settlement (1701); formed second Grand Alliance (1701); died as a result of a fall with his horse.

**William IV** and **William V** belong to another branch of the House of Nassau, the second line of Orange-Nassau, descended from Ernest Casimir (see NASSAU):

**William IV.** *Former name* **Charles Henry Fri′so** (frē′sō). 1711–1751. Son of John William Friso and grandson of a cousin of William III. Stadholder (1747–51); at first held the office in northern provinces; later (1747), accepted by all Holland as stadholder, practically a limited hereditary monarch; m. Anne, dau. of George II of England; under his brief rule, nothing effected toward strengthening country.

**William V.** 1748–1806. Son of William IV; succeeded father as stadholder (1751–95), but affairs of state controlled during his minority by queen mother (1751–59) and by regents (1759–66), Holland remaining neutral during Seven Years' War (1756–63); m. Wilhelmina of Prussia, who dominated him; under his weak rule, country weakened by taking part in European conflicts (1780, 1792–93), by party strife (1787), and finally by the general revolutionary spirit, which (1795) overthrew the stadholdership; fled to England; his rule followed by Batavian Republic (1795–1806) and, under French domination, the kingdom of Holland (1806–15); his son William became first king of the Netherlands (1815) as William I (*q.v.*).

**William.** *Dutch* **Willem.** Name of three kings of the Netherlands:

**William I.** *Full Dutch name* **Willem Frederik.** 1772–1843. King (1815–40). Son of William V, Prince of Orange, last stadholder of Holland. Commanded Dutch army against France (1793–95); joined army of Prussia; captured at Jena (1806); lost (1806) hereditary lands in Germany (see NASSAU); fought at Wagram in Austrian army (1809); recovered German territories (1813); made first king of new Kingdom of the Netherlands erected out of Belgium and Holland by the Congress of Vienna (1815); relinquished German duchy for Luxemburg (1815); unable to prevent separate establishment of Belgium as kingdom (1830); failed in attempt to coerce Belgians (1830–32) but granted more favorable terms by conference of Powers; finally ratified definitive treaty of separation (1839); abdicated (1840) in favor of his son.

**William II.** *Full Dutch name* **Willem Frederik George Lodewijk.** 1792–1849. King (1840–49). Son of William I. Fought in Spain under Wellington and commanded Dutch forces at Waterloo (1815); approved of separation of Belgium (1830); commanded Dutch army that was defeated (1832) by the French in attempt at coercion; made king on abdication of his father (1840); aided financial improvements; against a conservative States-General secured (1848) a new constitution with many liberal features.

**William III.** *Full Dutch name* **Willem Alexander Paul Frederik Lodewijk.** 1817–1890. King (1849–90). Son of William II. Abolished slavery in Dutch West Indies (1862); fought long against establishment of government by parliamentary ministries (1853–62), but finally forced to yield; during his reign: province of Limburg incorporated in the Netherlands (1866), neutrality of Luxemburg recognized by Treaty of London (1867), culture system in Java abolished (1870–72); m. (1879) as second wife, Emma (*q.v.*) of Waldeck-Pyrmont; succeeded by their daughter Wilhelmina (*q.v.*).

**William.** *Swed.* **Vilhelm.** 1884– . Prince of Sweden and Duke of **Sö′der·man·land′** (sû′dẽr·män·länd′). Second son of King Gustavus V; m. (1908) Grand Duchess Maria Pavlovna, daughter of Grand Duke Paul of Russia; divorced (1914). Writer and explorer; naval officer (1907–18); writings include three volumes of poetry (1916–22), short stories, plays (1924–27), and several books of travel; at first wrote under pseudonym **L. Wi′ca** (vē′kȧ).

**William Atheling.** See under WILLIAM, Dukes of Normandy.

**William Au·gus′tus** (ô·gŭs′tŭs). Duke of **Cum′ber·land** (kŭm′bẽr·lănd). 1721–1765. English military commander; 3d son of George II and Queen Caroline. Educ. for navy; privy councilor (1742); served on Main at Dettingen (1743); commander in chief of British, Hanoverian, Austrian, and Dutch forces, unsuccessfully engaged Marshal Saxe at Fontenoy (1745); quelled Jacobite uprising headed by Prince Charles Edward in victory of Culloden Moor (1746); suppressed Jacobitism with utmost severity (acquiring nickname of "the Butcher"); again in Flanders, defeated by Saxe at Lauffeld or Val (1747); defeated by d'Estrées at Hastenbeck (1757); capitulated and evacuated Hanover; retired to private life (1757).

**William Clito.** See under WILLIAM, Dukes of Normandy.

**William de Valence.** See de VALENCE.

**William Fitzosbern.** See FITZOSBERN.

**William Nich′o·las** (nĭk′ō·lăs). 1828–1896. Duke of **Würt′tem·berg** (vür′tĕm·bĕrk) and German general; son of Duke Eugen, of the younger line of the house of Württemberg; entered Austrian army and took part in many European campaigns (1849, 1859, 1864, 1866, and 1878).

**William of —.** See also GUILLAUME DE —.

**William of Alnwick.** See ALNWICK.

**William of Au′vergne′** (ō′vĕrn′y′). = GUILLAUME DE PARIS.

**William of Corbeil.** See CORBEIL.

**William of Hol′land** (hŏl′ănd). *Ger.* **Wil′helm von Hol′land** (vĭl′hĕlm fōn hōl′änt). 1227–1256. Count of Holland (1234–56). Chosen king of Germany (1247; crowned 1248) in opposition to Frederick II; generally acknowledged after death of Conrad IV (1254–56); killed in battle against the Frisians.

**William of Ju′mièges′** (zhü′myâzh′). *Fr.* **Guil′laume′ de Jumièges** (gē′yōm′ dē). d. about 1090. Benedictine monk and chronicler; wrote *Histoire des Normands*, dedicated to William the Conqueror.

**William of Longchamp.** = William LONGCHAMP.

**William of Malmes′bur·y** (mämz′bẽr·ĭ; -brĭ). Between 1090 and 1096–?1143. English historian. Librarian of Malmesbury Abbey. Compiler of *Gesta Regum Anglorum* ("Acts of the Kings of the English"; 1125) and its sequel *Historia Novella* ("Modern History") carrying narrative to 1142. Compiled also works on lives of English bishops and history of monastery of Glastonbury.

**William of New′burgh** (nū′bŭ·rŭ; -brŭ). 1136–?1198. English historian; chief work *Historia Rerum Anglicarum* ("History of English affairs"), narrating events from 1066 to 1198.

**William of Nor′wich** (nŏr′ĭj; -ĭch), Saint. 1132?–1144. English boy "saint and martyr." A tanner's apprentice; found dead (Easter, 1144) and, by popular rumor, made first victim of alleged Jewish "ritual murders."

**William of Ockham** *or* **Occam.** See OCKHAM.

**William of** [*or* **de**] **Saint Ca′ri′lef′** (ŭv[dē] săN′ kȧ′-

rē′lĕf′) *or* **Saint Ca′lais′** (kä′lĕ′). d. 1096. Norman prelate in England. Bishop of Durham (1081); adviser to William I and chief minister to William II (1088); gave aid to rebellion of Bishop Odo of Bayeux (*q.v.*); deprived of bishopric, took refuge in Normandy (1088); returned after pardon (1091) and carried rebuilding of Durham Cathedral far enough to determine its lasting form; aided William II in persecution of Archbishop Anselm (1095).

**William of Sic′i·ly** (sĭs′ĭ·lĭ). Name of line of kings of Sicily, including: **William I** (d. 1166), known as "the Bad"; succeeded to power (1154); pursued policy of excluding great nobles from share in administration; crushed revolt of nobles (1160); aided in installation of Pope Alexander III in the Lateran (1166). His son **William II** (d. 1189), who succeeded to throne at thirteen (1166), was placed under regency of his mother, Margaret of Navarre; later engaged in unsuccessful series of campaigns against neighboring regions, notably against Egypt and Constantinople.

**William of Tyre** (tīr). 1130?–?1190. French prelate and chronicler; in Palestine (1166 or 1167) and appointed archdeacon of Tyre (1167), chancellor of the kingdom of Jerusalem (1174–83), archbishop of Tyre (1175); author of *Historia Rerum in Partibus Transmarinis Gestarum*, covering the period between 1095 and 1184 and accepted as the standard narrative of the deeds of French warriors in the East.

**William of Wied** (vēt), Prince. *Full Ger. name* **Wilhelm Friedrich Heinrich.** 1876–1945. King of Albania (1914), b. Neuwied, Prussia. Cousin of the German emperor and of the czar of Russia and nephew of Queen Elizabeth of Rumania; m. Princess Sophie of Rumania. Offered (1913) throne of autonomous Albania by European powers; arrived (Feb., 1914); made Durazzo his capital; conditions immediately became disturbed; intrigue and insurrections; after outbreak of World War, forced to leave; fought in World War; later, retired to Neuwied.

**William of Wykeham.** See WYKEHAM.

**William Rufus.** See WILLIAM II, King of England.

**William the Clerk** (klärk; klûrk). fl. 1208–1226. Anglo-Norman poet; author of an Arthurian romance, *Frégus et Galienne.*

**William the Conqueror.** See WILLIAM I, King of England.

**William the Li′on** (lī′ŭn). 1143–1214. King of Scotland (1165–1214). Grandson of David I and brother of Malcolm IV, whom he succeeded. Attended Henry II of England to French wars; invaded Northumberland in assistance of Henry II's sons against him; captured near Alnwick (1174); received back Northumbrian districts and Scottish independence (1189) by payment of 10,000 marks to Richard I of England for expedition to Palestine. Successfully established Scottish Church independent of English Church and subject only to see of Rome; founded abbey of Arbroath (1178).

**William the Silent.** See WILLIAM I, Count of Nassau.

**Wil′liams** (wĭl′yămz), **Al′ford** (ăl′fôrd) **Joseph.** 1896–1958. American aviator, b. New York City; with U.S. navy as research aviator (1917–30).

**Williams, Anna.** 1706–1783. Welsh poet. Lost her sight (1740); befriended by Dr. Johnson and from 1752 a member of his household; published *Miscellanies in Prose and Verse* (1766), to which Dr. Johnson contributed the preface and several pieces.

**Williams, Ben Ames.** 1889–1953. American novelist and short-story writer, b. Macon, Miss.; A.B. Dartmouth (1910); author of *All the Brothers Were Valiant* (1919), *Audacity* (1924), *Great Oaks* (1930), *Hostile Valley* (1934), *The Strumpet Sea* (1938), *Come Spring* (1940), *Time of Peace* (1942), *Leave Her to Heaven* (1944), *House Divided* (1947), etc.

**Williams, Bert,** *in full* **Egbert Austin.** 1876?–1922. Negro comedian and song writer on American stage, b. in the Bahama Islands; to U.S. as a child. Partner with George Walker in vaudeville (1895–1903) and musical comedy (1903–09); leading comedian in Ziegfeld Follies (from 1909).

**Williams, Betty.** 1943– . Irish peace activist. Awarded (with Mairead Corrigan) Nobel prize for peace (1977, for 1976).

**Williams, Blanche Colton.** 1879–1944. American educator, b. in Attala Co., Miss.; A.B., Miss. State Coll. for Women (1898), Ph.D., Columbia (1913); taught English at Teachers Coll., Columbia U. (1908–39; prof. and head of dept., 1926–39; retired); editor of anthologies of short stories; author of works on short-story writing and a life of Keats, *Forever Young* (1943).

**Williams, Charles Hanson Greville.** 1829–1910. English chemist; credited with discovery of cyanine and isoprene.

**Williams, Daniel Hale.** 1858–1931. American Negro surgeon, b. Hollidaysburg, Pa. M.D., Northwestern (1883); practiced in Chicago. Organizer (1891) of Provident Hospital, Chicago, affording facilities for training colored men as internes and colored women as nurses; surgeon on staff of this hospital (1891–1912). Charter member, American Coll. of Surgeons (1913), only Negro so honored. Credited with performing (1893) first successful surgical closure of a wound of the heart and pericardium.

**Williams, Edward.** *Bardic name* **Io′lo Mor·gan′nwg** (yŏ′lō mŏr·găn′ŏŏg). 1746–1826. Welsh bard; stonemason; land surveyor; one of three editors of collection of Welsh prose and verse *Myvyrian Archaiology* (1801); author of *Poems, Lyric and Pastoral* (1794) and a treatise on the mystery of bardism.

**Williams, Edward Huntington.** 1868–1944. American physician and writer; coauthor, with his brother Henry Smith Williams (*q.v.*), of *A History of Science* (5 vols., 1904), and *Every Day Science* (11 vols., 1910).

**Williams,** Sir **Edward Leader.** 1828–1910. English waterway engineer; chief engineer of construction for Manchester Ship Canal.

**Williams, Eleazar.** 1789?–1858. Missionary among the American Indians, b. Caughnawaga, Canada. Descendant of an American Indian chief and an American girl, Eunice Williams (daughter of John Williams, 1664–1729), one of the captives made in the French and Indian raid on Deerfield, Mass. (1704). Began missionary work among Indians of northern New York (c. 1813). Asserted himself (from 1839) to be the lost dauphin of France, son of Louis XVI; achieved notoriety as a result of magazine article on the subject, written by an Episcopal clergyman (1853). Author of books on Indian subjects, some written in Iroquois; credited with simplifying the writing of the Mohawk language.

**Williams, Elisha.** 1694–1755. American Congregational clergyman and educator; rector of Yale Coll. (1726–39). His half brother **Israel** (1709–1788), grad. Harvard (1727), was a trader and businessman of Hampshire County, Mass.; judge of Hampshire County court of common pleas (1758–74); member of governor's council (1761–67); applied the bequest of his kinsman Ephraim Williams (*q.v.*) to the founding of the free school that became (1793) Williams Coll.

**Williams, Elkanah.** 1822–1888. American pioneer specialist in diseases of the eye and ear, and one of the first physicians in U.S. to use the ophthalmoscope.

**Williams, Emlyn.** 1905– . British playwright and

actor, b. in Wales; M.A., Oxon.; author of *A Murder Has Been Arranged* (1930), *Night Must Fall* (1935), *The Corn Is Green* (1938), *The Light of Heart* (1940), *Morning Star* (1942).

**Williams, Ephraim.** 1714–1755. American Colonial army officer, b. Newton, Mass.; captain of Massachusetts militia (1745); commanded troops along northern Massachusetts border; ambushed and killed (Sept. 8, 1755). Under terms of his will, a large part of his estate was bequeathed for the founding of a free school in a township in Massachusetts to be named Williamstown, which bequest his kinsman Israel Williams (see under Elisha WILLIAMS) applied to the founding of the free school that became (1793) Williams College.

**Williams, Frederick Ballard.** 1871–1956. American painter; best known for landscapes and figure paintings.

**Williams, Frederick Wells.** See under Samuel Wells WILLIAMS.

**Williams,** Sir **George.** 1821–1905. English dry-goods merchant; founder (1844) of Young Men's Christian Association, treasurer (1863–85), president (1886).

**Williams, George Henry.** 1820–1910. American lawyer and politician; chief justice, Oregon Territory (1853–57). U.S. senator from Oregon (1865–71); opposed President Andrew Johnson; introduced tenure of office bill in the U.S. Senate (Dec., 1866). U.S. attorney general (1871–75). Nominated for chief justice, U.S. Supreme Court (1873), but not confirmed. Sent to Florida by Republican National Committee in disputed election of 1876 and aided in presentation of evidence securing that state's electoral vote for Hayes.

**Williams, Glu'yas** (gloo'yăs). 1888– . American cartoonist, b. San Francisco; A.B., Harvard (1911); contributor of cartoons to *Collier's*, *The New Yorker*, and daily newspapers; illustrator of works of Robert Benchley (*q.v.*).

**Williams, H. J.** 1874–1924. British author of the song *Tipperary*, popular with soldiers of the World War (1914–18).

**Williams, Henry Shaler.** 1847–1918. American paleontologist; authority on American Devonian period; on staff of U.S. Geological Survey (1883–1918); author of *Geological Biology* (1895).

**Williams, Henry Smith.** 1863–1943. American physician and writer; specialist in nervous and mental diseases and hematology. See also Edward Huntington WILLIAMS.

**Williams, Henry Willard.** 1821–1895. American ophthalmologist, b. Boston; first professor of this subject (from 1871), Harvard Med. School; a founder of American Ophthalmological Society (1864) and its president (1868–75).

**Williams, Horace,** *in full* **Henry Horace.** 1858–1940. American philosopher, b. Sunbury, N.C.; educ. N.C. State U. (grad. 1883), Yale, Harvard, and in Germany; taught philosophy at U. of N.C. (1891–1939); author of *The Evolution of Logic, Modern Logic, The Education of Horace Williams,* etc.

**Williams,** Sir **Ifor.** 1881–1965. Welsh scholar; authority on early Welsh language and literature.

**Williams, Isaac.** 1802–1865. Welsh clergyman and Tractarian author and poet; associated with Keble and Richard Hurrell Froude in Tractarian movement; author of sacred poetry after model of Keble's, but known chiefly for his tract No. 80 on *Reserve in Communicating Religious Knowledge;* wrote and translated many hymns.

**Williams, Israel.** See under Elisha WILLIAMS.

**Williams, James Robert.** 1888–1957. American cartoonist; produced *Out Our Way*, a daily syndicated cartoon appearing in more than 700 papers.

**Williams, Jesse Lynch.** 1807–1886. American civil engineer, b. Westfield, N.C. Government director, Union Pacific Railroad (1864–69); submitted report showing cost of construction less than government subsidy, and thus brought about the Crédit Mobilier inquiry.
His grandson **Jesse Lynch Williams** (1871–1929) was an author and playwright; author of the novels *The Married Life of the Frederick Carrolls* (1910), *Not Wanted* (1923), *She Knew She Was Right* (1930), etc., and the plays *The Stolen Story* (1906), *Why Marry* (1917; winner of Pulitzer prize), *Why Not* (1922), *Lovely Lady* (1925).

**Williams, John.** 1664–1729. American clergyman; pastor at Deerfield (from 1688); one of the captives taken by raiding band of French and Indians (Feb. 29, 1704); released (Nov. 21, 1706) and returned to his pastorate (Jan., 1707). See Eleazar WILLIAMS.

**Williams, John.** *Pseudonym* **Anthony Pas'quin** (păs'kwĭn). 1761–1818. Writer, b. London, Eng.; dramatic critic in London (to c. 1798); to U.S. (1797 or 1798); heartily vilified by contemporaries and literary historians for his bitter and satirical criticisms.

**Williams, John.** 1796–1839. English missionary martyr; killed and eaten by natives of Erromanga in New Hebrides.

**Williams, John.** 1817–1899. American Protestant Episcopal clergyman and educator; president of Trinity College, Hartford, Conn. (1848–53); bishop (from 1865); presiding bishop of the Protestant Episcopal Church (1887–99); a founder, professor, and dean, Berkeley Divinity School, Middletown, Conn. (1854–99).

**Williams, Jonathan.** 1750–1815. Grandnephew of Benjamin Franklin. American diplomat, businessman, and army officer, b. Boston. Joined Franklin in Paris (1776); remained abroad (to 1785) engaged in business and occasionally acting as colonial purchasing agent. Successful merchant in Philadelphia (from 1785). Superintendent of West Point (1805); encountered great difficulties of administration and congressional indifference to West Point's needs, and resigned (1812). As army engineer, planned and supervised building of defenses in New York harbor.

**Williams,** Sir **Monier Monier-.** See MONIER-WILLIAMS.

**Williams, Patry.** Pseudonym of two English women **M. Patry** and **D. Williams,** living and writing together; collaborators in *The Gulf Invisible* (1925), *The Other Law* (1927), *I Am Canute* (1938), *God's Warrior* (1942), etc.

**Williams, Ralph Vaughan.** See VAUGHAN WILLIAMS.

**Williams, Rebecca,** *nee* **Yan'cey** (yăn'sĭ). 1899– . American writer, b. Lynchburg, Va.; author of *The Vanishing Virginian*, story of her father and his circle (1940), *Carry Me Back* (autobiography; 1942).

**Williams, Robert R.** 1886–1965. American chemist; known for work on constitution and synthesis of vitamin $B_1$.

**Williams, Roger.** 1603?–1683. Clergyman and founder of colony of Rhode Island in America, b. London, Eng.; sailed for America (Dec. 1, 1630). Pastorate in Salem, Mass. (1631), but incurred hostility of civil authorities by his doctrines and outspoken criticisms of what he deemed their abuse of their powers; banished by Massachusetts General Court (Oct., 1635). With a few faithful adherents, moved southward and founded Providence (c. June, 1636), earliest settlement in Rhode Island. Maintained good relations with the Indians and, by his friendship with the Narragansetts, aided in colonial success in the Pequot War. In religious creed, accepted Baptist doctrine for a time, but soon (from 1639) withdrew from all church connections, accepting no creed but maintaining a fundamental belief in Christianity. To England (1643) and secured a charter for the Providence Plantations in Narragansett Bay (Mar. 14, 1644). President of the colony (1654–57). Famous as apostle of religious toleration and an advocate of democracy and liberal government. Elected to Hall of Fame (1920).

**Williams, Roger John.** 1893– . American chemist, b. Ootacamund, India; professor, Oregon State College (1932–39), Texas (from 1939). Discoverer of pantothenic acid; author of textbooks of organic chemistry and biochemistry.

**Williams, Rowland.** *Bardic name* **Hw'fa Môn** (hōō'vȧ mōn'). 1823–1905. Welsh Congregational minister and poet; won chair, highest bardic award, at National Eisteddfod (1862, 1873, 1878); chief bardic adjudicator (1875–92); archdruid (from 1894).

**Williams, Samuel Wells.** 1812–1884. American missionary and scholar, b. Utica, N.Y. Sailed for China (1833) to take position as printer in Canton. Devoted himself to study of Chinese and Japanese languages; interpreter for Admiral Perry's expedition to Japan (1853–54); secretary and interpreter for American legation in China (1856–76). Professor of Chinese language and literature, Yale (1877–84). Compiled *A Tonic Dictionary of the Chinese Language in the Canton Dialect* (1856), *A Syllabic Dictionary of the Chinese Language* (1874). His son **Frederick Wells** (1857–1928) was teacher of Oriental history, Yale (1893–1925); associated (1901–28) also with the founding and development of Yale-in-China, an institution at Changsha.

**Williams, Tal'cott** (tôl'kŭt). 1849–1928. Nephew of Samuel Wells Williams. American journalist; first director, Columbia School of Journalism (1912–19); author of *Turkey, a World Problem of Today* (1921), *The Newspaper Man* (1922).

**Williams, Tennessee.** *Orig. name* **Thomas Lanier Williams.** 1911– . Amer. playwright, b. Columbus, Miss. Wrote *The Glass Menagerie* (1945), *A Streetcar Named Desire* (1947), *Cat on a Hot Tin Roof* (1955), *Sweet Bird of Youth* (1959), *The Night of the Iguana* (1961).

**Williams, William.** 1717–1791. Welsh hymn writer and itinerant Methodist minister; author of over 800 hymns, including the one translated as *Guide Me, O Thou Great Jehovah.*

**Williams, William.** 1731–1811. American merchant and politician, b. Lebanon, Conn.; member, Continental Congress (1776–78; 1783, 1784) and a signer of the Declaration of Independence.

**Williams, William Car'los** (kär'lōs). 1883–1963. American physician and writer, b. Rutherford, N.J. Author of verse collected in *The Complete Collected Poems of William Carlos Williams 1906–1938* (1939); of essays, and the novels *A Voyage to Pagany* (1928), *White Mule* (1937), *In the Money* (1940). Awarded *Dial* prize for services to American literature (1926).

**Williams,** Sir **William Fenwick.** 1800–1883. British army officer. As commander of Turkish force in Crimean War, hero of defense of Kars against Russians (1855).

**Wil'liam·son** (wĭl'yăm·s'n), **Alexander William.** 1824–1904. English chemist; known esp. for work on etherification and the constitution of ether.

**Williamson, Charles Norris** (1859–1920) and his wife **Alice Muriel,** *nee* **Liv'ing·ston** [lĭv'ĭng·stŭn] (1869?–1933). Joint authors of popular novels, including *The Lightning Conductor* (1902), *My Friend the Chauffeur* (1905), *The Lion's Mouse* (1919).

**Williamson, George Charles.** 1858–1942. English art editor and writer on art.

**Williamson, Henry.** 1895– . English novelist; served in Flanders in World War; began his career with an autobiographical tetralogy, *The Flax of Dream* (comprising *The Beautiful Years,* 1921; *Dandelion Days,* 1922; *The Dream of Fair Women,* 1924; *The Pathway,* 1928); won Hawthornden prize (1928) with *Tarka the Otter.*

**Williamson, Thames** (thāmz) **Ross.** 1894– . American fiction writer; variously, a tramp, sheepherder, social worker, and college teacher (to 1922); devoted himself to writing (from 1922). His many books include *Problems in American Democracy* (1922), *Civics at Work* (1928), *North After Seals* (1934); several novels, and mystery stories under pseudonym of **S. S. Smith.**

**Williamson, William Crawford.** 1816–1895. English naturalist; first professor of natural history, anatomy, and physiology, Owens College, Manchester (1851–92); carried on researches on development of the teeth and bones of fishes, and in paleobotany.

**Wil'liams–Tay'lor** (wĭl'yămz·tā'lẽr), Sir **Frederick.** 1863–1945. Canadian financier, b. Moncton, New Brunswick; associated with Bank of Montreal (from 1878); manager of its London office (1905); general manager of bank (1913–29); director (from 1929).

**Wil'li·bald** (wĭl'ĭ·bôld), Saint. 700?–786. English missionary in Germany; nephew and associate of Saint Boniface; bishop of Eichstätt (741).

**Wil'li·brord** (wĭl'ĭ·brôrd) *or* **Wil'brord** (wĭl'brôrd) *or* **Wil'brod** (wĭl'brŏd), Saint. 657?–?738. English missionary to Friesland and Denmark (from 690); called "Apostle of the Frisians"; archbishop of the Frisians (695?), residing at Utrecht.

**Wil'ling·don** (wĭl'ĭng·dŭn), 1st Marquis of. **Freeman Free'man–Thom'as** (frē'măn·tŏm'ăs). 1866–1941. British statesman; junior lord of treasury (1905–12); governor of Bombay (1913–19), of Madras (1919–24); governor general of Canada (1926–31); viceroy and governor general of India (1931–36); lord warden of Cinque Ports (from 1936).

**Wil'lis** (wĭl'ĭs), Sir **Algernon Us'borne** (?ŭz'bẽrn). 1889– . British naval officer; entered navy (1904); served in World War (1914–18), including battle of Jutland; chief of staff, Mediterranean fleet (1939–41); rear admiral (1940); commander in chief, African Station (1941–43); flag officer commanding force "H" (Mar., 1943).

**Willis, Bailey.** See under Nathaniel Parker WILLIS.

**Willis, Henry Parker.** 1874–1937. American economist, b. Weymouth, Mass. Assoc. editor (1912–14) and editor in chief (1919–31), New York *Journal of Commerce.* Also, secretary of the Federal Reserve Board, in Washington, D.C. (1914–18) and director of research (1918–22); consulting economist for the board (from 1922). Professor of banking, Columbia (from 1917). Author of books on banking and finance.

**Willis, Nathaniel Parker.** 1806–1867. American editor and writer, b. Portland, Me. Founded and edited *American Monthly* in Boston (1829–31). Traveled in Europe as correspondent of New York *Mirror* (1831–36); associate editor, with George Pope Morris, of the *Evening Mirror* (1844–46) and the *Home Journal* (1846–67). Settled (1853) at his country home, "Idlewild," on the Hudson River near Washington Irving's "Sunnyside." Author of *Poetical Scripture Sketches* (1827), *Fugitive Poetry* (1829), *Inklings of Adventure* (3 vols., 1836), *À l'Abri; or, the Tent Pitch'd* (1839), *Loiterings of Travel* (1840), *American Scenery* (3 vols., 1840), *Pencillings by the Way* (1844), *Dashes at Life with a Free Pencil* (1845), *Rural Letters* (1849), *Famous Persons and Places* (1854), *Paul Fane* (1856), *The Convalescent* (1859), and the play *Tortesa, or the Usurer Matched* (1839). His son **Bailey** (1857–1949), geologist; on staff of U.S. Geological Survey

(1884–1916); professor of geology, Stanford (1915–22); consulting geological engineer (from 1922).

**Willis, Thomas.** 1621–1675. English anatomist and physician; founder of the Royal Society; physician to Charles II. Distinguished diabetes mellitus from other forms of diabetes; discovered system of connecting arteries at base of brain known as *circle of Willis;* published works in Latin on the brain and nervous system.

**Wil'lis·ton** (wĭl'ĭs·tŭn), **Samuel.** 1861–1963. American legal scholar; professor of law, Harvard (1895–1938); author and editor of legal treatises and compilations.

**Williston, Samuel Wendell.** 1852–1918. American paleontologist; assistant to O. C. Marsh at Yale (1876–85); head of department of vertebrate paleontology, Univ. of Chicago (from 1902).

**Will'kie** (wĭl'kĭ), **Wendell Lewis.** 1892–1944. American lawyer and business executive, b. Elwood, Indiana, of German descent (family name originally Willcke); B.A. (1913) and LL.B. (1916), Indiana; served in U.S. army in World War; practiced law in Indiana; in New York as attorney (1929–33), president (1933–40), Commonwealth and Southern Corp.; Republican nominee for president of the United States (1940); practiced law in New York (1941 ff.); made tour of Egypt, Middle East, Russia, and China (Sept.–Oct., 1942), recording experiences and conclusions in *One World* (1943).

**Wil'lough·by** *or* **Wil'lo·bie** (wĭl'ō·bĭ), **Henry.** 1574?–?1596. Hero and probable author of an English poem, *Willobies Avisa* (1594), in which occurs earliest known reference to Shakespeare's name in print and in which a friend, W. S. (presumably William Shakespeare), relates his recent rebuff by a haughty mistress.

**Willoughby,** Sir **Hugh.** d. 1554. English arctic navigator. Commander of a fleet of three vessels, one captained by Richard Chancellor, sent out by Sebastian Cabot to search for northeastern passage to Cathay (China) and India (1553); ships dispersed in a storm, Willoughby's ship and another landing in a harbor in Lapland. During the winter all perished.

**Willoughby, Westel Woodbury.** 1867–1945. American political scientist; professor, Johns Hopkins (1897–1933); adviser to Chinese government (1916–17, 1921–22, 1924–25); author of *Government and Administration of the United States* (1891), *The Nature of the State...* (1896), *Social Justice* (1900), *Constitutional Law of the United States* (3 vols., 1929), etc. His twin brother **William Franklin** (1867–1960), economist; on staff of U.S. Department of Labor (1890–1901); treasurer (1901–07) and secretary (1907–09) of Puerto Rico; professor of jurisprudence and politics, Princeton (1912–17); director of Institute for Government Research (1916–32); author of *The Government of Modern States* (1919), *Principles of Public Administration* (1927), etc.

**Wills** (wĭlz), **Helen Newington.** 1906– . American tennis player, b. Centerville, Calif.; m. (1929; divorced) Frederick S. Moody; 2d (1939) Aidan Roark. Women's singles tennis champion of U.S. (1923–29; with exception of 1926), of France (4 times), of England (8 times).

**Wills, William Gorman.** 1828–1891. Irish playwright and poet; made great success with *Charles I* (1872), played by Henry Irving; other plays include *Medea in Corinth* (1872), *Olivia* (1873; based on Goldsmith's *Vicar of Wakefield*). Author of ballads, including *I'll Sing Thee Songs of Araby.*

**Wills,** Sir **William Henry.** 1st Baron **Win'ter·stoke** (wĭn'tẽr·stōk). 1830–1911. English tobacco manufacturer, son of **William Day Wills** (1797–1865) and grandson of **Henry Overton Wills** (1761–1826) who was partner with his father-in-law, William Day, in tobacco and snuff trade, in Bristol. W. H. Wills entered partnership (1858), along with two first cousins, in father's company to form the firm W. D. and H. O. Wills; M.P. (1880–85, 1895–1900); baronet (1893); established (1901), with aid of negotiations by his cousin Sir **George Alfred Wills** (1854–1928), combine of British manufacturers, Imperial Tobacco Company of Great Britain and Ireland.

**Wills, William John.** 1834–1861. Australian explorer, b. Devonshire; emigrated to Victoria (1852); second in command to Robert O'Hara Burke (*q.v.*) in ill-fated exploratory expedition to discover northward route across Australia (1860); died of starvation.

**Willsie, Honoré.** See Honoré MORROW.

**Will'son** (wĭl's'n), **Russell.** 1883–1948. American naval officer, b. Fredonia, N.Y.; grad. U.S.N.A., Annapolis (1906); in World War, organized code signal section of Navy Dept.; rear admiral (1939); chief of staff, U.S. fleet (1942).

**Will'stät'ter** (vĭl'shtĕt'ẽr), **Richard.** 1872–1942. German chemist; known for researches on complex organic substances, esp. on the coloring matter (anthocyanins and chlorophyll) in plants and on enzymes. Awarded 1915 Nobel prize in chemistry.

**Willughby, Francis.** 1635–1672. See under John RAY.

**Wil'lum·sen** (vĕl'ŏŏm·s'n), **Jens Ferdinand.** 1863–1958. Danish painter and sculptor.

**Wil'lys** (wĭl'ĭs), **John North.** 1873–1935. American industrialist; started in bicycle business (1890); bought Overland Automobile Company plant in Indianapolis (1907) and manufactured Willys-Overland and other automobiles. U.S. ambassador to Poland (1930–32).

**Wil'marth** (wĭl'märth), **Lemuel Everett.** 1835–1918. American painter; studio in New York; painter esp. of genre pictures.

**Wilmington,** Earl of. 1673?–1743. See Spencer COMPTON.

**Wil'mot** (wĭl'mŏt), **David.** 1814–1868. American politician; practiced law in Towanda, Pa. Member, U.S. House of Representatives (1845–51); introduced proviso (Wilmot Proviso) attached as an amendment to a bill in Congress for purchasing territory from Mexico, the amendment providing that slavery should be prohibited in any such territory thus acquired; the proviso was adopted in the House but defeated in the Senate. One of the founders of the Republican party; U.S. senator (1861–63); loyally supported Lincoln.

**Wilmot, Henry** and **John.** Earls of **Rochester.** See ROCHESTER.

**Wil'motte'** (vēl'mōt'), **Maurice.** 1861–1942. Belgian literary critic and scholar.

**Wilms** (vĭlms), **Jan Willem** *or* **Johann Wilhelm.** 1772–1847. Pianist, organist, composer, and teacher, b. near Solingen, Germany; resident in Amsterdam (from 1791); composed Dutch national anthem *Wien Neêrlands Bloed,* also sonatas, concertos, a string quartet, trios, etc.

**Wil'na** (vĭl'nȧ), **Elijah** *or* **Elias.** *Also* **Elijah** *or* **Elias ben Sol'o·mon** (bĕn sŏl'ō·mŭn). *Or* **Ga'on** (gä'ōn; gä·ōn') **Elijah of Wilna.** 1720–1797. Hebrew scholar; his critical researches in rabbinic literature introduced later scientific investigations; instrumental in reviving interest in the older Midrash and the Palestinian Talmud; rigorous opponent of the Hasidim; among his published commentaries are those on the Pentateuch, the Prophets, the Hagiographa.

**Wil'pert** (vĭl'pẽrt), **Joseph.** 1857–1944. German authority on early Christian art, vestments, etc.

**Wil'son** (wĭl's'n), **Alexander.** 1714–1786. Scottish astronomer; first professor of astronomy, Glasgow (1760–84); discovered nature of sunspots (1769).

**Wilson, Alexander.** 1766–1813. Ornithologist, b. Paisley, in Renfrewshire, Scotland. Weaver (1779–89) and itinerant peddler (1789–94); to U.S. (1794) and became schoolmaster in rural schools in New Jersey and eastern Pennsylvania. Encouraged by William Bartram, Philadelphia, began serious ornithological work (c. 1802). Aided by Alexander Lawson, who prepared plates of the birds described, began publication of *American Ornithology* (7 vols., 1808–13; vols. 8 and 9, 1814), universally recognized as a classic in its field. Author also of a volume of verse (1790) and a poetical account of a walking trip from Philadelphia to Niagara Falls and back, under the title of *The Foresters* (1805).

**Wilson, Allen Benjamin.** 1824–1888. American inventor, b. Willett, N.Y.; cabinetmaker by trade (from 1840); experimented with a sewing machine (from 1848); secured patent on his invention (Nov. 12, 1850), and on improvements on his machine (Aug. 12, 1851); associated with Nathaniel Wheeler in partnership, Wheeler, Wilson & Co., to manufacture the improved sewing machines, the Wheeler and Wilson sewing machines (from 1851); introduced further improvements, including a stationary bobbin and a four-motion feed.

**Wilson, Arthur.** 1595–1652. English historian and playwright; author of *The Inconstant Lady* (1653) and other plays, not preserved, and of a history (1653) of the reign of James I.

**Wilson,** Sir **Arthur Knyvet.** 1842–1921. British naval officer. Served in Crimean War, and in operations against Alexandria (1880); won V.C. at El Teb (1884); rear admiral (1895); vice-admiral (1901); commander in chief of home and channel fleets (1903–07); admiral of the fleet (1907); first sea lord (1910–12).

**Wilson, Augusta Jane,** *nee* **Evans.** See EVANS.

**Wilson, Charles Edward.** 1886–1972. American industrialist, b. New York City; with General Electric Co. (1899), president (1940–42; 1944–50); vice-chairman (1942), executive vice-chairman (1943–44), War Production Board.

**Wilson, Charles Erwin.** 1890–1961. American engineer and industrialist, b. Minerva, Ohio; with General Motors Corp. (1919 ff.), vice-president (1929–40), president (1941–53); U.S. secretary of defense (1953–57).

**Wilson, Charles Morrow.** 1905– . American writer, b. Fayetteville, Ark.; A.B., Arkansas (1926); author of *Acres of Sky* (1930), *Meriwether Lewis* (1934), *Backwoods America* (1935), *Roots of America* (1936), *America at Work* (1938), *Central America* (1941), *Trees and Test Tubes* (1943), etc.

**Wilson, Charles Thomson Rees.** 1869–1959. Scottish physicist, b. Glencorse, Midlothian. M.A., Cantab. Professor of natural philosophy, Cambridge (1925–34). Known for research on atmospheric electricity and development of a method for obtaining photographic data on the activity of ionized particles in a special container (Wilson cloud chamber). Awarded (jointly with A. H. Compton) 1927 Nobel prize for physics.

**Wilson, Clarence True.** 1872–1939. American Methodist Episcopal clergyman and prohibitionist; general secretary, board of temperance, prohibition, and morals, Methodist Episcopal Church (1916–36).

**Wilson,** Sir **Daniel.** 1816–1892. Archaeologist and educational reformer, b. in Scotland; professor of history and English literature (1853) and president (from 1881), Toronto U.; advocate of undenominational university education. Author of *Anthropology* (1885), *The Lost Atlantis* (1892), etc.

**Wilson, Dover.** See John Dover WILSON.

**Wilson, Edmund.** 1895–1972. American critic and miscellaneous writer, b. Red Bank, N.J.; A.B., Princeton (1916); author of *I Thought of Daisy* (novel; 1929), *Axel's Castle* (1931), *The Triple Thinkers* (1938), *To the Finland Station* (1940), *The Wound and the Bow* (1941), *Memoirs of Hecate County* (novel; 1946), *The Shores of Light* (1952), *The Scrolls from the Dead Sea* (1955), *A Piece of My Mind* (1956), *Apologies to the Iroquois* (1959), *Patriotic Gore* (1962), *O Canada . . .* (1965), *A Prelude* (1967), *Upstate* (1971), etc.

**Wilson, Edmund Beecher.** 1856–1939. American zoologist; specialized in cytology, embryology, and experimental morphology.

**Wilson, Edward Adrian.** 1872–1912. English physician and antarctic explorer. On Robert F. Scott's last antarctic expedition as chief of scientific staff; with party of five which reached South Pole (Jan., 1912) and perished of cold and starvation on return sledge journey.

**Wilson, Florence.** See Florence AUSTRAL.

**Wilson, Forrest,** *in full* **Robert Forrest.** 1883–1942. American journalist and writer, b. Warren, Ohio; educ. Allegheny Coll. and Cambridge U.; author of *Paris on Parade* (1925), *Rich Brat* (1929), *Crusader in Crinoline* (1941; Pulitzer prize biography), short stories, etc.; coauthor of *Blessed Event* (play; 1932).

**Wilson, George Grafton.** 1863–1951. American authority on international law; professor, Harvard (1910–36) and at U.S. Naval War Coll. (1900–37).

**Wilson, Halsey William.** 1868–1954. American publisher, b. Wilmington, Vt.; compiled (1898) *Cumulative Book Index;* president of H. W. Wilson Co. (*United States Catalog*, *Readers' Guide to Periodical Literature*, and *Book Review Digest*).

**Wilson, Harold,** *in full* **James Harold.** 1916– British politician; labor party leader (from 1963); prime minister (1964–69, 1974–76).

**Wilson, Harry Leon.** 1867–1939. American fiction writer, b. Oregon, Ill.; m. (1902) Rose C. O'Neill (*q.v.*); editor, *Puck* (1896–1902); author of *Zig Zag Tales* (1896), *Bunker Bean* (1912), *Ruggles of Red Gap* (1915), *Two Black Sheep* (1931), etc.

**Wilson, Henry.** *Orig. name* **Jeremiah Jones Col'bath** (kōl'bȧth). 1812–1875. Name changed on his application to New Hampshire legislature (c. 1834). American politician, b. Farmington, N.H. Engaged in manufacture of shoes (from c. 1833). Ardent antislavery advocate; headed group that bolted Whig national convention (1848) and called convention at Buffalo that founded the Free-Soil party; edited Free-Soil party journal, the Boston *Republican* (1848–51); chairman, Free-Soil convention (1852). Joined the American (Know-Nothing) party (1854) but soon withdrew from it because of its intolerance and its failure to take a positive stand on slavery issue. U.S. senator from Massachusetts (1855–73); one of founders of Republican party; chairman of Senate committee on military affairs through the Civil War; strongly opposed Andrew Johnson. Vice-president of the United States (1873–75).

**Wilson, Henry Braid.** 1861–1954. American naval officer; grad. U.S.N.A., Annapolis (1881). Commissioned rear admiral (July, 1917); commanded patrol force of the Atlantic fleet (1917–18), and U.S. naval forces in France (1918–19); commissioned admiral (June, 1919) and commander in chief of the Atlantic fleet (1919–21); superintendent, U.S. Naval Academy (1921–25).

**Wilson,** Sir **Henry Hughes.** 1864–1922. British army officer and builder of the entente with France, b. in Ireland. Commandant of Staff Coll. (1907); advocated co-operation with France in event of Continental war; as director of military operations (from 1910), instrumental in landing expeditionary force in France without loss of a man or horse (1914); principal liaison officer with French headquarters (1914–15). Advocate and member of Allied Supreme War Council (1917); chief of British general staff (1918–22); field marshal (1919). M.P. for North Down, Ireland (1922); advocate of drastic coercion against Sinn Fein; murdered by two Sinn Feiners.

**Wilson, Henry Lane.** 1857–1932. American lawyer and diplomat; practiced law, Spokane, Wash.; U.S. minister to Chile (1897–1904), Belgium (1905–09), Mexico (1909–13); author of *Diplomatic Episodes in Mexico, Belgium and Chile* (1927).

**Wilson, Henry Maitland.** 1st baron. 1881–1964. British army officer; served in Boer War, World War I; commander, forces in Egypt (1939); military governor of Cyrenaica (1941); commander in Greece (1941), in Palestine and Trans-Jordan (1941), in Persia-Iraq (1942–43), in Middle East (1943–44); supreme allied commander in Mediterranean (1944); field marshal (1944); chief of British joint staff mission in Washington (1944–47).

**Wilson, Henry Parke Custis.** 1827–1897. American surgeon and gynecologist, in Baltimore (from 1851).

**Wilson, Herbert Cou′per** (kōō′pẽr). 1858–1940. American astronomer; on teaching staff, Carleton Coll. (1887–1926), as professor and director of Goodsell Observatory (1908–26). Made special study of double and variable stars and of astronomical photography.

**Wilson, Horace Hayman.** 1786–1860. English Orientalist; professor of Sanskrit, Oxford (1832–60). Published edition of the *Meghadūta* (1813); compiled *Sanskrit-English Dictionary* (1819) and Sanskrit grammar (1841); translated *Vishnupurāna* (1840), part of *Rig-Veda* (6 vols., 1850 ff.).

**Wilson, Hugh Robert.** 1885–1946. American diplomat, b. Evanston, Ill. B.A., Yale (1906); in diplomatic service (from 1911); envoy to Switzerland (1927–37); ambassador to Germany (1938–39); adviser to secretary of state (1940; retired); author of *Education of a Diplomat* (1938), *Diplomat Between Wars* (1941).

**Wilson, J. Arbuthnot.** Pseudonym of Grant ALLEN.

**Wilson, Jack.** See WOVOKA.

**Wilson, James.** 1742–1798. Lawyer and politician in America, b. near St. Andrews, Scotland. To U.S. (1765) and settled in Philadelphia. Member of Continental Congress (1775), and prepared and published for distribution to his fellow members *Considerations on the Nature and Extent of the Legislative Authority of the British Parliament*, in which he adopted the extreme position that Parliament had no authority over the colonies. Member of Continental Congress again (1776, 1782, 1783, 1785–87), and a signer of the Declaration of Independence. Delegate from Pennsylvania to the Constitutional Convention (1787) and to the Pennsylvania ratification convention (1788), where he had important influence in securing ratification of Constitution. Largely drafted constitution of State of Pennsylvania (1790). Associate justice, U.S. Supreme Court (1789–98); also, first professor of law, U. of Pennsylvania (from 1790).

**Wilson, James.** 1805–1860. British economist; founded *The Economist* (1843); financial secretary to treasury (1853–58); in India as financial member of council of India (from 1859); established paper currency in India.

**Wilson, James.** 1836–1920. Farmer and politician, b. in Ayrshire, Scotland; to U.S. (1851) and settled on a farm in Iowa (1855); U.S. secretary of agriculture (1897–1913); increased scope and effectiveness of department.

**Wilson, James Falconer.** 1828–1895. American lawyer and politician; member, U.S. House of Representatives (1861–69), and one of managers appointed by the House to conduct impeachment proceedings against Andrew Johnson (1868); member, U.S. Senate (1883–95); secured passage of Original Package Act, sometimes called the Wilson Act or Law (1890).

**Wilson, James Grant.** See under William WILSON (1801–1860).

**Wilson, James Harrison.** 1837–1925. American army officer and author; served through Civil War; brigadier general of volunteers (Oct., 1863); commanded third division in Sheridan's cavalry corps, Army of the Potomac; chief of cavalry, military division of the Mississippi, and brevet major general (Oct., 1864); defeated Forrest at Franklin (Nov. 30, 1864), and again at Ebenezer Church (Apr. 1, 1865), captured Montgomery, Ala., and Columbus, Ga., and reached Macon when hostilities ended. Resigned from army (Dec. 31, 1870) to engage in railway engineering and management. Volunteered in Spanish-American War; second in command to Gen. Adna R. Chaffee of contingent sent to China at time of Boxer uprising (1900).

**Wilson, John.** 1595–1674. English composer and lute virtuoso. Musician to Charles I (1635) and to Charles II (1661); set to music Shakespeare's *Take, O Take Those Lips Away* and composed airs and glees, including *In the Merry Month of May*. Perhaps the Jack Willson of stage direction in *Much Ado about Nothing* II iii, in the folio edition of 1623, who sang *Sigh no More, Ladies*.

**Wilson, John.** *Pseudonym* **Christopher North** (nôrth). 1785–1854. Scottish poet, essayist, and critic. Friend of Wordsworth, Southey, Coleridge, and De Quincey; published two volumes of graceful poetry, *The Isle of Palms* (1812), *The City of the Plague* (1816). Joined (1817) J. G. Lockhart in *Blackwood's Magazine*, Tory magazine; on basis of his Toryism, appointed professor of moral philosophy, Edinburgh (1820–51); turned to prose fiction in *Lights and Shadows of Scottish Life* (1822), *Trials of Margaret Lyndsay* (1823), *The Foresters* (1825); contributed to *Blackwood's* critical essays on Homer and Spenser and greater number of *Noctes Ambrosianae* (1822–35), a symposium on literature, politics, philosophy, and topics of the day, in which he appears as "Christopher North" and James Hogg as "the Ettrick Shepherd."

**Wilson, John.** 1802–1868. Printer and author, b. Glasgow, Scotland; to U.S. (1846); founded firm of John Wilson & Son, for many years in charge of University Press, Cambridge. Author of *Treatise on Grammatical* [changed in subsequent editions to *English*] *Punctuation* (1826), first standard English treatise on this subject.

**Wilson, John.** 1804–1875. Scottish missionary and Orientalist. To Bombay as missionary (1829); established schools for native children, strove for legal and social reform; mastered languages of western India, made linguistic contributions, esp. in Avestan; aided government by knowledge of archaic alphabets and local dialects during Sepoy Mutiny (1857); author of *The Parsi Religion Unfolded* (1843), *Lands of the Bible* (1847).

**Wilson, John Dover.** 1881–1969. English educator and Shakespearean scholar; author of *Life in Shakespeare's England* (1911), *The Essential Shakespeare* (1932), and books upon problems in *Hamlet*.

**Wilson, John Mackay.** 1804–1835. English poet and originator of the *Tales of the Borders*, realistic narratives of stirring incident or sentiment, in weekly numbers (1834–35), continued by Alexander Leighton.

**Wilson, Margaret.** Mrs. **G. D. Turner.** 1882– . American novelist; m. (1923) G. D. Turner, of Oxford, Eng.; resident in England thereafter; author of *The Able McLaughlins* (awarded Pulitzer prize; 1923), *The Kenworthys* (1925), *Daughters of India* (1928), *Trousers of Taffeta* (1929), *The Valiant Wife* (1933), *Law and the McLaughlins* (1937), etc.

**Wilson, Richard.** 1714–1782. Welsh landscape painter. Best-known pictures: *Niobe* (1760) and *View of Rome from the Villa Madama* (1765).

**Wilson, Robert.** d. 1600. English comic actor and playwright; original member of earl of Leicester's company (1574); author of several morality plays including *Three Ladies of London* (1584), containing the incident of the Jew seeking to recover his debt, later used by Shakespeare in his *Merchant of Venice.*

**Wilson, Robert.** 1803–1882. Scottish engineer; inventor of screw propeller for vessels (c. 1827) and double-acting steam hammer (1861); his double-action screw propeller used by British War Department in fish torpedo (1880).

**Wilson, Robert Burns.** 1850–1916. American painter and author; as a painter, excelled in landscapes; author of several collections of verse and one novel, *Until the Day Break* (1900). His best-known poem, *Remember the Maine* (1898), supplied the slogan of the war with Spain.

**Wilson,** Sir **Robert Thomas.** 1777–1849. English army officer and military writer. Commanded brigade under Wellington in Peninsular War; British military commissioner attached to Russian army (1811); commanded Prussian reserve at Lützen (1813); M.P. (1818–31); general (1841); governor of Gibraltar (1842–49). Author of accounts of expedition to Egypt (1802) and campaigns in Poland (1811), and of a *Sketch of the Military and Political Power of Russia* (1817).

**Wilson, Robert Woodrow.** 1936– . American radio astronomer. With Bell Laboratories (1963– ); awarded (with Arno A. Penzias) Nobel prize for physics (1978).

**Wilson, Romer.** See under Edward Joseph Harrington O'BRIEN.

**Wilson, Rose Cecil O'Neill.** See Rose Cecil O'NEILL.

**Wilson, Samuel.** 1766–1854. American meat packer, b. Arlington, Mass.; resident of Troy, N.Y. (from 1789), where he was known as "Uncle Sam"; during War of 1812, acted as inspector for a government contractor and stamped barrels of meat with initials U.S. (for United States), from which, through misinterpretation, may have come the use of "Uncle Sam" for the U.S. government.

**Wilson, Samuel Alexander Kin·nier′** (kĭ·nēr′). 1877–1937. Neurologist, b. in New Jersey, U.S.A.; practiced in London, Eng. Wilson's disease, a rare disease characterized by degeneration in the cerebrum and cirrhosis of the liver, is named for him.

**Wilson, Thomas Woodrow.** See Woodrow WILSON.

**Wilson, William.** 1690–1741. See under Ebenezer ERSKINE.

**Wilson, William.** 1801–1860. Bookdealer and poet, b. in Perthshire, Scotland; to U.S. (1833) and became partner in a bindery and bookstore in Poughkeepsie, N.Y. (1834). His collected verse was published posthumously (1869). His son **James Grant** (1832–1914) was a bookdealer, editor, and army officer; served in Civil War; coeditor with John Fiske of Appleton's *Cyclopaedia of American Biography* (6 vols., 1886–89); author of *Life and Campaigns of Ulysses Simpson Grant* (1868), *Fitz-Greene Halleck* (1869), *The Poets and Poetry of Scotland ...* (1876), etc.

**Wilson, William Bau′chop** (?bô′kŭp). 1862–1934. Labor leader in America, b. Blantyre, Scotland; to U.S. (1870). Employed in Pennsylvania coal mines (from 1871); one of organizers of United Mine Workers of America (1890) and its secretary-treasurer (1900–08); prominent in coal strikes (1899, 1902). Member, U.S. House of Representatives (1907–13). First U.S. secretary of labor (1913–21); organized new department and did important work in promoting mediation in labor disputes and advocating collective bargaining.

**Wilson, William Lyne.** 1843–1900. American soldier, educator, and politician, b. Middleway, Va. (now W.Va.). Served in Confederate army through Civil War. Member, U.S. House of Representatives (1883–95); associated with tariff legislation, esp. with what became known as the Wilson Act (1894), or the Wilson-Gorman Act. U.S. postmaster general (1895–97). Vigorous advocate of the gold standard; opposed W. J. Bryan (1896). President, Washington and Lee (1897–1900).

**Wilson, Woodrow,** *in full* **Thomas Woodrow.** 1856–1924. Twenty-eighth president of the United States, b. Staunton, Va. B.A., Princeton (1879). Adm. to bar and practiced in Atlanta, Ga. (1882). Ph.D., Johns Hopkins (1886). Instructor in history, Bryn Mawr (1885–88), Wesleyan (1888–90); professor of jurisprudence and political economy, Princeton (1890–1902); president of Princeton (1902–10); developed preceptorial system and advocated a house system based on the English universities with their component colleges. Governor of New Jersey (1911–13); attracted national attention by pushing through legislature important reform measures, including a primary election law, a corrupt practices act, an employers' liability act. President of the United States (1913–21); in domestic affairs, administration noted for passage of three constitutional amendments (17th, providing for direct popular election of senators; 18th, providing for prohibition; 19th, extending suffrage to women), Underwood Tariff Act, Clayton Antitrust Act, establishment of Federal Reserve banking system, repeal of Panama Canal tolls, Workmen's Compensation Act, Eight-hour Railway Wage Law, Federal Child Labor Law, purchase of Danish West Indies (Virgin Islands). In foreign affairs, policies were determined by World War (1914–18) and its aftermath. Maintained neutrality with great difficulty (1914–1915, 1916) until Germany, contrary to pledges previously given, announced (Jan. 31, 1917) unrestricted submarine warfare in waters around Great Britain; sinking of American ships following the change in German policy led to Wilson's appearance before Congress (Apr. 2, 1917) recommending a declaration that a state of war existed with Germany (voted by Congress Apr. 6, 1917). Directed mobilization of full strength of U.S. for victory; supported unwaveringly the men selected for important military and administrative posts; approved draft law for increasing the armed forces, War Industries Board's measures for control of production, measures for control of fuel and food, and measures for national regulation of railroads for war uses. Contributed to Allied success by formulating war aims, including proposals for a league of nations, and culminating in a speech before Congress (Jan. 8, 1918) in which he outlined Fourteen Points on the basis of which a peace might be made. Received acceptance from the Germans (Oct., 1918) of an armistice based on these Fourteen Points and transmitted it to Allies; gained acceptance, with reservations, by the Allies of the same Fourteen Points, and transmitted this to the German government (Nov. 5, 1918); with this mutual understanding, the Armistice was signed (Nov. 11, 1918). Wilson personally participated in Peace Conference, and forced acceptance of League of Nations covenant as an integral part of the treaty of peace. Awarded Nobel peace prize for 1919. In U.S., found a strong opposition in the Senate to ratification of the treaty of peace; refused to compromise on the terms; attempted country-wide speechmaking campaign to put the issue before the people (Sept., 1919); suffered nervous collapse (Sept. 25, 1919) followed by stroke of paralysis (Oct. 1–2, 1919); remained an invalid through remainder of his term of office. Lived in retirement in Washington (from Mar. 4, 1921), nominally a law partner with Bainbridge Colby but physically unable to do any work. Among his books are *Congressional Government, A Study in American Politics* (1885), *The State...*(1889), *A History of the American People* (5 vols., 1902), *Constitutional Government in the United States* (1908). A biography of Wilson, *Woodrow Wilson—Life and Letters* (8 vols., 1927–39), was published by Ray Stannard Baker. Elected to American Hall of Fame (1950). Cf. also Edward Mandell HOUSE.

**Wiltshire,** Earl of. See (1) Sir Thomas BOLEYN; (2) *William le Scrope*, at SCROPE family; (3) *James Butler*, under earls, marquises, and dukes of ORMONDE.

**Wi′mar** (vē′mär), **Carl,** *orig.* **Karl Ferdinand.** 1828–1862. Painter, b. near Bonn, Ger.; to U.S. (1843); known esp. for his paintings of American Indians.

**Wimbledon,** Viscount. See CECIL family.

**Wim′mer** (vĕm′ẽr), **Ludvig Frands Adalbert.** 1839–1920. Danish authority on Norse philology and runes.

**Wimpf′fen′** (vēmp′fĕn′), **Emmanuel Félix de.** 1811–1884. French army commander; served in Crimean and Italian wars, and in Algeria; corps commander in Franco-Prussian War; succeeded MacMahon in command in the battle of Sedan (1870) and signed the capitulation.

**Wims′hurst** (wĭmz′hûrst), **James.** 1832–1903. English engineer; invented a duplex generator of static electricity, the Wimshurst machine; adapted his generators to exciting X rays (1896); invented an improved vacuum pump and other devices.

**Wi′nant** (wī′nănt), **John Gilbert.** 1889–1947. American politician, b. New York City; served in A.E.F. (1917–19; captain in air corps); governor of New Hampshire (1925–26; 1931–34); chairman of Social Security Board (1935–37); U.S. ambassador to Great Britain (1941–46); U.S. representative to UN (1946–47).

**Win′chell** (wĭn′chĕl), **Alexander.** 1824–1891. American geologist; professor, Michigan (1853–73; from 1879); author of *Sketches of Creation* (1870), *The Doctrine of Evolution* (1874), *World Life* (a world history, 1883), *Geological Studies* (1886). His brother **Newton Horace** (1839–1914), geologist and archaeologist, was professor at Minnesota (1874–1900); believed that man lived on American continent in latter part of Ice Age; founder and editor (1888–1905) of *American Geologist*, first American geological periodical.

**Win′chel·sea** (wĭn′chĕl·sē), **Robert de.** d. 1313. English prelate; chancellor of Oxford (1288); archbishop of Canterbury (1293); strenuously upheld privileges of clergy; bore papal mandate (1300) forbidding Edward I's attack on Scots, and otherwise upheld papal authority; aided barons in struggle against Edward II.

**Win′ches′ter** (wĭn′chĕs′tẽr; -chĭs·tẽr), Marquises of. See PAULET.

**Winchester, Elhanan.** 1751–1797. American clergyman; in Baptist ministry (1771–87); unorthodox beliefs in universal restoration caused loss of pastorate. Preached with success in England (1787–94), a pioneer in spreading Universalist teaching.

**Winchester, Oliver Fisher.** 1810–1880. American industrialist; bought control of an arms-manufacturing company in New Haven, Conn., and acquired repeating-rifle inventions of various inventors; incorporated improvements until new Winchester rifle was developed (c. 1866); reorganized company under name of Winchester Repeating Arms Co.

**Win·chev′sky** (vĭn·chĕf′skē), **Morris.** *Original name* **Lip′pe** (lĭp′ĕ) **Ben·zi′on** (bĕn·tsē′ôn) **No′va·cho′vitch** (nô′vä·kô′vĭch). *Name used in private life* **Leopold Ben′e·dict** (bĕn′ē·dĭkt). *Pseudonym* **Ben–Nez** (bĕn-nĕts′). 1856–1932. Author, b. Yanovo, Lithuania; to U.S. (1894); widely known for his contributions to Yiddish journals, esp. for his lyric poems; author also of dramas, fables, novels, and brochures.

**Winchilsea,** Earls and countess of. See FINCH family.

**Winck′el·mann** (vĭng′kĕl·män), **Johann Joachim.** 1717–1768. German classical archaeologist and art critic, founder of scientific archaeology and expounder of classic art. Teacher and librarian (1743–54); Roman Catholic convert (1754); to Rome (1755), where he studied art and classical antiquities; visited Florence, Pompeii, Naples, etc.; in charge of antiquities (from 1763) and scriptor of the Vatican; murdered (1768). Author of *Gedanken über die Nachahmung der Griechischen Werke* (1755), *Geschichte der Kunst des Altertums* (1764), *Monumenti Antichi Inediti* (1767), etc.

**Winck′ler** (vĭngk′lẽr), **Hugo.** 1863–1913. German Assyriologist; professor, Berlin (1904); took part in excavations of ancient Sidon (1903–04); in Boghazkeui (1906–12), where he uncovered the ancient Hittite capital and discovered tablets in Hittite and other languages. Author of works on cuneiform inscriptions and the culture and history of ancient Babylonia and Assyria.

**Winckler, Josef.** 1881– . German author of hymns on work and industry, songs of German military exploits, and novels.

**Win′daus** (vĭn′dous), **Adolf.** 1876–1959. German chemist; professor and head of chemical institute, U. of Göttingen (1915–44); known for researches on sterols, especially for experiments proving that ultraviolet light activates ergosterol, giving it antirachitic properties. Awarded 1928 Nobel prize for chemistry.

**Win′del·band** (vĭn′dĕl·bänt), **Wilhelm.** 1848–1915. German philosopher.

**Wind′ham** (wĭn′dăm). See also WYNDHAM.

**Windham, William.** 1750–1810. English statesman; friend of Dr. Johnson and Burke; M.P. (1784–1810). On outbreak of French Revolution turned reactionary with Burke and joined cabinet under Pitt as secretary for war (1794–1801); held secretaryships of war and of colonial office in Grenville's government (1806–07); carried measures for pensions and shorter terms of service for army; advocated protection of England with large navy.

**Win′disch** (vĭn′dĭsh), **Ernst.** 1844–1918. German Sanskrit and Celtic philologist.

**Win′disch–Graetz′** (-grâts′), Prince **Alfred Candidus Ferdinand zu.** 1787–1862. Austrian field marshal; commander in Bohemia (1840–48); suppressed Czech uprising in Prague (1848), defeated Hungarians at Schwechat and suppressed insurrection in Vienna; with Schwarzenberg, helped elevate Francis Joseph I to the throne (1848); occupied Budapest, defeated Hungarians at Käpolna, but was defeated at Gödöllö and removed from command (1849); governor of fortress at Mainz (1859); Conservative member, Austrian upper house (1861).

**Win′dle** (wĭn′d'l), Sir **Bertram Co′ghill** (kō′g'l) **Alan.** 1858–1929. English medical scientist and Roman Catholic apologist. President of University College, Cork (1904–19), and professor of archaeology (1904); organized National University of Ireland. Professor of cosmology and anthropology, St. Michael's College, Toronto U. (from 1919); as president of Catholic Truth Society of Canada, sought to reconcile in public mind scientific advance with teaching of the church.

**Win′dom** (wĭn′dŭm), **William.** 1827–1891. American lawyer and politician; practiced in Winona, Minn. Member, U.S. House of Representatives (1859–69), and U.S. Senate (1870–81; 1881–83); U.S. secretary of the treasury (1881; 1889–91).

**Wind'sor** (wĭn'zẽr). Official name of royal family of Great Britain since 1917, superseding family name of Wettin (*q.v.*) and dynastic designation of Saxe-Coburg-Gotha (*q.v.*). Its ruling members have been: George V (from 1917), Edward VIII, George VI, and Elizabeth II. See also WELF and *Table* (*in Appendix*) for GREAT BRITAIN.

**Windsor,** Duke of. See EDWARD VIII (of Great Britain).

**Windsor, Alice de.** See Alice PERRERS.

**Windt'horst** (vĭnt'hôrst), **Ludwig.** 1812–1891. German statesman, lawyer, and Roman Catholic party leader; member of Reichstag (1867) and Prussian Chamber of Deputies; became leader (1870) of newly organized Catholic Center party during Kulturkampf, champion of ultramontane cause; leading opponent of Bismarck government, but a supporter of its economic policy.

**Wine'bren'ner** (wīn'brĕn'ẽr), **John.** 1797–1860. American religious leader; ordained in German Reformed Church ministry (1820). Evangelistic methods caused dismissal from his church in Harrisburg, Pa.; became itinerant evangelist in Pennsylvania and Maryland. Organized new church (1830), known (from 1845) as the General Eldership of the Churches of God in North America, or briefly as the Church of God in North America; its members known as Winebrennerians.

**Winefride,** Saint. See WINIFRED.

**Winfield, Arthur M.** See Edward STRATEMEYER.

**Winfrid.** See Saint BONIFACE.

**Win'gate** (wĭn'gĭt; -gāt), Sir **Francis Reginald.** 1861–1953. British army officer and administrator. Served on Sudan frontier (1889, 1891), in reconquest of Sudan (1896–98); succeeded Kitchener as governor general of Sudan (1899); general (1913); high commissioner for Egypt (1916–19). Master of Arabic; author of *Mahdiism and the Egyptian Sudan* (1891).

**Win'gate** (wĭn'gāt), **George Wood.** 1840–1928. American lawyer; practiced in New York City. As an officer in New York National Guard regiment, formulated (1867) rules for systematic rifle practice; instrumental in organizing National Rifle Association of America (1871) and was its president for 25 years.

**Wing'field** (wĭng'fēld), **Edward Maria.** 1560?–?1613. English settler in Virginia; one of those to whom Virginia charter was issued (Apr. 10, 1606); accompanied first settlers and was chosen first president of Virginia colony (Apr., 1607); deposed (Sept., 1607); sent to England (1608) and published his defense, *A Discourse of Virginia* (1608).

**Win'i·fred** (wĭn'ĭ·frĕd; -frĭd) *or* **Win'e·fride** (wĭn'ĕ-frĭd), Saint. Legendary 7th-century Welsh saint. Her head, cut off by Caractacus, lodged at foot of a hill, whence, according to the legend, a spring gushed, the famous holy well in Flintshire.

**Win'kel** (vĭng'kĕl), **Jan te.** 1847–1927. Dutch literary historian and philologist.

**Winkel, Lambert Allard te.** 1806–1868. Dutch philologist, founder of modern Dutch grammar and, with Matthijs de Vries (see VRIES) of modern Dutch orthography. Coeditor with de Vries of *Groot Woordenboek der Nederlandsche Taal* (1864); author of *De Grondbeginselen der Nederlandsche Spelling* (1863), *Leerboek der Nederlandsche Spelling* (1865), *Woordenlijst voor de spelling der Nederlandsche Taal* (with de Vries, 1866), etc.

**Win'kel·man** (vĭng'kĕl·män), **Henri Gerard.** 1876–1952. Dutch general; commander in chief of land and sea forces (Feb.–July, 1940) at the time of the German invasion; interned at Troppau (from 1940).

**Win'kel·mann** (vĭng'kĕl·män), **Eduard.** 1838–1896. German historian.

**Win'kel·ried** (vĭng'kĕl·rēt), **Arnold von.** Swiss patriot; national hero of Switzerland. According to tradition, headed charge against Austrians in battle of Sempach (1386); gathered all the Austrian pikes he could reach and directed them into his own body, thus making breach in Austrian line through which Swiss rushed to gain victory which assured their independence.

**Win'neck·e** (vĭn'ĕ·kĕ), **Friedrich August Theodor.** 1835–1897. German astronomer; director of observatory, Strassburg (1872–86); investigated paths of double stars and comets; made determination of solar parallax.

**Win'ner** (wĭn'ẽr), **Septimus.** 1827–1902. American composer of popular songs, as *What Is Home Without a Mother?*, *Listen to the Mocking Bird*, *Give Us Back Our Old Commander*, *God Save Our President*, *Oh Where! Oh Where! Is My Little Dog Gone.*

**Winnington Ingram, Arthur Foley.** See Arthur Foley Winnington INGRAM.

**Wins'low** (wĭnz'lō), **Edward.** 1595–1655. A founder of Plymouth colony in Massachusetts, b. Droitwich, Eng. Arrived at Plymouth on the *Mayflower* (Dec. 21, 1620); wrote *A Relation or Iournall of the Beginning and Proceedings of the English Plantation Setled at Plimoth in New England* (printed in London, 1622), and *Good News from New England...* (1624). Engaged in trading and exploring along New England coast. Served as member of the governor's council (1624–46) and as governor (1633, 1636, 1644). In England (from 1646); appointed by Cromwell a commissioner on expedition to capture the Spanish West India colonies, and seized Jamaica (1655); died at sea on return trip. His son **Josiah** (1629?–1680), b. Plymouth, was member of the governor's council (1657–73) and governor of New Plymouth Colony (1673–80), first native-born governor in America. A grandson of Josiah Winslow, **John** (1703–1774), was a colonial army officer; captain (1740) of a company in Vernon's West Indian expedition; served in Nova Scotia (1744–51); major general commanding contingent on upper Kennebec River (1754); served under Monckton and Loudoun (1755–56).

**Winslow, Forbes Benignus.** 1810–1874. English alienist, lineal descendant of first governor of Plymouth Colony, Massachusetts. Author of treatises on insanity and a pioneer in the humane treatment of the insane and of the now generally accepted plea of insanity in criminal cases, in pursuit of which he testified before parliamentary committee (1872) and at numerous trials.

**Wins'low** (vĕns'lou), **Jakob Benignus.** 1669–1760. Danish naturalist; author of *Exposition Anatomique de la Structure du Corps Humain* (5 vols., 1732).

**Wins'low** (wĭnz'lō), **John Ancrum.** 1811–1873. American naval officer; zealous abolitionist, served on blockade duty in Civil War; commanded *Kearsarge* in victory over Raphael Semmes in Confederate raider *Alabama* off Cherbourg (June 19, 1864).

**Winslow, Miron.** 1789–1864. American missionary in India (1819–64). Served on committee revising Tamil Bible. His brother **Hubbard** (1799–1864) was a Congregational clergyman; succeeded Lyman Beecher in his Boston pastorate (1832–44); author of *Virtue and Happiness* (1837), *The Christian Doctrine* (1844), etc. Hubbard Winslow's son **William Copley** (1840–1925) was a Protestant Episcopal clergyman; interested in archaeological researches in Egypt and aided in gathering important collection of Egyptian relics for the Boston Museum.

**Win'sor** (wĭn'zẽr), **Justin.** 1831–1897. American librarian and historian, b. Boston. Librarian of Boston Public Library (1868–77), and of Harvard College (1877–97). A founder of American Library Association (1876) and its president (1876–85; 1897); also, a founder of the *Library Journal*. Author of *The Reader's Handbook of the American Revolution* (1879), *Christopher Columbus* (1891), *Cartier to Frontenac* (1894), *The Mississippi Basin* (1895), *The Westward Movement* (1897). Assembled a group of workers and co-ordinated their writing in producing *The Memorial History of Boston* (4 vols., 1880–81), and *Narrative and Critical History of America* (8 vols., 1884–89).

**Win'stan·ley** (wĭn'stăn·lĭ), **Gerrard.** 1609–1652. English Leveler. Leader of the Diggers, a group upholding right of common people to land rent free for cultivation and dwelling; alleged (by Thomas Comber, dean of Durham) to have been real founder of the Quaker sect.

**Winstanley, William.** 1628?–1698. English compiler; doubtless the author of almanacs published under pseudonym **Poor Rob'in** [po͝or rŏb'ĭn] (from 1662); compiled *The Loyall Martyrology* (1662), *Lives of the Most Famous English Poets* (1687).

**Win'ston** (wĭn'stŭn), **Joseph.** 1746–1815. American Revolutionary officer; commanded right wing against the British at King's Mountain (Oct. 7, 1780). Member, U.S. House of Representatives (1793–95; 1803–07). Winston, now Winston-Salem, N.C., was named in his honor.

**Wint, Peter de.** See DE WINT.

**Win'ter** (vĭn'tẽr), **De.** See DE WINTER.

**Win'ter** (wĭn'tẽr), Sir **James Spearman.** 1845–1911. Newfoundland statesman; attorney general (1885–89); judge of supreme court (1893–96); premier (1897–1900); representative at international conferences on fisheries questions (1887–88, 1890, 1898).

**Winter, John Strange.** Pseudonym of Henrietta STANNARD.

**Win'ter** (vĭn'tẽr), **Peter von.** 1754–1825. German composer of Italian and German operas, and of ballets, oratorios, church music, symphonies, chamber music, songs, etc.

**Win'ter** *or* **Win'tour** (wĭn'tẽr), **Thomas** (1572–1606) and **Robert** (d. 1606), brothers, conspirators involved in Gunpowder Plot; hanged.

**Win'ter** (wĭn'tẽr), **William.** 1836–1917. American writer, b. Gloucester, Mass. Dramatic critic, New York *Tribune* (1865–1909). Author of occasional verse, collected in the *Poems of William Winter* (1909), books of essays, and books on actors and the stage.

**Win'ter·feld** (vĭn'tẽr·fĕlt), **Karl Georg August Vivigens von.** 1784–1852. German writer on music.

**Win'ter·hal'ter** (vĭn'tẽr·häl'tẽr), **Franz Xaver.** 1805?–1873. German portrait painter; court painter, Karlsruhe (1828); lived in Paris (1834–70).

**Win'ter·nitz** (vĭn'tẽr·nĭts), **Moriz.** 1863–1937. Austrian Indologist and ethnologist, authority on ancient and medieval Indian literature.

**Winternitz, Wilhelm.** 1834–1917. German physician; pioneer in scientific hydrotherapy; a founder of first hydrotherapeutic clinic, Vienna.

**Winterstoke,** Baron. See Sir William Henry WILLS.

**Win'ther** (vĕn'tẽr), **Christian,** *in full* **Rasmus Villads Christian Ferdinand.** 1796–1876. Danish lyric and epic poet of the romantic school; author of the epic poem *Hjortens Flugt* (1855), prose tales and sketches of Danish life, etc.

**Win'throp** (wĭn'thrŭp), **John.** 1588–1649. First governor of Massachusetts Bay Colony, b. in Suffolk, Eng. Educ. Trinity College, Cambridge; studied law at Gray's Inn (1613) and practiced in London. Associated himself (c. 1629) with group obtaining charter from Charles I for settlement on a land grant in eastern Massachusetts; elected governor (Oct. 20, 1629) before the group set sail for America. Sailed in the *Arbella* (Apr. 8, 1630) and reached Salem (June 12, 1630); total community of about 1800 conveyed in the *Arbella* and in other ships arriving about the same time. Re-elected governor (1631, 1632, 1633, 1637–40, 1642–44, 1646–49); opposed Henry Vane; in period of Antinomian controversy, opposed Anne Hutchinson and presided at the court that found her guilty and sentenced her to banishment. Influential in organizing confederation of New England colonies (1645), and first president of the confederation. His *Journal*, often called *History of New England*, has been published: a convenient edition (*Winthrop's Journal*, 2 vols., 1908) was edited by J. K. Hosmer. His son **John** (1606–1676) was also a colonial governor, b. in Suffolk, Eng.; educ. at Trinity College, Dublin; studied law, and adm. as barrister at the Inner Temple (1625); landed at Boston (Nov. 4, 1631); leader of group that settled Ipswich (1633); in England (1634–35), where he was commissioned (July, 1635) governor of a new "plantation" in Connecticut sponsored by Lord Saye and Sele and Lord Brooke; acted as governor (1636) and then returned to Massachusetts; later, took up permanent abode in Connecticut and was governor (1657, 1659–76); obtained new liberal charter for Connecticut (1661–63). The Connecticut governor's son **John,** *often known as* **Fitz-John** (1638–1707), b. at Ipswich, Mass., was also a colonial governor; studied at Harvard; served as officer in the Parliamentary army in England and Scotland (1660); settled at New London, Conn. (1663); engaged as commander of Connecticut troops against the Dutch (1673) and the Indians (1675–76); again commanded Connecticut troops, against French (1690); governor of Connecticut (1698–1707). For other members of this Winthrop family, see John WINTHROP (1714–1779), Robert Charles WINTHROP, Theodore WINTHROP.

**Winthrop, John.** 1714–1779. Great-grandnephew of John Winthrop (1606–1676). American astronomer and physicist; professor, Harvard (1738–79). Did important research work in astronomy, observing sunspots (1739), transits of Mercury (1740, 1743, 1769); established (1746) first laboratory of experimental physics in America; introduced (1751) study of differential and integral calculus in the Harvard curriculum.

**Winthrop, Robert Charles.** 1809–1894. Descendant of John Winthrop (1588–1649). American politician, b. Boston. Member, U.S. House of Representatives (1840–50), and speaker of the house (1847–49); U.S. senator from Massachusetts (1850–51).

**Winthrop, Theodore.** 1828–1861. Descendant of John Winthrop (1588–1649). American writer and soldier, b. New Haven, Conn. At outbreak of Civil War, volunteered and joined 7th New York regiment; engaged in defense of Washington; killed in battle at Great Bethel (June 10, 1861). Author of novels, published posthumously, *Cecil Dreeme* (1861), *John Brent* (1862), *Edwin Brothertoft* (1862), *The Canoe and the Saddle* (1863), *Life in the Open Air* (1863).

**Winton,** Earl of. See (1) under SETON family; (2) 13th *earl of Eglinton*, under MONTGOMERIE family.

**Wintour, Thomas** and **Robert.** See WINTER.

**Win'tring·ham** (wĭn'trĭng·ăm), **Tom,** *in full* **Thomas Henry.** 1898–1949. English soldier and writer, b. Grimsby, Lincolnshire; served in air force in France (1916–18); to Spain as correspondent during civil war, later (1937) becoming commander of British battalion in International Brigade; on return to England advocated formation of a people's army; helped found (1940) Osterley Park training school for home guard; lecturer on War Office staff; author of *English Captain* (1939), *New Ways of War* (1940), *Armies of Freemen* (1940),

*Politics of Victory* (1941), *The Story of Weapons and Tactics* (1943), etc.

**Wint′zing·e·ro′de** (vĭn′tsĭng·ĕ·rō′dĕ), Baron **Ferdinand von.** 1770–1818. Russian field marshal and diplomat, b. Württemberg. Russian special ambassador (1805) charged with negotiations to form alliance against Napoleon; served in Russian army (1812–14).

**Win′wood** (wĭn′wo͝od), Sir **Ralph.** 1563?–1617. English diplomat; ambassador to France (1601–03); agent to States-General of Holland (1603–14); secretary of state for life (1614); defended in Parliament king's right to levy impositions; urged Sir Walter Raleigh to pillage Spanish settlements in South America.

**Wireker, Nigel.** See NIGEL.

**Wirnt von Gra′fen·berg** (vĭrnt′ fŏn grä′fĕn·bĕrk). b. about 1170. Middle High German epic poet; author of the epic romance in verse *Wigalois* (c. 1204 or 1230), after a French source.

**Wirt** (wûrt), **William.** 1772–1834. American lawyer, b. Bladensburg, Md. Practiced in Virginia. One of counsel for the prosecution in case against Aaron Burr (1807). U.S. attorney general (1817–29), and appeared in famous law cases, including McCulloch vs. Maryland, Gibbons vs. Ogden, and the Dartmouth College case. Antimasonic candidate for president of the United States (1832).

**Wirt, William Albert.** 1874–1938. American educator; superintendent of schools, Gary, Ind. (from 1907). Introduced new educational methods which resulted in what is known as the platoon school, or Gary plan, school, or system.

**Wirth** (vĭrt), **Albrecht.** 1866–1936. German historian; authority on Asiatic and Eastern history.

**Wirth, Joseph,** *in full* **Karl Joseph.** 1879–1956. German politician. Joined Catholic Center party; member of Reichstag (1914, 1920–33), and Weimar National Assembly (1919); minister of finance (1920–21) and chancellor (1921); accepted reparations terms of Allies (London ultimatum) and announced a policy of fulfillment (Erfüllungspolitik), but withdrew following disagreement over partition of Upper Silesia; formed second cabinet (1921) and acted as part-time foreign minister; represented Germany at Genoa Conference (1922); resigned as chancellor (1922) and was subsequently a leader of the left group of the Center party, Reichstag; minister of occupied provinces (1929–30) and minister of interior in Brüning's cabinet (1930–31).

**Wise** (wīz), **Aaron.** 1844–1896. Rabbi, b. Eger, Hungary. To U.S. (1874) and became rabbi of congregation in New York City (1875–96); a founder of Jewish Theol. Sem., New York City (1886). His son **Stephen Samuel** (1874–1949), b. Budapest, Hungary; founder (1907) and rabbi (from 1907), Free Synagogue, New York City; founder of first section of Federation of American Zionists, and of Zionist Organization of America; president of delegation of American Jewish Congress at the Peace Conference in Paris (1919); president of American Jewish Congress; founder and president of Jewish Institute of Religion.

**Wise** (wīz), **Henry Alexander.** 1806–1876. American lawyer and politician, b. Drummondtown, Va.; practiced in Virginia (from 1830). Member, U.S. House of Representatives (1833–44); U.S. minister to Brazil (1844–47); governor of Virginia (1856–60). Remained loyal to his state when it seceded (1861); brigadier general in Confederate army (May, 1861) and major general (Apr., 1865). His cousin **Henry Augustus Wise** (1819–1869) through his influence entered U.S. navy as a midshipman (1834); remained loyal to the Union in Civil War; on duty in the Bureau of Ordnance, U.S. Navy Department, Washington, D.C. (1862–68), and chief of the bureau (1864–68); author of books of travel and adventure. Henry Alexander Wise's son **John Sergeant** (1846–1913) was a lawyer and politician; served in Confederate army in Civil War; practiced law in Richmond, Va. (1867), New York (1888–?1907); author of *Diomed; The Life, Travels, and Observations of a Dog* (1897), *The End of the Era* (1899), *The Lion's Skin* (1905), etc.

**Wise, Isaac May′er** (mī′ẽr). *Orig. surname* **Weis** (vīs). 1819–1900. Rabbi, b. in Steingrub, Bohemia. To U.S. (1846); rabbi of congregations in Albany, N.Y. (1846–54) and Cincinnati (1854–1900). Prominent in organization of Union of American Hebrew Congregations (1873), and Hebrew Union College for the education of rabbis (1875); served as president of Hebrew Union College (1875–1900).

**Wise, John.** 1652–1725. American Congregational clergyman, b. Roxbury, Mass.; pastor in Ipswich, Mass. (1680–1725); known for his zeal in maintaining democratic rights; also, opposed the sentence of one of the witchcraft trial victims and signed a petition to the legislature (1703) asking it to reverse the convictions.

**Wise, Stephen Samuel.** See under Aaron WISE.

**Wise, Thomas James.** 1859–1937. English bibliographer, book collector, and forger.

**Wise′man** (wīz′măn), **Nicholas Patrick Stephen.** 1802–1865. English Roman Catholic prelate. Rector of English College, Rome (1828–40); bishop (1840); influenced Oxford Movement and confirmed Newman; vicar apostolic (coadjutor, 1839) of London district (1849); cardinal (1850) and archbishop of Westminster; preached and wrote *Appeal to English People* (1850), to allay storm of indignation at the papal establishment of hierarchy with territorial titles in England.

**Wiseman, Richard.** 1622?–1676. English surgeon; raised surgeon's profession to equality with that of physician; surgeon to Charles II (1672).

**Wish′art** (wĭsh′ärt; -ẽrt), **George.** 1513?–1546. Scottish reformer and martyr; convicted of heresy by convocation of bishops and burned.

**Wis′ler** (wĭs′lẽr), **Jacob.** 1808–1889. American Mennonite leader; separated from main Mennonite branch (c. 1870–74) and established group known as Old Order of the Mennonite Church.

**Wis′li·ce′nus** (vĭs′lē·tsā′no͞os), **Gustav Adolf.** 1803–1879. German Protestant theologian. His son **Johannes** (1835–1902), chemist, performed research on lactic acid, etc., of importance in development of stereochemistry.

**Wiss′ler** (wĭs′lẽr), **Clark.** 1870–1947. American anthropologist, b. Wayne Co., Indiana. Curator, American Museum of Natural History (1906–41); professor, Yale (1924–40). Author of *North American Indians of the Plains* (1912), *The American Indian* (1917), *Man and Culture* (1922), *Social Anthropology* (1929), etc.; special editor for anthropology, *Webster's New International Dictionary, Second Edition.*

**Wiss′mann** (vĭs′män), **Hermann von.** 1853–1905. German army officer and African explorer. Accompanied Pogge (1880) to Angola and Nyangwe (1882), and continued alone across continent to Zanzibar; made other journeys in equatorial Africa; proved navigability of Kasai River (1885); as German commissioner, suppressed Arab uprising in German East Africa (1888); founded Langenburg on Lake Nyasa; governor of German East Africa (1895–96).

**Wis·so′wa** (vĭ·sō′vä), **Georg.** 1859–1931. German classical philologist, authority on ancient Roman religion. His works include *Religion und Kultus der Römer* (1902) and revised editions of August Pauly's *Real-Encyclopädie der*

*Classischen Altertumswissenschaft* (books 1–6, 1894–1909) and Friedländer's *Darstellungen aus der Sittengeschichte Roms* (4 vols., 1919–23).

**Wis'tar** (wĭs'tẽr; *Ger.* vĭs'tär), **Caspar.** 1696–1752. Pioneer glass manufacturer in colonial America (from c. 1740), b. near Heidelberg, Ger.; to America (1717) and settled in Philadelphia. His grandson **Caspar Wistar** (1761–1818) was a physician; practiced in Philadelphia (from 1787); professor of anatomy, U. of Pennsylvania (1808–18) and author of *System of Anatomy* (1811), first American textbook on this subject; the genus of plants *Wistaria* was named (1818) by Thomas Nuttall in his honor and the Wistar Institute of Anatomy and Biology was founded and endowed by **Isaac Jones Wistar** (1827–1905), his grandnephew. A grandniece of Caspar Wistar (1696–1752), **Sarah Wis'ter** [wĭs'tẽr] (1761–1804), left an interesting *Journal of Life in Philadelphia* (Sept. 25, 1777–June 20, 1778).

**Wis'ter** (wĭs'tẽr), **Owen.** 1860–1938. American novelist, b. Philadelphia; author of *The Virginian* (1902), *Members of the Family* (1911), *The Pentecost of Calamity* (1915), *Roosevelt—The Story of a Friendship* (1930), and short stories and verse.

**Wister, Sarah.** See under Caspar WISTAR.

**Wis'ting** (vĭs'tĭng), **Oscar.** 1871–1936. Norwegian explorer; accompanied Amundsen across ice to South Pole (1911); led group (1928) in unsuccessful search for Amundsen after Amundsen was lost in attempt to rescue Nobile.

**Wit, Pieter de.** See Pietro CANDIDO.

**With'als** *or* **Whith'als** (wĭt''lz), **John.** fl. 1556. English lexicographer; compiler of English-Latin vocabulary for children (earliest ed. known, 1556), long reissued as textbook.

**With'er** (wĭth'ẽr) *or* **With'ers** (-ẽrz), **George.** 1588–1667. English poet and pamphleteer. Imprisoned in Marshalsea for satire, *Abuses Stript and Whipt* (1613), said to be libelous; during imprisonment wrote pastoral, *Shepherd's Hunting* (1615), containing famous passage in praise of poetry; after a love elegy, *Fidelia* (1615), including song "Shall I, wasting in despair," returned to satire in Wither's motto: *Nec habeo, nec careo, nec curo* (1621); after the fanciful lyric *Fair Virtue, The Mistress of Phil' Arete* (1622), became Puritan and devoted himself to religious poetry, the best of which is *Hallelujah* (1641), and controversial, often scurrilous, pamphlets. Raised troop of horse on Parliamentary side (1642); imprisoned (1660–63) for a verse pamphlet, *Vox Vulgi*, satirizing Parliament of 1661. His best verse collected in *Juvenilia* (1622).

**With'ers** (wĭth'ẽrz), **Hartley.** 1867–1950. English financial expert; editor of *Economist* (1916–21), of financial supplement of *Saturday Review* (1921–23); author of *The Meaning of Money* (1909), *Poverty and Waste* (1914), *The Case for Capitalism* (1920), *The Way to Wealth* (1935).

**With'er·spoon** (wĭth'ẽr·spōōn), **Herbert.** 1873–1935. American operatic and concert basso; member, Metropolitan Opera House Company (1908–16). Best known for his rendition of Wagnerian roles.

**Witherspoon, John.** 1723–1794. Presbyterian clergyman, b. near Edinburgh, Scotland; leader in the conservative group in the church. President, College of New Jersey, which became Princeton U. (1768–94). Member of Continental Congress (1776–79; 1780–81; 1782), and a signer of the Declaration of Independence; also, member of New Jersey constitutional ratification convention (1787). One of organizers of Presbyterian Church along national lines (1785–89), and moderator of the church's first General Assembly (May, 1789).

**Witkowski.** See Maximilian HARDEN.

**Wi'told** (vē'tôlt) *or, Russ.,* **Vi'tovt** (vyē'tôft). 1350–1430. Grand Duke of Lithuania; allied himself with Teutonic Order (1390) to curb power of Ladislas II of Poland; defeated by Tatars on the lower Dnieper (Aug. 12, 1399); turned to policy of alliance with Poland (1401) and fought Teutonic Order, defeating it in great battle of Grünewald, or Tannenberg (July, 1410) and breaking its power.

**Wi'tos** (vē'tôs), **Wincenty.** 1874–1945. Polish statesman; prime minister of Poland (1920–21, 1923–26); lived in voluntary exile (1926–39).

**Wits** (vĭts), **Hermann.** *Lat.* **Wit'si·us** (wĭt'sĭ·ŭs). 1636–1708. Dutch Calvinist theologian; author of *De Oeconomia Foederum Dei cum Hominibus* (1685), an unsuccessful attempt to strike a medium between the orthodox and the advocates of federal theology.

**Wit'te** (vĭt'ĕ), **Emanuel de.** 1617?–1692. Dutch painter; chief master of Dutch painters of church interiors.

**Wit'te** (vĭt'ĕ), **Karl.** 1800–1883. German jurist and Dante scholar; published (1862) a critical edition of original text of Dante's *Divina Commedia*, and translations of Dante and Boccaccio.

**Witte, Pieter de.** See Pietro CANDIDO.

**Wit'te** (vyĕt'tyĕ), Count **Sergei Yulievich.** 1849–1915. Russian statesman; minister of finance (1892–1903); president, council of ministers (1903). Negotiated Treaty of Portsmouth (1905) ending Russo-Japanese War. First constitutional Russian premier (Nov., 1905–May, 1906); resigned premiership (1906) and was appointed member of council of the empire.

**Wit'te·kind** (vĭt'ĕ·kĭnt) *or* **Wi'du·kind** (vē'dōō·kĭnt). d. about 807. Westphalian chieftain, leader of the Saxons against Charlemagne. Raided the Rhineland (778) and may have taken part in annihilation of Frankish army at Süntelberg (782); again led war until 785, when he submitted to Charlemagne, who became his patron, and was baptized at Attigny; said to have been appointed duke of the Saxons and to have died in battle (807).

**Wit'tels·bach** (vĭt'ĕls·bäk). A German family that ruled in Bavaria (12th century–1918) and in Rhenish Palatinate for part of that time. Count Otto VI became Duke Otto I of Bavaria (1180); family several times divided and reunited, but by 1559 some of branches were extinct; duchy became an electorate (1623) and Duke Maximilian was made elector. The following were electors: Maximilian the Great (ruled 1623–51), Ferdinand Maria (1651–79), Maximilian II Emanuel (1679–1726), Charles Albert (1726–45), and Maximilian III Joseph (1745–77), last of direct (younger) line. Duchy of Bavaria then (1777) passed to Palatinate branch, Elector Charles Theodore (1777–99) and Maximilian IV Joseph (1799–1805); electorate made a kingdom by Napoleon, Elector Maximilian continuing as King Maximilian I Joseph (1806–25); succeeding kings: Louis I (1825–48), Maximilian II Joseph (1848–64), Louis II (1864–86), Otto (1886–1913) under regency of princes Luitpold (d. 1912) and Louis (regent during interregnum, 1912–13), the latter becoming king as Louis III (1913–18; abdicated). Three of the kings of Germany have been members of Wittelsbach family: Louis IV of Bavaria (1287?–1347; Holy Roman emperor, 1314–47), Rupert of the Palatinate (1352–1410; king, 1400–10), and Charles VII of Bavaria [Elector Charles Albert, above] (1697–1745; Holy Roman emperor, 1742–45). See individual biographies.

**Wittenberg line.** See ALBERTINE LINE.

**Witt'gen·stein** (vĭt'gĕn·shtīn), **Ludwig Adolf Peter.** Prince of **Sayn'-Witt'gen·stein-Lud'wigs·burg**

(zĭn′, lo͞ot′vĭks·bo͝ork; lo͞od′vĭks·bo͝ork). 1769–1843. Russian soldier; served in 1807 campaign against Napoleon, and against Oudinot and Victor (1812); defeated by French (1813) and relieved of command after battle of Bautzen; commanded Russian contingent in later campaign (1813–14).

**Wittgenstein, Ludwig Josef Johan.** 1889–1951. Philosopher, b. Vienna. Ph.D., Cambridge U., 1929; taught at Cambridge, 1930–47. Influential student of logical positivism, linguistic analysis, and semantics. Major works include *Tractatus logico-philosophicus* (1921).

**Wittlesey, William.** See Simon Islip.

**Witt′lin** (vēt′lēn), **Józef.** 1896– . Polish novelist and poet; fled from Poland (1939) and from France (1940); resident in U.S. (from 1940); author of the novel *Salt of the Earth* (1925), awarded Polish Academy prize.

**Wit′wer** (wĭt′wẽr), **Harry Charles.** 1890–1929. American journalist and humorist.

**Witz′le′ben** (vĭts′lā′bĕn), **Karl August Friedrich von.** *Pseudonym* **A. von Trom′litz** (trôm′lĭts). 1773–1839. German army officer and novelist; author of the historical romances *Die Pappenheimer* (1827), *Franz von Sickingen* (1828), *Die Vierhundert von Pforzheim* (1830), etc., which appeared largely in his *Vielliebchen* (14 vols., 1828–41). His collected writings fill 108 volumes (1829–43).

**Wla·di′mir** (*Ger.* vlä·dē′mĭr). Variant of Vladimir.

**Wladislaus** *or* **Wladislaw** *or* **Władysław.** See Ladislas, Kings of Poland.

**Wode′house** (wo͝od′hous), **John.** 1st Earl of **Kimberley.** See Kimberley.

**Wode′house** (wo͝od′hous), **Pelham Grenville.** 1881–1975. English humorous novelist. Conducted column "By the Way" in London *Globe* (1903–09); spent year (1909) in America writing short stories, afterwards often half each year in U.S. Began as writer of stories for boys (including *The Pothunters,* 1902; *A Prefect's Uncle,* 1903), followed by humorous novels, many of which center about the following characters or groups: Psmith (as *Psmith in the City,* 1910, which gained him wide reputation), Bertie Wooster and his valet Jeeves (*The Inimitable Jeeves,* 1924; *The Code of the Woosters,* 1938), Stanley Featherstonehaugh Ukridge (*Ukridge,* 1924), Mr. Mulliner (*Meet Mr. Mulliner,* 1927; *Mulliner Omnibus,* 1935), Lord Emsworth and the family at Blandings Castle (*Blandings Castle,* 1935; *Lord Emsworth and Others,* 1937). Collaborator with Guy Bolton in musical comedies including *The Cabaret Girl* (1922), and with Ian Hay in plays including *Leave it to Psmith* (1930). Captured by Germans (1939) and interned in Germany; became U.S. citizen (1955).

**Wod′row** (wo͝od′rō), **Robert.** 1679–1734. Scottish ecclesiastical historian.

**Woer′mann** (vûr′män), **Adolf.** 1847–1911. German shipowner and colonial politician; founded (1884) African Steamship Company, forerunner of Woermann Line; helped Germany acquire Togo and Cameroons; aided in founding the German East Africa Line (1890).

**Woes·tij′ne** (vo͞os·tī′nĕ), **Karel van de.** 1879–1929. Belgian poet.

**Wof′fing·ton** (wŏf′ĭng·tŭn), **Margaret,** *known as* **Peg.** 1714?–1760. Irish actress; debut in London (1740) as Silvia in *The Recruiting Officer;* became a favorite as Sir Harry Wildair in *The Constant Couple* (1741) and in other "breeches parts." Played chief roles in comedy and tragedy, probably best as elegant women of fashion, Lady Betty Modish and Lady Townly. Subject of a successful play, *Masks and Faces* (1852) by Charles Reade and Tom Taylor, and of a romance, *Peg Woffington* (1853), by Reade.

**Wöh′ler** (vû′lẽr), **Friedrich.** 1800–1882. German chemist. First to synthesize an organic compound (urea, 1828); one of the first to isolate aluminum and beryllium, and to observe cases of isomerism; devised a process for manufacturing nickel. Author of *Grundriss der Unorganischen Chemie* (1831), *Grundriss der Organischen Chemie* (1840).

**Wohl′ge·muth** *or* **Wohl′ge·mut** *or* **Wol′ge·mut** (vōl′gĕ·mo͞ot), **Michel** *or* **Michael.** 1434–1519. German painter and designer for wood engraving; teacher of Albrecht Dürer. His works include many carved altarpieces with painted wings (executed with others), the Hofer altar (now in Munich), high altars of churches at Zwickau, Nuremberg, and Schwabach.

**Woj′cie·chow′ski** (voi′chĕ·kôf′skē), **Stanisław.** 1869–1953. Polish economist and statesman; joined Socialist party; political activities forced him to leave Poland (1892); returned to Poland (1906). During World War I (1914–18), headed Polish group favoring Allies. Minister of interior (1919–20); president of Poland (1922–26); deposed by coup d'etat effected by Marshal Pilsudski.

**Wol′cot** (wo͝ol′kŭt), **John.** *Pseudonym* **Peter Pin′dar** (pĭn′dẽr). 1738–1819. English satirist and poet. M.D., Aberdeen (1767); physician (1767–73) to Sir William Trelawny, governor of Jamaica; abandoned practice of medicine in England (1778) for writing pungent poetical satires, witty but coarse, on George III, Boswell and Mrs. Piozzi, Pitt, and many others.

**Wol′cott** (wo͝ol′kŭt), **Roger.** 1679–1767. American colonial administrator, b. Windsor, Conn. Deputy governor of Connecticut (1741–50); major general, and second in command of troops that captured Louisburg from the French (1745); governor of Connecticut (1751–54); author of *Poetical Meditations* (1725), first volume of verse published in Connecticut. His son **Oliver** (1726–1797) was a political leader in colonial America; member of Continental Congress (1775–78; 1780–84), and a signer of the Declaration of Independence; commander of fourteen Connecticut militia regiments reinforcing Gen. Putnam on the Hudson River (1776); also, commanded volunteer contingent joining Gates's army against Burgoyne, and as major general (1779) provided for defense of Connecticut coast against Tryon's raids; lieutenant governor of Connecticut (1787–96) and governor (1796–97). **Oliver** (1760–1833), son of Oliver, was a lawyer and politician; auditor of U.S. Treasury (1789–91); comptroller of U.S. Treasury (1791–95); U.S. secretary of the treasury, succeeding Hamilton (1795–1800); governor of Connecticut (1817–27).

**Woldemaras.** Variant of Voldemaras.

**Wolf.** See also Wolff.

**Wolf** (vôlf), **Charles Joseph Étienne.** 1827–1918. French astronomer. At Paris observatory (from 1863); with Georges Rayet (*q.v.*), discovered spectroscopically (1867) three stars, Wolf-Rayet stars, whose spectra indicate presence of hydrogen, helium, etc., but not metals.

**Wolf** (vôlf), **Ferdinand.** 1796–1866. Austrian Romance scholar and literary historian; authority on medieval Spanish and Portuguese literature.

**Wolf, Friedrich August.** 1759–1824. German classical philologist and Homeric critic; friend of Goethe and Wilhelm von Humboldt. Author of *Prolegomena ad Homerum* (1795), in which he argued that the *Iliad* and *Odyssey* are the work not of one but of several authors, and of *Darstellung der Altertumswissenschaft* (1807), in which he championed the study of classical antiquity; edited Homer, Plato, Cicero, and others.

**Wolf** (wo͝olf), **Henry.** 1852–1916. Wood engraver, b. Eckwersheim, in Alsace; to U.S. (1871) and worked in

New York City (from 1873). Engraved illustrations of E. A. Abbey, Joseph Pennell, Howard Pyle, and after paintings of Innes, Sargent, and others; excelled in half-tone photoengraving (after c. 1880).

**Wolf** (vôlf), **Hugo.** 1860–1903. Austrian composer; disciple of Wagner. Composer of over 200 songs, including musical settings for poems of Mörike, Eichendorff, Goethe, and other poets and for translations by Heyse and Geibel; also composed instrumental works including a string quartet (1880), the symphonic poem *Penthesilea* (1883), and *Italian Serenade* for small orchestra (1894).

**Wolf, Julius.** 1862–1935. German economist.

**Wolf, Max Franz Joseph Cornelius.** 1863–1932. German astronomer; director, Königstuhl observatory (1893): discovered periodical comet with course of seven years (1884); specialized in spectrum analysis and photography.

**Wolf, Rudolf.** 1816–1893. Swiss astronomer; discovered parallelism between sunspots and magnetic variations (1852).

**Wolfe** (wo͝olf), **Charles.** 1791–1823. Irish clergyman and poet; author of a short stirring poem, *The Burial of Sir John Moore*, appearing anonymously (1817).

**Wolfe, Humbert.** 1885–1940. English poet; attracted public notice with satires *Lampoons* (1925), *News of the Devil* (1926); gained recognition with *Requiem* (1927), *The Silver Cat* (1928), *This Blind Rose* (1928). More recent books: *Tennyson, Stings and Wings, The Upward Anguish.*

**Wolfe, James.** 1727–1759. British army officer. Served in Flanders and Germany and against Young Pretender (1742–47); present at Dettingen, Falkirk, and Culloden Moor; under Amherst played a brilliant part in siege of Louisburg (1758); commanded with rank of major general expedition against Quebec (1759); scaled heights to Plains of Abraham, routed French under Montcalm and thus completed British conquest of North America: fell mortally wounded on field.

**Wolfe, Reginald.** Pseudonym of Thomas Frognall Dibdin.

**Wolfe, Thomas Clayton.** 1900–1938. American novelist, b. Asheville, N.C.; A.B., North Carolina (1920); teacher of English, N.Y.U. (1924–30); author of *Look Homeward, Angel* (1929), *The Web of Earth* (1932), *A Portrait of Bascom Hawke* (1932), *Of Time and the River* (1935), *From Death to Morning* (1935), *The Story of a Novel* (1936), *I Have a Thing to Tell You* (1937), *The Web and the Rock* (pub. 1939), *You Can't Go Home Again* (pub. 1940), *The Hills Beyond* (pub. 1941), *Letters to His Mother* (ed. by John S. Terry, 1943).

**Wolfe–Barry,** Sir **John Wolfe.** See under Sir Charles Barry.

**Wol′fert** (wo͝ol′fẽrt), **Ira.** 1908– . American journalist, b. N.Y. City; LL.B., Columbia (1930); on staff of North American Newspaper Alliance; awarded 1942 Pulitzer prize for firsthand reporting of Solomons Islands campaign (pub. in book form as *Battle for the Solomons*, 1943); author of short stories, *Tucker's People* (novel, 1943), etc.

**Wolff.** See also Wolf.

**Wolff** (vôlf), **Albert.** 1814–1892. Cousin of Emil Wolff. German sculptor; works include statues of Frederick the Great (with Rauch; in Berlin) and Frederick William IV (in Königsberg) and equestrian statues of Ernest Augustus for Hanover (1861), Frederick William III for Berlin (1871), and Gen. Artigas for Montevideo (1885).

**Wolff** *or* **Wolf** (vôlf), Baron **Christian von.** 1679–1754. German philosopher and mathematician. Developed and popularized philosophy of Leibnitz (Leibnitz-Wolffian philosophy), and championed psycheometry and a deductive rationalistic system of philosophy. Author of numerous works, in Latin and German, on all branches of philosophy, and on mathematics and physics.

**Wolff, Emil.** 1802–1879. Cousin of Albert Wolff and nephew and pupil of Johann Gottfried Schadow. German sculptor of classical school, resident in Rome (from 1822); works include portrait busts of Thorvaldsen, Niebuhr, Bunsen, and other contemporaries, and Greek mythological and genre subjects.

**Wolff, Gustav.** 1865– . German biologist and psychologist.

**Wolff** (wo͝olf), Sir **Henry Drummond Charles.** 1830–1908. English diplomat; member of "Fourth Party" (1880); a founder of the Primrose League; minister to Persia (1888), Rumania (1891); ambassador to Spain (1892–1900).

**Wolff** (vôlf), **Kaspar Friedrich.** 1733–1794. German anatomist; founder of modern embryology. Several embryological structures (Wolffian bodies, etc.) are named after him.

**Wolff, Martin.** 1872–1953. German law scholar; authority on civil and commercial law.

**Wolff** (vôlf), **Pierre.** 1865–1944. French playwright; among his plays are *Le Boulet* (1898), *Le Béguin* (1900), *Le Secret de Polichinelle* (1903), *L'Âge d'Aimer* (1905), *Le Ruisseau* (1907), *Les Ailes Brisées* (1920), *La Belle de Nuit* (1932).

**Wolf′-Fer·ra′ri** (vôlf′fär·rä′rē), **Ermanno.** 1876–1948. Italian composer; settled at Munich (1909); composer of operas, as *I Gioielli della Madonna* ("Jewels of the Madonna"), a choral work (*La Vita Nuova*), *Kammersymphonie*, and compositions for piano and violin.

**Wölff′lin** (vûlf′lĭn), **Eduard.** 1831–1908. Classical scholar, b. in Switzerland. Professor, Munich (1880–1905); helped found and organize the *Thesaurus Linguae Latinae*, for which he prepared the *Archiv für Lateinische Lexikographie und Grammatik* (15 vols., 1884–1909); author of many philological works, esp. on colloquial Latin and the history of Latin. His son **Heinrich** (1864–1945), art historian, champion of formalistic art; author of *Renaissance und Barock* (1888), *Die Klassische Kunst* (1899; English trans., *The Art of the Italian Renaissance*, 1903), *Italien und das Deutsche Formgefühl* (1931), etc.

**Wolff′-Met′ter·nich** (vôlf′mĕt′ẽr·nĭĸ), **Paul.** Count **Wolff-Metternich zur Gracht** (tso͝or gräĸt′). 1853–1934. German diplomat; as ambassador to London (1901–12), attempted unsuccessfully to conclude relationships agreement between Great Britain and Germany; ambassador to Constantinople (1915–16).

**Wol′fram von E′schen·bach** (vôl′främ fôn ĕsh′ĕn·bäĸ). 1170?–?1220. Middle High German epic poet and minnesinger, descended from a Bavarian family of Eschenbach, near Ansbach. Lived (1202–17) at court of Hermann of Thuringia, where he met Walther von der Vogelweide. Author of lyrics (as *Tagelieder*), of *Parzival* (a metrical romance of the Holy Grail, which was based in part on Chrétien de Troyes's *Perceval* and from which Wagner derived the libretto of his *Parsifal*), of the *Titurel* fragments, and of an incomplete historical epic, *Willehalm.*

**Wolf′sohn** (wo͝olf′s'n; *Ger.* vôlf′zōn), **Carl.** 1834–1907. Musician, b. in Hesse, Ger.; to U.S. (1854); known esp. as a concert pianist; founded Beethoven Society (1869); conductor in Chicago (1874–84), and closely associated with Theodore Thomas.

**Wolgemut, Michel.** See Wohlgemuth.

**Wolkenstein, Oswald von.** See Oswald von Wolkenstein.

**Woll** (wōl), **Matthew.** 1880–1956. Labor leader, b. in

Luxemburg; to U.S. (1891); photoengraver by trade; president of International Photo-Engravers' Union of North America (1906–29); vice-president of American Federation of Labor and director of its legal bureau.

**Wol'las·ton** (wo͝ol'ăs·tŭn), **William Hyde.** 1766–1828. English chemist and physicist. In chemistry, discovered palladium (1804) and rhodium (1805); devised method of making platinum malleable; in optics, invented reflecting goniometer (1809), camera lucida (1812), Wollaston's doublet (a form of magnifying glass for correcting spherical aberrations); discovered dark lines in solar spectrum; in physics, showed identity of galvanic and frictional electricity. F.R.S. (1794); founded the Wollaston medal, awarded annually for mineralogical research.

**Wolle, John Frederick.** 1863–1933. American musician, b. Bethlehem, Pa. Organist of Moravian church in Bethlehem (1885–1905), and of Lehigh U. (1887–1905). Founded and conducted famous Bethlehem Bach Choir, which gave first complete American rendition of Bach's B-minor Mass (Mar. 27, 1900); also conducted Bach festivals in Bethlehem in later years (1901, 1903, 1905). Professor of music, U. of California (1905–11). Conducted largely-attended Bach festivals at Lehigh U. (1912–32).

**Wollstonecraft, Mary.** See Mary Wollstonecraft GODWIN.

**Wolmer,** Viscount. Title (cr. 1883) held by eldest son and heir of earl of Selborne. See under Roundell PALMER.

**Wo'low'ski'** (vô'lôf'skē'), **Louis François Michel Raymond.** 1810–1876. Polish-born French economist and politician; naturalized Frenchman (1836); member of the National Assembly (1848), Legislative Assembly (1849), National Assembly (1871); elected senator for life (1875). Founder of first crédit foncier in France (1852).

**Wolse'ley** (wo͝olz'lĭ), **Garnet Joseph.** 1st Viscount **Wolseley.** 1833–1913. British army officer; wounded and lost an eye at Sevastopol (1855); served in Sepoy Mutiny (1857–58); accompanied Anglo-French expedition into China (1860); in Canada (1861–71), commanded expedition to quell uprising in Red River (1870); as energetic reformer in army, put into effect Cardwell's short-service system and abolished the purchase of commissions; commanded Ashanti expedition (1873–74); held high command in Natal (1875), Cyprus (1878), southeast Africa (1879–80); suppressed rebellion in Egypt with victory at Tell el-Kebir (1882); commanded Nile expedition (1884) that arrived too late to relieve General Gordon at Khartoum; field marshal (1894); commander in chief of British army (1895–99).

**Wol'sey** (wo͝ol'zĭ), **Thomas.** 1475?–1530. English prelate and statesman; chaplain to Henry VII; rose rapidly to deanery of Lincoln (1509). Almoner to Henry VIII (1509); privy councilor in control of public and foreign affairs (1511); directed war preparations and campaign in northern France (1512–13); bishop of Tournai and of Lincoln, and archbishop of York (1514); cardinal (1515); lord chancellor (1515–29); repressed feudal jurisdiction and centered power in the monarch; papal legate a latere (1518), an office whose practical permanence he secured; affected extravagant pomp and arrogated to himself royal privileges. Reversed England's foreign policy of alliance with France on election of Charles V as emperor; concluded secret defensive and offensive alliance with Charles against France (1521); negotiated marriage of Princess Mary (later Mary I of England) and Charles (1522); endeavored to hold balance so that Francis I and Charles would by turns support England; aided Charles, according to his detractors, in order to obtain Charles's furtherance of his candidacy for papacy, but both in 1521 and 1524 failed to receive Charles's support; dealt England's prestige heavy blow by permitting emperor to defeat Francis at Pavia (1525) and before Naples (1528); aroused detestation of all classes by attempts to raise forced loans and benevolences (1526–28); concluded treaties with Francis I at Amiens (1527). Conducted negotiations with Pope Clement VII for consent to Henry VIII's divorce from Queen Catherine (1527); sat in judgment, along with Cardinal Campeggio, papal legate on divorce (1529); forced, partly by Catherine's intransigeance, to appeal to Rome; lost appeal because Emperor Charles, victorious in Italy over French, obliged papal refusal of appeal; deprived of king's support, stripped of all offices and honors, except archbishopric of York (1529); arrested on charge of high treason, on ground that he had invoked aid of Francis (1530); died on way to London. His zeal for learning borne out by conversion of monastery into Christ Church College, Oxford (1525).

**Wolstan,** Saint. See WULFSTAN.

**Wolverhampton,** Viscount. See Henry Hartley FOWLER.

**Wol'zo'gen** (vôl'tsō'gĕn), Baron **Karl August Alfred von.** 1823–1883. German writer and dramatist; author of *Aus Schinkels Nachlass* (4 vols., 1862–64), the drama *Sakuntala* (1869), several comedies, articles on music and the theater, etc. His sons: (1) Baron **Hans Paul** (1848–1938), poet and writer, esp. on Wagnerian music; editor (from 1878) of *Bayreuther Blätter*, founded by Richard Wagner; author of *Wagner und seine Werke* (1924), and other works promoting Wagner's ideas, and of adaptations and translations, as of the *Edda* and of Aeschylus, writings on German art and culture, operatic librettos, etc.; editor of Wagner's letters to his first wife (2 vols., 1908). (2) Baron **Ernst** (1855–1934), novelist, playwright, and poet; author of humorous and realistic novels and stories, the libretto of Richard Strauss's *Feuersnot* (1901), comedies, critical essays on George Eliot and Wilkie Collins (1885), antirevolutionary and anti-Semitic writings; composer of chamber music, songs, and orchestral pieces.

**Wolzogen,** Baroness **Karoline von,** *nee* **von Leng'e-feld** (fŏn lĕng'ĕ·fĕlt). 1763–1847. German poet and novelist; friend of Schiller, who later married her sister.

**Wood** (wo͝od). Family name of Viscounts HALIFAX.

**Wood, Anthony** *or* **Anthony à** (*ȧ*). 1632–1695. English antiquary and historian of Oxford and Oxford University. M.A., Oxon. (1655). Author of a history of Oxford U. (in Latin, 1674; in English, 1791–96); of *Athenae Oxonienses* (1691–92), a biographical dictionary of notable Oxford graduates (from 1500).

**Wood, Charles Erskine Scott.** 1852–1944. American writer; author of *A Book of Tales, Being Myths of the North American Indians* (1901), *The Poet in the Desert* (1915), *Maia* (1916), *Circe* (1919), *Heavenly Discourse* (1927), *Poems from the Ranges* (1929), etc.

**Wood, Clement.** 1888–1950. American lawyer and writer; practiced law in Birmingham, Ala.; teacher in New York schools (1915–23); vice-president, Bankers' Financial Trust (from 1934). Author of many novels, volumes of verse, comic operas, compilations (as *The Complete Rhyming Dictionary and Poet's Craft Book*, 1936), books of games, histories, and anthologies. Among his best-known poems are *The Glory Road, Short'nin' Bread, Jehovah*, and the song cycle *Cahawba Days*.

**Wood, Fernando.** 1812–1881. American politician; associated in politics with Tammany Hall (from 1834); member, U.S. House of Representatives (1841–43); mayor of New York (1855–58; 1861; 1862); associated with Vallandigham in organizing Peace Democrats

(1863); again member of U.S. House of Representatives (1863–65; 1867–81).

**Wood, Francis Asbury.** 1859–1948. American philologist; professor of Germanic philology, Chicago (1914–27).

**Wood, Francis Derwent.** 1871–1926. English sculptor; notable among his works: Machine Gun Corps memorial at Hyde Park Corner (1925), bronze statue *Psyche* (1919), statue of William Pitt in National Gallery of Art, Washington, D.C. (1920).

**Wood, George Bacon.** 1797–1879. American physician, b. Greenwich, N.J.; compiler, with Franklin Bache, of *The Dispensatory of the United States of America* (1833); author of *Treatise on the Practice of Medicine* (1847), etc. Bequeathed valuable collection of medicinal plants to U. of Pennsylvania for establishment of botanical garden. His nephew **Horatio Charles Wood** (1841–1920) was also a physician; professor of botany, U. of Pennsylvania (1866–76) and of materia medica, pharmacy, and general therapeutics (1876–1906); editor of the *Medical Times* (1873–80) and the *Therapeutic Gazette* (1884–1900); author of *A Treatise on Therapeutics* (1874), etc.

**Wood, Grant.** 1892–1942. American painter, b. Anamosa, Iowa; taught art in Cedar Rapids, Iowa, public schools (1919–24); artist in residence, School of Fine Arts, U. of Iowa. Among his notable paintings are *Daughters of Revolution; John B. Turner, Pioneer; Woman with Plants, American Gothic.* Often called America's "Painter of the Soil."

**Wood,** Mrs. **Henry,** *nee* **Ellen Price** (prīs). 1814–1887. English novelist; m. (1836) Henry Wood (d. 1866). Achieved success with *East Lynne* (1861), a melodramatic novel, several times dramatized; editor of the *Argosy* (from 1867), for which she wrote the *Johnny Ludlow* stories from 1868; author of over 30 other novels including *The Channings* (1862), *The Shadow of Ashlydyat* (1863), *Within the Maze* (1872), *Edina* (1876).

**Wood,** Sir **Henry Evelyn.** 1838–1919. British army officer; served in Crimean War in naval brigade; transferred to army and won V.C. in Sepoy Mutiny (1859); commanded a column through Zulu war (1878–79); first British sirdar of Egyptian army (1882–85); quartermaster general (1893); full general (1895); adjutant general to forces (1897–1901); field marshal (1903).

**Wood,** Sir **Henry Joseph.** 1869–1944. English orchestral conductor and composer. Won international reputation as conductor of Queen's Hall (London) symphony and promenade concerts (from 1897); conducted symphonies by living British composers in Hollywood Bowl, U.S. (1925, 1926). Composer of an oratorio, *Saint Dorothea* (1889), a comic opera, and operettas.

**Wood, Horatio Charles.** See under George Bacon Wood.

**Wood, James Rushmore.** 1813–1882. American surgeon; with associates, developed Bellevue Hospital (1847) and became its chief surgeon; introduced first hospital ambulance service (1869) and first training school for nurses (1873); one of organizers of Bellevue Hospital Medical College (1856).

**Wood, Jethro.** 1774–1834. American inventor, resident on a farm in Cayuga County, N.Y.; inventor of a cast-iron plow (patented Sept. 1, 1819), distinguished esp. by the shape of the moldboard.

**Wood, John George.** 1827–1889. English clergyman and popular writer and lecturer on natural history; author of *My Feathered Friends* (1856), *Man and Beast* (1874), etc.

**Wood,** Sir **Kingsley.** 1881–1943. English statesman; parliamentary secretary to ministry of health (1924–29); postmaster general (1931–35); minister of health (1935–38); secretary of state for air (1938–40); lord privy seal (1940); chancellor of exchequer (1940 ff.).

**Wood, Leonard.** 1860–1927. American physician, army officer, and colonial administrator, b. Winchester, N.H. Commissioned in U.S. army medical corps (1886). Close friend of Theodore Roosevelt (from 1897); co-operated with Roosevelt in raising and organizing the Rough Riders, and commanded the regiment as colonel (1898) in battle of Las Guasimas, Cuba (June 24, 1898); promoted to command cavalry brigade (July 1, 1898). Appointed military governor of Santiago and did notable work in cleaning it up and establishing order; appointed military governor of Cuba (Dec., 1899–May, 1902). Commissioned brigadier general (1901) and major general (1903). Governor of Mindanao and near-by islands in the Philippines (1903); commanded U.S. forces in the Philippines (1906–08). Chief of staff, U.S. army (1910–14). In command, department of the east (1914). Prominent candidate for Republican nomination for president of the United States (1916 and 1920). Governor general of the Philippines (1921–27). Awarded Medal of Honor.

**Wood, Mary Knight.** See Mary Knight Mason.

**Wood, Matilda Alice Victoria.** Real name of Marie Lloyd.

**Wood, Robert Elkington.** 1879–1969. American army officer and businessman, b. Kansas City, Mo. Grad. U.S.M.A., West Point (1900); officer in U.S. army (1900–15) and in National army (brigadier general) during World War; vice-president of Montgomery Ward & Co., Chicago (1919–24); vice-president (1924–28) and president (1928–39), Sears Roebuck & Co., Chicago; chairman, America First Committee (to 1941).

**Wood, Robert Williams.** 1868–1955. American physicist; professor, Johns Hopkins (1901–38). Developed a color-photography process, carried on researches in optics, spectroscopy, atomic and molecular radiation, and on the biological and physiological effects of high-frequency sound waves. Author of *Physical Optics* (1905), and of fiction including *The Man Who Rocked the Earth* (with Arthur Train, 1915), and illustrated nonsense verse *How to Tell the Birds from the Flowers* (1907)

**Wood, William.** 1671–1730. English ironmaster. Obtained (1722) patent to coin halfpence and farthings for circulation in Ireland (Wood's halfpence), sharing difference between bullion value and nominal value with George I's mistress, the duchess of Kendal. Also granted patent (1722) to strike halfpence, pence, and twopences for the American colonies, these coins, dated 1722 and 1723, of "Wood's metal," being known as the Rosa Americana coinage. Forced to surrender both patents before popular indignation, which was increased by *The Drapier's Letters* (1724) of Jonathan Swift.

**Wood'ber'ry** (wŏŏd'bĕr'ĭ; -bĕr·ĭ), **George Edward.** 1855–1930. American man of letters, b. Beverly, Mass. Frequent contributor to the *Atlantic Monthly* and *The Nation* (1876–91); literary editor, Boston *Post* (1888); professor of literature, Columbia U. (1891–1904). Remainder of life passed partly in traveling and partly in retirement. Author of *The North Shore Watch and Other Poems* (1890), *Wild Eden* (verse, 1899), *Heart of Man* (essays, 1899), *Makers of Literature* (essays, 1900), *The Torch* (1905), *The Appreciation of Literature* (1907), *Great Writers* (1907), *Ideal Passion* (verse, 1917), *The Roamer and Other Poems* (1920), etc.

**Wood'bridge** (wŏŏd'brĭj), **Frederick James Eugene.** 1867–1940. Educator, b. Windsor, Ontario, Can.; to U.S. as a boy; professor of philosophy, Columbia U. (from 1902), and dean of faculties of political science, philosophy, and pure science (1912–29).

**Wood'burn** (wŏŏd'bẽrn), **James Albert.** 1856–1943. American educator; professor of American history, Indiana U. (1890–1924); author of *The American Repub-*

*lic and Its Government* (1903), *Political Parties and Party Problems in the United States* (1903), etc.

**Wood'bur'y** (wŏŏd'bĕr'ĭ; -bēr·ĭ; *esp. Brit.*, -brĭ), **Charles Herbert.** 1864–1940. American marine painter; well-known paintings: *Mid-Ocean, A Heavy Sea, The Ground Swell, Maine Coast.*

**Woodbury, Levi.** 1789–1851. American jurist; practiced in New Hampshire; governor of New Hampshire (1823, 1824); U.S. senator (1825–31); U.S. secretary of the navy (1831–34); U.S. secretary of the treasury (1834–41); again U.S. senator (1841–45); associate justice, U.S. Supreme Court (1845–51).

**Woodbury, Walter Bentley.** 1834–1885. English photographer and inventor; migrated to Batavia, Java (1858), where he used collodion process of photography; settled in Birmingham; invented (1866) a new method of photoengraving, called *woodburytype*, and other photographic processes and devices.

**Wood'fall** (wŏŏd'fôl), **Henry Sampson.** 1739–1805. English printer and journalist; took over from his father and conducted (1758?–93) the *Public Advertiser*, in which he printed (1768–72), the *Letters of Junius* (see Sir Philip FRANCIS), without having acquaintance with their author.

**Wood'ford** (wŏŏd'fērd), **Stewart Lyndon.** 1835–1913. American lawyer, army officer, and diplomat, b. New York City; served in Union army in Civil War; lieutenant governor of New York (1867–69); member, U.S. House of Representatives (1873–74); U.S. minister to Spain (1897–98).

**Wood'house** (wŏŏd'hous), **Henry.** *Orig. name* **Mario Terenzio Enrico Ca'sa·le'gno** (kä'sä·lā'nyō). 1884– . Authority in America on aeronautics, b. Turin, Italy; to U.S. (1904), became naturalized and legally changed name (1917). Founded and published magazine *Flying* (1912–20); adviser of arctic and antarctic explorers who planned to use aircraft for their explorations. Author of *Textbook of Naval Aeronautics* (1917), *Textbook of Military Aeronautics* (1918), *Aerial Laws and Regulations for Air Traffic* (1920), etc.

**Wood'house** (wŏŏd'hous), **Robert.** 1773–1827. English mathematician and astronomer; one of first in England to explain and advocate use of the calculus.

**Woodhouselee,** Lord. See *Alexander Fraser Tytler,* under William TYTLER.

**Wood'hull** (wŏŏd'hŭl), **Victoria Claflin.** See CLAFLIN.

**Wood'in** (wŏŏd''n; -ĭn), **William Hartman.** 1868–1934. American industrialist and financier, b. Berwick, Pa.; president, American Car and Foundry Co. (from 1916); U.S. secretary of the treasury (1933).

**Wood'ring** (wŏŏd'rĭng), **Harry Hines.** 1890–1967. American banker and politician, b. Elk City, Kans.; governor of Kansas (1931–33); U.S. assistant secretary of war (1933–36), secretary of war (1936–40).

**Wood'row** (wŏŏd'rō), Mrs. **Wilson,** *nee* **Nancy Mann Wad·del'** (wŏ·dĕl'). 1870–1935. American writer, b. Chillicothe, Ohio; m. James Wilson Woodrow (1897); author of *The Bird of Time* (1907), *The Hornets' Nest* (1917), *Burned Evidence* (1925), *Pawns of Murder* (1932), etc.

**Wood'ruff** (wŏŏd'rŭf), **Wilford.** 1807–1898. American Mormon leader, b. Avon, Conn.; was in first group of Mormons to enter valley of Great Salt Lake (1847); president of the quorum of the Twelve Apostles (1880–89); succeeded John Taylor as president of the Mormon Church (1889–98).

**Woods** (wŏŏdz), **Frederick Adams.** 1873–1939. American biologist, b. Boston; author of *Mental and Moral Heredity in Royalty* (1906), *The Influence of Monarchs* (1913), etc.

**Woods, Leonard.** 1774–1854. American Congregational theologian; professor of theology, Andover Sem. (1808–46). His son **Leonard** (1807–1878) was a Presbyterian clergyman and educator; president of Bowdoin College (1839–66).

**Woods, Margaret Louisa,** *nee* **Brad'ley** (brăd'lĭ). 1856–1945. English poet and dramatist; m. (1879) Rev. H. G. Woods; author of *A Village Tragedy* (1887), *Pastels under the Southern Cross* (1911), *The Spanish Lady* (1927).

**Woods, Robert Archey.** 1865–1925. American social-settlement worker; head of Andover House, first social settlement in Boston (1891–1925); author of *The City Wilderness* (1898), *Americans in Process* (1902), *Neighborhood in Nation-Building* (1923), etc.

**Woods, William Burnham.** 1824–1887. American jurist, b. Newark, Ohio; served in Civil War; judge, U.S. circuit court, 5th circuit, including Georgia and the Gulf States (1869–80); associate justice, U.S. Supreme Court (1880–87).

**Woodstock, Edward of.** 1330–1376. See EDWARD, Prince of Wales.

**Woodstock, Thomas of.** See THOMAS OF WOODSTOCK.

**Wood'ville** (wŏŏd'vĭl) *or* **Wyde'ville** (wĭd'vĭl), **Richard.** 1st Earl **Riv'ers** (rĭv'ērz). d. 1469. English soldier; m. (1436?) secretly Jacquetta, widow of John of Lancaster, Duke of Bedford; accompanied duke of York to France (1441); helped to put down Jack Cade's Rebellion (1450); privy councilor (1450); fought for Lancastrians at Towton (1461), but quitted Henry VI after the battle and tendered allegiance to Edward IV; treasurer (1466) and so powerful at court as to arouse enmity of Richard Neville, Earl of Warwick; after Edward's defeat at Edgecot, executed, along with his son Sir John Woodville. Another son, **Anthony Woodville** *or* **Wyd'ville** [wĭd'vĭl] (1442?–1483), Baron **Scales** (skālz) and 2d Earl Rivers, tendered allegiance to Edward IV after Towton (1461); fought famous tournament with Anthony, bastard of Burgundy (1467); lieutenant of Calais (1470); aided Edward IV in victorious return from exile (1471); guardian and governor to Edward, Prince of Wales (1473); made pilgrimage to Rome (1475–76); protected and encouraged Caxton; his translations from French brought out by Caxton, one being *Dictes and Sayings of the Philosophers* (1477); beheaded at Pontefract by Richard III. For **Elizabeth Woodville** (1437?–1492) and her daughter **Elizabeth** (1465–1503), wife of Henry VII, see ELIZABETH, queen of Edward IV of England.

**Wood'ward** (wŏŏd'wērd; wŏŏd'ērd), **Sir Arthur Smith.** 1864–1944. English paleontologist; with British Museum (1882); keeper, department of geology (1901–24); known for research on extinct vertebrates, esp. fishes; associated with Charles Dawson in discovery and interpretation of the Piltdown skull (1912–14).

**Woodward, Calvin Milton.** 1837–1914. American educator; originated and directed St. Louis Manual Training School, opened (1880) under sponsorship of Washington U.; regarded as pioneer in manual-training high-school development.

**Woodward, John.** 1837–1898. Scottish clergyman; rector, Montrose, Scotland; fellow of Society of Antiquaries; coauthor, with George Burnett (1822–1890), of *Treatise on Heraldry, British and Foreign* (1892).

**Woodward, Joseph Janvier.** 1833–1884. American physician; entered U.S. army medical corps (June, 1861); in surgeon general's office, Washington, D.C. (1862–65). Prepared medical section, comprising first two volumes, of *Medical and Surgical History of the War of the Rebellion* (6 vols., 1870–88). On duty at Army

Medical Museum, Washington, D.C.; pioneer in applying photomicrography to the uses of pathology; developed improvements in photomicrographic camera. Attended President Garfield (1881).

**Woodward, Robert Burns.** 1917–1979. American chemist, b. Boston, Mass. At Harvard U. (1937–79); awarded Nobel prize in chemistry (1965) for work on organic synthesis.

**Woodward, Robert Simpson.** 1849–1924. American astronomer and mathematical physicist; professor, Columbia (1893–1904); president, Carnegie Institution, Washington, D.C. (1904–20).

**Woodward, Samuel Bayard.** 1787–1850. American physician; studied methods of caring for the insane.

**Woodward, William E.** 1874–1950. American writer; in business in New York City (1899–1920); author of *Bunk* (1923), *Lottery* (1924), *Bread and Circuses* (1925), *George Washington—the Image and the Man* (1926), *Meet General Grant* (1928), *A New American History* (1936), *Lafayette* (1938), etc.

**Wood'worth** (wŏŏd'wûrth; -wẽrth), **Robert Sessions.** 1869–1962. American psychologist; on teaching staff at Columbia U. (1903–42); wrote *Dynamic Psychology* (1917), *Adjustment and Mastery* (1933), *Experimental Psychology* (1938), etc.

**Woodworth, Samuel.** 1784–1842. American printer, journalist, and author, b. Scituate, Mass.; printing office in New York City (from 1809); wrote a novel, a few plays (including one success, *The Forest Rose*, 1825, the chief character being a Yankee, "Jonathan Ploughboy"), and much verse, including *The Old Oaken Bucket.*

**Wool** (wŏŏl), **John Ellis.** 1784–1869. American army officer, b. Newburgh, N.Y. Colonel and inspector general, U.S. army (1816–41); brigadier general (June, 1841). Organized (1846) and led volunteers in Mexican War; second in command at battle of Buena Vista, and brevetted major general for his service there. Commanded eastern military division (1848–53), department of the Pacific (1854–57), department of the East (1857–61) and sent reinforcements in time to save Fortress Monroe for the Union (1861). Commissioned major general (May, 1862); retired (1863).

**Wool'dridge** (wŏŏl'drĭj), **Harry Ellis.** 1845–1917. English painter and writer on musical history; professor of fine art, Oxford (1895–1904); contributed first two volumes (entitled *The Polyphonic Period;* 1901, 1905) of *Oxford History of Music.* Lifelong friend of Robert Bridges, with whom he collaborated in the *Yattendon Hymnal* (1895–99).

**Woolf** (wŏŏlf), **Arthur.** 1766–1837. English mining engineer; introduced the Woolf engine, first practical compound engine (1804; patented, 1810).

**Woolf, Leonard Sidney.** 1880–1969. English publicist; educ. Cambridge; with his wife founded (1917) the Hogarth Press; literary editor of *The Nation* (1923–30); joint editor of *Political Quarterly* (1931–59); author of *International Government* (1916), *Co-operation and the Future of Industry* (1918), *Socialism and Co-operation* (1921), *Imperialism and Civilization* (1928), *After the Deluge* (survey of contemporary political and social ideas; 2 vols., 1931, 1939), etc. His wife (m. 1912), **Virginia,** *in full* **Adeline Virginia** (1882–1941), dau. of Sir Leslie Stephen; author of fiction including *The Voyage Out* (1915), *Monday or Tuesday* (short stories; 1921), in which she launched a new method of revealing thoughts of characters by their effects on their surroundings, which is further developed in *Jacob's Room* (1922), *Mrs. Dalloway* (1925), in which she initiated bolder experimentation in the stream-of-consciousness technique, perfected in *To the Lighthouse* (1927), *Orlando* (1928), *The Waves* (1931), *Between the Acts* (1941), and of miscellaneous prose including *A Room of One's Own* (1930; championing independent life for women), *The Common Reader* (critical essays; 1925; second series 1932), *Flush* (1933; biography of Elizabeth Barrett Browning's cocker spaniel), *Roger Fry* (biography; 1940). For her sister Vanessa, see under Clive Bell.

**Woolf, Samuel Johnson.** 1880–1948. American painter, b. New York City; with A.E.F. in World War; painted portraits of leading American commanders and of scenes at the front.

**Wooll'cott** (wŏŏl'kŭt), **Alexander.** 1887–1943. American journalist and writer, b. Phalanx, N.J.; served in A.E.F. (1917–19); dramatic critic, New York *Times* (1914–22), New York *Herald* (1922), New York *World* (1925–28); radio broadcaster (1929–43). Author of *The Command is Forward* (1919), *Shouts and Murmurs* (1923), *Mr. Dickens Goes to the Play* (1923), *The Story of Irving Berlin* (1925), *Going to Pieces* (1928), *While Rome Burns* (1934); compiler of anthologies, *The Woollcott Reader* (1935), *Woollcott's Second Reader* (1937), *As You Were* (1943).

**Wool'lett** (wŏŏl'ĕt; -ĭt), **William.** 1735–1785. English draftsman and line engraver; established reputation with engravings *Temple of Apollo* (1760), after Claude Lorrain, and *Niobe*, after Richard Wilson; gained with his most famous work, *Death of General Wolfe* (1776), after Benjamin West, appointment of historical engraver to the king.

**Wool'ley** (wŏŏl'ĭ), **Celia,** *nee* **Parker.** 1848–1918. American social-settlement worker; m. Jefferson H. Woolley (1868); founded and served as resident head, Frederick Douglass Center (1904–18), a social settlement on Chicago's south side for work among Negroes.

**Woolley,** Sir **Charles Leonard.** 1880–1960. English archaeologist. Conducted excavations in Corbridge (1906–07), in Nubia (1907–11; 1912), Carchemish (1912–14; 1919), Sinai (1914), Tell el-Amarna (1921–22), Ur (1922–34), near Antioch, Syria (1936–38). Author of *The Sumerians* (1929), *Ur of the Chaldees, The Royal Cemetery* (2 vols., 1934), *Abraham* (1936), etc.

**Woolley, Mary Emma.** 1863–1947. American educator, b. South Norwalk, Conn.; president, Mount Holyoke College (1900–37); active in movements for world peace.

**Wool'man** (wŏŏl'măn), **John.** 1720–1772. American Quaker preacher and abolitionist, b. Rancocas, New Jersey; tailor by trade; itinerant Quaker preacher (1743–72), traveling through the colonies both northern and southern and inveighing against slavery; best known for his *Journal* (first published in 1774, after his death, and often reprinted).

**Wool'ner** (wŏŏl'nẽr), **Thomas.** 1825–1892. English sculptor and poet. Member of Pre-Raphaelite Brotherhood (1848) contributing the poem *My Lady Beautiful* to first number of their magazine, *The Germ.* Inspired, by his departure to Australian gold fields (1852–54), Ford Madox Brown's *The Last of England.* Began with bust of Tennyson (1857) success with portrait busts and medallions of eminent men; executed statues of Macaulay, John Stuart Mill, Captain Cook.

**Wool'sey** (wŏŏl'sĭ), **Theodore Dwight.** 1801–1889. American educator, b. New York City. Professor of Greek language and literature, Yale (1831–46); president of Yale (1846–71). Chairman, New Testament company of the American committee for revision of the English version of the Bible (1871–81). Author of editions of Greek classics, and *Political Science...* (1878), *Communism and Socialism* (1880), etc. His son **Theodore Salisbury** (1852–1929) was a jurist; professor of international law, Yale Law School (1878–1911). A niece of

Theodore Dwight Woolsey, **Sarah Chauncey Woolsey** (1835–1905), was a writer, under pseudonym **Susan Coo'lidge** (kōō'lĭj), of stories for girls (*What Katy Did*, etc.).

**Wool'son** (wŏŏl's'n), **Constance Fenimore.** 1840–1894. Grandniece of James Fenimore Cooper. American writer, b. Claremont, N.H.; resident abroad (after 1879). Author of *The Old Stone House* (1873, over pseudonym "Anne March" [märch]), *Castle Nowhere: Lake Country Sketches* (1875), *Rodman the Keeper: Southern Sketches* (1880), and the novels *Anne* (1883), *For the Major* (1883), *East Angels* (1886), *Jupiter Lights* (1889), *Horace Chase* (1894), *Dorothy* (1896).

**Wool'ston** (wŏŏl'stŭn), **Thomas.** 1670–1733. English deist; challenged clergy in freethinking tracts and lost fellowship; his series of six *Discourses* (1727–29), questioning the miracles of the New Testament, caused imprisonment until his death.

**Wool'ton** (wŏŏl't'n; -tŭn), 1st Earl. **Frederick James Mar'quis** (mär'kwĭs). 1883–1964. English businessman; M.A., B.Sc., Manchester; officer in banking, investment, and insurance firms; director-general of equipment and stores, ministry of supply (1939–40); minister of food (1940–43).

**Wool'worth** (wŏŏl'wûrth; -wẽrth), **Frank Winfield.** 1852–1919. American merchant, b. Rodman, N.Y. Opened first successful five-cent store, in Lancaster, Pa. (June, 1879); soon added ten-cent goods; expanded until the Woolworth five-and-ten-cent stores became famous in all large cities of U.S. Erected Woolworth Building, New York City (1913), 792 feet high and for a time the world's tallest building.

**Woos'ter** (wŏŏs'tẽr), **David.** 1711–1777. American Revolutionary officer, b. Stratford, Conn. Brigadier general (June, 1775); succeeded Montgomery as commander in Canada, but was recalled and put on inactive status (1776). Major general of Connecticut militia (1776); mortally wounded in action at Ridgefield, Conn. (Apr. 27, 1777) and died five days later. His grandson **Charles Whiting Wooster** (1780–1848) commanded American privateer *Saratoga* preying on British commerce in War of 1812; entered service of Chile as naval captain (1817–19) and chief of Chilean naval forces (1822–35); co-operated with land forces in successful attack on last stronghold of the Spaniards in Chile, the island of Chiloé (Jan. 11, 1826); commissioned rear admiral in Chilean navy (Nov., 1829); retired, with pension (1835).

**Worces'ter** (wŏŏs'tẽr). (1) Earl of. See *Thomas Percy* (1344?–1403), under PERCY family; John TIPTOFT. (2) Earls and marquises of. See SOMERSET family.

**Worcester, Dean Conant.** 1866–1924. American colonial administrator and author, b. Thetford, Vt. Member of scientific expeditions to Philippine Islands (1887–88; 1890–93); member, U.S. Philippine commission (1899–1901); secretary of the interior, Philippine insular government (1901–13). Author of *The Philippine Islands and Their People* (1899), *The Philippines Past and Present* (1913), etc.

**Worcester, Elwood.** 1862–1940. American Protestant Episcopal clergyman and writer, b. Massillon, Ohio; rector of Emmanuel Church, Boston (1904–29); associated with Samuel McComb in the Emmanuel movement (1906); author of *The Christian Religion as a Healing Power* (1909), *Body, Mind and Spirit* (with Samuel McComb; 1931), etc.

**Worcester, Joseph Emerson.** 1784–1865. American lexicographer, b. Bedford, N.H. Settled at Cambridge, Mass. (1819) and devoted himself to literary work. First of his series of dictionaries was an edition of *Johnson's English Dictionary...with Walker's Pronouncing Dictionary, Combined* (1828). His *Comprehensive Pronouncing and Explanatory Dictionary of the English Language* (1830) brought charges of plagiarism from Noah Webster and initiated what was known as "the War of the Dictionaries." Compiled *A Universal and Critical Dictionary of the English Language* (1846), *A Pronouncing, Explanatory, and Synonymous Dictionary of the English Language*, containing discrimination of synonyms (1855), *A Dictionary of the English Language*, an illustrated quarto (1860).

**Worcester, Noah.** 1758–1837. American theologian, b. Hollis, N.H. Pastor in Congregational church at Thornton, N.H. (1787–1810); first editor, *Christian Disciple*, a monthly Unitarian periodical (1813–18); founded and edited *The Friend of Peace* (1819–28), a pacifist magazine.

**Worde** (wôrd), **Wyn'kyn** (wĭng'kĭn) **de** (dĕ). *Real name* **Jan** (yän) **van Wynkyn.** d. 1534? English printer and stationer, b. in Alsace, prob. at Wörth. Became assistant to Caxton in Westminster (1477) and succeeded him (1491); removed to Fleet Street (1500); made improvements in the art of type cutting; issued over 400 distinct works.

**Wor'den** (wûr'd'n), **John Lorimer.** 1818–1897. American naval officer; commanded *Monitor* in passage from Greenpoint, Long Island, to Hampton Roads, Va., and in battle with Confederate *Merrimack* (Mar. 9, 1862); commanded monitor *Montauk* in attack on Fort McAllister (Jan. 27, 1863), in sinking Confederate cruiser *Nashville* (Feb., 1863), and in attack on Charleston (Apr. 7, 1863). Rear admiral (1872).

**Words'worth** (wûrdz'wûrth; -wẽrth), **Christopher.** 1774–1846. English clergyman and ecclesiastical biographer. Youngest brother of William Wordsworth. Chaplain to archbishop of Canterbury (1805); master of Trinity College, Cambridge (1820–41), a strict disciplinarian. Author of *Ecclesiastical Biography* (6 vols., 1810) and *Who Wrote Eikon Basilike* (1824), supporting authorship of Charles I. His three sons were: **John** (1805–1839), classical scholar. **Charles** (1806–1892), bishop of St. Andrews (1852); advocate of reunion of churches of England and Scotland; one of the New Testament revisers (1870); author of *Shakespeare's Knowledge and Use of the Bible* (1864). **Christopher** (1807–1885), headmaster of Harrow (1836–44); bishop of Lincoln (1868–85); author of *Athens and Attica* (1836) and other works of classical scholarship, of a commentary on the whole Bible (1856–70), and a church history to 451 A.D. (1881–83).

**John** (1843–1911), elder son of Christopher (1807–1885), bishop of Salisbury (1885–1911) and author of *Fragments of Early Latin* (1874). His daughter **Elizabeth** (1840–1932) was the first principal of Lady Margaret Hall, Oxford.

**Wordsworth, William.** 1770–1850. English poet, b. Cockermouth, Cumberland. B.A., Cantab. (1791); traveled in France (1792); sympathized with French revolutionary spirit; fell in love at Blois with a surgeon's daughter, Marie Anne ("Annette") Vallon, who bore him a daughter Anne Caroline (b. 1792, m. Jean Baptiste Martin Baudouin, 1816), an episode reflected in *Vaudracour and Julia*. Published (1793) first works, *The Evening Walk* and *Descriptive Sketches*, the latter an account of a walking tour in the Alps; began (1793) *Guilt and Sorrow*, showing Godwinian rationalistic influence; in a period of pessimism wrote (1795–96) a tragedy, *The Borderers*. On receipt of a £900 legacy settled, with sister Dorothy (see below) as constant companion, at Racedown, Dorsetshire; moved to Alfoxden, Somerset, to be near Samuel Taylor Coleridge, with whom he wrote *Lyrical Ballads* (1798, 1800, 1802, 1805), a collection of poems representing revolt against the artificial style and a vindication of the life of the senses, many of them written in a distinctive blank verse, reaching its height in *Lines composed a few miles above Tintern Abbey;* increased the hostility of the critics by the statement of his poetical principles and his theory of poetic diction. Lived (1798–99) in Goslar, Germany, where he wrote *Ruth* and *Lucy Gray* and other similar poems, and began *The Prelude* (completed 1805, publ. after his death), a spiritual autobiography. Settled (1799) at Grasmere with Dorothy; m. (1802) Mary Hutchinson (b. 1770), after revelation of the story of Annette. Became an opponent of liberalism; made tours in Scotland (1801, 1803) and began friendship with Walter Scott (1803); published two volumes of poems, including *Ode to Duty, Intimations of Immortality, Yarrow Unvisited, Solitary Reaper* (1807). Made Rydal Mount, Grasmere, his home (from 1813) for rest of his life, which was marked by few events of note beyond publishing of his works. After tour in Scotland, published *Yarrow Visited* and *The Excursion* (1814), the latter to be part of a projected poem, never completed, to be entitled *The Recluse.* Published *Laodamia* (1814) and other poems on classical subjects (1816, 1817); collected his poems (1815) and published (1815–19) *The White Doe of Rylstone* (a tragedy, written 1807), *Peter Bell* (written 1798), *The Waggoner* (written 1805); created in *Ecclesiastical Sonnets* (1822) some of his most perfect sonnets, in a period of declining power. After paying last visit to Scott at Abbotsford wrote *Yarrow Revisited* (1831); visited Italy (1837); succeeded Southey as poet laureate (1843); buried in Grasmere churchyard. His letters edited by Professor W. Knight (1907). His sister **Dorothy** (1771–1855) visited the Lakes with William (1794), began (1798) the first of her *Journals* (printed 1889, 1897, 1904) in which she described homely country life at Alfoxden and Grasmere; wrote also accounts of tours in Scotland and on the Continent, all of which have proved invaluable to biographers of her brother; suffered nervous breakdown (1829), from which she never recovered. His daughter **Dorothy [Dora]** (1804–1847), authoress, m. (1841) Edward Quillinan, poet, published a journal of a visit to Spain and Portugal (1847). See also Christopher WORDSWORTH.

**Work** (wûrk), **Henry Clay.** 1832–1884. American song writer, b. Middletown, Conn.; printer by trade; among his better-known songs were *Come Home, Father* (often sung in the famous play *Ten Nights in a Barroom*); *We're Coming, Sister Mary; Marching through Georgia; Kingdom Coming; Grandfather's Clock.*

**Work, Hubert.** 1860–1942. American physician and politician, b. Marion Center, Pa.; postmaster general of the United States (1922–23); U.S. secretary of the interior (1923–28).

**Work′man** (wûrk′măn), **Herbert Brook.** 1862–1951. English Wesleyan Methodist minister, educator, and church historian.

**Workman, William Hunter.** 1847–1937. American physician and explorer. With his wife (m. 1881), **Fanny,** *nee* **Bul′lock** [bo͝ol′ŭk] (1859–1925), traveled and explored widely throughout the world, esp. among the Himalayas, and collaborated in writing *Algerian Memories* (1895), *In the Ice World of Himálaya* (1900), *Peaks and Glaciers of Nun Kun* (1909), *The Call of the Snowy Hispar* (1910), etc.

**Worm** (vŏrm), **Ole.** *Lat.* **Olaus Wor′mi·us** (wôr′mĭ·ŭs). 1588–1654. Danish physician after whom the Wormian bones of the cranium were named.

**Worme′ley** (wûrm′lĭ), **Katharine Prescott.** 1830–1908. Writer and translator, b. in Ipswich, Eng.; to U.S. (c. 1848); author of *The Other Side of War* (1889), etc.; translator of works by Balzac, Dumas, Molière, Daudet, Saint-Simon, Sainte-Beuve, and other French authors.

**Wor′saae** (vôr′sô), **Jens Jacob Asmussen.** 1821–1885. Danish historian and archaeologist.

**Worth** (wûrth), **Charles Frederick.** 1825–1895. Anglo-French dressmaker, b. in Lincolnshire, England; as designer of women's clothes (from 1858) in Paris, gained notice of Empress Eugénie; arbiter of Paris fashions for 30 years.

**Worth, Nicholas.** Pseudonym of Walter Hines PAGE.

**Worth, William Jenkins.** 1794–1849. American army officer; colonel of infantry (1838) and in command at victory of Palaklaklaha against the Seminole Indians in Florida. In Mexican War, engaged at Palo Alto, Resaca de la Palma, and Monterey; brevetted major general; also engaged at Cerro Gordo, Churubusco, Chapultepec, and Mexico City. Commanded department of Texas at time of his death (May 7, 1849). His son **William Scott** (1840–1904) served through Civil War, with the Army of the Potomac (from 1862); served through Spanish-American War, and was wounded in battle of San Juan Hill (1898); brigadier general, U.S. army (1898).

**Wor′thing·ton** (wûr′thĭng·tŭn), **Henry Rossiter.** 1817–1880. American engineer and inventor; invented direct steam pump and established factory for its manufacture in New York (1859); also invented duplex steam feed pump, much used in waterworks and in oil pipe lines.

**Wort′ley** (wûrt′lĭ), **Stuart-.** See *earls of Bute,* under STEWART family.

**Wortley Montagu.** See under Mary Wortley MONTAGU.

**Wot′ton** (wŏt′'n), Sir **Henry.** 1568–1639. English diplomat and poet; friend of John Donne. Traveled on Continent seven years; confidential agent of Robert Devereux, Earl of Essex, supplying foreign intelligence (1595) until Essex's downfall (1601); sent from Italy by way of Norway to warn James VI of Scotland, afterwards James I of England, of a murder plot. Employed by James as ambassador (1604–24), mostly in Venice, whence he forwarded to James installments of Paolo Sarpi's history of the Council of Trent as fast as written. Financially ruined, made provost of Eton (1624); pensioned on agreement to write history of England; associated with Isaak Walton and John Hales. Author of oft-quoted poems *On his Mistris, the Queen of Bohemia* and *The Character of a Happy Life,* and of the famous description of an ambassador as an honest man sent abroad to lie for the good of his country.

**Wotton, William.** 1666–1727. English scholar of remarkable precocity; B.A., Cantab. (1679); published *Reflections upon Ancient and Modern Learning* (1694), on the side of the moderns.

**Wou′wer·man** (vou′vẽr·män), **Philips.** 1619–1668. Dutch painter, esp. of battle and hunting scenes, cavalry skirmishes, and landscapes.

**Wo·vo′ka** (wō·vō′kȧ). *Among the Whites known also as* **Jack Wil′son** (wĭl′s'n). 1856?–1932. American Paiute Indian mystic, b. in Esmeralda County, Nev.; originator of the ghost-dance religion (c. 1889); recognized by his Indian followers as a messiah (1890–91).

**Woyrsch** (voirsh), **Felix.** 1860–1944. Composer, b. Troppau, Austrian Silesia; professor (1901) and member (1917) of the Berlin Academy. His compositions include oratorios (*Passions-Oratorium; Totentanz*), choral works with orchestra, symphonies, a symphonic prologue to Dante's *Divina Commedia,* chamber music, songs, operas, etc.

**Wran'gel** *or* **Wran'gell** (vrän'gyĕl; *Angl.* răng'gĕl), Baron **Ferdinand Petrovich von.** 1794–1870. Russian explorer. On expeditions around world (1817–19, 1825–27); commanded expedition to polar regions north of Asiatic Russia (1820–24); governor general of Russian America (Alaska, 1829–34); opposed sale of Alaska to U.S. Wrangel Island sought for but not found by Wrangel (1823) after being first reported by native Siberians; it was sighted by Capt. (later Sir Henry) Kellett (1849) and named for Wrangel by T. Long, an American whaler, who discovered it in 1867.

**Wrang'el** (vräng'ĕl), Count **Friedrich Heinrich Ernst von.** 1784–1877. Called "Papa Wrangel." Prussian field marshal general; commanded allied and Prussian troops in Schleswig-Holstein (1848) and suppressed uprising in Berlin (1848); field marshal (1856); commanded Prussian and Austrian forces against Denmark (1864); ennobled (1864).

**Wrang'el** (vrång'ĕl), **Karl Gustav.** Count of **Sal'mis** and **Söl'ves·borg'** (sål'mĭs, sûl'vĕs·bŏr'y'). 1613–1676. Swedish admiral and marshal. Distinguished himself in army and in navy during Thirty Years' War; created count (1645); succeeded Torstenson (1646) as commander in chief of Swedish army in Germany; with Turenne defeated Imperialists and Bavarians at Zusmarshausen (1648); took part in Charles X's wars against Poland, Brandenburg, and Denmark (1655–58); member (1660–72) of regency council during minority of Charles XI; commanded Swedish army against Brandenburg (1674); defeated at Fehrbellin (1675).

**Wran'gel** (vrän'gyĕl), Baron **Pëtr Nikolaevich.** 1878–1928. Russian general; served in Russo-Japanese War (1904–05) and World War (1914–18). After Bolshevik coup d'état (Nov., 1917), joined Kaledin against Bolsheviks and later allied himself with Denikin; after Denikin's retreat (Apr., 1920), received appointment as commander in chief of volunteer anti-Bolshevik army. Took command in the Crimea; reorganized his army; after a few initial successes, lost Sevastopol (Nov. 15, 1920) and was forced to evacuate with such troops as he could save; retired to Yugoslavia; later (1926), to Belgium where he became mining engineer; died at Brussels.

**Wrat'ten** (răt''n), **F. C. L.** 1840–1926. English pioneer manufacturer of photographic plates. His son **S. H. Wratten** (1871– ) and C. E. K. Mees (*q.v.*) took over operation of firm (c. 1906); produced color-sensitive plates, filters, and safelights bearing trade-mark *Wratten.*

**Wrax'all** (răk'sôl), Sir **Nathaniel William.** 1751–1831. English writer of historical memoirs.

**Wray** (rā), **John.** See John RAY.

**Wre'de** (vrā'dĕ), Prince **Karl Philipp.** 1767–1838. Bavarian field marshal, b. Heidelberg. Major general at Hohenlinden (1800); commanded Bavarian division against Austria (1805); as cavalry general, in alliance with the French, led Bavarians in invasion of Russia (1812); negotiated alliance with Austria at Ried (1813) and commanded an Austro-Bavarian army against French at Hanau; defeated (1813); took part (1814) in battles at La Rothière, Rosny, Bar-sur-Aube, and Arcis-sur-Aube; made field marshal and prince (1814); represented Bavaria in Congress of Vienna (1814–15); led Bavarian forces in France (1815); generalissimo of Bavarian army (1822).

**Wren** (rĕn), Sir **Christopher.** 1632–1723. English architect, b. in Wiltshire. Professor of astronomy, Oxford (1661–73); a charter member of Royal Society; devoted himself to architecture (c. 1663). Proposed plans for rebuilding city of London after Great Fire (1666); designed and rebuilt St. Paul's Cathedral (1675–1716); built 52 churches in London. Other works include the Sheldonian Theatre (1664–69), Custom House (1668), Temple Bar (1670–72), monument commemorating the Great Fire (1671–78), library of Trinity College, Cambridge (1677–92), chapel of Queen's College, Oxford (1682), and additions to Hampton Court Palace.

**Wren, Percival Christopher.** 1885–1941. English novelist; educ. Oxford; world traveler; hunter; journalist; tramp; British cavalry trooper; legionary in French Foreign Legion; asst. director of education, Bombay. Author of Indian stories including *Dew and Mildew* (1912), series of novels of French Foreign Legion, *The Wages of Virtue* (1916), *Beau Geste* (1924), *Beau Sabreur* (1926), *Beau Ideal* (1928), *Good Gestes* (1929), and other novels, as *Port o' Missing Men* (1934), *None Are So Blind* (1939), *Two Feet from Heaven* (1940).

**Wright** (rīt), Sir **Almroth Edward. 1861–1947.** British physician and pathologist. Known for research on protective power of blood against bacteria; demonstrated, with others, that blood contains substances (opsonins) that render bacteria subject to phagocytosis; originated a system of antityphoid inoculation.

**Wright, Arthur Williams.** 1836–1915. American physicist; conducted researches in electricity, spectroscopy, astrophysics, and radioactivity.

**Wright, Carroll Davidson.** 1840–1909. American statistician; first commissioner, U.S. bureau of labor, Department of the Interior (1885–1905). First president, Clark College, Worcester, Mass. (1902–09).

**Wright, Elizur.** 1804–1885. American reformer and actuary; grad. Yale (1826); professor of mathematics, Western Reserve Coll. (1829–33); to New York (1833), where he participated in the antislavery movement and edited antislavery journals; to Boston (1838). Began lobbying (1853) in Massachusetts legislature for reform of life-insurance practices; secured legislation requiring life-insurance companies to maintain adequate reserves against their policies, and demonstrated how such reserves are computed; later (1861), secured legislation (nonforfeiture law) preventing companies from appropriating reserves for their own use, and finally (1880) secured legislation requiring companies to pay in cash the value of lapsed policies. Called "the father of legal-reserve life insurance."

**Wright, Frances** *or* **Fanny.** 1795–1852. Reformer, b. Dundee, Scotland. First toured U.S. (1818–20) and wrote book *Views of Society and Manners in America* (1821). Again toured U.S., accompanying Lafayette (1824). Settled in New York City (1829), and scandalized contemporary America by appearing on the lecture platform (from 1830) attacking religion, the existing system of education, and defending equal rights for women and a system of marriage based on moral obligation only; m. (1831) **William Phiquepal D'A'rus'mont'** *or* **Da'rus'mont'** (dȧ'rüs'môN') but later divorced him. Continued on lecture platform (after 1835), discussing birth control, emancipation of women, more equal distribution of wealth, emancipation of slaves and their colonization outside U.S. Was an important influence in securing free public schools in U.S.

**Wright, Frank Lloyd. 1869–1959.** American architect, b. Richland Center, Wis. Practiced in Chicago (from 1893), producing from the beginning of his practice strikingly original designs, both in private dwellings and public or quasi-public buildings. Among his notable works are: Oak Park Unity Temple, near Chicago (1904); his own residence "Taliesin" at Spring Green, Wis. (1911); Imperial Hotel at Tokyo, Japan (1916); the Millard House at Pasadena, Calif. (1923); and many private dwellings in and near Chicago. Founded and headed "the Taliesin Fellowship," a cultural experiment in the arts, on his estate at Spring Green, Wis. Author of *Experimenting with Human Lives* (1923), *Modern Architecture* (1931), etc.

**Wright, George Frederick.** 1838–1921. American Congregational clergyman and geologist; professor of New Testament language and literature, Oberlin (1881–92) and of harmony of science and religion (1892–1907). Editor, *Bibliotheca Sacra* (1883–1921). Interested himself in geology (from 1862); came into public notice with paper advancing theory that gravel ridges near Andover, Mass. were of glacial origin; conducted explorations to determine nature, period, and extent of glacial deposits; wrote *The Ice Age in North America* (1889).

**Wright, George Grover.** See under Joseph Albert WRIGHT.

**Wright, Harold Bell.** 1872–1944. American novelist, b. Rome, N.Y. In ministry of the Christian Church (1897–1908). Author of many popular novels, including: *The Shepherd of the Hills* (1907), *The Calling of Dan Matthews* (1909), *The Winning of Barbara Worth* (1911), *The Mine with the Iron Door* (1923), *God and the Groceryman* (1927), *Ma Cinderella* (1932).

**Wright, Horatio Gouverneur.** 1820–1899. American army officer; brigadier general of volunteers (Sept., 1861); commanded force capturing Florida coastal and river cities (Feb., 1862); commanded department of the Ohio (1862–63). Engaged at Gettysburg, Rappahannock Bridge (1863), and in the Wilderness campaign (1864). Major general (May, 1864); repulsed Jubal A. Early in his raid toward Washington (July, 1864); served under Sheridan in Shenandoah Valley. Commanded first troops to enter Confederate works at Petersburg (Apr. 2, 1865). Chief of engineers (1879); retired (1884).

**Wright, John.** 1770?–1844. English bookseller and literary hack, whose shop in Piccadilly, London, was the rallying place of friends of the Pitt ministry, as was Debrett's of the opposition; published the *Anti-Jacobin* (1797), failed; through debt forced to become William Cobbett's hack, editing Cobbett's *Parliamentary History*, *Parliamentary Debates*, etc.; literary editor for John Murray and Richard Bentley; his most important work the editing of *Debates of the House of Commons* (1839–43) from 48 vols. of shorthand notes of the parliamentary reporter Sir Henry Cavendish.

**Wright, John Henry.** 1852–1908. American Greek scholar; professor, Harvard (1887–1908).

**Wright, John Joseph.** 1909–1979. American Roman Catholic churchman, b. Boston, Mass. Ordained (1935); bishop (1947); cardinal (1969).

**Wright, Joseph.** 1734–1797. English genre and portrait painter; called "Wright of Derby," having passed virtually his whole life in Derby; known for candlelight or fireside scenes (1765–73).

**Wright, Joseph.** 1756–1793. American portrait painter; studio in New York (1787) and Philadelphia (1790).

**Wright, Joseph.** 1855–1930. English philologist. Mainly self-taught; deputy professor of comparative philology, Oxford (1891–1901) and professor, succeeding Max Müller (1901–24). Author of primers of Middle and Old High German (1888) and Gothic (1892) and comparative grammars of Old English (1908, 1923), Gothic (1910), Greek (1912), Middle English (1923), New English (1924). Editor of *English Dialect Dictionary* (6 vols., 1896–1905).

**Wright, Joseph Albert.** 1810–1867. American lawyer and politician; practiced Rockville, Ind. Member, U.S. House of Representatives (1843–45); governor of Indiana (1849–57); U.S. minister to Prussia (1857–61); U.S. senator from Indiana (1862–63); again, U.S. minister to Prussia (1865–67). His brother **George Grover** (1820–1896) was also a lawyer and politician; practiced in Keosauqua, Iowa (1840–65) and Des Moines (from 1865); U.S. senator from Iowa (1871–77).

**Wright, Luke Edward.** 1846–1922. American lawyer and administrator; member of Philippines commission (1900); vice-governor of the Philippines (1901–04); succeeded William H. Taft as governor (1904), becoming governor general (1905); first U.S. ambassador to Japan (1906–07); U.S. secretary of war (1908–09).

**Wright, Mabel,** *nee* **Os'good** (ŏz'go͝od). 1859–1934. American writer; m. James Osborne Wright (1884; d. 1920); best known as a writer of nature books. Author of *Birdcraft* (a field book of New England birds, 1895), *Four-footed Americans and Their Kin* (1898), *The Flowers and Ferns in Their Haunts* (1901), *Gray Lady and the Birds* (1907), *The Stranger at the Gate* (1913), *Captains of the Watch* (1927), *Eudora's Men* (1931), etc.

**Wright, Marcus Joseph.** 1831–1922. American army officer and historian; served in Confederate army through Civil War; brigadier general (1862); official U.S. agent for collection of Confederate records of Civil War (1878–1917).

**Wright, Orville.** See under Wilbur WRIGHT.

**Wright, Philip Green.** 1861–1934. American educator and poet, b. Boston; joined staff of Institute of Economics, which later became Brookings Institution (1922–31); published studies on economic questions; his verse includes *The Dial of the Heart* (1904), *The Dreamer* (1906), *A Baker's Dozen for a Few Score Friends*, and two long poems of radical nature, *The Captain of Industry* and *The Socialist*. His *The Cry of the Underlings* has been widely circulated through reprints in the labor journals.

**Wright, Richard.** 1908–1960. American Negro fiction writer, b. near Natchez, Miss. Variously, porter, messenger, ditchdigger, clerk. Awarded Guggenheim Fellowship (1939). Author of *Uncle Tom's Children* (1938), *Native Son* (1940), *Twelve Million Black Voices* (1941).

**Wright, Silas.** 1795–1847. American lawyer and politician; practiced in Canton, N.Y.; rose to political power in northern New York; member of Albany regency; member of U.S. House of Representatives (1827–29); comptroller, New York (1829–33); U.S. senator from New York (1833–44); supporter of Van Buren, and chairman of senate finance committee (1836–41); governor of New York (1845–47).

**Wright, Sydney Fowler.** 1874–1965. English writer; accountant in Birmingham (1895 ff.); author of verse including *The Ballad of Elaine* (1926), *The Riding of Lancelot* (1929), a translation of Dante's *Divina Commedia* (1942); political works; a *Life of Sir Walter Scott* (1932); novels and historical romances including *The Knights of Malta* (1941), *The Siege of Malta* (1942); short stories, as in *The New Gods Lead* (1932); and, under the pen name **Sydney Fowler,** detective fiction.

**Wright, Thomas.** 1810–1877. English antiquary and historian; collaborated with James Orchard Halliwell; compiled *Biographia Britannica Literaria* (1842–46); edited early English texts, *Piers Plowman*, and the *Canterbury Tales;* published works on literary subjects and on manners and customs.

**Wright, Wilbur** (1867–1912) and his brother **Orville** (1871–1948). American pioneers in aviation, Wilbur b. at Millville, Ind., and Orville at Dayton, Ohio. Brothers formed Wright Cycle Co. (c. 1892), a small concern manufacturing Van Cleve bicycles. Interested in aviation (from c. 1896); first experimented with kites and gliders (1896–1903). First successful flight in a motor-powered airplane made at Kitty Hawk, N.C., when the machine stayed in the air 59 seconds and traveled 852 ft. (Dec. 17, 1903). Continued experiments and improvements; made successful circular flight of 24¼ miles in 38 minutes and 3 seconds at Dayton, Ohio (Oct. 5, 1905); received patent for their flying machine (May 22, 1906). Made exhibition flights in France (1908) and won Michelin trophy (Dec. 31, 1908) by a flight of 124 kilometers in 2 hours and 20 minutes. Completed airplane for U.S. War Department (1908), but on test (Sept. 17, 1908) machine crashed, killing army officer passenger Lieut. Thomas E. Selfridge; machine repaired and successfully underwent army tests (June, 1909). Organized American Wright Company (1909) to manufacture airplanes under their patents. After Wilbur's death from typhoid fever (May 30, 1912), Orville sold his interest in the airplane manufacturing company (1915); became member of the U.S. naval consulting board; director of Wright Aeronautical Laboratory, Dayton, Ohio. Both were elected to American Hall of Fame (Wilbur in 1955; Orville in 1965).

**Wright, Willard Huntington.** 1888–1939. American writer and critic, b. Charlottesville, Va. Student at Pomona College, Calif., and Harvard. In journalistic work (1907–23), notably as literary critic for *Town Topics* (1910–14), art critic of *The Forum* (1915–16), *International Studio* (1916–17), and Hearst's *International Magazine* (1922–23). Creator, under pseudonym **S. S. Van Dine** (văn dīn′), of the detective Philo Vance, in various novels, including *The Canary Murder Case* (1927), *The Bishop Murder Case* (1929), *The Casino Murder Case* (1934), *The Powwow Murder Case* (1938).

**Wright, William.** 1830–1889. English Orientalist; prepared catalogue of Syriac mss., British Museum; member Old Testament revision committee; author of studies in Arabic, Syriac, and Ethiopic, and an Arabic grammar.

**Wright, William Aldis.** 1836?–1914. English Shakespearean and Biblical scholar; edited Bacon's *Essays* (1862); joint editor, with William George Clark, of *Cambridge Shakespeare* (1863–66), and sole editor of second edition (1891–93); edited, with Clark, the *Globe Shakespeare* (1864); carried on editing of Clarendon Press series (1874–97); published abridgment of Smith's *Dictionary of the Bible* (1865); secretary to (British) Old Testament Revision Company (1870–85); edited Psalms in *Hexaplar English Psalter* (1911); an editor of *Journal of Philology* (1868–1913).

**Wright, William Mason.** 1863–1943. American army officer, b. Newark, N.J. Engaged in Santiago campaign, in Spanish-American War (1898), and in suppression of Filipino insurrection (1899). Brigadier general, U.S. army (1917), and major general in the National army (Aug., 1917); in command of divisions of the A.E.F. in the Vosges and during the St. Mihiel and Meuse-Argonne offensives (1918–19). Deputy chief of staff, U.S. army (1920–21); major general, U.S. army (Mar., 1921). Commanded Philippine department (Feb.–Sept., 1922); retired (Dec., 1922).

**Wrig′ley** (rĭg′lĭ), **William, Jr.** 1861–1932. American industrialist; founded firm, William Wrigley, Jr., & Co., manufacturers of chewing gum, Chicago (1891), and served as president until his death.

**Wriothesley.** Family name of earls of SOUTHAMPTON.

**Wris′berg** (vrĭs′bĕrK), **Heinrich August.** 1739–1808. German anatomist, after whom were named *Wrisberg's cartilage, Wrisberg's ganglion,* etc.

**Wró·blew′ski** (vrōō·blĕf′skē), **Zygmunt Florenty.** 1845–1888. Polish physicist; known for work on the liquefaction of gases, esp. oxygen, nitrogen, and carbon monoxide.

**Wrong** (rŏng), **George MacKinnon.** 1860–1948. Canadian historian; author of *The Canadians: the Story of a People* (1938), etc.

**Wroń′ski** (vrôn′y′·skē), **Józef Maria.** *Real name* **Hoe′ne** (hĕ′nĕ). *Also known as* **Hoene–Wroński.** 1778–1853. Polish mathematician and philosopher; orig. a disciple of Kant, but later an advocate of a philosophic system of his own, which he termed Messianism. Author of *Prospectus of Messianism* (1831), *Messianism, Final Union of Philosophy and Religion* (1831–39), etc.

**Wu** (wōō). A Chinese dynasty (222–280 A.D.), ruling in the state of Wu, that one of the three kingdoms in the central part along the lower Yangtze and in the south; capital was Nanking; finally absorbed by the Western Chin.

**Wu, C. C.** *Orig.* **Wu Ch'ao-ch'u** (wōō′ chou′chōō′). 1886–1934. Chinese statesman, b. at Tientsin. Son of Wu T'ing-fang. Early education at Washington, D.C., and Atlantic City; three years at London U. (LL.B., 1911). Member of Parliament (1913); councilor to ministry of foreign affairs (1915–17); joined Canton government, supporting Sun Yat-sen; delegate to Paris Peace Conference (1919); vice-minister and minister for foreign affairs (1920–24); mayor of Canton (1925); minister for foreign affairs at Nanking (1927–29); minister to the United States (1929–31); China's delegate at The Hague and at the Assembly of the League of Nations (1930–31); member of Kuomintang Central Executive Committee (from 1926). Author of two works on politics.

**Wu Ch'êng–ên** (wōō′ chŭng′ŭn′). Sixteenth-century Chinese author of *Monkey* (trans. by Arthur Waley, 1942), based on the pilgrimage of Hsüan Tsang (*q.v.*).

**Wu Hou** (wōō′ hō′). Empress of China (684–704 A.D.) of the T'ang dynasty. See KAO TSUNG.

**Wu′jek** (vōō′yĕk), **Jakób.** 1540–1597. Polish Jesuit and translator; translated Bible into Polish (Wujek's Bible: Old Testament, 1593; New Testament, 1599), still the authorized Polish Roman Catholic version of the Bible.

**Wul′fen** (vŏŏl′fĕn), **Franz Xaver von.** 1728–1805. Austrian mineralogist, after whom wulfenite, or yellow lead ore, is named.

**Wulf′he′re** (wŏŏlf′hĕ′rĕ). d. 675. King of the Mercians (from 658); first Mercian king to be baptized; spread Christianity as he enlarged boundaries of kingdom.

**Wulfila.** = ULFILAS.

**Wulf′stan** (wŏŏlf′stăn; -stăn). d. 1023. English prelate; archbishop of York (from 1003), bishop of Worcester (1003–16); author of a homily in alliterative prose, *Sermo Lupi ad Anglos*, describing desperate conditions after Danish raids.

**Wulf′stan** (wŏŏlf′stăn; -stăn) *or* **Wol′stan** (wŏŏl′stăn; -stăn), Saint. 1012?–1095. English prelate; bishop of Worcester (1062); submitted to William the Conqueror and left in his see; supported William II against Welsh; put end to slave trade practiced at Bristol upon English men and women; canonized (1203).

**Wül′ker** (vül′kẽr), **Richard Paul.** *Orig. surname* **Wülck′er.** 1845–1910. German Anglicist; author of *Grundriss zur Geschichte der Angelsächsischen Literatur* (1885), etc.

**Wul′len·we′ver** (vŏŏl′ĕn·vā′vẽr) *or* **Wul′len·we′ber** (-vā′bẽr), **Jürgen.** 1488?–1537. Hanseatic statesman, b. Hamburg; moved to Lübeck; aimed to restore supremacy of Lübeck on Baltic, chiefly by subjection of Denmark and Sweden, and to spread Protestantism; imprisoned by Duke Henry of Brunswick-Wolfenbüttel, an anti-Lutheran; tortured into self-accusations, condemned to death, and executed (1537).

**Wüll′ner** (vül′nẽr), **Franz.** 1832–1902. German pianist, director, and composer; in Munich (1864–77), Dresden (1877–82), Berlin (1883–84), Cologne (from 1884); composer of choral works with and without orchestra (including the cantata *Heinrich der Finkler*, a Miserere, a

Stabat Mater, the 125th Psalm), chamber music, songs, piano pieces, etc. His son **Ludwig** (1858–1938), dramatic actor in Meiningen (1889–95), baritone lieder singer, and reciter.

**Wüllner, Friedrich Hugo Anton Adolph.** 1835–1908. German physicist; known for work on the vapor pressure of salt solutions and the spectral analysis of gases under pressure.

**Wundt** (vŏŏnt), **Wilhelm.** 1832–1920. German physiologist and psychologist; professor at Leipzig (1875–1917); founder of the first laboratory for experimental psychology (1879); believed that psychology must be based directly on experience; correlated the mathematical, psychophysical, physiological, and experimental principles in psychology; author of books on physiology, psychology, ethics, etc. His son **Max** (1879– ), idealistic philosopher.

**Wün'sche** (vün'shĕ), **Karl August.** 1838–1913. German theologian, Hebraist, and Talmudic scholar.

**Wu P'ei–fu** (wōō' pā'fōō'). 1878–1939. Chinese general, b. in Shantung. Educ. for military career; served under Gen. Ts'ao K'un; made commander of third division army (1916); conducted successful campaigns in northern and central China (1917–20), becoming leader of Peking government against Sun Yat-sen forces in the south and Marshal Chang Tso-lin in Manchuria; defeated Chang Tso-lin (1922); driven out of Peking by General Feng Yu-hsiang (1924); regained control temporarily (1926–27); opposed to Chiang Kai-shek; defeated by him and retired to Yochow (1927); refused to aid Japanese (1937–39).

**Wur'de·mann** (wûr'dĕ·măn), **Audrey May.** 1911–1960. American poet, b. Seattle, Wash.; A.B., Washington (1932); m. (1933) Joseph Auslander (*q.v.*); author of *The House of Silk* (1926), *Bright Ambush* (1934; awarded Pulitzer prize), *The Seven Sins* (1935), *Splendor in the Grass* (1936), *Testament of Love* (1938).

**Wurm'ser** (vŏŏrm'zĕr), Count **Dagobert Siegmund von.** 1724–1797. Austrian field marshal; distinguished himself at Habelschwerdt (1779) in War of Bavarian Succession; led an army corps in French Revolution (1793), defeated at Weissenburg, and forced to recross Rhine; defeated French and took Mannheim (1795); commander in Italy against Napoleon, and was defeated (1796) at Castiglione, Rovereto, and Bassano; besieged in Mantua and surrendered (1797).

**Würt'tem·berg** (vür'tĕm·bĕrk). Medieval German county and duchy, later (1806) a kingdom, and its ruling family, which originated in 12th century. County was a part of Swabia, ruled by Hohenstaufens (*q.v.*); first counts, Ulrich (1241–65), Eberhard I (1279–1325), and successors, ruled in valley of the Neckar and adjacent lands; divided into several lines (15th century); Count Eberhard V (1450–96) became duke (1495) as Eberhard I; succeeded by Duke Ulrich (1498–1550) and ten other dukes (1550–1797), most of them Protestant; lands suffered severely in Thirty Years' War and later conflicts; Duke Frederick II (1797–1806) made elector (1803), then proclaimed king as Frederick I (1805). Recent rulers (kings): Frederick I (1806–16), William I (1816–64), Charles I (1864–91), William II (1891–1918; abdicated). See also ALBERT, Duke of Württemberg, and TECK.

**Wurtz** (vürts), **Charles Adolphe.** 1817–1884. French chemist; author of a dictionary of chemistry and works on medical and biological chemistry. See Rudolf FITTIG.

**Wurz'bach** (vŏŏrts'bäk). A family of Austrian writers and scholars, including: **Constant** (1818–1893), pseudonym **W. Con·stant'** (kôn·stänt'), poet and biographer; author of both epic and lyric poetry; compiler of *Biographisches Lexikon des Kaisertums Österreich* (60 vols., 1857–92). His son **Alfred** (1846–1915), art critic and historian, authority on Dutch painting.

**Wu San–kuei** (wōō' sän'gwā'). d. 1678. Chinese general. Commanded imperial army in last days of Ming dynasty; called Manchus to his assistance and defeated (1644) rebel leader Li Tzŭ-ch'êng; helped establish Manchu (Ch'ing) dynasty (1644); served new rulers in subduing western and southwestern provinces; governor of Yünnan and Szechwan; led revolt against Manchus (1674–79) but overcome and killed by forces of K'anghsi.

**Wü'sten·feld** (vüs'tĕn·fĕlt), **Heinrich Ferdinand.** 1808–1899. German Arabic scholar.

**Wu Tao–tzŭ** (wōō' dou'dzŭ') *or* **Wu Tao–hsüan** (-shü·än'). c. 700–760 A.D. Chinese painter of the T'ang dynasty, generally regarded as greatest of all Chinese figure painters; known for his landscapes and Buddhist religious pictures, nearly all now lost; his influence on painters of China and Japan very great.

**Wu Ti** (wōō' dē'). 157–87 B.C. Chinese emperor (140–87 B.C.) of the Han dynasty; extended empire on the south and annexed parts of Korea and Tonkin; sent to the Yuechi an envoy, Chang Ch'ien (*q.v.*), who brought back much knowledge and also several new fruits (grape, pomegranate, walnut).

**Wu T'ing–fang** (wōō' tĭng'fäng'). 1842–1922. Chinese diplomat, b. in Kwangtung province. Father of C. C. Wu. Educ. at St. Paul's Coll., Hong Kong; in government service as interpreter in law courts; studied law at Lincoln's Inn, London (1874–77); on official staff (1882–96) of Li Hung-chang; member of peace embassy that negotiated Treaty of Shimonoseki (1895); minister to the United States (1897–1902, 1908–09); vice-president of board of commerce (1903); as minister of board of punishment remodeled penal code (1905–07); supported the Revolution (1911); active as official in several capacities in the Canton government (1916–21).

**Wutt'ke** (vŏŏt'kĕ), **Heinrich.** 1818–1876. German historian and politician; member, National Assembly, Frankfurt (1848) and cofounder of the "Great German" party.

**Wu Wang** (wōō' wäng'). First ruler (1122–1115 B.C.) of the Chou dynasty of China. See CHOU.

**Wu'yeck** *or* **Wu'yek** (vōō'yĕk). Variants of WUJEK.

**Wy'ant** (wī'ănt), **Alexander Hel'wig** (?hĕl'wĭg). 1836–1892. American landscape painter; studio in New York City (from c. 1864); one of painters of the Hudson River school.

**Wy'att** (wī'ăt), Sir **Francis.** 1575?–1644. Great-grandson of Sir Thomas Wyatt, English poet. British colonial governor in America, b. in Kent. Investor in Virginia Company, in London (1620); named governor of the colony; arrived in Virginia (1621) and remained as governor for Virginia Company until company's dissolution (1624) and thereafter as first royal governor of the colony (1624–26); again served as governor (1639–41); credited with promoting cause of representative government in the colony.

**Wyatt, James.** 1746–1813. English architect; restored cathedrals; R.A. (1785); succeeded Sir William Chambers as surveyor to board of works (1796); built Royal Military Academy, Woolwich (1796), and Fonthill Abbey for Beckford; revived interest in Gothic architecture. His eldest son, **Benjamin Dean** (1775–?1850), architect, designed Drury Lane theater (1811) and Crockford's clubhouse (1827), London; his youngest son, **Matthew Cotes** (1777–1862), sculptor, exhibited portraits and historical subjects at Royal Academy (1803–14), executed the equestrian statues of George III in

Pall Mall East and of Wellington at Aldershot. A nephew, **Richard James Wyatt** (1795–1850), was also a sculptor. Another nephew, Sir **Jeffry Wy'at·ville** [wī'ăt·vĭl] (1766–1840), augmented *Wyatt* to *Wyatville* (1824), practiced architecture with his uncle (1792–99); built additions to Sidney Sussex Coll., Cambridge (1821–32); remodeled Windsor Castle (1824–28).

**Wyatt,** Sir **Matthew Digby.** 1820–1877. English architect; published *Geometric Mosaics of the Middle Ages* (1848); surveyor to East India Company (1855); first Slade professor of fine Arts, Cambridge (1869); author of books on metalwork and fine art.

**Wy'att** *or* **Wy'at** (wī'ăt), Sir **Thomas.** 1503?–1542. English poet and diplomat. Privy councilor (1533); a lover of Anne Boleyn; courtier in favor of Henry VIII, who sent him on diplomatic missions; imprisoned as ally of Thos. Cromwell, Earl of Essex (1541). Translator of Petrarchan sonnets, and pioneer of the sonnet in England; contributed sonnets, rondeaus, satires in heroic couplets, and lyric poems to Tottel's *Miscellany* (1557). Author of *Penitential Psalms* (1549). His son Sir **Thomas** the younger (1521?–1554), soldier, joined volunteers raised by Henry Howard, Earl of Surrey, and was active at Landrecies and Boulogne (1543–44); joined Edward Courtenay, Earl of Devonshire, in a general insurrection to prevent the marriage of Queen Mary with Philip of Spain (1554); led forces from Kent into Southwark; executed for high treason.

**Wyatville,** Sir **Jeffry.** See under James WYATT.

**Wych'er·ley** (wĭch'ẽr·lĭ), **William.** 1640?–1716. English dramatist; on acting of his comedy *Love in a Wood, or St. James's Park* (1671), gained favor of duchess of Cleveland and duke of Buckingham. Produced *The Gentleman Dancing-Master* (acted 1671 or 1672), comedy of intrigue; *The Country Wife* (acted 1672 or 1673), notoriously coarse but strongly constructed, dexterous in turns of plot, and smart in dialogue; *The Plain Dealer* (acted ?1674), based on Molière's *Misanthrope.*

**Wyc'liffe** *or* **Wic'lif** (wĭk'lĭf), **John.** *Also* **Wyc'lif** *or* **Wick'liffe,** etc. 1320?–1384. Called "Morning Star of the Reformation." English religious reformer and theologian, b. Hipswell, Yorkshire; studied at Oxford; master of Balliol (1361?); grad. doctor of theology (c. 1372). Rector of Lutterworth (1374?), continuing to teach and write at Oxford (till 1382). Developed systematic attack upon the hierarchical system; won favor of John of Gaunt, Duke of Lancaster, and his party by justifying limitation of the Church's lordship over temporal affairs; presented in Latin pamphlets logical grounds for national refusal of certain tribute demanded by Rome. Expounded (c. 1376) doctrine of "dominion as founded in grace," by which all authority, both ecclesiastical and secular, is derived from God and is forfeited when its possessor falls into mortal sin; attacked friars and the worldliness of the medieval church; accused of heresy in bulls by Pope Gregory XI (1377) and summoned before bishop of London in St. Paul's to answer this charge (1377); escaped trial as court session was terminated by general rioting before he could be interrogated; protected by queen mother and by public opinion at second hearing at Lambeth (1378) and was not sentenced. Denied (after 1378) priestly power of absolution, and power to enforce confession; rejected penances and indulgences, insisting upon inward and practical religion as against formalism; denied doctrine of transubstantiation (1380); forbidden on ground of heretical doctrines to teach at Oxford and permitted to retire (1382). Initiated the first complete translation of the Bible into English in order to reach the people directly, translating himself the Gospels, probably the rest of the New Testament, and part of the Old Testament, entrusting the editing to John Purvey, who completed it (c. 1388). Died from paralytic stroke; subsequently condemned at Council of Constance (1415), his body disinterred, burned, and thrown into the River Swift.

**Wy'eth** (wī'ĕth), **Newell Convers.** 1882–1945. American illustrator and mural painter; very successful as illustrator of Stevenson's novels (*Treasure Island, Kidnapped, The Black Arrow*) and an edition of *Robin Hood.* Among his mural paintings are panels in the Missouri State Capitol, Federal Reserve Bank at Boston, etc. His son, **Andrew Nelson** (1917– ), was an artist; b. Chadds Ford, Pa.; painter of landscapes, interiors, and figures in acutely defined detail.

**Wyke'ham** *or* **Wick'ham** (wĭk'ăm), **William of.** 1324–1404. English prelate and statesman, b. at Wickham, Hants; royal chaplain (1349); chief warden of royal castles (1359); priest (1362); keeper of privy seal (1364); bishop of Winchester (1367–1404); lord chancellor (1368–71); because of his leading the opposition to John of Gaunt, deprived of offices and see (1373). Founded New Coll., Oxford (built 1380–86) and St. Mary's Coll. at Winchester (built 1387–94). Pardoned by Richard II; chancellor (1389–91); retired (1391).

**Wyld** (wīld), **Henry Cecil Kennedy.** 1870–1945. English philologist and lexicographer; professor of language and philology, Liverpool (1904–20), of language and literature, Oxford (from 1920). Author of works on phonetics, comparative philology, dialects, historical grammar (*History of Modern Colloquial English,* 1920), rhymes, place names. Editor of *The Universal Dictionary* (1932).

**Wy'lie** (wī'lĭ), **Alexander.** 1815–1887. English missionary and Chinese scholar; translator of the Gospels and of mathematical texts into Chinese and of a Chinese-Manchu grammar into English.

**Wylie, Elinor Morton,** *nee* **Hoyt** (hoit). 1885–1928. American poet and novelist, b. Somerville, N.J.; m. Philip Hichborn (1905); eloped with Horace Wylie (1910; m. 1915; divorced 1923); m. William Rose Benét (1923). Author of verse, as in *Nets to Catch the Wind* (1921), *Black Armour* (1923), *Trivial Breath* (1928), *Last Poems* (pub. 1943), and the novels *Jennifer Lorn* (1923), *The Venetian Glass Nephew* (1925), *The Orphan Angel* (1926), *Mr. Hodge and Mr. Hazard* (1928).

**Wylie, Ida Alexa Ross.** 1885–1959. English author of novels, short stories, and autobiographical works including *The Rajah's People* (1910), *The Red Mirage* (1913), *Towards Morning* (1920), *The Silver Virgin* (1929), *Furious Young Man* (1935), *The Young in Heart* (1939), *My Life With George* (1940), *Flight to England* (1943).

**Wylie, Philip Gordon.** 1902–1971. American author, b. Beverly, Mass. Wrote *Generation of Vipers* (1942), *An Essay on Morals* (1947), *Tomorrow* (1953), etc.

**Wy'man** (wī'măn), **Jeffries.** 1814–1874. American anatomist; professor, Harvard (1847–74). Instrumental in building up anatomical museum at Harvard; curator, Peabody Museum, Harvard (1866–74).

**Wy'nants** *or* **Wij'nants** (vī'nänts), **Jan.** 1625?–1682. Dutch landscape painter, esp. of dunes and of hills covered with vegetation, often with figures supplied by Wouwerman, Adriaen van de Velde, etc.

**Wynd'ham** *or* **Wind'ham** (wĭn'dăm), Sir **Charles.** 2d Earl of **Eg're·mont** (ĕg'rē·mŏnt). 1710–1763. English statesman; M.P. (1734–50); secretary of state for southern department (1761–63); acting in triumvirate with George Grenville, his brother-in-law, and George Montagu Dunk, Earl of Halifax, negotiated with Spain (1761–62) and with France (1762) in settlement of terms of peace.

**Wyndham,** Sir **Charles.** *Real name* **Charles Cul′ver·well** (kŭl′vẽr·wĕl; -wĕl). 1837–1919. English actor and manager; excelled in light comedy in England and U.S.; as manager, produced best-known plays of Henry Arthur Jones.

**Wyndham, George.** 1863–1913. English political administrator and man of letters. Chief secretary for Ireland (1900–05); adopted conciliatory program to maintain union and carry out economic development; made bold use of imperial credit in Irish land-purchase bill (1903); resigned (1905). Friend of W. E. Henley; edited North's version of Plutarch's *Lives* (1895–96) and Shakespeare's poems (1898).

**Wyndham-Quin.** See earls of DUNRAVEN.

**Wynn** (wĭn), **Ed.** *Real name* **Isaiah Edwin Le′o·pold** (lē′ō·pōld). 1886–1966. American comedian; wrote lyrics and music, and owned and starred in, *The Perfect Fool*, *Simple Simon*, *The Laugh Parade;* also starred in motion pictures and on the radio.

**Wynne** (wĭn), **Ellis.** 1671–1734. Welsh author; published (1703) the Welsh allegorical prose classic *Gweledigaethau y Bardd Cwsg* ("Visions of the Sleeping Bard"); took orders; edited Welsh prayer book (1710, London).

**Wyn′toun** (wĭn′t'n; -tŭn), **Andrew of.** 1350?–?1420. Scottish chronicler; canon of St. Andrews; elected prior of St. Serf's Inch in Loch Leven (c. 1395); wrote the *Oryginale Cronykil* of Scotland, a metrical account beginning with the mythical period and extending to 1406, which is philologically important as an example of old Scots vernacular.

**Wy′on** (wī′ŭn). Name of a family of English medalists and seal engravers descended from **George Wyon** (d. 1796), and including: his son **Thomas** the elder (1767–1830); **Thomas** the younger (1792–1817), son of Thomas the elder; **William** (1795–1851), nephew of Thomas the elder; his son **Leonard Charles** (1826–1891); **Benjamin** (1802–1858), son of Thomas the elder; his eldest son **Joseph Shepherd** (1836–1873); **Alfred Benjamin** (1837–1884), second son of Benjamin; **Allan** (1843–1907); his son **Allan Gairdner** (1882–1962),

**Wyse** (wīz), Sir **Thomas.** 1791–1862. British political leader and diplomat, b. Ireland; B.A., Dublin (1812); m. Laetitia, niece of Napoleon (1821). Active advocate of Catholic emancipation in Ireland (1825); M.P. (1835–47); lord of treasury (1839–41); privy councilor (1849). British minister at Athens (1849), credited with bringing King Otto to reason; during Crimean War, with French envoy, virtually governed Greece.

**Wys·pian′ski** (vĭs·pyän′y'·skē), **Stanisław.** 1869–1907. Polish painter, poet, and playwright.

**Wyss** (vēs), **Johann Rudolf.** 1781–1830. Swiss writer and philosopher; author of the Swiss national hymn, *Rufst Du, Mein Vaterland?* (1811), and collector of Swiss tales and folklore; published the story *Der Schweizerische Robinson* (1813; Eng. trans. *The Swiss Family Robinson*, 1820), first related orally by his father, **Johann David Wyss** (1743–1818).

**Wythe** (wĭth), **George.** 1726–1806. American jurist and statesman; member of Continental Congress (1775–77) and a signer of the Declaration of Independence. A judge, Virginia high court of chancery (1778–1806).

**Wyt′ten·bach** (vĭt′ĕn·bäκ), **Daniel Albert.** 1746–1820. German-Swiss classical scholar in Holland; authority on Greek; author of work in *Epistola Critica* (1769), and of *Praecepta Philosophiae Logicae* (1782), *De Philosophia Kantiana* (1821); prepared a critical edition of Plutarch's *Moralia* (15 vols., 1795–1830), and an edition of the *Phaedo* (1810).

# X

**Xan·thip′pe** (zăn·tĭp′ē; -thĭp′ē) *or* **Xan·tip′pe** (-tĭp′ē). Wife of Socrates (*q.v.*). Her peevish scolding and quarrelsome temper have become proverbial.

**Xan·thip′pus** (zăn·tĭp′ŭs; -thĭp′ŭs). Athenian commander; father of Pericles; commanded Athenian fleet in victory at Mycale (479 B.C.).

**Xanthippus.** Spartan general; reorganized Carthaginian army in First Punic War; defeated Regulus (255 B.C.).

**Xán′tus** (ksän′tōōsh), **János.** 1825–1894. Ornithologist, b. at Csokonya, Hungary. To U.S. (1851); on staff of U.S. Coast Survey, in California (1857–61); there made valuable collection of birds for Smithsonian Institution, Washington, D.C. Resident in Hungary (from 1864).

**Xa′ver** (ksä′vẽr; ksä·vär′). *In full* **Franz August Xaver.** 1730–1806. Prince of Saxony; younger son of Augustus III of Saxony and Poland; lieutenant general in French army during Seven Years' War (1756–63); administrator of Saxony (1763–68).

**Xa′vi·er** (zā′vĭ·ẽr; zăv′ĭ·ẽr), Saint **Francis.** *Span.* **Francisco Ja·vier′** (hä·vyĕr′). 1506–1552. Jesuit missionary to Orient, called "Apostle of the Indies"; b. near Pamplona, Navarre, youngest son of noble Basque family. Studied in Paris (1525–34), where he made acquaintance of Ignatius of Loyola, whom he aided in founding Jesuit order (1534); ordained priest at Venice (1537); in service of order at Rome (1537–40). Sent by John III of Portugal to Goa as missionary (1541–42); preached at Goa and on southwest coast of India (1542–45); visited Malacca and the Moluccas (1545–46); to Ceylon (1547) where he converted many. Sailed for Kagoshima, Japan (1549); worked in Japan with some success for two years; while returning (1552) to Goa to organize a mission to China, died on small island near Macao, discouraged and physically weakened by opposition to his China plans. Canonized (1622).

**Xe·noc′ra·tes** (zē·nŏk′rȧ·tēz). 396–314 B.C. Greek Platonic philosopher, b. at Chalcedon; succeeded Speusippus as head of the Academy (339–314).

**Xe·noph′a·nes** (zē·nŏf′ȧ·nēz). Greek philosopher of 6th century B.C., b. at Colophon in Asia Minor; reputed founder of the Eleatic school; only fragments of his works extant.

**Xen′o·phon** (zĕn′ō·fŭn). 434?–?355 B.C. Greek historian and essayist, b. at Athens; disciple of Socrates. Joined expedition of Cyrus the Younger against his brother Artaxerxes II of Persia (401 B.C.); after death of Cyrus in battle of Cunaxa (401) and murder by Persians of the Greek commanders, rose to leadership among the 10,000 Greek soldiers and guided them back to Black Sea. Served with Spartans at Coronea (394); resided thereafter at Elis, and finally at Corinth. Chief works: *Anabasis* (an account of Cyrus's expedition and the Greek retreat), *Memorabilia* (account of the life and teachings of Socrates), *Hellenica* (history of Greece from about 411 B.C.), *Symposium* (a dialogue representing Socrates as the chief figure), *Cyropaedia* (political romance based on life of Cyrus), and essays on horsemanship and hunting.

**Xé'rez** (hā'rāth), **Francisco de.** b. 1504. Spanish historian, b. at Seville; secretary to Francisco Pizarro (1530–34); author of *Verdadera Relación de la Conquista del Perú y de la Provincia de Cuzco Llamada la Nueva Castilla* (1534).

**Xer'xes** (zûrk'sēz). *Greek name for Persian* **Khsha-yār'shā** (KSHȧ·yär'shä). See also AHASUERUS. Name of two kings of the Achaemenidae of Persia:

**Xerxes I.** Called "the Great." 519?–465 B.C. King (486–465 B.C.). Son of Darius Hystaspis and Atossa. Suppressed revolt in Egypt (485–484); carried on task of Darius of punishing Greeks; prepared great expedition (483–481); bridged the Hellespont; marched through Thrace, Macedonia, and Thessaly; his fleet checked by Greek navy at Artemisium and his army by small force of Leonidas at Thermopylae; won at Thermopylae (480); burned Athens; his fleet defeated at Salamis (480); returned to Asia Minor, but left army in Greece under Mardonius; his army beaten by Greeks at Plataea (479) and his fleet at Mycale on same day; passed his later years at Susa in dissolute living; murdered by Artabanus, captain of the guards, who was in turn killed (464) by Xerxes' son Artaxerxes I.

**Xerxes II.** d. 424 B.C. King for few weeks only (424 B.C.). Son of Artaxerxes I. Murdered by his half brother Sogdianus.

**Xerxes III** is name given in some sources to Arses (*q.v.*).

**Xi·me'nes** (hē·mā'nās) *or* **Xi·me'nez** (-nāth; -nās). = JIMÉNEZ.

**Xo'ite** (zō'īt). Name, according to Manetho, of XIVth dynasty of Egyptian kings (ruling about seventeenth century B.C.) derived from Xoïs, their capital, city of the delta. See *Table* (*in Appendix*) *for* EGYPT.

**Xy·lan'der** (ksü·län'dẽr), **Wilhelm.** *Real surname* **Holtz'mann** (hôlts'män). 1532–1576. German classical scholar and philologist, first translator of Euclid into German (1562).

**Xystus.** See popes SIXTUS.

# Y

**Ya·hu'da** (yȧ·hōō'dȧ), **Abraham Shalom Ezekiel.** 1877–1951. British scholar, b. Palestine; educ. Heidelberg and Strassburg (Ph.D.); taught in Berlin (1905–14); professor of Hebrew, Madrid U. (1915–22); author of works in Hebrew, German, Spanish, French, and English on Biblical exegesis, Arabic poetry, Hebrew philology, etc.

**Yahya.** See BARMECIDES.

**Yah·ya' Mu·ham'mad Ha·mid' ed–Din'** (yă·yä' mŏŏ·hăm'măd hă·mē'-dōōd·dēn'). 1869?–1948. The Imam, king of the Yemen (1934–48). Descendant of Yahya family which personally (1904) took over control of Yemen; recognized as king by Treaty of Friendship with ibn-Saud.

**Ya·kub' Khan** (yä·kōōb' kän'), **Mo·ham'med** (mô·hŭm'mĕd). 1849–1923. Amir of Afghanistan (1879–80). Son of Shere Ali (*q.v.*). Governor of Herat (1863–74); aided (1867–68) his father to regain Kabul after the latter's defeat by Abd-er-Rahman Khan; lost favor with his father and imprisoned at Kabul four years (1874–78); on his father's flight from the country (1878) and death (1879) became amir; signed peace treaty with British but forced to abdicate when British resident was massacred at Kabul; surrendered (1880) to British; lived on pension in India.

**Yale** (yāl), **Elihu.** 1649–1721. English official in India, b. Boston, Mass.; to England (1652) and educ. in London. In employ of East India Company (from 1671); on duty in Madras, where he became president and governor of Fort Saint George (1687–92). Resident in England (from 1699). Made gift of books and goods to the Collegiate School, then located at Saybrook, Connecticut (1714 and 1718), and the school took his name, perpetuated in the Yale College charter (1745). His tomb is at Wrexham, Wales.

**Yale, Linus.** 1821–1868. American locksmith and manufacturer; invented types of bank locks, dial locks, and small cylinder locks (Yale locks). President of Yale Lock Manuf. Co., with plant at Stamford, Conn. (1868).

**Yal'ow** (yăl'ō), **Rosalyn Sussman.** 1921– . American physicist. With Veterans Administration hospital, Bronx, N.Y. (1947– ); awarded (with Roger Guillemin and Andrew V. Schally) Nobel prize for physiology or medicine (1977).

**Ya·ma·ga·ta** (yä·mä·gä·tä), Prince **Aritomo.** 1838–1922. Japanese army commander and statesman; minister of war (1873); chief of general staff (1878; 1904); minister of home affairs (1885); premier (1889–91; 1898–1900); president of privy council (1905).

**Ya·ma·mo·to** (yä·mä·mô·tô), **Gonnohyoe.** 1852–1933. Japanese admiral and statesman; minister of the navy (1898–1906); admiral (1904); premier of Japan (1913–14, 1923–24).

**Yamamoto, Isoroku.** 1884–1943. Japanese admiral, b. on island of Nagaoka; served in Russo-Japanese War (1904–05); vice-minister of navy (1936); chief of aviation department of navy (1938); commander in chief of 1st fleet (1939 ff.) and of combined fleet (Dec., 1941 ff.); reported killed in an air action in southwest Pacific.

**Yamamoto,** Baron **Tatsuo.** 1856–1947. Japanese financier and politician; governor, Bank of Japan (1898–1903); governor, Hypothec Bank of Japan (1910); minister of finance (1911–12); minister of agriculture and commerce (1913–14, 1918–22). Established new political party, the Seiyuhonto (1924); approved its merger with Kenseikai party to form the Minseito (1927), and remained in position of adviser to new party.

**Ya·ma·shi·ta** (yä·mä·shē·tä), **Tomoyuki.** 1885–1946. Japanese general, b. in Kochi Prefecture; educ. at Military Academy and in Germany. Lieutenant general (1937); commanded division in northern China (1939); leader of Japanese mission to Germany to study German war methods (1940); commanded Japanese forces in Malayan campaign, and received surrender of Singapore (Feb., 1942); took over command of Japanese campaign in Philippines (1944); surrendered (1945); tried and executed (1946) for war atrocities.

**Yan'cey** (yăn'sĭ), **William Lowndes.** 1814–1863. American lawyer and politician, b. Warren Co., Ga.; began practice in Greenville, S.C.; to Wetumpka, Ala. (1839). Member, U.S. House of Representatives (1844–46); resident of Montgomery, Ala. (from 1846) and a leader in secession movement; bolted Democratic National Convention (1860) and organized Constitutional Democratic party, nominating Breckinridge for presidency; prepared and reported ordinance of secession in Alabama convention (1861). Confederate commissioner to England and France (1861–62); member of Confederate Senate (1862–63).

**Yang** (yäng), **Chen Ning**. 1922– . American (Chinese-born) physicist. At Inst. for Advanced Study (1949–65); S.U.N.Y. (Stony Brook) (1965– ); awarded Nobel prize in physics (1957) with T. D. Lee.

**Yang Chu** (yäng′ jo͞o′). fl. 4th century B.C. Chinese philosopher; an individualist and hedonist, opposed to Confucianism; his teachings resemble those of Epicurus.

**Yao** (you). Semilegendary Chinese emperor, supposed to have reigned (2357–2258 B.C.) with a well-organized government; praised by Confucius for his virtues; in his reign occurred the great Chinese flood (2296 B.C.) and the beginning (2277 B.C.) of the Chinese Era of Yao.

**Yaqub al-Mansur.** See al-MANSUR.

**Ya'qu'bi** (yă·ko͞o′bĭ). *Arab.* **Aḥmad ibn-abi-Ya'qūb.** Arab historian and geographer of 9th century; author of a universal history (to 872) and a treatise on historical geography, first of its kind in Arabic literature.

**Ya·qut′** (yä·ko͞ot′). *Arab.* **Yāqūt ibn-'Abdullāh al-Ḥamawi.** 1179–1229. Arab geographer and biographer, of Greek descent. Prepared geographical dictionary, or gazetteer, regarded as most important Arabic work of its kind, and a biographical dictionary of men of letters.

**Yar′mo·lin′sky** (yär′mō·lĭn′skĭ), **A·vrahm′** (ä·vräm′). 1890–1975. Librarian and writer, b. Russia; to U.S. (1913), naturalized (1922); chief of Slavonic division, New York Public Library (1918–55); author of many books on Russian literature and authors. m. (1921) **Ba′bette Deutsch** [bă′bĕt doich′; bă·bĕt′] (1895– ), poet; author of *Banners* (1919), *Honey Out of the Rock* (1925), *Fire for the Night* (1930), *Epistle to Prometheus* (1930); the novel *Mask of Silenus* (1933); a volume of literary criticism, *This Modern Poetry.*

**Yarmouth,** Earls of. See PASTON family.

**Ya·ro·slav′** (yŭ·rŭ·slăf′). d. 1054. Grand prince of Kiev; inherited Novgorod (1015) and extended power over greater part of Russia.

**Yar′rell** (yăr′ĕl), **William.** 1784–1856. English zoologist; author of *History of British Fishes* (1836) and *History of British Birds* (1843).

**Ya·su·da** (yä·so͞o·dä), **Takeo.** 1889–1964. Japanese general; educ. Military Engineering School; studied aviation and served as director of the Military Aeronautic Technical Laboratory (1938–42); commander in chief of Japanese army air force (1942).

**Yasuhito Chichibu-no-miya.** See CHICHIBU.

**Yates** (yāts), **Frederick Henry.** 1797–1842. English actor and manager. His wife (m. 1823), **Elizabeth,** *nee* **Brun′ton** [brŭn′t′n; -tŭn] (1799–1860), was an actress. Their son **Edmund Hodgson** (1831–1894), journalist and novelist, was employed (1847–72) in general post office, London; as editor of *Town Talk* (1858), offended Thackeray and was dismissed from Garrick Club; as editor of society weekly *The World* (which he founded in 1874), was imprisoned for libel on Lord Lonsdale (1885); author of several novels, including *Broken to Harness* (1864), *The Black Sheep* (1867), *The Impending Sword* (1874), several farces, and an autobiography.

**Yates, Richard.** 1706?–1796. English comedian; played at Drury Lane, London (1742–67). His wife, **Mary Ann,** *nee* **Graham** (1728–1787), tragic actress, played at Drury Lane (1753–55, 1756–67), her chief parts including most of Shakespeare's tragic heroines.

**Yates, Richard.** 1815–1873. American lawyer and politician, b. Warsaw, Ky.; practiced in Jacksonville, Ill. Member, U.S. House of Representatives (1851–55); governor of Illinois (1861–64), strongly supporting Lincoln's policies throughout Civil War; U.S. senator from Illinois (1865–71).

**Yates, Robert.** 1738–1801. American jurist; practiced in Albany, N.Y. Member of provincial congresses (1775–77) and committee of safety (1776). Justice, New York supreme court (1777–98), and chief justice (1790–98). Leader of Antifederalists (from c. 1785); in Constitutional Convention (1787) opposed framing of a federal constitution on ground that convention was exceeding its powers; attacked constitution in campaign against its ratification (1787–88).

**Yates, William.** 1792–1845. English missionary and Orientalist; prepared manuals of Sanskrit, Hindustani, and Arabic; devoted whole time (after 1839) to translation and preparation of Sanskrit and Hindustani dictionaries, a complete version of Bible in Bengali, portions of Bible into Sanskrit, and an edition of the *Nalodaya* (1840), a piece of original research.

**Yaz′de·gerd′** (yăz′dĕ·gĕrd′) *or* **Yez′de·gerd′** (yĕz′-) *or* **Yez′de·gird′** (yĕz′dĕ·gĭrd′); *also* **Is′di·gird** (ĭz′dĭ·gûrd). Name of three Sassanid kings of Persia:

**Yazdegerd I.** Son of Bahram IV; king (399–420); kept peace with Roman Empire; tried to free country of domination by nobles and Magian priests; stopped persecution of Christians.

**Yazdegerd II.** Grandson of Yazdegerd I and son of Bahram V; king (440–457); persecuted Christians and Jews; at war with Rome (441).

**Yazdegerd III.** d. 651. Grandson of Khosrau II; last of dynasty of Sassanidae, reigned (632–641); too young actually to rule; country torn by civil war; Arab invasions began (633); overwhelmed by Arabs in battles of Kadisiya (637) and Nehavend (c. 641); fled to Media; his accession date (June 16, 632 A.D.) marked beginning of Jalalaean Era, still used in calendar of Parsis.

**Ya·zid′** (yă·zēd′). *Arab.* **Yazīd.** Name of three Ommiad caliphs: **Yazid I** (d. 683). Caliph (680–683). Son of Mu'awiyah I. Engaged in civil war with Husain (*q.v.*), son of Ali; faced with revolt of Meccans; in siege of Mecca, the Kaaba was burned. **Yazid II** (d. 724). Caliph (720–724). Son of Abd-al-Malik. **Yazid III** (d. 744). Caliph for a few months (744).

**Y·bar′ra** (ĭ·bär′ȧ), **Thomas Russell.** 1880–1971. Son of General Alejandro Ybarra of Venezuela. American writer, b. Boston, Mass. Wrote *Bolivar, the Passionate Warrior* (1929), *Cervantes* (1931), *Hindenburg, the Man with Three Lives* (1932), *America Faces South* (1939), *Young Man of Caracas* (autobiography; 1941).

**Yea′mans** (yē′mănz), Sir **John.** 1610?–1674. English colonial governor in America, b. Bristol, Eng. Emigrated to Barbados (1650). Granted right to establish colony in Carolina (1665); commissioned governor of projected colony; selected site on Cape Fear River but abandoned colony (1667); yielded up governorship (1669); again governor (1672–74).

**Yeard′ley** (yärd′lĭ), Sir **George.** 1587?–1627. English colonial governor in America, b. London. Landed in Virginia (1609); acting governor of Virginia (1616–17); governor (1619–21; 1626–27); during first administration summoned first representative assembly in American colonies.

**Yeats** (yāts), **William Butler.** 1865–1939. Irish poet and dramatist, b. near Dublin; spent boyhood in Sligo; began literary work with translations of Gaelic tales and compilations of Irish folklore; his early lyric verse, as in *The Wanderings of Oisin* (1889) and *The Wind among* *the Reeds* (1899) marked by decorative "embroideries," later given up for more austere style, as in *Responsibilities* (1914), *The Wild Swans at Coole* (1917), *The Tower* (1927); friend of William Morris, W. E. Henley, and Arthur Symons; a founder of Rhymer's Club; wrote first poetic plays *The Countess Kathleen* (1892) and *The Land of Heart's Desire* (1894) and essays, *Celtic Twilight* (1893), followed later by critical essays, as in *Ideas of Good and Evil* (1903), *The Cutting of an Agate* (1912), and *Per Amica Silentia Lunae* (1918); assumed leadership (1901) of Irish literary revival (see also George MOORE); began dramatic activities by writing plays according to his mystical theories of drama; with aid of Lady Gregory and Edward Martyn, staged first performance of Irish Literary Theatre (1899), which became established (1904) as the Abbey Theatre; brought J. M. Synge from Paris to write plays; produced three plays in prose, *Cathleen ni Houlihan* (1902), *The Pot of Broth* (1902), and *The Hour Glass* (1903); wrote verse plays of tragic force, including *The Shadowy Waters* (1900), *The King's Threshold* (1904), *Deirdre* (1907), and later prose plays, as *The Player Queen* (1919) and *The Cat and the Moon* (1924); m. (1917) **Georgie Lees** (1893–1968), whom he believed to have mediumistic powers; announced in *A Vision* (1926) theories professedly communicated to his wife by supernatural beings; chosen one of first senators of Irish Free State (1922–28); awarded Nobel prize for literature (1923). Later verse includes *Winding Stair* (1929), *Wheels and Butterflies* (1934), and *Dramatis Personae* (1936). Author also of the autobiographical *Reveries over Childhood* (1915) and *The Trembling of the Veil* (1922).

His father, **John Butler** (1839–1922), was a distinguished artist, member of Royal Hibernian Academy. His younger brother, **Jack Butler** (1871–1957); landscape and genre painter; author of *Sligo* (1930), *Apparitions* (1933), *The Amaranthers* (1936), *Harlequin's Positions* (play, 1939), *Ah Well* (novel, 1942), etc.

**Yeats-Brown** (yāts′broun′), **Francis.** 1886–1944. British army officer and writer; served in India (1906–13), France and Mesopotamia (1914–15); prisoner of war in Turkey (1915–18); author of *Bengal Lancer* (1930), *Dogs of War* (1934), *Lancer at Large* (1936), *The Confessions of a Thug* (1938), *European Jungle* (1939).

**Yee Chiang.** See CHIANG.

**Yehonala.** See TZU HSI.

**Yellowplush, Charles James.** Pseudonym of William Makepeace THACKERAY.

**Ye-lü Ch'u-ts'ai** (yĕ′lü′ chōō′tsī′). 1190–1244. Chinese statesman at Mongol court. An administrator of the Kin Tatars in China; called (1215) by Genghis Khan to serve as his minister; continued in office after Genghis Khan's death (1227).

**Yen** (yĕn), **James Y. C.** *Orig.* **Yen Yang-ch'u** (yĕn′ yäng′chōō′). 1894– . Chinese scholar; educ. in U.S., at Yale (B.A.), Princeton (M.A.). General director of mass-education movement in China (1924–51); member of People's Political Council (1938–45).

**Yen, W. W.** *Orig.* **Yen Hui-ch'ing** (yĕn′ hwā′chĭng′). 1877–1950. Chinese statesman, b. in Shanghai. Educ. in U.S. at Virginia U. (B.A., 1900); minister to Germany and Denmark (1913–20); acting prime minister and cabinet officer (1921–24); prime minister (1925–26); adviser, ministry of foreign affairs (1928–31); minister to United States (1931–32); to Russia (1933–36).

**Yendys, Sydney.** Pseudonym of Sydney DOBELL.

**Yen Hsi-shan** (yĕn′ shē′shän′). 1882–1960. Chinese general; military governor of "model province" of Shansi (1912–28); supported Gen. Chiang Kai-shek (1927–30); commander in chief, Peiping and Tientsin garrisons (1928–30); member, Central Executive Committee, Kuomintang (1930); joined Feng Yu-hsiang in revolt (1930); fled to Dairen, but sent back to Shansi by Japanese (1931) and reinstated in Kuomintang; successfully opposed Japanese in northern China (1935–37).

**Ye·re·men′ko** (*Russ.* yĕ·ryĕ·myân′kô; *Ukrain.* yĕ·ryā′-myĕn·kô), **Andrei Ivanovich.** 1892–1970. Russian army officer, b. in Ukraine; in World War I; organized guerrilla bands in Ukraine (1917); cavalry officer in civil war; army commander on central front and in defense of Moscow (1941); transferred to Stalingrad front, broke German siege of city, and participated in Russian offensive in Don area (1942–43).

**Yer′kes** (yûr′kēz; -kēz), **Charles Tyson.** 1837–1905. American financier, b. Philadelphia. To Chicago (1882); gained control of Chicago street-railway system; accused of political manipulation to secure franchises of great value; thwarted by public protests; sold out his interests (1899). To England (1900) and headed syndicate building London underground railways. His name memorialized in Yerkes Observatory, Lake Geneva, Wis.

**Yer′kes** (yûr′kēz), **Robert Mearns** (mûrnz). 1876–1956. American psychobiologist; professor, Minnesota (1917–19), Yale (1924–44); author of *Introduction to Psychology* (1911), *The Mental Life of Monkeys and Apes* (1916), *The Mind of a Gorilla* (1927), etc.

**Yermak Timofeiev.** Variant of ERMAK TIMOFEEV.

**Yer′sin′** (yĕr′săN′), **Alexandre Émile John.** 1863–1943. Swiss bacteriologist. Worked with Roux on diphtheria antitoxin at Pasteur Institute, Paris (see E. von BEHRING); discovered the plague bacillus in Hong Kong simultaneously with Kitazato (1894); developed a protective serum against the plague.

**Yes·se′nin** (yĭ·syā′nyĭn). Variant of ESENIN.

**Yev′tu·shen′ko** (yĕf′tŭ·shĕng′kŭ; -kō), **Yevgeny Aleksandrovich.** 1933– . Soviet poet. Wrote *A Precocious Autobiography* (1963), *Bratsk Station and Other New Poems* (1967); also the poem *Babii Yar* (1961).

**Yezdegerd** *or* **Yezdegird.** Variants of YAZDEGERD.

**Ye·zhov′** (yĕ·zhôf′), **Nikolai Ivanovich.** 1895– Soviet politician; people's commissar of internal defense (1936–37); commissar of state security (1937–38), of internal affairs (Jan.–Dec., 1938), of water transport (1938); head of Gay-Pay-Oo (1936–38; resigned).

**Ye·zier′ska** (yĕ·zyĕr′skȧ), **An·zia′** (?än·zyä′). 1885–1970. Writer, b. in Russia; to U.S. (1901); factory worker and domestic servant in New York City; wrote of life on New York's east side (1918); author of *Hungry Hearts* (1920), *Salome of the Tenements* (1922), *Arrogant Beggar* (1927), *All I Could Never Be* (1932), etc.

**Yin.** = SHANG (dynasty).

**Yoannitsa.** See KALOYAN.

**Yohn** (yŏn), **Frederick Cof′fay** (kŏf′ĭ). 1875–1933. American illustrator and painter.

**Yo′lande′** (yô′läNd′). d. after 1219. Empress of Eastern Empire (1217–19). Sister of Baldwin I and Henry, first two Latin emperors of Eastern Empire; m. Peter of Courtenay, third Latin emperor; after his death (1217) succeeded to throne; followed (1219) by her son Robert of Courtenay.

**Yolande.** d. 1478. Sister of Louis XI of France; m. Amadeus IX, Duke of Savoy. Regent (1472–78) for him and for their son Philibert I.

**Yolande.** d. 1227. Queen of Jerusalem (1212–27). Dau. of John of Brienne; m. (1225) as second wife, Frederick II, Holy Roman emperor.

**Yon** (yôn), **Pietro A.** 1886–1943. Organist and composer, b. Italy; to U.S. (1907); organist in St. Patrick's Cathedral, New York City (from 1926); composed choral and orchestral works and songs, chiefly religious.

**Yo·nai** (yô·nī), **Mitsumasa.** 1880–1948. Japanese naval officer and political leader; commander in chief, Imperial Fleet (1936); minister of navy (1937–39; 1944–45); prime minister (1940); deputy prime minister (1944–45).

**Yonge** (yŭng), **Charlotte Mary.** 1823–1901. English novelist. Influenced by her friend John Keble to convey morality and High Church teachings in fiction; gained popular success with *The Heir of Redclyffe* (1853), *Heartsease* (1854), and *The Daisy Chain* (1856). Wrote historical romances including *The Dove in the Eagle's Nest* (1866), and biographical and historical works.

**Yorck** (*or* **York**) **von War′ten·burg** (yôrk′ fôn vär′-tĕn·bŏŏrk), Count **Hans David Ludwig.** 1759–1830. Prussian field marshal; took part in Polish campaign (1794) and war against France (1806); imprisoned at Lübeck (1806); major general (1807). Governor general of East and West Prussia (1811); commanded Prussian contingent of Napoleon's army in Russian campaign (1812) and entered into neutrality convention of Tauroggen with the Russians (1812); corps commander in campaign of 1813–14; defeated Beauharnais at Möckern, and fought at Bautzen, on the Katzbach, and at Leipzig (1813); served in French campaign at Montmirail, Laon, and Paris (1814). Withdrew from army (1815); field marshal (1821).

**Yo·ri·to·mo** (yô·rē·tô·mô). 1147–1199. First Minamoto shogun of Japan (1192–99) and founder of Kamakura shogunate (1192); son of Yoshitomo. Became a leader of Minamoto clan; after annihilation (1185) of Taira clan by his brother Yoshitsune, left as virtual ruler; set up feudal system; caused death of Yoshitsune (1189) and of other leading members of his family (1184–93); crushed Fujiwara clan in the north (1189); appointed shogun by emperor (1192), which marked establishment of Kamakura shogunate; first of long line of actual rulers of Japan; control passed to Hojo family (1219).

**York** (yôrk), House of. English royal house, one branch of the Plantagenets, which was given prominence by Richard Plantagenet (1411–1460), 3d Duke of York, who was paternal grandson of the fifth son of King Edward III, Edmund of Langley (see under duke of YORK), but who derived claim to throne from descent through his mother from Lionel of Antwerp, 1st Duke of Clarence, who was third son of King Edward III. Symbol of house in Wars of the Roses was the white rose. Reigning York kings and their reign dates: Edward IV (1461–70; 1471–83), Edward V (April–June, 1483), Richard III (1483–85). See *Table* (*in Appendix*) for ENGLAND.

**York,** Duke of. Title frequently conferred by British sovereign upon his second son. Conferred (1385) by Edward III of the house of Plantagenet upon his fifth son, Edmund of Langley, progenitor of house of York, and borne by latter's son and grandson (see below). Conferred (1474) by Edward IV upon son Richard Plantagenet (see below). Borne by James Stuart until his accession (1685) as James II of England. Conferred (1784) by George III on second son, Frederick Augustus (see YORK AND ALBANY). Borne (1892) by George (later George V) as second son of Prince of Wales. Conferred (1920) upon George V's second son, who became George VI.

**Edmund of Lang′ley** (lăng′lĭ). 1st Duke of **York.** 1341–1402. Fifth son of Edward III of England. Took part in campaigns in France and Spain (1359, 1367, 1375, 1381) and in Scotland (1385); regent three times during Richard II's absences (1394–99); after feeble opposition (1399), submitted to Henry of Lancaster (Henry IV).

Edmund's elder son, **Edward of Nor′wich** (nŏr′ĭj; -ĭch) *or* **Edward Plan·tag′e·net** (plăn·tăj′ĕ·nĕt; -nĭt). 2d Duke of **York.** 1373?–1415. Admiral of the fleet; rewarded, for support of Richard II against Gloucester and other lords appellant, with grants of land, duchy of Albemarle, and office of constable of England; deprived of lands and offices by Henry IV for suspected complicity in conspiracy of Christmas (1399) and attempt to kidnap the Mortimers (1405); killed at Agincourt, where he commanded right wing.

**Richard Plantagenet.** 3d Duke of **York.** 1411–1460. English statesman. Grandson of Edmund of Langley. Inherited possessions of maternal uncle Edmund de Mortimer, 5th Earl of March. King's lieutenant in France and Normandy (1436–37, 1440–45); king's lieutenant in Ireland (1447–57); strove against queen and Somerset for place in king's counsels; protector during Henry VI's illnesses (1454–55; 1455–56); marched on London and declared heir apparent and protector by Parliament (1460); on expedition to quell rising in north, hemmed in by Lancastrians at Wakefield, gave battle and was killed. Three of his sons were Edward IV, Richard III, and George, Duke of Clarence.

**Richard Plantagenet.** Duke of **York.** 1472–1483. Second son of Edward IV of England. Given up (1483) by queen mother, in sanctuary of Westminster, through persuasion of Cardinal Bourchier; placed in Tower of London with his brother (Edward V), where both were murdered by Richard III's order.

**York,** Duchess of. See *Anne Hyde*, under Edward HYDE, 1st Earl of Clarendon.

**York,** Cardinal. **Henry Benedict Maria Clement Stuart.** 1725–1807. Last direct male descendant of Stuart (*q.v.*) royal line; second son of James Francis Edward, the Old Pretender, and brother of Charles Edward, the Young Pretender. Known as Cardinal York during brother's life; thereafter assumed title Henry IX, King of England (1788). After failure of rebellion at Culloden Moor (1746), went to Rome; made bishop of Ostia and cardinal (1747), bishop of Frascati (1761); allowed revenues of two abbeys by French court; stripped of fortune by French Revolution, took refuge in Venice; granted pension by George III of England; bequeathed crown jewels to George IV, then prince of Wales.

**York, Alvin C.** 1887–1964. American soldier, b. Tennessee. Hero of World War I. As a sergeant, led detachment in battle of Argonne (Oct. 8, 1918); after most of his detachment had been killed or wounded, charged German machine-gun nest and captured about 90 men; marched his prisoners ahead of him toward a second machine-gun position and captured it with 42 more prisoners; feat called by Marshal Foch greatest thing accomplished by any noncommissioned soldier in all the armies in Europe; named for valor in report of Gen. Pershing. On return to America, received gift of a farm in Tennessee; at his request, a York Foundation was established, proceeds to be used for support of primary schools in the Tennessee mountains.

**York and Al′ba·ny** (ôl′bȧ·nĭ), Duke of. **Frederick Augustus.** 1763–1827. Second son of George III of England. Prince-bishop of Osnabrück (1763–1802); commanded expedition to Netherlands against French (1793–95); commander in chief (1798–1809); removed (1809) because of traffic in appointments by his mistress; reinstated (1811).

**Yorke** (yôrk), **Philip.** 1st Earl of **Hard′wicke** (härd′-wĭk). 1690–1764. English judge; solicitor general (1720); attorney general (1724); chief justice and privy councilor (1733); lord chancellor (1737). His eldest son, **Philip** (1720–1790), 2d earl, wrote (1741), with his brother Charles (see below), most of *Athenian Letters*, historical fiction; privy councilor (1760); high steward of Cambridge U. (1764–90); edited *Walpoliana* (1783). **Charles** (1722–1770), second son of 1st earl, M.A., Cantab. (1749), was counsel to East India Company (1751); solicitor general (1756–61); attorney general (1762–63); deserted Pitt's party for Rockingham Whigs; again attorney general (1765–67); drafted constitution for Province of Quebec.

**Yo·shi·da** (yō·shē·dä), **Zengo.** 1885–1966. Japanese naval officer (1904–45); held posts successively as a chief of section in Naval Affairs Bureau, battleship commander, director of Tactical Affairs Bureau (1933–35); commander of training squadron; commander in chief of 1st fleet (1936–37); appointed (Nov., 1942) commander of Japanese fleet in China waters.

**Yo·shi·hi·to** (yō·shē·hē·tō). *Reign name* **Tai·sho** (tī·shō). 1879–1926. Emperor of Japan (1912–26), 123d in direct lineage. Son of Mutsuhito. m. (1900) Princess Sadako. During reign, Japan joined Allies in World War I and became world power of first rank. Succeeded by son Hirohito, who had acted as regent (1921–26).

**Yo·shi·ma·sa** (yō·shē·mä·sä). 1435–1490. Eighth shogun of Ashikaga shogunate (1443–74). Grandson of Yoshimitsu. During reign, plague and famine caused uprisings against him (1461), followed by disastrous civil war (1467–77); neglected welfare of people but was patron of the minor arts, established the tea ceremony (chanoyu), and encouraged painting and the drama.

**Yo·shi·mi·tsu** (yō·shē·mē·tso͝o). 1358–1395. Third shogun of Ashikaga shogunate (1367–95). Grandson of Takauji. Checked piracy and subdued Kyushu (1374); established order in country and put end (1392) to civil war between north and south; entered into correspondence with Ming emperor of China; retired and became a monk, but still ruled country from his palace (Kinkakuji, "Golden Temple") at Kyoto; brought Ashikaga shogunate to height of its power.

**Yo·shi·mu·ne** (yō·shē·mo͞o·nĕ). 1677–1751. Japanese Tokugawa shogun (1716–45); did much for agriculture, extending irrigation and establishing trade system; allowed Dutch at Deshima to bring in books.

**Yoshinobu.** See Hitotsubashi.

**Yo·shi·to·mo** (yō·shē·tō·mō). 1123–1160. Minamoto warrior of Japan, an ally of Taira leader Kiyomori in civil war (1156–60); with Nobuyori (Fujiwara leader) defeated by Kiyomori and the Taira clan (1160). Father of Yoritomo and Yoshitsune.

**Yo·shi·tsu·ne** (yō·shē·tso͞o·nĕ). 1159–1189. Japanese warrior and hero, of Minamoto clan, son of Yoshitomo and younger brother of Shogun Yoritomo. Trained in military skill; fought with Minamoto clan (1180–85) in war against the Taira; in battle of Dan no Ura (1185) completely defeated the Taira; killed by order of Yoritomo, who was jealous of his brother's fame; hero of many legends, esp. as told in the *Heike monogatari.*

**Yost** (yōst), **Charles Woodruff.** 1907– . American diplomat. U.S. ambassador to U.N. (1969–71).

**Yost** (yōst), **Fielding Harris.** 1871–1946. American athletic director; director of intercollegiate athletics, U. of Michigan (1921–41).

**You'mans** (yo͞o'mănz), **Edward Livingston.** 1821–1887. American author; largely self-educated; popular lecturer on science (1851–68); founded *Popular Science Monthly* (1872); planned and supervised publication of *International Scientific Series* (1871 ff.); correspondent and admirer of Herbert Spencer, and instrumental in promoting sale of Spencer's books in U.S. His brother **William Jay** (1838–1901) collaborated with him in promoting publication of scientific works; coeditor (1872–87) and editor (1887–1900), *Popular Science Monthly;* sponsored esp. works by Spencer and Huxley; author of *Pioneers of Science in America* (1896).

**You'mans** (yo͞o'mănz), **Vincent.** 1898–1946. American composer of light operas, including *Two Little Girls in Blue* (with P. Lannin, 1921), *Wildflower* (with Herbert Stothart, 1923), *Hit the Deck* (1927), *Rainbow* (1928), *Smiles* (1930), *Through the Years* (1932).

**Young** (yŭng), Sir **Allen William.** 1827–1915. English mariner; took part in polar expeditions (1857–59, 1860, 1875); as commander of the *Hope,* rescued the explorer Benjamin Leigh Smith and party on coast of Novaya Zemlya (1882).

**Young, Allyn Abbott.** 1876–1929. American economist; on teaching staff of Stanford (1906–11), Washington U., St. Louis (1911–13), Cornell (1913–20), Harvard (1920–27), U. of London, Eng. (1927–29); one of commission of experts at Paris during Peace Conference (1918–19); author of *Economic Problems New and Old* (1927).

**Young, Andrew.** 1807–1889. Scottish schoolmaster and poet; wrote hymn "There is a happy land" (1838); author of *The Scottish Highland and Other Poems* (1876).

**Young, Art,** *in full* **Arthur Henry.** 1866–1943. American cartoonist and writer, b. near Orangeville, Ill.; cartoons collected in *The Best of Art Young* (1936), *Art Young: His Life and Times* (1939), etc.

**Young, Arthur.** 1741–1820. English agriculturist and writer on agricultural economy. Edited *Annals of Agriculture* (1784–1809); reported political and social observations in *Political Arithmetic* (1774), *Tour in Ireland* (1780); reported pre-Revolutionary conditions in French provinces in *Travels in France* (1792).

**Young** *or* **Yong** (yŭng), **Bartholomew.** fl. 1577–1598. English translator of the *Diana Enamorada* of Jorge de Montemayor (*q.v.*).

**Young, Brigham.** 1801–1877. American Mormon leader, b. Whitingham, Vt. Journeyman painter and glazier by trade, settled in Mendon, Monroe Co., N.Y. (1829), near where Joseph Smith published *The Book of Mormon* (1830). Was converted and baptized in Mormon faith (Apr. 14, 1832); successful itinerant missionary (from 1833); member of the quorum of the Twelve Apostles (1835); directed Mormon settlement in Nauvoo, Ill. (1838). Missionary in England (1839–41). Succeeded Joseph Smith as head of the Mormon Church, being duly elected (Dec. 5, 1847); directed and superintended mass migration of Mormons to Great Salt Lake Valley in Utah; organized and directed with great skill the settlement there, assuming dictatorial powers. First governor of Territory of Utah (1849–57); proclaimed and practiced polygamy; at strife with U.S. government, and removed from governorship by President Buchanan, but remained dominant in community; indicted for polygamy (1871) but not convicted. Pioneers' Day, July 24, is legal holiday in Utah, celebrating arrival in 1847 of Brigham Young and his followers at Great Salt Lake.

**Young, Cecilia.** See under Thomas Augustine Arne.

**Young, Charles Augustus.** 1834–1908. American astronomer; professor, Dartmouth (1866–77), Princeton (1877–1905); first to observe spectrum of solar corona; discovered the reversing layer in solar atmosphere, and investigated other solar phenomena; author of *The Sun* (1881), *Manual of Astronomy* (1902), etc.

**Young, Charles Jac** (jăk). 1880–1940. Landscape painter and etcher, b. in Bavaria; to U.S. (1882); best known for realistic snow scenes.

**Young, Charles Mayne.** 1777–1856. English actor; played largely Shakespearean roles with John Philip Kemble (from 1808), with Kean (from 1822).

**Young, Charles Morris.** 1869–1964. American portrait and landscape painter.

**Young, Denton T.,** *known as* **Cy** (sī). 1867–1955. American professional baseball player, b. Gilmore, Ohio; pitcher, in National League with Cleveland (1890–98), St. Louis (1899–1900), and Boston (1911), and in American League, with Boston (1901–08) and Cleveland (1909–11).

**Young, Edward.** 1683–1765. English poet, b. Upham, Hampshire. Gained patronage of Philip, Duke of Wharton; had two tragedies of ungoverned passion produced, *Busiris* (1719) and *Revenge* (1721); published seven satires under title of *The Universal Passion* (1725–28). Became rector of Welwyn (1730); gained popularity with classic series of poems, *The Complaint; or, Night-Thoughts on Life, Death and Immortality,* commonly referred to as *Night Thoughts* (1742–45), which gave rise to a school of "graveyard poets." Had his tragedy *The Brothers* (written 1726) produced (1753); published last important poem, *Resignation* (1762).

**Young, Edward.** 1831–1896. English explorer. Commanded expedition in search for Livingstone (1867); explored Lake Nyassa region (1875) and wrote *Nyassa* (1878).

**Young, Ella,** *nee* **Flagg** (flăg). 1845–1918. American educator, b. Buffalo, N.Y.; m. (1868) William Young (d. 1869). District superintendent of schools in Chicago (1887–99); professor of education, U. of Chicago (1899–1904); principal, Chicago Normal School (1905–09); superintendent of Chicago public schools (1909–15). Associated with Jane Addams in Chicago social-settlement work.

**Young, Ella.** 1867–1956. Poet and authority on Celtic mythology, b. County Antrim, Ireland; to U.S. (1926), settled in California; author of *Celtic Wonder Tales* (1923), *Unicorn with Silver Shoes* (1932), etc.

**Young, Emily Hilda.** 1880–1949. English novelist; m. (1902) J. A. H. Daniell; author of *William* (1925), *Moor Fires* (1927), *The Vicar's Daughter* (1928), *Miss Mole* (awarded James Tait Black memorial prize, 1931), etc.

**Young, Ewing.** d. 1841. American trapper and guide, b. eastern Tennessee; trading headquarters at Taos, N.Mex. (1821 ff.); guided party including young Kit Carson from near Santa Fe across Mojave Desert to California (1829); to Oregon region (1834) and rose to leadership among Oregon pioneers.

**Young, Francis Brett.** 1884–1954. English novelist; M.B., Birmingham; traveled in Far East as ship's doctor (1906–08); officer in medical corps in East Africa, in World War; author of *Deep Sea* (1914; about fishing folk of South Devon), *Dark Tower* (1914), *The Tragic Bride* (1920), *Woodsmoke* (1924), *Portrait of Clare* (1927; awarded James Tait Black memorial prize), *Jim Redlake* (1930), *The Cage Bird and Other Stories* (1933), *They Seek a Country* (1937), *Dr. Bradley Remembers* (1938), *The City of Gold* (1939), *A Man About the House* (1942), etc., and of several volumes of poems, and the plays *Captain Swing* (1919) and *The Furnace* (1928); composer of music for *Songs of Robert Bridges* (1912).

**Young, George.** Lord **Young.** 1819–1907. Scottish judge; solicitor general for Scotland (1862–69); lord advocate (1869–74); judge of Court of Session (1874–1905); author of Scottish Education Act (1872) and Law Agents Act (1873).

**Young,** Sir **George.** 1837–1930. English scholar and administrator; chief charity commissioner of England and Wales (1903–06); author of *An English Prosody* (1928); translator of Sophocles and Victor Hugo's poetry; edited poems of his uncle Winthrop Mackworth Praed (1888).

**Young, Hugh Hampton.** 1870–1945. American surgeon; head of department of urological surgery at Johns Hopkins Hospital, and professor of urology at Johns Hopkins U.; author of *Hugh Young* (autobiography, 1940).

**Young, James.** 1811–1883. Scottish industrial chemist and originator of paraffin industry. Produced lubricating oil and burning oil from petroleum from spring at Alfreton, Derbyshire (1848–51); patented method of producing paraffin by dry distillation of coal (1850–51); manufactured naphtha, lubricating oils, paraffin oil (*i.e.* kerosene), and solid paraffin from Boghead coal, and later from shales, in Scotland.

**Young,** Sir **John.** Baron **Lis'gar** (?lĭs'gär). 1807–1876. British political administrator; chief secretary for Ireland (1852–55); commissioner of Ionian Islands (1855–59); governor general of New South Wales (1861–67); governor general of Canada (1869–72).

**Young, John Russell.** 1840–1899. Journalist, b. Tyrone County, Ireland; to U.S. in infancy. Civil War correspondent of Philadelphia *Press* (1861); famous for graphic account of Federal defeat and retreat after battle of Bull Run. Contributor to New York *Tribune;* on staff of New York *Herald* (1872). U.S. minister to China (1882–85). Foreign correspondent of New York *Herald* (1885 ff.), chiefly in London and Paris. Librarian of Congress (1897–99). Author of *Around the World with General Grant* (2 vols., 1879), and reminiscences.

**Young, John Wesley.** 1879–1932. American mathematician; coauthor, with Oswald Veblen, of *Projective Geometry* (2 vols., 1910–18).

**Young, Levi Edgar.** 1874– . American Mormon leader and educator; author of *The Founding of Utah* (1923), etc.

**Young, Mahonri Mackintosh.** 1877–1957. American sculptor, painter, and etcher, b. Salt Lake City, Utah. Well known for statuettes of workmen, cowboys, etc., the bronzes *Stevedore* and *Man with Pick* (Metropolitan Museum of Art, New York City), *Sea Gull Monument* in Salt Lake City. Modeled the Hopi and Apache Indian groups for American Museum of Natural History in New York City.

**Young, Owen D.** 1874–1962. American lawyer and corporation executive; practiced law in Boston (1896–1913); counsel for General Electric Co. (from 1913); chairman of board, General Electric Co. (1922–39; 1942–44). Associated with Charles G. Dawes as American representative to the Reparations Conference (1924); agent general for German reparations during inauguration of Dawes plan. Chairman of Reparations Conference (1929); cooperated in preparation of the Young plan for German reparations payments.

**Young, Rida,** *nee* **Johnson.** 1875–1926. American playwright; m. James Young (1904); author of *Brown of Harvard, Naughty Marietta, Maytime, Little Old New York,* and the novels *The Girl Who Came Out of the Night* and *Virginal.*

**Young, Robert.** 1822–1888. Scottish literary missionary and Orientalist; superintendent of missionary press, Surat (1856–61); known chiefly for his *Analytical Concordance to the Bible* (1879).

**Young, Stark.** 1881–1963. American journalist, essayist, and playwright, b. Como, Miss. Teacher of English (1904–21); on editorial staff, *New Republic* and *Theatre Arts Monthly* (1921–24); dramatic critic, New York *Times* (1924–25); again with *New Republic* (from 1925). Author of plays (*The Saint, The Colonnade,* etc.), a volume of poetry, books of dramatic criticism, and novels (*The Torches Flare,* 1927; *River House,* 1929; *So Red the Rose,* 1934).

**Young, Sydney.** 1857–1937. English chemist; professor,

**Trinity** College, Dublin (1903–28); known esp. for researches on the boiling-point laws.

**Young, Thomas.** 1587–1655. Scottish clergyman; tutor of John Milton; a leader in opposition to introduction of episcopacy into Scotland. See SMECTYMNUUS.

**Young, Thomas.** 1773–1829. English physician, physicist, and Egyptologist. Physician to St. George's Hospital, London (1811–29); superintendent of *Nautical Almanac* and secretary of board of longitude (1818). First to describe and measure astigmatism; first to explain color sensation as due to presence in retina of structures corresponding to colors red, green, and violet, respectively; discovered interference of light, thus contributing to establishment of wave theory of light; explained theory of capillarity (which was set forth independently by Laplace); assisted in translating the demotic text of the Rosetta stone.

**Young, Whitney Moore.** 1921–1971. American civil rights leader, b. Lincoln Ridge, Ky. Exec. director, National Urban League (1961–71); author of *To Be Equal* (1964), etc.

**Youn'ger** (yŭng'gẽr), **Cole,** *in full* **Thomas Coleman.** 1844–1916. American desperado, b. Jackson Co., Mo. A Confederate guerrilla officer in Civil War. Prominent member of Jesse James gang; shot, captured, tried, pleaded guilty, and sentenced to life imprisonment after bank robbery at Northfield, Minn., in course of which two citizens were killed (Sept. 7, 1876); pardoned (1903).

**Young'hus'band** (yŭng'hŭz'bănd), **Sir Francis Edward.** 1863–1942. British explorer and author; explored mountain barrier between China and Kashmir (1886); transferred from army to political department (1890); commissioner to Tibet (1902–04); led British expedition into forbidden city of Lhasa (1904); resident, Kashmir (1906–09). Author of *Heart of a Continent* (1898), *India and Tibet: Within* (1912), *Everest: The Challenge* (1936), *A Venture of Faith* (1937), *The Sum of Things* (1939).

**Young Pretender.** See Charles Edward Louis Philip Casimir STUART.

**Yount** (yŭnt), **Barton Kyle.** 1883–1949. American army officer, b. Troy, Ohio; assistant chief of air corps; commanded 3d air force (1941); appointed (1942) chief of Flying Training Command; retired (1946).

**Yount, George Con'cep·ción'** (kôn'sĕp·syôn'). 1794–1865. American pioneer in California, b. Burke Co., N.C. Trapper in New Mexico (from c. 1825); associate of Ewing Young (*q.v.*); extended trapping trips northward (1828–29), where Yount's Peak memorializes his presence at source of Yellowstone River. To California (1830–31); became Mexican citizen (1835); acquired ranch (Caymus Rancho) in Napa valley and established himself as guardian of frontier against Indian attacks.

**You'ville', Marie Marguerite d'** (dyōō'vĭl'), *nee* **Du'frost' de La'jem'me·rais'** (dü'frō' dē lȧ'zhȧm'rē'). 1701–1771. Canadian foundress of Grey Nuns of Montreal; reorganized General Hospital (1747 ff.).

**Yo·va'no·vich.** Variant of JOVANOVIĆ.

**Ypres,** Earl of. See John Denton Pinkstone FRENCH.

**Yp'si·lan'ti** (ĭp'sĭ·lăn'tĭ) *or* **Hy'pse·lan'tes** *or* **Hy'psi·lan'tis** (ē'psē·län'dēs). Distinguished Greek Phanariot family, including: **Alexander Ypsilanti** (1725?–1807), hospodar of Wallachia (1774–77; 1796–98) and Moldavia (1787); executed at Constantinople for conspiracy. His son **Constantine** (1760–1816), hospodar of Moldavia (1799–1806) and Wallachia (1802–06; 1807); encouraged Serbians in rebellion against Turkey and had to take refuge in Russia. Constantine's son **Alexander** (1792–1828); promoted cause of Greek freedom; proclaimed independence of Greece (1821); defeated by Turks (June 19, 1821); fled to Austria, where he was imprisoned (1821–27). His brother **Demetrius** (1793–1832); fought in war for Greek independence (1821 ff.); successfully defended Argos (1823) and Napoli (1825); commander in chief of Greek forces (1828–30).

**Y'riarte'** (ē'ryȧrt'), **Charles.** 1833–1898. French man of letters; editor in chief of *Le Monde Illustré;* interested himself esp. in Italian Renaissance period. His many books include histories of Venice (1877) and Florence (1880), biographies of Francesca da Rimini (1882) and Caesar Borgia (1889), and *La Sculpture Italienne au XV^e Siècle; Matteo Civitali* (1885).

**Y·riar'te** (ē·ryär'tā) **y Oropesa, Tomás de.** See Tomás de IRIARTE Y OROPESA.

**Yrjö-Koskinen, Yrjö Sakari.** See Georg Zachris FORSMAN.

**Y'sa'ye'** (ē'zȧ'ē'), **Eugène.** 1858–1931. Belgian violinist; professor at conservatory of music, Brussels (1886–98); made extensive tours in Europe and America and established himself as one of greatest virtuosos of his time; composed violin concertos, sonatas, etc.

**Yü** *or* **Ta Yü** (dä' yü'). Chinese emperor, called "the Great Yü." See HSIA (dynasty).

**Yüan** (yü·än') *or* **Mon'gol** (mŏng'gŏl; -gŭl). A Chinese dynasty (1280–1368) of Mongol origin, founded by Kublai Khan. It had eleven rulers and was superseded by the Ming dynasty. The Mongol dynasty in the north (capital at Karakorum) began with Genghis Khan (1206), followed by Ogadai, Mangu Khan, and Kublai Khan, who (1280) became Chinese emperor, proclaiming that *Yüan* should be the name of his dynasty.

**Yüan Chên** (yü·än' jŭn'). 779–831 A.D. Chinese poet of the T'ang dynasty; for many years an official of the state.

**Yüan Chwang** *or* **Yüan Tsang.** = HSÜAN TSANG.

**Yüan Shih-k'ai** (yü·än' shĭr'kī'). 1859–1916. Chinese statesman, b. in Honan province. Served in army (1882–85); appointed by Li Hung-chang Chinese resident at Seoul, Korea (1885–94); in command of an army corps (1897); adviser to the emperor Kuang Hsü (1898); received advancement from Empress Dowager Tzu Hsi for disclosing a plot; governor of Shantung (1900); remained neutral during Boxer uprising (1901); viceroy of Pechili (Pohai) province (1901–07); made grand councilor (1907) but banished on death of emperor and empress dowager (1908). On overthrow of the Manchus (1911) became commander in chief of northern forces and (Feb., 1912) by the last imperial edict was made premier and authorized to organize a republican form of government; became provisional president of all China (1912–13) by resignation of Sun Yat-sen in the south; president (1913–16); sought to be dictator, suppressing Sun and followers, dismissing parliament (1914), and appointing an advisory council; restored Confucianism; attempted to re-establish monarchy (1915) but prevented by strong opposition of southern provinces and foreign powers; manner of his death not certainly known. Succeeded as president by Li Yüan-hung.

**Yu·a·sa** (yōō·ä·sä), **Kurahei.** 1874–1940. Japanese politician and administrator; vice-minister for home affairs (1924); chief civil administrator, Chosen (Korea, 1925–29); minister of imperial household (1933–36); lord keeper of the privy seal (1936 ff.).

**Yu·de'nich** (yōō·dyā'nyĭch), **Nikolai Nikolaevich.** 1862–1933. Russian soldier; served in Russo-Japanese War (1904–05); major general (1907) and lieutenant general (1913); at beginning of World War (1914), commanded Russian forces in Caucasus; after Russian Revolution (1917), took command of an anti-Bolshevik army operating from Estonia (1919), but was defeated; retired to England and France.

**Yui** (yü), **David Z. T.** *Orig.* **Yü Jih-chang** (yü′ rĭr′jäng′). 1882–1936. Chinese Christian leader; educ. St. John's U., Shanghai, and at Harvard. Identified with the Revolution (1911–12); secretary to Vice-President Li Yüan-hung and editor of Peking *Daily News* (1912–15); head of Y.M.C.A. activities in China (1916–36); a founder of the Institute of Pacific Relations; head of delegation to Washington Conference (1921).

**Yu·ka′wa** (yŏŏ·kä′wä), **Hideki.** 1907– . Japanese physicist. Awarded Nobel prize in physics (1949) for his work on nuclear forces.

**Yule** (yōōl), Sir **Henry.** 1820–1889. British Orientalist and military engineer in India; wrote *Cathay and the Way Thither* (1866), *Diary of Sir William Hedges* (1887); compiled *Hobson Jobson, A Glossary of Anglo-Indian Colloquial Words and Phrases* (with A. Burnell; 1886).

**Yung Chêng** (yŏŏng′ jŭng′). 1678–1735. Chinese emperor (1723–35), third of the Ch'ing dynasty. Son of K'ang-hsi.

**Yung Lo** (yŏŏng′ lŭ′). *Dynastic name* **Ch'êng Tsu** (chŭng′ dzōō′). 1359–1424. Chinese emperor (1403–24), third of the Ming dynasty. Son of Hung Wu. Seized throne by revolt against his own nephew, but as emperor became one of the greatest China has had; transferred (1421) capital from Nanking to Peking; had a few wars in Indo-China and on the west but more interested in developments of peace; sought trade relations with islands to the south (see CHENG HO).

**Yung Wing** (yŭng′ wĭng′; *Pekingese pron.* rōōng′ hōōng′). 1828–1912. Chinese educator in America; grad. Yale (1854), first Chinese graduate of an American university; became naturalized U.S. citizen. Returned to China (1854–63); succeeded finally in having Chinese government send Chinese boys to U.S. to be educated (1870–81); failed to re-establish system of educational aid, which was ended by conservative Chinese influence (1881).

**Yu·pan′qui Pa′cha·cu·tec′** (yōō·päng′kē pä′chä·kōō·tĕk′). d. ?1440. Ninth Inca sovereign; deposed his brother and after victories over Chancas assumed title of Pachacutec ("he who changes the world"); established splendor of Inca empire.

**Yu′sef** (yōō′sōōf), **Mulai.** 1882–1927. Sultan of Morocco; succeeded to throne after abdication (1912) of brother Abd-al-Hafiz; pursued policy of friendship with France; succeeded (1927) by son Mulai **Mo·ham′med** [mōō·hăm′mĕd] (1913–1961).

**Yush·ke′vich** (yŏŏsh·kyā′vyĭch), **Semën Solomonovich.** 1868–1927. Russian Jewish novelist and playwright; author of *The Jews, The Street, Léon Drey, In the City, The King,* etc.

**Yust** (yōōst), **Walter.** 1894–1960. American editor, b. Philadelphia; A.B., Pennsylvania (1917); journalist, chiefly in N.Y. and Philadelphia (1917–30); advertising manager (1930–32), associate editor (1932–38), editor in chief (1938–60), *Encyclopaedia Britannica* publications.

**Yusuf ibn-Tashfin.** See IBN-TASHFIN.

**Yu·su′pov** (yŏŏ·sōō′pôf), **Nikolai Borisovich.** 1827–1891. Russian violinist and composer.

**Yutang, Lin.** See LIN YUTANG.

**Yver, Colette.** See Antoinette HUZARD.

**Yves de Chartres** (ēv′ dẽ shár′tr′). 1040?–1116. French ecclesiastic; bishop of Chartres (1090); upheld rights of the church against royal encroachment and maintained high standards of conduct among his clergy; compiled a collection of canon law.

**Yves of Brit′ta·ny** (ēv, brĭt′′n·ĭ), **Saint.** 1253–1303. French lawyer and cleric; became (1280) government official at Rennes. Ordained priest (1284); rector of Louannec (1292); by his many charities acquired title of "l'Avocat des Pauvres" (là′vô′kȧ′ dā pō′vr′). Known as the patron saint of lawyers.

**Y′von′** (ē′vôɴ′), **Adolphe.** 1817–1893. French painter; best known for his historical canvases, as *La Bataille de Koulikowo, L'Assaut de Malakof, Solferino, Magenta, Les États Unis d'Amérique* (an allegorical painting, in Washington); also painted a number of portraits.

**Yzaac** *or* **Yzac, Heinrich.** See ISAAK.

# Z

**Za·błoc′ki** (zä·blôts′kē), **Franciszek.** 1754–1821. Polish writer of satirical comedies.

**Zabulon.** See ZEBULUN.

**Zac′ca·ri′a** (dzäk′kä·rē′ä), **Antonio Maria.** 1500–1539. Italian religious; founded order, Regular Clerks of St. Paul, known as order of Barnabites (1530).

**Zac·co′ni** (dzäk·kō′nē), **Lodovico.** 1555–1627. Italian musical theorist and composer; known esp. for his *Prattica di Musica...* (2 parts, 1592, 1622), a standard work of the polyphonic period.

**Zach** (tsäκ), Baron **Franz Xaver von.** 1754–1832. German astronomer; director of observatory near Gotha (1787–1806); editor, *Monatliche Korrespondenz zur Beförderung der Erd- und Himmelskunde* (28 vols., 1800–13).

**Za′cha·ri′ae** (tsä′κä·rē′ā), **Theodor.** 1851–1934. German Sanskrit scholar and folklorist; published works on Indian lexicography, Indology, and Indian and comparative folklore.

**Zachariah** *or* **Zacharias.** See ZECHARIAH.

**Zach′a·ri′as** (zăk′ȧ·rī′ăs). *In Douay Version* **Zach′a·ry** (zăk′ȧ·rĭ). In Bible, father of John the Baptist (*Luke* i. 5 ff.).

**Zach′a·ri′as** (zăk′ȧ·rī′ăs) *or* **Zach′a·ry** (zăk′ȧ·rĭ), **Saint.** Pope (741–752), b. in Calabria, of Greek parentage. Had great personal influence over kings of the Lombards; prevented exarchate of Ravenna from becoming part of Lombard kingdom; encouraged missionary work of St. Boniface and confirmed his anointing of Pepin at Soissons (751) as king of the Franks, the first of the Carolingians.

**Za′cha·ri′ä von Ling′en·thal** (tsä′κä·rē′ā fŏn lĭng′ĕn·täl), **Karl Salomo.** 1769–1843. German jurist; professor, Wittenberg (1798) and Heidelberg (1807); member, Baden upper house (1820) and lower house (1825); ennobled (1842); author of *Handbuch des Französischen Zivilrechts* (1808), *Vierzig Bücher vom Staate* (5 vols., 1820–32). His son **Karl Eduard** (1812–1894) was professor of Roman law, Heidelberg (1842–45); author of *Jus Graeco-Romanum* (a collection of the sources of Byzantine law, 7 vols., 1856–84), etc.

**Za′chow** (tsä′κō) *or* **Za′chau** (tsä′κou), **Friedrich Wilhelm.** 1663–1712. German Protestant church musician and composer; teacher of Handel; organist, Halle (1684–1712); composer esp. of church cantatas, organ works, and choral arrangements.

**Zach′ris·son′** (sȧk′krĭ·sôn′), **Robert Eugen.** 1880–1937. Swedish philologist; professor of English, Uppsala U. (1921); author of works on English language and literature, Shakespearean pronunciation, etc. Invented (1930) *Anglic* (a method of writing English according to a system of simplified spelling) to promote English as an international language.

**Zadkiel.** Pseudonym of Richard James MORRISON.

**Za′dok** (zā′dŏk). *In Douay Version* **Sa′doc** (sā′dŏk). In Bible, a descendant of Eleazar; high priest of Israel; remained faithful to David during Absalom's rebellion.

**Zaehns′dorf** (tsâns′dôrf), **Joseph.** 1816–1886. Bookbinder, b. in Budapest, Austria-Hungary; employed in London (1837); naturalized (1855).

**Zafar Khan.** See under ALA-UD-DIN.

**Zaffanii.** See John ZOFFANY.

**Zagh·lul′ Pa′sha** (zăg·lōōl′ pȧ′shä), **Saad** (săd). 1860?–1927. Egyptian lawyer and statesman; minister of public instruction (1906) and later, minister of justice. After World War I (1914–18), became head of Nationalist party which demanded breaking of ties binding Egypt to Great Britain and achievement of complete Egyptian independence. Deported to Malta (1919) and then to Ceylon; returned to Egypt (1921). Premier of Egypt (1924); failed to conclude satisfactory negotiations with British prime minister Macdonald.

**Za·go′skin** (zŭ·gô′skyĭn), **Lavrenti Alekseev.** Russian mariner in service of Russian-American Trading Co.; discovered Yukon River (1842); published (1847–48) account of his discovery.

**Zagoskin, Mikhail Nikolaevich.** 1789–1852. Russian writer; theater director in St. Petersburg, and later in Moscow. Among his works are the novels *Yuri Miloslavski, or the Russians in 1612, The Muscovites.*

**Za·ha′roff** (zŭ·ĸȧ′rôf; *Angl.* zȧ·hä′rôf), Sir **Bas′il** (băz′'l). 1850–1936. International armament contractor, b. at Phanar, Turkey, supposedly of Russian father and Greek mother; agent of Vickers firm in Spain (in 1880's), director; chairman of Vickers-Maxim (in 1890's); said to be associated with the Krupps, Schneider-Creusot, Skoda; engaged also in banking, oil enterprises; established chairs of aviation and literature, universities of Paris, Petrograd, Oxford.

**Zah′le** (sȧ′lĕ), **Carl Theodor.** 1866–1946. Danish statesman; prime minister and minister of justice (1909–10); again prime minister (1913–20); minister of justice (from 1929).

**Zahn** (tsän), **Ernst.** 1867–1952. Swiss fiction writer.

**Zahn, Theodor von.** 1838–1933. German Lutheran theologian; representative of conservative New Testament scholarship.

**Zahn′-Har′nack** (tsän′här′näk), **Agnes von.** 1884–1950. Daughter of Adolf von Harnack. German leader in feminist movement; author of *Die Arbeitende Frau* (1924), *Die Frauenbewegung* (1928), etc.

**Zahrt′mann** (särt′mȧn), **Christian.** 1843–1917. Danish painter of historical subjects, figures, and landscapes.

**Za·ï′mes** *or* **Za·ï′mis** (zä·ē′mēs), **Alexandros.** 1855–1936. Greek statesman; minister of justice (1890–92); premier (1897–99, after Greco-Turkish war; again 1901–02, 1904–06); as high commissioner of the powers in Crete (1906–11), helped bring about its subsequent annexation by Greece (1913); governor of the Greek National Bank (1913 ff.); premier (briefly, 1915, 1916, 1917) and head of an ecumenical government and two succeeding coalition cabinets (1926–28); president of the Republic of Greece (1929–35); left Greece (1935); died in Vienna. His father, **Thrasyboulos Zaïmes** (1829–1880), was also a Greek statesman; took part in revolution which overthrew King Otto (1862) and became minister of the interior in the provisional government; seized the Ionian Islands on behalf of new king, George; president of the council (1869); minister of justice (1877–78).

**Zai′ner** *or* **Zey′ner** *or* **Zay′ner** (tsī′nẽr), **Günther** (1430?–1478) and **Johann** (d. 1523). Pioneer German printers, probably related. Günther established first press at Augsburg (1468) and introduced Roman type into Germany; Johann founded a printing, woodcut, and bookselling business in Ulm.

**Zajic, Giovanni von.** See ZAYTZ.

**Za·krzew′ska** (zä·kshĕf′skä), **Ma·rie′** (mȧ·rē′) **E·liz′a·beth** (ē·lĭz′ȧ·bĕth). 1829–1902. Physician, b. of Polish parentage, in Berlin, Ger. Emigrated to U.S. (1853); M.D., Cleveland Medical College in Western Reserve U. (1856). Founded and served as resident physician in a hospital of her own (1862–1902), which developed into New England Hospital for Women and Children.

**Za·les′ki** (zä·lĕs′kē), **August.** 1883–1972. Polish statesman; president, Polish Democratic Committee, during World War I (1914–18); took part in Peace Conference at Paris (1919); minister of foreign affairs (1926–32); minister in Polish government in exile (1939–41); became president, Polish Republic in Exile (1947).

**Zaleski, Bogdan.** 1802–1886. Polish poet; took part in Polish rebellion (1830–31) and lived thereafter in exile, chiefly in Paris.

**Za·leu′cus** (zȧ·lū′kŭs). Greek lawgiver of 7th century B.C., of Locri in Magna Graecia; reputed author of first written legal code among Greeks (the Locrian code). According to the legend, the Locrians in despair at their own lawlessness deputed Zaleucus, a slave, to draft a code of laws, which he did with aid of divine inspiration; later, discovering that he had unwittingly broken one of his own laws, he committed suicide.

**Za·lin′ski** (zȧ·lĭn′skĭ), **Edmund Louis Gray.** 1849–1909. Army officer and inventor, b. at Kurnik, Poland; to U.S. (1853); served in Union army during part of Civil War; commissioned officer, U.S. army (1866–94); inventor of a pneumatic dynamite gun.

**Za·lus′ki** (zä·lōōs′kē). Distinguished Polish family, including: **Andrzej** (1650–1711), prelate and statesman; supporter of Sobieski; bishop of Kiev (1683), Płock (1691), Varmie (1699); grand chancellor of Poland (1699); finally differed with King Augustus II and was imprisoned. His nephew **Andrzej Stanisław** (1694–1758), bishop of Płock and later of Cracow; grand chancellor of the crown (1735–45). Another nephew, brother of preceding, **Józef Andrzej** (1702–1774), bishop of Kiev; collected large library which he presented to nation (1748) and which was later (1795) taken to St. Petersburg where it became nucleus of Imperial Russian Library, but which, under terms of Treaty of Riga (1921), was to be restored to Poland.

**Za′ma·cois′** (thä′mä·kois′), **Eduardo.** 1843–1871. Spanish genre and figure painter.

**Za·makh′sha·ri, al-** (ăl′zä·măĸ′shă·rĭ). *Arab.* **abu-al-Qāsim Maḥmūd al-Zamakhshari.** 1074?–1143. Arab scholar, b. Khwarazm (Khiva); author of an Arabic grammar, an Arabic-Persian dictionary, and a collection of moral apothegms known as *The Golden Necklaces.*

**Za′men·hof** (*Russ.* zä′myĕn·hôf; *Pol.* zä′mĕn·hôf), **Laz′a·rus** (lăz′ȧ·rŭs) **Lud′wig** (lōōt′vĭĸ; lōōd′-). 1859–1917. Polish oculist and philologist; practiced as oculist in Warsaw. Known esp. for advocacy of an international language designed to promote international understanding and peace; inventor of Esperanto, an artificial language (1887).

**Za·moj′ski** (zä·moi′skē). Distinguished Polish family, including: **Jan** (1541–1605), grand chamberlain (1573–

75) and grand chancellor (1575 ff.); commander in chief of Polish armies against Russia (1580–82); successful in defending Poland against Turks, Cossacks, and Swedes. **Andrzej** (1716–1792); after service in Saxon army, returned to Poland (1754) and became chancellor (1764–67); drew up new code of laws (1776).

**Za·mo′ra** (thä·mō′rä), **Antonio de.** 1660?–before 1743. Spanish dramatist; court poet (1694 ff.); author of comedies, as *Mazariegos y Monsalves* and the farce *El Hechizado por Fuerza,* and dramas, as *Judas Iscariote.*

**Zamora y Tor′res** (ē tôr′rās), **Niceto Al′ca·lá′** (äl′kä·lä′). 1877–1949. Spanish politician; opponent of Primo de Rivera; active in overthrow of Alfonso XIII, supporting republic (1930); tried and sentenced to prison; president of republic (1931–36).

**Zampieri, Domenico.** See Il DOMENICHINO.

**Za′nar·del′li** (dzä′när·dĕl′lē), **Giuseppe.** 1829–1903. Italian lawyer and statesman; active in national movement (1848–49); minister of public works (1876–77), interior (1878), justice (1881–83, 1887–91, 1897–98); premier (Feb., 1901–Oct., 1903).

**Zand** (zănd) *or* **Zend** (zĕnd). Short-lived Persian dynasty (1750–94) with capital at Shiraz. Its chief ruler was Karim Khan (*q.v.*), overthrown by the Kajars.

**Zan′der** (sȧn′dẽr), **Jonas Gustaf Wilhelm.** 1835–1920. Swedish physician; founder of a therapeutical method consisting of exercises carried out by means of special apparatus.

**Zan′do·na′i** (dzän′dō·nä′ē), **Riccardo.** 1883–1944. Italian composer of operas, a cantata, a *Messa da Requiem,* and orchestral pieces.

**Zane** (zān), **Charles Shuster.** 1831–1915. American jurist; practiced in Springfield, Ill. Friend and admirer of Lincoln, and succeeded him as law partner of Herndon (1861). Circuit judge (1873–84); chief justice, Utah Territory (1884–88, 1889–94); enforced the Edmunds law against polygamy with combined rigor and tact; first chief justice of the State of Utah (1896–98).

**Zane, Ebenezer.** 1747–1812. American pioneer; established claim to land at junction of Wheeling Creek and Ohio River (1770) and there made first Ohio River permanent settlement; acquired additional lands in that region, including tracts on site of present Zanesville (laid out 1799) and Lancaster, Ohio (laid out 1800). His sister **Betty** was heroine of an attack by Indians on Fort Henry, near Wheeling, when she ran through enemy fire to a hut near by and brought back a keg of powder.

**Za·nel′la** (dzä·nĕl′lä), **Giacomo.** 1820–1888. Italian poet and critic; ordained priest (1843). Among his works are *Poesie,* including the poem *Conchiglia Fossile* (1885), *Storia della Letteratura Italiana della Metà del Settecento ai Giorni Nostri* (1880), etc.

**Zan·gi′** (zăng·gĭ′) *or* **Sen·gi′** (zĕng·gĭ′) *or* **Zen·gi′** (zĕng·gĭ′), **′I·mad′-al-Din′** (ĭ·mäd′ĕd·dēn′). d. 1146. Seljuk atabeg of Mosul (1127–46); successful in his battles with Crusaders; extended his rule over northern Syria; founded **Zan′gid** (zăng′gĭd) dynasty ruling over Mesopotamia and Syria (1127–1250). Succeeded by his son Nureddin (*q.v.*).

**Zan′gwill** (zăng′gwĭl; zăng′wĭl), **Israel.** 1864–1926. English playwright and novelist; b. London, son of a Russian Jewish refugee to England (1848). Edited *Ariel,* a comic journal, in which he published witty stories, including *The Bachelors' Club* (1891) and *The Old Maids' Club* (1892). Established reputation with *The Children of the Ghetto* (1892, dramatized 1899), a novel interpreting the Jewish race; followed with *Dreamers of the Ghetto* (1898) and *Ghetto Tragedies* (1893, 1899), exerting international influence upon status of Jewry. Joined in Zionist cause of Theodor Herzl (1896); on Herzl's death devoted himself to vain search for home for Jewish émigrés (1904–11). Scored immense American success with *The Melting Pot* (1908), a drama of race fusion in America; appealed for international amity in *The War God* (1911); produced tragicomedies including *The Grey Wig* (1903), *The Next Religion* (1912), *Plaster Saints* (1914), *The Cockpit* (1921), *The Forcing House* (1922). Returned to novel writing with *Jinny the Carrier* (1919; orig. a play, 1905), set in rural Essex. Produced his last play *We Moderns* (1924) in New York. Author of poems, *Blind Children* (1903), *Ibn Gabirol's Poems* (trans. 1923).

**Zan′kow** (tsȧn′kôf). Variant of TSANKOV.

**Zan′uck** (zăn′ŭk), **Dar′ryl** (dăr′ĭl) **Francis.** 1902– . American motion-picture producer, b. Wahoo, Nebr.; with Warner Bros. Pictures, Inc. (1924–33), supervisor of production (1929–33); with Joseph Schenck organized 20th Century Pictures; vice-president of company and, after merger with Fox Films (1935), vice-president of 20th Century Fox Film Corporation; officer in U.S. army signal corps reserve in charge of motion-picture production of educational shorts, later of official pictures of North African campaigns; author of *Tunis Expedition* (1943).

**Za·pa′ta** (sä·pä′tä), **Emiliano.** 1877?–1919. Mexican revolutionist, champion of agrarianism; active 1911–16; independent of other revolutionary movements of the period (Madero, Huerta, Carranza, Villa).

**Za·pol′ska** (zä·pôl′skä), **Gabryela,** *nee* **Pio·trow′ska** (pyô·trôf′skä). 1860–1921. Polish novelist and playwright.

**Zá′po·lya** (zä′pō·lyŏ) *or* **Sza′po·lyai** (sŏ′pō·lyoi). Powerful Hungarian family, including: **John Zápolya** (1487–1540), governor of Transylvania (1511–26); regent for Louis II in his minority (1516–26); rival of Stephen Báthory; after defeat by Turks, elected king of Hungary (1526–40); struggled with Ferdinand I of Germany, Holy Roman emperor (1526–38). His son **John (II) Sig′is·mund** [sĭj′ĭs·mŭnd; sĭg′-] (1540–1571), prince of Transylvania and king of Hungary (1540–71); rival of Ferdinand I and Maximilian II, kings of Germany; supported by Suleiman the Magnificent.

**Zárate, Antonio Gil y.** See Antonio GIL Y ZÁRATE.

**Zarathustra.** See ZOROASTER.

**Zar′co** (zȧr′ko͞o), **João Gon·cal′ves** (gōɴ·säl′vĕzh). 15th-century Portuguese navigator; discoverer of Madeira; founded Funchal (1421).

**Zar·li′no** (dzär·lē′nō), **Giuseppe.** 1517–1590. Italian composer and musical theorist; Franciscan monk (1537 ff.); maestro di cappella, St. Mark's, Venice (1565–1590).

**Zarnck′e** (tsärng′kĕ), **Friedrich.** 1825–1891. German philologist, literary historian, and critic; edited a Middle High German dictionary (with W. Müller; 3 vols., 1854–66); author of works on the *Nibelungenlied,* on Goethe, comparative literature, medieval German universities, etc.

**Zauditu.** *Eng.* **Judith.** 1876–1930. Empress of Ethiopia (1916–30). Daughter of Menelik II. Married three times before becoming ruler; succeeded to throne (1916) on deposition of her nephew Lij Yasu; crowned (1917) empress ("queen of kings"); reign much disturbed; Ethiopia admitted (1923) to League of Nations; rule merely nominal after coronation as king (1928) of Regent Ras Taffari (Haile Selassie, *q.v.*), a distant cousin.

**Za′yas y Al·fon′so** (sä′yäs ē äl·fôn′sō), **Alfredo.** 1861–1934. Cuban lawyer and political leader; with J. M. Gómez, behind Liberal revolution against Estrada Palma (1906); vice-president of Cuba (1909–13); president (1921–25).

**Zayner, Günther** and **Johann.** See ZAINER.

**Zaytz** (tsīts) *or* **Za'jic** (tsä'yĕts), **Gio·van'ni** (jō·vän'nē) **von.** 1832–1914. Austrian composer of masses, songs, and instrumental pieces, Italian and German operas and operettas, and the first Croatian operas.

**Zdzie·chow'ski** (z'jĕ·kôf'skē), **Marjan.** 1861– . Polish scholar; professor of Slav and comparative literature, Cracow (1894), Wilno (1919); rector, Wilno (1925–27).

**Ze'a** (sā'ä), **Francisco Antonio.** 1770–1822. Scientist and statesman of New Granada (Colombia). Associated with José Mutis in scientific explorations. Joined Bolívar (1815); president of congress of Angostura (1819); vice-president of Colombia (1819); envoy of Colombia in France and England (1820–22). Published many scientific treatises, and *Historia de Colombia* (1821).

**Zeb'e·dee** (zĕb'ĕ·dē). In Bible, husband of Salome and father of apostles James and John (*qq.v.*).

**Zebi** *or* **Zevi, Sabbatai.** See SABBATAI ZEBI.

**Zeb'u·lun** (zĕb'ū·lŭn; zĕ·bū'lŭn). *In Douay Version* **Zab'u·lon** (zăb'ū·lŏn; zȧ·bū'lŭn). In Bible, Jacob's tenth son (*Genesis* xxx. 19–20), ancestor of one of the twelve tribes of Israel.

**Zech'a·ri'ah** (zĕk'ȧ·rī'ȧ) *or* **Zach'a·ri'ah** (zăk'-). d. 744 B.C. King of Israel (744 B.C.), last ruler of dynasty of Jehu. Son of Jeroboam II. Murdered by Shallum soon after accession (*2 Kings* xv. 8–12).

**Zechariah.** *In Douay Bible* **Zach'a·ri'as** (zăk'ȧ·rī'ăs). One of the minor Hebrew prophets, of the period of the return to Palestine (c. 520 B.C.), who, with Haggai, persuaded the Jews to rebuild the temple. The Old Testament book of Zechariah contains his exhortations to the returned exiles and prophecy of Messianic deliverance.

**Zé'dé'** (zā'dā'), **Gustave Alexandre.** 1825–1891. French naval engineer; designer of first successful French naval submarine (the *Gymnote*, launched 1888).

**Zed'e·ki'ah** (zĕd'ē·kī'ȧ). *Original name* **Mat'ta·ni'ah** (măt'ȧ·nī'ȧ). Last king of Judah; uncle of Jehoiachin and placed by Nebuchadnezzar II on the throne in Jerusalem (597 B.C.); revolted against Nebuchadnezzar (588); defeated (586) and taken in chains to Babylon.

**Ze'dlitz** (tsā'dlĭts), Baron **Joseph Christian von.** 1790–1862. Austrian poet and dramatist; author of *Totenkränze* (1828), dramatic works (4 vols., 1830–36; including *Kerker und Krone*), a translation of Byron's *Childe Harold's Pilgrimage* (1836), the epic poems *Waldfräulein* (1843) and *Altnordische Bilder* (1850), *Soldatenbüchlein* (2 vols., 1848–50), etc.

**Zee'land** (zā'länt), **Paul van.** 1893–1973. Belgian economist and statesman; delegate to various economic conferences (1922–33) after World War; prime minister of Belgium (1935–37).

**Zee'man** (zā'män), **Pieter.** 1865–1943. Dutch physicist; educ. Leiden (1885–90); professor, U. of Amsterdam (from 1900). Discovered (with H. A. Lorentz) the phenomena known as the *Zeeman effect*, including the resolution of single spectral lines into several components, when a source of radiation is placed in a magnetic field (1896). Awarded (jointly with Lorentz) 1902 Nobel prize for physics.

**Ze·gris'** (thā·grēz'). *Span.* **Ze·grí'es** (thā·grē'ās). A 15th-century family of Moors from Aragon; supporters of Boabdil.

**Zeis'ber'ger** (tsīs'bĕr'gẽr; *Angl.* zīs'bûr'gẽr), **David.** 1721–1808. Moravian missionary in America; to America (c. 1739) and was present at official founding of Bethlehem, Pa., Moravian church settlement (Dec., 1741). Lived and labored among the Indians (from 1745).

**Zeis'ler** (zīs'lẽr), **Sig'mund** (sĭg'mŭnd). 1860–1931. Lawyer, b. in Bielsko, Silesia; to U.S. (1883); practiced in Chicago (1884). His wife (m. 1885), **Fannie,** *nee* **Bloom'field** (blo͞om'fēld), *orig.* **Blu'men·feld** [blo͞o'mĕn·fĕlt] (1863–1927), b. in Bielsko, and emigrated to U.S. (1867), was a pianist; made European tours (1893, 1894, 1898, 1902, 1911–12); last public appearance, with Chicago Symphony orchestra (Feb. 25, 1925).

**Zeiss** (tsīs; *Angl.* zīs), **Carl.** 1816–1888. German manufacturer of optical instruments; founded at Jena (1846) optical factory, taken over at his death by his partner, Ernst Abbe (*q.v.*).

**Zeiss'berg** (tsīs'bĕrk), **Heinrich von.** 1839–1899. Austrian historian.

**Zeit'blom** (tsīt'blôm), **Bartholomäus.** 1450?–?1518. German religious painter; chief master of the Swabian school of Ulm. Among his works are the Eschach altarpiece and the Heerberg altarpiece (in Stuttgart).

**Zeit'ler** (zīt'lẽr), **Max.** 1854–1922. Engraver, b. Frankfurt am Main, Ger.; to U.S. (1888) and settled in Philadelphia; engraved the Great Seal of the United States.

**Zeit'lin** (zīt'lĭn), **Jacob.** 1883–1937. Educator, b. at Gorki, Russia; to U.S. (1892); teacher of English, U. of Illinois (1907–37), and professor (from 1925); editor of Petrarch's *Life of Solitude* (1924), *Seventeenth Century Essays* (1926), and various anthologies; translator and editor, Montaigne's *Essays* (1934).

**Zeitz'ler** (tsīts'lẽr), **Kurt.** 1895–1963. German army officer, b. Lackau; served in World War (1914–18); attached to general staff in Poland (1939), France (1940), and Balkans (1941); chief of staff of Kleist's 1st Panzer army in Russia (1941–42); appointed head of German general staff (1942–44).

**Zelandus.** Pseudonym of Jacobus BELLAMY.

**Ze·la'ya** (sā·lä'yä), **José Santos.** 1853–1919. Nicaraguan politician, b. Managua; became president on overthrow of Roberto Sacasa (1893–1909; 3 terms); seized Mosquitia, autonomous Indian reserve on Caribbean coast (1893), and annexed it to Nicaragua; forced to resign (Dec., 1909).

**Ze'lea–Co'dre·a'nu** (zĕ'lyä·kŏ'drĕ·ä'no͞o), **Corneliu.** 1899?–1938. Rumanian Fascist leader; an organizer of original Iron Guard; charged with plotting revolution and imprisoned (May, 1938); shot with other political prisoners, allegedly while attempting to escape (Nov. 30, 1938).

**Że·leń'ski** (zhĕ·lĕn'y'·skē), **Tadeusz.** *Pseudonym* **Boy** (boi). 1874–1942. Polish writer, of novels, satiric verse, essays, and dramatic criticisms; also translator of French classics, as Molière, Rabelais, Montaigne.

**Zélide.** See Isabelle de CHARRIÈRE.

**Ze'li·gow'ski** (zĕ'lē·gôf'skē), **Lucian.** 1865–1947. Polish general; brigade commander in World War (1914–18); later, headed force that seized Wilno (Oct., 1920) and established a provisional government there; Polish minister of war (1925–26).

**Ze·lin'ski** (zyĭ·lyēn'skû·ĭ; *Angl.* zĕ·lĭn'skĭ), **Nikolai Dimitrievich.** 1861–1953. Russian chemist; head of department of organic chemistry, Moscow State U.; known esp. for researches in synthetic rubber and the chemistry of petroleum (Stalin prize, 1942).

**Zell** (tsĕl), **Ulrich.** d. after 1507. German printer; established first printing works in Cologne.

**Zel'ler** (tsĕl'ẽr), **Eduard.** 1814–1908. German philosopher and theologian; author of *Platonische Studien* (1839), *Die Philosophie der Griechen* (3 vols., 1845–52), *Geschichte der Deutschen Philosophie seit Leibniz* (1873), *Grundriss der Geschichte der Griechischen Philosophie* (1883), etc.

**Zel'ler'** (zĕ'lâr'), **Jules Sylvain.** 1819–1900. French historian; succeeded Duruy as professor at École Polytechnique (1863); professor at Académie des Sciences Morales et Politiques (1874). Among his historical works are *Ulric de Hutten* (1849), *Histoire de l'Italie*...(1852), *Les Empereurs Romains* (1863), *Pie IX et Victor Emmanuel* (1879), *Histoire d'Allemagne* (1872–94).

**Zel'ler** (tsĕl'ẽr), **Karl.** 1842–1898. Austrian jurist and composer of the operettas *Der Vogelhändler* (1891) and *Der Obersteiger* (1895), male choruses, songs, etc.

**Zelotes.** See SIMON (the apostle), 2.

**Zelpha.** See ZILPAH.

**Zel'ter** (tsĕl'tẽr), **Karl Friedrich.** 1758–1832. German music director, and composer of solos and choruses, music for poems by Goethe and Schiller, cantatas, etc. His correspondence with Goethe was edited by Riemer (6 vols., 1833–34), L. Geiger (3 vols., 1904), etc.

**Zem·lin'sky** (zĕm·lĭn'skē), **Alexander von.** 1872–1942. Composer and director, b. in Vienna, of Polish parentage; composer of operas, symphonies, chamber music, choral works, songs, etc.

**Zend.** See ZAND.

**Zeng'er** (zĕng'ẽr; *Ger.* tsĕng'ẽr), **John Peter.** 1697–1746. Printer and publisher, b. in Germany; to America (1710); in New York City (from 1726). Central figure in a seditious libel trial (1734–35), resulting from censures of the government published in his antiadministration newspaper, New York *Weekly Journal* (founded 1733); defended by Andrew Hamilton of Philadelphia; acquitted by a jury, the decision being regarded as fundamental in establishing freedom of the press in America. Public printer for New York (from 1737) and for New Jersey (from 1738).

**Zengi.** Variant of ZANGI.

**Zen'ker** (tsĕng'kẽr), **Friedrich Albert von.** 1825–1898. German pathologist; discovered that trichinae are the cause of the serious, sometimes fatal, disease trichinosis.

**Zenker, Hans.** 1870–1932. German admiral; commanded the cruiser *Von der Tann* in battle of Jutland (1916); chief of German naval general staff (1924–28).

**Ze'no** (zē'nō) *or* **Ze'non** (-nŏn). 426–491. Isaurian emperor of the Eastern Roman Empire (474–491), b. in Isauria; son-in-law of Emperor Leo I. Had to put down revolts; for two years (476–477) yielded to usurper Basiliscus; Western Roman Empire overthrown (476); issued letter, *Henoticon* (482), in unsuccessful attempt to settle differences between Eastern and Western churches (Monophysite controversy); conflicts with Ostrogoths in Balkan Peninsula; finally persuaded (488) Theodoric to invade Italy.

**Zeno.** Greek Eleatic philosopher of 5th century B.C.; native of Elea (Velia) in Italy; disciple of Parmenides whom he accompanied to Athens; taught in Athens. His teachings are mentioned in Plato's *Parmenides*.

**Zeno.** Greek philosopher of late 4th and early 3d centuries B.C., b. at Citium, Cyprus; studied in Athens under Cynic philosophers; founded Stoic school of philosophy, and taught in Athens for more than fifty years.

**Zeno.** 150?–?78 B.C. Epicurean philosopher, b. in Sidon, Phoenicia; instructor of Cicero; head of Epicurean school in Athens (from c. 100 B.C.).

**Ze'no** (dzâ'nō). Venetian family of navigators and explorers, including: **Carlo** (1338–1418), admiral in Venetian service. His brother **Niccolò** (1340?–1396), navigator in service of Sir Henry Sinclair, Earl or Prince of Orkney, who explored "Frislanda" variously thought to be the Faeroes Islands, Iceland, etc. Another brother, **Antonio** (d. 1406), accompanied Niccolò in his explorations (1391 ff.), and, after Niccolò's death, voyaged with Sir Henry Sinclair to "Engroeneland" thought to be Greenland. After Antonio's return to Venice (1405), he wrote an account of the voyage, published later (1558) by a descendant. Antonio's grandson **Caterino** (fl. 1472), diplomat in Venetian service.

**Zeno, Apostolo.** 1668–1750. Italian poet and scholar; cofounder of *Giornale dei Letterati d'Italia*, first Italian critical journal (1710); court poet and historiographer to Charles VI (Holy Roman emperor) at Vienna (1718–29); notable for his melodramatic librettos and oratorios.

**Ze·no'bi·a** (zē·nō'bĭ·ȧ). Wife of Odenathus, King of Palmyra, at whose death (267 A.D.) she succeeded to throne as regent for her son. Ambitious to extend power of Palmyra over all the Roman empire in the East, she occupied Egypt and fixed garrisons in Asia Minor, all supposedly in close alliance with Rome; shortly after Aurelian's accession (270), she discarded all pretexts of allegiance; was defeated (271–272) and captured by Emperor Aurelian, who took her to Rome.

**Ze·nod'o·tus** (zē·nŏd'ō·tŭs). Greek scholar of early 3d century B.C., b. in Ephesus; first superintendent of the library in Alexandria; first critical editor of Homer's *Iliad* and *Odyssey*.

**Zent'may'er** (tsĕnt'mī'ẽr; *Angl.* zĕnt'-), **Joseph.** 1826–1888. German-born instrument maker in U.S.; to U.S. (1848) and settled (1853) in Philadelphia; known for his microscopes and his invention of an improved photographic lens (patented 1865).

**Zeph'a·ni'ah** (zĕf'ȧ·nī'ȧ). *In Douay Bible* **Soph'o·ni'as** (sŏf'ō·nī'ăs). One of the minor Hebrew prophets, of the time of Josiah, King of Judah (c. 640 B.C.), whose prophetic warning to Judah the Old Testament book of Zephaniah records.

**Zeph'y·ri'nus** (zĕf'ĭ·rī'nŭs), Saint. Pope (bishop of Rome; 198–217); pontificate marked by many controversies on doctrine.

**Zep'pe·lin'** (tsĕp'ĕ·lēn'; tsĕp'ĕ·lēn; *Angl.* zĕp'ĕ·lĭn), Count **Ferdinand von.** 1838–1917. German soldier, aeronaut, and airship designer. Served in American Civil War (with Union army, 1863), Austro-Prussian War (1866), and Franco-Prussian War (1870–71). Founded manufactory for airships, at Friedrichshafen; constructed (1900) first airship of rigid type known as *Zeppelin*, which was wrecked in landing; active in building and flying airships (from 1906).

**Zer·kau'len** (tsĕr·kou'lĕn), **Heinrich.** 1892–1954. German writer; author of collections of poems, novels, the war drama *Jugend von Langemark* (1933), the comedy *Der Sprung aus dem Alltag* (1935), etc.

**Zer'ni·ke** (zĕr'nĭ·kĕ), **Frits.** 1888–1966. Dutch physicist. Awarded Nobel prize in physics (1953) for invention of the phase contrast microscope (1932).

**Że·rom'ski** (zhĕ·rôm'skē), **Stefan.** 1864–1925. Polish novelist, poet, and playwright.

**Zer·rahn'** (tsĕr·rän'; *Angl.* zĕ·rän'), **Carl.** 1826–1909. Musical conductor, b. in Mecklenburg-Schwerin, Ger.; to U.S. (1848); conductor, Handel and Haydn Society, Boston (1854–96); also, conductor of music festivals at Worcester, Mass. (1866–97).

**Ze·rub'ba·bel** (zĕ·rŭb'ȧ·bĕl). fl. 6th century B.C. Governor of Jerusalem, a prince of Judah and in direct line of house of David; led returning exiles from Babylon (c. 538 B.C.) and took charge of rebuilding the temple; contemporary of Haggai and Zechariah.

**Ze'sen** (tsā'zĕn), **Philipp von.** 1619–1689. German rhetorician and author; founded at Hamburg (1643) Deutschgesinnte Genossenschaft, literary society which aimed to purify German language of barbarisms; author of lyric verse and of the novels *Die Adriatische Rosemund* (1645) and *Assenat* (1679).

**Zetland,** Marquises of. See Lawrence DUNDAS.

**Zet'ter·stedt'** (sĕt'tẽr·stĕt'), **Johan Vilhelm.** 1785–1874. Swedish naturalist; professor of botany, Lund.

**Zeu'ner** (tsoi'nẽr), **Gustav.** 1828–1907. German physicist and engineer; specialist in mechanics, hydraulics, and thermodynamics; director, polytechnic institute, Dresden (1873–97).

**Zeuss** (tsois), **Johann Kaspar.** 1806–1856. German historian and philologist, founder of modern Celtic philology; edited *Grammatica Celtica* (2 vols., 1853), and wrote *Die Deutschen und die Nachbarstämme* (1837), *Die Herkunft der Baiern von den Markomannen* (1839), etc.

**Zeux'is** (zūk'sĭs). fl. late 5th century B.C. Greek painter; studied in Athens; studio in Ephesus; reputed to have excelled in coloring and expression. According to a legend (see PARRHASIUS) his painting of a bunch of grapes was so realistic that birds were deceived and tried to eat the fruit.

**Zevi, Sabbatai.** See SABBATAI ZEBI.

**Ze'vin** (zĕ'vĭn), **Israel Joseph.** *Pseudonym* **Tash·rak'** (tȧsh·rȧk'). 1872–1926. Journalist and short-story writer, b. in Russia; to U.S. (1889) and settled in New York. On staff of *Jewish Daily News* (from c. 1892), contributing humorous stories in Yiddish based on life in New York's crowded East Side; sometimes referred to as "the Yiddish Mark Twain."

**Zeyner, Günther** and **Johann.** See ZAINER.

**Zhda'nov** (zhdȧ'nôf), **Andrei Aleksandrovich.** 1896–1948. Russian politician; secretary, Central Committee of the All-Union Communist party (Bolsheviks); member, Politburo (1935), and Presidium of the Supreme Soviet of the U.S.S.R.; chairman, Presidium of the Supreme Soviet of the Russian Socialist Federated Soviet Republic; president, foreign affairs committee of the U.S.S.R. (1938); member of military council on Leningrad front; lieutenant general (Feb., 1943).

**Zhu'kov** (zhōō'kôf), **Georgi Konstantinovich.** 1896–1974. Russian army officer; entered army (1915); served in Bolshevik forces (1917–18); commanded against Japanese in Amur River region, Mongolia (1938–39); chief of staff (Feb., 1941); conducted defense of Moscow against Germans; commander in chief on central front (Oct., 1941); first vice-commissar of defense (Aug., 1942); as representative of the supreme command on southwestern front, then on northern front, responsible for Russian offensives breaking sieges of Stalingrad and Leningrad (Oct., 1942–Jan., 1943); promoted to marshal of the Soviet Union (Jan., 1943).

**Zhu·kov'ski** (zhŏŏ·kôf'skû·ĭ; *Angl.* -skĭ), **Vasili Andreevich.** 1783-1852. Russian poet; reader to Maria Feodorovna (1815); tutor to Alexander II (from 1818); friend of Pushkin. Known for his innovations in poetical language (in the manner of Karamzin) and for his translations, esp. of German and English poetry. Author of the words of the Russian national anthem *God Save the Czar* (see Aleksei F. Lvov).

**Zi'chy** (zĭ'chĭ), **Mihály.** 1827–1906. Hungarian painter; court painter in St. Petersburg (from 1859); painted historical pictures, genre scenes, and symbolical subjects; illustrated a number of works of great Hungarian authors.

**Zichy zu Zich und Vá'sony·keö'** (tsōō zĭch' ŏŏnt vä'shōn·y'·kû'). Hungarian noble family including: Count **Jenő** (1837–1906), political economist and explorer; led expeditions (1892, 1895–96, 1897–98) to Central Asia and Caucasus region to search for Hungarian origins. Count **Géza** (1849–1924), pianist and composer of operas, choral works, piano pieces, and songs.

**Zieg'feld** (zĭg'fĕld), **Flor'enz** (flŏr'ĕnz). 1869–1932. American theatrical producer, b. Chicago. Introduced new type of production, the "revue," with *The Follies of 1907*, followed by annual "follies," popularly known as "Ziegfeld's follies," year after year. m. Anna Held (1897; divorced 1913) and Billie Burke (1914). Among other productions managed by him were *Rio Rita* (1927), *Show Boat* (1927), *Bitter Sweet* (1929), *The Pink Lady.*

**Zie'gler** (zē'glẽr; *Ger.* tsē'-), **Karl.** 1898–1973. German chemist. Awarded Nobel prize in chemistry (1963) with G. Natta for studies in the field of chemistry and technology of high polymers.

**Ziegler, Theobald.** 1846–1918. German philosopher and writer on pedagogy and ethics.

**Zie'gler** (zē'glẽr), **William.** 1843–1905. American baking-powder manufacturer, b. in Beaver County, Pa. Interested himself in polar exploration; financed expedition led by E. B. Baldwin (1901–02) and one led by Anthony Fiala (1903–05).

**Zie'hen** (tsē'ĕn), **Theodor.** 1862–1950. German philosopher, psychologist, and psychiatrist; taught psychiatry (1887–1912); devoted himself to philosophy (from 1912).

**Ziehn** (tsēn), **Bernhard.** 1845–1912. Musician, b. at Erfurt, Ger.; to U.S. (1868). Devoted himself to study of musical theory; solved problem of the unfinished final fugue in Johann Sebastian Bach's *Art of Fugue;* demonstrated spurious nature of *St. Lucas Passion,* traditionally attributed to Bach.

**Zie·liń'ski** (zhĕ·lēn'y'·skē), **Tadeusz.** 1859–1944. Polish classical scholar; author of *Our Debt to Antiquity* (1909), *Religion of Ancient Greece* (1926), *Horace and Roman Society in the Time of Augustus* (1938), etc.

**Ziem** (zyĕm), **Félix.** 1821–1911. French painter, esp. of scenes of Venice and Constantinople.

**Ziems'sen** (tsēm'sĕn), **Hugo Wilhelm von.** 1829–1902. German physician; specialist in internal medicine, children's diseases, diseases of the larynx, esophagus, etc., and in electrotherapeutics. Founder, with F. A. von Zenker, of *Das Deutsche Archiv für Klinische Medizin* (1865).

**Zie'ten** *or* **Zie'then** (tsē'tĕn), Count **Hans Ernst Karl von.** 1770–1848. Prussian field marshal general; commanded a brigade (1813–14), a corps at Ligny and Waterloo (1815), and the Prussian army of occupation in France (until 1817).

**Zieten** *or* **Ziethen, Hans Joachim von.** 1699–1786. Prussian cavalry general under Frederick the Great. Distinguished in first two Silesian Wars; commander, Brandenburg regiment of Hussars (1741); marched through enemy's territory to Jägerndorf to join Margrave Charles (1745) and won victory at Hohenfriedeberg (1745). Served in Seven Years' War at Prague and Kolín (1757), Leuthen, and Liegnitz (1760); decided the victory of Torgau (1760).

**Zi'la·hy** (zĭ'lŏ·hĭ), **Lajos.** 1891– . Hungarian playwright; journalist in Paris, London, and Budapest.

**Zil'boorg** (zĭl'bôrg), **Gregory.** 1890–1959. Psychiatrist, b. Kiev, Russia; physician in Russian army (1915–16); held political post under Kerenski (1917); journalist in Kiev; to U.S. (1919); on staff of Bloomingdale hospital (1926–31); in private practice, N.Y. City (1931–59). Wrote *The Medical Man and the Witch During the Renaissance* (1935), *A History of Medical Psychology* (1941; coauthor), *Mind, Medicine, and Man* (1943).

**Zil'cher** (tsĭl'ĸẽr), **Hermann.** 1881–1948. German concert pianist, director, and composer of song cycles, orchestral and choral works, chamber music, concertos, etc.

**Zil'pah** (zĭl'pȧ). *In Douay Version* **Zel'pha** (zĕl'fȧ). In Bible, the handmaid of Jacob's wife Leah (*Genesis* xxix. 24). See JACOB.

**Zim'ba·list** (*Angl.* zĭm'bȧ·lĭst; *Russ.* zyĭm·bŭ·lyēst'), **Ef'rem** (*Angl.* ĕf'rĕm; *Russ.* yĭ·fryâm'). 1889– . Violinist, b. Rostov, Russia; m. (1914) Alma Gluck (*q.v.*), operatic soprano; debut, St. Petersburg (1906);

later, toured Europe; to U.S. (1911) and has played in all leading cities of the country; composer of orchestral and violin suites, piano pieces, and songs.

**Zimisces.** See *John I Zimisces* (page 784).

**Zim'mer** (tsĭm'ẽr), **Friedrich.** 1855–1919. German Protestant theologian and educator; disciple of Froebel; wrote on music, theology, education, and women in education and social service.

**Zimmer, Heinrich.** 1851–1910. German Celtic scholar.

**Zim'mer·mann** (tsĭm'ẽr·män), **Alfred F. M.** 1859–1925. German colonial statesman and historian; author of *History of European Colonies* (6 vols., 1895–1914).

**Zim'mer·mann, Arthur.** 1864–1940. German statesman; in consular service (1896–1901); chief counselor (1903) and undersecretary of state for foreign affairs (1911–1916); foreign minister (1916–1917); sent (Jan. 16, 1917) "Zimmermann Telegram" which informed German ambassador to Mexico of imminent unrestricted submarine warfare and directed him to offer Mexico alliance with Germany and support in reconquering lost territory in Texas, New Mexico, and Arizona and which was intercepted and decoded by British Naval Intelligence and published (Mar. 1, 1917) in U.S. and became one of determining factors leading U.S. to war.

**Zimmermann, Clemens von.** 1788–1869. German mural and historical painter; painted murals for the Glyptothek, Pinakothek, and dining hall of Royal Palace, Munich.

**Zimmermann, Johann Georg von.** 1728–1795. Swiss physician and philosopher; court physician in Hanover (1768); author of *Von der Einsamkeit* (1756), *Vom Nationalstolz* (1758), *Von der Erfahrung in der Arzneikunst* (2 vols., 1764).

**Zimmermann, Robert von.** 1824–1898. Austrian Herbartian philosopher and aesthetician; founder of so-called aesthetics of form; opponent of Hegel and Vischer; author of *Ästhetik* (2 vols., 1858–65), *Anthroposophie* (1882), etc.

**Zim'mern** (zĭm'ẽrn), Sir **Alfred.** 1879–1957. English political scientist; professor of international politics, University College of Wales (1919–21); deputy director, League of Nations Institute of Intellectual Co-operation, Paris (1926–30); professor of international relations, Oxford (1930–44). Author of *The Greek Commonwealth* (1911), *Nationality and Government* (1918), *Europe in Convalescence* (1922), *The Third British Empire* (1926), *Learning and Leadership* (1928), *The Prospects of Democracy* (1929), *Spiritual Values and World-Affairs* (1939), etc.

**Zim'mern** (tsĭm'ẽrn), **Heinrich.** 1862–1931. German Assyriologist.

**Zim'mern** (zĭm'ẽrn), **Helen.** 1846–1934. English author, b. Hamburg; resided in England (1850–87), in Italy (1887–1934); translator and interpreter of German and Italian authors; author of *Schopenhauer, His Life and Philosophy* (1878), *The Hansa Towns* (1889), *Tripoli and Young Italy* (1912).

**Zin'ga·rel'li** (tsēng'gä·rĕl'lē), **Nicola Antonio.** 1752–1837. Italian composer; maestro di cappella, Milan cathedral (1792 ff.), St. Peter's at Rome (1804–11), Naples cathedral (1816 ff.). Among his compositions are operas, as *Romeo e Giulietta*, masses, oratorios, requiems, motets, and hymns.

**Zing'er·le** (tsĭng'ẽr·lĕ), **Ignaz Vinzenz.** Edler **von Sum'mers·berg** (fŏn zōōm'ẽrs·bĕrk). 1825–1892. Austrian poet and writer; author of works on philology, and of poems and prose tales chiefly of the Tirol.

**Zinn** (tsĭn), **Johann Gottfried.** 1727–1759. German physician and botanist; author of *Descriptio Anatomica Oculi Humani Iconibus Illustrata* (1755), reputed to be the first book on the anatomy of the eye. Linnaeus named in his honor the plant genus *Zinnia.*

**Zinn, Walter Henry.** 1906– . American nuclear physicist, b. Kitchener, Canada. To U.S. (1930); received Enrico Fermi award (1969) for his work on atomic reactors.

**Zi·nov'iev** (zyĭ·nôf'yĕf), **Grigori Evseevich.** *Orig.* **Hirsch Ap'fel·baum** (hĭrsh äp'fĕl·boum). 1883–1936. Russian Communist leader. Joined Social Democratic party (1901); associated with Lenin in forming Bolshevik group (1903). Imprisoned and exiled (1908); with Lenin in Switzerland during early years of World War (1914 ff.). Returned to Russia (1917); president of Leningrad Soviet of Workers and member of Politburo (1918); president of Third International (1919); an alleged letter from him to British Communists was used in British political campaign to defeat Ramsay MacDonald's first Labor government (1924). After Lenin's death (1924), for a time allied with Kamenev and Stalin as a ruling triumvirate, but soon conspired with Kamenev and Trotsky against Stalin, and was expelled from his various offices (1926–27). Recanted his opposition (1928) and was readmitted to Communist party. Accused of complicity in murder of Sergei Kirov (1934), confessed and was executed (Aug. 25, 1936).

**Zins'ser** (zĭn'sẽr), **Hans** (häns). 1878–1940. American bacteriologist, b. New York City; professor, Columbia (1913–23), Harvard Medical School (from 1923). Member of American Red Cross Sanitary Commission to Serbia to investigate typhus (1915); officer in Medical Corps of American Expeditionary Forces (1917–19); sanitary commissioner in Russia for health section of the League of Nations to study cholera (1923). With associates demonstrated method of producing immunization against certain varieties of typhus fever (1930).

**Zin'zen·dorf** (tsĭn'tsĕn·dôrf), Count **Nikolaus Ludwig von.** 1700–1760. Religious leader, b. Dresden, Saxony. Interested himself in the fate of the Unitas Fratrum, or Bohemian Brethren, a sect so severely persecuted as almost to have lost its identity; invited members of this sect to settle on his estate at Herrnhut; reorganized the church, the denomination coming to be known as the Moravian Brethren, or more exactly, the Renewed Church of the United Brethren; ordained (1737) a bishop of the Moravian Brethren. Expelled from Saxony; went to London (1737). Encouraged by letters from Spangenberg (*q.v.*) and George Whitefield, went to America (1741); held conferences with German Protestant leaders in Pennsylvania; established Moravian congregations in several towns in Pennsylvania, notably Bethlehem, Nazareth, Philadelphia, Lancaster, Hebron, and York; returned to England (1743). His banishment from Saxony was repealed (1748); resident of Herrnhut until his death (May 9, 1760).

**Zi'per·now'sky** (zĭ'pẽr·nôv'skĭ), **Károly.** 1853–1942. Hungarian electrical engineer; discovered (with Max Déri and Otto Titus Bláthy), the system of connecting an alternating-current transformer in parallel.

**Zir'kel** (tsĭr'kĕl), **Ferdinand.** 1838–1912. German mineralogist; pioneer in microscopical investigation of rocks. The mineral *zirkelite* is named after him.

**Ziska, Johann.** See Jan Žižka.

**Zi'ta** (zē'tȧ; *Ital.* dzē'tä; *Ger.* tsē'tä). 1892– . Princess of Bourbon and Parma, b. Viareggio, Italy; empress of Austria and queen of Hungary (1916–18); m. (1911) Charles I of Austria, later emperor; driven out of Austria (1918); left a widow (1922).

**Zí'tek** (zē'tĕk), **Josef.** 1832–1909. Czech architect; designed the museum at Weimar, the National Theater at Prague, etc.

**Zi'tel·mann** (tsē'tĕl·män), **Konrad.** *Pseudonym* **Konrad Tel'mann** (tĕl'män). 1854–1897. German poet and novelist.

**Zit'tel** (tsĭt'ĕl), **Karl Alfred von.** 1839–1904. German paleontologist and geologist; took part in F. G. Rohlfs's expedition into Libyan desert (1873–74).

**Živ'ko·vić** (zhēv'kô·vēt'y'; *Angl.* zhĭv'kô·vĭch), **Petar.** 1880–1947. Yugoslav soldier and statesman; commanded cavalry division in Balkan War (1912–13) and World War (1914–18); supported Alexander I in antiparliamentary coup d'état (Jan., 1929); premier and minister of interior (1929).

**Zi'war** (zē'wăr), **Ah'mad Pa'sha** (ă'măd pȧ'shä). 1864–1945. Egyptian statesman; succeeded Zaghlul Pasha as premier of Egypt (1924–26); pursued policy of friendship with Great Britain.

**Zi·ya' Gök Alp** (zĭ·yä' gûk' älp'). 1875–1924. Turkish sociologist and politician; founder of Turkish nationalist movement and a leader in Young Turk party.

**Zizim.** See JEM.

**Žiž'ka** (zhĭsh'kȧ), **Jan.** *Ger.* **Johann Zis'ka** (tsĭs'kä). 1360?–1424. Bohemian general and Hussite leader; built stronghold of Tabor; repulsed imperialist armies at Witkow, just outside of Prague (1420), and continued victorious campaign against Sigismund's armies (1421–22); headed the Taborites during the Hussite civil wars (1423–24). Subject of an epic poem by A. Meissner.

**Zmaj.** Pseudonym of Jovan JOVANOVIĆ.

**Zo** (zō), **Jean Baptiste Achille.** 1826–1901. French painter, esp. of Spanish scenes. His son **Henri** (1873– ) is also a painter.

**Zo·bair'** (zo͝o·bīr'). *Arab.* **al-Zubayr ibn-al-'Awwām.** d. 656. A cousin of Mohammed and one of earliest converts to Islam; killed in battle near Basra (Dec. 9, 656).

**Zo·bei'dah** (zo͝o·bī'dă). *Arab.* **Zubaydah.** 765?–831. Wife of Harun al-Rashid (from 785); mother of Prince Amin; name mentioned many times with that of Harun al-Rashid in *Thousand and One Nights* (*Arabian Nights*).

**Zo·beir' Ra'ha·ma Pa'sha** (zo͝o·bīr' ră'mă pȧ'shä). 1830–1913. Egyptian pasha in region of the Sudan. Slave trader in White Nile region; appointed governor of White Nile district; conquered Darfur (1874), made pasha, and demanded governor generalship of Darfur (1876). British and Egyptian authorities distrusted his influence in White Nile region and detained him in Cairo (1876–99); recommended (1884) by Governor General C. G. Gordon (*q.v.*) to be sent to Sudan to stem Mahdist movement, but recommendation not adopted. After conquest of the Sudan, allowed to return to his estates (1899).

**Zo'bel·titz, von** (fôn tsō'bĕl·tĭts). A family of German writers, including: **Fedor** (1857–1934), cavalry officer (1874–81), author of novels of manners and historical tales. His brother **Hanns** (1853–1918), *pseudonym* **Hanns von Spiel'berg** (shpēl'bĕrĸ), army officer (1872–90), editor, and novelist. Hanns's son **Hans-Caspar** (1883– ), editor, author of stories, novels (as *Die Europag*, 1924), comedies (as *Das Grosse Objekt*, 1932; *Verfasser-Unbekannt*, 1934), a biography of Hindenburg (1926), etc.

**Zo'ë** (zō'ē). Name of three empresses of the Eastern Roman Empire: **Zoë Za·üt'za** [zȧ·o͞ot'sȧ] (d. 896), 2d wife of Emperor Leo VI. **Zoë Car'bo·nop·si'na** (kär'bô·nŏp·sī'nȧ) *or* **Car'bo·nup·si'na** (kär'bô·no͞op-) *i.e.* black-eyed (d. 919); mistress and later (906) wife of Leo VI; mother of Constantine VII; on Leo's death (912) driven out but returned as regent for son (913–919). **Zoë** (980–1050); daughter of Constantine VIII; married (1028) Romanus III Argyrus; empress (1028–34); conspired with Michael IV to have Romanus murdered (1034); married Michael IV and adopted Michael V (1040); after revolution had deposed Michael V (1042), became coempress with sister Theodora (1042); married as third husband, Constantine IX (1042); joint ruler with Theodora and Constantine (1042–50).

**Zoë.** Russian empress. See under IVAN III VASILIEVICH.

**Zo·ë'ga** (sô·ẹ'gȧ), **Jörgen.** 1755–1809. Danish archaeologist.

**Zof'fa·ny** (zŏf'ȧ·nĭ) *or* **Zoffanji** *or* **Zaffanii, John** *or* **Johann.** 1733–1810. British painter, b. in Germany; to England (1758); under royal patronage became success as painter of portraits and dramatic conversation pieces.

**Zog I** (zōg) *or* **Zog'u I** (zōg'w'). *Also known as* **Scan'der·beg III** (skăn'dẽr·bĕg). *Original name* **Ah·med'** (äĸ·mĕd') **Bey** (bā) **Zogu.** 1895–1961. King of the Albanians; educ. Constantinople; orthodox Sunni Moslem by faith; during World War (1914–18), served in Austrian army; minister of interior (1920, 1921–22); minister of war (1921); premier of Albania (1922–24); elected president of Albanian Republic (1925); proclaimed king of Albanians (1928); pursued policy of close collaboration with Italy; driven from Albania by Italian invasion (1939); deposed (1946).

**Zog'baum** (zŏg'bäm), **Rufus Fairchild.** 1849–1925. American illustrator, b. Charleston, S.C.; specialized in illustrations of military and naval subjects, as *Manila Bay, The First Minnesota Regiment at the Battle of Gettysburg* (in the State capitol at St. Paul), *Battle of Lake Erie.*

**Zo'ĭ·lus** (zō'ĭ·lŭs). Greek rhetorician and critic of 4th century B.C., or later; known as **Ho·me'ro·mas'tix** (hô·mē'rô·măs'tĭks; hô·mẹr'ô-), *i.e.* "scourge of Homer," because of severity of his criticisms of Homer's poems; also criticized Isocrates and Plato. From his name derives the term *Zoilism*, for carping criticism.

**Zo'la'** (zô'lȧ'; *Angl.* zō'lȧ, zô·lä'), **Émile.** 1840–1902. French novelist, b. at Paris. Employee in the Hachette bookstore, Paris (1862–65). Among his notable works are *Contes à Ninon* (1864), *La Confession de Claude* (1865), *Le Vœu d'une Morte* (1866), *Les Mystères de Marseille* (1867), *Thérèse Raquin* (1867), *Madeleine Férat* (1868); the series of 20 novels published under the collective title *Les Rougon-Macquart* (1871–93), and including *Le Ventre de Paris* (1873), *L'Assommoir* (1877), *Nana* (1880), *La Joie de Vivre* (1884), *Germinal* (1885), *La Bête Humaine* (1890), *La Débâcle* (1892), *Le Docteur Pascal* (1893); the *Trilogy of the Three Cities* (*Lourdes*, 1894; *Rome*, 1896; *Paris*, 1898). Achieved reputation as one of the great leaders of naturalism in French literature. Interested himself in the Dreyfus case and became convinced Dreyfus had been wrongfully convicted; used all his powers in attempts to secure new trial; sentenced (Feb. 23, 1898) to imprisonment and fine for libeling (in journalistic attacks under the heading *J'Accuse*) the court-martial which tried and acquitted Major Esterhazy; spent some time in exile in England. Author also of a number of works of criticism, as *Mes Haines* (1866), *La République Française et la Littérature* (1879), *Le Naturalisme au Théâtre* (1881), *Les Romanciers Naturalistes* (1881).

**Zöll'ner** (tsûl'nẽr), **Carl Friedrich.** 1800–1860. German composer of songs for male and mixed choruses; the folk song *Das Wandern ist des Müllers Lust*, etc. His son **Heinrich** (1854–1941), composer, conductor, and writer; composer of operas (*Frithjof*, 1884; *Faust*, 1887; *Matteo Falcone*, 1894; *Der Überfall*, 1895; *Die Versunkene Glocke*, 1899), choruses, a cantata (*Die Neue Welt*, 1892), symphonies, orchestral pieces, songs, etc.

**Zöllner, Johann Karl Friedrich.** 1834–1882. German

astrophysicist; known for photometric work, esp. the construction of an astrophotometer, for researches on mental delusions, esp. optical illusions, and expansion of the electrodynamical theory of W. Weber.

**Zon′a·ras** (zŏn′ȧ·răs; *as mod. Grk.*, zô·nä·räs′), **Joannes.** fl. 12th century. Byzantine historian; author of a compendium of general history (18 books), valued chiefly for work of Dio Cassius (*q.v.*) which he incorporated in his own book.

**Zonta.** See GIUNTA.

**Zopyrion.** See under PAMPHILUS.

**Zo′rach** (zō′räk), **William.** 1887–1966. Sculptor and painter, b. in Lithuania; to U.S. as a child; sculptor for U.S. Post Office Department building in Washington, D.C.

**Zorn** (sôrn), **Anders Leonhard.** 1860–1920. Swedish painter, etcher, and sculptor; traveled and painted in many countries, including the U.S.A. (1893 ff.), but resident chiefly in Mora, Sweden. His paintings are esp. of Swedish subjects, female nudes, figures, and portraits; his etchings include nudes, portraits of Renan, Anatole France, Paul Verlaine, Proust, Rodin, Strindberg, and the *Portrait of the Artist and his Wife;* his sculptures include *Alma* (a nude), a bronze statue of Gustavus Vasa (in Mora), *Faun and Nymph* (a bronze statuette, 1896), etc.

**Zorn** (tsôrn), **Philipp.** 1850–1928. German jurist; author of works on constitutional, church, and civil law.

**Zo′ro·as′ter** (zō′rō·ăs′tĕr; zŏr′ō-) *or* **Zar′a·thus′tra** (zăr′ȧ·thōōs′trȧ). *Old Iranian form of name* **Za′ra·thush′tra** (zȧ′rȧ·thōōsh′trȧ). fl. prob. about 6th cent. B.C. Founder of the religion (Zoroastrianism) of the ancient Persian peoples; its sacred literature is the Zend-Avesta.

**Zor·ril′la** (thôr·rē′lyä), **Manuel Ruiz** (rōō·ēth′). 1834–1895. Spanish statesman; practiced law at Madrid. Progressist deputy to the Cortes (1856 ff.); exiled (1866–68); minister of commerce and public instruction (1868–69), of justice (1869); president of Cortes (1870); supported election of Amadeus of Savoy; premier (1871, 1872–73); to France, later Geneva, as leader of the Republicans (1875–93).

**Zor·ril′la de San Mar·tín′** (sôr·rē′yä thā sän′ mär·tēn′), **Juan.** 1855–1931. Uruguayan poet; chief work, the epic poem *Tabaré* (1888).

**Zor·ril′la y Mo·ral′** (thôr·rē′lyä ē mō·räl′), **José.** 1817–1893. Spanish poet and dramatist; lived in France (1847–55), Mexico (1855–66), Spain (1866 ff.). Author of lyric poetry, the uncompleted epic *Granada* (1852), historical leyendas, plays, as *El Zapatero y el Rey, Don Juan Tenorio,* and *A Buen Juez Mejor Testigo,* and memoirs.

**Zo′ser** (zō′sĕr). *Gr.* **To·sor′thros** (tō·sôr′thrŏs). A king (c. 2980–2950 B.C.) and probable founder of IIId (first Memphite) dynasty of Egypt; powerful and wealthy ruler; with aid of his counselor Imhotep (*q.v.*), extended and strengthened kingdom; built tombs and temples, and esp. a terraced pyramid (the Step Pyramid) at Saqqara, first large structure of stone known in history.

**Zo′shchen·ko** (zô′shchĕn·kô), **Mikhail.** 1895–1958. Russian writer; served in World War (1914–18) and after the war in the Bolshevik armies; author esp. of humorous tales, including *The Merry Life* (1924), *The Joyous Adventure* (1927), *The Woman Who Could not Read and Other Tales* (1940), etc.

**Zo′si·mus** (zō′sĭ·mŭs; zŏs′ĭ-), Saint. Pope (bishop of Rome; 417–418). Involved in Pelagian controversy; condemned Pelagius and his doctrines.

**Zosimus.** Byzantine historian of 5th century A.D.; author of a history of Rome from period of early emperors to capture of Rome by Alaric (410).

**Zouche** (zōōsh; zōōch), **Richard.** 1590–1661. English authority on civil law; regius professor of civil law, Oxford (1620–61); judge of high court of admiralty (1641), deprived because of Royalist adherence (1649); restored (1661); author of *Elementa Jurisprudentiæ,* mapping whole field of law in departments (1629), and *Jus Feciale,* first treatise to exhibit law of nations as an orderly system.

**Zri′nyi** (zrĭ′nyĭ). Name of an ancient Croatian noble family, including: **Miklós** *or* **Nicholas** (1508–1566), Hungarian army commander; ban of Croatia (1542–61); famed for defense of Szigetvár against Turks (1566), and killed in final sally from castle of the city. Two of his great grandsons, **Miklós** *or* **Nicholas** (1620–1664), who was ban of Croatia (from 1647), campaigned with success against Turks, and published a volume of verse, *The Siren of the Adriatic* (1651), and **Péter** (1621–1671), who was ban of Croatia (from 1665), took a leading part in conspiracy of Hungarian magnates, and was beheaded, in Vienna. Péter's daughter **Ilona** *or* **Helen** (1643–1703) m. (1667) Prince Franz I Rakoczi von Siebenbürgen and (1681) Count Imre Thököly (*q.v.*), and defended Munkacs (1685–88) heroically against the Imperialists.

**Zschok′ke** (chôk′ē), **Johann Heinrich Daniel.** 1771–1848. German writer; author of the robber novel *Abällino* (1794, dramatized 1795) and of historical novels and short stories, as *Bilder aus der Schweiz* (5 vols., 1825–26, including *Der Flüchtling im Jura*), *Das Goldmacherdorf* (1817); also of *Stunden der Andacht* (a religious work, 8 vols., 1809–16; Eng. trans., *Hours of Meditation*), of studies in Bavarian and Swiss history, etc.

**Zsig′mon·dy** (zhĭg′mōn·dē), **Richard.** 1865–1929. German chemist; professor, Göttingen (from 1908); made researches on the nature of colloids; invented the ultramicroscope (with H. F. W. Siedentopf, 1903); awarded 1925 Nobel prize for chemistry (1926).

**Zu·biá′ur·re** (sōō·byä′ōōr·rē), **Valentín de** (1879– ) and his brother **Ramón de** (1882– ). Spanish painters, esp. of landscapes of their native Basque region.

**Zuc′ca** (tsōō′kä), **Ma′na** (mä′nä). *Known as* **Mana-Zucca.** 1894?– . American pianist and composer, b. New York City; composer of many vocal, violin, and orchestral pieces, and an opera (*Hypatia*).

**Zuc′ca·rel′li** (tsōōk′kä·rĕl′lē), **Francesco.** 1702–1788. Italian painter; employed in Venice and London; foundation member of British Royal Academy; known esp. for his landscapes.

**Zuc′ca·ro** (tsōōk′kä·rō), **Taddeo.** 1529–1566. Italian painter, esp. of decorative frescoes in the manner of the school of Raphael; among his works are the frescoes in Palazzo Farnese at Caprarola. His brother and pupil **Federigo** (1543–1609) was also a mannerist painter, employed at Rome, northern Italy, England (1574), and Spain (1585–89); among his works are the fresco *Last Judgment* (in dome of Florence cathedral; begun by Vasari), frescoes in the Pauline Chapel (Vatican), in the Doge's Palace (Venice), and in the church of the Escorial (Spain), and portraits, as of Queen Elizabeth and Mary Stuart.

**Zuck′may′er** (tsōōk′mī′ĕr), **Carl.** 1896– . German playwright, novelist, and poet.

**Zueb′lin** (?zōōb′lĭn), **Charles.** 1866–1924. American sociologist; founded Northwestern U. settlement, in Chicago (1891); teacher of sociology, U. of Chicago (1892–1908), professor (1902–08); author of *A Decade of Civic Development* (1905), *Democracy and the Overman* (1911), etc.

**Zü′gel** (tsü′gĕl), **Heinrich von.** 1850–1941. German animal and genre painter.

**Zu·hair′** (zōō·hīr′). *Arab.* **Zuhair ibn-abi-Sulmā.**

Arabic poet of 6th century A.D. One of his poems is in *Mu'allaqāt.*

**Zu'ker·tort** (tsōō'kĕr·tôrt), **Johannes Hermann.** 1842–1888. Polish chess master; winner of international tournament, Paris (1878), and of the chess congress (1883).

**Zu'kor** (zōō'kĕr), **Adolph.** 1873– . Motion-picture producer, b. in Hungary; to U.S. in his youth (1888); founder of Famous Players Film Co. (1912), and chairman of the Board of Paramount Pictures, Inc.

**Zu·ław'ski** (zhōō·läf'skē), **Jerzy.** 1874–1915. Polish playwright, poet, and novelist.

**Zu'lo·a'ga** (sōō'lō·ä'gä), **Félix.** 1814–1876. Mexican soldier and statesman; supported Comonfort in presidency (1855–58); seized Mexico City and was proclaimed president of Mexico (1858).

**Zu'lo·a'ga** (thōō'lō·ä'gä), **Ignacio.** 1870–1945. Spanish painter; known esp. for his landscapes, portrayals of popular Spanish types, as gypsies, bullfighters, beggars, etc., and portraits of women. Among his works are *Daniel Zuloaga and his Daughters* and *Doña Mercedes* (in the Luxembourg, Paris), *Market Scene* (at Ghent), *Promenade After the Bull Fight* (at Leipzig), *Gypsy Bull Fighter's Family,* and *Mlle. Lucienne Bréval as Carmen* (in Hispanic Society, N.Y.).

**Zu'ma·la·cár're·gui** (sōō'mä·lä·kär'rĕ·gē), **Tomás.** 1788–1835. Spanish general; served against Napoleon; dismissed from army as Carlist (1832); assumed leadership of Carlist forces in Biscay (1833); waged successful campaigns and guerrilla wars against the Cristinos.

**Zu·már'ra·ga** (thōō·mär'rä·gä; sōō-), **Juan de.** 1468–1548. Spanish prelate in Mexico; member of Franciscan order; first bishop of Mexico; burned collections of Aztec manuscripts as heretical books; championed rights of Indians; extended missionary stations to Spanish conquests in Mexico and Central America.

**Zum'busch** (tsŏŏm'bŏŏsh), **Kaspar von.** 1830–1915. German sculptor; works are chiefly portrait busts, monuments, statues, and decorative pieces.

**Zumpt** (tsŏŏmpt), **Karl Gottlob.** 1792–1849. German classical scholar; author of a Latin grammar (1818), *Annales Veterum Regnorum et Populorum* (1819), *Die Religion der Römer* (1845), and other works on classical antiquities. His nephew **August Wilhelm Zumpt** (1815–1877), also a classical scholar.

**Zum'steeg** (tsŏŏm'shtāK), **Johann Rudolf.** 1760–1802. German violoncellist and composer; pioneer of the ballad and precursor of Franz Schubert and Johann K. G. Loewe (*qq.v.*); composed songs and ballads, operas, musical plays, music for the *Räuber* of his friend and schoolmate Schiller, church cantatas, etc.

**Zú'ñi·ga** (thōō'nyē·gä), **Alonso de Ercilla y.** See Alonso de ERCILLA Y ZÚÑIGA.

**Zú'ñi·ga y A'ze·ve'do** (thōō'nyē·gä ē ä'thā·vā'thō; sōō'nyē·gä ē ä'sā-), **Gaspar de.** Conde de **Mon'ter·rey'** (mōn'tĕr·rē'ē), *Eng.* Count of **Mon'te·rey'** (mŏn'tĕ·rā'). 1540?–1606. Spanish colonial administrator; viceroy of Mexico (1595–1603); sent out exploring and colonizing expeditions to north and northwest. Monterey, Calif., and the Bay of Monterey are named in his honor.

**Zú'ñi·ga** (thōō'nyē·gä) **y Requeséns, Luis de.** See REQUESÉNS.

**Zun'ser** (tsŏŏn'zĕr), **El'ia·kim** (ĕl'yō·kĭm). *Known as* **Eliakim Bad'chen** (bäd'Kĕn). 1836–1913. Yiddish poet, b. Vilna, then in Russia; to U.S. (1889) and toured country reciting his verses with great success. Among favorite poems are *Der Potshtover Glekl, Di Soche,* and *Shivath Zion.*

**Zunz** (tsŏŏnts), **Leopold.** 1794–1886. German Jewish scholar; founder of the scientific study of Judaism; author of *Die Namen der Juden* (1836), *Die Synagogale Poesie des Mittelalters* (1853), *Die Ritus des Synagogalen Gottesdienstes* (1859), *Literaturgeschichte der Synagogalen Poesie* (1865), etc.

**Žu·pan'čič** (zhōō·pän'chēch), **Oton.** 1878–1949. Slovene poet; translator of Shakespeare's plays.

**Zu·pit'za** (tsōō·pĭt'sä), **Julius.** 1844–1895. German philologist; founder of the scientific study of English philology in Germany; edited Cynewulf, *Beowulf,* and other Middle English and Old English works, etc.

**Zur'ba·rán'** (thōōr'bä·rän'), **Francisco de.** 1598–1664. Spanish painter; court painter to Philip IV (1638); known for religious paintings and for monastic portraiture. Among his works are *Crucifixion, St. Francis of Assisi, St. Anselm, Labors of Hercules* (ten canvases), *Ecstasy of the Beatified Alonso Rodriguez, Life of St. Buenaventura* (four panels), *Life of St. Peter.*

**Zu·ri'ta y Cas'tro** (thōō·rē'tä ē käs'trō), **Jerónimo.** 1512–1580. Spanish historian; author of *Anales de la Corona de Aragón* (6 vols., 1562–80), etc.

**Zweig** (tsvīK), **Arnold.** 1887–1968. German Jewish novelist, playwright, and essayist. Served in World War I; exiled from Germany (1933); to Palestine (1934). Author of plays, as *Ritual Murder in Hungary* (1913) and *Die Sendung Semaels* (1915), the novels *Claudia* (1912), *The Case of Sergeant Grischa* (1927; dramatized 1930), *Young Woman of 1914* (1931), *De Vriendt Goes Home* (1932), *Education before Verdun* (1935), and *The Crowning of a King* (1937), etc.

**Zweig, Stefan.** 1881–1942. Austrian writer of Jewish parentage; resident in Salzburg, later in London (1934–40; naturalized), New York, and Brazil. Author of: lyric poems; novels and stories, including *Amok* (1923), *Conflicts* (1926), *Kaleidoscope* (1934), *The Buried Candelabrum* (1937), *Beware of Pity* (1939); plays including *Jeremiah* (1918), *Volpone* (adapted from Ben Jonson; 1927); biographical studies; *Brazil* (1941); and an autobiography *The World of Yesterday* (pub. 1943).

**Zwick'y** (tsvĭk'ē), **Fritz.** 1898–1974. Swiss physicist in U.S.; known for investigations of cosmic rays.

**Zwie'di·neck von Sü'den·horst** (tsvē'dē·nĕk fōn zü'dĕn·hôrst), **Hans.** 1845–1906. German historian in Austria; edited *Zeitschrift für Allgemeine Geschichte* (1884–86) and *Bibliothek Deutscher Geschichte* (from 1886); author of *Die Politik der Republik Venedig* (2 vols., 1882–85), *Maria Theresia* (1905), etc.

**Zwing'er** (tsvĭng'ĕr), **Theodor.** 1533–1588. Swiss physician; professor of Greek (1565), moral philosophy (1571), and theory of medicine, Basel.

**Zwing'li** (tsvĭng'lē), **Huldreich** *or* **Ulrich.** 1484–1531. Swiss religious reformer; pastor at Glarus (1506), and served as chaplain to Glarus troops in Italy, at the battles of Novara (1513) and Marignano (1515). Pastor at Einsiedeln (1516) and appointed to the Great Minster in Zurich (1519) where he was rector and teacher of religion. By his preaching, established Reformation in Zurich, legalized by council of Zurich (1523); became a leader in political and religious affairs throughout Switzerland; conferred at Marburg with Saxon reformers, including Luther (1529), but was at variance with Luther on some doctrinal points; accompanied Zurich troops as chaplain in their campaign against Catholic cantons; killed at the battle of Kappel (Oct. 11, 1531). Chief work, *De Vera ac Falsa Religione* (1525). Cf. John CALVIN.

**Zwor'y·kin** (zwôr'ĭ·kĭn; *Russ.* zvôr'y'·kyĭn), **Vlad'i·mir Kos·ma'** (*Russ.* kŭz·y'·mä'). 1889– . Television authority, b. in Russia; to U.S. (1919); with Radio Corporation of America Mfg. Co. (1929–42); associate research director, R.C.A. Laboratories (1942–45); author of *Photocells and Their Applications* (1932).

# PRONOUNCING LIST OF PRENAMES

### AND OTHER ELEMENTS, SUCH AS PATRONYMICS, TITLES, AND PARTICLES, THE PRONUNCIATION OF WHICH HAS USUALLY NOT BEEN SHOWN IN THE MAIN VOCABULARY

This list is not intended as an exhaustive list of prenames for the many languages represented in it. It merely aims to cover unpronounced prenames that appear in the vocabulary of this book. A few prenames about which no reliable information could be obtained are not pronounced in either the vocabulary or this list.

As in the vocabulary, both an orthographic and a phonetic division are shown. The former (appearing in the bold-faced name) shows how a word may be divided at the end of a line of print or writing. The latter (appearing in the respelled pronunciation) shows the syllable divisions that are believed to occur when the word is uttered in speech. Where the orthographic division of a name belonging to two or more languages is not the same for all these languages, the name is repeated in bold-faced type, after a dash, with changed division, as many times as may be necessary (cf. **Alice**).

English pronunciations are unlabeled (cf. **Adah**), except in a very few cases requiring special treatment (cf. **Esther**). If a name belongs to more than one language one of which is English, the English pronunciation is given first, usually without a label (cf. **Abraham**). When a name belongs to two or more foreign languages, the foreign pronunciations are usually arranged in the alphabetical order of the language names (cf. **Alberto**); exceptions occur chiefly when a name is reprinted in bold-faced type to show a change of orthographic division (cf. **Albert**), or when, in order to save space, two or more language labels are attached to a pronunciation respelling that is identical for these languages (cf. **Herman**).

Names identically spelled with respect to letters but differing with respect to a modifier or modifiers borne by one or more of these letters, are separately entered (cf. **Adele, Adèle; Adelaide, Adélaïde**).

The pronunciation shown for Latin names in this list (as in the vocabulary) is the Anglicized, not the ancient Roman, pronunciation. Where, as is often the case, the Anglicized pronunciation of a Latin name is the same as the pronunciation of an identically spelled English name, no separate pronunciation is shown for the Latin name, and the English and Latin pronunciation is unlabeled and appears first if the name belongs also to one or more other languages (cf. **Alexius**).

An explanation of the reason for two or more pronunciations for a letter or letter group in a foreign name may often be found in the Guide to Pronunciation, in the section entitled "Values of Specific Letters and Letter Groups." Thus the subentries *Portuguese* and *Spanish* under the entry **d** in that section explain why two pronunciations are shown for the *D* in Portuguese *Damião* and Spanish *Damián*, respectively.

For abbreviations see pages xxxiii–xxxvi.

**à** ȧ, ä
**Aa′bye** *Dan.* ô′bü
**Aa′ge** *Dan.* ô′gĕ
**Aag′je** *Du.* äᴋ′yĕ
**Aall** *Norw.* ôl
**Aar′on** âr′ŭn—**Aa′ron** *Dan.* ä′rŏn; *Ger.* ä′rōn—**Aa′ron′** *Fr.* ä′rôɴ′
**Aa·ro′no·vich** *Russ.* ŭ·rô′nŭ·vyĭch
**Aart** *Du.* ärt
**Aas′mund** *Norw.* ôs′mo͝on
**A′ba·dí′a** *Span.* ä′bä·t͟hē′ä
**Ab′a·ste′ni·a** ăb′ȧ·stē′nĭ·ȧ
**Ab′ba** ăb′ȧ; *Heb.* äb′bä
**ab′bé′** *Fr.* ȧ′bā′
**Ab′bot, Ab′bott** ăb′ŭt
**Ab′by** ăb′ĭ
**Abd′al·lah′** *Pers.* äbd′ăl·lä′
**Ab·dul′lah** ăb·dŭl′ȧ—**Abd·ul·lah′** *Arab.* äb·do͞ol·lä′
**Ab′dy** ăb′dĭ
**Abe** āb
**A′bel** ā′bĕl; *Dan., Du.* ä′bĕl—**A′bel′** *Fr.* ȧ′bĕl′
**A′be·lar′do** *Span.* ä′bā·lär′t͟hō
**A′bels** ā′bĕlz
**Ab′er·crom′bie, -by** ăb′ẽr·krŏm′bĭ, -krŭm′bĭ
**Ab′er·dour′** ăb′ẽr·dour′
**A·bi′a·thar** ȧ·bī′ȧ·thẽr
**A′bi·el** ā′bĭ·ĕl, ȧ·bī′ĕl
**Ab′i·gail** ăb′ĭ·gāl
**A·bi′jah** ȧ·bī′jȧ
**A·bi′lio** *Port.* ȧ·bē′lyo͞o
**Ab′ner** ăb′nẽr
**Ab′ney** ăb′nĭ
**A·boyne′** ȧ·boin′
**A′bra·ham** ā′brȧ·hăm; *Dan.* ä′brä·häm; *Du.* ä′brä·häm; *Ger.* ä′brä·häm; *Swed.* ä′brä·häm′—**A′bra′ham′** *Fr.* ȧ′brȧ′ȧm′—**A′bra·ham′** *Span.* ä′brä·än′
**A′bra·hân′** *Span.* ä′brä·än′
**A′bram** ā′brăm—**A·bram′** *Russ.* ŭ·bräm′
**A·bra′mo·vich** *Russ.* ŭ·brä′mŭ·vyĭch
**Ab′thorpe** ăb′thôrp
**A′bu** *Pers.* ä′bo͞o
**A′by** *Ger.* ä′bē
**Ac·cept′ed** ăk·sĕp′tĕd, -tĭd
**A·cha′tes** ȧ·kā′tēz; *Swed.* ä·kä′tĕs
**A′chille′** *Fr.* ȧ′shēl′—**A·chil′le** *Ital.* ä·kēl′lā
**A·chil′les** ȧ·kĭl′ēz; *Ger.* ä·ᴋĭl′ĕs
**A′chim** *Ger.* ä′ᴋĭm
**A·cis′clo** *Span.* ä·thēs′klō, ä·sēs′-
**A·cis′lo** *Span.* ä·thēs′lō, ä·sēs′-
**Ac′land** ăk′lănd
**Ac′ton** ăk′tŭn
**A′da** ā′dȧ; *Ital.* ä′dä—**A′da′** *Fr.* ȧ′dȧ′
**A′dah** ā′dȧ
**A·dair′** ȧ·dâr′
**A′dal·bert** *Dan.* ä′däl·bărt; *Ger.* ä′däl·bĕrt
**Ad′am** ăd′ăm—**A′dam** *Dan.* ä′däm; *Du.* ä′däm; *Ger., Pol., Yugo.* ä′däm—**A′dam′** *Fr.* ȧ′däɴ′—**A·dam′** *Russ.* ŭ·däm′—**A′dam′** *Swed.* ä′däm′
**A′da·man′tios** *Mod. Grk.* ä′t͟hä·män′dyôs
**A′da·mon′ti** *Ital.* ä′dä·mōn′tē
**A·da′mo·vich** *Russ.* ŭ·dä′mŭ·vyĭch
**Ad′ams** ăd′ămz
**A·dán′** *Span.* ä·t͟hän′
**A·dare′** ȧ·dâr′
**Ad′dams** ăd′ămz
**Ad′ding·ton** ăd′ĭng·tŭn
**Ad′dis** ăd′ĭs
**Ad′di·son** ăd′ĭ·s′n
**Ad′e·la** ăd′ĕ·lȧ—**A·de′la** *Span.* ä·t͟hā′lä
**Ad′e·laide** ăd′ĕ·lād—**A′de·la′i·de** *Ital.* ä′dā·lä′ē·dā
**A′dé′la′ïde′** *Fr.* ȧ′dā′lȧ′ēd′
**A′dé′lard′** *Fr.* ȧ′dā′lȧr′
**A′de·lar′do** *Span.* ä′t͟hā·lär′t͟hō
**Ad′el·bert** ăd′ĕl·bẽrt, ȧ·dĕl′bẽrt—**A′del·bert** *Ger.* ä′dĕl·bĕrt
**A·dele′** ȧ·dĕl′—**A·de′le** *Ger.* ä·dā′lĕ
**A·dèle′** ȧ·dĕl′—**A′dèle′** *Fr.* ȧ′dĕl′
**A′del·heid** *Ger.* ä′dĕl·hīt
**Ad′e·li′na** ăd′ĕ·lī′nȧ—**A′de·li′na** *Ital.* ä′dā·lē′nä
**Ad′e·line** ăd′ĕ·līn, -lēn, -lĭn—**A′de·li′ne** *Dan.* ä′dĕ·lē′nĕ
**A·delle′** ȧ·dĕl′
**A′del·steen** *Norw.* ä′dĕl·stān
**A′de′o·da′to** *Ital.* ä′dā′ō·dä′tō
**Adg′er** ăj′ẽr
**Ad′hé′mar′** *Fr.* ȧ′dā′mȧr′
**A′din** ā′dĭn, ā′d′n
**Ad′lai** ăd′lā; ăd′lī
**Ad′na** ăd′nȧ
**Ad′olf** ăd′ŏlf, ȧ·dŏlf′, ā′dŏlf—**A′dolf** *Czech* ä′dôlf; *Dan.* ä′dŏlf; *Ger.* ä′dôlf; *Norw.* ä′dŏlf; *Pol.* ä′dôlf—**A·dolf′** *Russ.* ŭ·dôl′y′f—**A′dolf′** *Swed.* ä′dôlf′
**A′dol·fi′ne** *Norw.* ä′dŏl·fē′nĕ
**A·dol′fo** *Ital.* ä·dôl′fō; *Span.* ä·t͟hôl′fō

āle, chāotic, câre (7), ădd, ăccount, ärm, ȧsk (11), sofȧ; ēve, hēre (18), ēvent, ĕnd, silĕnt, makẽr; īce, ĭll, charĭty; ōld, ōbey, ôrb, ŏdd (40), sŏft (41), cŏnnect; fo͞od, fo͝ot; out, oil; cūbe, ūnite, ûrn, ŭp, circŭs, ü = u in Fr. menu;

**Ad′olph** ăd′ŏlf, *ȧ*·dŏlf′, ā′dŏlf—**A′dolph** *Dan.* ȧ′dŏlf; *Ger.* ä′dŏlf
**Ad′olphe** ăd′ŏlf, *ȧ*·dŏlf′, ā′dŏlf—**A′dolphe′** *Fr.* ȧ′dôlf′
**A·dol′pho** *Port.* *ȧ*·thôl′fōō
**A·dol′phus** *ȧ*·dŏl′f*ŭ*s
**Ad′o·ni′jah** ăd′ô·nī′j*ȧ*
**Ad′o·ni′ram** ăd′ô·nī′r*ă*m
**A′dri·aan** *Du.* ȧ′drē·ȧn
**A′dri·aans′zoon** *Du.* ȧ′drē·ȧn′s*ŭ*n, -sôn, -sōn
**A′dri·aen** *Du.* ȧ′drē·ȧn
**A′dri·aensz** *Du.* ȧ′drē·ȧns
**A′dri·an** ā′drĭ·*ă*n; *Du.* ȧ′drē·än; *Ger.* ä′drē·än
**A′dri·a′no** *Ital.* ä′drē·ä′nô
**A′dri·a′nus** *Lat.* ā′drĭ·ā′n*ŭ*s, ăd′rĭ-
**A′dri·en** ā′drĭ·ĕn—**A′dri′en′** *Fr.* ȧ′drē′äɴ′
**A′dri·enne** ā′drĭ·ĕn—**A′dri′enne′** *Fr.* ȧ′drē′ĕn′
**Aedh** *Ir.* ā
**Ae·gi′di·us** *Ger.* â·gē′dē·ōōs
**Ælf′gi′fu** *Old Eng.* ălf′yĭ′vōō
**Ae′li·a** *Lat.* ē′lĭ·*ȧ*
**Ae′li·us** *Lat.* ē′lĭ·*ŭ*s
**Ae·mil′i·a′nus** *Lat.* ē·mĭl′ĭ·ā′n*ŭ*s
**Ae·mil′i·us** *Lat.* ē·mĭl′ĭ·*ŭ*s, ē·mĭl′y*ŭ*s
**Aer′nout** *Du.* ȧr′nout
**Aert** *Du.* ȧrt
**af** *Norw.*, *Swed.* äv
**A·fa·na′se·vich** *Russ.* ŭ·fŭ·nȧ′syĕ-vyĭch
**A·fa·na′si** *Russ.* ŭ·fŭ·nȧ′syû·ĭ
**A·fa·na′sie·vich** *Russ.* ŭ·fŭ·nȧ′syĕ-vyĭch
**Af·fon′so, A·fon′so** *Port.* *ȧ*·fōɴ′sōō
**A·fra′nio** *Port.* *ȧ*·fră′nyōō
**A·fra′ni·us** *Lat.* *ă*·frā′nĭ·*ŭ*s
**Af′ri·ca′nus** ăf′rĭ·kā′n*ŭ*s
**Ag′a·tha** ăg′*ȧ*·th*ȧ*
**A′gathe′** *Fr.* ȧ′gȧt′—**A·ga′the** *Ger.* ä·gä′tĕ
**A′ga′thon′** *Fr.* ȧ′gȧ′tôɴ′
**A·ge′nor** *Ger.* ä·gā′nôr
**A′gé′nor′** *Fr.* ȧ′zhā′nôr′
**A′gi·de** *Ital.* ä′jē·dā
**Ă·gi′di·us** *Ger.* â·gē′dē·ōōs
**Ag′nes** ăg′nĕs, -nĭs; *Ger.* äg′nĕs; *Norw.* äng′nĕs
**A′gnès′** *Fr.* ȧ′nyâs′
**Ag′new** ăg′nū
**A′gno·lo** *Ital.* ä′nyô·lō
**Ag′nus** ăg′n*ŭ*s
**Á′gost** *Hung.* ä′gôsht
**A·gos·ti′nho** *Port.* *ȧ*·gōōsh·tē′nyōō, (*Braz.*) *ă*·gōōs·tē′nyōō
**A′go·sti′no** *Ital.* ä′gô·stē′nô
**Á′gos·ton** *Hung.* ä′gôsh·tôn
**A·grip′pa** *ȧ*·grĭp′*ȧ*—**A′grip′pa′** *Fr.* ȧ′grēp′pȧ′
**A′gui·lar′** *Span.* ä′gē·lär′
**A′gus·tín′** *Span.* ä′gōōs·tēn′
**Ah′mad** *Arab.* ă′măd
**Ah·med′** *Alban.* äᴋ·mĕd′
**Ah·met′** *Turk.* ä·mĕt′
**Ai′dan** ā′d′n
**Ai′ken** ā′k*ĕ*n
**Aik′man** āk′m*ă*n
**Ai′ma′ble** *Fr.* ĕ′mȧ′bl′
**Ai·mé′** â·mā′—**Ai′mé′** *Fr.* ĕ′mā′
**Ai′mée′** *Fr.* ĕ′mā′
**Ai′no** *Finn.* ī′nô
**Ains′worth** ānz′wûrth, -wẽrth
**Aitch′e·son** āch′*ĕ*·s'n
**Ait′ken** āt′k*ĕ*n
**A·ki′ba** ä·kē′bä
**A′kim** *Pol.* ä′kēm—**A·kim′** *Russ.* ŭ·kyēm′
**A′kin** ā′kĭn
**A·kin′fi** *Russ.* ŭ·kyēn′fyû·ĭ
**A·ki·tsu·ne** *Jap.* ä·kē·tsōō·nĕ
**Ak′sel** *Finn.* ȧk′sĕl
**Al** ăl
**Al′ain** ăl′ĭn—**A′lain′** *Fr.* ȧ′lăɴ′
**Al′an** ăl′*ă*n
**Al′an·son** ăl′*ă*n·s'n
**Al′a·ric** ăl′*ȧ*·rĭk—**A′la′ric′** *Fr.* ȧ′lȧ′-rēk′
**A′la·rik′** *Swed.* ä′lȧ·rĭk′
**Al′as·tair′** ăl′*ă*s·târ′
**Al′ban** ôl′b*ă*n, ăl′- —**Al·ban′** *Ger.* äl·bän′, äl′bän
**Al′bans′** *Fr.* ȧl′bäɴ′
**Al′ba·ny** ôl′b*ȧ*·nĭ
**Al′ben** ăl′b*ĕ*n
**Al′be·rich** *Ger.* äl′b*ĕ*·rĭᴋ
**Al′be·ri′co** *Ital.* äl′bâ·rē′kô
**Al′be·ri′cus** *Lat.* ăl′b*ĕ*·rī′k*ŭ*s
**Al′be·rik** *Ger.* äl′b*ĕ*·rĭk
**Al′bert** ăl′bẽrt; *Dan.* ȧl′bĕrt; *Du.* äl′bẽrt; *Finn.* ȧl′bĕrt; *Ger.* äl′bĕrt; *Hung.* ŏl′bĕrt; *Norw.* äl′bẽrt, -bĕrt; *Swed.* ȧl′bẽrt—**Al′bert′** *Fr.* ȧl′bâr′
**Al′ber·ti′na** ăl′bẽr·tē′n*ȧ*
**Al′ber·tine** ăl′bẽr·tēn—**Al′ber′tine′** *Fr.* ȧl′bĕr′tēn′—**Al′ber·ti′ne** *Ger.* äl′bĕr·tē′nĕ
**Al·ber′to** *Ital.* äl·bĕr′tô; *Port.* äl-bĕr′tōō; *Span.* äl·bĕr′tō
**Al′berts** *Latvian* äl′bĕrts
**Al·ber′tus** ăl·bûr′t*ŭ*s; *Du.* äl·bĕr′tûs
**Al·bi′ci·us** *Lat.* ăl·bĭsh′ĭ·*ŭ*s, -bĭsh′*ŭ*s
**Al′bin** ăl′bĭn—**Al′bin′** *Fr.* ȧl′băɴ′—**Al·bin′** *Ger.* äl·bēn′, äl′bēn
**Al′bine′** *Fr.* ȧl′bēn′
**Al·bi′no** *Span.* äl·bē′nō
**Al′bi·on** ăl′bĭ·*ŭ*n
**Al′bi·us** *Lat.* ăl′bĭ·*ŭ*s
**Al′brecht** *Dan.* ȧl′brĕkt; *Ger.* äl′-brĕᴋt
**Al′bree** ôl′brē
**Al′can** ăl′k*ă*n
**Al·cán′ta·ra** *Span.* äl·kän′tä·rä
**Al′cée′** *Fr.* ȧl′sā′
**Al′cide′** *Fr.* ȧl′sēd′
**Al′ci·mus** *Lat.* ăl′sĭ·m*ŭ*s
**Al′ci·phron** ăl′sĭ·frŏn
**Al′de·gonde′** *Fr.* ȧl′dē·gôɴd′
**Al′den** ôl′d*ĕ*n
**Al′der·man** ôl′dẽr·m*ă*n
**Al′dert** *Du.* äl′dẽrt
**Al′dis** ôl′dĭs
**Al′do** *Ital.* äl′dô
**Al′donce′** *Fr.* ȧl′dôɴs′
**Al′dous** ôl′d*ŭ*s
**Al′dred** ôl′drĕd, -drĭd, ăl′-
**Al′drich** ôl′drĭch, *esp. Brit.* -drĭj
**Al′dridge** ôl′drĭj
**Al′dro** ăl′drō
**Al′dus** *Lat.* ôl′d*ŭ*s, ăl′-
**Ald′worth** ôld′wûrth, -wẽrth
**A′le·ar′do** *Ital.* ä′lȧ·är′dô
**Al′ec, Al′eck** ăl′ĕk, -ĭk
**A·le′cu** *Rum.* ä·lĕ′kōō
**A′le·jan′dro** *Span.* ä′lĕ·hän′drō
**A·lek′san′dar** *Yugo.* ä·lĕk′sän′där
**A′lek·san′der** *Pol.* ä′lĕk·sän′dĕr
**A′le·ksan′dr** *Bulg.* ä′lĕ·ksȧn′dẽr; *Russ.* ŭ·lyĭ·ksȧn′dẽr
**A·le·ksan′dra** *Russ.* ŭ·lyĭ·ksȧn′drŭ
**A·le·ksan′dro·vich** *Russ.* ŭ·lyĭ·ksȧn′-drŭ·vyĭch
**A·le·kse′ev** *Russ.* ŭ·lyĭ·ksyā′yĕf
**A·le·kse′e·vich** *Russ.* ŭ·lyĭ·ksyā′yĕ-vyĭch
**A·le·kse′ev·na** *Russ.* ŭ·lyĭ·ksyā′-yĕv·nŭ
**A·le·ksei′, A·le·ksyey′** *Russ.* ŭ·lyĭ-ksyā′ĭ
**Al′ers** ăl′ẽrz
**A′leš** *Czech* ȧ′lĕsh
**A′les·san′dro** *Ital.* ä′lȧs·sän′drô
**A·les′sio** *Ital.* ä·lĕs′syô
**A·let′ta** *Du.* ȧ·lĕt′ȧ
**Al′ex** ăl′ĕks, -ĭks—**A′lex′** *Fr.* ȧ′lĕks′—**A′lex** *Ger.* ä′lĕks
**A·lex′a** *ȧ*·lĕk′s*ȧ*
**Al′ex·an′der** ăl′ĕg·zăn′dẽr, ăl′ĭg-, *Brit. also* -zän′- —**A′lex·an′der** *Du.* ȧ′lĕk·sän′dẽr; *Finn.* ȧ′lĕk·sȧn′dĕr; *Norw.* ä′lĕk·sän′dẽr; *Pol.* ä′lĕk-sän′dĕr; *Swed.* ȧ′lĕk·sȧn′dẽr—**A′le-xan′der** *Ger.* ä′lĕ·ksän′dẽr; *Russ.* ŭ·lyĭ·ksȧn′dẽr
**Al′ex·an′dra** ăl′ĕg·zăn′dr*ȧ*, ăl′ĭg-, *Brit. also* -zän′- —**A′lex·an′dra** *Dan.* ȧ′lĕk·sȧn′drä
**Al′ex·an′dre** ăl′ĕg·zăn′dẽr, ăl′ĭg-, *Brit. also* -zän′- —**A′lex′an′dre** *Fr.* ȧ′lĕk′säɴ′dr′—**A·le·xan′dre** *Port.* *ȧ*·lĕ·shăɴn′drĕ
**Al′ex·an·dri′na** ăl′ĕg·zăn·drē′n*ȧ*, ăl′-ĭg-, *Brit. also* -zän-
**A′lex·an·dri′ne** *Du.* ȧ′lĕk·sän·drē′nĕ—**A′lex′an′drine′** *Fr.* ȧ′lĕk′säɴ′-drēn′
**A·le′xan·dros** *Mod. Grk.* ä·lâ′ksän-thrôs
**A·le·xan′dro·vich, -vitch** *Russ.* ŭ·lyĭ-ksȧn′drŭ·vyĭch
**A′lex·an′dru** *Rum.* ä′lĕk·sän′drōō
**A·le·xei′** *Russ.* ŭ·lyĭ·ksyā′ĭ
**A·le·xe′ie·vich** *Russ.* ŭ·lyĭ·ksyā′yĕ-vyĭch
**A·le·xe′iev·na** *Russ.* ŭ·lyĭ·ksyā′yĕv-nŭ
**A·le·xe′ye·vich** *Russ.* ŭ·lyĭ·ksyā′yĕ-vyĭch
**A′lex·i′ne** *Du.* ȧ′lĕk·sē′nĕ
**A·lex′is** *ȧ*·lĕk′sĭs; *Ger.* ä·lĕk′sĭs—**A′lex·is** *Finn.* ȧ′lĕk·sĭs—**A′lex′is′** *Fr.* ȧ′lĕk′sē′
**A·lex′i·us** *ȧ*·lĕk′sĭ·*ŭ*s; *Ger.* ä·lĕk′sē-ōōs
**Alf** ălf; *Norw.* älf
**Al·fa′ro** *Span.* äl·fä′rō
**Al′fons** *Ger.* äl′fôns
**Al′fonse** ăl′fŏns, -fŏnz
**Al·fon′so** ăl·fŏn′sō, -zō; *Ger.* äl-fôn′zō; *Ital.* äl·fôn′sô; *Span.* äl·fôn′-sō
**Al′ford** ôl′fẽrd, ăl′-, -fôrd

**Al′fred** ăl′frĕd, -frĭd; *Du.* äl′frĕt; *Ger.* äl′frāt; *Norw.* äl′frĕd; *Pol.* äl′frĕt; *Swed.* ȧl′frĕd—**Al′fred′** *Fr.* ȧl′frĕd′
**Al′fré′dine′** *Fr.* ȧl′frā′dēn′
**Al·fre′do** *Ital.* äl·frā′dō; *Span.* äl-frā′thō
**Al′ger·non** ăl′jẽr·nŭn—**Al′ger′non′** *Fr.* ȧl′zhĕr′nôɴ′
**Al′i** ăl′ĭ—**A·li′** *Arab.* ä·lĭ′; *Pers.* ȧ·lē′; *Russ.* ŭ·lyē′
**Al′ice** ăl′ĭs—**A′lice′** *Fr.* ȧ′lēs′—**A·li′ce** *Ger.* ä·lē′sĕ; *Ital.* ä·lē′chā
**A·li′ci·a** ȧ·lĭsh′ĭ·ȧ, -lĭsh′ȧ—**A·li′cia** *Ital.* ä·lē′chä; *Span.* ä·lē′thyä, -syä
**A·li′di·us** *Du.* ȧ·lē′dē·ûs
**A·lin′da** *Ital.* ä·lēn′dä
**A·line′** ȧ·lēn′, ăl′ēn
**Al′i·son** ăl′ĭ·s′n
**Al′is·ter** ăl′ĭs·tẽr
**Al′ix** ăl′ĭks—**A′lix′** *Fr.* ȧ′lēks′—**A′lix** *Ger.* ä′lĭks
**Al′la** *Russ.* ȧl′lŭ
**Al′lan** ăl′ăn
**Al′lard** *Du.* äl′ärt—**Al′lard′** *Fr.* ȧ′lȧr′
**Al′lar·dice, -dyce** ăl′ẽr·dīs
**Al′lart** *Du.* äl′ärt
**Al′le·mand′** *Fr.* ȧl′mäɴ′
**Al′len** ăl′ĕn, -ĭn
**Al′ler·ton** ăl′ẽr·t′n, -tŭn
**Al·leyne′** ă·lān′, ăl′ĭn
**Al′li·bone** ăl′ĭ·bōn
**Al′li·ott** ăl′ĭ·ŭt
**Al′li·son** ăl′ĭ·s′n
**Al′lis·ton** ôl′ĭs·tŭn
**All′son** ôl′s′n
**All′ston** ôl′stŭn
**All′var** *Swed.* ȧl′vȧr
**Al′lyn** ăl′ĭn
**Al′ma** ăl′mȧ; *Ger.* äl′mä
**Al·man′za** ăl·măn′zȧ
**Al′ma·rin** ăl′mȧ·rĭn
**Al′mer** ăl′mẽr
**Al′me·rin** ăl′mĕ·rĭn
**Al·mi′ra** ăl·mī′rȧ
**Al′mon** ăl′mŭn, ôl′-
**Alm′roth** ălm′rŏth
**Al′my** ăl′mĭ
**A·lois′** ȧ·lois′—**A′lois** *Czech* ȧ′lois—**A′lo·is** *Ger.* ä′lō·ēs, ä′lois
**A′lo·i′sio** *Ital.* ä′lō·ē′zyō
**Al′o·i′si·us** ăl′ō·ĭsh′ĭ·ŭs, -ĭsh′ŭs—**A′lo·i′si·us** *Ger.* ä′lō·ē′zē·ōōs
**A·lon′so** ȧ·lŏn′zō; *Ital.* ä·lôn′sō; *Span.* ä·lôn′sō
**A·lon′zo** ȧ·lŏn′zō
**A′lo′ys′** *Fr.* ȧ′lô′ēs′—**A′lo·ys** *Ger.* ä′lō·üs, ä′lois
**Al′o·y′si·a** ăl′ō·ĭsh′ĭ·ȧ, -ĭsh′ȧ
**A′lo·y′sio** *Ital.* ä′lō·ē′zyō
**Al′o·y′si·us** ăl′ō·ĭsh′ĭ·ŭs, -ĭsh′ŭs—**A′lo·y′si·us** *Du.* ȧ′lō·ē′sē·ûs; *Ger.* ä′lō·ü′zē·ōōs
**Al′phe·us** ăl′fē·ŭs, ăl·fē′ŭs—**Al·phe′-us** *Ger.* äl·fā′ōōs
**Al′phonse** ăl′fŏns, -fŏnz—**Al′phonse′** *Fr.* ȧl′fôɴs′
**Al·phon′so** ăl·fŏn′sō, -zō
**Al·phon′sus** ăl·fŏn′sŭs
**Al′pi′nien′** *Fr.* ȧl′pē′nyăɴ′
**Al′sop** ôl′sŭp
**Al′ton** ôl′t′n, -tŭn
**Al′u·red** ăl′ū·rĕd
**Al′va** ăl′vȧ; *Span.* äl′vä
**Al′vah** ăl′vȧ
**Al′van** ăl′văn
**Al′var** *Finn.* ȧl′vȧr
**Ál′var** *Span.* äl′vär
**Ál′va·res** *Port.* äl′vȧ·rĕsh, (*Braz.*) -rĕs
**Ál′va·rez** *Span.* äl′vä·rāth, -rās
**Ál′va·ro** *Port.* äl′vȧ·rōō; *Span.* äl′-vä·rō
**Al′ver·son** ăl′vẽr·s′n
**Al′ves** *Port.* äl′vĕsh, (*Braz.*) -vĕs
**Al·vil′de** *Norw.* äl·vĭl′dĕ
**Al′vin** ăl′vĭn
**Al·vi′se** *Ital.* äl·vē′zā
**Al′vord** ôl′vôrd, ăl′-, -vẽrd
**Al′win** ăl′wĭn; *Ger.* äl′vēn
**Am′a·bel** ăm′ȧ·bĕl
**A′ma′ble** *Fr.* ȧ′mȧ′bl′
**A′ma·de′o** *Ital.* ä′mä·dâ′ō; *Span.* ä′mä·thā′ō
**Am′a·de′us** ăm′ȧ·dē′ŭs—**A′ma·de′us** *Ger.* ä′mä·dā′ōōs; *Swed.* ȧ′mȧ·dā′ŭs
**A′ma′dieu′** *Fr.* ȧ′mȧ′dyû′
**Am′a·dis** ăm′ȧ·dĭs—**A′ma′dis′** *Fr.* ȧ′mȧ′dēs′
**A·ma′li·a** *Ger.* ä·mä′lē·ä; *Ital.* ä·mä′lyä
**A·ma′li·e** *Dan.* ȧ·mȧ′lē·ĕ; *Ger.* ä·mä′lē·ĕ
**A′mand′** *Fr.* ȧ′mäɴ′
**A·man′da** ȧ·măn′dȧ; *Ger.* ä·män′dä
**A′man′dine′** *Fr.* ȧ′mäɴ′dēn′
**A·man′dus** ȧ·măn′dŭs; *Ger.* ä·män′-dōōs
**A·ma′ra** *Ger.* ä·mä′rä
**Am′a·ri′ah** ăm′ȧ·rī′ȧ
**Am′a·sa** ăm′ȧ·sȧ, ȧ·mā′sȧ
**A′mau′ry′** *Fr.* ȧ′mô′rē′
**Am·bro′gio** *Ital.* äm·brô′jō
**Am′broise′** *Fr.* äɴ′brwȧz′
**Am′brose** ăm′brōz; *Du.* äm′brōs
**Am·bro′sio** äm·brō′syō
**Am·bro′si·us** ăm·brō′zhĭ·ŭs, -zhŭs; *Du.* äm·brō′sē·ûs; *Ger.* äm·brō′-zē·ōōs
**A′mé′dée′** *Fr.* ȧ′mā′dā′
**A′me·de′o** *Ital.* ä′mā·dâ′ō
**A·meen′** *Arab.* ä·mēn′
**A·mel′ia** ȧ·mēl′yȧ, -mē′lĭ·ȧ—**A·me′-lia** *Ital.* ä·mâ′lyä; *Span.* ä·mā′lyä
**A·me′li·e** *Ger.* ä·mā′lē·ĕ, ä′mā·lē
**A′mé′lie′** *Fr.* ȧ′mā′lē′
**A′me·li′ta** *Ital.* ä′mā·lē′tä
**A·mé′ri·co** *Span.* ä·mā′rē·kō
**A·mer′i·cus** ȧ·mĕr′ĭ·kŭs—**A·me′ri-cus** *Du.* ȧ·mā′rē·kûs
**A′me·ri′go** *Ital.* ä′mā·rē′gō
**Ames** āmz
**A′mi′** *Fr.* ȧ′mē′
**A′mi·as** ā′mĭ·ăs, ăm′ĭ-
**A·mi′co** *Ital.* ä·mē′kō
**Am′i·el** ăm′ĭ·ĕl, ā′mĭ·ĕl
**A·mil′ca·re** *Ital.* ä·mēl′kä·rā
**Ä·mi′li·us** *Ger.* â·mē′lē·ōōs
**A·min′** *Arab.* ä·mēn′
**Am′mi** ăm′ī
**A′mo·ry** ā′mō·rĭ
**A′mos** ā′mŏs; *Czech* ȧ′môs
**A′mour′** *Fr.* ȧ′mōōr′
**Am′schel** ăm′shĕl; *Ger.* äm′shĕl
**A′my** ā′mĭ—**A′my′** *Fr.* ȧ′mē′
**Am′zi** ăm′zī
**A′na** *Span.* ä′nä
**A′na′char′sis′** *Fr.* ȧ′nȧ′kȧr′sēs′
**A′nas′tase′** *Fr.* ȧ′nȧs′täz′
**An′as·ta′si·a** ăn′ăs·tā′shĭ·ȧ, -shȧ, -zhĭ·ȧ, -zhȧ—**A′na·sta′si·a** *Ger.* ä′nä·stä′zē·ä
**A′na·sta′sio** *Ital.* ä′nä·stä′zyō—**A′nas·ta′sio** *Span.* ä′näs·tä′syō
**An′as·ta′si·us** ăn′ăs·tā′shĭ·ŭs, -shŭs, -zhĭ·ŭs, -zhŭs—**A′na·sta′si·us** *Ger.* ä′nä·stä′zē·ōōs
**A·na·tol′** *Russ.* ŭ·nŭ·tôl′y′
**A′na′tole′** *Fr.* ȧ′nȧ′tôl′
**A·na·to′li** *Russ.* ŭ·nŭ·tô′lyû·ĭ
**An′crum** ăng′krŭm
**An′ders** *Dan.* ȧn′ẽrs; *Swed.* ȧn′dẽrs
**An′der·sen** *Dan.* ȧn′ẽr·s′n
**An′der·son** ăn′dẽr·s′n
**An·do** *Jap.* än·dō
**An′doche′** *Fr.* äɴ′dôsh′
**An′drás** *Hung.* ŏn′dräsh
**An′drault′** *Fr.* äɴ′drō′
**An′dré′** *Fr.* äɴ′drā′—**An·dré′** *Swed.* ȧn·drā′
**An·dre′a** *Ital.* än·drâ′ä
**An′dre·as** ăn′drē·ăs; *Lat.* ăn′drē·ăs, ăn·drē′ăs—**An·dre′as** *Dan.* ȧn-drē′ȧs; *Du.*, *Ger.*, *Norw.* än·drā′äs; *Mod. Grk.* än·thrā′äs; *Swed.* ȧn-drā′ȧs
**An′drée′** *Fr.* äɴ′drā′
**An·dre′e·vich** *Russ.* ŭn·dryā′yĕ·vyĭch
**An·drei′** *Bulg.* än·drĕ′ĭ; *Russ.* ŭn-dryā′ĭ
**An·dre′ie·vich** *Russ.* ŭn·dryā′yĕ-vyĭch
**An′drej** *Slovak* ȧn′drĕ·ĭ
**An·drés′** *Span.* än·drās′
**An·dreu′** *Span.* än·drā′ōō
**An′drew** ăn′drōō
**An′drewes, An′drews** ăn′drōōz
**An·dre′ye·vich** *Russ.* ŭn·dryā′yĕ-vyĭch
**An′dries** *Du.* än′drēs
**An′drus** ăn′drŭs
**An′drzej** *Pol.* än′jĕ·ē
**A′net′** *Fr.* ȧ′nĕ′
**Ange** *Fr.* äɴzh
**An′gel** ān′jĕl
**Án′gel** *Span.* äng′hĕl
**An′ge·la** ăn′jĕ·lȧ; *Ital.* än′jâ·lä
**An·gel′i·ca** ăn·jĕl′ĭ·kȧ—**An·ge′li·ca** *Ger.* äng·gā′lē·kä; *Ital.* än·jâ′lē·kä
**An·ge′li·co** *Ital.* än·jâ′lē·kō
**An·gel′i·cus** ăn·jĕl′ĭ·kŭs
**An′ge·li′na** ăn′jĕ·lē′nȧ
**An′gé′lique′** *Fr.* äɴ′zhā′lēk′
**An′gell** ān′jĕl
**An′ge·lo** ăn′jĕ·lō; *Ger.*, *Ital.* än′jâ·lō
**An′ge·lus** ăn′jĕ·lŭs
**An′gier** ăn′jẽr
**An′gio·lo** *Ital.* än′jō·lō
**An′gus** ăng′gŭs
**A·ní′bal** *Span.* ä·nē′bäl
**An′ice** ăn′ĭs
**A′ni·ce′to** *Ital.* ä′nē·châ′tō; *Span.* ä′nē·thā′tō, -sā′tō

**A·ni′ci·us** *Lat.* ȧ·nĭsh′ĭ·ŭs
**A·niel′lo** *Ital.* ä·nyĕl′lō
**A·ni′ka** *Russ.* ŭ·nyē′kŭ
**A·ni·ki′ta** *Russ.* ŭ·nyĭ·kyē′tŭ
**A·ni′si·mo·vich** ŭ·nyē′syĭ·mŭ·vyĭch
**A·ni′ta** ȧ·nē′tȧ; *Ger., Span.* ä·nē′tä
**Ann** ăn
**An′na** ăn′ȧ; *Du.* än′ä; *Ger.* än′ä; *Ital., Latvian, Pol.* än′nä; *Russ.* ȧn′nŭ; *Swed.* ȧn′nȧ—**An′na′** *Fr.* ȧn′nȧ′
**An′na·bel′la** ăn′ȧ·bĕl′ȧ
**An·nae′us** *Lat.* ă·nē′ŭs
**Anne** ăn; *Fr.* än, ȧn; *Swed.* ȧn—**An′ne** *Ger.* än′ĕ
**An′ne·ma·rie′** *Ger.* än′ĕ·mä·rē′
**Annes′ley** ănz′lĭ
**An·net′ta** ă·nĕt′ȧ; *Ital.* än·nāt′tä
**An·nette′** ă·nĕt′, ă-—**An′nette′** *Fr.* ȧ′nĕt′—**An·net′te** *Ger.* ä·nĕt′ĕ
**An′ni·a** *Lat.* ăn′ĭ·ȧ
**An′ni′bal′** *Fr.* ȧ′nē′bȧl′
**An·ni′ba·le** *Ital.* än·nē′bä·lā
**An′nie** ăn′ĭ; *Swed.* ȧn′nĭ
**An′ni·us** *Lat.* ăn′ĭ·ŭs
**An′nun·cia′ta** *Ital.* än′no͞on·chä′tä
**An·sa′no** *Ital.* än·sä′nō
**An′sel** ăn′s'l
**An′selm** ăn′sĕlm; *Ger.* än′zĕlm
**An′selme′** *Fr.* äɴ′sĕlm′
**An·sel′mo** *Ital.* än·sĕl′mō
**An′son** ăn′s'n
**An′stey** ăn′stĭ
**An′tal** *Hung.* ŏn′tŏl
**An·ta′nas** *Lith.* än·tä′näs
**An′te** *Yugo.* än′tĕ
**An′te·ro** *Finn.* ȧn′tĕ·rŏ—**An·te′ro** *Port.* ăɴn·tâ′ro͞o
**An′thelme′** *Fr.* äɴ′tĕlm′
**An·tho′nie** *Du.* än·tō′nē
**An·tho′nis, -nisz** *Du.* än·tō′nĭs
**An′tho·ny** ăn′thō·nĭ, -tô·nĭ—**An·tho′ny** *Du.* än·tō′nē
**An·ti·och′** *Russ.* ŭn·tyĭ·ôĸ′
**An′tioche′** *Fr.* äɴ′tyôsh′
**An·ti·po′vich** *Russ.* ŭn·tyĭ·pô′vyĭch
**An·tis′ti·us** *Lat.* ăn·tĭs′tĭ·ŭs, -chĭ·ŭs
**An′to** *Du.* än′tō
**An′toine** ăn′twăn—**An′toine′** *Fr.* äɴ′twȧn′
**An′toi·nette′** ăn′t(w)ŏ·nĕt′—**An′toi′nette′** *Fr.* äɴ′twȧ′nĕt′—**An′toi·net′te** *Ger.* än′tō·ä·nĕt′ĕ
**An′ton** ăn′t'n, -tŏn, -tōn; *Czech* ȧn′tôn; *Du., Estonian* än′tôn; *Ger.* ȧn′tōn; *Swed.* ȧn′tôn—**An·ton′** *Ital.* än·tôn′; *Russ.* ŭn·tôn′
**An·tón′** *Span.* än·tôn′
**An·to′ni** *Pol.* än·tô′nē
**An·to′ni·a** ăn·tō′nĭ·ȧ, -tōn′yȧ; *Ital.* än·tô′nyä; *Span.* än·tō′nyä—**An′to′nia′** *Fr.* äɴ′tô′nyȧ′
**An·to′ni·e** *Ger.* än·tō′nē·ĕ
**An′to′nin′** *Fr.* äɴ′tô′năɴ′
**An′to·nín** *Czech* ȧn′tô·nyēn
**An·to·ni′na** *Russ.* ŭn·tŭ·nyē′nŭ
**An′to·ni′nus** *Lat.* ăn′tō·nī′nŭs
**An·to′ni·o** ăn·tō′nĭ·ō, -tōn′yō; *Ger.* än·tō′nē·ō; *Ital.* än·tô′nyō; *Port.* ăɴn·tô′nyo͞o; *Span.* än·tō′nyō—**An′to′nio′** *Fr.* äɴ′tô′nyō′
**An·tô′ni·o** *Port.* ăɴn·tô′nyo͞o
**An·to′ni·os** *Mod. Grk.* än·dô′nyôs
**An·to′nisz** *Du.* än·tō′nĭs
**An·to′ni·us** ăn·tō′nĭ·ŭs, -tōn′yŭs; *Du.* än·tō′nē·ûs
**An·to·no·vich** *Russ.* ŭn·tô′nŭ·vyĭch
**An′to·ny** ăn′tō·nĭ—**An·to′ny** *Du.* än·tō′nē—**An′to′ny′** *Fr.* äɴ′tô′nē′
**An′toon** *Du.* än′tōn
**An′trim** ăn′trĭm
**Ant′ti** *Finn.* ȧnt′tĭ
**An′tun** *Yugo.* än′to͞on
**Ant′werp** ănt′wûrp
**An·zhe·li′ka** *Russ.* ŭn·zhĕ·lyē′kŭ
**A·o′nio** *Ital.* ä·ô′nyō
**A·po′li·na′ry** *Pol.* ä·pô′lē·nä′rĭ
**A′pol′li′naire′** *Fr.* ȧ′pô′lē′nâr′
**A·pol·lo′ni** *Russ.* ŭ·pŭl·lô′nyû·ĭ
**Ap′ol·lo′ni·us** ăp′ŏ·lō′nĭ·ŭs, -lōn′yŭs—**A′pol·lo′ni·us** *Ger.* ä′pô·lō′nē·o͞os
**A·pol·lo′no·vich** ŭ·pŭl·lô′nŭ·vyĭch
**A·po′sto·lo** *Ital.* ä·pôs′tō·lō
**Ap·pia′no** *Ital.* äp·pyä′nō
**Ap′pi·us** *Lat.* ăp′ĭ·ŭs
**Ap′ple·ton** ăp′'l·t'n, -tŭn
**Ap′po·lo′nia** *Pol.* äp′pô·lô′nyä
**Ap′pu·le′ius** *Lat.* ăp′ū·lē′yŭs
**Ap′thorp** ăp′thôrp
**Aq′ui·la** *Lat.* ăk′wĭ·lȧ
**Ar′a·bel′la** ăr′ȧ·bĕl′ȧ
**Ar′bo·gast** *Ger.* är′bō·gäst
**Ar·buth′not, Ar·buth′nott** är·bŭth′-nŭt, är′bŭth·nŏt
**Ar·can′ge·lo** *Ital.* är·kän′jā·lō
**Arch′dale** ärch′dāl
**Ar′cher** är′chẽr
**Ar′chey** är′chĭ
**Ar′chi·bald** är′chĭ·bôld, -b'ld
**Ar′chie** är′chĭ
**Ar′chi′mède′** *Fr.* ȧr′shē′mĕd′
**Ar′chi·me′des** är′kĭ·mē′dēz
**Ar′cisse′** *Fr.* ȧr′sēs′
**Ar·de′li·a** är·dē′lĭ·ȧ, -dēl′yȧ
**Ar′den** är′d'n
**A′rendt, A′rent** *Du.* ä′rĕnt
**Ar′e·tas** ăr′ĕ·tăs
**A′rey** *Ger.* ä′rī
**Ar′gen·ti′no** *Span.* är′hān·tē′nō
**A′rias** *Span.* ä′ryäs
**A′rild** *Dan.* ä′rēl
**Ar′i·o** ăr′ĭ·ō, är′-
**A′ri·star′co** *Ital.* ä′rē·stär′kō
**A′ris′tide′** *Fr.* ȧ′rēs′tēd′—**A·ri′sti·de** *Ital.* ä·rēs′tē·dā
**Ar′is·ti′des** ăr′ĭs·tī′dēz—**A′ris·ti′des** *Span.* ä′rēs·tē′thās
**A·ri·to·mo** *Jap.* ä·rē·tō·mō
**Ar·ka′de·vich** *Russ.* ŭr·kȧ′dyĕ·vyĭch
**Ar·ka′di** *Russ.* ŭr·kȧ′dyû·ĭ
**Ar′kle** är′k'l
**Ar′koll** är′kŏl
**Ark′wright** ärk′rīt
**Ar′la·ni·bä′us** *Ger.* är′lä·nē·bâ′o͞os
**Ar′ling·ton** är′lĭng·tŭn
**Ar′lo** är′lō
**Ar′man** är′măn—**Ar′man′** *Fr.* ȧr′-mäɴ′
**Ar′mand** *Ger.* är′mänt—**Ar·mand′** *Rum.* är·mänd′—**Ar′mand′** *Fr.* ȧr′mäɴ′
**Ar·man′do** *Ital.* är·män′dō; *Span.* är·män′dō
**Ar′mar** är′mẽr
**Ar′mas** *Finn.* ȧr′mȧs
**Ar′mau′er** *Norw.* är′mou′ẽr
**Ar·min′** *Ger.* är·mēn′
**Ár′min** *Hung.* är′mĭn
**Ar·min′da** är·mĭn′dȧ
**Ar′mi·stead** är′mĭ·stĕd, -stĭd
**Ar′mi·tage** är′mĭ·tĭj
**Ar′mos** *Finn.* ȧr′mŏs
**Ar′mour** är′mẽr
**Arms** ärmz
**Arm′strong** ärm′strŏng
**Ar′nail′** *Fr.* ȧr′nȧ′y′
**Ar·nal′dus** *Lat.* är·năl′dŭs
**Ar′naud′** *Fr.* ȧr′nō′
**Ar′nault′** *Fr.* ȧr′nō′
**Ar′naut′** *Fr.* ȧr′nō′
**Arndt** *Ger.* ärnt
**Ar′ne** *Norw.* är′nĕ
**Ár′ni** *Icel.* oud′'n·ĭ
**Ar′no** *Ger.* är′nō
**Ar′nold** är′n'ld; *Dan.* är′nŏl; *Du.* är′nŏlt; *Ger.* är′nōlt; *Norw.* är′nŏl—**Ar′nold′** *Fr.* ȧr′nôld′
**Ar·nol′do·vich** *Russ.* ŭr·nôl′y'·dŭ·vyĭch
**Ar·nol′dus** *Du.* är·nŏl′dûs
**Ar′nolt** *Ger.* är′nōlt
**Ar′not, Ar′nott** är′nŭt, -nŏt
**Ar′nould′** *Fr.* ȧr′no͞o′
**Ar′nulf** *Ger.* är′no͝olf; *Norw.* är′no͝olf
**Ar·nul′fo** *Span.* är·no͞ol′fō
**A′ron** *Latvian* ä′rwôn
**Ar·ri′go** *Ital.* är·rē′gō
**Ar′sène′** *Fr.* ȧr′sân′
**Ar·se′ni** *Russ.* ŭr·syā′nyû·ĭ
**Ar·se′nio** *Ital.* är·sâ′nyō; *Span.* är·sā′nyō
**Ar′senne′** *Fr.* ȧr′sĕn′
**Ar′te·mas** är′tē·măs
**Ar′te·mis′i·a** är′tē·mĭz′ĭ·ȧ, -mĭsh′ĭ·ȧ
**Ar′te·mus** är′tē·mŭs
**Ar′tha** *Ger.* är′tä
**Ar′thur** är′thẽr; *Ger.* är′to͝or; *Hung.* ŏr′to͝or—**Ar′thur′** *Fr.* ȧr′tür′—**Ar·thur′** *Port.* ẽr·to͞or′
**Ar′tur** *Ger.* är′to͝or; *Pol.* är′to͝or; *Swed.* ȧr′tŭr—**Ar·tur′** *Port.* ẽr-to͞or′; *Russ.* ŭr·to͞or′
**Ar·tu′ro** *Ital.* är·to͞o′rō; *Port.* ẽr-to͞o′ro͞o; *Span.* är·to͞o′rō
**Ar′tus** *Du.* är′tûs—**Ar′tus′** *Fr.* ȧr′-tüs′
**Ar′vid′** *Swed.* ȧr′vĭd′
**A′ry′** *Fr.* ȧ′rē′
**A′sa** ā′sȧ
**A′sa·hel** ā′sȧ·hĕl, ăs′ȧ-, -hĕl, ā′s'l
**A′saph** ā′săf, -săf, ăs′ăf, ăz′ăf
**As′bur′y** ăz′bĕr′ĭ, -bẽr·ĭ, -brĭ
**A·sca′nio** *Ital.* äs·kä′nyō
**As′ger** *Dan.* ȧs′kẽr
**Ash** ăsh
**Ash′bel** ăsh′bĕl
**Ash′bur′ton** ăsh′bûr′t'n
**Ash′bur′y** ăsh′bĕr′ĭ, -bẽr·ĭ, -brĭ
**Ash′down** ăsh′doun
**Ash′er** ăsh′ẽr
**Ashe′ton** ăsh′tŭn
**A·shi·hei** *Jap.* ä·shē·hā
**Ash′ley** ăsh′lĭ

**Ash′man** ăsh′măn
**Ash′ton** ăsh′tŭn
**Ash′ur** ăsh′ẽr
**Ash′ville** ăsh′vĭl
**A·sin′i·us** *Lat.* ȧ·sĭn′ĭ·ŭs
**As′kew** ăs′kū
**As′mus** *Dan.* ȧs′mōōs; *Ger.* äs′mōōs
**As′mus·sen** *Dan.* ȧs′mōō·s'n
**Asshe′ton** ăsh′tŭn
**Ass′mann** *Ger.* äs′män
**Ast′ley** ăst′lĭ
**As′ton** ăs′tŭn
**As′trid** *Dan.* ȧs′trĕth; *Swed.* ȧs′trĭd
**A′ta·na′sio** *Ital.* ä′tä·nä′zyô; *Span.* ä′tä·nä′syō
**A′tha′nase′** *Fr.* ȧ′tȧ′näz′
**A′tha·na′sios** *Mod. Grk.* ä′thä·nä′syôs
**Ath′a·na′si·us** ăth′ȧ·nā′shĭ·ŭs, -sĭ·ŭs, -shŭs—**A′tha·na′si·us** *Ger.* ä′tä·nä′zē·ōōs
**Ath′el·stane** ăth′ĕl·stān
**A′thé′na′ïs′** *Fr.* ȧ′tā′nȧ′ēs′
**Ath′er·ton** ăth′ẽr·t'n, -tŭn
**Ath′ole** ăth′ŭl
**A·til′i·us** *Lat.* ȧ·tĭl′ĭ·ŭs
**At′kins** ăt′kĭnz
**At′kin·son** ăt′kĭn·s'n
**At′lee** ăt′lē; -lē
**At′ter·bur′y** ăt′ẽr·bĕr′ĭ, -bẽr·ĭ, -brĭ
**At·ti′lio** *Ital.* ät·tē′lyô
**Att′wood, At′wood** ăt′wŏŏd
**Au′bert′** *Fr.* ō′bâr′
**Au′brey** ô′brĭ
**Auck′land** ôk′lănd
**Au′drey** ô′drĭ
**Auge** *Fr.* ōzh
**Au′gier′** *Fr.* ō′zhyā′
**Au′gur** ô′gẽr
**Au′gust** ô′gŭst; *Dan., Finn., Ger.* ou′gŏŏst; *Pol.* ou′gōōst; *Swed.* ou′gŭst
**Au·gus′ta** ô·gŭs′tȧ; *Span.* ou·gōōs′tä —**Au·gu′sta** *Ger.* ou·gōōs′tä; *Ital.* ou·gōōs′tä—**Au′gus′ta′** *Fr.* ō′güs′tȧ′
**Au′guste′** *Fr.* ō′güst′—**Au·gu′ste** *Ger.* ou·gōōs′tĕ
**Au·gus′tin** ô·gŭs′tĭn—**Au′gus·tin** *Czech* ou′gōōs·tyĭn—**Au′gu·stin** *Du.* ou′gü·stĭn—**Au′gus′tin′** ō′güs′tăN′ —**Au′gu·stin′** *Ger.* ou′gōōs·tēn′; *Swed.* ou′gŭ·stēn′
**Au′gus·ti′nas** *Lith.* ou′gōōs·tĭ′näs
**Au′gus·tine** ô′gŭs·tēn, ô·gŭs′tĭn—**Au′gus′tine′** *Fr.* ō′güs′tēn′
**Au′gu·sti′no** *Ital.* ou′gōōs·tē′nô
**Au′gus·ti′nus** *Lat.* ô′gŭs·tī′nŭs
**Au·gu′sto** *Ital.* ou·gōōs′tô—**Au·gus′to** *Port.* ou·gōōsh′tōō, (*Braz.*) -gōōs′-; *Span.* ou·gōōs′tō
**Au·gus′tus** ô·gŭs′tŭs—**Au·gu′stus** *Ger.* ou·gōōs′tōōs
**Au′lus** *Lat.* ô′lŭs
**Au·rel′** *Ger.* ou·rāl′
**Au′rèle′** *Fr.* ō′rĕl′
**Au′re·lia′no** *Span.* ou′rā·lyä′nō
**Au·re′lio** *Ital.* ou·râ′lyô; *Span.* ou·rā′lyō
**Au·re′li·us** ô·rē′lĭ·ŭs, -rēl′yŭs; *Ger.* ou·rā′lē·ōōs
**Au·re′o·lus** *Lat.* ô·rē′ô·lŭs
**Au′ro·bin′do** *Bengali* ô′rô·bĭn′dô
**Au·ro′ra** ô·rō′rȧ; *Ger.* ou·rō′rä; *Span.* ou·rō′rä
**Au′rore′** *Fr.* ō′rôr′
**Au·sí′as** *Span.* ou·sē′äs
**Au′sone′** *Fr.* ō′zôn′
**Au·so′nio** *Ital.* ou·zô′nyô
**Aus′ten** ôs′tĕn, -tĭn
**Aus′tin** ôs′tĭn
**A′ve·li′no** *Span.* ä′vā·lē′nō
**A′ver·y** ā′vẽr·ĭ
**Av′gou·sti′nos** *Mod. Grk.* äv′gōō·stē′nôs
**Av′gust** *Yugo.* äv′gōōst
**Av·gus·tin′** *Russ.* ŭv·gōōs·tyēn′
**A·vid′i·us** *Lat.* ȧ·vĭd′ĭ·ŭs
**Á′vi·la** *Span.* ä′vē·lä
**A·vra·am′** *Russ.* ŭ·vrŭ·ȧm′
**Ax′el** ăk′s'l; *Dan.* ȧk′sĕl; *Ger.* äk′sĕl; *Swed.* ȧk′sĕl
**Ax′ton** ăks′tŭn
**Ayer** âr
**Ayl′mer** āl′mẽr
**Ay′lott** ā′lŏt, -lŭt
**Ayl′ward** āl′wẽrd
**Ayres** ârz
**Ayr′ton** âr′t'n
**Ays′cough** ăs′kū, ăs′kŭ, ās′kŭf, ās′kō
**Az′a·ri′ah** ăz′ȧ·rī′ȧ

**Bab′bitt** băb′ĭt
**Bab′cock** băb′kŏk
**Bab′ing·ton** băb′ĭng·tŭn
**Bac′chus** băk′ŭs
**Bac′cio** *Ital.* bät′chô
**Bache** bāch
**Back′house** băk′hous
**Back′us** băk′ŭs
**Ba′con** bā′kŭn
**Bad′de·ley** băd′'l·ĭ
**Badg′er** băj′ẽr
**Baer′mann** bâr′măn
**Bag′nall** băg′n'l
**Bag′nell** băg′n'l
**Bag′ot** băg′ŭt
**Bag′shaw, Bag′shawe** băg′shô
**Ba·ha′dur** *Hind.* bȧ·hä′dŏŏr
**Bai′ley** bā′lĭ
**Bail′lie** bā′lĭ
**Bain′bridge** bān′brĭj
**Baird** bârd
**Ba′ker** bā′kẽr
**Bak′huis** *Du.* bäk′hois
**Balch** bôlch, bôlsh
**Bal′das·sa′re, -sar′re** *Ital.* bäl′däs·sä′râ, -sär′râ
**Bal′do·me′ro** *Span.* bäl′dô·mā′rō
**Bal′du·in** *Ger.* bäl′dōō·ēn
**Bal′dur** *Ger.* bäl′dŏŏr
**Bald′win** bôld′wĭn
**Bal′four** băl′fŏŏr
**Ba·lil′la** *Ital.* bä·lēl′lä
**Bá′lint** *Hung.* bä′lĭnt
**Bal′iol** bāl′yŭl
**Ball** bôl
**Bal′lard** băl′ẽrd
**Bal′lin·ger** băl′ĭn·jẽr
**Bal′ling·ton** băl′ĭng·tŭn
**Bal′loch** băl′ŭκ
**Bal·lou′** bȧ·lōō′
**Bal′ta·sar′** *Span.* bäl′tä·sär′
**Bal·tha′sar** băl·thā′zẽr, -thăz′ẽr—**Bal′tha′sar′** *Fr.* bȧl′tȧ′zȧr′—**Bal′tha·sar** *Du.* bäl′tȧ·sär; *Ger.* bäl′tä·zär
**Bal·tha′zar** băl·thā′zẽr, -thăz′ẽr—**Bal′tha′zar′** *Fr.* bȧl′tȧ′zȧr′
**Bal′zac′** *Fr.* bȧl′zȧk′
**Bam′fylde** băm′fēld
**Ban** băn
**Ban′as·tre** băn′ăs·tẽr
**Ban′croft** băn′krŏft, băng′-
**Ban′is·ter** băn′ĭs·tẽr
**Bank′head** băngk′hĕd
**Banks** băngks
**Ban′na·tyne** băn′ȧ·tīn
**Ban′ner·man** băn′ẽr·măn
**Ban′nis·ter** băn′ĭs·tẽr
**Bap′tist** băp′tĭst—**Bap·tist′** *Du., Ger.* bäp·tĭst′
**Bap·tis′ta** băp·tĭs′tȧ; *Flem.* bäp·tĭs′tȧ; *Port.* bȧ·tēsh′tȧ, (*Braz.*) -tēs′-
**Bap′tiste′** *Fr.* bȧ′tēst′
**Bar′ba·ra** bär′bȧ·rȧ; *Ger., Ital.* bär′bä·rä—**Bar·ba′ra** *Russ.* bŭr·bȧ′rŭ
**Bar′bee** bär′bē, -bē
**Bar′ber** bär′bẽr
**Bar′bour** bär′bẽr
**Bar′bra** *Norw.* bär′brä
**Bar′bu** *Rum.* bär′bōō
**Bar′by** bär′bĭ
**Bar′clay** bär′klĭ, -klā
**Ba′rend** *Du.* bä′rĕnt
**Bar′ing** bâr′ĭng
**Bar′ker** bär′kẽr
**Bar′low** bär′lō
**Bar′na·ba** *Ital.* bär′nä·bä
**Bar′na·be** bär′nȧ·bē
**Bar′na′bé′** *Fr.* bȧr′nȧ′bā′
**Bar′na·by** bär′nȧ·bĭ
**Bar′nard** bär′nẽrd
**Bar′nas** ?bär′năs
**Barnes** bärnz
**Bar′net** bär′nĕt, -nĭt
**Bar′nett** bär′nĕt, -nĭt, bär·nĕt′
**Bar′ney** bär′nĭ
**Barn′well** bärn′wĕl, -wĕl
**bar′on** băr′ŭn—**ba′ron′** *Fr.* bȧ′rôN′
**Bar′on** băr′ŭn
**ba·ro′ne** *Ital.* bä·rō′nâ
**bar′on·ess** băr′ŭn·ĕs, -ĭs
**ba′ronne′** *Fr.* bȧ′rôn′
**Barr** bär
**Bar′ret, Bar′rett** băr′ĕt, -ĭt
**Bar′ring·ton** băr′ĭng·tŭn
**Bar′ron** băr′ŭn
**Bar′ry** băr′ĭ
**Bar′stow** bär′stō
**Bart** bärt
**Bar′tel** *Yugo.* bär′tĕl
**Bar′thel** *Ger.* bär′tĕl
**Bar′thé′le·mi′** *Fr.* bȧr′tāl′mē′
**Bar′thé′le·my′** *Fr.* bȧr′tāl′mē′
**Bar′thold** *Du.* bär′tôlt; *Ger.* bär′tôlt
**Bar·thol′o·mae′us** *Lat.* bär·tŏl′ô·mē′ŭs, -thŏl′-
**Bar′tho·lo·mä′us** *Du.* bär′tô·lô·mā′ûs; *Ger.* bär′tô·lô·mâ′ōōs
**Bar′tho·lo·meu′** *Port.* bȧr′tōō·lōō·mā′ōō
**Bar′tho·lo·me′us** *Du.* bär′tô·lô·mā′ûs

**Bar·thol′o·mew** bär·thŏl′ō·mū
**Bar′tle** bär′t'l
**Bart′lett, Bart′lette** bärt′lĕt, -lĭt
**Bart′ley** bärt′lĭ
**Bart′lit** bärt′lĭt
**Bar′to·lo·mé′** *Span.* bär′tō·lō·mā′
**Bar′to·lo·me′o** *Ital.* bär′tō·lō·mâ′ō
**Bar′to·lo·meu′** *Port.* bär′tōō·lōō-mā′ōō
**Bar′to·lom·me′o** *Ital.* bär′tō·lōm-mâ′ō
**Bar′ton** bär′t'n
**Ba′ruch** *Du.* bä′rōōK
**Bar′wick** băr′ĭk
**Bar·zil′la·i** bär·zĭl′â·ī, -zĭl′ī
**Bas′com** băs′kŭm
**Bash′ford** băsh′fẽrd
**Bas′il** băz′ĭl, -'l, băs′-
**Ba′sile′** *Fr.* bä′zēl′
**Ba·si′lio** *Ital.* bä·zē′lyō
**Ba·sí′lio** *Port.* bȧ·zē′lyōō
**Ba·si′li·us** *Ger.* bä·zē′lē·ōōs, bä′zē-lē′ōōs—**Ba·sil′i·us** *Lat.* bȧ·sĭl′-ĭ·ŭs, -zĭl′-
**Bass** băs
**Bas′sett** băs′ĕt, -ĭt
**Ba·stia′no** *Ital.* bäs·tyä′nō
**Bas′tien′** *Fr.* bȧs′tyăN′
**Bat** băt
**Bate** bāt
**Bate′man** bāt′măn
**Bates** bāts
**Bat′ter·son** băt′ẽr·s'n
**Bat′tey** băt′ĭ
**Bat·ti′sta** *Ital.* bät·tēs′tä
**Bau·tis′ta** *Span.* bou·tēs′tä
**Bax′ter** băks′tẽr
**Bay′ard** bī′ärd, -ẽrd, bā′-
**Bayle** bāl
**Bayles** bālz
**Bay′ley** bā′lĭ
**Bay′nard** bā′nẽrd, -närd
**Baz′ley** băz′lĭ
**Beach** bēch
**Beale** bēl
**Be′a·trice** bē′ȧ·trĭs—**Be′a·tri′ce** *Ger.* bā′ä·trē′sĕ; *Ital.* bā′ä·trē′chā
**Be′a·trix** bē′ȧ·trĭks—**Be·a′trix** *Ger.* bā·ä′trĭks; *Lat.* bē·ā′trĭks
**Beat′tie** bē′tĭ
**Be·a′tus** *Ger.* bā·ä′tōōs; *Lat.* bē·ā′tŭs
**Beau′champ** bē′chăm
**Beau′fort** bō′fẽrt, bū′-
**Beau′mont** bō′mŏnt, -mŭnt
**Beau′voir** bē′vẽr, bō′vwär′
**Beck** bĕk
**Beck′et** bĕk′ĕt, -ĭt
**Beck′les** bĕk′'lz
**Bede** bēd
**Bed′ford** bĕd′fẽrd
**Be′dřich** bĕ′dẽr·zhĭK
**Bee′be, Bee′bee** bē′bē
**Bee′cher** bē′chẽr
**Beer** *Ger.* bār
**Beete** bēt
**Bee′ver** bē′vẽr
**Beh·ram′ji** *Parsi* bā·räm′jē
**Beil′by** ?bēl′bĭ
**Bel** bĕl
**Be′la** bē′lȧ
**Bé′la** *Hung.* bā′lŏ
**Bel′ding** bĕl′dĭng
**Bel′fort** bĕl′fẽrt
**Be′li·sa′rio** *Ital.* bā′lē·zä′ryō; *Span.* bā′lē·sä′ryō
**Bel′knap** bĕl′năp
**Bell** bĕl
**Bel′la** bĕl′ȧ; *Ger.* bĕl′ä; *Ital.* bĕl′lä
**Bel′la·my** bĕl′ȧ·mĭ
**Bel′las** bĕl′ăs
**Belle** bĕl
**Bel′lew** bĕl′ū, bē·lōō′, bē·lū′
**Bel′ton** bĕl′t'n, -tŭn
**Bel·trán′** *Span.* bĕl·trän′
**Bel′va** bĕl′vȧ
**ben** *Heb.* bĕn
**Ben** bĕn
**Be′ne·det′to** *Ital.* bā′nā·dāt′tō
**Ben′e·dict** bĕn′ē·dĭkt, *Brit. also* bĕn′ĭt—**Be′ne·dict** *Du.* bā′nē·dĭkt; *Ger.* bā′nā·dĭkt
**Bé′né′dict′** *Fr.* bā′nā′dēkt′
**Ben′e·dic′tus** *Lat.* bĕn′ē·dĭk′tŭs
**Be′ne·dikt** *Ger.* bā′nā·dĭkt
**Be′ne·dik′tus** *Ger.* bā′nā·dĭk′tōōs
**Benge** bĕnj
**Bengt** *Swed.* bĕngt
**Bengts′son** *Swed.* bĕngt′sôn
**Bé′ni** *Hung.* bā′nĭ
**Be′nia·mi′no** *Ital.* bā′nyä·mē′nō
**Bé′nigne′** *Fr.* bā′nēn′y′
**Be·nig′no** *Span.* bā·nēg′nō
**Be·nig′nus** bē·nĭg′nŭs; *Dan.* bĕ·nĕg′-nōōs; *Ger.* bā·nĭg′nōōs
**Be·ni′to** *Ital.* bā·nē′tō; *Span.* -tō
**Ben′ja·mim′** *Port.* bāN′zhȧ·mēN′
**Ben′ja·min** bĕn′jȧ·mĭn; *Du.* bĕn′yȧ-mĭn; *Ger.* bĕn′yä·mēn; *Hung.* bĕn′-yō·mĭn—**Ben′ja′min′** *Fr.* băN′-zhȧ′măN′
**Benn** bĕn
**Ben′net, Ben′nett** bĕn′ĕt, -ĭt
**Ben′ning** bĕn′ĭng
**Ben′no** *Ger.* bĕn′ō; *Russ.* bân′nō
**Be·noît′** *Fr.* bē·nwȧ′
**Be·noîte′** *Fr.* bē·nwȧt′
**Ben′o′ni** bĕn′ō′nī
**Be·noz′zo** *Ital.* bā·nôt′tsō
**Ben′son** bĕn′s'n
**Ben′tham** bĕn′thăm
**Bent′ley** bĕnt′lĭ
**Ben′to** *Port.* bāNn′tōō
**Ben′ton** bĕn′t'n, -tŭn
**Ben′ve·nu′to** *Ital.* bān′vā·nōō′tō
**Be′rend** *Ger.* bā′rĕnt
**Ber′es·ford** bĕr′ĭz·fẽrd, bĕr′ĭs-
**Ber′gen** bûr′gĕn
**Be·ri′ah** bē·rī′ȧ
**Berke′ley** bûrk′lĭ, *Brit. usu.* bärk′-
**Ber′na·bé′** *Span.* bĕr′nä·bā′
**Ber′na·bò′** *Ital.* bār′nä·bô′
**Ber′na·dotte** bûr′nȧ·dŏt
**Ber·nal′** *Span.* bĕr·näl′
**Ber′nard** bûr′närd, -nẽrd, bẽr·närd′, bûr·närd′; *Du.* bĕr′närt; *Pol.* bĕr′-närt—**Ber′nard′** *Fr.* bĕr′nȧr′
**Ber·nar·dim′** *Port.* bẽr·nẽr·dēN′
**Ber′nar·di′no** *Ital.* bār′när·dē′nō; *Span.* bĕr′när·thē′nō—**Ber·nar·di′-no** *Port.* bẽr·nẽr·dē′nōō
**Ber·nar′do** *Ital.* bār·när′dō; *Port.* bẽr·nȧr′dōō; *Span.* bĕr·när′thō
**Ber·nar′do·vich** *Russ.* byẽr·nȧr′dŭ-vyĭch
**Ber·nat′** *Catalan* bĕr·nät′
**Ber′nay** ?bûr′nā, ?bẽr·nā′
**Bern′hard** bûr′närd, bûrn′härd; *Dan.* bĕrn′härt; *Du.* bĕrn′härt; *Ger.* bĕrn′härt; *Swed.* bâr′nȧrd
**Bern′hardt** bûrn′härt
**Ber′nice** bûr′nĭs, bẽr·nēs′, bûr-, bẽr-
**Bernt** *Ger.* bĕrnt; *Norw.* bărnt
**Ber′nulf** bûr′nŭlf
**Ber′rie·dale** bĕr′ĭ·dāl
**Ber′ri·en** bĕr′ĭ·ĕn
**Ber′ry** bĕr′ĭ
**Ber′ry·man** bĕr′ĭ·măn
**Bert** bûrt; *Ger.* bĕrt
**Ber′ta** bûr′tȧ; *Ger.* bĕr′tä
**Ber′tel** *Dan.* băr′tĕl
**Ber′tha** bûr′thȧ; *Ger.* bĕr′tä
**Berthe** *Fr.* bĕrt
**Ber′thold** *Ger.* bĕr′tôlt—**Ber′thold′** *Fr.* bĕr′tôld′
**Ber′tho′let′** *Fr.* bĕr′tô′lĕ′
**Ber′tie** bûr′tĭ
**Ber·ti′ta** bẽr·tē′tȧ, bûr-
**Ber′told, Ber′tolt** *Ger.* bĕr′tôlt
**Ber′ton** bûr′t'n—**Ber′ton′** *Fr.* bĕr′-tôN′
**Ber′tram** bûr′trăm
**Ber′trand** bûr′trănd—**Ber′trand′** *Fr.* bĕr′träN′
**Ber′wick** bĕr′ĭk
**Bess** bĕs
**Bes′sie** bĕs′ĭ
**Be′thune** bē′t'n
**Bet′je** *Du.* bĕt′yĕ
**Bet′sy** bĕt′sĭ
**Bet·ti′na** bĕ·tē′nȧ; *Ger.* bĕ·tē′nä
**Bet·ti′no** *Ital.* bāt·tē′nō
**Bet′ton** bĕt′'n
**Betts** bĕts
**Bet′ty** bĕt′ĭ
**Beu′lah** bū′lȧ
**Bev′an** bĕv′ăn
**Bev′er·ley, Bev′er·ly** bĕv′ẽr·lĭ
**Bev′il** bĕv′'l, -ĭl
**Bhim′rao′** *Marathi* bēm′rä′ōō
**Bhu′la·bhai′** *Gujarati* bōō′lȧ·bä′ĭ, -bī′
**Bian′ca** *Ital.* byäng′kä
**Bibb** bĭb
**Bib′bins** bĭb′ĭnz
**Bick′er·steth** bĭk′ẽr·stĕth, -stĭth
**Bick′er·ton** bĭk′ẽr·t'n, -tŭn
**Bick′ford** bĭk′fẽrd
**Bick′nell** bĭk′n'l
**Bid′dell** bĭd′'l
**Bid′dulph** bĭd′'lf, -ŭlf
**Bid′well** bĭd′wĕl, -wĕl
**Bien′ai′mé′** *Fr.* byăN′nĕ′mā′
**Bien′ve·nu′** *Fr.* byăNv′nü′
**Big′e·low** bĭg′ē·lō
**Big′ham** bĭg′ăm
**Bill** bĭl
**Bil′lie** bĭl′ĭ
**Bil′lings** bĭl′ĭngz
**Bil′ly** bĭl′ĭ
**Bing′ham** bĭng′ăm
**Bin′ning** bĭn′ĭng
**Bi′on** bī′ŏn
**Birch** bûrch

**Bir′chard** bûr′chẽrd
**Bird** bûrd
**Birds′eye′** bûrdz′ī′
**Bird′wood′** bûrd′wo͝od′
**Birge** bûrj
**Birk′beck** bûr(k)′bĕk
**Bir′ket** bûr′kĕt, -kĭt
**Bir′ney** bûr′nĭ
**Bi′rô** *Hung.* bĭ′rō
**Bish′op** bĭsh′ŭp
**Bis′sell** bĭs′′l
**Bis′sett** bĭs′ĕt, -ĭt
**Bis′sot′** *Fr.* bē′sō′
**Björn** *Norw.* byûrn
**Björns′son** *Swed.* byûrn′sôn
**Björn′stjer′ne** *Norw.* byûrn′styâr′nĕ
**Black** blăk
**Black′er** blăk′ẽr
**Black′ford** blăk′fẽrd
**Black′ie** blăk′ĭ
**Black′man** blăk′măn
**Black′well** blăk′wĕl, -wĕl
**Blaine** blān
**Blair** blâr
**Blaise** *Fr.* blâz
**Blake** blāk
**Blan′chard** blăn′chẽrd, -shẽrd
**Blanche** blȧnch; *Fr.* bläNsh
**Bland** blănd
**Blan′ford** blăn′fẽrd
**Blas** *Span.* bläs
**Bled′soe** blĕd′sō
**Bleeck′er** blēk′ẽr
**Bliss** blĭs
**Blood** blŭd
**Bloom′field** blo͞om′fēld
**Blos′si·us** *Lat.* blŏs′ĭ·ŭs
**Blount** blŭnt
**Blythe** blīth
**Bo** *Swed.* bo͞o
**Board′man** bōrd′măn
**Bob** bŏb
**Bob′by** bŏb′ĭ
**Boc·cac′cio** *Ital.* bôk·kät′chō
**Bo·dae′us** *Du.* bô·dā′ûs
**Bod′ham** bŏd′ăm
**Bo′do** *Ger.* bō′dō
**Bo·e′ti·us** *Du.* bô·ā′tē·ûs
**Bog′dan** *Bulg.* bôg′dän; *Pol.* bôg′dän —**Bog·dan′** *Rum.* bŏg·dän′; *Russ.* bŭg·dàn′
**Bo′gert** ?bō′gẽrt
**Bo′gis·law** *Ger.* bō′gĭs·läf
**Bo′gu·mil** *Ger.* bō′go͞o·mēl
**Bo·gu′mił** *Pol.* bô·go͞o′mēl
**Bohn** bōn
**Bo′hu·slav** *Czech* bô′ho͞o·sláf
**Boies** boiz
**Bo·le′sław** *Pol.* bô·lĕ′släf
**Bol′i·var** bŏl′ĭ·vẽr
**Bol′ler** bŏl′ẽr
**Bol′ling** bōl′ĭng
**Bol′ton** bōl′t′n, -tŭn
**Bom·ba′stus** *Ger.* bôm·bäs′to͝os
**Bon** *Fr.* bôN
**Bo′na** *Ger.* bō′nä
**Bon′a·my** bŏn′ȧ·mĭ
**Bo′na·parte** bō′nȧ·pärt
**Bon′ar** bŏn′ẽr
**Bo′na·ven·tu′ra** *Ger.* bō′nä·vĕn·to͞o′- rä; *Ital.* bô′nä·vȧn·to͞o′rä
**Bon′a·ven′ture** bŏn′ȧ·vĕn′tūr—**Bo′-na′ven′ture′** *Fr.* bô′nȧ′väN′tür′
**Bo′na·wen·tu′ra** *Pol.* bô′nä·vĕn-to͞o′rä
**Bond** bŏnd
**Bon′i·face** bŏn′ĭ·fās—**Bo′ni′face′** *Fr.* bô′nē′fás′
**Bo′ni·fa′cio** *Ital.* bō′nē·fä′chō
**Bo·ni·fá′cio** *Port.* bo͞o·nē·fá′syo͞o
**Bon′i·fa′ci·us** bŏn′ĭ·fā′shĭ·ŭs—**Bo′ni-fa′ci·us** *Ger.* bō′nē·fä′tsē·o͞os
**Bon·nell′** bŏ·nĕl′
**Bon′ne·vie** *Norw.* bŏn′nĕ·vē
**Bon′not′** *Fr.* bô′nō′
**Boog** bōg
**Book′er** bo͝ok′ẽr
**Boor′man** bo͝or′măn
**Booth** bo͞oth, *Brit. usually* bo͞oth
**Boott** bo͞ot
**Bor′den** bôr′d′n
**Bo′ris** bō′rĭs, bŏr′ĭs—**Bo·ris′** *Bulg.* bô·rĭs′, bô′rĭs; *Russ.* bŭ·ryĕs′
**Bo·ri′so·vich** *Russ.* bŭ·ryē′sŭ·vyĭch
**Bor′lase** bôr′lăs
**Bor′ne·mann** *Norw.* bŏr′nĕ·män
**Bör′ri·es** *Ger.* bûr′ē·ĕs
**Borth′wick** bôrth′wĭk
**Bos′well** bŏz′wĕl, -wĕl
**Bos′wood** bŏz′wo͝od
**Bo′tho** *Ger.* bō′tō
**Bots′ford** bŏts′fẽrd
**Bou′chard′** *Fr.* bo͞o′shár′
**Bou′det′** *Fr.* bo͞o′dĕ′
**Bough′ton** bou′t′n
**Bourke** bûrk
**Bou′ver·ie** bo͞o′vẽr·ĭ
**Bow′ditch** bou′dĭch
**Bowd′ler** boud′lẽr
**Bow′en** bō′ĕn
**Bow′ers** bou′ẽrz
**Bowes** bōz
**Bow′ie** bo͞o′ĭ, bō′ĭ
**Bowles** bōlz
**Bow′ling** bō′lĭng
**Bow′man** bō′măn
**Bowne** boun
**Bow′yer** bō′yẽr
**Boyce** bois
**Boyd** boid
**Boyle** boil
**Boyn′ton** boin′t′n, -tŭn
**Bo′že·na** *Czech* bô′zhĕ·nȧ
**Brab′a·zon** brăb′ȧ·z′n
**Brace** brās
**Brack′en** brăk′ĕn
**Brack′ett** brăk′ĕt, -ĭt
**Brad′ford** brăd′fẽrd
**Brad′ley** brăd′lĭ
**Brad′shaw** brăd′shô
**Brad′street** brăd′strēt
**Brad′war·dine** brăd′wẽr·dēn
**Bragg** brăg
**Braid** brād
**Brai′nard** brā′nẽrd
**Brai′nerd** brā′nẽrd
**Braith′waite** brāth′wāt
**Bram** brăm
**Bram′well** brăm′wĕl, -wĕl
**Branch** brȧnch
**Brand, Brande** brănd
**Bran′der** brăn′dẽr
**Bran′don** brăn′dŭn
**Bran′dreth** brăn′drĕth, -drĭth
**Bran′ford** brăn′fẽrd
**Bran′ko** *Yugo.* brän′kō
**Bran′ston** brăn′stŭn
**Brant** brănt
**Brant′ley** brănt′lĭ
**Bran′well** brăn′wĕl, -wĕl
**Bran′white** brăn′hwīt
**Bras′sey** brăs′ĭ
**Brau′lio** *Span.* brou′lyō
**Brax′ton** brăks′tŭn
**Braz** *Port.* brȧsh, (*Braz.*) brȧs
**Breck** brĕk
**Breck′en·ridge** brĕk′ĕn·rĭj
**Breck′in·ridge** brĕk′ĭn·rĭj
**Bre′da** *Norw.* brā′dä
**Breese** brēz
**Brem′ner** brĕm′nẽr
**Bren′da** brĕn′dȧ
**Bren′dan** brĕn′dăn
**Brere′ton** brẹr′t′n, brâr′-
**Bret** brĕt
**Bret′land** brĕt′lănd
**Brett** brĕt
**Bret′ting·ham** brĕt′ĭng·ăm
**Bre·vard′** brĕ·värd′
**Bre·voort′** brĕ·vōrt′, -vôrt′
**Brew′er** bro͞o′ẽr
**Brew′er·ton** bro͞o′ẽr·t′n, -tŭn
**Brew′ing·ton** bro͞o′ĭng·tŭn
**Brew′ster** bro͞o′stẽr
**Bri′an** brī′ăn
**Brice** brīs
**Bri′cie** brī′sĭ
**Bridg′er** brĭj′ẽr
**Bridg′es** brĭj′ĕz, -ĭz
**Bridg′man** brĭj′măn
**Bri′dle** brī′d′l
**Brig′ham** brĭg′ăm
**Brigh′ty** brī′tĭ
**Bri·git′ta** *Ital.* brē·jēt′tä—**Bri·git′ta′** *Swed.* brĭ·gĭt′tȧ′
**Brin′dly** brĭn′dlĭ
**Brin′ker·hoff** brĭng′kẽr·hŏf
**Brin′ley** brĭn′lĭ
**Brins′ley** brĭnz′lĭ
**Brin′ton** brĭn′t′n, -tŭn
**Bris′ben** brĭz′bĕn
**Bris′bin** brĭz′bĭn
**Bris′tol** brĭs′t′l
**Bri′tes** *Port.* brē′tēsh
**Brit′on** brĭt′′n
**Brit′ten** brĭt′′n
**Brit′ton** brĭt′′n
**Broa′dus** brô′dŭs
**Brock′den** brŏk′dĕn
**Brock′holst** brŏk′hōlst
**Brock′man** brŏk′măn
**Brod′head** brŏd′hĕd
**Bro′die** brō′dĭ
**Brom′ley** brŏm′lĭ, brŭm′-
**Bro·ni′sław** *Pol.* brô·nē′släf
**Brön′num** *Dan.* brûn′o͝om
**Bron′son** brŏn′s′n
**Bron′wyn** brŏn′wĭn
**Brook** bro͝ok
**Brooke** bro͝ok
**Brooks** bro͝oks
**Bror** *Swed.* bro͞or
**Brougham** bro͞om, bro͞o′ăm

**Broun** bro͞on
**Brown, Browne** broun
**Brow·nell′** brou·nĕl′, brou′nĕl
**Brown′ing** broun′ĭng
**Brown′son** broun′s'n
**Bruce** bro͞os
**Brune** bro͞on
**Bru·net′to** *Ital.* bro͞o·nāt′tō̇
**Brun′lees** brŭn′lēz
**Bru′no** bro͞o′nō; *Ger.* bro͞o′nō; *Ital.* bro͞o′nō̇; *Swed.* bro͞o′nō̇—**Bru′no′** *Fr.* brü′nō′
**Bru′yn** bro͞o′ĭn
**Bry′an** brī′ăn
**Bry′ant** brī′ănt
**Brydg′es** brĭj′ĕz, -ĭz
**Bry′die** brī′dĭ
**Bryn′jolf** *Icel.* brĭn′yŏlv; *Norw.* brün′yŏlf
**Bry′son** brī′s'n
**Bubb** bŭb
**Bu′ben·heim** bo͞o′bĕn·hīm
**Bu·chan′an** bŭ·kăn′ăn, bŭ-
**Buck** bŭk
**Buck′hout** bŭk′out
**Buck′ing·ham** bŭk′ĭng·ăm, -hăm
**Buck′ley** bŭk′lĭ
**Buck′lin** bŭk′lĭn
**Buck′ner** bŭk′nẽr
**Budes** *Fr.* büd
**Bud′ing·ton** bŭd′ĭng·tŭn
**Bu′el, Bu′ell** bū′ĕl
**Bugge** bŭg
**Bulk′ley** bŭlk′lĭ
**Bul′lock** bo͝ol′ŭk
**Bü′low** *Dan.* bü′lou
**Bul′strode** bo͝ol′strōd
**Bunce** bŭns
**Bun′ker** bŭng′kẽr
**Buo′na·parte** ?bō′nȧ·pärt
**Bur′bank** bûr′băngk
**Bur′chard** bûr′chẽrd
**Bur·dett′** bûr·dĕt′, bẽr-
**Bur′don** bûr′d'n
**Bur′ford** bûr′fẽrd
**Bur′ges, Bur′gess** bûr′jĕs, -jĭs
**Bur′kard** *Ger.* bo͝or′kärt
**Burke** bûrk
**Burk′hard** *Ger.* bo͝ork′härt
**Bur′kitt** bûr′kĭt
**Bur′leigh** bûr′lĭ
**Bur′ley** bûr′lĭ
**Bur′lin·game** bûr′lĭn·gām, -lĭng·gām
**Bur′man** bûr′măn
**Bur′net** bûr′nĕt, -nĭt
**Bur·nett′** bûr·nĕt′, bẽr-, bûr′nĕt, -nĭt
**Burn′ham** bûr′năm
**Burns** bûrnz
**Burr** bûr
**Bur′rage** bûr′ĭj
**Bur′rill** bûr′ĭl
**Bur′ris** bûr′ĭs
**Bur′ritt** bûr′ĭt
**Bur′roughs** bûr′ōz
**Burt** bûrt
**Bur′ten·shaw** bûr′t'n·shô
**Bur′tis** bûr′tĭs
**Bur′ton** bûr′t'n
**Bush** bo͝osh
**Bush′nell** bo͝osh′nĕl
**Bush′rod** bo͝osh′rŏd
**Bus′sy** bŭs′ĭ
**But′ler** bŭt′lẽr
**But′ter·worth** bŭt′ẽr·wûrth, -wẽrth
**But′ton** bŭt′'n
**Bux′ton** bŭks′tŭn
**Bu·yo** *Jap.* bo͞o·yō
**By′am** bī′ăm
**By′ford** bī′fẽrd
**Byles** bīlz
**Byrne** bûrn
**By′ron** bī′rŭn
**Bysshe** bĭsh

**Cab′ell** kăb′ĕl
**Cab′ot** kăb′ŭt
**Cä·ci′li·a** *Ger.* tsâ·tsē′lē̇·ä
**Cad′mus** kăd′mŭs
**Ca·dog′an** kȧ·dŭg′ăn
**Cad·wal′la·der** kăd·wŏl′ȧ·dẽr
**Ca′dy** kā′dĭ
**Cae·cil′i·us** *Lat.* sē̇·sĭl′ĭ·ŭs, -sĭl′yŭs
**Cae′li·us** *Lat.* sē′lĭ·ŭs
**Cae′sar** sē′zẽr
**Cae′so** *Lat.* sē′zō, sē′sō
**Ca′ius** kā′yŭs, kī′ŭs
**Cal′der** kôl′dẽr
**Cald′well** kôld′wĕl, -wĕl, kŏld′-
**Cale** kāl
**Ca′leb** kā′lĕb
**Cal·houn′** kăl·ho͞on′, kȧ·ho͞on′
**Ca·lix′to** *Span.* kä·lē(k)s′tō
**Cal′kins** kô′kĭnz
**Call** kôl
**Cal′la·han** kăl′ȧ·hăn
**Call′cott** kôl′kŭt
**Cal′ly·han** kăl′ĭ·hăn
**Cal·pur′ni·us** *Lat.* kăl·pûr′nĭ·ŭs
**Cal′vagh** *Ir.* kăl′vȧK
**Cal′ver·ley** kăl′vẽr·lĭ
**Cal′vert** kăl′vẽrt
**Cal′vin** kăl′vĭn
**Cam** kăm
**Cam′er·on** kăm′ẽr·ŭn
**Ca·mil′la** kȧ·mĭl′ȧ; *Ital.* kä·mēl′lä; *Norw.* kä·mĭl′lä
**Ca·mille′** kȧ·mēl′—**Ca′mille′** *Fr.* kȧ′mē′y′
**Ca·mil′lo** *Ital.* kä·mēl′lō̇; *Port.* kȧ·mē′lo͞o
**Ca·mi′lo** *Span.* kä·mē′lō
**Cam′mer·mey′er** *Norw.* käm′mẽr·mā′ẽr
**Camp** kămp
**Camp′bell** kăm′bĕl; *in U.S., also* kăm′ĕl
**Can′di·do** *Ital.* kän′dē̇·dō
**Cán′di·do** *Span.* kän′dē̇·thō
**Can′di·dus** *Ger.* kän′dē̇·do͝os
**Can′field** kăn′fēld
**Can′ning** kăn′ĭng
**Cant′well** kănt′wĕl, -wĕl
**Ca′pell** kā′pĕl
**Ca·rad′oc** kȧ·răd′ŭk, kä·rä′dŏg
**Car′dale** kär′dāl
**Car′di′nal′** *Fr.* kȧr′dē′nȧl′
**Car·do′sa** *Port.* kẽr·dô′zȧ
**Car·do′zo** *Port.* kẽr·dō′zo͞o
**Card′well** kärd′wĕl, -wĕl
**Ca′rel** *Du.* kȧ′rĕl—**Ca′rel′** *Fr.* kȧ′-rĕl′
**Ca·rew′** kȧ·ro͞o′
**Car′ey** kâr′ĭ
**Ca·ril′lo** *Span.* kä·rē′lyō, -rē′yō
**Ca′rit** *Dan.* kä′rē̇t
**Carl** kärl; *Dan., Finn., Ger., Norw., Swed.* kärl
**Car′la** kär′lȧ
**Carle** kärl; *Fr.* kȧrl
**Car′less** kär′lĕs, -lĭs
**Carle′ton** kärl′tŭn, -t'n
**Car·let′to** *Ital.* kär·lāt′tō̇
**Car′lin** kär′lĭn
**Car·li′no** *Ital.* kär·lē′nō̇
**Carll** kärl
**Car′lo** kär′lō; *Ital.* kär′lō̇; *Swed.* kär′lō̇
**Car′lo′man′** *Fr.* kȧr′lō̇′mäN′
**Car′los** kär′lōs, -lŏs; *Ger.* kär′lō̇s; *Port.* kȧr′lo͞osh, (*Braz.*) -lo͞os; *Span.* kär′lōs
**Car·lot′ta** kär·lŏt′ȧ; *Ital.* kär·lôt′tä
**Carl′ton** kärl′tŭn, -t'n
**Car·lyle′** kär·līl′, kär′līl
**Car·mel′a** kär·mĕl′ȧ
**Car′mi** kär′mī
**Car′mi′chael** kär′mī′kĕl, -k'l, kär-mī′-
**Car′nac** kär′năk
**Car′ol** kăr′ŭl—**Ca′rol** *Rum.* kä′rŏl
**Car′o·li′na** kăr′ō̇·lī′nȧ—**Ca′ro·li′na** *Ital., Span.* kä′rō̇·lē′nä
**Car′o·line** kăr′ō̇·līn, -lĭn—**Ca′ro′line′** *Fr.* kȧ′rô′lēn′, kä′-
**Ca′ro′lus′** *Fr.* kȧ′rô′lüs′—**Car′o·lus** *Lat.* kăr′ō̇·lŭs
**Car′o·lyn** kăr′ō̇·lĭn
**Car′pen·ter** kär′pĕn·tẽr
**Carr** kär
**Car′rie** kăr′ĭ
**Car′roll** kăr′ŭl
**Car·ruth′ers** kă·rŭth′ẽrz
**Car′ry** kăr′ĭ
**Car′son** kär′s'n
**Car′sten** *Dan., Ger., Norw.* kär′stĕn
**Car′ter** kär′tẽr
**Car′ton′** *Fr.* kȧr′tôN′
**Cart′wright** kärt′rīt
**Car′ty** kär′tĭ
**Ca·ruth′ers** kȧ·rŭth′ẽrz
**Car·va′lho** kẽr·vȧ′lyo͞o
**Car′vell** kär′vĕl
**Car′vill** kär′vĭl
**Car′y** kâr′ĭ
**Car′yl** kăr′ĭl
**Cä′sar** *Ger.* tsâ′zär
**Ca′sey** kā′sĭ
**Cas′i·mir** kăz′ĭ·mĭr—**Ca′si′mir′** *Fr.* kȧ′zē′mēr′
**Ca′si′mire′** *Fr.* kȧ′zē′mēr′
**Cas′par** kăs′pẽr; *Dan.* kȧs′pär; *Du.* käs′pär; *Ger.* käs′pär
**Cas′pa·rus** *Lat.* kăs′pȧ·rŭs
**Cas′per** kăs′pẽr; *Ger.* käs′pẽr
**Cass** kăs
**Cas′sa·day** kăs′ȧ·dā
**Cas′sel** kăs′'l
**Cas′si·us** kăsh′ĭ·ŭs, kăsh′ŭs, kăs′ĭ·ŭs
**Cas′wall** kăz′wôl, -wȧl
**Cas′well** kăz′wĕl, -wĕl
**Ca′ta·ri′na** *Ital.* kä′tä·rē′nä
**Ca′te·ri′na** *Ital.* kä′tā·rē′nä
**Ca′te·ri′no** *Ital.* kä′tā·rē′nō̇

**Cates′by** kāts′bĭ
**Ca′thal** *Ir.* kä′hȧl
**Cath′a·rine** kăth′ȧ·rĭn
**Cath′er·ine** kăth′ẽr·ĭn—**Ca′the·rine′** *Fr.* kȧ′trēn′
**Ca′ti·us** *Lat.* kā′shĭ·ŭs, kā′shŭs
**Cat′lett** kăt′lĕt, -lĭt
**Ca′to** *Norw.* kä′tô
**Cat′te·ri′no** *Ital.* kät′tâ·rē′nô
**Ca′tulle′** *Fr.* kȧ′tül′
**ca′va·lie′re** *Ital.* kä′vä·lyâ′râ
**Cave** kāv
**Cav′en·dish** kăv′ĕn·dĭsh
**Cay′ley** kā′lĭ
**Cec′co** *Ital.* chāk′kô
**Ce′cil** sē′s'l, sĕs′'l, sĕs′ĭl, sĭs′'l
**Ce·cile′** sḗ·sēl′, sĕs′'l, sĕs′ĭl, sĭs′'l
**Cé′cile′** *Fr.* sā′sēl′, (*Canad.*) sā′sĭl′
**Ce·cil′i·a** sḗ·sĭl′ĭ·ȧ, -sĭl′yȧ, sḗ·sēl′- — **Ce·ci′li·a** *Span.* thā·thē′lyä, sā·sē′-
**Ce·ci′li·o** *Span.* thā·thē′lyō, sā·sē′-
**Ce·cil′i·us** sḗ·sĭl′ĭ·ŭs, -sĭl′yŭs
**Ce′dar** sē′dẽr
**Če′do·milj** *Yugo.* chĕ′dô·mēl′y'
**Ced′ric** sĕd′rĭk, sē′drĭk
**Ce·io′ni·us** *Lat.* sḗ·yō′nĭ·ŭs
**Ce·leste′** sḗ·lĕst′
**Cé′leste′** *Fr.* sā′lĕst′
**Cé′les′tin′** *Fr.* sā′lĕs′tăɴ′
**Ce′le·sti′no** *Ital.* chā′lās·tē′nô
**Cel′ia** sēl′yȧ
**Cel′so** *Span.* thĕl′sō, sĕl′-
**Cen′cio** *Ital.* chĕn′chô
**Cen·ni′no** *Ital.* chān·nē′nô
**Ce·nón′** *Span.* thā·nôn′; sā-
**Cen′zio** *Ital.* chĕn′tsyô
**Ce′phas** sē′făs
**Cer′tain′** *Fr.* sĕr′tăɴ′
**Cé′saire′** *Fr.* sā′zâr′
**Cé′sar′** *Fr.* sā′zȧr′—**Cé′sar** *Span.* thā′sär, sā′-
**Ce′sa·re** *Ital.* chā′zä·rā
**Ce·sá′re·o** *Span.* thā·sä′rā·ō, sā·sä′-
**Cha′bot′** *Fr.* shȧ′bō′
**Chace** chās
**Chad′wick** chăd′wĭk
**Cha·im′** *Heb.* kī·yĭm′, kī′yĭm; *Yid.* kī′yĭm
**Chal′mers** chăl′mẽrz, *esp. Brit.* chä′mẽrz
**Cham′bers** chām′bẽrz
**Champ′lin** chămp′lĭn
**Chance** chȧns
**Chan′cel·lor** chȧn′sĕ·lẽr
**Chan′dler** chȧn′dlẽr
**Chan′dra** *Bengali* chôn′drô; *Skr.* chŭn′drȧ
**Chan′ning** chăn′ĭng
**Cha′pin** chā′pĭn
**Chap′lin** chăp′lĭn
**Chap′man** chăp′măn
**Char′le·magne** shär′lē·mān—**Char′·le·magne′** *Fr.* shȧr′lē·mȧn′y'
**Charles** chärlz; *Du.* shärl; *Fr.* shȧrl
**Char′lie** chär′lĭ
**Char·lot′ta** *Swed.* shȧr·lôt′tȧ
**Char′lotte** shär′lŏt—**Char′lotte′** *Fr.* shȧr′lôt′—**Char·lot′te** *Ger.* shär·lôt′ĕ—**Char·lotte′** *Swed.* shȧr·lôt′
**Charl′ton** chärl′t'n, -tŭn
**Chase** chās
**Chat′ham** chăt′ăm
**Chat′man** chăt′măn
**Chaun′cey** chôn′sĭ, chän′-
**Chav′e·li′ta** chăv′ĕ·lē′tȧ
**Cha·yim′** *Heb.* kī·yĭm′, kī′yĭm; *Yid.* kī′yĭm
**Chee′ver** chē′vẽr
**Che′ney** chē′nĭ
**Ché′ri′** *Fr.* shā′rē′
**Ches′ter** chĕs′tẽr
**Chet′wynd** chĕt′wĭnd
**chev′a·lier′** shĕv′ȧ·lḗr′—**che·va′lier′** *Fr.* shē·vȧ′lyā′
**Chew** chōō
**Chich′es·ter** chĭch′ĭs·tẽr
**Childe** chīld
**Childs** chīldz
**Chip′man** chĭp′măn
**Chip′pen·dall** chĭp′ĕn·dôl
**Chit′ta** *Bengali* chĭt′tȧ
**Chit′ten·den** chĭt′'n·dĕn
**Chlod′wig** *Ger.* klōt′vĭĸ
**Chre′stos** *Mod. Grk.* krē′stôs
**Chré′tien′** *Fr.* krā′tyăɴ′
**Chris′ta·bel** krĭs′tȧ·bĕl, -bĕl
**Chris′ten** *Dan., Norw.* krĭs′tĕn
**Chris′ten·sen** *Dan.* krĭs′tĕn·s'n
**Chris′ti·aan** *Du.* krĭs′tḗ·ȧn
**Chris′ti·aan·szoon** *Du.* krĭs′tḗ·ȧn-sŭn, -sōn, -sōn
**Chris′tian** krĭs′chăn, krĭst′yăn; *Dan.* krḗs′tyȧn; *Norw.* krĭs′tyän—**Chris′·ti·an** *Du.* krĭs′tḗ·än; *Swed.* krĭs′tĭ·ȧn, krĭsh′ȧn—**Chris′tian′** *Fr.* krēs′tyäɴ′—**Chri′sti·an** *Ger.* krĭs′tḗ·än
**Chri′sti·a′na** *Ger.* krĭs′tḗ·ä′nä
**Chri′sti·a′ne** *Ger.* krĭs′tḗ·ä′nĕ
**Chris′ti·a′nus** *Du.* krĭs′tḗ·ȧ′nûs
**Chris′tie** krĭs′tĭ
**Chris′tiern** *Dan.* krḗs′tyĕrn
**Chris·ti′na** krĭs·tē′nȧ
**Chris·tine′** krĭs·tēn′, krĭs′tēn—**Chris′tine′** *Fr.* krēs′tēn′—**Chri·sti′ne** *Ger.* krĭ·stē′nĕ—**Chri·stine′** *Swed.* krĭ·stēn′
**Christ′lob** *Ger.* krĭst′lōp
**Christ′mas** krĭs′măs, krĭst′-
**Chris·to′fer** *Norw.* krĭs·tŏf′ẽr; *Swed.* krĭs·tôf′ẽr
**Chri′stoff** *Ger.* krĭs′tôf
**Chri·stof′fel** *Ger.* krĭ·stôf′ĕl
**Chris·tof′fer** *Swed.* krĭs·tôf′fẽr
**Chri·sto′fo·ro** *Ital.* krḗs·tô′fô·rō
**Chris′toph** *Du., Swed.* krĭs′tôf—**Chri′stoph** *Ger.* krĭs′tôf
**Chris′tophe′** *Fr.* krēs′tôf′
**Chris′to·pher** krĭs′tô·fẽr—**Chris·to′·pher** *Swed.* krĭs·tôf′ẽr
**Chris′ty** krĭs′tĭ
**Chrow′der** krou′dẽr
**Chry′sos′tome′** *Fr.* krē′zôs′tōm′
**Chry·so′sto·mus** *Ger.* krü·zôs′tô-mōōs
**Chrys′tal** krĭs′t'l
**Chry·zos′tom** *Pol.* krĭ·zôs′tôm
**Church** chûrch
**Church′ill** chûrch′(h)ĭl
**Chur′ton** chûr′t'n
**Cic′e·ly** sĭs′ĕ·lĭ; sĭs′lĭ
**Ci′cé′ron′** *Fr.* sē′sā′rôɴ′
**Cic′i·ly** sĭs′ĭ·lĭ
**Cil′ni·us** *Lat.* sĭl′nĭ·ŭs
**Cin′cin·nat′us** sĭn′sĭ·năt′ŭs, -nā′tŭs
**Ci′pri·a′no** *Ital.* chē′prḗ·ä′nô; *Span.* thē′prḗ·ä′nō, sē′-
**Ci·ri′lo** *Span.* thḗ·rē′lō, sḗ-
**Ci′ro** *Ital.* chē′rô
**Cis′sie** sĭs′ĭ
**Claes** *Du.* klȧs
**Claesz** *Du.* klȧs
**Clag′gett** klăg′ĕt, -ĭt
**Clair** klâr; *Fr.* klâr
**Claire** klâr; *Fr., Ger.* klâr
**Clapp** klăp
**Clar′a** klăr′ȧ, klâr′ȧ—**Cla′ra′** *Fr.* klȧ′rȧ′—**Cla′ra** *Ger.* klä′rä; *Span.* klä′rä
**Clare** klâr
**Clar′ence** klăr′ĕns—**Cla′rence′** *Fr.* klȧ′räɴs′
**Cla′ret′** *Fr.* klȧ′rĕ′
**Cla·ri′na** klă·rē′nȧ
**Cla′ris′** *Fr.* klȧ′rēs′
**Cla·ris′sa** klă·rĭs′ȧ
**Clark, Clarke** klärk
**Clark′son** klärk′s'n
**Clar′y** klâr′ĭ
**Clas′son** *Swed.* klä′sôn
**Claud** klôd
**Claude** klôd; *Fr.* klōd
**Clau′di·a** klô′dĭ·ȧ; *Ital.* klou′dyä
**Clau′di·a′nus** *Lat.* klô′dĭ·ā′nŭs
**Clau′din′** *Fr.* klō′dăɴ′
**Clau′dine′** *Fr.* klō′dēn′
**Clau′di·o** *Ital.* klou′dyô; *Span.* klou′thyō
**Cláu′di·o** *Port.* klou′thyōō
**Clau′di·us** klô′dĭ·ŭs; *Ger.* klou′dḗ·ōōs
**Claus** *Du., Norw.* klous
**Clav′er·ing** klăv′ẽr·ĭng
**Clay** klā
**Clay′poole** klā′pōōl
**Clay′ton** klā′t'n
**Clegg** klĕg
**Cleg′horn** klĕg′hôrn, ?-ẽrn
**Clem′ence** klĕm′ĕns
**Clé′mence′** *Fr.* klā′mäɴs′
**Clem′ens** klĕm′ĕnz; *Lat.* klĕm′ĕnz, klē′mĕnz—**Cle′mens** *Ger.* klā′mĕns
**Clem′ent** klĕm′ĕnt
**Clé′ment′** *Fr.* klā′mäɴ′
**Cle·men′te** *Ital.* klā·mĕn′tâ; *Span.* klā·män′tā
**Cle·men′ti·a′nus** *Lat.* klḗ·mĕn′shĭ·ā′-nŭs
**Clé′men′tine′** *Fr.* klā′mäɴ′tēn′
**Clem′ents** klĕm′ĕnts
**Clem′son** klĕm′s'n
**Cle′o·fon′te** *Ital.* klā′ô·fōn′tâ
**Clé′o′phas′** *Fr.* klā′ô′fäs′
**Cler′i·hew** klĕr′ĭ·hū
**Cle′to** *Span.* klā′tō
**Cleve′land** klēv′lănd
**Cleves** klēvz
**Cliffe** klĭf
**Clif′ford** klĭf′ẽrd
**Clif′ton** klĭf′tŭn
**Clinch** klĭnch
**Clin′ton** klĭn′t'n, -tŭn
**Clip′ston** klĭp′stŭn
**Clive** klīv

**Clo′di·us** *Lat.* klō′dĭ·ŭs
**Clop′ton** klŏp′tŭn
**Clo′rinne′** *Fr.* klô′rēn′
**Clo′tilde′** *Fr.* klô′tēld′—**Clo·til′de** *Ital.* klô·tēl′dâ
**Cloudes′ley** kloudz′lĭ
**Clough** klŭf, kloo
**Clo′vis′** *Fr.* klô′vēs′
**Clowdis′ley** kloudz′lĭ
**Cloyd** kloid
**Cloyne** kloin
**Clyde** klīd
**Cnae′us** *Lat.* nē′ŭs
**Cne′ius** *Lat.* nē′yŭs
**Coal′ter** kōl′tẽr
**Coape** kōp
**Coates** kōts
**Cob′ham** kŏb′ăm
**Coc·ce′ius** *Lat.* kŏk·sē′yŭs
**Coch′ran** kŏk′răn
**Coch′rane** kŏk′răn
**Cock·ayne′** kŏ·kān′
**Cock′burn** kō′bẽrn
**Cod′man** kŏd′măn
**Coe** kō
**Coe′li·us** *Lat.* sē′lĭ·ŭs
**Cof′fay** kŏf′ĭ
**Cof′fin** kŏf′ĭn
**Coff′man** kŏf′măn
**Cogs′well** kŏgz′wĕl, -wĕl
**Coit** koit
**Co′la** *Ital.* kô′lä
**Col′bert** kōl′bẽrt
**Col′burn** kōl′bẽrn
**Col′by** kōl′bĭ
**Col′den** kōl′dĕn
**Col′ding·ham** kōl′dĭng·ăm
**Cole** kōl
**Cole′brooke** kōl′brŏŏk
**Cole′man** kōl′măn
**Cole′ridge** kōl′rĭj
**Coles** kōlz
**Co′lette′** *Fr.* kô′lĕt′
**Co′ley** kō′lĭ
**Col′in** kŏl′ĭn, kō′lĭn—**Co′lin′** *Fr.* kô′lăɴ′—**Co′lin** *Ger.* kōl′ĭn, -ēn
**Col·leer′** kŏ·lēr′
**Col′let** kŏl′ĕt, -ĭt
**Col′lett** *Norw.* kŏl′lĕt
**Col′ley** kŏl′ĭ
**Col′lier** kŏl′yẽr, kŏl′ĭ·ẽr
**Col′ling·ham** kŏl′ĭng·ăm
**Col′lings** kŏl′ĭngz
**Col′ling·wood** kŏl′ĭng·wŏŏd
**Col′lins** kŏl′ĭnz
**Col′lis** kŏl′ĭs
**Co·lón′** *Span.* kō·lôn′
**Colt** kōlt
**Col′ton** kōl′t'n, -tŭn
**Col′trin** kōl′trĭn
**Co·lum′bus** kō·lŭm′bŭs
**Col′ville** kōl′vĭl, kŏl′-
**Com′fort** kŭm′fẽrt
**Com′mer·ford** kŭm′ẽr·fẽrd
**Comp′ton** kŏmp′tŭn, kŭmp′-
**comte** *Fr.* kôɴt
**com′tesse′** *Fr.* kôɴ′tĕs′
**Com′yn** kŭm′ĭn
**Com′yns** kŭm′ĭnz
**Con** kŏn
**Con′al** kŏn′'l
**Co′nant** kō′nănt
**Con′cep·ción′** *Span.* kôn′thĕp·thyôn′, kôn′sĕp·syôn′
**Con′cha** *Span.* kôn′chä
**Con·ci′no** *Ital.* kōn·chē′nō
**con′de** *Port.* kōɴn′dĕ; *Span.* kôn′dā
**Con′dé** kŏn′dā—**Con′dé′** *Fr.* kôɴ′dā′
**Con′ings·by** kŏn′ĭngz·bĭ
**Con′nel·ly** kŏn′'l·ĭ
**Con′nop** kŏn′ŭp
**Con′nor, Con′or** kŏn′ẽr
**Con′o·ver** kŏn′ō·vẽr
**Con′rad** kŏn′răd; *Dan.* kŏn′räth; *Du.* kôn′rät; *Ger.* kôn′rät
**Con·ra′do** *Span.* kôn·rä′thō
**Con′stance** kŏn′stăns—**Cons′tance′** *Fr.* kôɴs′täɴs′
**Con′stant** kŏn′stănt—**Cons′tant′** *Fr.* kôɴs′täɴ′—**Con·stant′** *Ger.* kôn·stänt′
**Con′stan·tijn** *Du.* kôn′stän·tīn
**Con′stan·tin** kŏn′stăn·tĭn—**Cons′-tan′tin′** *Fr.* kôɴs′täɴ′tăɴ′—**Con′-stan·tin′** *Ger.* kôn′stän·tēn′, kôn′-stän·tēn; *Rum.* kŏn′stän·tēn′
**Con′stan·tine** kŏn′stăn·tīn, -tēn
**Con′stan·ti′no** *Ital.* kōn′stän·tē′nō
**Con·stan′ze** *Ger.* kôn·stän′tsĕ
**con′te** *Ital.* kōn′tā
**Con′tee** kŏn′tē
**con·tes′sa** *Ital.* kōn·tās′sä
**Con′vers** kŏn′vẽrz
**Con′way** kŏn′wā
**Con′yers** kŏn′yẽrz
**Con′yng·ham** kŭn′ĭng·ăm, *in U.S. also* -hăm
**Cook** kŏŏk
**Coo′ley** kōō′lĭ
**Coo′lidge** kōō′lĭj
**Coombs** kōōmz
**Coo′per** kōō′pẽr, kŏŏp′ẽr
**Coote** kōōt
**Cope** kōp
**Cope′land** kōp′lănd
**Cop′ley** kŏp′lĭ
**Co′ra** kō′rȧ; *Norw.* kō′rä
**Cor′dell** kôr′dĕl, kôr·dĕl′
**Cor′dy** kôr′dĭ
**Co′ren′tin′** *Fr.* kô′räɴ′tăɴ′
**Co·rin′na** kō·rĭn′ȧ
**Co·rinne′** kō·rĭn′, -rēn′
**Cor′neille′** *Fr.* kôr′nâ′y′
**Cor·nel′ia** kôr·nēl′yȧ, -nē′lĭ·ȧ
**Cor·ne′lio** *Ital.* kōr·nâ′lyō
**Cor·ne′lis, Cor·ne′lisz** *Du.* kôr·nā′lĭs
**Cor·ne′lis·zoon** *Du.* kôr·nā′lĭ·sŭn, -sôn, -sōn
**Cor·ne′liu** *Rum.* kŏr·nĕ′lū
**Cor·nel′ius** kôr·nēl′yŭs, -nē′lĭ·ŭs—**Cor·ne′li·us** *Dan.* kŏr·nę′lē·ōōs; *Du.* kôr·nā′lē·ûs; *Ger.* kōr·nā′lē·ōōs
**Corne′wall** kôrn′wăl, -wôl
**Corn′wall** kôrn′wăl, -wôl
**Corn·wal′lis** kôrn·wŏl′ĭs
**Cor′ra** kŏr′ȧ
**Cor·ra′do** *Ital.* kōr·rä′dō
**Cor·rowr′** kŏ·rour′
**Cor′ry** kŏr′ĭ, kôr′-
**Cor′so** *Ital.* kôr′sō
**Cort** kôrt; *Dan.* kôrt
**Cor·tés′** *Span.* kôr·tās′
**Cor′win** kôr′wĭn
**Co′ry** kō′rĭ
**Cor′y·ton** kŏr′ĭ·tŭn
**Co′si·ma** *Ger.* kō′zē·mä
**Co′si·mo** *Ital.* kô′zē·mō
**Cos′mas** *Ger.* kŏs′mäs
**Cos′mo** kŏz′mō; *Ital.* kôz′mō
**Cos′sar** kŏs′ẽr
**Cos′ta, da** dȧ kŏs′tȧ
**Co·stan′zo** *Ital.* kō·stän′tsō
**Cotes** kōts
**Cotes′worth** kōts′wûrth, -wẽrth
**Cot′ter** kŏt′ẽr
**Cot′ton** kŏt′'n
**Cot′trell** kŏt′rĕl
**Coul′son** kōl′s'n, kōōl′s'n
**Coun′sel·man** koun′sĕl·măn
**Cou′per** kōō′pẽr
**Court** kōrt
**Courte′nay** kōrt′nĭ, kōr′t'n·ā
**Courte′ney** kōrt′nĭ
**Court′land** kōrt′lănd
**Court′ney** kōrt′nĭ
**Coutts** kōōts
**Cov′en·try** kŏv′ĕn·trĭ, kŭv′-
**Cow′an** kou′ăn
**Cow′den** kou′d'n
**Cowles** koulz, kōlz
**Cow′ley** kou′lĭ
**Cow′per** kou′pẽr, kōō′pẽr
**Cox** kŏks
**Coxe** kŏks
**Coy** koi
**Crabb** krăb
**Crace** krās
**Craig** krāg
**Crai′gie** krā′gĭ
**Cram** krăm
**Cranch** krȧnch
**Crane** krān
**Cran′field** krăn′fēld
**Cran′mer** krăn′mẽr
**Cran′nell** krăn′'l
**Cran′stoun** krăn′stŭn
**Cran′will** krăn′wĭl
**Crar′y** krâr′ĭ
**Crau′furd, Craw′ford** krô′fẽrd
**Craw′shay** krô′shā
**Cre·mu′ti·us** *Lat.* krē·mū′shĭ·ŭs, -shŭs
**Cres′ap** krĕs′ăp
**Cres·co′ni·us** *Lat.* krĕs·kō′nĭ·ŭs
**Cres′son** krĕs′'n
**Cres′sy** krĕs′ĭ
**Cres′wicke** krĕz′ĭk
**Crich′ton** krī′t'n
**Cris′ler** krĭs′lẽr
**Cri·sós′to·mo** *Span.* krē·sōs′tō·mō
**Cris′pus** krĭs′pŭs
**Cri·sti′na** *Ital.* krēs·tē′nä
**Cris·tó′bal** *Span.* krēs·tō′bäl
**Cri·sto′fa·no** *Ital.* krēs·tô′fä·nō
**Cri·sto′fo·ro** *Ital.* krēs·tô′fō·rō
**Cris′well** krĭs′wĕl, -wĕl, krĭz′-
**Crit′ten·den** krĭt′'n·dĕn
**Crock′er** krŏk′ẽr
**Crof′ton** krŏf′tŭn
**Crofts** krŏfts
**Crom′bie** krŏm′bĭ, krŭm′-
**Cromme′lin** krŭm′lĭn, krŏm′-
**Crom′well** krŏm′wĕl, -wĕl, krŭm′-

**Cro′nyn** krō′nĭn
**Crookes** kro͝oks
**Croom** kro͞om
**Cros′by** krŏz′bĭ, krŏs′-
**Cros′well** krŏz′wĕl, -wĕl
**Crowe** krō
**Crow′ell** krō′ĕl
**Crown′in·shield** kroun′ĭn·shēld
**Crum** krŭm
**Crun′dall** krŭn′d'l, -dôl
**Cruz** *Span.* kro͞oth, kro͞os
**Cu′bitt** kū′bĭt
**Cul′lem** kŭl′ĕm
**Cul′len** kŭl′ĕn
**Cul′ling** kŭl′ĭng
**Cul·ross′** kŭl·rŏs′
**Cum′ber·land** kŭm′bẽr·lănd
**Cum′ming** kŭm′ĭng
**Cun′liffe** kŭn′lĭf
**Cun′ning·ham** kŭn′ĭng·ăm, *in U.S. also* -hăm
**Cur·ba′stro** *Ital.* ko͞or·bäs′trō
**cu·ré′** kū·rā′—**cu′ré′** *Fr.* kü'rā′
**Cu′ri·us** *Lat.* kū′rĭ·ŭs
**Cur′son** kûr′s'n
**Cur′tis** kûr′tĭs
**Cur′zon** kûr′z'n
**Cush′ing** ko͝osh′ĭng
**Cush′man** ko͝osh′măn
**Cust** kŭst
**Cus′tance** kŭs′tăns
**Cus′tis** kŭs′tĭs
**Cus·to′dio** *Port.* ko͞osh·tô′thyo͞o, (*Braz.*) ko͞os·tô′-; *Span.* ko͞os·tō′-thyō
**Cut′cliffe** kŭt′klĭf
**Cuth′bert** kŭth′bẽrt
**Cutts** kŭts
**Cuy′ler** kī′lẽr
**Cy** sī
**Cyn′thi·a** sĭn′thĭ·ȧ
**Cyp′ri·an** sĭp′rĭ·ăn
**Cy′pri′en′** *Fr.* sē′prē′ăN′
**Cyp′rjan** *Pol.* tsĭp′ryän
**Cy·riel′** *Du.* sē·rēl′
**Cyr′il** sĭr′ĭl
**Cy′rus** sī′rŭs—**Cy′rus′** *Fr.* sē′rüs′

**d'** *Fr.* d-; *Ger.* d-; *Ital.* d-; *Port.* th-, d-
**da** dȧ; *Ital.* dä; *Port.* thȧ, dȧ
**Dab′ney** dăb′nĭ
**Da′comb** dā′kŭm
**da Cos′ta** dȧ kŏs′tȧ
**Da′cre** dā′kẽr
**Da′da·bha′i** *Parsi* dä′dä·bä′ē
**Dag′mar** dăg′mär; *Dan.* dȧg′mär
**Da′go′bert′** *Fr.* dȧ′gô′bâr′—**Da′go·bert** *Ger.* dä′gō·bĕrt
**Daines** dānz
**Dai′sy** dā′zĭ
**dal** *Ital.* däl
**Dale** dāl
**dal·l'** *Ital.* däl·l-, däl′l-
**Dal′las** dăl′ăs
**Dal·rym′ple** dăl·rĭm′p'l, dăl′rĭm′p'l
**Dal′ton, D'Al′ton** dôl′t'n, -tŭn
**Dal·zell′** dăl·zĕl′, dē·ĕl′
**Da′mi·an′** *Ger.* dä′mē·än′
**Da·mián′** *Span.* dä·myän′, thä-
**Da·mia′no** *Ital.* dä·myä′nō
**Da·mião′** *Port.* dȧ·myouN′, thȧ-
**Da′mon** dā′mŭn
**Dan** dăn
**Da′na** dā′nȧ
**Dan′dridge** dăn′drĭj
**Dane** dān
**Dan′forth** dăn′fōrth
**Dan′iel** dăn′yĕl—**Da′ni·el** *Du.* dȧ′-nē·ĕl; *Ger.* dä′nē·ĕl; *Swed.* dä′nĭ·ĕl—**Da′niel′** *Fr.* dȧ′nyĕl′—**Da·niel′** *Span.* dä·nyĕl′, thä-
**Dá′ni·el** *Hung.* dä′nĭ·ĕl
**Da·nie′le** *Ital.* dä·nyâ′lā
**Da·niel′lo** *Ital.* dä·nyĕl′lō
**Dan′te** dăn′tē; *Ital.* dän′tā
**Daph′ne** dăf′nē
**Darch** därch
**D'Ar′cy** där′sĭ
**Da′rio** *Ital.* dä′ryō
**Da·ri′us** dȧ·rī′ŭs—**Da′rius′** *Fr.* dȧ′-ryüs′
**Da′ri·ya** *Russ.* dȧ′ryĭ·yŭ
**Dar′ling** där′lĭng
**Dar′ling·ton** där′lĭng·tŭn
**Dar′rah** dăr′ȧ
**Dar′rell** dăr′ĕl
**Dart′mouth** därt′mŭth
**Dar′win** där′wĭn
**Da·shiell′** dă·shēl′
**Dash′wood** dăsh′wo͝od
**da Sil′va** dȧ sĭl′vȧ; *Port.* thȧ [dȧ] sĭl′vȧ
**Dau′mont′** *Fr.* dō′môN′
**Dav′en·port** dăv′ĕn·pōrt
**Da′vey** dā′vĭ
**Da′vid** dā′vĭd; *Du.* dȧ′vĭt; *Ger.* dä′-vēt, -vĭt, -fēt, -fĭt; *Ital.* dä′vēd—**Da′vid′** *Fr.* dä′vēd′—**Da·vid′** *Russ.* dŭ·vyēd′
**Da·vi′do·vich** *Russ.* dŭ·vyē′dŭ·vyĭch
**Da′vid·son** dā′vĭd·s'n
**Da′vidsz** *Du.* dȧ′vĭts
**Da′vies** dā′vēz, *esp. Brit.* -vĭs
**Da′vis** dā′vĭs
**Da′vi·son, Da′vis·son** dā′vĭ·s'n
**Da′vy** dā′vĭ—**Da′vy′** *Fr.* dȧ′vē′
**Da·vy′do·vich** *Russ.* dŭ·vĭ′dŭ·vyĭch
**Da′vys** dā′vĭs
**Dawn** dôn
**Daw′son** dô′s'n
**Day** dā
**Day′don** dā′d'n
**Day′ton** dā′t'n
**Day·yan′** *Heb.* dī·yän′
**de** dĕ, dē; *Du.* dĕ; *Fr.* dē; *Ger.* dĕ; *Ital.* dā, dā; *Lat.* dē, dē; *Port.* thĕ, dĕ, *before vowels*, thē, dē; *Russ.* dyĕ; *Span.* thā, thā, dā, dā
**de'** *Ital.* dā, dā
**De′al·try** dē′ăl·trĭ
**Dean, Deane** dēn
**Dear′ing** dēr′ĭng
**De·bau′fre′** ?dē·bō′frā′
**de Bow** dĕ bō′
**De·ca′tur** dē·kā′tẽr
**Dec′i·mus** dĕs′ĭ·mŭs
**De′ci·us** dē′shĭ·ŭs, -shŭs
**De Cour′cy** dĕ ko͞or′sĭ
**Dee** dē
**Deems** dēmz
**De·for′est** dĕ·fŏr′ĕst, -ĭst
**De For′est** dĕ fŏr′ĕst, -ĭst
**de′gli** *Ital.* dā′lyē
**De·hone′** dĕ·hōn′
**de′i** *Ital.* dā′ē
**del** *Ital.* dāl, dāl; *Span.* thĕl, dĕl
**Del′a·haye** dĕl′ȧ·hā
**De La·mar** dĕl′ȧ·mär
**de la Mer** dĕl′ȧ·mẽr
**Del′a·mere** dĕl′ȧ·mēr
**De Lan′cey** dĕ lăn′sĭ
**De Land** dĕ lănd′
**Del′a·no** dĕl′ȧ·nō
**de La·tour′** dĕl′ȧ·to͝or′
**Del′a·van** dĕl′ȧ·văn, -văn
**Del′e·van** dĕl′ĕ·văn, -văn
**Del·fim′** *Port.* dĕl·fēN′, thĕl-
**Del·fi′na** *Span.* dĕl·fē′nä, thĕl-
**Del′ia** dēl′yȧ, dē′lĭ·ȧ
**del·l'** *Ital.* dāl·l-, dāl′l-
**del′la** *Ital.* dāl′lä
**Del′phin′** *Fr.* dĕl′făN′
**Del′phine′** *Fr.* dĕl′fēn′
**Del′ta** dĕl′tȧ
**Del′u·cen′na** dĕl′ū·sĕn′ȧ
**dem** *Ger.* dĕm
**Dem′a·rest** dĕm′ȧ·rĕst
**De·me′tri·os** *Mod. Grk.* thē·mē′trē·ôs
**De·me′tri·us** dē·mē′trĭ·ŭs
**Dem′ing** dĕm′ĭng
**De·mós′te·nes** *Span.* dā·mōs′tā·nās, thā-
**Demp′ster** dĕm(p)′stẽr
**den** *Du., Ger.* dĕn
**Dene** dēn
**Den′ham** dĕn′ăm
**Den′is** dĕn′ĭs—**De·nis′** *Du.* dĕ·nēs′; *Fr.* dē·nē′; *Russ.* dyĭ·nyēs′
**Den′i·son** dĕn′ĭ·s'n
**Den′man** dĕn′măn
**Den′mark** dĕn′märk
**Den′nett** dĕn′ĕt, -ĭt
**Den′nis** dĕn′ĭs
**Den′ni·son** dĕn′ĭ·s'n
**Den′son** dĕn′s'n
**Dent** dĕnt
**Den′ton** dĕn′t'n, -tŭn
**De·nys′** *Fr.* dē·nē′
**Den′zil** dĕn′zĭl
**Dé′o′dat′** *Fr.* dā′ô′dȧt′
**De·o·do′ro** *Port.* dē·o͞o·thō′ro͞o, thē-
**de Pau′la** *Ger.* dā pou′lä
**der** *Du., Ger.* dẽr
**Der′mot** dûr′mŭt
**Der′rick** dĕr′ĭk
**Der′went** dûr′wĕnt
**des** *Fr.* dā; *before vowels or sometimes before h*, dāz
**De′si·de′ri·us** *Ger.* dā′zē·dā′rē·o͞os—**Des′i·de′ri·us** *Lat.* dĕs′ĭ·dēr′ĭ·ŭs
**Dé′si′ré′** *Fr.* dā′zē′rā′
**Dé′si′rée′** *Fr.* dā′zē′rā′
**Des′mond** dĕz′mŭnd
**de So′la** dĕ sō′lȧ
**Det′lev** *Ger.* dĕt′lĕf
**de Vane** dĕ vān′
**Dev′er·eux** dĕv′ẽr·o͞o, -o͞oks
**de Wa′ter** dĕ wô′tẽr, wŏt′ẽr
**Dew′ey** dū′ĭ
**de Witt, De Witt, De·witt′** dĕ·wĭt′
**De Wolf, De Wolfe** dĕ wo͝olf′
**Dex′ter** dĕks′tẽr
**De′zső** *Hung.* dĕ′zhû

**Dhan** *Bengali* dôn, dô′nô (*Angl.* dŭn)
**Dhu·leep′** *As. Ind.* d*ŭ*·lēp′
**di** *Ital.* dē̇, dē
**Di·an′a** dī·ăn′*ȧ*
**Diar′maid** dĭr′mĭd
**Diar′mid** dĭr′mĭd
**Dick** dĭk
**Dick′er·man** dĭk′ẽr·m*ă*n
**Dick′er·son** dĭk′ẽr·s'n
**Dick′in·son** dĭk′ĭn·s'n
**Dick′son** dĭk′s'n
**Di′de·rich** *Dan.* dē′d*ĕ*·rē̇k
**Di′de·ri′cus** *Du.* dē′d*ĕ*·rē′kûs
**Di′de·rik** *Du.* dē′d*ĕ*·rĭk
**Di′dier′** *Fr.* dē′dyā′
**Die′de·rich** *Ger.* dē′d*ĕ*·rĭᴋ
**Die′drich** dē′drĭk
**Die′go** *Span.* dyā′gō, t͟hyā′-
**Diehl** dēl
**Die′rik** *Du.* dē′rĭk
**Die′trich** *Ger.* dē′trĭᴋ
**Dieu** *Fr.* dyû
**Dieu′don′né′** *Fr.* dyû′dô′nā′
**Diez** *Fr.* dyĕz
**Dig′by** dĭg′bĭ
**Digh′ton** dī′t'n
**Dike′man** dīk′m*ă*n
**Dill** *Eng., Ger.* dĭl
**Dil′ler** dĭl′ẽr
**Dill′man** dĭl′m*ă*n
**Dil′lon** dĭl′*ŭ*n
**Dil′worth** dĭl′wûrth, -wẽrth
**Di·mi′tri** d*ĭ*·mē′trĭ; *Mod. Grk.* t͟hē̇-mē′trē̇; *Russ.* dyĭ·myē′tryû·ĭ
**Di·mi′tri·e** *Rum.* dē̇·mē′trē̇·yĕ
**Di·mi′tri·e·vich** *Russ.* dyĭ·myē′tryĭ-y*ĕ*·vyĭch
**Di·mi′tri·je** *Yugo.* dē̇·mē′trē̇·y*ĕ*
**Di′mond** dī′m*ŭ*nd
**Di′nah** dī′n*ȧ*
**Di′nes** *Dan.* dē′nĕs
**Din′ham** dĭn′*ă*m
**Di′no** *Ital.* dē′nō̇
**Di′o** dī′ō
**Dio′go** *Port.* dyō′go͞o, t͟hyō′-
**Di′o·me′de** *Ital.* dē′ō̇·mâ′dā̇
**Di′on** dī′ŏn, -*ŭ*n
**Di′o·ni′sio** *Ital.* dē′ō̇·nē′zyō̇—**Dio·ni′sio** *Span.* dyō̇·nē′syō, t͟hyō̇-
**Dio·ny′sios** *Mod. Grk.* t͟hyô·nyē′syôs
**Di′o·ny′si·us** dī′ō̇·nĭsh′ĭ·*ŭ*s, -nĭsh′*ŭ*s, -nĭs′ĭ·*ŭ*s, -nī′sĭ·*ŭ*s
**Dirck** *Du.* dĭrk
**Dirk** dûrk; *Du.* dĭrk
**Dit′lev** *Dan.* dē̇t′lĕv
**Dix** dĭks
**Dix′on** dĭk′s'n
**Dmi′tri** d*ŭ*·mē′trĭ; *Rum.* d'mē′trē̇; *Russ.* d'myē′tryû·ĭ
**Dmi′tri·e·vich** *Russ.* d'myē′tryĭ·y*ĕ*-vyĭch
**do** *Port.* t͟ho͞o, do͞o
**Dobbs** dŏbz
**Dob′in·son** dŏb′ĭn·s'n
**Do′cia** dō′sh*ȧ*, -shĭ·*ȧ*
**Dod′dridge** dŏd′rĭj
**Dodge** dŏj
**Do′die** dō′dĭ
**Dod′son** dŏd′s'n
**Dol′i·ver** dŏl′*ĭ*·vẽr
**Dol′ly** dŏl′ĭ
**Do·lo′res** dō̇·lō′rĕs, -rĭs; *Span.* dō̇-lō′rās, t͟hō̇-
**Dol′son** dŏl′s'n
**dom** dŏm; *Fr.* dôɴ; *Port.* dōɴ, t͟hōɴ
**Do′me·la** *Du.* dô′m*ĕ*·lȧ
**Do·me′ni·co** *Ital.* dō̇·mā′nē̇·kō
**Do·min′go** *Port.* do͞o·mēɴng′go͞o, t͟ho͞o-; *Span.* dō̇·mēng′gō, t͟hō̇-
**Do·min′gos** *Port.* do͞o·mēɴng′go͞osh, t͟ho͞o-, (*Braz.*) -go͞os
**Dom′i·nic, -nick** dŏm′*ĭ*·nĭk
**Do′mi·nik** *Ger.* dō′mē̇·nĭk
**Do·mi′ni·kus** *Ger.* dō̇·mē′nē̇·ko͝os
**Do′mi′nique′** *Fr.* dô′mē′nēk′
**Do·mi′ti·us** *Lat.* dō̇·mĭsh′ĭ·*ŭ*s, -mĭsh′-*ŭ*s
**Don** dŏn
**don** dŏn; *Ital.* dôn, dōn; *Span.* dôn, t͟hôn
**Do′nal** *Ir.* t͟hū′n*ȧ*l
**Don′ald** dŏn′'ld
**Do′na′tien′** *Fr.* dô′nȧ′syăɴ′
**Do·na′to** *Ital.* dō̇·nä′tō̇
**Do·na′tus** *Ger.* dō̇·nä′to͞os
**Don′is·thorpe** dŏn′ĭs·thôrp
**Donn** dŏn
**Don′na** dŏn′*ȧ*
**Don′ough** dŏn′ō̇; *Ir.* t͟hŭn′ō̇
**Doo′lit′tle** do͞o′lĭt′'l
**Do′ra** dō′r*ȧ*
**Do′reen** dō′rēn, dō̇·rēn′
**Do·re′mus** dō̇·rē′m*ŭ*s
**Dor′is** dŏr′ĭs, dō′rĭs
**Do′ri·us** *Ger.* dō′rē̇·o͝os
**Dor′man** dôr′m*ă*n
**Dor′mer** dôr′mẽr
**Dor′mont′** *Fr.* dôr′môɴ′
**Dorn** dôrn
**Dor·nel′les** *Port.* do͞or·nĕ′lē̇sh, t͟ho͞or-, (*Braz.*) -lē̇s
**Do′ro·te′o** *Span.* dō′rō̇·tā′ō, t͟hō′-
**Dor′o·the′a** dŏr′ō̇·thē′*ȧ*—**Do′ro·the′a** *Ger.* dō′rō̇·tā′ä
**Do′ro′thée′** *Fr.* dô′rô′tā′
**Dor′o·thy** dŏr′ō̇·thĭ
**Dorr** dôr
**Dor′sey** dôr′sĭ
**Dor′the** *Norw.* dŏr′t*ĕ*
**Doud** doud
**Dou′gal** do͞o′g*ă*l
**Doug′las, -lass** dŭg′l*ă*s
**Doust** doust
**Dou′ville** do͞o′vĭl
**Dou′wes** *Du.* dou′wĕs
**Do′ver** dō′vẽr
**Dove′ton** ?dŭv′t*ŭ*n
**Dow** dou
**Dow′ner** dou′nẽr
**Dow′nie** dou′nĭ
**Dow′ning** dou′nĭng
**Doyle** doil
**Dra′gan** *Bulg.* drȧ′găn
**Dra′gu·tin** *Yugo.* drä′go͞o·tēn
**Drake** drāk
**Dra′per** drā′pẽr
**Dra′ža** *Yugo.* drä′zhä
**Dred** drĕd
**Drew** dro͞o
**Drink′er** drĭngk′ẽr
**Dru** dro͞o
**Drum′mond** drŭm′*ŭ*nd
**Dru′ry** dro͝or′ĭ
**Dru′sus** *Lat.* dro͞o′s*ŭ*s
**Drys′dale** drīz′dāl
**du** *Fr.* dü
**Duar′te** *Port.* dwȧr′t*ĕ*, t͟hwȧr′t*ĕ*
**Du Bose** dū̇ bōz′, do͞o, d*ŭ*
**duc** *Fr.* dük
**du′ca** *Ital.* do͞o′kä
**du′chesse′** *Fr.* dü′shĕs′
**Du′clos′** *Fr.* dü′klō′
**Dud** dŭd
**Dud′ley** dŭd′lĭ
**Duer** dūr, dū′ẽr
**Duff** dŭf
**Duf′field** dŭf′ēld
**Duf′fle** dŭf′'l
**Du′gald** do͞o′g*ă*ld, dū′-
**Du·i′liu** *Rum.* do͞o·ē′lyo͞o
**Du·mas′** dū̇·mä′, do͞o-—**Du′mas′** *Fr.* dü′mȧ′
**Du·mi′tru** *Rum.* do͞o·mē′tro͞o
**Du′mont′** *Fr.* dü′môɴ′
**Dun·bar′** dŭn·bär′, dŭn′bär
**Dun′can** dŭng′k*ă*n
**Dun·glas′** dŭn·glȧs′
**Dun′gli·son** dŭng′glĭ·s'n
**Dun′lap** dŭn′lăp, -l*ă*p
**Dun′lop** dŭn′lŏp, dŭn·lŏp′
**Dunn** dŭn
**Dun′na·chie** dŭn′*ȧ*·kĭ
**Dun′ning** dŭn′ĭng
**Dun′stan** dŭn′st*ă*n
**Dun′wo′dy** dŭn′wo͝od′ĭ
**Dun′wood′y** dŭn′wo͝od′ĭ
**du Pré** *Fr.* dü prā′
**Du·Rant′** dū̇·rănt′
**Du′šan** *Yugo.* do͞o′shän
**Du′shan** *Yugo.* do͞o′shän
**Dus′tin** dŭs′tĭn
**Dut′ton** dŭt′'n
**Dwight** dwīt
**Dwy′er** dwī′ẽr
**Dyce** dīs
**Dy′er** dī′ẽr
**Dyke** dīk
**Dykes** dīks
**Dyl′an** dĭl′*ă*n
**Dyne′ley** dīn′lĭ
**Dy′o·ni′zy** *Pol.* dĭ′ô·nē′zĭ

**e** *Port.* ē̇
**Ead′weard** ĕd′wẽrd
**Ea′ger** ē′gẽr
**Ea′gle** ē′g'l
**Eames** ēmz, āmz
**Ea′mon** *Ir.* ā′m*ŭ*n
**Eard′ley** ûrd′lĭ
**Earl, Earle** ûrl
**Ear′nest** ûr′nĕst, -nĭst
**Ea′son** ?ē′s'n
**East′man** ēst′m*ă*n
**Ea′ton** ē′t'n
**Eb′ba′** *Swed.* ĕb′bȧ′
**Eb′be·sen** ĕb′*ĕ*·s'n
**Eb′en** ĕb′*ĕ*n
**Eb′en·e′zer** ĕb′*ĕ*n·ē′zẽr—**E′be′ne′-zer′** *Fr.* ā′bā′nā′zâr′
**E′ber·hard, -hardt** *Ger.* ā′bẽr·härt
**Ec′cles** ĕk′'lz
**Ec′cle·stone** ĕk′'l·stōn, *esp. Brit.* -st*ŭ*n
**Ec·di′ci·us** *Lat.* ĕk·dĭsh′ĭ·*ŭ*s

**Eck′ert** ĕk′ẽrt
**Eck′hard** *Ger.* ĕk′härt
**É′cou′chard′** *Fr.* ā′ko͞o′shȧr′
**Ec′tor** ĕk′tẽr
**Ed** ĕd
**Ed′da** *Ital.* ĕd′dä
**Ed′die, Ed′dy** ĕd′ĭ
**E′de** *Hung.* ĕ′dĕ
**E′de·les′tand′** *Fr.* ĕd′lĕs′täN′
**E′den** ē′d'n
**Ed′gar** ĕd′gẽr; *Ger.* ĕt′gär—**Ed′gar′** *Fr.* ĕd′gȧr′
**Ed′gard′** *Fr.* ĕd′gȧr′
**Edg′cumbe** ĕj′kŭm, -ko͞om
**Edge** ĕj
**Edge′worth** ĕj′wûrth, -wẽrth
**Ed′i·son** ĕd′ĭ·s'n
**E′dith** ē′dĭth; *Ger.* ā′dĭt
**E′dler** *Ger.* ā′dlẽr
**Ed′mands** ĕd′măndz
**Edme** *Fr.* ĕd′m′; *before a cons.*, ĕd′mē
**Ed′mée′** *Fr.* ĕd′mā′
**Ed′mond** ĕd′mŭnd—**Ed′mond′** *Fr.* ĕd′môN′
**Ed·mon′do** *Ital.* ȧd·mōn′dō̇
**Ed′monds** ĕd′mŭndz
**Ed′mon·stone** ĕd′mŭn·stōn, *esp. Brit.* -stŭn
**Ed′mund** ĕd′mŭnd; *Ger.* ĕt′mo͝ont
**Ed·mun′do·vich** *Russ.* ĕd·mo͞on′dŭ-vyĭch
**Ed′munds** ĕd′mŭndz
**Ed′mund·son** ĕd′mŭnd·s'n
**Ed′na** ĕd′nȧ
**E′do·ar′do** *Ital.* ā′dō̇·är′dō̇
**É′dou·ard′** *Fr.* ā′dwȧr′
**Ed′ric** ?ĕd′rĭk
**Ed′sel** ĕd′s'l
**Ed′son** ĕd′s'n
**E′du·ard** *Czech* ĕ′do͞o·ärt; *Du.* ā′dü-ärt; *Ger.* ā′do͞o·ärt—**Ed′uard** *Dan.* ĕd′värd—**E·du·ard′** *Russ.* ȧ·do͞o-ȧrt′
**E·duar′do** *Ital.* ȧ·dwär′dō̇; *Port.* ē̇·thwȧr′do͞o; *Span.* ȧ·thwär′thō
**Ed′vard** *Dan.* ĕd′värd; *Norw.* ĕd′-värt, ăd′-—**E′dvard** *Swed.* ā′dvȧrd
**Ed′vart** *Norw.* ĕd′värt, ăd′-
**Ed′ward** ĕd′wẽrd; *Dan.* ĕd′värd; *Ger.* ĕt′värt; *Pol.* ĕd′värt
**Ed′wards** ĕd′wẽrdz
**Ed′win** ĕd′wĭn; *Ger.* ĕt′vēn
**Ed·wi′na** ĕd·wē′nȧ, -wĭn′ȧ
**Ed′wyn** ĕd′wĭn
**Eel′co** *Du.* āl′kō
**Ee′mil** *Finn.* â′mĭl
**e·fen′di, ef·fen′di** *Angl. & Pers.* ĕ·fĕn′dĭ; *Turk.* ĕ·fĕn·dĭ′
**Ef′fie** ĕf′ĭ
**E·fim′** *Russ.* yĭ·fyēm′
**E·fi′mo·vich** *Russ.* yĭ·fyē′mŭ·vyĭch
**E·frem′** *Russ.* yĭ·fryâm′; *Angl.* ĕf′-rĕm
**E·fre′mo·vich** *Russ.* yĭ·fryâ′mŭ·vyĭch
**Eg′bert** ĕg′bẽrt; *Du.* ĕK′bẽrt
**Eg·ber′tus** *Du.* ĕK·bĕr′tûs
**E′ge·berg** *Norw.* ā′kĕ·băr
**Eg′er·ton** ĕj′ẽr·t'n, -tŭn
**Eg′gle·ston** ĕg′'l·stŭn
**E·gid′** *Ger.* ȧ·gēt′
**É′gide′** *Fr.* ā′zhēd′
**E·gi′dio** *Ital.* ȧ·jē′dyō̇
**Eg′le·ston** ĕg′'l·stŭn
**Eg′lin·ton** ĕg′lĭn·tŭn
**E′glon** *Du.* ā′glôn
**Eg′mont** *Ger.* ĕg′mȯnt
**Eg·na′ti·us** *Lat.* ĕg·nā′shĭ·ŭs, -shŭs
**E′gon** *Ger.* ā′gôn
**E·gor′** *Russ.* yĭ·gôr′
**E′gron** *Swed.* ā′grôn
**Eh′ren·fried** *Ger.* ā′rĕn·frēt; *Swed.* ā′rĕn·frēd
**Eh′ren·gard** *Ger.* ā′rĕn·gärt
**Eh′rich** ā′rĭK
**Ei-i·chi** *Jap.* ā·ē̇·chē̇
**Ei·ki** *Jap.* ā·kē̇
**Ei′leen** ī′lēn, ī·lēn′, ā′lēn, ȧ·lēn′
**Ei′lert** *Norw.* ĕ′ĭ·lĕrt
**Eil′hardt** *Ger.* īl′härt
**Ei′lif** *Norw.* ĕ′ĭ·lēf
**Ei′nar** *Dan.* ī′när; *Icel.* ĕ′ĭ·när; *Swed.* ĕ′ĭ·nȧr
**Ei′rik** *Norw.* ĕ′ĭ·rēk
**Ei′ríkr** *Icel.* ĕ′ĭ·rē′kẽr
**Ei′tel** *Ger.* ī′tĕl
**Ei·to·ku** *Jap.* ā·tō̇·ko͞o
**Ei′vind** *Norw.* ĕ′ĭ·vĭn
**Ej′nar** *Dan.* ī′när
**E·ka·te·ri′na** *Russ.* yĕ·kŭ·tyĭ·ryē′nŭ
**el** *Span.* ĕl
**E·laine′** ē̇·lān′
**El′bert** ĕl′bẽrt
**El′bridge** ĕl′brĭj
**El′don** ĕl′dŭn
**El′dredge** ĕl′drĭj
**El′dridge** ĕl′drĭj
**El′ea·nor** ĕl′ȧ·nẽr
**El′e·a·zar** ĕl′ē̇·ā′zẽr
**E′le·á′zar** *Span.* ā′lā̇·ä′thär, -sär
**E·lec′tus** ē̇·lĕk′tŭs
**E′lek** *Hung.* ĕ′lĕk
**É′lé′mir′** *Fr.* ā′lā′mēr′
**El′e·na** ĕl′ĕ·nȧ—**E′le·na** *Ger.* ā′lā̇-nä; *Ital.* â′lā̇·nä—**E·le′na** *Ruman.* ĕ·lĕ′nä; *Russ.* yĭ·lyâ′nŭ
**El′e·o·no′ra** ĕl′ē̇·ō̇·nō′rȧ—**E′le·o·no′-ra** *Ital.* ā′lā̇·ō̇·nô′rä
**E′le·o·no′re** *Ger.* ā′lā̇·ō̇·nō′rĕ
**É′lé′o′nore′** *Fr.* ā′lā′ô′nôr′
**E′lert** *Ger.* ā′lĕrt
**É′leu′thère′** *Fr.* ā′lû′târ′
**E′leu·the′rios** *Mod. Grk.* ā′lyĕf·thâ′-ryôs
**El′ford** ĕl′fẽrd
**El·ha′nan** ĕl·hā′năn
**E′li** ē′lī
**E·li′a·kim** ē̇·lī′ȧ·kĭm
**E·li′as** ē̇·lī′ăs; *Ger.* ȧ·lē′äs; *Swed.* ĕ·lē′ȧs—**E′li·as** *Finn.* ĕ′lyȧs
**E·lí′as** *Span.* ȧ·lē′äs
**É′lie′** *Fr.* ā′lē′
**E′li·el** *Finn.* ĕ′lyĕl
**E′li·e′ser** *Ger.* ā′lē̇·ā′zẽr
**E·li′gio** *Span.* ȧ·lē′hyō
**E·li′gi·us** *Ger.* ȧ·lē′gē̇·o͝os
**El′i·hu** ĕl′ĭ·hū, ē̇·lī′hū
**E·li′jah** ē̇·lī′jȧ
**El′i·nor** ĕl′ĭ·nẽr
**E′lio** *Span.* ā′lyō
**El′i·ot** ĕl′ĭ·ŭt, ĕl′yŭt
**E·liph′a·let** ē̇·lĭf′ȧ·lĕt, -lĭt
**E·li′sa** *Ger., Ital.* ȧ·lē′zä
**É′li′sa′** *Fr.* ā′lē′zȧ′
**E·li′sa·bet** *Ger.* ȧ·lē′zä·bĕt
**E·lis′a·beth** ē̇·lĭz′ȧ·bĕth—**E·li′sa·beth** *Ger.* ȧ·lē′zä·bĕt; *Swed.* ĕ·lē′sȧ·bĕt′
**É′li′sa′beth′** *Fr.* ā′lē′zȧ′bĕt′
**E′li·sä′us** *Norw.* ĕ′lĭ·sā′o͞os
**É′lise′** *Fr.* ā′lēz′
**É′li′sée′** *Fr.* ā′lē′zā′
**E·li′sha** ē̇·lī′shȧ
**E·li′za** ē̇·lī′zȧ
**E·liz′a·beth** ē̇·lĭz′ȧ·bĕth—**E·li′za·beth** *Du.* ȧ·lē′zȧ·bĕt
**E·li·za·ve′ta** *Russ.* yĕ·lyĭ·zŭ·vyâ′tŭ
**E·li′zur** ē̇·lī′zẽr
**El′kan** ĕl′kăn
**El·ka′nah** ĕl·kā′nȧ, -kä′nȧ
**El′king·ton** ĕl′kĭng·tŭn
**El′kins** ĕl′kĭnz
**El′la** ĕl′ȧ
**El′len** ĕl′ĕn, -ĭn; *Swed.* ĕl′lĕn
**El′ler·ker** ĕl′ẽr·kẽr
**El′ler·y** ĕl′ẽr·ĭ
**El′lett** ĕl′ĕt, -ĭt
**El′lice** ĕl′ĭs
**El′li·cott** ĕl′ĭ·kŏt
**El′lies′** *Fr.* ā′lē′
**El′ling** *Norw.* ĕl′lĭng
**El′ling·ton** ĕl′ĭng·tŭn
**El′ling·wood** ĕl′ĭng·wo͝od
**El′lin·wood** ĕl′ĭn·wo͝od
**El′li·ot** ĕl′ĭ·ŭt, ĕl′yŭt
**El′li·ott** ĕl′ĭ·ŭt, ĕl′yŭt
**El′lis** ĕl′ĭs
**El′li·son** ĕl′ĭ·s'n
**Ells′worth** ĕlz′wûrth, -wẽrth
**Ell′wood** ĕl′wo͝od
**Elme** *Fr.* ĕlm
**El′mer** ĕl′mẽr
**El′more** ĕl′mōr
**É′loi′** *Fr.* ā′lwȧ′
**E′lon** ē′lŏn
**E·loy′** *Span.* ȧ·loi′
**El′phin·stone** ĕl′fĭn·stōn, *esp. Brit.* -stŭn
**El′ring·ton** ĕl′rĭng·tŭn
**El′roy** ĕl′roi
**El′sa** ĕl′sȧ; *Ger.* ĕl′zä; *Swed.* ĕl′sȧ—**El′sa′** *Fr.* ĕl′sȧ′
**Els′beth** *Ger.* ĕls′bĕt
**El′se** *Ger.* ĕl′zĕ
**El·se′us** *Norw.* ĕl·sā′o͞os
**El′sie** ĕl′sĭ
**El′speth** ĕl′spĕth, -spēth
**Els′wyth** ĕlz′wĭth
**El′ton** ĕl′t'n, -tŭn
**El·vi′ra** ĕl·vī′rȧ, -vẹr′ȧ
**El′well** ĕl′wĕl, -wĕl
**El′win** *Ger.* ĕl′vēn
**El′wood** ĕl′wo͝od
**El′wyn** ĕl′wĭn
**E′ly** ē′lĭ
**El′zé′ar′** *Fr.* ĕl′zā′ȧr′
**El′zie** ĕl′zĭ
**E·man′u·el** ē̇·măn′ū̇·ĕl—**E·ma′nu·el** *Dan.* ĭ·mȧ′no͞o·ĕl; *Du.* ȧ·mȧ′nü·ĕl; *Finn.* ĕ·mä′no͞o·ĕl; *Ger.* ȧ·mä′-no͞o·ĕl; *Swed.* ĕ·mä′no͞o·ĕl—**E′ma-nu·el** *Czech* ĕ′mȧ·no͞o·ĕl—**E′ma′-nu·el′** *Fr.* ĕ′mȧ′nü·ĕl′
**E′ma·nue′le** *Ital.* ā′mä·nwâ′lā̇

**E·mel·yan′** *Russ.* yĕ·myĭl·yȧn′
**Em′er·ich** ĕm′ẽr·ĭk—**E′me·rich** *Ger.* ā′mĕ·rĭᴋ
**Em′er·son** ĕm′ẽr·s'n
**Em′er·y** ĕm′ẽr·ĭ
**E′mil** ē′mĭl, ā′mĭl, ĕm′ĭl; *Czech* ĕ′mĭl; *Finn.* ĕ′mĭl; *Ger.* ā′mēl; *Hung.* ĕ′mĭl; *Pol.* ĕ′mēl; *Swed.* ā′mĭl—**E·mil′** *Dan.* ĭ·mēl′
**É′mil′** *Fr.* ā′mēl′
**É·mile′** *Du.* ȧ·mēl′—**É′mile′** *Fr.* ā′mēl′
**E·mil′i·a** ė·mĭl′ĭ·ȧ, -mĭl′yȧ—**E·mi′lia** *Span.* ȧ·mē′lyä
**E′mi·lia′no** *Ital.* ā′mē·lyä′nō; *Span.* ā′mē·lyä′nō
**Em′i·lie** ĕm′ĭ·lĭ—**E·mi′li·e** *Ger.* ȧ·mē′lē·ĕ—**E·mi′lie** *Swed.* ĕ·mĭ′lē
**É′mi′lie′** *Fr.* ā′mē′lē′
**É′mi′lien′** *Fr.* ā′mē′lyăɴ′
**E·mil′ie·vich** *Russ.* ĕ·myēl′yĕ·vyĭch
**E·mi′lio** *Ital.* ȧ·mē′lyō; *Span.* ȧ·mē′lyō
**E·mi′li·us** *Dan.* ĭ·mē′lē·o͝os
**Em′i·ly** ĕm′ĭ·lĭ
**Em′lin** ĕm′lĭn
**Em′lyn** ĕm′lĭn
**Em′ma** ĕm′ȧ; *Du.* ĕm′ȧ; *Ger.* ĕm′ä; *Ital.* ĕm′mä—**Em′ma′** *Fr.* ĕm′mȧ′
**Em·man′u·el** ĕ·măn′ū·ĕl, ĭ- —**Em′ma′nu·el′** *Fr.* ĕ′mȧ′nü·ĕl′—**Em·ma′nu·el** *Ger.* ĕ·mä′no͞o·ĕl—**Em′ma·nuel′** *Mod. Grk.* â′mä·nwēl′
**Em′ma·nue′le** *Ital.* ām′mä·nwâ′lā
**Em′ma·nu·i′lo·vich** *Russ.* ĕm′mŭ·no͞o·ē′ĭŭ·vyĭch
**Em′me·line** ĕm′ĕ·lĭn, -lēn
**Em′me·rich** *Ger.* ĕm′ĕ·rĭᴋ
**Em′met, Em′mett** ĕm′ĕt, -ĭt
**Em′mi** *Ger.* ĕm′ē
**Em′mons** ĕm′ŭnz
**Em′mus·ka** *Hung.* ĕm′mo͞osh·kŏ
**Em′my** ĕm′ĭ; *Ger.* ĕm′ē
**Em′o·ry** ĕm′ō·rĭ
**Em′pie** ĕm′pĭ
**Em′roy** ĕm′roi
**Ems′ley** ĕmz′lĭ
**En′di·cott** ĕn′dĭ·kŭt
**En′dre** *Hung.* ĕn′drĕ
**End′sor** ĕn′zẽr
**En·dym′i·on** ĕn·dĭm′ĭ·ŭn
**E·ne′a** *Ital.* ȧ·nâ′ä
**En′field** ĕn′fēld
**Eng′el·bert** *Finn.* ĕng′ĕl·bĕrt; *Ger.* ĕng′ĕl·bĕrt
**Eng′el·hard** *Ger.* ĕng′ĕl·härt
**En′gle** ĕng′g'l
**Eng′lish** ĭng′glĭsh
**En′guer′rand′** *Fr.* äɴ′gĕ′räɴ′
**E′nid** ē′nĭd
**En′ne·mond′** *Fr.* ĕn′môɴ′
**En′nio** *Ital.* ĕn′nyō
**En′nis** ĕn′ĭs
**En′no** *Ger.* ĕn′ō
**E′noch** ē′nŭk
**E′nos** ē′nŏs
**En·ri′co** *Ital.* ān·rē′kō
**En·ri′ka** *Ger.* ĕn·rē′kä
**En·ri′que** *Span.* ān·rē′kā
**En′sor** ĕn′zẽr
**Eo′ghan** *Ir.* ō′ĕn
**Eoin** *Ir.* yōn, ō′ĕn
**E′pa·mei·non′das** *Mod. Grk.* â′pä-mē·nôn′thäs
**Epes** ĕps
**E′phra·im** ē′frȧ·ĭm, ē′frĭ·ŭm; *Ger.* ā′frä·ĭm, ȧ·frä′ĭm
**E·pi·ta′cio** *Port.* ė·pē·tȧ′syo͞o
**Ep′per·son** ĕp′ẽr·s'n
**É′rasme′** *Fr.* ā′rȧs′m'
**E·ras′mo** *Ital.* ȧ·räz′mō
**E·ras′mus** ė·răz′mŭs; *Dan.* ĭ·räs′-mo͞os; *Ger.* ȧ·räs′mo͞os
**E·ras′tus** ė·răs′tŭs
**E′razm** *Pol.* ĕ′räz'm
**Er′co·le** *Ital.* ĕr′kō·lā
**Erd′mann** *Ger.* ārt′män
**Er′hard** *Ger.* ār′härt
**Er′ic** ĕr′ĭk, ēr′ĭk—**E′ric** *Dan.* ē′rĕk; *Norw.* ā′rĕk—**E′ric′** *Swed.* ā′rĭk′
**E′rich** *Ger.* ā′rĭᴋ
**E·ri′co** *Port.* ?ė·rē′ko͞o
**E·rig′e·na** ė·rĭj′ĕ·nȧ
**E′rik** *Dan.* ē′rĕk; *Ger.* ā′rĭk; *Norw.* ā′rĕk—**E′rik′** *Fr.* ā′rēk′—**E′rik′** *Swed.* ā′rĭk′
**E′ri·ka** *Ger.* ā′rē·kä
**E′ri′kit′** *Fr.* ā′rē′kēt′
**E′ris** *Ger.* ā′rĭs
**Er′ken·bald** ûr′kĕn·bôld, -b'ld
**Erk′ki** *Finn.* ĕrk′kĭ
**Er′land′** *Swed.* âr′lȧnd′
**Erle** ûrl
**Er·man′no** *Ital.* âr·män′nō
**Er·me′te** *Ital.* âr·mâ′tā
**Er·mi′nia** *Ital.* âr·mē′nyä
**Er′mi·nie** ûr′mĭ·nĭ
**Er·min′nie** ûr·mĭn′ĭ
**Er′nald** ûr′n'ld
**Er′nest** ûr′nĕst, -nĭst; *Swed.* âr′nĕst —**Er·nest′** *Ger.* ĕr·nĕst′—**Er′nest′** *Fr.* ĕr′nĕst′
**Er·nes′tas** *Lith.* ĕr·nĕs′täs
**Er′nes·tine** ûr′nĕs·tēn, -nĭs- —**Er′ne-sti′ne** *Ger.* ĕr′nĕs·tē′nĕ
**Er·ne′sto** *Ital.* âr·nâ′stō—**Er·nes′to** *Port.* ĕr·nĕsh′to͞o, (*Braz.*) -nĕs′-; *Span.* ĕr·nās′tō
**Er·ne′stus** *Ger.* ĕr·nĕs′to͞os
**Ern′le** ûrn′'l
**Er′nő** *Hung.* ĕr′nû
**Ernst** ûrnst; *Du., Ger.* ĕrnst; *Norw.* ărnst; *Swed.* ârnst
**Er·ri′co** *Ital.* âr·rē′kō
**Er′ro** *Finn.* ĕr′rō
**Er·si′lio** *Ital.* âr·sē′lyō
**Er′skine** ûr′skĭn
**Er′vin** ûr′vĭn
**Er′win** ûr′wĭn; *Ger.* ĕr′vēn
**E·sa′ias** *Du.* ȧ·sȧ′yäs—**E·sai′as** *Swed.* ĕ·sī′ȧs
**E′sek** ē′sĕk
**Es′mé** ĕz′mē
**Es′mond** ĕz′mŭnd
**Es′prit′** *Fr.* ĕs′prē′
**Es′sex** ĕs′ĕks, -ĭks
**Es′ta·brook** ĕs′tȧ·bro͝ok
**Es·ta′cio** *Port.* ĕsh·tȧ′syo͞o, (*Braz.*) ĕs-
**Es′ta·nis·la′o** *Span.* ās′tä·nēs·lä′ō
**Es·te′ban** *Span.* ȧs·tā′bän
**Es′tell** ĕs′tĕl
**Es·telle′** ĕs·tĕl′; ĕs′tĕl
**Es′ten** ĕs′tĕn
**Es′tes** ĕs′tĕs
**Es′ther** *Eng., Ger.* ĕs′tẽr
**Es′tienne′** *Fr.* ĕs′tyĕn′
**Est′lin** ĕst′lĭn
**Es·tra′da** *Span.* ȧs·trä′thä
**E·su′vi·us** *Lat.* ė·sū′vĭ·ŭs
**et** *Fr.* ā
**E′than** ē′thăn
**Eth′el** ĕth′ĕl
**Eth′el·bert** ĕth′ĕl·bẽrt
**Eth′e·lin′da** ĕth′ĕ·lĭn′dȧ
**Eth′el·re′da** ĕth′ĕl·rē′dȧ
**É′tienne′** *Fr.* ā′tyĕn′
**É′tien′nette′** *Fr.* ā′tyĕ′nĕt′
**Et′to·re** *Ital.* ĕt′tō·rā
**Eudes** *Fr.* ûd
**Eu·gen′** *Ger.* oi·gān′
**Eu·gene′** ū·jēn′, ū′jēn
**Eu′gène′** *Fr.* û′zhân′, ü′zhân′
**Eu·ge′ni·a** ū·jē′nĭ·ȧ, ū·jēn′yȧ
**Eu·ge′ni·e** *Ger.* oi·gā′nē·ĕ
**Eu′gé′nie′** *Fr.* û′zhā′nē′, ü′zhā′nē′
**Eu·ge′nio** *Ital.* ȧ·o͞o·jâ′nyō; *Span.* ȧ·o͞o·hā′nyō
**Eu·gê′nio** *Port.* ȧ·o͞o·zhā′nyo͞o
**Eu·ge′ni·us** *Dan.* ĕ·o͞o·gē′nē·o͞os
**Eu′las** ū′lăs
**Eu′nice** ū′nĭs—**Eu·ni′ce** *Lat.* ū·nī′sē
**Eu′phra′sie′** *Fr.* û′frȧ′zē′, ü′frȧ′zē′
**Eu·phros′y·ne** ū·frŏs′ĭ·nē, -frŏz′-
**Eu·ret′ta** ū·rĕt′ȧ
**Eu·sa′pia** *Ital.* ȧ·o͞o·zä′pyä
**Eu·se′bio** *Ital.* ȧ·o͞o·zâ′byō; *Span.* ȧ·o͞o·sā′byō
**Eu·se′bi·us** *Ger.* oi·zā′bē·o͞os
**Eus′tace** ūs′tĭs
**Eus′tache′** *Fr.* ûs′tȧsh′, üs′tȧsh′
**Eu′trope′** *Fr.* û′trôp′, ü′trôp′
**Eu·tych′** *Ger.* oi·tüᴋ′
**E′va** ē′vȧ; *Ger., Norw.* ā′vä
**Ev′an** ĕv′ăn
**E·van′der** ė·văn′dẽr
**E·van′ge·line** ė·văn′jĕ·lēn, -līn, -lĭn
**E′van·ge·li′sta** *Ger.* ā′väng·gā·lĭs′tä; *Ital.* ā′vän·jā·lēs′tä
**Ev′ans** ĕv′ănz
**É′va′riste′** *Fr.* ā′vȧ′rēst′
**E·va·ris′to** *Port.* ė·vȧ·rēsh′to͞o, (*Braz.*) -rēs′-; *Span.* ā′vä·rēs′tō
**Ev′arts** ĕv′ẽrts
**Ev·do·ki′a, -ki′ya** *Russ.* yĭv·dŭ-kyē′yŭ
**E′ve·li′na** *Ital.* ā′vā·lē′nä
**Ev′e·lyn** ĕv′ĕ·lĭn, ēv′lĭn, ē′vĕ·lĭn
**Ev′er·ard** ĕv′ẽr·ärd
**Ev′er·ett** ĕv′ẽr·ĕt, -ĭt
**E′ver·har′dus** *Du.* ā′vẽr·här′dûs
**Ev′er·ley, -ly** ĕv′ẽr·lĭ
**Ev′ers** ĕv′ẽrz
**Ev′er·shed** ĕv′ẽr·shĕd
**Ev′ert** ĕv′ẽrt—**E′vert** *Du.* ā′vẽrt
**Ev′ert·son** ĕv′ẽrt·s'n
**Ev·ge′ni, -nii** *Russ.* yĕf·gyā′nyû·ĭ
**Ev·ge′nie·vich** *Russ.* yĕf·gyā′nyĕ-vyĭch
**Ev·ge′ni·os** *Mod. Grk.* ĕv·yâ′nyôs
**Ev·gra′fo·vich** *Russ.* yĕv·grȧ′fŭ·vyĭch
**E′vind** *Finn.* ā′vĭnd
**É′vrard′** *Fr.* ā′vrȧr′

**Ev·se'e·vich** *Russ.* yĕf·syā'yĕ·vyĭch
**E'wald** *Ger.* ā'vält
**Ew'art** ū'ẽrt
**Ew'banke** ū'băngk
**Ew'ell** ū'ĕl
**Ew'en** ū'ĕn
**Ew'ing** ū'ĭng
**Eyre** âr
**Ey'ster** ī'stẽr
**Ey'ton** ī't'n
**Ey'vind** *Norw.* ĕ'ĭ·vĭn
**E·ze'chi·el** *Ger.* ā·tsĕᴋ'ē·ĕl
**E·zek'iel** ē·zēk'yĕl, -zē'kĭ·ĕl
**E'ze·quiel'** *Span.* ā'thā·kyĕl', ā'sā-
**Ez'ra** ĕz'rȧ

**Fa'bi·an** fā'bĭ·ăn, fāb'yăn; *Ger.* fä'-bē·än
**Fa'bio** *Ital.* fä'byō
**Fa'bi·us** *Lat.* fā'bĭ·ŭs
**Fa'bre** *Fr.* fȧ'br'
**Fa'bri'** *Fr.* fȧ'brē'
**Fa'brice'** *Fr.* fȧ'brēs'
**Fa·bri'zio** *Ital.* fä·brē'tsyō
**Fa·cun'do** *Ital.* fä·ko͞on'dō
**Fad·de'e·vich** *Russ.* fŭ·dyā'yĕ·vyĭch
**Fad·de'i** *Russ.* fŭ·dyā'ĭ
**Fair** fâr
**Fair'child** fâr'chīld
**Fair'fax** fâr'făks
**Fair'field** fâr'fēld
**Fair'ly** fâr'lĭ
**Faith'ful** fāth'fo͝ol, -f'l
**Fal'con** fôl'kŭn, fô'kŭn
**Fal'con·er** fôk'nẽr, fô(l)'kŭn·ẽr
**Fales** fālz
**Fal'las** făl'ăs
**Fal'low** făl'ō
**Fan'nie** făn'ĭ
**Fan'ning** făn'ĭng
**Fan'ny** făn'ĭ; *Ger.* fän'ē—**Fan'ny'** *Fr.* fȧ'nē'
**Fan'shawe** făn'shô
**Far'a·day** făr'ȧ·dā, -dĭ
**Far'kas** *Hung.* fŏr'kŏsh
**Farn'ham** fär'năm
**Farns'worth** färnz'wûrth, -wẽrth
**Far'quhar** fär'kwẽr, -kẽr
**Far'quhar·son** fär'kwẽr·s'n, -kẽr·s'n
**Far'rar, Far'rer** făr'ẽr
**Far'thing** fär'thĭng
**Far'well** fär'wĕl, -wĕl
**Faulk'land** fôk'lănd, fôlk'-
**Faus'tin'** *Fr.* fōs'tăɴ'
**Fau·sti'na** *Ital.* fou·stē'nä
**Faus·ti'no** *Span.* fous·tē'nō
**Fau'sto** *Ital.* fou'stō
**Faus'tus** *Lat.* fôs'tŭs
**Fa'vre** *Fr.* fȧ'vr'
**Faw'cett** fô'sĕt, -sĭt
**Fay** fā
**Fay·ette'** fā·ĕt'
**Fa·zil'** *Turk.* fä·zûl'
**Fear'gus** fûr'gŭs
**Fear'on** fēr'ŭn
**Fé'dé'ric'** *Fr.* fā'dā'rēk'
**Fe'de·ri'co** *Ital.* fā'dā·rē'kō; *Span.* fā'thā·rē'kō
**Fe'de·ri'go** *Ital.* fā'dā·rē'gō; *Span.* fā'thā·rē'gō
**Fe'dor** *Ger.* fā'dōr, -dōr

**Fë'dor** *Russ.* fyô'dẽr
**Fë'do·ro'vich** *Russ.* fyô'dŭ·rô'vyĭch
**Fë'do·rov'na** *Russ.* fyô'dŭ·rôv'nŭ
**Fel'ia** *Russ.* fyâl'yŭ, fyā'lyĭ·yŭ
**Fe·li·ber'to** *Port.* fĕ·lē·bâr'to͞o
**Fe·li'ce** *Ital.* fā·lē'chā
**Fe·li'ci·a** fē·lĭsh'ĭ·ȧ, -lĭsh'ȧ, -lĭs'ĭ·ȧ; *Span.* fā·lē'thyä, -syä
**Fe·li·cia'no** *Port.* fĕ·lē·syă'no͞o; *Span.* fā'lē·thyä'nō, -syä'nō
**Fé'li'cien'** *Fr.* fā'lē'syăɴ'
**Fé'li'ci'té'** *Fr.* fā'lē'sē'tā'
**Fe'liks** *Pol.* fĕ'lēks; *Russ.* fyā'lyĭks
**Fe'lim** *Ir.* fā'lĭm
**Fe·li'pe** *Span.* fā·lē'pā
**Fe'lix** fē'lĭks; *Du., Ger.* fā'lĭks; *Russ.* fyā'lyĭks
**Fé'lix'** *Fr.* fā'lēks'—**Fé'lix** *Span.* fā'lēks
**Fel'lows** fĕl'ōz
**Fel'ton** fĕl't'n, -tŭn
**Fen'e·lon** fĕn''l·ŭn
**Fen'i·more** fĕn'ĭ·mōr
**Fen'no** fĕn'ō
**Fen'ton** fĕn't'n, -tŭn
**Fen'wick** fĕn'wĭk, *esp. Brit.* fĕn'ĭk
**Fe'o·dor** *Ger.* fā'ō·dōr—**Fe·o'dor** *Russ.* fyĭ·ô'dẽr
**Fe'o·do'ra** fē'ō·dō'rȧ
**Fe·o'do·ro'vich** *Russ.* fyĭ·ô'dŭ·rô'-vyĭch
**Fe·o'do·rov'na** *Russ.* fyĭ·ô'dŭ·rôv'nŭ
**Fe·o·fan'** *Russ.* fyĭ·ŭ·fȧn'
**Fe·o·fi·lak'to·vich** *Russ.* fyĭ·ŭ·fyĭ-lȧk'tŭ·vyĭch
**Fer'ber** fûr'bẽr
**Fer'chault'** *Fr.* fĕr'shō'
**Fer'di·nand** fûr'dĭ·nănd; *Dan.* făr'-dĭ·nȧn; *Du., Ger.* fĕr'dē·nänt; *Swed.* făr'dĭ·nȧnd—**Fer'di'nand'** *Fr.* fĕr'-dē'näɴ'—**Fer·di·nand'** *Russ.* fyĕr-dyĭ·nȧnt', fyăr'dyĭ·nŭnt
**Fer'di'nande'** *Fr.* fĕr'dē'näɴd'
**Fer'di·nan'do** fûr'dĭ·năn'dō; *Ital.* fār'dē·nän'dō
**Fer·dy'nand** *Pol.* fĕr·dĭ'nänt
**Fe'renc, Fe'rencz** *Hung.* fĕ'rĕnts
**Fé'ré'ol'** *Fr.* fā'rā'ôl'
**Fer'gus** fûr'gŭs
**Fer'gu·son, -gus·son** fûr'gŭ·s'n
**Fern** fûrn
**Fer·nam'** *Port.* fẽr·nouɴ'
**Fer·nán'** *Span.* fĕr·nän'
**Fer'nand'** *Fr.* fĕr'näɴ'
**Fer·nan'des** *Port.* fẽr·năɴn'dĕsh, (*Braz.*) -dēs
**Fer·nan'dez** fẽr·năn'dĕz, -dĭz; *Port.* fẽr·năɴn'dĕsh, (*Braz.*) -dēs
**Fer·nán'dez** *Span.* fĕr·nän'dāth, -dās
**Fer·nan'do** fẽr·năn'dō, fûr-; *Ital.* fār·nän'dō; *Port.* fẽr·năɴn'do͞o; *Span.* fĕr·nän'dō
**Fer·não'** *Port.* fẽr·nouɴ'
**Fer·ran'te** *Ital.* fār·rän'tā
**Fer'ris** fĕr'ĭs
**Fer·ruc'cio** *Ital.* fār·ro͞ot'chō
**Fes'sen·den** fĕs''n·dĕn
**Fes'tus** *Lat.* fĕs'tŭs
**Fet'tes** fĕt'ĭs
**Fè'vre, Le** *Fr.* lē fâ'vr'

**Fia'cre** *Fr.* fyȧ'kr'
**Fid'di·an** fĭd'ĭ·ăn
**Fi·del'** *Span.* fē·thĕl'
**Fi·de'li·o** *Ger.* fē·dā'lē·ō
**Fi·de'lis** *Ger.* fē·dā'lĭs
**Field** fēld
**Fiel'ding** fēl'dĭng
**Fields** fēldz
**Fiennes** fĭnz
**Fife** fīf
**Fi'li·ber'to** *Ital.* fē'lē·bĕr'tō
**Fi·lin'to** *Port.* fē·lēɴn'to͞o
**Fi·lipp'** *Russ.* fyĭ·lyēp'
**Fi'lip·pi'no** *Ital.* fē'lēp·pē'nō
**Fi·lip'po** *Ital.* fē·lēp'pō
**Fil'ley** fĭl'ĭ
**Fill'more** fĭl'mōr
**fils** *Fr.* fēs
**Finch** fĭnch
**Find'lay** fĭn(d)'lā, -lĭ
**Find'ley** fĭn(d)'lĭ
**Fin'gal** fĭng'găl
**Fin'lay** fĭn'lā, -lĭ
**Fin'ley** fĭn'lĭ
**Finn** *Eng., Swed.* fĭn; *Icel.* fĭd''n
**Fin'ne** *Swed.* fĭn'nĕ
**Fin'nur** *Icel.* fĭn'nẽr
**Fi·o'na** fī·ō'nȧ, fĭ-
**Fio·ren'zo** *Ital.* fyō·rĕn'tsō
**Fir'min'** *Fr.* fēr'măɴ'
**Fish** fĭsh
**Fish'er** fĭsh'ẽr
**Fisk, Fiske** fĭsk
**Fitch** fĭch
**Fitts** fĭts
**Fitz** fĭts
**Fitz·ed'ward** fĭts·ĕd'wẽrd
**Fitz·Ger'ald** fĭts·jĕr'ăld
**Fitz'-Greene'** fĭts'grēn', fĭts·grēn'
**Fitz'hugh'** fĭts'hū', fĭts·hū'
**Fitz'james', Fitz'-James'** fĭts'jāmz', fĭts·jāmz'
**Fitz'-John', Fitz'John'** fĭts'jŏn', fĭts-jŏn'
**Fitz·mau'rice** fĭts·mô'rĭs, -mŏr'ĭs
**Fitz·ran'dolph** fĭts·răn'dŏlf
**Fitz'Roy', Fitz'roy'** fĭts'roi', fĭts·roi'
**Fitz·si'mons** fĭt(s)·sĭ'mŭnz
**Fitz·wil'liam** fĭts·wĭl'yăm
**Flack** flăk
**Flagg** flăg
**Fla·mi'nio** *Ital.* flä·mē'nyō
**Fla'vi·a** *Lat.* flā'vĭ·ȧ
**Fla'vio** *Ital.* flä'vyō
**Fla'vi·us** flā'vĭ·ŭs
**Fleem'ing** flĕm'ĭng
**Flem'ing** flĕm'ĭng
**Fletch'er** flĕch'ẽr
**Flin'ders** flĭn'dẽrz
**Flood** flŭd
**Flo'ra** flō'rȧ
**Flor'ance** flŏr'ăns
**Flor'ence** flŏr'ĕns—**Flo'rence'** *Fr.* flô'räɴs'
**Flo·ren'cio** *Span.* flō·rān'thyō, -syō
**Flo'rens** *Ger.* flō'rĕns, *Lat.* flō'rĕnz
**Flo'rent'** *Fr.* flô'räɴ'; *Du.* flō·rĕnt'
**Flo'ren'tin'** *Fr.* flô'räɴ'tăɴ'
**Flo·ren'ty** *Pol.* flō·rĕn'tĭ
**Flo'res'tan'** *Fr.* flô'rĕs'täɴ'
**Flo're·sta'no** *Ital.* flō'rās·tä'nō

**Flo'ri·an** flō'rĭ·ăn; *Ger.* flō'rē·än—**Flo'rian'** *Fr.* flô'ryäN'
**Flo·rián'** *Span.* flô·ryän'
**Flo·ria'no** *Port.* flōō·ryă'nōō
**Flo'ri·mond** *Flem.* flō'rē·mônt—**Flo'-ri'mond'** *Fr.* flô'rē'môN'
**Flo'ri·mund** *Ger.* flō'rē·mōōnt
**Floyd** floid
**Flynt** flĭnt
**Fogg** fŏg
**Fol'co** *Ital.* fôl'kō
**Fol'ger** fōl'jẽr
**Folkes** fōlks
**Fol'len** fŏl'ĕn
**Fol'lett** fŏl'ĕt, -ĭt
**Fon·taine'** fŏn·tān', fŏn'tān
**Foot, Foote** fo͝ot
**Force** fōrs
**Ford** fōrd
**For'dyce** fōr'dīs
**For'est** fŏr'ĕst, -ĭst
**For'es·ter** fŏr'ĕs·tẽr, -ĭs·tẽr
**For'man** fôr'măn
**For'rest** fŏr'ĕst, -ĭst
**For'res·ter** fŏr'ĕs·tẽr, -ĭs·tẽr
**For'ster** fôr'stẽr
**Fort** fōrt
**For'tu'nat'** *Fr.* fôr'tü'nà'
**For'tu·na'to** *Ital.* fōr'tōō·nä'tō
**For'tu·na'tus** fôr'tū·nā'tŭs
**For'tune** fôr'tūn
**For'tu'né'** *Fr.* fôr'tü'nā'
**Foss** fôs
**Fos'ter** fôs'tẽr
**Foth'er·gill** fŏth'ẽr·gĭl
**Foun'tain** foun'tĭn, -tĕn
**Fow'ell** fou'ĕl
**Fowle** foul
**Fowl'er** foul'ẽr
**Fowles** foulz
**Fownes** founz
**Fox** fŏks
**Fox'croft** fŏks'krôft
**Fox'well** fŏks'wĕl, -wĕl
**fra** *Ital.* frä
**Fran'ces** från'sĕs, -sĭs
**Fran·ce'sca** *Ital.* frän·chās'kä
**Fran·ce'sco** *Ital.* frän·chās'kō
**Fran·chi'no** *Ital.* fräng·kē'nō
**Fran'cis** från'sĭs; *Du.* frän'sĭs; *Ger.* frän'tsĭs; *Norw.* frän'sĭs—**Fran'cis'** *Fr.* fräN'sēs'
**Fran·cis'ca** frăn·sĭs'kà; *Port.* fräN-sēsh'kà, (*Braz.*) -sēs'-; *Span.* frän-thēs'kä, -sēs'-
**Fran·cis'co** frăn·sĭs'kō; *Port.* fräN-sēsh'kōō, (*Braz.*) -sēs'-; *Span.* frän-thēs'kō, -sēs'-
**Fran·cis'cus** *Du.* frän·sĭs'kûs; *Lat.* frăn·sĭs'kŭs
**Fran'cisque'** *Fr.* fräN'sēsk'
**Fran·ci'szek** *Pol.* frän·tsē'shĕk
**Franck, Francke** frăngk
**Fran'co** *Ital.* fräng'kō
**Fran'çois'** *Fr.* fräN'swà'
**Fran'çoise'** *Fr.* fräN'swàz'
**Frands** *Dan.* fräns
**Frank** frăngk; *Fr.* fräNk; *Du.*, *Ger.* frängk
**Frank'fort** frăngk'fẽrt
**Frank'lin, -lyn** frăngk'lĭn
**Fra'nov** *Yugo.* frä'nôv
**Frans** *Du.* fräns; *Finn.*, *Swed.* fråns
**Fran'ti·šek** *Czech* från'tyĭ·shĕk
**Frants** *Norw.* fränts; *Russ.* frånts
**Fran'tse·vich** *Russ.* från'tsyĕ·vyĭch
**Frantz** *Fr.* fräNts
**Franz** frănts, frănz, fränts; *Fr.* fräNts; *Ger.* fränts; *Russ.* frånts
**Fran'ze·vich** *Russ.* från'tsyĕ·vyĭch
**Fran·zis'ka** *Ger.* frän·tsĭs'kä
**Fra'ser** frā'zẽr
**Frau** *Ger.* frou
**fray** *Span.* frä'ē
**Fra'zer** frā'zẽr
**Fra'zier** frā'zhẽr
**Fred** frĕd
**Fred'er·ic** frĕd'ẽr·ĭk, frĕd'rĭk—**Fre'-de·ric** *Norw.* frĕd'rĭk
**Fré'dé'ric'** *Fr.* frā'dā'rēk'
**Fre'de·ri'ca** *Ger.* frā'dā·rē'kä
**Fred'er·ick** frĕd'ẽr·ĭk, frĕd'rĭk—**Fre'de·rick** *Dan.* frĭth'rĭk
**Fré'dé'rick'** *Fr.* frā'dā'rēk'
**Fred'er·ick'a** frĕd'ẽr·ĭk'à
**Fre'de·rik** *Dan.* frĭth'rĭk; *Du.*, *Swed.* frā'dĕ·rĭk
**Fre'de·ri'ka** *Dan.* frĭ'thĕ·rē'kà
**Fred'ric** frĕd'rĭk—**Fre'dric** *Swed.* frā'drĭk
**Fred·ri'ca** frĕd·rē'kà
**Fred'rik** *Dan.* frĭth'rĭk; *Norw.* frĕd'-rĭk—**Fre'drik** *Du.*, *Finn.*, *Swed.* frā'drĭk
**Fred·ri'ka** *Swed.* frĕd·rē'kà
**Free'land** frē'lănd
**Free'man** frē'măn
**Free'mont** frē'mŏnt
**Freer** frēr
**frei** *Port.* frā'ē
**Frei'herr'** *Ger.* frī'hĕr'
**Fre'ling·huy'sen** frē'lĭng·hī'z'n
**Fre'man'tle** frē'măn't'l
**Fre'mont** frē'mŏnt, frē·mŏnt'
**French** frĕnch
**Frend** frĕnd
**Fres'nin'** *Fr.* frā'năN'
**Fri'da** *Ger.* frē'dä
**Fri'do·lin** *Du.* frē'dō·lĭn
**Fridt'jof** *Norw.* frĭt'yŏf
**Frie'da** *Ger.* frē'dä
**Frie'de·mann** *Ger.* frē'dĕ·män
**Frie'de·ri'ke** *Ger.* frē'dĕ·rē'kĕ
**Fried'lieb** *Ger.* frēt'lēp
**Frie'drich** frē'drĭk; *Ger.* frē'drĭK
**Fries** frēs
**Frink** frĭngk
**Fris'bie** frĭz'bĭ
**Frit'hiof** *Swed.* frĭt'yôf
**Frits** *Dan.* frĕts
**Fritz** *Eng.*, *Ger.* frĭts
**Frog'nall** frŏg'n'l
**Fro'men'tal'** *Fr.* frô'mäN'tàl'
**Fruc·tuo'so** *Span.* frōōk·twō'sō
**Fry·de'ryk** *Pol.* frĭ·dĕ'rĭk
**Fryn'i·wyd** frĭn'ĭ·wĭd
**Fuch** *Fr.* fo͞ok
**Fu'fi·us** *Lat.* fū'fĭ·ŭs
**Ful'cran'** *Fr.* fül'kräN'
**Ful'gence'** *Fr.* fül'zhäNs'
**Ful·gen'cio** *Span.* fōōl·hān'thyō, -syō
**Fulke** fo͝olk
**Ful'ler** fo͝ol'ẽr
**Ful'ler·ton** fo͝ol'ẽr·t'n, -tŭn
**Fü'löp** *Hung.* fü'lûp
**Ful'ton** fo͝ol't'n, -tŭn
**Ful'via** *Ital.* fōōl'vyä
**Ful'vi·us** *Lat.* fŭl'vĭ·ŭs
**Fu·mi·ma·ro** *Jap.* fōō·mē·mä·rō
**Funk** fŭngk
**Fürch'te·gott** *Ger.* fürK'tĕ·gôt
**Fu'rio** *Ital.* fōō'ryō
**Fu'ri·us** *Lat.* fū'rĭ·ŭs
**Fur'man** fûr'măn
**Fur'neaux** fûr'nō
**Fur'ni·fold** fûr'nĭ·fōld
**Fu'sée'** *Fr.* fü'zā'
**Fynes** fīnz
**Fyodor.** Variant transliteration of FËDOR.
**Fyodorovich.** Variant transliteration of FËDOROVICH.
**Fyodorovna.** Variant transliteration of FËDOROVNA.

**Gab'bert** găb'ẽrt
**Gá'bor** *Hung.* gä'bôr
**Ga'bri·el** gā'brĭ·ĕl; *Du.* gà'brē·ĕl; *Ger.* gä'brē·ĕl; *Norw.*, *Swed.* gä'-brĭ·ĕl—**Ga'bri'el'** *Fr.* gà'brē'ĕl' —**Ga·bri·el'** *Port.* gă·brē·ĕl'—**Ga'bri·el'** *Span.* gä'brē·ĕl'
**Ga'bri·e'la** *Span.* gä'brē·ā'lä
**Ga'bri·e'le** *Ger.* gä'brē·ā'lĕ; *Ital.* gä'-brē·â'lâ
**Ga'bri·el'la** gā'brĭ·ĕl'à, găb'rĭ-
**Ga'bri·elle'** gā'brĭ·ĕl', găb'rĭ-—**Ga'-bri'elle'** *Fr.* gà'brē'ĕl'
**Ga'bri·el'lo** *Ital.* gä'brē·ĕl'lō
**Ga'bri·els·son'** *Swed.* gä'brĭ·ĕl·sôn'
**Ga'brjel** *Pol.* gä'bryĕl
**Ga'bry·e'la** *Pol.* gä'brĭ·ĕ'lä
**Gad'do** *Ital.* gäd'dō
**Gads'by** gădz'bĭ
**gaek'war** gīk'wär
**Ga'é'tan'** *Fr.* gà'ā'täN'
**Ga'e·ta'na** *Ital.* gä'â·tä'nä
**Ga'e·ta'no** *Ital.* gä'â·tä'nō
**Gail** gāl
**Gaines** gānz
**Gaird'ner** gârd'nẽr, gärd'-
**Ga'ius** *Lat.* gā'yŭs, gī'ŭs
**Ga·lak·ti·o'no·vich** *Russ.* gŭ·lŭk·tyĭ-ô'nŭ·vyĭch
**Gal'bert'** *Fr.* gàl'bâr'
**Gal·braith'** găl·brāth', găl'brāth
**Gale** gāl
**Ga'le·az'zo** *Ital.* gä'lâ·ät'tsō
**Ga'len** gā'lĕn
**Ga·le'ri·a** *Lat.* gà·lēr'ĭ·à
**Ga·le'ri·us** *Lat.* gà·lēr'ĭ·ŭs
**Gal'i·le'o** găl'ĭ·lē'ō—**Ga'li·le'o** *Ital.* gä'lē·lâ'ō
**Ga'lis'sard'** *Fr.* gà'lē'sàr'
**Gal'la·tin** găl'à·tĭn
**Gal'lo·way** găl'ō·wā
**Gal'lus** *Ger.* gäl'ōōs
**Gal'ton** gôl't'n, -tŭn
**Ga·lu'sha** gà·lū'shà
**Gam'age** găm'ĭj
**Ga·ma'li·el** gà·mā'lĭ·ĕl, gà·māl'yĕl
**Gam'ble** găm'b'l
**Gan'na·way** găn'à·wā

**Gan′nett** găn′ĕt, -ĭt
**Gans** *Ger.* gäns
**Ga′on** *Heb.* gä′ōn, gä·ōn′
**Gar·ci′a** *Port.* gẽr·sē′ȧ
**Gar·cí′a** *Span.* gär·thē′ä, -sē′ä
**Gard** gärd
**Gar′di·ner** gärd′nẽr, gär′d′n·ẽr
**Gard′ner** gärd′nẽr
**Gar′et** găr′ĕt
**Gar′field** gär′fēld
**Gar′i** gâr′ĭ
**Gar′i·bal′di** găr′ĭ·bôl′dĭ, -băl′dĭ
**Gar′land** gär′lănd
**Gar′net, -nett** gär′nĕt, -nĭt
**Gar′ret, -rett** găr′ĕt
**Gar′rick** găr′ĭk
**Gar′ri·son** găr′ĭ·s′n
**Garth** gärth
**Garv** ?gärv
**Gar′ver** gär′vẽr
**Gar′y** gâr′ĭ
**Gas′par** găs′pẽr; *Lat.* găs′pär—**Gas·par′** *Port.* gȧsh·pȧr′, (*Braz.*) gȧs·pȧr′; *Span.* gäs·pär′
**Gas′pard′** *Fr.* gȧs′pȧr′
**Ga′spa·ro** *Ital.* gäs′pä·rō
**Gas′sa·way** găs′ȧ·wā
**Gas′sett** găs′ĕt, -ĭt
**Gas′ton** găs′tŭn—**Gas′ton′** *Fr.* gȧs′-tôɴ′
**Ga·sto′ne** *Ital.* gäs·tō′nā
**Gates** gāts
**Ga′thorne** gā′thôrn
**Gau′denz** *Ger.* gou′dĕnts
**Gau·den′zio** *Ital.* gou·dĕn′tsyō
**Gau′tier′** *Fr.* gō′tyā′
**Gav′an** găv′ăn
**Ga′vi·us** *Lat.* gā′vĭ·ŭs
**Ga·vri·il′** *Russ.* gŭ·vryĭ·ēl′
**Ga′vri′lo** *Yugo.* gä′vrē′lō
**Ga·vri′lo·vich, -vitch** *Russ.* gŭ·vryē′-lŭ·vyĭch
**Gay′lord** gā′lôrd
**Geb′hard** *Ger.* gĕp′härt
**Ged′ney** gĕd′nĭ
**Geer** gēr
**Geer·har′dus** *Du.* gār·här′dûs
**Geert** *Du.* gārt
**Geer·trui′da** *Du.* gār·troi′dȧ
**Ge·la′sio** *Ital.* jā·lä′zyō
**Ge·lett′** jĕ·lĕt′
**Gem′ma** *Ital.* jĕm′mä
**Ge′na** jē′nȧ
**Gene** jēn
**Gen′e·vieve′** jĕn′ĕ·vēv′, jĕn′ĕ·vēv
**Ge·ne·viève′** *Fr.* zhĕn·vyâv′
**Gen·na′ro** *Ital.* jān·nä′rō
**Gen·ta·ro** *Jap.* gĕn·tä·rō
**Gen·ti′le** *Ital.* jān·tē′lā
**Geof′frey** jĕf′rĭ
**Geof′froi′, Geof′froy′** *Fr.* zhô′frwä′
**Ge·org′** *Dan.* gĭ·ŏr(g)′; *Ger.* gā·ôrĸ′—**Ge′org** *Finn.* yĕ′ŏrg; *Norw.* gā′ŏrg; *Swed.* yā′ôr·y′
**George** jôrj; *Fr.* zhôrzh; *Ger.* zhôrsh; *Ruman.* zhŏrzh, jŏr′jĕ—**Geor′ge** *Du.* zhŏr′zhĕ
**Georges** *Fr.* zhôrzh
**Geor·gette′** jôr·jĕt′
**Ge·or′gi** *Russ.* gyĭ·ôr′gyû·ĭ
**Geor′gi·a** jôr′jĭ·ȧ, -jȧ
**Geor′gi·an′a** jôr′jĭ·ăn′ȧ, -ä′nȧ
**Geor′gie** jôr′jĭ
**Ge·or′gi·e·vich** *Russ.* gyĭ·ôr′gyĭ·yĕ-vyĭch
**Geor·gi′na** jôr·jē′nȧ
**Ge·or′gi·os** *Anc. Grk.* jē·ôr′jĭ·ŏs, jôr′-; *Mod. Grk.* yâ·ôr′yē·ôs
**Geor′gi·us** *Lat.* jôr′jĭ·ŭs; jē·ôr′-—**Ge·or′gi·us** *Swed.* yĕ·ôr′gĭ·ŭs
**Ge′raert** *Du.* gā′rȧrt
**Ger′ald** jĕr′ăld
**Gé′rald′** *Fr.* zhā′rȧld′
**Ger′al·dine** jĕr′ăl·dēn
**Ge·rard′** jĕ·rärd′, *esp. Brit.* jĕr′ärd, -ẽrd—**Ge′rard** *Du.* gā′rärt
**Gé′rard′** *Fr.* zhā′rȧr′
**Ge·rar′do** *Span.* hā·rär′thō
**Ge·rar′dus** *Du.* gā·rär′dûs; *Lat.* jĕ-rär′dŭs
**Ge·ra′sim** *Russ.* gyĕ·rȧ′syĭm
**Ge·ra′si·mo′vich** *Russ.* gyĕ·rȧ′syĭ-mô′vyĭch
**Gé′raud′** *Fr.* zhā′rō′
**Ger′bert′** *Fr.* zhĕr′bâr′
**Ger′brand** *Du.* gĕr′bränt
**Gerd** *Ger.* gĕrt
**Ger′gely** *Hung.* gĕr′gĕl·y′
**Ger′hard** *Du.* gā′rärt; *Ger.* gār′härt; *Norw.* gĕr′härt; *Swed.* yâr′hȧrd
**Ger′hardt** gĕr′härt
**Ger·har′dus** *Lat.* jûr·här′dŭs, jĕr-
**Ger′hart** *Ger.* gār′härt
**Ger′main′** *Fr.* zhĕr′măɴ′
**Ger·maine′** jûr·mān′, jĕr-—**Ger′-maine′** *Fr.* zhĕr′mân′
**Ger′man** jûr′măn
**Ger·mán′** *Span.* hĕr·män′
**Ger′ma·no·vich** *Russ.* gyâr′mŭ·nŭ-vyĭch
**Ge·ro′la·mo** *Ital.* jā·rô′lä·mō
**Ge′rold** *Ger.* gā′rôlt
**Ge·ro′ni·mo** *Ital.* jā·rô′nē·mō
**Ge·ró′ni·mo** *Span.* hā·rō′nē·mō
**Ger′rard** jĕr′ärd, -ẽrd, jĕ·rärd′
**Ger′rish** gĕr′ĭsh
**Ger′rit** gĕr′ĭt; *Du.* gĕr′ĭt
**Ger′rits, -ritsz** *Du.* gĕr′ĭts
**Ger′ry** gĕr′ĭ
**Ger′schon** gûr′shŏn
**Ger′shom** gûr′shŏm
**Ger′son** *Ger.* gĕr′zōn
**Ger′trud** *Dan.* găr′trōōth; *Ger.* gĕr′-trōōt
**Ger′trude** gûr′trōōd
**Ger·tru′dis** *Span.* hĕr·trōō′thēs
**Ger′vais′** *Fr.* zhĕr′vĕ′
**Ger′vase** jûr′văs
**Ger·va′sio** *Span.* hĕr·vä′syō
**Ge·si′nus** *Du.* gā·sē′nûs
**Ge·tu′lio** zhĕ·tōō′lyōō
**Gé′za** *Hung.* gā′zŏ
**Ghee′rardt** *Du.* gā′rärt
**Ghee′raert** *Du.* gā′rȧrt
**Gheor′ghe** *Rum.* gyŏr′gĕ
**Ghe·rar′do** *Ital.* gā·rär′dō
**Ghis′lain′** *Fr.* gē′lăɴ′
**Ghol′son** gōl′s′n
**Gia·cin′to** *Ital.* jä·chēn′tō
**Gia′co·mo** *Ital.* jä′kō·mō
**Gia′co·muz′zo** *Ital.* jä′kō·mōōt′tsō
**Gia′co·po** *Ital.* jä′kō·pō
**Giam′bat·ti′sta** *Ital.* jäm′bät·tēs′tä
**Giam′ma·ri′a** *Ital.* jäm′mä·rē′ä
**Gian′fran·ce′sco** *Ital.* jän′frän-chās′kō
**Gian′ga′le·az′zo** *Ital.* jäng′gä′lā·ät′-tsō
**Gian·gior′gio** *Ital.* jän·jōr′jō, -jôr′jō
**Gian′ma·ri′a** *Ital.* jäm′mä·rē′ä
**Gian′ni** *Ital.* jän′nē
**Gia′no** *Ital.* jä′nō
**Gib′bon** gĭb′ŭn
**Gib′bons** gĭb′ŭnz
**Gibbs** gĭbz
**Gib′son** gĭb′s′n
**Gid′e·on** gĭd′ē·ŭn—**Gi′de·on** *Ger.* gē′dā·ōn
**Gif′fard** gĭf′ẽrd
**Gif′ford** gĭf′ẽrd, jĭf′ẽrd
**Gi-i·chi** *Jap.* gē·ē·chē
**Gijs′bert** *Du.* gīs′bĕrt
**Gil** *Port.* zhĭl; *Span.* hēl
**Gi·lar′mi** *Ital.* jē·lär′mē
**Gil′bert** gĭl′bẽrt—**Gil′bert′** *Fr.* zhēl′-bâr′
**Gil·ber′tus** *Lat.* gĭl·bûr′tŭs
**Gil′christ** gĭl′krĭst
**Gil′der·sleeve** gĭl′dẽr·slēv
**Giles** jīlz
**Gilg** *Ger.* gĭlĸ
**Gill** gĭl
**Gil′les** *Du.* gĭl′ĕs—**Gilles** *Fr.* zhēl
**Gil·les′pie** gĭ·lĕs′pĭ
**Gil′lies** gĭl′ĭs, -ĭz
**Gil′lis** *Du.* gĭl′ĭs
**Gil′man** gĭl′măn
**Gil′more** gĭl′mōr
**Gi·nés′** *Span.* hē·nās′
**Gi′no** *Ital.* jē′nō
**Gio′ac·chi′no** *Ital.* jō′äk·kē′nō
**Gior·da′no** *Ital.* jōr·dä′nō
**Gior′gio** *Ital.* jōr′jō, jôr′jō
**Gio·suè′** *Ital.* jō·zwĕ′
**Gio·van′** *Ital.* jō·vän′
**Gio·van′ni** *Ital.* jō·vän′nē
**Gio·via′no** *Ital.* jō·vyä′nō
**Gip′sy** jĭp′sĭ
**Gi′raud′** *Fr.* zhē′rō′
**Gir′ja** *As. Ind.* gĭr′jä
**Gir′ling** gûr′lĭng
**Gi·ro′la·mo** *Ital.* jē·rô′lä·mō
**Gi·rón′** *Span.* hē·rôn′
**Gis′bert** *Du.* gĭs′bĕrt; *Ger.* gĭs′bĕrt
**Gis′le** *Norw.* gĭs′lĕ
**Gi′tha** gē′thȧ
**Giu·dit′ta** *Ital.* jōō·dēt′tä
**Giu′lia** *Ital.* jōō′lyä
**Giu·lia′no** *Ital.* jōō·lyä′nō
**Giu′lio** *Ital.* jōō′lyō
**Giu·sep′pe** *Ital.* jōō·zĕp′pā
**Giu′sep·pi′na** *Ital.* jōō′zāp·pē′nä
**Giu′sto** *Ital.* jōōs′tō
**Glad′heim** glăd′hīm
**Glad′stone** glăd′stōn, *esp. Brit.* -stŭn
**Glad′ys** glăd′ĭs
**Glas′gow** glȧs′gō, -kō, glăz′gō
**Glass** glȧs
**Glass′ford** glȧs′fẽrd
**Glea′son** glē′s′n
**Gleb** *Russ.* glyâp
**Glen, Glenn** glĕn

**Glen′ville** glĕn′vĭl
**Glen′way** glĕn′wā
**Glo′ri·a** glō′rĭ·ȧ
**Glov′er** glŭv′ẽr
**Glyn** glĭn
**Gnae′us** *Lat.* nē′ŭs
**God′dard** gŏd′ẽrd
**Go′de·fried** *Du.* gō′dĕ·frēt
**Go′de·froi′** *Fr.* gôd′frwä′
**Go′de·froid′** *Du.* gō′dĕ·frwȧ′—**Go′-de·froid′** *Fr.* gôd′frwä′
**Go′de·froy′** *Fr.* gôd′frwä′
**Go′dert** *Du.* gō′dẽrt
**God′frey** gŏd′frĭ
**God′fried** *Du.* gŏt′frēt
**God′ske** *Dan.* gŏth′skĕ
**God′win** gŏd′wĭn
**Goff** gŏf
**Gof·fre′do** *Ital.* gôf·frā′dô
**Gold** gōld
**Gol′den** gōl′dĕn
**Gol′die** gōl′dĭ
**Golds′bor′ough** gōldz′bûr′ō, *esp. Brit.* -bŭ·rŭ, -brŭ
**Gold′smith** gōld′smĭth
**Golds′wor′thy** gōldz′wûr′thĭ
**Gold′win** gōld′wĭn
**Gom′baud′** *Fr.* gôɴ′bō′
**Gom·bei** *Jap.* gôm·bā
**Go′mes** *Port.* gō′mĕsh, (*Braz.*) -mĕs
**Gó′mez** *Span.* gō′māth, -mās
**Gon·ça′lo** *Port.* gôɴ·sȧ′lōō
**Gon·su·ke** *Jap.* gôn·sōō·kĕ
**Gon·za′les** *Du.* gôn·zä′lĕs; *Span.* gôn·thä′lās, -sä′lās
**Gon·zá′lez** *Span.* gôn·thä′lāth, -sä′-lās
**Gon·za′lo** *Span.* gôn·thä′lō, -sä′lō
**Gon′zalve′** *Fr.* gôɴ′zȧlv′
**Good′all** gŏŏd′ôl
**Good′hue** gŏŏd′hū
**Good′loe** gŏŏd′lō
**Good′man** gŏŏd′măn
**Good′rich** gŏŏd′rĭch
**Good′will** gŏŏd′wĭl
**Good′win** gŏŏd′wĭn
**Good′year** gŏŏd′yẽr
**Goold** gōōld
**Go·pal′** *Bengali* gô·pô′lô (*Angl.* gô-pôl′); *Marathi* gō·päl′, gō·pä′lȧ (*Angl.* gô·päl′)
**Gö′ran′** *Swed.* yû′rȧn′
**Gorch** *Ger.* gôrᴋ
**Gor′don** gôr′d′n
**Gore** gōr
**Gor′ham** gôr′ăm
**Gor′ing** gōr′ĭng
**Gor′man** gôr′măn
**Go·ro** *Jap.* gô·rō
**Gor′ton** gôr′t′n
**Gos′combe** gŏs′kŭm
**Gö′sta** *Norw.* yû′stä
**Got′hard** *Dan.* gŏt′härd
**Go′ti·fre′do** *Ital.* gō′tē·frā′dô
**Gott′fried** *Ger.* gôt′frēt; *Swed.* gôt′-frēd
**Gott′hard** *Ger.* gôt′härt; *Swed.* gôt′-(h)ȧrd
**Gott′hardt** *Ger.* gôt′härt
**Gott′helf** *Ger.* gôt′hĕlf
**Gott′hilf** *Ger.* gôt′hĭlf
**Gott′hold** *Ger.* gôt′hôlt
**Gott′lieb** gŏt′lēb; *Finn.* gŏt′lēb; *Ger.* gôt′lēp; *Swed.* gôt′lēb
**Gott′lob** *Dan.* gŏt′lŏb; *Ger.* gôt′lōp
**Gotz** *Ger.* gûts
**Gough** gŏf
**Gould** gōōld
**Gou′ver·neur′** gŭv′ẽr·nẹr′, gŭv′ẽr-nẹr
**Go′vaert** *Du.* gō′vȧrt
**Gove** gōv
**Go·vind′** *Punjabi* gō·vĭnd′
**Go·vin′da** *Skr.* gō·vĭn′dȧ
**Gow′en** gou′ĕn
**Gow′land** gou′lănd
**Grace** grās
**Gra′cie** grā′sĭ
**Gra′dy** grā′dĭ
**Graeme** grām
**Graf′ton** grȧf′tŭn
**Gra′ham** grā′ăm, grâ′ăm
**Gram** grăm
**Gran′ber′ry** grăn′bĕr′ĭ, -bẽr·ĭ
**Gran′di·son** grăn′dĭ·s′n
**Gra′ni·us** *Lat.* grā′nĭ·ŭs
**Grant** grȧnt
**Gran′ville** grăn′vĭl
**Gra′ta** *Lat.* grā′tȧ
**Gra′tien′** *Fr.* grȧ′syăɴ′
**Grat′tan** grăt′′n
**Graves** grāvz
**Gray** grā
**Gra′zia** *Ital.* grä′tsyä
**Gra′zia·di′o** *Ital.* grä′tsyä·dē′ô
**Gree′ley** grē′lĭ
**Green, Greene** grēn
**Green′field** grēn′fēld
**Green′leaf** grēn′lēf
**Gree′nough** grē′nō
**Greer** grẹr
**Gregg** grĕg
**Gré′goire′** *Fr.* grā′gwȧr′
**Greg′or** grĕg′ẽr—**Gre′gor** *Ger.* grā′-gôr, grȧ·gôr′
**Gre·go′rio** *Ital.* grȧ·gô′ryô; *Span.* grȧ·gō′ryō
**Gre·go′ri·us** *Lat.* grē·gō′rĭ·ŭs
**Greg′o·ry** grĕg′ō·rĭ
**Gren′fell** grĕn′fĕl
**Gren′fill** grĕn′fĭl
**Gren′ville** grĕn′vĭl
**Gré′sinde′** *Fr.* grā′zăɴd′
**Gre′ta** grē′tȧ, grĕt′ȧ; *Swed.* grā′tȧ
**Gre′the** *Ger.* grā′tĕ
**Grev′ille** grĕv′ĭl, -′l
**Grey** grā
**Grid′ley** grĭd′lĭ
**Grier** grẹr
**Grif′fin** grĭf′ĭn
**Grif′fith** grĭf′ĭth
**Grif′fiths** grĭf′ĭths
**Griggs** grĭgz
**Gri·gor′e·vich** *Russ.* gryĭ·gôr′yĕ-vyĭch
**Gri·go′ri** *Russ.* gryĭ·gô′ryû·ĭ
**Gri·gor′ie·vich** *Russ.* gryĭ·gôr′yĕ-vyĭch
**Grimes** grīmz
**Grin′ling** grĭn′lĭng
**Gris′wold** grĭz′wŭld, -wōld, -wôld
**Gri·zel′** grĭ·zĕl′, grĭz′′l
**Gros′ve·nor** grōv′nẽr, grō′v′n·ẽr
**Grote** grōt
**Grove** grōv
**Gro′ver** grō′vẽr
**Groves** grōvz
**Grubb** grŭb
**Grze′gorz** *Pol.* gzhĕ′gôsh
**Gua′da·lu′pe** *Span.* gwä′thä·lōō′pā
**Gua·ri′no** *Ital.* gwä·rē′nô
**Gud′mund** *Swed.* gōōd′mŭnd
**Gud′mun′dur** *Icel.* gŭth′mûn′dẽr
**Guern′sey** gûrn′zĭ
**Guer′ra** *Port.* gâr′rȧ
**Gu·gliel′mo** *Ital.* gōō·lyĕl′mô
**Gui** *Fr.* gē
**Gui′chard′** *Fr.* gē′shȧr′
**Gui′do** gwē′dō; *Du.* gē′dō; *Ital.* gwē′dô—**Gu·i′do** *Ger.* gōō·ē′dō, gē′dō
**Gui′du·bal′do** *Ital.* gwē′dōō·bäl′dô
**Guild′ford** gĭl′fẽrd
**Gui·lher′me** *Port.* gē·lyâr′mĕ
**Guil′laume′** *Fr.* gē′yōm′
**Guil·lén′** *Span.* gē·lyān′, gē·yān′
**Guil·ler′mo** *Span.* gē·lyĕr′mō, gē-yĕr′mō
**Guit′ton·ci′no** *Ital.* gwēt′tôn·chē′nô
**Gu′li·el′mus** *Lat.* gū′lĭ·ĕl′mŭs
**Gun′nar** *Icel.* gûn′när; *Norw.* gōōn′-när; *Swed.* gŭn′nȧr
**Gun′ning** gŭn′ĭng
**Gun′no** *Swed.* gŭn′nô
**Gün′ther** *Ger.* gün′tẽr
**Gur′don** gûr′d′n
**Gur′ney** gûr′nĭ
**Gus′taf** *Finn.* gōōs′tȧf; *Swed.* gŭs′täv—**Gu′staf** *Ger.* gōōs′täf
**Gus′tafs·son** *Swed.* gŭs′täv·sôn
**Gus′tav** *Dan.* gōōs′tȧv; *Norw.* gōōs′-täv; *Swed.* gŭs′täv—**Gu′stav** *Ger.* gōōs′täf
**Gus′tave′** *Fr.* güs′tȧv′
**Gus·ta′vo** *Port.* gōōsh·tȧ′vōō, (*Braz.*) gōōs·tȧ′-; *Span.* gōōs·tä′vō
**Gus·ta′vus** gŭs·tā′vŭs, -tä′vŭs, gōōs-tä′-
**Gus′taw** *Pol.* gōōs′täf
**Guth′rie** gŭth′rĭ
**Gu·tier′re** *Span.* gōō·tyĕr′rā
**Guy** gī; *Fr.* gē
**Gwen** gwĕn
**Gwen′do·line** gwĕn′dô·lĭn, -lēn
**Gwi·nett′** gwĭ·nĕt′
**Gwlad′ys** glăd′ĭs
**Gwynne** gwĭn
**György** *Hung.* dyûrd′y′
**Gyp′sy** jĭp′sĭ
**Gyu′la** *Hung.* dyōō′lŏ

**Hab′dank** *Pol.* häb′dängk
**Ha·chi·ro** *Jap.* hä·chē·rô
**Ha·chi·ro·e·mon** *Jap.* hä·chē·rô·yĕ-môn
**Hack** hăk
**Hack′ett** hăk′ĕt, -ĭt
**Had′don** hăd′′n
**Ha′den** hā′d′n
**Ha′gar** hā′gẽr, -gär
**Hahn** hän
**Haigh** hāg, hā
**Ha·im′** *Heb.* ᴋĭ·yĭm′, ᴋĭ′yĭm

**Haines** hānz
**Ha·ji·me** *Jap.* hä·jĕ·mĕ
**Hal** hăl
**Hal′bert** hăl′bẽrt
**Hal′cott** ?hôl′kŭt
**Hal′cy·on** hăl′sĭ·ŭn
**Hale** hāl
**Ha′ley** hā′lĭ
**Half′dan** *Dan.* hȧlv′dȧn; *Norw.* hälv′dän
**Hall** hôl
**Hal′lam** hăl′ăm
**Hal′lett** hăl′ĕt, -ĭt
**Hal′li·day** hăl′ĭ·dā
**Hal′lie** hăl′ĭ
**Hal′lock** hăl′ŭk
**Hal′lo·well** hăl′ō·wĕl, -wĕl
**Hal′lowes** hăl′ōz
**Halse** hôls
**Hal′sey** hôl′sĭ, hăl′-
**Hal′stead, -sted** hôl′stĕd, -stĭd
**Halv′dan** *Norw.* hälv′dän
**Ha′mar** hā′mẽr
**Hame′lin** hăm′lĭn, hăm′ĕ·lĭn
**Ha′mer** hā′mẽr
**Ham′il·ton** hăm′ĭl·tŭn, -t′n
**Ha′mish** hā′mĭsh
**Ham′lin** hăm′lĭn
**Ham′mond** hăm′ŭnd
**Ha′mo** ?hā′mō
**Hamp′ton** hăm(p)′tŭn
**Hand** hănd
**Han′del** hăn′d′l
**Han′der·son** hăn′dẽr·s′n
**Hand′ley** hănd′lĭ
**Han′dy** hăn′dĭ
**Han′dy·side** hăn′dĭ·sīd
**Han′ford** hăn′fẽrd
**Han′kins** hăng′kĭnz
**Han′ley** hăn′lĭ
**Han′na, -nah** hăn′ȧ
**Han′nes** *Icel.* hän′nĕs
**Han′ni·bal** hăn′ĭ·băl
**Han′ning** hăn′ĭng
**Han′nis** hăn′ĭs
**Hanns** *Ger.* häns
**Hans** hănz, häns; *Dan.* hȧns; *Du., Ger., Norw.* häns; *Swed.* hȧns
**Han′sen** *Dan.* hȧn′s′n
**Han′son** hăn′s′n
**Ha′nuš** *Czech* hȧ′no͝osh
**Ha′rald** *Dan., Norw.* hä′räl; *Swed.* hä′rȧld′
**Har′butt** här′bŭt
**Har′court** här′kẽrt, -kōrt
**Har′de·man** här′dĕ·măn
**Har′die** här′dĭ
**Har′ding, -dinge** här′dĭng
**Hard′wicke** härd′wĭk
**Har′dy** här′dĭ
**Har′ford** här′fẽrd
**Har′i·ett** hăr′ĭ·ĕt
**Har′ing·ton** hăr′ĭng·tŭn
**Hark′ness** härk′nĕs, -nĭs
**Har′lan** här′lăn; *Span.* är′län
**Har′ley** här′lĭ
**Har′low, -lowe** här′lō
**Har′man** här′măn
**Har′mar** här′mẽr
**Har′men** *Du.* här′mĕn
**Har·mo′dio** *Span.* är·mō′thyō
**Har′mon** här′mŭn
**Har′nam** här′năm
**Har′old** hăr′ŭld
**Har′per** här′pẽr
**Har′perts·zoon** *Du.* här′pẽrt·sŭn, -sôn, -sōn
**Har′rell** hăr′ĕl
**Har′ri·et** hăr′ĭ·ĕt
**Har′ri·man** hăr′ĭ·măn
**Har′ring·ton** hăr′ĭng·tŭn
**Har′ri·ot, -ott** hăr′ĭ·ŭt
**Har′ris** hăr′ĭs
**Har′ri·son** hăr′ĭ·s′n
**Har′ry** hăr′ĭ; *Dan., Ger.* här′ē
**Hart, Harte** härt
**Hart′ley** härt′lĭ
**Hart′man** härt′măn
**Hart′mann** *Ger.* härt′män
**Hart′pole** ?härt′pōl
**Harts′horne** härts′hôrn
**Hart′well** härt′wĕl, -wĕl
**Hart′wick** härt′wĭk
**Hart′wig** *Ger.* härt′vĭᴋ
**Hart′zell** härt′s′l
**Har′vey** här′vĭ
**Har′wood** här′wo͝od
**Has′kell** hăs′kĕl
**Has′kins** hăs′kĭnz
**Has′tings** hās′tĭngz
**Has′ty** hās′tĭ
**Has′well** hăz′wĕl, -wĕl
**Hatch** hăch
**Hatch′er** hăch′ẽr
**Hat′field** hăt′fēld
**Have′lock** hăv′lŏk, -lŭk
**Ha′ven** hā′vĕn
**Hav′er·sham** hăv′ẽr·shăm, här′shăm
**Haw′ley** hô′lĭ
**Haw′thorne** hô′thôrn
**Hay** hā
**Hay′den** hā′d′n
**Hayes** hāz
**Hay′ley** hā′lĭ
**Hay′man** hā′măn
**Haynes** hānz
**Hays** hāz
**Hay′ward** hā′wẽrd
**Hay′wood** hā′wo͝od
**Hay·yim′** *Heb.* ᴋī·yĭm′, ᴋī′yĭm
**Haz′ard** hăz′ẽrd
**Ha′zle·hurst** hā′z′l·hûrst
**Haz′lett** hăz′lĕt, -lĭt
**Haz′litt** hăz′lĭt
**Head′land** hĕd′lănd
**Hea′ley** hē′lĭ
**Heard** hûrd
**Heas′lip** hēs′lĭp
**Heath** hēth
**Heath′cote** *Brit.* hĕth′kŭt
**He′ber** hē′bẽr
**Heck** hĕk
**Hec′tor** hĕk′tẽr—**Hec′tor′** *Fr.* ĕk′-tôr′
**Héc′tor** *Span.* ĕk′tôr
**Hedg′es** hĕj′ĕz, -ĭz
**Hed′vig** *Swed.* hĕd′vĭg
**Hed′wig** *Ger.* hāt′vĭᴋ
**Hed′worth** hĕd′wûrth, -wẽrth
**Hef′ner** *Ger.* hāf′nẽr
**Hei·ha·chi·ro** *Jap.* hā·hä·chē·rō
**Hei′ke** *Du.* hī′kĕ
**Heik′ki** *Finn.* hĕ′ĭk·kĭ
**Hein** *Du.* hīn
**Hein′rich** *Dan.* hīn′rĕᴋ; *Ger.* hīn′rĭᴋ
**Heinz** *Ger.* hīnts
**Heiss** hīs
**Hel′en** hĕl′ĕn, -ĭn
**Hel′e·na** hĕl′ĕ·nȧ, hĕ·lē′nȧ—**He·le′na** *Du.* hȧ·lā′nȧ—**He′le·na** *Ger.* hā′lȧ·nä
**He·le′ne** *Ger.* hȧ·lā′nĕ
**Hé′lène′** *Fr.* ā′lĕn′
**He·le′nus** *Swed.* hĕ·lā′nŭs
**Hel′ge** *Dan.* hĕl′gĕ
**He·lia′de** *Rum.* hĕ·lyä′dĕ
**Hé′li′dore′** *Fr.* ā′lē′dôr′
**Hé′lio′dore′** *Fr.* ā′lyô′dôr′
**Hell′muth** *Ger.* hĕl′mo͞ot
**Helm** hĕlm
**Hel′mich** *Swed.* hĕl′mĭk
**Hel·mi′ne** *Ger.* hĕl·mē′nĕ
**Hel′mut, -muth** *Ger.* hĕl′mo͞ot
**Hel·ve′ti·us** *Du.* hĕl·vā′(t)sē·ûs
**Hel′vi·us** *Lat.* hĕl′vĭ·ŭs
**He′man** hē′măn
**Hem′ing** hĕm′ĭng
**Hemp′stead** hĕmp′stĕd, -stĭd
**Hen′der·son** hĕn′dẽr·s′n
**Hen′dric** hĕn′drĭk
**Hen′drick** *Du.* hĕn′drĭk
**Hen′drick·je** *Du.* hĕn′drĭk·yĕ
**Hen′dricks** hĕn′drĭks
**Hen′dricksz** *Du.* hĕn′drĭks
**Hen·dri′cus** *Du.* hĕn·drē′kûs
**Hen′drik** hĕn′drĭk
**Hen′dry** hĕn′drĭ
**Hen′eage** hĕn′ĭj
**Hen′gist** hĕng′gĭst
**Hen′ley** hĕn′lĭ
**Henn** hĕn
**Hen′ney** hĕn′ĭ
**Hen′nig** *Ger.* hĕn′ĭᴋ
**Hen′ni·ker** hĕn′ĭ·kẽr
**Hen′ning** *Ger.* hĕn′ĭng; *Swed.* hĕn′-nĭng′
**Hen′ri** *Du.* häɴ′rĭ—**Hen′ri′** *Fr.* äɴ′rē′
**Hen′rick** *Dan.* hĕn′rĕk; *Du.* hĕn′rĭk
**Hen·ri′cus** *Du.* hĕn·rē′kûs; *Lat.* hĕn·rī′kŭs
**Hen′ri·et′ta** hĕn′rĭ·ĕt′ȧ
**Hen′ri·ette′** *Fr.* äɴ′ryĕt′—**Hen′ri-et′te** *Du., Ger.* hĕn′rē·ĕt′ĕ
**Hen′rik** *Eng., Finn., Ger., Hung., Norw., Swed.* hĕn′rĭk; *Dan.* hĕn′rĕk
**Hen·ri′que** *Port.* ãɴ·rē′kĕ; *Span.* ân·rē′kā
**Hen·ri′ques** *Port.* ãɴ·rē′kĕsh, (*Braz.*) -kĕs
**Hen′ry** hĕn′rĭ, *Du.* häɴ′rĭ; *Ger.* hĕn′rē—**Hen′ry′** *Fr.* äɴ′rē′
**Hen′ryk** *Pol.* hĕn′rĭk
**Hens′leigh** hĕnz′lĭ
**Hens′ley** hĕnz′lĭ
**Hep′burn** hĕp′bẽrn; *Brit. also* hĕb′-ẽrn, -ûrn
**Hep′ple** hĕp′′l
**Hep′worth** hĕp′wûrth, -wẽrth
**He·rac′li·us** *Lat.* hē·răk′lĭ·ŭs
**Hé′ra′cli′us′** *Fr.* ā′rȧ′klē′üs′
**Her′bert** hûr′bẽrt; *Ger.* hĕr′bĕrt; *Swed.* hăr′bĕrt

**Her'cule'** *Fr.* ĕr'kül'
**Her'cu·les** hûr'kû·lēz; *Du.* hĕr'kü·lĕs
**He·ren'ni·us** *Lat.* hĕ·rĕn'ĭ·ŭs
**Her'e·ward** hĕr'ĕ·wērd
**Her'holdt** *Dan.* hăr'hŏlt
**He'ri·bert** *Du., Ger.* hā'rê·bĕrt
**He'ri·ber'to** *Span.* ā'rê·bĕr'tō
**Her'man** hûr'măn; *Dan.* hăr'mȧn; *Du., Ger.* hĕr'män; *Finn.* hĕr'mȧn; *Norw.* hăr'män
**Her'mann** hûr'măn; *Dan.* hăr'mȧn; *Du., Ger., Icel.* hĕr'män—**Her'mann'** *Fr.* ĕr'mȧn'
**Her·ma'nus** *Du.* hĕr·mȧ'nûs
**Her'me·ne·gild** *Czech* hĕr'mĕ·nĕ·gĭlt
**Her'me·ne·gil'do** *Port.* âr'mĕ·nĕ·zhĭl'dōō; *Span.* ĕr'mā·nā·hēl'dō
**Her'mes** *Port.* âr'mĕsh, (*Braz.*) -mĕs
**Her·me'to** *Port.* ĕr·mā'tōō
**Her·mi'ne** *Ger.* hĕr·mē'nĕ
**Her'mione'** *Fr.* ĕr'myôn'
**Her·mog'e·nes** hûr·mŏj'ĕ·nēz
**Her'mon** hûr'mŭn
**Her·nán'** *Span.* ĕr·nän'
**Her·nán'dez** *Span.* ĕr·nän'dāth, -dās
**Her·nan'do** *Span.* ĕr·nän'dō
**Hern'don** hûrn'dŭn
**Her'rick** hĕr'ĭk
**Her'ries** hĕr'ĭs
**Her'ron** hĕr'ŭn
**Her'schel** hûr'shĕl
**Her'sey** hûr'sĭ
**Hers'leb** *Dan.* hărs'lĭb; *Norw.* hărs'lĕb
**Her'tha** ?hûr'thȧ
**Hertz'berg** hûrts'bûrg
**Her'vé'** *Fr.* ĕr'vā'
**Her'vey** hûr'vĭ, *esp. Brit.* här'vĭ
**Her'warth** *Ger.* hĕr'värt
**Hes'ba** hĕz'bȧ
**He'si·od** hē'sĭ·ŏd, hĕs'ĭ-
**Hes'keth** hĕs'kĕth, -kĭth
**Hes'sels** *Du.* hĕs'ĕls
**Hes'sin** hĕs'ĭn
**Hes'ter** hĕs'tēr
**Heth** hĕth
**Heth'er·ing·ton** hĕth'ĕr·ĭng·tŭn, hĕth'rĭng-
**Het'ty** hĕt'ĭ
**Hew** hū
**Hew'ard** hū'ērd
**Hew'ett** hū'ĕt, -ĭt
**Hew'itt** hū'ĭt
**Hew'lett** hū'lĕt, -lĭt
**Hew'son** hū's'n
**Heyl** hīl
**Hey'mann** *Ger.* hī'män
**Hey'ward** hā'wērd
**Hey'wood** hā'wŏŏd
**Hey'worth** hā'wûrth
**Hez'e·ki'ah** hĕz'ē·kī'ȧ
**Hib'bard** hĭb'ērd
**Hib'bert** hĭb'ērt
**Hice** hīs
**Hick'ey** hĭk'ĭ
**Hick'ling** hĭk'lĭng
**Hick'man** hĭk'măn
**Hicks** hĭks
**Hick'y** hĭk'ĭ
**Hic'ok** hĭk'ŏk
**Hid'den** hĭd''n
**Hi·de·ki** *Jap.* hê·dĕ·kê
**Hi·de·yo** *Jap.* hê·dĕ·yô
**Hi'er·on'y·mus** hī'ēr·ŏn'ĭ·mŭs—**Hi'e·ro'ny·mus** *Du.* hē'ĕ·rō'nē·mûs; *Ger.* hē'ā·rō'nü·mōōs
**Hig'gins** hĭg'ĭnz
**Hig'gin·son** hĭg'ĭn·s'n
**High'am** hī'ăm
**High'land** hī'lănd
**Hi·gi'nio** *Span.* ē·hē'nyō
**Hi·ko·i·chi** *Jap.* hê·kô·ê·chê
**Hi·ko·no·jo** *Jap.* hê·kô·nô·jō
**Hi·laire'** hĭ·lâr'—**Hi'laire'** *Fr.* ē'lâr'
**Hi·la'rio** *Span.* ē·lä'ryō
**Hi'la'rion'** *Fr.* ē'lȧ'ryôɴ'
**Hi'la·rión'** *Span.* ē'lä·ryôn'
**Hi·la'ri·us** *Ger.* hê·lä'rê·ōōs
**Hil'a·ry** hĭl'ȧ·rĭ
**Hil'borne** hĭl'bērn, -bôrn
**Hil'da** hĭl'dȧ
**Hil'de·bert** *Ger.* hĭl'dĕ·bĕrt
**Hil'de·brand** hĭl'dĕ·brănd; *Du., Ger.* hĭl'dĕ·bränt
**Hil'de·garde** hĭl'dĕ·gärd
**Hil'dreth** hĭl'drĕth, -drĭth
**Hill** hĭl
**Hil'lard** hĭl'ērd
**Hil'ler** hĭl'ēr
**Hil'lier** ?hĭl'yēr
**Hill'man** hĭl'măn
**Hil'ton** hĭl't'n, -tŭn
**Hinck'ley** hĭngk'lĭ
**Hines** hīnz
**Hin'rich** *Ger.* hĭn'rĭᴋ
**Hin'ton** hĭn't'n, -tŭn
**Hi'ob** *Ger.* hē'ôp
**Hi·pó'li·to** *Span.* ē·pō'lē·tō
**Hip'po'lyte'** *Fr.* ē'pô'lēt'
**Hipsch** *Ger.* hĭpsh
**Hi'ram** hī'răm
**Hi·ro·bu·mi** *Jap.* hê·rô·bōō·mê
**Hi·ro·shi** *Jap.* hê·rô·shê
**Hi·sa·ya** *Jap.* hê·sä·yä
**Hitch'cock** hĭch'kŏk
**Hjal'mar** *Dan.* yȧl'mär; *Finn., Swed.* yȧl'mȧr; *Norw.* yäl'mär
**Hjorth** *Norw.* yôrt
**Hoad'ley** hōd'lĭ
**Ho'bart** hō'bērt, -bärt, *esp. Brit.* hŭb'ērt
**Hob'son** hŏb's'n
**Hodg'don** hŏj'dŭn
**Hodges** hŏj'ĕz, -ĭz
**Hodg'son** hŏj's'n
**Hoff'man** hŏf'măn
**Hogg** hŏg
**Ho·jo** *Jap.* hō·jō
**Hoke** hōk
**Hol'brook** hōl'brŏŏk, hŏl'-
**Hol'burt** hŏl'bērt
**Hol'den** hōl'dĕn
**Holds'worth** hōldz'wûrth
**Hol'ger** *Dan.* hŏl'gēr
**Hol'la·day** hŏl'ȧ·dā
**Hol'land** hŏl'ănd
**Hol'ley** hŏl'ĭ
**Hol'li·day** hŏl'ĭ·dā
**Hol'lings·worth** hŏl'ĭngz·wûrth
**Hol'lis** hŏl'ĭs
**Hol'lis·ter** hŏl'ĭs·tēr
**Holl'way** hŏl'wā
**Hol'ly** hŏl'ĭ
**Holm** *Norw.* hŏlm
**Hol'man** hōl'măn
**Holmes** hōmz
**Holt** hōlt
**Ho'mans** hō'mănz
**Home** hōm, hūm
**Ho'mer** hō'mēr
**Hom'mel** *Dan.* hŏm'ĕl
**Hon-A·mi** *Jap.* hôn·ä·mê
**Hon'ey·wood** hŭn'ĭ·wŏŏd
**Ho'no'rat'** *Fr.* ô'nô'rȧ'
**Hon'o·ré'** ŏn'ô·rā'; ŏn'ô·rā'—**Ho'no'ré'** *Fr.* ô'nô'rā'
**Ho·no'rio** *Port.* ōō·nô'ryōō
**Ho·no'ri·us** *Lat.* hô·nō'rĭ·ŭs
**Hook** hŏŏk
**Hook'er** hŏŏk'ēr
**Hook'ham** hŏŏk'ăm
**Hope** hōp
**Hop'kin** hŏp'kĭn
**Hop'kins** hŏp'kĭnz
**Hop'kin·son** hŏp'kĭn·s'n
**Hop'wood** hŏp'wŏŏd
**Hor'ace** hŏr'ĭs—**Ho'race'** *Fr.* ô'rȧs'
**Ho·ra'tio** hô·rā'shō, -shĭ·ō
**Ho·ra'tius** hô·rā'shŭs, -shĭ·ŭs
**Horne** hôrn
**Hor·nell'** hôr·nĕl', hôr'nĕl
**Hors'ley** hôrz'lĭ, hôrs'lĭ
**Horst** *Ger.* hôrst
**Hor·tense'** hôr·tĕns', hôr'tĕns—**Hor'tense'** *Fr.* ôr'täɴs'
**Hor'ton** hôr't'n
**Ho·se'a** hô·zē'ȧ, -zā'ȧ
**Hos'mer** hŏz'mēr
**Hotch'kin** hŏch'kĭn
**Hotch'kiss** hŏch'kĭs
**Hoth'am** hŭth'ăm
**Hough'ton** hō't'n, hou'-, hô'-
**Hous'ton** hūs'tŭn, hōōs'-
**Hov'ey** hŭv'ĭ
**How'ard** hou'ērd
**How'arth** hou'ērth, -ärth
**Howe** hou
**How'el, -ell** hou'ĕl
**How'land** hou'lănd
**Hox'ie** hŏk'sĭ
**Hoyt** hoit
**Hub'bard** hŭb'ērd
**Hu'bert** hū'bērt; *Du.* hü'bĕrt; *Ger.* hōō'bĕrt—**Hu'bert'** *Fr.* ü'bâr'
**Hu·ber'tus** *Du.* hü·bĕr'tûs; *Ger.* hōō·bĕr'tōōs
**Hübsch** *Ger.* hüpsh
**Hucks** hŭks
**Hud'dle·ston** hŭd''l·stŭn
**Hud'son** hŭd's'n
**Hu'ey** hū'ĭ
**Huff** hŭf
**Huf'fam** hŭf''m
**Hu'ger** hū'gēr
**Hugh** hū
**Hughes** hūz
**Hugh'lings** hū'lĭngz
**Hu'go** hū'gō; *Du.* hü'gō; *Ger.* hōō'gō; *Pol.* hōō'gô; *Swed.* hōō'gô
**Hugues** *Fr.* üg
**Hui'bert** *Du.* hoi'bērt
**Huig** *Du.* hoiᴋ
**Hul'beart, -bert** hŭl'bērt

**Hul′dreich** *Ger.* hōōl′drĭk
**Hull** hŭl
**Hulse** hŭls
**Hultz** hŭlts
**Hum′bert** hŭm′bẽrt
**Hume** hūm
**Hum′mell** hŭm′ĕl
**Hum′phrey** hŭm′frĭ
**Hum′phreys** hŭm′frĭz
**Hum′phry** hŭm′frĭ
**Hun′ger·ford** hŭng′gẽr·fẽrd
**Hunt** hŭnt
**Hun′ter** hŭn′tẽr
**Hun′ting·ton** hŭn′tĭng·tŭn
**Hunt′ley, -ly** hŭnt′lĭ
**Hu′ot′** *Fr.* ü′ō′
**Hurd** hûrd
**Hur′rell** hûr′ĕl
**Hur·ta′do** *Span.* ōōr·tä′thō
**Hus·sein′** *Turk.* hü·sān′
**Hus′ton** hūs′tŭn
**Hutch′e·son** hŭch′ĕ·s'n
**Hutch′ings** hŭch′ĭngz
**Hutch′ins** hŭch′ĭnz
**Hutch′in·son** hŭch′ĭn·s'n
**Hutch′i·son** hŭch′ĭ·s'n
**Hut′tle·ston** hŭt′'l·stŭn
**Hut′ton** hŭt′'n
**Huy′brecht** *Du.* hoi′brĕKt
**Huy′ghen** *Du.* hoi′gĕn
**Hya′cinthe′** *Fr.* yȧ′săNt′
**Hy′att** hī′ăt
**Hyde** hīd
**Hy′der** hī′dẽr
**Hy′men** hī′mĕn
**Hy′nek** *Czech* hĭ′nĕk
**Hy′po′lite′** *Fr.* ē′pô′lēt′

**Ia′co·po** *Ital.* yä′kô·pō
**I′an** ē′än, ē′ăn, ī′ăn
**Ian′cu** *Rum.* yäng′kōō
**I′An·son** ī′ăn·s'n
**ibn** ĭb′'n
**Ib·ra·him′** *Turk.* ĭb·rä·hĭm′
**Ich′a·bod** ĭk′ȧ·bŏd
**I·chi·ro** *Jap.* ē·chē·rō
**I·chi·ta·ro** *Jap.* ē·chē·tä·rō
**I′ci′lius′** *Fr.* ē′sē′lyüs′
**I′da** ī′dȧ; *Ger.* ē′dä
**Ide** īd
**I′gnace′** *Fr.* ē′nyȧs′
**Ig·na′cio** *Port.* ēg·nȧ′syōō; *Span.* ēg·nä′thyō, -syō
**Ig·na′cy** *Pol.* ēg·nä′tsĭ
**Ig·na′ti·us** ĭg·nā′shĭ·ŭs, -shŭs
**Ig′naz** *Ger.* ĭg′näts, ĭg·näts′
**I·gna′zio** *Ital.* ē·nyä′tsyô
**I′gor** *Russ.* ē′gôr·y′
**Ih′no** *Ger.* ē′nō
**Ik** ĭk
**il** *Ital.* ēl
**I·la·ri·o′no·vich** *Russ.* ĭ·lŭ·ryĭ·ô′nŭ-vyĭch
**Il′de·bran′do** *Ital.* ēl′dā·brän′dô
**Il·ich′** *Russ.* ĭl·yēch′
**I′lo·na** *Hung.* ĭ′lô·nŏ
**Il′se** *Ger.* ĭl′zĕ
**Il·ya′** *Russ.* ĭl·yȧ′
**Il·yich′** *Russ.* ĭl·yēch′
**Im′bault′** *Fr.* ăN′bō′
**Im·man′u·el** ĭ·măn′ū·ĕl—**Im·ma′-nu·el** *Dan.* ē·mȧ′nōō·ĕl; *Ger.* ĭ·mä′nōō·ĕl
**Im′o·gen** ĭm′ō·jĕn, -jĕn
**Im′pey** ĭm′pĭ
**Im′re** *Hung.* ĭm′rĕ
**I′na** ī′nȧ
**I·na·zo** *Jap.* ē·nä·zō
**In′crease** ĭn′krēs
**In′da·le′cio** *Span.* ēn′dä·lā′thyō, -syō
**I·nés′** *Span.* ē·nās′
**I′nez** ī′nĕz, ē′nĕz, -nĭz—**I·nez′** *Span.* ē·nāth′, -nās′
**Ing′e·borg** *Dan.* ĕng′ĕ·bŏrg; *Ger.* ĭng′ĕ·bôrK
**Ing′e·bret′sen** *Norw.* ing′ĕ·brĕt′sĕn
**In′ger·soll** ĭng′gẽr·sŏl, -s'l
**Ing′ham** ĭng′ăm
**In′glis** ĭng′glĭs, *esp. Brit.* -g'lz
**In′gram** ĭng′grăm
**In′i·go** ĭn′ĭ·gō
**Í′ñi·go** *Span.* ē′nyē·gō
**In′nes, In′ness** ĭn′ĕs, -ĭs
**In′no·cen′zo** *Ital.* ēn′nô·chĕn′tsô
**I′no·cên′cio** *Port.* ē′nōō·sāN′syōō
**Ioan** *Rum.* ywän
**Io·ann′** *Russ.* yô·ȧn′
**Io·an′nes** *Mod. Grk.* yô·ä′nyēs
**Ion** *Rum.* yŏn
**Io·na′che** *Rum.* yŏ·nä′kĕ
**I·o′sif** *Russ.* ĭ·ô′syĭf, yô′syĭf
**I·o′si·fo′vich** *Russ.* ĭ·ô′syĭ·fô′vyĭch, yô′syĭ-
**Ip·po·lit′** *Russ.* ĭp·pŭ·lyēt′
**Ip·po′li·to** *Ital.* ēp·pô′lē·tō
**I′ra** ī′rȧ
**Ire′dell** īr′dĕl
**Ire′land** īr′lănd
**I′re·nae′us** ī′rē·nē′ŭs
**I′re·nä′us** *Ger.* ē′rā·nâ′ōōs
**I·rene′** ī·rēn′; *esp. Brit., and Lat.,* ī·rē′nē—**I·re′ne** *Ger.* ē·rā′nĕ
**I′rène′** *Fr.* ē′rĕn′
**I′ré′née′** *Fr.* ē′rā′nā′
**Ir′vin, Ir′vine** ûr′vĭn
**Ir′ving** ûr′vĭng
**Ir′win** ûr′wĭn
**I′saac** ī′zȧk, -zĭk; *Du.* ē′säk—**I′saac′** *Fr.* ē′zȧk′—**I′sa·ac** *Ger.* ē′zä·äk, ē′zäk—**I·saac′** *Russ.* ĭ·sȧk′—**I′sa-ac′** *Span.* ē′sä·äk′
**I′saacs** ī′zȧks, -zĭks
**I′saak** *Du.* ē′säk—**I′sa·ak** *Ger.* ē′zä·äk, ē′zäk
**Is′a·bel** ĭz′ȧ·bĕl—**I′sa·bel′** *Span.* ē′sä·bĕl′
**Is′a·bel′la** ĭz′ȧ·bĕl′ȧ—**I′sa·bel′la** *Du.* ē′sȧ·bĕl′ȧ; *Ital.* ē′zä·bĕl′lä
**I′sa′belle′** *Fr.* ē′zȧ′bĕl′—**I′sa·bel′le** *Ger.* ē′zä·bĕl′ĕ
**I′sack** *Du.* ē′säk
**Is′a·dor, Is′a·dore** ĭz′ȧ·dōr
**Is′a·do′ra** ĭz′ȧ·dō′rȧ
**I′sa·i′a** *Ital.* ē′zä·ē′ä
**I·sa′iah** ī·zā′yȧ, ī·zī′ȧ
**I′sa·i′as** *Span.* ē′sä·ē′äs
**I′sak** *Dan.* ē′sȧk
**I·sa·mu** *Jap.* ē·sä·mōō
**I′sham** ī′shăm
**Ish′bel** ĭsh′bĕl
**Is′i·dor** ĭz′ĭ·dôr—**I′si·dor** *Ger.* ē′zē-dōr, ē′zē·dōr′
**Is′i·dore** ĭz′ĭ·dōr—**I′si′dore′** *Fr.* ē′zē′dôr′
**I′si·do′ro** *Span.* ē′sē·thō′rō
**I·si′dro** *Span.* ē·sē′thrō
**Is′ma·el** *Ger.* ĭs′mä·ĕl—**Is′ma·el′** *Span.* ēs′mä·ĕl′
**Is′mar** *Ger.* ēs′mär
**İs·met′** *Turk.* ĭs·mĕt′
**I·so, I·soh** *Jap.* ē·sō
**I·sol′de** *Ger.* ē·zôl′dĕ
**I·so·ro·ku** *Jap.* ē·sô·rô·kōō
**Is′ra·el** ĭz′rȧ·ĕl, -rĭ·ĕl; *Du.* ĭs′rȧ·ĕl; *Swed.* ēs′rȧ·ĕl—**Is′ra′el′** *Fr.* ēs′-rȧ′ĕl′
**Is·ra′e·le·vich** *Russ.* ĭs·rȧ′ĭ·lyĕ·vyĭch
**Is′ra·hel** *Du.* ĭs′rȧ·ĕl
**Is′sa·char** ĭs′ȧ·kär
**Ist′ván** *Hung.* ĭsht′vän
**I′ta·lo** *Ital.* ē′tä·lō
**Ith′i·el** ĭth′ĭ·ĕl
**I·to** *Jap.* ē·tō
**I·tu′ri** *Span.* ē·tōō′rē
**Iu′liu** *Rum.* yōō′lyōō
**I′vah** ī′vȧ
**I′van** ī′văn; *Swed.* ē′vȧn; *Yugo.* ē′vän—**I·van′** *Bulg., Russ.* ĭ·vȧn′
**I·va′no·vich, -vitch** *Russ.* ĭ·vȧ′nŭ-vyĭch
**I′var** *Norw.* ē′vär; *Swed.* ē′vȧr
**Ives** īvz
**I′vey** ī′vĭ
**I′vor** ē′vẽr, ī′-
**I′vy** ī′vĭ
**I·wan′** *Ger.* ē·vän′, ē′vän
**I·wa·o** *Jap.* ē·wä·ô
**I·ye·sa·to** *Jap.* ē·yĕ·sä·tô
**I′zaak** ī′zȧk, ī′zĭk; *Du.* ē′zäk

**Jaak′ko** *Finn.* yäk′kô
**Jaan** *Eston.* yän
**Ja′bez** jā′bĕz, -bĭz
**Ja·cin′to** *Span.* hä·thēn′tō, -sēn′-
**Jack** jăk
**Jack′son** jăk′s'n
**Ja′cob** jā′kŭb; *Dan., Du.* yȧ′kŏp; *Ger.* yä′kŏp; *Norw., Sou. Afr. Du.* yä′kŏp; *Swed.* yä′kôp—**Ja′cob′** *Fr.* zhȧ′kôb′
**Ja′co·bi′na** *Ger.* yä′kô·bē′nä
**Ja′cobs** jā′kŭbz
**Ja·co′bus** jȧ·kō′bŭs; *Du.* yȧ·kō′bûs; *Ger.* yä·kō′bōōs
**Ja′comb** jā′kŭm
**Ja′co·po** *Ital.* yä′kô·pō
**Jac′que·line** jăk′wĕ·lĭn, -lēn—**Jac′-que·line′** *Fr.* zhä′klēn′
**Jacques** *Du., Fr., Ger.* zhäk
**Jaf′fray** jăf′rā, -rĭ
**Ja′gad·gu′ru** *Skr.* jŭ′gȧd·gōō′rōō
**Ja′gan·nath′** *As. Ind.* jŭ′gȧn·nät′
**Jai′me** *Span.* hī′mā
**Ja′kob** *Dan., Du.* yȧ′kŏp; *Ger.* yä′-kŏp; *Norw.* yä′kŏp; *Swed.* yä′kôp
**Ja′kób** *Pol.* yä′kōōp
**jam** *As. Ind.* jäm
**James** *Eng., Ger.* jāmz; *Fr.* zhāmz, zhȧm
**Jan** jăn; *Czech* yȧn; *Du., Ger., Latvian, Pol.* yän
**Jane** jān; *Fr.* zhȧn
**Janes** jānz

**Ja·net′** jȧ·nĕt′, jăn′ĕt, jăn′ĭt
**Jane′way** jān′wā
**Jā′nis** *Latvian* yä′nĭs
**Jan′kiew** *Pol.* yän′kyĕf, yäng′-
**Já′nos** *Hung.* yä′nôsh
**Jan′sen** *Du.* yän′sĕn
**Jans′zoon** *Du.* yän′sŭn, -sôn, -sōn
**Ja·nuá′rio** *Port.* zhȧ·nwȧ′ryōō
**Jan′u·ar′i·us** jăn′ū·âr′ĭ·ŭs—**Ja′nu·a′ri·us** *Ger.* yä′nōō·ä′rē·ōōs
**Ja′nus** jā′nŭs
**Ja·pe′tus** *Dan.* yȧ·pē′tōōs
**Jar′ed** jâr′ĕd, -ĭd
**Jarl** *Finn.* yȧrl; *Norw.* yärl
**Jar′mi·la** *Czech* yȧr′mĭ·lȧ
**Ja′ro·mír** *Czech* yȧ′rô·mēr
**Ja′ro·slav** *Czech* yȧ′rô·slȧf
**Ja′ro·slaw** *Ger.* yä′rô·släf
**Jar′vis** jär′vĭs
**Ja′son** jā′s'n
**Jas′par, Jas′per** jăs′pẽr
**Jas′want** *Marathi* jŭs′vȧnt
**Ja·vier′** *Span.* hä·vyĕr′
**Jay** jā
**Jayne** jān
**Jean** jēn; *Du., Fr., Ger.* zhäN; *Finn.* zhän
**Jeanne** jēn; *Fr.* zhän
**Jean·nette′** jĕ·nĕt′
**Jean′not′** *Fr.* zhȧ′nō′
**Jeb** jĕb
**Je·bu′sa** ?jĕ·bū′sȧ, ?jĕb′ū·sȧ
**Jed′e·di′ah, Jed′i·di′ah** jĕd′ĭ·dī′ȧ
**Jef** *Fr., Du.* zhĕf
**Jeff** jĕf
**Jef′fer·son** jĕf′ẽr·s'n
**Jef′fer·y** jĕf′rĭ, jĕf′ẽr·ĭ
**Jef′fer·ys** jĕf′rĭz, jĕf′ẽr·ĭz
**Jef′frey** jĕf′rĭ
**Jef′freys, Jef′fries** jĕf′rĭz
**Jef′fry** jĕf′rĭ
**Je·han′** *Fr.* zhäN
**Je·hosh′a·phat** jē·hŏsh′ȧ·făt
**Je·hu′da** jĕ·hōō′dȧ
**Jel′les** *Du.* yĕl′ĕs
**Jem** jĕm
**Je·mi′ma** jĕ·mī′mȧ
**Jem′i·son** jĕm′ĭ·s'n
**Jem′my** jĕm′ĭ
**Jen′ings** jĕn′ĭngz
**Jen′kin** jĕng′kĭn
**Jen′kins** jĕng′kĭnz
**Jen′kin·son** jĕng′kĭn·s'n
**Jen′ners** jĕn′ẽrz
**Jen·nette′** jĕ·nĕt′
**Jen′ni** *Du.* yĕn′ē
**Jen′nie** jĕn′ĭ, *Brit. also* jĭn′ĭ
**Jen′nings** jĕn′ĭngz
**Jen′ny** jĕn′ĭ, *Brit. also* jĭn′ĭ
**Je′nő** *Hung.* yĕ′nû
**Jens** *Dan., Ger., Norw.* yĕns
**Jeph′son** jĕf′s'n
**Jep′tha** jĕp′thȧ
**Jer′e·mi′ah** jĕr′ĕ·mī′ȧ
**Je′re·mi′as** *Du., Ger.* yā′rȧ·mē′äs
**Jé′ré′mie′** *Fr.* zhā′rā′mē′
**Jer′e·my** jĕr′ĕ·mĭ
**Jer′myn** jûr′mĭn
**Jer′nej** *Yugo.* yĕr′nĕ·ĭ
**Jer′ning·ham** jûr′nĭng·hăm, -nĭng-ăm
**Je·roen′** *Du.* yĕ·rōōn′
**Je·rome′** jĕ·rōm′, *Brit. also* jĕr′ŭm
**Jé′rôme′** *Fr.* zhā′rōm′
**Je·rô′ni·mo** *Port.* zhĕ·rô′nē·mōō
**Je·ró′ni·mo** *Span.* hā·rō′nē·mō
**Je·room′** *Du.* yĕ·rōm′
**Jer′rold** jĕr′ŭld
**Jer′ry** jĕr′ĭ
**Jer′vis** jûr′vĭs, *Brit. also* jär′vĭs
**Je′rzy** *Pol.* yĕ′zhĭ
**Jess** jĕs
**Jes′se** jĕs′ē
**Jes′sie** jĕs′ĭ
**Jes′up** jĕs′ŭp
**Je·sús′** *Span.* hā·sōōs′
**Jeth′ro** jĕth′rō, jē′thrō
**Jew′ett** jōō′ĕt, -ĭt
**Jim** jĭm
**Ji′ři** *Czech* yĭr′zhē
**Ji·ro** *Jap.* jē·rō
**Jo** jō; *Du.* yō
**Jo′a·chim** jō′ȧ·kĭm; *Dan.* yō′ȧ·kĕm; *Du.* yō′ȧ·kĭm; *Ger.* yō′ä·kĭm, yô·ä′-kĭm; *Norw.* yō′ä·kĭm—**Jo′a′chim′** *Fr.* zhō′ȧ′kēm′—**Jo·a′chim** *Pol.* yô·ä′kĕm
**Jo′a·kim** *Yugo.* yō′ä·kēm
**Joan** jōn; jō′ăn; jō·ăn′
**Jo·ann′** *Russ.* yŏ·ȧn′
**Jo·an′na** jō·ăn′ȧ
**Jo·an′nes** jō·ăn′ēz, -ĕs; *Du.* yō·än′ĕs; *Anc. Grk.* jō·ăn′ēz, -ĕs; *Mod. Grk.* yô·ä′nyĕs
**Jo·ão′** *Port.* zhwouN
**Joa·quim′** *Port.* zhwȧ·kēN′
**Joa·quín′** *Span.* hwä·kēn′
**Joa·qui′na** *Span.* hwä·kē′nä
**Job** jōb; *Du.* yôp
**Jobst** *Ger.* yôpst, yōpst
**Joce′lyn** jŏs′lĭn, jŏs′ĕ·lĭn
**Jo·do′cus** *Ger.* yō·dō′kōōs—**Jod′o·cus** *Lat.* jŏd′ō·kŭs
**Joe** jō
**Jo′el** jō′ĕl, -ĕl
**Jo′ël′** *Fr.* zhô′ĕl′
**Joest** *Du.* yōōst
**Jo·han′** *Dan.* yōō·hȧn′; *Du., Norw.* yō·hän′—**Jo′han** *Eston.* yō′hän; *Finn., Swed.* yōō′hȧn
**Jo·hann′** *Dan.* yōō·hȧn′; *Du.* yō·hän′; *Ger.* yō·hän′, yō′hän—**Jo′hann** *Finn., Swed.* yōō′hȧn
**Jó′hann** *Icelandic* yō′hän
**Jo·han′na** jō·hăn′ȧ; *Du.* yō·hän′ä; *Ger.* yō·hän′ä; *Swed.* yō·hȧn′nȧ′
**Jo·han′ne** *Dan.* yōō·hȧn′ĕ; *Ger.* yō·hän′ĕ
**Jo·han′nes** jō·hăn′ēz, -ĕs; *Dan.* yōō·hȧn′ĕs; *Du.* yō·hän′ĕs; *Finn.* yōō·hȧn′nĕs; *Ger.* yō·hän′ĕs, -ĕs; *Swed.* yō·hȧn′nĕs—**Jo′han′nes′** *Fr.* zhô′-ȧ′nĕs′
**John** jŏn; *Fr.* zhôn
**John′nie** jŏn′ĭ
**Johns** jŏnz
**John′son** jŏn′s'n
**John′ston, -stone** jŏn′stŭn, jŏn′s'n
**Jo·ki·chi** *Jap.* jō·kē·chē
**Jo′lán** *Hung.* yō′län
**Jon** jŏn; *Norw.* yōn, yŏn; *Rum.* yŏn
**Jón** *Icelandic* yōn
**Jo′nas** jō′năs; *Du., Ger., Norw.* yō′-näs; *Lith.* yô′näs; *Swed.* yōō′nȧs′
**Jó′nas** *Icelandic* yō′näs
**Jon′a·than** jŏn′ȧ·thăn—**Jo′na·than** *Ger.* yō′nä·tän
**Jones** jōnz
**jonk′heer** *Du.* yôngk′hār
**Jöns** *Swed.* yûns
**Jöns′son** *Swed.* yûn′sôn
**Joos** *Du.* yōs
**Joost** *Du., Ger.* yōst
**Jor′dan** jôr′d'n, *in sou. U.S. also* jûr′-
**Jörg** *Ger.* yûrK
**Jor′ge** *Port.* zhôr′zhĕ; *Span.* hôr′hā
**Jör′gen** *Dan., Norw.* yûr′gĕn
**Jo′ris** *Du.* yō′rĭs
**Jo′sa·phat** *Ger.* yō′zä·fät
**Jo·sé′** *Port.* zhōō·zâ′; *Span.* hō·sā′
**Jo′sef** jō′zĕf, -zĭf; *Czech* yô′sĕf; *Du.* yō′sĕf; *Ger.* yō′zĕf; *Swed.* yōō′sĕf
**Jo·se′fa** *Span.* hō·sā′fä
**Jo′seph** jō′zĕf; -zĭf; *Du.* yō′sĕf; *Ger.* yō′zĕf; *Swed.* yōō′sĕf—**Jo′seph′** *Fr.* zhō′zĕf′
**Jo·se′pha** jō·sē′fȧ
**Jo′sèphe′** *Fr.* zhō′zĕf′
**Jo′sé′phin′** *Fr.* zhō′zā′făN′
**Jo′se·phine** jō′zĕ·fēn, jō′zĕ·fēn′—**Jo′se·phi′ne** *Du.* yō′sĕ·fē′nĕ; *Ger.* yō′zĕ·fē′nĕ
**Jo′sé′phine′** *Fr.* zhō′zā′fēn′
**Jo·se′phus** jō·sē′fŭs; *Du.* yō·sā′fŭs
**Josh** jŏsh
**Josh′u·a** jŏsh′ū·ȧ
**Jo·si′ah** jō·sī′ȧ
**Jo·si′as** jō·sī′ăs; *Ger.* yō·zē′äs—**Jo′sias′** *Fr.* zhō′zyäs′
**Jo′sip** *Yugo.* yō′sēp
**Jos′lin** jŏs′lĭn, jŏz′-
**Jos′quin′** *Fr.* zhôs′kăN′
**Josse** *Fr.* zhôs
**Jos′se·lin′** *Fr.* zhôs′lăN′
**Josse′lyn** jŏs′lĭn, jŏs′ĕ·lĭn
**Joss′lyn** jŏs′lĭn
**Jost** *Ger.* yōst
**Jo′su·é′** *Fr.* zhō′zü·ā′
**Jo′van** *Serb.* yō′vän
**Jo′vi·a′nus** *Lat.* jō′vĭ·ā′nŭs
**Joy** joi
**Joyce** jois
**Jo′zef** *Du.* yō′zĕf
**Jó′zef** *Pol.* yōō′zĕf
**Jó′zsef** *Hung.* yō′zhĕf
**Juan** *Fr.* zhü·äN′; *Span.* hwän
**Jua′na** *Span.* hwä′nä
**Ju′bal** jōō′băl
**Ju′dah** jōō′dȧ
**Judd** jŭd
**Ju′dith** jōō′dĭth; *Du.* yü′dĭt; *Ger.* yōō′dĭt—**Ju′dith′** *Fr.* zhü′dēt′
**Jud′son** jŭd′s'n
**Ju′ha·ni** *Finn.* yōō′hȧ·nĭ
**Ju′ho** *Finn.* yōō′hŏ
**Ju·i·chi** *Jap.* jōō·ē·chē
**Jules** jōōlz; *Fr.* zhül
**Jul′ia** jōōl′yȧ—**Ju′li·a** *Du.* yü′lē·ä; *Finn.* yōō′lĭ·ȧ—**Ju′lia′** *Fr.* zü′lyȧ′
**Jul′ian** jōōl′yăn—**Ju′li·an′** *Ger.* yōō′lē·än′—**Ju′lian** *Pol.* yōō′lyän
**Ju·lián′** *Span.* hōō·lyän′

**Ju′li·an′a** jo͞o′lĭ·ăn′*ȧ*, -ä′n*ȧ*
**Ju′li·a′ne** *Ger.* yo͞o′lē̇·ä′n*ĕ*
**Ju′li·a′nus** *Lat.* jo͞o′lĭ·ā′n*ŭ*s
**Ju′lie** jo͞o′lĭ—**Ju′lie′** *Fr.* zhü′lē′—**Ju′li·e** *Ger.* yo͞o′lē̇·*ĕ*
**Ju′lien′** *Fr.* zhü′lyăɴ′
**Ju′li·et** jo͞o′lĭ·ĕt, -*ĕ*t, jo͞o′lĭ·ĕt′, jo͞ol′-yĕt
**Ju′li·ette′** jo͞o′lĭ·ĕt′; *Fr.* zhü′lyĕt′
**Ju′lio** *Span.* ho͞o′lyō
**Jú′lio** *Port.* zho͞o′lyo͞o
**Jul′ius** jo͞ol′y*ŭ*s—**Ju′li·us** *Czech* yo͝o′lĭ·o͝os; *Dan.* yo͞o′lē̇·o͝os; *Du.* yü′lē̇·ûs; *Ger.* yo͞o′lē̇·o͝os; *Swed.* yo͞o′lĭ·ŭs′
**Ju′liusz** *Pol.* yo͞o′lyo͞osh
**Jump** jŭmp
**June** jo͞on
**Ju′ni·a′nus** *Lat.* jo͞o′nĭ·ā′n*ŭ*s
**Ju·ní′pe·ro** *Span.* ho͞o·nē′pȧ·rō
**Jun′ius** jo͞on′y*ŭ*s; jo͞o′nĭ·*ŭ*s
**Jun·no·su·ke** *Jap.* jo͞on·nō̇·so͞o·kĕ
**Ju′raj** *Yugo.* yo͞o′rī
**Jürg** *Ger.* yürᴋ
**Jür′gen** *Ger.* yür′g*ĕ*n
**Ju′ri·aen** *Du.* yûr′ē̇·ȧn
**Ju′ri·an** *Du.* yûr′ē̇·än
**Ju·se′pe** *Span.* ho͞o·sā′pā
**Jus′si′** *Swed.* yŭs′sĭ′
**Just** *Fr.* zhüst
**Jus′ta** *Lat.* jŭs′t*ȧ*
**Juste** *Fr.* zhüst
**Jus′tice** jŭs′tĭs
**Jus′tin** jŭs′tĭn—**Jus′tin′** *Fr.* zhüs′-tăɴ′—**Ju·stin′** *Ger.* yo͝os·tēn′
**Jus′tine′** *Fr.* zhüs′tēn′
**Jus·tin′i·an** jŭs·tĭn′ĭ·*ă*n
**Jus′ti·nia′no** *Span.* ho͞os′tē̇·nyä′nō
**Ju·sti′nus** *Ger.* yo͝os·tē′no͝os—**Jus·ti′nus** *Lat.* jŭs·tī′n*ŭ*s
**Jus′to** *Span.* ho͞os′tō
**Jus′tus** jŭs′t*ŭ*s; *Du.* yûs′tûs—**Ju′-stus** *Ger.* yo͝os′to͝os
**Ju·ta·ro** *Jap.* jo͞o·tä·rō
**Ju·ven′ti·us** *Lat.* jo͞o·vĕn′shĭ·*ŭ*s, -sh*ŭ*s

**Kaar′lo** *Finn.* kär′lŏ
**Ka·a·ru** *Jap.* kä·ä·ro͞o
**Kae′so** *Lat.* kē′sō
**Ka·ge·a·ki** *Jap.* kä·gĕ·ä·kē̇
**Kaj** *Dan.* kī
**Ka·ki·chi** *Jap.* kä·kē̇·chē̇
**Ka·ku·zo** kä·ko͞o·zō
**Kál′mán** *Hung.* käl′män
**Kane** kān
**Kan·ji** *Jap.* kän·jē̇
**Ka·no** *Jap.* kä·nō
**Ka·o·ru** *Jap.* kä·ō̇·ro͞o
**Ka′ram·chand** *Gujarati* kŭ′r*ȧ*m-chŭnd
**Ka′rel** *Czech* kȧ′rĕl; *Du.* kȧ′r*ĕ*l
**Ka′ren** *Dan., Norw.* kä′r*ĕ*n
**Ka·ri** *Jap.* kä·rē̇
**Ka′rin** *Dan.* kä′rēn
**Kar′ker** kär′kẽr
**Karl** *Eng., Dan., Du., Ger., Norw., Swed.* kärl; *Finn., Fr., Russ.* kȧrl
**Kar′lo·vich** *Russ.* kȧr′lŭ·vyĭch
**Ka′rol** *Pol.* kä′rôl
**Ka′ro·li′na** *Swed.* kȧ′rô·lē′nȧ
**Ka′ro·li′ne** *Ger.* kä′rō̇·lē′n*ĕ*
**Ká′roly** *Hung.* kä′rôl·y′
**Ka′sim** *Pers.* kä′sĭm
**Ka′si·mir** *Ger.* kä′zē̇·mēr
**Kas′par** *Dan.* kȧs′pär; *Du., Ger.* käs′pär; *Hung.* kŏsh′pŏr
**Kas′per** *Pol.* käs′pĕr
**Kate** kāt
**Ka′tha·ri′na** *Ger.* kä′tä·rē′nä
**Kath′a·rine** kăth′*ȧ*·rĭn—**Ka′tha·ri′ne** *Ger.* kä′tä·rē′n*ĕ*
**Kä′the** *Ger.* kâ′t*ĕ*
**Kath′er·ine** kăth′ẽr·ĭn
**Kath′leen** kăth′lēn
**Kath′ryn** kăth′rĭn
**Ka·tri′na** k*ȧ*·trē′n*ȧ*
**Ka·tsu·no·ri** *Jap.* kä·tso͞o·nō̇·rē̇
**Ka·tsu·no·su·ke** *Jap.* kä·tso͞o·nō̇-so͞o·kĕ
**Kauff′man** kôf′m*ă*n, kouf′-
**Kay, Kaye** kā
**Ka·zi′mierz** *Pol.* kä·zē′myĕsh
**Ka·zi·mir′** *Russ.* kŭ·zyē̇·myēr′
**Káz′mér** *Hung.* käz′mār
**Kean** kēn
**Kears′ley** kẹrz′lĭ
**Kea′tinge** kē′tĭng
**Ke′ble** kē′b'l
**Ke′gan** kē′g*ă*n
**Keir** kẹr
**Kei·shi·ro** *Jap.* kā·shē̇·rō
**Kei·su·ke** *Jap.* kā·so͞o·kĕ
**Keith** kēth
**Kel′head** kĕl′hĕd
**Kel′logg** kĕl′ŏg, -*ŭ*g
**Kells** kĕlz
**Kel′ly** kĕl′ĭ
**Kel′sea** kĕl′sē̇
**Kel′sey** kĕl′sĭ
**Kel′vey** kĕl′vĭ
**Kem′ble** kĕm′b'l
**Kemp** kĕmp
**Ken′dall** kĕn′d'l
**Ken′drick** kĕn′drĭk
**Ken′elm** kĕn′ĕlm
**Ken·ji** *Jap.* kĕn·jē̇
**Ken′na·way** kĕn′*ȧ*·wā
**Ken′neth** kĕn′ĕth, -ĭth
**Ken′nett** kĕn′ĕt, -ĭt
**Ken′rick** kĕn′rĭk
**Ken′sing·ton** kĕn′zĭng·t*ŭ*n
**Ken·su·ke** *Jap.* kĕn·so͞o·kĕ
**Kent** kĕnt
**Ken·ta·ro** *Jap.* kĕn·tä·rō
**Ken′yon** kĕn′y*ŭ*n
**Ken·zo** *Jap.* kĕn·zō
**Ker** kûr, *esp. Brit.* kär, kâr
**Ker′che·ver** kûr′chĕ·vẽr
**Ker′mit** kûr′mĭt
**Kerr** kûr, *esp. Brit.* kär, kâr
**Ker′sey** kûr′zĭ
**Ker′stin** *Swed.* chăr′stĭn
**Ketch′um** kĕch′*ŭ*m
**Kev′in** kĕv′ĭn
**Key** kē
**khan** kän, kăn; *Afghan, Arab., Pers., Turk.* ᴋän
**Kha·ri′la·os** *Mod. Grk.* ᴋä·rē′lä·ôs
**Khri·sti·an′** *Russ.* ᴋryĭ·styĭ·ȧn′
**Khri·sti·a′no·vich** *Russ.* ᴋryĭ·styĭ·ȧ′-nŭ·vyĭch
**Khris′to** *Bulg.* ᴋrĭs′tô
**Khri·sto·fo′ro·vich** *Russ.* ᴋryĭ·stŭ-fô′rŭ·vyĭch
**Khri·sto·fo′rov·na** *Russ.* ᴋryĭ·stŭ-fô′rŭv·nŭ
**Khu′ri** *Arab.* ᴋo͞o′rē
**Ki** *Jap.* kē̇
**Kib′ble** kĭb′'l
**Ki·chi·sa·bu·ro** *Jap.* kē̇·chē̇·sä·bo͞o·rō
**Kid′der** kĭd′ẽr
**Kif′fin** kĭf′ĭn
**Ki·i·chi·ro** *Jap.* kē̇·ē̇·chē̇·rō
**Ki·ju·ro** *Jap.* kē̇·jo͞o·rō
**Ki·ku·ji·ro** *Jap.* kē̇·ko͞o·jē̇·rō
**Kil′burn** kĭl′bẽrn
**Ki′li·aen** *Du.* kē′lē̇·ȧn
**Kil′jan** *Icelandic* kyĭl′yän
**Kil′ling·worth** kĭl′ĭng·wûrth
**Kim′ball** kĭm′b'l
**Kim′ble** kĭm′b'l
**Kim′brough** kĭm′brō
**Kim·mo·chi** *Jap.* kēm·mō̇·chē̇
**Ki·mu·ra** *Jap.* kē̇·mo͞o·rä
**King** kĭng
**King′dom** kĭng′d*ŭ*m
**King′don** kĭng′d*ŭ*n
**Kin·go·ro** *Jap.* kēn·gō̇·rō
**Kings′ley** kĭngz′lĭ
**King′ston** kĭng′st*ŭ*n
**Kin·naird′** kĭ·nârd′
**Kin′ney** kĭn′ĭ
**Kin′ni·cut, -cutt** kĭn′ĭ·k*ŭ*t
**Kin·nier′** kĭ·nẹr′
**Ki·ril′** *Bulg.* kĭ·rĭl′
**Ki·rill′** *Russ.* kyĭ·ryēl′
**Kirk, Kirke** kûrk
**Kirk·pat′rick** kûrk·păt′rĭk
**Kir′sopp** kûr′s*ŭ*p
**Kir′sten** *Norw.* ᴋĭsh′t'n, ᴋĭr′st'n
**Kirt′land** kûrt′l*ă*nd
**Kirt′ley** kûrt′lĭ
**Kis′sam** kĭs′*ă*m
**Kit** kĭt
**Ki·ta·ga·wa** *Jap.* kē̇·tä·gä·wä
**Kitch′ell** kĭch′'l
**Kitch′en** kĭch′ĕn, -ĭn
**Kit′to** kĭt′ō
**Kit′ty** kĭt′ĭ
**Ki·yo·shi** *Jap.* kē̇·yō̇·shē̇
**Kjers′chow** *Norw.* ᴋărs′kŏv
**Klap′ka** klăp′k*ȧ*
**Kla′ra** *Ger.* klä′rä
**Klas** *Swed.* kläs
**Klaus** *Ger.* klous
**Klav′di·ya** *Russ.* klȧv′dyĭ·yŭ
**Kle′mens** *Ger.* klā′mĕns; *Pol.* klĕ′-mĕns
**Kle·men′ti** *Russ.* klyĭ·myān′tyû·ĭ
**Kle·o′fas** *Pol.* klĕ·ô′fäs
**Kli′ment** *Bulg.* klĭ′mȧnt; *Russ.* klyē′myĕnt
**Knick′er·bock′er** nĭk′ẽr·bŏk′ẽr
**Knight** nīt
**Knowles** nōlz
**Knox** nŏks
**Knud** *Dan.* k'no͞oth; *Norw.* k'no͞ot
**Knut** *Norw., Swed.* k'no͞ot
**Knyv′et** nĭv′ĕt, -ĭt
**Ko·go·ro** *Jap.* kō·gō̇·rō
**Ko·ki** *Jap.* kō·kē̇
**Ko·ko·ro** *Jap.* kō·gō̇·rō
**Kol′mar** *Ger.* kôl′mär

**Ko'lo·man** *Ger.* kō'lō·män
**Kon·dra'ti** *Russ.* kŭn·drȧ'tyû·ĭ
**Kon'rad** *Dan.* kŏn'räd; *Ger.* kôn'rät; *Pol.* kôn'rät; *Rum.* kŏn'räd
**Kon'ra·din** *Ger.* kôn'rä·dēn
**Kon'stan·tin** *Czech* kôn'stȧn·tyĭn; *Eston.* kôn'stȧn·tĭn—**Kon'stan·tin'** *Dan.* kŏn'stȧn·tēn'; *Ger.* kôn'stän-tēn', kôn'stän·tēn—**Kon·stan·tin'** *Russ.* kŭn·stŭn·tyēn'
**Kon'stan·ti'nos** *Mod. Grk.* kôn'stän-dē'nôs
**Kon·stan·ti'no·vich** *Russ.* kŭn·stŭn-tyē'nŭ·vyĭch
**Kon·stan·ti'nov·na** *Russ.* kŭn·stŭn-tyē'nôv·nŭ
**Kon·stan'ty** *Pol.* kôn·stän'tĭ
**Kon'stanz** *Ger.* kôn'stänts
**Koos** *Du.* kōs
**Ko·re·ki·yo** *Jap.* kō·rĕ·kē·yō
**Kor'nel** *Pol.* kôr'nĕl
**Kor·ne'lis** *Du.* kôr·nā'lĭs
**Kos·tes'** *Mod. Grk.* kôs·tēs'
**Kost'ka** *Pol.* kôst'kä
**Ko·wa** *Jap.* kō·wä
**Ko·ya·ta** *Jap.* kō·yä·tä
**Kraft** *Ger.* kräft
**Krish'na** *Marathi, Skr.* krĭsh'nȧ
**Kris'ti·an** *Dan.* krēs'tyän; *Du.* krĭs'-tē·än; *Finn.* krĭs'tĭ·ȧn
**Kri'sti·jo'nas** *Lith.* krĭ'stĭ·yō'näs
**Krist'mann** *Icel.* krĭst'män
**Kris·to'fer** *Norw.* krĭs·tŏf'ĕr; *Swed.* krĭs·tôf'ĕr
**Kris·tof'fer** *Dan.* krēs·tŏf'ĕr; *Norw.* krĭs·tŏf'fĕr; *Swed.* krĭs·tôf'fĕr
**Krom** krŏm
**Ksa'ver** *Yugo.* ksä'vĕr
**Ksa·we'ry** *Pol.* ksä·vĕ'rĭ
**Ku·ni·a·ki** *Jap.* kōō·nē·ä·kē
**Ku·ni·ma·tsu** *Jap.* kōō·nē·mä·tsōō
**Ku'no** *Ger.* kōō'nō
**Ku·ra·hei** *Jap.* kōō·rä·hā
**Kurd** *Ger.* kōōrt
**Kurt** *Ger.* kōōrt; *Swed.* kŭrt
**Kuz·ma'** *Russ.* kōōz·y'·mȧ'
**Kuz·mich'** *Russ.* kōōz·y'·myēch'
**Kwan-i·chi** *Jap.* kwän·ē·chē
**Kyle** *Eng.* kīl
**Kyös'ti** *Finn.* kü'ûs·tĭ
**Ky'ri·a·kos'** *Mod. Grk.* kyē'ryä·kôs'
**Ky'ril·los** *Mod. Grk.* kyē'rē·lôs
**Kyrle** kûrl

**l'** *Fr.* l-
**la** lȧ; *Fr.* lȧ; *Ital., Span.* lä
**La'cher'** *Fr.* lȧ'shâr'
**Lach'lan** lăk'lăn
**La'con** lā'kŭn
**La'cy** lā'sĭ
**Lad'is·las** lăd'ĭs·lăs, -läs—**La'dis'las'** *Fr.* lȧ'dēs'läs'
**La'dis·laus** *Ger.* lä'dĭs·lous
**La'di·slav** *Czech* lȧ'dyĭ·slȧf
**Lae'li·us** *Lat.* lē'lĭ·ŭs
**Lae·ti'ti·a** lē·tĭsh'ĭ·ȧ, -tĭsh'yȧ, -tĭsh'ȧ
**La Fay·ette', La'fay·ette'** lä'fĭ·ĕt', lăf'ĭ-
**Lafe** lāf
**Laird** lârd
**La'jos** *Hung.* lŏ'yōsh
**Lake** lāk
**La'lor** ?lā'lĕr
**La'man** lā'măn
**La·mar'** lȧ·mär'
**Lam'ar·tine** lăm'ĕr·tēn
**Lamb** lăm
**Lam'bert** lăm'bĕrt; *Du.* läm'bĕrt—**Lam'bert'** *Fr.* läɴ'bâr'
**Lam·ber'to** *Ital.* läm·bĕr'tō
**Lam·ber'tus** *Du.* läm·bĕr'tûs
**La'mo'ral'** *Fr.* lȧ'mô'rȧl'
**Lam'son** lăm's'n
**Lan'cas·ter** lăng'kăs·tĕr
**Lan'ce·lot** lȧn'sĕ·lŏt, lȧns'lŏt
**Lan'cy** lȧn'sĭ
**Land** lănd
**Lan'dey** lăn'dĭ
**Lan'dis** lăn'dĭs
**Lan'do** *Ital.* län'dō
**Lan'do·lin** *Ger.* län'dō·lēn
**Lan'don** lăn'dŭn
**Land'seer** lăn(d)'sēr, -syēr
**Lane** lān
**Lang'bridge** lăng'brĭj
**Lang'don** lăng'dŭn
**Lang'e** *Norw.* läng'ĕ
**Lang'ford** lăng'fĕrd
**Lang'horne** lăng'hôrn, lăng'ĕrn
**Lan'glois'** *Fr.* läɴ'glwȧ'
**Lang'son** lăng's'n
**Lang'ston** lăng'stŭn
**Lang'ton** lăng'tŭn
**Lan'sing** lăn'sĭng, *Brit.* län'-
**Lant** lănt
**La'o·ni'cus** *Lat.* lā'ō·nī'kŭs
**Lar'com** lär'kŭm
**Lar'kin** lär'kĭn
**La·roy'** lȧ·roi'
**Lar'ry** lăr'ĭ
**Lars** *Lat.* lärz; *Swed.* lärs, *Angl.* lärz
**Larz** lärz
**las** *Span.* läs
**La'scăr** *Rum.* lä'skĕr
**Las'celles** lăs''lz
**La'ska·ri'na** *Mod. Grk.* lä'skä·rē'nä
**Las'sen** *Dan.* lȧs''n
**Lász'ló** *Hung.* läs'lō
**La'tham** lā'thăm, -thăm
**La'throp** lā'thrŭp
**Lat'i·mer** lăt'ĭ·mĕr
**La'tour'** *Fr.* lȧ'tōōr'
**Lat'ta** lăt'ȧ
**Lau'der** lô'dĕr
**Lau'ge** *Dan.* lou'gĕ
**Laugh'ton** lô't'n
**Laun'ce·lot** lôn'sĕ·lŏt, län'-, lôns'lŏt, läns'-
**Launt** lônt, länt
**Lau'ra** lô'rȧ; *Ital.* lou'rä; *Swed.* lou'rȧ
**Laure** *Fr.* lôr
**Lau'rel** lô'rĕl, lŏr'ĕl
**Lau'rence** lô'rĕns, lŏr'ĕns
**Lau'rens** lô'rĕnz, -rĕns, lŏr'ĕnz, -ĕns; *Du.* lou'rĕns
**Lau'rent'** *Fr.* lô'räɴ'
**Lau'ren·tine** ?lô'rĕn·tĭn, -tēn
**Lau·ren'ti·us** *Lat.* lô·rĕn'shĭ·ŭs, -shŭs; *Swed.* lou·rĕn'tsĭ·ûs
**Lau·re'nus** lô·rē'nŭs
**Lau·rette'** lô·rĕt'
**Lau'ri** *Finn.* lou'rĭ
**Lau'rie** lô'rĭ, lŏr'ĭ
**Lau'rits, -ritz** *Dan.* lou'rēts
**Lau'ro** *Ital.* lou'rō
**La·val'** lȧ·văl'
**La Verne** lȧ vûrn'
**Lav'ing·ton** lăv'ĭng·tŭn
**La·vin'i·a** lȧ·vĭn'ĭ·ȧ—**La·vi'nia** *Ital.* lä·vē'nyä
**Lavr** *Russ.* lȧ'vĕr
**Lav·ren'ti** *Russ.* lŭv·ryān'tyû·ĭ
**Lav·rent'ie·vich** *Russ.* lŭv·ryānt'yĕ-vyĭch
**La'vro·vich** *Russ.* lȧ'vrŭ·vyĭch
**Law** lô
**Lawes** lôz
**Law'rence** lô'rĕns, lŏr'ĕns
**Law'ry** lô'rĭ
**Law'son** lô's'n
**Law'ton** lô't'n
**Lay'ton** lā't'n
**La'za** *Yugo.* lä'zä
**La'zar** *Russ.* lȧ'zŭr·y'
**Lá'zár** *Hung.* lä'zär
**La'zare'** *Fr.* lȧ'zȧr'
**Lá'za·ro** *Span.* lä'thä·rō, lä'sä-
**Laz'a·rus** lăz'ȧ·rŭs—**La'za·rus** *Ger.* lä'tsä·rōōs
**La·zelle'** lȧ·zĕl'
**Laz'za·ro** *Ital.* läd'dzä·rō
**le** lĕ, lē; *Fr.* lē
**Lea'der** lē'dĕr
**Le·an'der** lē·ăn'dĕr; *Ger.* lā·än'dĕr
**Le·an'dro** *Ital.* lā·än'drō; *Span.* lā-än'drō
**Lear'ned** lûr'nĕd, -nĭd
**Lea'tham** lē'thăm
**Leav'itt** lĕv'ĭt
**Le Bar'on** lĕ băr'ŭn
**Leb'by** lĕb'ĭ
**Le'be·recht** *Ger.* lā'bĕ·rĕkt
**Leb'recht** *Dan.* lĭb'rĕkt; *Ger.* lāp'-rĕkt, lā'brĕkt
**Le Bret'on** lĕ brĕt''n
**Le·clerc'** *Fr.* lē·klâr'
**Led'bet'ter** lĕd'bĕt'ĕr
**Led'yard** lĕd'yĕrd
**Lee** lē
**Leeds** lēdz
**Leete** lēt
**Lee'vi** *Finn.* lā'vĭ
**Leg'att** lĕg'ăt
**Legge** lĕg
**Legh** lē
**Le·grand'** *Fr.* lē·gräɴ'
**Leh'man** lā'măn, lē'-
**Leib** *Yiddish* lāb
**Leices'ter** lĕs'tĕr
**Leigh** lē
**Leigh'ton** lā't'n
**Lei'la** lē'lȧ
**Leith** lēth
**Le'land** lē'lănd
**Le'lio** *Ital.* lā'lyō
**Lem'bert'** *Fr.* läɴ'bâr'
**Le Me'su·rier** lĕ mĕzh'ŭ·rĕr
**Lem'on** lĕm'ŭn
**Lem'u·el** lĕm'û·ĕl
**Le'na** lē'nȧ
**Len'nart** *Swed.* lĕn'nȧrt
**Len'nox, Len'ox** lĕn'ŭks

**Lent** lĕnt
**Le′o** lē′ō; *Du., Ger.* lā′ō; *Finn.* lā′ô; *Ital.* lâ′ô
**Lé′o′** *Fr.* lā′ō′
**Lé′o′ca′die′** *Fr.* lā′ô′kȧ′dē′
**Le·of′ric** lē̇·ŏf′rĭk
**Le′o·line** lē′ô·lĭn
**Le′on** lē′ŏn; *Pol.* lĕ′ôn—**Le·on′** *Ital.* lâ·ōn′
**Lé′on′** *Fr.* lā′ôɴ′
**Le·ón′** *Span.* lâ·ôn′
**Le·o′na** lē̇·ō′nȧ
**Leon′ard** lĕn′ẽrd—**Le′o·nard** *Du., Ger.* lā′ô·närt; *Swed.* lā′ô·nȧrd—**Le·o′nard** *Pol.* lĕ·ô′närt
**Lé′o′nard′** *Fr.* lā′ô′nȧr′
**Le′o·nar′do** *Ital.* lā′ô·när′dô; *Span.* lā′ô·när′tho
**Le′o·nar′dus** *Du.* lā′ô·när′dûs
**Lé′once′** *Fr.* lā′ôɴs′
**Le·o′ne** *Ital.* lâ·ō′nâ
**Le′o·nel′lo** *Ital.* lā′ô·nĕl′lô
**Le′on·hard** *Ger.* lā′ôn·härt; *Swed.* lā′ô·nȧrd
**Le·o·nid′** *Russ.* lyĕ·ô·nyēt′
**Le·o′ni·da** *Ital.* lâ·ô′nē·dä
**Le·on′i·das** lē̇·ŏn′ĭ·dăs—**Le′o·ni′das** *Span.* lā′ô·nē′thäs
**Lé′o′nide′** *Fr.* lā′ô′nēd′
**Le·o·ni′do·vich** *Russ.* lyĕ·ô·nyē′dŭ·vyĭch
**Le′o·nor** lē′ô·nôr
**Le′o·no′ra** lē′ô·nō′rȧ
**Le′o·pold** lē′ô·pōld; *Du.* lā′ô·pŏlt; *Finn.* lĕ′ŏ·pŏld; *Ger.* lā′ô·pōlt—**Le·o′pold** *Pol.* lĕ·ô′pôlt
**Lé′o′pold′** *Fr.* lā′ô′pôld′
**Le′o·pol·di′ne** *Ger.* lā′ô·pôl·dē′nĕ
**Lé′o′pol′dine′** *Fr.* lā′ô′pôl′dēn′
**Le′o·pol′do** *Ital.* lā′ô·pôl′dô; *Span.* lā′ô·pôl′dō
**Le′os** *Czech* lĕ′ôsh
**Le·roy′, Le Roy** lĕ·roi′, lē̇-, lē′roi
**Les′ley, Les′lie** lĕs′lĭ, *esp. Brit.* lĕz′lĭ
**Les′ter** lĕs′tẽr
**Les′ton** lĕs′tŭn
**L′Es·trange′** lĕs·trānj′, lĕs-
**Leth′bridge** lĕth′brĭj
**Le·ti′ti·a** lē̇·tĭsh′ĭ·ȧ, -tĭsh′yȧ, -tĭsh′ȧ
**Le·ti′zia** *Ital.* lâ·tē′tsyä
**Let′tice** lĕt′ĭs
**Let′tie** lĕt′ĭ
**Lev** *Russ.* lyâf
**Lev′er·ett** lĕv′ẽr·ĕt, -ĭt, lĕv′rĕt, -rĭt
**Leve′son** lo͞o′s′n, lū′-
**Le′vi** lē′vī
**Lev′in** lĕv′ĭn
**Lev′ing·ton** lĕv′ĭng·tŭn
**Lew** lū, lo͞o
**Lew·el′yn** lo͝o·ĕl′ĭn
**Lew′is** lū′ĭs, lo͞o′-
**Leyces′ter** lĕs′tẽr
**Li′bé′ral′** *Fr.* lē′bā′rȧl′
**Li′be·ra′to** *Span.* lē′bâ·rä′tō
**Lib′er·ty** lĭb′ẽr·tĭ
**Li·cin′i·us** *Lat.* lī·sĭn′ĭ·ŭs
**Lieb′mann** *Ger.* lēp′män
**Light′foot** līt′fo͝ot
**Light′ner** līt′nẽr
**Li′gier′** *Fr.* lē′zhyā′
**Li′li′** *Fr.* lē′lē′—**Li′li** *Ger.* lĭ′lē̇
**Lil′i·an** lĭl′ĭ·ăn, lĭl′yăn
**Li′lio** *Ital.* lē′lyô
**Lil′lah** lĭl′ȧ
**Lill′burn** lĭl′bẽrn
**Lil′li** *Ger.* lĭ′lē̇
**Lil′li·an** lĭl′ĭ·ăn. lĭl′yăn
**Lil′lie** lĭl′ĭ
**Lil′y** lĭl′ĭ—**Li′ly′** *Fr.* lē′lē′—**Li′ly** *Ger.* lĭ′lē̇
**Li′na** *Ger., Ital.* lē′nä
**Lin′coln** lĭng′kŭn
**Lin′da** lĭn′dȧ
**Lin′den·berg** lĭn′dĕn·bûrg
**Lind′ley** lĭn(d)′lĭ
**Lin·dol′fo** *Span.* lēn·dôl′fō
**Lin′don** lĭn′dŭn
**Lind′say** lĭn′zĭ
**Lin′ley** lĭn′lĭ
**Linn** lĭn
**Lin·nae′us** lĭ·nē′ŭs
**Lins′ly** lĭnz′lĭ
**Lin′ton** lĭn′t′n, -tŭn
**Li′nus** lī′nŭs
**Li′on** lī′ŭn
**Lio·nar′do** *Ital.* lyô·när′dô
**Li′o·nel** lī′ô·nĕl, -n′l
**Lip′pin·cott** lĭp′ĭn·kŭt, -kŏt
**Lip·pi′no** *Ital.* lēp·pē′nô
**Lip′po** *Ital.* lēp′pô
**Lip′trot** ?lĭp′trŏt
**Li′sa** *Ital.* lē′zä
**Li·san′dro** *Span.* lē̇·sän′drō
**Li·sar′do** *Span.* lē̇·sär′thō
**Lis′beth** *Ger.* lēs′bĕt
**Li′se** *Ger.* lē′zĕ
**Li·set′te** *Ger.* lē̇·zĕt′ĕ
**Lisle** līl
**Lis′ter** lĭs′tẽr
**Li·tel′lus** lī·tĕl′ŭs, lĭ-
**Litt** lĭt
**Lit′tle** lĭt′′l
**Lit′tle·ton** lĭt′′l·tŭn
**Live** *Fr.* lēv
**Liv′er·more** lĭv′ẽr·mōr
**Liv′i·a** *Lat.* lĭv′ĭ·ȧ
**Liv′ing·ston** lĭv′ĭng·stŭn
**Li′viu** *Rum.* lē′vyo͞o
**Liv′i·us** *Lat.* lĭv′ĭ·ŭs
**Liv′sey** lĭv′zĭ, -sĭ
**Li′za** lī′zȧ
**Li·zar′do** *Span.* lē̇·thär′thō, -sär′thō
**Li·zette′** lĭ·zĕt′
**Li′zin′ka′** *Fr.* lē′zăɴ′kȧ′
**Liz′zie** lĭz′ĭ
**Lju′bo·mir** *Yugo.* lyo͞o′bô·mēr
**Lju′de·vit** *Yugo.* lyo͞o′dĕ·vēt
**Llew·el′lyn, Llew·el′yn** lo͝o·ĕl′ĭn
**Lloyd** loid
**lo** *Ital.* lō
**Lo·am′mi** lō̇·ăm′ī
**Löb** *Ger.* lûp
**Lock, Locke** lŏk
**Lock′hart** lŏk′härt, lŏk′ẽrt
**Lock′wood** lŏk′wo͝od
**Lo′de·wijk, -wyck** *Du.* lō′dĕ·vīk
**Lo′do·vi′co** *Ital.* lō′dô·vē′kô
**Lod′o·wick, -wicke** lŏd′ô·wĭk, lō′dô-
**Lof′tin** lŏf′tĭn
**Lo′gan** lō′găn
**Lo′gie** lō′gĭ
**Lo′ie** lō′ĭ
**Lo′la** lō′lȧ
**Lo′mer′** *Fr.* lô′mâr′
**Lon** lŏn
**Long′bourne** lŏng′bōrn, -bẽrn
**Lon′gi·no·vich** *Russ.* lôn′gyĭ·nŭ·vyĭch
**Long′streth** lŏng′strĕth
**Longue′ville** lŏng′vĭl
**Lons′bur′y** lŏnz′bĕr′ĭ, -bẽr·ĭ
**Loo′mis** lo͞o′mĭs
**Lo′pe** *Span.* lō′pā
**Ló′pez** *Span.* lō′pāth, -pās
**Ló′ránt** *Hung.* lō′ränt
**Lord** lôrd
**Lore** lōr
**Lo′rentz** *Dan., Norw.* lō′rĕnts
**Lo′renz** *Ger.* lō′rĕnts
**Lo′ren·zi′no** *Ital.* lō′rân·tsē′nô
**Lo·ren′zio** *Ital.* lô·rĕn′tsyô
**Lo·ren′zo** lô·rĕn′zō; *Ital.* lô·rĕn′tsô; *Span.* lô·rān′thō, -sō; *Swed.* lô-rĕn′(t)sô
**Lor′i·mer** lŏr′ĭ·mẽr
**Lo·rine′** lô·rēn′
**Lo′ring** lō′rĭng
**Lor′na** lôr′nȧ
**Lor·rain′, Lor·raine′** lô·rān′, lŏ-
**Lor′rin** lŏr′ĭn
**los** *Span.* lōs
**Lot** lŏt
**Lo·ta′rio** *Ital.* lô·tä′ryô
**Lo′thar** *Ger.* lō′tär, lô·tär′
**Lo′throp** lō′thrŭp
**Lott** lŏt
**Lot′ta** lŏt′ȧ; *Finn.* lŏt′tȧ
**Lot′te** *Ger.* lŏt′ĕ
**Lo′tus** lō′tŭs
**Lou** lo͞o
**Lou′don** lou′d′n
**Lough′bor′ough** lŭf′bûr′ô, *esp. Brit.* -bŭ·rŭ, -brŭ
**Lough′ton** lou′t′n
**Lou·iche′** *Fr.* lwēsh
**Lou′is** lo͞o′ĭs, lo͞o′ĭ; *Ger.* lo͞o′ē; *Norw.* lo͞o′ĭ, -ĭs; *Swed.* lo͞o′ē—**Lou·is′** *Du.* lo͞o·ē′; *Fr.* lwē
**Lou·i′sa** lo͞o·ē′zȧ; *Du.* lo͞o·ē′sȧ
**Lou·ise′** lo͞o·ēz′; *Fr.* lwēz—**Lou·i′se** *Dan.* lo͞o·ē′sĕ; *Du.* lo͞o·ē′sĕ; *Ger.* lo͞o·ē′zĕ
**Love** lŭv
**Love′good** lŭv′go͝od
**Lov′ell** lŭv′ĕl
**Lov′ett** lŭv′ĕt, -ĭt
**Lo′vis** *Ger.* lō′vĭs
**Lo′vi·sa′** *Swed.* lo͞o′vĭ·sȧ′
**Low, Lowe** lō
**Low′ell** lō′ĕl
**Lowes** lōz
**Lowndes** loundz
**Low′rie, Low′ry** lou′rĭ
**Low′ther** lou′thẽr
**Low′thi·an** lō′thĭ·ăn, -thyăn
**Loy** loi
**Loyd** loid
**Loy′set′** *Fr.* lwȧ′zĕ′
**Lub′bock** lŭb′ŭk
**Luc** *Fr.* lük
**Lu′ca** *Ital., Rum.* lo͞o′kä
**Lu′cas** lū′kăs; *Du.* lü′käs; *Ger., Span.* lo͞o′käs—**Lu′cas′** *Fr.* lü′kä′

**Luc·chi′no** *Ital.* lo͞ok·kē′nō̇
**Luce** lūs; *Fr.* lüs
**Lu′ci·a** lū′shĭ·*ȧ*, -sh*ȧ*; *Ger.* lo͞o′tsē̇·ä—**Lu·ci′a** *Ital.* lo͞o·chē′ä
**Lu′cian** lū′sh*ă*n; *Pol.* lo͞o′tsyän—**Lu′ci·an′** *Ger.* lo͞o′tsē̇·än′—**Lu-cian′** *Rum.* lo͞o·chän′
**Lu·cia′no** *Ital.* lo͞o·chä′nō̇; *Port.* lo͞o·syă′no͞o; *Span.* lo͞o·thyä′nō, -syä′-
**Lu′cie** lū′sĭ—**Lu′cie′** *Fr.* lü′sē′
**Lu′cien** lū′sh*ĕ*n—**Lu′cien′** *Fr.* lü′-syăɴ′
**Lu′cienne′** *Fr.* lü′syĕn′
**Lu·ci′la** *Span.* lo͞o·thē′lä, -sē′lä
**Lu·cile′** lů·sēl′—**Lu′cile′** *Fr.* lü′sēl′
**Lu·ci′lio** *Ital.* lo͞o·chē′lyō̇
**Lu·cille′** lů·sēl′
**Lu·cin′da** lů·sĭn′d*ȧ*
**Lu′cinde′** *Fr.* lü′săɴd′
**Lu′ci·us** lū′shĭ·*ŭ*s, lū′sh*ŭ*s
**Lu′cjan** *Pol.* lo͞o′tsyän
**Lu·cre′ti·a** lů·krē′shĭ·*ȧ*, -sh*ȧ*
**Lu·cre′zia** *Ital.* lo͞o·krâ′tsyä
**Lu′cy** lū′sĭ
**Lud′low** lŭd′lō
**Lu′do** *Ger.* lo͞o′dō
**Lu′dolf** *Dan.* lo͞o′dŏlf; *Du.* lü′dŏlf; *Ger.* lo͞o′dŏlf
**Lu′dolph** *Du.* lü′dŏlf; *Ger.* lo͞o′dŏlf
**Lu′do·vic** lū′dō̇·vĭk—**Lu′do′vic′** *Fr.* lü′dō̇′vēk′
**Lu′do·vi′ca** *Ger.*, *Ital.* lo͞o′dō̇·vē′kä
**Lu′do·vick** lū′dō̇·vĭk
**Lu′do·vi′co** *Ital.* lo͞o′dō̇·vē′kō̇
**Lu′do·vi′cus** *Lat.* lū′dō̇·vī′k*ŭ*s
**Lud′vig** *Dan.* lo͞oth′vē̇; *Swed.* lŭd′-vĭg
**Lud′well** lŭd′wĕl, -w*ĕ*l
**Lud′wig** lŭd′wĭg, lo͝od′-; *Dan.* lo͞oth′-vē̇; *Ger.* lo͞ot′vĭĸ, lo͝od′-; *Swed.* lŭd′-vĭg
**Lud′wik** *Pol.* lo͞od′vē̇k
**Luf′kin** lŭf′kĭn
**Lu·i′gi** *Ital.* lo͞o·ē′jē̇
**Luin′each** *Ir.* lĭn′*ȧ*ĸ
**Lu·is′** *Port.* lo͞o·ēsh′; *Span.* lo͞o·ēs′
**Lu·i′sa** *Ital.* lo͞o·ē′zä
**Lu·i′se** *Dan.* lo͝o·ē′sĕ; *Ger.* lo͞o·ē′z*ĕ*
**Lu′it·pold** *Ger.* lo͞o′ĭt·pō̇lt
**Lu·iz′** *Port.* lo͞o·ēsh′
**Lu′jo** *Ger.* lo͞o′yō
**Lu′kas** *Ger.* lo͞o′käs
**Lu′kasz** *Pol.* lo͞o′käsh
**Luke** lūk
**Lu′kens** lū′k*ĕ*nz
**Lu′kich** *Russ.* lo͞o′kyĭch
**Lu′la** lū′l*ȧ*
**Lu′lu** *Ger.* lo͞o′lo͞o
**Lum′ley** lŭm′lĭ
**Lum′mis** lŭm′ĭs
**Luns′ford** lŭnz′fẽrd
**Lu·per′cio** *Span.* lo͞o·pĕr′thyō, -syō
**Lu·ta′ti·us** *Lat.* lů·tā′shĭ·*ŭ*s, -sh*ŭ*s
**Lu′ther** lū′thẽr
**Lut′widge** lŭt′wĭj
**Lvo′vich** *Russ.* lyvô′vyĭch
**Ly·cur′gus** lī·kûr′g*ŭ*s
**Lyd′i·a** lĭd′ĭ·*ȧ*—**Ly′di·a** *Ger.* lü′dē̇·ä
**Ly′ell** lī′*ĕ*l
**Lyle** līl
**Ly′man** lī′m*ă*n
**Lynch** lĭnch
**Lynde** lĭnd
**Lyn′don** lĭn′d*ŭ*n
**Lyne** līn—**Ly′ne** *Dan.* lü′n*ĕ*
**Lynn** lĭn
**Ly′on** lī′*ŭ*n
**Lys′ter** lĭs′tẽr
**Lyt′tel·ton** lĭt′'l·t*ŭ*n
**Lyt′ton** lĭt′'n
**Ly′ulph** lī′*ŭ*lf, -ŭlf

**Maar′ten** *Du.* mär′t*ĕ*n
**Maas′tricht** *Ger.* mäs′trĭĸt
**Ma′bel** mā′b*ĕ*l
**Mac·al′lan** m*ă*k·ăl′*ă*n
**Mc·Al′lis·ter** m*ă*k·ăl′ĭs·tẽr
**Ma·cau′lay, -ley** m*ȧ*·kô′lĭ
**Mac·beth′** m*ă*k·bĕth′
**Mac·Bride′** m*ă*k·brīd′
**Mc·Cal′mont** ?m*ȧ*·kăl′mŏnt
**Mc·Car′rell** m*ȧ*·kăr′*ĕ*l
**Mc·Cau′ley** m*ȧ*·kô′lĭ
**Mc·Ches′ney** m*ă*k·chĕs′nĭ
**Mc·Chord′** m*ȧ*·kôrd′
**Mac′ci·us** *Lat.* măk′sĭ·*ŭ*s
**Mc·Clel′lan** m*ȧ*·klĕl′*ă*n
**Mc·Clel′land** m*ȧ*·klĕl′*ă*nd
**Mc·Clure′** m*ȧ*·klo͝or′
**Mc·Clurg′** m*ȧ*·klûrg′
**Mc·Coy′** m*ȧ*·koi′
**Mc·Cul′lagh** m*ȧ*·kŭl′*ȧ*
**Mc·Cune′** m*ȧ*·kūn′
**Mc·Don′ald** m*ă*k·dŏn′'ld
**Mc·Dou′all** m*ă*k·dou′*ă*l
**Mac·Dou′gal** m*ă*k·do͞o′g*ă*l
**Mc·Dow′ell** m*ă*k·dou′*ĕ*l
**Ma′ce·do′nio** *Ital.* mä′chā̇·dô′nyō̇
**Mc′El·der′ry** m*ă*k′'l·dĕr′ĭ
**Ma′cer** *Lat.* mā′sẽr
**Mc·Far′lan** m*ă*k·fär′l*ă*n
**Mc·Gar′el** m*ȧ*·găr′*ĕ*l
**Mc·Gav′ock** m*ȧ*·găv′*ŭ*k
**Mc·Gil′li·vray** m*ȧ*·gĭl′*ĭ*·vrā
**Mc·Greg′or** m*ȧ*·grĕg′ẽr
**Ma′ciej** *Pol.* mä′chā
**Mc′In·tyre** m*ă*k′ĭn·tīr
**Mac·kay′** m*ȧ*·kī′, m*ȧ*·kā′, m*ă*k′ĭ
**Mc·Kean′** m*ȧ*·kēn′
**Mc·Kee′** m*ȧ*·kē′
**Mc·Keen′** m*ȧ*·kēn′
**M′Kel′lar** m*ȧ*·kĕl′ẽr
**Mc·Ken′dree** m*ȧ*·kĕn′drē̇
**Mac·ken′zie** m*ȧ*·kĕn′zĭ
**Mac·Kin′lay** m*ȧ*·kĭn′lĭ
**Mc·Kin′ley** m*ȧ*·kĭn′lĭ
**Mc·Kin′ney** m*ȧ*·kĭn′ĭ
**Mac·Kin′non** m*ȧ*·kĭn′*ŭ*n
**Mack′in·tosh, Mac′Kin·tosh** m*ă*k′-ĭn·tŏsh
**Mack′lin** ?m*ă*k′lĭn
**Mac·Knight′** m*ă*k·nīt′
**Mack′worth** ?m*ă*k′wûrth, -wẽrth
**Mc·Lain′** m*ă*k·lān′
**Mc·Lane′** m*ă*k·lān′
**Mc·Lar′en** m*ă*k·lăr′*ĕ*n
**Mac·Lean′, Mc·Lean′** m*ă*k·lān′
**Mc·Lel′land** m*ă*k·lĕl′*ă*nd
**Mc·Len′dell** m*ă*k·lĕn′d'l
**Mc·Len′nan** m*ă*k·lĕn′*ă*n
**Mac·Leod′, Mc·Leod′** m*ă*k·loud′
**Mc·Ma′hon** m*ă*k·mä′*ŭ*n, m*ă*k·män′, m*ă*k′m*ȧ*·hŏn
**Mc·Mas′ters** m*ă*k·m*ȧ*s′tẽrz
**Mac·mil′lan** m*ă*k·mĭl′*ă*n
**Mc·Mur′trie** m*ă*k·mûr′trĭ
**M′Nair′** m*ă*k·nâr′
**Mc·Neal′** m*ă*k·nēl′
**Mc·Nee′ly** m*ă*k·nē′lĭ
**Mc·Neill′** m*ă*k·nēl′
**Ma′con** mā′k*ŭ*n
**Mc·Phail′** m*ă*k·fāl′
**Mac·pher′son** m*ă*k·fûr′s'n
**Mc·Pher′son** m*ă*k·fûr′s'n
**Mac·quorn′** m*ȧ*·kwôrn′
**Ma·crae′** m*ȧ*·krā′
**M′Tag′gart** m*ă*k·tăg′ẽrt
**Mc·Tag′gart** m*ă*k·tăg′ẽrt
**Mac·vey′** m*ă*k·vā′
**mad′ame** măd′*ă*m—**ma′dame′** *Fr.* m*ȧ*′d*ȧ*m′
**Mad′den** măd′'n
**Mad′dern** măd′ẽrn
**Mad′di·son** măd′*ĭ*·s'n
**Mad′dock** măd′*ŭ*k
**Mad′e·leine** măd′*ĕ*·lĭn, -lān—**Ma′-de·leine′** *Fr.* m*ȧ*′dlĕn′
**ma′de·moi′selle′** *Fr.* m*ȧ*d′mw*ȧ*′zĕl′, m*ȧ*m′zĕl′, *Angl.* măd′ē·mō̇·zĕl′
**Madge** măj
**Ma′dhu** *Bengali* mŏ′do͞o
**Mad′i·son** măd′*ĭ*·s'n
**Mad′ox** măd′*ŭ*ks
**Mae·cil′i·us** *Lat.* mē̇·sĭl′ĭ·*ŭ*s
**Maf·fe′o** *Ital.* mäf·fâ′ō̇
**Mag′da** *Rum.* mäg′dä
**Mag′de·leine′** *Fr.* m*ȧ*g′dē·lĕn′
**Mag′gie** măg′ĭ
**Ma·gill′** m*ȧ*·gĭl′
**Mag′nus** măg′n*ŭ*s; *Dan.* m*ȧ*g′no͝os; *Ger.* mäg′no͝os; *Norw.* mäng′no͝os; *Swed.* m*ȧ*ng′nŭs
**Ma′ha·de′o** *As. Ind.* mŭ′hä·dā′ō̇
**Ma′har·ban′ji** *Parsi* mŭ′h*ȧ*r·bän′jē
**Mah′lon** mā′l*ŭ*n, mä′-
**Mah·mud′** *Turk.* mä·mo͞od′
**Ma·ho′ney** m*ȧ*·hō′nĭ, mä′*ŭ*·nĭ, mä′nĭ
**Main** mān
**Main′wa·ring** măn′*ȧ*·rĭng
**Mair** mâr
**Mait′land** māt′l*ă*nd
**Ma′jor** mā′jẽr
**Mak·dou′gall** m*ă*k·do͞o′g*ă*l
**Make′peace′** māk′pēs′
**Ma·ko·to** *Jap.* mä·kō̇·tō̇
**Mak·sim′** *Russ.* mŭk·syēm′
**Mak·si′mo·vich** *Russ.* mŭk·syē′mŭ-vyĭch
**Mal′a·by** măl′*ȧ*·bĭ
**Mal′colm** măl′k*ŭ*m
**Mal·har′** *Marathi* m*ȧ*l·här′
**Ma′lik** *As. Ind.* mä′lĭk
**Ma′lin** mā′lĭn
**Mal′la·han** măl′*ȧ*·hăn
**Mal′lord** măl′ẽrd
**Mal′lo·ry** măl′ō̇·rĭ
**Ma′lo′** *Fr.* m*ȧ*′lō′
**Ma·lone′** m*ȧ*·lōn′
**Mal′vin** măl′vĭn
**Ma·mo·ru** *Jap.* mä·mō̇·ro͝o
**Ma·nas′seh** m*ȧ*·năs′*ĕ*
**Man′dé′** *Fr.* mäɴ′dā′

**Man′ford** măn′fẽrd
**Man′fred** *Ger.* män′frāt
**Man·fre′di** *Ital.* män·frā′dē
**Man·fre′do** *Ital.* män·frā′dō
**Ma′ni·us** *Lat.* mā′nĭ·ŭs
**Man′key** măng′kĭ
**Man′ley** măn′lĭ
**Man′li·us** măn′lĭ·ŭs
**Mann** măn
**Man′ne′** *Swed.* mȧn′nĕ′
**Man′ning** măn′ĭng
**Man′ning·ton** măn′ĭng·tŭn
**Ma·no·el′** *Port.* mȧ·nwĕl′
**Ma′non′** *Fr.* mȧ′nôɴ′
**Mans′field** măns′fēld
**Man′suète′** *Fr.* mäɴ′sü·ĕt′
**Man·sur′** *Pers.* män·sōōr′
**Man′u·el** măn′ū·ĕl—**Ma·nu·el′** *Port.* mȧ·nwĕl′; *Span.* mä·nwĕl′
**Man′us** măn′ŭs, mä′nŭs, mā′nŭs
**Man′ville** măn′vĭl
**Ma·phe′us** *Lat.* mȧ·fē′ŭs
**Marc** märk; *Fr.* mȧrk
**Marc An·to′nio, Marc′An·to′nio, Marc′-an·to′nio** *Ital.* mär′kän·tô′nyō
**Mar′cel′** *Fr.* mȧr′sĕl′
**Mar′ce·lin′** *Fr.* mȧr′sē·lăɴ′
**Mar′ce·line′** *Fr.* mȧr′sē·lēn′
**Mar′ce·li′no** *Span.* mär′thā·lē′nō, mär′sā-
**Mar′celle′** *Fr.* mȧr′sĕl′
**Mar′cel·lin′** *Fr.* mȧr′sē·lăɴ′
**Mar·cel′lo** *Ital.* mär·chĕl′lō
**Mar·cel′lus** mär·sĕl′ŭs; *Du.* mär-sĕl′ûs
**Mar·ce′lo** *Span.* mär·thā′lō, -sā′lō
**March** märch
**mar·che′sa** *Ital.* mär·kā′zä
**mar·che′se** *Ital.* mär·kā′zā
**Mar′cia** mär′shȧ
**Mar·cial′** *Span.* mär·thyäl′, -syäl′
**Mar′cien′** *Fr.* mȧr′syăɴ′
**Mar′cin** *Pol.* mär′tsēn
**Mar′ci·us** *Lat.* mär′shĭ·ŭs, -shŭs
**Mar′co** mär′kō; *Ital.* mär′kō; *Span.* mär′kō—**Mar′co′** *Fr.* mȧr′kō′
**Mar′cos** *Port.* mȧr′kōōsh; *Span.* mär′kōs
**Mar′cus** mär′kŭs; *Du.* mär′kûs; *Ger.*, *Norw.* mär′kōōs; *Swed.* mȧr′-kŭs
**Mar′cy** mär′sĭ
**ma′ré′chal′** *Fr.* mȧ′rā′shȧl′
**Ma·re·su·ke** *Jap.* mä·rĕ·sōō·kĕ
**Mar′fa** *Russ.* mȧr′fŭ
**Mar′ga·ret** mär′gȧ·rĕt, -rĭt
**Mar′ga·re′ta** *Swed.* mȧr′gȧ·rā′tȧ
**Mar′ga·re′te** *Ger.* mär′gä·rā′tĕ
**Mar′ga·ret′ta** mär′gȧ·rĕt′ȧ
**Mar′ga·ri′ta** mär′gȧ·rē′tȧ
**Mar′ger·y** mär′jẽr·ĭ
**Mar′ghe·ri′ta** *Ital.* mär′gā·rē′tä
**Mar′got** mär′gō, -gŭt
**Mar·gre′te** *Dan.* mär·grē′tĕ
**Mar′gue·rite′** mär′gē·rēt′; *Fr.* mȧr′-gē·rēt′
**Ma·ri′a** mȧ·rī′ȧ, -rē′ȧ; *Du.*, *Finn.* mȧ·rē′ȧ; *Ger.*, *Ital.* mä·rē′ä; *Port.* mȧ·rē′ȧ; *Russ.* mŭ·ryē′yŭ; *Swed.* mȧ·rē′ȧ—**Ma′ria** *Pol.* mä′ryä
**Ma·rí′a** *Span.* mä·rē′ä
**Mar′i·an** mâr′ĭ·ȧn, măr′-
**Mar′i·an′a** mâr′ĭ·ăn′ȧ, măr′-, -ä′nȧ
**Ma·ri·an′na** *Port.* mȧ·rē·ă′nȧ
**Mar′i·anne′** mâr′ĭ·ăn′, măr′-—**Ma′-ri·an′ne** *Ger.* mä′rē·än′ĕ
**Ma·ria′no** *Ital.* mä·ryä′nō; *Span.* mä·ryä′nō
**Ma·rie′** mȧ·rē′, *Brit. also* mä′rĭ, măr′ĭ; *Dan.*, *Du.*, *Swed.* mȧ·rē′—**Ma′rie′** *Fr.* mȧ′rē′—**Ma·ri′e** *Dan.*, *Norw.* mä·rē′ĕ; *Ger.* mä·rē′ĕ, mä·rē′
**Mar′i·et′ta** mâr′ĭ·ĕt′ȧ, măr′-—**Ma′-ri·et′ta** *Ital.* mä′rē·āt′tä
**Ma′rin′** *Fr.* mȧ′răɴ′
**Ma·ri′na** *Russ.* mŭ·ryē′nŭ
**Ma·ri′no** *Ital.* mä·rē′nō
**Ma·ri′nus** mȧ·rē′nŭs, -rī′nŭs; *Du.* mȧ·rē′nûs
**Ma′rio′** *Fr.* mȧ′ryō′—**Ma′rio** *Ital.* mä′ryō; *Span.* mä′ryō
**Mar′i·on** măr′ĭ·ŭn, mâr′-
**Mar′i·us** mâr′ĭ·ŭs—**Ma′ri·us** *Du.* mȧ′rē·ûs; *Ger.*, *Norw.* mä′rē·ōōs—**Ma′rius′** *Fr.* mȧ′ryüs′
**Ma·ri′ya** *Russ.* mŭ·ryē′yŭ
**Ma′rja** *Pol.* mä′ryä
**Ma′rjan** *Pol.* mä′ryän
**Mar′jo·rie, Mar′jo·ry** mär′jō·rĭ
**Mark** märk; *Du.* märk; *Russ.* mȧrk
**Mark′ham** mär′kăm
**Mar′kos** *Mod. Grk.* mär′kôs
**Mar′ko·vich** *Russ.* mȧr′kŭ·vyĭch
**Marks** märks
**Mar′kus** *Ger.* mär′kōōs
**Mar′land** mär′lănd
**Mar′ma·duke** mär′mȧ·dūk
**mar·qués′** *Span.* mär·kās′
**mar·quês′** *Port.* mȧr·kāsh′, (*Braz.*) -kās′
**Már′quez** *Span.* mär′kāth, -kās
**Mar′quis** mär′kwĭs
**mar′quis′** *Fr.* mȧr′kē′
**mar′quise′** *Fr.* mȧr′kēz′
**Marr** mär
**Mar′ri·ner** măr′ĭ·nẽr
**Mar′ri·ot, Mar′ri·ott** măr′ĭ·ŭt
**Mars′den** märz′dĕn
**Marsh** märsh
**Mar′shall** mär′shăl
**Marsh′man** märsh′măn
**Mar·si′lio** *Ital.* mär·sē′lyō
**Mar′tha** mär′thȧ
**Mar·thi′nus** *Du.* mär·tē′nûs
**Mar′tial′** *Fr.* mȧr′syȧl′
**Mar·tim′** *Port.* mȧr·tēɴ′
**Mar′tin** mär′tĭn, -t'n; *Dan.* mär′tēn; *Du.* mär′tĭn, mär·tĭn′; *Finn.* mȧr′-tĭn; *Ger.* mär′tēn; *Swed.* mȧr′tĭn—**Mar′tin′** *Fr.* mȧr′tăɴ′
**Mar·tín′** *Span.* mär·tēn′
**Mar′tine′** *Fr.* mȧr′tēn′
**Mar·tí′nez** *Span.* mär·tē′nāth, -nās
**Mar·ti·nia′no** *Port.* mȧr·tē·nyȧ′nōō
**Mar·ti′no** *Ital.* mär·tē′nō
**Mar·ti′nus** mär·tī′nŭs; *Du.* -tē′nûs
**Mar′tyn** mär′tĭn, -t'n
**Mar′tyr′** *Fr.* mȧr′tēr′
**Mar′vin** mär′vĭn
**Mar′y** mâr′ĭ
**Ma′rya** *Pol.* mä′ryä—**Mar′ya** *Russ.* mȧr′yŭ
**Mar·zia′le** *Ital.* mär·tsyä′lā
**Ma·sa·na·o** *Jap.* mä·sä·nä·ō
**Ma·sa·no·bu** *Jap.* mä·sä·nō·bōō
**Ma·sa·yo·shi** *Jap.* mä·sä·yō·shē
**Ma·sa·yu·ki** *Jap.* mä·sä·yōō·kē
**Mas′ke·lyne** măs′kē·lĭn, -lĭn
**Ma′so** *Ital.* mä′zō
**Ma′son** mā′s'n
**Mas′sey** măs′ĭ
**Mas′si·mi·lia′no** *Ital.* mäs′sē·mē-lyä′nō
**Mas′si·mo** *Ital.* mäs′sē·mō
**Mas·su′ri·us** *Lat.* mă·sū′rĭ·ŭs
**Mas′sy** măs′ĭ
**Mas′ter·man** mȧs′tẽr·măn
**Mas′ters** mȧs′tẽrz
**Ma·sti′no** *Ital.* mäs·tē′nō
**Ma·te′o** *Span.* mä·tā′ō
**Ma·thä′us** *Ger.* mä·tâ′ōōs
**Math′ew** măth′ū
**Math′ews** măth′ūz
**Math′ew·son** măth′ū·s'n
**Ma·thi′as** mȧ·thī′ăs; *Ger.*, *Norw.* mä·tē′äs; *Port.* mȧ·tē′ȧsh, (*Braz.*) -ȧs—**Ma′thias′** *Fr.* mȧ′tyäs′
**Ma′thieu′** *Fr.* mȧ′tyû′
**Ma′thilde′** *Fr.* mȧ′tēld′—**Ma·thil′de** *Ger.* mä·tĭl′dĕ
**Ma′thu′rin′** *Fr.* mȧ′tü′răɴ′
**Ma·thys′** *Du.* mä·tīs′
**Ma·tí′as** *Span.* mä·tē′äs
**Ma′ti·ja** *Yugo.* mä′tē·yä
**Ma·til′da** mȧ·tĭl′dȧ; *Ital.* mä·tēl′dä
**Ma′tilde′** *Fr.* mȧ′tēld′
**Matt** măt
**Mat·te′o** *Ital.* mät·tâ′ō
**Mat′te·son** măt′ĕ·s'n
**Mat·thä′us** *Ger.* mä·tâ′ōōs
**Mat′thew** măth′ū
**Mat′thews** măth′ūz
**Mat·thi′as** mă·thī′ăs; *Finn.* mȧ·tē′-ȧs; *Ger.*, *Norw.* mä·tē′äs
**Mat′thí·as** *Icel.* mät′tē·äs
**Mat′thieu′** *Fr.* mȧ′tyû′
**Mat·thijs′** *Du.* mä·tīs′
**Mat·ti′a** *Ital.* mät·tē′ä
**Mat·toon′** mă·tōōn′
**Mat′ty** măt′ĭ
**Mat·ve′e·vich** *Russ.* mŭt·vyā′yĕ-vyĭch
**Mat·vei′** *Russ.* mŭt·vyā′ĭ
**Má′tyás** *Hung.* mä′tyäsh
**Maud, Maude** môd
**Maule** môl
**Maunde** mônd
**Maun′sel** măn′s'l
**Maur** môr
**Mau′rice** mô′rĭs, mŏr′ĭs—**Mau′rice′** *Fr.* mō′rēs′
**Mau′ris** mô′rĭs, mŏr′ĭs
**Mau′ritz** *Du.*, *Norw.*, *Swed.* mou′rĭts
**Mau·ri′zio** *Ital.* mou·rē′tsyō
**Mau′rus** *Ger.* mou′rōōs; *Lat.* mô′rŭs
**Mau·ry′cy** *Pol.* mou·rĭ′tsĭ
**Max** măks; *Du.* mäks; *Fr.* mȧks; *Ger.* mäks
**Max′ence′** *Fr.* mȧk′säɴs′
**Max′field** măks′fēld
**Max·im′** *Russ.* mŭk·syēm′
**Max′ime′** *Fr.* mȧk′sēm′
**Max·im′i·a′na** *Lat.* măk·sĭm′ĭ·ā′nȧ

**Max′i·mil′ian** măk′sĭ·mĭl′yăn, -mĭl′ĭ·ăn—**Ma′xi·mi′li·an** *Ger.* mäk′sē·mē′lē·än; *Pol.* mäk′sĭ·mē′lyän—**Ma′xi·mi·li·an′** *Norw.* mäk′sē·mē·lē·än′
**Ma′xi·mi·li·a′na** *Ger.* mäk′sē·mē·lē·ä′nä
**Ma′xi·mi·li·a′ne** *Ger.* mäk′sē·mē·lē·ä′nĕ
**Ma′xi·mi·lia′no** *Span.* mäk′sē·mē·lyä′nō
**Max′i′mi′lien′** *Fr.* mȧk′sē′mē′lyăN′
**Max′i′min′** *Fr.* mȧk′sē′măN′
**Má′xi·mo** *Span.* mäk′sē·mō
**Max′i·mus** *Lat.* măk′sĭ·mŭs
**Max·ine′** măk·sēn′, măk′sēn
**Max′well** măks′wĕl, -wĕl
**May** mā
**May′er** mī′ẽr, mā′ẽr; *Ger.* mī′ẽr
**May′field** mā′fēld
**May′hew** mā′hū
**May′nard** mā′nẽrd, -närd
**Mayne** mān
**May′o** mā′ō
**Mead, Meade** mēd
**Mead′ows** mĕd′ōz
**Mearns** mûrnz
**Mech·til′de** *Ger.* mĕK·tĭl′dĕ
**Mé′dart′** *Fr.* mā′dȧr′
**Mé′dé′ric′** *Fr.* mā′dā′rēk′
**Me·dill′** mĕ·dĭl′
**Mee′ker** mē′kẽr
**Megh·nad′** māg·näd′
**Me·he·met′, Meh·med′, Meh·met′** *Turk.* mĕ·mĕt′
**Mein′dert** *Du.* mīn′dẽrt
**Mein′hard** *Ger.* mīn′härt
**Mein′rad** *Ger.* mīn′rät
**Meir** *Dan.* mīr
**Me·lanch′thon, Me·lanc′thon** mē·lăngk′thŭn
**Me·lanc′ton** mē·lăngk′tŭn
**Mel′ba** mĕl′bȧ
**Mel′bourne** mĕl′bẽrn, -bôrn
**Mel′chi·or** mĕl′kē·ôr; *Ger.* mĕl′Kē·ôr—**Mel′chior′** *Fr.* mĕl′kyôr′
**Mel·chior′re** *Ital.* mâl·kyôr′rā
**Mel′chis′sé′dech′** *Fr.* mĕl′kē′sā′dĕk′
**Mel·chor′** *Span.* mĕl·chôr′
**Mel′e·si′na** mĕl′ĕ·sē′nȧ
**Mel′len** mĕl′ĕn
**Mel′lin′** *Fr.* mĕ′lăN′
**Mel′ton** mĕl′t'n, -tŭn
**Me′lu·si′na** *Ger.* mā′lōō·zē′nä
**Mel′vil, Mel′vill, Mel′ville** mĕl′vĭl
**Mel′vin** mĕl′vĭn
**Mem, Men** *Port.* māēN, (*Braz.*) māēN
**Me′na·hem** *Ger.* mā′nä·hĕm, mȧ·nä′hĕm
**Men′des** *Port.* mäNn′dēsh, (*Braz.*) -dēs
**Men′no** *Du.* mĕn′ō
**Me·not′ti** *Ital.* mā·nôt′tē
**Men′tor** mĕn′tẽr, -tôr
**Mer′cer** mûr′sẽr
**Mer′chant** mûr′chănt
**Mer·cu′ri·us** *Du.* mĕr·kü′rē·ŭs
**Mer′cy** mûr′sĭ
**Mer′e·dith** mĕr′ĕ·dĭth
**Mé′ria′dec′** *Fr.* mā′ryȧ′dĕk′
**Mer′i·am** mĕr′ĭ·ăm
**Mer′i·an** mĕr′ĭ·ăn
**Mé′ric′** *Fr.* mā′rēk′
**Mer′i·weth′er** mĕr′ĭ·wĕth′ẽr
**Merle** mûrl
**Mer′lin** mûr′lĭn
**Me·ro′pi·us** *Lat.* mē·rō′pĭ·ŭs
**Mer′rill** mĕr′ĭl
**Mer′ri·ott** mĕr′ĭ·ŭt
**Mer′rit, Mer′ritt** mĕr′ĭt
**Mer′ry** mĕr′ĭ
**Mer′ton** mûr′t'n
**Mer′ven** mûr′vĕn
**Mer′vil** mûr′vĭl
**Mer′vyn** mûr′vĭn
**Mer·wan′gi, -ji** *Parsi* mār·vän′jē
**Mer′win** mûr′wĭn
**Me′shech** mē′shĕk
**Mes′sin·ger** ?mĕs′ĭn·jẽr
**Mes′si·us** *Lat.* mĕs′ĭ·ŭs
**met** *Du.* mĕt
**Me′ta** mē′tȧ
**Met′calfe** mĕt′kȧf, -kȧf
**Meth′u·en** mĕth′ū·ĭn
**Met′tus** *Lat.* mĕt′ŭs
**Mey′er** *Eng., Dan., Ger.* mī′ẽr
**Mey′rick** mĕr′ĭk, mā′rĭk, mī′rĭk
**Me′zio** *Ital.* mâ′tsyō
**Mi′cah** mī′kȧ
**Mi·ca′jah** mī·kā′yȧ
**Mi′chael** mī′kĕl, -k'l—**Mi′cha·el** *Du.* mē′Kȧ·ĕl; *Finn.* mē′kȧ·ĕl; *Ger.* mĭ′Kä·ĕl—**Mi·chael′** *Dan.* mē·kȧl′, mēk′kĕl; *Norw.* mē·käl′
**Mi′chał** *Pol.* mē′Käl
**Mi′chel** mī′kĕl, -k'l; *Ger.* mĭ′Kĕl—**Mi′chel′** *Fr.* mē′shĕl′
**Mi′chel·an′ge·lo** mī′kĕl·ăn′jĕ·lō, mĭk′ĕl-; *Ital.* mē′kȧl·än′jā·lō
**Mi·che′le** *Ital.* mē·kā′lā
**Mi′chelle′** *Fr.* mē′shĕl′
**Mi·chiel′** *Du.* mē·Kēl′
**Mi·chi·tsu·ra** *Jap.* mē·chē·tsōō·rä
**Mich′ler** mĭk′lẽr
**Mid′dle·ton** mĭd′'l·tŭn
**Mie·czy′sław** *Pol.* myĕ·chĭ′släf
**Mien′se** *Du.* mēn′sĕ
**Mi′ers** mī′ẽrz
**Miff′lin** mĭf′lĭn
**Mi·guel′** *Port.* mē·gâl′; *Span.* mē·gĕl′
**Mi·hai′** *Rum.* mē·hī′
**Mi′ha·il′** *Rum.* mē′hä·ēl′
**Mi′hály** *Hung.* mĭ′häl·y′
**Mi′ka·el** *Swed.* mē′kȧ·ĕl
**Mi·kal′** *Norw.* mē·käl′
**Mi·kha·il′** *Bulg.* mĭ·Kä·ĭl′; *Russ.* myĭ·Kŭ·ēl′
**Mi·khai′lo·vich** *Russ.* myĭ·Kī′lŭ·vyĭch
**Mi·khai′lov·na** *Russ.* myĭ·Kī′lŭv·nŭ
**Mik′kel** *Dan.* mēk′kĕl
**Mik′kjel** *Norw.* mĭK′Kĕl
**Mi′klós** *Hung.* mĭ′klōsh
**Mi·ko′łaj** *Pol.* mē·kô′lī
**Mi′lan** *Czech* mĭ′lȧn; *Yugo.* mē′län
**Mil′bry** mĭl′brĭ
**Mil′burn, -burne** mĭl′bẽrn
**Mil′dred** mĭl′drĕd, -drĭd
**Miles** mīlz
**Mi′li** *Russ.* myē′lyû·ĭ
**Mi′li′vo·je** *Yugo.* mē′lē′vô·yĕ
**Mil′ka** *Yugo.* mēl′kä
**Mil′lard** mĭl′ẽrd
**Mil′ledge** mĭl′ĭj
**Mil′ler** mĭl′ẽr
**Mil′li·cent** mĭl′ĭ·sĕnt, -s'nt
**Mil′li·gan** mĭl′ĭ·găn
**Mil′ling·ton** mĭl′ĭng·tŭn
**Mills** mĭlz
**Mil′more** mĭl′mōr
**Milne** mĭl, mĭln
**Mil′ner** mĭl′nẽr
**Mil′nor** mĭl′nẽr, -nôr
**Mi′lo** mī′lō
**Mi′lo·slav** *Czech* mĭ′lô·släf
**Mi′lo·van** *Yugo.* mē′lō·vän
**Mil′ton** mĭl′t'n, -tŭn
**Mi′mi′** *Fr.* mē′mē′
**Mi·nei·chi·ro** *Jap.* mē·nā·chē·rō
**Mi′ner** mī′nẽr
**Mi·ner′va** mĭ·nûr′vȧ
**Minge** mĭnj
**Min′na** *Finn.* mĭn′nȧ; *Ger.* mĭn′ä
**Min′nie** mĭn′ĭ
**Mi′no** *Ital.* mē′nō
**Mi′nor** mī′nẽr, -nôr
**Mi′not** mī′nŭt
**Min′ton** mĭn′t'n, -tŭn
**Min′turn** mĭn′tẽrn
**Mir′a·beau** mĭr′ȧ·bō
**Mi·ran′da** mĭ·răn′dȧ
**Mir′i·am** mĭr′ĭ·ăm
**Mi′ron** mī′rŭn
**Mi·ro′no·vich** *Russ.* myĭ·rô′nŭ·vyĭch
**mir·za′** *Pers.* mēr·zä′
**Mi′scha** mē′shȧ; *Russ.* myē′shŭ
**Mis′key** mĭs′kĭ
**Mitch′ell** mĭch′ĕl
**Mi′te** *Ger.* mē′tĕ
**Mi·tro·fan′** *Russ.* myĭ·trŭ·fȧn′
**Mi·tsu·ma·sa** *Jap.* mē·tsōō·mä·sä
**Mix** mĭks
**Mo′ber·ly** mō′bẽr·lĭ
**Mod′er·a′tus** *Lat.* mŏd′ẽr·ā′tŭs
**Mo·dest′** *Russ.* mŭ·dyâst′
**Mo′deste′** *Fr.* mô′dĕst′
**Mo·des′to** *Span.* mō·thās′tō
**Mof′fett** mŏf′ĕt, -ĭt
**Mo·ham′med** mō·hăm′ĕd, -ĭd; *Afghan* mō·hŭm′mĕd; *Arab.* mōō·hăm′măd; *Pers.* mō·hȧm′măd
**Mo′han·das** *Gujarati* mō′hȧn·däs
**Moi′ra** moi′rȧ
**Mo′ïse′** *Fr.* mô′ēz′
**Moi·se′e·vich** *Russ.* mŭ·ĭ·syā′yĕ·vyĭch
**Moi·sei′** *Russ.* mŭ·ĭ·syā′ĭ
**Moles′worth** mōlz′wûrth, -wẽrth
**Moll** mŏl
**Mol′ly** mŏl′ĭ
**Molt′ke** *Norw.* mōlt′kĕ
**Mom′či·lo** *Yugo.* mōm′chē·lō
**Mon·crieff′** mŏn·krēf′, mŭn-
**Mon·cure′** mŏn·kūr′, mŭn-, mŏn′kūr
**Mon′i·ca** mŏn′ĭ·kȧ
**Mon·roe′** mŭn·rō′, *Brit. also* mŭn′rō
**Mon′son** mŭn′s'n
**Mon′ta·cute** mŏn′tȧ·kūt, mŭn′-
**Mon′ta·gu, -gue** mŏn′tȧ·gū, mŭn′-
**Mon′te·fi·o′re** mŏn′tē·fĭ·ō′rē, -ô′rē
**Mon·teith′** mŏn·tēth′

**Mon'tes·quieu'** mŏn'tĕs·kū'
**Mont'fort** mŏnt'fĕrt
**Mont·gom'er·ie** mŏn(t)·gŭm'ĕr·ĭ, -gŭm'rĭ, -gŏm'-
**Moo'dy** mōō'dĭ
**Moor, Moore** mŏŏr, mōr
**Moors** mŏŏrz, mōrz
**Mór** *Hung.* mōr
**Mor'daunt** môr'd'nt
**Mor'de·cai** môr'dē·kī, môr'dē·kā'ī
**Mor'dey** môr'dĭ
**More** mōr
**Mo·reau'** ?mō·rō'
**Mo·rell'** ?mō·rĕl'
**More'ton** mōr't'n
**Mor'gan** môr'găn
**Mo·ri** *Jap.* mō·rē
**Mo·ri·no·bu** *Jap.* mō·rē·nō·bŏŏ
**Mor'i·son** mŏr'ĭ·s'n
**Mo'ritz** *Ger.* mō'rĭts
**Mo'ri·tzo·vich** *Russ.* mô'ryĭ·tsŭ-vyĭch
**Mo'riz** *Ger.* mō'rĭts
**Mor'ley** môr'lĭ
**Mor'rill** mŏr'ĭl
**Mor'ris** mŏr'ĭs; *Dan.* mŏ'rēs
**Mor'ri·son** mŏr'ĭ·s'n
**Mor'row** mŏr'ō
**Morse, Morss** môrs
**Mor'te·mart'** *Fr.* môr'tĕ·mȧr'
**Mor'ti·mer** môr'tĭ·mĕr
**Mor'ton** môr't'n
**Mose'ley** mōz'lĭ
**Mo·sén'** *Span.* mō·sān'
**Mo'ses** mō'zĕz, -zĭz; *Ger.* mō'zĕs
**Mo'she** *Yiddish* mō'shĕ
**Moss** mŏs
**Moss'man** mŏs'măn
**Mo'tier'** *Fr.* mô'tyā'
**Mo·to·no·bu** *Jap.* mō·tō·nō·bŏŏ
**Mott** mŏt
**mou·la'na** *Arab.* mou·lä'nä
**Moul'ton** mōl't'n, -tŭn
**Mount·stu'art** mount·stū'ĕrt
**Mow'bray** mō'brā, -brĭ
**Mu'ci·us** *Lat.* mū'shĭ·ŭs, -shŭs
**Mu·ḥam'mad** *Arab.* mŏŏ·hăm'măd; *Pers.* mŏ·hȧm'mȧd
**Muh'len·berg** mū'lĕn·bûrg
**Muir** mūr
**Muir'head** mūr'hĕd
**mu·lai'** *Arab.* mou·lī'
**Mul'drup** mŭl'drŭp
**Mü'lertz** *Norw.* mü'lĕrts
**Mul'ford** mŭl'fĕrd
**Mum'ford** mŭm'fĕrd
**Mu·na'ti·us** *Lat.* mū·nā'shĭ·ŭs, -shŭs
**Mu·ne·mi·tsu** *Jap.* mōō·nĕ·mē·tsōō
**Mun'go** mŭng'gō
**Mun·ro', Mun·roe'** mŭn·rō', *Brit. also* mŭn'rō
**Mu·rad'** *Ger.* mōō·rät'
**Mur'do** mûr'dō
**Mur'doch** mûr'dŏk
**Mu'ri·el** mū'rĭ·ĕl
**Mur'ray** mûr'ĭ
**Mur'rough** mûr'ō
**Mur'ry** mûr'ĭ
**Mur'ton** mûr't'n
**Mu'sa** *Ital.* mōō'zä
**Mus'kett** mŭs'kĕt, -kĭt
**Mus'ta·fa** *Arab.* mŏŏs'tä·fä—**Mus·ta·fa'** *Turk.* mŏŏs·tä·fä'
**Mu'zio** *Ital.* mōō'tsyō
**My'er** mī'ĕr
**My'ers** mī'ĕrz
**Myles** mīlz
**My'nors** mī'nĕrz, -nôrz
**My'ra** mī'rȧ
**My'rick** mī'rĭk
**Myr'na** mûr'nȧ
**My'ron** mī'rŭn
**Myr·til'la** mûr·tĭl'ȧ, mĕr-
**Myr'tle** mûr't'l

**Nach·man'** *Heb.* näk·män'
**Na·dine'** nȧ·dēn', nȧ-
**Na·dezh'da** *Russ.* nŭ·dyâzh'dŭ
**Na'few** nā'fū
**Na'gel** *Norw.* nä'gĕl
**Na'hum** nā'(h)ŭm, -hŭm
**Nance** năns
**Nan'cy** năn'sĭ
**Nan'nerl** *Ger.* nän'ĕrl
**Nan'ni** *Ital.* nän'nē
**Na'no** ?nā'nō
**Na'o·mi** nā'ō·mī, -mĭ, nā·ō'mī, -mĭ
**Na·o·ta·ke** *Jap.* nä·ō·tä·kĕ
**Naph'ta·li** năf'tȧ·lī
**Na'pi·er** nā'pĭ·ĕr, nȧ·pēr'
**Na·po'le·on** nȧ·pō'lē·ŭn, -pōl'yŭn; *Ger.* nä·pō'lā·ôn, -lā·ôɴ
**Na'po'lé'on'** *Fr.* nȧ'pô'lā'ôɴ'
**Na'po·le·o'ne** *Ital.* nä'pō·lā·ō'nā
**Nap'per** năp'ĕr
**Nar·ci'so** *Span.* när·thē'sō, -sē'sō
**Nar'cisse'** *Fr.* nȧr'sēs', (*Canad.*) -sĭs'
**Na·ri·a·ki·ra** *Jap.* nä·rē·ä·kē·rä
**Na·ri·man'** *Russ.* nŭ·ryĭ·mȧn'
**Nash** năsh
**Nas'sau** năs'ô
**Nat** năt
**Nat'a·lie** năt'ȧ·lĭ
**Na·ta'lio** *Span.* nä·tä'lyō
**Na·tal'ya** *Russ.* nŭ·tȧl'yŭ
**Na'than** nā'thăn, -th'n; *Ger.* nä'tän; *Swed.* nä'tȧn
**Na·than'a·el** nȧ·thăn'ā·ĕl—**Na·tha'na·el** *Ger.* nä·tä'nä·ĕl
**Na·than'iel** nȧ·thăn'yĕl, -ĭ·ĕl
**Na'zaire'** *Fr.* nȧ'zâr'
**Neal, Neale** nēl
**Ned** nĕd
**Need'ham** nēd'ăm
**Neeve** nēv
**Neg'ley** nĕg'lĭ
**Ne'he·mi'ah** nē'(h)ĕ·mī'ȧ
**Neil** nēl
**Neil'son** nēl's'n
**Neith** nēth
**Né'lie'** *Fr.* nā'lē'
**Nell** nĕl
**Nel'lie** nĕl'ĭ
**Nel'son** nĕl's'n
**Né'o'clès'** *Fr.* nā'ô'klâs'
**Né'po'mu'cène'** *Fr.* nā'pô'mü'sân'
**Ne'po·mu·ce'no** *Span.* nā'pō·mōō-thā'nō, -sā'nō
**Ne'po·muk** *Ger.* nā'pō·mŏŏk
**Ne'ri** *Ital.* nā'rē
**Ne'ro** nē'rō, nēr'ō
**Nes'ta** nĕs'tȧ
**Nes'tor** nĕs'tôr, -tĕr; *Finn.* nĕs'tŏr—**Nes'tor'** *Fr.* nĕs'tôr'
**Nés'tor** *Span.* nās'tôr
**Net'ty** *Ger.* nĕt'ē
**Neu'mann** *Norw.* nû'ĭ·män
**Nev'il, Nev'ile, Nev'ill, Nev'ille** nĕv'-'l, -ĭl
**Nev'ins** nĕv'ĭnz
**New** nū
**New'bold** nū'bōld
**New'ell** nū'ĕl
**New'en·ham** nū'ĕn·ăm
**New'ing·ton** nū'ĭng·tŭn
**New'man** nū'măn
**New'ton** nū't'n
**New'zam** nū'zăm
**Niall** *Ir.* nēl
**Ni'caise'** *Fr.* nē'kâz'
**Ni·ca'sio** *Span.* nē·kä'syō
**Nic·co'la** *Ital.* nēk·kō'lä
**Nic'co·lo** *Ital.* nēk'kō·lō
**Nic'co·lò'** *Ital.* nēk'kō·lô'
**Ni'cé'phore'** *Fr.* nē'sā'fôr'
**Ni·ceph'o·rus** *Lat.* nī·sĕf'ō·rŭs
**Ni·ce'to** *Span.* nē·thā'tō, -sā'tō
**Nich'ol** nĭk'ŭl, -'l
**Nich'o·las** nĭk'ō·lăs
**Nich'olls, Nich'ols** nĭk'ŭlz, -'lz
**Nick** nĭk
**Ni'co·de'mus** *Swed.* nĭ'kō·dā'mŭs
**Nic'ol** nĭk'ŭl, -'l
**Ni·co'la** *Ital.* nē·kô'lä
**Ni'co·laas** *Du.* nē'kō·läs
**Ni'co·lae'** *Rum.* nē'kŏ·lī'
**Ni'co·laes** *Du.* nē'kō·läs
**Ni·co·lai'** *Dan.* nē·kō·lī'—**Ni'co·la'i** *Du.* nē'kō·lȧ'ē; *Ger.* nē'kō·lä'ē, nē'-kō·lī
**Ni·co·lâ'o** *Port.* nē·kōō·lȧ'ōō
**Nic'o·las** nĭk'ō·lăs—**Ni'co·las** *Dan.* nē'kō·lȧs; *Du.* nē'kō·läs—**Ni'co'las'** *Fr.* nē'kô'lä'
**Ni'co·lás'** *Span.* nē'kō·läs'
**Ni'co·la'us** *Ger.* nē'kō·lä'ŏŏs, nē'kō-lous—**Nic'o·la'us** *Lat.* nĭk'ō·lā'ŭs
**Ni'cole'** *Fr.* nē'kôl'
**Nic'oll** nĭk'ŭl, -'l
**Ni'co·lò'** *Ital.* nē'kō·lô'
**Nic'ol·son** nĭk'ŭl·s'n, -'l·s'n
**Ni'co·me'de** *Ital.* nē'kō·mâ'dā
**Niel** nēl
**Niels** *Dan.* nēls; *Norw.* nēls
**Niel'sen** *Norw.* nēl'sĕn
**Ni'gel** nī'jĕl
**Ni·ki'fo·ro'vich** *Russ.* nyĭ·kyē'fŭ·rô'-vyĭch
**Ni·ki'ta** *Russ.* nyĭ·kyē'tŭ
**Ni·ki'tich** *Russ.* nyĭ·kyē'tyĭch
**Ni'klaas** *Du.* nē'klȧs
**Ni'klas** *Ger.* nē'kläs—**Nik'las** *Swed.* nĭk'lȧs
**Ni'ko·dem'** *Ger.* nē'kō·dām'
**Ni'ko·de'mus** *Ger.* nē'kō·dā'mŏŏs
**Ni'ko·la** *Yugo.* nē'kō·lä
**Ni'ko·laas** *Du.* nē'kō·läs
**Ni·ko·la'e·vich** *Russ.* nyĭ·kŭ·lȧ'yĕ-vyĭch
**Ni·ko·la'ev·na** *Russ.* nyĭ·kŭ·lȧ'yĕv-nŭ
**Ni·ko·lai'** *Dan.* nē·kō·lī'—**Ni·ko·lai'** *Russ.* nyĭ·kŭ·lī'

**Ni·ko·laj′** *Dan.* nē̇·kô̇·lī′
**Ni·ko′la·os** *Mod. Grk.* nyē̇·kô′lä·ôs
**Ni′ko·las** *Ger.* nē′kô̇·läs
**Ni′ko·la′us** *Ger.* nē′kô̇·lä′o͞os, nē′kô̇-lous
**Niles** nīlz
**Ni′lo** *Port.* nē′lo͞o
**Nils** *Dan.* nēls; *Norw.* nēls; *Swed.* nĭls
**Nils′son** *Swed.* nĭls′sôn
**Nim′mons** nĭm′ŭnz
**Ni′na** nī′nȧ, nē′-; *Russ.* nyē′nŭ
**Nin′i·an** nĭn′ĭ·ăn
**Ni′no** *Ital.* nē′nô̇
**Ni′non′** *Fr.* nē′nôɴ′
**Niv′en** nĭv′ĕn
**Nix′on** nĭk′s′n
**No′ah** nō′ȧ
**No′ble** nō′b′l
**No·bu·a·ki** *Jap.* nô̇·bo͞o·ä·kē̇
**No·bu·ma·sa** *Jap.* nô̇·bo͞o·mä·sä
**No·bu·shi·ge** *Jap.* nô̇·bo͞o·shē̇·gĕ
**No·bu·ta·ke** *Jap.* nô̇·bo͞o·tä·kĕ
**No·bu·yu·ki** *Jap.* nô̇·bo͞o·yo͞o·kē̇
**No′el** nō′ĕl
**No′ël′** *Fr.* nô′ĕl′
**No′é′mi′** *Fr.* nô′ā′mē′
**No′land** nō′lănd
**Noon** no͞on
**No′ra** nō′rȧ
**Nor′bert** nôr′bẽrt; *Ger.* nô̇r′bĕrt—**Nor′bert′** *Fr.* nôr′bâr′
**Nor′borne** nôr′bẽrn
**Nor′cliffe** nôr′klĭf
**Nor′dal** *Norw.* nô̇r′däl
**Nor′ma** nôr′mȧ
**Nor′man** nôr′măn
**Nor′reys** nŏr′ĭs, -ēz
**Nor′ris** nŏr′ĭs
**North** nôrth
**North′cote** nôrth′kŭt, -kōt
**North′more** nôrth′mōr
**Nor′throp** nôr′thrŭp
**Nor′ton** nôr′t′n
**Nor′val** nôr′văl
**Nor′vin** nôr′vĭn
**Nor′wood** nôr′wo͝od
**Nott** nŏt
**Not′tidge** nŏt′ĭj
**Not′ting·ham** nŏt′ĭng·ăm, -ĭng·ăm
**No·vel′lo** nô̇·vĕl′ō; *Ital.* nô̇·vĕl′lô̇
**Nuck′les** nŭk′′lz
**Nu′gent** nū′jĕnt
**Nu′ma′** *Fr.* nü′mȧ′—**Nu′ma** *Span.* no͞o′mä
**Nú′ñez** *Span.* no͞o′nyāth, -nyās
**Nu′nho** *Port.* no͞o′nyo͞o
**Nu′no** *Port.* no͞o′no͞o
**Nu′ño** *Span.* no͞o′nyō

**Oake′ley** ōk′lĭ
**Oakes** ōks
**Oa′key** ō′kĭ
**O′ba·di′ah** ō′bȧ·dī′ȧ
**O′bed** ō′bĕd, ō′bĭd
**O′biz·zo** *Ital.* ô′bē̇t·tsō; ô̇·bēt′tsô̇
**O′Bri′en** ô̇·brī′ĕn
**O′Con′nell** ô̇·kŏn′′l
**O′Con′or** ô̇·kŏn′ẽr
**Oc′tave** ŏk′tāv—**Oc′tave′** *Fr.* ôk′-tȧv′
**Oc·ta′vi·a** ŏk·tā′vĭ·ȧ
**Oc′ta·vian′** *Rum.* ŏk′tä·vyän′
**Oc·ta′vi·o** *Ger.* ô̇k·tä′vē̇·ō; *Span.* ôk-tä′vyō
**Oc·ta′vi·us** ŏk·tā′vĭ·ŭs
**Od·do′ne** *Ital.* ô̇d·dō′nā̇
**O·dell′** ô̇·dĕl′
**O′det′** *Fr.* ô′dĕ′
**O′di′lon′** *Fr.* ô′dē′lôɴ′
**O′do** ō′dō
**O′do·ar′do** *Ital.* ō′dô̇·är′dô̇
**Ö′dön** *Hung.* û′dûn
**Oe·no′ne** ē̇·nō′nē̇
**Off′ley** ô̆f′lĭ
**O′Fla′her·tie** ô̇·flă′hẽr·tĭ, ô̇·flâr′tĭ, ô̇·flä′(h)ẽr·tĭ
**O·fo′ni·us** *Lat.* ô̇·fō′nĭ·ŭs
**Og′den** ŏg′dĕn
**Ogg** ŏg
**O′gle·thorpe** ō′g′l·thôrp
**O′gni·be′ne** *Ital.* ō′nyē̇·bâ′nā̇
**O′Har′a** ô̇·hâr′ȧ, ô̇·hä′rȧ
**O′la′** *Swed.* o͞o′lȧ′
**O′laf** ō′lăf; *Dan.* ō′lȧf; *Norw.* ō′läf; *Swed.* o͞o′lȧf′, o͞o′lȧv′
**O′lafs·son** *Norw.* ō′läf·sŏn
**O·la′us** *Dan.* ô̇·lȧ′o͞os; *Ger.* ô̇·lä′o͞os, ō′lous; *Lat.* ô̇·lā′ŭs; *Swed.* o͞o·lä′ŭs
**O′lav** *Norw.* ō′läv, ō′läf
**Ol′cott** ŏl′kŭt
**Old′ham** ōl′dăm
**O′le** *Dan., Norw.* ō′lĕ
**O′ley** ō′lĭ
**Ol′ga** ŏl′gȧ; *Russ.* ôl′y′·gŭ
**O·lim′pia** *Ital.* ô̇·lēm′pyä
**O′lin** ō′lĭn
**O·lin′do** *Ital.* ô̇·lēn′dô̇
**O·lin′thus** ô̇·lĭn′thŭs
**O·lin′to** *Ital.* ô̇·lēn′tô̇
**Ol′ive** ŏl′ĭv
**Ol′i·ver** ŏl′ĭ·vẽr
**O·liv′i·a** ô̇·lĭv′ĭ·ȧ
**O′li·vier** *Du.* ō′lē̇·vēr—**O′li′vier′** *Fr.* ô′lē′vyā′
**Ol′lie** ŏl′ĭ
**Ol′ney** ŏl′nĭ, ōl′nĭ, ō′nĭ
**O′lof** *Swed.* o͞o′lôv, o͞o′lôf
**O′loff** *Du.* ō′lôf
**O′luf** *Dan., Ger., Norw.* ō′lo͝of
**O′lympe′** *Fr.* ô′lăɴp′
**O·lym′pi·a** ô̇·lĭm′pĭ·ȧ
**O′mo·bo′no** *Ital.* ō′mô̇·bô′nô̇
**O′Moore′** ô̇·mo͝or′, ô̇·mōr′
**On′no** *Ger.* ôn′ō
**O′no·ra′to** *Ital.* ō′nô̇·rä′tô̇
**Ons′low** ŏnz′lō
**O·nu′fri·e·vich** *Russ.* ŭ·no͞o′fryĭ·yĕ-vyĭch
**O·pe′li·us** *Lat.* ô̇·pē′lĭ·ŭs, -pēl′yŭs
**O′pid** *Pol.* ô′pēt
**O′pie** ō′pĭ
**Op·ta′ti·a′nus** *Lat.* ŏp·tā′shĭ·ā′nŭs
**Or′ace** ŏr′ĭs
**Or′ange** ŏr′ĕnj, -ĭnj
**O·ra′zio** *Ital.* ô̇·rä′tsyô̇
**Or′chard** ôr′chẽrd
**Ord′way** ôrd′wā
**O′ren** ō′rĕn
**O·rest′** *Russ.* ŭ·ryâst′
**O·re′ste** *Ital.* ô̇·rĕs′tā̇
**O·res′tes** ô̇·rĕs′tēz
**O′ri·el** ō′rĭ·ĕl
**Or′i·son** ŏr′ĭ·z′n
**Or′la** *Dan.* ŏr′lȧ
**Or·lan′do** ôr·lăn′dō; *Ital.* ôr·län′dô̇
**Or′ley** ôr′lĭ
**Or′lo** ôr′lō
**Orms′bee** ôrmz′bē̇
**Orms′by** ôrmz′bĭ
**Orne** ôrn
**O′ronce′** *Fr.* ô′rôɴs′
**O·ron′zo** *Ital.* ô̇·rôn′tsô̇
**O·roz′co** *Span.* ô̇·rôth′kō, -rōs′kō
**Or′pen** ôr′pĕn
**Or′pheus** ôr′fūs, ôr′fē̇·ŭs
**Or′ren** ŏr′ĕn
**Or′ridge** ŏr′ĭj
**Or′ris** ŏr′ĭs
**Or′son** ôr′s′n
**Or′ville** ôr′vĭl
**O′sa** ō′sȧ
**O·sa·mi** *Jap.* ô̇·sä·mē̇
**Os′bert** ŏz′bẽrt
**Os′born, Os′borne** ŏz′bẽrn
**Os′car** ŏs′kẽr; *Ger.* ô̇s′kär; *Norw.* ŏs′kär; *Pol.* ôs′kär; *Russ., Swed.* ôs′kȧr—**Os′car′** *Fr.* ôs′kȧr′—**Os-car′** *Port.* ôsh·kȧr′, (*Braz.*) ôs·kȧr′
**Ós′car** *Span.* ōs′kär
**Os′good** ŏz′go͝od
**O′sip** *Russ.* ô′syĭp
**O′si·po′vich** *Russ.* ô′syĭ·pô′vyĭch
**Os′kar** ŏs′kẽr; *Finn.* ŏs′kȧr; *Ger.* ô̇s′kär; *Norw.* ŏs′kär; *Swed.* ôs′kȧr
**Os·man′** *Turk.* ŏs·män′
**Os′mond** ŏz′mŭnd
**Os′sian** ŏsh′ăn, ŏs′ĭ·ăn—**Os′sian′** *Fr.* ô′syäɴ′
**Os′sip** *Russ.* ô′syĭp
**Ö′sten** *Swed.* û′stĕn
**Os′vald** *Swed.* ôs′vȧld
**Os′wald** ŏz′wȧld; *Ger.* ô̇s′vält
**Os·wal′do** *Port.* ôzh·wäl′do͞o, (*Braz.*) ôz·wäl′-
**O′ta·kar** *Czech* ô′tȧ·kȧr
**Ot′fried** *Ger.* ô̇t′frēt
**O′the·nin′** *Fr.* ôt′năɴ′
**Oth′mar** *Ger.* ô̇t′mär
**Oth′ni·el** ŏth′nĭ·ĕl
**O′tho** ō′thō
**O′thon′** *Fr.* ô′tôɴ′
**O′tis** ō′tĭs
**Ot′mar** *Ger.* ô̇t′mär
**O′ton** *Yugo.* ō′tôn
**O·tsu·zo** *Jap.* ô̇·tso͞o·zō
**Ot′ta·via′no** *Ital.* ōt′tä·vyä′nô̇
**Ot·ta′vio** *Ital.* ô̇t·tä′vyô̇
**Ot′ti·li·a′na′** *Swed.* ôt′tĭ·lĭ·ä′nȧ′
**Ot·ti′li·e** *Ger.* ô̇·tē′lē̇·ĕ
**Ott′mar** *Ger.* ô̇t′mär
**Ott′mer** ŏt′mẽr
**Ot′to** ŏt′ō; *Dan.* ŏt′ô̇; *Du.* ŏt′ō; *Eston.* ôt′tô; *Finn.* ŏt′tŏ; *Ger.* ô̇t′ō; *Norw.* ŏt′tô; *Swed.* ôt′to͞o′
**Ot′to·kar** *Ger.* ô̇t′ô̇·kär
**Ot′to·mar** *Ger.* ô̇t′ô̇·mär
**Ot·to′ne** *Ital.* ô̇t·tō′nā̇
**Ot′to·ri′no** *Ital.* ōt′tô̇·rē′nô̇
**Ot′way** ŏt′wā
**Ours** *Fr.* o͞ors
**O′ve** *Dan.* ō′vĕ
**O′ver·ton** ō′vẽr·t′n, -tŭn

**O·ve'ta** ō·vē'tȧ
**O'vide'** *Fr.* ô'vēd'
**Ow'en** ō'ĕn, -ĭn
**Ox'ley** ŏks'lĭ
**O·zi'as** ō·zī'ăs

**Paa'vo** *Finn.* pä'vŏ
**Pa'blo** *Span.* pä'blō
**Padh'raic, Pad'raic** *Ir.* pôth'rĭg
**Paf·nu'ti** *Russ.* pŭf·nōō'tyû·ĭ
**Page** pāj
**Pag'et** păj'ĕt, -ĭt
**Paige** pāj
**Paine** pān
**Pál** *Hung.* päl
**Pal'ma** *Ital.* päl'mä
**Pal·mel'la** păl·mĕl'ȧ
**Palm'er** päm'ẽr
**Pam'e·la** păm'ĕ·lȧ
**Pam'fi·lo** *Ital.* päm'fē·lō
**Pam'phile'** *Fr.* päɴ'fēl', (*Canad.*) -fĭl'
**Pa'na·ges', Pa'na·gis'** *Mod. Grk.* pä'nä·yēs'
**Pa'na·it'** *Rum.* pä'nä·ēt'
**Pan'cho** *Span.* pän'chō
**Pan'coast** păn'kōst, păng'-
**Pan·dol'fo** *Ital.* pän·dôl'fō
**Pán'fi·lo** *Span.* päm'fē·lō
**Pan'ta'lé'on'** *Fr.* päɴ'tȧ'lā'ôɴ'
**Pan·te·lei'mon** *Russ.* pŭn·tyĕ·lyā'ĭ·mŭn
**Pa'o·lo** *Ital.* pä'ō·lō
**Pa'pi·a'nus** *Lat.* pā'pĭ·ā'nŭs, păp'ĭ-
**Pa·pin'i·us** *Lat.* pȧ·pĭn'ĭ·ŭs
**Par'fait'** *Fr.* pȧr'fĕ'
**Par'is** păr'ĭs
**Par'ish** păr'ĭsh
**Park, Parke** pärk
**Par'ker** pär'kẽr
**Parkes** pärks
**Park'hurst** pärk'hûrst
**Par'kin·son** pär'kĭn·s'n
**Parks** pärks
**Par'ley** pär'lĭ
**Par'me·le, -lee** pär'mĕ·lē, -lē
**Par'mo** *Dan.* pär'mō
**Par·nell'** pär·nĕl', pär'n'l
**Parr** pär
**Par'rish** păr'ĭsh
**Par'ry** păr'ĭ
**Par'sons** pär's'nz
**Par'tridge** pär'trĭj
**pa·şa'** *Turk.* pä·shä'
**Pas'cal'** *Fr.* pȧs'kȧl'
**Pas'chal** pȧs'kăl
**Pas'coe** păs'kō
**Pas·cual'** *Span.* päs·kwäl'
**pa'sha** *Arab.* pȧ'shä—**pa·sha'** *Turk.* pä·shä'
**Pa·squa'le** *Ital.* päs·kwä'lā
**Pas'quier'** *Fr.* pȧ'kyā'
**Pass'more** pȧs'mōr
**Pas'ton** păs'tŭn
**Pas'tor** pȧs'tẽr—**Pas·tor'** *Span.* päs·tôr'
**Pat** păt
**Patch** păch
**Pa'tience** pā'shĕns
**Pa'ton** pā't'n
**Pa'trice'** *Fr.* pȧ'trēs'
**Pa·tri'cia** pȧ·trĭsh'ȧ, -ĭ·ȧ
**Pa·tri'cio** *Span.* pä·trē'thyō, -syō
**Pat'rick** păt'rĭk
**Pa'trik** *Swed.* pä'trĭk
**Pat'ten** păt''n
**Pat'ter·son** păt'ẽr·s'n
**Pat'ti·son** păt'ĭ·s'n
**Pat'ton** păt''n
**Pat'yn** păt''n, -ĭn
**Paul** *Eng.*, *Fr.* pôl; *Dan.*, *Du.*, *Ger.*, *Norw.*, *Swed.* poul; *Sou. Afr. Du.* pō'ŏŏl
**Pau'la** *Ger.*, *Span.* pou'lä; *Port.* pou'lȧ
**Paule** *Fr.* pôl
**Pau'lin'** *Fr.* pô'lăɴ'
**Pau·li'na** *Ital.* pou·lē'nä
**Pau·line'** pô·lēn', pô'lēn—**Pau·li'ne** *Du.*, *Ger.* pou·lē'nĕ—**Pau'line'** *Fr.* pô'lēn'
**Pau·li'nus** pô·lī'nŭs
**Pau'lus** *Ger.* pou'lŏŏs; *Lat.* pô'lŭs; *Sou. Afr. Du.* pō'ŏŏ·lûs
**Pa'vel** *Czech* pȧ'vĕl; *Russ.* pȧ'vyĕl
**Pav'los** *Mod. Grk.* päv'lôs
**Pa·vlo'vich** *Russ.* pŭ·vlô'vyĭch
**Pa'vol** *Slovak* pȧ'vôl
**Pax'son** păk's'n
**Pax'ton** păks'tŭn
**Payne** pān
**Pay'son** pā's'n
**Paz** *Span.* päth, päs
**Pea'bod'y** pē'bŏd'ĭ, -bŭd·ĭ
**Peace** pēs
**Peale** pēl
**Pearce** pērs
**Pearl** pûrl
**Pear'sall** pēr'sôl, -s'l
**Pearse** pērs
**Pear'son** pēr's'n
**Pease** pēz
**Peck** pĕk
**Pe·da'ni·us** *Lat.* pē·dā'nĭ·ŭs
**Pe'der** *Dan.* pē'thẽr
**Pe'do** *Lat.* pē'dō
**Pe·dra'rias** *Span.* pā·thrä'ryäs
**Pe'dro** *Port.* pā'thrōō; *Span.* pā'thrō
**Pef'fer** pĕf'ẽr
**Peg** pĕg
**Peg'gy** pĕg'ĭ
**Pehr** *Finn.*, *Swed.* pâr
**Peirce** pērs, pûrs
**Peire** *Fr.* pâr
**Pé'lage'** *Fr.* pā'lȧzh'
**Pel'a·ti'ah** pĕl'ȧ·tī'ȧ
**Pe·la'yo** *Span.* pā·lä'yō
**Pe'leg** pē'lĕg
**Pel'ham** pĕl'ăm
**Pell** pĕl
**Pel'le·gri'no** *Ital.* pāl'lā·grē'nō
**Pel'le·vé'** *Fr.* pĕl'vā'
**Pel·lio'ne** *Ital.* pāl·lyō'nā
**Pem'ber** pĕm'bẽr
**Pem'ell** pĕm'ĕl
**Pen·al'ver** pĕn·ăl'vẽr
**Pen'dle·ton** pĕn'd'l·tŭn
**Pe·nel'o·pe** pē·nĕl'ō·pē
**Pen'field** pĕn'fēld
**Pen·hal'low** pĕn·hăl'ō
**Penn** pĕn
**Pen'ne·fa'ther** pĕn'ē·fä'thẽr
**Pen'ni·man** pĕn'ĭ·măn
**Pen'rhyn** pĕn'rĭn, pĕn·rĭn'
**Pen'rose** pĕn'rōz, pĕn·rōz'
**Pent'land** pĕnt'lănd
**Pep'per·ell** pĕp'ẽr·ĕl
**Pep·pi'no** *Ital.* pāp·pē'nō
**Per** *Swed.* pâr
**Per'ce·val** pûr'sĕ·văl
**Per'cey** pûr'sĭ
**Per'ci·val, -vall** pûr'sĭ·văl
**Per'cy** pûr'sĭ
**Per'e·grine** pĕr'ĕ·grĭn, -grīn, -grēn
**Pé'rez** *Span.* pā'rāth, -rās
**Pe·ri'no** *Ital.* pā·rē'nō
**Per'kin** pûr'kĭn
**Per'kins** pûr'kĭnz
**Per'ley** pûr'lĭ
**Per'rin** pĕr'ĭn
**Per'rott** pĕr'ŭt
**Per'ry** pĕr'ĭ
**Per'si·for** pûr'sĭ·fẽr, -fôr
**Per'son** pûr's'n
**Per'so'nier'** *Fr.* pĕr'sô'nyā'
**Per'sonne'** *Fr.* pĕr'sôn'
**Pers'son** *Swed.* pârs'sôn
**Pe'tar** *Yugo.* pĕ'tär
**Pe'ter** pē'tẽr; *Dan.* pē'tẽr; *Du.*, *Ger.*, *Norw.*, *Swed.* pā'tẽr
**Pé'ter** *Hung.* pā'tĕr
**Pe'ter·field** pē'tẽr·fēld
**Pe'ters** pē'tẽrz
**Pe'ter·son** pē'tẽr·s'n
**Pe·til'li·us** *Lat.* pē·tĭl'ĭ·ŭs
**Pet'ko** *Bulg.* pĕt'kō
**Pëtr** *Russ.* pyô'tĕr
**Pe·tra'che** *Rum.* pĕ·trä'kĕ
**Pe'tre** pē'tẽr; *Rum.* pĕ'trĕ
**Pe'tri** *Ger.* pā'trē
**Pe'tri·cei'cu** *Rum.* pĕ'trē·chā'kōō
**Pé'tro'nille'** *Fr.* pā'trô'nē'y'
**Pe·tro'ni·us** *Lat.* pē·trō'nĭ·ŭs
**Pe'tros** *Mod. Grk.* pâ'trôs
**Pe'tro·vić** *Yugo.* pĕ'trō·vēt'y', *Angl.* -vĭch
**Pe·tro'vich** *Russ.* pyĭ·trô'vyĭch
**Pe·trov'na** *Russ.* pyĭ·trôv'nŭ
**Pe·truc'cio** *Ital.* pā·trōōt'chō
**Pe'trus** *Du.* pā'trûs; *Lat.* pē'trŭs; *Swed.* pā'trŭs
**Pé'trus'** *Fr.* pā'trüs'
**Pett** pĕt
**Pet'ter** *Norw.* pĕt'tẽr
**Pet'ti·bone** pĕt'ĭ·bōn
**Pet'tus** pĕt'ŭs
**Pevs'ner** *Russ.* pyāfs'nyẽr
**Pey'ton** pā't'n
**phar'aoh** fâr'ō, fā'rō
**Phe'lim** *Ir.* fā'lĭm
**Phé'lip'peaux'** *Fr.* fā'lē'pō'
**Phelps** fĕlps
**Phil** fĭl
**Phi·lan'der** fĭ·lăn'dẽr; *Du.*, *Ger.* fē·län'dẽr
**Phi'la'rète'** *Fr.* fē'lȧ'rĕt'
**Phil'brook** fĭl'brŏŏk
**Phi'lé'as'** *Fr.* fē'lā'äs'
**Phi·le'mon** fĭ·lē'mŏn, fī-
**Phi'li'bert'** *Fr.* fē'lē'bâr'
**Phil'ip** fĭl'ĭp—**Phi'lip** *Du.*, *Swed.* fē'lĭp; *Ger.* fē'lĭp, fĭl'ĭp

**Phi'lipp** *Ger.* fē'lĭp, fĭl'ĭp; *Swed.* fē'lĭp—**Phi·lipp'** *Russ.* fyĭ·lyēp'
**Phi'lippe'** *Fr.* fē'lēp'
**Phi'lip'pine'** *Fr.* fē'lē'pēn'—**Phi'lip·pi'ne** *Ger.* fē'lĭ·pē'nĕ
**Phil'ipps** fĭl'ĭps
**Phi·lip'pus** *Lat.* fĭ·lĭp'ŭs
**Phil'ips** fĭl'ĭps—**Phi'lips** *Du.* fē'-lĭps
**Phil'lipps, Phil'lips** fĭl'ĭps
**Phil'lis** fĭl'ĭs
**Phi'lo** fī'lō
**Phil'pot** fĭl'pŏt
**Phim'is·ter** fĭm'ĭs·tēr
**Phin'e·as** fĭn'ē·ăs
**Phin'ney** fĭn'ĭ
**Phipps** fĭps
**Pho'cas** *Lat.* fō'kăs
**Phoe'be** fē'bē
**Phoe'bus** fē'bŭs
**Phyl'lis** fĭl'ĭs
**Pic·co'ni** *Ital.* pēk·kō'nē
**Pick'ens** pĭk'ĕnz
**Pick'er·ing** pĭk'ēr·ĭng
**Pick'ett** pĭk'ĕt, -ĭt
**Pick'man** pĭk'măn
**Pier** *Dan.* pēr; *Ital.* pyĕr
**Pierce** pērs
**Pier'fran·ce'sco** *Ital.* pyĕr'frän·chās'-kō
**Pier'lu·i'gi** *Ital.* pyĕr'lōō·ē'jē
**Pie'ro** *Ital.* pyâ'rō
**Pier'pont** pēr'pŏnt
**Pierre** pyâr, pēr; *Du., Fr.* pyâr
**Pierre'pont** pēr'pŏnt
**Piers** pērz
**Pier'son** pēr's'n
**Piet** *Du.* pēt
**Pie'ta·ri** *Finn.* pyĕ'tȧ·rĭ
**Pie'ter** *Du.* pē'tēr
**Pie'ters** *Du.* pē'tērs
**Pie'ter·sen** *Du.* pē'tēr·sĕn
**Pie'tersz** *Du.* pē'tērs
**Pie'ters·zoon** *Du.* pē'tēr·sŭn, -sôn, -sōn
**Pietr** *Du.* pē'tēr
**Pie'tro** *Ital.* pyâ'trō
**Pig'ot** pĭg'ŭt
**Pike** pīk
**Pinck'ney** pĭngk'nĭ
**Pi'nel'** *Fr.* pē'nĕl'
**Pink'ham** pĭngk'ăm
**Pink'ney** pĭngk'nĭ
**Pink'stone** pĭngk'stōn, -stŭn
**Pi'not'** *Fr.* pē'nō'
**Pi'o** *Ital.* pē'ō
**Pí'o** *Span.* pē'ō
**Piotr** *Pol., Russ.* pyô'tēr
**Pir'ro** *Ital.* pēr'rō
**Pi·sco'pia** *Ital.* pē·skô'pyä
**Pi·ti·rim'** *Russ.* pyĭ·tyĭ·ryēm'
**Pitt** pĭt
**Pit'ton'** *Fr.* pē'tôN'
**Pitts** pĭts
**Pi'us** *Lat.* pī'ŭs
**Pla'cide'** *Fr.* plȧ'sēd'
**Plá'ci·do** *Span.* plä'thē·thō, plä'sē-
**Plan·ci'a·des** *Lat.* plăn·sī'ȧ·dēz
**Pla·ton'** *Russ.* plŭ·tôn'
**Pla·to'no·vich** *Russ.* plŭ·tô'nŭ·vyĭch
**Platt** plăt
**Play'fair** plā'fâr
**Plea'ter** plē'tēr
**Plim'mon** plĭm'ŭn
**Plin'y** plĭn'ĭ
**Plu'mer** plōō'mēr
**Plu·tar'co** *Span.* plōō·tär'kō
**Poer, de la** dĕl'ȧ·pōōr'
**Pol** *Du.* pŏl; *Fr.* pôl
**Po'li·car'po** *Span.* pō'lē·kär'pō
**Po'li·do'ro** *Ital.* pō'lē·dô'rō
**Pol'lard** pŏl'ērd
**Pol'lock** pŏl'ŭk
**Po'ly·carp'** *Ger.* pō'lü·kärp'
**Po'ly'carpe'** *Fr.* pô'lē'kȧrp'
**Pol'y·dore** pŏl'ĭ·dōr—**Po'ly'dore'** *Fr.* pô'lē'dôr'
**Po'ly·karp'** *Ger.* pō'lü·kärp'
**Pom'er·oy** pŏm'ēr·oi, pŏm'roi, pŭm'-ēr·oi, pŭm'roi
**Pom·pe'ia** *Lat.* pŏm·pē'(y)ȧ
**Pom·pe'ius** *Lat.* pŏm·pē'(y)ŭs
**Pom·pe'o** *Ital.* pôm·pâ'ō
**Pom·pi'lio** *Span.* pôm·pē'lyō
**Pom·po'nio** *Ital.* pôm·pô'nyō
**Pom·po'ni·us** *Lat.* pŏm·pō'nĭ·ŭs
**Ponce** *Fr.* pôNs
**Pon·cia'no** *Span.* pôn·thyä'nō, pôn-syä'-
**Pons** *Fr.* pôNs
**Pon'tas'** *Fr.* pôN'täs'
**Pon'ti·cus** *Lat.* pŏn'tĭ·kŭs
**Pon'tius** *Lat.* pŏn'shŭs, pŏn'tĭ·ŭs
**Pon'tus'** *Fr.* pôN'tüs'—**Pon'tus** *Swed.* pôn'tŭs
**Pope** pōp
**Po·pil'i·us** *Lat.* pō·pĭl'ĭ·ŭs
**Pó'po·lo** *Span.* pō'pō·lō
**Por'ci·us** *Lat.* pôr'shĭ·ŭs, -shŭs
**Por·fir'e·vich, Por·fir'ie·vich** *Russ.* pŭr·fyēr'yĕ·vyĭch
**Por·fi'rio** *Span.* pôr·fē'ryō
**Por'rett** pŏr'ĕt
**Por'ter** pōr'tēr
**Por'ter·field'** pōr'tēr·fēld'
**Port'land** pōrt'lănd
**Por'tus** pōr'tŭs
**Post** pōst
**Pos·tu'mi·us** *Lat.* pŏs·tū'mĭ·ŭs
**Pot'ter** pŏt'ēr
**Potts** pŏts
**Poul** *Dan.* poul
**Pou'lett** pô'lĕt, -lĭt
**Poult'ney** pōlt'nĭ
**Pow'el, -ell** pou'ĕl, *Brit. also* pō'ĕl
**Pow'er** pou'ēr
**Pow'ha·tan'** pou'ȧ·tăn'
**Pow'is** pō'ĭs, pou'-
**Poyntz** points
**Prae'co·ni'nus** *Lat.* prē'kō·nī'nŭs, prĕk'ō-
**Pra'ger** *Du.* prȧ'gēr
**Pra·san'no** *As. Ind.* prô·sôn'nô
**Pratt** prăt
**Pra·xe'de** *Ger.* prä·ksā'dĕ
**Prá'xe·des** *Span.* präk'sȧ·thās
**Pren'der·gast** prĕn'dēr·găst
**Pren'tiss** prĕn'tĭs
**Pres'cott** prĕs'kŭt
**Pre·serv'ed** prē·zûr'vĕd, -vĭd
**Pres'ton** prĕs'tŭn
**Prest'wich** prĕst'wĭch
**Price** prīs
**Prich'ard** prĭch'ērd
**Priest'ley** prēst'lĭ
**Pri'mo** *Span.* prē'mō
**Prince** prĭns
**prince** *Fr.* prăNs
**prin·ce'sa** *Span.* prēn·thā'sä, prēn-sā'-
**prin'cesse'** *Fr.* prăN'sĕs'
**prin'ci·pe** *Span.* prēn'thē·pā, prēn'-sē-
**prin'ci·pes'sa** *Ital.* prēn'chē·pās'sä
**Prin'dle** prĭn'd'l
**Prin'gle** prĭng'g'l
**Pri'or** prī'ēr
**Pris·cil'la** prĭ·sĭl'ȧ
**Pritch'ard** prĭch'ērd
**Probe** *Fr.* prôb
**Pro'by** prō'bĭ
**Pro·cof'ieff** *Russ.* prŭ·kôf'yĕf
**Pro·co'pi·us** *Ger.* prō·kō'pē·ōōs
**Proc'ter, -tor** prŏk'tēr
**Pro·me'theus** prō·mē'thūs, -thē·ŭs
**Pros'per** prŏs'pēr; *Ger.* prôs'pēr—**Pros'per'** *Fr.* prôs'pâr'
**Pro'spe·ro** *Ital.* prôs'pȧ·rō
**Prós'pe·ro** *Span.* prōs'pȧ·rō
**Prowse** prous
**Pru'dence** prōō'dĕns, -d'ns
**Pru·den'cio** *Span.* prōō·thān'thyō, -syō
**Pru'dens** *Du.* prü'dĕns
**Pru·den'te** *Port.* prōō·thăNn'tĕ
**Pry'or** prī'ēr
**Pub·lil'i·us** *Lat.* pŭb·lĭl'ĭ·ŭs
**Pub'li·us** *Lat.* pŭb'lĭ·ŭs
**Pue** pū
**Pun'chard** pŭn'chērd
**pun'dit** *As. Ind.* pŭn'dĭt
**Pur'die** pûr'dĭ
**Pur'don** pûr'd'n
**Pur'dy** pûr'dĭ
**Pur'ser** pûr'sēr
**Put'nam** pŭt'năm
**Pyke** pīk
**Pyne** pīn
**Pyotr** *Russ.* pyô'tēr
**Py'rame'** *Fr.* pē'rȧm'

**Quarles** kwôrlz, kwärlz
**Quayle** kwāl
**Quen'tin** kwĕn't'n, -tĭn; *Du.* kvĭn'-tĭn, kvĕn'tĭn, kvĭn·tĭn'—**Quen'tin'** *Fr.* käN'tăN'
**Quil'ler** kwĭl'ēr
**Quinc'ti·us** *Lat.* kwĭngk'shĭ·ŭs, -shŭs
**Quin'cy** kwĭn'sĭ, -zĭ
**Quin'ten** *Du.* kvĭn'tĕn
**Quin·til'i·a'nus** *Lat.* kwĭn·tĭl'ĭ·ā'nŭs
**Quin·til'i·us** *Lat.* kwĭn·tĭl'ĭ·ŭs, -tĭl'-yŭs
**Quin'tin** kwĭn't'n, -tĭn
**Quin·ti'no** *Ital.* kwēn·tē'nō
**Quin'ti·us** *Lat.* kwĭn'shĭ·ŭs, -shŭs, kwĭn'tĭ·ŭs
**Quin'tus** kwĭn'tŭs
**Qui·rijn'** *Du.* kvē·rīn'
**Qui'rin'** *Fr.* kē'răN'—**Qui·rin'** *Ger.* kvē·rēn'
**Qui·ri'no** *Ital.* kwē·rē'nō
**Qui·ri'nus** *Ger.* kvē·rē'nōōs; *Du.* -nûs

**rab** *Heb.* räv, *Angl.* răb
**Ra·bin′dra·nath′** *As. Ind.* rȧ·bēn′-drȧ·nät′
**Ra′chel** rā′chĕl; *Du.* rȧ′ᴋĕl—**Ra′-chel′** *Fr.* rȧ′shĕl′
**Rad′cliffe, -clyffe** răd′klĭf
**Rad′ko** *Bulg.* rȧt′kô
**Ra′dó** *Hung.* rŏ′dō
**Ra′do·mir** *Yugo.* rä′dô·mēr
**Rae** rā
**Ra′fa·el′** *Span.* rä′fä·ĕl′
**Rafe** rāf
**Ra′felsz** *Du.* rȧ′fĕls
**Raf′fa·e′le** *Ital.* räf′fä·â′lâ
**Raf′fa·el′lo** *Ital.* räf′fä·ĕl′lô
**Rag′nar′** *Swed.* rȧng′nȧr′
**Ra′hel** *Ger.* rä′hĕl, rä′ĕl
**Raikes** rāks
**Rail′ton** rāl′tŭn, -t′n
**Rai′mond′** *Fr.* rā′môɴ′
**Rai′mund** *Ger.* rī′mōōnt
**Rai·mun′do** *Port.* rī·mōōɴn′dōō; *Span.* rī·mōōn′dō
**Rai·mun′dus** *Lat.* rī·mŭn′dŭs
**Raine** rān
**Rai′ner** *Du., Ger.* rī′nēr
**Rai′ney** rā′nĭ
**Rains′ford** rānz′fērd
**Ra′is′sa′** *Fr.* rȧ′ē′sȧ′
**ra′ja** *As. Ind.* rä′jȧ
**Ra′leigh** rô′lĭ, rä′lĭ, răl′ĭ
**Ralls** rôlz
**Ralph** rălf; *Brit. also* rāf, rä(l)f; *Ger.* rälf
**Ra·mí′rez** *Span.* rä·mē′rāth, -rās
**Ram′ji** *Marathi* räm′jē
**Ra·món′** *Span.* rä·môn′
**Ram′say** răm′zĭ
**Ran′ald** răn′′ld
**Rand** rănd
**Ran′dal, -dall, -dle** răn′d′l
**Ran′dolph** răn′dŏlf, -d′lf
**Ran′don′** *Fr.* räɴ′dôɴ′
**Ran·fur′ly** ?răn·fûr′lĭ
**Ra·nie′ro** *Ital.* rä·nyâ′rô
**Ran′jan** *Bengali* rŭn′jȧn
**Ran′ken** răng′kĕn
**Ran′kin** răng′kĭn
**Rann** răn
**Ran′nulf** răn′ŭlf
**Rans′ford** răns′fērd
**Ran′som, -some** răn′sŭm
**Ra·nuc′cio** *Ital.* rä·nōōt′chô
**Ra′nulf, -nulph** rā′nŭlf, răn′ŭlf
**Rao** *Marathi* rä′ōō
**Ra′oul′** *Fr.* rȧ′ōōl′—**Ra·oul′** *Ger., Span.* rä·ōōl′
**Raph′a·el** răf′ā·ĕl, -ĭ·ĕl, rā′fā·ĕl, -fĭ·ĕl—**Ra′phael** *Du.* rȧ′fĕl—**Ra′-pha′el′** *Fr.* rȧ′fȧ′ĕl′—**Ra′pha·el** *Ger.* rä′fä·ĕl
**Rash** răsh
**Ras′mus** *Dan., Norw.* räs′mōōs
**Rat′cliffe** răt′klĭf
**Rath′bone** răth′bōn, -bŭn
**Rat′tray** răt′rā
**Ra·úl′** *Span.* rä·ōōl′
**Raw′don** rô′d′n
**Raw′lins** rô′lĭnz
**Raw′son** rô′s′n
**Ray** rā
**Ray′mond** rā′mŭnd—**Ray′mond′** *Fr.* rā′môɴ′
**Ray′mund** *Ger.* rī′mōōnt
**Ray′ner** rā′nēr
**Raynes** rānz
**Raynes′ford, Rayns′ford** rānz′fērd
**Read, Reade** rēd
**Read′y** rĕd′ĭ
**Reave′ley** rēv′lĭ
**Re′ba** rē′bȧ
**Re·bec′ca, Re·bek′ah** rē·bĕk′ȧ
**Red′cliffe** rĕd′klĭf
**Redd** rĕd
**Red′de·ford** rĕd′ĕ·fērd
**Red′den** rĕd′′n
**Red′ding** rĕd′ĭng
**Rede** rēd
**Red′fern** rĕd′fērn
**Red′field** rĕd′fēld
**Red′man** rĕd′măn
**Red′mond** rĕd′mŭnd
**Red′vers** rĕd′vērz
**Reed** rēd
**Rees** rēs
**Reeves** rēvz
**Re·gi′na** *Ital.* râ·jē′nä
**Reg′i·nald** rĕj′ĭ·n′ld
**Ré′gis′** *Fr.* rā′zhēs′
**Re·gnault′** *Fr.* rē·nyō′
**Reg·nier′** *Du.* rĭ·nēr′
**Reid** rēd
**Rei′gnier** ?rā′nyā
**Rei·ji·ro** *Jap.* rā·jē·rō
**Reil′ly** rī′lĭ
**Rei′na** *Span.* rĕ′ē·nä
**Rein′hard** *Ger.* rīn′härt
**Rein′hart** *Du.* rīn′härt
**Rein′hold** *Ger.* rīn′hôlt
**Rei·nier′** *Du.* rī·nēr′
**Rem′bert** *Du., Ger.* rĕm′bĕrt
**Rem·ber′tus** *Lat.* rĕm·bûr′tŭs
**Rem′brandt** rĕm′brănt
**Re′mi′** *Fr.* rā′mē′
**Rem′ick** rĕm′ĭk
**Re·mi′gio** *Span.* rĕ·mē′hyō
**Re·mi′gi·us** *Ger.* râ·mē′gē·ōōs
**Rem′ing·ton** rĕm′ĭng·tŭn
**Rem′sen** rĕm′s′n, -z′n
**Re′mus** *Ger.* rā′mōōs
**Ré′my′** *Fr.* rā′mē′
**Re′na** rē′nȧ
**Re·na′to** *Ital.* râ·nä′tô
**Re·na′tus** *Lat.* rē·nā′tŭs
**Re·naud′** *Fr.* rē·nō′
**Ren′del** rĕn′d′l
**Re·né′** *Eng., Fr., Ger.* rē·nā′
**Re·née′** *Fr.* rē·nā′
**Renn** rĕn
**Ren′nie** rĕn ĭ
**Rens′se·laer** rĕn′sē·lēr
**Reres′by** rẹrz′bĭ
**Reu′ben** rōō′bĕn
**Re′wi** rā′wē
**Rex** rĕks
**Rex′ford** rĕks′fērd
**Rey·nal′do** *Span.* rĕ·ē·näl′dō
**Rey′ner** *Ger.* rī′nēr
**Reyn′old** rĕn′′ld
**Reyn′olds** rĕn′′ldz
**Rhea** rā; *as a woman's name, also* rē′ȧ
**Rhijn′vis** *Du.* rīn′vĭs
**Rhine′land′er** rīn′lăn′dēr
**Rhoades** rōdz
**Rho′da** rō′dȧ
**Rhys** rēs
**Ri·car′da** *Ger.* rē·kär′dä
**Ri·car′do** *Span.* rē·kär′thō
**Ric·car′do** rĭ·kär′dō; *Ital.* rēk·kär′dô
**Ric·ciot′ti** *Ital.* rēt·chôt′tē
**Rice** rīs
**Rich** rĭch
**Rich′ard** rĭch′ērd—**Ri′chard** *Du.* rē′shärt; *Ger.* rĭᴋ′ärt—**Ri′chard′** *Fr.* rē′shȧr′
**Rich′ards** rĭch′ērdz
**Rich′ard·son** rĭch′ērd·s′n
**Rich′ford** rĭch′fērd
**Rich′mal** rĭch′măl
**Rich′mond** rĭch′mŭnd
**Rick′ard** rĭk′ērd
**Rick′art** *Swed.* rĭk′ärt
**Rick′et·son** rĭk′ĕt·s′n, -ĭt·s′n
**Rick′man** rĭk′măn
**Ri′da** ?rē′dȧ
**Rid′dell** rĭd′′l, rĭ·dĕl′
**Ri′der** rī′dēr
**Ridge′ly** rĭj′lĭ
**Ridge′way, Ridg′way** rĭj′wā
**Rid′ley** rĭd′lĭ
**Ri·dol′fo** *Ital.* rē·dôl′fô
**Rig′nall** rĭg′n′l
**Ri′kard** *Norw.* rĭk′ärd, -kärt
**Ri′ley** rī′lĭ
**Ri·nal′do** rĭ·năl′dō; *Ital.* rē·näl′dô
**Rip′ley** rĭp′lĭ
**Ritch′ie** rĭch′ĭ
**Rit′ten·house** rĭt′′n·hous
**Rit′ter** rĭt′ēr
**rit′ter** *Ger.* rĭt′ēr
**Riv′ers** rĭv′ērz
**Ri′vière′** *Fr.* rē′vyâr′
**Ri′zos** *Mod. Grk.* rē′zôs
**Roach** rōch
**Ro′ald** *Norw.* rō′äl
**Roark** rōrk
**Ro′bard** rō′bärd
**Rob′bins** rŏb′ĭnz
**Ro·be′na** rō·bē′nȧ
**Rob′ert** rŏb′ērt—**Ro′bert** *Dan.* rō′-bärt; *Du.* rŏb′ērt; *Finn.* rô′bĕrt; *Ger.* rō′bĕrt; *Swed.* rô′bĕrt—**Ro′-bert′** *Fr.* rô′bâr′—**Ro·bert′** *Russ.* rŭ·byârt′, rô′byĕrt
**Ro·ber′to** *Ital.* rō·bĕr′tô; *Span.* rô-bĕr′tō
**Rob′erts** rŏb′ērts
**Rob′ert·son** rŏb′ērt·s′n
**Ro′bey, Ro′bie** rō′bĭ
**Rob′in·son** rŏb′ĭn·s′n
**Rob′ley** rŏb′lĭ
**Rob′recht** *Du.* rŏb′rĕᴋt
**Rob′son** rŏb′s′n
**Roch** *Fr.* rôk
**Roche** rōch; *Fr.* rôsh
**Ro′chus** *Ger.* rôᴋ′ōōs
**Rock′hill** rŏk′hĭl
**Rock′ing·ham** rŏk′ĭng·hăm, *esp. Brit.* -ăm
**Rock′well** rŏk′wĕl, -wĕl
**Rock′wood** rŏk′wŏŏd
**Ro′den** rō′d′n

**Rod′er·ic** rŏd′ẽr·ĭk
**Ro′de·rich** *Ger.* rō′dĕ·rĭĸ
**Rod′er·ick** rŏd′ẽr·ĭk
**Rod′man** rŏd′măn
**Rod′ney** rŏd′nĭ
**Ro·dol′fo** *Ital.* rô·dôl′fô; *Span.* rô-thôl′fō
**Ro′dolphe′** *Fr.* rô′dôlf′
**Ro·dol′pho** *Ital.* rô·dôl′fô
**Ro·dol′phus** *Du.* rô·dŏl′fûs; *Lat.* rô-dŏl′fŭs
**Rod·ri′go** rŏd·rē′gō—**Ro·dri′go** *Ital.* rô·drē′gô; *Span.* rô·thrē′gō
**Ro′drigue′** *Fr.* rô′drēg′
**Ro·drí′guez** *Span.* rô·thrē′gāth, -gās
**Rod′well** rŏd′wĕl, -wĕl
**Roe** rō
**Roe′lof** *Du.* rōō′lôf
**Rof′fey** rŏf′ĭ
**Rog′er** rŏj′ẽr—**Ro′ger′** *Fr.* rô′zhā′
**Rog′ers** rŏj′ẽrz
**Ro·gier′** *Du.* rô·gēr′
**Ro′land** rō′lănd; *Ger.* rō′länt—**Ro′-land′** *Fr.* rô′läɴ′
**Rolf** rŏlf
**Ro·lin′da** rô·lĭn′dȧ
**Rolles** rōlz
**Rol′lin** rŏl′ĭn
**Rol′lin·son** rŏl′ĭn·s′n
**Rol′lo** rŏl′ō
**Ro′ma** rō′mȧ
**Ro′main′** *Fr.* rô′măɴ′
**Ro·maine′** rô·mān′
**Ro′man** *Pol.* rô′män—**Ro·man′** *Russ.* rŭ·mán′
**Ro·ma′no·vich** *Russ.* rŭ·má′nŭ·vyĭch
**Ro·ma′nov·na** *Russ.* rŭ·má′nŭv·nŭ
**Ro·man′za** rô·măn′zȧ
**Ro′mer** rō′mẽr
**Ro·me′ro** *Span.* rô·mā′rō
**Ro·meyn′** rô·mān′, -mīn′
**Ro′mo·al′do** *Ital.* rō′mô·äl′dô
**Rom′ney** rŏm′nĭ, rŭm′-
**Ro′mo·lo** *Ital.* rō′mô·lō
**Ro′mu·ald** *Ger.* rō′mōō·ält
**Rô′mu·lo** *Span.* rô′mōō·lō
**Rom′u·lus** rŏm′ū·lŭs
**Ron′ald** rŏn′′ld—**Ro′nald** *Norw.* rō′näl(d)—**Ro·nald′** *Port.* rōō-näld′
**Ro·nayne′** ?rô·nān′
**Rood** rōōd
**Rookes** rŏŏks
**Roo′ney** rōō′nĭ
**Root** rōōt
**Rootes** rōōts
**Ro′que** *Span.* rô′kā
**Ro′ry** rō′rĭ
**Ro′sa** rō′zȧ; *Ger.* rō′zä; *Ital.* rô′zä; *Span.* rô′sä—**Ro′sa′** *Fr.* rō′zȧ′
**Ros′a·belle** rŏz′ȧ·bĕl
**Ro·sal′ba** *Ital.* rô·zäl′bä
**Ros′a·lie** rŏz′ȧ·lē, rō′zȧ·lē—**Ro′sa′-lie′** *Fr.* rō′zȧ′lē′
**Ros′a·lind** rŏz′ȧ·lĭnd, rō′zȧ-, -līnd
**Ros′a·mond, -mund** rŏz′ȧ·mŭnd
**Ro·san′na** rô·zăn′ȧ
**Ros′coe** rŏs′kō
**Rose** *Eng., Fr.* rōz
**Ro′se·monde′** *Fr.* rôz′môɴd′
**Rose′well** rōz′wĕl, -wĕl
**Ro·si′na** rô·zē′nȧ
**Ro′sine′** *Fr.* rō′zēn′
**Ro·si′ta** rô·zē′tȧ
**Ross** rŏs
**Ros′set·ter** rŏs′ĕ·tẽr
**Ros′si·ter** rŏs′ĭ·tẽr
**Ross′keen** rŏs′kēn
**Ross′lyn** rŏs′lĭn
**Ros·trev′or** rŏs·trĕv′ẽr
**Ros′well** rŏz′wĕl, -wĕl
**Roun′dell** roun′d′l
**Rowe** rō
**Row′land** rō′lănd
**Row′ley** rou′lĭ, rō′lĭ
**Rox′burgh** rŏks′brŭ
**Rox′ey** rŏk′sĭ
**Roy** roi
**Roy′al, Roy′all** roi′ăl
**Royds** roidz
**Ru′adh** *Scot.* rōō′ăth
**Ru′aidh·ri** *Ir.* rōō′ȧ·rĭ
**Ru·bén′** *Span.* rōō·bān′
**Ru′bens** rōō′bĕnz
**Ru′bert** rōō′bẽrt
**Ru′bin** rōō′bĭn
**Ru′by** rōō′bĭ
**Ruck′er** rŭk′ẽr
**Rudd** rŭd
**Rü′di·ger** rü′dĭ·gẽr
**Ru′dolf** rōō′dŏlf; *Czech* rōō′dôlf; *Du.* rü′dŏlf; *Finn.* rōō′dŏlf; *Ger.* rōō′-dôlf; *Swed.* rōō′dôlf
**Ru′dolph** rōō′dŏlf; *Du.* rü′dŏlf; *Ger.* rōō′dôlf; *Norw.* rōō′dŏlf
**Ru′dulph** rōō′dŭlf
**Rud′yard** rŭd′yẽrd
**Ru·fi′no** *Span.* rōō·fē′nō
**Ru′fus** rōō′fŭs
**Rug·ge′ro, Rug·gie′ro** *Ital.* rōōd·jâ′rô
**Rug′gles** rŭg′′lz
**Rug′las** rŏŏg′lăs
**Ru·iz′** *Span.* rōō·ēth′, -ēs′
**Rulffs** rŏŏlfs
**Run′ci·man** rŭn′sĭ·măn
**Run′nell** rŭn′′l
**Ru′pert** rōō′pẽrt; *Ger.* rōō′pĕrt; *Swed.* rōō′pĕrt
**Ru·per′to** *Span.* rōō·pĕr′tō
**Ru′ry** rŏŏr′ĭ
**Rush** rŭsh
**Rush·di′** *Turk.* rüsh·tü′
**Rush′more** rŭsh′mōr
**Rush′ton** rŭsh′tŭn
**Rush′worth** rŭsh′wûrth, -wẽrth
**Russ** rŭs
**Rus′sa** rŭs′ȧ
**Rus′sel, Rus′sell** rŭs′′l
**Rüş·tü′** *Turk.* rüsh·tü′
**Rut′gers** rŭt′gẽrz
**Ruth** rōōth
**Ruth′er·ford** rŭth′ẽr·fẽrd
**Ru·til′i·us** *Lat.* rōō·tĭl′ĭ·ŭs
**Rut′land** rŭt′lănd
**Rut′sen** rŭt′s′n
**Rut′ter** rŭt′ẽr
**Ruy** *Port.* rōō′ē; *Span.* rōō·ē′
**Ry′an** rī′ăn
**Ry′der** rī′dẽr
**Ry′ley** rī′lĭ
**Ry′mer** rī′mẽr
**Ryo·kei** *Jap.* ryō·kā
**Rys′to** *Finn.* rüs′tŏ

**Sab·ba′ti·us** *Lat.* să·bā′shĭ·ŭs
**Sa′bès′** *Fr.* sȧ′bâs′
**Sa′bine′** *Fr.* sȧ′bēn′
**Sa·bi′nus** *Lat.* sȧ·bī′nŭs
**Sa·bu·ro** *Jap.* sä·bŏŏ·rō
**Sa′cha′** *Fr.* sȧ′shȧ′
**Sa·chev′er·ell** sȧ·shĕv′ẽr·ĕl
**Sack′ville** săk′vĭl
**Sa·da·na·ru** *Jap.* sä·dä·nä·rŏŏ
**Sa·da·o** *Jap.* sä·dä·ô
**Sa′di′** *Fr.* sȧ′dē′
**Sad′ler** săd′lẽr
**Saf′ford** săf′ẽrd
**Sa′gesse′** *Fr.* sȧ′zhĕs′
**Sa·ha·chi·ro** *Jap.* sä·hä·chē·rō
**sa′hib** *Arab., As. Ind.* sä′hĭb
**Saint, St.** sānt; *when preceding a name,* sȧnt *or, esp. Brit.,* sĭnt, s′nt; *Fr.* săɴ
**Saint Clair, St. Clair, StClair** sȧnt klâr′; *esp. Brit.,* sĭng′klâr, sĭn′klâr
**St. Hill** sȧnt hĭl′
**Saint John** sȧnt jŏn′, *esp. Brit.* sĭn′-jŭn
**St. Leg′er** sȧnt lĕj′ẽr, *Brit. also* sĕl′ĭn·jẽr
**St. Loe** sȧnt lōō′
**Sa′ka·ri** *Finn.* sȧ′kȧ·rĭ
**Sal′bi′go′ton′** *Fr.* sȧl′bē′gô′tôɴ′
**Sa·le′ius** *Lat.* sȧ·lē′yŭs
**Sa′lem** sā′lĕm
**Salis′bur·y** sôlz′bẽr·ĭ, -brĭ
**Sal′lie** săl′ĭ
**Sal′ly** săl′ĭ; *Finn.* sȧl′lĭ
**Sal′mon** săl′mŏn
**Sa·lo′me** sȧ·lō′mē
**Sa′lo·mo** *Ger.* zä′lô·mō
**Sa′lo·mon** *Du.* sȧ′lô·môn; *Ger.* zä′-lô·môn; *Swed.* sä′lōō·môn—**Sa′lo′-mon′** *Fr.* sȧ′lô′môɴ′
**Sa′lo·mo′ne** *Ital.* sä′lô·mō′nâ
**Sal′ter** sôl′tẽr
**Sal′ton·stall** sôl′t′n·stôl
**Sa′lus·tia′no** *Span.* sä′lōōs·tyä′nō
**Sal′va·dor′** *Span.* säl′vä·thôr′
**Sal′va·tor′** *Ital.* säl′vä·tōr′
**Sam** săm
**Samp′son** săm(p)′s′n
**Sam′son** săm′s′n; *Ger.* zäm′zôn
**Sam′u·el** săm′ū·ĕl—**Sa′mu·el** *Du.* sȧ′mü·ĕl; *Ger.* zä′mōō·ĕl; *Swed.* sä′-mōō·ĕl—**Sa′mu·el′** *Fr.* sȧ′mü·ĕl′—**Sa·mu′el** *Pol.* sä·mōō′ĕl—**Sa·muel′** *Span.* sä·mwĕl′
**Sa·mu·i′lo·vich** *Russ.* sŭ·mōō·ē′lŭ-vyĭch
**San** *Ital., Span.* sän
**Sán′chez** *Span.* sän′chāth, -chās
**San′ders** sȧn′dẽrz
**San′der·son** sȧn′dẽr·s′n
**Sand′field** săn(d)′fēld
**Sand′ford** săn(d)′fẽrd
**Sán′dor** *Hung.* shän′dôr
**Šan′dor** *Yugo.* shän′dôr
**San′dro** *Ital.* sän′drô
**Sands** săndz
**San′ford** săn′fẽrd
**Sang′er** săng′ẽr; săng′gẽr
**Sant′** *Ital.* sänt

**San′ta** *Ital., Span.* săn′tä
**San·tia′go** *Span.* săn·tyä′gō
**San·to′rio** *Ital.* săn·tô′ryō̇
**San′tos** *Span.* săn′tōs
**Sap′ping·ton** săp′ĭng·tŭn
**Sar′a, Sar′ah** sâr′ȧ, sā′rȧ
**Sar′geant, Sar′gent** sär′jĕnt
**Sar·mien′to** *Span.* sär·myān′tō
**Sa·ro′ji·ni** *As. Ind.* sȧ·rō′jĭ·nē
**Sars′field** särs′fēld
**Sas′ki·a** *Du.* săs′kē̇·ȧ
**Sa·tyen′dra** *As. Ind.* sô·tyān′drô
**Saul** sôl
**Saun′ders** sôn′dẽrz, săn′dẽrz
**Sau′ter′** *Fr.* sō′târ′
**Sa′va** *Yugo.* sä′vä
**Sav′age** săv′ĭj
**Sa·ve′rio** *Ital.* sä·vâ′ryō̇
**Sav′ile, Sav′ille** săv′ĭl
**Sa′vi′nien′** *Fr.* sȧ′vē′nyăN′
**Sav′vich** *Russ.* sȧv′vyĭch
**Saw′don** sô′d'n
**Saw′yer** sô′yẽr
**Sax** săks
**sa′yid, say′yid** *Arab.* sī′yĭd
**Sca′ra·muc′cia** *Ital.* skä′rä·mo͞ot′chä
**Sca·ve′ni·us** *Dan.* skȧ·vę̄′nē̇·o͞os
**Schack** *Dan.* shȧk
**Schaw** shô
**Schel′te** *Du.* sKĕl′tĕ
**Schil′ler** shĭl′ẽr
**Schley** shlī
**School′craft** sko͞ol′krȧft
**Schu′ma′cher** *Dan.* sho͞o′mȧ′Kẽr
**Schuy′ler** skī′lẽr
**Schwenck** shwĕngk
**Sciar′ra** *Ital.* shär′rä
**Sci′pion′** *Fr.* sē′pyôN′
**Sci·pio′ne** *Ital.* shē̇·pyō′nā
**Scott** skŏt
**Sco′tus** *Lat.* skō′tŭs
**Scri·bo′ni·us** *Lat.* skrĭ·bō′nĭ·ŭs
**Scull** skŭl
**Sea′ly** sē′lĭ
**Sea′man** sē′măn
**Sean, Seán** *Ir.* shôn, shăn
**Sear′gent** sär′jĕnt
**Sears** sẹ̄rz
**Sea′ton** sē′t'n
**Sea′ver** sē′vẽr
**Sea′vey** sē′vĭ
**Se′ba** sē′bȧ
**Se′bald** *Du.* sā′bält; *Ger.* zā′bält
**Se·bas′tian** sē̇·băs′chăn—**Se·bas′ti·an** *Du.* sȧ·bäs′tē̇·än; *Norw.* sȧ·bäs′tē̇·än; *Pol.* sĕ·bäs′tyän—**Se·ba′sti·an** *Ger.* zȧ·bäs′tē̇·än
**Se′bas·tián′** *Span.* sā′bäs·tyän′
**Se′ba·stia′no** *Ital.* sā′bäs·tyä′nō̇
**Se·bas′ti·a′nus** *Lat.* sē̇·băs′chĭ·ā′nŭs
**Se·bas·tião′** *Port.* sĕ·bȧsh·tyouN′, (*Braz.*) -bȧs·tyouN′
**Sé′bas′tien′** *Fr.* sā′bȧs′tyăN′
**Se·bas′tyan** *Pol.* sĕ·bäs′tyän
**Seck′el** sĕk′ĕl
**Sedg′wick** sĕj′wĭk
**See′bohm** sē′bōm
**See′ly, See′lye** sē′lĭ
**Sef′ton** sĕf′tŭn
**Se′gel·cke** *Norw.* sā′gĕl·kĕ
**sei′gneur′** *Fr.* sĕ′nyûr′
**Sei·hin** *Jap.* sā·hĭn
**Sei·i·ti·ro** *Jap.* sā·ē̇·tē̇·rō
**Sei·ji** *Jap.* sā·jē̇
**Sei·ki** *Jap.* sā·kē̇
**Sei·shi·ro** *Jap.* sā·shē̇·rō̇
**Se′lah** sē′lȧ
**Sel′by** sĕl′bĭ
**Sel′den** sĕl′dĕn
**Se′lim** sē′lĭm; *Finn.* sā′lĭm
**Se·li′na** sĕ·lē′nȧ, -lī′nȧ
**Sell** sĕl
**Sel′lif** *Swed.* sĕl′lĭf
**Sel′ma** *Swed.* sĕl′mȧ
**Sel′wyn** sĕl′wĭn
**Se·mën′** *Russ.* syĭ·myôn′
**Se·më′no·vich** *Russ.* syĭ·myô′nŭ·vyĭch
**Se·mion′** *Russ.* syĭ·myôn′
**Se·mio′no·vich** *Russ.* syĭ·myô′nŭ·vyĭch
**Sem·pro′ni·us** *Lat.* sĕm·prō′nĭ·ŭs
**Se·myon′** *Russ.* syĭ·myôn′
**Se·myo′no·vich** *Russ.* syĭ·myô′nŭ·vyĭch
**Sen·ju·ro** *Jap.* sĕn·jo͞o·rō
**Sep·tim′i·us** *Lat.* sĕp·tĭm′ĭ·ŭs
**Sep′ti·mus** sĕp′tĭ·mŭs
**ser** *Ital.* sĕr
**Se′ra·fín′** *Span.* sā′rä·fēn′
**Se′ra·fi′no** *Ital.* sā′rä·fē′nō̇
**Se′raph** *Ger.* zā′räf
**Sé′ra′phin′** *Fr.* sā′rȧ′făN′
**Sé′ra′phine′** *Fr.* sā′rȧ′fēn′
**Şer·ban′** *Rum.* shĕr·bän′
**Se·re′no** sĕ·rē′nō
**Serge** *Fr.* sĕrzh
**Ser′geant** sär′jĕnt
**Ser·ge′e·vich** *Russ.* syĭr·gyā′yĕ·vyĭch
**Ser·gei′** *Russ.* syĭr·gyā′ĭ
**Ser′gio** *Span.* sĕr′hyō
**Ser′gi·us** sûr′jĭ·ŭs
**Ser′vais′** *Fr.* sĕr′vĕ′
**Ser·vil′i·us** *Lat.* sûr·vĭl′ĭ·ŭs, sẽr-, -vĭl′yŭs
**Ser′vi·us** *Lat.* sûr′vĭ·ŭs
**Ses′sions** sĕsh′ŭnz
**Seth** sĕth; *Ger.* zāt
**Se′ton** sē′t'n
**Seu′mas** *Ir.* shā′mȧs
**Seu′se** *Ger.* zoi′zĕ
**Se′ve·rin′** *Norw.* sĕ′vĕ·rēn′
**Sé′ve·rin′** *Fr.* sā′vrăN′
**Se·ve·ri′no·vich** *Russ.* syĭ·vyĕ·ryē′-nŭ·vyĭch
**Sev′er·i′nus** *Lat.* sĕv′ẽr·ī′nŭs
**Se·ve′ro** *Span.* sȧ·vā′rō
**Sew′all** sū′ăl
**Sew′ard** sū′ẽrd, *Brit. also* sē′wẽrd
**Sew′ell** sū′ĕl
**Se·we′ryn** *Pol.* sĕ·vĕ′rĭn
**Sex′tus** *Lat.* sĕks′tŭs
**Sey′mour** sē′mōr, -môr, -mẽr
**sey′yid** *Arab.* sī′yĭd
**Sfor′za** *Ital.* sfôr′tsä
**Shack′er·ley** shăk′ẽr·lĭ
**Sha′drach** shā′drăk
**Shad′worth** shăd′wûrth, -wẽrth
**Shae′mas** *Ir.* shā′mȧs
**Shai′ler** shā′lẽr
**Shak′er·ley** shăk′ẽr·lĭ
**Shake′speare** shāk′spẹ̄r
**Sha′ler** shā′lẽr
**Sha·lom′** *Heb.* shä·lōm′
**Shane** *Ir.* shān
**Shan′kar** *As. Ind.* shŭng′kẽr
**Shan′non** shăn′ŭn
**Shar′on** shăr′ŭn, shâr′ŭn
**Sharp** shärp
**Shar′tle** shär′t'l
**Shaw** shô
**Shay** shā
**Sheaf** shēf
**Shed′den** shĕd′'n
**Shei′la** shē′lȧ
**Shel′by** shĕl′bĭ
**Shel′don** shĕl′dŭn
**Shel′ford** shĕl′fẽrd
**Shel′ton** shĕl′t'n
**Shep′ard** shĕp′ẽrd
**Shep′herd** shĕp′ẽrd
**Sher′ard** ?shĕr′ẽrd, -ärd
**Sher′burne** shûr′bẽrn
**Sher′i·dan** shĕr′ĭ·d'n
**Sher′man** shûr′măn
**Sher′ry** shĕr′ĭ
**Sher′win** shûr′wĭn
**Sher′wood** shûr′wo͝od
**Shi·ba·sa·bu·ro** *Jap.* shē̇·bä·sä·bo͝o·rō
**Shield** shēld
**Shields** shēldz
**Shi·ge·no·bu** *Jap.* shē̇·gĕ·nō̇·bo͝o
**Shi·ge·no·ri** *Jap.* shē̇·gĕ·nō̇·rē̇
**Shi·ge·ta·ro** *Jap.* shē̇·gĕ·tä·rō
**Shim·pei** *Jap.* shēm·pā
**Shin·i·chi·ro** *Jap.* shēn·ē̇·chē̇·rō
**Ship′ley** shĭp′lĭ
**Shir′ley** shûr′lĭ
**Shi·ro** *Jap.* shē̇·rō̇
**Sho′bal** shō′băl
**Sho′lem** *Yiddish* shō′lĕm
**Sho′lom** *Heb.* shô′lŭm
**Shol′to** shôl′tō
**Shrews′bur·y** shro͞oz′bẽr·ĭ, shrōz′-, -brĭ
**shri** *Skr.* shrē
**Shun·ro·ku** *Jap.* sho͞on·rō̇·ko͞o
**Shus′ter** sho͞os′tẽr
**Shute** sho͞ot
**Shu·zo** *Jap.* sho͞o·zō
**Si′bert** sī′bẽrt
**Sib′yl** sĭb′'l, -ĭl
**Si·byl′la** *Ger.* zē̇·bül′ä
**Si′bylle′** *Fr.* sē′bēl′
**Sid** sĭd
**Sid′dons** sĭd′'nz
**Si′dey** sī′dĭ
**Sid′ney** sĭd′nĭ
**Si′do′nie′** *Fr.* sē′dô′nē′—**Si·do′ni·e** *Ger.* zē̇·dō′nē̇·ĕ
**Si·dô′nio** *Port.* sē̇·thō′nyo͞o
**Sieg′bert** *Ger.* zēK′bĕrt
**Sieg′fried** sēg′frēd; *Ger.* zēK′frēt
**Sieg′mund** *Ger.* zēK′mo͞ont
**Sient′je** *Du.* sēnt′yĕ
**sieur** *Fr.* syûr
**Sif′frein′** *Fr.* sē′frăN′
**Si′ful** *Norw.* sĭf′fo͞ol
**Sig′björn** *Norw.* sĭg′byûrn
**Sig′frid** *Ger.* zēK′frēt
**Sig′fús** *Icelandic* sĭg′fo͞os
**Si′gis′bert′** *Fr.* sē′zhēz′bâr′

**Si′gis·mon′do** *Ital.* sē′jēz·mōn′dō
**Sig′is·mund** sĭj′ĭs·mŭnd, sĭg′- —**Si′-gis·mund** *Ger.* zē′gĭs·mo͝ont; *Swed.* sē′gĭs·mŭnd′
**Sig′mund** sĭg′mŭnd; *Ger.* zēK′mo͝ont
**Sig′ni·us** *Dan.* sĕg′nē·o͞os
**si·gno′re** *Ital.* sē·nyō′rā
**Si′grid** *Ger.* zē′grĭt, -grēt; *Norw.* sĭ′grĭ; *Swed.* sē′grĭd
**Si′gurd** *Norw.* sĭg′go͝ord
**Si′las** sī′lăs
**Silk** sĭlk
**Sil′li·man** sĭl′ĭ·măn
**Sil′vain′** *Fr.* sēl′văN′
**Sil′van** sĭl′văn
**Sil·va′nus** sĭl·vā′nŭs
**Sil′ves′tre** *Fr.* sēl′vĕs′tr′—**Sil·ves′-tre** *Span.* sēl·vās′trā
**Sil·ves′tro** *Ital.* sēl·vĕs′trō
**Sil′vi·o** *Ger.* zĭl′vē·ō—**Sil′vio** *Ital.* sēl′vyō
**Sim** sĭm
**Sime** sīm
**Sim′e·on** sĭm′ē·ŭn—**Si·me·on′** *Russ.* syĭ·myĕ·ôn′
**Si′mé′on′** *Fr.* sē′mā′ôN′
**Sim′mons** sĭm′ŭnz
**Si′mon** sī′mŭn; *Ger.* zē′mōn; *Russ.* syē′môn; *Yugo.* sē′mōn—**Si′mon′** *Fr.* sē′môN′
**Si·món′** *Span.* sē·môn′
**Si′monde′** *Fr.* sē′môNd′
**Si′monds** sī′mŭn(d)z, sĭm′ŭn(d)z
**Si·mo′ne** *Ital.* sē·mō′nā
**Si′mos** *Mod. Grk.* sē′môs
**Sim′plice′** *Fr.* săN′plēs′
**Simp′son** sĭm(p)′s′n
**Sims** sĭmz
**Sin′clair** sĭn′klâr, sĭng′-, sĭn·klâr′
**Sing′er** sĭng′ēr
**Sin′gle·ton** sĭng′g′l·tŭn
**Si′ni·bal′do** *Ital.* sē′nē·bäl′dō
**Sinks** sĭngks
**sir·dar′** *As. Ind.* sēr·där′
**sire** *Fr.* sēr
**Sis′ley** sĭs′lĭ
**Si′sto** *Ital.* sēs′tō
**Sit′ling·ton** sĭt′lĭng·tŭn
**Sjoerd** *Du.* sho͞ort
**Skar′bek** *Pol.* skär′bĕk
**Skeele** skēl
**Skel′ton** skĕl′t′n
**Skene** skēn
**Skin′ner** skĭn′ēr
**Sla′ter** slā′tēr
**Slee′per** slē′pēr
**Slings′by** slĭngz′bĭ
**Sloan, Sloane** slōn
**Sloat** slōt
**Slo·bo′dan** *Yugo.* slô·bō′dän
**Slo′cum** slō′kŭm
**Smed′ley** smĕd′lĭ
**Smi′ley** smī′lĭ
**Smith** smĭth; *Dan.* smēt
**Smyth** smĭth, smīth
**Smythe** smīth, smīth
**Snave′ly** snāv′lĭ
**Snell** *Du.* snĕl
**Snow** snō
**Snow′den** snō′d′n
**Sny′der** snī′dēr

**Soame** sōm
**Soc′ra·tes** sŏk′rā·tēz—**So·cra′tes** *Mod. Grk.* sô·krä′tēs
**So·fi′a** *Swed.* sô·fē′á
**So′fo·nis′ba** *Ital.* sō′fō·nēz′bä
**So′fus** *Dan., Norw.* sō′fo͞os
**Sof′ya** *Russ.* sôf′yá
**Sol** sŏl
**So·la′no** *Span.* sô·lä′nō
**So′lis** sō′lĭs
**Sol′li·us** *Lat.* sŏl′ĭ·ŭs
**Sol′o·mon** sŏl′ō·mŭn
**So·lo·mo′no·vich** *Russ.* sŭ·lŭ·mô′-nŭ·vyĭch
**So′lon** sō′lŏn, -lŭn
**Sol′y·man** sŏl′ĭ·măn
**Som′ers** sŭm′ērz
**Som′er·set** sŭm′ēr·sĕt, -sĭt
**Som′er·ville** sŭm′ēr·vĭl
**So′nya** *Russ.* sô′nyá
**So·phi′a** sô·fī′ȧ, sō′fĭ·ȧ; *Dan., Swed.* so͞o·fē′á; *Ger.* zô·fē′ä—**Soph′ia** *Russ.* sôf′yá
**So′phie** sō′fĭ—**So′phie′** *Fr.* sô′fē′—**So·phi′e** *Ger.* zô·fē′ĕ, zô·fē′—**So-phie′** *Swed.* so͞o·fē′
**So′phus** sō′fŭs; *Dan., Norw.* sō′fo͞os; *Ger.* zō′fo͞os
**Sö′ren** *Dan.* sû′rĕn
**So·to·ki·chi** *Jap.* sô·tô·kē·chē
**South′cote** south′kŭt, -kōt
**South′er·den** sŭth′ēr·d′n
**South′gate** south′gāt, -gĭt
**South′worth** south′wûrth, -wērth
**Sow′er·by** sō′ēr·bĭ
**Spar′row** spăr′ō
**Speak′man** spēk′măn
**Spear** spēr
**Spear′man** spēr′măn
**Speed** spēd
**Speirs** spērz
**Spence** spĕns
**Spen′cer, Spen′ser** spĕn′sēr
**Sper′ry** spĕr′ĭ
**Spi′cer** spī′sēr
**Sprague** sprāg
**Sprigg** sprĭg
**Spring** sprĭng
**Spu′ri·us** *Lat.* spū′rĭ·ŭs
**Spy·ri′don** *Mod. Grk.* spē·rē′thôn
**Squire** skwīr
**Sri** *As. Ind.* shrē, srē
**Sta′cey, Sta′cy** stā′sĭ
**Staf′ford** stăf′ērd
**Stan′bur′rough** stăn′bûr′ō
**Stan′dish** stăn′dĭsh
**Stan′ford** stăn′fērd
**Stan′hope** stăn′ŭp
**Sta′nis·la′o** *Ital.* stä′nēz·lä′ō
**Stan′is·las** stăn′ĭs·lăs, -läs—**Sta′nis′-las′** *Fr.* stá′nēs′läs′
**Stan′is·laus** stăn′ĭs·lôs—**Sta′nis·laus** *Ger.* shtä′nĭs·lous, stä′-
**Sta′ni·slav** *Czech* stá′nyĭ·sláf
**Sta·ni′sław** *Pol.* stä·nē′sláf
**Stan′ko** *Yugo.* stän′kō
**Stan′ley** stăn′lĭ
**Stan′nard** stăn′ērd
**Stans′bur′y** stănz′bĕr′ĭ, -bēr·ĭ, -brĭ
**Stan′ton** stăn′t′n, -tŭn, *Brit. also* stăn′-

**Stan′wood** stăn′wo͝od
**Stan′yan** stăn′yăn
**Sta′ples** stā′p′lz
**Sta′ple·ton** stā′p′l·tŭn
**Starck, Stark, Starke** stärk
**Star′key** stär′kĭ
**Star′ling** stär′lĭng
**Starr** stär
**Star′rett** stăr′ĕt, -ĭt
**Staugh′ton** stô′t′n
**Stearns** stûrnz
**Steb′bins** stĕb′ĭnz
**Sted′man** stĕd′măn
**Steel, Steele** stēl
**Steen** *Dan.* stēn
**Steen′berg** *Dan.* stēn′bărg
**Steen′sen** *Dan.* stēn′s′n
**Ste′fan** *Bulg. Pol., Yugo.* stĕ′fän; *Ger.* shtĕ′fän
**Ste′fa·no** *Ital.* stā′fä·nō, stā′-
**Ste·fa′no·vić** *Yugo.* stĕ·fä′nô·vēt′y′, *Angl.* -vĭch
**Stein** stīn; *Norw.* stĕ′ĭn
**Stei′ner** stī′nēr
**Stel′la** stĕl′ȧ
**Sten** *Norw., Swed.* stān
**Sté′nio′** *Fr.* stā′nyō′
**Ste·pan′** *Russ.* styĭ·pán′—**Ste′pan** *Yugo.* stĕ′pän
**Ste·pa′no·vich** *Russ.* styĭ·pá′nŭ·vyĭch
**Ste′phan** *Ger.* shtĕ′fän; *Norw.* stā′fän
**Sté′phane′** *Fr.* stā′fán′
**Sté′pha·nie′** *Fr.* stā′fá′nē′
**Ste′pha·nos** *Mod. Grk.* stâ′fä·nôs
**Ste·pha′nus** *Du.* stā·fá′nûs
**Ste′phen** stē′vĕn; *Ger.* shtĕ′fĕn—**Ste′phen′** *Fr.* stā′fĕn′
**Ste′phens** stē′vĕnz
**Ste′phen·son** stē′vĕn·s′n
**Ster′ling** stûr′lĭng
**Stern′dale** stûrn′dāl
**Ster′ry** stĕr′ĭ
**Steu′art** stū′ērt
**Ste′van** *Yugo.* stĕ′vän
**Ste′vens** stē′vĕnz
**Ste′ven·son** stē′vĕn·s′n
**Ste′vens·zen** *Du.* stā′vĕn·sĕn
**Ste′vens·zoon** *Du.* stā′vĕn·sŭn, -sôn, -sōn
**Stew′art** stū′ērt
**Stick′ney** stĭk′nĭ
**Stijn** *Du.* stīn
**Stiles** stīlz
**Stil′ling·fleet** stĭl′ĭng·flēt
**Still′man** stĭl′măn
**Still′son** stĭl′s′n
**Still′well, Stil′well** stĭl′wĕl, -wĕl
**Stim′son** stĭm′s′n
**Stir′ling** stûr′lĭng
**Stock′man** stŏk′măn
**Stock′ton** stŏk′tŭn
**Stod′art** stŏd′ērt
**Stod′dard** stŏd′ērd
**Stod′dert** stŏd′ērt
**Sto′jan** *Yugo.* stō′yän
**Stone** stōn
**Stop′ford** stŏp′fērd
**Storm** stôrm
**Stor′row** stŏr′ō
**Storrs** stôrz
**Sto′ry** stō′rĭ

**Stow′ell** stō′ĕl
**Sto·yan′** *Bulg.* stô·yȧn′
**Strachan** strôn
**Strat′ford** străt′fẽrd
**Stra·thern′** strȧ·thĕrn′; strȧ·thûrn′
**Strat′ton** străt′′n
**Street** strēt
**Stree′ter** strē′tẽr
**Strick′land** strĭk′lănd
**String′er** strĭng′ẽr
**Strong** strŏng
**Strud′wick** strŭd′wĭk
**Struth′ers** strŭth′ẽrz
**Strutt** strŭt
**Stu′art** stū′ẽrt
**Stud′dert** stŭd′ẽrt
**Sturge** stûrj
**Stur′ges** stûr′jĕs, -jĭs
**Styles** stīlz
**Su′dan** *Bengali* sōō′dôn
**Sud′dards** sŭd′ẽrdz
**Su′dre** *Fr.* sü′dr′
**Su·ke·no·ri** *Jap.* sōō·kĕ·nô·rē
**Şü·krü′** *Turk.* shü·krü′
**Su·lei·man′** *Turk.* sü·lā·män′
**Sul′li·van** sŭl′ĭ·văn
**Sul′pice′** *Fr.* sül′pēs′
**Sul·pi′ci·us** sŭl·pĭsh′ĭ·ŭs, -pĭsh′ŭs
**Sum′mers** sŭm′ẽrz
**Sum′ner** sŭm′nẽr
**Su·ren′dra·nath** *Bengali* sōō·rān′-drô·nät
**Sur′ridge** sûr′ĭj
**Sur′tees** sûr′tēz
**Su′san** sū′z′n
**Su·san′na, -nah** sū·zăn′ȧ
**Su·san′ne** *Ger.* zōō·zän′ĕ
**Su·te·ji·ro** *Jap.* sōō·tĕ·jē·rō
**Su·te·mi** *Jap.* sōō·tĕ·mē
**Suth′er·land** sŭth′ẽr·lănd
**Su·zanne′** sū·zăn′—**Su′zanne′** *Fr.* sü′zȧn′
**Su′zor′** *Fr.* sü′zôr′
**Su·zu·ki** *Jap.* sōō·zōō·kē
**Svan′te′** *Swed.* svȧn′tĕ′
**Sva′to·pluk** *Czech* svȧ′tô·plŏŏk
**Svein′björn** *Icelandic* svān′byûd·′n
**Sven** *Dan., Norw., Swed.* svĕn
**Svend** *Dan.* svĕn
**Sve′to·zar** *Slovak* svyĕ′tô·zȧr; *Yugo.* svĕ′tô·zär
**Swain** swān
**Swan, Swann** swŏn
**Swan′wick** swŏn′ĭk
**Sweet** swēt
**Sweet′ser** swēt′sẽr
**Swett** swĕt
**Swift** swĭft
**Swin′ner·ton** swĭn′ẽr·t′n, -tŭn
**Swin′ton** swĭn′t′n, -tŭn
**Swyn′fen** swĭn′fĕn
**Syb′il** sĭb′′l, -ĭl
**Syd′en·ham** sĭd′′n·ăm, sĭd′năm
**Syd′ney** sĭd′nĭ
**Syd′nor** sĭd′nẽr
**sy′ed** *Arab.* sĭ′yĭd
**Syl′vain′** *Fr.* sēl′văɴ′
**Syl′va′nie′** *Fr.* sēl′vȧ′nē′
**Syl·va′nus** sĭl·vā′nŭs
**Syl′vère′** *Fr.* sēl′vâr′
**Syl·ves′ter** sĭl·vĕs′tẽr
**Syl′ves′tre** *Fr.* sēl′vĕs′tr′
**Syl′vi·a** sĭl′vĭ·ȧ
**Syl′vio** *Ital.* sēl′vyô
**Sy′monds** sī′mŭn(d)z, sĭm′ŭn(d)z
**Syng, Synge** sĭng
**Szczęs′ny** *Pol.* shchĕɴs′nĭ
**Szy′mon** *Pol.* shĭ′môn

**Ta′ber** tā′bẽr
**Ta·da·su** *Jap.* tä·dä·sōō
**Tad·de′o** *Ital.* täd·dâ′ô
**Tá′dé** *Hung.* tä′dā
**Ta·de′o** *Span.* tä·thā′ō
**Ta·de′usz** *Pol.* tä·dĕ′ōōsh
**Tadhg** *Ir.* thīg, thāg, tāg
**Tag′gart** tăg′ẽrt
**Tai·su·ke** *Jap.* tī·sōō·kĕ
**Tait** tāt
**Ta·ka·a·ki·ra** *Jap.* tä·kä·ä·kē·rä
**Ta·ka·mi·ne** *Jap.* tä·kä·mē·nĕ
**Ta·ka·shi** *Jap.* tä·kä·shē
**Ta·ka·to·shi** *Jap.* tä·kä·tô·shē
**Ta·ka·ya·su** *Jap.* tä·kä·yä·sōō
**Ta′ke** *Rum.* tä′kĕ
**Ta·ke·o** *Jap.* tä·kĕ·ô
**Tal′bot, -but** tôl′bŭt, tăl′-
**Tal′ia·ferro** tŏl′ĭ·vẽr
**Tal·lu′lah** tă·lū′lȧ
**Tal′madge** tăl′mĭj
**Ta·ma′ra** *Russ.* tŭ·mȧ′rŭ
**Ta′más** *Hung.* tŏ′mäsh
**Ta·me·mo·to** *Jap.* tä·mĕ·mô·tô
**Ta·me·sa·da** *Jap.* tä·mĕ·sä·dä
**Tan′a·quil′lus** *Lat.* tăn′ȧ·kwĭl′ŭs
**Tan′cred** *Finn.* tȧn′krād
**Tan′crède′** *Fr.* täɴ′krĕd′
**Tan′natt** tăn′ăt
**Tan′ne·gui′** *Fr.* tȧn′gē′
**Tan′ner** tăn′ẽr
**Tan′worth** tăn′wûrth, -wẽrth
**Tan·yu** *Jap.* tän·yōō
**Tap′pan** tăp′ăn
**Tap′ping** tăp′ĭng
**Ta′ras** *Russ.* tȧ′rŭs
**Tar·ie′lo·vich** *Russ.* tŭr·yâ′lŭ·vyĭch
**Tarle′ton** tärl′tŭn
**Ta·ro** *Jap.* tä·rō
**Tar·qui′nio** *Port.* tẽr·kwē′nyōō
**Tar·quin′i·us** *Lat.* tär·kwĭn′ĭ·ŭs
**Tas′ker** tăs′kẽr
**Tas′si·lo** *Ger.* täs′ē·lō
**Tate** tāt
**Ta·tsu·o** *Jap.* tä·tsōō·ô
**Tat′ton** tăt′′n
**Tau′rus** *Lat.* tô′rŭs
**Tax′ile′** *Fr.* tȧk′sēl′
**Tay′ler, Tay′lor** tā′lẽr
**te** *Du.* tĕ
**Te·cum′seh** tē·kŭm′sĕ, -sē
**Ted** tĕd
**Tej** *As. Ind.* tāj
**Te·ja′da** *Span.* tĕ·hä′thä
**Te′les·fo′ro** *Span.* tā′lās·fō′rō
**Té′les′phore′** *Fr.* tā′lĕs′fôr′
**Tell** tĕl
**Tem′ple** tĕm′p′l
**Tem′pler** tĕm′plẽr
**ten** *Du.* tĕn
**Tench** tĕnch
**Ten′er** tĕn′ẽr
**Ten′i·son** tĕn′ĭ·s′n
**Ten′nant** tĕn′ănt
**Ten′nes·see′** tĕn′ĕ·sē′, tĕn′ĕ·sē
**Ten′ney** tĕn′ĭ
**Ten′ny·son** tĕn′ĭ·s′n
**Te′o·bal′do** *Ital.* tā′ô·bäl′dô
**Te·o′dor** *Pol.* tē·ô′dôr—**Te′o·dor** *Swed.* tā′ô·dôr
**Te′o·do′ro** *Ital.* tā′ô·dô′rô; *Span.* tā′ô·thō′rō
**Te·ó′du·lo** *Span.* tā·ō′thōō·lō
**Te·o′fil** *Pol.* tĕ·ô′fēl
**Te·o′fi·lo** *Ital.* tā·ô′fē·lō
**Te·ó′fi·lo** *Port.* tē·ô′fē·lōō
**ter** *Du.* tẽr
**Ter′ence** tĕr′ĕns
**Te·ren′ti·us** *Lat.* tĕ·rĕn′shĭ·ŭs, -shŭs
**Te·ren′zio** *Ital.* tā·rĕn′tsyô
**Te·re′sa** tĕ·rē′sȧ, -zȧ; *Ital.* tā·râ′zä; *Span.* tā·rā′sä
**Ter′rick** tĕr′ĭk
**Ter′rot** ?tĕr′ŭt
**Ter′ry** tĕr′ĭ
**Ter′zi** *Ital.* tĕr′tsē
**Tess** tĕs
**Tet′ley** tĕt′lĭ
**Tev·fik′, Tew·fik′** *Turk.* tĕv·fēk′
**Thack′er** thăk′ẽr
**Thad·dä′us** *Ger.* tä·dâ′ōōs
**Thad′de·us, Thad′e·us** thăd′ē·ŭs, thă·dē′ŭs
**Thas′ci·us** *Lat.* thăsh′ĭ·ŭs
**Thax′ter** thăks′tẽr
**Thayer** thâr
**The′o** thē′ō; *Du.* tā′ō
**The′o·bald** thē′ô·bôld, *now rarely* tĭb′ăld; *Ger.* tā′ô·bält
**Thé′o′bald′** *Fr.* tā′ô′bȧld′
**Thé′o′de·linde′** *Fr.* tā′ô′dlăɴd′
**The′o·door** *Du.* tā′ô·dōr
**The′o·dor** thē′ô·dôr; *Dan.* tẹ′ô·dôr; *Du.* tā′ô·dôr; *Ger.* tā′ô·dōr; *Norw.* tā′ô·dôr; *Swed.* tā′ô·dôr
**Thé′o′dor′** *Fr.* tā′ô′dôr′
**The′o·dore** thē′ô·dōr
**Thé′o′dore′** *Fr.* tā′ô′dôr′
**The·od′o·ric** thē·ŏd′ô·rĭk
**Thé′o′do′ric′** *Fr.* tā′ô′dô′rēk′
**The·o′do·ros** *Mod. Grk.* thâ·ô′thô-rôs
**The′o·do′rus** *Lat.* thē′ô·dō′rŭs
**The′o·do′si·a** thē′ô·dō′shĭ·ȧ, -shȧ
**The′o·do′si·us** *Ger.* tā′ô·dō′zē·ōōs
**The·od′ric** thē·ŏd′rĭk
**Thé′o′dule′** *Fr.* tā′ô′dül′
**The′o·phil** thē′ô·fĭl; *Ger.* tā′ô·fēl
**Thé′o′phile′** *Fr.* tā′ô′fēl′
**The·oph′i·lus** thē·ŏf′ĭ·lŭs—**The·o′-phi·lus** *Dan.* tĭ·ō′fē·lōōs; *Ger.* tā·ō′fē·lōōs
**Thé′o′phraste′** *Fr.* tā′ô′frȧst′
**The′o·phra′stus** *Ger.* tā′ô·fräs′tōōs
**The·re′sa** tĕ·rē′sȧ, -zȧ
**Thé′ré′sa′** *Fr.* tā′rā′zȧ′
**The·re′se** *Ger.* tā·rā′zĕ
**Thé′rèse′** *Fr.* tā′râz′
**Ther′kel** *Dan.* tăr′kĕl
**Theu′nis** *Du.* tû′nĭs
**Thier′ry′** *Fr.* tyĕ′rē′
**Thies** *Ger.* tēs
**Tho′by** ?thō′bĭ
**Thom′as** tŏm′ăs—**Tho′mas** *Dan.*

tô′mȧs; *Du.*, *Ger.* tō′mäs; *Norw.* tŏm′mäs; *Swed.* to͞o′mȧs′—**Tho′mas′** *Fr.* tô′mä′
**Tho′ma·si′ne** *Dan.* tŏ′mȧ·sē′nĕ
**Thom′a·son** tŏm′ȧ·s′n
**Thomp′son** tŏm(p)′s′n
**Thom′son** tŏm′s′n
**Thor′burn** thôr′bẽrn
**Thōr′dar·son** *Icelandic* thōr′där·sŏn
**Thor′kild** *Dan.* to͝or′kêl
**Thorn′dike** thôrn′dīk
**Thorne** thôrn
**Thor′ney·croft** thôr′nĭ·krôft
**Thorn′hill** thôrn′hĭl
**Thorn′ton** thôrn′t′n, -tŭn
**Thorn′well** thôrn′wĕl, -wĕl
**Thor′old** thûr′ŭld
**Thor′stein** thôr′stīn
**Thor′vald** *Dan.* to͝or′vȧl
**Thor′val′dur** *Icelandic* thŏr′väl′dẽr
**Thra·sy′bou·los** *Mod. Grk.* thrä·sē′vo͞o·lôs
**Thresh′ie** thrĕsh′ĭ
**Throck** thrŏk
**Thros′by** thrŏz′bĭ
**Thu′re′** *Swed.* to͞o′rĕ′
**Thur′low** thûr′lō
**Thur′man** thûr′măn
**Thurs′ton** thûrs′tŭn
**Thy′ra** thī′rȧ; *Swed.* tü′rȧ
**Tib′bitts** tĭb′ĭts
**Ti·be′rio** *Ital.* tē·bâ′ryô
**Ti·be′ri·us** tī·bẹr′ĭ·ŭs; *Du.* tē·bā′rē·ûs
**Ti·bur′cio** *Span.* tē·bo͞or′thyō, -syō
**Tick′nor** tĭk′nẽr, -nôr
**Tier′ney** tẹr′nĭ
**Tif′fa·ny** tĭf′ȧ·nĭ
**Tift** tĭft
**Ti′kho·no′vich** *Russ.* tyē′ᴋŭ·nô′vyĭch
**Til′ford** tĭl′fẽrd
**Till** *Ger.* tĭl
**Til′ling·hast** tĭl′ĭng·hăst
**Til′loch** tĭl′ŭᴋ
**Til′man** *Ger.* tĭl′män
**Til′ston, Til′stone** tĭl′stŭn
**Ti·mo·fe′e·vich** *Russ.* tyĭ·mŭ·fyā′yĕ·vyĭch
**Ti′mo′lé′on′** *Fr.* tē′mô′lā′ôɴ′
**Ti·mo′te·o** *Ital.* tē·mô′tā·ō
**Ti′mo′thée′** *Fr.* tē′mô′tā′
**Tim′o·thy** tĭm′ô·thĭ
**Tim′son** tĭm′s′n
**Ti′na** *Ger.* tē′nä
**Tin′ney** tĭn′ĭ
**Tip′la′dy** tĭp′lā′dĭ
**Tis′dale** tĭz′dāl
**Ti′tian** tĭsh′ăn
**Ti′to** *Ital.* tē′tô
**Tits′worth** tĭts′wûrth, -wẽrth
**Tit′ta** *Ital.* tēt′tä
**Ti′tus** tī′tŭs
**Ti′tusz** *Hung.* tĭ′to͞os
**Ti′va·dar** *Hung.* tĭ′vŏ·dŏr
**Ti·zia′no** *Ital.* tē·tsyä′nô
**To·bi′as** tô·bī′ăs; *Du.*, *Ger.* tô·bē′äs; *Swed.* to͞o·bē′ȧs′
**To′bie, To′by** tō′bĭ
**Tod, Todd** tŏd
**Tod′hun′ter** tŏd′hŭn′tẽr, tŏd′ŭn·tẽr

**Toirdhealbhach** *Ir.* thûr′lȧᴋ
**Tol′bert** tŏl′bẽrt
**Tom** tŏm; *Dan.* tŏm; *Ger.* tōm
**To′ma** *Rum.* tŏ′mä
**To·más′** *Span.* tô·mäs′
**To′máš** *Czech* tô′mäsh
**To′masz** *Pol.* tô′mäsh
**To·maz′** *Port.* to͞o·mȧsh′
**Tom′kyns** tŏm′kĭnz
**Tom′lin·son** tŏm′lĭn·s′n
**Tom·ma′so** *Ital.* tôm·mä′zô
**To·mo·mi** *Jap.* tô·mô·mê
**To·mo·sa·bu·ro** *Jap.* tô·mô·sä·bo͞o·rō
**To·mo·yu·ki** *Jap.* tô·mô·yo͞o·kê
**Tomp′kins** tŏm(p)′kĭnz
**To′ny** tō′nĭ—**To′ny′** *Fr.* tô′nē′
**Top′ham** tŏp′ăm
**Top′ping** tŏp′ĭng
**Tor** *Swed.* to͞or
**Tor′bern** *Swed.* tôr′bẽrn
**Tor·cua′to** *Span.* tôr·kwä′tō
**To′re** *Norw.* tō′rĕ
**To·ri′bio** *Span.* tô·rē′byō
**Tor·qua′to** *Ital.* tôr·kwä′tô
**Tor′rey** tŏr′ĭ
**To·sa** *Jap.* tô·sä
**To·shi·mi·chi** *Jap.* tô·shê·mê·chê
**To·shi·o** *Jap.* tô·shê·ô
**Tous′saint′** *Fr.* to͞o′săɴ′
**Town′send** toun′zĕnd, *esp. Brit.* -zĕnd
**To·yo·hi·ko** *Jap.* tô·yô·hê·kô
**To·yo·to·mi** *Jap.* tô·yô·tô·mê
**Tra′cey, Tra′cy** trā′sĭ
**Traf′ford** trăf′ẽrd
**Tra·ia′no** *Ital.* trä·yä′nô
**Traill** trāl
**Trau′gott** *Ger.* trou′gôt
**Trav′ers** trăv′ẽrz
**Trav′is** trăv′ĭs
**Treat** trēt
**Tre·bo′ni·a′nus** *Lat.* trê·bō′nĭ·ā′nŭs
**Tre·law′ney** trê·lô′nĭ
**Trem′bly** trĕm′blĭ
**Tren′chard** trĕn′chẽrd, -chärd, -shẽrd, -shärd
**Tre·vel′yan** trê·vĕl′yăn, -vĭl′yăn
**Trev′or** trĕv′ẽr
**Trick** trĭk
**Trigg** trĭg
**Trim′ble** trĭm′b′l
**Tris′tan′** *Fr.* trēs′täɴ′—**Tri·stan′** *Rum.* trê·stän′
**Tris·tán′** *Span.* três·tän′
**Tris·tão′** *Port.* trêsh·touɴ′, (*Braz.*) três·touɴ′
**Tris′tram** trĭs′trăm
**Triv′ett** trĭv′ĕt, -ĭt
**Trix′ie** trĭk′sĭ
**Tro′phime′** *Fr.* trô′fēm′
**Trot′wood** trŏt′wo͝od
**Trow′bridge** trō′brĭj
**Troy** troi
**True** tro͞o
**Tru′fant** tro͞o′fănt
**Tru′man** tro͞o′măn
**Trum′bull** trŭm′bŭl
**Trus′ler** trŭs′lẽr
**Tser·claes′** *Flem.* tsẽr·klȧs′
**Tse′zar** *Russ.* tsâ′zŭr·y′
**Tsu·ne·o** *Jap.* tso͞o·nĕ·ô

**Tsu·yo·shi** *Jap.* tso͞o·yô·shê
**Tuck′er** tŭk′ẽr
**Tu′dor** tū′dẽr
**Tuf′nell** tŭf′n′l
**Tuf′ton** tŭf′tŭn
**Tufts** tŭfts
**Tu′ka·ji** *Marathi* to͞o′kä·jē
**Tul′lio** *Ital.* to͞ol′lyô
**Tul′li·us** *Lat.* tŭl′ĭ·ŭs
**Tul′ly** tŭl′ĭ
**Tu′nis** tū′nĭs
**Tun′stall** tŭn′st′l
**Tur′ber·ville** tûr′bẽr·vĭl
**Tu′re′** *Swed.* to͞o′rĕ′
**Ture′man** tūr′măn
**Tur′lough** *Ir.* tho͝or′lô
**Tur′ner** tûr′nẽr
**Tur′ney** tûr′nĭ
**Tur′pin** tûr′pĭn
**Tut′tle** tŭt′′l
**Tu′ve′** *Swed.* to͞o′vĕ′
**Twi′ning** twī′nĭng
**Ty′as** tī′ăs
**Ty′cho** *Dan.* tü′kô; *Ger.* tü′ᴋō
**Ty′ler** tī′lẽr
**Tyng** tĭng
**Ty·ran′ni·us** *Lat.* tĭ·răn′ĭ·ŭs
**Ty·rone′** tĭ·rōn′
**Tyr′whitt** tĭr′ĭt
**Ty′son** tī′s′n

**U·bal′do** *Ital.* o͞o·bäl′dô
**Ub′bo** *Du.* ûb′ō
**U′ber·ti′no** *Ital.* o͞o′bâr·tē′nô
**U·ber′to** *Ital.* o͞o·bĕr′tô
**U′go** *Ital.* o͞o′gô
**U′go·li′no** *Ital.* o͞o′gô·lē′nô
**U′h′ler** ū′lẽr
**U′lick** ū′lĭk
**U·li′ses** *Span.* o͞o·lē′sās
**U·lis′se** *Ital.* o͞o·lēs′sâ
**Ul′pi·us** *Lat.* ŭl′pĭ·ŭs
**Ul′ric** ŭl′rĭk
**Ul′rich** ŭl′rĭk; *Ger.* o͝ol′rĭᴋ—**Ul′rich′** *Fr.* ül′rēk′
**Ul′rik** *Norw.* o͝ol′rĭk; *Swed.* ŭl′rĭk
**Ul′ri′ka** *Finn.* o͝ol′rē′kȧ—**Ul·ri′ka′** *Swed.* ŭl·rē′kȧ′
**Ul·ri′ke** *Ger.* o͝ol·rē′kĕ
**U′lysse′** *Fr.* ü′lēs′
**U·lys′ses** ū·lĭs′ēz; *Ger.* o͞o·lüs′ĕs
**Um·ber′to** *Ital.* o͞om·bĕr′tô
**U′na** ū′nȧ
**und** *Ger.* o͝ont
**Un′der·wood** ŭn′dẽr·wo͝od
**Un′win** ŭn′wĭn
**Up′ham** ŭp′ăm
**Up′ton** ŭp′tŭn
**Ur′bain′** *Fr.* ür′băɴ′
**Ur·ba′no** *Ital.* o͞or·bä′nô
**Ur·ba′nus** *Ger.* o͝or·bä′no͝os
**U·ri′ah** ū·rī′ȧ
**U′ri·an** ū′rĭ·ăn
**U·ri·el′** *Port.* o͞o·ryâl′
**Ur′jö** *Finn.* o͝or′yû
**Ur′su·la** ûr′sû·lȧ; *Ital.* o͞or′so͞o·lä
**Ur′syn** *Pol.* o͞or′sĭn
**Ush′er** ŭsh′ẽr
**Us′ta′zade′** *Fr.* üs′tȧ′zȧd′
**U′stick** ū′stĭk
**U·ta·ga·wa** *Jap.* o͝o·tä·gä·wä

**Va′chel** vā′chĕl
**Vá′clav** *Czech* vä′tsläf
**Vail** vāl
**Va·lan′cy** vȧ·lăn′sĭ
**Val′de·mar** *Dan.* vȧl′dĕ·mär; *Swed.* vȧl′dĕ·mȧr
**Va′len·tin** *Ger., Yugo.* vä′lĕn·tēn—**Va′len′tin′** *Fr.* vȧ′läɴ′tăɴ′
**Va′len·tín′** *Span.* vä′lȧn·tēn′
**Va′len·ti′na** *Ital.* vä′lȧn·tē′nä
**Val′en·tine** văl′ĕn·tīn—**Va′len·ti′ne** *Ger.* vä′lĕn·tē′nĕ
**Va′len·ti′no** *Ital.* vä′lȧn·tē′nō
**Va·len·ti′no·vich** *Russ.* vŭ·lyĕn·tyē′nŭ·vyĭch
**Va′lé′rand′** *Fr.* vȧ′lā′räɴ′
**Va′lère′** *Fr.* vȧ′lâr′
**Va·le′ri** *Russ.* vŭ·lyā′ryŭ·ĭ
**Va·le′ri·a** vȧ·lēr′ĭ·ȧ
**Va·le·ri·an′** *Russ.* vŭ·lyĕ·ryĭ·ȧn′
**Va′le·ria′no** *Span.* vä′lā·ryä′nō
**Va·le·ri·a′no·vich** *Russ.* vŭ·lyĕ·ryĭ·ȧ′nŭ·vyĭch
**Va·le′ri·a′nus** *Lat.* vȧ·lēr′ĭ·ā′nŭs
**Va′lé′rie′** *Fr.* vȧ′lā′rē′
**Va·le′rio** *Ital.* vä·lâ′ryō
**Va·le′ri·us** *Lat.* vȧ·lēr′ĭ·ŭs; *Ger.* vä·lā′rē·ŏŏs
**Va′lé′ry′** *Fr.* vȧ′lā′rē′
**Val′lance** văl′ăns
**Val′py** văl′pĭ
**Van** văn
**van** văn; *Du.* vän; *Ger.* vän, fän
**Van Bu′ren** văn bū′rĕn
**Vance** vȧns
**Van·cou′ver** văn·kōō′vẽr
**Van′der·burg** văn′dẽr·bûrg
**Van′de·veer** văn′dĕ·vēr
**Van Do′ren** văn dō′rĕn
**Van·dyke′, Van Dyke** văn·dīk′
**Van·es′sa** văn·ĕs′ȧ
**Van Ness** văn nĕs′
**Van Nest** văn nĕst′
**Van·ne′var** vă·nē′vär
**Van′ni** *Ital.* vän′nē
**Van·noy′** vă·noi′
**Van Rens′se·laer** văn rĕn′sĕ·lẽr
**Van·sit′tart** văn·sĭt′ẽrt
**Van Wyck** văn wīk′
**Var′dis** vär′dĭs
**Va·ri′na** vȧ·rē′nȧ
**Var′i·us** *Lat.* vâr′ĭ·ŭs
**Var′let′** *Fr.* vȧr′lĕ′
**Var′num** vär′nŭm
**Vas′co** *Port.* vȧsh′kōō, (*Braz.*) vȧs′kōō; *Span.* väs′kō
**Va·sil′** *Bulg.* vä·sĭl′
**Va·si′le** *Rum.* vä·sē′lĕ
**Va·si′li** *Russ.* vŭ·syē′lyŭ·ĭ
**Va·sil′ie·vich** *Russ.* vŭ·syēl′yĕ·vyĭch
**Va·sil′iev·na** *Russ.* vŭ·syēl′yĕv·nŭ
**Vás′quez** *Span.* väs′kāth, -kās
**Vas′sall** văs′'l
**Va′tro·slav** *Yugo.* vä′trō·släv
**Vaughan** vôn
**Vea′zey, Vea′zie** vē′zĭ
**Veik′ko** *Finn.* vāk′kŏ
**Ven′a·ble** vĕn′ȧ·b'l
**Ven′a·bles** vĕn′ȧ·b'lz
**Ve·nan′cio** *Span.* vā·nän′thyō, -syō
**Ve·nan′ti·us** *Lat.* vē·năn′shĭ·ŭs, -shŭs
**Ve·ne·dik′to·vich** *Russ.* vyĕ·nyĕ·dyēk′tŭ·vyĭch
**Venn** vĕn
**Ven·tu′ra** *Span.* vȧn·tōō′rä
**Ve′nus·tia′no** *Span.* vā′nōōs·tyä′nō
**Ve′ra** vēr′ȧ; *Russ.* vyâ′rŭ
**Ve·ra′nus** ?vĕ·rā′nŭs
**Vere** vēr
**Ver·mil′ye** vẽr·mĭl′yĕ
**Verne** vûrn
**Ver′ner** vûr′nẽr; *Swed.* văr′nẽr
**Ver′ney** vûr′nĭ
**Ver′non** vûr′nŭn
**Ver′rall** vĕr′ôl
**Ver′ri·us** *Lat.* vĕr′ĭ·ŭs
**Ver′tu′** *Fr.* vĕr′tü′
**Ve′rus** *Lat.* vēr′ŭs
**Ve′sey** vē′zĭ
**Ves′to** vĕs′tō
**Vet′ti·us** *Lat.* vĕt′ĭ·ŭs
**Vian′na** *Port.* vyă′nȧ
**Vib′i·us** *Lat.* vĭb′ĭ·ŭs
**Vic′ars** vĭk′ẽrz
**Vic′a·ry** vĭk′ȧ·rĭ
**Vi·cen′te** *Span.* vē·thān′tā, vē·sān′-
**Vi·cen′zo** *Ital.* vē·chĕn′tsō
**Vick′i** *Ger.* vĭk′ē
**vi′comte′** *Fr.* vē′kôɴt′
**vi′com′tesse′** *Fr.* vē′kôɴ′tĕs′
**Vic′toire′** *Fr.* vēk′twȧr′
**Vic′tor** vĭk′tẽr; *Dan.* vēk′tŏr; *Ger.* vĭk′tōr—**Vic′tor′** *Fr.* vēk′tôr′—**Vic·tor′** *Ruman.* vēk·tŏr′
**Víc′tor** *Span.* vēk′tôr
**Vic·to′ri·a** vĭk·tō′rĭ·ȧ; *Swed.* vĭk·tōō′rĭ·ȧ—**Vic′to′ria′** *Fr.* vēk′tô′ryȧ′
**Vic′to·ria′no** *Span.* vēk′tō·ryä′nō
**Vic′to′rien′** *Fr.* vēk′tô′ryăɴ′
**Vic′to′rine′** *Fr.* vēk′tô′rēn′
**Vic′to·ri′no** *Span.* vēk′tō·rē′nō
**Vic′tur′nien′** *Fr.* vēk′tür′nyăɴ′
**Vi′da** vē′dȧ, vī′-
**Vid′kun** *Norw.* vĭd′kōōn
**Viets** vēts
**Vig′go** *Dan.* vēg′ō
**Vih′to·ri** *Finn.* vĭᴋ′tŏ·rĭ
**Vi·ken′ti** *Russ.* vyĭ·kyān′tyŭ·ĭ
**Vi·kent′ie·vich** *Russ.* vyĭ·kyānt′yĕ·vyĭch
**Vik′tor** *Czech* vĭk′tôr; *Ger.* vĭk′tŏr; *Russ.* vyēk′tôr; *Swed.* vĭk′tôr
**Vik′to·ro′vich** *Russ.* vyēk′tŭ·rô′vyĭch
**Vil′brun′** *Russ.* vēl′brŭɴ′
**Vil·fre′do** *Ital.* vēl·frā′dō
**Vil′helm** *Dan., Norw.* vĭl′hĕlm; *Swed.* vĭl′(h)ĕlm
**Vil′hel·mi′na** *Finn.* vĭl′hĕl·mē′nȧ
**Vil′helms** *Latvian* vĭl′hĕlms
**Vil′lads** *Dan.* vĕl′ȧs
**Vil′liers** vĭl′ẽrz, vĭl′yẽrz
**Vil′mos** *Hung.* vĭl′mōsh
**Vin′cenc** *Czech* vĭn′tsĕnts
**Vin′cent** *Eng., Norw.* vĭn′sĕnt—**Vin·cent′** *Du.* vĭn·sĕnt′—**Vin′cent′** *Fr.* văɴ′säɴ′
**Vin·cen′ti·us** *Lat.* vĭn·sĕn′shĭ·ŭs, -shŭs
**Vin′cenz** *Ger.* vĭn′tsĕnts
**Vin·cen′zo** *Ital.* vēn·chĕn′tsō
**Vin′nie** vĭn′ĭ
**Vin·ti′lă** *Rum.* vēn·tē′lȧ
**Vin′ton** vĭn′t'n, -tŭn
**Vin′zenz** *Ger.* vĭn′tsĕnts
**Vi′o·la** vī′ō·lȧ, vē·ō′lȧ, vī·ō′-, vē′ō-
**Vi′o·let** vī′ō·lĕt, -lĭt
**Vip·sa′ni·us** *Lat.* vĭp·sā′nĭ·ŭs, -sān′yŭs
**Vir′gil** vûr′jĭl
**Vir′gile′** *Fr.* vēr′zhēl′
**Vir·gin′i·a** vẽr·jĭn′ĭ·ȧ, -jĭn′yȧ—**Vir·gi′nia** *Ital.* vēr·jē′nyä
**Vir′gi′nie′** *Fr.* vēr′zhē′nē′
**Vir·gi′nio** *Ital.* vēr·jē′nyō
**Vir·gin′i·us** vẽr·jĭn′ĭ·ŭs, -jĭn′yŭs
**vis·con′de** *Port.* vēsh·kōɴn′dĕ, (*Braz.*) vēs·kōɴn′dĕ
**vis′count** vī′kount
**Vis·sa·ri·on′** *Russ.* vyĭs·sŭ·ryĭ·ôn′
**Vis·sar·ri·o′no·vich** *Russ.* vyĭs·sŭ·ryĭ·ô′nŭ·vyĭch
**Vi′tal′** *Fr.* vē′tȧl′
**Vi·tal′ie·vich** *Russ.* vyĭ·tȧl′yĕ·vyĭch
**Ví′těz·slav** *Czech* vē′tyĕs·läf
**Vi′to** *Ital.* vē′tō
**Vit·to′re** *Ital.* vēt·tō′rā
**Vit·to′ria** *Ital.* vēt·tô′ryä
**Vit·to′rio** *Ital.* vēt·tô′ryō
**Vi′tus** *Dan.* vē′tōōs
**Vi′vant′** *Fr.* vē′väɴ′
**Viv′i·an** vĭv′ĭ·ăn, vĭv′yăn
**Vi′vi·gens** *Ger.* vē′vē·gĕns
**Vlad′i·mir** vlăd′ĭ·mĭr—**Vla·di′mir** *Russ.* vlŭ·dyē′myĭr
**Vla′di·mír** *Czech* vlȧ′dyĭ·mēr
**Vla·di′mi·ro′vich** *Russ.* vlŭ·dyē′myĭ·rô′vyĭch
**Vla′di·slav** *Czech* vlȧ′dyĭ·släf—**Vla·di·slav′** *Russ.* vlŭ·dyĭ·släf′
**Vla·di·sla′vo·vich** *Russ.* vlŭ·dyĭ·slȧ′vŭ·vyĭch
**Vlas′ti·mil** *Czech* vlȧs′tyĭ·mĭl
**Vo′ji·slav** *Yugo.* voi′yē·släv
**Voj′těch** *Czech* voi′tyĕᴋ
**Vo′kos** *Mod. Grk.* vô′kôs
**Vol′cher** *Du.* vŏl′ᴋẽr
**Volck′erts·zoon** *Du.* vŏl′kẽrt·sŭn, -sôn, -sōn
**Vol′e·ro** *Lat.* vŏl′ẽr·ō
**Volk′mar** *Ger.* fôlk′mär
**Vol′ko** *Ger.* fôl′kō
**Vol′lam** vŏl′ăm
**Vol′ney** vŏl′nĭ
**Vol′rath** *Ger.* fôl′rät
**vom** fôm
**von** *Dan.* vŏn; *Finn.* fŏn; *Ger.* fôn; *Hung.* fôn; *Pol.* fôn; *Russ.* fôn; *Swed.* fôn
**Vose** vōz
**Vse′vo·lod** *Russ.* fsyâ′vŭ·lôt
**Vuk** *Yugo.* vōōk
**Vya·che·slav′** *Russ.* vyĭ·chĕ·släf′
**Vy′ell** ?vī′ĕl
**Vy′ner** vī′nẽr

**Wa′cław** *Pol.* vä′tsläf
**Wad·dell′** wŏ·dĕl′
**Wad′dy** wŏd′ĭ
**Wade** wād
**Wad′leigh** wŏd′lĭ
**Wads′worth** wŏdz′wûrth, -wẽrth
**Wa′ger** wā′jẽr
**Wag′ga·man** wăg′ȧ·măn

**Wait** wāt
**Wake′field** wāk′fēld
**Wake′ley** wāk′lĭ
**Wake′lin** wāk′lĭn
**Wake′ly** wāk′lĭ
**Wake′lyn** wāk′lĭn
**Wake′man** wāk′măn
**Wal′bridge** wôl′brĭj
**Wal′cott** wôl′kŭt
**Walde′grave** wôl′grāv
**Wal′de·mar** wôl′dĕ·mär; *Ger.*, *Norw.* väl′dĕ·mär
**Wal′do** wôl′dō, wŏl′-
**Wal′dorf** wôl′dôrf
**Wal′er·an** wŏl′ēr·ăn
**Wa·le′ry** *Pol.* vä·lĕ′rĭ
**Wales** wālz
**Wal′ford** wôl′fērd
**Wal′house** wôl′hous
**Walk′er** wôk′ēr
**Wall** wôl
**Wal′lace** wŏl′ĭs
**Wal·len′sis** wŏ·lĕn′sĭs
**Wal′ler** wŏl′ēr
**Wal′let** wŏl′ĕt, -ĭt
**Wal′lis** wŏl′ĭs
**Wal′rod** wôl′rŏd
**Walsh** wôlsh
**Walt** wôlt
**Wal′ter** wôl′tēr; *Ger.* väl′tēr
**Wal′ters** wôl′tērz
**Wal′ther′** *Fr.* vȧl′târ′—**Wal′ther** *Ger.* väl′tēr
**Wal′ton** wôl′t'n, -tŭn
**Wan′da** wŏn′dȧ; *Pol.* vän′dä
**Ward** wôrd
**Ware** wâr
**War′ing** wâr′ĭng
**Wark** wôrk
**War·mol′dus** *Du.* vär·mŏl′dûs
**Warne** wôrn
**War′ner** wôr′nēr
**War′ren** wŏr′ĕn, -ĭn
**War′ren·der** wŏr′ĕn·dēr
**War′ring·ton** wŏr′ĭng·tŭn
**War′wick** wŏr′ĭk
**Wash′burn** wŏsh′bērn, -bûrn
**Wash′ing·ton** wŏsh′ĭng·tŭn
**Was·sil′ie·vitch** *Russ.* vŭ·syēl′yĕ-vyĭch
**Was′son** wŏs′'n
**Wat** wŏt
**Wat′cyn** *Welsh* wŏt′kĭn
**Wa′ter·house** wô′tēr·hous, wŏt′ēr-
**Wa′ter·man** wô′tēr·măn, wŏt′ēr-
**Wa′ters** wô′tērz, wŏt′ērz
**Wat′kin** wŏt′kĭn
**Wat′kins** wŏt′kĭnz
**Wat′kiss** wŏt′kĭs
**Wat′son** wŏt′s'n
**Watt** wŏt
**Wat′ter·son** wŏt′ēr·s'n
**Watts** wŏts
**Waugh** wô
**Way′land** wā′lănd
**Wayne** wān
**Webb, Webbe** wĕb
**Web′ber** wĕb′ēr
**Web′ley** wĕb′lĭ
**Web′ster** wĕb′stēr
**Wed′der·burn** wĕd′ēr·bûrn
**Wed′lake** wĕd′lāk
**Weeks** wēks
**Weet′man** wēt′măn
**Weight′man** wāt′măn
**Weir** wẹr
**Wel′bore** ?wĕl′bōr
**Wel′burn** wĕl′bērn
**Wel′by** wĕl′bĭ
**Welch** wĕlch, wĕlsh
**Weld** wĕld
**Wel′don** wĕl′dŭn
**Well′born** wĕl′bērn
**Welles** wĕlz
**Welles′ley** wĕlz′lĭ
**Wel′ling·ton** wĕl′ĭng·tŭn
**Well′man** wĕl′măn
**Wells** wĕlz
**Welsh** wĕlsh
**Wel′tach** *Ger.* vĕl′täĸ
**Wemyss** wēmz
**Wen′ces·lao′** *Span.* vān′thȧs·lä′ō, vān′sȧs-
**Wen′ces·lau′** *Port.* vāɴ′sĕzh·lä′o͝o, (*Braz.*) -sĕz·lä′o͝o
**Wen′ces·laus** *Ger.* vĕn′tsĕs·lous
**Wen′del** *Ger.* vĕn′dĕl
**Wen′de·lin** *Ger.* vĕn′dĕ·lēn
**Wen′dell** wĕn′d'l
**Wend′ling** *Ger.* vĕnt′lĭng
**Went′worth** wĕnt′wûrth, -wērth
**Wen′zel** *Ger.* vĕn′tsĕl
**Wen′zes·laus** *Ger.* vĕn′tsĕs·lous
**Wer′ner** *Ger.* vĕr′nēr
**Wes′ley** wĕs′lĭ, *esp. Brit.* wĕz′-
**Wes′sels** *Du.* vĕs′ĕls
**West** wĕst
**West′brook** wĕst′bro͝ok
**Wes′tel** wĕs′tĕl
**Wes′ter** wĕs′tēr
**West′land** wĕst′lănd
**West′ley** wĕst′lĭ
**Wes′ton** wĕs′tŭn
**Weth′er·bee** wĕth′ēr·bē
**Wet′more** wĕt′mōr
**Wex′els** *Norw.* vĕk′sĕls
**Wha′len** hwā′lĕn
**Whar′ton** hwôr′t'n
**Whee′ler** hwē′lēr
**Whee′lock** hwē′lŏk
**Wheel′ton** hwēl′t'n, -tŭn
**Whet′ten** hwĕt′'n
**Whip′ple** hwĭp′'l
**Whit** hwĭt
**Whit′a·ker** hwĭt′ȧ·kēr
**Whit′bread** hwĭt′brĕd
**Whit′comb** hwĭt′kŭm
**White** hwīt
**White′field** hwīt′fēld
**White′head** hwīt′hĕd
**White′hill** hwīt′hĭl
**White′law** hwīt′lô
**Whit′field** hwĭt′fēld
**Whit′ford** hwĭt′fērd
**Whit′ing** hwīt′ĭng
**Whit′ley** hwĭt′lĭ
**Whit′man** hwĭt′măn
**Whit′ney** hwĭt′nĭ
**Whi′ton** hwī′t'n
**Whit′ten** hwĭt′'n
**Whit′ti·er** hwĭt′ĭ·ēr
**Whit′ting·ham** hwĭt′ĭng·ăm, -'n·jăm
**Whit′well** hwĭt′wĕl, -wĕl
**Wi′chard** *Ger.* vĭĸ′ärt
**Wick′ham** wĭk′ăm
**Wide′man** wīd′măn
**Wi′gand** *Ger.* vē′gänt
**Wig′gin·ton** wĭg′ĭn·tŭn
**Wig′gles·worth** wĭg′'lz·wûrth
**Wight** wīt
**Wight′man** wīt′măn
**Wil′ber** wĭl′bēr
**Wil′ber·force** wĭl′bēr·fōrs
**Wil′bert** wĭl′bērt
**Wil′bor** wĭl′bēr
**Wil′bourne** wĭl′bērn
**Wil′bur** wĭl′bēr
**Wil′cox** wĭl′kŏks
**Wil′der** wīl′dēr
**Wilds** wīldz
**Wiles** wīlz
**Wi′ley** wī′lĭ
**Wil′ford** wĭl′fērd
**Wil′fred** wĭl′frĕd, -frĭd
**Wil′frid** wĭl′frĭd—**Wil′frid′** *Fr.* wēl′frēd′
**Wil′fried** *Ger.* vĭl′frēt
**Wil′helm** *Dan.*, *Ger.*, *Norw.* vĭl′hĕlm; *Swed.* vĭl′(h)ĕlm
**Wil·hel′ma** *Ger.* vĭl·hĕl′mä
**Wil′hel·mi′na** wĭl′hĕl·mē′nȧ, wĭl′ĕ-mē′nȧ; *Du.* vĭl′hĕl·mē′nȧ; *Ger.* vĭl′-hĕl·mē′nä
**Wil′hel′mine′** *Fr.* vē′lĕl′mēn′—**Wil′-hel·mi′ne** *Ger.* vĭl′hĕl·mē′nĕ
**Wil·hel′mus** *Du.* vĭl·hĕl′mûs
**Wi′li·bald** *Ger.* vĭl′ē·bält
**Wilkes** wĭlks
**Wil′kie** wĭl′kĭ
**Wil′kins** wĭl′kĭnz
**Wil′kin·son** wĭl′kĭn·s'n
**Will** wĭl
**Wil′la** wĭl′ȧ
**Wil′lans** wĭl′ănz
**Wil′lard** wĭl′ērd
**Will′cox** wĭl′kŏks
**Wil′le·brord** *Du.* vĭl′ĕ·brôrt
**Wil′lem** *Du.* vĭl′ĕm
**Wil′let** wĭl′ĕt
**Wil′ley** wĭl′ĭ
**Wil′li** *Ger.* vĭl′ē
**Wil′liam** wĭl′yăm—**Wil′liam′** *Fr.* wēl′yȧm′
**Wil′liams** wĭl′yămz
**Wil′liam·son** wĭl′yăm·s'n
**Wil′li·bald** *Ger.* vĭl′ē·bält
**Wil′lie** wĭl′ĭ
**Wil′lis** wĭl′ĭs
**Wil′lis·ton** wĭl′ĭs·tŭn
**Wil′lock** wĭl′ŭk
**Wil′lough·by** wĭl′ō·bĭ
**Wills** wĭlz
**Will′sie** wĭl′sĭ
**Will′son** wĭl′s'n
**Wil′ly** wĭl′ĭ; *Ger.* vĭl′ē
**Wil′marth** wĭl′märth
**Wil′mer** wĭl′mēr
**Wil′mot** wĭl′mŏt
**Wil′shere** wĭl′shēr, -shẹr
**Wil′son** wĭl′s'n
**Wilt′ber′ger** wĭlt′bûr′gēr
**Wil′ton** wĭl′t'n, -tŭn
**Wilts** wĭlts

**Win·cen′ty** *Pol.* vēn·tsĕn′tĭ
**Win′chell** wĭn′chĕl
**Win′ches′ter** wĭn′chĕs′tẽr, -chĭs·tẽr
**Winck′worth** wĭngk′wûrth, -wẽrth
**Wind′ham** wĭn′dăm
**Wind′sor** wĭn′zẽr
**Win′field** wĭn′fēld
**Win′ford** wĭn′fẽrd
**Win′fred** wĭn′frĕd, -frĭd
**Wing** wĭng
**Win′gate** wĭn′gāt, -gĭt
**Win′i·fred** wĭn′ĭ·frĕd, -frĭd
**Wink′worth** wĭngk′wûrth, -wẽrth
**Win′ni·fred** wĭn′ĭ·frĕd, -frĭd
**Win′ning·ton** wĭn′ĭng·tŭn
**Wi·no′na** wĭ·nō′nȧ
**Wins′low** wĭnz′lō
**Win′ston** wĭn′stŭn
**Win′ter** wĭn′tẽr
**Win′throp** wĭn′thrŭp
**Wirt** wûrt
**Wise** wīz
**Wis′tar, Wis′ter** wĭs′tẽr
**With′er·ell** wĭth′ẽr·ĕl
**With′er·le** wĭth′ẽr·lē
**With′ers** wĭth′ẽrz
**Wit′lam** wĭt′lăm
**Wit′mer** wĭt′mẽr
**Wit′ter** wĭt′ẽr
**Wix′om** wĭk′sŭm
**Wla·di′mir** *Ger.* vlä·dē′mĭr
**Wła·dy′sław** *Pol.* vlä·dĭ′släf
**Wło·dzi′mierz** *Pol.* vlô·jē′myĕsh
**Wode′house** wŏŏd′hous
**Woj′ciech** *Pol.* voi′chĕĸ
**Wol′cott** wŏŏl′kŭt
**Wol′de·mar** *Finn.* wŏl′dĕ·mȧr; *Ger.* vôl′dĕ·mär
**Wolf, Wolfe, Wolff** wŏŏlf
**Wolf′gang** *Ger.* vôlf′gäng
**Wolf·gang′us** *Ger.* vôlf·gäng′ōōs
**Wol′las·ton** wŏŏl′ăs·tŭn
**Woll′stone·craft** wŏŏl′stŭn·krȧft
**Wol′sey** wŏŏl′zĭ
**Wood** wŏŏd
**Wood′bine** wŏŏd′bīn
**Wood′bridge** wŏŏd′brĭj
**Wood′burn** wŏŏd′bẽrn
**Wood′bur′y** wŏŏd′bĕr′ĭ, -bẽr·ĭ
**Woodd** wŏŏd
**Woodes** wŏŏdz
**Wood′field** wŏŏd′fēld
**Wood′fin** wŏŏd′fĭn
**Wood′hill** wŏŏd′hĭl
**Wood′ley** wŏŏd′lĭ
**Wood′row** wŏŏd′rō
**Wood′ruff** wŏŏd′rŭf
**Woods** wŏŏdz
**Wood′son** wŏŏd′s′n
**Wood′ville** wŏŏd′vĭl
**Wood′ward** wŏŏd′wẽrd, wŏŏd′ẽrd

**Wood′worth** wŏŏd′wûrth, -wẽrth
**Woolf** wŏŏlf
**Wooll′gar** ?wŏŏl′gär
**Wool′sey** wŏŏl′zĭ
**Wool′ston** wŏŏl′stŭn
**Worces′ter** wŏŏs′tẽr
**Words′worth** wûrdz′wûrth, -wẽrth
**Work** wûrk
**Wor′rall** wŏr′ăl
**Worth** wûrth
**Wor′thing·ton** wûr′thĭng·tŭn
**Wort′ley** wûrt′lĭ
**Wou′ter** *Du.* vou′tẽr
**Wright** rīt
**Wrig′ley** rĭg′lĭ
**Wriothes′ley** rĭz′lĭ, rŏts′lĭ
**Wy′att** wī′ăt
**Wyc′liffe** wĭk′lĭf
**Wyke** ?wĭk
**Wyke′ham** wĭk′ăm
**Wy′lie** wī′lĭ
**Wyl′lis** wĭl′ĭs
**Wy′ly** wī′lĭ
**Wy′man** wī′măn
**Wy′mark** ?wī′märk
**Wym′ber·ley** wĭm′bẽr·lĭ
**Wynd′ham** wĭn′dăm
**Wynd′low** wĭnd′lō
**Wyn′kyn** wĭng′kĭn
**Wynne** wĭn
**Wys′tan** wĭs′tăn
**Wythe** wĭth

**Xan′thus** zăn′thŭs
**Xa′ver** *Ger.* ksä′vẽr, ksä·vär′
**Xa′vi·er** zā′vĭ·ẽr, zăv′ĭ- —**Xa′vier′** *Fr.* gzȧ′vyā′—**Xa·vier′** *Port.* shȧ·vyār′; *Span.* hä·vyĕr′

**y** *Span.* ē
**Ya′kov** *Russ.* yȧ′kŭf
**Ya′kov·le·vich** *Russ.* yȧ′kŭv·lyĕ·vyĭch
**Yá′ñez** *Span.* yä′nyāth, -nyās
**Ya·no·su·ke** *Jap.* yä·nō·sōō·kĕ
**Yard′ley** yärd′lĭ
**Ya·su·hi·to** *Jap.* yä·sōō·hē·tō
**Ya·su·ka·ta** *Jap.* yä·sōō·kä·tä
**Ya·su·ma·sa** *Jap.* yä·sōō·mä·sä
**Ya·su·ya** *Jap.* yä·sōō·yä
**Ya·ta·ro** *Jap.* yä·tä·rō
**Yates, Yeates** yāts
**Yel′ver·ton** yĕl′vẽr·t′n, -tŭn
**Yo·i·tsu** *Jap.* yō·ē·tsōō
**Yo′lande′** *Fr.* yô′läɴd′
**Yo·ne** *Jap.* yō·nĕ
**Yonge** yŭng
**York, Yorke** yôrk
**Yo·sa** *Jap.* yō·sä
**Yo·shi·mi·chi** *Jap.* yō·shē·mē·chē
**Yo·shi·no·ri** *Jap.* yō·shē·nō·rē

**Yo·shi·su·ke** *Jap.* yō·shē·sōō·kĕ
**Yo·su·ke** *Jap.* yō·sōō·kĕ
**Young** yŭng
**Youngs** yŭngz
**Y·si′dro** ?ĭ·sē′drō
**Yu′do·vich** *Russ.* yōō′dŭ·vyĭch
**Yu·ki·chi** *Jap.* yōō·kē·chē
**Yu·ko** *Jap.* yōō·kō
**Yu′li** *Russ.* yōō′lyû·ĭ
**Yul′ie·vich** *Russ.* yōōl′yĕ·vyĭch
**Yu′ri** *Russ.* yōō′ryû·ĭ
**Yur′ie·vich** *Russ.* yōōr′yĕ·vyĭch
**Yu′suf** *Arab.* yōō′sōōf
**Yves** *Fr.* ēv
**Y′vette′** *Fr.* ē′vĕt′
**Y′von′** *Fr.* ē′vôɴ′
**Y′vonne′** *Fr.* ē′vôn′

**Zá′boj** *Czech* zä′boi
**Zach′a·ri′ah** zăk′ȧ·rī′ȧ
**Za′cha·ri′as** *Du.* zȧ′ĸȧ·rē′äs; *Ger.* tsä′ĸä·rē′äs
**Zach′a·ry** zăk′ȧ·rĭ
**Zach′ris** *Swed.* sȧk′rĭs
**Za·de′** *Turk.* zä·dĕ′
**Za′dock** zā′dŏk
**Zane** zān
**Zden′ko** *Czech* zdĕng′kô
**Zeal′ous** zĕl′ŭs
**Zeb′u·lon** zĕb′ū·lŭn
**Zech′a·ri′ah** zĕk′ȧ·rī′ȧ
**Zel′ia** zēl′yȧ, zē′lĭ·ȧ
**Zé′lide′** *Fr.* zā′lēd′
**Zen·go** *Jap.* zĕn·gō
**Ze′nith** zē′nĭth
**Zé′nobe′** *Fr.* zā′nôb′
**Ze·no′bio** *Ital.* dzā·nô′byō
**Ze′non** *Pol.* zĕ′nôn
**Ze·nón′** *Span.* thā·nôn′, sā-
**Ze′nus** zē′nŭs
**Zeph′a·ni′ah** zĕf′ȧ·nī′ȧ
**Ze·shin** *Jap.* zĕ·shēn
**Zig′frids** *Latvian* zĭg′frĭdz
**Zi·na·i′da** *Russ.* zyĭ·nŭ·ē′dŭ
**Zi·no′vi** *Russ.* zyĭ·nô′vyû·ĭ
**Ži′vo′jin** *Yugo.* zhē′vō′yēn
**Zo′é′** *Fr.* zô′ā′
**Zo′ë** zō′ē
**Zo′fia, Zo′fja** *Pol.* zô′fyä
**Zoi′la** *Span.* thoi′lä, soi′-
**Zol′tán** *Hung.* zôl′tän
**Zo′na** zō′nȧ
**Zo′ra** zō′rȧ
**Zo′si·mo** *Ital.* dzô′zē·mō
**Zsig′mond** *Hung.* zhĭg′mōnd
**Zsolt** *Hung.* zhōlt
**zu** *Ger.* tsōō
**zum** *Ger.* tsŏŏm, tsōōm
**zur** *Ger.* tsōōr, tsōōr
**Zwier** *Du.* zvēr
**Zyg′munt** *Pol.* zĭg′mōōnt

## United States



## World

# Presidents of the United States of America

| NO. | NAME AND LIFE DATES | BIRTHPLACE | TERM | VOCATION | POLITICS | RESIDENCE WHEN ELECTED | WIFE'S NAME AND MARRIAGE YEAR |
|---|---|---|---|---|---|---|---|
| 1 | George Washington, 1732–1799 | Westmoreland Co., Va. | 1789–1797 | Planter | Federalist | Va. | Mrs. Martha D. Custis 1759 |
| 2 | John Adams, 1735–1826 | Quincy, Mass.[1] | 1797–1801 | Lawyer | Federalist | Mass. | Abigail Smith 1764 |
| 3 | Thomas Jefferson, 1743–1826 | Shadwell, Va.[2] | 1801–1809 | Lawyer | Dem.-Rep.[13] | Va. | Mrs. Martha W. Skelton 1772 |
| 4 | James Madison, 1751–1836 | Port Conway, Va.[3] | 1809–1817 | Lawyer | Dem.-Rep.[13] | Va. | Mrs. Dorothea (Dolley) P. Todd 1794 |
| 5 | James Monroe, 1758–1831 | Westmoreland Co., Va. | 1817–1825 | Statesman | Dem.-Rep.[13] | Va. | Eliza Kortright 1786 |
| 6 | John Quincy Adams, 1767–1848 | Quincy, Mass.[1] | 1825–1829 | Lawyer | Dem.-Rep.[13] | Mass. | Louisa C. Johnson 1797 |
| 7 | Andrew Jackson, 1767–1845 | Waxhaw settlement, S. C.[4] | 1829–1837 | Lawyer | Democrat | Tenn. | Mrs. Rachel D. Robards 1791, 1794[16] |
| 8 | Martin Van Buren, 1782–1862 | Kinderhood, N. Y.[5] | 1837–1841 | Lawyer | Democrat | N.Y. | Hannah Hoes 1807 |
| 9 | William Henry Harrison, 1773–1841 | Charles City Co., Va. | 1841 | Soldier | Whig | Ohio | Anna Symmes 1795 |
| 10 | John Tyler, 1790–1862 | Charles City Co., Va. | 1841–1845 | Lawyer | Democrat[14] | Va. | (1) Letitia Christian 1813<br>(2) Julia Gardiner 1844 |
| 11 | James Knox Polk, 1795–1849 | Mecklenburg Co., N. C. | 1845–1849 | Lawyer | Democrat | Tenn. | Sarah Childress 1824 |
| 12 | Zachary Taylor, 1784–1850 | Orange Co., Va. | 1849–1850 | Soldier | Whig | La. | Margaret Smith 1810 |
| 13 | Millard Fillmore, 1800–1874 | Locke, Cayuga Co., N. Y.[6] | 1850–1853 | Lawyer | Whig | N.Y. | (1) Abigail Powers 1826<br>(2) Mrs. Caroline C. McIntosh 1858 |
| 14 | Franklin Pierce, 1804–1869 | Hillsboro, N. H. | 1853–1857 | Lawyer | Democrat | N.H. | Jane Means Appleton 1834 |
| 15 | James Buchanan, 1791–1868 | Near Mercersburg, Pa. | 1857–1861 | Lawyer | Democrat | Pa. | Unmarried |
| 16 | Abraham Lincoln, 1809–1865 | Near Hodgenville, Ky.[7] | 1861–1865 | Lawyer | Republican | Ill. | Mary Todd 1842 |
| 17 | Andrew Johnson, 1808–1875 | Raleigh, N. C. | 1865–1869 | Statesman | Democrat[15] | Tenn. | Eliza McCardle 1827 |
| 18 | Ulysses Simpson Grant, 1822–1885 | Point Pleasant, Ohio[8] | 1869–1877 | Soldier | Republican | D.C. | Julia Dent 1848 |
| 19 | Rutherford Birchard Hayes, 1822–1893 | Delaware, Ohio | 1877–1881 | Lawyer | Republican | Ohio | Lucy Ware Webb 1852 |
| 20 | James Abram Garfield, 1831–1881 | Orange, Ohio[9] | 1881 | Lawyer | Republican | Ohio | Lucretia Rudolph 1858 |
| 21 | Chester Alan Arthur, 1829–1886 | Fairfield, Vt. | 1881–1885 | Lawyer | Republican | N.Y. | Ellen Lewis Herndon 1859 |
| 22 | Grover Cleveland, 1837–1908 | Caldwell, N. J. | 1885–1889 | Lawyer | Democrat | N.Y. | Frances Folsom 1886 |
| 23 | Benjamin Harrison, 1833–1901 | North Bend, Ohio[10] | 1889–1893 | Lawyer | Republican | Ind. | (1) Caroline Lavinia Scott 1853<br>(2) Mrs. Mary Scott Dimmick 1896 |
| 24 | Grover Cleveland, 1837–1908 | Caldwell, N. J. | 1893–1897 | Lawyer | Democrat | N.Y. | (see above) |
| 25 | William McKinley, 1843–1901 | Niles, Ohio | 1897–1901 | Lawyer | Republican | Ohio | Ida Saxton 1871 |
| 26 | Theodore Roosevelt, 1858–1919 | New York City, N. Y. | 1901–1909 | Statesman | Republican | N.Y. | (1) Alice H. Lee 1880<br>(2) Edith K. Carow 1886 |
| 27 | William Howard Taft, 1857–1930 | Cincinnati, Ohio | 1909–1913 | Lawyer | Republican | Ohio | Helen Herron 1886 |
| 28 | Woodrow Wilson, 1856–1924 | Staunton, Va. | 1913–1921 | Educator | Democrat | N.J. | (1) Ellen Louise Axson 1885<br>(2) Mrs. Edith Bolling Galt 1915 |
| 29 | Warren Gamaliel Harding, 1865–1923 | Corsica, Ohio | 1921–1923 | Editor | Republican | Ohio | Mrs. Florence Kling De Wolfe 1891 |
| 30 | Calvin Coolidge, 1872–1933 | Plymouth, Vt.[11] | 1923–1929 | Lawyer | Republican | Mass. | Grace A. Goodhue 1905 |
| 31 | Herbert Clark Hoover, 1874–1964 | West Branch, Iowa[12] | 1929–1933 | Engineer | Republican | Calif. | Lou Henry 1899 |
| 32 | Franklin Delano Roosevelt, 1882–1945 | Hyde Park, N. Y. | 1933–1945 | Lawyer | Democrat | N.Y. | Anna Eleanor Roosevelt 1905 |
| 33 | Harry S Truman, 1884–1972 | Lamar, Mo. | 1945–1953 | Lawyer | Democrat | Mo. | Elizabeth Virginia Wallace 1919 |
| 34 | Dwight David Eisenhower, 1890–1969 | Denison, Tex. | 1953–1961 | Soldier | Republican | N.Y. | Mamie Geneva Doud 1916 |
| 35 | John Fitzgerald Kennedy, 1917–1963 | Brookline, Mass. | 1961–1963 | Statesman | Democrat | Mass. | Jacqueline Lee Bouvier 1953 |
| 36 | Lyndon Baines Johnson, 1908–1973 | Stonewall, Texas | 1963–1969 | Statesman | Democrat | Texas | Claudia Alta Taylor 1934 |
| 37 | Richard Milhous Nixon, 1913– | Yorba Linda, Calif. | 1969–1974 | Lawyer | Republican | N.Y. | Patricia Ryan 1940 |
| 38 | Gerald Rudolph Ford, 1913– | Omaha, Nebr. | 1974–1977 | Lawyer | Republican | Mich. | Mrs. Elizabeth Bloomer Warren 1948 |
| 39 | Jimmy Carter, 1924– | Plains, Ga. | 1977– | Farmer | Democrat | Ga. | Rosalyn Smith 1946 |

[1] Formerly a part of Braintree.
[2] Four miles east of Charlottesville.
[3] About 18 miles southeast of Fredericksburg, on the Rappahannock.
[4] Now in Lancaster County, 12 miles southeast of Rock Hill.
[5] About 11 miles northeast of Hudson.
[6] Now Summerhill.
[7] Then in Hardin County, now in Larue County.
[8] About 22 miles southeast of Cincinnati, on the Ohio.
[9] About 10 miles southeast of Cleveland.
[10] About 16 miles west of Cincinnati on the Ohio.
[11] About 14 miles southeast of Rutland.
[12] About 10 miles east of Iowa City.
[13] The Democratic-Republican party.
[14] Elected Vice-president as a Whig, but on succeeding to the presidency acted with the Democratic party.
[15] He was a pro-Union Democrat nominated and elected with Lincoln.
[16] Because a legal divorce was not in effect in 1791, a second marriage ceremony was performed in 1794.

| NAME | TERM | POLITICS | RESIDENCE |
|---|---|---|---|
| John Adams[1,2] | 1789–1797 | Fed. | Mass. |
| Thomas Jefferson[1] | 1797–1801 | D.-R.[7] | Va. |
| Aaron Burr | 1801–1805 | D.-R.[7] | N.Y. |
| George Clinton[2,3] | 1805–1812 | D.-R.[7] | N.Y. |
| Elbridge Gerry[3] | 1813–1814 | D.-R.[7] | Mass. |
| Daniel D. Tompkins[2] | 1817–1825 | D.-R.[7] | N.Y. |
| John C. Calhoun[2,4] | 1825–1829 | D.-R.[7] | S.C. |
| John C. Calhoun[4] | 1829–1832 | Dem. | S.C. |
| Martin Van Buren[1] | 1833–1837 | Dem. | N.Y. |
| Richard M. Johnson | 1837–1841 | Dem. | Ky. |
| John Tyler[5] | 1841 | Whig | Va. |
| George M. Dallas | 1845–1849 | Dem. | Pa. |
| Millard Fillmore[5] | 1849–1850 | Whig | N.Y. |
| William R. King[3,6] | 1853 | Dem. | Ala. |
| John C. Breckinridge | 1857–1861 | Dem. | Ky. |
| Hannibal Hamlin | 1861–1865 | Rep. | Me. |
| Andrew Johnson[5] | 1865 | Rep. | Tenn. |
| Schuyler Colfax | 1869–1873 | Rep. | Ind. |
| Henry Wilson[3] | 1873–1875 | Rep. | Mass. |
| William A. Wheeler | 1877–1881 | Rep. | N.Y. |
| Chester A. Arthur[5] | 1881 | Rep. | N.Y. |
| Thomas A. Hendricks[3] | 1885 | Dem. | Ind. |
| Levi P. Morton | 1889–1893 | Rep. | N.Y. |
| Adlai E. Stevenson | 1893–1897 | Dem. | Ill. |
| Garrett A. Hobart[2] | 1897–1899 | Rep. | N.J. |
| Theodore Roosevelt[5,1] | 1901 | Rep. | N.Y. |
| Charles W. Fairbanks | 1905–1909 | Rep. | Ind. |
| James S. Sherman[3] | 1909–1912 | Rep. | N.Y. |
| Thomas R. Marshall[2] | 1913–1921 | Dem. | Ind. |
| Calvin Coolidge[5,1] | 1921–1923 | Rep. | Mass. |
| Charles G. Dawes | 1925–1929 | Rep. | Ill. |
| Charles Curtis | 1929–1933 | Rep. | Kans. |
| John N. Garner[2] | 1933–1941 | Dem. | Tex. |
| Henry A. Wallace | 1941–1945 | Dem. | Iowa |
| Harry S Truman[5,1] | 1945 | Dem. | Mo. |
| Alben W. Barkley | 1949–1953 | Dem. | Ky. |
| Richard M. Nixon[2,1] | 1953–1961 | Rep. | Calif. |
| Lyndon B. Johnson[5,1] | 1961–1963 | Dem. | Tex. |
| Hubert H. Humphrey | 1965–1969 | Dem. | So. Dak. |
| Spiro T. Agnew[8] | 1969–1973 | Rep. | Md. |
| Gerald R. Ford[9] | 1973–1974 | Rep. | Mich. |
| Nelson A. Rockefeller[10] | 1974–1977 | Rep. | N.Y. |
| Walter F. Mondale | 1977– | Dem. | Minn. |

[1] Later elected president.
[2] Elected vice-president for two terms.
[3] Died in office.
[4] Calhoun elected in 1824 as a Democratic-Republican with John Quincy Adams; in 1828 as a Democrat with Andrew Jackson; resigned in 1832, having been elected senator.
[5] Succeeded to the presidency on the death of the president.
[6] Took the oath of office but never served as vice-president.
[7] The Democratic-Republican party.
[8] Resigned Oct. 10, 1973.
[9] Appointed to the vice-presidency; succeeded to the presidency on the resignation of Richard M. Nixon.
[10] Appointed to the vice-presidency, and confirmed by the Senate Dec. 19, 1974.

## JUSTICES OF THE UNITED STATES SUPREME COURT

| NAME | TERM | YEARS OF SERVICE | RESIDENCE |
|---|---|---|---|
| CHIEF JUSTICES | | | |
| John Jay | 1789–1795 | 6 | N.Y. |
| John Rutledge[1] | 1795 | — | S.C. |
| Oliver Ellsworth | 1796–1799 | 4 | Conn. |
| John Marshall | 1801–1835 | 34 | Va. |
| Roger B. Taney | 1836–1864 | 28 | Md. |
| Salmon P. Chase | 1864–1873 | 9 | Ohio |
| Morrison R. Waite | 1874–1888 | 14 | Ohio |
| Melville W. Fuller | 1888–1910 | 22 | Ill. |
| Edward D. White | 1910–1921 | 11 | La. |
| William H. Taft | 1921–1930 | 9 | Conn. |
| Charles E. Hughes | 1930–1941 | 11 | N.Y. |
| Harlan F. Stone | 1941–1946 | 5 | N.Y. |
| Frederick M. Vinson | 1946–1953 | 7 | Ky. |
| Earl Warren | 1953–1969 | 16 | Calif. |
| Warren E. Burger | 1969– | | Minn. |
| ASSOCIATE JUSTICES | | | |
| John Rutledge | 1789–1791 | 2 | S.C. |
| William Cushing | 1789–1810 | 21 | Mass. |
| James Wilson | 1789–1798 | 9 | Pa. |
| John Blair | 1789–1796 | 7 | Va. |
| James Iredell | 1790–1799 | 9 | N.C. |
| Thomas Johnson | 1791–1793 | 2 | Md. |
| William Paterson | 1793–1806 | 13 | N.J. |
| Samuel Chase | 1796–1811 | 15 | Md. |
| Bushrod Washington | 1798–1829 | 31 | Va. |
| Alfred Moore | 1799–1804 | 5 | N.C. |
| William Johnson | 1804–1834 | 30 | S.C. |
| Henry B. Livingston | 1806–1823 | 17 | N.Y. |
| Thomas Todd | 1807–1826 | 19 | Ky. |
| Joseph Story | 1811–1845 | 34 | Mass. |
| Gabriel Duval | 1811–1836 | 25 | Md. |
| Smith Thompson | 1823–1843 | 20 | N.Y. |
| Robert Trimble | 1826–1828 | 2 | Ky. |
| John McLean | 1829–1861 | 32 | Ohio |
| Henry Baldwin | 1830–1844 | 14 | Pa. |
| James M. Wayne | 1835–1867 | 32 | Ga. |
| Philip P. Barbour | 1836–1841 | 5 | Va. |
| John Catron | 1837–1865 | 28 | Tenn. |
| John McKinley | 1837–1852 | 15 | Ala. |
| Peter V. Daniel | 1841–1860 | 19 | Va. |
| Samuel Nelson | 1845–1872 | 27 | N.Y. |
| Levi Woodbury | 1845–1851 | 6 | N.H. |
| Robert C. Grier | 1846–1870 | 23 | Pa. |
| Benjamin R. Curtis | 1851–1857 | 6 | Mass. |
| John A. Campbell | 1853–1861 | 8 | Ala. |
| Nathan Clifford | 1858–1881 | 23 | Me. |
| Noah H. Swayne | 1862–1881 | 19 | Ohio |
| Samuel F. Miller | 1862–1890 | 28 | Iowa |
| David Davis | 1862–1877 | 15 | Ill. |
| Stephen J. Field | 1863–1897 | 34 | Calif. |
| William Strong | 1870–1880 | 10 | Pa. |
| Joseph P. Bradley | 1870–1892 | 22 | N.J. |
| Ward Hunt | 1873–1882 | 9 | N.Y. |
| John M. Harlan | 1877–1911 | 34 | Ky. |
| William B. Woods | 1880–1887 | 7 | Ga. |
| Stanley Matthews | 1881–1889 | 8 | Ohio |
| Horace Gray | 1882–1902 | 20 | Mass. |
| Samuel Blatchford | 1882–1893 | 11 | N.Y. |
| Lucius Q. C. Lamar | 1888–1893 | 5 | Miss. |
| David J. Brewer | 1889–1910 | 21 | Kans. |
| Henry B. Brown | 1890–1906 | 16 | Mich. |
| George Shiras | 1892–1903 | 11 | Pa. |
| Howell E. Jackson | 1893–1895 | 2 | Tenn. |
| Edward D. White | 1894–1910 | 16 | La. |
| Rufus W. Peckham | 1896–1909 | 13 | N.Y. |
| Joseph McKenna | 1898–1925 | 27 | Calif. |
| Oliver W. Holmes | 1902–1932 | 30 | Mass. |
| William R. Day | 1903–1922 | 19 | Ohio |
| William H. Moody | 1906–1910 | 4 | Mass. |
| Horace H. Lurton | 1910–1914 | 5 | Tenn. |
| Charles E. Hughes | 1910–1916 | 6 | N.Y. |
| Willis Van Devanter | 1910–1937 | 27 | Wyo. |
| Joseph R. Lamar | 1911–1916 | 5 | Ga. |
| Mahlon Pitney | 1912–1922 | 11 | N.J. |
| James C. McReynolds | 1914–1941 | 26 | Tenn. |
| Louis D. Brandeis | 1916–1939 | 23 | Mass. |
| John H. Clarke | 1916–1922 | 6 | Ohio |
| George Sutherland | 1922–1938 | 16 | Utah |
| Pierce Butler | 1923–1939 | 17 | Minn. |
| Edward T. Sanford | 1923–1930 | 7 | Tenn. |
| Harlan F. Stone | 1925–1941 | 16 | N.Y. |
| Owen J. Roberts | 1930–1945 | 15 | Pa. |
| Benjamin N. Cardozo | 1932–1938 | 6 | N.Y. |
| Hugo L. Black | 1937–1971 | 34 | Ala. |
| Stanley F. Reed | 1938–1957 | 19 | Ky. |
| Felix Frankfurter | 1939–1962 | 23 | Mass. |
| William O. Douglas | 1939–1975 | 36 | Conn. |
| Frank Murphy | 1940–1949 | 9 | Mich. |
| Robert H. Jackson | 1941–1954 | 13 | N.Y. |
| James F. Byrnes | 1941–1942 | 1 | S.C. |
| Wiley B. Rutledge | 1943–1949 | 6 | Iowa |
| Harold H. Burton | 1945–1958 | 13 | Ohio |
| Tom C. Clark | 1949–1967 | 18 | Texas |
| Sherman Minton | 1949–1956 | 7 | Ind. |
| John Marshall Harlan | 1955–1971 | 16 | N.Y. |
| William J. Brennan, Jr. | 1956– | — | N.J. |
| Charles E. Whittaker | 1957–1962 | 5 | Mo. |
| Potter Stewart | 1958– | — | Ohio |
| Byron R. White | 1962– | — | Colo. |
| Arthur J. Goldberg | 1962–1965 | 3 | Ill. |
| Abe Fortas | 1965–1969 | 4 | Tenn. |
| Thurgood Marshall | 1967– | — | N.Y. |
| Harry A. Blackmun | 1970– | — | Minn. |
| Lewis F. Powell, Jr. | 1972– | — | Va. |
| William H. Rehnquist | 1972– | — | Ariz. |
| John Paul Stevens | 1975– | — | Ill. |

[1] Appointed chief justice (1795) but the U.S. Senate did not confirm. Meanwhile he had held one term of the Supreme Court.

| NAME | TERM | RESIDENCE |
|---|---|---|
| Frederick A. C. Muhlenberg | 1789–1791 | Pa. |
| Jonathan Trumbull | 1791–1793 | Conn. |
| Frederick A. C. Muhlenberg | 1793–1795 | Pa. |
| Jonathan Dayton | 1795–1799 | N.J. |
| Theodore Sedgwick | 1799–1801 | Mass. |
| Nathaniel Macon | 1801–1807 | N.C. |
| Joseph B. Varnum | 1807–1811 | Mass. |
| Henry Clay | 1811–1814 | Ky. |
| Langdon Cheves | 1814–1815 | S.C. |
| Henry Clay | 1815–1820 | Ky. |
| John W. Taylor | 1820–1821 | N.Y. |
| Philip P. Barbour | 1821–1823 | Va. |
| Henry Clay | 1823–1825 | Ky. |
| John W. Taylor | 1825–1827 | N.Y. |
| Andrew Stevenson | 1827–1834 | Va. |
| John Bell | 1834–1835 | Tenn. |
| James K. Polk | 1835–1839 | Tenn. |
| Robert M. T. Hunter | 1839–1841 | Va. |
| John White | 1841–1843 | Ky. |
| John W. Jones | 1843–1845 | Va. |
| John W. Davis | 1845–1847 | Ind. |
| Robert C. Winthrop | 1847–1849 | Mass. |
| Howell Cobb | 1849–1851 | Ga. |
| Linn (or Lynn) Boyd | 1851–1855 | Ky. |
| Nathaniel P. Banks | 1856–1857 | Mass. |
| James L. Orr | 1857–1859 | S.C. |
| William Pennington | 1860–1861 | N.J. |
| Galusha A. Grow | 1861–1863 | Pa. |
| Schuyler Colfax | 1863–1869 | Ind. |
| James G. Blaine | 1869–1875 | Me. |
| Michael C. Kerr | 1875–1876 | Ind. |
| Samuel J. Randall | 1876–1881 | Pa. |
| Joseph W. Keifer | 1881–1883 | Ohio |
| John G. Carlisle | 1883–1889 | Ky. |
| Thomas B. Reed | 1889–1891 | Me. |
| Charles F. Crisp | 1891–1895 | Ga. |
| Thomas B. Reed | 1895–1899 | Me. |
| David B. Henderson | 1899–1903 | Iowa |
| Joseph G. Cannon | 1903–1911 | Ill. |
| Champ Clark | 1911–1919 | Mo. |
| Frederick H. Gillett | 1919–1925 | Mass. |
| Nicholas Longworth | 1925–1931 | Ohio |
| John N. Garner | 1931–1933 | Tex. |
| Henry T. Rainey | 1933–1934 | Ill. |
| Joseph W. Byrns | 1935–1936 | Tenn. |
| William B. Bankhead | 1936–1940 | Ala. |
| Sam Rayburn | 1940–1946 | Tex. |
| Joseph W. Martin | 1947–1949 | Mass. |
| Sam Rayburn | 1949–1953 | Tex. |
| Joseph W. Martin | 1953–1955 | Mass. |
| Sam Rayburn | 1955–1961 | Tex. |
| John W. McCormack | 1962–1971 | Mass. |
| Carl B. Albert | 1971–1976 | Okla. |
| Thomas P. O'Neill, Jr. | 1976– | Mass. |

# UNITED STATES CABINET OFFICERS

(Ad interim appointees are generally omitted)

## SECRETARIES OF STATE

| NAME | PRESIDENT | DATE | RES. |
|---|---|---|---|
| John Jay | Washington | [1] | N.Y. |
| Thomas Jefferson | Washington | 1790 | Va. |
| Edmund Randolph | Washington | 1794 | Va. |
| Timothy Pickering | Washington | 1795 | Pa. |
| Timothy Pickering | J. Adams | 1797 | Pa. |
| John Marshall | J. Adams | 1800 | Va. |
| James Madison | Jefferson | 1801 | Va. |
| Robert Smith | Madison | 1809 | Md. |
| James Monroe | Madison | 1811 | Va. |
| Richard Rush | Monroe | 1817 | Pa. |
| John Quincy Adams | Monroe | 1817 | Mass. |
| Henry Clay | J. Q. Adams | 1825 | Ky. |
| Martin Van Buren | Jackson | 1829 | N.Y. |
| Edward Livingston | Jackson | 1831 | La. |
| Louis McLane | Jackson | 1833 | Del. |
| John Forsyth | Jackson | 1834 | Ga. |
| John Forsyth | Van Buren | 1837 | Ga. |
| Daniel Webster | W. H. Harrison | 1841 | Mass. |
| Daniel Webster | Tyler | 1841 | Mass. |
| Abel P. Upshur | Tyler | 1843 | Va. |
| John C. Calhoun | Tyler | 1844 | S.C. |
| James Buchanan | Polk | 1845 | Pa. |
| John M. Clayton | Taylor | 1849 | Del. |
| Daniel Webster | Fillmore | 1850 | Mass. |
| Edward Everett | Fillmore | 1852 | Mass. |
| William L. Marcy | Pierce | 1853 | N.Y. |
| Lewis Cass | Buchanan | 1857 | Mich. |
| Jeremiah S. Black | Buchanan | 1860 | Pa. |
| William H. Seward | Lincoln | 1861 | N.Y. |
| William H. Seward | Johnson | 1865 | N.Y. |
| Elihu B. Washburne | Grant | 1869 | Ill. |
| Hamilton Fish | Grant | 1869 | N.Y. |
| William M. Evarts | Hayes | 1877 | N.Y. |
| James G. Blaine | Garfield | 1881 | Me. |
| Fredk. T. Frelinghuysen | Arthur | 1881 | N.J. |
| Thomas F. Bayard | Cleveland | 1885 | Del. |
| James G. Blaine | B. Harrison | 1889 | Me. |
| John W. Foster | B. Harrison | 1892 | Ind. |
| Walter Q. Gresham | Cleveland | 1893 | Ill. |
| Richard Olney | Cleveland | 1895 | Mass. |
| John Sherman | McKinley | 1897 | Ohio |
| William R. Day | McKinley | 1898 | Ohio |
| John M. Hay | McKinley | 1898 | D.C. |
| John M. Hay | T. Roosevelt | 1901 | D.C. |
| Elihu Root | T. Roosevelt | 1905 | N.Y. |
| Robert Bacon | T. Roosevelt | 1909 | N.Y. |
| Philander C. Knox | Taft | 1909 | Pa. |
| William Jennings Bryan | Wilson | 1913 | Nebr. |
| Robert Lansing | Wilson | 1915 | N.Y. |
| Bainbridge Colby | Wilson | 1920 | N.Y. |
| Charles Evans Hughes | Harding | 1921 | N.Y. |
| Charles Evans Hughes | Coolidge | 1923 | N.Y. |
| Frank B. Kellogg | Coolidge | 1925 | Minn. |
| Henry Lewis Stimson | Hoover | 1929 | N.Y. |
| Cordell Hull | F. D. Roosevelt | 1933 | Tenn. |
| Edward R. Stettinius, Jr. | F. D. Roosevelt | 1944 | N.Y. |
| James Francis Byrnes | Truman | 1945 | S.C. |
| George C. Marshall | Truman | 1947 | Va. |
| Dean G. Acheson | Truman | 1949 | Md. |
| John Foster Dulles | Eisenhower | 1953 | N.Y. |
| Christian A. Herter | Eisenhower | 1959 | Mass. |
| Dean Rusk | Kennedy | 1861 | N.Y. |
| Dean Rusk | L. B. Johnson | 1963 | N.Y. |
| William P. Rogers | Nixon | 1969 | Md. |
| Henry A. Kissinger | Nixon | 1973 | Mass. |
| Henry A. Kissinger | Ford | 1974 | Mass. |
| Cyrus R. Vance | Carter | 1977 | N.Y. |

[1] John Jay was the Secretary for Foreign Affairs under the Continental Congress from Dec. 21, 1784 and continued unofficially to conduct the Department of State until Jefferson took office.

## SECRETARIES OF THE TREASURY

| NAME | PRESIDENT | DATE | RES. |
|---|---|---|---|
| Alexander Hamilton | Washington | 1789 | N.Y. |
| Oliver Wolcott | Washington | 1795 | Conn. |
| Oliver Wolcott | J. Adams | 1797 | Conn. |
| Samuel Dexter | J. Adams | 1801 | Mass. |
| Albert Gallatin | Jefferson | 1801 | Pa. |
| Albert Gallatin | Madison | 1809 | Pa. |
| George W. Campbell | Madison | 1814 | Tenn. |
| Alexander J. Dallas | Madison | 1814 | Pa. |
| William H. Crawford | Madison | 1816 | Ga. |
| William H. Crawford | Monroe | 1817 | Ga. |
| Richard Rush | J. Q. Adams | 1825 | Pa. |
| Samuel D. Ingham | Jackson | 1829 | Pa. |
| Louis McLane | Jackson | 1831 | Del. |
| William J. Duane | Jackson | 1833 | Pa. |
| Roger B. Taney | Jackson | 1833 | Md. |
| Levi Woodbury | Jackson | 1834 | N.H. |
| Levi Woodbury | Van Buren | 1837 | N.H. |
| Thomas Ewing | W. H. Harrison | 1841 | Ohio |
| Walther Forward | Tyler | 1841 | Pa. |
| John C. Spencer | Tyler | 1843 | N.Y. |
| George M. Bibb | Tyler | 1844 | Ky. |
| Robert J. Walker | Polk | 1845 | Miss. |
| William M. Meredith | Taylor | 1849 | Pa. |
| Thomas Corwin | Fillmore | 1850 | Ohio |
| James Guthrie | Pierce | 1853 | Ky. |
| Howell Cobb | Buchanan | 1857 | Ga. |
| Philip F. Thomas | Buchanan | 1860 | Md. |
| John A. Dix | Buchanan | 1861 | N.Y. |
| Salmon P. Chase | Lincoln | 1861 | Ohio |
| William P. Fessenden | Lincoln | 1864 | Me. |
| Hugh McCulloch | Lincoln | 1865 | Ind. |
| Hugh McCulloch | Johnson | 1865 | Ind. |
| George S. Boutwell | Grant | 1869 | Mass. |
| William A. Richardson | Grant | 1873 | Mass. |
| Benjamin H. Bristow | Grant | 1874 | Ky. |
| Lot M. Morrill | Grant | 1876 | Me. |
| John Sherman | Hayes | 1877 | Ohio |
| William Windom | Garfield | 1881 | Minn. |
| Charles J. Folger | Arthur | 1881 | N.Y. |
| Walter Q. Gresham | Arthur | 1884 | Ind. |
| Hugh McCulloch | Arthur | 1884 | Ind. |
| Daniel Manning | Cleveland | 1885 | N.Y. |
| Charles S. Fairchild | Cleveland | 1887 | N.Y. |
| William Windom | B. Harrison | 1889 | Minn. |

SECRETARIES OF THE TREASURY (Continued)

| NAME | PRESIDENT | DATE | RES. |
|---|---|---|---|
| Charles Foster | B. Harrison | 1891 | Ohio |
| John G. Carlisle | Cleveland | 1893 | Ky. |
| Lyman J. Gage | McKinley | 1897 | Ill. |
| Lyman J. Gage | T. Roosevelt | 1901 | Ill. |
| Leslie M. Shaw | T. Roosevelt | 1902 | Iowa |
| George B. Cortelyou | T. Roosevelt | 1907 | N.Y. |
| Franklin MacVeagh | Taft | 1909 | Ill. |
| William G. McAdoo | Wilson | 1913 | N.Y. |
| Carter Glass | Wilson | 1918 | Va. |
| David F. Houston | Wilson | 1920 | Mo. |
| Andrew W. Mellon | Harding | 1921 | Pa. |
| Andrew W. Mellon | Coolidge | 1923 | Pa. |
| Andrew W. Mellon | Hoover | 1929 | Pa. |
| Ogden L. Mills | Hoover | 1932 | N.Y. |
| William H. Woodin | F. D. Roosevelt | 1933 | N.Y. |
| Henry Morgenthau, Jr. | F. D. Roosevelt | 1934 | N.Y. |
| Frederick M. Vinson | Truman | 1945 | Ky. |
| John W. Snyder | Truman | 1946 | Mo. |
| George M. Humphrey | Eisenhower | 1953 | Ohio |
| Robert B. Anderson | Eisenhower | 1957 | Conn. |
| C. Douglas Dillon | Kennedy | 1961 | N.J. |
| C. Douglas Dillon | L. B. Johnson | 1963 | N.J. |
| Henry H. Fowler | L. B. Johnson | 1965 | Va. |
| David M. Kennedy | Nixon | 1969 | Ill. |
| John B. Connally, Jr. | Nixon | 1971 | Tex. |
| George P. Shultz | Nixon | 1972 | N.Y. |
| William E. Simon | Nixon | 1974 | N.J. |
| William E. Simon | Ford | 1974 | N.J. |
| W. Michael Blumenthal | Carter | 1977 | Mich. |
| G. William Miller | Carter | 1979 | Mass. |

SECRETARIES OF DEFENSE

| NAME | PRESIDENT | DATE | RES. |
|---|---|---|---|
| James V. Forrestal | Truman | 1947 | N.Y. |
| Louis A. Johnson | Truman | 1949 | Va. |
| George C. Marshall | Truman | 1950 | Va. |
| Robert A. Lovett | Truman | 1951 | N.Y. |
| Charles E. Wilson | Eisenhower | 1953 | Mich. |
| Neil H. McElroy | Eisenhower | 1957 | Ohio |
| Thomas S. Gates | Eisenhower | 1959 | Pa. |
| Robert S. McNamara | Kennedy | 1961 | Calif. |
| Robert S. McNamara | L. B. Johnson | 1963 | Calif. |
| Clark M. Clifford | L. B. Johnson | 1968 | D.C. |
| Melvin R. Laird | Nixon | 1969 | Wisc. |
| Elliot L. Richardson | Nixon | 1973 | Mass. |
| James R. Schlesinger | Nixon | 1973 | N.Y. |
| James R. Schlesinger | Ford | 1974 | N.Y. |
| Donald H. Rumsfeld | Ford | 1975 | Ill. |
| Harold Brown | Carter | 1977 | Calif. |

SECRETARIES OF WAR[1]

| NAME | PRESIDENT | DATE | RES. |
|---|---|---|---|
| Henry Knox | Washington | 1789 | Mass. |
| Timothy Pickering | Washington | 1795 | Pa. |
| James McHenry | Washington | 1796 | Md. |
| James McHenry | J. Adams | 1797 | Md. |
| Samuel Dexter | J. Adams | 1800 | Mass. |
| Henry Dearborn | Jefferson | 1801 | Mass. |
| William Eustis | Madison | 1809 | Mass. |
| John Armstrong | Madison | 1813 | N.Y. |
| James Monroe | Madison | 1814 | Va. |
| William H. Crawford | Madison | 1815 | Ga. |
| John C. Calhoun | Monroe | 1817 | S.C. |
| James Barbour | J. Q. Adams | 1825 | Va. |
| Peter B. Porter | J. Q. Adams | 1828 | N.Y. |
| John H. Eaton | Jackson | 1829 | Tenn. |
| Lewis Cass | Jackson | 1831 | Ohio |
| Benjamin F. Butler | Jackson | 1836 | N.Y. |
| Joel R. Poinsett | Van Buren | 1837 | S.C. |
| John Bell | W. H. Harrison | 1841 | Tenn. |
| John C. Spencer | Tyler | 1841 | N.Y. |
| James M. Porter | Tyler | 1843 | Pa. |
| William Wilkins | Tyler | 1844 | Pa. |
| William L. Marcy | Polk | 1845 | N.Y. |
| George W. Crawford | Taylor | 1849 | Ga. |
| Charles M. Conrad | Fillmore | 1850 | La. |
| Jefferson Davis | Pierce | 1853 | Miss. |
| John B. Floyd | Buchanan | 1857 | Va. |
| Joseph Holt | Buchanan | 1861 | Ky. |
| Simon Cameron | Lincoln | 1861 | Pa. |
| Edwin M. Stanton | Lincoln | 1862 | Ohio |
| Edwin M. Stanton | Johnson | 1865 | Ohio |
| U. S. Grant (ad int.) | Johnson | 1867 | Ill. |
| John M. Schofield | Johnson | 1868 | N.Y. |
| John A. Rawlins | Grant | 1869 | Ill. |
| William W. Belknap | Grant | 1869 | Iowa |
| Alphonso Taft | Grant | 1876 | Ohio |
| James D. Cameron | Grant | 1876 | Pa. |
| George W. McCrary | Hayes | 1877 | Iowa |
| Alexander Ramsey | Hayes | 1879 | Minn. |
| Robert T. Lincoln | Garfield | 1881 | Ill. |
| Robert T. Lincoln | Arthur | 1881 | Ill. |
| William C. Endicott | Cleveland | 1885 | Mass. |
| Redfield Proctor | B. Harrison | 1889 | Vt. |
| Stephen B. Elkins | B. Harrison | 1891 | W.Va. |
| Daniel S. Lamont | Cleveland | 1893 | N.Y. |
| Russell A. Alger | McKinley | 1897 | Mich. |
| Elihu Root | McKinley | 1899 | N.Y. |
| Elihu Root | T. Roosevelt | 1901 | N.Y. |
| William H. Taft | T. Roosevelt | 1904 | Ohio |
| Luke E. Wright | T. Roosevelt | 1908 | Tenn. |
| Jacob M. Dickinson | Taft | 1909 | Tenn. |
| Henry L. Stimson | Taft | 1911 | N.Y. |
| Lindley M. Garrison | Wilson | 1913 | N.J. |
| Newton D. Baker | Wilson | 1916 | Ohio |
| John W. Weeks | Harding | 1921 | Mass. |
| John W. Weeks | Coolidge | 1923 | Mass. |
| Dwight F. Davis | Coolidge | 1925 | Mo. |
| James W. Good | Hoover | 1929 | Iowa |
| Patrick J. Hurley | Hoover | 1929 | Okla. |
| George H. Dern | F. D. Roosevelt | 1933 | Utah |
| Harry H. Woodring | F. D. Roosevelt | 1936 | Kans. |
| Henry L. Stimson | F. D. Roosevelt | 1940 | N.Y. |
| Robert P. Patterson | Truman | 1945 | N.Y. |
| Kenneth C. Royall | Truman | 1947 | N.C. |

[1] By Act of Congress, July 25, 1947, the War Dept. became Dept. of the Army and a subdepartment of Dept. of Defense.

SECRETARIES OF THE NAVY[1]

| NAME | PRESIDENT | DATE | RES. |
|---|---|---|---|
| Benjamin Stoddert | J. Adams | 1798 | Md. |
| Benjamin Stoddert | Jefferson | 1801 | Md. |
| Robert Smith[2] | Jefferson | 1801 | Md. |
| Paul Hamilton | Madison | 1809 | S.C. |
| William Jones | Madison | 1813 | Pa. |
| Benjamin W. Crowninshield | Madison | 1814 | Mass. |
| Benjamin W. Crowninshield | Monroe | 1817 | Mass. |
| Smith Thompson | Monroe | 1819 | N.Y. |
| Samuel L. Southard | Monroe | 1823 | N.J. |
| Samuel L. Southard | J. Q. Adams | 1825 | N.J. |
| John Branch | Jackson | 1829 | N.C. |
| Levi Woodbury | Jackson | 1831 | N.H. |
| Mahlon Dickerson | Jackson | 1834 | N.J. |
| Mahlon Dickerson | Van Buren | 1837 | N.J. |
| James K. Paulding | Van Buren | 1838 | N.Y. |
| George E. Badger | W. H. Harrison | 1841 | N.C. |
| Abel P. Upshur | Tyler | 1841 | Va. |
| David Henshaw | Tyler | 1843 | Mass. |
| Thomas W. Gilmer | Tyler | 1844 | Va. |
| John Y. Mason | Tyler | 1844 | Va. |
| George Bancroft | Polk | 1845 | Mass. |
| John Y. Mason | Polk | 1846 | Va. |
| William B. Preston | Taylor | 1849 | Va. |
| William A. Graham | Fillmore | 1850 | N.C. |
| John P. Kennedy | Fillmore | 1852 | Md. |
| James C. Dobbin | Pierce | 1853 | N.C. |
| Isaac Toucey | Buchanan | 1857 | Conn. |
| Gideon Welles | Lincoln | 1861 | Conn. |
| Gideon Welles | Johnson | 1865 | Conn. |
| Adolph E. Borie | Grant | 1869 | Pa. |
| George M. Robeson | Grant | 1869 | N.J. |
| Richard W. Thompson | Hayes | 1877 | Ind. |
| Nathan Goff, Jr. | Hayes | 1881 | W.Va. |
| William H. Hunt | Garfield | 1881 | La. |
| William E. Chandler | Arthur | 1882 | N.H. |
| William C. Whitney | Cleveland | 1885 | N.Y. |
| Benjamin F. Tracy | B. Harrison | 1889 | N.Y. |
| Hilary A. Herbert | Cleveland | 1893 | Ala. |
| John D. Long | McKinley | 1897 | Mass. |
| John D. Long | T. Roosevelt | 1901 | Mass. |
| William H. Moody | T. Roosevelt | 1902 | Mass. |
| Paul Morton | T. Roosevelt | 1904 | N.Y. |
| Charles J. Bonaparte | T. Roosevelt | 1905 | Md. |
| Victor H. Metcalf | T. Roosevelt | 1906 | Calif. |
| Truman H. Newberry | T. Roosevelt | 1908 | Mich. |
| George von L. Meyer | Taft | 1909 | Mass. |
| Josephus Daniels | Wilson | 1913 | N.C. |
| Edwin Denby | Harding | 1921 | Mich. |
| Edwin Denby | Coolidge | 1923 | Mich. |
| Curtis D. Wilbur | Coolidge | 1924 | Calif. |
| Charles F. Adams | Hoover | 1929 | Mass. |
| Claude A. Swanson | F. D. Roosevelt | 1933 | Va. |
| Charles Edison | F. D. Roosevelt | 1939 | N.J. |
| Frank Knox | F. D. Roosevelt | 1940 | Ill. |
| James V. Forrestal | F. D. Roosevelt | 1944 | N.Y. |
| James V. Forrestal | Truman | 1945 | N.Y. |

[1] By Act of Congress, July 25, 1947, the Dept. of the Navy became a subdepartment of Dept. of Defense.
[2] Served briefly as Attorney General 1805 but resigned this post and resumed duties of Secretary of the Navy.

## ATTORNEYS GENERAL

| NAME | PRESIDENT | DATE | RES. | NAME | PRESIDENT | DATE | RES. |
|---|---|---|---|---|---|---|---|
| Edmund Randolph | Washington | 1789 | Va. | Benjamin H. Brewster | Arthur | 1881 | Pa. |
| William Bradford | Washington | 1794 | Pa. | Augustus H. Garland | Cleveland | 1885 | Ark. |
| Charles Lee | Washington | 1795 | Va. | William H. H. Miller | B. Harrison | 1889 | Ind. |
| Charles Lee | J. Adams | 1797 | Va. | Richard Olney | Cleveland | 1893 | Mass. |
| Levi Lincoln | Jefferson | 1801 | Mass. | Judson Harmon | Cleveland | 1895 | Ohio |
| John Breckinridge | Jefferson | 1805 | Ky. | Joseph McKenna | McKinley | 1897 | Calif. |
| Caesar A. Rodney | Jefferson | 1807 | Del. | John W. Griggs | McKinley | 1898 | N.J. |
| Caesar A. Rodney | Madison | 1809 | Del. | Philander C. Knox | McKinley | 1901 | Pa. |
| William Pinkney | Madison | 1811 | Md. | Philander C. Knox | T. Roosevelt | 1901 | Pa. |
| Richard Rush | Madison | 1814 | Pa. | William H. Moody | T. Roosevelt | 1904 | Mass. |
| William Wirt | Monroe | 1817 | Va. | Charles J. Bonaparte | T. Roosevelt | 1906 | Md. |
| William Wirt | J. Q. Adams | 1825 | Va. | George W. Wickersham | Taft | 1909 | N.Y. |
| John M. Berrien | Jackson | 1829 | Ga. | James C. McReynolds | Wilson | 1913 | Tenn. |
| Roger B. Taney | Jackson | 1831 | Md. | Thomas W. Gregory | Wilson | 1914 | Tex. |
| Benjamin F. Butler | Jackson | 1833 | N.Y. | A. Mitchell Palmer | Wilson | 1919 | Pa. |
| Benjamin F. Butler | Van Buren | 1837 | N.Y. | Harry M. Daugherty | Harding | 1921 | Ohio |
| Felix Grundy | Van Buren | 1838 | Tenn. | Harry M. Daugherty | Coolidge | 1923 | Ohio |
| Henry D. Gilpin | Van Buren | 1840 | Pa. | Harlan F. Stone | Coolidge | 1924 | N.Y. |
| John J. Crittenden | W. H. Harrison | 1841 | Ky. | John G. Sargent | Coolidge | 1925 | Vt. |
| Hugh S. Legaré | Tyler | 1841 | S.C. | William D. Mitchell | Hoover | 1929 | Minn. |
| John Nelson | Tyler | 1843 | Md. | Homer S. Cummings | F. D. Roosevelt | 1933 | Conn. |
| John Y. Mason | Polk | 1845 | Va. | Frank Murphy | F. D. Roosevelt | 1939 | Mich. |
| Nathan Clifford | Polk | 1846 | Me. | Robert H. Jackson | F. D. Roosevelt | 1940 | N.Y. |
| Isaac Toucey | Polk | 1848 | Conn. | Francis Biddle | F. D. Roosevelt | 1941 | Pa. |
| Reverdy Johnson | Taylor | 1849 | Md. | Thomas C. Clark | Truman | 1945 | Tex. |
| John J. Crittenden | Fillmore | 1850 | Ky. | J. Howard McGrath | Truman | 1949 | R.I. |
| Caleb Cushing | Pierce | 1853 | Mass. | James Patrick McGranery | Truman | 1952 | Pa. |
| Jeremiah S. Black | Buchanan | 1857 | Pa. | Herbert Brownell, Jr. | Eisenhower | 1953 | N.Y. |
| Edwin M. Stanton | Buchanan | 1860 | Ohio | William P. Rogers | Eisenhower | 1957 | N.Y. |
| Edward Bates | Lincoln | 1861 | Mo. | Robert F. Kennedy | Kennedy | 1961 | Mass. |
| James Speed | Lincoln | 1864 | Ky. | Robert F. Kennedy | L. B. Johnson | 1963 | Mass. |
| James Speed | Johnson | 1865 | Ky. | Nicholas Katzenbach | L. B. Johnson | 1965 | D.C. |
| Henry Stanbery | Johnson | 1866 | Ohio | Ramsey Clark | L. B. Johnson | 1967 | Va. |
| William M. Evarts | Johnson | 1868 | N.Y. | John N. Mitchell | Nixon | 1969 | N.Y. |
| Ebenezer R. Hoar | Grant | 1869 | Mass. | Richard G. Kleindienst | Nixon | 1972 | Ariz. |
| Amos T. Akerman | Grant | 1870 | Ga. | Elliot L. Richardson | Nixon | 1973 | Mass. |
| George H. Williams | Grant | 1871 | Ore. | William B. Saxbe | Nixon | 1974 | Ohio |
| Edwards Pierrepont | Grant | 1876 | N.Y. | William B. Saxbe | Ford | 1974 | Ohio |
| Alphonso Taft | Grant | 1876 | Ohio | Edward H. Levi | Ford | 1975 | Ill. |
| Charles Devens | Hayes | 1877 | Mass. | Griffin B. Bell | Carter | 1977 | Ga. |
| Wayne MacVeagh | Garfield | 1881 | Pa. | Benjamin R. Civiletti | Carter | 1979 | Md. |

## POSTMASTERS GENERAL[1]

| NAME | PRESIDENT | DATE | RES. | NAME | PRESIDENT | DATE | RES. |
|---|---|---|---|---|---|---|---|
| Samuel Osgood | Washington | 1789 | Mass. | Thomas L. James | Garfield | 1881 | N.Y. |
| Timothy Pickering | Washington | 1791 | Pa. | Timothy O. Howe | Arthur | 1882 | Wis. |
| Joseph Habersham | Washington | 1795 | Ga. | Walter Q. Gresham | Arthur | 1883 | Ind. |
| Joseph Habersham | J. Adams | 1797 | Ga. | Frank Hatton | Arthur | 1884 | Iowa |
| Joseph Habersham | Jefferson | 1801 | Ga. | William F. Vilas | Cleveland | 1885 | Wis. |
| Gideon Granger | Jefferson | 1801 | Conn. | Don M. Dickinson | Cleveland | 1888 | Mich. |
| Gideon Granger | Madison | 1809 | Conn. | John Wanamaker | B. Harrison | 1889 | Pa. |
| Return J. Meigs | Madison | 1814 | Ohio | Wilson S. Bissell | Cleveland | 1893 | N.Y. |
| Return J. Meigs | Monroe | 1817 | Ohio | William L. Wilson | Cleveland | 1895 | W.Va. |
| John McLean | Monroe | 1823 | Ohio | James A. Gary | McKinley | 1897 | Md. |
| John McLean | J. Q. Adams | 1825 | Ohio | Charles Emory Smith | McKinley | 1898 | Pa. |
| William T. Barry | Jackson | 1829 | Ky. | Charles Emory Smith | T. Roosevelt | 1901 | Pa. |
| Amos Kendall | Jackson | 1835 | Ky. | Henry C. Payne | T. Roosevelt | 1902 | Wis. |
| Amos Kendall | Van Buren | 1837 | Ky. | Robert J. Wynne | T. Roosevelt | 1904 | Pa. |
| John M. Niles | Van Buren | 1840 | Conn. | George B. Cortelyou | T. Roosevelt | 1905 | N.Y. |
| Francis Granger | W. H. Harrison | 1841 | N.Y. | George von L. Meyer | T. Roosevelt | 1907 | Mass. |
| Charles A. Wickliffe | Tyler | 1841 | Ky. | Frank H. Hitchcock | Taft | 1909 | Mass. |
| Cave Johnson | Polk | 1845 | Tenn. | Albert S. Burleson | Wilson | 1913 | Tex. |
| Jacob Collamer | Taylor | 1849 | Vt. | Will H. Hays | Harding | 1921 | Ind. |
| Nathan K. Hall | Fillmore | 1850 | N.Y. | Hubert Work | Harding | 1922 | Colo. |
| Samuel D. Hubbard | Fillmore | 1852 | Conn. | Harry S. New | Harding | 1923 | Ind. |
| James Campbell | Pierce | 1853 | Pa. | Harry S. New | Coolidge | 1923 | Ind. |
| Aaron V. Brown | Buchanan | 1857 | Tenn. | Walter F. Brown | Hoover | 1929 | Ohio |
| Joseph Holt | Buchanan | 1859 | Ky. | James A. Farley | F. D. Roosevelt | 1933 | N.Y. |
| Horatio King | Buchanan | 1861 | Me. | Frank C. Walker | F. D. Roosevelt | 1940 | Pa. |
| Montgomery Blair | Lincoln | 1861 | Md. | Robert E. Hannegan | Truman | 1945 | Mo. |
| William Dennison | Lincoln | 1864 | Ohio | Jesse M. Donaldson | Truman | 1947 | Mo. |
| William Dennison | Johnson | 1865 | Ohio | Arthur E. Summerfield | Eisenhower | 1953 | Mich. |
| Alexander W. Randall | Johnson | 1866 | Wis. | J. Edward Day | Kennedy | 1961 | Calif. |
| John A. J. Creswell | Grant | 1869 | Md. | John A Gronouski | Kennedy | 1963 | Wis. |
| James W. Marshall | Grant | 1874 | Va. | John A. Gronouski | L. B. Johnson | 1963 | Wis. |
| Marshall Jewell | Grant | 1874 | Conn. | Lawrence F. O'Brien | L. B. Johnson | 1965 | Mass. |
| James N. Tyner | Grant | 1876 | Ind. | William M. Watson | L. B. Johnson | 1968 | Tex. |
| David McK. Key | Hayes | 1877 | Tenn. | Winton M. Blount | Nixon | 1969 | Ala. |
| Horace Maynard | Hayes | 1880 | Tenn. | | | | |

[1] By act of Congress the Post Office Dept. became an independent agency on July 1, 1971.

## SECRETARIES OF THE INTERIOR

| NAME | PRESIDENT | DATE | RES. | NAME | PRESIDENT | DATE | RES. |
|---|---|---|---|---|---|---|---|
| Thomas Ewing | Taylor | 1849 | Ohio | Zachariah Chandler | Grant | 1875 | Mich. |
| Thomas M. T. McKennan | Fillmore | 1850 | Pa. | Carl Schurz | Hayes | 1877 | Mo. |
| Alexander H. H. Stuart | Fillmore | 1850 | Va. | Samuel J. Kirkwood | Garfield | 1881 | Iowa |
| Robert McClelland | Pierce | 1853 | Mich. | Henry M. Teller | Arthur | 1882 | Colo. |
| Jacob Thompson | Buchanan | 1857 | Miss. | Lucius Q. C. Lamar | Cleveland | 1885 | Miss. |
| Caleb B. Smith | Lincoln | 1861 | Ind. | William F. Vilas | Cleveland | 1888 | Wis. |
| John P. Usher | Lincoln | 1863 | Ind. | John W. Noble | B. Harrison | 1889 | Mo. |
| James Harlan | Johnson | 1865 | Iowa | Hoke Smith | Cleveland | 1893 | Ga. |
| Orville H. Browning | Johnson | 1866 | Ill. | David R. Francis | Cleveland | 1896 | Mo. |
| James Harlan | Johnson | 1865 | Iowa | Hoke Smith | Cleveland | 1893 | Ga. |
| Orville H. Browning | Johnson | 1866 | Ill. | David R. Francis | Cleveland | 1896 | Mo. |
| Jacob D. Cox | Grant | 1869 | Ohio | Cornelius N. Bliss | McKinley | 1897 | N.Y. |
| Columbus Delano | Grant | 1870 | Ohio | Ethan A. Hitchcock | McKinley | 1898 | Mo. |

## SECRETARIES OF THE INTERIOR (Continued)

| NAME | PRESIDENT | DATE | RES. |
|---|---|---|---|
| Ethan A. Hitchcock | T. Roosevelt | 1901 | Mo. |
| James R. Garfield | T. Roosevelt | 1907 | Ohio |
| Richard A. Balinger | Taft | 1909 | Wash. |
| Walter L. Fisher | Taft | 1911 | Ill. |
| Franklin K. Lane | Wilson | 1913 | Calif. |
| John Barton Payne | Wilson | 1920 | Ill. |
| Albert B. Fall | Harding | 1921 | N.Mex. |
| Hubert Work | Harding | 1923 | Colo. |
| Hubert Work | Coolidge | 1923 | Colo. |
| Roy O. West | Coolidge | 1928 | Ill. |
| Ray L. Wilbur | Hoover | 1929 | Calif. |
| Harold L. Ickes | F. D. Roosevelt | 1933 | Ill. |
| Julius A. Krug | Truman | 1946 | Tenn. |
| Oscar L. Chapman | Truman | 1949 | Colo. |
| Douglas McKay | Eisenhower | 1953 | Ore. |
| Fred A. Seaton | Eisenhower | 1956 | Nebr. |
| Stewart L. Udall | Kennedy | 1961 | Ariz. |
| Stewart L. Udall | L. B. Johnson | 1963 | Ariz. |
| Walter J. Hickel | Nixon | 1969 | Alaska |
| Rogers C. B. Morton | Nixon | 1971 | Md. |
| Rogers C. B. Morton | Ford | 1974 | Md. |
| Stanley E. Hathaway | Ford | 1975 | Wyo. |
| Thomas S. Kleppe | Ford | 1975 | N.D. |
| Cecil D. Andrus | Carter | 1977 | Ida. |

## SECRETARIES OF AGRICULTURE

| NAME | PRESIDENT | DATE | RES. |
|---|---|---|---|
| Norman J. Colman | Cleveland | 1889 | Mo. |
| Jeremiah M. Rusk | B. Harrison | 1889 | Wis. |
| J. Sterling Morton | Cleveland | 1893 | Nebr. |
| James Wilson | McKinley | 1897 | Iowa |
| James Wilson | T. Roosevelt | 1901 | Iowa |
| James Wilson | Taft | 1909 | Iowa |
| David F. Houston | Wilson | 1913 | Mo. |
| Edwin T. Meredith | Wilson | 1920 | Iowa |
| Henry C. Wallace | Harding | 1921 | Iowa |
| Henry C. Wallace | Coolidge | 1923 | Iowa |
| Howard M. Gore | Coolidge | 1924 | W.Va. |
| William M. Jardine | Coolidge | 1925 | Kans. |
| Arthur M. Hyde | Hoover | 1929 | Mo. |
| Henry A. Wallace | F. D. Roosevelt | 1933 | Iowa |
| Claude R. Wickard | F. D. Roosevelt | 1940 | Ind. |
| Clinton P. Anderson | Truman | 1945 | N.Mex. |
| Charles F. Brannan | Truman | 1948 | Colo. |
| Ezra Taft Benson | Eisenhower | 1953 | Utah |
| Orville L. Freeman | Kennedy | 1961 | Minn. |
| Orville L. Freeman | L. B. Johnson | 1963 | Minn. |
| Clifford M. Hardin | Nixon | 1969 | Neb. |
| Earl L. Butz | Nixon | 1971 | Ind. |
| Earl L. Butz | Ford | 1974 | Ind. |
| Robert S. Bergland | Carter | 1977 | Minn. |

## SECRETARIES OF COMMERCE AND LABOR[1]

| NAME | PRESIDENT | DATE | RES. |
|---|---|---|---|
| George B. Cortelyou | T. Roosevelt | 1903 | N.Y. |
| Victor H. Metcalf | T. Roosevelt | 1904 | Calif. |
| Oscar S. Straus | T. Roosevelt | 1906 | N.Y. |
| Charles Nagel | Taft | 1909 | Mo. |

[1] [By Act of Congress, effective March 3, 1913, the Dept. of Commerce and Labor was divided into two departments, the Dept. of Commerce and the Dept. of Labor.]

## SECRETARIES OF COMMERCE

| NAME | PRESIDENT | DATE | RES. |
|---|---|---|---|
| William C. Redfield | Wilson | 1913 | N.Y. |
| Joshua W. Alexander | Wilson | 1919 | Mo. |
| Herbert C. Hoover | Harding | 1921 | Calif. |
| Herbert C. Hoover | Coolidge | 1923 | Calif. |
| William F. Whiting | Coolidge | 1928 | Mass. |
| Robert P. Lamont | Hoover | 1929 | N.Y. |
| Roy D. Chapin | Hoover | 1932 | Mich. |
| Daniel C. Roper | F. D. Roosevelt | 1933 | S.C. |
| Harry L. Hopkins | F. D. Roosevelt | 1938 | Iowa |
| Jesse H. Jones | F. D. Roosevelt | 1940 | Tex. |
| Henry A. Wallace | F. D. Roosevelt | 1945 | Iowa |
| W. Averell Harriman | Truman | 1946 | N.Y. |
| Charles Sawyer | Truman | 1948 | Ohio |
| Sinclair Weeks | Eisenhower | 1953 | Mass. |
| Lewis L. Strauss | Eisenhower | 1958 | Va. |
| Frederick H. Mueller | Eisenhower | 1959 | Mich. |
| Luther H. Hodges | Kennedy | 1961 | N.C. |
| Luther H. Hodges | L. B. Johnson | 1963 | N.C. |
| John T. Connor | L. B. Johnson | 1965 | N.Y. |
| Alexander B. Trowbridge | L. B. Johnson | 1967 | N.J. |
| Cyrus Rowlett Smith | L. B. Johnson | 1968 | N.Y. |
| Maurice H. Stans | Nixon | 1969 | Minn. |
| Peter G. Peterson | Nixon | 1972 | Ill. |
| Frederick B. Dent | Nixon | 1973 | S.C. |
| Frederick B. Dent | Ford | 1974 | S.C. |
| Rogers C. B. Morton | Ford | 1975 | Md. |
| Elliot L. Richardson | Ford | 1976 | Mass. |
| Juanita M. Kreps | Carter | 1977 | N.C. |

## SECRETARIES OF LABOR

| NAME | PRESIDENT | DATE | RES. |
|---|---|---|---|
| William B. Wilson | Wilson | 1913 | Pa. |
| James J. Davis | Harding | 1921 | Pa. |
| James J. Davis | Coolidge | 1923 | Pa. |
| James J. Davis | Hoover | 1929 | Pa. |
| William N. Doak | Hoover | 1930 | Va. |
| Frances Perkins | F. D. Roosevelt | 1933 | N.Y. |
| Lewis B. Schwellenbach | Truman | 1945 | Wash. |
| Maurice J. Tobin | Truman | 1948 | Mass. |
| Martin P. Durkin | Eisenhower | 1953 | Ill. |
| James P. Mitchell | Eisenhower | 1953 | N.J. |
| Arthur J. Goldberg | Kennedy | 1961 | D.C. |
| W. Willard Wirtz | Kennedy | 1962 | Ill. |
| W. Willard Wirtz | Kennedy | 1962 | Ill. |
| W. Willard Wirtz | L. B. Johnson | 1963 | Ill. |
| George P. Shultz | Nixon | 1969 | Ill. |
| James D. Hodgson | Nixon | 1970 | Calif. |
| Peter J. Brennan | Nixon | 1973 | N.Y. |
| Peter J. Brennan | Ford | 1974 | N.Y. |
| John T. Dunlop | Ford | 1975 | Mass. |
| W. J. Usery, Jr. | Ford | 1976 | Fla. |
| F. Ray Marshall | Carter | 1977 | Tex. |

## SECRETARIES OF HEALTH, EDUCATION, AND WELFARE

| NAME | PRESIDENT | DATE | RES. |
|---|---|---|---|
| Oveta Culp Hobby | Eisenhower | 1953 | Tex. |
| Marion B. Folsom | Eisenhower | 1955 | N.Y. |
| Arthur S. Flemming | Eisenhower | 1958 | Ohio |
| Abraham A. Ribicoff | Kennedy | 1961 | Conn. |
| Anthony J. Celebrezze | Kennedy | 1962 | Ohio |
| Anthony J. Celebrezze | L. B. Johnson | 1963 | Ohio |
| John W. Gardner | L. B. Johnson | 1965 | N.Y. |
| Wilber J. Cohen | L. B. Johnson | 1968 | Wisc. |
| Robert H. Finch | Nixon | 1969 | Calif. |
| Elliot L. Richardson | Nixon | 1970 | Mass. |
| Caspar W. Weinberger | Nixon | 1973 | Calif. |
| Caspar W. Weinberger | Ford | 1974 | Calif. |
| F. David Mathews | Ford | 1975 | Ala. |
| Joseph A. Califano, Jr. | Carter | 1977 | D.C. |
| Patricia Roberts Harris | Carter | 1979 | D.C. |

## SECRETARIES OF HOUSING AND URBAN DEVELOPMENT

| NAME | PRESIDENT | DATE | RES. |
|---|---|---|---|
| Robert C. Weaver | L. B. Johnson | 1966 | Fla. |
| George W. Romney | Nixon | 1969 | Mich. |
| James T. Lynn | Nixon | 1973 | Ohio |
| James T. Lynn | Ford | 1974 | Ohio |
| Carla Anderson Hills | Ford | 1975 | Calif. |
| Patricia Roberts Harris | Carter | 1977 | D.C. |
| Moon Landrieu | Carter | 1979 | La. |

## SECRETARIES OF TRANSPORTATION

| NAME | PRESIDENT | DATE | RES. |
|---|---|---|---|
| Alan S. Boyd | L. B. Johnson | 1966 | Fla. |
| John A. Volpe | Nixon | 1969 | Mass. |
| Claude S. Brinegar | Nixon | 1973 | Calif. |
| Claude S. Brinegar | Ford | 1974 | Calif. |
| William T. Coleman | Ford | 1975 | Pa. |
| Brockman Adams | Carter | 1977 | Wash. |
| Neil E. Goldschmidt | Carter | 1979 | Ore. |

## SECRETARIES OF ENERGY

| NAME | PRESIDENT | DATE | RES. |
|---|---|---|---|
| James R. Schlesinger | Carter | 1977 | N.Y. |
| Charles W. Duncan, Jr. | Carter | 1979 | Tex. |

## SIGNERS OF THE U.S. DECLARATION OF INDEPENDENCE
as adopted by Congress, July 4, 1776

| NAME | DELEGATE FROM | NAME | DELEGATE FROM |
|---|---|---|---|
| Adams, John | Massachusetts | Lynch, Thomas, Jr. (1749–79) | South Carolina |
| Adams, Samuel | Massachusetts | McKean, Thomas[2] | Delaware |
| Bartlett, Josiah | New Hampshire | Middleton, Arthur | South Carolina |
| Braxton, Carter | Virginia | Morris, Lewis | New York |
| Carroll, Charles, of Carrollton | Maryland | Morris, Robert | Pennsylvania |
| Chase, Samuel | Maryland | Morton, John | Pennsylvania |
| Clark, Abraham | New Jersey | Nelson, Thomas, Jr.[1] | Virginia |
| Clymer, George | Pennsylvania | Paca, William | Maryland |
| Ellery, William | Rhode Island | Paine, Robert Treat | Massachusetts |
| Floyd, William | New York | Penn, John | North Carolina |
| Franklin, Benjamin | Pennsylvania | Read, George | Delaware |
| Gerry, Elbridge | Massachusetts | Rodney, Caesar | Delaware |
| Gwinnett, Button | Georgia | Ross, George | Pennsylvania |
| Hall, Lyman | Georgia | Rush, Benjamin | Pennsylvania |
| Hancock, John | Massachusetts | Rutledge, Edward | South Carolina |
| Harrison, Benjamin | Virginia | Sherman, Roger | Connecticut |
| Hart, John | New Jersey | Smith, James | Pennsylvania |
| Hewes, Joseph | North Carolina | Stockton, Richard | New Jersey |
| Heyward, Thomas, Jr.[1] | South Carolina | Stone, Thomas | Maryland |
| Hooper, William | North Carolina | Taylor, George | Pennsylvania |
| Hopkins, Stephen | Rhode Island | Thornton, Matthew | New Hampshire |
| Hopkinson, Francis | New Jersey | Walton, George | Georgia |
| Huntington, Samuel | Connecticut | Whipple, William | New Hampshire |
| Jefferson, Thomas | Virginia | Williams, William | Connecticut |
| Lee, Francis Lightfoot | Virginia | Wilson, James | Pennsylvania |
| Lee, Richard Henry | Virginia | Witherspoon, John | New Jersey |
| Lewis, Francis | New York | Wolcott, Oliver | Connecticut |
| Livingston, Philip | New York | Wythe, George | Virginia |

[1] Father's name not the same. Jr. was used in signing because another member of family had same name.
[2] McKean was with Washington's army when the Declaration was engrossed, so that his name does not appear in the list of signers printed by order of Congress on Jan. 18, 1777. He signed later.

## SIGNERS OF THE ARTICLES OF CONFEDERATION
as adopted by Congress, Nov. 15, 1777; signatures completed and in effect, March 1, 1781.

| NAME | DELEGATE FROM | NAME | DELEGATE FROM |
|---|---|---|---|
| Adams, Andrew | Connecticut | Langworthy, Edward | Georgia |
| Adams, Samuel | Massachusetts | Laurens, Henry | South Carolina |
| Adams, Thomas | Virginia | Lee, Francis Lightfoot | Virginia |
| Banister, John | Virginia | Lee, Richard Henry | Virginia |
| Bartlett, Josiah | New Hampshire | Lewis, Francis | New York |
| Carroll, Daniel | Maryland | Lovell, James | Massachusetts |
| Clingan, William | Pennsylvania | McKean, Thomas | Delaware |
| Collins, John | Rhode Island | Marchant, Henry | Rhode Island |
| Dana, Francis | Massachusetts | Mathews, John | South Carolina |
| Dickinson, John | Delaware | Morris, Gouverneur | New York |
| Drayton, William Henry | South Carolina | Morris, Robert | Pennsylvania |
| Duane, James | New York | Penn, John | North Carolina |
| Duer, William | New York | Reed, Joseph | Pennsylvania |
| Ellery, William | Rhode Island | Roberdeau, Daniel | Pennsylvania |
| Gerry, Elbridge | Massachusetts | Scudder, Nathaniel | New Jersey |
| Hancock, John | Massachusetts | Sherman, Roger | Connecticut |
| Hanson, John | Maryland | Smith, Jonathan Bayard | Pennsylvania |
| Harnett, Cornelius | North Carolina | Telfair, Edward | Georgia |
| Harvie, John | Virginia | Van Dyke, Nicholas | Delaware |
| Heyward, Thomas, Jr. | South Carolina | Walton, George | Georgia |
| Holten, Samuel | Massachusetts | Wentworth, John, Jr. | New Hampshire |
| Hosmer, Titus | Connecticut | Williams, John | North Carolina |
| Huntington, Samuel | Connecticut | Witherspoon, John | New Jersey |
| Hutson, Richard | South Carolina | Wolcott, Oliver | Connecticut |

## DELEGATES TO THE FEDERAL CONVENTION THAT PREPARED THE NATIONAL CONSTITUTION[1]
Philadelphia, May 25–Sept. 17, 1787

| NAME | DELEGATE FROM | NAME | DELEGATE FROM |
|---|---|---|---|
| Baldwin, Abraham | Georgia | Hamilton, Alexander | New York |
| Bassett, Richard | Delaware | *Houston, William C.* | New Jersey |
| Bedford, Gunning, Jr. | Delaware | *Houstoun, William* | Georgia |
| Blair, John | Virginia | Ingersoll, Jared | Pennsylvania |
| Blount, William | North Carolina | Jenifer, Daniel of St. Thomas | Maryland |
| Brearley, David | New Jersey | Johnson, William S. | Connecticut |
| Broom, Jacob | Delaware | King, Rufus | Massachusetts |
| Butler, Pierce | South Carolina | Langdon, John | New Hampshire |
| Carroll, Daniel | Maryland | *Lansing, John* | New York |
| Clymer, George | Pennsylvania | Livingston, William | New Jersey |
| *Davie, William R.* | North Carolina | *McClurg, James* | Virginia |
| Dayton, Jonathan | New Jersey | McHenry, James | Maryland |
| Dickinson, John | Delaware | Madison, James | Virginia |
| *Ellsworth, Oliver* | Connecticut | *Martin, Alexander* | North Carolina |
| Few, William | Georgia | *Martin, Luther* | Maryland |
| Fitzsimmons, Thomas | Pennsylvania | *Mason, George* | Virginia |
| Franklin, Benjamin | Pennsylvania | *Mercer, John Francis* | Maryland |
| *Gerry, Elbridge* | Massachusetts | Mifflin, Thomas | Pennsylvania |
| Gilman, Nicholas | New Hampshire | Morris, Gouverneur | Pennsylvania |
| Gorham, Nathaniel | Massachusetts | Morris, Robert | Pennsylvania |

[1] A total of 65 delegates was appointed to attend the Convention: 39 of these signed the Constitution; 16 members attended (names in italics in the Table) but did not sign; the following 10 never attended–John Pickering and Benjamin West (N.H.), Francis Dana (Mass.), John Neilson and Abraham Clark (N.J.), Patrick Henry (Va.), Richard Caswell and Willie Jones (N.C.), and George Walton and Nathaniel Pendleton (Ga.).

## Delegates to the Federal Convention that Prepared the National Constitution (Continued)

| NAME | DELEGATE FROM | NAME | DELEGATE FROM |
|---|---|---|---|
| Paterson, William | New Jersey | Spaight, Richard D. | North Carolina |
| *Pierce, William* | Georgia | *Strong, Caleb* | Massachusetts |
| Pinckney, Charles | South Carolina | Washington, George | Virginia |
| Pinckney, Charles C. | South Carolina | Williamson, Hugh | North Carolina |
| *Randolph, Edmund J.* | Virginia | Wilson, James | Pennsylvania |
| Read, George | Delaware | *Wythe, George* | Virginia |
| Rutledge, John | South Carolina | *Yates, Robert* | New York |
| Sherman, Roger | Connecticut | | |

## Hall of Fame for Great Americans

Established in 1900 at New York University through the generosity of Helen Miller Gould (Mrs. Finley J. Shepard)

| NAME | DATE ELECTED | PROFESSION OR OCCUPATION | NAME | DATE ELECTED | PROFESSION OR OCCUPATION |
|---|---|---|---|---|---|
| George Washington | 1900 | Statesman | Francis Parkman | 1915 | Historian |
| Abraham Lincoln | 1900 | Statesman | Louis Agassiz | 1915 | Scientist |
| Daniel Webster | 1900 | Statesman | Elias Howe | 1915 | Inventor |
| Benjamin Franklin | 1900 | Statesman | Joseph Henry | 1915 | Scientist |
| Ulysses S. Grant | 1900 | Soldier | Charlotte S. Cushman | 1915 | Actress |
| John Marshall | 1900 | Jurist | Daniel Boone | 1915 | Explorer |
| Thomas Jefferson | 1900 | Statesman | Rufus Choate | 1915 | Jurist |
| Ralph Waldo Emerson | 1900 | Author | Samuel L. Clemens | 1920 | Author |
| Robert Fulton | 1900 | Inventor | William T. G. Morton | 1920 | Dentist |
| Henry W. Longfellow | 1900 | Author | Augustus Saint-Gaudens | 1920 | Sculptor |
| Washington Irving | 1900 | Author | Roger Williams | 1920 | Colonizer |
| Jonathan Edwards | 1900 | Theologian | Patrick Henry | 1920 | Statesman |
| Samuel F. B. Morse | 1900 | Inventor | Alice Freeman Palmer | 1920 | Educator |
| David G. Farragut | 1900 | Sailor | James B. Eads | 1920 | Engineer |
| Henry Clay | 1900 | Statesman | Edwin Booth | 1925 | Actor |
| George Peabody | 1900 | Philanthropist | John Paul Jones | 1925 | Sailor |
| Nathaniel Hawthorne | 1900 | Author | J. A. McNeill Whistler | 1930 | Painter |
| Peter Cooper | 1900 | Philanthropist | Matthew F. Maury | 1930 | Scientist |
| Eli Whitney | 1900 | Inventor | James Monroe | 1930 | Statesman |
| Robert Edward Lee | 1900 | Soldier | Walt Whitman | 1930 | Author |
| Horace Mann | 1900 | Educator | William Penn | 1935 | Colonizer |
| John James Audubon | 1900 | Scientist | Simon Newcomb | 1935 | Scientist |
| James Kent | 1900 | Jurist | Grover Cleveland | 1935 | Statesman |
| Henry Ward Beecher | 1900 | Preacher | Stephen Collins Foster | 1940 | Ballad Composer |
| Joseph Story | 1900 | Jurist | Booker T. Washington | 1945 | Educator |
| John Adams | 1900 | Statesman | Thomas Paine | 1945 | Author |
| William Ellery Channing | 1900 | Preacher | Walter Reed | 1945 | Surgeon |
| Gilbert Charles Stuart | 1900 | Painter | Sidney Lanier | 1945 | Poet |
| Asa Gray | 1900 | Scientist | Susan B. Anthony | 1950 | Reformer |
| James Russell Lowell | 1905 | Author | Alexander Graham Bell | 1950 | Inventor |
| John Quincy Adams | 1905 | Statesman | Josiah Willard Gibbs | 1950 | Physicist |
| Mary Lyon | 1905 | Educator | Theodore Roosevelt | 1950 | Statesman |
| William Tecumseh Sherman | 1905 | Soldier | Woodrow Wilson | 1950 | Statesman |
| James Madison | 1905 | Statesman | William Crawford Gorgas | 1950 | Physician |
| John Greenleaf Whittier | 1905 | Author | Thomas Jonathan Jackson | 1955 | Soldier |
| Emma Willard | 1905 | Educator | George Westinghouse | 1955 | Inventor |
| Maria Mitchell | 1905 | Scientist | Wilbur Wright | 1955 | Inventor |
| Harriet Beecher Stowe | 1910 | Author | Thomas A. Edison | 1960 | Inventor |
| Edgar Allan Poe | 1910 | Author | Edward A. MacDowell | 1960 | Composer |
| Oliver Wendell Holmes | 1910 | Author | Henry D. Thoreau | 1960 | Writer |
| James Fenimore Cooper | 1910 | Author | Jane Addams | 1965 | Social Worker |
| Phillips Brooks | 1910 | Preacher | Oliver Wendell Holmes, Jr. | 1965 | Jurist |
| William Cullen Bryant | 1910 | Author | Sylvanus Thayer | 1965 | Military Educator |
| Frances Elizabeth Willard | 1910 | Reformer | Orville Wright | 1965 | Aviation Pioneer |
| George Bancroft | 1910 | Historian | Albert A. Michelson | 1970 | Physicist |
| Andrew Jackson | 1910 | Statesman | Lillian D. Wald | 1970 | Social Worker |
| John Lothrop Motley | 1910 | Historian | | | |
| Alexander Hamilton | 1915 | Statesman | | | |
| Mark Hopkins | 1915 | Educator | | | |

## Afghanistan

AMIRS

| | |
|---|---|
| Ahmad Shah | 1747-1773 |
| Timur Shah | 1773-1793 |
| Zaman Shah | 1793-1799 |
| Mahmud Shah | 1799-1803 |
| Shah Shuja | 1803-1810 |
| Mahmud Shah (restored) | 1810-1818 |
| [Period of unrest 1818-1826] | |
| Dost Mohammed | 1826-1839 |
| Shah Shuja (restored) | 1839-1842 |
| Dost Mohammed (restored) | 1842-1863 |
| Shere Ali | 1863-1878 |
| Yakub Khan | 1879-1880 |
| Abd-er-Rahman Khan | 1880-1901 |
| Habibullah Khan | 1901-1919 |
| Amanullah Khan | 1919-1929 |
| Inayatullah | 1929 |
| Mohammed Nadir Shah | 1929-1933 |
| Mohammed Zahir Shah | 1933-1973[1] |

PRESIDENT

| | |
|---|---|
| Mohammed Daud Khan | 1973-1978 |
| Nur Mohammed Taraki | 1978-1979 |
| Hafizullah Amin | 1979- |

[1]Republic proclaimed July 1973.

## Albania

| | |
|---|---|
| King William of Wied | 1914 |
| [World War I; Provisional Governments to 1925] | |

PRESIDENT

| | |
|---|---|
| Ahmed Zogu (later Zog I) | 1925-1928 |

KING

| | |
|---|---|
| Zog I (formerly Ahmed Zogu) | 1928-1939 |
| [World War II 1939-1944] | |

PRESIDENTS

| | |
|---|---|
| Omer Nishani | 1946-1953 |
| Haxhi Lleshi | 1953- |

PRIME MINISTERS

| | |
|---|---|
| Enver Hoxha | 1944-1954 |
| Mehmet Shehu | 1954- |

## Argentina

PRESIDENTS (since 1854)

| | |
|---|---|
| Justo José Urquiza | 1854-1860 |
| Santiago Derqui | 1860-1862 |
| Bartolomé Mitre | 1862-1868 |
| Domingo Faustino Sarmiento | 1868-1874 |
| Nicolás Avellaneda | 1874-1880 |
| Julio Argentino Roca | 1880-1886 |
| Miguel Juárez Celmán | 1886-1890 |
| Carlos Pellegrini | 1890-1892 |
| Luis Sáenz Peña | 1892-1895 |
| José Evaristo Uriburu | 1895-1898 |
| Julio Argentino Roca | 1898-1904 |
| Manuel Quintana | 1904-1906 |
| José Figueroa Alcorta | 1906-1910 |
| Roque Sáenz Peña | 1910-1914 |
| Victorino de la Plaza | 1914-1916 |
| Hipólito Irigoyen | 1916-1922 |
| Marcelo Torcuato de Alvear | 1922-1928 |
| Hipólito Irigoyen | 1928-1930 |
| José Francisco Uriburu (provisional) | 1930-1932 |
| Augustín P. Justo | 1932-1938 |
| Roberto M. Ortiz | 1938-1942 |
| Ramón S. Castillo | 1942-1943 |
| Pedro Ramírez | 1943-1944 |
| Edelmiro J. Farrell | 1944-1946 |
| Juan Domingo Perón | 1946-1955 |
| Pedro Eugenio Aramburu (provisional) | 1955-1958 |
| Arturo Frondizi | 1958-1962 |
| José María Guido | 1962-1963 |
| Arturo Umberto Illia | 1963-1966 |
| Juan Carlos Onganía | 1966-1970 |
| Roberto Marcelo Levingston | 1970-1971 |
| Alejandro Agustín Lanusse | 1971-1973 |
| Héctor Cámpora | 1973[1] |
| Juan Domingo Perón | 1973-1974 |
| Isabel (María Estela) Martinez de Perón | 1974-1976 |
| Jorge Rafael Videla | 1976- |

[1]Resigned to make way for return of Juan Domingo Perón.

## Australia

(Commonwealth established Jan. 1, 1901)

GOVERNORS-GENERAL

| | |
|---|---|
| John Adrian Louis Hope, Earl of Hopetoun, Marquis (1902) of Linlithgow | 1901-1902 |
| Hallam Tennyson, Baron Tennyson | 1902-1904 |
| Henry Stafford Northcote, Baron Northcote | 1904-1908 |
| William Humble Ward, Earl of Dudley | 1908-1911 |
| Thomas Denman, Baron Denman | 1911-1914 |
| Ronald Craufurd Munro-Ferguson, Viscount (1920) Novar of Raith | 1914-1920 |
| Henry William Forster, Baron Forster of Lepe | 1920-1925 |
| John Lawrence Baird, Baron Stonehaven | 1925-1930 |
| Isaac Alfred Isaacs | 1931-1936 |
| Alexander Gore Arkwright Hore-Ruthven, Baron Gowrie | 1936-1945 |
| Henry William Frederick Albert, Duke of Gloucester | 1945-1946 |
| William John McKell | 1947-1953 |
| William Slim | 1953-1960 |
| William Shepherd Morrison, Vis. Dunrossil | 1960-1961 |
| William Philip Sidney, Vis. De L'Isle | 1961-1965 |
| Richard Gardiner Casey, Baron Casey | 1965-1969 |
| Paul Meernaa Caedwalla Hasluck | 1969-1974 |
| John Robert Kerr | 1974-1977 |
| Zelman Cowen | 1977- |

PRIME MINISTERS

| | |
|---|---|
| Edmund Barton | 1901-1903 |
| Alfred Deakin | 1903-1904 |
| John C. Watson | 1904 |
| George Houstoun Reid | 1904-1905 |
| Alfred Deakin | 1905-1908 |
| Andrew Fisher | 1908-1909 |
| Alfred Deakin | 1909-1910 |
| Andrew Fisher | 1910-1913 |
| Joseph Cook | 1913-1914 |
| Andrew Fisher | 1914-1915 |
| William M. Hughes | 1915-1923 |
| Stanley M. Bruce | 1923-1929 |
| James H. Scullin | 1929-1931 |
| Joseph A. Lyons | 1932-1939 |
| Robert Gordon Menzies | 1939-1941 |
| Arthur William Fadden | 1941 |
| John Curtin | 1941-1945 |
| Joseph Benedict Chifley | 1945-1949 |
| Robert Gordon Menzies | 1949-1966 |
| Harold Edward Holt | 1966-1967 |
| John Grey Gorton | 1968-1971 |
| William McMahon | 1971-1972 |
| Edward Gough Whitlam | 1972-1975 |
| Malcolm Fraser | 1975- |

## Austria

DUCHY OF AUSTRIA

| | |
|---|---|
| Babenberg Dynasty | 976-1246 |
| [Interregnum, 1246-1250] | |
| Ottokar (*Ger.* Otakar) | 1251-1276 |
| Rudolf of Hapsburg, Holy Roman Emperor, gains control of duchy | 1276-1291 |
| Dukes of Austria appointed by Emperors (see HOLY ROMAN EMPERORS) | 1291-1740 |
| [Hungary added to Austria, 1687] | |
| [Death of Emperor Charles VI ends male Hapsburg line as rulers of Austria, 1740] | |

# Austria (Continued)

### SOVEREIGNS OF AUSTRIA-HUNGARY

| | |
|---|---|
| Maria Theresa (*Ger.* Maria Theresia), wife of Emperor Francis I | 1740–1780 |
| [War of Austrian Succession, 1740–1748] | |
| Joseph II (Holy Roman Emperor) | 1780–1790 |
| Leopold II (Holy Roman Emperor) | 1790–1792 |
| Francis II (Holy Roman Emperor) | 1792–1804 |
| Francis II, as Francis I, Emperor of Austria | 1804–1835 |
| Ferdinand I, Emperor | 1835–1848 |

### EMPERORS OF AUSTRIA AND KINGS OF HUNGARY

| | |
|---|---|
| Francis Joseph I | 1848–1916 |
| Charles I | 1916–1918 |

### REPUBLIC (1918–1938)[1]

|  |  |
|---|---|
| Karl Seitz | 1919–1920 |
| Michael Hainisch | 1920–1928 |
| Wilhelm Miklas | 1928–1938 |

### SECOND REPUBLIC[2]

|  |  |
|---|---|
| Karl Renner | 1945–1950 |
| Theodor Koerner | 1951–1957 |
| Adolf Schaerf | 1957–1965 |
| Franz Jonas | 1965–1974 |
| Rudolf Kirschschläger | 1974– |

[1] In 1938 Austria became a part of the German Reich.

[2] Established Dec. 19, 1945.

# Bahamas

### GOVERNOR-GENERAL

|  |  |
|---|---|
| Milo Broughton Butler | 1973–1979 |

### PRIME MINISTERS

|  |  |
|---|---|
| Lynden Oscar Pindling | 1973– |

# Bangladesh

### PRESIDENTS

|  |  |
|---|---|
| Abu Sayeed Chowdhury | 1972–1974 |
| Mohammed Ullah | 1974–1975 |
| Mujibur Rahman | 1975 |
| Mushtaque Ahmed | 1975 |
| Abu Sadat Mohammed Sayem | 1975–1977 |
| Ziaur Rahman | 1977– |

### PRIME MINISTERS

|  |  |
|---|---|
| Mujibur Rahman | 1972–1975 |
| Mohammed Mansoor Ali | 1975 |

# Barbados

### GOVERNORS-GENERAL

|  |  |
|---|---|
| John Montague Stow | 1966–1967 |
| Arleigh Winston Scott | 1967–1976 |
| Deighton Lisle Ward | 1976– |

### PRIME MINISTERS

|  |  |
|---|---|
| Errol Walton Barrow | 1966–1976 |
| J. M. G. Adams | 1976– |

# Belgium[1]

### KINGS

| | |
|---|---|
| Leopold I | 1831–1865 |
| Leopold II | 1865–1909 |
| Albert I | 1909–1934 |
| Leopold III | 1934–1951 |
| Baudouin I | 1951– |

[1] The early history of Belgium is part of the story of Flanders; from 1579, when the Hapsburgs lost the Netherlands, until 1713 it was a province of Spain, from 1713–1792 of Austria; in 1792 it became a dependency of France; in 1815 it was reunited with Holland; by a revolt of the people in 1830 the modern kingdom of Belgium was established.

# Bolivia

### PRESIDENTS (since 1825)

|  |  |
|---|---|
| Antonio José de Sucre | 1826–1828 |
| Andrés Santa Cruz | 1829–1839 |
| José Miguel de Velasco | 1839–1841 |
| José Ballivián | 1841–1848 |
| Manuel Isidoro Belzú | 1848–1855 |
| Jorge Córdoba | 1855–1857 |
| José María Linares (dictator) | 1857–1861 |
| José María de Achá | 1861–1864 |
| Mariano Melgarejo (dictator) | 1865–1871 |
| Augustín Morales | 1871–1872 |
| Adolfo Ballivián | 1873–1874 |
| Tomás Frías | 1874–1876 |
| Hilarión Daza | 1876–1880 |
| Narciso Campero | 1880–1884 |
| Gregorio Pacheco | 1884–1888 |
| Aniceto Arce | 1888–1892 |
| Mariano Baptista | 1892–1896 |
| Severo Fernández Alonso | 1896–1899 |
| José Manuel Pando | 1899–1904 |
| Ismael Montes | 1904–1909 |
| Eliodoro Villazón | 1909–1913 |
| Ismael Montes | 1913–1917 |
| José Gutiérrez Guerra (deposed) | 1917–1920 |
| [Provisional junta, 1920–1921] | |
| Bautista Saavedra | 1921–1925 |
| Felipe Guzmán (provisional) | 1925–1926 |
| Hernando Siles (deposed) | 1926–1930 |
| Carlos Blanco Galindo (provisional) | 1930–1931 |
| Daniel Salamanca | 1931–1934 |
| José Luis Tejada Sorzano (deposed) | 1934–1936 |
| José David Toro (deposed) | 1936–1937 |
| Germán Busch | 1937–1939 |
| Carlos Quintanilla (provisional) | 1939–1940 |
| Enrique Peñaranda | 1940–1943 |
| Gualberto Villarroel | 1943–1946 |
| Tomás Monje Gutiérrez (provisional) | 1946–1947 |
| Enrique Hertzog | 1947–1949 |
| Mamerto Urriolagoitia | 1949–1951 |
| Hugo Balliviáu R. | 1951–1952 |
| Victor Paz Estenssoro | 1952–1956 |
| Hernán Siles Zuazo | 1956–1960 |
| Victor Paz Estenssoro | 1960–1964 |
| René Barrientos Ortuño | 1966–1969 |
| Alfredo Ovando Candia | 1969–1970 |
| Juan José Torres Gonzáles | 1970–1971 |
| Hugo Banzer Suárez | 1971–1978 |
| Juan Pereda Asbún | 1978 |
| David Padilla Arancibia | 1978–1979 |
| Walter Guevara Arze (provisional) | 1979– |

# Brazil

### EMPERORS[1]

| | |
|---|---|
| Dom Pedro I (abdicated) | 1822–1831 |
| Dom Pedro II (dethroned) | 1831–1889[2] |

### PRESIDENTS[3]

|  |  |
|---|---|
| Manuel Deodoro da Fonesca | 1889–1891[4] |
| Floriano Peixoto | 1891–1894 |
| Prudente José de Moraes Barros | 1894–1898 |
| Manuel Ferraz de Campos Salles | 1898–1902 |
| Francisco de Paula Rodrigues Alves | 1902–1906 |
| Affonso Augusto Moreira Penna | 1906–1909 |
| Nilo Peçanha | 1909–1910 |
| Hermes da Fonseca | 1910–1914 |
| Wenceslau Braz Pereira Gomes | 1914–1918 |
| Francisco de Paula Rodrigues Alves[5] | 1918–1919 |
| Delfim Moreira (acting) | 1918–1919 |
| Epitacio da Silva Pessôa | 1919–1922 |

### PRESIDENTS (Continued)

|  |  |
|---|---|
| Arthur da Silva Bernardes | 1922–1926 |
| Washington Luiz Pereira de Souza (deposed) | 1926–1930 |
| Getulio Dornelles Vargas[6] | 1930–1945 |
| José Linhares (provisional) | 1945–1946 |
| Enrico Gaspar Dutra | 1946–1951 |
| Getúlio Dornelles Vargas | 1951–1954 |
| João Café Filho | 1954–1955 |
| Nereú Ramos (acting) | 1955–1956 |
| Jusceline Kubitschek de Oliveira | 1956–1961 |
| Jânio Quadros | 1961 |
| João Belchior Marques Goulart | 1961–1964 |
| Humberto Castelo Branco | 1964–1967 |
| Arthur Costa e Silva | 1967–1969 |
| Emilio Garrastazú Médici | 1969–1974 |
| Ernesto Geisel | 1974– |

[1] Independence proclaimed Sept. 7, 1822. [2] Regency, 1831–1840. [3] Republic, "United States of Brazil," proclaimed Nov. 15, 1889. [4] Provisional president 1889 to Feb. 24, 1891; elected president, Feb. 24–Nov. 23, 1891. [5] Died (Jan. 16, 1919) without taking office. [6] Provisional president 1930–1934; elected president 1934.

## Bulgaria[1]

| | |
|---|---|
| Prince Alexander of Battenberg, Prince of Bulgaria | 1879–1886 |
| [Eastern Rumelia united with Bulgaria, 1885] | |
| Prince Ferdinand of Saxe-Coburg | 1887–1908 |
| [Independence of Bulgaria proclaimed, 1908] | |
| Ferdinand as king (czar) | 1908–1918 |
| Boris III | 1918–1943 |
| Simeon II | 1943–1946[2] |

### CHAIRMEN OF THE PRESIDIUM

| | |
|---|---|
| Vasil Kolarov (provisional) | 1946–1947 |
| Mintcho Neytchev | 1947–1950 |
| Georgi Damyanov | 1950–1958 |
| Dimitur Ganev | 1958–1964 |
| Georgi Traikov | 1964–1971 |
| Todor Zhivkov | 1971– |

[1] Principality of Bulgaria and autonomous province of Eastern Rumelia constituted by the Treaty of Berlin, July 13, 1878.
[2] Proclaimed a republic in Sept. 1946.

## Burma

### PRESIDENTS

| | |
|---|---|
| Sao Shwe Thaike | 1948–1952 |
| Ba U | 1952–1957 |
| U Win Maung | 1957–1962 |
| Ne Win[1] | 1962– |

[1] 1962 coup d'état replaced the President with a Chairman of the Revolutionary Council. A new constitution in 1974 restored presidential rule.

## Canada

### GOVERNORS-GENERAL SINCE CONFEDERATION

| | |
|---|---|
| Charles Stanley Monck, Viscount Monck[1] | 1867–1868 |
| John Young, Baron Lisgar | 1869–1872 |
| Frederick T. H.-T. Blackwood, Marquis of Dufferin and Ava | 1872–1878 |
| John Douglas S. Campbell, Marquis of Lorne and Duke of Argyll | 1878–1883 |
| Henry C. K. Petty Fitzmaurice, Marquis of Lansdowne | 1883–1888 |
| Frederick A. Stanley, Earl of Derby | 1888–1893 |
| John C. Gordon, Marquis of Aberdeen and Temair | 1893–1898 |
| Gilbert John Elliot-Murray-Kynynmond, Earl of Minto | 1898–1904 |
| Albert H. G. Grey, Earl Grey | 1904–1911 |
| Prince Arthur William Patrick Albert, Duke of Connaught | 1911–1916 |
| Victor C. W. Cavendish, Duke of Devonshire | 1916–1921 |
| Julian H. G. Byng, Viscount Byng of Vimy | 1921–1926 |
| Freeman Freeman-Thomas, Marquis of Willingdon | 1926–1931 |
| Vere Brabazon Ponsonby, Earl of Bessborough | 1931–1935 |
| John Buchan, Baron Tweedsmuir | 1935–1940 |
| Alexander A. F. Cambridge, Earl of Athlone | 1940–1946 |
| Harold R. L. G. Alexander, Vis. Alexander of Tunis | 1946–1952 |
| Vincent Massey | 1952–1959 |
| Georges P. Vanier | 1959–1967 |
| Roland Michener | 1967–1974 |
| Jules Léger | 1974– |

### PRIME MINISTERS

| | |
|---|---|
| John A. Macdonald, Conservative | 1867–1873 |
| Alexander Mackenzie, Liberal | 1873–1878 |
| John A. Macdonald, Conservative | 1878–1891 |
| John J. C. Abbott, Conservative | 1891–1892 |
| John S. D. Thompson, Conservative | 1892–1894 |
| Mackenzie Bowell, Conservative | 1894–1896 |
| Charles Tupper, Conservative | 1896 |
| Wilfrid Laurier, Liberal | 1896–1911 |
| Robert L. Borden, Conservative | 1911–1920 |
| Arthur Meighen, Conservative | 1920–1921 |
| W. L. Mackenzie King, Liberal | 1921–1926 |
| Arthur Meighen, Conservative | 1926 |
| W. L. Mackenzie King, Liberal | 1926–1930 |
| Richard B. Bennett, Conservative | 1930–1935 |
| W. L. Mackenzie King, Liberal | 1935–1948 |
| Louis Stephen St. Laurent, Liberal | 1948–1957 |
| John George Diefenbaker, Conservative | 1957–1963 |
| Lester B. Pearson, Liberal | 1963–1968 |
| Pierre Elliott Trudeau, Liberal | 1968–1979 |
| Joe Clark, Progressive Conservative | 1979– |

[1] He had been governor general of British North America since 1861.

## Ceylon (since 1972 officially Sri Lanka)

### GOVERNORS-GENERAL

| | |
|---|---|
| Henry Monck-Mason Moore | 1948–1949 |
| Lord Soulbury | 1949–1954 |
| Oliver Goonetilleke | 1954–1962 |
| William Gopallawa | 1962–1972 |

### PRESIDENTS

| | |
|---|---|
| William Gopallawa | 1972–1978 |
| J. R. Jayawardene | 1978– |

### PRIME MINISTERS

| | |
|---|---|
| D. S. Senanayake | 1948–1954 |
| John Kotelawala | 1954–1956 |
| S. W. R. D. Bandaranaike | 1956–1959 |
| Sirimavo R. D. Bandaranaike | 1960–1965 |
| Dudley Senanayake | 1965–1970 |
| Sirimavo R. D. Bandaranaike | 1970–1977 |
| J. R. Jayawardene | 1977–1978 |
| Ranasingle Premadasa | 1978– |

## Chile

### PRESIDENTS (since 1831)

| | |
|---|---|
| Bernardo O'Higgins (dictator) | 1817–1823 |
| [Ten different presidents, 1823–1831] | |
| Joaquín Prieto | 1831–1841 |
| Manuel Bulnes | 1841–1851 |
| Manuel Montt | 1851–1861 |
| José Joaquín Pérez | 1861–1871 |
| Federico Errázuriz Zañartu | 1871–1876 |
| Aníbal Pinto | 1876–1881 |
| Domingo Santa María | 1881–1886 |
| José Manuel Balmaceda | 1886–1891 |
| Jorge Montt | 1891–1896 |
| Federico Errazuriz Echaurren | 1896–1901 |
| Germán Riesco | 1901–1906 |
| Pedro Montt | 1906–1910 |
| Elías Fernández Albano (acting) | 1910 |
| Emiliano Figueroa Larrain (acting) | 1910 |
| Ramón Barros Luco | 1910–1915 |
| Juan Luis Sanfuentes | 1915–1920 |
| Arturo Alessandri Palma | 1920–1924 |
| Luis Altamirano (acting) | 1924–1925 |
| Emilio Bello Codesido (acting) | 1925 |
| Arturo Alessandri Palma (restored) | 1925 |
| Luis Barros Borgoño (acting) | 1925 |
| Emiliano Figueroa Larrain | 1925–1927 |
| Carlos Ibáñez del Campo | 1927–1931 |
| Pedro Opazo Letelier (acting) | 1931 |
| Juan Esteban Montero (acting) | 1931 |
| Manuel Trucco (acting) | 1931 |
| Juan Esteban Montero | 1931–1932 |
| Carlos G. Dávila (acting) | 1932 |
| Bartolomé Blanche (acting) | 1932 |
| Abraham Oyanedel (acting) | 1932 |
| Arturo Alessandri Palma (re-elected) | 1932–1938 |
| Pedro Aguirre Cerda | 1938–1941 |
| Gerónimo Méndez (acting) | 1941–1942 |
| Juan Antonio Ríos | 1942–1946 |
| Gabriel González Videla | 1946–1952 |
| Carlos Ibáñez del Campo | 1952–1958 |
| Jorge Alessandri Rodríguez | 1958–1964 |
| Eduardo Frei Montalva | 1964–1970 |
| Salvador Allende Gossens | 1970–1973 |
| Augusto Pinochet Ugarte | 1973– |

# China

EMPIRE (DYNASTIES)

| | |
|---|---|
| Hsia | 2205–1766 B.C. |
| Shang (or Yin) | 1766–1122 B.C. |
| Chou (Chow) | 1122–255[1] B.C. |
| Ch'in (Ts'in) | 255[1]–206 B.C. |
| Han, Earlier, or Western | 202 B.C.–9 A.D. |
| Han, Later, or Eastern | 25 A.D.–220 |
| Wei | 220–264 |
| Chin or Tsin (Western Chin) | 265–317 |
| Chin or Tsin (Eastern Chin) | 317–419 |
| Sung (Liu Sung) | 420–479 |
| Ch'i (Tsi) | 479–502 |
| Liang | 502–557 |
| Ch'ên (Chen) | 557–589 |
| Sui | 589–618 |
| T'ang (Tang) | 618–907 |
| Five Dynasties | 907–960 |
| Sung | 960–1127[2] |
| Kin Tatar (in the North) | 1127–1234 |
| Southern Sung | 1127[2]–1280[3] |
| Yüan (Mongol) in the North | 1206–1280 |
| Kublai Khan | 1260–1294 |
| Yüan (Mongol) | 1280–1368 |
| Ming | 1368–1644 |
| Ch'ing or Ta Ch'ing (Manchu) | 1644–1912 |

RULERS OF CH'ING (MANCHU) DYNASTY

| | |
|---|---|
| Shun Chih | 1644–1662 |
| K'ang-hsi | 1662–1722 |
| Yung Chêng | 1723–1735 |
| Ch'ien Lung | 1736–1796 |
| Chia Ch'ing | 1796–1820 |
| Tao Kuang | 1821–1850 |
| Hsien Fêng | 1851–1861 |
| T'ung Chih | 1862–1875 |
| Kuang Hsü[4] | 1875–1908 |
| Hsüan T'ung[5] | 1908–1912 |

REPUBLIC

| | |
|---|---|
| Provisional President–Sun Yat-sen | 1911–1912 |
| Provisional President–Yüan Shih-k'ai | 1912–1913 |
| President Yüan Shih-k'ai | 1913–1916 |
| President Li Yüan-hung | 1916–1917 |
| President Gen. Feng Kuo-chang | 1917–1918 |
| President Hsü Shih-ch'ang | 1918–1922 |
| President Li Yüan-hung | 1922–1923 |
| President Tsao Kun | 1923–1924 |
| [Civil War] | |
| Pres. of Executive Yüan: Chiang Kai-shek | 1928–1945 |
| President of National Government: | |
| Lin Sên | 1932–1943 |
| Chiang Kai-shek | 1943–1949[6] |

REPUBLIC (NATIONALIST) PRESIDENTS

| | |
|---|---|
| Li Tsung-jen (acting) | 1949–1950 |
| Chiang Kai-shek | 1950–1975 |
| Yen Chia-kan | 1975–1978 |
| Chiang Ching-kuo | 1978– |

PEOPLE'S REPUBLIC (COMMUNIST) HEAD OF STATE

| | |
|---|---|
| Mao Tse-tung[7] | 1949–1959 |
| Liu Shao-ch'i[8] | 1959–1968[9] |
| Tung Pi-wu | 1972–1975[10] |
| Chu Teh | 1975–1976 |
| Yeh Chien-ying | 1978– |

[1] Or 221. [2] Or 1125. [3] Or 1260. [4] Tzu Hsi, Empress Dowager and actual ruler, 1898–1908. [5] Better known as Henry Pu-yi; later, as K'ang Te, Emperor of Manchukuo (1934–45). [6] Politically divided since 1949; mainland China under the People's Republic (Communist); Taiwan under the Republic (Nationalist). [7] Chairman of the Central People's Government Council. [8] Chairman of the People's Republic of China. [9] Dismissed in Oct. 1968. [10] Acting.

# Colombia

PRESIDENTS (since 1870)

| | |
|---|---|
| Eustorgio Salgar | 1870–1872 |
| Manuel Murillo Toro | 1872–1874 |
| Santiago Pérez | 1874–1876 |
| Aquileo Parra | 1876–1878 |
| Julián Trujillo | 1878–1880 |
| Rafael Núñez | 1880–1882 |
| Francisco Javier Zaldúa | 1882 |
| Climacho Calderón | 1882 |
| José Eusebio Otálora (acting) | 1882–1884 |
| Ezequiel Hurtado | 1884 |
| Rafael Núñez | 1884–1886 |
| José Maria Campo Serrano | 1886–1887 |
| Eliseo Payán | 1887 |
| Rafael Núñez | 1887–1888 |
| Carlos Holguín | 1888–1892 |
| Miguel Antonio Caro | 1892–1896 |
| Guillermo Quintero Calderón | 1896 |
| Miguel Antonio Caro | 1896–1898 |
| José Manuel Marroquín (acting) | 1898 |
| Manuel Antonio Sanclemente | 1898–1900 |
| José Manuel Marroquin | 1900–1904 |
| Rafael Reyes | 1904–1908 |
| Euclides de Angulo | 1908 |
| Rafael Reyes | 1908–1909 |
| Jorge Holguín (acting) | 1909 |
| Ramón González Valencia | 1909–1910 |
| Carlos E. Restrepo | 1910–1914 |
| José Vicente Concha | 1914–1918 |
| Marco Fidel Suárez | 1918–1921 |
| Jorge Holguín | 1921–1922 |
| Pedro Nel Ospina | 1922–1926 |
| Miguel Abadia Méndez | 1926–1930 |
| Enrique Olaya Herrera | 1930–1934 |
| Alfonso López | 1934–1938 |
| Eduardo Santos | 1938–1942 |
| Alfonso López | 1942–1945 |
| Alberto Lleras Camargo | 1945–1946 |
| Mariano Ospina Pérez | 1946–1950 |
| Laureano Gómez | 1950–1953 |
| Gustavo Rojas Pinilla | 1953–1957 |
| Gabriel Paris | 1957–1958 |
| Alberto Lleras Camargo | 1958–1962 |
| Guillermo León Valencia | 1962–1966 |
| Carlos Lleras Restrepo | 1966–1970 |
| Misael Pastrana Borrero | 1970–1974 |
| Alfonso López Michelsen | 1974–1978 |
| Julio César Turbay Ayala | 1978– |

# Costa Rica

PRESIDENTS (since 1893)

| | |
|---|---|
| Rafael Iglesias | 1893–1902 |
| Ascensión Esquivel | 1902–1906 |
| Cleto González Víquez | 1906–1910 |
| Ricardo Jiménez Oreamuno | 1910–1914 |
| Alfredo González Flores | 1914–1917 |
| Federico Tinoco Granados | 1917–1919 |
| Francisco Aguilar Barquero (provisional) | 1919–1920 |
| Julio Acosta | 1920–1924 |
| Ricardo Jiménez Oreamuno | 1924–1928 |
| Cleto González Víquez | 1928–1932 |
| Ricardo Jiménez Oreamuno | 1932–1936 |
| León Cortés Castro | 1936–1940 |
| Rafael Angel Calderón Guardia | 1940–1944 |
| Teodoro Picado Michalski | 1944–1948 |
| José Figueres Ferrer | 1948–1949 |
| Otilio Ulate | 1949–1953 |
| José Figueres Ferrer | 1953–1958 |
| Mario Echandi Jiménez | 1958–1962 |
| Francisco José Orlich Bolmarcich | 1962–1966 |
| José Joaquin Trejos Fernandez | 1966–1970 |
| José Figuéres Ferrer | 1970–1974 |
| Daniel Oduber Quirós | 1974–1978 |
| Rodrigo Carazo Odio | 1978– |

## Cuba

U. S. PROVISIONAL GOVERNORS

| | |
|---|---|
| Gen. John Rutter Brooke | 1899[1] |
| Gen. Leonard Wood | 1899–1902 |

PRESIDENT

| | |
|---|---|
| Tomás Estrada Palma | 1902–1906 |

U. S. PROVISIONAL GOVERNORS

| | |
|---|---|
| William Howard Taft | 1906[2] |
| Charles Edward Magoon | 1906–1909 |

PRESIDENTS

| | |
|---|---|
| José Miguel Gómes | 1909–1913 |
| Mario García Menocal | 1913–1921 |
| Alfredo Zayas y Alfonso | 1921–1925 |
| Gerardo Machado y Morales (deposed) | 1925–1933 |

PRESIDENTS (Continued)

| | |
|---|---|
| Carlos Manuel de Céspedes y Quesada (provisional) | 1933[3] |
| [Provisional junta, Sept. 5–10, 1933] | |
| Ramón Grau San Martín (provisional) | 1933–1934 |
| Carlos Mendieta (provisional) | 1934–1935 |
| José A. Barnet y Vinageras (provisional) | 1935–1936 |
| Miguel Mariano Gómez y Arias (deposed) | 1936 |
| Federico Laredo Bru | 1936–1940 |
| Fulgencio Batista y Zaldívar | 1940–1944 |
| Ramón Grau San Martín | 1944–1948 |
| Carlos Prío Socarrás | 1948–1952 |
| Fulgencio Batista y Zaldívar | 1952–1959 |
| Manuel Urrutia Lleo (provisional) | 1959 |
| Osvaldo Dorticós Torrado | 1959–1976 |
| Fidel Castro Ruz | 1976– |

[1] In office Jan. 1–Dec. 23, 1899. [2] In office Sept. 29–Oct. 13, 1906. [3] In office Aug. 12–Sept. 5, 1933.

## Czechoslovakia

PRESIDENTS

| | |
|---|---|
| Tomáš Garrigue Masaryk | 1918–1935 |
| Eduard Beneš | 1935–1938 |
| [Occupied by Germany, 1938–1945] | |
| Emil Hácha | 1938–1939 |
| Eduard Beneš[1] | 1940–1948 |
| Klement Gottwald | 1948–1953 |
| Antonín Zápotocký | 1953–1957 |
| Antonín Novotný | 1957–1968 |
| Ludvík Svoboda | 1968–1975 |
| Gustav Husak | 1975– |

PRIME MINISTERS

| | |
|---|---|
| Karel Kramář | 1918–1919 |
| Vlastimil Tusar | 1919–1920 |
| Jan Černý | 1920–1921 |
| Eduard Beneš[2] | 1921–1922 |
| Antonín Švehla | 1922–1926 |

PRIME MINISTERS (Continued)

| | |
|---|---|
| Jan Černý | 1926 |
| Antonín Švehla | 1926–1929 |
| František Udržal | 1929–1932 |
| Jan Malypetr | 1932–1935 |
| Milan Hodža | 1935–1938 |
| Jan Syrovy | 1938 |
| Rudolf Beran | 1938–1939 |
| Jan Srámek[3] | 1940–1945 |
| Zdenek Fierlinger | 1945–1946 |
| Klement Gottwald | 1946–1948 |
| Antonín Zápotocký | 1948–1953 |
| Viliam Široký | 1953–1963 |
| Jozef Lenárt | 1963–1968 |
| Oldřich Černík | 1968–1970 |
| Lubomír Štrougal | 1970– |

[1] Assumed presidency in London; elected 1946. [2] In all the ministries from 1918 to 1935 Eduard Beneš held the portfolio of Minister of Foreign Affairs. [3] With Beneš in London.

## Denmark

| | |
|---|---|
| Gorm the Old | 883?–?940 |
| Harold (or Harald) Bluetooth | 940?–?985 |
| Sweyn (or Svend) Forkbeard | 985?–1014 |
| Harold | 1014–1018 |
| Canute II[1] (or Cnut, Knut) | 1018–1035 |
| Hardecanute[2] (or Harthacnut), or Canute III | 1035–1042 |
| Magnus I (of Norway) | 1042–1047 |

ESTRITH DYNASTY (1047–1375)

| | |
|---|---|
| Sweyn II (or Sweyn Estrithsson) | 1047–1075 |
| Harold | 1076–1080 |
| Canute IV | 1080–1086 |
| Olaf I Hunger | 1086–1095 |
| Eric I the Evergood | 1095–1103 |
| Nicholas I (*Dan.* Niels) | 1104–1134 |
| Eric II the Memorable | 1134–1137 |
| Eric III the Lamb | 1137–1147 |
| Sweyn III and Canute V (Civil War) | 1147–1157 |
| Waldemar (or Valdemar) | 1157–1182 |
| Canute VI | 1182–1202 |
| Waldemar II | 1202–1241 |
| Waldemar III (coregent) | 1219–1231 |
| Eric IV | 1241–1250 |
| Abel | 1250–1252 |
| Christopher I | 1252–1259 |
| Eric V Klipping | 1259–1286 |
| Eric VI Menved | 1286–1319 |
| Christopher II | 1320–1326 and 1330–1332 |
| [Interregnum, 1332–1340] | |
| Waldemar IV Atterdag | 1340–1375 |
| [Interregnum, 1375–1376] | |
| Olaf II | 1376–1387 |
| Margaret, Queen of Denmark, Norway, and Sweden | 1387–1397 |
| [Union of Kalmar, 1397–1523] | |
| Margaret and Eric VII of Pomerania | 1397–1412 |
| Eric VII (alone) | 1412–1439 |
| [Interregnum, 1439–1440] | |
| Christopher III | 1440–1448 |

HOUSE OF OLDENBURG

| | |
|---|---|
| Christian I | 1448–1481 |
| John (*Dan.* Hans) | 1481–1513 |
| Christian II | 1513–1523[3] |

KINGS OF DENMARK AND NORWAY

| | |
|---|---|
| Frederick I (*Dan.* Frederik) | 1523–1533 |
| [Interregnum, 1533–1534] | |
| Christian III | 1534–1559 |
| Frederick II | 1559–1588 |
| Christian IV | 1588–1648 |
| Frederick III | 1648–1670 |
| Christian V | 1670–1699 |
| Frederick IV | 1699–1730 |
| Christian VI | 1730–1746 |
| Frederick V | 1746–1766 |
| Christian VII | 1766–1808 |
| Frederick VI (Regent) | 1784–1808 |
| Frederick VI (King) | 1808–1839 |
| [Norway annexed to Sweden, 1814] | |

SOVEREIGNS OF DENMARK

| | |
|---|---|
| Christian VIII | 1839–1848 |
| Frederick VII | 1848–1863 |
| Christian IX | 1863–1906 |
| Frederick VIII | 1906–1912 |
| Christian X | 1912–1947 |
| Frederick IX | 1947–1972 |
| Margrethe II | 1972– |

[1] King of England 1016–1035. [2] King of England 1040–1042. [3] Denmark and Sweden are separated, 1523.

## Dominican Republic

PRESIDENTS

| | |
|---|---|
| Pedro Santana | 1844–1848 |
| Manuel Jiménez | 1848–1849 |
| Buenaventura Báez | 1849–1853 |
| Pedro Santana | 1853–1856 |
| Manuel de Regla Mota | 1856 |
| Buenaventura Báez | 1856–1857 |
| José Desiderio Valaerde | 1857–1858 |
| Pedro Santana | 1858–1861 |
| [Under Spanish control 1861–1865] | |
| Antonio Pimentel | 1865 |
| José María Cabral | 1865 |
| Buenaventura Báez | 1865–1866 |

# Dominican Republic (Continued)

PRESIDENTS (Continued)

| | |
|---|---|
| José María Cabral | 1866–1868 |
| Buenaventura Báez | 1868–1873 |
| Ignacio María González | 1874–1876 |
| Ulises Espaillat | 1876 |
| Ignacio María González | 1876 |
| Buenaventura Báez | 1876–1878 |
| Ignacio María González | 1878 |
| Cesáreo Guillermo | 1879 |
| Gregório Luperón | 1879–1880 |
| Fernando A. Meriño | 1880–1882 |
| Ulises Heureaux | 1882–1883 |
| Francisco Gregorio Billini | 1883–1884 |
| Alejandro Woss y Gil | 1884–1887 |
| Ulises Heureaux | 1887–1899 |
| Horacio Vásquez | 1899 |
| Juan Isidro Jiménez | 1899–1902 |
| Horacio Vásquez | 1902–1903 |
| Alejandro Woss y Gil | 1903 |
| Carlos Morales | 1903–1906 |
| Ramón Cáceres | 1906–1911 |
| Eladio Victoria | 1911–1912 |
| Adolfo Nouel | 1912–1913 |
| José Bordas Valdes | 1913–1914 |
| Ramón Báez | 1914 |
| Juan Isidro Jiménez | 1914–1916 |
| Francisco Henríquez y Carvajal | 1916 |
| [U.S. military occupation 1916–1922] | |
| Vicini Burgos | 1922–1924 |
| Horacio Vásquez | 1924–1930 |
| Rafael Estrella Ureña | 1930 |
| Rafael Leonidas Trujillo Molina | 1930–1938 |
| Jacinto Bienvenido Peynado | 1938–1940 |
| Manuel de Jesús Troncoso de la Concha | 1940–1942 |
| Rafael Leonidas Trujillo Molina | 1942–1952 |
| Héctor Bienvenido Trujillo Molina | 1952–1960 |
| Joaquín Balaguer | 1960–1962 |
| Rafael Bonnelly | 1962–1963 |
| Juan Bosch | 1963 |
| [Military juntas 1963–1965] | |
| Héctor García Godoy | 1965–1966 |
| Joaquín Balaguer | 1966–1978 |
| Antonio Guzmán Fernández | 1978– |

[1] Not including many short term provisional governments since independence in 1844.

# Ecuador

PRESIDENTS (since 1830)

| | |
|---|---|
| Juan José Flores | 1830–1835 |
| Vincente Rocafuerte | 1835–1839 |
| Juan José Flores | 1839–1845 |
| Vicente Ramón Roca | 1845–1850 |
| Diego Noboa | 1851 |
| José María Urvina (or Urbina) | 1852–1856 |
| Francisco Robles | 1856–1859 |
| Gabriel García Moreno | 1861–1865 |
| Gerónimo Carrión | 1865–1867 |
| Javier Espinosa | 1868–1869 |
| Gabriel García Moreno | 1869–1875 |
| Antonio Borrero | 1875–1876 |
| Ignacio de Veintemilla | 1876–1883 |
| José María Plácido Caamaño | 1883–1888 |
| Antonio Flores | 1888–1892 |
| Luis Cordero | 1892–1895 |
| Eloy Alfaro | 1897–1901 |
| Leonidas Plaza Gutiérrez | 1901–1905 |
| Lisardo García (deposed) | 1905–1906 |
| Eloy Alfaro | 1907–1911 |
| Emilo Estrada | 1911 |
| Leonidas Plaza Gutiérrez | 1912–1916 |
| Alfredo Baquerizo Moreno | 1916–1920 |
| José Luis Tamayo | 1920–1924 |
| Gonzalo S. Córdoba (deposed) | 1924–1925 |
| [Provisional junta, July 9, 1925–Apr. 1, 1926] | |
| Isidro Ayora (provisional, 1926–1929) | 1926–1931 |
| Luis A. Larrea Alba (provisional) | 1931 |
| Alfredo Baquerizo Moreno (provisional) | 1931–1932 |
| [Period of revolution, Aug. 27–Sept. 2, 1932] | |
| Alberto Guerrero Martínez (provisional) | 1932 |
| Juan de Dios Martínez Mera (deposed) | 1932–1933 |
| Abelardo Montalvo (provisional) | 1933–1934 |
| José María Velasco Ibarra (deposed) | 1934–1935 |
| Antonio Pons (provisional) | 1935 |
| Federico Páez ("supreme chief") | 1935–1937 |
| G. Alberto Enríquez (provisional) | 1937–1938 |
| Manuel M. Borrero (provisional) | 1938 |
| Aurelio Mosquera Narváez | 1938–1939 |
| Carlos Alberto Arroyo del Río (acting, 1939) | 1940–1944 |
| José María Velasco Ibarra | 1944–1947 |
| Carlos Mancheno | 1947 |
| Carlos Julio Arosenna | 1947 |
| Galo Peaza Lasso | 1948–1952 |
| José María Velasco Ibarra | 1952–1956 |
| Camilo Ponce Enríquez | 1956–1960 |
| José María Velasco Ibarra | 1960–1961 |
| Carlos Julio Arosemena Monroy[1] | 1961–1963 |
| José María Velasco Ibarra | 1968–1972 |
| Guillermo Rodriguez Lara[2] | 1972–1976 |
| Jaime Roldós Aguilera | 1979– |

[1] Ousted July 1963; military junta set up to rule.

[2] Resigned; military junta ruled 1976–1979.

# Egypt[1] (Ancient)

OLD KINGDOM (Dynasties I-VI)

| | |
|---|---|
| Accession of Menes | 3400 (3500?) |
| Ist and IId Dynasties (Thinite) | 3400–2980 |
| IIId Dynasty (Memphite) | 2980–2900 |
| Zoser | |
| Sneiru | |
| IVth Dynasty (Memphite) | 2900–2750 |
| Khufu or Cheops, pyramid builder | |
| Khafre | |
| Menkure | |
| Vth Dynasty (Memphite) | 2750–2625 |
| VIth Dynasty (Memphite) | 2625–2475 |
| Pepi I | |
| Pepi II (reign of 90 years) | |
| VIIth and VIIIth Dynasties (Memphite) | 2475–2445 |

MIDDLE KINGDOM (IX–XVII)

| | |
|---|---|
| IXth and Xth Dynasties (Heracleopolitan) | 2445–2160 |
| XIth Dynasty (Theban) | 2160–2000 |
| Nibbepetre Mentuhotep IV | |
| XIIth Dynasty (Theban) | 2000–1788 |
| Amenemhet I | 2000–1970 |
| Sesostris (or Senusret or Usertesen) | 1980–1935 |
| Amenemhet II | 1938–1903 |
| Sesostris II | 1906–1887 |
| Sesostris III | 1887–1849 |
| Amenemhet III | 1849–1801 |
| XIIIth Dynasty (Theban) | 1778 |
| XIVth Dynasty (Xoite) | |
| XVth and XVIth Dynasties (Hyksos or "Shepherd Kings") | to |
| XVIIth Dynasty (Theban) | 1580 |

NEW KINGDOM or NEW EMPIRE (XVIII–XX)

| | |
|---|---|
| XVIIIth Dynasty (Diospolite) | 1580–1350 |
| Ahmose I (or Ahmes) | 1580–1557 |
| Amenhotep I (or Amenophis) | 1557 |
| Thutmose I (or Thothmes) | to |
| Thutmose II | 1501 |

NEW KINGDOM (Continued)

| | |
|---|---|
| Thutmose III and | 1501 |
| Queen Hatshepsut (or Hatasu) | to 1447 |
| Amenhotep II | 1447–1420 |
| Thutmose IV | 1420–1411 |
| Amenhotep III | 1411–1375 |
| Ikhnaton (or Amenhotep IV) | 1375–1358 |
| Tutankhamen (or Tutankhamon) | fl. c. 1358 |
| XIXth Dynasty (Diospolite) | 1350–1200 |
| Harmhab | 1350–1315 |
| Seti I | 1313–1292 |
| Ramses II (or Sesostris) | 1292–1225 |
| Merneptah (or Meneptah) | 1225–1215 |
| Seti II | 1209?–1205 |
| XXth Dynasty (Diospolite) | 1200–1090 |
| Ramessides (Ramses III–XII) esp. Ramses III (1198–1167) | 1198–1090 |
| XXIst Dynasty (Tanite) | 1090–945 |
| XXIId Dynasty (Bubastite) | 945–745 |
| Sheshonk I or Shoshenk or Shisak | 945–924 |
| Osorkon I | 924–895 |
| Osorkon II | 874–853 |
| XXIIId Dynasty (Tanite) | 745–718 |
| XXXIVth Dynasty (Saite) | 718–712 |
| XXVth Dynasty (Ethiopian) | 712–663 |
| XXVIth Dynasty (Saite) | 663–525 |
| Psamtik I | 663–609 |
| Necho II (or Niku) | 609–593 |
| Psamtik II | 593–588 |
| Apries (or Hophra) | 588–569 |
| XXVIIth to XXXth Dynasties (Persian) | 525–332 |
| [Egypt a Persian province] | |
| [Egypt conquered by Alexander the Great 332 B.C.] | |

PTOLEMIES

| | |
|---|---|
| Ptolemy I–XIV | 323–30 |
| Cleopatra VII (or VI) | 51–49, 48–30 |

[1] All dates in this table are B.C. The spelling of names and the chronology are based on Breasted. Under some of the Dynasties (names in parentheses) the more important rulers are mentioned; from the XIIth Dynasty their reign dates are also given. All dates before the XIIth Dynasty are problematical; after that they are determined with fair certainty by astronomical factors, although scholars do not agree on all of these. [2] These overlapping dates indicate coregency of father and son.

# EGYPT[1] (MODERN)

VICEROYS (KHEDIVES)[2]

| | |
|---|---|
| Mebemet Ali | 1805–1848 |
| Ibrahim Pasha | 1848 |
| Abbas I | 1848–1854 |
| Said Pasha | 1854–1863 |
| Ismail Pasha | 1863–1879 |
| Tewnk Pasha | 1879–1892 |
| Abbas II | 1892–1914 |

SULTANS

| | |
|---|---|
| Hussein Kamil | 1914–1917 |
| Ahmed Fuad Pasha | 1917–1922 |

KINGS

| | |
|---|---|
| Fuad I (Ahmed Fuad Pasha) | 1922–1936 |
| Faruk I | 1936–1952 |
| Faruk II | 1952–1953 |

PRESIDENTS

| | |
|---|---|
| Muhammad Naguib | 1953–1954 |
| Gámal Abdel Nasser (premier 1954–56) | 1956–1970 |
| Anwar el-Sadat | 1970– |

[1] For more than 19 centuries after 30 B.C. Egypt was under the control of different foreign powers: Roman province 30 B.C. to A.D. 640; conquered by Moslems 640–646; part of caliphate 646–968; Fatimid caliphs 968–1171; Mamelukes (sultans and beys) 1250–1798; French conquest 1798–1802; Turkish and British control 1803–1922. From 1958 to 1971 known as the United Arab Republic; in 1971 became the Arab Republic of Egypt. [2] The title *Khedive* first officially granted by the Ottoman Sultan in 1867; abolished by the British in 1914.

# EL SALVADOR

PRESIDENTS (since 1876)

| | |
|---|---|
| Rafael Zaldívar | 1876–1885 |
| Francisco Menéndez | 1885–1890 |
| Carlos Ezeta (provisional) | 1890–1894 |
| Rafael Antonio Gutiérrez | 1895–1899 |
| Tomás Regalado | 1899–1903 |
| Pedro José Escalón | 1903–1907 |
| Fernando Figueroa | 1907–1911 |
| Manuel Enrique Araújo | 1911–1913 |
| Carlos Meléndez (acting) | 1913–1914 |
| Alfonso Quiñónez Molina (provisional) | 1914–1915 |
| Carlos Meléndez | 1915–1919 |
| Jorge Meléndez | 1919–1923 |
| Alfonso Quiñónez Molina | 1923–1927 |
| Pío Romero Bosque | 1927–1931 |
| Arturo Araújo | 1931 |
| Maximiliano Hernández Martínez | 1931–1934 |
| Andrés Ignacio Menéndez (acting) | 1934–1935 |
| Maximiliano Hernández Martínez | 1935–1944 |
| Andrés Ignacio Menéndez (acting) | 1944 |
| Osmin Aguirre Salinas | 1944 |
| Salvador Castañeda Castro | 1945–1949 |
| Oscar Osorio | 1949–1956 |
| José María Lemus | 1956–1960[1] |
| Julio Adalberto Rivera | 1962–1967 |
| Fidel Sánchez Hernández | 1967–1972 |
| Arturo Armando Molina | 1972–1977 |
| Carlos Humberto Romero | 1977– |

[1] Military junta governed (1960–1961).

# ETHIOPIA (MODERN)

EMPERORS

| | |
|---|---|
| Theodore | 1855–1868 |
| Johannes IV | 1872–1889 |
| Menelik II | 1889–1913 |
| Lij Yasu | 1913–1916 |
| Zauditu | 1916–1930 |
| Haile Selassie (deposed) | 1930–1974 |

REVOLUTIONARY HEADS OF STATE

| | |
|---|---|
| Aman Michael Andom | 1974 |
| Teferi Benti | 1974–1977 |
| Mengistu Haile Mariam | 1977– |

# FINLAND

PRESIDENTS

| | |
|---|---|
| Kaarlo Juho Stahlberg | 1919–1925 |
| Lauri Kristian Relander | 1925–1931 |
| Pehr Evind Svinhufvud | 1931–1937 |
| Kyösti Kallio | 1937–1940 |
| Risto Heikki Ryti | 1940–1944 |
| Karl Gustav Mannerheim | 1944–1946 |
| Juho Kusti Paasikivi | 1946–1956 |
| Urho Kaleva Kekkonen | 1956– |

# FRANCE

MEROVINGIAN KINGS[1]
CAROLINGIANS[2]

| | |
|---|---|
| Pepin the Short (*Fr.* Pépin le Bref) | 751–768 |
| Charlemagne, or Charles the Great (Holy Roman Emperor, 800–814) | 768–814 |
| Louis I[3] the Pious; called also le Débonnaire | 814–840 |
| Charles I the Bald (Holy Roman Emperor as Charles II) | 840–877 |
| Louis II | 877–879 |
| Louis III[4] | 879–882 |
| Carloman[4] | 879–884 |
| Charles II the Fat (Holy Roman Emperor as Charles III) | 884–887 |
| Odo, Count of Paris (*Fr.* Eudes) | 888–898 |
| Charles III the Simple | 893–923 |
| Robert I (of the Capetian Line[5]) | 922–923 |
| Rudolf (or Raoul), Duke of Burgundy | 923–936 |
| Louis IV | 936–954 |
| Lothair | 934–986 |
| Louis V | 986–987 |

KINGDOM OF FRANCE
CAPETIAN LINE[5]

| | |
|---|---|
| Hugh Capet (*Fr.* Hugues Capet) | 987–996 |
| Robert II | 996–1031 |
| Henry I (*Fr.* Henri) | 1031–1060 |
| Philip I (*Fr.* Philippe) | 1060–1108 |
| Louis VI | 1108–1137 |
| Louis VII | 1137–1180 |
| Philip II, or Philip Augustus (*Fr.* Philippe Auguste) | 1180–1223 |
| Louis VIII | 1223–1226 |

CAPETIAN LINE (Continued)

| | |
|---|---|
| Louis IX (Saint Louis) | 1226–1270 |
| Philip III | 1270–1285 |
| Philip IV | 1285–1314 |
| Louis X | 1314–1316 |
| John I (*Fr.* Jean) | 1316 |
| Philip V | 1316–1322 |
| Charles IV | 1322–1328 |

HOUSE OF VALOIS

| | |
|---|---|
| Philip VI | 1328–1350 |
| John II | 1350–1364 |
| Charles V | 1364–1380 |
| Charles VI | 1380–1422 |
| Charles VII | 1422–1461 |
| Louis XI | 1461–1483 |
| Charles VIII | 1483–1498 |
| Louis XII | 1498–1515 |
| Francis I (*Fr.* François) | 1515–1547 |
| Henry II | 1547–1559 |
| Francis II | 1559–1560 |
| Charles IX | 1560–1574 |
| Henry III | 1574–1589 |

HOUSE OF BOURBON

| | |
|---|---|
| Henry IV | 1589–1610 |
| Louis XIII | 1610–1643 |
| Louis XIV | 1643–1715 |
| Louis XV | 1715–1774 |
| Louis XVI (executed 1793) | 1774–1792 |
| Louis XVII (nominal king only) | 1793–1795 |

[1] See MEROVINGIAN in this dictionary. [2] See CAROLINGIAN in this dictionary. [3] Also Holy Roman Emperor. [4] Joint rulers. [5] See CAPETIAN in this dictionary.

## France (Continued)

THE REPUBLIC

National Convention, Sept. 20, 1792–Oct. 26, 1795
The Directory (*Fr.* Directoire), Oct. 27, 1795–Nov. 9, 1799

THE CONSULATE (*FR.* CONSULAT) 1799–1804

FIRST EMPIRE

| | |
|---|---|
| Napoleon I, Bonaparte, Emperor of the French[6] | 1804–1815 |

THE RESTORATION

| | |
|---|---|
| Louis XVIII | 1814–1824 |
| Charles X | 1824–1830 |
| Louis Philippe | 1830–1848 |

THE SECOND REPUBLIC

| | |
|---|---|
| Louis Napoleon, President | 1848–1852 |

THE SECOND EMPIRE

| | |
|---|---|
| Napoleon III (Louis Napoleon), Emperor | 1852–1870 |

THE THIRD REPUBLIC
(*Presidents*)

| | |
|---|---|
| Louis Adolphe Thiers | 1871–1873 |
| Marshal MacMahon | 1873–1879 |
| Jules Grévy | 1879–1887 |
| Marie François Sadi Carnot | 1887–1894 |
| Jean Casimir-Périer | 1894–1895 |
| Francois Félix Faure | 1895–1899 |
| Émile Loubet | 1899–1906 |
| Armand Fallières | 1906–1913 |

THE THIRD REPUBLIC (Continued)

| | |
|---|---|
| Raymond Poincaré | 1913–1920 |
| Paul Deschanel | 1920 |
| Alexandre Mulerand | 1920–1924 |
| Gaston Doumergue | 1924–1931 |
| Paul Doumer | 1931–1932 |
| Albert Lebrun | 1932–1940 |

VICHY GOVERNMENT[7]

| | |
|---|---|
| Marshal Philippe Pétain, Chief of the State | 1940–1944 |
| Pierre Laval, Chief of Government | 1942–1944 |

PROVISIONAL GOVERNMENT
(*Presidents*)

| | |
|---|---|
| Charles de Gaulle | 1944–1946 |
| Félix Gouin (Jan. 23) | 1946 |
| Georges Bidault (June 19) | 1946 |
| Léon Blum (Dec. 12) | 1946 |

THE FOURTH REPUBLIC[8]
(*Presidents*)

| | |
|---|---|
| Vincent Auriol | 1947–1954 |
| René Coty | 1954–1959 |

THE FIFTH REPUBLIC[9]
(*Presidents*)

| | |
|---|---|
| Charles de Gaulle | 1959–1969 |
| Georges Pompidou | 1969–1974 |
| Valéry Giscard d'Estaing | 1974– |

[6] Abdicated (Apr. 11, 1814); retired to Elba; in France (Hundred Days), Mar. 20–June 29, 1815; defeated at Waterloo, June 18, 1815 abdicated again, June 22. Louis XVIII became king May 3, 1814. [7] On June 28, 1940, General de Gaulle became head of "Free France" in exile (London). On Dec. 1, 1942, Admiral Darian assumed authority of chief of state (in Algiers) and was succeeded on Dec. 24 by General Giraud. A Committee of National Liberation was set up on June 3, 1943, with de Gaulle and Giraud as copresidents; on Nov. 6, 1943, de Gaulle became sole president. [8] Established Dec. 24, 1946. [9] Established Sept. 28, 1958.

## Germany

| | |
|---|---|
| Charlemagne, or Charles the Great (*Ger.* Karl), ruler of Frankish Empire | 768–814 |
| Louis I (*Ger.* Ludwig) | 814–840 |
| Lothair I (*Ger.* Lothar) | 840–843 |
| Louis II the German | 843–876 |
| Charles II the Bald, reunites Frankish dominions | 875–877 |
| Holy Roman Emperors, as Kings of Germany (see HOLY ROMAN EMPERORS) | 881–1806 |
| Confederation of the Rhine | 1806–1813 |
| German Confederation (Bund) | 1815–1866 |
| North German Confederation (Bund) | 1866–1871 |

EMPERORS OF GERMANY

| | |
|---|---|
| William I (*Ger.* Wilhelm)[1] | 1871–1888 |
| Frederick III (*Ger.* Friedrich) | 1888 |
| William II | 1888–1918 |

HEADS OF THE REICH[2]

| | |
|---|---|
| Friedrich Ebert, President | 1919–1925 |
| Paul von Hindenburg, President | 1925–1934 |
| Adolf Hitler, Leader (*Ger.* Führer) and Chancellor (*Ger.* Reichskanzler) | 1934–1945 |

KINGS OF PRUSSIA

| | |
|---|---|
| Frederick I (Frederick III of Brandenburg) (*Ger.* Friedrich) | 1701–1713 |
| Frederick William I (*Ger.* Friedrich Wilhelm) | 1713–1740 |
| Frederick II the Great | 1740–1786 |
| Frederick William II | 1786–1797 |
| Frederick William III | 1797–1840 |
| Frederick William IV | 1840–1861 |
| William I (*Ger.* Wilhelm)[1] | 1861–1871 |

CHANCELLORS (REICHSKANZLERS) OF GERMAN EMPIRE

| | |
|---|---|
| Prince Otto von Bismarck | 1871–1890 |
| Count Leo von Caprivi | 1890–1894 |
| Prince Chlodwig Karl Viktor Hohenlohe-Schillingsfürst | 1894–1900 |
| Prince Bernhard von Bülow | 1900–1909 |
| Theobald von Bethmann-Hollweg | 1909–1917 |
| Georg Michaelis | 1917 |
| Count Georg von Hertling | 1917–1918 |
| Maximilian (Prince Max of Baden) | 1918 |

GERMAN REPUBLIC (REICH)[2]–PREMIERS OR CHANCELLORS

| | |
|---|---|
| Philipp Scheidemann | 1919 |
| Gustav Bauer | 1919–1920 |
| Hermann Müller | 1920 |
| Konstantin Fehrenbach | 1920–1921 |
| Karl J. Wirth | 1921–1922 |
| Wilhelm Cuno | 1922–1923 |
| Gustav Stresemann | 1923 |
| Wilhelm Marx | 1923–1924 |
| Hans Luther | 1925–1926 |
| Wilhelm Marx (2d & 3d terms) | 1926, 1927–1928 |
| Hermann Müller (2d term) | 1928–1930 |
| Heinrich Brüning | 1930–1932 |
| Franz von Papen | 1932 |
| Kurt von Schleicher | 1932–1933 |
| Adolf Hitler | 1933–1934[3] |
| Adolf Hitler, Führer (Leader) and Chancellor[4] | 1934–1945 |

## Federal Republic of Germany (West Germany)

PRESIDENTS

| | |
|---|---|
| Theodor Heuss | 1949–1959 |
| Heinrich Lübke | 1959–1969 |
| Gustav Heinemann | 1969–1974 |
| Walter Scheel | 1974– |

CHANCELLORS

| | |
|---|---|
| Konrad Adenauer | 1949–1963 |
| Ludwig Erhard | 1963–1966 |
| Kurt G. Kiesinger | 1966–1969 |
| Willy Brandt | 1969–1974 |
| Helmut H. W. Schmidt | 1974– |

## German Democratic Republic (East Germany)

PRESIDENT

| | |
|---|---|
| Wilhelm Pieck | 1949–1960[5] |

CHAIRMAN OF THE COUNCIL OF STATE

| | |
|---|---|
| Walter Ulbricht | 1960–1971 |
| Erich Honecker | 1971– |

PRIME MINISTERS

| | |
|---|---|
| Otto Grotewohl | 1949–1964 |
| Willi Stoph | 1964– |

[1] King William I of Prussia became Emperor William I of Germany.
[2] Literally, realm, empire: (1) the empire, 1871–1919; (2) a republic, 1919–1933; (3) a Fascist totalitarian state, 1933–1945.
[3] By decree of Aug. 2, 1934, the offices of president and chancellor were combined.
[4] See (Heads of the Reich).
[5] In Sept. 1960, the president was replaced by the Chairman of the Council of State.

# Great Britain[1]

RULERS OF ENGLAND

| NAME | DYNASTY OR HOUSE | REIGN |
|---|---|---|
| Egbert (or Ecgberht)[2] | Saxon | 828-839 |
| Ethelwulf | Saxon | 839-858 |
| Ethelbald | Saxon | 858-860 |
| Ethelbert | Saxon | 860-866 |
| Ethelred I | Saxon | 866-871 |
| Alfred the Great | Saxon | 871-899 |
| Edward the Elder | Saxon | 899-924 |
| Athelstan | Saxon | 924-940 |
| Edmund | Saxon | 940-946 |
| Edred | Saxon | 946-955 |
| Edwy | Saxon | 955-959 |
| Edgar | Saxon | 959-975 |
| Edward the Martyr | Saxon | 975-978 |
| Ethelred II the Unready | Saxon | 978-1016 |
| Edmund Ironside | Saxon | 1016 |
| Canute (or Cnut)[3] | Danish | 1016-1035 |
| Harold I Harefoot | Danish | 1035-1040 |
| Hardecanute[3] | Danish | 1040-1042 |
| Edward the Confessor | Saxon | 1042-1066 |
| Harold II | Saxon | 1066 |
| William I the Conqueror | Norman | 1066-1087 |
| William II Rufus | Norman | 1087-1100 |
| Henry I Beauclerc | Norman | 1100-1135 |
| Stephen | Norman | 1135-1154 |
| Henry II | Plantagenet[4] | 1154-1189 |
| Richard I Cœur de Lion | Plantagenet | 1189-1199 |
| John Lackland | Plantagenet | 1199-1216 |
| Henry III | Plantagenet | 1216-1272 |
| Edward I Longshanks | Plantagenet | 1272-1307 |
| Edward II | Plantagenet | 1307-1327 |
| Edward III | Plantagenet | 1327-1377 |
| Richard II | Plantagenet | 1377-1399 |
| Henry IV Bolingbroke | Lancaster | 1399-1413 |
| Henry V | Lancaster | 1413-1422 |
| Henry VI[5] | Lancaster | 1422-1461 |
| Edward IV[5] | York | 1461-1483 |
| Edward V | York | 1483 |
| Richard III | York | 1483-1485 |
| Henry VII | Tudor | 1485-1509 |
| Henry VIII | Tudor | 1509-1547 |
| Edward VI | Tudor | 1547-1553 |
| Mary | Tudor | 1553-1558 |
| Elizabeth I | Tudor | 1558-1603 |

RULERS OF SCOTLAND (from 1005)

| NAME | REIGN |
|---|---|
| Malcolm II | 1005-1034 |
| Duncan I | 1034-1040 |
| Macbeth (usurper) | 1040-1057 |
| Malcolm III Canmore | 1057-1093 |
| Donald Bane (or Donalbane) | 1093-1094 |
| Duncan II | 1094 |
| Donald Bane (restored) | 1095-1097 |
| Edgar | 1097-1107 |
| Alexander I the Fierce | 1107-1124 |
| David I the Saint | 1124-1153 |
| Malcolm IV the Maiden | 1153-1165 |
| William the Lion | 1165-1214 |
| Alexander II | 1214-1249 |
| Alexander III | 1249-1286 |
| Margaret of Norway | 1286-1290 |
| [Interregnum] | 1290-1292 |
| John de Baliol | 1292-1296 |
| [Interregnum] | 1296-1306 |
| Robert I (Bruce) | 1306-1329 |
| David II (Bruce) | 1329-1371 |
| HOUSE OF STUART | |
| Robert II | 1371-1390 |
| Robert III | 1390-1406 |
| James I | 1406-1437 |
| James II | 1437-1460 |
| James III | 1460-1488 |
| James IV | 1488-1513 |
| James V | 1513-1542 |
| Mary | 1542-1567 |
| James VI[6] | 1567-1625 |

[1] Officially the United Kingdom of Great Britain and Northern Ireland.
[2] King of Wessex and first king of all England.
[3] See Rulers of Denmark.
[4] Or Anjou.
[5] During the Wars of the Roses (1455-1485) Henry VI was restored to the throne for a short period, from Oct. 5, 1470 to his death May 21, 1471.
[6] Became James I of Great Britain at the Union of England and Scotland in 1603 (see next Table).

# Sovereigns of Great Britain (from 1603)

| NAME | DYNASTY OR HOUSE | REIGN |
|---|---|---|
| James I (VI of Scotland) | Stuart | 1603-1625 |
| Charles I | Stuart | 1625-1649 |
| [Commonwealth, 1649-1660] | | |
| [Oliver Cromwell, Lord Protector, 1653-1658] | | |
| [Richard Cromwell, Lord Protector, 1658-1659] | | |
| Charles II | Stuart | 1660-1685 |
| James II | Stuart | 1685-1688 |
| [Revolution of 1688] | | |
| William III and Mary | Stuart[1] | 1689-1702 |
| Anne | Stuart | 1702-1714 |
| George I[2] | Hanover | 1714-1727 |
| George II | Hanover | 1727-1760 |
| George III | Hanover | 1760-1820 |
| George IV[3] | Hanover | 1820-1830 |
| William IV | Hanover | 1830-1837 |
| Victoria[4] | Hanover | 1837-1901 |
| Edward VII | Saxe-Coburg | 1901-1910 |
| George V | Windsor | 1910-1936 |
| Edward VIII[5] | Windsor | 1936 |
| George VI | Windsor | 1936-1952 |
| Elizabeth II | Windsor | 1952- |

[1] William III was son of William Prince of Orange by Mary, daughter of Charles I; he married Mary, eldest daughter of James II. After Mary's death in 1694 William reigned alone until 1702. See footnote 2, Netherlands table.
[2] George I was son of the Elector of Hanover by Sophia, daughter of Elizabeth, who was the daughter of James I.
[3] Regent from Feb. 5, 1811.
[4] Daughter of Edward, Duke of Kent, fourth son of George III.
[5] Succeeded at death of his father (George V) Jan. 20, 1936; abdicated Dec. 11, before coronation.

| NAME | RULER | TERM |
|---|---|---|
| Sidney Godolphin, Earl (1706) of Godolphin | Anne | 1702-1710 |
| Robert Harley, Earl (1711) of Oxford | Anne | 1710-1714 |
| Charles Talbot, Duke (1694) of Shrewsbury | Anne | 1714[2] |
| Charles Montagu, Earl (1714) of Halifax | George I | 1714-1715 |
| Charles Howard, Earl (1692) of Carlisle | George I | 1715[3] |
| Robert Walpole, Earl (1742) of Orford | George I | 1715-1717 |
| James Stanhope, Earl (1718) Stanhope | George I | 1717-1718 |
| Charles Spencer, Earl (1702) of Sunderland | George I | 1718-1721 |
| Robert Walpole, Earl (1742) of Orford | George I | 1721-1727 |
| Robert Walpole, Earl (1742) of Orford | George II | 1727-1742 |
| Spencer Compton, Earl (1730) of Wilmington | George II | 1742-1743 |
| Henry Pelham | George II | 1743-1744 |
| Henry Pelham ("Broad-bottomed Administration") | George II | 1744-1746 |
| Henry Pelham | George II | 1746-1754 |
| Thomas Pelham-Holles, Duke (1715) of Newcastle | George II | 1754-1756 |
| William Cavendish, Duke (1755) of Devonshire[4] | George II | 1756-1757 |
| Thomas Pelham-Holles, Duke of Newcastle[4] | George II | 1757-1760 |
| Thomas Pelham-Holles, Duke of Newcastle | George III | 1760-1762 |
| John Stuart, Earl (1723) of Bute | George III | 1762-1763 |
| George Grenville | George III | 1763-1765 |
| Charles Watson-Wentworth, Marquis (1750) of Rockingham | George III | 1765-1766 |
| William Pitt, Earl (1766) of Chatham[5] | George III | 1766-1768 |
| Augustus Henry Fitzroy, Duke (1757) of Grafton[5] | George III | 1768-1770 |
| Frederick North, Earl (1790) of Guilford[6] | George III | 1770-1782 |
| Charles Watson-Wentworth, Marquis (1750) of Rockingham | George III | 1782 |
| William Petty, Earl of Shelburne, Marquis (1784) of Lansdowne | George III | 1782-1783 |
| William Henry Cavendish Bentinck, Duke (1762) of Portland (Coalition) | George III | 1783 |
| William Pitt (son of Earl of Chatham) | George III | 1783-1801 |
| Henry Addington, Viscount (1805) Sidmouth | George III | 1801-1804 |
| William Pitt (son of Earl of Chatham) | George III | 1804-1806 |
| William Wyndham Grenville, Baron (1790) Grenville All-the-Talents Administration) | George III | 1806-1807 |
| Wm. Bentinck, Duke of Portland | George III | 1807-1809 |
| Spencer Perceval | George III[7] | 1809-1812 |
| Robert Banks Jenkinson, Earl (1808) of Liverpool | George III, IV | 1812-1827 |
| George Canning[8] | George IV | 1827 |
| Frederick John Robinson, Viscount Goderich, Earl (1833) of Ripon | George IV | 1827-1828 |
| Arthur Wellesley, Duke (1814) of Wellington | George IV & William IV | 1828-1830 |
| Charles Grey, Earl (1807) Grey | William IV | 1830-1834 |
| William Lamb, Viscount (1828) Melbourne | William IV | 1834 |
| Robert Peel, Baronet (1830) | William IV | 1834-1835 |
| William Lamb, Viscount Melbourne | William IV & Victoria | 1835-1841 |
| Robert Peel | Victoria | 1841-1846 |
| John Russell, Earl (1861) Russell | Victoria | 1846-1852 |
| Edward George Geoffrey Smith Stanley, Earl (1851) of Derby | Victoria | 1852 |
| George Hamilton Gordon, Earl (1801) of Aberdeen | Victoria | 1852-1855 |
| Henry John Temple, Viscount (1802) Palmerston | Victoria | 1855-1858 |
| Edward Stanley, Earl of Derby | Victoria | 1858-1859 |
| Viscount Palmerston | Victoria | 1859-1865 |
| John Russell, Earl (1861) Russell | Victoria | 1865-1866 |
| Edward Stanley, Earl of Derby | Victoria | 1866-1868 |
| Benjamin Disraeli, Earl (1876) of Beaconsfield | Victoria | 1868 |
| William Ewart Gladstone | Victoria | 1868-1874 |
| Benjamin Disraeli, Earl of Beaconsfield | Victoria | 1874-1880 |
| William Ewart Gladstone | Victoria | 1880-1885 |
| Robert A. T. Gascoyne-Cecil, Marquis (1868) of Salisbury | Victoria | 1885-1886 |
| William Ewart Gladstone | Victoria | 1886 |
| Robert Gascoyne-Cecil, Marquis of Salisbury | Victoria | 1886-1892 |
| William Ewart Gladstone | Victoria | 1892-1894 |
| Archibald Philip Primrose, Earl (1868) of Rosebery | Victoria | 1894-1895 |
| Robert Gascoyne-Cecil, Marquis of Salisbury | Victoria & Edward VII | 1895-1902 |
| Arthur James Balfour, Earl (1922) Balfour | Edward VII | 1902-1905 |
| Henry Campbell-Bannerman | Edward VII | 1905-1908 |
| Herbert Henry Asquith, Earl (1925) of Oxford and Asquith | Edward VII & George V | 1908-1915 |
| Herbert Henry Asquith | George V | 1915-1916 |
| David Lloyd George | George V | 1916-1922 |
| Andrew Bonar Law | George V | 1922-1923 |
| Stanley Baldwin | George V | 1923-1924 |
| James Ramsay MacDonald | George V | 1924 |
| Stanley Baldwin | George V | 1924-1929 |
| James Ramsay MacDonald | George V | 1929-1935 |
| Stanley Baldwin, Earl (1937) Baldwin of Bewdley | George V, Edward VIII, & George VI | 1935-1937 |
| Neville Chamberlain | George VI | 1937-1940 |
| Winston Churchill | George VI | 1940-1945 |
| Clement Richard Attlee | George VI | 1945-1951 |
| Winston Churchill | George VI & Elizabeth II | 1951-1955 |
| Anthony Eden | Elizabeth II | 1955-1957 |
| Harold Macmillan | Elizabeth II | 1957-1963 |
| Alec Douglas-Home | Elizabeth II | 1963-1964 |
| Harold Wilson | Elizabeth II | 1964-1970 |
| Edward Heath | Elizabeth II | 1970-1974 |
| Harold Wilson | Elizabeth II | 1974-1976 |
| James Callaghan | Elizabeth II | 1976-1979 |
| Margaret Thatcher | Elizabeth II | 1979- |

[1] The prime minister usually holds the portfolio of first lord of the treasury in the cabinet. The term, used descriptively of Sir Robert Walpole and of Lord North as head of a ministry in the 18th century, came into common use in the 19th century. [2] Appointed head of ministry a few days before death of Queen Anne, was influential in bringing about succession of George I. [3] Held office of first lord of the treasury, a position he had also held in 1701-02. [4] In both these ministries William Pitt was the real leader. [5] Pitt remained as minister until Oct., 1768, but because of his illness Grafton acted as chief minister after Feb., 1767. [6] Lord North was prime minister during the entire period of the American Revolution. [7] The Prince of Wales (later George IV) became regent Feb., 1811. [8] The Canning ministry was formed Apr. 24-30, 1827; terminated Aug. 8 on his death.

## POETS LAUREATE OF ENGLAND

NOTE—The term *Laureate* had its origin in medieval universities in the practice of crowning with laurel candidates admitted to degrees in grammar, rhetoric, and poetry. Later, it came to be applied to any poet of notable achievement. It was used as a standard compliment to Chaucer, and was informally bestowed upon John Gower, John Lydgate, and John Skelton, among others. Edmund Spenser, Michael Drayton, and Samuel Daniel performed officially recognized court functions as did Ben Jonson, who considered himself a formal laureate since he received two pensions and considerable popular acclaim. William Davenant seems to have been tacitly recognized as poet laureate under both Charles I and II, but he held no official patent. The office received its first official recognition with the appointment of John Dryden in 1668.

| NAME | TERM | NAME | TERM |
|---|---|---|---|
| John Dryden | 1670–1689 | Robert Southey | 1813–1843 |
| Thomas Shadwell | 1689–1692 | William Wordsworth | 1843–1850 |
| Nahum Tate | 1692–1715 | Alfred Tennyson | 1850–1892 |
| Nicholas Rowe | 1715–1718 | [Vacant] | 1892–1896 |
| Laurence Eusden | 1718–1730 | Alfred Austin | 1896–1913 |
| Colley Cibber | 1730–1757 | Robert S. Bridges | 1913–1930 |
| William Whitehead | 1757–1785 | John Masefield | 1930–1967 |
| Thomas Warton | 1785–1790 | Cecil Day Lewis | 1968–1972 |
| Henry James Pye | 1790–1813 | John Betjeman | 1972– |

## ARCHBISHOPS OF CANTERBURY[1]

| | NAME | TERM | | NAME | TERM |
|---|---|---|---|---|---|
| 1 | Augustine (Saint) | 601–604 | 52 | Simon Meopham | 1327–1333 |
| 2 | Lawrence (or Laurentius) | 604–619 | 53 | John de Stratford | 1333–1348 |
| 3 | Mellitus | 619–624 | 54 | John de Offord (or Ufford)[1,2] | 1348–1349 |
| 4 | Justus | 624–627 | 55 | Thomas Bradwardine | 1349 |
| 5 | Honorius | 627–653 | 56 | Simon Islip | 1349–1366 |
| 6 | Deusdedit | 655–664 | 57 | Simon Langham | 1366–1368 |
| 7 | Theodore | 668–690 | 58 | William Whittlesey (or Wittlesey) | 1368–1374 |
| 8 | Brihtwald (or Berchtwald) | 692–731 | 59 | Simon of Sudbury | 1375–1381 |
| 9 | Tatwin (or Taetwine) | 731–734 | 60 | William Courtenay | 1381–1396 |
| 10 | Nothelm | 735–739 | 61 | Thomas Arundel[3] | 1396–1414 |
| 11 | Cuthbert | 740–758 | 62 | Henry Chichele (or Chicheley) | 1414–1443 |
| 12 | Bregwin (or Bregowine) | 759–765 | 63 | John Stafford | 1443–1452 |
| 13 | Jaenbert (or Lambert, etc.) | 766–791 | 64 | John Kemp | 1452–1454 |
| 14 | Ethelhard (or Æthelheard) | 791–805 | 65 | Thomas Bourchier | 1454 1486 |
| 15 | Wulfred | 805–832 | 66 | John Morton | 1486–1500 |
| 16 | Feologeld (or Fleogild) | 832 | 67 | Henry Deane | 1501–1503 |
| 17 | Ceolnoth | 843–870 | 68 | William Warham | 1504–1532 |
| 18 | Ethelred (or Æthelred) | 870–889 | 69 | Thomas Cranmer | 1533–1556 |
| 19 | Plegmund (or Plegemund) | 890–914 | 70 | Reginald Pole | 1556–1558 |
| 20 | Athelm | 914–923 | 71 | Matthew Parker | 1559–1575 |
| 21 | Wulfhelm | 923–942 | 72 | Edmund Grindal | 1576–1583 |
| 22 | Odo (or Oda) | 942–959 | 73 | John Whitgift | 1583–1604 |
| 23 | Ælfsige (or Aelfsige)[1] | 959 | 74 | Richard Bancroft | 1604–1610 |
| 24 | Dunstan | 961–988 | 75 | George Abbot | 1611–1633 |
| 25 | Ethelgar (or Æthelgar) | 988–990 | 76 | William Laud | 1633–1645 |
| 26 | Sigeric | 990–994 | 77 | William Juxon | 1660–1663 |
| 27 | Ælfric (or Aelfric) | 995–1005 | 78 | Gilbert Sheldon | 1663–1677 |
| 28 | Ælfheah (or St. Alphege) | 1006–1012 | 79 | William Sancroft | 1678–1690 |
| 29 | Lyfing | 1013–1020 | 80 | John Tillotson | 1691–1694 |
| 30 | Ethelnoth (or Æthelnoth) | 1020–1038 | 81 | Thomas Tenison | 1694–1715 |
| 31 | Eadsige | 1038–1050 | 82 | William Wake | 1716–1737 |
| 32 | Robert of Jumièges | 1051–1052 | 83 | John Potter | 1737–1747 |
| 33 | Stigand | 1052–1070 | 84 | Thomas Herring | 1747–1757 |
| 34 | Lanfranc | 1070–1089 | 85 | Matthew Hutton | 1757–1758 |
| 35 | Anselm | 1093–1109 | 86 | Thomas Secker | 1758–1768 |
| 36 | Ralph d'Escures (or Ralph de Turbine) | 1114–1122 | 87 | Frederick Cornwallis | 1768–1783 |
| 37 | William of Corbeil | 1123–1136 | 88 | John Moore | 1783–1805 |
| 38 | Theobald | 1138–1161 | 89 | Charles Manners-Sutton | 1805–1828 |
| 39 | Thomas à Becket | 1162–1170 | 90 | William Howley | 1828–1848 |
| 40 | Richard | 1173–1184 | 91 | John Bird Sumner | 1848–1862 |
| 41 | Baldwin | 1185–1190 | 92 | Charles Thomas Longley | 1862–1868 |
| 42 | Reginald Fitzjocelin[1,2] | 1191 | 93 | Archibald Campbell Tait | 1869–1882 |
| 43 | Hubert Walter | 1193–1205 | 94 | Edward White Benson | 1882–1896 |
| 44 | Stephen Langton | 1207–1228 | 95 | Frederick Temple | 1896–1902 |
| 45 | Richard Grant (or Richard of Wethershed) | 1229–1231 | 96 | Randall Thomas Davidson | 1903–1928 |
| 46 | Edmund Rich | 1234–1240 | 97 | Cosmo Gordon Lang | 1928–1942 |
| 47 | Boniface of Savoy | 1241–1270 | 98 | William Temple | 1942–1944 |
| 48 | Robert Kilwardby | 1272–1278 | 99 | Geoffrey Francis Fisher | 1945–1961 |
| 49 | John Peckham | 1279–1292 | 100 | Arthur Michael Ramsey | 1961–1974 |
| 50 | Robert de Winchelsea | 1293–1313 | 101 | Frederick Donald Coggan | 1974–1980 |
| 51 | Walter Reynolds | 1313–1327 | 102 | Robert Alexander Kennedy Runcie | 1980– |

[1] Nos. 23, 42, & 54 are omitted from some lists; this accounts for differences as to total number.
[2] Archbishop-elect; died before being consecrated.
[3] During Arundel's banishment from England by Richard II, Roger Walden was archbishop for about one year (1398), but with the accession of Henry IV (1399), Arundel was restored to the see.

# Greece (modern)

**KINGS**

| | |
|---|---|
| Otto I, prince of Bavaria | 1832–1862 |
| George I, of Denmark | 1863–1913 |
| Constantine I (abdicated) | 1913–1917 |
| Alexander | 1917–1920 |
| Constantine I (recalled) | 1920–1922 |
| George II | 1922–1923 |
| Admiral Paul Koundouriotes (regent) | 1923–1924 |
| [Republic declared Apr. 13, 1924] | |

**PRESIDENTS**

| | |
|---|---|
| Admiral Paul Koundouriotes (provisional) | 1924–1929 |
| Alexander Zaimis | 1929–1935 |
| [Monarchy reestablished Oct. 10, 1935] | |

**KINGS**

| | |
|---|---|
| George II | 1935–1947 |
| Paul I | 1947–1964 |
| Constantine | 1964–1973 |
| [Republic reestablished Aug. 13, 1973] | |

**PRESIDENTS**

| | |
|---|---|
| George Papadopoulos | 1973 |
| Phaedon Gizikis | 1973–1974 |
| Michael Stassinopoulos (ad interim) | 1974–1975 |
| Konstantinos Tsatsos | 1975– |

# Grenada

**GOVERNOR-GENERAL**

| | |
|---|---|
| Leo de Gale | 1974– |

**PRIME MINISTER**

| | |
|---|---|
| Eric Matthew Gairy | 1974– |

# Guatemala

**PRESIDENTS (since 1840)**

| | |
|---|---|
| Rafael Carrera[1] | 1840–1848, 1854–1865 |
| Vicente Cerna (deposed) | 1865–1871 |
| Miguel García Granados (provisional) | 1871–1873 |
| Justo Rufino Barrios | 1873–1885 |
| Manuel Lisandro Barillas | 1886–1892 |
| José María Reina Barrios | 1892–1898 |
| Manuel Estrada Cabrera | 1898–1920 |
| Carlos Herrera (deposed) | 1920–1921 |
| José María Orellana | 1921–1926 |
| Lázaro Chacón | 1921–1930 |
| José María Reyna Andrade (provisional) | 1931 |
| Jorge Ubico | 1931–1944 |
| Federico Ponce (provisional) | 1944 |
| [Revolutionary Junta, 1944–1945] | |
| Juan José Arévalo | 1945–1951 |
| Jacobo Arbenz Guzman | 1951–1954 |
| Carlos Castillo Armas | 1954–1957 |
| Guillermo Flores Avendaño (provisional) | 1957–1958 |
| Miguel Ydígoras Fuentes | 1958–1963 |
| Julio César Mendez Montenegro[2] | 1966–1970 |
| Carlos Arana Osorio | 1970–1974 |
| Kjell Laugerud García | 1974–1978 |
| Fernando Romeo Lucas García | 1978– |

[1] Virtually dictator from 1840 to 1865.
[2] Military rule (1963–1966).

# Guyana

**GOVERNOR-GENERAL[1]**

| | |
|---|---|
| David J. G. Rose | 1966–1970 |

**PRESIDENTS**

| | |
|---|---|
| Arthur Chung | 1970– |

**PRIME MINISTER**

| | |
|---|---|
| Lindon Forbes Sampson Burnham | 1966– |

[1] Became a republic Feb. 23, 1970.

# Haiti

**EMPEROR**

| | |
|---|---|
| Jean Jacques Dessalines | 1804–1806[1] |

**PRESIDENTS**

| | |
|---|---|
| Jean Pierre Boyer | 1820–1843 |
| Charles Hérard | 1843–1844 |
| Philippe Guerrier | 1844–1845 |
| Jean Louis Pierrot | 1845–1846 |
| Jean Baptiste Riche | 1846–1847 |
| Faustin Soulouque[2] | 1847–1859 |
| Fabre Geffrard | 1859–1867 |
| Sylvain Saenave | 1867–1869 |
| Nissage-Saget | 1870–1874 |
| Michel Domingue | 1874–1876 |
| Boisrond-Canal | 1876–1879 |
| Louis Etienne Félicité Salomon | 1879–1888 |
| Déus Légitime | 1888–1889 |
| Florvil Hyppolite | 1889–1896 |
| Tirésias Simon Sam | 1896–1902 |
| Nord Alexis | 1902–1908 |

**PRESIDENTS (Continued)**

| | |
|---|---|
| Antoine Simon | 1908–1911 |
| Cincinnatus Leconte | 1911–1912 |
| Tancrède Auguste | 1912–1913 |
| Michel Oreste | 1913–1914 |
| Oreste Zamor | 1914 |
| Joseph Davilmar Théodore | 1914–1915 |
| Jean Vilbrun Guillaume Sam | 1915 |
| Philippe Sudre Dartiguenave | 1915–1922 |
| Joseph Louis Borno | 1922–1930 |
| Eugène Roy | 1930 |
| Sténio Vincent | 1930–1941 |
| Élie Lescot | 1941–1946 |
| [Provisional Government Jan.-Aug. 1946] | |
| Dumarsais Estimé | 1946–1950 |
| [Provisional Government May-Oct. 1950] | |
| Paul Magloire | 1950–1956[3] |
| François Duvalier | 1956–1971 |
| Jean-Claude Duvalier | 1971– |

[1] Internally divided 1806–1820. [2] Emperor 1849–1859. [3] Five interim regimes Dec. 1956–Oct. 1957.

# Holy Roman Empire[1]

**FRANKISH KINGS AND EMPERORS (CAROLINGIAN)**

| | |
|---|---|
| Charlemagne, or Charles the Great (*Ger.* Karl); King of the Franks 768–814; crowned Emperor of the West 800[2] | 800–814 |
| Louis I the Pious (*Ger.* Ludwig); called also le Débonnaire | 814–840 |
| Lothair I (*Ger.* Lothar)[3] | 840–855 |
| Louis II | 855–875 |
| Charles II the Bald | 875–877 |
| [No Emperor, 877–881] | |
| Charles III the Fat[4] | 881–887 |
| Arnulf, King of Germany; crowned 896 | 887–899 |
| *Louis III the Child, King of Germany | 899–911 |
| *Conrad of Franconia, King of Germany (*Ger.* Konrad) | 911–918 |

**SAXON KINGS AND EMPERORS**

| | |
|---|---|
| *Henry I the Fowler, King of Germany (*Ger.* Heinrich) | 919–936 |
| Otto I the Great; crowned 962[1] | 936–973 |
| Otto II | 973–983 |
| Otto III | 983–1002 |
| Henry II the Saint; crowned 1014 | 1002–1024 |

**FRANCONIAN EMPERORS (SALIAN)**

| | |
|---|---|
| Conrad II; crowned 1027 | 1024–1039 |
| Henry III; crowned 1046 | 1039–1056 |
| Henry IV; crowned 1084[5] | 1056–1106 |
| Henry V; crowned 1111 | 1106–1125 |
| Lothair II (or III) of Saxony; crowned 1133 | 1125–1137 |

[1] Rulers of Germany and Northern Italy. The boundaries of the Holy Roman Empire were continually shifting; under Charlemagne it comprised Neustria, Austrasia, Aquitaine, and North Italy; from 843 to 888, the Western Frankish Kingdom and the Eastern Frankish Kingdom (including Lotharingia); from 900 to 1100, France (western two thirds of modern France), Burgundy, and all of central Europe (to the Oder and Hungary) and most of Italy; later, France and Italy increased at the expense of the Empire but the Empire gained new lands to the East. Rulers marked with an asterisk (*) were never crowned as emperors; after Maximilian I (1493) the Emperors took the title without the papal coronation.
[2] The year 800 is generally taken as the beginning of the Holy Roman Empire, in its wider form, but some scholars prefer to cite 962, the coronation of Otto I, as marking the date at which the continuous existence of the Empire began.
[3] King of Lorraine and Emperor after Treaty of Verdun, 843.
[4] His deposition in 887 marked the dismemberment of the empire of Charlemagne.
[5] Crowned by the antipope Clement III.

## Holy Roman Empire[1] (Continued)

### HOHENSTAUFEN KINGS AND EMPERORS

| | |
|---|---|
| *Conrad III | 1138–1152 |
| *Frederick I Barbarossa (*Ger.* Friedrich); crowned 1155 | 1152–1190 |
| Henry VI; crowned 1191 | 1190–1197 |
| *Philip of Swabia (*Ger.* Philipp)[2] | 1198–1208 |
| Otto IV of Brunswick; crowned 1209[2] | 1198–1215 |
| Frederick II; crowned 1220 | 1215–1250 |
| *Conrad IV | 1250–1254 |
| [The Great Interregnum, 1254–1273] | |

### RULERS FROM DIFFERENT HOUSES

| | |
|---|---|
| *Rudolf I of Hapsburg | 1273–1291 |
| *Adolf of Nassau | 1292–1298 |
| *Albert I of Austria (*Ger.* Albrecht) | 1298–1308 |
| Henry VII of Luxemburg | 1308–1313 |
| Louis IV of Bavaria[3] | 1314–1347 |
| *Frederick of Austria[3] | 1314–1326 |
| Charles IV of Luxemburg; crowned 1355 | 1347–1378 |
| Wenceslaus of Bohemia (*Ger.* Wenzel) | 1378–1400 |
| *Rupert of the Palatinate (*Ger.* Ruprecht) | 1400–1410 |
| Sigismund; crowned 1433 | 1411–1437 |

### HAPSBURG EMPERORS

| | |
|---|---|
| *Albert II | 1438–1439 |
| Frederick III; crowned 1452 | 1440–1493 |
| Maximilian I | 1493–1519 |
| Charles V; crowned 1520[4] | 1519–1556[5] |
| Ferdinand I | 1556–1564 |
| Maximilian II | 1564–1576 |
| Rudolph II | 1576–1612 |
| Matthias | 1612–1619 |
| Ferdinand II | 1619–1637 |
| Ferdinand III | 1637–1657 |
| Leopold I | 1658–1705 |
| Joseph I | 1705–1711 |
| Charles VI | 1711–1740 |
| Charles VII of Bavaria (*Ger.* Karl Albrecht) | 1742–1745 |

### HAPSBURG-LORRAINE EMPERORS

| | |
|---|---|
| Francis I (*Ger.* Franz) | 1745–1765 |
| Joseph II | 1765–1790 |
| Leopold II | 1790–1792 |
| Francis II[6] | 1792–1806 |

[1] Rulers marked with an asterisk (*) were never crowned as Emperors; after Maximilian I (1493) the Emperors took the title without the papal coronation.
[2] Rival kings of Ghibellines and Guelphs.
[3] Rival kings; 1325–26 joint kings.
[4] Also Charles I of Spain 1516–1556.
[5] Charles did not formally abdicate in favor of Ferdinand until 1558.
[6] Emperor of Austria 1804–1835. Holy Roman Empire officially declared ended, by Napoleon.

## Honduras

### PRESIDENTS (since 1864)

| | |
|---|---|
| José M. Medina | 1864–1872 |
| Celio Arias | 1872–1874 |
| Marco Aurelio Soto | 1874–1875 |
| Ponciano Leiva | 1875–1876 |
| Marco Aurelio Soto | 1877–1883 |
| Luis Bográn | 1883–1891 |
| Ponciano Leiva | 1891–1894 |
| Policarpo Bonilla | 1894–1900 |
| Terencio Sierra | 1900–1903 |
| Manuel Bonilla | 1903–1907 |
| Miguel R. Dávila | 1907–1911 |
| Francisco Bertrand (provisional) | 1911–1912 |
| Manuel Bonilla | 1912–1913 |
| Francisco Bertrand | 1913–1919 |
| Rafael López Gutiérrez | 1919–1924 |
| [Civil war, 1924] | |
| Vincente Tosta (provisional) | 1924–1925 |
| Miguel Paz Baraona | 1925–1929 |
| Vicente Mejía Colindres | 1929–1933 |
| Tiburcio Carías Andino | 1933–1949 |
| Juan Manuel Gálvez | 1949–1954 |
| Julio Lozano Diaz | 1954–1956 |
| Ramón Villeda Morales[1] | 1957–1963 |
| Oswaldo López Arellano[2] | 1965–1971 |
| Ramón Ernesto Cruz | 1971–1972[3] |
| Oswaldo López Arellano[3] (deposed) | 1972–1975 |
| Juan Alberto Melgar Castró | 1975– |

[1] Military junta (1956–1957)
[2] Military rule (1963–65)
[3] Military rule instituted.

## Hungary[1]

### REGENT

| | |
|---|---|
| Nicholas Horthy de Nagybánya | 1920–1944 |

### PRESIDENTS[2]

| | |
|---|---|
| Zoltán Tildy | 1946–1948 |
| Arpad Szakasits | 1948–1950 |
| Sándor Rónai | 1950–1952 |
| István M. Dobi | 1952–1967 |
| Pál Losonczi | 1967– |

[1] Part of Austria-Hungary to 1918; provisional governments 1918–1919.
[2] Declared a republic Feb. 1946.

## India

### EMPERORS OF MOGUL DYNASTY

| | |
|---|---|
| Baber (or Babar) | 1526–1530 |
| Humayun | 1530–1556 |
| Akbar the Great | 1556–1605 |
| [British East India Company chartered, 1600] | |
| Jahangir | 1605–1627 |
| [First English factory established at Surat, 1612] | |
| Shah Jahan | 1628–1658 |
| Aurangzeb | 1658–1707 |
| Bahadur Shah I | 1707–1712 |
| Jahandar Shah (or Jehandar Shah) | 1712–1713 |
| Farruk-Siar | 1713–1719 |
| Mohammed Shah | 1719–1748 |
| Ahmed (or Ahmad) | 1748–1754 |
| Alamgir | 1754–1759 |
| [Battle of Plassey, 1757] | |
| Shah Alam | 1759–1806 |
| Mohammed Akbar II | 1806–1837 |
| Bahadur Shah II | 1837–1857 |
| [Sepoy Mutiny, 1857–1858] | |
| [End of East India Company, 1858] | |

### GOVERNORS OF BENGAL

| | |
|---|---|
| Robert Clive, Baron Clive of Plassey | 1757–1760 |
| Henry Vansittart | 1760–1764 |
| Robert Clive, Baron Clive of Plassey | 1764–1767 |
| Harry Verelst | 1767–1769 |
| John Cartier | 1769–1772 |

### GOVERNORS-GENERAL OF BENGAL AND INDIA

| | |
|---|---|
| Warren Hastings | 1773–1785 |
| John Macpherson (acting) | 1785–1786 |
| Charles Cornwallis, Marquis (1792) Cornwallis | 1786–1793 |
| John Shore, Baron (1798) Teignmouth | 1793–1797 |
| Richard C. Wellesley, Earl of Mornington, Marquis (1799) Wellesley | 1797–1805 |
| Charles Cornwallis, Marquis (1792) Cornwallis | 1805 |
| George Hilaro Barlow (acting) | 1805–1807 |
| Gilbert Elliot-Murray-Kynynmond, Earl (1813) of Minto | 1807–1813 |
| Francis Rawdon Hastings, Earl of Moira, Marquis (1817) of Hastings | 1813–1822 |
| William Pitt Amherst, Earl (1826) Amherst of Arakan | 1823–1828 |
| William Cavendish Bentinck | 1828–1835 |
| Charles Metcalfe, Baron (1845) Metcalfe (acting) | 1835 |
| George Eden, Earl (1839) of Auckland | 1835–1841 |
| Edward Law, Earl (1844) of Ellenborough | 1841–1844 |
| Henry Hardinge, Viscount (1846) Hardinge of Lahore | 1844–1847 |
| Sir James Andrew Broun Ramsay, Marquis (1849) of Dalhousie | 1848–1856 |
| Charles John Canning, Earl (1859) Canning | 1850–1858 |

# INDIA (Continued)

VICEROYS AND GOVERNORS-GENERAL OF INDIA

| | |
|---|---|
| Charles John Canning, Earl (1859) Canning | 1858–1862 |
| James Bruce, Earl (1841) of Elgin | 1862–1863 |
| John Laird Mair Lawrence, Baron (1869) Lawrence | 1863–1869 |
| Richard Southwell Bourke, Earl (1867) of Mayo | 1869–1872 |
| Thomas George Baring, Earl (1876) of Northbrook | 1872–1876 |
| Edward Robert Bulwer Lytton, Earl (1880) of Lytton | 1876–1880 |
| George F. S. Robinson, Viscount Goderich, Marquis (1871) of Ripon | 1880–1884 |
| Frederick T. H.-T. Blackwood, Marquis (1888) of Dufferin and Ava | 1884–1888 |
| Henry Charles Keith Petty Fitzmaurice, Marquis (1866) of Lansdowne | 1888–1893 |
| Victor Alexander Bruce, Earl (1863) of Elgin and Kincardine | 1894–1899 |
| George Nathaniel Curzon, Marquis (1921) Curzon of Kedleston | 1899–1905 |
| Gilbert John Elliot-Murray-Kynynmond, Earl (1891) of Minto | 1905–1910 |
| Charles Hardinge, Baron (1910) Hardinge of Penshurst | 1910–1916 |
| Frederic John Napier Thesiger, Viscount (1921) of Chelmsford | 1916–1921 |
| Rufus Daniel Isaacs, Marquis (1926) of Reading | 1921–1926 |
| Edward Frederick Lindley Wood, Baron Irwin, Viscount (1934) Halifax | 1926–1931 |
| Freeman Freeman-Thomas, Marquis (1936) of Willingdon | 1931–1936 |
| Victor Alexander John Hope, Marquis (1908) of Linlithgow | 1936–1943 |
| Field Marshal Archibald Percival Wavell, Earl (1947) Wavell | 1943–1947 |
| Louis Mountbatten, Viscount (1946) Mountbatten of Burma | 1947–1948 |
| Shri Chakravarti Rajagopalachari | 1948–1950 |

REPUBLIC OF INDIA

PRESIDENTS

| | |
|---|---|
| Rajendra Prasad | 1950–1962 |
| Sarvepalli Radhakrishnan | 1962–1967 |
| Zakir Husain | 1967–1969 |
| Varahagiri Venkata Giri | 1969–1974 |
| Fahkruddin Ali Ahmed | 1974–1977 |
| Neelan Sanjiva Reddy | 1977– |

PRIME MINISTERS

| | |
|---|---|
| Jawaharlal Nehru | 1950–1964 |
| Lal Bahadur Shastri | 1964–1966 |
| Indira Gandhi | 1966–1977 |
| Morarji R. Desai | 1977–1979 |
| Charan Singh | 1979– |

# IRAN (PERSIA)

KINGS OR SHAHS (from 1794)

| | |
|---|---|
| Agha Mohammed Khan | 1794–1797 |
| Fath Ali | 1797–1835 |
| Mohammed Shah | 1835–1848 |
| Nasr-ed-Din | 1848–1896 |
| Muzaffar-ed-Din | 1896–1907 |
| Mohammed Ali | 1907–1909 |
| Ahmed Shah (or Ahmed Mirza)[1] | 1909–1925 |
| Riza Shah Pahlevi[2] | 1925–1941 |
| Mohammed Riza Pahlevi | 1941–1979 |

[1] Last of the Kajar Dynasty. [2] First of Pahlevi Dynasty; abdicated under Russian and British pressure.

# IRELAND

IRISH FREE STATE
(Established Dec. 6, 1921)

PRESIDENTS OF THE EXECUTIVE COUNCIL[1]

| | |
|---|---|
| William T. Cosgrave | 1922–1932 |
| Eamon de Valera | 1932–1937 |

GOVERNORS-GENERAL

| | |
|---|---|
| Timothy Michael Healy | 1922–1927 |
| James McNeill | 1928–1932 |
| Donal Buckley | 1932–1937 |

IRISH REPUBLIC[2]

PRESIDENTS

| | |
|---|---|
| Douglas Hyde | 1938–1945 |
| Sean T. O'Kelly | 1945–1959 |
| Eamon de Valera | 1959–1973 |
| Erskine Hamilton Childers | 1973–1974 |
| Cearbhall O Dalaigh | 1974–1976 |
| Patrick J. Hillery | 1976– |

PRIME MINISTERS

| | |
|---|---|
| Eamon de Valera | 1937–1948 |
| John A. Costello | 1948–1951 |
| Eamon de Valera | 1951–1954 |
| John A. Costello | 1954–1957 |
| Eamon de Valera | 1957–1959 |
| Sean F. Lemass | 1959–1966 |
| John M. Lynch | 1966–1973 |
| Liam Cosgrave | 1973–1977 |
| John Lynch | 1977– |

[1] Arthur Griffith was president of the Dail-Eireann, Jan. 10 to Aug. 12, 1922.
[2] New constitution approved by a plebiscite July 1, 1937; effective Dec. 29, 1937.

# ISRAEL

PRESIDENTS

| | |
|---|---|
| Chaim Wiezmann | 1949–1952 |
| Izhak Ben-Zvi | 1952–1963 |
| Zalman Shazar | 1963–1973 |
| Ephraim (Katchalski) Katzir | 1973– |

PRIME MINISTERS

| | |
|---|---|
| David Ben-Gurion | 1949–1963 |
| Levi Eshkol | 1963–1969 |
| Golda Meir | 1969–1974 |
| Yitzhak Rabin | 1974–1977 |
| Menahem Begin | 1977– |

# ITALY[1]

KINGS OF SARDINIA AND ITALY: HOUSE OF SAVOY

| | |
|---|---|
| Victor Amadeus II | 1720–1730 |
| Charles Emmanuel III | 1730–1773 |
| Victor Amadeus III | 1773–1796 |
| Charles Emmanuel IV | 1796–1802 |
| Victor Emmanuel I[2] | 1802–1821 |
| Charles Felix | 1821–1831 |
| Charles Albert | 1831–1849 |
| Victor Emmanuel II[3] | 1849–1878 |
| Humbert I | 1878–1900 |
| Victor Emmanuel III | 1900–1946 |
| Humbert II | 1946 |

[Republic declared June 9, 1946]

PRESIDENTS

| | |
|---|---|
| Enrico de Nicola | 1946–1948 |
| Luigi Einaudi | 1948–1955 |
| Giovanni Gronchi | 1955–1962 |
| Antonio Segni | 1962–1964 |
| Giuseppe Saragat | 1964–1971 |
| Giovanni Leone | 1971–1978 |
| Alessandro Pertini | 1978– |

[1] The Italian city-states of the 14th and 15th centuries were followed by more than three centuries of control over Italy by the Hapsburgs. In the 18th century the House of Savoy began the long struggle for a free Italy, finally successful in 1861.
[2] King of Sardinia only, 1805–1814, during which period Savoy and Piedmont were part of the kingdom of Italy under Napoleon I, Emperor of the French.
[3] Becomes King of Italy in 1861.

# Jamaica

## GOVERNORS-GENERAL

| | | | |
|---|---|---|---|
| Clifford Clarence Campbell | 1962–1973 | Florizel Augustus Glasspole | 1973– |

## PRIME MINISTERS

| | | | |
|---|---|---|---|
| Alexander Bustamante | 1962–1967 | Hugh L. Shearer | 1967–1972 |
| Donald Sangster | 1967 | Michael Manley | 1972– |

# Japan[1]

| | |
|---|---|
| [Early (Legendary) Period, 660 B.C.–710 A.D.] | |
| *Jimmu Tenno*, Emperor | 660–585 B.C. |
| *Jingo*, Empress | 360. A.D. |
| *Shōtoku Taishi*, Emperor | 593–621 |
| *Tenchi*, Emperor | 662–671 |
| Nara Period (capital at Nara) | 710–784 |
| *Kwammu*, Emperor | 782–805 |
| Heian Period (capital at Kyoto) | 794–1185 |
| FUJIWARA CLAN or FAMILY | 858–1156 |
| *Sanjo II*, Emperor | 1068–1072 |
| TAIRA CLAN or FAMILY | 1160–1185 |
| KAMAKURA SHOGUNATE | |
| (capital at Kamakura) | 1192–1333 |
| MINAMOTO CLAN or FAMILY | 1185–1219 |
| *Yoritomo*, First Shogun | 1192–1199 |
| *Yoriie*, Shogun | 1202–1204 |
| *Sanetomo*, Shogun | 1203–1219 |
| *Daigo II*, Emperor | 1318–1339 |
| ASHIKAGA SHOGUNATE (capital at Kyoto) | 1338–1568 |
| *Takauji*, Shogun | 1338–1358 |
| *Yoshimitsu*, Shogun | 1367–1395 |
| [Coming of the Portuguese, 1542] | |
| *Nobunaga*, or *Oda Nobunago*, Shogun | 1568–1582 |
| *Hideyoshi*, Shogun | 1585–1598 |
| TOKUGAWA SHOGUNATE | |
| (capital at Yedo, modern Tokyo) | 1603–1867 |
| *Iyeyasu*, Shogun | 1603–1616 |
| *Hidetada*, Shogun | 1616–1623 |
| *Iyemitsu*, Shogun | 1623–1651 |
| [Japan closed for over 200 years to all foreigners except Dutch at Deshima, 1641] | |
| *Iyetsuna*, Shogun | 1651–1680 |
| *Tsunayoshi*, Shogun | 1680–1709 |
| *Yoshimune*, Shogun | 1716–1745 |
| *Iyenari*, Shogun | 1793–1837 |
| *Komei*, Emperor | 1847–1867 |
| [Arrival of Commodore M. C. Perry, 1853] | |
| *Hitotsubashi* (or *Yoshinobu*), last Shogun | 1867 |
| MEIJI ERA—*Mutsuhito*, Emperor | 1867–1912 |
| TAISHO ERA—*Yoshihito*, Emperor | 1912–1926 |
| SHOWA ERA—*Hirohito*, Emperor | 1926– |

## PRIME MINISTERS

| | |
|---|---|
| Hirobumi Ito | 1885–1888 |
| Kiyotaka Kuroda | 1888–1889 |
| Aritomo Yamagata | 1889–1891 |
| Masayoshi Matsukata | 1891–1892 |
| Hirobumi Ito | 1892–1896 |
| Masayoshi Matsukata | 1896–1898 |
| Hirobumi Ito | 1898 |

## PRIME MINISTERS (Continued)

| | |
|---|---|
| Shigenobu Okuma | 1898 |
| Aritomo Yamagata | 1898–1900 |
| Hirobumi Ito | 1900–1901 |
| Taro Katsura | 1901–1906 |
| Kimmochi Saionge | 1906–1908 |
| Taro Katsura | 1908–1911 |
| Kimmochi Saionge | 1911–1912 |
| Tarō Katsura | 1912–1913 |
| Gonnohyoe Yamamoto | 1913–1914 |
| Shigenobu Okuma | 1914–1916 |
| Masatake Terauchi | 1916–1918 |
| Takashi Hara | 1918–1921 |
| Korekiyo Takahashi | 1921–1922 |
| Tomosaburō Kato | 1922–1923 |
| Gonnohyōe Yamamoto | 1923–1924 |
| Keigo Kiyoura | 1924 |
| Takaakira Kato | 1924–1926 |
| Reijirō Wakatsuki | 1926–1927 |
| Giichi Tanaka | 1927–1929 |
| Osachi Hamaguchi | 1929–1931 |
| Reijirō Wakatsuki | 1931 |
| Ki Tsuyoshi Inukai | 1931–1932 |
| Makoto Saito | 1932–1934 |
| Keisuki Okada | 1934–1936 |
| Kōki Hirota | 1936–1937 |
| Senjuro Hayashi | 1937 |
| Fumimaro Konoye | 1937–1939 |
| Kiichirō Hiranuma | 1939 |
| Nobuyuki Abe | 1939–1940 |
| Mitsumasa Yonai | 1940 |
| Fumimaro Konoye | 1940–1941 |
| Hideki Tojo | 1941–1944 |
| Kuniaki Koiso | 1944–1945 |
| Kantaro Suzuki | 1945 |
| Haruhiko Higashikuma | 1945 |
| Kijūrō Shidehira | 1945–1946 |
| Shigeru Yoshida | 1946–1947 |
| Tetsu Katayama | 1947–1948 |
| Hitoshi Ashida | 1948 |
| Shigeru Yoshida | 1948–1954 |
| Ichirō Hatoyama | 1954–1956 |
| Tanzan Ishibashi | 1956–1957 |
| Nobusuke Kishi | 1957–1960 |
| Hayato Ikeda | 1960–1964 |
| Eisaku Sato | 1964–1972 |
| Kakuei Tanaka | 1972–1974 |
| Takeo Miki | 1974–1976 |
| Takeo Fukuda | 1976–1978 |
| Masayoshi Ohira | 1978– |

[1] Clans and Shogunates are printed in small capitals; rulers in italics. Only the most important emperors and shoguns are given.

# Jordan

## KINGS

| | | | |
|---|---|---|---|
| Abdullah | 1946–1951 | Hussein | 1952– |
| Talal | 1951–1952 | | |

# Korea

## DEMOCRATIC PEOPLE'S REPUBLIC (NORTH)

## PREMIERS

| | |
|---|---|
| Kim Il Sung | 1948– |

## REPUBLIC (SOUTH)

## PRESIDENTS

| | | | |
|---|---|---|---|
| Syngman Rhee | 1948–1960 | Chung Hee Park | 1961– |
| Posun Yun | 1960–1961 | | |

# Lebanon

## PRESIDENTS

| | | | |
|---|---|---|---|
| Bechara el-Khoury | 1943–1952 | Charles Helou | 1964–1970 |
| Camille Chamoun | 1952–1958 | Suleiman Frangié | 1970–1976 |
| Fuad Chehab | 1958–1964 | Elias Sarkis | 1976– |

# Liberia

## PRESIDENTS

| | | | |
|---|---|---|---|
| Joseph J. Roberts | 1848–1856 | Joseph J. Cheeseman | 1892–1896 |
| Stephen A. Benson | 1856–1864 | William D. Coleman | 1896–1900 |
| Daniel B. Warner | 1864–1868 | Garretson W. Gibson | 1900–1904 |
| James S. Payne | 1868–1870 | Arthur Barclay | 1904–1912 |
| Edward J. Roye | 1870–1872 | Daniel E. Howard | 1912–1920 |
| Joseph J. Roberts | 1872–1876 | Charles D. B. King | 1920–1930 |
| James S. Payne | 1876–1878 | Edwin Barclay | 1930–1944 |
| Anthony W. Gardiner | 1878–1883 | William V. S. Tubman | 1944–1971 |
| Alfred F. Russell | 1883–1884 | William R. Tolbert | 1971– |
| Hilary Richard Wright Johnson | 1884–1892 | | |

# Mexico

## PRESIDENTS (since 1824)

| | |
|---|---|
| [First and Second Regencies, 1821-1822] | |
| Augustín de Iturbide, Emperor | 1822-1823 |
| [Republic established, 1823-1824] | |
| Guadalupe Victoria | 1824-1829 |
| Vicente Guerrero | 1829 |
| José María de Bocanegra (acting) | 1829 |
| Anastasio Bustamante | 1829-1832 |
| Melchor Múzquiz (acting) | 1832 |
| Manuel Gómez Pedraza | 1832-1833 |
| Antonio López de Santa Anna | 1833-1835 |
| Miguel Barragán | 1835-1836 |
| José Justo Corro | 1836-1837 |
| Anastasio Bustamante[1] | 1837-1841 |
| Javier Echeverría (acting) | 1841 |
| Antonio López de Santa Anna[2] | 1841-1842 |
| Nicolás Bravo[3] | 1842-1843 |
| Antonio López de Santa Anna (provisional) | 1843 |
| Valentin Canalizo[3] | 1843-1844 |
| Antonio López de Santa Anna | 1844 |
| José Joaquín Herrera (acting) | 1844 |
| Valentín Canalizo (acting) | 1844 |
| José Joaquín Herrera | 1844-1845 |
| Mariano Paredes y Arrillaga | 1846 |
| Nicolás Bravo | 1846 |
| José Mariano Salas (acting) | 1846 |
| [War with the United States, 1846-1848] | |
| Valentín Gómez Farias (acting) | 1846-1847 |
| Antonio López de Santa Anna | 1847 |
| Pedro María Anaya[3] | 1847 |
| Antonio López de Santa Anna | 1847 |
| Manuel de la Peña y Peña (provisional) | 1847 |
| Pedro María Anaya (acting) | 1847-1848 |
| Manuel de la Peña y Peña | 1848 |
| José Joaquín Herrera | 1848-1851 |
| Mariano Arista | 1851-1853 |
| Juan Bautista Ceballos (acting) | 1853 |
| Manuel M. Lombardine (acting) | 1853 |
| Antonio López de Santa Anna (dictator) | 1853-1855 |
| Martín Carrera (acting) | 1855 |
| Juan Alvarez (acting) | 1855 |
| Ignacio Comonfort[3] | 1855-1857 |
| Benito Juárez (provisional) | 1857-1861 |
| Benito Juárez | 1861-1872 |
| [Period of French intervention, 1861-1867. Austrian Archduke Maximilian crowned Emperor, June 12, 1864; executed June 19, 1867] | |
| Sebastián Lerdo de Tejada | 1872-1876 |
| Porfirio Díaz (provisional) | 1876 |
| Juan N. Méndez (acting) | 1876-1877 |
| Porfirio Díaz (provisional) | 1877 |
| Porfirio Díaz | 1877-1880 |
| Manuel González | 1880-1884 |
| Porfirio Díaz | 1884-1911 |
| Francisco León de la Barra (provisional) | 1911 |
| Francisco Indalecio Madero | 1911-1913 |
| Pedro Lascurain (provisional)[4] | 1913 |
| Victoriano Huerta (provisional) | 1913-1914 |
| Francisco Carbajal (provisional) | 1914 |
| Venustiano Carranza ("first chief") | 1914 |
| Eulalio Martín Gutiérrez | 1914-1915 |
| Roque González Garza (provisional) | 1915 |
| Francisco Lagos Cházaro (provisional) | 1915 |
| Venustiano Carranza (provisional)[5] | 1915-1917 |
| Venustiano Carranza | 1917-1920 |
| Adolfo de la Huerta (provisional) | 1920 |
| Alvaro Obregón | 1920-1924 |
| Plutarco Elías Calles | 1924-1928 |
| Emilio Portes Gil (provisional) | 1928-1930 |
| Pascual Ortiz Rubio | 1930-1932 |
| Abelardo L. Rodríguez (provisional) | 1932-1934 |
| Lázaro Cárdenas | 1934-1940 |
| Manuel Avila Camacho | 1940-1946 |
| Miguel Alemán Valdés | 1946-1952 |
| Adolfo Ruiz Cortines | 1952-1958 |
| Adolfo López Mateos | 1958-1964 |
| Gustavo Díaz Ordaz | 1964-1970 |
| Luis Echeverría Alvarez | 1970-1976 |
| José Lopez Portillo | 1976- |

[1] From March 18 to July 10, 1839, Santa Anna was in control; from July 10 to 17, 1839, Nicolas Bravo was acting president.
[2] Virtually dictator.
[3] Described as "substitute" president under the Constitution then in force.
[4] Was president for 46 minutes only, Feb. 19, 1913.
[5] Carranza recognized by the United States as head of the de facto government, Oct. 19, 1915, but not inaugurated until May 1, 1917. In 1915-1917 occurred the Villa raids and the Pershing expedition.

# The Netherlands[1] (Holland)

## PRINCES OF ORANGE, STADHOLDERS (since 1579)

| | |
|---|---|
| William I | 1579-1584 |
| Maurice | 1587-1625 |
| Frederick Henry | 1625-1647 |
| William II | 1647-1650 |
| [Stadholdership suspended, 1650-1672] | |
| Jan De Witt, Grand Pensionary | 1653-1672 |
| William of Nassau[2] | 1672-1702 |
| [Stadholdership suspended, 1702-1747] | |
| William IV | 1747-1751 |
| William V | 1751-1795 |
| [Batavian Republic established by France, 1795-1806] | |

## SOVEREIGNS

| | |
|---|---|
| Louis Bonaparte | 1806-1810 |
| [Holland again united to France, 1810-1813] | |
| [House of Orange restored, 1813] | |
| Willem Frederik, Prince of Orange, as William I | 1815-1840 |
| William II | 1840-1849 |
| William III | 1849-1890 |
| Wilhelmina[3] | 1890-1948 |
| Juliana | 1948- |

[1] Free cities of Holland and Zealand were important in Middle Ages; in 15th century they came under control of Burgundy but from 1477 to 1579 the Netherlands was ruled by the Hapsburgs. [2] William III of England, 1689-1702. See Sovereigns of Great Britain. [3] Seat of government established in London, May, 1940, after German occupation of Netherlands.

# New Zealand

## GOVERNORS

| | |
|---|---|
| Col. Thomas Gore Browne | 1855-1861 |
| George Grey | 1861-1868 |
| George Ferguson Bowen | 1868-1872 |
| George Alfred Arney: Administrator | 1873 |
| James Fergusson | 1873-1874 |
| George Augustus Constantine Phipps, Marquis of Normanby: Administrator | 1874-1875 |
| Marquis of Normanby: Governor | 1875-1879 |
| James Prendergast: Administrator | 1879 |
| Hercules George Robert Robinson, Baron Rosmead | 1879-1880 |
| Arthur Charles Hamilton-Gordon, Baron Stanmore | 1880-1883 |
| Lt. Gen. William Francis Drummond Jervois | 1883-1889 |
| William Hillier Onslow, Earl of Onslow | 1889-1892 |
| David Boyle, Earl of Glasgow | 1892-1897 |
| Uchter John Mark Knox, Earl of Ranfurly | 1897-1904 |
| William Lee Plunket, Baron Plunket | 1904-1910 |
| John Poynder Dickson-Poynder, Baron Islington | 1910-1912 |
| Arthur William de Brito Savile Foljambe, Earl of Liverpool | 1912-1917 |

GOVERNORS-GENERAL FROM 1917

|  |  |
|---|---|
| Arthur William de Brito Savile Foljambe, Earl of Liverpool | 1917-1920 |
| John Rushworth Jellicoe, Earl Jellicoe | 1920-1924 |
| Charles Fergusson | 1924-1930 |
| Charles Bathurst, Viscount Bledisloe | 1930-1935 |
| George Vere Arundell Monckton-Arundell, Viscount Galway | 1935-1941 |
| Cyril L. N. Newall | 1941-1945 |
| Bernard Cyril Freyberg | 1946-1952 |
| Willoughby Norrie | 1952-1957 |
| Charles John Lyttelton, Vis. Cobham | 1957-1962 |
| Bernard Fergusson | 1962-1967 |
| Arthur Porritt | 1967-1972 |
| Denis Blundell | 1972-1977 |
| Keith Holyoake | 1977- |

PRIME MINISTERS

|  |  |
|---|---|
| Henry Sewell | 1856 |
| William Fox | 1856 |
| Edward William Stafford | 1856-1861 |
| William Fox | 1861-1862 |
| Alfred Domett | 1862-1863 |
| Frederick Whitaker | 1863-1864 |
| Frederick Aloysius Weld | 1864-1865 |
| Edward William Stafford | 1865-1869 |
| William Fox | 1869-1872 |
| Edward William Stafford | 1872 |
| George Marsden Waterhouse | 1872-1873 |
| William Fox | 1873 |
| Julius Vogel | 1873-1875 |
| Daniel Pollen | 1875-1876 |
| Julius Vogel | 1876 |
| Harry Albert Atkinson | 1876-1877 |
| George Grey | 1877-1879 |
| John Hall | 1879-1882 |
| Frederick Whitaker | 1882-1883 |
| Harry Albert Atkinson | 1883-1884 |
| Robert Stout | 1884 |
| Harry Albert Atkinson | 1884 |
| Robert Stout | 1884-1887 |
| Harry Albert Atkinson | 1887-1891 |
| John Ballance | 1891-1893 |
| Richard John Seddon | 1893-1906 |
| William Hall-Jones | 1906 |
| Joseph George Ward | 1906-1912 |
| Thomas Mackenzie | 1912 |
| William Ferguson Massey | 1912-1925 |
| Francis Henry Dillon Bell | 1925 |
| Joseph Gordon Coates | 1925-1928 |
| Joseph George Ward | 1928-1930 |
| George William Forbes | 1930-1935 |
| Michael J. Savage | 1935-1940 |
| Peter Fraser | 1940-1949 |
| Sidney G. Holland | 1949-1957 |
| Walter Nash | 1957-1960 |
| Keith J. Holyoake | 1960-1972 |
| John R. Marshall | 1972 |
| Norman Eric Kirk | 1972-1974 |
| Wallace E. Rowling | 1974-1975 |
| Robert David Muldoon | 1975- |

## NICARAGUA

PRESIDENTS (since 1853)

|  |  |
|---|---|
| Frutos Chamorro | 1853-1855 |
| Tomás Martínez | 1857-1867 |
| Fernando Guzmán | 1867-1871 |
| Vincente Quadra | 1871-1875 |
| Pedro Joaquín Chamorro | 1875-1879 |
| Joaquín Zavala | 1879-1883 |
| Adán Cárdenas | 1883-1887 |
| Evaristo Carazo | 1887-1889 |
| Roberto Sacasa (deposed) | 1889-1893 |
| José Zelaya | 1893-1909 |
| José Madriz (provisional) | 1909-1910 |
| Juan J. Estrada | 1910-1911 |
| Adolfo Díaz (provisonal) | 1911 |
| Luis Mena | 1911-1912 |
| Adolfo Díaz | 1913-1916 |
| Emiliano Chamorro Vargas | 1917-1920 |
| Diego Manuel Chamorro | 1921-1923 |
| Bartolo Martínez (provisional) | 1923-1924 |
| Carlos Solórzano | 1925-1926 |
| Emiliano Chamorro Vargas | 1926 |
| Adolfo Díaz | 1926-1928 |
| José María Moncada | 1929-1932 |
| Juan Bautista Sacasa | 1933-1936 |
| Carlos Brenes Jarquín (provisional) | 1936 |
| Anastasio Somoza | 1937-1947 |
| Leonardo Argüello | 1947 |
| Benjamin Lacayo-Sacasa | 1947 |
| Victor Manuel Román y Reyes | 1947-1950 |
| Anastasio Somoza | 1950-1956 |
| Luis Somoza Debayle | 1956-1963 |
| René Schick Gutiérrez | 1963-1966 |
| Anastasio Somoza Debayle[1] | 1967-1972 |
| Anastasio Somoza Debayle[2] | 1974-1979 |

[1] Resigned 1972, succeeded by a three-man junta; reelected 1974. [2] Deposed 1979 by five-man junta.

## NORWAY

|  |  |
|---|---|
| Haakon (also Hakon, Hako) the Good | 935-961 |
| Harold II (or Harald) | 961-970 |
| Earl Haakon (or Hakon Jarl) | 970-995 |
| Olaf I (or Olav) Tryggvesson | 995-1000 |
| [Norway divided between Sweden and Denmark] | |
| Earls Eric (or Erik) and Sweyn | 1000-1015 |
| Olaf II (Saint Olaf) | 1016-1030 |
| Sweyn, son of King Canute of England | 1028-1035 |
| Magnus I the Good | 1035-1047 |
| Harold Haardraade (or Hardrada) | 1047-1066 |
| Olaf III and Magnus II | 1066-1069 |
| Olaf III (alone) | 1069-1093 |
| Magnus III | 1093-1103 |
| Olaf IV (d. 1115), Eystein (I) Magnusson (d. 1122), Sigurd I (joint rule) | 1103-1130 |
| Magnus IV and Harold Gille | 1130-1136 |
| Sigurd II and Inge I[1] | 1137-1161 |
| Eystein (II) Haraldsson, Haakon II, Magnus V[1] | 1142-1162 |
| Magnus V (alone) | 1162-1184 |
| Sverre (or Swerro) | 1184-1202 |
| Haakon III | 1202-1204 |
| Guthrum (or Guttorm) | 1204-1205 |
| Inge II (alone) | 1205-1217 |
| Haakon IV the Old | 1217-1263 |
| Magnus VI the Law-Mender | 1263-1280 |
| Eric Magnusson | 1280-1299 |
| Haakon V | 1299-1319 |
| Magnus VII (Magnus II of Sweden) | 1319-1343 |
| Haakon VI | 1343-1380 |
| Olaf V (Olaf II of Denmark) | 1380-1387[2] |
| Haakon VII | 1905-1957 |
| Olav V | 1957- |

[1] Period of civil wars—all contenders for the crown. [2] Norway united with Sweden and Denmark under Margaret (see rulers of DENMARK, 1387-1814). Norway and Sweden united 1814-1905 (see rulers of SWEDEN).

## PAKISTAN

GOVERNORS-GENERAL

|  |  |
|---|---|
| Mohammed Ali Jinnah | 1947-1948 |
| Khawaja Nazimuddin | 1948-1951 |
| Ghulam Mohammad | 1951-1955 |
| Iskander Mirza | 1955-1956[1] |

PRESIDENTS

|  |  |
|---|---|
| Iskander Mirza | 1956-1958 |
| Mohammed Ayub Khan | 1958-1969 |
| A. M. Yahya Khan | 1969-1971 |
| Zulfiqar Ali Bhutto | 1971-1973 |
| Fazal Elahi Chaudhry | 1973-1978 |
| Mohammed Zia-ul-Haq[3] | 1978- |

PRIME MINISTERS

|  |  |
|---|---|
| Liaquat Ali Khan | 1947-1951 |
| Khawaja Nazimuddin | 1951-1953 |
| Mohammed Ali | 1953-1956 |
| H. S. Suhrawady | 1956-1957 |
| Malik Firoz Khan Noon | 1957-1958[2] |
| Zulfiqar Ali Bhutto | 1973-1977 |

[1] Republic established March 23, 1956.
[2] Martial law imposed 1959 and government reorganized with the President acting as martial law administrator; civil government restored 1973.
[3] De facto ruler under martial law from 1977.

## PANAMA[1]

PRESIDENTS (since 1904)

| | | | |
|---|---|---|---|
| Manuel Amador Guerrero | 1904–1908 | Augusto Samuel Boyd (acting) | 1939–1940 |
| José Domingo de Obaldía | 1908–1910 | Arnulfo Arias | 1940–1941 |
| Carlos Antonio Mendoza (acting) | 1910 | Ricardo Adolfo de la Guardia | 1941–1945 |
| Pablo Arosemena (acting) | 1910–1912 | Enrique Adolfo Jiménez | 1945–1948 |
| Belisario Porras | 1912–1916 | Domingo Díaz Arosemena | 1948–1949 |
| Ramón Valdez | 1916–1918 | Arnulfo Arias | 1949–1951 |
| Ciro Luis Urriola (acting) | 1918 | Alcibíades Arosemena | 1951–1952 |
| Belisario Porras (acting) | 1918–1920 | José Antonio Remon Cantera | 1952–1955 |
| Ernesto Lefevre | 1920 | José Arias Espinosa | 1955–1956 |
| Belisario Porras | 1920–1924 | Ernesto de la Guardia, Jr. | 1956–1960 |
| Rodolfo Chiari | 1924–1928 | Roberto F. Chiari | 1960–1964 |
| Florencio Harmodio Arosemena | 1928–1931 | Marco A. Robles | 1964–1968 |
| Harmodio Arias (provisional) | 1931 | Arnulfo Arias | 1968 |
| Ricardo J. Alfaro | 1931–1932 | José María Pinilla | 1968–1969 |
| Harmodio Arias | 1932–1936 | Demetrio Basilio Lakas Bahas | 1969–1978 |
| Juan Demóstenes Arosemena | 1936–1939 | Aristides Royo | 1978– |

[1] Independence declared Nov. 3, 1903.

## PARAGUAY[1]

| DICTATORS (1814–1870) | |
|---|---|
| José Gaspar Rodríguez Francia | 1814–1840 |
| Carlos Antonio López[2] | 1844–1862 |
| Francisco Solano López | 1862–1870 |

| PRESIDENTS (since 1870) | |
|---|---|
| Cirilo Rivarola | 1870–1871 |
| Salvador Jovellanos | 1871–1874 |
| J. Bautista Gil | 1874–1877 |
| Higinio Uriarte (acting) | 1877–1878 |
| Cándido Barreiro | 1878–1880 |
| Bernardino Caballero | 1880–1885 |
| Patricio Escobar | 1886–1890 |
| Juan González | 1890–1894 |
| Juan Bautista Egusquiza | 1894–1898 |
| Emilio Aceval | 1898–1902 |
| Héctor Carvallo | 1902 |
| Juan B. Escurra | 1902–1904 |
| Juan Gaona (provisional) | 1904–1905 |
| Cecilio Baez (provisional) | 1906 |
| Benigno Ferreira | 1906–1908 |
| Emiliano González Navero (provisional) | 1908–1910 |
| Manuel Gondra | 1910–1911 |
| Albino Jara (provisional) | 1911 |
| Liberato Marcial Rojas (provisional) | 1911–1912 |

| PRESIDENTS (Continued) | |
|---|---|
| Pedro Peña (provisional) | 1912 |
| Emiliano González Navero (provisional) | 1912 |
| Eduardo Schaerer | 1912–1916 |
| Manuel Franco | 1916–1919 |
| José Montero (acting) | 1919–1920 |
| Manuel Gondra | 1920–1921 |
| Félix Paiva (acting) | 1921 |
| Eusebio Ayala (provisional) | 1921–1923 |
| Eligio Ayala (provisional) | 1923–1924 |
| Luis Riart (provisional) | 1924 |
| Eligio Ayala | 1924–1928 |
| José Patricio Guggiari | 1928–1931 |
| Emiliano González Navero (provisional) | 1931–1932 |
| José Patricio Guggiari | 1932 |
| Eusebio Ayala | 1932–1936 |
| Rafael Franco (provisional) | 1936–1937 |
| Félix Paiva (provisional, 1937) | 1937–1939 |
| José Félix Estigarribia | 1939–1940 |
| Higinio Morínigo | 1940–1949 |
| Raimundo Rolón (provisional) | 1949 |
| Felipe Molas López | 1949 |
| Federico Cháves | 1949–1954 |
| Alfredo Stroessner | 1954– |

[1] Republic declared Nov. 25, 1870.
[2] Upon death of Francia (1840) he became secretary of military junta and one of the consuls (1841–1844).

## PERU[1]

PRESIDENTS (since 1821)

| | | | |
|---|---|---|---|
| José de San Martín[2] | 1821–1822 | Nicolás de Piérola | 1895–1899 |
| José de la Riva Aguero | 1823 | Eduardo Lopez de Romaña | 1899–1903 |
| Simón Bolívar (dictator) | 1824–1827 | Manuel Candamo | 1903–1904 |
| José de Lamar | 1827–1829 | Serapio Calderón (acting) | May–Sept. 1904 |
| Agustín Gamarra | 1829–1833 | José Pardo y Barreda | 1904–1908 |
| Luis José Orbegosa | 1833–1835 | Augusto Bernardino Leguía y Salcedo | 1908–1912 |
| Felipe Santiago Salaverry | 1835–1836 | Guillermo Enrique Billinghurst | 1912–1914 |
| Andrés Santa Cruz[3] | 1836–1839 | Oscar Raimundo Benavides (provisional) | 1915 |
| Agustín Gamarra | 1839–1841 | José Pardo y Barreda | 1915–1919 |
| Manuel Menéndez[4] (acting) | 1841–1845 | Augusto Bernardino Leguía y Salcedo | 1919–1930 |
| Ramón Castilla | 1845–1851 | Manuel Ponce (provisional) | 1930 |
| José Rufino Echenique | 1851–1855 | Luis M. Sánchez Cerro (provisional) | 1930–1931 |
| Ramón Castilla | 1855–1862 | Ricardo Leoncio Elías (provisional) | 1931 |
| Miguel San Román | 1862–1863 | Gustavo Jiménez (provisional) | 1931 |
| Juan Antonio Pezet | 1863–1865 | David Samánez Ocampo (provisional) | 1931 |
| Mariano Ignacio Prado (dictator) | 1865–1868 | Luis M. Sánchez Cerro | 1931–1933 |
| José Balta | 1868–1872 | Oscar Raimundo Benavides | 1933–1939 |
| Manuel Pardo | 1872–1876 | Manuel Prado Ugarteche | 1939–1945 |
| Mariano Ignacio Prado | 1876–1879 | José Luis Bustamente Rivero | 1945–1948 |
| Nicolás de Piérola | 1879–1881 | Manuel Odría (provisional) | 1948–1950 |
| Francisco García Calderón | 1881 | Zenón Noriega | 1950 |
| Lizardo Montero | 1881–1883 | Manuel Odría | 1950–1956 |
| Miguel Iglesias | 1883–1886 | Manuel Prado y Ugarteche | 1956–1962 |
| Andrés Avelino Cáceres | 1886–1890 | Ricardo Pérez Godoy (provisional) | 1962 |
| Remigio Morales Bermúdez | 1890–1894 | Fernando Belaúnde Terry | 1963–1968 |
| Justiniano Borgoño | 1894 | Juan Velasco Alvarado | 1968–1975 |
| Andrés Avelino Cáceres | 1894–1895 | Francisco Morales Bermúdez | 1975– |

[1] Independence declared July 28, 1821.
[2] Assumed title of "Protector of Peru"; not generally listed as a president.
[3] President of the Peru-Bolivia Confederation; actually a dictator.
[4] The period 1841–1844 was one of civil war and confusion. Juan Crisóstomo Torrico and Manuel Vivanco were each for a short time in power.

## PHILIPPINES

PRESIDENTS

| | | | |
|---|---|---|---|
| Manuel Roxas | 1946–1948 | Carlos P. Garcia | 1957–1961 |
| Elpidio Quirino | 1948–1953 | Diosdado Macapagal | 1961–1965 |
| Ramon Magsaysay | 1953–1957 | Ferdinand E. Marcos | 1965– |

# Poland

## PRESIDENTS

| | |
|---|---|
| Jósef Pilsudski | 1919–1922 |
| Gabrjel Narutowicz | 1922 |
| Stanislaw Wojciechowski | 1922–1926 |
| Ignace Mościcki | 1926–1939[3] |
| Wladyslaw Raczkiewicz[1] | 1939–1945 |
| Boleslaw Bierut[2] | 1944–1952 |

## CHAIRMEN OF THE COUNCIL OF STATE[4]

| | |
|---|---|
| Aleksander Zawadzki | 1952–1964 |
| Edward Ochab | 1964–1968 |
| Marian Spychalski | 1968–1970 |
| Józef Cyrankiewicz | 1970–1972 |
| Henryk Jabloński | 1972– |

[1] Seat of government in London, England. [2] Assumed presidency in Moscow; elected 1947. [3] Conquered by Germany, 1939. [4] The constitution of 1952 replaced the President with a Chairman of the Council of State.

# Portugal

## HOUSE OF BURGUNDY

| | |
|---|---|
| Alfonso I (*Port.* Affonso) | 1139–1185 |
| Sancho I | 1185–1211 |
| Alfonso II | 1211–1223 |
| Sancho II | 1223–1248 |
| Alfonso III | 1248–1279 |
| Denis (or Dionysius) (*Port.* Diniz) | 1279–1325 |
| Alfonso IV | 1325–1357 |
| Peter I (*Port.* Pedro) | 1357–1367 |
| Ferdinand I (*Port.* Fernando) | 1367–1383 |
| [Interregnum, 1383–1385] | |

## HOUSE OR AVIZ (OR AVIS)

| | |
|---|---|
| John (*Port.* João) | 1385–1433 |
| Edward (*Port.* Duarte) | 1433–1438 |
| Alfonso V | 1438–1481 |
| John II | 1481–1495 |
| Emanuel (*Port.* Manuel or Manoel) | 1495–1521 |
| John III | 1521–1557 |
| Sebastian (*Port.* Sebastião) | 1557–1578 |
| Henry (*Port.* Henrique) | 1578–1580 |

## UNDER SPANISH DOMINATION[1]

| | |
|---|---|
| Philip I (II of Spain) | 1580–1598 |
| Philip II (III of Spain) | 1598–1621 |
| Philip III (IV of Spain) | 1621–1640 |

## HOUSE OF BRAGANZA

| | |
|---|---|
| John IV | 1640–1656 |
| Alfonso VI | 1656–1683 |
| Peter II | 1683–1706 |
| John V | 1706–1750 |

## HOUSE OF BRAGANZA (Continued)

| | |
|---|---|
| Joseph Emanuel (*Port.* José Manuel) | 1750–1777 |
| Maria I and Peter III | 1777–1786 |
| Maria I (alone) | 1786–1816 |
| John VI[2] | 1816–1826 |
| Peter IV (Dom Pedro)[3] | 1826 |
| Maria II da Gloria | 1826–1828 |
| Miguel | 1828–1833 |
| Maria II (restored) | 1833–1853 |

## HOUSE OF BRAGANZA-COBURG

| | |
|---|---|
| Peter V | 1853–1861 |
| Louis (*Port.* Luis) | 1861–1889 |
| Carlos I | 1889–1908 |
| Manuel II | 1908–1910 |
| [Revolution; Republic declared Oct. 5, 1910] | |

## PRESIDENTS OF THE REPUBLIC

| | |
|---|---|
| Teófilo Braga (provisional) | 1910–1911 |
| Manuel José de Arriaga | 1911–1915 |
| Teófilo Braga | 1915 |
| Bernardino Luiz Machado | 1915–1917 |
| Sidônio B. Cardoso da Silva Paes | 1917–1918 |
| João de Canto e Castro (provisional) | 1918–1919 |
| Antônio José de Almeida | 1919–1923 |
| Manuel Teixeira Gomes | 1923–1925 |
| Bernardino Luiz Machado | 1925–1926 |
| Antonio Oscar de Fragoso Carmona | 1926–1951 |
| Francisco Higino Craveiro Lopes | 1951–1958 |
| Américo de Deus Rodriguez Tomás | 1958–1974 |
| Antonio de Spinola | 1974 |
| Francisco da Costa Gomes | 1974–1976 |
| António dos Santos Ramalho Eanes | 1976– |

[1] See RULERS OF SPAIN. [2] John was regent from 1792 to 1816. [3] Dom Pedro I, Emperor of Brazil (see BRAZIL) became king of Portugal on the death of John VI, but abdicated in favor of his daughter Maria.

# Roman Empire

## THE CAESARS

| | |
|---|---|
| Augustus (Octavianus) | 27 B.C.–14 A.D. |
| Tiberius | 14 A.D.–37 A.D. |
| Caligula | 37–41 |
| Claudius | 41–54 |
| Nero | 54–68 |
| Galba | 68–69 |
| Otho | 69 |
| Vitellius | 69 |
| Vespasian | 69–79 |
| Titus | 79–81 |
| Domitian | 81–96 |

## THE GOOD EMPERORS

| | |
|---|---|
| Nerva | 96–98 |
| Trajan | 98–117 |
| Hadrian | 117–138 |
| Antoninus Pius | 138–161 |
| Marcus Aurelius[1] | 161–180 |
| Lucius Aurelius Verus[1] | 161–169 |

## MILITARY DESPOTS

| | |
|---|---|
| Commodus | 180–192 |
| Pertinax | 193 |
| Didius Julianus | 193 |
| Septimius Severus | 193–211 |
| Caracalla[2] | 211–217 |
| Geta[2] | 211–212 |
| Macrinus | 217–218 |
| Heliogabalus or Elagabalus | 218–222 |
| Alexander Severus | 222–235 |
| Maximinus | 235–238 |
| Gordianus I | 238 |
| Gordianus II | 238 |
| Balbinus and Pupienus | 238 |

## MILITARY DESPOTS (Continued)

| | |
|---|---|
| Gordianus III | 238–244 |
| Philip the Arabian | 244–249 |
| Decius | 249–251 |
| Gallus | 251–253 |
| Aemilianus | 253 |
| Valerian[3] | 253–260 |
| Gallienus[3] | 260–268 |
| Claudius II | 268–270 |
| Aurelian | 270–275 |
| Tacitus | 275–276 |
| Florian | 276 |
| Probus | 276–282 |
| Carus | 282–283 |

## LATER EMPERORS

| | |
|---|---|
| Carinus and Numerianus[4] | 283–285 |
| Diocletian[4] | 284–305 |
| Maximian[4] | 286–305 |
| Constantius[5] | 305–306 |
| Galerius[5] | 305–311 |
| Constantine the Great[6] | 306–337 |
| Constantine II[7] | 337–340 |
| Constans[7] | 337–350 |
| Constantius II[7] | 337–361 |
| Julian the Apostate | 361–363 |
| Jovian | 363–364 |
| Valentinian I (West) | 364–375 |
| Valens (East) | 364–378 |
| Gratian (West)[8] | 375–383 |
| Valentinian II (West) | 375–392 |
| Theodosius the Great (East) | 379–394 |
| Maximus (West) | 383–388 |
| Eugenius (West) | 392–394 |
| Theodosius sole emperor[9] | 394–395 |

[1] As colleagues sharing imperial powers in full equality. [2] Caracalla and Geta, brothers, were appointed joint emperors by their father, Septimius Severus, but Caracalla caused the death of Geta in 212. [3] Valerian and Gallienus, joint emperors (253–260), but Valerian was captured and imprisoned by the Persians in 260. [4] Joint emperors (Augusti). [5] Had been Caesars under the Augusti, Diocletian, and Maximian. [6] In the early part of the reign of Constantine there were six claimants to the title of Emperor: Constantine; Galerius, successor to Diocletian, as Augustus in the East, 305–311; Maxentius, self-proclaimed Caesar in the West, 306–312; Maximian (who had been emperor, 286–305) with reassumed imperial dignity in Rome, 306–308; Flavius Valerius Severus, favorite of Maximian, proclaimed Augustus, 306–307; and Licinius, joint emperor with, and successor to, Galerius in the East, 311–324. [7] Sons of Constantine; the empire divided. [8] Gratian was made Augustus by his father, Valentinian I, in 367, ruling jointly with him until the latter's death in 375. [9] Roman Empire divided, 395.

# Roman Empire (Continued)

### ROMAN EMPERORS OF THE WEST

|  |  |
|---|---|
| Honorius | 395–423 |
| Valentinian III | 425–455 |
| Petronius Maximus | 455 |
| Avitus | 455–456 |
| Majorian | 457–461 |
| Severus | 461–465 |
| Anthemius | 467–472 |
| Olybrius | 472 |
| Glycerius | 473 |
| Julius Nepos | 473–475 |
| Romulus Augustulus[10] | 475–476 |

### ROMAN EMPERORS OF THE EAST

|  |  |
|---|---|
| Arcadius | 395–408 |
| Theodosius II | 408–450 |
| Marcian | 450–467 |
| Leo I | 457–474 |
| Leo II | 473–474 |

### BYZANTINE EMPERORS

|  |  |
|---|---|
| Zeno the Isaurian | 474–491 |
| Anastasius I | 491–518 |
| Justin I | 518–527 |
| Justinian I | 527–565 |
| Justin II | 565–578 |
| Tiberius II | 578–582 |
| Maurice | 582–602 |
| Phocas | 602–610 |
| Heraclius | 610–641 |
| Constantine III | 641 |
| Constans II | 641–668 |
| Constantine IV | 668–685 |
| Justinian II | 685–695 |
| Leontius | 695–698 |
| Tiberius III | 698–705 |
| Justinian II (restored) | 705–711 |
| Philippicus | 711–713 |
| Anastasius II | 713–716 |
| Theodosius III | 716–717 |
| Leo III the Isaurian | 717–741 |
| Constantine V | 741–775 |
| Leo IV | 775–780 |
| Constantine VI | 780–797 |
| Irene (empress) | 797–802 |
| Nicephorus I | 802–811 |
| Stauracius | 811 |
| Michael I (Rhangabé) | 811–813 |
| Leo V the Armenian | 813–820 |
| Michael II | 820–829 |
| Theophilus I | 829–842 |
| Michael III | 842–867 |
| Bardas | 842–866 |
| Theophilus II | 867 |
| Basil I the Macedonian | 867–886 |
| Leo VI the Wise | 886–912 |
| Alexander, regent | 912–913 |
| Constantine VII (Porphyrogenitus) | 913–959 |
| Romanus I (Lecapenus), regent[11] | 919–944 |
| Romanus II | 959–963 |

### BYZANTINE EMPERORS (Continued)

|  |  |
|---|---|
| Basil II (Bulgaroctonus) | 963–1025 |
| Nicephorus II (Phocas)[12] | 963–969 |
| John I Zimisces[12] | 969–976 |
| Constantine VIII | 1025–1028 |
| Zoë (empress) | 1028–1050 |
| Romanus III Argyrus[13] | 1028–1034 |
| Michael IV the Paphlagonian[13] | 1034–1041 |
| Michael V (Kalaphates) | 1041–1042 |
| Constantine IX (Monomachus)[13] | 1042–1055 |
| Theodora (empress) | 1055–1056 |
| Michael VI (Stratioticus) | 1056–1057 |

### THE COMNENI AND ANGELI

|  |  |
|---|---|
| Isaac I (Comnenus) | 1057–1059 |
| Constantine X (Ducas) | 1059–1067 |
| Romanus IV (Diogenes) | 1067–1071 |
| Michael VII (Parapinakes) | 1071–1078 |
| Nicephorus III (Botaniates) | 1078–1081 |
| Alexius I (Comnenus) | 1081–1118 |
| John II (Comnenus) | 1118–1143 |
| Manuel I (Comnenus) | 1143–1180 |
| Alexius II (Comnenus) | 1180–1183 |
| Andronicus II (Comnenus) | 1183–1185 |
| Isaac II (Angelus-Comnenus) | 1185–1195 |
| Alexius III (Angelus) | 1195–1203 |
| Isaac II (restored)[14] | 1203–1204 |
| Alexius IV (Angelus)[14] | 1203–1204 |
| Alexius V (Ducas) | 1204 |

### LATIN EMPERORS

|  |  |
|---|---|
| Baldwin I | 1204–1205 |
| Henry | 1205–1216 |
| Peter of Courtenay | 1216–1217 |
| Robert of Courtenay | 1221–1228 |
| Baldwin II | 1228–1261 |

### NICAEAN EMPERORS

|  |  |
|---|---|
| Theodore I (Lascaris) | 1206–1222 |
| John III (Ducas or Vatatzes) | 1222–1254 |
| Theodore II (Lascaris) | 1254–1258 |
| John IV (Lascaris) | 1258–1261 |
| Michael VIII (Palaeologus)[15] | 1259–1261 |

### THE PALAEOLOGI (empire restored)

|  |  |
|---|---|
| Michael VIII | 1261–1282 |
| Andronicus II (the Elder) | 1282–1328 |
| Michael IX[16] | 1295–1320 |
| Andronicus III (the Younger) | 1328–1341 |
| John V | 1341–1347 |
| John VI (Cantacuzene) | 1347–1355 |
| John V (restored) | 1355–1376 |
| Andronicus IV | 1376–1379 |
| John V (restored) | 1379–1391 |
| John VII | 1390 |
| Manuel II | 1391–1425 |
| John VIII | 1425–1448 |
| Constantine XI[17] | 1448–1453 |

[10] End of the Western Roman Empire; Augustulus deposed and banished by Odoacer. [11] Coregent emperor with Constantine VII. [12] Coregent emperors with Basil II. [13] Husbands of Zoë, and corulers with her. [14] Corulers under the Crusaders. [15] Coemperor with John IV. [16] Coemperor with Andronicus II. [17] Constantinople captured by Mohammed—end of Eastern Empire, 1453.

# Romania[1]

|  |  |
|---|---|
| Prince Alexander John I (Col. Alexander Cuza of Moldavia) | 1861–1866 |
| Carol I (Prince Charles of Hohenzollern-Sigmaringen), as domu (lord) | 1866–1881 |
| Carol I, as king | 1881–1914 |
| Ferdinand I | 1914–1927 |
| Prince Michael (Mihai) | 1927–1930 |
| Carol II | 1930–1940 |
| Michael (reinstated by Germany)[2] | 1940–1947 |

### PRESIDENTS

|  |  |
|---|---|
| Constantin I. Parhon | 1948–1952 |
| Petru Groza | 1952–1958 |
| Ion Gheorghe Maurer | 1958–1961 |
| Gheorghe Gheorghiu-Dej | 1961–1965 |
| Chivu Stoica | 1965–1967 |
| Nicolae Ceausescu | 1967– |

[1] Two principalities, Walachia and Moldavia, united to form Romania (1862). [2] Forced to abdicate Dec. 30, 1947. Romania declared a Republic.

# Saudi Arabia

### KINGS

|  |  |
|---|---|
| Abdul-Aziz | 1932–1953 |
| Saud | 1953–1964 |
| Faisal | 1964–1975 |
| Khalid | 1975– |

# South Africa

### GOVERNORS-GENERAL

|  |  |
|---|---|
| Herbert John Gladstone, Viscount (1910) Gladstone | 1910–1914 |
| Sydney Charles Buxton, Earl (1920) Buxton | 1914–1920 |
| Prince Arthur Frederick Patrick Albert, Duke of Connaught | 1920–1923 |
| Alexander A. F. G. Cambridge, Earl (1917) of Athlone | 1923–1931 |
| George H. H. Villiers, Earl (1914) of Clarendon | 1931–1937 |
| Patrick Duncan | 1937–1943 |
| Gideon Brand van Zyl | 1946–1950 |
| Ernest George Jansen | 1951–1959 |
| Charles Robberts Swart | 1960–1961 |

PRESIDENTS[1]

| | |
|---|---|
| Charles Robberts Swart | 1961–1967 |
| Jozua Francois Naudé (acting) | 1967–1968 |
| Jacobus Johannes Fouché | 1968–1975 |
| Nicolaas J. Diederichs | 1975–1978 |
| Balthazar Johannes Vorster | 1978– |

PRIME MINISTERS

| | |
|---|---|
| Louis Botha | 1910–1919 |
| Jan Christiaan Smuts | 1919–1924 |
| James Barry Munnik Hertzog | 1924–1939 |
| Jan Christiaan Smuts | 1939–1948 |
| Daniel Francois Malan | 1948–1954 |
| Johannes Gerhardus Strijdom | 1954–1958 |
| Hendrik Frensch Verwoerd | 1958–1966 |
| Balthazar Johannes Vorster | 1966–1978 |
| Pieter W. Botha | 1978– |

[1] On May 31, 1961 South Africa was proclaimed a republic.

## Spain

| | |
|---|---|
| Gothic Kings | 412–711 |
| Kings of Asturias and León | 718–1027 |
| Kings of Navarre | 873–1512 |
| Kings of León and Castile | 1035–1504 |
| Kings of Aragon | 1035–1479 |
| [Union of Castile and Aragon, 1479] | |
| Ferdinand II of Aragon (*Span.* Fernando) and Isabella of Castile (*Span.* Isabel) | 1479–1504 |
| Philip I and Juanna, under regency of Ferdinand | 1504–1506 |
| Ferdinand V (II of Aragon) | 1506–1516 |
| **HOUSE OF HAPSBURG** | |
| Charles I[1] (*Span.* Carlos) | 1516–1556 |
| Philip II (*Span.* Felipe) | 1556–1598 |
| Philip III | 1598–1621 |
| Philip IV | 1621–1665 |
| Charles II | 1665–1700 |
| **HOUSE OF BOURBON** | |
| Philip V | 1700–1724 |
| Louis I (*Span.* Luis) (reigned only a few months) | 1724 |
| Philip V (again) | 1724–1746 |
| Ferdinand VI | 1746–1759 |
| Charles III | 1759–1788 |
| Charles IV | 1788–1808 |
| Ferdinand VII | 1808 |
| Joseph Bonaparte[2] | 1808–1813 |
| **HOUSE OF BOURBON (Continued)** | |
| Ferdinand VII (restored) | 1814–1833 |
| Isabella II | 1833–1868 |
| **HOUSE OF SAVOY** | |
| Amadeus (*Span.* Amadeo) | 1870–1873 |
| **REPUBLIC** | |
| Emilio Castelar y Ripoll, head of the government | 1873–1874 |
| **HOUSE OF BOURBON** | |
| Alfonso XII | 1874–1885 |
| Alfonso XIII[3] | 1886–1931 |
| **PRESIDENTS OF THE REPUBLIC** | |
| Niceto Alcalá Zamora y Torres | 1931–1936 |
| Manuel Azaña | 1936–1939 |
| [Civil War, 1936–1939] | |
| **CHIEF OF THE NEW STATE** | |
| Francisco Franco-Bahamonde | 1938–1975 |
| **CONSTITUTIONAL MONARCHY** | |
| Juan Carlos I | 1975– |

[1] Holy Roman Emperor as Charles V. [2] Not a Bourbon—placed on throne by his brother Napoleon. [3] Under regency (1886–1902) of his mother Queen Maria Christina.

## Sweden

| | |
|---|---|
| Houses of Sverker and Eric (or Erik) | 1130–1250 |
| **FOLKUNG DYNASTY (1250–1365)** | |
| Earl Birger (Regent) | 1250–1266 |
| Waldemar I (or Valdemar) | 1250–1275 |
| Magnus I | 1275–1290 |
| Birger II | 1290–1318 |
| Magnus II | 1319–1365[1] |
| Eric XII | 1356–1359[1] |
| Haakon VI | 1362–1363[1] |
| Albert of Mecklenburg | 1364–1389 |
| Margaret (Regent) | 1389–1412 |
| [Union with Denmark] | |
| Eric XIII (Eric VII of Denmark) | 1412–1439 |
| Engelbrekt[2] | 1435–1436 |
| Karl Knutsson[2] | 1436–1440 |
| Christopher of Bavaria[3] | 1440–1448 |
| Charles VIII (Karl Knutsson) | 1448–1457 |
| Christian I of Oldenburg[3] | 1457–1464 |
| Charles VIII | 1464–1465 and 1467–1470 |
| Sten Sture the Elder[2] | 1470–1503 |
| John II[3] | 1497–1501 |
| Svante Sture[2] | 1503–1512 |
| Sten Sture the Younger[2] | 1512–1520 |
| Christian II[3] | 1520–1523 |
| **VASA DYNASTY** | |
| Gustavus I (*Swed.* Gustaf) (Administrator) | 1521–1523 |
| Gustavus I (King) | 1523–1560 |
| Eric XIV | 1560–1568 |
| John III (or Johan) | 1568–1592 |
| **VASA DYNASTY (Continued)** | |
| Sigismund | 1592–1604 |
| Charles IX (or Carl) (Regent) | 1599–1604 |
| Charles IX (King) | 1604–1611 |
| Gustavus (II) Adolphus (or Gustaf Adolf) | 1611–1632 |
| Christina | 1632–1654 |
| **PALATINATE DYNASTY** | |
| Charles X Gustavus | 1654–1660 |
| Charles XI | 1660–1697 |
| Charles XII | 1697–1718 |
| Ulrica Eleanora | 1718–1720 |
| Frederick I of Hesse (*Swed.* Fredrik) | 1720–1751 |
| **HOLSTEIN-GOTTORP DYNASTY** | |
| Adolphus Frederick (*Swed.* Adolf Fredrik) | 1751–1771 |
| Gustavus III | 1771–1792 |
| Gustavus IV Adolphus | 1792–1809 |
| Charles XIII | 1809–1818 |
| [Sweden and Norway united, 1814–1905] | |
| **BERNADOTTE DYNASTY** | |
| Charles XIV John | 1818–1844 |
| Oscar I | 1844–1859 |
| Charles XV | 1859–1872 |
| Oscar II | 1872–1907 |
| [Norway becomes independent, 1905] | |
| Gustavus V (or Gustaf) | 1907–1950 |
| Gustaf VI Adolf | 1950–1973 |
| Charles XVI Gustaf | 1973– |

[1] 1355–1365—period of civil wars and disunion. [2] Swedish regents or protectors. [3] Danish kings.

## Trinidad and Tobago

GOVERNORS-GENERAL

| | |
|---|---|
| Solomon Hochoy | 1962–1973 |
| Ellis Emmanuel Innocent Clarke | 1973– |

PRIME MINISTER

| | |
|---|---|
| Eric Eustace Williams | 1962 |

| OTTOMAN SULTANS | | OTTOMAN SULTANS (Continued) | |
|---|---|---|---|
| Osman (or Othman) | c. 1299-1326 | Ahmed III | 1703-1730 |
| Orkhan | 1326-1359 | Mahmud I (or Mahmoud) | 1730-1754 |
| Murad I (or Amurath) | 1359-1389 | Osman III | 1754-1757 |
| Bajazet I (or Bayazid) | 1389-1403 | Mustafa III | 1757-1774 |
| Suleiman I (or Solyman) | 1403-1411 | Abdul-Hamid I | 1774-1789 |
| Prince Musa | 1411-1413 | Selim III | 1789-1807 |
| Mohammed I | 1413-1421 | Mustafa IV | 1807-1808 |
| Murad II | 1421-1451 | Mahmud II | 1808-1839 |
| Mohammed II | 1451-1481 | Abdul-Medjid I (or Abdul Mejid) | 1839-1861 |
| Bajazet II | 1481-1512 | Abdul-Aziz | 1861-1876 |
| Selim I | 1512-1520 | Murad V | 1876 |
| Suleiman I (or II) | 1520-1566 | Abdul-Hamid II | 1876-1909 |
| Selim II | 1566-1574 | Mohammed V (or Mehmed) | 1909-1918 |
| Murad III | 1574-1595 | Mohammed VI | 1918-1922 |
| Mohammed III | 1595-1603 | [Abolition of Sultanate, 1922; Turkey proclaimed a Republic, 1923] | - |
| Ahmed I (or Achmet) | 1603-1617 | | |
| Mustafa I (or Mustapha) | 1617-1618 | PRESIDENTS | |
| Osman II | 1618-1622 | Kemal Atatürk, orig. Mustafa Kemal Pasha | 1923-1938 |
| Mustafa I (restored) | 1622-1623 | İsmet İnönü | 1938-1950 |
| Murad IV | 1623-1640 | Celâl Bayar | 1950-1960 |
| Ibrahim | 1640-1648 | Cemal Gursel | 1960-1966 |
| Mohammed IV | 1648-1687 | Cevdet Sunay | 1966-1973 |
| Suleiman II (or III) | 1687-1691 | Fahri Korutürk | 1973- |
| Ahmed II | 1691-1695 | | |
| Mustafa II | 1695-1703 | | |

# UNION OF SOVIET SOCIALIST REPUBLICS

## RULERS OF RUSSIA

| HOUSE OF RURIK | | HOUSE OF ROMANOV (Continued) | |
|---|---|---|---|
| Ivan III the Great | 1462-1505 | Catherine I | 1725-1727 |
| Basil III | 1505-1533 | Peter II | 1727-1730 |
| Ivan IV the Terrible | 1533-1584 | Anna | 1730-1740 |
| Fëdor I | 1584-1598 | Ivan VI | 1740-1741 |
| Boris Godunov | 1598-1605 | Elizabeth | 1741-1762 |
| Fëdor II | 1605 | Peter III | 1762 |
| Demetrius (*Russ.* Dmitri)[1] | 1605-1606 | Catherine II | 1762-1796 |
| Basil (IV) Shuiski | 1606-1610 | Paul I | 1796-1801 |
| [Interregnum, 1610-1613] | | Alexander I | 1801-1825 |
| HOUSE OF ROMANOV | | Nicholas I | 1825-1855 |
| | | Alexander II | 1855-1881 |
| Michael Romanov | 1613-1645 | Alexander III | 1881-1894 |
| Alexis | 1645-1676 | Nicholas II | 1894-1917 |
| Fëdor III | 1676-1682 | [Revolution; Alexander Kerenski, Socialist leader, provisional head, Aug.-Nov. 1917] | |
| Ivan V and Peter the Great | 1682-1689 | | |
| Peter the Great (alone) | 1689-1725 | | |

## CHAIRMEN OF THE PRESIDIUM OF THE SUPREME SOVIET (PRESIDENTS)

| | | | |
|---|---|---|---|
| Mikhail I. Kalinin | 1923-1946 | Anastas I. Mikoyan | 1964-1965 |
| Nikolai M. Shvernik | 1946-1953 | Nikolai V. Podgorny | 1965-1977 |
| Kliment E. Voroshilov | 1953-1960 | Leonid I. Brezhnev | 1977- |
| Leonid I. Brezhnev | 1960-1964 | | |

## CHAIRMEN OF THE COUNCIL OF MINISTERS (PRIME MINISTERS)

| | | | |
|---|---|---|---|
| Nikolai Lenin | 1917-1924 | Georgii M. Malenkov | 1953-1955 |
| Aleksei Ivanovich Rykov | 1924-1930 | Nikolai A. Bulganin | 1955-1958 |
| Vyacheslav Mikhailovich Molotov | 1930-1941 | Nikita S. Khrushchev | 1958-1964 |
| Joseph Stalin | 1941-1953 | Aleksei N. Kosygin | 1964- |

[1] Usurped the throne. The period 1604-1613 is known as the "Time of Troubles."

# URUGUAY

## PRESIDENTS (since 1830)

| | | | |
|---|---|---|---|
| José Fructuoso Rivera | 1830-1835 | Juan Idiarte Borda | 1894-1897 |
| Manuel Oribe | 1835-1838 | Juan Lindolfo Cuestas | 1897-1903 |
| José Fructuoso Rivera | 1838-1842 | José Batlle y Ordóñez | 1903-1907 |
| [Civil War, 1842-1851][1] | | Claudio Williman | 1907-1911 |
| Venancio Flores | 1854-1855 | José Batlle y Ordóñez | 1911-1915 |
| Manuel Bustamante (provisional) | 1855-1856 | Feliciano Viera | 1915-1919 |
| Gabriel Antonio Pereira | 1856-1858 | Baltasar Brum | 1919-1923 |
| Manuel Freire (provisional) | 1858 | José Serrato | 1923-1927 |
| Bernardo Prudencio Berro | 1860-1864 | Juan Campísteguy | 1927-1931 |
| Atanasio Cruz Aguirre (provisional) | 1864 | Gabriel Terra | 1931-1938 |
| Venancio Flores[2] | 1865-1868 | Alfredo Baldomir | 1938-1943 |
| Pedro Varela (acting) | 1868 | Juan José Amézaga | 1943-1947 |
| Lorenzo Batlle | 1868-1872 | Tomás Berreta | 1947 |
| Tomás Gomensoro (acting) | 1872-1873 | Luis Batlle Berres | 1947-1951 |
| José Ellaury | 1874-1875 | Andrés Marténez Trueba | 1951 |
| Pedro Varela | 1875-1876 | Oscar Diego Gestido[3] | 1967 |
| Lorenzo Latorre | 1876-1880 | Jorge Pacheco Areco | 1967-1972 |
| F. M. Vidal | 1880-1882 | Juan María Bordaberry | 1972-1976 |
| Máximo Santos | 1882-1886 | Alberto Demicheli (ad interim) | 1976 |
| Máximo Tajes | 1886-1890 | Aparicio Méndez | 1976- |
| Julio Herrera y Obes | 1890-1894 | | |

[1] Following the Civil War of 1842-1851 affairs were extremely unstable, especially until 1864. The interference of Brazil and the domestic strife between the Colorados and Blancos made tenure in office of the presidents uncertain.
[2] Provisional president, 1865-66.
[3] National Council form of government (1951-66).

## POPES[1]

| | PONTIFF | PONTIFICATE |
|---|---|---|
| 1 | Saint Peter | 41?–?67 |
| 2 | Saint Linus | 67–?79 |
| 3 | Saint Anacletus | 79–?90 |
| 4 | Saint Clement I | 90–?99 |
| 5 | Saint Evaristus | 99–?107 |
| 6 | Saint Alexander I | 107–?116 |
| 7 | Saint Sixtus I | 116–?125 |
| 8 | Saint Telesphorus | 125–?136 |
| 9 | Saint Hyginus | 136–?140 |
| 10 | Saint Pius I | 140–?154 |
| 11 | Saint Anicetus | 154–?165 |
| 12 | Saint Soter | 165–174 |
| 13 | Saint Eleutherius | 174–189 |
| 14 | Saint Victor I | 189–198 |
| 15 | Saint Zephyrinus | 198–217 |
| 16 | Saint Calixtus I (or Callistus) | 217–222 |
| 17 | Saint Urban | 222–230 |
| 18 | Saint Pontian | 230–235 |
| 19 | Saint Anterus | 235–236 |
| 20 | Saint Fabian | 236–250 |
| 21 | Saint Cornelius | 251–253 |
| 22 | Saint Lucius I | 253–254 |
| 23 | Saint Stephen I | 254–257 |
| 24 | Saint Sixtus II | 257–258 |
| 25 | Saint Dionysius | 259–268 |
| 26 | Saint Felix I | 269–274 |
| 27 | Saint Eutychianus (or Eutychian) | 275–283 |
| 28 | Saint Gaius (or Caius) | 283–296 |
| 29 | Saint Marcellinus | 296–304 |
| 30 | Saint Marcellus I | 308–309 |
| 31 | Saint Eusebius | 309 (310) |
| 32 | Saint Miltiades (or Melchiades) | 310?–314 |
| 33 | Saint Sylvester (or Silvester) | 314–335 |
| 34 | Saint Mark | 336 |
| 35 | Saint Julius I | 337–352 |
| 36 | Saint Liberius | 352–366 |
| 37 | Saint Damasus I | 366–384 |
| 38 | Saint Siricius | 384–398 |
| 39 | Saint Anastasius I | 398–401 |
| 40 | Saint Innocent I | 402–417 |
| 41 | Saint Zosimus | 417–418 |
| 42 | Saint Boniface I | 418–422 |
| 43 | Saint Celestine I | 422–432 |
| 44 | Saint Sixtus III | 432–440 |
| 45 | Saint Leo I, "The Great" | 440–461 |
| 46 | Saint Hilarius | 461–468 |
| 47 | Saint Simplicius | 468–483 |
| 48 | Saint Felix II (or III) | 483–492 |
| 49 | Saint Gelasius I | 492–496 |
| 50 | Saint Anastasius II | 496–498 |
| 51 | Saint Symmachus | 498–514 |
| 52 | Saint Hormisdas | 514–523 |
| 53 | Saint John I | 523–526 |
| 54 | Saint Felix III (or IV) | 526–530 |
| 55 | Boniface II | 530–532 |
| 56 | John II | 533–535 |
| 57 | Saint Agapetus I | 535–536 |
| 58 | Saint Silverius | 536–?538 |
| 59 | Vigilius | 538–555 |
| 60 | Pelagius I | 556–561 |
| 61 | John III | 561–574 |
| 62 | Benedict I | 575–579 |
| 63 | Pelagius II | 579–590 |
| 64 | Saint Gregory I, "The Great" | 590–604 |
| 65 | Sabinianus | 604–606 |
| 66 | Boniface III | 607 |
| 67 | Saint Boniface IV | 608–615 |
| 68 | Saint Deusdedit | 615–618 |
| 69 | Boniface V | 619–625 |
| 70 | Honorius I | 625–638 |
| 71 | Severinus | 640 |
| 72 | John IV | 640–642 |
| 73 | Theodore I | 642–649 |
| 74 | Saint Martin I | 649–655 |
| 75 | Saint Eugenius I | 654–657 |
| 76 | Saint Vitalian | 657–672 |
| 77 | Saint Adeodatus II | 672–676 |
| 78 | Donus | 676–678 |
| 79 | Saint Agatho | 678–681 |
| 80 | Saint Leo II | 682–683 |
| 81 | Saint Benedict II | 684–685 |
| 82 | John V | 685–686 |
| 83 | Conon | 686–687 |
| 84 | Saint Sergius I | 687–701 |
| 85 | John VI | 701–705 |
| 86 | John VII | 705–707 |
| 87 | Sisinnius | 708 |
| 88 | Constantine (I) | 708–715 |
| 89 | Saint Gregory II | 715–731 |
| 90 | Saint Gregory III | 731–741 |
| 91 | Saint Zacharias | 741–752 |
| 92 | Stephen II (III) | 752–757 |
| 93 | Saint Paul I | 757–767 |
| 94 | Stephen III (IV) | 768–772 |
| 95 | Saint Adrian I (or Hadrian) | 772–795 |
| 96 | Saint Leo III | 795–816 |
| 97 | Stephen IV (V) | 816–817 |
| 98 | Saint Paschal I | 817–824 |
| 99 | Eugenius II | 824–827 |
| 100 | Valentine | 827 |
| 101 | Gregory IV | 827–844 |
| 102 | Sergius II | 844–847 |
| 103 | Saint Leo IV | 847–855 |
| 104 | Benedict III | 855–858 |
| 105 | Saint Nicholas I | 858–867 |
| 106 | Adrian II | 867–872 |
| 107 | John VIII | 872–882 |
| 108 | Marinus I (or Martin II) | 882–884 |
| 109 | Saint Adrian III | 884–885 |
| 110 | Stephen V (VI) | 885–891 |
| 111 | Formosus | 891–896 |
| 112 | Boniface VI | 896 |
| 113 | Stephen VI (VII) | 896–897 |
| 114 | Romanus | 897 |
| 115 | Theodore II | ?897 |
| 116 | John IX | 898–900 |
| 117 | Benedict IV | 900–903 |
| 118 | Leo V | 903 |
| 119 | Christopher | 903–904 |
| 120 | Sergius III | 904–911 |
| 121 | Anastasius III | 911–913 |
| 122 | Lando | 913–914 |
| 123 | John X | 914–928 |
| 124 | Leo VI | 928–929 |
| 125 | Stephen VII (VIII) | 929–931 |
| 126 | John XI | 931–936 |
| 127 | Leo VII | 936–939 |
| 128 | Stephen VIII (IX) | 939–942 |
| 129 | Marinus II (or Martin III) | 942–946 |
| 130 | Agapetus II | 946–955 |
| 131 | John XII | 955–964 |
| 132 | Leo VIII | 963–965 |
| 133 | Benedict V | 964 |
| 134 | John XIII | 965–972 |
| 135 | Benedict VI | 973–974 |
| 136 | Benedict VII | 974–983 |
| 137 | John XIV | 983–984 |
| 138 | Boniface VII | 984–985 |
| 139 | John XV[2] | 985–996 |
| 140 | Gregory V | 996–999 |
| 141 | Sylvester II | 999–1003 |
| 142 | John XVII | 1003 |
| 143 | John XVIII | 1003–1009 |
| 144 | Sergius IV | 1009–1012 |
| 145 | Benedict VIII | 1012–1024 |
| 146 | John XIX | 1024–1032 |
| 147 | Benedict IX | 1032–1045 |
| 148 | Gregory VI | 1045–1046 |
| 149 | Clement II | 1046–1047 |
| 150 | Damasus II | 1048 |
| 151 | Saint Leo IX | 1049–1054 |
| 152 | Victor II | 1055–1057 |
| 153 | Stephen IX (X) | 1057–1058 |
| 154 | Benedict X | 1058–1059 |
| 155 | Nicholas II | 1059–1061 |
| 156 | Alexander II | 1061–1073 |
| 157 | Saint Gregory VII | 1073–1085 |
| 158 | Victor III | 1086–1087 |
| 159 | Urban II | 1088–1099 |
| 160 | Paschal II | 1099–1118 |
| 161 | Gelasius II | 1118–1119 |
| 162 | Calixtus II | 1119–1124 |
| 163 | Honorius II | 1124–1130 |
| 164 | Innocent II | 1130–1143 |
| 165 | Celestine II | 1143–1144 |
| 166 | Lucius II | 1144–1145 |
| 167 | Eugenius III | 1145–1153 |
| 168 | Anastasius IV | 1153–1154 |
| 169 | Adrian IV[3] | 1154–1159 |
| 170 | Alexander III | 1159–1181 |
| 171 | Lucius III | 1181–1185 |
| 172 | Urban III | 1185–1187 |
| 173 | Gregory VIII | 1187 |
| 174 | Clement III | 1187–1191 |
| 175 | Celestine III | 1191–1198 |
| 176 | Innocent III | 1198–1216 |
| 177 | Honorius III | 1216–1227 |
| 178 | Gregory IX | 1227–1241 |
| 179 | Celestine IV | 1241 |
| 180 | Innocent IV | 1243–1254 |
| 181 | Alexander IV | 1254–1261 |
| 182 | Urban IV | 1261–1264 |
| 183 | Clement IV | 1265–1268 |
| 184 | Gregory X | 1271–1276 |

[1] Bishop of Rome is the more usual title for all popes before the fourth century. During that time Pope became the distinctive title of the bishop of Rome. Dates of pontificates for first ten popes after Peter are quite uncertain.
[2] For the confusion in numbering of popes named John from John XV to John XXI, see note under John XV in this dictionary.
[3] Nicholas Breakspear, the only English pope.

POPES (Continued)

| | PONTIFF | PONTIFICATE | | PONTIFF | PONTIFICATE |
|---|---|---|---|---|---|
| 185 | Innocent V | 1276 | 226 | Saint Pius V | 1566-1572 |
| 186 | Adrian V | 1276 | 227 | Gregory XIII | 1572-1585 |
| 187 | John XXI | 1276-1277 | 228 | Sixtus V | 1585-1590 |
| 188 | Nicholas III | 1277-1280 | 229 | Urban VII | 1590 |
| 189 | Martin IV | 1281-1285 | 230 | Gregory XIV | 1590-1591 |
| 190 | Honorius IV | 1285-1287 | 231 | Innocent IX | 1591 |
| 191 | Nicholas IV | 1288-1292 | 232 | Clement VIII | 1592-1605 |
| 192 | Saint Celestine V | 1294 | 233 | Leo XI | 1605 |
| 193 | Boniface VIII | 1294-1303 | 234 | Paul V | 1605-1621 |
| 194 | Benedict XI | 1303-1304 | 235 | Gregory XV | 1621-1623 |
| 195 | Clement V[4] | 1305-1314 | 236 | Urban VIII | 1623-1644 |
| 196 | John XXII | 1316-1334 | 237 | Innocent X | 1644-1655 |
| 197 | Benedict XII | 1334-1342 | 238 | Alexander VII | 1655-1667 |
| 198 | Clement VI | 1342-1352 | 239 | Clement IX | 1667-1669 |
| 199 | Innocent VI | 1352-1362 | 240 | Clement X | 1670-1676 |
| 200 | Urban V | 1362-1370 | 241 | Innocent XI | 1676-1689 |
| 201 | Gregory XI | 1370-1378 | 242 | Alexander VIII | 1689-1691 |
| 202 | Urban VI[5] | 1378-1389 | 243 | Innocent XII | 1691-1700 |
| 203 | Boniface IX | 1389-1404 | 244 | Clement XI | 1700-1721 |
| 204 | Innocent VII | 1404-1406 | 245 | Innocent XIII | 1721-1724 |
| 205 | Gregory XII | 1406-1415 | 246 | Benedict XIII | 1724-1730 |
| 206 | Alexander V | 1409-1410 | 247 | Clement XII | 1730-1740 |
| 207 | Martin V | 1417-1431 | 248 | Benedict XIV | 1740-1758 |
| 208 | Eugenius IV | 1431-1447 | 249 | Clement XIII | 1758-1769 |
| 209 | Nicholas V | 1447-1455 | 250 | Clement XIV | 1769-1774 |
| 210 | Calixtus III | 1455-1458 | 251 | Pius VI | 1775-1799 |
| 211 | Pius II | 1458-1465 | 252 | Pius VII | 1800-1823 |
| 212 | Paul II | 1464-1471 | 253 | Leo XII | 1823-1829 |
| 213 | Sixtus IV | 1471-1484 | 254 | Pius VIII | 1829-1830 |
| 214 | Innocent VIII | 1484-1492 | 255 | Gregory XVI | 1831-1846 |
| 215 | Alexander VI | 1492-1503 | 256 | Pius IX | 1846 1878 |
| 216 | Pius III | 1503 | 257 | Leo XIII | 1878-1903 |
| 217 | Julius II | 1503-1513 | 258 | Pius X | 1903-1914 |
| 218 | Leo X | 1513-1521 | 259 | Benedict XV | 1914-1922 |
| 219 | Adrian VI | 1522-1523 | 260 | Pius XI | 1922-1939 |
| 220 | Clement VII | 1523-1534 | 261 | Pius XII | 1939-1958 |
| 221 | Paul III | 1534-1549 | 262 | John XXIII | 1958-1963 |
| 222 | Julius III | 1550-1555 | 263 | Paul VI | 1963-1978 |
| 223 | Marcellus II | 1555 | 264 | John Paul I | 1978 |
| 224 | Paul IV | 1555-1559 | 265 | John Paul II | 1978- |
| 225 | Pius IV | 1559-1565 | | | |

[4] From 1309 to 1377, Clement V to Gregory XI, the popes resided at Avignon, France (the Babylonian captivity).
[5] From 1378 to 1417, Urban VI to Martin V, was the period of the Great, or Western Schism when there were rival popes at Rome and at Avignon. See list of antipopes below.

ANTIPOPES OR DOUBTFUL POPES

| | | | |
|---|---|---|---|
| Novatian | 251-?258 | Celestine II | 1124 |
| Felix II | 355-358 | Anacletus II | 1130-1138 |
| Eulalius | 418-419 | Victor IV | -1138 |
| Laurentius | 498-505 | Victor IV | 1139-1164 |
| Stephen (II) | 752 | Paschal III | 1164-1168 |
| Constantine (II) | 767-768 | Calixtus III (or Callistus) | 1168-1178 |
| Anastasius | 855 | Innocent III | 1179-1180 |
| Boniface VII | 974 | Nicholas V | 1328-1330 |
| John XVI | 997-998 | Clement VII[1] | 1378-1394 |
| Sylvester III | 1045 | Benedict XIII[1] | 1394-1423 |
| Benedict IX | 1047-1048 | John XXIII | 1410-1415 |
| Honorius II | 1061-1064 | Clement VIII | 1424?-1429 |
| Clement III | 1080, 1084-1100 | Benedict XIV | ?1424 |
| Sylvester IV | 1105-1111 | Felix V[2] | 1439-1449 |
| Gregory VIII | 1118-1121 | | |

[1] Antipopes of the Great, or Western, Schism, at Avignon. [2] Antipope of the Second Schism (1439-49), at Avignon.

## VENEZUELA

PRESIDENTS (since 1830)

| | | | |
|---|---|---|---|
| José Antonio Páez[1] | 1830-1846 | Juan Vicente Gómez | 1922-1929 |
| José Tadeo Monagas | 1846-1851 | Juan Bautista Pérez (provisional) | 1929-1931 |
| José Gregorio Monagas | 1851-1855 | Juan Vicente Gómez | 1931-1935 |
| José Tadeo Monagas | 1855-1858 | Eleázar López Contreras (provisional, 1935) | 1936-1941 |
| [Civil War, 1858-1863] | | Isaías Medina Angarita | 1941-1945 |
| Juan Crisóstomo Falcón | 1863-1868 | Rómulo Betancourt (provisional) | 1945-1947 |
| José Ruperto Monagas | 1868-1870 | Rómulo Gallegos | 1947-1948 |
| Antonio Guzmán Blanco[2] | 1870-1889 | Carlos Delgado Chalbaud (provisional) | 1948-1950 |
| José Pablo Rogas Paúl (provisional) | 1889-1890 | Germán Suárez Flamerich | 1950-1952 |
| Raimundo Andueza Palacio | 1890-1892 | Marcos Pérez Jiménez | 1952-1958 |
| Joaquín Crespo[3] | 1892-1898 | Military junta of six men | 1958 |
| Ignacio Andrade | 1898-1899 | Rómulo Betancourt | 1959-1963 |
| Cipriano Castro | 1899-1908 | Raúl Leoni | 1968-1969 |
| Juan Vicente Gómez[4] | 1908-1915 | Rafael Caldera | 1969-1974 |
| Victorino Márquez Bustillos (provisional) | 1915-1922 | Carlos Andrés Pérez | 1974- |

[1] Páez was practically dictator; two nominal presidents during the period were José Vargas (1835-1839) and Carlos Soublette (1843-1845).
[2] Guzmán Blanco was practically dictator from 1870 to 1889, causing himself to be elected for alternate periods of 2 years, with puppets for the intermediate terms.
[3] For the period 1892-94 practically a military dictatorship.
[4] Gómez was supreme dictator (1908-35), provisional president (1908-10), elected president (1910-15, 1922-29, 1931-35). He acted as commander in chief of the army, and dominated provisional presidents Bustillos and Pérez.

## YUGOSLAVIA

MONTENEGRO[1,2]

| | | | |
|---|---|---|---|
| Peter I, ruling prince | 1782-1830 | Nicholas I as king | 1910-1918 |
| Peter II | 1830-1851 | [United with Yugoslavia, 1919] | |
| Danilo | 1851-1860 | | |
| Nicholas I | 1860-1910 | | |

SERBIA[1,3]

| | | | |
|---|---|---|---|
| [Struggle for independence began, 1804] | | Michael (Obrenovich) (again) | 1860-1868 |
| Karageorge (Czerny Djordje, "Black George") founder of Karageorgevich Dynasty, and commander | 1804-1813 | Milan I | 1868-1889 |
| Miloš (Obrenovich), leader against the Turks, and Prince of Serbia | 1815-1830 | [Independence of Serbia recognized by Congress of Berlin, 1878; Milan proclaimed himself king, 1882] | |
| Miloš (Obrenovich), as hereditary prince | 1830-1839 | Alexander I (Obrenovich) | 1889-1903 |
| Milan (Obrenovich) | 1839 | Peter I (Karageorgevich)[4] | 1903-1919 |
| Michael (Obrenovich) | 1839-1842 | [Became part of Yugoslavia, 1919] | |
| Alexander (son of Karageorge) | 1842-1858 | | |
| Miloš (Obrenovich) (restored) | 1858-1860 | | |

| KINGS OF YUGOSLAVIA | | PRESIDENTS OF YUGOSLAVIA | |
|---|---|---|---|
| Peter I (of Serbia)[5] | 1919-1921 | Ivan Ribar (provisional) | 1945-1953 |
| Alexander I | 1921-1934 | Josip Broz (Tito) | 1953- |
| Peter II[6] | 1934-1945 | | |
| [Republic declared Nov. 29, 1945] | | | |

[1] Montenegro and Serbia became part of Yugoslavia in 1919.
[2] A Balkan state, never subdued by the Turks, 1389-1876; declared independent by the Treaty of Berlin, 1878.
[3] Under Turkish rule from 1389, battle of Kosovo, to 1878.
[4] Prince Alexander acted as Regent, 1914-1919.
[5] Prince Alexander of Serbia acted as Regent for his father King Peter I, 1914-1921 (Serbia and Yugoslavia).
[6] Born 1923; during his minority the country governed by a Regency Council; seat of government established in London, 1941.